RIA Federal Tax Regulations

For customer service or to obtain the name and telephone number of your local account representative, please call 1-800-431-9025, Option # 7. Additional copies of this product are available, at a fee. Please call 1-800-950-1216 or visit our Product Store at http://ria.thomson.com to order.

RIA

By
Thomson Reuters/RIA
195 Broadway
New York, NY 10007

RIA FEDERAL TAX REGULATIONS

Including Proposed Regulations

Current through January 16, 2009

VOLUME 1

Volume 1: TABLE OF CONTENTS

FOREWORD

REGULATIONS AND TREASURY DECISIONS EXPLAINED

TABLE OF FINAL AND TEMPORARY REGULATIONS

TABLE OF IRREGULARLY NUMBERED REGULATIONS

PROPOSED REGULATIONS FINDING LIST

AMENDING ACTS TABLE

TABLE OF CODE SECTIONS

FINAL AND TEMPORARY REGULATIONS TOPIC INDEX

PROPOSED REGULATIONS TOPIC INDEX

FINAL, TEMPORARY AND PROPOSED REGULATIONS
1.0-1 through 1.281-4

Volume 2: FINAL, TEMPORARY AND PROPOSED REGULATIONS
1.301-1 through 1.483-4

Volume 3: FINAL, TEMPORARY AND PROPOSED REGULATIONS
1.501(a)-1 through 7.999-1

Volume 4: FINAL, TEMPORARY AND PROPOSED REGULATIONS
1.1001-1 through 157.5891-1

Volume 5: FINAL, TEMPORARY AND PROPOSED REGULATIONS
1.6001-1 through END

CIRCULAR 230

PREAMBLES TO PROPOSED REGULATIONS

TABLE OF CONTENTS

	Volume	Starts at Page
Foreword	1	1,001
Regulations and Treasury Decisions explained	1	2,001
Table of final and temporary regulations	1	3,001
Table of irregularly numbered regulations	1	4,001
Proposed regulations finding list	1	5,001
Amending Acts Table	1	6,001
Table of Code Sections	1	7,001
Final and temporary regulations topic index	1	8,001
Proposed regulations topic index	1	9,001
Text of final and temporary regulations	1	10,001
Text of final and temporary regulations	2	20,001
Text of final and temporary regulations	3	30,001
Text of final and temporary regulations	4	40,001
Text of final and temporary regulations	5	50,001
Circular 230	5	52,001
Preambles to proposed regulations	5	53,001

FOREWORD

The five-volume Research Institute of America Federal Tax Regulations provides the exact text of all final, temporary and proposed regulations issued by the Treasury Department under Title 26 of the Code of Federal Regulations, on income tax, estate tax, gift tax, withholding, procedure, administration, and certain excise taxes.

Volume 1 contains finding aids and also separate topic indexes for the final/temporary and proposed regulations (see Table of Contents on previous page).

The final, temporary and proposed regulations are arranged in sequence, in Code Section order, with the prefix numbers arranged numerically. So for example, final regulation 1.401-1 would be followed by proposed regulation 1.401-1, which would be followed by final regulation 301.401-1, since all three regulations pertain to Code Section 401. The preambles to the proposed regulations appear in Volume 5, and are arranged in chronological order. Each proposed regulation contains a cross-reference to the preamble paragraph number.

This edition contains all regulations (final, temporary and proposed) published as of January 16, 2009.

Regulations and Treasury Decisions (T.D.s) Explained

IRS issues regulations that set forth its interpretation of the law. The regulations are issued over the signature of the Secretary of the Treasury (or his delegate) and carry more weight than any rulings or releases on tax matters otherwise issued by IRS or the Treasury.

New regulations are added and existing regulations are amended or withdrawn by Treasury Decisions (T.D. or TD) which are issued as the need arises.

Numbering of the regulations generally follows the Code, with a prefix number (before a decimal) indicating the Part of the regulations in which the section is included and a suffix number (after a hyphen) indicating the subdivision of the regulation covering a particular Code section. A suffix number followed by the letter "T" (e.g. *Reg § 1.441-1T)* indicates a temporary regulation.

The prefix numbers (Parts of the regulations) used are:

1.	Income tax
4. thru 18.	Income tax (temporary)
20.	Estate tax
22.	Estate tax (temporary)
25.	Gift tax
26.	Generation-skipping transfer tax
31.	Employment taxes and collection of income tax at source
32.	Employment taxes (temporary)
35., 35a.	Collection of income tax at source
36.	Employment taxes
40.–49.	Excise taxes
52.	Environmental taxes
53.	Foundation excise taxes
54.	Pension excise taxes
55.	Excise tax on certain REITs
56.	Public charity excise taxes
141. thru 157.	Excise taxes
300.	User fees
301.	Procedure and administration
305.	Procedure and administration
401. thru 404.	Procedure and administration (temporary)
500. thru 599.	Tax conventions
601.	Procedural rules
801.	Measuring performance within IRS

The various Code sections are generally covered in the particular Part of the regs as follows:

Code Secs.	*Are in regs. on*
1 to 1999	Income tax (1.)
2001 to 2299	Estate tax (20.)
2501 to 2599	Gift tax (25.)
2601 to 2622	Generation-skipping transfer tax (26.)
3101 to 3599	Employment tax (31.)
4001 to 4999	Excise tax (40.-153.)
5001 to 5899	Alcohol, tobacco and certain excise taxes (170.–299.)

6001 to end	Procedure and administration

illustration: *Reg § 1.165-4* is the fourth subdivision (-4) of the income tax regulations (1.) covering Code Sec. 165.

Treasury Decisions (TDs). TDs promulgate new regulations or amend or withdraw existing regulations. They are issued by IRS with the approval of the Secretary of the Treasury. In addition to amending, adding or withdrawing regulation sections, TDs include a preamble that summarizes the new regulatory material and sometimes gives additional insight into the change or addition.

Treasury Decisions are numbered consecutively with no break for a new year, etc.

Temporary Regulations. IRS issues some regulations as temporary regulations. Generally, temporary regulations are effective immediately upon publication and remain in effect until replaced by final regulations. Temporary regulations issued after November 20, 1988, however, must be simultaneously issued in proposed form, and are permitted to remain in effect for no more than 3 years from the date of issuance.

Proposed Regulations. Before being issued in final form in a TD, a change or addition to the regulations is generally issued in proposed form so that interested parties may offer comments or suggestions for amendments to be made before the proposal becomes final. At least 30 days must usually pass before the proposed regulation becomes final, and in some cases regulations remain in proposed form for many years. The final versions of regulation additions and changes are frequently quite different from the proposed version.

Proposed regulations are generally indicated by the date of publication in the Federal Register.

The proposed regulations and the proposed amendments to regulations are reproduced in sequence, along with the final and temporary regulations.

Publication of TDs and Proposed Regulations. Both proposed regulations and Treasury Decisions are first published in the Federal Register, the official publication for regulations and legal notices issued by the Executive Branch of the Federal Government, which is published daily Monday through Friday (except holidays).

For citation purposes, the Federal Register is cited by volume and page, with each year commencing a new volume. Thus, proposed regulations filed on 4/9/2003 or published on 4/10/2003, 68 F.R. 17569 means the proposed regulations were filed on 4/9/2003 with the Office of the Federal Register, and published on 4/10/2003 in Vol. 68 of the Federal Register at page 17569.

Final, Temporary and Proposed Regulations

The Final, temporary and proposed regulations are arranged in sequence, in Code section order, with the prefix numbers arranged numerically. So for example, final regulation 1.401-1 would be followed by proposed regulation 1.401-1, which would be followed by final regulation 301.401-1, since all three regulations pertain to Code Section 401. The preambles to the proposed regulations appear in Volume 5, and are arranged in chronological order. Each proposed regulation contains a cross-reference to the preamble paragraph number. The following table contains a list of regulation sections and topics covered. A table of irregularly numbered regulations appears at page 10,301.

Regulation section numbers	*Topics*
	Volume 1
1.0-1 through 1.58-9	Determination of tax liability
1.61-1 through 1.281-4	Computation of taxable income
	Volume 2
1.301-1 through 1.383-2	Corporate distributions and adjustments
1.401-0 through 1.425-1	Deferred compensation, etc.
1.441-0 through 1.483-4	Accounting periods and methods
	Volume 3
1.501(a)-1 through 1.528-10	Exempt organizations
1.531-1 through 1.565-6	Corporations used to avoid income tax on shareholders
1.581-1 through 1.601-1	Banking institutions
1.611-0 through 1.638-2	Natural resources
1.641(a)-0 through 1.692-1	Estates, trusts, beneficiaries and decedents
1.701-1 through 1.761-2	Partners and partnerships
1.801-2 through 1.848-3	Insurance companies
1.851-1 through 1.860G-3	Regulated Investment Companies, REITs, and REMICs
1.861-1 through 1.937-3T	Tax based on income from within or without the United States
1.951-1 through 7.999-1	Tax based on income from within or without the United States
	Volume 4
1.1001-1 through 1.1092(d)-2	Gain or loss on disposition of property
1.1201-1 through 1.1298-3T	Capital gains and losses

Regulation section numbers	*Topics*
1.1311(a)-1 through 1.1341-1	Readjustment of tax between years and special limitations
1.1361-0 through 18.1379-2	Subchapter S corporations
1.1381-1 through 1.1398-2	Cooperatives and their patrons; individual bankruptcy
1.1401-1 through 1.1403-1	Tax on self-employment income
1.1441-1 through 1.1464-1	Withholding of tax on nonresident aliens and foreign corporations and tax-free covenant bonds
1.1491-1 through 1.1494-2	Recovery of excessive profits on government contracts
1.1501-1 through 1.1563-4	Consolidated returns
20.0-1 through 20.2209-1	Estate taxes
25.0-1 through 25.2524-1	Gift taxes
26.2600-1 through 26.2663-2	Generation-skipping taxes
25.2701-0 through 25.2704-3	Valuation
31.3101-1 through 31.3308-1	Employment taxes
31.3401(a)-1 through 31.3507-2	Collection of income tax at source
48.4041-0 through 44.4906-1	Miscellaneous excise taxes
56.4911-0 through 56.4911-10	Public charities
53.4940-1 through 53.4963-1	Foundation and similar excise taxes
54.4971-1 through 54.4979-1	Qualified pension, etc. plans
55.4981-1 through 55.4981-2	REITs
54.4981A-1T	Qualified pension, etc. plans
55.4982-1	REITs
51.4989-1 through 51.4996-5	Miscellaneous excise taxes
156.5881-1	Greenmail
157.5891-1	Structured settlement factoring transactions

Volume 5

1.6001-1 through 1.7872-15	Procedure and administration
1.9101-1 through 801.8T	Irregularly numbered regulations
Circular 230	Practice before IRS

Table of Irregularly Numbered Regulations

Certain regulations do not follow the numbering scheme described in "Regulations and Treasury Decisions explained." The following table lists the irregularly numbered regulations and where they may be found in the five volume set.

Regulations that do not pertain to one specific Code Section are located in the Irregularly Numbered Regulations tab in Volume 5.

Regulation Section Number	*Subject*	*Location*
1.9101-1	Permission to submit information required by certain returns and statements on magnetic tape	Volume 5
3.1–3.11	Merchant Marine and Fisheries Capital Construction Funds	Volume 5
8.1	Charitable remainder trusts	After regulation 1.664-1
9.1	Investment credit—public utility property elections	After prop reg 1.46-6
12.3	Investment credit, public utility property elections	After regulation 9.1
12.8	Elections with respect to net leases of real property	After regulation 1.56A-5
12.9	Election to postpone determination with respect to the presumption described in section 183(d)	After regulation 1.183-4
13.4	Arbitrage bonds; temporary rules	After regulation 1.103-11
16.3-1	Returns as to the creation of or transfers to certain foreign trusts	After regulation 301.6048-1
17.1	Industrial development bonds used to provide solid waste disposal facilities; temporary rules	After prop reg 1.103-8
18.0	Effective date of temporary regulations under Subchapter S Revision Act of 1982	After regulation 1.1361-6
20.0-1; 20.0-2	Introduction (Estate taxes)	Before regulation 20.2001-1
22.0	Certain elections under the Economic Recovery Tax Act of 1981	After regulation 20.2209-1
25.0-1	Introduction (Gift taxes)	Before regulation 25.2501-1
31.0-1– 31.0-4	Introduction (Employment taxes)	After regulation 25.2704-3

Regulation Section Number	Subject	Location
32.1; 32.2	Employment taxes	After regulation 31.3123-1
40.0-1	Introduction (Excise tax procedures)	After regulation 49.6011(a)-1
41.0-1	Highway motor vehicle use tax regulations	After regulation 43.4472-1
43.0-1	Introduction (Excise tax on transportation by water)	After regulation 40.0-1
44.0-1	Introduction	Before regulation 44.4401-1
44.0-2	General definitions and use of terms	After regulation 44.0-1
44.0-3	Scope of regulations	After regulation 44.0-2
44.0-4	Extent to which the regulations in this part supersede prior regulations	After regulation 44.0-3
46.0-1	Introduction (Taxes on policies issued by foreign insurers)	After regulation 47.4362-1
48.0-1– 48.0-3	Manufacturers and Retailers Excise Tax Regulations	After prop reg 145.4051-1
48.9000-0	Paperwork Reduction Act	After regulation 48.6675-1
49.0-1	Introduction (facilities and services excise tax)	After regulation 48.4225-1
49.0-2	General definitions and use of terms	After regulation 49.0-1
52.0-1	Introduction (Environmental tax)	After regulation 41.4484-1
148.1-5	Constructive sale price	After regulation 48.4216(f)-1
300.0–300.3	User fees	After regulation 41.6156-1
301.9000-1	IRS procedures on requests for disclosure	Volume 5
301.9001-1– 301.9001-3	Outer continental shelf oil fee	Volume 5
301.9100-0	Outline of regulations	Volume 5
301.9100-1	Extensions of time to make elections	Volume 5
301.9100-2	Automatic extensions	Volume 5
301.9100-3	Other extensions	Volume 5
301.9100-4T	Time and manner of making certain elections under the Economic Recovery Tax Act of 1981	Volume 5

Regulation Section Number	*Subject*	*Location*
301.9100-5T	Time and manner of making certain elections under the Tax Equity and Fiscal Responsibility Act of 1982	Volume 5
301.9100-6T	Time and manner of making certain elections under the Deficit Reduction Act of 1984	Volume 5
301.9100-7T	Time and manner of making certain elections under the Tax Reform Act of 1986	Volume 5
301.9100-8	Time and manner of making certain elections under the Technical and Miscellaneous Revenue Act of 1988	Volume 5
301.9100-9T	Election by a bank holding company to forego grandfather provision for all property representing pre-June 30, 1968 activities	Volume 5
301.9100-10T	Election by certain family-owned bank holding companies to divest all banking and nonbanking property	Volume 5
301.9100-11T	Election by a qualified bank holding corporation to pay in installments the tax attributable to sales under the Bank Holding Act	Volume 5
301.9100-12T	Various elections under the Tax Reform Act of 1976	Volume 5
301.9100-14T	Individual's election to terminate taxable year when cases commences	Volume 5
301.9100-15T	Election to use retroactive effective date	Volume 5
301.9100-16T	Election to accrue vacation pay	Volume 5
301.9100-17T	Procedure applicable to certain elections	Volume 5
301.9100-18T	Election to include in gross income in year of transfer	Volume 5
301.9100-21	References to other temporary elections under various tax acts	Volume 5
601.101–601.702	Tax procedures	Volume 5
601.901	Missing children shown on penalty mail	Volume 5
801.1–801.7	System for measuring organizational and employee performance within the Internal Revenue Service	Volume 5
801.1T–801.8T	System for measuring organizational and employee performance within the Internal Revenue Service (temporary)	Volume 5

Proposed Regulations

Changes in or additions to Treasury regulations are made by Treasury Decisions (TDs). But before being issued in final form in a TD, a change or addition to the regulations is generally issued in proposed form so that interested parties may offer comments or suggestions for amendments to be made before the proposal becomes final. At least 30 days must usually pass before the proposed regulation becomes final, and in some cases regulations remain in proposed form for many years. The final versions of regulation additions and changes are frequently quite different from the proposed versions.

Proposed regulations are indicated by the date of publication in the Federal Register.

The proposed regulations are listed by Internal Revenue Code Section. The Code Section is the number following the (.) and preceding the hyphen (-). Thus proposed regulation § 1.61-6 covers Code Section 61. This makes it easy to check the listing to see if there are proposed regulations on a Code Section of interest.

For irregularly numbered regulations (i.e., the regulation number does not correspond to a Code section), see the beginning of the table.

Here is a list of regulations sections for which changes are being proposed and of new regulations sections which would be added if the proposed regulations become final.

Col. 1—lists the proposed changed or new regulations section in Code section order (and also indicates whether the proposed regulations were also issued as final regulations).

Col. 2—gives the date of publication in the Federal Register.

Col. 3—reports the paragraph number in Volume 5 at which the preamble to the proposed regulation is reproduced.

Col. 1 Regs. §	Col. 2 Pub. Date	Col. 3 Preamble ¶
40.0-1	7/29/2008	153,041
48.0-1	7/29/2008	153,041
48.0-2	1/2/91	151,211
48.0-3	1/2/91	151,211
48.0-4	7/29/2008	153,041
3.2	4/8/86	151,065
3.2	1/29/76	150,183
3.3	4/8/86	151,065
3.3	1/29/76	150,183
3.5	1/29/76	150,183
3.6	1/29/76	150,183
3.8	1/29/76	150,183
514.23	4/8/86	151,065
10.34	9/26/2007	152,913
10.35	12/20/2004	152,611
10.36	12/20/2004	152,611
10.38	12/20/2004	152,611
10.39	12/20/2004	152,611
10.52	12/20/2004	152,611
1.40-1	7/29/2008	153,041
1.40-2	7/29/2008	153,041
1.40A-1	7/29/2008	153,041
1.41-4	12/26/2001	152,211
1.41-6	6/17/2008	153,005
1.41-8	6/17/2008	153,005
1.41-9	6/17/2008	153,005
1.42-18	6/19/2007	152,871
1.45D-1	9/24/2008	153,063
1.45D-1	8/11/2008	153,049
1.46-3	12/20/85	151,041
1.47-1	12/20/85	151,041
1.48-4	9/21/87	151,105
1.48-9	1/26/82	150,725
1.48-9	12/20/85	151,041
1.56(g)-1	12/30/92	151,475
1.61-6	4/8/86	151,065
1.61-7	4/8/86	151,065
1.61-8	12/18/2002	152,347
1.61-16	2/3/78	150,305
1.61-21	6/15/2007	152,867

Col. 1 Regs. §	Col. 2 Pub. Date	Col. 3 Preamble ¶
1.61-21	10/9/92	151,421
1.62-1	7/14/81	150,703
1.67-3T	9/3/92	151,413
1.67-3T	9/30/91	151,317
1.67-4	7/27/2007	152,887
1.72-4	4/30/75	150,135
1.72-6	10/18/2006	152,809
1.72-13	4/30/75	150,135
1.72-15	8/20/2007	152,901
1.74-1	1/9/89	151,137
1.74-2	1/9/89	151,137
1.83-3	5/24/2005	152,663
1.83-6	5/24/2005	152,663
1.89(a)-1	3/7/89	151,141
1.89(k)-1	3/7/89	151,141
1.101-2	4/30/75	150,135
1.101-8	12/15/92	151,453
1.102-1	1/9/89	151,137
1.103-8	11/7/85	151,037
1.103-8	8/22/84	150,971
1.103-8	8/20/75	150,243
1.103-10	2/21/86	151,059
1.103-10	2/21/86	151,057
6a.103A-2	4/8/86	151,065
1.105-4	8/20/2007	152,901
1.105-6	8/20/2007	152,901
1.105-11	2/28/83	150,825
601.106	9/20/93	151,541
1.106-1	8/20/2007	152,901
1.106-1	6/15/87	151,085
1.108-7	8/6/2008	153,045
1.108-7	7/18/2003	152,431
1.108-8	10/31/2008	153,069
1.117-0	6/9/88	151,121
1.117-1	6/9/88	151,121
1.117-2	6/9/88	151,121
1.117-3	6/9/88	151,121
1.117-4	6/9/88	151,121
1.117-5	6/9/88	151,121
1.117-6	6/9/88	151,121
1.120-1	4/29/80	150,581
1.120-2	4/29/80	150,581
1.122-1	4/30/75	150,135
1.125-0	8/6/2007	152,897
1.125-1	8/6/2007	152,897
1.125-1	1/10/2001	152,127
1.125-2	8/6/2007	152,897
1.125-2	1/10/2001	152,127
1.125-2	3/7/89	151,141
1.125-5	8/6/2007	152,897
1.125-6	8/6/2007	152,897
1.125-7	8/6/2007	152,897
1.132-5	6/9/2008	153,001
1.141-0	9/26/2006	152,807
1.141-1	9/26/2006	152,807
1.141-6	9/26/2006	152,807
1.141-12	7/21/2003	152,439
1.141-13	9/26/2006	152,807
1.141-15	9/26/2006	152,807
1.141-15	7/21/2003	152,439
1.142(a)(6)-1	5/10/2004	152,527
1.145-2	9/26/2006	152,807
1.147(f)-1	9/9/2008	153,057
1.148-0	9/26/2007	152,909
1.148-3	9/26/2007	152,909
1.148-4	9/26/2007	152,909
1.148-5	9/26/2007	152,909
1.148-8	9/26/2007	152,909
1.148-11	9/26/2007	152,909
1.150-1	4/10/2002	152,255
1.152-2	11/15/2000	152,101
1.162-3	3/10/2008	152,973
1.162-4	3/10/2008	152,973
1.162-6	3/10/2008	152,973
1.162-24	3/31/2008	152,983
1.162-26	6/15/87	151,085
1.162-30	2/26/2004	152,497
5f.163-1	1/21/93	151,499
5f.163-1	4/8/86	151,065
1.163-4	4/8/86	151,065
1.163-5T	5/19/88	151,117
1.163(j)-0	6/18/91	151,279
1.163(j)-1	6/18/91	151,279
1.163(j)-2	6/18/91	151,279
1.163(j)-3	6/18/91	151,279
1.163(j)-4	6/18/91	151,279
1.163(j)-5	6/18/91	151,279
1.163(j)-6	6/18/91	151,279
1.163(j)-7	6/18/91	151,279
1.163(j)-8	6/18/91	151,279
1.163(j)-9	6/18/91	151,279
1.163(j)-10	6/18/91	151,279
1.166-4	12/19/83	150,911
1.167(a)-11	12/20/85	151,041
1.167(a)-11	2/16/84	150,941
1.167(a)-13	3/15/94	151,563
1.167(n)-0	5/31/2002	152,279
1.167(n)-1	5/31/2002	152,279
1.167(n)-2	5/31/2002	152,279
1.167(n)-3	5/31/2002	152,279
1.167(n)-4	5/31/2002	152,279
1.167(n)-5	5/31/2002	152,279
1.167(n)-6	5/31/2002	152,279
1.167(n)-7	5/31/2002	152,279
1.168-1	2/16/84	150,941
1.168-2	2/16/84	150,941
1.168-3	2/16/84	150,941
1.168-4	2/16/84	150,941
1.168-5	2/16/84	150,941
1.168-6	2/16/84	150,941
1.170-0	8/7/2008	153,047
1.170-2	8/7/2008	153,047
1.170A-9	9/9/2008	153,055
1.170A-13	8/7/2008	153,047
1.170A-13	5/5/88	151,114
1.170A-15	8/7/2008	153,047
1.170A-16	8/7/2008	153,047
1.170A-17	8/7/2008	153,047
1.170A-18	8/7/2008	153,047
1.178-1	2/16/84	150,941
1.179B-1	6/27/2008	153,015
1.179C-1	7/9/2008	153,025
1.181-0	2/9/2007	152,835
1.181-1	2/9/2007	152,835
1.181-2	2/9/2007	152,835
1.181-3	2/9/2007	152,835
1.181-4	2/9/2007	152,835
1.181-5	2/9/2007	152,835

Col. 1 Regs. §	Col. 2 Pub. Date	Col. 3 Preamble ¶
1.181-6	2/9/2007	152,835
1.183-1	8/7/80	150,615
1.195-1	7/8/2008	153,023
1.196-1	9/21/87	151,105
1.197-2	4/10/2006	152,747
1.199-0	11/4/2005	152,713
1.199-1	11/4/2005	152,713
1.199-2	11/4/2005	152,713
1.199-3	11/4/2005	152,713
1.199-4	11/4/2005	152,713
1.199-5	11/4/2005	152,713
1.199-6	11/4/2005	152,713
1.199-7	11/4/2005	152,713
1.199-8	11/4/2005	152,713
601.201	1/17/2001	152,147
1.212-1	2/26/2004	152,497
1.212-1	8/7/80	150,615
1.219-1	7/14/81	150,703
1.219-2	7/14/81	150,703
1.219-3	7/14/81	150,703
1.219(a)-1	1/23/84	150,933
1.219(a)-2	1/23/84	150,933
1.219(a)-3	1/23/84	150,933
1.219(a)-4	1/23/84	150,933
1.219(a)-5	1/23/84	150,933
1.219(a)-6	1/23/84	150,933
1.220-1	7/14/81	150,703
1.248-1	7/8/2008	153,023
1.249-1	4/8/86	151,065
1.262-1	8/7/80	150,615
1.263(a)-0	3/10/2008	152,973
1.263(a)-1	3/10/2008	152,973
1.263(a)-2	3/10/2008	152,973
1.263(a)-3	3/10/2008	152,973
1.263(g)-1	1/18/2001	152,157
1.263(g)-2	1/18/2001	152,157
1.263(g)-3	1/18/2001	152,157
1.263(g)-4	1/18/2001	152,157
1.263(g)-5	1/18/2001	152,157
1.263A-1	3/10/2008	152,973
1.263A-2	6/14/2001	152,181
1.263A-3	6/14/2001	152,181
1.265-2	5/7/2004	152,525
1.269A-1	3/31/83	150,847
1.274-1	1/9/89	151,137
1.274-3	1/9/89	151,137
1.274-5	6/9/2008	153,001
1.274-5T	6/9/2008	153,001
1.274-8	1/9/89	151,137
1.274-9	1/9/89	151,137
1.274-9	6/15/2007	152,867
1.274-10	6/15/2007	152,867
1.280A-1	7/21/83	150,873
1.280A-1	8/7/80	150,615
1.280A-2	7/21/83	150,873
1.280A-2	8/7/80	150,615
1.280A-3	7/21/83	150,873
1.280A-3	8/7/80	150,615
1.280F-6	6/9/2008	153,001
1.280G-1	5/5/89	151,143
1.312-10	11/15/2000	152,099
1.312-15	9/21/87	151,105
1.332-2	3/10/2005	152,637
1.336-0	9/9/2008	153,053
1.336-1	9/9/2008	153,053
1.336-2	9/9/2008	153,053
1.336-3	9/9/2008	153,053
1.336-4	9/9/2008	153,053
1.336-5	9/9/2008	153,053
1.337(d)-2	3/18/2004	152,509
1.337(d)-2	5/31/2002	152,283
1.337(d)-3	12/15/92	151,455
1.338-0	9/9/2008	153,053
1.338-1	9/9/2008	153,053
1.338-1	4/10/2006	152,747
1.338-5	9/9/2008	153,053
1.338-6	9/16/2004	152,597
1.338-11	4/10/2006	152,747
1.346-1	1/21/77	150,249
1.351-1	3/10/2005	152,637
1.355-0	5/8/2007	152,855
1.355-1	5/8/2007	152,855
1.355-2	12/15/2008	153,077
1.355-3	5/8/2007	152,855
1.355-8	11/22/2004	152,605
1.358-2	10/23/2006	152,815
1.358-6	8/20/2008	153,051
1.362-3	10/23/2006	152,815
1.362-4	10/23/2006	152,815
1.367(a)-1	1/5/2009	153,087
1.367(a)-1T	8/20/2008	153,051
1.367(a)-1T	8/29/2005	152,697
1.367(a)-2	7/3/2008	153,021
1.367(a)-3	8/20/2008	153,051
1.367(a)-3	5/27/2008	152,999
1.367(a)-3	2/5/2007	152,833
1.367(a)-4	7/3/2008	153,021
1.367(a)-5	7/3/2008	153,021
1.367(a)-7	8/20/2008	153,051
1.367(a)-8	2/5/2007	152,833
1.367(b)-4	8/20/2008	153,051
1.367(b)-5	11/15/2000	152,099
1.367(b)-6	8/20/2008	153,051
1.367(b)-6	6/19/98	151,865
1.367(b)-8	11/15/2000	152,099
1.367(b)-14	5/27/2008	152,999
1.367(e)-1	11/15/2000	152,099
1.367(e)-2T	4/1/92	151,369
1.368-1	3/20/2007	152,843
1.368-2	3/1/2007	152,837
1.386-2	12/19/2006	152,825
1.368-2	3/10/2005	152,637
1.368-2	8/12/2004	152,569
1.381(a)-1	11/16/2007	152,935
1.381(c)(4)-1	11/16/2007	152,935
1.381(c)(5)-1	11/16/2007	152,935
1.382-7	6/14/2007	152,865
1.401-1	8/20/2007	152,901
1.401(a)-13	10/09/2008	153,065
1.401(a)-20	10/09/2008	153,065
1.401(a)(4)-3	12/11/2002	152,345
1.401(a)(4)-9	12/11/2002	152,345
1.401(a)(9)-1	7/10/2008	153,027
1.401(a)(9)-1	12/30/97	151,831
1.401(a)(6)-1	7/10/2008	153,027
1.401(a)(31)-1	9/19/96	151,753
1.401(a)(35)-1	1/3/2008	152,955
1.401(k)-0	11/8/2007	152,927

Col. 1 Regs. §	Col. 2 Pub. Date	Col. 3 Preamble ¶
1.401(k)-1	11/8/2007	152,927
1.401(k)-2	11/8/2007	152,927
1.401(k)-3	11/8/2007	152,927
1.401(k)-6	11/8/2007	152,927
1.401(m)-0	11/8/2007	152,927
1.401(m)-1	11/8/2007	152,927
1.401(m)-2	11/8/2007	152,927
1.401(m)-3	11/8/2007	152,927
1.402(a)-1	8/20/2007	152,901
1.402(a)-1	5/31/79	150,475
1.402(a)-1	4/30/75	150,135
1.402(c)-2	11/8/2007	152,927
1.402(c)-2	8/20/2007	152,901
1.402(c)-2	9/19/96	151,753
1.402(e)-2	5/31/79	150,475
1.402(e)-2	4/30/75	150,135
1.402(e)-3	4/30/75	150,135
1.402(e)-14	5/31/79	150,475
11.402(e)(4)(B)-1	4/30/75	150,135
1.402(f)-1	10/09/2008	153,065
1.403(a)-1	8/20/2007	152,901
1.403(a)-1	4/30/75	150,135
1.403(a)-2	5/31/79	150,475
1.403(a)-2	4/30/75	150,135
1.403(b)-6	7/10/2008	153,027
1.403(b)-6	8/20/2007	152,901
1.404(h)-1	7/14/81	150,703
1.404A-0	5/7/93	151,519
1.404A-1	5/7/93	151,519
1.404A-2	5/7/93	151,519
1.404A-3	5/7/93	151,519
1.404A-4	5/7/93	151,519
1.404A-5	5/7/93	151,519
1.404A-6	5/7/93	151,519
1.404A-7	5/7/93	151,519
1.405-3	4/30/75	150,135
1.408-2	7/22/2004	152,545
1.408-2	1/23/84	150,933
1.408-2	7/14/81	150,703
1.408-3	1/23/84	150,933
1.408-3	7/14/81	150,703
1.408-4	7/14/81	150,703
1.408-5	11/16/84	151,003
1.408-6	7/14/81	150,703
1.408-7	7/14/81	150,703
1.408-8	7/14/81	150,703
1.408-9	7/14/81	150,703
1.408-10	1/23/84	150,933
1.409-1	4/8/86	151,065
1.409-1	7/14/81	150,703
1.409(p)-1	12/17/2004	152,609
1.409A-0	12/08/2008	153,075
1.409A-4	12/08/2008	153,075
1.410(a)-3T (also issued as temporary regs)	1/6/88	See Vol. 2
1.410(a)-4A	4/11/88	151,113
1.411(a)-1	4/11/88	151,113
1.411(a)-4	11/8/2007	152,927
1.411(a)-7	4/11/88	151,113
1.411(a)-11	10/09/2008	153,065
1.411(a)(13)-1	12/28/2007	152,945
1.411(b)-1	6/18/2008	153,009

Col. 1 Regs. §	Col. 2 Pub. Date	Col. 3 Preamble ¶
1.411(b)-2	12/11/2002	152,345
1.411(b)-2	4/11/88	151,113
1.411(b)(5)-1	12/28/2007	152,945
1.411(c)-1	12/22/95	151,705
1.411(c)-1	4/11/88	151,113
1.411(d)-1	4/9/80	150,571
1.411(d)-3	3/18/2008	152,975
1.412(a)-1	12/1/82	150,781
1.412(b)-1	12/1/82	150,781
1.412(b)-3	12/1/82	150,781
1.412(b)-4	12/1/82	150,781
1.412(c)(2)-2	12/1/82	150,781
1.412(c)(4)-1	12/1/82	150,781
1.412(c)(5)-1	12/1/82	150,781
1.412(c)(6)-1	12/1/82	150,781
1.412(c)(7)-1	12/1/82	150,781
1.412(c)(8)-1	12/1/82	150,781
1.412(c)(9)-1	12/1/82	150,781
1.412(c)(10)-1	12/1/82	150,781
11.412(c)-7	12/1/82	150,781
11.412(c)-11	12/1/82	150,781
11.412(c)-12	12/1/82	150,781
1.412(g)-1	12/1/82	150,781
1.413-1	12/1/82	150,781
1.413-2	12/1/82	150,781
1.414(m)-1	2/28/83	150,825
1.414(m)-2	2/28/83	150,825
1.414(m)-3	2/28/83	150,825
1.414(m)-4	2/28/83	150,825
1.414(o)-1	8/27/87	151,095
1.414(w)-1	11/8/2007	152,927
1.415-1	1/23/84	150,933
1.415-2	1/23/84	150,933
1.415-6	1/23/84	150,933
1.415-7	1/23/84	150,933
1.415-8	2/28/83	150,825
1.415-8	7/14/81	150,703
1.417(e)-1	10/09/2008	153,065
1.421-1	7/29/2008	153,039
1.422-2	7/29/2008	153,039
1.422-5	7/29/2008	153,039
1.423-1	7/29/2008	153,039
1.423-2	7/29/2008	153,039
1.430(a)-1	4/15/2008	152,985
1.430(d)-1	12/31/2007	152,949
1.430(f)-1	8/31/2007	152,907
1.430(g)-1	12/31/2007	152,949
1.430(h)(2)-1	12/31/2007	152,949
1.430(i)-1	12/31/2007	152,949
1.430(j)-1	4/15/2008	152,985
1.432(a)-1	3/18/2008	152,975
1.432(b)-1	3/18/2008	152,975
1.436-1	8/31/2007	152,907
1.441-1	2/3/87	151,083
1.441-1T	1/5/93	151,485
1.442-1	1/5/93	151,485
1.442-2T	1/5/93	151,485
1.446-1	11/16/2007	152,935
1.446-1	1/26/99	151,953
1.446-2	12/22/92	151,457
1.446-3	2/26/2004	152,497
1.451-1	4/8/86	151,065
1.451-2	4/8/86	151,065
1.453-1	5/3/84	150,947

Col. 1 Regs. §	Col. 2 Pub. Date	Col. 3 Preamble ¶
1.454-1	4/8/86	151,065
1.460-3	8/4/2008	153,043
1.460-4	8/4/2008	153,043
1.460-5	8/4/2008	153,043
1.460-6	8/4/2008	153,043
1.465-1	6/5/79	150,479
1.465-2	6/5/79	150,479
1.465-3	6/5/79	150,479
1.465-4	6/5/79	150,479
1.465-5	6/5/79	150,479
1.465-6	6/5/79	150,479
1.465-7	6/5/79	150,479
1.465-9	6/5/79	150,479
1.465-10	6/5/79	150,479
1.465-11	6/5/79	150,479
1.465-12	6/5/79	150,479
1.465-13	6/5/79	150,479
1.465-22	6/5/79	150,479
1.465-23	6/5/79	150,479
1.465-24	6/5/79	150,479
1.465-25	6/5/79	150,479
1.465-26	6/5/79	150,479
1.465-38	6/5/79	150,479
1.465-39	6/5/79	150,479
1.465-41	6/5/79	150,479
1.465-42	6/5/79	150,479
1.465-43	6/5/79	150,479
1.465-44	6/5/79	150,479
1.465-45	6/5/79	150,479
1.465-66	6/5/79	150,479
1.465-67	6/5/79	150,479
1.465-68	6/5/79	150,479
1.465-69	6/5/79	150,479
1.465-75	6/5/79	150,479
1.465-76	6/5/79	150,479
1.465-77	6/5/79	150,479
1.465-78	6/5/79	150,479
1.465-79	6/5/79	150,479
1.465-95	6/5/79	150,479
1.468A-0	12/31/2007	152,947
1.468A-1	12/31/2007	152,947
1.468A-2	12/31/2007	152,947
1.468A-3	12/31/2007	152,947
1.468A-4	12/31/2007	152,947
1.468A-5	12/31/2007	152,947
1.468A-6	12/31/2007	152,947
1.468A-7	12/31/2007	152,947
1.468A-8	12/31/2007	152,947
1.468A-9	12/31/2007	152,947
1.468B-0	2/7/2006	152,739
1.468B-6	2/7/2006	152,739
1.468B-8	2/1/99	151,955
1.471-12	1/26/99	151,953
1.472-2	2/10/83	150,819
1.475(a)-1	1/4/95	151,647
1.475(a)-2	1/4/95	151,647
1.475(b)-3	1/4/95	151,647
1.475(c)-1	1/26/99	151,953
1.475(c)-2	1/26/99	151,953
1.475(e)-1	1/26/99	151,953
1.475(f)-1	1/26/99	151,953
1.475(f)-2	1/26/99	151,953
1.475(g)-1	1/26/99	151,953
1.475(g)-2	3/6/98	151,855
1.482-0	1/5/2009	153,087
1.482-0	8/4/2006	152,783
1.482-0	8/29/2005	152,697
1.482-0	9/10/2003	152,461
1.482-0	3/6/98	151,855
1.482-1	1/5/2009	153,087
1.482-1	8/4/2006	152,783
1.482-1	8/29/2005	152,697
1.482-1	9/10/2003	152,461
1.482-1	3/6/98	151,855
1.482-2	1/5/2009	153,087
1.482-2	8/4/2006	152,783
1.482-2	9/10/2003	152,461
1.482-2	3/6/98	151,855
1.482-4	1/5/2009	153,087
1.482-4	8/4/2006	152,783
1.482-4	8/29/2005	152,697
1.482-4	9/10/2003	152,461
1.482-5	8/29/2005	152,697
1.482-6	8/4/2006	152,783
1.482-6	9/10/2003	152,461
1.482-7	1/5/2009	153,087
1.482-7	8/29/2005	152,697
1.482-8	1/5/2009	153,087
1.482-8	8/4/2006	152,783
1.482-8	8/29/2005	152,697
1.482-8	3/6/98	151,855
1.482-9	1/5/2009	153,087
1.482-9	8/4/2006	152,783
1.482-9	9/10/2003	152,461
1.501(c)(9)-2	8/7/92	151,401
1.501(c)(13)-1	11/29/78	150,405
1.501(c)(20)-1	4/29/80	150,581
1.507-2	9/9/2008	153,055
1.509(a)-3	9/9/2008	153,055
1.529-0	8/24/98	151,877
1.529-1	8/24/98	151,877
1.529-2	8/24/98	151,877
1.529-3	8/24/98	151,877
1.529-4	8/24/98	151,877
1.529-5	8/24/98	151,877
1.529-6	8/24/98	151,877
1.563-3	1/5/93	151,485
1.563-4	1/5/93	151,485
1.581-2	12/19/83	150,911
1.582-1	4/8/86	151,065
1.591-1	12/19/83	150,911
1.593-1	12/19/83	150,911
1.593-2	12/19/83	150,911
1.593-3	12/19/83	150,911
1.593-4	12/19/83	150,911
1.593-5	12/19/83	150,911
1.593-6	12/19/83	150,911
1.593-6A	12/19/83	150,911
1.593-7	12/19/83	150,911
1.593-8	12/19/83	150,911
1.593-9	12/19/83	150,911
1.593-10	12/19/83	150,911
1.593-11	12/19/83	150,911
1.593-12	7/12/2000	152,075
1.593-13	7/12/2000	152,075
1.593-14	7/12/2000	152,075
1.612-3	2/8/2000	152,051
1.613A-3	10/3/84	150,991

Col. 1 Regs. §	Col. 2 Pub. Date	Col. 3 Preamble ¶
1.636-1	4/8/86	151,065
1.642(c)-1	5/5/88	151,114
1.642(c)-2	5/5/88	151,114
1.642(c)-3	6/18/2008	153,011
1.643(a)-5	6/18/2008	153,011
1.652(b)-1	4/30/75	150,135
1.664-1	12/19/75	150,177
1.671-1	9/27/96	151,755
1.671-2	9/27/96	151,755
1.704-1	5/24/2005	152,663
1.704-1	1/22/2003	152,359
1.704-1	3/9/83	150,829
1.704-3	5/19/2008	152,997
1.704-3	8/22/2007	152,903
1.704-3	1/22/2003	152,359
1.704-4	8/22/2007	152,903
1.705-1	10/23/2006	152,815
1.705-1	9/21/87	151,105
1.706-1	8/4/2006	152,781
1.706-3	5/24/2005	152,663
1.707-0	11/26/2004	152,607
1.707-1	5/24/2005	152,663
1.707-3	11/26/2004	152,607
1.707-5	11/26/2004	152,607
1.707-6	11/26/2004	152,607
1.707-7	11/26/2004	152,607
1.707-8	11/26/2004	152,607
1.707-9	11/26/2004	152,607
1.709-1	7/8/2008	153,023
1.721-1	10/31/2008	153,069
1.721-1	5/24/2005	152,663
1.721-2	1/22/2003	152,359
1.737-1	8/22/2007	152,903
1.737-2	8/22/2007	152,903
1.737-5	8/22/2007	152,903
1.752-3	11/26/2004	152,607
1.761-1	5/24/2005	152,663
1.761-3	1/22/2003	152,359
1.801-4	1/2/97	151,777
1.818-3	4/8/86	151,065
1.846-2	4/10/2006	152,747
1.846-4	4/10/2006	152,747
1.856-1	12/7/72	150,099
1.856-2	12/7/72	150,099
1.856-3	12/7/72	150,099
1.856-4	12/7/72	150,099
1.860A-0	11/9/2007	152,929
1.860A-1	11/9/2007	152,929
1.860E-1	2/7/2000	152,047
1.860F-4	8/10/2004	152,563
1.860F-4	9/30/91	151,317
1.860G-2	11/9/2007	152,929
1.860H-0	2/7/2000	152,047
1.860H-1	2/7/2000	152,047
1.860H-2	2/7/2000	152,047
1.860H-3	2/7/2000	152,047
1.860H-4	2/7/2000	152,047
1.860H-5	2/7/2000	152,047
1.860H-6	2/7/2000	152,047
1.860I-1	2/7/2000	152,047
1.860I-2	2/7/2000	152,047
1.860J-1	2/7/2000	152,047
1.860L-1	2/7/2000	152,047
1.860L-2	2/7/2000	152,047
1.860L-3	2/7/2000	152,047
1.860L-4	2/7/2000	152,047
1.861-2	4/8/86	151,065
1.861-4	10/17/2007	152,921
1.861-8	8/4/2006	152,783
1.861-9	4/25/2006	152,753
1.861-9T	9/7/2006	152,801
1.861-9T (also issued as temporary regs)	2/7/2000	152,047
1.861-12	4/25/2006	152,753
1.861-17	8/29/2005	152,697
1.863-3	10/10/97	151,855
1.863-7	10/10/97	151,855
1.864-6	10/10/97	151,855
1.864(b)-1	6/12/98	151,863
1.881-3	12/22/2008	153,079
1.882-5	8/17/2006	152,789
1.882-5	3/8/96	151,713
1.883-0	6/25/2007	152,877
1.883-1	6/25/2007	152,877
1.883-2	6/25/2007	152,877
1.883-3	6/25/2007	152,877
1.883-4	6/25/2007	152,877
1.883-5	6/25/2007	152,877
1.884-1	8/17/2006	152,789
1.884-1	3/8/96	151,713
1.898-0	1/5/93	151,485
1.898-1	1/5/93	151,485
1.898-2	1/5/93	151,485
1.898-3	1/5/93	151,485
1.898-4	6/14/2001	152,177
1.898-4	1/5/93	151,485
1.901-1	7/16/2008	153,031
1.901-2	7/16/2008	153,031
1.901-2	8/4/2006	152,781
1.902-1	4/25/2006	152,753
1.904-0	12/21/2007	152,941
1.904-2	12/21/2007	152,939
1.904-2	4/25/2006	152,753
1.904-4	12/21/2007	152,939
1.904-4	4/25/2006	152,753
1.904-5	12/21/2007	152,939
1.904-5	4/25/2006	152,753
1.904-5	7/13/99	151,985
1.904-7	12/21/2007	152,939
1.904(f)-1	12/21/2007	152,941
1.904(f)-2	12/21/2007	152,941
1.904(f)-7	12/21/2007	152,941
1.904(f)-8	12/21/2007	152,941
1.904(f)-12	12/21/2007	152,939
1.904(f)-12	4/25/2006	152,753
1.904(g)-0	12/21/2007	152,941
1.904(g)-1	12/21/2007	152,941
1.904(g)-2	12/21/2007	152,941
1.904(g)-3	12/21/2007	152,941
1.905-3	11/7/2007	152,925
1.905-4	11/7/2007	152,925
1.905-5	11/7/2007	152,925
1.921-1T	2/3/87	151,083
7.936-1	1/21/86	151,049
1.936-2	1/21/86	151,049
1.936-3	1/21/86	151,049
1.936-3A	1/21/86	151,049

Col. 1 Regs. §	Col. 2 Pub. Date	Col. 3 Preamble ¶
1.936-10 (also issued as temporary regs)	5/13/91	151,269
1.952-2	7/1/92	151,393
1.953-0	4/17/91	151,253
1.953-1	4/17/91	151,253
1.953-2	4/17/91	151,253
1.953-3	4/17/91	151,253
1.953-4	4/17/91	151,253
1.953-5	4/17/91	151,253
1.953-6	4/17/91	151,253
1.953-7	4/17/91	151,253
1.954-0	7/13/99	151,985
1.954-1	7/13/99	151,985
1.954-2	7/3/2008	153,021
1.954-2	7/13/99	151,985
1.954-3	12/29/2008	153,083
1.954-9	7/13/99	151,985
1.956-1	6/24/2008	153,013
1.956-2	7/3/2008	153,021
1.959-1	8/29/2006	152,795
1.959-2	8/29/2006	152,795
1.959-3	8/29/2006	152,795
1.959-4	8/29/2006	152,795
1.961-1	8/29/2006	152,795
1.961-2	8/29/2006	152,795
1.961-3	8/29/2006	152,795
1.961-4	8/29/2006	152,795
1.964-1	4/25/2006	152,753
1.964-1	7/1/92	151,393
1.964-1	4/17/91	151,253
1.985-1	9/7/2006	152,801
1.985-5	9/7/2006	152,801
1.987-1	9/7/2006	152,801
1.987-2	9/7/2006	152,801
1.987-3	9/7/2006	152,801
1.987-4	9/7/2006	152,801
1.987-5	9/7/2006	152,801
1.987-6	9/7/2006	152,801
1.987-7	9/7/2006	152,801
1.987-8	9/7/2006	152,801
1.987-9	9/7/2006	152,801
1.987-10	9/7/2006	152,801
1.987-11	9/7/2006	152,801
1.988-1	9/7/2006	152,801
1.988-1	1/13/2000	152,031
1.988-4	9/7/2006	152,801
1.989(a)-1	9/7/2006	152,801
1.989(c)-1	9/7/2006	152,801
1.991-1	2/3/87	151,083
1.992-1	2/3/87	151,083
1.992-2	2/3/87	151,083
1.993-1	4/8/86	151,065
1.995-2	2/3/87	151,083
1.995-2A	2/3/87	151,083
1.995-8	2/3/87	151,083
1.995(f)-1	2/3/87	151,083
1.996-1	2/3/87	151,083
1.996-9	2/3/87	151,083
1.999-1	3/1/77	150,253
1.1001-1	10/18/2006	152,809
1.1012-2	4/8/86	151,065
1.1016-3	2/16/84	150,941
1.1016-4	2/16/84	150,941
1.1016-5	4/8/86	151,065
1.1017-1	7/18/2002	152,431
1.1031(k)-1	2/7/2006	152,739
1.1037-1	4/8/86	151,065
1.1058-1	7/26/83	150,875
1.1058-2	7/26/83	150,875
1.1060-1	9/16/2004	152,597
1.1092(d)-1	1/18/2001	152,157
1.1092(d)-2	5/2/95	151,667
1.1221-3	2/8/2008	152,961
1.1223-2	7/26/83	150,875
1.1232-1	4/8/86	151,065
1.1232-2	4/8/86	151,065
1.1232-3	4/8/86	151,065
1.1232-3A	4/8/86	151,065
1.1232-3A	7/5/79	150,485
1.1234A-1	2/26/2004	152,497
1.1248-1	8/20/2008	153,051
1.1248-1	4/17/91	151,253
1.1248-3	8/20/2008	153,051
1.1248-6	8/20/2008	153,051
1.1248-7	8/20/2008	153,051
1.1248-8	8/20/2008	153,051
1.1248(f)-1	8/20/2008	153,051
1.1248(f)-2	8/20/2008	153,051
1.1248(f)-3	8/20/2008	153,051
1.1271-0	8/25/2004	152,589
1.1272-1	1/22/2003	152,359
1.1273-2	1/22/2003	152,359
1.1275-2	8/25/2004	152,589
1.1275-4	1/22/2003	152,359
1.1291-0T	4/28/95	151,663
1.1291-1	4/1/92	151,369
1.1291-2	4/1/92	
1.1291-3	4/1/92	151,369
1.1291-4	4/1/92	151,369
1.1291-5	4/1/92	151,369
1.1291-6	4/1/92	151,369
1.1291-7	4/1/92	151,369
1.1293-1	4/1/92	151,369
1.1293-2	12/24/96	151,773
1.1295-1	4/1/92	151,369
1.1295-2	12/24/96	151,773
1.1296-4	4/28/95	151,663
1.1296-6	4/28/95	151,663
1.1297-4	9/27/96	151,755
1.1301-1	7/22/2008	153,037
1.1361-0	9/28/2007	152,915
1.1361-1	9/28/2007	152,915
1.1361-4	9/28/2007	152,915
1.1361-6	9/28/2007	152,915
1.1362-0	9/28/2007	152,915
1.1362-4	9/28/2007	152,915
1.1363-1	8/24/2006	152,793
1.1366-0	9/28/2007	152,915
1.1366-2	9/28/2007	152,915
1.1366-5	9/28/2007	152,915
1.1367-1	10/23/2006	152,815
1.1397E-1	7/16/2007	152,883
1.1402(a)-2	1/13/97	151,791
1.1441-3	10/17/2007	152,919
1.1502-1	12/30/92	151,475
1.1502-2	12/30/92	151,475
1.1502-5	12/30/92	151,475
1.1502-9	12/21/2007	152,941

Col. 1 Regs. §	Col. 2 Pub. Date	Col. 3 Preamble ¶	Col. 1 Regs. §	Col. 2 Pub. Date	Col. 3 Preamble ¶
1.1502-12	8/29/2006	152,795	31.3402(t)-1	12/05/2008	153,073
1.1502-13	3/7/2008	152,969	31.3402(t)-2	12/05/2008	153,073
1.1502-13	2/25/2008	152,965	31.3402(t)-3	12/05/2008	153,073
1.1502-13	2/22/2005	152,629	31.3402(t)-4	12/05/2008	153,073
1.1502-13	5/7/2004	152,525	31.3402(t)-5	12/05/2008	153,073
1.1502-20	8/26/2004	152,591	31.3402(t)-6	12/05/2008	153,073
1.1502-20	5/7/2003	152,381	31.3402(t)-7	12/05/2008	153,073
1.1502-20	5/31/2002	152,283	31.3406(g)-1	7/13/2007	152,881
1.1502-20	3/12/2002	152,251	31.3406(g)-1	8/2/2002	152,317
1.1502-21	3/14/2003	152,369	31.3406(g)-2	12/05/2008	153,073
1.1502-21	5/31/2002	152,281	31.3508-1	1/7/86	151,045
1.1502-32	4/10/2007	152,847	31.3509-1	1/7/86	151,045
1.1502-32	8/29/2006	152,795	48.4001-1	1/2/91	151,211
1.1502-32	8/26/2004	152,591	48.4002-1	1/2/91	151,211
1.1502-32	8/18/2004	152,581	48.4003-1	1/2/91	151,211
1.1502-32	5/7/2003	152,381	48.4004-1	1/2/91	151,211
1.1502-32	3/14/2003	152,369	48.4004-2	1/2/91	151,211
1.1502-32	3/12/2002	152,251	48.4004-3	1/2/91	151,211
1.1502-33	12/30/92	151,475	48.4004-4	1/2/91	151,211
1.1502-35	4/10/2007	152,847	48.4006-1	1/2/91	151,211
1.1502-35	3/18/2004	152,509	48.4007-1	1/2/91	151,211
1.1502-35	3/14/2003	152,369	48.4011-1	1/2/91	151,211
1.1502-43	12/22/2006	152,827	48.4011-2	1/2/91	151,211
1.1502-47	12/22/2006	152,827	48.4011-3	1/2/91	151,211
1.1502-55	12/30/92	151,475	48.4011-4	1/2/91	151,211
1.1502-80	3/18/2004	152,509	48.4011-5	1/2/91	151,211
1.1502-80	11/14/2001	152,195	48.4011-6	1/2/91	151,211
1.1552-1	12/30/92	151,475	48.4011-7	1/2/91	151,211
1.1561-0	12/26/2007	152,943	48.4011-8	1/2/91	151,211
1.1561-1	12/22/2006	152,827	48.4012-1	1/2/91	151,211
1.1561-2	12/26/2007	152,943	48.4041-0	7/29/2008	153,041
1.1561-2	12/22/2006	152,827	48.4041-18	7/29/2008	153,041
1.1561-3	12/22/2006	152,827	48.4041-19	7/29/2008	153,041
1.1563-1	12/26/2007	152,943	48.4041-20	7/29/2008	153,041
1.1563-1	12/22/2006	152,827	48.4052-1	7/1/98	151,869
1.1563-1	5/30/2006	152,759	48.4081-1	7/29/2008	153,041
20.2031-4	8/20/85	151,027	48.4081-1	7/1/98	151,869
20.2032-1	4/25/2008	152,993	48.4081-1	1/5/83	150,797
20.2036-2	8/3/83	150,877	48.4081-2	7/29/2008	153,041
20.2039-2	1/23/84	150,933	48.4081-3	7/29/2008	153,041
20.2039-4	1/23/84	150,933	48.4081-6	7/29/2008	153,041
20.2051-1	4/23/2007	152,851	48.4082-1	4/26/2005	152,651
20.2053-1	4/23/2007	152,851	48.4082-1	1/5/83	150,797
20.2053-3	4/23/2007	152,851	48.4082-4	7/29/2008	153,041
20.2053-4	4/23/2007	152,851	48.4083-1	1/5/83	150,797
20.2053-6	4/23/2007	152,851	48.4083-2	1/5/83	150,797
20.2053-9	4/23/2007	152,851	48.4084-1	1/5/83	150,797
20.2053-10	4/23/2007	152,851	48.4091-1	1/5/83	150,797
20.2055-2	12/19/75	150,177	48.4091-2	1/5/83	150,797
20.2056(b)-10	2/18/97	151,799	48.4091-3	1/5/83	150,797
25.2503-5	7/14/81	150,703	48.4091-4	1/5/83	150,797
25.2512-4	4/8/86	151,065	48.4091-5	1/5/83	150,797
25.2512-4	8/20/85	151,027	48.4092-1	1/5/83	150,797
25.2512-8	4/8/86	151,065	48.4093-1	1/5/83	150,797
25.2517-1	1/23/84	150,933	48.4101-1	7/29/2008	153,041
26.2600-1	8/2/2007	152,895	48.4101-1	4/26/2005	152,651
26.2642-6	8/2/2007	152,895	48.4101-1	1/5/83	150,797
26.2642-7	4/17/2008	152,987	48.4102-1	1/5/83	150,797
26.2654-1	8/2/2007	152,895	49.4252-0	4/1/2003	152,371
31.3121(a)(5)-1	7/14/81	150,703	53.4965-1	7/6/2007	152,879
31.3121(s)-1	8/4/2006	152,783	53.4965-2	7/6/2007	152,879
31.3121(s)-1	9/10/2003	152,461	53.4965-3	7/6/2007	152,879
31.3306(b)(5)-1	7/14/81	150,703	53.4965-4	7/6/2007	152,879
31.3402(t)-0	12/05/2008	153,073	53.4965-5	7/6/2007	152,879

Col. 1 Regs. §	Col. 2 Pub. Date	Col. 3 Preamble ¶
53.4965-6	7/6/2007	152,879
53.4965-7	7/6/2007	152,879
53.4965-8	7/6/2007	152,879
53.4965-9	7/6/2007	152,879
54.4971-1	12/1/82	150,781
54.4971-2	12/1/82	150,781
54.4971-3	12/1/82	150,781
54.4971(c)-1	4/15/2008	152,985
54.4973-1	7/14/81	150,703
54.4974-1	7/14/81	150,703
54.4979-1	11/8/2007	152,927
54.4980B-0	7/16/2008	153,033
54.4980B-2	7/16/2008	153,033
54.4980D-1	7/16/2008	153,033
54.4980E-1	7/16/2008	153,033
54.4980F-1	3/21/2008	152,977
54.4980G-1	7/16/2008	153,033
54.4980G-3	7/16/2008	153,033
54.4980G-4	7/16/2008	153,033
54.4980G-6	7/16/2008	153,033
54.4980G-7	7/16/2008	153,033
51.4989-1	9/30/86	151,075
51.4989-1	9/25/86	151,073
51.4991-1	1/20/83	150,815
51.4993-1	9/10/84	150,989
51.4993-2	9/10/84	150,989
51.4993-3	9/10/84	150,989
51.4993-4	9/10/84	150,989
51.4994-1	1/20/83	
51.4995-2	1/20/83	150,815
51.4996-1	9/30/86	151,075
51.4996-1	9/25/86	151,073
51.4996-3	9/25/86	151,073
51.4996-4	9/25/86	151,073
51.4996-5	9/30/86	151,075
54.6011-1	7/6/2007	152,879
1.6011-2	2/3/87	151,083
1.6011-4	9/26/2007	152,911
31.6011(a)-1	1/3/2006	152,731
31.6011(a)-4	12/05/2008	153,073
31.6011(a)-4	1/3/2006	152,731
31.6011(a)-1	12/29/2008	153,085
31.6011(a)-1	1/3/2006	152,731
31.6011(a)-4	12/29/2008	153,085
301.6011(g)-1	7/6/2007	152,879
1.6033-2	9/9/2008	153,055
1.6033-5	7/6/2007	152,879
301.6033-5	7/6/2007	152,879
1.6033-6	11/15/2007	152,933
1.6038A-3	8/4/2006	152,783
1.6038A-3	9/10/2003	152,461
1.6038B-1	8/20/2008	153,051
1.6039-1	7/17/2008	153,035
1.6039-2	7/17/2008	153,035
301.6039E-1	12/24/92	151,471
1.6039I-1	11/13/2007	152,931
1.6041A-1	1/7/86	151,045
1.6043-3	9/9/2008	153,055
1.6043-4	12/30/2003	152,483
1.6045-1	4/8/86	151,065
1.6045-3	12/30/2003	152,483
1.6045-4	11/29/2007	152,937
1.6046-1	4/17/91	151,253
1.6049-4	8/2/2002	152,317
1.6049-4	4/8/86	151,065
1.6049-5	4/8/86	151,065
1.6049-6	8/2/2002	152,317
1.6049-6	4/8/86	151,065
1.6049-7	5/19/99	151,971
1.6049-7	9/30/91	151,317
1.6049-8	8/2/2002	152,317
1.6050P-0	11/10/2008	153,071
1.6050P-1	11/10/2008	153,071
1.6050S-2	2/14/2001	152,165
31.6051-5	12/05/2008	153,073
53.6071-1	7/6/2007	152,879
31.6071(a)-1	12/05/2008	153,073
31.6071(a)-1	9/27/90	151,187
1.6081-2	7/1/2008	153,017
1.6081-6	7/1/2008	153,017
54.6081-1	7/1/2008	153,017
301.6103(j)(1)-1	12/31/2007	152,953
301.6103(j)(1)-1	3/11/2005	152,641
301.6103(n)-1	1/3/89	151,135
301.6103(n)-2	3/25/2008	152,981
301.6103(p)(4)-1	2/24/2006	152,743
301.6103(p)(7)-1	2/24/2006	152,743
301.6104(a)-1	8/14/2007	152,899
301.6109-3	8/31/92	151,411
301.6110-1	8/14/2007	152,899
301.6111-3	9/26/2007	152,911
301.6114-1	4/27/92	151,379
301.6159-0	3/5/2007	152,839
301.6159-1	3/5/2007	152,839
1.6164-4	3/26/84	150,943
1.6164-8	3/26/84	150,943
31.6205-1	12/10/92	151,449
31.6302-0	12/29/2008	153,085
31.6302-1	12/29/2008	153,085
31.6302-1	12/05/2008	153,073
31.6302-1	1/3/2006	152,731
31.6302-1	12/6/2000	152,103
31.6302-4	12/05/2008	153,073
31.6302(c)-1	9/27/90	151,187
40.6302(c)-1	7/29/2008	153,041
40.6302(c)-4	10/19/94	151,609
40.6302(c)-5 (also issued as temporary regs)	8/29/95	See Vol. 5
301.6323(b)-1	4/17/2008	152,989
301.6323(c)-2	4/17/2008	152,989
301.6323(f)-1	4/17/2008	152,989
301.6323(g)-1	4/17/2008	152,989
301.6323(h)-1	4/17/2008	152,989
301.6331-4	3/5/2007	152,839
301.6404-0	6/21/2007	152,875
301.6404-0	6/21/2007	152,873
301.6404-4	6/21/2007	152,875
301.6404-4	6/21/2007	152,873
1.6411-2	8/27/2007	152,905
1.6411-3	8/27/2007	152,905
48.6426-1	7/29/2008	153,041
48.6426-2	7/29/2008	153,041
48.6426-3	7/29/2008	153,041
48.6426-4	7/29/2008	153,041
48.6426-5	7/29/2008	153,041
48.6426-6	7/29/2008	153,041
48.6426-7	7/29/2008	153,041

Col. 1 Regs. §	Col. 2 Pub. Date	Col. 3 Preamble ¶
48.6427-8	7/29/2008	153,041
48.6427-10 (also issued as temporary regs)	7/1/98	See Vol. 5
48.6427-10	10/19/94	151,609
48.6427-11	7/1/98	151,869
48.6427-12	7/29/2008	153,041
301.6503(j)-1	4/28/2008	152,995
301.6601-1	10/9/84	150,995
301.6611-1	10/9/84	150,995
301.6652-4	1/23/84	150,933
1.6662-0 (also issued as temporary regs)	2/2/94	See Vol. 5
1.6662-5T (also issued as temporary regs)	2/2/94	See Vol. 5
1.6662-6	8/4/2006	152,783
1.6662-6	8/29/2005	152,697
1.6664-0 (also issued as temporary regs)	2/2/94	See Vol. 5
1.6664-4T (also issued as temporary regs)	2/2/94	See Vol. 5
301.6676-2	9/27/90	151,187
31.6682-1	9/27/90	151,187
301.6689-1	11/7/2007	152,925
301.6693-1	7/14/81	150,703
301.6707-1	12/22/2008	153,081
301.6707A-1	9/11/2008	153,059
301.6724-1	7/13/2007	152,881
301.6724-1	7/9/2003	152,421
301.7216-3	7/2/2008	153,019
1.7476-2	1/17/2001	152,147
301.7477-1	6/9/2008	153,003
301.7477-2	6/9/2008	153,003
301.7502-1	9/21/2004	152,599
301.7701-1	8/29/2005	152,697
301.7701-3	10/22/2003	152,463
301.7701-15	6/17/2008	151,923
301.7701(b)-7	4/27/92	151,379
1.7702-0	12/15/92	151,453
1.7702-0	7/5/91	151,287
1.7702-1	7/5/91	151,287
1.7702-2	12/15/92	151,453
1.7702A-1	12/15/92	151,453
301.7811-1	4/19/96	151,719
1.7872-1	8/20/85	151,027
20.7872-1	8/20/85	151,027
25.7872-1	8/20/85	151,027
1.7872-2	8/20/85	151,027
1.7872-3	8/20/85	151,027
1.7872-4	4/8/86	151,065
1.7872-4	8/20/85	151,027
1.7872-5	8/20/85	151,027
1.7872-6	8/20/85	151,027
1.7872-7	8/20/85	151,027
1.7872-8	8/20/85	151,027
1.7872-9	8/20/85	151,027
1.7872-10	8/20/85	151,027
1.7872-11	8/20/85	151,027
1.7872-12	8/20/85	151,027
1.7872-13	8/20/85	151,027
1.7872-14	8/20/85	151,027
1.7872-16	2/7/2006	152,739
1.7874-2	6/6/2006	152,765
1.9006-1	4/8/86	151,065
301.9100-3	4/17/2008	152,987
301.9100-4T	3/31/2008	152,983
1.9300-1	12/12/2006	152,823
54.9801-1	12/30/2004	152,615
54.9801-2	12/30/2004	152,615
54.9801-4	12/30/2004	152,615
54.9801-5	12/30/2004	152,615
54.9801-6	12/30/2004	152,615
54.9801-7	12/30/2004	152,615
54.9831-1	12/30/2004	152,615

Amending Acts

Additions and amendments to the Internal Revenue Code of 1954, enacted on August 16, 1954, and the Internal Revenue Code of 1986, enacted on October 22, 1986, are made by Public Laws. Some Public Laws bear special titles, such as "Revenue Act", "Reform Act", "Technical Changes Act", or "Technical Amendments Act" of a stated year. Others bear no title. The table below lists, in order of enactment, the Public Laws that have amended the Internal Revenue Code since August 16, 1954. Each entry contains the P.L. number, the enactment date, the title or subject, and the location of the reprint in either the Cumulative Bulletin or the Statute Books.

Finding List for Amending Acts

Public Law No.	Date	Title or Subject	Reprint
		Statutes Enacted by the 83rd Congress—2nd Session	
729	8-31-54	Filling oral prescriptions for certain drugs	1954-2 CB 599
746	8-31-54	Amending Railroad Retirement Act, etc.	1954-2 CB 602
761	9-1-54	Social Security Amendments of 1954	1954-2 CB 603
764	9-1-54	Extending and amending Renegotiation Act of 1951	1955-1 CB 620
767	9-1-54	Extending unemployment compensation program	1954-2 CB 612
		Statutes Enacted by the 84th Congress—1st Session	
1	1-20-55	Amending Code Sec. 7237	1955-1 CB 619
9	3-2-55	Amending Code Sec. 7443(c)	1955-2 CB 747
18	3-30-55	Tax Rate Extension Act of 1955	1955-1 CB 619
66	6-8-55	Continuing suspension of duties and import taxes on metal scrap	1955-2 CB 747
74	6-15-55	Repealing Code Secs. 452 and 462	1955-2 CB 748
91	6-21-55	Continuing suspension of certain import duties on copper	1955-2 CB 749
196	8-1-55	Revising Philippines trade agreement	1955-2 CB 750
216	8-3-55	Extending Renegotiation Act of 1951	1955-2 CB 754
285	8-9-55	Amending International Settlement Act of 1949	1955-2 CB 756
299	8-9-55	Extending retirement income tax credit to members of Armed Forces	1955-2 CB 758
303	8-9-55	Extending period for claiming floor tax refunds	1955-2 CB 758
306	8-9-55	Amending Code Sec. 3402	1955-2 CB 759
310	8-9-55	Amending Sec. 345 of the Revenue Act of 1951	1955-2 CB 759
317	8-9-55	Providing for maximum manufacturers' excise tax on leases of certain automobile utility trailers	1955-2 CB 760
319	8-9-55	Amending Agricultural Act of 1949	1955-2 CB 761
321	8-9-55	Amending Code Sec. 3401	1955-2 CB 761
323	8-9-55	Providing for bonding certain civilian officers and employees	1955-2 CB 763
333	8-9-55	Providing personal exemption with respect to certain dependents in the Philippines	1955-2 CB 764
354	8-11-55	Exempting admissions to certain athletic events	1955-2 CB 765
355	8-11-55	Amending Code with respect to cutting oils tax	1955-2 CB 765
363	8-11-55	Providing for refund of credit of taxes on distilled spirits and wines lost in hurricane	1955-2 CB 766
366	8-11-55	Providing for tax treatment of damages for patent infringements	1955-2 CB 767
367	8-11-55	Removing excise tax from certain radio and television equipment	1955-2 CB 768
370	8-11-55	Amending Sec. 223 of the Revenue Act of 1950	1955-2 CB 770
379	8-12-55	Repealing excise tax on motorcycles	1955-2 CB 770
383	8-12-55	Amending Railroad Retirement Act, etc.	1955-2 CB 770
384	8-12-55	Amending tax treatment on amounts recovered held by another under claim of right	1955-2 CB 771
385	8-12-55	Amending Code Secs. 542(a)(2) and 1233	1955-2 CB 772
		Statutes Enacted by the 84th Congress—2nd Session	
396	1-28-56	Providing for carryover of unused pension trust deductions in certain cases	1956-1 CB 852
397	1-28-56	Providing for claims limitation period by certain transferees and fiduciaries	1956-1 CB 852
398	1-28-56	Amending Code Sec. 37	1956-1 CB 853
399	1-28-56	Providing credits to corporation for computing alternative tax	1956-1 CB 853

Public Law No.	Date	Title or Subject	Reprint
400	1-28-56	Providing for documentary stamp tax on certain obligations paid for in installments	1956-1 CB 854
408	2-15-56	Relating to unlimited deduction for charitable contributions	1956-1 CB 854
414	2-20-56	Amending Sec. 208(b) of the Technical Changes Act of 1953	1956-1 CB 855
417	2-20-56	Providing credit against estate tax	1956-1 CB 857
429	3-13-56	Life Insurance Company Tax Act for 1955	1956-1 CB 858
458	3-29-56	Tax Rate Extension Act of 1956	1956-1 CB 869
466	4-2-56	Relieving farmers of tax on certain farm fuels	1956-1 CB 870
495	4-27-56	Amending Code Sec. 1237	1956-1 CB 874
511	5-9-56	Providing for treatment of distributions made under bank holding company act	1956-1 CB 875
545	5-29-56	Amending Sugar Act of 1948	1956-1 CB 887
627	6-29-56	Providing additional revenue from taxes on motor fuels, tires, etc.	1956-2 CB 1150
628	6-29-56	Relating to tax treatment of certain railroad reorganizations	1956-2 CB 1164
629	6-29-56	Relating to trademark and trade name expenditures, etc.	1956-2 CB 1165
700	7-11-56	Amending Code Secs. 852(b)(3) and 5217(c)	1956-2 CB 1169
723	7-16-56	Continuing suspension of import taxes on metal scrap, etc.	1956-2 CB 1169
726	7-18-56	Mutual Security Act of 1956	1956-2 CB 1170
728	7-18-56	Narcotic Control Act of 1956	1956-2 CB 1171
784	7-24-56	Providing 1955 formula for taxing life insurance companies	1956-2 CB 1179
796	7-25-56	Exempting certain foreign travel from transition tax	1956-2 CB 1180
870	8-1-56	Extending and amending Renegotiation Act of 1951	1956-2 CB 1182
880	8-1-56	Social Security Amendments of 1956	1956-2 CB 1188
881	8-1-56	Servicemen's and Veterans' Survivor Benefits Act	1956-2 CB 1196
896	8-1-56	Implementing Organic Act of Guam	1956-2 CB 1204
901	8-1-56	Amending provisions relating to estate tax	1956-2 CB 1205
1010	8-6-56	Providing for exemption from admissions tax	1956-2 CB 1205
1011	8-6-56	Allowing charitable deductions for certain bequests	1956-2 CB 1206
1015	8-7-56	Extending exemption for tax on transportation of persons	1956-2 CB 1207
1022	8-7-56	Providing for deduction of contributions to medical research organizations	1956-2 CB 1207

Statutes Enacted by the 85th Congress—1st Session

Public Law No.	Date	Title or Subject	Reprint
85-12	3-29-57	Tax Rate Extension Act of 1957	1957-1 CB 666
85-56	6-17-57	Veterans' Benefits Act of 1957	1957-2 CB 1055
85-74	6-29-57	Exempting furlough travel of service personnel from transportation tax	1957-2 CB 1057
85-165	8-26-57	Amending Internal Revenue Code to provide relief for amounts received for breach of contract and to restrict issuance of rapid amortization of emergency facilities	1957-2 CB 1058
85-235	8-30-57	Suspending tax on processing of coconut oil temporarily	1957-2 CB 1061
85-239	8-30-57	Extending time for ministers to elect coverage under Social Security program	1957-2 CB 1061
85-300	9-7-57	Providing tax exemption for certain bonds	1958-1 CB 626

Statutes Enacted by the 85th Congress—2nd Session

Public Law No.	Date	Title or Subject	Reprint
85-318	2-11-58	Amending 1939 Code Sec. 812(e)(1)(D)	1958-1 CB 627
85-319	2-11-58	Amending Sec. 223 of the Revenue Act of 1950	1958-1 CB 628
85-320	2-11-58	Providing basis of shares acquired by exercise of restricted stock options after death of employee	1958-1 CB 628
85-321	2-11-58	Relating to administration of certain collected taxes	1958-1 CB 629
85-323	2-11-58	Preventing unjust enrichment by precluding refunds of alcohol and tobacco taxes to persons who have not borne ultimate burden of tax	1958-1 CB 630
85-345	3-17-58	Extending 1955 formula for taxing life insurance companies	1958-1 CB 632
85-367	4-7-58	Amending definition of unrelated business taxable income	1958-1 CB 633
85-380	4-16-58	Extending exemption to admissions for certain musical, dramatic and athletic events	1958-1 CB 633
85-475	6-30-58	Tax Rate Extension Act of 1958	1958-3 CB 73
85-517	7-11-58	Extension of authority of distilled spirits transfers	1958-3 CB 75
85-595	8-6-58	Defining place at which certain income tax offenses take place	1958-3 CB 75
85-605	8-8-58	Allotting lands in Fort Belknap Indian Reservation	1958-3 CB 76
85-612	8-8-58	Benefitting Lummi Indian Tribe	1958-3 CB 76
85-671	8-18-58	Providing taxability of certain Indian land and income	1958-3 CB 77
85-688	8-20-58	Amending Organic Act of Guam	1958-3 CB 78
85-731	8-23-58	Providing for acquisition of Klamath Indian lands	1958-3 CB 80
85-758	8-25-58	Conveying certain lands to Makah Indians	1958-3 CB 82

Public Law No.	Date	Title or Subject	Reprint
85-791	8-28-58	Abbreviating records for review	1958-3 CB 83
85-840	8-28-58	Social Security Amendments of 1958	1958-3 CB 85
85-859	9-2-58	Excise Tax Technical Changes Act of 1958	1958-3 CB 92
85-866	9-2-58	Technical Amendments Act of 1958 Retirement-Straight Line Adjustment Act of 1958 Small Business Tax Revision Act of 1958	1958-3 CB 254
85-878	9-2-58	Reimbursing Pine Ridge Sioux Tribe	1958-3 CB 334
85-881	9-2-58	Amending certain Internal Revenue Code Secs	1958-3 CB 334
85-915	9-2-58	Rehabilitating Indians of Standing Rock Sioux Reservation	1958-3 CB 335
85-916	9-2-58	Providing payments to Indians of Crow Creek Sioux Reservation	1958-3 CB 336
85-920	9-2-58	Relating to venue of tax refund suits	1958-3 CB 337
85-923	9-2-58	Providing Payments to Indians of Lower Brule Sioux Reservation	1958-3 CB 338
		Statutes Enacted by the 86th Congress—1st Session	
86-28	5-19-59	Amending Railroad Retirement Act, etc	1959-2 CB 652
86-37	5-29-59	Suspending tax on processing palm oil, etc	1959-2 CB 654
86-69	6-25-59	Life Insurance Company Income Act of 1959	1959-2 CB 654
86-70	6-25-59	Alaskan Omnibus Act	1959-2 CB 678
86-75	6-30-59	Tax Rate Extension Act of 1959	1959-2 CB 679
86-89	7-15-59	Extension of 1951 Renegotiation Act	1959-2 CB 680
86-94	7-17-59	Providing payments to Potawatomi	1959-2 CB 682
86-95	7-17-59	Providing payments to Couer D'Alene Tribe	1959-2 CB 683
86-97	7-17-59	Providing per capita distribution of funds to Quapaw Tribe	1959-2 CB 684
86-125	7-31-59	Exempting from income tax certain payments to Indians	1959-2 CB 684
86-141	8-7-59	Amending Code Sec 2038	1959-2 CB 685
86-168	8-18-59	Farm Credit Act of 1959	1959-2 CB 685
86-175	8-21-59	Providing Federal Estate Tax deduction for certain transfers to charities subjected to foreign death taxes	1959-2 CB 686
86-245	9-9-59	Transferring funds to Ute Mountain Tribe	1959-2 CB 688
86-246	9-9-59	Providing per capita distribution of funds to Siletz Indians	1959-2 CB 688
86-280	9-16-59	Extending period for filing claims for credit or refund of overpayments of income taxes from renegotiation of government contracts	1959-2 CB 689
86-319	9-21-59	Exempting from the admissions tax certain athletic games	1959-2 CB 690
86-322	9-21-59	Providing a division of tribal assets of the Catawba Indians	1959-2 CB 691
86-330	9-21-59	Providing payments to the Kiowa, Comanche, and Apache tribes	1959-2 CB 693
86-339	9-21-59	Providing equalization of allotments on the Ague Caliente Reservation	1959-2 CB 694
86-342	9-21-59	Federal-Aid Highway Act of 1959	1959-2 CB 697
86-344	9-21-59	Amending certain excise tax laws	1959-2 CB 700
86-346	9-22-59	Permitting interest rate increases of series E and H savings bonds, and amending certain provisions relating to exchanges of government securities	1959-2 CB 703
86-368	9-22-59	Providing a Chief Counsel for the Internal Revenue Service	1959-2 CB 705
86-376	9-23-59	Providing for a personal exemption for children placed for adoption and clarifying certain provisions relating to the election of small business corporations	1959-2 CB 707
		Statutes Enacted by the 86th Congress—2nd Session	
86-413	4-8-60	Amending Code Sec 4021 to delete "Aromatic cachous"	1960-1 CB 786
86-416	4-8-60	Relating to tax on issuance of shares or certificates of regulated investment companies	1960-1 CB 786
86-418	4-8-60	Exempting bicycle tires and tubes used in manufacture of new bicycles	1960-1 CB 786
86-422	4-8-60	Reducing cabaret tax to 10%	1960-1 CB 788
86-428	4-22-60	Exempting certain non-profit corporations	1960-1 CB 789
86-429	4-22-60	Narcotics Manufacturing Act of 1960	1960-1 CB 789
86-432	4-22-60	Continuing suspension of tax on certain oils	1960-1 CB 792
86-435	4-22-60	Treatment of corporate royalties—personal holding company tax	1960-1 CB 792
86-437	4-22-60	Excluding certain payments to non-resident aliens from gross income	1960-1 CB 794
86-440	4-22-60	Tax of 1 cent per pound on laminated tires	1960-1 CB 795
86-459	5-13-60	Providing method of paying tax by dealers having reserve income	1960-1 CB 795
86-470	5-14-60	Procedure for assessing certain tax additions, and other purposes	1960-1 CB 800
86-478	6-1-60	Relating to the tax on firearms	1960-1 CB 801
86-496	6-8-60	Providing for nontaxability of certain discharge of indebtedness of railroads	1960-2 CB 680
86-564	6-30-60	Public Debt and Tax Rate Extension Act of 1960	1960-2 CB 681
86-592	7-6-60	Amending Sugar Act of 1948	1960-2 CB 685

Public Law No.	Date	Title or Subject	Reprint
86-594	7-6-60	Amending Code Sec. 615(c) relating to deduction of exploration expenditures	1960-2 CB 685
86-624	7-12-60	Hawaii Omnibus Act	1960-2 CB 686
86-631	7-12-60	Amending 11 U.S.C. 1078 Bankruptcy Act	1960-2 CB 687
86-667	7-14-60	Amending unemployment trusts tax provisions	1960-2 CB 687
86-707	9-6-60	Amending Code Sec. 912	1960-2 CB 690
86-723	9-8-60	Amending Foreign Service Act	1960-2 CB 691
86-733	9-8-60	Amending Menominee Termination Act	1960-2 CB 691
86-761	9-13-60	Conveying land to Potawatomi Indians	1960-2 CB 692
86-778	9-13-60	Social Security Amendments of 1960	1960-2 CB 693
86-779	9-14-60	Amending Code Sec. 5701 and other sections of the Internal Revenue Code of 1954	1960-2 CB 709
86-780	9-14-60	Amending foreign tax credit overall limitation	1960-2 CB 720
86-781	9-14-60	Relating to treatment of local advertising to fix manufacturers' sales price	1960-2 CB 726
86-791	9-14-60	Conveying land to Cheyenne and Arapaho Indians	1960-2 CB 730
		Statutes Enacted by the 87th Congress—1st Session	
87-4	3-22-61	Prescribes time for Joint Committee to file renegotiation report	1961-1 CB 854
87-6	3-24-61	Temporary Extended Unemployment Compensation Act of 1961	1961-1 CB 854
87-15	3-31-61	Amending Sugar Act of 1954	1961-1 CB 855
87-24	4-24-61	Providing Funds to Nez Perce Tribe	1960-1 CB 856
87-29	5-4-61	Exempting income derived by a foreign central bank	1960-2 CB 307
87-59	6-27-61	Qualification of Union Fund Code Sec. 401(a)	1961-2 CB 308
87-61	6-29-61	Federal-Aid Highway Act of 1961	1961-2 CB 309
87-64	6-30-61	Social Security Amendments of 1961	1961-2 CB 315
87-72	6-30-61	Tax Rate Extension Act of 1961	1961-2 CB 317
87-109	7-26-61	Prepaid dues of certain membership organizations as gross income	1961-2 CB 318
87-205	9-6-61	Providing funds to Potawatomi Tribe	1961-2 CB 320
87-235	9-14-61	Disposition of funds of the Omaha Tribe of Indians	1961-2 CB 320
87-256	9-21-61	Mutual Educational and Cultural Exchange Act of 1961	1961-2 CB 322
87-262	9-21-61	Defining employment in certain hospitals transferred	1961-2 CB 333
87-293	9-22-61	Peace Corps Act	1961-2 CB 336
87-298	9-26-61	Authorizing use of funds of Colville Tribe	1961-2 CB 338
87-312	9-26-61	Determining gross income manufacture of clay products	1961-2 CB 339
87-321	9-26-61	Amending unemployment tax credit; percentage depletion	1961-2 CB 341
87-370	10-4-61	Annuities for public school teachers and Tax Court judges' dependents	1961-2 CB 344
87-397	10-5-61	Taxpayer account numbers	1961-2 CB 348
		Statutes Enacted by the 87th Congress—2nd Session	
87-403	2-2-62	Distributors of stock pursuant to an order enforcing the antitrust laws	1962-1 CB 370
87-426	3-31-62	Treatment of casualty losses in disaster areas	1962-1 CB 374
87-456	5-24-62	Tariff Classification Act of 1962	1962-3 CB 57
87-508	6-28-62	Tax Rate Extension Act of 1962	1962-3 CB 58
87-520	7-3-62	Extension of the Renegotiation Act of 1951	1962-3 CB 64
87-535	7-13-62	Sugar Act Amendments of 1962	1962-3 CB 65
87-629	9-5-62	Division of tribal assets of Ponca Tribe	1962-3 CB 65
87-682	9-25-62	Estimated income tax treatment extended to fishermen	1962-3 CB 68
87-710	9-27-62	Providing a seven-year net operating loss carryover for certain regulated transportation corporations	1961-3 CB 69
87-722	9-28-62	Amending law concerning Currency Comptroller	1962-3 CB 70
87-734	10-3-62	Division of assets Lower Brule Sioux Tribe	1962-3 CB 71
87-735	10-3-62	Division of assets of Crow Creek Sioux Tribe	1962-3 CB 78
87-768	10-9-62	Relating to personal holding company tax on consumer finance companies	1962-3 CB 85
87-770	10-9-62	Relating to definition of "advertising" for excise tax purposes	1962-3 CB 86
87-775	10-9-62	Division of tribal assets of Cherokee Nation	1962-3 CB 86
87-790	10-10-62	Relating to tax on life insurance companies	1962-3 CB 88
87-792	10-10-62	Self employed Individuals Tax Retirement Act of 1962	1962-3 CB 89
87-794	10-11-62	Trade Expansion Act of 1962	1962-3 CB 107
87-834	10-15-62	Revenue Act of 1962	1962-3 CB 111
87-846	10-22-62	Amending 1948 War Claims Act	
87-858	10-23-62	Relating to manufacturers excise tax, charitable contributions, and life insurance companies taxes	1962-3 CB 206
87-859	10-23-62	Suspending the tax on palm and coconut oils	1962-3 CB 210

Public Law No.	Date	Title or Subject	Reprint
87-863	10-23-62	Increasing the amounts allowable on medical and dental expense deductions	1962-3 CB 210
87-870	10-23-62	Income tax treatment of terminal railroad corporations	1962-3 CB 213
87-876	10-24-62	Relating to limitation on retirement income	1962-3 CB 217
		Statutes Enacted by the 88th Congress—1st Session	
88-4	4-2-63	Child Care expenses for deserted wives	1963-1 CB 412
88-9	4-10-63	Tax treatment of redeemable ground rents	1963-1 CB 412
88-31	5-29-63	Federal unemployment rate change	1963-1 CB 414
88-36	6-4-63	Silver bullion transfer tax repeal	1963-2 CB 696
88-52	6-29-63	Tax Extension Act of 1963	1963-2 CB 697
88-133	10-5-63	Amending Railroad Retirement Tax Act, etc	1963-2 CB 698
88-153	10-17-63	Deductibility of accrual vacation pay	1963-2 CB 699
88-173	11-7-63	Amending Federal Unemployment Tax Act, etc	1963-2 CB 699
88-180	11-16-63	Implementing Organic Act of Guam	1963-2 CB 701
88-231	12-23-63	Division of tribal assets of Kootenai Tribe	1964-1 (Part 2) CB 5
		Statutes Enacted by the 88th Congress—2nd Session	
88-272	2-26-64	Revenue Act of 1964	1964-1 (Part 2) CB 6
88-300	4-29-64	American-Mexican Chamizal Convention Act of 1964	1964-1 (Part 2) CB 110
88-339	6-30-64	Extension of Renegotiation Act of 1951	1964-2 CB 593
88-342	6-30-64	Preventing double tax on tobacco	1964-2 CB 593
88-348	6-30-64	Excise Tax Rate Extension Act of 1964	1964-2 CB 594
88-380	7-17-64	Unrelated business taxable income	1964-2 CB 596
88-412	8-10-64	Division of assets of Lower Pend D'Oreille or Kailspel Indians	1964-2 CB 597
88-421	8-11-64	Division of assets of Potawatomi Indians	1964-2 CB 597
88-428	8-14-64	Amending Missing Persons Act	1964-2 CB 600
88-457	8-20-64	Division of assets of Shawnee Indians	1964-2 CB 602
88-461	8-20-64	Division of Assets of Cherokees	1964-2 CB 603
88-464	8-20-64	Division of assets of certain Oregon Indians	1964-2 CB 603
88-474	8-21-64	Division of judgement assets of Pawnee Indians	1964-2 CB 604
88-484	8-22-64	Collapsible corporations and inclusion of rents in personal holding company income	1964-2 CB 605
88-506	8-30-64	Division of assets of Tillamook Indians	1964-2 CB 607
88-528	8-31-64	Patronage refunds to be paid in cash	1962-2 CB 608
88-533	8-31-64	Division of Asset of members of Seneca Nation	1964-2 CB 608
88-539	8-31-64	Amending law relating to total contract price personalty sold on installment	1964-2 CB 610
88-551	8-31-64	Division of funds of Confederated Tribes of Colville Reservation	1964-2 CB 611
88-554	8-31-64	Continuing rule relating to deductibility of accrued vacation pay	1964-2 CB 612
88-559	9-1-64	Division of funds of Cheyene Tribe	1964-2 CB 615
88-563	9-2-64	Interest Equalization Tax Act	1964-2 CB 615
88-570	9-2-64	Amending law relating to reacquisitions of realty and to installment obligations	1964-2 CB 647
88-571	9-2-64	Amending law relating to life insurance company tax inequities	1964-2 CB 649
88-611	10-2-64	Exemption of gifts to Commerce Dept	1964-2 CB 655
88-650	10-13-64	Amending certain self-employment tax	1964-2 CB 656
88-653	10-13-64	Amending fruit-flavor concentrates provisions	1964-2 CB 658
88-663	10-13-64	Division of assets of Chippewas	1964-2 CB 659
		Statutes Enacted by the 89th Congress—1st Session	
89-28	5-27-65	Disposition of judgement funds of Quinaielt Tribe	1965-2 CB 568
89-44	6-21-65	Excise Tax Reduction Act of 1965	1965-2 CB 568
89-97	7-30-65	Social Security Amendments of 1965	1965-2 CB 601
89-130	8-19-65	Disposition of judgement funds of Tlingit and Haida Indians of Alaska	1965-2 CB 619
89-134	8-24-65	Peace Corps Act	1965-2 CB 621
89-184	9-15-65	Amending the Federal Firearms Act	1965-2 CB 621
89-209	9-29-65	National Foundation on the Arts and the Humanities Act of 1965	1965-2 CB 622
89-212	9-29-65	Amending the Railroad Retirement Act of 1937 and the Railroad Retirement Tax Act	1965-2 CB 623
89-224	10-1-65	Disposition of tribal assets of Klamath, Modoc, and Yakooskin Indians	1965-2 CB 626

Public Law No.	Date	Title or Subject	Reprint
89-243	10-9-65	Interest Equalization Tax Extension Act Of 1965	1965-2 CB 627
89-331	11-8-65	Sugar Act Amendments of 1965	1965-2 CB 639
89-332	11-8-65	To provide for the right persons to be represented in matters before Federal Agencies	1965-2 CB 640
		Statutes Enacted by the 89th Congress—2nd Session	
89-352	2-2-66	To expand exemption of credit unions	1966-1 CB 375
89-354	2-2-66	Fixing new method of Tax Court Judges retired pay	1966-1 CB 376
89-359	3-7-66	To amend certain estate tax provisions of the Internal Revenue Code of 1939	1966-1 CB 376
89-365	3-8-66	Tax treatment of amounts paid to certain members of uniformed services and their survivors	1966-1 CB 377
89-368	3-15-66	Tax Adjustment Act of 1966	1966-1 CB 379
89-384	4-8-66	To provide recovery of losses from foreign expropriation, etc	1966-1 CB 414
89-389	4-14-66	To amend subchapter S of the 1954 Code	1966-1 CB 419
89-429	5-24-66	To promote private financing of credit needs	1966-2 CB 593
89-480	6-30-66	To extend the Renegotiation Act of 1951	1966-2 CB 594
89-493	7-5-66	To transfer certain duties of U.S. District Court to other agencies	1966-2 CB 594
89-495	7-5-66	To amend the Bankruptcy Act	1966-2 CB 595
89-496	7-5-66	Limiting the priority and nondeductibility of taxes in bankruptcy	1966-2 CB 598
89-523	8-1-66	Amending excise taxes on tires and tubes	1966-2 CB 599
89-570	9-12-66	Treatment of exploration expenditures in the case of mining	1966-2 CB 600
89-621	10-4-66	Treatment of disclaimers in computing marital deduction for estate tax purposes	1966-2 CB 604
89-642	10-11-66	Child Nutrition Act of 1966	1966-2 CB 606
89-655	10-14-66	Disposition of Quileute tribal funds	1966-2 CB 606
89-656	10-14-66	Disposition of Nooksack tribal funds	1966-2 CB 608
89-659	10-14-66	Disposition of Miami tribal funds	1966-2 CB 609
89-660	10-14-66	Disposition of Dumanish tribal funds	1966-2 CB 611
89-661	10-14-66	Disposition of Otoe and Missouria tribal funds	1966-2 CB 612
89-663	10-14-66	Disposition of Skokomis tribal funds	1966-2 CB 612
89-670	10-15-66	Exemption of gifts to Department of Transportation	1966-2 CB 613
89-692	10-15-66	Continues rules on accrued vacation pay	1966-2 CB 614
89-699	10-30-66	Amends various railroad retirement provisions	1966-2 CB 614
89-700	10-30-66	Amends other railroad retirement provisions	1966-2 CB 615
89-713	11-2-66	Promotes savings under IRS data processing	1966-2 CB 617
89-717	11-2-66	Disposition of Omaha tribal funds	1966-2 CB 622
89-719	11-2-66	Federal Tax Lien Act of 1966	1966-2 CB 623
89-721	11-2-66	Interest on tax refunds	1966-2 CB 643
89-722	11-2-66	Reserve deduction for certain guaranteed debts	1966-2 CB 645
89-739	11-2-66	Increase excludible combat pay	1966-2 CB 647
89-774	11-6-66	Amending the Washington Metropolitan Area Transit Regulation Compact	1966-2 CB 647
89-793	11-8-66	Narcotic Addict Rehabilitation Act of 1966	1966-2 CB 648
89-800	11-8-66	Suspends investment credits and accelerated depreciation	1966-2 CB 649
89-809	11-13-66	Tax treatment of foreign investments in United States ("Foreign Investors Tax Act of 1966")	1966-2 CB 656
		Statutes Enacted by the 90th Congress—1st Session	
90-11	4-22-67	Disposition of Salish and Kootenai tribal funds	1967-1 CB 427
90-26	6-13-67	To restore the investment credit and the allowance of accelerated depreciation	1967-2 CB 481
90-59	7-31-67	Interest Equalization Tax Extension Act of 1967	1967-2 CB 482
90-60	8-1-67	Disposition of Ute Indian tribal funds	1967-2 CB 499
90-63	8-11-67	Disposition of Otawa tribal funds	1967-2 CB 500
90-73	8-29-67	Technical amendments to interest equalization tax	1967-2 CB 501
90-78	8-31-67	Dependency exemption for children of divorced parents	1967-2 CB 502
90-80	8-31-67	Disposition of Sac and Fox Tribal funds	1967-2 CB 503
90-93	9-27-67	Disposition of Emigrant New York Indian tribal funds	1967-2 CB 504
90-94	9-27-64	Disposition of Minnesota Chippewa tribal funds	1967-2 CB 505
90-114	10-24-67	Disposition of Chelais tribal funds	1967-2 CB 506
90-117	10-31-67	Disposition of Cheyene-Arapaho tribal funds	1967-2 CB 507
90-199	12-14-67	Disposition of Iowa Tribes of Kansas and Nebraska of Oklahoma tribal funds	1968-1 CB 639
90-209	12-18-67	To establish the National Park Foundation	1968-1 CB 639
90-225	12-27-67	Tax treatment of certain distributions pursuant to Bank Holding Company Act	1968-1 CB 640
90-237	1-2-68	To amend the Subversive Activities Control Act of 1950	1968-1 CB 643

Public Law No.	Date	Title or Subject	Reprint
90-240	1-2-68	Duty-free status of certain gifts by members of the Armed Forces and for other purposes	1968-1 CB 644
90-248	1-2-68	Social Security Act of 1967	1968-1 CB 648
		Statutes Enacted by the 90th Congress—2nd Session	
90-266	3-12-68	To authorize the consolidation and use of funds arising form judgement in favor of the Apache Tribe of the Mescalero Reservation and each of its constituent groups	1968-1 CB 657
90-278	3-30-68	Disposition of Yakima tribal funds	1968-1 CB 657
90-279	3-30-68	Disposition of Chilocco Indian school lands	1968-1 CB 658
90-285	4-12-68	To continue temporarily the excise tax rates on automobiles and communication services	1968-1 CB 659
90-310	5-18-68	To convey certain federally owned lands to the Cheyenne and Arapaho Tribes of Oklahoma	1968-1 CB 661
90-355	6-10-68	To authorize purchase, sale and exchange of lands on Spokane Indian Reservation	1968-2 CB 709
90-337	6-10-68	Distribution of Spokane tribal funds	1968-2 CB 710
90-346	6-18-68	Advertising in a convention program of a national political convention [Repealed by PL93-625, I-3-75]	1968-2 CB 711
90-364	6-28-68	Revenue and Expenditure Control Act of 1968	1968-2 CB 715
90-448	8-1-68	Housing and Urban Development Act of 1968	1968-2 CB 734
90-504	9-21-68	Disposition of tribal funds of Creek Nation of Indians	1968-2 CB 737
90-506	9-21-68	Disposition of tribal funds of Creek Nation of Indians	1968-2 CB 738
90-507	9-21-68	Disposition of California tribal funds	1968-2 CB 739
90-508	9-21-68	Disposition of Funds of Delaware Nation of Indians	1968-2 CB 741
90-527	9-28-68	Disposition of Kiowa, Comanche, and Apache tribal funds	1968-2 CB 742
90-529	9-28-68	Disposition of Quechan tribal funds	1968-2 CB 743
90-530	9-28-68	Disposition of Muchleshoot tribal funds	1968-2 CB 743
90-531	9-28-68	Disposition of funds of confederated tribes of Colville Reservation	1968-2 CB 746
90-537	9-30-68	Colorado River Basin Project Act	1968-2 CB 745
90-584	10-17-68	Disposition of Southern Paiute tribal funds	1968-2 CB 746
90-607	10-21-68	To provide an effective date for a 1966 law change	1968-2 CB 748
90-615	10-21-68	To continue existing suspension of duties on certain alumina and bauxite	1968-2 CB 748
90-618	10-22-68	Gun Control Act of 1968	1968-2 CB 749
90-619	10-22-68	To facilitate the production of wine	1968-2 CB 768
90-621	10-22-68	Treatment of certain statutory mergers of corporations	1968-2 CB 769
90-622	10-22-68	Treatment of income from operation of communications satellite	1968-2 CB 770
90-624	10-22-68	Amending the Railroad Retirement Tax Act	1968-2 CB 771
90-630	10-22-68	Amending certain provisions relating to distilled spirits	1968-2 CB 772
90-634	10-24-68	Renegotiation Amendments Act of 1968	1968-2 CB 775
		Statutes Enacted by the 91st Congress—1st Session	
91-36	6-30-69	To continue for one month the existing rates of withholding of income tax	1969-3 CB 1
91-50	8-2-69	To continue the existing interest equalization tax	1969-3 CB 1
91-53	8-7-69	Surcharge extension and collection of Federal unemployment tax	1969-3 CB 1
91-65	8-25-69	To continue the existing interest equalization tax	1969-3 CB 4
91-75	9-29-69	Disposition of Salish and Kootenai tribal funds	1969-3 CB 5
91-128	11-26-69	Interest Equalization Tax Extension Act of 1969	1969-3 CB 5
91-130	12-1-69	To amend the Second Liberty Bond Act	1969-3 CB 9
91-160	12-24-69	To organize and hold a diplomatic conference and to negotiate a Patent Cooperation Treaty	83 Stat. 443
91-172	12-30-69	Tax Reform Act of 1969	1969-3 CB 10
		Statutes Enacted by the 91st Congress—2nd Session	
91-215	3-17-70	To amend the Railroad Retirement Tax Act	1970-1 CB 360
91-235	4-24-70	To provide that individuals illegally detained in North Korea be treated as serving in combat zone	1970-1 CB 360
91-258	5-21-70	Airport and Airway Revenue Act of 1970	1970-1 CB 361
91-259	5-21-70	Disposition of Umatilla Indian tribal funds	1970-2 CB 343
91-264	5-22-70	To further the economic advancement of Hopi Indian tribe	1970-2 CB 344
91-283	6-19-70	Disposition of Sioux and tribal funds	1970-2 CB 345

Public Law No.	Date	Title or Subject	Reprint
91-290	6-25-70	Extending the period of restriction on Quapaw Indian Lands	84 Stat. 325
91-335	7-13-70	Disposition of tribal funds of Tlingit and Haida Indians of Alaska	1970-2 CB 347
91-346	7-20-70	To amend the National Foundation on the Arts and Humanities Act of 1965	84 Stat. 443
91-351	7-24-70	Emergency Home Finance Act of 1970	1970-2 CB 347
91-364	7-30-70	Disposition of tribal funds of Weas, Piankashaws, Peorias and Kaskaskias	1970-2 CB 347
91-373	8-10-70	Employment Security Amendments of 1970	1970-2 CB 348
91-400	9-16-70	Disposition of judgment funds of Hualapai tribe	1970-2 CB 361
91-401	9-16-70	Disposition of judgment funds of Potawatomi Indians	1970-2 CB 361
91-404	9-19-70	Disposition of Sac and Fox tribal funds	1970-2 CB 361
91-413	9-25-70	Disposition of Yakima tribal funds	1970-2 CB 361
91-417	9-25-70	Disposition of Chemehuevi tribal funds	1970-2 CB 362
91-420	9-25-70	Disposition of tribal funds of Confederated bands of Ute Indians	1970-2 CB 362
91-452	10-15-70	Control of organized crime in U.S.	1970-2 CB 363
91-469	10-21-70	To amend the Merchant Marine Act, 1936	1970-2 CB 372
91-478	10-21-70	To convey certain federally owned land to the Cherokee Tribe of Oklahoma	84 Stat. 1074
91-513	10-27-70	Comprehensive Drug Abuse Prevention and Control Act of 1970	1970-2 CB 376
91-518	10-30-70	Rail Passenger Service Act of 1970	1970-2 CB 381
91-575	12-24-70	Consenting to the Susquehanna River Basin Compact	1971-1 CB 529
91-598	12-30-70	Securities Investor Protection Act of 1970	1971-1 CB 530
91-605	12-31-70	Federal-Aid Highway Act of 1970	1971-1 CB 531
91-606	12-31-70	Disaster Relief Act of 1970	1971-1 CB 532
91-614	12-31-70	Excise, Estate and Gift Tax Adjustment Act of 1970	1971-1 CB 533
91-617	12-30-70	To provide interest on certain insured loans sold out of Agricultural Credit Insurance Fund	1971-1 CB 539
91-618	12-31-70	Clarifying exemption from income taxation of cemetery corporations	1971-1 CB 539
91-642	12-31-70	To extend the period for filing certain manufacturers claims for floor stocks refunds	1971-1 CB 539
91-646	1-2-71	Uniform Relocation Assistance and Real Property Acquisition Policies Act of 1970	1971-1 CB 540
91-659	1-8-71	To amend '54 Code relating to distilled spirits	1971-1 CB 542
91-673	1-12-71	To amend provisions of '54 Code relating to beer	1971-1 CB 544
91-675	1-12-71	To amend Sec. 905 of the '69 Tax Reform Act	1971-1 CB 545
91-676	1-12-71	To allow leasing of aircraft for temporary use outside the U.S. with recapture of investment credit	1971-1 CB 545
91-677	1-12-71	Treatment of losses sustained though confiscation of property by Cuban government	1971-1 CB 546
91-678	1-12-71	To provide floor stocks refunds in case of cement mixers	1971-1 CB 547
91-679	1-12-71	Relating to joint income tax returns by husband and wife	1971-1 CB 547
91-680	1-12-71	To extend the application of Code Sec. 2789 from citrus groves to almond groves	1971-1 CB 548
91-681	1-12-71	To amend 1954 Code Sec. 367 relating to foreign corporations	1971-1 CB 548
91-683	1-12-71	To amend Code Sec. 1372 relating to passive investment income	1971-1 CB 549
91-684	1-12-71	To amend 1954 Code Secs. 902(b) and (c) to reduce the 50-percent requirement to 10-percent between first and second levels and to include third level foreign corporations in the tax credit structure if the 10-percent test is met	1971-1 CB 550
91-686	1-12-71	Relating to the income tax treatment of certain sales of real property by a corporation	1971-1 CB 550
91-687	1-12-71	To provide for treatment of losses on worthless securities	1971-1 CB 551
91-688	1-12-71	Relating to consolidated returns of life insurance companies	1971-1 CB 552
91-691	1-12-71	Relating to period of qualification of certain union-negotiated pension plans	1971-1 CB 552
91-693	1-12-71	Relating to certain statutory mergers	1971-1 CB 553

Statutes Enacted by the 92nd Congress—1st Session

Public Law No.	Date	Title or Subject	Reprint
92-5	3-17-71	To increase the public debt limit	1971-1 CB 553
92-9	4-1-71	Interest Equalization Act of 1971	1971-1 CB 554
92-12	5-7-71	To amend the Rural Electrification Act of 1936, as amended	1971-2 CB 491
92-29	6-23-71	Disposition of funds of the Iowa Tribe of Oklahoma, Kansas and Nebraska Indians	1971-2 CB 491
92-30	6-23-71	Disposition of funds of the Snohomish, Upper Skagit, Snoquamic and Skykomish tribal funds	1971-2 CB 492
92-41	7-1-71	Amending the Renegotiation Act of 1951	1971-2 CB 492

Public Law No.	Date	Title or Subject	Reprint
92-59	7-29-71	Disposition of the funds of the Pembina Band of Chippewa Indians	1971-2 CB 494
92-138	10-14-71	Sugar Act Amendments of 1971	1971-2 CB 495
92-164	11-23-71	Disposition of funds of the Pueblo of Laguna Indians	1972-1 CB 442
92-178	12-10-71	Revenue Act of 1971	1972-1 CB 443
92-181	12-10-71	Farm Credit Act of 1971	1972-2 CB 663
92-203	12-18-71	Alaska Native Claims Settlement Act	1972-1 CB 490
92-206	12-18-71	Apportionment of Shoshone tribal funds	1972-1 CB 495
		Statutes Enacted by the 92nd Congress—2nd Session	
92-244	3-9-72	Disposition of funds of the Confederated Tribes of the Colville Reservation	1972-1 CB 496
92-253	3-17-72	Disposition of funds of the Salish and Kootenai Tribes	1972-1 CB 497
92-254	3-18-72	Disposition of funds of the Blackfeet and Gros Ventre Tribes	1972-1 CB 497
92-258	3-22-72	To amend the Older Americans Act of 1965	86 Stat. 88
92-279	4-26-72	Income tax exclusion for Vietnam prisoners of war	1972-1 CB 498
92-295	5-16-72	Disposition of funds of the Jicarilla Apache Tribe	1972-2 CB 669
92-309	6-2-72	Disposition of funds of the Miami Tribe of Oklahoma and the Miami Indians of Indiana	1972-2 CB 669
92-310	6-6-72	To provide that the Federal Government shall assume the risks of its fidelity losses	1972-2 CB 670
92-329	6-30-72	To extend the emergency unemployment compensation program	1972-2 CB 671
92-336	7-1-72	To increase Social Security benefits	1972-2 CB 672
92-349	7-13-72	To amend the National Transportation Act of 1969	1972-2 CB 674
92-418	8-29-72	Exempt status of veterans' organizations	1972-2 CB 675
92-419	8-30-72	Rural Development Act of 1972	1972-2 CB 676
92-438	9-29-72	Disposition of funds of Havasupai Tribe	1972-2 CB 678
92-442	9-29-72	Disposition of funds of Shoshone-Bannock tribal funds	1972-2 CB 678
92-456	10-3-72	Disposition of funds of Delaware Tribe	1972-2 CB 678
92-461	10-6-72	Disposition of Yavapai Apache tribal funds	1972-2 CB 679
92-462	10-6-72	Disposition of Pueblo de Acoma tribal funds	1972-2 CB 680
92-467	10-6-72	Disposition of Kickapoo tribal funds	1972-2 CB 680
92-468	10-6-72	Disposition of Yankton Sioux tribal funds	1972-2 CB 681
92-500	10-18-72	Federal Water Pollution Control Act Amendments of 1972	1972-2 CB 681
92-512	10-20-72	State and Local Assistance Act of 1972	1972-2 CB 684
92-526	10-21-72	Relating to the Administrative Conference of the U.S.	1972-2 CB 701
92-552	10-25-72	Authorizing the City of Clinton Bridge Commission to convey its bridge structures and other assets to the State of Iowa	1973-1 CB 707
92-555	10-25-72	Disposition of trial funds of Mississippi Sioux Indians	1973-1 CB 708
92-557	10-25-72	Disposition of tribal funds of the Assiniboine Indians	1973-1 CB 709
92-558	10-25-72	To provide funds for certain wildlife restoration projects	1972-2 CB 701
92-578	10-27-72	Pennsylvania Avenue Development Corporation Act of 1972	1973-1 CB 710
92-580	10-27-72	Personal exemption in the case of American Samoans	1972-2 CB 703
92-586	10-27-72	Disposition of tribal funds of the Osage Indians	1973-1 CB 711
92-603	10-30-72	Social Security Amendments of 1972	1972-2 CB 703
92-606	10-31-72	Coordination of U.S. and Guam individual income taxes	1972-2 CB 709
		Statutes Enacted by the 93rd Congress—1st Session	
93-17	4-10-73	Interest Equalization Tax Extension Act of 1973	1973-1 CB 712
93-29	5-3-73	"Older Americans Comprehensive Services Amendments of 1973"	1973-2 CB 437
93-53	7-1-73	Income tax treatment of payments to Presidential Election Campaign Fund	1973-2 CB 438
93-66	7-9-73	To extend the Renegotiation Act of 1951	1973-1 CB 439
93-69	7-10-73	To amend the Railroad Retirement Act of 1937 and the Railroad Retirement Tax Act	1973-2 CB 440
93-113	10-1-73	Domestic Volunteer Service Act of 1973	1973-2 CB 441
93-116	10-1-73	To amend the Merchant Marine Act, 1936	87 Stat. 421
93-129	10-19-73	Board for International Broadcasting Act of 1973	87 Stat. 456
93-133	10-19-73	National Foundation on the Arts and Humanities Amendments of 1973	87 Stat. 461
93-134	10-19-73	Disposition of funds of Indian claims	1973-2 CB 445
93-161	11-27-73	To amend the International Organizations Immunities Act	1974-1 CB 377
93-197	12-22-73	Menominee Restoration Act	1974-1 CB 377
93-198	12-24-73	District of Columbia Self-Government and Governmental Reorganization Act	1974-1 CB 378
93-203	12-28-73	Comprehensive Employment and Training Act of 1973	1974-1 CB 379
93-224	12-29-73	Federal Financing Bank Act of 1973	1974-1 CB 379

Public Law No.	Date	Title or Subject	Reprint
93-233	12-31-73	To increase Social Security benefits	1974-1 CB 380
		Statutes Enacted by the 93rd Congress—2nd Session	
93-236	1-2-74	Regional Rail Reorganization Act of 1973	1974-1 CB 383
93-286	5-21-74	To amend PL 90-335 relating to the purchase, sale and exchange of certain lands on the Spokane Indian Reservation	1974-2 CB 414
93-288	5-22-74	Disaster Relief Act of 1974	1974-2 CB 414
93-310	6-8-74	To amend Code Sec. 501 relating to exemption from tax on corporations, etc.	1974-2 CB 415
93-313	6-8-74	To delay for six months the taking effect of certain measures to provide additional funds for certain wildlife restoration projects	1974-2 CB 417
93-329	6-30-74	To extend the Renegotiation Act of 1951	1974-2 CB 417
93-355	7-25-74	To provide exemption for Legal Services Corp	1974-2 CB 417
93-368	8-7-74	Exempting from duty certain equipment and repairs for vessels, etc.	1974-2 CB 418
93-383	8-22-74	Housing and Community Development Act of 1974	1974-2 CB 418
93-387	8-24-74	Council on Wage and Price Stability Act	1974-2 CB 420
93-406	9-2-74	Employee Retirement Income Security Act of 1974 (ERISA)	1974-3 CB 1
93-443	10-15-74	Federal Election Campaign Act Amendments of 1974	1974-2 CB 421
93-445	10-16-74	To amend the Railroad Retirement Act of 1937	1974-2 CB 440
93-480	10-26-74	Treatment of life insurance company dividends for personal holding company consolidated return purposes	1974-2 CB 442
93-482	10-26-74	Accounts receivables of related DISCs and low income housing	1974-2 CB 444
93-483	10-26-74	Armed Forces Scholarships, Insurance Company guarantees and premature withdrawals from term accounts	1974-2 CB 447
93-490	10-26-74	Application of moving expense provisions to members of U.S. military services, etc.	1974-2 CB 451
93-496	10-28-74	To amend the Rail Passenger Service Act of 1970	88 Stat. 1526
93-497	10-29-74	Basis adjustment for property received in liquidation prior to 7-1-57	1974-2 CB 455
93-499	10-29-74	Wagering tax amendments	1974-2 CB 456
93-531	12-22-74	Providing for final settlement of the conflicting rights and interests of the Hopi and Navajo Tribes	1975-1 CB 425
93-597	1-2-75	Tax treatment of members of the Armed Forces of the United States and civilian employees who are prisoners of war or missing in action	1975-1 CB 495
93-618	1-3-75	Trade Act of 1974	1975-1 CB 501
93-625	1-3-75	To amend the tariff schedules of the U.S., etc.	1975-1 CB 510
96-644	1-4-75	Headstart, Economic Opportunity, and Community Partnership Act of 1974	1975-1 CB 542
93-647	1-4-75	Social Services Amendments of 1974	1975-1 CB 543
		Statutes Enacted by the 94th Congress—1st Session	
94-12	3-29-75	Tax Reduction Act of 1975	1975-1 CB 545
94-45	6-30-75	Emergency Compensation and Special Unemployment Assistance Extension Act of 1975	1975-2 CB 513
94-46	6-30-75	To amend PL 93-647	1975-2 CB 526
94-81	8-9-75	Treatment of Condemnation proceeds from forest lands held in trust for the Klamath Indian Tribe, etc.	1975-2 CB 526
94-92	8-9-75	To amend the Railroad Unemployment Insurance Act	1975-2 CB 528
94-93	8-9-75	Amendments to the Railroad Retirement Tax Act	1975-2 CB 528
94-114	10-17-75	Treatment of certain submarginal land held in trust for certain Indian tribes	1975-2 CB 529
94-118	10-20-75	Japan-United States Friendship Act	89 Stat. 603
94-129	11-13-75	Gifts or devises to the National Arboretum	1975-2 CB 531
94-164	12-23-75	Revenue Adjustment Act of 1975	1976-1 CB 486
94-168	12-23-75	Metric Conversion Act of 1975	1976-1 CB 502
94-182	12-31-75	To amend the Social Security Act	1976-1 CB 490
94-185	12-31-75	To extend the Renegotiation Act of 1951	1976-1 CB 502
94-189	12-31-75	Disposition of Sac and Fox Tribes fund	1976-1 CB 502
94-202	1-2-76	To amend the Social Security Act	1976-1 CB 503
94-204	1-2-76	To amend the Alaska Native Claims Settlement Act	89 Stat. 1145

Public Law No.	Date	Title or Subject	Reprint
		Statutes Enacted by the 94th Congress—2nd Session	
94-236	3-19-76	Application of certain provisions of the '54 Code to specified transactions by certain public employee retirement systems created by the State of New York or any of its political subdivisions	1976-1 CB 507
94-241	3-24-76	To approve the "Covenant to Establish a Commonwealth of the Northern Mariana Islands in Political Union with the U.S.A."	1976-1 CB 513
94-253	3-31-76	Tax treatment for exchanges under the final system plan for ConRail	1976-1 CB 520
94-267	4-15-76	To permit tax-free rollovers of distribution from employee retirement plans in the event of plan termination	1976-1 CB 527
94-273	4-21-76	Fiscal Year Adjustment Act	1976-2 CB 517
94-274	4-21-76	Fiscal Year Transition Act	1976-2 CB 518
94-280	5-5-76	Authorizing appropriations for the construction of certain highways in accordance with Title 23 of the U.S. Code	1976-2 CB 518
94-283	5-11-76	Federal Election Campaign Act Amendments of 1976	1976-2 CB 522
94-331	6-30-76	To amend '54 Code Sec 815	1976-2 CB 28
94-396	9-3-76	To amend '54 Code Sec 512(b)(5)	1976-2 CB 531
94-401	9-7-76	To facilitate and encourage the implementation by States of child day care services programs	1976-2 CB 533
94-414	9-17-76	To amend Code Sec. 584 relating to common trust funds; treatment of affiliated banks	1976-2 CB 535
94-444	10-1-76	Emergency Jobs Programs Extension Act of 1976	90 Stat. 1476
94-452	10-2-76	Bank Holding Company Tax Act of 1976	1976-2 CB 536
94-455	10-4-76	Tax Reform Act of 1976	1976-3 (Vol. 1) CB 1
94-514	10-15-76	Interest deduction on certain corporate indebtedness	1976-2 CB 551
94-528	10-17-76	To provide for a distribution deduction for certain cemetery perpetual care fund, etc.	1976-2 CB 553
94-529	10-17-76	To amend Code Sec. 5051 (relating to the Federal excise tax on beer)	90 Stat. 2485
94-530	10-17-76	Exempting from fuel tax certain aircraft museums	1976-2 CB 555
94-540	10-18-76	To provide for the disposition of funds for the Grand River Band of Ottowa Indians	1976-2 CB 557
94-547	10-18-76	To amend the Railroad Retirement Act of 1974	1976-2 CB 558
94-553	10-19-76	General revision of the Copyright Law	90 Stat. 2541
94-559	10-19-76	The Civil Rights Attorney's Fees Awards Act of 1976	90 Stat. 2641
94-563	10-19-76	To amend chapter 21 of the Internal Revenue Code and title II of the Social Security Act	1976-2 CB 558
94-566	10-20-76	Unemployment Compensation Amendments of 1976	1976-2 CB 564
94-568	10-20-76	To provide for tax treatment of social clubs and certain other membership organizations, and for other purposes	1976-2 CB 596
94-569	10-20-76	To permit the authorization of means other than stamp on containers of distilled spirits as evidence of tax payment, and for other purposes	1976-2 CB 603
		Statutes Enacted by the 95th Congress—1st Session	
95-19	4-12-77	Emergency Unemployment Compensation Extension Act of 1977	1977-1 CB 437
95-30	5-23-77	Tax Reduction and Simplification Act of 1977	1977-1 CB 451
95-125	10-7-77	To amend the Accounting and Auditing Act of 1950, to provide for the audit, by the Comptroller General, of the IRS and of the Bureau of Alcohol Tobacco, and Firearms	91 Stat. 1104
95-147	10-28-77	To authorize the Secretary to invest public money, and for other purposes	1978-1 CB 455
95-170	11-12-77	To suspend until July 1, 1978, the rate of duty on mattress blanks of latex rubber, etc.	1978-1 CB 456
95-171	11-12-77	To extend certain Social Security Act provisions, etc.	1978-1 CB 457
95-172	11-12-77	To extend for an additional temporary period the existing suspension of duties on certain classifications of years of silk, etc.	1978-1 CB 459
95-176	11-14-77	To amend certain provisions of the '54 Code relating to distilled spirits, etc.	91 Stat. 1363
95-195	11-18-77	Siletz Indian Tribe Restoration Act	91 Stat. 1415
95-210	12-13-77	To amend Titles XVIII and XIX of the Social Security Act, etc.	1978-1 CB 461
95-216	12-20-77	Social Security amendments of 1977	1978-1 CB 462

Public Law No.	Date	Title or Subject	Reprint
		Statutes Enacted by the 95th Congress—2nd Session	
95-227	2-10-78	The Black Lung Benefits Revenue Act of 1977	1978-1 CB 494
95-239	3-1-78	The Black Lung Benefits Reform Act of 1977	92 Stat. 95
95-258	4-7-78	Relating to the year for including in income certain payments under the Agricultural Act of 1949 received in 1978 but attributable to 1977, and to extend for one year the existing treatment of State legislators' travel expenses away from home	1978-1 CB 505
95-339	8-8-78	New York City Loan Guarantee Act of 1978	1978-2 CB 353
95-345	8-15-78	To amend the '54 Code with respect to the treatment of mutual or cooperative telephone company income, etc.	1978-2 CB 356
95-423	10-6-78	To amend '54 Code Sec. 5064	92 Stat. 935
95-427	10-7-78	To prohibit the issuance of Regs on the taxation of fringe benefits, etc.	1978-2 CB 363
95-458	10-14-78	To amend the '54 Code with respect to excise tax on certain trucks, buses, tractors, etc., home production of beer and wine, refunds of taxes on gasoline and special fuels to aerial applicators, and partial rollovers of lump sum distributions	1978-2 CB 367
95-472	10-17-78	To amend Code Sec. 7447 with respect to the revocation of an election to receive retired pay as a judge of the Tax Court	1978-2 CB 373
95-473	10-17-78	To revise, codify, and enact without substantive change the Interstate Commerce Act and related laws	1978-2 CB 377
95-479	10-18-78	Veterans' Disability Compensation and Survivors' Benefits Act of 1978	1978-2 CB 377
95-488	10-20-78	To amend the '54 Code to insure that the deduction for contributions to a black lung benefit trust be allowed for any such contributions which are made for the purpose of satisfying unfunded future liability, etc.	1978-2 CB 378
95-496	10-21-78	To amend certain laws relating to the Osage Tribe of Oklahoma, etc.	1978-2 CB 381
95-497	10-21-78	Relating to the application of certain provisions of the '54 Code to specified transactions by certain public employee retirement systems created by the State of New York or any of its political subdivisions	1978-2 CB 382
95-498	10-21-78	To declare that the U.S. holds in trust for the Pueblo of Santa Ana certain public domain lands	1978-2 CB 392
95-499	10-21-78	To declare that the U.S. holds in trust for the Pueblo of Zio certain public domain land	1978-2 CB 393
95-502	10-21-78	To amend the '54 Code to provide that income from the conducting of certain bingo games by certain tax-exempt organizations will not be subject to tax, etc.	1978-2 CB 393
95-565	11-1-78	U.S. Railway Association Amendments Act of 1978	1978-2 CB 399
95-599	11-6-78	Highway Revenue Act of 1978	1978-2 CB 403
95-600	11-6-78	Revenue Act of 1978	1978-3 CB 1
95-602	11-6-78	Rehabilitation, Comprehensive Services, and Developmental Disabilities Amendments of 1978	1978-2 CB 415
95-615	11-8-78	Tax Treatment Extension Act of 1977 (Foreign Earned Income)	1978-2 CB 415
95-616	11-8-78	Fish and Wildlife Improvement Act of 1978	1978-2 CB 435
95-618	11-9-78	Energy Tax Act of 1978	1978-3 CB 1
95-628	11-10-78	To revise miscellaneous timing requirements of the revenue laws, etc.	1978-2 CB 435
		Statutes Enacted by the 96th Congress—1st Session	
96-8	4-10-79	Taiwan Relations Act	1979-1 CB 459
96-39	7-26-79	Trade Agreements Act of 1979	93 Stat. 144
96-72	9-29-79	Export Administration Act of 1979	1979-2 CB 473
96-74	9-29-79	Treasury Department Appropriations Act of 1980	1979-2 CB 473
96-84	10-10-79	To amend the Unemployment Compensation Amendments of 1976 with respect to the National Commission on Unemployment Compensation	1979-2 CB 474
96-167	12-29-79	To continue through May 31, 1981, the existing prohibition on the issuance of fringe benefit regulations, etc.	1980-1 CB 483
96-178	1-2-80	To extend for one year the provision of law relating to the business expenses of State legislators	1980-1 CB 494

Public Law No.	Date	Title or Subject	Reprint
		Statutes Enacted by the 96th Congress—2nd Session	
96-187	1-8-80	Federal Election Campaign Act Amendments for 1979	93 Stat. 1339
96-222	4-1-80	Technical Corrections Act of 1979	1980-1 CB 499
96-223	4-2-80	Crude Oil Windfall Profit Tax Act of 1980	1980-3 CB 1
96-249	5-26-80	Food Stamp Act Amendments of 1980	1980-2 CB 414
96-265	6-9-80	Social Security Disability Amendments of 1980	1980-2 CB 418
96-272	6-17-80	Adoption Assistance and Child Welfare Act of 1980	1980-2 CB 419
96-283	6-28-80	Deep Seabed Hard Mineral Resources Act	1980-2 CB 422
96-294	6-30-80	Energy Security Act	1980-2 CB 428
96-298	7-1-80	To provide a three-month extension of the Taxes which are transferred to the Airport and Airway Trust fund	1980-2 CB 431
96-304	7-8-80	To make supplemental appropriations for the fiscal year ending 9-30-80, rescinding certain budget authority, etc.	1980-2 CB 433
96-318	8-1-80	Delaware Tribe of Indians judgement funds	94 Stat. 968
96-320	8-3-80	Ocean Thermal Energy Conversion Act of 1980 (To amend the '36 Merchant Marine Act)	1980-2 CB 433
96-330	8-26-80	Veteran's Administration Health-Care Amendments of 1980	1980-2 CB 435
96-364	9-26-80	Multiemployer Pension Plan Amendments Act of 1980	1980-2 CB 437
96-369	10-1-80	Continuing Appropriations, 1981	1980-2 CB 479
96-417	10-10-80	Customs Court Act of 1980	94 Stat. 1727
96-439	10-14-80	To authorize three additional judges for the Tax Court and to remove the age limitation on appointments to the Tax Court	94 Stat. 1878
96-449	10-14-80	Hostage Relief Act of 1980	1980-2 CB 479
96-451	10-14-80	Reforestation; Federal Boat Safety Act	1980-2 CB 485
96-454	10-15-80	Household Goods Transportation Act of 1980	94 Stat. 2011
96-465	10-17-80	Foreign Service Act of 1980	94 Stat. 2071
96-471	10-19-80	Installment Sales Revision Act of 1980	1980-2 CB 489
96-481	10-21-80	Equal Access to Justice Act	94 Stat. 2321
96-499	12-5-80	Omnibus Reconciliation Act of 1980	1980-2 CB 509
96-510	12-11-80	Comprehensive Environmental Response, Compensation, and Liability Act of 1980	1980-2 CB 589
96-536	12-16-80	Continuing appropriations for fiscal year '81	1980-2 CB 596
96-541	12-17-80	Tax Treatment Extension Act of 1980	1980-2 CB 596
96-589	12-24-80	Bankruptcy Tax Act of 1980	1980-2 CB 607
96-595	12-24-80	To amend the '54 Code with respect to net operating loss carryovers of taxpayers who cease to be REITs, etc.	1980-2 CB 647
96-596	12-24-80	To amend the '54 Code with respect to the determination of second tier taxes, etc.	1980-2 CB 653
96-598	12-24-80	Excise tax refunds in the case of certain uses of tread rubber, etc.	1980-2 CB 661
96-601	12-24-80	To simplify certain provisions of the '54 Code	1980-2 CB 666
96-603	12-28-80	To amend the '54 Code to simplify private foundation return and reporting requirements, etc.	1980-2 CB 684
96-605	12-28-80	Miscellaneous Revenue Act of 1980	1980-2 CB 702
96-608	12-28-80	To amend the '54 Code to waive in certain cases the residency requirements for deductions or exclusions of individuals living abroad, to allow the tax-free rollover of certain distributions from money purchase pension plans, etc.	1980-2 CB 37
96-611	12-28-80	To amend title XVIII of the Social Security Act	1980-2 CB 728
96-613	12-28-80	To make certain miscellaneous changes in the tax laws	1980-2 CB 737
		Statutes Enacted by the 97th Congress—1st Session	
97-34	8-13-81	Economic Recovery Tax Act of 1981	1981-2 CB 256
97-35	8-13-81	Omnibus Budget Reconciliation Act of 1981	1981-2 CB 528
97-51	10-1-81	Continuing appropriations for fiscal year 1982	1982-1 CB 306
97-92	12-15-81	Further continuing appropriations for fiscal year 1982	1982-1 CB 306
97-119	12-29-81	To provide a temporary increase in the tax imposed on Producers of Coal, etc.	1982-1 CB 307
97-123	12-29-81	To amend the '81 Omnibus Reconciliation Act to restore minimum benefits under the Social Security Act	1982-1 CB 314

Public Law No.	Date	Title or Subject	Reprint
		Statutes Enacted by the 97th Congress—2nd Session	
97-164	4-2-82	Federal Courts Improvement Act of 1982	1982-1 CB 316
97-216	7-18-82	To make supplemental appropriations for the fiscal year ending Sept. 30, 1982, etc.	1982-2 CB 461
97-248	9-3-82	Tax Equity and Fiscal Responsibility Act of 1982 (TEFRA)	1982-2 CB 462
97-258	9-13-82	To amend title 31, U.S.C., money and finance	96 Stat. 877
97-261	9-20-82	Bus Regulatory Reform Act of 1982	96 Stat. 1102
97-354	10-19-82	Subchapter S Revision Act of 1982	1982-2 CB 702
97-362	10-25-82	Miscellaneous Revenue Act of 1982	1983-1 CB 367
97-365	10-25-82	Debt Collection Act of 1982	1983-1 CB 390
97-402	12-31-82	To provide for the use and distribution of Clallam judgement funds	96 Stat. 2020
97-403	12-31-82	To provide for the use and distribution of funds awarded to the Pembina Chippewa Indians	96 Stat. 2022
97-408	1-3-83	To provide for the use and distribution of funds awarded to the Blackfeet and Gros Ventre Tribes, Assiniboine, and Papago Indians	96 Stat. 2035
97-414	1-4-83	Orphans Drug Act	1983-1 CB 403
97-424	1-6-83	Highway Revenue Act of 1982	1983-1 CB 405
97-436	1-8-83	To provide for the distribution of Warm Springs judgement funds awarded in docket numbered 198 before the Indian Claims Commission, and for other purposes	96 Stat. 2283
97-448	1-12-83	Technical Corrections Act of 1982	1983-1 CB 451
97-449	1-12-83	To revise, codify, and enact without substantive change certain general and permanent laws related to transportation as subtitle I and chapter 31 of subtitle II of title 49, United States Code, "Transportation"	96 Stat. 2413
97-452	1-12-83	To codify laws relating to money and finance	96 Stat. 2467
97-455	1-12-83	To reduce the rate of certain taxes paid to the Virgin Island on Virgin Islands' source income	1983-1 CB 507
97-473	1-14-83	To amend the Code for tax treatment of periodic payments for personal injury, etc.	1983-1 CB 510
		Statutes Enacted by the 98th Congress—1st Session	
98-4	3-11-83	Payment-in-Kind Tax Treatment Act of 1983	1983-2 CB 296
98-21	4-20-83	Social Security Amendments of 1983	97 Stat. 65
98-63	7-30-83	Supplemental Appropriations Act, 1983	1983-2 CB 351
98-67	8-5-83	Interest and Dividend Tax Compliance Act of 1983	97 Stat. 369
98-76	8-12-83	Railroad Retirement Solvency Act of 1983	1983-2 CB 375
98-118	10-11-83	To extend the Federal Supplemental Compensation Act of 1982	1983-2 CB 401
98-123	10-13-83	To provide for tax exempt distribution of judgement funds to members of the Red Lake Band of Chippewa Indians	1983-2 CB 401
98-124	10-13-83	To provide for tax exempt distribution of judgement funds to members of the Assiniboine Tribe	1983-2 CB 402
98-134	10-18-83	Mashantucket Pequot Indian Claims Settlement Act	1984-1 CB 310
98-135	10-24-83	Federal Supplemental Compensation Amendments of 1983	1984-1 CB 311
98-213	12-8-83	To authorize capital improvement projects on Guam	97 Stat. 1459
		Statutes Enacted by the 98th Congress—2nd Session	
98-216	2-14-84	To amend laws related to money and finance	98 Stat. 3
98-259	4-10-84	To exempt from Federal income taxes certain military and civilian employees of the U.S. dying as a result of injuries sustained overseas	1984-1 CB 313
98-355	7-11-84	To increase the Federal contribution for the Quadrennial Political Party Presidential National Nominating Conventions	98 Stat. 394
98-369	7-18-84	Deficit Reduction Act of 1984 [Tax Reform Act of 1984]	1984-3 CB 1
98-378	8-16-84	Child Support Enforcement Amendments of 1984	1984-2 CB 429
98-397	8-23-84	Retirement Equity Act of 1984	98 Stat. 1426
98-408	8-28-84	To convey certain lands to the Zuni Indian Tribe for religious purposes	1984-2 CB 462
98-432	9-28-84	Shoalwater Bay Indian Tribe—Dexter-by-the-Sea Claim Settlement Act	1984-2 CB 463
98-443	10-4-84	Civil Aeronautics Board Sunset Act of 1984	1985-1 CB 410
98-454	10-5-84	To enhance the economic development of Guam, the Virgin Islands, American Samoa, the Northern Mariana Islands, etc.	1985-1 CB 410
98-473	10-12-84	Making continuing appropriations for the fiscal year 1985, etc.	98 Stat. 1837
98-573	10-30-84	Trade and Tariff Act of 1984	87 Stat. 2948

Public Law No.	Date	Title or Subject	Reprint
98-601	10-30-84	To amend the Tax Equity and Fiscal Responsibility Act of 1982	1985-1 CB 411
98-611	10-31-84	To extend for two years the exclusion from gross income for educational assistance programs	1985-1 CB 413
98-612	10-31-84	To extend for one year the exclusion from gross income for group legal services plans	1985-1 CB 416
98-620	11-8-84	To amend Title 28, U.S.C., with respect to the places where court shall be held in certain judicial districts, and for other purposes	98 Stat. 3335
		Statutes Enacted by the 99th Congress—1st Session	
99-44	5-24-85	To amend the '54 Code to repeal the contemporaneous recordkeeping requirements added by the 1984 TRA, and for other purposes	1985-2 CB 350
99-92	8-16-85	Nurse Education Amendments of 1985	99 Stat. 393
99-107	9-30-85	Emergency Extension Act of 1985	1985-2 CB 366
99-121	10-11-85	To amend the '54 Code to simplify the imputed interest rules of Code Secs. 1274 and 483, etc.	1985-2 CB 367
99-155	11-14-85	To temporarily increase the limit on public debt and to restore the investment of the Social Security Trust Funds and other trust funds	99 Stat. 814
99-181	12-13-85	To extend until 12-18-85, the application of certain tobacco excise taxes, etc.	99 Stat. 1172
99-189	12-18-85	To extend until 12-20-85, the application of certain tobacco excise taxes, etc.	99 Stat. 1184
99-190	12-19-85	To make further continuing appropriations for the fiscal year 1986, etc.	99 Stat. 1185
99-201	12-23-85	To extend until 3-15-86, the application of certain tobacco excise taxes, etc.	99 Stat. 1665
99-221	12-26-85	Cherokee Leasing Act	99 Stat. 1735
99-234	1-2-86	Federal Civilian Employee Contractor Travel Expenses Act of 1985	99 Stat. 1755
99-239	1-14-86	Compact of Free Association Act of 1985	99 Stat. 1770
		Statutes Enacted by the 99th Congress—2nd Session	
99-272	4-7-86	Consolidated Omnibus Budget Reconciliation Act of 1985	1986-2 CB 298
99-308	5-19-86	Firearms Owners' Protection Act	100 Stat. 449
99-386	8-22-86	Congressional Reports Elimination Act of 1986	100 Stat. 821
99-335	6-6-86	Federal Employees' Retirement System Act of 1986	99 Stat. 514
99-346	6-30-86	Saginaw Chippewa Indian Tribe of Michigan Distribution of Judgement Funds Act	1987-2 CB 337
99-398	8-28-86	Klamath Indian Tribe Restoration Act	99 Stat. 849
99-499	10-17-86	Superfund Amendments and Reauthorization Act of 1986	1987-1 CB 373
99-509	10-21-86	Omnibus Budget Reconciliation Act of 1986	99 Stat. 1874
99-514	10-22-86	Tax Reform Act of 1986	1986-3 CB 1
99-595	10-31-86	To extend the exclusion from Federal unemployment tax wages paid to certain alien farmworkers	1987-1 CB 393
99-640	11-10-86	Coast Guard Authorization Act of 1986	99 Stat. 3545
99-662	11-17-86	Water Resources Development Act of 1986	1986-2 CB 364
		Statutes Enacted by the 100th Congress—1st Session	
100-17	4-2-87	Surface Transportation and Uniform Relocation Assistance Act of 1987	101 Stat. 132
100-202	12-22-87	To make further continuing appropriations for the '88 fiscal year, and for other purposes	101 Stat. 1329
100-203	12-22-87	Omnibus Budget Reconciliation Act of 1987	1987-3 CB-1
100-223	12-30-87	Airport and Airway Safety and Capacity Expansion Act of 1987	101 Stat. 1486
		Statutes Enacted by the 100th Congress—2nd Session	
100-360	7-1-88	Medicare Catastrophic Coverage Act of 1988	1989-1 CB 355
100-418	8-23-88	Omnibus Trade and Competitiveness Act of 1988	102 Stat. 1107
100-448	9-28-88	Coast Guard Authorization Act of 1988	102 Stat. 1836
100-485	10-13-88	Family Support Act of 1988	1989-2 CB 338
100-647	11-10-88	Technical and Miscellaneous Revenue Act of 1988 (TAMRA)	1988-3 CB 1
100-690	11-18-88	Anti-Drug Abuse Act of 1988	1989-2 CB 347
100-707	11-23-88	Disaster Relief and Emergency Assistance Amendments of 1988	102 Stat. 4689

Public Law No.	Date	Title or Subject	Reprint
		Statutes Enacted by the 101st Congress—1st Session	
101-73	8-9-89	Financial Institutions Reform, Recovery, and Enforcement Act of 1989	1989-2 CB 349
101-140	11-8-89	Repeal of Code Sec. 89 Non-discrimination Rules	1990-1 CB 207
101-179	11-28-89	Support for East European Democracy (SEED) Act of 1989	103 Stat. 1298
101-194	11-30-89	Ethics Reform Act of 1989	1990-1 CB 209
101-221	12-12-89	Steel Trade Liberalization Program Implementation Act	103 Stat. 1886
101-234	12-13-89	Medicare Catastrophic Coverage Repeal Act of 1989	103 Stat. 1979
101-239	12-19-89	Omnibus Budget Reconciliation Act of 1989	1990-1 CB 210
		Statutes Enacted by the 101st Congress—2nd Session	
101-280	5-4-90	Technical Corrections to the Ethics Reform Act of 1989	104 Stat. 149
101-380	8-18-90	Oil Pollution Act of 1990	104 Stat. 484
101-382	8-20-90	Customs and Trade Act of 1990	104 Stat. 629
101-508	11-5-90	Omnibus Budget Reconciliation Act of 1990	1991-2 CB 481
101-509	11-5-90	Treasury, Postal Service and General Government Appropriations Act of 1991	104 Stat. 3066
101-604	11-16-90	Aviation Security Improvement Act of 1990	104 Stat. 3066
101-624	11-28-90	Food, Agriculture, Conservation, and Trade Act of 1990	1991-1 CB 306
101-647	11-29-90	Crime Control Act of 1990	1992-1 CB 485
101-649	11-29-90	Immigration Act of 1990	104 Stat. 4978
		Statutes Enacted by the 102nd Congress—1st Session	
102-2	1-30-91	Armed Forces Taxes	1991-1 CB 307
102-40	5-7-91	Department of Veterans Affairs Health-Care Personnel Act of 1991	105 Stat. 187
102-54	6-13-91	Veterans programs for housing and memorial affairs	105 Stat. 267
102-90	8-14-91	Appropriations for the Legislative Branch for the fiscal year ending 9-30-92	1992-2 CB 330
102-107	8-17-91	Emergency Unemployment Compensation Act of 1991	105 Stat. 541
102-164	11-15-91	Emergency Unemployment Compensation Act of 1991	1992-2 CB 330
102-227	12-11-91	Tax Extension Act of 1991	1992-2 CB 333
102-240	12-18-91	Surface Transportation Revenue Act of 1991	1992-2 CB 335
		Statutes Enacted by the 102nd Congress—2nd Session	
102-244	2-7-92	Extension of Unemployment Benefits	1992-2 CB 337
102-318	7-3-92	Unemployment Compensation Amendments of 1992	1992-2 CB 339
102-393	10-6-92	Appropriations for the Treasury Department, U.S. Postal Service, Executive Office of President, etc. for the fiscal year ending September 30, 1993	106 Stat. 1729
102-486	10-24-92	Energy Policy Act of 1992	1993-1 CB 246
102-568	10-29-92	Veterans' Benefits Act of 1992	106 Stat. 4320
102-581	10-31-92	Airport and Airway Safety, Capacity, Noise Improvement, and Intermodal Transportation Act of 1992	106 Stat. 4872
		Statutes Enacted by the 103rd Congress—1st Session	
103-66	8-10-93	Omnibus Budget Reconciliation Act of 1993	1993-3 CB 1
103-149	11-23-93	South African Democratic Transition Support Act of 1993	107 Stat. 1503
103-178	12-3-93	Intelligence Authorization Act for Fiscal Year 1994	107 Stat. 2024
103-182	12-8-93	North American Free Trade Agreement Implementation Act	107 Stat. 2057
		Statutes Enacted by the 103rd Congress—2nd Session	
103-260	5-26-94	Airport Improvement Program Temporary Extension Act of 1994	108 Stat. 698
103-272	7-5-94	Codification of Certain U.S. Transportation Laws as Title 49, United States Code	108 Stat. 745
103-296	8-15-94	Social Security Independence and Program Improvements Act of 1994	1994-1 CB 543
103-305	8-23-94	Federal Aviation Administration Authorization Act of 1994	108 Stat. 1569
103-322	9-13-94	Violent Crime Control and Law Enforcement Act of 1994	108 Stat. 1799
103-337	10-5-94	National Defense Authorization Act for Fiscal Year 1995	108 Stat. 2663
103-387	10-22-94	Social Security Domestic Employment Reform Act of 1994	108 Stat. 4071
103-429	10-31-94	To codify without substantive change recent laws related to transportation and to improve the United States Code	108 Stat. 4377
103-465	12-8-94	Uruguay Round Agreements Act	1995-1 CB 230

Public Law No.	Date	Title or Subject	Reprint
		Statutes Enacted by the 104th Congress—1st Session	
104-7	4-11-95	Self-Employed Health Insurance Act	109 Stat. 93
104-88	12-29-95	ICC Termination Act of 1995	109 Stat. 803
		Statutes Enacted by the 104th Congress—2nd Session	
104-117	3-20-96	To provide that members of the Armed Forces performing services for the peacekeeping efforts in Bosnia and Herzegovina, Croatia, and Macedonia shall be entitled to tax benefits in the same manner as if such services were performed in a combat zone	1996-3 CB 1
104-134	4-26-96	Omnibus Consolidated Rescissions and Appropriations Act of 1996	1996-3 CB 17
104-168	7-30-96	Taxpayer Bill of Rights	1996-3 CB 19
104-188	8-20-96	Small Business Job Protection Act of 1996	1996-3 CB 155
104-191	8-21-96	Health Insurance Portability and Accountability Act of 1996	1996-3 CB 1111
104-193	8-22-96	Personal Responsibility and Work Opportunity Reconciliation Act of 1996	1996-3 CB 1179
104-201	9-23-96	National Defense Authorization Act for Fiscal Year 1997	110 Stat. 2422
104-264	10-9-96	Federal Aviation Reauthorization Act of 1996	110 Stat. 3213
104-316	10-19-96	General Accounting Office Act of 1996	110 Stat. 3826
		Statutes Enacted by the 105th Congress—1st Session	
105-2	2-28-97	Airport and Airway Trust Fund Tax Reinstatement Act of 1997	1997-1 CB 315
105-33	8-5-97	Balanced Budget Act of 1997	111 Stat. 251
105-34	8-5-97	Taxpayer Relief Act of 1997	111 Stat. 788
105-35	8-5-97	Taxpayer Browsing Protection Act	1997-2 CB 278
105-61	10-10-97	Appropriations for the Treasury Dept., the U.S. Postal Service, the Executive Office of the President, and certain Independent Agencies, for the fiscal year ending 9-30-98, and for other purposes	111 Stat. 1272
105-65	10-27-97	Departments of Veterans Affairs and Housing and Urban Development, and Independent Agencies Appropriations Act, 1998	111 Stat. 1344
105-78	11-13-97	Appropriations for the Depts. of Labor, Health and Human Services, and Education, and related agencies for the fiscal year ending 9-30-98, and for other purposes	111 Stat. 1467
105-102	11-20-97	To codify without substantive change laws related to transportation and to improve the United States Code	111 Stat. 2204
105-115	11-21-97	Food and Drug Administration Modernization Act of 1997	111 Stat. 2326
105-130	12-1-97	Surface Transportation Extension Act of 1997	111 Stat. 2552
		Statutes Enacted by the 105th Congress—2nd Session	
105-178	6-9-98	Transportation and Equity Act for the 21st Century	112 Stat. 107
105-206	7-22-98	IRS Restructuring and Reform Act of 1998	112 Stat. 685
105-277	10-21-98	Tax and Trade Relief Extension Act of 1998	112 Stat. 2681
105-306	10-28-98	Noncitizen Benefit Clarification and Other Technical Amendments Act of 1998	112 Stat. 2926
		Statutes Enacted by the 106th Congress—1st Session	
106-21	4-19-99	To extend the tax benefits available with respect to services performed in a combat zone to services performed in the Federal Republic of Yugoslavia (Serbia/Montenegro) and certain other areas	113 Stat. 34
106-36	6-25-99	Miscellaneous Trade and Technical Corrections Act of 1999	113 Stat. 127
106-78	10-22-99	Agriculture, Rural Development, Food and Drug Administration, and Related Agencies Appropriations Act, 2000	113 Stat. 1135
106-170	12-17-99	Ticket to Work and Work Incentives Improvement Act of 1999	113 Stat. 1860
		Statutes Enacted by the 106th Congress—2nd Session	
106-181	4-5-00	Wendell H. Ford Aviation and Investment Reform Act for the 21st Century	114 Stat. 196
106-200	5-18-00	Trade and Development Act of 2000	114 Stat. 251
106-230	7-1-00	To require Code Sec. 527 organizations to disclose their political activities	114 Stat. 477
106-408	11-1-00	Fish and Wildlife Programs Improvement and National Wildlife Refuge System Centennial Act of 2000	114 Stat. 1775
106-476	11-9-00	Tariff Suspension and Trade Act of 2000	114 Stat. 2101
106-519	11-15-00	FSC Repeal and Extraterritorial Income Exclusion Act of 2000	114 Stat. 2423
106-554	12-21-00	Consolidated Appropriations Act, 2001	114 Stat. 2763

Public Law No.	Date	Title or Subject	Reprint
106-573	12-28-00	Installment Tax Correction Act of 2000	114 Stat. 3061
		Statutes Enacted by the 107th Congress—1st Session	
107-15	6-5-01	Fallen Hero Survivor Benefit Fairness Act of 2001	115 Stat. 37
107-16	6-7-01	Economic Growth and Tax Relief Reconciliation Act of 2001	115 Stat. 38
107-22	7-26-01	To rename the education individual retirement accounts as the Coverdell education savings accounts	115 Stat. 196
107-67	11-12-01	Treasury and General Government Appropriations Act, 2002	115 Stat. 514
107-71	11-19-01	Aviation and Transportation Security Act	115 Stat. 597
107-90	12-21-01	Railroad Retirement and Survivors' Improvement Act of 2001	115 Stat. 878
107-110	1-8-02	No Child Left Behind Act of 2001	115 Stat. 1425
107-116	1-10-02	Departments of Labor, Health and Human Services, and Education, and Related Agencies Appropriations Act, 2002	115 Stat. 2177
107-131	1-16-02	To simplify the reporting requirements relating to higher education tuition and related expenses	115 Stat. 2410
107-134	1-23-02	Victims of Terrorism Tax Relief Act of 2001	115 Stat. 2427
		Statutes Enacted by the 107th Congress—2nd Session	
107-147	3-9-02	Job Creation and Worker Assistance Act of 2002	116 Stat. 21
107-181	5-20-02	Clergy Housing Allowance Clarification Act of 2002	116 Stat. 583
107-210	8-6-02	Trade Act of 2002	116 Stat. 933
107-217	8-21-02	To revise, codify, and enact without substantive change certain general and permanent laws, related to public buildings, property, and works, as title 40, United States Code, "Public Buildings, Property, and Works"	116 Stat. 1062
107-276	11-2-02	To amend section 527 of the Internal Revenue Code of 1986 to eliminate notification and return requirements for State and local party committees and candidate committees	116 Stat. 1929
107-296	11-25-02	Homeland Security Act of 2002	116 Stat. 2135
107-330	12-6-02	Veterans Benefits Act of 2002	116 Stat. 2820
107-358	12-17-02	Holocaust Restitution Tax Fairness Act of 2002	116 Stat. 3015
		Statutes Enacted by the 108th Congress—1st Session	
108-27	5-28-03	Jobs and Growth Tax Relief Reconciliation Act of 2003	117 Stat. 752
108-81	9-25-03	Museum and Library Services Act of 2003	117 Stat. 991
108-88	9-30-03	Surface Transportation Extension Act of 2003	117 Stat. 1110
108-89	10-1-03	To extend the Temporary Assistance for Needy Families block grant program, and certain tax and trade programs, and for other purposes	117 Stat. 1131
108-121	11-11-03	Military Family Tax Relief Act of 2003	117 Stat. 1335
108-173	12-8-03	Medicare Prescription Drug, Improvement, and Modernization Act of 2003	117 Stat. 2066
108-176	12-12-03	Vision 100—Century of Aviation Reauthorization Act	117 Stat. 2490
108-178	12-15-03	To improve the United States Code	117 Stat. 2637
108-189	12-19-03	Servicemembers Civil Relief Act	117 Stat. 2835
		Statutes Enacted by the 108th Congress—2nd Session	
108-202	2-29-04	Surface Transportation Extension Act of 2004	118 Stat. 478
108-203	3-2-04	Social Security Protection Act of 2004	118 Stat. 493
108-218	4-10-04	Pension Funding Equity Act of 2004	118 Stat. 596
108-224	4-30-04	Surface Transportation Extension Act of 2004, Part II	118 Stat. 627
108-263	6-30-04	Surface Transportation Extension Act of 2004, Part III	118 Stat. 698
108-280	7-30-04	Surface Transportation Extension Act of 2004, Part IV	118 Stat. 876
108-310	9-30-04	Surface Transportation Extension Act of 2004, Part V	118 Stat. 1144
108-311	10-4-04	Working Families Tax Relief Act of 2004	118 Stat. 1166
108-357	10-22-04	American Jobs Creation Act of 2004	118 Stat. 1418
108-375	10-28-04	Ronald W. Reagan Defense Authorization Act for Fiscal Year 2005	118 Stat. 1811
108-429	12-3-04	Miscellaneous Trade and Technical Corrections Act of 2004	118 Stat. 2434
108-476	12-21-04	To treat certain arrangements maintained by the YMCA Retirement Fund as church plans for the purposes of certain provisions of the Internal Revenue Code of 1986, and for other purposes	118 Stat. 3901
108-493	12-23-04	To amend the Internal Revenue Code of 1986 to modify the taxation of arrow components	118 Stat. 3984

Public Law No.	Date	Title or Subject	Reprint
		Statutes Enacted by the 109th Congress—1st Session	
109-1	1-7-05	To accelerate the income tax benefits for charitable cash contributions for the relief of victims of the Indian Ocean tsunami	119 Stat. 3
109-6	3-31-05	To amend the Internal Revenue Code of 1986 to extend the Leaking Underground Storage Tank Trust Fund financing rate	119 Stat. 20
109-7	4-15-05	To amend the Internal Revenue Code of 1986 to provide for the proper tax treatment of certain disaster mitigation payments	119 Stat. 21
109-14	5-31-05	Surface Transportation Extension Act of 2005	119 Stat. 324
109-20	7-1-05	Surface Transportation Extension Act of 2005, Part II	119 Stat. 346
109-35	7-20-05	Surface Transportation Extension Act of 2005, Part III	119 Stat. 379
109-37	7-22-05	Surface Transportation Extension Act of 2005, Part IV	119 Stat. 394
109-40	7-28-05	Surface Transportation Extension Act of 2005, Part V	119 Stat. 410
109-42	7-30-05	Surface Transportation Extension Act of 2005, Part VI	119 Stat. 435
109-58	8-8-05	Energy Tax Incentives Act of 2005 [title XIII of the Energy Policy Act of 2005]	119 Stat. 594
109-59	8-10-05	Safe, Accountable, Flexible, Efficient Transportation Act: A Legacy for Users [Transportation Act of 2005]	119 Stat. 1144
109-73	9-23-05	Katrina Emergency Tax Relief Act of 2005	119 Stat. 2016
109-74	9-29-05	Sportfishing and Recreational Boating Safety Amendments Act of 2005	119 Stat. 2030
109-135	12-21-05	Gulf Opportunity Zone Act of 2005	119 Stat. 2577
109-151	12-30-05	To amend title I of ERISA, title XXVII of the Public Health Service Act, and the Internal Revenue Code to extend by one year provisions requiring parity in the application of certain limits to mental health benefits	119 Stat. 2886
		Statutes Enacted by the 109th Congress—2nd Session	
109-171	2-8-06	Deficit Reduction Act of 2005	120 Stat. 4
109-222	5-17-06	Tax Increase Prevention and Reconciliation Act of 2005	120 Stat. 345
109-227	5-29-06	Heroes Earned Retirement Opportunities Act	120 Stat. 385
109-241	7-12-06	Coast Guard and Maritime Transportation Act of 2006	120 Stat. 516
109-280	8-17-06	Pension Protection Act of 2006	120 Stat. 780
109-432	12-20-06	Tax Relief and Health Care Act of 2006	120 Stat. 2922
		Statutes Enacted by the 110th Congress—1st Session	
110-28	5-25-07	Small Business and Work Opportunity Tax Act of 2007	121 Stat. 112
110-42	6-30-07	Andean Trade Preference Act	121 Stat. 235
110-52	8-1-07	Approving the renewal of import restrictions contained in the Burmese Freedom and Democracy Act of 2003	121 Stat. 982
110-138	12-14-07	United States-Peru Trade Promotion Agreement Implementation Act	121 Stat. 1492
110-140	12-19-07	Energy Independence and Security Act of 2007	121 Stat.
110-141	12-19-07	To exclude from gross income payments from the Hokie Spirit Memorial Fund to the victims of the tragic event, loss of life and limb, at Virginia Polytechnic Institute & State University	121 Stat.
110-142	12-20-07	Mortgage Forgiveness Debt Relief Act of 2007	121 Stat. 1803
110-161	12-26-07	Consolidated Appropriations Act, 2008	121 Stat. 1844
110-166	12-26-07	Tax Increase Prevention Act of 2007	121 Stat. 2461
110-172	12-29-07	Tax Technical Corrections Act of 2007	121 Stat. 2473
		Statutes Enacted by the 110th Congress—2nd Session	
110-185	2-13-08	Economic Stimulus Act of 2008	122 Stat. 613
110-190	2-28-08	Airport and Airway Extension Act of 2008	122 Stat. 643
110-233	5-21-08	Genetic Information Nondiscrimination Act of 2008	122 Stat. 881
110-234	5-22-08	Food, Conservation, and Energy Act of 2008	122 Stat. 923
110-245	6-17-08	Heroes Earnings Assistance and Relief Tax Act of 2008	122 Stat. 1624
110-246	5-22-08	Food, Conservation, and Energy Act of 2008	122 Stat.
110-253	6-30-08	Federal Aviation Administration Extension Act of 2008	122 Stat. 2417
110-289	7-30-08	Housing Assistance Tax Act of 2008	122 Stat. 2654
110-317	8-29-08	Hubbard Act	122 Stat. 3526
110-318	9-15-08	To amend the Internal Revenue Code of 1986 to restore the Highway Trust Fund balance.	122 Stat. 3532
110-328	9-30-08	SSI Extension for Elderly and Disabled Refugees Act	122 Stat. 3567
110-330	9-30-08	Federal Aviation Administration Extension Act of 2008, Part II	122 Stat. 3717

Public Law No.	Date	Title or Subject	Reprint
110-343	10-3-08	Emergency Economic Stabilization Act of 2008	122 Stat. 3765
110-351	10-7-08	Fostering Connections to Success and Increasing Adoptions Act of 2008	122 Stat. 3949
110-381	10-9-08	Michelle's Law	122 Stat. 4081
110-428	10-15-08	Inmate Tax Fraud Prevention Act of 2008	122 Stat. 4839
110-458	12-23-08	Worker, Retiree, and Employer Recovery Act of 2008	122 Stat. 5092

TABLE OF CODE SECTIONS

Internal Revenue Code

(as amended)

SUBTITLE A—INCOME TAXES

Chapter 1. Normal Taxes and Surtaxes

Subchapter A. Determination of Tax Liability

PART I. TAX ON INDIVIDUALS

Sec.	
1	Tax imposed
2	Definitions and special rules
3	Tax tables for individuals
4	Repealed [Rules for optional tax]
5	Cross references relating to tax on individuals

PART II. TAX ON CORPORATIONS

Sec.	
11	Tax imposed
12	Cross references relating to tax on corporations

PART III. CHANGES IN RATES DURING A TAXABLE YEAR

Sec.	
15	Effect of changes

PART IV. CREDITS AGAINST TAX

Subpart A. Nonrefundable personal credits

Sec.	
21	Expenses for household and dependent care services necessary for gainful employment
22	Credit for the elderly and the permanently and totally disabled
23	Adoption expenses
23	Repealed [Residential energy credit]
24	Child tax credit
24	Repealed [Contributions to candidates for public office]
25	Interest on certain home mortgages
25A	Hope and Lifetime Learning credits
25B	Elective deferrals and IRA contributions by certain individuals
25C	Nonbusiness energy property
25D	Residential energy efficient property
26	Limitation based on tax liability; definition of tax liability

Subpart B. Other credits

Sec.	
27	Taxes of foreign countries and possessions of the United States; possession tax credit
28	Repealed [Clinical testing expenses for certain drugs for rare diseases or conditions]
30	Credit for qualified electric vehicles
30A	Puerto Rico economic activity credit
30B	Alternative motor vehicle credit
30C	Alternative fuel vehicle refueling property credit

Subpart C. Refundable credits

Sec.	
31	Tax withheld on wages
32	Earned income
33	Tax withheld at source on nonresident aliens and foreign corporations
34	Certain uses of gasoline and special fuels
35	Health insurance costs of eligible individuals
36	First-time homebuyer credit
37	Overpayments of tax
36	Repealed [Credits not allowed to individuals taking standard deduction]

Subpart D. Business related credits

Sec.	
38	General business credit
38	Repealed [Investment in certain depreciable property]
39	Carryback and carryforward of unused credits
40	Alcohol used as fuel
40	Repealed [Expenses of work incentive programs]
40A	Biodiesel and renewable diesel used as fuel
41	Credit for increasing research activities
41	Repealed [Employee stock ownership credit]
42	Low-income housing credit
43	Enhanced oil recovery credit
44	Expenditures to provide access to disabled individuals
44	Repealed [Purchase of new principal residence]
44B	Repealed [Credit for employment of certain new employees]
45	Electricity produced from certain renewable resources, etc.
45A	Indian employment credit
45B	Credit for portion of employer social security taxes paid with respect to employee cash tips
45C	Clinical testing expenses for certain drugs for rare diseases or conditions
45D	New markets tax credit
45E	Small employer pension plan startup costs
45F	Employer-provided child care credit
45G	Railroad track maintenance credit
45H	Credit for production of low sulfur diesel fuel
45I	Credit for producing oil and gas from marginal wells
45J	Credit for production from advanced nuclear power facilities
45K	Credit for producing fuel from a nonconventional source
45L	New energy efficient home credit
45M	Energy efficient appliance credit
45N	Mine rescue training credit
45O	Agricultural chemicals security credit
45P	Employer wage credit for employees who are active duty members of the uniformed services

Subpart E. Rules for computing investment credit

Sec.	
46	Amount of credit
47	Rehabilitation credit
48	Energy credit
48A	Qualifying advanced coal project credit
48B	Qualifying gasification project credit
49	At-risk rules
50	Other special rules

Sec.

Subpart F. Rules for computing work opportunity credit

51 Amount of credit
51A Temporary incentives for employing long-term family assistance recipients
52 Special rules

Subpart G. Credit against regular tax for prior year minimum tax liability

53 Credit for prior year minimum tax liability
53 Repealed [Limitation based on amount of tax]

Subpart H. Nonrefundable credit to holders of certain bonds

54 Credit to holders of clean renewable energy bonds
54A Credit to holders of qualified tax credit bonds
54B Qualified forestry conservation bonds

PART V. REPEALED [TAX SURCHARGE]

PART VI. ALTERNATIVE MINIMUM TAX

55 Alternative minimum tax imposed
56 Adjustments in computing alternative minimum taxable income
57 Items of tax preference
58 Denial of certain losses
59 Other definitions and special rules

PART VII. ENVIRONMENTAL TAX

59A Environmental tax

PART VIII. REPEALED [SUPPLEMENTAL MEDICARE PREMIUM]

59B Repealed [Supplemental medicare premium]

Subchapter B. Computation of Taxable Income

PART I. DEFINITION OF GROSS INCOME, ADJUSTED GROSS INCOME, TAXABLE INCOME, ETC.

61 Gross income defined
62 Adjusted gross income defined
63 Taxable income defined
64 Ordinary income defined
65 Ordinary loss defined
66 Treatment of community income
67 2-percent floor on miscellaneous itemized deductions
68 Overall limitation on itemized deductions

PART II. ITEMS SPECIFICALLY INCLUDED IN GROSS INCOME

71 Alimony and separate maintenance payments
72 Annuities; certain proceeds of endowment and life insurance contracts
73 Services of child
74 Prizes and awards
75 Dealers in tax-exempt securities
76 Repealed [Mortgages made or obligations issued by joint-stock land banks]
77 Commodity credit loans
78 Dividends received from certain foreign corporations by domestic corporations choosing foreign tax credit
79 Group-term life insurance purchased for employees
80 Restoration of value of certain securities
81 Repealed [Increase in vacation pay suspense accounts]
82 Reimbursement for expenses of moving
83 Property transferred in connection with performance of services

Sec.

84 Transfer of appreciated property to political organization
85 Unemployment compensation
86 Social security and tier 1 railroad retirement benefits
87 Alcohol and biodiesel fuels credits
88 Certain amounts with respect to nuclear decommissioning costs
89 Repealed [Benefits provided under certain employee benefit plans]
90 Illegal federal irrigation subsidies

PART III. ITEMS SPECIFICALLY EXCLUDED FROM GROSS INCOME

101 Certain death benefits
102 Gifts and inheritances
103 Interest on State and local bonds
103A Repealed [Mortgage subsidy bonds]
104 Compensation for injuries or sickness
105 Amounts received under accident and health plans
106 Contributions by employer to accident and health plans
107 Rental value of parsonages
108 Income from discharge of indebtedness
109 Improvements by lessee on lessor's property
110 Qualified lessee construction allowances for short-term leases
110 Repealed [Income taxes paid by lessee corporation]
111 Recovery of tax benefit items
112 Certain combat zone compensation of members of the Armed Forces
113 Repealed [Mustering-out payments for members of the Armed Forces]
114 Repealed [Extraterritorial income]
114 Repealed [Sports programs conducted for the American National Red Cross]
115 Income of States, municipalities, etc.
116 Repealed [Partial exclusion of dividends received by individuals]
117 Qualified scholarships
118 Contributions to the capital of a corporation
119 Meals or lodging furnished for the convenience of the employer
120 Amounts received under qualified group legal services plans
121 Exclusion of gain from sale of principal residence
122 Certain reduced uniformed services retirement pay
123 Amounts received under insurance contracts for certain living expenses
124 Repealed [Qualified transportation provided by employer]
125 Cafeteria plans
126 Certain cost-sharing payments
127 Educational assistance programs
128 Repealed [Interest on certain savings certificates]
129 Dependent care assistance programs
130 Certain personal injury liability assignments
131 Certain foster care payments
132 Certain fringe benefits
133 Repealed [Interest on certain loans used to acquire employer securities]

Sec.	
134	Certain military benefits
135	Income from United States savings bonds used to pay higher education tuition and fees
136	Energy conservation subsidies provided by public utilities
137	Adoption assistance programs
138	Medicare Advantage MSA
139	Disaster relief payments
139A	Federal subsidies for prescription drug plans
139B	Benefits provided to volunteer firefighters and emergency medical responders.
140	Cross references to other Acts

PART IV. TAX EXEMPTION REQUIREMENTS FOR STATE AND LOCAL BONDS

Subpart A. Private activity bonds

141	Private activity bond; qualified bond
142	Exempt facility bond
143	Mortgage revenue bonds: qualified mortgage bond and qualified veterans' mortgage bond
144	Qualified small issue bond; qualified student loan bond; qualified redevelopment bond
145	Qualified 501(c)(3) bond
146	Volume cap
147	Other requirements applicable to certain private activity bonds

Subpart B. Requirements applicable to all State and local bonds

148	Arbitrage
149	Bonds must be registered to be tax exempt; other requirements

Subpart C. Definitions and special rules

150	Definitions and special rules

PART V. DEDUCTIONS FOR PERSONAL EXEMPTIONS

151	Allowance of deductions for personal exemptions
152	Dependent defined
153	Cross references

PART VI. ITEMIZED DEDUCTIONS FOR INDIVIDUALS AND CORPORATIONS

161	Allowance of deductions
162	Trade or business expenses
163	Interest
164	Taxes
165	Losses
166	Bad debts
167	Depreciation
168	Accelerated cost recovery system
168	Repealed [Amortization of emergency facilities]
169	Amortization of pollution control facilities
170	Charitable, etc., contributions and gifts
171	Amortizable bond premium
172	Net operating loss deduction
173	Circulation expenditures
174	Research and experimental expenditures
175	Soil and water conservation expenditures
176	Payments with respect to employees of certain foreign corporations
177	Repealed [Trademark and trade name expenditures]
178	Amortization of cost of acquiring a lease
179	Election to expense certain depreciable business assets
179A	Deduction for clean-fuel vehicles and certain refueling property
179B	Deduction for capital costs incurred in complying with Environmental Protection Agency sulfur regulations
179C	Election to expense certain refineries
179D	Energy efficient commercial buildings deduction
179E	Election to expense advance mine safety equipment
180	Expenditures by farmers for fertilizer, etc.
181	Treatment of certain qualified film and television productions
181	Repealed [Deduction for certain unused investment credit]
182	Repealed [Expenditures by farmers for clearing land]
183	Activities not engaged in for profit
184	Repealed [Amortization of certain railroad rolling stock]
185	Repealed [Amortization of railroad grading and tunnel bores]
186	Recoveries of damages for antitrust violations, etc.
187	Repealed [Amortization of certain coal mine safety equipment]
188	Repealed [Amortization of certain expenditures for child care facilities]
189	Repealed [Amortization of real property construction period interest and taxes]
190	Expenditures to remove architectural and transportation barriers to the handicapped and elderly
191	Repealed [Amortization of certain rehabilitation expenditures for certified historic structures]
192	Contributions to black lung benefit trust
193	Tertiary injectants
194	Treatment of reforestation expenditures
194A	Contributions to employer liability trusts
195	Start-up expenditures
196	Deduction for certain unused business credits
197	Amortization of goodwill and certain other intangibles
198	Expensing of environmental remediation costs
199	Income attributable to domestic production activities

PART VII. ADDITIONAL ITEMIZED DEDUCTIONS FOR INDIVIDUALS

211	Allowance of deductions
212	Expenses for production of income
213	Medical, dental, etc., expenses
214	Repealed [Expenses for household and dependent care services necessary for gainful employment]
215	Alimony, etc., payments
216	Deduction of taxes, interest, and business depreciation by cooperative housing corporation tenant-stockholder
217	Moving expenses
218	Repealed [Contributions to candidates for public office]
219	Retirement savings
220	Archer MSAs

Sec.
220 Repealed [Jury duty remitted to employer]
220 Repealed [Retirement savings for certain married individuals]
221 Interest on education loans
221 Repealed [Deduction for two-earner married couples]
222 Qualified tuition and related expenses
222 Repealed [Adoption expenses]
223 Health savings accounts
224 Cross reference

PART VIII. SPECIAL DEDUCTIONS FOR CORPORATIONS

241 Allowance of special deductions
242 Repealed [Partially tax-exempt interest]
243 Dividends received by corporations
244 Dividends received on certain preferred stock
245 Dividends received from certain foreign corporations
246 Rules applying to deductions for dividends received
246A Dividends received deduction reduced where portfolio stock is debt financed
247 Dividends paid on certain preferred stock of public utilities
248 Organizational expenditures
249 Limitation on deduction of bond premium on repurchase
250 Repealed [Certain payments to the national railroad passenger corporation]

PART IX. ITEMS NOT DEDUCTIBLE

261 General rule for disallowance of deductions
262 Personal, living, and family expenses
263 Capital expenditures
263A Capitalization and inclusion in inventory costs of certain expenses
264 Certain amounts paid in connection with insurance contracts
265 Expenses and interest relating to tax-exempt income
266 Carrying charges
267 Losses, expenses, and interest with respect to transactions between related taxpayers
268 Sale of land with unharvested crop
269 Acquisitions made to evade or avoid income tax
269A Personal service corporations formed or availed of to avoid or evade income tax
269B Stapled entities
270 Repealed [Limitation on deductions allowable to individuals in certain cases]
271 Debts owed by political parties, etc.
272 Disposal of coal or domestic iron ore
273 Holders of life or terminable interest
274 Disallowance of certain entertainment, etc., expenses
275 Certain taxes
276 Certain indirect contributions to political parties
277 Deductions incurred by certain membership organizations in transactions with members
278 Repealed [Capital expenditures incurred in planting and developing citrus and almond groves; certain capital expenditures of farming syndicates]
279 Interest on indebtedness incurred by corporation to acquire stock or assets of another corporation

Sec.
280 Repealed [Certain expenditures incurred in production of films, books, records, or similar property]
280A Disallowance or certain expenses in connection with business use of home, rental of vacation homes, etc.
280B Demolition of structures
280C Certain expenses for which credits are allowable
280D Repealed [Portion of chapter 45 taxes for which credit or refund is allowable under section 6429]
280E Expenditures in connection with the illegal sale of drugs
280F Limitation on depreciation for luxury automobiles; limitation where certain property used for personal purposes
280G Golden parachute payments
280H Limitation on certain amounts paid to employee-owners by personal service corporations electing alternative taxable years

PART X. TERMINAL RAILROAD CORPORATIONS AND THEIR SHAREHOLDERS

281 Terminal railroad corporations and their shareholders

PART XI. SPECIAL RULES RELATING TO CORPORATE PREFERENCE ITEMS

291 Special rules relating to corporate preference items

Subchapter C. Corporate Distributions and Adjustments

PART I. DISTRIBUTIONS BY CORPORATIONS

Subpart A. Effects on recipients

301 Distributions of property
302 Distributions in redemption of stock
303 Distributions in redemption of stock to pay death taxes
304 Redemption through use of related corporations
305 Distributions of stock and stock rights
306 Dispositions of certain stock
307 Basis of stock and stock rights acquired in distributions

Subpart B. Effects on corporation

311 Taxability of corporation on distribution
312 Effect on earnings and profits

Subpart C. Definitions; constructive ownership of stock

316 Dividend defined
317 Other definitions
318 Constructive ownership of stock

PART II. CORPORATE LIQUIDATIONS

Subpart A. Effects on recipients

331 Gain or loss to shareholders in corporate liquidations
332 Complete liquidations of subsidiaries
333 Repealed [Election as to recognition of gain in certain liquidations]
334 Basis of property received in liquidations

Subpart B. Effects on corporation

336 Gain or loss recognized on property distributed in complete liquidation
337 Nonrecognition for property distributed to parent in complete liquidation of subsidiary

Sec.
338 Certain stock purchases treated as asset acquisitions

Subpart C. Repealed [Collapsible corporations]

341 Repealed [Collapsible corporations]
342 Repealed [Liquidation of certain foreign personal holding companies]

Subpart D. Definition and special rule

346 Definition and special rule

PART III. CORPORATE ORGANIZATIONS AND REORGANIZATIONS

Subpart A. Corporate organizations

351 Transfer to corporation controlled by transferor

Subpart B. Effects on shareholders and security holders

354 Exchanges of stock and securities in certain reorganizations
355 Distribution of stock and securities of a controlled corporation
356 Receipt of additional consideration
357 Assumption of liability
358 Basis to distributees

Subpart C. Effects on corporations

361 Nonrecognition of gain or loss to corporations; treatment of distributions
362 Basis to corporations
363 Repealed [Effect on earnings and profits]

Subpart D. Special rule; definitions

367 Foreign corporations
368 Definitions relating to corporate reorganizations

PART IV. REPEALED [INSOLVENCY REORGANIZATIONS]

370 Repealed [Termination of part]
371 Repealed [Reorganization in certain receivership and bankruptcy proceedings]
372 Repealed [Basis in connection with certain receivership and bankruptcy proceedings]
373 Repealed [Loss not recognized in certain railroad reorganizations]
374 Repealed [Gain or loss not recognized in certain railroad reorganizations]

PART V. CARRYOVERS

381 Carryovers in certain corporate acquisitions
382 Limitation on net operating loss carryforwards and certain built-in losses following ownership change
383 Special limitations on certain excess credits, etc.
384 Limitation on use of preacquisition losses to offset built-in gains

PART VI. TREATMENT OF CERTAIN CORPORATE INTERESTS AS STOCK OR INDEBTEDNESS

385 Treatment of certain interests in corporations as stock or indebtedness

PART VII. REPEALED [MISCELLANEOUS CORPORATE PROVISIONS]

386 Repealed [Transfers of partnership and trust interests by corporations]

Subchapter D. Deferred Compensation, Etc.

PART I. PENSION, PROFIT-SHARING, STOCK BONUS PLANS, ETC.

Sec.

Subpart A. General rules

401 Qualified pension, profit-sharing, and stock bonus plans
402 Taxability of beneficiary of employees' trust
402A Optional treatment of elective deferrals as Roth contributions
403 Taxation of employee annuities
404 Deduction for contributions of an employer to an employees' trust or annuity plan and compensation under a deferred-payment plan
404A Deduction for certain foreign deferred compensation plans
405 Repealed [Qualified bond purchase plans]
406 Employees of foreign affiliates covered by section 3121(l) agreements
407 Certain employees of domestic subsidiaries engaged in business outside the United States
408 Individual retirement accounts
408A Roth IRAs
409 Qualifications for tax credit employee stock ownership plans
409 Repealed [Retirement bonds]
409A Inclusion in gross income of deferred compensation under nonqualified deferred compensation plans

Subpart B. Special rules

410 Minimum participation standards
411 Minimum vesting standards
412 Minimum funding standards
413 Collectively bargained plans, etc.
414 Definitions and special rules
415 Limitations on benefits and contributions under qualified plans
416 Special rules for top-heavy plans
417 Definitions and special rules for purposes of minimum survivor annuity requirements

Subpart C. Special rules for multiemployer plans

418 Reorganization status
418A Notice of reorganization and funding requirements
418B Minimum contribution requirement
418C Overburden credit against minimum contribution requirement
418D Adjustments in accrued benefits
418E Insolvent plans

Subpart D. Treatment of welfare benefit funds

419 Treatment of funded welfare benefit plans
419A Qualified asset account; limitation on additions to account

Subpart E. Treatment of transfers to retiree health accounts

420 Transfers of excess pension assets to retiree health accounts

PART II. CERTAIN STOCK OPTIONS

421 General rules
422 Incentive stock options
422 Repealed [Qualified stock options]
423 Employee stock purchase plans
424 Definitions and special rules
424 Repealed [Restricted stock options]

Sec.

PART III. RULES RELATING TO MINIMUM FUNDING STANDARDS AND BENEFIT LIMITATIONS

Subpart A. Minimum funding standards for pension plans

430 Minimum funding standards for single-employer defined benefit pension plans.
431 Minimum funding standards for multiemployer plans
432 Additional funding rules for multiemployer plans in endangered status or critical status

Subpart B. Benefit limitations under single-employer plans

436 Funding-based limitation on shutdown benefits and other unpredictable contingent event benefits under single-employer plans

Subchapter E. Accounting Periods and Methods of Accounting

PART I. ACCOUNTING PERIODS

441 Period for computation of taxable income
442 Change of annual accounting period
443 Returns for a period of less than 12 months
444 Election of taxable year other than required taxable year

PART II. METHODS OF ACCOUNTING

Subpart A. Methods of accounting in general

446 General rule for methods of accounting
447 Method of accounting for corporations engaged in farming
448 Limitation on use of cash method of accounting

Subpart B. Taxable year for which items of gross income included

451 General rule for taxable year of inclusion
452 Repealed [Prepaid income]
453 Installment method
453A Special rules for nondealers
453B Gain or loss on disposition of installment obligations
453C Repealed [Certain indebtedness treated as payments on installment obligations]
454 Obligations issued at discount
455 Prepaid subscription income
456 Prepaid dues income of certain membership organizations
457 Deferred compensation plans of State and local governments and tax-exempt organizations
457A Nonqualified deferred compensation from certain tax indifferent parties.
458 Magazines, paperbacks, and records returned after the close of the taxable year
460 Special rules for long-term contracts

Subpart C. Taxable year for which deductions taken

461 General rule for taxable year of deduction
462 Repealed [Reserves for estimated expenses, etc.]
463 Repealed [Accrual of vacation pay]
464 Limitations on deductions for certain farming [expenses]
465 Deductions limited to amount at risk
466 Repealed [Qualified discount coupons redeemed after close of taxable year]
467 Certain payments for the use of property or services

Sec.

468 Special rules for mining and solid waste reclamation and closing costs
468A Special rules for nuclear decommissioning costs
468B Special rules for designated settlement funds
469 Passive activity losses and credits limited
470 Limitation on deductions allocable to property used by governments or other tax-exempt entities

Subpart D. Inventories

471 General rule for inventories
472 Last-in, first-out inventories
473 Qualified liquidations of LIFO inventories
474 Simplified dollar-value LIFO method for certain small businesses
475 Mark to market accounting method for dealers in securities

PART III. ADJUSTMENTS

481 Adjustments required by changes in method of accounting
482 Allocation of income and deductions among taxpayers
483 Interest on certain deferred payments

Subchapter F. Exempt Organizations

PART I. GENERAL RULE

501 Exemption from tax on corporations, certain trusts, etc.
502 Feeder organizations
503 Requirements for exemption
504 Status after organization ceases to qualify for exemption under section 501(c)(3) because of substantial lobbying or because of political activities
505 Additional requirements for organizations described in paragraph (9), (17), or (20) of section 501(c)

PART II. PRIVATE FOUNDATIONS

507 Termination of private foundation status
508 Special rules with respect to section 501(c)(3) organizations
509 Private foundation defined

PART III. TAXATION OF BUSINESS INCOME OF CERTAIN EXEMPT ORGANIZATIONS

511 Imposition of tax on unrelated business income of charitable, etc., organizations
512 Unrelated business taxable income
513 Unrelated trade or business
514 Unrelated debt-financed income
515 Taxes of foreign countries and possessions of the United States

PART IV. FARMERS' COOPERATIVES

521 Exemption of farmers' cooperatives from tax
522 Repealed [Tax on farmers' cooperatives]

PART V. SHIPOWNERS' PROTECTION AND INDEMNITY ASSOCIATIONS

526 Shipowners' protection and indemnity associations

PART VI. POLITICAL ORGANIZATIONS

527 Political organizations

PART VII. CERTAIN HOMEOWNERS ASSOCIATIONS

528 Certain homeowners associations

Sec.

PART VIII. HIGHER EDUCATION SAVINGS ENTITIES

529 Qualified tuition programs
530 Coverdell education savings accounts

Subchapter G. Corporations Used to Avoid Income Tax on Shareholders

PART I. CORPORATIONS IMPROPERLY ACCUMULATING SURPLUS

531 Imposition of accumulated earnings tax
532 Corporations subject to accumulated earnings tax
533 Evidence of purpose to avoid income tax
534 Burden of proof
535 Accumulated taxable income
536 Income not placed on annual basis
537 Reasonable needs of the business

PART II. PERSONAL HOLDING COMPANIES

541 Imposition of personal holding company tax
542 Definition of personal holding company
543 Personal holding company income
544 Rules for determining stock ownership
545 Undistributed personal holding company income
546 Income not placed on annual basis
547 Deduction for deficiency dividends

PART III. REPEALED [FOREIGN PERSONAL HOLDING COMPANIES]

551 Repealed [Foreign personal holding company income taxed to United States shareholders]
552 Repealed [Definition of foreign personal holding company]
553 Repealed [Foreign personal holding company income]
554 Repealed [Stock ownership]
555 Repealed [Gross income of foreign personal holding companies]
556 Repealed [Undistributed foreign personal holding company income]
557 Repealed [Income not placed on annual basis]
558 Repealed [Returns of officers, directors, and shareholders of foreign personal holding companies]

PART IV. DEDUCTION FOR DIVIDENDS PAID

561 Definition of deduction for dividends paid
562 Rules applicable in determining dividends eligible for dividends paid deduction
563 Rules relating to dividends paid after close of taxable year
564 Dividend carryover
565 Consent dividends

Subchapter H. Banking Institutions

PART I. RULES OF GENERAL APPLICATION TO BANKING INSTITUTIONS

581 Definition of bank
582 Bad debts, losses, and gains with respect to securities held by financial institutions
583 Repealed [Deductions of dividends paid on certain preferred stock]
584 Common trust funds
585 Reserves for losses on loans of banks
586 Repealed [Reserves for losses on loans of small business investment companies, etc.]

Sec.

PART II. MUTUAL SAVINGS BANKS, ETC.

591 Deduction for dividends paid on deposits
592 Repealed [Deduction for repayment of certain loans]
593 Reserves for losses on loans
594 Alternative tax for mutual savings banks conducting life insurance business
595 Repealed [Foreclosure on property securing loans]
596 Repealed [Limitation on dividends received deduction]
597 Treatment of transactions in which federal financial assistance provided

PART III. REPEALED [BANK AFFILIATES]

601 Repealed [Special deduction for bank affiliates]

Subchapter I. Natural Resources

PART I. DEDUCTIONS

611 Allowance of deduction for depletion
612 Basis for cost depletion
613 Percentage depletion
613A Limitations on percentage depletion in case of oil and gas wells
614 Definition of property
615 Repealed [Pre-1970 exploration expenditures]
616 Development expenditures
617 Deduction and recapture of certain mining exploration expenditures

PART II. REPEALED [EXCLUSIONS FROM GROSS INCOME]

621 Repealed [Payments to encourage exploration, development, and mining for defense purposes]

PART III. SALES AND EXCHANGES

631 Gain or loss in the case of timber, coal, or domestic iron ore
632 Repealed [Sale of oil or gas properties]

PART IV. MINERAL PRODUCTION PAYMENTS

636 Income tax treatment of mineral production payments

PART V. CONTINENTAL SHELF AREAS

638 Continental shelf areas

Subchapter J. Estates, Trusts, Beneficiaries, and Decedents

PART I. ESTATES, TRUSTS, AND BENEFICIARIES

Subpart A. General rules for taxation of estates and trusts

641 Imposition of tax
642 Special rules for credits and deductions
643 Definitions applicable to subparts A, B, C, and D
644 Taxable year of trusts
644 Repealed [Special rule for gain on property transferred to trust at less than fair market value]
645 Certain revocable trusts treated as part of estate
646 Tax treatment of electing Alaska Native Settlement Trusts

Subpart B. Trusts which distribute current income only

651 Deduction for trusts distributing current income only
652 Inclusion of amounts in gross income of beneficiaries of trusts distributing current income only

Subpart C. Estates and trusts which may accumulate income or which distribute corpus

Sec.

661 Deduction for estates and trusts accumulating income or distributing corpus
662 Inclusion of amounts in gross income of beneficiaries of estates and trusts accumulating income or distributing corpus
663 Special rules applicable to sections 661 and 662
664 Charitable remainder trusts

Subpart D. Treatment of excess distributions by trusts

665 Definitions applicable to subpart D
666 Accumulation distribution allocated to preceding years
667 Treatment of amounts deemed distributed by trust in preceding years
668 Interest charge on accumulation distributions from foreign trusts
668 Repealed [Treatment of amounts deemed distributed in preceding years]
669 Repealed [Treatment of capital gain deemed distributed in preceding years]

Subpart E. Grantors and others treated as substantial owners

671 Trust income, deductions, and credits attributable to grantors and others as substantial owners
672 Definitions and rules
673 Reversionary interests
674 Power to control beneficial enjoyment
675 Administrative powers
676 Power to revoke
677 Income for benefit of grantor
678 Person other than grantor treated as substantial owner
679 Foreign trusts having one or more United States beneficiaries

Subpart F. Miscellaneous

681 Limitation on charitable deduction
682 Income of an estate or trust in case of divorce, etc.
683 Use of trust as an exchange fund
684 Recognition of gain on certain transfers to certain foreign trusts and estates [before 1/1/2010]
684 Recognition of gain on certain transfers to certain foreign trusts and estates and nonresident aliens [after 12/31/2009]
685 Treatment of funeral trusts

PART II. INCOME IN RESPECT OF DECEDENTS

691 Recipients of income in respect of decedents
692 Income taxes of members of Armed Forces, astronauts, and victims of certain terrorist attacks on death

Subchapter K. Partners and Partnerships

PART I. DETERMINATION OF TAX LIABILITY

701 Partners, not partnership, subject to tax
702 Income and credits of partner
703 Partnership computations
704 Partner's distributive share
705 Determination of basis of partner's interest
706 Taxable years of partner and partnership
707 Transactions between partner and partnership
708 Continuation of partnership

Sec.

709 Treatment of organization and syndication fees

PART II. CONTRIBUTIONS, DISTRIBUTIONS, AND TRANSFERS

Subpart A. Contributions to a partnership

721 Nonrecognition of gain or loss on contribution
722 Basis of contributing partner's interest
723 Basis of property contributed to partnership
724 Character of gain or loss on contributed unrealized receivables, inventory items, and capital loss property

Subpart B. Distributions by a partnership

731 Extent of recognition of gain or loss on distribution
732 Basis of distributed property other than money
733 Basis of distributee partner's interest
734 Adjustment to basis of undistributed partnership property where section 754 election or substantial basis reduction
735 Character of gain or loss on disposition of distributed property
736 Payments to a retiring partner or a deceased partner's successor in interest
737 Recognition of precontribution gain in case of certain distributions to contributing partner

Subpart C. Transfers of interests in a partnership

741 Recognition and character of gain or loss on sale or exchange
742 Basis of transferee partner's interest
743 Special rules where section 754 election or substantial built-in loss

Subpart D. Provisions common to other subparts

751 Unrealized receivables and inventory items
752 Treatment of certain liabilities
753 Partner receiving income in respect of decedent
754 Manner of electing optional adjustment to basis of partnership property
755 Rules for allocation of basis

PART III. DEFINITIONS

761 Terms defined

PART IV. SPECIAL RULES FOR ELECTING LARGE PARTNERSHIPS

771 Application of subchapter to electing large partnerships
772 Simplified flow-through
773 Computations at partnership level
774 Other modifications
775 Electing large partnership defined
776 Special rules for partnerships holding oil and gas properties
777 Regulations

PART IV. REPEALED [EFFECTIVE DATE FOR SUBCHAPTER]

771 Repealed [Effective date]

Subchapter L. Insurance Companies

PART I. LIFE INSURANCE COMPANIES

Subpart A. Tax imposed

801 Tax imposed

Subpart B. Life insurance gross income

803 Life insurance gross income

Sec.

Subpart C. Life insurance deductions

804 Life insurance deductions
805 General deductions
806 Small life insurance company deduction
807 Rules for certain reserves
808 Policyholder dividends deduction
809 Repealed [Reduction in certain deductions of mutual life insurance companies]
810 Operations loss deduction

Subpart D. Accounting, allocation, and foreign provisions

811 Accounting provisions
812 Definition of company's share and policyholders' share
813 Repealed [Foreign life insurance companies]
814 Contiguous country branches of domestic life insurance companies
815 Distributions to shareholders from pre-1984 policyholders surplus account

Subpart E. Definitions and special rules

816 Life insurance company defined
817 Treatment of variable contracts
817A Special rules for modified guaranteed contracts
818 Other definitions and special rules

PART II. REPEALED [MUTUAL INSURANCE COMPANIES (OTHER THAN LIFE AND CERTAIN MARINE INSURANCE COMPANIES AND OTHER THAN FIRE OR FLOOD INSURANCE COMPANIES WHICH OPERATE ON BASIS OF PERPETUAL POLICIES OR PREMIUM DEPOSITS)]

821 Repealed [Tax on mutual insurance companies to which part II applies]
823 Repealed [Determination of statutory underwriting income or loss]
824 Repealed [Adjustments to provide protection against losses]
825 Repealed [Unused loss deduction]

PART II. OTHER INSURANCE COMPANIES

831 Tax on insurance companies other than life insurance companies
832 Insurance company taxable income
833 Treatment of Blue Cross and Blue Shield organizations, etc.
834 Determination of taxable investment income
835 Election by reciprocal

PART III. PROVISIONS OF GENERAL APPLICATION

841 Credit for foreign taxes
842 Foreign companies carrying on insurance business
843 Annual accounting period
844 Special loss carryover rules
845 Certain reinsurance agreements
846 Discounted unpaid losses defined
847 Special estimated tax payments
848 Capitalization of certain policy acquisition expenses

Subchapter M. Regulated Investment Companies and Real Estate Investment Trusts

PART I. REGULATED INVESTMENT COMPANIES

851 Definition of regulated investment company
852 Taxation of regulated investment companies and their shareholders

Sec.

853 Foreign tax credit allowed to shareholders
854 Limitations applicable to dividends received from regulated investment company
855 Dividends paid by regulated investment company after close of taxable year

PART II. REAL ESTATE INVESTMENT TRUSTS

856 Definition of real estate investment trust
857 Taxation of real estate investment trusts and their beneficiaries
858 Dividends paid by real estate investment trust after close of taxable year
859 Adoption of annual accounting period
859 Repealed [Deduction for deficiency dividends]

PART III. PROVISIONS WHICH APPLY TO BOTH REGULATED INVESTMENT COMPANIES AND REAL ESTATE INVESTMENT TRUSTS

860 Deduction for deficiency dividends

PART IV. REAL ESTATE MORTGAGE INVESTMENT CONDUITS

860A Taxation of REMIC's
860B Taxation of holders of regular interests
860C Taxation of residual interests
860D REMIC defined
860E Treatment of income in excess of daily accruals on residual interests
860F Other rules
860G Other definitions and special rules

PART V. REPEALED [FINANCIAL ASSET SECURITIZATION INVESTMENT TRUSTS]

860H Repealed [Taxation of a FASIT; other general rules]
860I Repealed [Gain recognition on contributions to a FASIT and in other cases]
860J Repealed [Non-FASIT losses not to offset certain FASIT inclusions]
860K Repealed [Treatment of transfers of high-yield interests to disqualified holders]
860L Repealed [Definitions and other special rules]

Subchapter N. Tax Based on Income from Sources Within or Without the United States

PART I. DETERMINATION OF SOURCES OF INCOME

861 Income from sources within the United States
862 Income from sources without the United States
863 Special rules for determining source
864 Definitions and special rules
865 Source rules for personal property sales

PART II. NONRESIDENT ALIENS AND FOREIGN CORPORATIONS

Subpart A. Nonresident alien individuals

871 Tax on nonresident alien individuals
872 Gross income
873 Deductions
874 Allowance of deductions and credits
875 Partnerships; beneficiaries of estates and trusts
876 Alien residents of Puerto Rico, Guam, American Samoa, or the Northern Mariana Islands
877 Expatriation to avoid tax
878 Foreign educational, charitable, and certain other exempt organizations

Sec.
879 Tax treatment of certain community income in the case of nonresident alien individuals

Subpart B. Foreign corporations

881 Tax on income of foreign corporations not connected with United States business
882 Tax on income of foreign corporations connected with United States business
883 Exclusions from gross income
884 Branch profits tax
885 Cross references

Subpart C. Tax on gross transportation income

887 Imposition of tax on gross transportation income of nonresident aliens and foreign corporations

Subpart D. Miscellaneous provisions

891 Doubling of rates of tax on citizens and corporations of certain foreign countries
892 Income of foreign governments and of international organizations
893 Compensation of employees of foreign governments or international organizations
894 Income affected by treaty
895 Income derived by a foreign central bank of issue from obligations of the United States or from bank deposits
896 Adjustment of tax on nationals, residents, and corporations of certain foreign countries
897 Disposition of investment in United States real property
898 Taxable year of certain foreign corporations

PART III. INCOME FROM SOURCES WITHOUT THE UNITED STATES

Subpart A. Foreign tax credit

901 Taxes of foreign countries and of possessions of United States
902 Deemed paid credit where domestic corporation owns 10 percent or more of voting stock of foreign corporation
903 Credit for taxes in lieu of income, etc., taxes
904 Limitation on credit
905 Applicable rules
906 Nonresident alien individuals and foreign corporations
907 Special rules in case of foreign oil and gas income
908 Reduction of credit for participation in or cooperation with an international boycott

Subpart B. Earned income of citizens or residents of United States

911 Citizens or residents of the United States living abroad
912 Exemption for certain allowances
913 Repealed [Deduction for certain expenses of living abroad]

Subpart C. Repealed [Taxation of foreign sales corporations]

921 Repealed [Exempt foreign trade income excluded from gross income]
922 Repealed [FSC defined]
923 Repealed [Exempt foreign trade income]

Sec.
924 Repealed [Foreign trading gross receipts]
925 Repealed [Transfer pricing rules]
926 Repealed [Distributions to shareholders]
927 Repealed [Other definitions and special rules]

Subpart D. Possessions of the United States

931 Income from sources within Guam, American Samoa, or the Northern Mariana Islands
932 Coordination of United States and Virgin Islands income taxes
933 Income from sources within Puerto Rico
934 Limitation on reduction in income tax liability incurred to the Virgin Islands
934A Repealed [Income tax rate on Virgin Islands source income]
935 Repealed [Coordination of United States and Guam individual income taxes]
936 Puerto Rico and possession tax credit
937 Residence and source rules involving possessions

Subpart E. Repealed [Qualifying foreign trade income]

941 Repealed [Qualifying foreign trade income]
942 Repealed [Foreign trading gross receipts]
943 Repealed [Other definitions and special rules]

Subpart E. Repealed [China Trade Act corporations]

941 Repealed [Special deduction for China Trade Act corporations]
942 Repealed [Disallowance of foreign tax credit]
943 Repealed [Exclusion of dividends to residents of Formosa or Hong Kong]

Subpart F. Controlled foreign corporations

951 Amounts included in gross income of United States shareholders
952 Subpart F income defined
953 Insurance income
954 Foreign base company income
955 Withdrawal of previously excluded subpart F income from qualified investment
956 Investment of earnings in United States property
956A Repealed [Earnings invested in excess passive assets]
957 Controlled foreign corporations; United States persons
958 Rules for determining stock ownership
959 Exclusion from gross income of previously taxed earnings and profits
960 Special rules for foreign tax credit
961 Adjustments to basis of stock in controlled foreign corporations and of other property
962 Election by individuals to be subject to tax at corporate rates
963 Repealed [Receipt of minimum distributions by domestic corporations]
964 Miscellaneous provisions
965 Temporary dividends received deduction

Subpart G. Export trade corporations

970 Reduction of subpart F income of export trade corporations
971 Definitions

Sec.
972 Repealed [Consolidation of group of export trade corporations]

Subpart H. Repealed [Income of certain nonresident United States citizens subject to foreign community property laws]

981 Repealed [Election as to treatment of income subject to foreign community property laws]

Subpart I. Admissibility of documentation maintained in foreign countries

982 Admissibility of documentation maintained in foreign countries

Subpart J. Foreign currency transactions

985 Functional currency
986 Determination of foreign taxes and foreign corporation's earnings and profits
987 Branch transactions
988 Treatment of certain foreign currency transactions
989 Other definitions and special rules

PART IV. DOMESTIC INTERNATIONAL SALES CORPORATIONS

Subpart A. Treatment of qualifying corporations

991 Taxation of a domestic international sales corporation
992 Requirements of a domestic international sales corporation
993 Definitions
994 Inter-company pricing rules

Subpart B. Treatment of distributions to shareholders

995 Taxation of DISC income to shareholders
996 Rules for allocation in the case of distributions and losses
997 Special subchapter C rules

PART V. INTERNATIONAL BOYCOTT DETERMINATIONS

999 Reports by taxpayers; determinations

Subchapter O. Gain or Loss on Disposition of Property

PART I. DETERMINATION OF AMOUNT OF AND RECOGNITION OF GAIN OR LOSS

1001 Determination of amount of and recognition of gain or loss
1002 Repealed [Recognition of gain or loss]

PART II. BASIS RULES OF GENERAL APPLICATION

1011 Adjusted basis for determining gain or loss
1012 Basis of property—cost
1013 Basis of property included in inventory
1014 Basis of property acquired from a decedent
1015 Basis of property acquired by gifts and transfers in trust
1016 Adjustments to basis
1017 Discharge of indebtedness
1018 Repealed [Adjustment of capital structure before September 22, 1938]
1019 Property on which lessee has made improvements
1020 Repealed [Election in respect of depreciation, etc., allowed before 1952]
1021 Sale of annuities
1022 Treatment of property acquired from a decedent dying after December 31, 2009

Sec.
1022 Repealed [Increase in basis with respect to certain foreign personal holding company stock or securities]
1023 Cross references

PART III. COMMON NONTAXABLE EXCHANGES

1031 Exchange of property held for productive use or investment
1032 Exchange of stock for property
1033 Involuntary conversions
1034 Repealed [Rollover of gain on sale of principal residence]
1035 Certain exchanges of insurance policies
1036 Stock for stock of same corporation
1037 Certain exchanges of United States obligations
1038 Certain reacquisitions of real property
1039 Repealed [Certain sales of low-income housing projects]
1040 Transfer of certain farm, etc., real property [before 1/1/2010]
1040 Use of appreciated carryover basis property to satisfy pecuniary bequest [after 12/31/2009]
1041 Transfers of property between spouses or incident to divorce
1042 Sales of stock to employee stock ownership plans or certain cooperatives
1043 Sale of property to comply with conflict-of-interest requirements
1044 Rollover of publicly traded securities gain into specialized small business investment companies
1045 Rollover of gain from qualified small business stock to another qualified small business stock

PART IV. SPECIAL RULES

1051 Property acquired during affiliation
1052 Basis established by the Revenue Act of 1932 or 1934 or by the Internal Revenue Code of 1939
1053 Property acquired before March 1, 1913
1054 Certain stock of Federal National Mortgage Association
1055 Redeemable ground rents
1056 Repealed [Basis limitation for player contracts transferred in connection with the sale of a franchise]
1057 Repealed [Election to treat transfer to foreign trust, etc., as taxable exchange]
1058 Transfers of securities under certain agreements
1059 Corporate shareholder's basis in stock reduced by nontaxed portion of extraordinary dividends
1059A Limitation on taxpayer's basis or inventory cost in property imported from related persons
1060 Special allocation rules for certain asset acquisitions
1061 Cross references

PART V. REPEALED [CHANGES TO EFFECTUATE F.C.C. POLICY]

1071 Repealed [Gain from sale or exchange to effectuate policies of F.C.C.]

PART VI. REPEALED [EXCHANGES IN OBEDIENCE TO S.E.C. ORDERS]

1081 Repealed [Nonrecognition of gain or loss on exchanges or distributions in obedience to orders of S.E.C.]

Sec.
1082 Repealed [Basis for determining gain or loss]
1083 Repealed [Definitions]

PART VII. WASH SALES; STRADDLES

1091 Loss from wash sales of stock or securities
1092 Straddles

PART VIII. REPEALED [DISTRIBUTIONS PURSUANT TO BANK HOLDING COMPANY ACT]

1101 Repealed [Distributions pursuant to Bank Holding Company Act]
1102 Repealed [Special rules]
1103 Repealed [Definitions]

PART IX. REPEALED [DISTRIBUTIONS PURSUANT TO ORDER ENFORCING THE ANTITRUST LAWS]

1111 Repealed [Distribution of stock pursuant to order enforcing the antitrust laws]

Subchapter P. Capital Gains and Losses

PART I. TREATMENT OF CAPITAL GAINS

1201 Alternative tax for corporations
1202 Partial exclusion for gain from certain small business stock
1202 Repealed [Deduction for capital gains]

PART II. TREATMENT OF CAPITAL LOSSES

1211 Limitation on capital losses
1212 Capital loss carrybacks and carryovers

PART III. GENERAL RULES FOR DETERMINING CAPITAL GAINS AND LOSSES

1221 Capital asset defined
1222 Other terms relating to capital gains and losses
1223 Holding period of property

PART IV. SPECIAL RULES FOR DETERMINING CAPITAL GAINS AND LOSSES

1231 Property used in the trade or business and involuntary conversions
1232 Repealed [Bonds and other evidence of indebtedness]
1232A Repealed [Original issue discount]
1232B Repealed [Tax treatment of stripped bonds]
1233 Gains and losses from short sales
1234 Options to buy or sell
1234A Gains or losses from certain terminations
1234B Gains or losses from securities futures contracts
1235 Sale or exchange of patents
1236 Dealers in securities
1237 Real property subdivided for sale
1238 Repealed [Amortization in excess of depreciation]
1239 Gain from sale of depreciable property between certain related taxpayers
1240 Repealed [Taxability to employee of termination payments]
1241 Cancellation of lease or distributor's agreement
1242 Losses on small business investment company stock
1243 Loss of small business investment company
1244 Losses on small business stock
1245 Gain from dispositions of certain depreciable property
1246 Repealed [Gain on foreign investment company stock]

Sec.
1247 Repealed [Election by foreign investment companies to distribute income currently]
1248 Gain from certain sales or exchanges of stock in certain foreign corporations
1249 Gain from certain sales or exchanges of patents, etc., to foreign corporations
1250 Gain from dispositions of certain depreciable realty
1251 Repealed [Gain from disposition of property used in farming where farm losses offset nonfarm income]
1252 Gain from disposition of farm land
1253 Transfers of franchises, trademarks, and trade names
1254 Gain from disposition of interest in oil, gas, geothermal, or other mineral properties
1255 Gain from disposition of section 126 property
1256 Section 1256 contracts marked to market
1257 Disposition of converted wetlands or highly erodible croplands
1258 Recharacterization of gain from certain financial transactions
1259 Constructive sales treatment for appreciated financial positions
1260 Gains from constructive ownership transactions

PART V. SPECIAL RULES FOR BONDS AND OTHER DEBT INSTRUMENTS

Subpart A. Original issue discount

1271 Treatment of amounts received on retirement or sale or exchange of debt instruments
1272 Current inclusion in income of original issue discount
1273 Determination of amount of original issue discount
1274 Determination of issue price in the case of certain debt instruments issued for property
1274A Special rules for certain transactions where stated principal amount does not exceed $2,800,000.
1275 Other definitions and special rules

Subpart B. Market discount on bonds

1276 Disposition gain representing accrued market discount treated as ordinary income
1277 Deferral of interest deduction allocable to accrued market discount
1278 Definitions and special rules

Subpart C. Discount on short-term obligations

1281 Current inclusion in income of discount on certain short-term obligations
1282 Deferral of interest deduction allocable to accrued discount
1283 Definitions and special rules

Subpart D. Miscellaneous provisions

1286 Tax treatment of stripped bonds
1287 Denial of capital gain treatment for gains on certain obligations not in registered form
1288 Treatment of original issue discount on tax-exempt obligations

PART VI. TREATMENT OF CERTAIN PASSIVE FOREIGN INVESTMENT COMPANIES

Subpart A. Interest on tax deferral

1291 Interest on tax deferral

Sec.

Subpart B. Treatment of qualified electing funds

1293 Current taxation of income from qualified electing funds

1294 Election to extend time for payment of tax on undistributed earnings

1295 Qualified electing fund

Subpart C. Election of mark to market for marketable stock

1296 Election of mark to market for marketable stock

Subpart D. General provisions

1297 Passive foreign investment company

1298 Special rules

Subchapter Q. Readjustment of Tax Between Years and Special Limitations

Part I. Income Averaging

1301 Averaging of farm income

Part I. Repealed [Income Averaging]

1301 Repealed [Limitation on tax]

1302 Repealed [Definition of averageable income; related definitions]

1303 Repealed [Eligible individuals]

1304 Repealed [Special rules]

1305 Repealed [Regulations]

Part II. Mitigation of Effect of Limitations and Other Provisions

1311 Correction of error

1312 Circumstances of adjustment

1313 Definitions

1314 Amount and method of adjustment

1315 Repealed [Effective date]

Part III. Repealed [Involuntary Liquidation and Replacement of LIFO Inventories]

1321 Repealed [Involuntary liquidation of LIFO inventories]

Part IV. Repealed [War Loss Recoveries]

1331 Repealed [War loss recoveries]

1332 Repealed [Inclusion in gross income of war loss recoveries]

1333 Repealed [Tax adjustment measured by prior benefits]

1334 Repealed [Restoration of value of investments referable to destroyed or seized property]

1335 Repealed [Election by taxpayer for application of section 1333]

1336 Repealed [Basis of recovered property]

1337 Repealed [Applicable rules]

Part V. Claim of Right

1341 Computation of tax where taxpayer restores substantial amount held under claim of right

1342 Repealed [Computation of tax where taxpayer recovers substantial amount held by another under claim of right]

Part VI. Repealed [Maximum Rate on Personal Service Income]

1346 Repealed [Recovery of unconstitutional Federal taxes]

Sec.

1347 Repealed [Claims against United States involving acquisition of property]

1348 Repealed [50-percent maximum rate on personal service income]

Part VII. Recoveries of Foreign Expropriation Losses

1351 Treatment of recoveries of foreign expropriation losses

Subchapter R. Election to Determine Corporate Tax on Certain International Shipping Activities Using Per Ton Rate

1352 Alternative tax on qualifying shipping activities

1353 Notional shipping income

1354 Alternative tax election; revocation; termination

1355 Definitions and special rules

1356 Qualifying shipping activities

1357 Items not subject to regular tax; depreciation; interest

1358 Allocation of credits, income, and deductions

1359 Disposition of qualifying vessels

Subchapter R. Repealed [Election of Certain Partnerships as to Taxable Status]

1361 Repealed [Unincorporated business enterprises electing to be taxed as domestic corporations]

Subchapter S. Tax Treatment of S Corporations and Their Shareholders

Part I. In General

1361 S corporation defined

1362 Election; revocation; termination

1363 Effect of election on corporation

Part II. Tax Treatment of Shareholders

1366 Pass-thru of items to shareholders

1367 Adjustments to basis of stock of shareholders, etc.

1368 Distributions

Part III. Special Rules

1371 Coordination with subchapter C

1372 Partnership rules to apply for fringe benefit purposes

1373 Foreign income

1374 Tax imposed on certain built-in gains

1375 Tax imposed when passive investment income of corporation having accumulated earnings and profits exceeds 25 percent of gross receipts

Part IV. Definitions; Miscellaneous

1377 Definitions and special rule

1378 Taxable year of S corporation

1379 Transitional rules on enactment

Subchapter T. Cooperatives and Their Patrons

Part I. Tax Treatment of Cooperatives

1381 Organizations to which part applies

1382 Taxable income of cooperatives

1383 Computation of tax where cooperative redeems nonqualified written notices of allocation or nonqualified per-unit retain certificates

Part II. Tax Treatment by Patrons of Patronage Dividends and Per-Unit Retain Allocations

1385 Amounts includible in patron's gross income

Part III. Definitions, Special Rules

1388 Definitions; special rules

Sec.

Subchapter U. Designation and Treatment of Empowerment Zones, Enterprise Communities, and Rural Development Investment Areas

PART I. DESIGNATION

1391 Designation procedure
1392 Eligibility criteria
1393 Definitions and special rules

PART II. TAX-EXEMPT FACILITY BONDS FOR EMPOWERMENT ZONES AND ENTERPRISE COMMUNITIES

1394 Tax-exempt enterprise zone facility bonds

PART III. ADDITIONAL INCENTIVES FOR EMPOWERMENT ZONES

Subpart A. Empowerment zone employment credit

1396 Empowerment zone employment credit
1397 Other definitions and special rules

Subpart B. Additional expensing

1397A Increase in expensing under section 179

Subpart C. Nonrecognition of gain on rollover of empowerment zone investments

1397B Nonrecognition of gain on rollover of empowerment zone investments

Subpart D. General provisions

1397C Enterprise zone business defined
1397D Qualified zone property defined

PART IV. INCENTIVES FOR EDUCATION ZONES

1397E Credit to holders of qualified zone academy bonds

PART V. REGULATIONS

1397F Regulations

Subchapter U. Repealed [General Stock Ownership Corporations]

1391 Repealed [Definitions]
1392 Repealed [Election by GSOC]
1393 Repealed [GSOC taxable income taxed to shareholders]
1394 Repealed [Rules applicable to distributions of an electing GSOC]
1395 Repealed [Adjustments to basis of stock of shareholders]
1396 Repealed [Minimum distribution]
1397 Repealed [Special rules applicable to an electing GSOC]

Subchapter V. Title 11 Cases

1398 Rules relating to individuals' title 11 cases
1399 No separate taxable entities for partnerships, corporations, etc.

Subchapter W. District of Columbia Enterprise Zone

1400 Establishment of DC Zone
1400A Tax-exempt economic development bonds
1400B Zero percent capital gains rate
1400C First-time homebuyer credit for District of Columbia

Subchapter X. Renewal Communities

PART I. DESIGNATION

1400E Designation of renewal communities

PART II. RENEWAL COMMUNITY CAPITAL GAIN; RENEWAL COMMUNITY BUSINESS

1400F Renewal community capital gain

Sec.

1400G Renewal community business defined

PART III. ADDITIONAL INCENTIVES

1400H Renewal community employment credit
1400I Commercial revitalization deduction
1400J Increase in expensing under section 179

Subchapter Y. Short-Term Regional Benefits

PART I. TAX BENEFITS FOR NEW YORK LIBERTY ZONE

1400L Tax benefits for New York Liberty Zone

PART II. TAX BENEFITS FOR GO ZONES

1400M Definitions
1400N Tax benefits for Gulf Opportunity Zone
1400O Education tax benefits
1400P Housing tax benefits
1400Q Special rules for use of retirement funds
1400R Employment relief
1400S Additional tax relief provisions
1400T Special rules for mortgage revenue bonds

Chapter 2. Tax on Self-Employment Income

1401 Rate of tax
1402 Definitions
1403 Miscellaneous provisions

Chapter 3. Withholding of Tax on Nonresident Aliens and Foreign Corporations

Subchapter A. Nonresident Aliens and Foreign Corporations

1441 Withholding of tax on nonresident aliens
1442 Withholding of tax on foreign corporations
1443 Foreign tax-exempt organizations
1444 Withholding on Virgin Islands source income
1445 Withholding of tax on dispositions of United States real property interests
1446 Withholding tax on foreign partners' share of effectively connected income

Subchapter B. Repealed [Tax-Free Covenant Bonds]

1451 Repealed [Tax-free covenant bonds]

Subchapter B. Application of Withholding Provisions

1461 Liability for withheld tax
1462 Withheld tax as credit to recipient of income
1463 Tax paid by recipient of income
1464 Refunds and credits with respect to withheld tax
1465 Repealed [Definition of withholding agent]

Chapter 4. Repealed [Rules Applicable to Recovery of Excessive Profits on Government Contracts]

Subchapter A. Repealed [Recovery of Excessive Profits on Government Contracts]

1471 Repealed [Recovery of excessive profits on government contracts]

Subchapter B. Repealed [Mitigation of Effect of Renegotiation of Government Contracts]

1481 Repealed [Mitigation of effect of renegotiation of government contracts]
1482 Repealed [Readjustment for repayments made pursuant to price redeterminations]

Chapter 5. Repealed [Tax on Transfers to Avoid Income Tax]

1491 Repealed [Imposition of tax]
1492 Repealed [Nontaxable transfers]

Sec.
1493 Repealed [Definition of foreign trust]
1494 Repealed [Payment and collection]

Chapter 6. Consolidated Returns

Subchapter A. Returns and Payment of Tax

1501 Privilege to file consolidated returns
1502 Regulations
1503 Computation and payment of tax
1504 Definitions
1505 Cross references

Subchapter B. Related Rules

PART I. IN GENERAL

1551 Disallowance of the benefits of the graduated corporate rates and accumulated earnings credit
1552 Earnings and profits

PART II. CERTAIN CONTROLLED CORPORATIONS

1561 Limitations on certain multiple tax benefits in the case of certain controlled corporations
1562 Repealed [Privilege of groups to elect multiple surtax exemptions]
1563 Definitions and special rules
1564 Repealed [Transitional rules in the case of certain controlled corporations]

SUBTITLE B—ESTATE AND GIFT TAXES

Chapter 11. Estate Tax

Subchapter A. Estates of Citizens or Residents

PART I. TAX IMPOSED

2001 Imposition and rate of tax
2002 Liability for payment

PART II. CREDITS AGAINST TAX

2010 Unified credit against estate tax
2011 Credit for State death taxes
2012 Credit for gift tax
2013 Credit for tax on prior transfers
2014 Credit for foreign death taxes
2015 Credit for death taxes on remainders
2016 Recovery of taxes claimed as credit

PART III. GROSS ESTATE

2031 Definition of gross estate
2032 Alternate valuation
2032A Valuation of certain farm, etc., real property
2033 Property in which the decedent had an interest
2033A Repealed [Family-owned business exclusion]
2034 Dower or curtesy interests
2035 Adjustments for certain gifts made within 3 years of decedent's death
2036 Transfers with retained life estate
2037 Transfers taking effect at death
2038 Revocable transfers
2039 Annuities
2040 Joint interests
2041 Powers of appointment
2042 Proceeds of life insurance
2043 Transfers for insufficient consideration
2044 Certain property for which marital deduction was previously allowed
2045 Prior interests
2046 Disclaimers

Sec.

PART IV. TAXABLE ESTATE

2051 Definition of taxable estate
2052 Repealed [Exemption]
2053 Expenses, indebtedness, and taxes
2054 Losses
2055 Transfers for public, charitable, and religious uses
2056 Bequests, etc., to surviving spouse
2056A Qualified domestic trust
2057 Family-owned business interests
2057 Repealed [Sales of employer securities to employee stock ownership plans or worker-owned cooperatives]
2057 Repealed [Bequests, etc., to certain minor children]
2058 State death taxes

Subchapter B. Estates of Nonresidents Not Citizens

2101 Tax imposed
2102 Credits against tax
2103 Definition of gross estate
2104 Property within the United States
2105 Property without the United States
2106 Taxable estate
2107 Expatriation to avoid tax
2108 Application of pre-1967 estate tax provisions

Subchapter C. Miscellaneous

2201 Combat zone-related deaths of members of the Armed Forces, deaths of astronauts, and deaths of victims of certain terrorist attacks
2202 Repealed [Missionaries in foreign service]
2203 Definition of executor
2204 Discharge of fiduciary from personal liability
2205 Reimbursement out of estate
2206 Liability of life insurance beneficiaries
2207 Liability of recipient of property over which decedent had power of appointment
2207A Right of recovery in the case of certain marital deduction property
2207B Right of recovery where decedent retained interest
2208 Certain residents of possessions considered citizens of the United States
2209 Certain residents of possessions considered nonresidents not citizens of the United States
2210 Termination
2210 Repealed [Liability for payment in case of transfer of employer securities to an employee stock ownership plan or a worker-owned cooperative]

Chapter 12. Gift Tax

Subchapter A. Determination of Tax Liability

2501 Imposition of tax
2502 Rate of tax
2503 Taxable gifts
2504 Taxable gifts for preceding calendar periods
2505 Unified credit against gift tax

Subchapter B. Transfers

2511 Transfers in general
2512 Valuation of gifts
2513 Gift by husband or wife to third party
2514 Powers of appointment
2515 Treatment of generation-skipping transfer tax

Sec.
2515 Repealed [Tenancies by the entirety in real property]
2515A Repealed [Tenancies by the entirety in personal property]
2516 Certain property settlements
2517 Repealed [Certain annuities under qualified plans]
2518 Disclaimers
2519 Dispositions of certain life estates

Subchapter C. Deductions

2521 Repealed [Specific exemption]
2522 Charitable and similar gifts
2523 Gift to spouse
2524 Extent of deductions

Chapter 13. Tax on Certain Generation-Skipping Transfers

Subchapter A. Tax Imposed

2601 Tax imposed
2602 Amount of tax
2603 Liability for tax
2604 Credit for certain State taxes

Subchapter B. Generation-Skipping Transfers

2611 Generation-skipping transfer defined
2612 Taxable termination; taxable distribution; direct skip
2613 Skip person and non-skip person defined

Subchapter C. Taxable Amount

2621 Taxable amount in case of taxable distribution
2622 Taxable amount in case of taxable termination
2623 Taxable amount in case of direct skip
2624 Valuation

Subchapter D. GST Exemption

2631 GST exemption
2632 Special rules for allocation of GST exemption

Subchapter E. Applicable Rate; Inclusion Ratio

2641 Applicable rate
2642 Inclusion ratio

Subchapter F. Other Definitions and Special Rules

2651 Generation assignment
2652 Other definitions
2653 Taxation of multiple skips
2654 Special rules

Subchapter G. Administration

2661 Administration
2662 Return requirements
2663 Regulations
2664 Termination

Chapter 14. Special Valuation Rules

2701 Special valuation rules in case of transfers of certain interests in corporations or partnerships
2702 Special valuation rules in case of transfers of interests in trusts
2703 Certain rights and restrictions disregarded
2704 Treatment of certain lapsing rights and restrictions

Chapter 15. Gifts and Bequests From Expatriates

2801 Imposition of tax

SUBTITLE C—EMPLOYMENT TAXES AND COLLECTION OF INCOME TAX

Sec.

Chapter 21. Federal Insurance Contributions Act

Subchapter A. Tax on Employees

3101 Rate of tax
3102 Deduction of tax from wages

Subchapter B. Tax on Employers

3111 Rate of tax
3112 Instrumentalities of the United States
3113 Repealed [District of Columbia credit unions]

Subchapter C. General Provisions

3121 Definitions
3122 Federal service
3123 Deductions as constructive payments
3124 Estimate of revenue reduction
3125 Returns in the case of governmental employees in States, Guam, American Samoa, and the District of Columbia
3126 Return and payment by governmental employer
3127 Exemption for employers and their employees where both are members of religious faiths opposed to participation in Social Security Act programs
3128 Short title

Chapter 22. Railroad Retirement Tax Act

Subchapter A. Tax on Employees

3201 Rate of tax
3202 Deduction of tax from compensation

Subchapter B. Tax on Employee Representatives

3211 Rate of tax
3212 Determination of compensation

Subchapter C. Tax on Employers

3221 Rate of tax

Subchapter D. General Provisions

3231 Definitions
3232 Court jurisdiction
3233 Short title

Subchapter E. Tier 2 Tax Rate Determination

3241 Determination of tier 2 tax rate based on average account benefits ratio

Chapter 23. Federal Unemployment Tax Act

3301 Rate of tax
3302 Credits against tax
3303 Conditions of additional credit allowance
3304 Approval of State laws
3305 Applicability of State law
3306 Definitions
3307 Deductions as constructive payments
3308 Instrumentalities of the United States
3309 State law coverage of services performed for nonprofit organizations or governmental entities
3310 Judicial review
3311 Short title

Chapter 23A. Railroad Unemployment Repayment Tax

3321 Imposition of tax
3322 Definitions

Chapter 24. Collection of Income Tax at Source

Subchapter A. Withholding from Wages

3401 Definitions
3402 Income tax collected at source

Sec.
3403 Liability for tax
3404 Return and payment by governmental employer
3405 Special rules for pensions, annuities, and certain other deferred income
3406 Backup withholding

Subchapter B. Repealed [Withholding From Interest and Dividends]

3451 Repealed [Income tax collected at source on interest, dividends, and patronage dividends]
3452 Repealed [Exemptions from withholding]
3453 Repealed [Payor defined]
3454 Repealed [Definitions of interest, dividend, and patronage dividend]
3455 Repealed [Other definitions and special rules]
3456 Repealed [Administrative provisions]

Chapter 25. General Provisions Relating to Employment Taxes and Collection of Income Taxes at Source

3501 Collection and payment of taxes
3502 Nondeductibility of taxes in computing taxable income
3503 Erroneous payments
3504 Acts to be performed by agents
3505 Liability of third parties paying or providing for wages
3506 Individuals providing companion sitting placement services
3507 Advance payment of earned income credit
3508 Treatment of real estate agents and direct sellers
3509 Determination of employer's liability for certain employment taxes
3510 Coordination of collection of domestic service employment taxes with collection of income taxes
3510 Repealed [Credit for increased social security employee taxes and railroad retirement tier 1 employee taxes imposed during 1984]

SUBTITLE D—MISCELLANEOUS EXCISE TAXES

Chapter 31. Retail Excise Taxes

Subchapter A. Luxury Passenger Vehicles

4001 Imposition of tax
4002 1st retail sale; uses, etc. treated as sales; determination of price
4003 Special rules

Subchapter B. Special Fuels

4041 Imposition of tax
4042 Tax on fuel used in commercial transportation on inland waterways

Subchapter C. Heavy Trucks and Trailers

4051 Imposition of tax on heavy trucks and trailers sold at retail
4052 Definitions and special rules
4053 Exemptions

Chapter 32. Manufacturers Excise Taxes

Subchapter A. Automotive and Related Items

PART I. GAS GUZZLERS

4061 Repealed [Imposition of tax]
4062 Repealed [Articles classified as parts]
4063 Repealed [Exemptions]

Sec.
4064 Gas guzzler tax

PART II. TIRES

4071 Imposition of tax
4072 Definitions
4073 Exemptions

PART III. PETROLEUM PRODUCTS

Subpart A. Motor and aviation fuels

4081 Imposition of tax
4082 Exemptions for diesel fuel and kerosene
4083 Definitions; special rule; administrative authority
4084 Cross references

Subpart B. Repealed [Aviation fuel]

4091 Repealed [Imposition of tax]
4092 Repealed [Exemptions]
4093 Repealed [Definitions]

Subpart B. Repealed [Lubricating oil]

4091 Repealed [Imposition of tax]
4092 Repealed [Definitions]
4093 Repealed [Exemptions]
4094 Repealed [Cross reference]

Subpart B. Special provisions applicable to fuels tax

4101 Registration and bond
4102 Inspection of records by local officers
4103 Certain additional persons liable for tax where willful failure to pay
4104 Information reporting for persons claiming certain tax benefits
4105 Two-party exchanges

Subchapter B. Coal

4121 Imposition of tax

Subchapter C. Certain Vaccines

4131 Imposition of tax
4132 Definitions and special rules

Subchapter D. Recreational Equipment

PART I. SPORTING GOODS

4161 Imposition of tax
4162 Definitions; treatment of certain resales

PART II. REPEALED [PHOTOGRAPHIC EQUIPMENT]

PART III. FIREARMS

4181 Imposition of tax
4182 Exemptions

Subchapter E. Repealed [Other Items]

Subchapter F. Special Provisions Applicable to Manufacturers Tax

4216 Definition of price
4217 Leases
4218 Use by manufacturer or importer considered sale
4219 Application of tax in case of sales by other than manufacturer or importer

Subchapter G. Exemptions, Registration, Etc.

4221 Certain tax-free sales
4222 Registration
4223 Special rules relating to further manufacture
4224 Repealed [Exemption for articles taxable as jewelry]
4225 Exemption of articles manufactured or produced by Indians

Sec.
4226 Repealed [Floor stocks taxes]
4227 Cross references

Chapter 33. Facilities and Services

Subchapter A. Repealed [Admissions and Dues]

Subchapter B. Communications

4251 Imposition of tax
4252 Definitions
4253 Exemptions
4254 Computation of tax

Subchapter C. Transportation by Air

PART I. PERSONS

4261 Imposition of tax
4262 Definition of taxable transportation
4263 Special rules

PART II. PROPERTY

4271 Imposition of tax
4272 Definition of taxable transportation, etc.

PART III. SPECIAL PROVISIONS APPLICABLE TO TAXES ON TRANSPORTATION BY AIR

4281 Small aircraft on nonestablished lines
4282 Transportation by air for other members of affiliated group
4283 Repealed [Reduction in aviation-related taxes in certain cases]

Subchapter D. Repealed [Safe Deposit Boxes]

Subchapter E. Special Provisions Applicable to Services and Facilities Taxes

4291 Cases where persons receiving payment must collect tax
4292 Repealed [State and local governmental exemption]
4293 Exemption for United States and possessions
4294 Repealed [Exemption for nonprofit educational organizations]

Chapter 34. Policies Issued by Foreign Insurers

4371 Imposition of tax
4372 Definitions
4373 Exemptions
4374 Liability for tax

Chapter 35. Taxes on Wagering

Subchapter A. Tax on Wagers

4401 Imposition of tax
4402 Exemptions
4403 Record requirements
4404 Territorial extent
4405 Cross references

Subchapter B. Occupational Tax

4411 Imposition of tax
4412 Registration
4413 Certain provisions made applicable
4414 Cross references

Subchapter C. Miscellaneous Provisions

4421 Definitions
4422 Applicability of Federal and State laws
4423 Inspection of books
4424 Disclosure of wagering tax information

Sec.

Chapter 36. Certain Other Excise Taxes

Subchapter A. Harbor Maintenance Tax

4461 Imposition of tax
4462 Definitions and special rules

Subchapter B. Repealed [Occupational Tax on Coin-Operated Devices]

4461 Repealed [Imposition of tax]
4462 Repealed [Definition of coin-operated gaming device]
4463 Repealed [Administrative provisions]
4464 Repealed [Credit for State-imposed taxes]

Subchapter B. Transportation by Water

4471 Imposition of tax
4472 Definitions

Subchapter C. Repealed [Occupational Tax on Bowling Alleys, Billiard and Pool Tables]

Subchapter D. Tax on Use of Certain Vehicles

4481 Imposition of tax
4482 Definitions
4483 Exemptions
4484 Cross references

Subchapter E. Repealed [Tax on Use of Civil Aircraft]

4491 Repealed [Imposition of tax]
4492 Repealed [Definitions]
4493 Repealed [Special rules]
4494 Repealed [Cross reference]

Subchapter F. Repealed [Tax on Removal of Hard Mineral Resources from Deep Seabed]

4495 Repealed [Imposition of tax]
4496 Repealed [Definitions]
4497 Repealed [Imputed value]
4498 Repealed [Termination]

Chapter 37. Repealed [Sugar]

4501 Repealed [Imposition of tax]
4502 Repealed [Definitions]
4503 Repealed [Exemptions for sugar manufactured for home consumption]

Chapter 38. Environmental Taxes

Subchapter A. Tax on Petroleum

4611 Imposition of tax
4612 Definitions and special rules

Subchapter B. Tax on Certain Chemicals

4661 Imposition of tax
4662 Definitions and special rules

Subchapter C. Tax on Certain Imported Substances

4671 Imposition of tax
4672 Definitions and special rules

Subchapter C. Repealed [Tax on Hazardous Wastes]

4681 Repealed [Imposition of tax]
4682 Repealed [Definitions and special rules]

Subchapter D. Ozone-Depleting Chemicals, Etc.

4681 Imposition of tax
4682 Definitions and special rules

Chapter 39. Registration-Required Obligations

4701 Tax on issuer of registration-required obligation not in registered form

Sec.

Chapter 40. General Provisions Relating to Occupational Taxes

4901 Payment of tax
4902 Liability of partners
4903 Liability in case of business in more than one location
4904 Liability in case of different businesses of same ownership and location
4905 Liability in case of death or change of location
4906 Application of State laws
4907 Federal agencies or instrumentalities

Chapter 41. Public Charities

4911 Tax on excess expenditures to influence legislation
4912 Tax on disqualifying lobbying expenditures of certain organizations

Chapter 42. Private Foundations and Certain Other Tax-Exempt Organizations

Subchapter A. Private Foundations

4940 Excise tax based on investment income
4941 Taxes on self-dealing
4942 Taxes on failure to distribute income
4943 Taxes on excess business holdings
4944 Taxes on investments which jeopardize charitable purpose
4945 Taxes on taxable expenditures
4946 Definitions and special rules
4947 Application of taxes to certain nonexempt trusts
4948 Application of taxes and denial of exemption with respect to certain foreign organizations

Subchapter B. Black Lung Benefit Trusts

4951 Taxes on self-dealing
4952 Taxes on taxable expenditures
4953 Tax on excess contributions to black lung benefit trusts

Subchapter C. Political Expenditures of Section 501(c)(3) Organizations

4955 Taxes on political expenditures of section 501(c)(3) organizations

Subchapter D. Failure by Certain Charitable Organizations to Meet Certain Qualification Requirements

4958 Taxes on excess benefit transactions

Subchapter E. Abatement of First and Second Tier Taxes in Certain Cases

4961 Abatement of second tier taxes where there is correction
4962 Abatement of first tier taxes in certain cases
4963 Definitions

Subchapter F. Tax Shelter Transactions

4965 Excise tax on certain tax-exempt entities entering into prohibited tax shelter transactions

Subchapter F. Donor advised funds

4966 Taxes on taxable distributions
4967 Taxes on prohibited benefits

Chapter 43. Qualified Pension, Etc., Plans

4971 Taxes on failure to meet minimum funding standards
4972 Tax on nondeductible contributions to qualified employer plans
4972 Repealed [Tax on excess contributions for self-employed individuals]
4973 Tax on excess contributions to certain tax-favored accounts and annuities
4974 Excise tax on certain accumulations in qualified retirement plans
4975 Tax on prohibited transactions
4976 Taxes with respect to funded welfare benefit plans
4977 Tax on certain fringe benefits provided by an employer
4978 Tax on certain dispositions by employee stock ownership plans and certain cooperatives
4978A Repealed [Tax on certain dispositions of employer securities to which section 2057 applied]
4978B Repealed [Tax on disposition of employer securities to which section 133 applied]
4979 Tax on certain excess contributions
4979A Tax on certain prohibited allocations of qualified securities
4980 Tax on reversion of qualified plan assets to employer
4980A Repealed [Tax on excess distributions from qualified retirement plans]
4980B Failure to satisfy continuation coverage requirements of group health plans
4980C Requirements for issuers of qualified long-term care insurance contracts
4980D Failure to meet certain group health plan requirements
4980E Failure of employer to make comparable Archer MSA contributions
4980F Failure of applicable plans reducing benefit accruals to satisfy notice requirements
4980G Failure of employer to make comparable health savings account contributions

Chapter 44. Qualified Investment Entities

4981 Excise tax on undistributed income of real estate investment trusts
4982 Excise tax on undistributed income of regulated investment companies

Chapter 45. Provisions Relating to Expatriated Entities

4985 Stock compensation of insiders in expatriated corporations

Chapter 45. Repealed [Windfall Profit Tax on Domestic Crude Oil]

Subchapter A. Repealed [Imposition and Amount of Tax]

4986 Repealed [Imposition of tax]
4987 Repealed [Amount of tax]
4988 Repealed [Windfall profit; removal price]
4989 Repealed [Adjusted base price]
4990 Repealed [Phaseout of tax]

Subchapter B. Repealed [Categories of Oil]

4991 Repealed [Taxable crude oil; categories of oil]
4992 Repealed [Independent producer oil]
4993 Repealed [Incremental tertiary oil]

Sec.
4994 Repealed [Definitions and special rules relating to exemptions]

Subchapter C. Repealed [Miscellaneous Provisions]

4995 Repealed [Withholding; depositary requirements]
4996 Repealed [Other definitions and special rules]
4997 Repealed [Records and information; regulations]
4998 Repealed [Cross references]

Chapter 46. Golden Parachute Payments

4999 Golden parachute payments

Chapter 47. Certain Group Health Plans

5000 Certain group health plans

SUBTITLE E—ALCOHOL, TOBACCO, AND CERTAIN OTHER EXCISE TAXES

Chapter 51. Distilled Spirits, Wines, and Beer

Subchapter A. Gallonage and Occupational Taxes

PART I. GALLONAGE TAXES

Subpart A. Distilled spirits

5001 Imposition, rate, and attachment of tax
5002 Definitions
5003 Cross references to exemptions, etc.
5004 Lien for tax
5005 Persons liable for tax
5006 Determination of tax
5007 Collection of tax on distilled spirits
5008 Abatement, remission, refund, and allowance for loss or destruction of distilled spirits
5009 Repealed [Drawback]
5010 Credit for wine content and for flavors content
5011 Income tax credit for average cost of carrying excise tax

Subpart B. Repealed [Rectification]

5021 Repealed [Imposition and rate of tax]
5022 Repealed [Tax on cordials and liqueurs containing wine]
5023 Repealed [Tax on blending of beverage rums or brandies]
5024 Repealed [Definitions]
5025 Repealed [Exemption from rectification tax]
5026 Repealed [Determination and collection of rectification tax]

Subpart C. Wines

5041 Imposition and rate of tax
5042 Exemption from tax
5043 Collection of taxes on wines
5044 Refund of tax on wine
5045 Cross references

Subpart D. Beer

5051 Imposition and rate of tax
5052 Definitions
5053 Exemptions
5054 Determination and collection of tax on beer
5055 Drawback of tax
5056 Refund and credit of tax, or relief from liability

Subpart E. General provisions

5061 Method of collecting tax
5062 Refund and drawback in case of exportation

Sec.
5063 Repealed [Floor stocks tax refunds on distilled spirits, wines, cordials, and beer]
5064 Losses resulting from disaster, vandalism, or malicious mischief
5065 Territorial extent of law
5066 Distilled spirits for use of foreign embassies, legations, etc.
5067 Cross reference

PART II. OCCUPATIONAL TAX [BEFORE 7/1/2008]

Subpart A. Repealed effective 7/1/2008 [Proprietors of distilled spirits plants, bonded wine cellars, etc.]

5081 Repealed effective 7/1/2008 [Imposition and rate of tax]

Subpart A. Repealed [Rectifier]

5081 Repealed [Imposition and rate of tax]
5082 Repealed [Definition of rectifier]
5083 Repealed [Exemptions]
5084 Repealed [Cross references]

Subpart B. Repealed effective 7/1/2008 [Brewer]

5091 Repealed effective 7/1/2008 [Imposition and rate of tax]
5092 Repealed effective 7/1/2008 [Definition of brewer]
5093 Repealed effective 7/1/2008 [Cross references]

Subpart C. Manufacturers of stills [redesignated as Subpart A (on and after 7/1/2008)]

5101 Notice of manufacture of still; notice of set up of still
5102 Definition of manufacturer of stills

Subpart D. Generally repealed effective 7/1/2008 [Wholesale dealers]

5111 Repealed effective 7/1/2008 [Imposition and rate of tax]
5112 Repealed effective 7/1/2008 [Definitions]
5113 Repealed effective 7/1/2008 [Exemptions]
5114 Records
5115 Repealed [Sign required on premises]
5116 Packaging distilled spirits for industrial uses
5117 Repealed effective 7/1/2008 [Prohibited purchases by dealers]

Subpart E. Generally repealed effective 7/1/2008 [Retail dealers]

5121 Repealed effective 7/1/2008 [Imposition and rate of tax]
5122 Repealed effective 7/1/2008 [Definitions]
5123 Repealed effective 7/1/2008 [Exemptions]
5124 Records
5125 Repealed effective 7/1/2008 [Cross references]

Subpart F. Nonbeverage domestic drawback claimants [redesignated as Subpart B (on and after 7/1/2008)]

5131 Eligibility and rate of tax
5132 Registration and regulation
5133 Investigation of claims
5134 Drawback

Subpart G. Generally repealed effective 7/1/2008 [General provisions]

5141 Repealed effective 7/1/2008 [Registration]
5142 Payment of tax
5143 Provisions relating to liability for occupational taxes

Sec.
5144 Repealed [Supply of stamps]
5145 Application of State laws
5146 Preservation and inspection of records, and entry of premises for inspection
5147 Repealed effective 7/1/2008 [Application of subpart]
5148 Repealed effective 7/1/2008 [Suspension of occupational tax]
5149 Repealed effective 7/1/2008 [Cross references]

PART II. MISCELLANEOUS PROVISIONS [ON AND AFTER 7/1/2008]

Subpart A. Manufacturer of stills [on and after 7/1/2008]

5101 Notice of manufacture of still; notice of set up of still [on and after 7/1/2008]
5102 Defintion of manufacturer of stills [on and after 7/1/2008]

Subpart B. Nonbeverage domestic drawback claimants [on and after 7/1/2008]

5111 Eligibility [on and after 7/1/2008]
5112 Registration and regulation [on and after 7/1/2008]
5113 Investigation of claims [on and after 7/1/2008]
5114 Drawback [on and after 7/1/2008]

Subpart C. Recordkeeping and registration by dealers [on and after 7/1/2008]

5121 Recordkeeping by wholesale dealers [on and after 7/1/2008]
5122 Recordkeeping by retail dealers [on and after 7/1/2008]
5123 Preservation and inspection of records, and entry of premises for inspection [on and after 7/1/2008]
5124 Registration by dealers [on and after 7/1/2008]

Subpart D. Other provisions [on and after 7/1/2008]

5131 Packaging distilled spirits for industrial uses [on and after 7/1/2008]
5132 Prohibited purchases by dealers [on and after 7/1/2008]

Subchapter B. Qualification Requirements for Distilled Spirits Plants

5171 Establishment
5172 Application
5173 Bonds
5174 Repealed [Withdrawal bonds]
5175 Export bonds
5176 New or renewed bonds
5177 Other provisions relating to bonds
5178 Premises of distilled spirits plants
5179 Registration of stills
5180 Signs
5181 Distilled spirits for fuel use
5182 Cross references

Subchapter C. Operation of Distilled Spirits Plants

PART I. GENERAL PROVISIONS

5201 Regulation of operations
5202 Supervision of operations
5203 Entry and examination of premises
5204 Gauging
5205 Repealed [Stamps]
5206 Containers
5207 Records and reports

Sec.

PART II. OPERATIONS ON BONDED PREMISES

Subpart A. General

5211 Production and entry of distilled spirits
5212 Transfer of distilled spirits between bonded premises
5213 Withdrawal of distilled spirits from bonded premises on determination of tax
5214 Withdrawal of distilled spirits from bonded premises free of tax or without payment of tax
5215 Return of tax determined distilled spirits to bonded premises
5216 Regulation of operations

Subpart B. Production

5221 Commencement, suspension, and resumption of operations
5222 Production, receipt, removal, and use of distilling materials
5223 Redistillation of spirits, articles, and residues

Subpart C. Storage

5231 Entry for deposit
5232 Imported distilled spirits
5233 Repealed [Bottling of distilled spirits in bond]
5234 Repealed [Mingling and blending of distilled spirits]
5235 Bottling of alcohol for industrial purposes
5236 Discontinuance of storage facilities and transfer of distilled spirits

Subpart D. Denaturation

5241 Authority to denature
5242 Denaturing materials
5243 Sale of abandoned spirits for denaturation without collection of tax
5244 Cross references

Subchapter D. Industrial Use of Distilled Spirits

5271 Permits
5272 Bonds
5273 Sale, use, and recovery of denatured distilled spirits
5274 Applicability of other laws
5275 Records and reports
5276 Repealed effective 7/1/2008 [Occupational tax]

Subchapter E. General Provisions Relating to Distilled Spirits

PART I. RETURN OF MATERIALS USED IN THE MANUFACTURE OR RECOVERY OF DISTILLED SPIRITS

5291 General

PART II. REGULATION OF TRAFFIC IN CONTAINERS OF DISTILLED SPIRITS

5301 General

PART III. MISCELLANEOUS PROVISIONS

5311 Detention of containers
5312 Production and use of distilled spirits for experimental research
5313 Withdrawal of distilled spirits from customs custody free of tax for use of the United States
5314 Special applicability of certain provisions

Subchapter F. Bonded and Taxpaid Wine Premises

PART I. ESTABLISHMENT

5351 Bonded wine cellar
5352 Taxpaid wine bottling house

Sec.
5353 Bonded wine warehouse
5354 Bond
5355 General provisions relating to bonds
5356 Application
5357 Premises

PART II. OPERATIONS

5361 Bonded wine cellar operations
5362 Removals of wine from bonded wine cellars
5363 Taxpaid wine bottling house operations
5364 Wine imported in bulk
5364 Repealed [Standard wine premises]
5365 Segregation of operations
5366 Supervision
5367 Records
5368 Gauging and marking
5369 Inventories
5370 Losses
5371 Insurance coverage, etc.
5372 Sampling
5373 Wine spirits

PART III. CELLAR TREATMENT AND CLASSIFICATION OF WINE

5381 Natural wine
5382 Cellar treatment of natural wine
5383 Amelioration and sweetening limitations for natural grape wines
5384 Amelioration and sweetening limitations for natural fruit and berry wines
5385 Specially sweetened natural wines
5386 Special natural wines
5387 Agricultural wines
5388 Designation of wines

PART IV. GENERAL

5391 Exemption from distilled spirits taxes
5392 Definitions

Subchapter G. Breweries

PART I. ESTABLISHMENT

5401 Qualifying documents
5402 Definitions
5403 Cross references

PART II. OPERATIONS

5411 Use of brewery
5412 Removal of beer in containers or by pipeline
5413 Brewers procuring beer from other brewers
5414 Removals from one brewery to another belonging to the same brewer
5415 Records and returns
5416 Definitions of package and packaging
5417 Pilot brewing plants
5418 Beer imported in bulk

Subchapter H. Miscellaneous Plants and Warehouses

PART I. VINEGAR PLANTS

5501 Establishment
5502 Qualification
5503 Construction and equipment
5504 Operation
5505 Applicability of provisions of this chapter

Sec.

PART II. VOLATILE FRUIT-FLAVOR CONCENTRATE PLANTS

5511 Establishment and operation
5512 Control of products after manufacture

PART III. REPEALED [MANUFACTURING BONDED WAREHOUSES]

5521 Repealed [Establishment and operation]
5522 Repealed [Withdrawal of distilled spirits to manufacturing bonded warehouses]
5523 Repealed [Special provisions relating to distilled spirits and wines rectified in manufacturing bonded warehouses]

Subchapter I. Miscellaneous General Provisions

5551 General provisions relating to bonds
5552 Installation of meters, tanks, and other apparatus
5553 Supervision of premises and operations
5554 Pilot operations
5555 Records, statements, and returns
5556 Regulations
5557 Officers and agents authorized to investigate, issue search warrants, and prosecute for violations
5558 Authority of enforcement officers
5559 Determinations
5560 Other provisions applicable
5561 Exemptions to meet the requirements of the national defense
5562 Exemptions from certain requirements in cases of disaster

Subchapter J. Penalties, Seizures, and Forfeitures Relating to Liquors

PART I. PENALTY, SEIZURE, AND FORFEITURE PROVISIONS APPLICABLE TO DISTILLING, RECTIFYING, AND DISTILLED AND RECTIFIED PRODUCTS

5601 Criminal penalties
5602 Penalty for tax fraud by distiller
5603 Penalty relating to records, returns, and reports
5604 Penalties relating to marks, brands, and containers
5605 Penalty relating to return of materials used in the manufacture of distilled spirits, or from which distilled spirits may be recovered
5606 Penalty relating to containers of distilled spirits
5607 Penalty and forfeiture for unlawful use, recovery, or concealment of denatured distilled spirits, or articles
5608 Penalty and forfeiture for fraudulent claims for export drawback or unlawful relanding
5609 Destruction of unregistered stills, distilling apparatus, equipment, and materials
5610 Disposal of forfeited equipment and material for distilling
5611 Release of distillery before judgment
5612 Forfeiture of taxpaid distilled spirits remaining on bonded premises
5613 Forfeiture of distilled spirits not closed, marked, or branded as required by law
5614 Burden of proof in cases of seizure of spirits
5615 Property subject to forfeiture

PART II. PENALTY AND FORFEITURE PROVISIONS APPLICABLE TO WINE AND WINE PRODUCTION

Sec.
5661 Penalty and forfeiture for violation of laws and regulations relating to wine
5662 Penalty for alteration of wine labels
5663 Cross reference

PART III. PENALTY, SEIZURE, AND FORFEITURE PROVISIONS APPLICABLE TO BEER AND BREWING

5671 Penalty and forfeiture for evasion of beer tax and fraudulent noncompliance with requirements
5672 Penalty for failure of brewer to comply with requirements and to keep records and file returns
5673 Forfeiture for flagrant and willful removal of beer without tax payment
5674 Penalty for unlawful production or removal of beer
5675 Penalty for intentional removal or defacement of brewer's marks and brands

PART IV. PENALTY, SEIZURE, AND FORFEITURE PROVISIONS COMMON TO LIQUORS

5681 Penalty relating to signs
5682 Penalty for breaking locks or gaining access
5683 Penalty and forfeiture for removal of liquors under improper brands
5684 Penalties relating to the payment and collection of liquor taxes
5685 Penalty and forfeiture relating to possession of devices for emitting gas, smoke, etc., explosives and firearms, when violating liquor laws
5686 Penalty for having, possessing, or using liquor or property intended to be used in violating provisions of this chapter
5687 Penalty for offenses not specifically covered
5688 Disposition and release of seized property
5690 Definition of the term "person"

PART V. REPEALED EFFECTIVE 7/1/2008 [PENALTIES APPLICABLE TO OCCUPATIONAL TAXES]

5691 Repealed effective 7/1/2008 [Penalties for nonpayment of special taxes]
5692 Repealed [Penalties relating to posting of special tax stamps]

Chapter 52. Tobacco Products and Cigarette Papers and Tubes

Subchapter A. Definitions; Rate and Payment of Tax; Exemption From Tax; and Refund and Drawback of Tax

5701 Rate of tax
5702 Definitions
5703 Liability for tax and method of payment
5704 Exemption from tax
5705 Credit, refund, or allowance of tax
5706 Drawback of tax
5707 Repealed [Floor stocks refund on cigarettes]
5708 Losses caused by disaster

Subchapter B. Qualification Requirements for Manufacturers and Importers of Tobacco Products and Cigarette Papers and Tubes, and Export Warehouse Proprietors

5711 Bond
5712 Application for permit
5713 Permit

Sec.

Subchapter C. Operations by Manufacturers and Importers of Tobacco Products and Cigarette Papers and Tubes, and Export Warehouse Proprietors

5721 Inventories
5722 Reports
5723 Packages, marks, labels, and notices

Subchapter D. Occupational Tax

5731 Imposition and rate of tax
5732 Payment of tax [on and after 7/1/2008]
5733 Provisions relating to liability for occupational taxes [on and after 7/1/2008]
5734 Application of State laws [on and after 7/1/2008]

Subchapter D. Repealed [Operations by Dealers in Tobacco Materials]

5731 Repealed [Shipments and deliveries restricted]
5732 Repealed [Inventory, and statement of shipments and deliveries]

Subchapter E. Records of Manufacturers and Importers of Tobacco Products and Cigarette Papers and Tubes, and Export Warehouse Proprietors

5741 Records to be maintained

Subchapter F. General Provisions

5751 Purchase, receipt, possession, or sale of tobacco products and cigarette papers and tubes, after removal
5752 Restrictions relating to marks, labels, notices, and packages
5753 Disposal of forfeited, condemned, and abandoned tobacco products, and cigarette papers and tubes
5754 Restriction on importation of previously exported tobacco products

Subchapter G. Penalties and Forfeitures

5761 Civil penalties
5762 Criminal penalties
5763 Forfeitures

Chapter 53. Machine Guns, Destructive Devices, and Certain Other Firearms

Subchapter A. Taxes

PART I. SPECIAL (OCCUPATIONAL) TAXES

5801 Imposition of tax
5802 Registration of importers, manufacturers, and dealers

PART II. TAX ON TRANSFERRING FIREARMS

5811 Transfer tax
5812 Transfers

PART III. TAX ON MAKING FIREARMS

5821 Making tax
5822 Making

Subchapter B. General Provisions and Exemptions

PART I. GENERAL PROVISIONS

5841 Registration of firearms
5842 Identification of firearms
5843 Records and returns
5844 Importation
5845 Definitions
5846 Other laws applicable
5847 Effect on other laws
5848 Restrictive use of information

Sec.
5849 Citation of chapter

PART II. EXEMPTIONS

5851 Special (occupational) tax exemption
5852 General transfer and making tax exemption
5853 Transfer and making tax exemption available to certain governmental entities
5854 Exportation of firearms exempt from transfer tax

Subchapter C. Prohibited Acts

5861 Prohibited acts

Subchapter D. Penalties and Forfeitures

5871 Penalties
5872 Forfeitures

Chapter 54. Greenmail

5881 Greenmail

Chapter 55. Structured Settlement Factoring Transactions

5891 Structured settlement factoring transactions

SUBTITLE F—PROCEDURE AND ADMINISTRATION

Chapter 61. Information and Returns

Subchapter A. Returns and Records

PART I. RECORDS, STATEMENTS, AND SPECIAL RETURNS

6001 Notice or regulations requiring records, statements, and special returns

PART II. TAX RETURNS OR STATEMENTS

Subpart A. General requirement

6011 General requirement of return, statement, or list

Subpart B. Income tax returns

6012 Persons required to make returns of income
6013 Joint returns of income tax by husband and wife
6014 Income tax return—tax not computed by taxpayer
6015 Relief from joint and several liability on joint return
6015 Repealed [Declaration of estimated income tax by individuals]
6017 Self-employment tax returns
6017A Repealed [Place of residence]

Subpart C. Estate and gift tax returns [before 1/1/2010]

6018 Estate tax returns
6019 Gift tax returns

Subpart C. Returns relating to transfers during life or at death [after 12/31/2009]

6018 Returns relating to large transfers at death
6019 Gift tax returns

Subpart D. Miscellaneous provisions

6020 Returns prepared for or executed by Secretary
6021 Listing by Secretary of taxable objects owned by nonresidents of internal revenue districts

PART III. INFORMATION RETURNS

Subpart A. Information concerning persons subject to special provisions

6031 Return of partnership income
6032 Returns of banks with respect to common trust funds
6033 Returns by exempt organizations

Sec.
6034 Returns by trusts described in section 4947(a)(2) or claiming charitable deductions under section 642(c) [effective before 1/1/2007]
6034 Returns by certain trusts [effective after 12/31/2006]
6034A Information to beneficiaries of estates and trusts
6035 Repealed [Returns of officers, directors, and shareholders of foreign personal holding companies]
6036 Notice of qualification as executor or receiver
6037 Return of S corporation
6038 Information reporting with respect to certain foreign corporations and partnerships
6038A Information with respect to certain foreign-owned corporations
6038B Notice of certain transfers to foreign persons
6038C Information with respect to foreign corporations engaged in U.S. business
6039 Returns required in connection with certain options
6039A Repealed [Information regarding carryover basis property acquired from a decedent]
6039B Repealed [Return of general stock ownership corporation]
6039C Returns with respect to foreign persons holding direct investments in United States real property interests
6039D Returns and records with respect to certain fringe benefit plans
6039E Information concerning resident status
6039F Notice of large gifts received from foreign persons
6039G Information on individuals losing United States citizenship
6039H Information with respect to Alaska Native Settlement Trusts and sponsoring Native Corporations
6039I Returns and records with respect to employer-owned life insurance contracts
6039J Information reporting with respect to commodity credit corporation transactions
6040 Cross references

Subpart B. Information concerning transactions with other persons

6041 Information at source
6041A Returns regarding payments of remuneration for services and direct sales
6042 Returns regarding payments of dividends, and corporate earnings and profits
6043 Liquidating, etc., transactions
6043A Returns relating to taxable mergers and acquisitions
6044 Returns regarding payments of patronage dividends
6045 Returns of brokers
6046 Returns as to organization or reorganization of foreign corporations and as to acquisitions of their stock
6046A Returns as to interests in foreign partnerships
6047 Information relating to certain trusts and annuity plans
6048 Information with respect to certain foreign trusts
6049 Returns regarding payments of interest
6050 Repealed [Returns relating to certain transfers to exempt organizations]

Sec.

6050A Reporting requirements of certain fishing boat operators

6050B Returns relating to unemployment compensation

6050C Repealed [Information regarding windfall profit tax on domestic crude oil]

6050D Returns relating to energy grants and financing

6050E State and local income tax refunds

6050F Returns relating to social security benefits

6050G Returns relating to certain railroad retirement benefits

6050H Returns relating to mortgage interest received in trade or business from individuals

6050I Returns relating to cash received in trade or business, etc.

6050J Returns relating to foreclosures and abandonments of security

6050K Returns relating to exchanges of certain partnership interests

6050L Returns relating to certain donated property

6050M Returns relating to persons receiving contracts from Federal executive agencies

6050N Returns regarding payment of royalties

6050P Returns relating to the cancellation of indebtedness by certain entities

6050Q Certain long-term care benefits

6050R Returns relating to certain purchases of fish

6050S Returns relating to higher education tuition and related expenses

6050T Returns relating to credit for health insurance costs of eligible individuals

6050U Charges or payments for qualified long-term care insurance contracts under combined arrangements

6050V Returns relating to applicable insurance contracts in which certain exempt organizations hold interests

6050W Returns relating to payments made in settlement of payment card and third party network transactions

Subpart C. Information regarding wages paid employees

6051 Receipts for employees

6052 Returns regarding payment of wages in the form of group-term life insurance

6053 Reporting of tips

Subpart D. Repealed [Information concerning private foundations]

6056 Repealed [Annual reports by private foundations]

Subpart E. Registration of and information concerning pension, etc., plans

6057 Annual registration, etc.

6058 Information required in connection with certain plans of deferred compensation

6059 Periodic report of actuary

Subpart F. Information concerning income tax return preparers

6060 Information returns of income tax return preparers

PART IV. SIGNING AND VERIFYING OF RETURNS AND OTHER DOCUMENTS

6061 Signing of returns and other documents

Sec.

6062 Signing of corporation returns

6063 Signing of partnership returns

6064 Signature presumed authentic

6065 Verification of returns

PART V. TIME FOR FILING RETURNS AND OTHER DOCUMENTS

6071 Time for filing returns and other documents

6072 Time for filing income tax returns

6073 Repealed [Time for filing declarations of estimated income tax by individuals]

6075 Time for filing estate and gift tax returns

6076 Repealed [Time for filing return of windfall profit tax]

PART VI. EXTENSION OF TIME FOR FILING RETURNS

6081 Extension of time for filing returns

PART VII. PLACE FOR FILING RETURNS OR OTHER DOCUMENTS

6091 Place for filing returns or other documents

PART VIII. DESIGNATION OF INCOME TAX PAYMENTS TO PRESIDENTIAL ELECTION CAMPAIGN FUND

6096 Designation by individuals

Subchapter B. Miscellaneous Provisions

6101 Period covered by returns or other documents

6102 Computations on returns or other documents

6103 Confidentiality and disclosure of returns and return information

6104 Publicity of information required from certain exempt organizations and certain trusts

6105 Confidentiality of information arising under treaty obligations

6106 Repealed [Publicity of unemployment tax returns]

6107 Income tax return preparer must furnish copy of return to taxpayer and must retain a copy or list

6108 Statistical publications and studies

6109 Identifying numbers

6110 Public inspection of written determinations

6111 Disclosure of reportable transactions

6112 Material advisors of reportable transactions must keep lists of advisees, etc.

6113 Disclosure of nondeductibility of contributions

6114 Treaty-based return positions

6115 Disclosure related to quid pro quo contributions

6116 Cross reference

Chapter 62. Time and Place for Paying Tax

Subchapter A. Place and Due Date for Payment of Tax

6151 Time and place for paying tax shown on returns

6152 Repealed [Installment payments]

6153 Repealed [Installment payments of estimated income tax by individuals]

6154 Repealed [Installment payment of estimated income tax by corporations]

6155 Payment on notice and demand

6156 Repealed [Installment payments of tax on use of highway motor vehicles]

6157 Payment of Federal unemployment tax on quarterly or other time period basis

Sec.
6158 Repealed [Installment payment of tax attributable to divestitures pursuant to Bank Holding Company Act amendments of 1970]
6159 Agreements for payment of tax liability in installments

Subchapter B. Extensions of Time for Payment

6161 Extension of time for paying tax
6163 Extension of time for payment of estate tax on value of reversionary or remainder interest in property
6164 Extension of time for payment of taxes by corporations expecting carrybacks
6165 Bonds where time to pay tax or deficiency has been extended
6166 Extension of time for payment of estate tax where estate consists largely of interest in closely held business
6166A Repealed [Extension of time for payment of estate tax where estate consists largely of interest in closely held business]
6167 Extension of time for payment of tax attributable to recovery of foreign expropriation losses

Chapter 63. Assessment

Subchapter A. In General

6201 Assessment authority
6202 Establishment by regulations of mode or time of assessment
6203 Method of assessment
6204 Supplemental assessments
6205 Special rules applicable to certain employment taxes
6206 Special rules applicable to excessive claims under sections 6420, 6421, and 6427 [before 1/1/2006]
6206 Special rules applicable to excessive claims under certain sections [after 12/31/2005]
6207 Cross references

Subchapter B. Deficiency Procedures in the Case of Income, Estate, Gift, and Certain Excise Taxes

6211 Definition of a deficiency
6212 Notice of deficiency
6213 Restrictions applicable to deficiencies; petition to Tax Court
6214 Determinations by Tax Court
6215 Assessment of deficiency found by Tax Court
6216 Cross references

Subchapter C. Tax Treatment of Partnership Items

6221 Tax treatment determined at partnership level
6222 Partner's return must be consistent with partnership return or Secretary notified of inconsistency
6223 Notice to partners of proceedings
6224 Participation in administrative proceedings; waivers; agreements
6225 Assessments made only after partnership level proceedings are completed
6226 Judicial review of final partnership administrative adjustments
6227 Administrative adjustment requests
6228 Judicial review where administrative adjustment request is not allowed in full
6229 Period of limitations for making assessments

Sec.
6230 Additional administrative provisions
6231 Definitions and special rules
6232 Repealed [Extension of subchapter to windfall profit tax]
6233 Extension to entities filing partnership returns, etc.
6234 Declaratory judgment relating to treatment of items other than partnership items with respect to an oversheltered return

Subchapter D. Treatment of Electing Large Partnerships

PART I. TREATMENT OF PARTNERSHIP ITEMS AND ADJUSTMENTS

6240 Application of subchapter
6241 Partner's return must be consistent with partnership return
6242 Procedures for taking partnership adjustments into account

PART II. PARTNERSHIP LEVEL ADJUSTMENTS

Subpart A. Adjustments by Secretary

6245 Secretarial authority
6246 Restrictions on partnership adjustments
6247 Judicial review of partnership adjustment
6248 Period of limitations for making adjustments

Subpart B. Claims for adjustments by partnership

6251 Administrative adjustment requests
6252 Judicial review where administrative adjustment request is not allowed in full

PART III. DEFINITIONS AND SPECIAL RULES

6255 Definitions and special rules

Subchapter D. Repealed [Tax Treatment of Subchapter S Items]

6241 Repealed [Tax treatment determined at corporate level]
6242 Repealed [Shareholder's return must be consistent with corporate return or Secretary notified of inconsistency]
6243 Repealed [All shareholders to be notified of proceedings and given opportunity to participate]
6244 Repealed [Certain partnership provisions made applicable]
6245 Repealed [Subchapter S item defined]

Chapter 64. Collection

Subchapter A. General Provisions

6301 Collection authority
6302 Mode or time of collection
6303 Notice and demand for tax
6304 Fair tax collection practices
6305 Collection of certain liability
6306 Qualified tax collection contracts

Subchapter B. Receipt of Payment

6311 Payment of tax by commercially acceptable means
6313 Fractional parts of a cent
6314 Receipt for taxes
6315 Payments of estimated income tax
6316 Payment by foreign currency
6317 Payments of Federal unemployment tax for calendar quarter

Sec.

Subchapter C. Lien for Taxes

PART I. DUE PROCESS OF LIENS

6320 Notice and opportunity for hearing upon filing of notice of lien

PART II. LIENS

6321 Lien for taxes
6322 Period of lien
6323 Validity and priority against certain persons
6324 Special liens for estate and gift taxes
6324A Special lien for estate tax deferred under section 6166
6324B Special lien for additional estate tax attributable to farm, etc., valuation
6325 Release of lien or discharge of property
6326 Administrative appeal of liens
6327 Cross references

Subchapter D. Seizure of Property for Collection of Taxes

PART I. DUE PROCESS FOR COLLECTIONS

6330 Notice and opportunity for hearing before levy

PART II. LEVY

6331 Levy and distraint
6332 Surrender of property subject to levy
6333 Production of books
6334 Property exempt from levy
6335 Sale of seized property
6336 Sale of perishable goods
6337 Redemption of property
6338 Certificate of sale; deed of real property
6339 Legal effect of certificate of sale of personal property and deed of real property
6340 Records of sale
6341 Expense of levy and sale
6342 Application of proceeds of levy
6343 Authority to release levy and return property
6344 Cross references

Subchapter E. Repealed [Collection of State Individual Income Taxes]

6361 Repealed [General rules]
6362 Repealed [Qualified State individual income taxes]
6363 Repealed [State agreements; other procedures]
6364 Repealed [Regulations]
6365 Repealed [Definitions and special rules]

Chapter 65. Abatements, Credits, and Refunds

Subchapter A. Procedure in General

6401 Amounts treated as overpayments
6402 Authority to make credits or refunds
6403 Overpayment of installment
6404 Abatements
6405 Reports of refunds and credits
6406 Prohibition of administrative review of decisions
6407 Date of allowance of refund or credit
6408 State escheat laws not to apply

Subchapter B. Rules of Special Application

6411 Tentative carryback and refund adjustments
6412 Floor stocks refunds
6413 Special rules applicable to certain employment taxes

Sec.

6414 Income tax withheld
6415 Credits or refunds to persons who collected certain taxes
6416 Certain taxes on sales and services
6418 Repealed [Sugar]
6419 Excise tax on wagering
6420 Gasoline used on farms
6421 Gasoline used for certain nonhighway purposes, used by local transit systems, or sold for certain exempt purposes
6422 Cross references
6423 Conditions to allowance in the case of alcohol and tobacco taxes
6424 Repealed [Lubricating oil used for certain nontaxable purposes]
6425 Adjustment of overpayment of estimated income tax by corporation
6426 Credit for alcohol fuel and biodiesel mixtures [before 10/1/2006]
6426 Credit for alcohol fuel, biodiesel, and alternative fuel mixtures [after 9/30/2006]
6426 Repealed [Refund of aircraft use tax where plane transports for hire in foreign air commerce]
6427 Fuels not used for taxable purposes
6428 Acceleration of 10 percent income tax rate bracket benefit for 2001
6428 Repealed [1981 rate reduction tax credit]
6429 Advance payment of portion of increased child credit for 2003
6429 Repealed [Credit and refund of Chapter 45 taxes paid by royalty owners]
6430 Treatment of tax imposed at Leaking Underground Storage Tank Trust Fund financing rate
6430 Repealed [Credit or refund of windfall profit taxes to certain trust beneficiaries]

Chapter 66. Limitations

Subchapter A. Limitations on Assessment and Collection

6501 Limitations on assessment and collection
6502 Collection after assessment
6503 Suspension of running of period of limitation
6504 Cross references

Subchapter B. Limitations on Credit or Refund

6511 Limitations on credit or refund
6512 Limitations in case of petition to Tax Court
6513 Time return deemed filed and tax considered paid
6514 Credits or refunds after period of limitation
6515 Cross references

Subchapter C. Mitigation of Effect of Period of Limitations

6521 Mitigation of effect of limitation in case of related taxes under different chapters

Subchapter D. Periods of Limitation in Judicial Proceedings

6531 Periods of limitation on criminal prosecutions
6532 Periods of limitation on suits
6533 Cross references

Sec.

Chapter 67. Interest

Subchapter A. Interest on Underpayments

6601 Interest on underpayment, nonpayment, or extensions of time for payment, of tax
6602 Interest on erroneous refund recoverable by suit
6603 Deposits made to suspend running of interest on potential underpayments, etc.

Subchapter B. Interest on Overpayments

6611 Interest on overpayments
6612 Cross references

Subchapter C. Determination of Interest Rate; Compounding of Interest

6621 Determination of rate of interest
6622 Interest compounded daily

Subchapter D. Notice Requirements

6631 Notice requirements

Chapter 68. Additions to the Tax, Additional Amounts, and Assessable Penalties

Subchapter A. Additions to the Tax and Additional Amounts

PART I. GENERAL PROVISIONS

6651 Failure to file tax return or to pay tax
6652 Failure to file certain information returns, registration statements, etc.
6653 Failure to pay stamp tax
6654 Failure by individual to pay estimated income tax
6655 Failure by corporation to pay estimated income tax
6656 Failure to make deposit of taxes
6657 Bad checks
6658 Coordination with title 11
6659 Repealed [Addition to tax in the case of valuation overstatements for purposes of the income tax]
6659A Repealed [Addition to tax in case of overstatements of pension liabilities]
6660 Repealed [Addition to tax in the case of valuation understatement for purposes of estate or gift taxes]
6661 Repealed [Substantial understatement of liability]
6662 Repealed [Applicable rules]

PART II. ACCURACY-RELATED AND FRAUD PENALTIES

6662 Imposition of accuracy-related penalty on underpayments
6662A Imposition of accuracy-related penalty on understatements with respect to reportable transactions
6663 Imposition of fraud penalty
6664 Definitions and special rules

PART III. APPLICABLE RULES

6665 Applicable rules

Subchapter B. Assessable Penalties

PART I. GENERAL PROVISIONS

6671 Rules for application of assessable penalties
6672 Failure to collect and pay over tax, or attempt to evade or defeat tax
6673 Sanctions and costs awarded by courts
6674 Fraudulent statement or failure to furnish statement to employee

Sec.

6675 Excessive claims with respect to the use of certain fuels
6676 Erroneous claim for refund or credit
6677 Failure to file information returns with respect to certain foreign trusts
6678 Repealed [Failure to furnish certain statements]
6679 Failure to file returns, etc., with respect to foreign corporations or foreign partnerships
6682 False information with respect to withholding
6683 Repealed [Failure of foreign corporation to file return of personal holding company tax]
6684 Assessable penalties with respect to liability for tax under chapter 42
6685 Assessable penalty with respect to public inspection requirements for certain tax-exempt organizations
6686 Failure to file returns or supply information by DISC or FSC
6687 Repealed [Failure to supply information with respect to place of residence]
6688 Assessable penalties with respect to information required to be furnished under section 7654
6689 Failure to file notice of redetermination of foreign tax
6690 Fraudulent statement or failure to furnish statement to plan participant
6692 Failure to file actuarial report
6693 Failure to provide reports on certain tax-favored accounts or annuities; penalties relating to designated nondeductible contributions
6694 Understatement of taxpayer's liability by income tax return preparer
6694 Repealed [Failure to file information with respect to carryover basis property]
6695 Other assessable penalties with respect to the preparation of income tax returns for other persons
6695A Substantial and gross valuation misstatements attributable to incorrect appraisals
6696 Rules applicable with respect to sections 6694, 6695, and 6695A
6697 Assessable penalties with respect to liability for tax of regulated investment companies
6698 Failure to file partnership return
6698A Repealed [Failure to file information with respect to carryover basis property]
6699 Failure to file S corporation return.
6699 Repealed [Assessable penalties relating to tax credit employee stock ownership plan]
6700 Promoting abusive tax shelters, etc.
6701 Penalties for aiding and abetting understatement of tax liability
6702 Frivolous tax submissions
6703 Rules applicable to penalties under sections 6700, 6701, and 6702
6704 Failure to keep records necessary to meet reporting requirements under section 6047(d)
6705 Failure by broker to provide notice to payors
6706 Original issue discount information requirements
6707 Failure to furnish information regarding reportable transactions

Sec.

6707A Penalty for failure to include reportable transaction information with return

6708 Failure to maintain lists of advisees with respect to reportable transactions

6709 Penalties with respect to mortgage credit certificates

6710 Failure to disclose that contributions are nondeductible

6711 Failure by tax-exempt organization to disclose that certain information or service available from Federal government

6712 Failure to disclose treaty-based return positions

6713 Disclosure or use of information by preparers of returns

6714 Failure to meet disclosure requirements applicable to quid pro quo contributions

6715 Dyed fuel sold for use or used in taxable use, etc.

6715A Tampering with or failing to maintain security requirements for mechanical dye injection systems

6716 Failure to file information with respect to certain transfers at death and gifts

6717 Refusal of entry

6718 Failure to display tax registration on vessels

6719 Failure to register or reregister

6720 Fraudulent acknowledgments with respect to donations of motor vehicles, boats, and airplanes

6720A Penalty with respect to certain adulterated fuels

6720B Fraudulent identification of exempt use property

PART II. FAILURE TO COMPLY WITH CERTAIN INFORMATION REPORTING REQUIREMENTS

6721 Failure to file correct information returns

6722 Failure to furnish correct payee statements

6723 Failure to comply with other information reporting requirements

6724 Waiver; definitions and special rules

6725 Failure to report information under section 4101

Subchapter C. Procedural Requirements

6751 Procedural requirements

Chapter 69. General Provisions Relating to Stamps

6801 Authority for establishment, alteration, and distribution

6802 Supply and distribution

6803 Accounting and safeguarding

6804 Attachment and cancellation

6805 Redemption of stamps

6806 Occupational tax stamps

6807 Stamping, marking, and branding seized goods

6808 Special provisions relating to stamps

Chapter 70. Jeopardy, Receiverships, Etc.

Subchapter A. Jeopardy

PART I. TERMINATION OF TAXABLE YEAR

6851 Termination assessments of income tax

6852 Termination assessments in case of flagrant political expenditures of section 501(c)(3) organizations

PART II. JEOPARDY ASSESSMENTS

6861 Jeopardy assessments of income, estate, gift, and certain excise taxes

6862 Jeopardy assessment of taxes other than income, estate, gift, and certain excise taxes

Sec.

6863 Stay of collection of jeopardy assessments

6864 Termination of extended period for payment in case of carryback

PART III. SPECIAL RULES WITH RESPECT TO CERTAIN CASH

6867 Presumptions where owner of large amount of cash is not identified

Subchapter B. Receiverships, Etc.

6871 Claims for income, estate, gift, and certain excise taxes in receivership proceedings, etc.

6872 Suspension of period on assessment

6873 Unpaid claims

Chapter 71. Transferees and Fiduciaries

6901 Transferred assets

6902 Provisions of special application to transferees

6903 Notice of fiduciary relationship

6904 Prohibition of injunctions

6905 Discharge of executor from personal liability for decedent's income and gift taxes

Chapter 72. Licensing and Registration

Subchapter A. Licensing

7001 Collection of foreign items

Subchapter B. Registration

7011 Registration—persons paying a special tax

7012 Cross references

Chapter 73. Bonds

7101 Form of bonds

7102 Single bond in lieu of multiple bonds

7103 Cross references—other provisions for bonds

Chapter 74. Closing Agreements and Compromises

7121 Closing agreements

7122 Compromises

7123 Appeals dispute resolution procedures

7124 Cross references

Chapter 75. Crimes, Other Offenses, and Forfeitures

Subchapter A. Crimes

PART I. GENERAL PROVISIONS

7201 Attempt to evade or defeat tax

7202 Willful failure to collect or pay over tax

7203 Willful failure to file return, supply information, or pay tax

7204 Fraudulent statement or failure to make statement to employees

7205 Fraudulent withholding exemption certificate or failure to supply information

7206 Fraud and false statements

7207 Fraudulent returns, statements, or other documents

7208 Offenses relating to stamps

7209 Unauthorized use or sale of stamps

7210 Failure to obey summons

7211 False statements to purchasers or lessees relating to tax

7212 Attempts to interfere with administration of internal revenue laws

7213 Unauthorized disclosure of information

7213A Unauthorized inspection of returns or return information

Sec.
7214 Offenses by officers and employees of the United States
7215 Offenses with respect to collected taxes
7216 Disclosure or use of information by preparers of returns
7217 Prohibition on executive branch influence over taxpayer audits and other investigations
7217 Repealed [Civil damages for unauthorized disclosure of returns and return information]

PART II. PENALTIES APPLICABLE TO CERTAIN TAXES
7231 Failure to obtain license for collection of foreign items
7232 Failure to register or reregister under section 4101, false representations of registration status, etc.
7240 Repealed [Officials investing or speculating in sugar]
7241 Repealed [Willful failure to furnish certain information regarding windfall profit tax on domestic crude oil]

Subchapter B. Other Offenses
7261 Representation that retailers' excise tax is excluded from price of article
7262 Violation of occupational tax laws relating to wagering—failure to pay special tax
7268 Possession with intent to sell in fraud of law or to evade tax
7269 Failure to produce records
7270 Insurance policies
7271 Penalties for offenses relating to stamps
7272 Penalty for failure to register or reregister
7273 Penalties for offenses relating to special taxes
7275 Penalty for offenses relating to certain airline tickets and advertising

Subchapter C. Forfeitures

PART I. PROPERTY SUBJECT TO FORFEITURE
7301 Property subject to tax
7302 Property used in violation of internal revenue laws
7303 Other property subject to forfeiture
7304 Penalty for fraudulently claiming drawback

PART II. PROVISIONS COMMON TO FORFEITURES
7321 Authority to seize property subject to forfeiture
7322 Delivery of seized personal property to United States marshal
7323 Judicial action to enforce forfeiture
7324 Special disposition of perishable goods
7325 Personal property valued at $100,000 or less
7326 Disposal of forfeited or abandoned property in special cases
7327 Customs laws applicable
7328 Cross references

Subchapter D. Miscellaneous Penalty and Forfeiture Provisions
7341 Penalty for sales to evade tax
7342 Penalty for refusal to permit entry or examination
7343 Definition of term "person"
7344 Extended application of penalties relating to officers of the Treasury Department

Sec.

Chapter 76. Judicial Proceedings

Subchapter A. Civil Actions by the United States
7401 Authorization
7402 Jurisdiction of district courts
7403 Action to enforce lien or to subject property to payment of tax
7404 Authority to bring civil action for estate taxes
7405 Action for recovery of erroneous refunds
7406 Disposition of judgments and moneys recovered
7407 Action to enjoin income tax return preparers
7408 Actions to enjoin specified conduct related to tax shelters and reportable transactions
7409 Action to enjoin flagrant political expenditures of section 501(c)(3) organizations
7410 Cross references

Subchapter B. Proceedings by Taxpayers and Third Parties
7421 Prohibition of suits to restrain assessment or collection
7422 Civil actions for refund
7423 Repayments to officers or employees
7424 Intervention
7425 Discharge of liens
7426 Civil actions by persons other than taxpayers
7427 Income tax return preparers
7428 Declaratory judgments relating to status and classification of organizations under section 501(c)(3), etc.
7429 Review of jeopardy levy or assessment procedures
7430 Awarding of costs and certain fees
7431 Civil damages for unauthorized inspection or disclosure of returns and return information
7432 Civil damages for failure to release lien
7433 Civil damages for certain unauthorized collection actions
7433A Civil damages for certain unauthorized collection actions by persons performing services under qualified tax collection contracts
7434 Civil damages for fraudulent filing of information returns
7435 Civil damages for unauthorized enticement of information disclosure
7436 Proceedings for determination of employment status
7437 Cross references

Subchapter C. The Tax Court

PART I. ORGANIZATION AND JURISDICTION
7441 Status
7442 Jurisdiction
7443 Membership
7443A Special trial judges
7444 Organization
7445 Offices
7446 Times and places of sessions
7447 Retirement
7448 Annuities to surviving spouses and dependent children of judges and special trial judges

PART II. PROCEDURE
7451 Fee for filing petition

Sec.
7452 Representation of parties
7453 Rules of practice, procedure, and evidence
7454 Burden of proof in fraud, foundation manager, and transferee cases
7455 Service of process
7456 Administration of oaths and procurement of testimony
7457 Witness fees
7458 Hearings
7459 Reports and decisions
7460 Provisions of special application to divisions
7461 Publicity of proceedings
7462 Publication of reports
7463 Disputes involving $50,000 or less
7464 Intervention by trustee of debtor's estate
7465 Provisions of special application to transferees

PART III. MISCELLANEOUS PROVISIONS

7471 Employees
7472 Expenditures
7473 Disposition of fees
7474 Fee for transcript of record
7475 Practice fee

PART IV. DECLARATORY JUDGMENTS

7476 Declaratory judgments relating to qualification of certain retirement plans
7477 Declaratory judgments relating to value of certain gifts
7477 Repealed [Declaratory judgments relating to transfers of property from the United States]
7478 Declaratory judgments relating to status of certain governmental obligations
7479 Declaratory judgments relating to eligibility of estate with respect to installment payments under section 6166

Subchapter D. Court Review of Tax Court Decisions

7481 Date when Tax Court decision becomes final
7482 Courts of review
7483 Notice of appeal
7484 Change of incumbent in office
7485 Bond to stay assessment and collection
7486 Refund, credit, or abatement of amounts disallowed
7487 Cross references

Subchapter E. Burden of Proof

7491 Burden of proof

Subchapter E. Repealed [Miscellaneous Provisions]

7491 Repealed [Burden of proof in exemptions in the case of marijuana offenses]
7492 Repealed [Enforceability of cotton futures contracts]
7493 Repealed [Immunity of witnesses in cases relating to cotton futures]

Chapter 77. Miscellaneous Provisions

7501 Liability for taxes withheld or collected
7502 Timely mailing treated as timely filing and paying
7503 Time for performance of acts where last day falls on Saturday, Sunday, or legal holiday
7504 Fractional parts of a dollar
7505 Sale of personal property acquired by the United States

Sec.
7506 Administration of real estate acquired by the United States
7507 Exemption of insolvent banks from tax
7508 Time for performing certain acts postponed by reason of service in combat zone or contingency operation
7508A Authority to postpone certain deadlines by reason of Presidentially declared disaster or terroristic or military actions
7509 Expenditures incurred by the United States Postal Service
7510 Exemption from tax of domestic goods purchased for the United States
7511 Repealed [Exemption of consular officers and employees of foreign states from payment of internal revenue taxes on imported articles]
7512 Separate accounting for certain collected taxes, etc.
7513 Reproduction of returns and other documents
7514 Authority to prescribe or modify seals
7515 Repealed [Special statistical studies and compilations and other services on request]
7516 Supplying training and training aids on request
7517 Furnishing on request of statement explaining estate or gift evaluation
7518 Tax incentives relating to merchant marine capital constructions funds
7519 Required payments for entities electing not to have required taxable year
7520 Valuation tables
7521 Procedures involving taxpayer interviews
7522 Content of tax due, deficiency, and other notices
7523 Graphic presentation of major categories of federal outlays and income
7524 Annual notice of tax delinquency
7525 Confidentiality privileges relating to taxpayer communications
7526 Low income taxpayer clinics
7527 Advance payment of credit for health insurance costs of eligible individuals
7528 Internal Revenue Service user fees

Chapter 78. Discovery of Liability and Enforcement of Title

Subchapter A. Examination and Inspection

7601 Canvass of districts for taxable persons and objects
7602 Examination of books and witnesses
7603 Service of summons
7604 Enforcement of summons
7605 Time and place of examination
7606 Entry of premises for examination of taxable objects
7607 Repealed [Additional authority for Bureau of Customs]
7608 Authority of internal revenue enforcement officers
7609 Special procedures for third-party summonses
7610 Fees and costs for witnesses
7611 Restrictions on church tax inquiries and examinations
7612 Special procedures for summonses for computer software
7613 Cross references

Sec.

Subchapter B. General Powers and Duties

7621 Internal revenue districts
7622 Authority to administer oaths and certify
7623 Expenses of detection of underpayments and fraud, etc.
7624 Reimbursement to State and local law enforcement agencies

Subchapter C. Repealed [Supervision of Operations of Certain Manufacturers]

7641 Repealed [Supervision of operations of certain manufacturers]

Subchapter D. Possessions

7651 Administration and collection of taxes in possessions
7652 Shipments to the United States
7653 Shipments from the United States
7654 Coordination of United States and certain possession individual income taxes
7655 Cross references

Chapter 79. Definitions

7701 Definitions
7702 Life insurance contract defined
7702A Modified endowment contract defined
7702B Treatment of qualified long-term care insurance
7703 Determination of marital status
7704 Certain publicly traded partnerships treated as corporations

Chapter 80. General Rules

Subchapter A. Application of Internal Revenue Laws

7801 Authority of Department of the Treasury
7802 Internal Revenue Service Oversight Board
7803 Commissioner of Internal Revenue; other officials
7804 Other personnel
7805 Rules and regulations
7806 Construction of title
7807 Rules in effect upon enactment of this title
7808 Depositaries for collections
7809 Deposit of collections
7810 Revolving fund for redemption of real property
7811 Taxpayer Assistance Orders

Subchapter B. Effective Date and Related Provisions

7851 Applicability of revenue laws
7852 Other applicable rules

Subchapter C. Provisions Affecting More than One Subtitle

7871 Indian tribal governments treated as States for certain purposes
7872 Treatment of loans with below-market interest rates
7873 Income derived by Indians from exercise of fishing rights
7874 Rules relating to expatriated entities and their foreign parents

SUBTITLE G—THE JOINT COMMITTEE ON TAXATION

Chapter 91. Organization and Membership of the Joint Committee

8001 Authorization
8002 Membership

Sec.
8003 Election of chairman and vice chairman
8004 Appointment and compensation of staff
8005 Payment of expenses

Chapter 92. Powers and Duties of the Joint Committee

8021 Powers
8022 Duties
8023 Additional powers to obtain data

SUBTITLE H—FINANCING OF PRESIDENTIAL ELECTION CAMPAIGNS

Chapter 95. Presidential Election Campaign Fund

9001 Short title
9002 Definitions
9003 Condition for eligibility for payments
9004 Entitlement of eligible candidates to payments
9005 Certification by Commission
9006 Payments to eligible candidates
9007 Examinations and audits; repayments
9008 Payments for presidential nominating conventions
9009 Reports to Congress; regulations
9010 Participation by Commission in judicial proceedings
9011 Judicial review
9012 Criminal penalties
9013 Effective date of chapter

Chapter 96. Presidential Primary Matching Payment Account

9031 Short title
9032 Definitions
9033 Eligibility for payments
9034 Entitlement of eligible candidates to payments
9035 Qualified campaign expense limitations
9036 Certification by Commission
9037 Payments to eligible candidates
9038 Examinations and audits; repayments
9039 Reports to Congress; regulations
9040 Participation by Commission in judicial proceedings
9041 Judicial review
9042 Criminal penalties

SUBTITLE I—TRUST FUND CODE

Chapter 98. Trust Fund Code

9500 Short title

Subchapter A. Establishment of Trust Funds

9501 Black Lung Disability Trust Fund
9502 Airport and Airway Trust Fund
9503 Highway Trust Fund
9504 Aquatic Resources Trust Fund [before 10/1/2005]
9504 Sport Fish Restoration and Boating Trust Fund [on and after 10/1/2005]
9505 Harbor Maintenance Trust Fund
9506 Inland Waterways Trust Fund
9507 Hazardous Substance Superfund
9508 Leaking Underground Storage Tank Trust Fund
9509 Oil Spill Liability Trust Fund
9510 Vaccine Injury Compensation Trust Fund
9511 Repealed [National Recreational Trails Trust Fund]

Subchapter B. General Provisions

9601 Transfer of amounts
9602 Management of trust funds

Sec.

SUBTITLE J—COAL INDUSTRY HEALTH BENEFITS

Chapter 99. Coal Industry Health Benefits

Subchapter A. Definitions of General Applicability

9701 Definitions of general applicability

Subchapter B. Combined Benefit Fund

PART I. ESTABLISHMENT AND BENEFITS

9702 Establishment of the United Mine Workers of America Combined Benefit Fund
9703 Plan benefits

PART II. FINANCING

9704 Liability of assigned operators
9705 Transfers
9706 Assignment of eligible beneficiaries

PART III. ENFORCEMENT

9707 Failure to pay premium

PART IV. OTHER PROVISIONS

9708 Effect on pending claims or obligations

Subchapter C. Health Benefits of Certain Miners

PART I. INDIVIDUAL EMPLOYER PLANS

9711 Continued obligations of individual employer plans

PART II. 1992 UMWA BENEFIT PLAN

9712 Establishment and coverage of 1992 UMWA Benefit Plan

Subchapter D. Other Provisions

9721 Civil enforcement
9722 Sham transactions

SUBTITLE K—GROUP HEALTH PLAN PORTABILITY, ACCESS, AND RENEWABILITY REQUIREMENTS

Chapter 100. Group Health Plan Portability, Access, and Renewability Requirements

Subchapter A. Requirements Relating to Portability, Access, and Renewability

9801 Increased portability through limitation on pre-existing condition exclusions
9802 Prohibiting discrimination against individual participants and beneficiaries based on health status
9803 Guaranteed renewability in multiemployer plans and certain multiple employer welfare arrangements

Subchapter B. Other Requirements

9811 Standards relating to benefits for mothers and newborns
9812 Parity in the application of certain limits to mental health benefits

Subchapter C. General Provisions

9831 General exceptions
9832 Definitions
9833 Regulations
9834 Enforcement

Final and Temporary Regulations Topic Index

References are to Reg. § numbers

A

Abandonment
. natural resources
. . basis, holding period, and abandonment losses 1.614-6
. reporting for secured property 1.6050J-1T
. worthless securities .... 1.165-5(i)

Abatements, credits, and refunds (See also particular credit)
. accrued credits 1.905-4T
. accumulated earnings credit 1.535-3; 1.1502-43; 1.1502-43T; 1.1551-1
. assessment of tax .... 301.6501(a)-1 to 301.6503(g)-1
. aviation fuel
. . manufacturers excise taxes 48.4091-3
. bad debts, worthless securities, etc. .... 301.6511(d)-1
. capital gains and losses (See Capital gains and losses)
. carrybacks and carryovers (See Carrybacks and carryovers)
. claims for credit or refund 301.6402-2
. collection of tax ...... 301.6501(a)-1 to 301.6503(g)-1
. consolidated returns 1.6411-4
. corporations .... 1.78-1; 301.6501(g)-1
. death taxes, credit for state 20.2011-1; 20.2011-2
. deficiency notice .... 301.6503(a)-1
. depreciation (See Depreciation)
. diesel and special motor fuels tax (See Diesel and special motor fuels tax)
. double deduction or credit .... 1.642(g)-1; 1.642(g)-2; 1.818-7; 1.1312-1 to 1.1312-4
. earned income credit (See Earned income credit)
. elderly .... 1.37-1 to 1.37-3
. employment taxes ...... 31.6413(a)-1 to 31.6413(c)-1; 301.6413-1
. estate tax .... 1.641(b)-1 et seq.; 301.6503(d)-1
. estimated income tax .... 1.6425-1 to 1.6425-3
. excise taxes
. . exporters, refunds to .... 48.6416(e)-1
. . manufacturers (See subhead manufacturers excise taxes)
. . returns, credit on .... 48.6416(f)-1
. . shippers, refunds to .... 48.6416(e)-1
. . transportation of persons by air
. . . duty to collect .... 49.4264(b)-1
. extension of time by agreement .... 301.6511(c)-1
. farm use of gasoline
. . manufacturers excise taxes .... 48.6420-1 to 48.6420-6
. Federal Insurance Contributions Act, under .... 31.6402(a)-2

Abatements, credits, and refunds (See also particular credit) — Cont'd
. financial institutions, insolvent
. . consolidated group 301.6402-7
. floor stocks tax
. . amount paid on each article 48.6412-3
. . cement mixers 48.4061-1
. . definitions 48.6412-2
. . generally 48.6412-1
. foreign corporations 1.882-4; 1.6414-1
. . filing deadlines, waiver of .... 1.882-4(a)(ii)
. foreign tax credit (See Foreign tax credit)
. fuel, taxable 48.4081-7
. generally 1.31-1; 301.6404-1
. gift tax credit 20.2012-1
. household and dependent care services ... 1.44A-1 to 1.44A-4
. interest 301.6404-2
. investment credit (See Investment credit)
. jobs credit pass-through 1.53-1; 1.53-3
. judicial proceedings, limitation periods .... 301.6511(a)-1
. life insurance endowments or annuities 1.72-7
. limitations, generally .... 301.6511(a)-1 et seq.
. manufacturers excise taxes
. . exempt sales 48.6420-3
. . farm use of gasoline .... 48.6420-1 to 48.6420-6
. . gasoline, ultimate purchasers of 48.6420-1; 48.6420-2; 48.6420-4
. . off-highway business use ... 48.6420-1 to 48.6420-6
. . overpayments, claims for credit or refund .... 48.6416(a)-1; 48.6416(a)-3
. mutual insurance companies 1.826-6
. net operating loss ..... 301.6501(h)-1; 301.6511(d)-2
. new jobs credit (See New jobs credit)
. nonresident aliens 1.6414-1
. . allowance of credits 1.874-1
. . unified credit 20.2102-1
. overpayments .... 1.1464-1; 1.6425-1 to 1.6425-3; 301.6401-1; 301.6402-5; 301.6402-6; 301.6403-1; 301.6425-1; 301.6511(a)-1 et seq.
. partners and partnerships .... 301.6231(c)-2
. partnership items ..... 301.6501(o)-2; 301.6501(o)-3; 301.6511(g)-1
. payments in excess of amounts shown on return (See subhead overpayments)
. period of limitations .... 301.6511(a)-1
. personal holding companies ... 1.545-3; 301.6501(f)-1
. private foundations 1.507-9
. public retirement system income 1.37-3
. Railroad Retirement Tax Act .... 31.6402(a)-2

References are to Reg. § numbers

Abatements, credits, and refunds (See also particular credit) —Cont'd
. real estate investment trusts 1.860-4
. reports of refunds and credits 301.6405-1
. research activity, credit for increasing....... 1.280C-4
. self-employment tax .... 301.6511(a)-1
. Social Security tax .... 1.31-2; 301.6511(a)-1
. targeted jobs credit (See Targeted jobs credit)
. Tax Court.................. 301.6512-1; 301.7507-6
. tentative refund under claim of right adjustment 5.6411-1
. third party property, seizure of
. . official defined .... 301.6503(f)-1(c)
. . wrongful lien for substitution of value, discharge of .... 301.6503(f)-1(b)
. . wrongful seizure................. 301.6503(f)-1(a)
. time of allowance .... 301.6407-1; 301.6511(c)-1
. transferred property, credit for tax on prior 20.2013-1
. wage expenses deduction 1.280C-1
. wagering taxes 44.6419-1
. withholding .... 1.1462-1; 1.1464-1; 31.6402(a)-1; 31.6414-1; 301.6414-1
. work incentive programs ...... 1.40-1; 301.6501(o)-1; 301.6511(d)-7
. written advice of IRS, abatement of penalty or additional tax attributable to erroneous 301.6404-3

Absence from work
. generally 1.105-3

Abusive tax shelters
. penalties 301.6708-1T
. potentially 301.6112-1

Academic period
. education tax credits, defined for 1.25A-2

Accelerated cost recovery system (ACRS)
. additional first year depreciation deduction
. . MACRS property ...... 1.168(k)-1(a); 1.168(k)-1(b)
. conventions under .... 1.56(g)-1; 1.168(d)-1
. . half-year and mid-quarter conventions ... 1.168(d)-1
. . mid-quarter convention, additional rules of application of....................... 1.168(d)-1(b)
. definitions concerning.................... 1.168(b)-1
. disposition of property
. . half-year and mid-quarter conventions, subject to .... 1.168(d)-1(c)
. 50-percent bonus depreciation property .... 1.168(d)-1
. like-kind exchanges and involuntary conversions .... 1.168(d)-1
. modified accelerated cost recovery system .... 1.168(a)-1; 1.168(b)-1
. New York Liberty zone property .... 1.168(d)-1(b)
. property placed in service and disposed of in the same taxable year .... 1.168(d)-1(b)
. safe-harbor lease information returns concerning qualified mass commuting vehicles ...... 1.168(f)(8)-1T

Accident and health plans
. cost maintenance period, significant reduction of coverage during 1.420-1
. employer contributions 1.106-1
. exemptions .... 1.105-5; 1.106-1; 1.501(c)(9)-3
. life insurance endowments or annuities 1.72-15
. withholding .... 31.3402(o)-3; 31.6051-3

Accidental disability
. social security taxes 32.1

Accounting methods
. adoption or change, requirement respecting ....1.446-1(e)
. advance payments for goods and long-term contracts 1.451-5
. aggregation of certain activities 1.465-1T
. allocation, method of 1.455-3; 1.456-3
. allocation under new method.............. 1.481-2
. arbitrage transactions 1.148-6
. books and records, failure to maintain 1.148-6
. cash method, limitations.......... 1.448-1; 1.448-1T
. cessation of taxpayer's liability 1.455-4; 1.456-4
. change 601.204
. . allocation under new method 1.481-2
. . computer programs, transactions involving 1.861-18
. . costs subject to section 263A, for......... 1.263A-7
. . pre-1954 Code years.................. 1.481-3
. computation of taxable income 1.148-6
. consolidated returns 1.1502-17
. constructive receipt of income 1.451-2
. contested liabilities 1.461-2
. . transfer to provide for satisfaction of 1.461-2T
. contingent payments 1.483-4
. corporate, estimated tax
. . changes in .... 1.6655-6(b)
. . generally........................... 1.6655-6(a)
. . installment payments.................. 1.6655-6(a)
. corporate organizations and reorganizations .... 1.381(c)(21)-1
. coupons
. . discount 1.466-1
. . premium 1.451-4
. crop insurance proceeds 1.451-6
. dealers..................... 1.453A-1 to 1.453A-3
. deductions, taxable year for which taken ... 1.461-1 et seq.
. deferred compensation.................... 1.457-1
. . agreement for deferral ....1.457-4(b)
. . annual deferrals 1.457-4
. . death benefits.......................1.457-10(d)
. . definitions 1.457-2
. . distribution, taxation of 1.457-7
. . distribution, timing of 1.457-6
. . excess deferral under eligible plans...... 1.457-4(e)

References are to Reg. § numbers

Accounting methods —Cont'd
. *deferred compensation—Cont'd*
. . funding rules 1.457-8
. . government plans .... 1.457-9(a)
. . individual limitations 1.457-5
. . life insurance proceeds .... 1.457-10(d)
. . maximum deferral limitations .... 1.457-4(c)
. . plan termination .... 1.457-10; 1.457-10(a)
. . plan-to-plan transfers .... 1.457-10(b)
. . qualified domestic relations orders .... 1.457-10(c)
. . rollovers to eligible government plans ... 1.457-10(e)
. . sick, vacation and back pay .... 1.457-4(d)
. . taxation of annual deferrals .... 1.457-4(a)
. . tax-exempt plans .... 1.457-9(b)
. deferred periodic payments .... 1.453-4 to 1.453-6
. depreciation .... 1.167(a)-7
. disbursement method, limitations on 1.448-1
. discount coupons, redemption of 1.466-1
. economic performance requirement
. . fund, establishment of 1.461-6
. . generally 1.461-4
. evidence of indebtedness payable on demand or readily tradable 1.453-3
. functional currency 1.985-4
. gain or loss on disposition of installment obligations 1.453-9
. generally .. 1.446-1 et seq.; 1.461-0; 1.469-1; 601.204
. gross income included, taxable year for which items of .... 1.451-1 et seq.
. ineligible plan 1.457-3
. installment method (See Installment method of accounting)
. interest 1.446-2
. . accrual of interest other than qualified stated interest .... 1.446-2(c)
. . accrual of qualified stated interest .... 1.446-2(b)
. . debt instruments in currency other than U.S. dollars .... 1.446-2(g)
. . land exchanged between related individuals .... 1.483-3(b)
. . test rate of interest applicable to a contract 1.483-3
. life insurance companies .... 1.818-1 to 1.818-8
. like-kind property, funds used during deferred exchanges of .... 1.468B-6; 1.468B-6(b)(1); 1.468B-6(c)
. . definitions .... 1.468B-6(b)
. . earnings attributable to the taxpayer's exchange funds
. . . allocation of earning in commingled accounts .... 1.468B-6(c)(2)(ii)(B)
. . . separately identified account .... 1.468B-6(c)(2)(ii)(A)
. . . transactional expenses .... 1.468B-6(c)(2)(ii)(C)
. . effective date .... 1.468B-6(f); 1.468B-6(f)(1)

Accounting methods —Cont'd
. *like-kind property, funds used during deferred exchanges of—Cont'd*
. . examples .... 1.468B-6(e)
. . exchange facilitator .... 1.468B-6(b)(3)
. . exchange funds .... 1.468B-6(b)(2)
. . exchange funds generally treated as loaned to an exchange facilitator .... 1.468B-6(c)(1)
. . exchange funds not treated as loaned to an exchange facilitator .... 1.468B-6(c)(2); 1.468B-6(c)(2)(i)
. . . earnings attributable to the taxpayer's exchange funds .... 1.468B-6(c)(2)(ii)
. . . taxpayer treatment .... 1.468B-6(c)(2)(iii)
. . information reporting requirements .... 1.468B-6(d)
. . scope .... 1.468B-6(a)
. . transactional expenses .... 1.468B-6(b)(4); 1.468B-6(b)(4)(i)
. . . special rule for certain fees for exchange facilitator services .... 1.468B-6(b)(4)(ii)
. . transitional rule .... 1.468B-6(f)(2)
. limitations, cash method 1.448-1; 1.448-1T
. limitations on tax 1.481-2
. livestock sold on account of drought 1.451-7
. long-term contracts (See Long-term contracts)
. magazines, paperbacks, or records, exclusion for returned 1.458-1
. material participation 1.469-5; 1.469-5T
. more than one business, taxpayer with .... 1.446-1(d)
. notional principal contracts 1.446-3
. nuclear decommissioning costs .... 1.468A-0T to 1.468A-9T
. nuclear power plant 1.468A-6T
. obligations issued at discount 1.454-1
. outline of regulations under section 482 .... 1.482-0
. passive activity credit 1.469-3; 1.469-3T
. passive activity loss .... 1.469-0 to 1.469-11
. permissible methods .... 1.446-1(c)
. premium coupons, redemption of 1.451-4
. prepaid dues income .... 1.456-1 to 1.456-7
. prepaid subscription income .... 1.455-1 to 1.455-5
. recurring item exception 1.461-5
. regularly employ a method of accounting, taxpayer does not .... 1.446-1(b)
. self-charged interest and deductions 1.469-7
. service providers, nonaccrual of certain amounts by
. . accounts receivable defined .... 1.448-2(c)(1)
. . actual experience method .... 1.448-2(f)(2)
. . . uncollectible amounts .... 1.448-2(d)
. . alternative nonaccrual-experience method .... 1.448-2(f)(5)
. . applicable period defined .... 1.448-2(c)(2)
. . application of method .... 1.448-2(b)
. . bad debt defined .... 1.448-2(c)(3)
. . charge-offs defined .... 1.448-2(c)(4)

References are to Reg. § numbers

Accounting methods —Cont'd
. *service providers, nonaccrual of certain amounts by —Cont'd*
. . clear reflection of experience requirement . . . 1.448-2(e)
. . determination date defined . . . 1.448-2(c)(5)
. . fields of services . . . 1.448-1T(d)(2)(A); 1.448-1T(e)(4)
. . generally . . . 1.448-2(a)
. . modified Black Motor method . . . 1.448-2(f)(3)
. . modified moving average method . . . 1.448-2(f)(4)
. . recoveries defined . . . 1.448-2(c)(6)
. . revenue-based moving average methods . . . 1.448-2(f)(1)
. . safe harbors . . . 1.448-2(f)
. . special rules . . . 1.448-2(c)
. . uncollectible amount
. . . defined . . . 1.448-2(c)(7)
. . . estimate, use of experience to . . . 1.448-2(d)
. successor corporations . . . 1.381(c)(4)-1
. Tax Court . . . 301.7512-1
. taxable year (See also Taxable year)
. . affected years . . . 15a.453-0
. . deductions . . . 1.461-1 et seq.
. . gross income items to be included . . . 1.451-1
. . inclusion . . . 1.451-1 et seq.
. time and manner of making election . . . 1.455-6; 1.456-6
. trading stamps, redemption of . . . 1.451-4
. vacation pay . . . 1.463-1T

Accounting periods
. annual, change in . . . 1.442-1
. change . . . 601.204
. contingent payments . . . 1.483-4
. fiscal year (See Fiscal year)
. generally . . . 601.204
. newly married couples
. . change in annual accounting period . . . 1.442-1
. outline of regulations under section 482 . . . 1.482-0
. personal service corporations . . . 1.280H-1T
. S corporations (See S corporations, subhead tax year)
. short tax year (See Short tax year)
. subsidiary corporations
. . change in annual accounting period . . . 1.442-1
. tax year (See Tax year)
. taxable year (See Taxable year)

Accounting services
. nonaccrual of certain amounts by . . 1.448-1T(d)(2)(A); 1.448-1T(e)(4)

Accrued benefits
. burdensome, elimination of . . . 1.411(d)-3(e)
. de minimis, elimination of . . . 1.411(d)-3(e)
. defined benefit plans . . . 1.401(a)(4)-3
. ERISA . . . 1.411(b)-1; 1.411(c)-1

Accrued benefits —Cont'd
. *ERISA—Cont'd*
. . restrictions . . . 1.411(a)-11
. . Section 411(d)(6) protected benefits . . . 1.411(d)-4
. foreign tax credit . . . 1.905-4T
. noncore optional forms, elimination of . . 1.411(d)-3(d)
. pension plan amendment reducing rate of future benefit accrual, notice requirement for . . . 54,4980F-1
. protection of . . . 1.411(d)-3(a)
. redundant, elimination of . . . 1.411(d)-3(c)

Accumulated adjustments account
. S corporations . . . 1.1368-2

Accumulated earnings credit . . . 1.532-1; 1.563-1; 1.1502-43; 1.1502-43T; 1.1551-1

Accumulated earnings tax
. accumulated taxable income . . . 1.535-1
. burden of proof . . . 1.534-1; 1.534-2
. computation . . . 1.535-2
. consolidated groups . . . 1.1502-43; 1.1502-43T
. consolidated returns . . . 1.1502-43; 1.1502-43T; 1.1551-1
. corporations subject to . . . 1.532-1
. evidence of purpose to avoid tax . . . 1.533-1
. imposition of . . . 1.531-1
. jeopardy assessments . . . 1.534-3
. statement of accumulated earnings and profits . . . 1.533-2

Accumulated production expenditures
. capitalization of costs . . . 1.263A-15(b)
. unit of property for determining, real property . . . 1.263A-10

Accumulated profits
. foreign tax credit . . . 1.902-2

Accuracy related penalties
. Omnibus Budget Reconciliation Act of 1993 . . . 1.6662-7
. substantial understatement of income tax . . . 1.6662-4
. underpayment of tax
. . amount of income tax imposed . . . 1.6664-2(b)
. . amount shown as the tax by the taxpayer on his return . . . 1.6664-2(c)
. . amounts not so shown previously assessed . . . 1.6664-2(d)
. . carryback years not reduced by amount of carrybacks . . . 1.6664-2(f)
. . carrybacks and carryovers . . . 1.6662-3
. . charitable deduction, valuation misstatements of . . . 1.6664-4(h)
. . collected without assessment . . . 1.6664-2(d)
. . definitions . . . 1.6664-1
. . facts and circumstances taken into account . . . 1.6664-4(b)
. . generally . . . 1.6662-2
. . good faith exception . . . 1.6664-4

References are to Reg. § numbers

Accuracy related penalties —Cont'd
. *underpayment of tax —Cont'd*
. . negligence or disregard of rules or regulations 1.6662-3
. . opinion or advice, reliance on .... 1.6664-4(c)
. . overview 1.6662-1
. . qualified amended returns 1.6664-1
. . reasonable cause 1.6664-4
. . rebates .... 1.6664-2(e)
. . reportable transaction, due to .... 1.6664-4(d)
. . returns filed after December 31, 2002 ..... 1.6662-2
. . underpayment defined .... 1.6664-2(a)

ACP test (See Pension, profit-sharing, and stock bonus plans subhead actual contribution percentage test)

Acquisitions
. indebtedness (See Corporations)
. stock distributions, recognition of gain on certain 1.355-7

ACRS (See Accelerated cost recovery system)

Active conduct of business
. defined 1.355-3

Activities not engaged in for profit
. defined 1.183-2
. election to postpone determination of 12.9
. generally 1.183-1
. taxable years affected 1.183-4

Actual contribution percentage test (ACP)
. pension, profit-sharing, and stock bonus plans (See Pension, profit-sharing, and stock bonus plans)

Actual deferral percentage (ADP) testing (See Cash deferred arrangements (CODAs))

Actuarial reports and methods
. generally ..... 1.412(c)(2)-1; 301.6059-1; 301.6692-1

Actuarial services
. nonaccrual of certain amounts .... 1.448-1T(d)(2)(A); 1.448-1T(e)(4)

Additional first year depreciation deduction
. adjusted depreciable property defined .. 1.168(k)-1(a)
. computation of deduction .... 1.168(k)-1(d)
. computer software .... 1.168(k)-1(f)
. decrease in basis .... 1.168(k)-1(f)
. definitions .... 1.168(k)-1(a)
. depreciation deduction until September 4, 2006 .... 1.168(d)-1
. election not to deduct .... 1.168(k)-1(e)
. 50-percent bonus depreciation property ... 1.168(d)-1; 1.168(k)-1(b)
. . computation of depreciation .... 1.168(k)-1(d)
. improvements to property .... 1.168(k)-1(c)
. leasehold improvement property .... 1.168(k)-1(c)
. like-kind exchanges .... 1.168(k)-1(f)
. MACRS property .... 1.168(k)-1(a); 1.168(k)-1(b)

Additional first year depreciation deduction — Cont'd
. New York Liberty Zone leasehold property .... 1.168(k)-1(b); 1.1400L(b)-1T
. original use after September 10, 2001 .. 1.168(k)-1(b)
. pollution control facilities .... 1.169-3 et seq.
. property placed in service and disposed of in the same taxable year .... 1.168(k)-1(f)
. qualified property .... 1.168(k)-1(b)
. . computation of depreciation .... 1.168(k)-1(b)
. redetermination of basis .... 1.168(k)-1(f)
. section 168(i)(7) transactions .... 1.168(k)-1(f)
. technical termination of partnership ..... 1.168(k)-1(f)
. 30-percent property .... 1.168(k)-1(b)
. unadjusted depreciable property defined .... 1.168(k)-1(a)

Additions to tax, additional amounts, and assessable penalties
. actuarial report 301.6692-1
. annuities 301.6693-1
. bad checks 301.6657-1
. Chapter 42 liability, assessable penalties 301.6684-1
. computation of penalty .... 1.6661-2 et seq.
. corporations .... 1.6655-1 et seq.; 301.6679-1
. damages assessable for instituting proceedings before Tax Court merely for delay 301.6673-1
. deduction for fine or penalty, allowance of ... 1.162-21
. defined 301.6659-1
. DISC failure to file returns 301.6686-1
. erroneous written advice of IRS, abatement of additional tax attributable to 301.6404-3
. estimated tax 1.6654-4; 1.6654-5; 301.6654-1; 301.6655-1
. evasion or avoidance of tax 301.6672-1
. excessive adjustment 1.6655-7
. exempt and nonexempt organizations, failure to file returns 301.6652-2
. failure to file return or pay tax ..... 301.6651-1 et seq.
. false information 301.6682-1
. foreign corporations and partnerships 1.6038A-4; 301.6679-1
. fraud 301.6674-1; 301.6682-1; 301.6690-1
. generally .... 1.6654-1 et seq.
. gift or income tax 301.6653-1
. individual exceptions 1.6654-2
. individual retirement arrangements or annuities 301.6693-1
. information returns 301.6652-1
. itemized deductions 301.6682-1
. jeopardy 301.6658-1
. mortgage credit certificates 1.6709-1T
. payment of tax .... 301.6653-1 et seq.
. penalties, generally .... 301.6671-1 et seq.
. possession of the U.S. 301.6688-1

References are to Reg. § numbers

Additions to tax, additional amounts, and assessable penalties —Cont'd
. preparer 1.6694-1; 1.6694-2; 1.6695-1; 1.6696-1
. private foundations 301.6685-1
. real estate investment trusts 1.860-3
. retirement plans 301.6652-3
. returns .... 301.6651-1 et seq.
. safe harbor for installments of tax 1.6655-2T
. short taxable years, corporations 1.6655-3
. statements to payees 301.6678-1
. tax shelters 1.6661-5; 301.6707-1T; 301.6708-1T
. treaty-based return positions, failure to disclose 301.6712-1
. understatement of liability 1.6661-1; 1.6694-1; 1.6694-2
. verification of returns 20.6065-1
. waiver of penalty 1.6661-6
. withholding 301.6682-1

Adjusted basis
. allocation rules, partnerships 1.755-1
. gain or loss .... 1.1011-1; 1.1014-4 to 1.1014-7; 1.1016-5

Adjusted gross income
. deductions in computation, allowable .... 1.62-1(c)
. expense allowances 1.62-2
. foreign base company income 1.954-1
. generally 1.62-1T; 1.71-1T
. reimbursements .... 1.62-2; 31.3401(a)-4
. 2-percent floor of miscellaneous itemized deductions 1.67-1T

Adjusted taxable gifts
. determination of 20.2001-1

Adjustments
. corporate distributions (See Distributions by corporations)
. generally .... 1.481-1 et seq.; 1.912-1; 1.6655-7
. overpayment of tax (See Overpayment of tax)

Administrative costs and expenses
. Bankruptcy Code sections 362 or 524
. . damage actions concerning, costs incurred in 301.7430-8
. deductions for 20.2053-3
. estate taxes 20.2055-3
. management expenses 20.2055-3
. marital deduction .... 20.2056(b)-4
. reasonable costs
. . described .... 301.7430-4(b)
. . exclusion of certain costs .... 301.7430-4(c)
. . generally 301.7430-4
. recovery of reasonable
. . amount in controversy, determining ... 301.7430-5(d)
. . effective date 301.7430-5
. . most significant issue, presentation of .... 301.7430-5(e)

Administrative costs and expenses —Cont'd
. *recovery of reasonable —Cont'd*
. . net worth and size limitations .... 301.7430-5(f)
. . prevailing party determination of ...... 301.7430-5; 301.7430-5(g)
. . procedure .... 301.7430-2(c)
. . protraction, unreasonable .... 301.7430-2(d)
. . requirements for recovery .... 301.7430-2(b)
. . substantially justified position of IRS .... 301.7430-5(c)

Administrative proceeding
. collection actions .... 301.7430-3(b)
. date .... 301.7430-3(c)
. defined .... 301.7430-3(a)

Administrative review
. returns .... 301.6103(p)(7)-1

Administrator of plan
. defined .... 1.414(g)-1

Adoption
. taxpayer identification number (TIN) 301.6109-3

ADP testing (See Cash deferred arrangements subhead actual deferral percentage (ADP) testing)

Advance payments
. accounting methods 1.451-5
. arbitrage transactions 1.148-11
. income (See Prepaid income)
. royalties, natural resources 1.612-3

Advances
. determination of taxable income .... 1.482-2(a)

Advertising or promotion of good will
. itemized deductions ... 1.162-14; 1.162-20; 1.263(b)-1

Affiliated corporations
. expanded affiliated groups
. . domestic production activities (See Domestic production activities)
. groups, affiliated
. . charitable organizations lobbying expenditures .... 56.4911-7 to 56.4911-10
. . interest expense, allocation ... 1.861-14; 1.861-14T
. . . income from sources within or without U.S. 1.861-11T
. . taxable year determination, consolidated return filing 1.441-3
. limited affiliated groups
. . charitable organizations, lobbying expenditures 56.4911-10
. loss on worthless security of .... 1.165-5(d)
. manufacturers excise tax, constructive sale price .... 48.4216(b)-4

Affiliated subsidiaries
. dividends from, S corporations 1.1362-8

Age, minimum
. deferred compensation plans .... 1.410(a)-3T

References are to Reg. § numbers

Aged persons
. credits . . . 1.37-1 to 1.37-3
. exemption from sale or exchange of residence gains . . . 1.121-1 to 1.121-5
. itemized deductions for architectural or transportation barriers . . . 1.190-1 to 1.190-3
Agents
. collecting foreign items, license requirement . . . 301.7001-1
. consolidated returns
. . alternative agents for the group . . . 1.1502-77
. . common parent agents for subsidiaries . . . 1.1502-77A
. . termination of common parent . . . 1.1502-77(d)
. . termination of corporation's existence . . . 1.1502-77
. contractor for disclosure purposed, defined as . . . 301.6103(l)-1; 301.6103(m)-1
. fiduciaries (See Fiduciaries)
. foreign corporations
. . information returns, authorization of agent . . . 1.6038A-5
. nonresident aliens
. . withholding tax at source . . . 1.871-6
. subsidiaries
. . common parent agent . . . 1.1502-77A
. withholding . . . 1.871-6; 1.1441-1 et seq.; 1.1441-7; 31.3402(g)-3; 31.3504-1
Aggregation
. accounting methods . . . 1.465-1T
. employee retirement and benefit plans . . 1.401(a)(4)-9
. natural resources
. . nonoperating mineral interests . . . 1.614-5
. . separate operating mineral interests . . . 1.614-0 et seq.
. research expenditures, controlled corporations . . . 1.41-6
. . consolidated groups, special rules for . . . 1.41-6(d)
. . controlled group of corporations . . . 1.41-6(a)
. . group credit
. . . allocation of . . . 1.41-6(c)
. . . computation of . . . 1.41-6(b)
Agreements (See Contracts and agreements)
Agricultural matters (See Farming)
Agriculture, Department of
. disclosure of return information to officers and employee of . . . 301.6103(j)(5)-1
. . census of agriculture, conducting . . . 301.6103(j)(5)-1
Air passenger transportation, excise tax on (See Transportation of persons by air)
Aircraft
. aviation fuel (See Aviation fuel)
. commutation tickets, non-established lines . . . 49.4263-5
. entertainment, use for
Aircraft —Cont'd
. *entertainment, use for —Cont'd*
. . aggregation of aircraft . . . 1.274-10(d)(4)
. . allocation of expenses . . . 1.274-10(e)
. . basis determination . . . 1.274-10(f)(1)
. . business entertainment air travel . . . 1.274-10(b)(3)
. . deadhead flights . . . 1.274-10(f)(3)
. . depreciation allowance, straight-line method for . . . 1.274-10(d)(3)
. . disallowed amounts . . . 1.274-10(c)
. . entertainment air travel defined . . . 1.274-10(b)(2)
. . entertainment defined . . . 1.274-10(b)(1)
. . expenses defined . . . 1.274-10(d)
. . generally . . . 1.274-10(a)
. . leases or charters to third parties . . . 1.274-10(d)(2)
. . pro rata disallowance . . . 1.274-10(f)(2)
. . specified individual defined . . . 1.274-10(b)(5)
. . taxpayer-provided aircraft . . . 1.274-10(b)(4)
. income from sources within or without United States . . . 1.861-15; 1.861-16
. international operations, exclusion of income . . . 1.883-1; 1.883-1T
. museums
. . diesel and special motor fuels tax exemption . . . 48.4041-14
. supplies
. . diesel and special motor fuels tax exemption . . . 48.4041-10
. . exempt sales, manufacturers excise taxes . . . 48.4221-4
Alaska
. diesel and special motor fuels tax . . . 48.4082-5
Alaska native corporations
. consolidated returns . . . 1.1502-81T
Alcohol mixture fuels
. excise taxes (See Diesel and special motor fuels tax)
. gasoline mixed with alcohol . . . 48.4081-2; 48.4081-6
. generally . . . 48.4041-18
Aliens
. education tax credits . . . 1.25A-1
. investment in U.S. real property interests . . . 1.897-1
. nonresident (See Nonresident aliens)
. withholding tax at source . . . 1.897-5T; 1.970-1 to 1.970-3; 1.971-1; 1.1445-11T
Alimony and separate maintenance payments
. exemptions . . . 1.101-5
. gross income . . . 1.61-10; 1.71-1; 1.71-1T; 1.71-2
. itemized deductions . . . 1.215-1; 1.215-1T
Allocation
. accounting methods . . . 1.455-3; 1.456-3
. arbitrage transactions . . . 1.148-4; 1.148-6; 1.148-9
. arm's length standard . . . 1.482-1(b); 1.482-1T
. asset acquisitions . . . 1.1060-1
. basis adjustment, partnership . . . 1.755-1

References are to Reg. § numbers

Allocation —Cont'd
. best method rule .... 1.482-1(c)
. capitalization of costs 1.263A-2
. carryover allocation (See Carryover allocations)
. collateral adjustments with respect to allocation under sec. 482 .... 1.482-1(g)
. cost sharing arrangements 1.482-7; 1.482-7A
. cost sharing arrangements under sec. 482 .... 1.482-2T(e)
. debt issuance costs 1.446-5
. ERISA .... 1.411(c)-1
. exempt organizations .... 1.514(e)-1
. foreign corporations 1.959-3
. foreign taxes 1.904-6
. gain or loss
. . foreign sources .... 1.904(f)-3
. . personal property other than stock 1.865-1
. . stock 1.865-2
. . unrecaptured 1250 gain reported on installment method 1.453-12
. generation-skipping transfer tax exemption 26.2632-1
. income and deductions among taxpayers .... 1.482-1(a); 1.482-1T; 1.482-1T(a)
. income and loss; loss corporations 1.382-6
. . coordination of 1.382.6 and 1.1502-76(b) rules 1.382-6
. . credits .... 1.382-6(e)
. lobbying activity costs 1.162-28
. real estate mortgage investment conduit expenses 1.67-3T
. redering of services under sec. 482 ...... 1.482-2T(b)
. refunding issue proceeds 1.148-8; 1.148-9
. research and experimental expenditures, income from sources within or without U.S. 1.861-17

Allowance
. defined 1.269-1

Almond groves
. itemized deductions 1.278-1

Alternate valuation
. closely-held business property, material participation requirements for 20.2032A-3
. election of special use valuation 20.2032A-8
. farm property
. . material participation requirements 20.2032A-3
. . method of valuing 20.2032A-4
. generally 20.2032-1
. material participation requirements 20.2032A-3

Alternative minimum tax (AMT)
. annualization exemption, adjustments under 1.6655-7
. common trust funds 1.58-5
. computation of taxable income 1.55-1
. . consolidated groups 1.1502-55

Alternative minimum tax (AMT) —Cont'd
. electing small business corporations, apportionment rules 1.58-4
. estates and trusts 1.58-3
. exempt organizations 1.511-4
. exemption amounts 1.58-1
. foreign tax credit computation for .... 1.904(b)-2; 1.904-4(k)
. generally 1.57-0
. partners and partnerships 1.58-2
. preference items defined 1.57-1
. preferences attributable to foreign sources or possessions of United States 1.58-7; 1.58-8
. real estate investment trusts 1.58-6
. recordkeeping requirements 1.57-5
. regulated investment companies 1.58-6
. tax benefit rule 1.58-9

Alternative tax
. capital gains and losses 1.1201-1

American Samoa
. bona fide residency
. . alien individuals presence test .... 1.937-1(c)(2)
. . bona fide resident .... 1.937-1(b)
. . closer connection test .... 1.937-1(e)
. . days of presence .... 1.937-1(c)(3)
. . definitions concerning .... 1.937-1(a)
. . generally 1.937-1
. . information reporting .... 1.937-1(h)
. . medical treatment .... 1.937-1(c)(4)
. . presence test .... 1.937-1(c)
. . significant connection to the United States .... 1.937-1(c)(5)
. . tax home test .... 1.937-1(d)
. . year of move .... 1.937-1(f)
. generally 1.876-1
. gross income exclusions 1.931-1

Amortization
. basis for gain or loss 1.1016-3; 1.1016-4
. . adjustments to 1.1016-5
. bond premiums .... 1.171-1 to 1.171-5
. capital gains and losses 1.1238-1
. child care facilities 1.188-1
. computer software
. . excluded under section 197, intangibles .... 1.167(a)-14(b)
. corporate organizations and reorganizations .... 1.381(c)(9)-1
. ERISA .... 1.412(b)-2; 1.412(b)-5
. estates and trusts .... 1.642(f)-1
. goodwill 1.197-2; 1.197-2T
. group deferred annuities .... 1.412(b)-2; 1.818-3
. intangibles excluded under section 197 ... 1.167(a)-14
. interests or rights not acquired by purchase

References are to Reg. § numbers

Amortization —Cont'd
. *interests or rights not acquired by purchase —Cont'd*
. . excluded under section 197, intangibles .... 1.167(a)-14(c)
. itemized deductions .... 1.171-1 to 1.171-5
. life insurance companies
. . generally 1.79-4T
. mortgage servicing rights
. . excluded under section 197, intangibles .... 1.167(a)-14(d)
. start-up expenditures, election 1.195-1
. trademark and trade name expenditures 1.177-1

AMT (See Alternative minimum tax)

Animals
. capitalization 1.263A-4
. exempt organization for prevention of cruelty to animals .... 1.501(c)(3)-1
. livestock (See Livestock)

Annualized wages
. withholding .... 31.3402(h)(2)-1

Annuities and annuity contracts
. accident or health plans 1.72-15
. amortization, group deferred annuity contracts .... 1.412(b)-2; 1.818-3
. collection of income tax and withholding on pensions, annuities, and other deferred income 35.3405-1
. contract valuation 25.2512-6
. contributions
. . employer meeting section 401(a), (a)(2) requirements .... 1.404(a)-8
. . limitations under section 404(a)(1)(B) ... 1.404(a)-5; 1.404(a)-6
. corporate organizations and reorganizations .... 1.381(c)(11)-1
. deemed IRAs in employer plan .... 1.408(q)-1
. generally .... 1.72-1 et seq.; 20.2039-1
. generation-skipping transfer tax
. . charitable lead annuity trust rules........ 26.2642-3
. gross income 1.61-10
. individual retirement annuities 1.408-3
. individual retirement arrangements 20.2039-5
. information returns 301.6047-1
. joint and survivor
. . amounts received by surviving annuitant .... 1.691(d)-1
. . content requirements .... 1.417(a)(3)-1(b)
. . distribution restrictions...... 1.417(e)-1; 1.417(e)-1T
. . marital deduction, disallowance of ..... 25.2523(i)-1
. . participant specific requirement .... 1.417(a)(3)-1(c)
. . substitution of generally applicable information for participant information .... 1.417(a)(3)-1(d)
. . written explanation requirement ...... 1.401(a)(3)-1; 1.417(a)(3)-1(a)
. life insurance (See Life insurance)

Annuities and annuity contracts —Cont'd
. minimum distribution requirements ..... 1.401(a)(9)-5; 1.401(a)(9)-6
. . 501(c)(3) organization, account established by .... 1.401(a)(9)-5
. . public school, account established by .... 1.403(b)-3
. modified guaranteed contracts 1.817A-1
. nonannuity distributions .... 1.72(e)-1T
. nonresident aliens, withholding tax exemption 1.1441-4
. nontransferable contracts.................. 1.401-9
. penalties 301.6693-1
. preretirement survivor annuities .... 1.401(a)-20
. qualified interests, determining 25.2702-3
. qualified plans 20.2039-2
. qualified preretirement survivor annuities .... 1.401(a)(4)-3
. rollover distributions, eligible
. . questions and answers .... 1.403(b)-2
. . withholding on, questions and answers .... 31.3405(c)-1
. salary reduction agreements defined .... 31.3121(a)(5)-1T
. Section 403(b) annuities 20.2039-2
. Section 501(c)(3) organization or public school
. . minimum distribution requirements .... 1.403(b)-3
. self-employment income 1.72-17A; 1.72-18
. surviving spouse with power of appointment .... 20.2056(b)-6
. tax-sheltered annuities 20.2039-2
. valuation 1.7520-1; 20.2031-7A; 25.2512-5A; 25.7520-1
. . actuarial valuation .... 20.7520-1(a); 25.7520-1
. . charitable interests..................... 20.7520-2
. . contract valuation 25.2512-6
. . interest for life or term of years......... 20.2031-7; 20.2031-7A(a); 20.2031-7A(b); 20.2031-7A(c); 20.2031-7T
. withholding .... 31.3401(a)(12)-1; 31.3402(o)-2; 35.3405-1

Antitrust damage payments
. itemized deductions 1.162-22; 1.186-1

Apostolic associations
. exempt organizations .... 1.501(d)-1

Appeals (See Judicial review)

Applicable asset acquisitions
. consideration, allocation 1.1060-1
. depreciation .... 1.167(a)-5T

Appointment, power of (See Power of appointment)

Apportionment
. new jobs credit 1.53-2
. research and experimental expenditures, income from sources within or without U.S............ 1.861-17
. targeted jobs credit 1.53-2

References are to Reg. § numbers

Appreciated property
. generally . . . 1.170A-4
Arbitrage transactions
. accounting
. . hedges . . . 1.148-4
. . rules . . . 1.148-6
. advance refunding bonds, limitations on . . . 1.149(d)-1
. . aggregate bonds . . . 1.148-4
. allocation rules . . . 1.148-6
. anti-abuse rules . . . 1.148-10
. . advance refunding . . . 1.149(d)-1
. authority of Commissioner . . . 1.148-10
. computations
. . investments, yield and valuation of . . . 1.148-5
. . yield on issue . . . 1.148-4
. definitions . . . 1.148-1
. effective dates . . . 1.148-11
. elections . . . 1.148-1
. generally . . . 5c.103-3
. hedge bonds . . . 1.149(g)-1
. hedges . . . 1.148-4
. interest on, temporary rules . . . 13.4
. investments, yield and valuation of . . . 1.148-5
. investment-type property . . . 1.148-1
. materially higher yield defined . . . 1.148-2
. mortgage revenue . . . 1.148-4
. mortgage revenue bonds
. . mortgage interest rate bond yield not exceeding 1.125 percentage points . . . 1.143(g)-1(b)
. . owner-financing, reduction in . . . 1.143(g)-1(c)
. . requirements . . . 1.143(g)-1
. pooled financing . . . 1.148-8
. prepayments . . . 1.148-11
. qualified zone academy bonds restrictions . . . 1.1397E-1T(i)
. rebate rules, generally . . . 1.148-3
. refunding issues . . . 1.148-8
. . rules . . . 1.148-9
. replacement proceeds defined . . . 1.148-1
. reserve or replacement funds . . . 1.148-2
. restriction rules, generally . . . 1.148-2
. small issuers with general taxing powers, exception for . . . 1.148-8
. spending exceptions . . . 1.148-7
. student loan bonds . . . 1.148-4
. valuation of investments . . . 1.148-5
. yield on issue, computation . . . 1.148-4
. yield restriction rules . . . 1.148-2
Architectural and transportation barriers
. itemized deductions for removal of . . . 1.190-1 to 1.190-3
Architectural services
. accounting, nonaccrual of certain amounts by . . . 1.448-1T(d)(2)(A); 1.448-1T(e)(4)
. domestic production gross receipts . . . 1.199-3(n)
. foreign trading gross receipts . . . 1.924(a)-1T(e)
Armed Forces of the U.S.
. combat pay . . . 1.112-1
. combat zone compensation
. . exclusion . . . 1.112-1
. . exemption . . . 49.4253-4
. communications services, excise tax exemption
. . combat zone, military personnel in . . . 49.4253-4
. death of member during induction period . . . 20.2201-1
. fees and services as compensation . . . 1.61-2(b)
. fuel, military specifications . . . 48.4081-1
. generally . . . 1.113-1; 1.122-1; 1.501(c)(19)-1; 1.512(a)-4; 6a.103A-3; 31.3401(a)(1)-1; 301.7701-8
. hospitalization while in combat zone . . . 1.112-1
. income from military property . . . 1.995-6
. military property
. . domestic international sales corporations . . . 1.995-6
. pension, profit-sharing, and stock bonus plan loans . . . 1.72(p)-1
. retirement pay
. . exemptions . . . 1.122-1
. . withholding of tax . . . 31.6011(a)-4(b)(2)
Arm's length transactions
. best method rule . . . 1.482-1(b)
. . examples . . . 1.482-8; 1.482-8T
. capitalization of costs . . . 1.263A-1
. collateral adjustments allocation under sec. 482 . . . 1.482-1(g)
. comparability . . . 1.482-1(d)
. comparable profits method
. . determination of . . . 1.482-5
. . taxable income determination . . . 1.482-9T(f)
. comparable uncontrolled services price method
. . taxable income, determination of . . . 1.482-9T(c)
. contingent-payment contractual terms for services . . . 1.482-9T(i)
. controlled services transaction
. . taxable income, determination of . . . 1.482-9T et seq.
. . transfer pricing rules, coordination with . . . 1.482-9T(m); 1.6662-6T
. cost of services plus method
. . taxable income, determination of . . . 1.482-9T(e)
. cost-sharing arrangements consistent with . . . 1.482-7
. foreign legal restrictions, effect of . . . 1.482-1(h)(2)
. gross services margin method; determination of taxable income . . . 1.482-9T(d)
. profit split method
. . determination of . . . 1.482-6
. . taxable income determination . . . 1.482-9T(g)
. range, determination of arm's length . . . 1.482-1(e)

References are to Reg. § numbers

Arm's length transactions —Cont'd
. review, scope of . . . . 1.482-1(f)
. sec. 936, coordination with . . . . 1.482-1(h)(3)
. services cost method; determination of taxable income . . . . 1.482-9T(b)
. taxable income, determination of 1.482-3

Assembling costs
. capitalization of 1.263A-3

Assessable penalties (See Additions to tax, additional amounts, and assessable penalties)

Assessment of tax
. bankruptcy . . . . 301.6871(a)-1; 301.6871(a)-2; 301.6872-1
. collection after (See Collection of tax)
. generally 301.6201-1; 301.6305-1
. jeopardy assessments (See Jeopardy assessments)
. review 301.6305-1
. termination assessments of flagrant political expenditures 301.6852-1

Asset depreciation ranges
. class lives and asset depreciation ranges . . . . 1.167(a)-11; 1.167(a)-12; 1.167(m)-1

Assets (See also particular asset)
. acquisition allocation consideration 1.1060-1
. briefly held 1.6011-4
. unidentified assets
. . gift to spouse . . . . 25.2523(c)-1
. . marital deduction for . . . . 20.2056(b)-2

Associations (See also particular type of association)
. classification for tax purposes 301.7701-3
. entity classification election 301.7701-3
. . notice of election 301.7701-3
. homeowner association property . . . . 1.528-1 to 1.528-10

At risk amounts
. generally . . . . 7.465-1 to 7.465-5

ATIN
. generally 301.6109-3

Atomic energy communities
. itemized deductions 1.164-8

Attorney-in-fact
. mutual insurance companies 1.826-3

Attorneys
. federal government attorneys, disclosure of returns to . . . . 301.6103(a)-2

Attribution
. foreign corporations
. . information returns . . . . 1.6038-2(c)
. . removal of rules . . . . 1.367(b)-6(d)
. information returns
. . foreign corporations . . . . 1.6038-2(c)
. private foundations . . . . 1.509(a)-5

Automatic extensions (See Extension of time for filing return)

Automobiles
. general asset accounts
. . passenger automobiles, special rules for . . . . 1.168(i)-1(d)(2)
. investment tax credit
. . acquired passenger automobile . . . . . . 1.280F-2T(g)
. . exchanged passenger automobile . . . . 1.280F-2T(g)
. . improvements that qualify as capital expenditures . . . . 1.280F-2T(f)
. . leased 1.280F-5T
. leased
. . cost recovery deductions 1.280F-5T
. . December 31, 1986, after 1.280F-7
. . election, section 48 . . . . 1.280F-5T(b)
. . income inclusion of lessees . . . 1.280F-5T(d) et seq.
. . investment credit 1.280F-5T
. . recovery deduction of leased property 1.280F-5T
. . regularly engaged in the business of leasing . . . . 1.280F-5T(c)

Aviation fuel
. generally 48.4041-5
. inspection of IRS records, state . . . . 48.4102-1(b)
. inspection of taxpayer records, state 48.4102-1
. manufacturers excise taxes
. . kerosene, exemption for aviation grade 48.4082-8T
. . refunds 48.4091-3
. noncommercial aviation
. . exempt sales 48.4041-11
. . liquids for use as fuel, application of tax . . 48.4041-4
. . registered purchasers 48.4041-11

Avoidance of tax (See Evasion or avoidance of tax)

Avoided cost method
. capitalization of costs; interest calculation . . . 1.263A-9

Awards
. gross income 1.74-1

B

Back pay
. deferral of sick, vacation and back pay . . . . . 1.457-4(d)

Backup withholding
. accounts subject to . . . . 31.3406(a)-3
. alternative sources, special rules for withholdings . . . . 31.3406(h)-2
. barter exchanges . . . . 31.3406(b)(3)-2
. brokers 35a.9999-3A; 35a.9999-4T
. . defined . . . . 31.3406(h)-1
. business day defined . . . . 31.3406(h)-1
. certificates
. . failure to furnish . . . . 31.3406(h)-2
. . payee certification failure . . . . 31.3406(d)-2

References are to Reg. § numbers

Backup withholding —Cont'd
. commissions .... 31.3406(b)(3)-1
. commodities .... 31.3406(b)(3)-2
. confidentiality of information concerning .... 31.3406(f)-1
. day .... 31.3406(h)-1
. dividends ... 31.3406(b)(2)-4; 35a.3406-2; 35a.9999-1 to 35a.9999-5
. exceptions
. . payments to certain payees .... 31.3406(g)-1
. . reportable payments for which withholding is otherwise required .... 31.3406(g)-2
. exemptions
. . minimal payments .... 31.3406(b)(4)-1
. . principal payments made by brokers ... 35a.9999-3A
. . taxpayer identification numbers, payee waiting for .... 31.3406(g)-3
. federal tax deposit rules 31.6302-3
. fishing boat operators, payment by ... 31.3406(b)(3)-3
. foreign currency, conversion of amounts paid in .... 31.3406(h)-2
. generally 31.3406-0
. instruments acquired through a broker, special rules for .... 31.3406(d)-4
. interest ...... 1.6050H-1T; 35a.3406-2; 35a.9999-1 to 35a.9999-5
. interest payments, reportable .... 31.3406(b)(2)-1
. joint accounts, special rules for .... 31.3406(h)-2
. middleman
. . adjustment of prior withholding by ..... 31.3406(h)-2
. . defined for withholding obligation ...... 31.3406(a)-4
. nonemployee compensation .... 31.3406(b)(3)-1
. notice 35a.3406-2
. . underreporting of interest or dividend payments .... 31.3406(c)-1
. original issue discount (OID) .... 31.3406(b)(2)-2
. patronage dividends subject to ...... 31.3406(b)(2)-5
. payment card transactions, special rules for .... 31.3406(g)-1(f)
. payments deemed made, time when .... 31.3406(a)-4
. payments subject to, returns .... 31.6011(a)-4(b)(5)
. payor defined for withholding obligation .... 31.3406(a)-2
. period withholding is required .... 31.3406(e)-1
. premature withdrawal penalties ...... 31.3406(b)(2)-1
. qualified payment card agents .... 31.3406(g)-1(f)
. readily tradable instrument .... 31.3406(h)-1
. rents .... 31.3406(b)(3)-1
. requirement to invoke .... 31.3406(a)-1
. royalties .... 31.3406(b)(3)-4
. securities sales .... 31.3406(b)(3)-2
. special rules for certain payment card transactions .... 31.3406(g)-1(f)
. statement required in case of 31.6051-4
. taxpayer identification number .... 31.3406(d)-5

Backup withholding —Cont'd
. *taxpayer identification number—Cont'd*
. . defined .... 31.3406(h)-1
. . exemption for payee waiting for TIN ... 31.3406(g)-3
. . furnishing .... 31.3406(d)-1
. . incorrect .... 31.3406(d)-5
. TEFRA 5f.163-1
. 30 day rules .... 31.3406(d)-3
. trusts .... 31.3406(h)-2
. underreporting of interest or dividend payments .... 31.3406(c)-1
. window transactions .... 31.3406(b)(2)-3

Bad debts
. abatements, credits, and refunds ...... 301.6511(d)-1
. corporate organizations and reorganizations .... 1.381(c)(12)-1
. itemized deductions .... 1.166-1 to 1.166-10
. mutual savings banks .... 1.593-1 to 1.593-7
. reserve, denial of
. . large bank 1.585-5
. . recapture method 1.585-6
. securities, credit or refund for .... 301.6511(d)-1
. worthless securities 1.582-1

Balanced performance measurement system
. business results measures 801.6; 801.6T
. customer satisfaction measures 801.4; 801.4T
. employee performance, measuring
. . equitable taxpayer treatment ... 801.3(b); 801.3T(b)
. . general workforce .... 801.3(d); 801.3T(d)
. . generally .... 801.3(a); 801.3T(a)
. . limitations .... 801.3(d); 801.3T(d)
. . Senior Executive Service and special positions .... 801.3(c); 801.3T(c)
. employee satisfaction measures 801.5; 801.5T
. generally 801.1
. performance goals
. . basis, as 801.1T
. . limitations on measuring .... 801.2(b)
. . measuring .... 801.2(a); 801.2T

Bank for International Settlements
. generally 1.895-1
. withholding taxes 1.1441-8

Banking institutions
. affiliates of banks 1.601-1
. bad debt .... 1.582-1; 1.593-1 to 1.593-7
. . reserve, denial of 1.585-5
. . revoking election 1.585-8
. building and loan associations
. . definitions concerning .. 301.7701-13; 301.7701-13A
. checks 301.6311-1; 301.6657-1
. collection of foreign items 301.7001-1
. common trust funds .... 1.584-1 to 1.584-5; 1.6032-1; 301.6032-1

References are to Reg. § numbers

Banking institutions —Cont'd
. deferred exchanges .... 1.1031(k)-1
. defined, bank 1.581-1
. definitions 301.7701-14
. foreign central bank of issue 1.895-1
. foreign personal holding companies 1.552-4; 1.552-5
. gains and losses .... 1.582-1; 1.584-6; 1.585-1 to 1.585-4; 1.586-1; 1.586-2
. generally .... 1.581-1 et seq.
. income of participants in common trust fund .. 1.584-2
. information returns 1.6032-1; 301.6032-1
. international settlement banks 1.895-1
. large bank, bad debt reserve
. . changing from, cut-off method of 1.585-7
. . denial of reserve 1.585-5
. . . recapture method 1.585-6
. . . revoking election 1.585-8
. loans, reserve for losses on ...... 1.585-1 to 1.585-4; 1.586-1; 1.586-2
. mutual savings banks (See Mutual savings banks)
. net operating loss deduction 1.584-6
. returns, common trust funds 1.584-5
. securities 1.582-1
. small business investment company loans .. 1.586-1; 1.586-2
. Tax Court 301.7507-1
. worthless securities .... 1.165-5(h)

Bankruptcy
. administrative costs
. . damage actions for violations of Bankruptcy Code sections 362 or 524 .... 301.7430-8
. assessment of taxes ... 301.6871(a)-1; 301.6871(a)-2; 301.6872-1
. Bankruptcy Code section 362 or 524 violations
. . administrative costs, damage actions ... 301.7430-8
. . civil cause of action for 301.7433-2
. bonds issued by insolvent corporation ..... 1.165-5(e)
. collection of tax .... 301.6871(a)-2
. generally .... 1.6851-1 to 1.6851-3; 601.109
. partnership items .... 301.6231(c)-7
. passive activity losses and credits 1.1398-1; 1.1398-2
. pendency of Tax Court proceedings .... 301.6871(b)-1
. suspension of running of period of limitations on assessment 301.6872-1
. title 11 cases, debtor in .... 301.6229(b)-2
. unpaid claims 301.6873-1

Barter exchanges (See Broker and barter exchanges)

Basis
. allocation rules, partnership 1.755-1
. indebtedness to shareholder 1.1367-2
. shareholder's stock in S corporation 1.1367-1

Basis —Cont'd
. substituted transactions, allocation rules 1.755-1

Basis for gain or loss
. adjusted basis (See Adjusted basis)
. affiliation, property acquired during 1.1051-1
. amortization 1.1016-3; 1.1016-4
. bequest, devise, or inheritance of remainder interest 1.1014-8
. capital account 1.1016-2
. capital gains and losses .... 1.1244(d)-1; 1.1244(d)-2; 1.1245-2; 1.1245-5
. charitable organizations 1.1011-2
. consolidated returns .... 1.1502-31 to 1.1502-34
. corporate organizations and reorganizations .. 1.362-1
. decedent 1.1014-1; 1.1014-2; 1.1014-8
. depletion 1.1016-3; 1.1016-4
. depreciation .... 1.167(a)-5; 1.167(g)-1
. DISC stock 1.1014-9
. discharge of indebtedness 1.1017-1
. disposition of depreciable property 1.1245-1
. exhaustion, wear and tear, obsolescence, amortization, and depletion 1.1016-3; 1.1016-4
. Federal National Mortgage Association 1.1054-1
. foreign corporations, stock 1.961-1; 1.961-2
. generally .... 1.1011-1 et seq.; 1.1012-1
. gift 1.1015-1
. inventory 1.1013-1
. liquidation 1.334-1
. multiple interests 1.1014-7
. mutual insurance companies 1.832-6
. natural resources 1.614-6
. partners and partnerships (See Partners and partnerships)
. property acquired before March 1, 1913 ..... 1.1053-1
. readjustment of tax 1.1312-7
. redeemable ground rents .... 1.1055-1 to 1.1055-4
. Revenue Act of 1932 .... 1.1052-1
. Revenue Act of 1934 .... 1.1052-2
. Revenue Act of 1959 .... 1.1052-3
. SEC orders .... 1.1082-1 to 1.1082-6
. stock .... 1.307-1; 1.307-2; 1.961-1; 1.961-2; 1.1244(d)-2
. substituted basis 1.1016-10
. transfers, part sale and part gift 1.1012-2
. trusts .... 1.1015-2 to 1.1015-5

Below-market loans
. split-dollar loans (See Split-dollar loans)

Benevolent life insurance associations
. exempt organization .... 1.501(c)(12)-1

Best method rule
. allocation .... 1.482-1(c)
. arm's length transactions .... 1.482-1(b)
. . examples 1.482-8; 1.482-8T

References are to Reg. § numbers

Beverages
. domestic production gross receipts........1.199-3(o)
Bingo
. generally 1.513-5; 7.6041-1
Black lung benefit trusts
. generally .. 1.501(c)(21)-1; 1.501(c)(21)-2; 53.4951-1; 53.4952-1
Blocked pump
. kerosene 48.6427-11
Boards of trade
. exempt organizations .... 1.501(c)(6)-1
Boats
. diesel and special motor fuels tax 48.4041-3
. generally ... 1.861-15; 1.861-16; 1.871-3; 1.6050A-1; 31.3401(a)(14)-1; 301.6050A-1
Bond issue premium
. debt instrument issued with 1.163-13
Bond premiums
. interest expense allocation .... 1.861-9T(b)(5)
Bond purchase plans
. generally ....1.405-1; 1.405-2; 31.3401(a)(12)-1; 301.6047-1
. salary reduction agreements defined .... 31.3121(a)(5)-1T
Bonding requirements
. manufacturers excise taxes
. . trucks and trailers...................48.4061(a)-2
Bonds
. activity bonds, exemptions .... 1.103(n)-1T to 1.103(n)-7T
. advance refunding, limitations on ....1.149(d)-1
. amortization of premiums.......... 1.171-1 to 1.171-5
. . loss exception 1.865-1
. arbitrage (See Arbitrage transactions)
. capital gains and losses .... 1.1232-1 to 1.1232-4
. corporate organizations and reorganizations ....1.381(c)(9)-1
. covenant bonds................. 1.1451-1; 1.1451-2
. enterprise zone facility bonds 1.1394-1
. ERISA ....11.412(c)-11
. estate tax, payment of 20.6165-1
. exempt (See Tax-exempt bonds)
. extension of time for payment of tax 156.6165-1; 156.6165-1T
. federally guaranteed ....1.149(b)-1
. general obligation bonds refunding rules .. 1.141-13(f)
. gift tax, payment of 25.6165-1
. gross income 1.75-1
. hedge ....1.149(g)-1
. industrial development bonds 1.103-7; 1.103-10; 5c.103-2; 5f.103-2
. inflation-indexed debt instruments; special rules 1.171-3
. interest

Bonds —Cont'd
. *interest —Cont'd*
. . exempt facility bonds 1.103-8
. . federally guaranteed .... 1.149(b)-1
. IRS personnel 301.7803-1
. itemized deductions ..... 1.163-3 to 1.163-5; 1.166-7; 1.249-1
. . issuance premiums 1.163-13
. lien for estate tax treated as 20.2204-3
. maturity limitation-treatment of working capital ....1.147(b)-1
. mortgage bonds, qualified 1.103A-2; 6a.103A-2
. payment of taxes, for 1.6165-1; 1.6851-3; 53.6165-1; 53.7101-1; 301.6165-1; 301.7101-1; 301.7102-1
. pension, profit-sharing, and stock bonus plans 1.405-1; 1.405-2
. private activity (See Private activity bonds)
. reimbursement 1.150-2
. security for payment of tax (See Bonding requirements; Bonds for payment of taxes)
. substantial user bonds 1.103-11
. TEFRA 5f.103-3
. treasury bond exemptions 1.103-5
. valuation of 20.2031-2
. . gift tax 25.2512-2
. variable rate debt instruments; special rules .. 1.171-3
. withholding ... 1.1451-1; 1.1451-2; 31.3401(a)(12)-1; 35.3405-1
. yield on issue, computation 1.148-4
Bonus depreciation (See Additional first year depreciation deduction)
Bonuses
. itemized deductions 1.162-9
. natural resources 1.612-3
. stock bonus plans (See Pension, profit-sharing, and stock bonus plans)
Books and records
. defined for computation of taxable income 1.441-1
. failure to maintain
. . allocation of proceeds 1.148-6
. production of (See Production of books and records)
. property produced by taxpayer, rules concerning 1.263A-2
Boot
. intercompany reorganization .... 1.1502-13(f)
Bows and arrows
. manufacturers excise taxes
. . definitions ....48.4161(b)-2
. . effective dates ....48.4161(b)-5
. . exempt sales ....48.4161(b)-4
. . generally .... 48.4161(b)-1 to 48.4161(b)-5
. . imposition of tax ....48.4161(b)-1
. . use considered sale..................48.4161(b)-3

References are to Reg. § numbers

Boycotts, international, participation in
. foreign sales corporations .... 1.927(e)-2T
. international boycott factor, computation 7.999-1
. Tax Reform Act of 1976 .... 7.999-1

Branch profits tax
. foreign corporation liability 1.884-1
. reorganization 1.884-2; 1.884-2T
. termination of U.S. trade or business 1.884-2; 1.884-2T

Bribes
. deductibility of 1.162-18

Bridge banks
. federal financial assistance
. . consolidated groups .... 1.597-4(f)
. . single entity status .... 1.597-4(e)
. . transfers to .... 1.597-4(d)

Broker and barter exchanges
. backup withholding .... 31.3406(b)(3)-2
. . defined for.......................... 31.3406(h)-1
. . exemptions, principal payments made outside U.S. 35a.9999-3A
. generally 1.6045-1; 1.6045-2
. information returns 1.6045-1; 1.6045-2
. . original issue discount, reporting on....... 1.6049-5
. short sales, substitute payment 1.6045-2
. substitute payments 1.6045-2; 1.6045-2T

Building and loan associations
. definitions 301.7701-13; 301.7701-13A

Buildings
. carryover allocation, qualified for............ 1.42-6
. rehabilitation expenditures (See Rehabilitation expenditures)

Built-in losses (See Gain or loss)

Bulk sales
. compressed natural gas................ 48.4041-21

Burden of proof (See Presumptions and burden of proof)

Buses
. diesel and special motor fuels tax (See Diesel and special motor fuels tax)
. highway vehicles use tax
. . transit buses, exemptions 41.4483-2
. manufacturers excise taxes
. . intercity buses, exempt sales of tires, tubes and tread rubber 48.4221-8

Business credit (See Abatement, credits, and refunds; specific subject heading)

Business day
. backup withholding, defined for......... 31.3406(h)-1

Business deductions
. generally .... 1.162-1 et seq.

Business entities
. association defined as .... 301.7701-2(b)(2)

Business entities —Cont'd
. classification of certain 301.7701-3
. definitions 301.7701-2
. . multiple charters, entities with..... 301.7701-2(b)(9)
. entity classification election 301.7701-3
. . notice of election 301.7701-3
. foreign entity defined as .... 301.7701-2(b)(8)
. . special rules ....301.7701-2(d)
. insurance company defined as ..... 301.7701-2(b)(4)
. joint-stock company or association defined as .... 301.7701-2(b)(3)
. multiple charters, entities with ...... 301.7701-2(b)(9)
. noncorporate 301.7701-3
. partnerships defined as .... 301.7701-2(c)(1)

Business expenses
. substantiation of 1.162-17

Business gifts
. substantiation requirements....... 1.274-5; 1.274-5T

Business interests
. defined 20.6166A-2
. valuation of 20.2031-3
. . gift tax 25.2512-3

Business leagues
. exempt organizations .... 1.501(c)(6)-1

C

Cable services (See Telegraph and cable services)

Cafeteria plans
. election, revocation of 1.125-4
. Family and Medical Leave Act.............. 1.125-3

Campaigns (See Political campaigns)

Capital accounts
. generally 1.266-1; 1.551-5; 1.1016-2

Capital assets
. capital gains and losses 1.1223-1

Capital construction funds
. accounts, establishment of 3.4
. deposits
. . ceiling on 3.2
. . taxability of 3.3
. generally .... 3.1 to 3.9
. withdrawals, treatment of 3.5

Capital contributions
. generally 1.118-1; 1.362-2

Capital expenditures
. election to deduct or capitalize .... 1.263(a)-3
. examples .... 1.263(a)-2
. generally .... 1.263(a)-1 et seq.; 5c.103-1
. sulfur regulations, deduction for capital costs incurred in complying with EPA (See Environmental Protection Agency)

References are to Reg. § numbers

Capital gains and losses
. alternative tax 1.1201-1
. amortization in excess of depreciation 1.1238-1
. amount of gain where loss previously disallowed, sale or exchange . . . . 1.267(d)-1
. basis . . . . 1.1244(d)-1; 1.1244(d)-2; 1.1245-2; 1.1245-5
. bonds and other evidences of indebtedness . . . . 1.1232-1 to 1.1232-4
. carrybacks and carryovers 1.1212-1
. consolidated returns
. . determination of long term gains 1.1502-22A; 1.1502-41A
. contingent payment debt instruments 1.1275-4
. corporate organizations and reorganizations . . . . 1.381(c)(3)-1; 1.383-1
. debt instruments, gain on . . . . 1.1271-1(a)
. deductions . . . . 1.1202-1 et seq.
. definitions 1.1221-1; 1.1222-1
. depreciable property . . . 1.1238-1; 1.1239-1; 1.1239-2; 1.1250-1 to 1.1250-5
. dividends, recapitalization . . . . 1.1244(d)-3
. domestic corporations 1.1248-6
. election or choice to buy or sell . . . . 1.1234-1 to 1.1234-3
. estates and trusts . . . 1.643(a)-3 et seq.; 1.665(f)-1A et seq.; 1.669(f)-1A et seq.
. exceptions 1.1245-4
. exemption for persons over age 55 from residence sale or exchange gains . . . . 1.121-1 to 1.121-5
. farming . . . . . 1.1251-1 to 1.1251-4; 1.1252-1; 1.1252-2
. foreign corporations . . 1.1248-1 to 1.1248-7; 1.1249-1
. foreign investment companies . . . 1.1247-1 to 1.1247-5
. foreign tax credit . . . . 1.904(b)-1; 1.904(b)-2; 1.1247-4
. generally . . . . 1.1701-1 et seq.
. income from sources outside the U.S.
. . alternative tax rate defined . . . . 1.904(b)-1(f)
. . capital gain rate differential adjustment
. . . entire taxable income . . . . 1.904(b)-1(c)(2)
. . . foreign source taxable income . . . . 1.904(b)-1(c)(1)
. . capital losses . . . . 1.904(b)-1(a)(2)
. . . consolidated 1.1502-9T
. . capital losses rate differential adjustment
. . . determination . . . . 1.904(b)-1(d)(2)
. . . generally . . . . 1.904(b)-1(d)(1)
. . limitations . . . . 1.904(b)-1(a)(1)
. . net capital gain defined . . . . 1.904(b)-1(f)
. . overall domestic loss
. . . allocation and apportionment of deduction . . . . 1.904(g)-1T(c)(4)
. . . defined . . . . 1.904(g)-1T(c)(2)
. . . determination of . . . . . 1.904(g)-1T; 1.904(g)-1T(c)
. . . qualified year defined . . . . 1.904(g)-1T(c)(3)
. . overall domestic loss accounts
. . . additions to account . . . . 1.904(g)-1T(d); 1.904(g)-1T(e)

Capital gains and losses —Cont'd
. *income from sources outside the U.S. —Cont'd*
. . *overall domestic loss accounts —Cont'd*
. . . establishment of . . . . 1.904(g)-1T(b)
. . . ordering rules for allocation . . . 1.904(g)-3T et seq.
. . . recapture . . . . 1.904(g)-2T
. . . taxable year loss is sustained . . . 1.904(g)-1T(b)(2)
. . overall foreign loss
. . . ordering rules for allocation . . . 1.904(g)-3T et seq.
. . rate differential portion defined . . . . 1.904(b)-1(f)
. . separate limitation loss
. . . defined . . . . 1.904(f)-7T(b)
. . . determination of . . . . 1.904(f)-7T
. . . ordering rules for allocation . . . 1.904(g)-3T et seq.
. . . separate category defined . . . . 1.904(f)-7T(b)
. . . separate limitation defined . . . . 1.904(f)-7T(b)
. . separate limitation loss account
. . . additions to account . . . . 1.904(f)-7T(d)
. . . allocated to reduce separate limitation income . . . . 1.904(f)-7T(c)
. . . recapture of account . . . . 1.904(f)-8T
. . . reductions of account . . . . 1.904(f)-7T(e)
. investment company 1.1242-1; 1.1243-1
. lease or distributor's agreement, cancellation of 1.1241-1
. life insurance companies . . . 1.812-4; 1.812-8; 1.817-2 to 1.817-4; 1.818-8; 1.825-2; 1.825-3
. limitations 1.1211-1
. . assessment and collection . . . . 301.6501(h)-1
. livestock held for draft, breeding, dairy, or sporting purposes 1.1231-2
. look-through rule
. . partnerships, sales or exchanges of interest in . . . . 1.1(h)-1
. . S corporations, sales or exchanges of interest in . . . . 1.1(h)-1
. . trust, sales or exchanges of interest in . . . . . 1.1(h)-1
. minimum tax 1.58-8
. net operating loss deduction . . . . 1.1244(d)-4
. net unrealized built-in gain, S corporation . . . 1.1374-3
. obligations with excess coupons detached . . 1.1232-4
. partnerships
. . holding period, partnership interest 1.1223-3
. . look-through rule
. . . sales or exchanges of interest in partnership . . . . 1.1(h)-1
. . sale of 1.741-1
. . sales or exchanges of interest in . . . . 1.1(h)-1
. passive foreign investment companies . . . . 1.1291-1 et seq.
. patents 1.1235-1; 1.1235-2
. pension, profit-sharing, and stock bonus plans . . . . 1.403(a)-2
. principal amount not exceeding $2,8000.000
. . cash method debt instruments . . . . 1.1274A-1(b)

References are to Reg. § numbers

Capital gains and losses —Cont'd
. *principal amount not exceeding $2,8000.000 —Cont'd*
. . qualified and cash method debt instruments .... 1.1274A-1(b)
. qualifying debt instruments, integration of 1.1275-6
. rate of tax 1.1374-1
. real estate investment trusts .... 1.857-2 to 1.857-10
. real property subdivided for sale 1.1237-1
. recordkeeping requirements .... 1.1244(e)-1; 1.1247-5
. regulated investment companies (RICs) undistributed, designation of 1.852-9
. S corporations, sales or exchanges of interest in .... 1.1(h)-1
. Section 126 property .... 16A.1255-1 to 16A.1255-2
. Section 1244 stock defined .... 1.1244(c)-1
. Section 1245 property 1.1245-3
. Section 1274, application of
. . assumptions 1.1274-5
. . debt instruments 1.1274-1
. . issue price of debt instrument 1.1274-2
. . potentially abusive situations 1.1274-3
. . test rate of interest 1.1274-4
. securities dealers 1.1236-1
. short sales 1.1233-1
. short-term obligations, gain on .... 1.1271-1(b)
. small business investment company .... 1.1242-1; 1.1243-1; 1.1244(a)-1 to 1.1244(e)-1
. small business stock .... 1.1244(a)-1 to 1.1244(e)-1
. stock .... 1.1242-1; 1.1243-1; 1.1244(a)-1 to 1.1244(e)-1; 1.1248-5
. surcharge 1.56-1
. taxability 1.1374-1
. time period for which capital assets are held 1.1223-1
. trade or business 1.1231-1
. trust, sales or exchanges of interest in .... 1.1(h)-1
. variable rate debt instruments
. . applicability .... 1.1275-5(a)
. . floating rate, qualified .... 1.1275-5(b)
. . objective rate defined .... 1.1275-5(c)
. . reset bonds .... 1.1275-5(f)
. worthless securities .... 1.165-5(c)

Capitalization of costs
. accounting method, change in .... 1.263A-1T(k)
. accumulated production expenditures .... 1.263A-15(b)
. additional Sec. 263A costs .... 1.263A-1(d)
. allocating categories of costs .... 1.263A-1(g)
. allocation methods .... 1.263A-1(f)
. anti-abuse rules 1.263A-15
. avoided cost method use to calculate interest 1.263A-9
. creative expenses .... 1.263A-1(b)
. definitions concerning .... 1.263A-1(d)
. determination of .... 1.263A-1(c)

Capitalization of costs —Cont'd
. farming .... 1.263A-1(b); 1.263A-4
. generally .... 1.263A-1(a)
. intangible drilling and development costs .... 1.263A-1(b)
. long-term contracts .... 1.263A-1(b)
. natural gas acquired for resale .... 1.263A-1(b)
. not-for profit activities .... 1.263A-1(b)
. oil and gas activities 1.263A-13
. origination of loan exception .... 1.263A-1(b)
. production period 1.263A-12
. property produced by taxpayer, rules concerning 1.263A-2
. . books and teaching aids .... 1.263A-2(a)
. . contract defined .... 1.263A-2(a)
. . intellectual property .... 1.263A-2(a)
. . produce defined .... 1.263A-2(a)
. . routine purchase order exception .... 1.263A-2(a)
. . simplified production method .... 1.263A-2(b)
. . sound recordings .... 1.263A-2(a)
. resale 1.263A-3
. research and experimental expenditures .... 1.263A-1(b)
. scope, general 1.263A-1
. Sec. 471 costs .... 1.263A-1(d)
. self-constructed tangible personal property produced on a routine and repetitive basis .... 1.263A-1T(h)
. self-controlled assets .... 1.263A-1(d)
. service, property provided incident to .... 1.263A-1(b)
. simplified service cost method .... 1.263A-1(h)
. small resellers .... 1.263A-1(b)
. special rules .... 1.263A-1(j)
. subject to, costs .... 1.263A-1(e)
. substantially constructed property .... 1.263A-1(b)
. timber business, cost incurred in .... 1.263A-1(b)
. transitional rules 1.263A-15
. uniform 1.263A-1

Cargo, international operations
. exclusion of income; aircraft and ships 1.883-1; 1.883-1T

Caribbean basin countries
. investments 1.936-10

Carrybacks and carryovers
. capital gains and losses 1.1212-1
. charitable contributions 1.170A-10
. consolidated returns
. . net operating losses 1.1502-79A
. . tentative adjustments 1.1502-78
. . unused credits 1.1502-79
. corporate organizations and reorganizations, carryovers of predecessor (See Successor corporations, subhead carryovers of predecessor)
. decedent's property .... 7.1023(b)(3)-1; 7.6039A-1
. DISCs 1.996-7; 1.996-8

References are to Reg. § numbers

Carrybacks and carryovers —Cont'd
. dividends ... 1.564-1
. extensions of time for payment ... 1.6164-1; 301.6164-1
. financial institutions, insolvent
. . consolidated group, member of ... 301.6402-7
. foreign tax credit ... 1.904-2; 1.904-2T; 1.904-3; 301.6501(i)-1
. generally ... 1.6411-1 to 1.6411-4; 301.6411-1; 301.6501(m)-1
. governmental obligations, interest on ... 1.103(n)-4T
. investment credit ... 1.46-2; 301.6501(j)-1; 301.6511(d)-4
. life insurance companies ... 1.812-4; 1.812-8; 1.817-2 to 1.817-4; 1.825-2; 1.825-3
. mutual insurance company ... 1.825-2; 1.825-3
. net operating loss (See Net operating loss carrybacks and carryovers)
. partnership items ... 301.6231(c)-1
. successor corporations (See Successor corporations, subhead carryovers of predecessor)
. surcharge ... 1.53-2; 1.56A-2; 1.56A-5
. Tax Reform Act of 1976 ... 7.6039A-1
. tentative adjustment, computation of
. . allowance of adjustment ... 1.6411-3; 1.6411-3T
. . decrease, application of ... 1.6411-3(d); 1.6411-3T(d)
. . decrease in tax attributable to carryback ... 1.6411-2(b); 1.6411-2T(b)
. . disallowance of application for adjustment ... 1.6411-3(c); 1.6411-3T(c)
. . examination of application for adjustment ... 1.6411-3(b); 1.6411-3T(b)
. . previously determined tax ... 1.6411-2(a); 1.6411-2T(a)
. . time prescribed for allowance of adjustment ... 1.6411-3(a); 1.6411-3T(a)
. work incentive programs ... 301.6501(o)-1; 301.6511(d)-7

Carrying charges
. capital accounts ... 1.266-1

Carryover allocations
. election of appropriate percentage month ... 1.42-8
. estates and trust beneficiary ... 1.642(h)-4
. general public
. . buildings not used by ... 1.42-9(c)
. . buildings used by ... 1.42-9(a)
. qualifications for ... 1.42-6
. services, providing ... 1.42-11

Cars (See Motor vehicles)

Cash
. debt for cash, sale of
. . intercompany transactions ... 1.1502-13(g)
. owner of large amounts of cash not identified, presumptions where ... 301.6867-1

Cash —Cont'd
. trade or business receipts in excess of $10,000, information reporting ... 1.6050I-1
. valuation of cash on hand or on deposit ... 20.2031-5

Cash basis of accounting
. limitations on use ... 1.448-1; 1.448-1T

Cash in excess of $10,000, reporting
. cash defined for ... 1.6050I-2

Cash or deferred arrangements (CODAs)
. accounting requirements ... 1.401(k)-1
. actual deferral percentage ... 1.414(v)-1
. actual deferral percentage (ADP) testing
. . determination of ADP ... 1.401(k)-2
. . excess contributions ... 1.401(k)-2
. . generally ... 1.401(k)-2
. . inconsistent method, plan with ... 1.401(k)-1
. catch-up contributions ... 1.414(v)-1
. definitions concerning ... 1.401(k)-5; 1.401(k)-6
. distribution limitations ... 1.401(k)-1
. elective deferrals, limitations on exclusion for ... 1.402(g)-1
. excess contributions
. . ADP testing ... 1.401(k)-2
. generally ... 1.401(k)-0; 1.401(k)-1
. matching contributions
. . safe harbor requirements ... 1.401(k)-3
. multiemployer plans ... 1.401(k)-1
. nondiscrimination rules ... 1.401(a)-1
. nonforfeitability requirements ... 1.401(k)-1
. plan testing procedures, changes to ... 1.401(k)-1
. safe harbor requirements ... 1.401(k)-3
. . matching contributions ... 1.401(k)-3
. . suspension of matching contributions ... 1.401(k)-3
. self-employed individuals, payments to ... 1.401(k)-1
. SIMPLE 401(k) plan requirements ... 1.401(k)-4

Cash value
. defined ... 1.7702-2

Casualty losses
. itemized deductions ... 1.165-7

Catch-up contributions
. multiple plan, increased limit for ... 1.402(g)-2
. pension plan, to ... 1.414(v)-1a

CDE (See Community development entity (CDE)

Cement mixers, excise taxes
. floor stock refunds or credits ... 48.4061-1

Cemetery companies and crematoria
. exempt organizations ... 1.501(c)(13)-1

Census Bureau
. disclosure of return information to ... 301.6103(j)(1)-1

Certificates
. generally ... 1.25-3T to 1.25-6T; 1.401-9; 1.6851-2; 46.4701-1; 301.6338-1

References are to Reg. § numbers

Certificates —Cont'd

. qualified enhanced oil recovery project 1.43-3
. qualified mortgage credit certificates 1.25-3; 1.25-3T; 1.25-4T

Chambers of commerce

. exempt organizations . . . . 1.501(c)(6)-1

Charitable contributions

. allowance of deduction . . . . 1.170A-1(a)
. annuity purchases . . . . 1.170A-1(c)
. appreciated property, reduction in amount of charitable contributions of 1.170A-4
. carryovers
. . corporate . . . . 1.170A-11; 1.381(c)(19)-1
. . . election by corporation on accrual method; carry-over limitation 1.170A-11
. . individuals 1.170A-10
. church defined for section 170(b)(1)(A) organization 1.170A-9
. conservation contributions 1.170A-14
. consolidated returns 1.1502-24
. corporate
. . carryovers . . . . 1.170A-11; 1.381(c)(19)-1
. . . election by corporation on accrual method 1.170A-11
. . limitation on
. . . election by corporation on accrual method; carry-over limitation 1.170A-11
. deductions . . . . 25.2522(c)-1
. educational organization defined for section 170(b)(1)(A) organization 1.170A-9
. estates and trusts . . . . . . 1.170A-6; 1.642(c)-1 et seq.; 1.651(a)-4 et seq.; 1.664-1 et seq.
. future interests in tangible personal property 1.170A-5
. generally . . . . 1.170A-1 to 1.170A-14; 1.170-0
. hospital defined for section 170(b)(1)(A) organization 1.170A-9
. income in receipt of decedent
. . unlimited deduction, determination of . . . . 1.642(c)-3
. income interest in trust 1.170A-6
. information returns
. . donated property, disposition of 1.6050L-1
. interest on indebtedness 1.170A-3; 1.170A-5; 1.170A-12
. inventory and other property 1.170A-4A
. limitation 1.170A-8; 1.170-2
. medical research organization defined for section 170(b)(1)(A) organization 1.170A-9
. partial interests in property 1.170A-7
. possessions of the U.S. 1.170A-1
. private foundations 1.508-2
. quid pro quo contributions, disclosure of 1.6115-1
. recordkeeping requirements 1.170A-13
. reduction of deduction by amounts not included in gross income . . . . 1.642(c)-3

Charitable contributions —Cont'd

. remainder interests
. . real property 1.170A-12
. . trust 1.170A-6
. return requirements 1.170A-13
. Section 170(b)(1)(A) organization defined . . . 1.170A-9
. state and municipal college defined for section 170(b)(1)(A) organization 1.170A-9
. students 1.170A-2
. substantiation of contributions $250 or more . . . . 1.170A-13(f)
. time of making contribution . . . . 1.170A-1(b)
. trust 1.170A-6
. unlimited deduction, determination of . . . . . . 1.642(c)-3
. useful life of depreciable property, determination of 1.170A-12

Charitable interests

. limitation on application of section 7520 . . . . 1.7520-3; 20.7520-3
. valuation 1.7520-2; 25.7520-2; 25.7520-3
. . limitations 1.7520-2
. . transitional rules 1.7520-4

Charitable lead annuity trusts

. generation-skipping transfer tax 26.2642-3

Charitable organizations

. disclosure of listed transactions involvement 56.6011-4
. generally . . . . 1.501(c)(3)-1; 1.1011-2
. listed transactions involvement, disclosure of 56.6011-4
. public charities, lobbying expenditures (See Lobbying expenditures)

Charitable remainder annuity trusts

. general description 1.664-2

Charitable remainder interests

. valuation 1.664-4A

Charitable remainder trusts

. annual distributions to recipients, treatment of . . . . 1.664-1(d)
. . character of distributions . . . . 1.664-1(e)(1)
. . distributions in kind . . . . 1.664-1(e)(2)
. defined . . . . 1.664-1(a)
. excise tax on . . . . 1.664-1(c)
. foundation rules, application of certain . . . . . 1.664-1(b)
. general description 1.664-1
. surviving spouse
. . noncharitable beneficiaries, other . . 20.2056(b)-8(b)
. . noncharitable beneficiary, spouse is not only . . . . 25.2523(g)-1(b)
. . noncharitable beneficiary, spouse is only . . . . 25.2523(g)-1(a)
. . special rules for . . . . 20.2056(b)-8
. testamentary transfers . . . . 1.664-1(a)(5)(i)

References are to Reg. § numbers

Charitable remainder trusts —Cont'd
. transfers of interest special valuation rules 25.2702-1
Charitable remainder unitrusts
. general description 1.664-3
. remainder interests
. . calculation of fair market value 1.664-4
Charitable transfers
. death taxes 20.2055-3
. . December 31, 1969, death before 20.2055-5
. . January 1, 1970, death before 20.2055-4
. deductions for 20.2055-2
Checks
. generally 301.6311-1; 301.6657-1
Chemicals, ozone-depleting (See Ozone-depleting chemicals, taxes on)
Child care facilities
. amortization 1.188-1
Children and dependents (See also Minors)
. amortization 1.188-1
. credits for dependent care services . . . . 1.44A-1 to 1.44A-4
. cruelty to, organizations for prevention of . . . . 1.501(c)(3)-1
. defined, dependent 1.25A-2; 1.152-1; 1.152-2
. education tax credits, dependents defined for 1.25A-2
. exempt organization for prevention of cruelty to children . . . . 1.501(c)(3)-1
. gross income 1.73-1
. missing children, dissemination of materials to help locate 601.901
. personal exemptions 1.151-2; 1.152-3; 1.152-4T
. students 1.170A-2; 1.871-9
. unearned income, tax on . . . . 1.1(i)-1T
China Trade Act corporations
. returns 1.6072-3
Churches (See Religious organizations)
Circulation expenditures
. itemized deductions . . . . 1.173-1 to 1.174-4
. optional 10-year writeoff of certain tax preferences 1.59-1
Citrus and almond groves
. itemized deductions 1.278-1
Civic organizations
. exempt organizations . . . . 1.501(c)(4)-1
Class lives and asset depreciation ranges
. depreciation . . . . 1.167(a)-11; 1.167(a)-12; 1.167(m)-1
Class year plans
. ERISA . . . . 1.411(d)-5
Classifications for federal tax purposes
. business entities 301.7701-3
. changing . . . . 301.7701-3(g)
Classifications for federal tax purposes —Cont'd
. cost sharing arrangements . . . . 301.7701-1(c)
. determination of . . . . 301.7701-1(b)
. entities defined 301.7701-1
. . domestic and foreign entities 301.7701-1; 301.7701-5
. entity classification election 301.7701-3
. . notice of election 301.7701-3
. organizations for federal tax purposes . . . . 301.7701-1(a)
. state, District of Columbia defined as . . . . 301.7701-1(e)
Clergy (See Ministers or religious personnel)
Clinical testing expenses
. drugs 1.28-1; 1.280C-3
Closely-held corporations
. alternate valuation for business property, material participation requirements for 20.2032A-3
. extension of time to pay tax 20.6166-1
. interest defined 20.6166A-2
Closing agreements by IRS
. generally . . . . 1.1313(a)-2; 1.1313(a)-4; 301.7121-1; 601.202; 601.203
Coal, coal lands, and coal companies
. adjusted basis 1.1016-5
. depletion 48.4121-1
. generally 1.272-1; 1.631-3
. rate of tax 48.4121-1
COBRA
. beneficiaries 54.4980B-3
. compliance 54.4980B-2
. continuation coverage
. . compliance requirements 54.4980B-2
. . duration 54.4980B-7
. . electing 54.4980B-6
. . generally 54.4980B-1
. . paying for 54.4980B-8
. . requirements 54.4980B-5
. duration of continuation coverage 54.4980B-6
. electing continuation coverage 54.4980B-6
. FMLA and 54.4980B-10
. generally 54.4980B-1
. independent contractors 54.4980B-2
. paying for continuation coverage 54.4980B-8
. qualified beneficiaries defined 54.4980B-3
. qualifying events 54.4980B-4
. reorganization, employer withdrawal after 54.4980B-9
. self-employed individuals 54.4980B-2
. small employer plans 54.4980B-2
COD income
. depreciation
. . basis reduction, election for 1.108-4
. discharge of indebtedness 1.108-7T

References are to Reg. § numbers

COD income —Cont'd
. *discharge of indebtedness—Cont'd*
. . consolidated returns 1.1502-28
. . section 381, application of 1.1017-1
. reduction of tax attributions, order of 1.108-7T
CODAs (See Cash or deferred arrangements)
Coin-operated telephone services
. communications services, excise taxes
. . exemption 49.4253-1
. . payment for 49.4254-2
Collapsible corporations
. liquidation .... 1.341-1 to 1.341-6
Collection Due Process hearing
. notice and opportunity for hearing prior to levy 301.6320-1; 301.6330-1
Collection of tax
. abatements, credits, and refunds ... 301.6501(a)-1 to 301.6503(g)-1
. additions to tax (See Additions to tax, additional amounts, and assessable penalty)
. administrative proceeding .... 301.7430-3(b)
. annuities 35.3405-1
. assessment, after
. . court proceeding for collection .... 301.6502-1(c)
. . extension of limitation period, agreement on .... 301.6502-1(b)
. . generally 301.6502-1
. . levy date, determination of .... 301.6502-1(e)
. . statutory suspension of limitation period if executed collection extension agreement is in effect .... 301.6502-1(d)
. bankruptcy .... 301.6871(a)-2
. civil action for damages 301.7433-1
. . failure to release a lien 301.7432-1
. classification of IRS taxes 601.102
. deferred income 35.3405-1
. depositaries of government ...... 1.6302-1; 1.6302-2; 1.6361-1; 31.6302(c)-1
. employment taxes (See Employment taxes)
. fringe benefits .... 31.3501(a)-1T
. generally . . 1.6302-1; 1.6302-2; 1.6361-1; 301.6305-1; 601.101 to 601.106
. IRS, general purpose of 601.101
. jeopardy assessments (See Jeopardy assessments)
. methods of 601.104
. mode or time of 301.6302-1
. pensions 35.3405-1
. period of limitations, suspension of running of
. . outside the U.S., taxpayer or property held .... 301.6503(c)-1
. receivership .... 301.6871(a)-2
. review 301.6305-1
. seizure of property (See Seizure of property)
. state and local taxes 1.6361-1; 31.6361-1
Collection of tax —Cont'd
. Tax Equity and Fiscal Responsibility Act ... 35.3405-1
. unauthorized collection actions 301.7433-1
. withholding on pension, annuities, and other deferred income 35.3405-1
Collective bargaining agreements
. generally 1.413-1; 1.419A-1T; 301.7701-17T
. pension, profit-sharing, and stock bonus plans, nondiscrimination rules .... 1.401(a)(4)-1
. qualified asset account limitation 1.419A-2T
. . 10 or more employer plan exception ... 1.419A(f)(6)
Combat zone compensation
. exclusion 1.112-1
. exemption 49.4253-4
Commerce, chambers of (See Chambers of commerce)
Commerce, Department of
. disclosure of return information to .... 301.6103(j)(1)-1
Commissioner or other Internal Revenue officers
. returns prepared or executed by (See Internal Revenue Service)
Commissions
. backup withholding .... 31.3406(b)(3)-1
. compensation 1.61-2
. withholding .... 31.3402(j)-1
Commodities
. backup withholding on sales .... 31.3406(b)(3)-2
Commodity credit corporation loans
. gross income 1.77-1; 1.77-2
. loan, adjusted basis 1.1016-5
Common trust funds
. alternative minimum tax 1.58-5
. banking institutions ..... 1.584-1 to 1.584-5; 1.6032-1; 301.6032-1
. information returns 1.6032-1; 301.6032-1
Commonly controlled trades or businesses
. corporations (See Controlled corporations)
. ERISA .... 1.414(c)-1 to 1.414(c)-5
. stock acquisition 1.304-4T
Communications activity
. foreign communication income, source of . . 1.863-9(d)
. income derived from .... 1.863-9(a); 1.863-9(h)
. international communication income, source of .... 1.863-9(b)
. partnerships .... 1.863-9(i)
. reporting and documentation requirements .... 1.863-9(k)
. space/ocean communication income, source of .... 1.863-9(e)
. taxable income .... 1.863-9(g)
. taxpayer cannot establish the two points between which the taxpayer is paid to transmit the communications, source of .... 1.863-9(f)

References are to Reg. § numbers

Communications activity —Cont'd
. U.S. communication income, source of .... 1.863-9(c)
Communications services, excise taxes
. application of tax 49.4251-2
. certificates of exemption, use and retention of 49.4253-11
. common carriers exempt 49.4253-6
. communications companies exempt 49.4253-6
. computation of tax 49.4254-1
. exempt organizations 49.4253-3
. imposition of tax 49.4251-1
. installation charges, exemption for 49.4253-7
. interior communication system, exemption for certain 49.4253-9
. items otherwise taxed, exemptions for 49.4253-5
. payment of tax
. . time and place 49.6151-1
. private communications services, exemption for certain 49.4253-10
. rate of tax 49.4251-2
. returns .... 49.6011(a)-1
. . employer identification number 49.6109-1
. . time for filing .... 49.6071(a)-1
. Section 4251 to 4254, applicability 49.4251-3
. service personnel in combat zones, exemption for 49.4253-4
. states or political subdivisions 49.4253-12
. . generally 49.4252-3
. . provisions common to 49.4252-4
. telegraph services
. . generally 49.4252-3
. . provisions common to 49.4252-4
. telephone services 49.4252-1; 49.4252-2
. . coin-operated services
. . . exemption 49.4253-1
. . . payment for 49.4254-2
. . news services 49.4253-2
. . news services exemption 49.4253-2
. . provisions common to 49.4252-4
. . service personnel in combat zones exempt 49.4253-4
. . toll telephone services 49.4254-2
. teletypewriter exchange services 49.4252-5
. . items otherwise taxed, exemptions for.... 49.4253-5
. terminal facilities in case of wire mileage service, exemption for 49.4253-8
. wire mile service, exemption for terminal facility in case of 49.4253-8
Communist-controlled organizations
. exempt organizations .... 1.501(k)-1
Community development entity (CDE)
. new markets tax credit 1.45D-1
Community income
. definitions concerning 1.66-4
Community income —Cont'd
. denial of federal tax benefits 1.66-3
. failure to give notice to spouse 1.66-3
. fraud 1.66-4
. generally .... 1.66-1; 1.879-1; 1.1402(a)-8
. not electing to file joint federal income tax return, spouses 1.66-1
. offer in compromise, effect of 1.66-4
. prior closing agreement, effect of 1.66-4
. request for relief from federal income tax liability 1.66-4
. spouses living apart 1.66-2
. transferred income 1.66-2
Community property
. gift to spouse .... 25.2523(f)-1A
. income earned abroad by U.S. citizens 1.911-5
Commutation tickets, excise taxes
. aircraft on non-established lines 49.4263-5
. American Red Cross, transportation furnished to 49.4263-3
. Armed Forces, members of 49.4263-4
. charges not exceeding 60 cents 49.4263-2
. exemptions 49.4263-6
. generally .... 49.4263-1 et seq.
. international organizations, transportation furnished to 49.4263-3
. 60 cents, charges not exceeding........... 49.4263-2
Commuter highway vehicles (See Highway vehicles, subhead commuter vehicles)
Companion sitting placement services
. withholding 31.3506-1
Comparable profits method
. arm's length transactions
. . determination of taxable income........ 1.482-9T(f)
. . use in determination of 1.482-5
Comparable uncontrolled services price method
. arm's length transactions; determination of taxable income .... 1.482-9T(c)
Compensation (See kind and source or specific subject heading)
Composite returns
. generally .... 1.6012-5; 31.6011(a)-8
Compressed natural gas
. bulk sales 48.4041-21
. motor vehicle or motorboat, delivery to 48.4041-21
Compromise by IRS
. generally 301.7122-1T; 601.203
. offer to compromise fee 300.3
Computation of tax
. claims arising out of erroneous computation .... 301.6230(c)-1
Computer software
. amortization

References are to Reg. § numbers

Computer software —Cont'd
. *amortization —Cont'd*
. . exclusion under section 197, intangibles .... 1.167(a)-14(b)
. domestic production gross receipts ...... 1.199-8(i)(4)
. . Tax Increase Prevention and Reconciliation Act of 2005 .... 1.199-8(i)(5)

Condemnation (See also Involuntary conversions)
. gain or loss .... 1.1033(g)-1

Conduit entities
. financing arrangements 1.881-3
. . recordkeeping requirements 1.881-4
. . withhold, duty to 1.1441-7
. surcharge 1.58-2

Conference with IRS
. evidence 601.507
. generally .... 601.501 to 601.506; 601.521

Confidential transactions
. defined 1.6011-4

Confidentiality
. backup withholding, information concerning .... 31.3406(f)-1
. corporate tax shelters 301.6111-2

Confiscation of foreign property
. itemized deductions 1.172-9

Congress, members of
. travel expense deductions 5e.274-8

Consent dividends
. adjusted basis 1.1016-5
. consent filed for dividend paid deduction, time of filing 1.565-1
. consent stock defined 1.565-6
. definitions 1.565-6
. effect of 1.565-3
. generally .... 1.565-1 et seq.; 1.565-3; 1.565-4
. limitations 1.565-2
. nonresident aliens and foreign corporations .. 1.565-5
. preferred dividends defined 1.565-6

Conservation expenditures
. generally .. 1.170A-14; 1.175-1 to 1.175-7; 16A.126-0 to 16A.126-2

Consideration
. insufficient, disposition of property for 25.2512-8
. tenancy by entirety 25.2515-1

Consolidated groups
. agents
. . carryback adjustments, tentative 1.1502-78
. hedging transactions 1.1221-2
. structure change, stock basis after 1.1502-31

Consolidated returns
. abatements, credits, and refunds 1.6411-4
. accounting methods 1.1502-17

Consolidated returns —Cont'd
. accumulated earnings 1.1502-43; 1.1502-43T; 1.1551-1
. affiliated groups
. . taxable year, determination of 1.441-3
. agents
. . alternative agents for the group 1.1502-77
. . common parent agents for subsidiaries ... 1.1502-77
. . termination of common parent .... 1.1502-77(d)
. . termination of corporation's existence 1.1502-77
. Alaska Native Corporations 1.1502-81T
. allocation
. . coordination of 1.382.6 and 1.1502-76(b) rules 1.382-6
. alternative agents for the group 1.1502-77
. alternative minimum tax, computation of 1.1502-55
. basis .... 1.1502-31 to 1.1502-34
. capital construction funds 3.9
. capital gains and losses 1.1502-22; 1.1502-22A
. . long term gains, determination of 1.1502-41A
. carryback adjustments 1.1502-78
. ceasing to be consolidated group member
. . apportionment of section 382 limitation .... 1.1502-95(c)
. . . election, filing .... 1.1502-95(f)
. . June 25, 1999, before 1.1502-95A
. . loss subgroups, ceasing to be member of .... 1.1502-95(d)
. . net unrealized built-in loss, allocation of .... 1.1502-95(e)
. . reporting requirements .... 1.1502-95(e)
. . rules on, general .... 1.1502-95(a)
. . section 382, application of .... 1.1502-95(b)
. charitable contributions 1.1502-24
. circular stock basis adjustments .... 1.1502-11(b)
. common parent agents for subsidiaries ... 1.1502-77A
. computation .... 1.1502-2 et seq.
. consolidated taxable income, determining .... 1.1502-11(a)
. controlled group of corporations
. . brother-sister controlled group defined .... 1.1563-1T(a)(3)
. . . transitional rule during revision of brother-sister group control group definition ..... 1.1563-1T(d)
. . component members defined ...... 1.1563-1T(b)(1)
. . defined .... 1.1563-1T et seq.
. . excluded members defined .... 1.1563-1T(b)(2)
. . parent-subsidiary controlled group defined .... 1.1563-1T(a)(2)
. . transitional rule during revision of brother-sister group control group definition ..... 1.1563-1T(d)
. deconsolidation of subsidiary member, transfers of subsidiary member stock and 35
. . anti-avoidance rules .... 35(g)
. . loss suspension .... 35(c)

References are to Reg. § numbers

Consolidated returns —Cont'd
. *deconsolidation of subsidiary member, transfers of subsidiary member stock and—Cont'd*
. . redetermination of basis .... 35(b)
. . worthlessness not followed by separate return years .... 35(f)
. definitions .... 1.1502-1; 1.1502-1(h); 1.1504-1
. discharge of indebtedness income (COD), excluded 1.1502-28
. disposition or deconsolidation of subsidiary stock 1.1502-20
. . limitation of applicability of 1.1502-20 ... 1.1502-20T
. . revocation or amendment of prior elections 1.1502-20T
. dispositions of stock .... 1.1502-28(b)(7)
. dividends 1.1502-26
. due dates for separate returns .... 1.1502-76(c)
. earnings and profits 1.1552-1
. . anti-avoidance rule .... 1.1502-33(g)
. . deconsolidation .... 1.1502-33(e)
. . federal income tax liability .... 1.1502-33(d)
. . generally .... 1.1502-33(a)
. . intercompany transactions, special rules for .... 1.1502-33(c)
. . predecessors and successors .... 1.1502-33(h)
. . special rules .... 1.1502-33(c)
. . stock of members, special rules for .... 1.1502-33(c)
. . structure of group, changes in .... 1.1502-33(f)
. . tiering up earnings and profits .... 1.1502-33(b)
. ERTA .... 5c.168(f)(8)-11
. estimated tax 1.1502-5
. excess loss account .... 1.1502-28(b)(6)
. exemption of corporations from tax 1.1502-100
. filing 1.1502-75
. . first year filing form 1122 .... 1.1502-75
. financial institutions, insolvent
. . refund claims 301.6402-7
. . tentative carryback adjustments 301.6402-7
. foreign tax credit 1.1502-4
. form 1122, first year filing 1.1502-75
. franchised corporations 1.1563-4
. information statements
. . loss group ownership change .... 1.1502-92(d)
. insurance companies 1.1502-47
. intercompany agreements and liability for tax 1.1502-6
. inventory adjustment 1.1502-18
. investment adjustment
. . allocation among shares of stock ...... 1.1502-32(c)
. . anti-avoidance rule .... 1.1502-32(e)
. . definitions concerning .... 1.1502-32(d)
. . election to treat loss carryover as expiring .... 1.1502-32T(b)
. . predecessors and successors .... 1.1502-32(f)

Consolidated returns —Cont'd
. *investment adjustment —Cont'd*
. . recordkeeping .... 1.1502-32(g)
. . stock basis adjustments .... 1.1502-32(b)
. investment credit 1.1502-3
. items included in .... 1.1502-76(b)
. liability for tax .... 1.1502-2 et seq.; 1.1502-6
. life insurance companies 1.818-8
. life-nonlife groups 1.1502-47
. life-nonlife insurance groups 1.1502-47
. limitations on built-in deductions 1.1502-15A
. limitations on built-in losses .... 1.1502-15(b)
. losses
. . common parent of group, recognition by .... 1.1502-15(f)
. . generally 1.1502-19
. . limitations on .... 1.1502-15(b)
. . SRLY limitations on .... 1.1502-15(a)
. mine exploration expenditures 1.1502-16
. multiple debtor members .... 1.1502-28(b)(1)
. mutual savings banks 1.1502-42
. net operating loss 1.1502-21
. . carryover limitations .... 1.1502-21(c)
. . carryovers .... 1.1502-21(b)
. . carryovers and carrybacks .... 1.1502-21(c)
. . charge of ownership limitation, coordination with .... 1.1502-21(d)
. . defined 1.1502-21
. . generally 1.1502-21
. . Sec. 382 overlap .... 1.1502-21(g)
. . special rules 1.1502-21
. ownership change
. . built-in gain and loss, net unrealized ... 1.1502-91(g)
. . built-in gain and loss, recognized ...... 1.1502-91(h)
. . consolidated attribute, pre-change ..... 1.1502-91(e)
. . definitions .... 1.1502-91(b)
. . effect of .... 1.1502-91(a)
. . June 25, 1999, testing date before 1.1502-91A
. . loss group .... 1.1502-91(c)
. . . adjustments .... 1.1502-92(b)
. . . determination of ownership change .. 1.1502-92(b)
. . . information statements .... 1.1502-92(d)
. . . parent change .... 1.1502-92(b)
. . . rules .... 1.1502-92(a)
. . . supplemental rules .... 1.1502-92(c)
. . . testing period .... 1.1502-92(d)
. . loss subgroup .... 1.1502-91(d)
. . nomenclature .... 1.1502-91(b)
. . predecessor and successor corporations .... 1.1502-91(j)
. . subgroup attribute, pre-change .... 1.1502-91(f)
. percentage depletion for independent producers and royalty owners 1.1502-44
. personal holding companies 1.542-4

References are to Reg. § numbers

Consolidated returns —Cont'd
. reduction of basis of intercompany obligations and former intercompany obligations ..... 1.1502-28(b)(5)
. rules
. . testing dates before June 25, 1999 ..... 1.1502-96A
. Sec. 108(a), application of .... 1.1502-28(a)(1)
. Sec. 108(b)(5), elections under ...... 1.1502-28(b)(2)
. Sec. 163(e)(5), non-applicability of ...... 1.1502-80(e)
. Sec. 165, applicability of .... 1.1502-80(c)
. Sec. 247 deduction 1.1502-27
. Sec. 304, applicability of .... 1.1502-80(b)
. Sec. 332, applicability of .... 1.1502-80(g)
. Sec. 357(c), non-applicability of .... 1.1502-80(d)
. Sec. 382
. . coordination with corporation becomes a member of consolidated group before June 25, 1999 .... 1.1502-94A; 1.1502-98A
. . coordination with corporation leaving consolidated group before June 25, 1999 .... 1.1502-98A
. . coordination with regulations when corporation becomes a member of a consolidated group
. . . built-in gains and losses .... 1.1502-94(c)
. . . generally .... 1.1502-94(a)
. . . information statements .... 1.1502-94(d)
. . . new loss member, application of Sec. 382 to .... 1.1502-94(b)
. . limitation
. . . June 25, 1999, testing date before 1.1502-93A
. . ownership change
. . . June 25, 1999, testing date before 1.1502-91A
. Sec. 1017, application of .... 1.1502-28(b)(3)
. Sec. 1031, non-applicability of.......... 1.1502-80(f)
. Sec. 1231 net gain or loss 1.1502-23; 1.1502-23A
. Sec. 1245, application of .... 1.1502-28(b)(4)
. separate returns
. . carryback and carryover of net operating losses to 1.1502-79A
. . carryback and carryover of unused credits to 1.1502-79
. separate taxable income .... 1.1502-12 et seq.
. SRLY limitations on built-in losses ...... 1.1502-15(a)
. stock .... 1.1502-31 to 35; 1.1563-2
. stock basis adjustments .... 1.1502-32(b)
. stock ownership
. . component member, statement on treatment, special rules .... 1.1563-3(d)
. . constructive ownership .... 1.1563-3(b)
. . operating rules .... 1.1563-3(c)
. . rules, generally .... 1.1563-3(a)
. . Sec. 1563(f)(3)(B) special rules .... 1.1563-3(d)
. . special rules .... 1.1563-3(c)
. subsidiaries
. . disposition or deconsolidation of stock ... 1.1502-20
. . . limitations on applicability of 1.1502-20 .... 1.1502-20T

Consolidated returns —Cont'd
. *subsidiaries —Cont'd*
. . *disposition or deconsolidation of stock—Cont'd*
. . . revocation or amendment of prior elections 1:1502-20T
. . transfers of stock and deconsolidation of subsidiary 1.1502-35
. subsidiary member stock transfers and deconsolidations 35
. surtax exemption 1.1551-1
. taxable year, members of group 1.1502-76
. transfers of subsidiary stock and deconsolidation of subsidiary
. . anti-avoidance rules .... 1.1502-35(g); 1.1502-35(h)
. . application of other rules of law ..... 1.1502-35T(h)
. . definitions concerning .... 1.1502-35(d)
. . loss suspension .... 1.1502-35(c)
. . redetermination of basis .... 1.1502-35(b)
. . reduction of suspended loss .... 1.1502-35T(c)
. . tax benefits, avoidance of multiple ..... 1.1502-35(a)
. . worthlessness not followed by separate return years .... 1.1502-35(f)

Construction, aid of
. contributions 1.118-2

Construction allowances
. leases.................................... 1.110-1

Construction funds (See Capital construction funds)

Constructive ownership
. corporate distributions and adjustments .... 1.316-1 to 1.318-4
. personal holding companies ...... 1.544-1 to 1.544-6
. sale or exchange; accruable expenses..... 1.267(c)-1
. stock; successor corporations 1.382-4

Constructive receipt of income
. determining 1.451-2

Consulting services
. accounting
. . nonaccrual of certain amounts by .... 1.448-1T(d)(2)(A); 1.448-1T(e)(4)

Consumer protection
. qualified long-term care insurance contracts 1.7702B-1

Continental shelf areas
. natural resources 1.638-1; 1.638-2
. possessions of United States .... 1.1402(a)-12

Contingent payment debt instruments
. applicability .... 1.1275-4(a)
. effective date........................... 1.1275-4(f)
. losses.................................... 1.865-1
. method for nonpublicly traded property ... 1.1275-4(c)
. noncontingent bond method .... 1.1275-4(b)
. original issue discount, interest treated as .... 1.1275-4(e)
. tax-exempt obligations .... 1.1275-4(d)

References are to Reg. § numbers

Contingent payments
. arm's length transactions . . . . 1.482-9T(i)
. debt instruments . . . . 1.1001-1(g)(2); 1.1275-4
. generally 1.483-4

Contractors, independent (See Independent contractors)

Contracts and agreements
. amortization group deferred annuity contracts . . . . 1.412(b)-2; 1.818-3
. closing agreements of IRS . . 1.1313(a)-2; 1.1313(a)-4; 601.202; 601.203
. collective bargaining 1.413-1; 301.7701-17T
. federal agencies, information returns 1.6050M-1
. financing agreements . . . . 301.6323(c)-1
. gain recognition agreement requirements . . 1.367(a)-8
. inventories 1.471-10
. life insurance companies 1.801-8
. long-term contracts 1.451-5; 1.471-10
. multiple support agreements 1.152-3
. notional principal contracts 1.863-7
. pension, profit-sharing, and stock bonus plans 1.401-9
. property produced by taxpayer under 1.263A-2
. . resellers 1.263A-3
. readjustment of tax . . . . 1.1313(a)-2; 1.1313(a)-4
. resellers
. . property produced by taxpayer 1.263A-3
. treaties 1.871-12; 1.894-1; 1.1441-6

Contributions
. capital 1.118-1; 1.362-2
. catch-up contributions . . . . 1.414(v)-1a
. charitable (See Charitable contributions)
. construction, contribution in aid of 1.118-2
. employment taxes
. . additional credit
. . . generally . . . . 31.3302(b)-1
. . . proof of . . . . 31.3302(b)-2
. . credit against tax
. . . generally . . . . 31.3302(a)-1
. . . proof of . . . . 31.3302(a)-3
. . state contribution, refund of . . . . 31.3302(a)-2
. itemized deductions 1.162-15
. partners and partnerships . . 1.721-1; 1.722-1; 1.723-1
. pension, profit-sharing, and stock bonus plans . . . . 1.404(a)-1 et seq.

Contributory defined benefit plans
. nondiscrimination . . . . 1.401(a)(4)-6

Controlled corporations
. component members, tax benefits available to
. . allocation of Sec. 1561(a) tax benefit items
. . . apportionment plan in effect . . . . 1.1561-3T(c)
. . . filing form . . . . 1.1561-3T(a)
. . . no apportionment plan in effect . . . . . 1.1561-3T(b)

Controlled corporations —Cont'd
. *component members, tax benefits available to —Cont'd*
. . *allocation of Sec. 1561(a) tax benefit items —Cont'd*
. . . special rules 1.1561-2T
. . amount of benefit, determining
. . . short taxable years . . . . 1.1561-2(e)
. . corporation defined for . . . . 1.1561-1T(b)
. . evasion or avoidance of tax . . . . 1.1561-1T(c)
. . 52-53-week taxable year, corporation electing . . . . 1.1561-1T(b)
. . general rules . . . . 1.1561-1T(a)
. corporate organizations and reorganizations . . 1.355-1 to 1.355-7
. distributions of stock and securities . . . . 1.355-1 to 1.355-7
. . business purpose for distribution . . . . . 1.355-2(b)(3)
. . continuity of interest . . . . 1.355-2(c)
. . corporate business purpose . . . . 1.355-2(b)(2)
. . disqualified stock 1.355-6
. . earnings and profits, device distribution of . . . . 1.355-2(d)
. . independent business purpose . . . . 1.355-2(b)
. . limitations 1.355-0T; 1.355-2
. . nondevice, business purpose as evidence of . . . . 1.355-2(b)(4)
. . only stock received . . . . 1.355-2(f)(2)
. . property distributed, limitations on . . . . 1.355-2(a)
. . recently acquired controlled stock under sec. 355(a)(3)(B) . . . . 1.355-2(g)
. . recognition of gain 1.355-6
. . recordkeeping requirements
. . . distributing corporation . . . . 1.355-5(a)
. . . publicly traded stock defined . . . . 1.355-5(c)
. . . significant distributee . . . . 1.355-5(b)
. . . significant distributee defined . . . . 1.355-5(c)
. . . substantial information, retaining . . . . 1.355-5(d)
. . retroactive elections under sec. 355 . . . 1.355-2(i)(3)
. . securities received . . . . 1.355-2(f)(1)
. . separation of gain under sec. 355 . . . . 1.355-1(b)
. . stock rights . . . . 1.355-1(c)
. . transition elections under sec. 355 . . . . . 1.355-2(i)(2)
. ERISA . . . . 1.414(b)-1
. increase in earnings invested in U.S. property
. . shareholder's pro rata share
. . . aggregate amount of U.S. property . . 1.956-1(b)(2)
. . . amount attributable to property . . . . 1.956-1(e)
. . . determination, date and basis of . . . . 1.956-1(d)
. . . dividend limitations . . . . 1.956-1(b)(1)
. . . earning and profit, treatment of . . . . . 1.956-1(b)(3)
. . . general rule . . . . 1.956-1(c)(1)
. . . generally . . . . 1.956-1(a)
. . . investments of earnings in U.S. property, treatment of certain . . . . 1.956-1T(b)(4)

References are to Reg. § numbers

Controlled corporations —Cont'd
. *increase in earnings invested in U.S. property — Cont'd*
. . *shareholder's pro rata share —Cont'd*
. . . nonrecognition transactions, adjusted basis of property acquired in certain ...... 1.956-1T(b)(6)
. . . nonrecourse obligations, treatment of certain .... 1.956-1T(b)(5)
. . . recourse obligations, treatment of certain .... 1.956-1T(b)(5)
. Railroad track maintenance credit .... 1.45G-1(f)
. research expenditures, aggregation 1.41-6
. stock distributions (See subhead distributions of stock and securities)
. transfers to .... 1.351-1 et seq.

Controlled foreign corporations
. adjusted gross foreign base company income, computation of .... 1.954-1(b)
. adjusted gross insurance income, computation of .... 1.954-1(b)
. adjusted net foreign base company income, computation of .... 1.954-1(d)
. adjusted net insurance income, computation of .... 1.954-1(d)
. asset disposition, income or gain from
. . target affiliate consistency .... 1.338-8(h)
. deemed dividend election by shareholder of 1.1291-9
. defined .... 1.904-5(a); 1.957-1
. earnings and profits 1.964-1T
. . foreign tax credit
. . . high withholding tax defined for .... 1.904-7(d)
. . . installment sales .... 1.904-7(c)
. . . look-through rules, application of....... 1.904-7(b)
. . . non-look through pools in post 2002 taxable years .... 1.904-7T(f)
. . . recapture income .... 1.904-7(e)
. . . taxable years beginnings Jan. 1. 2007 .... 1.904-7T(g)
. foreign base company income.............. 1.954-1
. . related person defined for 1.954-1
. foreign personal holding companies (See Foreign personal holding companies)
. foreign tax credit 1.904-5
. . dividends .... 1.904-5(c)(4)
. . earnings and profits, distributions
. . . high withholding tax defined for .... 1.904-7(d)
. . . installment sales .... 1.904-7(c)
. . . look-through rules, application of....... 1.904-7(b)
. . . non-look through pools in post 2002 taxable years .... 1.904-7T(f)
. . . recapture income .... 1.904-7(e)
. . . taxable years beginnings Jan. 1. 2007 .... 1.904-7T(g)
. . high withholding tax interest .... 1.904-5(f)
. . interest payments................. 1.904-5(c)(2)

Controlled foreign corporations —Cont'd
. *foreign tax credit—Cont'd*
. . look-through rules 1.904-5; 1.904-5T
. . rents and royalties .... 1.904-5(c)(3)
. . subpart F exclusions .... 1.904-5(d)
. . subpart F inclusions................ 1.904-5(c)(1)
. . subpart F income in excess of 70 percent gross income .... 1.904-5(e)
. generally .... 1.883-3T(a)
. income inclusion test 1.883-3
. interest expense, allocation
. . income from sources within or without U.S. 1.861-10; 1.861-10T
. net foreign base company income, computation of .... 1.954-1(c)
. qualified electing fund.................... 1.1291-9
. qualified U.S. person ownership test...... 1.883-3T(b)
. reporting requirements .... 1.883-3; 1.883-3T(d)
. stock ownership test 1.883-3
. Subpart F income 1.952-1
. . look-through rules
. . . exclusions, subpart F .... 1.904-5(d)
. . . inclusions, subpart F............. 1.904-5(c)(1)
. . . income in excess of 70 percent gross income .... 1.904-5(e)
. substantiation of CFC stock ownership...... 1.883-3; 1.883-3T(c)
. trust, creating .... 1.672(f)-2
. underdeveloped countries, investments 1.954-5

Controlled foreign partnerships
. information returns 1.6038-3
. . overlap with section 6031 .... 1.6038-3

Controlled groups
. brother-sister controlled group defined .... 1.1563-1T(a)(3)
. . transitional rule during revision of brother-sister group control group definition ..... 1.1563-1T(d)
. component members defined .... 1.1563-1T(b)(1)
. deferred losses and deductions from sale .. 1.267(f)-1
. defined .... 1.1563-1T et seq.
. excluded members defined .... 1.1563-1T(b)(2)
. loss corporations
. . adjustments to value .... 1.382-8(a)
. . computation of value .... 1.382-8(c)
. . consolidated groups, coordination between .... 1.382-8(f)
. . controlled group loss defined .... 1.382-8(b)
. . information statement .... 1.382-11(a)
. . net operating loss carrybacks and carryovers 1.382-8
. . net unrealized built-in loss.............. 1.382-8(b)
. . reporting requirements .... 1.382-11(a)
. new jobs and targeted jobs credits apportionment 1.53-2

References are to Reg. § numbers

Controlled groups —Cont'd
. parent-subsidiary controlled group defined .... 1.1563-1T(a)(2)
. services, performances of 1.482-2
. successor corporations 1.382-8
. transitional rule during revision of brother-sister group control group definition .... 1.1563-1T(d)

Controlled services transactions
. arm's length transactions; determination of taxable income .... 1.482-9T et seq.

Controlled transfer
. arm's length transactions (See Arm's length transactions)

Conventions
. exempt organizations 1.513-3

Conversion transactions
. netting rule 1.1258-1

Conversions, involuntary (See Involuntary conversions)

Convertible securities
. personal holding companies 1.544-5

Cooperatives
. banks 301.7701-14
. definitions 1.1388-1; 301.7701-14
. enterprise zone facility bonds (See Enterprise zone facility bonds)
. excise tax on dispositions 54.4978-1T
. exemptions, generally 1.1382-7
. farmers .... 1.521-1 et seq.; 1.1381-2; 1.1382-3
. . domestic production activities (See Domestic production activities, subhead agricultural and horticultural cooperatives)
. gain or loss on stock sale 1.1042-1T
. generally .... 1.1381-1 et seq.
. gross income 1.61-5; 1.1382-1; 1.1385-1
. hospital service organizations, exempt ..... 1.501(e)-1
. housing corporations 1.216-1; 1.216-2
. patronage dividends 1.1382-2; 1.1382-6
. payment period for each taxable year 1.1382-4
. pooling arrangements, products marketed under 1.1382-5
. redemption of nonqualified written notices of allocation 1.1383-1

Copyrights
. computer programs, classification of transactions involving 1.861-18
. depreciation .... 1.167(a)-6
. nonresident aliens 1.871-11

Corporate organizations and reorganizations (See Reorganization; Successor corporations)

Corporations
. abatements, credits, and refunds ..... 1.77-1; 1.77-2; 301.6501(g)-1
. accumulating surplus (See Accumulated earnings tax)

Corporations —Cont'd
. acquiring corporations (See Successor corporations)
. acquisition indebtedness
. . annual interest, paid or incurred .... 1.279-5(e)
. . application of Sec. 279(b) 1.279-3
. . banks, special rules for .... 1.279-5(g)
. . defined 1.279-3
. . interest deductibility .... 1.279-1 to 1.279-6
. . lending or finance companies, special rules for .... 1.279-5(g)
. . ratio of debt to equity and projected earnings .... 1.279-5(d)
. . ration of debt to equity .... 1.279-5(f)
. . several corporation, of .... 1.279-5(c)
. additions to tax, additional amounts, and assessable penalties .... 1.6655-1 et seq.; 301.6679-1
. alternative minimum tax (See Alternative minimum tax)
. characteristics of 301.7701-2
. China Trade Act corporations 1.6072-3
. collapsible .... 1.341-1 to 1.341-6
. commodity credit corporation loans 1.77-1; 1.77-2
. consolidated returns 1.1502-81T; 1.1502-100
. controlled corporations (See Controlled corporations; Controlled foreign corporations)
. development corporations 1.851-6
. DISC (See Domestic international sales corporation)
. distributions (See Distributions by corporations; Dividends)
. dividends (See Dividends)
. domestic (generally)
. . capital gains and losses 1.1248-6
. . definitions 301.7701-5
. . foreign corporations election to be treated as domestic corporation under section 897(i) 1.897-3
. . foreign subsidiary, employ of .... 31.3121(l)-1
. . foreign tax credit 1.902-1; 1.902-1T
. . international sales corporations (See Domestic international sales corporations (DISC))
. export trade corporations .... 1.970-1 to 1.970-3; 1.971-1
. foreign corporations (See Foreign controlled corporations; Foreign corporations)
. freezing estate value, special valuation rules 25.2701-1
. gain or loss based on exchange of SEC order 1.1081-4
. housing corporations 1.216-1
. interest expense, allocation
. . income from sources within or without U.S. 1.861-9T
. investment companies (See Investment companies)
. itemized deductions 1.164-7
. life insurance companies (See Life insurance companies)
. liquidation (See Liquidation)

References are to Reg. § numbers

Corporations —Cont'd
. mutual insurance companies (See Mutual insurance companies other than life, marine, fire, or flood)
. net operating loss (See Net operating loss carrybacks and carryovers)
. personal holding companies (See Personal holding companies)
. personal service corporations 1.280H-1T
. public safety testing corporations ...... 1.501(c)(3)-1
. related corporations 1.304-2; 1.993-5
. reorganizations (See Reorganization)
. returns (See Returns)
. shareholders (See Shareholders)
. short tax year 1.6655-3
. small business corporations (See Small business corporations)
. stock (See Stock)
. stock options (See Stock options)
. subsidiaries (See Subsidiaries)
. successor (See Successor corporations)
. surcharge 1.56-1
. surplus (See Surplus)
. taxability, generally .... 1.11-1 et seq.
. transfer to corporation controlled by transferor 1.351-1
. transportation corporations 1.172-8; 1.863-4

Correlative deductions
. readjustment of tax 1.1312-5; 1.1312-6

Cost maintenance period
. accident and health plans
. . significant reduction of coverage during cost maintenance period 1.420-1

Cost of services plus method
. arm's length transactions; determination of taxable income .... 1.482-9T(e)

Cost recovery (See Recovery deductions)

Cost sharing arrangements
. allocation of costs 1.482-7
. arm's length transactions, consistent with 1.482-7
. classifications for federal tax purposes .... 301.7701-1(c)
. defined 1.482-7
. intangible development costs 1.482-7
. intangible property income 1.936-6
. possession of United States election to use ... 1.936-7
. qualified 1.482-7
. stock-based compensation 1.482-7
. taxable income determination under sec. 482 .... 1.482-2T(e)

Cost-of-living adjustments
. generally 1.912-1

Coupons, redemption cost accounting
. discount coupons 1.451-4; 1.466-1
. premium coupons 1.451-4

Covenant bonds
. generally 1.1451-1; 1.1451-2

Covenants not to compete
. amortization 1.197-2

Creative property (See Intellectual property)

Credit unions
. exempt organizations .... 1.501(c)(14)-1

Credits (See Abatements, credits, and refunds)

Crematorium
. exempt organizations .... 1.501(c)(13)-1

Crewmen
. information returns 301.6050A-1

Criminal investigations
. functions of IRS 601.107
. partnership items .... 301.6231(c)-5

Criminal penalties
. failure to file (See Failure to file tax return or to pay tax)
. failure to produce records 301.7269-1
. federal officers and employees, offenses under revenue laws 301.7214-1
. fraudulent returns, statements, or other documents 301.7207-1

Crops
. insurance proceeds, accounting method 1.451-6
. organizations organized to finance operations .... 1.501(c)(16)-1
. unharvested, sold with land 1.268-1
. . adjusted basis 1.1016-5

Crude oil windfall profit tax 1.6001-1

Cruelty to children or animals, organizations for prevention of
. exemption .... 1.501(c)(3)-1

Cumulative wages
. withholding .... 31.3402(h)(3)-1

Currency
. foreign (See Foreign currency)
. functional (See Functional currency)
. money (See Money)
. nonfunctional
. . recognition and computation of exchange gain or loss 1.988-2

Curtesy (See Dower and curtesy)

Custodial accounts
. pension, profit-sharing, and stock bonus plans .... 1.401(f)-1; 1.401-8
. . minimum distribution requirements
. . . 501(c)(3) organization, account established by .... 1.403(b)-3
. . . public school, account established by ... 1.403(b)-3

Customer-based intangibles
. amortization 1.197-2

References are to Reg. § numbers

Customs Service, United States
. disclosure of return information to . . . 301.6103(l)(14)-1

D

Damages
. Bankruptcy Code 362 or 524 violations
. . administrative costs 301.7430-8
. civil action
. . failure to release lien 301.7432-1
. . unauthorized collection 301.7433-1
. generally 301.6673-1
. recovery in certain cases 301.7426-2

DASTM (See Dollar Approximate Separate Transactions Method (DASTM))

Day
. backup withholding, defined for . . . . 31.3406(h)-1

De minimis fringe benefits
. exemptions 1.132-6; 1.132-6T

De minimis rules
. deposit rules for withheld income taxes . . 31.6302-1(f)

Dealers
. generally 1.75-1; 1.471-5; 1.1236-1
. installment reporting . . . . 1.453A-1 to 1.453A-3
. securities (See Securities dealers)

Death and death benefits
. exemptions 1.101-2
. joint returns 1.6013-3
. life insurance contracts, defined for 1.7702-2
. partners and partnerships 1.753-1

Death taxes
. credit
. . foreign death taxes (See subhead foreign death taxes credit)
. . recovery of taxes claimed as 20.2016-1
. . remainders 20.2015-1
. foreign death taxes credit
. . convention, cases involving 20.2014-4
. . generally 20.2014-1
. . limitations
. . . deduction allowed, when 20.2014-7
. . . first 20.2014-2
. . . period of 20.2014-6
. . . second 20.2014-3
. . proof of credit 20.2014-5
. recovery of taxes claimed as credit 20.2016-1
. remainders, credit for taxes on 20.2015-1
. state death taxes (See State and local taxes)

Debt
. bad (See Bad debts)
. generally (See Indebtedness)

Debt instruments (See also specific subject)
. currency other than U.S. dollars, in

Debt instruments (See also specific subject) — Cont'd
. *currency other than U.S. dollars, in —Cont'd*
. . accounting methods interest . . . . 1.446-2(g)
. . OID inclusion in income . . . . 1.1272-1(h)
. foreign currency
. . nonfunctional currency contingent payment debt instruments 1.988-6
. inflation-indexed (See Inflation-indexed debt instruments)
. modifications of (See Modifications of debt instruments)

Debt issuance costs
. allocation 1.446-5

Debt-financed property
. exempt organizations . . . . 1.514(b)-1
. partnerships, allocation . . . . 1.514(c)-2

Decedents
. estates (See Estates and trusts)
. interest of decedent, property which had . . . 20.2033-1
. marital deduction in respect of (See Marital deduction)
. nonresident aliens (See Nonresident aliens)
. passed from decedent
. . defined . . . . 20.2056(c)-1
. . person other than surviving spouse, to . . . . 20.2056(c)-3
. . surviving spouse, to . . . . 20.2056(c)-2
. return requirements (See Estates and trusts)
. returns of trust or part of trust owned by decedent, time for filing 1.6072-1
. taxes (See Death taxes)
. transfers taking effect at death 20.2037-1
. trust owned by
. . time for filing returns 1.6072-1
. . TIN following death, obtaining 301.6109-1

Deceit (See Fraud and deceit)

Declaratory judgments
. Tax Court . . . . 1.7476-1 to 1.7476-3; 301.7476-1; 301.7477-1

Declining balance method of depreciation
. application . . . . 1.167(b)-2
. change in . . . . 1.167(e)-1(b)
. limitations and use . . . . 1.167(c)-1

Deductions (See also particular item)
. accounting methods . . . . 1.461-1 et seq.
. business expenses, generally . . . . 1.162-1 et seq.
. capital gains and losses 1.1202-1
. charitable contributions (See Charitable contributions)
. charitable gifts 25.2524-1
. contested liabilities 1.461-2
. deferred from intercompany transaction . . . . 1.267(f)-1
. depreciation (See Depreciation)
. disallowance of items . . . . 1.261-1 et seq.

References are to Reg. § numbers

Deductions (See also particular item) —Cont'd
. dividends .... 1.561-1 et seq.
. double deductions or credits .... 1.818-7; 1.1312-1 to 1.1312-4
. education loans, payments of interest on qualified
. . Dec. 31, 2001, after 1.221-1
. . Jan. 1,2002, before 1.221-2
. fine or penalty, allowance for 1.162-21
. foreign corporations (See Foreign corporations)
. foreign personal holding companies 1.511-3
. foreign persons 1.1441-9
. generally .... 1.164-1 to 1.164-8; 1.275-1
. interest 1.163-1
. kickbacks 1.162-18
. marital (See Marital deduction)
. Medicaid and Medicare kickbacks and rebates 1.162-18
. moving expenses 1.217-2
. mutual insurance companies 1.832-2; 1.832-5
. nonresident aliens 1.873-1T; 1.874-1
. $1,000,000 remuneration, employees in excess of 1.162-27
. pass-thru entities section 199 deduction 1.199-5; 1.1312-6
. rebates 1.162-18
. recovery deductions .... 1.280F-1T; 1.280F-1T to 1.280F-3T
. stock, decline in valuation of 1.165-4
. taxes, generally .... 1.164-1 to 1.164-8
. worthless business debts 1.166-9

Defense programs
. natural resources 1.621-1

Deferral of tax liability
. surcharge 1.56A-2

Deferred annuity contracts
. generally .... 1.412(b)-2; 1.818-3

Deferred compensation
. accounting methods (See Accounting methods)
. accruals and allocations
. . restriction and valuation of .... 1.411(a)-11
. cash-out limits .... 1.401(a)(4)-4
. collection of income tax and withholding on pensions, annuities, and other deferred income 35.3405-1
. compensation defined .... 1.414(s)-1
. distributions
. . restriction and valuation of .... 1.411(a)-11
. gap agreements .... 31.3121(v)(2)-2
. independent contractors .... 1.404(d)-1T
. information returns 301.6058-1
. in-kind distributions; section 1.411(d)-4 protected benefits
. . defined contribution plan .... 1.411(d)-4
. methods of deferring receipt of compensation .... 1.404(b)-1T

Deferred compensation —Cont'd
. minimum age .... 1.410(a)-3T
. mortality tables .... 1.412(l)(7)-1
. nondiscriminatory availability of benefits .... 1.401(a)(4)-4
. nonqualified plans
. . amounts deferred under .... 31.3121(v)(2)-1; 31.3306(r)(2)-1
. notice
. . electronic medium, use of .... 1.401(a)-21
. pensions (See Pension, profit-sharing, and stock bonus plans)
. rollover distributions .... 1.403(b)-2
. service conditions .... 1.410(a)-3T

Deferred exchanges
. gain or loss .... 1.1031(b)-2
. sales and transfers .... 1.1031(k)-1

Deferred expenditures
. corporate organizations and reorganizations .... 1.381(c)(10)-1

Deferred income
. sec. 3405, under
. . withholding of tax .... 31.6011(a)-4(b)(4)

Deferred losses
. controlled groups .... 1.267(f)-1

Deferred payments
. accounting methods .... 1.453-4 to 1.453-6

Deficiency and deficiency procedures
. defined 301.6211-1
. estate tax 20.6161-2
. . bond, payment with 20.6165-1
. extension of time for payment .. 1.6161-1; 301.6165-1
. generally .... 301.6211-1 et seq.
. gift tax 25.6161-1
. . bond, payment with 25.6165-1
. notice, generally .... 301.6212-1; 301.6503(a)-1
. partnership .... 301.6221-1 to 301.6303-1
. readjustment of tax .... 1.1311(b)-3
. Tax Court 301.6213-1; 301.6215-1

Deficiency distributions
. domestic international sales corporations 1.992-3
. requirements for 1.963-6

Deficiency dividends
. generally .... 1.381(c)(25)-1; 1.547-1 et seq.; 1.860-1; 1.860-2

Defined benefit plans (See Pension, profit-sharing, and stock bonus plans; specific subject heading)

Defined contribution plans (See Pension, profit-sharing, and stock bonus plans; specific subject heading)

Definitions
. rules of general application ..... 1.141-1 et seq. (See also specific subject heading)

References are to Reg. § numbers

Delinquency
. successor corporations . . . . 1.381(c)(12)-1
Demolition of buildings
. itemized deductions 1.165-3; 1.280B-1
Dental expenses
. itemized deductions 1.213-1
Department of Agriculture (See Agriculture, Department of)
Department of Commerce (See Commerce, Department of)
Department of Justice (See Justice, Department of)
Dependency exemption (See Children and dependents)
Dependents and dependent care (See Children and dependents)
Depletion
. basis for gain or loss 1.1016-3; 1.1016-4
. minerals, mines, and mining . . . . 1.381(c)(18)-1
. natural resources . . . . 1.611-1; 1.611-4; 1.612-1; 1.612-3; 1.613A-1 et seq.; 1.613-1; 1.613-2; 1.613-6; 1.1502-44
. successor corporations . . . . 1.381(c)(18)-1
Depositaries of government
. backup withholding . . . . 31.6302(c)-3; 31.6302-3
. calendar months beginning after Dec. 31, 1980, but before Jan. 1, 1993 . . . . 31.6302(c)-1(a)
. collection of tax . . . 1.6302-1 to 1.6302-3; 31.6302(c)-1
. . nonpayroll payments made after December 31, 1993 . . . . 31.6302-4
. electronic fund transfers
. . FICA, deposit rules for withheld income taxes 31.6302-1
. . generally . . . . 40.6302(c)-1
. . made by . . . . 31.6302(c)-3(c)
. . nonresident alien income and estimated income taxes 1.6302-2
. . September deposits, persons not required to use . . . . 40.6302(c)-2
. . tax-exempt organization income and estimated income taxes 1.6302-1
. . voluntary payments . . . . 31.6302-1(j)
. failure to deposit
. . abatement of penalty 301.6656-1
. FICA, deposit rules for withheld income taxes . . . . 31.6302(c)-3; 31.6302-1
. . banking days . . . . 31.6302-1(c)(4)
. . employment taxes defined . . . . 31.6302-1(e)
. . interest free adjustments . . . . 31.6302-1(c)(7)
. . monthly deposit rules . . . . 31.6302-1(c)(1)
. . monthly depositor status, determination . . . . 31.6302-1(b)(2)
. . one day deposit rules . . . . 31.6302-1(c)(3)
. . semi-weekly deposit rules . . . . 31.6302-1(c)(2)
. . semi-weekly depositor status, determination . . . . 31.6302-1(b)(3)
Depositaries of government —Cont'd
. foreign corporations, withheld taxes on 1.6302-2
. FTD coupon, made by . . . . 31.6302(c)-3(b)
. general rules for use . . . . 40.6302(c)-1
. generally . . . . 31.6302-0 et seq.
. 9-day rule taxes . . . . 40.6302(c)-1
. nonpayroll payment made after December 31, 1993 . . . . 31.6302-4
. nonresident aliens, withheld taxes on 1.6302-2
. payment of tax . . . . 1.6302-1; 1.6302-2; 1.6361-1; 31.6302(c)-1; 31.6302-4
. payment of tax, backup withholding . . . . . 31.6302(c)-3
. quarterly returns . . . . 40.6302(c)-1
. . safe harbor rule modifications . . . . 40.6302(c)-1
. Railroad Retirement Tax Act taxes 31.6302-2
. requirement, general deposit . . . . 40.6302(c)-1
. September deposits
. . amount of deposit . . . . 40.6302(c)-2
. . chapter 33 . . . . 40.6302(c)-3
. . electronic funds transfers, persons not required to use . . . . 40.6302(c)-2
. . special rules . . . . 40.6302(c)-1
. special rules under chapter 33 . . . . 40.6302(c)-3
. tax-exempt organizations 1.6302-1
. 30-day rule taxes . . . . 40.6302(c)-1
. trusts, estimated tax 1.6302-3
Depositors' guaranty fund
. itemized deductions 1.162-13
Deposits
. timely mailing 301.7502-2
Depreciation
. accelerated cost recovery system (ACRS) . . . . . 1.168(k)-1(b) (See Accelerated cost recovery system (ACRS))
. accounting . . . . 1.167(a)-7
. additional first year depreciation deduction (See Additional first year depreciation deduction)
. adjusted current earnings, deduction for . . . . 1.56(g)-1
. basis . . . . 1.167(a)-5; 1.167(g)-1
. . election for reduction of
. . . COD income 1.108-4
. capital gains and losses . . . . 1.1238-1; 1.1239-1; 1.1239-2; 1.1250-1 to 1.1250-5
. . disposition of depreciable property 1.1245-1
. change in method . . . . 1.167(e)-1
. . declining balance method . . . . 1.167(e)-1(b)
. . section 1245 property . . . . 1.167(e)-1(c)
. . section 1250 property . . . . 1.167(e)-1(d)
. class lives and asset depreciation ranges . . . 1.167(a)-11; 1.167(a)-12; 1.167(c)-1; 1.167(m)-1
. computation methods . . . . 1.167(b)-0 et seq.
. corporate distributions and adjustments 1.312-15
. declining balance method
. . application . . . . 1.167(b)-2

References are to Reg. § numbers

Depreciation —Cont'd
. *declining balance method —Cont'd*
. . change in method .... 1.167(e)-1(b)
. . limitations and use .... 1.167(c)-1
. deduction, allowance of .... 1.167(a)-10
. election to expense (See Expensing in lieu of depreciation)
. estates and trusts .... 1.642(e)-1
. expensing in lieu of (See Expensing in lieu of depreciation)
. farmers .... 1.167(a)-6
. general asset accounts .... 1.56(g)-1
. generally ... 1.56(g)-1; 1.167(a)-1 et seq.; 1.167(a)-11
. intangibles .... 1.167(a)-3
. . safe harbor amortization .... 1.167(a)-3(b)
. leased property .... 1.48-4; 1.167(a)-4; 1.168(f)(8)-1T
. life tenants and beneficiaries .... 1.167(h)-1
. mine improvements .... 1.167(i)-1
. obsolescence .... 1.167(a)-9
. patents or copyrights .... 1.167(a)-6
. public utilities .... 1.167(l)-1 to 1.167(l)-4
. recovery (See Recovery deductions)
. rehabilitation expenditures 1.48-11
. retirement-replacement-betterment (RRB) property 1.168-5
. retirements .... 1.167(a)-8
. safe harbor lease information returns ... 1.168(f)(8)-1T
. salvage value .... 1.167(f)-1
. Section 179 property (See Expensing in lieu of depreciation)
. Section 1245 property
. . change in method .... 1.167(e)-1(c)
. Section 1250 property
. . change in method .... 1.167(e)-1(d)
. straight line method .... 1.167(b)-1; 7.57(d)-1
. successor corporations .... 1.381(c)(6)-1
. sum-of-the-years-digits method .... 1.167(b)-3
. tangible property .... 1.167(a)-2
. uniform capitalization rules 1.263A-1
. useful life and rates of depreciation, agreement as to .... 1.167(d)-1

Deregulated public utility property, disposition of
. excess deferred income tax reserve
. . December 21, 2005, after .... 1.168(i)-3(d)
. . generally .... 1.168(i)-3(a)
. . reduction, amount of .... 1.168(i)-3(b)
. . regulation property, application of ... 1.168(i)-3(d)(3)
. . sec. 203(e), application of .... 1.168(i)-3(a)(1)
. . transferee, property that becomes public of the .... 1.168(i)-3(d)(2)

Designees, taxpayer
. return information, disclosure of .... 301.6103(c)-1

Determination letters
. generally 601.201

Determination letters —Cont'd
. public inspection 301.6110-1

Development bonds, industrial (See Industrial development bonds)

Development corporations
. investment companies 1.851-6

Development costs
. generally .... 1.263(c)-1; 1.381(c)(10)-1; 1.616-1; 1.621-1

Diesel and special motor fuels tax
. abatements, credits, and refunds
. . buses, intercity, local or school buses .... 48.6427-2 et seq.
. . claims for credit or refund .... 48.6416(a)-1
. . farm use .... 48.6427-1 et seq.
. . generally 48.4041-13
. . overpayment of tax .... 48.6416(a)-2
. aircraft
. . museums, exemption for sale to or use by 48.4041-14
. . supplies, exemption 48.4041-10
. Alaska 48.4082-5
. alcohol mixture fuels 48.4041-18
. back-up tax 48.4082-4
. boats 48.4041-3
. buses, intercity, local or school buses, credits or payments to purchaser 48.6427-2
. . applicable laws 48.6427-4
. . limitations on 48.6427-6
. . recordkeeping requirements 48.6427-5
. . time for filing claims 48.6427-3
. common tanks 48.4042-2
. compressed natural gas 48.4041-21
. credits or refunds
. . buses, intercity, local or school buses 48.6427-2
. . . applicable laws 48.6427-4
. . . limitations on 48.6427-6
. . . recordkeeping requirements 48.6427-5
. . . time for filing claims 48.6427-3
. . claims .... 48.6416(a)-1
. . . filing of 48.6427-8
. . . fuel taxed after December 31,1993 .... 48.6427-8; 48.6427-9
. . farm use 48.6427-1
. . . applicable laws 48.6427-4
. . . recordkeeping requirements 48.6427-5
. . . time for filing claims 48.6427-3
. . generally 48.4041-13
. . overpayment of tax; credit or refund claims .... 48.6416(a)-1; 48.6416(a)-2
. . ultimate purchaser claims 48.6427-8
. defined prior to and after April 1, 1996 ... 48.4081-1(c)
. definitions 48.4041-8; 48.4082-1
. dual use by propulsion engine 48.4042-2

References are to Reg. § numbers

Diesel and special motor fuels tax —Cont'd
. dyeing requirement 48.4082-1; 48.4082-1T
. . notice requirement 48.4082-2; 48.4082-7T
. . penalty for misuse of dyed fuel 48.6715-1
. educational organizations, exempt retail sales to 48.4041-17
. ethanol fuel
. . generally 48.4041-19
. . partially exempt fuel 48.4041-20
. exempt organizations, exempt retail sales to 48.4041-17
. exemption 48.4082-1; 48.4082-4
. export sales 48.4041-16
. farm use
. . credits or payments to purchaser 48.6427-1
. . . applicable laws 48.6427-4
. . . recordkeeping requirements 48.6427-5
. . . time for filing claims 48.6427-3
. . exemption 48.4041-9
. liquid fuel
. . application of tax 48.4041-6
. . aviation fuel 48.4041-4
. . dual use of taxable liquid fuel 48.4041-7
. methanol fuel 48.4041-19
. motor boats 48.4041-3
. motor vehicles, sale of special motor fuel ... 48.4041-3
. overpayment of tax
. . claims for credit or refund .... 48.6416(a)-1; 48.6416(a)-2
. . exportations causing, evidence required .... 48.6416(b)(2)-4
. . resales causing, evidence determing .... 48.6416(b)(2)-4
. payment of tax, time and place 48.6151-1
. political subdivisions, exemptions for sales to 48.4041-15
. records and reports
. . farm use 48.6427-5
. . intercity, local or school buses 48.6427-5
. states, exemptions for sales to 48.4041-15
. United States, sales by 48.4041-12
. vessels, supplies for, exemption 48.4041-10

Disability benefits
. seizure and levy 301.6334-1
. self-insured medical reimbursement plans, exclusions 1.105-11
. social security taxes 32.1

Disabled persons
. generally .... 1.190-1 to 1.190-3; 7.105-1

Disallowance of deductions
. employee remuneration in excess of $1,000,000 .... 1.162-27
. entertainment, gift, and travel expenses 1.274-1; 1.274-2

Disallowance of deductions —Cont'd
. exempt-interest dividends of RICs 1.265-3
. passive activity losses and credits 1.469-1T
. uniform capitalization rules 1.263A-1

Disasters
. postponement of certain tax-related deadlines 301.7508A-1

Discharge of indebtedness
. adjusted current earnings computation .... 1.56(g)-1(c)
. basis, reduction in 1.1017-1
. COD income 1.108-7T
. . Section 381, under 1.1017-1
. generally 1.61-12; 1.1017-1
. information returns
. . certain entities 1.6050-1T
. . financial entities 1.6050P-1; 1.6050P-1T
. lending money, organization a significant trade or business is 1.6050P-2
. real property business
. . indebtedness in excess of value 1.108-6
. recognized built-in gain or loss 1.1374-4
. reduction of tax attributions, order of 1.108-7T

Discharge of lien (See Liens)

Discharge of property
. liens 301.6325-1

Disclaimed property
. transfers 20.2046-1

Disclosure
. Agriculture Department officers and employees, return information to .... 301.6103(j)(5)-1
. . census of agriculture, conducting ... 301.6103(j)(5)-1
. Commerce Department officers and employees, return information to .... 301.6103(j)(1)-1
. confidential transactions defined 1.6011-4
. contractually protected transactions 1.6011-4
. Customs Service, to U.S. .... 301.6103(l)(14)-1
. Economic Analysis Bureau, return information to .... 301.6103(j)(1)-1
. individual retirement arrangements 1.408-6
. IRS records or information
. . adverse ruling with respect to refusal to disclose, procedure in the event of .... 301.9000-4(g)
. . benefit or separate privilege ...... 301.9000 et seq.
. . Bivens matters .... 301.9000-4(d)
. . congressional matters .... 301.9000-4(e)
. . creation of .... 301.9000-4(i)
. . defined 301.9000-1
. . examples 301.9000-6
. . FTCA matters .... 301.9000-4(d)
. . government contract matters .... 301.9000-4(d)
. . labor relations matters .... 301.9000-4(d)
. . nonauthorization, situations for 301.9000-2
. . notification of disclosure officer ...... 301.9000-4(b)

References are to Reg. § numbers

Disclosure —Cont'd
. *IRS records or information —Cont'd*
. . opposition to a demand .... 301.9000-4(f)
. . personnel matters .... 301.9000-4(d)
. . request or demand procedure 301.9000-4
. . responding, considerations in 301.9000-2
. . safeguard tax returns or information, failure to .... 301.6103(p)(4)-1T
. . testimony authorizations 301.9000-3
. . U.S. Tax court request or demand procedure .... 301.9000-4(c)
. . waiver of written statement requirements for non-IRS matters .... 301.9000-5(b)
. . written statement requirements for non-IRS matters .... 301.9000-5(a)
. listed transactions (See Listed transactions)
. prohibited tax shelter transaction disclosure (See Prohibited tax shelter transaction disclosure)
. quid pro quo contributions 1.6115-1
. Reportable Transaction Disclosure Statement 1.6011-4
. . rulings and protective disclosures 1.6011-4T
. reportable transactions 301.6111-3
. returns and return information (See Returns under disclosure subheads)
. safeguard tax returns or information, failure to .... 301.6103(p)(4)-1T
. taxpayer identity information .... 301.6103(m)-1
. TIN, waiver of prohibition to disclose
. . acceptance agent................... 301.6109-1
. treaty-based return positions, failure to disclose 301.6712-1

Discount coupons
. redemption of, accounting method for 1.466-1

Discounts
. employee, exemption for 1.132-3; 1.132-3T

Discovery of liability and enforcement of title
. books and witnesses 301.7602-1
. canvass of districts for taxable persons and objects 301.7601-1
. church tax inquiries and examinations 301.7611-1
. entry of premises for examination of taxable objects 301.7606-1
. examination and inspection .... 301.7601-1 et seq.
. Internal Revenue districts.................. 301.7621-1
. intervene 301.7609-3
. oaths 301.7622-1
. possessions, coordinating of U.S. and Guam individual income taxes 301.7654-1
. rewards for information relating to violation of Internal Revenue laws 301.7623-1
. statutes of limitations 301.7609-5
. summons 301.7602-1; 301.7603-1; 301.7604-1; 301.7609-1; 301.7609-4
. third-party recordkeepers 301.7609-2

Discovery of liability and enforcement of title — Cont'd
. witness fees.......................... 301.7610-1

Discrimination rules
. group term life insurance 1.79-4T
. pension, profit-sharing, and stock bonus plans 1.401-4
. . special rules .... 1.401(a)(5)-1

DISCs (See Domestic international sales corporations)

Disparity in benefits and contributions (See Pension, profit-sharing, and stock bonus plans, subhead permitted disparity)

Disposal facilities
. industrial development bonds used to provide solid waste disposal facilities 17.1

Dispositions
. adjustments 1.52-2
. consolidated returns
. . stock disposition................. 1.1502-28(b)(7)
. . subsidiary disposition or deconsolidation of stock 1.1502-20
. . . disposition or deconsolidation of stock 1.1502-20T
. . . limitations on applicability of 1.1502-20 .... 1.1502-20T
. . . revocation or amendment of prior elections 1.1502-20T
. controlled foreign corporations
. . asset disposition, income or gain from
. . . target affiliate consistency .... 1.338-8(h)
. cooperative, excise tax on 54.4978-1T
. depreciable property
. . basis for gain or loss 1.1245-1
. . capital gains and losses 1.1245-1
. deregulated public utility property
. . excess deferred income tax reserve
. . . December 21, 2005, after .... 1.168(i)-3(d)
. . . generally .... 1.168(i)-3(a)
. . . reduction, amount of .... 1.168(i)-3(b)
. . . regulation property, application of .... 1.168(i)-3(d)(3)
. . . sec. 203(e), application of .... 1.168(i)-3(a)(1)
. . . transferee, property that becomes public of the .... 1.168(i)-3(d)(2)
. DISCs
. . gain on disposition of stock................ 1.995-4
. . previous disposition of DISC stock......... 1.996-4
. donated property, information returns 1.6050L-1
. energy property
. . nuclear decommissioning funds 1.468A-6T
. foreign partnerships, disposition of interest in 1.6046A-1
. foreign partnerships returns

References are to Reg. § numbers

Dispositions —Cont'd
. *foreign partnerships returns —Cont'd*
. . U.S. person disposition or acquiring interest in 1.6046A-1
. foreign sales corporations (FSCs)
. . export property, disposition of........... 1.924(e)-1
. gain or loss
. . coordination of section 1060 with section 1031 .... 1.1031(d)-1T
. . records and reports 1.1081-11
. general asset accounts
. . adjustments on prior dispositions .... 1.168(i)-1(j)
. . disposition of assets from .... 1.168(i)-1(e)
. information returns
. . donated property, disposition of 1.6050L-1
. installment obligations
. . accounting methods, gain or loss.......... 1.453-9
. insufficient consideration 25.2512-8
. investment credit
. . exceptions to disposition and cessation rules 1.47-3
. . Section 38 property, disposition or cessation of 1.47-1; 1.47-2
. . . exception to rules 1.48-3
. life estates
. . disposition of certain 25.2519-1
. . transfers, disposition as................ 25.2519-1
. mining property, gain from 1.617-4
. nonresident aliens, withholding tax at source
. . U.S. real property interests by foreign persons .... 1.1445-1 to 1.1445-7
. nuclear decommissioning funds dispositions or transfers.................................. 1.468A-6T
. ownership change, asset disposition .... 1.168(i)-1(e)
. partnerships, publicly traded
. . withholding
. . . U.S. real property interest, dispositions of 1.1445-8
. pension, profit-sharing, and stock bonus plans
. . minimum coverage requirements after 1993 .... 1.410(b)-2
. recapture .... 1.168(i)-1(g)
. records and reports, gain or loss.......... 1.1081-11
. REITs, withholding
. . U.S. real property interest, dispositions of 1.1445-8
. REMICs, inducement fees
. . residual interest, special rule for disposition of .... 1.446-6(d)
. rental agreements
. . Section 467 agreements 1.467-7
. self-employment income
. . gain or loss from disposition of property .... 1.1402(a)-6
. stock

Dispositions —Cont'd
. *stock —Cont'd*
. . nonrecognition provision, transactions not qualifying under any other 1.1032-3
. stock of subsidiary, consolidated group deduction on
. . anti-avoidance rules .. 1.337(d)-2(e); 1.337(d)-2T(e)
. . investment adjustments............. 1.337(d)-2(f); 1.337(d)-2T(f)
. . loss limitation window period .... 1.337(d)-2; 1.337(d)-2T
. . . basis reduction on deconsolidation .... 1.337(d)-2(b); 1.337(d)-2T(b)
. . . loss general rule .... 1.337(d)-2(c); 1.337(d)-2T(c)
. . . netting .... 1.337(d)-2; 1.337(d)-2T
. . successors .... 1.337(d)-2(d); 1.337(d)-2T(d)
. stock of subsidiary, disposition or deconsolidation
. . limitations of the applicability of 1.1502-20 .... 1.1502-20T
. . subsidiary stock, disposition or deconsolidation 1.1502-20T
. stock options
. . disqualifying dispositions................. 1.421-2
. . nonrecognition provision, transactions not qualifying under any other 1.1032-3
. . statutory
. . . disposition of stock 1.424-1
. surcharges
. . acquisitions and dispositions 1.52-2
. targeted jobs credit adjustment for acquisitions and dispositions.......................... 1.52-2
. triangular reorganization
. . stock of controlling corporation........... 1.1032-2
. withholding taxes
. . publicly traded partnerships
. . . U.S. real property interest, dispositions of 1.1445-8
. . real estate investment trusts
. . . U.S. real property interests, dispositions of 1.1445-8

Disputed ownership funds
. defined .... 1.468B-9(b)
. distributions to claimants other than transferor-claimants .... 1.468B-9(f)
. taxation of .... 1.468B-9(c)
. transferor-claimants rules.............. 1.468B-9(d)
. transfers of property other than cash, statements to fund and IRS concerning............ 1.468B-9(g)

Dissolution (See also Liquidation)
. information returns 301.6043-1

Distraint (See Seizure of property)

Distributions
. corporate distributions (See Distributions by corporations)
. deficiency distributions 1.963-6
. DISCs..................................... 1.995-3

References are to Reg. § numbers

Distributions —Cont'd
. excise taxes . . . 53.4942(a)-1 to 53.4942(b)-3
. life insurance companies . . . 1.809-8; 1.815-1 et seq.
. life insurance endowments or annuities . . . 1.72(e)-1T
. liquidation
. . gain or loss by shareholder . . . 1.331-1(b)
. . gain or loss recognition by shareholder . . . 1.367(e)-2
. . recharacterization . . . 1.331-1(c)
. . reporting requirements . . . 1.331-1(d)
. mutual savings banks . . . 1.593-10
. partners and partnerships (See Partners and Partnerships)
. pension, profit-sharing, and stock bonus plans (See Pension, profit-sharing, and stock bonus plans)
. records and reports
. . Commission orders, corporations subject to . . . 1.1081-11(b)
. . holders of stock or securities, significant . . . 1.1081-11(a)
. . publicly traded stock defined . . . 1.1081-11(d)
. . significant holder defined . . . 1.1081-11(d)
. . substantiation information, retaining . . . 1.1081-11(e)
. . system groups, sales by members of . . . 1.1081-11(c)
. stock and stock rights (See Stock)
. withholding taxes, special rules for . . . 1.1445-5

Distributions by corporation
. specified transfers of property
. . active conduct of a trade or business outside the United States . . . 1.36(a)-2T(b)(1)

Distributions by corporations
. active conduct of a trade or business, property for use in the . . . 1.367(a)-2T
. . active conduct of a trade or business outside the United States . . . 1.36(a)-2T(b)
. . . active conduct . . . 1.36(a)-2T(b)(3)
. . . outside of the United States . . . 1.36(a)-2T(b)(4)
. . . trade or business . . . 1.36(a)-2T(b)(2)
. . . use in the trade or business . . . 1.36(a)-2T(b)(5)
. . generally . . . 1.36(a)-2T(a)
. . May 2, 2006, transfers occurring on or after . . . 1.36(a)-2T(e)
. . . effective date . . . 1.36(a)-2T(e)(2)
. . . expiration date . . . 1.36(a)-2T(e)(3)
. . . general rule . . . 1.36(a)-2T(e)(1)
. . property transferred by transferee corporation . . . 1.36(a)-2T(c)
. . . exception . . . 1.36(a)-2T(c)(2)
. . . general rule . . . 1.36(a)-2T(c)(1)
. . transitional rule . . . 1.36(a)-2T(d)
. adjusted basis
. . target assets, allocation of adjusted grossed-up basis among . . . 1.338-8(h)
. adjustment to earnings and profits . . . 1.312-1
. . examples . . . 1.312-4

Distributions by corporations —Cont'd
. constructive ownership of stock . . . 1.316-1 to 1.318-4
. depreciated property in the U.S. . . . 1.367(a)-4T(b)
. . effective date . . . 1.367(a)-4T(b)(5)
. . generally . . . 1.367(a)-4T(b)(1)
. . property used within and without the U.S. . . . 1.367(a)-4T(b)(3)
. . U.S. depreciated property . . . 1.367(a)-4T(b)(2)
. depreciation on earnings and profits . . . 1.312-15
. DISCs (See subhead, domestic international sales corporations)
. disproportionate distributions . . . 1.305-3
. dividends . . . 1.316-1
. domestic international sales corporations . . . 1.992-3; 1.993-2; 1.995-1 to 1.995-3; 1.995-2; 1.996-1
. earnings and profits . . . 1.312-1; 1.312-6 to 1.312.15
. effective date . . . 1.367(a)-4T(i); 1.367(a)-4T(i)(1)
. estates, trusts, and options . . . 1.318-3
. exchange . . . 1.351-2
. . records to be kept and information to be held
. . . publicly traded stock defined . . . 1.351-3(d)
. . . significant transferor . . . 1.351-3(a)
. . . significant transferor defined . . . 1.351-3(d)
. . . substantiation information . . . 1.351-3(e)
. . . transferee corporation . . . 1.351-3(b)
. . . transferee corporation exceptions . . . 1.351-3(c)
. expiration date . . . 1.367(a)-4T(i)(2)
. fair market value date . . . 1.301-1
. foreign currency . . . 1.367(a)-5T(d)
. . exception for certain obligations . . . 1.367(a)-5T(d)(2)
. . generally . . . 1.367(a)-5T(d)(1)
. . limitation of gain required to be recognized . . . 1.367(a)-5T(d)(3)
. gain or loss recognition . . . 1.897-5T
. . foreign corporation, corporation distribution to . . . 1.367(e)-2
. gain recognition agreement requirements . . 1.367(a)-8
. generally . . . 1.301-1 et seq.; 1.355-3; 1.367(a)-4T(a); 1.367(b)-2 to 1.367(b)-13
. iInsurance company elections under section 338 . . . 1.338-11
. . adjusted grossed-up basis (AGUB) . . . 1.338-11(b)
. . aggregate deemed sale price (ADSP) . . . 1.338-11(b)
. . assumption reinsurance principles . . . 1.338-11(c)
. . new target election for retroactive application . . . 1.338-i-1(c)
. . old target election for retroactive application . . . 1.338-i-1(c)
. . policyholders surplus account, effect on . . . 1.338-11(g)
. . reserve increases by new target after deemed asset sale . . . 1.338-11(d); 1.338-11(d)T
. . Sec. 846(e) election, effect on . . . 1.338-11T(e)
. . Sec. 847 special estimated payments . . . 1.338-11(h)

References are to Reg. § numbers

Distributions by corporations —Cont'd
. *iInsurance company elections under section 338—Cont'd*
. . Sec. 848, old target capitalization under .... 1.338-11(f)
. income, subsequent treatment of amounts attributed or included in .... 1.367(b)-12
. installment obligations .... 1.367(a)-5T(c)
. intangible property .... 1.367(a)-5T(e)
. inventory .... 1.367(a)-5T(b)
. inventory assets 1.312-2
. leased, property to be .... 1.367(a)-4T(c)
. . aircraft and vessels leased in foreign commerce .... 1.367(a)-4T(c)(3)
. . de minimis leasing by transferee .. 1.367(a)-4T(c)(2)
. . leasing business of transferee .... 1.367(a)-4T(c)(1)
. leased tangible property .... 1.367(a)-5T(f)
. . leased by the transferee to third persons, property that will be leased .... 1.367(a)-5T(f)(2)
. . not be leased by the transferee to third persons, property that will .... 1.367(a)-5T(f)(1)
. . vessels and aircraft that will be leased by the transferee to third persons .... 1.367(a)-5T(f)(3)(i)
. liabilities 1.312-3
. loan proceed distributions guaranteed by United States 1.312-12
. money 1.301-1; 1.305-2
. oil and gas working interests .... 1.367(a)-4T(e)
. . active use of working interest ..... 1.367(a)-4T(e)(2)
. . generally .... 1.367(a)-4T(e)(1)
. . other applicable rules .... 1.367(a)-4T(e)(4)
. . start-up operations .... 1.367(a)-4T(e)(3)
. partial liquidation and certain redemptions 1.312-5
. preferred stock distributions .... 1.305-4 to 1.305-6
. property 1.301-1
. . regardless of use in trade or business .... 1.367(a)-5T; 1.367(a)-5T(a)
. property to be sold .... 1.367(a)-4T(d)
. recognition of gain 1.355-6
. . disqualified stock 1.355-6
. redemptions .... 1.302-2 to 1.302-4
. related corporation, acquisition by 1.304-2
. relationship to other sections .... 1.367(a)-4T(g)
. S corporations 1.1368-1; 1.1368-3
. Section 338, elections under
. . adjusted grossed-up basis 1.338-5
. . . allocation 1.338-6
. . . allocation of redetermined 1.338-7
. . . asset and stock consistency 1.338-8
. . . combined return 1.338-10
. . . insurance companies .... 1.338-11(b)
. . . nuclear decommissioning funds 1.338-6
. . . returns, filing of 1.338-10
. . aggregate deemed sale price
. . . allocation 1.338-6

Distributions by corporations —Cont'd
. *Section 338, elections under —Cont'd*
. . *aggregate deemed sale price —Cont'd*
. . . allocation of redetermined 1.338-7
. . . determination of 1.338-4
. . . insurance companies .... 1.338-11(b)
. . assumption reinsurance principles
. . . insurance companies .... 1.338-11(c)
. . basis of acquired assets .... 1.338-8(d)
. . consistency, asset and stock 1.338-8
. . deemed asset sale 1.338-4
. . deemed transactions 1.338-1
. . definitions 1.338-2
. . DISCs 1.338-2
. . dividends .... 1.338-9(c)
. . foreign corporations 1.338-2
. . foreign targets .... 1.338-9(b)
. . gain from disposition .... 1.338-8(c)
. . insurance companies (See subhead insurance companies)
. . international aspects 1.338-9
. . new target, liabilities of 1.338-5
. . nomenclature 1.338-2
. . old target, liabilities of 1.338-4
. . post-acquisition events, effect of 1.338-3
. . qualified stock purchases, rules relating to .. 1.338-3
. . target treatment under IRC 1.338-1; 1.338-1T
. Section 338(h)(10), elections under
. . deemed asset sale and liquidation ... 1.338(h)(10)-1
. special rules applicable to specified transfers of property .... 1.367(a)-4T
. . compulsory transfers .... 1.367(a)-4T(f)
. split-dollar life insurance arrangement ..... 1.301-1(q)
. stock and securities
. . controlled corporations .... 1.355-1 to 1.355-7
. . generally .... 1.305-4 to 1.306-3
. . nonqualified preferred stock, "other property " status of 1.356-6
. . Section 306 stock defined 1.306-3
. subsidiary, acquisition by 1.304-3
. target affiliates
. . controlled foreign corporations .... 1.338-8(h)
. termination of shareholder's interests 1.302-4
. transactions treated as 1.301-1
. transfers of certain property to FCSs .. 1.367(a)-4T(h)
. . exception .... 1.367(a)-4T(h)(2)
. . generally .... 1.367(a)-4T(h)(1)
. U.S. real property holding corporation 1.897-5T

Distributive shares
. partners and partnerships 1.704-1

District directors or other Internal Revenue officers
. definitions 301.7701-10

References are to Reg. § numbers

District of Columbia
. classification as state for federal tax purpose ....301.7701-1(e)

Dividends 18.1371-1
. accumulated earnings tax 1.563-1
. affiliated group distributions 1.562-3
. backup withholding . . . 1.6042-2 to 1.6042-5; 1.6044-2; 1.6044-5; 31.3406(b)(2)-4; 35a.3406-2; 35a.9999-1 to 35a.9999-5
. capital gains and losses ....1.1244(d)-3
. carryover 1.564-1
. consent dividends (See Consent dividends)
. consolidated dividends paid deduction 1.1502-43; 1.1502-43T
. consolidated returns 1.1502-26
. corporate distributions and adjustments .... 1.302-2 to 1.302-4; 1.305-2 to 1.305-8; 1.316-1
. corporate organizations and reorganizations .... 1.381(c)(25)-1
. deductions
. . dividend paid deduction, allowable......... 1.562-1
. . generally ....1.561-1 et seq.
. deficiency dividends .... 1.381(c)(25)-1; 1.547-2; 1.860-1; 1.860-2
. dividends considered as paid on last day of taxable year 1.563-3
. dividends-received deduction .... 1.56(g)-1(d)
. domestic corporations 1.861-3
. estates and trusts . . 1.643(a)-4; 1.643(a)-7; 1.643(b)-2
. exclusions 1.120-1
. exempt-interest dividends of RICs 1.265-3
. exemptions 1.103-2; 1.265-3
. foreign corporations 1.864-3; 1.960-2
. foreign sales corporations (FSC)........ 1.56(g)-1(d)
. generally ....1.561-1 et seq.
. gross income 1.61-9
. information returns ... 1.6042-1 to 1.6042-4; 1.6044-1 to 1.6044-5; 301.6042-1
. intercompany dividends, loss deduction ....1.1502-26(b)
. interest ....35a.9999-1 to 35a.9999-5
. investment companies 1.854-1; 1.855-1
. itemized deductions ..... 1.243-1 to 1.247-1; 1.265-3
. life insurance companies . . 1.811-2; 1.812-1; 1.823-2; 1.823-5
. limitations...............................1.565-2
. mutual insurance companies 1.823-2; 1.823-5
. mutual savings banks 1.591-1; 1.596-1
. patronage dividends (See Patronage dividends)
. pension, profit-sharing, and stock bonus plans ....1.404(k)-1T
. . disallowance of deduction on ESOP reacquisition payments.......................... 1.404(k)-3
. personal holding companies 1.547-2; 1.547.4; 1.563-2

Dividends—Cont'd
. preferential dividends 1.562-2
. preferred stock dividends, itemized deductions 1.244-1; 1.244-2
. public utilities............................ 1.247-1
. real estate investment trusts ..... 1.858-1; 1.860-1 to 1.860-4
. redemption not taxable as 1.302-2
. reporting, subject to 1.6042-3
. securities lending transactions.............. 1.861-3
. self-employment income ....1.1402(a)-5
. time considered paid 1.561-2
. United States, income from sources within or without 1.861-3

Dividends paid deduction
. dividend carryover .... 1.381(c)(14)-1
. public utilities............................ 1.247-1

Dividends received deduction
. holding period for stock 1.246-5

Divorce
. alimony (See Alimony or separate maintenance)
. transfers incident to, gain or loss on 1.1041-1T

Documents
. last-known address defined for 301.6212-2
. timely mailing as timely filing 301.7502-1

Dollar Approximate Separate Transactions Method (DASTM)
. foreign tax credit, gain or loss .... 1.904-4(j)
. functional currency
. . qualified business units (QBUs) 1.985-7

Dollar-value method of pricing
. LIFO inventories 1.472-8

Domestic building and loan associations
. distributions to shareholders 1.593-7
. mutual savings banks...................... 1.593-7

Domestic corporations (See Corporations)

Domestic international sales corporations (DISCs)
. basis.......................... 1.996-5; 1.1014-9
. carrybacks or carryovers 1.996-7; 1.996-8
. deficiency distributions 1.992-3
. definitions .... 1.993-1 to 1.993-7
. distributions .... 1.992-3; 1.993-2; 1.995-1 to 1.995-3; 1.995-2; 1.996-1
. earned income of U.S. citizens 1.921-1T
. earning and profits 1.996-3
. export property .... 1.993-1 to 1.993-3
. export receipts............................ 1.993-1
. failure to file 301.6686-1
. film rents 1.992-4
. gain on disposition of stock 1.995-4
. generally .... 1.991-1 et seq.
. gross receipts 1.993-6
. income from sources within or without U.S.

References are to Reg. § numbers

Domestic international sales corporations (DISCs) —Cont'd
. *income from sources within or without U.S. —Cont'd*
. . interest expense, allocation .... 1.861-12T(h)
. intercompany pricing rules 1.994-1
. losses 1.996-2
. marginal costing rules 1.994-2
. military property 1.995-6
. previous disposition of DISC stock 1.996-4
. producer's loans 1.993-4; 1.995-5
. qualified export assets 1.993-2
. qualified export receipts 1.993-1
. related foreign export corporation 1.993-5
. requirements 1.992-1
. returns 1.6011-2; 301.6686-1
. shareholders, taxation of income to 1.995-1
. termination 1.921-1T
. transitional rules 1.921-1T
. United States, defined 1.993-7

Domestic iron ore
. generally 1.272-1; 1.631-3

Domestic production activities
. adjusted gross income, taxable income and .... 1.199-1(b)
. agricultural and horticultural cooperatives
. . double counting .... 1.199-6(l)
. . exclusive nature of section 199 deduction .... 1.199-6(k)
. . generally .... 1.199-6(a)
. . marketing cooperative, special rules for .. 1.199-6(d)
. . passthrough of section 199 deduction, additional rules .... 1.199-6(h)
. . qualified payment defined .... 1.199-6(e)
. . recapture of section 199 deduction ...... 1.199-6(j)
. . section 1382 deduction, denial of .... 1.199-6(b)
. . specified agricultural or horticultural cooperative defined .... 1.199-6(f)
. . taxable income, determination of .... 1.199-6(c)
. . W-2 wages .... 1.199-6(h)
. . written notice to patrons .... 1.199-6(g)
. allocation of gross receipts .... 1.199-1(d)
. alternative minimum tax, coordination with .... 1.199-8(d)
. disallowed losses or deductions .... 1.199-8(h)
. expanded affiliated groups
. . allocation of deduction .... 1.199-7(c)
. . computation of deduction .... 1.199-7(b)
. . consolidated group, rules for members of same .... 1.199-7(d)
. . deduction corporate affiliated group member for some or all taxable year .... 1.199-7(g)
. . different taxable year, 199 deduction for member with .... 1.199-7(h)
. . generally .... 1.199-7(a)

Domestic production activities —Cont'd
. *expanded affiliated groups —Cont'd*
. . partnership owned by single expanded affiliated group .... 1.199-9(j)
. . portion of year, allocation of income and loss of member for .... 1.199-7(f)
. 52-53 week taxable year, taxpayer with .... 1.199-8(f)
. income attributable to .... 1.199-1(a)
. individuals .... 1.199-8(b)
. multiple year transactions .... 1.199-1(e)
. nonrecognition transactions .... 1.199-8(e)
. pass-thru entities, application of Sec. 199 to
. . attribution of qualified activities .... 1.199-9(h)
. . disposition of an interest in entity, gain or loss from .... 1.199-9(f)
. . generally .... 1.199-9(a)
. . grantor trusts .... 1.199-9(d)
. . in-kind partnership, qualifying .... 1.199-9(i)
. . May 17, 2006, on or before .... 1.199-9(a)
. . non-grantor trusts and estates
. . . allocation among trust or estate and beneficiaries .... 1.199-9(e)(2)
. . . cost allocation .... 1.199-9(e)(1)
. . . W-2 wages, beneficiaries share of .. 1.199-9(e)(3)
. . . W-2 wages, transition percentage rule for .... 1.199-9(e)(4)
. . partnerships
. . . disallowed losses or deductions .... 1.199-9(b)(2)
. . . entity level .... 1.199-9(b)(1)(ii)
. . . in-kind partnership, qualifying .... 1.199-9(i)
. . . partner level .... 1.199-9(b)(1)(i)
. . . single expanded affiliated group, partnership owned by .... 1.199-9(j)
. . . subchapter K, electing out of .... 1.199-9(b)(5)
. . . W-2 wages, partner share of .... 1.199-9(b)(3)
. . . W-2 wages, transition percentage rule for .... 1.199-9(b)(4)
. . S corporations
. . . disallowed losses or deductions .... 1.199-9(c)(2)
. . . entity level .... 1.199-9(c)(1)(ii)
. . . shareholder level .... 1.199-9(c)(1)(i)
. . . W-2 wages, shareholder's share of .. 1.199-9(c)(3)
. . . W-2 wages, transition percentage rule for .... 1.199-9(c)(4)
. . single expanded affiliated group, partnership owned by .... 1.199-9(j)
. . Tax Increase Prevention and Reconciliation Act of 2005 .... 1.199-9(a)
. . wage limitations and tiered structures .... 1.199-9(g)
. qualified domestic production activities income .... 1.199-1(c)
. Sec. 481(a) adjustments .... 1.199-8(g)
. taxable income and adjusted gross income .... 1.199-1(b)

References are to Reg. § numbers

Domestic production activities —Cont'd
. trade or businesses, application of 1.199-3 to .... 1.199-8(c)

Domestic production gross receipts
. agricultural and horticultural cooperatives .... 1.199-8(i)(7)
. by the taxpayer defined .... 1.199-3(f)
. computer software .... 1.199-8(i)(4)
. . Tax Increase Prevention and Reconciliation Act of 2005 .... 1.199-8(i)(5)
. construction performed in the United States defined .... 1.199-3(m)
. costs allocable to
. . average annual gross receipts .... 1.199-4(g)
. . charitable contributions .... 1.199-4(d)
. . deductions allocated or apportioned to gross receipts treated as DPGR .... 1.199-4(d)
. . deductions properly allocable to DPGR .... 1.199-4(c)
. . generally .... 1.199-4(a)
. . goods sold .... 1.199-4(b)
. . net operating losses .... 1.199-4(c)
. . pass-thru entities .... 1.199-4(d)
. . research and experimental expenditures .... 1.199-4(d)
. . section 861 allocation method .... 1.199-4(d)
. . simplified deduction method .... 1.199-4(e)
. . small business simplified overall method .... 1.199-4(f)
. . W-2 wages .... 1.199-4(c)
. defined .... 1.199-3(c)
. derived from the lease, rental, license, sale, exchange, or other disposition .... 1.199-3(i)
. . partnership owned by member of a single expanded affiliated group .... 1.199-3(i)(8)
. . qualifying in-kind partnership for taxable year beginning May 17, 2006 .... 1.199-3(i)(7)
. determining .... 1.199-3(d)
. electricity, natural gas, or potable water .... 1.199-3(l)
. engineering and architectural services defined .... 1.199-3(n)
. food and beverage sales .... 1.199-3(o)
. generally .... 1.199-3(a)
. guaranteed payments .... 1.199-3(p)
. in whole or in significant part defined .... 1.199-3(g)
. lease, rental, license, sale, exchange, or other disposition .... 1.199-3(a); 1.199-3(i)
. losses-used to reduce taxable income of expanded affiliated groups .... 1.199-8(i)(6)
. manufactured, produced, grown or extracted defined .... 1.199-3(e)
. non-consolidated EAG members .... 1.199-8(i)(3)
. pass-thru entities .... 1.199-8(i)(2)
. qualified film defined .... 1.199-3(k)
. qualifying production property defined .... 1.199-3(j)
. related persons .... 1.199-3(b)

Domestic production gross receipts —Cont'd
. United States defined .... 1.199-3(h)
. W-2 wages (See W-2 wages)

Domestic services
. withholding .... 31.3401(a)(3)-1
. . wages for domestic services .... 31.6011(a)-4(a)(2)

Domicile (See Residence and domicile)

Donated property (See Charitable contributions; Gifts)

Double deduction or credit
. denial of .... 20.2056(b)-9; 25.2523(h)-1
. generally .... 1.642(g)-1; 1.642(g)-2; 1.818-7; 1.1312-1 to 1.1312-4
. terminal interest property
. . disallowance of deduction .... 20.2055-6; 25.2522(c)-4

Double inclusion of item in gross income
. readjustment of tax 1.1312-1

Dower and curtesy
. interests 20.2034-1

Drilling costs
. capitalization of costs 1.263A-1
. itemized deductions .... 1.263(c)-1

Drought
. livestock sale, deferral of income 1.451-7

Drugs
. clinical testing expenses 1.28-1; 1.280C-3

Dual consolidated loss
. affiliated dual resident defined .... 1.1503(d)-1(b)(10)
. attribution of items .... 1.1503(d)-5 et seq.
. basis adjustments .... 1.1503(d)-5 et seq.
. certification period defined .... 1.1503(d)-1(b)(20)
. consolidated group defined .... 1.1503(d)-1(b)(8)
. defined .... 1.1503(d)-1(b)(5)
. disregarded entity defined .... 1.1503(d)-1(b)(17)
. domestic affiliate
. . limitation on use of 1.1503-2
. domestic affiliate defined .... 1.1503(d)-1(b)(12)
. domestic corporation defined .... 1.1503(d)-1(b)(1)
. domestic owner defined .... 1.1503(d)-1(b)(9)
. domestic use
. . annual certificate reporting requirement .... 1.1503(d)-6(g)
. . consolidated groups, effect on .... 1.1503(d)-4(c)
. . defined .... 1.1503(d)-1(b)(13)
. . election of .... 1.1503(d)-6(d)
. . elimination of loss after certain transactions .... 1.1503(d)-4(d)
. . foreign tax credit limitation, computation of .... 1.1503(d)-4(f)
. . limitations and related operating rules .... 1.1503(d)-4 et seq.
. . limitations rules, exceptions to .... 1.1503(d)-6 et seq.

References are to Reg. § numbers

Dual consolidated loss —Cont'd
. *domestic use —Cont'd*
. . no possibility of foreign use . . . . 1.1503(d)-6(c)
. . offset, loss made available for . . . . 1.1503(d)-2
. . tainted income, denial of use to offset . . . . 1.1503(d)-4(e)
. . triggering events requiring the recapture of dual consolidated loss . . . . 1.1503(d)-6(e)
. . unaffiliated domestic owner . . . . 1.1503(d)-4(c)
. . unaffiliated dual resident corporation . . . . 1.1503(d)-4(c)
. . U.S. and a foreign country, elective agreement in place between . . . . 1.1503(d)-6(b)
. dual resident corporation
. . defined . . . . 1.1503(d)-1(b)(2)
. . income or dual consolidated loss, determination of . . . . 1.1503(d)-5(b)
. elective relief provisions 1.1503-2
. foreign branch separate unit
. . income or dual consolidated loss, determination of . . . . 1.1503(d)-5(c)(2)
. foreign country defined . . . . 1.1503(d)-1(b)(7)
. foreign use
. . available for use . . . . 1.1503(d)-3(b)
. . defined . . . . . . 1.1503(d)-1(b)(14); 1.1503(d)-3(a)(1)
. . exceptions . . . . 1.1503(d)-3(c)
. . indirect use . . . . 1.1503(d)-3(a)(2)
. . mirror legislation rule . . . . 1.1503(d)-3(e)
. . ordering rule for determining . . . . 1.1503(d)-3(d)
. grantor trust defined . . . . 1.1503(d)-1(b)(15)
. hybrid entity defined . . . . 1.1503(d)-1(b)(3)
. hybrid entity separate unit
. . income or dual consolidated loss, determination of . . . . 1.1503(d)-5(c)(3)
. ownership defined . . . . 1.1503(d)-1(b)(19)
. partnership defined . . . . 1.1503(d)-1(b)(18)
. reasonable cause exception . . . . 1.1503(d)-1(c)
. recapture of loss and interest charge . . 1.1503(d)-6(h)
. reporting requirement, annual certificate . . . . 1.1503(d)-6(g)
. separate unit
. . defined . . . . 1.1503(d)-1(b)(4)
. . income or dual consolidated loss, determination of . . . . 1.1503(d)-5(c)
. subject to tax defined . . . . 1.1503(d)-1(b)(6)
. successor-in-interest, limitation on use of . . . 1.1503-2
. transparent entity
. . defined . . . . 1.1503(d)-1(b)(16)
. . income or dual consolidated loss, determination of . . . . 1.1503(d)-5(c)
. triggering event
. . domestic use; requiring the recapture of dual consolidated loss . . . . 1.1503(d)-6(e)
. . exception domestic use limitation . . . . 1.1503(d)-6(d)

Dual consolidated loss —Cont'd
. unaffiliated dual resident corporation defined . . . . 1.1503(d)-1(b)(11)

Due diligence requirements
. tax return preparer
. . earned income credit eligibility 1.6695-2

Dues
. prepaid 1.456-1

Duplication of returns or documents
. generally 301.7513-1; 601.525

Dwellings (See Residence and domicile)

Dyed fuels (See Diesel and special motor fuels tax)

E

Earned income
. credit (See Earned income credit)
. earned abroad by U.S. citizens (See Income earned abroad by U.S. citizens)

Earned income credit
. accumulated earnings credit 1.532-1; 1.535-3; 1.563-1; 1.1502-43; 1.1502-43T
. advance payments, coordination with . . . . 1.32-2(e)
. deficiency as basis for denial 1.32-3
. . subsequent claims 1.32-3
. denial 1.32-3
. generally 1.43-1; 1.43-2
. limitations on credit after December 31, 1978 . . . . 1.32-2(b)
. tax return preparer due diligence requirements 1.6695-2
. U.S. citizens abroad (See Income earned abroad by U.S. citizens)
. withholding 31.3507-1; 31.3507-2

Earnings and profits
. accumulated, tax on (See Accumulated earnings tax)
. adjusted current earnings . . . . 1.56(g)-1 et seq,
. commissions . . . . 31.3402(j)-1
. consolidated returns 1.1502-33; 1.1552-1
. controlled foreign corporations (See Controlled foreign corporations)
. corporate distributions and adjustments . . . . . 1.312-1; 1.312-6 to 1.312-15
. DISCs 1.996-3
. excess profits 301.6105-1
. foreign corporations (See Foreign corporations)
. investment companies 1.852-5
. itemized deductions for activities not engaged in for profit . . . . 1.183-1 to 1.183-4
. real estate investment trusts 1.857-7
. real estate investment trusts non-REIT 1.857-11
. regulated investment companies non-RIC . . . 1.852-12
. surplus, improper accumulation of 1.537-2
. Tax Court 301.7507-5

References are to Reg. § numbers

Eating facilities
. exemptions 1.119-1; 1.132-7; 1.132-7T
Economic Analysis Bureau
. disclosure of return information to .... 301.6103(j)(1)-1
Economic Recovery Tax Act of 1981 (ERTA)
. arbitrage 5c.103-3
. capital expenditures 5c.103-1
. consolidated returns .... 5c.168(f)(8)-11
. industrial development bonds 5c.103-2
. investment tax credit.... 5c.168(f)(8)-7; 5c.168(f)(8)-9
. leases.............. 5c.44F-1; 5c.103-1 to 5c.103-3; 5c.168(f)(8)-1 to 5c.168(f)(8)-10
. recapture .... 5c.168(f)(8)-8
. research expenses 5c.44F-1
Education (See Educational organizations; Schools and educational institutions)
Education loans
. deduction of interest payment on qualified 1.221-2
. . Dec. 31, 2001, after 1.221-1
. . Jan. 1, 2002, after 1.221-2
. information reporting
. . interest payments...................... 1.6050S-3
. information returns 1.6050S-2
. payments of interest on qualified
. . deduction, loans after Dec. 31, 2001 .... 1.221-1
. . deduction, loans before Jan. 1, 2002 .... 1.221-2
. . electronic furnishing of statements...... 31.6050S-4
Education tax credits
. adjustments 1.25A-5
. alien taxpayers 1.25A-1
. calculation and eligibility.................. 1.25A-1
. claimed dependent, expenses paid by 1.25A-5
. definitions concerning...................... 1.25A-2
. dependents 1.25A-1
. election 1.25A-1
. identification requirements 1.25A-1
. limitations, modified adjusted gross income as basis for 1.25A-1
. married taxpayers 1.25A-1
. refund of tuition and expenses 1.25A-5
. third party payment of expenses 1.25A-5
. timing rules 1.25A-5
Educational matters
. information returns 1.6041-3
Educational organizations
. diesel and special motor fuels tax, exemption from 48.4041-17
. domestic services provided by student for college organizations .... 31.3121(b)(2)-1
. nonprofit
. . manufacturers excise taxes, exempt sales 48.4221-6
Educational organizations —Cont'd
. research expenditures funded for taxable years beginning before January 1, 1987 .... 1.41-5A
. services for college organizations by student .... 31.3121(b)(10)-2; 31.3306(c)(10)-2
Effectively connected income
. withholding taxes 1.1441-4
Elderly persons (See Aged persons)
Electing small business corporation
. adjusted basis 1.1016-5
. returns 1.6037-1
. . criminal penalties for failure to file ...... 1.6037-1(d)
. . form 1120-S treatment .... 1.6037-1(c)
. . items to be included in return .... 1.6037-1(a)
. . magnetic media, requirement to use (See Magnetic media)
. . time and place for filing return .... 1.6037-1(b)
Electing small business trusts
. allocation of income 1.1361-1
. allocation of state and local taxes and administration expenses.......................... 1.641(c)-1
. beneficiary, S corporation shareholder treatment as 1.1361-1
. consents 1.1361-1; 1.1362-6
. conversions
. . ESTB to QSST 1.1361-1
. . pro rata share; shareholder trust conversion 1.1377-1
. . QSST to ESBT 1.1361-1
. definitions .... 1.641(c)-1; 1.1361-1
. distributions .... 1.641(c)-1
. effect of election 1.1361-1
. entity status 1.444-4
. generally .... 1.641(c)-1; 1.1361-1
. grantor portion, taxation of .... 1.641(c)-1
. non-S portion, taxation of .... 1.641(c)-1
. pro rata share, allocation of income 1.1377-1
. QSST conversion to 1.1361-1
. revocation of election .... 1.641(c)-1
. S corporation defined for 1.1361-1
. S portion .... 1.641(c)-1
. . exemption of......................... 1.641(c)-1
. . shareholder treatment of beneficiary 1.1361-1
. . taxation of .... 1.641(c)-1
. termination of election .... 1.641(c)-1
. termination of entire interest 1.1377-1
Election or choice (See also specific subject heading)
. alternate valuation, election of special use 20.2032A-8
. automatic extensions 301.9100-2
. capital gains and losses .... 1.1234-1 to 1.1234-3
. closely-held business, extension of time for 20.6166-1

References are to Reg. § numbers

Election or choice (See also specific subject heading) —Cont'd
. Deficit Reduction Act of 1984, elections under 301.9100-6T
. electronic medium, use of
. . pension, profit-sharing, and stock bonus plans .... 1.401(a)-21
. ERTA, elections under 301.9100-4T
. expensing in lieu of depreciation ... 1.179-1 to 1.179-5
. extensions of time to make elections
. . automatic extensions 301.9100-2
. . . requests not meeting requirements for 301.9100-3
. gross income 1.61-15
. individual, to terminate taxable year 301.9100-14T
. information returns 301.6039-1
. intangibles 1.197-1T
. lien for estate tax 20.2204-3
. life estate transferred to donee spouse .. 25.2523(f)-1
. lobbying expenditures, charitable organizations
. . expenditure test .... 1.501(h)-2
. personal holding companies 1.544-4
. procedure 301.9100-17T
. religious orders, coverage by .... 31.3121(r)-1
. Tax Reform Act of 1976, elections under 301.9100-12T
. Tax Reform Act of 1986, elections under 301.9100-7T
. TEFRA, elections under 301.9100-5T
. tenancy by entirety, treatment as 25.2515-2
. vacation pay 301.9100-16T
. various tax acts, elections under 301.9100-21

Election to amortize organizational expenditures 1.248-1; 1.248-1T
. determination of when corporation begins business .... 1.248-1T(d)
. effective date .... 1.248-1T(f)
. examples .... 1.248-1T(e)
. . expenditures of $5,000 or less ...... 1.248-1T(e)(1)
. . expenditures of more than $5,000 but less than or equal to $50,000 .... 1.248-1T(e)(2)
. . expenditures of more than $50,000 but less than or equal to $55,000 .... 1.248-1T(e)(5)
. . expenditures of more than $55,000 .. 1.248-1T(e)(6)
. . subsequent redetermination of year in which business begins .... 1.248-1T(e)(4)
. expiration date .... 1.248-1T(g)
. generally .... 1.248-1T(a)
. organizational expenditures defined 1.248-1b
. time and manner of making election .... 1.248-1c; 1.248-1T(c)

Election to amortize start-up expenditures .. 1.195-1

Electric railway corporation
. corporate organizations and reorganizations .. 1.374-4

Electric vehicles
. qualified electric vehicle defined .... 1.30-1(a)
. recapture of credit for .... 1.30-1(b)

Electricity, natural gas, or potable water
. domestic production gross receipts .... 1.199-3(l)

Electronic filing
. financial institutions 1.6302-4
. tips reported by employee to employer 31.6053-1
. withholding exemption certificate ...31.3402(f)(5)-1(c)

Electronic funds transfers
. depositaries of government
. . FICA, deposit rules for withheld income taxes 31.6302-1
. . generally .... 31.6302(c)-3(c); 40.6302(c)-1
. . nonresident alien income and estimated income taxes 1.6302-2
. . tax-exempt organization income and estimated income taxes 1.6302-1
. . voluntary payments .... 31.6302-1(j)

Electronic furnishing of statements
. education loans, payments of interest on qualified 31.6050S-4
. tuition and related expenses 1.6050S-2
. W-2 statements .... 31.6051-1(f)(2)(i)(f)

Electronic mediums
. notice and participant election, use for
. . pension, profit-sharing, and stock bonus plans .... 1.401(a)-21

Elevators
. investment credit 1.48-1

Eminent domain
. gain or loss .... 1.1033(g)-1

Employee benefits
. ERISA (See Employee Retirement Income Security Act)
. itemized deductions 1.162-10; 1.162-10T
. life insurance endowments or annuities 1.72-13
. pension, profit-sharing and stock bonus plans (See Pension, profit-sharing, and stock bonus plans)

Employee discounts
. exemption 1.132-3; 1.132-3T

Employee representative
. supplemental tax 31.3211-3

Employee retirement and benefit plans (See Pension, profit-sharing, and stock bonus plans; Railroad Retirement Tax Act (RRTA))

Employee Retirement Income Security Act (ERISA)
. accrued benefit requirements .. 1.411(b)-1; 1.411(c)-1
. . Section 411(d)(6) protected benefits ..... 1.411(d)-5
. accrued benefits, protection of .... 1.411(d)-3
. actuarial valuation methods .... 1.412(c)(2)-1
. age requirements
. . maximum .... 1.410(a)-4

References are to Reg. § numbers

Employee Retirement Income Security Act (ERISA) —Cont'd
. *age requirements —Cont'd*
. . minimum .... 1.410(a)-3
. allocation of accrued benefits .... 1.411(c)-1
. amortization .... 1.412(b)-2; 1.412(b)-5
. annuity contracts .... 1.412(b)-2
. bonds .... 11.412(c)-11
. break in service rules .... 1.410(a)-5; 1.410(a)-6; 1.411(a)-6; 1.411(a)-9
. church .... 1.410(d)-1
. class year plans .... 1.411(d)-5
. collectively bargained plans 1.413-1
. commonly controlled trades or businesses .... 1.414(c)-1 to 1.414(c)-5
. controlled group of corporations .... 1.414(b)-1
. deferred annuity contracts .... 1.412(b)-2
. definitions .... 1.411(a)-7
. determinations to be made under funding method .... 1.412(c)(1)-1
. elapsed time .... 1.410(a)-7
. employer-derived benefits, vesting in .... 1.411(a)-3; 1.411(a)-3T
. excise tax 141.4975-13
. exempt organizations .... 1.501(c)(9)-7
. extension of time to make contributions .... 11.412(c)-12
. forfeitures, suspensions, etc. .... 1.411(a)-4; 1.411(a)-4T
. funding methods .... 1.412(c)(3)-1; 1.412(c)(3)-2
. generally .... 1.410(a)-1 et seq.; 11.402(e)(4)(A)-1 et seq.
. insurance contract plans .... 1.412(i)-1
. lump sum distributions .... 11.402(e)(4)(A)-1; 11.402(e)(4)(B)-1
. maximum age conditions and time of participation .... 1.410(a)-4
. mergers and consolidation of plans or transfers of plan assets .... 1.414(l)-1
. minimum age and service conditions .... 1.410(a)-3
. minimum funding requirements
. . restored plans, application to .... 1.412(c)(1)-3T
. minimum participation standards .... 1.410(a)-1
. mortality tables .... 1.412(l)(7)-1
. multiemployer plan .... 1.413-2; 1.414(f)-1
. multiple employers 1.413-2
. nonforfeitable percentage .... 1.411(a)-5
. ownership .... 1.414(c)-4
. pension, profit-sharing, and stock bonus plans
. . special rules .... 1.404(a)-14
. plan administrator defined .... 1.414(g)-1
. restored plans, minimum funding requirements applied to .... 1.412(c)(1)-3T
. retroactive plan amendments .... 11.412(c)-7
. shortfall method .... 1.412(c)(1)-2

Employee Retirement Income Security Act (ERISA) —Cont'd
. termination or partial termination or discontinuance of contributions .... 1.411(d)-2
. time when contributions to H.R. 10 plans considered made .... 11.404(a)(6)-1
. top-heavy plans 1.416-1
. valuation of plan assets .... 1.412(c)(2)-1
. vesting schedule, changes in .... 1.411(a)-8
. vesting standards .... 1.411(a)-1 et seq.
. welfare benefit funds 1.419-1T
. year of service .... 1.410(a)-5; 1.410(a)-6; 1.411(a)-6; 1.411(a)-9

Employee stock ownership plans (ESOPs)
. gain or loss on sale of stock 1.1042-1T
. nondiscrimination .... 1.401(a)(4)-4
. pension excise taxes 54.4975-11; 54.4978-1T
. reacquired stock
. . disallowance of deduction on reacquisition payments .... 1.404(k)-3
. S corporation, holding shares in
. . deemed-owned ESOP shares .... 1.409(p)-1(e)
. . disqualified persons .... 1.409(p)-1(d)
. . nonallocation year, prohibited allocation in .... 1.409(p)-1(b)
. . nonallocation year defined .... 1.409(p)-1(c)
. . prohibited allocations .... 1.409(p)-1 et seq.; 1.409(p)-1T
. . synthetic equity
. . . avoidance or evasion of sec 409(p) .... 1.409(p)-1(g)

Employee stock purchase plan
. approval stockholder 1.423-2
. coverage 1.423-2
. defined 1.423-2
. restrictions on options 1.423-2

Employer contributions
. accident and health plans 1.106-1
. exemptions .... 1.105-1 to 1.105-6
. life insurance 1.72-8
. pension, profit-sharing, and stock bonus plans See Pension, profit-sharing, and stock bonus plans)

Employer identification number (EIN)
. returns 301.6109-1

Employment related expenses
. household services and care credit (See Household services and care credit)

Employment taxes
. abatements, credits, and refunds .... 31.6413(a)-1 to 31.6413(c)-1; 301.6413-1
. collection, mode or time of 301.6301-1
. collection and liability .... 31.3102-1 et seq.
. compensation
. . determination of 31.3212-1

References are to Reg. § numbers

Employment taxes —Cont'd
. *compensation —Cont'd*
. . generally .... 31.3231(e)-1
. computation of remuneration
. . cash remuneration for domestic service in private home .... 31.3121(i)-1(b)
. . domestic service .... 31.3121(i)-1
. . religious orders, members of .... 31.3121(i)-4
. . uniformed service, individual as a member of .... 31.3121(i)-2
. . volunteer service .... 31.3121(i)-3
. concurrent employment by related corporations with one paymaster .... 31.3121(s)-1
. contributions
. . credit against tax for (See subhead credit against tax for contributions)
. . state, refund of .... 31.3302(a)-2
. credit against tax for contributions
. . additional credit
. . . generally .... 31.3302(b)-1
. . . proof of .... 31.3302(b)-2
. . generally .... 31.3302(a)-1
. . limitation on total credits .... 31.3302(c)-1
. . . definitions and special rules relating to .... 31.3302(d)-1
. . proof of .... 31.3302(a)-3
. . successor employers .... 31.3302(e)-1
. deductions
. . remuneration of an employee, employer from 31.3123-1; 31.3307-1
. deposit rules for withheld income taxes, defined for .... 31.6302-1(e)
. depository requirements .... 36.3121(l)(10)-4
. disclosure of listed transactions 31.6011-4
. domestic corporations
. . employee of a foreign subsidiary ...... 31.3121(l)-1
. employee representative tax
. . computation of 31.3211-2
. . employee defined .... 31.3231(c)-1
. . measure of 31.3211-1
. . rates of 31.3211-2
. employees
. . compensation
. . . collection of, and liability for 31.3202-1
. . . computation of 31.3201-2
. . . rate of 31.3201-2
. . definition .. 31.3121(d)-1; 31.3231(b)-1; 31.3306(i)-1
. . measure of 31.3201-1
. . related corporations .... 31.3306(p)-1
. . tips .... 31.3102-3; 31.3121(q)-1
. . wages
. . . attachment of tax, time of 31.3101-3
. . . computation of 31.3101-2
. . . manner and time of payment of 31.3102-2

Employment taxes —Cont'd
. *employees —Cont'd*
. . *wages —Cont'd*
. . . measure of 31.3101-1
. . . rates of 31.3101-2
. employers
. . American employer .... 31.3121(h)-1
. . compensation
. . . computation of 31.3221-2
. . . measure of 31.3221-1
. . . rates of 31.3221-2
. . definition .... 31.3121(d)-2; 31.3231(a)-1; 31.3306(a)-1
. . wages
. . . attachment of tax, time of 31.3111-3
. . . computation of 31.3111-2; 31.3301-3
. . . exemption 31.3112-1
. . . liability for 31.3111-4
. . . manner and time of payment of 31.3111-5
. . . measure of 31.3111-1
. . . measure of tax 31.3301-2
. . . persons liable for tax 31.3301-1
. . . rate of 31.3301-3
. . . rates of 31.3111-2
. . . time of 31.3301-4
. erroneously collected, repayment of ..... 31.6413(a)-1
. exemption
. . individual employed before August 1, 1956 .... 31.3121(k)-3
. . instrumentalities of U.S. 31.3308-1
. . remuneration of less than $50 for calendar quarter .... 31.3121(b)(10)-1
. . waiver of .... 31.3121(k)-1
. . . effective date .... 31.3121(k)-2
. . . Social Security taxes, filing of .... 31.3121(k)-4
. failure to deposit; abatement of penalty ... 301.6656-1
. family employment .... 31.3121(b)(3)-1
. Federal Insurance Contributions Act 31.0-3
. generally 31.0-1
. listed transactions, disclosure of 31.6011-4
. payment of amounts equivalent to tax .... 36.3121(l)(10)-4
. religious orders
. . election of coverage by .... 31.3121(r)-1
. services
. . agricultural labor .... 31.3121(g)-1; 31.3306(c)(1)-1; 31.3306(k)-1
. . . crew leader .... 31.3121(o)-1
. . American vessels and aircraft .... 31.3121(f)-1; 31.3306(m)-1
. . . business conducted by Secretary of Commerce .... 31.3306(n)-1
. . communist organizations .... 31.3121(b)(17)-1
. . domestic service .... 31.3306(c)(2)-1

References are to Reg. § numbers

Employment taxes —Cont'd
. *services —Cont'd*
. . employees' beneficiary associations, before 1962 ... 31.3306(c)(10)-3
. . exception .... 31.3121(b)-4 et seq.; 31.3306(c)-3 et seq.
. . exempt organizations ... 31.3121(b)(8)-2; 31.3306(c)(10)-1
. . family employment ... 31.3121(b)(3)-1; 31.3306(c)(5)-1
. . farming ... 31.3121(b)(16)-1
. . fishing and fishing boats ... 31.3121(b)(20)-1; 31.3306(c)(17)-1
. . foreign agricultural workers ... 31.3121(b)(1)-1
. . foreign government ... 31.3121(b)(11)-1; 31.3306(c)(11)-1
. . generally ... 31.3231(d)-1
. . Guam, services performed by resident of Philippines in ... 31.3121(b)(18)-1
. . hospital intern or student nurse ... 31.3121(b)(13)-1; 31.3306(c)(13)-1
. . included and excluded services ... 31.3121(c)-1; 31.3306(d)-1
. . instrumentalities of U.S. ... 31.3121(b)(5)-1
. . insurance agent or solicitor ... 31.3306(c)(14)-1
. . international organization ... 31.3121(b)(15)-1; 31.3306(c)(16)-1
. . minister or member of religious order ... 31.3121(b)(8)-1
. . newspapers, shopping news or magazines, delivery or distribution of ... 31.3121(b)(14)-1; 31.3306(c)(15)-1
. . non-American vessels or aircraft ... 31.3121(b)(4)-1; 31.3306(c)(4)-1
. . nonresident aliens ... 31.3121(b)(19)-1; 31.3306(c)(18)-1
. . Philippines, resident of ... 31.3121(b)(18)-1
. . pre-1955 ... 31.3121(b)-1; 31.3121(b)-2; 31.3306(c)-1
. . public retirement system, employees who are not members of ... 31.3121(b)(7)-2
. . railroad industry employee representative ... 31.3121(b)(9)-1; 31.3306(c)(9)-1
. . religious, charitable, or educational organizations ... 31.3121(b)(8)-2; 31.3306(c)(8)-1
. . states or political subdivisions ... 31.3121(b)(7)-1; 31.3306(c)(7)-1
. . students for college organizations .. 31.3121(b)(2)-1; 31.3121(b)(10)-2; 31.3306(c)(10)-2
. . trade or business, not in course of .. 31.3306(c)(3)-1
. . transportation services ... 31.3121(j)-1
. . United States or instrumentalities ... 31.3121(b)(5)-1 et seq.; 31.3121(b)(6)-1; 31.3306(c)(6)-1
. . wholly owned instrumentality of foreign government ... 31.3121(b)(12)-1; 31.3306(c)(12)-1
. state and United States defined ... 31.3121(e)-1; 31.3306(j)-1

Employment taxes —Cont'd
. Tax Court ... 301.7507-11
. tips ... 31.3121(a)(12)-1
. wages
. . agricultural labor ... 31.3121(a)(8)-1
. . annual wage limitation ... 31.3121(a)(1)-1
. . annuity plans ..... 31.3121(a)(5)-1; 31.3306(b)(5)-1
. . bond purchase plans ... 31.3121(a)(5)-1; 31.3306(b)(5)-1
. . cash payment for service in private house ... 31.3121(a)(7)-1(c)
. . cash remuneration test for agricultural labor ... 31.3121(a)(8)-1(d); 31.3121(a)(8)-1(f)
. . cash remuneration to home workers ... 31.3121(a)(10)-1(d)
. . defined ... 31.3121(a)-1; 31.3121(a)-1T
. . disabled former employee ... 31.3121(a)(15)-1
. . domestic service ... 31.3121(a)(7)-1
. . educational assistance program, qualified ... 31.3121(a)(18)-1
. . employee contributions under a state law ... 31.3121(a)(6)-1; 31.3306(b)(6)-1
. . employer plans ... 31.3121(a)(2)-1 et seq.; 31.3306(b)(2)-1
. . exclusion, time of ... 31.3121(a)-3
. . generally ...... 31.3121(a)-1T et seq.; 31.3306(b)-1
. . home workers ... 31.3121(a)(10)-1
. . more than one employer, home workers with ... 31.3121(a)(10)-1(c)
. . moving expenses ... 31.3121(a)(11)-1; 31.3306(b)(9)-1
. . nonwork periods ... 31.3121(a)(9)-1; 31.3306(b)(8)-1
. . qualified educational assistance program ... 31.3306(b)(13)-1
. . questions and answers relating to ... 31.3306(b)-1T
. . reimbursement ... 31.3121(a)-3; 31.3306(b)-2
. . retirement, disability or death ... 31.3121(a)(3)-1; 31.3121(a)(13)-1; 31.3306(b)(3)-1; 31.3306(b)(10)-1
. . salary reduction agreement defined ... 31.3121(a)(5)-1T
. . sickness or accident disability, or medical or hospitalization expenses, account of .... 31.3121(a)(4)-1; 31.3306(b)(4)-1
. . survivor or estate of former employee ... 31.3121(a)(14)-1
. . tax-exempt trusts .. 31.3121(a)(5)-1; 31.3306(b)(5)-1
. . $3000 limitation ... 31.3306(b)(1)-1
. . time paid and received ... 31.3121(a)-2
. . trade or business, service not in the course of ... 31.3121(a)(7)-1; 31.3306(b)(7)-1
. . worker's compensation ... 31.3121(a)(2)-1(d)
. work incentive programs (See Work incentive programs)

Employment-related deductions
. generally ... 1.214A-5

References are to Reg. § numbers

Empowerment Zone Employment Credit
. qualified zone employees 1.1396-1
Endorsers
. generally 1.166-8
. guarantors, endorsers, and indemnitors 1.166-8; 1.166-9
Energy matters
. atomic energy communities 1.164-8
. information returns 1.6050D-1
. investment credit 1.47-1; 1.48-9
Energy property
. alternative tax energy preference deduction . . . . . 1.56(g)-1(s)
. investment credit 1.48-9
. nuclear decommissioning funds
. . dispositions or transfers 1.468A-6T
. . electing taxpayers 1.468A-2T
. . qualification requirements 1.468A-1T; 1.468A-5T
. . ruling amount 1.468A-3T
. . self-dealing 1.468A-5T
. . termination of fund 1.468A-5T
. . transitional rules 1.468A-9T
. . treatment of fund 1.468A-4T
Engineering services
. accounting
. . nonaccrual of certain amounts by . . . . . 1.448-1T(d)(2)(A); 1.448-1T(e)(4)
. domestic production gross receipts . . . . . 1.199-3(n)
. foreign trading gross receipts . . . . . 1.924(a)-1T(e)
Engineer's certificate
. qualified enhanced oil recovery project 1.43-3
England
. foreign tax credit 1.905-5T
Enterprise zone facility bonds
. generally 1.1394-1
Entertainment
. aircraft use for (See Aircraft subhead entertainment, use for)
. itemized deductions . . . . 1.274-1 to 1.274-6; 1.274-6T; 1.274-7; 1.274-8
. partners and partnership 1.702-2
. substantiation requirements 1.274-5; 1.274-5T
Environmental Protection Agency
. sulfur regulation, deduction for capital costs incurred in complying with . . . . . 1.179B-1T; 1.179B-1T(b)
. . basis, effect on . . . . . 1.179B-1T(c)
. . . generally . . . . . 1.179B-1T(c)(1)
. . . treatment as depreciation . . . . . 1.179B-1T(c)(2)
. . computation of deduction . . . . . 1.179B-1T(b)(2)
. . . example . . . . . 1.179B-1T(b)(3)
. . . generally . . . . . 1.179B-1T(b)(2)(i)
. . . reduced percentage . . . . . 1.179B-1T(b)(2)(ii)

Environmental Protection Agency —Cont'd
. *sulfur regulation, deduction for capital costs incurred in complying with—Cont'd*
. . definitions concerning . . . . . 1.179B-1T(a); 1.179B-1T(a)(1); 1.179B-1T(a)(2)
. . effective date . . . . . 1.179B-1T(f)
. . . application to taxable years ending on or after June 26, 2008 . . . . . 1.179B-1T(f)(2)
. . . expiration date . . . . . 1.179B-1T(f)(4)
. . . modifications applicable to taxable years ending before June 26, 2008 . . . . . 1.179B-1T(f)(3)
. . election to allocate deduction to cooperative owners . . . . . 1.179B-1T(e)
. . election to deduct qualified capital costs . . . . . 1.179B-1T(d); 1.179B-1T(d)(1)
. . . allocate of deduction to cooperative owners . . . . . 1.179B-1T(e); 1.179B-1T(e)(1)
. . . . cooperative small business refiner denied section 1382 . . . . . 1.179B-1T(e)(2)
. . . . irrevocable election . . . . . 1.179B-1T(e)(4)
. . . . manner of making election . . . 1.179B-1T(e)(3)(ii)
. . . . time and manner for making election . . . . . 1.179B-1T(e)(3)
. . . . time for making election . . . . . 1.179B-1T(e)(3)(i)
. . . . written notice to owners . . . . . 1.179B-1T(e)(5)
. . . cooperative small business refiners . . . . . 1.179B-1T(d)(1)(iii)
. . . failure to make election . . . . . 1.179B-1T(d)(4)
. . . information required in election statement . . . . . 1.179B-1T(d)(2)(ii)(B)
. . . manner of making election . . . . 1.179B-1T(d)(2)(ii); 1.179B-1T(d)(2)(ii)(A)
. . . revocation of election . . . . . 1.179B-1T(d)(3)
. . . section 179B election . . . . . 1.179B-1T(d)(1)(i)
. . . taxable years ending before June 26, 2008 . . . . . 1.179B-1T(d)(5)
. . . time and manner for making section 179B election . . . . . 1.179B-1T(d)(2)
. . . time for making election . . . . . 1.179B-1T(d)(2)(i)
. . . validity of election . . . . . 1.179B-1T(d)(2)(iii)
. . . year-by-year elections . . . . . 1.179B-1T(d)(1)(ii)
. . expiration date . . . . . 1.179B-1T(f)(4)
. . failure to make election to deduct qualified capital costs . . . . . 1.179B-1T(d)(4)
. . generally . . . . . 1.179B-1T(a); 1.179B-1T(b)(1)
. . June 26, 2008
. . . elections before . . . . . 1.179B-1T(d)(5)
. . . modifications applicable to taxable years ending before . . . . . 1.179B-1T(f)(3)
. . . taxable years ending on or after . . 1.179B-1T(f)(2)
. . revocation of election to deduct qualified capital costs . . . . . 1.179B-1T(d)(3)
. . time and manner of making election to deduct qualified capital costs . . . . . 1.179B-1T(d)(2)
Equity options (See also Stock options)
. covered calls . . . . . 1.1092(c)-1

References are to Reg. § numbers

Equity options (See also Stock options) —Cont'd
. definitions concerning . . . 1.1092(c)-4
. flexible terms . . . 1.1092(c)-2
. over-the-counter options . . . 1.1092(c)-3
. payment of income, received as . . . 1.61-15
. qualified call options . . . 1.1092(c)-1

ERISA (See Employee Retirement Income Security Act)

Errors (See Mistakes and errors)

ESBT (See Electing small business trust)

Escalators
. investment credit . . . 1.48-1

Escrow accounts
. pre-closing escrow
. . defined . . . 1.468B-7(b)
. . examples . . . 1.468B-7(e)
. . reporting obligations of the administrator . . . 1.468B-7(d)
. . taxation of . . . 1.468B-7(c)

ESOPs (See Employee stock ownership plans)

Estate tax
. administration expenses . . . 20.2053-3; 20.2055-3
. annuities
. . agreements or plans to which section 2039(a) and (b) applies . . . 20.2039-1(b)
. . amount includible in the gross estate . . . 20.2039-1(c)
. . effective dates . . . 20.2039-1(f)
. . generally . . . 20.2039-1(a)
. . insurance under policies on the life of the decedent . . . 20.2039-1(d)
. . no application to certain trusts . . . 20.2039-1(e)
. Armed Forces member dying during induction period . . . 20.2201-1
. charitable transfers (See Charitable transfers)
. defined . . . 20.2051-1
. disclaimed property . . . 20.2046-1
. disclosure of listed transactions . . . 20.6011-4
. extension of time for paying . . . 20.6161-1
. . acceleration of payment . . . 20.6166A-3
. . bond, use of . . . 20.6165-1
. . closely-held business . . . 20.6166-1
. . deficiencies . . . 20.6161-2
. generally . . . 20.0-1; 20.0-2
. gross estate, defined . . . 20.2031-1
. liability for payment . . . 20.2002-1
. lien for . . . 20.6324A-1
. . decedent dying after December 31, 1976 . . . 20.2204-3
. . farm, attributable to . . . 20.6324B-1
. . release or partial discharge . . . 20.6325-1
. listed transactions, disclosure of . . . 20.6011-4
. marital deduction (See Marital deduction)
. nonresident aliens (See Nonresident aliens)

Estate tax —Cont'd
. omission of gross income from return . . . 301.6501(e)-1
. payment of
. . duplicate receipts . . . 20.6314-1
. . extension of time . . . 20.6161-1
. persons required to file . . . 20.6018-2
. place for filing returns . . . 20.6091-1
. recovery
. . marital deduction property . . . 20.2207A-1
. retained life estate . . . 20.2036; 20.2036(a); 20.2036-1(a)
. . period not ascertainable without reference to his death . . . 20.2036-1(b)(1)
. . retained annuity, unitrust, and other income interests in trusts . . . 20.2036(c)(2); 20.2036(c)(2)(iii); 20.2036-1(c)(2); 20.2036-1(c)(2)(iii)
. . . graduated retained interests . . . 20.2036-1(c)(2)(ii)
. . retained or reserved interest . . . 20.2036(c); 20.2036-1(c)
. . . amount included in gross estate . . . 20.2036(c)(1); 20.2036(c)(1)(ii); 20.2036-1(c)(1); 20.2036-1(c)(1)(i); 20.2036-1(c)(3)
. . right to designate the persons who shall possess or enjoy the transferred property or the income therefrom . . . 20.2036-1(b)(3)
. . use, possession, right to the income, or other enjoyment of the transferred property . . . 20.2036-1(b)(2)
. retained or reserved interest
. . gross estate, amount included in . . . 20.2036(c)(1)(i); 20.2036-1(c)(1)(i)
. . retained annuity, unitrust, and other income interests in trusts . . . 20.2036(c)(2)(i); 20.2036-1(c)(2)(i)
. return requirements
. . filing . . . 20.6018-2
. . omission of gross income from . . . 301.6501(e)-1
. . verification of return . . . 20.6065-1
. section 2056A estate tax, imposition of . . . 20.2056A-5
. . amount, determining . . . 20.2056A-6
. . circumstances affecting imposition of tax . . . 20.2056A-10
. . decedents dying after August 22, 1995 . . . 20.2056A-13
. . filing requirements . . . 20.2056A-11
. . increased basis for tax . . . 20.2056A-12
. state death taxes (See State and local taxes)

Estates and trusts
. abatements, credits, and refunds . . 1.641(b)-1 et seq.; 301.6503(d)-1
. accumulating income . . . 1.661(a)-1
. alternative minimum tax . . . 1.58-3
. amortization . . . 1.642(f)-1
. automatic extension of time for filing returns . . . 1.6081-6T
. backup withholding . . . 1.671-4(e); 31.3406(h)-2
. banking institutions . . . 1.584-3

References are to Reg. § numbers

Estates and trusts —Cont'd

. basis for gain or loss... 1.1014-1; 1.1014-2; 1.1014-8; 1.1015-2 to 1.11015-5
. beneficiaries succeeding to the property of the estate or trust defined .... 1.642(h)-3
. black lung benefit trusts .... 1.501(c)(21)-1; 1.501(c)(21)-2
. business trusts .... 301.7701-4(b)
. capital gains and losses .... 1.643(a)-3 et seq.; 1.665(f)-1A et seq.; 1.669(f)-1A et seq.
. capital gains look-through rule
. . sales or exchanges of interest in S trust .... 1.1(h)-1
. carryover .... 1.642(h)-1 et seq.; 7.1023(b)(3)-1; 7.6039A-1
. . allocation among beneficiaries .... 1.642(h)-4
. charitable contributions ...... 1.170A-6; 1.642(c)-1 et seq.; 1.651(a)-4 et seq.; 1.664-1 et seq.
. common trust funds (See Common trust funds)
. corporate distributions and adjustments 1.318-3
. court test, satisfaction of 301.7701-7
. death, transfers taking effect at 20.2037-1
. decedents, trust owned by
. . time for filing returns 1.6072-1
. . TIN following death, obtaining 301.6109-1
. deductions, generally .... 1.641(b)-1 et seq.
. depositaries of government, estimated tax ... 1.6302-3
. distributing corpus .... 1.661(a)-1
. dividends .... 1.643(a)-4; 1.643(a)-7; 1.643(b)-2
. . received by beneficiaries, when deemed .... 1.642(a)(3)-2
. double deductions .... 1.642(g)-1; 1.642(g)-2; 1.663(a)-3
. environmental remediation trusts ...... 301.7701-4(e)
. excise taxes 53.4947-1; 53.4947-2
. executors and administrators (See Fiduciaries)
. exempt
. . entity status 1.444-4
. fiduciaries (See Fiduciaries)
. foreign corporations, created by .... 1.672(f)-2
. foreign taxes .... 1.642(a)(2)-1
. foreign trusts ... 1.643(a)-6 et seq.; 1.643(d)-1 et seq.; 1.665(c)-1A et seq.; 1.1493-1; 16.3-1; 301.6048-1
. generally .... 1.641(a)-0 to 1.692-1; 301.7701-4
. generation-skipping taxes 26.2654-1; 26.2654-6
. . division of a trust included in the gross estate .... 26.2654-1(b)
. . . allocation of exemption .... 26.2654-1(b)(3)
. . . effective date .... 26.2654-1(b)(4)
. . . examples .... 26.2654-1(b)(4)
. . . formula severance .... 26.2654-1(b)(4)
. . . generally .... 26.2654-1(b)(1)
. . . severance of revocable trust ..... 26.2654-1(b)(4)
. . . severance of single trust .... 26.2654-1(b)(4)
. . . special rule .... 26.2654-1(b)(2)

Estates and trusts —Cont'd

. generation-skipping taxes—Cont'd

. . single trust treated as separate trusts
. . . additional contributions .... 26.2654-1(a)(5)
. . . allocation of exemption .... 26.2654-1(a)(4)
. . . distributions from a separate share .... 26.2654-1(a)(5)
. . . examples .... 26.2654-1(a)(5)
. . . multiple transferors to single trust .... 26.2654-1(a)(5)
. . . multiple transferors with respect to single trust .... 26.2654-1(a)(2)
. . . pecuniary payment as separate share .... 26.2654-1(a)(5)
. . . separate share rule inapplicable .. 26.2654-1(a)(5)
. . . separate shares as separate trusts .... 26.2654-1(a)(5)
. . . severance of a single trust .... 26.2654-1(a)(3)
. . . subsequent mandatory division into separate trusts .... 26.2654-1(a)(5)
. . . substantially separate and independent shares .... 26.2654-1(a)(1)
. gift tax (See Gift tax)
. grantors, income for the benefit of .... 1.677(a)-1
. gross income 1.61-13
. . determination of .... 1.641(a)-2
. imposition of tax .... 1.641(a)-1
. inadvertent migrations 1.684-4
. inbound grantor trusts
. . foreign persons not treated as owners .... 1.672(f)-1
. . . exceptions to general rules .... 1.672(f)-3
. . recharacterization of purported gifts ...... 1.672(f)-4
. . special rules .... 1.672(f)-5
. information returns 1.6034-1; 301.6034-1; 301.6047-1
. interest .... 1.643(a)-5
. interest expense, allocation
. . income from sources within or without U.S. 1.861-9T
. investment companies 1.851-7
. investment credit 1.47-5; 1.48-6
. investment trusts .... 301.7701-4(c)
. liens 301.6324A-1; 301.6324-1
. life estates .... 1.167(h)-1; 1.273-1
. liquidating trusts .... 301.7701-4(d)
. migrations 1.684-4
. missionaries, death while in foreign missionary service 20.2202-1
. net operating loss .... 1.642(d)-1
. nonresident alien estates (See Nonresident aliens)
. ordinary trusts .... 301.7701-4(a)
. outbound migrations 1.684-4
. outside the United States, trusts created or organized .... 1.404(a)-11

References are to Reg. § numbers

Estates and trusts —Cont'd
. owned by one or more grantors or other person ... 1.671-4(b)
. pension, profit-sharing, and stock bonus plans (See Pension, profit-sharing, and stock bonus plans)
. personal exemption ... 1.642(b)-1; 1.643(a)-2
. pooled income funds ... 1.642(c)-5 et seq.
. . remainder, valuation of ... 1.642(c)-6
. . yearly rate of return, computation of ... 1.642(c)-6
. pre-existing transfers or interests ... 20.2045-1
. prior transfers, credit for ... 20.2013-1
. . definitions ... 20.2013-5
. . examples ... 20.2013-6
. . generally ... 20.2013-6
. . limitations
. . . first ... 20.2013-2
. . . second ... 20.2013-3
. . valuation of property ... 20.2013-4
. qualified domestic trusts (See Qualified domestic trusts)
. qualified subchapter S trust ... 1.1361-1
. real estate investment trusts (See Real estate investment trusts)
. reporting income, methods of (See Records and reports subhead trust income, methods of reporting)
. research expenditures ... 1.41-7
. returns ... 1.641(b)-2
. . chapter 42 taxes ... 301.6501(n)-1
. . contents of returns ... 20.6018-3
. . documents accompanying ... 20.6018-4
. . due date for filing ... 20.6075-1
. . persons required to file ... 20.6018-2
. revocable trust treatment as part of estate, election of ... 1.645-1
. separate share rule
. . computation of distributable net income for each separate share ... 1.663(c)-2
. . estates, applicability to ... 1.663(c)-4
. . multiple beneficiaries and beneficiaries of multiple shares ... 1.663(c)-4
. . multiple share beneficiaries ... 1.663(c)-4
. . qualified revocable trusts, applicability to ... 1.663(c)-4
. . separate trusts or estates, separate share treated as ... 1.663(c)-1
. . trusts, applicability to certain ... 1.663(c)-3
. situs trusts ... 1.402(c)-1
. small business corporation status ... 1.1361-1
. special rules
. . sections 661 and 662, applicable to ... 1.663(a)-1
. surcharge ... 1.58-3T
. termination of ... 1.641(b)-3
. . excess deduction on ... 1.642(h)-2
. transfer certificates ... 20.6325-1
. transfers ... 1.684-4

Estates and trusts —Cont'd
. treasury bond exemptions ... 1.103-5
. trusts (See Trusts)
. unit investment trust ... 1.851-7
. United States person, status as ... 301.7701-7
. widely held fixed investment trusts (See Widely held fix investment trusts)
. withholding ... 31.3401(a)(12)-1; 35.3405-1

Estimated tax
. abatements, credits, and refunds ... 1.6425-1 to 1.6425-3
. accounting methods, corporate
. . changes in ... 1.6655-6(b)
. . generally ... 1.6655-6(a)
. . installment payments ... 1.6655-6(a)
. adjustment of tax
. . allowance of adjustment ... 1.6425-3
. . computation of adjustment ... 1.6425-2
. consolidated returns ... 1.1502-5
. corporations ... 301.6655-1
. . declaration ... 1.6074-1; 1.6074-2
. . failure to pay ... 301.6655-1
. extension of time to pay ... 1.6153-4
. government depositaries ... 1.6302-3
. individuals
. . nonresident aliens ... 1.6654-6
. . overpayment by ... 1.6654-1
. . payment by, determination of ... 1.6654-5
. . short taxable year, determination of ... 1.6654-3
. nonresident aliens ... 1.6654-6
. overpayment of tax
. . computation of adjustment ... 1.6425-2
. payment by individual ... 1.6654-5
. penalties ... 1.6654-4; 1.6654-5; 301.6654-1; 301.6655-1
. receipt of payment ... 301.6315-1; 301.6316-6
. returns ... 1.1502-5; 1.6073-1 to 1.6073-4; 301.6073-1
. short tax year (See Short tax year)
. time and place for paying ... 1.6153-1 to 1.6153-4; 301.6153-1
. trusts, depositaries of government ... 1.6302-3

Ethanol fuel (See Diesel and special motor fuels tax)

European Monetary Union
. conversion to euro ... 1.985-8; 1.1001-5

Evasion or avoidance of tax
. allocation of deduction, credit, or other allowance in part by district director ... 1.269-4
. allowance defined for ... 1.269-1
. assessable penalties ... 301.6672-1
. control defined for ... 1.269-1
. definition, limitations on ... 1.269-1
. disallowance of deduction, credit, or other allowance ... 1.269-2; 1.269-3

References are to Reg. § numbers

Evasion or avoidance of tax —Cont'd
. expatriation 20.2107-1
. intercompany transactions .... 1.1502-13(h)
. person defined for 1.269-1
. shareholder, corporation used for income tax on .... 1.531-1 et seq.
. Tax Reform Act of 1986
. . Sec. 269 and Sec. 382 after Act, relationship of 1.269-7
. . Sec. 269 and Sec. 382 before Act, relationship of 1.269-6

Evidence
. corporations improperly accumulating surplus 1.533-1; 1.534-1; 1.534-2
. nonresident aliens, proof of residence 1.871-4
. presumptions and burden of proof (See Presumptions and burden of proof)
. production of books and records (See Production of books and records)
. seizure of property for collection of taxes 301.6333-1

Examination and inspection
. exempt organization
. . application for exemption .... 301.6104(d)-1
. . information returns, annual .... 301.6104(d)-1
. generally .... 301.7601-1 et seq.
. restrictions 301.7605-1
. time and place 301.7605-1

Exceptions
. capital gains and losses 1.1245-4
. corporate organizations and reorganizations .. 1.368-1 to 1.368-3
. investment credit 1.47-3
. life insurance endowments or annuities 1.72-14

Excess accumulations
. tax on 54.4981A-1T

Excess benefit transactions
. applicable tax-exempt organization defined 53.4958-2
. controlled entities 53.4958-4
. correction of transaction 53.4958-7
. defined 53.4958-4
. disqualified person
. . defined 53.4958-3
. . tax paid by 53.4958-1
. foundation manager, participation by 301.7454-2
. generally 53.4958-1
. intent to treat economic benefit as consideration for performance of service 53.4958-4
. non-fixed payments
. . presumption of reasonable payments 53.4958-6
. organization manager, tax paid by 53.4958-1
. organization no longer exists
. . correction of transaction 53.4958-7

Excess benefit transactions —Cont'd
. organization no longer tax-exempt
. . correction of transaction 53.4958-7
. partially performed contract
. . correction of transaction 53.4958-7
. rebuttable of presumption 53.4958-6
. valuation of economic benefit 53.4958-4

Excess business holdings
. excise taxes .... 53.4943-1 to 53.4943-11

Excess distributions
. tax on 54.4981A-1T

Excess expenditures
. related persons 1.263A-14

Excess loss accounts
. gain or loss
. . income or gain, taken into account as 1.1502-19
. . special allocation of basis in connection with adjustment or determination 1.1502-19

Excess profits tax
. generally 1.901-2; 301.6105-1
. income, war profits, or excess profits tax defined .... 1.901-2(a)
. . dual capacity taxpayers .... 1.901-2(a)(2)(ii)
. . . control of property .... 1.901-2(a)(2)(ii)(D)
. . . generally .... 1.901-2(a)(2)(ii)(A)
. . . indirect receipt of a benefit ..... 1.901-2(a)(2)(ii)(E)
. . . pension, unemployment, and disability fund payments .... 1.901-2(a)(2)(ii)(C)
. . . specific economic benefit ...... 1.901-2(a)(2)(ii)(B)
. . generally .... 1.901-2(a)(1); 1.901-2(a)(2)(i)
. . predominant character .... 1.901-2(a)(3)
. net gain .... 1.901-2(b)
. . generally .... 1.901-2(b)(1)
. . gross receipts .... 1.901-2(b)(3)
. net income .... 1.901-2(b)(4)
. . carryovers .... 1.901-2(b)(4)(iii)
. . consolidation of profits and losses .. 1.901-2(b)(4)(ii)
. . examples .... 1.901-2(b)(4)(iv)
. . generally .... 1.901-2(b)(4)(i)
. realization .... 1.901-2(b)(2)
. . certain deemed distributions .... 1.901-2(b)(2)(ii)
. . example .... 1.901-2(b)(2)(iv)
. . generally .... 1.901-2(b)(2)(i)
. . readily marketable property .... 1.901-2(b)(2)(iii)
. separate levies imposed by foreign country .... 1.901-2(d)
. . amount of income tax that is creditable ... 1.901-2(e)
. . . generally .... 1.901-2(e)(1)
. . . multiple levies ..... 1.901-2(e)(4); 1.901-2(e)(4)(i)
. . . noncompulsary amounts .... 1.901-2(e)(5); 1.901-2(e)(5)(ii)
. . . refunds and credits .... 1.901-2(e)(2)
. . . subsidies .... 1.901-2(e)(3); 1.901-2(e)(3)(ii)

References are to Reg. § numbers

Excess profits tax —Cont'd
. *separate levies imposed by foreign country—Cont'd*
. . contractual modifications .... 1.901-2(d)(2)
. . definitions .... 1.901-2(g)
. . effective date .... 1.901-2(h); 1.901-2(h)(1)
. . examples .... 1.901-2(d)(3)
. . generally .... 1.901-2(d)(1)
. . taxpayer .... 1.901-2(f)
. . . generally .... 1.901-2(f)(1)
. . . party undertaking tax as part of transaction .... 1.901-2(f)(2)
. soak-up taxes .... 1.901-2(c)
. . examples .... 1.901-2(c)(2)
. . generally .... 1.901-2(c)(1)

Excessive adjustments
. additions to tax, additional amounts, and assessable penalties 1.6655-7

Excessive compensation
. taxable income, and determination of 1.162-8

Excise taxes
. air transportation of passengers (See subhead transportation of persons by air)
. alcohol mixture fuels (See Diesel and special motor fuels tax)
. aviation fuel (See Aviation fuel)
. black lung trusts 53.4951-1; 53.4952-1
. bonds where time to pay tax or deficiency has been extended 53.6165-1; 53.7101-1
. charitable organizations
. . excess lobbying expenditures .... 56.4911-0 to 56.4911-10
. charitable remainder trusts, on .... 1.664-1(c)
. collection of tax
. . mode or time of 301.6302-1
. . persons receiving payment duty to collect 49.4291-1
. commercial waterway transportation, fuel used in .... 48.4042-1 et seq.
. . dual use of liquid fuel 48.4042-2
. . excluded types of transportation 48.4042-3
. . specified waterways, voyages crossing ... 48.4042-2
. communications services (See Communication services)
. commutation tickets (See Commutation tickets)
. correction period defined 53.4963-1
. credits and refunds
. . exporters, refunds to .... 48.6416(e)-1
. . returns, credit on .... 48.6416(f)-1
. . shippers, refunds to .... 48.6416(e)-1
. . transportation of persons by air
. . . duty to collect .... 49.4264(b)-1
. definitions 53.4946-1; 53.4963-1; 145.4052-1
. diesel and special motor fuels tax (See Diesel and special motor fuels tax)

Excise taxes —Cont'd
. distribute income, failure to .... 53.4942(a)-1 to 53.4942(b)-3
. duty to collect 49.4291-1
. employers (See Railroad Retirement Tax Act, subhead supplemental annuity tax; Railroad Unemployment Repayment Tax)
. ethanol fuel (See Diesel and special motor fuels tax)
. excess business holdings ... 53.4943-1 to 53.4943-11
. extension of time for paying tax or deficiency 53.6161-1; 53.6165-1; 53.6601-1
. first tier tax defined 53.4963-1
. floor stocks tax (See Floor stocks tax)
. foreign insurers (See Insurance)
. foreign organizations 53.4948-1
. gas guzzler tax 48.4064-1
. gasohol 48.4081-6
. gift tax, effect on 25.2512-7
. highway vehicles (See Highway vehicles)
. interest on underpayment, nonpayment, or extensions of time for payment of tax 53.6601-1
. investments ...... 53.4940-1; 53.4944-1 to 53.4944-6
. jeopardy 301.6861-1
. judicial proceedings 301.7422-1
. manufacturers excise taxes (See Manufacturers excise taxes; specific manufactured product e.g. Tires)
. methanol fuel (See Diesel and special motor fuels tax)
. notice or regulations requiring records, statements, and special returns 53.6001-1
. oil production
. . collection of fee 301.9001-1
. . definitions 301.9001-2
. omission of gross estate from return .... 301.6501(e)-1
. ozone-depleting chemicals (See Ozone-depleting chemicals, taxes on)
. payment of tax, extension .... 45.6161(a)(1)-1
. pension, profit-sharing, and stock bonus plans (See Pension, profit-sharing, and stock bonus plans, subhead penalties)
. pension excise taxes (See Pension excise taxes)
. real estate investment trusts ... 55.4981-1; 55.4981-2; 55.4982-1
. recordkeeping requirements, generally 45.6001-1
. refund proceedings 301.7422-1
. registration-required obligations 46.4701-1
. retail excise taxes (See Retail excise taxes)
. returns
. . black lung trusts, taxes related to ...... 53.6071-1(d)
. . excess benefits transactions .... 53.6071-1(f)
. . extension of time for filing 53.6081-1
. . failure to file return or to pay tax 53.6651-1
. . final return .... 40.6011(a)-2
. . 501(c)(3) organizations, expenditures of .... 53.6071-1(e)

References are to Reg. § numbers

Excise taxes —Cont'd
. *returns —Cont'd*
. . generally .... 45.6001-6; 53.6001-1; 53.6061-1; 53.6071-1(a)
. . identifying numbers .... 40.6109(a)-1
. . omission of gross estate from .... 301.6501(e)-1
. . pension excise tax 54.6011-1
. . . entity manager tax on prohibited tax shelter transactions .... 54.6011-1T(c)
. . . reversion of qualified plan assets to employer .... 54.6011-1T(a)
. . period covered by returns 41.6101-1; 45.6101-1
. . place for filing .... 41.6091-1; 41.6151(a)-1; 53.6091-1; 53.6091-2
. . prohibited tax shelter transactions to which tax-exempt entities are parties ... 53.6071-1T(g)
. . time and place for paying tax 53.6151-1
. . time for filing 53.6071-1
. . verification 53.6065-1
. second tier excise taxes ...... 53.4961-1 to 53.4963-1
. self-dealing .... 53.4941(a)-1 to 53.4941(f)-1
. special rules 145.4052-1
. stamp taxes (See Stamp taxes)
. structured settlement factoring transactions (See Structured settlement factoring transactions)
. . automatic extension on form 8876 ...... 157.6081-1
. taxable event defined 53.4963-1
. taxable expenditures .... 53.4945-1 to 53.4945-6
. temporary excise taxes 141.4975-13
. transportation of persons by air (See Transportation of persons by air)
. trucks, sale or resale of heavy 48.4052-1
. trusts 53.4947-1; 53.4947-2
. wagering taxes (See Wagering taxes)
. waterway transportation (See subhead commercial waterway transportation)

Exclusions (See also Exemptions)
. combat zone compensation 1.112-1
. employee achievement awards 1.74-2
. foreign corporations 1.959-1; 1.959-2
. . ships or aircraft 1.883-1; 1.883-1T
. foreign personal holding companies 1.552-4; 1.552-5
. life insurance endowments or annuities ..... 1.72-3 et seq.
. partners and partnerships 1.761-2
. private foundations .... 1.509(a)-2
. revenue Act of 1962 .... 16A.126-0 to 16A.126-2
. withholding .... 31.3401(a)-2

Execution of returns
. withholding .... 31.6011(a)-7

Executors and administrators (See Fiduciaries)

Exempt facility bonds
. interest on 1.103-8

Exempt facility bonds —Cont'd
. interest on, computation of taxable income ... 1.142-1
. . remedial actions 1.142-2

Exempt organizations
. acquisition indebtedness .... 1.514(c)-1
. allocation rules .... 1.514(e)-1
. apostolic associations or corporations ..... 1.501(d)-1
. application for exemption
. . availability .... 301.6104(d)-1
. . copies, requests for .... 301.6104(d)-1
. . public inspection and distribution of ... 301.6104(d)-1
. automatic extensions for filing returns 1.6081-9
. bingo games 1.513-5
. black lung trusts ...... 1.501(c)(21)-1; 1.501(c)(21)-2
. business income .... 1.511-1 et seq.
. business leagues, chambers of commerce, real estate boards, and boards of trade .... 1.501(c)(6)-1
. capitalization of costs 1.263A-1
. cemetery companies and crematoria .. 1.501(c)(13)-1
. charitable, scientific, testing for public safety, literary, or educational purposes, or for the prevention of cruelty to children or animals .... 1.501(c)(3)-1
. civic organizations and local associations of employees .... 1.501(c)(4)-1
. communications services, excise tax, exemption from 49.4253-3
. communist-controlled organizations .... 1.501(k)-1
. convention and trade show activity 1.513-3
. cooperative hospital service organization ... 1.501(e)-1
. corporate liquidation .... 1.514(d)-1
. credit unions and mutual insurance funds .... 1.501(c)(14)-1
. crop operators, corporations organized to finance .... 1.501(c)(16)-1
. debt-financed property .... 1.514(b)-1
. depositaries of government 1.6302-1
. device of exemption 1.504-1
. diesel and special motor fuels tax, exemption from 48.4041-17
. disclosure of listed transactions 53.6011-4
. ERISA .... 1.501(c)(9)-7
. excess benefit transactions (See Excess benefit transactions)
. farmers' cooperatives .... 1.521-1 et seq.
. feeder organizations 1.502-1
. foreign
. . unrelated business taxable income, computation of 1.1443-1
. . withholding at source .... 1.1441-1 et seq.
. . withholding exemption 1.1441-9
. fraternal beneficiary societies .... 1.501(c)(8)-1; 1.501(c)(10)-1
. funded pension trusts .... 1.501(c)(18)-1
. future status of organizations denied exemption .... 1.503(c)-1 to 1.503(e)-4

References are to Reg. § numbers

Exempt organizations —Cont'd
. generally ...... 1.501(a)-1 et seq.; 1.501(h)-1 et seq.
. grass roots expenditures .... 1.501(h)-3
. harassment campaigns against .... 301.6104(d)-3
. homeowner associations .... 1.528-1 to 1.528-10
. hospital services .... 1.501(e)-1; 1.513-6
. income, unrelated business (See subhead unrelated business taxable income)
. influencing legislation 1.504-1
. information returns ... 1.6033-1; 1.6033-2; 1.6050A-1; 301.6033-1
. . availability .... 301.6104(d)-2
. . copies, requests for .... 301.6104(d)-2
. . notification requirement for entities not required to file annual information return under sec. 6033(a)(1) 1.6033-6T
. . public inspection and distribution of ... 301.6104(d)-1
. labor, agricultural, and horticultural organizations .... 1.501(c)(5)-1
. leases .... 1.514(a)-2; 1.514(f)-1; 1.514(g)-1
. leasing rules, questions concerning ...... 1.168(j)-1T
. life, sick, accident, or other benefits .... 1.501(c)(9)-3
. listed transactions, disclosure of 53.6011-4
. loans by employers who are prohibited from pledging assets .... 1.503(f)-1
. lobbying expenditures
. . ceiling amount, expenditures in excess of .... 1.501(h)-3
. . denial of exemption 1.504-1
. . . transfers to avoid 1.504-2
. . expenditure test .... 1.501(h)-1
. . . election of test .... 1.501(h)-2
. local benevolent life insurance associations, mutual irrigation and telephone companies, and like organizations .... 1.501(c)(12)-1
. minimum tax for tax preferences 1.511-4
. modifications .... 1.512(b)-1
. mutual insurance companies or associations .... 1.501(c)(15)-1
. notification requirement for recognition of exemption .... 1.505(c)-1T
. partners and partnership .... 1.512(c)-1 et seq.
. penalties 301.6652-2
. political organizations (See Political organizations)
. private foundations (See Private foundations)
. prohibited tax shelter transaction disclosure (See Prohibited tax shelter transaction disclosure)
. prohibited transactions .... 1.503(a)-1; 1.503(b)-1
. public inspection
. . exemption application and information returns .... 301.6104(d)-1
. recordkeeping .... 1.501(c)(9)-5
. religious organizations ...... 1.501(c)(3)-1; 1.501(d)-1
. returns
. . magnetic media, use of (See Magnetic media)

Exempt organizations —Cont'd
. social clubs .... 1.501(c)(7)-1
. supplemental unemployment benefit trusts .... 1.501(c)(17)-1 to 1.501(c)(17)-3
. title to property .... 1.501(c)(2)-1
. transfers of assets from taxable corporation to .... 1.337(d)-4
. travel and tour activities 1.513-7
. unemployment compensation ...... 1.501(c)(17)-1 to 1.501(c)(17)-3
. unrelated business taxable income .... 1.512(a)-5T
. . defined .... 1.512(a)-1
. . generally .... 1.512(a)-1
. . sponsorship payments .... 1.512(a)-1
. unrelated debt-financed income and deductions .... 1.514(a)-1
. unrelated trade or business .... 1.512(a)-5T; 1.513-1; 1.513-2
. . sponsorships 1.513-4
. veterans' organizations .... 1.501(c)(19)-1; 1.512(a)-4
. voluntary employees' beneficiary associations .... 1.501(c)(9)-1 to 1.501(c)(9)-8; 1.501(c)(9)-2

Exemption certificates
. electronic .... 31.3402(f)(5)-1(c)
. withholding (See Withholding exemption certificates)

Exemptions (See also Exclusions)
. absence from work 1.105-3
. accident and health plans ..... 1.106-1; 1.501(c)(9)-3
. activity bonds .... 1.103(n)-1T to 1.103(n)-7T
. additions to tax 1.6654-2; 1.6655-2
. alimony 1.101-5
. Armed Forces members 1.112-1; 1.113-1
. backup withholding 35a.9999-3A
. bonds (See Tax-exempt bonds)
. capital contributions 1.118-1
. collapsible corporations 1.341-6
. cooperatives (See Cooperatives)
. covenant bonds 1.1451-2
. de minimis fringes 1.132-6; 1.132-6T
. death benefits 1.101-2
. dependency exemption (See Children and dependents)
. diesel and special motor fuels 48.4041-10, 48.4041.18
. dividends 1.103-2; 1.265-3
. domestic gas wells 1.613A-2
. eating facilities 1.119-1; 1.132-7; 1.132-7T
. educational assistance program .. 1.117-1 to 1.117-5; 1.127-1; 1.127-2; 1.501(c)(3)-1
. employee discounts 1.132-3; 1.132-3T
. employer contributions .... 1.105-1 to 1.105-6
. employer tax 31.3112-1
. excise taxes
. . common carriers 49.4253

References are to Reg. § numbers

Exemptions (See also Exclusions) —Cont'd
. *excise taxes —Cont'd*
. . communications services, generally .... 49.4253-3; 49.4253-5; 49.4253-6 to 49.4253-10
. . telephone services
. . . coin-operated phones 49.4253-1
. . . news services 49.4253-2
. . . service personnel in combat zones 49.4253-4
. . teletypewriter exchange services 49.4253-5
. . terminal facilities in case if wire mileage service 49.4253-8
. federal employees 1.117-5
. foreign corporations 1.1441-4; 1.1442-1; 1.1442-2
. foreign trade income 1.923-1T
. franchises, trademarks and trade names 1.1254-2
. fringe benefits .... 1.132-1 to 1.132-8T
. generally 20.2052-1
. gift tax
. . qualified disclaimer of property .... 25.2518-1 et seq.
. . settlements involving husband and wife ... 25.2516-1
. . specific exemption 25.2521-1
. highway vehicles use tax (See Highway vehicles, subhead exemptions)
. homeowners association 1.528-9
. independent producers and royalty owners 1.613A-3
. industrial development bonds 1.103-7; 1.103-10
. injuries or sickness 1.104-1
. insurance proceeds 1.123-1
. interest .... 1.103-1 to 1.103-9
. itemized deductions .... 1.265-1 to 1.265-3
. legal services plan 1.120-3
. lessee, value of improvements erected by 1.109-1
. life insurance contracts .... 1.101-1 to 1.101-6
. line-of-business limitations 1.132-4; 1.132-4T
. loans 1.133-1T; 1.7872-5T
. manufacturers excise taxes (See Manufacturers excise taxes)
. meals and lodging 1.119-1; 1.132-7; 1.132-7T
. medical care 1.105-2; 1.105-11
. natural resources .... 1.613A-2 to 1.1613A-4
. no-additional cost services 1.132-2; 1.132-2T
. nonresident aliens and foreign corporations, not engaged in business in the U.S. 1.103-6
. organizations (See Exempt organizations)
. parsonages, rental value of 1.107-1
. partnership items .... 301.6231(a)(1)-1
. pension excise taxes 54.4975-6; 54.4975-7
. personal exemptions (See Personal exemptions)
. political organizations 1.527-3
. previously deducted or credited items, recovery of 1.111-1
. public charities 56.4911-4

Exemptions (See also Exclusions) —Cont'd
. railroad corporations, income from discharge of indebtedness of .... 1.108(b)-1
. residence of individual who has attained age 55, gain from sale or exchange of .... 1.121-1 to 1.121-5
. . reduced exclusion 1.121-3
. retired employees 1.105-6
. retirement (See Retirement)
. scholarship or fellowship grants ... 1.117-1 to 1.117-5
. seizure of property for collection of taxes .... 301.6334-1 to 301.6334-4
. . amount, determination of 301.6334-3
. . wages, salary, and other incomes 301.6334-2
. self-insured medical reimbursement plans ... 1.105-11
. substantial user bonds 1.103-11
. surcharge .... 1.58-1 et seq.
. treasury bond, trusts or partnerships 1.103-5
. uniformed services retirement pay 1.122-1
. wage continuation plans 1.105-4
. withholding .... 31.3401(e)-1; 31.3402(f)(1)-1 to 31.3402(f)(6)-1

Exhaustion
. wear and tear, obsolescence, amortization, and depletion 1.1016-3

Exhaustion of administrative remedies
. basis for gain or loss 1.1016-4
. judicial proceedings 301.7430-1

Expanded affiliated groups
. domestic production activities (See Domestic production activities)

Expatriation
. tax avoidance 20.2107-1

Expenditure test
. homeowner associations 1.528-6

Expenditures (See specific item)

Expense allowance arrangements
. defined for determining "adjusted gross income" 1.62-2

Expenses (See also specific subject headings)
. administrative costs and expenses (See Administrative costs and expenses)
. business 1.162-17
. clinical testing (See Clinical testing expenses)
. deductions 20.2053-1
. . nonresident aliens 20.2106-2
. dental expenses 1.213-1
. funeral 20.2053-2
. moving expenses (See Moving expenses)
. travel expenses (See Travel expenses)
. wage expense deduction 1.280C-1

Expensing in lieu of depreciation
. carryover of disallowed deduction 1.179-3
. definitions 1.179-4

References are to Reg. § numbers

Expensing in lieu of depreciation —Cont'd
. election 1.179-1
. generally 1.179-1
. limitations on amounts subject to 1.179-2
. . dollar limitation 1.179-2
. refineries, election to expense certain refineries (See Refineries subhead election to expense certain refineries)
. time and manner of making election 1.179-5
. . property placed in service in a tax year beginning after 2002 and before 2006 .... 1.179-5
. 2002 and before 2006, property placed in service in a tax year beginning after 1.179-5

Experience-rating arrangements
. pension, profit-sharing, and stock bonus plans
. . 10 or more employees .... 1.419A(f)(6)

Experiments and tests
. expenditure test 1.528-6
. research expenditures (See Research expenditures)

Exploration expenditures
. deferred development, adjusted basis 1.1016-5
. generally ... 1.381(c)(10)-1; 1.617-1; 1.617-3; 1.621-1

Export trade corporations
. generally .... 1.970-1 to 1.970-3; 1.971-1

Exports
. diesel and special motor fuels tax 48.4041-16
. DISCs .... 1.993-1; 1.993-1 to 1.993-3
. earned income of U.S. citizens .... 1.924(e)-1; 1.927(a)-1T
. export trade corporations .... 1.970-1 to 1.970-3; 1.971-1
. manufacturers excise taxes
. . overpayment of tax, exportations causing .... 48.6416(b)(2)-1 to 48.6416(b)(2)-4
. ozone-depleting chemicals, taxes on 52.4682-5
. possessions corporation, section 936(h)(5) election by 1.936-7
. resale exemptions .... 48.4221-3; 48.6416(b)(2)-2
. supplies for vessels or aircraft .... 48.6416(b)(2)-2
. tires sold for further manufacture .... 48.6416(b)(2)-2
. vaccines .... 48.4221-3; 48.6416(b)(2)-2

Extension of time for filing returns ...... 1.6081-1 to 1.6081-9; 31.6081(a)-1; 156.6081-1; 301.6081-1
. automatic extensions
. . chapter 44 returns 55.6081-1
. . chapter 54 returns 156.6081-1
. . chapter 55 returns 157.6081-1
. . corporation income tax 1.6081-3
. . election or choice
. . . requests not meeting requirements for 301.9100-3
. . employee plan returns 1.6081-11
. . estates 20.6081-1

Extension of time for filing returns— Cont'd
. *automatic extensions —Cont'd*
. . excise tax on structured settlement factoring transactions 157.6081-1
. . exempt organization return 1.6081-9
. . foreign persons, U.S. source income of ... 1.6081-10
. . foreign trusts 301.6081-2
. . generation-skipping transfer tax returns 1.6081-1T; 26.6081-1
. . gift tax returns 25.6081-1
. . individual income tax 1.6081-4
. . information returns 1.6081-8
. . nuclear decommissioning fund taxes 53.6081-1
. . partners 1.6081-2T
. . REIT undistributed income, return on 55.6081-1
. . REMICs 1.6081-7
. . self-dealing with nuclear decommissioning fund, return reporting sec. 4951 taxes due for 53.6081-1
. . time and place for filing returns 1.6081-4
. . trust income returns 1.6081-6T
. good cause basis 20.6081-1
. partners and partnerships 1.6081-5; 301.6233-1
. payment of tax, effect on 20.6081-1
. Social Security Administration copy of W-2 .... 31.6081(a)-1T

Extension of time for payment of tax
. abatements, credits, and refunds ...... 301.6511(c)-1
. bonds 156.6165-1; 156.6165-1T
. bonds upon extension of time ... 1.6165-1; 55.6165-1; 301.6165-1
. carrybacks 1.6164-1; 301.6164-1
. deficiency 1.6161-1; 301.6165-1
. elections, extension of time for making 1.9100-1
. estate tax 20.6161-1
. . acceleration of payment 20.6166A-3
. . bonds, payment with 20.6165-1
. . closely-held businesses 20.6166-1
. . deficiency in 20.6161-2
. . remainders 20.6163-1
. estimated tax 1.6153-4
. excise taxes 53.6161-1; 53.6165-1; 53.6601-1
. generally .... 1.6161-1 to 1.6165-1; 55.6161-1; 301.6161-1
. gift tax 25.6081-1
. . bond, with 25.6165-1
. liquidation of personal holding companies .. 1.6162-1; 301.6162-1
. magnetic media returns 1.9101-1
. period of extension 1.6164-5
. remainders 1.6164-4; 20.6163-1
. returns, magnetic media 1.9101-1
. revised statements 1.6164-6
. termination 1.6164-7; 1.6164-8

References are to Reg. § numbers

Extension of time for payment of tax —Cont'd
. withholding .... 31.6161(a)(1)-1
Extension of time to make elections (See Election or choice)

F

Face-amount certificates
. pension, profit-sharing, and stock bonus plans 1.401-9
Failure to file tax return or pay tax
. excise taxes 53.6651-1
. generally 301.6651-1
. information return 301.6721-1
. penalties .... 301.6651-1 et seq.
. years ending on or after December 31, 1996 .... 301.6651-1
Fair market value (FMV)
. charitable remainder unitrusts, remainder interest in
. . calculation of fair market value 1.664-4
. notes 25.2512-4
. stocks and bonds 25.2512-2
False information
. penalties 301.6682-1
Family and Medical Leave Act
. cafeteria plans 1.125-3
. COBRA and 54.4980B-10
Family partnerships .... 1.704-1(e)
Farmers' cooperatives
. domestic production activities (See Domestic production activities, subhead agricultural and horticultural cooperatives)
. generally .... 1.521-1 et seq.; 1.1381-2; 1.1382-3
Farming
. almond groves 1.278-1
. alternate valuation for farms, material participation requirements for 20.2032A-3
. capital gains and losses .... 1.1251-1 to 1.1251-4; 1.1252-1; 1.1252-2
. capitalization of costs 1.263A-1; 1.263A-4
. crops .... 1.268-1; 1.451-6; 1.501(c)(16)-1
. deposit rules for withheld income taxes .... 31.6302-1(g)
. depreciation .... 1.167(a)-6
. diesel and special motor fuels tax (See Diesel and special motor fuels tax)
. domestic production activities (See Domestic production activities, subhead agricultural and horticultural cooperatives)
. exempt organizations .... 1.501(c)(5)-1
. gross income 1.61-4
. highway vehicles use tax
. . agricultural vehicles used for 7,500 or fewer miles on public highways, exemption for 41.4483-3

Farming —Cont'd
. inventories 1.471-6
. investment credit 1.48-10
. itemized deductions 1.162-12; 1.165-6; 1.175-3; 1.175-4; 1.180-1; 1.180-2
. lien for estate tax 20.6324B-1
. manufacturers excise taxes; gasoline
. . farm use of gasoline, refunds and credits .... 48.6420-1 to 48.6420-6
. . . recordkeeping requirements 48.6420-6
. . . ultimate purchasers of gasoline 48.6420-1; 48.6420-2; 48.6420-4
. self-employment income .... 1.1402(a)-13 to 1.1402(a)-16
. soil and water conservation expenditures .. 1.175-1 to 1.175-7
. uniform capitalization rules 1.263A-1
. valuing, method of 20.2032A-4
. withholding .... 31.3401(a)(2)-1
. . agricultural labor, wages for ..... 31.6011(a)-4(a)(3)
Fast-pay arrangements
. stock, recharacterizing financing arrangement involving .... 1.7701(l)-3
. withholding agents 1.1441-10
FCC (See Federal Communications Commission)
Federal agencies
. contracts, information returns 1.6050M-1
Federal Communications Commission (FCC)
. gain or loss .... 1.1071-1 to 1.1071-4
Federal employees
. exemptions 1.117-5
Federal financial assistance
. agency control 1.597-4
. agency obligations, original issue discount rules and 1.597-3
. anti-abuse rule 1.597-3
. bridge banks
. . consolidated groups .... 1.597-4(f)
. . single entity status .... 1.597-4(e)
. . transfers to .... 1.597-4(d)
. consolidated groups, rules for .... 1.597-4(f)
. debt treatment 1.597-3
. definitions 1.597-1
. effective date 1.597-7
. limitation on collection of tax 1.597-6
. losses 1.597-3
. ownership of assets 1.597-3
. residential entity
. . single entity status .... 1.597-4(b)
. successors 1.597-3
. taxable transfers 1.597-5
. taxation 1.597-2
. transitional rules 1.597-8

References are to Reg. § numbers

Federal financial assistance —Cont'd
. uncollected tax, reporting of . . . 1.597-6
Federal government (See United States)
Federal Insurance Contributions Act (FICA)
. credits and refunds under . . . 31.6402(a)-2
. deposit rules for withheld income taxes . . . 31.6302-1
. employment taxes . . . 31.0-3
. overpayment adjustments . . . 31.6413(a)-2
. returns under . . . 31.6011(a)-1 et seq.
. . requirement . . . 31.6011(a)-1T(a)
. time for filing returns and other documents . . . 31.6071(a)-1(a)
. underpayment adjustments . . . 31.6205-1
Federal National Mortgage Association (FNMA)
. generally . . . 1.162-19; 1.1054-1
Federal reserve bank
. withholding taxes deposits . . . 1.1461-1
Federal tax deposit (FTD) coupons
. depositaries of government . . . 31.6302(c)-3(b)
Federal Unemployment Tax Act
. time for filing returns and other documents . . . 31.6071(a)-1(c)
Feeder organizations
. exempt organizations . . . 1.502-1
Fees
. compensation . . . 1.61-2
. enrollment of enrolled actuary fee . . . 300.7
. imposition . . . 300.0
. installment agreement fees . . . 300.1
. offer to compromise fee . . . 300.3
. renewal of enrollment
. . enrolled actuary fee . . . 300.8
. . enrolled agent fee . . . 300.6
. special enrollment examination fee . . . 300.4
. witness . . . 301.7457-1; 301.7610-1
Fellowship grants (See Scholarships and fellowships)
Fiduciaries
. definitions . . . 301.7701-6
. discharge of executor from personal liability for decedent's income and gift taxes . . . 301.6905-1
. estates and trusts . . . 301.6905-1
. . defined . . . 20.2203-1
. . gift tax, liability for . . . 25.2502-2
. . lien, election of . . . 20.2204-3
. . notice of qualification, filing of . . . 20.6036-1; 20.6036-2
. . payment of tax, time and place . . . 20.6151-1
. . personal liability, discharge from . . . 20.2204-1
. . returns
. . . due date . . . 20.6075-1
. . . payment, time and place for . . . 20.6151-1
. . . place for filing . . . 20.6091-1
Fiduciaries —Cont'd
. *estates and trusts—Cont'd*
. . *returns —Cont'd*
. . . signing of . . . 20.6061-1
. . . verification . . . 20.6065-1
. . signature on returns . . . 20.6061-1
. . time for . . . 20.6071-1
. executor's status as . . . 301.6903-1
. information returns . . . 1.6036-1; 301.6036-1
. notice of fiduciary relationship . . . 301.6903-1
. personal liability, discharge from . . . 20.2204-2; 301.6905-1
. returns . . . 1.6012-3
. withholding . . . 31.3402(g)-3
50-percent bonus depreciation property (See Additional first year depreciation deduction)
Filing returns (See Time and place for filing returns)
Film (See Motion picture, television films and tapes)
Financial assistance, federal (See Federal financial assistance)
Financial counseling
. new markets tax credit . . . 1.45D-1
Financial institutions (See also Banking institutions; Mutual savings banks)
. agency control defined . . . 1.597-1
. bridge bank defined . . . 1.597-1
. electronic filing . . . 1.6302-4
. information returns
. . discharge of indebtedness by certain financial entities . . . 1.6050P-1; 1.6050P-1T
. insolvent consolidated group
. . refund claims . . . 301.6402-7
. insolvent member of consolidated group
. . tentative carryback adjustments . . . 301.6402-7
. taxable transfers defined . . . 1.597-1
Financial Institutions Reform, Recovery, and Enforcement Act (FIRREA)
. low-income housing projects funded by loan proceeds from . . . 1.42-3
Financial products
. alter effective cost of borrowing, that
. . interest expense allocation . . . 1.861-9T(b)(6)
Financial services income
. foreign tax credit . . . 1.904-4(e)
Financing agreements
. liens . . . 301.6323(c)-1; 301.6323(c)-2
Financing arrangements
. avoidance of tax through conduit financing arrangement . . . 1.881-3
. conduit entities . . . 1.881-3
Fines and penalties (See Additions to tax, additional amounts, and assessable penalties)

References are to Reg. § numbers

Fire
. basis of premium deposits, mutual insurance company 1.832-6
Fire departments, volunteer
. obligations issued by 1.103-16
Fiscal year
. defined 1.441-1
. grandfathered 1.441-1
Fishing boat crew members
. withholding on wages .... 31.3401(a)(17)-1; 31.3406(b)(3)-3
Fishing boat operators
. backup withholding .... 31.3406(b)(3)-3
. information returns 1.6050A-1; 301.6050A-1
Fishing equipment
. manufacturers excise taxes .... 48.4161(a)-1 to 48.4161(a)-5
. . definitions .... 48.4161(a)-2
. . exempt sales .... 48.4161(a)-5
. . generally .... 48.4161(a)-1
. . parts and accessories .... 48.4161(a)-3
. . use considered sale .... 48.4161(a)-4
Fixed investment trusts, widely held
. trust income, methods of reporting (See Records and reports under subhead trust income, methods of reporting)
Flood insurance
. basis of premium deposits, mutual insurance company 1.832-6
Floor stocks tax
. cement mixers, credits or refunds 48.4061-1
. final returns .... 40.6011(a)-2
. fuel (See Fuel floor stocks tax)
. manufacturers excise taxes, credit or refund 48.6412-1
. . amount of tax paid on each article 48.6412-3
. . definitions 48.6412-2
. ozone-depleting chemicals 52.4682-4
. returns .... 40.6011(a)-1
Flow-through entities
. withholding certificates; foreign entity 1.1441-1
FMV (See Fair market value)
FNMA (See Federal National Mortgage Association)
FOGEI and FORI
. foreign base company, income from 1.954-8
Food
. domestic production gross receipts .... 1.199-3(o)
. generally 1.119-1; 1.132-7; 1.132-7T
Food Stamp Act of 1977
. employer identification number collection for 301.6109-1
Foreclosures
. generally 1.595-1; 1.856-6; 1.857-3; 5.856-1

Foreclosures —Cont'd
. reporting 1.6050J-1T
Foreign affiliates (See Intercompany transactions, subhead transfer pricing)
Foreign base company income
. sales from foreign and U.S. sources
. . agricultural commodities grown in the US. in commercially marketable quantities, table of .... 1.954-3(a)(1)(b)
. . apportionment of income .... 1.954-3(a)(5)
. . branches of controlled foreign corporation treated as separate corporation
. . . allocation of income .... 1.954-3(b)(1)(i)(b)
. . . behalf of branch, activities treated as .... 1.954-3(b)(2)(c)
. . . general rules .... 1.954-3(b)(1)
. . . sales or purchase branch .... 1.954-3(b)(1)(i)
. . . wholly owned subsidiary corporation, determination of .... 1.954-3(b)(2)(i)
. . generally .... 1.954-3(a)
. . manufactured or produced by the controlled foreign corporation .... 1.954-3(a)(4)
. . partnership income, distributive share of .... 1.954-3(a)(6)
. . use, consumption, or disposition within the country controlled corporation is created or organized .... 1.954-3(a)(2)
Foreign central bank of issue
. generally 1.895-1
. withholding taxes 1.1441-8
Foreign corporations
. abatements, credits, and refunds 1.6414-1
. acquisition of foreign corporation stock or asset by foreign corporation .... 1.367(b)-4
. . generally .... 1.367(b)-4(a)
. . income inclusion .... 1.367(b)-4(b)
. . triangular reorganization .... 1.367(b)-4(b)
. actual United States risks 1.953-2
. adjusted current earnings, LIFO inventories .... 1.56(g)-1 et seq.
. affiliate-owned stock
. . book stock treatment .... 1.7874-1(d)
. . determination of ownership .... 1.7874-1(a); 1.7874-1(b)
. . one or more members of the expanded affiliated group, stock held by .... 1.7874-1(c)
. . partnership, stock held by .... 1.7874-1(e)
. allocation of distributions to earnings and profits 1.959-3
. assets, transfer of .... 7.367(b)-8
. attribution rules, removal of .... 1.367(b)-6(d)
. branch profits tax 1.884-1
. . reorganization 1.884-2; 1.884-2T
. . termination of U.S. trade or business 1.884-2; 1.884-2T

References are to Reg. § numbers

Foreign corporations —Cont'd
. branch-level interest tax 1.884-4
. capital gains and losses .... 1.1248-1 to 1.1248-7; 1.1249-1
. . death tax payments .... 1.1248-1(e)
. . foreign tax credits.................... 1.1248-1(d)
. . installment reporting .... 1.1248-1(f)
. . recognition of gain from sale or exchange of stock .... 1.1248-1(c)
. . reorganizations, section 356 .... 1.1248-1(e)
. . sale or exchange of stock in certain foreign corporations 1.1248-1
. compensation of employees of foreign governments or international organizations 1.893-1
. consent dividends 1.565-5
. constructive ownership of stock............. 1.958-2
. controlled foreign corporations (See Controlled foreign corporations)
. coordination rules .... 1.367(b)-6
. credits 1.882-4
. . filing deadlines, waiver of .... 1.882-4(a)(ii)
. deductions, generally 1.882-4; 1.882-5
. definitions ..... 1.956-2; 1.957-1; 1.957-4; 7.367(b)-2; 301.7701-5
. direct ownership of stock 1.958-1
. disposition of stock
. . basis, determination of .... 1.367(b)-13(b)
. . . triangular reorganization......... 1.367(b)-13(c)
. . divided shares .... 1.367(b)-13(d)
. . generally .... 1.367(b)-12
. . holding period, determination of
. . . triangular reorganization.......... 1.367(b)-13(c)
. distributions by
. . gain or loss recognition .... 1.367(e)-2
. . United States real property interests 1.897-5T
. distributions of stock
. . withholding at source 1.1445-5
. distributions to, corporation
. . gain or loss recognition .... 1.367(e)-2
. dividends 1.864-3; 1.960-2
. domestic corporation, election to be treated as 1.897-3; 1.1445-7
. earned income of U.S. citizens .... 1.921-2 et seq.
. earnings and profits .... 1.964-1; 7.367(b)-9; 7.367(b)-11
. . accounting adjustments............... 1.964-1(b)
. . allocation of distributions 1.959-3
. . determination .... 1.964-1T(a)
. . exchanges of stock .... 7.367(b)-9
. . functional currency, computation in ..... 1.964-1T(g)
. . previously taxed 1.959-1
. . tax adjustments .... 1.964-1(c)
. . taxable years, determination of .... 1.964-1T(c)
. earnings and profits attributable to stock

Foreign corporations —Cont'd
. earnings and profits attributable to stock —Cont'd
. . block, attributable to .... 1.1248-2(e)
. . block of stock .... 1.1248-2(b)
. . complex cases, stock sales in .... 1.1248-3(a)
. . establishment of, taxpayer 1.1248-7
. . lower tier corporation a less developed country corporation .... 1.1248-3(g)
. . non-recognition transactions, following certain 1.1248-8
. . . foreign liquidation corporation .... 1.1248-8(c)
. . . restructuring transaction............. 1.1248-8(b)
. . simple cases, stock sales in .... 1.1248-2(a)
. . subsidiaries of foreign corporation ...... 1.1248-3(f)
. . taxable year, attributable to
. . . complex case .... 1.1248-3(b)
. . . ratable share of earnings and profits accumulated for a taxable year .... 1.1248-3(e)
. . . simple case .... 1.1248-2(d)
. . . tentative ratable share if deficit in earning accumulated................................ 1.1248-3(d)
. . . tentative ratable share if earnings and profits not less than zero .... 1.1248-3(c)
. effectively connected income.............. 1.1441-4
. exchanges of stock .... 7.367(b)-1 et seq.
. . attribution rules, removal of.......... 1.367(b)-6(d)
. . carryover, capital loss .... 1.367(b)-3(e)
. . carryover, earnings and profit .... 1.367(b)-3(f)
. . . foreign-to-foreign nonrecognition transactions .... 1.367(b)-7
. . carryover, net operating loss .... 1.367(b)-3(e)
. . carryover of foreign taxes .... 1.367(b)-3(f)
. . definitions .... 1.367(b)-2; 7.367(b)-2
. . described in more than one Code provision .... 7.367(b)-4
. . described in Section 354
. . . controlled foreign corporation .... 7.367(b)-7
. . . more than one Code section, described in .... 7.367(b)-4
. . . reorganizations .... 7.367(b)-4
. . earnings and profits .... 7.367(b)-9; 7.367(b)-11
. . foreign corporation stock by foreign corporation in certain nonrecognition transactions ... 1.367(b)-4
. . foreign investment company, in .... 7.367(b)-6
. . nonrecognition transactions
. . . acquisition of foreign corporation stock or asset by foreign corporation .... 1.367(b)-4
. . . foreign-to-foreign nonrecognition transactions .... 1.367(b)-7
. . . repatriation of foreign corporate asset .... 1.367(b)-3; 1.367(b)-3T
. . notice (section 367(b)) requirements ..... 1.367(b)-1
. . prior published guidance, reasonable methods to comply with .... 1.367(b)-6(c)
. . recapitalizations .... 1.367(b)-6(b)

References are to Reg. § numbers

Foreign corporations —Cont'd
. *exchanges of stock—Cont'd*
. . repatriation of assets in nonrecognition transactions .... 1.367(b)-3; 1.367(b)-3T
. . special rules .... 7.367(b)-3
. . U.S. person that is not a U.S.shareholder .... 1.367(b)-3(c)
. . U.S. person to foreign corporation, transfer of stock from .... 1.367(a)-2
. . U.S. shareholder, owned directly by .. 1.367(b)-3(b)
. excise taxes............................ 53.4948-1
. exclusions from gross income 1.959-1; 1.959-2
. . ships or aircraft................ 1.883-1; 1.883-1T
. exemptions .... 1.1441-4; 1.1442-1 to 1.1442-3
. family ownership of stock 1.958-2
. foreign base company . . 1.954-3 to 1.954-6; 1.955A-1; 1.955A-2
. . income, computation of 1.954-1
. . oil related income....................... 1.954-8
. foreign central bank of issue or Bank for International Settlements........................... 1.895-1
. foreign government, income 1.893-1
. foreign investment companies 1.951-2
. . exchanges of stock in .... 7.367(b)-6
. . passive foreign investment company .... 1.1291-1 et seq.
. . qualified electing fund 1.1294-1T
. foreign personal holding companies (See Foreign personal holding companies)
. foreign tax credit .... 1.960-1 to 1.960-7
. gain or loss recognition
. . corporation of distribution of property to foreign corporation .... 1.367(e)-2
. gain recognition agreements .... 1.367(a)-8; 1.367(a)-8T
. . asset reorganization defined..... 1.367(a)-8T(a)(l)(i)
. . common parent defined........ 1.367(a)-8T(a)(l)(ii)
. . consolidated group defined..... 1.367(a)-8T(a)(l)(iii)
. . defined .... 1.367(a)-8T(a)(l)(v)
. . disposition defined............ 1.367(a)-8T(a)(l)(iv)
. . generally .... 1.367(a)-8T(b)
. . initial transfer defined .... 1.367(a)-8T(a)(l)(vi)
. . nonrecognition transaction defined .... 1.367(a)-8T(a)(l)(vii)
. . security, use of .... 1.367(a)-8T(c)
. . transferee foreign corporation defined .... 1.367(a)-8T(a)(l)(viii)
. . transferred corporation defined .... 1.367(a)-8T(a)(l)(ix)
. . triangular asset reorganization defined .... 1.367(a)-8T(a)(l)(i)(a)
. . triggering event .... 1.367(a)-8T(d)
. . . defined .... 1.367(a)-8T(a)(l)(x)
. . U.S. transferor defined .... 1.367(a)-8T(a)(l)(xi)
. generally .... 1.951-1 et seq.

Foreign corporations —Cont'd
. gross income .... 1.78-1; 1.882-3 et seq.
. . inclusions 1.951-1
. . taxable income, determination of 1.952-2
. gross-up of amounts included in income 1.960-3
. identifying numbers......................... 1.897-1
. income from within or without U.S. (See Income from sources within or without U.S.)
. information reporting rule, transitional....... 1.883-5; 1.883-5T
. information returns ..... 1.6038A-1 et seq.; 1.6038-2; 1.6046-1; 301.6038-1; 301.6046-1
. . attribution rules..........1.6038A-2(g); 1.6038-2(c)
. . authorization of agent 1.6038A-5
. . content of returns .... 1.6038A-2(b); 1.6038-2(f)
. . control ....1.6038-2(b)
. . controlled foreign corporations 1.6038-2
. . domestic reporting corporations, transactions solely with .... 1.6038-2A-2(f)
. . exceptions to filing .... 1.6038-2(l)
. . failure to furnish information .... 1.6038A-6; 1.6038-2(k)
. . financial statements ....1.6038-2(g)
. . foreign sale corporation, transactions with .... 1.6038-2A-2(f)
. . Form 5472 requirement.............1.6038A-2(a); 1.6038-2A-2(a)
. . generally 1.6038A-1
. . method, reporting.................. 1.6038-2A-2(c)
. . no reportable transactions.......... 1.6038-2A-2(f)
. . noncompliance 1.6038A-7
. . partnership attributed to a reporting transaction ....1.6038-2A-2(g)
. . penalty, monetary 1.6038A-4
. . period covered by return ....1.6038-2(e)
. . record maintenance 1.6038A-3
. . related parties, transactions with .... 1.6038-2(f)
. . reporting methods ....1.6038A-2(c); 1.6038-2(h)
. . requirements 1.6038A-1; 1.6038A-2
. . section 6038, corporation subject to reporting under .... 1.6038-2A-2(f)
. . time and place, filing ....1.6038-2A-2(d)
. . time and place for filing .... 1.6038A-2(d); 1.6038A-2T(d); 1.6038-2(i)
. . transfers 1.6038B-1; 1.6038B-1T
. . transfers of property to 1.6038B-1; 1.6038B-1T
. . transitional rules 1.883-5; 1.883-5T
. . two or more persons required to file..... 1.6038-2(j)
. . untimely filed .... 1.6038A-2(e); 1.6038-2A-2(d)
. . U.S. persons.........................1.6038-2(f)
. insurance ...... 1.819-1; 1.819-2; 1.953-1 to 1.954-6; 1.957-2
. insurance company stock................... 1.958-1
. interest 1.882-5
. . repeal of tax on 1.871-14

References are to Reg. § numbers

Foreign corporations —Cont'd
. interest deduction, determination of 1.882-5; 1.882-5T
. interest expense, allocation
. . income from sources within or without U.S. 1.861-9T
. international operations
. . exclusion of income; aircraft and ships 1.883-1; 1.883-1T
. international organizations, generally 1.893-1
. investment companies
. . passive foreign investment companies .. 1.1291-1 et seq.
. investments .... 1.367(b)-6; 1.897-1; 1.954-5; 1.954-7; 1.955A-3; 1.955A-4; 1.1247-1 to 1.1247-5
. itemized deductions 1.243-3; 1.245-1
. limitation of tax .... 1.962-1 to 1.962-3
. liquidation .... 1.367(b)-5; 1.884-2; 1.884-2T
. . distributions .... 1.367(e)-2
. manner of taxing 1.881-1
. noncontrolled section 902 corporation ..... 1.904-4(e)
. nonresident alien ownership of stock 1.958-2
. notice (section 367(b)) requirements ... 1.367(b)-1(c)
. penalties 301.6679-1
. personal holding corporations
. . adjusted basis of stock in 1.1016-5
. possessions of U.S. 1.957-3
. previously taxed earnings and profits 1.959-1; 1.959-2
. primarily traded stocks of 1.883-2
. prior published guidance, reasonable methods to comply with .... 1.367(b)-6(c)
. property use in trade or business
. . section 367(a), subject to .... 1.367(a)-5T
. publicly traded 1.883-2; 1.883-2T
. qualified foreign corporation status
. . application, election for retroactive 1.883-5
. qualified resident defined 1.884-4
. recapitalizations .... 1.367(b)-6(b)
. records 1.964-3
. regularly traded stocks of 1.883-2
. reorganization
. . branch profits tax 1.884-2; 1.884-2T
. reporting transfers to 1.6038B-1; 1.6038B-1T
. research expenditures
. . gross receipts defined 1.41-3
. sales corporations......... 1.367(b)-1; 1.921-2 et seq.
. securities lending transactions.............. 1.881-2
. shareholders 1.951-1
. . constructive ownership rules............ 1.883-4(c)
. . partnerships 1.883-4
. . qualified shareholder defined .... 1.883-4(b)
. . qualified shareholder stock ownership test .... 1.883-4(a); 1.883-4T

Foreign corporations —Cont'd
. *shareholders—Cont'd*
. . reporting requirements .... 1.883-4(e)
. . substantiation of stock ownership .... 1.883-4(d)
. shipping operations..... 1.954-7; 1.955A-1; 1.955A-2
. stapled corporations (See Stapled foreign corporations)
. stock..... 1.958-1; 1.958-2; 1.960-2; 1.961-1; 1.961-2
. subpart F income, U.S. shareholder pro rata (See Subpart F income)
. subsidiary, liquidation of................. 7.367(b)-5
. substantiation
. . corporation is publicly traded 1.883-2
. . stock ownership 1.883-4
. surrogate foreign corporation
. . acquisition by publicly traded foreign partnership .... 1.7874-2T(e)
. . acquisition of domestic corporation stock .... 1.7874-2T(b)(1)
. . acquisition of domestic corporation stock or assets by controlled corporation .... 1.7874-2T(b)(4)
. . acquisition of foreign corporation stock .... 1.7874-2T(b)(2)
. . acquisition of partnership interest... 1.7874-2T(b)(3)
. . acquisition of property, indirect....... 1.7874-2T(b)
. . determination of status .... 1.7874-2T(a)
. . domestic status, change from foreign to .... 1.7874-2T(g)
. . EAG, substantial business activities of .... 1.7874-2T(d)
. . expanded affiliated group, substantial business activities by .... 1.7874-2T(d)
. . former shareholder or partner, stock held by .... 1.7874-2T(c)
. . generally .... 1.7874-2T(a)
. . indirect acquisition of properties ...... 1.7874-2T(b)
. . options and similar interest treatment .. 1.7874-2T(f)
. . publicly traded foreign partnership, acquisition by .... 1.7874-2T(e)
. . sec. 367, nonapplicability of .... 1.7874-2T(h)
. tax credit 1.911-3
. Tax Reform Act of 1976 .... 1.367(b)-5
. termination of U.S. trade or business
. . branch profits tax 1.884-2; 1.884-2T
. transfers........ 1.367(a)-1T; 1.367(b)-1; 7.367(b)-1; 7.367(b)-8
. . branch, transfers to foreign .... 1.367(a)-6T
. . certain beneficiaries to foreign settlor .... 1.672(f)-5
. . exceptions, use in active conduct of trade or business .... 1.367(a)-2T
. . foreign branch with previously deducted loss .... 1.367(a)-6T
. . generally .... 1.367(a)-1T
. . intangible property .... 1.367(d)-1T
. . regardless of use in trade or business ... 1.367(a)-5T
. . reporting 1.6038B-1; 1.6038B-1T

References are to Reg. § numbers

Foreign corporations —Cont'd
. *transfers—Cont'd*
. . special rules for specific transfers of property .... 1.367(a)-4T
. . stock or securities .... 1.367(a)-3
. . . Sec. 361 exchange .... 1.367(a)-3T
. treaty 1.1441-6
. . income affected by 1.894-1
. triangular reorganization
. . acquisition of foreign corporation stock or asset by foreign corporation .... 1.367(b)-4(b)
. trust created by .... 1.672(f)-2
. United States real property holding corporations 1.897-2
. . distributions 1.897-5T
. U.S. business, taxation when not engaged in 1.881-2
. U.S. person defined 1.957-3; 1.957-3T
. verification of income 1.964-4
. withholding .... 1.1441-1 et seq.
. . agents 1.1441-7; 1.1445-4
. . depositaries of government 1.6302-2
. . distributions 1.1445-5
. . domestic corporation, foreign corporation's election to be treated as 1.1445-7
. . exemptions 1.1441-4; 1.1441-4T; 1.1442-2
. . generally .... 1.897-5T; 1.970-1 to 1.970-3; 1.971-1; 1.1445-11T
. . treaty 1.1441-6

Foreign countries
. dual consolidated loss
. . domestic use
. . . U.S. and a foreign country, elective agreement in place between .... 1.1503(d)-6(b)
. . foreign country defined .... 1.1503(d)-1(b)(7)
. income from sources within or without U.S.
. . foreign country, income partly from 1.863-3AT
. . foreign country or U.S. possession 1.863-6
. personal property income
. . income partly from foreign country 1.863-3AT
. returns
. . disclosure in preparation of foreign country obligations .... 301.7216-2(k)
. structured passive investment arrangements 1.901-2T

Foreign currency
. backup withholding; conversion of amounts paid in .... 31.3406(h)-2
. borrowing, interest expense allocation .... 1.861-9T(b)(2)
. European Monetary Union conversion to euro 1.985-8; 1.1001-5
. functional (See Functional currency)
. gain or loss on transactions
. . computation of 1.988-2

Foreign currency —Cont'd
. *gain or loss on transactions —Cont'd*
. . debt instruments and deposits denominated in hyperinflationary currencies 1.988-2
. . definitions 1.988-1
. . exchange or loss defined 1.988-1
. . fair market value defined 1.988-1
. . hyperinflationary currency defined 1.988-1
. . nonfunctional currency contingent payment debt instruments 1.988-6
. . nonfunctional currency defined 1.988-1
. . recognition of 1.988-2
. . section 988 transaction defined 1.988-1
. . spot contract defined 1.988-1
. . spot rate defined 1.988-1
. hedging transactions 1.988-5
. hyperinflationary currencies, debt instruments and deposits denominated in 1.988-2
. payment of tax 301.6316-1; 301.6316-3; 301.6316-5; 301.6316-7; 301.6316-8

Foreign death taxes credit (See Death taxes)

Foreign earned income (See Income earned abroad by U.S. citizens)

Foreign entities
. classifications for federal tax purposes .... 301.7701-2(b)(8)
. . special rules .... 301.7701-2(d); 301.7701-3(d)
. entity classification election 301.7701-3
. . notice of election 301.7701-3

Foreign estates
. withholding taxes 1.1441-5

Foreign exempt organizations
. unrelated business taxable income, computation of 1.1443-1
. withholding exemption 1.1441-9

Foreign expropriation loss
. itemized deductions 1.172-9

Foreign governments
. generally ..... 1.892-1T et seq.; 1.893-1; 1.1445-10T; 31.3401(a)(5)-1
. interest deduction, determination of 1.882-5
. withholding taxes .... 1.1441-1 et seq.; 1.1441-8

Foreign income
. FOGEI and FORI taxes (See FOGEI and FORI)

Foreign income taxes (See Foreign taxes)

Foreign investment companies
. deemed dividend election 1.1291-10
. generally ...... 1.367(b)-6; 1.897-1; 1.954-5; 1.954-7; 1.955A-3; 1.955A-4; 1.1247-1 to 1.1247-5
. identifying numbers 1.897-1
. passive, capital gains and losses of ..... 1.1291-10 to 1.1297-3
. qualified electing fund

References are to Reg. § numbers

Foreign investment companies —Cont'd
. *qualified electing fund —Cont'd*
. . election to extend time to pay tax on undistributed earnings 1.1294-1T

Foreign items
. backup withholding 1.6041-4
. license for collection of 301.7231-1

Foreign life insurance companies
. generally 1.819-1; 1.819-2

Foreign loss recapture
. consolidated returns 1.1502-9; 1.1502-9T

Foreign mineral income
. foreign tax credit 1.901-3

Foreign oil and gas extraction income (FOGEI) (See FOGEI and FORI)

Foreign oil related income (FORI) (See FOGEI and FORI)

Foreign partnerships
. acquiring interest in 1.6046A-1
. disposition of interest in 1.6046A-1
. effectively connected taxable income, withholding on
. . coordination with other withholdings .... 1.1446-3(c)
. . determination of foreign partnership status .... 1.1446-1(c)
. . determination of income allocable under section 704 .... 1.1446-2
. . failure to withhold, partnership liability for .... 1.1446-3(e)
. . generally 1.1446-1
. . installment payments .... 1.1446-3(b)
. . publicly traded partnership 1.1446-4
. . reporting and crediting .... 1.1446-3(d)
. . special rules 1.1446-6
. . tiered partnerships 1.1446-5
. . time and manner of paying over tax 1.1446-3
. proportional interest in, substantial change of 1.6046A-1
. reporting transfers to 1.6038B-2
. returns .... 1.6031(a)-1
. . disposition or acquiring interest in, U.S. person 1.6046A-1
. . exception, Commissioner .... 1.6031(a)-1
. . substantial change of interest in, U.S. person with 1.6046A-1
. . U.S. partner of foreign partner making section 1296 election .... 1.6031(a)-1(b)
. tiered partnerships
. . effectively connected taxable income, withholding on 1.1446-5
. transfers
. . reporting 1.6038B-2
. U.S. partner of foreign partner making section 1296 election .... 1.6031(a)-1(b)

Foreign personal holding companies
. adjustments to taxable income 1.556-2
. capital account 1.551-5
. deduction for U.S. obligations 1.511-3
. definitions 1.552-1; 1.556-1
. excluded banks 1.552-4; 1.552-5
. generally .... 1.551-1 et seq.
. gross income 1.551-2; 1.552-2; 1.555-2
. information returns .... 1.6035-1 to 1.6035-3; 301.6035-1
. returns 1.551-4
. stock ownership 1.552-3
. subpart F income 1.952-1
. undistributed income 1.556-3

Foreign personal holding company income
. bona fide hedging transaction
. . effect of identification and non-identification .... 1.954-2(a)(4)(ii)(C)
. . . anti-abuse rule .... 1.954-2(a)(4)(ii)(C)(4); 1.954-2(a)(4)(ii)(C)(5)
. . . inadvertent error .... 1.954-2(a)(4)(ii)(C)(4)
. . . inadvertent identification .... 1.954-2(a)(4)(ii)(C)(2)
. . . transactions identified .... 1.954-2(a)(4)(ii)(C)(1)
. . . transactions not identified .... 1.954-2(a)(4)(ii)(C)(3)
. . identification .... 1.954-2(a)(4)(ii)(B)
. certain property transactions .... 1.954-2(e)
. changes in the use or purpose for which property is held
. . anti-abuse rule .... 1.954-2(a)(3)(ii)(A)
. . hedging transactions .... 1.954-2(a)(3)(ii)(B)
. commodities transactions .... 1.954-2(f)
. . commodity defined .... 1.954-2(f)(2)(i)
. . defined .... 1.954-2(f)(2)(ii)
. . definitions concerning .... 1.954-2(f)(2)
. . exception .... 1.954-2(f)(1)(ii)
. . financial institution not a producer defined .... 1.954-2(f)(2)(vi)
. . generally .... 1.954-2(f)(1)
. . inclusion in foreign personal holding company income .... 1.954-2(f)(1)(i)
. . qualified active sale
. . . active conduct of a commodities business .... 1.954-2(f)(2)(iii)(B); 1.954-2(f)(2)(iv)(B)
. . . activities of employees of a related entity .... 1.954-2(f)(2)(iii)(D)
. . . defined .... 1.954-2(f)(2)(iii); 1.954-2(f)(2)(iii)(A)
. . . substantially all .... 1.954-2(f)(2)(iii)(C); 1.954-2(f)(2)(iv)(C)
. . qualified hedging transaction entered into on or after January 31, 2003 .... 1.954-2(f)(2)(iii)(D)(v); 1.954-2(f)(2)(v)(A)
. . . defined .... 1.954-2(f)(2)(v)
. . . effective date .... 1.954-2(f)(2)(iii)(D)(v)(D)
. . . examples .... 1.954-2(f)(2)(iii)(D)(v)(C); 1.954-2(f)(2)(v)(C)

References are to Reg. § numbers

Foreign personal holding company income —Cont'd
. *commodities transactions—Cont'd*
. . *qualified hedging transaction entered into on or after January 31, 2003—Cont'd*
. . . exception . . . . 1.954-2(f)(2)(iii)(D)(v)(B); 1.954-2(f)(2)(v)(B)
. . . financial institutions not a producer, etc. . . . . 1.954-2(f)(2)(iii)(D)(v)(D)(vi)
. . . generally . . . . 1.954-2(f)(2)(iii)(D)(v)(A)
. . qualified hedging transaction entered into prior to January 31, 2003 . . . . .1.954-2(f)(2)(iii)(D)(iv); 1.954-2(f)(2)(iv)(A)
. . . defined . . . . 1.954-2(f)(2)(iv)
. . . effective date . . . . 1.954-2(f)(2)(iii)(D)(iv)(C); 1.954-2(f)(2)(iv)(C)
. . . exception . . . . 1.954-2(f)(2)(iii)(D)(iv)(B); 1.954-2(f)(2)(iv)(B)
. . . generally . . . . .1.954-2(f)(2)(iii)(D)(iv)(A)
. . treatment of losses . . . . 1.954-2(f)(1)(iii)
. computation
. . bona fide hedging transactions . . . 1.954-2(a)(4)(ii)(A)
. . . defined . . . . 1.954-2(a)(4)(ii)(A)
. . . effect of identification and non-identification . . . . .1.954-2(a)(4)(ii)(C)
. . . identification . . . . 1.954-2(a)(4)(ii)(B)
. . categories of foreign personal holding company income . . . . 1.954-2(a)(1)
. . changes in the use or purpose for which property is held . . . . 1.954-2(a)(3)
. . . example . . . . 1.954-2(a)(3)(iii)
. . . generally . . . . .1.954-2(a)(3)(i)
. . . special rules . . . . 1.954-2(a)(3)(ii)
. . coordination of overlapping categories under foreign personal holding company provisions . . . . 1.954-2(a)(2)
. . . generally . . . . .1.954-2(a)(2)(i)
. . . priority of categories . . . . 1.954-2(a)(2)(ii)
. . dealer property
. . . hedging transactions . . . . .1.954-2(a)(4)(v)(C)
. . . securities dealers . . . . .1.954-2(a)(4)(v)(B)
. . dealer property defined . . . . .1.954-2(a)(4)(v)(A)
. . definitions and special rules . . . . 1.954-2(a)(4)
. . . bona fide hedging transaction . . . . 1.954-2(a)(4)(ii)
. . . dealer property . . . . 1.954-2(a)(4)(v)
. . . examples .1.954-2(a)(4)(vi)
. . . interest . . . . .1.954-2(a)(4)(i)
. . . inventory and similar property . . . . 1.954-2(a)(4)(iii)
. . . regular dealer . . . . .1.954-2(a)(4)(iv)
. . interest
. . . bona fide hedging transaction . . . . 1.954-2(a)(4)(ii)
. . . inventory and similar property . . . . 1.954-2(a)(4)(iii)
. . inventory and similar property
. . . defined . . . . 1.954-2(a)(4)(iii)(A)
. . . hedging transactions . . . . 1.954-2(a)(4)(iii)(B)
. . special rules applicable to distributive share of partnership income . . . . 1.954-2(a)(5)

Foreign personal holding company income —Cont'd
. *computation —Cont'd*
. . *special rules applicable to distributive share of partnership income—Cont'd*
. . . certain other exceptions applicable to foreign personal holding company income . . 1.954-2(a)(5)(ii)
. . . effective date . . . . 1.954-2(a)(5)(v)
. . . examples . . . . 1.954-2(a)(5)(iii)
. dividends, interest, rents, royalties, and annuities . . . . .1.954-2(b)
. . exclusion of certain export financing interest . . . . 1.954-2(b)(2)
. . . conduct of a banking business . . . 1.954-2(b)(2)(iii)
. . . conduct of banking business . . . . . 1.954-2(b)(2)(iii)
. . . examples . . . . 1.954-2(b)(2)(iv)
. . . exceptions . . . . 1.954-2(b)(2)(ii)
. . . generally . . . . 1.954-2(b)(2)(i)
. . exclusion of dividends or interest from related persons . . . . 1.954-2(b)(4)
. . . coordination with sections 864(d) and 881(c) . . . . .1.954-2(b)(4)(ii)(C)
. . . exceptions . . . 1.954-2(b)(4)(ii); 1.954-2(b)(4)(ii)(A); 1.954-2(b)(4)(ii)(B)(1)
. . . generally . . . . .1.954-2(b)(4)(i)
. . . interest paid out of adjusted foreign base company income or insurance income . . . . .1.954-2(b)(4)(ii)(B)
. . . . rule for corporations that are both recipients and payors of interest . . . . 1.954-2(b)(4)(ii)(B)(2)
. . . location of debt instruments . . . . . . 1.954-2(b)(4)(ix)
. . . location of intangible property . . . 1.954-2(b)(4)(vii); 1.954-2(b)(4)(vii)(A)
. . . location of inventory and dealer property . . . . 1.954-2(b)(4)(viii); 1.954-2(b)(4)(viii)(A)
. . . location of tangible property . . . . . 1.954-2(b)(4)(vi); 1.954-2(b)(4)(vi)(A); 1.954-2(b)(4)(vi)(B)
. . . substantial assets test . . . . .1.954-2(b)(4)(iv)
. . . trade or business requirement . . . . 1.954-2(b)(4)(iii)
. . . treatment of certain stock interests . . . . 1.954-2(b)(4)(x)
. . . valuation of assets . . . . 1.954-2(b)(4)(v)
. . exclusion of rents and royalties derived from related persons . . . . 1.954-2(b)(5)
. . . exceptions . . . . 1.954-2(b)(5)(ii)
. . . generally .1.954-2(b)(5)(i)
. . exclusion of rents and royalties derived in the active conduct of a trade or business . . . . 1.954-2(b)(6)
. . generally . . . . 1.954-2(b)(1)
. . treatment of tax exempt interest . . . . . . 1.954-2(b)(3)
. dual character property . . . . .1.954-2(e)(1)(iv)
. exceptions . . . . 1.954-2(e)(1)(ii)
. excluded rents . . . . 1.954-2(c)
. . active conduct of a trade or business . 1.954-2(c)(1)
. . examples . . . . 1.954-2(c)(3)
. . special rules . . . . 1.954-2(c)(2)
. . . active leasing expenses . . . . 1.954-2(c)(2)(iii)

References are to Reg. § numbers

Foreign personal holding company income —Cont'd
. *excluded rents—Cont'd*
. . *special rules—Cont'd*
. . . adding substantial value .... 1.954-2(c)(2)(i)
. . . adjusted leasing profit........... 1.954-2(c)(2)(iv)
. excluded royalties .... 1.954-2(d)
. . active conduct of a trade or business . 1.954-2(d)(1)
. . examples .... 1.954-2(d)(3)
. . special rules .... 1.954-2(d)(2)
. . . active licensing expenses .... 1.954-2(d)(2)(iii)
. . . adding substantial value.......... 1.954-2(d)(2)(i)
. . . adjusted licensing profit .... 1.954-2(d)(2)(iv)
. . . substantiality of foreign organization .... 1.954-2(d)(2)(ii)
. foreign currency gain or loss .... 1.954-2(g); 1.954-2(g)(2)
. . business needs .... 1.954-2(g)(2)(ii)(B)
. . capital gains and losses .... 1.954-2(g)(5)(i)
. . election to characterize foreign currency gain or loss that arises from a specific category of subpart F income as gain or loss in that category .... 1.954-2(g)(3)
. . . example .... 1.954-2(g)(3)(iv)
. . . generally .... 1.954-2(g)(3)(i)
. . . revocation of election .... 1.954-2(g)(3)(iii)
. . . time and manner of election...... 1.954-2(g)(3)(ii)
. . election to treat all foreign currency gains or losses as foreign personal holding company income .... 1.954-2(g)(4)
. . . generally .... 1.954-2(g)(4)(i)
. . . revocation of election .... 1.954-2(g)(4)(iii)
. . . time and manner of election...... 1.954-2(g)(4)(ii)
. . exclusions
. . . business needs .... 1.954-2(g)(2)(ii)
. . . . example .... 1.954-2(g)(2)(ii)(D)
. . . . general rule................ 1.954-2(g)(2)(ii)(A)
. . . . regular dealers .... 1.954-2(g)(2)(ii)(C)
. . . dealer property, interest-bearing liabilities treated as...................... 1.954-2(g)(2)(ii)(C)(2); 1.954-2(g)(2)(ii)(C)(2)(i); 1.954-2(g)(2)(ii)(C)(2)(iii)
. . . . failure to identify certain liabilities .... 1.954-2(g)(2)(ii)(C)(2)(ii)
. . . general rule .... 1.954-2(g)(2)(ii)(C)(1)
. . generally .... 1.954-2(g)(1)
. . inclusion .... 1.954-2(g)(2)(i)
. . income not subject to section 988 . . 1.954-2(g)(5)(ii)
. . income not subject to section 998 . . 1.954-2(g)(5)(ii)
. . qualified business units using the dollar approximate separate transaction method.... 1.954-2(g)(5)(iii)
. . qualified business units using the dollar approximate separate transactions method . . . 1.954-2(g)(5)(iii)
. generally .... 1.954-2(e)(1)
. hedging transactions .... 1.954-2(a)(4)(iii)(B)
. inclusions.......................... 1.954-2(e)(1)(i)
. income equivalent to interest

Foreign personal holding company income —Cont'd
. *income equivalent to interest —Cont'd*
. . defined .... 1.954-2(h)(2)
. . examples .... 1.954-2(h)(6)
. . exceptions .... 1.954-2(h)(1)(ii); 1.954-2(h)(1)(ii)(B)
. . generally .... 1.954-2(h)(1); 1.954-2(h)(1)(i); 1.954-2(h)(2)
. . inclusion in foreign personal holding company income .... 1.954-2(h)(1)(i)
. . income equivalent to interest from factoring .... 1.954-2(h)(4)
. . . examples .... 1.954-2(h)(4)(iv)
. . . exceptions .... 1.954-2(h)(4)(ii)
. . . factored receivable .... 1.954-2(h)(4)(iii)
. . . general rule .... 1.954-2(h)(4)(i)
. . interest .... 1.954-2(h)(1)(ii)(B)
. . liability hedging transactions ..... 1.954-2(h)(1)(ii)(A)
. . notional principal contracts .... 1.954-2(h)(3)
. . . generally .... 1.954-2(h)(3)(i)
. . . regular dealers .... 1.954-2(h)(3)(ii)
. . receivable arising from performance of services .... 1.954-2(h)(5)
. . receivables arising from performance of services .... 1.954-2(h)(5)
. income equivalent to interest defined .... 1.954-2(h)(2)(i)
. income from the sale of property ..... 1.954-2(h)(2)(ii)
. property that does not give rise to income .... 1.954-2(e)(3)
. property that gives rise to certain income .... 1.954-2(e)(2); 1.954-2(e)(2)(i)
. . gain or loss from the disposition of a debt instrument .... 1.954-2(e)(2)(ii)
. related persons, exclusion of dividends or interest from
. . corporate payor .... 1.954-2(b)(4)(i)(A); 1.954-2(b)(5)(i)(A)
. . interest paid out of adjusted foreign base company income or insurance income .... 1.954-2(b)(4)(ii)(B)(1)
. . inventory and dealer property located in part in the payor's country of incorporation .... 1.954-2(b)(4)(viii)(B)
. . partnership payments .... 1.954-2(b)(5)(i)(B)
. . property located in part in the payor's country of incorporation .... 1.954-2(b)(4)(vii)(B)
. . property used in part in the controlled foreign corporation's country of incorporation .... 1.954-2(b)(5)(ii)(B)
. . property used in part in the controlled foreign corporation's county of incorporation .... 1.954-2(b)(5)(ii)(B)
. . rents or royalties paid out of adjusted foreign base company income or insurance income .... 1.954-2(b)(5)(ii)(A)
. treatment of losses .... 1.954-2(e)(1)(iii)

Foreign personal holding corporations
. trust, creating .... 1.672(f)-2

References are to Reg. § numbers

Foreign persons
. deductions 1.1441-9
. taxpayer identification number (TIN) 301.6109-1
. U.S. real property interest, transfer of
. . nonrecognition 1.897-6T
. withholding .... 1.1441-1 et seq.

Foreign private foundations
. withholding .... 1.1441-1 et seq.
. withholding exemption 1.1441-9

Foreign related person
. amounts owed to, deduction of .... 1.267(a)-3

Foreign sales corporations (FSCs)
. boycotts, participation in international ..... 1.927(e)-2T
. definitions .... 1.927(d)-2T
. distributions to shareholders .. 1.926(a)-1; 1.926(a)-1T
. dividends-received deduction .... 1.56(g)-1(d)
. export property .... 1.927(a)-1T
. . disposition of .... 1.924(e)-1
. foreign trade income 1.923-1T
. foreign trading gross receipts
. . controlled group .... 1.924(a)-1T(a)
. . . defined .... 1.924(a)-1T(h)
. . defined .... 1.924(a)-1T
. . engineering and architectural services .... 1.924(a)-1T(e)
. . entitlement to income .... 1.924(a)-1T(i)
. . excluded receipts .... 1.924(a)-1T(g)
. . export property .... 1.924(a)-1T(a)
. . . leases of .... 1.924(a)-1T(c)
. . . sales of .... 1.924(a)-1T(b)
. . gross receipts .... 1.924(a)-1T(a)
. . managerial services .... 1.924(a)-1T(f)
. . related and subsidiary services ..... 1.924(a)-1T(d)
. . related supplier and related party .... 1.924(a)-1T(a)
. . sales and lease .... 1.924(a)-1T(a)
. . small FSC limitations .... 1.924(a)-1T(j)
. generally .... 1.367(b)-1; 1.921-2 et seq.
. gross receipts defined .... 1.927(b)-1T
. interest expense, allocation
. . income from sources within or without U.S. .... 1.861-12T(g)
. management outside of the U.S., requirements for
. . bank accounts, disbursements from .. 1.924(c)-1(d)
. . bank accounts outside the U.S., maintenance of .... 1.924(c)-1(c)
. . generally .... 1.924(c)-1(a)
. . meetings
. . . management .... 1.924(c)-1(b)
. . . shareholder .... 1.924(c)-1(b)
. marginal costing rules .... 1.925(b)-1T
. rules, generally .... 1.921-2 et seq.
. taxable year, determination of 1.441-1
. termination 1.921-1T

Foreign sales corporations (FSCs) —Cont'd
. transfer pricing rules .... 1.925(a)-1T
. . combined taxable income method ...... 1.925(a)-1T
. . gross receipts method, use of .... 1.925(a)-1T
. . grouping transactions .... 1.925(a)-1
. . related supplier, transfer from a .... 1.925(a)-1T
. transitional rules 1.921-1T

Foreign source income
. allocation .... 1.168(i)-1(f)
. amount of income tax that is creditable
. . noncompulsary amounts .... 1.901-2(e)(5)(i)
. . refunds and credits .... 1.901-2(e)(2)(i); 1.901-2(e)(2)(ii)
. . subsidies
. . . effective date .... 1.901-2(e)(3)(v)
. . . examples .... 1.901-2(e)(3)(iv)
. . . general rule .... 1.901-2(e)(3)(i)
. . . official exchange rate .... 1.901-2(e)(3)(iii)
. credit for tax, allowance of 1.901-1; 1.901-1T
. . alien resident of the United States or Puerto Rico .... 1.901-1T(a)(3)
. . citizens of the United States .... 1.901-1T(a)(1)
. . deduction denied if credit claimed .... 1.901-1(c)
. . dividends from a DISC treated as foreign .... 1.901-1(i)
. . domestic corporation .... 1.901-1T(a)(2)
. . effective applicability date .... 1.901-1T(j)
. . effective date .... 1.901-1(j)
. . expiration date .... 1.901-1T(k)
. . generally .... 1.901-1T(a)
. . joint return .... 1.901-1(e)
. . limitations .... 1.901-1T(b)
. . period during which election can be made or changed .... 1.901-1(d)
. . taxes against which credit not allowed .... 1.901-1(f)
. . taxpayers denied credit in a particular taxable year .... 1.901-1(h)
. . taxpayers to whom credit not allowed .... 1.901-1(g)
. income, war profits, or excess profits tax paid or accrued .... 1.901-2(T)
. . expiration date .... 1.901-2(T)(h)(3)
. . foreign payments paid under sec. 1.901-2(1) in taxable years ending on or after July 16, 2008 .... 1.901-2(T)(h)(2)
. party undertaking tax as part of transaction
. . examples .... 1.901-2(f)(2)(ii)
. . generally .... 1.901-2(f)(2)(i)

Foreign tax credit
. accrued, unpaid taxes 1.905-4T
. accumulated profits 1.902-2
. allocation and apportionment of taxes 1.904-6
. allowance, conditions for 1.905-2
. alternate minimum tax rates, use of .... 1.904(b)-1
. alternative minimum tax, computation of ... 1.904-4(k)

References are to Reg. § numbers

Foreign tax credit —Cont'd
. capital gains .... 1.904(b)-1; 1.904(b)-2; 1.1247-4
. carryback of deficit in post-1986 undistributed earnings .... 1.902-2(a)
. carrybacks and carryovers .... 1.904-2; 1.904-2T; 1.904-3; 301.6501(i)-1
. carryforward of pre-1987 accumulated profits .... 1.902-2(b)
. categories of income .... 1.904-4T(a)
. consolidated returns 1.1502-4
. controlled foreign corporations 1.904-5; 1.904-5T
. . dividends .... 1.904-5(c)(4)
. . earnings and profits, distributions
. . . high withholding tax defined for .... 1.904-7(d)
. . . installment sales .... 1.904-7(c)
. . . look-through rules, application of .... 1.904-7(b)
. . . non-look through pools in post 2002 taxable years .... 1.904-7T(f)
. . . recapture income .... 1.904-7(e)
. . . taxable years beginnings Jan. 1. 2007 .... 1.904-7T(g)
. . high withholding tax interest .... 1.904-5(f)
. . interest payments .... 1.904-5(c)(2)
. . look-through rules 1.904-5; 1.904-5T
. . rents and royalties .... 1.904-5(c)(3)
. . subpart F exclusions .... 1.904-5(d)
. . subpart F inclusions .... 1.904-5(c)(1)
. . subpart F income in excess of 70 percent gross income .... 1.904-5(e)
. DASTM gain or loss, special rules for ...... 1.904-4(j)
. deconsolidation to avoid credit limitations, limits on
. . definitions .... 1.904(i)-1(b)
. . effective date .... 1.904(i)-1(e)
. . foreign tax payments, consistency requirement .... 1.904(i)-1(d)
. . general rule .... 1.904(i)-1
. . special rules .... 1.904(i)-1(b)
. . taxable year .... 1.904(i)-1(c)
. deficit in post-1986 undistributed earnings 1.902-2
. disallowance 1.911-6
. domestic corporate shareholder ... 1.902-1; 1.902-1T
. exemption from limitation .... 1.904(j)
. export financing interest .... 1.904-4(h)
. financial services income .... 1.904-4(e)
. foreign corporations .... 1.960-1 to 1.960-7
. foreign earned income 1.911-3
. foreign mineral income 1.901-3
. generally .... 1.901-1 et seq.; 1.904-1 et seq.
. high-taxed income .... 1.904-4(c)
. housing cost 1.911-4
. interaction of section 907(c) and income in this section .... 1.904-4(i)
. limitation 1.904-1
. limitation exemption .... 1.904(j)

Foreign tax credit —Cont'd
. net operating losses and net capital losses .... 1.904(f)-3
. noncontrolled section 902 corporation ..... 1.904-4(e)
. overall foreign loss ... 1.904(f)-1(a); 1.904(f)-1 et seq.; 1.904(f)-1T
. . consolidated 1.1502-9T
. . determination of loss .... 1.904(f)-1(c)
. overall foreign loss accounts .... 1.904(f)-1 et seq.; 1.904(f)-1T
. . additions to .... 1.904(f)-1(d)
. . establishment of .... 1.904(f)-1(b)
. . reduction of .... 1.904(f)-1(e)
. overall foreign loss recapture
. . determination of taxable income .... 1.904(f)-2(b)
. . generally .... 1.904(f)-2(a)
. . sec. 904(f)(1) recapture .... 1.904(f)-2(c); 1.904(f)-2T
. . sec. 904(f)(3) recapture .... 1.904(f)-2(d)
. partial exclusion for earned income 1.911-1
. passive income
. . grouping of items .... 1.904-4T(b)
. pools of foreign taxes, adjustments to
. . currency translation
. . . accred taxes .... 1.905-3T(b)(1)
. . . allocation of refunds .... 1.905-3T(b)(4)
. . . basis of foreign currency refunded .... 1.905-3T(b)(5)
. . . election to translate using date of payment exchange rate .... 1.905-3T(b)(1)(D)
. . . functional currency liability ...... 1.905-3T(b)(5)(iv)
. . . gain or loss, foreign currency .... 1.905-3T(b)(5)(v)
. . . inflationary currency .... 1.905-3T(b)(1)(C)
. . . Jan. 1, 1987, taxable years beginning prior to .... 1.905-5T(b)
. . . nondollar functional currency .... 1.905-3T(b)(5)(iii)
. . . paid taxes .... 1.905-3T(b)(2)
. . . refund or other reductions of foreign tax liability .... 1.905-3T(b)(3)
. . . regulated investment companies .... 1.905-3T(b)(1)(E)
. . . U.S. dollar functional currency ... 1.905-3T(b)(5)(ii)
. . foreign tax redetermination .... 1.905-3T(a)(2)
. . . de minimis currency fluctuations, exceptions to .... 1.905-5T(e)
. . . defined .... 1.905-3T(c); 1.905-5T(c)
. . . foreign tax imposed on foreign refund .... 1.905-3T(e)
. . . Jan. 1, 1987, taxable years beginning prior to .... 1.905-5T(c)
. . U.S tax liability redetermination .... 1.905-3T(d)
. . . foreign tax paid direct by U.S. person .... 1.905-3T(d)(1)
. . . foreign tax paid under section 902 or 960 .... 1.905-3T(d)(2)
. . . Jan. 1, 1987, beginning prior to .... 1.905-5T(d)

References are to Reg. § numbers

Foreign tax credit —Cont'd
. procedural rules 1.911-7
. qualified individuals 1.911-2
. recapture .... 1.904(f)-2 to 1.904(f)-12
. . beginning after December 31, 2002 . . 1.904(f)-12(g); 1.904(f)-12T(g)
. . beginning before January 1, 1987 ...... 1.904(f)-12
. . beginning before January 1, 2003 ... 1.904(f)-12(g); 1.904(f)-12T(g)
. regulated investment companies 1.853-1
. sale of personal property .... 1.904(b)-3
. spouses 1.904-3; 1.911-5
. taxes in lieu of income taxes 1.903-1
. time for credit 1.905-1
. undistributed earnings, post-1986 .... 1.902-2
. United Kingdom income taxes paid with respect to royalties 1.905-5T
. U.S tax liability redetermination
. . Jan. 1, 1987, beginning prior to, foreign tax paid under section 902 or 960 .... 1.905-5T(d)
. . notification of foreign tax redetermination
. . . contents of notification .... 1.905-4T(c)(1)
. . . failure to file 301.6689-1T
. . . foreign taxes deemed paid .... 1.905-4T(c)(3)
. . . foreign taxes paid or accrued ..... 1.905-4T(c)(2)
. . . interest penalties .... 1.905-4T(e)
. . . large and midsize business division, taxpayers under jurisdiction of .... 1.905-4T(b)(3)
. . . payment or refund of U.S. taxes ...... 1.905-4T(d)
. . . pooling adjustment in lieu of redetermination .... 1.905-4T(b)(2)
. . . time and manner .... 1.905-4T(b)

Foreign taxes
. corporate organizations and reorganizations .... 1.381(a)-1
. estates .... 1.642(a)(2)-1
. partnership allocation of distributive share tax .... 1.704-1(b)
. redetermination
. . pools of foreign taxes, adjustments to (See Foreign tax credit)

Foreign trade income
. foreign sales corporations
. . distributions to shareholders .... 1.926(a)-1T
. . exemption 1.923-1T
. gross receipts .... 1.924(a)-1T et seq.

Foreign trusts
. agents, intermediary treatment as .... 1.643(h)-1
. automatic extension of time for filing returns 301.6081-2
. distributions through intermediaries .... 1.643(h)-1
. gain, recognition of
. . charitable trust, transfers to 1.684-3

Foreign trusts —Cont'd
. *gain, recognition of —Cont'd*
. . charitable trusts, transfers to 1.684-3
. . death, transfers at 1.684-3
. . distributions to trusts 1.684-3
. . exceptions to general rule 1.684-3
. . fair market value to unrelated trust, transfers for 1.684-3
. . grantor trust, transfers to 1.684-3
. . grantor trusts, transfers to 1.684-3
. . immediate 1.684-1
. . inadvertent migrations 1.684-4
. . indirect transfers 1.684-2
. . outbound migrations of domestic trusts 1.684-4
. . reporting requirements 1.684-1
. . transfer when foreign trust no longer treated as owned by U.S. person 1.684-2
. . unrelated trusts, transfers for fair market to 1.684-3
. generally ...... 1.643(a)-6 et seq.; 1.643(d)-1 et seq.; 1.665(c)-1A et seq.; 1.1493-1; 16.3-1; 301.6048-1
. information returns upon creation of 16.3-1
. transfers
. . constructive 1.684-2
. . deemed 1.684-2
. . entities owned by a foreign trust 1.684-2
. . indirect 1.684-2
. . recognition of gain (See subhead gain, recognition of)
. . U.S. beneficiaries, by (See subhead U.S. beneficiaries)
. U.S. beneficiaries
. . acquisition or loss of beneficiary 1.679-2
. . constructive transfers 1.679-3
. . definitions concerning transfers to trust 1.679-1
. . determination of treatment 1.679-2
. . entities owned by foreign trusts, transfers to 1.679-3
. . exceptions to general rule 1.679-4
. . failed qualified obligations, transfers resulting from 1.679-4
. . fair market value, transfers for 1.679-4
. . guarantee of trust obligations 1.679-3
. . indirect beneficiaries 1.679-2
. . indirect transfers 1.679-3
. . nonresident alien becoming U.S. person 1.679-5
. . outbound migrations of domestic trusts 1.679-6
. . owner status of U.S. transferor 1.679-1
. . partial consideration, transfers for 1.679-4
. . pre-immigration trusts, transfers for 1.679-5
. . tax avoidance 1.679-3
. . transfers 1.679-3
. withholding taxes 1.1441-5

References are to Reg. § numbers

Foreigners (See Aliens; Nonresident aliens)

Forfeitures

. ERISA .... 1.411(a)-4; 1.411(a)-4T

. pension, profit-sharing, and stock bonus plans 1.401-7

Former employees

. employment taxes

. . disabled former employee .... 31.3121(a)(15)-1

. . survivor or estate of former employee .... 31.3121(a)(14)-1

. minimum participation requirements, defined benefit plans .... 1.401(a)(26)-4

. pension, profit-sharing, and stock bonus plans (See also Pension, profit-sharing, and stock bonus plans)

. . nondiscrimination rules .... 1.401(a)(4)-1; 1.401(a)(4)-10

Forms

. guidance on, IRS 301.6011-1

Foundations, private (See Private foundations)

401(k) plans (See Cash or deferred arrangements)

Franchises, trademarks, and trade names

. generally .... 1.177-1; 1.1254-1 to 1.1254-5; 1.1563-4

Fraternal beneficiary societies

. exempt organizations ... 1.501(c)(8)-1; 1.501(c)(10)-1

Fraud and deceit

. imprisonment 301.7207-1

. penalties 301.6674-1; 301.6682-1; 301.6690-1

. personal holding companies 1.547-5

Freezing estate value

. special valuation rules

. . accumulated qualified payments 25.2701-4

. . adjustments 25.2701-5

. . applicable retained interests 25.2701-2

. . family-held gifts 25.2701-3

. . gift, determination of amount of 25.2701-3

. . guaranteed payments, applicable retained interests 25.2701-2

. . indirect holding of interests 25.2701-6

. . interests in corporations and partnerships 25.2701-1

. . limitations on assessment and collection, exceptions to .... 301.6501(c)-1

. . partnerships 25.2701-5

. . restrictive arrangements 25.2703-1

. . . effective date 25.2703-1

. . separate interests 25.2701-7

. . transfers of interests in trust ...... 25.2702-1 et seq.

. . . annuity interests 25.2702-3

. . . applicable restrictions, transfers subject to 25.2704-2

. . . definitions 25.2702-2

. . . effective date 25.2703-2; 25.2704-3

. . . gifts, reduction in taxable 25.2702-6

. . . held in trust, property treated as 25.2702-4

Freezing estate value —Cont'd

. *special valuation rules —Cont'd*

. . *transfers of interests in trust—Cont'd*

. . . joint purchases 25.2702-4

. . . lapse of certain rights 25.2704-1; 25.2704-3

. . . leases 25.2702-4

. . . personal residence trusts 25.2702-5

. . . qualified interests 25.2702-3

. . . remainder interests 25.2702-3

. . . unitrust interests 25.2702-3

Fringe benefits (See also particular benefit)

. generally ..... 1.61-2T; 1.61-21; 1.132-1 to 1.132-8T; 1.162-25T

. gross income exclusion 1.132-1; 1.132-1T

. line-of-business limitations 1.132-4; 1.132-4T

. no-additional cost services 1.132-2; 1.132-2T

. noncash, deduction for 1.162-25T

. nondiscrimination rules........... 1.132-8; 1.132-8T

. taxation of 1.61-21

. transportation

. . employer provided 1.132-5

. . qualified transportation fringes, questions concerning 1.132-9

. vehicle allocation rules 1.132-5

. working condition fringe benefits ... 1.132-5; 1.132-5T

Fuel, taxable

. administrative authority 48.4083-1

. alcohol blends 48.4081-2

. ASTM specifications 48.4081-1

. blended taxable fuel .... 48.4081-1(c)

. bulk transfers

. . from a terminal by an unregistered holder .... 48.4081-3(d)

. . not received at an approved terminal or refinery .... 48.4081-3(e)

. definitions concerning 48.4081-1

. entry into the U.S. .... 48.4081-3(c)

. information returns, registrant 48.4101-2

. inspection

. . IRS records, state .... 48.4102-1(b)

. . place of .... 48.4083-1(b)

. . refusal to submit to .... 48.4083-1(c)

. . taxpayer records, state 48.4102-1

. measurement 48.4081-8

. military specifications 48.4081-1

. notification certificate of taxable fuel registrant 48.4081-5

. persons required to register .... 48.4101-1(c)

. refund of 48.4081-7

. registration, rules relating to ... 48.4101-1; 48.4101-1T

. removal at terminal rack 48.4081-2

. . taxable events other than 48.4081-3

. removal from a refinery .... 48.4081-3(b)

References are to Reg. § numbers

Fuel, taxable —Cont'd
. removal or sale of blended taxable fuel by the blender . . . . 48.4081-3(g)
. sales within the bulk transfer/terminal system . . . . 48.4081-3(f)

Fuel floor stocks tax
. aviation fuel, imposition of tax . . . . 48.6416(b)(2)-2
. exemptions . . . . 48.4082-10T; 48.6416(b)(2)-2
. exports . . . . 48.6416(b)(2)-2
. government entities, applicability for . . 48.6416(b)(2)-2
. imposition of tax . . . . 48.6416(b)(2)-2
. kerosene exemption 48.4082-10T

Functional currency
. accounting methods 1.985-4
. dollar approximate separate transactions 1.985-3
. dollar as 1.985-2
. European Monetary Union conversion to euro 1.985-8; 1.1001-5
. generally . . . . 1.985-1 et seq.
. separate transactions method 1.985-3

Funeral expenses
. deductions 20.2053-2

Future interests
. charitable contributions 1.170A-5

Future status
. exempt organizations . . . . 1.503(c)-1 to 1.503(e)-4

G

Gain or loss
. accounting methods 1.453-9
. acquisitions
. . stock distributions, recognition of gain on certain 1.355-7
. alternative minimum tax 1.61-6
. assumption of liabilities . . . . 1.1031(d)-2
. banks . . . . 1.582-1; 1.584-6; 1.585-1 to 1.585-4; 1.586-1; 1.586-2
. basis (See Basis for gain or loss)
. built-in loss 1.865-1; 1.1258-1
. . consolidated group member, ceasing to be
. . . net unrealized built-in loss, allocation of . . . . 1.1502-95(e)
. . consolidated returns
. . . limitations on built-in losses . . . . 1.1502-15(b)
. . . SRLY limitations on built-in losses . . . 1.1502-15(a)
. . controlled groups; loss corporations . . . . 1.382-8(b)
. . loss group member, ceasing to be
. . . net unrealized built-in loss, allocation of . . . . 1.1502-95(e)
. . ownership change
. . . net operating loss carrybacks and carryovers loss limitations 1.382-2T
. . . net unrealized built-in losses . . . . 1.56(g)-1(k)

Gain or loss —Cont'd
. *built-in loss—Cont'd*
. . prepaid income . . . . 1.382-7T(a)
. capital gains and losses (See Capital gains and losses)
. carrybacks and carryovers (See Net operating loss carrybacks and carryovers)
. computation 1.1001-1
. condemnation of property . . . . 1.1033(g)-1
. consolidated returns (See Consolidated returns)
. controlled groups
. . deferring certain losses of . . . . 1.267(f)-1
. . loss corporations, net unrealized built-in loss . . . . 1.382-8(b)
. coordination of section 1060 with section 1031
. . disposition of property . . . . 1.1031(d)-1T
. deferred exchanges . . . . 1.1031(b)-2
. . coordination with section 453
. . . bona fide intent requirement . . 1.1031(k)-1(j)(2)(iv)
. . . disqualified property . . . . 1.1031(k)-1(j)(2)(v)
. . . effective date . . . . 1.1031(k)-1(j)(2)(vii)
. . . examples . . . 1.1031(k)-1(j)(2)(vi); 1.1031(k)-1(j)(3)
. . . qualified escrow accounts and qualified trusts . . . . 1.1031(k)-1(j)(2)(i)
. . . qualified intermediaries . . . . 1.1031(k)-1(j)(2)(ii)
. . . transferee indebtedness . . . . 1.1031(k)-1(j)(2)(iii)
. discharge of liabilities 1.1001-2
. DISCs 1.995-4; 1.996-2
. disposition of property (See Gain or loss on disposition of property)
. divorce, transfer of property incident to 1.1041-1T
. employee stock ownership plans, sale of stock 1.1042-1T
. excess loss accounts 1.1502-19
. . income or gain, taken into account as 1.1502-19
. . special allocation of basis in connection with adjustment or determination . . . . 1.1502-19T(d)
. exchange
. . recognition and computation of 1.988-2
. exempt exchange . . . . 1.1031(d)-1
. FCC policy . . . . 1.1071-1 to 1.1071-4
. foreign loss recapture 1.1502-9; 1.1502-9T
. franchises, trademarks and trade names 1.1254-1
. generally . . . . 1.1001-1 et seq.
. gross income 1.61-6
. insurance policies 1.1035-1
. intangible personal property and nondepreciable personal property
. . like-kind exchanges . . . . 1.1031(a)-2
. intercompany transactions 1.108-3
. intermediaries in transfers of like-kind property, safe harbor for . . . . 1.1031(b)-2
. inventories 1.472-2
. involuntary conversions . . . 1.1033(a)-1 to 1.1033(a)-3; 1.1033(b)-1; 1.1033(d)-1

References are to Reg. § numbers

Gain or loss —Cont'd
. irrigation projects ... 1.1033(c)-1
. itemized deductions ... 1.165-1 et seq.; 1.172.9; 1.172-13
. life insurance companies ... 1.809-1 to 1.812-6
. like-kind exchanges
. . coordination of section 1060 with section 1031 ... 1.1031(d)-1T
. . intangible personal property and nondepreciable personal property ... 1.1031(a)-2
. . sales or exchanges ... 1.1031(a)-1 et seq.
. liquidation ... 1.332-2
. livestock ... 1.1031(e)-1; 1.1033(d)-1; 1.1033(e)-1
. low-income housing projects ... 1.1039-1
. multiple properties, like-kind exchanges ... 1.1031(j)-1
. mutual savings banks, real property loans ... 1.593-4
. natural resources ... 1.617-4
. net operating loss (See Net operating losses)
. nonrecognition ... 1.1031(c)-1
. . real estate transfer by foreign person ... 1.897-6T
. nontaxable exchanges ... 1.1031(a)-1 to 1.1039-1
. obligations at discount ... 1.1232-3
. partners and partnerships ... 1.721-1; 1.731-1; 1.741-1; 301.6231(f)-1
. . allocation
. . . contributed property ... 1.704-3
. . . distributive share of partner ... 1.704-1
. . new partnership resulting from termination of partnership ... 1.704-3
. partnership items ... 301.6231(d)-1
. passive activity (See Passive activity losses and credits)
. personal property
. . like-kind exchanges
. . . intangible personal property and nondepreciable personal property ... 1.1031(a)-2
. . NAICS product classes ... 1.1031(a)-2
. . other than stock ... 1.865-1
. reacquisition of real property ... 1.1038-1; 1.1038-2
. recognition agreement requirements ... 1.367(a)-8
. . corporation on distributions to foreign corporation ... 1.367(e)-2
. residence, sale or exchange of ... 1.121-1 to 1.121-5; 1.165-9; 1.1033(a)-3; 1.1034-1; 1.1038-2
. S corporations (See S corporations)
. safe harbor for qualified intermediaries in transfers of like-kind property ... 1.1031(b)-2
. sales or exchanges
. . generally ... 1.1002-1
. . like-kind exchanges ... 1.1031(a)-1 et seq.
. SEC orders, exchanges in obedience to, generally ... 1.1081-1 et seq.
. self-employment income ... 1.1402(a)-6
. spouses, transfer of property between ... 1.1041-1T
. stock (See Stock)

Gain or loss —Cont'd
. tax-free exchange ... 1.1031(b)-1
. trade or business or investment, property held for productive use in ... 1.1031(a)-1
. transitional subsidiary loss limitation rule ... 1.337(d)-1
. United States obligations ... 1.1037-1

Gain or loss on disposition of property
. coordination of section 1060 with section 1031 ... 1.1031(d)-1T
. deferred exchanges, gain or loss recognition in ... 1.1031(k)-1; 1.1031(k)-1(j)
. . coordination with section 453 ... 1.1031(k)-1(j)(2)
. . disqualified person defined ... 1.1031(k)-1(k)
. . effective date ... 1.1031(k)-1(o)
. . example ... 1.1031(k)-1(k)(1)
. . examples ... 1.1031(k)-1(j)(3)
. . fair market value defined ... 1.1031(k)-1(m)
. . generally ... 1.1031(k)-1(j)(1)
. . identification and receipt of replacement property to be produced ... 1.1031(k)-1(e); 1.1031(k)-1(e)(2)
. . . additional rules ... 1.1031(k)-1(e)(4)
. . . example ... 1.1031(k)-1(e)(5)
. . . receipt of replacement property to be produced ... 1.1031(k)-1(e)(3)
. . identification and receipt requirements ... 1.1031(k)-1(b); 1.1031(k)-1(b)(1)
. . . example ... 1.1031(k)-1(b)(3)
. . . identification period and exchange period ... 1.1031(k)-1(b)(2)
. . identification or replacement property before the end of the identification period ... 1.1031(k)-1(c); 1.1031(k)-1(c)(1)
. . . alternative and multiple properties ... 1.1031(k)-1(c)(4)
. . . description of replacement property ... 1.1031(k)-1(c)(3)
. . . examples ... 1.1031(k)-1(c)(7)
. . . incidental property disregarded ... 1.1031(k)-1(c)(5)
. . . manner of identifying replacement property ... 1.1031(k)-1(c)(2)
. . . revocation of identification ... 1.1031(k)-1(c)(6)
. . interest and growth factors ... 1.1031(k)-1(h)
. . . generally ... 1.1031(k)-1(h)(1)
. . . treatment as interest ... 1.1031(k)-1(h)(2)
. . no inference with respect to actual or constructive receipt rules outside of section 1031 ... 1.1031(k)-1(n)
. . overview ... 1.1031(k)-1(a)
. . receipt of identified replacement property ... 1.1031(k)-1(d)
. . . examples ... 1.1031(k)-1(d)(2)
. . . generally ... 1.1031(k)-1(d)(1)
. . receipt of money or other property
. . . actual and constructive receipt ... 1.1031(k)-1(f)(2)
. . . example ... 1.1031(k)-1(f)(3)

References are to Reg. § numbers

Gain or loss on disposition of property —Cont'd
. *deferred exchanges, gain or loss recognition in—Cont'd*
. . *receipt of money or other property —Cont'd*
. . . generally .... 1.1031(k)-1(f)(1)
. . safe harbors .... 1.1031(k)-1(g)
. . . additional restrictions on safe harbors under paragraphs (g)(3) through (g)(5) .... 1.1031(k)-1(g)(6)
. . . examples .... 1.1031(k)-1(g)(8)
. . . generally .... 1.1031(k)-1(g)(1)
. . . interests and growth factors ..... 1.1031(k)-1(g)(5)
. . . items disregarded in applying safe harbors under paragraphs (g)(3) through (g)(5) .... 1.1031(k)-1(g)(7)
. . . qualified escrow accounts and qualified trusts .... 1.1031(k)-1(g)(3)
. . . qualified intermediaries .... 1.1031(k)-1(g)(4)
. . . security or guarantee arrangements .... 1.1031(k)-1(g)(2)
. records and reports.................... 1.1081-11

Gambling (See Wagering taxes)

Gap agreements
. deferred compensation............. 31.3121(v)(2)-2

Gas (See Oil and gas)

Gas guzzler tax
. generally 48.4064-1

Gasohol 48.4081-2
. generally 48.4041-18
. mixtures defined as, gasoline and alcohol .. 48.4081-6
. rate of tax............................ 48.4081-6

Gasoline tax (See also Aviation fuel; Diesel and special motor fuels tax; Fuel, taxable)
. alcohol blends 48.4041-18
. definitions 48.4081-1
. farm use of gasoline, refunds and credits... 48.6420-1 to 48.6420-6
. . ultimate purchasers of gasoline 48.6420-1; 48.6420-2; 48.6420-4
. gasoline blendstocks, special rules for 48.4081-4
. manufacturers excise taxes
. . farm use of gasoline, refunds and credits .... 48.6420-1 to 48.6420-6
. . off-highway business use
. . . refunds and credits .... 48.6421-0 to 48.6421-7
. . ultimate purchasers of gasoline exemption 48.4084-1
. off-highway business use, refunds and credits 48.6421-4; 48.6421-7
. . applicable laws....................... 48.6421-6
. . exempt sales 48.6421-5
. . recordkeeping requirements 48.6421-7
. . time for filing claim 48.6421-3
. . ultimate purchasers of gasoline 48.6421-1
. recordkeeping

Gasoline tax (See also Aviation fuel; Diesel and special motor fuels tax; Fuel, taxable) —Cont'd
. *recordkeeping —Cont'd*
. . state or local tax officers, inspection of records by 48.4102-1
. reduced rates of tax 48.4081-6
. ultimate purchasers of gasoline........... 48.4084-1
. . farm use of gasoline 48.6420-1; 48.6420-2; 48.6420-4
. . . credits or payments to ultimate purchaser 48.6420-1; 48.6420-2; 48.6420-4
. . off-highway business use, credits or payments 48.6421-1

General asset accounts
. adjustments on prior dispositions .... 1.168(i)-1(j)
. changes in use .... 1.168(i)-1(h)
. conversion to personal use .... 1.168(i)-1(h)
. definitions .... 1.168(i)-1
. depreciation allowance, determination of .... 1.168(i)-1(d)
. disposed or converted assets .... 1.168(i)-1(i)
. disposition of assets from.............. 1.168(i)-1(e)
. elections.............................. 1.168(i)-1(k)
. eligible assets for establishment of ...... 1.168(i)-1(c)
. establishment of .... 1.168(i)-1(c)
. foreign income assets generating .... 1.168(i)-1(f)
. foreign source income .... 1.168(i)-1(f)
. identification or disposed or converted asset .... 1.168(i)-1(i)
. passenger automobiles .... 1.168(i)-1(d); 1.168(i)-1(d)(2)

General obligation bonds
. refunding, special rules for.............. 1.141-13(f)

Generation-skipping transfer tax
. allocation of exemption.................. 26.2632-1
. assignment of generation
. . collateral heirs .... 26.2651-1(b)
. . deceased parents, persons with....... 26.2651-1(a)
. . more than one generation, individual assigned to 26.2651-2
. chapter 13 treatment
. . nonresident not citizen of United States .. 26.2663-2
. charitable lead annuity trust rules 26.2642-3
. definitions concerning 26.2612-1; 26.2652-1
. direct skip defined...................... 26.2612-1
. effective dates.......................... 26.2601-1
. executor defined 26.2652-1
. generation-skipping transfer defined....... 26.2611-1
. inclusion ratio 26.2642-1
. . finality of 26.2642-5
. interest in trust defined 26.2612-1
. lifetime transfers 26.2642-2
. multiple skip taxation 26.2653-1
. nonresident not citizen of United States

References are to Reg. § numbers

Generation-skipping transfer tax —Cont'd
. *nonresident not citizen of United States —Cont'd*
. . chapter 13 treatment 26.2663-2
. predeceased parent rule 26.2651-1
. . collateral heirs 26.2651-1
. . individual assigned to more than one generation 26.2651-2
. qualified severance..................... 26.2642-6
. . actuarial value of beneficial interests, based on .... 26.2642-6(j)(3)
. . beneficiary's interest dependent on inclusion ratio .... 26.2642-6(j)(10)
. . date of severance .... 26.2642-6(j)(11)
. . deemed to precede a taxable termination .... 26.2642-6(j)(8)
. . defined ....26.2642-6(b)
. . examples .... 26.2642-6(j)
. . 50% inclusion ratio, trust with .... 26.2642-6(j)(4)
. . funding of severed trusts
. . . common stocks, fair market value .... 26.2642-6(j)(6)(i); 26.2642-6(j)(6)(ii); 26.2642-6(j)(6)(iii)
. . . non-pro rata basis............. 26.2642-6(j)(5); 26.2642-6(j)(6); 26.2642-6(j)(6)(i)
. . generally ....26.2642-6(a)
. . non-qualified severance, following a .... 26.2642-6(j)(13)
. . regulatory qualified severance ...... 26.2642-6(j)(9)
. . reporting ....26.2642-6(e)
. . reporting a qualified severance
. . . generally .... 26.2642-6(e)(1)
. . . new trust .... 26.2642-6(e)(3)
. . . original trust.................. 26.2642-6(e)(2)
. . requirements ....26.2642-6(d)
. . requirements not met............. 26.2642-6(j)(12)
. . succession of interests .... 26.2642-6(j)(1)
. . . discretionary trust .... 26.2642-6(j)(2)
. . time for making...................... 26.2642-6(f)
. . transition rules .... 26.2642-6(k)(2)
. . trusts resulting non qualified severance ....26.2642-6(h)
. . trusts that were irrevocable on September 25, 1985 ....26.2642-6(g)
. . . generally .... 26.2642-6(g)(1)
. . . trusts in receipt of a post-September 25, 1985, addition .... 26.2642-6(g)(2)
. qualified terminable interest property election 26.2652-2
. rate of tax.............................. 26.2641-1
. recapture tax 26.2663-1
. redetermination of applicable fraction for trust 26.2642-4
. return requirements 26.2662-1
. skip person defined 26.2612-1
. taxable distribution defined 26.2612-1

Generation-skipping transfer tax —Cont'd
. taxable termination defined 26.2612-1
. transferor defined 26.2652-1
. transfers at death 26.2642-2
. trusted defined 26.2652-1
. trusts
. . defined 26.2652-1
. . gross estate, division of trust included in 26.2654-1
. . redetermination of applicable fraction 26.2642-4
. . single trust treatment as separate trust ... 26.2654-1
. valuation 26.2642-2

Geothermal wells
. natural resources 1.612-5

Gift splitting
. consent
. . events signifying 25.2513-2
. . revocation of.......................... 25.2513-3
. return requirements 25.6019-2

Gift tax
. adjusted basis 1.1016-5
. adjusted taxable gifts 20.2001-1
. annuity contract valuation 25.2512-6
. applicability of 25.2511-1
. bond, payment with 25.6165-1
. business, interests in 25.2512-3
. charitable gifts
. . citizens or residents (See subhead citizens or residents, charitable gifts by)
. . disallowance of deduction ....25.2522(c)-1
. . nonresidents not citizens............25.2522(b)-1
. . private and charitable purposes combined ....25.2522(c)-3
. citizens or residents, charitable gifts by
. . disallowance of deduction ....25.2522(c)-1
. . generally ....25.2522(a)-1
. . private and charitable purposes combined .... 25.2522(a)-2; 25.2522(c)-3
. community property ....25.2523(f)-1A
. credit for................................. 20.2012-1
. deductions 25.2524-1
. deficiencies, extension of time to pay 25.6161-1
. disclosure of listed transactions........... 20.6011-4
. donor's domination and control, cessation of 25.2511-2
. excise tax, purchases subject to 25.2512-7
. extension of time to pay
. . bond, with 25.6165-1
. . deficiencies, payment of 25.6161-1
. generally 25.0-1
. gift splitting 25.2513-1
. imposition 25.2501-1; 25.2511-1
. insufficient considerations, transfers for 25.2512-8

References are to Reg. § numbers

Gift tax —Cont'd
. interests in business 25.2512-3
. liability for 25.2502-2
. life estates (See Life estates)
. life insurance contract valuation 25.2512-6
. listed transactions, disclosure of 20.6011-4
. marital deduction .... 25.2523(e)-1
. minor, transfer for benefit of 25.2503-4
. nonresidents not citizens, transfers by 25.2511-3
. notes, valuation of 25.2512-4
. omission of gross estate from return .... 301.6501(e)-1
. open-end investment company shares 25.2512-6
. payment, extension of time 25.6161-1
. persons required to file 25.6019-1
. power of appointment
. . generally 25.2514-1
. . time of creation 25.2514-2; 25.2514-3
. preceding calendar periods
. . liability determination 25.2504-1
. . valuation 25.2504-2
. preceding calendar year, taxable gifts for ... 25.2504-1
. property settlements 25.2516-1
. qualified disclaimer of property
. . entire interest, disclaimer less than 25.2518-3
. . generally 25.2518-1
. . requirements for 25.2518-2
. rate of 25.2502-1
. record keeping requirements 25.6001-1
. recovery, marital deduction property 25.2207A-1
. . failure to exercise right of recover 25.2207A-1
. return requirements 25.6011-1
. . contents of return 25.6019-3
. . due date 25.6075-1
. . filing 25.6019-1
. . gifts made after Dec. 31, 1996 not adequately disclosed .... 301.6501(c)-1
. . omission of gross estate from return .... 301.6501(e)-1
. . place of filing returns and other documents 25.6091-1
. . property, description of 25.6019-4
. . signature 25.6061-1
. specific exemption 25.2521-1
. taxable gift
. . computation 25.2503-2
. . defined 25.2503-1
. tenancies by entirety
. . election and valuation 25.2515-2
. . generally 25.2515-1
. . termination of 25.2515-3
. time for filing 25.6075-1
. . extension of 25.6081-1
. total amount of gift

Gift tax —Cont'd
. *total amount of gift —Cont'd*
. . defined 25.2503-1
. . determination of 25.2503-2
. . future interest in property 25.2503-2
. valuation 25.2512-5
. . annuity contract 25.2512-6
. . business interests 25.2512-3
. . generally 25.2512-1
. . life estates 25.2512-5
. . life insurance 25.2512-6
. . notes 25.2512-4
. . open-end investment company shares ... 25.2512-6
. . preceding calendar periods 25.2504-2
. . remainders and reversions 25.2512-5
. . stocks and bonds 25.2512-2
. . tenancies by entirety 25.2515-2
. . terms for years 25.2512-5

Gifts
. adjusted taxable gifts 20.2001-1
. basis for gain or loss .... 1.1015-1; 1.1015-3 to 1.1015-5
. business gift substantiation requirement 1.274-5; 1.274-5T
. charitable (See Charitable contributions)
. corporate organizations and reorganizations .. 1.356-5
. deductibility 1.174-3
. failure to pay tax 301.6653-1
. gain, recognition of; Section 126 property .... 16A.1255-2(a)
. . death, transfer at .... 16A.1255-2(b)
. . non section 126 property .... 16A.1255-2(e)
. . sale or exchange .... 16A.1255-2(a)(2)
. . tax-free transfer ..... 16A.1255-2(c); 16A.1255-2(d)
. preceding calendar year, determination for 25.2504-2
. purported, recharacterization of .... 1.672(f)-4

Going concern value
. amortization 1.197-2

Golden parachutes
. questions and answers concerning 1.280G-1

Good faith
. section 6662 penalties, exception to 1.6664-4; 1.6664-4T

Goodwill
. amortization 1.197-2; 1.197-2T
. itemized deductions ... 1.162-14; 1.162-20; 1.263(b)-1

Government
. depositaries (See Depositaries of government)
. foreign .... 1.892-1T et seq.; 1.893-1; 1.1445-10T; 31.3401(a)(5)-1
. Indian Tribal Governmental Tax Status Act of 1982 .... 305.7701-1; 305.7871-1
. United States (See United States)

References are to Reg. § numbers

Government depositaries (See Depositaries of government)

Government pension plans
. nondiscrimination rules, application of . . 1.401(a)(4)-1

Governmental units
. trustee of deemed IRAs, special rules for 1.408-2

Gramm-Leach-Bliley Act
. returns, failure to disclosure or use of information in, penalty for . . . . . 301.7216-1(c)

Grantor trusts
. foreign person not treated as owners . . . . . . 1.672(f)-1
. owner treatment . . . . . 1.678(b)-1
. revocable trusts
. . exceptions to general rule . . . . . 1.672(f)-3
. substantial owner treatment . . . . . 1.678(a)-1
. support, for . . . . . 1.678(c)-1

Grants
. generally . . . 1.117-1 to 1.117-5; 1.6041-3; 1.6050D-1

Gratuities (See also Tips)
. reporting requirements 31.6053-1
. substantiation 31.6053-4
. withholding . . . . . 31.3401(a)(16)-1; 31.3401(f)-1; 31.3402(k)-1; 31.6053-1; 31.6053-3; 31.6053-4

Greenmail returns
. extension of time for filing returns 156.6081-1
. time and place for filing returns 156.6091-1

Gross estate
. decedent, interest of 20.2033-1
. defined 20.2031-1
. nonresident alien estate 20.2103-1; 20.2107-1

Gross income
. determination of taxable income 1.482-2
. estates and trust, determination for . . . . . 1.641(a)-2
. foreign corporations 1.952-2
. fringe benefits, exclusion for certain 1.132-1; 1.132-1T
. generally . . . . . 1.61-1 et seq.; 1.1312-1
. insurance companies 1.832-4
. miscellaneous items 1.61-14
. nonresident aliens . . . . . 1.6654-6(b)
. pass-through entities 1.67-2T
. sources within or without U.S. (See Income from sources within or without U.S.)
. state contracts 1.61-3
. substantial risk of forfeiture defined . . . . . 1.83-3(c)
. substantially vested defined . . . . . 1.83-3(b)
. transfers, inclusion in year of 1.83-2

Gross receipts
. domestic product gross receipts (See Domestic product gross receipts)

Gross services margin method
. arm's length transactions; determination of taxable income . . . . . 1.482-9T(d)

Group deferred annuity contracts
. generally . . . . . 1.412(b)-2; 1.818-3

Group health plans
. basis 54.9801-1
. creditable coverage
. . certification 54.9801-5
. . disclosure of previous 54.9801-5
. . generally 54.9801-4
. definitions concerning 54.9801-2
. dependent beneficiaries
. . enrollment, special 54.9801-6
. health status, discrimination based on 54.9802-1
. loss of coverage
. . enrollment, special 54.9801-6
. mental health benefits, parity in application of limits 54.9812-1T
. notice of enrollment rights 54.9801-6
. preexisting conditions, limitations 54.9801-3
. small group health plans, special rules 54.9831-1

Group legal services plans
. dividends exclusions 1.120-1
. exemptions 1.120-3

Group-term life insurance
. amount equal to cost of, determination of 1.79-3
. combined with other benefits . . . . . 1.79-1(b)
. defined 1.79-1
. fewer than 10 employees . . . . . 1.79-1(c)
. gross income . . . . . 1.79-0 to 1.79-4T
. information returns . . . 1.6052-1; 1.6052-2; 301.6052-1
. nondiscrimination rules 1.79-4T
. withholding . . . . . 31.3401(a)(14)-1

Guam
. bona fide residency
. . alien individuals presence test . . . . 1.937-1(c)(2)
. . bona fide resident . . . . . 1.937-1(b)
. . closer connection test . . . . . 1.937-1(e)
. . days of presence . . . . . 1.937-1(c)(3)
. . definitions concerning . . . . . 1.937-1(a)
. . generally 1.937-1
. . information reporting . . . . . 1.937-1(h)
. . medical treatment . . . . . 1.937-1(c)(4)
. . presence test . . . . . 1.937-1(c)
. . significant connection to the United States . . . . . 1.937-1(c)(5)
. . tax home test . . . . . 1.937-1(d)
. . year of move . . . . . 1.937-1(f)
. coordination of individual income taxes 1.935-1
. . definitions concerning . . . . . 1.935-1(a)
. . entity consistency status . . . . . 1.935-1(e)
. . estimated income tax special rules . . . . . 1.935-1(d)
. . extension of territory . . . . . 1.935-1(c)
. . filing requirements . . . . . 1.935-1(b)
. . individuals covered . . . . . 1.935-1(a)

References are to Reg. § numbers

Guam —Cont'd
. *coordination of individual income taxes—Cont'd*
. . liability to other jurisdictions . . . . 1.935-1(b)
. . payment of tax . . . . 1.935-1(b)
. generally 1.876-1; 1.935-1; 301.7654-1
. gross income exclusions 1.931-1
Guarantors, endorsers, and indemnitors
. itemized deductions 1.166-8; 1.166-9

H

Handicapped persons
. generally . . . . 1.190-1 to 1.190-3
Handling costs
. capitalization of 1.263A-3
Harassment campaigns
. exempt organizations, against . . . . 301.6104(d)-3
HCEs (See Highly compensated employees)
Head of household
. defined . . . . 1.2-2(b)
Health care providers
. accounting
. . nonaccrual of certain amounts by . . . . 1.448-1T(d)(2)(A); 1.448-1T(e)(4)
Health plans (See Accident and health plans)
Health Saving Accounts (HSA)
. contributions, comparable
. . cafeteria plans and waiver of excise tax 54.4980G-5
. . calculation 54.4980G-4
. . employee defined for comparability testing 54.4980G-3
. . employer contributions defined 54.4980G-2
. . failure of employer to make 54.4980G-1
Health status
. discrimination based on, group health plan 54.9802-1
Hedge bonds . . . . 1.149(g)-1
Hedging transactions
. consolidated groups . . . . 1.1221-2(e)
. debt instruments 1.446-4
. defined . . . . 1.446-4; 1.1221-2(b)
. foreign currency 1.988-5
. generally . . . . 1.446-3; 1.1221-2(a); 1.1221-2T(a)
. identification
. . description of program . . . . 1.1221-2(f)
. . effect of . . . . 1.1221-2(f)
. . members of same consolidated group . . . 1.1221-2(f)
. . nonidentification . . . . 1.1221-2(g)
. . requirements . . . . 1.1221-2(f); 1.1256(e)-1
. . timing of . . . . 1.1221-2(f)
. . transactions no identified . . . . 1.1221-2(g)
. notional principal contracts 1.446-3; 1.446-4

Hedging transactions —Cont'd
. recordkeeping . . . . 1.446-4; 1.1221-2(f)
. risk reduction transactions . . . . 1.1221-2(d)
. short sales and options, gains from . . . . . . 1.1221-2(a)
. termination payments 1.446-3
Highly compensated employees
. deferred compensation . . . . 1.414(q)-1T
. defined . . . . 1.401(l)-1
. nondiscrimination rules
. . pension, profit-sharing, and stock bonus plans (See Pension, profit-sharing, and stock bonus plans)
. number of employees in top-paid group . . . . 1.414(q)-1
. $1,000,000 remuneration, employees in excess of 1.162-27
. optional forms of benefits . . . . 1.401(a)-4
Highway vehicles
. commuter vehicles
. . investment credit 1.46-11
. . safe harbor lease information returns . . . . 1.168(f)(8)-1T
. highway motor vehicle defined . . . . 41.4482(a)-1
. use tax
. . agricultural vehicles used for 7,500 or fewer miles on public highways, exemption for 41.4483-3
. . contiguous foreign countries, vehicles registered in 41.4483-7
. . customary use defined . . . . 41.4482(c)-1
. . definitions . . . . 41.4482(b)-1; 41.4482(c)-1
. . exemptions
. . . agricultural vehicles used for 7,500 or fewer miles on public highways 41.4483-3
. . . application of 41.4483-4
. . . state and local government 41.4483-1
. . . transit buses 41.4483-2
. . . trucks used for 5,000 or fewer miles on public highways 41.4483-3
. . foreign countries, vehicles registered in . . 41.4483-7
. . generally . . . . 41.0-1 et seq.; 41.4481-1 et seq.
. . imposition 41.4481-1
. . liability for 41.4481-2
. . logging, reduction in tax for trucks used in 41.4483-6
. . payment of
. . . installment payment 41.6156-1
. . . state registration purposes, proof of payment for 41.6001-2
. . . time and place 41.6101-1
. . . United States, proof of for entry into 41.6001-3
. . recordkeeping 41.6001-1; 44.6001-1
. . registration
. . . proof of payment for state registration purposes 41.6001-2
. . . requirements 41.4481-3
. . returns . . . . 41.6011(a)-1

References are to Reg. § numbers

Highway vehicles —Cont'd
. *use tax —Cont'd*
. . *returns—Cont'd*
. . . identifying number 41.6109-1
. . . time for filing .... 41.6071(a)-1; 41.6151(a)-1
. . state
. . . defined .... 41.4482(c)-1
. . . government exemption 41.4483-1
. . taxable gross weights
. . . defined .... 41.4482(b)-1
. . taxable period defined .... 41.4482(c)-1
. . transit buses, exemptions 41.4483-2
. . trucks used for 5,000 or fewer miles on public highways, exemption for 41.4483-3
. . use defined .... 41.4482(c)-1

Holding companies
. foreign personal holding companies (See Foreign personal holding companies)
. personal holding companies (See Personal holding companies)

Holding periods
. briefly asset holding period 1.6011-4
. levied bank accounts 301.6332-3
. stock
. . dividends received deduction 1.246-5
. . reduction of period 1.246-5

Holidays
. time for performance of act where last day falls on Sunday 301.7503-1

Homeowner associations
. generally .... 1.528-1 to 1.528-10

Hope Scholarship credit
. amount, determination of 1.25A-3
. eligibility 1.25A-3
. Lifetime learning credit
. . coordination with education tax credits 1.25A-1
. per student 1.25A-3
. prepayments, academic period for 1.25A-3

Horticultural matters (See Farming)

Hospitals
. exempt organizations .... 1.501(e)-1; 1.513-6

House of Representatives
. travel expenses 5e.274-8

Household
. cost of maintaining defined .... 1.2-2(d)
. defined .... 1.2-2(c)

Household and personal effects
. valuation of 20.2031-6

Household care services
. credits .... 1.44A-1 to 1.44A-4

Household services and care credit
. amount of credit .... 1.21-1(a)
. care of qualifying individual and household services
. . allocation of expenses .... 1.21-1(d)(2)
. . day camps, employment related expense status of .... 1.21-1(d)(7)
. . defined .... 1.21-1(d)(1)
. . dependent care centers .... 1.21-1(e)(2)
. . employment taxes .... 1.21-1(d)(9)
. . household services .... 1.21-1(d)(3)
. . indirect expenses .... 1.21-1(d)(11)
. . manner of providing care .... 1.21-1(d)(4)
. . outside taxpayer's household, services .... 1.21-1(e)
. . overnight camps, employment related expense status of .... 1.21-1(d)(6)
. . room and board .... 1.21-1(d)(10)
. . school or school programs .... 1.21-1(d)(5)
. . transportation costs .... 1.21-1(d)(8)
. daily basis of employment .. 1.21-1(b)(3); 1.21-1(c)(2)
. divorced or separated parents, special test for .... 1.21-1(b)(5)
. employment related expenses .... 1.21-1(a)
. . medical expenses .... 1.21-1(j)
. . reimbursed .... 1.21-1(f)
. gainful employment requirement .... 1.21-1(c)
. generally .... 1.21-1(a)
. limitations on credit
. . annual dollar amount .... 1.21-2(a)
. . earned income limitations .... 1.21-2(b)
. maintenance of household .... 1.21-1(h)
. married taxpayers
. . death of named taxpayer .... 1.21-3(c)
. . joint returns .... 1.21-3(a)
. . taxpayer treated not as not married .... 1.21-3(b)
. medical expenses .... 1.21-1(j)
. parents living apart, special test for ...... 1.21-1(b)(5)
. physical or mental incapacity .... 1.21-1(b)(4)
. principal place of abode defined .... 1.21-1(g)
. qualifying individuals .... 1.21-1(b)
. related individual, payments to
. . generally .... 1.21-4(a)
. . partnership or other entities .... 1.21-4(b)

Housing corporations
. itemized deductions 1.216-1

Housing credit agencies
. correction of administrative errors 1.42-13

H.R. 10 plans
. ERISA, time when contributions made under .... 11.404(a)(6)-1

References are to Reg. § numbers

Husbands and wives (See Spouses)

I

Identification number (See Taxpayer identification number)

Immunity
. Tax Court .... 301.7507-7 to 301.7507-10

Importers
. manufacturers excise taxes
. . bonding of .... 48.4061(a)-2
. . use by importer .... 48.4218-1 to 48.4218-5
. . . business or personal use 48.4218-2
. . . computation of tax 48.4218-5
. . . events subsequent to taxable use 48.4218-3
. . . further manufacture, use in 48.4218-4
. ozone-depleting chemicals, taxes on 52.4682-3
. related persons, imports from
. . basis limitations 1.1059A-1

Improvements
. capitalization rules 1.263A-11
. natural resources 1.611-5

Incentive programs (See Work incentive programs (WIN))

Incentive stock options
. additional compensation 1.422-5
. approval, stockholder 1.422-2; 1.422-3
. cashless exercise 1.422-5
. condition, options subject to 1.422-5
. defined 1.422-2
. employment requirement, failure to satisfy 1.422-1
. generally 1.422-1; 14a.422A-1
. holding period requirement, failure to satisfy .. 1.422-1
. $100,000 limitations 1.422-4

Income, gross (See Gross income)

Income earned abroad by U.S. citizens
. cost-of-living allowances exclusion 1.912-1
. defined 1.911-3
. earned income exclusion .. 1.43-1; 1.911-1 to 1.911-8
. election as to exclusion 1.911-7
. employee retirement and benefit plans 1.406-1; 1.407-1
. filing in office other than required office 1.6091-4
. foreign service personnel 1.912-2
. foreign tax credit 1.911-3
. housing expenses 1.911-4
. international income tax returns, filing 1.6091-3
. married couples 1.911-5
. returns 1.6091-4
. withholding tax .... 31.3401(a)(8)(A)-1

Income from sources within or without U.S.
. aircraft or vessels 1.861-15; 1.861-16

Income from sources within or without U.S. — Cont'd
. allocation of gross income under section 863 .... 1.863-1
. . determination of taxable income .... 1.863-1(c)
. . effective / applicability date .... 1.863-1(f)
. . generally .... 1.863-1; 1.863-1(a)
. . inventory sales .... 1.863-3(a)
. . natural resources .... 1.863-1(b)
. . . additional production activities .... 1.863-1(b)(3)(ii)
. . . additional production prior to export terminal .... 1.863-1(b)(2)
. . . definitions .... 1.863-1(b)(3)
. . . determination of fair market value ... 1.863-1(b)(4)
. . . determination of gross income ...... 1.863-1(b)(5)
. . . examples .... 1.863-1(b)(7)
. . . export terminal .... 1.863-1(b)(3)(iii)
. . . generally .... 1.863-1(b)(1)
. . . production activity .... 1.863-1(b)(3)(i)
. . . tax return disclosure .... 1.863-1(b)(6)
. . personal property sales 1.863-3A
. . residual interest in a REMIC .... 1.863-1(e)
. . . excess inclusion income and net losses .... 1.863-1(e)(1)
. . . REMIC inducement fees .... 1.863-1(e)(1)
. . scholarships, fellowship, grants, prizes and awards .... 1.863-1(d)
. . . definitions .... 1.863-1(d)(3)
. . . foreign source income .... 1.863-1(d)(2)(ii)
. . . generally .... 1.863-1(d)(1)
. . . source of income .... 1.863-1(d)(2)
. . scholastic awards .... 1.863-1(d)
. . taxable income, source determination .... 1.863-2(b)
. . taxable income determination .... 1.863-1(c); 1.863-2(a)
. computation of taxable income .... 1.861-8; 1.861-8T; 1.861-8 to 1.861-14T
. . allocation of deductions .... 1.861-8T(a)(2); 1.861-8T(b)(1); 1.861-8T(e)
. . apportionment of deductions .... 1.861-8T(a)(2); 1.861-8T(c)(1); 1.861-8T(e)
. . excess of deductions and excluded and eliminated items of income .... 1.861-8T(d)(2)
. corporate distributions 1.897-5T
. dividends 1.861-3
. domestic international sales (See Domestic international sales corporations)
. earned income of U.S. citizens .... 1.921-2 et seq.
. effectively connected with U.S. business 1.864-4
. export trade corporations .... 1.970-1 to 1.970-3
. foreign country, income partly from 1.863-3AT
. foreign country or U.S. possession 1.863-6
. foreign source income effectively connected with U.S. business 1.864-5
. foreign tax credit (See Foreign tax credit)

References are to Reg. § numbers

Income from sources within or without U.S. — Cont'd
. generally .... 1.861-1 to 1.970-3
. gross income allocation 1.863-1
. interest 1.861-2
. interest expense, allocation
. . affiliated corporations 1.861-11T; 1.861-14; 1.861-14T
. . controlled foreign corporations 1.861-10; 1.861-10T
. . disallowed interest, assets funded by .. 1.861-12T(f)
. . domestic international sales corporation stock .... 1.861-12T(h)
. . foreign sales corporation stock .... 1.861-12T(g)
. . foreign sales corporations 1.861-13T
. . inventories .... 1.861-12T(b)
. . notes .... 1.861-12T(d)
. . partnerships 1.861-9T
. . portfolio securities, inventory or primarily gains .... 1.861-12T(e)
. . stock treatment .... 1.861-12T(c)
. labor or personal services 1.861-4
. leases 1.861-5; 1.861-15
. nonresident aliens or foreign corporations 1.864-3
. notional principal contracts 1.863-7
. office or other fixed place of business 1.864-6; 1.864-7
. partly within and partly without 1.863-2; 1.863-3
. personal property sales 1.863-3A
. possessions of U.S. 1.863-6; 1.864-5
. REMIC
. . inducement fees .... 1.863-1(e)
. rentals and royalties 1.861-5
. research and experimental expenditures, allocation and apportionment of 1.861-17
. sale of property ... 1.861-6; 1.861-7; 1.863-3; 1.864-1
. scholarships, fellowship, grants, prizes and awards
. . certain activities conducted outside the United States .... 1.863-1(d)(2)(ii)
. . United States source of income ..... 1.863-1(d)(2)(i)
. scholarships and fellowships(d) 1.863-1
. securities lending transactions 1.861-2; 1.861-3; 1.871-7; 1.881-2
. sources without U. S., generally 1.862-1
. trade or business within U. S. 1.864-2
. transportation services 1.863-4

Income through conduct of a trade or business in a possession 1.937-3

Indebtedness
. acquisition of
. . person related to debtor .... 1.108-2(a)
. . . amount of discharge of debt income realized .... 1.108-2(f)
. . . correlative adjustments .... 1.108-2(f)
. . . definitions concerning .... 1.108-2(d)

Indebtedness — Cont'd
. *acquisition of — Cont'd*
. . *person related to debtor — Cont'd*
. . . direct acquisition .... 1.108-2(b)
. assumption of
. . corporate acquisitions .... 1.381(c)(15)-1
. certificates of indebtedness (See Treasury certificates of indebtedness)
. corporate acquisitions .... 1.279-1 to 1.279-6
. deductibility, generally 20.2053-1
. discharge of indebtedness (See Discharge of indebtedness)
. S corporations shareholders, basis adjustment (See S corporations subhead indebtedness to shareholders)

Indemnitors
. generally 1.166-8; 1.166-9

Independent contractors
. deferred compensation and deferred benefits, deductibility of .... 1.404(d)-1T

Independent producers
. exemptions 1.613A-3

Indian Tribal Government Tax Status Act of 1982
. generally 305.7701-1; 305.7871-1

Indian tribal governments
. Alaska Native Corporations 1.1502-81T
. state treatment of tribe as state for certain purposes 305.7871-1
. withholding of tax on gaming profits ..... 31.3402(r)-1

Indians (See Indian tribal governments; Native Americans)

Individual income tax
. automatic extension of time for filing returns 1.6081-4
. generally .... 1.1-1 et seq.

Individual retirement annuities
. generally 1.408-3

Individual retirement arrangements (IRAs)
. annual reports by trustees and issuers 1.408-5
. annuities under 20.2039-5
. definitions .... 1.411(a)-7
. disclosure statements 1.408-6
. distribution requirements .... 1.408-4 et seq.; 1.408-8
. employer plan, deemed IRA in .... 1.408(q)-1
. generally .... 1.408-1 to 1.408-7; 1.408-2 et seq.
. governmental units, special rules for 1.408-2
. limitations and repeal of estate tax exclusion for 20.2039-1T
. penalties 301.6693-1
. pension excise tax 54.4974-1
. pension excise taxes 54.4974-1
. retirement bonds 1.409-1
. returned or recharacterized contributions, net income calculation for 1.408-11

References are to Reg. § numbers

Individual retirement arrangements (IRAs) —Cont'd
. simplified employee pensions .... 1.408-7 to 1.408-9; 301.6693-1
. vesting .... 1.411(a)-1 et seq.
. vesting schedule, changes in............. 1.411(a)-8
. withholding .... 31.3401(a)(12)-1; 35.3405-1
Indorsers
. generally 1.166-9
Inducement fees
. REMICs (See Real estate mortgage investment conduits (REMICs))
Industrial development bonds
. generally 1.103-7; 1.103-10; 5c.103-2; 5f.103-2
Inflation-indexed debt instruments
. income tax treatment of 1.1275-7
. stripped 1.1286-2
Influencing legislation (See Lobbying)
Information base
. amortization............................ 1.197-2
Information returns
. abandonment of security 1.6050J-1T
. acquisition of control in capital structure..... 1.6043-4
. actuary 301.6059-1
. annuity and bond purchase plans 301.6047-1
. attorneys, payment to
. . amount of payments defined .... 1.6045-5(d)
. . attorney defined .... 1.6045-5(d)
. . exception, filing .... 1.6045-5(c)
. . joint or multiple payees .... 1.6045-5(b)
. . legal services defined .... 1.6045-5(d)
. . payments defined..................... 1.6045-5(d)
. . payor defined .... 1.6045-5(d)
. . requirement 1.6045-5
. . TIN, furnishing .... 1.6045-5(e)
. automatic extensions of time for filing returns 1.6081-8
. backup withholding 1.6041-3; 1.6041-4; 1.6042-2; 1.6044-2; 1.6045-1
. banks 1.6032-1; 301.6032-1
. barter exchanges 1.6045-1; 1.6045-2
. . magnetic media 1.6045-1; 1.6045-1T
. brokers 1.6045-1; 1.6045-2
. . magnetic media 1.6045-1; 1.6045-1T
. Canadian residents...................... 1.6049-8
. capital structure, acquisition of control or substantial change in 1.6045-3
. cash in excess of $10,000 received in a trade or business.................................... 1.6050I-1
. common trust funds 1.6032-1; 301.6032-1
. controlled foreign partnerships 1.6038-3
. . overlap with section 6031 .... 1.6038-3
. corporate dissolution or liquidation .... 1.6043-1 to 1.6043-3

Information returns —Cont'd
. *corporate dissolution or liquidation—Cont'd*
. . acquisition of control of corporation 1.6043-4
. . capital structure changes 1.6043-4
. . shareholders........................... 1.6043-4
. crewmen on fishing boats 301.6050A-1
. deferred compensation................. 301.6058-1
. depreciation, safe harbor lease information returns .... 1.168(f)(8)-1T
. direct sales from sources outside the United States 1.6041A-1
. discharge of indebtedness
. . certain entities 1.6050-1T
. dividend payments .... 1.6042-1 to 1.6042-4
. dividends .... 1.6042-1 to 1.6044-6; 1.6044-1 to 1.6044-5; 301.6042-1
. dividends paid 1.6042-2
. donated property, disposition of 1.6050L-1
. education loans......................... 1.6050S-2
. . payments of interest on qualified 31.6050S-4
. employees, employer statements to 1.6041-2
. employees, payments to 1.6041-2
. energy grants and financing.............. 1.6050D-1
. executors and fiduciaries 1.6036-1; 301.6036-1
. exempt organizations 1.6033-1; 1.6033-2; 301.6033-1
. . notification requirement for entities not required to file annual information return under sec. 6033(a)(1) 1.6033-6T
. . public inspection and distribution of ... 301.6104(d)-1
. failure to file correct 301.6721-1
. . preparer, tax return 1.6695-1
. federal agencies, contracts from 1.6050M-1
. fiduciaries 1.6036-1; 301.6903-1
. financial institution, discharge of indebtedness by 1.6050P-1; 1.6050P-1T
. fishing boats 1.6050A-1; 301.6050A-1
. fixed or determinable income
. . payments of $600 or more 1.6041-1
. . widely held fixed investment trust reporting, coordination with 1.6041-8
. foreclosures.......................... 1.6050J-1T
. foreign corporations (See Foreign corporations)
. foreign personal holding companies ...... 1.6035-1 to 1.6035-3; 301.6035-1
. foreign trusts 16.3-1; 301.6048-1
. foreign-related items 1.6041-4
. forms 1096 and 1099 .... 1.6041-6; 1.6041-7
. fuel registrants, taxable 48.4101-2
. group-term life insurance 1.6052-1; 1.6052-2; 301.6052-1
. interest .... 1.6049-1 to 1.6049-6; 301.6049-1
. interest paid .... 1.6049-4(b)(1)
. . certificates of deposit issued on bearer form .... 1.6049-4(b)(4)

References are to Reg. § numbers

Information returns —Cont'd
. *interest paid—Cont'd*
. . December 31, 1982, includible in gross income after 1.6049-4
. . December 31, 1982, subject to reporting after 1.6049-5
. . documentation absent, determination of U.S. or foreign payee when .... 1.6049-5(d)
. . exclusions from reporting requirement ... 1.6049-5(b)
. . exempt recipient, payment made to .. 1.6049-4(c)(1)
. . foreign currency, conversion of amounts paid in .... 1.6049-4(d)(3)
. . governmental units, payments by .... 1.6049-4(d)(5)
. . middlemen, return by .... 1.6049-4(b)(3)
. . subject to reporting requirement .... 1.6049-5(a)
. . time and place for filing for payment .... 1.6049-4(g)
. . transactional reporting .... 1.6049-4(e)
. . widely held fixes investment trusts ... 1.6049-4(c)(3)
. liquidation, dissolution, termination, or contraction 301.6043-1
. liquidation distributions 1.6043-2
. magnetic media 1.6041-7
. money lending organizations 1.6050P-2
. monthly returns .... 31.6011(a)-5
. mortgages 1.6050H-1; 1.6050H-1T; 1.6050H-2
. no return required 1.6041-3
. notification requirement for entities not required to file annual information return under sec. 6033(a)(1) 1.6033-6T
. options 301.6039-1
. original issue discount .... 1.6049-4(b)(2)
. . middlemen, return by .... 1.6049-4(b)(3)
. . special rules .... 1.6049-4(d)(2)
. partnerships 1.6050K-1
. . controlled foreign partnerships 1.6038-3
. . nominee reporting .... 1.6031(c)-1T
. . statements to partners .... 1.6031(b)-1T
. patronage dividends .... 1.6044-1 to 1.6044-5; 301.6044-1
. . statements to recipients
. . . royalty payments 1.6050N-1
. payments made on behalf of another person
. . $600 or more 1.6041-1
. payments of $600 or more 1.6041-1
. penalties 301.6652-1
. . waiver based on reasonable cause 301.6724-1
. preparers 1.6060-1
. private foundations 1.6033-3
. . foreign organizations, special rules for .. 1.6033-3(d)
. . foundation manager duties .... 1.6033-3(a)
. . furnishing copies of State officers ...... 1.6033-3(c)
. . itemized statements and lists .... 1.6033-3(a)
. . notice to public of availability of annual return .... 1.6033-3(b)
. publicity of information .... 301.6104(b)-1

Information returns —Cont'd
. real estate mortgage investment conduits .... 1.6031(b)-2T
. . nominee reporting .... 1.6031(c)-2T
. real estate transactions 1.6045-4
. reasonable cause as basis for waiver of failure penalties 301.6724-1
. receipts for employees 301.6051-1
. receivers 1.6036-1; 301.6036-1; 301.6316-9
. REMICs 1.6049-7
. retirement plans ... 1.6047-1; 301.6057-1; 301.6057-2
. royalties 1.6050N-1
. Section 367 transactions .. 1.6038B-1T; 1.6038B-1TT
. securities dealers 1.6045-1
. $600 or more, payments of 1.6041-1
. small business corporation 1.6037-1; 301.6037-1
. state and local income tax refunds 1.6050E-1
. stock option transactions 1.6039-1
. stock options 1.6039-2
. . electronic statements .... 1.6039-1(f)
. . employee stock purchase plan, stock purchased under .... 1.6039-1(b)
. . incentive stock options .... 1.6039-1(a)
. . mail, statements furnished by .... 1.6039-1(d)
. . penalties for failure to furnish .... 1.6039-1(e)
. . statement of transaction, furnishing transferee with 1.6039-2
. . time to furnish statements .... 1.6039-1(c)
. substantial change in capital structure 1.6043-4
. substitute payments, broker 1.6045-2
. trade or business, persons engaged in
. . payments of $600 or more 1.6041-1
. trusts 1.6034-1; 301.6034-1; 301.6047-1
. tuition and related expenses 1.6050S-1
. unemployment compensation payments ... 1.6050B-1
. withholding 31.6051-2

Information statements
. consolidated returns
. . loss group ownership change .... 1.1502-92(d)
. . section 382 coordination with regulations when corporation becomes a member of a consolidated group .... 1.1502-94(d)
. controlled groups, loss corporations ...... 1.382-11(a)
. education loan interest
. . electronic information statement, furnishing 1.6050S-4

Injuries (See Sickness benefits)

In-kind distributions
. section 411(d)(6) protected benefits .... 1.411(d)-4

Inner tubes
. manufacturers excise taxes
. . further manufacture causing overpayments of tax .... 48.6416(b)(3)-2

References are to Reg. § numbers

Insolvency (See Bankruptcy)
Installment accounts
. manufacturers excise taxes
. . return of causing overpayment of tax .... 48.6416(b)(5)-1
. . sale of installment accounts .... 48.4216(d)-1
Installment agreements
. fees
. . amount of fee .... 300.1(b)
. . applicability .... 300.1(a)
. . liability for fee .... 300.1(c)
. . reinstatement of restructuring of fees 300.2
. restriction on levy while installment agreements are pending or in effect 301.6331-4
Installment method of accounting
. carryovers .... 1.381(c)(8)-1
. generally 1.453-9
. sales of real estate and personal property . . 15a.453-1
Installment payment of tax
. generally 1.6655-2T; 301.6159-1
Installment reporting
. allocation of unrecaptured section 1250 ..... 1.453-12
. dealers in personal property ... 1.453A-1 to 1.453A-3
. . adoption of or change to, requirements 1.453A-3
. . revolving credit plans 1.453A-2
Installment sales
. generally 15a.453-0; 15a.453-1
. liquidating corporation, installment obligations received from 1.453-11
. manufacturers excise taxes
. . computation of tax .... 48.4216(c)-1
. partners and partnerships 1.737-2
. S corporation built-in gain or loss 1.1374-10
. . revocation or reelection of S corporation status 1.1374-10T
Instructions
. guidance on, IRS 301.6011-1
Insurance
. accident and health plans (See Accident and health plans)
. crop insurance proceeds 1.451-6
. ERISA .... 1.412(i)-1
. exemptions 1.123-1
. flood insurance 1.832-6
. foreign corporations ..... 1.819-2; 1.953-1 to 1.954-6; 1.957-2
. foreign insurers, excise taxes
. . computation of tax 46.4371-3
. . generally .... 46.4371-1 to 46.4374-1
. . imposition of tax 46.4371-2
. . liability for tax 46.4374-1
. . payment of tax 46.4374-1
. . rate of tax 46.4371-3
Insurance —Cont'd
. *foreign insurers, excise taxes —Cont'd*
. . subpart, applicability 46.4371-1
. gain or loss 1.1035-1
. group term life insurance (See Group term life insurance)
. interinsurers .... 1.823-7; 1.826-1 to 1.826-6
. life insurance (See Life insurance)
. life insurance companies (See Life insurance companies)
. mutual insurance companies (See Mutual insurance companies other than life, marine, fire, or flood)
. partnerships 1.6050K-1; 301.6063-1
. qualified long-term care contracts
. . consumer protection 1.7702B-1
. religious organization's opposition to insurance .... 1.1402(c)-7; 1.1402(h)-1
. self-employment income .... 1.72-17A; 1.72-18; 1.1402(c)-7; 1.1402(h)-1
. split-dollar insurance arrangements (See Split-dollar insurance arrangements)
Insurance companies
. amortization 1.818-3
. . generally 1.79-4T
. asset acquisition .... 1.1060-1(b); 1.1060-1(c)
. consolidated returns 1.1502-47
. discounting unpaid losses
. . discount factors, application of 1.846-1
. . effective date 1.846-4
. . election to use 1.846-2
. . fresh start, computing 1.846-3
. . historical loss payment pattern use of 1.846-2; 1.846-2T
. . reserve strengthening, computing 1.846-3
. distributions
. . section 338, elections under (See Distributions by corporations, subhead Section 338, elections under)
. . successor life insurance companies ... 1.381(c)(22)
. generally 1.818-3
. life (See Life insurance companies)
. mortality tables (See Mortality and morbidity tables)
. mutual insurance companies 1.1502-47
. reinsurance of insurance contract as asset acquisition .... 1.1060-1(b)
Insurance income
. controlled foreign corporations .... 1.953-1 et seq.
Intangible development costs
. cost sharing arrangements 1.482-7; 1.482-7A
Intangible drilling and development expenditures
. optional 10-year writeoff of certain tax preferences 1.59-1
Intangible drilling costs
. adjusted current earnings................. 1.56(g)-1

References are to Reg. § numbers

Intangible drilling costs —Cont'd
. uniform capitalization rules 1.263A-1

Intangibles
. acquire or create, amount paid to .... 1.236(a)-4
. . accounting method changes .... 1.236(a)-4(p)
. . accrual method taxpayers .... 1.236(a)-4(j)
. . capitalization .... 1.236(a)-4(b)
. . capitalization of acquired intangible ... 1.236(a)-4(c)
. . capitalization of created intangible .... 1.236(a)-4(d)
. . capitalized cost, treatment of .... 1.236(a)-4(g)
. . indirect payments .... 1.236(a)-4(k)
. . related parties .... 1.236(a)-4(k)
. . transaction costs .... 1.236(a)-4(e)
. . 12 month rule .... 1.236(a)-4(f)
. amortization
. . excluded under section 197, intangibles .... 1.167(a)-14
. . goodwill 1.197-2
. depreciation allowance .... 1.167(a)-3
. election for 1.197-1T
. . straight line recovery of intangibles .... 7.57(d)-1
. foreign corporation, transfers to .... 1.367(d)-1T
. gain or loss, like-kind exchanges .... 1.1031(a)-2
. safe harbor amortization .... 1.167(a)-3(b)
. taxable income determination in connection with transfer of intangible property 1.482-4
. transfers
. . taxable income, determination of 1.482-4T
. uniform capitalization rules 1.263A-2

Intellectual property
. capitalization of costs 1.263A-1
. capitalization rules 1.263A-2
. information returns 1.6050L-2
. property produced by taxpayer, rules concerning 1.263A-2

Intercompany transactions
. abatement 301.6404-2
. acceleration rule .... 1.1502-13(d)
. . timing and attributes .... 1.1502-13(g)
. accounting for intercompany items ...... 1.1502-13(c)
. allocation of intercompany items .... 1.1502-13(c)
. anti-avoidance rules .... 1.1502-13(h)
. boot in reorganization .... 1.1502-13(f)
. debt for cash, sale of .... 1.1502-13(g)
. defined .... 1.1502-13(b)
. definitions concerning .... 1.1502-13(b)
. determination .... 1.469-1(h)(6); 1.1502-12
. excess loss accounts 1.1502-19
. . income or gain, taken into account as 1.1502-19
. income and deductions, allocation of
. . foreign legal restrictions, effect of 1.482-1
. losses and deductions 1.108-3
. . excess loss accounts 1.1502-19

Intercompany transactions —Cont'd
. losses and deductions—Cont'd
. . excess loss accounts—Cont'd
. . . income or gain, taken into account as .. 1.1502-19
. . . special allocation of basis in connection with adjustment or determination 1.1502-19
. . from sale, deferred .... 1.267(f)-1
. matching rule .... 1.1502-13(c)
. . timing and attributes .... 1.1502-13(g)
. obligations, intercompany .... 1.1502-13(g)
. . timing and attributes .... 1.1502-13(g)
. operating rules .... 1.1502-13(j)
. pricing rules 1.994-1
. recapture income .... 1.1502-13(c)
. section 301, application of .... 1.1502-13(f)
. simplifying rules .... 1.1502-13(e)
. single entity treatment .... 1.1502-13(a)
. stock basis of common parent, reduction of .... 1.1502-13(f)
. stock of members .... 1.1502-13(f)
. taxable income
. . determination 1.482-2
. . reflecting .... 1.1502-13(a)
. transfer pricing
. . allocation of income and deductions 1.482-1
. . taxable income, determination 1.482-2
. transitional subsidiaries .... 1.337(d)-1

Interest
. adjustments 1.483-4
. alternative minimum tax 1.61-7
. at risk provisions 1.465-8
. backup withholding .... 1.6049-4 to 1.6049-6; 1.6050H-1T; 35a.3406-2; 35a.9999-1 to 35a.9999-5
. bonds
. . exempt facility bonds 1.103-8
. . federally guaranteed .... 1.149(b)-1
. capitalization .... 1.263A-1; 1.263A-8 et seq.
. changes in rates 1.25-1T; 1.25-2T
. charitable contributions 1.170A-3; 1.170A-5; 1.170A-12
. closely-held business interest defined 20.6166A-2
. contingent payments 1.483-4
. corporate acquisition indebtedness .... 1.279-1 to 1.279-6; 1.279-2
. deductions
. . denial of deduction 1.163-5; 1.163-5T
. . generally 1.163-1
. defined for Canadian residents 1.6049-8
. disclaimer of property, requirements for 25.2518-3
. dividends .... 35a.9999-1 to 35a.9999-5
. education loan
. . electronic information statement, furnishing 1.6050S-4
. estates and trusts .... 1.643(a)-5

References are to Reg. § numbers

Interest —Cont'd
. excise taxes 53.6601-1
. exempt-interest dividends of RICs 1.265-3
. exemptions .... 1.103-1 to 1.103-9
. foreign corporations 1.871-14; 1.882-5
. generally .... 1.163-6T; 1.163-8T; 1.163-10T; 301.6601-1 et seq.
. governmental obligations
. . industrial development bonds 1.103-10
. gross income 1.61-7
. information returns .... 1.6049-1 to 1.6049-6; 301.6049-1
. joint interests, generally 20.2040-1
. mortgages .... 1.25-1T to 1.25-8T
. . points .... 1.6050H-1(f)
. . received, time and manner of reporting interest 1.6050H-1; 1.6050H-2
. nonresident aliens 1.871-14
. overpayments 301.6611-1
. partners and partnerships .... 301.6231(d)-1
. payment to securities lending transactions 1.861-2
. personal interest 1.163-9T
. portfolio debt investments 1.871-14
. rate of interest .... 301.6621-1 to 301.6622-1
. real estate investment trusts 1.856-5; 1.860-3
. receipt of payment of tax 301.6316-9
. registration-required obligations .. 1.165-12; 5f.103-1; 5f.163-1
. . questions and answers on withholding .. 35a.9999-5
. reporting, subjectivity to 1.6049-5
. self-employment .... 1.1402(a)-5
. sources of income 1.861-2
. tax-exempt income 1.265-2; 1.265-3
. unaccrued but unpaid
. . losses attributable to 1.865-1
. underpayments 301.6601-1; 301.6602-1; 301.6621-2T
. United States, income from sources within or without 1.861-2
. valuation of
. . estate tax 20.2031-3
. . gift tax 25.2512-3
. . reversionary interest transferred after November 30, 1983 .... 25.2512-4

Interest expense
. allocation among expenditures 1.163-8T
. allocation and apportionment 1.861-9; 1.861-10
. . affiliated group of corporations 1.861-11
. . alternate tax book value method .... 1.861-9(i)
. . asset method .... 1.861-9T(g)
. . bond premiums .... 1.861-9T(b)(5)
. . corporations
. . . controlled foreign corporations .... 1.861-9T(f)(3)
. . . domestic .... 1.861-9T(f)(1)

Interest expense —Cont'd
. *allocation and apportionment—Cont'd*
. . *corporations —Cont'd*
. . . foreign branches of domestic .... 1.861-9T(f)(2)
. . deductions, allowable .... 1.861-9T(c)
. . fair market value method .... 1.861-9T(h)
. . financial products that alter effective cost of borrowing .... 1.861-9T(b)(6)
. . foreign currency borrowing .... 1.861-9T(b)(2)
. . interest equivalent .... 1.861-9T(b)
. . interest expense defined .... 1.861-9T(a)
. . modified gross income method .... 1.861-9T(j)
. . partners and partnerships .... 1.861-9T(e)(1)
. . . aggregate rule .... 1.861-9T(e)(1)
. . . corporate partners .... 1.861-9T(e)(2)
. . . 10 percent interest in partnership, less than .... 1.861-9T(e)(4)
. . . 10 percent interest in partnership, more than .... 1.861-9T(e)(2); 1.861-9T(e)(3)
. . . tiered partnerships .... 1.861-9T(e)(5)
. . receivable, losses on sale of certain .... 1.861-9T(b)(3)
. . United States citizens, rules for .... 1.861-9T(d)(1)
. capitalization .... 1.263A-1; 1.263A-8 et seq.
. foreign corporations 1.882-5
. tiered partnerships
. . allocation and apportionment .... 1.861-9T(e)(5)

Interests or rights not acquired by purchase
. amortization
. . excluded under section 197, intangibles .... 1.167(a)-14(c)

Interinsurers
. mutual insurance companies .... 1.823-7; 1.826-1 to 1.826-6

Internal Revenue Service
. Commissioner or other Internal Revenue officers
. . returns prepared or executed by
. . . deficiency procedure .... 301.6020-1(b)(4)
. . . employment status procedure ... 301.6020-1(b)(5)
. . . execution of return .... 301.6020-1(b)
. . . form of return .... 301.6020-1(b)(2)
. . . preparation generally .... 301.6020-1(a)
. . . responsibilities of person for whom return is prepared .... 301.6020-1(a)(2)
. . . status of return .... 301.6020-1(b)(3)
. disclosure of IRS records or information (See Disclosure)
. guidance on forms, reports, and instructions 301.6011-1

International boycotts, participation in (See Boycotts, international, participation in)

International operations
. cargo
. . exclusion of income; aircraft and ships 1.883-1

References are to Reg. § numbers

International operations —Cont'd
. exclusion of income; aircraft and ships 1.883-1; 1.883-1T

International organizations
. foreign corporations (See Foreign corporations)
. nonresident aliens (See Nonresident aliens)
. withholding at source .... 1.1441-1 et seq.
. withholding taxes 1.1441-8

International sales corporations, domestic (See Domestic international sales corporations)

International settlements
. generally 1.895-1

Inventories
. accounting method change
. . costs subject to section 263A, for......... 1.263A-7
. acquiring corporation's inventories .. 1.471-9; 1.472-7
. alternative minimum tax computation ..... 1.56(g)-1(r)
. basis for gain or loss...................... 1.1013-1
. charitable contributions 1.170A-4A
. consolidated returns 1.1502-18
. corporate organizations and reorganizations .... 1.381(c)(5)-1
. cost, at 1.471-3
. cost or market, inventories at....... 1.471-3; 1.471-4
. dealers in securities 1.471-5
. distributions of assets 1.312-2
. farming 1.471-6
. fixed price contracts 1.471-4
. generally .... 1.471-1 et seq.
. interest expense, allocation
. . income from sources within or without U.S. .... 1.861-12T(b)
. LIFO
. . adjusted current earnings .... 1.56(g)-1
. . adjustments, taxpayer 1.472-4
. . alternative minimum tax computation.... 1.56(g)-1(r)
. . change from 1.472-6
. . change in pooling method.................. 1.472-8
. . change to dollar-value method from another pricing method 1.472-8
. . dollar-value method of pricing............. 1.472-8
. . recapture of benefits .... 1.56(g)-1(f); 1.1363-2
. . revocation of election..................... 1.472-5
. . S corporations 1.1374-7; 1.1374-10
. . time and manner of making election 1.472-3
. . treatment, permitted 1.472-1
. . uniform capitalization rules 1.263A-1; 1.263A-2; 1.263A-9
. livestock 1.471-6
. livestock raisers 1.471-6
. long-term contract methods 1.471-10
. loss exception 1.865-1
. manufacturers 1.471-7; 1.471-10; 1.471-11

Inventories —Cont'd
. market, inventories at 1.471-4
. miners 1.471-7
. partners and partnerships 1.751-1
. passive activity losses and credits limited 1.472-2
. property produced by taxpayer, rules concerning 1.263A-2
. records 1.852-6
. redemption of interests, distributions in 1.852-10
. retail merchants 1.471-8
. returns 1.852-7; 1.852-8
. S corporations 1.1374-7; 1.1374-10
. . revocation or reelection of S corporation status 1.1374-10T
. sales (See Domestic international sales corporations)
. securities transfers 1.1059A-1
. small business investment company......... 1.586-1; 1.586-2; 1.1242-1; 1.1243-1
. uniform capitalization rules 1.263A-1; 1.263A-2; 1.263A-9
. unit investment trusts 1.851-7
. valuation 1.471-2
. . capitalization of costs 1.263A-1
. worthless securities .... 1.165-5(g)

Investment companies
. capital gains and losses......... 1.1242-1; 1.1243-1
. definition 1.851-1
. development corporations 1.851-6
. dividends 1.854-1; 1.855-1
. foreign investment company ..... 1.367(b)-6; 1.897-1; 1.954-5; 1.954-7; 1.955A-3; 1.955A-4; 1.1247-1 to 1.1247-5
. foreign tax credit 1.853-1
. generally .... 1.851-1 et seq.
. limitations...................... 1.851-2; 1.854-1
. open-end company shares, valuation of ... 20.2031-8; 25.2512-6
. passive foreign investment companies ..... 1.1291-1 et seq.
. regulated investment companies (See Regulated investment companies (RICs))

Investment credit
. additional credit.................... 1.46-1 to 1.46-8
. agricultural or horticultural structures 1.48-10
. amortized property 1.48-1
. automobiles 1.280F-1T
. business use percentage of listed property is not greater than 50% 1.280F-3T
. carryback and carryover of unused credit ..... 1.46-2; 301.6501(j)-1; 301.6511(d)-4
. commuter highway vehicles 1.46-11
. consolidated returns 1.1502-3
. . carryovers and carrybacks 1.1502-3
. corporate organizations and reorganizations .... 1.381(c)(23)-1

References are to Reg. § numbers

Investment credit —Cont'd
. date Section 38 property placed in service 1.47-1
. designation of credits 1.46-1
. determination of amount 1.46-1
. disposition or cessation of Section 38 property 1.47-1; 1.47-2
. . exception to rules 1.48-3
. energy property 1.47-1; 1.48-9
. energy property, special rules for 1.46-1
. ERTA ..... 5c.168(f)(8)-7; 5c.168(f)(8)-9
. estates and trusts 1.47-5; 1.48-6
. exceptions to disposition and cessation rules .. 1.47-3
. generally 1.38-1
. identification of property 1.47-1
. improvements that qualify as capital expenditures ..... 1.280F-4T(b)
. itemized deductions ..... 1.280F-1T to 1.280F-3T
. leases 1.48-4
. limitations ..... 1.46-4 to 1.46-6
. . automobiles 1.280F-1T
. mass assets, treatment of 1.47-1
. mass commuter vehicles 1.46-11
. motion picture and television films and tapes 1.992-4
. new Section 38 property 1.48-2; 1.48-4
. nonqualifying property 1.48-1
. partnerships 1.47-6
. public utility property 1.47-1
. qualified investment 1.46-3
. qualifying Section 38 property 1.48-1
. recapture 1.47-1
. recomputation of credit ..... 1.47-1; 1.47-1 et seq.
. refundable energy credit, special rules for 1.46-1
. rehabilitated building 1.48-11
. rehabilitation expenditures 1.46-1
. restoration of credit 1.50-1
. Section 38 property defined 1.48-1
. small business corporation 1.47-4; 1.48-5
. TRASOP requirements for 1-percent additional credit 1.46-8
. used Section 38 property 1.48-2; 1.48-3

Investments
. adjustments 1.1502-32
. Caribbean basin countries 1.936-10
. consolidated returns 1.1502-32
. corporate organizations and reorganizations ..... 1.381(c)(25)-1
. credit (See Investment credit)
. excise taxes ..... 53.4940-1; 53.4944-1 to 53.4944-6
. foreign corporations .... 1.367(b)-6; 1.897-1; 1.954-5; 1.954-7; 1.955A-3; 1.955A-4; 1.1247-1 to 1.1247-5
. gain or loss, like-kind exchange of property held for investment ..... 1.1031(a)-1 et seq.
. investment companies (See Investment companies)

Investments —Cont'd
. joint operating agreements
. . subchapter K exclusion election 1.761-2
. life insurance 1.72-6; 1.72-7
. passive activity losses and credits (See Passive activity losses and credits)
. penalties, abusive tax shelters 301.6708-1T
. pension plans, tax on excess distributions and excess accumulations 54.4981A-1T
. private foundations ..... 1.509(e)-1
. Puerto Rico 1.936-10
. readjustment of tax 1.1375-1
. real estate investment trusts (See Real estate investment trusts)
. securities (See Securities)
. subsidiary-parent basis adjustment 1.1502-32
. yield and valuation 1.148-5

Investment-type property
. defined for arbitrage transaction 1.148-1

Involuntary conversions
. basis for gain or loss ..... 1.1033(b)-1
. corporate organizations and reorganizations ..... 1.381(c)(13)-1
. gain or loss .. 1.1033(a)-1 to 1.1033(a)-3; 1.1033(b)-1; 1.1033(d)-1
. MACRS property acquired through (See Modified accelerated cost recovery system subhead like-kind exchange or involuntary conversion, property acquired through)

IRAs (See Individual retirement arrangements)

Iron ore deposits (See also Minerals, mines, and mining)
. depletion ..... 1.381(c)(18)-1
. generally 1.272-1; 1.631-3

Irrigation
. exempt organizations ..... 1.501(c)(12)-1
. gain or loss ..... 1.1033(c)-1

ISOs (See Incentive stock options)

Itemized deductions (See also particular item)
. additional ..... 1.211-1 et seq.
. alimony or separate maintenance payments 1.215-1-1T
. amortization ..... 1.171-1 to 1.171-5
. bad debts reserve 1.166-4
. disaster losses 1.165-11
. generally ..... 1.161-1 et seq.
. lobbying, political campaigns, attempts to influence legislation, and advertising expenses 1.162-20
. original issue discount 1.163-4

J

Jeopardy assessments
. accumulated earnings tax 1.534-3

References are to Reg. § numbers

Jeopardy assessments —Cont'd
. additions to tax, additional amounts, and assessable penalties ... 301.6658-1
. collection ... 301.6863-1; 301.6863-2
. corporations improperly accumulating surplus ... 1.534-3
. excise taxes ... 301.6861-1
. generally .. 1.6851-1 to 1.6851-3; 301.6851-1 et seq.; 301.6863-1; 301.6863-2
. judicial appeal ... 301.7429-1 to 301.7429-3
. stay of collection ... 301.6863-1

Jobs and Growth Tax Relief Reconciliation Act of 2003
. elections under, time and manner of making ... 1.163(d)-1

Joint and survivor annuities (See Annuities and annuity contracts)

Joint interests
. generally ... 20.2040-1

Joint operating agreements
. natural gas producers ... 1.761-2(d)
. subchapter K exclusion election ... 1.761-2

Joint returns
. death of either spouse ... 1.6013-3
. generally ... 1.2-1; 1.6013-1 et seq.; 301.6013-1
. itemized deductions ... 1.172-7
. nonresident alien ... 1.6013-6; 1.6013-7
. optional tax ... 1.2-1
. separate return, joint return after filing of ... 1.6013-2
. surviving spouse ... 1.2-1

Joint tenancy
. noncitizen of United States
. . spouse not a citizen, one ... 25.2523(i)-2

Jointly-owned property, transfers of
. foreign corporations information returns ... 1.6038B-1; 1.6038B-1T

Judgment lien creditors
. generally ... 301.6323(a)-1

Judgments and money recovered
. declaratory judgments, Tax Court ... 1.7476-1 to 1.7476-3; 301.7476-1; 301.7477-1
. judicial proceedings ... 301.7406-1

Judicial proceedings
. abatements, credits, and refunds ... 301.6511(a)-1
. automatic stay violations, actions involving ... 301.7430-1
. civil actions
. . persons other than taxpayers, by ... 301.7426-1
. . United States, by ... 301.7401-1 to 301.7406-1
. excise taxes ... 301.7422-1
. exhaustion of administrative remedies ... 301.7430-1
. jeopardy and termination assessment procedures reviewed ... 301.7429-1 to 301.7429-3
. judgments and money recovered ... 301.7406-1

Judicial proceedings —Cont'd
. liens ... 301.7403-1; 301.7425-1 to 301.7425-4
. persons other than taxpayers, civil actions by ... 301.7426-1
. prevailing party
. . qualified offer, based on ... 301.7430-7
. . treatment as based on qualified offer ... 301.7430-7(b)
. qualified offers ... 301.7430-7
. . defined ... 301.7430-7(c)
. . prevailing party, treatment as ... 301.7430-7(b)
. Tax Court (See Tax Court)
. taxpayer and third party proceedings ... 301.7422-1 to 301.7430-1
. United States, civil actions by ... 301.7401-1 to 301.7406-1

Judicial review
. appeals office, procedure before ... 601.106
. jeopardy and termination assessment procedures ... 301.7429-1 to 301.7429-3
. partnership items ... 301.6226(f)-1
. Tax Court ... 301.7481-1 to 301.7484-1

Justice, Department of
. disclosure of returns and return information to ... 301.6103(a)-2 to 301.6103(p)(2)(B)-1

K

Keno
. Tax Reform Act of 1976 ... 7.6041-1

Kerosene
. aviation-grade ... 48.4082-6
. blocked pump ... 48.6427-11
. claims, ultimate vendor ... 48.6427-10; 48.6427-11
. feedstock exemption ... 48.4082-7
. fuel floor stocks tax exemption ... 48.4082-10T
. manufacturers excise taxes
. . aviation grade, exemption for ... 48.4082-8T
. . aviation grade kerosene, exemption ... 48.4082-8T
. . floor stock tax exemption ... 48.4082-10T
. . non-fuel feedstock exemption ... 48.4082-9T
. . registration ... 48.4101-1

Kickbacks
. deductibility of ... 1.162-18

Know-how
. amortization ... 1.197-2

L

Labor costs
. capitalization of ... 1.263A-3
. uniform capitalization rules ... 1.263A-1

Labor organizations
. exempt organizations ... 1.501(c)(5)-1

References are to Reg. § numbers

Laches and delay
. penalties 301.6673-1
Landlord and tenant (See Leases)
Last-in, first-out (LIFO) inventories (See Inventories subhead LIFO)
Last-known address
. defined 301.6212-2
Lease term
. changes in status .... 1.168(i)-2(e)
. effective date .... 1.168(i)-2(f)
. financial obligation, retention by lessee .. 1.168(i)-2(b)
. generally .... 1.168(i)-2(a)
. multiple leases .... 1.168(i)-2(c)
. related person .... 1.168(i)-2(d)
. subleases .... 1.168(i)-2(c)
Leases
. automobiles 1.280F-5T; 1.280F-7
. backup withholding, rents subject to .. 31.3406(b)(3)-1
. capital gains and losses 1.1241-1
. construction allowances 1.110-1
. depreciation .... 1.48-4; 1.167(a)-4; 1.168(f)(8)-1T
. Economic Recovery Tax Act of 1981 ...... 5c.44F-1; 5c.103-1 to 5c.103-3; 5c.168(f)(8)-1 to 5c.168(f)(8)-10
. exempt organizations .... 1.514(a)-2; 1.514(f)-1; 1.514(g)-1
. exemptions 1.109-1
. freezing estate value, special valuation rules 25.2702-4
. gross income 1.61-8
. investment credit 1.48-4
. itemized deductions .... 1.162-11; 1.178-1 to 1.178-3; 1.280F-4T to 1.280F-6
. lease term (See Lease term)
. manufacturers excise taxes
. . computation of tax .... 48.4216(c)-1
. . sale, lease considered
. . . generally 48.4217-1
. . . limitation on taxable amount 48.4217-2
. real estate investment trusts 1.856-4
. redeemable ground rents .... 1.1055-1 to 1.1055-4
. rental income activities, passive activity losses and credits 1.469-9
. Revenue Act of 1971 .... 12.8
. safe harbor leases .... 1.168(f)(8)-1T
. self-employment income .... 1.1402(a)-4
. tax-exempt entity rules, questions and answers concerning .... 1.168(j)-1T
. United States, income from sources within or without 1.861-5; 1.861-15
Legal holidays (See Holidays)
Legal services
. accounting

Legal services —Cont'd
. *accounting —Cont'd*
. . nonaccrual of certain amounts by .... 1.448-1T(d)(2)(A); 1.448-1T(e)(4)
Legal services plans (See Group legal services plans)
Length of service
. deferred compensation .... 1.410(a)-3T
Lessees
. exemption for value of improvements erected by 1.109-1
. retention of financial obligation .... 1.168(i)-2(b)
Levy and distraint (See Seizure of property)
Liability for tax (See also specific tax)
. executors and administrators 20.2204-1
. payment of estate tax 20.2002-1
. preceding calendar period 25.2504-1
Licenses
. collection of foreign items 301.7231-1
. generally 301.7001-1
Liens
. definitions .... 301.6323(h)-0; 301.6323(h)-1
. discharge
. . consent to sale .... 301.7425-3(b)
. . . application for consent .... 301.7425-3(b)(2)
. . . generally .... 301.7425-3(b)(1)
. . content of notice of sale .... 301.7425-3(d)
. . . acknowledgment of notice ...... 301.7425-3(d)(3)
. . . disclosure of adequacy notice ... 301.7425-3(d)(4)
. . . generally .... 301.7425-3(d)(1)
. . . inadequate notice .... 301.7425-3(d)(2)
. . effective date .... 301.7425-3(e)
. . generally 301.7425-3
. . notice of sale, content .... 301.7425-3(d)
. . notice of sale requirements .... 301.7425-3(a)
. . . generally .... 301.7425-3(a)(1)
. . . postponement of scheduled sale .... 301.7425-3(a)(2); 301.7425-3(a)(2)(iii)
. . . . where notice of sale is given .... 301.7425-3(a)(2)(i)
. . . . where notice of sale is not given .... 301.7425-3(a)(2)(ii)
. . perishable goods, sale of .... 301.7425-3(c)
. . redemption by United States 301.7425-4
. . release of levy 301.6343-1
. . sale of perishable goods .... 301.7425-3(c)
. . . generally .... 301.7425-3(c)(1)
. . . perishable goods defined .... 301.7425-3(c)(2)
. estate tax 20.6324A-1; 20.6324B-1; 301.6324A-1; 301.6324-1
. . release or discharge 20.6325-1
. failure to release 301.7432-1
. financing agreements ... 301.6323(c)-1; 301.6323(c)-2

References are to Reg. § numbers

Liens —Cont'd
. 45-day period for making disbursements ....301.6323(d)-1
. generally ....301.6321-1 et seq.
. hearing, opportunity for 301.6320-1
. judicial proceedings ....301.7403-1; 301.7425-1 to 301.7425-4
. mortgages (See Mortgages)
. notice ... 301.6323(b)-1; 301.6323(f)-1; 301.6323(g)-1
. . erroneous filing 301.6326-1
. obligatory disbursement agreements ...301.6323(c)-3
. personal property, place for filing notice ....301.6323(f)-1
. priority of interest and expenses ....301.6323(e)-1
. purchasers, holders of security interests, mechanic's lienors, and judgment lien creditors ....301.6323(a)-1
. real property construction or improvement financing agreements ....301.6323(c)-2
. release of lien or discharge of property ...301.6325-1
. special rules ....301.6323(i)-1

Life estates
. disposition of certain 25.2519-1
. generally ....1.167(h)-1; 1.273-1
. marital deduction ....20.2056(b)-1
. . donees spouse, power of appointment in ....25.2523(e)-1
. . surviving spouse, election ....20.2056(b)-7
. . surviving spouse, power of appointment in ....20.2056(b)-5
. spouse, gift to ....25.2523(b)-1
. surviving spouse ....20.2056(b)-7
. transferred to donee spouse, election ....25.2523(f)-1
. transfers, disposition as 25.2519-1
. transfers with retained 20.2036-1
. valuation 1.7520-1; 20.2031-7; 25.2512-5; 25.7520-1

Life insurance
. accident or health plans 1.72-15
. amounts not received as annuity payments ...1.72-11
. annuities, generally ....1.72-2 et seq.
. companies (See Life insurance companies)
. contract valuation 25.2512-6
. distributions
. . successor life insurance companies ...1.381(c)(22)
. employee contributions ....1.72(e)-1T; 1.72-13
. employer contributions 1.72-8
. exceptions 1.72-14
. excludable amounts ....1.72-3 et seq.
. exclusion ratio 1.72-4
. exempt organizations ...1.501(c)(9)-3; 1.501(c)(12)-1
. exemptions ....1.101-1 to 1.101-6
. expected return 1.72-5
. generally ....1.61-10; 1.72-1 et seq.

Life insurance —Cont'd
. group term life insurance (See Group term life insurance)
. investments 1.72-6; 1.72-7
. itemized deductions ....1.264-1 to 1.264-4
. lump sum, annuity in lieu of 1.72-12
. modified guaranteed contracts 1.817A-1
. mortality table 1.101-7; 1.807-1
. mutual savings banks 1.594-1
. notices .. 301.6323(b)-1; 301.6323(f)-1; 301.6323(g)-1
. owner-employees 1.72-17; 1.72-17A
. proceeds 20.2042-1
. . deferred compensation plans ....1.457-10(d)
. qualified employee plans 1.72-16
. securities dealer status ....1.475(c)-1(d)
. self-employed individuals 1.72-17A; 1.72-18
. split-dollar life insurance arrangements (See Split-dollar insurance arrangements)
. surviving spouse with power of appointment, proceeds to ....20.2056(b)-6
. tables 1.72-9
. transfer of contracts on investment in contract 1.72-10
. valuation of 20.2031-8

Life insurance companies
. accounting methods ....1.818-1 to 1.818-8
. adjusted basis 1.1016-5
. adjusted current earnings ....1.56(g)-1(h)
. adjusted life insurance reserves ...1.806-1 to 1.806-4
. amortization of premium and accrual of discount 1.818-3
. basis in computing reserves 1.806-4
. capital gains and losses ....1.812-4; 1.812-8; 1.817-2 to 1.817-4; 1.818-8; 1.825-2; 1.825-3
. carrybacks and carryovers ....1.812-4; 1.812-8; 1.817-2 to 1.817-4; 1.825-2; 1.825-3
. consolidated returns 1.818-8
. . life-nonlife groups, by 1.1502-47
. contracts and agreements 1.801-8
. . variable annuities, diversification requirements 1.817-5
. corporate organizations and reorganizations ....1.381(c)(22)-1; 1.381(d)-1
. deductions ....1.809-5 et seq.
. definitions 1.801-3; 1.809-3
. dividends 1.811-2; 1.812-1; 1.823-2; 1.823-5
. double deductions 1.818-7
. endowment diversification requirements 1.817-5
. exempt organization ....1.501(c)(12)-1
. foreign life insurance companies 1.819-1; 1.819-2
. gain and loss from operations ....1.809-1 to 1.812-6
. generally ....1.801-2 et seq.; 1.818-3
. gross income 1.832-4
. gross investment income 1.804-3

References are to Reg. § numbers

Life insurance companies —Cont'd
. investment income 1.72-6; 1.72-7
. mutualization distributions 1.809-8
. offset 1.812-5
. operations loss deduction .... 1.812-2 to 1.812-5
. policy acquisition expenses .... 1.56(g)-1(h)
. policyholders' surplus account.............. 1.815-4
. reserves .... 1.801-4 to 1.801-8; 1.810-2 to 1.810-4
. shareholders .... 1.815-1 to 1.815-4
. short tax years.......................... 1.818-5
. successor, carryovers of predecessor
 .... 1.381(c)(22)-1
. variable annuities 1.801-7
. . diversification requirements 1.817-5

Life insurance contracts
. adjusted current earnings................1.56(g)-1(c)
. attained age of insured
. . generally ....1.7702-3(a)
. . multiple lives on first-to-die basis ....1.7702-3(d)
. . multiple lives on last-to-die basis ....1.7702-3(c)
. . single life contract ....1.7702-3(b)

Life interests
. valuation 1.7520-1; 25.2512-5A

Life-nonlife groups
. consolidated returns 1.1502-47

Lifetime learning credit
. amount of............................... 1.25A-4
. eligibility 1.25A-4
. Hope Scholarship credit
. . coordination with education tax credits 1.25A-1

LIFO (See Inventories)

Like-kind exchanges
. gain or loss
. . multiple properties ....1.1031(j)-1
. . safe harbor for qualified intermediaries
 ....1.1031(b)-2
. . trade or business or investments, property held for productive use in, generally ....1.1031(a)-1
. investment property ....1.1031(a)-1
. MACRS property acquired through (See Modified accelerated cost recovery system subhead like-kind exchange or involuntary conversion, property acquired through)
. tax-exempt use property
. . allowable depreciation deductions .... 1.168(h)-1(b)
. . effective date .... 1.168(h)-1(e)
. . generally ....1.168(h)-1; 1.168(h)-1(a)
. . related tax-exempt use property ...... 1.168(h)-1(c)
. trade or business, property held for productive use in
 ....1.1031(a)-1

Limitation of actions (See Statute of limitations)

Limited liability company
. tax matters partner, designation of .. 301.6231(a)(7)-2

Line-of-business limitations, fringe benefits
 .... 1.132-4; 1.132-4T

Liquidation (See also Dissolution)
. basis..................................... 1.334-1
. collapsible corporations .... 1.341-1 to 1.341-6
. consenting corporations, sales of stock of 1.341-7
. distributions
. . gains of loss recognition by shareholder
 ....1.367(e)-2
. . gains or loss by shareholder ....1.331-1(b)
. . information returns 1.6043-2
. . recharacterization ....1.331-1(c)
. . reporting requirements ....1.331-1(d)
. exempt organizations ....1.514(d)-1
. foreign corporations 1.884-2; 1.884-2T
. foreign subsidiary ....1.367(b)-5
. gain or loss, nonrecognition of.............. 1.332-2
. generally ....1.331-1 et seq.
. indebtedness of subsidiary to parent 1.332-7
. information returns .... 1.6043-1 to 1.6043-4; 301.6043-1
. installment obligations received from 1.453-11
. loss limitation rule
. . transitional rule.......................1.337(d)-1
. minority interests......................... 1.332-5
. partial .... 1.312-5; 1.346-1 to 1.346-3
. personal holding companies ... 1.6162-1; 301.6162-1
. presumptions 1.341-3
. records
. . liquidating distributions defined ....1.332-6(c)
. . liquidation corporation, filings by ....1.332-6(b)
. . plan defined ....1.332-6(c)
. . recipient corporation, statement filed by .. 1.332-6(a)
. . recipient corporation defined.............1.332-6(c)
. . substantiation information ....1.332-6(d)
. redemptions 1.346-2
. stock......... 1.305-4 to 1.306-3; 1.316-1 to 1.318-4
. subsidiary corporation .... 1.332-1 to 1.332-7; 1.367(b)-5
. time to complete 1.332-3; 1.332-4
. U.S. real property holding corporations 1.897-5T

Listed property
. employee use of 1.280F-6
. generally .... 1.280F-1T to 1.280F-6

Listed transactions
. charitable organization involvement, disclosure of
 ....56.6011-4
. employment tax involvement, disclosure of
 ....31.6011-4
. estate tax involvement, disclosure of 20.6011-4
. exempt organization involvement, disclosure of
 ....53.6011-4
. gift tax involvement, disclosure of 25.6011-4
. participation in 1.6011-4

References are to Reg. § numbers

Listed transactions —Cont'd
. pension plan involvement, disclosure of 54.6011-4
. private foundation involvement, disclosure of 53.6011-4
. Reportable Transaction Disclosure Statement 1.6011-4

Lists
. material advisors (See Material advisors)
. private foundations 53.6011-1

Literary organizations
. exemption .... 1.501(c)(3)-1

Livestock
. accounting methods 1.451-7
. capital gains and losses 1.1231-2
. capitalization 1.263A-4
. drought, sale due to 1.451-7
. gain or loss .... 1.1031(e)-1; 1.1033(d)-1; 1.1033(e)-1
. inventories 1.471-6
. investment credit 1.48-1

Living expenses
. generally 1.262-1; 5e.274-8
. members of Congress 5e.274-8

Loans
. at risk provisions
. . interest other than of a creditor 1.465-8
. . personal liability for repayment 1.465-8
. bad debts (See Bad debts)
. banking institutions .... 1.585-1 to 1.585-4; 1.586-1; 1.586-2
. Commodity Credit Corporation loans 1.77-1; 1.77-2
. construction loans
. . interest, reporting of 1.6050H-1
. determination of taxable income .... 1.482-2(a)
. DISCs 1.993-4; 1.995-5
. education loans (See Education loans)
. employee-relocation loans .... 1.7872-5T(c)(1)(i)
. employer plan participants .... 1.72(p)-1
. exempt organizations .... 1.503(f)-1
. exemptions 1.133-1T; 1.7872-5; 1.7872-5T
. . below-market loans involving foreign persons .... 1.7872-5T(c)(2)
. . employee-relocation loans .... 1.7872-5T(c)(1)
. . general rule .... 1.7872-5(a)(1); 1.7872-5T(a)(1)
. . list of exemptions .... 1.7872-5(b); 1.7872-5T(b)
. . loans without significant tax effect .. 1.7872-5T(c)(3)
. . special rules .... 1.7872-5T(c)
. . tax avoidance loans .... 1.7872-5(a)(2); 1.7872-5T(a)(2)
. information returns
. . money lending organizations 1.6050P-2
. interest in activity other than that of creditor
. . generally .... 1.465-8(a)
. . nonrecourse loan secured by asset

Loans —Cont'd
. interest in activity other than that of creditor —Cont'd
. . nonrecourse loan secured by asset —Cont'd
. . . ascertainable market value .... 1.465-8(c)
. . . nonascertainable market value .... 1.465-8(d)
. . personal liability, borrower .... 1.465-8(b)
. loss, amount protected against 1.465-20
. mineral production payments 1.636-1
. mortgages (See Mortgages)
. mutual savings banks 1.593-4; 1.593-6A; 1.593-7; 1.593-11
. no personal liability 1.465-20
. no security pledged 1.465-20
. nonrecourse financing, qualified
. . real property, secured by .... 1.465-27(b)
. nonrecourse loan secured by asset
. . generally .... 1.465-27(a)
. . interest in activity other than that of creditor
. . . ascertainable market value .... 1.465-8(c)
. . . nonascertainable market value .... 1.465-8(d)
. . real property, secured by .... 1.465-27(b)
. reserves for losses (See Banking institutions, subhead bad debt)
. split-dollar (See Split-dollar loans)

Lobbying
. grass roots communications
. . record keeping 56.4911-6
. influencing legislation 1.162-29
. . communication, activity supporting lobbying .... 1.162-29(d)
. . communication not made, lobbying .... 1.162-29(e)
. . purpose of activity as basis for determining .... 1.162-29(c)

Lobbying expenditures
. allocation of costs incurred in 1.162-28
. ceiling amount, expenditures in excess of .. 1.501(h)-3
. excess .... 56.4911-0 to 56.4911-10
. . affiliated groups .... 56.4911-7 to 56.4911-10
. . communication with members 56.4911-5
. . direct lobbying communications 56.4911-2; 56.4911-3
. . exempt purpose expenditures 56.4911-4
. . grass roots lobbying communications ... 56.4911-2; 56.4911-3
. . . records of expenditures 56.4911-6
. . limited affiliated groups 56.4911-10
. . records of expenditures 56.4911-6; 56.6001-1
. . returns 56.6001-1; 56.6011-1
. exempt organizations .... 1.501(h)-3
. expenditure test .... 1.501(h)-1
. . election of test .... 1.501(h)-2
. grass roots communications 56.4911-3
. itemized deductions 1.162-20
. limited affiliated groups 56.4911-10

References are to Reg. § numbers

Lobbying expenditures —Cont'd
. public charities 56.4911-1; 56.4911-2; 56.4911-6; 56.4911-8
Local taxes (See State and local taxes)
Lodging and meals (See Meals and lodging)
Long-term contracts
. accounting methods 1.451-5; 1.471-10
. . allocable costs 1.460-1
. . alternate minimum taxable income.......... 1.460-4
. . capitalized-cost method.................. 1.460-4
. . change in method, consent to.............. 1.460-4
. . completed contract method (CCM), use of 1.460-1; 1.460-4
. . consolidated groups 1.460-4
. . definitions concerning 1.460-1
. . exempt-contract method 1.460-4
. . manufacturing contracts 1.460-2
. . mid-contract change in taxpayer 1.460-4
. . percentage of completion method (PCM), use of 1.460-1; 1.460-4
. . ship contract 1.460-2
. . step-in-the-shoes transactions 1.460-4
. . uniform capitalization rules 1.263A-1
. capitalization of costs 1.263A-1
. completion date, contract 1.460-1
. defined 1.460-1
. entering into 1.460-1
. generally 1.451-5; 1.471-10
. hybrid contracts 1.460-1
. insurance
. . consumer protection 1.7702B-1
. manufacturing contracts
. . accounting methods 1.460-1
. related parties 1.460-1
. . production by 1.460-2
. ship contract
. . accounting methods 1.460-2
Long-term home construction contracts
. accounting methods
. . alternative minimum taxable income ..... 1.460-4(f)
. . . election to use regular completion factors .... 1.460-4(f)(2)
. . . generally .... 1.460-4(f)(1)
. . completed-contract method .... 1.460-4(d)
. . . contracts with disputed claims ...... 1.460-4(d)(4); 1.460-4(d)(4)(i); 1.460-4(d)(4)(iv)
. . . generally .... 1.460-4(d)(1)
. . . gross contract price .... 1.460-4(d)(3)
. . . post-completion-year income and costs .... 1.460-4(d)(2)
. . consolidated groups and controlled groups .... 1.460-4(j)
. . . intercompany transactions .... 1.460-4(j)(1); 1.460-4(j)(1)(i)
Long-term home construction contracts —Cont'd
. *accounting methods —Cont'd*
. . examples .... 1.460-4(h)
. . exempt contract methods .. 1.460-4(c); 1.460-4(c)(1)
. . . exempt-contract percentage-of-completion method .... 1.460-4(c)(1); 1.460-4(c)(1)(i)
. . generally .... 1.460-4; 1.460-4(g); 1.460-4(g)(1)
. . mid-contract change in taxpayer .... 1.460-4(k); 1.460-4(k)(1)
. . . anti-abuse rule .... 1.460-4(k)(4)
. . . constructive completion transactions .... 1.460-4(k)(2)(i)
. . . effective date .... 1.460-4(k)(6)
. . . examples .... 1.460-4(k)(5)
. . . step-in-the-shoes transactions...... 1.460-4(k)(3); 1.460-4(k)(3)(i)
. . overview .... 1.460-4(a)
. . percentage of completion / capitalized-cost method .... 1.460-4(e)
. . percentage of completion method .... 1.460-4(b)
. . . completion factor .... 1.460-4(b)(5)
. . . computations .... 1.460-4(b)(2)
. . . generally .... 1.460-4(b)(1)
. . . post-completion-year income........ 1.460-4(b)(3)
. . . 10-percent method .... 1.460-4(b)(5); 1.460-4(b)(5)(i); 1.460-4(b)(6)(ii)
. . . terminated contract .... 1.460-4(b)(7)
. . . total contract price .... 1.460-4(b)(4)
. . taxpayer-initiated change in method of accounting .... 1.460-4(g)(2)
. . . change from a permissible PCM method to another permissible PCM method....... 1.460-4(g)(2)(ii)
. . . change to an exempt contract method for exempt contracts other than home construction contracts .... 1.460-4(g)(2)(iv)
. . . change to an exempt contract method for home construction contracts .... 1.460-4(g)(2)(iii)
. . . change to PCM for long-term contracts for which PCM is required .... 1.460-4(g)(2)(i)
. disputed claims
. . taxpayer assured of profit or loss ... 1.460-4(d)(4)(ii)
. . taxpayer unable to determine profit or loss .... 1.460-4(d)(4)(iii)
. exempt-contract percentage-of-completion method
. . determination of work performed ... 1.460-4(c)(1)(ii)
. intercompany transactions
. . consent to change method of accounting .... 1.460-4(j)(4)
. . definitions and nomenclature .... 1.460-4(j)(1)(ii)
. . effective dates .... 1.460-4(j)(3)
. . example .... 1.460-4(j)(2)
. mid-contract change in taxpayer
. . constructive completion transactions
. . . new taxpayer .... 1.460-4(k)(2)(iii)
. . . old taxpayer .... 1.460-4(k)(2)(ii)

References are to Reg. § numbers

Long-term home construction contracts —Cont'd
. *mid-contract change in taxpayer —Cont'd*
. . *constructive completion transactions —Cont'd*
. . . special rules relating to distributions of certain contracts by a partnership .... 1.460-4(k)(2)(iv)
. . step-in-the-shoes transactions
. . . new taxpayer .... 1.460-4(k)(3)(iii)
. . . old taxpayer .... 1.460-4(k)(3)(ii)
. . . special rules related to certain corporate and partnership transactions .... 1.460-4(k)(3)(iv)
. . . special rules related to certain partnership transactions .... 1.460-4(k)(3)(v)
. percentage of completion method
. . allocable contract costs .... 1.460-4(b)(5)(i)
. . cumulative allocable contract costs .... 1.460-4(b)(5)(ii)
. . estimating total allocable contract costs .... 1.460-4(b)(5)(iii)
. . pre-contracting-year costs .... 1.460-4(b)(5)(iv)
. terminated contract
. . adjusted basis .... 1.460-4(b)(7)(ii)
. . look-back method .... 1.460-4(b)(7)(iii)
. . reversal of income .... 1.460-4(b)(7)(i)
. total contract price, estimating .... 1.460-4(b)(4)(ii)

Look-through rules
. capital gains, estates and trusts
. . sales or exchanges of interest in S trust .... 1.1(h)-1
. capital gains and losses
. . partnerships, sales or exchanges of interest in .... 1.1(h)-1
. . S corporations, sales or exchanges of interest in .... 1.1(h)-1
. . trust, sales or exchanges of interest in ..... 1.1(h)-1
. foreign tax credit
. . controlled foreign corporations ... 1.904-5; 1.904-5T
. . . dividends .... 1.904-5(c)(4)
. . . earnings and profits .... 1.904-7(b)
. . . high withholding tax interest .... 1.904-5(f)
. . . interest payments .... 1.904-5(c)(2)
. . . rents and royalties .... 1.904-5(c)(3)
. . . subpart F inclusions .... 1.904-5(c)(1)
. . . subpart F income in excess of 70 percent gross income .... 1.904-5(e)
. . domestic corporations .... 1.904-5(g)
. . partnerships .... 1.904-5(h)
. . passive foreign investment company inclusions .... 1.904-5(j)
. . pass-through entities .... 1.904-5(h)
. . related person, ordering rules .... 1.904-5(k)
. partners and partnerships
. . capital gains and losses
. . . sales or exchanges of interest in partnership .... 1.1(h)-1
. . foreign tax credit .... 1.904-5(h)

Look-through rules —Cont'd
. passive foreign investment company inclusions
. . foreign tax credit .... 1.904-5(j)
. pass-through entities
. . foreign tax credit .... 1.904-5(h)
. S corporations, capital gains
. . sales or exchanges of interest in S corporation .... 1.1(h)-1

Loss corporations (See Net operating loss carrybacks and carryovers)

Losses
. capital (See Capital gains and losses)
. gain or loss (See Gain or loss)
. net operating (See Net operating losses; Net operating loss carrybacks and carryovers)
. passive activity (See Passive activity losses and credits)

Low-income housing
. Affordable Housing Program; FIRREA loan proceeds 1.42-3
. allocation rules for post-2000 state housing credit ceiling amounts 1.42-14
. carryover allocations (See Carryover allocations)
. compliance monitoring requirements 1.42-5
. credit ceilings and limitations 1.42-1T
. existing buildings, credit for 1.42-2
. filing form 8586, Low-Income Housing Credit .... 1.42-1(h)
. general public, use by
. . credit under section 42, eligibility for 1.42-9
. generally 1.42-1T; 1.1039-1
. housing credit dollar amount allocation 1.42-17
. not-for-profit rules, application of 1.42-4
. qualified allocation plan 1.42-17

Lubricating oil
. manufacturers excise taxes
. . cutting oil 48.4091-3
. . records and reports
. . . state or local tax officers, inspection of records by 48.4102-1
. . registration 48.4101-1

Lump sum distributions
. ERISA .... 11.402(e)(4)(A)-1; 11.402(e)(4)(B)-1
. . explanation requirement .... 1.402(f)-1
. life insurance endowments or annuities 1.72-12
. qualified plans 20.2039-3; 20.2039-4

M

MACRS (See Modified accelerated cost recovery system)

Magazines
. exclusion for returned 1.458-1

References are to Reg. § numbers

Magazines —Cont'd
. generally .... 31.3401(a)(10)-1
Magnetic media returns
. corporate 1.6011-5; 301.6011-5
. . controlled group of corporations defined .... 301.6011-5(d)(3)
. . corporate income tax return defined .... 301.6011-5(d)(4)
. . corporation defined .... 301.6011-5(d)(2)
. . determination of 250 returns ...... 301.6011-5(d)(5)
. . magnetic media defined .... 301.6011-5(d)(1)
. . requirement to file magnetically ......301.6011-5(a)
. . waiver of requirement to file magnetically ....301.6011-5(b)
. electing small business corporation 1.6037-2; 301.6037-2
. . corporation defined .... 301.6037-2(d)(2)
. . determination of 250 returns ...... 301.6037-2(d)(5)
. . electing small business corporation defined .... 301.6037-2(d)(4)
. . electing small business corporation return define .... 301.6037-2(d)(3)
. . failure to file return magnetically......301.6037-2(c)
. . form 1120S.......................301.6037-2(a)
. . magnetic media defined .... 301.6037-2(d)(1)
. . requirement to file magnetically ....301.6037-2(a)
. . waiver of requirement to file magnetically ....301.6037-2(b)
. exempt organizations 301.6033-4
. . determination of 250 returns ...... 301.6033-4(d)(3)
. . failure to file return magnetically......301.6033-4(c)
. . form 990/990-PF ....301.6033-4(a)
. . magnetic media defined .... 301.6033-4(d)(1)
. . notification requirement for entities not required to file annual information return under sec. 6033(a)(1) 1.6033-6T
. . requirement to file magnetically ......301.6033-4(a)
. . returned required under Sec. 6033 .... 301.6033-4(d)(2)
. . waiver of requirement to file magnetically ....301.6033-4(b)
. extension of time for payment of tax 1.9101-1
. generally 301.6011-2
. information returns 1.6041-7
. . brokers and barter exchanges 1.6045-1; 1.6045-1T
. partnership returns 301.6011-3
Mailing
. timely filing........................... 301.7502-1
. . documents and payments 301.7502-1
. timely mailing
. . deposits 301.7502-2
Manufacturers
. inventories 1.471-7; 1.471-10; 1.471-11
Manufacturers excise taxes
. accounting procedures
. . like articles ....48.6416(h)-1
. advertising charges
. . local, exclusion from ....48.4216(e)-1
. advertising charges, readjustments for .... 48.6416(b)(1)-3
. aggregate of exclusions, limitations .....48.4216(e)-2
. aircraft, exempt sales of articles for use as supplies for 48.4221-4
. aviation fuel
. . kerosene, exemption for aviation grade 48.4082-8T
. . refunds 48.4091-3
. bonding requirements
. . importers..........................48.4061(a)-2
. bows and arrows (See Bows and arrows)
. buses, parts or accessories
. . further manufacture causing overpayments of tax .... 48.6416(b)(3)-2
. coal....................................48.4121-1
. credits and refunds
. . claims for ....48.6416(a)-1; 48.6416(a)-3
. . floor stocks tax 48.6412-1
. . . amount of tax paid on each article 48.6412-3
. . . definitions 48.6412-2
. definitions 48.0-2
. determination of price readjustments .... 48.6416(b)(1)-2
. exempt sales
. . aircraft, supplies for 48.4221-4
. . credits and refunds 48.6420-3
. . educational organizations, nonprofit 48.4221-6
. . export, articles used for 48.4221-3
. . fishing equipment....................48.4161(a)-5
. . further manufacture, articles to be used or resold for 48.4221-2
. . gasoline, ultimate purchasers of.........48.4084-1
. . generally ....48.4221-1 et seq.
. . Indians, articles produced by 48.4225-1
. . nonprofit organizations, articles to 48.4221-6
. . registration and ....48.4222(d)-1
. . school buses tires, tubes and tread rubber 48.4221-8
. . state and local governments, articles for exclusive use of.............................48.4221-5
. . tires 48.4073-4; 48.4221-7; 48.4221-8
. . trucks and trailers..........48.4063-1 to 48.4063-3
. . vessels, supplies for 48.4221-4
. exemption certificates.......................48.0-3
. exemptions (See subhead exempt sales)
. exports
. . overpayments of tax, exportation causing .... 48.6416(b)(2)-1 to 48.6416(b)(2)-4
. . tax free sales 48.4221-3

References are to Reg. § numbers

Manufacturers excise taxes —Cont'd
. firearms, exempt sales 48.4182-1
. fishing equipment (See Fishing equipment)
. floor stocks tax, credit or refund 48.6412-1
. . amount of tax paid on each article 48.6412-3
. . definitions 48.6412-2
. further manufacture, overpayments of tax caused by .... 48.6416(b)(3)-1 et seq.
. . bus parts or accessories .... 48.6416(b)(3)-2
. . evidence in support of .... 48.6416(b)(3)-3
. . included manufactures .... 48.6416(b)(3)-2
. . inner tubes .... 48.6416(b)(3)-2
. . tires .... 48.6416(b)(3)-2
. . truck parts or accessories .... 48.6416(b)(3)-2
. further manufacture, special rules 48.4223-1
. gas guzzler tax (See Gas guzzler tax)
. gasoline (See Gasoline)
. importers (See Importers)
. imposition of tax 48.4081-1
. Indians, exemption for articles produced by 48.4225-1
. inner tubes.......................... 48.6416(b)(3)-2
. installment accounts
. . return of causing overpayment of tax .... 48.6416(b)(5)-1
. . sale of ....48.4216(d)-1
. installment accounts, sale of ....48.4216(d)-1
. installment sales, computation of tax ....48.4216(c)-1
. kerosene (See Kerosene)
. leases
. . computation of tax ....48.4216(c)-1
. . sale, lease considered....... 48.4217-1; 48.4217-2
. . . generally 48.4217-1
. . . limitation on taxable amount 48.4217-2
. like articles, accounting procedures for...48.6416(h)-1
. lubricating oil (See Lubricating oil)
. nonprofit organizations, exempt sales of articles to 48.4221-6
. overpayment of tax
. . claims for credit or refund .... 48.6416(a)-1; 48.6416(a)-3
. . exportations causing .... 48.6416(b)(2)-1 to 48.6416(b)(2)-4
. . . evidence required .... 48.6416(b)(2)-3
. . . included exportations .... 48.6416(b)(2)-2
. . further manufacture causing ..... 48.6416(b)(3)-1 et seq.
. . . evidence in support of .... 48.6416(b)(3)-3
. . included manufactures .... 48.6416(b)(3)-2
. . installment accounts, return of causing .... 48.6416(b)(5)-1
. . price readjustments causing
. . . advertising charges, readjustment for .... 48.6416(b)(1)-3

Manufacturers excise taxes —Cont'd
. overpayment of tax —Cont'd
. . price readjustments causing —Cont'd
. . . determination of price readjustments .... 48.6416(b)(1)-2
. . . evidence in support of .... 48.6416(b)(1)-4
. . resales causing .... 48.6416(b)(2)-1 to 48.6416(b)(2)-4
. . . evidence required .... 48.6416(b)(2)-3
. . . included resales .... 48.6416(b)(2)-2
. parts or accessories
. . fishing equipment...................48.4161(a)-3
. . imposition of tax ....48.4061(b)-1
. . rebuilt or reconditioned ....48.4061(b)-3
. . . exchange basis, sale on............48.4062(b)-1
. person other than manufacturer, importer or producer, sales of taxable articles by 48.4219-1
. producer, use by ....48.4218-1 to 48.4218-5
. . business or personal use 48.4218-2
. . computation of tax 48.4218-5
. . events subsequent to taxable use 48.4218-3
. . further manufacture, use in 48.4218-4
. rates of tax.............................48.4081-1
. readjustments limitation ....48.4216(e)-2
. records and reports
. . state or local tax officers, inspection of records by 48.4102-1
. registration..........................48.4222(a)-1
. . exception to requirements..............48.4222(b)-1
. . exempt sales and.....................48.4222(d)-1
. . revocation of........................48.4222(c)-1
. . suspension of.......................48.4222(c)-1
. resale
. . exempt sales to manufacturers for
. . . parts or accessories sold in connection with 48.4063-2
. . overpayment of tax, resales causing .... 48.6416(b)(2)-1 to 48.6416(b)(2)-4
. . tax-free sales for further manufacture 48.4221-2
. sale price
. . advertising charges ....48.4216(e)-3
. . . local, exclusion from ....48.4216(e)-1
. . . price readjustments for local advertising causing overpayment .... 48.6416(b)(1)-3
. . affiliated corporations ....48.4216(b)-4
. . arms-length sales....................48.4216(b)-3
. . charges to be included in ....48.4216(a)-1
. . constructive sale price ... 48.4216(b)-1; 48.4216(b)-1 to 48.4216(b)-4
. . . affiliated corporations ....48.4216(b)-4
. . . application of......................48.4216(b)-1
. . . arms-length sales ....48.4216(b)-3
. . . basic rules ....48.4216(b)-2
. . exchanges and......................48.4216(a)-3
. . exclusions from ....48.4216(a)-2

References are to Reg. § numbers

Manufacturers excise taxes —Cont'd
. *sale price —Cont'd*
. . readjustments .... 48.4216(a)-3
. . . limitations .... 48.4216(e)-2
. . . overpayments of tax caused by ... 48.6416(b)(1)-1
. . replacements under warranty .... 48.4216(a)-3
. . trucks and trailers, value of used components excluded from price .... 48.4216(f)-1
. school bus tires, tubes and tread rubber ... 48.4221-8
. state and local governments, articles for exclusive use of 48.4221-5
. tires (See Tires)
. trucks and trailers (See Trucks and trailers)
. use by manufacturer, importer or producer .... 48.4218-1 to 48.4218-5
. . business or personal use 48.4218-2
. . computation of tax 48.4218-5
. . events subsequent to taxable use 48.4218-3
. . further manufacture, use in 48.4218-4
. vessels, exempt sales of articles for use as supplies for 48.4221-4

Marginal costing rules
. foreign sales corporations .... 1.925(b)-1T

Marital deduction
. administration expenses .... 20.2056(b)-4
. citizen
. . spouse not .... 25.2523(i)-1
. . surviving spouse not 20.2056A-1
. disallowance
. . spouse not a citizen .... 25.2523(i)-1
. disclaimers
. . effect of .... 20.2056(d)-2
. . pre-January 1, 1977 transfers......... 20.2056(d)-3
. generally .... 20.2056(a)-1
. interest in property resulting from disclaimer, surviving spouse.......................... 20.2056(d)-2
. interests deductible.................. 20.2056(a)-2
. life estate .... 20.2056(b)-1
. . donee spouse, power of appointment in .... 25.2523(e)-1
. . surviving spouse
. . . election .... 20.2056(b)-7
. . . power of appointment in .... 20.2056(b)-5
. nondeductible interests .... 20.2056(a)-2
. passed from decedent defined .... 20.2056(c)-1
. . person other than surviving spouse .... 20.2056(c)-3
. . surviving spouse, to .... 20.2056(c)-2
. power of appointment in surviving spouse
. . annuity payments .... 20.2056(b)-6
. . life estate .... 20.2056(b)-5
. . life insurance .... 20.2056(b)-6
. previously allowed 20.2044-1

Marital deduction —Cont'd
. qualified domestic trusts (See also Qualified domestic trusts)
. . election 20.2056A-3
. . imposition of section 2056A estate tax .. 20.2056A-5
. . marital trusts and nontrust transfers, conforming 20.2056A-4
. . requirements for 20.2056A-2
. . transfer credits, allowance of 20.2056A-7
. recovery
. . estate tax 20.2207A-1
. . failure to exercise right of recover 25.2207A-1
. . gift tax 25.2207A-1
. terminable interest limitation .... 20.2056(b)-1
. . exceptions to .... 20.2056(b)-3
. treaties, transfers subject to estate and gift tax 20.2056A-1
. unidentified assets, interest in .... 20.2056(b)-2
. valuation of interest .... 20.2056(b)-4

Marital status
. determination 1.7703-1

Market value, decline in
. worthless securities .... 1.165-5(f)

Mark-to-market
. securities
. . hedges .... 1.475(b)-1(d)
. . held for investment .... 1.475(b)-1(c)
. . identified as held for investment .... 1.475(b)-(b)
. . section 1296 stock 1.1296-1
. . transition issues .... 1.475(b)-1(e)
. securities dealers exemption .... 1.475(b)-1

Married persons (See Spouses)

Mass transit vehicles (See Highway vehicles, subhead commuter vehicles)

Material advisors
. list of investors
. . content .... 301.6112-1(b)(3)
. . definitions concerning .... 301.6112-1(c)
. . designation agreements .... 301.6112-1(f)
. . furnishing .... 301.6112-1(e)
. . persons required to be included on list .... 301.6112-1(b)(2)
. . preparation of list .... 301.6112-1(b)(1)
. . requirement to maintain............. 301.6112-1(a)
. . retention of list .... 301.6112-1(d)
. reportable transactions .... 301.6111-3(b)
. . designation agreements .... 301.6111-3(f)
. . disclosure statement, form of .... 301.6111-3(d)
. . protective disclosure .... 301.6111-3(g)
. . time of providing .... 301.6111-3(e)

References are to Reg. § numbers

Material participation 1.469-5; 1.469-5T
. alternate valuation of certain farm and closely-held business, material participation requirements 20.2032A-3

Materials, cost of
. net income and 1.162-3

Maternity leave
. service requirements .... 1.410(a)-9

MCCs (See Mortgage credit certificates)

Meals and lodging
. generally 1.119-1; 1.132-7; 1.132-7T

Mechanic's lien
. generally .... 301.6323(a)-1

Medicaid
. kickbacks and rebates, deductibility of 1.162-18

Medical care
. generally 1.105-2; 1.105-11; 1.213-1

Medicare
. kickbacks and rebates, deductibility of 1.162-18

Medicines
. drugs (See Drugs)
. vaccines (See Vaccines)

Mental health benefits
. group health plans, parity in application of limits 54.9812-1T

Merchants
. qualified payment card agents
. . backup withholding .... 31.3406(g)-1(f)

Mergers
. confidential transactions 1.6011-4
. generally .... 1.414(l)-1

Methanol fuel (See Diesel and special motor fuels tax)

Military personnel (See Armed Forces of U.S.)

Military property
. domestic international sales corporations 1.995-6

Mineral production payments
. character of amounts .... 1.652(b)-1
. loans, treatment of production payments as .. 1.636-1

Minerals, mines, and mining
. aggregate separate interests, election to 1.614-2
. basis 1.614-6
. capital additions 1.612-2
. coal or domestic iron ore 1.272-1; 1.631-3
. depletion .... 1.381(c)(18)-1
. depreciation .... 1.167(i)-1
. exploration expenditures, consolidated returns 1.1502-16
. foreign tax credit 1.901-3
. generally 1.611-2
. inventories 1.471-7
. natural resources 1.621-1

Minerals, mines, and mining —Cont'd
. oil and gas (See Oil and gas)
. production payments .... 1.636-1 to 1.636-4
. separate operating mineral interests 1.614-3; 1.614-4; 1.614-8

Minimum age
. deferred compensation plans .... 1.410(a)-3T

Minimum funding requirements
. restored pension plan .... 1.412(c)(1)-3

Minimum tax on preference income (See Alternative minimum tax)

Mining exploration
. optional 10-year writeoff of certain tax preferences 1.59-1

Ministers or religious personnel
. self-employment income .. 1.1402(a)-11; 1.1402(c)-5; 1.1402(c)-7; 1.1402(e)-2A to 1.1402(e)-4A; 1.1402(h)-1
. withholding .... 31.3401(a)(9)-1

Minority interests
. liquidation 1.332-5

Minors
. missing children, dissemination of materials to help locate 601.901
. transfers for benefit of 25.2503-4

Misrepresentations (See Fraud and deceit)

Missing children
. dissemination of materials to help locate 601.901

Missionaries
. death while in foreign missionary service ... 20.2202-1

Mistakes and errors
. accuracy related penalty, Omnibus Reconciliation Act of 1993 .... 1.6662-7
. claims arising out of erroneous computation .... 301.6230(c)-1
. correction not be made, request that ... 301.6230(b)-1
. employment taxes, repayment of erroneously collected .... 31.6413(a)-1
. housing credit agency correction of administrative errors 1.42-13
. written advice of IRS, abatement of penalty or additional tax attributable to erroneous 301.6404-3

Modifications of debt instruments
. effective date .... 1.1001-3(h)
. examples .... 1.1001-3(d)
. generally .... 1.1001-3(a); 1.1001-3(b)
. modification defined .... 1.1001-3(c)
. significant modifications .... 1.1001-3(e)
. . applicable rules .... 1.1001-3(f)
. . examples .... 1.1001-3(g)

Modified accelerated cost recovery system
. changes in use
. . accounting method, no change in ...... 1.168(i)-4(f)

References are to Reg. § numbers

Modified accelerated cost recovery system —Cont'd
. *changes in use —Cont'd*
. . business or income-producing use, conversion to .... 1.168(i)-4(b)
. . depreciation method computation as change in accounting method, change in .... 1.168(i)-4(f)
. . MACRS property during the placed-in-service year .... 1.168(i)-4(e)
. . personal use, conversion to .... 1.168(i)-4(c)
. . placed in service year, change in use of property during .... 1.168(i)-4(e)
. . recovery period and/or depreciation method, resulting in different .... 1.168(i)-4(d)
. like-kind exchanges and involuntary conversions
. . definitions concerning .... 1.168(i)-6(b)
. . depreciation allowance, computation of .... 1.168(i)-6(c)
. . depreciation allowance, special rules for determining .... 1.168(i)-6(d)
. . generally .... 1.168(i)-6
. . MACRS property elections .... 1.168(i)-6(h)(1); 1.168(i)-6(j)
. . mid-quarter convention .... 1.168(i)-6(f)
. . optional depreciation tables, use of .... 1.168(i)-6(e)
. . replacement property as MACRS property, election to treat .... 1.168(i)-6(h)(2)
. . Sec. 179 election .... 1.168(i)-6(g)

Modified guaranteed contracts
. equity-indexed 1.817A-1
. interest rates for 1.817A-1
. non-equity-indexed 1.817A-1

Money
. distributions by corporations 1.301-1
. foreign (See Foreign currency)

Money lending organizations
. information returns 1.6050P-2

Money orders
. receipt of tax payment 301.6311-1

Money purchase pension plans
. cash or deferred arrangements .... 1.401(k)-1

Monopolies
. generally 1.162-22; 1.186-1

Monthly returns
. information returns .... 31.6011(a)-5
. withholding .... 31.6011(a)-5

Mortality and morbidity tables
. construction of combined tables for small plans .... 1.430(h)(3)-1(c)(2)
. current liability, used to determine...... 1.431(c)(6)-1
. . effective date .... 1.431(c)(6)-1(b)
. . mortality tables used to detmine current liability .... 1.431(c)(6)-1(a); 1.431(c)(6)-1(b)
. deferred compensation plans .... 1.412(l)(7)-1
. generational mortality tables .... 1.430(h)(3)-1(a)(4)(ii)

Mortality and morbidity tables —Cont'd
. insurance contracts 1.807-1
. life insurance 1.101-7
. present value, use to determine .... 1.430(h)(3)-1
. . base mortality tables and projection factors .... 1.430(h)(3)-1(d)
. . basis for mortality tables
. . . construction of static tables ...... 1.430(h)(3)-1(c)
. . . generally .... 1.430(h)(3)-1(a)(1)
. . . generational mortality tables .. 1.430(h)(3)-1(a)(4); 1.430(h)(3)-1(a)(4)(i)
. . . static tables .... 1.430(h)(3)-1(a)(3)
. . . static tables or generational tables permitted .... 1.430(h)(3)-1(a)(2)
. . effective/applicability date .... 1.430(h)(3)-1(f)
. . small plan tables .... 1.430(h)(3)-1(b)(2)
. . static mortality tables with respect to valuation dates occurring during 2008 .... 1.430(h)(3)-1(e)
. . use of the tables .... 1.430(h)(3)-1(b)
. . . separate tables for annuitants and nonannuitants .... 1.430(h)(3)-1(b)(1); 1.430(h)(3)-1(b)(1)(i)
. projected mortality improvements .... 1.430(h)(3)-1(c)(2)
. separate tables for annuitants and nonannuitants
. . examples of calculation .... 1.430(h)(3)-1(b)(1)(ii)
. separate tables for specified populations
. . annuitant and nonannuitant separate populations .... 1.430(h)(3)-2(c)(4)(ii)
. . credible mortality experience for separate populations .... 1.430(h)(3)-2(c)(4)(iii)
. source of basic rates .... 1.430(h)(3)-1(c)(1)
. substitute mortality tables
. . aggregation
. . . permissive aggregation of plans .... 1.430(h)(3)-2(d)(3)(i)
. . . required aggregation of plans .... 1.430(h)(3)-2(d)(3)(ii)
. . analysis of mortality experience .... 1.430(h)(3)-2(d)(ii)(B)
. . approval to use
. . . deemed approval .... 1.430(h)(3)-2(b)(iii)
. . . request for additional information .... 1.430(h)(3)-2(b)(ii)
. . . written request, requirements .... 1.430(h)(3)-2(b)(1)(i)
. . base table and base year
. . . base year requirements .... 1.430(h)(3)-2(c)(2)(iii)
. . . change in number of individuals covered by table .... 1.430(h)(3)-2(c)(2)(iv)
. . . experience study and base table requirements .... 1.430(h)(3)-2(c)(2)(i)
. . . . amounts weighted mortality rates .... 1.430(h)(3)-2(c)(2)(ii)(B)
. . . . base table construction .... 1.430(h)(3)-2(c)(2)(ii)(D)
. . . . grouping of ages ...... 1.430(h)(3)-2(c)(2)(ii)(C)

References are to Reg. § numbers

Mortality and morbidity tables —Cont'd
. *substitute mortality tables —Cont'd*
. . demonstration of credible mortality experience for newly affiliated plan
. . . demonstration of credible mortality experience .... 1.430(h)(3)-2(d)(iv)(B)
. . . demonstration of lack of credible mortality experience .... 1.430(h)(3)-2(d)(iv)(C)
. . . example .... 1.430(h)(3)-2(d)(iv)(D)
. . determination; example of calculation .... 1.430(h)(3)-2(c)(3)(ii)
. . early termination of use of tables .... 1.430(h)(3)-2(d)(4)(A)(i)
. . . change in coverage from time of certification .... 1.430(h)(3)-2(d)(4)(A)(ii)(B)
. . . change in coverage from time of experience study .... 1.430(h)(3)-2(d)(4)(A)(ii)(A)
. . morality experience requirements
. . . credible mortality experience .... 1.430(h)(3)-2(c)(1)(ii)
. . . disabled individuals .... 1.430(h)(3)-2(c)(1)(iv)
. . . gender without credible mortality experience .... 1.430(h)(3)-2(c)(1)(iii)
. . newly affiliated plan defined .... 1.430(h)(3)-2(d)(B)
. . present value determination .... 1.430(h)(3)-2(c)
. . . aggregation .... 1.430(h)(3)-2(d)(3)
. . . all plans in controlled group must use substitute mortality table .... 1.430(h)(3)-2(d)(i)
. . . approval to use, procedures for
. . . . Commissioner's review of request .... 1.430(h)(3)-2(b)(i)
. . . . extension of time permitted .. 1.430(h)(3)-2(b)(iv)
. . . . written request to use substitute mortality tables .... 1.430(h)(3)-2(b)(1); 1.430(h)(3)-2(b)(1)(ii)
. . . base table and base year .... 1.430(h)(3)-2(c)(2); 1.430(h)(3)-2(c)(2)(i)
. . . . experience study and base table requirements .. 1.430(h)(3)-2(c)(2)(ii); 1.430(h)(3)-2(c)(2)(ii)(A)
. . . . generally .... 1.430(h)(3)-2(c)(2)(i)
. . . demonstration of credible mortality experience for newly affiliated plan .... 1.430(h)(3)-2(d)(iv); 1.430(h)(3)-2(d)(iv)(A)
. . . determination of substitute mortality tables .... 1.430(h)(3)-2(c)(3); 1.430(h)(3)-2(c)(3)(i)
. . . duration of use of tables .... 1.430(h)(3)-2(d)(2)
. . . early termination of use of tables .... 1.430(h)(3)-2(d)(4)
. . . gender without credible mortality experience
. . . . demonstration of lack of credible mortality experience for a gender .... 1.430(h)(3)-2(c)(1)(iii)(B)
. . . . generally .... 1.430(h)(3)-2(c)(1)(iii)(A)
. . . generally .... 1.430(h)(3)-2; 1.430(h)(3)-2(a); 1.430(h)(3)-2(d)
. . . morality experience requirements .... 1.430(h)(3)-2(c)(1); 1.430(h)(3)-2(c)(1)(i)
. . . newly affiliated plans not using substitute mortality tables ... 1.430(h)(3)-2(d)(A); 1.430(h)(3)-2(d)(iii)

Mortality and morbidity tables —Cont'd
. *substitute mortality tables —Cont'd*
. . *present value determination—Cont'd*
. . . plans without credible experience .... 1.430(h)(3)-2(d)(ii); 1.430(h)(3)-2(d)(ii)(A)
. . . separate tables for specified populations .... 1.430(h)(3)-2(c)(4); 1.430(h)(3)-2(c)(4)(i)
. . . substitute mortality tables
. . . . written request to use substitute mortality tables .... 1.430(h)(3)-2(b)(1)(ii)(A)
. . written request to use
. . . October 1, 2007, submitted on or before .... 1.430(h)(3)-2(b)(1)(ii)(B)
. . . October 1, 2008, with respect to plan years beginning during 2009, submitted on or before .... 1.430(h)(3)-2(b)(1)(ii)(C)

Mortgage bonds, qualified 1.103A-2; 6a.103A-2

Mortgage credit certificates (MCCs)
. penalties with respect to 1.6709-1T

Mortgage revenue bonds
. arbitrage transactions (See Arbitrage transactions)

Mortgage servicing rights
. amortization
. . excluded under section 197, intangibles .... 1.167(a)-14(d)

Mortgages
. basis for gain or loss 1.1054-1
. exempt qualified mortgage bonds 1.103A-2; 6a.103A-2
. Federal National Mortgage Association 1.162-19; 1.1054-1
. foreclosure 1.595-1; 1.856-6; 1.857-3; 5.856-1
. information returns 1.6050H-1; 1.6050H-1T; 1.6050H-2
. interest .... 1.25-1T to 1.25-8T
. . reporting of interest received 1.6050H-1; 1.6050H-2
. interest received
. . time and manner of reporting 1.6050H-1; 1.6050H-2
. itemized deductions 1.166-6
. Omnibus Reconciliation Act of 1980 ..... 6a.103A-1 to 6a.103A-3
. penalties 1.6709-1T
. points 1.6050H-1
. qualified mortgage credit certificates 1.25-3; 1.25-3T; 1.25-4T
. rate changes .... 1.25-1T to 1.25-8T
. revenue yield, arbitrage transactions 1.148-4
. subsidiary bonds 6a.103A-1
. taxable mortgage pools (See Taxable mortgage pools)
. veterans' mortgage bonds 6a.103A-3

Motion picture, television films and tapes
. generally 1.992-4

References are to Reg. § numbers

Motion picture, television films and tapes —Cont'd
. qualified film and production costs, deduction for 1.181-1T
. . acquired productions .... 1.181-3T(e)
. . actor defined .... 1.181-3T(f)(1)
. . compensation defined .... 1.181-3T(c)
. . depreciation or amortization, nonallowance of other .... 1.181-1T(c)
. . generally .... 1.181-3T(a)
. . limits, cost and deduction amount ...... 1.181-1T(b)
. . owner defined for deduction .... 1.181-1T(a)(2)
. . production costs defined for deduction .... 1.181-1T(a)(3)
. . production defined .... 1.181-3T(b)
. . production personnel defined .... 1.181-3T(f)(2)
. . qualified compensation defined .... 1.181-3T(d)
. . recapture 1.181-4T
. . time and manner of election .... 1.181-2T(a)
. . . entity, election by .... 1.181-2T(b)
. . . information requirements .... 1.181-2T(c)
. . . revocation of election .... 1.181-2T(d)
. . . transition rules .... 1.181-2T(e)
. . United States defined .... 1.181-3T(f)(3)

Motor fuels tax (See Diesel and special motor fuels tax)

Motor vehicles (See also Highway vehicles; Trailers; Trucks)
. compressed natural gas 48.4041-21
. gasoline or fuel taxes 1.164-5
. investment credit 1.46-11; 1.280F-1T
. itemized deductions 1.280F-1T; 1.280F-2T
. leased 1.280F-7
. limitations on recovery deductions 1.280F-2T
. manufacturers excise taxes
. . tires 48.4071-1
. recovery deductions 1.280F-1T
. safe harbor lease information returns ... 1.168(f)(8)-1T
. transportation corporations 1.172-8; 1.863-4

Motorboats (See also Ships and shipping; Vessels)
. compressed natural gas 48.4041-21

Movies (See Motion picture, television films and tapes)

Moving expenses
. generally .... 1.82-1 et seq.
. itemized deductions 1.217-1; 1.217-2
. withholding .... 31.3401(a)(15)-1

Multiple employers
. ERISA .... 1.413-2; 1.414(f)-1

Multiple support agreements
. personal exemptions 1.152-3

Municipal bonds
. adjusted basis 1.1016-5

Museums, aircraft
. diesel and special motor fuels tax, exemption 48.4041-14

Mutual insurance companies other than life, marine, fire, or flood
. attorney-in-fact of electing reciprocals 1.826-3
. basis of premium deposits, policyholders of mutual fire or flood insurance companies operating on 1.832-6
. carrybacks and carryovers 1.825-2; 1.825-3
. credit or refund 1.826-6
. deductions, generally 1.832-2; 1.832-5
. dividends to policyholders 1.823-2; 1.823-5
. exempt organizations .. 1.501(c)(14)-1; 1.501(c)(15)-1
. gross income .... 1.832-1 to 1.832-6
. multiple line companies taxed on total income 1.831-4
. net premiums .... 1.823-1 to 1.823-8
. perpetual policies .... 1.831-1 to 1.831-3
. reciprocal underwriters and interinsurers .... 1.823-7; 1.826-1 to 1.826-6
. Section 82 taxes 1.821-4
. subscribers of reciprocal underwriters and interinsurers 1.823-7
. underwriting ..... 1.823-6; 1.823-7; 1.826-1 to 1.826-6
. unused loss deduction .... 1.825-1 to 1.825-3

Mutual irrigation organizations
. exempt organizations .... 1.501(c)(12)-1

Mutual savings banks (See also Financial institutions; Banking institutions)
. additions to reserves for bad debts 1.593-5; 1.593-6; 1.593-6A
. bad debts ..... 1.582-1; 1.593-1 to 1.593-3; 1.593-1 to 1.593-7
. consolidated returns 1.1502-42
. distributions to shareholders 1.593-10
. distributions to shareholders by domestic building and loan associations 1.593.7
. dividends 1.591-1; 1.596-1
. foreclosed property 1.595-1
. generally .... 1.581-2; 1.591-1 et seq.
. life insurance business 1.594-1
. loans 1.593-6A; 1.593-11
. real estate 1.593-11
. real property loans, addition to reserve for losses on qualifying 1.593-4

Mutualization distributions
. life insurance companies 1.809-8

N

Native Americans
. excise tax exemption for articles manufactured by 48.4225-1
. tribal government (See Indian tribal governments)

References are to Reg. § numbers

Natural resources
. allocation of gross income under section 863 .... 1.863-1(b)
. basis, holding period, and abandonment losses 1.614-6
. bonuses and advanced royalties 1.612-3
. coal or domestic iron ore 1.272-1; 1.631-3
. continental shelf areas 1.638-1; 1.638-2
. deductions, generally .... 1.611-0 et seq.
. defense purposes 1.621-1
. deferral of expenditures 1.616-2
. depletion .... 1.611-1; 1.611-4; 1.612-1; 1.612-3; 1.613A-1 et seq.; 1.613-1; 1.613-2; 1.613-6; 1.1502-44
. development expenditures 1.616-1; 1.621-1
. election under section 613A(c)(4) 1.613A-5
. exclusions under subchapter K 1.761-2
. exemptions .... 1.613A-2 to 1.613A-4
. exploration expenditures .... 1.381(c)(10)-1; 1.617-1; 1.617-3; 1.621-1
. . deduction limitations 1.617-2
. extension of time for performing certain acts .. 1.614-7
. gain from disposition of mining property 1.617-4
. gas wells, domestic 1.613A-2
. generally .... 1.611-0 et seq.
. geothermal wells 1.612-5
. gross income 1.613-4
. improvements 1.611-5
. independent producers and royalty owners 1.613A-3
. limitations on exemptions 1.613A-4
. mines and mining (See Minerals, mines, and mining)
. nonoperating mineral interests, aggregation .. 1.614-5
. oil and gas (See Oil and gas)
. percentage depletion .... 1.613A-1 et seq.; 1.613-1; 1.613-2; 1.613-6; 1.1502-44
. property defined 1.614-1
. recordkeeping requirements 1.613A-6
. returns due on or before May 2, 1960 .... 1.616-3
. royalties 1.543-12; 1.612-3; 1.613A-3
. sales and exchanges .... 1.631-1 to 1.631-3
. separate operating mineral interests, aggregation .... 1.614-0 et seq.
. taxable income 1.613-5
. timber 1.611-3; 1.631-2

Negligence
. rules or regulations; underpayment of tax ... 1.6662-3

Net operating loss carrybacks and carryovers
. abatements, credits, and refunds .... 301.6501(h)-1; 301.6511(d)-2
. banking institutions 1.584-6
. capital gains and losses .... 1.1244(d)-4
. consolidated returns 1.1502-21; 1.1502-79A
. . carryovers and carrybacks 1.1502-21

Net operating loss carrybacks and carryovers — Cont'd
. corporations, generally 1.172-2
. domestic international sales corporations 1.996-8
. dual consolidated loss 1.1503-2; 1.1503-2A
. . elective relief provisions 1.1503-2
. estates and trusts .... 1.642(d)-1
. foreign tax credit .... 1.904(f)-3
. generally .... 1.172-4 et seq.
. itemized deductions .... 1.172-1 to 1.172-13
. limitations on assessment and collection .... 301.6501(h)-1
. loss corporations
. . allocation of income and loss to periods before and after change date 1.382-6
. . controlled groups 1.382-8
. . determination of net operating loss .... 1.382-6(c)
. . ownership changes 1.382-2
. . time and manner of acquisition of interest in, determination of 1.382-10
. net recognized built-in gain or loss 1.1374-5; 1.1374-8
. ownership change
. . defined 1.382-2T
. . limitations on built-in losses 1.382-2T; 1.382-5
. . predecessor corporations 1.382-2
. . successor corporations 1.382-2
. partners and partnerships 1.702-2
. self-employment income .... 1.1402(a)-7
. successor corporations (See Successor corporations)
. surcharge 1.56A-2

Net operating losses
. carrybacks and carryovers (See Net operating loss carrybacks and carryovers)
. consolidated returns .... 1.1502-0 et seq.; 1.1502-21
. . carryovers and carrybacks .... 1.1502-21(b)

Netting rule
. conversion transactions 1.1258-1

New jobs credit
. apportionment among members of controlled groups 1.52-1
. carrybacks and carryovers .... 1.381(c)(26)-1
. generally 1.44B-1
. limitation 1.53-1
. pass-through of 1.53-3

New lines of business
. possessions corporation claiming credits 1.936-11

New markets tax credit
. allowance .... 1.45D-1(b)
. anti-abuse .... 1.45D-1(g)
. basis reduction .... 1.45D-1(f)
. community development entity .... 1.45D-1(d)
. equity investments .... 1.45D-1(c)

References are to Reg. § numbers

New markets tax credit —Cont'd
. financial counseling and other services . . . 1.45D-1(d)
. low-income community investments . . . . . . 1.45D-1(d)
. notification by CDE to taxpayer of equity investment . . . . . . 1.45D-1(g)
. qualified active low-income community business . . . . . . 1.45D-1(d)
. qualified low-income community investments . . . . . . 1.45D-1(d)
. recapture . . . . . . 1.45D-1(e)
. reporting requirements . . . . . . 1.45D-1(g)

New York Liberty Zone leasehold property
. additional first year depreciation deduction . . . . . . 1.168(k)-1(b); 1.1400L(b)-1T

New York Liberty Zone property
. additional first year depreciation deduction . . . . . . 1.1400L(b)-1
. . computation of deduction of qualified New York Liberty zone property . . . . . . 1.1400L(b)-1(d)
. . definitions concerning . . . . . . 1.1400L(b)-1(b)
. . qualified New York Liberty zone property . . . . . . 1.1400L(b)-1(c)
. distributions by corporations
. . depreciation on earnings and profits 1.312-15
. mid-quarter convention, rules for applying . . . . . . 1.168(d)-1(b)
. pollution control facilities, depreciation deduction . . . . . . 1.169-3(b)
. rehabilitation expenditures incurred after December 31, 1981 . . . . . . 1.48-12

Newly married couples
. change in annual accounting period 1.442-1

News services
. excise tax exemption 49.4253-2

Newspapers
. generally . . . . . . 31.3401(a)(10)-1

9-day rule taxes
. depositaries of government . . . . . . 40.6302(c)-1

No-additional cost services 1.132-2; 1.132-2T

Nonbusiness expenses
. generally 1.212-1

Noncash remuneration
. retail commission salesperson, services by . . . . . . 31.3402(j)-1(c)

Noncitizen of United States
. gift tax, nonresidents not citizens
. . charitable gifts . . . . . . 25.2522(b)-1
. . transfers by 25.2511-3
. joint tenancy
. . spouse not a citizen, one . . . . . . 25.2523(i)-2
. marital deduction
. . citizen, spouse not . . . . . . 25.2523(i)-1
. . disallowance
. . . spouse not a citizen . . . . . . 25.2523(i)-1

Noncitizen of United States —Cont'd
. *marital deduction —Cont'd*
. . surviving spouse not citizen 20.2056A-1
. possessions of United States
. . nonresidents not citizen 20.2209-1
. qualified domestic trust election
. . citizen after, surviving spouse becoming 20.2056A-10

Nondiscrimination rules
. cash or deferred arrangements . . . . . . 1.401(a)-1; 1.401(k)-1
. fringe benefits 1.132-8; 1.132-8T
. group term life insurance 1.79-4T
. pension, profit-sharing, and stock bonus plans (See Pension, profit-sharing, and stock bonus plans)
. . protected benefits . . . . . . 1.411(d)-4

Nonemployee compensation
. backup withholding . . . . . . 31.3406(b)(3)-1

Nonpayroll payments
. withholding of tax . . . . . . 31.6011(a)-4(b)

Nonprofit organizations (See Exempt organizations)

Nonqualified deferred compensation plans
. aggregation rules . . . . . . 1.409A-1(c)(2)
. amounts deferred, statutory application of . . . . . . 1.409A-6(a)(1)
. calculation of amount of compensation, statutory application of . . . . . . 1.409A-6(a)(3)
. compensation
. . specified employee . . . . . . 1.409A-2(i)(2)
. date of deferral, identification of, statutory application of . . . . . . 1.409A-6(a)(2)
. deferral elections
. . annualize recurring part-year compensation . . . . . . 1.409A-2(a)(14)
. . cafeteria plan, election change under . . . . . . 1.409A-2(a)(10)
. . commissions . . . . . . 1.409A-2(a)(12)
. . final payroll period, compensation paid for . . . . . . 1.409A-2(a)(13)
. . first year of eligibility . . . . . . 1.409A-2(a)(7)
. . fiscal year compensation . . . . . . 1.409A-2(a)(6)
. . forfeitable rights . . . . . . 1.409A-2(a)(5)
. . general rule . . . . . . 1.409A-2(a)(3)
. . initial . . . . . . 1.409A-2(a)(1) et seq.
. . performance-based compensation . . . 1.409A-2(a)(8)
. . qualified employer plans, nonqualified plan linked to . . . . . . 1.409A-2(a)(9)
. . separation pay . . . . . . 1.409A-2(a)(11)
. . service recipient election . . . . . . 1.409A-2(a)(2)
. . short-term deferrals . . . . . . 1.409A-2(a)(4)
. . subsequent change in time and form of payment . . . . . . 1.409A-2(b)(1)
. deferral of compensation
. . customary payment timing arrangements . . . . . . 1.409A-1(b)(3)

References are to Reg. § numbers

Nonqualified deferred compensation plans —Cont'd
. *deferral of compensation —Cont'd*
. . earnings . . . . . 1.409A-1(b)(2)
. . equity based compensation . . . . . 1.409A-1(b)(5)
. . foreign plans . . . . . 1.409A-1(b)(8)
. . forfeiture, risk of . . . . . 1.409A-1(d)
. . generally . . . . . 1.409A-1(b)(1)
. . performance based compensation . . . . . 1.409A-1(e)
. . restricted property . . . . . 1.409A-1(b)(6)
. . section 402(b) trusts . . . . . 1.409A-1(b)(6)
. . section 403(c) annuities . . . . . 1.409A-1(b)(6)
. . separation pay plans . . . . . 1.409A-1(b)(9)
. . short-term . . . . . 1.409A-1(b)(4)
. . stock appreciation rights . . . . . 1.409A-1(b)(5)
. . stock options . . . . . 1.409A-1(b)(5)
. defined . . . . . 1.409A-1(c)(1); 1.409A-1(1)
. earnings defined . . . . . 1.409A-1(o)
. established securities markets
. . defined . . . . . 1.409A-1(k)
. foreign plans . . . . . 1.409A-1(3)
. involuntary separation from service
. . defined . . . . . 1.409A-1(n)
. material modifications, statutory application of . . . . . 1.409A-6(a)(4)
. permissible payments
. . acceleration of payments, prohibitions against . . . . . 1.409A-3(j)
. . alternative specified payment date or schedule based upon permissible payment event . . . . 1.409A-3(c)
. . definitions concerning . . . . . 1.409A-3(i)
. . designated payment date . . . . . 1.409A-3(d)
. . disputed payments . . . . . 1.409A-3(g)
. . generally . . . . . 1.409A-3(a)
. . permissible payment event, upon . . . . . 1.409A-3(b)
. . refusals to pay . . . . . 1.409A-3(g)
. . resident aliens . . . . . 1.409A-3(h)
. . special rules . . . . . 1.409A-3(i)
. . specified time and fixed schedule . . . . . 1.409A-3(i)
. . substitutions . . . . . 1.409A-3(f)
. . time and form of payment . . . . . 1.409A-3(e)
. qualified employer plan status . . . . . 1.409A-1(2)
. separation from service
. . asset purchase transactions . . . . . 1.409A-2(h)(4)
. . collectively bargained plans . . . . . 1.409A-2(h)(6)
. . defined . . . . . 1.409A-1(h)
. . dual status . . . . . 1.409A-2(h)(5)
. . independent contractors . . . . . 1.409A-2(h)(2)
. . service recipient and employer . . . . . 1.409A-2(h)(3)
. . termination of employment . . . . . 1.409A-1(h)(ii)
. separation pay plan . . . . . 1.409A-1(m)
. service recipient defined . . . . . 1.409A-1(g)
. six-month delay rule
. . alternative methods of satisfying . . . . . 1.409A-2(i)(5)

Nonqualified deferred compensation plans —Cont'd
. specified employee
. . compensation . . . . . 1.409A-2(i)(2)
. . defined . . . . . 1.409A-2(i)(1)
. . effective date . . . . . 1.409A-2(i)(4)
. . identification date . . . . . 1.409A-2(i)(3)
. . six-month delay rule, alternative methods of satisfying . . . . . 1.409A-2(i)(5)
. stock right defined . . . . . 1.409A-1(l)
. subsequent change in time and form of payment
. . acceleration of payments, coordination with . . . . . 1.409A-2(b)(5)
. . beneficiaries . . . . . 1.409A-2(b)(3)
. . delay of payments . . . . . 1.409A-2(b)(7)
. . domestic relations orders . . . . . 1.409A-2(b)(4)
. . multiple payment events . . . . . 1.409A-2(b)(6)
. . payment for defined . . . . . 1.409A-2(b)(2)
. . USERRA rights . . . . . 1.409A-2(b)(8)

Nonrefundable personal credits
. generally 1.871-7; 301.6402-3

Nonresident aliens
. abatements, credits, and refunds 1.6414-1
. Bank for International Settlements 1.895-1
. Canadian residents
. . interest paid to 1.6049-8
. . OID paid to 1.6049-8
. . reportable payments made to . . . . . 31.3406(g)-1
. change of U.S. citizenship or residence 1.871-13
. classification and manner of taxing 1.871-1
. closer connection exception . . . . . 301.7701(b)-2
. collection of tax at source . . . 1.6302-2; 31.3401(a)(6)-1
. community income 1.879-1
. compensation of employees of foreign governments or international organizations 1.893-1
. consent dividends 1.565-5
. credits 1.874-1
. days of presence in the United States . . 301.7701(b)-3
. deductions 1.873-1; 1.874-1
. definitions 301.7701-5
. departing aliens, certificate of compliance with income tax laws 1.6851-2
. dividends 1.565-5
. estates
. . credits 20.2102-1
. . deductions
. . . determination of taxable estate 20.2106-1
. . . expenses and losses 20.2106-2
. . entire gross estate defined 20.2103-1
. . expatriation to avoid tax 20.2107-1
. . gross estate
. . . entire gross estate, determination of 20.2103-1
. . . expatriation to avoid tax 20.2107-1
. . property within United States 20.2104-1

References are to Reg. § numbers

Nonresident aliens —Cont'd
. *estates —Cont'd*
. . property without United States 20.2105-1
. . tax avoidance 20.2107-1
. . taxable estate, determination 20.2106-1
. . unified credit 20.2102-1
. estimated tax 1.6654-6
. exemption, income subject to 1.1441-2
. foreign central bank of issue or Bank for International Settlements 1.895-1
. foreign governments, income of .... 1.892-1T et seq.; 1.893-1
. foreign investment in United States real property 1.897-1
. generally .... 1.871-1; 1.871-1 et seq.; 301.7701(b)-0
. gross income 1.872-1; 1.872-2
. . determination .... 1.6654-6(b)
. income from sources within or without U.S. 1.864-3
. interest, repeal of tax on 1.871-14
. joint returns 1.6013-6; 1.6013-7
. lawful permanent resident .... 301.7701(b)-1
. loss of residence 1.871-5
. mortgage interest, reporting of 1.6050H-1
. partnerships 1.875-1
. patents, copyrights, or similar property 1.871-11
. possessions of United States .... 301.7701(b)-1
. procedural rules .... 301.7701(b)-8
. proof of residence 1.871-4
. Puerto Rico 1.876-1
. real property .... 1.871-10; 1.1445-1 to 1.1445-7
. related person factoring income 1.864-8T
. remuneration for services .... 31.3401(a)(6)-1
. residency, time period .... 301.7701(b)-4
. returns 1.6013-6; 1.6013-7
. scholarships or fellowships
. . withholding tax exemption 1.1441-4
. seamen 1.871-3
. Section 877, coordination with .... 301.7701(b)-5
. securities lending transactions 1.871-7
. small business corporations 1.1361-1
. students or trainees 1.871-9
. taxable year .... 301.7701(b)-6
. treaty .... 1.1441-6; 301.7701(b)-7
. . income affected by 1.894-1
. treaty income 1.871-12
. U.S. business, alien individuals engaged in .. 1.871-7; 1.871-8
. U.S. real property holding corporations 1.897-2
. . distributions 1.897-5T
. withholding . . 1.441-2; 1.1441-1 to 1.1441-9; 1.1441-2
. . depositaries of government 1.6302-2
. . determinability of amount .... 1.441-2(b)(1)(iii); 1.1441-2(b)(1)(iii)
. . effective date .... 1.441-2(f); 1.1441-2(f)

Nonresident aliens —Cont'd
. *withholding—Cont'd*
. . fixed or determinable annual or periodical income .... 1.441-2(b); 1.1441-2(b)
. . . definition .... 1.441-2(b)(1)(i); 1.1441-2(b)(1)(i)
. . . exceptions .... 1.441-2(b)(2); 1.1441-2(b)(2)
. . . generally .... 1.441-2(b)(1); 1.1441-2(b)(1)
. . . original issue discount .... 1.441-2(b)(3); 1.1441-2(b)(3)
. . . . exceptions to withholding ..... 1.441-2(b)(3)(iii); 1.1441-2(b)(3)(iii)
. . . REMIC residual .... 1.441-2(b)(5)
. . . REMIC residual interests .... 1.1441-2(b)(5)
. . . securities lending transactions and equivalent transactions .... 1.441-2(b)(4); 1.1441-2(b)(4)
. . generally .... 1.441-2(a); 1.1441-2(a)
. . manner of payment .... 1.441-2(b)(1)(ii); 1.1441-2(b)(1)(ii)
. . no money or property is paid or lack of knowledge, exception .... 1.441-2(d); 1.1441-2(d)
. . . cancellation of debt .... 1.441-2(d)(2); 1.1441-2(d)(2)
. . . general rule .... 1.441-2(d)(1); 1.1441-2(d)(1)
. . . inapplicable, withholding exemption .... 1.1441-2(d)(4)
. . . satisfaction of liability following underwithholding by withholding agent . . 1.441-2(d)(3); 1.1441-2(d)(3)
. . original issue discount
. . . amount subject to tax .... 1.441-2(b)(3)(i); 1.1441-2(b)(3)(i)
. . . amount subject to withholding .... 1.441-2(b)(3)(ii); 1.1441-2(b)(3)(ii)
. . other income .... 1.441-2(c)
. . other income subject to withholding ..... 1.1441-2(c)
. . payment .... 1.441-2(e); 1.1441-2(e)
. . . blocked income ..... 1.441-2(e)(3); 1.1441-2(e)(3)
. . . certain interest accrued by a foreign corporation .... 1.441-2(e)(5); 1.1441-2(e)(5)
. . . general rule .... 1.441-2(e)(1); 1.1441-2(e)(1)
. . . income allocated under section 482 .... 1.441-2(e)(2); 1.1441-2(e)(2)
. . . payments other than in U.S. dollars .... 1.441-2(e)(6); 1.1441-2(e)(6)
. . . special rules for dividends .... 1.441-2(e)(4); 1.1441-2(e)(4)
. withholding tax at source
. . agents 1.871-6; 1.1441-7
. . amounts subject to withholding 1.1441-2
. . claiming to be not subject to withholding ... 1.1441-5
. . determination of amounts to be withheld ... 1.1441-3
. . disposition of U.S. real property interests by foreign persons .... 1.1445-1 to 1.1445-7
. . distributions 1.1445-5
. . exemptions .... 1.1441-4; 1.1441-4T; 1.1442-2; 1.1443-1; 31.3402(f)(6)-1

References are to Reg. § numbers

Nonresident aliens —Cont'd
. *withholding tax at source —Cont'd*
. . generally .... 31.3401(a)(6)-1; 31.3401(a)(6)-1A; 31.3401(a)(7)-1
. . tax treaty, application of 1.1441-6
Nontaxable exchanges
. gain or loss .... 1.1031(a)-1 to 1.1039-1
Nontrade or nonbusiness expenses
. itemized deduction 1.212-1
Normal taxes
. generally .... 1.1-1 et seq.
North American Industry Classification System (NAICS)
. manual and classes .... 1.1031(a)-2
. personal property exchanges .... 1.1031(a)-2
Northern Mariana Islands
. bona fide residency
. . alien individuals presence test .... 1.937-1(c)(2)
. . bona fide resident .... 1.937-1(b)
. . closer connection test .... 1.937-1(e)
. . days of presence .... 1.937-1(c)(3)
. . definitions concerning .... 1.937-1(a)
. . generally 1.937-1
. . information reporting .... 1.937-1(h)
. . medical treatment .... 1.937-1(c)(4)
. . presence test .... 1.937-1(c)
. . significant connection to the United States .... 1.937-1(c)(5)
. . tax home test .... 1.937-1(d)
. . year of move .... 1.937-1(f)
. coordination of individual income taxes 1.935-1
. . definitions concerning .... 1.935-1(a)
. . entity consistency status .... 1.935-1(e)
. . estimated income tax special rules ...... 1.935-1(d)
. . extension of territory .... 1.935-1(c)
. . filing requirements .... 1.935-1(b)
. . individuals covered .... 1.935-1(a)
. . liability to other jurisdictions .... 1.935-1(b)
. . payment of tax .... 1.935-1(b)
. generally 1.876-1
. gross income exclusions 1.931-1
Not for profit activities (See also Charitable contributions; Exempt organizations)
. generally 1.183-1
. uniform capitalization rules 1.263A-1
Notes
. fair market value; gift tax 25.2512-4
. interest expense, allocation
. . income from sources within or without U.S. .... 1.861-12T(d)
. valuation of 20.2031-4; 25.2512-4
Notice
. backup withholding 35a.3406-2
Notice —Cont'd
. *backup withholding—Cont'd*
. . underreporting of interest or dividend payments .... 31.3406(c)-1
. deficiency .... 301.6212-1; 301.6503(a)-1
. diesel fuel tax; dyeing 48.4082-2
. electronic medium, use of
. . pension, profit-sharing, and stock bonus plans .... 1.401(a)-21
. excise taxes 53.6001-1
. exempt organizations .... 1.505(c)-1T
. . notification requirement for entities not required to file annual information return under sec. 6033(a)(1) 1.6033-6T
. federal tax lien, withdrawal of notice .... 301.6323(j)-1
. fiduciaries 301.6903-1
. last-known address defined for 301.6212-2
. liens .... 301.6323(b)-1; 301.6823(f)-1; 301.6323(g)-1
. mortgage rates 1.25-7T
. partnership items ..... 301.6222(b)-1; 301.6222(b)-2; 301.6223(a)-1; 301.6223(a)-2; 301.6223(e)-1; 301.6223(e)-2
. . notice group .... 301.6223(b)-1
. . withdrawal of notice .... 301.6223(a)-2
. pension plan amendment
. . future benefit accrual, reducing rate of .. 54.4980F-1
. private foundations 1.508-1
. recognized representative, to 601.506
. records, statements, and special returns ... 56.6001-1
. returns 301.6001-1; 301.6110-5
. . notification requirement for entities not required to file annual information return under sec. 6033(a)(1) 1.6033-6T
. seizure and of property 301.6335-1
. Tax Court; to interested parties 1.7476-2
. tax matters partner .... 301.6223(a)-1
. . IRS failure to provide notice .... 301.6223(e)-1
. . IRS failure to provide timely notice .... 301.6223(e)-2
. time and place for paying tax 301.6155-1
. TIN matching program .... 31.3406(j)-1(b)
. withholding 35a.3406-2
Notional principal contracts
. allocation of income attributable to 1.863-7
. derivatives, and
. . securities dealers .... 1.475(b)-1(c)
. . treatment .... 1.475(d)-1(b)
. generally 1.446-3
. hedging transactions 1.446-3; 1.446-4
. income and deductions, reflection of 1.446-3
. modification of certain contracts 1.1001-4
. source of income .... 1.863-7(b)
. timing of income and deductions 1.451-1
Nuclear decommissioning costs
. generally 1.88-1

References are to Reg. § numbers

Nuclear decommissioning funds
. allocation; section 338, elections under
. . adjusted grossed-up basis (AGUB) 1.338-6
. dispositions or transfers 1.468A-6T
. disqualification of fund 1.468A-5T
. electing taxpayers 1.468A-2T
. manner and time for making election for deduction 1.468A-7T
. qualification requirements 1.468A-1T; 1.468A-5T
. ruling amount 1.468A-3T
. self-dealing 1.468A-5T
. special transfers 1.468A-8T
. termination of fund 1.468A-5T
. treatment of fund 1.468A-4T

Nuclear power plants
. accounting methods 1.468A-6T
. decommissioning costs, generally . . . . . . 1.468A-1T to 1.468A-9T
. disposition of interest in 1.468A-6

O

Oaths
. generally 301.7456-1; 301.7622-1

Obligations
. installment
. . liquidating corporation, received from 1.453-11
. registration requirements
. . generally 5f.163-1; 35a.9999-5
. . interest deduction 5f.163-1
. . questions and answers on withholding tax on interest 35a.9999-5
. volunteer fire departments 1.103-16
. withholding, foreign persons 1.1441-3

Obsolescence
. accounting method change . . . . 1.1016-3(h)
. basis for gain or loss 1.1016-3; 1.1016-4
. depreciation . . . . 1.167(a)-9
. itemized depreciation 1.165-2

Offenses (See headings beginning Criminal)

Offer to compromise fee 300.3
. amount of fee . . . . 300.3(b)
. applicability . . . . 300.3(a)
. liability . . . . 300.3(c)

Offset
. life insurance company 1.812-5

OID (See Original issue discount)

Oil and gas (See also Windfall profit tax on domestic crude oil)
. capitalization of costs 1.263A-1; 1.263A-13
. capitalization rules 1.263A-1; 1.263A-13
. cumulative gas balancing method 1.761-2
. election under section 613A(c)(4) 1.613A-5

Oil and gas (See also Windfall profit tax on domestic crude oil) —Cont'd
. enhanced oil recovery credit . . . . 1.43-0 et seq.
. . election 1.43-6
. . generally 1.43-1
. . qualifying costs 1.43-4
. exempt facility bonds
. . termination of financing, manner an making election . . . . 1.142(f)(4)-1T
. exemptions 1.613A-2
. floor stocks tax (See Fuel floor stocks tax)
. foreign base company, income from 1.954-8
. . verification of income 1.964-4
. foreign source income taxes (See FOGEI and FORI)
. franchises, trademarks and trade names 1.1254-1
. gas balancing method, annual and cumulative 1.761-2
. generally 1.164-5; 1.611-2; 1.612-4; 1.613-4
. gross income from the property defined 1.612-3
. itemized deduction . . . . 1.263(c)-1
. joint operating agreements . . . . 1.761-2(d)
. percentage depletion . . . . 1.613A-1 et seq.
. percentage depletion, limitations
. . cumulative method . . . . 1.761-2(d)
. . domestic gas, exemptions 1.613-2
. . exemptions generally 1.613-2
. . partner's distributive share 1.704-1
. petroleum tax on natural gas 52.4612-1
. qualified enhanced oil recovery project 1.43-2
. . engineer's certification 1.43-3
. recognized built-in gain or loss 1.1374-4
. sale of property 1.613-1
. separate operating mineral interests 1.614-4; 1.614-8
. tertiary injectant expenses 1.193-1

Older persons (See Aged persons)

Omnibus Budget Reconciliation Act of 1993
. elections under, time and manner of making . . . . 1.163(d)-1

Omnibus Reconciliation Act of 1980
. generally . . . . 6a.103A-1 et seq.
. mortgages . . . . 6a.103A-1 to 6a.103A-3
. veterans' mortgage bonds 6a.103A-3

Omnibus Reconciliation Act of 1993
. accuracy related penalty 1.6662-7
. time and manner of making election under . . 1.108-5; 1.1044(a)-1; 1.6655(e)-1

$1,000,000 remuneration
. employees in excess of, deduction 1.162-27

Optional 10-year writeoff of certain tax preferences 1.59-1

Optional tax
. generally 1.2-1

References are to Reg. § numbers

Options
. equity (See Equity options)
. stock (See Stock options)
Ore (See Minerals, mines, and mining)
Organizational expenses and syndication costs
. election to amortize .... 1.709-1T(b)
. . effective date .... 1.709-1T(b)(5)
. . examples .... 1.709-1T(b)(4)
. . expenditures of more than $55,000 .... 1.709-1T(b)(4)(6)
. . expiration date .... 1.709-1T(b)(6)
. . $5,000 but less than or equal to $50,000, expenditures of more than .... 1.709-1T(b)(4)(2)
. . $5,000 or less, expenditures of .... 1.709-1T(b)(4)(1)
. . $50,000 but less than or equal to $55,000, expenditures of more than .... 1.709-1T(b)(4)(5)
. . generally .... 1.709-1T(b)(1)
. . liquidation of partnership .... 1.709-1T(b)(3)
. . subsequent change in the characterization of an item .... 1.709-1T(b)(4)(3)
. . subsequent redetermination of year in which business begins .... 1.709-1T(b)(4)(4)
. . time and manner of making election .... 1.709-1T(b)(2)
. generally 1.248-1; 1.709-1
Organizations
. classification for tax purposes 301.7701-2
. cooperative (See Cooperatives)
. exempt (See Exempt organizations)
Original issue discount (OID)
. accrual of .... 1.1272-1(b)
. adjusted basis 1.1016-5
. aggregation of debt instruments .... 1.1275-2(c)
. anti-abuse rule .... 1.1275-2(g)
. backup withholding .... 1.6049-4 to 1.6049-6; 31.3406(b)(2)-2
. bond houses, sales to .... 1.1273-2(e)
. Canadian nonresident aliens 1.6049-8
. cash payments incident to lending .... 1.1273-2(g)
. contingent payment debt instruments 1.1275-4
. de minimis .... 1.1273-1(d)
. debt instruments, deduction 1.163-7
. . accrual period choice of .... 1.163-7(d)
. . de minimus OID, special rules for .... 1.163-7(b)
. . reopening, qualified .... 1.163-7(e)
. . repurchase .... 1.163-7(c)
. defined 1.1273-1
. definitions 1.1275-1
. disclosure of certain information to holders .... 1.1275-2(e)
. distribution, stock .... 1.1275-2(b)
. election to treat all interest as 1.1272-3
. incidental contingencies .... 1.1275-2(h)
. income, current inclusion in 1.1272-1
Original issue discount (OID) —Cont'd
. information returns .... 1.1275-3; 1.6049-4 et seq.
. investment units .... 1.1273-2(h)
. issue price, determination of 1.1273-2
. itemized deductions 1.163-4
. premium, instruments purchased at 1.1272-2
. principal payment uncertain as to time .... 1.1272-1(d)
. pro rata prepayments .... 1.1275-2(f)
. publicly traded issued for property .... 1.1273-2(b)
. publicly traded property, instrument issued for .... 1.1273-2(c)
. related foreign person, held by 1.163-12
. remote contingencies .... 1.1275-2(h)
. reopenings .... 1.1275-2(k)
. reporting 1.6049-5
. short term obligation, determination of .... 1.1272-1(f)
. Treasury securities .... 1.1275-2(d)
. treatment of certain modifications .... 1.1275-2(j)
. variable rate debt instruments
. . qualified stated interest and .... 1.1275-5(e)
. yield and maturity of debt instruments .... 1.1272-1(c)
Output facilities
. private activity bonds
. . allocation and accounting rules 1.141-6
. . $15 million limitation for 1.141-8
. . private business test 1.141-7
. refunding bonds 1.141-15
Overpayment of tax
. abatements, credits, and refunds .... 1.1464-1; 1.6425-1 to 1.6425-3; 301.6401-1; 301.6402-5; 301.6402-6; 301.6403-1; 301.6425-1; 301.6511(a)-1 et seq.
. adjustments
. . after return is filed .... 31.6413(a)-2(c)(2)
. . before return is filed .... 31.6413(a)-2(c)(1)
. . FICA .... 31.6413(a)-2; 31.6413(a)-2(b)
. . generally .... 31.6413(a)-2
. . not permitted .... 31.6413(a)-2(d)
. . RRTA .... 31.6413(a)-2; 31.6413(a)-2(b)
. estimated tax adjustment, computation of 1.6425-2
. excise taxes (See specific tax)
. FICA overpayment adjustments .... 31.6413(a)-2
. generally 301.6402-4; 301.6611-1
. interest 301.6611-1
. review by IRS of overpayment exceeding $200,000 .... 601.108
. RRTA overpayment adjustments .... 31.6413(a)-2
Owner-employees
. life insurance endowments or annuities 1.72-17; 1.72-17A
. pension, profit-sharing, and stock bonus plans .... 1.401(e)-3; 1.401-12; 1.401-13
Ownership
. affiliate-owned stock 1.7874-1

References are to Reg. § numbers

Ownership —Cont'd
. constructive (See Constructive ownership)
. corporate organizations and reorganizations (See Successor corporations)
. discovery of liability and enforcement of title (See Discovery of liability and enforcement of title)
. ownership change defined 1.383-2
. personal holding companies . . . . . . 1.544-1 to 1.544-6
. property produced by taxpayer 1.263A-2
Ownership change
. consolidated return 1.1502-1
. corporate organizations and reorganizations (See Successor corporations)
. credit limitations
. . limitation, determination of 1.1502-93
. disposition of assets . . . . 1.168(i)-1(e)
. foreign corporation stock acquisitions 1.6046-1
. net unrealized built-in losses . . . . 1.56(g)-1(k)
. reverse acquisitions 1.1502-1
Ozone-depleting chemicals, taxes on
. exports 52.4682-5
. floor stocks tax 52.4682-4
. generally 52.4681-0; 52.4682-1
. imported taxable products 52.4682-3
. imposition of tax 52.4681-1
. qualifying sales 52.4682-2

P

Paperwork Reduction Act 48.9000-0
Parachute payments
. questions and answers concerning 1.280G-1
Parsonages
. exemptions 1.107-1
Partial liquidations
. generally . . . . 1.312-5; 1.346-1 to 1.346-3
Partners and partnerships
. abatements, credits, and refunds . . . . . 301.6501(o)-2; 301.6501(o)-3; 301.6511(g)-1
. abusive tax shelter . . . . 301.6231(c)-2
. additional information regarding partners furnished to IRS . . . . 301.6223(c)-1
. adjusted current earnings . . . . 1.56(g)-1(p)
. administrative adjustments . . . . 301.6227(c)-1
. . IRS duplicate . . . . 301.6223(f)-1
. . limitations on . . . . 301.6231(c)-3
. administrative proceedings . . . . 301.6224(a)-1
. . participation in, right of . . . . 301.6224(a)-1
. alternative minimum tax 1.58-2
. automatic extension of time for filing returns 1.6081-2T
. bankruptcy and receivership . . . . 301.6231(c)-7
. basis

Partners and partnerships —Cont'd
. *basis —Cont'd*
. . allocation of 1.755-1
. . contributing partner's interest 1.722-1
. . distributed property 1.732-1; 1.732-2; 1.732-3
. . distributee partner's interest 1.733-1
. . generally 1.755-1
. . optional adjustment 1.743-1
. . partner's interest 1.705-1
. . partnership property 1.754-1
. . property contributed to partnership 1.723-1
. . transferee partner's interest 1.742-1
. . undistributed partnership property 1.734-1; 1.734-2; 1.735-1; 1.736-1
. C corporation status . . . . 301.6231(a)(2)-1
. capital gains and losses
. . holding period, partnership interest 1.1223-3
. . look-through rule
. . . sales or exchanges of interest in partnership . . . . 1.1(h)-1
. . sale of 1.741-1
. carrybacks and carryovers . . . . 301.6231(c)-1
. classification for tax purposes 301.7701-3
. communications activity . . . . 1.863-9(i)
. computations . . . . 1.704-1; 301.6231(a)(6)-1
. consistent treatment . . . . 301.6222(a)-1
. continuation of partnership 1.708-1
. . mergers or consolidations 1.708-1
. contributed contracts 1.737-2
. contributed property . . . . 1.704-1(c); 1.704-3
. contributions to partnership 1.721-1; 1.722-1; 1.723-1
. . distributions of previously contributed property 1.737-2
. . distributions of section 704(c) property 1.704-4
. . recognition of precontribution gain 1.737-1
. correction not be made, request that . . . 301.6230(b)-1
. criminal investigations . . . . 301.6231(c)-5
. debt, allocation of partnership
. . assumption of Sec. 1.752-7 liability by partnership on or after June 24, 2003 . . . . 1.752-7
. . assumption of Sec. 358(h) liability after Oct. 18, 1999 and before June 24, 2003 . . . . 1.752-6T
. . nonrecourse liability 1.752-1
. . partner's share of nonrecourse liabilities 1.752-3
. . recourse liability 1.752-1
. . . anti-abuse rules . . . . 1.752-2(j)
. . . de minimis exceptions . . . . 1.752-2(d)
. . . disregarded entity . . . . 1.752-2(k)
. . . nonrecourse liability with interest guaranteed by a partner . . . . 1.752-2(e)
. . . obligation to make payment . . . . 1.752-2(b)
. . . partner or related person as lender . . . . . 1.752-2(c)
. . . partner' share 1.752-2

References are to Reg. § numbers

Partners and partnerships —Cont'd
. *debt, allocation of partnership —Cont'd*
. . *recourse liability—Cont'd*
. . . security for partnership liability, property provided as .... 1.752-2(h)
. . . tiered partnerships .... 1.752-2(i)
. . single nonrecourse liability among multiple properties 1.752-3
. . special rules 1.752-4
. debt-financed real property, allocations .... 1.514(c)-2
. decedent, partner receiving income in respect of 1.753-1
. deficiency procedures .... 301.6221-1 et seq.
. definitions .... 1.709-2; 301.6231(a)(5)-1
. determination of partnership item, nonpartnership item and.... 301.6231(e)-1
. distributions
. . aggregate stock ownership rules 1.732-3; 1.1502-34
. . anti-abuse rules 1.737-4
. . basis adjustments 1.737-3
. . contributed property 1.704-4
. . foreign base personal holding company income 1.737-4
. . generally 1.731-1; 1.732-1; 1.733-1
. . liquidations 1.732-1
. . marketable securities 1.732-2
. . optional adjustment to basis of undistributed property 1.734-1
. . previously contributed property 1.737-2
. . property other than money 1.732-1
. . recognition of precontribution gain 1.737-1
. . recovery rules 1.737-3
. . Sec. 708(b)(1)(B) termination 1.737-2
. . special rules 1.737-2
. distributive shares 1.704-1
. . foreign tax expenditures .... 1.704-1T(b)
. . limitation on allowance of losses .... 1.704-1(d)
. division of partnership
. . continuation of partnership status 1.708-1
. domestic production activities (See Domestic production activities subhead pass-thru entities)
. entity classification election 301.7701-3
. . notice of election 301.7701-3
. exclusion of unincorporated organizations 1.761-2
. exemptions .... 1.512(c)-1 et seq.
. extension of time to file returns 301.6233-1
. family partnerships .... 1.704-1(e)
. 5-percent group .... 301.6226(b)-1
. . notice group status as .... 301.6223(b)-1
. foreign partnerships (See Foreign partnerships)
. franchises, trademarks and trade names 1.1254-5
. freezing estate value, special valuation rules 25.2701-1; 25.2701-5
. gain or loss 1.721-1; 1.731-1; 1.741-1

Partners and partnerships —Cont'd
. *gain or loss—Cont'd*
. . allocations .... 301.6231(f)-1
. . . contributed property .. 1.167(c)-1; 1.704-1; 1.704-3
. . . distributive share of partner 1.704-1
. . . limitation on loss allowances .... 1.704-1(e)
. . disallowance of losses and credits .... 301.6231(f)-1
. . new partnership resulting from termination of partnership 1.704-3
. generally .... 1.701-1 et seq.
. gross income 1.61-13
. income and credits of partner 1.702-1
. inconsistent treatment . 301.6222(b)-1; 301.6222(b)-2
. incorporation 1.737-2
. incorrect schedule, receipt of .... 301.6222(b)-3
. indirect partners .... 301.6222(a)-2; 301.6222(b)-2; 301.6224(c)-2
. indirect tax liability based on partnership items .... 301.6231(a)(2)-1
. information returns 1.6050K-1
. . controlled foreign partnerships 1.6038-3
. installment sales 1.737-2
. insurance 1.6050K-1; 301.6063-1
. interest expense allocation
. . aggregate rule .... 1.861-9T(e)(1)
. . corporate partners .... 1.861-9T(e)(2)
. . foreign partners 1.861-9T
. . income from sources within or without U.S. 1.861-9T
. . 10 percent interest in partnership, less than .... 1.861-9T(e)(4)
. . 10 percent interest in partnership, more than .... 1.861-9T(e)(2); 1.861-9T(e)(3)
. . tiered partnerships .... 1.861-9T(e)(5)
. inventory items 1.751-1
. investment credit 1.47-6
. investment partnerships
. . defined .... 1.704-3(e)
. . Subchapter K exclusion election 1.761-2
. joint interest, spouses holding .... 301.6231(a)(12)-1
. judicial decision not to bar certain adjustments .... 301.6231(e)-2
. judicial review .... 301.6226(f)-1
. jurisdiction, District Court or Claims Court .... 301.6226(e)-1
. liabilities, determination of 1.704-1
. . nonrecourse debt 1.704-2
. marketable securities, distributions 1.732-2
. mergers or consolidations
. . assets-over form, sales characterized as 1.708-1
. . continuation of partnership, consideration as 1.708-1
. net operating loss deduction of partner 1.702-2
. newly-formed partnership, taxable year of 1.706-1
. nominee reporting .... 1.6031(c)-1T

References are to Reg. § numbers

Partners and partnerships —Cont'd
. nonpartnership item . . . . 301.6231(e)-1
. . determination of partnership item, and . . . . 301.6231(e)-1
. nonrecourse debt, allocation of 1.704-2
. . deduction determination . . . . 1.704-2(c)
. . definitions concerning . . . . 1.704-2(b)
. . economic risk of loss, partner bearing . . . . 1.704-2(i)
. . examples . . . . 1.704-2(m)
. . minimum gain, distribution of proceeds allocable to increase in . . . . 1.704-2(h)
. . minimum gain, shares of partnership . . . . . 1.704-2(g)
. . minimum gain chargeback requirement . . . 1.704-2(f)
. . ordering rules . . . . 1.704-2(j)
. . requirements . . . . 1.704-2(e)
. . tiered partnership . . . . 1.704-2(k)
. nonresident aliens 1.875-1
. notice group
. . 5-percent group, status as . . . . 301.6223(b)-1; 301.6226(b)-1
. notices . . . . 301.6222(b)-1; 301.6222(b)-2; 301.6223(a)-1; 301.6223(a)-2; 301.6223(e)-1; 301.6223(e)-2
. . group, notice . . . . 301.6223(b)-1
. oil and gas properties 1.704-1
. organization and syndication costs 1.709-1
. partnership level of taxes 301.6221-1
. pass-thru partner . . . . . . 301.6223(e)-1; 301.6223(h)-1; 301.6224(c)-2
. . responsibilities
. . . notices and information . . . . 301.6223(h)-1
. principal place of business . . . . 301.6226(a)-1
. profits interest . . . . 301.6231(d)-1
. prompt assessment, request for . . . . 301.6231(c)-8
. proof of income . . . . 301.6231(c)-6
. publicly traded partnerships
. . defined 1.469-10
. . investment income 1.7704-3
. . transition provisions 301.7704-2
. . withholding
. . . U.S. real property interest, dispositions of 1.1445-8
. recognition of precontribution gain 1.737-1
. research expenditures 1.41-2; 1.41-7
. retiring partner or a deceased partner's successor in interest 1.706-1; 1.736-1
. return of income
. . automatic extension 1.6081-2T
. returns . . . . 1.6031(a)-1; 1.6050K-1; 301.6063-1
. . exception, Commissioner . . . . 1.6031(a)-1
. . extension of time for filing 1.6081-5
. . magnetic media, use of 301.6011-3
. S corporation interests

Partners and partnerships —Cont'd
. S corporation interests —Cont'd
. . recognized built-in gain or loss, determination of 1.1374-4; 1.1374-10
. . . revocation or re-election of S corporation status 1.1374-10T
. sale or exchange; accruable expenses . . . . . 1.267(b)-1
. securities partnership . . . . 1.704-3(e)
. self-employment income . . . 1.1402(a)-17; 1.1402(f)-1
. settlement agreements . . . . 301.6224(c)-3
. . consistent terms . . . . 301.6224(c)-3
. . partial agreements, special rules . . . . . 301.6229(f)-1
. small partnerships . . . . 301.6231(a)(1)-1
. space and ocean activity . . . . 1.863-8(e)
. spouse filing joint return with individual holding separate interest . . . . 301.6231(a)(2)-1
. spouses . . . . 301.6231(a)(12)-1
. statements to partners . . . . 1.6031(b)-1T
. subchapter K (See Subchapter K)
. tax matters partner . . . . 301.6230(e)-1
. . designation of . . . . 301.6231(a)(7)-1
. . indirect partners and . . . . 301.6224(c)-1
. . . nonnotice partner and . . . . 301.6224(c)-1
. . IRS failure to provide notice to . . . . 301.6223(e)-1
. . IRS failure to provide timely notice . . . . 301.6223(e)-2
. . responsibilities . . . . 301.6223(g)-1
. . . notices and information . . . . 301.6223(g)-1
. . selection of . . . . 301.6231(a)(7)-1
. Tax Reform Act 1976 . . . . 1.706-2T; 7.704-1
. tax shelters . . . . 301.6231(c)-2
. tax years 1.702-3T
. . other than required, election . . . 1.444-1T to 1.444-3T
. . . required payments . . . . . . 1.7519-1T to 1.7519-3T
. . . tiered structure entities 1.444-2T
. . tiered structure status 1.444-2T
. taxable year 1.706-1
. termination and jeopardy assessment . . 301.6231(c)-4
. termination of partnership
. . jeopardy assessment and . . . . 301.6231(c)-4
. . sec 708(b)(1)(B) termination 1.737-2
. termination partnership
. . general rule 1.708-1
. tiered partnerships
. . debt, allocation of partnership
. . . recourse liability . . . . 1.752-2(i)
. . interest expense allocation . . . . 1.861-9T(e)(5)
. . nonrecourse debt, allocation of . . . . 1.704-2(k)
. tiered structure status 1.444-2T
. transactions between
. . disclosure of information 1.707-8
. . disguised sales of property to partnership . . . 1.707-3 et seq.
. . effective dates and transitional rules 1.707-9
. . generally 1.707-1

References are to Reg. § numbers

Partners and partnerships —Cont'd
. *transactions between —Cont'd*
. . guaranteed payments 1.707-4
. . liabilities, disguised sales of property to partnership 1.707-5; 1.707-6
. . operating cash flow distributions 1.707-4
. . preferred returns 1.707-4
. . reimbursements of preformation expenditures 1.707-4
. transfers of partnership interests 1.741-1; 1.742-1
. transfers to another 1.737-2
. transfers to corporation 1.358-7
. Treasury bond exemptions 1.103-5
. unidentified partner ....301.6229(e)-1
. unrealized receivables 1.751-1
. waiver of rights ....301.6224(b)-1
. withholding
. . U.S. real property interest, dispositions of 1.1445-8

Passive activity losses and credits
. activity defined .... 1.469-1T(e); 1.469-4
. consolidated returns ....1.469-1T(h)
. credits
. . title 11 cases 1.1398-1; 1.1398-2
. disallowed 1.469-1T
. generally 1.469-0
. inventories 1.472-2
. livestock raisers and other farmers 1.471-6
. losses
. . accounting methods .... 1.469-0 to 1.469-11
. . activity defined 1.469-4T
. . generally 1.469-2; 1.469-2T
. . title 11 case, treatment of 1.1398-1; 1.1398-2
. rental income activities 1.469-9
. self-charged items of income and expense ... 1.469-7

Passive foreign investment companies
. capital gains and losses ....1.1291-1 et seq.
. deemed dividend election
. . basis adjustments .... 1.1291-9(f)
. . former PFIC, shareholders of .... 1.1291-9(i)
. . holding period treatment ....1.1291-9(g)
. . manner of election ....1.1291-9(d)
. . qualification date ....1.1291-9(e)
. . section 959(e) coordination............1.1291-9(h)
. . shareholders who may make .... 1.1291-9(b); 1.1291-10
. . time for election ....1.1291-9(c)
. deemed sale election 1.1297-3
. . CFC qualification date ....1.1297-3(d)
. . deemed dividend election rules, application of ....1.1297-3(c)
. . late purging elections requiring consent ....1.1297-3(e)
. . rules, application of ....1.1297-3(b)

Passive foreign investment companies —Cont'd
. deemed sale or dividend election
. . shareholder of former PFIC
. . . deemed dividend rules, application of ....1.1298-3(c)
. . . deemed sale rules, application of .....1.1298-3(b)
. . . generally 1.1298-3
. . . late purging elections requiring consent ....1.1298-3(e)
. exempt organization as shareholder 1.1291-1
. generally ....1.1291-1 et seq.
. marketable stock defined 1.1296-1; 1.1296-2
. mark-to-market election for marketable stock 1.1296-1
. . U.S. partner of foreign partner making section 1296 election .... 1.6031(a)-1(b)
. qualified electing fund 1.1291-1; 1.1291-10
. section 1296 stock defined 1.1296-1
. shareholders that are not pedigreed QEF's, taxation ....1.1291-1 et seq.
. . coordination with other PFIC rules ......1.1291-1(c)
. trust, creating .... 1.672(f)-2
. U.S. partner of foreign partner making section 1296 election .... 1.6031(a)-1(b)

Passive investment arrangements
. foreign country, amount paid to 1.901-2T

Pass-through entities
. domestic production activities (See Domestic production activities)
. gross income 1.67-2T
. qualified production activities 1.199-5
. self-charged items of interest income and deductions, accounting treatment of 1.469-7

Pass-through of jobs credit
. surcharge 1.53-3

Patents
. depreciation ....1.167(a)-6
. generally 1.871-11; 1.1235-1; 1.1235-2

Paternity leave
. service requirements ....1.410(a)-9

Patronage dividends
. backup withholding .... 31.3406(b)(2)-5
. cooperatives 1.1382-2; 1.1382-6
. generally ....1.6044-2 to 1.6044-5
. information returns .... 1.6044-1 to 1.6044-5; 301.6044-1

Payment card transactions
. backup withholding ....31.3406(g)-1(f)

Payment of tax
. abatements, credits, and refunds (See Abatements, credits, and refunds)
. advance payments 1.451-5
. backup withholding 1.6041-3

References are to Reg. § numbers

Payment of tax —Cont'd
. bonds for payment of taxes 1.6165-1; 1.6851-3; 53.6165-1; 53.7101-1; 301.6165-1; 301.7101-1; 301.7102-1
. deferred payments (See Deferred payments)
. depositaries of government (See Depositaries of government)
. duplicate receipts 20.6314-1
. estate tax 20.2002-1; 20.6151-1
. executors, discharge from personal liability 301.6905-1
. executors and administrators discharge from personal liability 20.2204-1
. extension of time (See Extension of time for payment of tax)
. failure to pay (See Failure to file return or pay tax)
. fiduciaries, discharge from personal liability 20.2204-1
. foreign currency 301.6316-1; 301.6316-3; 301.6316-5; 301.6316-7; 301.6316-8
. information returns 1.6041-1
. installment payments 1.6655-2T
. overpayment of tax (See Overpayment of tax)
. penalties ....301.6653-1 et seq.
. receipt of payment ....301.6311-1 to 301.6316-9
. time and place for paying (See Time and place for paying tax)
. underpayments (See Underpayment of tax)
. withholding of tax 1.6041-3

Payor
. defined for backup withholding obligation ....31.3406(a)-2

Payroll period
. withholding .... 31.3401(b)-1; 31.3402(g)-2 (See also specific tax)

Peace Corps volunteers
. withholding from .... 31.3401(a)(13)-1

Penalties (See also Additions to tax, additional amounts, and assessable penalties)
. accumulating surplus (See Accumulated earnings tax)
. dyed diesel fuel, misuse of................ 48.6715-1
. erroneous written advice of IRS, abatement of additional tax attributable to 301.6404-3
. failure to deposit; abatement of penalty ... 301.6656-1
. foreign tax credit
. . information return, failure to file 1.6038-2
. individual retirement accounts and annuities, and simplified employee pensions 301.6693-1
. mortgage interest reporting requirements, failure to comply with 1.6050H-2
. negligence
. . rules or regulations; underpayment of tax .. 1.6662-3
. pension, profit-sharing, and stock bonus plans (See Pension, profit-sharing, and stock bonus plans)
. tax return preparers (See Tax return preparers)

Penalties (See also Additions to tax, additional amounts, and assessable penalties) —Cont'd
. understatement of tax liability
. . reasonable cause and good faith exception 1.6662-4
. . substantial defined 1.6662-4

Pendency of Tax Court proceedings
. generally ....301.6871(b)-1

Pension, profit-sharing, and stock bonus plans
. active participant defined 1.219-2
. actual contribution percentage test (ACP) .... 1.401(m)-2
. . mergers, and acquisitions .... 1.401(m)-4
. . safe harbor requirements .... 1.401(m)-3
. affiliated groups......................1.404(a)-10
. aggregation ....1.410(b)-7
. . excise tax on excessive aggregate contributions 54.4979-1
. . nondiscrimination .... 1.401(a)(4)-9
. alternate limitation, multiple use of .... 1.401(m)-2
. amendment to plan
. . future benefit accrual, reducing rate of . . 54.4980F-1
. annuities, generally...................... 1.403(a)-1
. annuity contracts
. . limitations on benefits and contributions . . 1.415(b)-3
. . minimum distribution requirements
. . . 501(c)(3) organization, account established by .... 1.401(a)(9)-5
. . . public school, account established by . . . 1.403(b)-3
. annuity plan, employee
. . Sec. 403(b) contract status . . . 1.415(b)-2; 1.415(b)-3
. . Sec. 415, status under .... 1.415(b)-1
. average benefit percentage test ....1.410(b)-5
. beneficiaries (See also other subheads)
. . taxation ....1.402(a)-1
. benefiting under plan
. . employee and former employees who benefit under plan ....1.410(b)-3
. . employees .... 1.401(a)(26)-5
. benefits (See other subheads)
. bond purchase plans 1.405-1; 1.405-2
. bonds, taxation of 1.409-1
. breaks in service (See subhead service requirements)
. capital gains ....1.403(a)-2
. . explanation requirement .... 1.402(f)-1
. capital gains and losses 1.1232-2
. catch-up contributions .... 1.414(v)-1
. church plans .... 1.410(d)-1; 1.414(e)-1
. . minimum coverage requirements after 1993 .... 1.410(b)-2
. collection and withholding 35.3405-1
. compensation
. . defined .... 1.414(s)-1
. . limitations .... 1.401(a)(17)-1; 1.404(a)-4

References are to Reg. § numbers

Pension, profit-sharing, and stock bonus plans — Cont'd

. contributions .... 1.404(a)-1 et seq.
. . limitations under section 404(a)(1)(B) .... 1.404(a)-5
. . limitations under section 404(a)(1)(C) .... 1.404(a)-6
. contributions, employer
. . deductions .... 1.404(a)-3
. . pension trusts .... 1.404(a)-3
. contributory defined benefit plans
. . nondiscrimination .... 1.401(a)(4)-6
. coverage requirements, generally .. 1.410(b)-1 et seq.
. custodial accounts .... 1.401(f)-1; 1.401-8
. . minimum distribution requirements
. . . 501(c)(3) organization, account established by .... 1.403(b)-3
. . . public school, account established by ... 1.403(b)-3
. deferred payment plan .... 1.404(a)-1T
. defined benefit excess plans
. . railroad plans, special rules .... 1.401(l)-4
. defined benefit plans
. . equivalent employer-provided contributions .... 1.401(a)(4)-8
. . former employees, minimum participation .... 1.401(a)(26)-4
. . fresh-start rules .... 1.401(a)(4)-13
. . minimum distribution requirements ... 1.401(a)(9)-6
. . . participants in more than one plan .. 1.401(a)(9)-8
. . nondiscrimination .... 1.401(a)(4)-3
. . prior benefit structure, rules applicable to .... 1.401(a)(26)-3
. . rate disparity for, permitted .... 1.401(l)-3
. defined contribution plans
. . disparity limits, overall permitted .... 1.401(l)-5
. . employee and matching contributions ... 1.401(m)-1
. . in-kind distributions; section 1.411(d)-4 protected benefits .... 1.411(d)-4
. . minimum distribution requirements ... 1.401(a)(9)-5
. . . participants in more than one plan .. 1.401(a)(9)-8
. . new comparability plans
. . . aggregation and restructuring ...... 1.401(a)(4)-9
. . . nondiscrimination requirement...... 1.401(a)(4)-8
. . nondiscrimination requirement
. . . allocation rate, broadly available .... 1.401(a)(4)-8
. . . new comparability plans .... 1.401(a)(4)-8
. . nondiscrimination rules .... 1.401(a)(4)-2
. . railroad plans, special rules .... 1.401(l)-4
. . rate disparity for, permitted .... 1.401(l)-2
. definitions .... 1.410(b)-9
. disaggregation of plan .... 1.410(b)-7
. disclosure of listed transactions........... 54.6011-4
. disclosure statements 1.408-6
. discrimination .... 1.401-4 (See also subhead, nondiscrimination)
. . nondiscriminatory classification test...... 1.410(b)-4

Pension, profit-sharing, and stock bonus plans — Cont'd

. disparity, permitted (See subhead permitted disparity)
. dispositions
. . minimum coverage requirements after 1993 .... 1.410(b)-2
. distributions
. . contributions, all employee .... 1.72(e)-1T
. . loans to employer plan participants as..... 1.72(p)-1
. . minimum distribution requirements (See subhead minimum distribution requirements)
. . restrictions and valuation of
. . . accrued benefits .... 1.401(a)-11(a)
. . . consent, without participant's...... 1.401(a)-11(a)
. . . consent requirements .... 1.401(a)-11(c)
. . . general consent rules .... 1.401(a)-11(b)
. . . notice .... 1.401(a)-11(f)
. . . termination of plan .... 1.401(a)-11(e)
. . . valuation requirements .... 1.401(a)-11(d)
. diversion under trust instrument 1.401-2
. dividend distributions .... 1.404(k)-1T
. . disallowance of deduction on ESOP reacquisition payments.......................... 1.404(k)-3
. domestic subsidiaries' employees........... 1.407-1
. early retirement
. . nondiscrimination ...... 1.401(a)(4)-3; 1.401(a)(4)-4
. electronic medium use, notice and participant election .... 1.401(a)-21.
. employee and matching contributions
. . defined contribution plans .... 1.401(m)-1
. employee contributions
. . disparity, permitted .... 1.401(l)-1
. . early implementation of new rules ...... 1.401(m)-1
. . matching contributions .... 1.401(m)-1
. . nondiscrimination rules .... 1.401(m)-1
. Employee Retirement Income Security Act (ERISA)
. . special rules .... 1.404(a)-14
. employees
. . minimum coverage requirements after 1993 .... 1.410(b)-2
. employer contributions .... 1.404(a)-1 et seq.; 1.404(a)-1T
. . deductions allowable under section 401(a)(1) .... 1.404(a)-13
. . definitions concerning .... 1.401(l)-1
. . section 401(a) requirements, not meeting .... 1.404(a)-12
. employer liability payments .... 1.404(g)-1
. employer provided benefits, determination of
. . nondiscrimination .... 1.401(a)(4)-6
. ERISA (See Employee Retirement Income Security Act)
. excess contributions .... 1.401(e)-4
. . excise tax on 54.4979-1

References are to Reg. § numbers

Pension, profit-sharing, and stock bonus plans — Cont'd
. excess distributions and excess accumulations, tax on 54.4981A-1T
. excise taxes (See Pension excise taxes)
. excludable employees .... 1.401(a)(26)-6
. . former employees .... 1.401(a)(26)-4
. exempt organizations .... 1.501(c)(18)-1
. experience-rating arrangements .... 1.419A(f)(6)
. face-amount certificates 1.401-9
. floor-offset arrangements .... 1.401(a)(4)-8
. . fresh-start rules .... 1.401(a)(4)-13
. foreign subsidiaries 1.406-1
. forfeitures 1.401-7
. former employees
. . cash-out limits .... 1.401(a)(26)-4
. . minimum coverage requirements after 1993 .... 1.410(b)-2
. . minimum participation requirements .... 1.401(a)(26)-4
. . minimum participation rule .... 1.401(a)(26)-4
. generally .... 1.401-0 et seg.
. government plans
. . minimum coverage requirements after 1993 .... 1.410(b)-2
. gross income 1.61-11
. highly compensated employees .... 1.414(q)-1T
. . nondiscrimination rules .... 1.401(a)(4)-1
. . optional forms of benefits .... 1.401(a)-4
. independent contractors, deductibility of deferred compensation and deferred benefits .... 1.404(d)-1T
. individual retirement accounts (See Individual retirement arrangements)
. individual retirement arrangements (See Individual retirement arrangements)
. information furnished by employer claiming deductions .... 1.404(a)-2; 1.404(a)-2A
. information returns 1.6047-1; 301.6057-1; 301.6057-2
. . failure to file 301.6652-3
. in-kind distributions; section 1.411(d)-4 protected benefits .... 1.411(d)-4
. insurance contract plans
. . nondiscrimination .... 1.401(a)(4)-3
. limitations on benefits and contributions
. . aggregating plans
. . . affiliated employers, affiliated service groups and leased employees .... 1.415(f)-1(b)
. . . generally .... 1.415(f)-1(a)
. . . multiemployer plans .... 1.415(f)-1(g)
. . . predecessor employer .... 1.415(f)-1(c)
. . . previously unaggregated plans .... 1.415(f)-1(e)
. . . Sec. 403(b) annuity contracts .... 1.415(f)-1(f)
. . . special rules .... 1.415(f)-1(d); 1.415(f)-1(h)
. . annual benefit

Pension, profit-sharing, and stock bonus plans — Cont'd
. *limitations on benefits and contributions — Cont'd*
. . *annual benefit — Cont'd*
. . . adjustment to form of benefit .... 1.415(b)-1(c)
. . . adjustment to Sec. 415(b)(1)(A) dollar limit for commencement after age 65 .... 1.415(b)-1(e)
. . . adjustment to Sec. 415(b)(1)(A) dollar limit for commencement before age 62 .... 1.415(b)-1(d)
. . . defined .... 1.415(b)-1(b)(1)
. . . employee contributions and rollover contributions, attributable to .... 1.415(b)-1(b)(2)
. . . qualified governmental excess benefit arrangements .... 1.415(b)-1(b)(4)
. . . special rule for participation or service of less than 10 years .... 1.415(b)-1(g)
. . . $10,000, total annual payment not in excess of .... 1.415(b)-1(f)
. . . transferred benefits .... 1.415(b)-1(b)(3)
. . church plans
. . . alternative contribution limitations .... 1.415(d)(1)
. . . church, convention or association of churches .... 1.415(d)(4)
. . . foreign ministries .... 1.415(d)(3)
. . . special rules .... 1.415(d)
. . . years of service for ministers or lay employees .... 1.415(d)(2)
. . compensation
. . . aggregation of Sec. 403(b) annuity with qualified plan of controlled employer .... 1.415(c)-2(g)(3)
. . . controlled groups of corporations, employees of .... 1.415(c)-2(g)(2)
. . . defined .... 1.415(c)-2(a)
. . . defined contribution plan participant, disability of .... 1.415(c)-2(g)(3)
. . . items includible as .... 1.415(c)-2(b)
. . . safe harbor rules and definition of .... 1.415(c)-2(d)
. . . Sec. 401(a)(17), interaction with .... 1.415(c)-2(f)
. . . Sec. 403(b) annuity contracts .... 1.415(c)-2(g)(1)
. . . special rules .... 1.415(c)-2(g)
. . . timing rules .... 1.415(c)-2(e)
. . cost-of-living adjustments
. . . defined benefit plans .... 1.415(d)-1(a)
. . . defined contribution plans .... 1.415(d)-1(b)
. . . implementation .... 1.415(d)-1(d)
. . defined benefit plans
. . . adjustments to dollar limitation for commencement before age 62 or after age 65 ... 1.415(b)-1(a)(4)
. . . annual benefit exceeding limitations, plan provisions precluding possibility of ... 1.415(b)-1(a)(3)
. . . average compensation for high 3-years of service .... 1.415(d)-1(a)(2)
. . . average compensation for period of high-3 years of service .... 1.415(b)-1(a)(5)
. . . cost-of-living adjustments dollar limitations .... 1.415(d)-1(a)

References are to Reg. § numbers

Pension, profit-sharing, and stock bonus plans — Cont'd
. *limitations on benefits and contributions —Cont'd*
. . *defined benefit plans —Cont'd*
. . . defined for .... 1.415(b)-1(a)(2)
. . . exceptions, compensation limit ... 1.415(b)-1(a)(6)
. . . maximum limitations .... 1.415(b)-1(a)(1)
. . . special rules .... 1.415(b)-1(a)(7)
. . defined contribution plans
. . . annual additions defined for Sec. 415 purposes .... 1.415(c)-1(b)(1)
. . . cost-of-living adjustments dollar limitations .... 1.415(d)-1(b)
. . . defined for Sec. 415 purposes .... 1.415(c)-1(a)(2)
. . . disability of participant, permanent and total .... 1.415(c)-2(g)(3)
. . . employee contributions .... 1.415(c)-1(b)(3)
. . . employer contributions treated as annual additions .... 1.415(c)-1(b)(2)
. . . general rules .... 1.415(c)-1(a)
. . . loan repayments .... 1.415(c)-1(b)(3)(ii)
. . . maximum limitations .... 1.415(c)-1(a)(1)
. . . other than cash, contributions .... 1.415(c)-1(b)(5)
. . . repayments .... 1.415(c)-1(b)(3)(ii)
. . . rollover contributions .... 1.415(c)-1(b)(3)(i)
. . . timing rules .... 1.415(c)-1(b)(6)
. . . transactions with plans .... 1.415(c)-1(b)(4)
. . disqualification of plans
. . . generally .... 1.415(g)-1(a)
. . . plan year for certain annuity contracts and individual retirement plans .... 1.415(g)-1(c)
. . . rules for disqualification of plans and trusts .... 1.415(g)-1(b)
. . employee stock ownership plans, special rules for .... 1.415(f)
. . general rules in apply section 415 .... 1.415(c)
. . incorporation by reference, plan provisions for .... 1.415(d)(3)
. . limitation year
. . . alternative limitation year election .... 1.415(j)-1(b)
. . . change of limitation year .... 1.415(j)-1(d)
. . . generally .... 1.415(j)-1(a)
. . . individual retirement plans are maintained, individuals for which .... 1.415(j)-1(f)
. . . multiple limitation years .... 1.415(j)-1(c)
. . . Sec. 403(b) annuity contracts have been purchased on behalf of, individuals which .... 1.415(j)-1(e)
. . medical benefits, special rules for .... 1.415(e)
. . more than one employer, plan maintained by .... 1.415(e)
. . plan provision precluding possibility of exceeding Sec. 415 limitations .... 1.415(d)
. . profit-sharing and stock bonus plan provisions, special rules for

Pension, profit-sharing, and stock bonus plans — Cont'd
. *limitations on benefits and contributions —Cont'd*
. . *profit-sharing and stock bonus plan provisions, special rules for —Cont'd*
. . . freeze or reduction in annual additions, automatic .... 1.415(d)(2)
. listed transactions, disclosure of 54.6011-4
. loans to employer plan participants .... 1.72(p)-1
. lump sum distributions
. . explanation requirement .... 1.402(f)-1
. medical benefits 1.401-14
. mergers, and acquisitions
. . actual contribution percentage test (ACP) .... 1.401(m)-4
. method deferring receipt of compensation .... 1.404(b)-1T
. method of contribution .... 1.404(b)-1; 1.404(b)-1T
. minimum age and service requirements
. . excluded employees .... 1.410(b)-6
. minimum coverage requirements after 1993 .... 1.410(b)-2
. minimum distribution requirements
. . age 70 1/2, determination of .... 1.401(a)(9)-2
. . annuity contracts ...... 1.401(a)(9)-5; 1.401(a)(9)-6
. . . 501(c)(3) organization, account established by .... 1.401(a)(9)-5
. . . public school, account established by ... 1.403(b)-3
. . beginning date, required .... 1.401(a)(9)-2
. . contingent beneficiary .... 1.401(a)(9)-5
. . custodial accounts
. . . 501(c)(3) organization, account established by .... 1.403(b)-3
. . . public school, account established by ... 1.403(b)-3
. . death before required distributions date .... 1.401(a)(9)-3; 1.401(a)(9)-5
. . death benefits .... 1.401(a)(9)-6
. . defined benefit plans .... 1.401(a)(9)-6
. . . participants in more than one plan .. 1.401(a)(9)-8
. . defined contribution plans .... 1.401(a)(9)-5
. . . participants in more than one plan .. 1.401(a)(9)-8
. . designated beneficiaries
. . . deceased beneficiary .... 1.401(a)(9)-4
. . . determination .... 1.401(a)(9)-4
. . . surviving spouse .... 1.401(a)(9)-4
. . 501(c)(3) organization, account established by .... 1.403(b)-3
. . incidental benefit requirement........ 1.401(a)(9)-5
. . joint and survivor annuity .... 1.401(a)(9)-6
. . life expectancy .... 1.401(a)(9)-3; 1.401(a)(9)-5
. . lifetime of employee, distributions commencing during .... 1.401(a)(9)-2
. . participants in more than one plan .... 1.401(a)(9)-8
. . public school, account established by .... 1.403(b)-3
. . spousal beneficiary .... 1.401(a)(9)-3

References are to Reg. § numbers

Pension, profit-sharing, and stock bonus plans — Cont'd
. *minimum distribution requirements —Cont'd*
. . successor beneficiary .... 1.401(a)(9)-5
. . time for distributions for defined contribution plans .... 1.401(a)(9)-5
. minimum funding standards
. . failure to meet 54.4971-1
. . owner-employee plans 1.401-12
. minimum participation requirements ... 1.401(a)(26)-1
. . disaggregation .... 1.401(a)(26)-2
. . effective date .... 1.401(a)(26)-9
. . excludable employees .... 1.401(a)(26)-6
. . former employees .... 1.401(a)(26)-4
. . frozen plans .... 1.401(a)(26)-2
. . testing methods .... 1.401(a)(26)-7
. modified guaranteed contracts 1.817A-1
. multiemployer plans
. . nondiscrimination .... 1.401(a)(4)-3
. multiple plans
. . catch-up contributions .... 1.414(v)-1
. negotiated plans .... 1.404(c)-1
. . nondiscrimination requirements .... 1.401(a)-4
. nondiscrimination .... 1.401(a)(4)-1
. . accrual rates, determination of equivalent .... 1.401(a)(4)-8
. . aggregation .... 1.401(a)(4)-9
. . aggregation of benefits, rights or features .... 1.401(a)(4)-4
. . allocation rates, broad based .... 1.401(a)(4)-8
. . amendment of plan .... 1.401(a)(4)-5
. . ancillary benefits .... 1.401(a)(4)-4
. . benefits .... 1.401(a)(4)-4
. . cash-outs, mandatory .... 1.401(a)(4)-4
. . compensation .... 1.401(a)(17)-1
. . contributory defined benefit plans .... 1.401(a)(4)-6
. . cross-testing .... 1.401(a)(4)-8
. . defined benefit plans .... 1.401(a)(4)-3
. . defined contribution plans .... 1.401(a)(4)-2
. . definitions .... 1.401(a)(4)-12
. . disparities, permitted .... 1.401(a)(4)-7
. . distribution formulas, differences in ... 1.401(a)(4)-4
. . dollar limits .... 1.401(a)(4)-4
. . early retirement .... 1.401(a)(4)-4
. . elimination of benefits .... 1.401(a)(4)-4
. . employee stock ownership plans (ESOPs) .... 1.401(a)(4)-4
. . employer provided benefits, determination of .... 1.401(a)(4)-6
. . equivalent allocations .... 1.401(a)(4)-8
. . equivalent employer-provided benefits, testing of .... 1.401(a)(4)-8
. . features, plan .... 1.401(a)(4)-4
. . floor-offset arrangements .... 1.401(a)(4)-8

Pension, profit-sharing, and stock bonus plans — Cont'd
. *nondiscrimination—Cont'd*
. . former employees .... 1.401(a)(4)-10
. . fresh-start rules .... 1.401(a)(4)-13
. . hypothetical allocations, provisions for .... 1.401(a)(4)-8
. . imputed service .... 1.401(a)(4)-11
. . insurance contract plans .... 1.401(a)(4)-3
. . investments, direction of .... 1.401(a)(4)-4
. . loans .... 1.401(a)(4)-4
. . make-up of missed employee contributions .... 1.401(a)(4)-11
. . normal retirement age .... 1.401(a)(4)-4
. . part-time employee, imputed service for .... 1.401(a)(4)-11
. . protected benefits .... 1.411(d)-4
. . rights .... 1.401(a)(4)-4
. . rollover contributions rights .... 1.401(a)(4)-4
. . rules for determining satisfaction ..... 1.401(a)(4)-11
. . service conditions .... 1.401(a)(4)-4
. . servicing credit rules .... 1.401(a)(4)-11
. . special rules .... 1.401(a)(5)-1
. . spousal benefits .... 1.401(a)(4)-4
. . target benefit allocations .... 1.401(a)(4)-8
. . target benefit plans .... 1.401(a)(4)-8
. . termination of plan .... 1.401(a)(4)-5
. . time-limited age .... 1.401(a)(4)-4
. . vesting .... 1.401(a)(4)-11
. . widow benefits, early retirement ...... 1.401(a)(4)-4
. nondiscriminatory classification test .... 1.410(b)-4
. nonqualified annuity .... 1.403(c)-1
. optional forms of benefits .... 1.401(a)-4
. owner-employees ..... 1.401(e)-3; 1.401-12; 1.401-13
. participants in more than one plan
. . minimum distribution requirements ... 1.401(a)(9)-8
. permitted disparity
. . generally .... 1.401(l)-1
. . primary insurance amount offsets .... 1.401(l)-5
. post-ERISA plans and trusts .... 1.401(a)-2
. post-ERISA qualified plans and qualified trusts
. . definitely determinable benefits .... 1.401(a)-1(b)(1)
. . distributions prior to retirement ..... 1.401(a)-1(b)(3)
. . generally .... 1.401(a)-1(a)
. . normal retirement age .... 1.401(a)-1(b)(2)
. . pension plan requirements .... 1.401(a)-1(b)
. protected benefits
. . elimination of .... 1.411(d)-4(a)
. . section 411(d)(6), under .... 1.411(d)-4
. public retirement system income, credit for 1.37-3
. qualified asset account limitation 1.419A-1T; 1.419A-2T
. . 10 or more employer plan exception ... 1.419A(f)(6)
. qualified separate line of business .... 1.414(r)-5

References are to Reg. § numbers

Pension, profit-sharing, and stock bonus plans — Cont'd
. railroad plans, special rules .... 1.401(l)-4
. railroad retirement benefits (See Railroad Retirement Tax Act (RRTA))
. reduced uniformed services retirement pay ... 1.122-1
. reports 1.408-7
. restored plans, minimum funding requirements to .... 1.412(c)(1)-3
. retirement bonds 1.405-3; 1.409-1
. retroactive changes in plan .... 1.401(b)-1
. returns .... 301.6104(a)-2 to 301.6104(a)-4
. rollovers .... 1.402(a)(5)-1T
. . direct, questions and answers relating to .... 1.401(a)-(31)-1
. . eligible distributions, questions and answers relating to .... 1.402(c)-2
. . explanation requirements .... 1.402(f)-1
. . withholding on eligible distributions, questions and answers relating to .... 31.3405(c)-1
. safe harbor requirements
. . actual contribution percentage test (ACP) .... 1.401(m)-3
. savings deduction .... 1.219-1 to 1.219-2
. Section 402(d) .... 1.402(d)-1
. Section 501(c)(3) organization or public school .... 1.403(b)-1
. self-employed individuals ..... 1.401(e)-1; 1.401(e)-2; 1.401(e)-5; 1.401(e)-6; 1.401-10; 1.401-11; 1.404(e)-1; 1.404(e)-1A
. service requirements
. . breaks in service .... 1.410(a)-8
. . . maternity or paternity leave .... 1.410(a)-9
. . year of service .... 1.410(a)-8T
. simplified pensions (See Simplified employee pensions)
. situs trusts .... 1.402(c)-1
. subsidiaries 1.406-1; 1.407-1
. successor corporations .... 1.381(c)(11)-1
. target benefit allocations
. . nondiscrimination .... 1.401(a)(4)-8
. target benefit plans
. . nondiscrimination .... 1.401(a)(4)-8
. 10 or more employer plans, characteristics of .... 1.419A(f)(6)
. termination .... 1.401-6; 1.402(e)-1
. testing options and methods .... 1.410(b)-8
. trusts
. . qualified plan status under Sec. 401(a)(16) .... 1.415(a)-1
. trusts, generally ... 1.401(a)-1; 1.401(a)-2; 1.402(b)-1; 1.402(c)-1; 1.404(a)-9; 1.404(a)-11; 11.401(d)(1)-1
. . distributed ownership interests from 1.382-10T
. United States, trusts created or organized outside .... 1.404(a)-11
. vesting, generally .... 1.411(a)-1 et seq.

Pension, profit-sharing, and stock bonus plans — Cont'd
. vesting schedule, changes in .... 1.411(a)-8
. withholding .... 31.3401(a)(12)-1; 35.3405-1
. . questions and answers regarding 35.3405-1T

Pension excise taxes
. accumulations
. . distributions less than required 54.4974-2
. . individual retirement accounts or annuities 54.4974-1
. cooperatives 54.4978-1T
. employer securities, qualifying 54.4975-12
. entity manager tax on prohibited tax shelter transactions .... 54.6011-1T(c)
. ESOPs 54.4975-11; 54.4978-1T
. exemptions 54.4975-6; 54.4975-7
. generally .... 54.4971-1 et seq.
. individual retirement arrangements or annuities 54.4974-1
. lines of business 54.4977-1T
. minimum funding standards, failure to meet 54.4971-1
. prohibited transactions 54.4975-1; 54.4975-14
. return, statement, or list 54.6011-1
. reversion of qualified plan assets to employer .... 54.6011-1T(a)
. self-employed individuals 54.4972-1
. welfare benefit funds 54.4976-1T

Percentage depletion
. natural resources .... 1.613A-1 et seq.; 1.613-1; 1.613-2; 1.613-6; 1.1502-44

Percentage method
. withholding of tax .... 31.3402(b)-1

Performance measurement (See Balanced performance measurement system)

Performing arts
. accounting, nonaccrual of certain amounts by .... 1.448-1T(d)(2)(A); 1.448-1T(e)(4)

Periods of accounting (See Accounting periods)

Perishable goods
. seizure for forfeiture 301.6336-1; 301.7324-1

Perpetual policies
. mutual insurance companies ...... 1.831-1 to 1.831-3

Person
. defined 1.269-1; 301.7701-6

Personal, living, and family expenses
. generally 1.262-1; 5e.274-8

Personal and household effects (See Household and personal effects)

Personal exemptions
. amount of deduction for each exemption 1.151-4
. definitions 1.151-3
. dependents 1.151-2; 1.152-3; 1.152-4T

References are to Reg. § numbers

Personal exemptions —Cont'd
. divorced parents, dependency exemption ... 1.152-4; 1.152-4T
. estates ... 1.642(b)-1; 1.643(a)-2
. generally ... 1.151-1 to 1.153-1
. live apart, parents who ... 1.152-4
. marital status 1.152-3; 1.152-4; 1.152-4T; 1.153-1
. multiple support agreements ... 1.152-3
. self-employment income ... 1.1402(a)-10
. separated parents ... 1.152-4
. short taxable year, deduction adjustment for .. 1.443-1

Personal expenses
. nondeductible items ... 1.262-1

Personal holding companies
. abatements, credits, and refunds ... 1.545-3; 301.6501(f)-1
. adjustments to taxable income ... 1.545-3
. claim for credit or refund ... 1.547-3
. consolidated returns ... 1.542-4
. constructive ownership ... 1.544-1 to 1.544-6
. convertible securities ... 1.544-5
. corporate acquisitions, dividends ..... 1.381(c)(14)-1; 1.381(c)(15)-1; 1.381(c)(17)-1
. deduction for deficiency dividends, effective date of ... 1.547-7
. defined ... 1.545-1
. dividends ... 1.547-2; 1.547-4; 1.563-2
. . deficiency dividends ... 1.547-1 et seq.
. extension of time for payment .. 1.6162-1; 301.6162-1
. foreign personal holding companies (See Foreign personal holding companies)
. fraud or willful failure to file timely return 1.547-5
. generally ... 1.541-1 et seq.
. gross income
. . computing, general rule for ... 1.555-1
. . requirement ... 1.542-2; 1.543-2
. income, generally ... 1.543-1
. limitation on income ... 1.543-2
. liquidation ... 301.6162-1
. natural resources ... 1.543-12
. options ... 1.544-4
. . family and partnership rule, option rule in lieu of ... 1.544-7
. returns ... 1.542-4; 1.547-5
. sale or exchange; accruable expenses ..... 1.267(b)-1
. statute of limitations and stay of collection 1.547-6
. stock ownership requirement ... 1.542-3
. tax years
. . other than required, election ... 1.444-1T to 1.444-3T
. . . required payments ...... 1.7519-0T to 1.7519-3T
. . . tiered structure entities ... 1.444-2T
. tiered structure status ... 1.444-2T

Personal interest
. generally ... 1.163-9T

Personal property
. capitalization rules ... 1.263A-2
. gain or loss, like-kind exchanges ... 1.1031(a)-2
. . intangible personal property and nondepreciable personal property ... 1.1031(a)-2
. income from sale derived partly from within and without U.S. ... 1.863-3A
. . foreign country, income partly from 1.863-3AT
. lien on, place for filing notice ... 301.6323(f)-1
. loss with respect to ... 1.865-1
. stock, special rules ... 1.1092(d)-2
. tangible, investment credit ... 1.48-1

Personal residence trusts
. generally ... 25.2702-5

Personal service corporation
. compensation costs ... 1.441-3
. deduction limitations ... 1.280H-1T
. defined ... 1.441-3
. employee-owner defined ... 1.441-3
. generally ... 1.162-7; 1.280H-0T; 1.280H-1T
. limitation on amount paid employee-owners ... 1.280H-1T
. services performed by employee-owners 1.441-3
. services treated as personal service ... 1.441-3
. tax years
. . other than required, election ... 1.444-1T to 1.444-3T
. . tiered structure status ... 1.444-2T
. taxable year
. . calendar year requirement ... 1.441-3
. . determination of PSC ... 1.441-1
. tiered structure status ... 1.444-2T
. withholding tax exemption ... 1.1441-4

Place and time for filing returns (See Time and place for filing returns)

Political campaigns
. committees ... 1.527-9
. generally ... 1.162-20
. itemized deduction ... 1.162-20

Political expenditures
. flagrant
. . enjoin, action to ... 301.7409-1
. . termination assessments ... 301.6852-1
. initial (first tier) tax, abatement of ... 53.4955-1
. organizational managers, tax on ... 53.4955-1
. tax on ... 53.4955-1

Political organizations
. appreciated property transferred to ... 1.84-1
. communist-controlled organization as exempt ... 1.501(k)-1
. generally ... 1.162-20; 1.527-1 to 1.527-9
. itemized deductions ... 1.271-1; 1.276-1

References are to Reg. § numbers

Political organizations —Cont'd
. returns 1.6012-6
Political subdivisions
. diesel and special motor fuels tax, exemptions for sales to 48.4041-15
Pollution facilities
. amortizable basis for deductions under section 169 .... 1.169-3; 1.169-3(a)
. . cases exceeding 15 years .... 1.169-3(d)
. . generally .... 1.169-3(a)
. . post-1968 construction, reconstruction or erection limitations .... 1.169-3(b)
. . profit making abatement work, modifications for .... 1.169-3(c)
. itemized deductions .... 1.169-1 to 1.169-4
Pooled income funds
. estates and trusts .... 1.642(c)-5 et seq.
. . remainder, valuation of .... 1.642(c)-6
. transitional rules .... 1.642(c)-7
. yearly rate of return, computation of .... 1.642(c)-6
Pooling arrangements
. cooperatives 1.1382-5
Portfolio securities
. inventory or primarily gains
. . interest expense, allocation .... 1.861-12T(e)
Possessions of the United States
. American Samoa (See American Samoa)
. bona fide residency
. . alien individuals presence test .... 1.937-1(c)(2)
. . bona fide resident .... 1.937-1(b)
. . closer connection test .... 1.937-1(e)
. . days of presence .... 1.937-1(c)(3)
. . definitions concerning .... 1.937-1(a)
. . generally 1.937-1
. . information reporting .... 1.937-1(h)
. . medical treatment .... 1.937-1(c)(4)
. . presence test .... 1.937-1(c)
. . significant connection to the United States .... 1.937-1(c)(5)
. . tax home test .... 1.937-1(d)
. . year of move .... 1.937-1(f)
. charitable contributions 1.170A-1
. citizens, residents considered as 20.2208-1
. corporation claiming credits
. . new lines of business, prohibitions against 1.936-11
. corporation created or organized in 1.881-5; 1.881-5T; 1.884-0
. cost-sharing or profit split method, election to use 1.936-7
. export sales, section 936(h)(5) election 1.936-7
. generally .... 1.931-1 to 1.936-7
. Guam (See Guam)
. income from sources within a possession 1.937-2

Possessions of the United States —Cont'd
. income from sources within or without United States 1.863-6
. income through conduct of a trade or business in a possession 1.937-3
. information returns 301.6688-1
. intangible property income 1.936-6
. investment income 7.936-1
. nonresidents not citizens 20.2209-1
. partly within and partly without, income 1.863-3
. personal property sales, income from .... 1.863-3A(c)
. Puerto Rico (See Puerto Rico)
. self-employment income .... 1.1402(a)-9; 1.1402(a)-12
. status of citizens 1.932-1
. U.S. person defined 1.957-3T
. Virgin Islands (See Virgin Islands)
. withholding .... 31.3401(a)(8)(B)-1
Power of appointment
. donee spouse, in .... 25.2523(e)-1
. generally 20.2041-1
. gift, transfer of property as .... 25.2514-1 et seq.
. October 21, 1942
. . created after 20.2041-3; 25.2514-3
. . created on or before 20.2041-2
. surviving spouse, in
. . life estate, interest in .... 20.2056(b)-5
. . life insurance or annuity payments .... 20.2056(b)-6
Power of attorney
. acts requiring 601.522
. execution and filing 601.524
. generally .... 601.503 et seq.
. revocation 601.526
Practical capacity
. property produced by taxpayer, rules concerning 1.263A-2
Predecessor corporations
. carryovers of predecessor
. . net operating loss limitations
. . . ownership change defined 1.382-2
Preexisting conditions
. group health plans, limitations 54.9801-3
Preferential dividends
. defined 1.565-6
. generally 1.562-2
Preferred stock
. generally .... 1.244-1; 1.244-2; 1.247-1; 1.305-4 to 1.305-6
Premium, instruments purchased at
. original issue discount (OID) 1.1272-2
Premium coupons
. accounting methods 1.451-4

References are to Reg. § numbers

Prepaid income
. built-in, gain or loss . . . . . 1.382-7T(a)
. membership dues, accounting methods . . . . 1.456-1 to 1.456-7
. subscriptions, accounting methods . . . . . 1.455-1 to 1.455-5

Preparers of returns (See Tax return preparers)

Prepayments (See Advance payments)

Preretirement survivor annuities
. Retirement Equity Act of 1984 . . . . . 1.401(a)-20

President and Vice Presidential Nominee Account
. Presidential Election Campaign Fund transfer of amounts to . . . . . 301.9006-1(d)

Presidential Election Campaign Fund
. additional deposits, limits on . . . . . 301.9006-1(e)
. President and Vice Presidential Nominee Account, transfer of amounts to . . . . . 301.9006-1(d)
. Presidential Nominating Convention Account, transfer of amounts to . . . . . 301.9006-1(c)
. Presidential Primary Matching Payment Account, transfer of amounts to . . . . . 301.9006-1(f)
. separate accounts within, creation of . . . 301.9006-1(b)
. transfers of amounts to . . . . . 301.9006-1(a)

Presidential Primary Matching Payment Account
. guidance, possible IRS . . . . . 702.9037-2(b)
. payments from . . . . . 702.9037-2(a)
. . certification of, Federal Election Commission . . . . . 702-9037-2(a); 702-9037-2T(a)
. . guidance, IRS publication of . . . . . 702-9037-2T(b)
. . notification to Federal Election Commission of . . . . . 702-9037-2(b)
. . shortfall, to candidates in the case of . . . . . 702-9037-2(c)
. Presidential Election Campaign Fund transfer of amounts to . . . . . 301.9006-1(f)
. transfer of amounts to . . . . . 702.9037-1(a)

Presidentially declared disasters
. postponement of certain tax-related deadlines 301.7508A-1

Presumptions and burden of proof
. corporations improperly accumulating surplus 1.534-1; 1.534-2
. itemized deductions for disproportionate purchase price 1.269-5
. liquidations 1.341-3
. owner of large amounts of cash not identified 301.6867-1
. property transfers 301.6902-1
. Tax Court 301.7454-1; 301.7454-2

Prevention of cruelty to children or animals, organizations for
. exempt organizations . . . . . 1.501(c)(3)-1

Priests (See Ministers or religious personnel)

Primary insurance amount offsets
. pension, profit-sharing, and stock bonus plans permitted disparity . . . . . 1.401(l)-5

Private activity bonds
. allocation
. . certification of no consideration . . . . . 1.103(n)-5T
. . nonqualified bonds 1.141-2
. . output facilities 1.141-6
. . population determination . . . . . 1.103(n)-6T
. computation of taxable income, other requirements 1.147-1
. definition 1.141-2
. deliberate actions 1.141-2
. effective after 11/22/2002, tests 1.141-2
. effective before 11/23/2002, tests 1.141-2
. electric output facilities used to provide open access 1.141-6
. exclusion of interest 1.141-2
. exempt bonds, change in use of facilities financed with 1.150-4
. exempt facility, interest on 1.103-8
. exemptions . . . . . 1.103(n)-1T et seq.; 1.103(n)-1 to 1.103(n)-7T
. $15 million limitation
. . output facilities 1.141-8
. generally . . . . . 1.103(n)-1T et seq.
. no consideration certification for allocation . . . . . 1.103(n)-5T
. nonqualified bonds 1.141-2
. output contracts 1.141-6
. output facilities
. . allocation and accounting rules 1.141-6
. . $15 million limitation 1.141-8
. . private business test 1.141-7
. . refunding bonds 1.141-15
. population determination, allocation of private activity bond ceiling . . . . . 1.103(n)-6T
. private business use test . . . . . 1.145-2(b)
. . issuance costs . . . . . 1.145-2(c)
. private loan defined 1.141-5
. private loan financing test 1.141-5
. reasonable expectations test 1.141-2
. refunding
. . advance, limitations on . . . . . 1.149(d)-1(g)

Private business use test
. general rule 1.141-3
. private activity bonds . . . . . 1.145-2(b)
. . issuance costs . . . . . 1.145-2(c)
. refunding . . . . . 1.141-13(b)

Private foundations
. abatement of taxes 1.507-9
. aggregate tax benefit, generally 1.507-5
. attribution . . . . . 1.509(a)-5

References are to Reg. § numbers

Private foundations —Cont'd
. broadly, publicly supported organizations . . 1.509(a)-3
. Chapter 42 liability, assessable penalties 301.6684-1
. classification . . . . 1.509(a)-6
. continuation of status . . . . 1.509(b)-1
. defined . . . . 1.509(a)-1
. disallowance of certain deductions 1.508-2
. disclosure of listed transactions 53.6011-4
. exclusions . . . . 1.509(a)-2
. failure to file 53.6651-1
. foreign
. . withholding at source . . . . 1.1441-1 et seq.
. . withholding exemption 1.1441-9
. generally . . . . 1.507-1 to 1.509(e)-1; 53.4941(d)-2; 53.4945-2
. governing instruments 1.508-3
. gross investment income . . . . 1.509(e)-1
. information returns (See Information returns)
. list requirements 53.6011-1
. listed transactions, disclosure of 53.6011-4
. notices 1.508-1
. penalties 301.6685-1
. propaganda influencing legislation 53.4945-2
. . lobbying expenditures 56.4911-1; 56.4911-3
. returns 55.6091-2
. . chapter 42 taxes . . . . 301.6501(n)-1
. . requirements 53.6011-1
. self-dealing . . . . 53.4941(d)-2
. self-dealing tax, overpayment of . . . . 301.6511(f)-1
. statement requirements 53.6011-1
. substantial contributor defined 1.507-6
. support defined . . . . 1.509(d)-1
. supporting organizations . . . . 1.509(a)-4
. termination of status . . . . 1.509(c)-1
. transfers 1.507-2; 1.507-3; 1.507-8
. trust treated as
. . charitable contribution deductions . . . . 1.642(c)-4
. value of assets 1.507-7

Private loan financing test
. generally 1.141-5
. refunding . . . . 1.141-13(b)

Private loans
. defined 1.141-5

Private security or payment test
. refunding . . . . 1.141-13(c)

Prizes
. gross income 1.74-1

Pro rata shares
. S corporations 1.1377-1

Processing costs
. capitalization of 1.263A-3

Producers
. loans
. . domestic international sales corporations . . 1.993-4; 1.995-5
. manufacturers excise taxes, use by producer . . . . 48.4218-1 to 48.4218-5
. . business or personal use 48.4218-2
. . computation of tax 48.4218-5
. . events subsequent to taxable use 48.4218-3
. . further manufacture, use in 48.4218-4

Product liability losses
. itemized deductions 1.172-13

Production of books and records
. criminal penalty for failure to produce records concerning estate of decedent 301.7269-1
. seizure of property for collection of taxes 301.6333-1

Professional expenses
. itemized deductions 1.162-6

Profit split method
. arm's length transactions
. . determination of 1.482-6
. . taxable income determination . . . . 1.482-9T(g)

Profit split options
. intangible property income 1.936-6
. possession of United States election to use . . . 1.936-7

Profits (See Earnings and profits)

Profit-sharing plans (See Pension, profit-sharing, and stock bonus plans)

Prohibited tax shelter transaction disclosure
. tax-exempt entities that are parties to reportable transactions
. . by whom disclosure is made . . . . 1.6033-5T(d)
. . defined . . . . 1.6033-5T(b)
. . frequency of disclosure . . . . 1.6033-5T(c)
. . generally 1.6033-5T
. . penalty for failure to provide statement . . . . 1.6033-5T(f)
. . time and place for filing . . . . 1.6033-5T(e)

Prohibited transactions
. generally . . . . 1.503(a)-1; 1.503(b)-1; 54.4975-1; 54.4975-14

Proof (See Evidence)

Property produced by taxpayer (See Produced by taxpayer, property)

Public charities
. lobbying by (See Lobbying; Lobbying expenditures)
. organizations, charitable (See Charitable organizations)

Public inspection
. exempt organizations
. . exemption application and information returns . . . . 301.6104(d)-1
. fuel taxpayer records by state 48.4102-1

References are to Reg. § numbers

Public inspection —Cont'd
. generally 601.702
. returns .... 301.6104(a)-1 to 301.6104(a)-6
Public office
. self-employment income .... 1.1402(c)-2
Public retirement system income
. credits 1.37-3
Public safety testing organizations
. exempt organizations .... 1.501(c)(3)-1
Public schools (See Schools and educational institutions)
Public utilities
. allowances .... 1.42-10; 1.42-10(b)
. . carryover allocations .... 1.42-12(c)
. . changes in applicable utility allowances .. 1.42-10(c)
. . . annual reviews .... 1.42-10(c)(2)
. . . generally .... 1.42-10(c)(1)
. . Community Renewal Tax Relief Act of 2000 .... 1.42-12(a)(2)
. . Department of Housing and Urban Development, building assisted by .... 1.42-10(b)(3)
. . electronic filing simplification changes .... 1.42-12(a)(3)
. . generally .... 1.42-12(a)(1)
. . inclusion of utility allowances in gross rent .... 1.42-10(a)
. . other buildings .... 1.42-10(b)(4)
. . other tenants .... 1.42-10(b)(4)(ii)
. . . agency estimate .... 1.42-10(b)(4)(ii)(C)
. . . Energy consumption model .... 1.42-10(b)(4)(ii)(E)
. . . general rule .... 1.42-10(b)(4)(ii)(A)
. . . HUD Utility Schedule Model .... 1.42-10(b)(4)(ii)(D)
. . . utility company estimate .... 1.42-10(b)(4)(ii)(B)
. . prior period .... 1.42-12(b)
. . record retention .... 1.42-10(c)
. . Rural Housing Service, building assisted by .... 1.42-10(b)(1)
. . Rural Housing Service assisted tenants, building with .... 1.42-10(b)(2)
. . tenants receiving HUD rental assistance .... 1.42-10(b)(4)(i)
. . utility allowances .... 1.42-12(a)(4)
. depreciation .... 1.167(l)-1 to 1.167(l)-4
. deregulated (See Deregulated public utility property)
. dividends paid deduction 1.247-1
. energy property 1.47-1
. investment credit 1.47-1
Publicity
. generally 601.702
. Tax Court 301.7461-1
. unemployment tax returns 301.6106-1
Publicly traded partnerships
. defined 1.7704-1

Publicly traded partnerships —Cont'd
. investment income 1.7704-3
. transition provisions 301.7704-2
. withholding
. . U.S. real property interest, dispositions of 1.1445-8
Puerto Rico
. bona fide residency
. . alien individuals presence test .... 1.937-1(c)(2)
. . bona fide resident .... 1.937-1(b)
. . closer connection test .... 1.937-1(e)
. . days of presence .... 1.937-1(c)(3)
. . definitions concerning .... 1.937-1(a)
. . generally 1.937-1
. . information reporting .... 1.937-1(h)
. . medical treatment .... 1.937-1(c)(4)
. . presence test .... 1.937-1(c)
. . significant connection to the United States .... 1.937-1(c)(5)
. . tax home test .... 1.937-1(d)
. . year of move .... 1.937-1(f)
. generally ... 1.876-1; 1.1402(a)-9; 31.3401(a)(8)(C)-1
. gross income exclusions 1.933-1
. investments 1.936-10
Purchasing, handling and storage costs
. capitalization of 1.263A-3
Purported gifts
. recharacterization of .... 1.672(f)-4

Q

QBUs (See Qualified business units)
QRT (See Qualified revocable trusts)
QSub elections
. S corporations 1.1361-4
Qualified business units (QBUs)
. defined .... 1.989(a)-1
. functional currency .... 1.985-1 et seq.
. . accounting methods 1.985-4
. . dollar, use as 1.985-2
. . dollar approximate separate transactions .. 1.985-3; 1.985-7
. . foreign corporations, adjustments to 1.985-7
. . separate transactions method 1.985-3
. . U.S. shareholders of controlled foreign corporations 1.985-7
Qualified clean-fuel recapture property
. recapture of deduction for 1.179A-1
Qualified clean-fuel refueling property
. recapture 1.179A-1
Qualified clean-fuel vehicle
. recapture of deduction for 1.179A-1

References are to Reg. § numbers

Qualified construction allowances
. leases . . . 1.110-1
Qualified domestic relations orders (QDROS)
. accounting methods
. . deferred compensation plans . . . 1.457-10(c)
Qualified domestic trusts
. election . . . 20.2056A-3
. . citizen after, surviving spouse becoming . . . 20.2056A-10
. . filer, designated . . . 20.2056A-9
. . joint property, special rules for . . . 20.2056A-8
. . transfer credits, allowance of . . . 20.2056A-7
. estate tax under section 2056A (See Estate tax, subhead imposition of section 2056A estate tax)
. marital deduction
. . marital trusts and nontrust transfers, conforming . . . 20.2056A-4
. . requirements . . . 20.2056A-2
Qualified electing funds
. controlled foreign corporations . . . 1.1291-9
. . deemed dividend election . . . 1.1291-9
. election to recognize gain . . . 1.1291-10
. foreign investment companies . . . 1.1294-1T
. generally . . . 1.1295-1
. income from . . . 1.1293-1
. retroactive elections . . . 1.1295-3
Qualified electric vehicles
. defined . . . 1.30-1(a)
. recapture of credit for . . . 1.30-1(b)
Qualified interests
. annuities and annuity contracts . . . 25.2702-3
Qualified mortgage credit certificates
. certificates . . . 1.25-3T
Qualified payment card agents
. backup withholding . . . 31.3406(g)-1(f)
Qualified plans (generally) (See also particular plans, e.g., Pension, profit-sharing, and stock bonus plans)
. annuities contracts, Section 403(b) . . . 20.2039-2
. limitations and repeal of estate tax exclusion for . . . 20.2039-1T
. lump sum distributions under . . . 20.2039-3; 20.2039-4
Qualified preretirement survivor annuities
. nondiscrimination, defined benefit plan . 1.401(a)(4)-3
Qualified production activities
. grantor trusts . . . 1.199-5(d)
. non-grantor trusts and estates . . . 1.199-5(e)
. partnership section 199 deduction . . . 1.199-5(b)
. pass-thru entities . . . 1.199-5
. S corporation section 199 deduction . . . 1.199-5(c)
Qualified rehabilitation expenditures (See Rehabilitation expenditures)
Qualified residence interest
. generally . . . 1.163-9T; 1.163-10T
Qualified resident
. foreign corporation as, status of . . . 1.884-4
Qualified revocable trusts
. estate, election filed for treatment as part of . . 1.645-1
Qualified separate line of business
. pension, profit-sharing, and stock bonus plans . . . 1.414(r)-5
Qualified small business stock
. defined . . . 1.1045-1(g)(1)
. months defined . . . 1.1045-1(g)(4)
. partner sale of QSB stock
. . eligible partner defined . . . 1.1045-1(g)(3)
. . Sec. 1045, election to apply . . . 1.1045-1(c)(1)
. partnerships
. . contribution of QSB stock or replacement stock to a partnership . . . 1.1045-1(f)
. . distribution of QSB stock to a partner . . . 1.1045-1(e)
. . holding QSB stock for more than six month . . . 1.1045-1(a)
. . notice requirements . . . 1.1045-1(b)(5)
. . purchase of QSB stock, partner's share of cost . . . 1.1045-1(c)(3)
. . replacement QSB stock, purchase of . . . 1.1045-1(a); 1.1045-1(b)(1)
. . . basis adjustment . . . 1.1045-1(b)(3)(ii)
. . . defined, replacement QSB stock . . . 1.1045-1(g)(2)
. . . election, time and manner of . . . 1.1045-1(h)(1)
. . . information reporting requirements . . . 1.1045-1(h)(2)
. . sale of QSB stock
. . . amount realized by, eligible partner's share on . . . 1.1045-1(c)(2)
. . . basis adjustment . . . 1.1045-1(b)(2); 1.1045-1(c)(4)
. . . information reporting requirements . . . 1.1045-1(h)(2)
. . . nonrecognition limitation . . . 1.1045-1(d); 1.1045-1(h)(3)
. . . recognition of gain, partner's . . . 1.1045-1(c)(5)
. . . Sec. 1045 gain, partner's distributive share of . . . 1.1045-1(b)(2)
. . Sec. 1045, eligible partner opting out of . . . 1.1045-1(b)(4)
. replacement QSB stock defined . . . 1.1045-1(g)(2)
Qualified stock purchase
. sec. 338 consistency rules . . . 1.338-8
Qualified Subchapter S trust
. defined . . . 1.1361-1
. electing small business trust, conversion to . . . 1.1361-1
. revocation of election . . . 1.1361-1
Qualified terminable interest property (QTIP)
. generation-skipping transfer tax . . . 26.2652-2

References are to Reg. § numbers

Qualified zone academy bonds
. arbitrage investment restrictions .... 1.1397E-1T(i)
. contribution requirements............. 1.1397E-1(c)
. credit allowance as payment of interest .. 1.1397E-1(f)
. credit rate.......................... 1.1397E-1(b)
. defined .... 1.1397E-1(a); 1.1397E-1T(a)
. information returns .... 1.1397E-1T(j)
. interest exemption 1.1397E-1
. maximum term, determination of .... 1.1397E-1(d); 1.1397E-1T(d)
. private entity defined .... 1.1397E-1(c)
. reimbursement .... 1.1397E-1(h)
. state or local government defined ...... 1.1397E-1(k)
. tax-exempt obligation status .... 1.1397E-1(g)
. use of proceeds .... 1.1397E-1T(h)
Qualifying debt instruments
. defined .... 1.1275-6(b)
. identification requirements .... 1.1275-6(e)
. integrated transactions
. . effective date .... 1.1275-6(j)
. . examples .... 1.1275-6(h)
. . generally .... 1.1275-6(c)
. . legging .... 1.1275-6(d)
. . taxation of .... 1.1275-6(f)
. integration of .... 1.1275-6(a)
. predecessors............................. 1.1275-6(g)
. successors .... 1.1275-6(g)
Qualifying employer security
. pension excise taxes 54.4975-12
Qualifying productions property
. domestic production gross receipts (See Domestic production gross receipts)
Quid pro quo contributions
. disclosure requirements 1.6115-1

R

Railroad Retirement Tax Act (RRTA)
. compensation
. . excluded remuneration .... 31.3231(e)-2
. . received both as employee and employee representative 31.3211-2
. . wages defined as .... 31.3121(a)-1; 31.3121(e)-1
. contribution base rule .... 31.3231(e)-2
. credits and refunds under .... 31.6402(a)-2
. employee representative tax
. . computation of 31.3211-2
. . measure of 31.3211-1
. . rates 31.3211-2
. . supplemental annuity tax 31.3211-2
. employee tax
. . backup withholding 31.3202-1
. . computation of 31.3201-2

Railroad Retirement Tax Act (RRTA) —Cont'd
. *employee tax —Cont'd*
. . measure of 31.3201-1
. . rates 31.3201-2
. . underpayment adjustments.............. 31.6205-1
. employer tax
. . computation of 31.3221-2
. . measure of 31.3221-1
. . rates 31.3221-2
. employers defined .... 31.3231(a)-1
. excise tax on employers (See subhead supplemental annuity tax)
. federal tax deposit rules 31.6302-1
. more than one employer 31.3202-1
. overpayment adjustments .... 31.6413(a)-2
. self-employment income .... 1.1402(c)-4
. supplemental annuity tax
. . employee representatives.............. 31.3211-2
. . generally 31.3211-2
. time for filing returns and other documents .... 31.6071(a)-1(b)
. wages and compensation given same meaning .... 31.3121(a)-1
. withholding taxes
. . federal tax deposit rules 31.6302-2
Railroad track maintenance credit
. adjustment to basis.................. 1.45G-1(e)(1)
. assignment of information statement (form 8900) .... 1.45G-1(d)(4)
. class II and class II railroad defined .... 1.45G-1(b)(1)
. controlled groups .... 1.45G-1(f)
. coordination with section 61 .... 1.45G-1(e)(2)
. definitions concerning.................. 1.45G-1(b)
. determination of credit amount .... 1.45G-1(c)
. eligible railroad track defined.......... 1.45G-1(b)(2)
. eligible taxpayer defined .... 1.45G-1(b)(3)
. form 8900, revised .... 1.45G-1(b)(10)
. generally .... 1.45G-1(a)
. limitations on credit.................. 1.45G-1(c)(2)
. multiple assignment of eligible railroad track made during the same taxable year .... 1.45G-1(d)(5)
. QRTME paid, determination of .... 1.45G-1(c)(3)
. qualified railroad track maintenancy expenditures defined.......................... 1.45G-1(b)(5)
. qualifying railroad structure defined .... 1.45G-1(b)(4)
. rail facilities defined .... 1.45G-1(b)(6)
. railroad track property defined .... 1.45G-1(b)(9)
. railroad-related property defined .... 1.45G-1(b)(7)
. subsequent dispositions of eligible railroad track during assignment year .... 1.45G-1(d)(5)
. track miles, assignment of .... 1.45G-1(d)
Railroad Unemployment Insurance Act (RUIA) (See Railroad Unemployment Repayment Tax)

References are to Reg. § numbers

Railroad Unemployment Repayment Tax
. government depositaries, use of ...... 31.6302(c)-2A

Railroads
. employment taxes (See Railroad Retirement Tax Act)
. itemized deductions .... 1.263(e)-1
. rolling stock .... 1.263(e)-1
. terminal railroad corporations and shareholders .... 1.281-1 to 1.281-4

Rates of tax
. capital gains or losses 1.1374-1
. changes .... 1.1-3; 1.25-1T to 1.25-8T; 1.441-2
. changes during taxable year 1.15-1
. coal.................................. 48.4121-1
. communications services 49.4251-2
. employee representative 31.3211-2
. foreign insurers 46.4371-3
. gasohol 48.4081-6
. generation-skipping transfer tax 26.2641-1
. railroad employee 31.3201-2
. railroad employer 31.3221-1; 31.3221-2
. telegraph and cable services 49.4251-2
. telephone services 49.4251-2

Readily tradable instrument
. backup withholding, defined for ....31.3406(h)-1

Readjustment of tax
. claim of right 1.341-1

Real estate (See Real property)

Real estate boards
. exempt organizations .... 1.501(c)(6)-1

Real estate investment trusts (REITs)
. additions to tax 1.860-3
. alternative minimum tax 1.58-6
. C corporation assets
. . new transitional rules for tax on ....1.337(d)-6
. . old transitional rules for tax on ....1.337(d)-5
. . tax on property owned by C corporation ..1.337(d)-7
. capital gains .... 1.857-2 to 1.857-10
. credit or refund 1.860-4
. deficiency dividends 1.860-1; 1.860-2
. definitions 1.856-1; 1.856-3
. dividends .... 1.858-1; 1.860-1 to 1.860-4
. earnings and profits 1.857-7
. earnings and profits, non-REIT 1.857-11
. excise tax......... 55.4981-1; 55.4981-2; 55.4982-1; 55.6081-1
. foreclosure property 1.856-6; 1.857-3; 5.856-1
. generally .... 1.856-0 et seq.
. gross income 1.856-7
. income and net capital gain ...... 1.857-2 to 1.857-10
. interest 1.856-5; 1.860-3
. itemized deductions 1.172-10
. limitation.................................. 1.856-2

Real estate investment trusts (REITs) —Cont'd
. prohibited transactions, net income and loss from 1.857-5
. qualified REIT subsidiary, treatment of 1.856-9
. records 1.857-8
. rents 1.856-4
. returns 1.857-9; 1.857-10; 55.6151-1
. revocation or termination of election 1.856-8
. shareholders, method of taxation 1.857-6
. source-of-income requirements 1.857-4
. subsidiaries, treatment of 1.856-9
. time and place for paying of tax shown on returns 55.6151-1
. undistributed income
. . automatic extension of time to file return 55.6081-1
. withholding
. . U.S. real property interest, dispositions of 1.1445-8

Real estate mortgage investment conduits (REMICs)
. administrative rules........................ 1.860F-4
. allocation of expenses 1.67-3; 1.67-3T
. automatic extension of time for filing returns 1.6081-7
. defined ....1.446-6(b)
. excise taxes.......................... 1.860A-1(b)(3)
. foreign persons 1.860G-3
. . accounting for REMIC net income ...1.860A-1(b)(5); 1.860G-3(b)
. . . allocation of partnership income to a foreign partner .... 1.860G-3(b)(1)
. . . excess inclusion income allocate by certain pass-through entities .... 1.860G-3(b)(2)
. . transfer of a residual interest with tax avoidance .... 1.860G-3(a)
. . . effectively connected income...... 1.860G-3(a)(3)
. . . generally .... 1.860G-3(a)(1)
. . . tax avoidance potential........... 1.860G-3(a)(2)
. . . . defined .... 1.860G-3(a)(2)(i)
. . . . safe harbor .... 1.860G-3(a)(2)(ii)
. . . transfer by a foreign holder .... 1.860G-3(a)(4)
. . transfers 1.860G-3
. inducement fees
. . accounting methods .... 1.446-6(f)
. . book method of recognition.............1.446-6(e)
. . defined ....1.446-6(b)
. . disposition of a residual interest, special rule for ....1.446-6(d)
. . general rule for recognition .... 1.446-6(c)
. . income from sources within the United States, status as ....1.863-1(e)
. . modified REMIC method of recognition ...1.446-6(e)
. . noneconomic residual interest defined ... 1.446-6(b)
. . reflection of income from becoming holder of noneconomic ....1.446-6(a)

References are to Reg. § numbers

Real estate mortgage investment conduits (REMICs) —Cont'd
. *inducement fees —Cont'd*
. . safe harbor methods of recognition ...... 1.446-6(e)
. information returns .... 1.6031(b)-2T; 1.6049-7
. . nominee reporting .... 1.6031(c)-2T
. information returns for persons engaged in trade or business .... 1.6041-1(b)(2)
. rate based on current interest rate .... 1.860A-1(b)(4)
. . generally .... 1.860A-1(b)(4)(i)
. . rate based on index .... 1.860A-1(b)(4)(ii)
. regular and residual interests defined 1.860G-1
. reporting and regulations .... 1.860A-1(b)(1)
. reporting requirements 1.860F-4
. residual interests
. . defined 1.860G-1
. . excess inclusions 1.860E-1
. . non-economic residual interests, transfers of 1.860E-1
. . transfer 1.860G-3
. residual interests, notice to holders of .... 1.860F-4(e)
. returns .... 1.860F-4(b)
. returns, signing .... 1.860F-4(c)
. tax avoidance rules .... 1.860A-1(b)(2)
. . transfers of certain residential interests .... 1.860A-1(b)(2)(i)
. . transfers to foreign holders .... 1.860A-1(b)(2)(ii)
. tax matters person, designation of .... 1.860F-4(d)
. transition rules 1.860A-1
Real property
. accumulated production expenditures, unit of property for determining 1.263A-10
. capital gains and losses 1.1237-1
. discharge of indebtedness in excess of value 1.108-6
. foreign person, transfer by 1.897-6T
. gain or loss 1.1038-1; 1.1038-2
. . foreign person, transfer by 1.897-6T
. homeowners' association .... 1.528-1 to 1.528-10
. information returns 1.6045-4
. investment trusts (See Real estate investment trusts)
. lien, discharged
. . redemption by United States 301.7425-4
. liens .... 301.6323(c)-2
. mortgages (See Mortgages)
. mutual savings banks 1.593-11
. nonresident aliens .... 1.871-10; 1.1445-1 to 1.1445-7
. U.S.-acquired, administration of 301.7506-1
Reasonable cause
. information returns 301.6724-1
. section 6662 penalties, exception to 1.6664-4; 1.6664-4T
Rebates
. arbitrage profits (See Arbitrage transactions)
Rebates —Cont'd
. Medicaid and Medicare, deductibility of 1.162-18
Recapture
. asset dispositions .... 1.168(i)-1(g)
. ERTA .... 5c.168(f)(8)-8
. exemptions 1.111-1
. foreign losses 1.1502-9; 1.1502-9T
. foreign tax credit .... 1.904(f)-2 to 1.904(f)-12
. . beginning after December 31, 2002 .. 1.904(f)-12(g); 1.904(f)-12T(g)
. . beginning before January 1, 1987 ...... 1.904(f)-12
. . beginning before January 1, 2003 ... 1.904(f)-12(g); 1.904(f)-12T(g)
. investment credit 1.47-1
. LIFO benefits .... 1.56(g)-1(f); 1.1363-2
. natural resources exploration expenditures ... 1.617-3
. overall domestic loss accounts
. . income from sources outside the U.S. ... 1.904(g)-2T
. qualified clean-fuel refueling property 1.179A-1
. qualified clean-fuel vehicle 1.179A-1
. qualified electric vehicle, recapture of credit for .... 1.30-1(b)
. separate limitation loss account
. . income from sources outside the U.S. ... 1.904(f)-8T
Receipt for payment of tax
. generally .... 301.6311-1 to 301.6316-9
Receivables
. foreign personal holding company income
. . income equivalent to interest from factoring
. . . factored receivable .... 1.954-2(h)(4)(iii)
. . performance of services, receivable arising from .... 1.954-2(h)(5)
. losses on sale of certain
. . interest expense allocation .... 1.861-9T(b)(3)
. service providers, nonaccrual of certain amounts by
. . accounts receivable defined .... 1.448-2(c)(1)
. unrealized, partners and partnerships 1.751-1
Receivership
. assessment of claims for income, estate, and gift taxes .... 301.6871(a)-1
. collection of assessed taxes .... 301.6871(a)-2
. generally .... 1.6851-1 to 1.6851-3; 601.109
. information returns 1.6036-1; 301.6036-1; 301.6316-9
. partnership items .... 301.6231(c)-7
. pendency of Tax Court proceedings .... 301.6871(b)-1
. suspension of running of period of limitations on assessment 301.6872-1
. unpaid claims 301.6873-1
Recharacterization
. purported gifts .... 1.672(f)-4
Recharacterizing financing arrangements
. fast-pay stock .... 1.7701(l)-3

References are to Reg. § numbers

Reciprocal underwriters and interinsurers
. mutual insurance companies ..... 1.823-7; 1.826-1 to 1.826-6

Records and reports
. abatements, credits, and refunds 301.6405-1
. actuarial reports and methods .... 1.412(c)(2)-1; 301.6059-1; 301.6692-1
. alternative minimum tax 1.57-5
. backup withholding for notified payee under reporting of reportable interest or dividend payments 35a.3406-2
. capital gains and losses .... 1.1244(e)-1; 1.1247-5
. charitable contributions 1.170A-13
. charitable organizations
. . lobbying expenditures
. . . excess lobbying expenditures, excise tax 56.4911-6; 56.6001-1
. communications activity .... 1.863-9(k)
. conduit financing arrangements 1.881-4
. controlled corporations
. . distributions of stock and securities (See Controlled corporation subhead distributions of stock and securities, recordkeeping requirements)
. . transfers to 1.351-3
. corporate organizations and reorganizations (See Reorganizations)
. diesel and special motor fuels tax
. . credits and refunds
. . . buses, intercity, local or school buses .. 48.6427-5
. . . farm use 48.6427-5
. disposition of property
. . gain or loss 1.1081-11
. distributions and exchanges
. . Commission orders, corporations subject to .... 1.1081-11(b)
. . holders of stock or securities, significant .... 1.1081-11(a)
. . publicly traded stock defined .... 1.1081-11(d)
. . significant holder defined .... 1.1081-11(d)
. . substantiation information, retaining ... 1.1081-11(e)
. . system groups, sales by members of ... 1.1081-11(c)
. dividends subject to reporting 1.6042-3
. exempt organizations .... 1.501(c)(9)-5
. fast-pay stock arrangements .... 1.7701(l)-3
. foreign corporations 1.964-3; 1.6038A-3
. gift tax 25.6001-1
. highway vehicles
. . use tax 41.6001-1; 44.6001-1
. individual retirement arrangements 1.408-7
. investment companies 1.852-6
. IRS records or information, disclosure of (See Disclosure)
. liquidations (See Liquidation subhead records)
. manufacturers excise taxes
. . farm use of gasoline 48.6420-6

Records and reports —Cont'd
. *manufacturers excise taxes —Cont'd*
. . state or local tax officers, inspection of records by 48.4102-1
. mortgage loans 1.25-8T
. natural resources 1.613A-6
. new markets tax credit allowance 1.45D-1
. production of (See Production of books and records)
. real estate investment trusts 1.857-8
. reorganizations (See Reorganizations)
. seizure of property for collection of taxes 301.6340-1
. space and ocean activity .... 1.863-8(g)
. structured settlement factoring transactions 157.6001-1
. surcharge 1.57-5
. trust income
. . widely held fixed investment trusts (See Widely held fixed investment trusts)
. wagering taxes 44.4403-1
. widely held fixed investment trusts (See Widely held fix investment trusts)
. windfall profits 1.6001-1

Recovery deductions
. automobiles 1.280F-1T
. business use percentage of listed property is not greater than 50% 1.280F-3T
. itemized deductions .... 1.280F-1T to 1.280F-3T
. leased property 1.280F-5T
. limitations 1.280F-2T
. listed property, special rules for 1.280F-4T

Redemption
. accounting methods 1.451-4; 1.466-1
. constructive distribution 1.1041-2
. cooperatives 1.1383-1
. corporate distributions and adjustments .... 1.302-2 to 1.302-4
. discharged lien
. . United States, redemption by 301.7425-4
. distribution
. . control requirement 1.304-5
. . dividends 1.305-1
. . gross estate of decedent, inclusion in determining .... 1.303-1 et seq.
. dividend
. . not taxable as 1.302-2
. investment companies 1.852-10
. liquidations 1.346-2
. non-pro rata .... 1.1059(e)-1
. related corporations, shareholder stock sales to 1.304-1
. seizure of property for collection of taxes 301.6337-1
. small business stock 1.1202-2
. spousal agreements 1.1041-2

References are to Reg. § numbers

Redemption —Cont'd
. trading stamps and coupons, accounting method 1.451-4
Redetermination of foreign taxes
. pools of foreign taxes, adjustments to (See Foreign tax credit)
Refineries
. election to allocate section 179C deduction to cooperative owners
. . generally .... 1.179C-1T(e)(1)
. . irrevocable election .... 1.179C-1T(e)(4)
. . time and manner for making elections .... 1.179C-1T(e)(2)
. . . manner of making election .... 1.179C-1T(e)(2)(ii)
. . . time for making election .... 1.179C-1T(e)(2)(i)
. . written notice to owners .... 1.179C-1T(e)(3)
. election to expense certain refineries
. . Clean Air Act waiver .... 1.179C-1T(b)(6)(ii)
. . computation of expense deduction for qualified refinery property .... 1.179C-1T(c)
. . construction of property
. . . binding contract defined .... 1.179C-1T(b)(7)(ii); 1.179C-1T(b)(7)(ii)(A)
. . . . components .... 1.179C-1T(b)(7)(ii)(E)
. . . . conditions .... 1.179C-1T(b)(7)(ii)(B)
. . . . options .... 1.179C-1T(b)(7)(ii)(C)
. . . generally .... 1.179C-1T(b)(7)(i); 1.179C-1T(b)(7)(ii)(A)
. . . self-constructed components .... 1.179C-1T(b)(7)(ii)(C)(2)
. . . self-constructed property .... 1.179C-1T(b)(7)(ii)
. . . . acquired components .... 1.179C-1T(b)(7)(ii)(C)(1)
. . . . components of self-constructed property .... 1.179C-1T(b)(7)(ii)(C)
. . . supply agreements .... 1.179C-1T(b)(7)(ii)(D)
. . . when construction begins .... 1.179C-1T(b)(7)(ii)(B)
. . definitions .... 1.179C-1T(a); 1.179C-1T(a)(2)
. . effective date .... 1.179C-1T(g)
. . environmental laws
. . . applicable .... 1.179C-1T(b)(6); 1.179C-1T(b)(6)(i)
. . . Clean Air Act waiver .... 1.179C-1T(b)(6)(ii)
. . expiration date .... 1.179C-1T(h)
. . generally .... 1.179C-1T; 1.179C-1T(b)(1); 1.179C-1T(d); 1.179C-1T(d)(1)
. . manner of making election .... 1.179C-1T(d)(2)(ii)
. . nonqualified refinery property .... 1.179C-1T(b)(2)(ii)
. . original use .... 1.179C-1T(b)(3)
. . . generally .... 1.179C-1T(b)(3)(i)
. . . sale-leaseback .... 1.179C-1T(b)(3)(ii)
. . placed-in-service date .... 1.179C-1T(b)(4)
. . . generally .... 1.179C-1T(b)(4)(i)
. . . sale-leaseback .... 1.179C-1T(b)(4)(ii)
. . production capacity
. . . generally .... 1.179C-1T(b)(5)(i)

Refineries —Cont'd
. election to expense certain refineries —Cont'd
. . production capacity —Cont'd
. . . multi-stage projects .... 1.179C-1T(b)(5)(iii)
. . . when production capacity is tested .... 1.179C-1T(b)(5)(ii)
. . qualified refinery property .... 1.179C-1T(b)(2); 1.179C-1T(b)(2)(i)
. . . nonqualified refinery property .... 1.179C-1T(b)(2)(ii)
. . reporting requirements .... 1.179C-1T(f)
. . . generally .... 1.179C-1T(f)(1)
. . . information to be included in the report .... 1.179C-1T(f)(2)
. . . manner of submitting report .... 1.179C-1T(f)(3)(ii)
. . . time and manner for submitting report .... 1.179C-1T(f)(3)
. . . . time for submitting report .... 1.179C-1T(f)(3)(i)
. . revocation of election to expense .... 1.179C-1T(d)(3); 1.179C-1T(d)(3)(i)
. . . after the revocation deadline .... 1.179C-1T(d)(3)(iii)
. . . cooperative taxpayer, by .... 1.179C-1T(d)(3)(iii)
. . . prior to the revocation deadline .... 1.179C-1T(d)(3)(ii)
. . time and manner for making election .... 1.179C-1T(d)(2)
. . time for making election .... 1.179C-1T(d)(2)(i)
Reforestation expenditures
. itemized deductions .... 1.194-1 to 1.194-4
Refunding obligations
. advance, limitations on
. . abusive devices .... 1.149(d)-1(b)
. . arbitrage regulations .... 1.149(d)-1(d)
. . future eligibility .... 1.149(d)-1(c)
. . private activity bonds limitations .... 1.149(d)-1(g)
. arbitrage bonds 1.148-8; 1.148-9
. effective dates for sections 141 .... 1.141-15
. multipurpose issue allocations .... 1.141-13(d)
. private business use test .... 1.141-13(b)
. private security or payment test .... 1.141-13(c)
. reasonable expectations test for certain bonds .... 1.141-13(e)
. special rules for certain generally obligation bonds .... 1.141-13(f)
Refunds (See Abatements, credits, and refunds)
Registration-required obligations
. capital gains treatment 1.1287-1
. excise taxes 46.4701-1
. generally 1.165-12; 5f.103-1; 5f.163-1; 35a.9999-5
. interest deduction 5f.163-1
. questions and answers on withholding tax on interest 35a.9999-5
Regulated investment companies (RICs)
. alternative minimum tax 1.58-6
. C corporation assets

References are to Reg. § numbers

Regulated investment companies (RICs) —Cont'd
. *C corporation assets —Cont'd*
. . new transitional rules for tax on .... 1.337(d)-6
. . old transitional rules for tax on .... 1.337(d)-5
. . tax on C corporation property .... 1.337(d)-7
. earnings and profits 1.852-5
. earnings and profits, non-RIC 1.852-12
. election of taxable year foreign income/war profits/excess profits
. . company, by .... 1.853-2(a)
. . dividends paid after close of the taxable year .... 1.853-2(c)
. . information, time and manner of providing .... 1.853-4(d)
. . information required .... 1.853-4(c)
. . irrevocability of election .... 1.853-4(b)
. . manner of making election .... 1.853-4(a)
. . shareholders, by .... 1.853-2(b)
. exempt-interest dividends 1.265-3
. foreign tax credit allowed to shareholders
. . generally .... 1.853-1(a)
. . qualifications for election .... 1.853-1(b)
. income 1.852-3
. losses 1.852-11
. market to market election for marketable stock 1.1296-1
. marketable stock defined 1.1296-1; 1.1296-2
. method of taxation .... 1.852-2 to 1.852-10
. notice to shareholders
. . foreign tax credit, creditable .... 1.853-3(a)
. . shareholder of record custodian of certain unit investment trusts .... 1.853-3(b)
. records 1.852-6
. returns 1.852-7; 1.852-8
. section 1296 stock defined 1.1296-1
. shareholders 1.852-4; 1.854-2
. . election of taxable year .... 1.853-2(b)
. . notice to shareholders
. . . foreign tax credit, creditable .... 1.853-3(a)
. . . shareholder of record custodian of certain unit investment trusts .... 1.853-3(b)
. status determination 1.851-4; 1.851-5
. undistributed capital gains, designation of 1.852-9
. withholding, foreign company 1.1441-3

Rehabilitation expenditures
. December 31, 1981, incurred after 1.48-12
. defined 1.48-12
. generally 1.48-11; 1.1012-2
. January 1, 1982, incurred before 1.48-11
. New York Liberty Zone property 1.48-12
. qualified rehabilitation building defined 1.48-12
. substantial rehabilitation test 1.48-12

Reimbursement
. bonds 1.150-2

Reimbursement —Cont'd
. expense allowance arrangements 1.62-2
. gross income .... 31.3401(a)-4
. medical expenses, self-insured medical plans 1.105-11
. tuition and related expenses 1.6050S-1T

Reinstatement of fees
. installment agreement fees 300.2

REITs (See Real estate investment trusts)

Related corporations
. concurrent employment with common paymaster .... 31.3121(s)-1
. employment taxes .... 31.3306(p)-1
. generally 1.304-2; 1.993-5

Related persons or parties
. domestic production gross receipts .... 1.199-3(b)
. excess expenditures, allocation of 1.263A-14
. information returns
. . foreign corporations .... 1.6038-2(f)
. notional principal contracts 1.446-3

Related taxpayers
. children (See Children and dependents)
. debt obligations to foreign related persons .. 1.163-12; 1.267(a)-3
. deductions disallowed .... 1.267(a)-1 et seq.
. husband and wife (See Spouses)
. imported property from
. . basis limitations 1.1059A-1
. land exchanged between related individuals, interest for a contract .... 1.483-3(b)
. nonresident aliens, factoring income 1.864-8T
. readjustment of tax .... 1.1313(c)-1
. resellers, property produced by taxpayer 1.263A-3
. sales between, basis 1.1012-2

Releases
. levy and return of property 301.6343-1
. lien for taxes 301.6325-1

Religious organizations
. clergy (See Ministers or religious personnel)
. discovery of liability and enforcement of title 301.7611-1
. ERISA .... 1.410(d)-1
. examination of books and activities 301.7605-1
. exempt organizations .... 1.501(c)(3)-1; 1.501(d)-1
. insurance, opposition to .... 1.1402(c)-7; 1.1402(h)-1
. ministers or religious personnel (See Ministers or religious personnel)
. pension, profit-sharing, and stock bonus plans .... 1.410(d)-1; 1.414(e)-1
. self-employment income .. 1.1402(a)-11; 1.1402(c)-5; 1.1402(c)-7; 1.1402(e)-2A to 1.1402(e)-4A; 1.1402(h)-1

Remainders
. charitable contributions 1.170A-12

References are to Reg. § numbers

Remainders —Cont'd
. death taxes on, credit for 20.2015-1
. estate tax, extension of time to pay........ 20.6163-1
. valuation of 1.7520-1; 20.2031-7; 25.2512-5; 25.2702-3; 25.7520-1
. . pooled income fund, transfers to .... 1.642(c)-6
. valuation of charitable remainder ....1.642(c)-6A
REMICs (See Real estate mortgage investment conduits)
Renewal of enrollment
. enrolled actuary fee
. . applicability.......................... 300.8(a)
. . fee .... 300.8(b)
. . liability for fee .... 300.8(c)
. enrolled agent fee
. . amount of fee .... 300.6(b)
. . applicability.......................... 300.6(a)
. . liability for fee .... 300.6(c)
Rental agreements, Section 467
. accounting methods 1.467-1
. accrual without adequate interest 1.467-2
. AFR 1.467-2
. avoidance of tax 1.467-3
. constant rental accrual method, automatic consent to change 1.467-8; 1.467-9
. deferred and prepaid rents, agreements with 1.467-2
. dispositions 1.467-7
. exchanges and conversions 1.467-7
. fixed rent, adequate interest on 1.467-2
. interest determination...................... 1.467-1
. leasebacks, disqualified 1.467-3
. loan rules 1.467-4
. long-term agreements, disqualified 1.467-3
. modification of agreement 1.467-1
. recapture rules 1.467-7
. variable interest.................. 1.467-2; 1.467-5
. variable rate treated as fixed 1.467-5
Rental property (See Leases)
Reorganization
. active business requirements 1.355-3
. asset continuity .... 1.368-1(d)(3)
. assumption of liabilities 1.357-1; 1.357-2; 1.358-3
. . partnership assumption after Oct. 18, 1999 and before June 24, 2003 .... 1.752-6
. . partnership transfers to corporation 1.358-7
. . special rules 1.358-5T
. basis to corporations 1.362-1
. basis to distributees
. . allocation 1.358-2
. . assumption of liabilities 1.358-3
. . . partnership assumption after Oct. 18, 1999, and before June 24, 2003 .... 1.752-6

Reorganization —Cont'd
. *basis to distributees —Cont'd*
. . exceptions 1.358-4
. . generally 1.358-1
. . reverse triangular merger 1.358-6
. . triangular reorganization 1.358-6
. capital construction fund 3.8
. capital contributions 1.362-2
. combining entity .... 1.368-2(b)
. consideration in connection with an exchange .... 1.356-1 to 1.356-5
. continuity of business enterprise .... 1.358-1(d); 1.368-1(d)(1)
. continuity of interest .... 1.358-1(e); 1.368-1(e)
. controlled corporations .... 1.355-1 to 1.355-7
. corporate acquisitions, carryovers......... 1.381(a)-1
. . closing of taxable year............. 1.381(b)-1(a)
. . date of distribution or transfer .... 1.381(b)-1(b)
. . net operating loss, carryback of .... 1.381(b)-1(d)
. . return of distributor or transferor corporation .... 1.381(b)-1(c)
. defined .... 1.358-1(a); 1.368-1(a); 1.368-2(a)
. disregarded entity .... 1.368-2(b)
. distributions
. . non pro rata 1.355-4
. electric railway corporation 1.374-4
. exchanges .... 1.368-1 et seq.
. . receipt of additional consideration 1.356-1
. . security holders 1.371-2
. . stock and securities 1.354-1
. gain or loss
. . accounting for....................... 1.358-1(a)
. . nonrecognition of .... 1.358-1(c)
. . recognition 1.361-1
. nonrecognition of gain or loss .... 1.368-1(c)
. other property
. . securities 1.356-3
. partnership transfers to corporation 1.358-7
. party to reorganization defined .... 1.358-1(a)
. purpose .... 1.368-1(b)
. real property transfer by foreign person 1.897-6T
. records
. . parties to the organization.............. 1.368-3(a)
. . publicly traded stock .... 1.368-3(c)
. . significant holder defined .... 1.368-3(c)
. . significant holders .... 1.368-3(b)
. . substantial information .... 1.368-3(d)
. redemption, non-pro rata .... 1.1059(e)-1
. reverse triangular merger.................. 1.358-6
. transactions treated as .... 1.368-2T(l)
. triangular reorganization (See Triangular reorganizations)

References are to Reg. § numbers

Repackaging costs
. capitalization of 1.263A-3

Repairs
. itemized deductions .... 1.162-4; 1.263(f)-1

Repatriation of assets
. foreign corporations stock exchange, nonrecognition transactions .... 1.367(b)-3

Reportable transactions
. disclosure 301.6111-3
. exempt organizations prohibited tax shelter transaction disclosure (See Prohibited tax shelter transaction disclosure)
. material advisor .... 301.6111-3(b)
. . designation agreements .... 301.6111-3(f)
. . disclosure statement, form of .... 301.6111-3(d)
. . protective disclosure .... 301.6111-3(g)
. . time of providing .... 301.6111-3(e)
. statements concerning 1.6011-4

Reports (See Records and reports)

Representation of parties
. contest between representatives 601.508
. fiduciaries (See Fiduciaries)
. IRS appearance .... 601.501 et seq.
. Tax Court 301.7452-1

Reproduction of returns or documents
. Tax Court 301.7513-1

Resale
. capitalization of costs 1.263A-1; 1.263A-3
. manufacturers excise taxes (See Manufacturers excise taxes)

Resale cases facility
. defined 1.263A-3

Research credits
. optional 10-year writeoff of certain tax preferences 1.59-1

Research expenditures
. adjusted basis 1.1016-5
. aggregation
. . accounting periods used 1.41-6
. . controlled corporations .... 1.41-6; 1.41-6T(b)
. . . group alternative simplified credit ...... 1.41-6T(e)
. . . single taxpayer treatment as .... 1.41-6T(b)(1)
. . . stand-alone entity credit .... 1.41-6T(c)(2)
. . intra-group transactions 1.41-6
. allocation and apportionment, income from sources within or without U.S. 1.861-17
. alternate incremental credit 1.41-8
. . controlled groups .... 1.41-8(b)(4); 1.41-8T(b)(4)
. . determination of credit .... 1.41-8(a)
. . revocation .... 1.41-8(b)(3); 1.41-8T(b)(3)
. . time and manner of credit .... 1.41-8(b)(2); 1.41-8T(b)(2)
. alternative simplified credit

Research expenditures — Cont'd
. alternative simplified credit — Cont'd
. . controlled groups ...... 1.41-9T(b)(4); 1.41-9T(c)(5)
. . determination of credit 1.41-9T
. . election .... 1.41-9T(b)
. . qualified research expenses year requirements .... 1.41-9T(c)(1)
. . revocation .... 1.41-9T(b)(3)
. . sec. 41(c), applicability of .... 1.41-9T(c)(2)
. . sec. 41(h), applicability of .... 1.41-9T(c)(3)
. . short taxable years .... 1.41-9T(c)(4)
. . time and manner of credit .... 1.41-9T(b)(2)
. base amount for taxable year beginning on or after January 3, 2001 .... 1.41-3
. base period research expense 1.41-3A
. basic research for taxable years beginning before January 1, 1987 .... 1.41-5A
. capitalization of costs 1.263A-1
. consistency requirement
. . increasing research activities 1.41-3
. contract expenses 1.41-2
. credit for increasing research activities 1.41-1; 1.280C-4
. documentation 1.41-4
. excluded activities 1.41-4
. foreign corporations
. . gross receipts defined 1.41-3
. generally .. 1.41-0 et seq.; 1.174-1; 1.174-2; 5c.44F-1
. gross receipts defined 1.41-3
. leases 5c.44F-1
. personal property use 1.41-2
. qualified expenditures paid or incurred on or after December 31, 2003 .... 1.41-4
. short taxable year special rules 1.41-3
. special rules
. . short taxable years 1.41-3
. . taxable year ending on or after November 9, 2006 .... 1.41-8
. supplies used 1.41-2
. trade or business requirements 1.41-2; 1.41-5A
. treatment of 1.174-3
. wage paid for services 1.41-2
. written agreement requirement 1.41-5A

Reserves
. guaranty debt obligation, itemized deduction 1.166-10
. life insurance companies .... 1.801-4 to 1.801-8; 1.810-2 to 1.810-4
. loans .... 1.585-1 to 1.585-4; 1.586-1; 1.586-2

Residence and domicile
. certification of; TIN 1.1441-6
. gain or loss on sale or exchange . 1.121-1 to 1.121-5; 1.165-9; 1.1033(a)-3; 1.1034-1; 1.1038-2
. . section 121 exclusion 1.1398-3

References are to Reg. § numbers

Residence and domicile —Cont'd
. low-income housing 1.1039-1
. missionaries in foreign service 20.2202-1
. nonresident aliens.............. 1.871-2 to 1.871-13
. possessions of United States
. . nonresidents not citizens of United States 20.2209-1
. . residents of 20.2208-1
. qualified residence interest 1.163-10T

Residential property
. personal residence trusts, freezing estate value 25.2702-5

Resources (See Natural resources)

Restructuring of fees
. installment agreement fees 300.2

Retail commission salespersons
. defined .... 31.3402(j)-1(b)
. withholding .... 31.3402(j)-1

Retail customer
. defined 1.263A-3

Retail excise taxes
. definitions 48.0-2
. diesel and special motor fuels tax (See Diesel and special motors fuel tax)
. exemption certificates..................... 48.0-3
. returns .... 48.4061(a)-4
. . place for filing 49.6091-1

Retail merchants
. inventories 1.471-8

Retail sales taxes
. itemized deductions 1.164-5

Retirement
. depreciation.......................... 1.167(a)-8
. ERISA (See Employee Retirement Income Security Act)
. exemptions for retired employees, generally . . 1.105-6
. individual retirement accounts (See Individual retirement arrangements)
. information returns 1.6047-1; 301.6057-1; 301.6057-2
. itemized deductions 1.219-1
. partners and partnerships 1.736-1
. penalties 301.6652-3
. pension, profit-sharing, and stock bonus plans (See Pension, profit-sharing, and stock bonus plans)
. self-employment income .... 1.1402(a)-17
. Tax Court.................... 1.7476-1 to 1.7476-3
. uniformed services retirement pay 1.122-1

Retirement Equity Act of 1984
. joint and survivor annuities .... 1.401(a)-20
. preretirement survivor annuities .... 1.401(a)-20

Retirement-replacement-betterment (RRB) property
. depreciation.............................. 1.168-5

Returns
. accounting period of less than 12 months 1.443-1
. administrative review .... 301.6103(p)(7)-1
. affiliated groups......................... 1.6012-2(d)
. attorneys of Justice Department and Office of Chief Counsel of IRS employees .... 301.6103(a)-2
. automatic extension of time for filing (See Extension of time for filing return)
. banking institutions 1.584-5
. charitable contributions 1.170A-13
. charitable organizations .... 1.6012-2(e)
. China Trade Act Corporations 1.6072-3
. claims arising out of erroneous computation .... 301.6230(c)-1
. Commissioner or other IRS officers preparing or executing 301.6020-1
. communications services, excise taxes .... 49.6011(a)-1
. . payment of tax shown on return, time and place for 49.6151-1
. . time for filing .... 49.6071(a)-1
. composite returns .... 1.6012-5; 31.6011(a)-8
. computations, generally 1.6014-2; 1.6102-1; 301.6102-1
. confidential transactions defined 1.6011-4
. consolidated returns (See Consolidated returns)
. copy of return 301.7513-1
. . form and manner of furnishing 1.6707-2T
. corporations....... 1.1502-100; 1.6072-2; 301.6062-1
. . extension of time for filing 1.6081-5
. . requirement to make .... 1.6012-2(a)
. disclosure, penalties for
. . attorney or accountant............. 301.7216-2(h)
. . commission of a crime, disclosure for reporting .... 301.7216-2(q)
. . corporate fiduciary .... 301.7216-2(i)
. . court order, demand, request, summon or subpoena, pursuant to .... 301.7216-2(f)
. . disclosure defined .... 301.7216-1(b)(5)
. . foreign country obligations, preparation of .... 301.7216-2(k)
. . generally .... 301.7216-1(a)
. . Gramm-Leach-Bliley Act requirements, superseded .... 301.7216-1(c)
. . hyperlink defined .... 301.7216-1(b)(6)
. . IRS, disclosure to.................. 301.7216-2(b)
. . lists for solicitation of tax return business .... 301.7216-2(n)
. . other provisions of the Code......... 301.7216-2(a)
. . other tax return preparers, disclosure to .... 301.7216-2(d)
. . preparation of a taxpayer's return .... 301.7216-2(c)
. . preparer death of incapacity .... 301.7216-2(r)
. . quality or peer review .... 301.7216-2(p)
. . related taxpayers .... 301.7216-2(e)

References are to Reg. § numbers

Returns —Cont'd
. *disclosure, penalties for —Cont'd*
. . request for consent defined ...... 301.7216-1(b)(7)
. . retention of records .... 301.7216-2(m)
. . securing legal advice .... 301.7216-2(g)
. . statistical information produced in connection with tax return preparation business .... 301.7216-2(o)
. . tax preparation service payments .... 301.7216-2(l)
. . tax return defined .... 301.7216-1(b)(1)
. . tax return information defined ..... 301.7216-1(b)(3)
. . tax return preparer defined .... 301.7216-1(b)(2)
. . taxpayer fiduciary, disclosure to ...... 301.7216-2(j)
. . use of return information defined .. 301.7216-1(b)(4)
. disclosure, taxpayer consent for
. . copy, providing taxpayer with ..... 301.7216-3(c)(3)
. . duration of consent .... 301.7216-3(b)(5)
. . entire return, disclosure of........ 301.7216-3(c)(2)
. . generally .... 301.7216-3(a)(1)
. . multiple disclosures or uses within one single consent form .... 301.7216-3(c)(1)
. . other tax return preparers, disclosure to .... 301.7216-3(a)(2)
. . retroactive consent .... 301.7216-3(b)(1)
. . social security number to return preparer outside of the U.S. with respect to Form 1040 .... 301.7216-3(b)(4)
. . solicitation context .... 301.7216-3(b)(2)
. . unsuccessful request, after .... 301.7216-3(b)(3)
. disclosure of information in .... 301.6103(a)-1 to 301.6103(p)(2)(B)-1; 301.6104(c)-1; 301.7216-1 to 1.7216-3
. . Agriculture Department, to .... 301.6103(j)(5)-1
. . . census of agriculture, conducting .... 301.6103(j)(5)-1
. . Census Bureau, to .... 301.6103(j)(1)-1
. . Commerce Department, to .... 301.6103(j)(1)-1
. . confidential transactions 1.6011-4
. . contractually protected transactions....... 1.6011-4
. . credit cards, payment of tax by .... 301.6103(k)(9)-1; 301.6311-2
. . criminal investigations .... 301.6301(k)(6)-1T
. . Customs Service (United States), to .... 301.6103(l)(14)-1
. . debit cards, payment of tax by .... 301.6103(k)(9)-1; 301.6311-2
. . designee of taxpayer, to .... 301.6103(c)-1
. . Economic Analysis Bureau, to ..... 301.6103(j)(1)-1
. . investigative purposes, to certain officers for .... 301.6103(k)(6)-1
. . Justice Department, to .... 301.6103(a)-2 to 301.6103(p)(2)(B)-1
. . mergers............................... 1.6011-4
. . misconduct .... 301.6103(k)(6)-1
. . procurement of property and services for tax administration purposes .... 301.6103(n)-1; 301.6103(n)-2T

Returns —Cont'd
. *disclosure of information in—Cont'd*
. . reportable transactions 1.6011-4
. . tax administration, for purposes other than .... 301.6103(l)-1
. . United States Customs Service ... 301.6103(l)(14)-1
. Domestic international sales corporations .. 1.6011-2; 301.6686-1
. electing small business corporation 1.6037-1
. . criminal penalties for failure to file ...... 1.6037-1(d)
. . form 1120-S treatment .... 1.6037-1(c)
. . items to be included in return .... 1.6037-1(a)
. . magnetic media (See Magnetic media)
. . time and place for filing return .... 1.6037-1(b)
. employer identification number
. . communications services, excise taxes ... 49.6109-1
. . definitions 301.7701-12
. . Food Stamp Act of 1977, collection for .. 301.6109-1
. estate tax due date 20.6075-1
. estates and trusts .... 1.641(b)-2
. estimated tax .... 1.1502-5; 1.6073-1 to 1.6073-4; 301.6073-1
. excess profits tax cases 301.6105-1
. excise tax
. . federal .... 40.6011(a)-1
. . final return......................... 40.6011(a)-2
. . identifying numbers .... 40.6109(a)-1
. . period covered by returns 41.6101-1; 45.6101-1
. . place for filing 41.6091-1
. extension agreements .... 301.6229(b)-1
. extension of time for filing (See Extension of time for filing return)
. failure to sign return;
. . tax return preparers 1.6695-1
. federal agency officers and employees, generally .... 301.6103(a)-1
. fiduciaries 1.6012-3
. final................................ 31.6011(a)-6
. final returns .... 40.6011(a)-2
. floor stocks .... 40.6011(a)-1
. foreign corporations .... 1.6012-2(g)
. foreign personal holding companies 1.551-4
. foreign trusts with United States beneficiary 404.6048-1
. form and manner of furnishing 1.6707-2T
. foundation excise taxes 53.6011-1
. gambling winnings 1.6011-3
. generation-skipping transfer tax 26.2662-1
. gift tax 25.6011-1
. . contents of return 25.6019-3
. . due date 25.6075-1
. . gift splitting 25.6019-2
. . persons required to file 25.6019-1
. . property, description of 25.6019-4

References are to Reg. § numbers

Returns —Cont'd
. *gift tax—Cont'd*
. . signature 25.6061-1
. guidance on, IRS 301.6011-1
. highway vehicles use tax . . . . . 41.6011(a)-1
. . identifying number 41.6109-1
. . time for filing . . . . . 41.6071(a)-1
. husband and wife (See Spouses)
. identifying number
. . highway vehicles use tax 41.6109-1
. individuals, generally 1.6012-1
. information returns (See Information returns)
. insurance companies . . . . . 1.6012-2(c)
. investment companies 1.852-7; 1.852-8
. joint returns (See Joint returns)
. listed transactions, participation in (See Listed transactions)
. lobbying expenditures, charitable organizations
. . excess lobbying expenditures, excise tax 56.6001-1; 56.6011-1
. magnetic media (See Magnetic media)
. miscellaneous returns 1.6012-4
. monthly or semimonthly
. . place for filing 40.6091-1
. nonresident aliens 1.6013-6; 1.6013-7
. nonresidents of Internal Revenue districts 301.6021-1
. notice 301.6001-1; 301.6110-5
. partners and partnerships . . . 1.6031(a)-1; 1.6050K-1; 1.6081-5; 301.6063-1
. . exception, Commissioner . . . . . 1.6031(a)-1
. pension excise taxes 54.6011-1; 54.6011-1T
. . entity manager tax on prohibited tax shelter transactions . . . . . 54.6011-1T(c)
. . return, statement, or list 54.6011-1
. . reversion of qualified plan assets to employer . . . . . 54.6011-1T(a)
. pension plans . . . . . 301.6104(a)-2 to 301.6104(a)-4
. period covered . . . . . 31.6101-1; 40.6011(a)-1(a)(2); 40.6101-1; 301.6101-1
. personal holding companies . . . . . 1.542-4; 1.547-5; 1.6012-2(b)
. persons required to make returns 301.6012-1
. place for filing returns (See Time and place for filing returns)
. political organizations 1.6012-6
. private foundations . . . 1.6033-3; 53.6011-1; 55.6091-2
. public inspection of material . . . . . 301.6104(a)-1 to 301.6104(a)-6
. quarterly
. . depositaries of government . . . . . 40.6302(c)-1
. . place for filing 40.6091-1
. . time for filing . . . . . 40.6071(a)-1
. real estate investment trusts 1.857-9; 1.857-10; 55.6151-1

Returns —Cont'd
. *real estate investment trusts—Cont'd*
. . excise taxes 55.6011-1
. receipt of payment 301.6316-4
. record of, form and manner of furnishing . . . 1.6707-2T
. reportable transactions defined 1.6011-4
. reproduction of 301.7513-1
. retail excise taxes . . . . . 48.4061(a)-4
. . place for filing 49.6091-1
. . trucks and trailers . . . . . 48.4061(a)-4; 48.6109-1
. self-employment tax returns 1.6017-1; 301.6017-1
. separate returns 1.6013-2
. signature on and verification of returns (See Signature on and verification of returns)
. spouse (See Spouses)
. statistics of income 301.6108-1
. tax shelter registration 301.6111-1T
. taxpayer identifying numbers 1.6109-1; 1.6109-2; 301.6109-1
. third parties 301.6110-4
. time and place for filing returns (See Time and place for filing returns)
. trailers, retail excise taxes . . . . . 48.4061(a)-4
. transfers to avoid income tax 1.1494-1; 1.1494-2
. treaty-based return positions 301.6114-1
. . failure to disclose 301.6712-1
. trucks, retail excise taxes . . . . . 48.4061(a)-4
. unemployment tax returns 301.6106-1
. unrelated business income, organizations with . . . . . 1.6012-2(e)
. verification 20.6065-1
. wagering taxes . . . . . 44.6011(a)-1; 45.6001-6
. . place for filing 44.6091-1
. . stamp taxes 45.6001-11
. . time for filing 44.6071-1
. withholding of information from public inspection . . . . . 301.6104(a)-5
. withholding of tax . . . . 31.6011(a)-4 et seq.; 31.6061-1
. . agricultural labor, wages for . . . . . 31.6011(a)-4(a)(3)
. . annuities . . . . . 31.6011(a)-4(b)(3)
. . armed forces retirement pay . . . . . 31.6011(a)-4(b)(2)
. . backup withholding, payments subject to . . . . . 31.6011(a)-4(b)(5)
. . deferred income under sec. 3405 . . . . . 31.6011(a)-4(b)(4)
. . domestic services, wages for . . . . 31.6011(a)-4(a)(2)
. . gambling . . . . . 31.6011(a)-4(b)(1)
. . nonpayroll payments . . . . . 31.6011(a)-4(b)
. . wages . . . . . 31.6011(a)-4(a); 31.6011(a)-4T(a)
. written determinations and background file documents 301.6110-1; 301.6110-6

Revenue Act of 1962
. generally . . . . . 16A.126-0 to 16A.126-2; 16.3-1

References are to Reg. § numbers

Revenue Act of 1971
. generally 12.8; 12.9
Revenue Act of 1978
. foreclosure property 5.856-1
Reversionary interests
. valuation 1.7520-1; 25.2512-5A
Revocable trusts
. estate, election filed for treatment as part of .. 1.645-1
Revolving credit plans
. installment reporting 1.453A-2
Rewards
. information relating to violation of Internal Revenue laws 301.7623-1
RICs (See Regulated investment companies)
Rollovers
. annuities
. . distributions, eligible rollover .... 1.401(a)(4)-1
. . distributions, withholding on eligible rollover .... 31.3405(c)-1
. deferred compensation plans
. . government plans, to eligible .... 1.457-10(e)
. pension, profit-sharing, and stock bonus plans ..... 1.401(a)(4)-1; 1.401(a)(31)-1; 1.402(a)(5)-1T; 1.402(c)-2; 1.402(f)-1; 31.3405(c)-1
Roth IRAs
. adjusted opening balance defined 1.408A-5
. contributions 1.408A-3
. . special rules .... 1.401(k)-1
. conversions to ...... 1.408A-4; 1.409A-4; 1.409A-4(a)
. . annuity contract surrendered .... 1.409A-4(a)(2)
. . definitions .... 1.409A-4(a)(3)
. . distribution fair market value upon conversion .... 1.409A-4(a)(1)
. . fair market value, determination of ..... 1.409A-4(b)
. . . accumulation method .... 1.409A-4(b)(3)
. . . additional guidance .... 1.409A-4(b)(1)(ii)
. . . effective date .... 1.409A-4(c)
. . . gift tax method .. 1.409A-4(b)(2); 1.409A-4(b)(2)(i); 1.409A-4(b)(2)(ii)
. . . overview .... 1.409A-4(b)(1)
. . . use of alternative methods ...... 1.409A-4(b)(1)(i)
. default elections, special rules for .... 1.408(k)-1(f)
. definitions concerning 1.408A-8
. designated account defined .... 1.401(k)-6
. direct rollovers, special rules for .... 1.408(k)-1(f)
. distributions 1.408A-6
. establishing 1.408A-2
. recharacterized contributions 1.408A-5
. reporting requirements 1.408A-7
Royalties
. backup withholding .... 31.3406(b)(3)-4
. gross income 1.61-8
. information returns 1.6050N-1
Royalties —Cont'd
. natural resources 1.543-12; 1.612-3; 1.613A-3
. sources within or without United States 1.861-5
RRTA (See Railroad Retirement Tax Act)
Rules of general application
. definitions .... 1.141-1 et seq.
Rural electric cooperatives
. cash or deferred arrangements .... 1.401(k)-1
Rural property
. gain or loss 1.1038-1; 1.1038-2

S

S corporations (See also Small business corporations)
. accounting periods
. . tax year (See subhead tax year)
. accumulated adjustments account 1.1368-2
. affiliated subsidiaries, dividends from 1.1362-8
. capital gains look-through rule
. . sales or exchanges of interest in S corporation .... 1.1(h)-1
. conversions
. . pro rata shares, computation of 1.1377-1
. . QSST to ESBT 1.1361-1
. defined 1.1361-1
. distributions 1.1368-1
. . examples 1.1368-3
. dividends 18.1371-1
. domestic production activities (See Domestic production activities subhead pass-thru entities)
. electing small business trusts (See Electing small business trusts)
. elections and consents 1.1362-6
. employee stock ownership plans (ESOPs)
. . allocation of securities, prohibited .... 1.409(p)-1
. generally 301.6241-1T
. indebtedness to shareholders, basis adjustment
. . generally 1.1367-2
. . reduction in basis of indebtedness ...... 1.1367-2(b)
. . restoration of basis .... 1.1367-2(c)
. . timing of effective date .... 1.1367-2(d)
. items 301.6245-1T
. net unrealized built-in gain 1.1374-3
. prior elections and terminations 18.1379-1
. pro rata shares
. . character of 1.1366-1
. . computation of 1.1377-1
. . officer signature on election statement, verification of 1.1377-1
. . post-termination transition periods 1.1377-2
. . terminate year, election to .... 1.1377-1(b)
. QSub elections 1.1361-3; 1.1361-4

References are to Reg. § numbers

S corporations (See also Small business corporations) —Cont'd
. *QSub elections—Cont'd*
. . termination of 1.1361-5
. qualified production activities; section 199 deduction .... 1.199-5(c)
. research expenditures 1.41-7
. revocation of S election 1.1362-6
. section 444 election, procedures for making 1.1378-1
. section 1374(d)(8) transactions . . 1.1374-8; 1.1374-8T
. shareholders
. . carryover of disallowed losses and deductions 1.1366-2
. . deduction limitations of passthrough items of corporation to 1.1366-2
. . determination of shareholder items 1.1366-1
. . family group treatment.................. 1.1366-3
. . gross income of 1.1366-1
. . passthrough of items of corporation to, limitations on 1.1366-4
. shareholder's consents 1.1362-6
. short period tax returns 1.1378-1
. special rules for elections, consents, and refusals 18.1379-2
. Subchapter S Revision Act of 1982 .... 18.0 to 18.1379-2
. subsidiaries, definitions concerning 1.1361-2
. tax attributes, reduction of
. . allocation of excess losses or deductions .... 1.108-7(d)(2)
. . . generally .... 1.108-7(d)(2)(i)
. . . multiple shareholders .... 1.108-7(d)(2)(ii)
. . . terminating shareholders .... 1.108-7(d)(2)(iii)
. . carryovers and carrybacks .... 1.108-7(b)
. . character of excess losses or deduction allocated to a shareholder .... 1.108-7(d)(3)
. . effective date .... 1.108-7(f)
. . examples .... 1.108-7(e)
. . generally .... 1.108-7(a); 1.108-7(d)(1)
. . information requirements .... 1.108-7(d)(4)
. . special rules .... 1.108-7(d)
. . transactions to which section 381 applies .... 1.108-7(c)
. tax year
. . other than required, election . . . 1.444-1T to 1.444-3T
. . . required payments ...... 1.7519-0T to 1.7519-3T
. . . tiered structure entities 1.444-2T
. . tiered structure status 1.444-2T
. taxable mortgage pools .... 301.7701(i)-4
. taxable year 1.1378-1
. termination of election 1.1362-2
. termination year treatment 1.1362-3
. tiered structure status 1.444-2T

Safe harbor leases
. generally .... 1.168(f)(8)-1T; 5f.168(f)(8)-1

Safety testing organizations
. generally .... 1.501(c)(3)-1

Salary reduction agreements
. defined for employment taxes ...... 31.3121(a)(5)-1T
. employer contributions to purchase Sec. 403(b) contract .... 1.402(g)(3)-1

Sales and transfers (See also Reorganization; Successor corporations)
. appreciated property transfers............... 1.84-1
. assets.................... 301.6901-1; 301.6902-1
. avoidance of income tax, use of transfer for 1.1491-1; 1.1494-2
. basis for gain or loss..................... 1.1016-2
. capital gains and losses (See Capital gains and losses)
. charitable (See Charitable transfers)
. corporate organizations and reorganizations . . 1.351-1 et seq.
. corporation 1.742-2
. death, on (See Estates and trusts)
. deductions disallowed .... 1.267(a)-1 et seq.
. deferred exchanges .... 1.1031(k)-1
. disclaimed property...................... 20.2046-1
. DISCs (See Domestic international sales corporations)
. exemption for persons over age 55 from sale or residence gains .... 1.121-1 to 1.121-5
. . reduced exclusion 1.121-3
. foreign corporations . . . 1.367(a)-1T et seq.; 1.921-2 et seq.
. . information returns 1.6038B-1; 1.6038B-1T
. foreign tax credit .... 1.904(b)-3
. foreign trust 1.1493-1
. gain or loss (See Gain or loss)
. holding period for section 83 property.......... 1.83-4
. income from sources within or without United States 1.861-6; 1.861-7; 1.863-3; 1.864-1
. installment of sales .... 15A.453-0 to 15A.453-1
. insufficient consideration, for 20.2043-1
. jointly-owned property
. . foreign corporations information returns 1.6038B-1; 1.6038B-1T
. life estates, transfers with retained 20.2036-1
. life insurance endowments or annuities 1.72-10
. like-kind exchanges .... 1.1031(a)-1 et seq.
. marital deduction (See Marital deduction)
. natural resources .... 1.631-1 to 1.631-3
. nonresident aliens, gift tax on 25.2511-3
. nontaxable transfers 1.1492-1
. outside the United States
. . information returns.................... 1.6041A-1
. partners and partnerships 1.741-1; 1.742-1
. private foundations 1.507-2; 1.507-3; 1.507-8

References are to Reg. § numbers

Sales and transfers (See also Reorganization; Successor corporations) —Cont'd
. private purposes, charitable purposes combined 20.2055-2
. records and reports
. . Commission orders, corporations subject to .... 1.1081-11(b)
. . holders of stock or securities, significant .... 1.1081-11(a)
. . publicly traded stock defined .... 1.1081-11(d)
. . significant holder defined .... 1.1081-11(d)
. . substantiation information, retaining .... 1.1081-11(e)
. . system groups, sales by members of .... 1.1081-11(c)
. residential property sales .... 1.121-1 to 1.121-5; 1.165-9; 1.1033(a)-3; 1.1034-1; 1.1038-2
. retail commission salesman .... 31.3402(j)-1
. returns 1.1494-1; 1.1494-2
. seizure of property for collection of taxes (See Seizure of property)
. services, transfers in connection with .. 1.83-1 et seq.; 13.1
. . debt, forgiveness of 1.83-4
. . deduction allowance 1.83-6
. . deduction by employer 1.83-6
. . definitions relating to 1.83-3
. . election to include in gross income 1.83-2
. . employee 1.83-7
. . holding periods 1.83-4
. . independent contractor 1.83-7
. . nonqualified stock options, taxation of 1.83-7
. . restrictions, nonlapsing 1.83-5
. . special rules 1.83-4
. . transitional rules 1.83-8
. . valuation of section 83 property 1.83-5
. Tax Court 301.7505-1
. valuation of section 83 property 1.83-5
. wash sales (See Wash Sales)

Sales for resale (See Resale)

Salvage value
. depreciation .... 1.167(f)-1

Saturdays
. time for performance of act where last day falls on Saturday 301.7503-1

Savings banks
. mutual savings bank (See Mutual savings banks)

Scholarships and fellowships
. allocation of gross income under section 863 .... 1.863-1(d)
. exemptions .... 1.117-1 to 1.117-5
. nonresident aliens
. . withholding tax exemption 1.1441-4

School buses
. diesel and special motor fuels tax, credits or payments to purchaser

School buses —Cont'd
. *diesel and special motor fuels tax, credits or payments to purchaser —Cont'd*
. . applicable laws 48.6427-4
. . generally 48.6427-2
. . limitations on 48.6427-6
. . recordkeeping requirements 48.6427-5
. . time for filing claims 48.6427-3
. manufacturers excise tax, exempt sales
. . tires, tubes and tread rubber 48.4221-8

Schools and educational institutions
. annuity contract distributions .... 1.403(b)-3
. exemptions .... 1.117-1 to 1.117-5; 1.127-1; 1.127-2; 1.501(c)(3)-1
. itemized deductions 1.162-5
. pension, profit-sharing, and stock bonus plans .... 1.403(b)-1
. . distribution requirements .... 1.403(b)-3
. students 1.170A-2; 1.871-9
. withholding .... 31.3401(a)(18)-1

Scientific organizations
. exemption .... 1.501(c)(3)-1

Seals, official
. description and illustration 301.7514-1

Seamen
. nonresident aliens 1.871-3

SEC (See Securities and Exchange Commission (SEC) orders)

Second tier excise taxes
. generally .... 53.4961-1 to 53.4963-1

Secretary of Agriculture
. Food Stamp Act of 1977, employer identification number collection for 301.6109-1

Secretary of Treasury or delegate
. definitions 301.7701-9

Section 23 credit
. adjusted basis 1.1016-5

Section 38 property (See also Investment credit)
. adjusted basis 1.1016-5
. defined 1.48-1

Section 179 property (See Expensing in lieu of depreciation)

Section 199 deduction
. domestic production activities (See Domestic production activities)
. domestic production gross receipts (See Domestic production gross receipts)

Section 247 deduction
. consolidated returns 1.1502-27

Section 306 stock
. corporate distributions and adjustments 1.306-3
. defined 1.306-3

References are to Reg. § numbers

Section 333 elections (See Distributions by corporations)

Section 367 transactions
. information returns 1.6038B-1T; 1.6038B-1TT

Section 403(b) annuities
. generally 20.2039-2

Section 411(d)(6) protected benefits
. generally .... 1.411(d)-4

Section 444 election
. generally .... 1.444-1T to 1.444-3T
. required payments .... 1.7519-0T to 1.7519-3T

Section 467 rental agreements (See Rental agreements, Section 467)

Section 902 corporations
. foreign tax credit
. . earnings and profits, distributions
. . . non-look through pools in post 2002 taxable years .... 1.904-7T(f)
. . . taxable years beginnings Jan. 1. 2007 .... 1.904-7T(g)
. noncontrolled section 902 corporation ..... 1.904-4(e)

Section 988 transactions (See Foreign currency)

Section 1231 gains or losses
. consolidated returns 1.1502-23; 1.1502-23A

Section 1244 stock
. capital gains and losses .... 1.1244(c)-1

Section 1245 property
. capital gains and losses 1.1245-3
. depreciation
. . change in method .... 1.167(e)-1(c)

Section 1296 stock
. mark to market election 1.1296-1

Securities
. backup withholding on sales .... 31.3406(b)(3)-2
. bad debts .... 1.582-1; 301.6511(d)-1
. banks 1.582-1
. bonds (See Bonds)
. corporate organizations and reorganizations . . 1.355-1 to 1.355-7
. dealers (See Securities dealers)
. gross income period 1.75-1
. held for investment .... 1.475(b)-1
. information returns 1.6045-1
. itemized deductions for both the security 1.165-5
. mark-to-market (See Mark-to-market)
. personal holding companies 1.544-5
. stock (See Stock)
. straddle positions ...... 1.1092(b)-2T to 1.1092(b)-5T
. synthetic debt instruments .... 1.475(c)-2(b)
. wash sales (See Wash Sales)
. worthless, refund or credit for ....301.6511(d)-1

Securities and Exchange Commission (SEC) orders
. basis for .... 1.1082-1 et seq
. gain or loss .... 1.1081-1 et seq.

Securities dealers
. dealer-customer relationships .... 1.475(c)-1
. definitions .... 1.475(c)-1
. gain or loss as factor in definition of .... 1.475(d)-1
. generally 1.471-5; 1.1236-1
. information returns 1.6045-1
. life insurance products, sellers of ...... 1.475(c)-1(d)
. mark-to-market exemption .... 1.475(b)-1
. negligible sales .... 1.475(c)-1(c)
. nonfinancial goods and services, sellers of .... 1.475(c)-1(b)
. notional principal contracts and derivatives .... 1.475(b)-1(c)
. . treatment, ordinary .... 1.475(d)-1(b)
. valuation safe harbor
. . applicable financial statement ...... 1.475(a)-4(h)(1)
. . certified audited financial statement .... 1.475(a)-4(h)(7)
. . compliance with other rules .... 1.475(a)-4(e)
. . consolidated groups .... 1.475(a)-4(h)(5)
. . dealer business model as basis .... 1.475(a)-4(a)(2)
. . different values, use of .... 1.475(a)-4(m)
. . eligible method defined .... 1.475(a)-4(d)
. . eligible position defined .... 1.475(a)-4(g)
. . eligible taxpayer defined .... 1.475(a)-4(c)
. . financial statement of equal priority .... 1.475(a)-4(h)(4)
. . generally .... 1.475(a)-4
. . primary financial statement .... 1.475(a)-4(h)(2)
. . retention and production of records ... 1.475(a)-4(k)
. . safe harbor general rule .... 1.475(a)-4(b)
. . significant business use .... 1.475(a)-4(j)
. . supplement or amendment to a financial statement .... 1.475(a)-4(h)(6)

Security interest
. liens .... 301.6323(a)-1

Segregated or transferred assets
. Tax Court 301.7507-3

Seizure of property
. certificate of sale of personal property and deed of real property 301.6338-1; 301.6339-1
. Collection Due Process hearing 301.6320-1; 301.6330-1
. exempt property ....301.6334-1 to 301.6334-4
. expense of levy and sale 301.6341-1
. generally .... 301.6331-1 et seq.; 301.7321-1; 301.7322-1
. levy and distraint 301.6331-1; 301.6331-2; 301.6341-1; 301.6342-1; 301.6343-1
. . notice and opportunity for hearing prior to levy 301.6330-1

References are to Reg. § numbers

Seizure of property —Cont'd
. *levy and distraint—Cont'd*
. . procedures and restrictions on 301.6331-2
. . recovery of damages in certain cases . . . 301.7426-2
. . restriction on levy while installment agreements are pending or in effect 301.6331-4
. . substitute sale proceeds . . . . 301.7426-1(a)(3)
. . substitution of value . . . . 301.7426-1(a)(4)
. . surplus proceeds . . . . 301.7426-1(a)(2)
. . wrongful levy 301.7426-2
. . . on person other than taxpayer . . . . . . 301.7426-1(a)
. notice of seizure 301.6335-1
. perishable goods 301.6336-1; 301.7324-1
. proceeds of levy 301.6342-1
. production of books 301.6333-1
. records of sale 301.6340-1
. redemption of property 301.6337-1
. release of levy and return of property 301.6343-1
. return of wrongfully levied property 301.6343-3
. sale of property, generally 301.6335-1
. surrender of property 301.6332-1; 301.6332-2
. third party property
. . official defined . . . . 301.6503(f)-1(c)
. . wrongful lien for substitution of value, discharge of . . . . 301.6503(f)-1(b)
. . wrongful seizure . . . . 301.6503(f)-1(a)
. wages, salary, and other income 301.6334-2

Self-constructed assets
. capitalization of costs 1.263A-2

Self-dealing
. excise taxes . . . . 53.4941(a)-1 to 53.4941(f)-1
. foundation manager 301.7454-2
. private foundations . . . . . . 53.4941(d)-2; 301.6511(f)-1

Self-employment income
. community income . . . . 1.1402(a)-8
. dividends and interest . . . . 1.1402(a)-5
. erroneously reported net earnings . . . . 1.1402(g)-1
. farmers . . . . 1.1402(a)-13 to 1.1402(a)-16
. gain or loss from disposition of property . . . 1.1402(a)-6
. generally . . . . 1.1401-1 et seq.; 1.1402(a)-1 et seq.
. insurance . . . . 1.72-17A; 1.72-18; 1.1402(c)-7; 1.1402(h)-1
. life insurance endowments or annuities 1.72-17A; 1.72-18
. ministers and members of religious orders . . . . 1.1402(a)-11; 1.1402(c)-5; 1.1402(c)-7; 1.1402(e)-2A to 1.1402(e)-4A; 1.1402(h)-1
. net earnings
. . computation . . . . 1.1402(a)-2; 1.1402(a)-3
. . defined . . . . 1.1402(a)-1
. net operating loss deduction . . . . 1.1402(a)-7
. partnerships . . . . 1.1402(a)-17; 1.1402(f)-1

Self-employment income —Cont'd
. pension, profit-sharing, and stock bonus plans . . . . . 1.401(e)-1; 1.401(e)-2; 1.401(e)-5; 1.401(e)-6; 1.401-10; 1.401-11; 1.404(e)-1; 1.404(e)-1A
. pension excise taxes 54.4972-1
. personal exemption . . . . 1.1402(a)-10
. possessions of United States . . . . 1.1402(a)-9; 1.1402(a)-12
. professions . . . . 1.1402(c)-6
. public office . . . . 1.1402(c)-2
. Puerto Rico . . . . 1.1402(a)-9
. railroad retirement system, individuals covered under . . . . 1.1402(c)-4
. rentals from real estate . . . . 1.1402(a)-4
. retirement payments to retired partners . . . . 1.1402(a)-17
. returns 1.6017-1; 301.6017-1
. trade or business . . . . 1.1402(c)-1

Self-employment tax (See Self-employment income)

Self-insured medical reimbursement plan
. exemptions 1.105-11

Senators, U.S.
. travel expenses 5e.274-8

Separate line of business
. pension, profit-sharing, and stock bonus plans . . . . 1.414(r)-5

Separate maintenance (See Alimony or separate maintenance)

Separate share rule (See Estates and trusts)

Separate taxable income
. consolidated returns . . . . 1.1502-12 et seq.

Service providers
. nonaccrual of certain amounts by (See Accounting methods subhead service providers, nonaccrual of certain amounts by)

Services, performances of
. controlled groups 1.482-2
. taxable income determination
. . rendering of services . . . . 1.482-2T(b)

Services, transfers in connection with (See Sales and transfers)

Services cost method
. arm's length transactions; determination of taxable income . . . . 1.482-9T(b)

Settlement funds
. appraisal prior to transfer 1.468B-3
. designated settlement funds 1.468B
. distributions to claimants 1.468B-4
. gross income 1.468B-2
. partnership interest held in fund 1.468B-2
. qualified funds, requirements for 1.468B-1
. subpart E trust, election to treat as . . . . 1.468B-1(k)
. taxation of qualified funds 1.468B-2
. transfers 1.468B-3

References are to Reg. § numbers

Settlement funds —Cont'd
. transitional rules 1.468B-5
Settlements
. consistency .... 301.6224(c)-3
. gift tax, exemption from 25.2516-2
. partnership settlement agreements ..... 301.6224(c)-3
. partnerships
. . partial, special rule .... 301.6229(f)-1
. structured settlement factoring transactions (See Structured settlement factoring transactions)
Shareholders (See also specific business entity)
. avoidance of income tax on shareholder, corporation used for .... 1.531-1 et seq.
. DISCs 1.995-1
. distributive share 1.704-1
. domestic corporations
. . foreign tax credit 1.902-1; 1.902-1T
. foreign corporations 1.951-1
. foreign sales corporations, distributions from .... 1.926(a)-1; 1.926(a)-1T
. foreign tax credit
. . domestic corporation shareholder 1.902-1; 1.902-1T
. investment companies 1.852-4; 1.854-2
. liquidations, minority interest 1.332-5
. pension, profit-sharing, and stock bonus plans .... 1.401(e)-6
. real estate investment trusts 1.857-6
. terminal railroad corporations ..... 1.281-1 to 1.281-4
. termination of interests, distributions by corporations 1.302-4
Ships and shipping (See also Motorboats; Vessels)
. covered voyages, excise taxes 43-4471-1T
. foreign corporations 1.955A-1; 1.955A-2
. generally ... 1.861-15; 1.861-16; 1.871-3; 1.6050A-1; 31.3401(a)(17)-1; 301.6050A-1
. international operation
. . exclusion of income 1.883-1; 1.883-1T
Shopping news distributors
. withholding .... 31.3401(a)(10)-1
Short sales
. capital gains and losses 1.1233-1
Short tax year
. change of annual accounting period
. . computation of tax 1.443-1
. corporations 1.6655-3
. . accumulated taxable income 1.536-1
. estimated tax
. . amount due for required installment..... 1.6655-5(b)
. . annualized income or seasonal installment method .... 1.6655-5(g)
. . exceptions to payments............... 1.6655-5(b)
. . 52 or 53 week taxable year............ 1.6655-5(f)
. . generally 1.6655-5

Short tax year —Cont'd
. *estimated tax —Cont'd*
. . installment due dates................. 1.6655-5(c)
. individuals 1.6654-3
. . personal exemption, adjustment in deduction for 1.443-1
. life insurance companies 1.818-5
. returns for period of less than 12 months 1.443-1
. S corporation changing taxable year........ 1.1378-1
Shortfall method
. ERISA .... 1.412(c)(1)-2
Sickness benefits
. accident and health plans (See Accident and health plans)
. deferral of sick, vacation and back pay ..... 1.457-4(d)
. exempt organizations .... 1.501(c)(9)-3
. generally 1.104-1
. Social security taxes 32.1
. withholding .... 31.3402(o)-3; 31.6051-3
Signature verification
. pro rata share election, S corporation 1.1377-1
. returns
. . generally ...... 1.6061-1 to 1.6065-1; 31.6065(a)-1; 301.6061-1 to 301.6065-1
. . partnership documents and returns 1.6063-1
Situs trusts
. pension, profit-sharing, and stock bonus plans .... 1.402(c)-1
Slot machines
. Tax Reform Act of 1976 .... 7.6041-1
Small business corporations (See also S corporations)
. activities not engaged in for profit
. . election to postpone determination of 12.9
. alternative minimum tax 1.58-4
. capital gains and losses .... 1.1242-1; 1.1243-1; 1.1244(a)-1 to 1.1244(e)-1
. classes of stock 1.1361-1
. defined 1.1361-1
. information returns 1.6037-1; 301.6037-1
. investment credit 1.47-4; 1.48-5
. nonresident alien shareholders or estate 1.1361-1
. shareholders for qualification as, number of 1.1361-1
. trusts 1.1361-1
Small business investment companies 1.586-1; 1.586-2; 1.1242-1; 1.1243-1
Small business stock
. capital gains and losses 1.1245-3
. qualified small business stock (See Qualified small business stock)
Small group health plans
. special rules 54.9831-1

References are to Reg. § numbers

Small issuer exception to rebate requirement 1.148-8

Social clubs
. exempt organizations . . . . . 1.501(c)(7)-1

Social Security
. generally . . . . . 1.31-2; 301.6511(a)-1

Social Security benefit number as identifying number
. definition 301.7701-11

Social security taxes
. accidental disability 32.1
. sickness benefits 32.1

Software
. classification of transactions involving 1.861-18

Soil and water conservation expenditures
. itemized deductions . . . . . 1.175-1 to 1.175-7

Solid waste disposal facilities
. bonds 17.1

Sound recordings
. property produced by taxpayer, rules concerning 1.263A-2

Space and ocean activity
. defined . . . . . 1.863-8(d)
. generally . . . . . 1.863-8(a)
. gross income sources . . . . . 1.863-8(b)
. partnerships . . . . . 1.863-8(e)
. reporting and documentation . . . . . 1.863-8(g)
. taxable income . . . . . 1.863-8(c)

Special enrollment examination fee
. amount of fee . . . . . 300.4(b)
. applicability . . . . . 300.4(a)
. liability for fee . . . . . 300.4(c)

Special motor fuels tax (See Diesel and special motor fuels tax)

Split-dollar life insurance arrangements
. amounts received under contract . . . . . 1.61-22(e)
. defined . . . . . 1.61-22(b)
. distributions by corporations . . . . . 1.301-1(q)
. economic benefits of . . . . . 1.61-22(d)
. generally 1.61-22
. loans (See Split-dollar loans)
. taxation 1.61-22
. transfers . . . . . 1.61-22(g)

Split-dollar loans 1.7872-15
. adjustments for interest paid at less than the stated rate
. . application . . . . . 1.7872-15(h)(1)
. . certain split-dollar term loans . . . . . 1.7872-15(h)(1)(ii)
. . deferral charge . . . . . 1.7872-15(h)(4)
. . . split-dollar demand loan . . . . . 1.7872-15(h)(4)(ii)
. . . split-dollar term loan . . . . . 1.7872-15(h)(4)(i)
. . examples . . . . . 1.7872-15(h)(5)

Split-dollar loans—Cont'd
. *adjustments for interest paid at less than the stated rate —Cont'd*
. . generally . . . . . 1.7872-15(h)(1)(i)
. . payments treated as a waiver, cancellation, or forgiveness . . . . . 1.7872-15(h)(1)(iii)
. . split-dollar demand loans . . . . . 1.7872-15(h)(3)
. . split-dollar term loans . . . . . 1.7872-15(h)(2)
. . treatment of certain nonrecourse spli-dollar loans . . . . . 1.7872-15(h)(1)(iv)
. application of section 7872 . . . . . 1.7872-15(j)(4)
. . adjustment upon the resolution of contingent payment . . . . . 1.7872-15(j)(4)(ii)
. . below-market status, determination of . . . . . 1.7872-15(j)(4)(i)
. . examples . . . . . 1.7872-15(j)(5)
. below-market loans . . . . . 1.7872-15(e); 1.7872-15(e)(i)
. . demand loans
. . . significant-effect split-dollar loans . . . . . 1.7872-15(e)(3)
. . . sufficient interest test . . . . . 1.7872-15(e)(3)(ii)
. . indirect split dollar loans
. . . application . . . . . 1.7872-15(e)(2)(ii)
. . . examples . . . . . 1.7872-15(e)(2)(iv)
. . . generally . . . . . 1.7872-15(e)(2)(i)
. . . limitations on investment interest for purposes of section 163(d) . . . . . 1.7872-15(e)(2)(iii)
. . limited application . . . 1.7872-15(e)(3)(iii)(B)(5)(iv)(D)
. . significant-effect split-dollar loans . . 1.7872-15(e)(ii)
. . special rules . . . . . 1.7872-15(e)(3)(iii)(B)(5)(iv); 1.7872-15(e)(3)(iii)(B)(5)(iv)(A); 1.7872-15(e)(3)(iii)(B)(5)(vi)
. . term loans (See subhead term loans)
. certain contingencies . . . . . 1.7872-15(j)(2)(i)
. certain interest provisions disregarded . . . . . 1.7872-15(a)(4)
. . examples . . . . . 1.7872-15(a)(4)(ii)
. . generally . . . . . 1.7872-15(a)(4)(i)
. contingent payments . . . . 1.7872-15(j); 1.7872-15(j)(3)
. . generally . . . . . 1.7872-15(j)(3)(i)
. . negative adjustments . . . . . 1.7872-15(j)(3)(iii)
. . projected payment schedule . . . . . 1.7872-15(j)(3)(ii)
. . . borrower / lender consistency . . . . . 1.7872-15(j)(3)(ii)(E)
. . . certain split-dollar term loans conditioned on the future performance of substantial services by an individual . . . . . 1.7872-15(j)(3)(ii)(C)
. . . demand loans . . . . . 1.7872-15(j)(3)(ii)(D)
. . . determination of schedule . . . 1.7872-15(j)(3)(ii)(A)
. death of an individual, payable not later than . . . . . 1.7872-15(e)(3)(iii)(B)(5)(ii)
. . applicability . . . . . 1.7872-15(e)(3)(iii)(B)(5)(ii)(A)
. . retirement and reissuance of loan . . . . . 1.7872-15(e)(3)(iii)(B)(5)(ii)(D)
. . term of loan . . . . . 1.7872-15(e)(3)(iii)(B)(5)(ii)(C)
. . treatment of loan . . . . 1.7872-15(e)(3)(iii)(B)(5)(ii)(B)

References are to Reg. § numbers

Split-dollar loans—Cont'd
. defined . . . . 1.7872-15(b)
. demand loans
. . generally . . . . 1.7872-15(e)(3)(i)
. . special rules . . . . 1.7872-15(e)(3)(iii)(B)(5); 1.7872-15(e)(3)(iii)(B)(5)(i)
. demand loans, imputations . . . . 1.7872-15(e)(3)(iii)
. . amount of forgone interest . . . 1.7872-15(e)(3)(iii)(A)
. . timing of transfers of forgone interest . . . . 1.7872-15(e)(3)(iii)(B); 1.7872-15(e)(3)(iii)(B)(1)
. . . death, liquidation, or termination of the borrower . . . . 1.7872-15(e)(3)(iii)(B)(2)
. . . repayment of below-market split dollar loan . . . . 1.7872-15(e)(3)(iii)(B)(3)
. exceptions . . . . 1.7872-15(j)(2); 1.7872-15(j)(2)(iv)
. exchange facilitator under sec. 1.468B-6, to 1.7872-16
. . AFR for exchange facilitator loans . . . . 1.7872-16(d)
. . approximate method, use of . . . . 1.7872-16(e)
. . compensation-related loan treatment . . . 1.7872-16(c)
. . demand loan treatment . . . . 1.7872-16(b)
. . effective date . . . . 1.7872-16(g)
. . example . . . . 1.7872-16(h)
. . exchange facilitator loans . . . . 1.7872-16(a)
. . exemption for certain below-market exchange facilitator loans . . . . 1.7872-16(f)
. future performance of substantial services by and individual . . . . 1.7872-15(e)(3)(iii)(B)(5)(iii)
. . applicability . . . . 1.7872-15(e)(3)(iii)(B)(5)(iii)(A); 1.7872-15(e)(3)(iii)(B)(5)(iii)(A)(1)
. . . exception . . . . 1.7872-15(e)(3)(iii)(B)(5)(iii)(A)(2)
. . retirement and issuance of loan . . . . 1.7872-15(e)(3)(iii)(B)(5)(iii)(D)
. . term of loan . . . . 1.7872-15(e)(3)(iii)(B)(5)(iii)(C)
. . treatment of loan . . . . 1.7872-15(e)(3)(iii)(B)(5)(iii)(B)
. general rules . . . . 1.7872-15(a)(1)
. . effective date . . . . 1.7872-15(n)(1); 1.7872-15(n)(2)
. generally . . . 1.7872-15; 1.7872-15(a); 1.7872-15(j)(1)
. insolvency and default . . . . 1.7872-15(j)(2)(ii)
. insurance arrangements generally (See Split-dollar insurance arrangements)
. interest deductions . . . . 1.7872-15(c)
. interest deductions for split-dollar loans . . . . 1.7872-15(c)
. loan treatment . . . . 1.7872-15(a)(2)
. no de minimis exceptions . . . . 1.7872-15(a)(3)
. nonrecourse payments . . . . 1.7872-15(d); 1.7872-15(d)(1)
. . contingent payments . . . . 1.7872-15(d)(2); 1.7872-15(d)(2)(i)
. . written representation
. . . time and manner for providing written representation . . . . 1.7872-15(d)(2)(ii)
. payment ordering rule

Split-dollar loans—Cont'd
. *payment ordering rule —Cont'd*
. . applicability . . . . 1.7872-15(g)(2); 1.7872-15(g)(2)(i)
. . . interest rate restrictions . . . . 1.7872-15(g)(2)(ii)
. . . testing for sufficient interest . . . . 1.7872-15(g)(3)
. . example . . . . 1.7872-15(g)(5)
. . generally . . . . 1.7872-15(g)(1)
. . interest accruals and imputed transfers . . . . 1.7872-15(g)(4)
. . testing for sufficient interest
. . . demand loan . . . . 1.7872-15(g)(3)(i)
. . . term loan . . . . 1.7872-15(g)(3)(ii)
. projected payment schedule
. . death of individual, loans payable upon . . . . 1.7872-15(j)(3)(ii)(B)
. remote and incidental contingencies . . . . 1.7872-15(j)(2)(iii)
. repayments received by a lender . . . . 1.7872-15(m)
. stated interest and OID . . . . 1.7872-15(f)
. . generally . . . . 1.7872-15(f)(1)
. . term, payment schedule, yield . . . . 1.7872-15(f)(2)
. term certain and another specified date, payable on the later of a . . . . 1.7872-15(e)(3)(iii)(B)(5)(v)
. . applicability . . . . 1.7872-15(e)(3)(iii)(B)(5)(v)(A)
. . retirement and reissuance . . . . 1.7872-15(e)(3)(iii)(B)(5)(v)(C)
. . treatment of a loan . . . 1.7872-15(e)(3)(iii)(B)(5)(v)(B)
. . . appropriate AFR . . . . 1.7872-15(e)(3)(iii)(B)(5)(v)(B)(3)
. . . generally . . . . 1.7872-15(e)(3)(iii)(B)(5)(v)(B)(2)
. . . term of the loan . . . . 1.7872-15(e)(3)(iii)(B)(5)(v)(B)(2)
. term loans . . . . 1.7872-15(e)(3)(iii)(B)(4)(i)
. . determining loan term . . 1.7872-15(e)(3)(iii)(B)(4)(iii)
. . . change in circumstances . . . . 1.7872-15(e)(3)(iii)(B)(4)(iii)(B)(2)
. . . death of an individual, payable on . . . . 1.7872-15(e)(3)(iii)(B)(4)(iii)(D)
. . . examples . . . . 1.7872-15(e)(3)(iii)(B)(4)(iii)(B)(3)
. . . future performance of substantial services by an individual as condition . . . . 1.7872-15(e)(3)(iii)(B)(4)(iii)(E)
. . . generally . . . . 1.7872-15(e)(3)(iii)(B)(4)(iii)(A)
. . . payment schedule that minimizes yield . . . . 1.7872-15(e)(3)(iii)(B)(4)(iii)(B)(1)
. . . special rules for certain options . . . . 1.7872-15(e)(3)(iii)(B)(4)(iii)(B)
. . . variable rate of interest, providing . . . . 1.7872-15(e)(3)(iii)(B)(4)(iii)(C)
. . sufficient interest test . . . . 1.7872-15(e)(3)(iii)(B)(4)(ii)
. term of loan . . . . 1.7872-15(e)(3)(iii)(B)(5)(iv)(C)
. treatment of loan . . . . 1.7872-15(e)(3)(iii)(B)(5)(iv)(B)

Sponsorship payments
. exempt organization unrelated trade or business 1.513-4

References are to Reg. § numbers

Sporting goods
. manufacturers excise taxes
. . bows and arrows ..... 48.4161(b)-1 to 48.4161(b)-5
. . fishing equipment ..... 48.4161(a)-1 to 48.4161(a)-5

Spouses
. alimony or separate maintenance (See Alimony or separate maintenance)
. education tax credits 1.25A-1
. foreign tax credit 1.904-3; 1.911-5
. gain or loss or transfer of property 1.1041-1T
. gift splitting 25.2513-1
. income earned abroad 1.911-5
. itemized deductions 1.214A-4
. joint interests, gift of ..... 25.2523(d)-1
. joint returns (See Joint returns)
. joint tenancy (See Joint tenancy; Tenancies by entirety)
. marital deduction (See Marital deduction)
. newly married couples
. . change in annual accounting period 1.442-1
. partnership items ..... 301.6231(a)(12)-1
. personal exemptions 1.152-3; 1.152-4; 1.152-4T; 1.153-1
. power of appointment in donee ..... 25.2523(e)-1
. property settlements 25.2516-1
. returns
. . joint returns (See Joint returns)
. . separate, joint return after filing of 1.6013-2
. terminable interest property, gift of ..... 25.2523(b)-1
. unidentified assets, interest in ..... 25.2523(c)-1
. withholding ..... 31.3402(l)-1

Stamp taxes
. redemption of stamps 301.6805-1
. wagering taxes
. . generally ..... 44.4901-1 et seq.
. . payment of tax 44.4901-1

Stapled foreign corporations
. assessment of tax ..... 1.269B-1(f)
. changes in status ..... 1.269B-1(c)
. collection of tax ..... 1.269B-1(f)
. defined ..... 1.269B-1(b)
. domestic corporation, treatment as ..... 1.269B-1(a)
. foreign owned exception to treatment as domestic corporation ..... 1.269B-1(a)
. includible corporations ..... 1.269B-1(d)
. subjectivity to tax 1.269B-
. U.S. treaties ..... 1.269B-1(e)

Start-up expenditures
. amortization, election 1.195-1
. election to amortize 1.195-1T
. . effective dates ..... 1.195-1T(d)
. . examples ..... 1.195-1T(c)
. . expenditures of $5,000 or less ..... 1.195-1T(c)(1)

Start-up expenditures —Cont'd
. *election to amortize—Cont'd*
. . expenditures of more than $5,000 but less than or equal to $50,000 ..... 1.195-1T(c)(2)
. . expenditures of more than $50,000 but less than or equal to $55,000 ..... 1.195-1T(c)(5)
. . expenditures of more than $55,000 ..... 1.195-1T(c)(6)
. . expiration date ..... 1.195-1T(e)
. . generally ..... 1.195-1T(a)
. . subsequent change in the characterization of an item ..... 1.195-1T(c)(3)
. . subsequent redetermination of year in which business begins ..... 1.195-1T(c)(4)
. . time and manner of making election ..... 1.195-1T(b)

State and local governments
. employee retirement plans
. . reporting transfers to certain foreign partnerships 1.6038B-2

State and local taxes
. communications services, excise taxes 49.4253-12
. death tax credit
. . deduction allowed, limitation on 20.2011-2
. . generally 20.2011-1
. . limitation when deduction allowed 20.2011-2
. . nonresident aliens 20.2102-1
. diesel and special motor fuels, exemptions for sales to 48.4041-15
. generally 1.6050E-1; 31.6361-1
. highway vehicles use tax, exemption ..... 41.4482(c)-1; 41.4483-1
. manufacturers excise taxes, articles for exclusive use of 48.4221-5
. refunds, reporting 1.6050E-1
. unified credit
. . nonresident aliens 20.2102-1

State law enforcement agencies
. highway vehicles use tax, registration 41.6001-2

State laws
. wagering tax, violations 44.4422-1

State taxes (See State and local taxes)

Statements
. electronic furnishing of (See Electronic furnishing of statements)
. guidance on, IRS 301.6011-1
. last-known address defined for 301.6212-2
. private foundations 53.6011-1

Statute of limitations
. bankruptcy 301.6872-1
. discovery of liability 301.7609-5
. generally ..... 301.6532-1 et seq.
. mitigation of effect of limitation period ..... 301.6514(a)-1
. personal holding companies 1.547-6
. receivership 301.6872-1
. suspension of assessment period 301.6872-1

References are to Reg. § numbers

Stay of collection
. personal holding companies 1.547-6
Stock
. affiliate-owned stock 1.7874-1
. basis
. . adjustments, consolidated returns . . . . . 1.1502-32(b)
. . group restructure change
. . . adjustments, additional . . . . 1.1502-31(d)
. . . asset acquisitions . . . . 1.1502-31(b)
. . . generally . . . . 1.307-2; 1.961-1; 1.961-2; 1.1016-5; 1.1244(d)-2; 1.1502-31(a)
. . . net asset basis . . . . 1.1502-31(c)
. . . predecessors and successors . . . . 1.1502-31(f)
. . . stock acquisitions . . . . 1.1502-31(b)
. . . waiver of loss carryovers of former common parent . . . . 1.1502-31(e)
. bonus plans (See Pension, profit-sharing, and stock bonus plans)
. capital gains and losses . . . . 1.1242-1; 1.1243-1; 1.1244(a)-1 to 1.1244(e)-1; 1.1248-5
. commonly owned business 1.304-4T
. consent stock defined 1.565-6
. consolidated returns . . . . 1.1502-31 to 35; 1.1563-2
. . component member, statement on treatment, special rules . . . . 1.1563-3(d)
. . constructive ownership . . . . 1.1563-3(b)
. . operating rules . . . . 1.1563-3(c)
. . rules, generally . . . . 1.1563-3(a)
. . Sec. 1563(f)(3)(B) special rules . . . . 1.1563-3(d)
. . special rules . . . . 1.1563-3(c)
. . subsidiary stock, disposition or deconsolidation 1.1502-20
. . . disposition or deconsolidation of stock 1.1502-20T
. . . limitations on the applicability of 1.1502-20 . . . . 1.1502-20T
. constructive ownership
. . consolidated returns . . . . 1.1563-3(b)
. . foreign corporations 1.958-2
. corporate distributions and adjustments . . . . 1.305-4 et seq.; 1.316-1 to 1.318-4
. corporate organizations and reorganizations . . 1.355-1 to 1.355-7
. DISCs 1.996-4
. disposition
. . nonrecognition provision, transactions not qualifying under any other 1.1032-3
. distributions
. . acquisition, gain recognition in connection with 1.355-7
. dividends (See Dividends)
. election or choice (See Stock options)
. equity options
. . covered calls . . . . 1.1092(c)-1
. . definitions concerning . . . . 1.1092(c)-4

Stock — Cont'd
. *equity options — Cont'd*
. . flexible terms, with . . . . 1.1092(c)-2
. . over-the-counter options . . . . 1.1092(c)-3
. . qualified call options . . . . 1.1092(c)-1
. family member, owned by 1.958-2
. fast-pay arrangements
. . recharacterizing . . . . 1.7701(l)-3
. . withholding agents 1.1441-10
. foreign corporations 1.958-1; 1.958-2; 1.960-2; 1.961-1; 1.961-2
. . affiliate-owned stock 1.7874-1
. . transfers . . . . 1.367(a)-3; 7.367(b)-1 et seq.
. . . Sec. 361 exchange . . . . 1.367(a)-3T
. foreign investment company . . . . 1.367(b)-6
. foreign mutual insurance company 1.958-1
. foreign personal holding companies 1.552-3
. gain or loss
. . allocation of loss against gain 1.865-2
. . capital gain or loss . . . . 1.1242-1; 1.1243-1; 1.1244(a)-1 to 1.1244(e)-1; 1.1248-5
. . dividend recapture 1.865-2
. . foreign office, stock attributable to 1.865-2
. . foreign tax home, U.S. citizen or resident with 1.865-2
. . nontaxable exchange 1.1032-1; 1.1036-1; 1.1042-1T
. . partnership loss 1.865-2
. . real property interest, stock constituting 1.865-2
. . SEC orders, exchanges and obedience to 1.1081-3; 1.1081-5; 1.1081-7
. holding periods
. . reduction of period 1.246-5
. information returns 1.6039-1
. interest expense, allocation
. . income from sources within or without U.S. . . . . 1.861-12T(c)
. itemized deductions . . . . 1.263(e)-1; 1.267(c)-1
. less developed country corporations 1.1248-5
. marketable stock defined 1.1296-1; 1.1296-2
. nonresident alien, owned by 1.958-2
. options (See Stock options)
. patronage dividends (See Patronage dividends)
. pension, profit-sharing, and stock bonus plans (See Pension, profit-sharing, and stock bonus plans)
. personal holding companies 1.542-3
. preferred stock . . . 1.244-1; 1.244-2; 1.247-1; 1.305-4 to 1.305-6
. redemption (See Redemption)
. section 1296 stock defined 1.1296-1; 1.1296-2
. shareholders (See Shareholders)
. straddle positions . . . . . . 1.1092(b)-2T to 1.1092(b)-5T
. . special rules . . . . 1.1092(d)-2
. valuation of stock 20.2031-2

References are to Reg. § numbers

Stock —Cont'd
. *valuation of stock—Cont'd*
. . decline, deduction for 1.165-4
. . gift tax 25.2512-2
. wash sales (See Wash Sales)
Stock bonus plans (See Pension, profit-sharing, and stock bonus plans)
Stock options (See also Equity options)
. definitions 1.421-1
. . statutory options, concerning 1.421-1; 1.425-1
. disposition
. . nonrecognition provision, transactions not qualifying under any other 1.1032-3
. disqualifying dispositions 1.421-2
. employee stock purchase plan defined 1.423-2
. incentive 14a.422A-1
. information returns
. . electronic statements .... 1.6039-1(f)
. . employee stock purchase plan, stock purchased under .... 1.6039-1(b)
. . incentive stock options .... 1.6039-1(a)
. . mail, statements furnished by .... 1.6039-1(d)
. . penalties for failure to furnish .... 1.6039-1(e)
. . statement of transaction, furnishing transferee with 1.6039-2
. . time to furnish statements .... 1.6039-1(c)
. minimum tax 1.58-8
. payment of income, received as 1.61-15
. qualifying transfers 1.421-2
. statutory 1.425-1
. . acquisition of new stock 1.424-1
. . attribution of stock ownership 1.424-1
. . definitions 1.424-1
. . disposition of stock 1.424-1
. . modification, extension or renewal of option 1.424-1
. . substitutions and assumptions of options ... 1.424-1
. stock-based compensation 1.482-7
. taxation of nonqualified 1.83-7
Stock ownership requirement
. foreign corporation as qualified resident .... 1.884-4(b)
. personal holding companies 1.542-3
Stock-based compensation
. cost sharing arrangements 1.482-7; 1.482-7A
. defined 1.482-7
Storage costs
. capitalization of 1.263A-3
Storage facility
. defined 1.263A-3
Straddle transactions
. itemized deductions, ERTA 1.165-13T
. wash sales of stock or securities ..... 1.1092(b)-2T to 1.1092(b)-5T
Straight line method of depreciation .... 7.57(d)-1
. application .... 1.167(b)-1
Structured passive investment arrangements
. foreign countries 1.901-2T
Structured settlement factoring transactions
. coordination with other provisions ...... 157.5891-1(d)
. defined 157.5891-1
. excise tax on 157.5891-1
. . bonds where time for paying extended .. 157.6165-1
. . definitions concerning .... 157.6061-1(c)
. . extension of time for paying 157.6161-1
. . returns
. . . extension of time for filing 157.6081-1
. . . February 19, 2003, rights received before .... 157.6071-1(b)
. . . general requirement to file 157.6011-1
. . . place for filing 157.6091-1
. . . signatures 157.6061-1
. . . time for filing 157.6071-1
. . . verification 157.6065-1
. . time and place for payment 157.6151-1
. . verification of returns 157.6065-1
. recordkeeping requirements 157.6001-1
. . IRS requirement .... 157.6001-1(b)
. . retention .... 157.6001-1(c)
Student loan bonds
. arbitrage transactions 1.148-4
Students
. defined for employment services .... 31.3121(b)(10)-2
. domestic services provided for college organizations .... 31.3121(b)(2)-1
. generally 1.170A-2; 1.871-9
. services for college organizations ... 31.3121(b)(10)-2; 31.3306(c)(10)-2
Subchapter K
. anti-abuse rules 1.701-2
. application of rules .... 1.701-2(b)
Subpart F income
. controlled foreign corporations, look-through rules
. . exclusions, subpart F .... 1.904-5(d)
. . inclusions, subpart F .... 1.904-5(c)(1)
. . income in excess of 70 percent gross income .... 1.904-5(e)
. foreign personal holding companies 1.952-1
. U.S. shareholder pro rata share in .... 1.951-1(b)
. . holding period .... 1.951-1(f)
. . limitations .... 1.951-1(b); 1.951-1(c)
. . pro rata share defined .... 1.951-1(e)
. . U.S. shareholder defined .... 1.951-1(g)
Subscriptions
. prepaid, accounting methods for 1.455-1
Subsidiaries
. agent, common parent 1.1502-77A

References are to Reg. § numbers

Subsidiaries —Cont'd
. change in annual accounting period 1.442-1
. consolidated returns
. . liability for tax after withdrawal 1.1502-6
. . stock of subsidiary, disposition or deconsolidation 1.1502-20
. . . limitations of the applicability of 1.1502-20 .... 1.1502-20T
. . . subsidiary stock, disposition or deconsolidation 1.1502-20T
. distributions and adjustments 1.304-3
. liquidations .... 1.332-1 to 1.332-7; 1.367(b)-5
. pension, profit-sharing, and stock bonus plans 1.406-1; 1.407-1
. S corporation subsidiaries, definitions concerning 1.1361-2
. withdrawal, liability for tax after 1.1502-6

Substantial and gross valuation misstatements
. chapter 1, under (See Valuation)

Substantial understatement of income tax
. underpayment of taxes................... 1.6662-4

Substantial user bonds
. exemptions 1.103-11

Substantiation requirements
. business gift 1.274-5; 1.274-5T
. entertainment 1.274-5; 1.274-5T
. travel expenses................. 1.274-5; 1.274-5T

Successor corporations
. carryovers of predecessor
. . accounting method ... 1.381(c)(4)-1; 1.381(c)(21)-1
. . acquisitions.......................... 1.381(b)-1
. . allocation of income and loss to periods before and after change date 1.382-6
. . amortization of bond discount or premium .... 1.381(c)(9)-1
. . bad debts, prior taxes or delinquency amounts .... 1.381(c)(12)-1
. . capital losses .... 1.381(c)(3)-1; 1.383-1
. . charitable contributions .... 1.381(c)(19)-1
. . closing of the book elections............ 1.382-6(b)
. . contributions to employee retirement and benefit plans .... 1.381(c)(11)-1
. . deferred exploration and development expenditures .... 1.381(c)(10)-1
. . deficiency dividend of investment entity .... 1.381(c)(25)-1
. . depletion, waste, or residue of prior mining .... 1.381(c)(18)-1
. . depreciation method .... 1.381(c)(6)-1
. . distributor or transferor corporation .. 1.381(c)(16)-1
. . earnings and profits .... 1.381(c)(2)-1
. . exploration and development expenditures, deferred .... 1.381(c)(10)-1
. . foreign taxes.......................... 1.383-1

Successor corporations —Cont'd
. *carryovers of predecessor —Cont'd*
. . generally .... 1.381(a)-1
. . indebtedness of personal holding companies .... 1.381(c)(15)-1
. . installment method................ 1.381(c)(8)-1
. . inventories .... 1.381(c)(5)-1
. . investment credit .... 1.381(c)(23)-1
. . involuntary conversions........... 1.381(c)(13)-1
. . life insurance companies.......... 1.381(c)(22)(a); 1.381(c)(22)-1; 1.381(d)-1
. . net operating loss................. 1.381(c)(1)-2
. . net operating loss limitations .... 1.381(c)(1)-1; 1.381(c)(1)-1 et seq.; 1.381(d)-1
. . . 5% shareholders 1.382-3
. . . life insurance companies .... 1.381(c)(22)-1
. . . ownership change...................... 1.383-2
. . . ownership change defined 1.382-2T
. . . special limitations 1.383-1
. . . two or more dates of distribution or transfer in the taxable year .... 1.381(c)(1)-2
. . new jobs credit .... 1.381(c)(26)-1
. . obligations assumed by........... 1.381(c)(16)-1
. . personal holding companies .... 1.381(c)(14)-1; 1.381(c)(15)-1; 1.381(c)(17)-1
. . targeted jobs credit .... 1.381(c)(26)-1
. . unused credits .... 1.381(c)(24)-1
. constructive ownership of stock............ 1.382-4
. controlled groups 1.382-8
. employee retirement and benefit plans .... 1.381(c)(11)-1
. jurisdiction of a court in a title 11 .... 1.382-9
. obligations assumed by .... 1.381(c)(16)-1

Sulfur regulations
. deduction for capital costs incurred in complying with EPA (See Environmental Protection Agency)

Summoned party, duties and protections
.... 301.7609-3

Summons
. generally 301.7603-1; 301.7604-1; 301.7609-1; 301.7609-4

Sum-of-the-years-digits method of depreciation
. application .... 1.167(b)-3

Sundays
. time for performance of act where last day falls on Sunday 301.7503-1

Supplemental taxes
. employee representative 31.3211-3
. safe harbor election in lieu of calculation work-hours .... 31.3221-3(d)
. work-hours
. . calculation of .... 31.3221-3(c)
. . defined .... 31.3221-3(b)

References are to Reg. § numbers

Supplemental unemployment benefit trusts
. exempt organizations .... 1.501(c)(17)-1 to 1.501(c)(17)-3
Supplemental wage payments
. aggregate withholding exemption exceeds wages paid .... 31.3402(g)-1(b)
. $1,000,000, in excess of .... 31.3402(g)-1(a)
. vacation allowances .... 31.3402(g)-1(c)
. withholding .... 31.3402(g)-1(a)
Supplier-based intangibles
. amortization 1.197-2
Surcharges
. acquisitions and dispositions 1.52-2
. carrybacks and carryovers ... 1.53-2; 1.56A-2; 1.56A-5
. common trust funds 1.58-5
. commonly controlled trade or business 1.52-1
. conduit entities 1.58-2
. corporations 1.56-1
. deferral of tax liability for net operating losses 1.56A-2
. estates and trusts 1.58-3; 1.58-3T
. exemptions .... 1.58-1 et seq.
. generally .... 1.52-1 et seq.
. imposition of tax 1.56A-1
. minimum tax exemption .... 1.58-1 et seq.
. partnerships and partners 1.58-2
. pass-through of jobs credit 1.53-3
. real estate investment trusts 1.58-6
. records, tax preference 1.57-5
. regulated investment companies 1.58-6
. small business corporations 1.58-4
. tax preference items .... 1.57-1 to 1.57-5; 1.58-7
Surety on bonds (See Bonding requirements; Bonds for payment of taxes)
Surplus
. accumulated earnings credit 1.532-1; 1.535-3
. adjustments to taxable income 1.535-2
. burden of proof 1.534-1; 1.534-2
. business of corporation 1.537-3
. defined 1.535-1
. earnings and profits 1.537-2
. evidence 1.533-1; 1.534-1; 1.534-2
. generally .... 1.531-1 et seq.
. imposition of tax 1.531-1
. jeopardy assessments 1.534-3
. reasonable business needs 1.537-1
. short tax years 1.536-1
. statement required 1.533-2
. tax years 1.536-1
Surrender of property
. seizure of property for collection of taxes 301.6332-1; 301.6332-2
Surtax exemption
. consolidated returns 1.1551-1
Surviving spouse
. defined .... 1.2-2(a)
. life estate for .... 20.2056(b)-7
Survivors
. joint returns 1.2-1
Synthetic debt instruments
. security status .... 1.475(c)-2(b)
Synthetic equity
. ESOP ownership .... 1.409(p)-1(f)
. . avoidance or evasion of sec 409(p) .... 1.409(p)-1(g)

T

Tangible personal property
. investment credit 1.48-1
. property produced by taxpayer, rules concerning 1.263A-2
Tangible property
. depreciation allowance .... 1.167(a)-2
Targeted jobs credit
. adjustment for acquisitions and dispositions 1.52-2
. allowance .... 1.51-1 to 1.53-2
. apportionment among commonly controlled trades or businesses .... 1.52-2 et seq.
. generally 1.44B-1
. limitations 1.52-3; 1.53-1
. pass-through of 1.52-3; 1.53-3
. unused
. . carrybacks and carryovers 1.53-2
Tax assessment bonds
. private business use test 1.141-3
Tax attributes for S corporations
. reduction of tax attributes for S corporations 1.108
Tax benefit rule
. alternative minimum tax, applicability to 1.58-9
Tax Court
. abatements, credits, and refunds 301.6512-1; 301.7507-6
. accounting for collected taxes 301.7512-1
. bankruptcy .... 301.6871(b)-1
. banks and trust companies 301.7507-1
. burden of proof 301.7454-1; 301.7454-2
. declaratory judgments .... 1.7476-1 to 1.7476-3; 301.7476-1; 301.7477-1
. deficiency procedures 301.6213-1; 301.6215-1
. earnings 301.7507-5
. employment taxes 301.7507-11
. generally .... 301.7452-1 et seq.
. hearings 301.7458-1
. immunity .... 301.7507-7 to 301.7507-10
. judicial review .... 301.7481-1 to 301.7484-1

References are to Reg. § numbers

Tax Court —Cont'd
. notice to interested parties 1.7476-2
. oaths and procurement of testimony, production of records of foreign corporations, foreign trusts or estates, and nonresident alien individuals 301.7456-1
. penalties 301.6673-1
. pendency of Tax Court proceedings . . . . 301.6871(b)-1
. power of attorney . . . . . . 601.503 to 601.505; 601.509
. publicity of proceedings 301.7461-1
. readjustment of tax . . . . 1.1313(a)-1
. real estate acquired by the United States 301.7506-1
. representation of parties 301.7452-1
. reproduction of returns and other documents 301.7513-1
. retirement plans . . . . 1.7476-1 to 1.7476-3
. sale of personal property acquired by United States 301.7505-1
. segregated or transferred assets 301.7507-3
. statistical studies and compilations on request 301.7515-1
. time for performance of acts where last day falls on Saturday, Sunday, or legal holiday 301.7503-1
. timely mailing treated as timely filing 301.7502-1
. training and training aids on request 301.7516-1
. unsegregated assets 301.7507-4
. witness fees 301.7457-1

Tax Equity and Fiscal Responsibility Act (TEFRA)
. bonds 5f.103-3
. elections, time and manner of 301.9100-5T
. generally . . . . 35.3405-1; 301.9100-5T et seq.
. industrial development bonds 5f.103-2
. interest deduction 5f.163-1
. safe harbor leases . . . . 5f.168(f)(8)-1

Tax Increase Prevention and Reconciliation Act of 2005
. computer software; domestic production gross receipts . . . . 1.199-8(i)(5)
. enactment date 1.199-5
. pass-thru entities, application of Sec. 199 to . . . . 1.199-9(a)
. W-2 wage limitations . . . . 1.199-2(e)

Tax matters partner
. generally . . . . 301.6224(c)-1
. responsibilities . . . . 301.6223(g)-1

Tax on self-employment income
. outline of regulation provisions for section 1441 . . . . 1.441-0

Tax preference items (See Alternative minimum tax)

Tax Reform Act of 1976
. at risk amounts . . . . 7.465-1 to 7.465-5
. carryover basis property acquired from decedent 7.6039A-1
. disability income payments 7.105-1

Tax Reform Act of 1976 —Cont'd
. elections under 301.9100-12T
. foreign corporations . . . . 1.367(b)-5
. foreign investment companies . . . . 1.367(b)-6
. generally . . . . 301.9100-12T et seq.
. international boycott factor 7.999-1
. investment income 7.936-1
. liquidation of foreign subsidiary . . . . 1.367(b)-5
. partner's distributive share 7.704-1
. returns for foreign trusts 404.6048-1
. straight line depreciation . . . . 7.57(d)-1
. substantial gainful activity 7.105-2
. winnings from bingo, keno, and slot machines 7.6041-1

Tax Reform Act of 1984
. questions and answers arising under . . . . . 1.267(a)-2T

Tax Reform Act of 1986
. elections, time and manner of 301.9100-7T

Tax return preparers
. credit or refund claims
. . claims filed by preparers . . . . 1.6696-1(b)
. . content of claim . . . . 1.6696-1(d)
. . notice and demand for payment . . . . 1.6696-1(a)
. . separation and consolidation of . . . . 1.6696-1(c)
. defined 301.7701-15
. due diligence requirements
. . earned income credit eligibility 1.6695-2
. earned income credit eligibility
. . due diligence requirements 1.6695-2
. failure to file correct information returns . . . 1.6695-1(e)
. failure to furnish copies to taxpayer . . . . . . 1.6695-1(a)
. failure to furnish identifying number . . . . . . 1.6695-1(c)
. failure to retain copy of return . . . . 1.6695-1(d)
. failure to sign return 1.6695-1; 1.6695-1T
. form and manner of furnishing copy of return and retaining copy 1.6107-2
. generally 1.6107-1
. information returns 1.6060-1
. negotiation of check . . . . 1.6695-1(f)
. penalties 1.6694-1; 1.6694-2; 1.6695-1
. . claims filed by preparers . . . . 1.6696-1(b)
. . content of claim . . . . 1.6696-1(d)
. . notice and demand for payment . . . . 1.6696-1(a)
. . separation and consolidation of . . . . 1.6696-1(c)
. sign return, failure to sign . . . . 1.6695-1(b)
. understatement due to unreasonable position
. . adequate disclosure with reasonable basis . . . . 1.6694-2(d)
. . advice of others, reliance on . . . . 1.6694-2(e)(5)
. . frequency of errors . . . . 1.6694-2(e)(2)
. . generally . . . . 1.6694-2(a)
. . generally accepted administrative or industry practice, reliance on . . . . 1.6694-2(e)(6)

References are to Reg. § numbers

Tax return preparers —Cont'd
. *understatement due to unreasonable position — Cont'd*
. . materiality of errors .... 1.6694-2(e)(3)
. . merits, more likely than not be sustained on .... 1.6694-2(b)
. . normal office practices .... 1.6694-2(e)(4)
. . reasonable basis, adequate disclosure of positions with .... 1.6694-2(d)
. . reasonable cause and good faith exception .... 1.6694-2(e)
. understatement due to willful, reckless or intention conduct
. . burden of proof...................... 1.6694-3(g)
. . corporations, partnerships, and other firms .... 1.6694-3(a)(2)
. . employment taxes 31.6694-3
. . highway motor vehicles, excise tax on.... 41.6694-3
. . proscribed conduct .... 1.6694-3(a)(1)
. . reckless or intentional disregard........ 1.6694-3(c)
. . rules or regulations defined............ 1.6694-3(e)
. . sec. 6694(b) penalty reduced by sec. 6694(a) .... 1.6694-3(f)
. understatement liability
. . 15% of a penalty, extension of collection period when preparer has paid .... 1.6694-4 et seq.
. . . employment taxes.................. 31.6694-4
. . . highway motor vehicles, excise tax on .. 41.6694-4

Tax shelters
. abusive
. . penalties for 301.6708-1T
. . potentially 301.6112-1
. confidential corporate tax shelters........ 301.6111-2
. evasion of tax, structured for 301.6111-2
. generally 1.6661-5; 301.6111-1T; 301.6707-1T
. list of investors, requirement to maintain .. 301.6112-1
. material advisors........................ 301.6112-1
. organizer or seller of interest in 301.6112-1
. potentially abusive 301.6112-1
. prohibited tax shelter transaction disclosure (See Prohibited tax shelter transaction disclosure)
. promoter defined.......................... 301.6111-2
. registration............................. 301.6112-1
. registration of confidential 301.6111-2

Tax year (See also Taxable year)
. gross income items includible .... 1.455-1 et seq.
. partners and partnerships (See Partners and partnerships)
. personal holding companies 1.444-1T
. S corporations (See S corporations, subhead tax year)

Taxable entities
. classifications for federal tax purposes 301.7701-1
. . domestic and foreign entities 301.7701-1; 301.7701-5

Taxable mortgage pools
. assets, composition of .... 301.7701(i)-1(c)
. credit enhancement assets .... 301.7701(i)-2(b)
. defined .... 301.7701(i)-1
. duration of classification .... 301.7701(i)-3
. portions of entities...................... 301.7701(i)-2
. real estate mortgage defined for ..... 301.7701(i)-1(d)
. S corporations .... 301.7701(i)-4
. special rules .... 301.7701(i)-4
. transitional rules .... 301.7701(i)-3

Taxable year
. adoption of............................. 1.441-1
. affected years 15a.453-0
. change in tax rate during 52-53 week taxable year 1.441-2
. change of.................................. 1.441-1
. change to or from 52-53 week taxable year ... 1.441-2
. deductions .... 1.461-1 et seq.
. defined 1.441-1
. determination by entity 1.441-1
. election of 52-53 taxable year 1.441-2
. 52-53 taxable year 1.441-2
. gross income items to be included 1.451-1
. inclusion .... 1.451-1 et seq.
. nonresident aliens.................... 301.7701(b)-6
. partnership income 1.706-1
. personal service corporation
. . calendar year requirement 1.441-3
. . determination of PSC 1.441-1
. required taxable year, use of 1.441-1
. retention of 1.441-1
. S corporations 1.1378-1
. tax rate change during 52-53 week taxable year 1.441-2

Taxes deductible (See Deductions)

Tax-exempt bonds
. arbitrage restrictions....................... 1.148-5
. carryover allocations.................... 1.42-8(b)
. change in use of facilities financed with 1.150-4
. covenant bonds 1.1451-2
. definitions 1.150-1
. industrial development bonds 1.103-7; 1.103-10
. interest derived by nonresident aliens and foreign corporations 1.103-6
. mortgage bonds, qualified 1.103A-2; 6a.103A-2
. notices and elections, filing 1.150-5
. private activity bonds ..... 1.103(n)-1T to 1.103(n)-7T
. reporting requirements .... 1.149(e)-1
. rules, special 1.150-1
. substantial user bonds 1.103-11
. termination of election for financing ..... 1.142(f)(4)-1
. Treasury bonds 1.103-5

References are to Reg. § numbers

Tax-exempt use property
. like-kind exchanges .... 1.168(h)-1
Taxpayer identification number (TIN)
. adoption taxpayer number, IRS 301.6109-3
. backup withholding .... 31.3406(d)-1; 31.3406(d)-5
. . incorrect TIN .... 31.3406(d)-5
. certification of 1.1441-6
. disclosure
. . acceptance agent.................... 301.6109-1
. foreign investment companies 1.897-1
. foreign person 301.6109-1
. information return, missing on
. . reasonable cause..... 301.6724-1(e); 301.6724-1(f)
. matching program
. . confidentiality of information .... 31.3406(j)-1(c)
. . establishment of program .... 31.3406(j)-1
. . failure to file information return ...... 31.3406(j)-1(d)
. . incorrect TIN, notice of .... 31.3406(j)-1(b)
. returns 1.6109-1; 1.6109-2; 301.6109-1
. trust follow death of individual treated as owner
.... 301.6109-1
. withholding .... 31.6011(b)-1; 31.6109-1
Taxpayer identity information
. disclosure .... 301.6103(m)-1
Tax-sheltered annuities
. generally 20.2039-2
TEFRA (See Tax Equity and Fiscal Responsibility Act)
Telegraph and cable services
. excise taxes
. . application of 49.4251-2
. . generally 49.4252-3
. . imposition 49.4251-1
. . items otherwise taxed, exemptions for 49.4253-5
. . provisions common to 49.4252-4
. . rate of 49.4251-2
. . Section 4251 to 4254, applicability 49.4251-3
Telephone companies
. exemption requirements............. 1.501(c)(12)-1
Telephone services
. application of 49.4251-2
. coin-operated services
. . exemption 49.4253-1
. . payment for 49.4254-2
. general service 49.4252-1
. imposition of 49.4251-1
. items otherwise taxed, exemptions for 49.4253-5
. news services, exemption for 49.4253-2
. provisions common to 49.4252-4
. rate 49.4251-2
. Section 4251 to 4254, applicability 49.4251-3
Teletypewriter exchange services
. excise taxes............................ 49.4252-5
. . items otherwise taxed, exemptions for.... 49.4253-5
Television films
. generally 1.992-4
Tenancies by entirety
. election 25.2515-2
. generally 25.2515-1
. noncitizen of United States
. . spouse not a citizen, one .... 25.2523(i)-2
. termination.................. 25.2515-3; 25.2515-4
. valuation 25.2515-2
Tenant and landlord (See Leases)
Tentative refunds
. under claim of right adjustment 5.6411-1
Term life insurance
. group term life insurance (See Group term life insurance)
Terminal interest property
. double deduction disallowance 20.2055-6
Terminal railroad corporations and shareholders
. generally .... 1.281-1 to 1.281-4
Termination and jeopardy assessment
. partnership items .... 301.6231(c)-4
Termination assessments
. flagrant political expenditures 301.6852-1
Tertiary injectant expenses
. itemized deductions 1.193-1
Tests (See Experiments and Tests)
Theft losses
. itemized deductions 1.165-8
Third parties
. discovery of liability and enforcement of title
.... 301.7609-2
. judicial proceedings .... 301.7422-1 to 301.7430-1
. recordkeepers 301.7603-2
. returns 301.6110-4
. withholding 31.3505-1
Third party summonses
. notification of persons identified 301.7609-2
. right to intervene 301.7609-4
. special procedures 301.7609-1
. suspensions of period of limitations 301.7609-5
Third-party contacts
. IRS officers, by 301.7602-2
. post-contact reports 301.7602-2
. pre-contact notice 301.7602-2
30-day rule taxes
. depositaries of government .... 40.6302(c)-1
Tiered structure, member of
. defined 1.444-2T

References are to Reg. § numbers

Timber
. capitalization of costs 1.263A-1
. depletion 1.611-3
. generally 1.611-3; 1.631-2
. investment credit 1.48-1

Time and place for filing returns
. automatic extension 1.6081-4
. Chapter 42 returns 53.6091-1
. Chapter 44 returns 55.6091-1
. Chapter 54 (Greenmail) returns 156.6091-1
. decedent, trust or part of trust owned by a . . . 1.6072-1
. extension of time for filing . . . . . 1.6081-1 to 1.6081-9; 31.6081(a)-1; 55.6081-1; 301.6081-1
. . Social Security Administration copy of W-2 . . . . . 31.6081(a)-1T
. generally . . . . . 1.6071-1 to 1.6073-4; 40.6151(a)-1; 301.6071-1 to 301.6073-1; 301.6091-1 to 301.6096-2
. individuals, estates, and trusts 1.6072-1
. limitations on credit or refund 301.6513-1
. other documents, and
. . extension agreement . . . . . 301.6229(b)-1
. . partnership return extensions 301.6233-1
. partnership returns, extension to entities filing 301.6233-1
. postponement; Presidentially declared disaster 301.7508A-1
. quarterly . . . . . 40.6071(a)-1
. withholding taxes 31.6091-1

Time and place for paying tax
. estimated tax . . . . . 1.6153-1 to 1.6153-4; 301.6153-1
. excise taxes 53.6151-1
. extension (See Extension of time for payment of tax)
. generally . . . . . 1.6151-1 et seq.; 301.6151-1 et seq.
. installment payments 1.6655-2T
. notice and demand 301.6155-1
. real estate investment trusts 55.6151-1
. receipt of payment . . . . . 301.6311-1 to 301.6316-9
. withholding . . 31.6071(a)-1; 31.6081(a)-1; 31.6151-1; 31.6161(a)(1)-1

TIN (See Taxpayer identification number)

Tips (See also Gratuities)
. electronic tip reports 31.6053-1
. employee tax . . . . . 31.3102-3; 31.3121(q)-1
. employment taxes . . . . . 31.3121(a)(12)-1
. reporting requirements 31.6053-1
. substantiation requirements 31.6053-4
. wages . . . . . 31.3121(a)(12)-1
. withholding . . . . . 31.3401(a)(16)-1; 31.3401(f)-1; 31.3402(k)-1; 31.6053-1; 31.6053-3; 31.6053-4

Tires
. manufacturers excise taxes
. . definitions 48.4072-1

Tires —Cont'd
. *manufacturers excise taxes —Cont'd*
. . delivery of tires and tubes to manufacturer's retail outlet 48.4071-3
. . exempt sales 48.4073-4; 48.4221-7
. . . buses, tires, tubes and tread rubber, exempt sales of 48.4221-8
. . exemptions . . . . . 48.4073-1 et seq.; 48.4221-7
. . further manufacture causing overpayments of tax . . . . . 48.6416(b)(3)-2
. . generally 48.4071-1
. . imported articles 48.4071-4
. . . original equipment tires 48.4071-4
. . internal wire fastening, exemption of tires with 48.4073-2
. . nonhighway tires, exemption of treat rubber used for recapping 48.4073-3
. . original equipment tires on imported articles 48.4071-4
. . sizes, exemptions for 48.4073-1
. . weight, determination of 48.4071-2

Title (See Ownership)

Tort claims
. generally 601.205

Trade boards
. exempt . . . . . 1.501(c)(6)-1

Trade corporations, export
. generally . . . . . 1.970-1 to 1.970-3; 1.971-1

Trade or business
. acquire or create, amount paid to
. . capitalization generally . . . . . 1.236(a)-5(a)
. . generally . . . . . 1.236(a)-5(a)
. cash receipts in excess of $10,000, information reporting 1.6050I-1
. gain or loss, like-kind exchange of property held for productive use . . . . . 1.1031(a)-1 et seq.
. property produced by taxpayer 1.263A-2

Trade shows
. exempt organizations 1.513-3

Trademarks, trade names, and franchises
. adjusted basis 1.1016-5
. generally 1.177-1; 1.1563-4

Trading stamps
. accounting methods 1.451-4

Trailers (See Trucks and trailers)

Trainees
. nonresident aliens 1.871-9

Training aids
. Tax Court 301.7516-1

Transfer certificates
. nonresident estates 20.6325-1

Transfer pricing rules
. arm's length transactions

References are to Reg. § numbers

Transfer pricing rules —Cont'd
. *arm's length transactions —Cont'd*
. . controlled services transaction; determination of taxable income .... 1.482-9T(m); 1.6662-6T
. foreign sales corporations (See Foreign sales corporations (FSC))

Transfers (See also Sales and transfers)
. computer programs, classification of transactions involving 1.861-18
. death, taking effect at 20.2037-1
. defined for taxable income purposes .... 1.83-3(a)
. divorce, incident to 1.1041-1T
. foreign partnership, reporting certain transfers to 1.6038B-2
. life estates disposition as 25.2519-1
. performance of service, property transferred in connection with .... 1.83-3(f)
. U.S. beneficiaries to foreign trust (See Foreign trusts, subhead U.S. beneficiaries)

Transfers in contemplation of death
. generally 20.2037-1

Transportation, employer provided
. working condition fringe benefits, as 1.132-5

Transportation barriers
. itemized deductions for removal of .... 1.190-1 to 1.190-3

Transportation corporations
. generally 1.172-8; 1.863-4

Transportation costs
. capitalization of 1.263A-3

Transportation of persons by air, excise taxes
. applicability of 49.4261-2
. application of tax 49.4261-2
. . seats and berths 49.4261-9
. definitions .... 49.4262(c)-1
. duty to collect
. . outside U.S. .... 49.4264(a)-1
. . refunds, special rules .... 49.4264(b)-1
. excluded travel .... 49.4262(b)-1
. generally .... 49.4261-1 to 49.4264(f)-1
. imposition of tax 49.4261-1
. outside U.S., duty to collect .... 49.4264(a)-1
. payments
. . examples of 49.4261-7
. . exemptions from tax, examples of 49.4261-8
. . outside U.S. 49.4261-5; 49.4261-6
. . persons liable for 49.4261-10
. . special rules .... 49.4264(c)-1
. . within U.S. 49.4261-3; 49.4261-4
. refunds, special rules .... 49.4264(b)-1
. round trips .... 49.4264(e)-1
. seats and berths 49.4261-9
. taxable transportation .... 49.4262(a)-1

Transportation of persons by air, excise taxes — Cont'd
. Western Hemisphere, transportation outside northern portion of .... 49.4264(f)-1

Travel and tour activities
. exempt organizations 1.513-7

Travel expenses
. foreign travels 1.274-4
. generally ...... 1.162-2; 1.274-1 to 1.274-8; 1.702-2; 5e.274-8
. substantiation requirements 1.274-5; 1.274-5T

Treasury bonds
. exemptions 1.103-5

Treasury certificates of indebtedness
. generally 301.6312-1; 301.6312-2

Treasury securities
. original issue discount (OID) .... 1.1275-2(d)

Treaties
. entities, special rules for income received by 1.894-1
. generally 1.894-1; 1.1441-6
. income affected by 1.894-1
. marital deduction; transfers subject to estate and gift tax 20.2056A-1
. nonresident aliens coordination with income tax treaties .... 301.7701(b)-7
. return position, treaty-based
. . disclosure of 301.6114-1
. . failure to disclose 301.6712-1
. stapled foreign corporations............. 1.269B-1(e)
. taxation of treaty income 1.871-12
. withholding reduced by income tax treaty ... 1.1441-6

Treble damages
. itemized deductions 1.162-22

Triangular reorganizations
. acquisition of foreign corporation stock or asset by foreign corporation .... 1.367(b)-4(b)
. acquisition of parent stock for property
. . collateral adjustments
. . . deemed contributions .... 1.367(b)-14T(c)(2)
. . . deemed distributions .... 1.367(b)-14T(c)(1)
. . deemed contributions
. . . acquisition from person other than foreign corporation .... 1.367(b)-14T(b)(3)
. . . collateral adjustments .... 1.367(b)-14T(c)(2)
. . deemed distributions .... 1.367(b)-14T(b)(1)
. . . collateral adjustments .... 1.367(b)-14T(c)(1)
. . definitions concerning .... 1.367(b)-14T(a)(2)
. . generally .... 1.367(b)-14T(a)
. . timing and deemed contribution in case of acquisition from person other than foreign corporation .... 1.367(b)-14T(b)(3)
. . timing in case of acquisition from foreign corporation .... 1.367(b)-14T(b)(2)

References are to Reg. § numbers

Triangular reorganizations —Cont'd
. basis to distributees 1.358-6
. . reverse triangular merger 1.358-6
. dispositions
. . foreign corporations disposition of stock
. . . basis, determination of .... 1.367(b)-13(c)
. . . holding period, determination of ... 1.367(b)-13(c)
. . stock of controlling corporation 1.1032-2
. foreign corporations
. . acquisition of foreign corporation stock or asset by foreign corporation .... 1.367(b)-4(b)
. . acquisition of parent stock for property
. . . timing .... 1.367(b)-14T(b)(2)
. . disposition of stock
. . . basis, determination of .... 1.367(b)-13(c)
. . . holding period, determination of ... 1.367(b)-13(c)
. . gain recognition agreements
. . . triangular asset reorganization defined .... 1.367(a)-8T(a)(l)(i)(a)
. reverse triangular merger 1.358-6

Tribal government (See Indian tribal governments)

Trucks and trailers
. chassis, bodies
. . parts or accessories sold in connection with .... 48.4061(a)-3; 48.4061(b)-2
. heavy, sale or resale of, certification 48.4052-1
. highway vehicles use tax (See Highway vehicles)
. light-duty trucks
. . parts or accessories sold in connection with. exempt sales 48.4063-2
. manufacturers excise taxes
. . bonding of importers .... 48.4061(a)-2
. . chassis, bodies, etc.
. . . parts or accessories sold in connection with .... 48.4061(a)-4
. . . sale of .... 48.4061(a)-5
. . definitions .... 48.4061(a)-3
. . exempt sales .... 48.4063-1 to 48.4063-3
. . importers, bonding of .... 48.4061(a)-2
. . light-duty trucks .... 48.4061(a)-1
. . . parts or accessories sold in connection with. exempt sales 48.4063-2
. . . parts or accessories sold in connection with exempt 48.4063-2
. . parts or accessories
. . . chassis, bodies, etc., sold in connection with .... 48.4061(a)-4
. . . light-duty trucks, exempt sales 48.4063-2
. . used components, value excluded from sale price .... 48.4216(f)-1
. parts or accessories .... 48.4061(a)-3
. . chassis, bodies .... 48.4061(a)-4
. . defined .... 48.4061(b)-2
. . exempt sales 48.4063-1

Trucks and trailers —Cont'd
. *parts or accessories—Cont'd*
. . further manufacture, sold in connection with
. . . overpayment of tax caused by .... 48.6416(b)(3)-2
. . resale, exempt sales of parts or accessories sold for 48.4063-2
. parts or accessories sold in connection with
. . exempt sales 48.4063-1
. . resale, exempt sales of parts or accessories sold for 48.4063-2
. retail excise tax returns .... 48.4061(a)-4

Trustees
. nonbank trustees of trusts benefiting owner-employees .... 11.401(d)(1)-1

Trusts and estates
. qualified severance
. . generation-skipping transfer tax (See Generation-skipping transfer tax subhead trusts)

Tuition and related expenses
. education tax credits
. . defined for 1.25A-2
. . refund of tuition and related expenses 1.25A-5
. electronic furnishing of statements 1.6050S-2
. information returns 1.6050S-1
. reimbursement 1.6050S-1T

U

Uncollected employee tax
. withholding 31.6053-2

Underpayment of taxes
. adjustments 31.6205-1
. generally 31.6205-1; 31.6205-2; 301.6602-1; 301.6621-2T
. interest 301.6601-1
. substantial understatement of income tax ... 1.6662-4

Underreporting of tax
. backup withholding 35a.3406-2
. penalties 1.6661-1; 1.6694-1; 1.6694-2

Underwriting
. mutual insurance companies .... 1.823-6; 1.823-7; 1.826-1 to 1.826-6

Undistributed income
. generally 1.556-3

Unemployment compensation
. exempt organizations .... 1.501(c)(17)-1 to 1.501(c)(17)-3
. gross income, inclusion in 1.85-1
. information returns 1.6050B-1
. returns 301.6106-1
. withholding .... 31.3402(o)-1

Uniform capitalization rules
. additional section 263A costs .... 1.263A-1(d)(3)
. allocating categories of costs .... 1.263A-1(g)

References are to Reg. § numbers

Uniform capitalization rules —Cont'd
. change in method of accounting . . . . 1.263A-1(k)
. costs subject to capitalization . . . . 1.263A-1(e)
. creative expenses . . . . 1.263A-1(b)(5)
. de minimus rule for certain producers with total indirect costs of $200,000 or less . . . . 1.263A-1(b)(12)
. depreciation 1.263A-1
. direct labor, allocation of . . . . 1.263A-1(g)(2)
. direct materials, allocation of . . . . 1.263A-1(g)(1)
. disallowance of deductions 1.263A-1
. drilling and development costs . . . . 1.263A-1(b)(7)
. farming . . . . 1.263A-1(b)(3)
. incident to services, property that is . . 1.263A-1(b)(11)
. indirect costs, allocation of . . . . 1.263A-1(g)(3)
. intangible drilling costs 1.263A-1
. intangibles 1.263A-2
. interest
. . avoided cost method 1.263A-9
. inventories 1.263A-1; 1.263A-2; 1.263A-9
. . LIFO 1.263A-1; 1.263A-2; 1.263A-9
. labor costs 1.263A-1
. long-term contracts . . . . 1.263A-1(b)(2)
. natural gas acquired for resale . . . . 1.263A-1(b)(8)
. not for profit activities . . . . 1.263A-1(b)(6)
. operation of section 263A . . . . 1.263A-1(c)
. optional capitalization of period costs . . 1.263A-1(h)(2)
. origination of loan, exception for . . . . . 1.263A-1(b)(13)
. related person, costs provided by a . . . 1.263A-1(h)(1)
. research and experimental expenditures . . . . 1.263A-1(b)(9)
. section 263A costs . . . . 1.263A-1(d)(4)
. section 471 costs . . . . 1.263A-1(d)(2)
. self constructed assets . . . . 1.263A-1(d)(1)
. service costs, allocation of . . . . 1.263A-1(g)(4)
. simplified service cost method . . . . 1.263A-1(h)
. small resellers . . . . 1.263A-1(b)(1)
. substantially constructed, property that is . . . . 1.263A-1(b)(10)
. tax avoidance, transfers for . . . . 1.263A-1(h)(4)
. timber, raising, harvesting or growing . . 1.263A-1(b)(4)
. trade or business application . . . . 1.263A-1(h)(3)

Uniformed services (See Armed Forces of U.S.)

Unit investment trusts
. investment companies 1.851-7

United Kingdom
. foreign tax credit 1.905-5T

United States
. citizen defined 20.2208-1
. civil actions . . . . 301.7401-1 to 301.7406-1
. crime of U.S. officer or employee 301.7214-1
. Customs Service, disclosure of return information to . . . . 301.6103(l)(14)-1
. deductions for obligations of U.S. 1.551-3

United States —Cont'd
. defined . . . . . 1.956-2; 1.956-2T; 1.956-2T(e); 1.956-3T
. defined for domestic production gross receipts . . . . 1.199-3(h)
. DISCs 1.993-7
. exceptions . . . . 1.956-2(b)
. . statement required . . . . 1.956-2(b)(2)
. foreign corporations 1.953-2
. foreign earned income (See Income earned abroad by U.S. citizens)
. foreign personal holding companies 1.552-5
. gain or loss on obligations of U.S. 1.1037-1
. income from sources within and without (See Income from sources within or without U.S.)
. loans guaranteed by, distribution of proceeds 1.312-12
. noncitizen of (See Noncitizen of United States)
. nonresident aliens 1.871-7; 1.871-8
. . estates of 20.2104-1; 20.2105-1
. offenses by officers 301.7214-1
. pension, profit-sharing, and stock bonus plans . . . . 1.404(a)-11
. pledges and guarantees . . . . 1.956-2(c); 1.956-2(c)(1); 1.956-2(d)
. . acquired . . . . 1.956-2(d)(1)
. . . applicable rules . . . . 1.956-2(d)(1)(i)
. . . illustrations . . . . 1.956-2(d)(1)(ii)
. . illustrations . . . . 1.956-2(c)(3)
. . indirect pledge or guarantee . . . . 1.956-2(c)(2)
. . special rule for certain conduit financing arrangements . . . . 1.956-2(c)(4)
. possessions (See Possessions of United States)
. property (See United States property)
. real estate acquired by, administration of 301.7506-1

United States person
. trust status as 301.7701-7

United States property
. excluded property . . . . 1.956-2(b)(1)
. generally 1.956-2T; 1.956-3T
. included property . . . . 1.956-2(a)
. . generally . . . . 1.956-2(a)(1)
. . illustrations . . . . 1.956-2(a)(2)
. real property holding corporations 1.897-2
. . distributions 1.897-5T
. . liquidations 1.897-5T

Unitrusts
. valuation of interests 1.7520-1; 25.2512-5A; 25.2702-3; 25.7520-1

User fees
. generally 300.0
. imposition 300.0
. installment agreements 300.1
. offer to compromise fee 300.3

References are to Reg. § numbers

User fees —Cont'd
. renewal of enrollment of enrolled agent fee 300.6
. special enrollment examination fee 300.4
Utilities, public (See Public utilities)

V

Vacation pay
. deferral of sick, vacation and back pay . . . . . 1.457-4(d)
. election or choice 301.9100-16T
. vested accrued, accounting methods for 1.463-1T
Vaccines
. exports . . . . 48.4221-3; 48.6416(b)(2)-2
Valuation
. alternate (See Alternate valuation)
. annuities . . . . 20.2031-7; 20.2031-7A; 20.2031-7A(a); 20.2031-7A(b); 20.2031-7A(c); 20.2031-7T; 20.2031-8
. . actuarial valuation . . . . 20.7520-1(a)
. . charitable interests 20.7520-2
. . components of valuation . . . . 20.7520-1(b)
. bonds 20.2031-2
. cash on hand or on deposit 20.2031-5
. charitable interests . . . 1.7520-2; 25.7520-2; 25.7520-3
. . limitations 1.7520-2
. . transitional rules 1.7520-4
. charitable quid pro quo contributions 1.6115-1
. charitable remainder . . . . 1.642(c)-6A
. charitable remainder interests 1.664-4; 1.664-4A
. generally 20.2031-1
. household and personal effects 20.2031-6
. interest passing to surviving spouse . . . . . 20.2056(b)-4
. interests in businesses 20.2031-3
. investment company, open-end, shares in 20.2031-8
. investments 1.148-5
. joint and survivor annuity distributions . . . . 1.417(e)-1T
. life estates 20.2031-7
. life insurance 20.2031-8
. notes 20.2031-4
. property, generally 20.2031-9
. property produced by taxpayer, rules concerning 1.263A-2
. remainders 20.2031-7
. shares in open-end investment company . . . 20.2031-8
. stock 20.2031-2
. . deduction for decline in valuation 1.165-4
. substantial and gross valuation misstatements under chapter 1 . . . . 1.6662-5T
. . carryback and carryovers . . . . 1.6662-6(e)
. . net adjustment penalties . . . . 1.6662-6(c)
. . transaction penalties . . . . 1.6662-6(b)
. . . net adjustment penalty coordination and . . . . 1.6662-6(f)

Valuation —Cont'd
. transferred property 20.2013-4
Variable annuities
. life insurance companies 1.801-7
VEBAs (See Voluntary employees' beneficiary associations)
Vehicles
. automobiles (See Automobiles)
. electric (See Electric vehicles)
. motor (See Motor vehicles)
. qualified clean-fuel vehicle (See Qualified clean-fuel vehicle property; Qualified clean-fuel vehicle refueling property)
. qualified electric (See Qualified electric vehicles)
Verification of and signature on returns
. generally . . . . 1.6061-1 to 1.6065-1; 31.6065(a)-1; 301.6061-1 to 301.6065-1
Vessels (See also Motorboats; Ships and shipping)
. capital construction funds . . . . 3.1 to 3.0
. deep draft ocean going vessels
. . diesel and special motor fuels tax 48.4042-3
. generally . . . 1.861-15; 1.861-16; 1.871-3; 1.6050A-1; 31.3401(a)(17)-1; 301.6050A-1
. passenger vessels defined 43.4472-1
. supplies for
. . diesel and special motor fuels tax
. . . exemption from 48.4041-10
. . manufacturers excise taxes
. . . exempt sales of articles for use as supplies for 48.4221-4
Veterans
. generally . . . . . . 1.501(c)(19)-1; 1.512(a)-4; 6a.103A-3
Virgin Islands
. bona fide residency
. . alien individuals presence test . . . . 1.937-1(c)(2)
. . bona fide resident . . . . 1.937-1(b)
. . closer connection test . . . . 1.937-1(e)
. . days of presence . . . . 1.937-1(c)(3)
. . definitions concerning . . . . 1.937-1(a)
. . generally 1.937-1
. . information reporting . . . . 1.937-1(h)
. . medical treatment . . . . 1.937-1(c)(4)
. . presence test . . . . 1.937-1(c)
. . significant connection to the United States . . . . 1.937-1(c)(5)
. . tax home test . . . . 1.937-1(d)
. . year of move . . . . 1.937-1(f)
. coordination of income tax with United States income tax 1.932-1
. generally 1.934-1
Voluntary employees' beneficiary associations (VEBAs)
. exempt organizations . . . 1.501(c)(9)-1 to 1.501(c)(9)-8

References are to Reg. § numbers

Voluntary withholding agreements .... 31.3401(a)-3; 31.3402(p)-1
Volunteer fire departments
. obligations issued by 1.103-16
Volunteers, Peace Corps
. withholding .... 31.3401(a)(13)-1
Voyage defined 43.4472-1

W

W-2 wages
. defined .... 1.199-2(e)
. limitations
. . acquisition of disposition of trade or business .... 1.199-2(c)
. . common law employer, paid by other than .... 1.199-2(a)(2)
. . generally .... 1.199-2(a)(1)
. . joint returns .... 1.199-2(a)(4)
. . non-duplication rule .... 1.199-2(d)
. . short taxable year, taxpayer with .... 1.199-2(b)
. . Social Security Administration return, wages reported on .... 1.199-2(a)(3)
. limitations under Tax Increase Prevention and Reconciliation Act of 2005
. . grantor trusts .... 1.199-5(d)
. . non-grantor trusts and estates .... 1.199-5(e)
. . S corporations .... 1.199-5(c)
Wage bracket withholding .... 31.3402(c)-1
Wage continuation plans
. exemptions 1.105-4
Wagering taxes
. attachment of tax, time of.............. 44.4401-3
. credit or refund
. . generally 44.6419-1
. . laid-off wagers 44.6419-2
. definitions 44.4421-1
. exemptions 44.4402-1
. federal laws, violations of 44.4422-1
. generally .... 7.6041-1; 44.4401-1 to 44.4421-1
. imposition of 44.4401-1; 44.4411-1
. liability for 44.4401-2
. losses, itemized deductions 1.165-10
. overpayment
. . generally 44.6419-1
. payees of winnings, statement from 1.6011-3
. payment of tax
. . time and place 44.6151-1
. provisions made applicable 44.4413-1
. recordkeeping 44.4403-1
. registration requirements 44.4412-1
. returns .... 1.6011-3; 44.6011(a)-1; 45.6001-6
. . place for filing 44.6091-1
Wagering taxes —Cont'd
. *returns—Cont'd*
. . time for filing 44.6071-1
. special tax (See subhead stamp taxes)
. stamp taxes
. . federal agencies or instrumentalities 45.4907-1
. . generally ....44.4901-1 et seq.
. . payment of 44.4901-1
. state laws
. . violations of 44.4422-1
. territorial extent 44.4404-1
. violations of state or federal laws 44.4422-1
. winnings, generally 1.6011-3
. withholding .... 31.3402(q)-1; 31.6011(a)-4(b)(1)
Wages
. withholding of tax .... 31.6011(a)-4(a)
Waiver
. penalties 1.6661-6
War profits tax
. dual capacity taxpayers .... 1.901-2(a)(2)(ii)
. . control of property .... 1.901-2(a)(2)(ii)(D)
. . generally .... 1.901-2(a)(2)(ii)(A)
. . indirect receipt of a benefit ...... 1.901-2(a)(2)(ii)(E)
. . pension, unemployment, and disability fund payments .... 1.901-2(a)(2)(ii)(C)
. . specific economic benefit .... 1.901-2(a)(2)(ii)(B)
. generally .... 1.901-2(a)(1); 1.901-2(a)(2)(i)
. income, war profits, or excess profits tax defined .... 1.901-2(a)
. multiple levies imposed by foreign country .... 1.901-2(e)(4)
. net gain .... 1.901-2(b)
. . generally .... 1.901-2(b)(1)
. . gross receipts .... 1.901-2(b)(3)
. net income .... 1.901-2(b)(4)
. . carryovers .... 1.901-2(b)(4)(iii)
. . consolidation of profits and losses .. 1.901-2(b)(4)(ii)
. . examples .... 1.901-2(b)(4)(iv)
. . generally .... 1.901-2(b)(4)(i)
. predominant character .... 1.901-2(a)(3)
. realization .... 1.901-2(b)(2)
. . certain deemed distributions .... 1.901-2(b)(2)(ii)
. . example .... 1.901-2(b)(2)(iv)
. . generally .... 1.901-2(b)(2)(i)
. . readily marketable property .... 1.901-2(b)(2)(iii)
. separate levies imposed by foreign country .... 1.901-2(d)
. . amount of income tax that is creditable .. 1.901-2(e); 1.901-2(e)(1)
. . contractual modifications .... 1.901-2(d)(2)
. . definitions .... 1.901-2(g)
. . effective date .... 1.901-2(h); 1.901-2(h)(1)
. . examples .... 1.901-2(d)(3)

References are to Reg. § numbers

War profits tax —Cont'd
. *separate levies imposed by foreign country—Cont'd*
. . generally .... 1.901-2(d)(1)
. . multiple levies .... 1.901-2(e)(4); 1.901-2(e)(4)(i)
. . noncompulsary amounts .... 1.901-2(e)(5); 1.901-2(e)(5)(ii)
. . party undertaking tax as part of transaction .... 1.901-2(f)(2)
. . refunds and credits .... 1.901-2(e)(2)
. . subsidies .... 1.901-2(e)(3); 1.901-2(e)(3)(ii)
. . taxpayer .... 1.901-2(f); 1.901-2(f)(1)
. soak-up taxes .... 1.901-2(c)
. . examples .... 1.901-2(c)(2)
. . generally .... 1.901-2(c)(1)

Wash sales
. basis 1.1091-2
. deferral of loss rules .... 1.1092(b)-1T
. losses, generally 1.1091-1
. mixed straddles .... 1.1092(b)-3T; 1.1092(b)-4T
. straddle positions ...... 1.1092(b)-2T to 1.1092(b)-5T

Waste disposal facilities
. industrial development bonds 17.1

Water and soil conservation expenditures
. itemized deductions .... 1.175-1 to 1.175-7

Wear and tear
. accounting method change .... 1.1016-3(h)
. basis for gain or loss 1.1016-3; 1.1016-4

Welfare benefits
. generally 1.419-1T; 54.4976-1T

Widely held fixed investment trusts
. trust income, methods of reporting 1.671-5
. . backup withholding requirements .... 1.671-5(l)
. . coordination with other reporting rules .... 1.671-5(k)
. . definitions concerning .... 1.671-5(b)
. . exempt recipients .... 1.671-5(h)
. . failure to comply .... 1.671-5(l)
. . form 1099 requirements .... 1.671-5(d)
. . middlemen that hold trust interest, filings of .... 1.671-5(h)
. . non-calendar-year beneficial owners ..... 1.671-5(h)
. . obligation to report, trustee .... 1.671-5(c)
. . penalties for failure to comply .... 1.671-5(m)
. . safe harbors ...... 1.671-5(f); 1.671-5(g); 1.671-5(h)
. . written statement requirement .... 1.671-5(e)

WIN (See Work incentive programs (WIN))

Windfall profit tax on domestic crude oil
. records 1.6001-1

Window transactions
. backup withholding .... 31.3406(b)(2)-3

Winnings
. gambling winnings .... 31.3402(g)-1

Withdrawal of notice
. federal tax lien .... 301.6323(j)-1
. partnership items .... 301.6223(a)-2

Withholding agents
. fast-pay arrangements 1.1441-10

Withholding exemption certificates
. account number, inclusion of ...... 31.3402(f)(2)-1(d)
. change in status .... 31.3402(f)(2)-1(b); 31.3402(f)(2)-1(c)
. commencing at employment ...... 31.3402(f)(2)-1(a)
. electronic filing .... 31.3402(f)(5)-1(c)
. exemptions, maximum .... 31.3402(f)(2)-1(g)
. form and content of .... 31.3402(f)(5)-1
. invalid .... 31.3402(f)(2)-1(e); 31.3402(f)(5)-1(b)
. state individual taxes, applicability to .... 31.3402(f)(2)-1(f)

Withholding taxes
. abatements, credits, or refunds ... 1.1462-1; 1.1464-1; 31.6414-1; 301.6414-1
. additional withholding .... 31.3402(i)-1
. adjustments for over or underwithholding 1.1461-2
. agents .... 1.871-6; 1.1441-1 et seq.; 1.1441-7; 31.3402(g)-3; 31.3504-1
. . adjustments for over or underwithholding .. 1.1461-2
. . liability of withholding agents 1.1441-7
. . multiple 1.1461-1
. . returns 1.1461-1
. aggregate withholding exemption exceeds wages paid .... 31.3402(g)-1(b)
. agricultural labor .... 31.3401(a)(2)-1
. aliens (See Nonresident aliens)
. annualized wages .... 31.3402(h)(2)-1
. annuities .... 31.3401(a)(12)-1; 31.3402(o)-2
. Armed Forces personnel .... 31.3401(a)(1)-1
. average wages .... 31.3402(h)(1)-1
. backup withholding (See Backup withholding)
. Bank for International Settlements 1.1441-8
. bonds .... 1.1451-1; 1.1451-2; 31.3401(a)(12)-1
. certificates 1.1441-4; 1.1441-5
. citizens of U. S., services performed outside U. S. by .... 31.3401(a)(8)(A)-1
. companion sitting placement services 31.3506-1
. composite return in lieu of specified form .... 31.6011(a)-8
. conduit financing arrangements 1.1441-7
. covenant bonds 1.1451-1; 1.1451-2
. creditable taxes 1.1462-1
. cumulative wages .... 31.3402(h)(3)-1
. deposits, federal reserve bank 1.1461-1
. distributions, special rules for 1.1445-5
. domestic service .... 31.3401(a)(3)-1
. earned income credit 31.3507-1; 31.3507-2
. educational assistance program .... 31.3401(a)(18)-1
. effectively connected income 1.1441-4

References are to Reg. § numbers

Withholding taxes —Cont'd

. employee account number .... 31.6011(b)-2
. employee defined .... 31.3401(c)-1
. employer defined .... 31.3401(d)-1
. employer identification number .... 31.6011(b)-1
. estates and trusts .... 31.3401(a)(12)-1
. exclusions .... 31.3401(a)-2
. execution of returns .... 31.6011(a)-7
. exemption certificate, form and content of .... 31.3402(f)(5)-1
. exemptions .. 1.1441-9; 31.3401(e)-1; 31.3402(f)(1)-1 to 31.3402(f)(6)-1
. . foreign persons 1.1441-4
. . partnerships 1.1441-5
. export trade corporations .... 1.970-1 to 1.970-3; 1.971-1
. extension of time for filing returns or paying tax .... 31.6081(a)-1; 31.6161(a)(1)-1
. . Social Security Administration copy of W-2 .... 31.6081(a)-1T
. failure to withhold .... 31.3402(d)-1
. federal tax deposit rules
. . generally 31.6302-0
. . nonpayroll payments made after December 31, 1993 .... 31.6302-4
. FICA, federal tax deposit rules 31.6302-1
. fiduciary .... 31.3402(g)-3
. final returns .... 31.6011(a)-6
. fishing boats .... 31.3401(a)(17)-1
. foreign central banks 1.1441-8
. foreign corporations (See Foreign corporations)
. foreign governments ...... 1.1441-1 et seq.; 1.1441-8; 1.1445-10T; 31.3401(a)(5)-1
. foreign partnerships 1.1441-5
. foreign persons .... 1.970-1 to 1.970-3; 1.971-1; 1.1441-9; 1.1445-11T
. . exemptions 1.1441-4
. foreign private foundations 1.1441-9
. gambling winnings .... 31.3402(q)-1
. government depositaries .. 31.6302(c)-1; 31.6302(c)-4
. . nonpayroll payments made after December 31, 1993 .... 31.6302-4
. governmental employer 31.3404-1
. group-term life insurance .... 31.3401(a)(14)-1
. included and excluded wages .... 31.3402(e)-1
. increases or decreases in withholding ... 31.3402(i)-2
. Indian gaming profits to tribal members .. 31.3402(r)-1
. individual retirement arrangements .. 31.3401(a)(12)-1
. information returns on Form W-3 and Social Security Administration copies of Forms W-2..... 31.6051-2
. international organizations 1.1441-8
. marital status .... 31.3402(l)-1
. ministers or religious personnel ...... 31.3401(a)(9)-1
. monthly returns .... 31.6011(a)-5
. moving expenses .... 31.3401(a)(15)-1

Withholding taxes —Cont'd

. newspapers, shopping news, or magazines .... 31.3401(a)(10)-1
. no income tax liability, employee incurring .... 31.3402(n)-1
. nonaccountability of taxes in computing taxable income 31.3502-1
. noncash fringe benefits .... 31.3501(a)-1T
. nonresident aliens (See Nonresident aliens, subhead withholding tax at source)
. notice 35a.3406-2
. $1,000,000, in excess of .... 31.3402(g)-1(a)
. overwithholding 1.1461-2
. partnerships
. . domestic 1.1441-5
. . U.S. real property interest, dispositions of 1.1445-8
. payment by recipient of income 1.1463-1
. payments in other than U.S. dollars 1.1441-3
. payroll period .... 31.3401(b)-1; 31.3402(g)-2
. Peace Corps volunteers .... 31.3401(a)(13)-1
. penalties 301.6682-1
. pension, profit-sharing, and stock bonus plans .... 31.3401(a)(12)-1; 35.3405-1
. . questions and answers regarding 35.3405-1T
. percentage method of withholding ...... 31.3402(b)-1
. place for filing returns 31.6091-1
. possessions of U. S. .... 31.3401(a)(8)(B)-1
. publicly traded partnerships
. . U.S. real property interest, dispositions of 1.1445-8
. Puerto Rico .... 31.3401(a)(8)(C)-1
. Railroad Retirement Tax Act
. . federal tax deposit rules 31.6302-2
. real estate investment trusts
. . U.S. real property interests, dispositions of 1.1445-8
. recipient of income paying tax 1.1463-1
. reduced withholding; income tax treaty 1.1441-6
. retail commission salespersons .... 31.3402(j)-1
. returns .. 31.6011(a)-4 et seq.; 31.6011(a)-4T et seq.; 31.6061-1
. . withholding agents 1.1461-1
. service not in the course of employer's trade or business .... 31.3401(a)(4)-1; 31.3401(a)(11)-1
. sick pay .... 31.3402(o)-3; 31.6051-3
. signing of returns 31.6061-1
. state individual income taxes 31.6361-1
. statements for employees 31.6051-1
. . wages not subject to withholding ...... 31.6051-1(b)
. supplemental wage payments .... 31.3402(g)-1
. tax treaty reduction 1.1441-6
. taxpayer identifying numbers .... 31.6011(b)-1; 31.6109-1

References are to Reg. § numbers

Withholding taxes —Cont'd

. third parties paying or providing for wages 31.3505-1

. time for filing returns or paying tax ..... 31.6071(a)-1; 31.6081(a)-1; 31.6151-1; 31.6161(a)(1)-1

. time period covered by returns 31.6101-1

. tips .... 31.3401(a)(16)-1; 31.3401(f)-1; 31.3402(k)-1; 31.6053-1; 31.6053-3; 31.6053-4

. uncollected employee tax................ 31.6053-2

. underpayment adjustments 31.6205-1

. underwithholding........................ 1.1461-2

. unemployment compensation ....31.3402(o)-1

. vacation allowances .... 31.3402(g)-1(c)

. verification of returns or other documents ....31.6065(a)-1

. voluntary withholding agreements...... 31.3401(a)-3; 31.3402(p)-1

. wage bracket withholding..............31.3402(c)-1

. wages

. . defined .... 31.3401(a)-1T

. . generally...........................31.3401(a)-1

. wrong chapter, payment under 31.3503-1

Witness fees

. generally 301.7457-1; 301.7610-1

Wives and husbands (See Spouses)

Work incentive program (WIN)

. abatements, credits, and refunds ..... 301.6501(o)-1; 301.6511(d)-7

. carrybacks and carryovers........... 301.6501(o)-1; 301.6511(d)-7

. carryovers of predecessor .... 1.381(c)(24)-1

. corporate organizations and reorganizations .... 1.381(c)(24)-1

Worker's compensation law

. wage payments.................. 31.3121(a)(2)-1(d)

Workforce in place

. amortization.............................. 1.197-2

Work-hours

. defined for supplemental taxes ....31.3221-3(b)

Working condition fringe benefits (See Fringe benefits)

Worthless business debt

. banks and other regulated corporations 1.166-2

. evidence of.............................. 1.166-2

. generally 1.166-9

. partial or total 1.166-3

Worthless securities

. abandoned securities .... 1.165-5(i)

. affiliated corporation, loss on security of.... 1.165-5(d)

. banks, special rules for................. 1.165-5(h)

. capital loss............................ 1.165-5(c)

. decline in market value.................. 1.165-5(f)

. insolvent corporation, bonds issued by..... 1.165-5(e)

. inventories............................ 1.165-5(g)

. itemized deductions 1.165-5

. ordinary loss .... 1.165-5(b)

. security defined........................ 1.165-5(a)

Z

Zero bracket amount

. gross income.............................1.63-1

Proposed Regulations Topic Index

References are to Reg. § numbers

A

Abandonment, security
. electronic filing
. . information returns 1.6050J-1T
. worthless securities 1.165-5

Abatements, credits and refunds
. allowance of credit for taxes 1.901-1
. . deduction denied if credit claimed .... 1.901-1(c)
. . dividends from a DISC treated as foreign .... 1.901-1(i)
. . effective / applicability date .... 1.901-1(j)
. . joint return .... 1.901-1(e)
. . period during which election can be made or changed .... 1.901-1(d)
. . taxes against which credit not allowed .... 1.901-1(f)
. . taxpayers denied credit in a particular taxable year .... 1.901-1(h)
. . taxpayers to whom credit not allowed .... 1.901-1(g)
. amount of income tax that is creditable .... 1.901-2(e)
. . multiple levies .... 1.901-2(e)(4)
. . noncompulsory amounts .... 1.901-2(e)(5); 1.901-2(e)(5)(ii)
. . refunds and credits .. 1.901-2(e)(2); 1.901-2(e)(2)(ii)
. . subsidies .... 1.901-2(e)(3); 1.901-2(e)(3)(iv)
. . . general rule .... 1.901-2(e)(3)(i)
. . . official exchange rate .... 1.901-2(e)(3)(iii)
. . . subsidy .... 1.901-2(e)(3)(ii)
. definition of income, war profits, or excess profits tax .... 1.901-2(a)
. . predominant character .... 1.901-2(a)(3)
. . tax .... 1.901-2(a)(2)
. definitions .... 1.901-2(g)
. education tax credits (See Education tax credits)
. effective / applicability date .... 1.901-2(h)
. foreign tax credits (See Foreign tax credits)
. gasoline used to produce gasohol 48.6427-10
. generally 1.901-2
. investment credit, energy property 1.48-9
. net gain .... 1.901-2(b)
. . consolidation of profits and losses .. 1.901-2(b)(4)(ii)
. . examples .... 1.901-2(b)(4)(iv)
. . gross receipts .... 1.901-2(b)(3)
. . . carryovers .... 1.901-2(b)(4)(iii)
. . . examples .... 1.901-2(b)(3)(ii)
. . . net income .... 1.901-2(b)(4)
. . realization .... 1.901-2(b)(2)
. . . certain deemed distributions ..... 1.901-2(b)(2)(ii)
. . . examples .... 1.901-2(b)(2)(iv)
. . . readily marketable property ...... 1.901-2(b)(2)(iii)

Abatements, credits and refunds —Cont'd
. passive activity credit (See Passive activity losses and credit)
. qualified retirement plans .... 1.401(a)-3
. research activities, credits for (See Research credits)
. seizure of property of third party .... 301.6503(f)-1
. separate levies .... 1.901-2(d)
. . contractual modifications .... 1.901-2(d)(2)
. . examples .... 1.901-2(d)(3)
. soak-up taxes .... 1.901-2(c)
. . examples .... 1.901-2(c)(2)
. Tax Refund Offset Program .. 301.6402-5; 301.6402-6
. taxpayer .... 1.901-2(f)
. . defined for credits 1.901-2
. . party undertaking tax obligation as part of transaction .... 1.901-2(f)(2)
. . . examples .... 1.901-2(f)(2)(ii)
. withholding .... 31.6402(a)-1; 31.6414-1

Academy zone bonds (See Qualified academy zone bonds)

Accelerated Cost Recovery System
. deduction allowance 1.168-1
. . computation of recovery allowance 1.168-2
. depreciation allowance .... 1.168(a)-1
. exclusions from ACRS 1.168-4
. exhaustion, wear and tear, obsolescence, and depletion
. . periods since February 28, 1913 .... 1.1016-3
. . periods when income was not subject to tax 1.1016-4
. recovery property 1.168-3
. retirement-replacement-betterment (RBR) property 1.168-5

Accelerated death benefits
. terminally ill individuals 1.101-8

Accident and health plans
. employer contributions 1.106-1
. . benefits attributable to .... 1.72-15(d)
. . gross income exclusion 1.106-1
. retired employees, medical benefits for
. . special rules .... 1.72-15(h)
. Section 89, qualification requirements ...... 1.89(k)-1

Accounting methods
. cash method, limitations
. . simplification of 481(a) adjustment periods .... 1.448-1(g)(2)(i)
. change
. . costs subject to section 263A, for
. . . simplification of 481(a) adjustment periods .... 1.263A-7(b)(2)(ii)

References are to Reg. § numbers

Accounting methods —Cont'd
. *change —Cont'd*
. . wear and tear, obsolescence, amortization and depletion 1.1016-3
. deferred compensation plans 1.457-1; 1.457-2
. disbursement method, limitations on
. . simplification of 481(a) adjustment periods .... 1.448-1(g)(2)(i)
. functional currency of business unit different from taxpayer 1.987-1
. general rule 1.446-1
. gross income determination
. . income from sources within or without U.S. 1.952-2
. ineligible plan 1.457-3
. installment method 1.453-1
. limitations, cash method
. . simplification of 481(a) adjustment periods .... 1.448-1(g)(2)(i)
. long-term home construction contracts (See Long-term home construction contracts)
. mark-to-market
. . commodity derivatives deemed not held for investment .... 1.475(e)-1
. . election by commodities dealers .... 1.475(e)-1
. . election by commodities traders .... 1.475(f)-1
. . general rule 1.446-1
. . nonfinancial customer paper
. . . inventory .... 1.475(c)-2
. obligations issued at discount 1.454-1
. service providers, nonaccrual of certain amounts by 1.448-2

Accounting periods
. change of annual accounting period 1.442-1
. controlled foreign corporations 1.441-1
. foreign personal holding corporations 1.441-1
. newly married couples
. . change of annual accounting period 1.442-1
. subsidiary corporation
. . change of annual accounting period 1.442-1
. taxable year 1.441-1

Accounts receivable
. capital asset exclusion 1.1221-1

Accrued benefits
. ERISA .... 1.411(b)-1
. . restrictions .... 1.411(a)-11

Accumulated deferred investment tax credit
. public utility, deregulated 1.46-6

Accumulated earnings tax
. consolidated returns 1.1502-43

Accuracy related penalties
. invalidity of a regulation, reliance on 1.6662-4
. opinion or advice from professional tax advisor, reliance on 1.6662-4

Accuracy related penalties —Cont'd
. reportable transactions, reliance on advice relating to 1.6662-4

Acquisitions
. dividends, amounts constituting 1.304-6
. gain or loss
. . stock distributions, recognition of gain on certain 1.355-7; 1.355-7T
. stock basis after group structure change 1.1502-31

ACRS (See Accelerated cost recovery system)

Activities not engaged in for profit 1.183-1

Actuarial valuations
. individual retirement accounts .... 1.412(c)(9)-1

ADADP (See Aggregate deemed asset disposition price)

Additions to tax
. corporations .... 1.6655-1 to 1.6655-5; 301.6655-1
. exceptions 1.6654-2; 1.6655-2
. voluntary employee contributions 301.6652-4

Adjusted gross income
. generally 1.62-1
. reimbursements
. . withholding rates .... 31.3401(a)-4(c)

Adjusted grossed-up basis
. allocation of .... 1.336-4(a)
. determination of .... 1.336-4(a)
. disposition date .... 1.336-4(b)(2)
. new target .... 1.336-4(b)(4)
. nonrecently disposed stock .... 1.336-4(b)(6)
. nonrecently purchased stock .... 1.336-4(b)(6)
. old target .... 1.336-4(b)(4)
. purchaser .... 1.336-4(b)(1)
. purchasing corporation .... 1.336-4(b)(1)
. recently disposed stock .... 1.336-4(b)(5)
. recently purchased stock .... 1.336-4(b)(5)
. section 336(e) election .... 1.336-4(b)(3)
. section 338 election .... 1.336-4(b)(3)
. section 338 election(h)(10 election .... 1.336-4(b)(3)

Administrative costs and expenses
. deductions for 20.2053-3

Affiliated group of corporations
. expanded affiliated groups
. . domestic production activities (See Domestic production activities)
. interest deductions, earnings stripping .... 1.163(j)-1 et seq.
. taxable year
. . personal service corporations filing consolidated returns 1.441-3

Affiliated service groups
. employee benefit requirements .... 1.414(m)-3
. ERISA .... 1.414(m)-1
. generally .... 1.414(m)-1

References are to Reg. § numbers

Agents
. contractor for disclosure purposed, defined as .... 301.6103(l)-1; 301.6103(m)-1
. real estate agents, collection and payment of taxes 31.3508-1

Aggregate deemed asset disposition price
. allocation of 1.336-3
. deemed disposition consequences .... 1.336-3(e)
. determination of .... 1.336-3(b)
. grossed-up amount realized on sale .... 1.336-3(c)(1)
. liabilities of old target .... 1.336-3(d)(1)

Agricultural and horticultural cooperatives
. domestic production activities (See Domestic production activities)

Agriculture (See Farming)

Agriculture, Department of
. disclosure of return information to officers and employee of .... 301.6103(j)(5)-1
. . census of agriculture, conducting ... 301.6103(j)(5)-1

AGUB (See Adjusted grossed-up basis)

Aircraft
. bareboat charters defined 1.883-1
. code-sharing arrangements 1.883-1
. entertainment use of business aircraft
. . allocation of expenses .... 1.274-10(e)
. . basis, determination of .... 1.274-10(f)(1)
. . deadhead flights .... 1.274-10(f)(3)
. . generally 1.274-10
. . pro rate expense disallowance ....1.274-10(f)(2)
. . specified individual, entertainment provided to 1.274-9
. international operations, exclusion of income from 1.883-1
. luxury tax 48.4003-1

Alcohol fuel and biodiesel ...... 1.40-2(a) (See Small ethanol producer credit)
. alcohol used as fuel 1.40-1
. . questions and answers relating to the meaning of the term "qualified mixture" in section 40(b)(1) 1.40-1
. biodiesel 1.40A-1
. . definitions .... 1.40A-1(b)
. . effective / applicability date .... 1.40A-1(c)
. election to expense certain refineries (See Election to expense certain refineries)
. generally .... 1.40A-1(a); 40.0-1(a)
. government depositaries .... 40.6302(c)-1
. . amount of deposit .... 40.6302(c)-b(1); 40.6302(c)-1(b)
. . chapter 33, tax imposed by ...... 40.6302(c)-1(a)(2)
. . computation of net tax liability for a semimonthly period .... 40.6302(c)-1(a)(4)
. . effective date .... 40.6302(c)-1(f)
. . exceptions .... 40.6302(c)-1(e)

Alcohol fuel and biodiesel—Cont'd
. *government depositaries—Cont'd*
. . *exceptions—Cont'd*
. . . de minimis exception .... 40.6302(c)-1(e)(3)
. . . one-time filings .... 40.6302(c)-1(e)(2)
. . . taxes excluded .... 40.6302(c)-1(e)(1)
. . generally .... 40.6302(c)-1(a)
. . net tax liability defined .... 40.6302(c)-1(a)(3)
. . remittance of deposits .... 40.6302(c)-1(d)
. . . deposits by electronic funds transfer .... 40.6302(c)-1(d)(2)
. . . deposits by federal tax deposit coupon .... 40.6302(c)-1(d)(1)
. . safe harbor rules .... 40.6302(c)-1(b)(2)
. . . alternative method taxes ... 40.6302(c)-1(b)(2)(iii)
. . . applicability .... 40.6302(c)-1(b)(2)(i)
. . . failure to comply with deposit requirements .... 40.6302(c)-1(b)(2)(v)
. . . modification for tax rate increase .... 40.6302(c)-1(b)(2)(iv)
. . . regular method taxes .... 40.6302(c)-1(2)(ii)
. . semimonthly deposits required ... 40.6302(c)-1(a)(1)
. . time to deposit .. 40.6302(c)-1(c); 40.6302(c)-1(c)(1)
. . . exceptions .... 40.6302(c)-1(c)(2)
. person .... 40.0-1(d)
. references to forms .... 40.0-1(b)
. semimonthly period defined .... 40.0-1(c)
. taxable events other than removal at the terminal rack 48.4081-3
. . bulk transfers .... 48.4081-3(f)(3)(i)
. . bulk transfers from a terminal by and unregistered position holder .. 48.4081-3(d); 48.4081-3(d)(2)(i)
. . . conditions for avoidance of liability .... 48.4081-3(d)(2)(iii)
. . . imposition of tax .... 48.4081-3(d)(1)
. . . joint and several liability of terminal operator .... 48.4081-3(d)(2)(ii)
. . . liability for tax .... 48.4081-3(d)(2)
. . bulk transfers not received at an approved terminal or refinery ...... 48.4081-3(e); 48.4081-3(e)(2)(i)
. . . conditions for avoidance of liability .... 48.4081-3(e)(2)(ii)
. . . imposition of tax .... 48.4081-3(e)(1)
. . . liability for tax .... 48.4081-3(e)(2)
. . . liability of the operator of the facility where the taxable fuel is received ...... 48.4081-3(e)(2)(iii)
. . effective / applicability date .... 48.4081-3(j)
. . entry into the United States .... 48.4081-3(c); 48.4081-3(c)(2)(i)
. . . conditions for avoidance of liability .... 48.4081-3(c)(2)(iii)
. . . customs bond .... 48.4081-3(c)(2)(iv)
. . . imposition of tax .... 48.4081-3(c)(1)
. . . joint a several liability of the importer of record .... 48.4081-3(c)(2)(ii)
. . exemptions .... 48.4081-3(i)

References are to Reg. § numbers

Alcohol fuel and biodiesel—Cont'd
. *taxable events other than removal at the terminal rack—Cont'd*
. . overview .... 48.4081-3(a)
. . rate of tax .... 48.4081-3(h)
. . removal or sale of blended taxable fuel by the blender .... 48.4081-3(g)
. . . examples .... 48.4081-3(g)(3)
. . . imposition of tax .... 48.4081-3(g)(1)
. . . liability for tax.................. 48.4081-3(g)(2)
. . . liability of seller of untaxed liquid .... 48.4081-3(g)(2)(ii)
. . . liability of the blender .... 48.4081-3(g)(2)(i)
. . renewal from a refinery .... 48.4081-3(b)
. . . exception for certain refineries.... 48.4081-3(b)(2)
. . . imposition of tax .... 48.4081-3(b)(1)
. . . liability for tax.................. 48.4081-3(b)(3)
. . sales within the bulk transfer / terminal system .... 48.4081-3(f)
. . . conditions for avoidance of liability .... 48.4081-3(f)(3)(ii)
. . . example .... 48.4081-3(f)(4)
. . . exception for certain sales of taxable fuel for export .... 48.4081-3(f)(2)
. . . imposition of tax .... 48.4081-3(f)(1)
. . . liability for tax.................. 48.4081-3(f)(3)
. . . liability of the buyer .... 48.4081-3(f)(3)(iii)

Aliens, nonresident (See Nonresident aliens)

Allocation and apportionment
. charitable contributions 1.861-8
. controlled group of corporations
. . insurance income expenses 1.953-5
. . investment income expenses 1.953-4
. expenses
. . alternative method for determining tax book value 1.861-9
. foreign corporations 1.959-3
. global dealing operations
. . notional principal contracts 1.863-7
. interest expenses
. . qualified business unit 1.861-9T
. inventory, sales of.......................... 1.863-3
. loss
. . at risk provisions 1.465-77
. . personal property.......................... 1.861-8
. . stock 1.861-8
. low-income housing; rules for post-2000 state housing credit ceiling amounts 1.42-14
. partnerships, built in gain or loss on contributions to
. . distributive share or partner 1.704-1
. S corporation stock
. . prohibited allocations.................. 1.409(p)-1
. state housing credit, allocation of (See Low-income housing subhead State housing credit)

Alternative minimum tax (AMT)
. compensation reduction plans or arrangements 1.61-16
. gains for property dealings.................. 1.61-6
. interest 1.61-7

American Samoa
. exclusion, income 1.931-1; 1.931-1T
. individual income tax
. . nonresident alien individual who is resident of U.S. possession or Puerto Rico, taxation of ... 1.1-1(b)
. nonresident aliens.......................... 1.876-1

Amortization
. leased property, depreciation or amortization of improvements 1.178-1
. life insurance companies 1.818-3

AMT (See Alternative minimum tax (AMT))

Annuities and annuity contracts
. accrual of benefits, reduction of rate of future
. . notice requirements 54.4980F-1
. beneficiaries, taxability of................ 1.403(a)-1
. contribution limitations .... 1.415(a)-1
. distributions
. . capital gains treatment .... 1.403(a)-2
. . required................................ 1.403(b)-2
. employee trusts .... 1.403(b)-2
. employee's annuities
. . gift, limitation on amount excludable from 25.2517-1
. exchange for property, received in .... 1.72-6(e); 1.1001-1
. generally 1.72-4; 1.72-13
. guaranteed annuity interest defined .... 1.170A-6; 25.2522(c)-3
. joint and survivor
. . explanations provided to participants, required .... 1.417(a)(3)-1
. . REA 1984 requirements .... 1.401(a)-20
. . substitution of generally applicable information for participant information .... 1.417(a)(3)-1(d)
. . written explanation requirement ...... 1.417(a)(3)-1
. lump-sum distributions
. . accumulated deductible employee contributions 20.2039-4
. modified guaranteed contracts 1.817A-1
. notice requirements
. . accrual of benefits, reduction of rate of future 54.4980F-1
. preretirement survivor annuities .... 1.401(a)-20
. . explanation provided to participants, required .... 1.417(a)(3)-1
. public school purchase of; taxability (See subhead section 501(c)(3) organization purchase of)
. salary reduction agreement
. . section 403(b) contract under, employer contribution to purchase .... 1.402(g)(3)-1

References are to Reg. § numbers

Annuities and annuity contracts —Cont'd
. section 501(c)(3) organization purchase of
. . aggregation of contracts .... 1.403(b)-3
. . church plans .... 1.403(b)-10
. . combining assets .... 1.403(b)-8
. . contracts not meeting definition of annuity contract .... 1.403(b)-8
. . contribution limitations .... 1.403(b)-4
. . contributions to the plan .... 1.403(b)-8
. . corrective distributions .... 1.403(b)-7
. . custodial account defined .... 1.403(b)-8
. . definitions concerning .... 1.403(b)-2; 1.403(b)-8
. . domestic relations orders, distributions from .... 1.403(b)-7; 1.403(b)-10
. . exclusion from gross income .... 1.403(b)-3
. . failure to satisfy nonforfeitability requirement .... 1.403(b)-3
. . frozen plan .... 1.403(b)-10
. . funding .... 1.403(b)-8
. . individual retirement arrangements, rollover to .... 1.403(b)-7
. . investments .... 1.403(b)-8
. . loans .... 1.403(b)-7
. . nondiscrimination rules for contributions other than section 403(b) elective deferrals ...... 1.403(b)-5
. . plan-to-plan transfers .... 1.403(b)-10
. . retirement income accounts .. 1.403(b)-8; 1.403(b)-9
. . rollover contributions .... 1.403(b)-7; 1.403(b)-10
. . section 72(p)(1) loans .... 1.403(b)-7
. . section 403(b) elective deferrals .... 1.403(b)-4
. . taxability .... 1.403(b)-1
. . taxation of distributions and benefits ..... 1.403(b)-7
. . tax-exempt organizations .... 1.414(c)-5
. . termination of plan .... 1.403(b)-10
. . years of service, determination of .... 1.403(b)-4

Appeal
. procedure, taxpayer 601.106

Apportionment (See Allocation and apportionment)

Arbitrage bonds
. investment-type property defined 1.148-1
. mortgage bonds .... 1.143(g)-1
. yield and valuation of investments 1.148-5

Arm's length transactions
. controlled services transactions
. . comparable profits method to determine taxable income .... 1.482-9(e)
. . comparable uncontrolled services to determine taxable income .... 1.482-9(b)
. . cost of services plus method to determine taxable income .... 1.482-9(d)
. . gross services margin method to determine taxable income .... 1.482-9(c)
. . profit split method to determine taxable income .... 1.482-6; 1.482-9(g)

Arm's length transactions —Cont'd
. controlled services transactions —Cont'd
. . simplified cost-basis method to determine taxable income .... 1.482-9(f)
. . taxable income determination ... 1.482-9; 1.482-9(h)
. profit split method use in determination of
. . comparable profits method 1.482-6
. . market returns for routine contribution, determination of 1.482-6
. . residual profits, allocation of 1.482-6

At risk provisions
. activities applicable to section 1.465-1 ..... 1.465-1(a)
. activity, use of term .... 1.465-9(c)
. affected taxpayers .... 1.465-1(d)
. allocation of loss 1.465-77
. allowance of deductions 1.465-2
. amounts borrowed for use in an activity .... 1.465-9(b)
. amounts loaned to the activity by the taxpayer 1.465-7
. amounts protected against loss .... 1.465-9(a); 1.465-20
. avoidance, attempts at 1.465-4
. capital loss, allowance of .... 1.465-38(a)
. certain persons, amounts borrowed from 1.465-20
. contingent repayment liabilities .... 1.465-6(c)
. double counting of additions and reductions to amount at risk .... 1.465-9(e)
. effective date, amount at risk with respect to activities begun prior to .... 1.465-75 to 1.465-95
. examples, illustrative 1.465-41
. exploring for or exploiting oil and gas resources 1.465-45
. farming 1.465-43
. foreclosure .... 1.465-9(g)
. generally .... 1.465-1 et seq.
. guarantors, repayment .... 1.465-6(d)
. increases and decreases in amount of risk, timing of 1.465-39
. insufficient records 1.465-78
. interest other than of a creditor 1.465-8
. leasing Section 1245 property 1.465-44
. loan creation and personal liability 1.465-24
. loss, amounts protected against 1.465-6
. losses .... 1.465-11 to 1.465-13
. money transactions 1.465-22
. motion picture films or video tapes, holding, producing or distributing 1.465-42
. nonrecourse liability by a partnership ..... 1.465-25(c)
. nonrecourse loan for which taxpayer pledges property not used in the activity .... 1.465-25(a)
. nonrecourse loan for which taxpayer pledges property used in the activity .... 1.465-25(b)
. ordering rules, deduction 1.465-38
. partnership liability .... 1.465-24(a)(2)

References are to Reg. § numbers

At risk provisions —Cont'd
. *partnership liability—Cont'd*
. . repayment of nonrecourse liability by a partnership .... 1.465-25(c)
. personal funds or personal assets .... 1.465-9(f)
. personal liability for repayment 1.465-8
. property transactions 1.465-23
. record insufficient 1.465-78
. recourse liabilities which become nonrecourse 1.465-5
. rules of construction 1.465-9
. S corporations and shareholders 1.465-10
. single activity, use of term .... 1.465-9(d)
. substance over form in application, prevalence of .... 1.465-1(b)
. tax preference items, allowance of .... 1.465-38(a)
. taxpayer, loans to the activity by the 1.465-7
. transfers and dispositions .... 1.465-66 through 1.465-69; 1.465-66 to 1.465-69
. unencumbered property contributions 1.465-23
. zero, amount at risk below 1.465-3

Averaging of income (See Income averaging)

Aviation gasoline
. defined 48.4081-1

Avoided cost method
. capitalization of costs; interest calculation 1.263A-9

Awards
. employee achievement special exclusion 1.74-2
. income exclusion 1.74-1

B

Backup withholding
. deposits and deposit forms .... 31.6302(c)-1
. diligence defense 301.6676-2
. dividends 1.6042-5
. remuneration for services and direct sales 1.6041A-1
. reportable payments .... 31.3406(b)(1)-1
. returns 1.6041A-1
. taxpayer identification number incorrect .... 31.3406(d)-5
. 30-day rules .... 31.3406(d)-3

Bad debt
. former thrift institution
. . change by 1.593-13
. . generally .... 1.593-12 et seq.
. . ineligible to use reserve method of Sec. 593 .... 1.593-12
. . requalification for Sec. 593 .... 1.593-14
. generally .... 1.166-4; 1.582-1; 1.593-1 to 1.593-3

Balanced performance measurement system
. performance goals
. . basis, as 801.1T

Balanced performance measurement system — Cont'd
. *performance goals —Cont'd*
. . business results measures 801.6T
. . customer satisfaction measures 801.4T
. . employee performance 801.3T
. . employee satisfaction measures 801.5T
. . organizational performance 801.2T

Banking institutions
. mutual savings banks (See Mutual saving banks)
. S corporations
. . taxable income, computation of .... 1.1363-1(b)(2)

Basis
. adjusted grossed-up basis (See Adjusted grossed-up basis)
. indebtedness to shareholder 1.1367-2
. related parties, sales or exchanges between 1.1012-2
. shareholder's stock in S corporation 1.1367-1
. successor corporations
. . stock basis after group structure change 1.1502-31
. . unified rule for loss on subsidiary stock 1.1502-36

Basis for gain or loss
. built-in loss duplication, limitations on
. . election, sec. 362(e)(2)(C) .... 1.362-4(c)
. . generally .... 1.362-4(b)
. . multiple transferors .... 1.362-4(b)(2)
. . net built-in loss .... 1.362-4(b)(4)
. . reorganizations, sec. 362(e)(2) .... 1.362-4(b)(5)
. . transactions described in sec. 362(e)(1) .... 1.362-4(b)(3)
. . transfer of property .... 1.362-4(a)
. . U.S. person, neither party .... 1.362-4(b)(7)
. corporate organizations and reorganizations
. . limitations on loss importation 1.362-3
. discharge of indebtedness 1.1017-1
. foreign corporations
. . adjustment in basis of stock held by 1.961-3
. . increase in basis of stock in CFC 1.961-1
. . redemption of stock treated as distribution 1.961-4
. . reduction in basis of stock in CFC 1.961-2

Below-market loans
. generally .... 1.7872-1 to 1.7872-13
. split-dollar 1.7872-15

Boats
. luxury tax 48.4002-1

Bond premiums
. repurchase, corporation 1.249-1

Bonds
. capital gains and losses 1.1232-1
. corporations 1.249-1

References are to Reg. § numbers

Bonds —Cont'd
. general obligation bonds refunding special rules .... 1.141-13(f)
. individual retirement accounts .... 1.412(c)(2)-2
. pension excise tax 54.4973-1
. qualified bond purchase plans 1.405-3
. retirement bonds 1.405-3; 1.409-1

Boycotts, international, participation in
. computation of international boycott factor 1.999-1

Branch profits tax
. hedging transactions 1.884-1

Buildings
. carryover allocation, qualified for 1.42-6

Bullet swaps
. notional principal contracts 1.1234A-1

Bureau of Census
. disclosure of information .... 301.6103(j)(1)-1

Bureau of Economic Analysis
. disclosure of information .... 301.6103(j)(1)-1

Business entities
. classifications for federal tax purposes 301.7701-3
. . partial withdrawal of regulation concerning .... 301.7701-3(h)
. definitions
. . entity with single owner disregarded as entity separate from owner 301.7701-2
. foreign eligible entities 301.7701-3

C

Cafeteria plans
. Family and Medical Leave Act, effect of 1.125-3
. generally 1.125-1; 1.125-2
. questions and answers 1.125-1; 1.125-2

Camp
. dependent care services
. . employment related expenses, credit for ... 1.21-1(d)

Cancellation of indebtedness
. information reports 1.6050P-1
. organization which lends money 1.6050P-2

Capital asset exclusion
. accounts receivable 1.1221-1
. notes receivable 1.1221-1

Capital assets
. musical works, capital asset treatment of self-created 1.1221-3

Capital construction funds
. generally 3.2; 3.3; 3.5; 3.6; 3.8

Capital gains and losses
. annuity contract .... 1.403(a)-2
. bonds and other evidence of indebtedness .. 1.1232-1
. charitable contributions included in distributable net income .... 1.643(a)-3

Capital gains and losses —Cont'd
. charitable purposes
. . set asides for long-term capital gains ..... 1.642(c)-2
. employee trusts .... 1.403(a)-2
. foreign corporations, special rules
. . overall domestic loss .... 1.904(g)-1
. . . ordering rules for separate limitation losses, overall foreign losses and overall domestic losses .... 1.904(g)-3
. . overall domestic loss account .... 1.904(g)-1
. . . recapture .... 1.904(g)-2
. . overall foreign loss .... 1.904(f)-1(a)(1); 1.904(f)-1(d)(4)
. . . ordering rules for separate limitation losses, overall foreign losses and overall domestic losses .... 1.904(g)-3
. . . recapture .... 1.904(f)-2
. . overall foreign loss accounts ...... 1.904(f)-1(a)(1); 1.904(f)-1(d)(4)
. . recapture
. . . overall domestic loss account .... 1.904(g)-2
. . . overall foreign loss .... 1.904(f)-2
. . . separate limitation loss accounts ...... 1.904(f)-8
. . section 904 corporations 1.904-4
. . separate limitation loss .... 1.904(f)-7
. . . ordering rules for separate limitation losses, overall foreign losses and overall domestic losses .... 1.904(g)-3
. . separate limitation loss accounts .... 1.904(f)-7
. . . recapture .... 1.904(f)-8
. long-term capital gains
. . permanent set asides for charitable purposes .... 1.642(c)-2
. net capital losses
. . ordering rules for net operating losses, net capital losses, U.S. source losses .... 1.904(g)-3
. net operating losses
. . ordering rules for net operating losses, net capital losses, U.S. source losses .... 1.904(g)-3
. obligations issued at discount 1.1232-3
. retirement benefits 1.1232-2
. U.S. source losses
. . ordering rules for net operating losses, net capital losses, U.S. source losses .... 1.904(g)-3

Capitalization of costs
. anti-abuse rules 1.263A-15
. avoided cost method use to calculate interest 1.263A-9
. property produced by taxpayer 1.263A-2
. transitional rules 1.263A-15
. uniform 1.263A-1

Caribbean basin countries
. investments 1.936-10

Carrybacks and carryovers
. foreign tax credit 1.904-2

References are to Reg. § numbers

Carryover allocations
. basis .... 1.42-6(b)
. defined .... 1.42-6(a)
. election of appropriate percentage month 1.42-8
. partnerships or other flow-through entities ... 1.42-6(e)
. qualifications for 1.42-6
. requirements .... 1.42-6(d)
. state housing credit, allocation of (See Low-income housing subhead State housing credit)
. transfers after allocation, treatment of ...... 1.42-6(e)
. verification of basis .... 1.42-6(c)

Cash balance plans
. accruals .... 1.401(a)(4)-3
. attainment of age as factor in accruals or allocations .... 1.411(b)-2

Cash basis of accounting
. limitations on use
. . simplification of 481(a) adjustment periods .... 1.448-1(g)(2)(i)

Cash or deferred arrangements (CODAs)
. automatic contribution arrangements
. . ADP test
. . . corrective distributions .... 1.401(k)-2(b)(2)(vi)
. . . default elective contributions .. 1.401(k)-2(a)(5)(vi)
. . . early participation rules .... 1.401(k)-3(h)(3)
. . . excess contributions, income allocable to .... 1.401(k)-2(b)(2)(iv)
. . . 401-1(k)(12) safe harbor .... 1.401(k)-3(a)(1)
. . . 401-1(k)(13) safe harbor .... 1.401(k)-3(a)(2)
. . . 401-1(m)(11) safe harbor .... 1.401(m)-3(a)(1)
. . . 401-1(m)(12) safe harbor .... 1.401(m)-3(a)(2)
. . . Jan. 1, 2008, plans before .. 1.401(k)-2(b)(2)(iv)(D)
. . . matching contributions .... 1.401(m)-2(a)(5)
. . . nonelective contributions to satisfy other discrimination tests, use of .... 1.401(k)-3(h)(2)
. . . QMAC forfeiture, permitted .... 1.401(k)-2(b)(2)(B)(4)
. . . safe harbor contribution and ADP testing .... 1.401(k)-1(e)(7)
. . . safe harbor contributions requirements .... 1.401(k)-3(a)(3); 1.401(m)-3(a)(3)
. . . special rules for automatic contributions .... 1.401(k)-2(b)(2)(B)(5)
. . applicable employer plan defined ... 1.414(w)-1(e)(1)
. . default elective contribution .... 1.414(w)-1(e)(3)
. . defined .... 1.414(w)-1(e)(2)
. . distributions, permissible .... 1.402(c)-2
. . eligible employee .... 1.414(w)-1(e)(4)
. . employee contributions and matching contributions
. . . ACP test for matching contributions .... 1.401(m)-2(a)(5)
. . . forfeiture, matching contributions treatment as .... 1.411(a)-4(b)(7)
. . . plan provision requirements ...... 1.401(m)-1(c)(2)
. . . safe harbor provisions .... 1.401(m)-1(b)(1)(iii)

Cash or deferred arrangements (CODAs) —Cont'd
. *automatic contribution arrangements —Cont'd*
. . excess distribution, no tax on ...... 1.414(w)-1(c)(1)
. . forfeiture, matching contributions treatment as .... 1.411(a)-4(b)(7)
. . qualified automatic contribution arrangement
. . . automatic requirement .... 1.401(k)-3(j)(1)
. . . qualified percentage .... 1.401(k)-3(j)(2)
. . qualified matching contributions defined .. 1.401(k)-6
. . safe harbor provisions
. . . ADP testing and safe harbor contributions .... 1.401(k)-1(e)(7)
. . . employee contributions and matching contributions .... 1.401(m)-1(b)(1)(iii)
. . . 401-1(k)(12) safe harbor, ADP test .... 1.401(k)-3(a)(1)
. . . 401-1(k)(13) safe harbor, ADP test .... 1.401(k)-3(a)(2)
. . . 401-1(m)(11) safe harbor, ADP test ....1.401(m)-3(a)(1)
. . . 401-1(m)(12) safe harbor, ADP test ....1.401(m)-3(a)(2)
. . . modifications to contribution requirements .... 1.401(k)-3(k)
. . withdrawals, permissible
. . . amount of distribution .... 1.414(w)-1(c)(3)
. . . consent rules .... 1.414(w)-1(d)(3)
. . . consequences of withdrawal ..... 1.414(w)-1(d)(1)
. . . eligible automatic contribution arrangement .... 1.414(w)-1(b)(1)
. . . forfeiture of matching contributions .... 1.414(w)-1(d)(2)
. . . generally .... 1.414(w)-1(a); 1.414(w)-1(c)(1)
. . . income tax consequences of withdrawal .... 1.414(w)-1(d)(1)
. . . notice requirements .... 1.414(w)-1(b)(3)
. . . timing .... 1.414(w)-1(c)(2)
. . . uniformity requirements .... 1.414(w)-1(b)(2)
. benefit limitations .... 1.401(k)-1

Cash value
. defined 1.7702-2

Catch-up contributions
. individual retirement arrangements (IRAs), individuals over age 50 .... 1.414(v)-1
. pension plans for individuals over age 50 .. 1.414(v)-1

Cemetery companies and crematoria
. exemption .... 1.501(c)(13)-1

Census Bureau
. disclosure of return information to .... 301.6103(j)(1)-1

Charitable contributions
. allocation and apportionment............... 1.861-8
. carryovers
. . corporate
. . . election by corporation on accrual method; carryover limitation 1.170A-11

References are to Reg. § numbers

Charitable contributions —Cont'd
. estates and trusts, unlimited deduction
. . substantiation .... 1.642(c)-2
. long-term capital gains
. . permanent set asides for charitable purposes .... 1.642(c)-2

Charitable organizations
. excess benefit transactions
. . church tax inquiries 53.4958-7
. . cooperatives, allocation or return of net margins or capital to members of.............. 53.4958-5
. . defined 53.4958-4
. . disqualified persons
. . . defined 53.4958-3
. . . statutory categories 53.4958-3
. . . tax paid by 53.4958-1
. . economic benefit provided by tax-exempt organizations 53.4958-5
. . excess benefits
. . . defined 53.4958-1
. . . identification standards............. 53.4958-4
. . facts and circumstances effecting 53.4958-3
. . imposition of tax, effective date for....... 53.4958-1
. . intent 53.4958-4
. . organization manager, tax paid by 53.4958-1
. . rebutting presumption of transaction 53.4958-6
. . substantial influence, persons having 53.4958-3
. . tax exemption, effects on statutory standards for 53.4958-7
. public charity, special rules
. . form 990 .... 1.170A-9

Charitable remainder annuity trusts
. distributions
. . annual distributions, treatment of 1.664-1
. . ordering rule 1.664-1

Charitable remainder trusts
. distributions
. . annual distributions, treatment of 1.664-1
. . anti-abuse rules, application of............ 1.664-1
. . deemed sale by trust, determination of ... 1.643(a)-8
. . ordering rule 1.664-1
. excise tax on .... 1.664-1(c)
. unlimited deduction, substantiation .... 1.642(c)-2
. unrelated business taxable income, effect of .. 1.664-1

Charitable remainder unitrusts
. distributions
. . annual distributions, treatment of 1.664-1
. . ordering rule 1.664-1
. income defined for trusts 1.664-3

Circulation expenditures
. optional 10-year writeoff of certain tax preferences 1.59-1

Classifications for federal tax purposes
. business entities 301.7701-3
. . association taxable as corporation for a qualified electing S corporation 301.7701-3
. . partial withdrawal of regulation concerning .... 301.7701-3(h)

COD income
. discharge of indebtedness
. . consolidated returns 1.1502-28
. . consolidated returns, excess loss accounts 1.1502-28

Collateralized debt obligations
. information returns, electronic filing
. . time and place for filing 1.6049-7

Collection Due Process hearing
. notice and opportunity for hearing prior to levy 301.6330-1

Collection of taxes
. assessment, after
. . continued effectiveness of extension limitations period of collection entered into on or before December 31, 1999 .... 301.6502-1(c)
. . court proceeding for collection .... 301.6502-1(c)
. . extension of limitation period, agreement on .... 301.6502-1(b)
. . generally .... 301.6502-1(a)
. . levy date, determination of .... 301.6502-1(f)
. . statutory suspension of limitation period if executed collection extension agreement is in effect .... 301.6502-1(e)
. assessments under IRC sec. 6502 .... 301.6502-1
. backup withholding (See Backup withholding)
. installment payments
. . assessments under IRC sec. 6502 ..... 301.6502-1
. liability of employer, determination of 31.3509-1
. real estate agents and direct sellers as nonemployees 31.3508-1
. unauthorized collection actions
. . administrative claim for recovery of damages 301.7426-2
. . administrative costs, recovery of 301.7430-8
. . administrative proceedings 301.7430-3
. . Bankruptcy Code
. . . automatic stay violations under section 362 .... 301.7430-1
. . . civil cause of action for violation of sections 362 or 524 .... 301.7433-2
. . civil cause of action 301.7433-1
. . exhaustion of administrative remedies... 301.7433-1
. . recovery of damages in certain cases ... 301.7426-2
. unlawful collection actions (See subhead unauthorized collection actions)
. withholding (See Withholding of tax)

Collectively bargained funds
. generally 1.413-1

References are to Reg. § numbers

Commodities dealers
. derivatives
. . trading for taxpayer's own account . . . . 1.864(b)-1
Common nontaxable exchanges
. generally 1.1037-1
Communications activity
. gross income derived from 1.863-9
. taxable income 1.863-9
Communications services, excise taxes
. distance sensitivity 49.4252-0
Community income
. fraudulent schemes 1.66-4
. general treatment 1.66-1
. living apart, spouses 1.66-2
. marital status and effect on 1.66-1
. notification of spouses 1.66-3
. relief from operation of law 1.66-4
. request for relief from community property law 1.66-4
. transferee liability 1.66-1
. transferred income
. . liability, transferee 1.66-1
. . living apart, spouses 1.66-2
Community property law income (See Community income)
Community Renewal Tax Relief Act of 2000
. effective dates 1.42-12
Compensation
. deferred (See Deferred compensation)
. pension, profit-sharing, and stock bonus plans (See Pension, profit-sharing, and stock bonus plans)
. personal services (See Personal services)
. wages (See Wages)
Compensation reduction plans or arrangements
. alternative minimum tax (AMT) 1.61-16
Computer software
. domestic production gross receipts . . 1.199-3; 1.199-8
Conduit debtors
. Financial Asset Securitization Investment Trusts
. . regular interests 1.860H-5
Consent dividends
. consent filed for dividend paid deduction, time of filing 1.565-1
Consolidated groups
. agents
. . common parent as 1.1502-77
. . matters subject to 1.1502-77
. intercompany obligations, transfer or extinguishment of rights under 1.1502-13
. triangular reorganizations . . . . 1.358-6(e)
. . group structure change, stock basis after 1.1502-30
. . stock basis 1.1502-30
Consolidated returns
. accumulated earnings tax 1.1502-43
. circular stock basis elimination when there is excluded COD income . . . . 1.1502-11(c)
. circular stock basis elimination when there is no excluded COD income . . . . 1.1502-11(b)
. consolidated taxable income, determining . . 1.1502-11
. discharge of indebtedness income (COD), excluded 1.1502-28
. . excess loss accounts 1.1502-28
. filing 1.1502-75
. investment adjustment
. . allocation of adjustments among shares of stock . . . . 1.1502-32(c)
. . previously taxed earnings 1.1502-32
. life-nonlife insurance groups 1.1502-47
. net operating loss
. . generally 1.1502-21
. provisions of other law, applicability of
. . section 332 applied, liquidations to which . . . . 1.1502-80(g)
. separate taxable income 1.1502-12
. taxable year
. . personal service corporations; affiliated groups filing consolidated returns 1.441-3
. transfers of subsidiary stock and deconsolidation of subsidiary
. . anti-avoidance rules . . . . 1.1502-35(g); 1.1502-35(h)
. . definitions concerning . . . . 1.1502-35(d)
. . loss suspension . . . . 1.1502-35(c)
. . on or before date regulations published as final in Federal Register, anti-loss reimportation rules applicable . . . . 1.1502-35(b)
. . prior to date regulations published as final in Federal Register, losses on transfers or deconsolidations . . . . 1.1502-35(a)
. . redetermination of basis . . . . 1.1502-35(b)
. . tax benefits, avoidance of multiple . . . . . 1.1502-35(a)
. . unified rule for loss on subsidiary stock . . . 1.1502-36
. . worthlessness not followed by separate return years . . . . 1.1502-35(f)
. unified rule for loss on subsidiary stock 1.1502-36
Constructive receipt of income
. accounting methods 1.451-2
Contracts and agreements
. gain recognition agreement requirements . . 1.367(a)-8
Contributions
. charitable (See Charitable contributions)
. pension, profit-sharing, and stock bonus plans (See Pension, profit-sharing, and stock bonus plans)
Controlled corporations
. component members, tax benefits available to
. . allocation of reductions to certain 1561(a) tax benefit items 1.1561-3
. . amount of benefit, determining 1.1561-2

References are to Reg. § numbers

Controlled corporations —Cont'd
. *component members, tax benefits available to —Cont'd*
. . component members defined 1.1561-1
. . controlled group defined 1.1561-1
. . defined, component members 1.1563-1
. . . additional members . . . . 1.1563-1(b)(3)
. . . constructive ownership rule, application of . . . . 1.1563-1(b)(5)
. . . excluded members . . . . 1.1563-1(b)(2)
. . . generally . . . . 1.1563-1(b)
. . defined, controlled group 1.1563-1
. . . brother-sister . . . . 1.1563-1(a)(3)
. . . generally . . . . 1.1563-1(a)(1)
. . . life insurance . . . . 1.1563-1(a)(5)
. . . parent-subsidiary . . . . 1.1563-1(a)(2)
. . general rules 1.1561-1
. . overlapping groups . . . . 1.1563-1(c)
. . transitional rules . . . . 1.1563-1(d)
. increase in earnings invested in U.S. property
. . shareholder's pro rata share
. . . amount attributable to property . . . . 1.956-1(e)
. reorganization
. . distribution of stock and securities . . . . 1.367(b)-5
. research credits 1.41-6
. stock distributions
. . active trade or business
. . . defined, active conduct of a trade or business . . . . 1.355-3(b)
. . . definitions concerning . . . . 1.355-3(c)
. . . examples . . . . 1.355-3(d)
. . . generally . . . . 1.355-3(a)
. . limitations . . . . 1.355-2(g)
. . predecessors and successors under section 355(e) 1.355-8
. transfers to . . . . . . 1.351-1 et seq.; 1.351-1 to 1.351-3
. voting rights, retained 20.2036-2

Controlled foreign corporations
. accounting period 1.441-1
. acquisition of stock, returns 1.6046-1
. earnings and profits 1.964-1; 1.964-1T
. foreign base company income 1.954-1
. gross income exclusions 1.883-3
. hybrid branch payments 1.954-9
. insurance income
. . computation 1.953-6
. . expenses, allocation and apportionment of 1.953-5
. . generally 1.953-1
. . investment income, allocating items of 1.953-4
. . premiums 1.953-3
. . related person insurance income (RPII) . . . 1.953-3; 1.953-7
. . subchapters L and N 1.953-6

Controlled foreign corporations —Cont'd
. liability on or after January 1, 1963, requirement of returns 1.6046-1
. look-through rules
. . income received or accrued, characterization of 1.904-5
. mark-to-market election for marketable stock
. . basis, adjustment to . . . . 1.1296-1(d)
. . coordination rules for first year of election . . . . 1.1296-1(i)
. . disposition of stock . . . . 1.1296-1(g)
. . effect of section 1296 election . . . . 1.1296-1(c)
. . elections . . . . 1.1296-1(h)
. . holding period . . . . 1.1296-1(f)
. . section 1296 election . . . . 1.1296-1(b)
. . stock owned by certain foreign entities . . 1.1296-1(e)
. . U.S. person, treatment of CFC as . . . . . . 1.1296-1(g)
. organization or reorganization, returns 1.6046-1
. partnership income, distributive share of 1.952-1
. returns 1.6046-1
. sales or exchanges, treatment of gain 1.1248-1
. subpart F income
. . pro rata share, determination of 1.951-1

Controlled services transactions
. arm's length (See Arm's length transactions)

Controlled trades and businesses
. generally . . . . 1.367(b)-5

Cooperative housing corporation
. tenant-shareholder
. . principal residence sales, exclusion of gain from sale or exchange 1.121-4

Corporate organizations and reorganization
. capital construction funds 3.8
. controlled corporations reorganization
. . distribution of stock and securities . . . . 1.367(b)-5
. controlled foreign corporations
. . returns 1.6046-1
. reorganization defined 1.368-2

Corporations
. additions to tax . . . . 1.6655-1 to 1.6655-5; 301.6655-1
. bond premium on repurchase 1.249-1
. controlled corporations . . . . 1.367(b)-5
. DISCs (See Domestic international sales corporations)
. distributions (See Distributions by corporations)
. earnings stripping . . . . 1.163(j)-1 et seq.
. estimated tax 301.6655-1
. foreign branches (See Foreign deferred compensation plans)
. foreign corporations (See Foreign corporations)
. personal service corporations 1.269A-1
. reorganizations (See Corporate organizations and reorganizations)

References are to Reg. § numbers

Corporations —Cont'd

. transfer to corporation controlled by transferor 1.351-1

Cost sharing arrangements

. coordination of 1.481 with 1.482-7 .... 1.482-1
. coordination with 1.482-1 .... 1.482-7
. defined 1.482-7
. intangible development costs 1.482-7
. qualified 1.482-7
. taxable income, determination of
. . accounting requirements .... 1.482-7(k)
. . allocations .... 1.482-7(i)
. . arms-length amount charged to PCT ..... 1.482-7(g)
. . arms-length standard, coordination with .. 1.482-7(h)
. . benefits defined .... 1.482-7(j)
. . best method rule, examples of .... 1.482-(8)
. . classification of organization for federal tax 301.7701-1
. . controlled participant defined .... 1.482-7(j)
. . controlled participant's reasonably anticipated benefits defined .... 1.482-7(j)
. . cost shared intangible defined .... 1.482-7(j)
. . CSA activity defined .... 1.482-7(j)
. . defined .... 1.482-7(b)
. . documentation .... 1.482-7(k)
. . intangible development costs .... 1.482-7(d)
. . interest in an intangible defined .... 1.482-7(j)
. . make-or-sell rights, exclusion of .... 1.482-7(c)
. . methodology 1.482-7
. . net transfer price adjustments 1.6662-6
. . participation, changes in .... 1.482-7(f)
. . reasonably anticipated benefits share .... 1.482-7(e)
. . reporting requirements .... 1.482-7(k)
. . research and development expenditures, allocation of 1.461-17
. . special rules .... 1.482-7(j)
. . territorial operating profit or loss defined .. 1.482-7(j)

Credits (See Abatements, credits, and refunds- specific credit)

Crude oil

. tiers 51.4991-1

Custodial accounts

. employee trusts .... 1.403(b)-2
. pension, profit-sharing, and stock bonus plans
. . gross income exclusion .... 1.403(b)-3

D

Death

. married taxpayer, dependent care services
. . employment related expenses, credit for ... 1.21-3(c)
. transfers at 3.8

Death benefits

. exclusion from gross income 1.101-2
. life insurance contracts, defined for 1.7702-2
. qualified accelerated death benefits
. . amounts paid with respect to terminally ill individuals 1.7702A-1

Death taxes

. December 31, 2004, decedents dying on or before
. . state death tax deduction, exercise of .... 20.2053-9(c)
. deduction for .... 20.2053-6(c)
. foreign death taxes, deduction for ...... 20.2053-10(c)

Debt

. bad (See Bad debt)
. cancellation of (See Cancellation of indebtedness)

Debt instruments

. disposition of security by a dealer .... 1.475(a)-2
. mark-to-market .... 1.475(a)-1
. nonfunctional currency contingent payment
. . accrual of interest 1.988-6
. . adjusted basis .... 1.988-6(b)
. . denomination currency determination, multicurrency instruments .... 1.988-6(d)
. . gain or loss, character of 1.988-6
. . gain or loss not attributable to foreign currency .... 1.988-6(b)
. . multicurrency instruments .... 1.988-6(d)
. . noncontingent bond method of interest accrual .... 1.988-6(b)
. . nonpublicly traded property .... 1.988-6(e)
. original issue discount (See Original issue discount)

Debt obligations

. registration requirements (See Registration-required obligations)

Decedents

. December 31, 2004, dying on or before
. . generally .... 20.2053-9(a)
. . state death tax deduction, exercise of .... 20.2053-9(c)
. gross estate, computation of
. . deduction for taxes .... 20.2053-6(a)
. post-death adjustments of deductible tax liability .... 20.2053-6(g)

Declaratory judgments

. gift valuation for gift tax purposes 301.7477-1

Deductions (See also specific topics)

. at risk provisions general rules 1.465-2

Deferred compensation

. accounting methods 1.457-1; 1.457-2
. accruals and allocations
. . employer and employee contributions, allocation of accrued benefits between .... 1.411(c)-1
. . restriction and valuation of .... 1.411(a)-11
. . specified age, after a .... 1.411(b)-2

References are to Reg. § numbers

Deferred compensation —Cont'd
. alternate maximum funding standard account .... 1.412(g)-1
. definitions 1.457-2
. discrimination requirements
. . vesting schedule requirements coordination with .... 1.411(d)-1
. distributions
. . defer, consequences of failure to .... 1.411(a)-11(h)
. . restriction and valuation of .... 1.411(a)-11
. eligible compensation plans
. . administration not in accordance with eligibility requirements 1.457-9
. . annual deferrals 1.457-4
. . catch-up, age 50 .... 1.457-4
. . . multiple eligible plan rules 1.457-5
. . deferral limitations 1.457-4
. . definitions 1.457-2
. . distributions
. . . taxation of 1.457-7
. . . timing of 1.457-6
. . emergency distributions 1.457-6
. . excess deferral 1.457-4
. . frozen plans 1.457-10
. . funding rules 1.457-8
. . generally 1.457-3
. . gross estate, distributions included in 1.457-7
. . independent contractor severance from employment 1.457-6
. . individual limitations for combined annual deferrals 1.457-5
. . loans from 1.457-6
. . maximum deferral limitations 1.457-4
. . plan-to-plan transfers 1.457-10
. . severance from employment 1.457-6
. . sick, vacation, and back pay deferral 1.457-4
. . tax treatment of noneligible plans 1.457-11
. . termination of plan 1.457-10
. foreign plans (See Foreign deferred compensation plans)
. full funding limitation .... 1.412(c)(6)-1
. funding method, change in .... 1.412(c)(5)-1
. nonqualified plans 1.457-1
. . amount includible in income
. . . additional 20 percent tax under sec. 409A(a)(1)(B)(i)(II) .... 1.409A-4(c)
. . . application of amounts included in income under sec. 409A to payment of amounts deferred .... 1.409A-4(f)
. . . failure to meet requirements of sec. 409A(a) .... 1.409A-4(a)
. . . forfeiture or other permanent loss of right to deferred compensation .... 1.409A-4(g)
. . . premium interest tax under sec. 409A(a)(1)(B)(i)(I) .... 1.409A-4(d)

Deferred compensation —Cont'd
. *nonqualified plans—Cont'd*
. . *amount includible in income —Cont'd*
. . . total amount deferred under a plan for a taxable year .... 1.409A-4(b)
. . deferral compensation generally .... 1.409A-1(b)
. . defined 1.409A-1
. . election
. . . changes in time and form of payment .... 1.409A-2(b)
. . . initial .... 1.409A-2(a)
. . established securities market .... 1.409A-1(k)
. . forfeiture, substantial risk of .... 1.409A-1(d)
. . nonresident alien .... 1.409A-1(j)
. . payments, permissible 1.409A-3
. . . acceleration, prohibition on .... 1.409A-3(h)
. . . alternate dates, designation of .... 1.409A-3(c)
. . . change in ownership of assets .... 1.409A-3(g)(5)
. . . change in ownership or control .... 1.409A-3(g)(5)
. . . definitions concerning .... 1.409A-3(g)
. . . delay in payment to specified employee pursuant to a separation from service .... 1.409A-3(g)(2)
. . . designation of .... 1.409A-3(b)
. . . disability .... 1.409A-3(g)(4)
. . . disputed .... 1.409A-3(e)
. . . effective dates, statutory .... 1.409A-6(a)
. . . emergency, unforeseeable .... 1.409A-3(g)(3)
. . . fixed schedule .... 1.409A-3(g)(1)
. . . made, treatment as .... 1.409A-3(d)
. . . resident aliens .... 1.409A-3(f)
. . . specified time .... 1.409A-3(g)(1)
. . performance based compensation .... 1.409A-1(e)
. . plan defined for .... 1.409A-1(c)
. . separation from service .... 1.409A-1(h)
. . separation pay arrangement .... 1.409A-1(m)
. . service recipient .... 1.409A-1(g)
. . specified employee .... 1.409A-1(i)
. . stock right .... 1.409A-1(l)
. notice
. . electronic medium, use of .... 1.401(a)-21
. plan year, change in .... 1.412(c)(5)-1
. retroactive amendments, treatment of .... 1.412(c)(8)-1
. state plans, eligible (See subhead eligible compensation plans)
. vesting schedule requirements
. . discrimination requirements coordination with .... 1.411(d)-1

Defined benefit plans (See Pension, profit-sharing, and stock bonus plans)

Defined contribution plans (See Pension, profit-sharing, and stock bonus plans)

Dependent
. definition, general rules regarding 1.152-2

References are to Reg. § numbers

Dependent care services
. employment related expenses, credit for
. . allocation of expenses .... 1.21-1(d)
. . amount of credit, determination of .... 1.21-1(a)
. . camp, child at .... 1.21-1(d)
. . death of married taxpayer .... 1.21-3(c)
. . divorced or separated persons, special tests for .... 1.21-1(b)
. . dollar limitation, annual .... 1.21-2(a)
. . earned income limitation .... 1.21-2(b)
. . gainful employment defined .... 1.21-1(c)
. . generally .... 1.21-1(a)
. . household services, expenses for .... 1.21-1(d)
. . indirect expenses .... 1.21-1(d)
. . joint return requirement .... 1.21-3(a)
. . maintenance of household .... 1.21-1(h)
. . medical expenses, qualifying .... 1.21-1(j)
. . partnerships or other entities .... 1.21-4(b)
. . principal place of abode defined .... 1.21-1(g)
. . qualifying individuals .... 1.21-1(b)
. . reimbursed expenses .... 1.21-1(f)
. . related individuals, payments to .... 1.21-4(a)
. . room and board .... 1.21-1(d)
. . school below level of kindergarten, care of child in .... 1.21-1(d)
. . self-care, individuals incapable of .... 1.21-1(b)
. . separated on not married taxpayer .... 1.21-3(b)
. . services outside taxpayer's household .... 1.21-1(e)
. . spousal earned income .... 1.21-2(b)
. . student earned income attribution .... 1.21-2(b)
. . substantiation .... 1.21-1(k)
. . transportation expenses .... 1.21-1(d)
. . two or more families occupying same living quarters .... 1.21-1(h)

Depletion
. Accelerated Cost Recovery System
. . periods since February 28, 1913 .... 1.1016-3

Depositaries of government
. collection of taxes .... 31.6302(c)-1
. special rules under chapter 33 .... 40.6302(c)-3

Depreciation
. accelerated cost recovery system (ACRS)
. . generally .... 1.168-4 et seq.
.. additional first year depreciation deduction .... 1.168(k)-1
. change in method .... 1.167(e)-1
. changes in computation .... 1.446-1(e)-1
. class lives and ADR property placed in service after December 31, 1970
. . repairs .... 1.167(a)-11
. first year deduction .... 1.168(k)-1
. income forecast method
. . accounting method .... 1.167(n)-1

Depreciation —Cont'd
. *income forecast method —Cont'd*
. . aggregations, treatment of .... 1.167(n)-5
. . basis .... 1.167(n)-2
. . computation of depreciation .... 1.167(n)-4
. . costs treated as separate property .... 1.167(n)-5
. . current year income .... 1.167(n)-3
. . disposal of forecast property .... 1.167(n)-6
. . failure to generate income, forecast property .... 1.167(n)-6
. . final year depreciation .... 1.167(n)-4
. . forecasted total income .... 1.167(n)-3
. . generally .... 1.167(n)-1
. . look-back interest, treatment of .... 1.167(n)-6
. . look-back method, application of .... 1.167(n)-6
. . overpayment of tax .... 1.167(n)-6
. . property for which method may be used .... 1.167(n)-5
. . redetermination of basis .... 1.167(n)-2
. . underpayment of tax .... 1.167(n)-6
. . unrecoverable depreciable basis .... 1.167(n)-2
. leased property, depreciation or amortization of improvements 1.178-1
. New York Liberty zone first year deduction .... 1.1400L(b)-1

Derivatives
. commodities dealers
. . trading for taxpayer's own account .... 1.864(b)-1

Designated or related summons
. defined .... 301.6503(j)-1(b)
. limitations on assessment
.. period of suspension .... 301.6503(j)-1
. . special rules .... 301.6503(j)-1(d)
. number of summons that may be issued .... 301.6503(j)-1(d)

Diesel fuel
. dyed fuel exemption 48.4082-1

Disability benefits
. self-insured medical reimbursement plans, exclusions 1.105-11
. sickness or accident disability payments .... 31.3121(a)(2)-1

Discharge of indebtedness
. basis, reduction in 1.1017-1

Disclosure
. Agriculture Department officers and employees, return information to .... 301.6103(j)(5)-1
. . census of agriculture, conducting ... 301.6103(j)(5)-1
. Bureau of Economic Analysis .... 301.6103(j)(1)-1
. Census Bureau, to .... 301.6103(j)(1)-1
. electronically filed tax information administration (See Electronic filing subhead disclosure of tax information)

References are to Reg. § numbers

Disclosure —Cont'd
. investigative purposes, to certain officers for .... 301.6103(k)(6)-1
. IRS records or information
. . adverse ruling with respect to refusal to disclose, procedure in the event of ....301.9000-4(g)
. . benefit or separate privilege .... 301.9000 et seq.
. . Bivens matters ....301.9000-4(d)
. . congressional matters ....301.9000-4(e)
. . creation of .... 301.9000-4(i)
. . defined 301.9000-1
. . examples 301.9000-6
. . FTCA matters ....301.9000-4(d)
. . government contract matters ....301.9000-4(d)
. . labor relations matters ....301.9000-4(d)
. . nonauthorization, situations for 301.9000-2
. . notification of disclosure officer ......301.9000-4(b)
. . opposition to a demand .... 301.9000-4(f)
. . personnel matters ....301.9000-4(d)
. . request or demand procedure 301.9000-4
. . responding, considerations in 301.9000-2
. . safeguard tax returns or information, failure to .... 301.6103(p)(4)-1; 301.6103(p)(7)-1
. . testimony authorizations 301.9000-3
. . U.S. Tax court request or demand procedure ....301.9000-4(c)
. . waiver of written statement requirements for non-IRS matters ....301.9000-5(b)
. . written statement requirements for non-IRS matters ....301.9000-5(a)
. procurement of property or services for tax administration ....301.6103(n)-1
. safeguard tax returns or information, failure to .... 301.6103(p)(4)-1; 301.6103(p)(7)-1
. taxpayer consent, section 7216
. . copy of consent taxpayer, providing .... 301.7216-3(c)(3)
. . disclosure of entire return .... 301.7216-3(c)(2)
. . duration of consent .... 301.7216-3(b)(5)
. . effective / applicability date ....301.7216-3(d)
. . form and content consent ....301.7216-3(a)(3); 301.7216-3(a)(3)(i)
. . . examples ....301.7216-3(a)(3)(iv)
. . . Form 1040 series .... 301.7216-3(a)(3)(ii)
. . . with respect to all other taxpayers ....301.7216-3(a)(3)(iii)
. . furnishing tax return information to another tax return preparer .... 301.7216-3(a)(2)
. . generally .... 301.7216-3; 301.7216-3(a); 301.7216-3(a)(1)
. . multiple disclosures within a single consent form or multiple uses with a single consent form .... 301.7216-3(c)(1)
. . retroactive consent .... 301.7216-3(b)(1)
. . special rules ....301.7216-3(c)

Disclosure —Cont'd
. *taxpayer consent, section 7216 —Cont'd*
. . time limitations on requesting consent in solicitation context .... 301.7216-3(b)(2)
. . timing requirements and limitations . . .301.7216-3(b)
. . unsuccessful requests .... 301.7216-3(b)(3)
. whistleblowers and their legal representative, written contracts among IRS ....301.6103(n)-2

Discrimination
. generally .... 1.408-8; 1.411(d)-1

DISCs (See Domestic international sales corporations)

Disputed ownership funds
. defined .... 1.468B-9(b)
. distributions to claimants other than transferor-claimants .... 1.468B-9(f)
. escrow account status as 1.468B-9
. taxation of ....1.468B-9(c)
. transferor-claimants rules.............. 1.468B-9(d)
. transfers of property other than cash, statements to fund and IRS concerning .... 1.468B-9(g)

Distributions
. corporate (See Distributions by corporations)
. lump sum distributions (See Lump-sum distributions)
. pension, profit-sharing, and stock bonus plans (See Pension, profit-sharing, and stock bonus plans)
. stock and stock rights (See Stock)

Distributions by corporations
. domestic international sales corporations ... 1.995-2; 1.995-2A; 1.996-1
. fair market value date 1.301-1
. foreign persons, stock distributions to
. . gain, recognition of .... 1.367(e)-1
. gain recognition agreement requirements .. 1.367(a)-8
. generally .... 1.301-1 et seq.
. money 1.301-1
. property 1.301-1
. S corporations 1.1368-1
. Section 338, elections under
. . adjusted grossed-up basis (AGUB)
. . . insurance companies ....1.338-11(b)
. . aggregate deemed sale price (ADSP)
. . . insurance companies ....1.338-11(b)
. . assumption reinsurance principles
. . . insurance companies .... 1.338-11(c)
. . insurance companies...................... 1.338-11
. . . adjusted grossed-up basis (AGUB) .... 1.338-11(b)
. . . aggregate deemed sale price (ADSP) ....1.338-11(b)
. . . assumption reinsurance principles .... 1.338-11(c)
. . . policyholders surplus account, effect on .... 1.338-11(f)
. . . reserve increases by new target after deemed asset sale ....1.338-11(d)

References are to Reg. § numbers

Distributions by corporations —Cont'd
. *Section 338, elections under —Cont'd*
. . *insurance companies—Cont'd*
. . . sec. 847 special estimated payments ..... 1.338-11(g)
. . . sec. 848, old target capitalization under ..... 1.338-11(e)
. split-dollar life insurance arrangement ..... 1.301-1(q)
. transactions treated as 1.301-1
District of Columbia
. withholding under sec. 3402(t) ..... 31.3402(t)-2(c)
Dividends
. backup withholding 1.6042-5
. exclusions 1.120-1; 1.120-2
. intercompany dividends, loss deduction 1.6044-6
. mutual savings banks 1.591-1
. pension, profit-sharing, and stock bonus plans
. . disallowance of deduction on ESOP reacquisition payments ..... 1.404(k)-3
. qualified dividend income as investment income, election to make ..... 1.163(d)-1
Divorced or separated persons
. child of, dependency deduction for
. . apart, parents who live 1.152-4
. . custodial parent
. . . defined ..... 1.152-4(c)
. . . release of claim by ..... 1.152-4(b)
. . . written declaration of release of claim by ..... 1.152-4(d)
. . . written declaration of release of claim by, revocation of ..... 1.152-4(d)(3)
. . generally ..... 1.152-4(a)
. . qualifying child or relative of noncustodial parent ..... 1.152-4(e)
. . residency of child ..... 1.152-4(c)
. dependent care services
. . employment related expenses, credit for ..... 1.21-1(b)
Documentation
. space or ocean activity income 1.863-8
Documents
. timely mailing as timely filing 301.7502-1
Domestic building and loan associations
. distributions to shareholders 1.593-7
. mutual savings banks 1.593-7
Domestic international sales corporations (DISCs)
. adjustments 1.996-9
. distributions 1.995-2; 1.995-2A; 1.996-1
. export receipts 1.993-1; 1.995-7; 1.995-8
. generally ..... 1.991-1 et seq.
. interest, deferred tax liability 1.6011-2
. interest charge
. . deferred tax liability after 1984 ..... 1.995(f)-1
Domestic production activities
. adjusted gross income ..... 1.199-1(b)

Domestic production activities —Cont'd
. agricultural and horticultural cooperatives
. . double counting ..... 1.199-6(h)
. . generally ..... 1.199-6(a)
. . pass-through of 199 deduction, rules for ..... 1.199-6(d)
. . patronage dividend deductions ..... 1.199-6(g)
. . qualified production activities income, determining ..... 1.199-6(c)
. . recapture of 199 deduction ..... 1.199-6(f)
. . section, exclusivity of 1.199-6(g) ..... 1.199-6(g)
. . W-2 wages ..... 1.199-6(e)
. . written notice to patrons ..... 1.199-6(b)
. allocation of gross receipts ..... 1.199-1(d)
. alternative minimum tax, coordination with ..... 1.199-8(c)
. domestic production gross receipts
. . by the taxpayer defined ..... 1.199-3(e)
. . construction performed in the United States defined ..... 1.199-3(l)
. . costs allocable to
. . . average annual gross receipts ..... 1.199-4(g)
. . . deductions allocable or apportioned, other ..... 1.199-4(c)
. . . generally ..... 1.199-4(a)
. . . goods sold ..... 1.199-4(b)
. . . section 861 allocation method ..... 1.199-4(d)
. . . simplified deduction method ..... 1.199-4(e)
. . . small business simplified overall method ..... 1.199-4(f)
. . defined ..... 1.199-3(a)
. . derived from the lease, rental, license, sale exchange, or other disposition defined ..... 1.199-3(h)
. . electricity, natural gas, or potable water ..... 1.199-3(k)
. . engineering and architectural services defined ..... 1.199-3(m)
. . food and beverage exception ..... 1.199-3(n)
. . gross receipts defined ..... 1.199-3(c)
. . in whole or in significant part defined ..... 1.199-3(f)
. . manufactured, produced, grown or extracted defined ..... 1.199-3(d)
. . qualified film defined ..... 1.199-3(k)
. . qualifying production property defined ..... 1.199-3(i)
. . related persons ..... 1.199-3(b)
. . United States defined ..... 1.199-3(g)
. expanded affiliated groups
. . allocation of deduction ..... 1.199-7(c)
. . allocation of income and loss of corporate affiliated group member for only a portion of year ..... 1.199-7(f)
. . computation of deduction ..... 1.199-7(b)
. . consolidated group, rules for members of same ..... 1.199-7(d)
. . deduction corporate affiliated group member for some or all taxable year ..... 1.199-7(g)

References are to Reg. § numbers

Domestic production activities —Cont'd
. *expanded affiliated groups —Cont'd*
. . deduction corporate affiliated group member with different taxable year . . . . 1.199-7(h)
. . generally . . . . 1.199-7(a)
. 52-53 week taxable year, taxpayer with . . . . 1.199-8(e)
. individuals . . . . 1.199-8(a)
. nonrecognition transactions . . . . 1.199-8(d)
. pass-thru entities, application of sec. 199 to
. . attribution of qualified activities . . . . 1.199-5(g)
. . gain or loss from disposition of entity . . . . 1.199-5(e)
. . grantor trusts . . . . 1.199-5(c)
. . non-grantor trusts and estates . . . . 1.199-5(d)
. . partnerships . . . . 1.199-5(a)
. . S corporations . . . . 1.199-5(b)
. . wage limitations and tiered structures . . . . 1.199-5(f)
. QPAI, timing rules for determining . . . . 1.199-1(e)
. qualified production activities income . . . . 1.199-1(c)
. sec. 481(a) adjustments . . . . 1.199-8(f)
. taxable income . . . . 1.199-1(b)
. trade or businesses, application of 1.199-3 to . . . . 1.199-8(b)
. wage limitations
. . acquisition or disposition of a trade or business . . . . 1.199-2(d)
. . application, rules of . . . . 1.199-2(a)
. . employment tax purposes, rules of application for . . . . 1.199-2(a)
. . non-duplication rule . . . . 1.199-2(e)
. . short taxable year, application for . . . . 1.199-2(a)
. . W-2 wages defined . . . . 1.199-2(f)

Domestic service
. payments for . . . . 31.3121(a)(7)-1
. . computation . . . . 31.3121(i)-1
. wages paid for, withholding . . . . 31.6011(a)-4

Donated property (See Charitable contributions-Gifts)

Dual consolidated losses
. accounting rules . . . . 1.1503(d)-3
. definitions concerning . . . . 1.1503(d)-1
. denial of use . . . . 1.1503(d)-2(d)
. dual resident corporation or domestic owner members of consolidated groups 1.1503-2
. elimination of loss after certain transactions . . . . 1.1503(d)-2(c)
. examples for application of . . . . 1.1503(d)-5
. exceptions to domestic use limitation rule . . . . 1.1503(d)-4
. foreign tax credit limitation, computation of . . . . 1.1503(d)-2(e)
. net operating loss carrybacks and carryovers 1.1503-2
. operating rules . . . . 1.1503(d)-2
. recapture events 1.1503-2

Dual consolidated losses —Cont'd
. special filing rules . . . . 1.1503(d)-1(c)

Dwelling units
. business use
. . expenses of unit used as residence 1.280A-2
. . rental of dwelling unit 1.280A-3
. limitation of deductions with respect to 1.280A-1

E

Earnings stripping
. affiliated group rules . . . . 1.163(j)-5
. carryforward of tax attributes, limitations on . . . . 1.163(j)-6
. debt-equity ratio, computation of . . . . 1.163(j)-3
. deductibility of interest expense, relationship to other provisions affecting . . . . 1.163(j)-7
. definitions . . . . 1.163(j)-2
. effective dates . . . . 1.163(j)-10
. foreign corporations . . . . 1.163(j)-1; 1.163(j)-8
. generally . . . . 1.163(j)-1
. interest not subject to tax . . . . 1.163(j)-4
. S corporations, exception to disallowance rule . . . . 1.163(j)-1

Economic Growth and Tax Relief Reconciliation Act of 2001 (EGTRRA)
. alternate forms of payment under defined contribution plans . . . . 1.411(d)-1
. catch-up contributions for individuals over age 50 . . . . 1.414(v)-1

Education loans
. information reporting of interest payments
. . failure to file, penalties for 1.6050S-2
. . magnetic media requirements 301.6011-2
. . return, requirement to file 1.6050S-2
. . special rules 1.6050S-2
. . statement, requirement to furnish 1.6050S-2

Education tax credits
. calculation of 1.25A-1
. definitions concerning 1.25A-2
. HOPE and Lifetime Learning credit, coordination 1.25A-1

EGTRRA (See Economic Growth and Tax Relief Reconciliation Act of 2001)

Election or choice (See specific subject heading)
. electronic medium, use of
. . pension, profit-sharing, and stock bonus plans . . . . 1.401(a)-21

Election to expense certain refineries
. computation of expense deduction for qualified refinery property . . . . 1.179C-1(c)
. effective / applicability date . . . . 1.179C-1(g)
. election to allocate section 179C deduction to cooperative owners . . . . 1.179C-1(e); 1.179C-1(e)(1)

References are to Reg. § numbers

Election to expense certain refineries —Cont'd
. *election to allocate section 179C deduction to cooperative owners—Cont'd*
. . irrevocable election . . . . 1.179C-1(e)(4)
. . time and manner for making election . . . . 1.179C-1(e)(2)
. . . manner for making election . . . . . 1.179C-1(e)(2)(ii)
. . . time for making election . . . . 1.179C-1(e)(2)(i)
. . written notice to owners . . . . 1.179C-1(e)(3)
. election to amortize organizational expenditures 1.248-1
. . organizational expenditures defined . . . . . 1.248-1(b)
. . time and manner of making election . . . . . 1.248-1(c)
. election to amortize start-up expenditures 1.195-1
. expiration date . . . . 1.179C-1(h)
. generally . . . . 1.179C-1(d)(1)
. qualified refinery property . . . . 1.179C-1(b); 1.179C-1(b)(1)
. . applicable environmental laws . . . . . 1.179C-1(b)(6); 1.179C-1(b)(6)(i)
. . . Clean Air Act waiver . . . . 1.179C-1(b)(6)(iii)
. . construction of property . . . . 1.179C-1(b)(7); 1.179C-1(b)(7)(i)
. . . definition of a binding contract . . . 1.179C-1(b)(7)(ii)
. . . self-constructed property . . . . . . 1.179C-1(b)(7)(iii)
. . description of qualified refinery property . . . . 1.179C-1(b)(2); 1.179C-1(b)(2)(i)
. . . nonqualified refinery property . . . 1.179C-1(b)(2)(ii)
. . original use . . . . 1.179C-1(b)(3); 1.179C-1(b)(3)(i)
. . . nonqualified refinery property . . . 1.179C-1(b)(3)(ii)
. . placed-in-service date . . . . 1.179C-1(b)(4); 1.179C-1(b)(4)(i)
. . . sale-leaseback . . . . 1.179C-1(b)(4)(ii)
. . production capacity . . . . 1.179C-1(b)(5); 1.179C-1(b)(5)(i)
. . . multi-stage projects . . . . 1.179C-1(b)(5)(iii)
. . . when production capacity is tested . . . . 1.179C-1(b)(5)(ii)
. reporting requirement . . . . . 1.179C-1(f); 1.179C-1(f)(1)
. . information to be included in the report . . . . 1.179C-1(f)(2)
. . time and manner for submitting report . . . . 1.179C-1(f)(3)
. revocation of election . . . . 1.179C-1(d)(3)(i)
. . after the revocation deadline . . . . 1.179C-1(d)(3)(iii)
. . cooperative taxpayer, by . . . . 1.179C-1(d)(3)(iv)
. . prior to the revocation deadline . . . 1.179C-1(d)(3)(ii)
. scope and definitions . . . . 1.179C-1(a)
. . definitions . . . . 1.179C-1(a)(2)
. . scope . . . . 1.179C-1(a)(1)
. time and manner for making election . . 1.179C-1(d)(2)
. . manner of making election . . . . 1.179C-1(d)(2)(ii)
. . time for making election . . . . 1.179C-1(d)(2)(i)
. treatment of organization and syndication costs 1.709-1

Election to expense certain refineries —Cont'd
. *treatment of organization and syndication costs—Cont'd*
. . general rule . . . . 1.709-1(a)

Electronic filing
. disclosure of tax information
. . accountant, by . . . . 301.7216-2(h)
. . administrative order, pursuant to . . . . . 301.7216-2(f)
. . attorney, by . . . . 301.7216-2(h)
. . audit preparation . . . . 301.7216-2(k)
. . Congressional subpoena, pursuant to . . . . 301.7216-2(f)
. . court order, pursuant to . . . . 301.7216-2(f)
. . crime, to report . . . . 301.7216-2(q)
. . death or incapacity of tax preparer . . . . 301.7216-2(r)
. . definitions concerning . . . . 301.7216-1(b)
. . demand or summons, pursuant to . . . . 301.7216-2(f)
. . ethics board subpoena, pursuant to . . . 301.7216-2(f)
. . facilitate electronic administration, to . . . . 301.7216-2(b)
. . federal or state agency subpoena, pursuant to . . . . 301.7216-2(f)
. . fiduciaries . . . . 301.7216-2(i); 301.7216-2(j)
. . Gramm-Leach-Bliley Act requirements . . . . 301.7216-1(c)
. . lists for solicitation of business . . . . . . 301.7216-2(n)
. . payment for tax preparation services . . 301.7216-2(l)
. . penalties . . . . 301.7216-1(a)
. . permissible 301.7216-2
. . preparation of return, for . . . . 301.7216-2(c)
. . Public Company Accounting Oversight Board subpoena, pursuant to . . . . 301.7216-2(f)
. . quality for peer review, for . . . . 301.7216-2(p)
. . related taxpayers . . . . 301.7216-2(e)
. . retention of records . . . . 301.7216-2(m)
. . statistical information for tax return business . . . . 301.7216-2(o)
. . tax return preparer, to other . . . . 301.7216-2(d)
. . Treasury investigation, for use in . . . . . 301.7216-2(g)
. form 5472 . . . . 1.6038A-1; 1.6038A-2
. information returns
. . collateralized debt obligations
. . . time and place for filing 1.6049-7
. . REMIC regular interest
. . . time and place for filing 1.6049-7
. . time and place for filing
. . . collateralized debt obligations 1.6049-7
. . . REMIC regular interest 1.6049-7

Electronic mediums
. notice and participant election, use for
. . pension, profit-sharing, and stock bonus plans . . . . 1.401(a)-21

Employee achievement awards
. special exclusion 1.74-2

References are to Reg. § numbers

Employee retirement and benefit plans (See Pension, profit-sharing, and stock bonus plans)

Employee Retirement Income Security Act of 1974 (ERISA)
. accrued benefit requirements .... 1.411(b)-1
. affiliated service groups .... 1.414(m)-1
. collectively bargained plans 1.413-1
. definitions .... 1.414(m)-2
. maximum age conditions .... 1.410(a)-4A
. multiple employers 1.413-2
. vesting .... 1.411(a)-1

Employee stock ownership plans (ESOPs)
. gain or loss on sale of stock
. . notarized statement of purchase 1.1042-1T
. reacquired stock
. . disallowance of deduction on reacquisition payments .... 1.404(k)-3

Employee stock purchase plan
. corporations defined .... 1.421-1(i)(1)
. defined .... 1.423-2(a)
. incentive stock option defined
. . amendment of option terms .... 1.422-2(a)(3)
. . option requirements .... 1.422-2(a)(2)
. . terms provide option not an incentive stock option .... 1.422-2(a)(4)
. incentive stock options
. . defined .... 1.422-2(a)(1)
. . option plan .... 1.422-2(b)(1)
. income taxes
. . applicability of section 421(a) 1.423-1
. . . cross-references .... 1.423-1(b)
. . . general rule .... 1.423-1(a)
. . employee stock purchase plan defined 1.423-2
. . . annual $25,000 limitation .... 1.423-2(i)
. . . effective / applicability date .... 1.423-2(l)
. . . employees covered by plan .... 1.423-2(e)
. . . equal rights and privileges .... 1.423-2(f)
. . . option period .... 1.423-2(h)
. . . option price .... 1.423-2(g)
. . . options granted to certain shareholders .... 1.423-2(d)
. . . options restricted to employees .... 1.423-2(b)
. . . restriction on transferability .... 1.423-2(j)
. . . special rule where option price is between 85 percent and 100 percent of value of stock .... 1.423-2(k)
. . . stockholder approval .... 1.423-2(c)
. . incentive stock options defined 1.422-2
. . . duration of option grants under the plan .... 1.422-2(c)
. . . incentive stock option defined .... 1.422-2(a)
. . . option plan .... 1.422-2(b)
. . . option price .... 1.422-2(e)

Employee stock purchase plan —Cont'd
. *income taxes —Cont'd*
. . *incentive stock options defined—Cont'd*
. . . options granted to certain stockholders .... 1.422-2(f)
. . . period for exercising options .... 1.422-2(d)
. . meaning and use of certain terms 1.421-1
. . . additional definitions .... 1.421-1(i)
. . . effective date .... 1.421-1(j)
. . . employment relationship .... 1.421-1(h)
. . . exercise .... 1.421-1(f)
. . . option .... 1.421-1(a)
. . . option price .... 1.421-1(e)
. . . statutory options .... 1.421-1(b)
. . . stock and voting stock .... 1.421-1(d)
. . . time and date of granting option .... 1.421-1(c)
. . . transfer .... 1.421-1(g)
. . permissible provisions 1.422-5
. . . additional compensation .... 1.422-5(c)
. . . cashless exercise .... 1.422-5(b)
. . . effective date .... 1.422-5(f)
. . . examples .... 1.422-5(e)
. . . general rule .... 1.422-5(a)
. . . option subject to a condition .... 1.422-5(d)
. option plan
. . conflicting option terms .... 1.422-2(b)(5)
. . designation of employees .... 1.422-2(b)(4)
. . examples illustrating principles of this paragraph .... 1.422-2(b)(6)
. . maximum aggregate number of shares .... 1.422-2(b)(3)
. . stockholder approval .... 1.422-2(b)(2)
. parent corporation and subsidiary corporation defined .... 1.421-1(i)(2)
. permissible provisions
. . effective date .... 1.422-5(f)(1)
. reliance and transition period .... 1.422-5(f)(2)

Employer comparable contributions
. pension excise taxes
. . calculating comparable contributions ... 54.4980G-4
. . failure of employer to make comparable health savings account contributions 54.4980G-3
. . plans that must comply 54.4980B-2
. . requirement of return and time for filing of the excise tax under section 4980D 54.4980D-1
. . requirement of return and time for filing of the excise tax under section 4980E 54.4980E-1
. . special comparability rules for qualified HSA distributions contributed to HSAs on or after December 20, 2006 and before January 1, 2012 .... 54.4980G-7
. . special rule for contributions made to the HSAs of nonhighly compensated employees 54.4980G-6
. . table of contents 54.4980B-0

References are to Reg. § numbers

Employer contributions
. accident and health plans 1.106-1
. simplified employee pensions . . . . 1.404(h)-1
Employer-owned life insurance
. reporting on 1.6039I-1
Employment taxes
. adjustments to
. . domestic services, payments for . . . . 31.6011(a)-4(a)(2)
. . FICA under collected or underpaid . . . . . 31.6025-1(a)
. agricultural labor, payments for . . . . . . 31.3121(a)(8)-1
. business entity defined 301.7701-2
. collection of, and liability for 31.3102-1
. credits or refunds
. . FICA claim for overpayment paid to IRS . . . . 31.6402(a)-2(a)
. . Railroad Retirement Tax Act tax claim for overpayment paid to IRS . . . . 31.6402(a)-2(a)
. deposit rules for withheld income, and FICA taxes to payment made after Dec. 31, 1992 . . . . . 31.6302-1
. domestic services, payments for . . . . . 31.3121(a)(7)-1
. . computation . . . . 31.3121(i)-1
. home workers, payments to . . . . 31.3121(a)(10)-1
. Qsub election, effect of 1.1361-4
. services not in the course of employer's trade or business . . . . 31.3121(a)(7)-1
. wages
. . annual wage limitation
. . . workers' compensation . . . . 31.3121(a)(2)-1
. . payments
. . . employer plans . . . . 31.3121(a)(2)-1 et seq.
. . . workers' compensation . . . . 31.3121(a)(2)-1
. wages, paid and received . . . . 31.3121(a)-2
Endowment contract
. transfer of contract, treatment as property 1.83-3
Energy property
. investment credit 1.48-9
Environmental Protection Agency
. sulfur regulation, deduction for capital costs incurred in complying with
. . generally 1.179B-1
ERISA (See Employee Retirement Income Security Act of 1974)
Escrow accounts
. contingent at-closing escrow's 1.468B-8
. deferred exchanges of like-kind property, used in 1.468B-6
. disputed ownership fund status 1.468B-9
. preclosing 1.468B-7
Estate tax
. administrative costs and expenses
. . attorney's fees . . . . 20.2053-3(c)
. . deductions for 20.2053-3
. . executors commissions . . . . 20.2053-3(b)
Estate tax —Cont'd
. defined 20.2051-1
. lien for
. . release or partial discharge 20.6325-1
Estates and trusts
. automatic extension of time for filing returns 1.6081-6
. claims against the estate, deduction for
. . contested claims . . . . 20.2053-4(b)(2)
. . family members, related entities, or beneficiaries, claims by . . . . 20.2053-4(b)(4)
. . generally . . . . 20.2053-4(a)
. . interest on claims . . . . 20.2053-4(c)
. . multiple parties, claims against . . . . . 20.2053-4(b)(3)
. . potential and unmatured claims . . . . 20.2053-4(b)(1)
. . promise, claims founded upon a . . . . 20.2053-4(b)(6)
. . recurring payments . . . . 20.2053-4(b)(7)
. . unenforceable claims . . . . 20.2053-4(b)(5)
. deferred exchanges of like-kind property, used in 1.468B-6
. income
. . defined for trust purposes . . . . . . 1.643(b)-1; 1.664-3
. . distribution requirement . . . . 1.651(a)-2
. . distributions to beneficiaries . . . . 1.661(a)-2
. . in kind distributions . . . . 1.651(a)-2
. section 67 limitations
. . bundled fees . . . . 1.67-4(c)
. . costs paid or incurred . . . . 1.67-4(a)
. . 2-percent floor on itemized deductions, exception to . . . . 1.67-4(a)
. . unique costs, determination of . . . . 1.67-4(b)
Estimated tax
. consolidated returns
. . large corporations . . . . 1.6655-4(f)
. . underpayment of tax, corporate . . . . 1.6655-1(g)
. corporations 1.6655-4; 301.6655-1
. . accounting method . . . . 1.6655-6(a)
. . . automatic changes . . . . 1.6655-6(b)(1)
. . . non-automatic changes . . . . 1.6655-6(b)(2)
. . additions to tax 1.6655-1
. . . consolidated returns . . . . 1.6655-1(g)
. . . definitions concerning . . . . 1.6655-1(g)
. . . due dates, installment . . . . 1.6655-1(f)
. . . excessive adjustment under sec. 6425 . . . 1.6655-7
. . . installment requirement . . . . 1.6655-1(d)
. . . large corporations requirement to pay 100 percent of current year tax . . . . 1.6655-1(c)
. . . subsequent taxable year, overpayments applied to . . . . 1.6655-1(i)
. . . underpayment requirement . . . . 1.6655-1(b)
. . adjusted seasonal installments 1.6655-3
. . . amount determination . . . . 1.6655-3(c)
. . . limitations . . . . 1.6655-3(b)
. . . special rules . . . . 1.6655-3(d)

References are to Reg. § numbers

Estimated tax —Cont'd
. *corporations—Cont'd*
. . adjustments, effect of .... 1.6425-3(f)
. . . excessive adjustment under sec. 6425 . . . 1.6655-7
. . annualized income installments
. . . determination .... 1.6655-2(b)
. . . election of different annualization periods .... 1.6655-2(d)
. . . events arising after installment due date, unforeseeable .... 1.6655-2(h)
. . . 52-53 week taxable year .... 1.6655-2(e)
. . . generally .... 1.6655-2(a)
. . . items substantially affecting taxable income .... 1.6655-2(g)
. . . special rules .... 1.6655-2(c)
. . . taxable income determination .... 1.6655-2(f)
. . book income estimates 1.56-1
. . excessive adjustment under sec. 6425
. . . additions to tax 1.6655-7
. . failure to pay
. . . adjustment, effect of 1.6425-3
. . overpayment of tax
. . . income tax liability 1.6425-2
. . . subsequent taxable year, applied to . . . 1.6655-1(i)
. . short taxable year 1.6655-5
. . . amount due for required installment . . . 1.6655-5(d)
. . . annualized income method .... 1.6655-5(g)
. . . due date, installment .... 1.6655-5(c)
. . . exceptions to payment .... 1.6655-5(b)
. . . 52-53 week taxable year .... 1.6655-5(f)
. . . preceding taxable year is short taxable year .... 1.6655-5(h)
. . . seasonal income method .... 1.6655-5(g)
. . underpayment of tax .... 1.6655-1(a)
. . . amount of .... 1.6655-1(b)
. . . amount of required installment .... 1.6655-1(d)
. . . consolidated returns .... 1.6655-1(h)
. . . definitions concerning .... 1.6655-1(g)
. . . installment due dates .... 1.6655-1(f)
. . . large corporations .... 1.6655-1(d)
. . . overpayment applied to .... 1.6655-1(i)
. . . period of .... 1.6655-1(c)
. large corporations
. . additions to tax
. . . requirement to pay 100 percent of current year tax .... 1.6655-1(c)
. . carryback or carry over from other taxable year, effect of .... 1.6655-4(e)
. . consolidated returns .... 1.6655-4(f)
. . controlled group members .... 1.6655-4(d)
. . defined .... 1.6655-4(a)
. . testing period .... 1.6655-4(b)
. . . taxable income computation during . . . . 1.6655-4(c)
. . underpayment of tax .... 1.6655-1(d)

Exceptions
. corporate organizations and reorganizations
. . definition of terms 1.368-2
. . special rules 1.368-1

Excess benefit transactions
. applicable tax-exempt organization defined 53.4958-2
. charitable organizations (See Charitable organizations)

Excess deferred income tax reserve
. public utility deregulation
. . disposition of property, treatment upon . . . 1.168(i)(3)

Excess loss accounts
. consolidated returns
. . discharge of indebtedness income (COD), excluded 1.1502-28
. redemption, dividends 1.1502-19

Excess profits tax (See Income, war profits, or excess profits tax paid or accrued)

Exchange
. gain or loss
. . global dealing operations 1.988-4
. personal property .... 1.1031(a)-2

Exchange for property
. annuities and annuity contracts . . . 1.72-6(e); 1.1001-1

Excise taxes
. collection of tax
. . persons receiving payment duty to collect 49.4291-1
. duty to collect 49.4291-1
. employers (See Railroad Unemployment Repayment Tax)
. first retail sale 48.4011-3
. pension, profit-sharing, and stock bonus plans (See Pension, profit-sharing, and bonus plans subhead penalties)
. sales price 48.4011-4

Exclusions
. foreign corporations 1.959-1; 1.959-2

Exempt facilities bonds
. interest paid to 1.103-8
. solid waste disposal facility .... 1.142(a)(6)-1

Exempt organizations
. contributions distinguished from gross receipts .... 1.509(a)-3
. excess benefit transactions
. . applicable tax-exempt organization defined 53.4958-2
. exemptions
. . withholding under sec. 3402(t), government entities .... 31.3402(t)-4(d)
. form 990 .... 1.6033-2
. group legal services plan trust .... 1.501(c)(20)-1
. income, unrelated business (See subhead unrelated business taxable income)

References are to Reg. § numbers

Exempt organizations —Cont'd
. information returns
. . notification requirement for entities not required to file annual information return under sec. 6033(a)(1) . . . 1.6033-6
. pension, profit-sharing, and stock bonus plans
. . excludable employees . . . 1.410(b)-6(g)
. public inspections
. . documents included in the term "application for exemption for Federal income tax" . . . 301.6104(a)-1(e)
. . exemption application . . . 301.6104(a)-1
. . IRS letters or documents with respect to application for exemption . . . 301.6104(a)-1(c)
. . material open unde section 6110 . . . 301.6104(a)-1(f)
. . notice of status filed by political organization . . . 301.6104(a)-1(b)
. . procedures for inspection . . . 301.6104(a)-1(k)
. . publication of exempt status . . . 301.6104(a)-1(i)
. . requirement of exempt status . . . 301.6104(a)-1(d)
. . statement of exempt status . . . 301.6104(a)-1(h)
. . supporting documents defined . . . 301.6104(a)-1(g)
. . withholding of certain information . . . 301.6104(a)-1(j)
. . written determinations and background file documents . . . 301.6110-1(a)
. public *versus* private interest requirement . . . 1.501(c)(3)-1(d)
. section 4958, interaction with . . . 1.501(c)(3)-1(g)
. sponsorship payments . . . 1.513-4
. trade or business activities
. . sponsorship payments . . . 1.513-4
. unrelated business taxable income
. . defined . . . 1.512(a)-1
. . generally . . . 1.512(a)-1
. . questions concerning organizations described in 501(c) paragraphs (9), (17) or (20) . . . 1.512(a)-5T
. . sponsorship payments . . . 1.512(a)-1; 1.513-4
. voluntary employees' beneficiary associations . . . 1.501(c)(9)-2

Exemptions
. additions to tax . . . 1.6654-2; 1.6655-2
. organizations (See Exempt organizations)

Exhaustion
. Accelerated Cost Recovery System
. . periods since February 28, 1913 . . . 1.1016-3
. . periods when income was not subject to tax . . . 1.1016-4

Expanded affiliated groups
. domestic production activities (See Domestic production activities)

Expatriated entities
. foreign corporate parents . . . 1.7874-2

Expenditures (See specific item)

Expenses
. deductions . . . 20.2053-1

Expensing in lieu of depreciation
. definitions . . . 1.179-4
. limitations on amounts subject to . . . 1.179-2
. time and manner of making election . . . 1.179-5

Experimental expenditures (See Research credits)

Exports
. DISCs . . . 1.993-1; 1.995-7; 1.995-8

Extension of time for filing returns
. automatic extensions
. . chapter 43 returns
. . . generally . . . 54.6081-1(a)
. . . payment of tax, no extension for . . . 54.6081-1(c)
. . . penalties . . . 54.6081-1(e)
. . . requirements . . . 54.6081-1(b)
. . . termination of automatic extension . . . 54.6081-1(d)
. . partners . . . 1.6081-2
. . trust income returns . . . 1.6081-6

Extension of time for payment of tax
. generally . . . 1.6164-4; 1.6164-8
. installment payment of tax . . . 301.6502-1

F

False information
. withholding of tax . . . 31.6682-1

Family and Medical Leave Act
. cafeteria plans and . . . 1.125-3

Farm income, averaging
. effective / applicability date . . . 1.1301-1(g)
. electable farm income . . . 1.1301-1(e)
. . determination of amount that may be elected farm income . . . 1.1301-1(e)(2)
. . gain or loss on sale or other disposition of property
. . . cessation of a farming business . . . 1.1301-1(e)(1)(ii)(B)
. . . generally . . . 1.1301-1(e)(1)(ii)(A)
. . identification of items attributable to a farming business
. . . gain or loss on sale or other disposition of property . . . 1.1301-1(e)(1)(ii)
. . . generally . . . 1.1301-1(e)(1); 1.1301-1(e)(1)(i)
. generally . . . 1.1301-1
. guidelines for calculation of section 1 tax . . . 1.1301-1(d)
. . actual taxable income not affected . . . 1.1301-1(d)(1)
. . computation in base years . . . 1.1301-1(d)(2)
. . . example . . . 1.1301-1(d)(2)(ii)
. . . generally . . . 1.1301-1(d)(2)(i)
. . effect on subsequent elections . . . 1.1301-1(d)(3)
. . . example . . . 1.1301-1(d)(3)(ii)

References are to Reg. § numbers

Farm income, averaging —Cont'd
. *guidelines for calculation of section 1 tax—Cont'd*
. . *effect on subsequent elections—Cont'd*
. . . generally .... 1.1301-1(d)(3)(i)
. individual engaged in a farming business .... 1.1301-1(b)
. . certain landlords .... 1.1301-1(b)(2)
. . generally .... 1.1301-1(b)(1)
. making, changing, or revoking an election .... 1.1301-1(c)
. . changing or revoking an election .... 1.1301-1(c)(2)
. . generally .... 1.1301-1(c)(1)
. miscellaneous rules .... 1.1301-1(f)
. . alternative minimum tax .... 1.1301-1(f)(4)
. . changes in filing status .... 1.1301-1(f)(2)
. . employment tax .... 1.1301-1(f)(3)
. . short taxable year .... 1.1301-1(f)(1)
. . . base year is a short taxable year .... 1.1301-1(f)(1)(ii)
. . . election year is a short taxable year .... 1.1301-1(f)(1)(iii)
. . . generally .... 1.1301-1(f)(1)(i)
. . unearned income of minor child ...... 1.1301-1(f)(5)
. overview .... 1.1301-1(a)

Farmer's cooperatives
. returns .... 1.6012-2(f)(1)

Farming
. agricultural labor, payments for ...... 31.3121(a)(8)-1
. at risk provisions 1.465-43

FASIT (See Financial Asset Securitization Investment Trusts)

Federal Insurance Contributions Act (FICA)
. erroneous collection, repayment or reimbursement for .... 31.6413(a)-1(a)
. federal deposit rules for withheld income taxes
. . exception to monthly and semi-weekly deposit rules .... 31.6302-1(c)(7)
. . lookback period .... 31.6302-1(g)(4)
. overpaid taxes
. . adjustments of overpayment....... 31.6403(a)-2(a)
. returns under .... 31.6011(a)-1 et seq.
. under collected or underpaid taxes ..... 31.6025-1(a); 31.6025-1(b)
. . deduction from employee remuneration .... 31.6025-1(d)(1)
. underpayment adjustments 31.6205-1

Fellowship grants (See Scholarships and fellowships)

Film (See Motion picture and television films and tapes)

Financial Asset Securitization Investment Trusts
. allocation and apportionment of interest expense 1.861-10T
. annual reporting requirement.......... 1.860H-6
. anti-abuse rule 1.860L-2

Financial Asset Securitization Investment Trusts — Cont'd
. assets, permitted 1.860H-2
. cash and cash equivalents 1.860H-2
. cessation 1.860H-3
. debt instruments
. . disposition of 1.860L-1
. . permitted asset status 1.860H-2
. defined 1.860H-1
. elections 1.860H-1
. foreclosure property 1.860H-2
. gain, election to defer 1.860L-3
. gain on transfers, recognition of 1.860I-1
. hedges and guarantee contracts
. . accounting for 1.860H-6
. . disposition, exclusion of prohibited transaction tax to 1.860L-1
. . permitted asset status 1.860H-2
. intent of FASIT provision 1.860L-2
. interest expense
. . special allocations 1.861-10T
. lines of credit
. . origination of contract or agreement 1.860L-1
. loan originated by FASIT, transaction tax on 1.860L-1
. mark-to market asset transfers to 1.860H-6
. offset of non-FASIT losses 1.860J-1
. prohibited transactions tax 1.860L-1
. regular interests
. . conduit debtors 1.860H-5
. . foreign resident holders of yield 1.860H-5
. . generally 1.860H-4
. . high-yield 1.860H-4
. . issue price 1.860H-4
. . pass-thru, high-yield held by 1.860H-4
. . securities dealer, high-yield held by 1.860H-4
. taxation of owner 1.860H-6
. transfers of interests 1.860H-6
. transition rule 1.860L-3
. valuation of property 1.860I-2

Financial institutions
. mutual savings banks (See Mutual savings banks)

Fishing income, averaging
. alternative minimum tax .... 1.1301-1T(f)(4)
. changed in filing status .... 1.1301-1T(f)(2)
. effective / applicability date .... 1.1301-1(g); 1.1301-1T(g)
. electable farm income .... 1.1301-1(e)
. . determination of amount that may be elected farm income .... 1.1301-1(e)(2)
. . . electible farm income .... 1.1301-1(e)(2)(i)
. . . examples .... 1.1301-1(e)(2)(ii)
. . identification of items attributable to a farming business .... 1.1301-1(e)(1)

References are to Reg. § numbers

Fishing income, averaging —Cont'd
. *electable farm income—Cont'd*
. . *identification of items attributable to a farming business—Cont'd*
. . . gain or loss on sale or other disposition of property .... 1.1301-1(e)(1)(ii)
. electible farm income .... 1.1301-1T(e)
. . determination of amount that may be elected farm income .... 1.1301-1T(e)(2)
. . . electable farm income .... 1.1301-1T(e)(2)(i)
. . . examples .... 1.1301-1T(e)(2)(ii)
. . gain or loss on sale or other disposition of property
. . . cessation of a farming or fishing business .... 1.1301-1T(e)(1)(ii)(B)
. . . generally .... 1.1301-1T(e)(1)(ii)(A)
. . identification of items attributable to a farming or fishing business .... 1.1301-1T(e)(1)
. . . gain or loss on sale or other disposition of property .... 1.1301-1T(e)(1)(ii)
. . . generally .... 1.1301-1T(e)(1)(i)
. generally 1.1301-1; 1.1301-1T
. guidelines for calculation of section 1 tax .... 1.1301-1(d)
. . actual taxable income not affected ... 1.1301-1(d)(1)
. . computation in base years .... 1.1301-1(d)(2)
. . . example .... 1.1301-1(d)(2)(ii)
. . effect on subsequent elections ...... 1.1301-1(d)(3)
. . . example .... 1.1301-1(d)(3)(ii)
. individual engaged in a farming business .... 1.1301-1(b)
. . certain landlords................. 1.1301-1(b)(2)
. individuals engaged in a farming or fishing business .... 1.1301-1T(b)
. . deposits into Merchant Marine Capital Construction Fund .... 1.1301-1T(b)(4)
. . . example .... 1.1301-1T(b)(4)(ii)
. . . reduction to taxable income and electible farm income .... 1.1301-1T(b)(4)(i)
. . generally .... 1.1301-1T(b)(1)
. . . base years .... 1.1301-1T(b)(1)(iii)
. . . farming or fishing business .... 1.1301-1T(b)(1)(i)
. . . form of business .... 1.1301-1T(b)(1)(ii)
. . lessors of vessels used in fishing ... 1.1301-1T(b)(3)
. information reporting.............. 1.1301-1(e)(1)(i)
. . guidelines for calculation of section 1 tax
. . . base years computation .... 1.1301-1(d)(2)(i)
. . . effect on subsequent elections ... 1.1301-1(d)(3)(i)
. . individual engaged in a farming business .... 1.1301-1(b)(1)
. . making, changing, or revoking an election .... 1.1301-1(c)(1)
. . short taxable year .... 1.1301-1(f)(1)(i)
. making, changing, or revoking an election .... 1.1301-1(c); 1.1301-1T(c)
. . changing or revoking an election .... 1.1301-1(c)(2)
. . example .... 1.1301-1T(c)(3)

Fishing income, averaging —Cont'd
. *making, changing, or revoking an election—Cont'd*
. . generally .... 1.1301-1T(c)(1)
. miscellaneous rules .... 1.1301-1(f)
. . alternative minimum tax .... 1.1301-1(f)(4)
. . changes in filing status .... 1.1301-1(f)(2)
. . employment tax .... 1.1301-1(f)(3)
. . short taxable year .... 1.1301-1(f)(1)
. . . base year is a short taxable year .... 1.1301-1(f)(1)(ii)
. . . election year is a short taxable year .... 1.1301-1(f)(1)(iii)
. . unearned income of minor child ...... 1.1301-1(f)(5)
. overview.................. 1.1301-1(a); 1.1301-1T(a)

Fixed investment trusts
. widely held fixed investment trusts (See Widely held fixed investment trusts)

Foreign banks
. withholding of tax 1.1441-1

Foreign base company income
. deductible payments to nonfiscally transparent entities 1.954-1
. partnership income, distributive shares of 1.954-1
. sales income
. . guidance concerning .... 1.954-3(b)
. . partnership income, distributive shares of ... 1.954-3
. service income
. . partnership income, distributive shares of ... 1.954-4

Foreign corporations
. allocation of earnings and profits and foreign income taxes after section 355 distribution ...... 1.367(b)-8
. assets
. . repatriation of .... 1.367(b)-3
. . transfer of .... 1.367(b)-8; 7.367(b)-8
. capital gains and losses, special rules
. . overall domestic loss .... 1.904(g)-1
. . overall domestic loss account........... 1.904(g)-1
. . . recapture .... 1.904(g)-2
. . overall foreign loss .... 1.904(f)-1(a)(1); 1.904(f)-1(d)(4)
. . . recapture .... 1.904(f)-2
. . overall foreign loss accounts ...... 1.904(f)-1(a)(1); 1.904(f)-1(d)(4)
. . recapture
. . . overall domestic loss account .... 1.904(g)-2
. . . overall foreign loss .... 1.904(f)-2
. . . separate limitation loss accounts....... 1.904(f)-8
. . section 904 corporations 1.904-4
. . separate limitation loss .... 1.904(f)-7
. . separate limitation loss accounts .... 1.904(f)-7
. . . recapture .... 1.904(f)-8
. controlled foreign corporations (See Controlled foreign corporations)

References are to Reg. § numbers

Foreign corporations —Cont'd
. deferred compensation plans (See Foreign deferred compensation plans)
. domestic corporate shareholder
. . credits for paid foreign income taxes 1.902-1
. domestic subsidiary
. . termination or incorporation 1.884-2
. earnings and profits
. . attribution of .... 1.367(b)-9
. . carryover to surviving corporation after acquisitions .... 1.367(b)-7
. . determination .... 1.964-1T(a)
. . distributions of amounts excluded under 959(a) 1.959-4
. . foreign-to-foreign nonrecognition transactions .... 1.367(b)-7
. . functional currency, computation in ..... 1.964-1T(g)
. . maintenance and adjustment 1.959-3
. . previously taxed 1.959-1
. . taxable years, determination of .... 1.964-1T(c)
. earnings stripping .... 1.163(j)-1; 1.163(j)-8
. exchanges of stock
. . basis and holding period, special rules for determining .... 1.367(b)-13
. . definitions .... 1.367(b)-2
. . described in Sec. 354 .... 1.367(b)-7
. . foreign corporation stock by foreign corporation in certain nonrecognition transactions ... 1.367(b)-4
. . nonrecognition transactions
. . . acquisition of foreign corporation stock or asset by foreign corporation .... 1.367(b)-4
. . . repatriation of foreign corporate asset .... 1.367(b)-3; 1.367(b)-3T
. . repatriation of assets in nonrecognition transactions .... 1.367(b)-3; 1.367(b)-3T
. exclusions from gross income 1.959-1; 1.959-2
. expatriated entities and their foreign parents 1.7874-2
. gain recognition agreement requirements . . 1.367(a)-8
. gross income exclusions
. . constructive stock ownership test 1.883-4
. . controlled foreign corporations, treatment of 1.883-3
. . equivalent exemptions 1.883-1
. . income inclusion test 1.883-3
. . ownership test 1.883-1
. . possession of U.S. foreign country status ... 1.883-1
. . publicly-traded corporations 1.883-2
. . qualified shareholder stock ownership test .. 1.883-4
. . reporting requirements ... 1.883-1; 1.883-2; 1.883-3
. . retroactive application of rules 1.883-5
. . ships or aircraft, international operations of 1.883-1
. . substantiation of CFC ownership 1.883-3
. . substantiation of stock ownership 1.883-4

Foreign corporations —Cont'd
. *gross income exclusions —Cont'd*
. . substantiation that corporation is publicly-traded 1.883-2
. . transitional information reporting rule 1.883-5
. income from sources outside the United States
. . capital amounts included in .... 1.904(b)-1
. information returns
. . U.S. persons with annual accounting period 1.6038-2
. interest, portfolio
. . 10% shareholders .... 1.871-14(g)
. . 30% flat tax 1.881-2
. investments .... 1.367(b)-6
. maintenance and adjustment of earnings and profits 1.959-3
. nonrecognition transactions
. . assets, repatriation of .... 1.367(b)-3
. personal holding corporations
. . accounting period 1.441-1
. previously taxed earnings and profits 1.959-1; 1.959-2
. . maintenance and adjustment 1.959-3
. QBUs
. . gains or loss 1.987-2
. . termination of branch 1.987-3
. required year
. . changes in 1.898-4
. . determination of 1.898-3
. specified foreign corporation defined 1.898-2
. taxable year 1.898-1
. termination or incorporation 1.884-2
. 30% flat tax
. . interest, portfolio 1.881-2
. transfers
. . active conduct of a trade or business outside the United States .... 1.367(a)-2(b)(1)
. . exception for transfers of property for use in the active conducts of a trade or business, outside the United States .... 1.367(a)-2(b)(1)
. . generally .... 1.367(a)-1T; 7.367(b)-8
. . reporting 1.6038B-1
. . section 367(a)(1), property subject to .... 1.367(a)-5(a) .... 1.367(a)-5(d)(1)
. . specified transfers of property, special rules
. . . depreciated property used in the U.S. .... 1.367(a)-4(b)(1)
. . . FSCs, transfers of certain property to .... 1.367(a)-4(h)(1)
. . . generally .... 1.367(a)-4(a)
. . . oil and gas working interests ..... 1.367(a)-4(e)(1)
. . stock or securities .... 1.367(a)-3
. . . foreign corporation, domestic corporation to .... 1.367(a)-3(c)

References are to Reg. § numbers

Foreign corporations —Cont'd
. *transfers —Cont'd*
. . *stock or securities—Cont'd*
. . . foreign corporation, foreign corporation to .... 1.367(a)-3(b)
. . United States property defined .... 1.956-2(a)(1)
. . use in the active conduct of a trade or business .... 1.367(a)-2(a)

Foreign currency
. profit and loss method accounting
. . functional currency of business unit different from taxpayer 1.987-1

Foreign death taxes
. deduction for .... 20.2053-10(c)

Foreign deferred compensation plans
. effective date 1.404A-7
. general rules 1.404A-1
. limitations on amounts taken into account for qualified plans
. . accounting changes 1.404A-6
. . additional 1.404A-5
. . election, section 404A 1.404A-6
. . retroactive elections 1.404A-7
. . United States and foreign laws 1.404A-4
. 90% test 1.404A-1
. qualified funded plans, rules for 1.404A-2
. qualified reserve plans 1.404A-3
. retroactive effective date elections 1.404A-7
. transitional rules 1.404A-7

Foreign entities
. classifications for federal tax purposes 301.7701-2

Foreign governments
. withholding under sec. 3402(t), government entities .... 31.3402(t)-4(d)

Foreign income taxes
. foreign corporations
. . allocation of earnings and profits and foreign income taxes after section 355 distribution .... 1.367(b)-8
. . domestic corporate shareholders, credits for
. . . foreign income taxes 1.902-1

Foreign insurance companies
. stock held by, treatment of 1.864-4
. withholding of tax 1.1441-1

Foreign investment companies
. generally .... 1.367(b)-6

Foreign partnerships
. U.S. partner of foreign partner making section 1296 election .... 1.6031(a)-1(b)

Foreign personal holding company income
. adjustments to taxable income 1.556-2
. certain property transactions
. . property that gives rise to certain income .... 1.954-2(e)(2)(i)
. commodities transactions .... 1.954-2(f)(1)

Foreign personal holding company income —Cont'd
. *commodities transactions—Cont'd*
. . defined .... 1.954-2(f)(2)(ii)
. . financial institutions not a producer .... 1.954-2(f)(2)(vi)
. . qualified active sale .... 1.954-2(f)(2)(iii)
. . qualified hedging transaction entered into after January 31, 2003 .... 1.954-2(f)(2)(v)
. . qualified hedging transaction entered into prior to January 31, 2003 .... 1.954-2(f)(2)(iv)
. computation of foreign holding company income
. . bona fide hedging transaction ...... 1.954-2(a)(4)(ii)
. . changes in the use or purpose for which property is held .... 1.954-2(a)(3)(i); 1.954-2(a)(3)(ii); 1.954-2(a)(3)(iii)
. . distributive shares of partnership income .... 1.954-2(a)(5)(ii); 1.954-2(a)(5)(iii)
. currency gains or losses as foreign personal holding company income, election to treat all foreign .... 1.954-2(g)(4)(i)
. dividends, interests, rents, royalties, and annuities .... 1.954-2(b)(1)
. . exclusion of dividends or interest from related persons .... 1.954-2(b)(4)(i)
. . . location of debt instruments ...... 1.954-2(b)(4)(ix)
. . . location of intangible property ... 1.954-2(b)(4)(vii)
. . . location of inventory and dealer property .... 1.954-2(b)(4)(viii)
. . . location of tangible property ...... 1.954-2(b)(4)(vi)
. . . substantial assets test .... 1.954-2(b)(4)(iv)
. . . trade or business requirement .... 1.954-2(b)(4)(iii)
. . . treatment of certain stock interests .... 1.954-2(b)(4)(x)
. . . valuation of assets .... 1.954-2(b)(4)(v)
. . exclusion of rents and royalties derived from related persons .... 1.954-2(b)(5)(i)
. dual character property .... 1.954-2(e)(1)(iv)
. exceptions .... 1.954-2(e)(1)(ii)
. excluded rents
. . active leasing expenses .... 1.954-2(c)(2)(iii)
. . adding substantial value .... 1.954-2(c)(2)(i)
. . adjusting leasing profit .... 1.954-2(c)(2)(iv)
. excluded royalties
. . active licensing expenses .... 1.954-2(d)(2)(iii)
. . adding substantial value .... 1.954-2(d)(2)(i)
. . adjusted licensing profit .... 1.954-2(d)(2)(iv)
. . substantiality of foreign organization .... 1.954-2(d)(2)(ii)
. foreign currency gain or loss .... 1.954-2(g)(2); 1.954-2(g)(3)(i)
. . election to characterize foreign currency gain or loss that arises from a specific category of subpart F income as gain or loss in that category
. . . example .... 1.954-2(g)(3)(iv)
. . . revocation of election .... 1.954-2(g)(3)(iii)
. . . time and manner of election ...... 1.954-2(g)(3)(ii)

References are to Reg. § numbers

Foreign personal holding company income —Cont'd
. *foreign currency gain or loss—Cont'd*
. . election to treat all foreign currency gains or losses as foreign personal holding company income
. . . time and manner of election . . . . . 1.954-2(g)(4)(ii)
. . exclusion for business needs . . . . . 1.954-2(g)(2)(ii)
. . gains and losses not subject to this paragraph
. . . capital gains and losses . . . . . 1.954-2(g)(5)(i)
. . . qualified business units using the dollar approximate separate transactions method . . . . . 1.954-2(g)(5)(iii)
. . inclusion . . . . . 1.954-2(g)(2)(i)
. gain or loss from the disposition of a debt instrument . . . . . 1.954-2(e)(2)(ii)
. generally . . . . . 1.954-2(e)(1)
. inclusions . . . . . 1.954-2(e)(1)(i)
. income equivalent to interest
. . defined . . . . . 1.954-2(h)(2)(i)
. . generally . . . . . 1.954-2(h)(1)
. . income from the sale of property . . . 1.954-2(h)(2)(ii)
. . notational principal contracts . . . . . 1.954-2(h)(3)(i)
. income equivalent to interest form factoring
. . examples . . . . . 1.954-2(h)(4)(iv); 1.954-2(h)(6)
. . factored receivable . . . . . 1.954-2(h)(4)(iii)
. . general rule . . . . . 1.954-2(h)(4)(i)
. . receivables arising from performance of services . . . . . 1.954-2(h)(5)
. notational principal contracts
. . regular dealers . . . . . 1.954-2(h)(3)(ii)
. treatment of losses . . . . . 1.954-2(e)(1)(iii)

Foreign personal holding corporations
. accounting period 1.441-1
. designation of dividend taken into account under sec. 563(c), procedure for 1.563-3

Foreign persons
. stock distributions to
. . gain, recognition of . . . . . 1.367(e)-1
. withholding of tax
. . amounts subject to withholding 1.1441-3
. . disposition of U.S. real property 1.1445-1

Foreign plans (See Foreign deferred compensation plans)

Foreign tax credit
. carrybacks and carryovers 1.904-2
. export financing interest . . . . . 1.904-4(h)
. limitations
. . individuals exempt from . . . . . 1.904(j)-1
. noncontrolled section 902 corporation and non-look-through 10/50 corporation 1.904-4
. passive foreign investment companies 1.1291-5
. pools of foreign taxes, adjustments to
. . foreign tax redetermination
. . . Jan. 1, 1987, taxable years beginning prior to 1.905-5T

Foreign tax credit —Cont'd
. recapture
. . beginning after December 31, 2002 . . . . . 1.904(f)-12T(g)
. . beginning before January 1, 2003 . . . 1.904(f)-12T(g)
. redeterminations
. . currency translation rules 1.905-5
. . Jan. 1, 1987, taxable years beginning prior to 1.905-5
. . notification 1.905-4
. . pools of post-1986 undistributed earnings and post-1986 undistributed earnings 1.905-3
. . U.S. tax liability 1.905-3
. regulated investment companies (RICs)
. . country-by-country reporting, elimination of . . . . . 1.853-1 et seq.
. . manner of making 853(a) election 1.853-4
. . notice to shareholders of 853(a) election 1.853-3
. . shareholders, allowed to 1.853-1; 1.853-2
. taxpayer defined for
. . income, war profits, or excess profits tax paid or accrued 1.901-2

Fringe benefits
. taxation of 1.61-21

Fuel, taxable
. aviation gasoline defined 48.4081-1
. blender liability for tax 48.4081-3
. crude oil
. . incremental tertiary oil 51.4993-1
. . tiers 51.4991-1
. definitions 48.4081-1
. exempt Indian oil 51.4995-2
. exemption
. . definitions relating to 51.4994-1
. imputed oil 51.4996-5
. incremental tertiary oil 51.4993-1
. lubricating oil
. . cutting oil sales 48.4091-3
. . defined 48.4091-2
. . manufacturers 48.4092-1
. . records inspection 48.4102-1
. . seldom used as a lubricant, oil 48.4091-4
. . tax on 48.4091-1
. newly discovered oil 51.4996-1
. producer's certificate 51.4995-2
. property defined 51.4996-4
. registration 48.4101-1
. seller of blended taxable fuel 48.4081-3
. tertiary recovery projects
. . IRS rulings 51.4993-4
. . self-certification 51.4993-2
. unitized properties, production from 51.4996-5

References are to Reg. § numbers

Functional currency
. change in
. . adjustments required upon 1.985-5
. . . qualified business unit .... 1.985-5(a)
. generally .... 1.985-1 et seq.
. qualified business units, section 987 (See Qualified business units subhead currency gain or loss, section 987)
. separate transactions method 1.985-3

Furs
. luxury tax 48.4007-1

G

Gain or loss
. acquisitions
. . stock distributions, recognition of gain on certain 1.355-7
. at risk provisions ..... 1.465-11 to 1.465-13; 1.465-77
. capital (See Capital gains and losses)
. exchange
. . global dealing operations 1.988-4
. global dealing operations 1.864-6
. inventories 1.472-2
. liquidations 1.332-2
. mutual savings banks, real property loans 1.593-4
. obligations at discount 1.1232-3
. partners and partnerships
. . allocation
. . . contributed property 1.704-3
. . . distributive share of partner 1.704-1
. passive activity (See Passive activity losses and credits)
. principal residence sales (See Principal residence sales)
. QBUs 1.987-2
. recognition agreement requirements ...... 1.367(a)-8
. S corporations
. . net unrealized built-in gain, adjustments to .... 1.1374-3(b)

Gas (See Oil and Gas)

Gasohol
. credit or payment; gasoline used to produce gasohol 48.6427-10

General obligation bonds
. refunding obligations
. . special rules .... 1.141-13(f)

Generation-skipping transfer tax
. allocation of exemption
. . automatic allocation to indirect skips made after December 31, 2000 .... 26.2632-1(b)(2)
. . death of transferor, after ....26.2632-1(d)
. . election to have automatic allocation rules not apply .... 26.2632-1(b)(2)

Generation-skipping transfer tax —Cont'd
. *allocation of exemption —Cont'd*
. . termination of election .... 26.2632-1(b)(2)
. predeceased parent rule 26.2651-1
. . collateral heirs 26.2651-1
. . individual assigned to more than one generation 26.2651-2
. qualified severance of trust
. . gain or loss computation 1.1001-1
. . generally 26.2642-6
. . irrevocable trusts 26.2642-6
. . requirements for a qualified severance ... 26.2642-6
. . single trust treated as separate trust ... 26.2654-1(a)
. . time for making 26.2642-6
. qualified state tuition programs, rules for 1.529-5

Gift taxes
. marital deduction property
. . right of recovery, failure to exercise 25.2207A-1
. qualified state tuition programs 1.529-5

Gifts
. below-market loans............. 1.7872-6; 1.7872-8
. charitable (See Charitable contributions)
. employee's annuities
. . limitation on amount excludable from..... 25.2517-1
. valuation for gift tax purposes
. . declaratory judgments relating to 301.7477-1

Global dealing operations
. allocation of income
. . notional principal contracts 1.863-7
. exchange gain or loss 1.988-4
. gain or loss 1.864-6
. risk transfer agreements .... 1.475(g)-2
. U.S. source income, special rules 1.864-4

Golden parachute payments 1.280G-1

Government bond
. defined 1.141-1

Government depositaries (See Depositaries of government)

Government entities
. withholding under sec. 3402(t)
. . crediting of withheld taxes .... 31.3402(t)-6
. . deposit and reporting requirements .. 31.3402(t)-1(c)
. . District of Columbia defined as a state .... 31.3402(t)-2(c)
. . exception for reportable payment for which withholding is otherwise required ....31.3406(g)-2
. . exemptions
. . . chapter 3 or chapter 24 (other than sec. 3406), payments subject to .... 31.3402(t)-4(a)
. . . classified or confidential contracts, payments pursuant to .... 31.3402(t)-4(f)
. . . disaster situation payments .... 31.3402(t)-4(l)
. . . emergency payments .... 31.3402(t)-4(l)

References are to Reg. § numbers

Government entities —Cont'd
. *withholding under sec. 3402(t) —Cont'd*
. . *exemptions —Cont'd*
. . . foreign corporations, payments received by .... 31.3402(t)-4(j)
. . . foreign government, payments to .... 31.3402(t)-4(e)(3)
. . . government employee services, payments for .... 31.3402(t)-4(i)
. . . government entities, payments to .... 31.3402(t)-4(e)(1)
. . . Indian tribal governments, payments to .... 31.3402(t)-4(k)
. . . nonresident alien individuals, payments received by .... 31.3402(t)-4(j)
. . . political subdivisions making payments less than $100,000,000 for property or services annually .... 31.3402(t)-4(g)
. . . public assistance or welfare programs, payments connected with .... 31.3402(t)-4(h)
. . . real property payments .... 31.3402(t)-4(d)
. . . sec. 3406 with backup withholding deducted, subject to .... 31.3402(t)-4(b)
. . . tax-exempt organizations, payments to .... 31.3402(t)-4(e)(2)
. . existing written binding contract payments, exception for .... 31.3402(t)-7(b)
. . FICA taxes attributable to payments made after Dec. 31, 1992 .... 31.6302-1
. . generally .... 31.3402(t)-1(a)
. . good faith exception for interest and penalties on payments before Jan. 1, 2012 .... 31.3402(t)-7(c)
. . government of the United States defined .... 31.3402(t)-2(b)
. . information returns, statements and
. . . information required .... 31.6051-5(d)
. . . prescribed form .... 31.6051-5(c)
. . . required information returns .... 31.6051-5(b)
. . . required statements .... 31.6051-5(a)
. . . time for filing .... 31.6071-(a)-1
. . . time for furnishing .... 31.6051-5(e)
. . nonpayroll payments made after Dec. 31, 1992 .... 31.6302-4
. . passthrough entities
. . . defined .... 31.3402(t)-5(b)(1)
. . . generally .... 31.3402(t)-2(g); 31.3402(t)-5(a)
. . . owner defined .... 31.3402(t)-5(b)(2)
. . . ownership percentage defined .. 31.3402(t)-5(b)(3)
. . . payments from .... 31.3402(t)-5(c)
. . . payments to .... 31.3402(t)-5(d)
. . . testing day defined .... 31.3402(t)-5(b)(4)
. . payments subject to
. . . credit card payments .... 31.3402(t)-3(e)
. . . generally .... 31.3402(t)-3(a)
. . . payment administrator or contractor, payments made through .... 31.3402(t)-3(d)

Government entities —Cont'd
. *withholding under sec. 3402(t) —Cont'd*
. . *payments subject to —Cont'd*
. . . payment card payments .... 31.3402(t)-3(e)
. . . successive payments .... 31.3402(t)-3(c)
. . . $10,000 payment threshold .... 31.3402(t)-3(b)
. . political subdivisions .... 31.3402(t)-2(d)
. . possessions of the United States .... 31.3402(t)-2(f)
. . returns of income tax withheld .... 31.6011(a)-4
. . small entity exception .... 31.3402(t)-2(h)
. . special rules for entities required to withhold .... 31.3402(t)-2; 31.3402(t)-3; 31.3402(t)-4
. . state defined .... 31.3402(t)-2(c)
. . transition rules .... 31.3402(t)-7

Governmental or tax-exempt entities
. pension, profit-sharing, and stock bonus plans
. . minimum age and service requirements .. 1.410(b)-6

Gramm-Leach-Bliley Act
. disclosure of tax information .... 301.7216-1(c)

Grantor trusts
. election 1.468B-5
. . settlement funds 1.468B-5

Grants
. generally .... 1.117-0 to 1.117-6

Gross estates
. decedents
. . alternative valuation method 20.2032-1; 301.9100-6T

Gross income
. adjusted gross income 1.62-1
. Real Estate Investment Trusts (REITs) 1.856-2
. sources within or without U.S. (See Income from sources within or without U.S.)

Group health plans
. average number of employee, determination of 54.9831-1
. continuation coverage 1.162-26
. number of plans employer or organization can maintain 54.9831-1

Group legal services plans
. dividends exclusions 1.120-1; 1.120-2
. exempt organizations .... 1.501(c)(20)-1

Group term life insurance
. deemed death benefits, formula to determine .. 1.79-1
. general rules 1.79-1

Guam
. exclusion, income 1.931-1; 1.931-1T
. individual income tax
. . nonresident alien individual who is resident of U.S. possession or Puerto Rico, taxation of ... 1.1-1(b)
. nonresident aliens 1.876-1
. Northern Mariana Islands, coordination of individual income taxes with 1.935-1

References are to Reg. § numbers

H

Health Insurance Portablility and Accountability Act of 1996 (HIPAA)
. creditable coverage
. . evidence of 54.9801-5
. . rules concerning 54.9801-4
. . significant breaks in 54.9801-4
. . special enrollment for certain individuals who lose coverage 54.9801-6
. . special enrollment with respect to certain dependent beneficiaries 54.9801-6
. Family and Medical Leave Act, interaction with 54.9801-7
. group health plans 54.9831-7
Health plans (See Accident and health plans)
Health Savings accounts
. contributions under section 4980G
. . Archer MSAs and HSAs 54.4980G-3
. . cafeteria plans 54.4980G-4; 54.4980G-5
. . comparable contributions 54.4980G-4
. . . calculating 54.4980G-0
. . employee defined for comparable testing 54.4980G-3
. . employer contributions defined 54.4980G-2
. . employer provided HDHP coverage 54.4980G-3
. . failure of employer to make comparable contributions 54.4980G-1
. . . computation for tax .... 54.4980G-1(a)
. . former employees 54.4980G-3
. . full-time employees 54.4980G-3
. . look-back basis contributions 54.4980G-4
. . management 54.4980G-3
. . partners, employee status of 54.4980G-3
. . part-time employees 54.4980G-3
. . pay-as-you-go contributions 54.4980G-4
. . waiver of excise tax 54.4980G-5
Hedging transactions
. branch profits tax 1.884-1
. interest deduction, determination of 1.882-5
Highway vehicle
. defined 48.4051-1
Home construction contracts
. cost allocation rules 1.460-5
. . costs incurred for non-long-term contract activities .... 1.460-5(f)(2)
. . exempt construction contracts reported using the CCM (See subhead exempt construction contracts reported using the CCM)
. . method of accounting .... 1.460-5(g)
. . nondeductible costs .... 1.460-5(f)(1)
. . overview .... 1.460-5(a)
. . PCCM, contracts subject to .... 1.460-5(e)
. . PCM, contracts subject to (See subhead PCM, contracts subject to)

Home construction contracts —Cont'd
. *cost allocation rules—Cont'd*
. . special rules .... 1.460-5(f)
. exempt construction contracts reported using the CCM
. . generally .... 1.460-5(d); 1.460-5(d)(1)
. . indirect costs
. . . allocable to exempt construction contracts .... 1.460-5(d)(2)(i)
. . . generally .... 1.460-5(d)(2)
. . . not allocable to exempt construction contracts .... 1.460-5(d)(2)(ii)
. long-term contracts .... (Long-term home contructions contracts)
. look back method
. . alternative minimum tax .... 1.460-6(h)(5)
. . alternative minimum tax credit .... 1.460-6(h)(8)
. . credit carryovers .... 1.460-6(h)(6)
. . delayed reapplication method
. . . examples .... 1.460-6(e)(3)
. . . generally .... 1.460-6(e)(1)
. . . time and manner of making election .... 1.460-6(e)(2)
. . election not to apply look-back method in de minimis cases .... 1.460-6(j)
. . examples .... 1.460-6(h)
. . net operating losses .... 1.460-6(h)(7)
. . operation of the look-back method
. . . overview .... 1.460-6(c)(1); 1.460-6(c)(1)(i)
. . . post-completion revenue and expenses .... 1.460-6(c)(1)(ii)
. . overview .... 1.460-6(h)(1)
. . period for interest .... 1.460-6(h)(9)
. . post-completion adjustments .... 1.460-6(h)(4)
. . procedure .... 1.460-6(f)(1)
. . scope of look-back method
. . . alternative minimum tax .... 1.460-6(b)(4)
. . . de minimis exception .... 1.460-6(b)(3)
. . . effective date .... 1.460-6(b)(5)
. . . exceptions from section 460 .... 1.460-6(b)(2)
. . . generally .... 1.460-6(b)(1)
. . statue of limitations and compounding of interest on look-back interest .... 1.460-6(f)(3)
. . Step One .... 1.460-6(c)(2)
. . . amount treated as contract price .... 1.460-6(c)(2)(vi)
. . . costs incurred prior to contract execution; 10-percent method .... 1.460-6(c)(2)(v)
. . . hypothetical reallocation of income among prior tax years .... 1.460-6(c)(2)(i)
. . . interim restimates not considered .... 1.460-6(c)(2)(iii)
. . . tax years in which income is affected .... 1.460-6(c)(2)(iv)
. . . treatment of estimated future costs in year of completion .... 1.460-6(c)(2)(ii)

References are to Reg. § numbers

Home construction contracts —Cont'd
. *look back method —Cont'd*
. . Step Three: calculation of interest on underpayment or overpayment of tax .... 1.460-6(c)(3)
. . . changes in the amount of a loss or credit carryback or carryover .... 1.460-6(c)(4)(ii)
. . . generally .... 1.460-6(c)(3)(i)
. . Step Two: computation of hypothetical overpayment or underpayment of tax .... 1.460-6(c)(3)
. . . cumulative determination of tax liability .... 1.460-6(c)(3)(iv)
. . . definition of tax liability .... 1.460-6(c)(3)(vi)
. . . generally .... 1.460-6(c)(3)(i)
. . . hypothetical underpayment or overpayment .... 1.460-6(c)(3)(iii)
. . . redetermination of tax liability .... 1.460-6(c)(3)(ii)
. . . Section 481(a) adjustments ..... 1.460-6(c)(3)(vii)
. . . years affected by look-back only . . 1.460-6(c)(3)(v)
. . treatment of interest on return .... 1.460-6(f)(2)
. . . general rule .... 1.460-6(f)(2)(i)
. . . timing of look-back interest .... 1.460-6(f)(2)(ii)
. mid-contract change in taxpayer
. . constructive completion transactions . . 1.460-6(g)(2)
. . generally ....1.460-6(g); 1.460-6(g)(1)
. . step-in-the-shoes transactions .... 1.460-6(g)(3)
. . . application of look-back method to post-transaction years .... 1.460-6(g)(3)(iii)
. . . application of look-back method to pre-transcription period .... 1.460-6(g)(3)(ii)
. . . effective date .... 1.460-6(g)(3)(iv)
. . . general rules .... 1.460-6(g)(3)(i)
. PCM, contracts subject to
. . components and subassemblies ... 1.460-5(b)(2)(ii)
. . costs identified under cost-plus long-term contracts and federal long-term contracts .... 1.460-5(b)(2)(iv)
. . direct material costs .... 1.460-5(b)(2)(i)
. . generally ....1.460-5(b); 1.460-5(b)(1)
. . interest .... 1.460-5(b)(2)(v)
. . . application .... 1.460-5(b)(2)(v)(C)
. . . production period .... 1.460-5(b)(2)(v)(B)
. . research and experimental expenses .... 1.460-5(b)(2)(vi)
. . service costs .... 1.460-5(b)(2)(vii)
. . . jobsite costs .... 1.460-5(b)(2)(vii)(B)
. . . limitation on other reasonable cost allocation methods .... 1.460-5(b)(2)(vii)(C)
. . . simplified service cost method .... 1.460-5(b)(2)(vii)(A)
. . simplified cost-to-cost method for contracts subject to the PCM .... 1.460-5(c); 1.460-5(c)(1)
. . . election .... 1.460-5(c)(2)
. . simplified production methods ..... 1.460-5(b)(2)(iii)
. . special rules ..... 1.460-5(b)(2); 1.460-5(b)(2)(v)(A)
. simplified marginal impact method

Home construction contracts —Cont'd
. *simplified marginal impact method —Cont'd*
. . anti-abuse rule .... 1.460-6(d)(3)
. . application .... 1.460-6(d)(4)
. . . elective use .... 1.460-6(d)(4)(ii)
. . . required use by certain pass-through entities .... 1.460-6(d)(4)(i)
. . generally .... 1.460-6(d)
. . introduction .... 1.460-6(d)(1)
. . operation .... 1.460-6(d)(2); 1.460-6(d)(2)(i)
. . . applicable tax rate .... 1.460-6(d)(2)(ii)
. . . example .... 1.460-6(d)(2)(v)
. . . overpayment ceiling .... 1.460-6(d)(2)(iii)
. . . Section 481(a) adjustments ...... 1.460-6(d)(2)(iv)

Home workers
. payments to .... 31.3121(a)(10)-1

HOPE scholarship credit
. amount of credit 1.25A-3
. education tax credit coordination 1.25A-1

Household expenses
. employment related expenses, credit for (See Dependent care services, subhead employment related expenses, credit for)

Husbands and wives (See Spouses)

Hybrid branches
. foreign tax reduction giving rise to subpart F income 1.954-9

I

Improvements
. leased property, depreciation or amortization of improvements 1.178-1

Incentive stock options .... 1.422A-1 to 1.422A-3
. bifurcation of options .... 1.422-4(c)
. defined 1.422-2
. duration of option grants under plans ...... 1.422-2(c)
. general rules 1.422-1
. holding period requirements .... 1.422-1(b)
. $100,000 limitation 1.422-4
. plans, option .... 1.422-2(b)
. statement requirement under sec. 6039(a)(1) 1.6039-1
. statutory option defined as 1.421-1
. transfers to individuals 1.422-1

Income
. community income (See Community income)
. gross (See Gross income)
. sources within or without U.S. (See Income from sources within or without U.S.)

Income, war profits, or excess profits tax paid or accrued
. amount of income tax that is creditable .... 1.901-2(e)(1)

References are to Reg. § numbers

Income, war profits, or excess profits tax paid or accrued —Cont'd

. *amount of income tax that is creditable—Cont'd*

. . multiple levies .... 1.901-2(e)(4)(i)

. . noncompulsory amounts .... 1.901-2(e)(5)(i)

. . refunds and credits .... 1.901-2(e)(2)(i)

. credits against tax (See Abatements, credits and refunds)

. defined .... 1.901-2(a)(1)

. net gain .... 1.901-2(b)(1)

. . gross receipts

. . . generally .... 1.901-2(b)(3)(i)

. . . net income .... 1.901-2(b)(4)(i)

. . realization .... 1.901-2(b)(2)(i)

. separate levies .... 1.901-2(d)(1)

. soak-up taxes .... 1.901-2(c)(1)

. taxpayers

. . generally .... 1.901-2(f)(1)

. . party undertaking tax obligation as part of transaction .... 1.901-2(f)(2)(i)

Income averaging

. generally 1.1304-2

Income forecast method of depreciation (See Depreciation)

Income from sources within or without U.S.

. foreign insurance companies, stock held by . . 1.864-4

. gross income determination

. . tax accounting method 1.952-2

. interest 1.861-2

. REMIC inducement fees .... 1.863-1(e)

. securities lending transactions............. 1.861-2

Income ordering rules

. income taxes

. . adjustments and other special rules for determining unlimited charitable contributions deduction .... 1.642(c)-3

. . . capital gains included in charitable contribution .... 1.642(c)-3(c)

. . . disallowance of deduction for amounts allocable to unrelated business income .... 1.642(c)-3(d)

. . . disallowance of deduction in certain cases .... 1.642(c)-3(e)

. . . income in respect of a decedent .... 1.642(c)-3(a)

. . . information returns .... 1.642(c)-3(f)

. . . reduction of charitable contributions deduction by amounts not included in gross income .... 1.642(c)-3(b)

Indebtedness

. deductibility, generally 20.2053-1

. partnership interest, satisfaction by

. . fair market value determination .... 1.108-8(b)

. . generally 1.108-8

Indian oil, exempt

. fuel, taxable 51.4995-2

Individual income tax

. nonresident alien individual who is resident of U.S. possession or Puerto Rico, taxation of..... 1.1-1 et seq.

Individual retirement arrangements (IRAs)

. accrued liability changes .... 1.412(c)(4)-1

. actuarial valuations .... 1.412(c)(9)-1

. annual reports by trustees and issuers 1.408-5

. bond valuation election............... 1.412(c)(2)-2

. catch-up contributions for individuals over age 50 .... 1.414(v)-1

. collectibles, investment in 1.408-10

. deemed IRA in qualified employer plan .... 1.408(q)-1

. disclosure statements...................... 1.408-6

. discrimination .... 1.408-8; 1.411(d)-1

. distribution requirements .... 1.408-4 et seq.

. funding standard requirements ..... 1.412(a)-1 et seq.

. generally .... 1.408-2 et seq.

. net income calculations

. . recharacterized contributions ... 1.408A-5; 1.408-11

. . returned contributions 1.408-11

. pension excise tax 54.4974-1

. recharacterized contributions

. . net income calculations for 1.408A-5; 1.408-11

. retirement bonds 1.409-1

. retirement savings deduction ... 1.219(a)-1; 1.219(a)-2

. retroactive plan amendments .... 1.412(c)(8)-1

. returned contributions, net income calculations for 1.408-11

. simplified employee pensions .... 1.219(a)-4; 1.219-3; 1.408-7 to 1.408-9; 301.6693-1

. spouse, plan for 25.2503-5

. termination............................ 1.412(b)-4

. time for making contributions .... 1.412(c)(10)-1

. vesting .... 1.411(a)-1 et seq.

Inducement fees

. REMICs (See Real estate mortgage investment conduits (REMICs))

Information returns and reports

. attorneys, payment to .... 1.6045-5(a)

. cancellation of indebtedness 1.6050P-1

. capital structure, acquisition of control or substantial change in 1.6045-3

. correction of failure, prompt 301.6724-1

. education loan (See Education loans)

. electronic filing (See Electronic filing)

. foreign corporations

. . U.S. persons with annual accounting period 1.6038-2

. foreign owned domestic corporations 1.6038-2

. intellectual property contributions 1.6050L-2

. magnetic media, returns on (See Magnetic media, returns on)

. monthly returns .... 31.6011(a)-5

References are to Reg. § numbers

Information returns and reports —Cont'd
. no return required . . . 1.6041-3
. notification requirement
. . entities not required to file annual information return under sec. 6033(a)(1) . . . 1.6033-6
. passport applicants . . . 301.6039E-1
. patronage dividends
. . statements to recipients . . . 1.6044-6
. . . royalty payments . . . 1.6050N-1
. payments of $600 or more . . . 1.6041-1
. Possessions of the U.S. . . . 1.6038-2
. returns required in connection with certain options . . . 1.6039-1
. . effective / applicability date . . . 1.6039-1(e); 1.6039-1(e)(1)
. . . transition period . . . 1.6039-1(e)(2)
. . penalty . . . 1.6039-1(d)
. . requirement of return with respect to incentive stock options . . . 1.6039-1(a)
. . requirement of return with respect to stock purchased under an employee stock purchase plan under section 6039(a)(2) . . . 1.6039-1(b)
. . time for filing returns . . . 1.6039-1(c); 1.6039-1(c)(1)
. . . extension of time . . . 1.6039-1(c)(2)
. sec. 6011 disclosures
. . reportable transactions, failure to include . . . 301.6767A-1
. $600 or more, payments of . . . 1.6041-1
. statements to persons with respect to whom information is reported . . . 1.6039-2
. . effective / applicability date . . . 1.6039-2(e); 1.6039-2(e)(1)
. . . reliance and transition period . . . 1.6039-2(e)(2)
. . penalty . . . 1.6039-2(d)
. . requirement of statement with respect to incentive stock options under section 6039(b) . . . 1.6039-2(a)
. . requirement of statement with respect to stock purchased under an employee stock purchase plan under section 6039(a)(2) . . . 1.6039-2(b)
. . time for furnishing statements . . . 1.6039-2(c); 1.6039-2(c)(1)
. . . extension of time . . . 1.6039-2(c)(2)
. stock option transactions . . . 1.6039-1
. . statement of transaction, furnishing transferee with . . . 1.6039-1
. tuition payment, reimbursement or refunds (See Tuition)
. widely held fixed investment trusts . . . 1.6049-7

Initial public offerings
. marketable stock, special rules . . . 1.1296(e)-1(b)(2)

Installment accounting methods
. generally . . . 1.453-1

Installment agreements
. reinstatement of fees . . . 300.2

Installment agreements —Cont'd
. restructuring of fees . . . 300.2
. user fees . . . 300.1

Installment payment of tax
. agreements for . . . 301.6159-1
. . acceptance, for and terms of agreement . . . 301.6159-1(c)
. . annual statement . . . 301.6159-1(h)
. . authority . . . 301.6159-1(a)
. . collection activity, effect of agreement on . . . 301.6159-1(f)
. . modification of agreement . . . 301.6159-1(e)
. . rejection of agreement . . . 301.6159-1(d)
. . review of partial payment agreements, biannual . . . 301.6159-1(i)
. . submission and consideration of proposed, procedure for . . . 301.6159-1(b)
. . suspension of statute of limitations on collection . . . 301.6159-1(g)
. . termination of agreement . . . 301.6159-1(e)
. extension agreements . . . 301.6502-1
. generally . . . 1.6152-1

Installment sales
. luxury tax . . . 48.4011-6

Insurance companies
. amortization . . . 1.818-3
. asset acquisition . . . 1.1060-1(b); 1.1060-1(c)
. generally . . . 1.818-3
. life (See Life insurance companies)
. reinsurance of insurance contract as asset acquisition . . . 1.1060-1(b)
. Sec. 338, application of (See Distributions by corporations)
. sec. 338, application of . . . 1.338-1

Insurance income
. controlled foreign corporations . . . 1.953-1 et seq.

Insurance premium excise tax
. liability . . . 46.4374-1

Intangible development costs
. cost sharing arrangements . . . 1.482-7

Intangible drilling and development expenditures
. optional 10-year writeoff of certain tax preferences . . . 1.59-1

Intangibles
. amortization
. . safe harbor . . . 1.167(a)-3
. . useful life period . . . 1.167(a)-3
. amounts paid to acquire, create, or enhance assets . . . 1.263(a)-4
. capitalization of intangible assets . . . 1.263(a)-4
. depreciation allowance . . . 1.167(a)-3
. intangible asset defined . . . 1.263(a)-4
. taxable income determination in connection with transfer of intangible property

References are to Reg. § numbers

Intangibles —Cont'd
. *taxable income determination in connection with transfer of intangible property —Cont'd*
. . contribution of value to property 1.482-4
. . ownership of property, determination of 1.482-4
Intellectual property
. information returns concerning contributions 1.6050L-2
Intercompany dividends
. loss deduction 1.6044-6
Intercompany obligations
. transfer or extinguishment of rights under .. 1.1502-13
Intercompany transactions
. operating rules .... 1.1502-13(j)
. sec. 362(e)(2) transactions .... 1.1502-13(e)(4)
. successor companies .... 1.1502-13(j)
Interest
. at risk provisions 1.465-8
. below-market loans........... 1.7872-12; 1.7872-13
. deduction, determination of
. . hedging transactions 1.882-5
. exempt facilities bonds 1.103-8
. expense; earnings stripping .... 1.163(j)-1 et seq.
. governmental obligations
. . industrial development bonds 1.103-10
. nonresident aliens, deposit interest paid to (See Nonresident aliens subhead deposit interest paid to)
. notice of amount of increased tax liability, IRS failure to provide
. . suspension of interest ....301.6404-4(a)
. overpayments 301.6611-1
. payment to securities lending transactions.... 1.861-2
. registration required obligations 5f.163-1
. sources of income........................ 1.861-2
. underpayments 301.6601-1
Interest expense
. allocation and apportionment............... 1.861-9
. . qualified business unit.................. 1.861-9T
Internal Revenue Service
. Administrative Law Judge
. . appointment .... 10.70(a)
. . decisions.................................. 10.76
. . discretionary review..................... 10.77(c)
. . failure to comply with order of........... 10.71(e)
. . interlocutory review .... 10.77(g)
. . notice of review .... 10.77(e)
. . petition for review...................... 10.77(a)
. . record of review .... 10.78(b)
. . reply and supplemental briefs............. 10.78(c)
. . scope of review .... 10.78(a)
. . Secretary review of decision .... 10.77(d)
. . standard of proof .... 10.76(b)
. practice before

Internal Revenue Service —Cont'd
. *practice before —Cont'd*
. . Acting Director of the Office of Professional Responsibility..................................10.1(c)
. . adequate procedures for all firm members providing federal tax advice, provisions for 10.36
. . Administrative Law Judge
. . . appointment......................... 10.70(a)
. . advisory committees, maintenance of 10.38
. . affidavits 10.34
. . best practices 10.33
. . censure, suspend, or disbar, authority to... 10.50(a)
. . conflicting interests 10.29
. . contingent fees..............................10.27
. . cross-examinations .... 10.72(b)
. . depositions .... 10.73(b)
. . depositions upon oral examination........ 10.71(b)
. . Director of the Office of Professional Responsibility 10.1
. . discovery 10.71
. . documentation 10.34
. . evidence 10.73
. . expedited suspension 10.82
. . failure to comply with order of ALJ .... 10.71(e)
. . fees 10.27
. . firm representation.................... 10.25(c)
. . former government employees, partners and associates 10.25
. . . definitions concerning................ 10.25(a)
. . hearings .... 10.72(a)
. . incompetent and disreputable conduct .... 10.51(a)
. . information furnished by client, relying on .. 10.34(d)
. . monetary penalty, authority to impose ..... 10.50(c)
. . motion filed with ALG
. . . oral motions and arguments .... 10.68(c)
. . . response to, filing .... 10.68(b)
. . Office of Professional Responsibility
. . . answer to complaints, demands of ...... 10.62(c)
. . . application for enrollment....................10.5
. . . change of address ....10.6(c)
. . . complaints 10.62
. . . continuing professional education .... 10.6(e)
. . . evidence in support of complaint, service of .... 10.63(d)
. . . form of application for enrollment .... 10.5(a)
. . . inactive retirement responsibility .... 10.6(l)
. . . institution of proceedings for misconduct 10.60
. . . renewal of enrollment .... 10.6(d)
. . . resignation or voluntary sanction........ 10.61(b)
. . . service of complaint .... 10.63(a)
. . . supplemental charges, filing .... 10.65(a)
. . party in matter .... 10.25(b)
. . pending provisions..................... 10.25(c)
. . potential penalties, advising clients on..... 10.34(c)

References are to Reg. § numbers

Internal Revenue Service —Cont'd
. *practice before —Cont'd*
. . prehearing memorandum . . . . . 10.72(c)
. . proof . . . . . 10.73(d)
. . publicity of proceedings . . . . . 10.72(d)
. . request for admission . . . . . 10.71(c); 10.73(c)
. . returns 10.34
. . saving provision 10.91
. . state and local bond offering materials 10.35
. . tax advisors, best practices for 10.36
. . tax shelter opinions 10.33; 10.36
. . Treasury Department, appearance before . 10.25(b)
. . U.S.C. 207 . . . . . 10.25(b)
. . violations subject to sanction 10.52
. . written advice 10.39
. suspension of interest and penalties
. . notice of amount of increased tax liability, IRS failure to provide . . . . . 301.6404-4(a)

International boycotts, participation in (See Boycotts, international, participation in)

International operations
. aircraft and ship exclusion of income from 1.883-1

International sales corporations (See Domestic international sales corporations)

Inventories
. accounting method change
. . costs subject to section 263A, for
. . . simplification of 481(a) adjustment periods . . . . . 1.263A-7(b)(2)(ii)
. allocation and apportionment of sales of inventory 1.863-3
. corporate organizations and reorganizations . . . . . 1.381(c)(5)-1
. LIFO
. . recapture 1.1363-2
. nonfinancial customer paper
. . mark-to-market accounting methods . . . . . 1.475(c)-2
. passive activity losses and credits limited 1.472-2

Investment companies
. foreign investment company . . . . . 1.367(b)-6

Investment credit
. energy property 1.48-9
. public utility, deregulated
. . accumulated deferred investment tax credit . . 1.46-6

Investment income
. dividend income treatment as . . . . . 1.163(d)-1

Investment trusts
. widely held fixed investment trusts (See Widely held fixed investment trusts)

Investments
. Caribbean basin countries 1.936-10
. foreign corporations . . . . . 1.367(b)-6
. individual retirement accounts 1.408-10

Investments —Cont'd
. securities (See Securities)

Investment-type property
. . defined 1.148-1

IRAs (See Individual retirement arrangements)

Itemized deductions
. bad debts reserve 1.166-4
. group health plans 1.162-26
. original issue discount 1.163-4

J

Jewelry
. luxury tax 48.4006-1

Jobs and Growth Tax Relief Reconciliation Act of 2003
. qualified dividend income as investment income, election to make
. . time and manner of making . . . . . 1.163(d)-1

Joint and survivor annuities
. explanations provided to participants, required . . . . . 1.417(a)(3)-1

Joint returns
. community income (See Community income)
. dependent care services
. . employment related expenses, credit for . . . 1.21-3(a)
. principal residence sales
. . exclusion of gain from sale or exchange 1.121-2

K

Kerosene
. dyed fuel exemption 48.4082-1

L

Labor
. compensation (See Personal services subhead compensation)

Last known address
. defined
. . foreclosure property 1.856-2

Leased property
. improvements, depreciation or amortization of 1.178-1

Leases
. advance rentals, gross income status of . . . . 1.61-8(b)
. cancellation payments . . . . . 1.61-8(b)
. expenditures by lessee . . . . . 1.61-8(c)
. gross income 1.61-8

Legal services plans (See Group legal services plans)

Lending institutions
. cancellation of indebtedness 1.6050P-2

References are to Reg. § numbers

Levy and distraint (See Seizure of property)

Liens

. estate tax

. . release or discharge 20.6325-1

. release of lien or discharge of property ... 301.6325-1

Life estates

. surviving spouse

. . income and principle, trustee adjustments between ....20.2056(b)-7

Life insurance

. additional benefits

. . terminal illness 1.7702A-1

. employer-owned life insurance, reporting on 1.6039I-1

. modified guaranteed contracts 1.817A-1

. split-dollar life insurance arrangements

. . below-market loans 1.7872-15

. . compensations ....31.3121(a)-1

. . contingent payment, loan 1.7872-15

. . current term protection, valuation of........ 1.61-22

. . deductions, employer 1.86-6

. . deductions for loans 1.7872-15

. . defined 1.61-22

. . distributions of money and other property ... 1.301-1

. . economic benefits 1.61-22

. . loans 1.7872-15

. . loans, policy 1.61-22

. . nonrecourse payments, loans with....... 1.7872-15

. . payment ordering rules, loan 1.7872-15

. . policy cash value 1.61-22

. . repayment received by lender, loan 1.7872-15

. . special tax rules 1.61-22

. . taxation, rules for 1.61-22

. . transfer part of 1.83-3

. . transfers of entire contract or interests 1.61-22; 1.86-6

. . valuation of current term protection 1.61-22

. . valuation of economic benefits 1.61-22; 1.83-6; 1.301-1

. . wages .... 1.61-22; 31.3121(a)-1

. split-dollar loans 1.7872-15

. transfer of contract, treatment as property 1.83-3

Life insurance companies

. consolidated returns

. . life-nonlife groups, by 1.1502-47

. contracts and agreements

. . variable annuities, diversification requirements 1.817-5

. generally 1.818-3

. variable annuities

. . diversification requirements 1.817-5

Life insurance contracts

. addition of certain benefits...............1.7702A-1

Life insurance contracts —Cont'd

. attained age of insured

. . generally ....1.7702-2(a); 1.7702-3(a)

. . multiple lives on first-to-die basis ...... 1.7702-2(d); 1.7702-3(d)

. . multiple lives on last-to-die basis ...... 1.7702-2(c); 1.7702-3(c)

. . single life contract ....1.7702-2(b); 1.7702-3(b)

. definitions concerning death benefits 1.7702-2

. mortality charges, determination of 1.7702-1

Life-nonlife groups

. consolidated returns 1.1502-47

Lifetime Learning credit

. amount of credit 1.25A-4

. education tax credit coordination............1.25A-1

Liquidation

. gain or loss, nonrecognition of............. 1.332-2

Loans

. at risk provisions ... 1.465-7; 1.465-24; 1.465-25 (See also At risk provisions)

. . amounts protected against loss 1.465-20

. . certain persons, amounts borrowed from .. 1.465-20

. . interest other than of a creditor............1.465-8

. . personal liability for repayment............1.465-8

. bad debts (See Bad debt)

. below-market loans...........1.7872-1 to 1.7872-13

. distributions, treated as ....1.72(p)-1

. mineral production payments...............1.636-1

. mutual savings bank.............. 1.593-4; 1.593-7

Long-term home construction contracts

. accounting methods

. . alternative minimum taxable income ... 1.460-4(f)(1)

. . . election to use regular completion factors ....1.460-4(f)(2)

. . capitalized-cost method.................1.460-4

. . change in method, consent to.............1.460-4

. . completed-contract method .... 1.460-4(d); 1.460-4(d)(1)

. . consolidated groups ....1.460-4; 1.460-4(j)

. . controlled groups .... 1.460-4(j)

. . examples ....1.460-4(h)

. . exempt contract methods ...... 1.460-4; 1.460-4(c); 1.460-4(c)(1)

. . exempt-contract percentage-of-completion method ....1.460-4(c)(1); 1.460-4(c)(1)(i)

. . . determination of work performed . . 1.460-4(c)(1)(ii)

. . generally .... 1.460-3; 1.460-4; 1.460-4(g); 1.460-4(g)(1)

. . home construction contracts.............. 1.460-3

. . intercompany transactions

. . . consent to change method of accounting ....1.460-4(j)(4)

. . . definitions and nomenclature .... 1.460-4(j)(1)(ii)

. . . effective dates .... 1.460-4(j)(3)

References are to Reg. § numbers

Long-term home construction contracts —Cont'd
. *accounting methods —Cont'd*
. . *intercompany transactions —Cont'd*
. . . example .... 1.460-4(j)(2)
. . . generally .... 1.460-4(j)(1); 1.460-4(j)(1)(i)
. . look-back method 1.460-6
. . mid-year change (See subhead mid-year contract change in taxpayer)
. . taxpayer-initiated change in method of accounting (See subhead taxpayer-initiated change in method of accounting)
. de minimis cases
. . look-back method, election not to apply 1.460-6
. exempt construction contracts
. . common improvements .... 1.460-3(b)(2)(iv)
. . generally ... 1.460-3(b); 1.460-3(b)(1); 1.460-3(b)(2); 1.460-3(b)(2)(i)
. . land improvements .... 1.460-3(b)(2)(ii)
. . mixed use costs .... 1.460-3(b)(2)(v)
. . $10,000,000 gross receipts test ...... 1.460-3(b)(3); 1.460-3(b)(3)(i)
. . . attribution of gross receipts ...... 1.460-3(b)(3)(iii)
. . . single employer .... 1.460-3(b)(3)(ii)
. . townhouses and rowhouses .... 1.460-3(b)(2)(iii)
. generally .... 1.460-3; 1.460-3(a); 1.460-6
. look-back accounting method 1.460-6
. mid-contract change in taxpayer
. . anti-abuse rule .... 1.460-4(k)(4)
. . constructive completion transactions
. . . new taxpayer .... 1.460-4(k)(2)(iii)
. . . old taxpayer .... 1.460-4(k)(2)(ii)
. . . scope .... 1.460-4(k)(2)(i)
. . . special rules relating to distributions of certain contracts by a partnership .... 1.460-4(k)(2)(iv)
. . effective date .... 1.460-4(k)(6)
. . examples .... 1.460-4(k)(5)
. . generally .... 1.460-4; 1.460-4(k); 1.460-4(k)(1); 1.460-6
. . step-in-the-shoes transactions
. . . generally .... 1.460-4(k)(3)
. . . new taxpayer .... 1.460-4(k)(3)(iii)
. . . old taxpayer .... 1.460-4(k)(3)(ii)
. . . scope .... 1.460-4(k)(3)(i)
. . . special rules related to certain corporate and partnership transactions .... 1.460-4(k)(3)(iv)
. . . special rules related to certain partnership transactions .... 1.460-4(k)(3)(v)
. mixed-use construction contracts 1.460-3
. . accounting methods 1.460-3
. overview .... 1.460-4(a)
. partnerships, look-back accounting method ... 1.460-6
. percentage of completion / capitalized-cost method .... 1.460-4(e)
. percentage of completion method
. . completion factor .... 1.460-4(b)(5)

Long-term home construction contracts —Cont'd
. *percentage of completion method —Cont'd*
. . *completion factor—Cont'd*
. . . allocable contract costs .... 1.460-4(b)(5)(i)
. . . cumulative allocable contract costs .... 1.460-4(b)(5)(ii)
. . . estimating total allocable contract costs .... 1.460-4(b)(5)(iii)
. . . pre-contracting-year costs .... 1.460-4(b)(5)(iv)
. . computations .... 1.460-4(b)(2)
. . generally .... 1.460-4(b); 1.460-4(b)(1)
. . post-completion-year income .... 1.460-4(b)(3)
. . 10-percent method ... 1.460-4(b)(5); 1.460-4(b)(5)(i)
. . . election .... 1.460-4(b)(6)(ii)
. . terminated contract .... 1.460-4(b)(7)
. . . adjusted basis .... 1.460-4(b)(7)(ii)
. . . look-back method .... 1.460-4(b)(7)(iii)
. . . reversal of income .... 1.460-4(b)(7)(i)
. . total contract price .... 1.460-4(b)(4)
. . . estimating total contract price .... 1.460-4(b)(4)(ii)
. percentage of completion method (PCM), use of 1.460-4
. residential construction contracts .... 1.460-3(C)
. step-in-the-shoes transactions.............. 1.460-4
. taxpayer-initiated change in method of accounting
. . change from a permissible PCM method to another permissible PCM method...... 1.460-4(g)(2)(ii)
. . change to an exempt contract method for exempt contracts other than home construction contracts .... 1.460-4(g)(2)(iv)
. . change to an exempt contract method for home construction contracts .... 1.460-4(g)(2)(iii)
. . change to PCM for long-term contracts for which PCM is required .... 1.460-4(g)(2)(i)
. . generally .... 1.460-4(g)(2)

Losses
. at risk provisions; amounts protected against 1.465-6
. capital (See Capital gains and losses)
. gain or loss (See Gain or Loss)
. passive activity (See Passive activity losses and credits)

Low-income housing
. allocation rules for post-2000 state housing credit ceiling amounts 1.42-14
. Community Renewal Tax Relief Act of 2000 .. 1.42-12
. qualified contract formula
. . adjusted investor equity............. 1.42-18(c)(4)
. . administrative responsibilities .... 1.42-18(d)
. . cash distributions .... 1.42-18(c)(6)
. . extended low-income housing commitment .... 1.42-18(a)
. . generally 1.42-18
. . low-income portion amount.......... 1.42-18(c)(2)
. . other capital contributions .... 1.42-18(c)(5)

References are to Reg. § numbers

Low-income housing —Cont'd
. *qualified contract formula —Cont'd*
. . outstanding indebtedness .... 1.42-18(c)(3)
. . purchase price formula, qualified contract .... 1.42-18(c)
. . special rules .... 1.42-18(b)
. State housing credit
. . agency coordination .... 1.42-14(j)
. . ceiling .... 1.42-14(a)
. . ceiling determination .... 1.42-14(f)
. . national pool component ..... 1.42-14(e); 1.42-14(i)
. . nonprofit set-aside .... 1.42-14(h)
. . population component .... 1.42-14(c)
. . returned credit component .... 1.42-14(d)
. . stacking order .... 1.42-14(g)
. . unused carryforward component .... 1.42-14(b)
. utility allowance
. . changes in allowance .... 1.42-10(c)
. . HUD regulated buildings .... 1.42-10(b)(3)
. . Rural Housing Service assisted buildings .... 1.42-10(b)(1)
. . Rural Housing Service assisted tenants .... 1.42-10(b)(2)
. . tenant, utility cost paid directly by .... 1.42-10(a)

Low-Income Taxpayer Clinic
. income tax return preparer defined 301.7701-15

Lubricating oil
. taxability (See Fuel, taxable)

Lump-sum distributions
. annuities
. . accumulated deductible employee contributions 20.2039-4
. employee trusts .... 1.402(e)-2; 1.402(e)-3
. pre-1974 participation as post-1973 participation, election to treat .... 1.402(e)-14

Luxury tax
. aircraft 48.4003-1
. boats 48.4002-1
. exemption certificate 48.4011-7
. exemptions 48.4011-2
. furs 48.4007-1
. generally 48.4011-1
. installment sales 48.4011-6
. jewelry 48.4006-1
. lease, qualified 48.4011-6
. passenger vehicles 48.4001-1
. use of article before first retail sale 48.4011-5
. vehicles, taxable 48.4004-1
. . exemptions 48.4004-2
. . resales, nonexempt 48.4004-4
. . subsequent 48.4004-3

M

MACRS (See Modified accelerated cost recovery system)

Magnetic media, returns on
. information returns
. . education loan interest 301.6011-2
. . electronic filing (See Electronic filing)
. . tuition payments, reimbursements and refunds 301.6011-2
. required use
. . corporate income tax 1.6011-5; 301.6011-5
. . electing small business corporations 301.6037-2
. . organizations filing under sec. 6033...... 1.6033-4; 301.6033-4
. . small business corporation 301.6037-2

Mailing
. timely filing
. . documents and payments 301.7502-1

Manufacturers and retailers excise taxes
. alcohol, alternative fuel, biodiesel and renewable diesel 48.6426-12
. . coordination with excise tax credit .... 48.6426-12(b)
. . effective / applicability date .... 48.6426-12(d)
. . generally .... 48.6426-12(a)
. . payment computation for certain blenders .... 48.6426-12(c); 48.6426-12(c)(1)
. . . example .... 48.6426-12(c)(2)
. alcohol fuel mixtures 48.6426-2
. . conditions to allowance .... 48.6426-2(b)
. . . ETBE; sold for use or used as a fuel .... 48.6426-2(b)(3)
. . . excise tax credit .... 48.6426-2(b)(1)
. . . overall limitations on credit and payments .... 48.6426-2(b)(4)
. . . payment or income tax credit..... 48.6426-2(b)(2)
. . content of claim .... 48.6426-2(c)
. . effective / applicability date .... 48.6426-2(d)
. . overview .... 48.6426-2(a)
. alternative fuel 48.6426-6
. . conditions to allowance .... 48.6426-6(b)
. . . excise tax credit .... 48.6426-6(b)(1)
. . . overall limitations on credits and payments .... 48.6426-6(b)(3)
. . . payment or income tax credit..... 48.6426-6(b)(2)
. . content of claim .... 48.6426-6(c)
. . effective / applicability date .... 48.6426-6(d)
. . overview .... 48.6426-6(a)
. alternative fuel mixtures 48.6426-5
. . allowances .... 48.6426-5(b)
. . . excise tax credit .... 48.6426-5(b)(1)
. . . overall limitations on credits and payments .... 48.6426-5(b)(3)
. . . payment or income tax credit..... 48.6426-5(b)(2)
. . content of claim .... 48.6426-5(c)

References are to Reg. § numbers

Manufacturers and retailers excise taxes —Cont'd
. *alternative fuel mixtures—Cont'd*
. . effective / applicability date ....48.6426-5(e)
. . overview ....48.6426-5(a)
. applicability of regulation relating to diesel fuel after December 31, 1993 ....48.4041-0
. ASTM and military specifications ....48.4081-1(d)
. biodiesel mixtures 48.6426-3
. . biodiesel reseller statement ....48.6426-3(f)(1)
. . certificate .... 48.6426-3(e); 48.6426-3(e)(1)
. . . certificate identification number ... 48.6426-3(e)(2)
. . . model certificate .... 48.6426-3(e)(4)
. . . multiple certificates for single sale ....48.6426-3(e)(3)
. . commingled biodiesel; accounting method ....48.6426-3(d)
. . conditions to allowance ....48.6426-3(b)
. . . excise tax credit ....48.6426-3(b)(1)
. . . overall limitations on credits and payments ....48.6426-3(b)(3)
. . . payment or income tax credit..........48.6426-3(b)(2)
. . content of claim ....48.6426-3(c)
. . effective / applicability date ....48.6426-3(h)
. . erroneous certificates; reasonable cause ....48.6426-3(g)
. . overview ....48.6426-3(a)
. . statement of biodiesel reseller ....48.6426-3(f)
. . . model statement of biodiesel reseller ....48.6426-3(f)(4)
. . . multiple resales ....48.6426-3(f)(2)
. . . withdrawal of the right to provide a certificate ....48.6426-3(f)(3)
. blended taxable fuel ....48.4081-1(c)(1)
. . defined ....48.4081-1(c)
. . exclusion; minor blending .... 48.4081-1(c)(1)(ii)
. . gasohol exclusion ....48.4081-1(c)(1)(iii)
. blended taxable fuel defined ....48.4081-1(c)(1)(i)
. credits and payment limitations..........48.6426-7
. . alternative fuel ....48.6426-7(b)
. . effective / applicability dates ....48.6426-7(c)
. . mixtures ....48.6426-7(a)
. definitions ....48.4081-1(b)
. diesel fuel ....48.4081-1(c)(2)
. . defined .... 48.4081-1(c); 48.4081-1(c)(1)(i)
. . exclusion..........48.4081-1(c)(2)(ii)
. diesel fuel or kerosene, back-up tax 48.4082-4
. . buses and trains..........48.4082-4(b)(1)
. . . buses, rate of tax ....48.4082-4(b)(3)(i)
. . . liability for tax..........48.4082-4(b)(2); 48.4082-4(b)(2)(i)
. . . rate of tax..........48.4082-4(b)(3)
. . . special rule for certain train operators ....48.4082-4(b)(2)(ii)
. . . trains, rate of tax ....48.4082-4(b)(3)(ii)
. . effective date ....48.4082-4(d)

Manufacturers and retailers excise taxes —Cont'd
. *diesel fuel or kerosene, back-up tax—Cont'd*
. . exemptions ....48.4082-4(c)
. . imposition of tax .... 48.4082-4(a); 48.4082-4(a)(1)
. . liability for tax .... 48.4082-4(a)(2)
. . rate of tax .... 48.4082-4(a)(3)
. effective date ....48.4081-1(f)
. forms 48.0-4
. fuels containing alcohol ... 48.4041-18; 48.4041-18(a)
. . alcohol mixture fuels qualifying for special tax treatment..........48.4041-18(b)
. . April 1, 1983, sale or use before... 48.4041-18(a)(3)
. . December 31, 1984, sale or use after ....48.4041-18(a)(1)
. . exemption for fuels sold or used in noncommercial aircraft .... 48.4041-18(d); 48.4041-18(d)(1)
. . . failure to use alcohol mixture fuel ....48.4041-18(d)(2)
. . later separation ....48.4041-18(c)
. . March 31, 1983, sale or use after ....48.4041-18(a)(2)
. . rate of tax for mixtures which fail to qualify ....48.4041-18(a)(4)
. . records required to be furnished by the taxpayer ....48.4041-18(f)
. . . mixtures within the tank of a vehicle before April 1, 1983..........48.4041-18(f)(1)
. . . mixtures within the tank of a vehicle before January 1, 1985 ....48.4041-18(f)(2)
. . refunds relating to diesel, special motor and noncommercial aviation fuels ....48.4041-18(e)
. gasohol defined..........48.4081-6(b)(1)(i); 48.4081-6(b)(2)(i)
. gasoline
. . defined ....48.4081-6(b)(2)(i)
. . removed or entered for gasohol production ....48.4081-6(c)(2)(i)
. gasoline blendstocks ....48.4081-1(c)(3)
. . defined ....48.4081-1(c)
. . exclusion..........48.4081-1(c)(3)(ii)
. gasoline/gasohol..........48.4081-6
. . alcohol..........48.4081-6(b)(1)
. . . products derived from alcohol ....48.4081-6(b)(1)(iii)
. . . proof and denaturants ....48.4081-6(b)(1)(ii)
. . defined ....48.4081-6(b)
. . failure to blend
. . . example ....48.4081-6(f)(2)(iv)
. . . imposition of tax ....48.4081-6(f)(2)(i)
. . . liability for tax..........48.4081-6(f)(2)(ii)
. . . rate of tax..........48.4081-6(f)(2)(iii)
. . gasohol ....48.4081-6(b)(2)
. . . examples ....48.4081-6(b)(2)(vi)
. . . 5.7 percent gasohol ....48.4081-6(b)(2)(iv)
. . . 7.7 percent gasohol ....48.4081-6(b)(2)(iii)

References are to Reg. § numbers

Manufacturers and retailers excise taxes —Cont'd
. *gasoline/gasohol—Cont'd*
. . *gasohol—Cont'd*
. . . tax on excess liquid .... 48.4081-6(b)(2)(v)
. . . 10 percent gasohol .... 48.4081-6(b)(2)(ii)
. . gasoline removed or entered for gasohol production
. . . certificate .... 48.4081-6(c)(2)
. . . Form 637 or letter of registration as a gasohol blender's certificate, use of ... 48.4081-6(c)(2)(iii)
. . . model certificate .... 48.4081-6(c)(2)(ii)
. . later separation
. . . imposition of tax .... 48.4081-6(f)(1)(i)
. . . liability for tax................ 48.4081-6(f)(1)(ii)
. . . rate of tax.................. 48.4081-6(f)(1)(iii)
. . later separation and failure to blend
. . . failure to blend................... 48.4081-6(f)(2)
. . . later separation .... 48.4081-6(f)(1)
. . overview .... 48.4081-6(a)
. . tax rates .... 48.4081-6(e)
. . . gasoline removed or entered .... 48.4081-6(d)
. . . gasoline removed or entered for gasohol production .... 48.4081-6(c)
. introduction 48.0-1
. other definitions...................... 48.4081-1(e)
. overview.............................. 48.4081-1(a)
. qualified methanol and ethanol fuel and partially exempt methanol or ethanol fuel .... 48.4041-19; 48.4041-19(a)
. . defined .... 48.4041-19(b)
. registration
. . action on the application by the district director .... 48.4101-1(g)
. . . approval .... 48.4101-1(g)(3)
. . . denial .... 48.4101-1(g)(2)
. . . review of application .... 48.4101-1(g)(1)
. . adverse actions by the district director against a registrant...................... 48.4101-1(i)
. . . action by the district director to revoke or suspend a registration .... 48.4101-1(i)(3)
. . . mandatory revocation or suspension .... 48.4101-1(i)(1)
. . . remedial action permitted in other cases .... 48.4101-1(i)(2)
. . applicant defined .... 48.4101-1(b)(1)
. . application instructions .... 48.4101-1(e)
. . bonded registrant defined .... 48.4101-1(b)(2)
. . bonds .... 48.4101-1(j)
. . . amount of bond .... 48.4101-1(j)(2)
. . . collection of taxes from
. . . . other bonds................. 48.4101-1(j)(3)(ii)
. . . . surety bonds............... 48.4101-1(j)(3)(i)
. . . collection of taxes from a bond .... 48.4101-1(j)(3)
. . . form .... 48.4101-1(j)(1)
. . . termination of bonds .... 48.4101-1(j)(4)
. . effective dates .... 48.4101-1(l)

Manufacturers and retailers excise taxes —Cont'd
. *registration —Cont'd*
. . gasohol bonding amount defined ... 48.4101-1(b)(3)
. . generally .... 48.4101-1; 48.4101-1(a)
. . other operator defined .... 48.4101-1(b)(9)
. . penalized for a wrongful act defined .... 48.4101-1(b)(4)
. . persons required to be registered .... 48.4101-1(c); 48.4101-1(c)(1)
. . . bus and train operators .... 48.4101-1(c)(2)
. . . consequences of failing to register .... 48.4101-1(c)(3)
. . persons that may, but are not required to, be registered .... 48.4101-1(d)
. . pipeline operator defined.......... 48.4101-1(b)(7)
. . registrant defined .... 48.4101-1(b)(6)
. . registration tests...... 48.4101-1(f); 48.4101-1(f)(1)
. . . acceptable risk test .... 48.4101-1(f)(3); 48.4101-1(f)(3)(i)
. . . activity test...................... 48.4101-1(f)(2)
. . . adequate security test .... 48.4101-1(f)(4); 48.4101-1(f)(4)(i)
. . . persons other than ultimate vendors, pipeline operators, and vessel operators .... 48.4101-1(f)(1)(i)
. . . ultimate vendors, pipeline operators, and vessel operators .... 48.4101-1(f)(1)(ii)
. . related person defined............. 48.4101-1(b)(5)
. . terms and conditions of registration .... 48.4101-1(h)
. . . additional terms and conditions for terminal operators........................ 48.4101-1(h)(3)
. . . affirmative duties .... 48.4101-1(h)(1)
. . . prohibited actions .... 48.4101-1(h)(2)
. . vessel operator defined .... 48.4101-1(b)(8)
. registration tests
. . acceptable risk test .... 48.4101-1(f)(3)(ii)
. . adequate security test
. . . adequate financial resources .... 48.4101-1(f)(4)(ii)
. . . satisfactory tax history .... 48.4101-1(f)(4)(iii)
. removal at a terminal rack 48.4081-2
. . effective date .... 48.4081-2(f)
. . exemptions .... 48.4081-2(e)
. . imposition of tax .... 48.4081-2(b)
. . joint and several liability of terminal operator
. . . conditions for avoidance of liability .... 48.4081-2(c)(2)(ii)
. . . incorrect information provided .... 48.4081-2(c)(3)
. . . unregistered position holder...... 48.4081-2(c)(2)
. . liability for tax .... 48.4081-2(c); 48.4081-2(c)(1); 48.4081-2(c)(4)
. . overview .... 48.4081-2(a)
. . rate of tax .... 48.4081-2(d)
. . terminal operator; unregistered position holder .... 48.4081-2(c)(2)(i)
. renewable and alternative fuels........... 48.6426-1
. . alcohol

References are to Reg. § numbers

Manufacturers and retailers excise taxes —Cont'd
. *renewable and alternative fuels—Cont'd*
. . *alcohol —Cont'd*
. . . defined .... 48.6426-1(c)
. . . ETBE .... 48.6426-1(c)(3)
. . . proof and denaturants .... 48.6426-1(c)(3)
. . . source of the alcohol .... 48.6426-1(c)(2)
. . defined .... 48.6426-1(c)(1)
. . definitions, other .... 48.6426-1(f)
. . effective / applicability date .... 48.6426-1(g)
. . explanation of terms .... 48.6426-1(b)
. . overview .... 48.6426-1(a)
. . renewable diesel mixture; definition .... 48.6426-1(d)
. . . special rules .... 48.6426-1(d)(2)
. . use as a fuel .... 48.6426-1(e)
. renewable diesel mixtures 48.6426-4
. . certificate for renewable diesel .... 48.6426-4(e); 48.6426-4(e)(1)
. . . identification number .... 48.6426-4(e)(2)
. . . model certificate .... 48.6426-4(e)(4)
. . . multiple certificates for single sale .... 48.6426-4(e)(3)
. . claim, content of .... 48.6426-4(c)
. . commingled renewable diesel, accounting method .... 48.6426-4(d)
. . conditions to allowance .... 48.6426-4(b)
. . . excise tax credit .... 48.6426-4(b)(1)
. . . overall limitations on credits and payments .... 48.6426-4(b)(3)
. . . payment or income tax credit ..... 48.6426-4(b)(2)
. . defined .... 48.6426-1(d)(1)
. . effective / applicability date .... 48.6426-4(h)
. . erroneous certificates; reasonable cause .... 48.6426-4(g)
. . overview .... 48.6426-4(a)
. . renewable diesel reseller statement .... 48.6426-4(f); 48.6426-4(f)(1)
. . . model statement of renewable diesel reseller .... 48.6426-4(f)(4)
. . . multiple resales .... 48.6426-4(f)(2)
. . . withdrawal of the right to provide a certificate .... 48.6426-4(f)(3)
. taxable fuels 48.4081-1
. ultimate purchasers, claims by 48.6426-8
. . blended taxable fuels .... 48.6426-8(b)(1)(vii)(E)

Marital deduction
. gift taxes
. . right of recovery, failure to exercise 25.2207A-1
. life estate
. . surviving spouse
. . . income, spouse entitled to .... 20.2056(b)-5
. power of appointment in surviving spouse
. . life estate .... 20.2056(b)-5

Marketable stock
. defined .... 1.1296(e)-1
. initial public offerings, special rules for .... 1.1296(e)-1(b)(2)
. mark-to-market election for 1.1296-1

Mark-to-market
. accounting methods (See Accounting methods)
. controlled foreign corporations, election for marketable stock (See Controlled foreign corporations subhead mark-to-market election for marketable stock)
. debt instruments .... 1.475(a)-1
. marketable stocks 1.1296-1

Married persons (See Spouses)

Material advisors
. reportable transactions .... 301.6111-3(b)
. . designation agreements .... 301.6111-3(f)
. . disclosure statement, form of .... 301.6111-3(d)
. . list of advisors .... 301.6112-1(a)
. . . definitions concerning .... 301.6112-1(c)
. . . designation agreements .... 301.6112-1(f)
. . . furnishing of lists .... 301.6112-1(e)
. . . preparation and maintenance ...... 301.6112-1(b)
. . . retention of lists .... 301.6112-1(d)
. . protective disclosure .... 301.6111-3(g)
. . time of providing .... 301.6111-3(e)

Medical expenses
. dependent care services
. . employment related expenses, credit for ... 1.21-1(j)

Mental self-care incapability
. principal residence sales, exclusion of gain from sale or exchange 1.121-4

Mineral production payments
. character of amounts .... 1.652(b)-1
. loans, treatment of production payments as .. 1.636-1

Minimum tax on preference income (See Alternative minimum tax (AMT))

Mining exploration
. optional 10-year writeoff of certain tax preferences 1.59-1

Modified accelerated cost recovery system
. depreciation allowance for MACRS property
. . accounting method, change in .... 1.168(i)-4(f)
. . change in use as factor in recovery period or depreciation method .... 1.168(i)-4(d)
. . change in use of property during the placed-in-service year .... 1.168(i)-4(e)
. . conversions to business or income-producing use .... 1.168(i)-4(b)
. . conversions to personal use .... 1.168(i)-4(c)
. . half-year and mid quarter year conventions .... 1.168(d)-1
. . use changes in the hands of the same taxpayer .... 1.168(i)-4
. general asset account rules .... 1.168(i)-1

References are to Reg. § numbers

Modified accelerated cost recovery system —Cont'd
. like-kind exchanges and involuntary conversions .... 1.168(i)-6
Modified Guaranteed Contracts
. defined 1.817A-1
. equity-indexed, interest rates for 1.817A-1
Money
. distributions by corporations 1.301-1
Monthly returns
. information returns .... 31.6011(a)-5
. withholding .... 31.6011(a)-5
Mortality charges
. life insurance contracts, determining for 1.7702-1
Mortality tables
. determination of current liability .... 1.431(c)(6)-1; 1.1412(1)(7)-1; 1.1412(1)(7)-1(d)
. . construction of table .... 1.1412(1)(7)-1(c)
. . use of table .... 1.1412(1)(7)-1(b)
. determination of present value
. . base mortality tables and projection factors .... 1.430(h)(3)-1(d)
. . basis .... 1.430(h)(3)-1(a)
. . construction of static tables .... 1.430(h)(3)-1(c)
. . use of table .... 1.430(h)(3)-1(b)
Mortgage revenue bonds
. arbitrage .... 1.143(g)-1
. private activity bonds, public approval
. . defined for .... 1.147(f)-1(c)(5)
. . special rules .... 1.147(f)-1(b)(3)
Motion picture and television films and tapes
. at risk provisions 1.465-42
. deduction for qualified film and television production costs .... 1.181-1 et seq.
Musical works
. self-created, capital asset treatment of 1.1221-3
Mutual savings banks
. bad debts .... 1.582-1; 1.593-1 to 1.593-3
. distributions to shareholders by domestic building and loan associations 1.593-7
. dividends paid on deposits 1.591-1
. real property loans, addition to reserve for losses on qualifying 1.593-4

N

Natural resources
. oil and gas (See Oil and gas)
Net capital losses
. foreign corporations
. . ordering rules for net operating losses, net capital losses, U.S. source losses .... 1.904(g)-3
Net operating losses
. consolidated returns 1.1502-21

Net operating losses —Cont'd
. dual consolidated loss 1.1503-2
. foreign corporations
. . ordering rules for net operating losses, net capital losses, U.S. source losses .... 1.904(g)-3
New comparability plans (See Pension, profit-sharing, and stock bonus plans subhead defined contribution plans)
New markets tax credit
. active conduct of a trade or business .... 1.45D-1(d)(4)(iv)
. generally 1.45D-1
. low-income persons .... 1.45D-1(d)(9)(i)
. qualified active low-income community business defined .... 1.45D-1(d)(4)(i)
. targeted populations .... 1.45D-1(d)(9)
New York Liberty zone
. additional first year depreciation deduction .... 1.1400L(b)-1
. first year depreciation deduction .... 1.1400L(b)-1
Nondiscrimination rules
. questions and answers relating to .... 1.89(a)-1
Nonfinancial customer paper
. mark-to-market accounting methods
. . inventory .... 1.475(c)-2
Nonqualified deferred compensation plans (See Deferred compensation subhead nonqualified plans)
Nonresident aliens
. deposit interest paid
. . exceptions, reportable payment .... 31.3406(g)-1
. . interest subject to reporting requirements 1.6049-8
. . payee statements 1.6049-6
. . reportable payments made to nonresident aliens .... 31.3406(g)-1
. . reporting requirements, interest subject to 1.6049-8
. original issue discount
. . reporting requirements, interest subject to 1.6049-8
. . statements, payee 1.6049-6
. possessions of the U.S. 1.871-1; 1.876-1
Northern Mariana Islands
. exclusion, income 1.931-1; 1.931-1T
. Guam coordination of individual income taxes with 1.935-1
. individual income tax
. . nonresident alien individual who is resident of U.S. possession or Puerto Rico, taxation of .... 1.1-1(b)
. nonresident aliens 1.876-1
Not for profit activities (See also Charitable contributions; Exempt organizations)
. generally 1.183-1
Notarized statements
. replacement property under sec. 1042 .... 1.1042-1T

References are to Reg. § numbers

Notes receivable
. capital asset exclusion 1.1221-1
Notice
. amount of increased tax liability, IRS failure to provide notice of
. . interest, suspension of ....301.6404-4(a)
. electronic medium, use of
. . pension, profit-sharing, and stock bonus plans ....1.401(a)-21
. exempt organizations
. . notification requirement for entities not required to file annual information return under sec. 6033(a)(1) 1.6033-6
. pension plan, amendments to
. . benefit accruals, reductions to 54.4980F-1
. returns
. . notification requirement for entities not required to file annual information return under sec. 6033(a)(1) 1.6033-6
. Tax Court; to interested parties 1.7476-2
. TIN, incorrect; multiple notices .... 31.3406(d)-5; 301.6724-1
Notional principal contracts
. bullet swaps, and forward contracts 1.1234A-1
. gain or loss, adjustment of .... 1.446-3(d)
. global dealing operations
. . allocation of income 1.863-7
. nontrade and nonbusiness expenses, payment 1.212-1
. ordinary and necessary business expenses, deductibility as 1.162-30
. recognition rules .... 1.446-3(d)
. taxable year of inclusion.................. 1.446-3(d)
Nuclear decommissioning funds
. allocations
. . ADSP and AGUB 1.338-6
. . asset acquisitions...................... 1.1060-1
. costs.. 1.468A-1
. disposition of interest in 1.468A-6
. electing taxpayer treatment 1.468A-2
. manner and time of making election 1.468A-7
. miscellaneous provisions 1.468A-5
. ruling amount 1.468A-3
. treatment of fund............................ 1.468A-4

O

Obligations
. registration requirements
. . generally 5f.163-1
. . interest deduction........................ 5f.163-1
Obsolescence
. Accelerated Cost Recovery System
. . periods since February 28, 1913 .... 1.1016-3
Obsolescence —Cont'd
. *Accelerated Cost Recovery System —Cont'd*
. . periods when income was not subject to tax 1.1016-4
. accounting method change .... 1.1016-3(h)
Offshore accounts
. documentary evidence for reporting 1.6049-5
Oil and gas
. at risk provisions 1.465-45
. taxable fuel (See Fuel, taxable)
Omnibus Budget Reconciliation Act of 1993
. qualified dividend income as investment income, election to make
. . time and manner of making .... 1.163(d)-1
Open account debt
. shareholder, indebtedness to 1.1367-2
. . adjustment of basis of .... 1.1367-2(a)
. . multiple indebtedness .... 1.1367-2(c)(2)
. . time at which adjustment of basis of indebtedness is effective .... 1.1367-2(d)
Optional 10-year writeoff of certain tax preferences 1.59-1
Options
. stock (See Stock options)
Original issue discount (OID)
. reporting
. . offshore accounts and possessions accounts, documentary evidence of 1.6049-5
. split-dollar loans 1.7872-15
Overpayment of tax
. adjustments of
. . generally ....31.6413(a)-2
. . not permitted .... 31.6413(a)-2(d)
. . Railroad Retirement Tax Act (RRTA) .... 31.6413(a)-2; 31.6413(a)-2(b)
. Federal Insurance Contributions Act (FICA)
. . overpayment adjustments ....31.6413(a)-2
. generally 301.6611-1
. Railroad Retirement Tax Act (RRTA)
. . overpayment adjustments ....31.6413(a)-2
Ownership
. affiliate-owned stock 1.7874-1

P

Partial liquidation
. generally 1.346-1
Partners and partnerships
. allocation of basis adjustments
. . coordination of section 755 and 1060
. . . gross value, partnership 1.755-2
. . . information statements 1.755-2
. . . residual method.......................... 1.755-2

References are to Reg. § numbers

Partners and partnerships —Cont'd
. automatic extension of time for filing returns 1.6081-2
. communications activity 1.863-9
. contributions by partnerships .... 1.358-7(b)
. contributions of partnership interest .... 1.358-7(a)
. contributions to partnership
. . distributions of previously contributed property 1.737-2
. . transfers to another partner .... 1.737-2(b)
. debt, allocation of partnership
. . assumption of sec. 1.752-7 liability on or after June 24, 2003 .... 1.752-7
. dependent care services
. . employment related expenses, credit for .... 1.21-4(b)
. disguised sales
. . disclosure of transfer 1.707-7; 1.707-8; 1.707-9
. . general rules 1.707-6
. . liabilities 1.707-7
. . liquidation of partner interest 1.707-7
. . transfers as sale 1.707-7
. . transfers before effective date 1.707-9
. . transfers presumed not to be sale 1.707-7
. distributions
. . controlled foreign corporations 1.952-1
. . foreign base company income 1.954-1
. . foreign base company income sales income 1.954-3
. . foreign base company income service income 1.954-4
. . interest in partnership 1.704-1
. domestic production activities .... 1.199-5(a)
. gain or loss, allocation of
. . contributed property 1.704-3
. . distributive share of partner 1.704-1
. hybrid branch payments; controlled foreign corporations 1.954-9
. income and credits
. . subpart F income 1.702-1
. indebtedness satisfied by partnership interest
. . fair market value determination .... 1.108-8(b)
. . generally 1.108-8
. installment sales
. . disposition of 704(c) property in 1.704-3
. . installment obligation received in 1.704-4
. . nonrecognition transactions 1.704-4; 1.737-2
. interest, determination of partner's 1.705-1
. . basis adjustments coordinating sec. 705 and 1032 .... 1.705-2
. . conversions and refinancing 1.704-2
. . disregarded 1.752-2
. . gain or loss, recognition of .... 1.83-6(b)
. . liabilities 1.704-2

Partners and partnerships —Cont'd
. *interest, determination of partner's—Cont'd*
. . nonrecourse debt into nonrecourse debt, conversions of 1.704-2; 1.752-2
. . property .... 1.83-3(e)
. . transfer of interest .... 1.83-3(l)
. liability, assumption of partnership .... 1.358-7(c)
. LIFO benefits, recapture of 1.1363-2
. limited partner defined for self-employment tax .... 1.1402(a)-2
. nonrecognition of gain or loss on contribution 1.721-1
. private activity bonds
. . private business use test
. . . regulations, application of .... 1.145-2(c)(3)
. property, partnership interest as .... 1.83-3(e)
. qualified small business stock, acquisition of 1.1045-1
. space or ocean activity income 1.863-8
. taxable year 1.706-1
. 358(h) liability
. . assumption .... 1.358-7(c)
. . basis determination 1.705-1
. . defined .... 1.358-7(d)
. transactions between partner and partnership 1.707-1
. transfers by partner to corporation 1.358-7
. transfers of property
. . performance of service, connected with 1.706-3

Passenger vehicles
. luxury tax 48.4001-1

Passive activity losses and credits
. inventories 1.472-2

Passive foreign investment companies
. deferred tax amount 1.1291-4
. dispositions 1.1291-3
. . section 1291 funds 1.1291-3
. foreign tax credit rules 1.1291-5
. generally .... 1.1291-1 et seq.
. mark-to-market election for marketable stock
. . definitions concerning .... 1.1296-1(a)
. . U.S. partner of foreign partner making section 1296 election .... 1.6031(a)-1(b)
. nonrecognition transfers 1.1291-6
. qualified electing fund
. . automatic termination of election .... 1.1291-1(i)(3)
. section 1291 funds
. . dispositions 1.1291-3
. . shareholders, taxation of 1.1291-1
. section 1291 stock
. . mark-to-market election 1.1296-1
. shareholders
. . deferred taxes 1.1291-4

References are to Reg. § numbers

Passive foreign investment companies —Cont'd
. shareholders that are not pedigreed QEF's, taxation .... 1.1291-1 et seq.
. . coordination with other PFIC rules ...... 1.1291-1(c)
. special election 1.1291-8
. taxation of
. . distributions 1.1291-2
. U.S. partner of foreign partner making section 1296 election .... 1.6031(a)-1(b)

Passport applicants
. information reporting.... 301.6039E-1

Pass-thru entities
. domestic production activities (See Domestic production activities)
. withholding under sec. 3402(t) .... 31.3402(t)-2(g)

Patronage dividends 1.6044-6

Payment cards
. reasonable cause based on reliance on a QPCA 301.6724-1
. withholding on reportable payments ..... 31.3406(g)-1

Payment of tax
. depositaries of government
. . backup withholding .... 31.6302(c)-3
. extensions of time for payment ... 1.6164-4; 1.6164-8
. installments
. . generally 1.6152-1
. insurance premium excise tax 46.4374-1
. overpayments 301.6611-1
. time and place (See Time and place for paying taxes)
. underpayments, interest.... 301.6601-1

Payments in lieu of taxes (PILOT)
. private activity bonds
. . private security or payment test ...... 1.141-4(e)(5)

Penalties
. individual retirement accounts and annuities, and simplified employee pensions 301.6693-1
. insurance premium excise tax, failure to pay 46.4374-1
. IRS suspension of interest and penalties
. . notice of amount of increased tax liability, IRS failure to provide .... 301.6404-4(a)
. pension, profit-sharing, and stock bonus plans (See Pension, profit-sharing, and stock bonus plans)

Pension, profit-sharing, and stock bonus plans
. age of participant
. . reduction of accruals or allocations, as factor in .... 1.411(b)-2
. aggregation and combining of plans
. . compensation when employer maintains for than one defined benefit plan .... 1.415(f)-1(d)
. . generally .... 1.415(f)-1
. . multiemployer plans.... 1.415(f)-1(h)
. . predecessor employers .... 1.415(f)-1(c)
. . previously unaggregated plans........ 1.415(f)-1(f)

Pension, profit-sharing, and stock bonus plans — Cont'd
. *aggregation and combining of plans —Cont'd*
. . sec. 403(b) annuity contracts .... 1.415(f)-1(g)
. . special rules for certain plans .... 1.415(f)-1(j)
. . years of participation when employer maintains for than one defined benefit plan ...... 1.415(f)-1(e)
. allocations
. . accrued benefits derived from mandatory employee contributions to .... 1.411(c)-1
. amendment reducing benefit accrual
. . notice requirement 54.4980F-1
. annual benefits determination
. . before current determination date, distributions occurred .... 1.415(b)-2(a)
. . form, change in distribution .... 1.415(b)-2(c)
. . prior distributions, attributable........ 1.415(b)-2(b)
. annual deferrals
. . individual limitation for combines deferral under multiple plans 1.457-5
. . severance from employment, after 1.457-4
. annuities
. . contribution limitations .... 1.415(a)-1
. at-risk status, plans in
. . funding target, determination of
. . . determination of at-risk status .... 1.430(i)-1(b)
. . . generally .... 1.430(i)-1(a)(1); 1.430(i)-1(c)
. . . multiple employer plans .... 1.430(i)-1(a)(2)
. . . target normal cost of plans in at-risk status .... 1.430(i)-1(d)
. . . transition between applicable funding targets and applicable target normal costs ..... 1.430(i)-1(e)
. attainment of age
. . defined .... 1.411(b)-2
. . reduction of accruals or allocations, as factor in .... 1.411(b)-2
. beneficiaries (See also other subheads)
. . taxation .... 1.402(a)-1
. benefits (See other subheads)
. bonds, taxation of 1.409-1
. capital gains and losses 1.1232-2
. cash balance plans
. . accruals .... 1.401(a)(4)-3
. . attainment of age as factor in accruals or allocations .... 1.411(b)-2
. catch-up contributions for individuals age 50 or over .... 1.414(v)-1
. compensation
. . defined .... 1.415(c)-2
. . exclusions from .... 1.415(c)-2(c)
. . included items .... 1.415(c)-2(b)
. . safe harbor rules and definition of .... 1.415(c)-2(d)
. . sec. 401(a)(17), interaction with .... 1.415(c)-2(f)
. contribution limitations .... 1.415(a)-1
. . church plans .... 1.415(c)-1(d)

References are to Reg. § numbers

Pension, profit-sharing, and stock bonus plans — Cont'd
. *contribution limitations—Cont'd*
. . limitation years .... 1.415(c)-1(d); 1.415(j)-1
. . . alternative .... 1.415(j)-1(b)
. . . change in .... 1.415(j)-1(d)
. . . individual retirement accounts maintained .... 1.415(j)-1(f)
. . . multiple years .... 1.415(j)-1(c)
. . . sec. 403(b) annuity contracts purchases .... 1.415(j)-1(e)
. . medical benefits .... 1.415(c)-1(e)
. . plan provisions .... 1.415(a)-1
. . stock ownership plans .... 1.415(c)-1(f)
. cost of living adjustments
. . defined benefit plans .... 1.415(d)-1(a)
. . defined contribution plans .... 1.415(d)-1(b)
. . implementation .... 1.415(d)-1(d)
. . rounding rules .... 1.415(d)-1(c)
. deemed IRA in qualified employer plan .... 1.408(q)-1
. defined benefit plans
. . adjustment to dollar limit for commencement before age 62 .... 1.415(b)-1(d); 1.415(b)-1(e)
. . adjustment to form of benefit .... 1.415(b)-1(c)
. . annual additions .... 1.415(c)-1(b)
. . annual benefits .... 1.415(b)-1(b)
. . benefit limitations .... 1.415(c)-1(a)
. . cost of living adjustments .... 1.415(d)-1(a)
. . participation and service less than 10 years .... 1.415(b)-1(g)
. . payments not in excess of $10,000 .... 1.415(b)-1(f)
. . statutory hybrid plans
. . . marked rate of return .... 1.411(b)(5)-1(d)
. . . plan conversion amendments .... 1.411(b)(5)-1(c)
. . . reduction in rate of benefit accrual .... 1.411(b)(5)-1(a)
. defined contribution plans
. . accrued benefits, protection of .... 1.411(d)-3(a)
. . ancillary benefits defined .... 1.411(d)-3(f)
. . burdensome and de minimis value, elimination or reduction of benefits of .... 1.411(d)-3(e)
. . core options defined .... 1.411(d)-3(f)
. . cost of living adjustments .... 1.415(d)-1(b)
. . definitions concerning section 411(d)(6)(B) protected benefits .... 1.411(d)-3(f)
. . diversification requirements
. . . applicable defined contribution plans defined .... 1.401(a)(35)(f)(2)
. . . elective deferrals and employee contributions in employer securities .... 1.401(a)(35)(b)
. . . employer securities, restrictions or conditions on investments in .... 1.401(a)(35)(e)
. . . employer security defined ...... 1.401(a)(35)(f)(3)
. . . generally .... 1.401(a)(35)(a)
. . . investment options .... 1.401(a)(35)(d)

Pension, profit-sharing, and stock bonus plans — Cont'd
. *defined contribution plans —Cont'd*
. . *diversification requirements —Cont'd*
. . . nonelective deferrals and employee contributions in employer securities .... 1.401(a)(35)(c)
. . . parent corporation defined ...... 1.401(a)(35)(f)(4)
. . . publicly traded defined .... 1.401(a)(35)(f)(5)
. . elimination of forms of distribution .... 1.411(d)-4
. . elimination of noncore optional benefits .... 1.411(d)-3(d)
. . elimination of redundant optional benefits .... 1.411(d)-3(c)
. . section 411(d)(6)(b) protected benefits, protection of .... 1.411(d)-3(b)
. disqualification of plan
. . generally .... 1.415(g)-1(a)
. . plan year, annuity contract .... 1.415(g)-1(c)
. . rules .... 1.415(g)-1(b)
. distributions
. . emergencies .... 1.457-6(c)
. . forms, elimination of .... 1.411(d)-4
. . generally 1.457-6
. . required minimum distributions (See Required minimum distributions)
. dividend distributions
. . disallowance of deduction on ESOP reacquisition payments .... 1.404(k)-3
. electronic medium use, notice and participant election .... 1.401(a)-21.
. employee contributions
. . deductions for .... 1.219(a)-5
. employer contributions
. . accident and health plans 1.106-1
. . simplified employee pensions .... 1.404(h)-1
. ERISA (See Employee Retirement Income Security Act of 1974)
. excise tax (See subhead penalties)
. excludable employees
. . government plans .... 1.410(b)-6(g)
. . tax-exempt entities .... 1.410(b)-6(g)
. government plans
. . excludable employees .... 1.410(b)-6(g)
. hybrid plans, statutory
. . calculation of benefits .... 1.411(a)(13)-1(b)
. . defined benefit plans
. . . marked rate of return .... 1.411(b)(5)-1(d)
. . . plan conversion amendments .... 1.411(b)(5)-1(c)
. . . reduction in rate of benefit accrual .... 1.411(b)(5)-1(a)
. . . safe harbor for certain plan designs .... 1.411(b)(5)-1(b)
. . lump sum-based benefit formula defined .... 1.411(a)(13)-1(d)(2)
. . rules applicable to .... 1.411(a)(13)-1(a)

References are to Reg. § numbers

Pension, profit-sharing, and stock bonus plans — Cont'd
. *hybrid plans, statutory — Cont'd*
. . statutory hybrid plans ....1.411(a)(13)-1(d)(3)
. . three-year vesting requirements ... 1.411(a)(13)-1(c)
. . variable annuity benefit formula ....1.411(a)(13)-1(d)(4)
. individual retirement accounts (See Individual retirement arrangements)
. limitation on benefits and contributions
. . cash or deferred arrangements
. . . section 415 compensation requirement .... 1.401(k)-1(e)(8)
. . section 403(b) contracts
. . . former employees, contributions made for .... 1.403(b)-3(b)(4)(ii)
. lump sum distributions .... 1.402(e)-2; 1.402(e)-3
. medical, accident benefits paid from .... 1.402(a)-1(e)
. minimum age and service requirements
. . excluded employees
. . . governmental or tax-exempt entities .... 1.410(b)-6
. minimum distribution incidental benefit requirement .... 1.401(a)(9)-2
. modified guaranteed contracts 1.817A-1
. more than one employer, plans maintained by
. . contribution limitations ....1.415(a)-1
. multiemployer plans, funding guidance
. . accumulated funding deficiency defined .... 1.432(a)-1(b)(1)
. . active participant .... 1.432(a)-1(b)(2)
. . annual certification by the plan's enrolled actuary .... 1.432(b)-1(d)
. . bargained and nonbargained participants, plans covering.............. 1.432(a)-1(c)(2)
. . bargained participants, plans covering .... 1.432(a)-1(c)(3)
. . bargaining party .... 1.432(a)-1(b)(3)
. . benefit commencement date....... 1.432(a)-1(b)(4)
. . critical status
. . . determination of .... 1.432(b)-1(c)
. . . general rule .... 1.432(a)-1(b)(5)
. . . plans in .... 1.432(a)-1(a)(3)
. . determination of plan status ....1.432(b)-1
. . endangered status
. . . defined .... 1.432(a)-1(b)(6)
. . . determination of .... 1.432(b)-1(b)
. . . plans in .... 1.432(a)-1(a)(2)
. . funded percentage .... 1.432(a)-1(b)(7)
. . funding improvement period for endangered or seriously endangered plans........ 1.432(a)-1(b)(8)
. . funding plan adoption period ...... 1.432(a)-1(b)(9)
. . generally ....1.432(a)-1
. . inactive participant .... 1.432(a)-1(b)(10)
. . initial critical year .... 1.432(a)-1(b)(11)
. . initial endangered year .... 1.432(a)-1(b)(12)

Pension, profit-sharing, and stock bonus plans — Cont'd
. *multiemployer plans, funding guidance — Cont'd*
. . nonbargained participant......... 1.432(a)-1(b)(13)
. . notice of endangered or critical status .... 1.432(b)-1(e)
. . obligation to contribute .... 1.432(a)-1(b)(14)
. . plan sponsor .... 1.432(a)-1(b)(15)
. . rehabilitation period .... 1.432(a)-1(b)(16)
. . rehabilitation plan adoption period .... 1.432(a)-1(b)(17)
. . seriously endangered status ...... 1.432(a)-1(b)(18)
. new comparability plans (See subhead defined contribution plans)
. notice requirement
. . amendment reducing benefit accrual 54.4980F-1
. penalties
. . accounts, contracts and bonds, excess contributions to 54.4973-1
. . accumulations
. . . generally 54.4974-2
. . . individual retirement accounts or annuities 54.4974-1
. . minimum funding standards, failure to meet .... 54-4971-1 to 54-4971-3
. phased retirement, benefits during .... 1.401(a)-3
. plan provisions
. . contribution limitations ....1.415(a)-1
. plan-to-plan transfers 1.457-10
. post-ERISA qualified plans and qualified trusts .... 1.401(a)-1 et seq.
. prefunding balance and funding standard carryover balance
. . defined benefit plans, application to .... 1.430(f)-1(a)
. . election to maintain balances .... 1.430(f)-1(b)
. . elections generally .... 1.430(f)-1(f)
. . minimum required contribution, election to apply balances to.......................... 1.430(f)-1(d)
. . multiple employer plans, special rules for ....1.430(f)-1(a)(2)
. . plan assets, effect on................... 1.430(f)-1(c)
. . reduce balances, election to .... 1.430(f)-1(e)
. . transition rules .... 1.430(f)-1(h)
. present value, interest rates used to determine
. . dates, applicable .... 1.430(h)2-1(g)(1)
. . delay effective date, plan with..... 1.430(h)2-1(g)(2)
. . elections .... 1.430(h)2-1(e)
. . liabilities, rates for determining plan .. 1.430(h)2-1(b)
. . monthly corporate bond yield curve .. 1.430(h)2-1(d)
. . multiple employer plans, special rules for .... 1.430(h)2-1(a)(2)
. . rules for............................ 1.430(h)2-1(a)(1)
. . segment rates .... 1.430(h)2-1(c)
. . shortfall amortization installments ..1.430(h)2-1(f)(2)
. . transitional rules.................. 1.430(h)2-1(g)(3)

References are to Reg. § numbers

Pension, profit-sharing, and stock bonus plans — Cont'd

. *present value, interest rates used to determine — Cont'd*

. . waiver amortization installments . . . . 1.430(h)2-1(f)(2)

. reduced uniformed services retirement pay . . . 1.122-1

. reduction of accruals or allocations, as factor in

. . age of participant . . . . 1.411(b)-2

. refund of mistaken employer contributions and withdrawal liability payments . . . . 1.401(a)-3

. required . . . . 1.401(a)(9)-1

. required minimum distribution

. . accrued benefits, actuarially increased, retirement after the calendar year employee attains age 70 1/2 . . . . 1.401(a)(9)-6(Q-7)

. . . actuarial increase ending date . . . . 1.401(a)(9)-6(A-7)(b)

. . . actuarial increase starting date . . . . 1.401(a)(9)-6(A-7)(a)

. . . nonapplication to government and church plans . . . . 1.401(a)(9)-6(A-7)(d)

. . . nonapplication to plan providing same required beginning date for all employees . . . . 1.401(a)(9)-6(A-7)(c)

. . actuarial increase in section 401(a)(9)(C)(iii), relationship to the actuarial increase required under section 411 . . . . 1.401(a)(9)-6(Q-9)

. . . nonforfeitable accrued benefit under section 411, defined benefit plan actuarial adjustment to an accrued benefit . . . . 1.401(a)(9)-6(A-9)

. . additional benefits accrued after the employee's first distribution calendar year . . . . 1.401(a)(9)-6(A-5)(a); 1.401(a)(9)-6(Q-5)

. . . administrative delay in the commencement of the distribution . . . . 1.401(a)(9)-6(A-5)(b)

. . additional guidance . . . . 1.401(a)(9)-6(A-1)(f)

. . amount of actuarial increase . . . . . 1.401(a)(9)-6(Q-8)

. . . requirements . . . . 1.401(a)(9)-6(A-8)

. . annuity commencement . . . . . . 1.401(a)(9)-6(A-1)(c)

. . annuity contract purchased from an insurance company . . . . . . 1.401(a)(9)-6(A-4); 1.401(a)(9)-6(Q-4)

. . annuity contract that has not yet been annualized . . . . 1.401(a)(9)-6(Q-12)

. . . entire interest . . . . 1.401(a)(9)-6(A-12)(b)

. . . examples . . . . 1.401(a)(9)-6(A-12)(d)

. . . exclusions . . . . 1.401(a)(9)-6(A-12)(c)

. . . general rule . . . . 1.401(a)(9)-6(A-12)(a)

. . annuity distributions, additional benefits accrued after employee's first distribution calendar year . . . . 1.401(a)(9)-6(Q-5)

. . . administrative delay in the commencement of the distribution . . . . 1.401(a)(9)-6(A-5)(b)

. . . first payment interval ending in the calendar year immediately following the calendar year in which such amount accrues . . . . . . 1.401(a)(9)-6(A-5)(a)

. . beneficiaries . . . . 1.401(a)(9)-1(A-2)(b)

Pension, profit-sharing, and stock bonus plans — Cont'd

. *required minimum distribution — Cont'd*

. . changing of annuity payment . . . 1.401(a)(9)-6(A-13)(a); 1.401(a)(9)-6(A-13)(c); 1.401(a)(9)-6(Q-13)

. . . examples . . . . 1.401(a)(9)-6(A-13)(d)

. . . reannuitization . . . . 1.401(a)(9)-6(A-13)(b)

. . death benefits . . . . 1.401(a)(9)-6(A-1)(e)

. . defined benefit plan permitted to extend, period certain under . . . . 1.401(a)(9)-6(Q-3)

. . . distributions commencing after the employee's death . . . . 1.401(a)(9)-6(A-3)(b)

. . . distributions commencing during the employee's life . . . . 1.401(a)(9)-6(A-3)(a)

. . defined period, extension of . . . . . 1.401(a)(9)-6(Q-3)

. . . distributions commencing during the employee's life . . . . 1.401(a)(9)-6(A-3)(a)

. . distributions under section 401(a)(9)

. . . additional guidance . . . . 1.401(a)(9)-6(A-1)(f)

. . . annuity commencement . . . . . 1.401(a)(9)-6(A-1)(c)

. . . death benefits . . . . 1.401(a)(9)-6(A-1)(e)

. . . general rules . . . . 1.401(a)(9)-6(A-1)(a)

. . . life annuity with period certain . . . . 1.401(a)(9)-6(A-1)(b)

. . employee, distributions commence to . . . . 1.401(a)(9)-6(Q-10)

. . . adjustment to employee / beneficiary age difference . . . . 1.401(a)(9)-6(A-10)(c)

. . . general rule . . . . 1.401(a)(9)-6(A-10)(a)

. . . period certain . . . . 1.401(a)(9)-6(A-10)(b)

. . employee's death, commencing after . . . . 1.401(a)(9)-6(A-3)(b)

. . generally . . . . . 1.401(a)(9)-1; 1.401(a)(9)-1(A-2)(a); 1.401(a)(9)-6(A-1)(a); 1.401(a)(9)-6(Q-1)

. . government plans . . . . 1.401(a)(9)-1(A-2)(d)

. . governmental plan within the meaning of section 414(d), annuity payments that do not satisfy section 401(a)(9)

. . . annuity payments under a governmental plan . . . . 1.401(a)(9)-6(A-16)(a)

. . increasing annuity payment . . . . 1.401(a)(9)-6(Q-14)

. . . additional permitted increases for annuity payments from a qualified trust . . . . . . 1.401(a)(9)-6(A-14)(d)

. . . additional permitted increases for annuity payments under annuity contracts purchased from insurance companies . . . . 1.401(a)(9)-6(A-14)(c)

. . . cost-of-living index . . . . 1.401(a)(9)-6(A-14)(b)

. . . definitions . . . . 1.401(a)(9)-6(A-14)(e)

. . . examples . . . . 1.401(a)(9)-6(A-14)(f)

. . . general rules . . . . 1.401(a)(9)-6(A-14)(a)

. . . surviving child, payments to . . 1.401(a)(9)-6(Q-15); 1.401(a)(9)-6(Q-15)(a)

. . life annuity with period certain . . . . 1.401(a)(9)-6(A-1)(b)

. . life (or joint and survivor), annuity incidental benefit requirements

References are to Reg. § numbers

Pension, profit-sharing, and stock bonus plans — Cont'd
. *required minimum distribution —Cont'd*
. . *life (or joint and survivor), annuity incidental benefit requirements —Cont'd*
. . . deemed satisfaction of incidental benefit rule .... 1.401(a)(9)-6(A-2)(e)
. . . life annuity for employee .... 1.401(a)(9)-6(A-2)(a)
. . . nonspouse beneficiary ...... 1.401(a)(9)-6(A-2)(c)
. . . period certain and annuity features .... 1.401(a)(9)-6(A-2)(d)
. . . spousal beneficiary .... 1.401(a)(9)-6(A-2)(b)
. . life (or joint and survivor) annuity .... 1.401(a)(9)-6(Q-2)
. . MDIB requirement of section 401(a)(9)(G) .... 1.401(a)(9)-6(Q-2)
. . . deemed satisfaction of incidental benefit rule .... 1.401(a)(9)-6(A-2)(e)
. . . joint and survivor annuity, nonspouse beneficiary .... 1.401(a)(9)-6(A-2)(c)
. . . joint and survivor annuity, spouse beneficiary .... 1.401(a)(9)-6(A-2)(b)
. . . life annuity for the employee .... 1.401(a)(9)-6(A-2)(a)
. . . period certain and annuity features .... 1.401(a)(9)-6(A-2)(d)
. . non vested benefits as of December 31 of a distribution calendar year .... 1.401(a)(9)-6(Q-6)
. . . portion not vested .... 1.401(a)(9)-6(A-6)
. . plans subject to .... 1.401(a)(9)-1(A-1); 1.401(a)(9)-1(Q-1)
. . portion of employee's benefit not vested as of December 31 of a distribution calendar year .... 1.401(a)(9)-6(Q-6)
. . . annuity distribution from a defined benefit plan .... 1.401(a)(9)-6(A-6)
. . rules for determining (calendar years 2003, 2004, 2005) . . 1.401(a)(9)-6(A-17); 1.401(a)(9)-6(Q-17)
. . single sum distributions .... 1.401(a)(9)-6(A-1)(d)
. . specific provisions a plan must contain to satisfy .... 1.401(a)(9)-1(Q-3)
. . . absence of optional provisions .... 1.401(a)(9)-1(A-3)(c)
. . . optional provisions .... 1.401(a)(9)-1(A-3)(b)
. . . required provisions .... 1.401(a)(9)-1(A-3)(a)
. . surviving spouse, distributions commence to .... 1.401(a)(9)-6(Q-11)
. . . annuity distributions .... 1.401(a)(9)-6(A-11)
. . trust documentation .... 1.401(a)(9)-1(A-2)(c)
. retirement bonds, taxation of 1.405-3
. savings deduction . . . 1.219(a)-1 to 1.219(a)-6; 1.219-1 to 1.219-3
. simplified pensions (See Simplified employee pensions)
. single employer defined benefit plans
. . benefits, limits on
. . . accelerated benefit payments .... 1.436-1(a)(5)(d)

Pension, profit-sharing, and stock bonus plans — Cont'd
. *single employer defined benefit plans —Cont'd*
. . *benefits, limits on —Cont'd*
. . . accruals for plans with severe funding shortfalls .... 1.436-1(a)(5)(e)
. . . avoidance of limitations, methods for .... 1.436-1(a)(5)(f)
. . . certification, operational rules for periods prior to and after .... 1.436-1(a)(5)(g)
. . . close of prohibited or cessation period, at .... 1.436-1(a)(4)
. . . generally .... 1.436-1(a)
. . . increasing liability for benefits, plan amendments .... 1.436-1(a)(5)(c)
. . . presumed underfunding .... 1.436-1(a)(5)(h)
. . . qualification requirements .... 1.436-1(a)(1)
. . . shutdown benefits .... 1.436-1(a)(5)(b)
. . . special rules .... 1.436-1(a)(3)
. . . unpredictable contingent event benefits .... 1.436-1(a)(5)(b)
. spouses .... 1.219(a)-3
. statutory hybrid plans (See subhead hybrid plans, statutory)
. target normal cost and funding target
. . actuarial assumptions .... 1.430(d)-1(f)(1)
. . anticipated future participants ..... 1.430(d)-1(e)(3)
. . asset value .... 1.430(g)-1(1)(c)
. . at-risk status, plans in .... 1.430(i)-1(d)
. . benefits taken into account .... 1.430(d)-1(c)(1)
. . changes in actuarial assumption .... 1.430(d)-1(f)(6)
. . contribution receipts, accounting for .... 1.430(g)-1(1)(d)
. . determination of .... 1.430(d)-1(a)
. . funding method .... 1.430(d)-1(f)(1)
. . funding target attainment percentage defined .... 1.430(d)-1(b)(3)
. . funding target defined .... 1.430(d)-1(b)(2)
. . insurance, benefits provided by .... 1.430(d)-1(c)(3)
. . interest and mortality rates .... 1.430(d)-1(f)(2)
. . optional forms of payment, probability of .... 1.430(d)-1(f)(4)
. . payment of expenses from plan assets .... 1.430(d)-1(c)(2)
. . plan population taken into account .... 1.430(d)-1(e)
. . plan provisions taken into account .... 1.430(d)-1(d)
. . reasonable techniques .... 1.430(d)-1(f)(5)
. . rule of parity cases .... 1.430(d)-1(e)(2)
. . rules for .... 1.430(d)-1(a)
. . target normal cost defined .... 1.430(d)-1(b)(1)
. . valuation date .... 1.430(g)-1(1)(b)
. trusts
. . contribution limitations .... 1.415(a)-1

Personal expenses
. non-deductible items 1.262-1

References are to Reg. § numbers

Personal property
. exchanges .... 1.1031(a)-2
Personal service corporations
. affiliated groups filing consolidated returns
. . taxable year 1.441-3
. generally 1.269A-1
. taxable year 1.441-3
Personal services
. compensation
. . artists 1.861-4
. . athletes 1.861-4
. . employee compensation 1.861-4
. . fringe benefits 1.861-4
. . generally 1.861-4
. . hazardous or hardship duties 1.861-4
. . individual services 1.861-4
. . moving expenses 1.861-4
. . multi-year arrangements 1.861-4
. . partly within or partly without the United States 1.861-4
. . transportation fringe benefits 1.861-4
. . within the United States 1.861-4
Phased retirements
. benefits during, pension
. . bona fide phased retirement program .... 1.401(a)-3(c)
. . commencement of phased retirement benefits, conditions for .... 1.401(a)-3(d)
. . definitions concerning .... 1.401(a)-3(b)
. . generally .... 1.401(a)-3(a)
. . highly compensated employees .... 1.401(a)-3(e)(1)
. . multiple phased retirement benefits permitted .... 1.401(a)-3(e)(2)
. . nondiscrimination rules .... 1.401(a)-3(e)(4)
. . sec. 411(d)(6) .... 1.401(a)-3(e)(3)
Physical self-care incapability
. principal residence sales, exclusion of gain from sale or exchange 1.121-4
Political subdivisions
. withholding under sec. 3402(t) .... 31.3402(t)-2(d)
Possessions accounts
. documentary evidence for reporting 1.6049-5
Possessions corporations tax credit
. generally 1.936-2; 1.936-3; 1.936-3A
Possessions of the U.S.
. alien individuals, taxation of 1.871-1
. bona fide residency in 1.937-1
. charitable contributions 1.170A-1
. computation of taxable income 1.861-8
. continental shelf .... 1.1402(a)-12
. corporation created or organized in
. . mirror code jurisdiction .... 1.881-5T(g)
. credits against tax 1.901-1
Possessions of the U.S. —Cont'd
. effectively connected income 1.937-3
. exclusion, income 1.931-1; 1.931-1T
. export sales, section 936(h)(5) election 1.936-7
. foreign country status for corporate gross income exclusion 1.883-1
. income from sources within 1.937-2
. individual income tax
. . nonresident alien individual who is resident of U.S. possession or Puerto Rico, taxation of ... 1.1-1(b)
. information returns 1.6038-2
. qualified possession source investment income 1.883-1
. United States person defined 1.957-3
Power of appointment
. surviving spouse, in
. . income, spouse entitled to .... 20.2056(b)-5
Preretirement survivor annuities
. explanation provided to participants, required .... 1.417(a)(3)-1
. Retirement Equity Act of 1984 .... 1.401(a)-20
Presidential primary matching account
. payments from 702.9037-2
. transfers to 702.9037-1
Presidentially declared disasters
. postponement of certain tax-related deadlines
. . acts performed by taxpayers .... 301.7508A-1(c)(1)
. . acts performed by the government .... 301.7508A-1(c)(2)
. . additional relief .... 301.7508A-1(b)(5)
. . due date not extended .... 301.7508A-1(b)(4)
. . effect of postponement period ... 301.7508A-1(b)(2)
. . generally .... 301.7508A-1(b)(1)
. . interaction between postponement period and extensions of time to file or pay .... 301.7508A-1(b)(3)
Principal place of abode
. dependent care services
. . employment related expenses, credit for ... 1.21-1(g)
Principal residence sales
. exclusion of gain from sale or exchange 1.121-1
. . deceased spouse 1.121-4
. . dollar limitations 1.121-2
. . expatriates 1.121-4
. . joint returns 1.121-2
. . limitations on 1.121-2
. . physical or mental self-care incapability 1.121-4
. . reduced exclusion 1.121-3
. . remainder interest sales 1.121-4
. . rollovers under section 1034 .... 1.121-4
. . spousal property 1.121-4
. . tenant-shareholder, cooperative housing corporation 1.121-4
. . 2-year sale or exchange requirement 1.121-2

References are to Reg. § numbers

Private activity bonds
. allocation and accounting rules
. . bond redemption in anticipation of unqualified use .... 1.141-6(f)
. . common cost of issue .... 1.141-6(i)
. . discrete physical allocation method .... 1.141-6(c)
. . expenditures, property and uses .... 1.141-6(a)
. . mixed-use projects .... 1.141-6(b); 1.141-6(e)
. . mix-us output facilities .... 1.141-6(g)
. . private payments .... 1.141-6(h)
. . proceeds to bond .... 1.141-6(j)
. . undivided portion allocation method .... 1.141-6(d)
. payments in lieu of taxes .... 1.141-4(e)(5)
. private business use test
. . issuance costs .... 1.145-2(c)
. . regulations, application of
. . . partnerships .... 1.145-2(c)(3)
. private security or payment test
. . payments in lieu of taxes .... 1.141-4(e)(5)
. public approval
. . deviations in public approval information .... 1.147(f)-1(b)(6)
. . facility defined .... 1.147(f)-1(c)(1)
. . 501(c)(3) bonds, special rules for .... 1.147(f)-1(b)(5)
. . generally .... 1.147(f)-1(a)
. . government unit approval requirement, special rules on .... 1.147(f)-1(d)
. . mortgage revenue bonds
. . . defined .... 1.147(f)-1(c)(5)
. . . special rules for .... 1.147(f)-1(b)(3)
. . public heading defined .... 1.147(f)-1(c)(2)
. . reasonable public notice
. . . defined .... 1.147(f)-1(c)(3)
. . . information required for .... 1.147(f)-1(b)(2)
. . student loan bonds, special rules for .... 1.147(f)-1(b)(4)
. . timing requirements .... 1.147(f)-1(b)(7)
. . writing defined .... 1.147(f)-1(c)(4)
. refunding
. . advance, limitations on .... 1.149(d)-1(g)
. tax equivalency payments .... 1.141-4(e)(5)

Private business use test
. refunding .... 1.141-13(b)

Private loan financing test
. refunding .... 1.141-13(b)

Private security or payment test
. refunding .... 1.141-13(c)

Pro rata shares
. S corporations 1.1377-1

Profit split method
. arm's length transactions, use in determination of
. . comparable profits method 1.482-6

Profit split method —Cont'd
. *arm's length transactions, use in determination of —Cont'd*
. . market returns for routine contribution, determination of 1.482-6
. . residual profits, allocation of 1.482-6

Profit-sharing plans (See Pension, profit-sharing, and stock bonus plans)

Prohibited tax shelter transactions
. approves or otherwise causes defined .... 53.4965-5(c)
. defined .... 53.4965-3(a)
. disclosure
. . designation agreements .... 301.6011(g)-1(h)
. . failure to provide, penalty for .... 301.6011(g)-1(i)
. . form and content .... 301.6011(g)-1(f)
. . frequency .... 301.6011(g)-1(e)
. . statements .... 301.6011(g)-1(d)
. . taxable party to entity to tax-exempt entities, by .... 301.6011(g)-1
. . tax-exempt entities that are parties to reportable transactions 301.6033-5
. . to whom disclosure is made .... 301.6011(g)-1(g)
. entity manager
. . knows or has reason to know .... 53.4965-6(b)
. . non-plan entity .... 53.4965-5(a)
. . plan entity, of .... 53.4965-5(b)
. entity-level excise tax
. . non-plan entities .... 53.4965-7(a)
. . tax-exempt entities .... 53.4965-1(a)
. knows or has reason to know defined 53.4965-6
. manager-level excise tax
. . amount of tax .... 53.4965-1(b)(1)
. . separate liability .... 53.4965-1(b)(4)
. . tax-exempt entities .... 53.4965-1(b)
. . timing of tax .... 53.4965-1(b)(2)
. net income and proceeds
. . allocation of .... 53.4965-8(c)
. . allocation to pre- and post-listing periods .... 53.4965-8(e)
. . defined .... 53.4965-8(b)
. . generally .... 53.4965-8(a)
. . transition year rules .... 53.4965-8(d)
. profession advise, reliance on .... 53.4965-6(c)
. subsequently listed transactions .... 53.4965-3(b)
. taxable party defined .... 301.6011(g)-1(c)
. tax-exempt entities
. . defined .... 53.4965-2(a)
. . disclosure by taxable party to entity .... 301.6011(g)-1
. . entity-level excise tax .... 53.4965-1(a)
. . manager-level excise tax .... 53.4965-1(b)
. . non-plan entities .... 53.4965-2(b)
. . plan entities defined .... 53.4965-2(c)
. tax-exempt party defined .... 301.6011(g)-1(b)
. tax-exempt party to .... 53.4965-4(a)

References are to Reg. § numbers

Public highway
. defined 48.4051-1
Public schools (See Schools, public)
Public utilities
. deregulation
. . accumulated deferred investment tax credit . . 1.46-6
. . excess deferred income tax reserve upon disposition of property .... 1.168(i)(3)
Publicly supported organizations
. form 990 .... 1.509(a)-3
Publicly-traded corporations
. foreign corporations, gross income exclusions 1.883-2
Puerto Rico
. corporation created or organized in .... 1.881-5T; 1.881-5T(e)
. exclusion of income from sources within 1.933-1
. individual income tax
. . nonresident alien individual who is resident of U.S. possession or Puerto Rico, taxation of . . . 1.1-1(b)
. nonresident aliens 1.876-1
. qualified possession source investment income 7.936-1
Purchase price allocations
. deemed actual asset acquisitions
. . adjusted gross-up basis 1.338-5
. . allocation
. . . ADSP and AGUB 1.338-6
. . . redetermined ADSP and AGUB 1.338-7
. . . special rules 1.1060-1
. . deemed sale gain 1.338-4
. . deemed sale price 1.338-4
. . definitions concerning 1.338-2
. . election, availability of 1.338-1
. . election, qualifications for 1.338-3
. . old target new target status 1.338-1
. . post-acquisition events, effect of 1.338-3
. . returns, filing of 1.338-10
. . stock purchases, rules relating to qualified . . 1.338-3

Q

Qualified academy zone bonds
. maximum term .... 1.1397E-1(d)
. proceeds, use of .... 1.1397E-1(h)
Qualified business units (QBUs)
. allocation and apportionment
. . interest expenses 1.861-9T
. currency gain or loss, section 987
. . attribution of assets and liabilities .... 1.987-2(a)
. . attribution of items to eligible QBU .... 1.987-2(b)
. . character and source of gain or loss
. . . generally .... 1.987-6(b)

Qualified business units (QBUs) —Cont'd
. *currency gain or loss, section 987 —Cont'd*
. . *character and source of gain or loss —Cont'd*
. . . ordinary income or loss .... 1.987-6(a)
. . definitions concerning .... 1.987-1(b); 1.988-1(a)
. . election, section 987 .... 1.987-1(e)
. . election to apply rules .... 1.987-11(b)
. . eligible QBU defined .... 1.987-1(b)(3)
. . exchange rates
. . . defined .... 1.987-1(c)
. . . translating items of income, gain, deduction or loss into functional currency .... 1.987-3(b)
. . functional currency, items that are denominated in the .... 1.987-3(c)
. . functional currency net value, determination of
. . . net unrecognized gain or loss .... 1.987-4(e)
. . historic item, section 987 .... 1.987-1(e)
. . marked item, section 987 .... 1.987-1(d)
. . net unrecognized gain or loss
. . . calculation .... 1.987-4(b)
. . . functional current net value, determination of .... 1.987-4(e)
. . . generally 1.987-4
. . . net accumulated for a taxable years .... 1.987-4(d)
. . . net accumulated for all prior taxable years .... 1.987-4(c)
. . nonfunctional currency, items that are denominated in the .... 1.987-3(d)
. . owner defined .... 1.987-1(b)(4)
. . partnerships, section 987
. . . assets and liabilities held indirectly through .... 1.987-7(b)
. . . generally .... 1.987-7(a)
. . . subchapter K, coordination with .... 1.987-7(c)
. . recognition of gain or loss by QBU owner
. . . adjusted basis determination in transferred assets .... 1.987-5(f)
. . . generally .... 1.987-5(a)
. . . remittance .... 1.987-5(c)
. . . remittance proportion .... 1.987-5(b)
. . . total of all amounts transferred from owner .... 1.987-5(e)
. . . total of all amounts transferred to owner .... 1.987-5(d)
. . section 987 QBU defined .... 1.987-1(b)(2)
. . section 988 transactions .... 1.987-3(e)
. . source of gain or loss realized on section 988 transfer 1.988-4
. . taxable income, determination of .... 1.987-1(a)
. . . loss of an owner of QBU .... 1.987-3(a)
. . taxpayers subject of section 987 ..... 1.987-1(b)(1)
. . termination of section 987 QBU
. . . effect of .... 1.987-8(d)
. . . generally .... 1.987-8(a); 1.987-8(b)
. . . reorganization .... 1.987-8(c)

References are to Reg. § numbers

Qualified business units (QBUs) —Cont'd
. *currency gain or loss, section 987 —Cont'd*
. . *termination of section 987 QBU —Cont'd*
. . . retention of records . . . 1.987-9(c)
. . . supplemental information . . . 1.987-9(b)
. . transfers to and from 987 QBU . . . 1.987-2(c)
. . transition date . . . 1.987-10(b)
. . transition method . . . 1.987-10(c)
. . transition rules . . . 1.987-10
. . translation of items transfers to 987 QBU . . . 1.987-2(d)
. . . exchange rates to be used . . . 1.987-3(b)
. defined
. . currency gain or loss, section 987 . . . 1.989(a)-1
. functional currency . . . 1.985-1 et seq.
. . dollar approximate separate transactions . . . 1.985-3
. . separate transactions method . . . 1.985-3
. Interest expense
. . allocation and apportionment . . . 1.861-9T

Qualified electing funds
. automatic termination . . . 1.1295-1
. passive foreign investment companies
. . automatic termination of election . . . 1.1291-1(i)(3)
. special preferred QEF election
. . special inclusion rules . . . 1.1293-2

Qualified nonpersonal use vehicles
. generally . . . 1.132-5
. listed property defined . . . 1.280F-6
. substantiation requirements
. . exceptions to . . . 1.174-5

Qualified plans (See Pension, profit-sharing, and stock bonus plans- particular plan)

Qualified possession source investment income
. Puerto Rico . . . 7.936-1

Qualified small business stock
. defined . . . 1.1045-1
. partner election . . . 1.1045-1
. partnership acquisition . . . 1.1045-1
. partnership election . . . 1.1045-1
. partnerships
. . election
. . . basis adjustments . . . 1.1045-1(b)(3)
. . . replacement QSB stock . . . 1.1045-1(b)(3)
. . holding stock for more than six months . . . 1.1045-1(a)
. . replacement QSB stock, purchase of . . . 1.1045-1(b)
. . section 1045 gain . . . 1.1045-1(b)(2)

Qualified state tuition programs
. account owner defined . . . 1.529-1
. accounts
. . aggregation of . . . 1.529-3
. . defined . . . 1.529-1
. . separate . . . 1.529-2

Qualified state tuition programs —Cont'd
. administrative fees . . . 1.529-1
. aggregation of accounts . . . 1.529-3
. contributions
. . defined . . . 1.529-1
. . permissible uses of . . . 1.529-2
. definitions concerning . . . 1.529-1
. description, general . . . 1.529-1; 1.529-2
. designated beneficiary
. . change in . . . 1.529-3
. . defined . . . 1.529-1
. distributee defined . . . 1.529-1
. distributions
. . defined . . . 1.529-1
. . final distribution defined . . . 1.529-1
. . income tax treatment of . . . 1.529-3
. . rollover distribution defined . . . 1.529-1
. . taxable, reporting . . . 1.529-4
. . verification of . . . 1.529-2
. earnings defined . . . 1.529-1
. earnings ratio defined . . . 1.529-1
. eligible educational institution defined . . . 1.529-1
. establishment of program . . . 1.529-2
. estate taxes . . . 1.529-5
. final distribution defined . . . 1.529-1
. forfeit defined . . . 1.529-1
. generation-skipping transfer tax rules . . . 1.529-5
. gift tax treatment . . . 1.529-5
. investment in the account defined . . . 1.529-1
. member of the family defined . . . 1.529-1
. penalties and forfeitures . . . 1.529-1
. qualified higher education defined . . . 1.529-1
. reporting taxable distributions . . . 1.529-4
. retroactive taxes . . . 1.529-6
. returns . . . 1.529-4
. rollover distribution defined . . . 1.529-1
. taxable earnings, computation of . . . 1.529-3
. total account balance defined . . . 1.529-1
. transition rules . . . 1.529-6
. unrelated business income tax . . . 1.529-1

R

Railroad Retirement Tax Act (RRTA)
. employee tax
. . underpayment adjustments . . . 31.6205-1
. erroneous collection, repayment or reimbursement for . . . 31.6413(a)-1(a)
. overpaid taxes
. . adjustments of overpayment . . . 31.6403(a)-2(a)
. . claim for overpayment paid to IRS . . 31.6402(a)-2(a)
. overpayment adjustments . . . 31.6413(a)-2
. under collected or underpaid taxes . . . 31.6025-1(b)

References are to Reg. § numbers

Railroad Retirement Tax Act (RRTA) —Cont'd
. *under collected or underpaid taxes—Cont'd*
. . deduction from employee remuneration .... 31.6025-1(d)(1)

Railroad track maintenance
. credit 1.45G

Railroad Unemployment Insurance Act (RUIA) (See Railroad Unemployment Repayment Tax)

Railroad Unemployment Repayment Tax
. quarterly payments .... 31.6302(c)-2A

Real estate agents
. collection and payment of taxes 31.3508-1

Real Estate Investment Trusts (REITs)
. gross income requirements 1.856-2
. real property defined 1.856-3
. rent, amounts not includable as 1.856-4
. status requirements, rules applicable to 1.856-1
. subsidiary corporation treatment as separate corporation 1.856-9

Real estate mortgage investment conduits (REMICs)
. inducement fees
. . income from sources within the United States, status as .... 1.863-1(e)
. . residual interest in REMIC .... 1.863-1(e)
. interest accrual 1.67-3T; 1.1275-2
. modification of commercial mortgage loans held by
. . conversion of interest rate by mortgagor pursuant to convertible mortgage terms ... 1.860G-2(b)(3)(iv)
. . effective dates 1.860A-1
. . principally secured test .... 1.860G-2(b)(7)
. . recourse to nonrecourse, change in obligation from .... 1.860G-2(b)(3)(vi)
. . release of interest in real property securing and qualified mortgage .... 1.860G-2(a)(8)
. waiver of due-on-sale clause or a due on encumbrance clause .... 1.860G-2(b)(3)(iii)

Real property
. exemptions
. . withholding under sec. 3402(t), government entities .... 31.3402(t)-4(d)
. foreign persons
. . disposition of U.S. real property interests .. 1.1445-1

Recapture
. foreign corporations
. . ordering rules for separate limitation losses, overall foreign losses and overall domestic losses .... 1.904(g)-3
. . overall domestic loss account........... 1.904(g)-2
. . overall foreign loss .... 1.904(f)-2
. . separate limitation loss accounts .... 1.904(f)-8
. foreign tax credit
. . beginning after December 31, 2002 .... 1.904(f)-12T(g)
. . beginning before January 1, 2003 ... 1.904(f)-12T(g)

Recapture —Cont'd
. LIFO benefits
. . partnership 1.1363-2

Records and reports
. at risk provisions, insufficient records 1.465-78
. lubricating oil, records inspection 48.4102-1
. trust income, methods of reporting
. . portion of trust treated as owned by the grantor or another person .... 1.671-4(a)
. . widely held fixed investment trusts 1.671-5
. . . backup withholding requirements ...... 1.671-5(k)
. . . coordination with other reporting rules .. 1.671-5(j)
. . . definitions concerning .... 1.671-5(b)
. . . exempt recipients .... 1.671-5(h)
. . . failure to comply .... 1.671-5(l)
. . . form 1099 requirements .... 1.671-5(d)
. . . middlemen that hold trust interest, filings of .... 1.671-5(h)
. . . non-calendar-year beneficial owners ... 1.671-5(h)
. . . obligation to report, trustee .... 1.671-5(c)
. . . safe harbors ... 1.671-5(f); 1.671-5(g); 1.671-5T(f)
. . . written statement requirement .... 1.671-5(e)

Redemption of stock
. constructive distribution to spouse 1.1041-2
. dividends
. . characterization rules and adjustments for certain assets 1.861-12
. . excess loss accounts 1.1502-19
. . intercompany transactions 1.1502-13
. . loss attributable to basis of redeemed stock 1.302-5; 1.1371-1
. . returns statements to be filed with 1.302-5
. . taxability 1.302-5
. loss attributable to basis of redeemed stock . 1.302-5; 1.1371-1
. redeemed shareholder defined 1.302-5
. redeeming corporation defined 1.302-5

Refineries
. election to expense certain refineries (See Election to expense certain refineries)

Refunding obligations
. advance, limitations on
. . private activity bonds limitations ...... 1.149(d)-1(g)
. effective dates for sections 141 .... 1.141-15
. multipurpose issue allocations .... 1.141-13(d)
. private business use test .... 1.141-13(b)
. private security or payment test.......... 1.141-13(c)
. reasonable expectations test for certain bonds .... 1.141-13(e)
. special rules for certain obligation bonds .. 1.141-13(f)

Refunds (See Abatements, credits, and refunds)

Registration-required obligations
. generally 5f.163-1

References are to Reg. § numbers

Registration-required obligations —Cont'd
. interest deduction ... 5f.163-1
Regulated investment companies (RICs)
. election of taxable year foreign income/war profits/excess profits
. . examples ... 1.853-2(d)
. . information, time and manner of providing ... 1.853-4(d)
. . information required ... 1.853-4(c)
. . irrevocability of election ... 1.853-4(b)
. . manner of making election ... 1.853-4(a)
. foreign tax credits
. . country-by-country reporting, elimination of ... 1.853-1 et seq.
. . manner of making 853(a) election ... 1.853-4
. . notice to shareholders of 853(a) election ... 1.853-3
. . shareholders, allowed to ... 1.853-1; 1.853-2
. market to market election for marketable stock
. . definitions concerning ... 1.1296-1(a)
. mark-to-market election ... 1.1291-8; 1.1296-1
. notice to shareholders
. . foreign tax credit, creditable ... 1.853-3(a)
. . shareholder of record custodian of certain unit investment trusts ... 1.853-3(b)
Rehabilitation costs
. generally ... 1.1012-2
Reimbursements
. dependent care services
. . employment related expenses, credit for ... 1.21-1(f)
. withholding rates ... 31.3401(a)-4(c)
Reinstatement of fees
. installment agreement fees ... 300.2
Related corporations
. acquisitions, stock ... 1.304-2
Related individuals
. dependent care services
. . employment related expenses, credit for ... 1.21-4(a)
Related taxpayers
. sales between, basis ... 1.1012-2
Releases
. lien for taxes ... 301.6325-1
REMICs (See Real estate mortgage investment conduits)
Remuneration
. backup withholding, services and direct sales ... 1.6041A-1
. deferred compensation (See Deferred compensation)
. pension, profit-sharing, and stock bonus plans (See Pension, profit-sharing, and stock bonus plans)
. wages (See Wages)
Rental of dwelling unit
. business use of home ... 1.280A-3
Reorganization
. assumption of liabilities ... 1.358-5
. . partnership assumption on or after June 24, 2003 ... 1.752-7
. basis to distributees
. . allocation ... 1.358-2
. . assumption of liabilities
. . . partnership assumption on or after June 24, 2003 ... 1.752-7
. . generally ... 1.358-1
. corporate (See Corporate organizations and reorganizations)
. definitions concerning
. . statutory mergers or consolidations ... 1.368-2
. exchanges
. . definitions concerning ... 1.368-2
. . purpose and scope of exception of
. . . definition of terms ... 1.368-2
. . . special rule ... 1.368-1
. section 368(a)(1)(F) ... 1.368-2
. statutory mergers or consolidations
. . definitions concerning ... 1.368-2
. triangular
. . consolidated group members ... 1.358-6(e)
. . . group structure change, stock basis after ... 1.1502-30
. . . stock basis ... 1.1502-30
. . parent stock, acquisition of ... 1.367(b)-14
. . transfers with exceptions provided by 1.367(a)-7(c) ... 1.358-6(a)
Repairs
. itemized deductions ... 1.162-4
Reportable transactions
. material advisors ... 301.6111-3(b)
. . designation agreements ... 301.6111-3(f)
. . disclosure statement, form of ... 301.6111-3(d)
. . list of advisors ... 301.6112-1(a)
. . . definitions concerning ... 301.6112-1(c)
. . . designation agreements ... 301.6112-1(f)
. . . furnishing of lists ... 301.6112-1(e)
. . . preparation and maintenance ... 301.6112-1(b)
. . . retention of lists ... 301.6112-1(d)
. . protective disclosure ... 301.6111-3(g)
. . time of providing ... 301.6111-3(e)
. material advisors failure to furnish information
. . assessment of penalty
. . . designation agreements ... 301.6767-1(c)(2)
. . . individual liability ... 301.6767-1(c)(1)
. . derive defined ... 301.6767-1(b)(7)
. . false information defined ... 301.6767-1(b)(5)
. . fines and penalties ... 301.6767-1(a)
. . generally ... 301.6767-1(a)
. . incomplete information defined ... 301.6767-1(b)(4)
. . intentional defined ... 301.6767-1(b)(6)

References are to Reg. § numbers

Reportable transactions —Cont'd
. *material advisors failure to furnish information — Cont'd*
. . listed transaction defined .... 301.6767-1(b)(2)
. . material advisor defined .... 301.6767-1(b)(3)
. . reportable transaction defined .... 301.6767-1(b)(1)
. . rescission authority ....301.6767-1(e)
. statements concerning
. . definitions concerning .... 1.6011-4(c)
. . form and content of disclosure statement ....1.6011-4(e)
. . requirement 20.6011-4; 25.6011-4; 31.6011-4; 53.6011-4; 56.6011-4
. . retention of document ....1.6011-4(g)

Reports
. FASIT requirements 1.860H-6
. individual retirement accounts 1.408-5

Research credits
. aggregation of expenditures 1.41-6
. allocation of controlled group credit .... 1.41-6(c)
. alternate incremental credit 1.41-8
. computation of controlled group credit ...... 1.41-6(b)
. controlled group credit 1.41-6
. discovery requirements 1.41-4
. excluded activities........................ 1.41-4
. expenditures paid or incurred in taxable years ending on or after December 26, 2001 ...... 1.41-4; 1.41-8
. optional 10-year writeoff of certain tax preferences 1.59-1
. qualified research 1.41-4
. shrinking-back rule 1.41-4
. taxable years ending on or after December 26, 2001
. . expenditures paid or incurred in 1.41-4
. . special rules for 1.41-8
. technology requirements 1.41-4

Residence
. business use expenses of dwelling unit used as residence.............................. 1.280A-2
. dwelling unit, limitation of deductions with respect to 1.280A-1
. sale of principal residence (See Principal residence sales)

Restructuring of fees
. installment agreement fees 300.2

Retired employees
. medical benefits; accident and health plans
. . special rules ....1.72-15(h)

Retirement bonds
. generally 1.405-3; 1.409-1

Retirement Equity Act of 1984
. joint and survivor annuities ....1.401(a)-20
. preretirement survivor annuities ....1.401(a)-20

Retirement income accounts
. employee trusts...........................1.403(b)-2

Retirement income contract
. transfer of contract, treatment as property 1.83-3

Retirement plans (See Pension, profit-sharing, stocks bonus plans- particular plan)

Retirement savings deduction
. generally ....1.219(a)-1 to 1.219(a)-6; 1.219-1 to 1.219-3; 1.220-1

Returns
. amended
. . notice of amount of increased tax liability, IRS failure to provide ....301.6404-4(a)(2)
. backup withholding 1.6041A-1
. claims arising out of erroneous computation ....301.6230(c)-1
. consolidated (See Consolidated returns)
. disclosure of information in
. . Agriculture Department, to .... 301.6103(j)(5)-1
. . . census of agriculture, conducting ....301.6103(j)(5)-1
. . investigative purposes, to certain officers for ....301.6103(k)(6)-1
. . reportable transactions ....1.6011-4(b)
. . . 1.6011-4(c) ..... statements concerningdefinitions concerning
. . . definitions concerning...............1.6011-4(c)
. . . form and content of disclosure statement ....1.6011-4(d)
. . . requirement 20.6011-4; 25.6011-4; 31.6011-4; 53.6011-4; 56.6011-4
. . . retention of document...............1.6011-4(g)
. . sec. 6011 disclosures
. . . reportable transactions, failure to include 301.6767A-1
. DISCs and former DISCs 1.6011-2
. failure to treat individual as employee .... 31.6025-1(c)(3)
. farmer's cooperatives ....1.6012-2(f)(1)
. foreign transactions 1.6041A-1
. information returns (See Information returns)
. joint returns
. . principal residence sales, exclusion of gain from sale or exchange 1.121-2
. qualified state tuition programs 1.529-4
. reportable transactions defined ....1.6011-4(b)
. sec. 6011 disclosures
. . reportable transactions, failure to include 301.6767A-1
. space or ocean activity income 1.863-8
. subchapter T cooperative................1.6012-2(f)
. subchapter T corporations ....1.6012-1(f)
. treaty-based return positions
. . January 1, 2001, amounts received after 301.6114-1
. withholding

References are to Reg. § numbers

Returns —Cont'd
. *withholding —Cont'd*
. . domestic service, wages paid for .... 31.6011(a)-4(a)(2)
. . reportable payments .... 31.6011(a)-11
. . undercollection
. . . after return is filed, error ascertained .... 31.6025-1(c)(2)
. . . before return is filed, ascertained .... 31.6025-1(c)(1)

RICs (See Regulated investment companies)

Risk transfer agreements
. global dealing operations .... 1.475(g)-2

Rollovers
. principal residence sales, exclusion of gain from sale or exchange 1.121-4

Room and board
. dependent care services
. . employment related expenses, credit for ... 1.21-1(d)

Roth IRAs
. conversions to 1.401A-4
. designated Roth accounts
. . contributions .... 1.401(k)(f)
. . contributions to purchase sec. 403(b) contracts .... 1.403(b)-3
. . coordination with designation and regular Roth account 1.408A-10
. . defined 1.402A-1
. . definitions concerning .... 1.403(b)-2
. . distributions .... 1.403(b)-7
. . . special rules .... 1.403(b)-7(e)
. . distributions, taxation of 1.402A-1
. . elective deferrals, limitation on exclusion for .... 1.402(g)-1
. . employer security distributions, taxability of 1.402A-1
. . 5-year-taxable-year period 1.402A-1
. . nondiscrimination rules .... 1.4039(b)-5
. . reporting and recordkeeping requirements 1.402A-2
. . sec. 403(b) contracts, exclusions for purchase of .... 1.403(b)-3

Royalties
. gross income 1.61-8

RUIA (See Railroad Unemployment Repayment Tax)

S

S corporations
. allocations, prohibited .... 1.409(p)-1
. at risk provisions 1.465-10
. defined
. . number of shareholders as basis for qualification as small business corporation ...... 1.1361-1(e)(1)
. distributions 1.1368-1

S corporations —Cont'd
. domestic production activities .... 1.199-5(b)
. earnings stripping, exception to disallowance rule .... 1.163(j)-1
. family members
. . common ancestry .... 1.1361-1(e)(3)
. . spouse and former spouses .... 1.1361-1(e)(3)
. income tax treaties, coordination with ... 301.7701(b)-7
. net unrealized built-in gain, adjustments to .... 1.1374-3(b)
. number of shareholders as basis for qualification as small business corporation .... 1.1361-1(e)(1)
. pro rata shares 1.1377-1
. QSub elections 1.1361-4
. special rules .... 1.108-7(d)(1)
. stock owned by member of a family ... 1.1361-1(e)(3)
. tax attributes
. . allocation of excess losses or deductions
. . . multiple shareholders .... 1.108-7(d)(2)(ii)
. . . terminating shareholders .... 1.108-7(d)(2)(iii)
. . reduction of
. . . allocation of excess losses or deductions .... 1.108-7(d)(2)(i)
. . . generally .... 1.108-7(a)
. . . special rules .... 1.108-7(d)(1)
. taxable income, computation of .... 1.1363-1(b)
. taxable year 1.1378-1

Salary reduction agreements
. section 403(b) contract under, employer contribution to purchase .... 1.402(g)(3)-1

Salary reduction plans 1.61-16

Sales and transfers
. accounting methods 1.453-1
. at risk provisions .... 1.465-66 to 1.465-69
. backup withholding 1.6041A-1
. basis, sales between related parties 1.1012-2
. corporation controlled by transferor, to
. . nonrecognition of gain 1.351-1
. foreign corporations .... 1.367(a)-1T et seq.
. international sales corporations (See Domestic international sales corporations (DISC))
. net value
. . exchanges of 1.368-1
. . nonrecognition of gain 1.332-2; 1.351-1
. nonrecognition of gain
. . corporation controlled by transferor, to 1.351-1
. principal residence (See Principal residence sales)
. reorganization exchanges 1.368-1
. securities 1.1058-1; 1.1058-2

Scholarships and fellowships
. generally .... 1.117-0 to 1.117-6

Schools
. dependent care services

References are to Reg. § numbers

Schools —Cont'd
. *dependent care services —Cont'd*
. . employment related expenses, credit for . . . 1.21-1(d)
. public
. . annuity contract, purchase of (See Annuities and annuity contracts subhead section 501(c)(3) organization purchase of)
. . generally . . . . 1.117-0 to 1.117-6

SCI income
. premiums attributable to 1.953-2

Section 38 property
. new property
. . lessor treatment of lessee as purchaser 1.48-4
. useful life/recovery period 1.46-3

Section 89 requirements
. nondiscrimination rules . . . . 1.89(a)-1
. qualification requirements
. . welfare benefit plans . . . . 1.89(k)-1

Section 199 deduction
. domestic production activities (See Domestic production activities)

Section 403(b) annuities
. distributions
. . contracts other than custodial accounts or amounts attributable to section 403(b) elective deferrals . . . . 1.403(b)-6(b)
. . custodial accounts that are not attributable to section 403(b) elective deferrals, from . . . . 1.403(b)-6(c)
. . elective deferrals . . . . 1.403(b)-6(c)
. . . death benefits and other incidental benefits . . . . 1.403(b)-6(g)
. . . hardship rules . . . . 1.403(b)-6(d)(2)
. . . rollover contribution, limitations . . . . . . 1.403(b)-6(i)
. . limitation on distributions . . . . 1.403(b)-6(d)(1)
. . . general rule . . . . 1.403(b)-6(d)(1)(i)
. . . special rule for pre-1989 section 403(b) elective deferrals . . . . 1.403(b)-6(d)(1)(ii)
. . loans . . . . 1.403(b)-6(f)
. . minimum required distribution for eligible plans . . . . 1.403(b)-6(e); 1.403(b)-6(e)(1)
. . . application to multiple contracts for an employee . . . . 1.403(b)-6(e)(7)
. . . required beginning date . . . . 1.403(b)-6(e)(3)
. . . retirement income accounts . . . . 1.403(b)-6(e)(5)
. . . special rules for benefits accruing before December 31, 1986 . . . . 1.403(b)-6(e)(6)
. . . surviving spouse rule does not apply . . . . 1.403(b)-6(e)(4)
. . . treatment as IRAs . . . . 1.403(b)-6(e)(2)
. . special rule regarding severance from employment . . . . 1.403(b)-6(h)
. . timing of distributions and benefits . . . . 1.403(b)-6

Section 3402(t) withholdings (See Government entities)

Section 7216
. Subpart F, aircraft and vessel leasing income (See Subpart F, aircraft and vessel leasing income)

Section 7216 disclosures (See Disclosure subhead taxpayer consent, section 7216)

Securities
. bonds (See Bonds)
. diversification requirements, defined contribution plan (See Pension, profit-sharing, and stock bonus plans)
. stock (See Stock)
. transfers 1.1058-1; 1.1058-2

Securities dealer or broker
. income, characterization of certain 1.1296-6
. mark-to-market
. . disposition of security by a dealer . . . . 1.475(a)-2
. valuation of securities held by
. . safe harbor valuation, section 475 . . . . 1.475(a)-4

Seizure of property
. Collection Due Process hearing 301.6330-1
. discharge of lien
. . special rules 301.7425-3
. exempt property
. . books, and tools of a trade . . . . 301.6334-1(a)(3)
. . fuel, provisions, furniture and personal effects . . . . 301.6334-1(a)(2)
. . inflation adjustment . . . . 301.6334-1(g)
. . judgments for support of minor children . . . . 301.6334-1(a)(8)
. . principal residences . . . . 301.6334-1(d)
. . residences . . . . 301.6334-1(a)(13)
. levy and distraint
. . notice and opportunity for hearing prior to levy 301.6330-1
. return of wrongfully levied property 301.6343-3
. third party property . . . . 301.6503(f)-1
. wrongfully levied, return of property 301.6343-2

Self-employment tax
. limited partner defined . . . . 1.1402(a)-2
. net earnings computation from . . . . 1.1402(a)-2

Self-insured medical reimbursement plans
. disability benefits 1.105-11

Separate taxable income
. consolidated returns 1.1502-12

SEPs (See Simplified employee pensions)

Settlement funds
. grantor trust election 1.468B-5
. subpart E trust 1.468B-1
. . election to treat as . . . . 1.468B-1(k)
. transitional rules
. . grantor trust elections under sec. 1.468B-1(k) . . . . 1.468B-5(c)

References are to Reg. § numbers

Shareholders
. at risk provisions 1.465-10
. RICs
. . notice to shareholders
. . . foreign tax credit, creditable .... 1.853-3(a)
. . . shareholder of record custodian of certain unit investment trusts .... 1.853-3(b)
. 10% shareholder
. . portfolio interest .... 1.871-14(g)

Ships
. bareboat charters defined 1.883-1
. code-sharing arrangements defined 1.883-1
. international operations, exclusion of income from 1.883-1

Short tax years
. additions to tax 1.6655-5

Sickness or accident disability payments .... 31.3121(a)(2)-1

Simplified employee pensions (SEPs)
. catch-up contributions for individuals over age 50 .... 1.414(v)-1
. deduction limitations 1.219-3
. employer contributions .... 1.404(h)-1
. individual retirement accounts .... 1.219(a)-4; 1.219-3; 1.408-7 to 1.408-9; 301.6693-1
. retirement savings deduction ..... 1.219(a)-4; 1.219-3

Small business stock (See Qualified small business stock)

Small ethanol producer credit
. denial of credit for ethanol produced at certain facilities .... 1.40-2(c)
. effective / applicability date .... 1.40-2(e)
. examples .... 1.40-2(d)
. generally .... 1.40-2; 1.40-2(a)
. qualified ethanol production .... 1.40-2(b)

Software
. research credits (See Research credits)

Solid waste disposal facility
. exempt facilities bond .... 1.142(a)(6)-1

Space or ocean activity
. determination of activity 1.863-8
. gross income derived from 1.863-8

Split-dollar life insurance arrangements (See Life insurance)
. distributions by corporations .... 1.301-1(q)

Spouses
. community income (See Community income)
. IRA plan for spouse 25.2503-5
. life estates
. . surviving spouse
. . . income, spouse entitled to .... 20.2056(b)-5
. . . income and principle, trustee adjustments between .... 20.2056(b)-7

Spouses —Cont'd
. newly married couples
. . change of annual accounting period 1.442-1
. pension, profit-sharing, and stock bonus plans .... 1.219(a)-3
. power of appointment
. . surviving spouse, in
. . . income, spouse entitled to .... 20.2056(b)-5
. power of appointment, surviving spouse
. . life estate .... 20.2056(b)-5
. principal residence sales
. . exclusion of gain from sale or exchange
. . . deceased spouse 1.121-4
. retirement savings deduction ..... 1.219(a)-3; 1.220-1
. stock redemption
. . constructive distribution to spouse 1.1041-2
. surviving spouses
. . income to defined as unitrust amount ... 20.2056A-5
. . life estates
. . . income and principle, trustee adjustments between .... 20.2056(b)-7

Stapled foreign corporations
. assessment and collection procedures 1.269B-1
. change in domestic or foreign status 1.269B-1
. defined 1.269B-1
. domestic corporations 1.269B-1
. subjectivity to tax 301.269B-1

State housing credit, allocation of (See Low-income housing subhead State housing credit)

State obligations
. government bond defined 1.141-1
. prior issue 1.141-13
. private activity bonds, limitations on advance funding of .... 1.149(d)-1
. private business test 1.141-13; 1.145.2
. private security or payment test 1.141-13
. private use test 1.141-13
. reasonable expectations test 1.141-13
. refunding bonds 1.141-15
. refunding issue 1.141-13

Statutory options
. defined 1.421-1
. definitions and special rules 1.424-1

Stock
. acquisition
. . basis after group structure change, stock 1.1502-31
. affiliate-owned stock 1.7874-1
. aggregate deemed asset disposition price (See Aggregate deemed asset disposition price)
. distributions
. . acquisition, gain recognition in connection with 1.355-7

References are to Reg. § numbers

Stock —Cont'd
. foreign corporations
. . basis adjustment of stock held by 1.961-3
. . increase in basis of stock in CFC 1.961-1
. . redemption treatment as distribution 1.961-4
. . reduction in basis of stock in CFC 1.961-2
. . transfers .... 1.367(a)-3
. . . foreign corporation, domestic corporation to .... 1.367(a)-3(c)
. . . foreign corporation, foreign corporation to .... 1.367(a)-3(b)
. foreign insurance companies, stock held by .. 1.864-4
. foreign investment company .... 1.367(b)-6
. foreign persons, distributions to
. . gain, recognition of .... 1.367(e)-1
. marketable stock defined .... 1.1296(e)-1
. mark-to-market election for marketable stocks 1.1296-1
. options (See Stock options)
. purchase price allocations (See Purchase price allocations)
. redemption (See Redemption of stock)
. small business stock (See Qualified small business stock)

Stock bonus plans (See Pension, profit-sharing, and stock bonus plans)

Stock options
. definitions 1.421-1; 1.425-1
. generally .... 1.421-8 et seq.
. incentive stock options .... 1.422A-1 to 1.422A-3
. information returns 1.6039-1

Stockholders (See Shareholders)

Straddle rules
. personal property
. . defined for straddle rule............... 1.1092(d)-2

Student loan bonds
. private activity bonds, public approval
. . special rules .... 1.147(f)-1(b)(4)

Students
. domestic service provided by for college organization .... 31.3121(b)(10)-1(d)
. earned income attribution, dependent care services
. . employment related expenses, credit for ... 1.21-2(b)
. employee with student status ... 31.3121(b)(10)-2(d); 31.3306(c)(10)-2(d)
. FICA exemption .. 31.3121(b)(2)-1; 31.3121(b)(10)-2; 31.3306(c)(10)-2
. school, college or university defined .... 31.3121(b)(10)-2(c)

Subchapter T corporations
. returns .... 1.6012-1(f)

Subsidiary corporations
. accounting period, change of............... 1.442-1
. acquisitions, stock........................ 1.304-3

Subsidiary corporations —Cont'd
. adjusted grossed-up basis (See Adjusted grossed-up basis)
. stock; sale, exchange or distributions of
. . aggregate deemed asset disposition price (See Aggregate deemed asset disposition price)
. . asset sale, treatment as
. . . adjusted grossed-up basis (See Adjusted grossed-up basis)
. . . aggregate deemed asset disposition price (See Aggregate deemed asset disposition price)
. . . deemed asset disposition defined .. 1.336-1(b)(13)
. . . deemed disposition tax consequences defined .... 1.336-1(b)(14)
. . . disposition date assets defined ..... 1.336-1(b)(8)
. . . disposition date defined .... 1.336-1(b)(7)
. . . disposition defined .... 1.336-1(b)(4)
. . . domestic corporation defined....... 1.336-1(b)(9)
. . . 80-percent purchaser defined ..... 1.336-1(b)(15)
. . . liquidation defined .... 1.336-1(b)(12)
. . . new target defined .... 1.336-1(b)(3)
. . . nonrecently disposed stock defined .... 1.336-1(b)(17)
. . . old target defined .... 1.336-1(b)(3)
. . . purchaser defined .... 1.336-1(b)(2)
. . . qualified stock disposition defined... 1.336-1(b)(5)
. . . recently disposed stock defined ... 1.336-1(b)(16)
. . . related persons defined .... 1.336-1(b)(11)
. . . seller defined .... 1.336-1(b)(1)
. . . target corporation defined .... 1.336-1(b)(3)
. . . target defined .... 1.336-1(b)(3)
. . . 12 month disposition period defined .... 1.336-1(b)(6)
. . section 336 election
. . . actual asset disposition treatment, and .... 1.336-2(e)
. . . availability of election .... 1.336-2(a)
. . . consolidated group members, treatment of .... 1.336-2(g)(2)
. . . deemed transaction .... 1.336-2(b)
. . . defined .... 1.336-1(b)(10)
. . . dispositions described in sec. 335(d)(2), or (e)(2) .... 1.336-2(b)(2)(i)(A)
. . . foreign taxes, allocation of .... 1.336-2(g)(3)(ii)
. . . gain, old target recognition of . 1.336-2(b)(1)(B)(1)
. . . loss, old target recognition of .. 1.336-2(b)(1)(B)(2)
. . . making election .... 1.336-2(h)
. . . minority shareholders .... 1.336-2(d)
. . . protective election, making............ 1.336-2(j)
. . . purchaser, federal income tax consequences to .... 1.336-2(c)
. . . source and foreign tax credits ..... 1.336-2(g)(3)(i)
. . . target, treatment under IRC .... 1.336-2(f)
. . . target, two corporations treatment... 1.336-2(g)(1)

References are to Reg. § numbers

Successor corporations
. carryovers of predecessor
. . inventories .... 1.381(c)(5)-1
. . life insurance companies .... 1.381(c)(22)-1
. stock basis after group structure change ... 1.1502-31

Summons
. designated or related summons (See Designated or related summons)
. disclosing summoned party not liable ... 301.7609-3(b)
. duty of summoned party .... 301.7609-3(a)
. intervention in proceeding .... 301.7609-4(a)
. John Doe
. . suspension of limitation periods, notification of .... 301.7609-3(d)
. no notice has been mailed, presumption .... 301.7609-4(c)
. quash, right to institute proceeding to ... 301.7609-4(b)
. service 301.7603-1
. suspension of periods of limitation 301.7609-5
. . agent defined .... 301.7609-5(e)
. . failure to resolve response to summons after intervention in action to enforce summons .... 301.7609-5(d)
. . final resolution of the summoned third party's response to summons .... 301.7609-5(e)
. . intervention in action to enforce summons .... 301.7609-5(b)
. . quash a summons, institution of proceeding to .... 301.7609-5(c)
. third-party
. . notification of persons identified in 301.7609-2
. . reimbursement of costs .... 301.7609-3(c)
. . special procedures 301.7609-1
. third-party recordkeepers 301.7603-2

Supplemental wage payments
. withholding
. . agents, payments made by .... 31.3401(a)-1
. . no income tax liability, employees incurring .... 31.3401(n)-1
. . $1,000,000, wages in excess of .... 31.3402(g)-1
. . reimbursements and other expense allowance .... 31.3401(a)-4
. . retail commission salesman, remuneration other than in cash .... 31.3402(j)-1

Surviving spouse
. income to defined as unitrust amount 20.2056A-5
. life estates
. . income and principle, trustee adjustments between .... 20.2056(b)-7

T

Tangible property
. amounts paid to acquire or produce
. . amount paid defined .... 1.263(a)-2(b)(1)

Tangible property — Cont'd
. *amounts paid to acquire or produce — Cont'd*
. . capital expenditures .... 1.263(a)-2(e)
. . . amount paid defined .... 1.263(a)-2(b)
. . . amounts required for capitalization .. 1.263(a)-2(e)
. . . coordination with other provisions of the IRC .... 1.263(a)-2(c)
. . . personal property defined .... 1.263(a)-2(b)
. . . real property defined .... 1.263(a)-2(b)
. . . recovery of capitalized amounts ..... 1.263(a)-2(f)
. . capitalization requirements ...... 1.263(a)-2(d)(1) et seq.
. . capitalize, election to ...... 1.263(a)-2(d)(3)(ii)(B)(2)
. . capitalized amounts, recover of .... 1.263(a)-2(f)
. . coordination with other provision of the IRC .... 1.263(a)-2(c)
. . de minimis rule .... 1.263(a)-2(d)(4)
. . defense or perfection of title to property .... 1.263(a)-2(d)(2)(i)
. . material and supplies treatment under 1.163-3 .... 1.263(a)-2(c)(2)
. . personal property defined .... 1.263(a)-2(b)(2)
. . produce defined .... 1.263(a)-2(b)(4)
. . real property defined .... 1.263(a)-2(b)(3)
. . rules, general .... 1.263(a)-2(a)
. . shipping costs .... 1.263(a)-2(d)(3)(ii)(B)(1)
. . shipping fees .... 1.263(a)-2(d)(3)(ii)(B)(1)
. . transaction costs .... 1.263(a)-2(d)(3)(i)
. . transporting the property ... 1.263(a)-2(d)(3)(ii)(B)(1)
. amounts paid to improve .... 1.263(a)-3(i)
. . amounts paid defined .... 1.263(a)-3(b)(1)
. . applicable financial statement defined .... 1.263(a)-3(b)(4)
. . capital expenditures
. . . amount paid defined .... 1.263(a)-3(b)
. . . amounts required for capitalization .. 1.263(a)-3(h)
. . . capitalization rule .... 1.263(a)-3(d)
. . . coordination with other provisions of the IRC .... 1.263(a)-3(c)
. . . generally .... 1.263(a)-3(a)
. . . personal property defined .... 1.263(a)-3(b)
. . . real property defined .... 1.263(a)-3(b)
. . . repair allowance .... 1.263(a)-3(g)
. . . restoration .... 1.263(a)-3(f)
. . . treatment of .... 1.263(a)-3(k)
. . capitalization of amounts to adapt property to a new of different use .... 1.263(a)-3(h)
. . capitalization of betterments .... 1.263(a)-3(f)
. . capitalization of restorations .... 1.263(a)-3(g)
. . capitalization rules, improved property
. . . aggregate of related amounts .... 1.263(a)-3(d)(5)
. . . regulatory requirements, compliance with .... 1.263(a)-3(d)(3)
. . . repairs and maintenance performed during improvement .... 1.263(a)-3(d)(4)

References are to Reg. § numbers

Tangible property —Cont'd
. *amounts paid to improve—Cont'd*
. . capitalized amount, recovery of .... 1.263(a)-3(l)
. . coordination with other provision of the IRC .... 1.263(a)-3(c)
. . generally .... 1.263(a)-3(a)
. . optional regulatory accounting method .... 1.263(a)-3(i)
. . personal property defined .... 1.263(a)-3(b)(2)
. . real property defined .... 1.263(a)-3(b)(3)
. . repair allowance .... 1.263(a)-3(j)
. . routine maintenance safe harbor
. . . class life .... 1.263(a)-3(e)(4)
. . . exception to routine maintenance inclusion .... 1.263(a)-3(e)(2)
. . . generally .... 1.263(a)-3(e)(1)
. . . spare parts, rotable or temporary .... 1.263(a)-3(e)(3)
. . uniform capitalization of costs
. . . de minimis rule, property subject to .... 1.263A-1(b)(14)

Tapes (See Motion picture and television films and tapes)

Tax attributes for S corporations
. reduction of tax attributes for S corporations
. . carryovers and carrybacks .... 1.108-7(b)
. . effective / applicability date .... 1.108-7(f)
. . examples .... 1.108-7(e)
. . special rules for S corporations .... 1.108-7(d)
. . . allocation of excess losses or deductions .... 1.108-7(d)(2)
. . . character of excess losses or deduction allocated to a shareholder .... 1.108-7(d)(3)
. . . information requirements .... 1.108-7(d)(4)
. . transactions to which section 381 applies .... 1.108-7(c)

Tax Court
. notice to interested parties 1.7476-2

Tax equivalency payments
. private activity bonds .... 1.141-4(e)(5)

Tax Increase and Prevention and Reconciliation Act of 2005 (TIPRA)
. amendment to section 199 .... 1.199-2; 1.199-3; 1.199-5; 1.199-7; 1.199-8

Tax Reform Act of 1976
. foreign investment companies .... 1.367(b)-6

Tax return preparers
. compensation paid to .... 1.6694-1(f)
. copies of returns
. . failure to furnish a copy, penalty for .... 1.6107-1(d)
. . retaining by signer of return .... 1.6107-1(b)
. . taxpayer, furnishing to
. . . employment taxes .... 31.6107-1(a)
. . . excise tax 40.6107-1

Tax return preparers —Cont'd
. *copies of returns —Cont'd*
. . *taxpayer, furnishing to —Cont'd*
. . . foundation and similar excise taxes .... 53.6107-1(a)
. . . generation-skipping transfer tax .... 26.6107-1(a)
. . . greenmail, excise tax on .... 156.6107-1(a)
. . . highway motor vehicles, excise tax on .... 41.6107-1(a)
. . . pension excise taxes .... 54.6107-1(a)
. . . public charity excise taxes .... 56.6107-1(a)
. . . REITs and RIC, excise tax on .... 55.6107-1(a)
. . . structured settlement factoring transactions, excise tax on .... 157.6107-1(a)
. . . wagering taxes .... 44.6107-1(a)
. defined 20.7701-1; 25.7701-1; 41.7701-1; 44.7701-1; 54.7701-1; 55.7701-1; 56.7701-1; 156.7701-1; 157.7701-1; 301.7701-15
. definitions concerning .... 301.7701-1(b)
. due diligence requirements
. . earned income credit eligibility 1.6695-2
. earned income credit eligibility
. . due diligence requirements 1.6695-2
. educational qualifications for .... 301.7701-1(d)
. electronic filing 1.6107-2; 1.6695-1
. failure to file correct information returns .... 1.6695-1(e)
. failure to furnish copies to taxpayer .... 1.6695-1(a)
. failure to furnish identifying number .... 1.6695-1(c)
. failure to retain copy of return .... 1.6695-1(d)
. failure to sign return 1.6695-1
. form and manner of furnishing copy of return and retaining copy 1.6107-2
. generally 1.6107-1
. identifying number, furnishing .... 1.6109-2(a); 25.6109-1
. . employment taxes 31.6109-2
. . estate tax return .... 20.6109-2(a)
. . excise tax 40.6109-1
. . foundation and similar excise taxes 53.6109-1
. . generation-skipping transfer tax .... 26.6109-2(a)
. . greenmail, excise tax on 156.6109-1
. . highway motor vehicles, excise tax on .... 41.6109-2(a)
. . pension excise taxes 54.6109-1
. . public charity excise taxes 56.6109-1
. . REITs and RIC, excise tax on 55.6109-1
. . structured settlement factoring transactions, excise tax on 157.6109-1
. . wagering taxes 44.6109-1
. income derived with respect to return or refund claim .... 1.6694-1(f)
. information returns 1.6060-1
. Low-Income Taxpayer Clinic, defined for 301.7701-15
. mechanical or clerical assistance .... 301.7701-1(c)
. negotiation of check .... 1.6695-1(f)

References are to Reg. § numbers

Tax return preparers —Cont'd
. nonsigning tax return preparer defined .... 301.7701-1(b)(2)
. outside the U.S., preparation of return .... 301.7701-1(e)
. penalties
. . abatement of penalty .... 1.6694-1(d)
. . date return is deemed prepared ..... 1.6694-1(a)(2)
. . employment taxes 26.7701-1; 31.6694-1; 31.6696-1
. . estate tax return 20.6694-1;,20.6695-1
. . excise tax 40.6060-1; 40.6694-1
. . failure to file correct information returns .... 1.6695-1(e)
. . failure to furnish copies to taxpayer ..... 1.6695-1(a)
. . failure to furnish identifying number ..... 1.6695-1(c)
. . failure to retain copy of return .... 1.6695-1(d)
. . failure to sign return 1.6695-1
. . firm responsibilities .... 1.6694-1(b)(4)
. . foundation and similar excise taxes 53.6694-1; 53.6695-1
. . generally 1.6694-1; 1.6694-2; 1.6695-1
. . generation-skipping transfer tax 26.6694-1; 26.6695-1
. . gift tax 25.6694-1
. . greenmail, excise tax on .... 156.6694-1; 156.6695-1(d)
. . highway motor vehicles, excise tax on .... 41.6694-1(a)
. . negotiation of check .... 1.6695-1(f)
. . nonsigning tax return preparers responsibilities .... 1.6694-1(b)(3)
. . pension excise taxes 54.6694-1; 54.6695-1
. . preparation of return .... 1.6695-1 et seq.
. . public charity excise taxes ... 56.6694-1; 56.6695-1
. . REITs and RIC, excise tax on 55.6694-1; 55.6695-1
. . sign return, failure to .... 1.6695-1(b)
. . signing tax return preparers responsibilities .... 1.6694-1(b)(2)
. . structured settlement factoring transactions, excise tax on 157.6694-1; 157.6695-1
. . suits for refund of penalty .... 1.6696-1(j)
. . tax return preparers defined .... 1.6694-1(b)(1)
. persons who are not tax return preparers, listing of .... 301.7701-1(f)
. refund or credit claims
. . content of claims .... 1.6696-1(d)
. . defined .... 301.7701-1(b)(4)
. . employment taxes 31.6060-1
. . estate tax return .... 20.6109-2(a); 20.6694-1; 20.6696-1
. . failure to furnish a copy, penalty for ..... 1.6107-1(d)
. . filed by preparer or appraiser .... 1.6696-1(b)
. . form of claims .... 1.6696-1(e)

Tax return preparers —Cont'd
. refund or credit claims —Cont'd
. . foundation and similar excise taxes 53.6696-1
. . generation-skipping transfer tax 26.6696-1
. . gift tax 25.6696-1
. . greenmail, excise tax on 156.6696-1
. . highway motor vehicles, excise tax on 41.6696-1
. . interest .... 1.6696-1(h)
. . notice and demand .... 1.6696-1(a)
. . outstanding liability, application of refund to .... 1.6696-1(h)
. . pension excise taxes 54.6696-1
. . place for filing .... 1.6696-1(f)
. . public charity excise taxes 56.6696-1
. . REITs and RIC, excise tax on 55.6696-1
. . separation and consolidation of claims .. 1.6696-1(c)
. . structured settlement factoring transactions, excise tax on 157.6696-1
. . suits for refund of penalty .... 1.6696-1(j)
. . time for filing .... 1.6696-1(g)
. . wagering taxes 44.6696-1
. reporting requirements
. . employers or engagers of one or more preparers 25.6060-1
. . employment taxes 31.6060-1
. . excise tax 40.6060-1
. . failure to retain and make records available, penalties for .... 1.6060-1(c)
. . foundation and similar excise taxes 53.6060-1
. . furnishing completed copy requirement .... 20.6107-1(a)
. . generation-skipping transfer tax .... 26.6060-1(a)
. . greenmail, excise tax on 156.6060-1
. . highway motor vehicles, excise tax on .... 41.6060-1(a)
. . information returns 1.6060-1
. . pension excise taxes 54.6060-1
. . public charity excise taxes 56.6060-1
. . REITs and RIC, excise tax on 55.6060-1
. . structured settlement factoring transactions, excise tax on 157.6060-1
. . wagering taxes .... 44.6060-1(a)
. return and claim for refund defined .. 301.7701-1(b)(4)
. sign return
. . failure to .... 1.6695-1(b)
. . requirement for preparer to 25.6109-1
. . signing tax return preparer defined ..... 1.6107-1(c)
. signing tax return preparer defined .. 301.7701-1(b)(1)
. substantial portion defined .... 301.7701-1(b)(3)
. understatement due to unreasonable position
. . adequate disclosure exception for position with reasonable basis .... 1.6694-2(c)
. . burden of proof .... 1.6694-2(e)
. . corporations, partnerships, and other firms .... 1.6694-2(a)(2)

References are to Reg. § numbers

Tax return preparers —Cont'd
. *understatement due to unreasonable position — Cont'd*
. . employment taxes 31.6694-2
. . estate tax return 20.6694-2
. . excise tax 40.6694-2
. . foundation and similar excise taxes 53.6694-2
. . generation-skipping transfer tax 26.6694-2
. . gift tax 25.6694-2; 25.6694-3
. . greenmail, excise tax on 156.6694-2
. . highway motor vehicles, excise tax on 41.6694-2
. . merits, position more likely than not be sustained on .... 1.6694-2(b)
. . pension excise taxes 54.6694-2
. . proscribed conduct .... 1.6694-2(a)(1)
. . public charity excise taxes 56.6694-2
. . reasonable cause and good faith exception .... 1.6694-2(d)
. . REITs and RIC, excise tax on 55.6694-2
. . structured settlement factoring transactions, excise tax on 157.6694-2
. . wagering taxes .... 44.6694-2(a)
. understatement due to willful, reckless or intention conduct
. . burden of proof .... 1.6694-3(g)
. . corporations, partnerships, and other firms .... 1.6694-3(a)(2)
. . employment taxes 31.6694-3
. . estate tax return 20.6694-3
. . excise tax 40.6694-3
. . foundation and similar excise taxes 53.6694-3
. . generation-skipping transfer tax 26.6694-3
. . greenmail, excise tax on 156.6694-3
. . highway motor vehicles, excise tax on 41.6694-3
. . pension excise taxes 54.6694-3
. . proscribed conduct .... 1.6694-3(a)(1)
. . public charity excise taxes 56.6694-3
. . reckless or intentional disregard .... 1.6694-3(c)
. . REITs and RIC, excise tax on 55.6694-3
. . rules or regulations defined .... 1.6694-3(e)
. . sec. 6694(b) penalty reduced by sec. 6694(a) .... 1.6694-3(f)
. . structured settlement factoring transactions, excise tax on 157.6694-3
. . wagering taxes 44.6694-3
. understatement liability .... 1.6694-1(c)
. . 15% of a penalty, extension of collection period when preparer has paid .... 1.6694-4 et seq.
. . . employment taxes 31.6694-4
. . . estate tax return 20.6694-4
. . . excise tax 40.6694-4
. . . foundation and similar excise taxes 53.6694-4
. . . generation-skipping transfer tax 26.6694-4
. . . gift tax 25.6694-4
. . . greenmail, excise tax on 156.6694-4

Tax return preparers —Cont'd
. *understatement liability—Cont'd*
. . *15% of a penalty, extension of collection period when preparer has paid—Cont'd*
. . . highway motor vehicles, excise tax on .. 41.6694-4
. . . pension excise taxes 54.6694-4
. . . public charity excise taxes 56.6694-4
. . . REITs and RIC, excise tax on 55.6694-4
. . . structured settlement factoring transactions, excise tax on 157.6694-4
. . . wagering taxes 44.6694-4
. understatement of liability on return ... 1.6694-1(a)(1)
. understatements (See understatement subheadings)
. verification of information furnished by taxpayer or other part
. . previously filed returns .... 1.6694-1(e)
. verification of information furnished by taxpayer or other party .... 1.6694-1(e)
. wagering taxes .... 44.6694-1(a)

Tax shelters
. list of investors, requirement to maintain .. 301.6112-1
. material advisors 301.6112-1

Taxable year
. defined 1.441-1
. 52-53 weeks, election of year consisting of ... 1.441-2
. foreign corporations 1.898-1
. partners and partnerships 1.706-1
. personal service corporations 1.441-3
. S corporations 1.1378-1

Tax-exempt bonds
. definitions 1.150-1

Taxpayer
. defined
. . foreign tax credits 1.901-2
. . income, war profits, or excess profits tax paid or accrued 1.901-2

Taxpayer assistance orders
. modification or rescinding authority 301.7811-1

Taxpayer identification number (TIN)
. collection for Federal Crop Insurance Act 301.6109-3
. incorrect
. . backup withholding .... 31.3406(d)-5
. . multiple notices .... 31.3406(d)-5; 301.6724-1
. real property interests by foreign persons, withholdings on U.S. 1.1445-1

Tax-related deadlines
. procedures and administration
. . postponement of certain tax-related deadlines by reason of Presidentially declared disaster or terroristic or military action 301.7508A-1
. . . acts for which a period may be disregarded .... 301.7508A-1(c)
. . . definitions .... 301.7508A-1(d)

References are to Reg. § numbers

Tax-related deadlines —Cont'd
. *procedures and administration —Cont'd*
. . *postponement of certain tax-related deadlines by reason of Presidentially declared disaster or terroristic or military action—Cont'd*
. . . examples .... 301.7508A-1(f)
. . . notice of postponement of certain acts .... 301.7508A-1(e)
. . . postponed deadlines .... 301.7508A-1(b)
. . . proposed effective date .... 301.7508A-1(g)
. . . scope .... 301.7508A-1(a)

Technology
. research credits (See Research credits)

Television (See Motion picture and television films and tapes)

10 or more employer plan
. welfare benefit funds .... 1.419A(f)(6)-1

Terminally ill individuals
. amounts paid to 1.101-8
. life insurance, additional benefits 1.7702A-1

Third-party contacts
. defined 301.7602-2
. notice 301.7602-2
. reports 301.7602-2

Timber sales
. lump-sum
. . information reporting with dates of closing on or after Jan. 1, 1991 .... 1.6045-4

Time and place for paying taxes
. extension of time 1.6164-4; 1.6164-8
. government depositaries (See Depositaries of government)
. installment payments 1.6152-1

Time for filing returns and other documents
. generally 301.6233-1

Timely mailing as timely filing
. documents and payments 301.7502-1

TIN (See Taxpayer identification number)

Transfers (See Sales and transfers)

Transportation expenses
. dependent care services
. . employment related expenses, credit for . . . 1.21-1(d)

Travel expenses
. state legislators away from home
. . committee of the legislation .... 1.162-24(d)(4)
. . election .... 1.162-24(e)
. . election, effect of .... 1.162-24(f)
. . federal per diem .... 1.162-24(d)(5)
. . fifty mile rule .... 1.162-24(c)
. . generally .... 1.162-24(a)
. . in session .... 1.162-24(d)(3)
. . legislative day .... 1.162-24(b)
. . living expenses defined .... 1.162-24(d)(2)

Travel expenses —Cont'd
. *state legislators away from home —Cont'd*
. . state legislator define .... 1.162-24(d)(1)

Treaties
. coordination with income tax treaties
. . S corporations .... 301.7701(b)-7
. return position, treaty-based
. . disclosure of, amounts received after January 1, 2001 .... 301.6114-1
. returns
. . treaty-based return positions 301.6114-1

Trusts (See also Pension, profit sharing, and stock bonus plans)
. charitable remainder trusts (See Charitable remainder trusts)
. control test for treatment as domestic trust 301.7701-7
. distributions, required .... 1.401(a)(9)-1
. exempt organizations .... 1.501(c)(20)-1
. grantor treatment as substantial owners 1.671-1
. individual retirement accounts 1.408-5
. qualified retirement plans .... 1.401(a)-1
. United States person, status as 301.7701-7
. valuation of gift when donor or family member retains interest in trust
. . contingencies 25.2702-3
. . definitions concerning 25.2702-2
. . holders 25.2702-2
. . qualified interests 25.2702-3
. . terms of annuity of unitrust interest 25.2702-3
. widely held fixed investment trusts (See Widely held fixed investment trusts)

Tuition
. information reporting 1.6050S-1
. . filing requirements 1.6050S-1
. payments, reimbursements or refunds
. . information reporting
. . . magnetic media requirements 301.6011-2
. qualified state tuition programs (See Qualified state tuition programs)

U

Unauthorized tax collection actions (See Collection of taxes subhead unauthorized collection actions)

Undercollection
. withholding
. . after return is filed, error ascertained .... 31.6025-1(c)(2)

Underpayment of taxes
. adjustments 31.6205-1
. generally 31.6205-1
. interest 301.6601-1

References are to Reg. § numbers

Uniform capitalization rules
. interest
. . avoided cost method 1.263A-9
United States obligations
. common nontaxable exchanges 1.1037-1
United States person
. defined 1.957-3
United States source income
. global dealing operations, special rules 1.864-4
Unitrust interest
. charitable interest in the form of .... 1.170A-6; 25.2522(c)-3
Unlawful tax collection actions (See Collection of taxes subhead unauthorized collection actions)
Unrelated business taxable income (See Exempt organizations)
Useful life/recovery period
. section 38 property 1.46-3
User fees
. enrollment
. . agent fee, enrolled 300.5; 300.6
. . examination 300.4
. enrollment to perform actuarial services
. . applicability .... 300.7(a)
. . fee .... 300.7(b)
. . person liable for fee .... 300.7(c)
. . renewal
. . . applicability .... 300.8(a)
. . . fee .... 300.8(b)
. . . person liable for fee .... 300.8(c)
. generally 300.0
. imposition 300.0
. installment agreements 300.1; 300.2

V

Valuation
. decedent's gross estate
. . alternative valuation method 20.2032-1; 301.9100-6T
. FASIT property 1.860I-2
. securities held by dealer or broker
. . safe harbor valuation, section 475 .... 1.475(a)-4
VEBAs (See Voluntary employees' beneficiary associations)
Vehicles, taxable
. luxury tax 48.4004-1
. . exemptions 48.4004-2
. . resales, nonexempt 48.4004-4
. . subsequent 48.4004-3
Vesting
. individual retirement accounts ..... 1.411(a)-1 et seq.
Virgin Islands
. corporation created or organized in ...... 1.881-5T(c)
. income tax reduction 1.934-1
. U.S. income tax coordination 1.932-1
Voluntary employee contributions
. additions to tax 301.6652-4
Voluntary employees' beneficiary associations (VEBAs)
. exempt organizations .... 1.501(c)(9)-2
. qualification, geographic locale restriction .... 1.501(c)(9)-2

W

Wages
. paid and received
. . employment taxes .... 31.3121(a)-2
. salary reduction plans 1.61-16
War profits tax (See Income, war profits, or excess profits tax paid or accrued)
Wear and tear
. Accelerated Cost Recovery System
. . periods since February 28, 1913 .... 1.1016-3
. . periods when income was not subject to tax 1.1016-4
. accounting method change .... 1.1016-3(h)
Welfare benefit fund
. 10 or more employer plan .... 1.419A(f)(6)-1
Welfare benefit plans
. Section 89 qualification requirements .... 1.89(k)-1
Whistleblowers
. disclosure of written contracts among IRS and whistleblowers and their legal representatives .... 301.6103(n)-2
Widely held fixed investment trusts
. backup withholdings 1.671-5
. exempt recipients of income 1.671-5
. form 1041 filings 1.671-4; 1.671-5
. information returns 1.6049-7
. interest paid, reporting 1.6049-5
. original issue discount subject to reporting ... 1.6049-5
. reporting requirements 1.671-5; 1.6042-5
. safe harbor for providing information for NMWHFIT .... 1.671-5T(g)
. trustee obligation to furnish information 1.671-5
. unit interest holder, statements to 1.671-5
Withdrawal liability payments
. retirement plans, qualified .... 1.401(a)-3
Withdrawals
. capital construction funds 3.5; 3.6
Withholding
. false information 31.6682-1
. foreign banks or insurance companies 1.1441-1

References are to Reg. § numbers

Withholding —Cont'd
. foreign partner
. . effectively connected taxable income 1.1446-1
. . . allocations under section 704 .... 1.1446-2
. . . calculation of 1446 tax 1.1446-3
. . . credits, 1446 tax .... 1.1446-3(d)
. . . designation of nominees to withhold under section 1446 .... 1.1446-4(d)
. . . determination of foreign partner status .... 1.1446-1(c)
. . . determination of obligation .... 1.1446-1(b)
. . . distributions subject to withholding .... 1.1446-4(f)
. . . ECTI allocation, election based on .... 1.1446-4(g)
. . . failure to withhold .... 1.1446-3(e)
. . . foreign status of partner, determination of .... 1.1446-4(e)
. . . installment payments of 1446 tax ..... 1.1446-3(b)
. . . look through rules, upper-tier partnerships .... 1.1446-5(c)
. . . publicly traded partnerships 1.1446-4
. . . reporting 1446 tax .... 1.1446-3(d)
. . . tiered partnerships 1.1446-5
. foreign person, payments to
. . amounts subject to withholding 1.1441-3
. no income tax liability, employee incurring .... 31.3402(n)-1
. regulated investment company
. . determination of amount to be withheld, special rules 1.1441-3
. returns
. . domestic service, wages paid for .... 31.6011(a)-4(a)(2)
. . undercollection
. . . before return is filed, ascertained .... 31.6025-1(c)(1)

Withholding —Cont'd
. Section 3402(t) withholdings (See Government entities)
. supplemental wage payments
. . flat rate
. . . agents, payments made by .... 31.3401(a)-1
. . . no income tax liability, employees incurring .... 31.3401(n)-1
. . . $1,000,000, wages in excess of ..... 31.3402(g)-1
. . . reimbursements and other expense allowance .... 31.3401(a)-4
. . . retail commission salesman, remuneration other than in cash .... 31.3402(j)-1
. . $1,000,000, in excess of .... 31.3402(g)-1(a)
. tax treaty reduction
. . reliance on claim of .... 1.1441-6(b)
. undercollection
. . after return is filed, error ascertained .... 31.6025-1(c)(2)
. . before return is filed, ascertained ... 31.6025-1(c)(1)
. . due date to collect .... 31.6025-1(d)(2)

Withholding taxes
. abatements, credits, or refunds 31.6414-1
. monthly returns .... 31.6011(a)-5
. underpayment adjustments 31.6205-1

Wives and husbands (See Spouses)

Workers' compensation
. sickness or accident disability payments .... 31.3121(a)(2)-1

Worthless securities
. abandonment of securities 1.165-5

§ 1.0-1 Internal Revenue Code of 1954 and regulations.

(a) Enactment of law. The Internal Revenue Code of 1954 which became law upon enactment of Pub. L. 591, 83d Congress, approved August 16, 1954, provides in part as follows:

Be it enacted by the Senate and House of Representatives of the United States of America in Congress assembled, That (a) Citation. (1) The provisions of this Act set forth under the heading "Internal Revenue Title" may be cited as the "Internal Revenue Code of 1954"

(2) The Internal Revenue Code enacted on February 10, 1939, as amended, may be cited as the "Internal Revenue Code of 1939".

(b) Publication. This Act shall be published as volume 68A of the United States Statutes at Large, with a comprehensive table of contents and an appendix; but without an index or marginal references. The date of enactment, bill number, public law number, and chapter number, shall be printed as a headnote.

(c) Cross reference. For saving provisions, effective date provisions, and other related provisions, see chapter 80 (sec. 7801 and following) of the Internal Revenue Code of 1954.

(d) Enactment of Internal Revenue Title into law. The Internal Revenue Title referred to in subsection (a)(1) is as follows:

* * * * *

In general, the provisions of the Internal Revenue Code of 1954 are applicable with respect to taxable years beginning after December 31, 1953, and ending after August 16, 1954. Certain provisions of that Code are deemed to be included in the Internal Revenue Code of 1939. See section 7851.

(b) Scope of regulations. The regulations in this part deal with (1) the income taxes imposed under subtitle A of the Internal Revenue Code of 1954, and (2) certain administrative provisions contained in subtitle F of such Code relating to such taxes. In general, the applicability of such regulations is commensurate with the applicability of the respective provisions of the Internal Revenue Code of 1954 except that with respect to the provisions of the Internal Revenue Code of 1954 which are deemed to be included in the Internal Revenue Code of 1939, the regulations relating to such provisions are applicable to certain fiscal years and short taxable years which are subject to the Internal Revenue Code of 1939. Those provisions of the regulations which are applicable to taxable years subject to the Internal Revenue Code of 1939 and the specific taxable years to which such provisions are so applicable are identified in each instance. The regulations in 26 CFR (1939) Part 39 (Regulations 118) are continued in effect until superseded by the regulations in this part. See Treasury Decision 6091, approved August 16, 1954 (19 FR 5167, C.B. 1954-2, 47).

§ 1.1-1 Income tax on individuals.

Caution: The Treasury has not yet amended Reg § 1.1-1 to reflect changes made by P.L. 108-311, P.L. 108-27, P.L. 107-16, P.L. 105-206, P.L. 105-34, P.L. 103-66, P.L. 101-508, P.L. 100-647, P.L. 97-448, P.L. 97-34, P.L. 95-600, P.L. 95-30.

(a) General rule. *(1)* Section 1 of the Code imposes an income tax on the income of every individual who is a citizen or resident of the United States and, to the extent provided by section 871(b) or 877(b), on the income of a nonresident alien individual. For optional tax in the case of taxpayers with adjusted gross income of less than $10,000 (less than $5,000 for taxable years beginning before January 1, 1970) see section 3. The tax imposed is upon taxable income (determined by subtracting the allowable deductions from gross income). The tax is determined in accordance with the table contained in section 1. See subparagraph (2) of this paragraph for reference guides to the appropriate table for taxable years beginning on or after January 1, 1964, and before January 1, 1965, taxable years beginning after December 31, 1964, and before January 1, 1971, and taxable years beginning after December 31, 1970. In certain cases credits are allowed against the amount of the tax. See part IV (section 31 and following), subchapter A, chapter 1 of the Code. In general, the tax is payable upon the basis of returns rendered by persons liable therefor (subchapter A (sections 6001 and following), chapter 61 of the Code) or at the source of the income by withholding. For the computation of tax in the case of a joint return of a husband and wife, or a return of a surviving spouse, for taxable years beginning before January 1, 1971, see section 2. The computation of tax in such a case for taxable years beginning after December 31, 1970, is determined in accordance with the table contained in section 1(a) as amended by the Tax Reform Act of 1969. For other rates of tax on individuals, see section 5(a). For the imposition of an additional tax for the calendar years 1968, 1969, and 1970, see section 51(a).

(2) (i) For taxable years beginning on or after January 1, 1964, the tax imposed upon a single individual, a head of a household, a married individual filing a separate return, and estates and trusts is the tax imposed by section 1 determined in accordance with the appropriate table contained in the following subsection of section 1:

	Taxable years beginning in 1964	Taxable years beginning after 1964 but before 1971	Taxable years beginning after Dec. 31, 1970 (references in this column are to the Code as amended by the Tax Reform Act of 1969)
Single individual	Sec. 1(a)(1)	Sec. 1(a)(2)	Sec. 1(c).
Head of a household	Sec. 1(b)(1)	Sec. 1(b)(2)	Sec. 1(b).
Married individual filing a separate return	Sec. 1(a)(1)	Sec. 1(a)(2)	Sec. 1(d).
Estates and trusts	Sec. 1(a)(1)	Sec. 1(a)(2)	Sec. 1(d).

(ii) For taxable years beginning after December 31, 1970, the tax imposed by section 1(d), as amended by the Tax Reform Act of 1969, shall apply to the income effectively connected with the conduct of a trade or business in the United States by a married alien individual who is a nonresident of the United States for all or part of the taxable year or by a foreign estate or trust. For such years the tax imposed by section 1(c), as amended by such Act, shall apply to the income effectively connected with the conduct of a trade or business in the United States by an unmarried alien individual (other than a surviving spouse) who is a nonresident of the United States for all or part of the taxable year. See paragraph (b)(2) of § 1.871-8.

(3) The income tax imposed by section 1 upon any amount of taxable income is computed by adding to the income tax for the bracket in which that amount falls in the appropriate table in section 1 the income tax upon the excess of that amount over the bottom of the bracket at the rate indicated in such table.

(4) The provisions of section 1 of the Code, as amended by the Tax Reform Act of 1969, and of this paragraph may be illustrated by the following examples:

Example (1). A, an unmarried individual, had taxable income for the calendar year 1964 of $15,750. Accordingly, the tax upon such taxable income would be $4,507.50, computed as follows from the table in section 1(a)(1):

Tax on $14,000 (from table)	$3,790.00
Tax on $1,750 (at 41 percent as determined from the table)	717.50
Total tax on $15,750	4,507.50

Example (2). Assume the same facts as in example (1), except the figures are for the calendar year 1965. The tax upon such taxable income would be $4,232.50, computed as follows from the table in section 1(a)(2):

Tax on $14,000 (from table)	$3,550.00
Tax on $1,750 (at 39 percent as determined from the table)	682.50
Total tax on $15,750	4,232.50

Example (3). Assume the same facts as in example (1), except the figures are for the calendar year 1971. The tax upon such taxable income would be $3,752.50, computed as follows from the table in section 1(c), as amended:

Tax on $14,000 (from table)	$3,210.00
Tax on $1,750 (at 31 percent as determined from the table)	542.50
Total tax on $15,750	3,752.50

(b) Citizens or residents of the United States liable to tax. In general, all citizens of the United States, wherever resident, and all resident alien individuals are liable to the income taxes imposed by the Code whether the income is received from sources within or without the United States. Pursuant to section 876, a nonresident alien individual who is a bona fide resident of a section 931 possession (as defined in § 1.931-1(c)(1) of this chapter) or Puerto Rico during the entire taxable year is, except as provided in section 931 or 933 with respect to income from sources within such possessions, subject to taxation in the same manner as a resident alien individual. As to tax on nonresident alien individuals, see sections 871 and 877.

(c) Who is a citizen. Every person born or naturalized in the United States and subject to its jurisdiction is a citizen. For other rules governing the acquisition of citizenship, see chapters 1 and 2 of title III of the Immigration and Nationality Act (8 U.S.C. 1401–1459). For rules governing loss of citizenship, see sections 349 to 357, inclusive, of such Act (8 U.S.C. 1481–1489), Schneider v. Rusk, (1964) 377 U.S. 163, and Rev. Rul. 70-506, C.B. 1970–2, 1. For rules pertaining to persons who are nationals but not citizens at birth, e.g., a person born in American Samoa, see section 308 of such Act (8 U.S.C. 1408). For special rules applicable to certain expatriates who have lost citizenship with a principal purpose of avoiding certain taxes, see section 877. A foreigner who has filed his declaration of intention of becoming a citizen but who has not yet been admitted to citizenship by a final order of a naturalization court is an alien.

(d) Effective/applicability date. The second sentence of paragraph (b) of this section applies to taxable years ending after April 9, 2008.

T.D. 6161, 2/3/56, amend T.D. 7117, 5/24/71, T.D. 7332, 12/20/74, T.D. 9391, 4/4/2008.

§ 1.1-2 Limitation on tax.

(a) Taxable years ending before January 1, 1971. For taxable years ending before January 1, 1971 the tax imposed by section 1 (whether by subsection (a) or subsection (b) thereof) shall not exceed 87 percent of the taxable income for the taxable year. For purposes of determining this limitation the tax under section 1(a) or (b) and the tax at the 87-percent rate shall each be computed before the allowance of any credits against the tax. Where the alternative tax on capital gains is imposed under section 1201(b), the 87-percent limitation shall apply only to the partial tax computed on the taxable income reduced by 50 percent of the excess of net long-term capital gains over net short-term capital losses. Where, for purposes of computations under the income averaging provisions, section 1201(b) is treated as imposing the alternative tax on capital gains computed under section 1304(e)(2), the 87-percent limitation shall apply only to the tax equal to the tax imposed by section 1, reduced by the amount of the tax imposed by section 1 which is attributable to capital gain net income for the computation year.

(b) Taxable years beginning after December 31, 1970. If, for any taxable year beginning after December 31, 1970, an individual has earned taxable income which exceeds his taxable income as defined by section 1348, the tax imposed by section 1, as amended by the Tax Reform Act of 1969, shall not exceed the sum computed under the provisions of section 1348. For imposition of minimum tax for tax preferences see sections 56 through 58.

T.D. 6161, 2/3/56, amend T.D. 6885, 6/1/66, T.D. 7117, 5/24/71.

§ 1.1-3 Change in rates applicable to taxable year.

For computation of the tax for a taxable year during which a change in the tax rates occurs, see section 21 and the regulations thereunder.

Regs. § 1.1-4, deleted by T.D. 7117, 5/24/71, Regs. § 1.1-5, redesignated § 1.1-3 by T.D. 7117, 5/24/71, Regs. § 1.1-4, added by T.D. 6161, 2/3/56, Regs. § 1.1-5, added by T.D. 6161, 2/3/56.

§ 1.1(h)-1 Capital gains look-through rule for sales or exchanges of interests in a partnership, S corporation, or trust.

Caution: The Treasury has not yet amended Reg § 1.1(h)-1 to reflect changes made by P.L. 108-27.

(a) In general. When an interest in a partnership held for more than one year is sold or exchanged, the transferor may recognize ordinary income (e.g., under section 751(a)), collectibles gain, section 1250 capital gain, and residual long-term capital gain or loss. When stock in an S corporation held for more than one year is sold or exchanged, the transferor may recognize ordinary income (e.g., under sections 304, 306, 341, 1254), collectibles gain, and residual long-term capital gain or loss. When an interest in a trust held for more than one year is sold or exchanged, a transferor who is not treated as the owner of the portion of the trust attributable to the interest sold or exchanged (sections 673 through

679) (a non-grantor transferor) may recognize collectibles gain and residual long-term capital gain or loss.

(b) Look-through capital gain. *(1) In general.* Look-through capital gain is the share of collectibles gain allocable to an interest in a partnership, S corporation, or trust, plus the share of section 1250 capital gain allocable to an interest in a partnership, determined under paragraphs (b)(2) and (3) of this section.

(2) Collectibles gain. (i) Definition. For purposes of this section, collectibles gain shall be treated as gain from the sale or exchange of a collectible (as defined in section 408(m) without regard to section 408(m)(3)) that is a capital asset held for more than 1 year.

(ii) Share of collectibles gain allocable to an interest in a partnership, S corporation, or a trust. When an interest in a partnership, S corporation, or trust held for more than one year is sold or exchanged in a transaction in which all realized gain is recognized, the transferor shall recognize as collectibles gain the amount of net gain (but not net loss) that would be allocated to that partner (taking into account any remedial allocation under § 1.704-3(d)), shareholder, or beneficiary (to the extent attributable to the portion of the partnership interest, S corporation stock, or trust interest transferred that was held for more than one year) if the partnership, S corporation, or trust transferred all of its collectibles for cash equal to the fair market value of the assets in a fully taxable transaction immediately before the transfer of the interest in the partnership, S corporation, or trust. If less than all of the realized gain is recognized upon the sale or exchange of an interest in a partnership, S corporation, or trust, the same methodology shall apply to determine the collectibles gain recognized by the transferor, except that the partnership, S corporation, or trust shall be treated as transferring only a proportionate amount of each of its collectibles determined as a fraction that is the amount of gain recognized in the sale or exchange over the amount of gain realized in the sale or exchange. With respect to the transfer of an interest in a trust, this paragraph (b)(2) applies only to transfers by non-grantor transferors (as defined in paragraph (a) of this section). This paragraph (b)(2) does not apply to a transaction that is treated, for Federal income tax purposes, as a redemption of an interest in a partnership, S corporation, or trust.

(3) Section 1250 capital gain. (i) Definition. For purposes of this section, section 1250 capital gain means the capital gain (not otherwise treated as ordinary income) that would be treated as ordinary income if section 1250(b)(1) included all depreciation and the applicable percentage under section 1250(a) were 100 percent.

(ii) Share of section 1250 capital gain allocable to interest in partnership. When an interest in a partnership held for more than one year is sold or exchanged in a transaction in which all realized gain is recognized, there shall be taken into account under section 1(h)(7)(A)(i) in determining the partner's unrecaptured section 1250 gain the amount of section 1250 capital gain that would be allocated (taking into account any remedial allocation under § 1.704-3(d)) to that partner (to the extent attributable to the portion of the partnership interest transferred that was held for more than one year) if the partnership transferred all of its section 1250 property in a fully taxable transaction for cash equal to the fair market value of the assets immediately before the transfer of the interest in the partnership. If less than all of the realized gain is recognized upon the sale or exchange of an interest in a partnership, the same methodology shall apply to determine the section 1250 capital gain recognized by the transferor, except that the partnership shall be treated as transferring only a proportionate amount of each section 1250 property determined as a fraction that is the amount of gain recognized in the sale or exchange over the amount of gain realized in the sale or exchange. This paragraph (b)(3) does not apply to a transaction that is treated, for Federal income tax purposes, as a redemption of a partnership interest.

(iii) Limitation with respect to net section 1231 gain. In determining a transferor partner's net section 1231 gain (as defined in section 1231(c)(3)) for purposes of section 1(h)(7)(B), the transferor partner's allocable share of section 1250 capital gain in partnership property shall not be treated as section 1231 gain, regardless of whether the partnership property is used in the trade or business (as defined in section 1231(b)).

(c) Residual long-term capital gain or loss. The amount of residual long-term capital gain or loss recognized by a partner, shareholder of an S corporation, or beneficiary of a trust on account of the sale or exchange of an interest in a partnership, S corporation, or trust shall equal the amount of long-term capital gain or loss that the partner would recognize under section 741, that the shareholder would recognize upon the sale or exchange of stock of an S corporation, or that the beneficiary would recognize upon the sale or exchange of an interest in a trust (pre-look-through long-term capital gain or loss) minus the amount of look-through capital gain determined under paragraph (b) of this section.

(d) Special rule for tiered entities. In determining whether a partnership, S corporation, or trust has gain from collectibles, such partnership, S corporation, or trust shall be treated as owning its proportionate share of the collectibles of any partnership, S corporation, or trust in which it owns an interest either directly or indirectly through a chain of such entities. In determining whether a partnership has section 1250 capital gain, such partnership shall be treated as owning its proportionate share of the section 1250 property of any partnership in which it owns an interest, either directly or indirectly through a chain of partnerships.

(e) Notification requirements. Reporting rules similar to those that apply to the partners and the partnership under section 751(a) shall apply in the case of sales or exchanges of interests in a partnership, S corporation, or trust that cause holders of such interests to recognize collectibles gain and in the case of sales or exchanges of interests in a partnership that cause holders of such interests to recognize section 1250 capital gain. See § 1.751-1(a)(3).

(f) Examples. The following examples illustrate the requirements of this section:

Example (1). Collectibles gain.

(i) A and B are equal partners in a personal service partnership (PRS). B transfers B's interest in PRS to T for $15,000 when PRS's balance sheet (reflecting a cash receipts and disbursements method of accounting) is as follows:

ASSETS	Adjusted basis	Market value
Cash	$ 3,000	$ 3,000
Loans Owed to Partnership	10,000	10,000
Collectibles	1,000	3,000
Other Capital Assets	6,000	2,000
Capital Assets	7,000	5,000
Unrealized Receivables	0	14,000
Total	20,000	32,000

	LIABILITIES AND CAPITAL	
	Adjusted basis	Market value
Liabilities	2,000	2,000
Capital:		
A...........	9,000	15,000
B...........	9,000	15,000
Total	20,000	32,000

(ii) At the time of the transfer, B has held the interest in PRS for more than one year, and B's basis for the partnership interest is $10,000 ($9,000 plus $1,000, B's share of partnership liabilities). None of the property owned by PRS is section 704(c) property. The total amount realized by B is $16,000, consisting of the cash received, $15,000, plus $1,000, B's share of the partnership liabilities assumed by T. See section 752. B's undivided one-half interest in PRS includes a one-half interest in the partnership's unrealized receivables and a one-half interest in the partnership's collectibles.

(iii) If PRS were to sell all of its section 751 property in a fully taxable transaction for cash equal to the fair market value of the assets immediately prior to the transfer of B's partnership interest to T, B would be allocated $7,000 of ordinary income from the sale of PRS's unrealized receivables. Therefore, B will recognize $7,000 of ordinary income with respect to the unrealized receivables. The difference between the amount of capital gain or loss that the partner would realize in the absence of section 751 ($6,000) and the amount of ordinary income or loss determined under § 1.751-1(a)(2) ($7,000) is the partner's capital gain or loss on the sale of the partnership interest under section 741. In this case, the transferor has a $1,000 pre-look-through long-term capital loss.

(iv) If PRS were to sell all of its collectibles in a fully taxable transaction for cash equal to the fair market value of the assets immediately prior to the transfer of B's partnership interest to T, B would be allocated $1,000 of gain from the sale of the collectibles. Therefore, B will recognize $1,000 of collectibles gain on account of the collectibles held by PRS.

(v) The difference between the transferor's pre-look-through long-term capital gain or loss (-$1,000) and the look-through capital gain determined under this section ($1,000) is the transferor's residual long-term capital gain or loss on the sale of the partnership interest. Under these facts, B will recognize a $2,000 residual long-term capital loss on account of the sale or exchange of the interest in PRS.

Example (2). Special allocations. Assume the same facts as in Example 1, except that under the partnership agreement, all gain from the sale of the collectibles is specially allocated to B, and B transfers B's interest to T for $16,000. All items of income, gain, loss, or deduction of PRS, other than the gain from the collectibles, are divided equally between A and B. Under these facts, B's amount realized is $17,000, consisting of the cash received, $16,000, plus $1,000, B's share of the partnership liabilities assumed by T. See section 752. B will recognize $7,000 of ordinary income with respect to the unrealized receivables (determined under § 1.751-1(a)(2)). Accordingly, B's pre-look-through long-term capital gain would be $0. If PRS were to sell all of its collectibles in a fully taxable transaction for cash equal to the fair market value of the assets immediately prior to the transfer of B's partnership interest to T, B would be allocated $2,000 of gain from the sale of the collectibles. Therefore, B will recognize $2,000 of collectibles gain on account of the collectibles held by PRS. B will recognize a $2,000 residual long-term capital loss on account of the sale of B's interest in PRS.

Example (3). Net collectibles loss ignored. Assume the same facts as in Example 1, except that the collectibles held by PRS have an adjusted basis of $3,000 and a fair market value of $1,000, and the other capital assets have an adjusted basis of $4,000 and a fair market value of $4,000. (The total adjusted basis and fair market value of the partnership's capital assets are the same as in Example 1.) If PRS were to sell all of its collectibles in a fully taxable transaction for cash equal to the fair market value of the assets immediately prior to the transfer of B's partnership interest to T, B would be allocated $1,000 of loss from the sale of the collectibles. Because none of the gain from the sale of the interest in PRS is attributable to unrealized appreciation in the value of collectibles held by PRS, the net loss in collectibles held by PRS is not recognized at the time B transfers the interest in PRS. B will recognize $7,000 of ordinary income (determined under § 1.751-1(a)(2)) and a $1,000 long-term capital loss on account of the sale of B's interest in PRS.

Example (4). Collectibles gain in an S corporation.

(i) A corporation (X) has always been an S corporation and is owned by individuals A, B, and C. In 1996, X invested in antiques. Subsequent to their purchase, the antiques appreciated in value by $300. A owns one-third of the shares of X stock and has held that stock for more than one year. A's adjusted basis in the X stock is $100. If A were to sell all of A's X stock to T for $150, A would realize $50 of pre-look-through long-term capital gain.

(ii) If X were to sell its antiques in a fully taxable transaction for cash equal to the fair market value of the assets immediately before the transfer to T, A would be allocated $100 of gain on account of the sale. Therefore, A will recognize $100 of collectibles gain (look-through capital gain) on account of the collectibles held by X.

(iii) The difference between the transferor's pre-look-through long-term capital gain or loss ($50) and the look-through capital gain determined under this section ($100) is the transferor's residual long-term capital gain or loss on the sale of the S corporation stock. Under these facts, A will recognize $100 of collectibles gain and a $50 residual long-term capital loss on account of the sale of A's interest in X.

Example (5). Sale or exchange of partnership interest where part of the interest has a short-term holding period.

(i) A, B, and C form an equal partnership (PRS). In connection with the formation, A contributes $5,000 in cash and a capital asset with a fair market value of $5,000 and a basis of $2,000; B contributes $7,000 in cash and a collectible with a fair market value of $3,000 and a basis of $3,000; and C contributes $10,000 in cash. At the time of the contribution, A had held the contributed property for two years. Six months later, when A's basis in PRS is $7,000, A transfers A's interest in PRS to T for $14,000 at a time when PRS's balance sheet (reflecting a cash receipts and disbursements method of accounting) is as follows:

	ASSETS	
	Adjusted basis	Market value
Cash	$22,000	$22,000
Unrealized Receivables	0	6,000
Capital Asset	2,000	5,000
Collectible	3,000	9,000
Capital Assets	5,000	14,000

Total	27,000	42,000

(ii) Although at the time of the transfer A has not held A's interest in PRS for more than one year, 50 percent of the fair market value of A's interest in PRS was received in exchange for a capital asset with a long-term holding period. Therefore, 50 percent of A's interest in PRS has a long-term holding period. See § 1.1223-3(b)(1).

(iii) If PRS were to sell all of its section 751 property in a fully taxable transaction immediately before A's transfer of the partnership interest, A would be allocated $2,000 of ordinary income. Accordingly, A will recognize $2,000 ordinary income and $5,000 ($7,000-$2,000) of capital gain on account of the transfer to T of A's interest in PRS. Fifty percent ($2,500) of that gain is long-term capital gain and 50 percent ($2,500) is short-term capital gain. See § 1.1223-3(c)(1).

(iv) If the collectible were sold or exchanged in a fully taxable transaction immediately before A's transfer of the partnership interest, A would be allocated $2,000 of gain attributable to the collectible. The gain attributable to the collectible that is allocable to the portion of the transferred interest in PRS with a long-term holding period is $1,000 (50 percent of $2,000). Accordingly, A will recognize $1,000 of collectibles gain on account of the transfer of A's interest in PRS.

(v) The difference between the amount of pre-look-through long-term capital gain or loss ($2,500) and the look-through capital gain ($1,000) is the amount of residual long-term capital gain or loss that A will recognize on account of the transfer of A's interest in PRS. Under these facts, A will recognize a residual long-term capital gain of $1,500 and a short-term capital gain of $2,500.

(g) Effective date. This section applies to transfers of interests in partnerships, S corporations, and trusts that occur on or after September 21, 2000.

T.D. 8902, 9/20/2000.

§ 1.1(i)-1T Questions and answers relating to the tax on unearned income of certain minor children (temporary).

Caution: The Treasury has not yet amended Reg § 1.1(i)-1T to reflect changes made by P.L. 110-28, P.L. 109-222, P.L. 108-311, P.L. 108-27, P.L. 107-16.

In general.

Q-1. To whom does section 1(i) apply?

A-1. Section 1(i) applies to any child who is under 14 years of age at the close of the taxable year, who has at least one living parent at the close of the taxable year, and who recognizes over $1,000 of unearned income during the taxable year.

Q-2. What is the effective date of section 1(i)?

A-2. Section 1(i) applies to taxable years of the child beginning after December 31, 1986.

Computation of tax.

Q-3. What is the amount of tax imposed by section 1 on a child to whom section 1(i) applies?

A-3. In the case of a child to whom section 1(i) applies, the amount of tax imposed by section 1 equals the greater of (A) the tax imposed by section 1 without regard to section 1(i) or (B) the sum of the tax that would be imposed by section 1 if the child's taxable income was reduced by the child's net unearned income, plus the child's share of the allocable parental tax.

Q-4. What is the allocable parental tax?

A-4. The allocable parental tax is the excess of (A) the tax that would be imposed by section 1 on the sum of the parent's taxable income plus the net unearned income of all children of such parent to whom section 1(i) applies, over (B) the tax imposed by section 1 on the parent's taxable income. Thus, the allocable parental tax is not computed with reference to unearned income of a child over 14 or a child under 14 with less than $1,000 of unearned income. *See* A-10 through A-13 for rules regarding the determination of the parent(s) whose taxable income is taken into account under section 1(i). *See* A-14 for rules regarding the determination of children of the parent whose net unearned income is taken into account under section 1(i).

Q-5. What is the child's share of the allocable parental tax?

A-5. The child's share of the allocable parental tax is an amount that bears the same ratio to the total allocable parental tax as the child's net unearned income bears to the total net unearned income of all children of such parent to whom section 1(i) applies. See A-14.

Example (1). During 1988, D, a 12 year old, receives $5,000 of unearned income and no earned income. D has no itemized deductions and is not eligible for a personal exemption. D's parents have two other children, E, a 15 year old, and F, a 10 year old. E has $10,000 of unearned income and F has $100 of unearned income. D's parents file a joint return for 1988 and report taxable income of $70,000. Neither D's nor his parent's taxable income is attributable to net capital gain. D's tax liability for 1988, determined without regard to section 1(i), is $675 on $4,500 of taxable income ($5,000 less $500 allowable standard deduction). In applying section 1(i), D's tax would be equal to the sum of (A) the tax that would be imposed on D's taxable income if it were reduced by any net unearned income, plus (B) D's share of the allocable parental tax. Only D's unearned income is taken into account in determining the allocable parental tax because E is over 14 and F has less than $1,000 of unearned income. *See* A-4. D's net unearned income is $4,000 ($4,500 taxable unearned income less $500). The tax imposed on D's taxable income as reduced by D's net unearned income is $75 ($500 × 15%). The allocable parental tax is $1,225, the excess of $16,957.50 (the tax on $74,000, the parent's taxable income plus D's net unearned income) over $15,732.50 (the tax on $70,000, the parent's taxable income). *See* A-4. Thus, D's tax under section 1(i)(1)(B) is $1,300 ($1,225 + $75). Since this amount is greater than the amount of D's tax liability as determined without regard to section 1(i), the amount of tax imposed on D for 1988 is $1,300. *See* A-3.

Example (2). H and W have 3 children, A, B, and C, who are all under 14 years of age. For the taxable year 1988, H and W file a joint return and report taxable income of $129,750. The tax imposed by section 1 on H and W is $35,355. A has $5,000 of net unearned income and B and C each have $2,500 of net unearned income during 1988. The allocable parental tax imposed on A, B, and C's combined net unearned income of $10,000 is $3,300. This tax is the excess of $38,655, which is the tax imposed by section 1 on $139,750 ($129,750 + 10,000), over $35,355 (the tax imposed by section 1 on H and W's taxable income of $129,750). *See* A-4. Each child's share of the allocable parental tax is an amount that bears the same ratio to the total allocable parental tax as the child's net unearned income bears to the total net unearned income of A, B, and C. Thus, A's share of the allocable parental tax is $1,650

$$\left(\frac{5,000}{10,000} \times 3,300\right)$$

and B and C's share of the tax is $825

$$\left(\frac{2,500}{10,000} \times 3,300\right)$$

each. *See* A-5.

Definition of net unearned income.

Q-6. What is net unearned income?

A-6. Net unearned income is the excess of the portion of adjusted gross income for the taxable year that is not "earned income" as defined in section 911(d)(2) (income that is not attributable to wages, salaries, or other amounts received as compensation for personal services), over the sum of the standard deduction amount provided for under section 63(c)(5)(A) ($500 for 1987 and 1988; adjusted for inflation thereafter), plus the greater of (A) $500 (adjusted for inflation after 1988) or (B) the amount of allowable itemized deductions that are directly connected with the production of unearned income. A child's net unearned income for any taxable year shall not exceed the child's taxable income for such year.

Example (3). A is a child who is under 14 years of age at the end of the taxable year 1987. Both of A's parents are alive at this time. During 1987, A receives $3,000 of interest from a bank savings account and earns $1,000 from a paper route and performing odd jobs. A has no itemized deductions for 1987. A's standard deduction is $1,000, which is an amount equal to A's earned income for 1987. Of this amount, $500 is applied against A's unearned income and the remaining $500 is applied against A's earned income. Thus, A's $500 of taxable earned income ($1,000 less the remaining $500 of the standard deduction) is taxed without regard to section 1(i); A has $2,500 of taxable unearned income ($3,000 gross unearned income less $500 of the standard deduction) of which $500 is taxed without regard to section 1(i). The remaining $2,000 of taxable unearned income is A's net unearned income and is taxed under section 1(i).

Example (4). B is a child who is subject to tax under section 1(i). B has $400 of earned income and $2,000 of unearned income. B has itemized deductions of $800 (net of the 2 percent of adjusted gross income (AGI) floor on miscellaneous itemized deductions under section 67) of which $200 are directly connected with the production of unearned income. The amount of itemized deductions that B may apply against unearned income is equal to the greater of $500 or the deductions directly connected with the production of unearned income. *See* A-6. Thus, $500 of B's itemized deductions are applied against the $2,000 of unearned income and the remaining $300 of deductions are applied against earned income. As a result, B has taxable earned income of $100 and taxable unearned income of $1,500. Of these amounts, all of the earned income and $500 of the unearned income are taxed without regard to section 1(i). The remaining $1,000 of unearned income is net unearned income and is taxed under section 1(i).

Unearned income subject to tax under section 1(i).

Q-7. Will a child be subject to tax under section 1(i) on net unearned income (as defined in section 1(i) (4) and A-6 of this section) that is attributable to property transferred to the child prior to 1987?

A-7. Yes. The tax imposed by section 1(i) on a child's net unearned income applies to any net unearned income of the child for taxable years beginning after December 31, 1986, regardless of when the underlying assets were transferred to the child.

Q-8. Will a child be subject to tax under section 1(i) on net unearned income that is attributable to gifts from persons other than the child's parents or attributable to assets resulting from the child's earned income?

A-8. Yes. The tax imposed by section 1(i) applies to all net unearned income of the child, regardless of the source of the assets that produced such income. Thus, the rules of section 1(i) apply to income attributable to gifts not only from the parents but also from any other source, such as the child's grandparents. Section 1(i) also applies to unearned income derived with respect to assets resulting from earned income of the child, such as interest earned on bank deposits.

Example (5). A is a child who is under 14 years of age at the end of the taxable year beginning on January 1, 1987. Both of A's parents are alive at the end of the taxable year. During 1987, A receives $2,000 in interest from his bank account and $1,500 from a paper route. Some of the interest earned by A from the bank account is attributable to A's paper route earnings that were deposited in the account. The balance of the account is attributable to cash gifts from A's parents and grandparents and interest earned prior to 1987. Some cash gifts were received by A prior to 1987. A has no itemized deductions and is eligible to be claimed as a dependent on his parent's return. Therefore, for the taxable year 1987, A's standard deduction is $1,500, the amount of A's earned income. Of this standard deduction amount, $500 is allocated against unearned income and $1,000 is allocated against earned income. A's taxable unearned income is $1,500 of which $500 is taxed without regard to section 1(i). The remaining taxable unearned income of $1,000 is net unearned income and is taxed under section 1(i). The fact that some of A's unearned income is attributable to interest on principal created by earned income and gifts from persons other than A's parents or that some of the unearned income is attributable to property transferred to A prior to 1987, will not affect the tax treatment of this income under section 1(i). *See* A-8.

Q-9. For purposes of section 1(i), does income which is not earned income (as defined in section 911(d) (2)) include social security benefits or pension benefits that are paid to the child?

A-9. Yes. For purposes of section 1(i), earned income (as defined in section 911(d)(2)) does not include any social security or pension benefits paid to the child. Thus, such amounts are included in unearned income to the extent they are includible in the child's gross income.

Determination of the parent's taxable income.

Q-10. If a child's parents file a joint return, what is the taxable income that must taken into account by the child in determining tax liability under section 1(i)?

A-10. In the case of parents who file a joint return, the parental taxable income to be taken into account in determining the tax liability of a child is the total taxable income shown on the joint return.

Q-11. If a child's parents are married and file separate tax returns, which parent's taxable income must be taken into account by the child in determining tax liability under section 1(i)?

A-11. For purposes of determining the tax liability of a child under section 1(i), where such child's parents are married and file separate tax returns, the parent whose taxable income is the greater of the two for the taxable year shall be taken into account.

Q-12. If the parents of a child are divorced, legally separated, or treated as not married under section 7703(b), which parent's taxable income is taken into account in computing the child's tax liability?

A-12. If the child's parents are divorced, legally separated, or treated as not married under section 7703(b), the taxable income of the custodial parent (within the meaning of section 152(e)) of the child is taken into account under section 1(i) in determining the child's tax liability.

Q-13. If a parent whose taxable income must be taken into account in determining a child's tax liability under section 1(i) files a joint return with a spouse who is not a parent of the child, what taxable income must the child take into account?

A-13. The amount of a parent's taxable income that a child must take into account for purposes of section 1(i) where the parent files a joint return with a spouse who is not a parent of the child is the total taxable income shown on such joint return.

Children of the parent.

Q-14. In determining a child's share of the allocable parental tax, is the net unearned income of legally adopted children, children related to such child by half-blood, or children from a prior marriage of the spouse of such child's parent taken into account in addition to the natural children of such child's parent?

A-14. Yes. In determining a child's share of the allocable parental tax, the net unearned income of all children subject to tax under section 1(i) and who use the same parent's taxable income as such child to determine their tax liability under section 1(i) must be taken into account. Such children are taken into account regardless of whether they are adopted by the parent, related to such child by half-blood, or are children from a prior marriage of the spouse of such child's parent.

Rules regarding income from a trust or similar instrument.

Q-15. Will the unearned income of a child who is subject to section 1(i) that is attributable to gifts given to the child under the Uniform Gift to Minors Act (UGMA) be subject to tax under section 1(i)?

A-15. Yes. A gift under the UGMA vests legal title to the property in the child although an adult custodian is given certain rights to deal with the property until the child attains majority. Any unearned income attributable to such a gift is the child's unearned income and is subject to tax under section 1(i), whether distributed to the child or not.

Q-16. Will a child who is a beneficiary of a trust be required to take into account the income of a trust in determining the child's tax liability under section 1(i)?

A-16. The income of a trust must be taken into account for purposes of determining the tax liability of a beneficiary who is subject to section 1(i) only to the extent it is included in the child's gross income for the taxable year under sections 652(a) or 662(a). Thus, income from a trust for the fiscal taxable year of a trust ending during 1987, that is included in the gross income of a child who is subject to section 1(i) and who has a calendar taxable year, will be subject to tax under section 1(i) for the child's 1987 taxable year.

Subsequent adjustments.

Q-17. What effect will a subsequent adjustment to a parent's taxable income have on the child's tax liability if such parent's taxable income was used to determine the child's tax liability under section 1(i) for the same taxable year?

A-17. If the parent's taxable income is adjusted and if, for the same taxable year as the adjustment, the child paid tax determined under section 1(i) with reference to that parent's taxable income, then the child's tax liability under section 1(i) must be recomputed using the parent's taxable income as adjusted.

Q-18. In the case where more than one child who is subject to section 1(i) uses the same parent's taxable income to determine their allocable parental tax, what effect will a subsequent adjustment to the net unearned income of one child have on the other child's share of the allocable parental tax?

A-18. If, for the same taxable year, more than one child uses the same parent's taxable income to determine their share of the allocable parental tax and a subsequent adjustment is made to one or more of such children's net unearned income, each child's share of the allocable parental tax must be recomputed using the combined net unearned income of all such children as adjusted.

Q-19. If a recomputation of a child's tax under section 1(i), as a result of an adjustment to the taxable income of the child's parents or another child's net unearned income, results in additional tax being imposed by section 1(i) on the child, is the child subject to interest and penalties on such additional tax?

A-19. Any additional tax resulting from an adjustment to the taxable income of the child's parents or the net unearned income of another child shall be treated as an underpayment of tax and interest shall be imposed on such underpayment as provided in section 6601. However, the child shall not be liable for any penalties on the underpayment resulting from additional tax being imposed under section 1 (i) due to such an adjustment.

Example (6). D and M are the parents of C, a child under the age of 14. D and M file a joint return for 1988 and report taxable income of $69,900. C has unearned income of $3,000 and no itemized deductions for 1988. C properly reports a total tax liability of $635 for 1988. This amount is the sum of the allocable parental tax of $560 on C's net unearned income of $2,000 (the excess of $3,000 over the sum of $500 standard deduction and the first $500 of taxable unearned income) plus $75 (the tax imposed on C's first $500 of taxable unearned income). *See* A-3. One year later, D and M's 1988 tax return is adjusted on audit by adding an additional $1,000 of taxable income. No adjustment is made to the amount reported as C's net unearned income for 1988. However, the adjustment to D and M's taxable income causes C's tax liability under section 1 (i) for 1988 to be increased by $50 as a result of the phase-out of the 15 percent rate bracket. *See* A-20. In addition to this further tax liability, C will be liable for interest on the $50. However, C will not have to pay any penalty on the delinquent amount.

Miscellaneous rules.

Q-20. Does the phase-out of the parent's 15 percent rate bracket and personal exemptions under section 1 (g), if applicable, have any effect on the calculation of the allocable parental tax imposed on a child's net unearned income under section 1(i)?

A-20. Yes. Any phase-out of the parent's 15 percent rate bracket or personal exemptions under section 1(g) is given full effect in determining the tax that would be imposed on the sum of the parent's taxable income and the total net unearned income of all children of the parent. Thus, any additional tax on a child's net unearned income resulting from the phase-out of the 15 percent rate bracket and the personal exemptions is reflected in the tax liability of the child.

Q-21. For purposes of calculating a parent's tax liability or the allocable parental tax imposed on a child, are other phase-outs, limitations, or floors on deductions or credits, such as the phase-out of the $25,000 passive loss allowance for rental real estate activities under section 469(i)(3) or the 2 percent of AGI floor on miscellaneous itemized deductions under section 67, affected by the addition of a child's net unearned income to the parent's taxable income?

A-21. No. A child's net unearned income is not taken into account in computing any deduction or credit for purposes of determining the parent's tax liability or the child's allocable parental tax. Thus, for example, although the amounts allowable to the parent as a charitable contribution deduction, medical expense deduction, section 212 deduction, or a miscellaneous itemized deduction are affected by the amount of the parent's adjusted gross income, the amount of these deductions that is allowed does not change as a result of the application of section 1(i) because the amount of the parent's adjusted gross income does not include the child's net unearned income. Similarly, the amount of itemized deductions that is allowed to a child does not change as a result of section 1(i) because section 1(i) only affects the amount of tax liability and not the child's adjusted gross income.

Q-22. If a child is unable to obtain information concerning the tax return of the child's parents directly from such parents, how may the child obtain information from the parent's tax return which is necessary to determine the child's tax liability under section 1(i)?

A-22. Under section 6103(e)(1)(A)(iv), a return of a parent shall, upon written request, be open to inspection or disclosure to a child of that individual (or the child's legal representative) to the extent necessary to comply with section 1(i). Thus, a child may request the Internal Revenue Service to disclose sufficient tax information about the parent to the child so that the child can properly file his or her return.

T.D. 8158, 9/4/87.

§ 1.2-1 Tax in case of joint return of husband and wife or the return of a surviving spouse.

Caution: The Treasury has not yet amended Reg § 1.2-1 to reflect changes made by P.L. 108-311, P.L. 99-514, P.L. 97-34, P.L. 95-600, P.L. 95-30, P.L. 94-455, P.L. 94-164, P.L. 94-12.

(a) Taxable year ending before January 1, 1971. *(1)* For taxable years ending before January 1, 1971, in the case of a joint return of husband and wife, or the return of a surviving spouse as defined in section 2(b), the tax imposed by section 1 shall be twice the tax that would be imposed if the taxable income were reduced by one-half. For rules relating to the filing of joint returns of husband and wife, see section 6013 and the regulations thereunder.

(2) The method of computing, under section 2(a), the tax of husband and wife in the case of a joint return, or the tax of a surviving spouse, is as follows:

(i) First, the taxable income is reduced by one-half. Second, the tax is determined as provided by section 1 by using the taxable income so reduced. Third, the tax so determined, which is the tax that would be determined if the taxable income were reduced by one-half, is then multiplied by two to produce the tax imposed in the case of the joint return or the return of a surviving spouse, subject, however, to the allowance of any credits against the tax under the provisions of sections 31 through 38 and the regulations thereunder.

(ii) The limitation under section 1(c) of the tax to an amount not in excess of a specified percent of the taxable income for the taxable year is to be applied before the third step above, that is, the limitation to be applied upon the tax is determined as the applicable specified percent of one-half of the taxable income for the taxable year (such one-half of the taxable income being the actual aggregate taxable income of the spouses, or the total taxable income of the surviving spouse, as the case may be, reduced by one-half). For the percent applicable in determining the limitation of the tax under section 1(c), see § 1.1-2(a). After such limitation is applied, then the tax so limited is multiplied by two as provided in section 2(a) (the third step above).

(iii) The following computation illustrates the method of application of section 2(a) in the determination of the tax of a husband and wife filing a joint return for the calendar year 1965. If the combined gross income is $8,200, and the only deductions are the two exemptions of the taxpayers under section 151(b) and the standard deduction under section 141, the tax on the joint return for 1965, without regard to any credits against the tax, is $1,034.20 determined as follows:

1. Gross income		$8,200.00
2. Less:		
Standard deduction, section 141	$ 820	
Deduction for personal exemption, section 151	1,200	2,020.00
3. Taxable income		6,180.00
4. Taxable income reduced by one-half		3,090.00
5. Tax computed by the tax table provided under section 1(a)(2) ($310 plus 19 percent of excess over $2,000)		517.10
6. Twice the tax in item 5		1,034.20

(b) Taxable years beginning after December 31, 1970. *(1)* For taxable years beginning after December 31, 1970, in the case of a joint return of husband and wife, or the return of a surviving spouse as defined in section 2(a) of the Code as amended by the Tax Reform Act of 1969, the tax shall be determined in accordance with the table contained in section 1(a) of the Code as so amended. For rules relating to the filing of joint returns of husband and wife see section 6013 as amended and the regulations thereunder.

(2) The following computation illustrates the method of computing the tax of a husband and wife filing a joint return for calendar year 1971. If the combined gross income is $8,200, and the only deductions are the two exemptions of the taxpayers under section 151(b), as amended, and the standard deduction under section 141, as amended, the tax on the joint return for 1971, without regard to any credits against the tax, is $968.46, determined as follows:

1. Gross income		$8,200.00
2. Less:		
Standard deduction, section 141	$1,066.00	
Deduction for personal exemption, section 151	1,300.00	2,366.00
3. Taxable income		5,834.00
4. Tax computed by the tax table provided under section 1(a) ($620 plus 19 percent of excess over $4,000)		968.46

(3) The limitation under section 1348 with respect to the maximum rate of tax on earned income shall apply to a married individual only if such individual and his spouse file a joint return for the taxable year.

(c) Death of a spouse. If a joint return of a husband and wife is filed under the provisions of section 6013 and if the husband and wife have different taxable years solely because of the death of either spouse, the taxable year of the deceased spouse covered by the joint return shall, for the purpose of the computation of the tax in respect of such joint return, be deemed to have ended on the date of the closing of the surviving spouse's taxable year.

(d) Computation of optional tax. For computation of optional tax in the case of a joint return or the return of a surviving spouse, see section 3 and the regulations thereunder.

(e) Change in rates. For treatment of taxable years during which a change in the tax occurs see section 21 and the regulations thereunder.

T.D. 6161, 2/3/56, amend T.D. 7117, 5/24/71.

§ 1.2-2 Definitions and special rules.

Caution: The Treasury has not yet amended Reg § 1.2-2 to reflect changes made by 108-311, P.L. 107-147, P.L. 104-117, P.L. 99-514, P.L. 97-448, P.L. 94-569, P.L. 93-597.

(a) Surviving spouse. *(1)* If a taxpayer is eligible to file a joint return under the Internal Revenue Code of 1954 without regard to section 6013(a)(3) thereof for the taxable year in which his spouse dies, his return for each of the next 2 taxable years following the year of the death of the spouse shall be treated as a joint return for all purposes if all three of the following requirements are satisfied:

(i) He has not remarried before the close of the taxable year the return for which is sought to be treated as a joint return, and

(ii) He maintains as his home a household which constitutes for the taxable year the principal place of abode as a member of such household of a person who is (whether by blood or adoption) a son, stepson, daughter, or stepdaughter of the taxpayer, and

(iii) He is entitled for the taxable year to a deduction under section 151 (relating to deductions for dependents) with respect to such son, stepson, daughter, or stepdaughter.

(2) See paragraphs (c)(1) and (d) of this section for rules for the determination of when the taxpayer maintains as his home a household which constitutes for the taxable year the principal place of abode, as a member of such household, of another person.

(3) If the taxpayer does not qualify as a surviving spouse he may nevertheless qualify as a head of a household if he meets the requirements of § 1.2-2(b).

(4) The following example illustrates the provisions relating to a surviving spouse:

Example. Assume that the taxpayer meets the requirements of this paragraph for the years 1967 through 1971, and that the taxpayer, whose wife died during 1966 while married to him, remarried in 1968. In 1969, the taxpayer's second wife died while married to him, and he remained single thereafter. For 1967 the taxpayer will qualify as a surviving spouse, provided that neither the taxpayer nor the first wife was a nonresident alien at any time during 1966 and that she (immediately prior to her death) did not have a taxable year different from that of the taxpayer. For 1968 the taxpayer does not qualify as a surviving spouse because he remarried before the close of the taxable year. The taxpayer will qualify as a surviving spouse for 1970 and 1971, provided that neither the taxpayer nor the second wife was a nonresident alien at any time during 1969 and that she (immediately prior to her death) did not have a taxable year different from that of the taxpayer. On the other hand, if the taxpayer, in 1969, was divorced or legally separated from his second wife, the taxpayer will not qualify as a surviving spouse for 1970 or 1971, since he could not have filed a joint return for 1969 (the year in which his second wife died).

(b) Head of household. *(1)* A taxpayer shall be considered the head of a household if, and only if, he is not married at the close of his taxable year, is not a surviving spouse (as defined in paragraph (a) of this section), and (i) maintains as his home a household which constitutes for such taxable year the principal place of abode, as a member of such household, of at least one of the individuals described in subparagraph (3), or (ii) maintains (whether or not as his home) a household which constitutes for such taxable year the principal place of abode of one of the individuals described in subparagraph (4).

(2) Under no circumstances shall the same person be used to qualify more than one taxpayer as the head of a household for the same taxable year.

(3) Any of the following persons may qualify the taxpayer as a head of a household:

(i) A son, stepson, daughter, or stepdaughter of the taxpayer, or a descendant of a son or daughter of the taxpayer. For the purpose of determining whether any of the stated relationships exist, a legally adopted child of a person is considered a child of such person by blood. If any such person is not married at the close of the taxable year of the taxpayer, the taxpayer may qualify as the head of a household by reason of such person even though the taxpayer may not claim a deduction for such person under section 151, for example, because the taxpayer does not furnish more than half of the support of such person. However, if any such person is married at the close of the taxable year of the taxpayer, the taxpayer may qualify as the head of a household by reason of such person only if the taxpayer is entitled to a deduction for such person under section 151 and the regulations thereunder. In applying the preceding sentence there shall be disregarded any such person for whom a deduction is allowed under section 151 only by reason of section 152(c) (relating to persons covered by a multiple support agreement).

(ii) Any other person who is a dependent of the taxpayer, if the taxpayer is entitled to a deduction for the taxable year for such person under section 151 and paragraphs (3) through (8) of section 152(a) and the regulations thereunder. Under section 151 the taxpayer may be entitled to a deduction for any of the following persons:

(a) His brother, sister, stepbrother, or stepsister;

(b) His father or mother, or an ancestor of either;

(c) His stepfather or stepmother;

(d) A son or a daughter of his brother or sister;

(e) A brother or sister of his father or mother; or

(f) His son-in-law, daughter-in-law, father-in-law, mother-in-law, brother-in-law, or sister-in-law;

if such person has a gross income of less than the amount determined pursuant to § 1.151-2 applicable to the calendar year in which the taxable year of the taxpayer begins, if the taxpayer supplies more than one-half of the support of such person for such calendar year and if such person does not make a joint return with his spouse for the taxable year beginning in such calendar year. The taxpayer may not be considered to be a head of a household by reason of any person for whom a deduction is allowed under section 151 only by reason of sections 152(a)(9), 152(a)(10), or 152(c) (relating to persons not related to the taxpayer, persons receiving institutional care, and persons covered by multiple support agreements).

(4) The father or mother of the taxpayer may qualify the taxpayer as a head of a household, but only if the taxpayer is entitled to a deduction for the taxable year for such father or mother under section 151 (determined without regard to section 152(c)). For example, an unmarried taxpayer who maintains a home for his widowed mother may not qualify as the head of a household by reason of his maintenance of a home for his mother if his mother has gross income equal to or in excess of the amount determined pursuant to § 1.151-2 applicable to the calendar year in which the taxable year of the taxpayer begins, or if he does not furnish more than one-half of the support of his mother for such calendar year. For this purpose, a person who legally adopted the taxpayer is considered the father or mother of the taxpayer.

(5) For the purpose of this paragraph, the status of the taxpayer shall be determined as of the close of the taxpayer's taxable year. A taxpayer shall be considered as not married if at the close of his taxable year he is legally separated from his spouse under a decree of divorce or separate maintenance, or if at any time during the taxable year the spouse to whom the taxpayer is married at the close of his taxable year was a nonresident alien. A taxpayer shall be considered married at the close of his taxable year if his spouse (other than a spouse who is a nonresident alien) dies during such year.

(6) If the taxpayer is a nonresident alien during any part of the taxable year he may not qualify as a head of a household even though he may comply with the other provisions of this paragraph. See the regulations prescribed under section 871 for a definition of nonresident alien.

(c) Household. *(1)* In order for a taxpayer to be considered as maintaining a household by reason of any individual described in paragraph (a)(1) or (b)(3) of this section, the household must actually constitute the home of the taxpayer for his taxable year. A physical change in the location of such home will not prevent a taxpayer from qualifying as a head of a household. Such home must also constitute the principal place of abode of at least one of the persons specified in such paragraph (a)(1) or (b)(3) of this section. It is not sufficient that the taxpayer maintain the household without being its occupant. The taxpayer and such other person must occupy the household for the entire taxable year of the taxpayer. However, the fact that such other person is born or dies within the taxable year will not prevent the taxpayer from qualifying as a head of household if the household constitutes the principal place of abode of such other person for the remaining or preceding part of such taxable year. The taxpayer and such other person will be considered as occupying the household for such entire taxable year notwithstanding temporary absences from the household due to special circumstances. A nonpermanent failure to occupy the common abode by reason of illness, education, business, vacation, military service, or a custody agreement under which a child or stepchild is absent for less than 6 months in the taxable year of the taxpayer, shall be considered temporary absence due to special circumstances. Such absence will not prevent the taxpayer from being considered as maintaining a household if (i) it is reasonable to assume that the taxpayer or such other person will return to the household, and (ii) the taxpayer continues to maintain such household or a substantially equivalent household in anticipation of such return.

(2) In order for a taxpayer to be considered as maintaining a household by reason of any individual described in paragraph (b)(4) of this section, the household must actually constitute the principal place of abode of the taxpayer's dependent father or mother, or both of them. It is not, however, necessary for the purposes of such subparagraph for the taxpayer also to reside in such place of abode. A physical change in the location of such home will not prevent a taxpayer from qualifying as a head of a household. The father or mother of the taxpayer, however, must occupy the household for the entire taxable year of the taxpayer. They will be considered as occupying the household for such entire year notwithstanding temporary absences from the household due to special circumstances. For example, a nonpermanent failure to occupy the household by reason of illness or vacation shall be considered temporary absence due to special circumstances. Such absence will not prevent the taxpayer from qualifying as the head of a household if (i) it is reasonable to assume that such person will return to the household, and (ii) the taxpayer continues to maintain such household or a substantially equivalent household in anticipation of such return. However, the fact that the father or mother of the taxpayer dies within the year will not prevent the taxpayer from qualifying as a head of a household if the household constitutes the principal place of abode of the father or mother for the preceding part of such taxable year.

(d) Cost of maintaining a household. A taxpayer shall be considered as maintaining a household only if he pays more than one-half the cost thereof for his taxable year. The cost of maintaining a household shall be the expenses incurred for the mutual benefit of the occupants thereof by reason of its operation as the principal place of abode of such occupants for such taxable year. The cost of maintaining a household shall not include expenses otherwise incurred. The expenses of maintaining a household include property taxes, mortgage interest, rent, utility charges, upkeep and repairs, property insurance, and food consumed on the premises. Such expenses do not include the cost of clothing, education, medical treatment, vacations, life insurance, and transportation. In addition, the cost of maintaining a household shall not include any amount which represents the value of services rendered in the household by the taxpayer or by a person qualifying the taxpayer as a head of a household or as a surviving spouse.

(e) Certain married individuals living apart. For taxable years beginning after December 31, 1969, an individual who is considered as not married under section 143(b) shall be considered as not married for purposes of determining whether he or she qualifies as a single individual, a married individual, a head of household or a surviving spouse under sections 1 and 2 of the Code.

T.D. 6161, 2/3/56, amend T.D. 6792, 1/24/65, T.D. 7117, 5/24/71.

---

§ 1.3-1 Application of optional tax.

(a) General rules.

(1) For taxable years ending before January 1, 1970, an individual whose adjusted gross income is less than $5,000 (or a husband and wife filing a joint return whose combined adjusted gross income is less than $5,000) may elect to pay

the tax imposed by section 3 in place of the tax imposed by section 1 (a) or (b). For taxable years beginning after December 31, 1969 and before January 1, 1971 an individual whose adjusted gross income is less than $10,000 (or a husband and wife filing a joint return whose combined adjusted gross income is less than $10,000) may elect to pay the tax imposed by section 3 as amended by the Tax Reform Act of 1969 in place of the tax imposed by section 1 (a) or (b). For taxable years beginning after December 31, 1970 an individual whose adjusted gross income is less than $10,000 (or a husband and wife filing a joint return whose combined adjusted gross income is less than $10,000) may elect to pay the tax imposed by section 3 as amended in place of the tax imposed by section 1 as amended. See § 1.4-2 for the manner of making such election. A taxpayer may make such election regardless of the sources from which his income is derived and regardless of whether his income is computed by the cash method or the accrual method. See section 62 and the regulations thereunder for the determination of adjusted gross income. For the purpose of determining whether a taxpayer may elect to pay the tax under section 3, the amount of the adjusted gross income is controlling, without reference to the number of exemptions to which the taxpayer may be entitled. See section 4 and the regulations thereunder for additional rules applicable to section 3.

(2) The following examples illustrate the rule that section 3 applies only if the adjusted gross income is less than $10,000 ($5,000 for taxable years ending before January 1, 1970).

Example (1). A is employed at a salary of $9,200 for the calendar year 1970. In the course of such employment, he incurred travel expenses of $1,500 for which he was reimbursed during the year. Such items constitute his sole income for 1970. In such case the gross income is $10,700 but the amount of $1,500 is deducted from gross income in the determination of adjusted gross income and thus A's adjusted gross income for 1970 is $9,200. Hence, the adjusted gross income being less than $10,000, he may elect to pay his tax for 1970 under section 3. Similarly, in the case of an individual engaged in trade or business (excluding from the term "engaged in trade or business" the performance of personal services as an employee), there may be deducted from gross income in ascertaining adjusted gross income those expenses directly relating to the carrying on of such trade or business.

Example (2). If B has, as his only income for 1970, a salary of $11,600 and his spouse has no gross income, then B's adjusted gross income is $11,600 (not $11,600 reduced by exemptions of $1,250) and he is not for such year, entitled to pay his tax under section 3. If, however, B has for 1970 a salary of $13,000 and incident to his employment he incurs expenses in the amount of $3,400 for travel, meals, and lodging while away from home, for which he is not reimbursed, the adjusted gross income is $13,000 minus $3,400 or $9,600. In such case his adjusted gross income being less than $10,000, B may elect to pay the tax under section 3. However, if B's wife has adjusted gross income of $400, the total adjusted gross income is $10,000. In such case, if B and his wife file a joint return, they may not elect to pay the optional tax since the combined adjusted gross income is not less than $10,000. B may nevertheless elect to pay the optional tax, but if he makes this election he must file a separate return and, since his wife has gross income, he may not claim an exemption for her in computing the optional tax.

(b) Surviving spouse. The return of a surviving spouse is treated as a joint return for purposes of section 3. See section 2, and the regulations thereunder, with respect to the qualifications of a taxpayer as a surviving spouse. Accordingly, if the taxpayer qualifies as a surviving spouse and elects to pay the optional tax, he shall use the column in the tax table, appropriate to his number of exemptions, provided for cases in which a joint return is filed.

(c) Use of tax table. *(1)* To determine the amount of the tax, the individual ascertains the amount of his adjusted gross income, refers to the appropriate table set forth in section 3 or the regulations thereunder, ascertains the income bracket into which such income falls, and, using the number of exemptions applicable to his case, finds the tax in the vertical column having at the top thereof a number corresponding to the number of exemptions to which the taxpayer is entitled.

(2) Section 3(b) (relating to taxable years beginning after Dec. 31, 1964 and ending before Jan. 1, 1970) contains 5 tables for use in computing the tax. Table I is to be used by a single person who is not a head of household. Table II is to be used by a head of household. Table III is to be used by married persons filing joint returns and by a surviving spouse. Table IV is to be used by married persons filing separate returns using the 10 percent standard deduction. Table V is to be used by married persons filing separate returns using the minimum standard deduction. For an explanation of the standard deduction see section 141 and the regulations thereunder.

(3) 30 tables are provided for use in computing the tax under the Tax Reform Act of 1969. Tables I through XV apply for taxable years beginning after December 31, 1969 and ending before January 1, 1971. Tables XVI through XXX apply for taxable years beginning after December 31, 1970. The standard deduction for Tables I through XV, applicable to taxable years beginning in 1970, is 10 percent. The standard deduction for Tables XVI through XXX, applicable to taxable years beginning in 1971, is 13 percent. For an explanation of the standard deduction and the low income allowance see section 141 as amended by the Tax Reform Act of 1969.

(4) In the case of married persons filing separate returns who qualify to use the optional tax imposed by section 3, such persons shall use the tax imposed by the table for the applicable year in accordance with the rules prescribed by sections 4(c) and 141 and the regulations thereunder governing the use and application of the standard deduction and the low income allowance.

(5) The tax shown in the tax tables set forth in section 3 or the regulations thereunder reflects full income splitting in the case of a joint return (including the return of a surviving spouse) and lesser income splitting in the case of a head of household. Therefore, it is possible for the tax shown in the tables relating to joint returns, or relating to a return of a head of a household, to be lower than that shown in the table for separate returns even though the amounts of adjusted gross income and the number of exemptions are the same.

T.D. 7117, 5/25/71.

§ 1.11-1 Tax on corporations.

Caution: The Treasury has not yet amended Reg § 1.11-1 to reflect changes made by P.L. 103-66, P.L. 100-647, P.L. 100-203, P.L. 99-514, P.L. 98-369, P.L. 97-34, P.L. 95-600, P.L. 95-30, P.L. 94-455, P.L. 94-164.

(a) Every corporation, foreign or domestic, is liable to the tax imposed under section 11 except (1) corporations specifically excepted under such section from such tax; (2) corporations expressly exempt from all taxation under subtitle A of the Code (see section 501); and (3) corporations subject to tax under section 511(a). For taxable years beginning after December 31, 1966, foreign corporations engaged in trade or business in the United States shall be taxable under section 11 only on their taxable income which is effectively connected with the conduct of a trade or business in the United States (see section 882(a)(1)). For definition of the terms "corporation," "domestic," and "foreign," see section 7701(a)(3), (4), and (5), respectively. It is immaterial that a domestic corporation, and for taxable years beginning after December 31, 1966, a foreign corporation engaged in trade or business in the United States, which is subject to the tax imposed by section 11 may derive no income from sources within the United States. The tax imposed by section 11 is payable upon the basis of the returns rendered by the corporations liable thereto, except that in some cases a tax is to be paid at the source of the income. See subchapter A (sections 6001 and following), chapter 61 of the Code, and section 1442.

(b) The tax imposed by section 11 consists of a normal tax and a surtax. The normal tax and the surtax are both computed upon the taxable income of the corporation for the taxable year, that is, upon the gross income of the corporation minus the deductions allowed by chapter 1 of the Code. However, the deduction provided in section 242 for partially tax-exempt interest is not allowed in computing the taxable income subject to the surtax.

(c) The normal tax is at the rate of 22 percent and is applied to the taxable income for the taxable year. However, in the case of a taxable year ending after December 31, 1974, and before January 1, 1976, the normal tax is at the rate of 20 percent of so much of the taxable income as does not exceed $25,000 and at the rate of 22 percent of so much of the taxable income as does exceed $25,000 and is applied to the taxable income for the taxable year.

(d) The surtax is at the rate of 26 percent and is upon the taxable income (computed without regard to the deduction, if any, provided in section 242 for partially tax-exempt interest) in excess of $25,000. However, in the case of a taxable year ending after December 31, 1974, and before January 1, 1976, the surtax is upon the taxable income (computed as provided in the preceding sentence) in excess of $50,000. In certain circumstances the exemption from surtax may be disallowed in whole or in part. See sections 269, 1551, 1561, and 1564 and the regulations thereunder. For purposes of sections 244, 247, 804, 907, 922 and §§ 1.51-1 and 1.815-4, when the phrase "the sum of the normal tax rate and the surtax rate for the taxable year" is used in any such section, the normal tax rate for all taxable years beginning after December 31, 1963, and ending before January 1, 1976, shall be considered to be 22 percent.

(e) The computation of the tax on corporations imposed under section 11 may be illustrated by the following example:

Example. The X Corporation, a domestic corporation, has gross income of $86,000 for the calendar year 1964. The gross income includes interest of $5,000 on United States obligations for which a deduction under section 242 is allowable in determining taxable income subject to the normal tax. It has other deductions of $11,000. The tax of the X Corporation under section 11 for the calendar year is $28,400 ($15,400 normal tax and $13,000 surtax) computed as follows:

Computation of Normal Tax

Gross income		$86,000
Deductions:		
Partially tax-exempt interest	$ 5,000	
Other	11,000	16,000
Taxable income		70,000
Normal tax (22 percent of $70,000)		15,400

Computation of Surtax

Taxable income	$70,000
Add: Amount of partially tax-exempt interest deducted in computing taxable income	5,000
Taxable income subject to surtax	75,000
Less: Exemption from surtax	25,000
Excess of taxable income subject to surtax over exemption	50,000
Surtax (26 percent of $50,000)	13,000

(f) For special rules applicable to foreign corporations engaged in trade or business within the United States, see section 882 and the regulations thereunder. For additional tax on personal holding companies, see part II (section 541 and following), subchapter G, chapter 1 of the Code, and the regulations thereunder. For additional tax on corporations improperly accumulating surplus, see part I (section 531 and following), subchapter G, chapter 1 of the Code, and the regulations thereunder. For treatment of China Trade Act corporations, see sections 941 and 942 and the regulations thereunder. For treatment of Western Hemisphere trade corporations, see sections 921 and 922 and the regulations thereunder. For treatment of capital gains and losses, see subchapter P (section 1201 and following), chapter 1 of the Code. For computation of the tax for a taxable year during which a change in the tax rates occurs, see section 21 and the regulations thereunder.

T.D. 6161, 2/3/56, amend T.D. 6237, 6/10/57, T.D. 6350, 1/6/59, T.D. 6407, 8/14/59, T.D. 6610, 8/30/62, T.D. 6681, 10/16/63, T.D. 7100, 3/19/71, T.D. 7181, 4/24/72, T.D. 7293, 11/27/73, T.D. 7413, 3/25/76.

§ 1.15-1 Changes in rate during a taxable year.

Caution: The Treasury has not yet amended Reg § 1.15-1 to reflect changes made by P.L. 105-34, P.L. 100-647, P.L. 95-600, P.L. 95-30.

(a) Section 21 applies to all taxpayers, including individuals and corporations. It provides a general rule applicable in any case where (1) any rate of tax imposed by chapter 1 of the Code upon the taxpayer is increased or decreased, or any such tax is repealed, and (2) the taxable year includes the effective date of the change, except where that date is the first day of the taxable year. For example, the normal tax on corporations might, under section 11(b), was decreased from 30 percent to 22 percent in the case of a taxable year beginning after December 31, 1963. Accordingly, the tax for a taxable year of a corporation beginning on January 1, 1964, would be computed under section 11(b) at the new rate without regard to section 21. However, for any taxable year beginning before January 1, 1964, and ending on or after that date, the tax would be computed under section 21. For additional circumstances under which section 21 is not applicable, see paragraph (k) of this section.

(b) In any case in which section 21 is applicable, a tentative tax shall be computed by applying to the taxable income for the entire taxable year the rate for the period within the taxable year before the effective date of change, and another tentative tax shall be computed by applying to the taxable income for the entire taxable year the rate for the period within the taxable year on or after such effective date. The tax imposed on the taxpayer is the sum of—

(1) An amount which bears the same ratio to the tentative tax computed at the rate applicable to the period within the taxable year before the effective date of the change that the number of days in such period bears to the number of days in the taxable year, and

(2) An amount which bears the same ratio to the tentative tax computed at the rate applicable to the period within the taxable year on and after the effective date of the change that the number of days in such period bears to the number of days in the taxable year.

(c) If the rate of tax is changed for taxable years "beginning after" or "ending after" a certain date, the following day is considered the effective date of the change for purposes of section 21. If the rate is changed for taxable years "beginning on or after" a certain date, that date is considered the effective date of the change for purposes of section 21. This rule may be illustrated by the following examples:

Example (1). Assume that the law provides that a change in a certain rate of tax shall be effective only with respect to taxable years beginning after December 31, 1969. The effective date of change for purposes of section 21 is January 1, 1970, and section 21 must be applied to any taxable year which begins before and ends on or after January 1, 1970.

Example (2). Assume that the law provides that a change in a certain rate of tax shall be applicable only with respect to taxable years ending after December 31, 1970. For purposes of section 21, the effective date of change is January 1, 1971, and section 21 must be applied to any taxable year which begins before and ends on or after January 1, 1971.

Example (3). Assume that the law provides that a change in a certain rate of tax shall be effective only with respect to taxable years beginning on or after January 1, 1971. The effective date of change for purposes of section 21 is January 1, 1971, and section 21 must be applied to any taxable year which begins before and ends on or after January 1, 1971.

(d) If a tax is repealed, the repeal will be treated as a change of rate for purposes of section 21, and the rate for the period after the repeal (for the purpose of computing the tentative tax with respect to that period) will be considered zero. For example, the Tax Reform Act of 1969 repealed section 1562, which imposed a 6 percent additional tax on controlled corporations electing multiple surtax exemptions, effective for taxable years beginning after December 31, 1974. For such controlled corporations having taxable years beginning in 1974 and ending in 1975, the rate for the period ending before January 1, 1975, would be 6 percent; the rate for the period beginning after December 31, 1974, would be zero. However, subject to the rules stated in this section, section 21 does not apply to the imposition of a new tax. For example, if a new tax is imposed for taxable years beginning on or after July 1, 1972, a computation under section 21 would not be required with respect to such new tax in the case of taxable years beginning before July 1, 1972, and ending on or after that date. If the effective date of the imposition of a new tax and the effective date of a change in rate of such tax fall in the same taxable year, section 21 is not applicable in computing the taxpayer's liability for such tax for such year unless the new tax is expressly imposed upon the taxpayer for a portion of his taxable year prior to the change in rate.

(e) If a husband and wife have different taxable years because of the death of either spouse, and if a joint return is filed with respect to the taxable year of each, then, for purposes of section 21, the joint return shall be treated as if the taxable years of both spouses ended on the date of the closing of the surviving spouse's taxable year. See section 6013(c), relating to treatment of joint return after death of either spouse. Accordingly, if a change in the rate of tax is effective during the taxable year of the surviving spouse, the tentative taxes with respect to the joint return shall be computed on the basis of the number of days during which each rate of tax was in effect for the taxable year of the surviving spouse.

(f) Section 21 applies whether or not the taxpayer has a taxable year of less than 12 months. Moreover, section 21 applies whether or not the taxable income for a taxable year of less than 12 months is required to be placed on an annual basis under section 443. If the taxable income is required to be computed under section 443(b) then the tentative taxes under section 21 are computed as provided in paragraph (1) or (2) of section 443(b) and are reduced as provided in those paragraphs. The tentative taxes so computed and reduced are then apportioned as provided in section 21(a)(2) to determine the tax for such taxable year as computed under section 21.

(g) If a taxpayer has made the election under section 441(f) (relating to computation of taxable income on the basis of an annual accounting period varying from 52 to 53 weeks), the rules provided in section 441(f)(2) shall be applicable for purposes of determining whether section 21 applies to the taxable year of the taxpayer. Where a taxpayer has made the election under section 441(f) and where section 21 applies to the taxable year of the taxpayer the computation under section 21(a)(2) shall be made upon the basis of the actual number of days in the taxable year and in each period thereof.

(h) *(1)* Section 21 is applicable only if a rate of tax imposed by chapter 1 changes. Sections in which rates of tax are specified or incorporated by reference include the following: 1, 2, 3, 11, 511, 531, 541, 821, 831, 871, 881, 1201 and 1348 (for taxable years beginning after December 31, 1970). Except as provided in subparagraph (3) of this paragraph, section 21 is not applicable with respect to changes in the law relating to deductions from gross income, exclusions from or inclusions in gross income, or other items taken into account in determining the amount or character of income subject to tax. Moreover, section 21 is not applicable with respect to changes in the law relating to credits against the tax or with respect to changes in the law relating to limitations on the amount of tax. Section 21 is applicable, however, to all those computations specified in the section providing the rate of tax which are implicit in determining the rate. For example, if one of the tax brackets in the tax tables under section 3 were to be changed, section 21 would be applicable to that change. Thus, if the bracket relating to "at least $4,200 but not less than $4,250" for heads of households should be changed to increase or decrease the last sum specified, with corresponding changes being made in subsequent brackets, section 21 would be applicable. The enactment of sections 1561 and 1562 is considered a change in section 11(d) which constitutes a change in rate for the period ending after December 31, 1963. The amendment of section 1561 and the repeal of section 1562 by the Tax Reform Act of 1969 is considered a change in section 11(d) which constitutes a change in rate for the period ending after December 31, 1974. The repeal of the 2 percent additional tax imposed under section 1503 on corporations filing consolidated returns constitutes a change in rate for the period ending after December 31, 1963. The addition to the Code of section 1348 (relating to 50 percent maximum rate on earned income) is a change in rate to which section 21(a) is applicable. The amendment of section 11(d) by the Tax Reduction Act of 1975 which increases to $50,000 the surtax exemption for a taxable year ending during 1975 constitutes a change in rate for such portion of the taxable year (if less than the entire taxable year) as follows December 31, 1974. Similarly, the return of the surtax exemption to $25,000 for a taxable year ending during 1976 constitutes a change in rate for such portion of the taxable year (if less than the entire taxable year) as follows December 31, 1975.

(2) Ordinarily, both the old and the new rates are applied to the same amount of taxable income. However, where the rate of tax is itself taken into account in determining taxable income (for example, the special deduction for Western Hemisphere trade corporations under section 922), the taxable income used in determining the tentative tax employing the rate before the effective date of change shall be determined by reference to that rate of tax, and the taxable income for the purpose of determining the tentative tax employing the rate for the period on and after the effective date of the change shall be determined by reference to the new tax rate.

(3) Section 21 is applicable with respect to changes in the law relating to the standard deduction for individuals provided in part IV of subchapter B and to the deduction for personal exemptions for individuals provided in part V of subchapter B.

(i) If the rate of tax changes more than once during the taxable year, section 21 is applicable to each change in rate. For example, if the rate of normal tax changed for taxable years beginning on or after March 1, 1954, and changed again for taxable years beginning on or after June 1, 1954, section 21 requires computation of 3 tentative taxes for any taxable year which began before March 1, 1954, and ended on or after June 1, 1954: One tentative tax at the rate in effect before the March 1 change; another tentative tax at the rate in effect from March 1 to May 31; and a third tentative tax at the rate in effect from June 1 to the end of the taxable year. The proportion of each such tentative tax taken into account in determining the tax imposed on the taxpayer is computed by reference to the portion of the taxable year before March 1, 1954, by reference to the portion of the taxable year from March 1, 1954, through May 31, 1954, and by reference to the portion of the taxable year from June 1, 1954, to the end of the taxable year, respectively.

(j) *(1)* If a change in the rate of one tax imposed by chapter 1 of the Code does not affect the amount of other taxes imposed by chapter 1 of the Code the other taxes may be determined without regard to section 21 and section 21 will be applied only to the tax for which a change in rate is made. However, if the change of rate of one tax does affect the amount of other taxes imposed under chapter 1 of the Code, then the computation of the taxes under chapter 1 of the Code so affected shall be made by applying section 21. For example, if section 1201 applies to an individual taxpayer for a taxable year containing the effective date of a change in a rate of tax provided in section 1, then under section 21 the taxpayer must compute a tentative tax for each period for which a different rate of tax is effective under section 1. The tentative tax for each such period as computed under section 1201 will reflect the rate of tax provided by section 1 for such period.

(2) In certain cases chapter 1 of the Code provides that the particular tax to be imposed upon the taxpayer shall be one of several taxes, the basis of selection being the tax that is greater or lesser. See, for example, sections 821 and 1201. If in any such case the rate of any one of these taxes changes, then the tentative taxes computed as provided by section 21 for each period shall be computed employing the tax selected in accordance with the general rule of selection for such a case, at the rate of tax in effect for such period. Thus, if a change in the rate of the alternative tax under section 1201 is such that the alternative tax under section 1201 is applicable if the old rate is used and is not applicable if the new rate is used, one tentative tax will consist of the alternative tax under section 1201 and the other tentative tax will consist of the tax imposed by the other applicable sections of chapter 1 of the Code. The two tentative taxes so computed are then prorated in accordance with section 21(a)(2) and the sum of the proportionate amounts is the tax imposed for the taxable year under chapter 1 of the Code. See the examples in paragraph (n) of this section.

(k) Section 21 does not apply in the following situations:

(1) The provisions of section 21 do not apply to the imposition of the tax surcharge by section 51. The proration rules of section 51(a) apply in the case of a taxable year ending on or after the effective date of the surcharge and beginning before July 1, 1970.

(2) The provisions of section 21 do not apply to the imposition of the minimum tax for tax preferences by section 56. The proration rules of section 301(c) of the Tax Reform Act of 1969 (83 Stat. 586) apply in the case of a taxable year beginning in 1969 and ending in 1970.

(l) In computing the number of days each rate of tax is in effect during the taxable year for purposes of section 21 (a)(2), the effective date of the change in rate shall be counted in the period for which the new rate is in effect.

(m) Any credits against tax, and any limitation in any credit against tax, shall be based upon the tax computed under section 21. For credits against tax, see part IV (section 31 and following), subchapter A, chapter 1 of the Code.

(n) The application of section 21 may be illustrated by the following examples: (See also the examples in § 1.1561-2A(a)(3).)

Example (1). A, a married taxpayer filing a joint return, reports his income on the basis of a fiscal year ending June 30, 1970. For his fiscal year ending June 30, 1970, A reports taxable income (exclusive of capital gains and losses) of $50,000 and net long-term capital gain (section 1201 gain (net capital gain for taxable years beginning after December 31, 1976)) of $75,000. The rate of tax on capital gains under section 1201(b) relating to the alternative tax has been increased from 25 percent to a maximum rate of 29½ percent with respect to gain in excess of $50,000 and the effective date of the change in rate is January 1, 1970. The income tax for the taxable year ended June 30, 1970, would be computed under section 21 as follows:

Tentative Tax

Taxable income exclusive of capital gains and losses	$50,000
Long-term capital gain	75,000
	125,000
Deduct 50% of long-term capital gain	37,500
Taxable income	87,500
Tax under section 1 (1969 and 1970 rates)	37,690

Alternative Tax Under Section 1201(b) (1969 Rates)

Taxable income ($50,000 + 50% of $75,000)	$87,500
Less 50% of long-term capital gain	37,500
Taxable income exclusive of capital gains	50,000
Partial tax (tax on $50,000)	17,060
Plus 25% of $75,000	18,750
Alternative tax under section 1201(b) at 1969 rates	2.65,810

Alternative Tax Under Section 1201(b) (1970 Rates)

Step I

Taxable income ($50,000 + 50% of $75,000)	$87,500	
Deduct 50% of net section 1201 gain (net capital gain for taxable years beginning after December 31, 1976)	37,500	
	50,000	
Tax on $50,000 (taxable income exclusive of capital gains)		$17,060

Step II

(a) Net section 1201 gain (net capital gain for taxable years beginning after December 31, 1976)	75,000	
(b) Subsection (d) gain	50,000	
25% of $50,000 (lesser of (a) or (b))		12,500

Step III

(c) 29½% of $25,000 (excess of (a) over (b))	7,375	
(d) Ordinary income	$50,000	
50% of net section 1201 gain (net capital gain for taxable years beginning after December 31, 1976)	37,500	
	87,500	
Tax on $87,500		37,690
Ordinary income	$50,000	
50% of subsection (d) gain	25,000	
	75,000	
Tax on $75,000	30,470	
Difference	7,220	
Lesser of (c) or (d)		7,220
Alternative tax (total of 3 Steps) at rates effective on and after January 1, 1970		36,780

Since the alternative tax is less than the tax imposed under section 1 for both the period in 1969 and the period in 1970, the alternative tax applies for both periods. Thus, since the effective date of the change in the rate of tax on capital gains is January 1, 1970, the old rate of alternative tax is effective for 184 days of the taxable year and the new rate of alternative tax is effective for 181 days of the taxable year. The alternative taxes are apportioned as follows:

1969--184/365 of $35,810	$18,052.16
1970--181/365 of $36,780	18,238.85
	36,291.01
Tax surcharge (See § 1.51-1(d)(1)(i))	2,729.28
Total tax for the taxable year	39,020.29

Example (2). B, a single individual not a head of a household, has a taxable year ending March 31. For the taxable year ending March 31, 1971, B has adjusted gross income of $18,500. His computation of the tax imposed is as follows:

1970--275/365 of $4,697.50	3,539.21
1971--90/365 of $3,949.00	973.73
	4,512.94
Tax surcharge (see § 1.51-1(d)(1)(i))	56.26
Total tax for the taxable year	4,569.20

Example (3). H and W, husband and wife, have a foster child, C, who qualifies as a dependent under section 152(b)(2) for the period beginning after December 31, 1969. H and W file a joint return on the basis of a taxable year ending August 31. For the taxable year ending August 31, 1970, H and W have adjusted gross income of $12,500. Their computation of the tax imposed is as follows:

1969--122/365 of $1,886.00	$ 630.39
1970--243/365 of $1,737.50	1,156.75
	1,787.14
Tax surcharge (See § 1.51-1(d)(1)(i))	104.05
Total tax for the taxable year	1,891.19

Example (4). B, a single individual with one exemption, reports his income on the basis of a fiscal year ending June 30. For fiscal year ending June 30, 1971, B reports adjusted gross income of $250,000, consisting of earned net income of $240,000 and investment income of $10,000. In addition, on April 24, 1971, stock was transferred to B pursuant to his exercise of a qualified stock option, and the fair market value of such stock at that time exceeded the option price by $175,000. Thus $175,000 constitutes an item of tax preference described in section 57(a)(6). B claims itemized deductions in the amount of $34,000. By reason of section 1348, the maximum rate of tax on earned taxable income for a taxable year beginning after 1970 but before 1972 is 60 percent. The income tax for the taxable year ending June 30, 1971, would be computed under section 21 as follows:

1970 Tentative Tax

Adjusted gross income		$250,000.00
Less:		
Itemized deductions	$ 34,000.00	
Personal exemption	625.00	34,625.00
Taxable income under 1970 deduction provisions		215,375.00
Tax on $215,375 (1970 rates)		
Tax on first $100,000	$ 55,490.00	
70 percent of $115,375	80,762.50	
Tentative tax at rates and deduction provisions effective on or after January 1, 1970		136,252.50

Minimum tax:

Total tax preference items		175,000.00
Less:		
Exemption	$ 30,000.00	
Income tax	136,252.50	166,252.50
Subject to 10 percent tax		8,747.50
10 percent tax		874.75
Total tentative tax ($136,252.50 + $874.75)		137,127.25

1971 Tentative Tax

Adjusted gross income		$250,000.00
Less:		
Itemized deductions	$ 34,000.00	
Personal exemption	650.00	34,650.00
Taxable income under 1971 deduction provisions		215,350.00
(a) Tax on highest amount of taxable income on which rate does not exceed 60 percent ($50,000) (1971 rates)		20,190.00
(b) Earned taxable income: ($215,350 × $240,000/$250,000)		206,736.00
Less: Tax preference offset: ($175,000 – $30,000)	145,000.00	
	$ 61,736.00	
(c) 60% of the amount by which $61,736 exceeds $50,000		7,041.00
(d) Tax on $215,350 (1971 rates)		
Tax on first $100,000	$ 53,090.00	
70% of $115,350	80,745.00	
Total	$133,835.00	
(e) Tax on $61,736 (1971 rates)		
Tax on first $60,000	$ 26,390.00	
64% of $1,736	1,111.04	
Total	$ 27,501.04	
(f) Excess of $133,835 over $27,501.04		106,333.96
Tentative tax (total of Steps (a), (c), and (f)) at rates and deduction provisions effective on or after January 1, 1971		133,565.56
Minimum tax:		
Total tax preference items		175,000.00
Less:		
Exemption	$ 30,000.00	
Income tax	133,565.56	163,565.56
Subject to 10 percent tax		11,434.44
10 percent tax		1,143.44
Total tentative tax $133,565.56 + $1,143.44)		134,709.00

The 1970 and 1971 tentative taxes are apportioned as follows:

1970--184/365 of $137,127.25	69,127.16
1971--181/365 of $134,709.00	66,800.90
Total tax for the taxable year	135,928.06

Example (5). The surtax exemption of corporation M (one of 4 subsidiary corporations of W corporation), which files its income tax returns on the basis of a fiscal year ending March 31, 1964, is less than $25,000, by reason of section 1561 of the Code applicable to taxable years ending after December 31, 1963, and beginning before January 1, 1975. The taxable income of corporation M is $100,000, and the amount of the surtax exemption determined under the new rule for the 1964 taxable year is $5,000 ($25,000 ÷ 5). M's income tax liability for the taxable year ending March 31, 1964, is computed as follows:

1963 Tentative Tax

Taxable income		$100,000
Normal tax on $100,000 (1963 rates)		
30 percent of $100,000	$30,000	
Surtax on $75,000 (1963 rates and $25,000 surtax exemption)		
22 percent of $75,000	16,500	
Total tentative tax at rates and surtax exemption effective before January 1, 1964		46,500

1964 Tentative Tax

Taxable income		$100,000
Normal tax on $100,000 (1964 rates)		
22 percent of $100,000	$22,000	
Surtax on $95,000 (1964 rates and a $5,000 surtax exemption)		
28 percent of $95,000	26,600	
Total tentative tax at rates and surtax exemption effective after January 1, 1964		46,600

The 1963 and 1964 tentative taxes are apportioned as follows:

1963--275/366 of $46,500	$34,938.52
1964--91/366 of $48,600	12,083.61
Total tax for the taxable year	47,022.13

M has the same amount of taxable income in 1965. Its income tax liability for the fiscal year ending March 31, 1965, is computed as follows:

1964 Tentative Tax

Taxable income		$100,000
Normal tax on $100,000 (1964 rates)		
22 percent of $100,000	$ 22,000	
Surtax on $95,000 (1964 rates and a $5,000 surtax exemption) 28 percent of $95,000	26,600	
Total tentative tax at the 1964 rates		48,600

1965 Tentative Tax

Taxable income		$100,000
Normal tax on $100,000 (1965 rates)		
22 percent of $100,000	$ 22,000	

Surtax on $95,000 (1965 rates and a $5,000 surtax exemption) 26 percent of $95,000	24,700	
Total tentative tax at the 1965 rates		46,700

The 1964 and 1965 tentative taxes are apportioned as follows:

1964--275/365 of $48,600.00	$36,616.44
1965--90/365 of $46,700.00	11,515.07
Total tax for the taxable year	48,131.51

Example (6). Assume the same facts as in example (5), except that M elected the additional tax under section 1562 for its fiscal year ending March 31, 1964. M's tax liability is completed as follows:

1963 Tentative Tax

Taxable income		$100,000
Normal tax on $100,000 (1963 rates) 30 percent of $100,000	$30,000	
Surtax on $75,000 (1963 rates and $25,000 surtax exemption) 22 percent of $75,000	16,500	
Total tentative tax at rates and surtax exemption effective before January 1, 1964		46,500

1964 Tentative Tax

Taxable income		$100,000
Normal tax on $100,000 (1964 rates) ... 22 percent of $100,000	$22,000	
Surtax on $75,000 (1964 rates and $25,000 surtax exemption) 28 percent of $75,000	21,000	
Additional tax on $25,000 6 percent of $25,000	1,500	
Total tentative tax at rates and surtax exemption effective on and after January 1, 1964		44,500

1963--275/366 of $46,500.00	$34,938.52
1964--91/366 of $44,500.00	11,064.21
Total tax for the taxable year	46,002.73

The 1963 and 1964 tentative taxes are apportioned as follows:

Example (7). Corporation N files its income tax returns on the basis of a fiscal year ending June 30. For its taxable year ending in 1976, the taxable income of N is $100,000. N's income tax liability is determined for the period July 1, 1975, through December 31, 1975, by taking into account two rates of normal tax under section 11(b)(2)(A) and (B) and the increase to $50,000 in the surtax exemption under section 11(d). For the period January 1, 1976, through June 30, 1976, N's income tax liability is determined by taking into account the single normal tax rate under section 11(b)(1) and the $25,000 surtax exemption under section 11(d). N's tax liability for the taxable year ending June 30, 1976, is computed as follows:

1975 Tentative Tax

Taxable income		$100,000
Normal tax on $100,000 (1975 rates) 20 percent of $25,000	$ 5,000	
22 percent of $75,000	16,500	
Surtax on $50,000 (1975 rates and $50,000 surtax exemption) 26 percent of $50,000	13,000	
Total tentative tax at rates and surtax exemption effective on and after January 1, 1975		$ 34,500

1976 Tentative Tax

Taxable income		$100,000
Normal tax on $100,000 (1976 rates) 22 percent of $100,000	$22,000	
Surtax on $75,000 (1976 rates and $25,000 surtax exemption) 26 percent of $75,000	19,500	
Total tentative tax at rates and surtax exemption effective on and after January 1, 1976		$ 41,500

The 1975 and 1976 tentative taxes are apportioned as follows:

1975--184/366 of $34,500	$17,344
1976--182/366 of $41,500	20,637
Total tax for the taxable year	37,981

T.D. 6161, 2/3/56, amend T.D. 6237, 6/10/57, T.D. 6350, 1/6/59, T.D. 6407, 8/14/59, T.D. 7164, 2/8/72, T.D. 7413, 3/25/76, T.D. 7528, 12/27/77, T.D. 7728, 10/31/80, T.D. 9354, 8/13/2007.

§ 1.21-1 Expenses for household and dependent care services necessary for gainful employment.

(a) In general. *(1)* Section 21 allows a credit to a taxpayer against the tax imposed by chapter 1 for employment-related expenses for household services and care (as defined in paragraph (d) of this section) of a qualifying individual (as defined in paragraph (b) of this section). The purpose of the expenses must be to enable the taxpayer to be gainfully employed (as defined in paragraph (c) of this section). For taxable years beginning after December 31, 2004, a qualifying individual must have the same principal place of abode (as defined in paragraph (g) of this section) as the taxpayer for more than one-half of the taxable year. For taxable years beginning before January 1, 2005, the taxpayer must maintain a household (as defined in paragraph (h) of this section) that includes one or more qualifying individuals.

(2) The amount of the credit is equal to the applicable percentage of the employment-related expenses that may be taken into account by the taxpayer during the taxable year (but subject to the limits prescribed in § 1.21-2). Applicable percentage means 35 percent reduced by 1 percentage point for each $2,000 (or fraction thereof) by which the taxpayer's adjusted gross income for the taxable year exceeds $15,000, but not less than 20 percent. For example, if a taxpayer's adjusted gross income is $31,850, the applicable percentage is 26 percent.

(3) Expenses may be taken as a credit under section 21, regardless of the taxpayer's method of accounting, only in the taxable year the services are performed or the taxable year the expenses are paid, whichever is later.

(4) The requirements of section 21 and §§ 1.21-1 through 1.21-4 are applied at the time the services are performed, regardless of when the expenses are paid.

(5) Examples. The provisions of this paragraph (a) are illustrated by the following examples.

Example (1). In December 2007, B pays for the care of her child for January 2008. Under paragraph (a)(3) of this section, B may claim the credit in 2008, the later of the years in which the expenses are paid and the services are performed.

Example (2). The facts are the same as in Example 1, except that B's child turns 13 on February 1, 2008, and B pays for the care provided in January 2008 on February 3, 2008. Under paragraph (a)(4) of this section, the determination of whether the expenses are employment-related expenses is made when the services are performed. Assuming other requirements are met, the amount B pays will be an employment-related expense under section 21, because B's child is a qualifying individual when the services are performed, even though the child is not a qualifying individual when B pays the expenses.

(b) Qualifying individual. *(1) In general.* For taxable years beginning after December 31, 2004, a qualifying individual is—

(i) The taxpayer's dependent (who is a qualifying child within the meaning of section 152) who has not attained age 13;

(ii) The taxpayer's dependent (as defined in section 152, determined without regard to subsections (b)(1), (b)(2), and (d)(1)(B)) who is physically or mentally incapable of self-care and who has the same principal place of abode as the taxpayer for more than one-half of the taxable year; or

(iii) The taxpayer's spouse who is physically or mentally incapable of self-care and who has the same principal place of abode as the taxpayer for more than one-half of the taxable year.

(2) Taxable years beginning before January 1, 2005. For taxable years beginning before January 1, 2005, a qualifying individual is—

(i) The taxpayer's dependent for whom the taxpayer is entitled to a deduction for a personal exemption under section 151(c) and who is under age 13;

(ii) The taxpayer's dependent who is physically or mentally incapable of self-care; or

(iii) The taxpayer's spouse who is physically or mentally incapable of self-care.

(3) Qualification on a daily basis. The status of an individual as a qualifying individual is determined on a daily basis. An individual is not a qualifying individual on the day the status terminates.

(4) Physical or mental incapacity. An individual is physically or mentally incapable of self-care if, as a result of a physical or mental defect, the individual is incapable of caring for the individual's hygiene or nutritional needs, or requires full-time attention of another person for the individual's own safety or the safety of others. The inability of an individual to engage in any substantial gainful activity or to perform the normal household functions of a homemaker or care for minor children by reason of a physical or mental condition does not of itself establish that the individual is physically or mentally incapable of self-care.

(5) Special test for divorced or separated parents or parents living apart. (i) Scope. This paragraph (b)(5) applies to a child (as defined in section 152(f)(1) for taxable years beginning after December 31, 2004, and in section 151(c)(3) for taxable years beginning before January 1, 2005) who—

(A) Is under age 13 or is physically or mentally incapable of self-care;

(B) Receives over one-half of his or her support during the calendar year from one or both parents who are divorced or legally separated under a decree of divorce or separate maintenance, are separated under a written separation agreement, or live apart at all times during the last 6 months of the calendar year; and

(C) Is in the custody of one or both parents for more than one-half of the calendar year.

(ii) Custodial parent allowed the credit. A child to whom this paragraph (b)(5) applies is the qualifying individual of only one parent in any taxable year and is the qualifying child of the custodial parent even if the noncustodial parent may claim the dependency exemption for that child for that taxable year. See section 21(e)(5). The custodial parent is the parent having custody for the greater portion of the calendar year. See section 152(e)(4)(A).

(6) Example. The provisions of this paragraph (b) are illustrated by the following examples.

Example. C pays $420 for the care of her child, a qualifying individual, to be provided from January 2 through January 31, 2008 (21 days of care). On January 20, 2008, C's child turns 13 years old. Under paragraph (b)(3) of this section, C's child is a qualifying individual from January 2 through January 19, 2008 (13 days of care). C may take into account $260, the pro rata amount C pays for the care of her child for 13 days, under section 21. See § 1.21-2(a)(4).

(c) Gainful employment. *(1) In general.* Expenses are employment-related expenses only if they are for the purpose of enabling the taxpayer to be gainfully employed. The expenses must be for the care of a qualifying individual or household services performed during periods in which the taxpayer is gainfully employed or is in active search of gainful employment. Employment may consist of service within or outside the taxpayer's home and includes self-employment. An expense is not employment-related merely because it is paid or incurred while the taxpayer is gainfully employed. The purpose of the expense must be to enable the taxpayer to be gainfully employed. Whether the purpose of an expense is to enable the taxpayer to be gainfully employed depends on the facts and circumstances of the particular case. Work as a volunteer or for a nominal consideration is not gainful employment.

(2) Determination of period of employment on a daily basis. (i) In general. Expenses paid for a period during only part of which the taxpayer is gainfully employed or in active search of gainful employment must be allocated on a daily basis.

(ii) Exception for short, temporary absences. A taxpayer who is gainfully employed is not required to allocate expenses during a short, temporary absence from work, such as for vacation or minor illness, provided that the care-giving arrangement requires the taxpayer to pay for care during the absence. An absence of 2 consecutive calendar weeks is a short, temporary absence. Whether an absence longer than 2 consecutive calendar weeks is a short, temporary absence is determined based on all the facts and circumstances.

(iii) Part-time employment. A taxpayer who is employed part-time generally must allocate expenses for dependent care between days worked and days not worked. However, if a taxpayer employed part-time is required to pay for dependent care on a periodic basis (such as weekly or monthly) that includes both days worked and days not worked, the taxpayer is not required to allocate the expenses. A day on which the taxpayer works at least 1 hour is a day of work.

(3) Examples. The provisions of this paragraph (c) are illustrated by the following examples:

Example (1). D works during the day and her husband, E, works at night and sleeps during the day. D and E pay for care for a qualifying individual during the hours when D is working and E is sleeping. Under paragraph (c)(1) of this section, the amount paid by D and E for care may be for the purpose of allowing D and E to be gainfully employed and may be an employment-related expense under section 21.

Example (2). F works at night and pays for care for a qualifying individual during the hours when F is working. Under paragraph (c)(1) of this section, the amount paid by F for care may be for the purpose of allowing F to be gainfully employed and may be an employment-related expense under section 21.

Example (3). G, the custodial parent of two children who are qualifying individuals, hires a housekeeper for a monthly salary to care for the children while G is gainfully employed. G becomes ill and as a result is absent from work for 4 months. G continues to pay the housekeeper to care for the children while G is absent from work. During this 4-month period, G performs no employment services, but receives payments under her employer's wage continuation plan. Although G may be considered to be gainfully employed during her absence from work, the absence is not a short, temporary absence within the meaning of paragraph (c)(2)(ii) of this section, and her payments for household and dependent care services during the period of illness are not for the purpose of enabling her to be gainfully employed. G's expenses are not employment-related expenses, and she may not take the expenses into account under section 21.

Example (4). To be gainfully employed, H sends his child to a dependent care center that complies with all state and local requirements. The dependent care center requires payment for days when a child is absent from the center. H takes 8 days off from work as vacation days. Because the absence is less than 2 consecutive calendar weeks, under paragraph (c)(2)(ii) of this section, H's absence is a short, temporary absence. H is not required to allocate expenses between days worked and days not worked. The entire fee for the period that includes the 8 vacation days may be an employment-related expense under section 21.

Example (5). J works 3 days per week and her child attends a dependent care center (that complies with all state and local requirements) to enable her to be gainfully employed. The dependent care center allows payment for any 3 days per week for $150 or 5 days per week for $250. J enrolls her child for 5 days per week, and her child attends the care center for 5 days per week. Under paragraph (c)(2)(iii) of this section, J must allocate her expenses for dependent care between days worked and days not worked. Three-fifths of the $250, or $150 per week, may be an employment-related expense under section 21.

Example (6). The facts are the same as in Example 5, except that the dependent care center does not offer a 3-day option. The entire $250 weekly fee may be an employment-related expense under section 21.

(d) Care of qualifying individual and household services. *(1) In general.* To qualify for the dependent care credit, expenses must be for the care of a qualifying individual. Expenses are for the care of a qualifying individual if the primary function is to assure the individual's well-being and protection. Not all expenses relating to a qualifying individual are for the individual's care. Amounts paid for food, lodging, clothing, or education are not for the care of a qualifying individual. If, however, the care is provided in such a manner that the expenses cover other goods or services that are incidental to and inseparably a part of the care, the full amount is for care.

(2) Allocation of expenses. If an expense is partly for household services or for the care of a qualifying individual and partly for other goods or services, a reasonable allocation must be made. Only so much of the expense that is allocable to the household services or care of a qualifying individual is an employment-related expense. An allocation must be made if a housekeeper or other domestic employee performs household duties and cares for the qualifying children of the taxpayer and also performs other services for the taxpayer. No allocation is required, however, if the expense for the other purpose is minimal or insignificant or if an expense is partly attributable to the care of a qualifying individual and partly to household services.

(3) Household services. Expenses for household services may be employment-related expenses if the services are performed in connection with the care of a qualifying individual. The household services must be the performance in and about the taxpayer's home of ordinary and usual services necessary to the maintenance of the household and attributable to the care of the qualifying individual. Services of a housekeeper are household services within the meaning of this paragraph (d)(3) if the services are provided, at least in part, to the qualifying individual. Such services as are performed by chauffeurs, bartenders, or gardeners are not household services.

(4) Manner of providing care. The manner of providing care need not be the least expensive alternative available to the taxpayer. The cost of a paid caregiver may be an expense for the care of a qualifying individual even if another caregiver is available at no cost.

(5) School or similar program. Expenses for a child in nursery school, pre-school, or similar programs for children below the level of kindergarten are for the care of a qualifying individual and may be employment-related expenses. Expenses for a child in kindergarten or a higher grade are not for the care of a qualifying individual. However, expenses for before- or after-school care of a child in kindergarten or a higher grade may be for the care of a qualifying individual.

(6) Overnight camps. Expenses for overnight camps are not employment-related expenses.

(7) Day camps. (i) The cost of a day camp or similar program may be for the care of a qualifying individual and an employment-related expense, without allocation under paragraph (d)(2) of this section, even if the day camp specializes in a particular activity. Summer school and tutoring programs are not for the care of a qualifying individual and the costs are not employment-related expenses.

(ii) A day camp that meets the definition of dependent care center in section 21(b)(2)(D) and paragraph (e)(2) of this section must comply with the requirements of section 21(b)(2)(C) and paragraph (e)(2) of this section.

(8) Transportation. The cost of transportation by a dependent care provider of a qualifying individual to or from a place where care of that qualifying individual is provided may be for the care of the qualifying individual. The cost of transportation not provided by a dependent care provider is not for the care of the qualifying individual.

(9) Employment taxes. Taxes under sections 3111 (relating to the Federal Insurance Contributions Act) and 3301 (relating to the Federal Unemployment Tax Act) and similar state payroll taxes are employment-related expenses if paid in respect of wages that are employment-related expenses.

(10) Room and board. The additional cost of providing room and board for a caregiver over usual household expenditures may be an employment-related expense.

(11) Indirect expenses. Expenses that relate to, but are not directly for, the care of a qualifying individual, such as application fees, agency fees, and deposits, may be for the care of a qualifying individual and may be employment-related expenses if the taxpayer is required to pay the expenses to obtain the related care. However, forfeited deposits and other payments are not for the care of a qualifying individual if care is not provided.

(12) Examples. The provisions of this paragraph (d) are illustrated by the following examples:

Example (1). To be gainfully employed, K sends his 3-year old child to a pre-school. The pre-school provides lunch and snacks. Under paragraph (d)(1) of this section, K is not required to allocate expenses between care and the lunch and snacks, because the lunch and snacks are incidental to and inseparably a part of the care. Therefore, K may treat the full amount paid to the pre-school as for the care of his child.

Example (2). L, a member of the armed forces, is ordered to a combat zone. To be able to comply with the orders, L places her 10-year old child in boarding school. The school provides education, meals, and housing to L's child in addition to care. Under paragraph (d)(2) of this section, L must allocate the cost of the boarding school between expenses for care and expenses for education and other services not constituting care. Only the part of the cost of the boarding school that is for the care of L's child is an employment-related expense under section 21.

Example (3). To be gainfully employed, M employs a full-time housekeeper to care for M's two children, aged 9 and 13 years. The housekeeper regularly performs household services of cleaning and cooking and drives M to and from M's place of employment, a trip of 15 minutes each way. Under paragraph (d)(3) of this section, the chauffeur services are not household services. M is not required to allocate a portion of the expense of the housekeeper to the chauffeur services under paragraph (d)(2) of this section, however, because the chauffeur services are minimal and insignificant. Further, no allocation under paragraph (d)(2) of this section is required to determine the portion of the expenses attributable to the care of the 13-year old child (not a qualifying individual) because the household expenses are in part attributable to the care of the 9-year-old child. Accordingly, the entire expense of employing the housekeeper is an employment-related expense. The amount that M may take into account as an employment-related expense under section 21, however, is limited to the amount allowable for one qualifying individual.

Example (4). To be gainfully employed, N sends her 9-year-old child to a summer day camp that offers computer activities and recreational activities such as swimming and arts and crafts. Under paragraph (d)(7)(i) of this section, the full cost of the summer day camp may be for care.

Example (5). To be gainfully employed, O sends her 9-year-old child to a math tutoring program for two hours per day during the summer. Under paragraph (d)(7)(i) of this section, the cost of the tutoring program is not for care.

Example (6). To be gainfully employed, P hires a full-time housekeeper to care for her 8-year old child. In order to accommodate the housekeeper, P moves from a 2-bedroom apartment to a 3-bedroom apartment that otherwise is comparable to the 2-bedroom apartment. Under paragraph (d)(10) of this section, the additional cost to rent the 3-bedroom apartment over the cost of the 2-bedroom apartment and any additional utilities attributable to the housekeeper's residence in the household may be employment-related expenses under section 21.

Example (7). Q pays a fee to an agency to obtain the services of an au pair to care for Q's children, qualifying individuals, to enable Q to be gainfully employed. An au pair from the agency subsequently provides care for Q's children. Under paragraph (d)(11) of this section, the fee may be an employment-related expense.

Example (8). R places a deposit with a pre-school to reserve a place for her child. R sends the child to a different pre-school and forfeits the deposit. Under paragraph (d)(11) of this section, the forfeited deposit is not an employment-related expense.

(e) Services outside the taxpayer's household. *(1) In general.* The credit is allowable for expenses for services performed outside the taxpayer's household only if the care is for one or more qualifying individuals who are described in this section at—

(i) Paragraph (b)(1)(i) or (b)(2)(i); or

(ii) Paragraph (b)(1)(ii), (b)(2)(ii), (b)(1)(iii), or (b)(2)(iii) and regularly spend at least 8 hours each day in the taxpayer's household.

(2) Dependent care centers. (i) In general. The credit is allowable for services performed by a dependent care center only if—

(A) The center complies with all applicable laws and regulations, if any, of a state or local government, such as state or local licensing requirements and building and fire code regulations; and

(B) The requirements provided in this paragraph (e) are met.

(ii) Definition. The term dependent care center means any facility that provides full-time or part-time care for more than six individuals (other than individuals who reside at the facility) on a regular basis during the taxpayer's taxable year, and receives a fee, payment, or grant for providing services for the individuals (regardless of whether the facility is operated for profit). For purposes of the preceding sentence, a facility is presumed to provide full-time or part-time care for six or fewer individuals on a regular basis during the taxpayer's taxable year if the facility has six or fewer individuals (including the taxpayer's qualifying individual) enrolled for full-time or part-time care on the day the qualifying individual is enrolled in the facility (or on the first day of the taxable year the qualifying individual attends the facility if the qualifying individual was enrolled in the facility in the preceding taxable year) unless the Internal Revenue Service demonstrates that the facility provides full-time or part-time care for more than six individuals on a regular basis during the taxpayer's taxable year.

(f) Reimbursed expenses. Employment-related expenses for which the taxpayer is reimbursed (for example, under a dependent care assistance program) may not be taken into account for purposes of the credit.

(g) Principal place of abode. For purposes of this section, the term principal place of abode has the same meaning as in section 152.

(h) Maintenance of a household. *(1) In general.* For taxable years beginning before January 1, 2005, the credit is available only to a taxpayer who maintains a household that includes one or more qualifying individuals. A taxpayer maintains a household for the taxable year (or lesser period) only if the taxpayer (and spouse, if applicable) occupies the household and furnishes over one-half of the cost for the taxable year (or lesser period) of maintaining the household. The household must be the principal place of abode for the taxable year of the taxpayer and the qualifying individual or individuals.

(2) Cost of maintaining a household. (i) Except as provided in paragraph (h)(2)(ii) of this section, for purposes of this section, the term cost of maintaining a household has the same meaning as in § 1.2-2(d) without regard to the last sentence thereof.

(ii) The cost of maintaining a household does not include the value of services performed in the household by the taxpayer or by a qualifying individual described in paragraph (b) of this section or any expense paid or reimbursed by another person.

(3) Monthly proration of annual costs. In determining the cost of maintaining a household for a period of less than a taxable year, the cost for the entire taxable year must be prorated on the basis of the number of calendar months within that period. A period of less than a calendar month is treated as a full calendar month.

(4) Two or more families. If two or more families occupy living quarters in common, each of the families is treated as maintaining a separate household. A taxpayer is maintaining a household if the taxpayer provides more than one-half of the cost of maintaining the separate household. For example, if two unrelated taxpayers with their respective children occupy living quarters in common and each taxpayer pays more than one-half of the household costs for each respective family, each taxpayer is treated as maintaining a household.

(i) Reserved.

(j) Expenses qualifying as medical expenses. *(1) In general.* A taxpayer may not take an amount into account as both an employment-related expense under section 21 and an expense for medical care under section 213.

(2) Examples. The provisions of this paragraph (j) are illustrated by the following examples:

Example (1). S has $6,500 of employment-related expenses for the care of his child who is physically incapable of self-care. The expenses are for services performed in S's household that also qualify as expenses for medical care under section 213. Of the total expenses, S may take into account $3,000 under section 21. S may deduct the balance of the expenses, or $3,500, as expenses for medical care under section 213 to the extent the expenses exceed 7.5 percent of S's adjusted gross income.

Example (2). The facts are the same as in Example 1, however, S first takes into account the $6,500 of expenses under section 213. S deducts $500 as an expense for medical care, which is the amount by which the expenses exceed 7.5 percent of his adjusted gross income. S may not take into account the $6,000 balance as employment-related expenses under section 21, because he has taken the full amount of the expenses into account in computing the amount deductible under section 213.

(k) Substantiation. A taxpayer claiming a credit for employment-related expenses must maintain adequate records or other sufficient evidence to substantiate the expenses in accordance with section 6001 and the regulations thereunder.

(l) Effective/applicability date. This section and §§ 1.21-2 through 1.21-4 apply to taxable years ending after August 14, 2007.

T.D. 9354, 8/13/2007.

---

§ 1.21-2 Limitations on amount creditable.

(a) Annual dollar limitation. *(1)* The amount of employment-related expenses that may be taken into account under § 1.21-1(a) for any taxable year cannot exceed—

(i) $2,400 ($3,000 for taxable years beginning after December 31, 2002, and before January 1, 2011) if there is one qualifying individual with respect to the taxpayer at any time during the taxable year; or

(ii) $4,800 ($6,000 for taxable years beginning after December 31, 2002, and before January 1, 2011) if there are two or more qualifying individuals with respect to the taxpayer at any time during the taxable year.

(2) The amount determined under paragraph (a)(1) of this section is reduced by the aggregate amount excludable from gross income under section 129 for the taxable year.

(3) A taxpayer may take into account the total amount of employment-related expenses that do not exceed the annual dollar limitation although the amount of employment-related expenses attributable to one qualifying individual is disproportionate to the total employment-related expenses. For example, a taxpayer with expenses in 2007 of $4,000 for one qualifying individual and $1,500 for a second qualifying individual may take into account the full $5,500.

(4) A taxpayer is not required to prorate the annual dollar limitation if a qualifying individual ceases to qualify (for example, by turning age 13) during the taxable year. However, the taxpayer may take into account only amounts that qualify as employment-related expenses before the disqualifying event. See also § 1.21-1(b)(6).

(b) Earned income limitation. *(1) In general.* The amount of employment-related expenses that may be taken into account under section 21 for any taxable year cannot exceed—

(i) For a taxpayer who is not married at the close of the taxable year, the taxpayer's earned income for the taxable year; or

(ii) For a taxpayer who is married at the close of the taxable year, the lesser of the taxpayer's earned income or the earned income of the taxpayer's spouse for the taxable year.

(2) Determination of spouse. For purposes of this paragraph (b), a taxpayer must take into account only the earned income of a spouse to whom the taxpayer is married at the close of the taxable year. The spouse's earned income for the entire taxable year is taken into account, however, even though the taxpayer and the spouse were married for only part of the taxable year. The taxpayer is not required to take into account the earned income of a spouse who died or was divorced or separated from the taxpayer during the taxable year. See § 1.21-3(b) for rules providing that certain married taxpayers legally separated or living apart are treated as not married.

(3) Definition of earned income. For purposes of this section, the term earned income has the same meaning as in section 32(c)(2) and the regulations thereunder.

(4) Attribution of earned income to student or incapacitated spouse. (i) For purposes of this section, a spouse is deemed, for each month during which the spouse is a full-time student or is a qualifying individual described in § 1.21-1(b)(1)(iii) or (b)(2)(iii), to be gainfully employed and to have earned income of not less than—

(A) $200 ($250 for taxable years beginning after December 31, 2002, and before January 1, 2011) if there is one qualifying individual with respect to the taxpayer at any time during the taxable year; or

(B) $400 ($500 for taxable years beginning after December 31, 2002, and before January 1, 2011) if there are two or more qualifying individuals with respect to the taxpayer at any time during the taxable year.

(ii) For purposes of this paragraph (b)(4), a full-time student is an individual who, during each of 5 calendar months of the taxpayer's taxable year, is enrolled as a student for the number of course hours considered to be a full-time course of study at an educational organization as defined in section 170(b)(1)(A)(ii). The enrollment for 5 calendar months need not be consecutive.

(iii) Earned income may be attributed under this paragraph (b)(4), in the case of any husband and wife, to only one spouse in any month.

(c) Examples. The provisions of this section are illustrated by the following examples:

Example (1). In 2007, T, who is married to U, pays employment-related expenses of $5,000 for the care of one qualifying individual. T's earned income for the taxable year is $40,000 and her husband's earned income is $2,000. T did not exclude any dependent care assistance under section 129. Under paragraph (b)(1) of this section, T may take into account under section 21 only the amount of employment-related expenses that does not exceed the lesser of her earned income or the earned income of U, or $2,000.

Example (2). The facts are the same as in Example 1 except that U is a full-time student at an educational organization within the meaning of section 170(b)(1)(A)(ii) for 9 months of the taxable year and has no earned income. Under paragraph (b)(4) of this section, U is deemed to have earned income of $2,250. T may take into account $2,250 of employment-related expenses under section 21.

Example (3). For all of 2007, V is a full-time student and W, V's husband, is an individual who is incapable of self-care (as defined in § 1.21-1(b)(1)(iii)). V and W have no earned income and pay expenses of $5,000 for W's care. Under paragraph (b)(4) of this section, either V or W may be deemed to have $3,000 of earned income. However, earned income may be attributed to only one spouse under paragraph (b)(4)(iii) of this section. Under the limitation in paragraph (b)(1)(ii) of this section, the lesser of V's and W's earned income is zero. V and W may not take the expenses into account under section 21.

(d) Cross-reference. For an additional limitation on the credit under section 21, see section 26.

T.D. 9354, 8/13/2007.

§ 1.21-3 Special rules applicable to married taxpayers.

(a) Joint return requirement. No credit is allowed under section 21 for taxpayers who are married (within the meaning of section 7703 and the regulations thereunder) at the close of the taxable year unless the taxpayer and spouse file a joint return for the taxable year. See section 6013 and the regulations thereunder relating to joint returns of income tax by husband and wife.

(b) Taxpayers treated as not married. The requirements of paragraph (a) of this section do not apply to a taxpayer who is legally separated under a decree of divorce or separate maintenance or who is treated as not married under section 7703(b) and the regulations thereunder (relating to certain married taxpayers living apart). A taxpayer who is treated as not married under this paragraph (b) is not required to take into account the earned income of the taxpayer's spouse for purposes of applying the earned income limitation on the amount of employment-related expenses under § 1.21-2(b).

(c) Death of married taxpayer. If a married taxpayer dies during the taxable year and the survivor may make a joint return with respect to the deceased spouse under section 6013(a)(3), the credit is allowed for the year only if a joint return is made. If, however, the surviving spouse remarries before the end of the taxable year in which the deceased spouse dies, a credit may be allowed on the decedent spouse(s separate return.

T.D. 9354, 8/13/2007.

§ 1.21-4 Payments to certain related individuals.

(a) In general. A credit is not allowed under section 21 for any amount paid by the taxpayer to an individual—

(1) For whom a deduction under section 151(c) (relating to deductions for personal exemptions for dependents) is allowable either to the taxpayer or the taxpayer's spouse for the taxable year;

(2) Who is a child of the taxpayer (within the meaning of section 152(f)(1) for taxable years beginning after December 31, 2004, and section 151(c)(3) for taxable years beginning before January 1, 2005) and is under age 19 at the close of the taxable year;

(3) Who is the spouse of the taxpayer at any time during the taxable year; or

(4) Who is the parent of the taxpayer's child who is a qualifying individual described in § 1.21-1(b)(1)(i) or (b)(2)(i).

(b) Payments to partnerships or other entities. In general, paragraph (a) of this section does not apply to services performed by partnerships or other entities. If, however, the partnership or other entity is established or maintained primarily to avoid the application of paragraph (a) of this section to permit the taxpayer to claim the credit, for purposes of section 21, the payments of employment-related expenses are treated as made directly to each partner or owner in proportion to that partner's or owner's ownership interest. Whether a partnership or other entity is established or maintained to avoid the application of paragraph (a) of this section is determined based on the facts and circumstances, including whether the partnership or other entity is established for the primary purpose of caring for the taxpayer's qualifying individual or providing household services to the taxpayer.

(c) Examples. The provisions of this section are illustrated by the following examples:

Example (1). During 2007, X pays $5,000 to her mother for the care of X's 5-year old child who is a qualifying individual. The expenses otherwise qualify as employment-related expenses. X's mother is not her dependent. X may take into account under section 21 the amounts paid to her mother for the care of X's child.

Example (2). Y is divorced and has custody of his 5-year old child, who is a qualifying individual. Y pays $6,000 during 2007 to Z, who is his ex-wife and the child's mother, for the care of the child. The expenses otherwise qualify as employment-related expenses. Under paragraph (a)(4) of this section, Y may not take into account under section 21 the amounts paid to Z because Z is the child's mother.

Example (3). The facts are the same as in Example 2, except that Z is not the mother of Y's child. Y may take into account under section 21 the amounts paid to Z.

T.D. 9354, 8/13/2007.

§ 1.23-1 Residential energy credit.

(a) General rule. Section 23 or former section 44C provides a residential energy credit against the tax imposed by chapter 1 of the Internal Revenue Code. The credit is an amount equal to the individual's qualified energy conservation expenditures (set out in paragraph (b)) plus the individual's qualified renewable energy source expenditures (set out in paragraph (c)) for the taxable year. However, the credit is subject to the limitations described in paragraph (d) and the special rules contained in § 1.23-3. The credit is nonrefundable (that is, the credit may not exceed an individual's tax liability for the taxable year). However, any unused credit may be carried over to succeeding years to the extent permitted under paragraph (e). Renters as well as owners of a dwelling unit may qualify for the credit. See § 1.23-3(h) for the rules relating to the allocation of the credit in the case of joint occupants of a dwelling unit.

(b) Qualified energy conservation expenditures. In the case of any dwelling unit, the qualified energy conservation expenditures are 15 percent of the energy conservation expenditures made by the taxpayer with respect to the dwelling unit during the taxable year, but not in excess of $2,000 of such expenditures. See § 1.23-2(a) for the definition of energy conservation expenditures.

(c) Qualified renewable energy source expenditures. In the case of taxable years beginning after December 31, 1979, the qualified renewable energy source expenditures are 40 percent of the renewable energy source expenditures made by the taxpayer during the taxable year (and before January 1, 1986) with respect to the dwelling units that do not exceed $10,000. In the case of taxable years beginning before January 1, 1980, the qualified renewable energy source expenditures are the renewable energy source expenditures made by the taxpayer with respect to the dwelling unit during the taxable year, but not in excess of-

(1) 30 percent of the expenditures up to $2,000, plus

(2) 20 percent of the expenditures over $2,000, but not more than $10,000.

See § 1.23-2(b) for the definition of renewable energy source expenditures.

(d) Limitations. *(1) Minimum dollar amount.* No residential energy credit shall be allowed with respect to any return (whether joint or separate) for any taxable year if the amount of the credit otherwise allowable (determined without regard to the tax liability limitation imposed by paragraph (d)(3) of this section) is less than $10.

(2) Prior expenditures taken into account. (i) In general. For purposes of determining the credit for expenditures made during a taxable year, the taxpayer must reduce the maximum amount of allowable expenditures with respect to the dwelling until in computing qualified energy conservation expenditures (under paragraph (b)) or qualified renewable energy conservation expenditures (under paragraph (c)) by prior expenditures which were made by the taxpayer or by joint occupants (see § 1.23-3(h)) with respect to the same dwelling unit, and which were taken into account in computing the credit for prior taxable years. In the case of expenditures made during taxable years beginning before January 1, 1980, the reduction of the maximum amount under paragraph (c) must first be made with respect to the first $2,000 of expenditures (to which a 30 percent rate applies) and then with respect to the next $8,000 of expenditures (to which a 20 percent rate applies). This reduction must be made if all or any part of the credit was allowed in or was carried over from a prior taxable year.

(ii) Change of principal residence. A taxpayer is eligible for the maximum credit for qualifying expenditures made with respect to a new principal residence notwithstanding the allowance of a credit for qualifying expenditures made with respect to the taxpayer's previous principal residence. Furthermore, except in certain cases involving joint occupancy (see § 1.23-3(h)), a taxpayer is eligible for the maximum credit notwithstanding the allowance of a credit to a prior owner of the taxpayer's new principal residence.

(iii) Example. The rules with respect to the reduction for prior expenditures are illustrated by the following example:

Example. In 1978, A has $1,000 of energy conservation expenditures and $5,000 of renewable energy source expenditures in connection with A's principal residence. A's residential energy credit for 1978 is $1,350, made up of $150 of qualified energy conservation expenditures (15 percent of $1,000) plus $1,200 of qualified renewable energy source expenditures (30 percent of the first $2,000 plus 20 percent of the next $3,000). In 1979 A has an additional $2,000 of energy conservation expenditures and $3,000 of renewable energy source expenditures in connection with the same principal residence. A's residential energy credit for 1979 is $750, made up of $150 of qualified energy conservation expenditures (15 percent of the new maximum $1,000, which was reduced from $2,000 by $1,000 of energy conservation expenditures taken into account in 1978) plus $600 of qualified renewable energy source expenditures (20 percent of $3,000, which reflects the reduction of the maximum allowable expenditures by the $5,000 of renewable energy source expenditures taken into account in 1978). The maximum residential energy credit allowable to A with respect to the same principal residence in subsequent years in which the credit is allowable is $400 (20 percent of the new maximum of $2,000 for renewable energy source expenditures and none for energy conservation expenditures).

(3) Effects of grants and subsidized energy financing. (i) In general. Qualified expenditures financed with Federal, State, or local grants shall be taken into account for purposes of computing the residential energy credit only if the amount of such grants is taxable as gross income to the taxpayer under section 61 (relating to the definition of gross income) and the regulations thereunder. In the case of taxable years beginning after December 31, 1980, qualified expenditures made from subsidized energy financing (as defined in § 1.23-2(i)) shall not be taken into account (except as provided in the following sentence) for purposes of computing the residential energy credit. In addition, the taxpayer must reduce the maximum amount allowable expenditures (reduced as provided in paragraph (d)(2) of this section) with respect to the dwelling unit in computing qualified energy conservation expenditures (under paragraph (b) of this section) or qualified renewable energy source expenditures

(under paragraph (c) of this section), whichever is appropriate, by an amount equal to the sum of—

(A) The amount of expenditures from subsidized energy financing (as defined in § 1.23-2(i)) that were made by the taxpayer during the taxable year or any prior taxable year beginning after December 31, 1980, with respect to the same dwelling unit, and

(B) The amount of any funds received by the taxpayer during the taxable year or any prior taxable year beginning after December 31, 1980, as a Federal, State, or local government grant made in taxable years beginning after December 31, 1980, that were used to make qualified expenditures with respect to the same dwelling unit and that were not included in the gross income of the taxpayer.

(ii) Example. The provisions of this paragraph (d)(3) may be illustrated by the following example:

Example. A had in 1979 made a renewable energy source expenditure of $2,000 in connection with A's residence for which he took the then allowed credit of $600. In 1981 A made additional renewable energy source expenditures of $9,000 with respect to which he received a loan of $5,000 from the Federal Solar-Energy and Energy Conservation Bank. Assume that the loan is subsidized energy financing. A computes the credit as follows: The initial maximum allowable dollar limit is $10,000 which is reduced by the sum of the prior year expenditures of $2,000 and the subsidized energy financing loan of $5,000 leaving a dollar limit of $3,000 ($10,000?($2,000+$5,000)). The $5,000 portion of the $9,000 funded by the subsidized energy financing loan is not allowed as a renewable energy source expenditure. The remaining expenditures in 1981 are $4,000 ($9,000?$5,000). However, this amount exceeds the allowed maximum dollar limit of $3,000. Therefore, A's creditable expenses for 1981 are only $3,000 on which the credit is $1,200 (40 percent of $3,000).

(4) Tax liability limitation.

(i) For taxable years beginning after December 31, 1983. For taxable years beginning after December 31, 1983, the credit allowed by this section shall not exceed the amount of tax imposed by chapter 1 of the Internal Revenue Code of 1954 for the taxable year, reduced by the sum of credits allowable under—

(A) Section 21 (relating to expenses for household and dependent care services necessary for gainful employment),

(B) Section 22 (relating to credit for the elderly and the permanently and totally disabled), and

(C) Section 24 (relating to contributions to candidates for public office).

See section 26 (b) and (c) for certain taxes that are not treated as imposed by chapter 1.

(ii) For taxable years beginning before January 1, 1984. For taxable years beginning before January 1, 1984, the credit allowed by this section shall not exceed the amount of the tax imposed by chapter 1 of the Internal Revenue Code of 1954 for the taxable year, reduced by the sum of the credits allowable under—

(A) Section 32 (relating to tax withheld at source on nonresident aliens and foreign corporations and on tax-free covenant bonds),

(B) Section 33 (relating to the taxes of foreign countries and possessions of the United States),

(C) Section 37 (relating to retirement income),

(D) Section 38 (relating to investment in certain depreciable property),

(E) Section 40 (relating to expenses of work incentive programs),

(F) Section 41 (relating to contributions to candidates for public office),

(G) Section 42 (relating to the general tax credit),

(H) Section 44 (relating to purchase of new personal residence),

(I) Section 44A (relating to expenses for household and dependent care services), and

(J) Section 44B (relating to employment of certain new employees).

(e) Carryforward of unused credit. If the credit allowable by this section exceeds the tax liability limitation imposed by section 23(b)(5) (or former section 44C(b)(5)) and paragraph (d)(4) of this section, the excess credit shall be carried forward to the succeeding taxable year and added to the credit allowable under this section for the succeeding taxable year. A carryforward that is not used in the succeeding year because it exceeds the tax liability limitation shall be carried forward to later taxable years until used, except that no excess credit may be carried forward to any taxable year beginning after December 31, 1987.

T.D. 7717, 8/29/80, amend T.D. 8146, 7/16/87.

§ 1.23-2 Definitions.

For purposes of section 23 or former section 44C and regulations thereunder-

(a) Energy conservation expenditures.

(1) In general. The term "energy conservation expenditure" means an expenditure made on or after April 20, 1977, and before January 1, 1986, by a taxpayer for insulation or any other energy-conserving component, or for labor costs allocable to the original installation of such insulation or other component, if all of the following conditions are satisfied:

(i) The insulation (as defined in paragraph (c)) or other energy-conserving component (as defined in paragraph (d)) is installed in or on a dwelling unit that is used as the taxpayer's principal residence when the installation is completed. See § 1.23-3(e) for the definition of principal residence.

(ii) The dwelling unit is located in the United States (as defined in section 7701(a)(9)).

(iii) The construction of the dwelling unit was substantially completed before April 20, 1977. See § 1.23-3(f) for the definition of the terms "construction" and "substantially completed". In the case of expenditures made with respect to the enlargement of a dwelling unit, the construction of the enlargement must have been substantially completed before April 20, 1977.

(2) Examples. The application of this paragraph may be illustrated by the following examples:

Example (1). In 1978, A spent $500 for the purchase and installation of new storm windows to replace old storm windows, $100 to reinstall old storm windows, and $150 to transfer a A's house insulation which had been installed in A's garage. Only the $500 spent for new storm windows qualifies as an energy conservation expenditure. The $100 spent to reinstall storm windows and the $150 spent to transfer insulation to A's house do not qualify since the only installation costs that qualify are those for the original installation of energy conservation property the original use of which commences with the taxpayer.

Example (2). In June 1977, B purchased for B's principal residence a new house that was substantially completed before April 20, 1977. Pursuant to B's request the builder installed storm windows on May 1, 1977, the cost of this option being included in the purchase price of the house. The portion of the purchase price of the residence allocable to the storm windows constitutes an energy conservation expenditure. However, no other part of the purchase price may be allocated to energy conservation property (insulation and other energy conserving components) installed before April 20, 1977. To qualify as an energy conservation expenditure, an expenditure must be made (i.e., installation of the energy conservation property must be completed) on or after April 20, 1977.

(b) Renewable energy source expenditures. The term "renewable energy source expenditures" means an expenditure made on or after April 20, 1977, and before January 1, 1986, by a taxpayer for renewable energy source property (as defined in paragraph (e)), or for labor costs properly allocable to the on-site preparation, assembly, or original installation such property, if both of the following conditions are satisfied:

(1) The renewable energy source property is installed in connection with a dwelling unit that is used as the taxpayer's principal residence when the installation is completed. See § 1.23-3(e).

(2) The dwelling unit is located in the United States (as defined in section 7701(a)(9)).

Additionally, the term "renewable energy source expenditures" includes expenditures made after December 31, 1979, and before January 1, 1986, for an onsite well drilled for any geothermal deposit (as defined in paragraph (h)), or for labor costs properly allocable to onsite preparation, assembly, or original installation of such well, but only if the requirements of paragraphs (b) (1) and (2) of this section are met and the taxpayer has not elected under section 263(c) to deduct any portion of such expenditures or allocable labor costs.

Eligibility as a renewable energy source expenditure does not depend on the date of construction of the dwelling unit. Thus, such an expenditure may be made in connection with either a new or an existing dwelling unit. Renewable energy source expenditures need only be made in connection with a dwelling, rather than in or on a dwelling unit. For example, a solar collector that otherwise constitutes renewable energy source property is not ineligible merely because it is installed separately from the dwelling unit. The term "renewable energy source expenditure" does not include any expenditure allocable to a swimming pool even when used as an energy storage medium or to any other energy storage medium whose primary function is other than the storage of energy. It also does not include the cost of maintenance of an installed system or the cost of leasing renewable energy source property.

(c) Insulation. The term "insulation" means any item that satisfies all of the following conditions:

(1) The item is specifically and primarily designed to reduce, when installed in or on a dwelling or on a water heater, the heat loss or gain of such dwelling or water heater. To qualify as insulation the item must be installed between a conditioned area and a nonconditioned area (except when installed on a water heater, water pipe, or heating/cooling duct). Thus for example, awnings do not qualify as insulation. For purposes of this section the term "conditioned area" means an area that has been heated or cooled by conventional or renewable energy source means. Insulation includes materials made of fiberglass, rock wool, cellulose, urea based foam, urethane, vermiculite, perlite, polystyrene, and extruded polystyrene foam.

(2) The original use of the item begins with the taxpayer.

(3) The item can reasonably be expected to remain in operation at least 3 years.

(4) The item meets the applicable performance and quality standards prescribed in § 1.23-4 (if any) that are in effect at the time the taxpayer acquires the item. The term "insulation" shall not include items whose primary purpose is not insulation (e.g., whose function is primarily structural, decorative, or safety-related). For example, carpeting, drapes (including linings), shades, wood paneling, fireplace screens (including those made of glass), new or replacement walls (except for qualifying insulation therein) and exterior siding do not qualify although they may have been designed in part to have an insulating effect.

(d) Other energy-conserving components. The term "other energy-conserving component" means any item (other than insulation) that satisfies all of the following conditions:

(1) The original use of the item begins with the taxpayer.

(2) The item can reasonably be expected to remain in operation for at least 3 years.

(3) The item meets the applicable performance and quality standards prescribed in § 1.23-4 (if any) that are in effect at the time of the taxpayer's acquisition of the item.

(4) The item is one of the following items:

(i) A furnace replacement burner. The term "furnace replacement burner" means a device (for oil and gas-fired furnaces or boilers) that is designed to achieve a reduction in the amount of fuel consumed as a result of increased combustion efficiency. The burner must replace an existing burner. It does not qualify if it is acquired as a component of, or for use in, a new furnace or boiler.

(ii) A device for modifying flue openings. The term "device for modifying flue openings" means an automatically operated damper that—

(A) Is designed for installation in the flue, between the barometric damper or draft hood and the chimney, of a furnace; and

(B) Conserves energy by substantially reducing the flow of conditioned air through the chimney when the furnace is not in operation. Conditioned air is air that has been heated or cooled by conventional or renewable energy source means.

(iii) A furnace ignition system. The term "furnace ignition system" means an electrical or mechanical device, designed for installation in a gas-fired furnace or boiler that automatically ignites the gas burner. In order to qualify, the device must replace a gas pilot light. Furthermore, it does not qualify if it is acquired as a component of, or for use in, a new furnace or boiler.

(iv) A storm or thermal window or door. The terms "storm or thermal window" and "storm or thermal door" mean the following:

(A) (1) A window placed outside or inside an ordinary or prime window, creating an insulating air space.

(2) A window with enhanced resistance to heat flow through the glazed area by multi-glazing.

(3) A window that consists of glass or other glazing materials that have exceptional heat-absorbing or heat-reflecting properties. For purposes of this subdivision (iv), the term "glazing material" does not include films and coatings applied on the surface of a window.

(B) (1) A second door, installed outside or inside a prime exterior door, creating an insulating air space.

(2) A door with enhanced resistance to heat flow through the glazed area by multi-glazing.

(3) A prime exterior door that has an R-value (a measurement of the ability of insulation to resist the flow of heat) of at least 2 throughout.

For purposes of this subdivision, "multi-glazing" is an arrangement in which two or more sheets of glazing material are affixed in a window or door frame to create one or more insulating air spaces. Multi-glazing can be achieved by installing a preassembled, sealed insulating glass unit or by affixing one or more additional sheets of glazing onto an existing window (or sash) or door. For purposes of this subdivision, a storm or thermal window or door does not include any film applied on or over the surface of a window or door.

(v) Automatic energy-saving setback thermostat. The term "automatic energy-saving setback thermostat" means a device that is designed to reduce energy consumption by regulating the demand on the heating or cooling system in which it is installed, and uses—

(A) A temperature control device for interior spaces incorporating more than one temperature control level, and

(B) A clock or other automatic mechanism for switching from one control level to another.

(vi) Caulking and weatherstripping. The term "caulking" means pliable materials used to fill small gaps at fixed joints on buildings to reduce the passage of air and moisture. Caulking includes, but is not limited to, materials commonly known as "sealants", "putty", and "glazing compounds". The term "weatherstripping" means narrow strips of material placed over or in movable joints of windows and doors to reduce the passage of air and moisture.

(vii) Energy usage display meter. The term "energy usage display meter" means a device the sole purpose of which is to display the cost (in money) of energy usage in the dwelling. It may show cost information for electricity usage, gas usage, oil usage, or any combination thereof. The device may measure energy usage of the whole dwelling, or individual appliances or systems on an instantaneous or cumulative basis.

(viii) Components specified by the Secretary. The Secretary (or his delegate) may, in his discretion, after consultation with the Secretary of Energy and the Secretary of Housing and Urban Development (or their delegates), and any other appropriate Federal officers, specify by regulation other energy-conserving components for addition to the list of qualified items. See § 1.23-6 for the procedures and criteria to be used in determining whether an item will be considered for addition to the list of qualified items by the Secretary.

The term "other energy-conserving component" is limited to items in a category specifically listed in section 44(c)(4)(A) (i) through (vii) or added by the Secretary.

(e) Renewable energy source property. *(1) In general.* The term "renewable energy source property" includes any solar energy property, wind energy property, geothermal energy property, or property referred to in subparagraph (2), which meets the following conditions:

(i) The original use of the property begins with the taxpayer.

(ii) The property can reasonably be expected to remain in operation for at least 5 years.

(iii) The property meets the applicable performance and quality standards prescribed in § 1.23-4 (if any) that are in effect at the time of the taxpayer's acquisition of the property.

Renewable energy source property does not include heating or cooling systems, nor systems to provide hot water or electricity, which serve to supplement renewable energy source equipment in heating, cooling, or providing hot water or electricity to a dwelling unit, and which employ a form of energy (such as oil or gas) other than solar, wind, or geothermal energy (or other forms of renewable energy provided in paragraph (e)(2) of this section. Thus, heat pumps or oil or gas furnaces, used in connection with renewable energy source property, are not eligible for the credit. In order to be eligible for the credit for renewable energy source property, the property (as well as labor costs properly allocable to onsite preparation, assembly or installation of equipment) must be clearly identifiable. See § 1.23-3(l) for recordkeeping rules.

(2) Renewable energy source specified by the Secretary. In addition to solar, wind, and geothermal energy property, renewable energy source property includes property that transmits or uses another renewable energy source that the Secretary (or his delegate) specifies by regulations, after consultation with the Secretary of Energy and the Secretary of Housing and Urban Development (or their delegates), and any other appropriate Federal officers, to be of a kind that is appropriate for the purpose of heating or cooling the dwelling or providing hot water or (in the case of expenditures made after December 31, 1979) electricity for use within the dwelling. For purposes of this section, references to the transmission or use of energy include its collection and storage. See § 1.23-6 for the procedures and criteria to be used in determining when another energy source will be considered for addition to the list of qualified renewable energy sources.

(f) Solar energy property.

(1) In general. The term "solar energy property" means equipment and materials of a solar energy system as defined in this paragraph (and parts solely related to the functioning of such equipment) which, when installed in connection with a dwelling, transmits or uses solar energy to heat or cool the dwelling or to provide hot water or (in the case of expenditures made after December 31, 1979) electricity for use within the dwelling. For this purpose, solar energy is energy derived directly from sunlight (solar radiation). Property which uses, as an energy source, fuel or energy which is indirectly derived from sunlight (solar radiation), such as fossil fuel or wood or heat in underground water, is not considered solar energy property. Materials and components of "passive solar systems" as well as "active solar systems", or a combination of both types of systems may qualify as solar energy property.

(2) Active solar system. An active solar system is based on the use of mechanically forced energy transfer, such as the use of fans or pumps to circulate solar generated energy, or thermal energy transfer, such as systems utilizing thermal siphon principles. Generally, this is accomplished through

the use of equipment such as collectors (to absorb sunlight and create hot liquids or air), storage tanks (to store hot liquids), rockbeds (to store hot air), thermostats (to activate pumps or fans which circulate the hot liquids or air), and heat exchangers (to utilize hot liquids or air to heat air or water).

(3) Passive solar system. A passive solar system is based on the use of conductive, convective, or radiant energy transfer. In order to qualify as a passive solar system, a solar system used for heating purposes must contain all of the following: a solar collection area, an absorber, a storage mass, a heat distribution method, and heat regulation devices. The term "solar collection area" means an expanse of transparent or translucent material, such as glass which is positioned in such a manner that the rays of the sun directly strike an absorber. The term "absorber" means a surface, such as a floor, that is exposed to the rays of the sun admitted through the solar collection area, which converts solar radiation into heat, and then transfers the heat to a storage mass. The term "storage mass" means material, such as masonry, that receives and holds heat from the absorber and later releases the heat to the interior of the dwelling. The storage mass must be of sufficient volume, depth, and thermal energy capacity to store and deliver adequate amounts of solar heat for the relative size of the dwelling. In addition, the storage mass must be located so that it is capable of distributing the stored heat directly to the habitable areas of the dwelling through a heat distribution method. The term "heat distribution method" means the release of radiant heating from the storage mass within the habitable areas of the dwelling, or convective heating from the storage mass through airflow paths provided by openings or by ducts in the storage mass, to habitable areas of the dwelling. The term "heat regulations devices" means shading or venting mechanisms (such as awnings or insulated drapes) to control the amount of solar heat admitted through the solar collection areas and nighttime insulation or its equivalent to control the amount of heat permitted to escape from the interior of the dwelling.

(4) Components with dual function. To the extent that a passive or active solar system utilizes portions of the structure of a residence, only the materials and components whose sole purpose is to transmit or use solar radiation (and labor costs associated with installing such materials and components) are included within the term "solar energy property". Accordingly, materials and components that serve a dual purpose, e.g., they have a significant structural function or are structural components of the dwelling (and labor costs associated with installing such materials and components) are not included within the term "solar energy property". For example, roof ponds that form part of a roof (including additional structural components to support the roof), windows (including clerestories and skylights), and greenhouses do not qualify as solar energy property. However, with respect to expenditures made after December 31, 1979, a solar collector panel installed as a roof or portion thereof (including additional structural components to support the roof attributable to the collector) does not fail to qualify as solar energy property solely because it constitutes a structural component of the dwelling on which it is installed. For this purpose, the term "solar collector panel" does not include a skylight or other type of window. In the case of a trombe wall (a south facing wall composed of a mass wall and exterior glazing), the mass wall (and labor costs associated with installing the mass wall) will not qualify. However, the exterior (non-window) glazing will qualify. Any shading, venting and heat distribution mechanisms or storage systems that do not have a dual function will also qualify.

(g) Wind energy property. The term "wind energy property" means equipment (and parts solely related to the functioning of such equipment) which, when installed in connection with a dwelling, transmits or uses wind energy to produce energy in a useful form for personal residential purposes. Examples of equipment using wind energy to produce energy in a useful form are windmills, wind-driven generators, power conditioning and storage devices that use wind to generate electricity or mechanical forms of energy. Devices that use wind merely to ventilate do not qualify as wind energy property.

(h) Geothermal energy property. The term "geothermal energy property" means equipment (and parts solely related to the functioning of such equipment) necessary to transmit or use energy from a geothermal deposit to heat or cool a dwelling or provide hot water for use within the dwelling. With respect to expenditures made after December 31, 1979, the term "geothermal energy property" also means equipment (and parts solely related to the functioning of such equipment) necessary to transmit or use energy from a geothermal deposit to produce electricity for use within the dwelling. Equipment such as a pipe that serves both a geothermal function (by transmitting hot geothermal water within a dwelling) and a non-geothermal function (by transmitting hot water from a water heater within a dwelling) does not qualify as geothermal property. A geothermal deposit is a geothermal reservoir consisting of natural heat which is from an underground source and is stored in rocks or in an aqueous liquid or vapor (whether or not under pressure), having a temperature exceeding 50 degrees Celsius as measured at the wellhead or, in the case of a natural hot spring (where no well is drilled), at the intake to the distribution system.

(i) Subsidized energy financing. *(1) In general.* The term "subsidized energy financing" means financing (e.g., a loan) made directly or indirectly (such as in association with, or through the facilities of, a bank or other lender) during a taxable year beginning after December 31, 1980, under a Federal, State, or local program, a principal purpose of which is to provide subsidized financing for projects designed to conserve or produce energy. For purposes of this paragraph (i), financing is made when funds that constitute subsidized energy financing are disbursed. Subsidized energy financing includes financing under a Federal, State, or local program having two or more principal purposes (provided that at least one of the principal purposes is to provide subsidized financing for projects designed to conserve or produce energy), but only to the extent that the financing—

(i) Is to be used for energy production or conservation purposes, or

(ii) Is provided out of funds designated specifically for energy production or conservation.

Loan proceeds meet the use test of paragraph (i)(l)(i) of this section only to the extent that the loan application, the loan instrument, or any other loan-related documents indicate that the funds are intended for such use. However, loan proceeds designated for the purchase either of property that contains "insulation" or any "other energy-conserving component" or of "renewable energy source property" as defined in paragraphs (c), (d), and (e), respectively, of this section meet the test of paragraph (i)(l)(i) of this section. Financing is subsidized if the interest rate or other terms of the financing (including any special tax treatment) provided to the taxpayer in connection with the program or used to raise funds for the program are more favorable than the terms generally available commercially. In addition, financing is subsidized if the principal obligation of the financing provided to the taxpayer is reduced by funds provided under the program. The source from which the funds for the program are derived is not a factor to be taken into account in determining whether the financing is subsidized. If a public utility disburses funds for the financing of energy conservation or renewable energy source property under a program that obtains the funds through sales to the utility's ratepayers, the program is not considered to be a Federal, State or local program even though the utility is a governmental agency, and, thus, the funds are not subsidized energy financing. Subsidized energy financing does not include a grant includible in gross income under section 61, nontaxable grants, a credit against State or local taxes made directly to the taxpayer claiming the credit provided for in section 23, or a loan guarantee made directly to the taxpayer claiming the credit provided for in section 23.

(2) Examples. The provisions of this paragraph (i) may be illustrated by the following examples:

Example (1). State A has a farm and home loan program. The program is used to provide low interest mortgage loans. In 1984 State A's legislature enacted statutory amendments to its farm and home loan program in an effort to encourage energy conservation-type measures. Low interest loans for such improvements were made available to qualified purchasers and owners under the farm and home loan program. The energy conservation measures subsidized by the program include energy conserving components and renewable energy source devices. State A's tax exempt bonds are the source of funds for loans under the program. Although the 1984 legislation authorizing loans for energy conserving components and renewable energy source improvements did not diminish the original purpose of the farm and home loan program, the 1984 legislation added another principal purpose to the program. Therefore, State A's program which has two principal purposes, one of which is the conservation or production of energy, is considered as providing subsidized energy financing for purposes of section 23 (c)(10) of the Code, to the extent that financing is provided by State A out of funds designated specifically for energy production or conservation. State A's program will also be considered as providing subsidized energy financing to the extent that the loan proceeds are to be used for energy production or conservation purposes. Loan proceeds meet the use test of the preceding sentence only to the extent that loan application, the loan instruments, or any other loan-related documents indicate that the funds are intended for such use.

Example (2). The United States Department of Energy disburses funds to State B that the Department received from settlements from alleged petroleum pricing and allocation violations. State B establishes a program under which B will use the funds to make loans at below market interest rates directly to qualified applicants for the purchase of renewable energy source property. B's loans are subsidized energy financing.

Example (3). State C establishes a program under which C will make loans at below market interest rates directly to qualified applicants for the purchases of renewable energy source property. The program is funded with money that State C was able to borrow after it obtained a loan guarantee from a Federal agency. C's loans provided under the program are subsidized energy financing.

Example (4). Company D is an electric utility that is a Federal agency. D purchases its electricity from another federal agency, transmits the electricity over its own distribution system, and sells the electricity to numerous local public utilities that in turn sell the electricity to their customers. D wishes to start a program under which D will make loans at below market interest rates directly to customers of the local utilities for the purchase of renewable energy source property from D. The local public utility will act as the collection agent for repayment of the loans. The loans will be repayable over a period of time not in excess of 15 years. Under law, D must cover its full costs through its own revenues derived from the sale of power and other services. While D may borrow by sale of bonds to the United States Treasury, D must borrow at rates comparable to the rates prevailing in the market for similar bonds. Thus, the subsidized loans made under D's program will be financed by the profits from the sale of electricity to consumers and not by the federal government. D's program, which is substantially the same as that carried out by private (investor-owned) utilities, is not considered to be a Federal, State or local governmental program. Therefore, D's loans are not subsidized energy financing.

Example (5). The Solar Energy and Energy Conservation Bank (Bank) disburses funds to State E. E disburses a portion of the funds to Financial Institution F. Both the Bank and State E make these disbursements under a program the principal purpose of which is to provide subsidized financing for projects designed to conserve or produce energy. F uses the funds to reduce a portion of the principal obligation on loans it issues to finance energy conservation or solar energy expenditures. Taxpayer G borrows $3,000 from F in order to purchase a solar water heating system. F uses $500 of the funds it received from the Bank to reduce the principal obligation of the loan to G to $2,500. The amount of subsidized energy financing to G is $3,000.

Example (6). State H allows a tax credit to Financial Institution J under a program the principal purpose of which is to provide loans at below market interest rates directly to qualified applicants for the purchase of renewable energy source property. J receives a credit each year in the amount of the excess of the interest that would have been paid at private market rates over the actual interest paid on such loans. The State H tax credit arrangement is an interest subsidy. Thus, any low-interest loans made pursuant to this credit arrangement are subsidized energy financing.

T.D. 7717, 8/29/80, amend T.D. 8146, 7/16/87.

§ 1.23-3 Special rules.

(a) When expenditures are treated as made. *(1) Timeliness of an expenditure for the energy credit.* In general, for the purpose of determining whether an expenditure qualifies as being timely for the residential energy credit under section 23 or former section 44C (i.e., is made after April 19, 1977, and before January 1, 1986), the expenditure is treated as made when original installation of the item is completed. Thus, solely for that purpose, the time of payment or accrual is irrelevant.

(2) Special rule for renewable energy source expenditures in the case of construction or reconstruction of a dwelling. In the case of renewable energy source expenditures in connection with the construction or reconstruction of a dwelling that becomes the taxpayer's new principal residence, the expenditures are to be treated as made (for the purpose of determining the timeliness of an expenditure for the residential energy credit) when the taxpayer commences use of the dwelling as his or her principal residence following its con-

struction or reconstruction. The term "reconstruction" means the replacement of most of a dwelling's major structural components such as floors, walls, and ceiling. When a taxpayer reoccupies a reconstructed dwelling that was the taxpayer's principal residence prior to reconstruction, a renewable energy source expenditure is considered made when the original installation of the renewable energy source property is completed.

(3) Taxable year in which credit is allowable. For the purpose of determining the taxable year in which the credit for an expenditure is allowable (once it has qualified as timely under subparagraph (1) or (2)), an expenditure is treated as made on the later of (i) the date on which it qualifies as timely; or (ii) the date on which it is paid or incurred by the taxpayer.

(b) Expenditures in 1977. No credit under section 23 or former section 44C shall be allowed for any taxable year beginning before 1978. However, the amount of any credit under section 23 or former section 44C for the taxpayer's first taxable year beginning after December 31, 1977, shall take into account qualified energy conservation expenditures and qualified renewable energy source expenditures made during the period beginning April 20, 1977, and ending on the last day of such first taxable year.

(c) Cross reference. For rules relating to expenditures financed with Federal, State, or local government grants or subsidized financing see paragraph (d)(3) of § 1.23-1 and paragraph (i) of § 1.23-2.

(d) Expenditures qualifying both as energy conservation expenditures and renewable source expenditures. In the case of an expenditure which meets both the definition of an energy conservation expenditure (as defined in § 1.23-2(a)) and a renewable energy source expenditure (as defined in § 1.23-2(b)), the taxpayer may claim either a credit under § 1.23-1(b) (relating to qualified energy conservation expenditures) or § 1.23-1(c) (relating to qualified renewable energy source expenditures) but may not claim both credits with respect to the same expenditure.

(e) Principal residence. For purposes of section 23 or former section 44C the determination of whether a dwelling unit is the taxpayer's principal residence shall be made under principles similar to those applicable to section 1034 and the regulations thereunder (relating to sale or exchange of a principal residence) except that ownership of the dwelling unit is not required. In making this determination, the period for which a dwelling is treated as a taxpayer's principal residence includes the 30-day period ending on the first day on which the dwelling unit would (but for this sentence) be treated as being used as the taxpayer's principal residence under principles similar to those applicable to section 1034. Thus, installation that are completed within that 30-day period may be eligible for the credit although, in the absence of the 30-day rule, the date of habitation of the dwelling unit by the taxpayer would mark the beginning of the taxpayer's use of the unit as a principal residence.

(f) Construction substantially completed. Construction of a dwelling unit is substantially completed when construction has progressed to the point where the unit could be put to use as a personal residence, even though comparatively minor items remain to be finished or performed in order to conform to the plans or specifications of the completed building. For this purpose, construction includes reconstruction as defined in paragraph (a)(2). This rule may be illustrated by the following example:

Example. On January 1, 1979, A purchases a dwelling that is to become A's principal residence. The dwelling unit was originally constructed in 1950. A spends $50,000 to reconstruct the dwelling by replacing most of the dwelling's major structural components such as floors, walls, and ceilings. Included in the cost is $3,000 attributable to energy-conserving components. Reconstruction is substantially completed on April 1, 1979, and A moves into the reconstructed residence on May 1, 1979. Since construction includes reconstruction, A's reconstructed residence is not considered substantially completed before April 20, 1977. Thus, amounts spent with respect to A's reconstructed residence for energy-conserving components do not qualify as energy conservation expenditures.

(g) Residential use of property. To be eligible for the residential energy credit, expenditures must be made for personal residential purposes. If at least 80 percent of the use of a component or item of property is for personal residential purposes, the entire amount of the energy conservation expenditure or the renewable energy source expenditure is taken into account in computing the credit under this section. If less than 80 percent of the use of a component or item of property is for personal residential purposes, the amount of an expenditure taken into account is the amount that bears the same ratio to the amount of the expenditure as the amount of personal residential use of the component or item bears to its total use. For purposes of this paragraph, use of a component or an item of property with respect to a swimming pool is not a use for a personal residential purpose. The rules with respect to residential use of property are illustrated by the following examples:

Example (1). In 1978 A makes an expenditure of $3,000 for the installation of storm windows of which 50 percent is on the portion of A's dwelling used as the principal family residence and 50 percent is on the portion of the dwelling used as an office. A has made no other energy conservation expenditures for the residence. The allowable energy conservation expenditure is $1,500 (50 percent of $3,000), the portion attributable to residential use. Therefore, the residential energy credit is $225 (the qualified conservation expenditure of 15 percent of $1.500).

Example (2). During 1979, B makes $10,000 of renewable energy source expenditures on solar energy property for B's principal residence. Approximately 60 percent of the use of the solar energy property will be for heating B's swimming pool; the other 40 percent will be for heating the dwelling unit. B had not previously made renewable energy source expenditures with respect to the residence. Since use for a swimming pool is not considered a residential use, less than 80 percent of the use of B's solar energy property is considered used for personal residential purposes. Therefore, only $4,000 (40 percent of $10,000), the proportionate part of B's expenditures representing personal residential use, is treated as a renewable energy source expenditure. B is allowed a $1,000 residential energy credit (30 percent of $2,000 plus 20 percent of $2,000) for 1979.

(h) Joint occupancy. *(1) In general.* If two or more individuals jointly occupied and used a dwelling unit as their principal residence during any portion of a calendar year—

(i) The amount of the credit allowable under section 23 or former section 44C by reason of energy conservation expenditures or by reason of renewable energy source expenditures shall be determined by treating all of the joint occupants as one taxpayer whose taxable year is such calendar year; and

(ii) The credit under section 23 or former section 44C allowable to each joint occupant for the taxable year with which or in which such calendar year ends shall be an amount which bears the same ratio to the amount determined under paragraph (h)(1)(i) of this section as the amount of energy conservation expenditures or renewable energy source expenditures made by that occupant bears to the total amount of each type of such expenditures made by all joint occupants during such calendar year. The provisions of this subparagraph may be illustrated by the following example:

Example. A, a calendar year taxpayer, and B, a June 1 fiscal year taxpayer, make energy conservation exenditures of $2,000 (A making expenditures of $500 and B making expenditures of $1,500) on their principal and jointly occupied residence in 1978. A and B have not previously make energy conservation expenditures with respect to this residence. Of the $300 credit (15 percent of $2,000), $75 will be allocated to A ($500/$2,000×$300) and $225 to B ($1,500/$2,000×300). A will claim the allocable share of the credit on A's 1978 tax return and B will claim the allocable share of the credit on B's tax return for the fiscal year ending May 31, 1979.

(2) Minimum credit. The fact that one joint occupant may be unable to claim all or part of the credit under section 23 of former section 44C because of insufficient tax liability or because that occupant's allowable credit does not exceed the $10 minimum credit (as set forth in paragraph (d)(1) of § 1.23-1) shall have no effect upon the computation of the amount of the allowable credits for the other joint occupants.

(3) Prior expenditures. Because joint occupants are treated as one taxpayer for purposes of determining the residential energy credit, the maximum amount of energy conservation expenditures or renewable energy source expenditures must be reduced by the total amount of such expenditures made in connection with the dwelling unit during prior calendar years in which any one of the residents of the unit during the current calendar year was a resident (whether made by the current resident or by an individual previously occupying the dwelling with the current resident). However, the preceding sentence shall not apply to prior expenditures no part of which was taken into account in computing the credits under section 23 of former section 44C for such years. Prior years' expenditures are not to be allocated among joint occupants to take into account the specific expenditures of each of the occupants in prior years.

(4) The rules of this paragraph may be illustrated by the following examples:

Example (1). Assume A and B have together made prior years' energy conservation expenditures of $1,600 (A having made $1,200 of expenditures and B having made $400) on their principal and jointly occupied residence. In the current year, each makes energy conservation expenditures of $300 with respect to the same residence. The maximum qualified expenditure with respect to the residence is reduced by the $1,600 of prior expenditures made by A and B. Therefore, only $400 of the $600 current expenditures are eligible as energy conservation expenditures. The resulting residential energy credit is $60 (15 percent of $400) of which $30 apiece will be allocated to A and B ($300/$600 × $60). The fact that A had previously computed the credit in prior years with respect to $1,200 of the total $1,600 of expenditures is irrelevant to the apportionment of the credit in the current year.

Example (2). In 1978, spouses C and D make $10,000 of renewable energy source expenditures with respect to their principal residence, half of which is paid by each spouse. No prior renewable energy source expenditures have been taken into account with respect to that residence by either C or D. C and D file separate returns for the calendar year. Under the joint occupancy rule, the maximum allowable renewable energy source credit with respect to C and D's principal residence is $2,200 (30 percent of the first $2,000, and 20 percent of the next $8,000 of expenditures). Half of this amount or $1,100, will be allowed to each spouse. If either spouse makes renewable energy source expenditures with respect to the same principal residence in future years, none of those expenditures would be qualified renewable energy source expenditures for which a credit can be claimed. That is, not more than $2,200 may be taken in the aggregate by C and D as a renewable energy source credit with respect to their principal residence.

Example (3). In 1978, E and F make energy conservation expenditures of $1,500 on their principal and jointly occupied residence. In 1979, E moves away and G becomes the other joint occupant of the residence. F and G make energy conservation expenditures of $1,000 in 1979. In 1980 F moves away and H moves in with G. G and H make energy conservation expenditures of $500. The maximum qualified expenditure made by F and G with respect to the residence is reduced by the $1,500 of prior expenditures made in 1978 by E and F. The maximum qualified expenditures made by G and H with respect to the residence is reduced only by the expenditures in prior years in connection with the residence during which either G or H was a joint occupant. Accordingly, the maximum qualified expenditures made by G and H with respect to the residence is reduced only by the $1,000 of prior expenditures made in 1979 by F and G.

(i) Condominiums and cooperative housing corporations. An individual who is a tenant stockholder in a cooperative housing corporation (as defined in section 216) or who is a member of a condominium management association with respect to a condominium which he or she owns shall be treated as having made a proportionate share of the energy conservation expenditures or renewable energy source expenditures of such corporation or association. The cooperative stockholder's allocable share of the expenditures is to be the same as his or her proportionate share of the cooperative's total outstanding stock (including any stock held by the corporation). However, in the case where only certain cooperative stockholders are assessed for the expenditures made by the cooperative housing corporation, only those cooperative stockholders that are assessed shall be treated as having made a share of the expenditures of such corporation. In such case, the cooperative stockholder's share of the expenditures is the amount that the stockholder is assessed. The allocable share of a condominium management association member's energy conservation of renewable energy source expenditures is the amount that the member is assessed (or would be assessed in the case where expenditures are from general funds) by the association as a result of such expenditures. The residential energy credit for a qualified expenditure is allowable for the year in which the association or corporation has completed original installation of the item (or has paid or incurred the expenditure, if later). For purposes of this paragraph, the term "condominium management association" means an organization meeting the requirements of section 528(c)(1) of the Code (other than subparagraph (E) of that section), with respect to a condominium project substantially all the units of which are used as residences.

(j) Joint ownership of energy conservation property or renewable energy source property. *(1) In general.* Energy conservation property renewable energy source property include property which is jointly owned by the taxpayer and another person (or persons) and installed in connection with two or more dwelling units. For example, the fact that a windmill, solar collector, or geothermal well and distribution system is owned by two or more individuals does not preclude its qualification as renewable energy source property. The amount of the credit allowable under section 23 shall be computed separately with respect to the amount of the expenditures made by each individual, subject to the limitations of $2,000 imposed by section 23(b)(1) and $10,000 imposed by section 23(b)(2), per dwelling units of jointly owned property. For example, in 1982, A, B, and C purchased as joint owners renewable energy source property that serviced two houses. One of the houses is jointly owned and occupied by A and B and the other is owned and occupied by C alone. The renewable energy source property cost $30,000 of which A paid $9,000, B paid $6,000, and C paid $15,000. A and B must share the $4,000 credit (40% of $10,000 maximum) with respect to the expenditures for the jointly owned house. Therefore, A is allowed a $2,400 credit ($4,000 times $9,000 divided by $9,000 plus $6,000) and B is allowed a $1,600 credit ($4,000 times $6,000 divided by $9,000 plus $6,000) with respect to the expenditures attributable to the jointly owned house. C is entitled to a credit of $4,000 with respect to the expenditures attributable to the other house.

(2) Example. The application of this subparagraph may be illustrated by the following example:

Example. A, B, and C each has a separate principal residence. They agree to finance jointly the construction of a solar collector, each providing one-third of the costs and taking one-third of the output of the collector. Each will separately pay for the costs of connecting the solar collector with his or her principal residence. Provided the solar collector and connection equipment otherwise qualify as renewable energy source property, A, B, and C will each be considered to have made renewable energy source expenditures equal to one-third of the cost of the collector plus his or her separate connection costs. Such expenditures will be subject to the limitations and other rules separately applicable to A, B, and C with respect to each principal residence, such as those with respect to the $10 minimum (§ 1.23-1(d)(1)), prior expenditures (§ 1.23-1(d)(2)), residential use (paragraph (g) of this section), and joint occupancy (paragraph (h) of this section).

(k) Basic adjustments. If a credit is allowed under section 23 or former section 44C for any expenditure with respect to any property, the increase in the basis of that property which would (but for this paragraph) result from such expenditure shall be reduced by the amount of the credit allowed.

(l) Recordkeeping. *(1) In general.* No residential energy credit is allowable unless the taxpayer maintains the records described in paragraph (l)(2) of this section. The records shall be retained so long as the contents thereof may become material in the administration of any internal revenue law.

(2) Records. The taxpayer must maintain records that clearly identify the energy-conserving components and renewable energy source property with respect to which a residential energy credit is claimed, and substantiate their cost to the taxpayer, any labor costs properly allocable to them paid for by the taxpayer, and the method used for allocating such labor costs.

T.D. 7717, 8/29/80, amnd T.D. 8146, 7/16/87.

---

§ 1.23-4 Performance and quality standards.

[Reserved]

§ 1.23-5 Certification procedures.

(a) Certification that an item meets the definition of an energy-conserving component or renewable energy source property. Upon the request of a manufacturer of an item pursuant to paragraph (b) of this section which is supported by proof that the item is entitled to be certified, the Assistant Commissioner (Technical) shall certify (or shall notify the manufacturer that the request is denied) that:

(1) The item meets the definition of insulation (see § 1.23-2(c)(1)).

(2) The item meets the definition of an other energy-conserving component specified in section 23(c)(4) or former section 44C(c)(4) see (§ 1.23-2(d)(4)).

(3) The item meets the definition of solar energy property (see § 1.23-2(f)), wind energy property (see § 1.23-2(g)), or geothermal energy property (see § 1.23-2(h)).

(4) The item meets the definition of a category of energy-conserving component that has been added to the list of approved items pursuant to paragraph (d)(4)(viii) of § 1.23-2.

(5) The item meets the definition of renewable energy source property that transmits or uses a renewable energy source that has been added to the list of approved renewable energy sources pursuant to paragraph (e)(2) of § 1.23-2.

(b) Procedure. *(1) In general.* A manufacturer of an item desiring to apply under paragraph (a) shall submit the application to the Commissioner of Internal Revenue, Attention: Associate Chief Counsel (Technical), CC:C:E, 1111 Constitution Avenue NW., Washington, DC 20224. Upon being advised by the National Office, orally or in writing, that an adverse decision is contemplated a manufacturer may request a conference. The conference must be held within 21 calendar days from the date of that advice. Procedures for requesting an extension of the 21-day period and notifying the manufacturer of the Service's decision on that request are the same as those applicable to conferences on ruling requests by taxpayers (see section 9.05 of Rev. Proc. 80-20).

(2) Contents of application. The application shall include a description of the item (including appropriate design drawings and specifications) and an explanation of the purpose and function of the item. There shall accompany the application a declaration in the following form: "Under penalties of perjury, I declare that I have examined this application, including accompanying documents and, to the best of my knowledge and belief, the facts presented in support of the application are true, correct, and complete." The statement must be signed by the person or persons making the application.

(c) Effect of certification under paragraph (a). Certifications granted under paragraph (a)(1), (2), or (3) will be applied retroactively to April 20, 1977. However, certifications granted under paragraph (a) (4) or (5) will be applied retroactively only to the date the applicable energy-conserving component or renewable energy source was added by Treasury decision to the list of qualifying components or sources. Certification of an item under this section means that the applicable definitional requirement of § 1.23-2 is considered satisfied in the case of any person claiming a residential energy credit with respect to such item. However, it does not relieve manufacturers of the need to establish that their items conform to performance and quality standards (if any) provided under § 1.23-4 and that their items can reasonably be expected to remain in operation at least 3 years, in the case of insulation and other energy-conserving components, or at least 5 years, in the case of renewable energy source property.

T.D. 7717, 8/29/80, amend T.D. 8146, 7/16/87.

§ 1.23-6 Procedure and criteria for additions to the approved list of energy-conserving components or renewable energy sources.

(a) Procedures for additions to the list of energy-conserving components or renewable energy sources. *(1) In general.* A manufacturer of an item (or a group of manufacturers) desiring to apply for addition to the approved list of energy-conserving components or renewable energy sources pursuant to paragraph (d)(4)(viii) or (e)(2) of § 1.23-2 shall submit an application to the Internal Revenue Service, Attention: Associate Chief Counsel (Technical), CC:C:E, 1111 Constitution Avenue, NW., Washington, DC 20224. The term "manufacturer" includes a person who assembles an item or a system from components manufactured by other persons. The application shall provide the information required under paragraph (b) of this section. An application may request that more than one item be added to the approved list. It will be the responsibility of the Office of the Associate Chief Counsel (Technical) upon receipt of the application to determine whether all the information required under paragraph (b) of this section has been furnished with the application. If an application lacks essential information, the applicant will be advised of the additional information required. If the information (or a reasonable explanation of the reason why the information cannot be made available) is not forthcoming within 30 days of the date of that advice, the application will be closed and the applicant will be so informed. Any resubmission of information beyond the 30-day period will be treated as a new application. If the Office of the Associate Chief Counsel (Technical) already is considering an application with respect to the same or a similar item, it may consolidate applications. The Office of the Associate Chief Counsel will make a report and recommendation to the ad hoc advisory board as to whether each item that is the subject to an application should be added in accordance with the manufacturer's request to the approved list of energy-conserving components or renewable energy sources in light of the applicable criteria provided in paragraph (c) and the standards for Secretarial determination provided in paragraph (d) of this section. In making this recommendation, the Office of the Associate Chief Counsel shall consult with the Secretary of Energy and the Secretary of Housing and Urban Development (or their delegates) and any other appropriate Federal officers to obtain their views concerning the item in question. In addition, the Office of the Associate Chief Counsel may request from the manufacturer clarification of information submitted with the application. The Office of the Associate Chief Counsel shall report its recommendation and forward the application to the ad hoc advisory board for further consideration.

(2) Ad hoc advisory board. The Commissioner of Internal Revenue and the Assistant Secretary (Tax Policy) shall establish an ad hoc advisory board to consider applications and recommendations forwarded by the Office of the Associate Chief Counsel (Technical). If a finding in favor of addition of any item is made, the board shall report its recommendation and forward the application to the Commissioner for further consideration. If the item is approved by the Commissioner, the application will be forwarded to the Secretary (or his delegate) for further consideration. The application will be closed with respect to an item if the board, the Commissioner, or the Secretary (or his delegate) determines that, under the applicable criteria or the standards for Secretarial determination, the item should not be added to the list of energy-conserving components or renewable energy sources.

(3) Action on application. (i) A final decision to grant or deny any application filed under paragraph (a)(1) shall be made within 1 year after the application and all information required to be filed with such request under paragraph (b) have been received by the Office of the Associate Chief Counsel (Technical). The applicant manufacturer shall be notified in writing of the final decision. In the event of a favorable determination, a regulation will be issued in accordance with the procedures contained in § 601.601 to include the item as an energy-conserving component or as a renewable energy source. A final decision to grant approval of an application is made when a Treasury decision adding the item (that is subject of the application) as an energy-conserving component or as a renewable energy source is published in theFederal Register.

(ii) The applicant manufacturer shall be entitled to a conference and be so notified anytime an adverse action is contemplated by the Office of the Associate Chief Counsel, the ad hoc advisory board, the Commissioner of Internal Revenue, or the Secretary (or his delegate) and no conference was previously conducted. Upon being advised in writing that an adverse recommendation or decision as to any item that is the subject of an application is contemplated, a manufacturer may request a conference. The conference must be held within 21 calendar days from the mailing of that advice. Procedures for requesting an extension of the 21-day period and notifying the manufacturer of the recommendation or decision with respect to that request are the same as those applicable to conferences on ruling requests by taxpayers. The applicant is entitled to only one conference. There is no right to another conference when a favorable recommendation or decision is reversed at a higher level.

(iii) A report of any application which has been denied during the preceding month and the reasons for the denial shall be published each month.

(b) Contents of application. The application by the manufacturer shall include the following information:

(1) A description of the item and the generic class to which it belongs, including any features relating to safe installation and use of the item. This description shall include appropriate design drawings and technical specifications (or representative drawings and specifications when application by a group of manufacturers).

(2) An explanation of the purpose, function, and each recommended use of the item.

(3) An estimate (and explanation of the estimation methods employed and the assumptions made) of the total number of units that would be sold for each recommended use during the first 4 years following the addition of the item to the approved list and of the total number that would be sold for each recommended use during that period in the absence of addition. If the item is sold in more than one size, the estimate shall indicate the projected sales for each size. This estimate shall reflect total industry sales of the item. Past industry sales information for each recommended use for the previous two years shall also be provided.

(4) Whether sufficient capacity is available to increase production to meet any increase in demand for the item, or for associated fuels and materials, caused by such addition. This determination shall be based on industry-wide data and not just the manufacturing capability of the applicant. If the

applicant has the exclusive right to manufacture the item, this information shall also be provided in the application.

(5) An estimate (including estimation methods and assumptions) of the energy in Btu's of oil and natural gas used directly or indirectly per unit by the applicant in the manufacture of the item and other items necessary for its use, the type of energy source (e.g., oil, natural gas, coal, electricity), and the extent of its use in the manufacturing process of the item. The applicant must also provide a list of the major components of the item and their composition and weight.

(6) Test data and experience data (where experience data is available) to substantiate for each recommended use the energy savings in Btu's that are claimed will be achieved by one unit during a period of one year. The data shall be obtained by controlled tests in which, if possible, the addition of the item is the only variable. If the item may be sold in various configurations, data shall be provided with respect to energy savings from each configuration with significantly different energy use characteristics. Test methods are to conform to recognized industry or government standards. This determination shall take into account the seasonal use of the item. If the energy savings of the item varies with climatic conditions, data shall be provided with respect to each climate zone. The applicant may use the Department of Energy's climatic zones for heating and cooling (see § 450.35 of 10 CFR part 450 (1980)).

(7) The impact of increased demand on the price of the item and the energy source used by the item.

(8) The energy source which will be replaced or conserved by the item, and, in the case of a request for addition to the approved list of renewable energy sources, data establishing that the energy source is inexhaustible.

(9) Data to show the total estimated savings of energy in Btu's attributable to reduced consumption of oil or natural gas whether directly or indirectly from use of the item, including assumptions underlying this estimate. If the consumption of both oil and natural gas will be reduced, data to show the energy savings in Btu's attributable to each shall be provided. The estimate is to be based on energy savings in Btu's per unit determined under paragraph (b)(6) of this section for the first four years of the useful life of the item and is to take into account only the additional units of the item estimated to be placed in service as a result of the addition using data obtained under paragraph (b)(3) of this section. If the item will result in reduction of oil or natural gas consumption by replacing an item which uses such an energy source, the application shall indicate the item replaced and the extent to which this reduction will occur.

(10) Geographical information if required under paragraph (b)(6) of this section to show the climatic zones of the country where the item is expected to be used, including an estimate of the total number of additional units to be placed in service during the first 4 years following the addition of the item in the area as a result of the addition of the item to the list of qualifying items.

(11) The retail cost of the item (or items if the item is sold in more than one size) including all installation costs necessary for safe and effective use.

(12) Whether the item is designed for residential use.

(13) The estimated useful life of the item and associated equipment necessary for its use.

(14) The type and amount of waste and emissions in weight per unit of energy saved resulting from use of the item.

(15) If the item might reasonably be suspected of presenting any health or safety hazard, test data to show that the item does not present such hazard.

With respect to applications for addition to the approved list of renewable energy sources, the term "item" as used in this paragraph refers to the property which uses the energy source and not the energy source itself. The application should clearly indicate whether the request is for addition to the approved list of energy-conserving components or renewable energy sources, identify the provisions for which data is being submitted, and present the data in the order requested. The tests required under this paragraph may be conducted by independent laboratories but the underlying data must be submitted along with the test results. There shall accompany the request a declaration in the following form: "Under penalties of perjury, I declare that I have examined this application, including accompanying documents, and, to the best of my knowledge and belief, the facts presented in support of the application are true, correct and complete." The statement must be signed by the person or persons making the application. The declaration shall not be made by the taxpayer's representative.

(c) Criteria for additions. *(1) Additions to the approved list of energy-conserving components.* For an item to be considered for addition to the approved list of energy-conserving components, the manufacturer must show that the item increases the energy efficiency of a dwelling. For an item to be considered as increasing the energy efficiency of a dwelling, all of the following criteria must be met:

(i) The use of the item must improve the energy efficiency of the dwelling structure, structural components of the dwelling, hot water heating, or heating or cooling systems.

(ii) The use of the item must result, directly or indirectly, in a significant reduction in the consumption of oil or natural gas.

(iii) The increase in energy efficiency must be established by test data and in accordance with accepted testing standards.

(iv) The item must not present a safety, fire, environmental, or health hazard when properly installed.

(2) Additions to the approved list of renewable energy sources. For an energy source to be considered for addition to the approved list of renewable energy sources, the manufacturer must show that the following criteria are met:

(i) As in the case of solar, wind, and geothermal energy, the energy source must be an inexhaustible energy supply. Accordingly, wood and agricultural products and by-products are not considered renewable energy sources. Similarly, no exhaustible or depletable energy source (such as sources that are depletable under 611) will be considered.

(ii) The energy source must be capable of being used for heating or cooling a residential dwelling or providing hot water or electricity for use in such a dwelling.

(iii) A practical working device, machine, or mechanism, etc., must exist and be commercially available to use such renewable energy source.

(iv) The use of the renewable energy source must not present a significant safety, fire, environmental, or health hazard.

(d) Standards for Secretarial determination. *(1) In general.* The Secretary will not make any addition to the approved list of energy-conserving components or renewable energy sources unless the Secretary determines that—

(i) There will be a reduction in the total consumption of oil or natural gas as a result of the addition, and that reduction is sufficient to justify any resulting decrease in Federal revenues.

(ii) The addition will not result in an increased use of any item which is known to be, or reasonably suspected to be, environmentally hazardous or a threat to public health or safety, and

(iii) Available Federal subsidies do not make the addition unnecessary or inappropriate (in the light of the most advantageous allocation of economic resources).

(2) Factors taken into account. In making any determination under paragraph (d)(1)(i) of this section, the Secretary will— (i) Make an estimate of the amount by which the addition will reduce oil and natural gas consumption, and

(ii) Determine whether the addition compares favorably, on the basis of the reduction in oil and natural gas consumption per dollar of cost to the Federal Government (including revenue loss), with other Federal programs in existence or being proposed.

(3) Factors taken into account in making estimates. In making any estimate under subparagraph (2)(i), the Secretary will take into account (among other factors)—

(i) The extent to which the use of any item will be increased as a result of the addition,

(ii) Whether sufficient capacity is available to increase production to meet any increase in demand for the item or associated fuels and materials caused by the addition,

(iii) The amount of oil and natural gas used directly or indirectly in the manufacture of the item and other items necessary for its use,

(iv) The estimated useful life of the item, and

(v) The extent additional use of the item leads, directly or indirectly, to the reduced use of oil or natural gas. Indirect uses of oil or natural gas include use of electricity derived from oil or natural gas.

(e) Effective date of addition to approved lists. In the case of additions to the approved list of energy-conserving components or renewable energy sources, the credit allowable by § 1.23-1 shall apply with respect to expenditures which are made on or after the date a Treasury decision amending the regulations pursuant to the application is published in theFederal Register.However, the Secretary may prescribe by regulations that expenditures for additions made on or after the date referred to in the preceding sentence and before the close of the taxable year in which such date occurs shall be taken into account in the following taxable year. Additions to the list will be subject to the performance and quality standards (if any) provided under § 1.23-4 which are in effect at the time of the addition. Furthermore, any addition made to the approved list will be subject to reevaluation by the Secretary for the purpose of determining whether the item still meets the requisite criteria and standards for addition to the list. If it is determined by the Secretary that an item no longer meets the requisite criteria, the Secretary will amend the regulations to delete the item from the approved list. Removal of an item from the list will be prospective from the date a Treasury decision amending the regulations is published in theFederal Register.

(Secs. 44C and 7805 of the Internal Revenue Code of 1954 (92 Stat. 3175, 26 U.S.C. 44C; 68A Stat. 917, 26 U.S.C. 7805). The amendments to the Statement of Procedural Rules are issued under the authority contained in 5 U.S.C. 301 and 552)

T.D. 7861, 12/16/82, amnd T.D. 8146, 7/16/87.

---

§ 1.25-1T Credit for interest paid on certain home mortgages (temporary).

Caution: The Treasury has not yet amended Reg § 1.25-1T to reflect changes made by P.L. 103-66, P.L. 101-239, P.L. 100-647, P.L. 99-514.

(a) In general. Section 25 permits States and political subdivisions to elect to issue mortgage credit certificates in lieu of qualified mortgage bonds. An individual who holds a qualified mortgage credit certificate (as defined in § 1.25-3T) is entitled to a credit against his Federal income taxes. The amount of the credit depends upon (1) the amount of mortgage interest paid or accrued during the year and (2) the applicable certificate credit rate. See § 1.25-2T. The amount of the deduction under section 163 for interest paid or accrued during any taxable year is reduced by the amount of the credit allowable under section 25 for such year. See § 1.163-6T. The holder of a qualified mortgage credit certificate may be entitled to additional withholding allowances. See section 3402(m) and the regulations thereunder.

(b) Definitions. For purposes of §§ 1.25-2T through 1.25-8T and this section, the following definitions apply:

(1) Mortgage. The term "mortgage" includes deeds of trust, conditional sales contracts, pledges, agreements to hold title in escrow, and any other form of owner financing.

(2) State. (i) The term "State" includes a possession of the United States and the District of Columbia.

(ii) Mortgage credit certificates issued by or on behalf of any State or political subdivision ("governmental unit") by constituted authorities empowered to issue such certificates are the certificates of such governmental unit.

(3) Qualified home improvement loan. The term "qualified home improvement loan" has the meaning given that term under section 103A(1)(6) and the regulations thereunder.

(4) Qualified rehabilitation loan. The term "qualified rehabilitation loan" has the meaning given that term under section 103A(1)(7)(A) and the regulations thereunder.

(5) Single-family and owner-occupied residences. The terms "single-family" and "owner-occupied" have the meaning given those terms under section 103A(1)(9) and the regulations thereunder.

(6) Constitutional home rule city. The term "constitutional home rule city" means, with respect to any calendar year, any political subdivision of a State which, under a State constitution which was adopted in 1970 and effective on July 1, 1971, had home rule powers on the 1st day of the calendar year.

(7) Targeted area residence. The term "targeted area residence" has the meaning given that term under section 103A(k) and the regulations thereunder.

(8) Acquisition cost. The term "acquisition cost" has the meaning given that term under section 103A(1)(5) and the regulations thereunder.

(9) Average area purchase price. The term "average area purchase price" has the meaning given that term under subparagraphs (2), (3), and (4) of section 103A(f) and the regulations thereunder. For purposes of this paragraph (b)(9), all determinations of average area purchase price shall be made with respect to residences as that term is defined in section 103A and the regulations thereunder.

(10) Total proceeds. The "total proceeds" of an issue is the sum of the products determined by multiplying—

(i) The certified indebtedness amount of each mortgage credit certificate issued pursuant to such issue, by

(ii) The certificate credit rate specified in such certificate. Each qualified mortgage credit certificate program shall be treated as a separate issue of mortgage credit certificates.

(11) Residence. The term "residence" includes stock held by a tenant-stockholder in a cooperative housing corporation (as those terms are defined in section 216(b)(1) and (2)). It does not include property such as an appliance, a piece of furniture, a radio, etc., which, under applicable local law, is not a fixture. The term also includes any manufactured home which has a minimum of 400 square feet of living space and a minimum width in excess of 102 inches and which is of a kind customarily used at a fixed location. The preceding sentence shall not apply for purposes of determining the average area purchase price for single-family residences, nor shall it apply for purposes of determining the State ceiling amount. The term "residence" does not, however, include recreational vehicles, campers, and other similar vehicles.

(12) Related person. The term "related person" has the meaning given that term under section 103(b)(6)(C)(i) and § 1.103-10(e)(1).

(13) Date of issue. A mortgage credit certificate is considered issued on the date on which a closing agreement is signed with respect to the certified indebtedness amount.

(c) Affidavits. For purposes of §§ 1.25-1T through 1.25-8T, an affidavit filed in connection with the requirements of §§ 1.25-1T through 1.25-8T shall be made under penalties of perjury. Applicants for mortgage credit certificates who are required by a lender or the issuer to sign affidavits must be informed that any fraudulent statement will result in (1) the revocation of the individual's mortgage credit certificate, and (2) a $10,000 penalty under section 6709. Other persons required by a lender or an issuer to provide affidavits must receive similar notice. A person may not rely on an affidavit where that person knows or has reason to know that the information contained in the affidavit is false.

T.D. 8023, 5/3/85.

---

§ 1.25-2T Amount of credit (temporary).

> ***Caution:*** The Treasury has not yet amended Reg § 1.25-2T to reflect changes made by P.L. 106-170, P.L. 103-66, P.L. 101-239, P.L. 100-647, P.L. 99-514.

(a) In general. Except as otherwise provided, the amount of the credit allowable for any taxable year to an individual who holds a qualified mortgage credit certificate is equal to the product of the certificate credit rate (as defined in paragraph (b)) and the amount of the interest paid or accrued by the taxpayer during the taxable year on the certified indebtedness amount (as defined in paragraph (c)).

(b) Certificate credit rate. *(1) In general.* For purposes of §§ 1.25-1T through 1.25-8T, the term "certificate credit rate" means the rate specified by the issuer on the mortgage credit certificate. The certificate credit rate shall not be less than 10 percent nor more than 50 percent.

(2) Limitation in certain States. (i) In the case of a State which—

(A) Has a State ceiling for the calendar year in which an election is made that exceeds 20 percent of the average annual aggregate principal amount of mortgages executed during the immediately preceding 3 calendar years for single-family owner-occupied residences located within the jurisdiction of such State, or

(B) Issued qualified mortgage bonds in an aggregate amount less than $150 million for calendar year 1983,

the certificate credit rate for any mortgage credit certificate issued under such program shall not exceed 20 percent unless the issuing authority submits a plan to the Commissioner to ensure that the weighted average of the certificate credit rates in such mortgage credit certificate program does not exceed 20 percent and the Commissioner approves such plan. For purposes of determining the average annual aggregate principal amount of mortgages executed during the immediately preceding 3 calendar years for single-family owner-occupied residences located within the jurisdiction of such State, an issuer may rely upon the amount published by the Treasury Department for such calendar years. An issuer may rely on a different amount from that safe-harbor limitation where the issuer has made a more accurate and comprehensive determination of that amount. The weighted average of the certificate credit rates in a mortgage credit certificate program is determined by dividing the sum of the products obtained by multiplying the certificate credit rate of each certificate by the certified indebtedness amount with respect to that certificate by the sum of the certified indebtedness amounts of the certificates issued. See section 103A(g) and the regulations thereunder for the definition of the term "State ceiling".

(ii) The following example illustrates the application of this paragraph (b)(2):

Example. City Z issues four qualified mortgage credit certificates pursuant to its qualified mortgage credit certificate program. H receives a certificate with a certificate credit rate of 30 percent and a certified indebtedness amount of $50,000. I receives a certificate with a certificate credit rate of 25 percent and a certified indebtedness amount of $100,000. J and K each receive certificates with certificate credit rates of 10 percent; their certified indebtedness amounts are $50,000 and $100,000, respectively. The weighted average of the certificate credit rates is determined by dividing the sum of the products obtained by multiplying the certificate credit rate of each certificate by the certified indebtedness amount with respect to that certificate ((.3 × $50,000) + (.25 × $100,000) + (.1 × $50,000) + (.1 x $100,000)) by the sum of the certified indebtedness amounts of the certificates issued ($50,000 + $100,000 + $50,000 + $100,000)). Thus, the weighted average of the certificate credit rates is 18.33 percent ($55,000/$300,000).

(c) Certified indebtedness amount. *(1) In general.* The term "certified indebtedness amount" means the amount of indebtedness which is—

(i) Incurred by the taxpayer—

(A) To acquire his principal residence, § 1.25-2T(c)(1)(i)

(B) As a qualified home improvement loan, or

(C) As a qualified rehabilitation loan, and

(ii) Specified in the mortgage credit certificate.

(2) Example. The following example illustrates the application of this paragraph:

Example. On March 1, 1986, State X, pursuant to its qualified mortgage credit certificate program, provides a mortgage credit certificate to B. State X specifies that the maximum amount of the mortgage loan for which B may claim a credit is $65,000. On March 15, B purchases for $67,000 a single-family dwelling for use as his principal residence. B obtains from Bank M a mortgage loan for $60,000. State X, or Bank M acting on behalf of State X, indicates on B's mortgage credit certificate that the certified indebtedness amount of B's loan is $60,000. B may claim a credit under section 25(e) based on this amount.

(d) Limitation on credit. *(1) Limitation where certificate credit rate exceeds 20 percent.* (i) If the certificate credit rate of any mortgage credit certificate exceeds 20 percent, the amount of the credit allowed to the taxpayer by section 25(a)(1) for any year shall not exceed $2,000. Any amount denied under this paragraph (d)(1) may not be carried forward under section 25(e)(1) and paragraph (d)(2) of this section.

(ii) If two or more persons hold interests in any residence, the limitation of paragraph (d)(1)(i) shall be allocated among such persons in proportion to their respective interests in the residence.

(2) Carryforward of unused credit. (i) If the credit allowable under section 25(a) and § 1.25-2T for any taxable year exceeds the applicable tax limit for that year, the excess (the "unused credit") will be a carryover to each of the 3 succeeding taxable years and, subject to the limitations of paragraph (d)(2)(ii), will be added to the credit allowable by section 25(a) and § 1.25-2T for that succeeding year.

(ii) The amount of the unused credit for any taxable year (the "unused credit year") which may be taken into account under this paragraph (d)(2) for any subsequent taxable year may not exceed the amount by which the applicable tax limit for that subsequent taxable year exceeds the sum of (A) the amount of the credit allowable under section 25(a) and § 1.25-1T for the current taxable year, and (B) the sum of the unused credits which, by reason of this paragraph (d)(2), are carried to that subsequent taxable year and are attributable to taxable years before the unused credit year. Thus, if by reason of this paragraph (d)(2), unused credits from 2 prior taxable years are carried forward to a subsequent taxable year, the unused credit from the earlier of those 2 prior years must be taken into account before the unused credit from the later of those 2 years is taken into account.

(iii) For purposes of this paragraph (d)(2) the term "applicable tax limit" means the limitation imposed by section 26(a) for the taxable year reduced by the sum of the credits allowable for that year under section 21, relating to expenses for household and dependent care services necessary for gainful employment, section 22, relating to the credit for the elderly and the permanently disabled, section 23, relating to the residential energy credit, and section 24, relating to contributions to candidates for public office. The limitation imposed by section 26(a) for any taxable year is equal to the taxpayer's tax liability (as defined in section 26(b)) for that year.

(iv) The following examples illustrate the application of this paragraph (d)(2):

Example (1). (i) B, a calendar year taxpayer, holds a qualified mortgage credit certificate. For 1986 B's applicable tax limit (i.e., tax liability) is $1,100. The amount of the credit under section 25(a) and § 1.25-2T for 1986 is $1,700. For 1986 B is not entitled to any of the credits described in sections 21 through 24. Under § 1.25-2T(d)(2), B's unused credit for 1986 is $600, and B is entitled to carry forward that amount to the 3 succeeding years.

(ii) For 1987 B's applicable tax limit is $1,500, the amount of the credit under section 25(a) and § 1.25-2T is $1,700, and the unused credit is $200. For 1988 B's applicable tax limit is $2,000, the amount of the credit under section 25(a) and § 1.25-2T is $1,300, and there is no unused credit. For 1987 and 1988 B is not entitled to any of the credits described in sections 21 through 24. No portion of the unused credit for 1986 my be used in 1987. For 1988 B is entitled to claim a credit of $2,000 under section 25(a) and § 1.25-2T, consisting of a $1,300 credit for 1988, the $600 unused credit for 1986, and $100 of the $200 unused credit for 1987. In addition, B may carry forward the remaining unused credit for 1987 ($100) to 1989 and 1990.

Example (2). The facts are the same as in Example (1) except that for 1988 B is entitled to a credit of $400 under section 23. B's applicable tax limit for 1988 is $1,600 ($2,000 less $400). For 1988 B is entitled to claim a credit of $1,600 under section 25(a) and § 1.25-2T, consisting of a $1,300 credit for 1988 and $300 of the unused credit for 1986. In addition, B may carry forward the remaining unused credits of $300 for 1986 to 1989 and of $200 for 1987 to 1989 and 1990.

T.D. 8023, 5/3/85.

---

§ 1.25-3 Qualified mortgage credit certificate.

(a) through (g)(1)(ii) [Reserved] For further guidance, see § 1.25-3T(a) through (g)(1)(ii).

(g) *(1)* (iii) Reissued certificate exception. See paragraph (p) of this section for rules regarding the exception in the case of refinancing existing mortgages.

(2) through (o) [Reserved] For further guidance, see § 1.25-3T(g)(2) through (o).

(p) Reissued certificates for certain refinancings. *(1) In general.* If the issuer of a qualified mortgage credit certificate reissues a certificate in place of an existing mortgage credit certificate to the holder of that existing certificate, the reissued certificate is treated as satisfying the requirements of this section. The period for which the reissued certificate is in effect begins with the date of the refinancing (that is, the date on which interest begins accruing on the refinancing loan).

(2) Meaning of existing certificate. For purposes of this paragraph (p), a mortgage credit certificate is an existing certificate only if it satisfies the requirements of this section. An existing certificate may be the original certificate, a certificate issued to a transferee under § 1.25-3T(h)(2)(ii), or a certificate previously reissued under this paragraph (p).

(3) Limitations on reissued certificate. An issuer may reissue a mortgage credit certificate only if all of the following requirements are satisfied:

(i) The reissued certificate is issued to the holder of an existing certificate with respect to the same property to which the existing certificate relates.

(ii) The reissued certificate entirely replaces the existing certificate (that is, the holder cannot retain the existing certificate with respect to any portion of the outstanding balance of the certified mortgage indebtedness specified on the existing certificate).

(iii) The certified mortgage indebtedness specified on the reissued certificate does not exceed the remaining outstanding balance of the certified mortgage indebtedness specified on the existing certificate.

(iv) The reissued certificate does not increase the certificate credit rate specified in the existing certificate.

(v) The reissued certificate does not result in an increase in the tax credit that would otherwise have been allowable to the holder under the existing certificate for any taxable year.

The holder of a reissued certificate determines the amount of tax credit that would otherwise have been allowable by multiplying the interest that was scheduled to have been paid on the refinanced loan by the certificate rate of the existing certificate. In the case of a series of refinancings, the tax credit that would otherwise have been allowable is determined from the amount of interest that was scheduled to have been paid on the original loan and the certificate rate of the original certificate.

(A) In the case of a refinanced loan that is a fixed interest rate loan, the interest that was scheduled to be paid on the refinanced loan is determined using the scheduled interest method described in paragraph (p)(3)(v)(C) of this section.

(B) In the case of a refinanced loan that is not a fixed interest rate loan, the interest that was scheduled to be paid on the refinanced loan is determined using either the scheduled interest method described in paragraph (p)(3)(v)(C) of this section or the hypothetical interest method described in paragraph (p)(3)(v)(D) of this section.

(C) The scheduled interest method determines the amount of interest for each taxable year that was scheduled to have been paid in the taxable year based on the terms of the refinanced loan including any changes in the interest rate that would have been required by the terms of the refinanced loan and any payments of principal that would have been required by the terms of the refinanced loan (other than repayments required as a result of any refinancing of the loan).

(D) The hypothetical interest method (which is available only for refinanced loans that are not fixed interest rate loans) determines the amount of interest treated as having been scheduled to be paid for a taxable year by constructing an amortization schedule for a hypothetical self-amortizing loan with level payments. The hypothetical loan must have a principal amount equal to the remaining outstanding balance of the certified mortgage indebtedness specified on the existing certificate, a maturity equal to that of the refinanced loan, and interest equal to the annual percentage rate (APR) of the refinancing loan that is required to be calculated for the Federal Truth in Lending Act.

(E) A holder must consistently apply the scheduled interest method or the hypothetical interest method for all taxable years beginning with the first taxable year the tax credit is claimed by the holder based upon the reissued certificate.

(4) Examples. The following examples illustrate the application of paragraph (p)(3)(v) of this section:

Example (1). A holder of an existing certificate that meets the requirements of this section seeks to refinance the mortgage on the property to which the existing certificate relates. The final payment on the holder's existing mortgage is due on December 31, 2000; the final payment on the new mortgage would not be due until January 31, 2004. The holder requests that the issuer provide to the holder a reissued mortgage credit certificate in place of the existing certificate. The requested certificate would have the same certificate credit rate as the existing certificate. For each calendar year through the year 2000, the credit that would be allowable to the holder with respect to the new mortgage under the requested certificate would not exceed the credit allowable for that year under the existing certificate. The requested certificate, however, would allow the holder credits for the years 2001 through 2004, years for which, due to the earlier scheduled retirement of the existing mortgage, no credit would be allowable under the existing certificate. Under paragraph (p)(3)(v) of this section, the issuer may not reissue the certificate as requested because, under the existing certificate, no credit would be allowable for the years 2001 through 2004. The issuer may, however, provide a reissued certificate that limits the amount of the credit allowable in each year to the amount allowable under the existing certificate. Because the existing certificate would allow no credit after December 31, 2000, the reissued certificate could expire on December 31, 2000.

Example (2). (a) The facts are the same as Example 1 except that the existing mortgage loan has a variable rate of interest and the refinancing loan will have a fixed rate of interest. To determine whether the limit under paragraph (p)(3)(v) of this section is met for any taxable year, the holder must calculate the amount of credit that otherwise would have been allowable absent the refinancing. This requires a determination of the amount of interest that would have been payable on the refinanced loan for the taxable year. The holder may determine this amount by—

(1) Applying the terms of the refinanced loan, including the variable interest rate or rates, for the taxable year as though the refinanced loan continued to exist; or

(2) Obtaining the amount of interest, and calculating the amount of credit that would have been available, from the schedule of equal payments that fully amortize a hypothetical loan with the principal amount equal to the remaining outstanding balance of the certified mortgage indebtedness specified on the existing certificate, the interest equal to the annual percentage rate (APR) of the refinancing loan, and the maturity equal to that of the refinanced loan.

(b) The holder must apply the same method for each taxable year the tax credit is claimed based upon the reissued mortgage credit certificate.

(5) Coordination with section 143(m)(3). A refinancing loan underlying a reissued mortgage credit certificate that replaces a mortgage credit certificate issued on or before December 31, 1990, is not a federally subsidized indebtedness for the purposes of section 143(m)(3) of the Internal Revenue Code.

T.D. 8692, 12/16/96.

§ 1.25-3T Qualified mortgage credit certificate (temporary).

Caution: The Treasury has not yet amended Reg § 1.25-3T to reflect changes made by P.L. 103-66, P.L. 101-239, P.L. 100-647, P.L. 99-514.

(a) Definition of qualified mortgage credit certificate. For purposes of §§ 1.25-1T through 1.25-8T, the term "qualified mortgage credit certificate" means a certificate that meets all of the requirements of this section.

(b) Qualified mortgage credit certificate program. A certificate meets the requirements of this paragraph if it is issued under a qualified mortgage credit certificate program (as defined in § 1.25-4T).

(c) Required form and information. A certificate meets the requirements of this paragraph if it is in the form specified in § 1.25-6T and if all the information required by the form is specified on the form.

(d) Residence requirement. *(1) In general.* A certificate meets the requirements of this paragraph only if it is provided in connection with the acquisition, qualified rehabilitation, or qualified home improvement of a residence, that is—

(i) A single-family residence (as defined in § 1.25-1T(b)(5)) which, at the time the financing on the residence is executed or assumed, can reasonably be expected by the issuer to become (or, in the case of a qualified home improvement loan, to continue to be) the principal residence (as defined in section 1034 and the regulations thereunder) of the holder of the certificate within a reasonable time after the financing is executed or assumed, and

(ii) Located within the jurisdiction of the governmental unit issuing the certificate.

See section 103a(d) and the regulations thereunder for further definitions and requirements.

(2) Certification procedure. The requirements of this paragraph will be met if the issuer or its agent obtains from the holder of the certificate an affidavit stating his intent to use (or, in the case of a qualified home improvement loan, that he is currently using and intends to continue to use) the residence as his principal residence within a reasonable time (e.g., 60 days) after the mortgage credit certificate is issued and stating that the holder will notify the issuer of the mortgage credit certificate if the residence ceases to be his principal residence. The affidavit must also state facts that are sufficient for the issuer or his agent to determine whether the residence is located within the jurisdiction of the issuer that issued the mortgage credit certificate.

(e) 3-year requirement. *(1) In general.* A certificate meets the requirements of this paragraph only if the holder of the certificate had no present ownership interest in a principal residence at any time during the 3-year period prior to the date on which the mortgage on the residence in connection with which the certificate is provided is executed. For purposes of the preceding sentence, the holder's interest in the residence with respect to which the certificate is being provided shall not be taken into account. See section 103A(e) and the regulations thereunder for further definitions and requirements.

(2) Exceptions. Paragraph (e)(1) shall not apply with respect to—

(i) Any certificate provided with respect to a targeted area residence (as defined in § 1.25-1T(b)(7)),

(ii) Any qualified home improvement loan (as defined in § 1.25-1T(b)(3)), and

(iii) Any qualified rehabilitation loan (as defined in § 1.25-1T(b)(4)).

(3) Certification procedure. The requirements of paragraph (e)(1) will be met if the issuer or its agent obtains from the holder of the certificate an affidavit stating that he had no present ownership interest in a principal residence at any time during the 3-year period prior to the date of which the certificate is issued and the issuer or its agent obtains from the applicant copies of the applicant's Federal tax returns for the preceding 3 years and examines each statement to determine whether the applicant has claimed a deduction for taxes on property which was the applicant's principal residence pursuant to section 164(a)(1) or a deduction pursuant to section 163 for interest paid on a mortgage secured by property which was the applicant's principal residence. Where the mortgage is executed during the period between January 1 and February 15 and the applicant has not yet filed has Federal income tax return with the Internal Revenue Service, the issuer may, with respect to such year, rely on a affidavit of the applicant that the applicant is not entitled to claim deductions for taxes or interest on indebtedness with respect to property constituting his principal residence for the preceding calendar year. In the alternative, when applicable, the holder may provide an affidavit stating that one of the exceptions provided in paragraph (e)(2) applies.

(4) Special rule. An issuer may submit a plan to the Commissioner for distributing certificates, in an amount not to exceed 10 percent of the proceeds of the issue, to individuals who do not meet the requirements of this paragraph. Such plan must described a procedure for ensuring that no more than 10 percent of the proceeds of a such issue will be used to provide certificates to such individuals. If the Commissioner approves the issuer's plan, certificates issued in accordance with the terms of the plan to holders who do not meet the 3-year requirement do not fail to satisfy the requirements of this paragraph.

(f) Purchase price requirement. *(1) In general.* A certificate meets the requirements of this paragraph only if the acquisition cost (as defined in § 1.25-1T(b)(8)) of the residence, other than a targeted area residence, in connection with which the certificate is provided does not exceed 110 percent of the average area purchase price (as defined in § 1.25-1T(b)(9)) applicable to that residence. In the case of a targeted area residence (as defined in § 1.251T(b)(7)) the acquisition cost may not exceed 120 percent of the average area purchase price applicable to such residence. See section 1093A(f) and the regulations thereunder for further definitions and requirements. § 1.25-3T(f)(1)

(2) Certification procedure. The requirements of paragraph (f)(1) will be met if the issuer or its agent obtains affidavits executed by the seller and the buyer that state these requirements have been met. Such affidavits must include an itemized list of—

(i) Any payments made by the buyer (or a related person) or for the benefit of the buyer,

(ii) If the residence is incomplete, an estimate of the reasonable cost of completing the residence, and

(iii) If the residence is purchased subject to a ground rent, the capitalized value of the ground rent.

The issuer or his agent must examine such affidavits and determine whether, on the basis of information contained therein, the purchase price requirement is met.

(g) New mortgage requirement. *(1) In general.* (i) A certificate meets the requirements of this paragraph only if the certificate is not issued in connection with the acquisition or replacement of an existing mortgage. Except in the case of a qualified home improvement loan, the certificate must be issued to an individual who did not have a mortgage (whether or not paid off) on the residence with respect to which the certificate is issued at any time prior to the execution of the mortgage.

(ii) Exceptions. For purposes of this paragraph, a certificate used in connection with the replacement of—

(A) Construction period loans,

(B) Bridge loans or similar temporary initial financing, and

(C) In the case of a qualified rehabilitation loan, an existing mortgage, shall not be treated as being used to acquire or replace an existing mortgage. Generally, temporary initial financing is any financing which has a term of 24 months or less. See section 103A(j)(1) and the regulations thereunder for examples illustrating the application of these requirements.

(2) Certification procedure. The requirements of paragraph (g)(1) will be met if the issuer or its agent obtains from the holder of the certificate an affidavit stating that the mortgage being acquired in connection with the certificate will not be used to acquire or replace an existing mortgage (other than

one that falls within the exceptions described in paragraph (g)(1)(ii)).

(h) Transfer of mortgage credit certificates. *(1) In general.* A certificate meets the requirements of this paragraph only if it is (i) not transferable or (ii) transferable only with the approval of the issuer.

(2) Transfer procedure. A certificate that is transferred with the approval of the issuer is a qualified mortgage credit certificate in the hands of the transferee only if each of the following requirements is met:

(i) The transferee assumed liability for the remaining balance of the certified indebtedness amount in connection with the acquisition of the residence from the transferor,

(ii) The issuer issues a new certificate to the transferee, and

(iii) The new certificate meets each of the requirements of paragraphs (d), (e), (f), and (i) of this section based on the facts as they exist at the time of the transfer as if the mortgage credit certificate were being issued for the first time. For example, the purchase price requirement is to be determined by reference to the average area purchase price at the time of the assumption and not when the mortgage credit certificate was originally issued.

(3) Statement on certificate. The requirements of paragraph (h)(1) will be met if the mortgage credit certificate states that the certificate may not be transferred or states that the certificate may not be transferred unless the issuer issues a new certificate in place of the original certificate.

(i) Prohibited mortgages. *(1) In general.* A certificate meets the requirements of this paragraph only if it is issued in connection with the acquisition of a residence none of the financing of which is provided from the proceeds of—

(i) A qualified mortgage bond (as defined under section 103A(c)(1) and the regulations thereunder), or

(ii) A qualified veterans' mortgage bond (as defined under section 103A(c)(3) and the regulations thereunder).

Thus, for example, if a mortgagor has a mortgage on his principal residence that was obtained from the proceeds of a qualified mortgage bond, a mortgage credit certificate issued to such mortgagor in connection with a qualified home improvement loan with respect to such residence is not a qualified mortgage credit certificate. If, however, the financing provided from the proceeds of the qualified mortgage bond had been paid off in full, the certificate would be a qualified mortgage credit certificate (assuming all the requirements of this paragraph are met).

(2) Certification procedure. The requirements of paragraph (i)(1) will be met if the issuer or its agent obtains from the holder of the certificate an affidavit stating that no portion of the financing of the residence in connection with which the certificate is issued is provided from the proceeds of a qualified mortgage bond or a qualified veterans' mortgage bond.

(j) Particular lenders. *(1) In general.* Except as otherwise provided in paragraph (j)(2), a certificate meets the requirements of this paragraph only if the certificate is not limited to indebtedness incurred from particular lenders. A certificate is limited to indebtedness from particular lenders if the issuer, directly or indirectly, prohibits the holder of a certificate from obtaining financing from one or more lenders or requires the holder of a certificate to obtain financing from one or more lenders. For purposes of this paragraph, a lender is any person, including an issuer of mortgage credit certificates, that provides financing for the acquisition, qualified rehabilitation, or qualified home improvement of a residence.

(2) Exception. A mortgage credit certificate that is limited to indebtedness incurred from particular lenders will not cease to meet the requirements of this paragraph if the Commissioner approves the basis for such limitation. The Commissioner may approve the basis for such limitation if the issuer establishes to the satisfaction of the Commissioner that it will result in a significant economic benefit to the holders of mortgage credit certificates (e.g., substantially lower financing costs) compared to the result without such limitation.

(3) Taxable bonds. The requirements of this paragraph do not prevent an issuer of mortgage credit certificates from issuing mortgage subsidy bonds (other than obligations described in section 103(a)) the proceeds of which are to be used to provide mortgages to holders of mortgage credit certificates provided that the holders of such certificates are not required to obtain financing from the proceeds of the bond issue. See § 1.25-4T(h) with respect to permissible fees.

(4) Lists of participating lenders. The requirements of this paragraph do not prohibit an issuer from maintaining a list of lenders that have stated that they will make loans to qualified holders of mortgage credit certificates, provided that (i) the issuer solicits such statements in a public notice similar to the notice described in § 1.25-7T, (ii) lenders are provided a reasonable period of time in which to express their interest in being included in such a list, and (iii) holders of mortgage credit certificates are not required to obtain financing from the lenders on the list. If an issuer maintains such a list, it must update the list at least annually.

(5) Certification procedure. The requirements of this paragraph will be met if (i) the issuer or its agent obtains from the holder of the certificate an affidavit stating that the certificate was not limited to indebtedness incurred from particular lenders or (ii) the issuer obtains a ruling from the Commissioner under paragraph (j)(2).

(6) Examples. The following examples illustrate the application of this paragraph:

Example (1). Under its mortgage credit certificate program, County Z distributes all the certificates to be issued to a group of 60 participating lenders. Residents of County Z may obtain mortgage credit certificates only from the participating lenders and only in connection with the acquisition of mortgage financing from that lender or one of the other participating lenders. Certificates issued under this program do not meet the requirements of this paragraph since the certificates are limited to indebtedness incurred from particular lenders. The certificates, therefore, are not qualified mortgage credit certificates.

Example (2). In connection with its mortgage credit certificate program, County Y arranges with Bank P for a line of credit to be used to provide mortgage financing to holders of mortgage credit certificates. County Y, pursuant to paragraph (j)(4), maintains a list of lenders participating in the mortgage credit certificate program. County Y distributes the certificates directly to applicants. Holders of the certificates are not required to obtain mortgage financing through the line of credit or through a lender on the list of participating lenders. Certificates issued pursuant to County Y's program satisfy the requirements of this paragraph.

(k) Developer certification. *(1) In general.* A mortgage credit certificate that is allocated by the issuer to any particular development meets the requirements of this paragraph only if the developer provides a certification to the purchaser of the residence and the issuer stating that the purchase price of that residence is not higher than the price would be if the issuer had not allocated mortgage credit certificates to the development. The certification must be made by the developer if a natural person or, if not, by a duly authorized official of the developer.

(2) Certification procedure. The requirements of this paragraph will be met if the issuer or its agent obtains from the holder of the certificate and affidavit stating that the has received from the developer the certification described in this paragraph.

(l) Expiration. *(1) In general.* A certificate meets the requirements of this paragraph if the certified indebtedness amount is incurred prior to the close of the second calendar year following the calendar year for which the issuer elected not to issue qualified mortgage bonds under § 1.25-4T with respect to that issue of mortgage credit certificates. Thus, for example, if on October 1, 1984, and issuing authority elects under § 1.25-4T not to issue qualified mortgage bonds, a mortgage credit certificate provided under that program does not meet the requirements of this paragraph unless the indebtedness is incurred on or before December 31, 1986.

(2) Issuer-imposed expiration dates. An issuer of mortgage credit certificates may provide that a certificate shall expire if the holder of the certificate does not incur certified indebtedness by a date that is prior to the expiration date provided in paragraph (l)(1). A certificate that expires prior to the date provided in paragraph (l)(1) may be reissued provided that the requirements of this paragraph are met.

(m) Revocation. A certificate meets the requirements of this paragraph only if it has not been revoked. Thus, the credit provided by section 25 and § 1.25-1T does not apply to interest paid or accrued following the revocation of a certificate. A certificate is treated as revoked when the residence to which the certificate relates ceases to be the holder's principal residence. An issuer may revoke a mortgage credit certificate if the certificate does not meet all the requirements of § 1.25-3T(d), (e), (f), (g), (h), (i), (j), (k), and (n). The certificate is revoked by the issuer's notifying the holder of the certificate and the Internal Revenue Service that the certificate is revoked. The notice to the Internal Revenue Service shall be made as part of the report required by § 1.25-8T(b)(2).

(n) Interest paid to related person. *(1) In general.* A certificate does not meet the requirements of this paragraph if interest on the certified indebtedness amount is paid to a person who is a related person to the holder of the certificate.

(2) Certification procedure. The requirements of this paragraph will be met if the issuer or its agent obtains from the holder of the certificate an affidavit stating that a related person does not have, and is not expected to have, an interest as a creditor in the certified indebtedness amount.

(o) Fraud. Notwithstanding any other provision of this section, a mortgage credit certificate does not meet the requirements of this section and, therefore, the certificate is not a qualified mortgage credit certificate for any calendar year, if the holder of the certificate provides a certification or any other information to the lender providing the mortgage or to the issuer of the certificate containing a material misstatement and such misstatement is due to fraud. In determining whether any misstatement is due to fraud, the rules generally applicable to underpayments of tax due to fraud (including rules relating to the statute of limitations) shall apply. See § 1.6709-1T with respect to the penalty for filing negligent or fraudulent statements.

T.D. 8023, 5/3/85, amend T.D. 8502, 12/22/93, T.D. 8692, 12/16/96.

§ 1.25-4T Qualified mortgage credit certificate program (temporary).

Caution: The Treasury has not yet amended Reg § 1.25-4T to reflect changes made by P.L. 103-66, P.L. 101-239, P.L. 100-647, P.L. 99-514.

(a) In general. *(1) Definition of qualified mortgage credit certificate program.* For purposes of §§ 1.25-1T through 1.25-8T, the term "qualified mortgage credit certificate program" means a program to issue qualified mortgage credit certificates which meets all of the requirements of paragraphs (b) through (i) of this section.

(2) Requirements are a minimum. Except as otherwise provided in this section, the requirements of this section are minimum requirements. Issuers may establish more stringent criteria for participation in a qualified mortgage credit certificate program. Thus, for example, an issuer may target 30 percent of the proceeds of an issue of mortgage credit certificates to targeted areas. Further, issuers may establish additional eligibility criteria for participation in a qualified mortgage credit certificate program. Thus, for example, issuers may impose an income limitation designed to ensure that only those individuals who could not otherwise purchase a residence will benefit from the credit.

(3) Except as otherwise provided in this section and § 1.25-3T, issuers may use mortgage credit certificates in connection with other Federal, State, and local programs provided that such use complies with the requirements of § 1.25-3T(j). Thus, for example, a mortgage credit certificate may be issued in connection with the qualified rehabilitation of a residence part of the cost of which will be paid from the proceeds of a State grant.

(b) Establishment of program. A program meets the requirements of this paragraph only if it is established by a State or political subdivision thereof for any calendar year for which it has the authority to issue qualified mortgage bonds.

(c) Election not to issue qualified mortgage bonds. *(1) In general.* A program meets the requirements of this paragraph only if the issuer elects, in the time and manner specified in this paragraph, not to issue an amount of qualified mortgage bonds that it may otherwise issue during the calendar year under section 103A and the regulations thereunder.

(2) Manner of making election. On or before the earlier of the date of distribution of mortgage credit certificates under a program or December 31, 1987, the issuer must file an election not to issue an amount of qualified mortgage bonds. The election (and the certification (or affidavit) described in paragraph (d)) shall be filed with the Internal Revenue Service Center, Philadelphia, Pennsylvania 19255. The election should be titled "Mortgage Credit Certificate Election" and must include—

(i) The name, address, and TIN of the issuer,

(ii) The issuer's applicable limit, as defined in section 103A(g) and the regulations thereunder,

(iii) The aggregate amount of qualified mortgage bonds issued by the issuing authority during the calendar year,

(iv) The amount of the issuer's applicable limit that it has surrendered to other issuers during the calendar year,

(v) The date and amount of any previous elections under this paragraph for the calendar year, and

(vi) The amount of qualified mortgage bonds that the issuer elects not to issue.

(3) Revocation of election. Any election made under this paragraph may be revoked, in whole or in part, at any time during the calendar year in which the election was made. The revocation, however, may not be made with respect to any part of the nonissued bond amount that has been used to issue mortgage credit certificates pursuant to the election. The revocation shall be filed with the Internal Revenue Service Center, Philadelphia, Pennsylvania 19255. The revocation should be titled "Revocation of Mortgage Credit Certificate Election" and must include—

(i) The name, address, and TIN of the issuer,

(ii) The nonissued bond amount as originally elected, and

(iii) The portion of the nonissued bond amount with respect to which the election is being revoked.

(4) Special rule. If at the time that an issuer makes an election under this paragraph it does not know its applicable limit, the issuer may elect not to use all of its remaining authority to issue qualified mortgage bonds; this form of election will be treated as meeting the requirements of paragraph (c)(2) if, prior to the later of the end of the calendar year and December 31, 1985, the issuer amends its election so as to indicate the exact amount of qualified mortgage bond authority that it elected not to issue.

(5) Limitation on nonissued bond amount. The amount of qualified mortgage bonds which an issuer elects not to issue may not exceed the issuer's applicable limit (as determined under section 103A(g) and the regulations thereunder). For example, a governmental unit that, pursuant to section 103A(g)(3), may issue $10 million of qualified mortgage bonds that elects to trade in $11 million in qualified mortgage bond authority has not met the requirements of this paragraph, and mortgage credit certificates issued pursuant to such election are not qualified mortgage credit certificates.

(d) State certification requirement. *(1) In general.* A program meets the requirements of this paragraph only if the State official designated by law (or, where there is no State official, the Governor) certifies, based on facts and circumstances as of the date on which the certification is requested, following a request for such certification, that the issue meets the requirements of section 103A(g) (relating to volume limitation) and the regulations thereunder. A copy of the State certification must be attached to the issuer's election not to issue qualified mortgage bonds, except that, in the case of elections made during calendar year 1984, the certification may be filed with the Service prior to July 8, 1985 provided that mortgage credit certificates may not be distributed until the certification is filed. In the case of any constitutional home rule city, the certification shall be made by the chief executive officer of the city.

(2) Certification procedure. The official making the certification described in this paragraph (d) need not perform an independent investigation to determine whether the issuer has met the requirements of section 103A(g). In determining the aggregate amount of qualified mortgage bonds previously issued by that issuer during the calendar year the official may rely on copies of prior elections under paragraph (c) of this section made by the issuer for that year, together with an affidavit executed by an official of the issuer who is responsible for issuing bonds stating that the issuer has not, to date, issued any other issues of qualified mortgage bonds during the calendar year and stating the amount, if any, of the issuer's applicable limit that it has surrendered to other issuers during the calendar year; for any calendar year prior to 1985, the official may rely on an affidavit executed by a duly authorized official of the issuer who states the aggregate amount of qualified mortgage bonds issued by the issuer during the year. In determining the aggregate amount of qualified mortgage bonds that the issuer has previously elected not to issue during that calendar year, the official may rely on copies of any elections not to issue qualified mortgage bonds filed by the issuer for that calendar year, together with an affidavit executed by an official of the issuer responsible for issuing mortgage credit certificates stating that the issuer has not, to date, made any other elections not to issue qualified mortgage bonds. If, based on such information, the certifying official determines that the issuer has not, as of the date on which the certification is provided, exceeded its applicable limit for the year, the official may certify that the issue meets the requirements of section 103A(g). The fact that the certification described in this paragraph (d) is provided does not ensure that the issuer has met the requirements of section 103A(g) and the regulations thereunder, nor does it preclude the application of the penalty for over-issuance of mortgage credit certificates if such over-issuance actually occurs. See § 1.25-5T.

(3) Special rule. If within 30 days after the issuer files a proper request for the certification described in this paragraph (d) the issuer has not received from the State official designated by law (or, if there is no State official, the Governor) certification that the issue meets the requirements of section 103A(g) or, in the alternative, a statement that the issue does not meet such requirements, the issuer may submit, in lieu of the certification required by this paragraph (d), an affidavit executed by an officer of the issuer responsible for issuing mortgage credit certificates stating that—

(i) The issue meets the requirements of section 103A(g) and the regulations thereunder,

(ii) At least 30 days before the execution of the affidavit the issuer filed a proper request for the certification described in this paragraph (d), and

(iii) The State official designated by law (or, if there is no State official, the Governor) has not provided the certification described in this paragraph (d) or a statement that the issue does not meet such requirements.

For purposes of this paragraph, a request for certification is proper if the request includes the reports and affidavits described in paragraph (d)(2).

(e) Information reporting requirement. *(1) Reports.* With respect to mortgage credit certificates issued after September 30, 1985, a program meets the requirements of this paragraph only if the issuer submits a report containing the information concerning the holders of certificates issued during the preceding reporting period required by this paragraph. The report must be filed for each reporting period in which certificates (other than transferred certificates) are issued under the program. The issuer is not responsible for false information provided by a holder if the issuer did not know or have reason to know that the information was false. The report must be filed on the form prescribed by the Internal Revenue Service. If no form is prescribed, or if the form prescribed is not readily available, the issuer may use its own form provided that such form is in the format set forth in this paragraph and contains the information required by this paragraph. The report must be titled "Mortgage Credit Certificate Information Report" and must include the name, address, and TIN of the issuer, the reporting period for which the information is provided, and the following tables containing information concerning the holders of certificates issued during the reporting period for which the report is filed:

(i) A table titled "Number of Mortgage Credit Certificates by Income and Acquisition Cost" showing the number of mortgage credit certificates issued (other than those issued in connection with qualified home improvement and rehabilitation loans) according to the annualized gross income of the holders (categorized in the following intervals of income: $0-$9,999; $10,000-$19,999; $20,000-$29,999; $30,000-$39,999; $40,000-$49,999; $50,000-$74,999; and $75,000 or more) and according to the acquisition cost of the residences acquired in connection with the mortgage credit certificates (categorized in the following intervals of acquisition cost: $0-$19,999; $20,000-$39,999; $40,000-$59,999; $60,000-$79,999; $80,000-$99,999; $100,000-$119,999; $120,000-$149,999; $150,000-$199,999; and $200,000 or more). For each interval of income and acquisition cost the table must also be categorized according to—

(A) The aggregate amount of fees charged to holders to cover any administrative costs incurred by the issuer in issuing mortgage credit certificates, and

(B) The number of holders that—

(1) Did not have a present ownership interest in a principal residence at any time during the 3-year period ending on the date the mortgage credit certificate is executed (i.e., satisfied the 3-year requirement) and purchased residences in targeted areas,

(2) Satisfied the 3-year requirement and purchased residences not located in targeted areas,

(3) Did have a present ownership interest in a principal residence at any time during the 3-year period ending on the date the mortgage credit certificate is executed (i.e., did not satisfy the 3-year requirement) and purchased residences in targeted areas, and

(4) Did not satisfy the 3-year requirement and purchased residences not located in targeted areas.

(ii) (A table titled "Volume of Mortgage Credit Certificates by Income and Acquisition Cost" containing data on—

(A) The total of the certified indebtedness amounts of the certificates issued (other than those issued in connection with qualified home improvement and rehabilitation loans);

(B) The sum of the products of the certified indebtedness amount and the certificate credit rate for each certificate (other than those issued in connection with qualified home improvement and rehabilitation loans) according to annualized gross income (categorized in the same intervals of income as the preceding table) and according to the acquisition cost of the residences acquired in connection with mortgage credit certificates (categorized in the same intervals of acquisition cost as the preceding table); and

(C) For each interval of income and acquisition cost, the information described in paragraph (e)(1)(ii)(A) and (B) categorized according to the holders that—

(1) Satisfied the 3-year requirement and purchased residences in targeted areas,

(2) Satisfied the 3-year requirement and purchased residences not located in targeted areas,

(3) Did not satisfy the 3-year requirement and purchased residences in targeted areas, and

(4) Did not satisfy the 3-year requirement and purchased residences not located in targeted areas.

(iii) A table titled "Mortgage Credit Certificates for Qualified Home Improvement and Rehabilitation Loans" showing the number of mortgage credit certificates issued in connection with qualified home improvement loans and qualified rehabilitation loans, the total of the certified indebtedness amount with respect to such certificates, and the sum of the products of the certified indebtedness amount and the certificate credit rate for each certificate; the information contained in the table must also be categorized according to whether the residences with respect to which the certificates were provided are located in targeted areas.

(2) Format. If no form is prescribed by the Internal Revenue Service, or if the prescribed form is not readily available, the issuer must submit the report in the format specified in this paragraph (e)(2). The specified format of the report is the following:

Mortgage Credit Certificate Information Report

Name of issuer:

Address of issuer:

TIN of issuer:

Reporting period:

Number of Mortgage Credit Certificates by Income and Acquisition Cost

3-year requirement:	Satisfied		Not Satisfied		
Annualized gross monthly income of borrowers	Nontargeted area	Targeted area	Nontargeted area	Targeted area	Totals fees
$0 to $9,999					
$10,000 to 19,999					
$20,000 to $29,999					
$30,000 to $39,999					
$40,000 to $49,999					
$50,000 to $74,999					
$75,000 or more					
Total					

3-year requirement:	Satisfied		Not Satisfied		
Annualized gross monthly income of borrowers	Nontargeted area	Targeted area	Nontargeted area	Targeted area	Totals fees
Acquisition Cost					
$0 to $19,999					
$20,000 to 39,999					
$40,000 to $59,999					
$60,000 to $79,999					
$80,000 to $99,999					

$100,000 to $119,999
$120,000 to $149,000
$150,000 to $199,000
$200,000 or more
Total

Volume of Mortgage Credit Certificates by Income and Acquisition Cost

	Holders satisfying the 3-year requirement				3-year requirement not satisfied				Totals	
	Nontargeted area		Targeted area		Nontargeted area		Targeted area			
Annualized gross monthly income of holders	Total of the certified indebtedness amounts	Sum of products certified indebtedness amounts and credit rates	Total of the certified indebtedness amounts	Sum of products certified indebtedness amounts and credit rates	Total of the certified indebtedness amounts	Sum of products certified indebtedness amounts and credit rates	Total of the certified indebtedness amounts	Sum of products certified indebtedness amounts and credit rates	Total of the certified indebtedness amounts	Sum of products certified indebtedness amounts and credit rates
$0 to $9,999										
$10,000 to $19,999										
$20,000 to $29,999										
$30,000 to $39,999										
$40,000 to $49,999										
$50,000 to $74,999										
$75,000 to more										
Total										
Acquisition Cost										
$0 to $19,999										
$20,000 to $39,999										
$40,000 to $59,999										
$60,000 to $79,999										
$80,000 to $99,999										
$100,000 to $119,999										
$120,000 to $149,999										
$150,000 to $199,999										
$200,000 to or more										
Total										

Mortgage Credit Certificates for Qualified Home Improvement and Rehabilitation Loans

	Nontargeted area	Targeted area	Totals
Home Improvement Loans			
Number of mortgage credit certificates			
Total of the certified indebtedness amounts			
Product of certified indebtedness amounts and credit rates			
Rehabilitation Loans			
Number of mortgage credit certificates			
Total of the certified indebtedness amounts			
Product of certified indebtedness amounts and credit rates			

(3) Definitions and special rules. (i) For purposes of this paragraph the term "annualized gross income" means the borrower's gross monthly income multiplied by 12. Gross monthly income is the sum of monthly gross pay, any additional income from investments, pensions, Veterans' Administration (VA) compensation, part-time employment, bonuses, dividends, interest, current overtime pay, net rental income, etc., and other income (such as alimony and child support, if the borrower chooses to disclose such income). Information with respect to gross monthly income may be obtained from available loan documents, e.g., the sum of lines 23D and 23E on the Application for VA or Fame Home Loan Guaranty or for HUD/FHA Insured Mortgage (VA Form 26-1802a, HUD 92900, Jan. 1982), or the total line from the Gross Monthly Income section of FHLMC Residential Loan Application form (FHLMC 65 Rev. 8/78).

(ii) For purposes of this paragraph, the term "reporting period" means each one year period beginning July 1 and ending June 30, except that issuers need not provide data with respect to the period prior to October 1, 1985.

(iii) For purposes of this paragraph, verification of information concerning a holder's gross monthly income by utilizing other available information concerning the holder's income (e.g., Federal income tax returns) is not required. In determining whether the holder of a mortgage credit certificate acquiring a residence in a targeted area satisfies the 3-year requirement, the issuer may rely on a statement signed by the holder.

(4) Time for filing. The report required by this paragraph shall be filed not later than the 15th day of the second calendar month after the close of the reporting period. The Commissioner may grant an extension of time for the filing of a report required by this paragraph if there is reasonable cause for the failure to file such report in a timely fashion. The report may be filed at any time before such date but must be complete based on facts and reasonable expectations as of the date the report is filed. The report need not be amended to reflect information learned subsequent to the date of fil-

ing, or to reflect changed circumstances with respect to any holder.

(5) Place for filing. The report required by this paragraph is to be filed at the Internal Revenue Service Center, Philadelphia, Pennsylvania 19255.

(f) Policy statement. A program established pursuant to an election under paragraph (c) made after 1984 meets the requirements of this paragraph only if the applicable elected representative of the governmental unit—

(1) Which is the issuer, or

(2) On whose behalf the certificates were issued, has published (after a public hearing following reasonable public notice) a policy statement described in § 1.103A-2(1) by the last day of the year preceding the year in which the election under paragraph (c) is made, and a copy of such report has been submitted to the Commissioner on or before such last day. See § 1.103A-2(1) for further definitions and requirements.

(g) Targeted areas requirement. *(1) In general.* A program meets the requirements of this paragraph only if—

(i) The portion of the total proceeds of the issue specified in paragraph (g)(2) is made available to provide mortgage credit certificates in connection with owner financing of targeted area residents for at least 1 year after the date on which mortgage credit certificates are first made available with respect to targeted area residences, and

(ii) The issuer attempts with reasonable diligence to place such proceeds with qualified persons.

Mortgage credit certificates are considered first made available with respect to targeted area residences on the date on which the issuer first begins to accept applications for mortgage credit certificates provided under that issue.

(2) Specified portion. (i) The specified portion of the total proceeds of an issue is the lesser of—

(A) 20 percent of the total proceeds, or

(B) 8 percent of the average annual aggregate principal amount of mortgages executed during the immediately preceding 3 calendar years for single-family, owner-occupied residences in targeted areas within the jurisdiction of the issuing authority.

For purposes of computing the required portion of the total proceeds specified in paragraph (g)(2)(i)(B) where such provision is applicable, an issuer may rely upon the safe-harbor formula provided in the regulations under section 103A(h).

(ii) See § 1.25-1T(b)(10)(ii) for the definition of "total proceeds".

(h) Fees. *(1) In general.* A program meets the requirements of this paragraph only if each applicant is required to pay, directly or indirectly, no fee other than those fees permitted under this paragraph.

(2) Permissible fees. Applicants may be required to pay the following fees provided that they are reasonable:

(i) Points, origination fees, servicing fees, and other fees in amounts that are customarily charged with respect to mortgages not provided in connection with mortgage credit certificates,

(ii) Application fees, survey fees, credit report fees, insurance fees, or similar settlement or financing costs to the extent such amounts do not exceed the amounts charged in the area in cases where mortgages are not provided in connection with mortgage credit certificates. For example, amounts charged for FHA, VA, or similar private mortgage insurance on an individual's mortgage are permissible so long as such amounts do not exceed the amounts charged in the area with respect to a similar mortgage that is not provided in connection with a mortgage credit certificate, and

(iii) Other fees that, taking into account all the facts and circumstances, are reasonably necessary to cover any administrative costs incurred by the issuer or its agent in issuing mortgage credit certificates.

(i) Qualified mortgage credit certificate. A program meets the requirements of this paragraph only if each mortgage credit certificate issued under the program meets each of the requirements of paragraphs (c) through (o) of § 1.25-3T.

(j) Good faith compliance efforts. *(1) Eligibility requirements.* (i) A program under which each of the mortgage credit certificates issued does not meet each of the requirements of paragraphs (c) through (o) of § 1.25-3T shall be treated as meeting the requirements of paragraph (i) of this section if each of the requirements of this paragraph (j)(1) is satisfied. A mortgage credit certificate program meets the requirements of this paragraph (j)(1) only if each of the following provisions is met:

(A) The issuer in good faith attempted to issue mortgage credit certificates only to individuals meeting each of the requirements of paragraphs (c) through (o) of § 1.25-3T. Good faith requires that agreements with lenders and agents and other relevant instruments contain restrictions that permit the approval of mortgage credit certificates only in accordance with the requirements of paragraphs (c) through (o) of § 1.25-3T. In addition, the issuer must establish reasonable procedures to ensure compliance with those requirements. Reasonable procedures include reasonable investigations by the issuer to determine whether individuals satisfy the requirements of paragraphs (c) through (o) of § 1.25-3T.

(B) 95 percent or more of the total proceeds of the issue were devoted to individuals with respect to whom, at the time that the certificate was issued, all the requirements of paragraphs (c) through (o) of § 1.25-3T were met. If a holder of a mortgage credit certificate fails to meet more than one of these requirements, the amount of the certificate (i.e., the certificate credit rate multiplied by the certified indebtedness amount) issued to that individual will be taken into account only once in determining whether the 95-percent requirement is met. However, all of the defects in that individual's certificate must be corrected pursuant to paragraph (j)(1)(i)(C).

(C) Any failure to meet the requirements of paragraphs (c) through (o) of § 1.25-3T is corrected within a reasonable period after that failure is discovered. For example, if an individual fails to meet one or more of such requirements those failures can be corrected by revoking that individual's certificate.

(ii) Examples. The following examples illustrate the application of this paragraph (j)(1):

Example (1). County X only distributes mortgage credit certificates to individuals who have contracted to purchase a principal residence. County X requires that applicants for mortgage credit certificates present the following information:

(i) An affidavit stating that the applicant intends to use the residence in connection with which the mortgage credit certificate is issued as his principal residence within a reasonable time after the certificate is issued by County X, that the applicant will notify the County if the residence ceases to be his principal residence, and facts that are sufficient for

County X to determine whether the residence is located within the jurisdiction of County X,

(ii) An affidavit stating that the applicant had no present ownership interest in a principal residence at any time during the 3-year period prior to the date on which the certificate is issued,

(iii) Copies of the applicant's Federal tax returns for the preceding 3 years,

(iv) Affidavits from the seller of the residence with respect to which the certificate is issued and the applicant stating the purchase price of the residence, including an itemized list of (A) payments made by or for the benefit of the applicant, (B) if the residence is incomplete, an estimate of the reasonable cost of completing the residence, and (C) if the residence is subject to a ground rent, the capitalized value of the ground rent,

(v) An affidavit executed by the applicant stating that the mortgage being acquired in connection with the certificate will not be used to acquire or replace an existing mortgage,

(vi) An affidavit executed by the applicant stating that no portion of the financing for the residence in connection with which the certificate is issued is provided from the proceeds of a qualified mortgage bond or qualified veterans' mortgage bond and that no portion of the mortgage for the residence is provided by a person related to the applicant (as defined in § 1.25-3T(n)),

(vii) An affidavit executed by the applicant stating that the certificate was not limited to indebtedness incurred from particular lenders, and

(viii) In the case of a mortgage credit certificate allocated for use in connection with a particular development, and affidavit executed by the applicant stating that the applicant received from the developer a certification stating that the price of the residence with respect to which the certificate was issued is no higher than it would be without the use of a mortgage credit certificate.

County X examines the information submitted by the applicant to determine whether the requirements of paragraphs (c), (d), (e), (f), (g), (i), (j), (k), and (n) of § 1.25-3T are met. County X determines that the certificate has not expired. The mortgage credit certificates issued by County X are in the form prescribed by § 1.25-6T and County X provides all the required information and statements. After determining that the applicant meets all these requirements County X issues a mortgage credit certificate to the applicant. This procedure for issuing mortgage credit certificates is sufficient evidence of the good faith of County X to meet the requirements of § 1.25-4T(j)(1)(i)(A).

Example (2). County W distributes preliminary mortgage credit certificates to individuals who have not entered into contracts to purchase a principal residence. County W issues preliminary certificates in the form prescribed by § 1.25-6T to those applicants that have submitted statements that they (i) intend to purchase a single-family residence located within the jurisdiction of County W which they will occupy as a principal residence, (ii) have had no present ownership interest in a principal residence within the preceding 3-year period, and (iii) will not use the certificate in connection with the acquisition or replacement of an existing mortgage. The certificates contain a maximum purchase price, the certificate credit rate, and a statement that the certificate will expire if the applicant does not enter into a closing agreement with respect to a loan within 6 months from the date of preliminary issuance. Holders of these certificates may apply for a mortgage loan from any lender. When the holder of the certificate applies for a loan the lender requires that he submit the following:

(i) An affidavit stating that the applicant intends to use the residence in connection with which the mortgage credit certificate is issued as his principal residence within a reasonable time after the certificate is issued by County W, that the applicant will notify the County if the residence ceases to be his principal residence, and facts that are sufficient for County W to determine whether the residence is located within the jurisdiction of County W.

(ii) An affidavit stating that the applicant had no present ownership interest in a principal residence at any time during the 3-year period prior to the date on which the certificate is issued.

(iii) Copies of the applicant's Federal tax returns for the preceding 3 years,

(iv) Affidavits from the seller of the residence with respect to which the certificate is issued and the applicant stating the purchase price of the residence, including an itemized list of (A) payments made by or for the benefit of the applicant, (B) if the residence is incomplete, an estimate of the reasonable cost of completing the residence, and (C) if the residence is subject to a ground rent, the capitalized value of the ground rent,

(v) An affidavit executed by the applicant stating that the mortgage being acquired in connection with the certificate will not be used to acquire or replace an existing mortgage,

(vi) An affidavit executed by the applicant stating that no portion of the financing for the residence in connection with which the certificate is issued in provided from the proceeds of a qualified mortgage bond or qualified veterans' mortgage bond and that no portion of the mortgage for the residence is provided by a person related to the applicant (as defined in § 1.25-3T(n)),

(vii) An affidavit executed by the applicant stating that the certificate was not limited to indebtedness incurred from particular lenders, and

(viii) In the case of a mortgage credit certificate allocated for use in connection with a particular development, an affidavit executed by the applicant stating that the applicant received from the developer a certification stating that the price of the residence with respect to which the certificate was issued is no higher than it would be without the use of a mortgage credit certificate.

The lender then submits those affidavits, together with its statement as to the amount of the indebtedness incurred, to County W. After determining that the requirements of paragraphs (c), (d), (e), (f), (g), (i), (j), (k) and (n) of § 1.25-3T are met and determining that the certificate has not expired, County W completes the mortgage credit certificate. This procedure for issuing mortgage credit certificates is sufficient evidence of the good faith of County W to meet the requirements of § 1.25-4T(j)(1)(i)(A).

(2) Program requirements. (i) A mortgage credit certificate program which fails to meet one or more of the requirements of paragraphs (b) through (h) of this section shall be treated as meeting such requirements if the requirements of this paragraph (j)(2) are satisfied. A mortgage credit certificate program meets the requirements of this paragraph (j)(2) only if each of the following provisions is met:

(A) The issuer in good faith attempted to meet all of the requirements of paragraphs (b) through (h) of this section. This good faith requirement will be met if all reasonable steps are taken by the issuer to ensure that the program complies with these requirements.

(B) Any failure to meet such requirements is due to inadvertent error, e.g., mathematical error, after taking reasonable steps to comply with such requirements.

(ii) The following example illustrates the application of this paragraph (j)(2):

Example. City X issues an issue of mortgage credit certificates. However, despite taking all reasonable steps to determine accurately the size of the applicable limit, as provided in section 103A(g)(3) and the regulations thereunder, the limit is exceeded because the amount of the mortgages, originated in the area during the past 3 years is incorrectly computed as a result of mathematical error. Such facts are sufficient evidence of the good faith of the issuer to meet the requirements of paragraph (j)(2).

T.D. 8023, 5/3/85, amend T.D. 8048, 8/29/85.

---

§ 1.25-5T Limitation on aggregate amount of mortgage credit certificates (temporary).

Caution: The Treasury has not yet amended Reg § 1.25-5T to reflect changes made by P.L. 103-66, P.L. 101-239, P.L. 100-647, P.L. 99-514.

(a) In general. If the aggregate amount of qualified mortgage credit certificates (as defined in paragraph (b)) issued by an issuer under a qualified mortgage credit certificate program exceeds 20 percent of the nonissued bond amount (as defined in paragraph (c)), the provisions of paragraph (d) shall apply.

(b) Aggregate amount of mortgage credit certificates. *(1) In general.* The aggregate amount of qualified mortgage credit certificates issued under a qualified mortgage credit certificate program is the sum of the products determined by multiplying—

(i) The certified indebtedness amount of each qualified mortgage credit certificate issued under that program, by

(ii) The certificate credit rate with respect to such certificate.

(2) Examples. The following examples illustrate the application of this paragraph (b):

Example (1). For 1986 City Q has a nonissued bond amount of $100 million. After making a proper election, Q issues 2,000 qualified mortgage credit certificates each with a certificate credit rate of 20 percent and a certified indebtedness amount of $50,000. The aggregate amount of qualified mortgage credit certificates is $20 million (2,000 × (.2 × $50,000)). Since this amount does not exceed 20 percent of the nonissued bond amount (.2 × $100 million = $20 million), Q has complied with the limitation on the aggregate amount of mortgage credit certificates, provided that it does not issue any additional certificates.

Example (2). The facts are the same as in example (1) except that instead of issuing all its certificates at the 20 percent rate, Q issues (i) qualified mortgage credit certificates with a certificate credit rate of 10 percent and an aggregate principal amount of $25 million, (ii) qualified mortgage credit certificates with a certificate credit rate of 40 percent and an aggregate principal amount of $25 million, and (iii) qualified mortgage credit certificates with a certificate credit rate of 30 percent and an aggregate principal amount of $25 million. The aggregate amount of qualified mortgage credit certificates is $20 million ((10 percent of $25 million) plus (40 percent of $25 million) plus (30 percent of $25 million)). Q has complied with the limitation on the aggregate amount of qualified mortgage credit certificates, provided that it does not issue any additional certificates pursuant to the same program.

(c) Nonissued bond amount. The term "nonissued bond amount" means, with respect to any qualified mortgage credit certificate program, the amount of qualified mortgage bonds (as defined in section 103A(c)(1) and the regulations thereunder) which the issuer is otherwise authorized to issue and elects not to issue under section 25(c)(2) and § 1.25-4T(b). The amount of qualified mortgage bonds which an issuing authority is authorized to issue is determined under section 103A(g) and the regulations thereunder; such determination shall take into account any prior elections by the issuer not to issue qualified mortgage bonds, the amount of any reduction in the State ceiling under paragraph (d) of this section, and the aggregate amount of qualified mortgage bonds issued by the issuer prior to its election not to issue qualified mortgage bonds.

(d) Noncompliance with limitation on aggregate amount of mortgage credit certificates. *(1) In general.* If the provisions of this paragraph apply, the State ceiling under section 103A(g)(4) and the regulations thereunder for the calendar year following the calendar year in which the Commissioner determines the correction amount for the State in which the issuer which exceeded the limitation on the aggregate amount of mortgage credit certificates is located shall be reduced by 1.25 times the correction amount with respect to such failure.

(2) Correction amount. (i) The term "correction amount" means an amount equal to the excess credit amount divided by .20.

(ii) The term "excess credit amount" means the excess of—

(A) The credit amount for any mortgage credit certificate program, over

(B) The amount which would have been the credit amount for such program had such program met the requirements of section 25(d)(2) and paragraph (a) of this section.

(iii) The term "credit amount" means the sum of the products determined by multiplying—

(A) The certified indebtedness amount of each qualified mortgage credit certificate issued under the program, by

(B) The certificate credit rate with respect to such certificate.

(3) Example. The following example illustrates the application of this paragraph:

Example. For 1987 City R has a nonissued bond amount of $100 million. City R issues all of its mortgage credit certificates with a certificate credit rate of 20 percent. City R issues certificates with an aggregate certified indebtedness amount of $120 million. The aggregate amount of mortgage credit certificates issued by City R is $24 million, which exceeds 20 percent of the nonissued bond amount. The State ceiling for the calendar year following the calendar year in which the Commissioner determines the correction amount is reduced by $25 million (the correction amount multiplied by 1.25). The correction amount is determined as follows: The credit amount is $24 million (.2 x $120 million); the amount which would have been the credit amount for the program had it met the requirements of section 25(d)(2) is $20 million (.2 × $100 million); the excess credit amount is $4 million ($24 million – $20 million); therefore, the correction amount is $20 million ($4 million/.2).

(4) Cross references. See section 103A(g)(4) and the regulations thereunder with respect to the reduction of the applicable State ceiling.

T.D. 8023, 5/3/85.

§ 1.25-6T Form of qualified mortgage credit certificate (temporary).

Caution: The Treasury has not yet amended Reg § 1.25-6T to reflect changes made by P.L. 103-66, P.L. 101-239, P.L. 100-647, P.L. 99-514.

(a) In general. Qualified mortgage credit certificates are to be issued on the form prescribed by the Internal Revenue Service. If no form is prescribed by the Internal Revenue Service, or if the form prescribed by the Internal Revenue Service is not readily available, the issuer may use its own form provided that such form contains the information required by this section. Each mortgage credit certificate must be issued in a form such that there are at least three copies of the form. One copy of the certificate shall be retained by the issuer; one copy shall be retained by the lender; and one copy shall be forwarded to the State official who issued the certification required by § 1.25-4T(d), unless that State official has stated in writing that he does not want to receive such copies.

(b) Required information. Each qualified mortgage credit certificate must include the following information:

(1) The name, address, and TIN of the issuer,

(2) The date of the issuer's election not to issue qualified mortgage bonds pursuant to which the certificate is being issued,

(3) The number assigned to the certificate,

(4) The name, address, and TIN of the holder of the certificate,

(5) The certificate credit rate,

(6) The certified indebtedness amount,

(7) The acquisition cost of the residence being acquired in connection with the certificate,

(8) The average area purchase price applicable to the residence,

(9) Whether the certificate meets the requirements of § 1.25-3T(d), relating to residence requirement,

(10) Whether the certificate meets the requirements of § 1.25-3T(e), relating to 3-year requirement,

(11) Whether the certificate meets the requirements of § 1.25-3T(g), relating to new mortgage requirement,

(12) Whether the certificate meets the requirements of § 1.25-3T(i), relating to prohibited mortgages,

(13) Whether the certificate meets the requirements of § 1.25-3T(j), relating to particular lenders,

(14) Whether the certificate meets the requirements of § 1.25-3T(k), relating to allocations to particular developments,

(15) Whether the certificate meets the requirements of § 1.25-3T(n), relating to interest paid to related persons,

(16) Whether the residence in connection with which the certificate is issued is a targeted area residence,

(17) The date on which a closing agreement is signed with respect to the certified indebtedness amount,

(18) The expiration date of the certificate,

(19) A statement that the certificate is not transferable or a statement that the certificate may be transferred only if the issuer issues a new certificate, and

(20) A statement, signed under penalties of perjury by an authorized official of the issuer or its agent, that such person has made the determinations specified in paragraph (b)(9) through (16).

T.D. 8023, 5/3/85.

§ 1.25-7T Public notice (Temporary).

Caution: The Treasury has not yet amended Reg § 1.25-7T to reflect changes made by P.L. 103-66, P.L. 101-239, P.L. 100-647, P.L. 99-514.

(a) In general. At least 90 days prior to the issuance of any mortgage credit certificate under a qualified mortgage credit certificate program, the issuer shall provide reasonable public notice of—

(1) The eligibility requirements for such certificate,

(2) The methods by which such certificates are to be issued, and

(3) The other information required by this section.

(b) Reasonable public notice. *(1) In general.* Reasonable public notice means published notice which is reasonably designed to inform individuals who would be eligible to receive mortgage credit certificates of the proposed issuance. Reasonable public notice may be provided through newspapers of general circulation.

(2) Contents of notice. The public notice required by paragraph (a) must include a brief description of the principal residence requirement, 3-year requirement, purchase price requirement, and new mortgage requirement. The notice must also provide a brief description of the methods by which the certificates are to be issued and the address and telephone number for obtaining further information.

T.D. 8023, 5/3/85.

§ 1.25-8T Reporting requirements (Temporary).

Caution: The Treasury has not yet amended Reg § 1.25-8T to reflect changes made by P.L. 103-66, P.L. 101-239, P.L. 100-647, P.L. 99-514.

(a) Lender. *(1) In general.* Each person who makes a loan that is a certified indebtedness amount with respect to any mortgage credit certificate must file the report described in paragraph (a)(2) and must retain on its books and records the information described in paragraph (a)(3). The report described in paragraph (a)(2) is an annual report and must be filed on or before January 31 of the year following the calendar year to which the report relates. See section 6709(c) and the regulations thereunder for the applicable penalties with respect to failure to file reports.

(2) Information required. The report shall be submitted on Form 8329 and shall contain the information required therein. A separate Form 8329 shall be filed for each issue of mortgage credit certificates with respect to which the lender made mortgage loans during the preceding calendar year. Thus, for example, if during 1986 Bank M makes three mortgage loans which are certified indebtedness amounts with respect to State Z's January 15, 1986, issue of mortgage credit certificates, and two mortgage loans which are certified indebtedness amounts with respect to State Z's April 15, 1986, issue of mortgage credit certificates, and fifty mortgage loans which are certified indebtedness

amounts with respect to County X's December 31, 1985, issue of mortgage credit certificates, Bank M must file three separate reports for calendar year 1986. The lender must submit the Form 8329 with the information required therein, including—

(i) The name, address, and TIN of the issuer of the mortgage credit certificates,

(ii) The date on which the election not to issue qualified mortgage bonds with respect to that mortgage credit certificate was made,

(iii) The name, address, and TIN of the lender, and

(iv) The sum of the products determined by multiplying—

(A) The certified indebtedness amount of each mortgage credit certificate issued under such program, by

(B) The certificate credit rate with respect to such certificate.

(3) Recordkeeping requirements. Each person who makes a loan that is a certified indebtedness amount with respect to any mortgage credit certificate must retain the information specified in this paragraph (a)(3) on its books and records for 6 years following the year in which the loan was made. With respect to each loan the lender must retain the following information:

(i) The name, address, and TIN of each holder of a qualified mortgage credit certificate with respect to which a loan is made,

(ii) The name, address, and TIN of the issuer of such certificate, and

(iii) The date the loan for the certified indebtedness amount is closed, the certified indebtedness amount, and the certificate credit rate of such certificate.

(b) Issuers. *(1) In general.* Each issuer of mortgage credit certificates shall file the report described in paragraph (b)(2).

(2) Quarterly reports. (i) Each issuer which elects to issue mortgage credit certificates shall file reports on Form 8330. These reports shall be filed on a quarterly basis, beginning with the quarter in which the election is made, and are due on the following dates: April 30 (for the quarter ending March 31), July 31 (for the quarter ending June 30), October 31 (for the quarter ending September 30), and January 31 (for the quarter ending December 31). For elections made prior to May 8, 1985, the first report need not be filed until July 31, 1985. An issuer shall file a separate report for each issue of mortgage credit certificates. In the quarter in which the last qualified mortgage credit certificate that may be issued under a program is issued, the issuer must state that fact on the report to be filed for that quarter; the issuer is not required to file any subsequent reports with respect to that program. See section 6709(c) for the penalties with respect to failure to file a report.

(ii) The report shall be submitted on Form 8330 and shall contain the information required therein, including—

(A) The name, address, and TIN of the issuer of the mortgage credit certificates,

(B) The date of the issuer's election not to issue qualified mortgage bonds with respect to the mortgage credit certificate program and the nonissued bond amount of the program,

(C) The sum of the products determined by multiplying—

(1) The certified indebtedness amount of each qualified mortgage credit certificate issued under that program during the calendar quarter, by

(2) The certificate credit rate with respect to such certificate, and

(D) A listing of the name, address, and TIN of each holder of a qualified mortgage credit certificate which has been revoked during the calendar quarter.

(c) Extensions of time for filing reports. The Commissioner may grant an extension of time for the filing of a report required by this section if there is reasonable cause for the failure to file such report in a timely fashion.

(d) Place for filing. The reports required by this section are to be filed at the Internal Revenue Service Center, Philadelphia, Pennsylvania 19225.

(e) Cross reference. See section 6709 and the regulations thereunder with respect to the penalty for failure to file a report required by this section.

T.D. 8023, 5/3/85.

---

§ 1.25A-0 Table of contents.

This section lists captions contained in §§ 1.25A-1, 1.25A-2, 1.25A-3, 1.25A-4, and 1.25A-5.

§ 1.25A-1 Calculation of education tax credit and general eligibility requirements.

(a) Amount of education tax credit.

(b) Coordination of Hope Scholarship Credit and Lifetime Learning Credit.

(1) In general.

(2) Hope Scholarship Credit.

(3) Lifetime Learning Credit.

(4) Examples.

(c) Limitation based on modified adjusted gross income.

(1) In general.

(2) Modified adjusted gross income defined.

(3) Inflation adjustment.

(d) Election.

(e) Identification requirement.

(f) Claiming the credit in the case of a dependent.

(1) In general.

(2) Examples.

(g) Married taxpayers.

(h) Nonresident alien taxpayers and dependents.

§ 1.25A-2 Definitions.

(a) Claimed dependent.

(b) Eligible educational institution.

(1) In general.

(2) Rules on federal financial aid programs.

(c) Academic period.

(d) Qualified tuition and related expenses.

(1) In general.

(2) Required fees.

(i) In general.

(ii) Books, supplies, and equipment.

(iii) Nonacademic fees.

(3) Personal expenses.

(4) Treatment of a comprehensive or bundled fee.

(5) Hobby courses.

(6) Examples.

§ 1.25A-3 *Hope Scholarship Credit.*
(a) Amount of the credit.
(1) In general.
(2) Maximum credit.
(b) Per student credit.
(1) In general.
(2) Example.
(c) Credit allowed for only two taxable years.
(d) Eligible student.
(1) Eligible student defined.
(i) Degree requirement.
(ii) Work load requirement.
(iii) Year of study requirement.
(iv) No felony drug conviction.
(2) Examples.
(e) Academic period for prepayments.
(1) In general.
(2) Example.
(f) Effective date.
§ 1.25A-4 *Lifetime Learning Credit.*
(a) Amount of the credit.
(1) Taxable years beginning before January 1, 2003.
(2) Taxable years beginning after December 31, 2002.
(3) Coordination with the Hope Scholarship Credit.
(4) Examples.
(b) Credit allowed for unlimited number of taxable years.
(c) Both degree and nondegree courses are eligible for the credit.
(1) In general.
(2) Examples.
(d) Effective date.
§ 1.25A-5 *Special rules relating to characterization and timing of payments.*
(a) Educational expenses paid by claimed dependent.
(b) Educational expenses paid by a third party.
(1) In general.
(2) Special rule for tuition reduction included in gross income of employee.
(3) Examples.
(c) Adjustment to qualified tuition and related expenses for certain excludable educational assistance.
(1) In general.
(2) No adjustment for excludable educational assistance attributable to expenses paid in a prior year.
(3) Scholarships and fellowship grants.
(4) Examples.
(d) No double benefit.
(e) Timing rules.
(1) In general.
(2) Prepayment rule.
(i) In general.
(ii) Example.
(3) Expenses paid with loan proceeds.
(4) Expenses paid through third party installment payment plans.
(i) In general.
(ii) Example.
(f) Refund of qualified tuition and related expenses.
(1) Payment and refund of qualified tuition and related expenses in the same taxable year.
(2) Payment of qualified tuition and related expenses in one taxable year and refund in subsequent taxable year before return filed for prior taxable year.
(3) Payment of qualified tuition and related expenses in one taxable year and refund in subsequent taxable year.
(i) In general.
(ii) Recapture amount.
(4) Refund of loan proceeds treated as refund of qualified tuition and related expenses.
(5) Excludable educational assistance received in a subsequent taxable year treated as a refund.
(6) Examples.

T.D. 9034, 12/24/2002.

---

§ 1.25A-1 Calculation of education tax credit and general eligibility requirements.

(a) Amount of education tax credit. An individual taxpayer is allowed a nonrefundable education tax credit against income tax imposed by chapter 1 of the Internal Revenue Code for the taxable year. The amount of the education tax credit is the total of the Hope Scholarship Credit (as described in § 1.25A-3) plus the Lifetime Learning Credit (as described in § 1.25A-4). For limitations on the credits allowed by subpart A of part IV of subchapter A of chapter 1 of the Internal Revenue Code, see section 26.

(b) Coordination of Hope Scholarship Credit and Lifetime Learning Credit. *(1) In general.* In the same taxable year, a taxpayer may claim a Hope Scholarship Credit for each eligible student's qualified tuition and related expenses (as defined in § 1.25A-2(d)) and a Lifetime Learning Credit for one or more other students' qualified tuition and related expenses. However, a taxpayer may not claim both a Hope Scholarship Credit and a Lifetime Learning Credit with respect to the same student in the same taxable year.

(2) Hope Scholarship Credit. Subject to certain limitations, a Hope Scholarship Credit may be claimed for the qualified tuition and related expenses paid during a taxable year with respect to each eligible student (as defined in § 1.25A-3(d)). Qualified tuition and related expenses paid during a taxable year with respect to one student may not be taken into account in computing the amount of the Hope Scholarship Credit with respect to any other student. In addition, qualified tuition and related expenses paid during a taxable year with respect to any student for whom a Hope Scholarship Credit is claimed may not be taken into account in computing the amount of the Lifetime Learning Credit.

(3) Lifetime Learning Credit. Subject to certain limitations, a Lifetime Learning Credit may be claimed for the aggregate amount of qualified tuition and related expenses paid during a taxable year with respect to students for whom no Hope Scholarship Credit is claimed.

(4) Examples. The following examples illustrate the rules of this paragraph (b):

Example (1). In 1999, Taxpayer A pays qualified tuition and related expenses for his dependent, B, to attend College Y during 1999. Assuming all other relevant requirements are met, Taxpayer A may claim either a Hope Scholarship

Credit or a Lifetime Learning Credit with respect to dependent B, but not both. See § 1.25A-3(a) and § 1.25A-4(a).

Example (2). In 1999, Taxpayer C pays $2,000 in qualified tuition and related expenses for her dependent, D, to attend College Z during 1999. In 1999, Taxpayer C also pays $500 in qualified tuition and related expenses to attend a computer course during 1999 to improve Taxpayer C's job skills. Assuming all other relevant requirements are met, Taxpayer C may claim a Hope Scholarship Credit for the $2,000 of qualified tuition and related expenses attributable to dependent D (see § 1.25A-3(a)) and a Lifetime Learning Credit (see § 1.25A-4(a))for the $500 of qualified tuition and related expenses incurred to improve her job skills.

Example (3). The facts are the same as in Example 2, except that Taxpayer C pays $3,000 in qualified tuition and related expenses for her dependent, D, to attend College Z during 1999. Although a Hope Scholarship Credit is available only with respect to the first $2,000 of qualified tuition and related expenses paid with respect to D (see § 1.25A-3(a)), Taxpayer C may not add the $1,000 of excess expenses to her $500 of qualified tuition and related expenses in computing the amount of the Lifetime Learning Credit.

(c) Limitation based on modified adjusted gross income. *(1) In general.* The education tax credit that a taxpayer may otherwise claim is phased out ratably for taxpayers with modified adjusted gross income between $40,000 and $50,000 ($80,000 and $100,000 for married individuals who file a joint return). Thus, taxpayers with modified adjusted gross income above $50,000 (or $100,000 for joint filers) may not claim an education tax credit.

(2) Modified adjusted gross income defined. The term modified adjusted gross income means the adjusted gross income (as defined in section 62) of the taxpayer for the taxable year increased by any amount excluded from gross income under section 911, 931, or 933 (relating to income earned abroad or from certain U.S. possessions or Puerto Rico).

(3) Inflation adjustment. For taxable years beginning after 2001, the amounts in paragraph (c)(1) of this section will be increased for inflation occurring after 2000 in accordance with section 1(f)(3). If any amount adjusted under this paragraph (c)(3) is not a multiple of $1,000, the amount will be rounded to the next lowest multiple of $1,000.

(d) Election. No education tax credit is allowed unless a taxpayer elects to claim the credit on the taxpayer's federal income tax return for the taxable year in which the credit is claimed. The election is made by attaching Form 8863, "Education Credits (Hope and Lifetime Learning Credits)," to the Federal income tax return.

(e) Identification requirement. No education tax credit is allowed unless a taxpayer includes on the federal income tax return claiming the credit the name and the taxpayer identification number of the student for whom the credit is claimed. For rules relating to assessment for an omission of a correct taxpayer identification number, see section 6213(b) and (g)(2)(J).

(f) Claiming the credit in the case of a dependent. *(1) In general.* If a student is a claimed dependent of another taxpayer, only that taxpayer may claim the education tax credit for the student's qualified tuition and related expenses. However, if another taxpayer is eligible to, but does not, claim the student as a dependent, only the student may claim the education tax credit for the student's qualified tuition and related expenses.

(2) Examples. The following examples illustrate the rules of this paragraph (f):

Example (1). In 1999, Taxpayer A pays qualified tuition and related expenses for his dependent, B, to attend University Y during 1999. Taxpayer A claims B as a dependent on his federal income tax return. Therefore, assuming all other relevant requirements are met, Taxpayer A is allowed an education tax credit on his federal income tax return, and B is not allowed an education tax credit on B's federal income tax return. The result would be the same if B paid the qualified tuition and related expenses. See § 1.25A-5(a).

Example (2). In 1999, Taxpayer C has one dependent, D. In 1999, D pays qualified tuition and related expenses to attend University Z during 1999. Although Taxpayer C is eligible to claim D as a dependent on her federal income tax return, she does not do so. Therefore, assuming all other relevant requirements are met, D is allowed an education tax credit on D's federal income tax return, and Taxpayer C is not allowed an education tax credit on her federal income tax return, with respect to D's education expenses. The result would be the same if C paid the qualified tuition and related expenses on behalf of D. See § 1.25A-5(b).

(g) Married taxpayers. If a taxpayer is married (within the meaning of section 7703), no education tax credit is allowed to the taxpayer unless the taxpayer and the taxpayer's spouse file a joint Federal income tax return for the taxable year.

(h) Nonresident alien taxpayers and dependents. If a taxpayer or the taxpayer's spouse is a nonresident alien for any portion of the taxable year, no education tax credit is allowed unless the nonresident alien is treated as a resident alien by reason of an election under section 6013(g) or (h). In addition, if a student is a nonresident alien, a taxpayer may not claim an education tax credit with respect to the qualified tuition and related expenses of the student unless the student is a claimed dependent (as defined in § 1.25A-2(a)).

T.D. 9034, 12/24/2002.

§ 1.25A-2 Definitions.

(a) Claimed dependent. A claimed dependent means a dependent (as defined in section 152) for whom a deduction under section 151 is allowed on a taxpayer's federal income tax return for the taxable year. Among other requirements under section 152, a nonresident alien student must be a resident of a country contiguous to the United States in order to be treated as a dependent.

(b) Eligible educational institution. *(1) In general.* In general, an eligible educational institution means a college, university, vocational school, or other postsecondary educational institution that is—

(i) Described in section 481 of the Higher Education Act of 1965 (20 U.S.C. 1088) as in effect on August 5, 1997, (generally all accredited public, nonprofit, and proprietary postsecondary institutions); and

(ii) Participating in a federal financial aid program under title IV of the Higher Education Act of 1965 or is certified by the Department of Education as eligible to participate in such a program but chooses not to participate.

(2) Rules on federal financial aid programs. For rules governing an educational institution's eligibility to participate in federal financial aid programs, see 20 U.S.C. 1070; 20 U.S.C. 1094; and 34 CFR 600 and 668.

(c) Academic period. Academic period means a quarter, semester, trimester, or other period of study as reasonably determined by an eligible educational institution. In the case of an eligible educational institution that uses credit hours or clock hours, and does not have academic terms, each payment period (as defined in 34 CFR 668.4, revised as of July 1, 2002) may be treated as an academic period.

(d) Qualified tuition and related expenses. *(1) In general.* Qualified tuition and related expenses means tuition and fees required for the enrollment or attendance of a student for courses of instruction at an eligible educational institution.

(2) Required fees. (i) In general. Except as provided in paragraph (d)(3) of this section, the test for determining whether any fee is a qualified tuition and related expense is whether the fee is required to be paid to the eligible educational institution as a condition of the student's enrollment or attendance at the institution.

(ii) Books, supplies, and equipment. Qualified tuition and related expenses include fees for books, supplies, and equipment used in a course of study only if the fees must be paid to the eligible educational institution for the enrollment or attendance of the student at the institution.

(iii) Nonacademic fees. Except as provided in paragraph (d)(3) of this section, qualified tuition and related expenses include fees charged by an eligible educational institution that are not used directly for, or allocated to, an academic course of instruction only if the fee must be paid to the eligible educational institution for the enrollment or attendance of the student at the institution.

(3) Personal expenses. Qualified tuition and related expenses do not include the costs of room and board, insurance, medical expenses (including student health fees), transportation, and similar personal, living, or family expenses, regardless of whether the fee must be paid to the eligible educational institution for the enrollment or attendance of the student at the institution.

(4) Treatment of a comprehensive or bundled fee. If a student is required to pay a fee (such as a comprehensive fee or a bundled fee) to an eligible educational institution that combines charges for qualified tuition and related expenses with charges for personal expenses described in paragraph (d)(3) of this section, the portion of the fee that is allocable to personal expenses is not included in qualified tuition and related expenses. The determination of what portion of the fee relates to qualified tuition and related expenses and what portion relates to personal expenses must be made by the institution using a reasonable method of allocation.

(5) Hobby courses. Qualified tuition and related expenses do not include expenses that relate to any course of instruction or other education that involves sports, games, or hobbies, or any noncredit course, unless the course or other education is part of the student's degree program, or in the case of the Lifetime Learning Credit, the student takes the course to acquire or improve job skills.

(6) Examples. The following examples illustrate the rules of this paragraph (d). In each example, assume that the institution is an eligible educational institution and that all other relevant requirements to claim an education tax credit are met. The examples are as follows:

Example (1). University V offers a degree program in dentistry. In addition to tuition, all students enrolled in the program are required to pay a fee to University V for the rental of dental equipment. Because the equipment rental fee must be paid to University V for enrollment and attendance, the tuition and the equipment rental fee are qualified tuition and related expenses.

Example (2). First-year students at College W are required to obtain books and other reading materials used in its mandatory first-year curriculum. The books and other reading materials are not required to be purchased from College W and may be borrowed from other students or purchased from off-campus bookstores, as well as from College W's bookstore. College W bills students for any books and materials purchased from College W's bookstore. The fee that College W charges for the first-year books and materials purchased at its bookstore is not a qualified tuition and related expense because the books and materials are not required to be purchased from College W for enrollment or attendance at the institution.

Example (3). All students who attend College X are required to pay a separate student activity fee in addition to their tuition. The student activity fee is used solely to fund on-campus organizations and activities run by students, such as the student newspaper and the student government (no portion of the fee covers personal expenses). Although labeled as a student activity fee, the fee is required for enrollment or attendance at College X. Therefore, the fee is a qualified tuition and related expense.

Example (4). The facts are the same as in Example 3, except that College X offers an optional athletic fee that students may pay to receive discounted tickets to sports events. The athletic fee is not required for enrollment or attendance at College X. Therefore, the fee is not a qualified tuition and related expense.

Example (5). College Y requires all students to live on campus. It charges a single comprehensive fee to cover tuition, required fees, and room and board. Based on College Y's reasonable allocation, sixty percent of the comprehensive fee is allocable to tuition and other required fees not allocable to personal expenses, and the remaining forty percent of the comprehensive fee is allocable to charges for room and board and other personal expenses. Therefore, only sixty percent of College Y's comprehensive fee is a qualified tuition and related expense.

Example (6). As a degree student at College Z, Student A is required to take a certain number of courses outside of her chosen major in Economics. To fulfill this requirement, Student A enrolls in a square dancing class offered by the Physical Education Department. Because Student A receives credit toward her degree program for the square dancing class, the tuition for the square dancing class is included in qualified tuition and related expenses.

T.D. 9034, 12/24/2002.

§ 1.25A-3 Hope Scholarship Credit.

(a) Amount of the credit. *(1) In general.* Subject to the phaseout of the education tax credit described in § 1.25A-1(c), the Hope Scholarship Credit amount is the total of—

(i) 100 percent of the first $1,000 of qualified tuition and related expenses paid during the taxable year for education furnished to an eligible student (as defined in paragraph (d) of this section) who is the taxpayer, the taxpayer's spouse, or any claimed dependent during any academic period beginning in the taxable year (or treated as beginning in the taxable year, see § 1.25A-5(e)(2)); plus

(ii) 50 percent of the next $1,000 of such expenses paid with respect to that student.

(2) Maximum credit. For taxable years beginning before 2002, the maximum Hope Scholarship Credit allowed for each eligible student is $1,500. For taxable years beginning after 2001, the amounts used in paragraph (a)(1) of this section to determine the maximum credit will be increased for inflation occurring after 2000 in accordance with section 1(f)(3). If any amount adjusted under this paragraph (a)(2) is not a multiple of $100, the amount will be rounded to the next lowest multiple of $100.

(b) Per student credit. *(1) In general.* A Hope Scholarship Credit may be claimed for the qualified tuition and related expenses of each eligible student (as defined in paragraph (d) of this section).

(2) Example. The following example illustrates the rule of this paragraph (b). In the example, assume that all the requirements to claim an education tax credit are met. The example is as follows:

Example. In 1999, Taxpayer A has two dependents, B and C, both of whom are eligible students. Taxpayer A pays $1,600 in qualified tuition and related expenses for dependent B to attend a community college. Taxpayer A pays $5,000 in qualified tuition and related expenses for dependent C to attend University X. Taxpayer A may claim a Hope Scholarship Credit of $1,300 ($1,000 + (.50 x $600)) for dependent B, and the maximum $1,500 Hope Scholarship Credit for dependent C, for a total Hope Scholarship Credit of $2,800.

(c) Credit allowed for only two taxable years. For each eligible student, the Hope Scholarship Credit may be claimed for no more than two taxable years.

(d) Eligible student. *(1) Eligible student defined.* For purposes of the Hope Scholarship Credit, the term eligible student means a student who satisfies all of the following requirements—

(i) Degree requirement. For at least one academic period that begins during the taxable year, the student enrolls at an eligible educational institution in a program leading toward a postsecondary degree, certificate, or other recognized postsecondary educational credential;

(ii) Work load requirement. For at least one academic period that begins during the taxable year, the student enrolls for at least one-half of the normal full-time work load for the course of study the student is pursuing. The standard for what is half of the normal full-time work load is determined by each eligible educational institution. However, the standard for half-time may not be lower than the applicable standard for half-time established by the Department of Education under the Higher Education Act of 1965 and set forth in 34 CFR 674.2(b) (revised as of July 1, 2002) for a half-time undergraduate student;

(iii) Year of study requirement. As of the beginning of the taxable year, the student has not completed the first two years of postsecondary education at an eligible educational institution. Whether a student has completed the first two years of postsecondary education at an eligible educational institution as of the beginning of a taxable year is determined based on whether the institution in which the student is enrolled in a degree program (as described in paragraph (d)(1)(i) of this section) awards the student two years of academic credit at that institution for postsecondary course work completed by the student prior to the beginning of the taxable year. Any academic credit awarded by the eligible educational institution solely on the basis of the student's performance on proficiency examinations is disregarded in determining whether the student has completed two years of postsecondary education; and

(iv) No felony drug conviction. The student has not been convicted of a federal or state felony offense for possession or distribution of a controlled substance as of the end of the taxable year for which the credit is claimed.

(2) Examples. The following examples illustrate the rules of this paragraph (d). In each example, assume that the student has not been convicted of a felony drug offense, that the institution is an eligible educational institution unless otherwise stated, that the qualified tuition and related expenses are paid during the same taxable year that the academic period begins, and that a Hope Scholarship Credit has not previously been claimed for the student (see paragraph (c) of this section). The examples are as follows:

Example (1). Student A graduates from high school in June 1998 and is enrolled in an undergraduate degree program at College U for the 1998 Fall semester on a full-time basis. For the 1999 Spring semester, Student A again is enrolled at College U on a full-time basis. For the 1999 Fall semester, Student A is enrolled in less than half the normal full-time course work for her degree program. Because Student A is enrolled in an undergraduate degree program on at least a half-time basis for at least one academic period that begins during 1998 and at least one academic period that begins during 1999, Student A is an eligible student for taxable years 1998 and 1999 (including the 1999 Fall semester when Student A enrolls at College U on less than a half-time basis).

Example (2). Prior to 1998, Student B attended college for several years on a full-time basis. Student B transfers to College V for the 1998 Spring semester. College V awards Student B credit for some (but not all) of the courses he previously completed, and College V classifies Student B as a first-semester sophomore. During both the Spring and Fall semesters of 1998, Student B is enrolled in at least one-half the normal full-time work load for his degree program at College V. Because College V does not classify Student B as having completed the first two years of postsecondary education as of the beginning of 1998, Student B is an eligible student for taxable year 1998.

Example (3). The facts are the same as in Example 2. After taking classes on a half-time basis for the 1998 Spring and Fall semesters, Student B is enrolled at College V for the 1999 Spring semester on a full-time basis. College V classifies Student B as a second-semester sophomore for the 1999 Spring semester and as a first-semester junior for the 1999 Fall semester. Because College V does not classify Student B as having completed the first two years of postsecondary education as of the beginning of 1999, Student B is an eligible student for taxable year 1999. Therefore, the qualified expenses and required fees paid for the 1999 Spring semester and the 1999 Fall semester are taken into account in calculating any Hope Scholarship Credit.

Example (4). Prior to 1998, Student C was not enrolled at another eligible educational institution. At the time that Student C enrolls in a degree program at College W for the 1998 Fall semester, Student C takes examinations to demonstrate her proficiency in several subjects. On the basis of Student C's performance on these examinations, College W classifies Student C as a second-semester sophomore as of the beginning of the 1998 Fall semester. Student C is enrolled at College W during the 1998 Fall semester and during the 1999 Spring and Fall semesters on a full-time basis and is classified as a first-semester junior as of the beginning of the 1999 Spring semester. Because Student C was not enrolled in a college or other eligible educational institution prior to 1998 (but rather was awarded three semesters of academic credit solely because of proficiency examinations), Student C is not treated as having completed the first two years of postsecondary education at an eligible educational institution as of the beginning of 1998 or as of the beginning of 1999. Therefore, Student C is an eligible student for both taxable years 1998 and 1999.

Example (5). During the 1998 Fall semester, Student D is a high school student who takes classes on a half-time basis at College X. Student D is not enrolled as part of a degree program at College X because College X does not admit students to a degree program unless the student has a high school diploma or equivalent. Because Student D is not enrolled in a degree program at College X during 1998, Student D is not an eligible student for taxable year 1998.

Example (6). The facts are the same as in Example 5. In addition, during the 1999 Spring semester, Student D again attends College X but not as part of a degree program. Student D graduates from high school in June 1999. For the 1999 Fall semester, Student D enrolls in College X as part of a degree program, and College X awards Student D credit for her prior course work at College X. During the 1999 Fall semester, Student D is enrolled in more than one-half the normal full-time work load of courses for her degree program at College X. Because Student D is enrolled in a degree program at College X for the 1999 Fall term on at least a half-time basis, Student D is an eligible student for all of taxable year 1999. Therefore, the qualified tuition and required fees paid for classes taken at College X during both the 1999 Spring semester (during which Student D was not enrolled in a degree program) and the 1999 Fall semester are taken into account in computing any Hope Scholarship Credit.

Example (7). Student E completed two years of undergraduate study at College S. College S is not an eligible educational institution for purposes of the education tax credit. At the end of 1998, Student E enrolls in an undergraduate degree program at College Z, an eligible educational institution, for the 1999 Spring semester on a full-time basis. College Z awards Student E two years of academic credit for his previous course work at College S and classifies Student E as a first-semester junior for the 1999 Spring semester. Student E is treated as having completed the first two years of postsecondary education at an eligible educational institution as of the beginning of 1999. Therefore, Student E is not an eligible student for taxable year 1999.

Example (8). Student F received a degree in 1998 from College R. College R is not an eligible educational institution for purposes of the education tax credit. During 1999, Student F is enrolled in a graduate-degree program at College Y, an eligible educational institution, for the 1999 Fall semester on a full-time basis. By admitting Student F to its graduate degree program, College Y treats Student F as having completed the first two years of postsecondary education as of the beginning of 1999. Therefore, Student F is not an eligible student for taxable year 1999.

Example (9). Student G graduates from high school in June 2001. In January 2002, Student G is enrolled in a one-year postsecondary certificate program on a full-time basis to obtain a certificate as a travel agent. Student G completes the program in December 2002 and is awarded a certificate. In January 2003, Student G enrolls in a one-year postsecondary certificate program on a full-time basis to obtain a certificate as a computer programer. Student G meets the degree requirement, the work load requirement, and the year of study requirement for the taxable years 2002 and 2003. Therefore, Student G is an eligible student for both taxable years 2002 and 2003.

(e) Academic period for prepayments. *(1) In general.* For purposes of determining whether a student meets the requirements in paragraph (d) of this section for a taxable year, if qualified tuition and related expenses are paid during one taxable year for an academic period that begins during January, February or March of the next taxable year (for taxpayers on a fiscal taxable year, use the first three months of the next taxable year), the academic period is treated as beginning during the taxable year in which the payment is made.

(2) Example. The following example illustrates the rule of this paragraph (e). In the example, assume that all the requirements to claim a Hope Scholarship Credit are met. The example is as follows:

Example. Student G graduates from high school in June 1998. After graduation, Student G works full-time for several months to earn money for college. Student G is enrolled on a full-time basis in an undergraduate degree program at University W, an eligible educational institution, for the 1999 Spring semester, which begins in January 1999. Student G pays tuition to University W for the 1999 Spring semester in December 1998. Because the tuition paid by Student G in 1998 relates to an academic period that begins during the first three months of 1999, Student G's eligibility to claim a Hope Scholarship Credit in 1998 is determined as if the 1999 Spring semester began in 1998. Thus, assuming Student G has not been convicted of a felony drug offense as of December 31, 1998, Student G is an eligible student for 1998.

(f) Effective date. The Hope Scholarship Credit is applicable for qualified tuition and related expenses paid after December 31, 1997, for education furnished in academic periods beginning after December 31, 1997.

T.D. 9034, 12/24/2002.

§ 1.25A-4 Lifetime Learning Credit.

(a) Amount of the credit. *(1) Taxable years beginning before January 1, 2003.* Subject to the phaseout of the education tax credit described in § 1.25A-1(c), for taxable years beginning before 2003, the Lifetime Learning Credit amount is 20 percent of up to $5,000 of qualified tuition and related expenses paid during the taxable year for education furnished to the taxpayer, the taxpayer's spouse, and any claimed dependent during any academic period beginning in the taxable year (or treated as beginning in the taxable year, see § 1.25A-5(e)(2)).

(2) Taxable years beginning after December 31, 2002. Subject to the phaseout of the education tax credit described in § 1.25A-1(c), for taxable years beginning after 2002, the Lifetime Learning Credit amount is 20 percent of up to $10,000 of qualified tuition and related expenses paid during the taxable year for education furnished to the taxpayer, the taxpayer's spouse, and any claimed dependent during any academic period beginning in the taxable year (or treated as beginning in the taxable year, see § 1.25A-5(e)(2)).

(3) Coordination with the Hope Scholarship Credit. Expenses paid with respect to a student for whom the Hope Scholarship Credit is claimed are not eligible for the Lifetime Learning Credit.

(4) Examples. The following examples illustrate the rules of this paragraph (a). In each example, assume that all the requirements to claim a Lifetime Learning Credit or a Hope Scholarship Credit, as applicable, are met. The examples are as follows:

Example (1). In 1999, Taxpayer A pays qualified tuition and related expenses of $3,000 for dependent B to attend an eligible educational institution, and Taxpayer A pays qualified tuition and related expenses of $4,000 for dependent C to attend an eligible educational institution. Taxpayer A does not claim a Hope Scholarship Credit with respect to either B or C. Although Taxpayer A paid $7,000 of qualified tuition and related expenses during the taxable year, Taxpayer A may claim the Lifetime Learning Credit with respect to only $5,000 of such expenses. Therefore, the maximum Lifetime Learning Credit Taxpayer A may claim for 1999 is $1,000 (.20 x $5,000).

Example (2). In 1999, Taxpayer D pays $6,000 of qualified tuition and related expenses for dependent E, and $2,000 of qualified tuition and related expenses for dependent F, to attend eligible educational institutions. Dependent F has already completed the first two years of postsecondary education. For 1999, Taxpayer D claims the maximum $1,500 Hope Scholarship Credit with respect to dependent E. In computing the amount of the Lifetime Learning Credit, Taxpayer D may not include any of the $6,000 of qualified tuition and related expenses paid on behalf of dependent E but may include the $2,000 of qualified tuition and related expenses of dependent F.

(b) Credit allowed for unlimited number of taxable years. There is no limit to the number of taxable years that a taxpayer may claim a Lifetime Learning Credit with respect to any student.

(c) Both degree and nondegree courses are eligible for the credit. *(1) In general.* For purposes of the Lifetime Learning Credit, amounts paid for a course at an eligible educational institution are qualified tuition and related expenses if the course is either part of a postsecondary degree program or is not part of a postsecondary degree program but is taken by the student to acquire or improve job skills.

(2) Examples. The following examples illustrate the rule of this paragraph (c). In each example, assume that all the requirements to claim a Lifetime Learning Credit are met. The examples are as follows:

Example (1). Taxpayer A, a professional photographer, enrolls in an advanced photography course at a local community college. Although the course is not part of a degree program, Taxpayer A enrolls in the course to improve her job skills. The course fee paid by Taxpayer A is a qualified tuition and related expense for purposes of the Lifetime Learning Credit.

Example (2). Taxpayer B, a stockbroker, plans to travel abroad on a "photo-safari" for his next vacation. In preparation for the trip, Taxpayer B enrolls in a noncredit photography class at a local community college. Because Taxpayer B is not taking the photography course as part of a degree program or to acquire or improve his job skills, amounts paid by Taxpayer B for the course are not qualified tuition and related expenses for purposes of the Lifetime Learning Credit.

(d) Effective date. The Lifetime Learning Credit is applicable for qualified tuition and related expenses paid after June 30, 1998, for education furnished in academic periods beginning after June 30, 1998.

T.D. 9034, 12/24/2002.

§ 1.25A-5 Special rules relating to characterization and timing of payments.

(a) Educational expenses paid by claimed dependent. For any taxable year for which the student is a claimed dependent of another taxpayer, qualified tuition and related expenses paid by the student are treated as paid by the taxpayer to whom the deduction under section 151 is allowed.

(b) Educational expenses paid by a third party. *(1) In general.* Solely for purposes of section 25A, if a third party (someone other than the taxpayer, the taxpayer's spouse if the taxpayer is treated as married within the meaning of section 7703, or a claimed dependent) makes a payment directly to an eligible educational institution to pay for a student's qualified tuition and related expenses, the student is treated as receiving the payment from the third party and, in turn, paying the qualified tuition and related expenses to the institution.

(2) Special rule for tuition reduction included in gross income of employee. Solely for purposes of section 25A, if an eligible educational institution provides a reduction in tuition to an employee of the institution (or to the spouse or dependent child of an employee, as described in section 132(h)(2)) and the amount of the tuition reduction is included in the employee's gross income, the employee is treated as receiving payment of an amount equal to the tuition reduction and, in turn, paying such amount to the institution.

(3) Examples. The following examples illustrate the rules of this paragraph (b). In each example, assume that all the requirements to claim an education tax credit are met. The examples are as follows:

Example (1). Grandparent D makes a direct payment to an eligible educational institution for Student E's qualified tuition and related expenses. Student E is not a claimed dependent in 1999. For purposes of claiming an education tax credit, Student E is treated as receiving the money from her grandparent and, in turn, paying her qualified tuition and related expenses.

Example (2). Under a court-approved divorce decree, Parent A is required to pay Student C's college tuition. Parent A makes a direct payment to an eligible educational institution for Student C's 1999 tuition. Under paragraph (b)(1) of this section, Student C is treated as receiving the money from Parent A and, in turn, paying the qualified tuition and related expenses. Under the divorce decree, Parent B has custody of Student C for 1999. Parent B properly claims Student C as a dependent on Parent B's 1999 federal income tax return. Under paragraph (a) of this section, expenses paid by Student C are treated as paid by Parent B. Thus, Parent B may claim an education tax credit for the qualified tuition and related expenses paid directly to the institution by Parent A.

Example (3). University A, an eligible educational institution, offers reduced tuition charges to its employees and their dependent children. F is an employee of University A. F's dependent child, G, enrolls in a graduate-level course at University A. Section 117(d) does not apply, because it is limited to tuition reductions provided for education below the graduate level. Therefore, the amount of the tuition reduction received by G is treated as additional compensation from University A to F and is included in F's gross income. For purposes of claiming a Lifetime Learning Credit, F is treated as receiving payment of an amount equal to the tuition reduction from University A and, in turn, paying such amount to University A on behalf of F's child, G.

(c) Adjustment to qualified tuition and related expenses for certain excludable educational assistance. *(1) In general.* In determining the amount of an education tax credit, qualified tuition and related expenses for any academic period must be reduced by the amount of any tax-free educational assistance allocable to such period. For this purpose, tax-free educational assistance means—

(i) A qualified scholarship that is excludable from income under section 117;

(ii) A veterans' or member of the armed forces' educational assistance allowance under chapter 30, 31, 32, 34 or 35 of title 38, United States Code, or under chapter 1606 of title 10, United States Code;

(iii) Employer-provided educational assistance that is excludable from income under section 127; or

(iv) Any other educational assistance that is excludable from gross income (other than as a gift, bequest, devise, or inheritance within the meaning of section 102(a)).

(2) No adjustment for excludable educational assistance attributable to expenses paid in a prior year. A reduction is not required under paragraph (c)(1) of this section if the amount of excludable educational assistance received during the taxable year is treated as a refund of qualified tuition and related expenses paid in a prior taxable year. See paragraph (f)(5) of this section.

(3) Scholarships and fellowship grants. For purposes of paragraph (c)(1)(i) of this section, a scholarship or fellowship grant is treated as a qualified scholarship excludable under section 117 except to the extent—

(i) The scholarship or fellowship grant (or any portion thereof) may be applied, by its terms, to expenses other than qualified tuition and related expenses within the meaning of section 117(b)(2) (such as room and board) and the student reports the grant (or the appropriate portion thereof) as income on the student's federal income tax return if the student is required to file a return; or

(ii) The scholarship or fellowship grant (or any portion thereof) must be applied, by its terms, to expenses other than qualified tuition and related expenses within the meaning of section 117(b)(2) (such as room and board) and the student reports the grant (or the appropriate portion thereof) as income on the student's federal income tax return if the student is required to file a return.

(4) Examples. The following examples illustrate the rules of this paragraph (c). In each example, assume that all the requirements to claim an education tax credit are met. The examples are as follows:

Example (1). University X charges Student A, who lives on University X's campus, $3,000 for tuition and $5,000 for room and board. University X awards Student A a $2,000 scholarship. The terms of the scholarship permit it to be used to pay any of a student's costs of attendance at University X, including tuition, room and board, and other incidental expenses. University X applies the $2,000 scholarship against Student A's $8,000 total bill, and Student A pays the $6,000 balance of her bill from University X with a combination of savings and amounts she earns from a summer job. University X does not require A to pay any additional fees beyond the $3,000 in tuition in order to enroll in or attend classes. Student A does not report any portion of the scholarship as income on her federal income tax return. Since Student A does not report the scholarship as income, the scholarship is treated under paragraph (c)(3) of this section as a qualified scholarship that is excludable under section 117. Therefore, for purposes of calculating an education tax credit, Student A is treated as having paid only $1,000 ($3,000 tuition - $2,000 scholarship) in qualified tuition and related expenses to University X.

Example (2). The facts are the same as in Example 1, except that Student A reports the entire scholarship as income on the student's federal income tax return. Since the full amount of the scholarship may be applied to expenses other than qualified expenses (room and board) and Student A reports the scholarship as income, the exception in paragraph (c)(3) of this section applies and the scholarship is not treated as a qualified scholarship excludable under section 117. Therefore, for purposes of calculating an education tax credit, Student A is treated as having paid $3,000 of qualified tuition and related expenses to University X.

Example (3). The facts are the same as in Example 1, except that the terms of the scholarship require it to be used to pay tuition. Under paragraph (c)(3) of this section, the scholarship is treated as a qualified scholarship excludable under section 117. Therefore, for purposes of calculating an education tax credit, Student A is treated as having paid only $1,000 ($3,000 tuition - $2,000 scholarship) in qualified tuition and related expenses to University X.

Example (4). The facts are the same as in Example 1, except that the terms of the scholarship require it to be used to pay tuition or room and board charged by University X, and the scholarship amount is $6,000. Under the terms of the scholarship, Student A may allocate the scholarship between tuition and room and board in any manner. However, because room and board totals $5,000, that is the maximum amount that can be applied under the terms of the scholarship to expenses other than qualified expenses and at least $1,000 of the scholarship must be applied to tuition. Therefore, the maximum amount of the exception under paragraph (c)(3) of this section is $5,000 and at least $1,000 is treated as a qualified scholarship excludable under section 117 ($6,000 scholarship - $5,000 room and board). If Student A reports $5,000 of the scholarship as income on the student's federal income tax return, then Student A will be treated as having paid $2,000 ($3,000 tuition - $1,000 qualified scholarship excludable under section 117) in qualified tuition and related expenses to University X.

Example (5). The facts are the same as in Example 1, except that in addition to the scholarship that University X awards to Student A, University X also provides Student A with an education loan and pays Student A for working in a work/study job in the campus dining hall. The loan is not excludable educational assistance within the meaning of paragraph (c) of this section. In addition, wages paid to a student who is performing services for the payor are neither a qualified scholarship nor otherwise excludable from gross income. Therefore, Student A is not required to reduce her qualified tuition and related expenses by the amounts she receives from the student loan or as wages from her work/study job.

Example (6). In 1999, Student B pays University Y $1,000 in tuition for the 1999 Spring semester. University Y does not require Student B to pay any additional fees beyond the $1,000 in tuition in order to enroll in classes. Student B is an employee of Company Z. At the end of the academic period and during the same taxable year that Student B paid tuition to University Y, Student B provides Company Z with proof that he has satisfactorily completed his courses at University Y. Pursuant to an educational assistance program described in section 127(b), Company Z reimburses Student B for all of the tuition paid to University Y. Because the reimbursement from Company Z is employer-provided educational assistance that is excludable from Student B's gross income under section 127, the reimbursement reduces Student B's qualified tuition and related expenses. Therefore, for purposes of calculating an education tax credit, Student B is treated as having paid no qualified tuition and related expenses to University Y during 1999.

Example (7). The facts are the same as in Example 6 except that the reimbursement from Company Z is not pursuant to an educational assistance program described in section 127(b), is not otherwise excludable from Student B's gross income, and is taxed as additional compensation to Student B. Because the reimbursement is not excludable educational assistance within the meaning of paragraph (c)(1) of this section, Student B is not required to reduce his qualified tuition and related expenses by the $1,000 reimbursement he received from his employer. Therefore, for purposes of calculating an education tax credit, Student B is treated as paying $1,000 in qualified tuition and related expenses to University Y during 1999.

(d) No double benefit. Qualified tuition and related expenses do not include any expense for which a deduction is allowed under section 162, section 222, or any other provision of chapter 1 of the Internal Revenue Code.

(e) Timing rules. *(1) In general.* Except as provided in paragraph (e)(2) of this section, an education tax credit is allowed only for payments of qualified tuition and related expenses for an academic period beginning in the same taxable year as the year the payment is made. Except for certain individuals who do not use the cash receipts and disbursements method of accounting, qualified tuition and related expenses are treated as paid in the year in which the expenses are actually paid. See § 1.461-1(a)(1).

(2) Prepayment rule. (i) In general. If qualified tuition and related expenses are paid during one taxable year for an academic period that begins during the first three months of the taxpayer's next taxable year (i.e., in January, February, or March of the next taxable year for calendar year taxpayers), an education tax credit is allowed with respect to the qualified tuition and related expenses only in the taxable year in which the expenses are paid.

(ii) Example. The following example illustrates the rule of this paragraph (e)(2). In the example, assume that all the requirements to claim an education tax credit are met. The example is as follows:

Example. In December 1998, Taxpayer A, a calendar year taxpayer, pays College Z $1,000 in qualified tuition and related expenses to attend classes during the 1999 Spring semester, which begins in January 1999. Taxpayer A may claim an education tax credit only in 1998 for payments made in 1998 for the 1999 Spring semester.

(3) Expenses paid with loan proceeds. An education tax credit may be claimed for qualified tuition and related expenses paid with the proceeds of a loan only in the taxable year in which the expenses are paid, and may not be claimed in the taxable year in which the loan is repaid. Loan proceeds disbursed directly to an eligible educational institution will be treated as paid on the date the institution credits the proceeds to the student's account. For example, in the case of any loan issued or guaranteed as part of a federal student loan program under Title IV of the Higher Education Act of 1965, loan proceeds will be treated as paid on the date of disbursement (as defined in 34 CFR 668.164(a), revised as of July 1, 2002) by the eligible educational institution. If a taxpayer does not know the date the institution credits the student's account, the taxpayer must treat the qualified tuition and related expenses as paid on the last date for payment prescribed by the institution.

(4) Expenses paid through third party installment payment plans. (i) In general. A taxpayer, an eligible educational institution, and a third party installment payment company may enter into an agreement in which the company agrees to collect installment payments of qualified tuition and related expenses from the taxpayer and to remit the installment payments to the institution. If the third party installment payment company is the taxpayer's agent for purposes of paying qualified tuition and related expenses to the eligible educational institution, the taxpayer is treated as paying the qualified expenses on the date the company pays the institution. However, if the third party installment payment company is the eligible educational institution's agent for purposes of collecting payments of qualified tuition and related expenses from the taxpayer, the taxpayer is treated as paying the qualified expenses on the date the taxpayer pays the company.

(ii) Example. The following example illustrates the rule of this paragraph (e)(4). The example is as follows:

Example. Student A, Company B, and College C enter into a written agreement in which Student A agrees to pay the tuition required to attend College C in 10 equal monthly installments to Company B. Under the written agreement, Student A is not relieved of her obligation to pay College C until Company B remits the payments to College C. Under the written agreement, Company B agrees to disburse the monthly installment payments to College C within 30 days of receipt. Because Company B acts as Student A's agent for purposes of paying qualified expenses to College C, Student A is treated as paying qualified expenses on the date Company B disburses payments to College C.

(f) Refund of qualified tuition and related expenses. *(1) Payment and refund of qualified tuition and related expenses in the same taxable year.* With respect to any student, the amount of qualified tuition and related expenses for a taxable year is calculated by adding all qualified tuition and related expenses paid for the taxable year, and subtracting any refund of such expenses received from the eligible educational institution during the same taxable year (including refunds of loan proceeds described in paragraph (f)(4) of this section).

(2) Payment of qualified tuition and related expenses in one taxable year and refund in subsequent taxable year before return filed for prior taxable year. If, in a taxable year, a taxpayer or someone other than the taxpayer receives a refund (including refunds of loan proceeds described in paragraph (f)(4) of this section) of qualified tuition and related expenses paid on behalf of a student in a prior taxable year and the refund is received before the taxpayer files a federal income tax return for the prior taxable year, the amount of the qualified tuition and related expenses for the prior taxable year is reduced by the amount of the refund.

(3) Payment of qualified tuition and related expenses in one taxable year and refund in subsequent taxable year. (i) In general. If, in a taxable year (refund year), a taxpayer or someone other than the taxpayer receives a refund (including refunds of loan proceeds described in paragraph (f)(4) of this section) of qualified tuition and related expenses paid on behalf of a student for which the taxpayer claimed an education tax credit in a prior taxable year, the tax imposed by

chapter 1 of the Internal Revenue Code for the refund year is increased by the recapture amount.

(ii) Recapture amount. The recapture amount is the difference in tax liability for the prior taxable year (taking into account any redetermination of such tax liability by audit or amended return) that results when the tax liability for the prior year is calculated using the taxpayer's redetermined credit. The redetermined credit is computed by reducing the amount of the qualified tuition and related expenses taken into account in determining any credit claimed in the prior taxable year by the amount of the refund of the qualified tuition and related expenses (redetermined qualified expenses), and computing the allowable credit using the redetermined qualified expenses and the relevant facts and circumstances of the prior taxable year, such as modified adjusted gross income (redetermined credit).

(4) Refund of loan proceeds treated as refund of qualified tuition and related expenses. If loan proceeds used to pay qualified tuition and related expenses (as described in paragraph (e)(3) of this section) during a taxable year are refunded by an eligible educational institution to a lender on behalf of the borrower, the refund is treated as a refund of qualified tuition and related expenses for purposes of paragraphs (f)(1), (2), and (3) of this section.

(5) Excludable educational assistance received in a subsequent taxable year treated as a refund. If, in a taxable year, a taxpayer or someone other than the taxpayer receives any excludable educational assistance (described in paragraph (c)(1) of this section) for the qualified tuition and related expenses paid on behalf of a student during a prior taxable year (or attributable to enrollment at an eligible educational institution during a prior taxable year), the educational assistance is treated as a refund of qualified tuition and related expenses for purposes of paragraphs (f)(2) and (3) of this section. If the excludable educational assistance is received before the taxpayer files a Federal income tax return for the prior taxable year, the amount of the qualified tuition and related expenses for the prior taxable year is reduced by the amount of the excludable educational assistance as provided in paragraph (f)(2) of this section. If the excludable educational assistance is received after the taxpayer has filed a federal income tax return for the prior taxable year, any education tax credit claimed for the prior taxable year is subject to recapture as provided in paragraph (f)(3) of this section.

(6) Examples. The following examples illustrate the rules of this paragraph (f). In each example, assume that all the requirements to claim an education tax credit are met. The examples are as follows:

Example (1). In January 1998, Student A, a full-time freshman at University X, pays $2,000 for qualified tuition and related expenses for a 16-hour work load for the 1998 Spring semester. Prior to beginning classes, Student A withdraws from 6 course hours. On February 15, 1998, Student A receives a $750 refund from University X. In September 1998, Student A pays University X $1,000 to enroll half-time for the 1998 Fall semester. Prior to beginning classes, Student A withdraws from a 2-hour course, and she receives a $250 refund in October 1998. Student A computes the amount of qualified tuition and related expenses she may claim for 1998 by:

(i) Adding all qualified expenses paid during the taxable year ($2,000 + 1,000 = $3,000);

(ii) Adding all refunds of qualified tuition and related expenses received during the taxable year ($750 + $250 = $1,000); and, then

(iii) Subtracting paragraph (ii) of this Example 1 from paragraph (i) of this Example 1 ($3,000 - $1,000 = $2,000). Therefore, Student A's qualified tuition and related expenses for 1998 are $2,000.

Example (2). (i) In December 1998, Student B, a senior at College Y, pays $2,000 for qualified tuition and related expenses for a 16-hour work load for the 1999 Spring semester. Prior to beginning classes, Student B withdraws from a 4-hour course. On January 15, 1999, Student B files her 1998 income tax return and claims a $400 Lifetime Learning Credit for the $2,000 qualified expenses paid in 1998, which reduces her tax liability for 1998 by $400. On February 15, 1999, Student B receives a $500 refund from College Y.

(ii) Student B calculates the increase in tax for 1999 by—

(A) Calculating the redetermined qualified expenses for 1998 ($2,000 - $500 = $1,500);

(B) Calculating the redetermined credit for the redetermined qualified expenses ($1,500 x .20 = $300); and

(C) Calculating the difference in tax liability for 1998 resulting from the redetermined credit. Because Student B's tax liability for 1998 was reduced by the full amount of the $400 education tax credit claimed on her 1998 income tax return, the difference in tax liability can be determined by subtracting the redetermined credit from the credit claimed in 1998 ($400 - $300 = $100).

(iii) Therefore, Student B must increase the tax on her 1999 Federal income tax return by $100.

Example (3). In September 1998, Student C pays College Z $1,200 in qualified tuition and related expenses to attend evening classes during the 1998 Fall semester. Student C is an employee of Company R. On January 15, 1999, Student C files a federal income tax return for 1998 claiming a Lifetime Learning Credit of $240 (.20 x $1,200), which reduces Student C's tax liability for 1998 by $240. Pursuant to an educational assistance program described in section 127(b), Company R reimburses Student C in February 1999 for the $1,200 of qualified tuition and related expenses paid by Student C in 1998. The $240 education tax credit claimed by Student C for 1998 is subject to recapture. Because Student C paid no net qualified tuition and related expenses for 1998, the redetermined credit for 1998 is zero. Student C must increase the amount of Student C's 1999 tax by the recapture amount, which is $240 (the difference in tax liability for 1998 resulting from the redetermined credit for 1998 ($0)). Because the $1,200 reimbursement relates to expenses for which the taxpayer claimed an education tax credit in a prior year, the reimbursement does not reduce the amount of any qualified tuition and related expenses that Student C paid in 1999.

T.D. 9034, 12/24/2002.

---

§ 1.28-0 Credit for clinical testing expenses for certain drugs for rare diseases or conditions; table of contents.

• ***Caution:*** Reg. § 1.28-0, following, relates to Code Sec. 45C as so redesignated by Sec. 1205(a)(1) of P.L. 104-188 (8/20/1996).

Caution: The Treasury has not yet amended Reg § 1.28-0 to reflect changes made by 110-458.

In order to facilitate use of § 1.28-1, this section lists the paragraphs, subparagraphs, and subdivisions contained in § 1.28-1.

(a) General rule.

(b) Qualified clinical testing expenses.

(1) In general.

(2) Modification of section 41(b).

(3) Exclusion for amounts funded by another person.

(i) In general.

(ii) Clinical testing in which taxpayer retains no rights.

(iii) Clinical testing in which taxpayer retains substantial rights.

(A) In general.

(B) Drug by drug determination.

(iv) Funding for qualified clinical testing expenses determinable only in subsequent taxable years.

(4) Special rule governing the application of section 41(b) beyond its expiration date.

(c) Clinical testing.

(1) In general.

(2) Definition of "human clinical testing".

(3) Definition of "carried out under" section 505(i).

(d) Definition and special rules.

(1) Definition of "rare disease or condition".

(i) In general.

(ii) Cost of developing and making available the designated drug.

(A) In general.

(B) Exclusion of costs funded by another person.

(C) Computation of cost.

(D) Allocation of common costs. Costs for developing and making available the designated drug for both the disease or condition for which it is designated and one or more other diseases or conditions.

(iii) Recovery from sales.

(iv) Recordkeeping requirements.

(2) Tax liability limitation.

(i) Taxable years beginning after December 31, 1986.

(ii) Taxable years beginning before January 1, 1987 and after December 31, 1983.

(iii) Taxable years beginning before January 1, 1984.

(3) Special limitations on foreign testing.

(i) Clinical testing conducted outside the United States—In general.

(ii) Insufficient testing population in the United States.

(A) In general.

(B) "Insufficient testing population".

(C) "Unrelated to the taxpayer".

(4) Special limitation for certain corporations.

(i) Corporations to which section 936 applies.

(ii) Corporations to which section 934(b) applies.

(5) Aggregation of expenditures.

(i) Controlled group of corporations: organizations under common control.

(A) In general.

(B) Definition of controlled group of corporations.

(C) Definition of organization.

(D) Determination of common control.

(ii) Tax accounting periods used.

(A) In general.

(B) Special rule where the timing of clinical testing is manipulated.

(iii) Membership during taxable year in more than one group.

(iv) Intra-group transactions.

(A) In general.

(B) In-house research expenses.

(C) Contract research expenses.

(D) Lease payments and payments for supplies.

(6) Allocations.

(i) Pass-through in the case of an S corporation.

(ii) Pass-through in the case of an estate or trust.

(iii) Pass-through in the case of a partnership.

(A) In general.

(B) Certain partnership non-business expenditures.

(C) Apportionment.

(iv) Year in which taken into account.

(v) Credit allowed subject to limitation.

(7) Manner of making an election.

T.D. 8232, 9/30/88.

§ 1.28-1 Credit for clinical testing expenses for certain drugs for rare diseases or conditions.

• ***Caution:*** Reg. § 1.28-1, following, relates to Code Sec. 45C as so redesignated by Sec. 1205(a)(1) of P.L. 104-188 (8/20/1996).

Caution: The Treasury has not yet amended Reg § 1.28-1 to reflect changes made by 110-458, P.L. 105-277, P.L. 105-34, P.L. 104-188, P.L. 103-66, P.L. 101-508.

(a) General rule. Section 28 provides a credit against the tax imposed by chapter 1 of the Internal Revenue Code. The amount of the credit is equal to 50 percent of the qualified clinical testing expenses (as defined in paragraph (b) of this section) for the taxable year. The credit applies to qualified clinical testing expenses paid or incurred by the taxpayer after December 31, 1982, and before January 1, 1991. The credit may not exceed the taxpayer's tax liability for the taxable year (as determined under paragraph (d)(2) of this section).

(b) Qualified clinical testing expenses. *(1) In general.* Except as otherwise provided in paragraph (b)(3) of this section, the term "qualified clinical testing expenses" means the amounts which are paid or incurred during the taxable year which would constitute "qualified research expenses" within the meaning of section 41(b) (relating to the credit for increasing research activities) as modified by section 28(b)(1)(B) and paragraph (b)(2) of this section. For example, amounts paid or incurred for the acquisition of depreciable property used in the conduct of clinical testing (as defined in paragraph (c) of this section) are not qualified clinical testing expenses.

(2) Modification of section 41(b). For purposes of paragraph (b)(1) of this section, section 41(b) is modified by substituting "clinical testing" for "qualified research" each place it appears in paragraph (2) of section 41(b) (relating to in-house research expenses) and paragraph (3) of section 41(b) (relating to contract research expenses). In addition, "100 percent" is substituted for "65 percent" in paragraph (3)(A) of section 41(b).

(3) Exclusion for amounts funded by another person. (i) In general. The term "qualified clinical testing expenses" shall not include any amount which would otherwise constitute qualified clinical testing expenses, to the extent such amount is funded by a grant, contract, or otherwise by another person (or any governmental entity). The determination of the extent to which an amount is funded shall be made in light of all the facts and circumstances. For a special rule regarding funding between commonly controlled businesses, see paragraph (d)(5)(iv) of § 1.28-1.

(ii) Clinical testing in which taxpayer retains no rights. If a taxpayer conducting clinical testing with respect to the designated drug for another person retains no substantial rights in the clinical testing under the agreement providing for the clinical testing the taxpayer's clinical testing expenses are treated as fully funded for purposes of section 28(b)(1)(C). Thus, for example, if the taxpayer incurs clinical testing expenses under an agreement that confers on another person the exclusive right to exploit the results of the clinical testing, those expenses do not constitute qualified clinical testing expenses because they are fully funded under this paragraph (b)(3)(ii). Incidental benefits to the taxpayer from the conduct of the clinical testing (for example, increased experience in the field of human clinical testing) do not constitute substantial rights in the clinical testing.

(iii) Clinical testing in which taxpayer retains substantial rights. (A) In general. If a taxpayer conducting clinical testing with respect to the designated drug for another person retains substantial rights in the clinical testing under the agreement providing for the clinical testing, the clinical testing expenses are funded to the extent of the payments (and fair market value of any property at the time of transfer) to which the taxpayer becomes entitled by conducting the clinical testing. The taxpayer shall reduce the amount paid or incurred by the taxpayer for the clinical testing expenses that would, but for section 28(b)(1)(C) constitute qualified clinical testing expenses of the taxpayer by the amount of the funding determined under the preceding sentence. Rights retained in the clinical testing are not treated as property for purposes of this paragraph (b)(3)(iii)(A). If the property that is transferred to the taxpayer is to be consumed in the clinical testing (for example, supplies), the taxpayer should exclude the value of that property from both the payments received and the expenses paid or incurred for the clinical testing.

(B) Drug by drug determination. The provisions of this paragraph (b)(3) shall be applied separately to each designated drug tested by the taxpayer.

(iv) Funding for qualified clinical testing expenses determinable only in subsequent taxable years. If, at the time the taxpayer files its return for a taxable year, it is impossible to determine to what extent some or all of the qualified clinical testing expenses may be funded, the taxpayer shall treat the clinical testing expenses as fully funded for purposes of that return. When the amount of funding for qualified clinical testing expenses in finally determined, the taxpayer should amend the return and any interim returns to reflect the amount of funding for qualified clinical testing expenses.

(4) Special rule governing the application of section 41(b) beyond its expiration date. For purposes of section 23 and this section, section 41(b), as amended, and the regulations thereunder shall be deemed to remain in effect after December 31, 1988.

(c) Clinical testing. *(1) In general.* The term "clinical testing" means any human clinical testing which—

(i) Is carried out under an exemption under section 505(i) of the Federal Food, Drug, and Cosmetic Act (21 U.S.C. 355(i)) and the regulations relating thereto (21 CFR Part 312) for the purpose of testing a drug for a rare disease or condition as defined in paragraph (d)(1) of this section,

(ii) Occurs after the date the drug is designated as a drug for a rare disease or condition under section 526 of the Federal Food, Drug, and Cosmetic Act (21, U.S.C. 360bb),

(iii) Occurs before the date on which an application for the designated drug is approved under section 505(b) of the Federal Food, Drug, and Cosmetic Act (21 U.S.C. 335(b)) or, if the drug is a biological product (other than a radioactive biological product intended for human use), before the date on which a license for such drug is issued under section 351 of the Public Health Services Act (42 U.S.C. 262), and

(iv) Is conducted by or on behalf of the taxpayer to whom the designation under section 526 of the Federal Food, Drug, and Cosmetic Act applies.

Human clinical testing shall be taken into account under this paragraph (c)(1) only to the extent that the testing relates to the use of a drug for the rare disease or condition for which the drug was designated under section 526 of the Federal Food, and Cosmetic Act. For purposes of paragraph (c)(1)(i) of this section the testing under section 505(i) exemption procedures (21 CFR part 312) of a biological product (other than a radioactive biological product intended for human use) pursuant to 21 CFR 601.21 is deemed to be carried out under an exemption under section 505(i) of the Federal Food, Drug, and Cosmetic Act.

(2) Definition of "human clinical testing." Testing is considered to be human clinical testing only to the extent that it uses human subjects to determine the effect of the designated drug on humans and is necessary for the designated drug either to be approved under section 505(b) of the Federal Food, Drug, and Cosmetic Act and the regulations thereunder (21 CFR Part 314), or if the designated drug is a biological product (other than a radioactive biological product intended for human use), to be licensed under section 351 of the Public Health Services Act and the regulations thereunder (21 CFR Part 601). For purposes of this paragraph (c)(2), a human subject is an individual who is a participant in research, either as a recipient of the drug or as a control. A subject may be either a health individual or a patient.

(3) Definition of "carried out under" section 505(i). Human clinical testing is not carried out under section 505(i) of the Federal Food, Drug, and Cosmetic Act and the regulations thereunder (21 CFR Part 312) unless the primary purpose of the human clinical testing is to ascertain the data necessary to qualify the designated drug for sale in the United States, and not to ascertain data unrelated or only incidentally related to that needed to qualify the designated drug. Whether or not this primary purpose test is met shall be determined in light of all of the facts and circumstances.

(d) Definition and special rules. *(1) Definition of "rare disease or condition".* (i) In general. The term "rare disease or condition" means any disease or condition which—

(A) Afflicts 200,000 or fewer persons in the United States, or

(B) Afflicts more than 200,000 persons in the United States but for which there is no reasonable expectation that the cost of developing and making available in the United States (as defined in section 7701(a)(9)) a drug for such disease or condition will be recovered from sales in the United States (as so defined) or such drug.

Determinations under paragraph (d)(1)(i)(B) of this section with respect to any drug shall be made on the basis of the facts and circumstances as of the date such drug is designated under section 526 of the Federal Food, Drug, and Cosmetic Act. Examples of diseases or conditions which in 1987 afflicted 200,000 or fewer persons in the United States are Duchenne dystrophy, one of the muscular dystrophies; Huntington's disease, a hereditary chorea; myoclonus; Tourette's syndrome; and amyotrophic lateral sclerosis (ALS or Lou Gehrig's disease).

(ii) Cost of developing and making available the designated drug. (A) In general. Except as otherwise provided in this subdivision, the taxpayer's computation of the cost of developing and making available in the United States the designated drug shall include only the costs that the taxpayer for any person whose right to make sales of the drug is directly or indirectly derived from the taxpayer, e.g., a licensee or transferee) has incurred or reasonably expects to incur in developing and making available in the United States the designated drug for the disease or condition for which it is designated. For example, if, prior to designation under section 526, the taxpayer incurred costs of $125,000 to test the drug for the rare disease or condition for which it is subsequently designated and incurred $500,000 to test the same drug for other diseases, and if, on the date of designation, the taxpayer expects to incur costs of $1.2 million to test the drug for the rare disease or condition for which it is designated, the taxpayer shall include in its cost computation both the $125,000 incurred prior to designation and the $1.2 million expected to be incurred after designation to test the drug for the rare disease or condition for which it is designated. The taxpayer shall not include the $500,000 incurred to test the drug for other diseases.

(B) Exclusion of costs funded by another person. In computing the cost of developing and making available in the United States the designated drug, the taxpayer shall not include any cost incurred or expected to be incurred by the taxpayer to the extent that the cost is funded or is reasonably expected to be funded (determined under the principles of paragraph (b)(3)) by a grant, contract, or otherwise by another person (or any governmental entity).

(C) Computation of cost. The cost computation shall use only reasonable costs incurred after the first indication of an orphan application for the designated drug. Such costs shall include the costs of obtaining data needed, and of meetings to be held, in connection with a request for FDA assistance under section 525 of the Federal, Food, Drug, and Cosmetic Act (21 U.S.C. 360aa) or a request for orphan designation under section 526 of that Act; costs of determining patentability of the drug; costs of screening, animal and clinical studies; costs associated with preparation of a Notice of Claimed Investigational Exemption for a New Drug (IND) and a New Drug Application (NDA); costs of possible distribution of drug under a "treatment" protocol; costs of development of a dosage form; manufacturing costs; distribution costs; promotion costs; costs to maintain required records and reports; and costs of the taxpayer in acquiring the right to market a drug from the owner of that right prior to designation. The taxpayer shall also include general overhead, depreciation costs and premiums for insurance against liability losses to the extent that the taxpayer can demonstrate that these costs are properly allocable to the designated drug under the established standards of financial accounting and reporting of research and development costs.

(D) Allocation of common costs. Costs for developing and making available the designated drug for both the disease or condition for which it is designated and one or more other diseases or conditions. In the case where the costs incurred or expected to be incurred in developing and making available the designated drug for the disease or condition for which it is designated are also incurred or expected to be incurred in developing and making available in the United States the same drug for one or more other diseases or conditions (whether or not they are also designated or expected to be designated), the costs shall be allocated between the cost of developing and making available the designated drug for the disease or condition for which the drug is designated and the cost of developing and making available the designated drug for the other diseases or conditions. The amount of the common costs to be allocated to the cost of developing and making available the designated drug for the disease or condition for which it is designated is determined by multiplying the common costs by a fraction the numerator of which is the sum of the expected amount of sales in the United States of the designated drug for the disease or condition for which the drug is designated and the denominator of which is the total expected amount of sales in the United States of the designated drug. For example, if prior to designation, the taxpayer incurs (among other costs) costs of $100,000 in testing the designated drug for its toxic effect on animals (without reference to any disease or condition), and if the taxpayer expects to recover $500,000 from sales in the United States of the designated drug for disease X, the disease for which the drug is designated, and further expects to recover another $1.5 million from the sales in the United States of the designated drug for disease Y, the taxpayer must allocate a proportionate amount of the common costs of $100,000 to the cost of developing and making available the designated drug for both disease X and disease Y. Since the ratio of the expected amount of sales in the United States of the designated drug for disease X to the total of both the expected amount of sales in the United States of the designated drug for disease X and the expected amount of sales in the United States of the designated drug for disease Y is $500,000/$2,000,000 25% of the common costs of $100,000 (i.e., $25,000) is allocated to the cost of developing and making available the designated drug for disease X.

(iii) Recovery from sales. In determining whether the taxpayer's cost described in paragraph (d)(1)(ii) of this section will be recovered from sales in the United States of the designated drug for the disease or condition for which the drug is designated, the taxpayer shall include anticipated sales by the taxpayer or any person whose right to make such sales is directly or indirectly derived from the taxpayer (such as a licensee or transferee). The anticipated sales shall be based upon the size of the anticipated patient population for which the designated drug would be useful, including the following factor: the degree of effectiveness and safety of the designated drug, if known: the projected fraction of the anticipated patient population expected to be given the designated drug and to continue to take it; other available agents and other types of therapy the likelihood that superior agents will become available within a few years; and the number of years during which the designated drug would be exclusively available, e.g., under a patent.

(iv) Recordkeeping requirements. The taxpayer shall keep records sufficient to substantiate the cost and sales estimates made pursuant to this paragraph (d)(1). The records required by this paragraph (d)(1)(iv) shall be retained so long as the contents thereof may become material in the administration of section 28.

(2) Tax liability limitation. (i) Taxable years beginning after December 31, 1986. The credit allowed by section 28 shall not exceed the excess (if any) of—

(A) The taxpayer's regular tax liability for the taxable year (as defined in section 26(b)), reduced by the sum of the credits allowable under—

(1) Section 21 (relating to expenses for household and dependent care services necessary for gainful employment),

(2) Section 22 (relating to the elderly and permanently and totally disabled),

(3) Section 23 (relating to residential energy),

(4) Section 25 (relating to interest on certain home mortgages), and

(5) Section 27 (relating to taxes on foreign countries and possessions of the United States), over

(B) The tentative minimum tax for the taxable year (as determined under section 55(b)(1)).

(ii) Taxable years beginning before January 1, 1987, and after December 31, 1983. The credit allowed by section 28 shall not exceed the taxpayer's tax liability for the taxable year (as defined in section 26 (b) prior to its amendment by the Tax Reform Act of 1986 (Pub. L. 99-514)), reduced by the sum of the credits allowable under—

(A) Section 21 (relating to expenses for household dependent care services necessary for gainful employment),

(B) Section 22 (relating to the elderly and permanently and totally disabled),

(C) Section 23 (relating to residential energy),

(D) Section 24 (relating to contributions to candidates for public office),

(E) Section 25 (relating to interest on certain home mortgages), and

(F) Section 27 (relating to the taxes on foreign countries and possessions of the United States).

(iii) Taxable years beginning before January 1, 1984. The credit allowed by section 28 shall not exceed the amount of the tax imposed by chapter 1 of the Internal Revenue Code for the taxable year, reduced by the sum of the credits allowable under the following sections as designated prior to the enactment of the Tax Reform Act of 1984 (Pub. Law 98-369):

(A) Section 32 (relating to tax withheld at source on nonresident aliens and foreign corporations and on tax-free convenant bonds),

(B) Sections 33 (relating to taxes of foreign countries and possessions of the United States),

(C) Section 37 (relating to the retirement income),

(D) Section 38 (relating to investment in certain depreciable property),

(E) Section 40 (relating to expenses of work incentive programs),

(F) Section 41 (relating to contributions to candidates for public office),

(G) Section 44 (relating to purchase of new principal residence),

(H) Section 44A (relating to expenses for household and dependent care services necessary for gainful employment),

(I) Section 44B (relating to employment of certain new employees),

(J) Section 44C (relating to residential energy),

(K) Section 44D (relating to producing fuel from a nonconventional source),

(L) Section 44E (relating to alcohol used as fuel),

(M) Section 44F (relating to increasing research activities), and

(N) Section 44G (relating to employee stock ownership). The term "tax imposed by chapter 1" as used in this paragraph (d)(2)(iii) does not include any tax treated as not imposed by chapter 1 of the Internal Revenue Code under the last sentence of section 53(a)

(3) Special limitations on foreign testing. (i) Clinical testing conducted outside of the United States—In general. Except as otherwise provided in this paragraph (d)(3), expenses paid or incurred with respect to clinical testing conducted outside the United States (as defined in section 7701(a)(9)) are not eligible for credit under this section. Thus, for example, wages paid an employee clinical investigator for clinical testing conducted in medical facilities in the United States and Mexico generally must be apportioned between the clinical testing conducted within the United States and the clinical testing conducted outside the United States, and only the wages apportioned to the clinical testing conducted within the United States are qualified clinical testing expenses.

(ii) Insufficient testing population in the United States. (A) In general. If clinical testing is conducted outside of the United States because there is an insufficient testing population in the United States, and if the clinical testing is conducted by a United States person (as defined in section 7701(a)(30)) or is conducted by any other person unrelated to the taxpayer to whom the designation under section 526 of the Federal Food, Drug, and Cosmetic Act applies, then the expenses paid or incurred for clinical testing conducted outside of the United States are eligible for the credit provided by section 28.

(B) "Insufficient testing population." The testing population in the United States is insufficient if there are not within the United States the number of available and appropriate human subjects needed to produce reliable data from the clinical investigation.

(C) "Unrelated to the taxpayer." For the purpose of determining whether a person is unrelated to the taxpayer to whom the designation under section 526 of the Federal Food, Drug, and Cosmetic Act and the regulations thereunder applies, the rules of section 613A(d)(3) shall apply except that the number "5" in section 613A(d)(3)(A), (B), and (C) shall be deleted and the number "10" inserted in lieu thereof.

(4) Special limitations for certain corporations. (i) Corporations to which section 936 applies. Expenses paid or incurred for clinical testing conducted either inside or outside the United States by a corporation to which section 936 (related to Puerto Rico and possessions tax credit) applies are not eligible for the credit under section 28.

(ii) Corporations to which section 934(b) applies. For taxable years beginning before January 1, 1987, expenses paid or incurred for clinical testing conducted either inside or outside the United States by a corporation to which section 934(b) (relating to the limitation on reduction in income tax liability incurred to the Virgin Islands), as in effect prior to its amendment by the Tax Reform Act of 1986, applies are not eligible for the credit under section 28. For taxable years beginning after December 31, 1986, see section 1277(c)(1) of the Tax Reform Act of 1986 (100 Stat. 2600) which makes the rule set forth in the preceding sentence inapplicable with respect to corporations created or organized in the Virgin Islands only if (and so long as) an implementing agreement described in that section is in effect between the United States and the Virgin Islands.

(5) Aggregation of expenditures. (i) Controlled group of corporations; organizations under common control.

(A) In general. In determining the amount of the credit allowable with respect to an organization that at the end of its taxable year is a member of a controlled group of corporations or a member of a group of organizations under common control, all members of the group are treated as a single taxpayer and the credit (if any) allowable to the member is determined on the basis of its proportionate share of the qualified clinical testing expenses of the aggregated group.

(B) Definition of controlled group of corporations. For purposes of this section, the term "controlled group of corporations" shall have the meaning given to the term by section 41(f)(5).

(C) Definition of organization. For purposes of this section, an organization is a sole proprietorship, a partnership, a trust, an estate, or a corporation, that is carrying on a trade or business (within the meaning of section 162). For purposes of this section, any corporation that is a member of a commonly controlled group shall be deemed to be carrying on a trade or business if any other member of that group is carrying on any trade or business.

(D) Determination of common control. Whether organizations are under common control shall be determined under the principles set forth in paragraphs (b)-(g) of 26 CFR § 1.52-1.

(ii) Tax accounting periods used. (A) In general. The credit allowable to a member of a controlled group of corporations or a group of organizations under common control is that member's share of the aggregate credit computed as of the end of such member's taxable year.

(B) Special rule where the timing of clinical testing is manipulated. If the timing of clinical testing by members using different tax accounting periods is manipulated to generate a credit in excess of the amount that would be allowable if all members of the group used the same tax accounting period, the district director may require all members of the group to calculate the credit in the current taxable year and all future years by using the "conformed years" method. Each member computing a credit under the "conformed years" method shall compute the credit as if all members of the group had the same taxable year as the computing member.

(iii) Membership during taxable year in more than one group. An organization may be a member of only one group for a taxable year. If, without application of this paragraphs (d)(5)(iii), an organization would be a member of more than one group at the end of its taxable year, the organization shall be treated as a member of the group in which it was included for its preceding taxable year. If the organization was not included for its preceding taxable year in any group in which it could be included as of the end of its taxable year, the organization shall designate in its timely filed return the group in which it is being included. If the return for a taxable year is due before May 1, 1985, the organization may designate its group membership through an amended return for that year filed on or before April 30, 1985. If the organization does not so designate, then the district director with audit jurisdiction of the return will determine the group in which the business is to be included.

(iv) Intra-group transactions. (A) In general. Because all members of a group under common control are treated as a single taxpayer for purposes of determining the credit, transactions between members of the group are generally disregarded.

(B) In-house research expenses. If one member of a group conducts clinical testing on behalf of another member, the member conducting the clinical testing shall include in its qualified clinical testing expenses any in-house research expenses for that work and shall not treat any amount received or accrued from the other member as funding the clinical testing. Conversely, the member for whom the clinical testing is conducted shall not treat any part of any amount paid or incurred as a contract research expense. For purposes of determining whether the in-house research for that work is clinical testing, the member performing the clinical testing shall be treated as carrying on any trade or business carried on by the member on whose behalf the clinical testing is performed.

(C) Contract research expenses. If a member of a group pays or incurs contract research expenses to a person outside the group in carrying on the member's trade or business, that member shall include those expenses as qualified clinical testing expenses. However, if the expenses are not paid or incurred in carrying on any trade or business of that member, those expenses may be taken into account as contract research expenses by another member of the group provided that the other member—

(1) Reimburses the member paying or incurring the expenses, and

(2) Carries on a trade or business to which the clinical testing relates.

(D) Lease payments. Amounts paid or incurred to another member of the group for the lease of personal property owned by a person outside the group shall be taken into account as in-house research expenses for purposes of section 28 only to the extent of the lesser of—

(1) The amount paid or incurred to the other member, or

(2) The amount of the lease expense paid to a person outside the group.

The amount paid or incurred to another member of the group for the lease of personal property owned by a member of the group is not taken into account for purposes of section 28.

(E) Payment for supplies. Amounts paid or incurred to another member of the group for supplies shall be taken into account as in-house research expenses for purposes of section 28 only to the extent of the lesser of—

(1) The amount paid or incurred to the other member, or

(2) The amount of the other member's basis in the supplies.

(6) Allocations. (i) Pass-through in the case of an S corporation. In the case of an S corporation (as defined in section 1361), the amount of the credit for qualified clinical testing expenses computed for the corporation for any taxable year shall be allocated among the persons who are shareholders

of the corporation during the taxable year according to the provisions of section 1366 and section 1377.

(ii) Pass-through in the case of an estate or a trust. In the case of an estate or a trust, the amount of the credit for qualified clinical testing expenses computed for the estate or trust for any taxable year shall be apportioned between the estate or trust and the beneficiaries on the basis of the income of the estate or trust allocable to each.

(iii) Pass-through in the case of a partnership. (A) In general. In the case of a partnership, the credit for qualified clinical testing expenses computed for the partnership for any taxable year shall be apportioned amount the persons who are partners during the taxable year in accordance with section 704 and the regulations thereunder.

(B) Certain partnership non-business expenditures. A partner's share of an in-house research expense or contract research expense paid or incurred by a partnership other than in carrying on a trade or business of the partnership constitutes a qualified clinical testing expense of the partner if—

(1) The partner is entitled to make independent use of the result of the clinical testing, and

(2) The clinical testing expense paid or incurred in carrying on the clinical testing would have been paid or incurred by the partner in carrying on a trade or business of the partner if the partner had carried on the clinical testing that was in fact carried on by the partnership.

(C) Apportionment. Qualified clinical testing expenses to which paragraph (d)(6)(iii)(B) of this section applies shall be apportioned among the persons who are partners during the taxable year in accordance with section 704 and the regulations thereunder. For purposes of section 28, these expenses shall be treated as paid or incurred directly by the partners rather than by the partnership. Thus, the partnership shall disregard these expenses in computing the credit to be apportioned under paragraph (d)(6)(iii)(A) of this section, and each partner shall aggregate the portion of these expenses allocated to the partner with other qualified clinical testing expenses of the partner in making the computations under section 28.

(iv) Year in which taken into account. An amount apportioned to a person under paragraph (d)(6) of this section shall be taken into account by the person in the taxable year of such person in which or with which the taxable year of the corporation, estate, trust, or partnership (as the case may be) ends.

(v) Credit allowed subject to limitation. Any person to whom any amount has been apportioned under paragraph (d)(6)(i), (ii), or (iii) of this section is allowed, subject to the limitation provided in section 28(d)(2), a credit for that amount.

(7) Manner of making an election. To make an election to have section 28 apply for its taxable year, the taxpayer shall file Form 6765 (Credit for Increasing Research Activities (or for claiming the orphan drugs credit)) containing all the information required by that form.

T.D. 8232, 9/30/88.

---

§ 1.30-1 Definition of qualified electric vehicle and recapture of credit for qualified electric vehicle.

Caution: The Treasury has not yet amended Reg § 1.30-1 to reflect changes made by P.L. 107-147, P.L. 104-188.

(a) Definition of qualified electric vehicle. A qualified electric vehicle is a motor vehicle that meets the requirements of section 30(c). Accordingly, a qualified electric vehicle does not include any motor vehicle that has ever been used (for either personal or business use) as a non-electric vehicle.

(b) Recapture of credit for qualified electric vehicle. *(1) In general.* (i) Addition to tax. If a recapture event occurs with respect to a taxpayer's qualified electric vehicle, the taxpayer must add the recapture amount to the amount of tax due in the taxable year in which the recapture event occurs. The recapture amount is not treated as income tax imposed on the taxpayer by chapter 1 of the Internal Revenue Code for purposes of computing the alternative minimum tax or determining the amount of any other allowable credits for the taxable year in which the recapture event occurs.

(ii) Reduction of carryover. If a recapture event occurs with respect to a taxpayer's qualified electric vehicle, and if a portion of the section 30 credit for the cost of that vehicle was disallowed under section 30(b)(3)(B) and consequently added to the taxpayer's minimum tax credit pursuant to section 53(d)(1)(B)(iii), the taxpayer must reduce its minimum tax credit carryover by an amount equal to the portion of any minimum tax credit carryover attributable to the disallowed section 30 credit, multiplied by the recapture percentage for the taxable year of recapture. Similarly, the taxpayer must reduce any other credit carryover amounts (such as under section 469) by the portion of the carryover attributable to section 30, multiplied by the recapture percentage.

(2) Recapture event. (i) In general. A recapture event occurs if, within 3 full years from the date a qualified electric vehicle is placed in service, the vehicle ceases to be a qualified electric vehicle. A vehicle ceases to be a qualified electric vehicle if—

(A) The vehicle is modified so that it is no longer primarily powered by electricity;

(B) The vehicle is used in a manner described in section 50(b); or

(C) The taxpayer receiving the credit under section 30 sells or disposes of the vehicle and knows or has reason to know that the vehicle will be used in a manner described in paragraph (b)(2)(i)(A) or (B) of this section.

(ii) Exception for disposition. Except as provided in paragraph (b)(2)(i)(C) of this section, a sale or other disposition (including a disposition by reason of an accident or other casualty) of a qualified electric vehicle is not a recapture event.

(3) Recapture amount. The recapture amount is equal to the recapture percentage times the decrease in the credits allowed under section 30 for all prior taxable years that would have resulted solely from reducing to zero the cost taken into account under section 30 with respect to such vehicle, including any credits allowed attributable to section 30 (such as under sections 53 and 469).

(4) Recapture date. The recapture date is the actual date of the recapture event unless a recapture event described in paragraph (b)(2)(i)(B) of this section occurs, in which case the recapture date is the first day of the recapture year.

(5) Recapture percentage. For purposes of this section, the recapture percentage is—

(i) 100, if the recapture date is within the first full year after the date the vehicle is placed in service;

(ii) 66⅔, if the recapture date is within the second full year after the date the vehicle is placed in service; or

(iii) 33⅓, if the recapture date is within the third full year after the date the vehicle is placed in service.

(6) Basis adjustment. As of the first day of the taxable year in which the recapture event occurs, the basis of the qualified electric vehicle is increased by the recapture amount and the carryover reductions taken into account under paragraphs (b)(1)(i) and (ii) of this section, respectively. For a vehicle that is of a character that is subject to an allowance for depreciation, this increase in basis is recoverable over the remaining recovery period for the vehicle beginning as of the first day of the taxable year of recapture.

(7) Application of section 1245 for sales and other dispositions. For purposes of section 1245, the amount of the credit allowable under section 30(a) with respect to any qualified electric vehicle that is (or has been) of a character subject to an allowance for depreciation is treated as a deduction allowed for depreciation under section 167. Therefore, upon a sale or other disposition of a depreciable qualified electric vehicle, section 1245 will apply to any gain recognized to the extent the basis of the depreciable vehicle was reduced under section 30(d)(1) net of any basis increase described in paragraph (b)(6) of this section.

(8) Examples. The following examples illustrate the provisions of this section:

Example (1). A, a calendar-year taxpayer, purchases and places in service for personal use on January 1, 1995, a qualified electric vehicle costing $25,000. On A's 1995 federal income tax return, A claims a credit of $2,500. On January 2, 1996, A sells the vehicle to an unrelated third party who subsequently converts the vehicle into a non-electric vehicle on October 15, 1996. There is no recapture upon the sale of the vehicle by A provided A did not know or have reason to know that the purchaser intended to convert the vehicle to non-electric use.

Example (2). B, a calendar-year taxpayer, purchases and places in service for personal use on October 11, 1994, a qualified electric vehicle costing $20,000. On B's 1994 federal income tax return, B claims a credit of $2,000, which reduces B's tax by $2,000. The basis of the vehicle is reduced to $18,000 ($20,000 – $2,000). On March 8, 1996, B sells the vehicle to a tax-exempt entity. Because B knowingly sold the vehicle to a tax-exempt entity described in section 50(b) in the second full year from the date the vehicle was placed in service, B must recapture $1,333 ($2,000 × 66⅔ percent). This recapture amount increases B's tax by $1,333 on B's 1996 federal income tax return and is added to the basis of the vehicle as of January 1, 1996, the beginning of the taxable year in which the recapture event occurred.

Example (3). X, a calendar-year taxpayer, purchases and places in service for business use on January 1, 1994, a qualified electric vehicle costing $30,000. On X's 1994 federal income tax return, X claims a credit of $3,000, which reduces X's tax by $3,000. The basis of the vehicle is reduced to $27,000 ($30,000 – $3,000) prior to any adjustments for depreciation. On March 8, 1995, X converts the qualified electric vehicle into a gasoline-propelled vehicle. Because X modified the vehicle so that it is no longer primarily powered by electricity in the second full year from the date the vehicle was placed in service, X must recapture $2,000 ($3,000 × 66⅔ percent). This recapture amount increases X's tax by $2,000 on X's 1995 federal income tax return. The recapture amount of $2,000 is added to the basis of the vehicle as of January 1, 1995, the beginning of the taxable year of recapture, and to the extent the property remains depreciable, the adjusted basis is recoverable over the remaining recovery period.

Example (4). The facts are the same as in Example 3. In 1996, X sells the vehicle for $31,000, recognizing a gain from this sale. Under paragraph (b)(7) of this section, section 1245 will apply to any gain recognized on the sale of a depreciable vehicle to the extent the basis of the vehicle was reduced by the section 30 credit net of any basis increase from recapture of the section 30 credit. Accordingly, the gain from the sale of the vehicle is subject to section 1245 to the extent of the depreciation allowance for the vehicle plus the credit allowed under section 30 ($3,000), less the previous recapture amount ($2,000). Any remaining amount of gain may be subject to other applicable provisions of the Internal Revenue Code.

(c) Effective date. This section is effective on October 14, 1994. If the recapture date is before the effective date of this section, a taxpayer may use any reasonable method to recapture the benefit of any credit allowable under section 30(a) consistent with section 30 and its legislative history. For this purpose, the recapture date is defined in paragraph (b)(4) of this section.

T.D. 8606, 8/2/95.

---

§ 1.31-1 Credit for tax withheld on wages.

Caution: The Treasury has not yet amended Reg § 1.31-1 to reflect changes made by P.L. 99-514.

(a) The tax deducted and withheld at the source upon wages under chapter 24 of the Internal Revenue Code of 1954 (or in the case of amounts withheld in 1954, under subchapter D, chapter 9 of the Internal Revenue Code of 1939) is allowable as a credit against the tax imposed by subtitle A of the Internal Revenue Code of 1954, upon the recipient of the income. If the tax has actually been withheld at the source, credit or refund shall be made to the recipient of the income even though such tax has not been paid over to the Government by the employer. For the purpose of the credit, the recipient of the income is the person subject to tax imposed under subtitle A upon the wages from which the tax was withheld. For instance, if a husband and wife domiciled in a State recognized as a community property State for Federal tax purposes makes separate returns, each reporting for income tax purposes one-half of the wages received by the husband, each spouse is entitled to one-half of the credit allowable for the tax withheld at source with respect to such wages.

(b) The tax withheld during any calendar year shall be allowed as a credit against the tax imposed by subtitle A for the taxable year of the recipient of the income which begins in that calendar year. If such recipient has more than one taxable year beginning in that calendar year, the credit shall be allowed against the tax for the last taxable year so beginning.

T.D. 6161, 2/3/56.

---

§ 1.31-2 Credit for "special refunds" of employee social security tax.

Caution: The Treasury has not yet amended Reg § 1.31-2 to reflect changes made by P.L. 99-514.

(a) In general. *(1)* In the case of an employee receiving wages from more than one employer during the calendar year, amounts may be deducted and withheld as employee social security tax with respect to more than $3,600 of wages received during the calendar year 1954, and with respect to more than $4,200 of wages received during a calendar year after 1954. For example, employee social security tax may be deducted and withheld on $5,000 of wages received by an employee during a particular calendar year if the employee is paid wages in such year in the amount of $3,000 by one employer and in the amount of $2,000 by another employer. Section 6413(c) (as amended by section 202 of the Social Security Amendments of 1954 (68 Stat 1089)), permits, under certain conditions, a so-called "special refund" of the amount of employee social security tax deducted and withheld with respect to wages paid to an employee in a calendar year after 1954 in excess of $4,200 ($3,600 for the calendar year 1954) by reason of the employee receiving wages from more than one employer during the calendar year. For provisions relating to the imposition of the employee tax and the limitation on wages, see with respect to the calendar year 1954, sections 1400 and 1426(a)(1) of the Internal Revenue Code of 1939 and, with respect to calendar years after 1954, sections 3101 and 3121(a)(1) of the Internal Revenue Code of 1954, as amended by sections 208(b) and 204(a), respectively, of the Social Security Amendments of 1954 (68 Stat 1094, 1091).

(2) An employee who is entitled to a special refund of employee tax with respect to wages received during a calendar year and who is also required to file an income tax return for such calendar year (or for his last taxable year beginning in such calendar year) may obtain the benefits of such special refund only by claiming credit for such special refund in the same manner as if such special refund were an amount deducted and withheld as income tax at the source. For provisions for claiming special refunds for 1955 and subsequent years in the case of employees not required to file income tax returns, see section 6413(c) and the regulations thereunder. For provisions relating to such refunds for 1954, see 26 CFR (1939) $408.802 (Regulations 128).

(3) The amount of the special refund allowed as a credit shall be considered as an amount deducted and withheld as income tax at the source under chapter 24 of the Internal Revenue Code of 1954 (or, in the case of a special refund for 1954, subchapter D, chapter 9 of the Internal Revenue Code of 1939). If the amount of such special refund when added to amounts deducted and withheld as income tax exceeds the taxes imposed by subtitle A of the Internal Revenue Code of 1954, the amount of the excess constitutes an overpayment of income tax under subtitle A, and interest on such overpayment is allowed to the extent provided under section 6611 upon an overpayment of income tax resulting from a credit for income tax withheld at source. See section 6401(b).

(b) Federal and State employees and employees of certain foreign corporations. The provisions of this section shall apply to the amount of a special refund allowable to an employee of a Federal agency or a wholly owned instrumentality of the United States, to the amount of a special refund allowable to an employee of any State or political subdivision thereof (or any instrumentality of any one or more of the foregoing), and to the amount of a special refund allowable to employees of certain foreign corporations. See, with respect to such special refunds for 1954, section 1401(d)(4) of the Internal Revenue Code of 1939, and with respect to such special refunds for 1955 and subsequent years, section 6413(c)(2) of the Internal Revenue Code of 1954, as amended by section 202 of the Social Security amendments of 1954.

T.D. 6161, 2/3/56.

§ 1.32-2 Earned income credit for taxable years beginning after December 31, 1978.

Caution: The Treasury has not yet amended Reg § 1.32-2 to reflect changes made by P.L. 108-311.

(a) [Reserved].

(b) Limitations. *(1)* [Reserved].

(2) Married individuals. No credit is allowed by section 32 in the case of an eligible individual who is married (within the meaning of section 7703 and the regulations thereunder) unless the individual and spouse file a single return jointly (a joint return) for the taxable year (see section 6013 and the regulations thereunder relating to joint returns of income tax by husband and wife). The requirements of the preceding sentence do not apply to an eligible individual who is not considered as married under section 7703(b) and the regulations thereunder (relating to certain married individuals living apart).

(3) Length of taxable year. No credit is allowed by section 32 in the case of a taxable year covering a period of less than 12 months. However, the rule of the preceding sentence does not apply to a taxable year closed by reason of the death of the eligible individual.

(c) Definitions. *(1)* [Reserved].

(2) Earned income. For purposes of this section, earned income is computed without regard to any community property laws which may otherwise be applicable. Earned income is reduced by any net loss in earnings from self-employment. Earned income does not include amounts received as a pension, an annuity, unemployment compensation, or workmen's compensation, or an amount to which section 871(a) and the regulations thereunder apply (relating to income of nonresident alien individuals not connected with United States business).

(d) [Reserved].

(e) Coordination of credit with advance payments. *(1) Recapture of excess advance payments.* If any advance payment of earned income credit under section 3507 is made to an individual by an employer during any calendar year, then the total amount of these advance payments to the individual in that calendar year is treated as an additional amount of tax imposed (by chapter 1 of the Code) upon the individual on the tax return for the individual's last taxable year beginning in that calendar year.

(2) Reconciliation of payments advanced and credit allowed. Any additional amount of tax under paragraph (e)(1) of this section is not treated as a tax imposed by chapter 1 of the Internal Revenue Code for purposes of determining the amount of any credit (other than the earned income credit) allowable under part IV, subchapter A, chapter 1 of the Internal Revenue Code.

T.D. 7683, 3/12/80, amend T.D. 8448, 11/20/92, T.D. 9045, 3/5/2003.

§ 1.32-3 Eligibility requirements after denial of the earned income credit.

(a) In general. A taxpayer who has been denied the earned income credit (EIC), in whole or in part, as a result of the deficiency procedures under subchapter B of chapter 63 (deficiency procedures) is ineligible to file a return claiming the EIC subsequent to the denial until the taxpayer demonstrates eligibility for the EIC in accordance with paragraph

(c) of this section. If a taxpayer demonstrates eligibility for a taxable year in accordance with paragraph (c) of this section, the taxpayer need not comply with those requirements for any subsequent taxable year unless the Service again denies the EIC as a result of the deficiency procedures.

(b) Denial of the EIC as a result of the deficiency procedures. For purposes of this section, denial of the EIC as a result of the deficiency procedures occurs when a tax on account of the EIC is assessed as a deficiency (other than as a mathematical or clerical error under section 6213(b)(1)).

(c) Demonstration of eligibility. In the case of a taxpayer to whom paragraph (a) of this section applies, and except as otherwise provided by the Commissioner in the instructions for Form 8862, "Information To Claim Earned Income Credit After Disallowance," no claim for the EIC filed subsequent to the denial is allowed unless the taxpayer properly completes Form 8862, demonstrating eligibility for the EIC, and otherwise is eligible for the EIC. If any item of information on Form 8862 is incorrect or inconsistent with any item on the return, the taxpayer will be treated as not demonstrating eligibility for the EIC. The taxpayer must follow the instructions for Form 8862 to determine the income tax return to which Form 8862 must be attached. If the taxpayer attaches Form 8862 to an incorrect tax return, the taxpayer will not be relieved of the requirement that the taxpayer attach Form 8862 to the correct tax return and will, therefore, not be treated as meeting the taxpayer's obligation under paragraph (a) of this section.

(d) Failure to demonstrate eligibility. If a taxpayer to whom paragraph (a) of this section applies fails to satisfy the requirements of paragraph (c) of this section with respect to a particular taxable year, the IRS can deny the EIC as a mathematical or clerical error under section 6213(g)(2)(K).

(e) Special rule where one spouse denied EIC. The eligibility requirements set forth in this section apply to taxpayers filing a joint return where one spouse was denied the EIC for a taxable year prior to marriage and has not established eligibility as either an unmarried or married taxpayer for a subsequent taxable year.

(f) Effective date. This section applies to returns claiming the EIC for taxable years beginning after December 31, 1997, where the EIC was denied for a taxable year beginning after December 31, 1996.

T.D. 8953, 6/22/2001.

§ 1.34-1 Special rule for owners of certain business entities.

Amounts payable under sections 6420, 6421, and 6427 to a business entity that is treated as separate from its owner under § 1.1361-4(a)(8) (relating to certain qualified subchapter S subsidiaries) or § 301.7701-2(c)(2)(v) of this chapter (relating to certain wholly-owned entities) are, for purposes of section 34, treated as payable to the owner of that entity.

T.D. 6500, 11/26/60, amend T.D. 6777, 12/15/64, T.D. 9356, 8/15/2007.

§ 1.37-1 General rules for the credit for the elderly.

Caution: The Treasury has not yet amended Reg § 1.37-1 to reflect changes made by P.L. 99-514, P.L. 98-369, P.L. 98-21.

(a) In general. In the case of an individual, section 37 provides a credit against the tax imposed by chapter 1 of the Internal Revenue Code of 1954. This section and §§ 1.37-2 and 1.37-3 provide guidance in the computation of the credit for the elderly provided under section 37 for taxable years beginning after 1975. For rules relating to the computation of the retirement income credit provided under section 37 for taxable years beginning before 1976, see 26 CFR 1.37-1 through 1.37-5 (Rev. as of April 1, 1980). Note that section 403 of the Tax Reduction and Simplification Act of 1977 provides that a taxpayer may elect to compute the credit under section 37 for the taxpayer's first taxable year beginning in 1976 in accordance with the rules applicable to taxable years beginning before 1976.

(b) Limitation on the amount of the credit. The credit allowed by section 37 for a taxable year shall not exceed the tax imposed by chapter 1 of the Code for the taxable year (reduced, in the case of a taxable year beginning before 1979, by the general tax credit allowed by section 42).

(c) Married couples must file joint returns. If the taxpayer is married at the close of the taxable year, the credit provided by section 37 shall be allowed only if the taxpayer and the taxpayer's spouse file a joint return for the taxable year. The preceding sentence shall not apply in the case of a husband and wife who are not members of the same household at any time during the taxable year. For the determination of marital status, see section 143 and § 1.143-1.

(d) Nonresident aliens ineligible. No credit is allowed under section 37 to any individual for any taxable year during which that individual is at any time a nonresident alien unless the individual is treated, by reason of an election under section 6013(g) or (h), as a resident of the United States for that taxable year.

T.D. 6161, 2/3/56, amend T.D. 6633, 1/14/63, T.D. 6791, 1/5/65, T.D. 7743, 12/19/80.

§ 1.37-2 Credit for individuals age 65 or over.

Caution: The Treasury has not yet amended Reg § 1.37-2 to reflect changes made by P.L. 99-514, P.L. 98-369, P.L. 98-21.

(a) In general. This section illustrates the computation of the credit for the elderly in the case of an individual who has attained the age of 65 before the close of the taxable year. This section shall not apply to an individual for any taxable year for which the individual makes the election described in section 37(e)(2) and paragraph (b) of § 1.37-3.

(b) Computation of credit. The credit for the elderly for an individual to whom this section applies equals 15 percent of the individual's "section 37 amount" for the taxable year. An individual's "section 37 amount" for a taxable year is the initial amount determined under section 37(b)(2), reduced as provided in section 37(b)(3) and (c)(1).

(c) Examples. The computation of the credit for the elderly for individuals to whom this section applies may be illustrated by the following examples:

Example (1). A, a single individual who is 67 years old, has adjusted gross income of $8,000 for the calendar year 1977. A also receives social security payments of $1,450 during 1977. A does not itemize deductions. A's credit for the elderly is $120, computed as follows:

Initial amount under section 37(b)(2)		$2,500
Reductions required by section 37 (b)(3) and (c)(1)		
Social security payments	$1,450	
One-half the excess of adjusted gross income over $7,500	250	1,700
Section 37 amount		800
15 pct of $800		$ 120

A's tax from the tax tables, which reflect the allowance of the general tax credit, is $662. Accordingly, the limitation of section 37(c)(2) and paragraph (b) of § 1.37-1 does not reduce A's credit for the elderly.

Example (2). H and W, who have both attained the age of 65, file a joint return for calendar year 1977. For that year H and W have adjusted gross income of $8,120; H also receives a railroad retirement pension of $1,550, and W receives social security payments of $1,200. H and W do not itemize deductions. The credit for the elderly allowed to H and W for 1977 is $139, computed as follows:

Initial amount under section 37(b)(2)		$3,750
Reductions required by section 37 (b)(3):		
Railroad retirement pension	$1,550	
Social Security payments	1,200	2,750
Section 37 amount		1,000
15 pct of $1,000		150
Limitation based upon amount of tax (derived from table reflecting allowance of general tax credit)		$ 139

T.D. 6161, 2/3/56, amend T.D. 6791, 1/5/65, T.D. 7743, 12/19/80.

§ 1.37-3 Credit for individuals under age 65 who have public retirement system income.

Caution: The Treasury has not yet amended Reg § 1.37-3 to reflect changes made by P.L. 99-514, P.L. 98-369, P.L. 98-21.

(a) In general. This section provides rules for the computation of the credit for the elderly under section 37(e) in the case of an individual who has not attained the age of 65 before the close of the taxable year and whose gross income for the taxable year includes retirement income within the meaning of paragraph (d)(1)(ii) of this section (*i.e.*, under a public retirement system). If such an individual is married within the meaning of section 143 at the close of the taxable year and the spouse of the individual has attained the age of 65 before the close of the taxable year, this section shall apply to the individual for the taxable year only if both spouses make the election described in paragraph (b) of this section. If both spouses make the election described in paragraph (b) of this section for the taxable year, the credit of each spouse shall be determined under the rules of this section. See paragraph (f)(2) of this section for a limitation on the effects of community property laws in making determinations and computations under section 37(e) and this section.

(b) Election by certain married taxpayers. If a married individual under age 65 at the close of the taxable year has retirement income and the spouse of that individual has attained the age of 65 before the close of the taxable year, both spouses may elect to compute the credit provided by section 37 under the rules of section 37(e) and this section. The spouses shall signify the election on the return (or amended return) for the taxable year in the manner prescribed in the instructions accompanying the return. The election may be made at any time before the expiration of the period of limitation for filing claim for credit or return for the taxable year. The election may be revoked without the consent of the Commissioner at any time before the expiration of that period by filing an amended return.

(c) Computation of credit. The credit of an individual under section 37(e) and this section equals 15 percent of the individual's credit base for the taxable year. The credit base of an individual for a taxable year is the lesser of—

(1) The retirement income of the individual for the taxable year, or

(2) The amount determined under section 37(e)(5), as modified by section 37(e)(6) and (7).

(d) Retirement income. *(1) General rule.* (i) For individuals 65 or over. Section 37(e)(4)(A) enumerates the kinds of income which may be treated as the retirement income of an individual who has attained the age of 65 before the close of the taxable year. They include income from pensions and annuities, interest, rents, dividends, certain bonds received under a qualified bond purchase plan, and certain individual retirement accounts or annuities.

(ii) For individuals under 65. In the case of an individual who has not attained the age of 65 before the close of the taxable year, retirement income consists only of income from pensions and annuities (including disability annuity payments) under a public retirement system which arises from services performed by that individual or by a present or former spouse of that individual. The term "public retirement system" means a pension, annuity, or retirement, or similar fund or system established by the United States, a State, a possession of the United States, any political subdivision of any of the foregoing, or the District of Columbia.

(2) Rents. For purposes of section 37(e)(4)(A)(iii), income from rents shall be the gross amount received, not reduced by depreciation or other expenses, except that beneficiaries of a trust or estate shall treat as retirement income only their proportionate shares, of the taxable rents of the trust or estate. In the case of an amount received for board and lodging, only the portion of the amount received for lodging is income from rents.

(3) Disability annuity payments received by individual under age 65. Disability annuity payments received under a public retirement system by an individual under age 65 at the close of the taxable year shall not be treated as retirement income unless the payments are for periods after the date on which the individual reached minimum retirement age, that is, the age at which the individual would be eligible to receive a pension or annuity without regard to disability, and any of the following conditions is satisfied—

(i) The individual is precluded from seeking the benefits of section 105(d) (relating to certain disability payments) for that taxable year by reason of an irrevocable election;

(ii) The individual was not permanently and totally disabled at the time of retirement (and was not permanently and totally disabled either on January 1, 1976, or on January 1, 1977, if the individual retired before the later date on disability or under circumstances which entitled the individual to retire on disability; or

(iii) The payments are for periods after the individual reached mandatory retirement age. For purposes of this paragraph, disability annuity payments include payments to an individual who retired on partial or temporary disability.

(4) Compensation of personal services rendered during taxable year. Retirement income does not include any

amount representing compensation for personal services rendered during the taxable year. For this purpose, amounts received as a pension shall not be treated as representing compensation for personal services rendered during the taxable year if the period of service during the taxable year is not substantial when compared with the total years of service. For example, an individual on the calendar year basis retires on November 30 after 5 years of service and receives a pension during the remainder of his taxable year. The pension is not treated as representing compensation for personal services rendered during such taxable year merely because it is paid by reason of the services of the individual for a period of 5 years which includes a portion of the taxable year.

(5) Amounts not includible in gross income. Retirement income does not include any amount not includible in the gross income of the individual for the taxable year. For example, if a portion of an annuity is excluded from gross income under section 72, relating to annuities, that portion of the annuity is not retirement income; similarly, the portion of dividend income excluded from gross income under section 116, relating to the partial exclusion of dividends received by individuals is not retirement income.

(e) Earned income. *(1) In general.* The term "earned income" in section 37(e)(5)(B) generally has the same meaning as in section 911(b), except that earned income does not include any amount received as a pension or annuity. See section 911(b) and the regulations thereunder. Section 911(b) provides, in general, that earned income includes wages, salaries, professional fees, and other amounts received as compensation for personal services rendered.

(2) Earned income from self-employment. For purposes of section 37(e)(5)(B), the earned income of a taxpayer from self-employment in a trade or business shall not exceed—

(i) The taxpayer's share of the net profits from the trade or business if capital is not a material income-producing factor in that trade or business; or

(ii) Thirty percent of the taxpayer's share of the net profits from the trade or business if capital is a material income-producing factor in that trade or business.

For other rules relating to the determination of earned income from self-employment in a trade or business, see section 911(b) and the regulations thereunder.

(3) Disability annuity payments received by individuals under age 65. Disability annuity payments received under a public retirement system by an individual under age 65 at the close of the taxable year shall be treated as earned income for purposes of section 37(e)(5)(B) unless the payments are treated as retirement income under paragraph (d)(3) of this section.

(f) Computation of credit under section 37(e) in the case of joint returns. *(1) In general.* In the case of a joint return of husband and wife, the credit base of each spouse under section 37(e) is computed separately. The spouses then combine their credit bases and compute a single credit. The limitation in section 37(c)(2) and paragraph (b) of § 1.37-1 on the amount of the credit is determined by reference to the joint tax liability of the spouses. Thus, regardless of whether a spouse would be liable for the tax imposed by chapter 1 of the Code if the joint return had not been filed, the credit base of that spouse is taken into account in computing the credit.

(2) Community property laws. For taxable years beginning after 1977, married individuals filing joint returns shall disregard community property laws in making any determination or computation required under section 37(e) or this section. Each item of income is attributed in full to the spouse whose income it would have been in the absence of community property laws. Thus, if a 67-year old individual files a joint return with a 62-year old spouse for 1979 and the only income of the couple is from a public pension of the older spouse, that public pension is attributed in full to the older spouse for purposes of section 37(e) even though the applicable community property law may treat one-half of the pension as the income of the 62-year old spouse. Since the younger spouse consequently has no retirement income within the meaning of paragraph (d) of this section, the couple may not make the election described in paragraph (b) of this section.

(g) Examples. The computation of the credit for the elderly under section 37(e) and this section is illustrated by the following examples:

Example (1). B, who is 62 years old and single, receives a fully taxable pension of $2,400 from a public retirement system during 1977. B performed the services giving rise to the pension. During that year, B also earns $2,650 from a part-time job. B receives no tax-exempt pension or annuity in 1977. Subject to the limitation of section 37(c)(2) and paragraph (b) of § 1.37-1, B's credit for the elderly for 1977 under section 37(e) is $195, computed as follows:

Maximum retirement income level under section 37(e)(5)		$2,500
Earned income offset under section 37(e)(5)(B)(ii):		
Earned income in excess of $1,700	$950	
One-half of earned income in excess of $1,200, but not in excess of $1,700	250	1,200
Amount determined under section 37(e)(5)		1,300
Retirement income		2,400
Credit for the elderly (15 pct. of $1,300)		195

Example (2). During 1978 H, who is 67 years old, has earnings of $1,300 and retirement income (rents, interest, etc.) of $6,000. H also receives social security payments totalling $1,400. During 1978 W, who is 63 years old, earns $1,600 and receives a fully taxable pension of $1,400 from a public retirement system that constitutes retirement income. W performed the services giving rise to the pension. H and W file a joint return for 1978 and elect to compute the credit for the elderly under section 37(e). Under the applicable law these items of income are community income, and both spouses share equally in each item. Because H and W are filing a joint return, they disregard community property laws in computing their credit under section 37(e). The couple allocates $1,600 of the $3,750 referred to in section 37(e)(6) to W and $2,150 to H. Subject to the limitation of section 37(c)(2) and paragraph (b) of § 1.37-1, their credit for the elderly is $315, computed as follows:

Credit base of H:		
Amount allocated to H under section 37(e)(6)		$2,150
Reductions required by section 37(e)(5):		
Social Security payments	$1,400	
One-half of excess of earnings over $1,200	$ 50	$1,450
Amount determined under section 37(e)(5)		700
Retirement income		6,000

Credit base of H		700
Credit base of W:		
Amount allocated to W under section 37(e)(6)		$1,600
Reduction required by section 37(e)(5)(B): One-half of excess of earnings over $1,200		$ 200
Amount determined under section 37(e)(5)		1,400
Retirement income		1,400
Credit base of W		1,400
Computation of credit:		
Credit base of H		700
Credit base of W		1,400
Combined credit base		2,100
Credit for the elderly (15 pct. of $2,100)		315

Example (3). (a) Assume the same facts as in example (2) of this paragraph, except that H and W live apart at all times during 1978 and file separate returns. Under these circumstances, H and W must give effect to the applicable community property law in determining their credits under section 37(e). Thus, each spouse must take into account one-half of each item of income.

(b) Subject to the limitation of section 37(c)(2) and paragraph (b) of § 1.37-1, H's credit for the elderly is $157.50, computed as follows:

Maximum retirement income level under section 37(e)(7)		$1,875
Reductions required by section 37(e)(5):		
Social security payments	$700	
One-half of excess of earnings over $1,200 (taking into account one-half of combined earnings of $2,900)	125	825
Amount determined under section 37(e)(5)		1,050
Retirement income		3,700
Credit of H (15 pct. of $1,050)		157.50

(c) Subject to the limitation of section 37(c)(2) and paragraph (b) of § 1.37-1, W's credit for the elderly is computed as follows:

Maximum retirement income level under section 37(e)(7)		$1,875
Reductions required by section 37(e)(5):		
Social security payments	$700	
One/half of excess of earnings over $1,200	125	825
Amount determined under section 37(e)(5)		1,050
Retirement income (limited to W's share of public pension)		700
Credit of W (15 pct. of $700)		105

T.D. 6161, 2/3/56, amend T.D. 6722, 4/13/64, T.D. 6791, 1/5/65, T.D. 7743, 12/19/80.

§ 1.38-1 Investment in certain depreciable property.

Caution: The Treasury has not yet amended Reg § 1.38-1 to reflect changes made by P.L. 101-508.

Regulations under sections 46 through 50 are prescribed under the authority granted the Secretary by section 38(b) to prescribe regulations as may be necessary to carry out the purposes of section 39 and subpart B, part IV, subchapter A, chapter 1 of the Code.

T.D. 6931, 10/9/67, amend T.D. 7609, 4/4/79.

§ 1.40-1 Questions and answers relating to the meaning of the term "qualified mixture" in section 40(b)(1).

Caution: The Treasury has not yet amended Reg § 1.40-1 to reflect changes made by P.L. 101-508, P.L. 101-239.

Q-1. What is a "qualified mixture" within the meaning of section 40(b)(1)?

A-1. A "qualified mixture" is a mixture of alcohol and gasoline or of alcohol and special fuel which (1) is sold by the taxpayer producing such mixture to any person for use as a fuel, or (2) is used as a fuel by the taxpayer producing such mixture.

Q-2. Must alcohol be present in a product in order for that product to be considered a mixture of alcohol and either gasoline or a special fuel?

A-2. No. A product is considered to be a mixture of alcohol and gasoline or of alcohol and a special fuel if the product is derived from alcohol and either gasoline or a special fuel even if the alcohol is chemically transformed in producing the product so that the alcohol is no longer present as a separate chemical in the final product, provided that there is no significant loss in the energy content of the alcohol. Thus, a product may be considered to be "mixture of alcohol and gasoline or of alcohol and a special fuel" within the meaning of section 40(b)(1)(B) if such product is produced in a chemical reaction between alcohol and either gasoline or a special fuel. Similarly a product may be considered to be a "mixture of alcohol and gasoline or of alcohol and a special fuel" if such product is produced by blending a chemical compound derived from alcohol with either gasoline or a special fuel.

Thus, for example, a blend of gasoline and ethyl tertiary butyl ether (ETBE), a compound derived from ethanol (a qualified alcohol), in a chemical reaction in which there is no significant loss in the energy content of the ethanol, is considered for purposes of section 40(b)(1)(B) to be a mixture of gasoline and the ethanol used to produce the ETBE, even though the ethanol is chemically transformed in the production of ETBE and is not present in the final product.

T.D. 7263, 3/2/73, amend T.D. 8291, 3/6/90.

PAR. 2. Section 1.40-1 is revised to read as follows:

Proposed § 1.40-1 Alcohol used as a fuel. [*For Preamble, see ¶ 153,041*]

For the definition of "alcohol" for purposes of the credits allowed by section 40, see § 48.6426-1(c) of this chapter.

Proposed § 1.40-2 Small ethanol producer credit. [*For Preamble, see ¶ 153,041*]

(a) In general. Section 40 provides a small ethanol producer credit for each gallon of qualified ethanol production of an eligible small ethanol producer. Section 40(b)(4)(B) defines "qualified ethanol production". Section 40(g)(1) defines "eligible small ethanol producer". Section 40(g)(5) provides authority to prescribe such regulations as may be necessary to prevent the credit from directly or indirectly benefiting any person with a direct or indirect productive capacity of more than 60 million gallons of alcohol during the taxable year. A person has produced ethanol if the person has title to the ethanol immediately after it is created.

(b) Qualified ethanol production. Section 40(b)(4)(B) limits qualified ethanol production to ethanol that is produced by an eligible small ethanol producer. Ethanol is "produced" for this purpose only when a feedstock other than ethanol is transformed into ethanol.

(c) Denial of credit for ethanol produced at certain facilities. The person at whose facilities ethanol is produced is treated for purposes of section 40(g)(5) as an indirect beneficiary of any credit allowed with respect to the ethanol. Accordingly, the small ethanol producer credit is not allowed with respect to ethanol that is produced at the facilities of a contract manufacturer or other person if such contract manufacturer or other person has a direct or indirect productive capacity of more than 60 million gallons of alcohol during the taxable year. Similarly, if the manufacturer does not have a productive capacity of more than 60 million gallons but more than 15 million gallons of ethanol is produced at the manufacturer's facilities during the taxable year, the small ethanol producer credit is allowed with respect to only the first 15 million gallons of ethanol produced at the facilities during the taxable year.

(d) Examples. The following examples illustrate the application of this section:

Example (1). X purchases hydrous ethanol and processes it into anhydrous ethanol. X is not the producer of the ethanol because X does not transform a feedstock other than ethanol into ethanol.

Example (2). Y arranges with contract manufacturer Z to produce 10 million gallons of ethanol. Y is not related to Z. Y provides the raw materials and retains title to them and to the finished ethanol. Z has the capacity to produce 100 million gallons of alcohol per year. The small producer credit is not allowed with respect to the 10 million gallons of ethanol because it is produced at the facilities of a contract manufacturer that has a productive capacity of more than 60 million gallons of alcohol during the taxable year.

(e) Effective/applicability date. This section is applicable on and after the date of publication of these regulations in the Federal Register as final regulations.

Proposed § 1.40A-1 Biodiesel. [*For Preamble, see ¶ 153,041*]

(a) In general. Rules similar to the rules of § 1.40-2 apply for purposes of the small agri-biodiesel producer credit allowed by section 40A.

(b) Definitions. For the definitions of "biodiesel" and "renewable diesel" for purposes of the credits allowed by section 40A, see § 48.6426-1(b) of this chapter.

(c) Effective/applicability date. This section is applicable on and after the date of publication of these regulations in the Federal Register as final regulations.

§ 1.41-0 Table of contents.

• ***Caution:*** In Notice 2001-19, 2001-10 IRB, IRS announced that these final regs, issued as TD 8930, are under review. Notice 2001-19 says that "[U]pon completion of the review, Treasury and IRS will announce changes to the regulations, if any, in the form of proposed regulations. In addition, TD 8930 will be revised so that the provisions of the regulations, including any changes to TD 8930, will be effective no earlier than the date when the completion of this review is announced, except that the provisions related to internal-use computer software (including any revisions) generally will be applicable for taxable years beginning after December 31, 1985." Notice 2001-19 also says that taxpayers may continue to rely on these final regs during the pendency of this review."

Caution: The Treasury has not yet amended Reg § 1.41-0 to reflect changes made by 110-458, P.L. 98-369.

This section lists the table of contents for §§ 1.41-1 through 1.41-9.

§ 1.41-1 Credit for increasing research activities.

(a) Amount of credit.

(b) Introduction to regulations under section 41.

§ 1.41-2 Qualified research expenses.

(a) Trade or business requirement.

(1) In general.

(2) New business.

(3) Research performed for others.

(i) Taxpayer not entitled to results.

(ii) Taxpayer entitled to results.

(4) Partnerships.

(i) In general.

(ii) Special rule for certain partnerships and joint ventures.

(b) Supplies and personal property used in the conduct of qualified research.

(1) In general.

(2) Certain utility charges.

(i) In general.

(ii) Extraordinary expenditures.

(3) Right to use personal property.

(4) Use of personal property in taxable years beginning after December 31, 1985.

(c) Qualified services.

(1) Engaging in qualified research.

(2) Direct supervision.

(3) Direct support.

(d) Wages paid for qualified services.

(1) In general.

(2) "Substantially all."

(e) Contract research expenses.

(1) In general.

(2) Performance of qualified research.

(3) "On behalf of."

(4) Prepaid amounts.

(5) Examples.

§ 1.41-3 Base amount for taxable years beginning on or after January 3, 2001.

(a) New taxpayers.

(b) Special rules for short taxable years.

(1) Short credit year.

(2) Short taxable year preceding credit year.

(3) Short taxable year in determining fixed-base percentage.

(c) Definition of gross receipts.
(1) In general.
(2) Amounts excluded.
(3) Foreign corporations.
(d) Consistency requirement.
(1) In general.
(2) Illustrations.
(e) Effective date.

§ 1.41-4 Qualified research for expenditures paid or incurred in taxable years ending on or after December 31, 2003.

(a) Qualified research.
(1) General rule.
(2) Requirements of section 41(d)(1).
(3) Undertaken for the purpose of discovering information.
(i) In general.
(ii) Application of the discovering information requirement.
(iii) Patent safe harbor.
(4) Technological in nature.
(5) Process of experimentation.
(i) In general.
(ii) Qualified purpose.
(6) Substantially all requirement.
(7) Use of computers and information technology.
(8) Illustrations.
(b) Application of requirements for qualified research.
(1) In general.
(2) Shrinking-back rule.
(3) Illustration.
(c) Excluded activities.
(1) In general.
(2) Research after commercial production.
(i) In general.
(ii) Certain additional activities related to the business component.
(iii) Activities related to production process or technique.
(iv) Clinical testing.
(3) Adaptation of existing business components.
(4) Duplication of existing business component.
(5) Surveys, studies, research relating to management functions, etc.
(6) Internal use software for taxable years beginning on or after December 31, 1985. [Reserved].
(7) Activities outside the United States, Puerto Rico, and other possessions.
(i) In general.
(ii) Apportionment of in-house research expenses.
(iii) Apportionment of contract research expenses.
(8) Research in the social sciences, etc.
(9) Research funded by any grant, contract, or otherwise.
(10) Illustrations.
(d) Recordkeeping for the research credit.
(e) Effective dates.

§ 1.41-5 Basic research for taxable years beginning after December 31, 1986. [Reserved]

§ 1.41-6 Aggregation of expenditures.

(a) Controlled groups of corporations; trades or businesses under common control.
(1) In general.
(2) Consolidated groups.
(3) Definitions.
(b) Computation of the group credit.
(1) In general.
(2) Start-up companies.
(c) Allocation of the group credit.
(1) In general.
(2) Stand-alone entity credit.
(d) Special rules for consolidated groups.
(1) In general.
(2) Start-up company status.
(3) Special rule for allocation of group credit among consolidated group members.
(e) Examples.
(f) For taxable years beginning before January 1, 1990.
(g) Tax accounting periods used.
(1) In general.
(2) Special rule when timing of research is manipulated.
(h) Membership during taxable year in more than one group.
(i) Intra-group transactions.
(1) In general.
(2) In-house research expenses.
(3) Contract research expenses.
(4) Lease payments.
(5) Payment for supplies.
(j) Effective/applicability date.
(1) In general.
(2) Consolidated group rule.
(3) Taxable years ending on or before December 31, 2006.

§ 1.41-7 Special rules.

(a) Allocations.
(1) Corporation making an election under subchapter S.
(i) Pass-through, for taxable years beginning after December 31, 1982, in the case of an S corporation.
(ii) Pass-through, for taxable years beginning before January 1, 1983, in the case of a subchapter S corporation.
(2) Pass-through in the case of an estate or trust.
(3) Pass-through in the case of a partnership.
(i) In general.
(ii) Certain expenditures by joint ventures.
(4) Year in which taken into account.
(5) Credit allowed subject to limitation.
(b) Adjustments for certain acquisitions and dispositions--Meaning of terms.
(c) Special rule for pass-through of credit.
(d) Carryback and carryover of unused credits.

§ 1.41-8 Alternative incremental credit.

(a) Determination of credit.
(b) Election.
(1) In general.

(2) Time and manner of election.

(3) Revocation.

(4) Special rules for controlled groups.

(5) Effective/applicability dates.

§ 1.41-9 Alternative simplified credit. [Reserved]. For further guidance, see the entries for § 1.41-9T in § 1.41-0T.

T.D. 8251, 5/16/89, amend T.D. 8930, 12/27/2000, T.D. 9104, 12/30/2003, T.D. 9205, 5/20/2005, T.D. 9296, 11/8/2006, T.D. 9401, 6/13/2008.

§ 1.41-0A Table of contents.

• ***Caution:*** In Notice 2001-19, 2001-10 IRB, IRS announced that these final regs, issued as TD 8930, are under review. Notice 2001-19 says that "[U]pon completion of the review, Treasury and IRS will announce changes to the regulations, if any, in the form of proposed regulations. In addition, TD 8930 will be revised so that the provisions of the regulations, including any changes to TD 8930, will be effective no earlier than the date when the completion of this review is announced, except that the provisions related to internal-use computer software (including any revisions) generally will be applicable for taxable years beginning after December 31, 1985." Notice 2001-19 also says that taxpayers may continue to rely on these final regs during the pendency of this review."

Caution: The Treasury has not yet amended Reg § 1.41-0A to reflect changes made by 110-458.

This section lists the paragraphs contained in §§ 1.41-0A, 1.41-3A, 1.41-4A and 1.41-5A.

§ 1.41-0A Table of contents.

§ 1.41-3A Base period research expense.

(a) Number of years in base period.

(b) New taxpayers.

(c) Definition of base period research expenses.

(d) Special rules for short taxable years.

(1) Short determination year.

(2) Short base period year.

(3) Years overlapping the effective dates of section 41 (section 44F).

(i) Determination years.

(ii) Base period years.

(4) Number of months in a short taxable year.

(e) Examples.

§ 1.41-4A Qualified research for taxable years beginning before January 1, 1986.

(a) General rule.

(b) Activities outside the United States.

(1) In-house research.

(2) Contract research.

(c) Social sciences or humanities.

(d) Research funded by any grant, contract, or otherwise.

(1) In general.

(2) Research in which taxpayer retains no rights.

(3) Research in which the taxpayer retains substantial rights.

(i) In general.

(ii) Pro rata allocation.

(iii) Project-by-project determination.

(4) Independent research and development under the Federal Acquisition Regulations System and similar provisions.

(5) Funding determinable only in subsequent taxable year.

(6) Examples.

§ 1.41-5A Basic research for taxable years beginning before January 1, 1987.

(a) In general.

(b) Trade or business requirement.

(c) Prepaid amounts.

(1) In general.

(2) Transfers of property.

(d) Written research agreement.

(1) In general.

(2) Agreement between a corporation and a qualified organization after June 30, 1983.

(i) In general.

(ii) Transfers of property.

(3) Agreement between a qualified fund and a qualified educational organization after June 30, 1983.

(e) Exclusions.

(1) Research conducted outside the United States.

(2) Research in the social sciences or humanities.

(f) Procedure for making an election to be treated as a qualified fund.

T.D. 7603, 3/26/79, amend T.D. 8251, 5/16/89, T.D. 8930, 12/27/2000.

§ 1.41-0T Table of contents (temporary).

Caution: The Treasury has not yet amended Reg § 1.41-0T to reflect changes made by 110-458.

This section lists the table of contents for Sec. § 1.41-6T, 1.41-8T, and 1.41-9T.

§ 1.41-6T Aggregation of expenditures (temporary).

(a) [Reserved]. For further guidance, see the entry for § 1.41-6(a) in § 1.41-0.

(b) Computation of the group credit.

(1) In general.

(2) [Reserved]. For further guidance, see the entry for § 1.41-6(b)(2) in § 1.41-0.

(c) Allocation of the group credit.

(1) [Reserved]. For further guidance, see the entry for § 1.41-6(c)(1) in § 1.41-0.

(3) Stand-alone entity credit.

(d) [Reserved]. For further guidance, see the entry for § 1.41-6(d) in § 1.41-0.

(e) Example.

(f) through (i) [Reserved]. For further guidance, see the entries for § 1.41-6(f) through (i) in § 1.41-0.

(j) Effective/applicability dates.

* * * * *

§ 1.41-8T Alternative incremental credit (temporary).

(a) [Reserved]. For further guidance, see the entry for § 1.41-8(a) in § 1.41-0.

(b) Election.

(1) In general.

(2) Time and manner of election.

(3) Revocation.

(4) Special rules for controlled groups.

(i) In general.

(ii) Designated member.

(5) Effective/applicability dates.

§ 1.41-9T Alternative simplified credit (temporary).

(a) Determination of credit.

(b) Election.

(1) In general.

(2) Time and manner of election.

(3) Revocation.

(4) Special rules for controlled groups.

(i) In general.

(ii) Designated member.

(c) Special rules.

(d) Effective/applicability dates.

(e) Expiration date.

T.D. 9401, 6/13/2008.

§ 1.41-1 Credit for increasing research activities.

• ***Caution:*** In Notice 2001-19, 2001-10 IRB, IRS announced that these final regs, issued as TD 8930, are under review. Notice 2001-19 says that "[U]pon completion of the review, Treasury and IRS will announce changes to the regulations, if any, in the form of proposed regulations. In addition, TD 8930 will be revised so that the provisions of the regulations, including any changes to TD 8930, will be effective no earlier than the date when the completion of this review is announced, except that the provisions related to internal-use computer software (including any revisions) generally will be applicable for taxable years beginning after December 31, 1985." Notice 2001-19 also says that taxpayers may continue to rely on these final regs during the pendency of this review."

Caution: The Treasury has not yet amended Reg § 1.41-1 to reflect changes made by 110-458.

(a) Amount of credit. The amount of a taxpayer's credit is determined under section 41(a). For taxable years beginning after June 30, 1996, and at the election of the taxpayer, the portion of the credit determined under section 41(a)(1) may be calculated using the alternative incremental credit set forth in section 41(c)(4). For taxable years ending after December 31, 2006, and at the election of the taxpayer, the portion of the credit determined under section 41(a)(1) may be calculated using either the alternative incremental credit set forth in section 41(c)(4), or the alternative simplified credit set forth in section 41(c)(5).

(b) Introduction to regulations under section 41.

(1) Sections 1.41-2 through 1.41-8 and 1.41-3A through 1.41-5A address only certain provisions of section 41. The following table identifies the provisions of section 41 that are addressed, and lists each provision with the section of the regulations in which it is covered.

Section of the regulation	Section of the Internal Revenue Code
§ 1.41-2	41(b).
§ 1.41-3	41(c).
§ 1.41-4	41(d).
§ 1.41-5	41(e).
§ 1.41-6	41(f).
§ 1.41-7	41(f). 41(g).
§ 1.41-8	41(c).
§ 1.41-3A	41(c) (taxable years beginning before January 1, 1990).
§ 1.41-4A	41(d) (taxable years beginning before January 1, 1986).
§ 1.41-5A	41(e) (taxable years beginning before January 1, 1987).

(2) Section 1.41-3A also addresses the special rule in section 221(d)(2) of the Economic Recovery Tax Act of 1981 relating to taxable years overlapping the effective dates of section 41. Section 41 was formerly designated as sections 30 and 44F. Sections 1.41-0 through 1.41-8 and 1.41-0A through 1.41-5A refer to these sections as section 41 for conformity purposes. Whether section 41, former section 30, or former section 44F applies to a particular expenditure depends upon when the expenditure was paid or incurred.

T.D. 8251, 5/16/89, amend T.D. 8930, 12/27/2000, T.D. 9401, 6/13/2008.

§ 1.41-2 Qualified research expenses.

Caution: The Treasury has not yet amended Reg § 1.41-2 to reflect changes made by 110-458, P.L. 105-34, P.L. 99-514, P.L. 98-369, P.L. 101-239.

• ***Caution:*** In Notice 2001-19, 2001-10 IRB, IRS announced that these final regs, issued as TD 8930, are under review. Notice 2001-19 says that "[U]pon completion of the review, Treasury and IRS will announce changes to the regulations, if any, in the form of proposed regulations. In addition, TD 8930 will be revised so that the provisions of the regulations, including any changes to TD 8930, will be effective no earlier than the date when the completion of this review is announced, except that the provisions related to internal-use computer software (including any revisions) generally will be applicable for taxable years beginning after December 31, 1985." Notice 2001-19 also says that taxpayers may continue to rely on these final regs during the pendency of this review."

(a) Trade or business requirement. *(1) In general.* An in-house research expense of the taxpayer or a contract research expense of the taxpayer is a qualified research expense only if the expense is paid or incurred by the taxpayer in carrying on a trade or business of the taxpayer. The phrase "in carrying on a trade or business" has the same meaning for purposes of section 41(b)(1) as it has for purposes of section 162; thus, expenses paid or incurred in connection with a trade or business within the meaning of section 174(a) (relating to the deduction for research and experimental expenses) are not necessarily paid or incurred in carrying on a trade or business for purposes of section 41. A research expense must relate to a particular trade or business being carried on by the taxpayer at the time the expense is paid or incurred in order to be a qualified research expense. For purposes of section 41, a contract research expense of the taxpayer is not a qualified research expense if the product or result of the research is intended to be transferred to another in return for license or royalty payments and the taxpayer does not use the product of the research in the taxpayer's trade or business.

(2) New business. Expenses paid or incurred prior to commencing a new business (as distinguished from expanding an existing business) may be paid or incurred in connection with a trade or business but are not paid or incurred in carrying on a trade or business. Thus, research expenses paid or incurred by a taxpayer in developing a product the sale of which would constitute a new trade or business for the taxpayer are not paid or incurred in carrying on a trade or business.

(3) Research performed for others. (i) Taxpayer not entitled to results. If the taxpayer performs research on behalf of another person and retains no substantial rights in the research, that research shall not be taken into account by the taxpayer for purposes of section 41. See § 1.41-A(d)(2).

(ii) Taxpayer entitled to results. If the taxpayer in carrying on a trade or business performs research on behalf of other persons but retains substantial rights in the research, the taxpayer shall take otherwise qualified expenses for that research into account for purposes of section 41 to the extent provided in § 1.41-4A(d)(3).

(4) Partnerships. (i) In general. An in-house research expense or a contract research expense paid or incurred by a partnership is a qualified research expense of the partnership if the expense is paid or incurred by the partnership in carrying on a trade or business of the partnership, determined at the partnership level without regard to the trade or business of any partner.

(ii) Special rule for certain partnerships and joint ventures. (A) If a partnership or a joint venture (taxable as a partnership) is not carrying on the trade or business to which the research relates, then the general rule in paragraph (a)(4)(i) of this section would not allow any of such expenditures to qualify as qualified research expenses.

(B) Notwithstanding paragraph (a)(4)(ii)(A) of this section, if all the partners or venturers are entitled to make independent use of the results of the research, this paragraph (a)(4)(ii) may allow a portion of such expenditures to be treated as qualified research expenditures by certain partners or venturers.

(C) First, in order to determine the amount of credit that may be claimed by certain partners or venturers, the amount of qualified research expenditures of the partnership or joint venture is determined (assuming for this purpose that the partnership or joint venture is carrying on the trade or business to which the research relates).

(D) Second, this amount is reduced by the proportionate share of such expenses allocable to those partners or venturers who would not be able to claim such expenses as qualified research expenditures if they had paid or incurred such expenses directly. For this purpose such partners' or venturers' proportionate share of such expenses shall be determined on the basis of such partners' or venturers' share of partnership items of income or gain (excluding gain allocated under section 704(c)) which results in the largest proportionate share. Where a partner's or venturer's share of partnership items of income or gain (excluding gain allocated under section 704 (c)) may vary during the period such partner or venturer is a partner or venturer in such partnership or joint venture, such share shall be the highest share such partner or venturer may receive.

(E) Third, the remaining amount of qualified research expenses is allocated among those partners or venturers who would have been entitled to claim a credit for such expenses if they had paid or incurred the research expenses in their own trade or business, in the relative proportions that such partners or venturers share deductions for expenses under section 174 for the taxable year that such expenses are paid or incurred.

(F) For purposes of section 41, research expenditures to which this paragraph (a)(4)(ii) applies shall be treated as paid or incurred directly by such partners or venturers. See § 1.41-7(a)(3)(ii) for special rules regarding these expenses.

(iii) The following examples illustrate the application of the principles contained in paragraph (a)(4)(ii) of this section.

Example (1). A joint venture (taxable as a partnership) is formed by corporations A, B, and C to develop and market a supercomputer. A and B are in the business of developing computers, and each has a 30 percent distributive share of each item of income, gain, loss, deduction, credit and basis of the joint venture. C, which is an investment banking firm, has a 40 percent distributive share of each item of income, gain, loss, deduction, credit and basis of the joint venture. The joint venture agreement provides that A's, B's and C's distributive shares will not vary during the life of the joint venture, liquidation proceeds are to be distributed in accordance with the partners' capital account balances, and any partner with a deficit in its capital account following the distribution of liquidation proceeds is required to restore the amount of such deficit to the joint venture. Assume in Year 1 that the joint venture incurs $100x of "qualified research expenses." Assume further that the joint venture cannot claim the research credit for such expenses because it is not carrying on the trade or business to which the research relates. In addition A, B, and C are all entitled to make independent use of the results of the research. First, the amount of qualified research expenses of the joint venture is $100x. Second, this amount is reduced by the proportionate share of such expenses allocable to C, the venturer which would not have been able to claim such expenses as qualified research expenditures if it had paid or incurred them directly, C's proportionate share of such expenses is $40x (40% of $100x). The reduced amount is $60x. Third, the remaining $60x of qualified research expenses is allocated between A and B in the relative proportions that A and B share deductions for expenses under section 174. A is entitled to treat $30x ((30%/(30% × 30%)) $60x) as a qualified research expense. B is also entitled to treat $30x ((30%/(30% × 30%)) $60x) as a qualified research expense.

Example (2). Assume the same facts as in example (1) except that the joint venture agreement provides that during the first 2 years of the joint venture, A and B are each allocated 10 percent of each item of income, gain, loss, deduction, credit and basis, and C is allocated 80 percent of each item of income, gain, loss, deduction, credit and basis. Thereafter the allocations are the same as in example (1). Assume for purposes of this example that such allocations have substantial economic effect for purposes of section 704(b). C's highest share of such items during the life of the joint venture is 80 percent. Therefore C's proportionate share of the joint venture's qualified research expenses is $80x (80% of $100x). The reduced amount of qualified research expenses is $20x ($100x − $80x). A is entitled to treat $10x ((10%/(10% + 10%)) $20x) as a qualified research expense in Year 1. B is also entitled to treat $10x ((10%/(10% + 10%)) $20x) as a qualified research expense in Year 1.

(b) Supplies and personal property used in the conduct of qualified research. *(1) In general.* Supplies and personal property (except to the extent provided in paragraph (b)(4) of this section) are used in the conduct of qualified research if they are used in the performance of qualified services (as defined in section 41(b)(2)(B), but without regard to the last sentence thereof) by an employee of the taxpayer (or by a person acting in a capacity similar to that of an employee of the taxpayer; see example (6) of § 1.41-2(e)(5)). Expenditures for supplies or for the use of personal property that are indirect research expenditures or general and administrative expenses do not qualify as in-house research expenses.

(2) Certain utility charges. (i) In general. In general, amounts paid or incurred for utilities such as water, electricity, and natural gas used in the building in which qualified research is performed are treated as expenditures for general and administrative expenses.

(ii) Extraordinary expenditures. To the extent the taxpayer can establish that the special character of the qualified research required additional extraordinary expenditures for utilities, the additional expenditures shall be treated as amounts paid or incurred for supplies used in the conduct of qualified research. For example, amounts paid for electricity used for general laboratory lighting are treated as general and administrative expenses, but amounts paid for electricity used in operating high energy equipment for qualified research (such as laser or nuclear research) may be treated as expenditures for supplies used in the conduct of qualified research to the extent the taxpayer can establish that the special character of the research required an extraordinary additional expenditure for electricity.

(3) Right to use personal property. The determination of whether an amount is paid to or incurred for another person for the right to use personal property in the conduct of qualified research shall be made without regard to the characterization of the transaction as a lease under section 168(f)(8) (as that section read before it was repealed by the Tax Reform Act of 1986). See § 5c.168(f)(8)-1(b).

(4) Use of personal property in taxable years beginning after December 31, 1985. For taxable years beginning after December 31, 1985, amounts paid or incurred for the use of personal property are not qualified research expenses, except for any amount paid or incurred to another person for the right to use (time-sharing) computers in the conduct of qualified research. The computer must be owned and operated by someone other than the taxpayer, located off the taxpayer's premises, and the taxpayer must not be the primary user of the computer.

(c) Qualified services. *(1) Engaging in qualified research.* The term "engaging in qualified research" as used in section 41(b)(2)(B) means the actual conduct of qualified research (as in the case of a scientist conducting laboratory experiments).

(2) Direct supervision. The term "direct supervision" as used in section 41(b)(2)(B) means the immediate supervision (first-line management) of qualified research (as in the case of a research scientist who directly supervises laboratory experiments, but who may not actually perform experiments). "Direct supervision" does not include supervision by a higher-level manager to whom first-line managers report, even if that manager is a qualified research scientist.

(3) Direct support. The term "direct support" as used in section 41(b)(2)(B) means services in the direct support of either—

(i) Persons engaging in actual conduct of qualified research, or

(ii) Persons who are directly supervising persons engaging in the actual conduct of qualified research. For example, direct support of research includes the services of a secretary for typing reports describing laboratory results derived from qualified research, of a laboratory worker for cleaning equipment used in qualified research, of a clerk for compiling research data, and of a machinist for machining a part of an experimental model used in qualified research. Direct support of research activities does not include general administrative services, or other services only indirectly of benefit to research activities. For example, services of payroll personnel in preparing salary checks of laboratory scientists, of an accountant for accounting for research expenses, of a janitor for general cleaning of a research laboratory, or of officers engaged in supervising financial or personnel matters do not qualify as direct support of research. This is true whether general administrative personnel are part of the research department or in a separate department. Direct support does not include supervision. Supervisory services constitute "qualified services" only to the extent provided in paragraph (c)(2) of this section.

(d) Wages paid for qualified services. *(1) In general.* Wages paid to or incurred for an employee constitute in-house research expenses only to the extent the wages were paid or incurred for qualified services performed by the employee. If an employee has performed both qualified services and nonqualified services, only the amount of wages allocated to the performance of qualified services constitutes an in-house research expense. In the absence of another method of allocation that the taxpayer can demonstrate to be more appropriate, the amount of in-house research expense shall be determined by multiplying the total amount of wages paid to or incurred for the employee during the taxable year by the ratio of the total time actually spent by the employee in the performance of qualified services for the taxpayer to the total time spent by the employee in the performance of all services for the taxpayer during the taxable year.

(2) "Substantially all." Notwithstanding paragraph (d)(1) of this section, if substantially all of the services performed by an employee for the taxpayer during the taxable year consist of services meeting the requirements of section 41(b)(2)(B)(i) or (ii), then the term "qualified services" means all of the services performed by the employee for the taxpayer during the taxable year. Services meeting the requirements of section 41(b)(2)(B)(i) or (ii) constitute substantially all of the services performed by the employee during a taxable year only if the wages allocated (on the basis

used for purposes of paragraph (d)(1) of this section) to services meeting the requirements of section 41(b)(2)(B)(i) or (ii) constitute at least 80 percent of the wages paid to or incurred by the taxpayer for the employee during the taxable year.

(e) Contract research expenses. *(1) In general.* A contract research expense is 65 percent of any expense paid or incurred in carrying on a trade or business to any person other than an employee of the taxpayer for the performance on behalf of the taxpayer of—

(i) Qualified research as defined in § 1.41-4 or 1.41-4A, whichever is applicable, or

(ii) Services which, if performed by employees of the taxpayer, would constitute qualified services within the meaning of section 41(b)(2)(B).

Where the contract calls for services other than services described in this paragraph (e)(1), only 65 percent of the portion of the amount paid or incurred that is attributable to the services described in this paragraph (e)(1) is a contract research expense.

(2) Performance of qualified research. An expense is paid or incurred for the performance of qualified research only to the extent that it is paid or incurred pursuant to an agreement that—

(i) Is entered into prior to the performance of the qualified research,

(ii) Provides that research be performed on behalf of the taxpayer, and

(iii) Requires the taxpayer to bear the expense even if the research is not successful.

If an expense is paid or incurred pursuant to an agreement under which payment is contingent on the success of the research, then the expense is considered paid for the product or result rather than the performance of the research, and the payment is not a contract research expense. The previous sentence applies only to that portion of a payment which is contingent on the success of the research.

(3) "On behalf of." Qualified research is performed on behalf of the taxpayer if the taxpayer has a right to the research results. Qualified research can be performed on behalf of the taxpayer notwithstanding the fact that the taxpayer does not have exclusive rights to the results.

(4) Prepaid amounts. Notwithstanding paragraph (e)(1) of this section, if any contract research expense paid or incurred during any taxable year is attributable to qualified research to be conducted after the close of such taxable year, the expense so attributable shall be treated for purposes of section 41(b)(1)(B) as paid or incurred during the period during which the qualified research is conducted.

(5) Examples. The following examples illustrate provisions contained in paragraphs (e)(1) through (4) of this section.

Example (1). A, a cash-method taxpayer using the calendar year as the taxable year, enters into a contract with B Corporation under which B is to perform qualified research on behalf of A. The contract requires A to pay B $300x, regardless of the success of the research. In 1982, B performs all of the research, and A makes full payment of $300x under the contract. Accordingly, during the taxable year 1982, $195x (65 percent of the payment of $300x) constitutes a contract research expense of A.

Example (2). The facts are the same as in example (1), except that B performs 50 percent of the research in 1983. Of the $195x of contract research expense paid in 1982, paragraph (e)(4) of this section provides that $97.5x (50 percent of $195x) is a contract research expense for 1982 and the remaining $97.5x is contract research expense for 1983.

Example (3). The facts are the same as in example (1), except that instead of calling for a flat payment of $300x, the contract requires A to reimburse B for all expenses plus pay B $100x. B incurs expenses attributable to the research as follows:

Labor	$90x
Supplies	20x
Depreciation on equipment	50x
Overhead	40x
Total	200x

Under this agreement A pays B $300x during 1982. Accordingly, during taxable year 1982, $195x (65 percent of $300x) of the payment constitutes a contract research expense of A.

Example (4). The facts are the same as in example (3), except that A agrees to reimburse B for all expenses and agrees to pay B an additional amount of $100x, but the additional $100x is payable only if the research is successful. The research is successful and A pays B $300x during 1982. Paragraph (e)(2) of this section provides that the contingent portion of the payment is not an expense incurred for the performance of qualified research. Thus, for taxable year 1982, $130x (65 percent of the payment of $200x) constitutes a contract research expense of A.

Example (5). C conducts in-house qualified research in carrying on a trade or business. In addition, C pays D Corporation, a provider of computer services, $100x to develop software to be used in analyzing the results C derives from its research. Because the software services, if performed by an employee of C, would constitute qualified services, $65x of the $100x constitutes a contract research expense of C.

Example (6). C conducts in-house qualified research in carrying on C's trade or business. In addition, C contracts with E Corporation, a provider of temporary secretarial services, for the services of a secretary for a week. The secretary spends the entire week typing reports describing laboratory results derived from C's qualified research. C pays E $400 for the secretarial service, none of which constitutes wages within the meaning of section 41(b)(2)(D). These services, if performed by employees of C, would constitute qualified services within the meaning of section 41(b)(2)(B). Thus, pursuant to paragraph (e)(1) of this section, $260 (65 percent of $400) constitutes a contract research expense of C.

Example (7). C conducts in-house qualified research in carrying on C's trade or business. In addition, C pays F, an outside accountant, $100x to keep C's books and records pertaining to the research project. The activity carried on by the accountant does not constitute qualified research as defined in section 41(d). The services performed by the accountant, if performed by an employee of C, would not constitute qualified services (as defined in section 41(b)(2)(B)). Thus, under paragraph (e)(1) of this section, no portion of the $100x constitutes a contract research expense.

T.D. 8251, 5/16/89, amend T.D. 8930, 12/27/2000.

---

§ 1.41-3 Base amount for taxable years beginning on or after January 3, 2001.

• ***Caution:*** In Notice 2001-19, 2001-10 IRB, IRS announced that these final regs, issued as TD 8930, are under review. Notice 2001-19 says that "[U]pon completion of the review, Treasury and IRS will announce changes to the regulations, if any, in the form of proposed regulations. In addition, TD 8930 will be revised so that the provisions of the regulations, including any changes to TD 8930, will be effective no earlier than the date when the completion of this review is announced, except that the provisions related to internal-use computer software (including any revisions) generally will be applicable for taxable years beginning after December 31, 1985." Notice 2001-19 also says that taxpayers may continue to rely on these final regs during the pendency of this review."

Caution: The Treasury has not yet amended Reg § 1.41-3 to reflect changes made by 110-458.

(a) New taxpayers. If, with respect to any credit year, the taxpayer has not been in existence for any previous taxable year, the average annual gross receipts of the taxpayer for the four taxable years preceding the credit year shall be zero. If, with respect to any credit year, the taxpayer has been in existence for at least one previous taxable year, but has not been in existence for four taxable years preceding the taxable year, then the average annual gross receipts of the taxpayer for the four taxable years preceding the credit year shall be the average annual gross receipts for the number of taxable years preceding the credit year for which the taxpayer has been in existence.

(b) Special rules for short taxable years. *(1) Short credit year.* If a credit year is a short taxable year, then the base amount determined under section 41(c)(1) (but not section 41(c)(2)) shall be modified by multiplying that amount by the number of months in the short taxable year and dividing the result by 12.

(2) Short taxable year preceding credit year. If one or more of the four taxable years preceding the credit year is a short taxable year, then the gross receipts for such year are deemed to be equal to the gross receipts actually derived in that year multiplied by 12 and divided by the number of months in that year.

(3) Short taxable year in determining fixed-base percentage. No adjustment shall be made on account of a short taxable year to the computation of a taxpayer's fixed-base percentage.

(c) Definition of gross receipts.

(1) In general. For purposes of section 41, gross receipts means the total amount, as determined under the taxpayer's method of accounting, derived by the taxpayer from all its activities and from all sources (e.g., revenues derived from the sale of inventory before reduction for cost of goods sold).

(2) Amounts excluded. For purposes of this paragraph (c), gross receipts do not include amounts representing—

(i) Returns or allowances;

(ii) Receipts from the sale or exchange of capital assets, as defined in section 1221;

(iii) Repayments of loans or similar instruments (e.g., a repayment of the principal amount of a loan held by a commercial lender);

(iv) Receipts from a sale or exchange not in the ordinary course of business, such as the sale of an entire trade or business or the sale of property used in a trade or business as defined under section 1221(2);

(v) Amounts received with respect to sales tax or other similar state and local taxes if, under the applicable state or local law, the tax is legally imposed on the purchaser of the good or service, and the taxpayer merely collects and remits the tax to the taxing authority; and

(vi) Amounts received by a taxpayer in a taxable year that precedes the first taxable year in which the taxpayer derives more than $25,000 in gross receipts other than investment income. For purposes of this paragraph (c)(2)(vi), investment income is interest or distributions with respect to stock (other than the stock of a 20-percent owned corporation as defined in section 243(c)(2).

(3) Foreign corporations. For purposes of section 41, in the case of a foreign corporation, gross receipts include only gross receipts that are effectively connected with the conduct of a trade or business within the United States, the Commonwealth of Puerto Rico, or other possessions of the United States. See section 864(c) and applicable regulations thereunder for the definition of effectively connected income.

(d) Consistency requirement. *(1) In general.* In computing the credit for increasing research activities for taxable years beginning after December 31, 1989, qualified research expenses and gross receipts taken into account in computing a taxpayer's fixed-base percentage and a taxpayer's base amount must be determined on a basis consistent with the definition of qualified research expenses and gross receipts for the credit year, without regard to the law in effect for the taxable years taken into account in computing the fixed-base percentage or the base amount. This consistency requirement applies even if the period for filing a claim for credit or refund has expired for any taxable year taken into account in computing the fixed-base percentage or the base amount.

(2) Illustrations. The following examples illustrate the application of the consistency rule of paragraph (d)(1) of this section:

Example (1). (i) X, an accrual method taxpayer using the calendar year as its taxable year, incurs qualified research expenses in 2001. X wants to compute its research credit under section 41 for the tax year ending December 31, 2001. As part of the computation, X must determine its fixed-base percentage, which depends in part on X's qualified research expenses incurred during the fixed-base period, the taxable years beginning after December 31, 1983, and before January 1, 1989.

(ii) During the fixed-base period, X reported the following amounts as qualified research expenses on its Form 6765:

1984	$100x
1985	120x
1986	150x
1987	180x
1988	170x
Total	720x

(iii) For the taxable years ending December 31, 1984, and December 31, 1985, X based the amounts reported as qualified research expenses on the definition of qualified research in effect for those taxable years. The definition of qualified research changed for taxable years beginning after December 31, 1985. If X used the definition of qualified research applicable to its taxable year ending December 31, 2001, the credit year, its qualified research expenses for the taxable years ending December 31, 1984, and December 31, 1985, would be reduced to $ 80x and $ 100x, respectively. Under the consistency rule in section 41(c)(5) and paragraph (d)(1) of this section, to compute the research credit for the tax year ending December 31, 2001, X must reduce its qualified research expenses for 1984 and 1985 to reflect the change in the definition of qualified research for taxable years beginning after December 31, 1985. Thus, X's total qualified research expenses for the fixed-base period (1984-1988) to be used in computing the fixed-base percentage is $80 + 100 + 150 + 180 + 170 = $680x.

Example (2). The facts are the same as in Example 1, except that, in computing its qualified research expenses for the taxable year ending December 31, 2001, X claimed that a certain type of expenditure incurred in 2001 was a qualified research expense. X's claim reflected a change in X's position, because X had not previously claimed that similar expenditures were qualified research expenses. The consistency rule requires X to adjust its qualified research expenses in computing the fixed-base percentage to include any similar expenditures not treated as qualified research expenses during the fixed-base period, regardless of whether the period for filing a claim for credit or refund has expired for any year taken into account in computing the fixed-base percentage.

(e) Effective date. The rules in paragraphs (c) and (d) of this section are applicable for taxable years beginning on or after the date final regulations are published in the Federal Register.

T.D. 8930, 12/27/2000.

§ 1.41-3A Base period research expense.

Caution: The Treasury has not yet amended Reg § 1.41-3A to reflect changes made by 110-458, P.L. 105-34, P.L. 103-66, P.L. 101-239.

• ***Caution:*** In Notice 2001-19, 2001-10 IRB, IRS announced that these final regs, issued as TD 8930, are under review. Notice 2001-19 says that "[U]pon completion of the review, Treasury and IRS will announce changes to the regulations, if any, in the form of proposed regulations. In addition, TD 8930 will be revised so that the provisions of the regulations, including any changes to TD 8930, will be effective no earlier than the date when the completion of this review is announced, except that the provisions related to internal-use computer software (including any revisions) generally will be applicable for taxable years beginning after December 31, 1985." Notice 2001-19 also says that taxpayers may continue to rely on these final regs during the pendency of this review."

(a) Number of years in base period. The term "base period" generally means the 3 taxable years immediately preceding the year for which a credit is being determined ("determination year"). However, if the first taxable year of the taxpayer ending after June 30, 1981, ends in 1981 or 1982, then with respect to that taxable year the term "base period" means the immediately preceding taxable year. If the second taxable year of the taxpayer ending after June 30, 1981, ends in 1982 or 1983, then with respect to that taxable year the term "base period" means the 2 immediately preceding taxable years.

(b) New taxpayers. If, with respect to any determination year, the taxpayer has not been in existence for the number of preceding taxable years that are included under paragraph (a) of this section in the base period for that year, then for purposes of paragraph (c)(1) of this section (relating to the determination of average qualified research expenses during the base period), the taxpayer shall be treated as—

(1) Having been in existence for that number of additional 12-month taxable years that is necessary to complete the base period specified in paragraph (a) of this section, and

(2) Having had qualified research expenses of zero in each of those additional years.

(c) Definition of base period research expenses. For any determination year, the term "base period research expenses" means the greater of—

(1) The average qualified research expenses for taxable years during the base period, or

(2) Fifty percent of the qualified research expenses for the determination year.

(d) Special rules for short taxable years. *(1) Short determination year.* If the determination year for which a research credit is being taken is a short taxable year, the amount taken into account under paragraph (c)(1) of this section shall be modified by multiplying that amount by the number of months in the short taxable year and dividing the result by 12.

(2) Short base period year. For purposes of paragraph (c)(1) of this section, if a year in the base period is a short taxable year, the qualified research expenses paid or incurred in the short taxable year are deemed to be equal to the qualified research expenses actually paid or incurred in that year multiplied by 12 and divided by the number of months in that year.

(3) Years overlapping the effective dates of section 41 (section 44F). (i) Determination years. If a determination year includes months before July 1981, the determination year is deemed to be a short taxable year including only the months after June 1981. Accordingly, paragraph (d)(1) of this section is applied for purposes of determining the base period expenses for such year. See section 221(d)(2) of the Economic Recovery Tax Act of 1981.

(ii) Base period years. No adjustment is required in the case of a base period year merely because it overlaps June 30, 1981.

(4) Number of months in a short taxable year. The number of months in a short taxable year is equal to the number of whole calendar months contained in the year plus fractions for any partially included months. The fraction for a partially included month is equal to the number of days in the month that are included in the short taxable year divided by the total number of days in that month. Thus, if a short taxable year begins on January 1, 1982, and ends on June 9, 1982, it consists of 5 and 9/30 months.

(e) Examples. The following examples illustrate the application of this section.

Example (1). X Corp., an accrual-method taxpayer using the calendar year as its taxable year, is organized and begins carrying on a trade or business during 1979 and subsequently incurs qualified research expenses as follows:

1979	$ 10x
1980	150x
1/1/81—6/30/81	90x
7/1/81—12/31/81	110x
1982	250x
1983	450x

(i) Determination year 1981. For determination year 1981, the base period consists of the immediately preceding taxable year, calendar year 1980. Because the determination year includes months before July 1981, paragraph (d)(3)(i) requires that the determination year be treated as a short taxable year. Thus, for purposes of paragraph (c)(1), as modified by paragraph (d)(1), the average qualified research expenses for taxable years during the base period are $75x ($150x, the average qualified research expenses for the base period, multiplied by 6, the number of months in the determination year after June 30, 1981, and divided by 12). Because this amount is greater than the amount determined under paragraph (c)(2) (50 percent of the determination year's qualified research expense of $110x, or $55x), the amount of base period research expenses is $75x. The credit for determination year 1981 is equal to 25 percent of the excess of $110x (the qualified research expenditures incurred during the determination year including only expenditures accrued on or after July 1, 1981, through the end of the determination year) over $75x (the base period research expenses).

(ii) Determination year 1982. For determination year 1982, the base period consists of the 2 immediately preceding taxable years, 1980 and 1981. The amount determined under paragraph (c)(1) of this section (the average qualified research expenses for taxable years during the base period) is $175x (($150x + $90x + $110x)/2). This amount is greater than the amount determined under paragraph (c)(2) (50 percent of $250x, or $125x). Accordingly, the amount of base period research expenses is $175x. The credit for determination year 1982 is equal to 25 percent of the excess of $250x (the qualified research expenses incurred during the determination year) over $175x (the base period research expenses).

(iii) Determination year 1983. For determination year 1983, the base period consists of the 3 immediately preceding taxable years 1980, 1981 and 1982. The amount determined under paragraph (c)(1) of this section (the average qualified research expenses for taxable years during the base period) is $200x (($150x + $200x + $250x)/3). The amount determined under paragraph (c)(2) is $225x (50 percent of the $450x of qualified research expenses in 1983). Accordingly, the amount of base period research expenses is $225x. The credit for determination year 1983 is equal to 25 percent of the excess of $450x (the qualified research expenses incurred during the determination year) over $225x (the base period research expenses).

Example (2). Y, an accrual-basis corporation using the calendar year as its taxable year comes into existence and begins carrying on a trade or business on July 1, 1983. Y incurs qualified research expenses as follows:

7/1/83—12/31/83	$ 80x
1984	200x
1985	200x

(i) Determination year 1983. For determination year 1983, the base period consists of the 3 immediately preceding taxable years: 1980, 1981 and 1982. Although Y was not in existence during 1980, 1981 and 1982, Y is treated under paragraph (b) of this section as having been in existence during those years with qualified research expenses of zero. Thus, the amount determined under paragraph (c)(1) of this section (the average qualified research expenses for taxable years during the base period) is $0x (($0x + $0x + $0x)/3). The amount determined under paragraph (c)(2) of this section is $40x (50 percent of $80x). Accordingly, the amount of base period research expenses is $40x. The credit for determination year 1983 is equal to 25 percent of the excess of $80x (the qualified research expenses incurred during the determination year) over $40x (the base period research expenses).

(ii) Determination year 1984. For determination year 1984, the base period consists of the 3 immediately preceding taxable years: 1981, 1982, and 1983. Under paragraph (b) of this section, Y is treated as having been in existence during years 1981 and 1982 with qualified research expenses of zero. Because July 1 through December 31, 1983 is a short taxable year, paragraph (d)(2) of this section requires that the qualified research expenses for that year be adjusted to $160x for purposes of determining the average qualified research expenses during the base period. The $160x results from the actual qualified research expenses for that year ($80x) multiplied by 12 and divided by 6 (the number of months in the short taxable year). Accordingly, the amount determined under paragraph (c)(1) of this section (the average qualified research expenses for taxable years during the base period) is $53⅓x (($0x + $0x + $160x)/3). The amount determined under paragraph (c)92) of this section is $100x (50 percent of $200x). The amount of the base period research expenses is $100x. The credit for determination year 1984 is equal to 25 percent of the excess of $200x (the qualified research expenses incurred during the determination year) over $100x (the base period research expenses).

(iii) Determination year 1985. For determination year 1985, the base period consists of the 3 immediately preceding taxable years: 1982, 1983, and 1984. Pursuant to paragraph (b) of this section, Y is treated as having been in existence during 1982 with qualified research expenses of zero. Because July 1 through December 31, 1982, is a short taxable year, paragraph (d)(2) of this section requires that the qualified research expense for that year be adjusted to $160x for purposes of determining the average qualified research expenses for taxable years during the base period. This $160x is the actual qualified research expense for that year ($80x) multiplied by 12 and divided by 6 (the number of months in the short taxable year). Accordingly, the amount determined under paragraph (c)(1) of this section (the average qualified research expenses for taxable years during the base period) is $120x (($0x + $160x + $200x)/3). The amount determined under paragraph (c)(2) of this section is $100x (50 percent of $200x). The amount of base period research expenses is $120x. The credit for determination year 1985 is equal to 25 percent of the excess of $200x (the qualified research expenses incurred during the determination year) over $120x (the base period research expenses).

T.D. 8251, 5/16/89, amend T.D. 8930, 12/27/2000.

§ 1.41-4 Qualified research for expenditures paid or incurred in taxable years ending on or after December 31, 2003.

Caution: The Treasury has not yet amended Reg § 1.41-4 to reflect changes made by 110-458, P.L. 98-369, P.L. 101-239.

(a) Qualified research. *(1) General rule.* Research activities related to the development or improvement of a business component constitute qualified research only if the research activities meet all of the requirements of section 41(d)(1) and this section, and are not otherwise excluded under section 41(d)(3)(B) or (d)(4), or this section.

(2) Requirements of section 41(d)(1). Research constitutes qualified research only if it is research—

(i) With respect to which expenditures may be treated as expenses under section 174, see § 1.174-2;

(ii) That is undertaken for the purpose of discovering information that is technological in nature, and the application of which is intended to be useful in the development of a new or improved business component of the taxpayer; and

(iii) Substantially all of the activities of which constitute elements of a process of experimentation that relates to a qualified purpose.

For certain recordkeeping requirements, see paragraph (d) of this section.

(3) Undertaken for the purpose of discovering information. (i) In general. For purposes of section 41(d) and this section, research must be undertaken for the purpose of discovering information that is technological in nature. Research is undertaken for the purpose of discovering information if it is intended to eliminate uncertainty concerning the development or improvement of a business component. Uncertainty exists if the information available to the taxpayer does not establish the capability or method for developing or improving the business component, or the appropriate design of the business component.

(ii) Application of the discovering information requirement. A determination that research is undertaken for the purpose of discovering information that is technological in nature does not require the taxpayer be seeking to obtain information that exceeds, expands or refines the common knowledge of skilled professionals in the particular field of science or engineering in which the taxpayer is performing the research. In addition, a determination that research is undertaken for the purpose of discovering information that is technological in nature does not require that the taxpayer succeed in developing a new or improved business component.

(iii) Patent safe harbor. For purposes of section 41(d) and paragraph (a)(3)(i) of this section, the issuance of a patent by the Patent and Trademark Office under the provisions of 35 U.S.C. 151 (other than a patent for design issued under the provisions of 35 U.S.C. 171) is conclusive evidence that a taxpayer has discovered information that is technological in nature that is intended to eliminate uncertainty concerning the development or improvement of a business component. However, the issuance of such a patent is not a precondition for credit availability.

(4) Technological in nature. For purposes of section 41(d) and this section, information is technological in nature if the process of experimentation used to discover such information fundamentally relies on principles of the physical or biological sciences, engineering, or computer science. A taxpayer may employ existing technologies and may rely on existing principles of the physical or biological sciences, engineering, or computer science to satisfy this requirement.

(5) Process of experimentation. (i) In general. For purposes of section 41(d) and this section, a process of experimentation is a process designed to evaluate one or more alternatives to achieve a result where the capability or the method of achieving that result, or the appropriate design of that result, is uncertain as of the beginning of the taxpayer's research activities. A process of experimentation must fundamentally rely on the principles of the physical or biological sciences, engineering, or computer science and involves the identification of uncertainty concerning the development or improvement of a business component, the identification of one or more alternatives intended to eliminate that uncertainty, and the identification and the conduct of a process of evaluating the alternatives (through, for example, modeling, simulation, or a systematic trial and error methodology). A process of experimentation must be an evaluative process and generally should be capable of evaluating more than one alternative. A taxpayer may undertake a process of experimentation if there is no uncertainty concerning the taxpayer's capability or method of achieving the desired result so long as the appropriate design of the desired result is uncertain as of the beginning of the taxpayer's research activities. Uncertainty concerning the development or improvement of the business component (e.g., its appropriate design) does not establish that all activities undertaken to achieve that new or improved business component constitute a process of experimentation.

(ii) Qualified purpose. For purposes of section 41(d) and this section, a process of experimentation is undertaken for a qualified purpose if it relates to a new or improved function, performance, reliability or quality of the business component. Research will not be treated as conducted for a qualified purpose if it relates to style, taste, cosmetic, or seasonal design factors.

(6) Substantially all requirement. In order for activities to constitute qualified research under section 41(d)(1), substantially all of the activities must constitute elements of a process of experimentation that relates to a qualified purpose. The substantially all requirement of section 41(d)(1)(C) and paragraph (a)(2)(iii) of this section is satisfied only if 80 percent or more of a taxpayer's research activities, measured on a cost or other consistently applied reasonable basis (and without regard to section 1.41-2(d)(2)), constitute elements of a process of experimentation for a purpose described in section 41(d)(3). Accordingly, if 80 percent (or more) of a taxpayer's research activities with respect to a business component constitute elements of a process of experimentation for a purpose described in section 41(d)(3), the substantially all requirement is satisfied even if the remaining 20 percent (or less) of a taxpayer's research activities with respect to the business component do not constitute elements of a process of experimentation for a purpose described in section 41(d)(3), so long as these remaining research activities satisfy the requirements of section 41(d)(1)(A) and are not otherwise excluded under section 41(d)(4). The substantially all requirement is applied separately to each business component.

(7) Use of computers and information technology. The employment of computers or information technology, or the reliance on principles of computer science or information technology to store, collect, manipulate, translate, disseminate, produce, distribute, or process data or information, and similar uses of computers and information technology does not itself establish that qualified research has been undertaken.

(8) Illustrations. The following examples illustrate the application of paragraph (a)(5) of this section:

Example (1). (i) Facts. X is engaged in the business of developing and manufacturing widgets. X wants to change the color of its blue widget to green. X obtains from various suppliers several different shades of green paint. X paints several sample widgets, and surveys X's customers to determine which shade of green X's customers prefer.

(ii) Conclusion. X's activities to change the color of its blue widget to green are not qualified research under section 41(d)(1) and paragraph (a)(5) of this section because substantially all of X's activities are not undertaken for a qualified purpose. All of X's research activities are related to style, taste, cosmetic, or seasonal design factors.

Example (2). (i) Facts. The facts are the same as in Example 1, except that X chooses one of the green paints. X obtains samples of the green paint from a supplier and determines that X must modify its painting process to accommodate the green paint because the green paint has different characteristics from other paints X has used. X obtains detailed data on the green paint from X's paint supplier. X also consults with the manufacturer of X's paint spraying machines. The manufacturer informs X that X must acquire a new nozzle that operates with the green paint X wants to use. X tests the nozzles to ensure that they work as specified by the manufacturer of the paint spraying machines.

(ii) Conclusion. X's activities to modify its painting process are a separate business component under section 41(d)(2)(A). X's activities to modify its painting process to change the color of its blue widget to green are not qualified research under section 41(d)(1) and paragraph (a)(5) of this section. X did not conduct a process of evaluating alternatives in order to eliminate uncertainty regarding the modification of its painting process. Rather, the manufacturer of the paint machines eliminated X's uncertainty regarding the modification of its painting process. X's activities to test the nozzles to determine if the nozzles work as specified by the manufacturer of the paint spraying machines are in the nature of routine or ordinary testing or inspection for quality control.

Example (3). (i) Facts. X is engaged in the business of manufacturing food products and currently manufactures a large-shred version of a product. X seeks to modify its current production line to permit it to manufacture both a large-shred version and a fine-shred version of one of its food products. A smaller, thinner shredding blade capable of producing a fine-shred version of the food product, however, is not commercially available. Thus, X must develop a new shredding blade that can be fitted onto its current production line. X is uncertain concerning the design of the new shredding blade, because the material used in its existing blade breaks when machined into smaller, thinner blades. X engages in a systematic trial and error process of analyzing various blade designs and materials to determine whether the new shredding blade must be constructed of a different material from that of its existing shredding blade and, if so, what material will best meet X's functional requirements.

(ii) Conclusion. X's activities to modify its current production line by developing the new shredding blade meet the requirements of qualified research as set forth in paragraph (a)(2) of this section. Substantially all of X's activities constitute elements of a process of experimentation because X evaluated alternatives to achieve a result where the method of achieving that result, and the appropriate design of that result, were uncertain as of the beginning of the taxpayer's research activities. X identified uncertainties related to the development of a business component, and identified alternatives intended to eliminate these uncertainties. Furthermore, X's process of evaluating identified alternatives was technological in nature, and was undertaken to eliminate the uncertainties.

Example (4). (i) Facts. X is in the business of designing, developing and manufacturing automobiles. In response to government-mandated fuel economy requirements, X seeks to update its current model vehicle and undertakes to improve aerodynamics by lowering the hood of its current model vehicle. X determines, however, that lowering the hood changes the air flow under the hood, which changes the rate at which air enters the engine through the air intake system, and which reduces the functionality of the cooling system. X's engineers are uncertain how to design a lower hood to obtain the increased fuel economy, while maintaining the necessary air flow under the hood. X designs, models, simulates, tests, refines, and re-tests several alternative designs for the hood and associated proposed modifications to both the air intake system and cooling system. This process enables X to eliminate the uncertainties related to the integrated design of the hood, air intake system, and cooling system, and such activities constitute eighty-five percent of X's total activities to update its current model vehicle. X then engages in additional activities that do not involve a process of evaluating alternatives in order to eliminate uncertainties. The additional activities constitute only fifteen percent of X's total activities to update its current model vehicle.

(ii) Conclusion. In general, if eighty percent or more of a taxpayer's research activities measured on a cost or other consistently applied reasonable basis constitute elements of a process of experimentation for a qualified purpose under section 41(d)(3)(A) and paragraph (a)(5)(ii) of this section, then the substantially all requirement of section 41(d)(1)(C) and paragraph (a)(2)(iii) of this section is satisfied. Substantially all of X's activities constitute elements of a process of experimentation because X evaluated alternatives to achieve a result where the method of achieving that result, and the appropriate design of that result, were uncertain as of the beginning of X's research activities. X identified uncertainties related to the improvement of a business component and identified alternatives intended to eliminate these uncertainties. Furthermore, X's process of evaluating the identified alternatives was technological in nature and was undertaken to eliminate the uncertainties. Because substantially all (in this example, eighty-five percent) of X's activities to update its current model vehicle constitute elements of a process of experimentation for a qualified purpose described in section 41(d)(3)(A), all of X's activities to update its current model vehicle meet the requirements of qualified research as set forth in paragraph (a)(2) of this section, provided that X's remaining activities (in this example, fifteen percent of X's total activities) satisfy the requirements of section 41(d)(1)(A) and are not otherwise excluded under section 41(d)(4).

(b) Application of requirements for qualified research. *(1) In general.* The requirements for qualified research in section 41(d)(1) and paragraph (a) of this section, must be applied separately to each business component, as defined in section 41(d)(2)(B). In cases involving development of both a product and a manufacturing or other commercial production process for the product, research activities relating to development of the process are not qualified research unless the requirements of section 41(d) and this section are met for the research activities relating to the process without taking into account the research activities relating to development of the product. Similarly, research activities relating to development of the product are not qualified research unless the requirements of section 41(d) and this section are met for the research activities relating to the product without taking into account the research activities relating to development of the manufacturing or other commercial production process.

(2) Shrinking-back rule. The requirements of section 41(d) and paragraph (a) of this section are to be applied first at the level of the discrete business component, that is, the product, process, computer software, technique, formula, or invention to be held for sale, lease, or license, or used by the taxpayer in a trade or business of the taxpayer. If these requirements are not met at that level, then they apply at the most significant subset of elements of the product, process, computer software, technique, formula, or invention to be held for sale, lease, or license. This shrinking back of the product is to continue until either a subset of elements of the product that satisfies the requirements is reached, or the most basic element of the product is reached and such element fails to satisfy the test. This shrinking-back rule is applied only if a taxpayer does not satisfy the requirements of section 41(d)(1) and paragraph (a)(2) of this section with respect to the overall business component. The shrinking-back rule is not itself applied as a reason to exclude research activities from credit eligibility.

(3) Illustration. The following example illustrates the application of this paragraph (b):

Example. X, a motorcycle engine builder, develops a new carburetor for use in a motorcycle engine. X also modifies an existing engine design for use with the new carburetor. Under the shrinking-back rule, the requirements of section 41(d)(1) and paragraph (a) of this section are applied first to the engine. If the modifications to the engine when viewed as a whole, including the development of the new carburetor, do not satisfy the requirements of section 41(d)(1) and paragraph (a) of this section, those requirements are applied to the next most significant subset of elements of the business component. Assuming that the next most significant subset of elements of the engine is the carburetor, the research activities in developing the new carburetor may constitute qualified research within the meaning of section 41(d)(1) and paragraph (a) of this section.

(c) Excluded activities. *(1) In general.* Qualified research does not include any activity described in section 41(d)(4) and paragraph (c) of this section.

(2) Research after commercial production. (i) In general. Activities conducted after the beginning of commercial production of a business component are not qualified research. Activities are conducted after the beginning of commercial production of a business component if such activities are conducted after the component is developed to the point where it is ready for commercial sale or use, or meets the basic functional and economic requirements of the taxpayer for the component's sale or use.

(ii) Certain additional activities related to the business component. The following activities are deemed to occur after the beginning of commercial production of a business component—

(A) Preproduction planning for a finished business component;

(B) Tooling-up for production;

(C) Trial production runs;

(D) Trouble shooting involving detecting faults in production equipment or processes;

(E) Accumulating data relating to production processes; and

(F) Debugging flaws in a business component.

(iii) Activities related to production process or technique. In cases involving development of both a product and a manufacturing or other commercial production process for the product, the exclusion described in section 41(d)(4)(A) and paragraphs (c)(2)(i) and (ii) of this section applies separately for the activities relating to the development of the product and the activities relating to the development of the process. For example, even after a product meets the taxpayer's basic functional and economic requirements, activities relating to the development of the manufacturing process still may constitute qualified research, provided that the development of the process itself separately satisfies the requirements of section 41(d) and this section, and the activities are conducted before the process meets the taxpayer's basic functional and economic requirements or is ready for commercial use.

(iv) Clinical testing. Clinical testing of a pharmaceutical product prior to its commercial production in the United States is not treated as occurring after the beginning of commercial production even if the product is commercially available in other countries. Additional clinical testing of a pharmaceutical product after a product has been approved for a specific therapeutic use by the Food and Drug Administration and is ready for commercial production and sale is not treated as occurring after the beginning of commercial production if such clinical testing is undertaken to establish new functional uses, characteristics, indications, combinations, dosages, or delivery forms for the product. A functional use, characteristic, indication, combination, dosage, or delivery form shall be considered new only if such functional use, characteristic, indication, combination, dosage, or delivery form must be approved by the Food and Drug Administration.

(3) Adaptation of existing business components. Activities relating to adapting an existing business component to a particular customer's requirement or need are not qualified research. This exclusion does not apply merely because a business component is intended for a specific customer.

(4) Duplication of existing business component. Activities relating to reproducing an existing business component (in whole or in part) from a physical examination of the business component itself or from plans, blueprints, detailed specifications, or publicly available information about the business component are not qualified research. This exclusion does not apply merely because the taxpayer examines an existing business component in the course of developing its own business component.

(5) Surveys, studies, research relating to management functions, etc. Qualified research does not include activities relating to—

(i) Efficiency surveys;

(ii) Management functions or techniques, including such items as preparation of financial data and analysis, development of employee training programs and management organization plans, and management-based changes in production processes (such as rearranging work stations on an assembly line);

(iii) Market research, testing, or development (including advertising or promotions);

(iv) Routine data collections; or

(v) Routine or ordinary testing or inspections for quality control.

(6) Internal use software for taxable years beginning on or after December 31, 1985. [Reserved].

(7) Activities outside the United States, Puerto Rico, and other possessions. (i) In general. Research conducted outside the United States, as defined in section 7701(a)(9), the Commonwealth of Puerto Rico and other possessions of the United States does not constitute qualified research.

(ii) Apportionment of in-house research expenses. In-house research expenses paid or incurred for qualified services performed both in the United States, the Commonwealth of Puerto Rico and other possessions of the United States and outside the United States, the Commonwealth of Puerto Rico and other possessions of the United States must be apportioned between the services performed in the United States, the Commonwealth of Puerto Rico and other possessions of the United States and the services performed outside the United States, the Commonwealth of Puerto Rico and other possessions of the United States. Only those in-house research expenses apportioned to the services performed within the United States, the Commonwealth of Puerto Rico and other possessions of the United States are eligible to be treated as qualified research expenses, unless the in-house research expenses are wages and the 80 percent rule of § 1.41-2(d)(2) applies.

(iii) Apportionment of contract research expenses. If contract research is performed partly in the United States, the Commonwealth of Puerto Rico and other possessions of the United States and partly outside the United States, the Commonwealth of Puerto Rico and other possessions of the United States, only 65 percent (or 75 percent in the case of amounts paid to qualified research consortia) of the portion of the contract amount that is attributable to the research activity performed in the United States, the Commonwealth of Puerto Rico and other possessions of the United States may qualify as a contract research expense (even if 80 percent or more of the contract amount is for research performed in the United States, the Commonwealth of Puerto Rico and other possessions of the United States).

(8) Research in the social sciences, etc. Qualified research does not include research in the social sciences (including economics, business management, and behavioral sciences), arts, or humanities.

(9) Research funded by any grant, contract, or otherwise. Qualified research does not include any research to the extent funded by any grant, contract, or otherwise by another person (or governmental entity). To determine the extent to which research is so funded, § 1.41-4A(d) applies.

(10) Illustrations. The following examples illustrate provisions contained in paragraphs (c)(1) through (9) (excepting paragraphs (c)(6) of this section) of this section. No inference should be drawn from these examples concerning the application of section 41(d)(1) and paragraph (a) of this section to these facts. The examples are as follows:

Example (1). (i) Facts. X, a tire manufacturer, develops a new material to use in its tires. X conducts research to determine the changes that will be necessary for X to modify its existing manufacturing processes to manufacture the new tire. X determines that the new tire material retains heat for a longer period of time than the materials X currently uses for tires, and, as a result, the new tire material adheres to the manufacturing equipment during tread cooling. X evaluates several alternatives for processing the treads at cooler temperatures to address this problem, including a new type of belt for its manufacturing equipment to be used in tread cooling. Such a belt is not commercially available. Because X is uncertain of the belt design, X develops and conducts sophisticated engineering tests on several alternative designs for a new type of belt to be used in tread cooling until X successfully achieves a design that meets X's requirements. X then manufactures a set of belts for its production equipment, installs the belts, and tests the belts to make sure they were manufactured correctly.

(ii) Conclusion. X's research with respect to the design of the new belts to be used in its manufacturing of the new tire may be qualified research under section 41(d)(1) and paragraph (a) of this section. However, X's expenses to implement the new belts, including the costs to manufacture, install, and test the belts were incurred after the belts met the taxpayer's functional and economic requirements and are excluded as research after commercial production under section 41(d)(4)(A) and paragraph (c)(2) of this section.

Example (2). (i) Facts. For several years, X has manufactured and sold a particular kind of widget. X initiates a new research project to develop a new or improved widget.

(ii) Conclusion. X's activities to develop a new or improved widget are not excluded from the definition of qualified research under section 41(d)(4)(A) and paragraph (c)(2) of this section. X's activities relating to the development of a new or improved widget constitute a new research project to develop a new business component. X's research activities relating to the development of the new or improved widget, a new business component, are not considered to be activities conducted after the beginning of commercial production under section 41(d)(4)(A) and paragraph (c)(2) of this section.

Example (3). (i) Facts. X, a computer software development firm, owns all substantial rights in a general ledger accounting software core program that X markets and licenses to customers. X incurs expenditures in adapting the core software program to the requirements of C, one of X's customers.

(ii) Conclusion. Because X's activities represent activities to adapt an existing software program to a particular customer's requirement or need, X's activities are excluded from the definition of qualified research under section 41(d)(4)(B) and paragraph (c)(3) of this section.

Example (4). (i) Facts. The facts are the same as in Example 3, except that C pays X to adapt the core software program to C's requirements.

(ii) Conclusion. Because X's activities are excluded from the definition of qualified research under section 41(d)(4)(B) and paragraph (c)(3) of this section, C's payments to X are not for qualified research and are not considered to be contract research expenses under section 41(b)(3)(A).

Example (5). (i) Facts. The facts are the same as in Example 3, except that C's own employees adapt the core software program to C's requirements.

(ii) Conclusion. Because C's employees' activities to adapt the core software program to C's requirements are excluded from the definition of qualified research under section 41(d)(4)(B) and paragraph (c)(3) of this section, the wages C paid to its employees do not constitute in-house research expenses under section 41(b)(2)(A).

Example (6). (i) Facts. X manufacturers and sells rail cars. Because rail cars have numerous specifications related to performance, reliability and quality, rail car designs are subject to extensive, complex testing in the scientific or laboratory sense. B orders passenger rail cars from X. B's rail car requirements differ from those of X's other existing customers only in that B wants fewer seats in its passenger cars and a higher quality seating material and carpet that are commercially available. X manufactures rail cars meeting B's requirements.

(ii) Conclusion. X's activities to manufacture rail cars for B are excluded from the definition of qualified research. The rail car sold to B was not a new business component, but merely an adaptation of an existing business component that did not require a process of experimentation. Thus, X's activities to manufacture rail cars for B are excluded from the definition of qualified research under section 41(d)(4)(B) and paragraph (c)(3) of this section because X's activities represent activities to adapt an existing business component to a particular customer's requirement or need.

Example (7). (i) Facts. X, a manufacturer, undertakes to create a manufacturing process for a new valve design. X determines that it requires a specialized type of robotic equipment to use in the manufacturing process for its new valves. Such robotic equipment is not commercially available, and X, therefore, purchases the existing robotic equipment for the purpose of modifying it to meet its needs. X's engineers identify uncertainty that is technological in nature concerning how to modify the existing robotic equipment to meet its needs. X's engineers develop several alternative designs, and conduct experiments using modeling and simulation in modifying the robotic equipment and conduct extensive scientific and laboratory testing of design alternatives. As a result of this process, X's engineers develop a design for the robotic equipment that meets X's needs. X constructs and installs the modified robotic equipment on its manufacturing process.

(ii) Conclusion. X's research activities to determine how to modify X's robotic equipment for its manufacturing process are not excluded from the definition of qualified research under section 41(d)(4)(B) and paragraph (c)(3) of this section, provided that X's research activities satisfy the requirements of section 41(d)(1).

Example (8). (i) Facts. An existing gasoline additive is manufactured by Y using three ingredients, A, B, and C. X seeks to develop and manufacture its own gasoline additive that appears and functions in a manner similar to Y's additive. To develop its own additive, X first inspects the composition of Y's additive, and uses knowledge gained from the inspection to reproduce A and B in the laboratory. Any differences between ingredients A and B that are used in Y's additive and those reproduced by X are insignificant and are not material to the viability, effectiveness, or cost of A and B. X desires to use with A and B an ingredient that has a materially lower cost than ingredient C. Accordingly, X engages in a process of experimentation to develop, analyze and test potential alternative formulations of the additive.

(ii) Conclusion. X's activities in analyzing and reproducing ingredients A and B involve duplication of existing business components and are excluded from the definition of qualified research under section 41(d)(4)(C) and paragraph (c)(4) of this section. X's experimentation activities to develop potential alternative formulations of the additive do not involve duplication of an existing business component and are not excluded from the definition of qualified research under section 41(d)(4)(C) and paragraph (c)(4) of this section.

Example (9). (i) Facts. X, a manufacturing corporation, undertakes to restructure its manufacturing organization. X organizes a team to design an organizational structure that will improve X's business operations. The team includes X's employees as well as outside management consultants. The team studies current operations, interviews X's employees, and studies the structure of other manufacturing facilities to determine appropriate modifications to X's current business operations. The team develops a recommendation of proposed modifications which it presents to X's management. X's management approves the team's recommendation and begins to implement the proposed modifications.

(ii) Conclusion. X's activities in developing and implementing the new management structure are excluded from the definition of qualified research under section 41(d)(4)(D) and paragraph (c)(5) of this section. Qualified research does not include activities relating to management functions or techniques including management organization plans and management-based changes in production processes.

Example (10). (i) Facts. X, an insurance company, develops a new life insurance product. In the course of developing the product, X engages in research with respect to the effect of pricing and tax consequences on demand for the product, the expected volatility of interest rates, and the expected mortality rates (based on published data and prior insurance claims).

(ii) Conclusion. X's activities related to the new product represent research in the social sciences (including economics and business management) and are thus excluded from the definition of qualified research under section 41(d)(4)(G) and paragraph (c)(8) of this section.

(d) Recordkeeping for the research credit. A taxpayer claiming a credit under section 41 must retain records in sufficiently usable form and detail to substantiate that the expenditures claimed are eligible for the credit. For the rules governing record retention, see § 1.6001-1. To facilitate compliance and administration, the IRS and taxpayers may agree to guidelines for the keeping of specific records for purposes of substantiating research credits.

(e) Effective dates. This section is applicable for taxable years ending on or after December 31, 2003.

T.D. 8930, 12/27/2000, amend T.D. 9104, 12/30/2003.

PAR. 4. Section 1.41-4 is revised to read as follows:

Proposed § 1.41-4 Qualified research for expenditures paid or incurred in taxable years ending on or after December 26, 2001. [*For Preamble, see ¶ 152,211*]

• ***Caution:*** This Notice of Proposed Rulemaking was partially finalized by TD 9104, 12/30/2003, except for proposed regulation § 1.41-4(c)(6).

(a) Qualified research. *(1) General rule.* Research activities related to the development or improvement of a business component constitute qualified research only if the research activities meet all of the requirements of section 41(d)(1) and this section, and are not otherwise excluded under section 41(d)(3)(B) or (d)(4), or this section.

(2) Requirements of section 41(d)(1). Research constitutes qualified research only if it is research—

(i) With respect to which expenditures may be treated as expenses under section 174, see § 1.174-2;

(ii) That is undertaken for the purpose of discovering information that is technological in nature, and the application of which is intended to be useful in the development of a new or improved business component of the taxpayer; and

(iii) Substantially all of the activities of which constitute elements of a process of experimentation that relates to a new or improved function, performance, reliability or quality.

(3) Undertaken for the purpose of discovering information. (i) In general. For purposes of section 41(d) and this section, research must be undertaken for the purpose of discovering information that is technological in nature. Research is undertaken for the purpose of discovering information if it is intended to eliminate uncertainty concerning the development or improvement of a business component. Uncertainty exists if the information available to the taxpayer does not establish the capability or method for developing or improving the business component, or the appropriate design of the business component.

(ii) Application of the discovering information requirement. A determination that research is undertaken for the purpose of discovering information that is technological in nature does not require the taxpayer be seeking to obtain information that exceeds, expands or refines the common knowledge of skilled professionals in the particular field of science or engineering in which the taxpayer is performing the research. In addition, a determination that research is undertaken for the purpose of discovering information that is technological in nature does not require that the taxpayer succeed in developing a new or improved business component.

(iii) Patent safe harbor. For purposes of section 41(d) and paragraph (a)(3)(i) of this section, the issuance of a patent by the Patent and Trademark Office under the provisions of 35 U.S.C. 151 (other than a patent for design issued under the provisions of 35 U.S.C. 171) is conclusive evidence that a taxpayer has discovered information that is technological in nature that is intended to eliminate uncertainty concerning the development or improvement of a business component. However, the issuance of such a patent is not a precondition for credit availability.

(4) Technological in nature. For purposes of section 41(d) and this section, information is technological in nature if the process of experimentation used to discover such information fundamentally relies on principles of the physical or biological sciences, engineering, or computer science. A taxpayer may employ existing technologies and may rely on existing principles of the physical or biological sciences, engineering, or computer science to satisfy this requirement.

(5) Process of experimentation. (i) In general. For purposes of section 41(d) and this section, a process of experimentation is a process designed to evaluate one or more alternatives to achieve a result where the capability or the method of achieving that result, or the appropriate design of that result, is uncertain as of the beginning of the taxpayer's research activities. Thus, a taxpayer may undertake a process of experimentation if there is no uncertainty concerning the taxpayer's capability or method of achieving the desired result so long as the appropriate design of the desired result is uncertain as of the beginning of the taxpayer's research activities. However, a process of experimentation does not include the evaluation of alternatives to achieve the desired result if the capability and method of achieving the desired result, and the appropriate design of the desired result, are readily discernible and applicable as of the beginning of the taxpayer's research activities. A process of experimentation may include developing one or more hypotheses designed to achieve the desired result, designing and conducting an experiment to test and analyze those hypotheses, and refining or discarding the hypotheses as part of a design process to develop or improve the business component. For purposes of this paragraph (a)(5), factors that tend to indicate that the taxpayer has engaged in a process of experimentation are listed in paragraph (a)(5)(iv) of this section.

(ii) Readily discernible capability, method and appropriate design. A taxpayer's activities do not constitute elements of a process of experimentation where the capability and method of achieving the desired new or improved business component, and the appropriate design of the desired new or improved business component, are readily discernible and applicable as of the beginning of the taxpayer's research activities, so that true experimentation in the scientific or laboratory sense would not have to be undertaken to test, analyze, and choose among viable alternatives. A process of experimentation does not include any activities to select among several alternatives that are readily discernible and applicable.

(iii) Qualified purpose. For purposes of section 41(d) and this section, a process of experimentation is undertaken for a qualified purpose if it relates to a new or improved function, performance, reliability or quality of the business component. Research will not be treated as conducted for a qualified purpose if it relates to style, taste, cosmetic, or seasonal design factors.

(iv) Factors tending to indicate that the taxpayer has engaged in a process of experimentation. For purposes of section 41(d) and this section, in determining whether a taxpayer has undertaken a process of experimentation, all facts and circumstances with respect to a taxpayer's research activities are taken into account. No one factor is dispositive in making this determination. Further, it is not intended that only the factors described in this paragraph are to be taken into account in making the determination. Thus, no inference should be drawn from the taxpayer's failure to satisfy any or all of the factors. Among the factors that tend to indicate that the taxpayer has engaged in a process of experimentation are—

(A) The taxpayer tests and analyzes numerous alternative hypotheses to develop a new or improved business component;

(B) The taxpayer engages in extensive, comprehensive, intricate or complex scientific or laboratory testing; or

(C) The taxpayer evaluates numerous or complex specifications related to the function, performance, reliability or quality of a new or improved business component.

(6) Substantially all requirement. (i) General rule. The substantially all requirement of section 41(d)(1)(C) and paragraph (a)(2)(iii) of this section is satisfied only if 80 percent or more of the research activities, measured on a cost or other consistently applied reasonable basis (and without regard to § 1.41-2(d)(2)), constitute elements of a process of experimentation for a purpose described in section 41(d)(3). The substantially all requirement is applied separately to each business component.

(ii) Illustrations. [Reserved]

(7) Use of computers and information technology. The employment of computers or information technology, or the reliance on principles of computer science or information technology to store, collect, manipulate, translate, disseminate, produce, distribute, or process data or information, and similar uses of computers and information technology does not itself establish that qualified research has been undertaken.

(8) Illustrations. The following examples illustrate the application of paragraph (a)(5) of this section:

Example (1). (i) Facts. X is engaged in the business of developing and manufacturing widgets. X wants to change the color of its blue widget to green. X obtains from various suppliers several different shades of green paint. X paints several sample widgets, and surveys X's customers to determine which shade of green X's customers prefer.

(ii) Conclusion. X's activities to change the color of its blue widget to green are not qualified research under section 41(d)(1) and paragraph (a)(5) of this section because substantially all of X's activities are not undertaken for a qualified purpose. All of X's research activities are related to style, taste, cosmetic, or seasonal design factors.

Example (2). (i) Facts. X is engaged in the business of manufacturing widgets and wants to change the color of its blue widget to green. X obtains samples of green paint from a supplier and determines that X must modify its painting process to accommodate the green paint because the green paint has different characteristics from other paints X has used. X obtains detailed data on the green paint from X's paint supplier. X also consults with the manufacturer of X's paint spraying machines and determines that X must acquire new nozzles that are designed to operate with paints similar to the green paint X wants to use. X installs the new nozzles on its paint spraying machines and tests the nozzles to ensure that they work as specified by the manufacturer of the paint spraying machines.

(ii) Conclusion. X's activities to modify its painting process relate to a separate business component under section 41(d)(2)(A). X's activities to modify its painting process by installing new nozzles on its paint spraying machines to change the color of its blue widget to green are not qualified research under section 41(d)(1) and paragraph (a)(5) of this section. The capability, method and appropriate design of the changes to X's painting process are readily discernible and applicable to X as of the beginning of X's activities. X's activities to test the nozzles to determine if the nozzles work as specified by the manufacturer of the paint spraying machines are not the type of testing activities that tend to indicate that a process of experimentation was undertaken.

Example (3). (i) Facts. X is engaged in the business of manufacturing food products and currently manufactures a large-shred version of a product. Because X's competitors manufacture both a large-shred and fine-shred version of comparable food products, X seeks to modify its current production line to permit it to manufacture both a large-shred version and fine-shred version of one of its own food products. A shredding blade capable of producing a fine-shred version of the food product is not commercially available. Thus, X must develop a new shredding blade that can be fitted onto X's current production line. X must test and analyze numerous alternative hypotheses to determine whether a new shredding blade must be constructed of a different material from that of its existing shredding blade. In addition, X must engage in comprehensive and complex scientific or laboratory testing to ensure that its modified production process, with the newly-developed shredding blade, can accommodate the manufacture of both the large-shred and fine-shred versions of X's food products.

(ii) Conclusion. X's activities to modify its current production line meet the requirements of qualified research as set forth in paragraph (a)(2) of this section. Substantially all of X's activities constitute elements of a process of experimentation because X must evaluate more than one alternative to achieve a result where the method and appropriate design are uncertain as of the beginning of the taxpayer's research activities. X must test and analyze numerous alternative hypotheses and engage in comprehensive and complex scientific or laboratory testing to ensure that its modified production process, with a newly-developed shredding blade, can accommodate the manufacture of both the large-shred and fine-shred versions of X's food products.

Example (4). (i) Facts. X operates wireless networks in several U.S. cities. X discovers in City a service problem and collects data on the nature of the problem. X analyzes the data and knows, based on its previous experience with wireless networks in other cities, that the installation of a new type of gateway will eliminate the problem. X installs the new gateway in its City network.

(ii) Conclusion. X's activities to determine a solution to its service problem are not qualified research under section 41(d)(1) and paragraph (a)(5) of this section. Substantially all of X's research activities do not constitute elements of a process of experimentation because the solution to the service problem is readily discernible and applicable by X as of the beginning of X's research activities.

Example (5). (i) Facts. X is engaged in the business of manufacturing and selling automobiles. X incorporated into one of its new vehicles a new exhaust system that it designed. After X offered the vehicle for sale, X received complaints of a rattling noise that could be heard in the passenger compartment. X's engineers determined that the cause of the noise was the exhaust system coming into contact with the undercarriage of the vehicle. Based on previous experience with similar noise problems, X's engineers knew of two safe, effective, reliable solutions that would eliminate the noise. X's engineers selected one of the solutions based on cost studies that indicated it would be the less expensive alternative.

(ii) Conclusion. X's activities to eliminate the rattling noise are not qualified research under section 41(d)(1) and paragraph (a)(5) of this section. Substantially all of X's research activities do not constitute elements of a process of experimentation because the solution is readily discernible and applicable to X as of the beginning of X's activities.

Example (6). (i) Facts. X is in the business of designing, developing and manufacturing automobiles and decides to update one of its current model vehicles. In response to government-mandated fuel economy requirements, X undertakes to improve aerodynamics by lowering the hood of the current model vehicle. X determines that lowering the hood changes the air flow under the hood, which changes the rate at which air enters the engine through the air intake system, and which reduces the functionality of the cooling system. X designs, models, tests, refines, and re-tests proposed modifications to both the air intake system and cooling system until modifications are developed that meet X's requirements. X then integrates the modified air intake and cooling systems into a current model vehicle with a lower hood, modifying in the process the new air intake and cooling systems as well as the underhood wiring, brake lines and fuel line. X conducts extensive and complex scientific or laboratory testing (including simulations and crash tests) to determine if the current model vehicle meets X's requirements.

(ii) Conclusion. X's activities to update its vehicle meet the requirements of qualified research as set forth in paragraph (a)(2) of this section. X must test and analyze numerous alternative hypotheses, engage in extensive testing and analysis, and evaluate complex specifications related to the functionality of several of the vehicle's underhood systems and to the vehicle's overall performance. These activities indicate that X undertook a process of experimentation to achieve the appropriate design of the updated vehicle.

(b) Application of requirements for qualified research. *(1) In general.* The requirements for qualified research in section 41(d)(1) and paragraph (a) of this section, must be applied separately to each business component, as defined in section 41(d)(2)(B). In cases involving development of both a product and a manufacturing or other commercial production process for the product, research activities relating to development of the process are not qualified research unless the requirements of section 41(d) and this section are met for the research activities relating to the process without taking into account the research activities relating to development of the product. Similarly, research activities relating to development of the product are not qualified research unless the requirements of section 41(d) and this section are met for the research activities relating to the product without taking into account the research activities relating to development of the manufacturing or other commercial production process.

(2) Shrinking-back rule. The requirements of section 41(d) and paragraph (a) of this section are to be applied first at the level of the discrete business component, that is, the product, process, computer software, technique, formula, or invention to be held for sale, lease, or license, or used by the taxpayer in a trade or business of the taxpayer. If the requirements for credit eligibility are met at that first level, then some or all of the taxpayer's qualified research expenses are eligible for the credit. If all aspects of such requirements are not met at that level, the test applies at the most significant subset of elements of the product, process, computer software, technique, formula, or invention to be held for sale, lease, or license. This shrinking back of the product is to continue until either a subset of elements of the product that satisfies the requirements is reached, or the most basic element of the product is reached and such element fails to satisfy the test. This shrinking-back rule is applied only if a taxpayer does not satisfy the requirements of section 41(d)(1) and paragraph (a)(2) of this section with respect to the overall business component. The shrinking-back rule is not itself applied as a reason to exclude research activities from credit eligibility.

(3) Illustration. The following example illustrates the application of this paragraph (b):

Example. X, a motorcycle engine builder, develops a new carburetor for use in a motorcycle engine. X also modifies an existing engine design for use with the new carburetor. Under the shrinking-back rule, the requirements of section 41(d)(1) and paragraph (a) of this section are applied first to the engine. If the modifications to the engine when viewed as a whole, including the development of the new carburetor, do not satisfy the requirements of section 41(d)(1) and paragraph (a) of this section, those requirements are applied to the next most significant subset of elements of the business component. Assuming that the next most significant subset of elements of the engine is the carburetor, the research activities in developing the new carburetor may constitute qualified research within the meaning of section 41(d)(1) and paragraph (a) of this section.

(c) Excluded activities. *(1) In general.* Qualified research does not include any activity described in section 41(d)(4) and paragraph (c) of this section.

(2) Research after commercial production. (i) In general. Activities conducted after the beginning of commercial production of a business component are not qualified research. Activities are conducted after the beginning of commercial production of a business component if such activities are conducted after the component is developed to the point where it is ready for commercial sale or use, or meets the basic functional and economic requirements of the taxpayer for the component's sale or use.

(ii) Certain additional activities related to the business component. The following activities are deemed to occur after the beginning of commercial production of a business component—

(A) Preproduction planning for a finished business component;

(B) Tooling-up for production;

(C) Trial production runs;

(D) Trouble shooting involving detecting faults in production equipment or processes;

(E) Accumulating data relating to production processes; and

(F) Debugging flaws in a business component.

(iii) Activities related to production process or technique. In cases involving development of both a product and a manufacturing or other commercial production process for the product, the exclusion described in section 41(d)(4)(A) and paragraphs (c)(2)(i) and (ii) of this section applies separately for the activities relating to the development of the product and the activities relating to the development of the process. For example, even after a product meets the taxpayer's basic functional and economic requirements, activities relating to the development of the manufacturing process still may constitute qualified research, provided that the development of the process itself separately satisfies the requirements of section 41(d) and this section, and the activities are conducted before the process meets the taxpayer's basic functional and economic requirements or is ready for commercial use.

(iv) Clinical testing. Clinical testing of a pharmaceutical product prior to its commercial production in the United States is not treated as occurring after the beginning of commercial production even if the product is commercially available in other countries. Additional clinical testing of a pharmaceutical product after a product has been approved for a specific therapeutic use by the Food and Drug Administration and is ready for commercial production and sale is not treated as occurring after the beginning of commercial production if such clinical testing is undertaken to establish new functional uses, characteristics, indications, combinations, dosages, or delivery forms for the product. A functional use, characteristic, indication, combination, dosage, or delivery form shall be considered new only if such functional use, characteristic, indication, combination, dosage, or delivery form must be approved by the Food and Drug Administration.

(3) Adaptation of existing business components. Activities relating to adapting an existing business component to a particular customer's requirement or need are not qualified research. This exclusion does not apply merely because a business component is intended for a specific customer.

(4) Duplication of existing business component. Activities relating to reproducing an existing business component (in whole or in part) from a physical examination of the business component itself or from plans, blueprints, detailed specifications, or publicly available information about the business component are not qualified research. This exclusion does not apply merely because the taxpayer examines an existing business component in the course of developing its own business component.

(5) Surveys, studies, research relating to management functions, etc. Qualified research does not include activities relating to—

(i) Efficiency surveys;

(ii) Management functions or techniques, including such items as preparation of financial data and analysis, development of employee training programs and management organization plans, and management-based changes in production processes (such as rearranging work stations on an assembly line);

(iii) Market research, testing, or development (including advertising or promotions);

(iv) Routine data collections; or

(v) Routine or ordinary testing or inspections for quality control.

(6) Internal use software for taxable years beginning on or after December 31, 1985. (i) General rule. Research with respect to computer software that is developed by (or for the benefit of) the taxpayer primarily for the taxpayer's internal use is eligible for the research credit only if the software satisfies the requirements of paragraph (c)(6)(ii) of this section.

(ii) Requirements. The requirements of this paragraph (c)(6)(ii) are—

(A) The software satisfies the requirements of section 41(d)(1);

(B) The software is not otherwise excluded under section 41(d)(4) (other than section 41(d)(4)(E)); and

(C) One of the following conditions is met—

(1) The taxpayer develops the software for use in an activity that constitutes qualified research (other than the development of the internal-use software itself);

(2) The taxpayer develops the software for use in a production process that satisfies the requirements of section 41(d)(1);

(3) The taxpayer develops the software for use in providing computer services to customers; or

(4) The software satisfies the high threshold of innovation test of paragraph (c)(6)(vi) of this section.

(iii) Computer software and hardware developed as a single product. This paragraph (c)(6) does not apply to the development costs of a new or improved package of computer software and hardware developed together by the taxpayer as a single product (or to the costs to modify an acquired computer software and hardware package), of which the software is an integral part, that is used directly by the taxpayer in providing services in its trade or business to customers. In these cases, eligibility for the research credit is to be determined by examining the combined software-hardware product as a single product.

(iv) Primarily for internal use. Unless computer software is developed to be commercially sold, leased, licensed, or otherwise marketed, for separately stated consideration to unrelated third parties, computer software is presumed developed by (or for the benefit of) the taxpayer primarily for the taxpayer's internal use. For example, the computer software may serve general and administrative functions of the taxpayer, or may be used in providing a noncomputer service. General and administrative functions include, but are not limited to, functions such as payroll, bookkeeping, financial management, financial reporting, personnel management, sales and marketing, fixed asset accounting, inventory management and cost accounting. Computer software that is developed to be commercially sold, leased, licensed or otherwise marketed, for separately stated consideration to unrelated third parties is not developed primarily for the taxpayer's internal use. The requirements of this paragraph (c)(6) apply to computer software that is developed primarily for the taxpayer's internal use even though the taxpayer subsequently sells, leases, licenses, or otherwise markets the computer software for separately stated consideration to unrelated third parties.

(v) Software used in the provision of services. (A) Computer services. For purposes of this section, a computer service is a service offered by a taxpayer to customers who conduct business with the taxpayer primarily for the use of the taxpayer's computer or software technology. A taxpayer does not provide a computer service merely because customers interact with the taxpayer's software.

(B) Noncomputer services. For purposes of this section, a noncomputer service is a service offered by a taxpayer to customers who conduct business with the taxpayer primarily to obtain a service other than a computer service, even if such other service is enabled, supported, or facilitated by computer or software technology.

(vi) High threshold of innovation test. Computer software satisfies this paragraph (c)(6)(vi) only if the taxpayer can establish that—

(A) The software is innovative in that the software is intended to be unique or novel and is intended to differ in a significant and inventive way from prior software implementations or methods;

(B) The software development involves significant economic risk in that the taxpayer commits substantial resources to the development and there is substantial uncertainty, because of technical risk, that such resources would be recovered within a reasonable period; and

(C) The software is not commercially available for use by the taxpayer in that the software cannot be purchased, leased, or licensed and used for the intended purpose without modifications that would satisfy the requirements of paragraphs (c)(6)(vi)(A) and (B) of this section.

(vii) Application of high threshold of innovation test. The costs of developing internal use software are eligible for the research credit only if the software satisfies the high threshold of innovation test of paragraph (c)(6)(vi) of this section. This test takes into account only the results attributable to the development of the new or improved software independent of the effect of any modifications to related hardware or other software.

(viii) Illustrations. The following examples illustrate provisions contained in this paragraph (c)(6) of this section. No inference should be drawn from these examples concerning the application of section 41(d)(1) and paragraph (a) of this section to these facts. The examples are as follows:

Example (1). (i) Facts. X, an insurance company, has increased its number of insurance policies in force. In recent years, regulatory and financial accounting rules for computing actuarial reserves on these insurance policies have changed several times. In order to compute actuarial reserves in a more timely and cost-effective manner, X undertakes to create an improved reserve valuation software that will generate data for regulatory and financial accounting purposes.

(ii) Conclusion. The improved reserve valuation software created by X is internal use software because the software is not developed to be commercially sold, leased, licensed, or otherwise marketed, for separately stated consideration to unrelated third parties. The improved reserve valuation software was developed by X to serve X's general and administrative functions. X's costs of developing the reserve valuation software are eligible for the research credit only if the software satisfies the high threshold of innovation test of paragraph (c)(6)(vi) of this section.

Example (2). (i) Facts. Assume the same facts as in Example 1. Also assume that in order to create the improved reserve valuation software, X purchases updated hardware with a new operating system to build the new software system. Several other insurance companies using the same updated hardware and new operating system have in place software systems that can handle the volume of transactions that X seeks to handle, provide reserve computations within a similar time frame, and accommodate the most current regulatory and financial accounting requirements.

(ii) Conclusion. X's reserve valuation software system is internal use software that does not satisfy the high threshold of innovation test of paragraph (c)(6)(vi) of this section. The software is not intended to be unique or novel in that it is intended to be merely comparable to software developed by other insurance companies. The software does not differ in a significant or inventive way from prior software implementations because X's reserve valuation software system was developed using the same technologies and methods that were employed by other insurance companies. Further, X's reserve valuation software is not excluded from the application of paragraph (c)(6) of this section by the rule of paragraph (c)(6)(iii) of this section.

Example (3). (i) Facts. In 1986, X, a large regional bank with hundreds of branch offices, maintained separate software systems for each of its customer's accounts, including checking, deposit, loan, lease, and trust. X determined that improved customer service could be achieved by redesigning its disparate systems into one customer-centric system. X also determined that commercially available database management systems did not meet all of the critical requirements of the proposed system. Specifically, available relational database management systems were well suited for the proposed system's data modeling requirements but not the data integrity and transaction throughput (transactions-per-second) requirements. Rather than waiting several years for vendor offerings to mature and become viable for its purpose, X decided to embark upon the project utilizing older technology that satisfied the data integrity and transaction throughput requirements but that was severely challenged with respect to the data modeling capabilities. X commits substantial resources to this project and, because of technical risk, X cannot determine if it will recover its resources in a reasonable period. Early in the course of the project, industry analysts observed that the project appeared highly ambitious and risky. The limitations of the technology X was attempting to utilize required that X develop a new database architecture that could accommodate transaction volumes unheard-of in the industry. X was unable to successfully develop the system and X abandoned the project.

(ii) Conclusion. X intended to develop a computer software system primarily for X's internal use because X did not intend to commercially sell, lease, license, or otherwise market the software, for separately stated consideration to unrelated third parties, and X intended to use the software in providing noncomputer services to its customers. X's software development activities satisfy the high threshold of innovation test of paragraph (c)(6)(vi) of this section because the system was intended to be innovative in that it was intended to be novel and it was intended to differ in a significant and inventive way from prior software implementations. In addition, X's development activities involved significant economic risk in that X committed substantial resources to the development and there was substantial uncertainty, because of technical risk, that such resources would be recovered within a reasonable period. Finally, at the time X undertook the development of the system, software meeting X's requirements was not commercially available for use by X.

Example (4). (i) Facts. X wishes to improve upon its capabilities in the area of insurance fraud prevention, detection and control. X believes that it can exceed the capabilities of current commercial offerings in this area by developing and applying pattern matching algorithms that are not implemented in current vendor offerings. X has determined that many insurance fraud perpetrators can evade detection because its current system relies too heavily on exact matches and scrubbed data. Because a computer software system that will accomplish these objectives is not commercially available, X undertakes to develop and implement advanced pattern matching algorithms that would significantly improve upon the capabilities currently available from vendors. X commits substantial resources to the development of the software system and cannot determine, because of technical risk, if it will recover its investment within a reasonable period.

(ii) Conclusion. X's computer software system is developed primarily for X's internal use because X did not intend to sell, lease, license or otherwise market the software, for separately stated consideration to unrelated third parties. X's software development activities satisfy the high threshold of innovation test of paragraph (c)(6)(vi) of this section because the software system is innovative in that it was intended to be novel and it was intended to differ in a significant and inventive way from prior software implementations. In addition, X's development activities involved significant economic risk in that X committed substantial resources to the development and there was substantial uncertainty, because of technical risk, that such resources would be recovered within a reasonable period. Finally, at the time X undertook the development of the software, software satisfying X's requirements was not commercially available for use by X.

Example (5). (i) Facts. X is engaged in the business of designing, manufacturing, and selling widgets. X delivers its widgets in the same manner and time as its competitors. To improve customer service, X undertakes to develop computer software that will monitor the progress of the manufacture and delivery of X's widgets to enable X's customers to track their widget orders from origination to delivery, whether by air, land or ship. In addition, at the request of a customer, X will be able to intercept and return or reroute packages prior to delivery. At the time X undertakes its software development activities, X is uncertain whether it can develop the real-time communication software necessary to achieve its objective. None of X's competitors have a comparable tracking system. X commits substantial resources to the development of the system and, because of technical risk, X cannot determine if it will recover its investment within a reasonable period.

(ii) Conclusion. X's computer software is developed primarily for X's internal use because the software is not developed to be commercially sold, leased, licensed, or otherwise marketed, for separately stated consideration to unrelated third parties. X's computer software was developed to be used by X in providing noncomputer services to its customers. X's software satisfies the high threshold of innovation test of paragraph (c)(6)(vi) of this section because, at the time the research is undertaken, X's software is designed to provide a new tracking capability that is novel in that none of X's competitors have such a capability. Further, the new capability differs in a significant and inventive way from prior software implementations. In addition, X's development activities involved significant economic risk in that X committed substantial resources to the development and there was substantial uncertainty, because of technical risk, that such resources would be recovered within a reasonable period. Finally, at the time X undertook the development of the software, software satisfying X's requirements was not commercially available for use by X.

Example (6). (i) Facts. X, a multinational chemical manufacturer with different business and financial systems in each of its divisions, undertakes a software development project aimed at integrating the majority of the functional areas of its major software systems into a single enterprise resource management system supporting centralized financial systems, inventory, and management reporting. This project involves the detailed analysis of X's (as well as each of X's divisions) legacy systems to understand the actual current business processes and data requirements. X also has to develop programs to fill in the gaps between the software features and X's system requirements. X hires Y, a systems consulting firm to assist with this development effort. Y has experience in developing similar systems. X, working jointly with Y, evaluates its needs, establishes goals for the new system, re-engineers the business processes that will be made concurrently with the implementation of the new system, and chooses and purchases a software system upon which to base its enterprise-wide system.

(ii) Conclusion. X's enterprise-wide computer software is developed primarily for internal use because the software is not developed to be commercially sold, leased, licensed, or otherwise marketed, for separately stated consideration to unrelated third parties. X's computer software was developed to be used by X to serve X's general and administrative functions. However, the development of X's enterprise management system does not satisfy the high threshold of innovation test of paragraph (c)(6)(vi) of this section because the system that X is seeking to develop is not intended to be unique or novel. Further, the software does not differ in a significant or inventive way from software implemented by other manufacturers.

Example (7). (i) Facts. X, a financial services company specializing in commercial mortgages, decides to support its ongoing expansion by upgrading its information technology infrastructure. In order to accommodate its expanding efforts to acquire and maintain corporate borrowers and draw securitized loan investors, X builds a scalable and modular enterprise network to run its latest business applications, including web-based portfolio access for investors and staff, document imaging for customer service personnel, desktop access to information services for in-house securities traders and multimedia on-line training and corporate information delivery for all company personnel. As a result, X is able to access market information faster and function more efficiently and effectively than before. The new network is based on a faster local area network technology which is better able to meet the higher bandwidth requirements of X's current multimedia applications.

(ii) Conclusion. X's software is developed primarily for X's internal use because the software is not developed to be commercially sold, leased, licensed, or otherwise marketed, for separately stated consideration to unrelated third parties. X's software development activities do not meet the high threshold of innovation test of paragraph (c)(6)(vi) of this section because the system is not intended to be unique or novel. Further, the software does not differ in a significant or inventive way from other existing software implementations.

Example (8). (i) Facts. X, a corporation, undertook a software project to rewrite a legacy mainframe application using an object-oriented programming language, and to move the new application off the mainframe to a client/server environment. Both the object-oriented language and client/server technologies were new to X. This project was undertaken to develop a more maintainable application, and to be able to implement new features more quickly. X had to perform a detailed analysis of the old legacy application in order to determine the requirements of the rewritten application. To accomplish this task, X had to train the legacy mainframe programmers in the new object-oriented and client/server technologies that they would have to utilize. Several of X's competitors had successfully implemented similar systems using object-oriented programming language and client/server technologies.

(ii) Conclusion. X's software is developed primarily for internal use because the software is not developed to be commercially sold, leased, licensed, or otherwise marketed, for separately stated consideration to unrelated third parties. X's activities to rewrite a legacy mainframe application using an object-oriented programming language, and to move the application from X's mainframe to a client/server environment do not satisfy the high threshold of innovation test of paragraph (c)(6)(vi) of this section. The software developed is not intended to be either unique or novel and is not intended to differ in a significant and inventive way from prior software implementations or methods.

Example (9). (i) Facts. X, a retail and distribution company, wants to upgrade its warehouse management software. Therefore, X performs an analysis of the warehouse management products and vendors in the marketplace. X selects vendor V's software and, in turn, develops the software interfaces between X's legacy systems and V's warehouse management software in order to integrate the new warehouse management system with X's financial and inventory systems. The development of these interfaces requires a detailed understanding of all the input and output fields and their data formats, and how they map from the old system to the new system and vice-versa. Once X develops the interfaces, X has to perform extensive testing and validation work to ensure that the interfaces work correctly and accurately.

(ii) Conclusion. X's software is developed primarily for internal use because the software is not developed to be commercially sold, leased, licensed, or otherwise marketed, for separately stated consideration to unrelated third parties. X's software development activities do not satisfy the high threshold of innovation test of paragraph (c)(6)(vi) of this section because the software development does not involve significant economic risk in that there is no substantial uncertainty, because of technical risk, that such resources will be recovered within a reasonable period.

Example (10). (i) Facts. X, a credit card company, knows that its customers are not comfortable with purchasing products over the Internet because they feel the Web is not secure. X decides to build a payment system that provides customers with a single use, automatically generated, short-term time-based, transaction number. This single-use transaction number has a short expiration period that is just long enough to allow a merchant to process and fill the customer's order. Thus, when a customer wishes to make a purchase over the

Internet, the customer requests X to generate automatically a single-use transaction number that merchant systems will accept as a legitimate card number. All purchases using single-use transaction numbers are automatically linked back to the customer's credit card account. X commits substantial resources to the development of the system and X cannot determine, because of technical risk, if it will recover its investment within a reasonable period. At the time of this project, nothing exists in the market that has these capabilities.

(ii) Conclusion. X's software is developed primarily for internal use because the software is not developed to be commercially sold, leased, licensed, or otherwise marketed, for separately stated consideration to unrelated third parties. X's computer software is developed primarily for X's internal use because it was intended to be used by X in providing noncomputer services to its customers. X's software satisfies the high threshold of innovation test of paragraph (c)(6)(vi) of this section because the system is a novel way to solve the security issue of making purchases over the Internet. Further, because of the secure payment capability, the software differs in a significant and inventive way from prior software implementations. In addition, X's development activities involved significant economic risk in that X committed substantial resources to the development and there was substantial uncertainty, because of technical risk, that such resources would be recovered within a reasonable period. Finally, at the time X undertook the development of the software, software satisfying X's requirements was not commercially available for use by X.

Example (11). (i) Facts. X, a corporation, wants to expand its internal computing power, and is aware that its PCs and workstations are idle at night, on the weekends, and for a significant part of any business day. Because the corporate computations that X needs to make could be done on workstations as well as PCs, X develops a screen-saver like application that runs on employee computers. When employees' computers have been idle for an amount of time set by each employee, the "screen-saver" starts to execute. However, instead of displaying moving lines, like the typical screen-saver, X's application goes back to a central server to get a new job to execute. This job will execute on the idle employee's computer until it has either finished, or the employee resumes working on his computer. X wants to ensure that it can manage all of the computation jobs distributed across its thousands of PCs and workstations. In addition, X wants to ensure that the additional load on its network caused by downloading the jobs and uploading the results, as well as in monitoring and managing the jobs, does not adversely impact the corporate computing infrastructure. At the time X undertook this software development project, X was uncertain, because of technical risk, it could develop a server application that could schedule and distribute the jobs across thousands of PCs and workstations, as well as handle all the error conditions that occur on a user's machine. Also, at the time X undertook this project, there was no commercial application available with such a capability.

(ii) Conclusion. X's computer software is developed primarily for internal use because the software is not developed to be commercially sold, leased, licensed, or otherwise marketed, for separately stated consideration to unrelated third parties. X's computer software was developed to be used by X to serve X's general and administrative functions. X's software satisfies the high threshold of innovation test of paragraph (c)(6)(vi) of this section because making use of idle corporate computing resources through what is ostensibly a screen-saver, was a novel approach to solving X's need for more computer intensive processing time. In addition, X's software development involves significant economic risk in that there was substantial uncertainty, because of technical risk, that the server application that schedules and distributes the jobs across thousands of PCs and workstations, as well as handles all the error conditions that can occur on a user's machine, amounts to developing a new operating system with new capabilities. Finally, at the time X undertook the development of the software, software satisfying X's requirements was not commercially available for use by X.

Example (12). (i) Facts.

(A) X, a corporation, wants to protect its internal documents without building a large public key infrastructure. In addition, X needs to implement a new highly secure encryption algorithm that has a ''back-door'' such that X can decrypt and read any document, even when the employee is on vacation or leaves the company. X wants to develop a new encryption algorithm that is both secure, easy to use, and difficult to break. Current commercial encryption/decryption products are too slow for high-level secure encryption processing. Furthermore, no commercial product exists that provides the capability of having a secure back-door key to decrypt files when the owner is unavailable.

(B) The development of the encryption/decryption software requires specialized knowledge of cryptography and computational methods. Due to the secret nature of X's work, the encryption algorithm has to be unbreakable, yet recoverable should the employee forget his key. X commits substantial resources to the development of the system and, because of technical risk, cannot estimate whether it will recover its investment within a reasonable period.

(ii) Conclusion. X's back-door file encryption software is developed primarily for internal use because the software is not developed to be commercially sold, leased, licensed, or otherwise marketed, for separately stated consideration to unrelated third parties. X's back-door file encryption software was developed to be used by X to serve X's general and administrative functions. X's encryption software satisfies the high threshold of innovation test of paragraph (c)(6)(vi) of this section because, at the time the research is undertaken, X's software is designed to provide encryption and back-door decryption capabilities that are unique in that no other product has these capabilities, which indicates the software encryption system differs in a significant way from prior software implementations. Further, the encryption and back-door decryption capabilities indicate that the software differs in a significant and inventive way from prior software implementations. In addition, X's development activities involved significant economic risk in that X committed substantial resources to the development and there was substantial uncertainty, because of technical risk, that such resources would be recovered within a reasonable period. Finally, at the time X undertook the development of the software, software satisfying X's requirements was not commercially available for use by X.

Example (13). (i) Facts. X, a large regional telephone company, is experiencing rapidly increasing customer demand. X would like to determine whether evolutionary algorithms such as genetic algorithms may improve its ability to design cost-effective networks and extend existing networks. X would also like to determine whether such adaptive algorithms may be used to optimize the routing of call traffic across existing networks in order to use efficiently the resources available without causing congestion. X first explores the use of evolutionary algorithms for the call routing task, because X determines that this type of complex, unpredictable problem is most appropriate for an adaptive algorithm solution. X develops and tests genetic algorithms until it determines that it has developed a software system it can test on a pilot basis on its existing networks. X commits substantial resources to the project, and cannot predict, because of technical risk, whether it will recover its resources within a reasonable period. Finally, at the time X undertook the development of the software, software satisfying X's requirements was not commercially available for use by X.

(ii) Conclusion. X's software is developed primarily for internal use because the software is not developed to be commercially sold, leased, licensed, or otherwise marketed, for separately stated consideration to unrelated third parties. X's computer software is intended to be used by X in providing noncomputer services to its customers. X's software satisfies the high threshold of innovation test of paragraph (c)(6)(vi) of this section because the software is intended to be novel and is intended to differ in a significant and inventive way from other existing software implementations. In addition, X's development activities involved significant economic risk in that X committed substantial resources to the development and there was substantial uncertainty, because of technical risk, that such resources would be recovered within a reasonable period. Finally, at the time X undertook the development of the software, software satisfying X's requirements was not commercially available.

(ix) Effective date. This paragraph (c)(6) is applicable for taxable years beginning after December 31, 1985.

(7) Activities outside the United States, Puerto Rico, and other possessions. (i) In general. Research conducted outside the United States, as defined in section 7701(a)(9), the Commonwealth of Puerto Rico and other possessions of the United States does not constitute qualified research.

(ii) Apportionment of in-house research expenses. In-house research expenses paid or incurred for qualified services performed both in the United States, the Commonwealth of Puerto Rico and other possessions of the United States and outside the United States, the Commonwealth of Puerto Rico and other possessions of the United States must be apportioned between the services performed in the United States, the Commonwealth of Puerto Rico and other possessions of the United States and the services performed outside the United States, the Commonwealth of Puerto Rico and other possessions of the United States. Only those in-house research expenses apportioned to the services performed within the United States, the Commonwealth of Puerto Rico and other possessions of the United States are eligible to be treated as qualified research expenses, unless the in-house research expenses are wages and the 80 percent rule of § 1.41-2(d)(2) applies.

(iii) Apportionment of contract research expenses. If contract research is performed partly in the United States, the Commonwealth of Puerto Rico and other possessions of the United States and partly outside the United States, the Commonwealth of Puerto Rico and other possessions of the United States, only 65 percent (or 75 percent in the case of amounts paid to qualified research consortia) of the portion of the contract amount that is attributable to the research activity performed in the United States, the Commonwealth of Puerto Rico and other possessions of the United States may qualify as a contract research expense (even if 80 percent or more of the contract amount is for research performed in the United States, the Commonwealth of Puerto Rico and other possessions of the United States).

(8) Research in the social sciences, etc. Qualified research does not include research in the social sciences (including economics, business management, and behavioral sciences), arts, or humanities.

(9) Research funded by any grant, contract, or otherwise. Qualified research does not include any research to the extent funded by any grant, contract, or otherwise by another person (or governmental entity). To determine the extent to which research is so funded, § 1.41-4A(d) applies.

(10) Illustrations. The following examples illustrate provisions contained in paragraphs (c)(1) through (9) (excepting (c)(6)) of this section. No inference should be drawn from these examples concerning the application of section 41(d)(1) and paragraph (a) of this section to these facts. The examples are as follows:

Example (1). (i) Facts. X, a tire manufacturer, develops a new material to use in its tires. X conducts research to determine the changes that will be necessary for X to modify its existing manufacturing processes to manufacture the new tire. X determines that the new material retains heat for a longer period of time than the materials X currently uses and, as a result, adheres to the manufacturing equipment during tread cooling. X evaluates numerous options for processing the treads at cooler temperatures. X designs, develops, and conducts sophisticated tests on the numerous options for a new type of belt to be used in tread cooling. X then manufactures a set of belts for its production equipment, installs the belts, and tests the belts to make sure they were manufactured correctly.

(ii) Conclusion. X's research with respect to the design of the new belts to be used in its manufacturing of the new tire may be qualified research under section 41(d)(1) and paragraph (a) of this section. However, X's expenses to implement the design, including the costs to manufacture, install, and test the belts were incurred after the belts met the taxpayer's functional and economic requirements and are excluded as research after commercial production under section 41(d)(4)(A) and paragraph (c)(2) of this section. In addition, amounts expended on component materials of the production belts and the costs of labor or other elements involved in the manufacture and installation of the production belts are not qualified research expenses. These expenses are not for expenditures that may be treated as expenses under section 174 and thus are not qualified research under section 41(d)(1)(A) and paragraph (a)(2)(i) of this section. See section 174(c) and § 1.174-2(b). Further, testing or inspection to determine whether the production belts were manufactured correctly is quality control testing under § 1.174-2(a)(4) and thus is not qualified research under section 41(d)(1)(A) and paragraph (a)(2)(i) of this section.

Example (2). (i) Facts. For several years, X has manufactured and sold a particular kind of widget. X initiates a new research project to develop a new or improved widget.

(ii) Conclusion. X's activities to develop a new or improved widget are not excluded from the definition of qualified research under section 41(d)(4)(A) and paragraph (c)(2) of this section. X's activities relating to the development of a new or improved widget constitute a new research project to develop a new business component. X's research activities relating to the development of the new or improved widget, a new business component, are not considered to be activities conducted after the beginning of commercial production under section 41(d)(4)(A) and paragraph (c)(2) of this section.

Example (3). (i) Facts. X, a computer software development firm, owns all substantial rights in a general ledger accounting software core program that X markets and licenses to customers. X incurs expenditures in adapting the core software program to the requirements of C, one of X's customers.

(ii) Conclusion. Because X's activities represent activities to adapt an existing software program to a particular customer's requirement or need, X's activities are excluded from the definition of qualified research under section 41(d)(4)(B) and paragraph (c)(3) of this section.

Example (4). (i) Facts. The facts are the same as in example 3, except that C pays X to adapt the core software program to C's requirements.

(ii) Conclusion. Because X's activities are excluded from the definition of qualified research under section 41(d)(4)(B) and paragraph (c)(3) of this section, C's payments to X are not for qualified research and are not considered to be contract research expenses under section 41(b)(3)(A).

Example (5). (i) Facts. The facts are the same as in example 3, except that C's own employees adapt the core software program to C's requirements.

(ii) Conclusion. Because C's employees' activities to adapt the core software program to C's requirements are excluded from the definition of qualified research under section 41(d)(4)(B) and paragraph (c)(3) of this section, the wages C paid to its employees do not constitute in-house research expenses under section 41(b)(2)(A).

Example (6). (i) Facts. X manufacturers and sells rail cars. Because rail cars have numerous specifications related to performance, reliability and quality, rail car designs are subject to extensive, complex testing in the scientific or laboratory sense. B orders passenger rail cars from X. B's rall car requirements differ from those of X's other customers in that B wants fewer seats in its passenger cars and a higher quality seating material and carpet. X manufactures rail cars meeting B's requirements. X does not conduct complex testing in the scientific or laboratory sense on the rail cars manufactured for B.

(ii) Conclusion. X's activities to manufacture rail cars for B are excluded from the definition of qualified research. The rail cars designed for B were not subject to the type of complex testing that is indicative of a process of experimentation. Further, the rail car sold to B was not a new business component, but merely an adaptation of an existing business component. Thus, X's activities to manufacture rail cars for B are excluded from the definition of qualified research under section 41(d)(4)(B) and paragraph (c)(3) of this section because X's activities represent activities to adapt an existing business component to a particular customer's requirement or need.

Example (7). (i) Facts. X, a manufacturer, undertakes to create a manufacturing process for a new valve design. X determines that it requires a specialized type of robotic equipment to use in the manufacturing process for its new valves. X is unable to locate robotic equipment that meets X's precise specifications, and, therefore, purchases existing robotic equipment for the purpose of modifying it to meet its needs. X's engineers conduct experiments using modeling and simulation in modifying the robotic equipment and conduct extensive scientific and laboratory testing of design alternatives. As a result of this process, X's engineers develop a design for the robotic equipment that meets X's specifications. X constructs and installs the modified robotic equipment on its manufacturing process.

(ii) Conclusion. X's research activities to determine how to modify X's robotic equipment for its manufacturing process are not excluded from the definition of qualified research under section 41(d)(4)(B) and paragraph (c)(3) of this section.

Example (8). (1) Facts. An existing gasoline additive is manufactured by Y using three ingredients, A, B, and C. X seeks to develop and manufacture its own gasoline additive that appears and functions in a manner similar to Y's additive. To develop its own additive, X first inspects the composition of Y's additive, and uses knowledge gained from the inspection to reproduce A and B in the laboratory. Any differences between ingredients A and B that are used in Y's additive and those reproduced by X are insignificant and are not material to the viability, effectiveness, or cost of A and B. X desires to use with A and B an ingredient that has a materially lower cost than ingredient C. Accordingly, X engages in a process of experimentation to develop, analyze and test potential alternative formulations of the additive.

(ii) Conclusion. X's activities in analyzing and reproducing ingredients A and B involve duplication of existing business components and are excluded from the definition of qualified research under section 41(d)(4)(C) and paragraph (c)(4) of this section. X's experimentation activities to develop potential alternative formulations of the additive do not involve duplication of an existing business component and are not excluded from the definition of qualified research under section 41(d)(4)(C) and paragraph (c)(4) of this section.

Example (9). (1) Facts. X, a manufacturing corporation, undertakes to restructure its manufacturing organization. X organizes a team to design an organizational structure that will improve X's business operations. The team includes X's employees as well as outside management consultants. The team studies current operations, interviews X's employees, and studies the structure of other manufacturing facilities to determine appropriate modifications to X's current business operations. The team develops a recommendation of proposed modifications which it presents to X's management. X's management approves the team's recommendation and begins to implement the proposed modifications.

(ii) Conclusion. X's activities in developing and implementing the new management structure are excluded from the definition of qualified research under section 41(d)(4)(D) and paragraph (c)(5) of this section. Qualified research does not include activities relating to management functions or techniques including management organization plans and management-based changes in production processes.

Example (10). (1) Facts. X, an insurance company, develops a new life insurance product. In the course of developing the product, X engages in research with respect to the effect of pricing and tax consequences on demand for the product, the expected volatility of interest rates, and the expected mortality rates (based on published data and prior insurance claims).

(ii) Conclusion. X's activities related to the new product represent research in the social sciences (including economics and business management) and are thus excluded from the definition of qualified research under section 41(d)(4)(G) and paragraph (c)(8) of this section.

(d) Recordkeeping for the research credit. A taxpayer claiming a credit under section 41 must retain records in sufficiently usable form and detail to substantiate that the expenditures claimed are eligible for the credit. For the rules governing record retention, see § 1.6001-1. To facilitate compliance and administration, the IRS and taxpayers may agree to guidelines for the keeping of specific records for purposes of substantiating research credits.

(e) Effective dates. In general, the rules of this section are applicable for taxable years ending on or after December 26, 2001.

§ 1.41-4A Qualified research for taxable years beginning before January 1, 1986.

Caution: The Treasury has not yet amended Reg § 1.41-4A to reflect changes made by 110-458, P.L. 99-514, P.L. 98-369, P.L. 101-239.

• ***Caution:*** In Notice 2001-19, 2001-10 IRB, IRS announced that these final regs, issued as TD 8930, are under review. Notice 2001-19 says that "[U]pon completion of the review, Treasury and IRS will announce changes to the regulations, if any, in the form of proposed regulations. In addition, TD 8930 will be revised so that the provisions of the regulations, including any changes to TD 8930, will be effective no earlier than the date when the completion of this review is announced, except that the provisions related to internal-use computer software (including any revisions) generally will be applicable for taxable years beginning after December 31, 1985." Notice 2001-19 also says that taxpayers may continue to rely on these final regs during the pendency of this review."

(a) General rule. Except as otherwise provided in section 30(d) (as that section read before amendment by the Tax Reform Act of 1986) and in this section, the term "qualified research" means research, expenditures for which would be research and experimental expenditures within the meaning of section 174. Expenditures that are ineligible for the section 174 deduction elections are not expenditures for qualified research. For example, expenditures for the acquisition of land or depreciable property used in research, and mineral exploration costs described in section 174(d), are not expenditures for qualified research.

(b) Activities outside the United States. *(1) In-house research.* In-house research conducted outside the United States (as defined in section 7701(a)(9)) cannot constitute qualified research. Thus, wages paid to an employee scientist for services performed in a laboratory in the United States and in a test station in Antarctica must be apportioned between the services performed within the United States and the services performed outside the United States, and only the wages apportioned to the services conducted within the United States are qualified research expenses unless the 80 percent rule of § 1.41-2(d)(2) applies.

(2) Contract research. If contract research is performed partly within the United States and partly without, only 65 percent of the portion of the contract amount that is attributable to the research performed within the United States can qualify as contract research expense (even if 80 percent or more of the contract amount was for research performed in the United States).

(c) Social sciences or humanities. Qualified research does not include research in the social sciences or humanities. For purposes of section 30(d)(2) (as that section read before amendment by the Tax Reform Act of 1986) and of this section, the phrase "research in the social sciences or humanities" encompasses all areas of research other than research in a field of laboratory science (such as physics or biochemistry), engineering or technology. Examples of research in the social sciences or humanities include the development of a new life insurance contract, a new economic model or theory, a new accounting procedure or a new cookbook.

(d) Research funded by any grant, contract, or otherwise. *(1) In general.* Research does not constitute qualified research to the extent it is funded by any grant, contract, or otherwise by another person (including any governmental entity). All agreements (not only research contracts) entered into between the taxpayer performing the research and other persons shall be considered in determining the extent to which the research is funded. Amounts payable under any agreement that are contingent on the success of the research and thus considered to be paid for the product or result of the research (see § 1.41-2(e)(2)) are not treated as funding. For special rules regarding funding between commonly controlled businesses, see § 1.41-6(e).

(2) Research in which taxpayer retains no rights. If a taxpayer performing research for another person retains no substantial rights in research under the agreement providing for the research, the research is treated as fully funded for purposes of section 41(d)(4)(H), and no expenses paid or incurred by the taxpayer in performing the research are qualified research expenses. For example, if the taxpayer performs research under an agreement that confers on another person the exclusive right to exploit the results of the research, the taxpayer is not performing qualified research because the research is treated as fully funded under this paragraph (d)(2). Incidental benefits to the taxpayer from performance of the research (for example, increased experience in a field of research) do not constitute substantial rights in the research. If a taxpayer performing research for another person retains no substantial rights in the research and if the payments to the researcher are contingent upon the success of the research, neither the performer nor the person paying for the research is entitled to treat any portion of the expenditures as qualified research expenditures.

(3) Research in which the taxpayer retains substantial rights. (i) In general. If a taxpayer performing research for another person retains substantial rights in the research under the agreement providing for the research, the research is funded to the extent of the payments (and fair market value of any property) to which the taxpayer becomes entitled by performing the research. A taxpayer does not retain substantial rights in the research if the taxpayer must pay for the right to use the results of the research. Except as otherwise provided in paragraph (d)(3)(ii) of this section, the taxpayer shall reduce the amount paid or incurred by the taxpayer for the research that would, but for section 41(d)(4)(H), constitute qualified research expenses of the taxpayer by the amount of funding determined under the preceding sentence.

(ii) Pro rata allocation. If the taxpayer can establish to the satisfaction of the district director—

(A) The total amount of research expenses,

(B) That the total amount of research expenses exceed the funding, and

(C) That the otherwise qualified research expenses (that is, the expenses which would be qualified research expenses if there were no funding) exceed 65 percent of the funding, then the taxpayer may allocate the funding pro rata to nonqualified and otherwise qualified research expenses, rather than allocating it 100 percent to otherwise qualified research expenses (as provided in paragraph (d)(3)(i) of this section). In no event, however, shall less than 65 percent of the funding be applied against the otherwise qualified research expenses.

(iii) Project-by-project determination. The provisions of this paragraph (d)(3) shall be applied separately to each research project undertaken by the taxpayer.

(4) Independent research and development under the Federal Acquisition Regulations System and similar provisions. The Federal Acquisition Regulations System and similar rules and regulations relating to contracts (fixed price, cost plus, etc.) with government entities provide for allocation of certain "independent research and development costs" and "bid and proposal costs" of a contractor to contracts entered into with that contractor. In general, any "independent research and development costs" and "bid and proposal costs" paid to a taxpayer by reason of such a contract shall not be treated as funding the underlying research activities except to the extent the "independent research and development costs" and "bid and proposal costs" are properly severable from the contract. See § 1.451-3(e); see also section 804(d)(2) of the Tax Reform Act of 1986.

(5) Funding determinable only in subsequent taxable year. If at the time the taxpayer files its return for a taxable year, it is impossible to determine to what extent particular research performed by the taxpayer during that year may be funded, then the taxpayer shall treat the research as completely funded for purposes of completing that return. When the amount of funding is finally determined, the taxpayer should amend the return and any interim returns to reflect the proper amount of funding.

(6) Examples. The following examples illustrate the application of the principles contained in this paragraph.

Example (1). A enters into a contract with B Corporation, a cash-method taxpayer using the calendar year as its taxable year, under which B is to perform research that would, but for section 41(d)(3)(H), be qualified research of B. The agreement calls for A to pay B $120x, regardless of the outcome of the research. In 1982, A makes full payment of $120x under the contract, B performs all the research, and B pays all the expenses connected with the research, as follows:

In-house research expenses	$100x
Outside research: (Amount B paid to third parties for research, 65 percent of which ($26x) is treated as a contract research expense of B)	40x
Overhead and other expenses	10x
Total	150x

If B has no rights to the research, B is fully funded. Alternatively, assume that B retains the right to use the results of the research in carrying on B's business. Of B's otherwise qualified research expenses of $126x + § 26x), $120x is treated as funded by A. Thus $6x ($126x − $120x) is treated as a qualified research expense of B. However, if B establishes the facts required under paragraph (d)(3) of this section, B can allocate the funding pro rata to nonqualified and otherwise qualified research expenses. Thus $100.8x ($120x ($126x/$150x)) would be allocated to otherwise qualified research expenses. B's qualified research expenses would be $25.2x ($126x − $100.8x). For purposes of the following examples (2), (3) and (4) assume that B retains substantial rights to use the results of the research in carrying on B's business.

Example (2). The facts are the same as in example (1) (assuming that B retains the right to use the results of the research in carrying on B's business) except that, although A makes full payment of $120x during 1982, B does not perform the research or pay the associated expenses until 1983. The computations are unchanged. However, B's qualified research expenses determined in example (1) are qualified research expenses during 1983.

Example (3). The facts are the same as in example (1) (assuming that B retains the right to use the results of the research in carrying on B's business) except that although B performs the research and pays the associated expenses during 1982. A does not pay the $102x until 1983. The computations are unchanged and the amount determined in example (1) is a qualified research expense of B during 1982.

Example (4). The facts are the same as in example (1) (assuming that B retains the right to use the results of the research in carrying on B's business) except that, instead of agreeing to pay B $120x, A agrees to pay $100x regardless of the outcome and an additional $20x only if B's research produces a useful product. B's research produces a useful product and A pays B $120x during 1982. The $20x payment that is conditional on the success of the research is not treated as funding. Assuming that B establishes to the satisfaction of the district director the actual research expenses, B can allocate the funding to nonqualified and otherwise qualified research expenses. Thus $84x ($100x ($126x/$150x)) would be allocated to otherwise qualified research expenses. B's qualified research expenses would be $42x ($126x − $84x).

Example (5). C enters into a contract with D, a cash-method taxpayer using the calendar year as its taxable year, under which D is to perform research in which both C and D will have substantial rights. C agrees to reimburse D for 80 percent of D's expenses for the research. D performs part of the research in 1982 and the rest in 1983. At the time that D files its return for 1982, D is unable to determine the extent to which the research is funded under the provisions of this paragraph. Under these circumstances, D may not treat any of the expenses paid by D for this research during 1982 as qualified expenses on its 1982 return. When the project is complete and D can determine the extent of funding, D should file an amended return for 1982 to take into account any qualified research expense for 1982.

T.D. 8251, 5/16/89, amend T.D. 8930, 12/27/2000.

§ 1.41-5 Basic research for taxable years beginning after December 31, 1986.

• ***Caution:*** Reg. § 1.41-5 is redesignated as § 1.41-4A by T.D. 8930. However, in Notice 2001-19, 2001-10 IRB, IRS announced that these final regs, issued as TD 8930, are under review. Notice 2001-19 says that "[U]pon completion of the review, Treasury and IRS will announce changes to the regulations, if any, in the form of proposed regulations. In addition, TD 8930 will be revised so that the provisions of the regulations, including any changes to TD 8930, will be effective no earlier than the date when the completion of this review is announced, except that the provisions related to internal-use computer software (including any revisions) generally will be applicable for taxable years beginning after December 31, 1985." Notice 2001-19 also says that taxpayers may continue to rely on these final regs during the pendency of this review."

Caution: The Treasury has not yet amended Reg § 1.41-5 to reflect changes made by 110-458, P.L. 99-514, P.L. 98-369, P.L. 101-239.

[Reserved]

T.D. 8930, 12/27/2000.

§ 1.41-5A Basic research for taxable years beginning before January 1, 1987.

• ***Caution:*** In Notice 2001-19, 2001-10 IRB, IRS announced that these final regs, issued as TD 8930, are under review. Notice 2001-19 says that "[U]pon completion of the review, Treasury and IRS will announce changes to the regulations, if any, in the form of proposed regulations. In addition, TD 8930 will be revised so that the provisions of the regulations, including any changes to TD 8930, will be effective no earlier than the date when the completion of this review is announced, except that the provisions related to internal-use computer software (including any revisions) generally will be applicable for taxable years beginning after December 31, 1985." Notice 2001-19 also says that taxpayers may continue to rely on these final regs during the pendency of this review."

Caution: The Treasury has not yet amended Reg § 1.41-5A to reflect changes made by 110-458, P.L. 99-514, P.L. 98-369, P.L. 101-239.

(a) In general. The amount expended for basic research within the meaning of section 30(e) (before amended by the Tax Reform Act of 1986) equals the sum of money plus the taxpayer's basis in tangible property (other than land) transferred for use in the performance of basic research.

(b) Trade or business requirement. Any amount treated as a contract research expense under section 30(e) (before amendment by the Tax Reform Act of 1986) shall be deemed to have been paid or incurred in carrying on a trade or business, if the corporation that paid or incurred the expenses is actually engaged in carrying on some trade or business.

(c) Prepaid amounts. *(1) In general.* If any basic research expense paid or incurred during any taxable year is attributable to research to be conducted after the close of such taxable year, the expense so attributable shall be treated for purposes of section 30(b)(1)(B) (before amendment by the Tax Reform Act of 1986) as paid or incurred during the period in which the basic research is conducted.

(2) Transfers of property. In the case of transfers of property to be used in the performance of basic research, the research in which that property is to be used shall be considered to be conducted ratably over a period beginning on the day the property is first so used and continuing for the number of years provided with respect to property of that class under section 168(c)(2) (before amendment by the Tax Reform Act of 1986). For example, if an item of property which is 3-year property under section 168(c) is transferred to a university for basic research on January 12, 1983, and is first so used by the university on March 1, 1983, then the research in which that property is used is considered to be conducted ratably from March 1, 1983, through February 28, 1986.

(d) Written research agreement. *(1) In general.* A written research agreement must be entered into prior to the performance of the basic research.

(2) Agreement between a corporation and a qualified organization after June 30, 1983. (i) In general. A written research agreement between a corporation and a qualified organization (including a qualified fund) entered into after June 30, 1983, shall provide that the organization shall inform the corporation within 60 days after the close of each taxable year of the corporation what amount of funds provided by the corporation pursuant to the agreement was expended on basic research during the taxable year of the corporation. In determining amounts expended on basic research, the qualified organization shall take into account the exclusions specified in section 30(e)(3) (before amendment by the Tax Reform Act of 1986) and in paragraph (e) of this section.

(ii) Transfers of property. In the case of transfers of property to be used in basic research, the agreement shall provide that substantially all use of the property is to be for basic research, as defined in section 30(e)(3) (before amendment by the Tax Reform Act of 1986).

(3) Agreement between a qualified fund and a qualified educational organization after June 30, 1983. A written research agreement between a qualified fund and a qualified educational organization (see section 30(e)(4)(B)(iii) (before amendment by the Tax Reform Act of 1986)) entered into after June 30, 1983, shall provide that the qualified educational organization shall furnish sufficient information to the qualified fund to enable the qualified fund to comply with the written research agreements it has entered into with grantor corporations, including the requirement set forth in paragraph (d)(2) of this section.

(e) Exclusions. *(1) Research conducted outside the United States.* If a taxpayer pays or incurs an amount for basic research to be performed partly within the United States and partly without, only 65 percent of the portion of the amount attributable to research performed within the United States can be treated as a contract research expense (even if 80 percent or more of the contract amount was for basic research performed in the United States).

(2) Research in the social sciences or humanities. Basic research does not include research in the social sciences or humanities, within the meaning of § 1.41-4A(c).

(f) Procedure for making an election to be treated as a qualified fund. In order to make an election to be treated as a qualified fund within the meaning of section 30(e)(4)(B)(iii) (before amendment by the Tax Reform Act of 1986) or as an organization described in section 41(e)(6)(D), the organization shall file with the Internal Revenue Service center with which it files its annual return a statement that—

(1) Sets out the name, address, and taxpayer identification number of the electing organization (the "taxpayer") and of

the organization that established and maintains the electing organization (the "controlling organization"),

(2) Identifies the election as an election under section 41(e)(6)(D) of the Code,

(3) Affirms that the controlling organization and the taxpayer are section 501(c)(3) organizations,

(4) Provides that the taxpayer elects to be treated as a private foundation for all Code purposes other than section 4940,

(5) Affirms that the taxpayer satisfies the requirement of section 41(e)(6)(D)(iii), and

(6) Specifies the date on which the election is to become effective. If an election to be treated as a qualified fund is filed before February 1, 1982, the election may be made effective as of any date after June 30, 1981, and before January 1, 1986. If an election is filed on or after February 1, 1982, the election may be made effective as of any date on or after the date on which the election is filed.

T.D. 8251, 5/16/89, amend T.D. 8930, 12/27/2000.

§ 1.41-6 Aggregation of expenditures.

Caution: The Treasury has not yet amended Reg § 1.41-6 to reflect changes made by 110-458, P.L. 110-172, P.L. 109-432.

(a) Controlled group of corporations; trades or businesses under common control. *(1) In general.* To determine the amount of research credit (if any) allowable to a trade or business that at the end of its taxable year is a member of a controlled group, a taxpayer must—

(i) Compute the group credit in the manner described in paragraph (b) of this section; and

(ii) Allocate the group credit among the members of the group in the manner described in paragraph (c) of this section.

(2) Consolidated groups. For special rules relating to consolidated groups, see paragraph (d) of this section.

(3) Definitions. For purposes of this section—

(i) Consolidated group has the meaning set forth in § 1.1502-1(h).

(ii) Controlled group and group mean a controlled group of corporations, as defined in section 41(f)(5), or a group of trades or businesses under common control. For rules for determining whether trades or businesses are under common control, see § 1.52-1 (b) through (g).

(iii) Credit year means the taxable year for which the member is computing the credit.

(iv) Group credit means the research credit (if any) allowable to a controlled group.

(v) Trade or business means a sole proprietorship, a partnership, a trust, an estate, or a corporation that is carrying on a trade or business (within the meaning of section 162). Any corporation that is a member of a commonly controlled group shall be deemed to be carrying on a trade or business if any other member of that group is carrying on any trade or business.

(b) Computation of the group credit. *(1) In general.* All members of a controlled group are treated as a single taxpayer for purposes of computing the research credit. The group credit is computed by applying all of the section 41 computational rules on an aggregate basis. All members of a controlled group must use the same method of computation, either the method described in section 41(a) or the alternative incremental research credit (AIRC) method described in section 41(c)(4), in computing the group credit for a credit year.

(2) Start-up companies. (i) In general. For purposes of computing the group credit, a controlled group is treated as a start-up company for purposes of section 41(c)(3)(B)(i) if—

(A) There was no taxable year beginning before January 1, 1984, in which a member of the group had gross receipts and either the same member or another member also had qualified research expenditures (QREs); or

(B) There were fewer than three taxable years beginning after December 31, 1983, and before January 1, 1989, in which a member of the group had gross receipts and either the same member or another member also had QREs.

(ii) Example. The following example illustrates the principles of paragraph (b)(2)(i) of this section:

Example. A, B, and C, all of which are calendar year taxpayers, are members of a controlled group. During the 1983 taxable year, A had QREs, but no gross receipts; B had gross receipts, but no QREs; and C had no QREs or gross receipts. The 1984 taxable year was the first taxable year for which each of A, B, and C had both QREs and gross receipts. A, B, and C had both QREs and gross receipts in 1985, 1986, 1987, and 1988. Because the first taxable year for which each of A, B, and C had both QREs and gross receipts began after December 31, 1983, each of A, B, and C is a start-up company under section 41(c)(3)(B)(i) and each is a start-up company for purposes of computing the stand-alone entity credit. During the 1983 taxable year, at least one member of the group, A, had QREs and at least one member of the group, B, had gross receipts, thus, the group had both QREs and gross receipts in 1983. Therefore, the controlled group is not a start-up company because the first taxable year for which the group had both QREs and gross receipts did not begin after December 31, 1983, and there were not fewer than three taxable years beginning after December 31, 1983, and before January 1, 1989, in which a member of the group had gross receipts and QREs.

(iii) First taxable year after December 31, 1993, for which the controlled group had QREs. In the case of a controlled group that is treated as a start-up company under section 41(c)(3)(B)(i) and paragraph (b)(2)(i) of this section, for purposes of determining the group's fixed-base percentage under section 41(c)(3)(B)(ii), the first taxable year after December 31, 1993, for which the group has QREs is the first taxable year in which at least one member of the group has QREs.

(iv) Example. The following example illustrates the principles of paragraph (b)(2)(iii) of this section:

Example. D, E, and F, all of which are calendar year taxpayers, are members of a controlled group. The group is treated as a start-up company under section 41(c)(3)(B)(i) and paragraph (b)(2)(i) of this section. The first taxable year after December 31, 1993, for which D had QREs was 1994. The first taxable year after December 31, 1993, for which E had QREs was 1995. The first taxable year after December 31, 1993, for which F had QREs was 1996. Because the 1994 taxable year was the first taxable year after December 31, 1993, for which at least one member of the group, D, had QREs, for purposes of determining the group's fixed-based percentage under section 41(c)(3)(B)(ii), the 1994 taxable year was the first taxable year after December 31, 1993, for which the group had QREs.

(c) Allocation of the group credit. *(1) In general.* (i) To the extent the group credit (if any) computed under paragraph (b) of this section does not exceed the sum of the stand-alone entity credits of all of the members of a controlled group, computed under paragraph (c)(2) of this section, such group credit shall be allocated among the members of the controlled group in proportion to the stand-alone entity credits of the members of the controlled group, computed under paragraph (c)(2) of this section:

group credit that does not exceed sum of all the members' stand-alone entity credits ×

$$\frac{\text{member's stand-alone entity credit}}{\text{sum of all the members' stand-alone entity credits.}}$$

(2) Stand-alone entity credit. The term stand-alone entity credit means the research credit (if any) that would be allowable to a member of a controlled group if the credit were computed as if section 41(f)(1) did not apply, except that the member must apply the rules provided in paragraphs (d)(1) (relating to consolidated groups) and (i) (relating to intragroup transactions) of this section. Each member's stand-alone entity credit for any credit year must be computed under whichever method (the method described in section 41(a) or the method described in section 41(c)(4)) results in the greater stand-alone entity credit for that member, without regard to the method used to compute the group credit.

(d) Special rules for consolidated groups. *(1) In general.* For purposes of applying paragraph (c) of this section, a consolidated group whose members are members of a controlled group is treated as a single member of the controlled group and a single stand-alone entity credit is computed for the consolidated group.

(2) Start-up company status. A consolidated group's status as a start-up company and the first taxable year after December 31, 1993, for which a consolidated group has QREs are determined in accordance with the principles of paragraph (b)(2) of this section.

(3) Special rule for allocation of group credit among consolidated group members. The portion of the group credit that is allocated to a consolidated group is allocated to the members of the consolidated group in accordance with the principles of paragraph (c) of this section. However, for this purpose, the stand-alone entity credit of a member of a consolidated group is computed without regard to section 41(f)(1), but with regard to paragraph (i) of this section.

(ii) To the extent that the group credit (if any) computed under paragraph (b) of this section exceeds the sum of the stand-alone entity credits of all of the members of the controlled group, computed under paragraph (c)(2) of this section, such excess shall be allocated among the members of a controlled group in proportion to the QREs of the members of the controlled group:

$$\text{(group credit sum of all the members'stand-alone entity credits)} \times \frac{\text{member's QREs}}{\text{sum of all the member's QREs}}$$

(e) Examples. The following examples illustrate the provisions of this section. Unless otherwise stated, no members of a controlled group are members of a consolidated group, no member of the group made any basic research payments or paid or incurred any amounts to an energy research consortium, and the group has not made an AIRC election (except as provided in Example 6) or an ASC election. For an example illustrating the calculation of the alternative simplified credit under section 41(c)(5), which is applicable for taxable years ending after December 31, 2006, see § 1.41-6T(e).

Example (1). Group credit is less than sum of members' stand-alone entity credits. (i) Facts. A, B, and C, all of which are calendar-year taxpayers, are members of a controlled group. For purposes of computing the group credit for the 2004 taxable year (the credit year), A, B, and C had the following:

	A	B	C	Group aggregate
Credit Year QREs	$200x	20x	110x	330x
1984-1988 QREs	$40x	10x	100x	150x
1984-1988 Gross Receipts	$1,000x	350x	150x	1,500x
Average Annual Gross Receipts for 4 Years Preceding the Credit Year	$1,200x	200x	300x	1,700x

(ii) Computation of the group credit. (A) In general. The research credit allowable to the group is computed as if A, B, and C were one taxpayer. The group credit is equal to 20 percent of the excess of the group's aggregate credit year QREs ($330x) over the group's base amount ($170x). The group credit is 0.20 x ($330x-$170x), which equals $32x.

(B) Group's base amount. (1) Computation. The group's base amount equals the greater of: The group's fixed-base percentage (10 percent) multiplied by the group's aggregate average annual gross receipts for the 4 taxable years preceding the credit year ($1,700x), or the group's minimum base amount ($165x). The group's base amount, therefore, is $170x, which is the greater of: 0.10 x $1,700x, which equals $170x, or $165x.

(2) Group's minimum base amount. The group's minimum base amount is 50 percent of the group's aggregate credit year QREs. The group's minimum base amount is 0.50 x $330x, which equals $165x.

(3) Group's fixed-base percentage. The group's fixed-base percentage is the lesser of: The ratio that the group's aggregate QREs for the taxable years beginning after December 31, 1983, and before January 1, 1989, bear to the group's aggregate gross receipts for the same period, or 16 percent (the statutory maximum). The group's fixed-base percentage, therefore, is 10 percent, which is the lesser of: $150x/$1,500x, which equals 10 percent, or 16 percent.

(iii) Allocation of the group credit. Under paragraph (c)(2) of this section, each member's stand-alone entity credit must be computed using the method that results in the greater stand-alone entity credit for that member. The stand-alone entity credit for each of A, B, and C is greater using the method described in section 41(a). Therefore, the stand-alone entity credit for each of A, B, and C must be computed using the method described in section 41(a). A's stand-alone entity credit is $20x. B's stand-alone entity credit is $2x. C's stand-alone entity credit is $11x. The sum of the members' stand-alone entity credits is $33x. Because the group credit of $32x is less than the sum of the stand-alone entity credits of all the members of the group ($33x), the group credit is allocated among the members of the group based on the ratio that each member's stand-alone entity credit bears to the sum of the stand-alone entity credits of all the members of the group. The $32x group credit is allocated as follows:

	A	B	C	Total
Stand-Alone Entity Credit	$20x	$2x	$11x	$33x
Allocation Ratio (Stand-Alone Entity Credit/Sum of Stand-Alone Entity Credits).	20/33	2/33	11/33	
Multiplied by: Group Credit	$32x	$32x	$32x	
Equals: Credit Allocated to Member.	$19.39x	$1.94x	$10.67x	$32x

Example (2). Group credit exceeds sum of members' stand-alone entity credits. (i) Facts. D, E, F, and G, all of which are calendar-year taxpayers, are members of a controlled group. For purposes of computing the group credit for the 2004 taxable year (the credit year), D, E, F, and G had the following:

	D	E	F	G	Group Aggregate
Credit Year (QREs).	$580x	$10x	$70x	$15x	$675x
1984-1988 QREs	$500x	$25x	$100x	$25x	$650x
1984-1988 Gross Receipts	$4,000x	$5,000x	$2,000x	$10,000x	$21,000x
Average Annual Gross Receipts for 4 Years Preceding the Credit Year.	$5,000x	$5,000x	$2,000x	$5,000x	$17,000x

(ii) Computation of the group credit. (A) In general. The research credit allowable to the group is computed as if D, E, F, and G were one taxpayer. The group credit is equal to 20 percent of the excess of the group's aggregate credit year QREs ($675x) over the group's base amount ($527x). The group credit is 0.20 x ($675x-$527x), which equals $29.76x.

(B) Group's base amount. (1) Computation. The group's base amount equals the greater of: The group's fixed-base percentage (3.10 percent) multiplied by the group's aggregate average annual gross receipts for the 4 taxable years preceding the credit year ($17,000x), or the group's minimum base amount ($337.50x). The group's base amount, therefore, is $527x, which is the greater of: 0.031 x $17,000x, which equals $527x, or $337.50x.

(2) Group's minimum base amount. The group's minimum base amount is 50 percent of the group's aggregate credit year QREs. The group's minimum base amount is 0.50 x $675x, which equals $337.50x.

(3) Group's fixed-base percentage. The group's fixed-base percentage is the lesser of: The ratio that the group's aggregate QREs for the taxable years beginning after December 31, 1983, and before January 1, 1989, bear to the group's aggregate gross receipts for the same period, or 16 percent (the statutory maximum). The group's fixed-base percentage, therefore, is 3.10 percent, which is the lesser of: $650x/$21,000x, which equals 3.10 percent, or 16 percent.

(iii) Allocation of the group credit. Under paragraph (c)(2) of this section, each member's stand-alone entity credit must be computed using the method that results in the greater stand-alone entity credit for that member. The stand-alone entity credits for D ($19.46x) and F ($1.71x) are greater using the AIRC method. Therefore, the stand-alone entity credits for D and F must be computed using the AIRC method. The stand-alone entity credit for G ($0.50x) is greater using the method described in section 41(a). Therefore, the stand-alone entity credit for G must be computed using the method described in section 41(a). E's stand-alone entity credit computed under either method is zero. The sum of the members' stand-alone entity credits is $21.67x. Because the group credit of $29.76x is greater than the sum of the stand-alone entity credits of all the members of the group ($21.67x), each member of the group is allocated an amount of the group credit equal to that member's stand-alone entity credit. The excess of the group credit over the sum of the members' stand alone entity credits ($8.09x) is allocated among the members of the group based on the ratio that each member's QREs bear to the sum of the QREs of all the members of the group. The $29.76x group credit is allocated as follows:

	D	E	F	G	Total
Group Credit					$29.76x
Minus: Sum of Stand-Alone Entity Credits.	$19.467x	$0.00x	$1.71x	$0.50x	$21.67x
Equals: Excess Group Credit					$8.09x
Excess Group Credit.	$8.09x	$8.09x	$8.09x	$8.09x	....
Multiplied By Allocation Ratio: QREs/Sum of QREs.	580/675	10/675	70/675	15/675	....
Excess Group Credit Allocated	$6.95x	$0.12x	$0.84x	$0.18x	....
Plus: Stand-Alone Entity Credit.	$19.46x	$0.00x	$1.71x	$0.50x	....
Equals: Credit Allocated to Member.	$26.41x	$0.12x	$2.55x	$0.68x	$29.76x

Example (3). Consolidated group within a controlled group. (i) Facts. The facts are the same as in Example 2, except that D and E file a consolidated return.

(ii) Allocation of the group credit. (A) In general. For purposes of allocating the controlled group's research credit of $29.76x among the members of the controlled group, D and E are treated as a single member of the controlled group.

(B) Computation of stand-alone entity credits. The stand-alone entity credit for the consolidated group is computed by treating D and E as a single entity. Under paragraph (c)(2) of this section, the stand-alone entity credit for each member must be computed using the method that results in the greater stand-alone entity credit for that member. The stand-alone entity credit for each of the DE consolidated group ($17.55x) and F ($1.71x) is greater using the AIRC method. Therefore, the stand-alone entity credit for each of the DE consolidated group and F must be computed using the AIRC method. The stand-alone entity credit for G ($0.50x) is greater using the method described in section 41(a). Therefore, the stand-alone entity credit for G must be computed using the method described in section 41(a). The sum of the members' stand-alone entity credits is $19.76x.

(C) Allocation of controlled group credit. Because the group credit of $29.76x is greater than the sum of the stand-alone entity credits of all the members of the group ($19.76x), each member of the group is allocated an amount of the group credit equal to that member's stand-alone entity credit. The excess of the group credit over the sum of the members' stand-alone entity credits ($10.00x) is allocated among the members of the group based on the ratio that each member's QREs bear to the sum of the QREs of all the members of the group. The group credit of $29.76x is allocated as follows:

	DE	F	G	Total
Group Credit				$29.76x
Minus: Sum of Stand-Alone Entity Credits	$17.55x	$1.71x	$0.50x	$19.76x
Equals: Excess Group Credit				$10.00x
Excess Group Credit	$10.00x	$10.00x	$10.00x	....
Multiplied By Allocation Ratio: QREs/Sum of QREs	590/675	70/675	15/675	....
Excess Group Credit Allocated	$8.74x	$1.04x	$0.22x	....
Plus: Stand-Alone Entity Credit	$17.55x	$1.71x	$0.50x	....
Equals: Credit Allocated to Member	$26.29x	$2.75x	$0.72x	$29.76x

(iii) Allocation of the group credit allocated to consolidated group.

(A) In general. The group credit that is allocated to a consolidated group is allocated among the members of the consolidated group in accordance with the principles of paragraph (c) of this section.

(B) Computation of stand-alone entity credits. Under paragraph (c)(2) of this section, the stand-alone entity credit for each member of the consolidated group must be computed using the method that results in the greater stand-alone entity credit for that member. The stand-alone entity credit for D ($19.46x) is greater using the AIRC method. Therefore, the stand-alone entity credit for D must be computed using the AIRC method. The stand-alone entity credit for E is zero under either method. The sum of the stand-alone entity credits of the members of the consolidated group is $19.46x.

(C) Allocation among members of consolidated group. Because the amount of the group credit allocated to the consolidated group ($26.29x) is greater than $19.46x, the sum of the stand-alone entity credits of all the members of the consolidated group, each member of the consolidated group is allocated an amount of the group credit allocated to the consolidated group equal to that member's stand-alone entity credit The excess of the group credit allocated to the consolidated group over the sum of the consolidated group members' stand alone entity credits ($6.83x) is allocated among the members of the consolidated group based on the ratio that each member's QREs bear to the sum of the QREs of all the members of the consolidated group. The group credit of $26.29x allocated to the DE consolidated group is allocated between D and E as follows:

	D	E	Total
Group Credit			$26.29x
Minus: Sum of Stand-Alone Entity Credits	$19.46x	$0.00x	$19.46x
Excess Group Credit			$6.83x
Excess Group Credit	$6.83x	$6.83x	
Multiplied By Allocation Ratio: QREs/Sum of QREs	580/590	10/590	
Excess Group Credit Allocated	$6.71x	$0.12x	
Plus: Stand-Alone Entity Credit	$19.46x	$0.00x	
Equals: Credit Allocated to Member	$26.17x	$0.12x	$26.29x

Example (4). Member is a start-up company. (i) Facts. H, I, and J, all of which are calendar-year taxpayers, are members of a controlled group. The first taxable year for which J has both QREs and gross receipts begins after December 31, 1983, therefore, J is a start-up company under section 41(c)(3)(B)(i). The first taxable year for which H and I had both QREs and gross receipts began before December 31, 1983, therefore, H and I are not start-up companies under section 41(c)(3)(B)(i). For purposes of computing the group credit for the 2004 taxable year (the credit year), H, I, and J had the following:

	H	I	J	Group Aggregate
Credit Year QREs	$200x	$20x	$50x	$270x
1984-1988 QREs	$55x	$15x	$0x	$70x
1984-1988 Gross Receipts	$1,000x	$400x	$0x	$1,400x
Average Annual Gross Receipts for 4 Years Preceding the Credit Year	$1,200x	$200x	$0x	$1,400x

(ii) Computation of the group credit. (A) In general. The research credit allowable to the group is computed as if H, I, and J were one taxpayer. The group credit is equal to 20 percent of the excess of the group's aggregate credit year QREs ($270x) over the group's base amount ($135x). The group credit is 0.20 x ($270x--$135x), which equals $27x.

(B) Group's base amount. (1) Computation. The group's base amount equals the greater of: the group's fixed-base percentage (5 percent) multiplied by the group's aggregate average annual gross receipts for the 4 taxable years preceding the credit year ($1,400x), or the group's minimum base amount ($135x). The group's base amount, therefore, is $135x, which is the greater of: 0.05 x $1,400x, which equals $70x, or $135x.

(2) Group's minimum base amount. The group's minimum base amount is 50 percent of the group's aggregate credit year QREs. The group's minimum base amount is 0.50 x $270x, which equals $135x.

(3) Group's fixed-base percentage. Because the first taxable year in which at least one member of the group has QREs and at least one member of the group has gross receipts does not begin after December 31, 1983, the group is not a start-up company. Therefore, the group's fixed-base percentage is the lesser of: the ratio that the group's aggregate QREs for the taxable years beginning after December 31, 1983, and before January 1, 1989, bear to the group's aggregate gross receipts for the same period, or 16 percent (the statutory maximum). The group's fixed-base percentage, therefore, is 5 percent, which is the lesser of: $70x/$1,400x, which equals 5 percent, or 16 percent.

(iii) Allocation of the group credit. Under paragraph (c)(2) of this section, the stand-alone entity credit for each member of the group must be computed using the method that results in the greater stand-alone entity credit for that member. The stand-alone entity credits for H ($20x), I ($2x), and J ($5x) are greater using the method described in section 41(a). Therefore, the stand-alone entity credits for each of H, I, and J must be computed using the method described in section 41(a). The sum of the stand-alone entity credits of the members of the group is $27x. Because the group credit of $27x is equal to the sum of the stand-alone entity credits of all the members of the group ($27x), the group credit is allocated among the members of the group based on the ratio that each member's stand-alone entity credit bears to the sum of the stand-alone entity credits of all the members of the group. The group credit of $27x is allocated as follows:

	H	I	J	Total
Stand-Alone Entity Credit	$20x	$2x	$5x	$27x
Allocation Ratio (Stand-Alone Entity Credit/Sum of Stand-Alone Entity Credits)	20/27	2/27	5/27	
Multiplied by: Group Credit	$27x	$27x	$27x	
Equals: Credit Allocated to Member	$20x	$2x	$5x	$27x

Example (5). Group is a start-up company. (i) Facts. K, L, and M, all of which are calendar-year taxpayers, are members of a controlled group. The taxable year ending on December 31, 1999, is the first taxable year in which a member of the group had QREs and either the same member or another member also had gross receipts. In that year, each of K, L, and M had both QREs and gross receipts. The 2004 taxable year is the fifth taxable year beginning after December 31, 1993, for which at least one member of the group had QREs For purposes of computing the group credit for the 2004 taxable year (the credit year), K, L, and M had the following:

	K	L	M	Group Aggregate
Credit Year QREs	$255x	$25x	$100x	$380x
1984-1988 QREs	$0x	$0x	$0x	$0x
1984-1988 Gross Receipts	$0x	$0x	$0x	$0x
Average Annual Gross Receipts for 4 Years Preceding the Credit Year	$1,600x	$340x	$300x	$2,240x

(ii) Computation of the group credit. (A) In general. The research credit allowable to the group is computed as if K, L, and M were one taxpayer. The group credit is equal to 20 percent of the excess of the group's aggregate credit year QREs ($380x) over the group's base amount ($190x). The group credit is 0.20x ($380x--$190x), which equals $38x.

(B) Group's base amount. (1) Computation. The group's base amount equals the greater of: the group's fixed-base percentage (3 percent) multiplied by the group's aggregate average annual gross receipts for the 4 taxable years preceding the credit year ($2,240x), or the group's minimum base amount ($190x). The group's base amount, therefore, is $190x, which is the greater of: 0.03 x $2,240x, which equals $67.20x, or $190x.

(2) Group's minimum base amount. The group's minimum base amount is 50 percent of the group's aggregate credit year QREs. The group's minimum base amount is 0.50 x $380x, which equals $190x.

(3) Group's fixed-base percentage. Because the first taxable year in which at least one member of the group has

QREs and at least one member of the group has gross receipts begins after December 31, 1983, the group is treated as a start-up company under section 41(c)(3)(B)(i) and paragraph (b)(2)(i) of this section. Because the 2004 taxable year is the fifth taxable year beginning after December 31, 1993, for which at least one member of the group had QREs, under section 41(c)(3)(B)(ii)(I), the group's fixed-base percentage is 3 percent.

(iii) Allocation of the group credit. Under paragraph (c)(2) of this section, the stand-alone entity credit for each member of the group must be computed using the method that results in the greater stand-alone entity credit for that member. The stand-alone entity credit for each of K ($25.5x), L ($2.5x), and M ($10x) is greater using the method described in section 41(a). Therefore the stand-alone entity credits for each of K, L, and M must be computed using the method described in section 41(a). The sum of the stand-alone entity credits of all the members of the group is $38x. Because the group credit of $38x is equal to sum of the stand-alone entity credits of all the members of the group ($38x), the group credit is allocated among the members of the group based on the ratio that each member's stand-alone entity credit bears to the sum of the stand-alone entity credits of all the members of the group. The $38x group credit is allocated as follows:

	K	L	M	Total
Stand-Alone Entity Credit	$25.5x	$2.5x	$10x	$38x
Allocation Ratio (Stand-Alone Entity Credit/Sum of Stand-Alone Entity Credits).	25.5/38	2.5/38	10/38	
Multiplied by: Group Credit	$38x	$38x	$38x	
Equals: Credit Allocated to Member.	$25.5x	$2.5x	$10x	$38x

Example (6). Group alternative incremental research credit. (i) Facts. N, O, and P, all of which are calendar-year taxpayers, are members of a controlled group. The research credit under section 41(a) is not allowable to the group for the 2004 taxable year because the group's aggregate QREs for the 2004 taxable year are less than the group's base amount. The group credit is computed using the AIRC rules of section 41(c)(4). For purposes of computing the group credit for the 2004 taxable year (the credit year), N, O, and P had the following:

	N	O	P	Group aggregate
Credit Year QREs	$0x	$20x	$110x	$130x
Average Annual Gross Receipts for 4 Years Preceding the Credit Year	$1,200x	$200x	$300x	$1,700x

(ii) Computation of the group credit. The research credit allowable to the group is computed as if N, O, and P were one taxpayer. The group credit is equal to the sum of: 2.65 percent of so much of the group's aggregate QREs for the taxable year as exceeds 1 percent of the group's aggregate average annual gross receipts for the 4 taxable years preceding the credit year, but does not exceed 1.5 percent of such average; 3.2 percent of so much of the group's aggregate QREs as exceeds 1.5 percent of such average but does not exceed 2 percent of such average; and 3.75 percent of so much of such QREs as exceeds 2 percent of such average. The group credit is [0.0265 x [($1,700x x 0.015)--($1,700x x 0.01)]] + [0.032 x [($1,700x x 0.02)--($1,700x x 0.015)]] + [0.0375 x [$130x--($1,700x x 0.02)]], which equals $4.10x.

(iii) Allocation of the group credit. Under paragraph (c)(2) of this section, the stand-alone entity credit for each member of the group must be computed using the method that results in the greater stand-alone entity credit for that member. The stand-alone entity credit for N is zero under either method. The stand-alone entity credit for each of O ($0.66x) and P ($3.99x) is greater using the AIRC method. Therefore, the stand-alone entity credits for each of O and P must be computed using the AIRC method. The sum of the stand-alone entity credits of the members of the group is $4.65x. Because the group credit of $4.10x is less than the sum of the stand-alone entity credits of all the members of the group ($4.65x), the group credit is allocated among the members of the group based on the ratio that each member's stand-alone entity credit bears to the sum of the stand-alone entity credits of all the members of the group. The $4.10x group credit is allocated as follows:

	N	O	P	Total
Stand-Alone Entity Credit	$0.00x	$0.66x	$3.99x	$4.65x
Allocation Ratio (Stand-Alone Entity Credit/Sum of Stand-Alone Entity Credits).	0/4.65	0.66/4.65	3.99/4.65	
Multiplied by: Group Credit	$4.10x	$4.10x	$4.10x	
Equals: Credit Allocated to Member	$0.00x	$0.58x	$3.52x	$4.10x

(f) For taxable years beginning before January 1, 1990. For taxable years beginning before January 1, 1990, see § 1.41-6 as contained in 26 CFR part 1, revised April 1, 2005.

(g) Tax accounting periods used. *(1) In general.* The credit allowable to a member of a controlled group is that member's share of the group credit computed as of the end of that member's taxable year. In computing the group credit for a group whose members have different taxable years, a member generally should treat the taxable year of another member that ends with or within the credit year of the computing member as the credit year of that other member. For example, Q, R, and S are members of a controlled group of corporations. Both Q and R are calendar year taxpayers. S files a return using a fiscal year ending June 30. For purposes of computing the group credit at the end of Q's and R's taxable year on December 31, S's fiscal year ending June 30, which ends within Q's and R's taxable year, is treated as S's credit year.

(2) Special rule when timing of research is manipulated. If the timing of research by members using different tax accounting periods is manipulated to generate a credit in excess of the amount that would be allowable if all members of the group used the same tax accounting period, then the appropriate Internal Revenue Service official in the operating division that has examination jurisdiction of the return may require each member of the group to calculate the credit in the current taxable year and all future years as if all members of the group had the same taxable year and base period as the computing member.

(h) Membership during taxable year in more than one group. A trade or business may be a member of only one group for a taxable year. If, without application of this paragraph, a business would be a member of more than one group at the end of its taxable year, the business shall be treated as a member of the group in which it was included for its preceding taxable year. If the business was not included for its preceding taxable year in any group in which it could be included as of the end of its taxable year, the business shall designate in its timely filed (including extensions) return the group in which it is being included. If the return for a taxable year is due before July 1, 1983, the business may designate its group membership through an amended return for that year filed on or before June 30, 1983. If the business does not so designate, then the appropriate Internal Revenue Service official in the operating division that has examination jurisdiction of the return will determine the group in which the business is to be included.

(i) Intra-group transactions. *(1) In general.* Because all members of a group under common control are treated as a single taxpayer for purposes of determining the research credit, transfers between members of the group are generally disregarded.

(2) In-house research expenses. If one member of a group performs qualified research on behalf of another member, the member performing the research shall include in its QREs any in-house research expenses for that work and shall not treat any amount received or accrued as funding the research. Conversely, the member for whom the research is performed shall not treat any part of any amount paid or incurred as a contract research expense. For purposes of determining whether the in-house research for that work is qualified research, the member performing the research shall be treated as carrying on any trade or business carried on by the member on whose behalf the research is performed.

(3) Contract research expenses. If a member of a group pays or incurs contract research expenses to a person outside the group in carrying on the member's trade or business, that member shall include those expenses as QREs. However, if the expenses are not paid or incurred in carrying on any trade or business of that member, those expenses may be taken into account as contract research expenses by another member of the group provided that the other member—

(i) Reimburses the member paying or incurring the expenses; and

(ii) Carries on a trade or business to which the research relates.

(4) Lease Payments. The amount paid or incurred to another member of the group for the lease of personal property owned by a member of the group is not taken into account for purposes of section 41. Amounts paid or incurred to another member of the group for the lease of personal property owned by a person outside the group shall be taken into account as in-house research expenses for purposes of section 41 only to the extent of the lesser of—

(i) The amount paid or incurred to the other member; or

(ii) The amount of the lease expenses paid to the person outside the group.

(5) Payment for supplies. Amounts paid or incurred to another member of the group for supplies shall be taken into account as in-house research expenses for purposes of section 41 only to the extent of the lesser of—

(i) The amount paid or incurred to the other member; or

(ii) The amount of the other member's basis in the supplies.

(j) Effective/applicability dates. *(1) In general.* Except for paragraph (d) of this section, these regulations are applicable for taxable years ending on or after May 24, 2005. Generally, a taxpayer may use any reasonable method of computing and allocating the credit (including use of the consolidated group rule contained in paragraph (d) of this section) for taxable years ending before May 24, 2005. However, paragraph (b) of this section, relating to the computation of the group credit, and paragraph (c) of this section, relating to the allocation of the group credit, (applied without regard to paragraph (d) of this section) will apply to taxable years ending on or after December 29, 1999, if the members of a controlled group, as a whole, claimed more than 100 percent of the amount that would be allowable under paragraph (b) of this section. In the case of a controlled group whose members have different taxable years and whose members use inconsistent methods of allocation, the members of the controlled group shall be deemed to have, as a whole, claimed more than 100 percent of the amount that would be allowable under paragraph (b) of this section.

(2) Consolidated group rule. Paragraph (d) of this section is applicable for taxable years ending on or after November 9, 2006. For taxable years ending on or after May 24, 2005, and before November 9, 2006, see § 1.41-6T(d) as contained in 26 CFR part 1, revised April 1, 2006.

(3) Taxable years ending on or before December 31, 2006. Paragraphs (b)(1) and (c)(2) of this section are applicable for taxable years ending on or before December 31, 2006. For taxable years ending after December 31, 2006, see § 1.41-6T.

T.D. 9296, 11/8/2006, amend T.D. 9401, 6/13/2008.

PAR. 2. Section 1.41-6 is amended by revising paragraphs (b)(1), (c)(2), (e) and (j) to read as follows:

Proposed § 1.41-6 Aggregation of expenditures. [*For Preamble, see ¶ 153,005*]

* * * * *

(b) *(1)* [The text of the proposed amendment to § 1.41-6(b)(1) is the same as the text of § 1.41-6T(b)(1) published elsewhere in this issue of the Federal Register.] [*See T.D. 9401, 06/17/2008, 73 Fed. Reg. 117.*]

* * * * *

(c) * * *

(2) [The text of the proposed amendment to § 1.41-6(c)(2) is the same as the text of § 1.41-6T(c)(2) published elsewhere in this issue of the Federal Register]. [*See T.D. 9401, 06/17/2008, 73 Fed. Reg. 117.*]

* * * * *

(e) [The text of the proposed amendment to § 1.41-6(e) is the same as the text of § 1.41-6T(e) published elsewhere in this issue of the Federal Register]. [*See T.D. 9401, 06/17/2008, 73 Fed. Reg. 117.*]

* * * * *

(j) [The text of the proposed amendment to § 1.41-6(j) is the same as the text of § 1.41-6T(j) published elsewhere in this issue of the Federal Register]. [*See T.D. 9401, 06/17/2008, 73 Fed. Reg. 117.*]

§ 1.41-6T Aggregation of expenditures.

Caution: The Treasury has not yet amended Reg § 1.41-6T to reflect changes made by 110-458.

(a) [Reserved]. For further guidance, see § 1.41-6(a).

(b) Computation of the group credit. *(1) In general.* All members of a controlled group are treated as a single taxpayer for purposes of computing the research credit. The group credit is computed by applying all of the section 41 computational rules on an aggregate basis. All members of a controlled group must use the same method of computation, either the method described in section 41(a)(1), the alternative incremental credit (AIRC) method described in section 41(c)(4), or the alternative simplified credit (ASC) method described in section 41(c)(5), in computing the group credit for a credit year.

(2) [Reserved]. For further guidance, see § 1.41-6(b)(2).

(c) Allocation of the group credit. *(1)* [Reserved]. For further guidance, see § 1.41-6(c)(1).

(2) Stand-alone entity credit. The term stand-alone entity credit means the research credit (if any) that would be allowable to a member of a controlled group if the credit were computed as if section 41(f)(1) did not apply, except that the member must apply the rules provided in § 1.41-6(d)(1) (relating to consolidated groups) and § 1.41-6(i) (relating to intra-group transactions). Each member's stand-alone entity credit for any credit year must be computed under whichever method (the method described in section 41(a), the method described in section 41(c)(4), or the method described in section 41(c)(5)) results in the greatest stand-alone entity credit for that member, without regard to the method used to compute the group credit.

(d) [Reserved]. For further guidance see § 1.41-6(d).

(e) Example. Group alternative simplified credit. The following example illustrates a group computation in a year for which the ASC method under section 41(c)(5) is in effect. No members of the controlled group are members of a consolidated group and no member of the group made any basic research payments or paid or incurred any amounts to an energy research consortium.

Example. (i) Facts. Q, R, and S, all of which are calendar-year taxpayers, are members of a controlled group. The research credit under section 41(a)(1) is not allowable to the group for the 2008 taxable year (the credit year) because the group's aggregate QREs for the credit year are less than the group's base amount. The group does not use the AIRC method of section 41(c)(4) because its aggregate QREs for the credit year do not exceed 1 percent of the average annual gross receipts for the four years preceding the credit year. The group credit is computed using the ASC rules of section 41(c)(5). Assume that each member of the group had QREs in each of the three years preceding the credit year. For purposes of computing the group credit for the credit year, Q, R, and S had the following:

	Q	R	S	Group aggregate
Credit Year QREs	$0x	$20x	$30x	$50x
Average QREs for 3 Years Preceding the Credit Year	10x	20x	10x	40x

(ii) Computation of the group credit. The research credit allowable to the group is computed as if Q, R, and S are one taxpayer. The group credit is equal to 12 percent of so much of the QREs for the credit year as exceeds 50 percent of the average QREs for the three taxable years preceding the credit year. The group credit is 0.12 x ($50x-(0.5 x $40x)), which equals $3.6x.

(iii) Allocation of the group credit. Under paragraph (c)(2) of this section, the stand-alone entity credit for each member of the group must be computed using the method that results in the greatest stand-alone entity credit for that member. The stand-alone entity credit for Q is zero under all three methods. Assume that the stand-alone entity credit for each of R ($1.2x) and S ($3x) is greatest using the ASC method. Therefore, the stand-alone entity credits for each of R and S must be computed using the ASC method. The sum of the stand-alone entity credits of the members of the group is $4.2x. Because the group credit of $3.6x is less than the sum of the stand-alone entity credits of all the members of the group ($4.2x), the group credit is allocated among the members of the group based on the ratio that each member's stand-alone entity credit bears to the sum of the stand-alone entity credits of all the members of the group. The $3.6x group credit is allocated as follows:

	Q	R	S	Total
Stand-Alone Entity Credit	$0x	$1.2x	$3x	$4.2x
Allocation Ratio (Stand-Alone Entity Credit/Sum of Stand-Alone Entity Credits)	0/4.2	1.2/4.2	3/4.2	
Multiplied by: Group Credit	$3.6x	$3.6x	$3.6x	
Equals: Credit Allocated to Member	$0x	$1.03x	$2.57x	$3.6x

(f) through (i) [Reserved]. For further guidance see § 1.41-6(f) through (i).

(j) Effective/applicability dates. This section is applicable for taxable years ending after December 31, 2006. For taxable years ending on or before December 31, 2006, see § 1.41-6.

(k) Expiration date. The applicability of this section will expire on or before June 13, 2011.

T.D. 9296, 11/8/2006, amend T.D. 9401, 6/13/2008.

§ 1.41-7 Special rules.

Caution: The Treasury has not yet amended Reg § 1.41-7 to reflect changes made by 110-458, P.L. 110-172, P.L. 101-239.

• ***Caution:*** In Notice 2001-19, 2001-10 IRB, IRS announced that these final regs, issued as TD 8930, are under review. Notice 2001-19 says that "[U]pon completion of the review, Treasury and IRS will announce changes to the regulations, if any, in the form of proposed regulations. In addition, TD 8930 will be revised so that the provisions of the regulations, including any changes to TD 8930, will be effective no earlier than the date when the completion of this review is announced, except that the provisions related to internal-use computer software (including any revisions) generally will be applicable for taxable years beginning after December 31, 1985." Notice 2001-19 also says that taxpayers may continue to rely on these final regs during the pendency of this review."

(a) Allocations. *(1) Corporation making an election under subchapter S.* (i) Pass-through, for taxable years beginning after December 31, 1982, in the case of an S corporation. In the case of an S corporation (as defined in section 1361) the amount of research credit computed for the corporation shall be allocated to the shareholders according to the provisions of section 1366 and section 1377.

(ii) Pass-through, for taxable years beginning before January 1, 1983, in the case of a subchapter S corporation. In the case of an electing small business corporation (as defined in section 1371 as that section read before the amendments made by the Subchapter S Revision Act of 1982), the amount of the research credit computed for the corporation for any taxable year shall be apportioned pro rata among the persons who are shareholders of the corporation on the last day of the corporation's taxable year.

(2) Pass-through in the case of an estate or trust. In the case of an estate or trust, the amount of the research credit computed for the estate or trust for any taxable year shall be apportioned among the estate or trust and the beneficiaries on the basis of the income of the estate or trust allocable to each.

(3) Pass-through in the case of a partnership. (i) In general. In the case of a partnership, the research credit computed for the partnership for any taxable year shall be apportioned among the persons who are partners during the taxable year in accordance with section 704 and the regulations thereunder. See, for example, § 1.704-1(b)(4)(ii). Because the research credit is an expenditure-based credit, the credit is to be allocated among the partners in the same proportion as section 174 expenditures are allocated for the year.

(ii) Certain expenditures by joint ventures. Research expenses to which § 1.41-2(a)(4)(ii) applies shall be apportioned among the persons who are partners during the taxable year in accordance with the provisions of that section. For purposes of section 41, these expenses shall be treated as paid or incurred directly by the partners rather than by the partnership. Thus, the partnership shall disregard these expenses in computing the credit to be apportioned under paragraph (a)(3)(i) of this section, and in making the computations under section 41 each partner shall aggregate its distributive share of these expenses with other research expenses of the partner. The limitation on the amount of the credit set out in section 41(g) and in paragraph (c) of this section shall not apply because the credit is computed by the partner, not the partnership.

(4) Year in which taken into account. An amount apportioned to a person under this paragraph shall be taken into account by the person in the taxable year of such person which or within which the taxable year of the corporation, estate, trust, or partnership (as the case may be) ends.

(5) Credit allowed subject to limitation. The credit allowable to any person to whom any amount has been apportioned under paragraph (a)(1), (2) or (3)(i) of this section is subject to section 41(g) and sections 38 and 39 of the Code, if applicable.

(b) Adjustments for certain acquisitions and dispositions—Meaning of terms. For the meaning of "acquisition," "separate unit," and "major portion," see paragraph (b) of § 1.52-2. An "acquisition" includes an incorporation or a liquidation.

(c) Special rule for pass-through of credit. The special rule contained in section 41(g) for the pass-through of the credit in the case of an individual who owns an interest in an unincorporated trade or business, is a partner in a partnership, is a beneficiary of an estate or trust, or is a shareholder in an S corporation shall be applied in accordance with the principles set forth in § 1.53-3.

(d) Carryback and carryover of unused credits. The taxpayer to whom the credit is passed through under paragraph (c) of this section shall not be prevented from applying the unused portion in a carryback or carryover year merely because the entity that earned the credit changes its form of conducting business.

T.D. 8251, 5/16/89, amend T.D. 8930, 12/27/2000.

§ 1.41-8 Alternative incremental credit.

Caution: The Treasury has not yet amended Reg § 1.41-8 to reflect changes made by 110-458, P.L. 109-432.

(a) Determination of credit. At the election of the taxpayer, the credit determined under section 41(a)(1) equals the amount determined under section 41(c)(4).

(b) Election. *(1) In general.* A taxpayer may elect to apply the provisions of the alternative incremental research credit (AIRC) in section 41(c)(4) for any taxable year of the taxpayer beginning after June 30, 1996. If a taxpayer makes an election under section 41(c)(4), the election applies to the taxable year for which made and all subsequent taxable years unless revoked in the manner prescribed in paragraph (b)(3) of this section.

(2) Time and manner of election. An election under section 41(c)(4) is made by completing the portion of Form 6765, "Credit for Increasing Research Activities," relating to the election of the AIRC, and attaching the completed form to the taxpayer's timely filed (including extensions) original return for the taxable year to which the election applies. An election under section 41(c)(4) may not be made on an amended return.

(3) Revocation. An election under this section may not be revoked except with the consent of the Commissioner. A taxpayer is deemed to have requested, and to have been granted, the consent of the Commissioner to revoke an election under section 41(c)(4) if the taxpayer completes the portion of Form 6765 relating to the regular credit and attaches the completed form to the taxpayer's timely filed (including extensions) original return for the year to which the revocation applies. An election under section 41(c)(4) may not be revoked on an amended return.

(4) Special rules for controlled groups. (i) In general. In the case of a controlled group of corporations, all the members of which are not included on a single consolidated return, an election (or revocation) must be made by the designated member by satisfying the requirements of paragraph (b)(2) or (b)(3) of this section (whichever applies), and such election (or revocation) by the designated member shall be binding on all the members of the group for the credit year to which the election (or revocation) relates. If the designated member fails to timely make (or revoke) an election, each member of the group must compute the group credit using the method used to compute the group credit for the immediately preceding credit year.

(ii) Designated member. For purposes of this paragraph (b)(4) of this section, for any credit year, the term designated member means that member of the group that is allocated the greatest amount of the group credit under § 1.41-6(c) based on the amount of credit reported on the original timely filed Federal income tax return (even if that member subsequently is determined not to be the designated member). If the members of a group compute the group credit using different methods (either the method described in section 41(a) or the AIRC method of section 41(c)(4)) and at least two members of the group qualify as the designated member, then the term designated member means that member that computes the group credit using the method that yields the greater group credit. For example, A, B, C, and D are members of a controlled group but are not members of a consolidated group. For the 2005 taxable year, the group credit using the method described in section 41(a) is $10x. Under this method, A would be allocated $5x of the group credit, which would be the largest share of the group credit under this method. For the 2005 taxable year, the group credit using the AIRC method is $15x. Under the AIRC method, C would be allocated $5x of the group credit, which is the largest share of the group credit computed using the AIRC method. Because the group credit is greater using the AIRC method and C is allocated the greatest amount of credit under that method, C is the designated member. Therefore, C's section 41(c)(4) election is binding on all the members of the group for the 2005 taxable year.

(5) Effective/applicability dates. These regulations are applicable for taxable years ending on or after November 9, 2006. For taxable years ending on or after May 24, 2005, and before November 9, 2006, see § 1.41-8T(b)(5) as contained in 26 CFR part 1, revised April 1, 2006. Paragraphs (b)(3) and (b)(4)(ii) of this section are applicable for taxable years ending on or before December 31, 2006. For taxable years ending after December 31, 2006, see § 1.41-8T.

T.D. 9296, 11/8/2006, amend T.D. 9401, 6/13/2008.

PAR. 3. Section 1.41-8 is amended by revising paragraphs (b)(2), (b)(3), (b)(4) and (b)(5) to read as follows:

Proposed § 1.41-8 Alternative incremental credit. [*For Preamble, see ¶ 153,005*]

* * * * *

(b) *(2)* through (b)(5) [The text of proposed § 1.41-8(b)(2) through (b)(5) is the same as the text of § 1.41-8T(b)(2) through (b)(5) published elsewhere in this issue of the Federal Register.] [*See T.D. 9401, 06/17/2008, 73 Fed. Reg. 117.*]

* * * * *

§ 1.41-8T Alternative incremental credit (temporary).

Caution: The Treasury has not yet amended Reg § 1.41-8T to reflect changes made by 110-458.

(a) [Reserved]. For further guidance, see § 1.41-8(a).

(b) Election. *(1)* [Reserved]. For further guidance, see § 1.41-8(b)(1).

(2) Time and manner of election. An election under section 41(c)(4) is made by completing the portion of Form 6765, "Credit for Increasing Research Activities," (or successor form) relating to the election of the AIRC, and attaching the completed form to the taxpayer's timely filed (including extensions) original return for the taxable year to which the election applies. An election under section 41(c)(4) may not be made on an amended return. An extension of time to make an election under section 41(c)(4) will not be granted under § 301.9100-3 of this chapter.

(3) Revocation. An election under this section may not be revoked except with the consent of the Commissioner. A taxpayer is deemed to have requested, and to have been granted, the consent of the Commissioner to revoke an election under section 41(c)(4) if the taxpayer completes the portion of Form 6765, "Credit For Increasing Research Activities," (or successor form) relating to the amount determined under section 41(a)(1) (the regular credit) or the alternative simplified credit (ASC) and attaches the completed form to the taxpayer's timely filed (including extensions) original return for the year to which the revocation applies. An election under section 41(c)(4) may not be revoked on an amended return. An extension of time to revoke an election under sec-

tion 41(c)(4) will not be granted under § 301.9100-3 of this chapter.

(4) Special rules for controlled groups. (i) [Reserved]. For further guidance, see § 1.41-8(b)(4)(i).

(ii) Designated member. For purposes of this paragraph (b)(4), for any credit year, the term designated member means that member of the group that is allocated the greatest amount of the group credit under § 1.41-6(c) based on the amount of credit reported on the original timely-filed Federal income tax return (even if that member subsequently is determined not to be the designated member). If the members of a group compute the group credit using different methods (the method described in section 41(a)(1), the AIRC method of section 41(c)(4), or the ASC method of section 41(c)(5)) and at least two members of the group qualify as the designated member, then the term designated member means that member that computes the group credit using the method that yields the greatest group credit. For example, A, B, C, and D are members of a controlled group but are not members of a consolidated group. For the 2008 taxable year (the credit year), the group credit using the method described in section 41(a)(1) is $10x. Under this method, A would be allocated $5x of the group credit, which would be the largest share of the group credit under this method. For the credit year, the group credit using the AIRC method is $15x. Under the AIRC method, B would be allocated $5x of the group credit, which is the largest share of the group credit computed using the AIRC method. For the credit year, the group credit using the ASC method is $10x. Under the ASC method, C would be allocated $5x of the group credit, which is the largest share of the group credit computed using the ASC method. Because the group credit is greatest using the AIRC method and B is allocated the greatest amount of credit under that method, B is the designated member. Therefore, if B makes a section 41(c)(4) election on its original timely-filed return for the credit year, that election is binding on all members of the group for the credit year.

(5) Effective/applicability dates. This section is applicable for taxable years ending after December 31, 2006. For taxable years ending on or before December 31, 2006, see § 1.41-8.

(6) Expiration date. This applicability of this section expires on or before June 13, 2011.

T.D. 9401, 6/13/2008.

§ 1.41-9 Alternative simplified credit.

Caution: The Treasury has not yet amended Reg § 1.41-9 to reflect changes made by 110-458.

[Reserved]. For further guidance, see § 1.41-9T.

T.D. 9401, 6/13/2008.

Proposed § 1.41-9 Alternative simplified credit. [*For Preamble, see ¶ 153,005*]

[The text of proposed § 1.41-9 is the same as the text of § 1.41-9T (a) through (d) published elsewhere in this issue of the Federal Register.] [*See T.D. 9401, 06/17/2008, 73 Fed. Reg. 117.*]

§ 1.41-9T Alternative simplified credit (temporary).

Caution: The Treasury has not yet amended Reg § 1.41-9T to reflect changes made by 110-458.

(a) Determination of credit. At the election of the taxpayer, the credit determined under section 41(a)(1) equals the amount determined under section 41(c)(5).

(b) Election. *(1) In general.* A taxpayer may elect to apply the provisions of the alternative simplified credit (ASC) in section 41(c)(5) for any taxable year of the taxpayer ending after December 31, 2006. If a taxpayer makes an election under section 41(c)(5), the election applies to the taxable year for which made and all subsequent taxable years unless revoked in the manner prescribed in paragraph (b)(3) of this section.

(2) Time and manner of election. An election under section 41(c)(5) is made by completing the portion of Form 6765, "Credit for Increasing Research Activities," (or successor form) relating to the election of the ASC, and attaching the completed form to the taxpayer's timely filed (including extensions) original return for the taxable year to which the election applies. An election under section 41(c)(5) may not be made on an amended return. An extension of time to make an election under section 41(c)(5) will not be granted under § 301.9100-3 of this chapter.

(3) Revocation. An election under this section may not be revoked except with the consent of the Commissioner. A taxpayer is deemed to have requested, and to have been granted, the consent of the Commissioner to revoke an election under section 41(c)(5) if the taxpayer completes the portion of Form 6765 (or successor form) relating to the credit determined under section 41(a)(1) (the regular credit) or the alternative incremental credit (AIRC) and attaches the completed form to the taxpayer's timely filed (including extensions) original return for the year to which the revocation applies. An election under section 41(c)(5) may not be revoked on an amended return. An extension of time to revoke an election under section 41(c)(5) will not be granted under § 301.9100-3 of this chapter.

(4) Special rules for controlled groups. (i) In general. In the case of a controlled group of corporations, all the members of which are not included on a single consolidated return, an election (or revocation) must be made by the designated member by satisfying the requirements of paragraph (b)(2) or (b)(3) of this section (whichever applies), and such election (or revocation) by the designated member shall be binding on all the members of the group for the credit year to which the election (or revocation) relates. If the designated member fails to timely make (or revoke) an election, each member of the group must compute the group credit using the method used to compute the group credit for the immediately preceding credit year.

(ii) Designated member. For purposes of this paragraph (b)(4), for any credit year, the term designated member means that member of the group that is allocated the greatest amount of the group credit under § 1.41-6(c) based on the amount of credit reported on the original timely-filed Federal income tax return (even if that member subsequently is determined not to be the designated member). If the members of a group compute the group credit using different methods (the method described in section 41(a), the AIRC method of section 41(c)(4), or the ASC method of section 41(c)(5)) and at least two members of the group qualify as the designated member, then the term designated member means that member that computes the group credit using the method that yields the greatest group credit. For example, A, B, C, and

D are members of a controlled group but are not members of a consolidated group. For the 2008 taxable year (the credit year), the group credit using the method described in section 41(a)(1) is $10x. Under this method, A would be allocated $5x of the group credit, which would be the largest share of the group credit under this method. For the credit year, the group credit using the AIRC method is $10x. Under the AIRC method, B would be allocated $5x of the group credit, which is the largest share of the group credit computed using the AIRC method. For the credit year, the group credit using the ASC method is $15x. Under the ASC method, C would be allocated $5x of the group credit, which is the largest share of the group credit computed using the ASC method. Because the group credit is greatest using the ASC method and C is allocated the greatest amount of credit under that method, C is the designated member. Therefore, if C makes a section 41(c)(5) election on its original timely-filed return for the credit year, that election is binding on all members of the group for the credit year.

(c) Special rules. *(1) Qualified research expenses (QREs) required in all years.* Unless a taxpayer has QREs in each of the three taxable years preceding the taxable year for which the credit is being determined, the credit equals that percentage of the QREs for the taxable year provided by section 41(c)(5)(B)(ii).

(2) Section 41(c)(6) applicability. QREs for the three taxable years preceding the credit year must be determined on a basis consistent with the definition of QREs for the credit year, without regard to the law in effect for the three taxable years preceding the credit year. This consistency requirement applies even if the period for filing a claim for credit or refund has expired for any of the three taxable years preceding the credit year.

(3) Section 41(h)(2) applicability. Solely for purposes of the computation under section 41(h)(2), the average QREs for the three taxable years preceding the taxable year for which the credit is being determined shall be treated as the base amount.

(4) Short taxable years. If one or more of the three taxable years preceding the credit year is a short taxable year, then the QREs for such year are deemed to be equal to the QREs actually paid or incurred in that year multiplied by 12 and divided by the number of months in that year. If a credit year is a short taxable year, then the average QREs for the three taxable years preceding the credit year are modified by multiplying that amount by the number of months in the short taxable year and dividing the result by 12.

(5) Controlled groups. For purposes of computing the group credit under § 1.41-6, a controlled group must apply the rules of this paragraph (c) on an aggregate basis. For example, if the controlled group has QREs in each of the three taxable years preceding the taxable year for which the credit is being determined, the controlled group applies the credit computation provided by section 41(c)(5)(A) rather than section 41(c)(5)(B)(ii).

(d) Effective/applicability dates. This section is applicable for taxable years ending after December 31, 2006. For certain transitional rules, see Division A, section 104(b)(3), (c)(2), and (c)(4) of the Tax Relief and Health Care Act of 2006 (Pub. L. 109-432, 120 Stat. 2922).

(e) Expiration date. The applicability of this section expires on or before June 13, 2011.

T.D. 9401, 6/13/2008.

§ 1.42-0 Table of contents.

This section lists the paragraphs contained in §§ 1.42-1 and 1.42-2.

§ 1.42-1 [Reserved]

§ 1.42-2 Waiver of requirement that an existing building eligible for the low-income housing credit was last placed in service more than 10 years prior to acquisition by the taxpayer.

(a) Low-income housing credit for existing building

(b) Waiver of 10-year holding period requirement

(c) Waiver requirements

(1) Federally-assisted building

(2) Federal mortgage funds at risk

(3) Statement by the Department of Housing and Urban Development or the Farmers' Home Administration

(4) No prior credit allowed

(d) Application for waiver

(1) Time and manner

(2) Information required

(3) Other rules

(4) Effective date of waiver

(5) Attachment to return

(e) Effective date of regulations

T.D. 8302, 5/22/90.

§ 1.42-1 Limitation on low-income housing credit allowed with respect to qualified low-income buildings receiving housing credit allocations from a State or local housing credit agency.

(a) through (g) [Reserved]. For further guidance, see § 1.42-1T(a) through (g).

(h) Filing of forms. Unless otherwise provided in forms or instructions, a completed Form 8586, "Low-Income Housing Credit," (or any successor form) must be filed with the owner's Federal income tax return for each taxable year the owner of a qualified low-income building is claiming the low-income housing credit under section 42(a). Unless otherwise provided in forms or instructions, a completed Form 8609, "Low-Income Housing Credit Allocation and Certification," (or any successor form) must be filed by the building owner with the IRS. The requirements for completing and filing Forms 8586 and 8609 are addressed in the instructions to the forms.

(i) [Reserved]. For further guidance, see § 1.42-1T(i).

(j) Effective dates. Section 1.42-1(h) applies to forms filed on or after November 7, 2005. The rules that apply for forms filed before November 7, 2005 are contained in § 1.42-1T(h) and § 1.42-1(h) (see 26 CFR part 1 revised as of April 1, 2003, and April 1, 2005).

T.D. 9112, 1/26/2004, amend T.D. 9228, 11/4/2005.

§ 1.42-1T Limitation on low-income housing credit allowed with respect to qualified low-income buildings receiving housing credit allocations from a State or local housing credit agency (temporary).

Caution: The Treasury has not yet amended Reg § 1.42-1T to reflect changes made by P.L. 110-343, P.L. 106-554, P.L. 103-66, P.L. 101-508, P.L. 101-239, P.L. 100-647.

(a) In general. *(1) Determination of amount of low-income housing credit.* Section 42 provides that, for purposes of section 38, a low-income housing credit is determined for a building in an amount equal to the applicable percentage of the qualified basis of the qualified low-income building. In general, the credit may be claimed annually for a 10-year credit period, beginning with the taxable year in which the building is placed in service or, at the election of the taxpayer, the succeeding taxable year. If, after the first year of the credit period, the qualified basis of a building is increased in excess of the qualified basis upon which the credit was initially determined, the allowable credit with respect to such additional qualified basis is determined using a credit percentage equal to two-thirds of the applicable percentage for the initial qualified basis. The credit for additions to qualified basis is generally allowable for the remaining years in the 15-year compliance period which begins with the first taxable year of the credit period for the building. In general, the low-income housing credit is available with respect to buildings placed in service after December 31, 1986, in taxable years ending after that date. See section 42 for the definitions of "qualified low-income building", "applicable percentage", "qualified basis", "credit period", "compliance period", and for other rules relating to determination of the amount of the low-income housing credit.

(2) Limitation on low-income housing credit allowed. Generally, the low-income housing credit determined under section 42 is allowed and may be claimed for any taxable year if, and to the extent that, the owner of a qualified low-income building receives a housing credit allocation from a State or local housing credit agency. The aggregate amount of housing credit allocations that may be made in any calendar year by all housing credit agencies within a State is limited by a State housing credit ceiling, or volume cap, described in paragraph (b) of this section. The authority to make housing credit allocations within the State housing credit ceiling may be apportioned among the State and local housing credit agencies, under the rules prescribed in paragraph (c) of this section. Upon apportionment of the State housing credit volume cap, each State or local housing credit agency receives an aggregate housing credit dollar amount that may be used to make housing credit allocations among qualified low-income buildings located within an agency's geographic jurisdiction. The rules governing the making of housing credit allocations by any state or local housing credit agency are provided in paragraph (d) of this section. Housing credit allocations are required to be taken into account by owners of qualified low-income buildings under the rules prescribed in paragraph (e) of this section. Exceptions to the requirement that a qualified low-income building receive a housing credit allocation from a State or local housing credit agency are provided in paragraph (f) of this section. Rules regarding termination of the authority of State and local housing credit agencies to make housing credit allocations after December 31, 1989, are specified in paragraph (g) of this section. Rules concerning information reporting by State and local housing credit agencies and owners of qualified low-income buildings are provided in paragraph (h) of this section. Special statutory transitional rules are incorporated into this section of the regulations as described in paragraph (i) of this section.

(b) The State housing credit ceiling. The aggregate amount of housing credit allocations that may be made in any calendar year by all State and local housing credit agencies within a State may not exceed the State's housing credit ceiling for such calendar year. The State housing credit ceiling for each State for any calendar year is equal to $1.25 multiplied by the State's population. A State's population for any calendar year is determined by reference to the most recent census estimate (whether final or provisional) of the resident population of the State released by the Bureau of the Census before the beginning of the calendar year for which the State's housing credit ceiling is set. Unless otherwise prescribed by applicable revenue procedure, determinations of population are based on the most recent estimates of population contained in the Bureau of the Census publication, "Current Population Reports, Series P-25: Population Estimates and Projections, Estimates of the Population of States". For purposes of this section, the District of Columbia and United States possessions are treated as States.

(c) Apportionment of State housing credit ceiling among State and local housing credit agencies. *(1) In general.* A State's housing credit ceiling for any calendar year is apportioned among the State and local housing credit agencies within such State under the rules prescribed in this paragraph. A "State housing credit agency" is any State agency specifically authorized by gubernatorial act or State statute to make housing credit allocations on behalf of the State and to carry out the provisions of section 42(h). A "local housing credit agency" is any agency of a political subdivision of the State that is specifically authorized by a State enabling act to make housing credit allocations on behalf of the State or political subdivision and to carry out the provisions of section 42(h). A "State enabling act" is any gubernatorial act, State statute, or State housing credit agency regulation (if authorized by gubernatorial act or State statute). A State enabling act enacted on or before October 22, 1986, the date of enactment of the Tax Reform Act of 1986, shall be given effect for purposes of this paragraph if such State enabling act expressly carries out the provision of section 42(h).

(2) Primary apportionment. Except as otherwise provided in paragraphs (c)(3) and (4) of this section, a State's housing credit ceiling is apportioned in its entirety to the State housing credit agency. Such an apportionment is the "primary apportionment" of a State's housing credit ceiling. There shall be no primary apportionment of the State housing credit ceiling and no grants of housing credit allocations in such State until a State housing credit agency is authorized by gubernatorial act or State statute. If a State has more than one State housing credit agency, such agencies shall be treated as a single agency for purposes of the primary apportionment. In such a case, the State housing credit ceiling may be divided among the multiple State housing credit agencies pursuant to gubernatorial act or State statute.

(3) States with 1 or more constitutional home rule cities. (i) In general. Notwithstanding paragraph (c)(2) of this section, in any State with 1 or more constitutional home rule cities, a portion of the State housing credit ceiling is apportioned to each constitutional home rule city. In such a State, except as provided in paragraph (c)(4) of this section, the remainder of the State housing credit ceiling is apportioned to the State housing credit agency under paragraph (c)(2) of this section. See paragraph (c)(3)(iii) of this section. The term "constitutional home rule city" means, with respect to any calendar year, any political subdivision of a State that, under a State constitution that was adopted in 1970 and effective on July 1, 1971, had home rule powers on the first day of the calendar year.

(ii) Amount of apportionment to a constitutional home rule city. The amount of the State housing credit ceiling apportioned to a constitutional home rule city for any calendar year is an amount that bears the same ratio to the State housing credit ceiling for that year as the population of the constitutional home rule city bears to the population of the entire State. The population of any constitutional home rule city for any calendar year is determined by reference to the most recent census estimate (whether final or provisional) of the resident population of the constitutional home rule city released by the Bureau of the Census before the beginning of the calendar year for which the State housing credit ceiling is apportioned. However, determinations of the population of a constitutional home rule city may not be based on Bureau of the Census estimates that do not contain estimates for all of the constitutional home rule cities within the State. If no Bureau of the Census estimate is available for all such constitutional home rule cities, the most recent decennial census of population shall be relied on. Unless otherwise prescribed by applicable revenue procedure, determinations of population for constitutional home rule cities are based on estimates of population contained in the Bureau of the Census publication, "Current Population Reports, Series P-26: Local Population Estimates".

(iii) Effect of apportionments to constitutional home rule cities on apportionments to other housing credit agencies. The aggregate amounts of the State housing credit ceiling apportioned to constitutional home rule cities under this paragraph (c)(3) reduce the State housing credit ceiling available for apportionment under paragraph (c)(2) or (4) of this section. Unless otherwise provided in a State constitutional amendment or by law changing the home rule provisions adopted in a manner provided by the State constitution, the power of the governor or State legislature to apportion the State housing credit ceiling among local housing credit agencies under paragraph (c)(4) of this section shall not be construed as allowing any reduction of the portion of the State housing credit ceiling apportioned to a constitutional home rule city under this paragraph (c)(3). However, any constitutional home rule city may agree to a reduction in its apportionment of the State housing credit ceiling under this paragraph (c)(3), in which case the amount of the State housing credit ceiling not apportioned to the constitutional home rule city shall be available for apportionment under paragraph (c)(2) or (4) of this section.

(iv) Treatment of governmental authority within constitutional home rule city. For purposes of determining which agency within a constitutional home rule city receives the apportionment of the State housing credit ceiling under this paragraph (c)(3), the rules of this paragraph (c) shall be applied by treating the constitutional home rule city as a "State", the chief executive officer of a constitutional home rule city as a "governor", and a city council as a "State legislature". A constitutional home rule city is also treated as a "State" for purposes of the set-aside requirement for housing credit allocations to projects involving a qualified nonprofit organization. See paragraph (c)(5) of this section for rules governing set-aside requirements. In this connection, a constitutional home rule city may agree with the State housing credit agency to exchange an apportionment set aside for projects involving a qualified nonprofit organization for an apportionment that is not so restricted. In such a case, the authorizing gubernatorial act, State statute, or State housing credit agency regulation (if authorized by gubernatorial act or State statute) must ensure that the set-aside apportionment transferred to the State housing credit agency be used for the purposes described in paragraph (c)(5) of this section.

(4) Apportionment to local housing credit agencies. (i) In general. In lieu of the primary apportionment under paragraph (c)(2) of this section, all or a portion of the State housing credit ceiling may be apportioned among housing credit agencies of governmental subdivisions. Apportionments of the State housing credit ceiling to local housing credit agencies must be made pursuant to a State enabling act as defined in paragraph (c)(1) of this section. Apportionments of the State housing credit ceiling may be made to housing credit agencies of constitutional home rule cities under this paragraph (c)(4), in addition to apportionments made under paragraph (c)(3) of this section. Apportionments of the State housing credit ceiling under this paragraph (c)(4) need not be based on the population of political subdivisions and may, but are not required to, give balanced consideration to the low-income housing needs of the entire State.

(ii) Change in apportionments during a calendar year. The apportionment of the State housing credit ceiling among State and local housing credit agencies under this paragraph (c)(4) may be changed after the beginning of a calendar year, pursuant to a State enabling act. No change in apportionments shall retroactively reduce the housing credit allocations made by any agency during such year. Any change in the apportionment of the State housing credit ceiling under this paragraph (c)(4) that occurs during a calendar year is effective only to the extent housing credit agencies have not previously made housing credit allocations during such year from their original apportionments of the State housing credit ceiling for such year. To the extent apportionments of the State housing credit ceiling to local housing credit agencies made pursuant to this paragraph (c)(4) for any calendar year are not used by such local agencies before a certain date (e.g., November 1) to make housing credit allocations in such year, the amount of unused apportionments may revert back to the State housing credit agency for reapportionment. Such reversion must be specifically authorized by the State enabling act.

(iii) Exchanges of apportionments. Any State or local housing credit agency that receives an apportionment of the State housing credit ceiling for any calendar year under this paragraph (c)(4) may exchange part or all of such apportionment with another State or local housing credit agency to the extent no housing credit allocations have been made in such year from the exchanged portions. Such exchanges must be made with another housing credit agency in the same State and must be consistent with the State enabling act. If an apportionment set aside for projects involving a qualified nonprofit organization is transferred or exchanged, the transferee housing credit agency shall be required to use the set-aside apportionment for the purposes described in paragraph (c)(5) of this section.

(iv) Written records of apportionments. All apportionments, exchanges of apportionments, and reapportionments of the State housing credit ceiling which are authorized by this paragraph (c)(4) must be evidenced in the written records maintained by each State and local housing credit agency.

(5) Set-aside apportionments for projects involving a qualified nonprofit organization. (i) In general. Ten percent of the State housing credit ceiling for a calendar year must be set aside exclusively for projects involving a qualified nonprofit organization (as defined in paragraph (c)(5)(ii) of this section). Thus, at least 10 percent of apportionments of the State housing credit ceiling under paragraphs (c)(2) and (3) of this section must be used only to make housing credit allocations to buildings that are part of projects involving a qualified nonprofit organization. In the case of apportionments of the State housing credit ceiling under paragraph (c)(4) of this section, the State enabling act must ensure that

the apportionment of at least 10 percent of the State housing credit ceiling be used exclusively to make housing credit allocations to buildings that are part of projects involving a qualified nonprofit organization. The State enabling act shall prescribe which housing credit agencies in the State receive apportionments that must be set aside for making housing credit allocations to buildings that are part of projects involving a qualified nonprofit organization. These set-aside apportionments may be distributed disproportionately among the State or local housing credit agencies receiving apportionments under paragraph (c)(4) of this section. The 10-percent set-aside requirement of this paragraph (c)(4) is a minimum requirement, and the State enabling act may set aside more than 10 percent of the State housing credit ceiling for apportionment to housing credit agencies for exclusive use in making housing credit allocations to buildings that are part of projects involving a qualified nonprofit organization.

(ii) Projects involving a qualified nonprofit organization. The term "projects involving a qualified nonprofit organization" means projects with respect to which a qualified nonprofit organization is to materially participate (within the meaning of section 469(h)) in the development and continuing operation of the project throughout the 15-year compliance period. The term "qualified nonprofit organization" means any organization that is described in section 501(c)(3) or (4), is exempt from tax under section 501(a), and includes as one of its exempt purposes the fostering of low-income housing.

(6) Expiration of unused apportionments. Apportionments of the State housing credit ceiling under this paragraph (c) for any calendar year may be used by housing credit agencies to make housing credit allocations only in such calendar year. Any part of an apportionment of the State housing credit ceiling for any calendar year that is not used for housing credit allocations in such year expires as of the end of such year and does not carry over to any other year. However, any part of an apportionment for 1989 that is not used to make a housing credit allocation in 1989 may be carried over to 1990 and used to make a housing credit allocation to a qualified low-income building described in section 42(n)(2)(B). See paragraph (g)(2) of this section.

(d) Housing credit allocations made by State and local housing credit agencies. *(1) In general.* This paragraph governs State and local housing credit agencies in making housing credit allocations to qualified low-income buildings. The amount of the apportionment of the State housing credit ceiling for any calendar year received by any State or local housing credit agency under paragraph (c) of this section constitutes the agency's aggregate housing credit dollar amount for such year. The aggregate amount of housing credit allocations made in any calendar year by a State or local housing credit agency may not exceed such agency's aggregate housing credit dollar amount for such year. A State or local housing credit agency may make housing credit allocations only to qualified low-income buildings located within the agency's geographic jurisdiction.

(2) Amount of a housing credit allocation. In making a housing credit allocation, a State or local housing credit agency must specify a credit percentage, not to exceed the building's applicable percentage determined under section 42(b), and a qualified basis amount. The amount of the housing credit allocation for any building is the product of the specified credit percentage and the specified qualified basis amount. In specifying the credit percentage and qualified basis amount, the State or local housing credit agency shall not take account of the first-year conventions described in section 42(f)(2)(A) and (3)(B). A State or local housing credit agency may adopt rules or regulations governing conditions for specification of less than the maximum credit percentage and qualified basis amount allowable under section 42(b) and (c), respectively. For example, an agency may specify a credit percentage and a qualified basis amount of less than the maximum credit percentage and qualified basis amount allowable under section 42(b) and (c), respectively, when the financing and rental assistance from all sources for the project of which the building is a part is sufficient to provide the continuing operation of the building without the maximum credit amount allowable under section 42.

(3) Counting housing credit allocations against an agency's aggregate housing credit dollar amount. The aggregate amount of housing credit allocations made in any calendar year by a State or local housing credit agency may not exceed such agency's aggregate housing credit dollar amount (i.e., the agency's apportionment of the State housing credit ceiling for such year). This limitation on the aggregate dollar amount of housing credit allocations shall be computed separately for set-aside apportionments received pursuant to paragraph (c)(5) of this section. Housing credit allocations count against an agency's aggregate housing credit dollar amount without regard to the amount of credit allowable to or claimed by an owner of a building in the taxable year in which the allocation is made or in any subsequent year. Thus, housing credit allocations (which are computed without regard to the first-year conventions as provided in paragraph (d)(2) of this section) count in full against an agency's aggregate housing credit dollar amount, even though the first-year conventions described in section 42(f)(2)(A) and (3)(B) may reduce the amount of credit claimed by a taxpayer in the first year in which a credit is allowable. See also paragraph (e)(2) of this section. Housing credit allocations count against an agency's aggregate housing credit dollar amount only in the calendar year in which made and not in subsequent taxable years in the credit period or compliance period during which a taxpayer may claim a credit based on the original housing credit allocation. Since the aggregate amount of housing credit allocations made in any calendar year by a State or local housing credit agency may not exceed such agency's aggregate housing credit dollar amount, an agency shall at all times during a calendar year maintain a record of its cumulative allocations made during such year and its remaining unused aggregate housing credit dollar amount.

(4) Rules for when applications for housing credit allocations exceed an agency's aggregate housing credit dollar amount. A State or local housing credit agency may adopt rules or regulations governing the awarding of housing credit allocations when an agency expects that applicants during a calendar year will seek aggregate allocations in excess of the agency's aggregate housing credit dollar amount. The State enabling act may provide uniform standards for the awarding of housing credit allocations when there is actual or anticipated excess demand from applicants in any calendar year.

(5) Reduced or additional housing credit allocations. (i) In general. A State or local housing credit agency may not reduce or rescind a housing credit allocation made to a qualified low-income building in the manner prescribed in paragraph (d)(8) of this section. Thus, a housing credit agency may not reduce or rescind a housing credit allocation made to a qualified low-income building which is acquired by a new owner who is entitled to a carryover of the allowable credit for such building under section 42(d)(7). A housing credit agency may make additional housing credit allocations

to a building in any year in the building's compliance period, whether or not there are additions to qualified basis for which an increased credit is allowable under section 42(f)(3). Each additional housing credit allocation made to a building is treated as a separate allocation and is subject to the rules and requirements of this section. However, in the case of an additional housing credit allocation made with respect to additions to qualified basis for which an increased credit is allowable under section 42(f)(3), the amount of the allocation that counts against the agency's aggregate housing credit dollar amount shall be computed as if the specified credit percentage were unreduced in the manner prescribed in section 42(f)(3)(A) and the specified qualified basis amount were unreduced by the first-year convention prescribed in section 42(f)(3)(B).

(ii) Examples. The rules of paragraph (d)(5)(i) of this section may be illustrated by the following examples:

Example (1). For 1987, the County L Housing Credit Agency has an aggregate housing credit dollar amount of $2 million. D, an individual, places in service on July 1, 1987, a new qualified low-income building. As of the close of each month in 1987 in which the building is in service, the building consists of 100 residential rental units, of which 20 units are both rent-restricted and occupied by individuals whose income is 50 percent or less of area median gross income. The total floor space of the residential rental units is 120,000 square feet, and the total floor space of the low-income units is 20,000 square feet. The building is not Federally subsidized within the meaning of section 42(i)(2). As of the end of 1987, the building has eligible basis under section 42(d) of $1 million. Thus, the qualified basis of the building determined without regard to the first-year convention provided in section 42(f) is $166,666.67 (i.e., $1 million eligible basis times 1/6, the floor space fraction which is required to be used instead of the larger unit fraction). However, the amount of the low-income housing credit determined for 1987 under section 42 reflects the first-year convention provided in section 42(f)(2). Since the building has the same floor space and unit fractions as of the close of each of the six months in 1987 during which it is in service, upon applying the first-year convention in section 42(f)(2), the qualified basis of the building in 1987 is $83,333.33 (i.e., $1 million eligible basis times 1/12, the fraction determined under section 42(f)(2)(A)). Under paragraph (d)(2) of this section, the County L Housing Credit Agency may make a housing credit allocation by specifying a credit percentage, not to exceed 9 percent, and a qualified basis amount, which may be greater or less than the qualified basis of the building in 1987 as determined under section 42(c), without regard to the first-year convention provided in section 42(f)(2). If the County L Housing Credit Agency specifies a credit percentage of 8 percent and a qualified basis amount of $100,000, the amount of the housing credit allocation is $8,000. Under paragraph (d)(3) of this section, the County L Housing Credit Agency's aggregate housing credit dollar amount for 1987 is reduced by $8,000, notwithstanding that D is entitled to claim less than $8,000 of the credit in 1987 under the rules in paragraph (e) of this section. Under paragraph (e)(2) of this section, in 1987 D is entitled to claim only $4,000 of the credit, determined by applying the first-year convention of 6/12 to the specified qualified basis amount contained in the housing credit allocation (i.e., .08 × $100,000)

Example (2). The facts are the same as in Example (1) except that on July 1, 1988, the number of occupied low-income units increases to 50 units and the floor space of the occupied low-income units increases to 48,000 square feet. These occupancy fractions remain unchanged as of the close of each month remaining in 1988. Under section 42(c), the qualified basis of the building in 1988, without regard to the first-year convention in section 42(f)(3)(B), is $400,000 (i.e., $1 million eligible basis times .4, the floor space fraction which is required to be used instead of the larger unit fraction). D's 1987 housing credit allocation from the County L Housing Credit Agency remains effective in 1988 and entitles D to a credit of $8,000 (i.e., .08, the specified credit percentage, times $100,000, the specified qualified basis amount). With respect to the additional $300,000 of qualified basis which the 1987 housing credit allocation does not cover, D must apply to the County L Housing Credit Agency for an additional housing credit allocation. Assume that the County L Housing Credit Agency has a sufficient aggregate housing credit dollar amount for 1988 to make a housing credit allocation to D in 1988 by specifying a credit percentage of 9 percent and a qualified basis amount of $300,000. The amount of the housing credit allocation that counts against the County L Housing Credit Agency's aggregate housing credit dollar amount is $27,000 (i.e., the amount counted (.09 times $300,000) is unreduced in the manner prescribed in section 42(f)(3)(A) and (B)). Since D's qualified basis in 1987 was $166,666.67, D is entitled to claim a credit in 1988 with respect to such basis of $14,000 (i.e., .08 × $100,000, the 1987 credit allocation, + .09 × $66,666.67, the 1988 credit allocation). In addition, D is entitled to claim a credit in 1988 and subsequent years in the 15-year compliance period with respect to the additional $233,333.33 of qualified basis covered by the 1988 housing credit allocation. However, the allowable credit for 1988 with respect to this amount of additional qualified basis is subject to reductions prescribed in section 42(f)(3)(A) and (B). Thus, D is entitled in 1988 to a credit at a 6-percent rate applied to $116,666.67 of additional qualified basis, which is reduced to reflect the first-year convention. D's total allowable low-income housing credit in 1988 is $21,000 (i.e., $14,000 with respect to original qualified basis + $7,000 with respect to 1988 additions to qualified basis). If the County L Housing Credit Agency had specified an 8-percent credit percentage in 1988 with respect to the qualified basis not covered by the 1987 housing credit allocation to D, D's allowable credit with respect to the $233,333.33 of additions to qualified basis would not exceed, in 1988 and subsequent years, an amount determined by applying a specified credit percentage of 5.33 percent (i.e., two-thirds of 8 percent). In 1988, D's specified qualified basis amount would be adjusted for the first-year convention.

(6) No carryover of unused aggregate housing credit dollar amount. Any portion of a State or local housing credit agency's aggregate housing credit dollar amount for any calendar year that is not used to make a housing credit allocation in such year may not be carried over to any other year, except as provided in paragraph (g) of this section. An agency may not permit owners of qualified low-income buildings to transfer housing credit allocations to other buildings. However, an agency may provide a procedure whereby owners may return to the agency, prior to the end of the calendar year in which housing credit allocations are made, unusable portions of such allocations. In such a case, an owner's housing credit allocation is deemed reduced by the amount of the allocation returned to the agency, and the agency may reallocate such amount to other qualified low-income buildings prior to the end of the year.

(7) Effect of housing credit allocations in excess of an agency's aggregate housing credit dollar amount. In the

event that a State or local housing credit agency makes housing credit allocations in excess of its aggregate housing credit dollar amount for any calendar year, the allocations shall be deemed reduced (to the extent of such excess) for buildings in the reverse order in which such allocations were made during such year.

(8) Time and manner for making housing credit allocations. (i) Time. Housing credit allocations are effective for the calendar year in which made in the manner prescribed in paragraph (d)(8)(ii) of this section. A State or local housing credit agency may not make a housing credit allocation to a qualified low-income building prior to the calendar year in which such building is placed in service. An agency may adopt its own procedures for receiving applications for housing credit allocations from owners of qualified low-income buildings. An agency may provide a procedure for making, in advance of a building's being placed in service, a binding commitment (e.g., by contract, inducement resolution, or other means) to make a housing credit allocation in the calendar year in which a qualified low-income building is placed in service or in a subsequent calendar year. Any advance commitment shall constitute a housing credit allocation for purposes of this section.

(ii) Manner. Housing credit allocations are deemed made when Part I of IRS Form 8609, Low-Income Housing Credit Allocation Certification, is completed and signed by an authorized official of the housing credit agency and mailed to the owner of the qualified low-income building. A copy of all completed (as to Part I) Form 8609 allocations along with a single completed Form 8610, Annual Low-Income Housing Credit Agencies Report, must also be mailed to the Internal Revenue Service not later than the 28th day of the second calendar month after the close of the calendar year in which the housing credit was allocated to the qualified low-income building. Housing credit allocations to a qualified low-income building must be made on Form 8609 and must include—

(A) The address of the building;

(B) The name, address, and taxpayer identification number of the housing credit agency making housing credit allocation;

(C) The name, address, and taxpayer identification number of the owner of the qualified low-income building;

(D) The date of the allocation of housing credit;

(E) The housing credit dollar amount allocated to the building on such date;

(F) The specified maximum applicable credit percentage allocated to the building on such date;

(G) The specified maximum qualified basis amount;

(H) The percentage of the aggregate basis financed by tax-exempt bonds taken into account for purposes of the volume cap under section 146;

(I) A certification under penalties of perjury by an authorized State or local housing credit agency official that the allocation is made in compliance with the requirements of section 42(h); and

(J) Any additional information that may be required by Form 8609 or by an applicable revenue procedure.

See paragraph (h) of this section for additional rules concerning filing of forms.

(iii) Certification. The certifying official for the State or local housing credit agency need not perform an independent investigation of the qualified low-income building in order to certify on Part I of Form 8609 that the housing credit allocation meets the requirements of section 42(h). For example, the certifying official may rely on information contained in an application for a low-income housing credit allocation submitted by the building owner which sets forth facts necessary to determine that the building is eligible for the low-income housing credit under section 42.

(iv) Fee. A State or local housing credit agency may charge building owners applying for housing credit allocations a reasonable fee to cover the agency's administrative expenses for processing applications.

(v) No continuing agency responsibility. The State or local housing credit agency need not monitor or investigate the continued compliance of a qualified low-income building with the requirements of section 42 throughout the applicable compliance period.

(e) Housing credit allocation taken into account by owner of a qualified low-income building. *(1) Time and manner for taking housing credit allocation into account.* An owner of a qualified low-income building may not claim a low-income housing credit determined under section 42 in any year in excess of an effective housing credit allocation received from a State or local housing credit agency. A housing credit allocation made to a qualified low-income building is effective with respect to any owner of the building beginning with the owner's taxable year in which the housing credit allocation is received. A housing credit allocation is deemed received in a taxable year, except as modified in the succeeding sentence, if that allocation is made (in the manner described in paragraph (d)(8) of this section) not later than the earlier of (i) the 60th day after the close of the taxable year, or (ii) the close of the calendar year in which such taxable year ends. A housing credit allocation is deemed received in a taxable year ending in 1987, if such allocation is made (in the manner described in paragraph (d)(8) of this section) on or before December 31, 1987. A housing credit allocation is not effective for any taxable year if received in a calendar year which ends prior to when the qualified low-income building is placed in service. A housing credit allocation made to a qualified low-income building remains effective for all taxable years in the compliance period.

(2) First-year convention limitation on housing credit allocation taken into account. For purposes of the limitation that the allowable low-income housing credit may not exceed the effective housing credit allocation received from a State or local housing credit agency, as provided in paragraph (e)(1) of this section, the amount of the effective housing credit allocation shall be adjusted by applying the first-year convention provided in section 42(f)(2)(A) and (3)(B) and the percentage credit reduction provided in section 42(f)(3)(A). Under paragraphs (d)(2) and (5) of this section, the State of local housing credit agency must specify the credit percentage and qualified basis amount, the product of which is the amount of the housing credit allocation, without taking account of the first-year convention described in section 42(f)(2)(A) and (3)(B) or the percentage credit reduction prescribed in section 42(f)(3)(A). However, for purposes of the limitation on the amount of the allowable low-income housing credit, as provided in paragraph (e)(2) of this section, in a taxable year in which the first-year convention applies to the amount of credit determined under section 42(a), the specified qualified basis amount shall be adjusted by the first-year convention fraction which is equal to the number of full months (during the first taxable year) in which the building was in service divided by 12. In addition, for pur-

poses of the limitation on the amount of the allowable low-income housing credit, as provided in paragraph (e)(1) of this section, in a taxable year in which the reduction in credit percentage applies to additions to qualified basis, as prescribed in section 42(f)(3), the specified credit percentage shall be reduced by one-third. See examples in paragraphs (d)(5)(ii) and (e)(3)(ii) of this section.

(3) Use of excess housing credit allocation for increases in qualified basis. (i) In general. If the housing credit allocation made to a qualified low-income building exceeds the amount of credit allowable with respect to such building in any taxable year (without regard to the first-year conventions under section 42(f)), such excess is not transferable to another qualified low-income building. However, if in a subsequent year there are increases in the qualified basis for which an increased credit is allowable under section 42(f)(3) at a reduced credit percentage, the original housing credit allocation (including the specified credit percentage and qualified basis amount) would be effective with respect to such increased credit.

(ii) Example. The provisions of this paragraph (e)(3) may be illustrated by the following example:

Example. In 1987, a newly-constructed qualified low-income building receives a housing credit allocation of $90,000 based on a specified credit percentage of 9 percent and a specified qualified basis amount of $1,000,000. The building is placed in service in 1987, but the qualified basis in such year is only $800,000, resulting in an allowable credit in 1987 (determined without regard to the first-year conventions) of $72,000. In 1988, the qualified basis is increased to $1,100,000, resulting in an additional credit allowable under section 42(f)(3) (without regard to the first-year conventions) of $18,000 (i.e., $300,000 × .06 or ⅔ of .09). The unused portion of the 1987 housing credit allocation ($18,000) is effective in 1988 and in each subsequent year in the compliance period only with respect to the specified qualified basis for the 1987 housing credit allocation ($1,000,000). Thus, the owner is allowed to claim a credit in 1988 and in each subsequent year (without regard to the first-year conventions), based on the effective housing credit allocation from 1987, of $84,000 (i.e., $72,000 + ($200,000 × .06)). The owner of the qualified low-income building must obtain a new housing credit allocation in 1988 with respect to the additional $100,000 of qualified basis in order to claim a credit on such basis in 1988 and in each subsequent year. If the applicable first-year convention under section 42(f)(3)(B) entitled the owner in 1988 to only ½ of the otherwise applicable credit for the additions to qualified basis, under paragraph (e)(2) of this section the owner is allowed to claim a credit in 1988, based on the effective housing credit allocation from 1987, of $78,000 (i.e., $72,000)

(4) Separate housing credit allocations for new buildings and increases in qualified basis. Separate housing credit allocations must be received for each building with respect to which a housing credit may be claimed. Rehabilitation expenditures with respect to a qualified low-income building are treated as a separate new building under section 42(e) and must receive a separate housing credit allocation. Increases in qualified basis in a qualified low-income building are not generally treated as a new building for purposes of section 42. To the extent that a prior housing credit allocation received with respect to a qualified low-income building does not allow an increased credit with respect to an increase in the qualified basis of such building, an additional housing credit allocation must be received in order to claim a credit with respect to that portion of increase in qualified basis. See paragraph (e)(3) of this section. The amount of credit allowable with respect to an increase in qualified basis is subject to the credit percentage limitation of section 42(f)(3)(A) and the first-year convention of section 42(f)(3)(B). See paragraph (d)(5) of this section for a rule requiring that the State or local housing credit agency count a housing credit allocation made with respect to an increase in qualified basis as if the specified credit percentage were unreduced in the manner prescribed in section 42(f)(3) and the specified basis amount were unreduced by the first-year convention prescribed in section 42(f)(3)(B).

(5) Acquisition of building for which a prior housing credit allocation has been made. If a carryover credit would be allowable to an acquirer of a qualified low-income building under section 42(d)(7), such acquirer need not obtain a new housing credit allocation with respect to such building. Under section 42(d)(7), the acquirer would be entitled to claim only such credits as would have been allowable to the prior owner of the building.

(6) Multiple housing credit allocations. A qualified low-income building may receive multiple housing credit allocations from different housing credit agencies having overlapping jurisdictions. A qualified low-income building that receives a housing credit allocation set aside exclusively for projects involving a qualified nonprofit organization may also receive a housing credit allocation from a housing credit agency's aggregate housing credit dollar amount that is not so set aside.

(f) Exception to housing credit allocation requirement. *(1) Tax-exempt bond financing.* (i) In general. No housing credit allocation is required in order to claim a credit under section 42 with respect to that portion of the eligible basis (as defined in section 42(d)) of a qualified low-income building that is financed with the proceeds of an obligation described in section 103(a) ("tax-exempt bond") which is taken into account for purposes of the volume cap under section 146. In addition, no housing credit allocation is required in order to claim a credit under section 42 with respect to the entire qualified basis (as defined in section 42(c)) of a qualified low-income building if 70 percent or more of the aggregate basis of the building and the land on which the building is located is financed with the proceeds of tax-exempt bonds which are taken into account for purposes of the volume cap under section 146. For purposes of this paragraph, "land on which the building is located" includes only land that is functionally related and subordinate to the qualified low-income building. See § 1.103-8(b)(4)(iii) for the meaning of the term "functionally related and subordinate". For purposes of this paragraph, the basis of the land shall be determined using principles that are consistent with the rules contained in section 42(d).

(ii) Determining use of bond proceeds. For purposes of determining the portion of proceeds of an issue of tax-exempt bonds used to finance (A) the eligible basis of a qualified low-income building, and (B) the aggregate basis of the building and the land on which the building is located, the proceeds of the issue must be allocated in the bond indenture or a related document (as defined in § 1.103-13(b)(8)) in a manner consistent with the method used to allocate the net proceeds of the issue for purposes of determining whether 95 percent or more of the net proceeds of the issue are to be used for the exempt purpose of the issue. If the issuer is not consistent in making this allocation throughout the bond indenture and related documents, or if neither the bond indenture nor a related document provides an allocation, the proceeds of the issue will be allocated on a pro rata basis to all of the property financed by the issue, based on the relative cost of the property.

(iii) Example. The provisions of this paragraph may be illustrated by the following example:

Example. In 1987, County K assigns $500,000 of its volume cap for private activity bonds under section 146 to a $500,000 issue of exempt facility bonds to provide a qualified residential rental project to be owned by A, an individual. The aggregate basis of the building and the land on which the building is located is $700,000. Under the terms of the bond indenture, the net proceeds of the issue are to be used to finance $490,000 of the eligible basis of the building. More than 70 percent of the aggregate basis of the qualified low-income building and the land on which the building is located is financed with the proceeds of tax-exempt bonds to which a portion of the volume cap under section 146 was allocated. Accordingly, A may claim a credit under section 42 without regard to whether any housing credit dollar amount was allocated to that building. If, instead, the aggregate basis of the building and land were $800,000, A would be able to claim the credit under section 42 without receiving a housing credit allocation for the building only to the extent that the credit was attributable to eligible basis of the building financed with tax-exempt bonds.

(g) Termination of authority to make housing credit allocation. *(1) In general.* No State or local housing credit agency shall receive an apportionment of a State housing credit ceiling for calendar years after 1989. Consequently, no housing credit allocations may be made after 1989, except as provided in paragraph (g)(2) of this section. Housing credit allocations made prior to January 1, 1990, remain effective after such date.

(2) Carryover of unused 1989 apportionment. Any State or local housing credit agency that has an unused portion of its apportionment of the State housing credit ceiling for 1989 from which housing credit allocations have not been made in 1989 may carry over such unused portion into 1990. Such carryover portion of the 1989 apportionment shall be treated as the agency's apportionment for 1990. From this 1990 apportionment, the State or local housing credit agency may make housing credit allocations only to a qualified low-income building meeting the following requirements:

(i) The building must be constructed, reconstructed, or rehabilitated by the taxpayer seeking the allocation;

(ii) More than 10 percent of the reasonably anticipated cost of such construction, reconstruction, or rehabilitation must have been incurred as of January 1, 1989; and

(iii) The building must be placed in service before January 1, 1991.

(3) Expiration of exception for tax-exempt bond financed projects. The exception to the requirement that a housing credit allocation be received with respect to any portion of the eligible basis of a qualified low-income building, as provided in paragraph (f) of this section, shall not apply to any building placed in service after 1989, unless such building is described in paragraph (g)(2)(i), (ii), and (iii) of this section.

(h) Filing of forms. For further guidance, see § 1.42-1(h).

(i) Transitional rules. The transitional rules contained in section 252(f)(1) of the Tax Reform Act of 1986 are incorporated into this section of the regulations for purposes of determining whether a qualified low-income building is entitled to receive a housing credit allocation or is excepted from the requirement that a housing credit allocation be received. Housing credit allocations made to qualified low-income buildings described in section 252(f)(1) shall not count against the State or local housing credit agency's aggregate housing credit dollar amount. The transitional rules contained in section 252(f)(2) of the Tax Reform Act of 1986 are incorporated into this section of the regulations for purposes of determining, amounts available to certain State or local housing credit agencies for the making of housing credit allocations to certain qualified low-income housing projects. Amounts available to housing credit agencies under section 252(f)(2) shall be treated as special apportionments unavailable for housing credit allocations to qualified low-income buildings not described in section 252(f)(2). Housing credit allocations made from the special apportionments shall not count against the State or local credit agency's aggregate housing credit dollar amount. The set-aside requirements shall not apply to these special apportionments. The transitional rules contained in section 252(f)(3) of the Tax Reform Act 1986 are incorporated in this section of the regulations for purposes of determining the amount of housing credit allocations received by certain qualified low-income buildings. Housing credit allocations deemed received under section 252(f)(3) shall not count against the State or local housing credit agency's aggregate housing credit dollar amount.

T.D. 8144, 6/17/87, amend T.D. 9112, 01/26/2004.

§ 1.42-2 Waiver of requirement that an existing building eligible for the low-income housing credit was last placed in service more than 10 years prior to acquisition by the taxpayer.

Caution: The Treasury has not yet amended Reg § 1.42-2 to reflect changes made by P.L. 110-289.

(a) Low-income housing credit for existing building. Section 42 provides that, for purposes of section 38, new and existing qualified low-income buildings are eligible for a low-income housing credit. The eligibility rules for new and existing buildings differ. Under section 42(d)(2), an existing building may be eligible for the low-income housing credit based upon the acquisition cost and amounts chargeable to capital account (to the extent properly included in eligible basis) if—

(1) The taxpayer acquires the building by purchase (as defined in section 179(d)(2), as applicable under section 42(d)(2)(D)(iii)(I)),

(2) There is a period of at least 10 years between the date of the building's acquisition by the taxpayer and the later of—

(i) The date the building was last placed in service, or

(ii) The date of the most recent nonqualified substantial improvement of the building, and

(3) The building was not previously placed in service by the taxpayer, or by a person who was a related person (as defined in section 42(d)(2)(D)(iii)(II)) with respect to the taxpayer as of the time the building was last previously placed in service.

(b) Waiver of 10-year holding period requirement. Section 42(d)(6) provides that a taxpayer may apply for a waiver of the 10-year holding period requirement specified in paragraph (a)(2) of this section. The Internal Revenue Service will grant a waiver only if—

(1) The existing building satisfies all of the requirements in paragraph (c) of this section, and

(2) The taxpayer makes an application in conformity with the requirements in paragraph (d) of this section.

(c) Waiver requirements. *(1) Federally-assisted building.* To satisfy the requirement of this paragraph, a building must be a Federally-assisted building. The term "Federally assisted building" means any building which is substantially assisted, financed, or operated under section 8 of the United States Housing Act of 1937, section 221(d)(3) or 236 of the National Housing Act, or section 515 of the Housing Act of 1949, as such acts were in effect on October 22, 1986.

(2) Federal mortgage funds at risk. To satisfy the requirement of this paragraph, Federal mortgage funds must be at risk with respect to a mortgage that is secured by the building or a project of which the building is a part. For purposes of this paragraph, Federal mortgage funds are at risk if, in the event of a default by the mortgagor on the mortgage secured by the building or the project of which the building is a part—

(i) The mortgage could be assigned to the Department of Housing and Urban Development or the Farmers' Home Administration, or

(ii) There could arise a claim against a Federal mortgage insurance fund (or such Department or Administration).

(3) Statement by the Department of Housing and Urban Development or the Farmers' Home Administration. (i) To satisfy the requirement of this paragraph, a letter or other written statement must be made or received and approved by the national office of the Department of Housing and Urban Development or the Farmers Home Administration ("the Federal agency"). This letter or statement shall include the following:

(A) A statement that, as of the earlier of the time of the taxpayer's acquisition of the building or the taxpayer's application for a waiver, the building is a Federally-assisted building within the meaning of paragraph (c)(1) of this section and identifies the source of Federal assistance;

(B) A statement that a waiver of the 10-year holding period requirement is necessary to avert Federal mortgage funds being at risk within the meaning of paragraph (c)(2) of this section; and

(C) A statement that the Federal agency has taken a Federal agency action as described in paragraph (c)(3)(ii) of this section.

(ii) The following specified Federal agency actions shall be the only means of satisfying the requirement of this paragraph:

(A) The Federal agency intends to accept an assignment of a mortgage secured by the building or the project of which the building is a part, and such assignment requires payments by the agency or a mortgage insurance fund maintained by the agency to the prior mortgagee;

(B) The Federal agency or a mortgage insurance fund maintained by the agency intends to accept, as a consequence of foreclosure proceedings or otherwise, conveyance of the building or the project of which the building is a part;

(C) The Federal agency or a mortgage insurance fund maintained by the agency intends, as a consequence of default, to take possession of, hold title to, or otherwise assume ownership of the building or the project of which the building is a part; or

(D) The Federal agency has designated the building or the project of which the building is a part as a troubled building or project. A designation of a troubled building or project must satisfy the following requirements:

(1) Designation of troubled status must be based on a review by the Federal agency of the financial condition of the building or project and on a determination by the Federal agency of a history of financial distress or mortgage defaults;

(2) Designation of troubled status must be made or received and approved by the national office of the Federal agency; and

(3) Federal agency regulations or procedures must provide that, in the event of transfer of the ownership of a designated troubled building or project, the building or project may be subject to continued review by the Federal agency. Each Federal agency may prescribe its own standards and procedures for designating a troubled building or project so long as such standards are consistent with the requirements of this paragraph (c)(3)(ii)(D).

(4) No prior credit allowed. The requirement of this paragraph is satisfied only if no prior owner was allowed a low-income housing credit under section 42 for the building.

(d) Application for waiver. *(1) Time and manner.* In order to receive a waiver of the 10-year holding period requirement specified in paragraph (a)(2) of this section, a taxpayer must file an application (including the applicable user fee) that complies with the requirements of this paragraph (d) and Rev. Proc. 90-1, 1990-1 I.R.B. 8 (or any subsequent applicable revenue procedure). The application must be filed by a taxpayer who has acquired the building by purchase or who has a binding contract to purchase the building. Such binding contract may be conditioned upon the granting of a waiver under this section. The application may be filed at any time after a binding contract has been entered into, but no later than 12 months after the taxpayer's acquisition of the building. An application for a waiver of the 10-year holding period requirement must not contain a request for a ruling on any other issue arising under section 42 or other sections of the Internal Revenue Code. An application for a waiver of the 10-year holding period requirement must be mailed or delivered to the address listed in section 3.01 of Rev. Proc. 90-1 (or any subsequent applicable revenue procedure).

(2) Information required. An application for a waiver of the 10-year holding period requirement must contain the following information:

(i) The taxpayer's name, address and taxpayer identification number;

(ii) The name (if any) and address of the acquired building and the project (if any) of which it is a part;

(iii) The date of acquisition or the date of the binding contract for acquisition of the building by the taxpayer and the expected date of acquisition, the amount of consideration paid or to be paid for the acquisition (including the value of any liabilities assumed by the taxpayer), and the taxpayer's certification that such acquisition is by purchase (as defined in section 179(d)(2), as applicable under section 42(d)(2)(D)(iii)(I));

(iv) The identity of the person from whom the building is acquired, and whether such person is a Federal agency, a mortgagee holding title to the building, or the mortgagor or prior owner;

(v) The date the building was last placed in service and the date of the most recent (if any) nonqualified substantial improvement of the building (as defined in section 42(d)(2)(D)(i));

(vi) The taxpayer's certification that the building was not previously placed in service by the taxpayer, or by a person who was a related person (as defined in section

42(d)(2)(D)(iii)(II)) with respect to the taxpayer as of the time the building was last placed in service;

(vii) The amount and disposition (e.g., discharge, assignment, assumption, or refinance) of the outstanding mortgage at the time of acquisition and the identities of the mortgagee and mortgagor;

(viii) The taxpayer's certification that no prior owner was allowed a low-income housing credit under section 42 for the building (made to the best of the taxpayer's knowledge, with no documentation from other persons needed to be submitted); and

(ix) The statement from the Federal agency required by paragraph (c)(3)(i) of this section.

(3) Other rules. (i) In the event that an acquired building will be owned by more than one taxpayer, a single application for waiver may be filed by one taxpayer on behalf of the co-owners if the application contains the names, addresses and taxpayer identification numbers of the other owners. A general partner or a designated limited partner may file an application for waiver on behalf of a partnership.

(ii) In the event that multiple Federally-assisted buildings in a project are being acquired by the taxpayer, a single application for waiver with respect to such buildings may be filed if the application contains the required information set out for the address of each Federally-assisted building involved.

(iii) In the event that specific Federally-assisted buildings are being acquired by the taxpayer in a project consisting of multiple buildings that may or may not be Federally-assisted, a single application for waiver with respect to the Federally-assisted buildings being acquired may be filed if the application contains the required information set out for the address of each Federally-assisted building being acquired.

(4) Effective date of waiver. A waiver will be effective when granted in writing by the Internal Revenue Service after submission of a completed application for waiver filed under this paragraph (d).

(5) Attachment to return. A waiver letter granted by the Internal Revenue Service shall be filed with the taxpayer's Federal income tax return for the first taxable year the low-income housing credit is claimed by the taxpayer.

(e) Effective date of regulations. The provisions of § 1.42-2 are effective for buildings placed in service by the taxpayer after December 31, 1986.

T.D. 8302, 5/22/90.

---

§ 1.42-3 Treatment of buildings financed with proceeds from a loan under an Affordable Housing Program established pursuant to section 721 of the Financial Institutions Reform, Recovery, and Enforcement Act of 1989 (FIRREA).

(a) Treatment under sections 42(i) and 42(b). A below market loan funded in whole or in part with funds from an Affordable Housing Program established under section 721 of FIRREA is not, solely by reason of the Affordable Housing Program funds, a below market Federal loan as defined in section 42(i)(2)(D). Thus, any building with respect to which the proceeds of the loan are used during the tax year is not, solely be reason of the Affordable Housing Program funds, treated as a federally subsidized building for that tax year and subsequent tax years for purposes of determining the applicable percentage for the building under section 42(b).

(b) Effective date. The rules set forth in paragraph (a) of this section are effective for loans made after August 8, 1989.

T.D. 8368, 9/25/91.

---

§ 1.42-4 Application of not-for-profit rules of section 183 to low-income housing credit activities.

(a) Inapplicability to section 42. In the case of a qualified low-income building with respect to which the low-income housing credit under section 42 is allowable, section 183 does not apply to disallow losses, deductions, or credits attributable to the ownership and operation of the building.

(b) Limitation. Notwithstanding paragraph (a) of this section, losses, deductions, or credits attributable to the ownership and operation of a qualified low-income building with respect to which the low-income housing credit under section 42 is allowable may be limited or disallowed under other provisions of the Code or principles of tax law. See, e.g., sections 38(c), 163(d), 465, 469; Knetsch v. United States, 364 U.S. 361 (1960), 1961-1 C.B. 34 ("sham" or "economic substance" analysis); and Frank Lyon Co. v Commissioner, 435 U.S. 561 (1978), 1978-1 C.B. 46 ("ownership" analysis).

(c) Effective date. The rules set forth in paragraphs (a) and (b) of this section are effective with respect to buildings placed in service after December 31, 1986.

T.D. 8420, 6/10/92.

---

§ 1.42-5 Monitoring compliance with low-income housing credit requirements.

(a) Compliance monitoring requirement. *(1) In general.* Under section 42(m)(1)(B)(iii), an allocation plan is not qualified unless it contains a procedure that the State or local housing credit agency ("Agency") (or an agent of, or other private contractor hired by, the Agency) will follow in monitoring for noncompliance with the provisions of section 42 and in notifying the Internal Revenue Service of any noncompliance of which the Agency becomes aware. These regulations only address compliance monitoring procedures required of Agencies. The regulations do not address forms and other records that may be required by the Service on examination or audit. For example, if a building is sold or otherwise transferred by the owner, the transferee should obtain from the transferor information related to the first year of the credit period so that the transferee can substantiate credits claimed.

(2) Requirements for a monitoring procedure. (i) In general. A procedure for monitoring for noncompliance under section 42(m)(1)(B)(iii) must include—

(A) The recordkeeping and record retention provisions of paragraph (b) of this section;

(B) The certification and review provisions of paragraph (c) of this section;

(C) The inspection provision of paragraph (d) of this section; and

(D) The notification-of-noncompliance provisions of paragraph (e) of this section.

(ii) Order and form. A monitoring procedure will meet the requirements of section 42(m)(1)(B)(iii) if it contains the substance of these provisions. The particular order and form of the provisions in the allocation plan is not material. A monitoring procedure may contain additional provisions or requirements.

(b) Recordkeeping and record retention provisions. *(1) Recordkeeping provision.* Under the recordkeeping provision, the owner of a low-income housing project must be required to keep records for each qualified low-income building in the project that show for each year in the compliance period—

(i) The total number of residential rental units in the building (including the number of bedrooms and the size in square feet of each residential rental unit);

(ii) The percentage of residential rental units in the building that are low-income units;

(iii) The rent charged on each residential rental unit in the building (including any utility allowances);

(iv) The number of occupants in each low-income unit, but only if rent is determined by the number of occupants in each unit under section 42(g)(2) (as in effect before the amendments made by the Omnibus Budget Reconciliation Act of 1989);

(v) The low-income unit vacancies in the building and information that shows when, and to whom, the next available units were rented;

(vi) The annual income certification of each low-income tenant per unit. For an exception to this requirement, see section 42(g)(8)(B) (which provides a special rule for a 100 percent low-income building);

(vii) Documentation to support each low-income tenant's income certification (for example, a copy of the tenant's federal income tax return, Forms W-2, or verifications of income from third parties such as employers or state agencies paying unemployment compensation). For an exception to this requirement, see section 42(g)(8)(B) (which provides a special rule for a 100 percent low-income building). Tenant income is calculated in a manner consistent with the determination of annual income under section 8 of the United States Housing Act of 1937 ("Section 8"), not in accordance with the determination of gross income for federal income tax liability. In the case of a tenant receiving housing assistance payments under Section 8, the documentation requirement of this paragraph (b)(1)(vii) is satisfied if the public housing authority provides a statement to the building owner declaring that the tenant's income does not exceed the applicable income limit under section 42(g);

(viii) The eligible basis and qualified basis of the building at the end of the first year of the credit period; and

(ix) The character and use of the nonresidential portion of the building included in the building's eligible basis under section 42(d) (e.g., tenant facilities that are available on a comparable basis to all tenants and for which no separate fee is charged for use of the facilities, or facilities reasonably required by the project).

(2) Record retention provision. Under the record retention provision, the owner of a low-income housing project must be required to retain the records described in paragraph (b)(1) of this section for at least 6 years after the due date (with extensions) for filing the federal income tax return for that year. The records for the first year of the credit period, however, must be retained for at least 6 years beyond the due date (with extensions) for filing the federal income tax return for the last year of the compliance period of the building.

(3) Inspection record retention provision. Under the inspection record retention provision, the owner of a low-income housing project must be required to retain the original local health, safety, or building code violation reports or notices that were issued by the State or local government unit (as described in paragraph (c)(1)(vi) of this section) for the Agency's inspection under paragraph (d) of this section. Retention of the original violation reports or notices is not required once the Agency reviews the violation reports or notices and completes its inspection, unless the violation remains uncorrected.

(c) Certification and review provisions. *(1) Certification.* Under the certification provision, the owner of a low-income housing project must be required to certify at least annually to the Agency that, for the preceding 12-month period—

(i) The project met the requirements of:

(A) The 20-50 test under section 42(g)(1)(A), the 40-60 test under section 42(g)(1)(B), or the 25-60 test under sections 42(g)(4) and 142(d)(6) for New York City, whichever minimum set-aside test was applicable to the project; and

(B) If applicable to the project, the 15-40 test under sections 42(g)(4) and 142(d)(4)(B) for "deep rent skewed" projects;

(ii) There was no change in the applicable fraction (as defined in section 42(c)(1)(B)) of any building in the project, or that there was a change, and a description of the change;

(iii) The owner has received an annual income certification from each low-income tenant, and documentation to support that certification; or, in the case of a tenant receiving Section 8 housing assistance payments, the statement from a public housing authority described in paragraph (b)(1)(vii) of this section. For an exception to this requirement, see section 42(g)(8)(B) (which provides a special rule for a 100 percent low-income building);

(iv) Each low-income unit in the project was rent-restricted under section 42(g)(2);

(v) All units in the project were for use by the general public (as defined in Sec. 1.42-9), including the requirement that no finding of discrimination under the Fair Housing Act, 42 U.S.C. 3601-3619, occurred for the project. A finding of discrimination includes an adverse final decision by the Secretary of the Department of Housing and Urban Development (HUD), 24 CFR 180.680, an adverse final decision by a substantially equivalent state or local fair housing agency, 42 U.S.C. 3616a(a)(1), or an adverse judgment from a federal court;

(vi) The buildings and low-income units in the project were suitable for occupancy, taking into account local health, safety, and building codes (or other habitability standards), and the State or local government unit responsible for making local health, safety, or building code inspections did not issue a violation report for any building or low-income unit in the project. If a violation report or notice was issued by the governmental unit, the owner must attach a statement summarizing the violation report or notice or a copy of the violation report or notice to the annual certification submitted to the Agency under paragraph (c)(1) of this section. In addition, the owner must state whether the violation has been corrected;

(vii) There was no change in the eligible basis (as defined in section 42(d)) of any building in the project, or if there was a change, the nature of the change (e.g., a common area has become commercial space, or a fee is now charged for a tenant facility formerly provided without charge);

(viii) All tenant facilities included in the eligible basis under section 42(d) of any building in the project, such as swimming pools, other recreational facilities, and parking areas, were provided on a comparable basis without charge to all tenants in the building;

(ix) If a low-income unit in the building became vacant during the year, that reasonable attempts were or are being made to rent that unit or the next available unit of comparable or smaller size to tenants having a qualifying income before any units in the project were or will be rented to tenants not having a qualifying income;

(x) If the income of tenants of a low-income unit in the project increased above the limit allowed in section 42(g)(2)(D)(ii), the next available unit of comparable or smaller size in the project was or will be rented to tenants having a qualifying income; and

(xi) An extended low-income housing commitment as described in section 42(h)(6) was in effect (for buildings subject to section 7108(c)(1) of the Omnibus Budget Reconciliation Act of 1989, 103 Stat. 2106, 2308-2311), including the requirement under section 42(h)(6)(B)(iv) that an owner cannot refuse to lease a unit in the project to an applicant because the applicant holds a voucher or certificate of eligibility under section 8 of the United States Housing Act of 1937, 42 U.S.C. 1437f (for buildings subject to section 13142(b)(4) of the Omnibus Budget Reconciliation Act of 1993, 107 Stat. 312, 438-439); and

(xii) All low-income units in the project were used on a nontransient basis (except for transitional housing for the homeless provided under section 42(i)(3)(B)(iii) or single-room-occupancy units rented on a month-by-month basis under section 42(i)(3)(B)(iv)).

(2) Review. The review provision must—

(i) Require that the Agency review the certifications submitted under paragraph (c)(1) of this section for compliance with the requirements of section 42;

(ii) Require that with respect to each low-income housing project—

(A) The Agency must conduct on-site inspections of all buildings in the project by the end of the second calendar year following the year the last building in the project is placed in service and, for at least 20 percent of the project's low-income units, inspect the units and review the low-income certifications, the documentation supporting the certifications, and the rent records for the tenants in those units; and

(B) At least once every 3 years, the Agency must conduct on-site inspections of all buildings in the project and, for at least 20 percent of the project's low-income units, inspect the units and review the low-income certifications, the documentation supporting the certifications, and the rent records for the tenants in those units; and

(iii) Require that the Agency randomly select which low-income units and tenant records are to be inspected and reviewed by the Agency. The review of tenant records may be undertaken wherever the owner maintains or stores the records (either on-site or off-site). The units and tenant records to be inspected and reviewed must be chosen in a manner that will not give owners of low-income housing projects advance notice that a unit and tenant records for a particular year will or will not be inspected and reviewed. However, an Agency may give an owner reasonable notice that an inspection of the building and low-income units or tenant record review will occur so that the owner may notify tenants of the inspection or assemble tenant records for review (for example, 30 days notice of inspection or review).

(3) Frequency and form of certification. A monitoring procedure must require that the certifications and reviews of paragraph (c)(1) and (2) of this section be made at least annually covering each year of the 15-year compliance period under section 42(i)(1). The certifications must be made under penalty of perjury. A monitoring procedure may require certifications and reviews more frequently than on a 12-month basis, provided that all months within each 12-month period are subject to certification.

(4) Exception for certain buildings. (i) In general. The review requirements under paragraph (c)(2)(ii) of this section may provide that owners are not required to submit, and the Agency is not required to review, the tenant income certifications, supporting documentation, and rent records for buildings financed by the Rural Housing Service (RHS), formerly known as Farmers Home Administration, under the section 515 program, or buildings of which 50 percent or more of the aggregate basis (taking into account the building and the land) is financed with the proceeds of obligations the interest on which is exempt from tax under section 103 (tax-exempt bonds). In order for a monitoring procedure to except these buildings, the Agency must meet the requirements of paragraph (c)(4)(ii) of this section.

(ii) Agreement and review. The Agency must enter into an agreement with the RHS or tax-exempt bond issuer. Under the agreement, the RHS or tax-exempt bond issuer must agree to provide information concerning the income and rent of the tenants in the building to the Agency. The Agency may assume the accuracy of the information provided by RHS or the tax-exempt bond issuer without verification. The Agency must review the information and determine that the income limitation and rent restriction of section 42(g)(1) and (2) are met. However, if the information provided by the RHS or tax-exempt bond issuer is not sufficient for the Agency to make this determination, the Agency must request the necessary additional income or rent information from the owner of the buildings. For example, because RHS determines tenant eligibility based on its definition of "adjusted annual income," rather than "annual income" as defined under Section 8, the Agency may have to calculate the tenant's income for section 42 purposes and may need to request additional income information from the owner.

(iii) Example. The exception permitted under paragraph (c)(4)(i) and (ii) of this section is illustrated by the following example.

Example. An Agency selects for review buildings financed by the RHS. The Agency has entered into an agreement described in paragraph (c)(4)(ii) of this section with the RHS with respect to those buildings. In reviewing the RHS-financed buildings, the Agency obtains the tenant income and rent information from the RHS for 20 percent of the low-income units in each of those buildings. The Agency calculates the tenant income and rent to determine whether the tenants meet the income and rent limitation of section 42(g)(1) and (2). In order to make this determination, the Agency may need to request additional income or rent information from the owners of the RHS buildings if the information provided by the RHS is not sufficient.

(5) Agency reports of compliance monitoring activities. The Agency must report its compliance monitoring activities annually on Form 8610, "Annual Low-Income Housing Credit Agencies Report."

(d) Inspection provision. *(1) In general.* Under the inspection provision, the Agency must have the right to perform an on-site inspection of any low-income housing project at least through the end of the compliance period of the buildings in the project. The inspection provision of this paragraph (d) is a separate requirement from any tenant file review under paragraph (c)(2)(ii) of this section.

(2) Inspection standard. For the on-site inspections of buildings and low-income units required by paragraph (c)(2)(ii) of this section, the Agency must review any local health, safety, or building code violations reports or notices retained by the owner under paragraph (b)(3) of this section and must determine—

(i) Whether the buildings and units are suitable for occupancy, taking into account local health, safety, and building codes (or other habitability standards); or

(ii) Whether the buildings and units satisfy, as determined by the Agency, the uniform physical condition standards for public housing established by HUD (24 CFR 5.703). The HUD physical condition standards do not supersede or preempt local health, safety, and building codes. A low-income housing project under section 42 must continue to satisfy these codes and, if the Agency becomes aware of any violation of these codes, the Agency must report the violation to the Service. However, provided the Agency determines by inspection that the HUD standards are met, the Agency is not required under this paragraph (d)(2)(ii) to determine by inspection whether the project meets local health, safety, and building codes.

(3) Exception from inspection provision. An Agency is not required to inspect a building under this paragraph (d) if the building is financed by the RHS under the section 515 program, the RHS inspects the building (under 7 CFR part 1930), and the RHS and Agency enter into a memorandum of understanding, or other similar arrangement, under which the RHS agrees to notify the Agency of the inspection results.

(4) Delegation. An Agency may delegate inspection under this paragraph (d) to an Authorized Delegate retained under paragraph (f) of this section. Such Authorized Delegate, which may include HUD or a HUD-approved inspector, must notify the Agency of the inspection results.

(e) Notification-of-noncompliance provision. *(1) In general.* Under the notification-of-noncompliance provisions, the Agency must be required to give the notice described in paragraph (e)(2) of this section to the owner of a low-income housing project and the notice described in paragraph (e)(3) of this section to the Service.

(2) Notice to owner. The Agency must be required to provide prompt written notice to the owner of a low-income housing project if the Agency does not receive the certification described in paragraph (c)(1) of this section, or does not receive or is not permitted to inspect the tenant income certifications, supporting documentation, and rent records described in paragraph (c)(2)(ii) of this section, or discovers by inspection, review, or in some other manner, that the project is not in compliance with the provisions of section 42.

(3) Notice to Internal Revenue Service. (i) In general. The Agency must be required to file Form 8823, "Low-Income Housing Credit Agencies Report of Noncompliance," with the Service no later than 45 days after the end of the correction period (as described in paragraph (e)(4) of this section, including extensions permitted under that paragraph) and no earlier than the end of the correction period, whether or not the noncompliance or failure to certify is corrected. The Agency must explain on Form 8823 the nature of the noncompliance or failure to certify and indicate whether the owner has corrected the noncompliance or failure to certify. Any change in either the applicable fraction or eligible basis under paragraph (c)(1)(ii) and (vii) of this section, respectively, that results in a decrease in the qualified basis of the project under section 42(c)(1)(A) is noncompliance that must be reported to the Service under this paragraph (e)(3). If an Agency reports on Form 8823 that a building is entirely out of compliance and will not be in compliance at any time in the future, the Agency need not file Form 8823 in subsequent years to report that building's noncompliance. If the noncompliance or failure to certify is corrected within 3 years after the end of the correction period, the Agency is required to file Form 8823 with the Service reporting the correction of the noncompliance or failure to certify.

(ii) Agency retention of records. An Agency must retain records of noncompliance or failure to certify for 6 years beyond the Agency's filing of the respective Form 8823. In all other cases, the Agency must retain the certifications and records described in paragraph (c) of this section for 3 years from the end of the calendar year the Agency receives the certifications and records.

(4) Correction period. The correction period shall be that period specified in the monitoring procedure during which an owner must supply any missing certifications and bring the project into compliance with the provisions of section 42. The correction period is not to exceed 90 days from the date of the notice to the owner described in paragraph (e)(2) of this section. An Agency may extend the correction period for up to 6 months, but only if the Agency determines there is good cause for granting the extension.

(f) Delegation of Authority. *(1) Agencies permitted to delegate compliance monitoring functions.* (i) In general. An Agency may retain an agent or other private contractor (" Authorized Delegate") to perform compliance monitoring. The Authorized Delegate must be unrelated to the owner of any building that the Authorized Delegate monitors. The Authorized Delegate may be delegated all of the functions of the Agency, except for the responsibility of notifying the Service under paragraphs (5) and (e)(3) of this section. For example, the Authorized Delegate may be delegated the responsibility of reviewing tenant certifications and documentation under paragraph (c)(1) and (2) of this section, the right to inspect buildings and records as described in paragraph (d) of this section, and the responsibility of notifying building owners of lack of certification or noncompliance under paragraph (e)(2) of this section. The Authorized Delegate must notify the Agency of any noncompliance or failure to certify.

(ii) Limitations. An Agency that delegates compliance monitoring to an Authorized Delegate under paragraph (f)(1)(i) of this section must use reasonable diligence to ensure that the Authorized Delegate properly performs the delegated monitoring functions. Delegation by an Agency of compliance monitoring functions to an Authorized Delegate does not relieve the Agency of its obligation to notify the Service of any noncompliance of which the Agency becomes aware.

(2) Agencies permitted to delegate compliance monitoring functions to another Agency. An Agency may delegate all or some of its compliance monitoring responsibilities for a building to another Agency within the State. This delegation may include the responsibility of notifying the Service under paragraph (e)(3) of this section.

(g) Liability. Compliance with the requirements of section 42 is the responsibility of the owner of the building for which the credit is allowable. The Agency's obligation to monitor for compliance with the requirements of section 42 does not make the Agency liable for an owner's noncompliance.

(h) Effective date. Allocation plans must comply with these regulations by June 30, 1993. The requirement of section 42(m)(1)(B)(iii) that allocation plans contain a procedure for monitoring for noncompliance becomes effective on January 1, 1992, and applies to buildings for which a low-income housing credit is, or has been, allowable at any time. Thus, allocation plans must comply with section 42(m)(1)(B)(iii) prior to June 30, 1993, the effective date of these regulations. An allocation plan that complies with these regulations, with the notice of proposed rulemaking published in the FEDERAL REGISTER on December 27, 1991, or with a reasonable interpretation of section 42(m)(1)(B)(iii) will satisfy the requirements of section 42(m)(1)(B)(iii) for periods before June 30, 1993. Section 42(m)(1)(B)(iii) and these regulations do not require monitoring for whether a building or project is in compliance with the requirements of section 42 prior to January 1, 1992. However, if an Agency becomes aware of noncompliance that occurred prior to January 1, 1992, the Agency is required to notify the Service of that noncompliance. In addition, the requirements in paragraphs (b)(3) and (c)(1)(v), (vi), and (xi) of this section (involving recordkeeping and annual owner certifications) and paragraphs (c)(2)(ii)(B), (c)(2)(iii), and (d) of this section (involving tenant file reviews and physical inspections of existing projects, and the physical inspection standard) are applicable January 1, 2001. The requirement in paragraph (c)(2)(ii)(A) of this section (involving tenant file reviews and physical inspections of new projects) is applicable for buildings placed in service on or after January 1, 2001. The requirements in paragraph (c)(5) of this section (involving Agency reporting of compliance monitoring activities to the Service) and paragraph (e)(3)(i) of this section (involving Agency reporting of corrected noncompliance or failure to certify within 3 years after the end of the correction period) are applicable January 14, 2000.

T.D. 8430, 9/1/92, amend T.D. 8563, 9/30/94, T.D. 8859, 1/13/2000.

§ 1.42-6 Buildings qualifying for carryover allocations.

Caution: The Treasury has not yet amended Reg § 1.42-6 to reflect changes made by P.L. 110-289, P.L. 106-554.

(a) Carryover allocations. *(1) In general.* A carryover allocation is an allocation that meets the requirements of section 42(h)(1)(E) or (F). If the requirements of section § 42(h)(1)(E) or (F) that are required to be satisfied by the close of a calendar year are not satisfied, the allocation is not valid and is treated as if it had not been made for that calendar year. For example, if a carryover allocation fails to satisfy a requirement in § 1.42-6(d) for making an allocation, such as failing to be signed or dated by an authorized official of an allocating agency by the close of a calendar year, the allocation is not valid and is treated as if it had not been made for that calendar year.

(2) 10 percent basis requirement. A carryover allocation may only be made with respect to a qualified building. A qualified building is any building which is part of a project if, by the date specified under paragraph (a)(2)(i) or (ii) of this section, a taxpayer's basis in the project is more than 10 percent of the taxpayer's reasonably expected basis in the project as of the close of the second calendar year following the calendar year the allocation is made. For purposes of meeting the 10 percent basis requirement, the determination of whether a building is part of a single-building project or multi-building project is based on whether the carryover allocation is made under section 42(h)(1)(E) (building-based allocation) or section 42(h)(1)(F) (project-based allocation). In the case of a multi-building project that receives an allocation under section 42(h)(1)(F), the 10 percent basis requirement is satisfied by reference to the entire project.

(i) Allocation made before July 1. If a carryover allocation is made before July 1 of a calendar year, a taxpayer must meet the 10 percent basis requirement by the close of that calendar year. If a taxpayer does not meet the 10 percent basis requirement by the close of the calendar year, the carryover allocation is not valid and is treated as if it had not been made.

(ii) Allocation made after June 30. If a carryover allocation is made after June 30 of a calendar year, a taxpayer must meet the 10 percent basis requirement by the close of the date that is 6 months after the date the allocation was made. If a taxpayer does not meet the 10 percent basis requirement by the close of the required date, the carryover allocation must be returned to the Agency. Unlike a carryover allocation made before July 1, if a taxpayer does not meet the 10 percent basis requirement by the close of the required date, the carryover allocation is treated as a valid allocation for the calendar year of allocation, but is included in the "returned credit component" for purposes of determining the State housing credit ceiling under section 42(h)(3)(C) for the calendar year following the calendar year of the allocation. See § 42-14(d)(1).

(b) Carryover-allocation basis. *(1) In general.* Subject to the limitations of paragraph (b)(2) of this section, a taxpayer's basis in a project for purposes of section 42(h)(1)(E)(ii) or (F) (carryover-allocation basis) is the taxpayer's adjusted basis in land or depreciable property that is reasonably expected to be part of the project, whether or not these amounts are includible in eligible basis under section 42(d). Thus, for example, if the project is to include property that is not residential rental property, such as commercial space, the basis attributable to the commercial space, although not includible in eligible basis, is includible in carryover-allocation basis. The adjusted basis of land and depreciable property is determined under sections 1012 and 1016, and generally includes the direct and indirect costs of acquiring, constructing, and rehabilitating the property. Costs otherwise includible in carryover-allocation basis are not excluded by reason of having been incurred prior to the calendar year in which the carryover allocation is made.

(2) Limitations. For purposes of determining carryover-allocation basis under paragraph (b)(1) of this section, the following limitations apply.

(i) Taxpayer must have basis in land or depreciable property related to the project. A taxpayer has carryover-allocation basis to the extent that it has basis in land or depreciable property and the land or depreciable property is reasonably expected to be part of the project for which the carryover allocation is made. This basis includes all items that are properly capitalizable with respect to the land or depreciable property. For example, a nonrefundable downpayment for, or an amount paid to acquire an option to purchase, land or depreciable property may be included in carryover-allocation basis if properly capitalizable into the basis of land or depreciable property that is reasonably expected to be part of a project.

(ii) High cost areas. Any increase in eligible basis that may result under section 42(d)(5)(C) from a building's location in a qualified census tract or difficult development area is not taken into account in determining carryover-allocation basis or reasonably expected basis.

(iii) Amounts not treated as paid or incurred. An amount is not includible in carryover-allocation basis unless it is treated as paid or incurred under the method of accounting used by the taxpayer. For example, a cash method taxpayer cannot include construction costs in carryover-allocation basis unless the costs have been paid, and an accrual method taxpayer cannot include construction costs in carryover-allocation basis unless they have been properly accrued. See paragraph (b)(2)(iv) of this section for a special rule for fees.

(iv) Fees. A fee is includible in carryover-allocation basis only to the extent the requirements of paragraph (b)(2)(iii) of this section are met and—

(A) The fee is reasonable;

(B) The taxpayer is legally obligated to pay the fee;

(C) The fee is capitalizable as part of the taxpayer's basis in land or depreciable property that is reasonably expected to be part of the project;

(D) The fee is not paid (or to be paid) by the taxpayer to itself; and

(E) If the fee is paid (or to be paid) by the taxpayer to a related person, and the taxpayer uses the cash method of accounting, the taxpayer could properly accrue the fee under the accrual method of accounting (considering, for example, the rules of section 461(h)). A person is a related person if the person bears a relationship to the taxpayer specified in sections 267(b) or 707(b)(1), or if the person and the taxpayer are engaged in trades or businesses under common control (within the meaning of subsections (a) and (b) of section 52).

(3) Reasonably expected basis. Rules similar to the rules of paragraphs (a) and (b) of this section apply in determining the taxpayer's reasonably expected basis in a project (land and depreciable basis) as of the close of the second calendar year following the calendar year of the allocation.

(4) Examples. The following examples illustrate the rules of paragraphs (a) and (b) of this section.

Example (1). (i) Facts. C, an accrual-method taxpayer, receives a carryover allocation from Agency, the state housing credit agency, in May of 2003. As of that date, C has not begun construction of the low-income housing building C plans to build. However, C has owned the land on which C plans to build the building since 1985. C's basis in the land is $100,000. C reasonably expects that by the end of 2005, C's basis in the project of which the building is to be a part will be $2,000,000. C also expects that because the project is located in a qualified census tract, C will be able to increase its basis in the project to $2,600,000. Before the close of 2003, C incurs $150,000 of costs for architects' fees and site preparation. C properly accrues these costs under its method of accounting and capitalizes the costs.

(ii) Determination of carryover-allocation basis. C's $100,000 basis in the land is includible in carryover-allocation basis even though C has owned the land since 1985. The $150,000 of costs C has incurred for architects' fees and site preparation are also includible in carryover-allocation basis. The expected increase in basis due to the project's location in a qualified census tract is not taken into account in determining C's carryover-allocation basis. Accordingly, C's carryover-allocation basis in the project of which the building is a part is $250,000.

(iii) Determination of whether building is qualified. C's reasonably expected basis in the project at the close of the second calendar year following the calendar year of allocation is $2,000,000. The expected increase in eligible basis due to the project's location in a qualified census tract is not taken into account in determining this amount. Because C's carryover-allocation basis is more than 10 percent of C's reasonably expected basis in the project of which the building is a part, the building for which C received the carryover allocation is a qualified building for purposes of section 42(h)(1)(E)(ii) and paragraph (a) of this section.

Example (2). (i) Facts. D, an accrual-method taxpayer, received a carryover allocation from Agency, the state housing credit agency of State X, on September 12, 2003. As of that date, D has not begun construction of the low-income housing building D plans to build and D does not have basis in the land on which D plans to build the building. From September 12, 2003, to the close of March 12, 2004, D incurs some costs related to the planned building, including architects' fees. As of the close of March 12, 2004, these costs do not exceed 10 percent of D's reasonably expected basis in the single-building project as of the close of 2005.

(ii) Determination of whether building is qualified. Because D's carryover-allocation basis as of the close of March 12, 2004, is not more than 10 percent of D's reasonably expected basis in the single-building project, the building is not a qualified building for purposes of section 42(h)(1)(E)(ii) and paragraph (a) of this section. Accordingly, the carryover allocation to D must be returned to the Agency. The allocation is valid for purposes of determining the amount of credit allocated by Agency from State X's 2003 State housing credit ceiling, but is included in the returned credit component of State X's 2004 housing credit ceiling.

(c) Verification of basis by Agency. *(1) Verification requirement.* An Agency that makes a carryover allocation to a taxpayer must verify that the taxpayer has met the 10 percent basis requirement of paragraph (a)(2) of this section.

(2) Manner of verification. An Agency may verify that a taxpayer has incurred more than 10 percent of its reasonably expected basis in a project by obtaining a certification from the taxpayer, in writing and under penalty of perjury, that the taxpayer has incurred by the close of the calendar year of the allocation (for allocations made before July 1) or by the close of the date that is 6 months after the date the allocation is made (for allocations made after June 30) more than 10 percent of the reasonably expected basis in the project. The certification must be accompanied by supporting documentation that the Agency must review. Supporting documentation may include, for example, copies of checks or other records of payments. Alternatively, an Agency may verify that the taxpayer has incurred adequate basis by requiring that the taxpayer obtain from an attorney or certified public accountant a written certification to the Agency, that the attorney or accountant has examined all eligible costs incurred with respect to the project and that, based upon this examination, it is the attorney's or accountant's belief that the taxpayer has incurred more than 10 percent of its reasonably expected basis in the project by the close of the calendar year of the allocation (for allocations made before July 1) or by the close of the date that is 6 months after the date the allocation is made (for allocations made after June 30).

(3) Time of verification. (i) Allocations made before July 1. For a carryover allocation made before July 1, an Agency

may require that the basis certification be submitted to or received by the Agency prior to the close of the calendar year of allocation or within a reasonable time following the close of the calendar year of allocation. The Agency will need to verify basis as provided in paragraph (c)(2) of this section to accurately complete the Form 8610, "Annual Low-Income Housing Credit Agencies Report," and the Schedule A (Form 8610), "Carryover Allocation of Low-Income Housing Credit," for the calendar year of the allocation. If the basis certification is not timely made, or supporting documentation is lacking, inadequate, or does not actually support the certification, the Agency should notify the taxpayer and try to get adequate documentation. If the Agency cannot verify before the Form 8610 is filed that the taxpayer has satisfied the 10 percent basis requirement for a carryover allocation made before July 1, the allocation is not valid and is treated as if it had not been made and the carryover allocation should not be reported on the Schedule A (Form 8610).

(ii) Allocations made after June 30. An Agency may require that the basis certification be submitted to or received by the Agency prior to the close of the date that is 6 months after the date the allocation was made or within a reasonable period of time following the close of the date that is 6 months after the date the allocation was made. The Agency will need to verify basis as provided in paragraph (c)(2) of this section. If the basis certification is not timely made, or supporting documentation is lacking, inadequate, or does not actually support the certification, the Agency should notify the taxpayer and try to get adequate documentation. If the Agency cannot verify that the taxpayer has satisfied the 10 percent basis requirement for a carryover allocation made after June 30, the allocation must be returned to the Agency. The carryover allocation is a valid allocation for the calendar year of the allocation, but is included in the returned credit component of the State housing credit ceiling for the calendar year following the calendar year of the allocation.

(d) Requirements for making carryover allocations. *(1) In general.* Generally, an allocation is made when an Agency issues the Form 8609, "Low-Income Housing Credit Allocation Certification," for a building. See § 1.42-1T(d)(8)(ii). An Agency does not issue the Form 8609 for a building until the building is placed in service. However, in cases where allocations of credit are made pursuant to section 42(h)(1)(E) (relating to carryover allocations for buildings) or section 42(h)(1)(F) (relating to carryover allocations for multiple-building projects), Form 8609 is not used as the allocating document because the buildings are not yet in service. When an allocation is made pursuant to section 42(h)(1)(E) or (F), the allocating document is the document meeting the requirements of paragraph (d)(2) of this section. In addition, when an allocation is made pursuant to section 42(h)(1)(F), the requirements of paragraph (d)(3) of this section must be met for the allocation to be valid. An allocation pursuant to section 42(h)(1)(E) or (F) reduces the state housing credit ceiling for the year in which the allocation is made, whether or not the Form 8609 is also issued in that year.

(2) Requirements for allocation. An allocation pursuant to section 42(h)(1)(E) or (F) is made when an allocation document containing the following information is completed, signed, and dated by an authorized official of the Agency—

(i) The address of each building in the project, or if none exists, a specific description of the location of each building;

(ii) The name, address, and taxpayer identification number of the taxpayer receiving the allocation;

(iii) The name and address of the Agency;

(iv) The taxpayer identification number of the Agency;

(v) The date of the allocation;

(vi) The housing credit dollar amount allocated to the building or project, as applicable;

(vii) The taxpayer's reasonably expected basis in the project (land and depreciable basis) as of the close of the second calendar year following the calendar year in which the allocation is made;

(viii) For carryover allocations made before July 1, the taxpayer's basis in the project (land and depreciable basis) as of the close of the calendar year of the allocation and the percentage that basis bears to the reasonably expected basis in the project (land and depreciable basis) as of the close of the second calendar year following the calendar year of allocation;

(ix) The date that each building in the project is expected to be placed in service; and

(x) The Building Identification Number (B.I.N.) to be assigned to each building in the project. The B.I.N. must reflect the year an allocation is first made to the building, regardless of the year that the building is placed in service. This B.I.N. must be used for all allocations of credit for the building. For example, rehabilitation expenditures treated as a separate new building under section 42(e) should not have a separate B.I.N. if the building to which the rehabilitation expenditures are made has a B.I.N. In this case, the B.I.N. used for the rehabilitation expenditures shall be the B.I.N. previously assigned to the building, although the rehabilitation expenditures must have a separate Form 8609 for the allocation. Similarly, a newly constructed building that receives an allocation of credit in different calendar years must have a separate Form 8609 for each allocation. The B.I.N. assigned to the building for the first allocation must be used for the subsequent allocation.

(3) Special rules for project-based allocations. (i) In general. An allocation pursuant to section 42(h)(1)(F) (a project-based allocation) must meet the requirements of this section as well as the requirements of section 42(h)(1)(F), including the minimum basis requirement of section 42(h)(1)(E)(ii).

(ii) Requirement of section 42(h)(1)(F)(i)(III). An allocation satisfies the requirement of section 42(h)(1)(F)(i)(III) if the Form 8609 that is issued for each building that is placed in service in the project states the portion of the project-based allocation that is applied to that building.

(4) Recordkeeping requirements. (i) Taxpayer. When an allocation is made pursuant to section 42(h)(1)(E) or (F), the taxpayer must retain a copy of the allocation document. The Form 8609 that reflects the allocation must be filed for the first taxable year that the credit is claimed and for each taxable year thereafter throughout the compliance period, whether or not a credit is claimed for the taxable year.

(ii) Agency. The Agency must retain the original carryover allocation document made under paragraph (d)(2) of this section and file Schedule A (Form 8610), with the Agency's Form 8610 for the year the allocation is made. The Agency must also retain a copy of the Form 8609 that is issued to the taxpayer and file the original with the Agency's Form 8610 that reflects the year the form is issued.

(5) Separate procedure for election of appropriate percentage month. If a taxpayer receives an allocation under section 42(h)(1)(E) or (F) and wishes to elect under section 42(b)(2)(A)(ii) to use the appropriate percentage for a month other than the month in which a building is placed in ser-

vice, the requirements specified in § 1.42-8 must be met for the election to be effective.

(e) Special rules. The following rules apply for purposes of this section.

(1) Treatment of partnerships and other flow-through entities. With respect to taxpayers that own projects through partnerships or other flow-through entities (e.g., S corporations, estates, or trusts), carryover-allocation basis is determined at the entity level using the rules provided by this section. In addition, the entity is responsible for providing to the Agency the certification and documentation required under the basis verification requirement in paragraph (c) of this section.

(2) Transferees. If land or depreciable property that is expected to be part of a project is transferred after a carryover allocation has been made for a building that is reasonably expected to be part of the project, but by the close of the calendar year of the allocation (for allocations made before July 1) or by the close of the date that is 6 months after the date the allocation is made (for allocations made after June 30), the transferee's carryover-allocation basis is determined under the principles of this section and section 42(d)(7). See also Rev. Rul. 91-38, 1991-2 C.B. 3 (see § 601.601(d)(2)(ii)(b) of this chapter). In addition, the transferee is treated as the taxpayer for purposes of the basis verification requirement of this section, and therefore, is responsible for providing to the Agency the required certifications and documentation.

T.D. 8520, 3/2/94, amend T.D. 8859, 1/13/2000, T.D. 9110, 1/2/2004.

§ 1.42-7 Substantially bond-financed buildings. [Reserved]

§ 1.42-8 Election of appropriate percentage month.

(a) Election under section 42(b)(2)(A)(ii)(I) to use the appropriate percentage for the month of a binding agreement. *(1) In general.* For purposes of section 42(b)(2)(A)(ii)(I), an agreement between a taxpayer and an Agency as to the housing credit dollar amount to be allocated to a building is considered binding if it—

(i) Is in writing;

(ii) Is binding under state law on the Agency, the taxpayer, and all successors in interest;

(iii) Specifies the type(s) of building(s) to which the housing credit dollar amount applies (i.e., a newly constructed or existing building, or substantial rehabilitation treated as a separate new building under section 42(e));

(iv) Specifies the housing credit dollar amount to be allocated to the building(s); and

(v) Is dated and signed by the taxpayer and the Agency during the month in which the requirements of paragraphs (a)(1)(i) through (iv) of this section are met.

(2) Effect on state housing credit ceiling. Generally, a binding agreement described in paragraph (a)(1) of this section is an agreement by the Agency to allocate credit to the taxpayer at a future date. The binding agreement may include a reservation of credit or a binding commitment (under section 42(h)(1)(C)) to allocate credit in a future taxable year. A reservation or a binding commitment to allocate credit in a future year has no effect on the state housing credit ceiling until the year the Agency actually makes an allocation. However, if the binding agreement is also a carryover allocation under section 42(h)(1)(E) or (F), the state housing credit ceiling is reduced by the amount allocated by the Agency to the taxpayer in the year the carryover allocation is made. For a binding agreement to be a valid carryover allocation, the requirements of paragraph (a)(1) of this section and § 1.42-6 must be met.

(3) Time and manner of making election. An election under section 42(b)(2)(A)(ii)(I) may be made either as part of the binding agreement under paragraph (a)(1) of this section to allocate a specific housing credit dollar amount or in a separate document that references the binding agreement. In either case, the election must—

(i) Be in writing;

(ii) Reference section 42(b)(2)(A)(ii)(I);

(iii) Be signed by the taxpayer;

(iv) If it is in a separate document, reference the binding agreement that meets the requirements of paragraph (a)(1) of this section; and

(v) Be notarized by the 5th day following the end of the month in which the binding agreement was made.

(4) Multiple agreements. (i) Rescinded agreements. A taxpayer may not make an election under section 42(b)(2)(A)(ii)(I) for a building if an election has previously been made for the building for a different month. For example, assume a taxpayer entered into a binding agreement for allocation of a specific housing credit dollar amount to a building and made the election under section 42(b)(2)(A)(ii)(I) to apply the appropriate percentage for the month of the binding agreement. If the binding agreement subsequently is rescinded under state law, and the taxpayer enters into a new binding agreement for allocation of a specific housing credit dollar amount to the building, the taxpayer must apply to the building the appropriate percentage for the elected month of the rescinded binding agreement. However, if no prior election was made with respect to the rescinded binding agreement, the taxpayer may elect the appropriate percentage for the month of the new binding agreement.

(ii) Increases in credit. The election under section 42(b)(2)(A)(ii)(I), once made, applies to any increase in the credit amount allocated for a building, whether the increase occurs in the same or in a subsequent year. However, in the case of a binding agreement (or carryover allocation that is treated as a binding agreement) to allocate a credit amount under section 42(e)(1) for substantial rehabilitation treated as a separate new building, a taxpayer may make the election under section 42(b)(2)(A)(ii)(I) notwithstanding that a prior election under section 42(b)(2)(A)(ii)(I) is in effect for a prior allocation of credit for a substantial rehabilitation that was previously placed in service under section 42(e).

(5) Amount allocated. The housing credit dollar amount eventually allocated to a building may be more or less than the amount specified in the binding agreement. Depending on the Agency's determination pursuant to section 42(m)(2) as to the financial feasibility of the building (or project), the Agency may allocate a greater housing credit dollar amount to the building (provided that the Agency has additional housing credit dollar amounts available to allocate for the calendar year of the allocation) or the Agency may allocate a lesser housing credit dollar amount. Under section 42(h)(7)(D), in allocating a housing credit dollar amount, the Agency must specify the applicable percentage and maximum qualified basis of the building. The applicable percentage may be less, but not greater than, the appropriate percentage for the month the building is placed in service, or the month elected by the taxpayer under section 42(b)(2)(A)(ii)(I). Whether the appropriate percentage is the

appropriate percentage for the 70-percent present value credit or the 30-percent present value credit is determined under section 42(i)(2) when the building is placed in service.

(6) Procedures. (i) Taxpayer. The taxpayer must give the original notarized election statement to the Agency before the close of the 5th calendar day following the end of the month in which the binding agreement is made. The taxpayer must retain a copy of the binding agreement and the election statement.

(ii) Agency. The Agency must retain the original of the binding agreement and election statement and, to the extent required by Schedule A (Form 8610), "Carryover Allocation of Low-Income Housing Credit," account for the binding agreement and election statement on that schedule.

(7) Examples. The following examples illustrate the provisions of this section. In each example, X is the taxpayer, Agency is the state housing credit agency, and the carryover allocations meet the requirements of § 1.42-6 and are otherwise valid.

Example (1). (i) In August 2003, X and Agency enter into an agreement that Agency will allocate $100,000 of housing credit dollar amount for the low-income housing building X is constructing. The agreement is binding and meets all the requirements of paragraph (a)(1) of this section. The agreement is a reservation of credit, not an allocation, and therefore, has no effect on the state housing credit ceiling. On or before September 5, 2003, X signs and has notarized a written election statement that meets the requirements of paragraph (a)(3) of this section. The applicable percentage for the building is the appropriate percentage for the month of August 2003.

(ii) Agency makes a carryover allocation of $100,000 of housing credit dollar amount for the building on October 2, 2003. The carryover allocation reduces Agency's state housing credit ceiling for 2003. Due to unexpectedly high construction costs, when X places the building in service in July 2004, the product of the building's qualified basis and the applicable percentage for the building (the appropriate percentage for the month of August 2003) is $150,000, rather than $100,000. Notwithstanding that only $100,000 of credit was allocated for the building in 2003, Agency may allocate an additional $50,000 of housing credit dollar amount for the building from its state housing credit ceiling for 2004. The appropriate percentage for the month of August 2003 is the applicable percentage for the building for the entire $150,000 of credit allocated for the building, even though separate allocations were made in 2003 and 2004. Because allocations were made for the building in two separate calendar years, Agency must issue two Forms 8609, "Low-Income Housing Credit Allocation Certification," to X. One Form 8609 must reflect the $100,000 allocation made in 2003, and the other Form 8609 must reflect the $50,000 allocation made in 2004.

(iii) X gives the original notarized statement to Agency on or before September 5, 2003, and retains a copy of the binding agreement, election statement, and carryover allocation document.

(iv) Agency retains the original of the binding agreement, election statement, and 2003 carryover allocation document. Agency accounts for the binding agreement, election statement, and 2003 carryover allocation on the Schedule A (Form 8610) that it files for the 2003 calendar year. After the building is placed in service in 2004, and assuming other necessary requirements for issuing a Form 8609 are met (for example, taxpayer has certified all sources and uses of funds and development costs for the building under § 1.42-17), Agency issues to X a copy of the Form 8609 reflecting the 2003 carryover allocation of $100,000. Agency files the original of this Form 8609 with the Form 8610, "Annual Low-Income Housing Credit Agencies Report," that it files for the 2004 calendar year. Agency also issues to X a copy of the Form 8609 reflecting the 2004 allocation of $50,000 and files the original of this Form 8609 with the Form 8610 that it files for the 2004 calendar year. Agency retains copies of the Forms 8609 that are issued to X.

Example (2). (i) In September 2003, X and Agency enter into an agreement that Agency will allocate $70,000 of housing credit dollar amount for rehabilitation expenditures that X is incurring and that X will treat as a new low-income housing building under section 42(e)(1). The agreement is binding and meets all the requirements of paragraph (a)(1) of this section. The agreement is a reservation of credit, not an allocation, and therefore, has no effect on Agency's state housing credit ceiling. On or before October 5, 2003, X signs and has notarized a written election statement that meets the requirements of paragraph (a)(3) of this section. The applicable percentage for the building is the appropriate percentage for the month of September 2003. Agency makes a carryover allocation of $70,000 of housing credit dollar amount for the building on November 15, 2003. The carryover allocation reduces by $70,000 Agency's state housing credit ceiling for 2003.

(ii) In October 2004, X and Agency enter into another binding agreement meeting the requirements of paragraph (a)(1) of this section. Under the agreement, Agency will allocate $50,000 of housing credit dollar amount for additional rehabilitation expenditures by X that qualify as a second separate new building under section 42(e)(1). On or before November 5, 2004, X signs and has notarized a written election statement meeting the requirements of paragraph (a)(3) of this section. On December 1, 2004, X receives a carryover allocation under section 42(h)(1)(E) for $50,000. The carryover allocation reduces by $50,000 Agency's state housing credit ceiling for 2004. The applicable percentage for the rehabilitation expenditures treated as the second separate new building is the appropriate percentage for the month of October 2004, not September 2003. The appropriate percentage for the month of September 2003 still applies to the allocation of $70,000 for the rehabilitation expenditures treated as the first separate new building. Because allocations were made for the building in two separate calendar years, Agency must issue two Forms 8609 to X. One Form 8609 must reflect the $70,000 allocation made in 2003, and the other Form 8609 must reflect the $50,000 allocation made in 2004.

(iii) X gives the first original notarized statement to Agency on or before October 5, 2003, and retains a copy of the first binding agreement, election statement, and carryover allocation document issued in 2003. X gives the second original notarized statement to Agency on or before November 5, 2004, and retains a copy of the second binding agreement, election statement, and carryover allocation document issued in 2004.

(iv) Agency retains the original of the binding agreements, election statements, and carryover allocation documents. Agency accounts for the binding agreement, election statement, and 2003 carryover allocation on the Schedule A (Form 8610) that it files for the 2003 calendar year. Agency also accounts for the binding agreement, election statement, and 2004 carryover allocation on the Schedule A (Form 8610) that it files for the 2004 calendar year. After each separate new building is placed in service, and assuming other necessary requirements for issuing a Form 8609 are met (for example, taxpayer has certified all sources and uses of funds and development costs for the building under § 1.42-17), the Agency will issue to X a copy of the Form 8609 reflecting the 2003 carryover allocation of $70,000 and a copy of the Form 8609 reflecting the 2004 carryover allocation of $50,000, respectively. Agency files the original of each Form 8609 with the Form 8610 that reflects the calendar year each Form 8609 is issued. Agency retains copies of the Forms 8609 that are issued to X.

(b) Election under section 42(b)(2)(A)(ii)(II) to use the appropriate percentage for the month tax-exempt bonds are issued. *(1) Time and manner of making election.* In the case of any building to which section 42(h)(4)(B) applies, an election under section 42(b)(2)(A)(ii)(II) to use the appropriate percentage for the month tax-exempt bonds are issued must—

(i) Be in writing;

(ii) Reference section 42(b)(2)(A)(ii)(II);

(iii) Specify the percentage of the aggregate basis of the building and the land on which the building is located that is financed with the proceeds of obligations described in section 42(h)(4)(A) (tax-exempt bonds);

(iv) State the month in which the tax-exempt bonds are issued;

(v) State that the month in which the tax-exempt bonds are issued is the month elected for the appropriate percentage to be used for the building;

(vi) Be signed by the taxpayer; and

(vii) Be notarized by the 5th day following the end of the month in which the bonds are issued.

(2) Bonds issued in more than one month. If a building described in section 42(h)(4)(B) (substantially bond-financed building) is financed with tax-exempt bonds issued in more than one month, the taxpayer may elect the appropriate percentage for any month in which the bonds are issued. Once the election is made, the appropriate percentage elected applies for the building even if all bonds are not issued in that month. The requirements of this paragraph (b), including the time limitation contained in paragraph (b)(1)(vii) of this section, must also be met.

(3) Limitations on appropriate percentage. Under section 42(m)(2)(D), the credit allowable for a substantially bond-financed building is limited to the amount necessary to assure the project's feasibility. Accordingly, in making the determination under section 42(m)(2), an Agency may use an applicable percentage that is less, but not greater than, the appropriate percentage for the month the building is placed in service, or the month elected by the taxpayer under section 42(b)(2)(A)(ii)(II).

(4) Procedures. (i) Taxpayer. The taxpayer must provide the original notarized election statement to the Agency before the close of the 5th calendar day following the end of the month in which the bonds are issued. If an authority other than the Agency issues the tax-exempt bonds, the taxpayer must also give the Agency a signed statement from the issuing authority that certifies the information described in paragraphs (b)(1)(iii) and (iv) of this section. The taxpayer must also retain a copy of the election statement.

(ii) Agency. The Agency must retain the original of the election statement and a copy of the Form 8609 that reflects the election statement. The Agency must file an additional copy of the Form 8609 with the Agency's Form 8610 that reflects the calendar year the Form 8609 is issued.

T.D. 8520, 3/2/94, amend T.D. 9110, 1/2/2004.

§ 1.42-9 For use by the general public.

Caution: The Treasury has not yet amended Reg § 1.42-9 to reflect changes made by P.L. 110-289.

(a) General rule. If a residential rental unit in a building is not for use by the general public, the unit is not eligible for a section 42 credit. A residential rental unit is for use by the general public if the unit is rented in a manner consistent with housing policy governing non-discrimination, as evidenced by rules or regulations of the Department of Housing and Urban Development (HUD) (24 CFR subtitle A and chapters I through XX). See HUD Handbook 4350.3 (or its successor). A copy of HUD Handbook 4350.3 may be requested by writing to: HUD, Directives Distribution Section, room B-100, 451 7th Street, SW., Washington, DC 20410.

(b) Limitations. Notwithstanding paragraph (a) of this section, if a residential rental unit is provided only for a member of a social organization or provided by an employer for its employees, the unit is not for use by the general public and is not eligible for credit under section 42. In addition, any residential rental unit that is part of a hospital, nursing home, sanitarium, lifecare facility, trailer park, or intermediate care facility for the mentally and physically handicapped is not for use by the general public and is not eligible for credit under section 42.

(c) Treatment of units not for use by the general public. The costs attributable to a residential rental unit that is not for use by the general public are not excludable from eligible basis by reason of the unit's ineligibility for the credit under this section. However, in calculating the applicable fraction, the unit is treated as a residential rental unit that is not a low-income unit.

T.D. 8520, 3/2/94.

§ 1.42-10 Utility allowances.

(a) Inclusion of utility allowances in gross rent. If the cost of any utility (other than telephone, cable television, or Internet) for a residential rental unit is paid directly by the tenant(s), and not by or through the owner of the building, the gross rent for that unit includes the applicable utility allowance determined under this section. This section only applies for purposes of determining gross rent under section 42(g)(2)(B)(ii) as to rent-restricted units.

(b) Applicable utility allowances. *(1) Buildings assisted by the Rural Housing Service.* If a building receives assistance from the Rural Housing Service (RHS-assisted building), the applicable utility allowance for all rent-restricted units in the building is the utility allowance determined under the method prescribed by the Rural Housing Service (RHS) for the building (whether or not the building or its tenants also receive other state or federal assistance).

(2) Buildings with Rural Housing Service assisted tenants. If any tenant in a building receives RHS rental assistance payments (RHS tenant assistance), the applicable utility allowance for all rent-restricted units in the building (including any units occupied by tenants receiving rental assistance payments from the Department of Housing and Urban Development (HUD)) is the applicable RHS utility allowance.

(3) Buildings regulated by the Department of Housing and Urban Development. If neither a building nor any tenant in

the building receives RHS housing assistance, and the rents and utility allowances of the building are reviewed by HUD on an annual basis (HUD-regulated building), the applicable utility allowance for all rent-restricted units in the building is the applicable HUD utility allowance.

(4) Other buildings. If a building is neither an RHS-assisted nor a HUD-regulated building, and no tenant in the building receives RHS tenant assistance, the applicable utility allowance for rent-restricted units in the building is determined under the following methods.

(i) Tenants receiving HUD rental assistance. The applicable utility allowance for any rent-restricted units occupied by tenants receiving HUD rental assistance payments (HUD tenant assistance) is the applicable Public Housing Authority (PHA) utility allowance established for the Section 8 Existing Housing Program.

(ii) Other tenants. (A) General rule. If none of the rules of paragraphs (b)(1), (2), (3), and (4)(i) of this section apply to any rent-restricted units in a building, the appropriate utility allowance for the units is the applicable PHA utility allowance. However, if a local utility company estimate is obtained for any unit in the building in accordance with paragraph (b)(4)(ii)(B) of this section, that estimate becomes the appropriate utility allowance for all rent-restricted units of similar size and construction in the building. This local utility company estimate procedure is not available for and does not apply to units to which the rules of paragraph (b)(1), (2), (3), or (4)(i) of this section apply. However, if a local utility company estimate is obtained for any unit in the building under paragraph (b)(4)(ii)(B) of this section, a State or local housing credit agency (Agency) provides a building owner with an estimate for any unit in a building under paragraph (b)(4)(ii)(C) of this section, a cost estimate is calculated using the HUD Utility Schedule Model under paragraph (b)(4)(ii)(D) of this section, or a cost estimate is calculated by an energy consumption model under paragraph (b)(4)(ii)(E) of this section, then the estimate under paragraph (b)(4)(ii)(B), (C), (D), or (E) becomes the applicable utility allowance for all rent-restricted units of similar size and construction in the building. Paragraphs (b)(4)(ii)(B), (C), (D), and (E) of this section do not apply to units to which the rules of paragraphs (b)(1), (2), (3), or (4)(i) of this section apply.

(B) Utility company estimate. Any interested party (including a low-income tenant, a building owner, or an Agency) may obtain a local utility company estimate for a unit. The estimate is obtained when the interested party receives, in writing, information from a local utility company providing the estimated cost of that utility for a unit of similar size and construction for the geographic area in which the building containing the unit is located. In the case of deregulated utility services, the interested party is required to obtain an estimate only from one utility company even if multiple companies can provide the same utility service to a unit. However, the utility company must offer utility services to the building in order for that utility company's rates to be used in calculating utility allowances. The estimate should include all component deregulated charges for providing the utility service. The local utility company estimate may be obtained by an interested party at any time during the building's extended use period (see section 42(h)(6)(D)) or, if the building does not have an extended use period, during the building's compliance period (see section 42(i)(1)). Unless the parties agree otherwise, costs incurred in obtaining the estimate are borne by the initiating party. The interested party that obtains the local utility company estimate (the initiating party) must retain the original of the utility company estimate and must furnish a copy of the local utility company estimate to the owner of the building (where the initiating party is not the owner), and the Agency that allocated credit to the building (where the initiating party is not the Agency). The owner of the building must make available copies of the utility company estimate to the tenants in the building.

(C) Agency estimate. A building owner may obtain a utility estimate for each unit in the building from the Agency that has jurisdiction over the building provided the Agency agrees to provide the estimate. The estimate is obtained when the building owner receives, in writing, information from the Agency providing the estimated per-unit cost of the utilities for units of similar size and construction for the geographic area in which the building containing the units is located. The Agency estimate may be obtained by a building owner at any time during the building's extended use period (see section 42(h)(6)(D)). Costs incurred in obtaining the estimate are borne by the building owner. In establishing an accurate utility allowance estimate for a particular building, an Agency (or an agent or other private contractor of the Agency that is a qualified professional within the meaning of paragraph (b)(4)(ii)(E) of this section) must take into account, among other things, local utility rates, property type, climate and degree-day variables by region in the State, taxes and fees on utility charges, building materials, and mechanical systems. If the Agency uses an agent or other private contractor to calculate the utility estimates, the agent or contractor and the owner must not be related within the meaning of section 267(b) or 707(b). An Agency may also use actual utility company usage data and rates for the building. However, use of the Agency estimate is limited to the building's consumption data for the twelve-month period ending no earlier than 60 days prior to the beginning of the 90-day period under paragraph (c)(1) of this section and utility rates used for the Agency estimate must be no older than the rates in place 60 days prior to the beginning of the 90-day period under paragraph (c)(1) of this section. In the case of newly constructed or renovated buildings with less than 12 months of consumption data, the Agency (or an agent or other private contractor of the Agency that is a qualified professional within the meaning of paragraph (b)(4)(ii)(E) of this section) may use consumption data for the 12-month period of units of similar size and construction in the geographic area in which the building containing the units is located.

(D) HUD Utility Schedule Model. A building owner may calculate a utility estimate using the "HUD Utility Schedule Model" that can be found on the Low-Income Housing Tax Credits page at http:// www.huduser.org/datasets/lihtc.html (or successor URL). Utility rates used for the HUD Utility Schedule Model must be no older than the rates in place 60 days prior to the beginning of the 90-day period under paragraph (c)(1) of this section.

(E) Energy consumption model. A building owner may calculate utility estimates using an energy and water and sewage consumption and analysis model (energy consumption model). The energy consumption model must, at a minimum, take into account specific factors including, but not limited to, unit size, building orientation, design and materials, mechanical systems, appliances, and characteristics of the building location. The utility consumption estimates must be calculated by either a properly licensed engineer or a qualified professional approved by the Agency that has jurisdiction over the building (together, qualified professional), and the qualified professional and the building owner must not be related within the meaning of section 267(b) or 707(b). Use of the energy consumption model is limited to the building's consumption data for the twelve-month period ending no earlier than 60 days prior to the beginning of the 90-day period under paragraph (c)(1) of this section, and utility rates used for the energy consumption model must be no older than the rates in place 60 days prior to the beginning of the 90-day period under paragraph (c)(1) of this section. In the case of newly constructed or renovated buildings with less than 12 months of consumption data, the qualified professional may use consumption data for the 12-month period of units of similar size and construction in the geographic area in which the building containing the units is located.

(c) Changes in applicable utility allowance. *(1) In general.* If, at any time during the building's extended use period (as defined in section 42(h)(6)(D)), the applicable utility allowance for units changes, the new utility allowance must be used to compute gross rents of the units due 90 days after the change (the 90-day period). For example, if rent must be lowered because a local utility company estimate is obtained that shows a higher utility cost than the otherwise applicable PHA utility allowance, the lower rent must be in effect for rent due at the end of the 90-day period. A building owner using a utility company estimate under paragraph (b)(4)(ii)(B) of this section, the HUD Utility Schedule Model under paragraph (b)(4)(ii)(D) of this section, or an energy consumption model under paragraph (b)(4)(ii)(E) of this section must submit copies of the utility estimates to the Agency that has jurisdiction over the building and make the estimates available to all tenants in the building at the beginning of the 90-day period before the utility allowances can be used in determining the gross rent of rent-restricted units. An Agency may require additional information from the owner during the 90-day period. Any utility estimates obtained under the Agency estimate under paragraph (b)(4)(ii)(C) of this section must also be made available to all tenants in the building at the beginning of the 90-day period. The building owner must pay for all costs incurred in obtaining the estimates under paragraphs (b)(4)(ii)(B), (C), (D), and (E) of this section and providing the estimates to the Agency and the tenants. The building owner is not required to review the utility allowances, or implement new utility allowances, until the building has achieved 90 percent occupancy for a period of 90 consecutive days or the end of the first year of the credit period, whichever is earlier.

(2) Annual review. A building owner must review at least once during each calendar year the basis on which utility allowances have been established and must update the applicable utility allowance in accordance with paragraph (c)(1) of this section. The review must take into account any changes to the building such as any energy conservation measures that affect energy consumption and changes in utility rates.

(d) Record retention. The building owner must retain any utility consumption estimates and supporting data as part of the taxpayer's records for purposes of § 1.6001-1(a).

T.D. 8520, 3/2/94, amend T.D. 9420, 7/28/008.

§ 1.42-11 Provision of services.

(a) General rule. The furnishing to tenants of services other than housing (whether or not the services are significant) does not prevent the units occupied by the tenants from qualifying as residential rental property eligible for credit under section 42. However, any charges to low-income tenants for services that are not optional generally must be included in gross rent for purposes of section 42(g).

(b) Services that are optional. *(1) General rule.* A service is optional if payment for the service is not required as a condition of occupancy. For example, for a qualified low-income building with a common dining facility, the cost of meals is not included in gross rent for purposes of section 42(g)(2)(A) if payment for the meals in the facility is not required as a condition of occupancy and a practical alternative exists for tenants to obtain meals other than from the dining facility.

(2) Continual or frequent services. If continual or frequent nursing, medical, or psychiatric services are provided, it is presumed that the services are not optional and the building is ineligible for the credit, as is the case with a hospital, nursing home, sanitarium, lifecare facility, or intermediate care facility for the mentally and physically handicapped. See also § 1.42-9(b).

(3) Required services. (i) General rule. The cost of services that are required as a condition of occupancy must be included in gross rent even if federal or state law requires that the services be offered to tenants by building owners.

(ii) Exceptions. (A) Supportive services. Section 42(g)(2)(B)(iii) provides an exception for certain fees paid for supportive services. For purposes of section 42(g)(2)(B)(iii), a supportive service is any service provided under a planned program of services designed to enable residents of a residential rental property to remain independent and avoid placement in a hospital, nursing home, or intermediate care facility for the mentally or physically handicapped. For a building described in section 42(i)(3)(B)(iii) (relating to transitional housing for the homeless) or section 42(i)(3)(B)(iv) (relating to single-room occupancy), a supportive service includes any service provided to assist tenants in locating and retaining permanent housing.

(B) Specific project exception. Gross rent does not include the cost of mandatory meals in any federally-assisted project for the elderly and handicapped (in existence on or before January 9, 1989) that is authorized by 24 CFR part 278 to provide a mandatory meals program.

T.D. 8520, 3/2/94, amend T.D. 8859, 1/13/2000.

§ 1.42-12 Effective dates and transitional rules.

(a) Effective dates. *(1) In general.* Except as provided in paragraphs (a)(2) and (a)(3) of this section, the rules set forth in Sec. § 1.42-6 and 1.42-8 through 1.42-12 are applicable on May 2, 1994. However, binding agreements, election statements, and carryover allocation documents entered into before May 2, 1994, that follow the guidance set forth in Notice 89-1, 1989-1 C.B. 620 (see § 601.601(d)(2)(ii)(b) of this chapter) need not be changed to conform to the rules set forth in Sec. § 1.42-6 and 1.42-8 through 1.42-12.

(2) Community Renewal Tax Relief Act of 2000. (i) In general. Section 1.42-6 (a), (b)(4)(iii) Example 1 and Example 2, (c), (d)(2)(viii), and (e)(2) are applicable for housing credit dollar amounts allocated after January 6, 2004. However, the rules in § 1.42-6 (a), (b)(4)(iii) Example 1 and Example 2, (c), (d)(2)(viii), and (e)(2) may be applied by Agencies and taxpayers for housing credit dollar amounts allocated after December 31, 2000, and on or before January 6, 2004. Otherwise, subject to the applicable effective dates of the corresponding statutory provisions, the rules that apply for housing credit dollar amounts allocated on or before January 6, 2004 are contained in § 1.42-6 in effect on and

before January 6, 2004 (see 26 CFR part 1 revised as of April 1, 2003).

(3) Electronic filing simplification changes. Sections 1.42-6(d)(4) and 1.42-8(a)(6)(i), (a)(6)(ii), (a)(7) Example 1 and Example 2, (b)(4)(i), and (b)(4)(ii) are applicable for forms filed after January 6, 2004.

(4) Utility allowances. The first sentence in § 1.42-10(a), § 1.42-10(b)(1), (2), (3), and (4), the last two sentences in § 1.42-10(b)(4)(ii)(A), the third, fourth, and fifth sentences in § 1.42-10(b)(4)(ii)(B), § 1.42-10(b)(4)(ii)(C), (D), and (E), and § 1.42-10(c) and (d) are applicable to a building owner's taxable years beginning on or after July 29, 2008. Taxpayers may rely on these provisions before the beginning of the building owner's taxable year beginning on or after July 29, 2008 provided that any utility allowances calculated under these provisions are effective no earlier than the first day of the building owner's taxable year beginning on or after July 29, 2008. The utility allowances provisions that apply to taxable years beginning before July 29, 2008 are contained in § 1.42-10 (see 26 CFR part 1 revised as of April 1, 2008).

The rules that apply for forms filed on or before January 6, 2004 are contained in § 1.42-6 and § 1.42-8 in effect on and before January 6, 2004 (see 26 CFR part 1 revised as of April 1, 2003).

(b) Prior periods. Notice 89-1, 1989-1 C.B. 620 and Notice 89-6, 1989-1 C.B. 625 (see § 601.601(d)(2)(ii)(b) of this chapter) may be applied for periods prior to May 2, 1994.

(c) Carryover allocations. The rule set forth in § 1.42-6(d)(4)(ii) relating to the requirement that state and local housing agencies file Schedule A (Form 8610), "Carryover Allocation of the Low-Income Housing Credit," is applicable for carryover allocations made after December 31, 1999.

T.D. 8520, 3/2/94, amend T.D. 8859, 1/13/2000, T.D. 9110, 1/2/2004, T.D. 9420, 7/28/008.

---

§ 1.42-13 Rules necessary and appropriate; housing credit agencies' correction of administrative errors and omissions.

(a) Publication of guidance. Under section 42(n), the Secretary has authority to prescribe regulations as may be necessary or appropriate to carry out the purposes of section 42. The Secretary may also provide guidance through various publications in the Internal Revenue Bulletin. (See § 601.601(d)(2)(ii)(b) of this chapter.)

(b) Correcting administrative errors and omissions. *(1) In general.* An Agency may correct an administrative error or omission with respect to allocations and recordkeeping, as described in paragraph (b)(2) of this section, within a reasonable period after the Agency discovers the administrative error or omission. Whether a correction is made within a reasonable period depends on the facts and circumstances of each situation. Except as provided in paragraph (b)(3)(iii) of this section, an Agency need not obtain the prior approval of the Secretary to correct an administrative error or omission, if the correction is made in accordance with paragraph (b)(3)(i) of this section. The administrative errors and omissions to which this paragraph (b) applies are strictly limited to those described in paragraph (b)(2) of this section, and, thus, do not include, for example, any misinterpretation of the applicable rules and regulations under section 42. Accordingly, an Agency's allocation of a particular calendar year's low-income housing credit dollar amount made after the close of that calendar year, or the use of an incorrect population amount in calculating a State's housing credit ceiling for a calendar year are not administrative errors that can be corrected under this paragraph (b).

(2) Administrative errors and omissions described. An administrative error or omission is a mistake that results in a document that inaccurately reflects the intent of the Agency at the time the document is originally completed or, if the mistake affects a taxpayer, a document that inaccurately reflects the intent of the Agency and the affected taxpayer at the time the document is originally completed. Administrative errors and omissions described in this paragraph (b)(2) include the following—

(i) A mathematical error;

(ii) An entry on a document that is inconsistent with another entry on the same or another document regarding the same property, or taxpayer;

(iii) A failure in tracking the housing credit dollar amount an Agency has allocated (or that remains to be allocated) in the current calendar year (e.g., a failure to include in its State housing credit ceiling a previously allocated credit dollar amount that has been returned by a taxpayer);

(iv) An omission of information that is required on a document; and

(v) Any other type of error or omission identified by guidance published in the Internal Revenue Bulletin (see § 601.601(d)(2)(ii)(b) of this chapter) as an administrative error or omission covered by this paragraph (b).

(3) Procedures for correcting administrative errors or omissions. (i) In general. An Agency's correction of an administrative error or omission, as described in paragraph (b)(2) of this section, must amend the document so that the corrected document reflects the original intent of the Agency, or the Agency and the affected taxpayer, and complies with applicable rules and regulations under section 42.

(ii) Specific procedures. If a document corrects a document containing an administrative error or omission that has not yet been filed with the Internal Revenue Service, the Agency, or the Agency and the affected taxpayer, should complete and file the corrected document as the original. When a document containing an administrative error or omission has already been filed with the Service, the Agency, or the Agency and the affected taxpayer, should refile a copy of the document containing the administrative error or omission, and prominently and clearly note the correction thereon or on an attached new document. The Agency should indicate at the top of the document(s) that the correction is being made under § 1.42-13 of the Income Tax Regulations.

(iii) Secretary's prior approval required. Except as provided in paragraph (b)(3)(vi) of this section, an Agency must obtain the Secretary's prior approval to correct an administrative error or omission, as described in paragraph (b)(2) of this section, if the correction is not made before the close of the calendar year of the error or omission and the correction—

(A) Is a numerical change to the housing credit dollar amount allocated for the building or project;

(B) Affects the determination of any component of the State's housing credit ceiling under section 42(h)(3)(C); or

(C) Affects the State's unused housing credit carryover that is assigned to the Secretary under section 42(h)(3)(D).

(iv) Requesting the Secretary's approval. To obtain the Secretary's approval under paragraph (b)(3)(iii) of this section, an Agency must submit a request for the Secretary's approval within a reasonable period after discovering the administrative error or omission, and must agree to any conditions that may be required by the Secretary under paragraph (b)(3)(v) of this section. When requesting the Secretary's approval, the Agency, or the Agency and the affected taxpayer, must file an application that complies with the requirements of this paragraph (b)(3)(iv). For further information on the application procedure see Rev. Proc. 93-1, 1993-1 I.R.B. 10 (or any subsequent applicable revenue procedure). (See § 601.601(d)(2)(ii)(b) of this chapter.) The application requesting the Secretary's approval must contain the following information—

(A) The name, address, and identification number of each affected taxpayer;

(B) The Building Identification Number (B.I.N.) and address of each building or project affected by the administrative error or omission;

(C) A statement explaining the administrative error or omission and the intent of the Agency, or of the Agency and the affected taxpayer, when the document was originally completed;

(D) Copies of any supporting documentation;

(E) A statement explaining the effect, if any, that a correction of the administrative error or omission would have on the housing credit dollar amount allocated for any building or project; and

(F) A statement explaining the effect, if any, that a correction of the administrative error or omission would have on the determination of the components of the State's housing credit ceiling under section 42(h)(3)(C) or on the State's unused housing credit carryover that is assigned to the Secretary under section 42(h)(3)(D).

(v) Agreement to conditions. To obtain the Secretary's approval under paragraph (b)(3)(iii) of this section, an Agency, or the Agency and the affected taxpayer, must agree to the conditions the Secretary considers appropriate.

(vi) Secretary's automatic approval. The Secretary grants automatic approval to correct an administrative error or omission described in paragraph (b)(2) of this section if—

(A) The correction is not made before the close of the calendar year of the error or omission and the correction is a numerical change to the housing credit dollar amount allocated for the building or multiple-building project;

(B) The administrative error or omission resulted in an allocation document (the Form 8609, "Low-Income Housing Credit Allocation Certification," or the allocation document under the requirements of section 42(h)(1)(E) or (F), and § 1.42-6(d)(2)) that either did not accurately reflect the number of buildings in a project (for example, an allocation document for a 10-building project only references 8 buildings instead of 10 buildings), or the correct information (other than the amount of credit allocated on the allocation document);

(C) The administrative error or omission does not affect the Agency's ranking of the building(s) or project and the total amount of credit the Agency allocated to the building(s) or project; and

(D) The Agency corrects the administrative error or omission by following the procedures described in paragraph (b)(3)(vii) of this section.

(vii) How Agency corrects errors or omissions subject to automatic approval. An Agency corrects an administrative error or omission described in paragraph (b)(3)(vi) of this section by—

(A) Amending the allocation document described in paragraph (b)(3)(vi)(B) of this section to correct the administrative error or omission. The Agency will indicate on the amended allocation document that it is making the "correction under § 1.42-13(b)(3)(vii)." If correcting the allocation document requires including any additional B.I.N.(s) in the document, the document must include any B.I.N.(s) already existing for buildings in the project. If possible, the additional B.I.N.(s) should be sequentially numbered from the existing B.I.N.(s);

(B) Amending, if applicable, the Schedule A (Form 8610), "Carryover Allocation of the Low-Income Housing Credit," and attaching a copy of this schedule to Form 8610, "Annual Low-Income Housing Credit Agencies Report," for the year the correction is made. The Agency will indicate on the schedule that it is making the "correction under § 1.42-13(b)(3)(vii)." For a carryover allocation made before January 1, 2000, the Agency must complete Schedule A (Form 8610), and indicate on the schedule that it is making the "correction under § 1.42-13(b)(3)(vii)";

(C) Amending, if applicable, the Form 8609 and attaching the original of this amended form to Form 8610 for the year the correction is made. The Agency will indicate on the Form 8609 that it is making the "correction under § 1.42-13(b)(3)(vii)"; and

(D) Mailing or otherwise delivering a copy of any amended allocation document and any amended Form 8609 to the affected taxpayer.

(viii) Other approval procedures. The Secretary may grant automatic approval to correct other administrative errors or omissions as designated in one or more documents published either in the Federal Register or in the Internal Revenue Bulletin (see § 601.601(d)(2) of this chapter).

(c) Examples. The following examples illustrate the scope of this section:

Example (1). Individual B applied to Agency X for a reservation of a low-income housing credit dollar amount for a building that is part of a low-income housing project. When applying for the low-income housing credit dollar amount, B informed Agency X that B intended to form Partnership Y to finance the project. After receiving the reservation letter and prior to receiving an allocation, B formed Partnership Y and sold partnership interests to a number of limited partners. B contributed the low-income housing project to Partnership Y in exchange for a partnership interest. B and Partnership Y informed Agency X of the ownership change. When actually allocating the housing credit dollar amount, Agency X sent Partnership Y a document listing B, rather than Partnership Y, as the building's owner. Partnership Y promptly notified Agency X of the error. After reviewing related documents, Agency X determined that it had incorrectly listed B as the building's owner on the allocation document. Since the parties originally intended that Partnership Y would receive the allocation as the owner of the building, Agency X may correct the error without obtaining the Secretary's approval, and insert Partnership Y as the building's owner on the allocation document.

Example (2). Agency Y allocated a lower low-income housing credit dollar amount for a low-income housing building than Agency Y originally intended. After the close of the calendar year of the allocation, B, the building's owner, discovered the error and promptly notified Agency Y. Agency Y reviewed relevant documents and agreed that an error had occurred. Agency Y and B must apply, as provided in paragraph (b)(3)(iv) of this section, for the Secretary's approval before Agency Y may correct the error.

(d) Effective date. This section is effective February 24, 1994. However, an Agency may elect to apply these regulations to administrative errors or omissions that occurred before the publication of these regulations. Any reasonable method used by a State or local housing credit agency to correct an administrative error or omission prior to February 24, 1994, will be considered proper, provided that the method is consistent with the rules of section 42. Paragraphs (b)(3)(vi), (vii), and (viii) of this section are effective January 14, 2000.

T.D. 8521, 2/23/94, amend T.D. 8859, 1/13/2000.

§ 1.42-14 Allocation rules for post-2000 State housing credit ceiling amount.

Caution: The Treasury has not yet amended Reg § 1.42-14 to reflect changes made by P.L. 110-343, P.L. 110-289, P.L. 106-554.

(a) State housing credit ceiling. *(1) In general.* The State housing credit ceiling for a State for any calendar year after 2000 is comprised of four components. The four components are—

(i) The unused State housing credit ceiling, if any, of the State for the preceding calendar year (the unused carryforward component);

(ii) The greater of—

(A) $1.75 ($1.50 for calendar year 2001) multiplied by the State population; or (B) $2,000,000 (the population component);

(iii) The amount of State housing credit ceiling returned in the calendar year (the returned credit component); plus

(iv) The amount, if any, allocated to the State by the Secretary under section 42(h)(3)(D) from a national pool of unused credit (the national pool component).

(2) Cost of Living Adjustment. (i) General rule. For any calendar year after 2002, the $2,000,000 and $1.75 amounts in paragraph (a)(1)(ii) of this section are each increased by an amount equal to—

(A) The dollar amount; multiplied by

(B) The cost-of-living adjustment determined under section 1(f)(3) for the calendar year by substituting "calendar year 2001" for "calendar year 1992" in section 1(f)(3)(B).

(ii) Rounding. Any increase resulting from the application of paragraph (a)(2)(i) of this section which, in the case of the $2,000,000 amount, is not a multiple of $5,000, is rounded to the next lowest multiple of $5,000, and which, in the case of the $1.75 amount, is not a multiple of 5 cents, is rounded to the next lowest multiple of 5 cents.

(b) The unused carryforward component. The unused carryforward component of the State housing credit ceiling for any calendar year is the unused State housing credit ceiling, if any, of the State for the preceding calendar year. The unused State housing credit ceiling for any calendar year is the excess, if any, of—

(1) The sum of the population, returned credit, and national pool components for the calendar year; over

(2) The aggregate housing credit dollar amount allocated for the calendar year reduced by the housing credit dollar amounts allocated from the unused carryforward component for the calendar year.

(c) The population component. The population component of the State housing credit ceiling of a State for any calendar year is determined pursuant to section 146(j). Thus, a State's population for any calendar year is determined by reference to the most recent census estimate, whether final or provisional, of the resident population of the State released by the Bureau of the Census before the beginning of the calendar year for which the State's housing credit ceiling is set. Unless otherwise prescribed by applicable revenue procedure, determinations of population are based on the most recent estimates of population contained in the Bureau of the Census publication, *Current Population Report, Series P-25; Population Estimates and Projections, Estimates of the Population of States.* For convenience, the Internal Revenue Service publishes the population estimates annually in the Internal Revenue Bulletin. (See § 601.601(d)(2)(ii)(b)).

(d) The returned credit component. *(1) In general.* The returned credit component of the State housing credit ceiling of a State for any calendar year equals the housing credit dollar amount returned during the calendar year that was validly allocated within the State in a prior calendar year to any project that does not become a qualified low-income housing project within the period required by section 42, or as required by the terms of the allocation. The returned credit component also includes credit allocated in a prior calendar year that is returned as a result of the cancellation of an allocation by mutual consent or by an Agency's determination that the amount allocated is not necessary for the financial feasibility of the project. For purposes of this section, credit is allocated within a State if it is allocated from the State's housing credit ceiling by an Agency of the State or of a constitutional home rule city in the State.

(2) Limitations and special rules. The following limitations and special rules apply for purposes of this paragraph (d).

(i) General limitations. Notwithstanding any other provision of this paragraph (d), returned credit does not include any credit that was—

(A) Allocated prior to calendar year 1990;

(B) Allowable under section 42(h)(4) (relating to the portion of credit attributable to eligible basis financed by certain tax-exempt bonds under section 103); or

(C) Allocated during the same calendar year that it is received back by the Agency.

(ii) Credit period limitation. Notwithstanding any other provision of this paragraph (d), an allocation of credit may not be returned any later than 180 days following the close of the first taxable year of the credit period for the building that received the allocation. After this date, credit that might otherwise be returned expires, and cannot be returned to or reallocated by any Agency.

(iii) Three-month rule for returned credit. An Agency may, in its discretion, treat any portion of credit that is returned from a project after September 30 of a calendar year and that is not reallocated by the close of the calendar year as returned on January 1 of the succeeding calendar year. In this case, the returned credit becomes part of the returned credit component of the State housing credit ceiling for the succeeding calendar year. Any portion of credit that is returned from a project after September 30 of a calendar year that is reallocated by the close of the calendar year is treated as part of the returned credit component of the State housing credit ceiling for the calendar year that the credit was returned.

(iv) Returns of credit. Subject to the limitations of paragraphs (d)(2)(i) and (ii) of this section, credit is returned to the Agency in the following instances in the manner described in paragraph (d)(3) of this section.

(A) Building not qualified within required time period. If a building is not a qualified building within the time period required by section 42, it loses its credit allocation and the credit is returned. For example, a building is not qualified within the required time period if it is not placed in service within the period required by section 42 or if the project of which the building is a part fails to meet the minimum set-aside requirements of section 42(g)(1) by the close of the first year of the credit period. Also, a building that has received a post-June 30 carryover allocation is not qualified within the required time period if the taxpayer does not meet the 10 percent basis requirement by the date that is 6 months after the date the allocation was made (as described in § 1.42-6(a)(2)(ii)).

(B) Noncompliance with terms of the allocation. If a building does not comply with the terms of its allocation, it loses the credit allocation and the credit is returned. The terms of an allocation are the written conditions agreed to by the Agency and the allocation recipient in the allocation document.

(C) Mutual consent. If the Agency and the allocation recipient cancel an allocation of an amount of credit by mutual consent, that amount of credit is returned.

(D) Amount not necessary for financial feasibility. If an Agency determines under section 42(m)(2) that an amount of credit allocated to a project is not necessary for the financial feasibility of the project and its viability as a qualified low-income housing project throughout the credit period, that amount of credit is returned.

(3) Manner of returning credit. (i) Taxpayer notification. After an Agency determines that a building or project no longer qualifies under paragraph (d)(2)(iv)(A), (B), or (D) of this section for all or part of the allocation it received, the Agency must provide written notification to the allocation recipient, or its successor in interest, that all or part of the allocation is no longer valid. The notification must also state the amount of the allocation that is no longer valid. The date of the notification is the date the credit is returned to the Agency. If an allocation is cancelled by mutual consent under paragraph (d)(2)(iv)(C) of this section, there must be a written agreement signed by the Agency, and the allocation recipient, or its successor in interest, indicating the amount of the allocation that is returned to the Agency. The effective date of the agreement is the date the credit is returned to the Agency.

(ii) Internal Revenue Service notification. If a credit is returned within 180 days following the close of the first taxable year of a building's credit period as provided in paragraph (d)(2)(ii) of this section, and a Form 8609, *Low-Income Housing Credit Allocation Certification,* has been issued for the building, the Agency must notify the Internal Revenue Service that the credit has been returned. If only part of the credit has been returned, this notification requirement is satisfied when the Agency attaches to an amended Form 8610, *Annual Low-Income Housing Credit Agencies Report,* the original of an amended Form 8609 reflecting the correct amount of credit attributed to the building together with an explanation for the filing of the amended Forms. The Agency must send a copy of the amended Form 8609 to the taxpayer that owns the building. If the building is not issued an amended Form 8609 because all of the credit allocated to the building is returned, notification to the Internal Revenue Service is satisfied by following the requirements prescribed in § 1.42-5(e)(3) for filing a Form 8823, *Low-Income Housing Credit Agencies Report of Noncompliance.*

(e) The national pool component. The national pool component of the State housing credit ceiling of a State for any calendar year is the portion of the National Pool allocated to the State by the Secretary for the calendar year. The national pool component for any calendar year is zero unless a State is a qualified State. (See paragraph (i) of this section for rules regarding the National Pool and the description of a qualified State.) A national pool component credit that is allocated during a calendar year and returned after the close of the calendar year may qualify as part of the returned credit component of the State housing credit ceiling for the calendar year that the credit is returned.

(f) When the State housing credit ceiling is determined. For purposes of accounting for the State housing credit ceiling on Form 8610 and for purposes of determining the set-aside apportionment for projects involving qualified nonprofit organizations described in section 42(h)(5) and § 1.42-1T(c)(5), the State housing credit ceiling for any calendar year is determined at the close of the calendar year.

(g) Stacking Order. Credit is treated as allocated from the various components of the State housing credit ceiling in the following order. The first credit allocated for any calendar year is treated as credit from the unused carryforward component of the State housing credit ceiling for the calendar year. After all of the credit in the unused carryforward component has been allocated, any credit allocated is treated as allocated from the sum of the population, returned credit, and national pool components of the State housing credit ceiling.

(h) Nonprofit set-aside. *(1) Determination of set-aside.* Under section 42(h)(5) and § 1.42-1T(c)(5), at least 10 percent of a State housing credit ceiling in any calendar year must be set aside exclusively for projects involving qualified nonprofit organizations (the nonprofit set-aside). However, credit allocated from the nonprofit set-aside in a calendar year and returned in a subsequent calendar year does not retain its nonprofit set-aside character. The credit becomes part of the returned credit component of the State housing credit ceiling for the calendar year that the credit is returned and must be included in determining the nonprofit set-aside of the State housing credit ceiling for that calendar year. Similarly, credit amounts that are not allocated from the nonprofit set-aside in a calendar year and are returned in a subsequent calendar year become part of the returned credit component of the State housing credit ceiling for that year and are also included in determining the set-aside for that year.

(2) Allocation rules. An Agency may allocate credit from any component of the State housing credit ceiling as part of the nonprofit set-aside and need not reserve 10 percent of each component for the nonprofit set-aside. Thus, an Agency may satisfy the nonprofit set-aside requirement of section 42(h)(5) and § 1.42-1T(c)(5) in any calendar year by setting aside for allocation an amount equal to at least 10 percent of the total State housing credit ceiling for the calendar year.

(i) National Pool. *(1) In general.* The unused housing credit carryover of a State for any calendar year is assigned to the Secretary for inclusion in a national pool of unused housing credit carryovers (National Pool) that is reallocated among qualified States the succeeding calendar year. The assignment to the Secretary is made on Form 8610.

(2) Unused housing credit carryover. The unused housing credit carryover of a State for any calendar year is the excess, if any, of—

(i) The unused carryforward component of the State housing credit ceiling for the calendar year; over

(ii) The total housing credit dollar amount allocated for the calendar year.

(3) Qualified State. (i) In general. The term qualified State means, with respect to any calendar year, any State that has allocated its entire State housing credit ceiling for the preceding calendar year and for which a request is made by the State, not later than May 1 of the calendar year, to receive an allocation of credit from the National Pool for that calendar year. Except as provided in paragraph (i)(3)(ii) of this section, a State is not a qualified State in a calendar year if there remains any unallocated credit in its State housing credit ceiling at the close of the preceding calendar year that was apportioned to any Agency within the State for the calendar year.

(ii) Exceptions. (A) De minimis amount. If the amount remaining unallocated at the close of a calendar year is only a de minimis amount of credit, the State is a qualified State eligible to participate in the National Pool. For that purpose, a credit amount is de minimis if it does not exceed 1 percent of the aggregate State housing credit ceiling of the State for the calendar year.

(B) Other circumstances. Pursuant to the authority under section 42(n), the Internal Revenue Service may determine that a State is a qualified State eligible to participate in the National Pool even though the State's unallocated credit is in excess of the 1 percent safe harbor set forth in paragraph (A) of this section. The Internal Revenue Service will make this determination based on all the facts and circumstances, weighing heavily the interests of the States who would otherwise qualify for the National Pool. The Internal Revenue Service will generally grant relief under this paragraph only where a State's unallocated credit is not substantial.

(iii) Time and manner for making request. For further guidance as to the time and manner for making a request of housing credit dollar amounts from the National Pool by a qualified State, see Rev. Proc. 92-31, 1992-1 C.B. 775. (See 601.601(d)(2)(ii)(b)).

(4) Formula for determining the National Pool. The amount allocated to a qualified State in any calendar year is an amount that bears the same ratio to the aggregate unused housing credit carryovers of all States for the preceding calendar year as that State's population for the calendar year bears to the population of all qualified States for the calendar year.

(j) Coordination between Agencies. The Agency responsible for filing Form 8610 on behalf of all Agencies within a State and making any request on behalf of the State for credit from the National Pool (the Filing Agency) must coordinate with each Agency within the State to ensure that the various requirements of this section are complied with. For example, the Filing Agency of a State must ensure that all Agencies within the State that were apportioned a credit amount for the calendar year have allocated all of their respective credit amounts for the calendar year before the Filing Agency can make a request on behalf of the State for a distribution of credit from the National Pool.

(k) Example. *(1)* The operation of the rules of this section is illustrated by the following examples. Unless otherwise stated in an example, Agency A is the sole Agency authorized to make allocations of housing credit dollar amounts in State M, all of Agency A's allocations are valid, and for calendar year 2003, Agency A has available for allocation a State housing credit ceiling consisting of the following housing credit dollar amounts:

A. unused carryforward component	$50
B. population component	110
C. returned credit component	10
D. national pool component	0
Total	170

(2) In addition, the $10 of returned credit component was returned before October 1, 2003.

Example (1). (i) Additional facts. By the close of 2003, Agency A had allocated $80 of the State M housing credit ceiling. Of the $80 allocated, $17 was allocated to projects involving qualified nonprofit organizations.

(ii) Application of stacking rules. The $80 of allocated credit is first treated as allocated from the unused carryforward component of the State housing credit ceiling. The $80 of allocated credit exceeds the $50 attributable to the unused carryforward component by $30. Because the unused carryforward component is fully utilized no credit will be forfeited by State M to the 2004 National Pool. The remaining $30 of allocated credit will next be treated as allocated from the $120 in credit determined by aggregating the population, returned credit, and national pool components ($110 + 10 + 0 = $120). The $90 of unallocated credit remaining in State M's 2003 State housing credit ceiling ($120 - 30 = $90) represents the unused carryforward component of State M's 2004 State housing credit ceiling. Under paragraph (i)(3) of this section, State M does not qualify for credit from the 2004 National Pool.

(iii) Nonprofit set-aside. Agency A allocated exactly the amount of credit to projects involving qualified nonprofit organizations as necessary to meet the nonprofit set-aside requirement ($17, 10% of the $170 ceiling).

Example (2). (i) Additional facts. By the close of 2003, Agency A had allocated $40 of the State M housing credit ceiling. Of the $40 allocated, $20 was allocated to projects involving qualified nonprofit organizations.

(ii) Application of stacking rules. The $40 of allocated credit is first treated as allocated from the unused carryforward component of the State housing credit ceiling. Because the $40 of allocated credit does not exceed the $50 attributable to the unused carryforward component, the remaining components of the State housing credit ceiling are unaffected. The $10 remaining in the unused carryforward component is assigned to the Secretary for inclusion in the 2004 National Pool. The $120 in credit determined by aggregating the population, returned credit, and national pool components becomes the unused carryforward component of State M's 2004 State housing credit ceiling. Under paragraph (i)(3) of this section, State M does not qualify for credit from the 2004 National Pool.

(iii) Nonprofit set-aside. Agency A allocated $3 more credit to projects involving qualified nonprofit organizations than necessary to meet the nonprofit set-aside requirement. This does not reduce the application of the 10% nonprofit set-aside requirement to the State M housing credit ceiling for calendar year 2004.

Example (3). (i) Additional fact. None of the applications for credit that Agency A received for 2003 are for projects involving qualified nonprofit organizations.

(ii) Nonprofit set-aside. Because at least 10% of the State housing credit ceiling must be set aside for projects involving a qualified nonprofit organization, Agency A can allocate only $153 of the $170 State housing credit ceiling for calendar year 2003 ($170 -17 = $153). If Agency A allocates $153 of credit, the credit is treated as allocated $50 from the unused carryforward component and $103 from the sum of the population, returned credit, and national pool components. The $17 of unallocated credit that is set aside for projects involving qualified nonprofit organizations becomes the unused carryforward component of State M's 2004 State housing credit ceiling. Under paragraph (i)(3) of this section, State M does not qualify for credit from the 2004 National Pool.

Example (4). (i) Additional facts. The $10 of returned credit component was returned prior to October 1, 2003. However, a $40 credit that had been allocated in calendar year 2002 to a project involving a qualified nonprofit organization was returned to the Agency by a mutual consent agreement dated November 15, 2003. By the close of 2003, Agency A had allocated $170 of the State M's housing credit ceiling, including $17 of credit to projects involving qualified nonprofit organizations.

(ii) Effect of three-month rule. Under the three-month rule of paragraph (d)(2)(iii) of this section, Agency A may treat all or part of the $40 of previously allocated credit as returned on January 1, 2004. If Agency A treats all of the $40 amount as having been returned in calendar year 2004, the State M housing credit ceiling for 2003 is $170. This entire amount, including the $17 nonprofit set-aside, has been allocated in 2003. Under paragraph (i)(3) of this section, State M qualifies for the 2004 National Pool.

(iii) If three-month rule not used. If Agency A treats all of the $40 of previously allocated credit as returned in calendar year 2003, the State housing credit ceiling for the 2003 calendar year will be $210 of which $50 will be attributable to the returned credit component ($10 + $40 = $50). Because credit amounts allocated to a qualified nonprofit organization in a prior calendar year that are returned in a subsequent calendar year do not retain their nonprofit character, the nonprofit set-aside for calendar year 2003 is $21 (10% of the $210 State housing credit ceiling). The $170 that Agency A allocated during 2003 is first treated as allocated from the unused carryforward component of the State housing credit ceiling. The $170 of allocated credit exceeds the $50 attributable to the unused carryforward component by $120. Because the unused carryforward component is fully utilized no credit will be forfeited by State M to the 2004 National Pool. The remaining $120 of allocated credit will next be treated as allocated from the $160 in credit determined by aggregating the population, returned credit, and national pool components ($110 + 50 + 0 = $160). The $40 of unallocated credit (which includes $4 of unallocated credit from the $21 nonprofit set-aside) remaining in State M's 2003 housing credit ceiling ($160-120 = $40) represents the unused carryforward component of State M's 2004 housing credit ceiling. Under paragraph (i)(3) of this section, State M does not qualify for credit from the 2004 National Pool.

(l) Effective dates. *(1) In general.* Except as provided in paragraph (l)(2) of this section, the rules set forth in § 1.42-14 are applicable on January 1, 1994.

(2) Community Renewal Tax Relief Act of 2000 changes. Paragraphs (a), (b), (c), (e), (i)(2) and (k) of this section are applicable for housing credit dollar amounts allocated after January 6, 2004. However, paragraphs (a), (b), (c), (e), (i)(2) and (k) of this section may be applied by Agencies and taxpayers for housing credit dollar amounts allocated after December 31, 2000, and on or before January 6, 2004. Otherwise, subject to the applicable effective dates of the corresponding statutory provisions, the rules that apply for housing credit dollar amounts allocated on or before January 6, 2004 are contained in this section in effect on and before January 6, 2004 (see 26 CFR part 1 revised as of April 1, 2003).

T.D. 8563, 9/30/94, amend T.D. 9110, 1/2/2004.

§ 1.42-15 Available unit rule.

(a) Definitions. The following definitions apply to this section:

Applicable income limitation means the limitation applicable under section 42(g)(1) or, for deep rent skewed projects described in section 142(d)(4)(B), 40 percent of area median gross income.

Available unit rule means the rule in section 42(g)(2)(D)(ii).

Comparable unit means a residential unit in a low-income building that is comparably sized or smaller than an over-income unit or, for deep rent skewed projects described in section 142(d)(4)(B), any low-income unit. For purposes of determining whether a residential unit is comparably sized, a comparable unit must be measured by the same method used to determine qualified basis for the credit year in which the comparable unit became available.

Current resident means a person who is living in the low-income building.

Low-income unit is defined by section 42(i)(3)(A).

Nonqualified resident means a new occupant or occupants whose aggregate income exceeds the applicable income limitation.

Over-income unit means a low-income unit in which the aggregate income of the occupants of the unit increases above 140 percent of the applicable income limitation under section 42(g)(1), or above 170 percent of the applicable income limitation for deep rent skewed projects described in section 142(d)(4)(B).

Qualified resident means an occupant either whose aggregate income (combined with the income of all other occupants of the unit) does not exceed the applicable income limitation and who is otherwise a low-income resident under section 42, or who is a current resident.

(b) General section 42(g)(2)(D)(i) rule. Except as provided in paragraph (c) of this section, notwithstanding an increase in the income of the occupants of a low-income unit above the applicable income limitation, if the income of the occupants initially met the applicable income limitation, and the unit continues to be rent-restricted—

(1) The unit continues to be treated as a low-income unit; and

(2) The unit continues to be included in the numerator and the denominator of the ratio used to determine whether a project satisfies the applicable minimum set-aside requirement of section 42(g)(1).

(c) Exception. A unit ceases to be treated as a low-income unit if it becomes an over-income unit and a nonqualified resident occupies any comparable unit that is available or that subsequently becomes available in the same low-income building. In other words, the owner of a low-income building must rent to qualified residents all comparable units that are available or that subsequently become available in the same building to continue treating the over-income unit as a low-income unit. Once the percentage of low-income units in a building (excluding the over-income units) equals the percentage of low-income units on which the credit is based, failure to maintain the over-income units as low-income units has no immediate significance. The failure to maintain the over-income units as low-income units, however, may affect the decision of whether or not to rent a particular available unit at market rate at a later time. A unit is not available for purposes of the available unit rule when the unit is no longer available for rent due to contractual arrangements that are binding under local law (for example, a unit is not available if it is subject to a preliminary reservation that is binding on the owner under local law prior to the date a lease is signed or the unit is occupied).

(d) Effect of current resident moving within building. When a current resident moves to a different unit within the building, the newly occupied unit adopts the status of the vacated unit. Thus, if a current resident, whose income exceeds the applicable income limitation, moves from an over-income unit to a vacant unit in the same building, the newly occupied unit is treated as an over-income unit. The vacated unit assumes the status the newly occupied unit had immediately before it was occupied by the current resident.

(e) Available unit rule applies separately to each building in a project. In a project containing more than one low-income building, the available unit rule applies separately to each building.

(f) Result of noncompliance with available unit rule. If any comparable unit that is available or that subsequently becomes available is rented to a nonqualified resident, all over-income units for which the available unit was a comparable unit within the same building lose their status as low-income units; thus, comparably sized or larger over-income units would lose their status as low-income units.

(g) Relationship to tax-exempt bond provisions. Financing arrangements that purport to be exempt-facility bonds under section 142 must meet the requirements of sections 103 and 141 through 150 for interest on the obligations to be excluded from gross income under section 103(a). This section is not intended as an interpretation under section 142.

(h) Examples. The following examples illustrate this section:

Example (1). This example illustrates noncompliance with the available unit rule in a low-income building containing three over-income units. On January 1, 1998, a qualified low-income housing project, consisting of one building containing ten identically sized residential units, received a housing credit dollar amount allocation from a state housing credit agency for five low-income units. By the close of 1998, the first year of the credit period, the project satisfied the minimum set-aside requirement of section 42(g)(1)(B). Units 1, 2, 3, 4, and 5 were occupied by individuals whose incomes did not exceed the income limitation applicable under section 42(g)(1) and were otherwise low-income residents under section 42. Units 6, 7, 8, and 9 were occupied by market-rate tenants. Unit 10 was vacant. To avoid recapture of credit, the project owner must maintain five of the units as low-income units. On November 1, 1999, the certificates of annual income state that annual incomes of the individuals in Units 1, 2, and 3 increased above 140 percent of the income limitation applicable under section 42(g)(1), causing those units to become over-income units. On November 30, 1999, Units 8 and 9 became vacant. On December 1, 1999, the project owner rented Units 8 and 9 to qualified residents who were not current residents at rates meeting the rent restriction requirements of section 42(g)(2). On December 31, 1999, the project owner rented Unit 10 to a market-rate tenant. Because Unit 10, an available comparable unit, was leased to a market-rate tenant, Units 1, 2, and 3 ceased to be treated as low-income units. On that date, Units 4, 5, 8, and 9 were the only remaining low-income units. Because the project owner did not maintain five of the residential units as low-income units, the qualified basis in the building is reduced, and credit must be recaptured. If the project owner had rented Unit 10 to a qualified resident who was not a current resident, eight of the units would be low-income units. At that time, Units 1, 2, and 3, the over-income units, could be rented to market-rate tenants because the building would still contain five low-income units.

Example (2). This example illustrates the provisions of paragraph (d) of this section. A low-income project consists of one six-floor building. The residential units in the building are identically sized. The building contains two over-income units on the sixth floor and two vacant units on the first floor. The project owner, desiring to maintain the over-income units as low-income units, wants to rent the available units to qualified residents. J, a resident of one of the over-income units, wishes to occupy a unit on the first floor. J's income has recently increased above the applicable income limitation. The project owner permits J to move into one of the units on the first floor. Despite J's income exceeding the applicable income limitation, J is a qualified resident under the available unit rule because J is a current resident of the building. The unit newly occupied by J becomes an over-income unit under the available unit rule. The unit vacated by J assumes the status the newly occupied unit had immediately before J occupied the unit. The over-income units in the building continue to be treated as low-income units.

(i) Effective date. This section applies to leases entered into or renewed on and after September 26, 1997.

T.D. 8732, 9/25/97.

§ 1.42-16 Eligible basis reduced by federal grants.

(a) In general. If, during any taxable year of the compliance period (described in section 42(i)(1)), a grant is made with respect to any building or the operation thereof and any portion of the grant is funded with federal funds (whether or not includible in gross income), the eligible basis of the building for the taxable year and all succeeding taxable years is reduced by the portion of the grant that is so funded.

(b) Grants do not include certain rental assistance payments. A federal rental assistance payment made to a building owner on behalf or in respect of a tenant is not a grant made with respect to a building or its operation if the payment is made pursuant to—

(1) Section 8 of the United States Housing Act of 1937;

(2) A qualifying program of rental assistance administered under section 9 of the United States Housing Act of 1937; or

(3) A program or method of rental assistance as the Secretary may designate by publication in the Federal Register or in the Internal Revenue Bulletin (see § 601.601(d)(2) of this chapter).

(c) Qualifying rental assistance program. For purposes of paragraph (b)(2) of this section, payments are made pursuant to a qualifying rental assistance program administered under section 9 of the United States Housing Act of 1937 to the extent that the payments—

(1) Are made to a building owner pursuant to a contract with a public housing authority with respect to units the owner has agreed to maintain as public housing units (PH-units) in the building;

(2) Are made with respect to units occupied by public housing tenants, provided that, for this purpose, units may be considered occupied during periods of short term vacancy (not to exceed 60 days); and

(3) Do not exceed the difference between the rents received from a building's PH-unit tenants and a pro rata portion of the building's actual operating costs that are reasonably allocable to the PH-units (based on square footage, number of bedrooms, or similar objective criteria), and provided that, for this purpose, operating costs do not include any development costs of a building (including developer's fees) or the principal or interest of any debt incurred with respect to any part of the building.

(d) Effective date. This section is effective September 26, 1997.

T.D. 8731, 9/25/97.

§ 1.42-17 Qualified allocation plan.

(a) Requirements. *(1) In general. [Reserved]*

(2) Selection criteria. [Reserved]

(3) Agency evaluation. Section 42(m)(2)(A) requires that the housing credit dollar amount allocated to a project is not to exceed the amount the Agency determines is necessary for the financial feasibility of the project and its viability as a qualified low-income housing project throughout the credit period. In making this determination, the Agency must consider—

(i) The sources and uses of funds and the total financing planned for the project. The taxpayer must certify to the Agency the full extent of all federal, state, and local subsidies that apply (or which the taxpayer expects to apply) to the project. The taxpayer must also certify to the Agency all other sources of funds and all development costs for the project. The taxpayer's certification should be sufficiently detailed to enable the Agency to ascertain the nature of the costs that will make up the total financing package, including subsidies and the anticipated syndication or placement proceeds to be raised. Development cost information, whether or not includible in eligible basis under section 42(d), that should be provided to the Agency includes, but is not limited to, site acquisition costs, construction contingency, general contractor's overhead and profit, architect's and engineer's fees, permit and survey fees, insurance premiums, real estate taxes during construction, title and recording fees, construction period interest, financing fees, organizational costs, rent-up and marketing costs, accounting and auditing costs, working capital and operating deficit reserves, syndication and legal fees, and developer fees;

(ii) Any proceeds or receipts expected to be generated by reason of tax benefits;

(iii) The percentage of the housing credit dollar amount used for project costs other than the costs of intermediaries. This requirement should not be applied so as to impede the development of projects in hard-to-develop areas under section 42(d)(5)(C); and

(iv) The reasonableness of the developmental and operational costs of the project.

(4) Timing of Agency evaluation. (i) In general. The financial determinations and certifications required under paragraph (a)(3) of this section must be made as of the following times—

(A) The time of the application for the housing credit dollar amount;

(B) The time of the allocation of the housing credit dollar amount; and

(C) The date the building is placed in service.

(ii) Time limit for placed-in-service evaluation. For purposes of paragraph (a)(4)(i)(C) of this section, the evaluation for when a building is placed in service must be made not later than the date the Agency issues the Form 8609, "Low-Income Housing Credit Allocation Certification." The Agency must evaluate all sources and uses of funds under paragraph (a)(3)(i) of this section paid, incurred, or committed by the taxpayer for the project up until date the Agency issues the Form 8609.

(5) Special rule for final determinations and certifications. For the Agency's evaluation under paragraph (a)(4)(i)(C) of this section, the taxpayer must submit a schedule of project costs. Such schedule is to be prepared on the method of accounting used by the taxpayer for federal income tax purposes, and must detail the project's total costs as well as those costs that may qualify for inclusion in eligible basis under section 42(d). For projects with more than 10 units, the schedule of project costs must be accompanied by a Certified Public Accountant's audit report on the schedule (an Agency may require an audited schedule of project costs for projects with fewer than 11 units). The CPA's audit must be conducted in accordance with generally accepted auditing standards. The auditor's report must be unqualified.

(6) Bond-financed projects. A project qualifying under section 42(h)(4) is not entitled to any credit unless the governmental unit that issued the bonds (or on behalf of which the bonds were issued), or the Agency responsible for issuing the Form(s) 8609 to the project, makes determinations under rules similar to the rules in paragraphs (a) (3), (4), and (5) of this section.

(b) Effective date. This section is effective on January 1, 2001.

T.D. 8859, 1/13/2000.

Proposed § 1.42-18 Qualified contracts. [*For Preamble, see ¶ 152,871*]

(a) Extended low-income housing commitment. *(1) In general.* No credit under section 42(a) is allowed by reason of section 42 and this section with respect to any building for the taxable year unless an extended low-income housing commitment (commitment) (as defined in section 42(h)(6)(B)) is in effect as of the end of such taxable year. A commitment must be in effect for the extended use period (as defined in paragraph (a)(1)(i) of this section).

(i) Extended use period. The term extended use period means the period beginning on the first day in the compliance period (as defined in section 42(i)(1)) on which the building is part of a qualified low-income housing project (as defined in section 42(g)(1)) and ending on the later of—

(A) The date specified by the low-income housing credit agency (Agency) in the commitment; or

(B) The date that is 15 years after the close of the compliance period.

(ii) Termination of extended use period. The extended use period under paragraph (a)(1)(i) of this section for any building will terminate—

(A) On the date the building is acquired by foreclosure (or instrument in lieu of foreclosure) unless the Secretary determines that such acquisition is part of an arrangement with the taxpayer a purpose of which is to terminate such period; or

(B) On the last day of the one-year period beginning on the date (after the 14th year of the compliance period) the owner submits a written request to the Agency to find a person to acquire the owner's interest in the low-income portion of the building and the Agency is unable to present during such period a qualified contract for the acquisition of the low-income portion of the building by any person who will continue to operate such portion as a qualified low-income building (as defined in section 42(c)(2)). This paragraph (a)(1)(ii)(B) shall not apply to the extent more stringent requirements are provided in the commitment or under state law. If the Agency provides a qualified contract within the one-year period and the owner rejects or fails to act upon the contract, the building remains subject to the existing commitment.

(iii) Eviction, gross-rent increase concerning existing low-income tenants not permitted. During the three-year period following the termination of a commitment, no owner shall be permitted to evict or terminate the tenancy (other than for good cause) of an existing tenant of any low-income unit, or increase the gross rent for such unit in a manner or amount not otherwise permitted by section 42.

(2) [Reserved]

(b) Special rules. For purposes of this section, the following terms are defined:

(1) Base calendar year means the calendar year with or within which the first taxable year of the credit period ends.

(2) The low-income portion of a building is the portion of the building equal to the applicable fraction (as defined in section 42(c)(1)) specified in the commitment for the building.

(3) The fair market value of the non low-income portion of the building is determined at the time of the Agency's offer of sale of the project to the general public. This valuation must take into account the existing and continuing requirements contained in the commitment for the building. The non low-income portion also includes the fair market value of the land underlying the entire building, both the non low-income portion and the low-income portion regardless of whether the project is entirely low-income. The non low-income portion also includes the fair market value of items of personal property not included in eligible basis under section 42(d)(1) that convey under the contract with the building.

(4) A qualifying building cost is—

(i) A cost that is included in eligible basis of a low-income housing building under section 42(d)(1) which is—

(A) Included in the adjusted basis of depreciable property subject to section 168 and the property qualifies as residential rental property under section 142(d) and § 1.103-8(b)(4)(iii); or

(B) Included in the adjusted basis of depreciable property subject to section 168 that is used in a common area or provided as a comparable amenity to all residential rental units in the building; and

(ii) Of the type described in paragraph (b)(4)(i) of this section incurred after the first year of the low-income building's credit period under section 42(f).

(c) Qualified contract purchase price formula. *(1) In general.* For purposes of this section, the term qualified contract means a bona fide contract to acquire (within a reasonable period after the contract is entered into) the non low-income portion of the building for fair market value (as defined in paragraph (b)(3) of this section) and the low-income portion of the building (as defined in paragraph (b)(2) of this section) for the low-income portion amount as calculated in paragraph (c)(2) of this section. The qualified contract amount is determined at the time of the Agency's offer of sale of the project to the general public. An Agency must, however, adjust the amount of the low-income portion of the qualified contract formula to reflect changes in the components of the qualified contract formula such as mortgage payments which reduce outstanding indebtedness between the time of the seller's request to the Agency to obtain a buyer and the project's actual sale closing date. In addition, the Agency may adjust the fair market value of the building if, after a reasonable period of time within the one-year offer of sale period, no buyer has made an offer or market values have adjusted downward.

(2) Low-income portion amount. The low-income portion amount is an amount not less than the applicable fraction specified in the commitment, as defined in section 42(h)(6)(B)(i), multiplied by the total of—

(i) The outstanding indebtedness for the building (as defined in paragraph (c)(3) of this section); plus

(ii) The adjusted investor equity in the building (as defined in paragraph (c)(4) of this section); plus

(iii) Other capital contributions (as defined in paragraph (c)(5) of this section), not including any amounts described in paragraphs (c)(2)(i) and (ii) of this section; minus

(iv) Cash distributions from (or available for distribution from) the building (as defined in paragraph (c)(6) of this section).

(3) Outstanding indebtedness. (i) For purposes of paragraph (c)(2)(i) of this section, except as provided in paragraph (c)(3)(ii) of this section, the term outstanding indebtedness for the building means the remaining stated principal balance, at the time of the Agency's offer of sale of the project to the general public, of any indebtedness secured by, or with respect to, the building that does not exceed the amount of qualifying building costs described in paragraph (b)(4) of this section. Examples of such indebtedness include certain mortgages and developer fee notes (excluding developer service costs not included in eligible basis). Outstanding indebtedness does not include debt used to finance non-depreciable land costs, syndication costs, legal and accounting costs, and operating deficit payments. The term outstanding indebtedness for the building only includes obligations that are indebtedness under general principles of Federal income tax law.

(ii) For purposes of paragraph (c)(2)(i) of this section, if the indebtedness had a yield to maturity below the applicable Federal rate (as determined under section 1274(d)) at the time of issuance, the term outstanding indebtedness for the building is the imputed principal amount of the indebtedness, secured by, or with respect to, the building, at the time of the Agency's offer of sale of the project to the general public, that does not exceed the amount of qualifying building costs described in paragraph (b)(4) of this section. The imputed principal amount of the indebtedness is the sum of the present values, as of the Agency's offer of sale of the project to the general public, of all the remaining payments of principal and interest payable on the indebtedness after the Agency's offer of sale of the project to the general public. The present value of each payment is determined by using a discount rate equal to the applicable Federal rate (as determined under section 1274(d)) at the time of issuance of the indebtedness. In the case of a variable rate debt instrument, rules similar to those in § 1.1274-2(f) are used to determine the instrument's imputed principal amount.

(4) Adjusted investor equity. (i) For purposes of paragraph (c)(2)(ii) of this section, the term adjusted investor equity for any calendar year means the aggregate amount of cash invested by owners for qualifying building costs described in paragraph (b)(4)(i) of this section. Thus, equity paid for land, credit adjuster payments, Agency low-income housing credit application and allocation fees, operating deficit contributions, and legal, syndication, and accounting costs all are examples of cost payments that do not qualify as adjusted investor equity under this section.

(ii) The adjusted investor equity as determined under paragraph (c)(4)(i) of this section is increased by an amount equal to the adjusted investor equity multiplied by the cost-of-living adjustment for such calendar year, determined under section 1(f)(3) by substituting for the language in section 1(f)(3)(B), the Consumer Price Index for all urban consumers (CPI) (not seasonally adjusted, U.S. City Average) as specified in paragraph (c)(4)(v) of this section for the base calendar year (as defined in paragraph (b)(1) of this section).

(iii) Adjusted investor equity is taken into account under this section only to the extent there existed an obligation to invest the amount as of the beginning of the low-income building's credit period (as defined in section 42(f)(1)).

(iv) Adjusted investor equity does not include amounts included in the calculation of outstanding indebtedness as defined in paragraph (c)(3) of this section.

(v) The cost-of-living adjustment is based on the CPI as of the close of the 12-month period ending on August 31 of the calendar year. The cost-of-living adjustment is the percent by which the CPI for the year preceding the written request to find a person to acquire the taxpayer's project (CPIp) exceeds the CPI for the base calendar year (CPIb). If the CPI for any calendar year during this period (after the base calendar year) exceeds the CPI for the preceding calendar year by more than 5 percent, the CPI for the base calendar year shall be increased such that such excess shall never be taken into account under paragraph (c)(4) of this section. The adjusted investor equity equals the aggregate amount of cash invested by the taxpayer in the building multiplied by the ratio of CPIp to CPIb.

(vi) Example. The following example illustrates the CPI calculation:

Example. Owner contributed $600,000 in equity to a building in 1991, which was the first year of the credit period for the project. In year 2005, owner requests Agency to find a buyer to purchase the building. The CPIb (at the close of the 12-month period ending on August 31, 1991) is 136.6. The CPIp for the close of the 12-month period ending August 31, 2004, is 189.5. At no time during this period (after the base calendar year) did the CPI for any calendar year exceed the CPI for the preceding calendar year by more than 5 percent. The owner's adjusted investor equity is $600,000 multiplied by 189.5/136.6, or $832,357.

(5) Other capital contributions. For purposes of paragraph (c)(2)(iii) of this section, other capital contributions to a low-income building are qualifying building costs described in paragraph (b)(4)(ii) of this section paid or incurred by the owner of the low-income building other than amounts included in the calculation of outstanding indebtedness or adjusted investor equity as defined in this section. For example, other capital contributions may include amounts incurred to replace a furnace after the first year of a low-income housing credit building's credit period under section 42(f), provided any loan used to finance the replacement of the furnace is not secured by the furnace or the building. Other capital contributions do not include expenditures for land costs, operating deficit payments, credit adjuster payments, and payments for legal, syndication, and accounting costs.

(6) Cash distribution. (i) In general. For purposes of paragraph (c)(2)(iv) of this section, the term cash distributions from (or available for distribution from) the project include—

(A) All distributions from the project to the owners or to related parties within the meaning of section 267(b) or section 707(b)), including distributions under section 301 (relating to distributions by a corporation), section 731 (relating to distributions by a partnership), or section 1368 (relating to distributions by a S corporation); and

(B) All cash and cash equivalents available for distribution at the time of sale, including for example, reserve funds whether operating or replacement reserves.

(ii) Anti-abuse rule. The Commissioner will interpret and apply the rules in this paragraph (c)(6) as necessary and appropriate to prevent manipulation of the qualified contract amount. For example, cash distributions include payments to owners or related parties within the meaning of section 267(b) or section 707(b) for any operating expenses in excess of amounts reasonable under the circumstances.

(d) Administrative responsibilities of the Agency. *(1) In general.* An Agency may exercise administrative discretion in evaluating and acting upon an owner's request to find a buyer to acquire the building. Examples of administrative discretion may include but are not limited to the following:

(i) Concluding that the owner's request lacks essential information and denying the request until such information is provided.

(ii) Refusing to consider an owner's representations without substantiating documentation verified with the Agency's records.

(iii) Suspending the one-year period for finding a buyer until the owner provides requested information.

(iv) Determining how many subsequent requests to find a buyer, if any, may be submitted if the owner has previously submitted a request for a qualified contract and then rejects or fails to act upon the qualified contract furnished by the Agency.

(v) Assessing and charging the seller certain administrative fees for the performance of services in obtaining a qualified contract (for example, real estate appraiser costs).

(vi) Requiring other conditions applicable to the qualified contract consistent with this section.

(2) Actual offer. Upon receipt of a written request from the owner to find a person to acquire the building, the Agency must offer the building for sale at the determined qualified contract amount to the general public in order for the qualified contract to satisfy the requirements of this section unless the Agency has already identified a willing buyer who submitted a contract to purchase the building.

(e) Effective/applicability date. This section is applicable on the date the final regulations are published in the Federal Register.

§ 1.43-0 Table of contents.

This section lists the captions contained in §§ 1.43-0 through 1.43-7.

§ 1.43-1 The enhanced oil recovery credit—general rules.

(a) Claiming the credit.

(1) In general.
(2) Examples.
(b) Amount of the credit.
(c) Phase-out of the credit as crude oil prices increase.
(1) In general.
(2) Inflation adjustment.
(3) Examples.
(d) Reduction of associated deductions.
(1) In general.
(2) Certain deductions by an integrated oil company.
(e) Basis adjustment.
(f) Passthrough entity basis adjustment
(1) Partners' interests in a partnership.
(2) Shareholders' stock in an S corporation.
(g) Examples.

§ 1.43-2 Qualified enhanced oil recovery project.
(a) Qualified enhanced oil recovery project.
(b) More than insignificant increase.
(c) First injection of liquids, gases, or other matter.
(1) In general.
(2) Example.
(d) Significant expansion exception.
(1) In general.
(2) Substantially unaffected reservoir volume.
(3) Terminated projects.
(4) Change in tertiary recovery method.
(5) Examples.
(e) Qualified tertiary recovery methods.
(1) In general.
(2) Tertiary recovery methods that qualify.
(3) Recovery methods that do not qualify.
(4) Examples.

§ 1.43-3 Certification.
(a) Petroleum engineer's certification of a project.
(1) In general.
(2) Timing of certification.
(3) Content of certification.
(b) Operator's continued certification of a project.
(1) In general.
(2) Timing of certification.
(3) Content of certification.
(c) Notice of project termination.
(1) In general.
(2) Timing of notice.
(3) Content of notice.
(d) Failure to submit certification.
(e) Effective date.

§ 1.43-4 Qualified enhanced oil recovery costs.
(a) Qualifying costs.
(1) In general.
(2) Costs paid or incurred for an asset which is used to implement more than one qualified enhanced oil recovery project or for other activities.
(b) Costs defined.
(1) Qualified tertiary injectant expenses.
(2) Intangible drilling and development costs.
(3) Tangible property costs.
(4) Examples.
(c) Primary purpose.
(1) In general.
(2) Tertiary injectant costs.
(3) Intangible drilling and development costs.
(4) Tangible property costs.
(5) Offshore drilling platforms.
(6) Examples.
(d) Costs paid or incurred prior to first injection.
(1) In general.
(2) First injection after filing of return for taxable year costs are allowable.
(3) First injection more than 36 months after close of taxable year costs are paid or incurred.
(4) Injections in volumes less than the volumes specified in the project plan.
(5) Examples.
(e) Other rules.
(1) Anti-abuse rule.
(2) Costs paid or incurred to acquire a project.
(3) Examples.

§ 1.43-5 At-risk limitation. [Reserved]

§ 1.43-6 Election out of section 43.
(a) Election to have the credit not apply.
(1) In general.
(2) Time for making the election.
(3) Manner of making the election.
(b) Election by partnerships and S corporations.

§ 1.43-7 Effective date of regulations.

T.D. 8448, 11/20/92.

§ 1.43-1 The enhanced oil recovery credit—general rules.

(a) Claiming the credit. *(1) In general.* The enhanced oil recovery credit (the "credit") is a component of the section 38 general business credit. A taxpayer that owns an operating mineral interest (as defined in § 1.614-2(b)) in a property may claim the credit for qualified enhanced oil recovery costs (as described in § 1.43-4) paid or incurred by the taxpayer in connection with a qualified enhanced oil recovery project (as described in § 1.43-2) undertaken with respect to the property. A taxpayer that does not own an operating mineral interest in a property may not claim the credit. To the extent a credit included in the current year business credit under section 38(b) is unused under section 38, the credit is carried back or forward under the section 39 business credit carryback and carryforward rules.

(2) Examples. The following examples illustrate the principles of this paragraph (a).

Example (1). Credit for operating mineral interest owner. In 1992, A, the owner of an operating mineral interest in a property, begins a qualified enhanced oil recovery project using cyclic steam. B, who owns no interest in the property, purchases and places in service a steam generator. B sells A steam, which A uses as a tertiary injectant described in section 193. Because A owns an operating mineral interest in the property with respect to which the project is undertaken, A may claim a credit for the cost of the steam. Although B owns the steam generator used to produce steam for the project, B may not claim a credit for B's costs because B does not own an operating mineral interest in the property.

Example (2). Credit for operating mineral interest owner. C and D are partners in CD, a partnership that owns an operating mineral interest in a property. In 1992, CD begins a qualified enhanced oil recovery project using cyclic steam. D purchases a steam generator and sells steam to CD. Because CD owns an operating mineral interest in the property with respect to which the project is undertaken, CD may claim a credit for the cost of the steam. Although D owns the steam generator used to produce steam for the project, D may not claim a credit for the costs of the steam generator because D paid these costs in a capacity other than that of an operating mineral interest owner.

(b) Amount of the credit. A taxpayer's credit is an amount equal to 15 percent of the taxpayer's qualified enhanced oil recovery costs for the taxable year, reduced by the phase-out amount, if any, determined under paragraph (c) of this section.

(c) Phase-out of the credit as crude oil prices increase. *(1) In general.* The amount of the credit (determined without regard to this paragraph (c)) for any taxable year is reduced by an amount which bears the same ratio to the amount of the credit (determined without regard to this paragraph (c)) as—

(i) The amount by which the reference price determined under section 29(d)(2)(C) for the calendar year immediately preceding the calendar year in which the taxable year begins exceeds $28 (as adjusted under paragraph (c)(2) of this section); bears to

(ii) $6.

(2) Inflation adjustment. (i) In general. For any taxable year beginning in a calendar year after 1991, an amount equal to $28 multiplied by the inflation adjustment factor is substituted for the $28 amount under paragraph (c)(1)(i) of this section.

(ii) Inflation adjustment factor. For purposes of this paragraph (c), the inflation adjustment factor for any calendar year is a fraction, the numerator of which is the GNP implicit price deflator for the preceding calendar year and the denominator of which is the GNP implicit price deflator for 1990. The "GNP implicit price deflator" is the first revision of the implicit price deflator for the gross national product as computed and published by the Secretary of Commerce. As early as practicable, the inflation adjustment factor for each calendar year will be published by the Internal Revenue Service in the Internal Revenue Bulletin.

(3) Examples. The following examples illustrate the principles of this paragraph (c).

Example (1). Reference price exceeds $28. In 1992, E, the owner of an operating mineral interest in a property, incurs $100 of qualified enhanced oil recovery costs. The reference price for 1991 determined under section 29(d)(2)(C) is $30 and the inflation adjustment factor for 1992 is 1. E's credit for 1992 determined without regard to the phase-out for crude oil price increases is $15 ($100 × 15%). In determining E's credit, the credit is reduced by $5 ($15 × ($30 – ($28 × 1))/6). Accordingly, E's credit for 1992 is $10 ($15 – $5).

Example (2). Inflation adjustment. In 1993, F, the owner of an operating mineral interest in a property, incurs $100 of qualified enhanced oil recovery costs. The 1992 reference price is $34, and the 1993 inflation adjustment factor is 1.10. F's credit for 1993 determined without regard to the phase-out for crude oil price increases is $15 ($100 × 15%). In determining F's credit, $30.80 (1.10 × $28) is substituted for $28, and the credit is reduced by $8 ($15 × ($34 – $30.80)/6). Accordingly, F's credit for 1993 is $7 ($15 – $8).

(d) Reduction of associated deductions. *(1) In general.* Any deduction allowable under chapter 1 for an expenditure taken into account in computing the amount of the credit determined under paragraph (b) of this section is reduced by the amount of the credit attributable to the expenditure.

(2) Certain deductions by an integrated oil company. For purposes of determining the intangible drilling and development costs that an integrated oil company must capitalize under section 291(b), the amount allowable as a deduction under section 263(c) is the deduction allowable after paragraph (d)(1) of this section is applied. See § 1.43-4(b)(2) (extent to which integrated oil company intangible drilling and development costs are qualified enhanced oil recovery costs).

(e) Basis adjustment. For purposes of subtitle A, the increase in the basis of property which would (but for this paragraph (e)) result from an expenditure with respect to the property is reduced by the amount of the credit determined under paragraph (b) of this section attributable to the expenditure.

(f) Passthrough entity basis adjustment. *(1) Partners' interests in a partnership.* To the extent a partnership expenditure is not deductible under paragraph (d)(1) of this section or does not increase the basis of property under paragraph (e) of this section, the expenditure is treated as an expenditure described in section 705(a)(2)(B) (concerning decreases to basis of partnership interests). Thus, the adjusted bases of the partners' interests in the partnership are decreased (but not below zero).

(2) Shareholders' stock in an S corporation. To the extent an S corporation expenditure is not deductible under paragraph (d)(1) of this section or does not increase the basis of property under paragraph (e) of this section, the expenditure is treated as an expenditure described in section 1367(a)(2)(D) (concerning decreases to basis of S corporation stock). Thus, the basis of the shareholders' S corporation stock are decreased (but not below zero).

(g) Examples. The following examples illustrate the principles of paragraphs (d) through (f) of this section.

Example (1). Deductions reduced for credit amount. In 1992, G, the owner of an operating mineral interest in a property, incurs $100 of intangible drilling and development costs in connection with a qualified enhanced oil recovery project undertaken with respect to the property. G elects under section 263(c) to deduct these intangible drilling and development costs. The amount of the credit determined under paragraph (b) of this section attributable to the $100 of intangible drilling and development costs is $15 ($100 × 15%). Therefore, G's otherwise allowable deduction of $100 for the intangible drilling and development costs is reduced by $15. Accordingly, in 1992, G may deduct under section 263(c) only $85 ($100 – $15) for these costs.

Example (2). Integrated oil company deduction reduced. The facts are the same as in Example 1, except that G is an integrated oil company. As in Example 1, the amount of the credit determined under paragraph (b) of this section attributable to the $100 of intangible drilling and development costs is $15, and G's allowable deduction under section

263(c) is $85. Because G is an integrated oil company, G must capitalize $25.50 ($85 × 30%) under section 291(b). Therefore, in 1992, G may deduct under section 263(c) only $59.50 ($85 − $25.50) for these intangible drilling and development costs.

Example (3). Basis of property reduced. In 1992, H, the owner of an operating mineral interest in a property, pays $100 to purchase tangible property that is an integral part of a qualified enhanced oil recovery project undertaken with respect to the property. The amount of the credit determined under paragraph (b) of this section attributable to the $100 is $15 ($100 × 15%). Therefore, for purposes of subtitle A, H's basis in the tangible property is $85 ($100 − $15).

Example (4). Basis of interest in passthrough entity reduced. In 1992, I is a 50% partner in IJ, a partnership that owns an operating mineral interest in a property. IJ pays $200 to purchase tangible property that is an integral part of a qualified enhanced oil recovery project undertaken with respect to the property. The amount of the credit determined under paragraph (b) of this section attributable to the $200 is $30 ($200 × 15%). Therefore, for purposes of subtitle A, IJ's basis in the tangible property is $170 ($200 − $30). Under paragraph (f) of this section, the amount of the purchase price that does not increase the basis of the property ($30) is treated as an expenditure described in section 705(a)(2)(B). Therefore, I's basis in the partnership interest is reduced by $15 (I's allocable share of the section 704(a)(2)(B) expenditure ($30 × 50%)).

T.D. 8448, 11/20/92.

§ 1.43-2 Qualified enhanced oil recovery project.

Caution: The Treasury has not yet amended Reg § 1.43-2 to reflect changes made by P.L. 100-647, P.L. 99-514, P.L. 98-369, P.L. 98-21, P.L. 97-34, P.L. 96-222.

(a) Qualified enhanced oil recovery project. A "qualified enhanced oil recovery project" is any project that meets all of the following requirements—

(1) The project involves the application (in accordance with sound engineering principles) of one or more qualified tertiary recovery methods (as described in paragraph (e) of this section) that is reasonably expected to result in more than an insignificant increase in the amount of crude oil that ultimately will be recovered;

(2) The project is located within the United States (within the meaning of section 638(1));

(3) The first injection of liquids, gases, or other matter for the project (as described in paragraph (c) of this section) occurs after December 31, 1990; and

(4) The project is certified under § 1.43-3.

(b) More than insignificant increase. For purposes of paragraph (a)(1) of this section, all the facts and circumstances determine whether the application of a tertiary recovery method can reasonably be expected to result in more than an insignificant increase in the amount of crude oil that ultimately will be recovered. Certain information submitted as part of a project certification is relevant to this determination. See § 1.43-3(a)(3)(i)(D). In no event is the application of a recovery method that merely accelerates the recovery of crude oil considered an application of one or more qualified tertiary recovery methods that can reasonably be expected to result in more than an insignificant increase in the amount of crude oil that ultimately will be recovered.

(c) First injection of liquids, gases, or other matter. *(1) In general.* The "first injection of liquids, gases, or other matter" generally occurs on the date a tertiary injectant is first injected into the reservoir. The "first injection of liquids, gases, or other matter" does not include—

(i) The injection into the reservoir of any liquids, gases, or other matter for the purpose of pretreating or preflushing the reservoir to enhance the efficiency of the tertiary recovery method; or

(ii) Test or experimental injections.

(2) Example. The following example illustrates the principles of this paragraph (c).

Example. Injections to pretreat the reservoir. In 1989, A, the owner of an operating mineral interest in a property, began injecting water into the reservoir for the purpose of elevating reservoir pressure to obtain miscibility pressure to prepare for the injection of miscible gas in connection with an enhanced oil recovery project. In 1992, A obtains miscibility pressure in the reservoir and begins injecting miscible gas into the reservoir. The injection of miscible gas, rather than the injection of water, is the first injection of liquids, gases, or other matter into the reservoir for purposes of determining whether the first injection of liquids, gases, or other matter occurs after December 31, 1990.

(d) Significant expansion exception. *(1) In general.* If a project for which the first injection of liquids, gases, or other matter (within the meaning of paragraph (c)(1) of this section) occurred before January 1, 1991, is significantly expanded after December 31, 1990, the expansion is treated as a separate project for which the first injection of liquids, gases, or other matter occurs after December 31, 1990.

(2) Substantially unaffected reservoir volume. A project is considered significantly expanded if the injection of liquids, gases, or other matter after December 31, 1990, is reasonably expected to result in more than an insignificant increase in the amount of crude oil that ultimately will be recovered from reservoir volume that was substantially unaffected by the injection of liquids, gases, or other matter before January 1, 1991.

(3) Terminated projects. Except as otherwise provided in this paragraph (d)(3), a project is considered significantly expanded if each qualified tertiary recovery method implemented in the project prior to January 1, 1991, terminated more than 36 months before implementing an enhanced oil recovery project that commences after December 31, 1990. Notwithstanding the provisions of the preceding sentence, if a project implemented prior to January 1, 1991, is terminated for less than 36 months before implementing an enhanced oil recovery project that commences after December 31, 1990, a taxpayer may request permission to treat the project that commences after December 31, 1990, as a significant expansion. Permission will not be granted if the Internal Revenue Service determines that a project was terminated to make an otherwise nonqualifying project eligible for the credit. For purposes of section 43, a qualified tertiary recovery method terminates at the point in time when the method no longer results in more than an insignificant increase in the amount of crude oil that ultimately will be recovered. All the facts and circumstances determine whether a tertiary recovery method has terminated. Among the factors considered is the project plan, the unit plan of development, or other similar plan. A tertiary recovery method is not necessarily terminated merely because the injection of the tertiary injectant has ceased. For purposes of this paragraph (d)(1), a project is implemented when costs that will be taken into account in

determining the credit with respect to the project are paid or incurred.

(4) Change in tertiary recovery method. If the application of a tertiary recovery method or methods with respect to an enhanced oil recovery project for which the first injection of liquids, gases, or other matter occurred before January 1, 1991, has not been terminated for more than 36 months, a taxpayer may request a private letter ruling from the Internal Revenue Service whether the application of a different tertiary recovery method or methods after December 31, 1990, that does not affect reservoir volume substantially unaffected by the previous tertiary recovery method or methods, is treated as a significant expansion. All the facts and circumstances determine whether a change in tertiary recovery method is treated as a significant expansion. Among the factors considered are whether the change in tertiary recovery method is in accordance with sound engineering principles and whether the change in method will result in more than an insignificant increase in the amount of crude oil that would be recovered using the previous method. A more intensive application of a tertiary recovery method after December 31, 1990, is not treated as a significant expansion.

(5) Examples. The following examples illustrate the principles of this paragraph (d).

Example (1). Substantially unaffected reservoir volume. In January 1988, B, the owner of an operating mineral interest in a property, began injecting steam into the reservoir in connection with a cyclic steam enhanced oil recovery project. The project affected only a portion of the reservoir volume. In 1992, B begins cyclic steam injections with respect to reservoir volume that was substantially unaffected by the previous cyclic steam project. Because the injection of steam into the reservoir in 1992 affects reservoir volume that was substantially unaffected by the previous cyclic steam injection, the cyclic steam injection in 1992 is treated as a separate project for which the first injection of liquids, gases, or other matter occurs after December 31, 1990.

Example (2). Tertiary recovery method terminated more than 36 months. In 1982, C, the owner of an operating mineral interest cyclic steam injection as a method for the recovery of crude oil. The project was certified as a tertiary recovery project for purposes of the windfall profit tax. In May 1988, the application of the cyclic steam tertiary recovery method terminated. In July 1992, C begins drilling injection wells as part of a project to apply the steam drive tertiary recovery method with respect to the same project area affected by the cyclic steam method. C begins steam injections in September 1992. Because C commences an enhanced oil recovery project more than 36 months after the previous tertiary recovery method was terminated, the project is treated as a separate project for which the first injection of liquids, gases, or other matter occurs after December 31, 1990.

Example (3). Change in tertiary recovery method affecting substantially unaffected reservoir volume. In 1984, D, the owner of an operating mineral interest in a property, implemented a tertiary recovery project using cyclic steam as a method for the recovery of crude oil. The project was certified as a tertiary recovery project for purposes of the windfall profit tax. D continued the cyclic steam injection until 1992, when the tertiary recovery method was changed from cyclic steam injection to steam drive. The steam drive affects reservoir volume that was substantially unaffected by the cyclic steam injection. Because the steam drive affects reservoir volume that was substantially unaffected by the cyclic steam injection, the steam drive is treated as a separate project for which the first injection of liquids, gases, or other matter occurs after December 31, 1990.

Example (4). Change in tertiary recovery method not affecting substantially unaffected reservoir volume. In 1988, E, the owner of an operating mineral interest in a property, undertook an immiscible nitrogen enhanced oil recovery project that resulted in more than an insignificant increase in the ultimate recovery of crude oil from the property. E continued the immiscible nitrogen project until 1992, when the project was converted from immiscible nitrogen displacement to miscible nitrogen displacement by increasing the injection of nitrogen to increase reservoir pressure. The miscible nitrogen displacement affects the same reservoir volume that was affected by the immiscible nitrogen displacement. Because the miscible nitrogen displacement does not affect reservoir volume that was substantially unaffected by the immiscible nitrogen displacement nor was the immiscible nitrogen displacement project terminated for more than 36 months before the miscible nitrogen displacement project was implemented, E must obtain a ruling whether the change from immiscible nitrogen displacement to miscible nitrogen displacement is treated as a separate project for which the first injection of liquids, gases, or other matter occurs after December 31, 1990. If E does not receive a ruling, the miscible nitrogen displacement project is not a qualified project.

Example (5). More intensive application of a tertiary recovery method. In 1989, F, the owner of an operating mineral interest in a property, undertook an immiscible carbon dioxide displacement enhanced oil recovery project. F began injecting carbon dioxide into the reservoir under immiscible conditions. The injection of carbon dioxide under immiscible conditions resulted in more than an insignificant increase in the ultimate recovery of crude oil from the property. F continues to inject the same amount of carbon dioxide into the reservoir until 1992, when new engineering studies indicate that an increase in the amount of carbon dioxide injected is reasonably expected to result in a more than insignificant increase in the amount of crude oil that would be recovered from the property as a result of the previous injection of carbon dioxide. The increase in the amount of carbon dioxide injected affects the same reservoir volume that was affected by the previous injection of carbon dioxide. Because the additional carbon dioxide injected in 1992 does not affect reservoir volume that was substantially unaffected by the previous injection of carbon dioxide and the previous immiscible carbon dioxide displacement method was not terminated for more than 36 months before additional carbon dioxide was injected, the increase in the amount of carbon dioxide injected into the reservoir is not a significant expansion. Therefore, it is not a separate project for which the first injection of liquids, gases, or other matter occurs after December 31, 1990.

(e) Qualified tertiary recovery methods. *(1) In general.* For purposes of paragraph (a)(1) of this section, a "qualified tertiary recovery method" is any one or any combination of the tertiary recovery methods described in paragraph (e)(2) of this section. To account for advances in enhanced oil recovery technology, the Internal Revenue Service may by revenue ruling prescribe that a method not described in paragraph (e)(2) of this section is a "qualified tertiary recovery method." In addition, a taxpayer may request a private letter ruling that a method not described in paragraph (e)(2) of this section or in a revenue ruling is a qualified tertiary recovery method. Generally, the methods identified in revenue rulings or private letter rulings will be limited to those methods that involve the displacement of oil from the reservoir rock by means of modifying the properties of the fluids in the reservoir or providing the energy and drive mechanism to force the oil to flow to a production well. The recovery methods described in paragraph (e)(3) of this section are not "qualified tertiary recovery methods."

(2) Tertiary recovery methods that qualify. (i) Thermal recovery methods. (A) Steam drive injection. The continuous injection of steam into one set of wells (injection wells) or other injection source to effect oil displacement toward and production from a second set of wells (production wells);

(B) Cyclic steam injection. The alternating injection of steam and production of oil with condensed steam from the same well or wells; and

(C) In situ combustion. The combustion of oil or fuel in the reservoir sustained by injection of air, oxygen-enriched air, oxygen, or supplemental fuel supplied from the surface to displace unburned oil toward producing wells. This process may include the concurrent, alternating, or subsequent injection of water.

(ii) Gas flood recovery methods. (A) Miscible fluid displacement. The injection of gas (e.g., natural gas, enriched natural gas, a liquefied petroleum slug driven by natural gas, carbon dioxide, nitrogen, or flue gas) or alcohol into the reservoir at pressure levels such that the gas or alcohol and reservoir oil are miscible;

(B) Carbon dioxide augmented waterflooding. The injection of carbonated water, or water and carbon dioxide, to increase waterflood efficiency;

(C) Immiscible carbon dioxide displacement. The injection of carbon dioxide into an oil reservoir to effect oil displacement under conditions in which miscibility with reservoir oil is not obtained. This process may include the concurrent, alternating, or subsequent injection of water; and

(D) Immiscible nonhydrocarbon gas displacement. The injection of nonhydrocarbon gas (e.g., nitrogen) into an oil reservoir, under conditions in which miscibility with reservoir oil is not obtained, to obtain a chemical or physical reaction (other than pressure) between the oil and the injected gas or between the oil and other reservoir fluids. This process may include the concurrent, alternating, or subsequent injection of water.

(iii) Chemical flood recovery methods. (A) Microemulsion flooding. The injection of a surfactant system (e.g., a surfactant, hydrocarbon, cosurfactant, electrolyte, and water) to enhance the displacement of oil toward producing wells; and

(B) Caustic flooding. The injection of water that has been made chemically basic by the addition of alkali metal hydroxides, silicates, or other chemicals.

(iv) Mobility control recovery method. Polymer augmented waterflooding. The injection of polymeric additives with water to improve the aerial and vertical sweep efficiency of the reservoir by increasing the viscosity and decreasing the mobility of the water injected. Polymer augmented waterflooding does not include the injection of polymers for the purpose of modifying the injection profile of the wellbore or the relative permeability of various layers of the reservoir, rather than modifying the water-oil mobility ratio.

(3) Recovery methods that do not qualify. The term "qualified tertiary recovery method" does not include—

(i) Waterflooding. The injection of water into an oil reservoir to displace oil from the reservoir rock and into the bore of the producing well;

(ii) Cyclic gas injection. The increase or maintenance of pressure by injection of hydrocarbon gas into the reservoir from which it was originally produced;

(iii) Horizontal drilling. The drilling of horizontal, rather than vertical, wells to penetrate hydrocarbon bearing formations;

(iv) Gravity drainage. The production of oil by gravity flow from drainholes that are drilled from a shaft or tunnel dug within or below the oil bearing zones; and

(v) Other methods. Any recovery method not specifically designated as a qualified tertiary recovery method in either paragraph (e)(2) of this section or in a revenue ruling or private letter ruling described in paragraph (e)(1) of this section.

(4) Examples. The following examples illustrate the principles of this paragraph (e).

Example (1). Polymer augmented waterflooding. In 1992 G, the owner of an operating mineral interest in a property, begins a waterflood project with respect to the property. To reduce the relative permeability in certain areas of the reservoir and minimize water coning, G injects polymers to plug thief zones and improve the areal and vertical sweep efficiency of the reservoir. The injection of polymers into the reservoir does not modify the water-oil mobility ratio. Accordingly, the injection of polymers into the reservoir in connection with the waterflood project does not constitute polymer augmented waterflooding and the project is not a qualified enhanced oil recovery project.

Example (2). Polymer augmented waterflooding. In 1993 H, the owner of an operating mineral interest in a property, begins a caustic flooding project with respect to the property. Engineering studies indicate that the relative permeability of various layers of the reservoir may result in the loss of the injectant to thief zones, thereby reducing the areal and vertical sweep efficiency of the reservoir. As part of the caustic flooding project, H injects polymers to plug the thief zones and improve the areal and vertical sweep efficiency of the reservoir. Because the polymers are injected into the reservoir to improve the effectiveness of the caustic flooding project, the project is a qualified enhanced oil recovery project.

T.D. 8448, 11/20/92.

---

§ 1.43-3 Certification.

(a) Petroleum engineer's certification of a project. *(1) In general.* A petroleum engineer must certify, under penalties of perjury, that an enhanced oil recovery project meets the requirements of section 43(c)(2)(A). A petroleum engineer's certification must be submitted for each project. The petroleum engineer certifying a project must be duly registered or certified in any state.

(2) Timing of certification. The operator of an enhanced oil recovery project or any other operating mineral interest owner designated by the operator ("designated owner") must submit a petroleum engineer's certification to the Internal Revenue Service Center, Austin, Texas, or such other place as may be designated by revenue procedure or other published guidance, not later than the last date prescribed by law (including extensions) for filing the operator's or designated owner's federal income tax return for the first taxable year for which the enhanced oil recovery credit (the "credit") is allowable. The operator may designate any other operating mineral interest owner (the "designated owner") to file the petroleum engineer's certification.

(3) Content of certification. (i) In general. A petroleum engineer's certification must contain the following information—

(A) The name and taxpayer identification number of the operator or the designated owner submitting the certification;

(B) A statement identifying the project, including its geographic location;

(C) A statement that the project involves a tertiary recovery method (as defined in section 43(c)(2)(A)(i)) and a description of the process used, including—

(1) A description of the implementation and operation of the project sufficient to establish that it is implemented and operated in accordance with sound engineering practices;

(2) If the project involves the application of a tertiary recovery method approved in a private letter ruling described in paragraph (e)(1) of § 1.43-2, a copy of the private letter ruling, and

(3) The date on which the first injection of liquids, gases, or other matter occurred or is expected to occur.

(D) A statement that the application of a qualified tertiary recovery method or methods is expected to result in more than an insignificant increase in the amount of crude oil that ultimately will be recovered, including—

(1) Data on crude oil reserve estimates covering the project area with and without the enhanced oil recovery process,

(2) Production history prior to implementation of the project and estimates of production after implementation of the project, and

(3) An adequate delineation of the reservoir, or portion of the reservoir, from which the ultimate recovery of crude oil is expected to be increased as a result of the implementation and operation of the project; and

(E) A statement that the petroleum engineer believes that the project is a qualified enhanced oil recovery project within the meaning of section 43(c)(2)(A).

(ii) Additional information for significantly expanded projects. The petroleum engineer's certification for a project that is significantly expanded must in addition contain—

(A) If the expansion affects reservoir volume that was substantially unaffected by a previously implemented project, an adequate delineation of the reservoir volume affected by the previously implemented project;

(B) If the expansion involves the implementation of an enhanced oil recovery project more than 36 months after the termination of a qualified tertiary recovery method that was applied before January 1, 1991, the date on which the previous tertiary recovery method terminated and an explanation of the data or assumptions relied upon to determine the termination date;

(C) If the expansion involves the implementation of an enhanced oil recovery project less than 36 months after the termination of a qualified tertiary recovery method that was applied before January 1, 1991, a copy of a private letter ruling from the Internal Revenue Service that the project implemented after December 31, 1990 is treated as a significant expansion; or

(D) If the expansion involves the application after December 31, 1990, of a tertiary recovery method or methods that do not affect reservoir volume that was substantially unaffected by the application of a different tertiary recovery method or methods before January 1, 1991, a copy of a private letter ruling from the Internal Revenue Service that the change in tertiary recovery method is treated as a significant expansion.

(b) Operator's continued certification of a project. *(1) In general.* For each taxable year following the taxable year for which the petroleum engineer's certification is submitted, the operator or designated owner must certify, under penalties of perjury, that an enhanced oil recovery project continues to be implemented substantially in accordance with the petroleum engineer's certification submitted for the project. An operator's certification must be submitted for each project.

(2) Timing of certification. The operator or designated owner of an enhanced oil recovery project must submit an operator's certification to the Internal Revenue Service Center, Austin, Texas, or such other place as may be designated by revenue procedure or other published guidance, not later than the last date prescribed by law (including extensions) for filing the operator's or designated owner's federal income tax return for any taxable year after the taxable year for which the petroleum engineer's certification is filed.

(3) Content of certification. An operator's certification must contain the following information—

(i) The name and taxpayer identification number of the operator or the designated owner submitting the certification;

(ii) A statement identifying the project, including its geographic location and the date on which the petroleum engineer's certification was filed;

(iii) A statement that the project continues to be implemented substantially in accordance with the petroleum engineer's certification (as described in paragraph (a) of this section) submitted for the project; and

(iv) A description of any significant change or anticipated change in the information submitted under paragraph (a)(3) of this section, including a change in the date on which the first injection of liquids, gases, or other matter occurred or is expected to occur.

(c) Notice of project termination. *(1) In general.* If the application of a tertiary recovery method is terminated, the operator or designated owner must submit a notice of project termination to the Internal Revenue Service.

(2) Timing of notice. The operator or designated owner of an enhanced oil recovery project must submit the notice of project termination to the Internal Revenue Service Center, Austin, Texas, or such other place as may be designated by revenue procedure or other published guidance, not later than the last date prescribed by law (including extensions) for filing the operator's or designated owner's federal income tax return for the taxable year in which the project terminates.

(3) Content of notice. A notice of project termination must contain the following information—

(i) The name and taxpayer identification number of the operator or the designated owner submitting the notice;

(ii) A statement identifying the project, including its geographic location and the date on which the petroleum engineer's certification was filed; and

(iii) The date on which the application of the tertiary recovery method was terminated.

(d) Failure to submit certification. If a petroleum engineer's certification (as described in paragraph (a) of this section) or an operator's certification (as described in paragraph (b) of this section) is not submitted in the time or manner prescribed by this section, the credit will be allowed only after the appropriate certifications are submitted.

(e) Effective date. Section 1.43-3T is effective for taxable years beginning after December 31, 1990.

T.D. 8384, 12/27/91, amend T.D. 8448, 11/20/92.

§ 1.43-4 Qualified enhanced oil recovery costs.

Caution: The Treasury has not yet amended Reg § 1.43-4 to reflect changes made by P.L. 106-554.

(a) Qualifying costs. *(1) In general.* Except as provided in paragraph (e) of this section, amounts paid or incurred in any taxable year beginning after December 31, 1990, that are qualified tertiary injectant expenses (as described in paragraph (b)(1) of this section), intangible drilling and development costs (as described in paragraph (b)(2) of this section), and tangible property costs (as described in paragraph (b)(3) of this section) are "qualified enhanced oil recovery costs" if the amounts are paid or incurred with respect to an asset which is used for the primary purpose (as described in paragraph (c) of this section) of implementing an enhanced oil recovery project. Any amount paid or incurred in any taxable year beginning before January 1, 1991, in connection with an enhanced oil recovery project is not a qualified enhanced oil recovery cost.

(2) Costs paid or incurred for an asset which is used to implement more than one qualified enhanced oil recovery project or for other activities. Any cost paid or incurred during the taxable year for an asset which is used to implement more than one qualified enhanced oil recovery project is allocated among the projects in determining the qualified enhanced oil recovery costs for each qualified project for the taxable year. Similarly, any cost paid or incurred during the taxable year for an asset which is used to implement a qualified enhanced oil recovery project and which is also used for other activities (for example, an enhanced oil recovery project that is not a qualified enhanced oil recovery project) is allocated among the qualified enhanced oil recovery project and the other activities to determine the qualified enhanced oil recovery costs for the taxable year. See § 1.613-5(a). Any cost paid or incurred for an asset which is used to implement a qualified enhanced oil recovery project and which is also used for other activities is not required to be allocated under this paragraph (a)(2) if the use of the property for nonqualifying activities is de minimis (e.g, not greater than 10%). Costs are allocated under this paragraph (a)(2) only if the asset with respect to which the costs are paid or incurred is used for the primary purpose of implementing an enhanced oil recovery project. See paragraph (c) of this section. Any reasonable allocation method may be used. A method that allocates costs based on the anticipated use in a project or activity is a reasonable method.

(b) Costs defined. *(1) Qualified tertiary injectant expenses.* For purposes of this section, "qualified tertiary injectant expenses" means any costs that are paid or incurred in connection with a qualified enhanced oil recovery project and that are deductible under section 193 for the taxable year. See section 193 and § 1.193-1. Qualified tertiary injectant expenses are taken into account in determining the credit with respect to the taxable year in which the tertiary injectant expenses are deductible under section 193.

(2) Intangible drilling and development costs. For purposes of this section, "intangible drilling and development costs" means any intangible drilling and development costs that are paid or incurred in connection with a qualified enhanced oil recovery project and for which the taxpayer may make an election under section 263(c) for the taxable year. Intangible drilling and development costs are taken into account in determining the credit with respect to the taxable year in which the taxpayer may deduct the intangible drilling and development costs under section 263(c). For purposes of this paragraph (b)(2), the amount of the intangible drilling and development costs for which an integrated oil company may make an election under section 263(c) is determined without regard to section 291(b).

(3) Tangible property costs. (i) In general. For purposes of this section, "tangible property costs" means an amount paid or incurred during a taxable year for tangible property that is an integral part of a qualified enhanced oil recovery project and that is depreciable or amortizable under chapter 1. An amount paid or incurred for tangible property is taken into account in determining the credit with respect to the taxable year in which the cost is paid or incurred.

(ii) Integral part. For purposes of this paragraph (b), tangible property is an integral part of a qualified enhanced oil recovery project if the property is used directly in the project and is essential to the completeness of the project. All the facts and circumstances determine whether tangible property is used directly in a qualified enhanced oil recovery project and is essential to the completeness of the project. Generally, property used to acquire or produce the tertiary injectant or property used to transport the tertiary injectant to a project site is property that is an integral part of the project.

(4) Examples. The following examples illustrate the principles of this paragraph (b). Assume for each of these examples that the qualified enhanced oil recovery costs are paid or incurred with respect to an asset which is used for the primary purpose of implementing an enhanced oil recovery project.

Example (1). Qualified costs—in general.

(i) In 1992, X, a corporation, acquires an operating mineral interest in a property and undertakes a cyclic steam enhanced oil recovery project with respect to the property. X pays a fee to acquire a permit to drill and hires a contractor to drill six wells. As part of the project implementation, X constructs a building to serve as an office on the property and purchases equipment, including downhole equipment (e.g., casing, tubing, packers, and sucker rods), pumping units, a steam generator, and equipment to remove gas and water from the oil after it is produced. X constructs roads to transport the equipment to the wellsites and incurs costs for clearing and draining the ground in preparation for the drilling of the wells. X purchases cars and trucks to provide transportation for monitoring the wellsites. In addition, X contracts with Y for the delivery of water to produce steam to be injected in connection with the cyclic steam project, and purchases storage tanks to store the water.

(ii) The leasehold acquisition costs are not qualified enhanced oil recovery costs. However, the costs of the permit to drill are intangible drilling and development costs that are qualified costs. The costs associated with hiring the contractor to drill, constructing roads, and clearing and draining the ground are intangible drilling and development costs that are qualified enhanced oil recovery costs. The downhole equipment, the pumping units, the steam generator, and the equipment to remove the gas and water from the oil after it is produced are used directly in the project and are essential to the completeness of the project. Therefore, this equipment is an integral part of the project and the costs of the equipment are qualified enhanced oil recovery costs. Although the building that X constructs as an office and the cars and trucks X purchases to provide transportation for monitoring the wellsites are used directly in the project, they are not essential to the completeness of the project. Therefore, the building and the cars and trucks are not an integral part of the project and their costs are not qualified enhanced oil recovery costs. The cost of the water X purchases from Y is a tertiary injectant expense that is a qualified enhanced oil recovery cost. The storage tanks X acquires to store the water are required to provide a proximate source of water for the production of steam. Therefore, the water storage tanks are an integral part of the project and the costs of the water storage tanks are qualified enhanced oil recovery costs.

Example (2). Diluent storage tanks. In 1992, A, the owner of an operating mineral interest, undertakes a qualified enhanced oil recovery project with respect to the property. A acquires diluent to be used in connection with the project. A stores the diluent in a storage tank that A acquires for that purpose. The storage tank provides a proximate source of diluent to be used in the tertiary recovery method. Therefore, the storage tank is used directly in the project and is essential to the completeness of the project. Accordingly, the storage tank is an integral part of the project and the cost of the storage tank is a qualified enhanced oil recovery cost.

Example (3). Oil storage tanks. In 1992, Z, a corporation and the owner of an operating mineral interest in a property, undertakes a qualified enhanced oil recovery project with respect to the property. Z acquires storage tanks that Z will use solely to store the crude oil that is produced from the enhanced oil recovery project. The storage tanks are not used directly in the project and are not essential to the completeness of the project. Therefore, the storage tanks are not an integral part of the enhanced oil recovery project and the costs of the storage tanks are not qualified enhanced oil recovery costs.

Example (4). Oil refinery. B, the owner of an operating mineral interest in a property, undertakes a qualified enhanced oil recovery project with respect to the property. Located on B's property is an oil refinery where B will refine the crude oil produced from the project. The refinery is not used directly in the project and is not essential to the completeness of the project. Therefore, the refinery is not an integral part of the enhanced oil recovery project.

Example (5). Gas processing plant. C, the owner of an operating mineral interest in a property, undertakes a qualified enhanced oil recovery project with respect to the property. A gas processing plant where C will process gas produced in the project is located on C's property. The gas processing plant is not used directly in the project and is not essential to the completeness of the project. Therefore, the gas processing plant is not an integral part of the enhanced oil recovery project.

Example (6). Gas processing equipment. The facts are the same as in Example 5 except that C uses a portion of the gas processing plant to separate and recycle the tertiary injectant. The gas processing equipment used to separate and recycle the tertiary injectant is used directly in the project and is essential to the completeness of the project. Therefore, the gas processing equipment used to separate and recycle the tertiary injectant is an integral part of the enhanced oil recovery project and the costs of this equipment are qualified enhanced oil recovery costs.

Example (7). Steam generator costs allocated. In 1988, D, the owner of an operating mineral interest in a property, undertook a steam drive project with respect to the property. In 1992, D decides to undertake a steam drive project with respect to reservoir volume that was substantially unaffected by the 1988 project. The 1992 project is a significant expansion that is a qualified enhanced oil recovery project. D purchases a new steam generator with sufficient capacity to provide steam for both the 1988 project and the 1992 project. The steam generator is used directly in the 1992 project and is essential to the completeness of the 1992 project. Accordingly, the steam generator is an integral part of the 1992 project. Because the steam generator is also used to provide steam for the 1988 project, D must allocate the cost of the steam generator to the 1988 project and the 1992 project. Only the portion of the cost of the steam generator that is allocable to the 1992 project is a qualified enhanced oil recovery cost.

Example (8). Carbon dioxide pipeline. In 1992, E, the owner of an operating mineral interest in a property, undertakes an immiscible carbon dioxide displacement project with respect to the property. E constructs a pipeline to convey carbon dioxide to the project site. E contracts with F, a producer of carbon dioxide, to purchase carbon dioxide to be injected into injection wells in E's enhanced oil recovery project. The cost of the carbon dioxide is a tertiary injectant expense that is a qualified enhanced oil recovery cost. The pipeline is used by E to transport the tertiary injectant, that is, the carbon dioxide to the project site. Therefore, the pipeline is an integral part of the project. Accordingly, the cost of the pipeline is a qualified enhanced oil recovery cost.

Example (9). Water source wells. In 1992, G the owner of an operating mineral interest in a property, undertakes a polymer augmented waterflood project with respect to the property. G drills water wells to provide water for injection in connection with the project. The costs of drilling the water wells are intangible drilling and development costs that are paid or incurred in connection with the project. Therefore, the costs of drilling the water wells are qualified enhanced oil recovery costs.

Example (10). Leased equipment. In 1992, H, the owner of an operating mineral interest in a property undertakes a steam drive project with respect to the property. H contracts with I, a driller, to drill injection wells in connection with the project. H also leases a steam generator to provide steam for injection in connection with the project. The drilling costs are intangible drilling and development costs that are paid in connection with the project and are qualified enhanced oil recovery costs. The steam generator is used to produce the tertiary injectant. The steam generator is used directly in the project and is essential to the completeness of the project; therefore, it is an integral part of the project. The costs of leasing the steam generator are tangible property costs that are qualified enhanced oil recovery costs.

(c) Primary purpose. *(1) In general.* For purposes of this section, a cost is a qualified enhanced oil recovery cost only if the cost is paid or incurred with respect to an asset which is used for the primary purpose of implementing one or more enhanced oil recovery projects, at least one of which is a qualified enhanced oil recovery project. All the facts and circumstances determine whether an asset is used for the primary purpose of implementing an enhanced oil recovery project. For purposes of this paragraph (c), an enhanced oil recovery project is a project that satisfies the requirements of paragraphs (a)(1) and (2) of section 1.43-2.

(2) Tertiary injectant costs. Tertiary injectant costs generally satisfy the primary purpose test of this paragraph (c).

(3) Intangible drilling and development costs. Intangible drilling and development costs paid or incurred with respect to a well that is used in connection with the recovery of oil by primary or secondary methods are not qualified enhanced oil recovery costs. Except as provided in this paragraph (c)(3), a well used for primary or secondary recovery is not used for the primary purpose of implementing an enhanced

oil recovery project. A well drilled for the primary purpose of implementing an enhanced oil recovery project is not considered to be used for primary or secondary recovery, notwithstanding that some primary or secondary production may result when the well is drilled, provided that such primary or secondary production is consistent with the unit plan of development or other similar plan. All the facts and circumstances determine whether primary or secondary recovery is consistent with the unit plan of development or other similar plan.

(4) Tangible property costs. Tangible property costs must be paid or incurred with respect to property which is used for the primary purpose of implementing an enhanced oil recovery project. If tangible property is used partly in a qualified enhanced oil recovery project and partly in another activity, the property must be primarily used to implement the qualified enhanced oil recovery project.

(5) Offshore drilling platforms. Amounts paid or incurred in connection with the acquisition, construction, transportation, erection, or installation of an offshore drilling platform (regardless of whether the amounts are intangible drilling and development costs) that is used in connection with the recovery of oil by primary or secondary methods are not qualified enhanced oil recovery costs. An offshore drilling platform used for primary or secondary recovery is not used for the primary purpose of implementing an enhanced oil recovery project.

(6) Examples. The following examples illustrate the principles of this paragraph (c).

Example (1). Intangible drilling and development costs. In 1992, J incurs intangible drilling and development costs in drilling a well. J intends to use the well as an injection well in connection with an enhanced oil recovery project in 1994, but in the meantime will use the well in connection with a secondary recovery project. J may not take the intangible drilling and development costs into account in determining the credit because the primary purpose of a well used for secondary recovery is not to implement a qualified enhanced oil recovery project.

Example (2). Offshore drilling platform. K, the owner of an operating mineral interest in an offshore oil field located within the United States, constructs an offshore drilling platform that is designed to accommodate the primary, secondary, and tertiary development of the field. Subsequent to primary and secondary development of the field, K commences an enhanced oil recovery project that involves the application of a qualified tertiary recovery method. As part of the enhanced oil recovery project, K drills injection wells from the offshore drilling platform K used in the primary and secondary development of the field and installs an additional separator on the platform. Because the offshore drilling platform was used in the primary and secondary development of the field and was not used for the primary purpose of implementing tertiary development of the field, costs incurred by K in connection with the acquisition, construction, transportation, erection, or installation of the offshore drilling platform are not qualified enhanced oil recovery costs. However, the costs K incurs for the additional separator are qualified enhanced oil recovery costs because the separator is used for the primary purpose of implementing tertiary development of the field. In addition, the intangible drilling and development costs K incurs in connection with drilling the injection wells are qualified enhanced oil recovery costs with respect to which K may claim the enhanced oil recovery credit.

(d) Costs paid or incurred prior to first injection. *(1) In general.* Qualified enhanced oil recovery costs may be paid or incurred prior to the date of the first injection of liquids, gases, or other matter (within the meaning of § 1.43-2(c)). If the first injection of liquids, gases, or other matter occurs on or before the date the taxpayer files the taxpayer's federal income tax return for the taxable year with respect to which the costs are allowable, the costs may be taken into account on that return. If the first injection of liquids, gases, or other matter is expected to occur after the date the taxpayer files that return, costs may be taken into account on that return if the Internal Revenue Service issues a private letter ruling to the taxpayer that so permits.

(2) First injection after filing of return for taxable year costs are allowable. Except as provided in paragraph (d)(3) of this section, if the first injection of liquids, gases, or other matter occurs or is expected to occur after the date the taxpayer files the taxpayer's federal income tax return for the taxable year with respect to which the costs are allowable, the costs may be taken into account on an amended return (or in the case of a Coordinated Examination Program taxpayer, on a written statement treated as a qualified return) after the earlier of—

(i) The date the first injection of liquids, gases, or other matter occurs; or

(ii) The date the Internal Revenue Service issues a private letter ruling that provides that the taxpayer may take costs into account prior to the first injection of liquids, gases, or other matter

(3) First injection more than 36 months after close of taxable year costs are paid or incurred. If the first injection of liquids, gases, or other matter occurs more than 36 months after the close of the taxable year in which costs are paid or incurred, the taxpayer may take the costs into account in determining the credit only if the Internal Revenue Service issues a private letter ruling to the taxpayer that so provides.

(4) Injections in volumes less than the volumes specified in the project plan. For purposes of this paragraph (d), injections in volumes significantly less than the volumes specified in the project plan, the unit plan of development, or another similar plan do not constitute the first injection of liquids, gases, or other matter.

(5) Examples. The following examples illustrate the provisions of paragraph (d) of this section.

Example (1). First injection before return filed. In 1992, L, a calendar year taxpayer, undertakes a qualified enhanced oil recovery project on a property in which L owns an operating mineral interest. L incurs $1,000 of intangible drilling and development costs, which L may elect to deduct under section 263(c) for 1992. The first injection of liquids, gases, or other matter (within the meaning of § 1.43-2(c)) occurs in March 1993. L files a 1992 federal income tax return in April 1993. Because the first injection occurs before the filing of L's 1992 federal income tax return, L may take the $1,000 of intangible drilling and development costs into account in determining the credit for 1992 on that return.

Example (2). First injection after return filed. In 1993, M, a calendar year taxpayer, undertakes a qualified enhanced oil recovery project on a property in which M owns an operating mineral interest. M incurs $2,000 of intangible drilling and development costs, which M elects to deduct under section 263(c) for 1993. The first injection of liquids, gases, or other matter is expected to occur in 1995. M files a 1993 federal income tax return in April 1994. Because the first injection of liquids, gases, or other matter occurs after the date on which M's 1993 federal income tax return is filed in April 1994, M may take the $2,000 of intangible drilling and development costs into account on an amended return for 1993 after the earlier of the date the first injection of liquids, gases, or other matter occurs, or the date the Internal Revenue Service issues a private letter ruling that provides that M may take the $2,000 into account prior to first injection.

Example (3). First injection more than 36 months after taxable year. N, a calendar year taxpayer, owns an operating mineral interest in a property on which N undertakes an immiscible carbon dioxide displacement project. In 1994, N incurs $5,000 in connection with the construction of a pipeline to transport carbon dioxide to the project site. The first injection of liquids, gases, or other matter is expected to occur after the pipeline is completed in 1998. Because the first injection of liquids, gases, or other matter occurs more than 36 months after the close of the taxable year in which the $5,000 is incurred, N may take the $5,000 into account in determining the credit only if N receives a private letter ruling from the Internal Revenue Service that provides that N may take the $5,000 into account prior to first injection.

(e) Other rules. *(1) Anti-abuse rule.* Costs paid or incurred with respect to an asset that is acquired, used, or transferred in a manner designed to duplicate or otherwise unreasonably increase the amount of the credit are not qualified enhanced oil recovery costs, regardless of whether the costs would otherwise be creditable for a single taxpayer or more than one taxpayer.

(2) Costs paid or incurred to acquire a project. A purchaser of an existing qualified enhanced oil recovery project may claim the credit for any section 43 costs in excess of the acquisition cost. However, costs paid or incurred to acquire an existing qualified enhanced oil recovery project (or an interest in an existing qualified enhanced oil recovery project) are not eligible for the credit.

(3) Examples. The following examples illustrate the principles of paragraph (e) of this section.

Example (1). Duplicating or unreasonably increasing the credit. O owns an operating mineral interest in a property with respect to which a qualified enhanced oil recovery project is implemented. O acquires pumping units, rods, casing, and separators for use in connection with the project from an unrelated equipment dealer in an arm's length transaction. The equipment is used for the primary purpose of implementing the project. Some of the equipment acquired by O is used equipment. The costs paid by O for the used equipment are qualified enhanced oil recovery costs. O does not need to determine whether the equipment has been previously used in an enhanced oil recovery project.

Example (2). Duplicating or unreasonably increasing the credit. P and Q are co-owners of an oil property with respect to which a qualified enhanced oil recovery project is implemented. In 1992, P and Q jointly purchase a nitrogen plant to supply the tertiary injectant used in the project. P and Q claim the credit for their respective costs for the plant. In 1994, X, a corporation unrelated to P or Q, purchases the nitrogen plant and enters into an agreement to sell nitrogen to P and Q. Because this transaction duplicates or otherwise unreasonably increases the credit, the credit is not allowable for the amounts incurred by P and Q for the nitrogen purchased from X.

Example (3). Duplicating or unreasonably increasing the credit. The facts are the same as in Example 2. In addition, in 1995, P and Q reacquire the nitrogen plant from X. This constitutes the acquisition of property in a manner designed to duplicate or otherwise unreasonably increase the amount of the credit. Therefore, the credit is not allowable for amounts incurred by P and Q for the nitrogen plant purchased from X.

Example (4). Duplicating or unreasonably increasing the credit. R owns an operating mineral interest in a property with respect to which a qualified enhanced oil recovery project is implemented. R acquires a pump that is installed at the site of the project. After the pump has been placed in service for 6 months, R transfers the pump to a secondary recovery project and acquires a replacement pump for the tertiary project. The original pump is suited to the needs of the secondary recovery project and could have been installed there initially. The pumps have been acquired in a manner designed to duplicate or otherwise unreasonably increase the amount of the credit. Depending on the facts, the cost of one pump or the other may be a qualified enhanced oil recovery cost; however, R may not claim the credit with respect to the cost of both pumps.

Example (5). Acquiring a project. In 1993, S purchases all of T's interest in a qualified enhanced oil recovery project, including all of T's interest in tangible property that is an integral part of the project and all of T's operating mineral interest. In 1994, S incurs costs for additional tangible property that is an integral part of the project and which is used for the primary purpose of implementing the project. S also incurs costs for tertiary injectants that are injected in connection with the project. In determining the credit for 1994, S may take into account costs S incurred for tangible property and tertiary injectants. However, S may not take into account any amount that S paid for T's interest in the project in determining S's credit for any taxable year.

T.D. 8448, 11/20/92.

§ 1.43-5 At-risk limitation. [Reserved]

§ 1.43-6 Election out of section 43.

(a) Election to have the credit not apply. *(1) In general.* A taxpayer may elect to have section 43 not apply for any taxable year. The taxpayer may revoke an election to have section 43 not apply for any taxable year. An election to have section 43 not apply (or a revocation of an election to have section 43 not apply) for any taxable year is effective only for the taxable year to which the election relates.

(2) Time for making the election. A taxpayer may make an election under paragraph (a) of this section to have section 43 not apply (or revoke an election to have section 43 not apply) for any taxable year at any time before the expiration of the 3-year period beginning on the last date prescribed by law (determined without regard to extensions) for filing the return for the taxable year. The time for making the election (or revoking the election) is prescribed by section 43(e)(2) and may not be extended under § 1.9100-1.

(3) Manner of making the election. An election (or revocation) under paragraph (a)(1) of this section is made by attaching a statement to the taxpayer's federal income tax return or an amended return (or, in the case of a Coordinated Examination Program taxpayer, on a written statement treated as a qualified amended return) for the taxable year for which the election (or revocation) applies. The taxpayer must indicate whether the taxpayer is electing to not have section 43 apply or is revoking such an election and designate the project or projects to which the election (or revocation) applies. For any taxable year, the last election (or revocation) made by a taxpayer within the period prescribed in

paragraph (a)(2) of this section determines whether section 43 applies for that taxable year.

(b) Election by partnerships and S corporations. For partnerships and S corporations, an election to have section 43 not apply (or a revocation of an election to have section 43 not apply) for any taxable year is made, in accordance with the requirements of paragraph (a) of this section, by the partnership or S corporation with respect to the qualified enhanced oil recovery costs paid or incurred by the partnership or S corporation for the taxable year to which the election relates.

T.D. 8448, 11/20/92.

§ 1.43-7 Effective date of regulations.

The provisions of §§ 1.43-1, 1.43-2 and 1.43-4 through 1.43-7 apply with respect to costs paid or incurred after December 31, 1991, in connection with a qualified enhanced oil recovery project. The provisions of § 1.43-3 apply with respect to taxable years beginning after December 31, 1990. For costs paid or incurred after December 31, 1990, and before January 1, 1992, in connection with a qualified enhanced oil recovery project, taxpayers must take reasonable return positions taking into consideration the statute and its legislative history.

T.D. 8448, 11/20/92.

§ 1.44B-1 Credit for employment of certain new employees.

Caution: The Treasury has not yet amended Reg § 1.44B-1 to reflect changes made by P.L. 98-369.

(a) In general. *(1) Targeted jobs credit.* Under section 44B a taxpayer may elect to claim a credit for wages (as defined in section 51(c) paid or incurred to members of a targeted group (as defined in section 51(d)). Generally, to qualify for the credit, the wages must be paid or incurred to members of a targeted group first hired after September 26, 1978. However, wages paid of incurred to a vocational rehabilitation referral (as defined in section 51(d)(2)) hired before September 27, 1978, may qualify for the credit if a credit under section 44B (as in effect prior to enactment of the Revenue Act of 1978) was claimed for the individual by the taxpayer for a taxable year beginning before January 1, 1979. The amount of the credit shall be determined under section 51. Section 280C(b) (relating to the requirement that the deduction for wages be reduced by the amount of the credit) and the regulations thereunder will not apply to taxpayers who do not elect to claim the credit.

(2) New jobs credit. Under section 44B (as in effect prior to enactment of the Revenue Act of 1978) a taxpayer may elect to claim as a credit the amount determined under sections 51, 52, and 53 (as in effect prior to enactment of the Revenue Act of 1978). Section 280C(b) (relating to the requirement that the deduction for wages be reduced by the amount of the credit) and the regulations thereunder will not apply to taxpayers who do not elect to claim the credit.

(b) Time and manner of making election. The election to claim the targeted jobs credit and the new jobs credit is made by claiming the credit on an original return, or on an amended return, at any time before the expiration of the 3-year period beginning on the last date prescribed by law for filing the return for the taxable year (determined without regard to extensions). The election may be revoked within the above-described 3-year period by filing an amended return on which the credit is not claimed.

(c) Election by partnership, electing small business corporation, and members of a controlled group. In the case of a partnership, the election shall be made by the partnership. In the case of an electing small business corporation (as defined in section 1371(a)), the election shall be made by the corporation. In the case of a controlled group of corporations (within the meaning of section 52(a) and the regulations issued thereunder) not filing a consolidated return under section 1501, the election shall be made by each member of the group. In the case of an affiliated group filing a consolidated return under section 1501, the election shall be made by the group.

T.D. 7921, 11/18/83.

§ 5c.44F-1 Leases and qualified research expenses.

Caution: The Treasury has not yet amended Reg § 5c.44F-1 to reflect changes made by 110-458, P.L. 99-514, P.L. 98-369.

For purposes of section 44F(b)(2)(A)(iii), the determination of whether any amount is paid or incurred to another person for the right to use personal property in the conduct of qualified research shall be made without regard to the characterization of the transaction as a lease under section 168(f)(8). See § 5c.168(f)(8)-1(b).

T.D. 7791, 10/20/81.

§ 1.45D-1 New markets tax credit.

Caution: The Treasury has not yet amended Reg § 1.45D-1 to reflect changes made by P.L. 110-343, P.L. 109-135, P.L. 108-357.

(a) Table of contents. This paragraph lists the headings that appear in § 1.45D-1.

(a) Table of contents.
(b) Allowance of credit.
(1) In general.
(2) Credit allowance date.
(3) Applicable percentage.
(4) Amount paid at original issue.
(c) Qualified equity investment.
(1) In general.
(2) Equity investment.
(3) Equity investments made prior to allocation.
(i) In general.
(ii) Exceptions.
(A) Allocation applications submitted by August 29, 2002.
(B) Other allocation applications.
(iii) Failure to receive allocation.
(iv) Initial investment date.
(4) Limitations.
(i) In general.
(ii) Allocation limitation.
(5) Substantially all.
(i) In general.
(ii) Direct-tracing calculation.
(iii) Safe harbor calculation.
(iv) Time limit for making investments.
(v) Reduced substantially-all percentage.
(vi) Examples.

(6) Aggregation of equity investments.
(7) Subsequent purchasers.
(d) Qualified low-income community investments.
(1) In general.
(i) Investment in a qualified active low-income community business.
(ii) Purchase of certain loans from CDEs.
(A) In general.
(B) Certain loans made before CDE certification.
(C) Intermediary CDEs.
(D) Examples.
(iii) Financial counseling and other services.
(iv) Investments in other CDEs.
(A) In general.
(B) Examples.
(2) Payments of, or for, capital, equity or principal.
(i) In general.
(ii) Subsequent reinvestments.
(iii) Special rule for loans.
(iv) Example.
(3) Special rule for reserves.
(4) Qualified active low-income community business.
(i) In general.
(A) Gross-income requirement.
(B) Use of tangible property.
(1) In general.
(2) Example.
(C) Services performed.
(D) Collectibles.
(E) Nonqualified financial property.
(1) In general.
(2) Construction of real property.
(ii) Proprietorships.
(iii) Portions of business.
(A) In general.
(B) Examples.
(iv) Active conduct of a trade or business.
(A) Special rule.
(B) Example.
(5) Qualified business.
(i) In general.
(ii) Rental of real property.
(iii) Exclusions.
(A) Trades or businesses involving intangibles.
(B) Certain other trades or businesses.
(C) Farming.
(6) Qualifications.
(i) In general.
(ii) Control.
(A) In general.
(B) Definition of control.
(C) Disregard of control.
(7) Financial counseling and other services.
(8) Special rule for certain loans.
(i) In general.
(ii) Example.
(e) Recapture.
(1) In general.
(2) Recapture event.
(3) Redemption.
(i) Equity investment in a C corporation.
(ii) Equity investment in an S corporation.
(iii) Capital interest in a partnership.
(4) Bankruptcy.
(5) Waiver of requirement or extension of time.
(i) In general.
(ii) Manner for requesting a waiver or extension.
(iii) Terms and conditions.
(6) Cure period.
(7) Example.
(f) Basis reduction.
(1) In general.
(2) Adjustment in basis of interest in partnership or S corporation.
(g) Other rules.
(1) Anti-abuse.
(2) Reporting requirements.
(i) Notification by CDE to taxpayer.
(A) Allowance of new markets tax credit.
(B) Recapture event.
(ii) CDE reporting requirements to Secretary.
(iii) Manner of claiming new markets tax credit.
(iv) Reporting recapture tax.
(3) Other Federal tax benefits.
(i) In general.
(ii) Low-income housing credit.
(4) Bankruptcy of CDE.
(h) Effective dates.
(1) In general.
(2) Exception.

(b) Allowance of credit. *(1) In general.* For purposes of the general business credit under section 38, a taxpayer holding a qualified equity investment on a credit allowance date which occurs during the taxable year may claim the new markets tax credit determined under section 45D and this section for such taxable year in an amount equal to the applicable percentage of the amount paid to a qualified community development entity (CDE) for such investment at its original issue. Qualified equity investment is defined in paragraph (c) of this section. Credit allowance date is defined in paragraph (b)(2) of this section. Applicable percentage is defined in paragraph (b)(3) of this section. A CDE is a qualified community development entity as defined in section 45D(c). The amount paid at original issue is determined under paragraph (b)(4) of this section.

(2) Credit allowance date. The term credit allowance date means, with respect to any qualified equity investment—

(i) The date on which the investment is initially made; and

(ii) Each of the 6 anniversary dates of such date thereafter.

(3) Applicable percentage. The applicable percentage is 5 percent for the first 3 credit allowance dates and 6 percent for the other 4 credit allowance dates.

(4) Amount paid at original issue. The amount paid to the CDE for a qualified equity investment at its original issue consists of all amounts paid by the taxpayer to, or on behalf of, the CDE (including any underwriter's fees) to purchase the investment at its original issue.

(c) Qualified equity investment. *(1) In general.* The term qualified equity investment means any equity investment (as defined in paragraph (c)(2) of this section) in a CDE if—

(i) The investment is acquired by the taxpayer at its original issue (directly or through an underwriter) solely in exchange for cash;

(ii) Substantially all (as defined in paragraph (c)(5) of this section) of such cash is used by the CDE to make qualified low-income community investments (as defined in paragraph (d)(1) of this section); and

(iii) The investment is designated for purposes of section 45D and this section by the CDE on its books and records using any reasonable method.

(2) Equity investment. The term equity investment means any stock (other than nonqualified preferred stock as defined in section 351(g)(2)) in an entity that is a corporation for Federal tax purposes and any capital interest in an entity that is a partnership for Federal tax purposes. See §§ 301.7701-1 through 301.7701-3 of this chapter for rules governing when a business entity, such as a business trust or limited liability company, is classified as a corporation or a partnership for Federal tax purposes.

(3) Equity investments made prior to allocation. (i) In general. Except as provided in paragraph (c)(3)(ii) of this section, an equity investment in an entity is not eligible to be designated as a qualified equity investment if it is made before the entity enters into an allocation agreement with the Secretary. An allocation agreement is an agreement between the Secretary and a CDE relating to a new markets tax credit allocation under section 45D(f)(2).

(ii) Exceptions. Notwithstanding paragraph (c)(3)(i) of this section, an equity investment in an entity is eligible to be designated as a qualified equity investment under paragraph (c)(1)(iii) of this section if—

(A) Allocation applications submitted by August 29, 2002.

(1) The equity investment is made on or after April 20, 2001;

(2) The designation of the equity investment as a qualified equity investment is made for a credit allocation received pursuant to an allocation application submitted to the Secretary no later than August 29, 2002; and

(3) The equity investment otherwise satisfies the requirements of section 45D and this section; or

(B) Other allocation applications.

(1) The equity investment is made on or after the date the Secretary publishes a Notice of Allocation Availability (NOAA) in the Federal Register;

(2) The designation of the equity investment as a qualified equity investment is made for a credit allocation received pursuant to an allocation application submitted to the Secretary under that NOAA; and

(3) The equity investment otherwise satisfies the requirements of section 45D and this section.

(iii) Failure to receive allocation. For purposes of paragraph (c)(3)(ii)(A) of this section, if the entity in which the equity investment is made does not receive an allocation pursuant to an allocation application submitted no later than August 29, 2002, the equity investment will not be eligible to be designated as a qualified equity investment. For purposes of paragraph (c)(3)(ii)(B) of this section, if the entity in which the equity investment is made does not receive an allocation under the NOAA described in paragraph (c)(3)(ii)(B)(1) of this section, the equity investment will not be eligible to be designated as a qualified equity investment.

(iv) Initial investment date. If an equity investment is designated as a qualified equity investment in accordance with paragraph (c)(3)(ii) of this section, the investment is treated as initially made on the effective date of the allocation agreement between the CDE and the Secretary.

(4) Limitations. (i) In general. The term qualified equity investment does not include—

(A) Any equity investment issued by a CDE more than 5 years after the date the CDE enters into an allocation agreement (as defined in paragraph (c)(3)(i) of this section) with the Secretary; and

(B) Any equity investment by a CDE in another CDE, if the CDE making the investment has received an allocation under section 45D(f)(2).

(ii) Allocation limitation. The maximum amount of equity investments issued by a CDE that may be designated under paragraph (c)(1)(iii) of this section by the CDE may not exceed the portion of the limitation amount allocated to the CDE by the Secretary under section 45D(f)(2).

(5) Substantially all. (i) In general. Except as provided in paragraph (c)(5)(v) of this section, the term substantially all means at least 85 percent. The substantially-all requirement must be satisfied for each annual period in the 7-year credit period using either the direct-tracing calculation under paragraph (c)(5)(ii) of this section, or the safe harbor calculation under paragraph (c)(5)(iii) of this section. For the first annual period, the substantially-all requirement is treated as satisfied if either the direct-tracing calculation under paragraph (c)(5)(ii) of this section, or the safe-harbor calculation under paragraph (c)(5)(iii) of this section, is performed on a single testing date and the result of the calculation is at least 85 percent. For each annual period other than the first annual period, the substantially-all requirement is treated as satisfied if either the direct-tracing calculation under paragraph (c)(5)(ii) of this section, or the safe harbor calculation under paragraph (c)(5)(iii) of this section, is performed every six months and the average of the two calculations for the annual period is at least 85 percent. For example, the CDE may choose the same two testing dates for all qualified equity investments regardless of the date each qualified equity investment was initially made under paragraph (b)(2)(i) of this section, provided the testing dates are six months apart. The use of the direct-tracing calculation under paragraph (c)(5)(ii) of this section (or the safe harbor calculation under paragraph (c)(5)(iii) of this section) for an annual period does not preclude the use of the safe harbor calculation under paragraph (c)(5)(iii) of this section (or the direct-tracing calculation under paragraph (c)(5)(ii) of this section) for another annual period, provided that a CDE that switches to a direct-tracing calculation must substantiate that the taxpayer's investment is directly traceable to qualified low-income community investments from the time of the CDE's initial investment in a qualified low-income community investment. For purposes of this paragraph (c)(5)(i), the 7-year credit period means the period of 7 years beginning on the date the qualified equity investment is initially made. See paragraph (c)(6) of this section for circumstances in which a

CDE may treat more than one equity investment as a single qualified equity investment.

(ii) Direct-tracing calculation. The substantially-all requirement is satisfied if at least 85 percent of the taxpayer's investment is directly traceable to qualified low-income community investments as defined in paragraph (d)(1) of this section. The direct-tracing calculation is a fraction the numerator of which is the CDE's aggregate cost basis determined under section 1012 in all of the qualified low-income community investments that are directly traceable to the taxpayer's cash investment, and the denominator of which is the amount of the taxpayer's cash investment under paragraph (b)(4) of this section. For purposes of this paragraph (c)(5)(ii), cost basis includes the cost basis of any qualified low-income community investment that becomes worthless. See paragraph (d)(2) of this section for the treatment of amounts received by a CDE in payment of, or for, capital, equity or principal with respect to a qualified low-income community investment.

(iii) Safe harbor calculation. The substantially-all requirement is satisfied if at least 85 percent of the aggregate gross assets of the CDE are invested in qualified low-income community investments as defined in paragraph (d)(1) of this section. The safe harbor calculation is a fraction the numerator of which is the CDE's aggregate cost basis determined under section 1012 in all of its qualified low-income community investments, and the denominator of which is the CDE's aggregate cost basis determined under section 1012 in all of its assets. For purposes of this paragraph (c)(5)(iii), cost basis includes the cost basis of any qualified low-income community investment that becomes worthless. See paragraph (d)(2) of this section for the treatment of amounts received by a CDE in payment of, or for, capital, equity or principal with respect to a qualified low-income community investment.

(iv) Time limit for making investments. The taxpayer's cash investment received by a CDE is treated as invested in a qualified low-income community investment as defined in paragraph (d)(1) of this section only to the extent that the cash is so invested within the 12-month period beginning on the date the cash is paid by the taxpayer (directly or through an underwriter) to the CDE.

(v) Reduced substantially-all percentage. For purposes of the substantially-all requirement (including the direct-tracing calculation under paragraph (c)(5)(ii) of this section and the safe harbor calculation under paragraph (c)(5)(iii) of this section), 85 percent is reduced to 75 percent for the seventh year of the 7-year credit period (as defined in paragraph (c)(5)(i) of this section).

(vi) Examples. The following examples illustrate an application of this paragraph (c)(5):

Example (1). X is a partnership and a CDE that has received a $1 million new markets tax credit allocation from the Secretary. On September 1, 2004, X uses a line of credit from a bank to fund a $1 million loan to Y. The loan is a qualified low-income community investment under paragraph (d)(1) of this section. On September 5, 2004, A pays $1 million to acquire a capital interest in X. X uses the proceeds of A's equity investment to pay off the $1 million line of credit that was used to fund the loan to Y. X's aggregate gross assets consist of the $1 million loan to Y and $100,000 in other assets. A's equity investment in X does not satisfy the substantially-all requirement under paragraph (c)(5)(i) of this section using the direct-tracing calculation under paragraph (c)(5)(ii) of this section because the cash from A's equity investment is not used to make X's loan to Y. However, A's equity investment in X satisfies the substantially-all requirement using the safe harbor calculation under paragraph (c)(5)(iii) of this section because at least 85 percent of X's aggregate gross assets are invested in qualified low-income community investments.

Example (2). X is a partnership and a CDE that has received a new markets tax credit allocation from the Secretary. On August 1, 2004, A pays $100,000 for a capital interest in X. On August 5, 2004, X uses the proceeds of A's equity investment to make an equity investment in Y. X controls Y within the meaning of paragraph (d)(6)(ii)(B) of this section. For the annual period ending July 31, 2005, Y is a qualified active low-income community business (as defined in paragraph (d)(4) of this section). Thus, for that period, A's equity investment satisfies the substantially-all requirement under paragraph (c)(5)(i) of this section using the direct-tracing calculation under paragraph (c)(5)(ii) of this section. For the annual period ending July 31, 2006, Y no longer is a qualified active low-income community business. Thus, for that period, A's equity investment does not satisfy the substantially-all requirement using the direct-tracing calculation. However, during the entire annual period ending July 31, 2006, X's remaining assets are invested in qualified low-income community investments with an aggregate cost basis of $900,000. Consequently, for the annual period ending July 31, 2006, at least 85 percent of X's aggregate gross assets are invested in qualified low-income community investments. Thus, for the annual period ending July 31, 2006, A's equity investment satisfies the substantially-all requirement using the safe harbor calculation under paragraph (c)(5)(iii) of this section.

Example (3). X is a partnership and a CDE that has received a new markets tax credit allocation from the Secretary. On August 1, 2004, A and B each pay $100,000 for a capital interest in X. X does not treat A's and B's equity investments as one qualified equity investment under paragraph (c)(6) of this section. On September 1, 2004, X uses the proceeds of A's equity investment to make an equity investment in Y and X uses the proceeds of B's equity investment to make an equity investment in Z. X has no assets other than its investments in Y and Z. X controls Y and Z within the meaning of paragraph (d)(6)(ii)(B) of this section. For the annual period ending July 31, 2005, Y and Z are qualified active low-income community businesses (as defined in paragraph (d)(4) of this section). Thus, for the annual period ending July 31, 2005, A's and B's equity investments satisfy the substantially-all requirement under paragraph (c)(5)(i) of this section using either the direct-tracing calculation under paragraph (c)(5)(ii) of this section or the safe harbor calculation under paragraph (c)(5)(iii) of this section. For the annual period ending July 31, 2006, Y, but not Z, is a qualified active low-income community business. Thus, for the annual period ending July 31, 2006—

(1) X does not satisfy the substantially-all requirement using the safe harbor calculation under paragraph (c)(5)(iii) of this section;

(2) A's equity investment satisfies the substantially-all requirement using the direct-tracing calculation because A's equity investment is directly traceable to Y; and

(3) B's equity investment does not satisfy the substantially-all requirement because B's equity investment is traceable to Z.

Example (4). X is a partnership and a CDE that has received a new markets tax credit allocation from the Secretary. On November 1, 2004, A pays $100,000 for a capital interest in X. On December 1, 2004, B pays $100,000 for a capital interest in X. On December 31, 2004, X uses $85,000 from A's equity investment and $85,000 from B's equity investment to make a $170,000 equity investment in Y, a qualified active low-income community business (as defined in paragraph (d)(4) of this section). X has no assets other than its investment in Y. X determines whether A's and B's equity investments satisfy the substantially-all requirement under paragraph (c)(5)(i) of this section on December 31, 2004. The calculation for A's and B's equity investments is 85 percent using either the direct-tracing calculation under paragraph (c)(5)(ii) of this section or the safe harbor calculation under paragraph (c)(5)(iii) of this section. Therefore, for the annual periods ending October 31, 2005, and November 30, 2005, A's and B's equity investments, respectively, satisfy the substantially-all requirement under paragraph (c)(5)(i) of this section. For the subsequent annual period, X performs its calculations on December 31, 2005, and June 30, 2006. The average of the two calculations on December 31, 2005, and June 30, 2006, is 85 percent using either the direct-tracing calculation under paragraph (c)(5)(ii) of this section or the safe harbor calculation under paragraph (c)(5)(iii) of this section. Therefore, for the annual periods ending October 31, 2006, and November 30, 2006, A's and B's equity investments, respectively, satisfy the substantially-all requirement under paragraph (c)(5)(i) of this section.

(6) Aggregation of equity investments. A CDE may treat any qualified equity investments issued on the same day as one qualified equity investment. If a CDE aggregates equity investments under this paragraph (c)(6), the rules in this section shall be construed in a manner consistent with that treatment.

(7) Subsequent purchasers. A qualified equity investment includes any equity investment that would (but for paragraph (c)(1)(i) of this section) be a qualified equity investment in the hands of the taxpayer if the investment was a qualified equity investment in the hands of a prior holder.

(d) Qualified low-income community investments. *(1) In general.* The term qualified low-income community investment means any of the following:

(i) Investment in a qualified active low-income community business. Any capital or equity investment in, or loan to, any qualified active low-income community business (as defined in paragraph (d)(4) of this section).

(ii) Purchase of certain loans from CDEs. (A) In general. The purchase by a CDE (the ultimate CDE) from another CDE (whether or not that CDE has received an allocation from the Secretary under section 45D(f)(2)) of any loan made by such entity that is a qualified low-income community investment. A loan purchased by the ultimate CDE from another CDE is a qualified low-income community investment if it qualifies as a qualified low-income community investment either—

(1) At the time the loan was made; or

(2) At the time the ultimate CDE purchases the loan.

(B) Certain loans made before CDE certification. For purposes of paragraph (d)(1)(ii)(A) of this section, a loan by an entity is treated as made by a CDE, notwithstanding that the entity was not a CDE at the time it made the loan, if the entity is a CDE at the time it sells the loan.

(C) Intermediary CDEs. For purposes of paragraph (d)(1)(ii)(A) of this section, the purchase of a loan by the ultimate CDE from a CDE that did not make the loan (the second CDE) is treated as a purchase of the loan by the ultimate CDE from the CDE that made the loan (the originating CDE) if—

(1) The second CDE purchased the loan from the originating CDE (or from another CDE); and

(2) Each entity that sold the loan was a CDE at the time it sold the loan.

(D) Examples. The following examples illustrate an application of this paragraph (d)(1)(ii):

Example (1). X is a partnership and a CDE that has received a new markets tax credit allocation from the Secretary. Y, a corporation, made a $500,000 loan to Z in 1999. In January of 2004, Y is certified as a CDE. On September 1, 2004, X purchases the loan from Y. At the time X purchases the loan, Z is a qualified active low-income community business under paragraph (d)(4)(i) of this section. Accordingly, the loan purchased by X from Y is a qualified low-income community investment under paragraphs (d)(1)(ii)(A) and (B) of this section.

Example (2). The facts are the same as in Example 1 except that on February 1, 2004, Y sells the loan to W and on September 1, 2004, W sells the loan to X. W is a CDE. Under paragraph (d)(1)(ii)(C) of this section, X's purchase of the loan from W is treated as the purchase of the loan from Y. Accordingly, the loan purchased by X from W is a qualified low-income community investment under paragraphs (d)(1)(ii)(A) and (C) of this section.

Example (3). The facts are the same as in Example 2 except that W is not a CDE. Because W was not a CDE at the time it sold the loan to X, the purchase of the loan by X from W is not a qualified low-income community investment under paragraphs (d)(1)(ii)(A) and (C) of this section.

(iii) Financial counseling and other services. Financial counseling and other services (as defined in paragraph (d)(7) of this section) provided to any qualified active low-income community business, or to any residents of a low-income community (as defined in section 45D(e)).

(iv) Investments in other CDEs. (A) In general. Any equity investment in, or loan to, any CDE (the second CDE) by a CDE (the primary CDE), but only to the extent that the second CDE uses the proceeds of the investment or loan—

(1) In a manner—

(i) That is described in paragraph (d)(1)(i) or (iii) of this section; and

(ii) That would constitute a qualified low-income community investment if it were made directly by the primary CDE;

(2) To make an equity investment in, or loan to, a third CDE that uses such proceeds in a manner described in paragraph (d)(1)(iv)(A)(1) of this section; or

(3) To make an equity investment in, or loan to, a third CDE that uses such proceeds to make an equity investment in, or loan to, a fourth CDE that uses such proceeds in a manner described in paragraph (d)(1)(iv)(A)(1) of this section.

(B) Examples. The following examples illustrate an application of paragraph (d)(1)(iv)(A) of this section:

Example (1). X is a partnership and a CDE that has received a new markets tax credit allocation from the Secretary. On September 1, 2004, X uses $975,000 to make an equity investment in Y. Y is a corporation and a CDE. On October 1, 2004, Y uses $950,000 from X's equity investment to make a loan to Z. Z is a qualified active low-income community business under paragraph (d)(4)(i) of this section.

Of X's equity investment in Y, $950,000 is a qualified low-income community investment under paragraph (d)(1)(iv)(A)(1) of this section.

Example (2). W is a partnership and a CDE that has received a new markets tax credit allocation from the Secretary. On September 1, 2004, W uses $975,000 to make an equity investment in X. On October 1, 2004, X uses $950,000 from W's equity investment to make an equity investment in Y. X and Y are corporations and CDEs. On October 5, 2004, Y uses $925,000 from X's equity investment to make a loan to Z. Z is a qualified active low-income community business under paragraph (d)(4)(i) of this section. Of W's equity investment in X, $925,000 is a qualified low-income community investment under paragraph (d)(1)(iv)(A)(2) of this section because X uses proceeds of W's equity investment to make an equity investment in Y, which uses $925,000 of the proceeds in a manner described in paragraph (d)(1)(iv)(A)(1) of this section.

Example (3). U is a partnership and a CDE that has received a new markets tax credit allocation from the Secretary. On September 1, 2004, U uses $975,000 to make an equity investment in V. On October 1, 2004, V uses $950,000 from U's equity investment to make an equity investment in W. On October 5, 2004, W uses $925,000 from V's equity investment to make an equity investment in X. On November 1, 2004, X uses $900,000 from W's equity investment to make an equity investment in Y. V, W, X, and Y are corporations and CDEs. On November 5, 2004, Y uses $875,000 from X's equity investment to make a loan to Z. Z is a qualified active low-income community business under paragraph (d)(4)(i) of this section. U's equity investment in V is not a qualified low-income community investment because X does not use proceeds of W's equity investment in a manner described in paragraph (d)(1)(iv)(A)(1) of this section.

(2) Payments of, or for, capital, equity or principal. (i) In general. Except as otherwise provided in this paragraph (d)(2), amounts received by a CDE in payment of, or for, capital, equity or principal with respect to a qualified low-income community investment must be reinvested by the CDE in a qualified low-income community investment no later than 12 months from the date of receipt to be treated as continuously invested in a qualified low-income community investment. If the amounts received by the CDE are equal to or greater than the cost basis of the original qualified low-income community investment (or applicable portion thereof), and the CDE reinvests, in accordance with this paragraph (d)(2)(i), an amount at least equal to such original cost basis, then an amount equal to such original cost basis will be treated as continuously invested in a qualified low-income community investment. In addition, if the amounts received by the CDE are equal to or greater than the cost basis of the original qualified low-income community investment (or applicable portion thereof), and the CDE reinvests, in accordance with this paragraph (d)(2)(i), an amount less than such original cost basis, then only the amount so reinvested will be treated as continuously invested in a qualified low-income community investment. If the amounts received by the CDE are less than the cost basis of the original qualified low-income community investment (or applicable portion thereof), and the CDE reinvests an amount in accordance with this paragraph (d)(2)(i), then the amount treated as continuously invested in a qualified low-income community investment will equal the excess (if any) of such original cost basis over the amounts received by the CDE that are not so reinvested. Amounts received by a CDE in payment of, or for, capital, equity or principal with respect to a qualified low-income community investment during the seventh year of the 7-year credit period (as defined in paragraph (c)(5)(i) of this section) do not have to be reinvested by the CDE in a qualified low-income community investment in order to be treated as continuously invested in a qualified low-income community investment.

(ii) Subsequent reinvestments. In applying paragraph (d)(2)(i) of this section to subsequent reinvestments, the original cost basis is reduced by the amount (if any) by which the original cost basis exceeds the amount determined to be continuously invested in a qualified low-income community investment.

(iii) Special rule for loans. Periodic amounts received during a calendar year as repayment of principal on a loan that is a qualified low-income community investment are treated as continuously invested in a qualified low-income community investment if the amounts are reinvested in another qualified low-income community investment by the end of the following calendar year.

(iv) Example. The application of paragraphs (d)(2)(i) and (ii) of this section is illustrated by the following example:

Example. On April 1, 2003, A, B, and C each pay $100,000 to acquire a capital interest in X, a partnership. X is a CDE that has received a new markets tax credit allocation from the Secretary. X treats the 3 partnership interests as one qualified equity investment under paragraph (c)(6) of this section. In August 2003, X uses the $300,000 to make a qualified low-income community investment under paragraph (d)(1) of this section. In August 2005, the qualified low-income community investment is redeemed for $250,000. In February 2006, X reinvests $230,000 of the $250,000 in a second qualified low-income community investment and uses the remaining $20,000 for operating expenses. Under paragraph (d)(2)(i) of this section, $280,000 of the proceeds of the qualified equity investment is treated as continuously invested in a qualified low-income community investment. In December 2008, X sells the second qualified low-income community investment and receives $400,000. In March 2009, X reinvests $320,000 of the $400,000 in a third qualified low-income community investment. Under paragraphs (d)(2)(i) and (ii) of this section, $280,000 of the proceeds of the qualified equity investment is treated as continuously invested in a qualified low-income community investment ($40,000 is treated as invested in another qualified low-income community investment in March 2009).

(3) Special rule for reserves. Reserves (not in excess of 5 percent of the taxpayer's cash investment under paragraph (b)(4) of this section) maintained by the CDE for loan losses or for additional investments in existing qualified low-income community investments are treated as invested in a qualified low-income community investment under paragraph (d)(1) of this section. Reserves include fees paid to third parties to protect against loss of all or a portion of the principal of, or interest on, a loan that is a qualified low-income community investment.

(4) Qualified active low-income community business. (i) In general. The term qualified active low-income community business means, with respect to any taxable year, a corporation (including a nonprofit corporation) or a partnership engaged in the active conduct of a qualified business (as defined in paragraph (d)(5) of this section), if the requirements in paragraphs (d)(4)(i)(A), (B), (C), (D), and (E) of this section are met. Solely for purposes of this section, a nonprofit corporation will be deemed to be engaged in the active con-

duct of a trade or business if it is engaged in an activity that furthers its purpose as a nonprofit corporation.

(A) Gross-income requirement. At least 50 percent of the total gross income of such entity is derived from the active conduct of a qualified business (as defined in paragraph (d)(5) of this section) within any low-income community (as defined in section 45D(e)). An entity is deemed to satisfy this paragraph (d)(4)(i)(A) if the entity meets the requirements of either paragraph (d)(4)(i)(B) or (C) of this section, if "50 percent" is applied instead of 40 percent. In addition, an entity may satisfy this paragraph (d)(4)(i)(A) based on all the facts and circumstances. See paragraph (d)(4)(iv) of this section for certain circumstances in which an entity will be treated as engaged in the active conduct of a trade or business.

(B) Use of tangible property. (1) In general. At least 40 percent of the use of the tangible property of such entity (whether owned or leased) is within any low-income community. This percentage is determined based on a fraction the numerator of which is the average value of the tangible property owned or leased by the entity and used by the entity during the taxable year in a low-income community and the denominator of which is the average value of the tangible property owned or leased by the entity and used by the entity during the taxable year. Property owned by the entity is valued at its cost basis as determined under section 1012. Property leased by the entity is valued at a reasonable amount established by the entity.

(2) Example. The application of paragraph (d)(4)(i)(B)(1) of this section is illustrated by the following example:

Example. X is a corporation engaged in the business of moving and hauling scrap metal. X operates its business from a building and an adjoining parking lot that X owns. The building and the parking lot are located in a low-income community (as defined in section 45D(e)). X's cost basis under section 1012 for the building and parking lot is $200,000. During the taxable year, X operates its business 10 hours a day, 6 days a week. X owns and uses 40 trucks in its business, which, on average, are used 6 hours a day outside a low-income community and 4 hours a day inside a low-income community (including time in the parking lot). The cost basis under section 1012 of each truck is $25,000. During non-business hours, the trucks are parked in the lot. Only X's 10-hour business days are used in calculating the use of tangible property percentage under paragraph (d)(4)(i)(B)(1) of this section. Thus, the numerator of the tangible property calculation is $600,000 (4/10 of $1,000,000 (the $25,000 cost basis of each truck times 40 trucks) plus $200,000 (the cost basis of the building and parking lot)) and the denominator is $1,200,000 (the total cost basis of the trucks, building, and parking lot), resulting in 50 percent of the use of X's tangible property being within a low-income community. Consequently, X satisfies the 40 percent use of tangible property test under paragraph (d)(4)(i)(B)(1) of this section.

(C) Services performed. At least 40 percent of the services performed for such entity by its employees are performed in a low-income community. This percentage is determined based on a fraction the numerator of which is the total amount paid by the entity for employee services performed in a low-income community during the taxable year and the denominator of which is the total amount paid by the entity for employee services during the taxable year. If the entity has no employees, the entity is deemed to satisfy this paragraph (d)(4)(i)(C), and paragraph (d)(4)(i)(A) of this section, if the entity meets the requirement of paragraph (d)(4)(i)(B) of this section if "85 percent" is applied instead of 40 percent.

(D) Collectibles. Less than 5 percent of the average of the aggregate unadjusted bases of the property of such entity is attributable to collectibles (as defined in section 408(m)(2)) other than collectibles that are held primarily for sale to customers in the ordinary course of business.

(E) Nonqualified financial property. (1) In general. Less than 5 percent of the average of the aggregate unadjusted bases of the property of such entity is attributable to nonqualified financial property. For purposes of the preceding sentence, the term nonqualified financial property means debt, stock, partnership interests, options, futures contracts, forward contracts, warrants, notional principal contracts, annuities, and other similar property except that such term does not include—

(i) Reasonable amounts of working capital held in cash, cash equivalents, or debt instruments with a term of 18 months or less (because the definition of nonqualified financial property includes debt instruments with a term in excess of 18 months, banks, credit unions, and other financial institutions are generally excluded from the definition of a qualified active low-income community business); or

(ii) Debt instruments described in section 1221(a)(4).

(2) Construction of real property. For purposes of paragraph (d)(4)(i)(E)(1)(i) of this section, the proceeds of a capital or equity investment or loan by a CDE that will be expended for construction of real property within 12 months after the date the investment or loan is made are treated as a reasonable amount of working capital.

(ii) Proprietorships. Any business carried on by an individual as a proprietor is a qualified active low-income community business if the business would meet the requirements of paragraph (d)(4)(i) of this section if the business were incorporated.

(iii) Portions of business. (A) In general. A CDE may treat any trade or business (or portion thereof) as a qualified active low-income community business if the trade or business (or portion thereof) would meet the requirements of paragraph (d)(4)(i) of this section if the trade or business (or portion thereof) were separately incorporated and a complete and separate set of books and records is maintained for that trade or business (or portion thereof). However, the CDE's capital or equity investment or loan is not a qualified low-income community investment under paragraph (d)(1)(i) of this section to the extent the proceeds of the investment or loan are not used for the trade or business (or portion thereof) that is treated as a qualified active low-income community business under this paragraph (d)(4)(iii)(A).

(B) Examples. The following examples illustrate an application of paragraph (d)(4)(iii) of this section:

Example (1). X is a partnership and a CDE that receives a new markets tax credit allocation from the Secretary. A pays $1 million for a capital interest in X. Z is a corporation that operates a supermarket that is not in a low-income community (as defined in section 45D(e)). X uses the proceeds of A's equity investment to make a loan to Z that Z will use to construct a new supermarket in a low-income community. Z will maintain a complete and separate set of books and records for the new supermarket. The proceeds of X's loan to Z will be used exclusively for the new supermarket. Assume that Z's new supermarket in the low-income community would meet the requirements to be a qualified active low-income community business under paragraph (d)(4)(i) of this section if it were separately incorporated. Pursuant to paragraph (d)(4)(iii)(A) of this section, X treats Z's new supermarket as the qualified active low-income community business. Accordingly, X's loan to Z is a qualified low-income community investment under paragraph (d)(1)(i) of this section.

Example (2). X is a partnership and a CDE that receives a new markets tax credit allocation from the Secretary. A pays $1 million for a capital interest in X. Z is a corporation that operates a liquor store in a low-income community (as defined in section 45D(e)). A liquor store is not a qualified business under paragraph (d)(5)(iii)(B) of this section. X uses the proceeds of A's equity investment to make a loan to Z that Z will use to construct a restaurant next to the liquor store. Z will maintain a complete and separate set of books and records for the new restaurant. The proceeds of X's loan to Z will be used exclusively for the new restaurant. Assume that Z's restaurant would meet the requirements to be a qualified active low-income community business under paragraph (d)(4)(i) of this section if it were separately incorporated. Pursuant to paragraph (d)(4)(iii) of this section, X treats Z's restaurant as the qualified active low-income community business. Accordingly, X's loan to Z is a qualified low-income community investment under paragraph (d)(1)(i) of this section.

Example (3). X is a partnership and a CDE that receives a new markets tax credit allocation from the Secretary. A pays $1 million for a capital interest in X. Z is a corporation that operates an insurance company in a low-income community (as defined in section 45D(e)). Five percent or more of the average of the aggregate unadjusted bases of Z's property is attributable to nonqualified financial property under paragraph (d)(4)(i)(E) of this section. Z's insurance operations include different operating units including a claims processing unit. X uses the proceeds of A's equity investment to make a loan to Z for use in Z's claims processing operations. Z will maintain a complete and separate set of books and records for the claims processing unit. The proceeds of X's loan to Z will be used exclusively for the claims processing unit. Assume that Z's claims processing unit would meet the requirements to be a qualified active low-income community business under paragraph (d)(4)(i) of this section if it were separately incorporated. Pursuant to paragraph (d)(4)(iii) of this section, X treats Z's claims processing unit as the qualified active low-income community business. Accordingly, X's loan to Z is a qualified low-income community investment under paragraph (d)(1)(i) of this section.

(iv) Active conduct of a trade or business. (A) Special rule. For purposes of paragraph (d)(4)(i) of this section, an entity will be treated as engaged in the active conduct of a trade or business if, at the time the CDE makes a capital or equity investment in, or loan to, the entity, the CDE reasonably expects that the entity will generate revenues (or, in the case of a nonprofit corporation, engage in an activity that furthers its purpose as a nonprofit corporation) within 3 years after the date the investment or loan is made.

(B) Example. The application of paragraph (d)(4)(iv)(A) of this section is illustrated by the following example:

Example. X is a partnership and a CDE that receives a new markets tax credit allocation from the Secretary on July 1, 2004. X makes a ten-year loan to Y. Y is a newly formed entity that will own and operate a shopping center to be constructed in a low-income community. Y has no revenues but X reasonably expects that Y will generate revenues beginning in December 2005. Under paragraph (d)(4)(iv)(A) of this section, Y is treated as engaged in the active conduct of a trade or business for purposes of paragraph (d)(4)(i) of this section.

(5) Qualified business. (i) In general. Except as otherwise provided in this paragraph (d)(5), the term qualified business means any trade or business. There is no requirement that employees of a qualified business be residents of a low-income community.

(ii) Rental of real property. The rental to others of real property located in any low-income community (as defined in section 45D(e)) is a qualified business if and only if the property is not residential rental property (as defined in section 168(e)(2)(A)) and there are substantial improvements located on the real property. However, a CDE's investment in or loan to a business engaged in the rental of real property is not a qualified low-income community investment under paragraph (d)(1)(i) of this section to the extent a lessee of the real property is described in paragraph (d)(5)(iii)(B) of this section.

(iii) Exclusions. (A) Trades or businesses involving intangibles. The term qualified business does not include any trade or business consisting predominantly of the development or holding of intangibles for sale or license.

(B) Certain other trades or businesses. The term qualified business does not include any trade or business consisting of the operation of any private or commercial golf course, country club, massage parlor, hot tub facility, suntan facility, racetrack or other facility used for gambling, or any store the principal business of which is the sale of alcoholic beverages for consumption off premises.

(C) Farming. The term qualified business does not include any trade or business the principal activity of which is farming (within the meaning of section 2032A(e)(5)(A) or (B)) if, as of the close of the taxable year of the taxpayer conducting such trade or business, the sum of the aggregate unadjusted bases (or, if greater, the fair market value) of the assets owned by the taxpayer that are used in such a trade or business, and the aggregate value of the assets leased by the taxpayer that are used in such a trade or business, exceeds $500,000. For purposes of this paragraph (d)(5)(iii)(C), two or more trades or businesses will be treated as a single trade or business under rules similar to the rules of section 52(a) and (b).

(6) Qualifications. (i) In general. Except as provided in paragraph (d)(6)(ii) of this section, an entity is treated as a qualified active low-income community business for the duration of the CDE's investment in the entity if the CDE reasonably expects, at the time the CDE makes the capital or equity investment in, or loan to, the entity, that the entity will satisfy the requirements to be a qualified active low-income community business under paragraph (d)(4)(i) of this section throughout the entire period of the investment or loan.

(ii) Control. (A) In general. If a CDE controls or obtains control of an entity at any time during the 7-year credit period (as defined in paragraph (c)(5)(i) of this section), the entity will be treated as a qualified active low-income community business only if the entity satisfies the requirements of paragraph (d)(4)(i) of this section throughout the entire period the CDE controls the entity.

(B) Definition of control. Control means, with respect to an entity, direct or indirect ownership (based on value) or control (based on voting or management rights) of more than 50 percent of the entity. For purposes of the preceding sentence, the term management rights means the power to influence the management policies or investment decisions of the entity.

(C) Disregard of control. For purposes of paragraph (d)(6)(ii)(A) of this section, the acquisition of control of an entity by a CDE is disregarded during the 12-month period following such acquisition of control (the 12-month period) if—

(1) The CDE's capital or equity investment in, or loan to, the entity met the requirements of paragraph (d)(6)(i) of this section when initially made;

(2) The CDE's acquisition of control of the entity is due to financial difficulties of the entity that were unforeseen at the time the investment or loan described in paragraph (d)(6)(ii)(C)(1) of this section was made; and

(3) If the acquisition of control occurs before the seventh year of the 7-year credit period (as defined in paragraph (c)(5)(i) of this section), either—

(i) The entity satisfies the requirements of paragraph (d)(4) of this section by the end of the 12-month period; or

(ii) The CDE sells or causes to be redeemed the entire amount of the investment or loan described in paragraph (d)(6)(ii)(C)(1) of this section and, by the end of the 12-month period, reinvests the amount received in respect of the sale or redemption in a qualified low-income community investment under paragraph (d)(1) of this section. For this purpose, the amount treated as continuously invested in a qualified low-income community investment is determined under paragraphs (d)(2)(i) and (ii) of this section.

(7) Financial counseling and other services. The term financial counseling and other services means advice provided by the CDE relating to the organization or operation of a trade or business.

(8) Special rule for certain loans. (i) In general. For purposes of paragraphs (d)(1)(i), (ii), and (iv) of this section, a loan is treated as made by a CDE to the extent the CDE purchases the loan from the originator (whether or not the originator is a CDE) within 30 days after the date the originator makes the loan if, at the time the loan is made, there is a legally enforceable written agreement between the originator and the CDE which—

(A) Requires the CDE to approve the making of the loan either directly or by imposing specific written loan underwriting criteria; and

(B) Requires the CDE to purchase the loan within 30 days after the date the loan is made.

(ii) Example. The application of paragraph (d)(8)(i) of this section is illustrated by the following example:

Example. (i) X is a partnership and a CDE that has received a new markets tax credit allocation from the Secretary. On October 1, 2004, Y enters into a legally enforceable written agreement with W. Y and W are corporations but only Y is a CDE. The agreement between Y and W provides that Y will purchase loans (or portions thereof) from W within 30 days after the date the loan is made by W, and that Y will approve the making of the loans.

(ii) On November 1, 2004, W makes an $825,000 loan to Z pursuant to the agreement between Y and W. Z is a qualified active low-income community business under paragraph (d)(4) of this section. On November 15, 2004, Y purchases the loan from W for $840,000. On December 31, 2004, X purchases the loan from Y for $850,000.

(iii) Under paragraph (d)(8)(i) of this section, the loan to Z is treated as made by Y. Y's loan to Z is a qualified low-income community investment under paragraph (d)(1)(i) of this section. Accordingly, under paragraph (d)(1)(ii)(A) of this section, X's purchase of the loan from Y is a qualified low-income community investment in the amount of $850,000.

(e) Recapture. *(1) In general.* If, at any time during the 7-year period beginning on the date of the original issue of a qualified equity investment in a CDE, there is a recapture event under paragraph (e)(2) of this section with respect to such investment, then the tax imposed by Chapter 1 of the Internal Revenue Code for the taxable year in which the recapture event occurs is increased by the credit recapture amount under section 45D(g)(2). A recapture event under paragraph (e)(2) of this section requires recapture of credits allowed to the taxpayer who purchased the equity investment from the CDE at its original issue and to all subsequent holders of that investment.

(2) Recapture event. There is a recapture event with respect to an equity investment in a CDE if—

(i) The entity ceases to be a CDE;

(ii) The proceeds of the investment cease to be used in a manner that satisfies the substantially-all requirement of paragraph (c)(1)(ii) of this section; or

(iii) The investment is redeemed or otherwise cashed out by the CDE.

(3) Redemption. (i) Equity investment in a C corporation. For purposes of paragraph (e)(2)(iii) of this section, an equity investment in a CDE that is treated as a C corporation for Federal tax purposes is redeemed when section 302(a) applies to amounts received by the equity holder. An equity investment is treated as cashed out when section 301(c)(2) or section 301(c)(3) applies to amounts received by the equity holder. An equity investment is not treated as cashed out when only section 301(c)(1) applies to amounts received by the equity holder.

(ii) Equity investment in an S corporation. For purposes of paragraph (e)(2)(iii) of this section, an equity investment in a CDE that is an S corporation is redeemed when section 302(a) applies to amounts received by the equity holder. An equity investment in an S corporation is treated as cashed out when a distribution to a shareholder described in section 1368(a) exceeds the accumulated adjustments account determined under § 1.1368-2 and any accumulated earnings and profits of the S corporation.

(iii) Capital interest in a partnership. In the case of an equity investment that is a capital interest in a CDE that is a partnership for Federal tax purposes, a pro rata cash distribution by the CDE to its partners based on each partner's capital interest in the CDE during the taxable year will not be treated as a redemption for purposes of paragraph (e)(2)(iii) of this section if the distribution does not exceed the CDE's operating income for the taxable year. In addition, a non-pro rata de minimis cash distribution by a CDE to a partner or partners during the taxable year will not be treated as a redemption. A non-pro rata de minimis cash distribution may not exceed the lesser of 5 percent of the CDE's operating income for that taxable year or 10 percent of the partner's capital interest in the CDE. For purposes of this paragraph (e)(3)(iii), with respect to any taxable year, operating income is the sum of:

(A) The CDE's taxable income as determined under section 703, except that—

(1) The items described in section 703(a)(1) shall be aggregated with the non-separately stated tax items of the partnership; and

(2) Any gain resulting from the sale of a capital asset under section 1221(a) or section 1231 property shall not be included in taxable income;

(B) Deductions under section 165, but only to the extent the losses were realized from qualified low-income community investments under paragraph (d)(1) of this section;

(C) Deductions under sections 167 and 168, including the additional first-year depreciation under section 168(k);

(D) Start-up expenditures amortized under section 195; and

(E) Organizational expenses amortized under section 709.

(4) Bankruptcy. Bankruptcy of a CDE is not a recapture event.

(5) Waiver of requirement or extension of time. (i) In general. The Commissioner may waive a requirement or extend a deadline if such waiver or extension does not materially frustrate the purposes of section 45D and this section.

(ii) Manner for requesting a waiver or extension. A CDE that believes it has good cause for a waiver or an extension may request relief from the Commissioner in a ruling request. The request should set forth all the relevant facts and include a detailed explanation describing the event or events relating to the request for a waiver or an extension. For further information on the application procedure for a ruling, see Rev. Proc. 2005-1 (2005-1 I.R.B. 1) or its successor revenue procedure (see § 601.601(d)(2) of this chapter).

(iii) Terms and conditions. The granting of a waiver or an extension to a CDE under this section may require adjustments of the CDE's requirements under section 45D and this section as may be appropriate.

(6) Cure period. If a qualified equity investment fails the substantially-all requirement under paragraph (c)(5)(i) of this section, the failure is not a recapture event under paragraph (e)(2)(ii) of this section if the CDE corrects the failure within 6 months after the date the CDE becomes aware (or reasonably should have become aware) of the failure. Only one correction is permitted for each qualified equity investment during the 7-year credit period under this paragraph (e)(6).

(7) Example. The application of this paragraph (e) is illustrated by the following example:

Example. In 2003, A and B acquire separate qualified equity investments in X, a partnership. X is a CDE that has received a new markets tax credit allocation from the Secretary. X uses the proceeds of A's qualified equity investment to make a qualified low-income community investment in Y, and X uses the proceeds of B's qualified equity investment to make a qualified low-income community investment in Z. Y and Z are not CDEs. X controls both Y and Z within the meaning of paragraph (d)(6)(ii)(B) of this section. In 2003, Y and Z are qualified active low-income community businesses. In 2007, Y, but not Z, is a qualified active low-income community business and X does not satisfy the substantially-all requirement using the safe harbor calculation under paragraph (c)(5)(iii) of this section. A's equity investment satisfies the substantially-all requirement of paragraph (c)(1)(ii) of this section using the direct-tracing calculation of paragraph (c)(5)(ii) of this section because A's equity investment is traceable to Y. However, B's equity investment fails the substantially-all requirement using the direct-tracing calculation because B's equity investment is traceable to Z. Therefore, under paragraph (e)(2)(ii) of this section, there is a recapture event for B's equity investment (but not A's equity investment).

(f) Basis reduction. *(1) In general.* A taxpayer's basis in a qualified equity investment is reduced by the amount of any new markets tax credit determined under paragraph (b)(1) of this section with respect to the investment. A basis reduction occurs on each credit allowance date under paragraph (b)(2) of this section. This paragraph (f) does not apply for purposes of sections 1202, 1400B, and 1400F.

(2) Adjustment in basis of interest in partnership or S corporation. The adjusted basis of either a partner's interest in a partnership, or stock in an S corporation, must be appropriately adjusted to take into account adjustments made under paragraph (f)(1) of this section in the basis of a qualified equity investment held by the partnership or S corporation (as the case may be).

(g) Other rules. *(1) Anti-abuse.* If a principal purpose of a transaction or a series of transactions is to achieve a result that is inconsistent with the purposes of section 45D and this section, the Commissioner may treat the transaction or series of transactions as causing a recapture event under paragraph (e)(2) of this section.

(2) Reporting requirements. (i) Notification by CDE to taxpayer. (A) Allowance of new markets tax credit. A CDE must provide notice to any taxpayer who acquires a qualified equity investment in the CDE at its original issue that the equity investment is a qualified equity investment entitling the taxpayer to claim the new markets tax credit. The notice must be provided by the CDE to the taxpayer no later than 60 days after the date the taxpayer makes the investment in the CDE. The notice must contain the amount paid to the CDE for the qualified equity investment at its original issue and the taxpayer identification number of the CDE.

(B) Recapture event. If, at any time during the 7-year period beginning on the date of the original issue of a qualified equity investment in a CDE, there is a recapture event under paragraph (e)(2) of this section with respect to such investment, the CDE must provide notice to each holder, including all prior holders, of the investment that a recapture event has occurred. The notice must be provided by the CDE no later than 60 days after the date the CDE becomes aware of the recapture event.

(ii) CDE reporting requirements to Secretary. Each CDE must comply with such reporting requirements to the Secretary as the Secretary may prescribe.

(iii) Manner of claiming new markets tax credit. A taxpayer may claim the new markets tax credit for each applicable taxable year by completing Form 8874, "New Markets Credit," and by filing Form 8874 with the taxpayer's Federal income tax return.

(iv) Reporting recapture tax. If there is a recapture event with respect to a taxpayer's equity investment in a CDE, the taxpayer must include the credit recapture amount under section 45D(g)(2) on the line for recapture taxes on the taxpayer's Federal income tax return for the taxable year in which the recapture event under paragraph (e)(2) of this section occurs (or on the line for total tax, if there is no such line for recapture taxes) and write NMCR (new markets credit recapture) next to the entry space.

(3) Other Federal tax benefits. (i) In general. Except as provided in paragraph (g)(3)(ii) of this section, the availability of Federal tax benefits does not limit the availability of the new markets tax credit. Federal tax benefits that do not limit the availability of the new markets tax credit include, for example:

(A) The rehabilitation credit under section 47;

(B) All deductions under sections 167 and 168, including the additional first-year depreciation under section 168(k), and the expense deduction for certain depreciable property under section 179; and

(C) All tax benefits relating to certain designated areas such as empowerment zones and enterprise communities under sections 1391 through 1397D, the District of Columbia Enterprise Zone under sections 1400 through 1400B, renewal communities under sections 1400E through 1400J, and the New York Liberty Zone under section 1400L.

(ii) Low-income housing credit. If a CDE makes a capital or equity investment or a loan with respect to a qualified low-income building under section 42, the investment or loan is not a qualified low-income community investment under paragraph (d)(1) of this section to the extent the building's eligible basis under section 42(d) is financed by the proceeds of the investment or loan.

(4) Bankruptcy of CDE. The bankruptcy of a CDE does not preclude a taxpayer from continuing to claim the new markets tax credit on the remaining credit allowance dates under paragraph (b)(2) of this section.

(h) Effective dates. *(1) In general.* Except as provided in paragraph (h)(2) of this section, this section applies on or after December 22, 2004, and may be applied by taxpayers before December 22, 2004. The provisions that apply before December 22, 2004, are contained in § 1.45D-1T (see 26 CFR part 1 revised as of April 1, 2003, and April 1, 2004).

(2) Exception. Paragraph (d)(5)(ii) of this section as it relates to the restriction on lessees described in paragraph (d)(5)(iii)(B) of this section applies to qualified low-income community investments made on or after June 22, 2005.

T.D. 9171, 12/22/2004.

PAR. 2. 2. Section 1.45D-1 is amended by:

1. Redesignating the paragraph (a) entries for paragraphs (e)(4), (e)(5), (e)(6), and (e)(7) as paragraphs (e)(5), (e)(6), (e)(7), and (e)(8), respectively, adding a new entry for paragraph (e)(4), and revising the entry for paragraph (h)(2).

3. Revising paragraph (d)(6)(i).

4. Revising paragraph (e)(3)(iii) introductory text.

5. Redesignating paragraphs (e)(3)(iii)(B), (e)(3)(iii)(C), (e)(3)(iii)(D), and (e)(3)(iii)(E) as paragraphs (e)(3)(iii)(C), (e)(3)(iii)(D), (e)(3)(iii)(E), and (e)(3)(iii)(F), respectively, and adding new paragraph (e)(3)(iii)(B).

6. Revising newly-designated paragraph (e)(3)(iii)(D).

7. Redesignating paragraphs (e)(4), (e)(5), (e)(6), and (e)(7) as paragraphs (e)(5), (e)(6), (e)(7), and (e)(8), respectively, and adding new paragraph (e)(4).

8. Revising the heading for paragraph (h)(2) and adding a sentence at the end of the paragraph.

The additions and revisions read as follows:

Proposed § 1.45D-1 New markets tax credit. [*For Preamble, see ¶ 153,049*]

(a) * * *

(e) * * *

(4) Section 708(b)(1)(B) termination.

* * * * *

(h) * * *

(2) Exception for certain provisions.

* * * * *

(d) * * *

(6) * * *

(i) * * * Except as provided in paragraph (d)(6)(ii) of this section, an entity is treated as a qualified active low-income community business for the duration of the qualified community development entity's (CDE's) investment in the entity if the CDE reasonably expects, at the time the CDE makes the capital or equity investment in, or loan to, the entity, that the entity will satisfy the requirements to be a qualified active low-income community business under paragraphs (d)(4)(i) and (d)(5) of this section (including, if applicable, portions of business under paragraph (d)(4)(iii) of this section) throughout the entire period of the investment or loan. A CDE may rely on this paragraph (d)(6)(i) to treat an entity as a qualified active low-income community business even if the CDE's investment in or loan to the entity is made through other CDEs under paragraph (d)(1)(iv)(A) of this section.

(e) * * *

(3) * * *

(iii) Capital interest in a partnership. In the case of an equity investment that is a capital interest in a CDE that is a partnership for Federal tax purposes, a pro rata cash distribution by the CDE to its partners based on each partner's capital interest in the CDE during the taxable year will not be treated as a redemption for purposes of paragraph (e)(2)(iii) of this section if the distribution does not exceed the sum of the CDE's "operating income" for the taxable year and the CDE's undistributed "operating income" (if any) for the prior taxable year. For purposes of this paragraph (e)(3)(iii), § 1.704-1(b)(1)(vii) applies to treat an allocation to a partner of its share of partnership net or "bottom line" taxable income or loss as an allocation to such partner of the same share of each item of income, gain, loss, and deduction that is taken into account in computing the partner's net or "bottom line" taxable income or loss. In addition, a non-pro rata "de minimis" cash distribution by a CDE to a partner or partners during the taxable year will not be treated as a redemption. A non-pro rata "de minimis" cash distribution may not exceed the lesser of 5 percent of the CDE's "operating income" for that taxable year or 10 percent of the partner's capital interest in the CDE. For purposes of this paragraph (e)(3)(iii), with respect to any taxable year, "operating income" is the sum of:

* * * * *

(B) Tax-exempt income under section 103;

* * * * *

(D) Deductions under sections 167 and 168, including the additional first-year depreciation under section 168(k), and any other depreciation and amortization deductions under the Code;

* * * * *

(4) Section 708(b)(1)(B) termination. A termination under section 708(b)(1)(B) of a CDE that is a partnership is not a recapture event.

* * * * *

(h) * * *

(2) Exception for certain provisions. * * * Paragraph (d)(6)(i) of this section as it relates to a CDE's investment under paragraph (d)(1)(iv)(A), paragraph (e)(3)(iii) of this section as it relates to the distribution of undistributed "operating income" for the prior taxable year and to the appli-

cation of § 1.704-1(b)(1)(vii), paragraph (e)(3)(iii)(B) of this section, paragraph (e)(3)(iii)(D) of this section as it relates to any other depreciation and amortization deductions under the Code, and paragraph (e)(4) of this section apply to taxable years ending on or after the date of publication of the Treasury decision adopting these rules as final regulation in the Federal Register.

PAR. 2. Section 1.45D-1 is amended by:

1. In paragraph (a), revising the entry for paragraph (h) and adding new entries for (d)(9), (d)(9)(i), (d)(9)(i)(A), (d)(9)(i)(B), (d)(9)(i)(B)(1), (d)(9)(i)(B)(2), (d)(9)(i)(B)(3), (d)(9)(i)(C), (d)(9)(i)(C)(1), (d)(9)(i)(C)(2), (d)(9)(i)(D), (d)(9)(ii), (d)(9)(ii)(A), (d)(9)(ii)(B), (d)(9)(ii)(C), (d)(9)(ii)(C)(1), (d)(9)(ii)(C)(2), (d)(9)(ii)(C)(2)(i), (d)(9)(ii)(C)(2)(ii), (d)(9)(ii)(D), (d)(9)(ii)(D)(1), (d)(9)(ii)(D)(2), (d)(9)(ii)(E), and (h)(3).

2. Revising paragraph (d)(4)(i) introductory text.

3. Adding the language "See paragraph (d)(9) of this section for rules relating to targeted populations." to the end of paragraph (d)(4)(i)(A).

4. Adding the language "See paragraph (d)(9) of this section for rules relating to targeted populations." to the end of paragraph (d)(4)(i)(B)(1).

5. Adding the language "See paragraph (d)(9) of this section for rules relating to targeted populations." to the end of paragraph (d)(4)(i)(C).

6. Adding a new sentence at the end of paragraph (d)(4)(iv)(A).

7. Adding new paragraph (d)(9).

8. Revising the heading for paragraph (h) and adding new paragraph (h)(3).

The additions and revisions read as follows:

Proposed § 1.45D-1 New markets tax credit. [*For Preamble, see ¶ 153,063*]

(a) * * *

(d) * * *

(9) Targeted populations.

(i) Low-income persons.

(A) Definition.

(B) Qualified active low-income community business requirements for low-income targeted populations.

(1) In general.

(2) Employee.

(3) Owner.

(C) 120-percent-income restriction.

(1) In general.

(2) Population census tract location.

(D) Rental of real property for low-income targeted populations.

(ii) Individuals who otherwise lack adequate access to loans or equity investments.

(A) In general.

(B) GO Zone Targeted Population.

(C) Qualified active low-income community business requirements for the GO Zone Targeted Population.

(1) In general.

(2) Location.

(i) In general.

(ii) Determination.

(D) 200-percent-income restriction.

(1) In general.

(2) Population census tract location.

(E) Rental of real property for the GO Zone Targeted Population.

* * * * *

(h) Effective/applicability dates

(3) Targeted populations.

* * * * *

(d) * * *

(4) * * *

(i) In general. The term qualified active low-income community business means, with respect to any taxable year, a corporation (including a nonprofit corporation) or a partnership engaged in the active conduct of a qualified business (as defined in paragraph (d)(5) of this section), if the requirements of (d)(4)(i)(A), (B), (C), (D), and (E) of this section are met (or in the case of an entity serving targeted populations, if the requirements of paragraphs (d)(4)(i)(D), (E), and (d)(9)(i) or (ii) of this section are met). Solely for purposes of this section, a nonprofit corporation will be deemed to be engaged in the active conduct of a trade or business if it is engaged in an activity that furthers its purpose as a nonprofit corporation.

* * * * *

(iv) Active conduct of a trade or business. (A) * * * This paragraph (d)(4)(iv) applies only for purposes of determining whether an entity is engaged in the active conduct of a trade or business and does not apply for purposes of determining whether the gross-income requirement under paragraph (d)(4)(i)(A), (d)(9)(i)(B)(1)(i), or (d)(9)(ii)(C)(1)(i) of this section is satisfied.

* * * * * *(9) Targeted populations.* As determined by the Treasury Department, for purposes of section 45D(e)(2), targeted populations that will be treated as a low-income community are individuals, or an identifiable group of individuals, including an Indian tribe, who are low-income persons as defined in paragraph (d)(9)(i) of this section or who are individuals who otherwise lack adequate access to loans or equity investments as defined in paragraph (d)(9)(ii) of this section.

(i) Low-income persons. (A) Definition. For purposes of section 45D(e)(2), an individual shall be considered to be low-income if the individual's family income, adjusted for family size, is not more than—

(1) For metropolitan areas, 80 percent of the area median family income; and

(2) For non-metropolitan areas, the greater of 80 percent of the area median family income, or 80 percent of the statewide non-metropolitan area median family income.

(B) Qualified active low-income community business requirements for low-income targeted populations. (1) In general. An entity will not be treated as a qualified active low-income community business for low-income targeted populations unless—

(i) At least 50 percent of the entity's total gross income for any taxable year is derived from sales, rentals, services, or other transactions with individuals who are low-income persons for purposes of section 45D(e)(2) and this paragraph (d)(9),

(ii) At least 40 percent of the entity's employees are individuals who are low-income persons for purposes of section 45D(e)(2) and this paragraph (d)(9), or

(iii) At least 50 percent of the entity is owned by individuals who are low-income persons for purposes of section 45D(e)(2) and this paragraph (d)(9).

(2) Employee. The determination of whether an employee is a low-income person must be made at the time the employee is hired. If the employee is a low-income person at the time of hire, that employee is considered a low-income person for purposes of section 45D(e)(2) and this paragraph (d)(9) throughout the time of employment, without regard to any increase in the employee's income after the time of hire.

(3) Owner. The determination of whether an owner is a low-income person must be made at the time the qualified low-income community investment is made. If an owner is a low-income person at the time the qualified low-income community investment is made, that owner is considered a low-income person for purposes of section 45D(e)(2) and this paragraph (d)(9) throughout the time the ownership interest is held by that owner.

(C) 120-percent-income restriction. (1) In general. (i) In no case will an entity be treated as a qualified active low-income community business under paragraph (d)(9)(i) of this section if the entity is located in a population census tract for which the median family income exceeds 120 percent of—

(A) In the case of a tract not located within a metropolitan area, the statewide median family income, or

(B) In the case of a tract located within a metropolitan area, the greater of statewide median family income or metropolitan area median family income (120-percent-income restriction).

(ii) The 120-percent-income restriction shall not apply to an entity located within a population census tract with a population of less than 2,000 if such tract is not located in a metropolitan area.

(iii) The 120-percent-income restriction shall not apply to an entity located within a population census tract with a population of less than 2,000 if such tract is located in a metropolitan area and more than 75 percent of the tract is zoned for commercial or industrial use. For this purpose, the 75 percent calculation should be made using the area of the population census tract. For purposes of this paragraph (d)(9)(i)(C)(1)(iii), property for which commercial or industrial use is a permissible zoning use will be treated as zoned for commercial or industrial use.

(2) Population census tract location. (i) For purposes of the 120-percent-income restriction, an entity will be considered to be located in a population census tract for which the median family income exceeds 120 percent of the applicable median family income under paragraph (d)(9)(i)(C)(1)(i)(A) or (B) of this section (non-qualifying population census tract) if—

(A) At least 50 percent of the total gross income of the entity is derived from the active conduct of a qualified business (as defined in paragraph (d)(5) of this section) within one or more non-qualifying population census tracts (non-qualifying gross income amount);

(B) At least 40 percent of the use of the tangible property of the entity (whether owned or leased) is within one or more non-qualifying population census tracts (non-qualifying tangible property usage); and

(C) At least 40 percent of the services performed for the entity by its employees are performed in one or more non-qualifying population census tracts (non-qualifying services performance).

(ii) The entity is considered to have the non-qualifying gross income amount if the entity has non-qualifying tangible property usage or non-qualifying services performance of at least 50 percent instead of 40 percent.

(iii) If the entity has no employees, the entity is considered to have the non-qualifying gross income amount as well as non-qualifying services performance if at least 85 percent of the use of the tangible property of the entity (whether owned or leased) is within one or more non-qualifying population census tracts.

(D) Rental of real property for low-income targeted populations. The rental to others of real property for low-income targeted populations that otherwise satisfies the requirements to be a qualified business under paragraph (d)(5) of this section will be treated as located in a low-income community for purposes of paragraph (d)(5)(ii) of this section if at least 50 percent of the entity's total gross income is derived from rentals to individuals who are low-income persons for purposes of section 45D(e)(2) and this paragraph (d)(9) and/or to a qualified active low-income community business that meets the requirements for low-income targeted populations under paragraphs (d)(9)(i)(B)(1)(i) or (ii) and (d)(9)(i)(B)(2) of this section.

(ii) Individuals who otherwise lack adequate access to loans or equity investments. (A) In general. Paragraph (d)(9)(ii) of this section may be applied only with regard to qualified low-income community investments made under the increase in the new markets tax credit limitation pursuant to section 1400N(m)(2). Therefore, only CDEs with a significant mission of recovery and redevelopment of the Gulf Opportunity Zone (GO Zone) that receive an allocation from the increase described in section 1400N(m)(2) may make qualified low-income community investments from that allocation pursuant to the rules in paragraph (d)(9)(ii) of this section.

(B) GO Zone Targeted Population. As determined by the Treasury Department, for purposes of targeted populations under section 45D(e)(2), an individual is considered to otherwise lack adequate access to loans or equity investments only if the individual was displaced from his or her principal residence as a result of Hurricane Katrina and/or the individual lost his or her principal source of employment as a result of Hurricane Katrina (GO Zone Targeted Population). In order to meet this definition, the individual's principal residence or principal source of employment, as applicable, must have been located in a population census tract within the GO Zone that contains one or more areas designated by the Federal Emergency Management Agency (FEMA) as flooded, having sustained extensive damage, or having sustained catastrophic damage as a result of Hurricane Katrina.

(C) Qualified active low-income community business requirements for the GO Zone Targeted Population. (1) In general. An entity will not be treated as a qualified active low-income community business for the GO Zone Targeted Population unless—

(i) At least 50 percent of the entity's total gross income for any taxable year is derived from sales, rentals, services, or other transactions with the GO Zone Targeted Population, low-income persons as defined in paragraph (d)(9)(i) of this section, or some combination thereof;

(ii) At least 40 percent of the entity's employees consist of the GO Zone Targeted Population, low-income persons as defined in paragraph (d)(9)(i) of this section, or some combination thereof; or

(iii) At least 50 percent of the entity is owned by the GO Zone Targeted Population, low-income persons as defined in paragraph (d)(9)(i) of this section, or some combination thereof.

(2) Location. (i) In general. In order to be a qualified active low-income community business under paragraph (d)(9)(ii)(C) of this section, the entity must be located in a population census tract within the GO Zone that contains one or more areas designated by FEMA as flooded, having sustained extensive damage, or having sustained catastrophic damage as a result of Hurricane Katrina (qualifying population census tract).

(ii) Determination. (A) For purposes of the preceding paragraph, an entity will be considered to be located in a qualifying population census tract if—

(I) At least 50 percent of the total gross income of the entity is derived from the active conduct of a qualified business (as defined in paragraph (d)(5) of this section) within one or more qualifying population census tracts (gross income requirement);

(II) At least 40 percent of the use of the tangible property of the entity (whether owned or leased) is within one or more qualifying population census tracts (use of tangible property requirement); and

(III) At least 40 percent of the services performed for the entity by its employees are performed in one or more qualifying population census tracts (services performed requirement).

(B) The entity is deemed to satisfy the gross income requirement if the entity satisfies the use of tangible property requirement or the services performed requirement on the basis of at least 50 percent instead of 40 percent.

(C) If the entity has no employees, the entity is deemed to satisfy the services performed requirement as well as the gross income requirement if at least 85 percent of the use of the tangible property of the entity (whether owned or leased) is within one or more qualifying population census tracts.

(D) 200-percent-income restriction. (1) In general. (i) In no case will an entity be treated as a qualified active low-income community business under paragraph (d)(9)(ii) of this section if the entity is located in a population census tract for which the median family income exceeds 200 percent of—

(A) In the case of a tract not located within a metropolitan area, the statewide median family income, or

(B) In the case of a tract located within a metropolitan area, the greater of statewide median family income or metropolitan area median family income (200-percent-income restriction).

(ii) The 200-percent-income restriction shall not apply to an entity located within a population census tract with a population of less than 2,000 if such tract is not located in a metropolitan area.

(iii) The 200-percent-income restriction shall not apply to an entity located within a population census tract with a population of less than 2,000 if such tract is located in a metropolitan area and more than 75 percent of the tract is zoned for commercial or industrial use. For this purpose, the 75 percent calculation should be made using the area of the population census tract. For purposes of this paragraph (d)(9)(ii)(D)(1)(iii), property for which commercial or industrial use is a permissible zoning use will be treated as zoned for commercial or industrial use.

(2) Population census tract location. (i) For purposes of the 200-percent-income restriction, an entity will be considered to be located in a population census tract for which the median family income exceeds 200 percent of the applicable median family income under paragraph (d)(9)(ii)(D)(1)(i)(A) or (B) of this section (non-qualifying population census tract) if—

(A) At least 50 percent of the total gross income of the entity is derived from the active conduct of a qualified business (as defined in paragraph (d)(5) of this section) within one or more non-qualifying population census tracts (non-qualifying gross income amount);

(B) At least 40 percent of the use of the tangible property of the entity (whether owned or leased) is within one or more non-qualifying population census tracts (non-qualifying tangible property usage); and

(C) At least 40 percent of the services performed for the entity by its employees are performed in one or more non-qualifying population census tracts (non-qualifying services performance).

(ii) The entity is considered to have the non-qualifying gross income amount if the entity has non-qualifying tangible property usage or non-qualifying services performance of at least 50 percent instead of 40 percent.

(iii) If the entity has no employees, the entity is considered to have the non-qualifying gross income amount as well as non-qualifying services performance if at least 85 percent of the use of the tangible property of the entity (whether owned or leased) is within one or more non-qualifying population census tracts.

(E) Rental of real property for the GO Zone Targeted Population. The rental to others of real property for the GO Zone Targeted Population that otherwise satisfies the requirements to be a qualified business under paragraph (d)(5) of this section will be treated as located in a low-income community for purposes of paragraph (d)(5)(ii) of this section if at least 50 percent of the entity's total gross income is derived from rentals to the GO Zone Targeted Population, low-income persons as defined in paragraph (d)(9)(i) of this section and/or to a qualified active low-income community business that meets the requirements for the GO Zone Targeted Population under paragraphs (d)(9)(ii)(C)(1)(i) or (ii) of this section.

* * * * *

(h) Effective/applicability dates * * *.

* * * * *

(3) Targeted populations. The rules in paragraph (d)(9) of this section apply to taxable years ending on or after the date of publication of the Treasury decision adopting these rules as final regulation in the Federal Register.

§ 1.45G-0 Table of contents for the railroad track maintenance credit rules.

This section lists the table of contents for § 1.45G-1.

§ 1.45G-1 Railroad track maintenance credit.

(a) In general.

(b) Definitions.

(1) Class II railroad and Class III railroad.

(2) Eligible railroad track.

(3) Eligible taxpayer.

(4) Qualifying railroad structure.
(5) Qualified railroad track maintenance expenditures.
(6) Rail facilities.
(7) Railroad-related property.
(8) Railroad-related services.
(9) Railroad track.
(10) Form 8900.
(11) Examples.
(c) Determination of amount of railroad track maintenance credit for the taxable year.
(1) General amount.
(2) Limitation on the credit.
(i) Eligible taxpayer is a Class II railroad or Class III railroad.
(ii) Eligible taxpayer is not a Class II railroad or Class III railroad.
(iii) No carryover of amount that exceeds limitation.
(3) Determination of amount of QRTME paid or incurred.
(i) In general.
(ii) Effect of reimbursements received from persons other than a Class II or Class III railroad.
(4) Examples.
(d) Assignment of track miles.
(1) In general.
(2) Assignment eligibility.
(3) Effective date of assignment.
(4) Assignment information statement.
(i) In general.
(ii) Assignor.
(iii) Assignee.
(iv) Special rule for returns filed prior to November 9, 2007.
(5) Special rules.
(i) Effect of subsequent dispositions of eligible railroad track during the assignment year.
(ii) Effect of multiple assignments of eligible railroad track miles during the same taxable year.
(6) Examples.
(e) Adjustments to basis.
(1) In general.
(2) Basis adjustment made to railroad track.
(3) Examples.
(f) Controlled groups.
(1) In general.
(2) Definitions.
(i) Trade or business.
(ii) Group and controlled group.
(iii) Group credit.
(iv) Consolidated group.
(v) Credit year.
(3) Computation of the group credit.
(4) Allocation of the group credit.
(i) In general.
(ii) Stand-alone entity credit.
(5) Special rules for consolidated groups.
(i) In general.
(ii) Special rule for allocation of group credit among consolidated group members.
(6) Tax accounting periods used.
(i) In general.
(ii) Special rule when timing of QRTME is manipulated.
(7) Membership during taxable year in more than one group.
(8) Intra-group transactions.
(i) In general.
(ii) Payment for QRTME.
(g) Effective/applicability date.
(1) In general.
(2) Taxable years ending before September 7, 2006.
(3) Special rules for returns filed prior to November 9, 2007.

T.D. 9365, 11/9/2007.

§ 1.45G-1 Railroad track maintenance credit.

(a) In general. For purposes of section 38, the railroad track maintenance credit (RTMC) for qualified railroad track maintenance expenditures (QRTME) paid or incurred by an eligible taxpayer during the taxable year is determined under this section. A taxpayer claiming the RTMC must do so by filing Form 8900, "Qualified Railroad Track Maintenance Credit," with its timely filed (including extensions) Federal income tax return for the taxable year the RTMC is claimed. Paragraph (b) of this section provides definitions of terms. Paragraph (c) of this section provides rules for computing the RTMC, including rules regarding limitations on the amount of the credit. Paragraph (d) of this section provides rules for assigning miles of railroad track. Paragraph (e) of this section contains rules for adjusting basis for the amount of the RTMC claimed by an eligible taxpayer. Paragraph (f) of this section contains rules for computing the amount of the RTMC in the case of a controlled group, and for the allocation of the group credit among members of the controlled group.

(b) Definitions. For purposes of section 45G and this section, the following definitions apply:

(1) Class II railroad and Class III railroad have the respective meanings given to these terms by the Surface Transportation Board (STB) without regard to the controlled group rules under section 45G(e)(2).

(2) Eligible railroad track is railroad track (as defined in paragraph (b)(9) of this section) located within the United States that is owned or leased by a Class II railroad or Class III railroad at the close of its taxable year. For purposes of section 45G and this section, a Class II railroad or Class III railroad owns railroad track if the railroad track is subject to the allowance for depreciation under section 167 by the Class II railroad or Class III railroad.

(3) Eligible taxpayer is—

(i) A Class II railroad or Class III railroad during the taxable year;

(ii) Any person that transports property using the rail facilities (as defined in paragraph (b)(6) of this section) of a Class II railroad or Class III railroad during the taxable year, but only is an eligible taxpayer with respect to the miles of eligible railroad track assigned to the person for that taxable year by that Class II railroad or Class III railroad under paragraph (d) of this section; or

(iii) Any person that furnishes railroad-related property (as defined in paragraph (b)(7) of this section) or railroad-related services (as defined in paragraph (b)(8) of this section), to a Class II railroad or Class III railroad during the taxable year, but only is an eligible taxpayer with respect to the miles of eligible railroad track assigned to the person for that taxable year by that Class II railroad or Class III railroad under paragraph (d) of this section.

(4) Qualifying railroad structure is property located within the United States that is described in the following STB property accounts in 49 CFR Part 1201, Subpart A:

(i) Property Account 3, Grading.

(ii) Property Account 4, Other right-of-way expenditures.

(iii) Property Account 5, Tunnels and subways.

(iv) Property Account 6, Bridges, trestles, and culverts.

(v) Property Account 7, Elevated structures.

(vi) Property Account 8, Ties.

(vii) Property Account 9, Rails and other track material.

(viii) Property Account 11, Ballast.

(ix) Property Account 13, Fences, snowsheds, and signs.

(x) Property Account 27, Signals and interlockers.

(xi) Property Account 39, Public improvements; construction.

(5) Qualified railroad track maintenance expenditures (QRTME) are expenditures for maintaining, repairing, and improving qualifying railroad structure (as defined in paragraph (b)(4) of this section) that is owned or leased as of January 1, 2005, by a Class II railroad or Class III railroad. These expenditures may or may not be chargeable to a capital account.

(6) Rail facilities of a Class II railroad or Class III railroad are railroad yards, tracks, bridges, tunnels, wharves, docks, stations, and other related assets that are used in the transport of freight by a railroad and that are owned or leased by the Class II railroad or Class III railroad.

(7) Railroad-related property is property that is provided directly to, and is unique to, a railroad and that, in the hands of a Class II railroad or Class III railroad, is described in—

(i) The following STB property accounts in 49 CFR Part 1201, Subpart A:

(A) Property Account 3, Grading;

(B) Property Account 5, Tunnels and subways;

(C) Property Account 22, Storage warehouses; and

(ii) Asset classes 40.1 through 40.54 in the guidance issued by the Internal Revenue Service under section 168(i)(1) (for further guidance, for example, see Rev. Proc. 87-56 (1987-2 CB 674), and § 601.601(d)(2)(ii)(b) of this chapter), except that any office building, any passenger train car, and any miscellaneous structure if such structure is not provided directly to, and is not unique to, a railroad are excluded from the definition of railroad-related property.

(8) Railroad-related services are services that are provided directly to, and are unique to, a railroad and that relate to railroad shipping, loading and unloading of railroad freight, or repairs of rail facilities (as defined in paragraph (b)(6) of this section) or railroad-related property (as defined in paragraph (b)(7) of this section). Examples of railroad-related services are the transport of freight by rail; the loading and unloading of freight transported by rail; railroad bridge services; railroad track construction; providing railroad track material or equipment; locomotive leasing or rental; maintenance of railroad's right-of-way (including vegetation control); piggyback trailer ramping; rail deramping services; and freight train cars repair services. Examples of services that are not railroad-related services are general business services, such as, accounting and bookkeeping, marketing, legal services; janitorial services; office building rental; banking services (including financing of railroad-related property); and purchasing of, or services performed on, property not described in paragraph (b)(7) of this section.

(9) Except as provided in paragraph (e)(2) of this section, railroad track is property described in STB property accounts 8 (ties), 9 (rails and other track material), and 11 (ballast) in 49 CFR part 1201, Subpart A. Double track is treated as multiple lines of railroad track, rather than as a single line of railroad track. Thus, one mile of single track is one mile, but one mile of double track is two miles.

(10) Form 8900. If Form 8900 is revised or renumbered, any reference in this section to that form shall be treated as a reference to the revised or renumbered form.

(11) Examples. The application of this paragraph (b) is illustrated by the following examples. In all examples, the taxpayers use a calendar taxable year, and are not members of a controlled group.

Example (1). A is a manufacturer that in 2006, transports its products by rail using the railroad tracks owned by B, a Class II railroad that owns 500 miles of railroad track within the United States on December 31, 2006. B properly assigns for purposes of section 45G 100 miles of eligible railroad track to A in 2006. A is an eligible taxpayer for 2006 with respect to the 100 miles of eligible railroad track.

Example (2). C is a bank that loans money to several Class III railroads. In 2006, C loans money to D, a Class III railroad, who in turn uses the loan proceeds to purchase track material. Because providing loans is not a service that is unique to a railroad, C is not providing railroad-related services and, thus, C is not an eligible taxpayer, even if D assigns miles of eligible railroad track to C for purposes of section 45G.

Example (3). E leases locomotives directly to Class I, Class II, and Class III railroads. In 2006, E leases locomotives to F, a Class II railroad that owns 200 miles of railroad track within the United States on December 31, 2006. F properly assigns for purposes of section 45G 200 miles of eligible railroad track to E. Because locomotives are property that is unique to a railroad, and E leases these locomotives directly to F in 2006, E is an eligible taxpayer for 2006 with respect to the 200 miles of eligible railroad track assigned to E by F.

Example (4). The facts are the same as in Example 3, except that E leases passenger trains, not locomotives, to F. Because passenger trains are not railroad-related property for purposes of section 45G, E is not an eligible taxpayer even if F assigns miles of eligible railroad track to E for purposes of section 45G.

(c) Determination of amount of railroad track maintenance credit for the taxable year. *(1) General amount.* Except as provided in paragraph (c)(2) of this section, for purposes of section 38, the RTMC determined under section 45G(a) for the taxable year is equal to 50 percent of the QRTME paid or incurred (as determined under paragraph (c)(3) of this section) by an eligible taxpayer during the taxable year.

(2) Limitation on the credit. (i) Eligible taxpayer is a Class II railroad or Class III railroad. If an eligible taxpayer is a Class II railroad or Class III railroad, the RTMC determined under paragraph (c)(1) of this section for the Class II

railroad or Class III railroad for any taxable year must not exceed $3,500 multiplied by the sum of—

(A) The number of miles of eligible railroad track owned or leased by the Class II railroad or Class III railroad, reduced by the number of miles of eligible railroad track assigned under paragraph (d) of this section by the Class II railroad or Class III railroad to another eligible taxpayer for that taxable year; and

(B) The number of miles of eligible railroad track owned or leased by another Class II railroad or Class III railroad that are assigned under paragraph (d) of this section to the Class II railroad or Class III railroad for the taxable year.

(ii) Eligible taxpayer is not a Class II railroad or Class III railroad. If an eligible taxpayer is not a Class II railroad or Class III railroad, the RTMC determined under paragraph (c)(1) of this section for the eligible taxpayer for any taxable year must not exceed $3,500 multiplied by the number of miles of eligible railroad track assigned under paragraph (d) of this section by a Class II railroad or Class III railroad to the eligible taxpayer for the taxable year.

(iii) No carryover of amount that exceeds limitation. Amounts that exceed the limitation under paragraph (c)(2)(i) of this section or paragraph (c)(2)(ii) of this section, may never be carried over to another taxable year.

(3) Determination of amount of QRTME paid or incurred. (i) In general. The term paid or incurred means, in the case of a taxpayer using an accrual method of accounting, a liability incurred (within the meaning of § 1.446-1(c)(1)(ii)). A liability may not be taken into account under section 45G and this section prior to the taxable year during which the liability is incurred. Any amount that an eligible taxpayer (assignee) pays a Class II railroad or Class III railroad (assignor) in exchange for an assignment of one or more miles of eligible railroad track under paragraph (d) of this section, is treated, for purposes of this section, as QRTME paid or incurred by the assignee, and not by the assignor, at the time and to the extent the assignor pays or incurs QRTME.

(ii) Effect of reimbursements received from persons other than a Class II or Class III railroad. The amount of QRTME treated as paid or incurred during the taxable year by an eligible taxpayer under paragraphs (b)(3)(ii) and (iii) of this section shall be reduced by any amount to which the eligible taxpayer is entitled to be reimbursed, directly or indirectly, from persons other than a Class II or Class III railroad.

(4) Examples. The application of this paragraph (c) is illustrated by the following examples. In all examples, the taxpayers use an accrual method of accounting and a calendar taxable year, and are not members of a controlled group.

Example (1). Computation of RTMC; section 45G credit limitation is not exceeded. (i) G is a Class II railroad that owns or has leased to it 1,000 miles of railroad track within the United States on December 31, 2006. H is a manufacturer that in 2006, transports its products by rail using the rail facilities of G. In 2006, for purposes of section 45G, G assigns 100 miles of eligible railroad track to H and does not make any other assignments of railroad track miles. H did not receive any other assignments of railroad track miles in 2006. During 2006, G incurred QRTME in the amount of $2.5 million and H incurred QRTME in the amount of $200,000.

(ii) For 2006, G determines the tentative amount of RTMC under paragraph (c)(1) of this section to be $1,250,000 (50% multiplied by $2,500,000 QRTME incurred by G during 2006). G further determines G's credit limitation under paragraph (c)(2)(i) of this section for 2006 to be $3,150,000 ($3,500 multiplied by 900 miles of eligible railroad track (1,000 miles owned by, or leased to, G on December 31, 2006, less 100 miles assigned by G to H in 2006)). Because G's tentative amount of RTMC does not exceed G's credit limitation amount for 2006, G may claim a RTMC for 2006 in the amount of $1,250,000.

(iii) For 2006, H determines the tentative amount of RTMC under paragraph (c)(1) of this section to be $100,000 (50% multiplied by $200,000 QRTME incurred by H during 2006). H further determines H's credit limitation under paragraph (c)(2)(ii) of this section for 2006 to be $350,000 ($3,500 multiplied by 100 miles of eligible railroad track assigned by G to H in 2006). Because H's tentative amount of RTMC does not exceed H's credit limitation amount for 2006, H may claim a RTMC in the amount of $100,000.

Example (2). Computation of RTMC; section 45G credit limitation is exceeded. (i) The facts are the same as in Example 1, except that G assigned for purposes of section 45G only 50 miles of railroad track to H in 2006 and, during 2006, H incurred QRTME in the amount of $400,000.

(ii) For 2006, G determines the tentative amount of RTMC under paragraph (c)(1) of this section to be $1,250,000 (50% multiplied by $2,500,000 QRTME incurred by G during 2006). G further determines G's credit limitation under paragraph (c)(2)(i) of this section for 2006 to be $3,325,000 ($3,500 multiplied by 950 miles of eligible railroad track (1,000 miles owned by, or leased to, G on December 31, 2006, less 50 miles assigned by G to H in 2006)). Because G's tentative amount of RTMC does not exceed G's credit limitation amount for 2006, G may claim a RTMC in the amount of $1,250,000.

(iii) For 2006, H determines the tentative amount of RTMC under paragraph (c)(1) of this section to be $200,000 (50% multiplied by $400,000 QRTME incurred by H during 2006). H further determines H's credit limitation under paragraph (c)(2)(ii) of this section for 2006 to be $175,000 ($3,500 multiplied by 50 miles of eligible railroad track assigned by G to H in 2006). Because H's tentative amount of RTMC exceeds H's credit limitation amount for 2006, H may claim a RTMC in the amount of $175,000 (the credit limitation amount). Under paragraph (c)(2)(iii) of this section, there is no carryover of the $25,000 (the tentative amount of $200,000 less the credit limitation amount of $175,000) that exceeds the limitation.

Example (3). Railroad track miles assigned for payment. (i) J is a Class II railroad that owns or has leased to it 1,000 miles of railroad track within the United States on December 31, 2006. K is a corporation that sells ties, ballast, and other track material to Class I, Class II, and Class III railroads. During 2006, K sold these items to J and J incurred QRTME in the amount of $1 million. Also, on December 6, 2006, J assigned for purposes of section 45G 150 miles of eligible railroad track to K and K paid J $800,000 for that assignment. K did not pay or incur any other QRTME during 2006.

(ii) For 2006, in accordance with paragraph (c)(3)(ii) of this section, J is treated as having incurred QRTME in the amount of $200,000 ($1 million QRTME actually incurred by J less the $800,000 paid by K to J for the assignment of the railroad track miles in 2006). For 2006, J determines the tentative amount of RTMC under paragraph (c)(1) of this section to be $100,000 (50% multiplied by $200,000 QRTME treated as incurred by J during 2006). J further determines J's credit limitation amount under paragraph (c)(2)(i) of this section for 2006 to be $2,975,000 ($3,500 multiplied by 850 miles of eligible railroad track (1,000 miles owned by, or leased to, J on December 31, 2006, less 150 miles assigned by J to K in 2006)). Because J's tentative amount of RTMC does not exceed J's credit limitation amount for 2006, J may claim a RTMC in the amount of $100,000.

(iii) For 2006, K is an eligible taxpayer because, during 2006, K provided railroad-related property to J and received an assignment of eligible railroad track miles from J. Under paragraph (c)(3)(ii) of this section, K is treated as having incurred QRTME in the amount of $800,000 (the amount paid by K to J for the assignment of the railroad track miles in 2006). For 2006, K determines the tentative amount of RTMC under paragraph (c)(1) of this section to be $400,000 (50% multiplied by $800,000 QRTME treated as incurred by K during 2006). K further determines K's credit limitation amount under paragraph (c)(2)(ii) of this section for 2006 to be $525,000 ($3,500 multiplied by 150 miles of eligible railroad track assigned by J in 2006). Because K's tentative amount of RTMC does not exceed K's credit limitation amount for 2006, K may claim a RTMC in the amount of $400,000.

(iv) The results in this Example 3 would be the same if K sold the ties, ballast, and other track material with a fair market value of $1 million to J for $200,000 in exchange for the assignment by J of 150 miles of eligible railroad track to K.

Example (4). Reimbursement of QRTME. (i) L is a Class III railroad that owns or has leased to it 500 miles of railroad track within the United States on December 31, 2006. M is a manufacturer that in 2006 transports its products by rail using the rail facilities of L. During 2006, L did not incur any QRTME. Also, in 2006, L assigned for purposes of section 45G 200 miles of eligible railroad track to M and agreed to reduce L's freight shipping rates to M by $250,000 in exchange for M upgrading these railroad track miles. Consequently, during 2006, M incurred QRTME of $500,000 to upgrade these 200 miles of railroad track and L reduced L's freight shipping rates for M by $250,000.

(ii) For 2006, M is an eligible taxpayer because, during 2006, M transported property using the rail facilities of L and received an assignment of eligible railroad track miles from L. The amount of QRTME paid or incurred by M during 2006 is $500,000 and is not reduced by the reimbursement of $250,000 by L to M because, under paragraph (c)(3)(ii) of this section, QRTME is not reduced by reimbursements from Class II or Class III railroads. For 2006, M determines the tentative amount of RTMC under paragraph (c)(1) of this section to be $250,000 (50% multiplied by $500,000 QRTME incurred by M during 2006). M further determines M's credit limitation amount under paragraph (c)(2)(ii) of this section for 2006 to be $700,000 ($3,500 multiplied by 200 miles of eligible railroad track assigned by L to M in 2006). Because M's tentative amount of RTMC does not exceed M's credit limitation amount for 2006, M may claim a RTMC in the amount of $250,000.

(d) Assignment of track miles. *(1) In general.* An assignment of any mile of eligible railroad track under this paragraph (d) is a designation by a Class II railroad or Class III railroad that is made solely for purposes of section 45G and this section of a specific number of miles of eligible railroad track as being assigned to another eligible taxpayer for a taxable year. A designation must be in writing and must include the name and taxpayer identification number of the assignee, and the information required under the rules of paragraph (d)(4)(iii)(B) of this section. A designation requires no transfer of legal title or other indicia of ownership of the eligible railroad track, and need not specify the location of any assigned mile of eligible railroad track. Further, an assigned mile of eligible railroad track need not correspond to any specific mile of eligible railroad track with respect to which the eligible taxpayer actually pays or incurs the QRTME.

(2) Assignment eligibility. Only a Class II railroad or Class III railroad may assign a mile of eligible railroad track. If a Class II railroad or Class III railroad assigns a mile of eligible railroad track to an eligible taxpayer, the assignee is not permitted to reassign any mile of eligible railroad track to another eligible taxpayer. The maximum number of miles of eligible railroad track that may be assigned by a Class II railroad or Class III railroad for any taxable year is its total miles of eligible railroad track less the miles of eligible railroad track that the Class II railroad or Class III railroad retains for itself in determining its RTMC for the taxable year.

(3) Effective date of assignment. If a Class II railroad or Class III railroad assigns a mile of eligible railroad track, the assignment is treated as being made by the Class II railroad or Class III railroad at the close of its taxable year in which the assignment was made. With respect to the assignee, the assignment of a mile of eligible railroad track is taken into account for the taxable year of the assignee that includes the date the assignment is treated as being made by the assignor Class II railroad or Class III railroad under this paragraph (d)(3).

(4) Assignment information statement. (i) In general. A taxpayer must file Form 8900, "Qualified Railroad Track Maintenance Credit," with its timely filed (including extensions) Federal income tax return for the taxable year for which the taxpayer assigns any mile of eligible railroad track, even if the taxpayer is not itself claiming the RTMC for that taxable year.

(ii) Assignor. Except as provided in paragraph (d)(4)(iv) of this section, a Class II railroad or Class III railroad (assignor) that assigns one or more miles of eligible railroad track during a taxable year to one or more eligible taxpayers must attach to the assignor's Form 8900 for that taxable year an information statement providing—

(A) The name and taxpayer identification number of each assignee;

(B) The total number of miles of the assignor's eligible railroad track;

(C) The number of miles of eligible railroad track assigned by the assignor to each assignee for the taxable year; and

(D) The total number of miles of eligible railroad track assigned by the assignor to all assignees for the taxable year.

(iii) Assignee. Except as provided in paragraph (d)(4)(iv) of this section, an eligible taxpayer (assignee) that has received an assignment of miles of eligible railroad track during its taxable year from a Class II railroad or Class III railroad, and that claims the RTMC for that taxable year, must attach to the assignee's Form 8900 for that taxable year a statement—

(A) Providing the total number of miles of eligible railroad track assigned to the assignee for the assignee's taxable year; and

(B) Attesting that the assignee has in writing, and has retained as part of the assignee's records for purposes of § 1.6001-1(a), the following information from each assignor:

(1) The name and taxpayer identification number of each assignor.

(2) The date of each assignment made by each assignor (as determined under paragraph (d)(3) of this section) to the assignee;

(3) The number of miles of eligible railroad track assigned by each assignor to the assignee for the assignee's taxable year.

(iv) Special rules for returns filed prior to November 9, 2007. If an eligible taxpayer's Federal income tax return for a taxable year beginning after December 31, 2004, and ending before November 9, 2007, was filed before December 13, 2007, and the eligible taxpayer is not filing an amended Federal income tax return for that taxable year pursuant to paragraph (g)(2) of this section before the eligible taxpayer's next filed original Federal income tax return, and the eligible taxpayer wants to apply paragraph (g)(2) of this section but did not include with that return the information specified in paragraph (d)(4)(ii) or (iii) of this section, as applicable, the eligible taxpayer must attach a statement containing the information specified in paragraph (d)(4)(ii) or (iii) of this section, as applicable, to either—

(A) The eligible taxpayer's next filed original Federal income tax return; or

(B) The eligible taxpayer's amended Federal income tax return that is filed pursuant to paragraph (g)(2) of this section, provided that amended Federal income tax return is filed by the eligible taxpayer before its next filed original Federal income tax return.

(5) Special rules. (i) Effect of subsequent dispositions of eligible railroad track during the assignment year. If a Class II railroad or Class III railroad assigns one or more miles of eligible railroad track that it owned or leased as of the actual date of the assignment, but does not own or lease any eligible railroad track at the close of the taxable year in which the assignment is made by the Class II railroad or Class III railroad, the assignment is not valid for that taxable year for purposes of section 45G and this section.

(ii) Effect of multiple assignments of eligible railroad track miles during the same taxable year. If a Class II railroad or Class III railroad assigns more miles of eligible railroad track than it owned or leased as of the close of the taxable year in which the assignment is made by the Class II railroad or Class III railroad, the assignment is valid for purposes of section 45G and this section only with respect to the name of the assignee and the number of miles listed by the assignor Class II railroad or Class III railroad on the statement required under paragraph (d)(4)(ii) of this section and only to the extent of the maximum miles of eligible railroad track that may be assigned by the assignor Class II railroad or Class III railroad as determined under paragraph (d)(2) of this section. If the total number of miles on this statement exceeds the maximum miles of eligible railroad track that may be assigned by the assignor Class II railroad or Class III railroad (as determined under paragraph (d)(2) of this section), the total number of miles on the statement shall be reduced by the excess amount of miles. This reduction is allocated among each assignee listed on the statement in proportion to the total number of miles listed on the statement for that assignee.

(6) Examples. The application of this paragraph (d) is illustrated by the following examples. In none of the examples are the taxpayers members of a controlled group:

Example (1). Assignor and assignee have the same taxable year. (i) N, a calendar year taxpayer, is a Class II railroad that owns 500 miles of railroad track within the United States on December 31, 2006. O, a calendar year taxpayer, is not a railroad, but is a taxpayer that provides railroad-related property to N during 2006. On November 7, 2006, N assigns for purposes of section 45G 300 miles of eligible railroad track to O. O receives no other assignment of eligible railroad track in 2006. O pays or incurs QRTME in the amount of $100,000 in November 2006, and $50,000 in February 2007. N and O each file Form 8900 with their timely filed Federal income tax returns for 2006 and attach the statement required by paragraph (d)(4)(ii) and (iii), respectively, of this section reporting the assignment of the 300 miles of eligible railroad track to O.

(ii) The assignment of the 300 miles of eligible railroad track made by N to O on November 7, 2006, is treated as made on December 31, 2006 (at the close of the N's taxable year). Consequently, the assignment is taken into account by O for O's taxable year ending on December 31, 2006. For 2006, O is an eligible taxpayer because, during 2006, O provides railroad-related property to N and receives an assignment of 300 eligible railroad track miles from N. For 2006, O determines the tentative amount of RTMC under paragraph (c)(1) of this section to be $50,000 (50% multiplied by $100,000 QRTME paid or incurred by O during 2006). O further determines the credit limitation amount under paragraph (c)(2)(i) of this section for 2006 to be $1,050,000 ($3,500 multiplied by 300 miles of eligible railroad track assigned by N to O on December 31, 2006). Because O's tentative amount of RTMC does not exceed O's credit limitation amount for 2006, O may claim a RMTC for 2006 in the amount of $50,000.

Example (2). Assignor and assignee have different taxable years. (i) The facts are the same as in Example 1, except that O's taxable year ends on March 31.

(ii) The assignment of the 300 miles of eligible railroad track made by N to O on November 7, 2006, is treated as made on December 31, 2006. As a result, the assignment is taken into account by O for O's taxable year ending on March 31, 2007. Thus, for the taxable year ending on March 31, 2007, O determines the tentative amount of RMTC under paragraph (c)(1) of this section to be $75,000 (50% multiplied by $150,000 QRTME incurred by O during its taxable year ending March 31, 2007). Because O's tentative amount of RTMC does not exceed O's credit limitation amount for the taxable year ending March 31, 2007, O may claim a RMTC for the taxable year ending March 31, 2007, in the amount of $75,000.

Example (3). Assignment location differs from QRTME location. (i) P, a calendar-year taxpayer, is a Class III railroad that owns or has leased to it 200 miles of railroad track within the United States on December 31, 2006. P owns 50 miles of this railroad track and leases 150 miles of this railroad track from Q, a Class I railroad. On February 8, 2006, P assigns for purposes of section 45G 50 miles of eligible railroad track to R. R is not a railroad, but is a taxpayer that ships products using the 50 miles of eligible railroad track owned by P, and R paid $100,000 in 2006 to P to enable P to upgrade these 50 miles of eligible railroad track. In March 2006, P also assigns for purposes of section 45G 150 miles of eligible railroad track to S. S is not a railroad, but is a taxpayer that provides railroad-related property to P, and S paid $400,000 to P to enable P to upgrade P's 200 miles of eligible railroad track. For 2006, P pays or incurs QRTME in the amount of $500,000 to upgrade the 150 miles of eligible railroad track that it leases from Q and pays or incurs no QRTME on the 50 miles of eligible railroad track that it owns. For 2006, P receives no other assignment of eligible railroad track miles and did not retain any eligible railroad track miles for itself. Also, R and S do not pay or incur any other amounts that would qualify as QRTME during 2006. P, R, and S each file Form 8900 with their timely filed Federal income tax returns for 2006 and attach the statement required by paragraph (d)(4) (ii) or (iii) of this section, whichever applies, reporting the assignment of eligible railroad track by P to R or S in 2006.

(ii) For 2006, in accordance with paragraph (c)(3)(ii) of this section, P is treated as having incurred QRTME in the amount of $0 ($500,000 QRTME actually incurred by P less the $100,000 paid by R to P for the assignment of the 50 miles of eligible railroad track and the $400,000 paid by S to P for the assignment of the 150 miles of eligible railroad track). Further, P assigned all of its eligible railroad track miles to R and S for 2006. Accordingly, for 2006, P may not claim any RTMC.

(iii) For 2006, R is an eligible taxpayer because, during 2006, R ships property using the rail facilities of P and receives an assignment of 50 eligible railroad track miles from P. In accordance with paragraph (c)(3)(ii) of this section, R is treated as having incurred QRTME in the amount of $100,000 (the amount paid by R to P for the assignment of the eligible railroad track miles in 2006) even though no work was performed on the 50 miles of eligible railroad track that was assigned by P to R. For 2006, R determines the tentative amount of RTMC under paragraph (c)(1) of this section to be $50,000 (50% multiplied by $100,000 QRTME treated as incurred by R during 2006). R further determines the credit limitation amount under paragraph (c)(2)(ii) of this section to be $175,000 ($3,500 multiplied by 50 miles of eligible railroad track assigned by P to R in 2006). Because R's tentative amount of RTMC does not exceed R's credit limitation amount for 2006, R may claim a RTMC for 2006 in the amount of $50,000.

(iv) For 2006, S is an eligible taxpayer because, during 2006, S provides railroad-related property to P and receives an assignment of 150 eligible railroad track miles from P. In accordance with paragraph (c)(3)(ii) of this section, S is treated as having incurred QRTME in the amount of $400,000 (amount paid by S to P for the assignment of the eligible railroad track miles in 2006). For 2006, S determines the tentative amount of RTMC under paragraph (c)(1) of this section to be $200,000 (50% multiplied by $400,000 QRTME treated as incurred by S during 2006). S further determines the credit limitation amount under paragraph (c)(2)(ii) of this section to be $525,000 ($3,500 multiplied by 150 miles of eligible railroad track assigned by P to S in 2006). Because S's tentative amount of RTMC does not exceed S's credit limitation amount for 2006, S may claim a RTMC for 2006 in the amount of $200,000.

Example (4). Multiple assignments of track miles. (i) T, a calendar-year taxpayer, is a Class III railroad that owns or has leased to it 200 miles of railroad track within the United States on December 31, 2006. T owns 75 miles of this railroad track and leases 125 miles of this railroad track from U, a Class I railroad. V and W are not railroads, but are both taxpayers that provide railroad-related services to T during 2006. On January 15, 2006, T assigns for purposes of section 45G 200 miles of eligible railroad track to V. V agrees to incur, in 2006, $1.4 million of QRTME to upgrade a portion of/segment of these 200 miles of eligible railroad track. Due to unexpected financial difficulties, V only incurs $250,000 of QRTME during 2006 and on May 15, 2006, T learns that V is unable to incur the remainder of the QRTME. On June 15, 2006, T assigns for purposes of section 45G the 200 miles of railroad track to W. In 2006, W incurs $1,100,000 of QRTME to upgrade a portion of/segment of the railroad track. For 2006, T receives no other assignment of eligible railroad track miles and did not retain any eligible railroad track miles for itself. V and W do not receive any other assignments of miles of eligible railroad track miles from a Class II railroad or Class III railroad during 2006. T and W each file Form 8900 with their timely filed Federal income tax returns for 2006, and attach the statement required by paragraph (d)(4) (ii) and (iii), respectively, of this section, reporting the assignment of 200 miles of eligible railroad track to W.

(ii) Because T did not retain any miles of eligible railroad track for itself for 2006, the maximum miles of eligible railroad track that may be assigned by T for 2006 is 200 miles pursuant to paragraph (d)(2) of this section. On the statement required by paragraph (d)(4)(ii) of this section, T assigned a total of 200 miles of eligible railroad track to W. Consequently, because T did not list V as an assignee on T's statement required by paragraph (d)(4)(ii) of this section, V did not receive an assignment of eligible railroad track miles from T during 2006 and V is not an eligible taxpayer for 2006. Thus, for 2006, V may not claim any RTMC even though V incurred QRTME in the amount of $250,000.

(iii) For 2006, W is an eligible taxpayer because, during 2006, W provides railroad-related services to T and receives an assignment of 200 eligible railroad track miles from T. W determines the tentative amount of RTMC under paragraph (c)(1) of this section to be $550,000 (50% multiplied by $1,100,000 QRTME incurred by W during 2006). W further determines the credit limitation amount under paragraph (c)(2)(ii) of this section to be $700,000 ($3,500 multiplied by the 200 miles of eligible railroad track assigned by T to W in 2006). Because W's tentative amount of RTMC does not exceed W's credit limitation amount for 2006, W may claim a RTMC for 2006 in the amount of $550,000.

Example (5). Multiple assignments of track miles. (i) Same facts as in Example 4, except T, to its Form 8900 for 2006, attaches the statement required by paragraph (d)(4)(ii) of this section assigning 200 miles of eligible railroad track to W and 200 miles of eligible railroad track to V.

(ii) Because T did not retain any miles of eligible railroad track for itself for 2006, the maximum miles of eligible railroad track that may be assigned by T for 2006 is 200 miles pursuant to paragraph (d)(2) of this section. However, on the statement required by paragraph (d)(4)(ii) of this section, T assigned a total of 400 miles of eligible railroad track (200 miles to W and 200 miles to V). Consequently, the 400 miles of eligible railroad track on this statement must be reduced to the 200 maximum miles of eligible railroad track available for assignment for 2006. Because the statement reports 200 miles of eligible railroad track assigned to each W and V, the reduction of 200 miles (400 total miles of eligible railroad track on the statement less 200 maximum miles of eligible railroad track available for assignment) is allocated pro-rata between W and V and, therefore, 100 miles each to W and V. Thus, pursuant to paragraph (d)(5)(ii) of this section, the number of miles of eligible railroad track assigned by T to W and V for 2006 is 100 miles each.

(iii) For 2006, V is an eligible taxpayer because, during 2006, V provides railroad-related services to T and receives an assignment of 100 eligible railroad track miles from T. V determines the tentative amount of RTMC under paragraph (c)(1) of this section to be $125,000 (50% multiplied by $250,000 QRTME incurred by V during 2006). V further determines the credit limitation amount under paragraph (c)(2)(ii) of this section to be $350,000 ($3,500 multiplied by the 100 miles of eligible railroad track assigned by T to V in 2006). Because V's tentative amount of RTMC does not exceed W's credit limitation amount for 2006, V may claim a RTMC for 2006 in the amount of $125,000.

(iv) For 2006, W is an eligible taxpayer because, during 2006, W provides railroad-related services to T and receives an assignment of 100 eligible railroad track miles from T. W determines the tentative amount of RTMC under paragraph (c)(1) of this section to be $550,000 (50% multiplied by $1,100,000 QRTME incurred by W during 2006). W further determines the credit limitation amount under paragraph (c)(2)(ii) of this section to be $350,000 ($3,500 multiplied by the 100 miles of eligible railroad track assigned by T to W in 2006). Because W's tentative amount of RTMC exceeds W's credit limitation amount for 2006, W may claim a RTMC for 2006 in the amount of $350,000 (the credit limitation). There is no carryover of the amount of $200,000 (the tentative amount of $550,000 less the credit limitation amount of $350,000).

(e) Adjustments to basis. *(1) In general.* All or some of the QRTME paid or incurred by an eligible taxpayer during the taxable year may be required to be capitalized under section 263(a) as a tangible asset or as an intangible asset. See, for example, § 1.263(a)-4(d)(8), which requires capitalization of amounts paid or incurred by a taxpayer to produce or improve real property owned by another (except to the extent the taxpayer is selling services at fair market value to produce or improve the real property) if the real property can reasonably be expected to produce significant economic benefits for the taxpayer. The basis of the tangible asset or intangible asset includes the capitalized amount of the QRTME.

(2) Basis adjustment made to railroad track. An eligible taxpayer must reduce the adjusted basis of any railroad track with respect to which the eligible taxpayer claims the RTMC. For purposes of section 45G(e)(3) and this paragraph (e)(2), the adjusted basis of any railroad track with respect to which the eligible taxpayer claims the RTMC is limited to the amount of QRTME, if any, that is required to be capitalized into the qualifying railroad structure or an intangible asset. The adjusted basis of the railroad track is reduced by the amount of the RTMC allowable (as determined under paragraph (c) of this section) by the eligible taxpayer for the taxable year, but not below zero. This reduction is taken into account at the time the QRTME is paid or incurred by an eligible taxpayer and before the depreciation deduction with respect to such railroad track is determined for the taxable year for which the RTMC is allowable. If all or some of the QRTME paid or incurred by an eligible taxpayer during the taxable year is capitalized under section 263(a) to more than one asset, whether tangible or intangible (for example, railroad track and bridges), the reduction to the basis of these assets under this paragraph (e)(2) is allocated among each of the assets subject to the reduction in proportion to the unadjusted basis of each asset at the time the QRTME is paid or incurred during that taxable year.

(3) Examples. The application of this paragraph (e) is illustrated by the following examples. In each example, all taxpayers use a calendar taxable year, and no taxpayers are members of a controlled group.

Example (1). (i) X is a Class II railroad that owns 500 miles of railroad track within the United States on December 31, 2006. During 2006, X incurs $1 million of QRTME for maintaining this railroad track. X uses the track maintenance allowance method for track structure expenditures (for further guidance, see Rev. Proc. 2002-65 (2002-2 CB 700) and § 601.601(d)(2)(ii)(b) of this chapter). Assume all of the $1 million QRTME is track structure expenditures and none of it was expended for new track structure.

(ii) For 2006, X determines the tentative amount of RTMC under paragraph (c)(1) of this section to be $500,000 (50% multiplied by $1 million QRTME incurred by X during 2006). X further determines the credit limitation amount under paragraph (c)(2)(i) of this section for 2006 to be $1,750,000 ($3,500 multiplied by 500 miles of eligible railroad track). Because X's tentative amount of RTMC does not exceed X's credit limitation amount for 2006, X may claim a RTMC for 2006 in the amount of $500,000.

(iii) Of the $1 million QRTME incurred by X during 2006, X determines under the track maintenance allowance method that $750,000 is the track maintenance allowance under section 162 and $250,000 is the capitalized amount for the track structure. In accordance with paragraph (e)(2) of this section, X reduces the capitalized amount of $250,000 by the RTMC of $500,000 claimed by X for 2006, but not below zero. Thus, the capitalized amount of $250,000 is reduced to zero. X also deducts under section 162 a track maintenance allowance of $750,000 on its 2006 Federal income tax return.

Example (2). (i) Y is a Class II railroad that owns or has leased to it 500 miles of eligible railroad track within the United States on December 31, 2006. Z is not a railroad, but is a taxpayer that, in 2006, transports its products using the rail facilities of Y. In 2006, Y assigns for purposes of section 45G 300 miles of eligible railroad track to Z. Z does not receive any other assignments of eligible railroad track miles in 2006. During 2006, Z incurs QRTME in the amount of $1 million, and Y does not incur any QRTME. Y and Z each file Form 8900 with their timely filed Federal income tax returns for 2006 and attach the statement required by paragraph (d)(4)(ii) and (iii), respectively, of this section reporting the assignment of the 300 miles of eligible railroad track to Z.

(ii) For 2006, Z determines the tentative amount of RTMC under paragraph (c)(1) of this section to be $500,000 (50% multiplied by $1 million QRTME incurred by Z during 2006). Z further determines the credit limitation amount under paragraph (c)(2)(ii) of this section for 2006 to be $1,050,000 ($3,500 multiplied by 300 miles of eligible railroad track assigned by Y to Z in 2006). Because Z's tentative amount of RTMC does not exceed Z's credit limitation amount for 2006, Z may claim a RTMC for 2006 in the amount of $500,000.

(iii) For 2006, Z also must determine the portion of the $1 million QRTME that Z incurs that is required to be capitalized under section 263(a), and the portion that is a section 162 expense. Because Z is not a Class II railroad or Class III railroad, Z cannot use the track maintenance allowance method. Assume that all of the QRTME constitutes an intangible asset under § 1.263(a)-4(d)(8) and, therefore, is required to be capitalized by Z under section 263(a) as an intangible asset. In accordance with paragraph (e)(2) of this section, Z reduces the capitalized amount of $1 million by the RTMC of $500,000 claimed by Z for 2006. Thus, the capitalized amount of $1 million for the intangible asset is reduced to $500,000. Further, pursuant to § 1.167(a)-3(b)(1)(iv), Z may treat this intangible asset with an adjusted basis of $500,000 as having a useful life of 25 years for purposes of the depreciation allowance under section 167(a).

(f) Controlled groups. *(1) In general.* Pursuant to section 45G(e)(2), if an eligible taxpayer is a member of a controlled group of corporations, rules similar to the rules in

§ 1.41-6T apply for determining the amount of the RTMC under section 45G(a) and this section. To determine the amount of RTMC (if any) allowable to a trade or business that at the end of its taxable year is a member of a controlled group, a taxpayer must—

(i) Compute the group credit in the manner described in paragraph (f)(3) of this section; and

(ii) Allocate the group credit among the members of the group in the manner described in paragraph (f)(4) of this section.

(2) Definitions. For purposes of section 45G(e)(2) and paragraph (f) of this section—

(i) A trade or business is a sole proprietorship, a partnership, a trust, an estate, or a corporation that is carrying on a trade or business (within the meaning of section 162). Any corporation that is a member of a commonly controlled group shall be deemed to be carrying on a trade or business if any other member of that group is carrying on any trade or business;

(ii) Group and controlled group means a controlled group of corporations, as defined in section 41(f)(5), or a group of trades or businesses under common control. For rules for determining whether trades or businesses are under common control, see § 1.52-1(b) through (g);

(iii) Group credit means the RTMC (if any) allowable to a controlled group;

(iv) Consolidated group has the meaning set forth in § 1.1502-1(h); and

(v) Credit year means the taxable year for which the member is computing the RTMC.

(3) Computation of the group credit. All members of a controlled group are treated as a single taxpayer for purposes of computing the RTMC. The group credit is computed by applying all of the section 45G computational rules (including the rules set forth in this section) on an aggregate basis.

(4) Allocation of the group credit. (i) In general. (A) To the extent the group credit (if any) computed under paragraph (f)(3) of this section does not exceed the sum of the stand-alone entity credits of all of the members of a controlled group, computed under paragraph (f)(4)(ii) of this section, such group credit shall be allocated among the members of the controlled group in proportion to the stand-alone entity credits of the members of the controlled group, computed under paragraph (f)(4)(ii) of this section:

$$\text{group credit that does not exceed sum of all the members' stand-along entity credits} \times \frac{\text{member's stand-along entity credits}}{\text{Sum of all the members' standalone entity credits.}}$$

(B) To the extent that the group credit (if any) computed under paragraph (f)(3) of this section exceeds the sum of the stand-alone entity credits of all of the members of the controlled group, computed under paragraph (f)(4)(ii) of this section, such excess shall be allocated among the members of a controlled group in proportion to the QRTMEs of the members of the controlled group:

$$\text{(group credit less the sum of all the members' stand-alone entity credits)} \times \frac{\text{QRTMEs of members that are eligble taxpayers}}{\text{sum of QRTMEs of all members that are eligible taxpayers.}}$$

(ii) Stand-alone entity credit. The term stand-alone entity credit means the RTMC (if any) that would be allowable to a member of a controlled group if the credit were computed as if section 45G(e)(2) did not apply, except that the member must apply the rules provided in paragraphs (f)(5) (relating to consolidated groups) and (f)(8) (relating to intra-group transactions) of this section.

(5) Special rules for consolidated groups. (i) In general. For purposes of applying paragraph (f)(4) of this section, a consolidated group whose members are members of a controlled group is treated as a single member of the controlled group and a single stand-alone entity credit is computed for the consolidated group.

(ii) Special rule for allocation of group credit among consolidated group members. The portion of the group credit that is allocated to a consolidated group is allocated to the members of the consolidated group in accordance with the principles of paragraph (f)(4) of this section. However, for this purpose, the stand-alone entity credit of a member of a consolidated group is computed without regard to section 45G(e)(2).

(6) Tax accounting periods used. (i) In general. The credit allowable to a member of a controlled group is that member's share of the group credit computed as of the end of that member's taxable year. In computing the group credit for a group whose members have different taxable years, a member generally should treat the taxable year of another member that ends with or within the credit year of the computing member as the credit year of that other member. For example, Q, R, and S are members of a controlled group of corporations. Both Q and R are calendar year taxpayers. S files a return using a fiscal year ending June 30. For purposes of computing the group credit at the end of Q's and R's taxable year on December 31, S's fiscal year ending June 30, which ends within Q's and R's taxable year, is treated as S's credit year.

(ii) Special rule when timing of QRTME is manipulated. If the timing of QRTME by members using different tax accounting periods is manipulated to generate a credit in excess of the amount that would be allowable if all members of the group used the same tax accounting period, then the appropriate Internal Revenue Service official in the operating division that has examination jurisdiction of the return may require each member of the group to calculate the credit in the current taxable year and all future years as if all members of the group had the same taxable year and base period as the computing member.

(7) Membership during taxable year in more than one group. A trade or business may be a member of only one group for a taxable year. If, without application of this paragraph (f)(7), a business would be a member of more than one group at the end of its taxable year, the business shall be treated as a member of the group in which it was included for its preceding taxable year. If the business was not included for its preceding taxable year in any group in which it could be included as of the end of its taxable year, the business shall designate in its timely filed (including extensions) federal income tax return for the taxable year the

group in which it is being included. If the business does not so designate, then the appropriate Internal Revenue Service official in the operating division that has examination jurisdiction of the return will determine the group in which the business is to be included. If the Federal income tax return for a taxable year beginning after December 31, 2004, and ending before November 9, 2007, was filed before December 13, 2007, and the business wants to apply paragraph (g)(2) of this section but did not designate its group membership in that return, the business must designate its group membership for that year either—

(i) In its next filed original Federal income tax return; or

(ii) In its amended Federal income tax return that is filed pursuant to paragraph (g)(2) of this section, provided that amended Federal income tax return is filed by the business before its next filed original Federal income tax return.

(8) Intra-group transactions. (i) In general. Because all members of a group under common control are treated as a single taxpayer for purposes of determining the RTMC, transfers between members of the group are generally disregarded.

(ii) Payment for QRTME. Amounts paid or incurred by the owner (or lessor) of eligible railroad track to another member of the group for QRTME shall be taken into account as QRTME by the owner (or lessor) of the eligible railroad track for purposes of section 45G only to the extent of the lesser of—

(A) The amount paid or incurred to the other member; or

(B) The amount that would have been considered paid or incurred by the other member for the QRTME, if the QRTME was not reimbursed by the owner (or lessor) of the eligible railroad track.

(g) Effective/applicability date. *(1) In general.* Except as provided in paragraphs (g)(2) and (g)(3) of this section, this section applies to taxable years ending on or after September 7, 2006.

(2) Taxable years ending before September 7, 2006. A taxpayer may apply this section to taxable years beginning after December 31, 2004, and ending before September 7, 2006, provided that the taxpayer applies all provisions in this section to the taxable year.

(3) Special rules for returns filed prior to November 9, 2007. If a taxpayer's Federal income tax return for a taxable year beginning after December 31, 2004, and ending before November 9, 2007, was filed before December 13, 2007, and the taxpayer is not filing an amended Federal income tax return for that taxable year pursuant to paragraph (g)(2) of this section before the taxpayer's next filed original Federal income tax return, see paragraphs (d)(4)(iv) and (f)(7) of this section for the statements that must be attached to the taxpayer's next filed original Federal income tax return.

T.D. 9365, 11/9/2007.

§ 1.46-1 Determination of amount.

Caution: The Treasury has not yet amended Reg § 1.46-1 to reflect changes made by P.L. 104-188, P.L. 101-508, P.L. 101-239, P.L. 100-647.

(a) Effective dates. *(1) In general.* This section is effective for taxable years beginning after December 31, 1975. However, transitional rules under paragraph (g) of this section are effective for certain earlier taxable years.

(2) Acts covered. This section reflects changes made by the following Acts of Congress:

Act and Section

Tax Reduction Act of 1975, section 301.

Tax Reform Act of 1976, section 802, 1701, 1703.

Revenue Act of 1978, section 311, 312, 315.

Energy Tax Act of 1978, section 301.

Economic Recovery Tax Act of 1981, section 212.

Technical Corrections Act of 1982, section 102(f).

Tax Reform Act of 1986, section 251.

(3) Prior regulations. For taxable years beginning before January 1, 1976, see 26 CFR § 1.46-1 (Rev. as of April 1, 1979). Those regulations do not reflect changes made by Pub. L. 89-384, Pub. L. 89-389, and Pub. L. 91-172.

(b) General rule. The amount of investment credit (credit) allowed by section 38 for the taxable year is the portion of credit available under section 46(a)(1) that does not exceed the limitation based on tax under section 46(a)(3).

(c) Credit available. The credit available for the taxable year is the sum of—

(1) Unused credit carried over from prior taxable years under section 46(b) (carryovers).

(2) Amount of credit determined under section 46(a)(2) for the taxable year (credit earned), and

(3) Unused credit carried back from succeeding taxable years under section 46(b) (carrybacks).

(d) Credit earned. The credit earned for the taxable year is the sum of the following percentages of qualified investment (as determined under section 46(c) and (d))—

(1) The regular percentage (as determined under section 46),

(2) For energy property, the energy percentage (as determined under section 46), and

(3) For the portion of the basis of a qualified rehabilitated building (as defined in § 1.48-12(b)) that is attributable to qualified rehabilitation expenditures (as defined in § 1.48-12(c)), the rehabilitation percentage (as determined under section 46(b)(4)).

(e) Designation of credits. The credit available for the taxable year is designated as follows:

(1) The credit attributable to the regular percentage is the "regular credit".

(2) The credit attributable to the ESOP percentage is the "ESOP credit".

(3) The credit attributable to the energy percentage for energy property other than solar or wind is the "nonrefundable energy credit".

(4) The credit attributable to the energy percentage for solar or wind energy property is the "refundable energy credit".

(5) The credit attributable to the rehabilitation percentage for qualified rehabilitation expenditures is the rehabilitation investment credit.

(f) Special rules for certain energy property. Energy property is defined in section 48(l). Under section 46(a)(2)(D), energy property that is section 38 property solely by reason of section 48(l)(1) qualifies only for the energy credit. Other energy property qualifies for both the regular credit (and, if applicable, the ESOP credit) and the energy credit. For limitation on the energy percentage for property financed by industrial development bonds, see section 48(l)(11).

(g) Transitional rule for regular and ESOP credit. *(1) In general.* Although section 46(a)(2) was amended by section 301(a)(1) of the Energy Tax Act of 1977 to eliminate the transitional rules under section 46(a)(2)(D), those rules still apply in certain instances. Section 46(a)(2)(D) was added by section 301(a) of the Tax Reduction Act of 1975 and amended by section 802(a) of the Tax Reform Act of 1976.

(2) Regular credit. Under section 46(a)(2)(D), the regular credit is 10 percent and applies for the following property:

(i) Property to which section 46(d) does not apply, the construction, reconstruction, or erection of which is completed by the taxpayer after January 21, 1975, but only to the extent of basis attributable to construction, reconstruction, or erection after that date.

(ii) Property to which section 46(d) does not apply, acquired by the taxpayer after January 21, 1975.

(iii) Qualified progress expenditures (as defined in section 46(d)) made after January 21, 1975.

(3) ESOP credit. See section 48(m) for transitional rules limiting the period for which the ESOP percentage under section 46(a)(2)(E) applies. For prior statutes, see section 46(a)(2)(B) and (D), as added by section 301 of the Tax Reduction Act of 1975 and amended by section 802 of the Tax Reform Act of 1976.

(4) Cross reference. (i) The principles of § 1.48-2(b) and (c) apply in determining the portion of basis attributable to construction, reconstruction, or erection after January 21, 1975, and in determining the time when property is acquired.

(ii) Section 311 of the Revenue Act of 1978 made the 10 percent regular credit permanent.

(5) Seven percent credit. To the extent that, under paragraph (g)(1) of this section, the 10 percent does not apply, the regular credit, in general, is 7 percent. For a special limitation on qualified investment for public utility property (other than energy property), see section 46(c)(3)(A).

(6) Qualified progress expenditures. For progress expenditure property that is constructed, reconstructed, or erected by the taxpayer within the meaning of § 1.48-2(b), the ten-percent credit applies in the year the property is placed in service to the portion of the qualified investment that remains after reduction for qualified progress expenditures under section 46(c)(4), but only to the extent that the remaining qualified investment is attributable to construction, reconstruction, or erection after January 21, 1975. For progress expenditure property that is acquired by the taxpayer (within the meaning of § 1.48-2(b)) after January 21, 1975, and placed in service after that date, the ten-percent credit applies in the year the property is placed in service to the entire portion of qualified investment that remains after reduction for qualified progress expenditures.

(h) Tax liability limitation. *(1) In general.* Section 46(a)(3) provides a tax liability limitation on the amount of credit allowed by section 38 (other than the refundable energy credit) for any taxable year. See section 46(a)(10)(C)(i). Tax liability is defined in paragraph (j) of this section. The excess of available credit over the applicable tax liability limitation for the year is an unused credit which may be carried forward or carried back under section 46(b).

(2) Regular and ESOP tax liability limitation. In general, the tax liability limitation for the regular and ESOP credits is the portion of tax liability that does not exceed $25,000 plus a percentage of the excess, as determined under section 46(a)(3)(B).

(3) Nonrefundable energy credit tax liability limitation. (i) For nonrefundable energy credit carrybacks to a taxable year ending before October 1, 1978, the tax liability limitation is the portion of tax liability that does not exceed $25,000 plus a percentage of the excess, as determined under section 46(a)(3)(B).

(ii) For a taxable year ending after September 30, 1978, the tax liability limitation for available nonrefundable energy credit is 100 percent of the year's tax liability.

(4) Alternative limitations. Alternative limitations apply for certain utilities, railroads, and airlines in determining the regular tax liability limitation and, for nonrefundable energy credit carrybacks to taxable years ending before October 1, 1978, the nonrefundable energy credit tax liability limitation. These alternative limitations do not apply in determining the energy tax liability limitation for a taxable year ending after October 1, 1978. The provisions listed below set forth the alternative limitations:

Code section, type, and years applicable

46(a)(6),[1] Utilities, Taxable years ending in 1975–1978.

46(a)(7),[2] Utilities, Taxable year ending in 1979.

46(a)(8), Railroads and Airlines, Taxable year ending in 1979 or 1980.

46(a)(8),[3] Railroads, Taxable years ending in 1977 or 1978.

46(a)(9),[3] Airlines, Taxable years ending in 1977 or 1978.[123]

(i) [Reserved]

(j) Tax liability. *(1) In general.* "Tax liability" for purposes of the regular and ESOP credit and carrybacks of nonrefundable energy credit to a taxable year ending before October 1, 1978, means the liability for tax as defined in section 46(a)(4). For ordering of regular, ESOP, and nonrefundable energy credits, see paragraph (m) of this section. In addition to taxes excluded under section 46(a)(4), tax liability does not include tax resulting from recapture of credit under section 47 and the alternative minimum tax imposed by section 55. See sections 47(c) and 55(c)(1).

(2) Certain nonrefundable energy credit. For a taxable year ending after September 30, 1978, "tax liability" for purposes of the nonrefundable energy credit is liability for tax, as defined in section 46(a)(4) and paragraph (j)(1) of this section, reduced by the regular and ESOP credit allowed for the taxable year. Thus, carrybacks of regular or ESOP credit to a taxable year may displace nonrefundable energy carryovers or credit earned taken into account in that year. However, carrybacks of regular, ESOP, or nonrefundable energy credit do not affect refundable energy credit which is treated as an overpayment of tax under section 6401(b). See paragraph (k) of this section.

(k) Special rule for refundable energy credit. The amount of the refundable energy credit is determined under the rules of section 46 (other than section 46(a)(3)). However, to permit the refund, the refundable energy credit for

1. Section 46(a)(6) was added by section 301(b)(2) of the Tax Reduction Act of 1975 and redesignated as section 46(a)(7) by section 302(a)(1) of the Tax Reform Act of 1976.

2. Section 46(a)(7) was amended by section 312(b)(1) of the Revenue Act of 1978.

3. These provisions were repealed by section 312(b)(2) of the Revenue Act of 1978.

purposes of the Internal Revenue Code (other than section 38, part IVB, and chapter 63 of the Code) is treated as allowed by section 39 and not by section 38. The refundable credit is not applied against tax liability for purposes of determining the tax liability limitation for other investment credits. Rather, it is treated as an overpayment of tax under section 6401(b).

(l) FIFO rule. If the credit available for a taxable year is not allowed in full because of the tax liability limitation, special rules determine the order in which credits are applied. Under the first-in-first-out rule of section 46(a)(1) (FIFO), carryovers are applied against the tax liability limitation first. To the extent the tax liability limitation exceeds carryovers, credit earned, and carrybacks are then applied.

(m) Special ordering rule. *(1) In general.* Under section 46(a)(1)(A), the FIFO rule applies separately—

(i) First, with respect to regular and ESOP credits, and

(ii) Second, with respect to nonrefundable energy credit.

(2) Regular and ESOP credit. Under § 1.46-8(c)(9)(ii), regular and ESOP credits available are applied in the following order:

(i) Regular carryovers;

(ii) ESOP carryovers;

(iii) Regular credit earned;

(iv) ESOP credit earned;

(v) Regular carrybacks; and

(vi) ESOP carrybacks.

(3) Example. For an example of the order of application of regular and ESOP credits, see § 1.46-8(c)(9)(iii).

(n) Examples. The following examples illustrate paragraphs (a) through (m) of this section.

Example (1). (a) Corporation M's regular credit available for its taxable year ending December 31, 1979 is as follows:

Regular carryovers	$ 5,000
Regular credit earned	10,000
Regular carrybacks	15,000
Credit available	30,000

(b) M's "tax liability" for 1979 is $30,000. M's tax liability limitation for 1979 for the regular credit is $28,000, consisting of $25,000 plus 60 percent of the $5,000 of "tax liability" in excess of $25,000.

(c) The regular carryovers and credit earned are allowed in full. However, only $13,000 of the regular carryback is allowed for 1979. The remaining $2,000 must be carried to the next year to which it may be carried under section 46(b).

Example (2). (a) For its taxable year ending December 31, 1980, corporation N has $30,000 regular credit earned and $9,000 nonrefundable energy credit earned. N has no carryovers to 1980 and no "tax liability" for pre-1980 years.

(b) N's "tax liability" for 1980 for the regular credit is $35,000. N's tax liability limitation for 1980 for the regular credit is $32,000, consisting of $25,000 plus 70 percent of the $10,000 of "tax liability" in excess of $25,000.

(c) The entire regular credit is allowed in 1980.

(d) N's "tax liability" for 1980 for the nonrefundable energy credit is $5,000, consisting of $35,000 less $30,000 regular credit allowed for 1980. N's tax liability limitation for 1980 for the nonrefundable energy credit is 100 percent of $5,000.

(e) $5,000 of the nonrefundable energy credit is allowed for 1980. The remaining $4,000 energy credit is an unused nonrefundable energy credit which must be carried to the next year to which it may be carried under section 46(b).

Example (3). (a) Assume the same facts as in example (2) except that in its taxable year ending December 31, 1981, N earns a regular credit of which it may carry back $2,000 to 1980.

(b) The $30,000 regular credit earned and $2,000 of the regular carryback is allowed for 1980. N's "tax liability" for 1980 for the nonrefundable energy credit is reduced to $3,000, consisting of $35,000 less $32,000 regular credit allowed for 1980. The nonrefundable energy credit allowed for 1980 is reduced to $3,000. The remaining $6,000 is an unused nonrefundable energy credit which must be carried to the next year to which it may be carried under section 46(b).

Example (4). (a) For its taxable year ending December 31, 1980, corporation P's regular credit earned is $20,000. P also has a $9,000 refundable energy credit for 1980. There are no carryovers or carrybacks to 1980.

(b) P's "tax liability" for 1980 for the regular credit is $25,000 which is also the tax liability limitation for the regular credit.

(c) The entire $20,000 regular credit is allowed for 1980. The entire $9,000 refundable energy credit is treated as an overpayment of tax under section 6401(b), even though "tax liability" remains.

Example (5). Assume the same facts as in example (4), except that in the following year P earns a regular credit, $5,000 of which it may carry back to 1980. The $5,000 carryback is allowed in full in 1980.

Example (6). (i) Corporation X, a calendar year taxpayer, constructs a ship on which it begins construction on January 1, 1973, and which, when placed in service on December 31, 1980, has a basis of $450,000. Of that amount $100,000 is attributable to construction before January 22, 1975. X makes an election under section 46(d) (qualified progress expenditures) for taxable years after 1975.

(ii) For 1976, 1977, 1978, and 1979, qualified progress expenditures total $200,000. The ten-percent credit applies to those expenditures.

(iii) For 1980, qualified investment for the ship is $450,000. Under section 46(c)(4), X must reduce this amount by $200,000, the amount of qualified progress expenditures taken into account. The ten-percent credit applies to the portion of the remaining qualified investment attributable to construction after January 21, 1975 ($150,000). The seven-percent credit applies to the portion of qualified investment attributable to construction before January 22, 1975 ($100,000).

Example (7). (i) Corporation Y agrees to build a ship for Corporation X, which uses the calendar year. In 1973, Y begins construction of the ship which X acquires and places in service on December 31, 1980. X makes an election under section 46(d) for taxable years after 1974. The contract price is $400,000.

(ii) For 1975, 1976, 1977, 1978, and 1979, qualified progress expenditures total $250,000. The ten-percent credit applies to those expenditures.

(iii) For 1980, qualified investment for the ship is $400,000, which is the contract price. X must reduce qualified investment by $250,000, the amount of qualified progress expenditures. The ten-percent credit applies to the $150,000 of qualified investment that remains after reduction for qualified progress expenditures.

(o) Married individuals. If a separate return is filed by a husband or wife, the tax liability limitation is computed by substituting a $12,500 amount for the $25,000 that applies under section 46(a)(3). However, this reduction of the $25,000 amount to $12,500 applies only if the taxpayer's spouse is entitled to a credit under section 38 for the taxable year of such spouse which ends with, or within, the taxpayer's taxable year. The taxpayer's spouse is entitled to a credit under section 38 either because of investment made in qualified property for such taxable year of the spouse (whether directly made by such spouse or whether apportioned to such spouse, for example, from an electing small business corporation, as defined in section 1371(b)), or because of an investment credit carryback or carryover to such taxable year. The determination of whether an individual is married shall be made under the principles of section 143 and the regulations thereunder.

(p) Apportionment of $25,000 amount among component members of a controlled group. *(1) In general.* In determining the tax liability limitation under section 46(a)(3) for corporations that are component members of a controlled group on a December 31, only one $25,000 amount is available to those component members for their taxable years that include that December 31. See subparagraph (2) of this paragraph for apportionment of such amount among such component members. See subparagraph (3) of this paragraph for definition of "component member".

(2) Manner of apportionment. (i) In the case of corporations which are component members of a controlled group on a particular December 31, the $25,000 amount may be apportioned among such members for their taxable years that include such December 31 in any manner the component members may select, provided that each such member less than 100 percent of whose stock is owned, in the aggregate, by the other component members of the group on such December 31 consents to an apportionment plan. The consent of a component member to an apportionment plan with respect to a particular December 31 shall be made by means of a statement, signed by a person duly authorized to act on behalf of the consenting member, stating that such member consents to the apportionment plan with respect to such December 31. The statement shall set forth the name, address, employer identification number, and taxable year of each component member of the group on such December 31, the amount apportioned to each such member under the plan, and the location of the Service Center where the statement is to be filed. The consent of more than one component member may be incorporated in a single statement. The statement shall be timely filed with the Service Center where the component member having the taxable year first ending on or after such December 31 files its return for such taxable year and shall be irrevocable after such filing. If two or more component members have the same such taxable year, a statement of consent may be filed by any one of such members. However, if the due date (including any extensions of time) of the return of such member is on or before December 15, 1971, the required statement shall be considered as timely filed if filed on or before March 15, 1972. Each component member of the group on such December 31 shall keep as a part of its records a copy of the statement containing all the required consents.

(ii) An apportionment plan adopted by a controlled group with respect to a particular December 31 shall be valid only for the taxable year of each member of the group which includes such December 31. Thus, a controlled group must file a separate consent to an apportionment plan with respect to each taxable year which includes a December 31 as to which an apportionment plan is desired.

(iii) If the apportionment plan is not timely filed, the $25,000 amount specified in section 46(a)(3) shall be reduced for each component member of the controlled group, for its taxable year which includes a December 31, to an amount equal to $25,000 divided by the number of component members of such group on such December 31.

(iv) If a component member of the controlled group makes its income tax return on the basis of a 52-53-week taxable year, the principles of section 441(f)(2)(A)(ii) and § 1.441-2 apply in determining the last day of such taxable year.

(3) Definitions of controlled group of corporations and component member of controlled group. For the purpose of this paragraph, the terms "controlled group of corporations" and "component member" of a controlled group of corporations shall have the same meaning assigned to those terms in section 1563(a) and (b). For purposes of applying § 1.1563-1(b)(2)(ii) *(c)*, an electing small business corporation shall be treated as an excluded member whether or not it is subject to the tax imposed by section 1378.

(4) Members of a controlled group filing a consolidated return. If some component members of a controlled group join in filing a consolidated return pursuant to § 1.1502-(3a)(3), and other component members do not join, then, unless a consent is timely filed apportioning the $25,000 amount among the group filing the consolidated return and the other component members of the controlled group, each component member of the controlled group (including each component member which joins in filing the consolidated return) shall be treated as a separate corporation for purposes of equally apportioning the $25,000 amount under subparagraph (2)(iii) of this paragraph. In that case, the tax liability limitation for the group filing the consolidated return is computed by substituting for the $25,000 amount under section 46(a)(3) the total amount apportioned to each component member that joins in filing the consolidated return. If the affiliated group filing the consolidated return and the other component members of the controlled group adopt an apportionment plan, the affiliated group shall be treated as a single member for the purpose of applying subparagraph (2)(i) of this paragraph. Thus, for example, only one consent executed by the common parent to the apportionment plan is required for the group filing the consolidated return. If any component member of the controlled group which joins in the filing of the consolidated return is an organization to which section 593 applies or a cooperative organization described in section 1381(a), see paragraph (a)(3)(ii) of § 1.1502-3.

(5) Examples. The provisions of this paragraph may be illustrated by the following examples:

Example (1). At all times during 1970 Smith, an individual, owns all the stock of corporations X, Y, and Z. Corporation X files an income tax return on a calendar year basis. Corporation Y files an income tax return on the basis of a fiscal year ending June 30. Corporation Z files an income tax return on the basis of a fiscal year ending September 30. On December 31, 1970, X, Y, and Z are component members of the same controlled group, X, Y, and Z all consent to an apportionment plan in which the $25,000 amount is apportioned entirely to Y for its taxable year ending June 30, 1971 (Y's taxable year which includes December 31, 1970). Such consent is timely filed. For purposes of computing the credit under section 38, Y's limitation based on amount of tax for its taxable year ending June 30, 1971, is so much of

Y's liability for tax as does not exceed $25,000, plus 50 percent of Y's liability for tax in excess of $25,000. X's and Z's limitations for their taxable years ending December 31, 1970, and September 30, 1971, respectively, are equal to 50 percent of X's liability for tax and 50 percent of Z's liability for tax. On the other hand, if an apportionment plan is not timely filed, X's limitation would be so much of X's liability for tax as does not exceed $8,333.33, plus 50 percent of X's liability in excess of $8,333.33, and Y's and Z's limitation would be computed similarly.

Example (2). At all times during 1970, Jones, an individual, owns all the outstanding stock of corporations P, Q, and R. Corporations Q and R both file returns for taxable years ending December 31, 1970. P files a consolidated return as a common parent for its fiscal year ending June 30, 1971, with its two wholly-owned subsidiaries N and O. On December 31, 1970, N, O, P, Q, and R are component members of the same controlled group. No consent to an apportionment plan is filed. Therefore, each member is apportioned $5,000 of the $25,000 amount ($25,000 divided equally among the five members). The limitation based on the amount of tax for the group filing the consolidated return (P, N, and O) for the year ending June 3, 1971 (the consolidated taxable year within which December 31, 1970, falls) is computed by using $15,000 instead of the $25,000 amount. The $15,000 is arrived at by adding together the $5,000 amounts apportioned to P, N, and O.

(q) Rehabilitation percentage *(1) General rule.* (i) In general. Due to amendments made by the Tax Reform Act of 1986, different rules apply depending on when the property attributable to the qualified rehabilitated expenditures (as defined in § 1.48-12(c)) is placed in service. Paragraph (q)(1)(ii) of this section contains the general rule relating to property placed in service after December 31, 1986. Paragraph (q)(1)(iii) of this section contains rules relating to property placed in service before January 1, 1987. Paragraph (q)(1)(iv) of this section contains rules relating to property placed in service after December 31, 1986, that qualifies for a transition rule.

(ii) Property placed in service after December 31, 1986. Except as otherwise provided in paragraph (q)(1)(iv) of this section, in the case of section 38 property described in section 48(a)(1)(E) placed in service after December 31, 1986, the term "rehabilitation percentage" means—

(A) 10 percent in the case of qualified rehabilitation expenditures with respect to a qualified rehabilitated building other than a certified historic structure, and

(B) 20 percent in the case of qualified rehabilitation expenditures with respect to a certified historic structure.

(iii) Property placed in service before January 1, 1987. For qualified rehabilitation expenditures (as defined in § 1.48-12(c)) with respect to property placed in service before January 1, 1987, section 46(b)(4)(A) as in effect prior to the enactment of the Tax Reform Act of 1986 provided for a three-tier rehabilitation percentage. The applicable rehabilitation percentage for such expenditures depends on whether the qualified rehabilitated building is a "30-year building," a "40-year building," or a certified historic structure (as defined in section 48(g)(3) and § 1.48-12(d)(1)). The rehabilitation percentage for such qualified rehabilitation expenditures incurred with respect to a qualified rehabilitated building is 15 percent to the extent that the building is a 30-year building *(i.e.,* at least 30 years, but less than 40 years, has elapsed between the date the physical work on the rehabilitation began and the date the building was first placed in service), 20 percent to the extent that the building is a 40-year building *(i.e.,* at least 40 years has so elapsed), and 25 percent for certified historic structures, regardless of age. See paragraph (q)(2)(ii) of this section for rules concerning buildings to which additions have been added.

(iv) Property placed in service after December 31, 1986, that qualifies under the transition rules. In the case of section 38 property described in section 48(a)(1)(E) placed in service after December 31, 1986, and to which the amendments made by section 251 of the Tax Reform Act of 1986 do not apply because the transition rules in section 251(d) of that Act and § 1.48-12(a)(2)(iv)(B) or (C) apply, the rehabilitation percentage for a "30-year building" (within the meaning of paragraph (q)(1)(iii) of this section) shall be 10 percent, the rehabilitation percentage for a "40-year building" (within the meaning of paragraph (q)(1)(iii) of this section) shall be 13 percent, and the rehabilitation percentage for a certified historic structure shall be 25 percent.

(2) Special rules. (i) Moved buildings. With respect to paragraph (q)(1)(ii) of this section, § 1.48-12(b)(5) provides that a building (other than a certified historic structure) is not a qualified rehabilitated building unless it has been at the location where it is being rehabilitated since January 1, 1936. In addition, for purposes of paragraph (q)(1)(iii) and (iv) of this section, a building is not a "30-year building" unless it has been at the location where it is being rehabilitated for the thirty-year period immediately preceding the beginning of the rehabilitation process, and is not a "40-year building" unless it has been at the location where it is being rehabilitated for the forty-year period immediately preceding the beginning of the rehabilitation process.

(ii) Building to which additions have been added. (A) Property placed in service after December 31, 1986. For purposes of paragraph (q)(1)(ii) of this section, if part of a building meets the definition of a qualified rehabilitated building, and part of the building does not meet the definition of a qualified rehabilitated building because such part is an addition that was placed in service after December 31, 1935, the qualified rehabilitation expenditures made to the building must be allocated to the pre-1936 portion of the building and the post-1935 portion of the building using the principles in § 1.48-12(c)(10)(ii). Qualified rehabilitation expenditures attributable to the post-1935 addition shall not qualify for the 10 percent rehabilitation percentage.

(B) Property placed in service before January 1, 1987, and property qualifying for a transitional rule. For purposes of paragraph (q)(1)(iii) and (iv) of this section, if part of a building meets the definition of a "40-year building" and part of the building is an addition that was placed in service less than forty years before physical work on the rehabilitation began but more than thirty years before such date, then the qualified rehabilitation expenditures made to the building shall be allocated between the forty year old portion of the building and the thirty year old portion of the building, and a 20 percent rehabilitation percentage shall be applied to the forty year old portion of the building and a 15 percent rehabilitation percentage shall be applied to the thirty year old portion. This allocation shall be made using the principles in § 1.48-12(c)(10)(ii). If an allocation cannot be made between the expenditures to the forty year old portion of the building and the thirty year old portion of the building, then the building will be considered to be a 30-year building. Furthermore, for purposes of this paragraph (q), a building (other than a certified historic structure) is not a qualified rehabilitated building to the extent of that portion of the building that is less than 30 years old. If rehabilitation expenditures are incurred with respect to an addition to a qualified rehabilitated building, but the addition is not considered to be part of the qualified rehabilitated building because the addition does not meet the age requirement in section 48(g)(1)(B) (as in effect prior to its amendment by the Tax Reform Act of 1986) and § 1.48-12(b)(4)(i)(B), then no rehabilitation percentage will be applied to the expenditures attributable to the rehabilitation of the addition. Thus, for purposes of paragraph (q)(1)(iii) and (iv) of this section, it may be necessary to allocate rehabilitation expenditures incurred with respect to a building between the original portion of the building and the addition.

(iii) Mixed-use buildings. If qualified rehabilitation expenditures are incurred for property that is excluded from section 38 property described in section 48(a)(1)(E) (because, for example, they are made with respect to a portion of the building used for lodging within the meaning of section 48(a)(3) and § 1.48-1(h)), an allocation of the expenditures must be made be made between the expenditures that result in an addition to basis that is section 38 property and the expenditures that result in an addition to basis that is excluded from the definition of section 38 property since the rehabilitation percentage is applicable only to section 38 property. These allocations should be made using the principles contained in § 1.48-12(c)(10)(ii).

(3) Regular and energy percentages not to apply. The regular percentage and the energy percentage shall not apply to that portion of the basis of any building that is attributable to qualified rehabilitation expenditures (as defined in § 1.48-12(c)).

(4) Effective date. The rehabilitation percentage is applicable only to qualified rehabilitation expenditures (as defined in § 1.48-12(c)). For rules relating to applicability of the regular percentage to qualified rehabilitation expenditures (as defined in § 1.48-11(c)), see § 1.48-11.

T.D. 6731, 5/7/64, amend T.D. 6931, 10/9/67, T.D. 6958, 6/20/68, T.D. 7181, 4/24/72, T.D. 7203, 8/24/72, T.D. 7564, 9/11/78, T.D. 7636, 8/9/79, T.D. 7751, 12/30/80, T.D. 8183, 3/1/88, T.D. 8233, 10/7/88, T.D. 8996, 5/16/2002.

Proposed § 1.46-1 [*For Preamble, see ¶ 152,177*]

§ 1.46-2 Carryback and carryover of unused credit.

Caution: The Treasury has not yet amended Reg § 1.46-2 to reflect changes made by P.L. 101-508, P.L. 101-239, P.L. 100-647, P.L. 99-514, P.L. 98-369, P.L. 97-354, P.L. 97-248, P.L. 97-34, P.L. 96-223, P.L. 96-222.

(a) Effective date. This section is effective for taxable years beginning after December 31, 1975. For taxable years beginning before January 1, 1976, see 26 CFR 1.46-2 (Rev. as of April 1, 1979).

(b) In general. Under section 46(b)(1), unused credit may be carried back and carried over. Carrybacks and carryovers of unused credit are taken into account in determining the amount of credit available and the credit allowed for the taxable years to which they may be carried. In general, the application of the rules of this section to regular and ESOP credits are separate from their application to nonrefundable energy credits. For example, the limitations on carrybacks and carryovers of unused nonrefundable energy credit under section 46(b)(2) and (3), respectively, differ in amount from the limitations on the regular and ESOP credits because the tax liability limitations for those credits differ. See § 1.46-1(h). For a further example, see the special ordering rule in § 1.46-1(m). Section 46(b) does not apply to the refundable energy credit.

(c) Unused credit. If carryovers and credit earned (as defined in § 1.46-1(c)(1)) exceed the applicable tax liability limitation, the excess attributable to credit earned is an unused credit. The taxable year in which an unused credit arises is referred to as the "unused credit year".

(d) Taxable years to which unused credit may be carried. An unused credit is a carryback to each of the 3 taxable years preceding the unused credit year and a carryover to each of the 7 taxable years succeeding the unused credit year. An unused credit must be carried first to the earliest of those 10 taxable years. An unused credit then must be carried to each of the other 9 taxable years (in order of time) to the extent that the unused credit was not absorbed during a prior taxable year because of the limitations under section 46(b)(2) and (3).

(e) Special rule for pre-1971 years. *(1) In general.* For unused credit years ending before January 1, 1971, unused credit is allowed a 10-year carryover rather than the 7-year carryover. The principles of paragraph (d) of this section apply to this 10-year carryover.

(2) Cross reference. For limitations on the taxable years to which unused credit from pre-1971 credit years may be carried, see paragraph (g) of this section.

(f) Limitations on carrybacks. Under the FIFO rule to section 46(a)(1), carryovers and credit earned are applied against the tax liability limitation before carrybacks. Thus, carrybacks to a taxable year may not exceed the amount by which the applicable tax liability limitation for that year exceeds the sum of carryovers to and credit earned for that year. Carrybacks from an unused credit year are applied against tax liability before carrybacks from a later unused credit year. To the extent an unused credit cannot be carried back to a particular preceding taxable year, the unused credit must be carried to the next succeeding taxable year to which it may be carried.

(g) Limitations on carryovers. *(1) General rule.* Carryovers to a taxable year may not exceed the applicable tax liability limitation for that year. Carryovers from an unused credit year are applied before carryovers from a later unused credit year.

(2) Exception. A 10-year carryover from a pre-1971 unused credit year may, under certain circumstances, be postponed to prevent a later-earned 7-year carryover from expiring. This exception does not extend the 10-year carryover period for pre-1971 unused credit. See section 46(b)(1)(D).

(h) Examples. The following examples illustrate paragraphs (a) through (g) of this section.

Example (1). (a) Corporation M is organized on January 1, 1977 and files its income tax return on a calendar year basis. Assume the facts set forth in columns (1) and (2) of the following table. The determination of the regular credit allowed for each of the taxable years indicated is set forth in the remaining portions of the table.

	(1) Credit available	(2) Tax liability	(3) Percent	(4) Tax liability limitation*(remaining, from Col. (6) on preceding line)	(5) Credit allowed (lower of (1) or (4))	(6) Remaining tax liability limitation ((4)-(5))	(7) Unused credit ((1)-(5)) or (amount absorbed)
1977:							
A. Credit earned	$20,000	$45,000	50	$ 35,000	$20,000	$15,000	0
B. Carryback from 1978	15,000*			[15,000]	15,000		
1978:							
A. Credit earned	80,000	55,000	50	40,000	40,000	0	$20,000
Carryback to 1977							(15,000*)
Carryback to 1979							(5,000*)
1979:							
A. Carryover from 1978	5,000*	50,000	60	40,000	6,000	35,000	
B. Credit earned	50,000			[35,000]	35,000	0	15,000
Carryover to 1980							(15,000*)
1980:							
A. Carryover from 1979	15,000*	55,000	70	46,000	15,000	31,000	
B. Credit earned	25,000			[31,000]	25,000	6,000	0

* For line "A" each year: Lesser of (1) tax liability or (2) $25,000 + (percentage in col. (3) × [col. (2) − $25,000]). See, § 1.46-1(h). For other lines: Amount in col. (6) on preceding line.

Example (2). (a) Assume the same facts as in example (1) except for 1979 M earns a $35,000 nonrefundable energy credit. The following table shows the determinations for each year.

	(1) Credit available	(2) Tax liability (a) Regular	(2) Tax liability (b) Energy ((2)(a)-(5)(R))	(3) Percent	(4) Tax Liability limitation* (remaining, from Col. (6) on preceding line)	(5) Credit allowed (lower of (1) or (4))	(6) Remaining Tax Liability limitation ((4)-(5))	(7) Unused credit ((1)-(5)) or (amount absorbed)
1977:								
Regular:								
A. Credit earned	$20,000	$45,000		50	$35,000	$20,000R	$15,000	0
B. Carryback from 1978	15,000*				[15,000]	15,000R	0	
1978:								
Regular:								
A. Credit earned	60,000	55,000		50	40,000	40,000R	0	$20,000
Carryback to 1977								(15,000*)
Carryover to 1979								(5,000*)
Energy:								
A. Carryback from 1979	15,000*		$15,000	100	15,000	15,000E	0	
1979:								
Regular:								
A. Carryover from 1978	5,000*	50,000		60	40,000	5,000R	35,000	
B. Credit Earned	50,000				[35,000]	35,000R	0	15,000
Carryover to 1980							(15,000*)	
Energy:								
A. Credit Earned	35,000		10,000	100	10,000	10,000E	0	25,000
Carryback to 1978								(15,000*)
Carryover to 1980								(10,000*)
1980:								
Regular:								
A. Carryover from 1979	15,000*	55,000		70	46,000	15,000R	31,000	
B. Credit Earned	25,000				[31,000]	25,000R	6,000	0
Energy:								

A. Carryover from 1979	10,000*		15,000	100	15,000	10,000E	5,000	

* See footnote to the chart in example (1).

(b) Although, in general, a nonrefundable energy credit may be carried back to taxable years ending before October 1, 1978, in this example the unused nonrefundable energy credit from 1979 may not be absorbed in 1977. The 1977 tax liability limitation for the nonrefundable energy credit is the same as it is for the regular credit, reduced by regular credit previously allowed for 1977. See §§ 1.46-1(h)(3) and 1.46-1(m).

Example (3). (a) Assume the same facts as in example (2) except M has regular credit of $37,000 for 1981 and M's tax liability for 1981 is $32,500. The determinations for 1980 and 1981 are set forth in the following table.

	(1)	(2)		(3)	(4)	(5)	(6)	(7)
		Tax liability						
	Credit available	(a) Regular	(b) Energy ((2)(a)-(5)R)	Percent	Tax Liability limitation* (remaining, from Col. (6) on preceding line)	Credit allowed (lower of (1) or (4))	Remaining Tax Liability limitation ((4)-(5))	Unused credit ((1)-(5)) or (amount absorbed)
1979 (restated):								
Energy:								
To be carried over								$10,000
Carryover to 1980								(9,000*)
Carryover to 1981								(1,000*)
1980 (restated):								
Regular:								
A. Carryover from 1979	$15,000	$55,000		70	$46,000	$15,000R	$31,000	
B. Credit earned	25,000*				[31,000]	25,000R	6,000	0
C. Carryback from 1981	6,000*				[6,000]	6,000R	0	
Energy:								
A. Carryover from 1979	9,000*		$9,000	100	9,000	9,000E		
1981:								
Regular:								
A. Credit earned	37,000	32,500		80	31,000	31,000R	0	6,000
Carryback to 1980								(6,000*)
Energy:								
A. Carryover from 1979	1,000*		1,500	100	1,500	1,000E	500	0

* See footnote to chart under example (1).

(b) Allowance of the regular carryback in 1980 from 1981 requires that the computations for 1980 be restated. The energy tax liability limitation for 1980 is reduced from $15,000 (as determined in example (2)) to $9,000. Thus, $1,000 of the $10,000 energy credit allowed for 1980 is displaced by the regular carryback. That amount may not be carried back because there is no remaining energy tax liability limitation for the prior 3 years (see table in example (2)). It may be carried over to 1981 and allowed in full in that year.

(i) [Reserved]

(j) Electing small business corporation. A shareholder of an electing small business corporation (as defined in section 1371(b)) may not take into account unused credit of the corporation attributable to unused credit years for which the corporation was not an electing small business corporation. However, a taxable year for which the corporation is an electing small business corporation is counted as a taxable year for determining the taxable years to which that unused credit may be carried.

(k) Periods of less than 12 months. A fractional part of a year that is considered a taxable year under sections 441(b) and 7701(a)(23) is treated as a preceding or succeeding taxable year for determining under section 46(b) the taxable years to which an unused credit may be carried.

(l) Corporation acquisitions. For carryover of unused credits in the case of certain corporate acquisitions, see section 381(c)(23).

T.D. 6731, 5/7/64, amend T.D. 6931, 10/9/67, T.D. 6958, 6/20/68, T.D. 7126, 6/9/71, T.D. 7203, 8/24/72, T.D. 7289, 11/5/73, T.D. 7751, 12/30/80.

§ 1.46-3 Qualified investment.

Caution: The Treasury has not yet amended Reg § 1.46-3 to reflect changes made by P.L. 104-188, P.L. 101-508, P.L. 100-647, P.L. 99-514, P.L. 98-369, P.L. 97-34, P.L. 96-222, P.L. 95-618, P.L. 95-600, P.L. 94-455, P.L. 94-12.

(a) In general. *(1)* With respect to any taxable year, the qualified investment of the taxpayer is the aggregate (expressed in dollars) of (i) the applicable percentage of the basis of each new section 38 property placed in service by the taxpayer during such taxable year, plus (ii) the applicable percentage of the cost of each used section 38 property placed in service by the taxpayer during such taxable year. With respect to any section 38 property, qualified investment means the applicable percentage of the basis (or cost) of such property. Section 38 property placed in service by the taxpayer during the taxable year includes the taxpayer's share of the basis (or cost) of section 38 property placed in service by a partnership in the taxable year of such partnership ending with or within the taxpayer's taxable year. In the case of a shareholder of an electing small business corporation (as defined in section 1371(b)), or a beneficiary of an estate or trust, see §§ 1.48-5 and 1.48-6, respectively, for apportionment of the basis (or cost) of section 38 property placed in service by such corporation, estate, or trust. For the definitions of new section 38 property and used section 38 property, see §§ 1.48-2 and 1.48-3, respectively. See § 1.46-5 for special rules for progress expenditure property.

(2) The basis (or cost) of section 38 property placed in service during a taxable year shall not be taken into account in determining qualified investment for such year if such property is disposed of or otherwise ceases to be section 38 property during such year, except where § 1.47-3 applies. Thus, if individual A places in service during a taxable year section 38 property and later in the same year sells such property, the basis (or cost) of such property shall not be taken into account in determining A's qualified investment. On the other hand, if A places in service section 38 property during a taxable year and dies later in the same year, the basis (or cost) of such property would be taken into account in computing qualified investment. Similarly, if section 38 property is destroyed by fire in the same year in which it is placed in service and paragraph (h) of this section applies to reduce the basis (or cost) of replacement property, the basis (or cost) of the destroyed property would be taken into account in computing qualified investment. In order to determine whether section 38 property is disposed of or otherwise ceases to be section 38 property see § 1.47-2.

(3) Qualified investment is reduced in the case of property which is "public utility property" (see paragraph (h) of this section), and in the case of property of organizations to which section 593 applies, regulated investment companies or real estate investment trusts subject to taxation under subchapter M, chapter 1 of the Code, and cooperative organizations described in section 1381(a) (see § 1.46-4).

(b) Applicable percentage. The applicable percentage to be applied to the basis (or cost) of property is 33⅓ percent if the estimated useful life of the property is 3 years or more but less than 7 years; 66⅔ percent if the estimated useful life is 5 years or more but less than 7 years; or 100 percent if the estimated useful life is 7 years or more. In the case of property which is not described in section 50, the preceding sentence shall be applied by substituting "4 years" for "3 years", "6 years" for "5 years", and "8 years" for "7 years". The provisions of this paragraph may be illustrated by the following example:

Example. Corporation Y acquires and places in service during 1972 the following new and used section 38 properties:

Property	Estimated useful life	Basis (or cost)
A (new)	4 years	$ 60,000
B (new)	10 years	90,000
C (new)	6 years	150,000
D (used)	3 years	30,000

Corporation Y's qualified investment for 1972 is $220,000 determined in the following manner:

Property	Basis (or cost)	Applicable percentage	Qualified investment
A	$ 60,000	33⅓	$ 20,000
B	90,000	100	90,000
C	150,000	66⅔	100,000
D	30,000	33⅓	10,000
Total			220,000

(c) Basis or cost. *(1)* The basis of any new section 38 property shall be determined in accordance with the general rules for determining the basis of property. Thus, the basis of property would generally be its cost (see section 1012), unreduced by the adjustment to basis provided by section 48(g)(1) with respect to property placed in service before January 1, 1964, and any other adjustment to basis, such as that for depreciation, and would include all items properly included by the taxpayer in the depreciable basis of the property, such as installation and freight costs. However, for purposes of determining qualified investment, the basis of new section 38 property constructed, reconstructed, or erected by the taxpayer shall not include any depreciation sustained with respect to any other property used in the construction, reconstruction, or erection of such new section 38 property. (See paragraph (b)(4) of § 1.48-1.)

If new section 38 property is acquired in exchange for cash and other property in a transaction described in section 1031 in which no gain or loss is recognized, the basis of the newly acquired property for purposes of determining qualified investment would be equal to the adjusted basis of the other property plus the cash paid. See § 1.48-4 for the basis of property to a lessee where the lessor has elected to treat such lessee as a purchaser.

(2) The cost of any used section 38 property shall be determined in accordance with paragraph (b) of § 1.48-3. However, the aggregate cost of used section 38 property which may be taken into account in any taxable year in computing qualified investment cannot exceed $50,000 (see paragraph (c) of § 1.48-3).

(3) For reduction in the basis (or cost) of certain property which replaces other property which was destroyed or damaged by fire, storm, shipwreck, or other casualty, or which was stolen, see paragraph (h) of this section.

(d) Placed in service. *(1)* For purposes of the credit allowed by section 38, property shall be considered placed in service in the earlier of the following taxable years:

(i) The taxable year in which, under the taxpayer's depreciation practice, the period for depreciation with respect to such property begins; or

(ii) The taxable year in which the property is placed in a condition or state of readiness and availability for a specifically assigned function, whether in a trade or business, in the production of income, in a tax-exempt activity, or in a personal activity.

Thus, if property meets the conditions of subdivision (ii) of this subparagraph in a taxable year, it shall be considered placed in service in such year notwithstanding that the period for depreciation with respect to such property begins in a succeeding taxable year because, for example, under the taxpayer's depreciation practice such property is accounted for in a multiple asset account and depreciation is computed under an "averaging convention" (see § 1.167(a)-(10)), or depreciation with respect to such property is computed under the completed contract method, the unit of production method, or the retirement method.

(2) In the case of property acquired by a taxpayer for use in his trade or business (or in the production of income), the following are examples of cases where property shall be

considered in a condition or state of readiness and availability for a specifically assigned function:

(i) Parts are acquired and set aside during the taxable year for use as replacements for a particular machine (or machines) in order to avoid operational time loss.

(ii) Operational farm equipment is acquired during the taxable year and it is not practicable to use such equipment for its specifically assigned function in the taxpayer's business of farming until the following year.

(iii) Equipment is acquired for a specifically assigned function and is operational but is undergoing testing to eliminate any defects.

However, fruitbearing trees and vines shall not be considered in a condition or state of readiness and availability for a specifically assigned function until they have reached an income-producing stage. Moreover, materials and parts acquired to be used in the construction of an item of equipment shall not be considered in a condition or state of readiness and availability for a specifically assigned function.

(iv) Reforestation expenditures (as defined in § 1.194-3(c)) are incurred during the taxable year in connection with qualified timber property (as defined in § 1.194-3(a)).

(3) Notwithstanding subparagraph (1) of this paragraph, property with respect to which an election is made under § 1.48-4 to treat the lessee as having purchased such property shall be considered placed in service by the lessor in the taxable year in which possession is transferred to such lessee.

(4) (i) The credit allowed by section 38 with respect to any property shall be allowed only for the first taxable year in which such property is placed in service by the taxpayer. The determination of whether property is section 38 property in the hands of the taxpayer shall be made with respect to such first taxable year. Thus, if a taxpayer places property in service in a taxable year and such property does not qualify as section 38 property (or only a portion of such property qualifies as section 38 property) in such year, no credit (or a credit only as to the portion which qualifies in such year) shall be allowed to the taxpayer with respect to such property notwithstanding that such property (or a greater portion of such property) qualifies as section 38 property in a subsequent taxable year. For example, if a taxpayer places property in service in 1963 and uses the property entirely for personal purposes in such year, but in 1964 begins using the property in a trade or business, no credit is allowable to the taxpayer under section 38 with respect to such property. See § 1.48-1 for the definition of section 38 property.

(ii) Notwithstanding subdivision (i) of this subparagraph, if, for the first taxable year in which property is placed in service by the taxpayer, the property qualifies as section 38 property but the basis of the property does not reflect its full cost for the reason that the total amount to be paid or incurred by the taxpayer for the property is indeterminate, a credit shall be allowed to the taxpayer for such first taxable year with respect to so much of the cost as is reflected in the basis of the property as of the close of such year, and an additional credit shall be allowed to the taxpayer for any subsequent taxable year with respect to the additional cost paid or incurred during such year and reflected in the basis of the property as of the close of such year. The estimated useful life used in computing each additional credit with respect to the property shall be the same as the estimated useful life used in computing the credit for the first taxable year in which the property was placed in service by the taxpayer. Assume, for example, that in 1964 X Corporation, a utility company which makes its return on the basis of a calendar year, enters into an agreement with Y Corporation, a builder, to construct certain utility facilities for a housing development built by Y. Assume further that part of the funds for the construction of the utility facilities is advanced by Y under a contract providing that X will repay the advances over a 10-year period in accordance with an agreed formula, after which no further amounts will be repayable by X even though the full amount advanced by Y has not been repaid. Assuming that the utility facilities are placed in service in 1964 and qualify as section 38 property, X is allowed a credit for 1964 with respect to its basis in the utility facilities at the close of 1964. For each succeeding taxable year X is allowed an additional credit with respect to the increase in the basis of the utility facilities resulting from the repayments to Y during such year.

(e) Estimated useful life. *(1) In general.* (i) With respect to assets placed in service by the taxpayer during any taxable year, for the purpose of computing qualified investment the estimated useful lives assigned to all assets which fall within a particular guideline class (within the meaning of Revenue Procedure 62-21) may be determined, at the taxpayer's option, under either subparagraph (2) or (3) of this paragraph. Thus, the taxpayer may assign estimated useful lives to all the assets falling in one guideline class in accordance with subparagraph (2) of this paragraph, and may assign estimated useful lives to all the assets falling within another guideline class in accordance with subparagraph (3) of this paragraph. See subparagraphs (4) and (5) of this paragraph for determination of estimated useful lives of assets not subject to subparagraph (2) or (3) of this paragraph.

(ii) Except as provided in subparagraph (7), this paragraph shall not apply to property described in section 50.

(2) Class life system. The taxpayer may assign to each asset falling within a guideline class, which is placed in service during the taxable year, the class life of the taxpayer for the guideline class for such year as determined under section 4, Part II of Revenue Procedure 62-21. The preceding sentence may be applied to the assets falling within a guideline class irrespective of whether the taxpayer uses single asset accounts or multiple asset accounts in computing depreciation with respect to such assets and irrespective of whether the taxpayer chooses to have his depreciation allowance with respect to such assets examined under the rules provided in Revenue Procedure 62-21.

(3) Individual useful life system. (i) The taxpayer may assign an individual estimated useful life to each asset falling within a guideline class which is placed in service during the taxable year. With respect to the assets falling within the guideline class which are placed in single asset accounts for purposes of computing depreciation, the estimated useful life used for each asset for that purpose shall be used in determining qualified investment. With respect to the assets falling within the guideline class which are placed in multiple asset accounts (including a guideline class account described in Revenue Procedure 62-21) for which a group, classified, or composite rate is used in computing depreciation (or in single asset accounts for which an average life rate is used), the determination of estimated useful life for each asset in the account shall be made individually on the best estimate obtainable on the basis of all the facts and circumstances. The individual estimated useful lives used for all the assets placed in a multiple asset account, when viewed together, must be consistent with the group, classified, or composite

life used for the account for purposes of computing depreciation.

(ii) In determining the individual estimated useful lives of assets similar in kind contained in a multiple asset account (or in single asset accounts for which an average life rate is used), the taxpayer may (a) assign to each of such assets the average useful life of such assets used for purposes of computing depreciation, or (b) assign separate lives to such assets based on the estimated range of years taken into consideration in establishing the average useful life. Thus, for example, if a taxpayer places 9 similar trucks with an average estimated useful life of 7 years, based on an estimated range of 6 to 8 years (two trucks with a useful life of 6 years, five trucks with a useful life of 7 years, and two trucks with a useful life of 8 years), in a multiple asset account for which a group rate is used in computing depreciation, he may either assign a useful life of 6 years to two of the trucks, 7 years to five of the trucks, and 8 years to two of the trucks, or he may assign the average useful life of the trucks (7 years) to each of the nine trucks. Likewise, if a taxpayer places 100 similar telephone poles with an average useful life of 28 years, based on an estimated range of 3 to 40 years (two with a useful life of less than 4 years, three with a useful life of 4 to 6 years, four with a useful life of 6 to 8 years, and 91 with a useful life of more than 8 years), in a multiple asset account for which a group rate is used in computing depreciation, he may either assign useful lives corresponding to the estimated range of years of the poles (i.e., a useful life of less than 4 years to two of the poles, etc.), or he may assign the average useful life of the poles (28 years) to each of the poles.

(iii) Reserved.

(iv) For purposes of subdivision (ii) of this subparagraph, assets (other than "mass assets") shall not be considered as "similar in kind" in respect of other assets unless all such assets are substantially of the same value, nor shall used section 38 property be considered as "similar in kind" to new section 38 property.

(4) Useful life of property subject to amortization. (i) In general. In the case of property with respect to which amortization in lieu of depreciation is allowable, the term over which amortization deductions are taken shall be considered as the estimated useful life of such property.

(ii) Qualified timber property. In the case of qualified timber property (within the meaning of section 194(c)(1)), the normal growing period of such property shall be considered its estimated useful life.

(5) Useful life of property subject to certain methods of depreciation. If a taxpayer is using a method of depreciation, such as the unit of production or retirement method, which does not measure the useful life of the property in terms of years, he must estimate such useful life in years in order to compute his qualified investment.

(6) Record requirements. The taxpayer shall maintain sufficient records to determine whether section 47 (relating to certain dispositions, etc., of section 38 property) applies with respect to any asset.

(7) Section 50 property. (i) The provisions of this subparagraph and subparagraphs (4) and (6) of this paragraph shall apply to property which is described in section 50.

(ii) The estimated useful life of property for purposes of computing qualified investment shall be the useful life used or to be used by the taxpayer in computing the allowance for depreciation with respect to such property under section 167 for the taxable year in which the property is placed in service. Thus, if property is placed in service by a taxpayer in a taxable year but the period for depreciation with respect to such property does not begin until a succeeding taxable year (see paragraph (d)(1) of this section), the estimated useful life for purposes of computing qualified investment must be the estimated useful life that the taxpayer uses in computing the allowance for depreciation. See subdivision (iv) of this subparagraph for rules for determining the estimated useful life of property with respect to which the allowance for depreciation under section 167 is computed under the unit of production method, the income-forecast method, or any other method which does not measure the useful life of the property in terms of years.

(iii) (a) The estimated useful life of any section 38 property to which an election under section 167(m) applies shall be the asset depreciation period selected for such property under § 1.167(a)-11(b)(4), whether or not such property constitutes mass assets (as defined in § 1.47-1(e)(4)).

(b) The estimated useful life of any section 38 property to which an election under section 167(m) does not apply and which is placed in a multiple asset account for which a group, classified, or composite rate is used in computing depreciation (or in single asset accounts for which an average life rate is used) shall be determined individually for each asset on the best estimate obtainable on the basis of all the facts and circumstances. The individual estimated useful life for each asset placed in a multiple asset account (including a mass asset account) must be the same as the useful life of such asset used in determining the group, classified, or composite life for the account for purposes of computing depreciation. The individual estimated useful lives of assets similar in kind may be determined in accordance with subdivisions (ii) and (iv) of subparagraph (3) of this paragraph. In the case of mass assets, subdivision (iii) of subparagraph (3) of this paragraph shall apply.

(iv) [Reserved]

(f) Partnerships. *(1) In general.* In the case of a partnership, each partner shall take into account separately, for his taxable year with or within which the partnership taxable year ends, his share of the basis of partnership new section 38 property and his share of the cost of partnership used section 38 property placed in service by the partnership during such partnership taxable year. Each partner shall be treated as the taxpayer with respect to his share of the basis of partnership new section 38 property and his share of the cost of partnership used section 38 property. The estimated useful life to each partner of such property shall be deemed to be the estimated useful life of the property in the hands of the partnership. Partnership section 38 property shall not, by reason of each partner taking his share of the basis or cost into account, lose its character as either new section 38 property or used section 38 property, as the case may be. For computation of each partner's qualified investment for the energy credit for a qualified intercity bus, see § 1.48-9(q)(9)(iv).

(2) Determination of partner's share. (i) Each partner's share of the basis (or cost) of any section 38 property shall be determined in accordance with the ratio in which the partners divide the general profits of the partnership (that is, the taxable income of the partnership as described in section 702(a)(9) regardless of whether the partnership has a profit or a loss for its taxable year during which the section 38 property is placed in service. However, if the ratio in which the partners divide the general profits of the partnership changes during the taxable year of the partnership, the ratio effective for the date on which the property is placed in service shall apply.

(ii) Notwithstanding subdivision (i) of this subparagraph, if all related items of income, gain, loss, and deduction with respect to any item of partnership section 38 property are specially allocated in the same manner and if such special allocation is recognized under section 704(a) and (b) and paragraph (b) of § 1.704-1, then each partner's share of the basis of such item of new section 38 property or the cost of such item of used section 38 property shall be determined by reference to such special allocation effective for the date on which the property is placed in service.

(iii) Notwithstanding subdivisions (i) and (ii) of this subparagraph, if with respect to a partnership's taxable year the conditions set forth in (a) through *(c)* of this subdivision are satisfied with respect to a partner, then such partner shall not take into account the basis (or cost) of any section 38 property placed in service by the partnership during such taxable year. The conditions referred to in the preceding sentence are:

(a) Such partner's interest in the general profits of the partnership during the taxable year is 5 percent or less;

(b) Under the partnership agreement, such partner will retire from the partnership during the taxable year or within 7 years after the end of such year; and

(c) The partnership agreement provides that the basis (or cost) of section 38 property placed in service by the partnership during the taxable year shall not be taken into account by a partner described in *(a)* and *(b)* of this subdivision.

Any basis (or cost) of section 38 property which is not taken into account by a partner because of the provisions of this subdivision shall be taken into account by the other partners in accordance with subdivision (i) of this subparagraph.

(3) Examples. This paragraph may be illustrated by the following examples:

Example (1). Partnership ABCD acquires and places in service on January 1, 1962, an item of new section 38 property, and acquires and places in service on September 1, 1962, another item of new section 38 property. The ABCD partnership and each of its partners reports income on the basis of the calendar year. Partners A, B, C, and D share partnership profits equally. Each partner's share of the basis of each new partnership section 38 property is 25 percent.

Example (2). Assume the same facts as in example (1) and the following additional facts: A dies on June 30, 1962, and B purchases A's interest as of such date. Each partner's share of the profits from January 1 to June 30 is 25 percent. From July 1 to December 31, B's share of the profits is 50 percent, and C and D's share of the profits is 25 percent each. For A's last taxable year (January 1 to June 30, 1962), A shall take into account 25 percent of the basis of the section 38 property placed in service on January 1. B shall take into account 25 percent of the basis of the section 38 property placed in service on January 1 and 50 percent of the basis of the section 38 property placed in service on September 1, C and D shall each take into account 25 percent of the basis of each new section 38 property placed in service by the partnership in 1962.

Example (3). Partnership MR is engaged in the business of renting soda fountain equipment and icemakers to restaurants. The partnership makes no elections under § 1.48-4 to treat its lessees as having purchased such property. Under the terms of the partnership agreement, the income, gain or loss on disposition, depreciation, and other deductions attributable to the icemakers are specially allocated 70 percent to partner M and 30 percent to partner R. In all other respects M and R share profits and losses equally. If the special allocation with respect to the icemakers is recognized under section 704(a) and (b) and paragraph (b) of § 1.704-1, the basis (or cost) of the icemakers which qualify as partnership section 38 property shall be taken into account 70 percent by M and 30 percent by R. The basis (or cost) of partnership section 38 property not subject to the special allocation shall be taken into account equally by M and R.

Example (4). Assume the same facts as in example (3) and the following additional facts: During November 1962, the partnership, which reports its income on the basis of a fiscal year ending May 31, acquires and places in service two items which qualify as new section 38 property, an icemaker and a soda fountain. The icemaker has an estimated useful life of 8 years to the partnership and a basis of $1,000. The soda fountain has an estimated useful life of 6 years to the partnership and a basis of $600. Partner M also owns and operates a business as a sole proprietorship and reports income on the calendar year basis. During 1963, M acquires and places in service in his sole proprietorship a machine which qualifies as new section 38 property. This machine has an estimated useful life of 4 years and a basis of $300. M owns no interest in any other partnerships, electing small business corporations, estates, or trusts. M's total qualified investment for 1963 is $1,000, computed as follows:

Property	Estimated useful life	Basis	M's share of basis	Applicable percentage	Qualified investment
Partnership MR					
Icemaker	8	$1,000	$700	100	$ 700
Soda fountain	6	600	300	66⅔	200
Machine	4	300		33⅓	100
Total					1,000

(g) Public utility property. *(1) In general.* (i) Scope of paragraph. This paragraph only applies to property described in section 50. For rules relating to public utility property not described in section 50, see 26 CFR Part 1 § 1.46-3(g) (as revised April 1, 1977). This paragraph does not reflect amendments to section 46(c) made after enactment of the Revenue Act of 1971.

(ii) Amount of qualified investment. A taxpayer's qualified investment in section 38 property that is public utility property is 4/7 of the amount otherwise determined under this section.

(2) Meaning and uses of certain terms. For purposes of this paragraph—

(i) Public utility property. "Public utility property" is property used by a taxpayer predominantly in a trade or business that is a public utility activity and property that is nonregulated communication property.

(ii) Public utility activity. A "public utility activity" is any activity in which the goods or services described in section 46(c)(3)(B)(i), (ii), or (iii) are furnished or sold at regulated rates. If property is used by a taxpayer both in a public utility activity and in another activity, the characterization of such property is based on the predominant use of such property during the taxable year in which it is placed in service.

(iii) Regulated rates. A taxpayer's rates are "regulated" if they are established or approved on a rate-of-return basis. Rates regulated on a rate-of-return basis are an authorization to collect revenues that cover the taxpayer's cost of providing goods or services, including a fair return on the taxpayer's investment in providing such goods or services, where the taxpayer's costs and investment are determined by use of a uniform system of accounts prescribed by the regulatory body. A taxpayer's rates are not "regulated" if they are established or approved on the basis of maintaining competition within an industry, insuring adequate service to customers of an industry, or charging "reasonable" rates within an industry since the taxpayer is not authorized to collect revenues based on the taxpayer's cost of providing goods or services. Rates are considered to have been "established or approved" if a schedule of rates is filed with a regulatory body that has the power to approve such rates, even though the regulatory body takes no action on the filed schedule or generally leaves undisturbed rates filed by the taxpayer.

(iv) Nonregulated communication property. "Nonregulated communication property" is property that is clearly the same type of property (and is used by the taxpayer predominantly for the same type of communication purposes) as communication property, but it is used by the taxpayer predominantly in a trade or business that is not a public utility activity. For purposes of this subdivision (iv), communication property is property ordinarily used for communication purposes by persons who provide regulated telephone or microwave communication services described in section 46(c)(3)(B)(iii). The determination of whether property is clearly of this same type and is used predominantly for these same communication purposes as communication property is made on the basis of the facts and circumstances of each particular case, including the current state of technology in the communications industry and the range and type of services permitted or required to be provided by the regulated telephone and microwave communication industry. As of 1978, wires or cables used predominantly to distribute to subscribers the signals of one or more television broadcast stations or cablecast stations (such as in a CATV system) are not used for the same type of communication purposes as communication property. Communication property includes microwave transmission equipment, private communication equipment (other than land mobile radio equipment for which the operator must obtain a license from the Federal Communications Commission), private switchboard (PBX) equipment, communications terminal equipment connected to telephone networks, data transmission equipment, and communications satellites. Communication property does not include (as of 1978) computer terminals or facsimile reproduction equipment that is connected to telephone lines to transmit data. It also does not include office furniture stands for communication property, tools, repair vehicles, and similar property, even if such property is exclusively used in providing regulated telephone or microwave communication services.

(3) Leased property. Public utility property includes property which is leased to others by a taxpayer where the leasing of such property is part of the lessor's public utility activity. Thus, such leased property is public utility property even though the lessee uses such property in an activity which is not a public utility activity, and whether or not the lessor of such property makes a valid election under § 1.48-4 to treat the lessee as having purchased such property for purposes of the credit allowed by section 38. Property leased by a lessor, where the leasing is not part of a public utility activity, to a lessee who uses such property predominantly in a public utility activity is public utility property for purposes of computing the lessor's or lessee's qualified investment with respect to such property.

(4) Property used in both the production or transmission of gas and the local distribution of gas. (i) With respect to properties of a taxpayer engaged in both the production or transmission of gas and the local distribution of gas, section 38 property shall be considered as used predominantly in the trade or business of the furnishing or sale of gas through a local distribution system if expenditures for such property are chargeable to any of the following accounts under either the uniform system of accounts prescribed for natural gas companies (class A and class B) by the Federal Power Commission, effective January 1, 1961, or the uniform system of accounts for class A and B gas utilities adopted in 1958 by the National Association of Railroad and Utility Commissioners (or would be chargeable to any of the following accounts if the taxpayer used either of such systems):

(a) Accounts 360 through 363, inclusive (Local Storage Plant), or

(b) Accounts 374 through 387, inclusive (Distribution Plant).

(ii) If expenditures for section 38 property are chargeable (or would be chargeable) to any of the following accounts under either of the systems named in subdivision (i) of this subparagraph, the determination of whether or not such property is used predominantly in the trade or business of the furnishing or sale of gas through a local distribution system shall be made under all the facts and circumstances relating to the actual use of such property in the year such property is placed in service:

(a) Accounts 304 through 320, inclusive (Manufactured Gas Production Plant), or

(b) Accounts 389 through 399, inclusive (General Plant).

For example, if an office machine is used 55 percent of the time for billing customers of the taxpayer's local distribution system in the year in which it is placed in service, such office machine shall be considered as used predominantly in the trade or business of the furnishing or sale of gas through a local distribution system.

(5) Certain submarine cable property. In the case of any interest in a submarine cable circuit which is property described in section 50 used to furnish telegraph service between the United States and a point outside the United States of a taxpayer engaged in furnishing international telegraph service (if the rates for such furnishing have been established or approved by a governmental unit, agency, instrumentality, commission, or similar body described in subparagraph (2) of this paragraph), the qualified investment shall not exceed the qualified investment attributable to so much of the interest of the taxpayer in the circuit as does not exceed 50 percent of all interests in the circuit.

(h) Certain replacement property. *(1)* (i) if section 38 property is placed in service by the taxpayer to replace property (whether or not section 38 property) similar or related in service or use which was destroyed or damaged before August 16, 1971 by fire, storm, shipwreck, or other casualty, or stolen before such date, then for purposes of paragraph (a) of this section the basis (or cost) of the replacement section 38 property otherwise determined under paragraph (c) of this section shall be reduced by an amount equal to the lesser of—

(a) The amount of money, or the fair market value of other property, received as compensation, by insurance or otherwise, for the property which was destroyed, damaged, or stolen, or

(b) The adjusted basis of such destroyed, damaged, or stolen property (immediately before such destruction, damage, or theft).

(ii) For purposes of subdivision (i) of this subparagraph—

(a) Section 38 property placed in service after the due date (including extensions of time thereof) for filing the taxpayer's income tax return for the taxable year in which the other property was destroyed, damaged, or stolen shall not be considered as replacement section 38 property, and

(b) If the property which is destroyed, damaged, or stolen, is leased property, no other leased property shall be considered as replacement property with respect to the property destroyed, damaged, or stolen, in any case in which the lessor makes or made an election under section 48(d) (relating to election with respect to certain leased property) with respect to either the property destroyed, damaged, or stolen, the other leased property, or both.

(2) Subparagraph (1) of this paragraph shall not apply to replacement property if the reduction, under such subparagraph (1), in the basis (or cost) of such replacement property is less than the excess of—

(i) The qualified investment with respect to the destroyed, damaged, or stolen property, over

(ii) The recomputed qualified investment with respect to such property (determined under the principles of paragraph (a) of § 1.47-1).

(3) This paragraph may be illustrated by the following examples:

Example (1). (i) A acquired and placed in service on January 1, 1962, machine No. 1, which qualified as section 38 property, with a basis of $30,000 and an estimated useful life of 6 years. The amount of qualified investment with respect to such machine was $20,000. On January 2, 1963, machine No. 1 is completely destroyed by fire. On January 1, 1963, the adjusted basis of such machine in A's hands is $24,500. On November 1, 1963, A receives $23,000 in insurance proceeds as compensation for the destroyed machine, and on December 15, 1963, A acquires and places in service machine No. 2, which qualifies as section 38 property, with a basis of $41,000 and an estimated useful life of 6 years to replace machine No. 1.

(ii) Under subparagraph (1) of this paragraph, the $41,000 basis of machine No. 2 is reduced, for purposes of paragraph (a) of this section, by $23,000 (that is, the $23,000 insurance proceeds since such amount is less than the $24,500 adjusted basis of machine No. 1 immediately before it was destroyed) to $18,000 since such reduction (that is, $23,000) is greater than the $20,000 reduction in qualified investment which would be made if paragraph (a) of § 1.47-1 were to apply to machine No. 1 ($20,000 qualified investment less zero recomputed qualified investment).

Example (2). (i) The facts are the same as in example (1) except that on November 1, 1963, A receives only $19,000 in insurance proceeds as compensation for the destroyed machine.

(ii) The $41,000 basis of machine No. 2 is not reduced, for purposes of paragraph (a) of this section, under this paragraph since the $19,000 reduction which would have been made under this paragraph had it applied (that is, the $19,000 insurance proceeds since such amount is less than the $24,500 adjusted basis of machine No. 1 immediately before it was destroyed) is less than the $20,000 reduction in qualified investment which is made since paragraph (a) of § 1.47-1 applies to machine No. 1 ($20,000 qualified investment less zero recomputed qualified investment).

T.D. 6731, 5/7/64, amend T.D. 6931, 10/9/67, T.D. 7203, 8/24/72, T.D. 7602, 3/20/79, T.D. 7927, 12/15/83, T.D. 7982, 10/5/84, T.D. 8183, 3/1/88, T.D. 8474, 4/26/93.

PAR. 2. Section 1.46-3 is amended as follows:

1. Paragraph (i) is added and reserved.

2. Paragraphs (e)(1) through (e)(6) are redesignated paragraphs (j)(1) through (j)(6), respectively.

3. The heading of paragraph (j), as redesignated, is revised to read: "(j) *Estimated useful life of property not described in paragraph (e)(8) of this section*—".

4. Paragraph (e)(7) is removed.

5. A new paragraph (e) is added to read as follows:

Proposed § 1.46-3 Qualified investment. [*For Preamble, see ¶ 151,041*]

* * * * *

(e) Useful life/recovery period. *(1) In general.* For purposes of computing qualified investment in property that is not recovery property (within the meaning of section 168) the useful life of such property to be used in determining the applicable percentage to be applied to its basis or cost is the life used or to be used by the taxpayer in computing their allowance for depreciation with respect to such property for the taxable year in which the property is placed in service. Thus, if property is placed in service by a taxpayer in a taxable year but the period for depreciation with respect to such property does not begin until a succeeding taxable year (see paragraph (d)(1) of this section), the useful life for purposes of computing qualified investment must be the useful life that the taxpayer uses in computing the allowances for depreciation. See paragraph (e)(6) of this section for rules for determining the useful life of property with respect to which the allowance for depreciation is computed under the unit of production method, the income-forecast method, or any other method which does not measure the useful life of the property in terms of years. For purposes of computing qualified investment in recovery property (within the meaning of section 168) the class of recovery property which applies to such property (as determined under section 168(c)) is determinative of the applicable percentage to be applied to its basis or cost.

(2) Individual life. (i) In order to determine qualified investment for multiple asset accounts (or single asset accounts for which an average life rate is used) it is necessary to determine the average life of the account. In order to determine average life, each asset which is section 38 property must be assigned an individual life. The rules for assigning individual lives to section 38 property are set forth below.

(ii) The individual life of any section 38 property to which an election under section 167(m) applies is the present class life selected for such property under § 1.167(a)-11(b)(4), whether or not such property constitutes mass assets (as defined in § 1.47-1(g)(2)).

(iii) The individual life of section 38 property described in this paragraph (e)(2)(iii) is determined for each asset on the best estimate obtainable on the basis of all the facts and circumstances. The individual life for each asset placed in a multiple asset account (including a mass asset account) must be the same as the useful life of such asset used in determining the group, classified, or composite life for the account for purposes of computing depreciation. Property is described in this paragraph (e)(2)(iii) if:

(a) it is not recovery property within the meaning of section 168;

(b) no election under section 167(m) is applicable to the property; and

(c) it is placed in a multiple asset account for which a group, classified, or composite rate is used in computing depreciation (or in single asset accounts for which an average life rate is used).

(iv) The individual life for recovery property within the meaning of section 168 is the recovery period which applies to such property as determined under section 168(c).

(3) Assets similar in kind. (i) For assets similar in kind contained in a multiple asset account (or in a single asset account for which an average life rate is used) and placed in service in taxable years beginning on or after [30 days after publication of this Treasury Decision in the FEDERAL REGISTER], the taxpayer must assign to each of those assets the average life of those assets used in computing the allowance for depreciation. Thus no assets may receive investment credit for a life longer than the average life of the assets in the account. For example, assume the taxpayer places 10 similar trucks in a multiple asset account for which a group rate is used in computing the allowance for depreciation. The trucks have an average useful life of 6 years, based on an estimated range of 5 to 7 years. The taxpayer must assign each asset a useful life of 6 years, even though some assets in the account are expected to remain in service for more than 6 years. For assets similar in kind that are placed in service in taxable years beginning before [30 days after publication of this Treasury Decision in the FEDERAL REGISTER], the rules contained in paragraph (e)(3)(ii) and (iv) of 26 CFR 1.46-3 (revised as of April 1, 1983) apply.

(ii) For purposes of paragraph (e)(3)(i) of this section, assets shall not be considered as "similar in kind" in respect of other assets unless all such assets are substantially of the same value, nor shall used section 38 property be considered as "similar in kind" to new section 38 property.

(4) Mass assets. For "mass assets" (as defined in paragraph (g)(2) of § 1.47-1) placed in service in taxable years beginning on or after [30 days after publication of this Treasury Decision in the FEDERAL REGISTER], each asset must be assigned the life of the account, even if a mortality dispersion table indicates that some assets are expected to remain in service longer than the life of the account. See paragraphs (g)(3) and (h)(2) of § 1.47-1 regarding the grouping of mass assets. For mass assets placed in service in taxable years beginning before [30 days after publication of this Treasury Decision in the FEDERAL REGISTER], the rules contained in paragraph (j)(3)(iii) of this section apply.

(5) Useful life of property subject to amortization. In the case of property with respect to which amortization in lieu of depreciation is allowable, the term over which amortization deductions are taken shall be considered as the useful life of such property.

(6) Useful life of property subject to certain methods of depreciation. If a taxpayer is using a method of depreciation, such as the unit of production or retirement method, which does not measure the useful life of the property in terms of years, he must estimate such useful life in years in order to compute his qualified investment.

(7) Record requirements. The taxpayer shall maintain sufficient records to determine whether section 47 (relating to certain dispositions, etc., of section 38 property) applies with respect to any asset.

(8) Effective dates. The provisions in paragraphs (e)(1) through (7) of this section apply only to property—

(i) the construction, reconstruction, or erection of which—

(a) Is completed by the taxpayer after August 15, 1971, or

(b) Is begun by the taxpayer after March 31, 1971, or

(ii) which is acquired by the taxpayer—

(a) After August 15, 1971, or

(b) After March 31, 1971, and before August 16, 1971, pursuant to an order which the taxpayer establishes was placed after March 31, 1971.

For property not described in this paragraph (e)(8), the rules in paragraphs (j)(1) through (6) of this section apply.

* * * * *

§ 1.46-4 Limitations with respect to certain persons.

• ***Caution:*** Reg. § 1.46-4, following, was issued under Code Sec. 46 before amendment by P.L. 101-508 (11/5/90). The relative provisions of Code Sec. 46 before such amendment were adopted by reference in current Code Sec. 50.

Caution: The Treasury has not yet amended Reg § 1.46-4 to reflect changes made by P.L. 104-188, P.L. 101-508, P.L. 100-647, P.L. 99-514, P.L. 98-369, P.L. 97-34.

(a) Mutual savings institutions. In the case of an organization to which section 593 applies (that is, a mutual savings bank, a cooperative bank, or a domestic building and loan association)—

(1) The qualified investment with respect to each section 38 property shall be 50 percent of the amount otherwise determined under § 1.46-3, and

(2) The $25,000 amount specified in section 46(a)(2), relating to limitation based on amount of tax, shall be reduced by 50 percent of such amount.

For example, if a domestic building and loan association places in service on January 1, 1963, new section 38 property with a basis of $30,000 and an estimated useful life of 6 years, its qualified investment for 1963 with respect to such property computed under § 1.46-3 is $20,000 (66⅔ percent of $30,000). However, under this paragraph such amount is reduced to $10,000 (50 percent of $20,000). If an organization to which section 593 applies is a member of an affiliated group (as defined in section 46(a)(5)), the $25,000 amount specified in section 46(a)(2) shall be reduced in accordance with the provisions of paragraph (f) of § 1.46-1 before such amount is further reduced under this paragraph.

(b) Regulated investment companies and real estate investment trusts. *(1)* In the case of a regulated investment company or a real estate investment trust subject to taxation under subchapter M, chapter 1 of the Code—

(i) The qualified investment with respect to each section 38 property otherwise determined under § 1.46-3, and

(ii) The $25,000 amount specified in section 46(a)(2), relating to limitation based on amount of tax,

shall be reduced to such person's ratable share of each such amount. If a regulated investment company or a real estate investment trust is a member of an affiliated group (as defined in section 46(a)(5)), the $25,000 amount specified in section 46(a)(2) shall be reduced in accordance with the provisions of paragraph (f) of § 1.46-1 before such amount is further reduced under this paragraph.

(2) A person's ratable share of the amount described in subparagraph (1)(i) and the amount described in subparagraph (1)(ii) of this paragraph shall be the ratio which—

(i) Taxable income for the taxable year, bears to

(ii) Taxable income for the taxable year plus the amount of the deduction for dividends paid taken into account under section 852(b)(2)(D) in computing investment company taxable income, or under section 857(b)(2)(B) (section 857(b)(2)(C), as then in effect, for taxable years ending before October 5, 1976) in computing real estate investment trust taxable income, as the case may be.

For purposes of the preceding sentence, taxable income means, in the case of a regulated investment company its investment company taxable income (within the meaning of section 852(b)(2)), and in the case of a real estate investment trust its real estate investment trust taxable income (within the meaning of section 857(b)(2)). For purposes of this paragraph only, in computing taxable income for a taxable year beginning before January 1, 1964, a regulated investment company or a real estate investment trust may compute depreciation deductions with respect to section 38 property placed in service before January 1, 1964, without regard to the reduction in basis of such property required under § 1.48-7. The amount of the deduction for dividends paid includes the amount of deficiency dividends (other than capital gains deficiency dividends) taken into account in computing investment company taxable income or real estate investment trust taxable income for the taxable year. In the case of a real estate investment trust, the amount of the deduction for dividends paid includes the amount of deficiency dividends (other than capital gains deficiency dividends) taken into account in computing real estate investment trust taxable income for the taxable year. See section 860(f) for the definition of deficiency dividends.

(3) This paragraph may be illustrated by the following example:

Example. (i) Corporation X, a regulated investment company subject to taxation under section 852 of the Code which makes its return on the basis of the calendar year, places in service on January 1, 1964, section 38 property with a basis of $30,000 and an estimated useful life of 6 years. Corporation X's investment company taxable income under section 852(b)(2) is $10,000 after taking into account a deduction for dividends paid of $90,000.

(ii) Under this paragraph, corporation X's qualified investment for the taxable year 1964 with respect to such property is $2,000, computed as follows: (a) $20,000 (qualified investment under § 1.46-3), multiplied by (b) $10,000 (taxable income), divided by (c) $100,000 (taxable income plus the deduction for dividends paid). For 1964, the $25,000 amount specified in section 46(a) is reduced to $2,500.

(c) Cooperatives. *(1)* In the case of a cooperative organization described in section 1381(a)—

(i) The qualified investment with respect to each section 38 property otherwise determined under § 1.46-3, and

(ii) The $25,000 amount specified in section 46(a), relating to limitation based on amount of tax,

shall be reduced to such cooperative's ratable share of each such amount. If a cooperative organization described in section 1381(a) is a member of an affiliated group (as defined in section 46(a)(5)), the $25,000 amount specified in section 46(a)(2) shall be reduced in accordance with the provisions of paragraph (f) of § 1.46-1 before such amount is further reduced under this paragraph.

(2) A cooperative's ratable share of the amount described in subparagraph (1)(i) and the amount described in subparagraph (1)(ii) of this paragraph shall be the ratio which—

(i) Taxable income for the taxable year, bears to

(ii) Taxable income for the taxable year plus the sum of (a) the amount of the deductions allowed under section 1382(b), (b) the amount of the deductions allowed under section 1382(c), and (c) amounts similar to the amounts described in (a) and (b) of this subdivision the tax treatment of which is determined without regard to subchapter T, chapter 1 of the Code and the regulations thereunder.

Amounts similar to deductions allowed under section 1382(b) or (c) are, for example, in the case of a taxable year of a cooperative organization beginning before January 1, 1963, the amount of patronage dividends which are excluded or deducted and any nonpatronage distributions which are deducted under section 522(b)(1). In the case of a taxable year of a cooperative organization beginning after December 31, 1962, such amounts are the amount of patronage dividends and nonpatronage distributions which are excluded or deducted without regard to section 1382(b) or (c) because they are paid with respect to patronage occurring before 1963. For purposes of this paragraph only, in computing taxable income for a taxable year beginning before January 1, 1964, a cooperative may compute depreciation deductions with respect to section 38 property placed in service before January 1, 1964, without regard to the reduction in basis of such property required under § 1.48-7.

(3) This paragraph may be illustrated by the following example:

Example. (i) Cooperative X, an organization described in section 1381(a) which makes its return on the basis of the calendar year, places in service on January 1, 1964, section 38 property with a basis of $30,000 and an estimated useful life of 6 years. Cooperative X's taxable income is $10,000 after taking into account deductions of $20,000 allowed under section 1382(b), deductions of $60,000 allowed under section 1382(c), and deductions of $10,000 allowed under section 522(b)(1)(B).

(ii) Under this paragraph, cooperative X's qualified investment for the taxable year 1964 with respect to such property is $2,000, computed as follows: (a) $20,000 (qualified investment under § 1.46-3), multiplied by (b) $10,000 (taxable income), divided by (c) $100,000 (taxable income plus the sum of the deductions allowed under sections 1382(b), 1382(c), and 522(b)(1)(B)). For 1964, the $25,000 amount specified in section 46(a)(2) is reduced to $2,500.

(d) Noncorporate lessors. *(1)* In the case of a lease entered into after September 22, 1971, a credit is allowed under section 38 to a noncorporate lessor of property with respect to the leased property only if—

(i) Such property has been manufactured or produced by the lessor in the ordinary course of his business, or

(ii) The term of the lease (taking into account any options to renew) is less than 50 percent of the estimated useful life of the property (determined under § 1.46-3(e), and for the period consisting of the first 12 months after the date on which the property is transferred to the lessee the sum of the deductions with respect to such property which are allowable to the lessor solely by reason of section 162 (other than rents and reimbursed amounts with respect to such property) exceeds 15 percent of the rental income produced by such property. In the case of property of which a partnership is the lessor, the credit otherwise allowable under section 38 with respect to such property to any partner which is a corporation shall be allowed notwithstanding the first sentence of this subparagraph. For purposes of this subparagraph, an electing small business corporation (as defined in section 1371) shall be treated as a person which is not a corporation. This paragraph shall not apply to property used by the taxpayer in his trade or business (other than the leasing of property) for a period of at least 24 months preceding the day on which any lease of such property is entered into.

(2) For purposes of subparagraph (1)(ii) of this paragraph, if at the time the lessor files his income tax return for the taxable year in which the property is placed in service, the lessor is unable to show that the more-than-15-percent test has been satisfied, then no credit may be claimed by the lessor on such return with respect to such property unless (i) taking into account the lessor's obligations under the lease it is reasonable to believe that the more-than-15-percent test will be satisfied, and (ii) the lessor files a statement with his return from which it may be determined that he expects to satisfy the more-than-15-percent test. If the more-than-15-percent test is not satisfied with respect to the property, the taxpayer must file an amended return for the year in which the property is placed in service.

(3) (i) The more-than-15-percent test described in subparagraph (1)(ii) of this paragraph is based on the relationship of the expense of the lessor relating to or attributable to the property to the gross income from rents of the taxpayer produced by the property. The test is applied with respect to such expenses and gross income as are properly attributable to the period consisting of the first 12 months after the date on which the property is transferred to the lessee. When more than one property is subject to a single lease and, pursuant to subparagraph (4) of this paragraph, the arrangement is considered to be a separate lease of each property, the test is applied separately to each such lease by making an apportionment of the payments received and expenses incurred with respect to each such property, considering all relevant factors. Such apportionment is made in accordance with any reasonable method selected and consistently applied by the taxpayer. For example, under subparagraph (4) of this paragraph, where a taxpayer leases an airplane which he owns to an airline along with a baggage truck, he is treated as having made two separate leases, one covering the airplane and one covering the baggage truck. Thus, the test will be applied by apportioning the related income and expenses between the two leases. Similarly, where a taxpayer leases a factory building erected by him containing section 38 property (machinery and equipment), the test will be applied to the taxpayer as though he had leased (to the lessee) the building and the section 38 property separately. Thus, the rental income and expenses are apportioned between the building and the section 38 property.

(ii) Only those deductions allowable solely by reason of section 162 are taken into account in applying the more-than-15-percent test. Hence, depreciation allowable by reason of section 167 (including amortization allowable in lieu of depreciation): interest allowable by reason of section 163: taxes allowable by reason of section 164; and depletion allowable by reason of section 611 are examples of deductions which are not taken into account in applying the test. Moreover, rents and reimbursed amounts paid or payable by the lessor are not taken into account notwithstanding that a deduction in respect of such rents or reimbursed amounts is allowable solely by reason of section 162. For purposes of this paragraph, a reimbursed amount is an expense for which the lessee or some other party is obligated to reimburse the lessor. Section 162 expenses paid or payable by any person other than the lessor are not taken into account unless the lessor is obligated to reimburse the person paying the expense. Further, if the lessee is obligated to pay to the lessor a charge for services which is separately stated or determinable, the expenses incurred by the lessor with respect to those services are not taken into account.

(iii) For purposes of the more-than-15-percent test, the gross income from rents of the lessor produced by the property is the total amount which is payable to the lessor by reason of the lease agreement other than reimbursements of section 162 expenses and charges for services which are separately stated or determinable. The fact that such amount depends, in whole or in part, on the sales or profits of the lessee or the performance of significant services by the lessor shall not affect the characterization of such amounts as gross income from rents for purposes of this paragraph. Gross income from rents also includes any taxes imposed on the lessor by local law but which are paid directly by the lessee on behalf of the lessor.

(4) For purposes of determining under this paragraph whether property is subject to a lease, the provisions of § 1.57-3(d)(1) (relating to definition of a lease) shall apply. If a noncorporate lessor enters into two or more successive leases with respect to the same or substantially similar items of section 38 property, the terms of such leases shall be aggregated and such leases shall be considered one lease for the purpose of determining whether the term of such leases is less than 50 percent of the estimated useful life of the property subject to such leases. Thus, for example, if an individual owns an airplane with an estimated useful life of 7 years and enters into three successive 3-year leases of such airplane, such leases will be considered to be one lease for a term of nine years for the purpose of determining whether the term of the lease is less than 3½ years (50 percent of the 7-year estimated useful life).

(5) The requirements of this paragraph shall not apply with respect to any property which is treated as section 38 property by reason of section 48(a)(1)(E).

T.D. 6731, 5/7/64, amend T.D. 6958, 6/20/68, T.D. 7203, 8/24/72, T.D. 7767, 2/3/81, T.D. 7936, 1/17/84, T.D. 8031, 6/18/85.

§ 1.46-5 Qualified progress expenditures.

• ***Caution:*** Reg. § 1.46-5, following, was issued under Code Sec. 46 before amendment by P.L. 101-508 (11/5/90). The relative provisions of Code

Sec. 46 before such amendment were adopted by reference in current Code Sec. 48.

Caution: The Treasury has not yet amended Reg § 1.46-5 to reflect changes made by P.L. 101-508, P.L. 100-647, P.L. 99-514, P.L. 98-369, P.L. 97-34.

(a) Effective date. This section applies to taxable years ending after December 31, 1974. This section reflects amendments to the Internal Revenue Code made only by the Tax Reduction Act of 1975, the Tax Reform Act of 1976, and the Revenue Act of 1978.

(b) General rule. Under section 46(d), a taxpayer may elect to take the investment credit for qualified progress expenditures (as defined in paragraph (g) of this section). In general, qualified progress expenditures are amounts paid (paid or incurred in the case of self-constructed property) for construction of progress expenditure property. The taxpayer must reasonably estimate that the property will take at least 2 years to construct and that the useful life of the property will be 7 year or more. Qualified progress expenditures may not be taken into account if made before the later of January 22, 1975, or the first taxable year to which an election under section 46(d) applies. In general, qualified progress expenditures are not allowed for the year property is placed in service, nor for the first year or any subsequent year recapture is required under section 47(a)(3). There is a percentage limitation on qualified progress expenditures for taxable years beginning before January 1, 1980. For a special rule relating to transfers of progress expenditure property, see paragraph (r) of this section.

(c) Reduction of qualified investment. Under section 46(c)(4), a taxpayer must reduce qualified investment for the year property is placed in service by qualified progress expenditures taken into account by that person or a predecessor. A "predecessor" of a taxpayer is a person whose election under section 46(d) carries over to the taxpayer under paragraph (o)(3) of this section.

(d) Progress expenditure property. Progress expenditure property is property constructed by or for the taxpayer, with a normal construction period of 2 years or more. The taxpayer must reasonably believe that the property will be new section 38 property with a useful life of 7 years or more when placed in service. Whether property is progress expenditure property is determined on the basis of facts know at the close of the taxable year of the taxpayer in which construction begins (or, if later, at the close of the first taxable year to which an election under section 46(d) applies). For purposes of this paragraph (d), property is constructed by or for the taxpayer only if it is built or manufactured from materials and component parts. Accordingly, progress expenditure property does not include property such as orchards, vineyards, livestock, or motion picture films or videotapes.

(e) Normal construction period. *(1) In general.* (i) The normal construction period is the period the taxpayer reasonably expects will be required to construct the property. The period begins on the date physical work on construction of the property commences and ends on the date the property is available to be placed in service. The normal construction period does not include, however, construction before January 22, 1975, nor construction before the first day of the first taxable year for which an election under section 46(d) is in effect. Physical work on construction of property does not include preliminary activities such as planning, designing, preparing blueprints, exploring, or securing financing.

(ii) The determination of the time when physical work on construction commences is based on the facts and circumstances of each case. Physical work on construction of property may include the physical work done by a subcontractor on a component specifically designated as part of the property. Also, the commencement of physical work on construction may occur at a site different from the main site of construction of the property. For example, if a shipyard orders a turbine before it begins work on building a ship, the normal construction period of the ship is measured from the time the subcontractor commences physical work on construction of the turbine (if it is normal for such work to precede the work of the main contractor).

(iii) Generally, physical work on construction does not include physical activity that is not necessary to complete construction of the property, nor does it include physical work on construction of a building or other property that will not be new section 38 property when placed in service. Physical work on construction also does not include research and development activities in a laboratory or experimental setting.

(iv) The normal construction period of property ends on the date it is expected the property will be available to be placed in service. Property is considered available to be placed in service when construction is completed and the property is available for delivery to the site of its assigned function. It is not necessary that property be in a state of readiness for a specifically assigned function. Nor is it necessary that it actually be delivered to the site of its assigned function.

(2) Estimates. Taxpayers should refer to normal industry practice in estimating the normal construction period of particular items. A different period may be used if special circumstances exist making it impractical to make the estimate on the basis of normal industry practice. The estimate must be based on information available at the close of the taxable year in which physical work on construction of the property begins, or, if later, at the close of the first taxable year for which an election under section 46(d) is in effect for the taxpayer. If the estimate is reasonable when made, the actual time it takes to complete the work is, in general, irrelevant in determining whether property is progress expenditure property. However, if there is a significant error in estimating the normal construction period, it may be evidence that the estimate was unreasonable when made. For taxable years ending after April 1, 1988, a taxpayer not relying on normal industry practice to estimate the normal construction period of particular property must attach to the tax return for the taxable year in which physical work on construction of the property begins (or, if later, the first taxable year for which an election under section 46(d) is in effect) a statement of the basis relied upon in estimating the normal construction period of the property.

(3) Integrated unit. (i) In determining whether property has a normal construction period of 2 years or more, property that will be placed in service separately is to be considered separately. For example, if two ships are contracted for at the same time, each ship is considered separately under this paragraph. However, for property that will be placed in service as an integrated unit, the taxpayer must determine the normal construction period of the integrated unit. If the normal construction period of the integrated unit is 2 years or more, the normal construction period of each item of new section 38 property that is a part of the integrated unit is considered to be 2 years or more. Thus, the normal construc-

tion period of an integrated unit may be 2 years or more even if no part of the unit has a normal construction period of 2 years or more.

(ii) Property is part of an integrated unit only if the operation of that item is essential to the performance of the function to which the unit is assigned. Property essential to the performance of the function to which the unit is assigned includes property the use of which is significantly connected to that function and which effects the safe, proper, or efficient performance of the unit. Generally, property must be placed in service at the same time to be considered part of the same integrated unit. Properties are not an integrated unit, however, solely because they are to be placed in service at the same time.

(iii) The normal construction period for an integrated unit begins on the date the normal construction period of the first item of new section 38 property that is part of the unit begins. It is not necessary that physical work commence at the main construction site of the integrated unit.

The period ends on the date the last item of new section 38 property that is part of that unit is available to be placed in service. Property that is not new section 38 property, such as a building, is not considered part of an integrated unit for purposes of determining the normal construction period of that unit. For example, if a manufacturing plant has a normal construction period of two years or more but the equipment (i.e., new section 38 property) to be installed in the plant has a normal construction period of less than two years, the plant and the equipment do not constitute an integrated unit with a construction period of two years or more and the equipment is not progress expenditure property.

(4) Examples. The following examples illustrate this paragraph (e).

Example (1). On July 1, 1974, corporation X begins physical work on construction of a machine with an estimated useful life when placed in service of more than 7 years. For its taxable year ending June 30, 1975, X makes an election under section 46(d). For purposes of determining on June 30, 1975, whether the machine is "progress expenditure property", the normal construction period is treated as having begun on January 22, 1975. Thus, the machine will be considered to be progress expenditure property on June 30, 1975, only if the estimated time required to complete construction after June 30 is at least 18 months and 22 days (i.e., 2 years less the period January 22, 1975, through June 30, 1975).

Example (2). (i) Corporation X constructs a pipeline in two sections and simultaneously begins physical work on construction of each section on January 1, 1976. One section extends from city M to city N. The other extends from city N to city O. Oil will be transferred to storage tanks at both city N and city O. Corporation X also begins construction on January 1, 1976, of a pumping station necessary to the operation of the pipeline from city M to city N. Construction of a pumping station necessary to the operation of the pipeline from city N to city O begins on June 30, 1977. For 1976, corporation X makes an election under section 46(d).

(ii) The section of pipeline from city M to city N and the associated pumping station will be available to be placed in service on January 1, 1977. Construction of the section of the pipeline from city N to city O will be completed on June 30, 1977. However, that section of the pipeline will not be available to be placed in service until completion of the associated pumping station on January 1, 1978.

(iii) The section of pipeline from city M to city N and the section from city N to city O must be considered separately in determining the normal construction period of the property. Each section will be placed in service separately. However, each section of the pipeline and the associated pumping station may be considered an integrated unit. The pumping stations are essential to the operation of each section of pipeline. Each section of pipeline and the associated pumping station are placed in service at the same time.

(iv) The section of pipeline from city M to city N and the associated pumping station are not progress expenditure property, because the normal construction period of that unit is only 1 year (January 1, 1976 to January 1, 1977).

(v) The section of pipeline from city N to city O and the associated pumping station are progress expenditure property, because the normal construction of that integrated unit is 2 years (January 1, 1976 to January 1, 1978). It is immaterial that neither the construction period of that section of pipeline (January 1, 1976 to June 30, 1977) nor the construction period of the associated pumping station (June 30, 1977 to January 1, 1978) is 2 years.

(vi) Assume the pumping station associated with the pipeline from city N to city O includes backup pumping equipment that will be used only if the primary pumping equipment fails. The backup equipment is part of the integrated unit because it serves to effect the safe or efficient performance of the unit.

(f) New section 38 property with a 7-year useful life. *(1) In general.* The taxpayer must determine if property will be new section 38 property with a useful life of 7 years or more when placed in service. The determination must be made at the close of the taxable year in which construction begins or, if later, at the close of the first taxable year to which an election under section 46(d) applies for the taxpayer.

(2) Determination based on reasonably expected use. The determination of whether property will be "new section 38 property" (within the meaning of §§ 1.48-1 and 1.48-2) when placed in service must be based on the reasonably expected use of the property by the taxpayer. There is a presumption that property will be new section 38 property if it would be new section 38 property if placed in service by the taxpayer when the determination is made. For example, in determining if property is an integral part of manufacturing under section 48(a)(1)(B)(i), it will be presumed that property will be new section 38 property if the taxpayer is engaged in manufacturing when the determination is made. Also, significant steps taken to establish a trade or business will be evidence the taxpayer will be engaged in that trade or business when the property is placed in service.

(3) Estimated useful life. The determination of whether property will have an estimated useful life of 7 years or more when placed in service must be made by applying the principles of § 1.46-3(e). If the estimated useful life is less than 7 years when the property is actually placed in service, the credit previously allowed under section 46(d) must be recomputed under section 47(a)(3)(B).

(g) Definition of qualified progress expenditures. *(1) In general.* A taxpayer's qualified progress expenditures are the sum of qualified progress expenditures for self-constructed property (determined under paragraph (h) of this section), plus qualified progress expenditures for non-self-constructed property (determined under paragraph (j) of this section). Only amounts includible under § 1.46-3(c) in the basis of new section 38 property may be considered as qualified progress expenditures.

(2) Excluded amounts. Qualified progress expenditures do not include:

(i) In the case of non-self-constructed property, amounts incurred (whether or not paid)—

(A) Before the normal construction period begins, or

(B) Before the later of January 22, 1975, or the first day of the first taxable year for which an election under section 46(d) applies for the taxpayer;

(ii) In the case of self-constructed property, amounts chargeable to capital account—

(A) Before the normal construction period begins, or

(B) Before the later of January 22, 1975, or the first day of the first taxable year for which an election under section 46(d) applies for the taxpayer,

(See, however, section 46(d)(4)(A) and paragraph (h)(3)(i) of this section, relating to the time when amounts for component parts and materials are properly chargeable to capital account);

(iii) Expenditures with respect to particular property in the earlier of—

(A) The taxable year in which the property is placed in service, or

(B) The taxable year in which the taxpayer must recapture investment credit under section 47(a)(3) for the property or any subsequent year;

(iv) Expenditures for construction, reconstruction, or erection of property that is not section 38 property; or

(v) Amounts treated as an expense and deducted in the year paid or accrued.

(h) Qualified progress expenditures for self-constructed property. *(1) In general.* Qualified progress expenditures for self-constructed property (as defined in paragraph (k) of this section) are amounts properly chargeable to capital account in connection with that property. In general, amounts paid or incurred are chargeable to capital account if under the taxpayer's method of accounting they are properly includible in computing basis under § 1.46-3. Qualified progress expenditures for self-constructed property include both direct costs (e.g., labor, material, parts) and indirect costs (e.g., overhead, insurance) associated with construction of property to the extent those costs are properly chargeable to capital account.

(2) Property partially non-self constructed. If an item of property is self-constructed because more than half of the construction expenditures are made directly by the taxpayer, then any expenditures (whether or not made directly by the taxpayer) for construction of that item of property are not subject to the limitations of section 46(d)(3)(B) and paragraph (j) of this section (relating to actual payment and progress in construction).

(3) Time when amounts paid or incurred are properly chargeable to capital account. (i) In general, expenditures for component parts and materials to be used in construction of self-constructed property are not properly chargeable to capital account until consumed or physically attached in the construction process. Component parts and materials that have been neither consumed nor physically attached in the construction process, but which have been irrevocably allocated to construction of that property are properly chargeable to capital account. Component parts and materials designed specifically for the self-constructed property may be considered irrevocably allocated to construction of that property at the time of manufacture of the component parts and materials. Component parts and materials not designed specifically for the property may be considered irrevocably allocated to construction at the time of delivery to the construction site if they would be economically impractical to remove. For example, pumps delivered to sites of construction of a tundra pipeline may be treated as irrevocably allocated to that pipeline on the date of delivery, even if they would be usable, but for their location on the tundra, in connection with other property. Component parts and materials are not to be considered irrevocably allocated to use in self-constructed property until physical work on construction of that property has begun (as determined under paragraph (e)(1)(ii) of this section). Mere bookkeeping notations are not sufficient evidence that the necessary allocation has been made.

(ii) A taxpayer's procedure for determining the time when an expenditure is properly chargeable to capital account for self-constructed property is a method of accounting. Under section 446(e), the method of accounting, once adopted, may not be changed without consent of the Secretary.

(4) Records requirement. The taxpayer shall maintain detailed records which permit specific identification of the amounts properly chargeable by the taxpayer during each taxable year to capital account for each item of self-constructed property.

(i) [Reserved]

(j) Qualified progress expenditures for non-self-constructed property. *(1) In general.* Qualified progress expenditures for non-self-constructed property (as defined in paragraph (l) of this section) are amounts actually paid by the taxpayer to another person for construction of the property, but only to the extent progress is made in construction. For example, such expenditures may include payments to the manufacturer of an item of progress expenditure property, payments to a contractor building progress expenditure property, or payments for engineering designs or blueprints that are drawn up during the normal construction period.

(2) Property partially self-constructed. If an item of property is non-self-constructed, but a taxpayer uses its own employees to construct a portion of the property, expenditures for construction of that portion are made directly by the taxpayer (see § 1.46-5(h)(1)). Subject to the limitations of paragraph (g) of this section, those expenditures are qualified progress expenditures for non-self-constructed property if they satisfy the requirements of paragraph (j)(4), (5), and (6) of this section. Wages actually paid to the taxpayer's employees are presumed to correspond to progress in construction. Other amounts, including expenditures for materials, parts, and overhead, must be actually paid, not borrowed from the payee, and attributable to progress made in construction by the taxpayer.

(3) Property constructed by more than one person. The percentage of completion limitation (as prescribed in paragraph (j)(6) of this section), including the presumption of ratable progress in construction, applies to an item of progress expenditure property as a whole. However, if several manufacturers or contractors do work in connection with the same property, the progress that each person makes toward completion of construction of the property must be determined separately. Section 46(d)(3)(B) is then applied separately to amounts paid to each manufacturer or contractor based on each person's progress in construction. For example, assume the taxpayer contracts with three persons to build an item of equipment. The taxpayer contracts with A to build the frame, B to build the motor, and C to assemble the frame and motor. Assume each contract represents 33⅓

percent of the construction costs of the property. If, within the taxable year in which construction begins, A and B each complete 50 percent of the construction of the frame and motor, respectively, amounts paid to A during that taxable year not in excess of 16⅔ percent of the overall cost of the property, and amounts paid to B during that taxable year not in excess of 16⅔ percent of the overall cost of the property, are qualified progress expenditures. Section 46(d)(3)(B) does not apply, however, to persons, such as lower-tier subcontractors, that do not have a direct contractual relationship with the taxpayer. If, in the above example, A engages a subcontractor to construct part of the frame, section 46(d)(3)(B) is applied only to amounts paid by the taxpayer to A, B, and C, but the portion of construction completed by A during a taxable year includes the portion completed by A's subcontractor.

(4) Requirement of actual payment. Qualified progress expenditures for non-self-constructed property must be actually paid and not merely incurred. Amounts paid during the taxable year to another person for construction of non-self-constructed property may be in the form of money or property (e.g., materials). However, property given as payment may be considered only to the extent it will be includible under § 1.46-3(c) in the basis of the non-self-constructed property when it is placed in service.

(5) Certain borrowing disregarded. Qualified progress expenditures for non-self-constructed property do not include any amount paid to another person (the "payee") for construction if the amount is paid out of funds borrowed directly or indirectly from the payee. Amounts borrowed directly or indirectly from the payee by any person that is related to the taxpayer (within the meaning of section 267) or that is a member of the same controlled group of corporations (as defined in section 1563(a)) will be considered borrowed indirectly from the payee. Similarly, amounts borrowed under any financing arrangement that has the effect of making the payee a surety will be considered amounts borrowed indirectly by the taxpayer from the payee.

(6) Percentage of completion limitation. (i) Under section 46(d)(3)(B)(ii), payments made in any taxable year may be considered qualified progress expenditures for non-self-constructed property only to the extent they are attributable to progress made in construction (percentage of completion limitation). Progress will generally be measured in terms of the manufacturer's incurred cost, as a fraction of the anticipated cost (as adjusted from year to year). Architectural or engineering estimates will be evidence of progress made in construction. Cost accounting records also will be evidence of progress. Progress will be presumed to occur not more rapidly than ratably over the normal construction period. However, the taxpayer may rebut the presumption by clear and convincing evidence of a greater percentage of completion.

(ii) If, after the first year of construction, there is a change in either the total cost to the taxpayer or the total cost of construction by another person, the taxpayer must recompute the percentage of completion limitation on the basis of revised cost. However, the recomputation will affect only amounts allowed as qualified progress expenditures in the taxable year in which the change occurs and in subsequent taxable years. The recomputation remains subject to the presumption of pro rata completion.

(iii) If, for any taxable year, the amount paid to another person for construction of an item of property under section 46(d)(3)(B)(i) exceeds the percentage of completion limitation in section 46(d)(3)(B)(ii), the excess is treated as an amount paid to the other person for construction for the succeeding taxable year. If for any taxable year the percentage of completion limitation for an item of property exceeds the amount paid to another during the taxable year for construction, the excess is added to the percentage of completion limitation for that property for the succeeding taxable year.

(iv) The taxpayer must maintain detailed records which permit specific identification of the amounts paid to each person for construction of each item of property and the percentage of construction completed by each person for each taxable year.

(7) Example. The following example illustrates paragraph (j)(6) of this section.

Example. (i) Corporation X agrees to build an airplane for corporation Y, a calendar year taxpayer. The airplane is non-self-constructed progress expenditure property. Physical work on construction begins on January 1, 1980. The normal construction period for the airplane is five years and the airplane is delivered and placed in service on December 31, 1984.

(ii) The cost of construction to corporation X is $500,000. The contract price is $550,000. Corporation Y makes a $110,000 payment in each of the years 1980 and 1981, an $85,000 payment in 1982, a $135,000 payment in 1983, and a $110,000 payment in 1984.

(iii) For 1980, corporation Y makes an election under section 46(d). Progress is presumed to occur ratably over the 5-year construction period, which is 20 percent in each year. Twenty percent of the contract price is $110,000. The percentage of completion limitation for each year, thus, is $110,000.

(iv) For each of the years 1980 and 1981, the $110,000 payments may be treated as qualified progress expenditures. The payments equal the percentage of completion limitation.

(v) For 1982, the $85,000 payment may be treated as a qualified progress expenditure, because it is less than the percentage of completion limitation. The excess of the percentage of completion limitation ($110,000) over the 1982 payment ($85,000) is added to the percentage of completion limitation for 1983. One hundred and ten thousand dollars minus $85,000 equals $25,000. Twenty-five thousand dollars plus $110,000 equals $135,000, which is the percentage of completion limitation for 1983.

(vi) For 1983, the entire $135,000 payment may be treated as a qualified progress expenditure. The payment equals the percentage of completion limitation for 1983.

(vii) For 1984, no qualified progress expenditures may be taken into account, because the airplane is placed in service in that year.

(viii) See example (2) of paragraph (r)(4) of this section for the result if Y sells its contract rights to the property on December 31, 1982.

(k) Definition of self-constructed property. *(1) In general.* Property is self-constructed property if it is reasonable to believe that more than half of the construction expenditures for the property will be made directly by the taxpayer. Construction expenditures made directly by the taxpayer include direct costs such as wages and materials and indirect costs such as overhead attributable to construction of the property. Expenditures for direct and indirect costs of construction will be treated as construction expenditures made directly by the taxpayer only to the extent that the expenditures directly benefit the construction of the property by employees of the taxpayer. Thus, wages paid to taxpayer's employees and expenditures for basic construction materials, such as sheet metal, lumber, glass, and nails, which are used by employees of the taxpayer to construct progress expenditure property, will be considered made directly by the taxpayer. Construction expenditures made by the taxpayer to a contractor or manufacturer, in general, will not be considered made directly by the taxpayer. Thus, the cost of component parts, such as boilers and turbines, which are purchased and merely installed or assembled by the taxpayer, will not be considered expenditures made directly by the taxpayer for construction. (See paragraph (h)(3) of this section to determine when such cost is properly chargeable to capital account.)

(2) Time when determination made. The determination of whether property is self-constructed is to be made at the close of the taxable year in which physical work on construction of the property begins, or, if later, the close of the first taxable year to which an election under this section applies. Once it is reasonably estimated that more than half of construction expenditures will be made directly by the taxpayer, the fact the taxpayer actually makes half, or less than half, of the expenditures directly will not affect classification of the property as self-constructed property. Similarly, once a determination has been made, classification of property as self-constructed property is not affected by a change in circumstances in a later taxable year. However, a significant error unrelated to a change in circumstances may be evidence that the estimate was unreasonable when made.

(3) Determination based on certain expenditures. For purposes of determining whether more than half of the expenditures for construction of an item of property will be made directly by the taxpayer, the taxpayer may take into account only expenditures properly includable by the taxpayer in the basis of the property under the provisions of § 1.46-3(c). Thus, property is self-constructed property only if more than half of the estimated basis of the property to be used for purposes of determining the credit allowed by section 38 is attributable to expenditures made directly by the taxpayer.

(l) Definition of non-self-constructed property. Non-self-constructed property is property that is not self-constructed property. Thus, property is non-self-constructed property if it is reasonable to believe that only half, or less than half, of the expenditures for construction will be made directly by the taxpayer.

(m) Alternative limitations for public utility, railroad, or airline property. The alternative limitations on qualified investment under section 46(a)(7) and (8) for public utility, railroad, or airline property (whichever applies) apply in determining the credit for qualified progress expenditures. The determination of whether progress expenditure property will be public utility, railroad, or airline property (whichever applies) when placed in service must be made at the close of the taxable year in which physical work on construction begins or, if later, at the close of the first taxable year for which an election under section 46(d) is in effect. If, at that time, the taxpayer is in a trade or business as a public utility, railroad, or airline (as described in section 46(c)(3)(B) and 46(a)(8)(D) and (E), respectively), it is evidence the property will be public utility, railroad, or airline property when placed in service.

(n) Leased property. A lessor of progress expenditure property may not elect under section 48(d) to treat a lessee (or a person who will be a lessee) as having made qualified progress expenditures.

(o) Election. *(1) In general.* The election under section 46(d)(6) to increase qualified investment by qualified progress expenditures may be made for any taxable year ending after December 31, 1974. Except as provided in paragraph (o)(2) of this section, the election is effective for the first taxable year for which it is made and for all taxable years thereafter unless it is revoked with the consent of the Commissioner. Except as provided in paragraphs (o)(2) and (3) of this section, the election applies to all qualified progress expenditures made by the taxpayer during the taxable year for construction of any progress expenditure property. Thus, the taxpayer may not make the election for one item of progress expenditure property and not for other items. If progress expenditure property is being constructed by or for a partnership, S corporation (as defined in section 1361(a)), trust, or estate, an election under section 46(d)(6) must be made separately by each partner or shareholder, or each beneficiary if the beneficiary, in determining his tax liability, would be allowed investment credit under section 38 for property subject to the election. The election may not be made by a partnership or S corporation, and may be made by a trust or estate only if the trust or estate, in determining its tax liability, would be allowed investment credit under section 38 for property subject to the election. The election of any partner, shareholder, beneficiary, trust, or estate will be effective for that person, even if a related partner, shareholder, beneficiary, trust, or estate does not make the election. An election made by a partner, shareholder, beneficiary, trust, or estate applies to all progress expenditure property of that person. For example, an election made by corporation X, which is a partner in the XYZ partnership, applies to progress expenditure property the corporation holds in its own capacity and also to its interest in progress expenditure property of the partnership.

(2) Time and manner of making election. An election under section 46(d)(6) must be made on Form 3468 and filed with the original income tax return for the first taxable year ending after December 31, 1974 to which the election will apply. An election made before March 2, 1988, by filing a written statement (whether or not attached to the income tax return) will be considered valid. The election may not be made on an amended return filed after the time prescribed for filing the original return (including extensions) for that taxable year. However, an election under this section may be made or revoked by filing a statement with an amended return filed on or before May 31, 1988, if the due date for filing a return for the first taxable year to which the election applies is before May 31, 1988.

(3) Carryover of election in certain transactions. In general, and election under section 46(d)(6) does not carry over to the transferee of progress expenditure property (or an interest therein). However, if under section 47(b) the property does not cease to be progress expenditure property because of the transfer, the election will carry over to the transferee. If so, the election will apply only to the property transferred. For rules relating to the determination of qualified progress expenditures of the transferee, see paragraph (r) of this section.

(p) Partnerships, S corporations, trusts, or estates. *(1) In general.* Each partner, shareholder, trust estate, or beneficiary of a trust or estate that makes an election under section 46(d) shall take into account its share of qualified progress expenditures (determined under paragraph (p)(2) of this section) made by the partnership, S corporation, trust, or estate. In determining qualified investment for the year in which the property is placed in service, the basis of the property is apportioned as provided in §§ 1.46-3(f), 1.48-6, or 1.48-5 (whichever applies). Each partner, shareholder, trust, estate, or beneficiary that made the election must reduce qualified investment under section 46(c)(4) for the year the property is placed in service by qualified progress expenditures taken into account by that person.

(2) Determination of share of qualified progress expenditures. The share of qualified progress expenditures of each partner, shareholder, trust, estate, or beneficiary that makes an election under section 46(d) must be determined in accordance with the same ratio used under §§ 1.46-3(f)(2), 1.48-5(a)(1), or 1.48-6(a)(1) (whichever applies) to determine its share of basis (or cost). The last sentence of § 1.46-3(f)(2)(i) must be applied by referring to the date on which qualified progress expenditures are paid or chargeable to capital amount (whichever is applicable).

(3) Examples. The following examples illustrate this paragraph (p).

Example (1). (i) Corporation X contracts to build a ship for partnership AB that qualifies as progress expenditure property. The contract price is $100,000. Physical work on construction of the ship begins on January 1, 1980. The ship is placed in service on December 31, 1983.

(ii) The AB partnership reports income on the calendar year basis. Partners A and B share profits equally. For A's taxable year ending December 31, 1980, A makes an election under section 46(d) B does not make the election.

(iii) For each of the years 1980, 1981, 1982, and 1983, the AB partnership makes $25,000 payments to corporation X. The payments made in 1980, 1981, and 1982 are qualified progress expenditures. The 1983 payment is not a qualified progress expenditure, because the ship is placed in service in that year.

(iv) For each of the years 1980, 1981, and 1982, A may take into account qualified progress expenditures of $12,500 because A had a 50 percent partnership interest in each of those years.

(v) For 1983, qualified investment for the ship is $100,000. A and B's share are $50,000 each, because each had a 50 percent partnership interest in 1983. However, A must reduce its $50,000 share for 1983 by $37,500, the amount of qualified progress expenditures taken into account by A. B's share is not reduced, because B did not take into account qualified progress expenditures.

Example (2). (i) The facts are the same as in example (1) except that on June 30, 1983, the partnership agreement is amended to admit a new partner, C. The partners agree to share profits equally. There is no special allocation in effect under section 704 with respect to the ship.

(ii) For each of the years 1980, 1981, and 1982, A may take into account qualified progress expenditures of $12,500 because A has a 50 percent partnership interest in those years.

(iii) For 1983, A, B, and C's share of qualified investment is $33,333 each, because each had a 33⅓ percent partnership interest in that year. A must reduce its share to zero, because it took $37,500 into account as qualified progress expenditures. In addition, the excess of the $37,500 over the $33,333 applied as a reduction is subject to recapture under section 47(a)(3)(B). B and C's shares are not reduced, because neither taxpayer took into account qualified progress expenditures.

(q) Limitation on qualified progress expenditures for taxable years beginning before 1980. *(1) In general.* (i) Under section 46(d)(7), qualified progress expenditures for any taxable year beginning before January 1, 1980, are limited. The taxpayer must apply the limitation under section 46(d)(7) on an item by item basis. In general, the taxpayer may take into account the applicable percentage (as determined under the table in section 46(d)(7)(A)) of qualified progress expenditures for each of those years. In addition, the taxpayer may take into account for each of those years 20 percent of qualified investment for each of the preceding taxable years determined without applying the limitations of section 46(d)(7).

(ii) The applicable percentage under section 46(d)(7)(A) may be applied only for one taxable year that ends within a calendar year in determining qualified investment for an item of progress expenditure property. For example, calendar year partners of a calendar year partnership may increase qualified investment for 1976 by 20 percent of qualified progress expenditures made in 1975 for an item of property. If the partnership incorporates in 1976 and the taxable year of the corporation begins on July 1, 1976, and ends on June 30, 1977, qualified investment of the corporation for its taxable year beginning on July 1, 1976, cannot be increased by 20 percent of the 1975 expenditure.

(2) Example. The following example illustrates this paragraph (q).

Example. (i) Corporation X contracts with A on January 1, 1976, to build an electric generator that qualifies as non-self-constructed progress expenditure property. A will build the generator at a cost of $125,000. Corporation X agrees to pay A $150,000. Corporation X reports income on the calendar year basis. Corporation X makes an election under section 46(d) for 1976. Physical work on construction begins on January 1, 1976. Corporation X makes payments of $30,000 to A for construction of the generator in each of the years 1976, 1977, 1978, 1979, and 1980. A incurs a cost of $25,000 in each of those years for construction of the property. The property is placed in service in 1980.

(ii) For 1976, X may increase qualified investment by $12,000, 40 percent of the payment made in 1976.

(iii) For 1977, corporation X may increase qualified investment by $24,000. Eighteen thousand dollars of that amount is 60 percent of the 1977 payment. The remaining $6,000 is 20 percent of the $30,000 payment made in 1976.

(iv) For 1978, corporation X may increase qualified investment by $36,000. Twenty-four thousand dollars of that amount is 80 percent of the 1978 payment. The remaining $12,000 is 20 percent of the $30,000 payment made in 1976, plus 20 percent of the $30,000 payment made in 1977.

(v) For 1979, corporation X may increase qualified investment by $48,000. Thirty thousand dollars of that amount is 100 percent of the 1979 payment. The remaining $18,000 of that amount is 20 percent of the $30,000 payments made in each of the years 1976, 1977, and 1978.

(vi) Qualified investment for corporation X for 1980 is $30,000. The $30,000 is the basis (or cost) of the generator ($150,000), reduced by qualified progress expenditures allowed with respect to that property ($120,000).

(r) Special rules for transferred property. *(1) In general.* A transferee of progress expenditure property (or an interest therein) may take into account qualified progress expenditures for the property only if—

(i) The property is progress expenditure property in the hands of the transferee, and

(ii) The transferee makes an election under section 46(d) or the election made by the transferor (or its predecessor) carries over to the transferee under paragraph (o)(3) of this section.

(2) Status as progress expenditure property. (i) If the transfer requires recapture under section 47(a)(3) and § 1.47-1(g) (or would require recapture if the transferor had made an election under section 46(d)), then—

(A) For purposes of determining if the property is progress expenditure property in the hands of the transferee, the normal construction period for the property begins on the date of the transfer, or, if later, on the first day of the first taxable year for which the transferee makes an election under section 46(d), and

(B) For purposes of determining whether the property is self-constructed or non-self-constructed in the hands of the transferee, the amount paid or incurred for the transfer of the property will not be considered a construction expenditure made directly by the transferee.

(ii) If the transfer does not require recapture under section 47(a)(3) and § 1.47-1(g), and the election carries over to the taxpayer under paragraph (o)(3) of this section, the property does not lose its status as progress expenditure property because of the transfer.

(3) Amount of qualified progress expenditures for transferee. (i) If the transfer does not require recapture under section 47(a)(3) and § 147-1(g), and the election carries over to the taxpayer under paragraph (o)(3) of this section, the transferee must determine its qualified progress expenditures—

(A) By using the same normal construction period used by the transferor,

(B) By treating the property as having the same status as self-constructed or non-self-constructed as the property had in the hands of the transferor, and

(C) In the case of non-self-constructed property, by taking into account any excess described in section 46(d)(4)(C)(i) (relating to the excess of payments over the percentage-of-completion limitation) or section 46(d)(4)(C)(ii) (relating to the excess of the percentage-of-completion limitation over the amount of payments) that the transferor would have taken into account with respect to that property.

(ii) If the transfer requires recapture under section 47(a)(3) and § 1.47-1(g) (or would require recapture if the transferor had made an election under section 46(d)), the amount paid or incurred for the transfer will be considered a payment for construction of that property to the extent that—

(A) It is properly includible in the basis of the property under § 1.46-3(c),

(B) The taxpayer can show the amount is attributable to construction costs paid or chargeable to capital account by the transferor or other person after physical work on construction of the property began, and

(C) It does not exceed the amount by which the transferor has increased qualified investment for qualified progress expenditures incurred with respect to the property (or would have increased qualified investment but for the "lesser of" limitation of section 46(d)(3)(B) or the absence of an election under section 46(d)), plus any amount that would have been treated as a qualified progress expenditure by the transferor had the property not been transferred.

Once the status of the property as self-constructed or non-self-constructed property in the hands of the transferee has been determined, all rules under this section for determining the amount of qualified progress expenditures for that type of property apply. For example, if the property is non-self-constructed in the hands of the transferee, amounts merely incurred (but not paid) for the transfer are not taken into account as qualified progress expenditures. Actual payment is necessary (see paragraph (j)(3) of this section). In applying section 46(d)(3)(B)(ii), the amount paid or incurred for the transfer (to the extent that it qualifies as a payment for construction under the first sentence of this paragraph (r)(3)(ii)) is considered to be part of the overall cost to the transferee of construction by another person, and the portion of construction which is completed during the taxable year is determined by taking into account construction that was completed before the constructed property was acquired by the transferee. If the transferee makes an election under section 46(d) and this section for the taxable year in which the transfer occurs, then for purposes of applying the presumption in section 46(d)(4)(D) that construction is deemed to occur not more rapidly than ratably over the normal construction period, the transferee's normal construction period is considered to have begun on the date on which physical work on construction of the acquired property began.

(4) Examples. The following examples illustrate this paragraph (r).

Example (1). Corporation X begins physical work on construction of progress expenditure property for corporation Y on January 1, 1976. Y accurately estimates a 3-year normal construction period and elects under section 46(d) on its return for its taxable year ending December 31, 1976. On January 1, 1978, Y sells the contract rights for construction of the property to corporation Z, which uses a fiscal year ending June 30. Qualified progress expenditures allowed to Y in 1976 and 1977 are subject to recapture under section 47(a)(3). Because Z's normal construction period for the property is less than 2 years (January 1, 1978 to January 1, 1979), the property is not progress expenditure property in Z's hands. Z may not elect progress expenditure treatment for the property.

Example (2). (i) Assume the same facts as in the example in paragraph (j)(7) of this section, except on, December 31, 1982, Y sells its contract rights to the property for $340,000 to corporation Z, which also uses the calendar year. Z pays Y the full $340,000 on that date. The property is still to be placed in service on December 31, 1984, and will not be available for placing in service at an earlier date. Z makes payments to X of $135,000 on December 31, 1983, and $110,000 on December 31, 1984.

(ii) The investment credit allowed Y in 1980 and 1981 for qualified progress expenditures is subject to recapture under section 47(a)(3) and Y may not treat its $85,000 payment in 1982 as a qualified progress expenditure.

(iii) For purposes of determining if the airplane is qualified progress expenditure property with respect to Z, the normal construction period for the property for Z begins on December 31, 1982, the date of transfer. Since the remaining construction period is two years, the property is progress expenditure property if it otherwise qualifies in Z's hands.

(iv) Only $305,000 of the $340,000 payment to Y can qualify as a qualified progress expenditure, because only that amount is attributable to construction costs paid by Y and does not exceed the sum of the amount by which Y increased qualified investment in 1980 and 1981 for qualified progress expenditures ($220,000) and the amount that Y would have treated as a qualified progress expenditure in 1982 ($85,000).

(v) Assume that Z cannot establish that progress in construction has been completed more rapidly than ratably. If Z makes an election under section 46(d) for 1982, then for purposes of applying the percentage of completion limitation, Z's normal construction period is considered to begin on January 1, 1980. Progress is presumed to occur ratably over the 5-year construction period, which is 20 percent in each year.

(vi) For 1982, Z may treat the full $305,000 as a qualified progress expenditure because it is less than the percentage of completion limitation, $330,000 ($110,000 a year for 1980, 1981, and 1982).

(vii) For 1983, Z may treat the entire $135,000 payment as a qualified progress expenditure, since it does not exceed the percentage of completion limitation for that year, $135,000 ($110,000 plus the $25,000 excess from 1982).

(viii) For Z's taxable year ending December 31, 1984, no qualified progress expenditures may be taken into account because the property is placed in service during that year.

T.D. 8183, 3/1/88.

§ 1.46-6 Limitation in case of certain regulated companies.

• ***Caution:*** Reg. § 1.46-6, following, was issued under Code Sec. 46 before amendment by P.L. 101-508 (11/5/90). The relative provisions of Code Sec. 46 before such amendment were adopted by reference in current Code Sec. 50.

Caution: The Treasury has not yet amended Reg § 1.46-6 to reflect changes made by P.L. 101-508, P.L. 99-514, P.L. 98-369.

(a) In general. *(1) Scope of section.* This section does not reflect amendments made to section 46 after enactment of the Revenue Act of 1971, other than the redesignation of section 46(e) as section 46(f) by the Tax Reduction Act of 1975.

(2) Disallowance of credit. Under section 46(f), a credit otherwise allowable under section 38 ("credit") will be disallowed in certain cases with respect to "section 46(f) property" as defined in paragraph (b)(1) of this section. Paragraph (f) of this section describes circumstances under which a determination put into effect by a regulatory body will result in the disallowance of the credit. Such a determination will result in a disallowance only if section 46(f)(1) or (2) applies to such property and such determination affects the taxpayer's cost of service or rate base in a manner inconsistent with section 46(f)(1) or (2) (whichever is applicable).

(3) General rules. The provisions of section 46(f)(1) and (2) are limitations on the treatment of the credit for ratemaking purposes and for purposes of the taxpayer's regulated books of account only. Under the provisions of section 46(f)(1), the credit may not be flowed through to income *(i.e.,* used to reduce taxpayer's cost of service) but in certain circumstances may be used to reduce rate base (provided that such reduction is restored not less rapidly than ratably). If an election is made under section 46(f)(2), the credit may be flowed through to income (but not more rapidly than ratably) and there may not be any reduction in rate base. If an election is made under section 46(f)(3), none of the limitations of section 46(f)(1) or (2) apply to certain section 46(f) property of the taxpayer. Thus, under the provisions of section 46(f)(3), no credit is disallowed if the credit is treated in any manner for ratemaking purposes, including any manner of treatment permitted under the limitations of section 46(f)(1) or (2).

(4) Elections. For rules relating to the manner of making, on or before March 9, 1972, the three elections listed in section 46(f)(1), (2), and (3), see 26 CFR 12.3. For rules relating to the application of such elections, see paragraph (h) of this section.

(5) Cross references. For rules with respect to the treatment of corporate reorganizations, asset acquisitions, and taxpayers subject to the jurisdiction of more than one regulatory body, etc., see paragraph (j) of this section.

(6) Nonapplication of prior law. Under section 105(e) of the Revenue Act of 1971, section 203 (e) of the Revenue Act of 1964, 78 Stat. 35, does not apply to section 46(f) property.

(b) Definitions. For purposes of this section, the following definitions apply:

(1) Section 46(f) property. "Section 46(f) property" is property described in section 50 that is—

(i) Public utility property within the meaning of section 46(c)(3)(B) (other than nonregulated communication property described in § 1.46-3(g)(2)(iv)) or

(ii) Property used predominantly in the trade or business of the furnishing or sale of steam through a local distribution system or of the transportation of gas or steam by pipeline, if the rates for the trade or business are regulated within the meaning of § 1.46-3(g)(2)(iii).

For purposes of determining whether property is used predominantly in the trade or business of transportation of gas by pipeline (or of transportation of gas by pipeline and of furnishing or sale of gas through a local distribution system), the rules prescribed in § 1.46-3(g)(4) apply except that accounts 365 through 371 inclusive (Transmission Plant) are added to the accounts listed in § 1.46-3(g)(4)(i).

(2) Cost of service. (i) (A) For purposes of this section, "cost of service" is the amount required by a taxpayer to provide regulated goods or services. Cost of service includes operating expenses (including salaries, cost of materials, etc.) maintenance expenses, depreciation expenses, tax expenses, and interest expenses. For purposes of this section, any effect on a taxpayer's permitted return on investment that results from a reduction in the taxpayer's rate base does not constitute a reduction in cost of service, even though, as a technical ratemaking term, "cost of service" ordinarily includes a permitted return on investment. In addition, taking into account a deduction for the additional interest that the taxpayer would pay or accrue if the credit were unavailable in determining Federal income tax expense ("synchronization of interest") does not constitute a reduction in cost of service for purposes of section 46(f)(2). This adjustment to Federal income tax expense may be taken into account in determining cost of service for the regulated accounting period or periods that include the taxable year to which the adjustment relates or for any subsequent regulated accounting period.

(B) See paragraph (b)(3)(ii)(B) of this section for rules relating to the amount of additional interest that the taxpayer would pay or accrue if the credit were unavailable.

(ii) In determining whether, or to what extent, a credit has been used to reduce cost of service, reference shall be made to any accounting treatment that affects cost of service. Examples of such treatment include reducing by all or a portion of the credit the amount of Federal income tax expense taken into account for ratemaking purposes and reducing the depreciable bases of property by all or a portion of the credit for ratemaking purposes.

(3) Rate base. (i) For purposes of this section, "rate base" is the monetary amount that is multiplied by a rate of return to determine the permitted return on investment.

(ii) (A) In determining whether, or to what extent, a credit has been used to reduce rate base, reference shall be made to any accounting treatment that affects rate base. In addition, in those cases in which the rate of return is based on the taxpayer's cost of capital, reference shall be made to any accounting treatment that reduces the permitted return on investment by treating the credit less favorably than the capital that would have been provided if the credit were unavailable. Thus, the credit may not be assigned a "cost of capital" rate that is less than the overall cost of capital rate, determined on the basis of a weighted average, for the capital that would have been provided if the credit were unavailable.

(B) For purposes of determining the cost of capital rate assigned to the credit and the amount of additional interest that the taxpayer would pay or accrue, the composition of the capital that would have been provided if the credit were unavailable may be determined—

(1) On the basis of all the relevant facts and circumstances; or

(2) By assuming for both such purposes that such capital would be provided solely by common shareholders, preferred shareholders, and long-term creditors in the same proportions and at the same rates of return as the capital actually provided to the taxpayer by such shareholders and creditors.

For purposes of this section, capital provided by long-term creditors does not include deferred taxes as described in section 167(e)(3)(G) or 168(e)(3)(B)(ii).

(C) If a taxpayer's overall rate of return is based on a deemed or hypothetical capital structure, paragraph (b)(3)(ii)(B) of this section shall be applied by treating the deemed or hypothetical capital as if it were the capital actually provided to the taxpayer and determining the composition of the capital that would have been provided if the credit were unavailable in a manner consistent with such treatment.

(iii) Whether or to what extent, a credit has been used to reduce rate base for any period to which pre-June 23, 1986 rates apply will be determined under 26 CFR 1.46-6(b)(3) and (4) (revised as of April 1, 1985) if such a determination avoids disallowance of a credit that would be disallowed under paragraph (b)(3)(ii) or (4)(ii) of this section. For this purpose, a period of which pre-June 23, 1986 rates apply is any period for which the effect of the credit on rate base for ratemaking purposes is established under a determination put into effect (within the meaning of paragraph (f) of this section) before June 23, 1986.

(4) Indirect reductions to cost of service or rate base. (i) Cost of service or rate base is also considered to have been reduced by reason of all or a portion of a credit if such reduction is made in an indirect manner.

(ii) One type of such indirect reduction is any ratemaking decision in which the credit is treated as operating income (subject to ratemaking regulation) or is treated less favorably than the capital that would have been provided if the credit were unavailable. For example, if the credit is accounted for as nonoperating income on a company's regulated books of account but a ratemaking decision has the effect of treating the credit as operating income in determining rate of return to common shareholders, then cost of service has been indirectly reduced by reason of the credit.

(iii) A second type of indirect reduction is any ratemaking decision intended to achieve an effect similar to a direct reduction to cost of service or rate base. In determining whether a ratemaking decision is intended to achieve this effect, consideration is given to all the relevant facts and circumstances of each case, including, but not limited to—

(A) The record of the proceeding,

(B) The regulatory body's orders or opinions (including any dissenting views), and

(C) The anticipated effect of the ratemaking decision on the company's revenues in comparison to a direct reduction to cost of service or rate base by reason of the investment tax credits available to the regulated company.

(iv) This subdivision (iv) describes a situation that is not an indirect reduction to cost of service or rate base by reason of all or a portion of a credit. The ratemaking treatment of credits may affect the financial condition of a company, including the company's ability to attract new capital, the cost of that capital, the company's future financial requirements, the market price of the company's securities, and the degree of risk attributable to investment in those securities. The financial condition may be reflected in certain customary financial indicators such as the comparative capital structure of the company, coverage ratios, price/earnings ratios, and price/book ratios. Under the facts and circumstances test of paragraph (b)(4)(iii) of this section, the consideration of a company's financial condition by a regulatory body is not an indirect reduction to cost of service or rate base, even though such condition, as affected by the ratemaking treatment of the company's investment tax credits, is considered in the development of a reasonable rate of return on common shareholders' investment.

(c) General rule. *(1) In general.* Section 46(f)(1) applies to all of the taxpayer's section 46(f) property except property to which an election under section 46(f)(2) or (3) applies. Under section 46(f)(1), the credit for the taxpayer's section 46(f) property will be disallowed if—

(i) the taxpayer's cost of service for ratemaking purposes is reduced by reason of any portion of such credit, or

(ii) The taxpayer's rate base is reduced by reason of any portion of the credit and such reduction in rate base is not restored or is restored less rapidly than ratably within the meaning of paragraph (g) of this section.

(2) Insufficient natural domestic supply. The provisions of paragraph (c)(1)(ii) of this section shall not apply to permit any reduction in taxpayer's rate base with respect to its "short supply property" if it made an election under the last sentence of section 46(f)(1) on or before March 9, 1972.

(3) Short supply property. For purposes of this section, section 46(f) property is "short supply property" if—

(i) The property is described in paragraph (b)(1)(ii) of this section,

(ii) The regulatory body described in section 46(c)(3)(B) that has jurisdiction for ratemaking purposes with respect to such trade or business is an agency or instrumentality of the United States, and

(iii) This regulatory body makes a short supply determination and the determination is in effect on the date such property is placed in service.

(4) Short supply determination. A short supply determination is made or revoked on the date of its publication in the FEDERAL REGISTER.It is a determination that the natural domestic supply of gas or steam is insufficient to meet the present and future requirements of the domestic economy.

(5) Dates short supply determination in effect. A short supply determination is considered to be in effect with respect to section 46(f) property placed in service at any time before the determination is revoked. However, a short supply determination made after [90 days after publication of this T.D.] is not considered to be in effect with respect to section 46(f) property placed in service before such determination was made.

(d) Special rule for ratable flow-through. If an election was made under section 46(f)(2) on or before March 9, 1972, section 46(f)(2) applies to all of the taxpayer's section 46(f) property except property to which an election under section 46(f)(3) applies. Under section 46(f)(2), the credit for the taxpayer's section 46(f) property will be disallowed if—

(1) The taxpayer's cost of service, for ratemaking purposes or in its regulated books of account, is reduced by more than a ratable portion of such credit within the meaning of paragraph (g) of this section or

(2) The taxpayer's rate base is reduced by reason of any portion of such credit.

(e) Flow-through property. If a taxpayer made an election under section 46(f)(3) on or before March 9, 1972, section 46(f)(1) and (2) do not apply to the taxpayer's section 46(f) property to which section 167(1)(2)(C) applies. In the case of an election under section 46(f)(3), a credit will not be disallowed, notwithstanding a determination by a regulatory body having jurisdiction over such taxpayer that reduces the taxpayer's cost of service or rate base by reason of such credit. In general, section 167(1)(2)(C) applies to property with respect to which a taxpayer may use a flow-through method of accounting (within the meaning of section 167(1)(3)(H)) to take into account the allowance for depreciation under section 167(a). Section 167(1)(2)(C) applies to property even though the taxpayer does not use a flow-through method of accounting with respect to the property. Section 167(1)(2)(C) does not apply to property if the taxpayer can not use a flow-through method of accounting with respect to the property. For example, section 167(1)(2)(C) does not apply to property with respect to which an election under section 167(1)(4)(A) applies. Thus, such property does not qualify for an election under section 46(f)(3).

(f) Limitations. *(1) In general.* This paragraph provides rules relating to limitations on the disallowance of credits under section 46(f)(4). Key terms are defined in paragraphs (f)(7), (8), and (9) of this section.

(2) Disallowance postponed. There is no disallowance of a credit before the first final inconsistent determination is put into effect for the taxpayer's section 46(f) property.

(3) Time of disallowance. A credit is disallowed—

(i) When the first final inconsistent determination is put into effect and

(ii) When any inconsistent determination (whether or not final) is put into effect after the first final inconsistent determination is put into effect.

(4) Credits disallowed. A credit is disallowed for section 46(f) property placed in service (within the meaning of § 1.46-3(d)) by the taxpayer—

(i) Before the date any inconsistent determination described in paragraph (f)(2) of this section is put into effect and

(ii) On or after such date and before the date a subsequent consistent determination (whether or not final) is put into effect.

(5) Barred years. No amount of credit for a taxable year is disallowed under paragraph (f)(3) of this section if, for such year, assessment of a deficiency is barred by any law or rule of law.

(6) Notification and other requirements. The taxpayer shall notify the district director of a disallowance of a credit under paragraph (f)(3) of this section within 30 days of the date that the applicable determination is put into effect. In the case of such a disallowance, the taxpayer shall recompute its tax liability for any affected taxable year, and such recomputation shall be made in the form of an amended return where necessary.

(7) Determinations. For purposes of this paragraph, the term "determination" refers to a determination made with respect to section 46(f) property (other than property to which an election under section 46(f)(3) applies) by a regulatory body described in section 46(c)(3)(B) that determines the effect of the credit—

(i) For purposes of section 46(f)(1), on the taxpayer's cost of service or rate base for ratemaking purposes or

(ii) In the case of a taxpayer that made an election under section 46(f)(2), on the taxpayer's cost of service, for ratemaking purposes or in its regulated books of account, or on the taxpayer's rate base for ratemaking purposes.

A regulatory body does not have to take affirmative action to make a determination. Thus, a regulatory body's failure to take action on a rate schedule filed by a taxpayer is a determination if the rates can be put into effect without further action by the regulatory body.

(8) Types of determinations. For purposes of this paragraph—

(i) The term "inconsistent" refers to a determination that is inconsistent with section 46(f)(1) or (2) (as the case may be). Thus, for example, a determination to reduce the taxpayer's cost of service by more than a ratable portion of the credit would be a determination that is inconsistent with section 46(f)(2). As a further example, such a determination would also be inconsistent if section 46(f)(1) applied because no reduction in cost of service is permitted under section 46(f)(1).

(ii) The term "consistent" refers to a determination that is consistent with section 46(f)(1) or (2) (as the case may be).

(iii) The term "final determination" means a determination with respect to which all rights to appeal or to request a review, a rehearing, or a redetermination have been exhausted or have lapsed.

(iv) The term "first final inconsistent determination" means the first final determination put into effect after December 10, 1971, that is inconsistent with section 46(f)(1) or (2) (as the case may be).

(9) Put into effect. A determination is put into effect on the latter of—

(i) The date it is issued (or, if a first final inconsistent determination, the date it becomes final) or

(ii) The date it becomes operative.

(10) Examples. The provisions of this paragraph may be illustrated by the following examples:

Example (1). Corporation X, a calendar-year taxpayer engaged in a public utility activity is subject to the jurisdiction of regulatory body A. On September 15, 1971, X purchases section 46(f) property and places it in service on that date. For 1971, X takes the credit allowable by section 38 with respect to such property. X does not make any election permitted by section 46(f). On October 9, 1972, A makes a determination that X must account for the credit allowable under section 38 in a manner inconsistent with section 46(f)(1). The determination, which was the first determination by A after December 10, 1971, becomes final on January 1, 1973, and holds that X must retroactively adjust the manner in which it accounted for the credit allowable under section 38 starting with the taxable year that began on January 1, 1972. Since, under the provisions of paragraph (f)(8) of this section, the determination by A is put into effect on January 1, 1973 (the date it becomes final), the credit is retroactively disallowed with respect to any of X's section 46(f) property placed in service before January 1, 1973, on any date which occurs during a taxable year with respect to which an assessment of a deficiency has not been barred by any law or rule of law. In addition, the credit is disallowed with respect to X's section 46(f) property placed in service on or after January 1, 1973, and before the date that a subsequent determination by A, which as to X is consistent with section 46(f)(1), is put into effect. Thus, X must amend its income tax return for 1971 to reflect the retroactive disallowance of the credit otherwise allowable under section 38 with respect to the section 46(f) property placed in service on September 15, 1971.

Example (2). The facts are the same as in example (1), except that the first inconsistent determination by A becomes final on April 5, 1972, and requires X to account for the credit for all taxable years beginning on or after January 1, 1973, in a manner inconsistent with section 46(f)(1). Under the provisions of paragraph (f)(8) of this section, the determination was put into effect on January 1, 1973 (the date it became operative). The result is the same as in example (1).

Example (3). The facts are the same as in example (1), except that on June 1, 1975, A issues a determination that X shall retroactively account for the credit allowable by section 38 in a manner consistent with the provisions of section 46(f)(1) for taxable years beginning on or after January 1, 1971. The determination becomes final on January 5, 1976, in the same form as originally issued. The result is the same as in example (1) with respect to property X places in service before June 1, 1975. The credit is allowed with respect to property X places in service on or after June 1, 1975 (the date that the consistent determination is put into effect).

(g) Ratable methods. *(1) In general.* Under this paragraph (g), rules are prescribed for purposes of determining whether or not, under section 46(f)(1), a reduction in the taxpayer's rate base with respect to the credit is restored less rapidly than ratably and whether or not under section 46(f)(2) the taxpayer's cost of service for ratemaking purposes is reduced by more than a ratable portion of such credit.

(2) Regulated depreciation expense. What is "ratable" is determined by considering the period of time actually used in computing the taxpayer's regulated depreciation expense for the property for which a credit is allowed. "Regulated depreciation expense" is the depreciation expense for the property used by a regulatory body for purposes of establishing the taxpayer's cost of service for ratemaking purposes. Such period of time shall be expressed in units of years (or shorter periods), units of production, or machine hours and shall be determined in accordance with the individual useful life system or composite (or other group asset) account system actually used in computing the taxpayer's regulated depreciation expense. A method of restoring, or reducing, is ratable if the amount to be restored to rate base, or to reduce cost of service (as the case may be), is allocated ratably in proportion to the number of such units. Thus, for example, assume that the regulated depreciation expense is computed under the straight line method by applying a composite annual percentage rate to "original cost" (as defined for purposes of computing regulated depreciation expense). If, with respect to an item of section 46(f) property, the amount to be restored annually to rate base is computed by applying a composite annual percentage rate to the amount by which the rate base was reduced, then the restoration is ratable. Similarly, if cost of service is reduced annually by an amount computed by applying a composite annual percentage rate to the amount of the credit, cost of service is reduced by a ratable portion. If such composite annual percentage rate were revised for purposes of computing regulated depreciation expense beginning with a particular accounting period, the computation of ratable restoration or ratable portion (as the case may be) must also be revised beginning with such period. A composite annual percentage rate is determined solely by reference to the period of time actually used by the taxpayer in computing its regulated depreciation expense without reduction for salvage or other items such as over and under accruals. A composite annual percentage rate determined by taking into account salvage value or other items shall be considered to be ratable in the case of a determination (whether or not final) issued before March 22, 1979, and any rate order (whether or not final) that is entered into before June 20, 1979, in response to a rate case filed before April 23, 1979. For this purpose, the term "rate order" does not include an order by a regulatory body that perfunctorily adopts rates as filed if such rates are suspended or subject to rebate.

(h) Elections. *(1) Applicability of elections.* (i) Any election under section 46(f) applies to all of the taxpayer's property eligible for the election, whether or not the taxpayer is regulated by more than one regulatory body.

(ii) Section 46(f)(1) applies to all of the taxpayer's section 46(f) property in the absence of an election under either section 46(f)(2) or (3). If an election is made under section 46(f)(2), section 46(f)(1) does not apply to any of the taxpayer's section 46(f) property.

(iii) An election made under the last sentence of section 46(f)(1) applies to that portion of the taxpayer's section 46(f) property to which section 46(f)(1) applies and which is short supply property within the meaning of paragraph (c)(2) of this section.

(iv) If a taxpayer makes an election under section 46(f)(2) and makes no election under section 46(f)(3), the election under section 46(f)(2) applies to all of the taxpayer's section 46(f) property.

(v) If a taxpayer makes an election under section 46(f)(3), such election applies to all of the taxpayer's section 46(f) property to which section 167(1)(2)(C) applies. Section 46(f)(1) or (2) (as the case may be) applies to that portion of the taxpayer's section 46(f) property that is not property to which section 167(f)(2)(C) applies. Thus, for example, if a taxpayer makes an election under section 46(f)(2) and also makes an election under section 46(f)(3), section 46(f)(3) applies to all of the taxpayer's section 46(f) property to which section 167(1)(2)(C) applies, and section 46(f)(2) applies to the remainder of the taxpayer's section 46(f) property.

(2) Method of making elections. See 26 CFR 12.3 for rules relating to the method of making the elections described in section 46(f)(1), (2), or (3).

(i) [Reserved]

(j) Reorganizations, asset acquisitions, multiple regulation, etc. *(1) Taxpayers not entirely subject to jurisdiction of one regulatory body.* (i) If a taxpayer is required by a regulatory body having jurisdiction over less than all of its property to account for the credit under a determination that is inconsistent with section 46(f)(1) or (2) (as the case may be), such credit shall be disallowed only with respect to property subject to the jurisdiction of such regulatory body.

(ii) For purposes of this paragraph (j), a regulatory body is considered to have jurisdiction over property of a taxpayer if the property is included in the rate base for which the regulatory body determines an allowable rate of return for ratemaking purposes or if expenses with respect to the property are included in cost of service as determined by the regulatory body for ratemaking purposes. For example, if regulatory body A, having jurisdiction over 60 percent of an item of corporation X's section 46(f) property, makes a determination which is inconsistent with section 46(f), and if regulatory body B, having jurisdiction over the remaining 40 percent of such item of property, makes a consistent determination (or if the remaining 40 percent is not subject to the jurisdiction of any regulatory body), then 60 percent of the credit for such item will be disallowed. For a further example, if regulatory body A, having jurisdiction over 60 percent of X's section 46(f) property, has jurisdiction over 100 percent of a particular generator, 100 percent of the credit for such generator will be disallowed.

(iii) For rules which provide that the 3 elections under section 46(f) may not be made with respect to less than all of the taxpayer's property eligible for the election, see paragraph (h)(1)(i) of this section.

(2) [Reserved]

(k) Treatment of accumulated deferred investment tax credits upon the deregulation of public utility property. *(1) Scope.* (i) In general. This paragraph (k) provides rules for the application of former sections 46(f)(1) and 46(f)(2) of the Internal Revenue Code to a taxpayer with respect to public utility property that ceases, whether by disposition, deregulation, or otherwise, to be public utility property with respect to the taxpayer and that is not described in paragraph (k)(1)(ii) of this section (deregulated public utility property).

(ii) Exception. This paragraph (k) does not apply to property that ceases to be public utility property with respect to the taxpayer on account of an ordinary retirement within the meaning of § 1.167(a)-11(d)(3)(ii).

(2) Ratable amount. (i) Restoration of rate base reduction. A reduction in the taxpayer's rate base on account of the credit with respect to public utility property that becomes deregulated public utility property is restored ratably during the period after the property becomes deregulated public utility property if the amount of the reduction remaining to be restored does not, at any time during the period, exceed the restoration percentage of the recoverable stranded cost of the property at such time.

For this purpose —

(A) The stranded cost of the property is the cost of the property reduced by the amount of such cost that the taxpayer has recovered through regulated depreciation expense during the period before the property becomes deregulated public utility property;

(B) The recoverable stranded cost of the property at any time is the stranded cost of the property that the taxpayer will be permitted to recover through rates after such time; and

(C) The restoration percentage for the property is determined by dividing the reduction in rate base remaining to be restored with respect to the property immediately before the property becomes deregulated public utility property by the stranded cost of the property.

(ii) Cost of service reduction. Reductions in the taxpayer's cost of service on account of the credit with respect to public utility property that becomes deregulated public utility property are ratable during the period after the property becomes deregulated public utility property if the cumulative amount of the reduction during such period does not, at any time during the period, exceed the flowthrough percentage of the cumulative stranded cost recovery for the property at such time. For this purpose—

(A) The stranded cost of the property is the cost of the property reduced by the amount of such cost that the taxpayer has recovered through regulated depreciation expense during the period before the property becomes deregulated public utility property;

(B) The cumulative stranded cost recovery for the property at any time is the stranded cost of the property that the taxpayer has been permitted to recover through rates on or before such time; and

(C) The flowthrough percentage for the property is determined by dividing the amount of credit with respect to the property remaining to be used to reduce cost of service immediately before the property becomes deregulated public utility property by the stranded cost of the property.

(3) Cross reference. See § 1.168(i)-(3) for rules relating to the treatment of balances of excess deferred income taxes when public utility property becomes deregulated public utility property.

(4) Effective/applicability dates. (i) In general. Except as provided in paragraph (k)(4)(ii) of this section, this paragraph (k) applies to public utility property that becomes deregulated public utility property with respect to a taxpayer after December 21, 2005.

(ii) Property that becomes public utility property of the transferee. This paragraph (k) does not apply to property that becomes deregulated public utility property with respect to a taxpayer an account of a transfer on or before March 20, 2008 if after the transfer the property is public utility property of the transferee.

(iii) Application of regulation project (REG-104385-01). A reduction in the taxpayer's cost of service will be treated as ratable if it is consistent with the proposed rules in regulation project (REG-104385-01) (68 FR 10190) March 4, 2003, and occurs during the period beginning on March 5, 2003, and ending on the earlier of—

(A) The last date on which the utility's rates are determined under the rate order in effect on December 21, 2005; or

(B) December 21, 2007.

T.D. 7602, 3/20/79, amend T.D. 8089, 5/21/86, T.D. 9387, 3/19/2008.

---

§ 9.1 Investment credit—public utility property elections.

(a) Applicability of prior election under section 46(f). *(1) In general.* Except as provided in paragraph (a)(2) of this section, an election made before March 10, 1972 (hereinafter referred to as a 1972 election) under section 46(f) (redesignated from section 46(e) by the Tax Reduction Act of 1975) applies to the credit allowable for a taxable year with respect to public utility property described in section 46(f)(5) by reason of sections 301 and 302 of the Tax Reduction Act of 1975.

(2) 1972 immediate flow-through election. A 1972 election under section 46(f)(3) (hereinafter referred to as an election for immediate flow-through) does not apply to the additional credit allowed under section 38 with respect to limited property (public utility property described in section 46(c)(3)(B) to which section 167(l)(2)(C) applies, other than nonregulated communication property of the type described in the last sentence of section 46(c)(3)(B) by reason of the Tax Reduction Act of 1975. However, a 1972 election for immediate flow-through does apply to the additional credit allowed for a taxable year with respect to property described in section 46(f)(5)(B). See paragraph (b) of this section for a new election under section 46(f)(3) with regard to the additional credit with respect to limited property allowed by reason of the Tax Reduction Act of 1975. See paragraph (a)(3) of this section for determination of additional credit. For purposes of this section the phrase "determined as if the Tax Reduction Act had not been enacted" means the following amendments shall be disregarded in determining credit allowable or allowed:

(i) The increase in the amount of credit from 7 percent to 10 or 11 percent under section 46(a)(1)(A), (B), and (D), (ii) the increase in the amount of qualified investment from 4/7 to 7/7 under section 46(a)(1)(C) and (c)(3)(A), (iii) the increase in the dollar limitation from $50,000 to $100,000 on used property under section 48(c)(2), and (iv) the increase in the limitation based on tax under section 46(a)(6) for certain public utilities. In determining the amount of credit attributable to limited property possible disallowance under section 46(f) shall be disregarded.

(A) The credit allowed by section 38 for the taxable year (determined without regard to section 46(b)) multiplied by a fraction, the numerator of which is the amount of credit earned for limited property for the taxable year and the denominator of which is the amount of credit earned for all section 38 property for the taxable year, over

(B) The amount of normal credit allowed for limited property for the taxable year (determined without regard to section 46(b)). The amount of normal credit allowed for limited property is the amount of credit that would be allowed for the taxable year determined as if the Tax Reduction Act had not been enacted multiplied by a fraction, the numerator of which is the amount of credit earned for limited property for the taxable year determined as if the Tax Reduction Act had not been enacted and the denominator of which is the credit earned for all section 38 property for the taxable year determined as if the Tax Reduction Act had not been enacted.

(ii) Carryover or carryback to taxable year. The amount of additional credit allowed for limited property attributable to a carryover or a carryback of any unused credit to any taxable year in an amount equal to the excess of—

(A) The amount of credit allowed by section 38 for the taxable year by reason of section 46(b) multiplied by the fraction contained in paragraph (a)(3)(i)(A) of this section for the unused credit year, over

(B) The amount of unused normal credit allowed for limited property for the taxable year. The amount of unused normal credit allowed for limited property is the amount of unused credit that would be allowed for the taxable year under section 38 by reason of section 46(b), taking into account the amount of unused credit that would be allowed for any preceding year, determined as if the Tax Reduction Act had not been enacted, multiplied by the fraction contained in paragraph (a)(3)(i)(B) of this section for the unused credit year.

(b) New election. *(1) In general.* A taxpayer who made a 1972 election for immediate flow-through under section 46(f)(3) with respect to limited property may elect to apply section 46(f)(3) to the additional credit allowed by the Tax Reduction Act of 1975 with respect to such property, or, if eligible, may make the election in paragraph (b)(2) of this section to apply section 46(f)(2) to such additional credit. The election to apply section 46(f)(2) or (3) must be made before June 28, 1975, in the manner provided in paragraph (c) of this section. If the taxpayer does not make a new election, section 46(f)(1) shall apply to additional credit for limited property. However, if the taxpayer made a 1972 election under section 46(f)(2) with respect to property to which section 46(f)(3) does not apply, then section 46(f)(2) shall apply to such additional credit notwithstanding any prohibition in section 46(f)(3) to the contrary.

(2) Special section 46(f)(2) election. A taxpayer who:

(i) Made a 1972 election under section 46(f)(3),

(ii) Did not make an election to apply section 46(f)(2) with respect to property to which section 46(f)(3) does not apply, and

(iii) Did not acquire property to which section 46(f)(1) applied in any taxable year ending before January 1, 1975, may elect to apply section 46(f)(2) to the additional credit allowed by the Tax Reduction Act of 1975 with respect to limited property notwithstanding any prohibition in section 46(f)(3) to the contrary.

(c) Method of making election. A taxpayer may make an election described in paragraph (b) of this section by filing a statement before June 28, 1975, with the district director or director of the internal revenue service center with whom the taxpayer ordinarily files its income tax return. For rules with respect to taxpayers filing consolidated returns, see § 1.1502-77(a) of part 1 of this chapter. The statement shall contain the following information: (1) the name, address, and taxpayer identification number of the taxpayer, and (2) the election which the taxpayer is making under paragraph (b) of this section. If a taxpayer is electing flow-through under section 46(f)(3), the statement shall also contain a written recitation that the election is made at the taxpayer's own option and without regard to any requirement imposed by an agency described in section 46(c)(2)(B) having jurisdiction over the taxpayer. The recitation shall be verified by a written declaration that it is made under the penalties of perjury.

T.D. 7360, 6/13/75.

§ 12.3 Investment credit, public utility property elections.

(a) Elections. *(1) In general.* Under section 46(e), three elections may be made on or before March 9, 1972, with respect to section 46(e) property (as defined in subparagraph

(3) of this paragraph). An election made under the provisions of section 46(e) shall be irrevocable.

(2) Applicability of elections. (i) Any election under section 46(e) shall be made with respect to all of the taxpayer's property eligible for the election whether or not the taxpayer is regulated by more than one regulatory body.

(ii) (a) Paragraph (1) of section 46(e) shall apply to all of the taxpayer's section 46(e) property in the absence of an election under paragraph (2) or (3) of section 46(e). If an election is made under paragraph (2) of section 46(e), paragraph (1) of such section shall not apply to any of the taxpayer's section 46(e) property.

(b) An election made under the last sentence of section 46(e)(1) shall apply to that portion of the taxpayer's section 46(e) property to which paragraph (1) of section 46(e) applies and which is short supply property within the meaning of § 1.46-5(b)(2) of this chapter (Income Tax Regulations) as set forth in a notice of proposed rule making published in 37 F.R. 3526 on February 17, 1971.

(iii) If a taxpayer makes an election under paragraph (2) of section 46(e), and makes no election under paragraph (3) of such section, the election under paragraph (2) of section 46(e) shall apply to all of its section 46(e) property.

(iv) If a taxpayer makes an election under paragraph (3) of section 46(e), such election shall apply to all of the taxpayer's section 46(e) property to which section 167(1)(2)(C) applies. Paragraph (1) or (2) of section 46(e) (as the case may be) shall apply to that portion of the taxpayer's section 46(e) property which is not property to which section 167(1)(2)(C) applies. Thus, for example, if a taxpayer makes an election under paragraph (2) of section 46(e), and also makes an election under paragraph (3) of section 46(e), paragraph (3) shall apply to all of the taxpayer's section 46(e) property to which section 167(1)(2)(C) applies and paragraph (2) shall apply to the remainder of the taxpayer's section 46(e) property.

(3) Section 46(e) property. "Section 46(e) property is section 38 property which is both property described in section 50 and is—

(i) Public utility property within the meaning of section 46(c)(3)(B) (other than nonregulated communication property of the type described in the last sentence of section 46(c)(3)(B)), or

(ii) Property used predominantly in the trade or business of the furnishing or sale of (a) steam through a local distribution system or (b) the transportation of gas or steam by pipeline, if the rates for such furnishing or sale are established or approved by a governmental unit, agency, instrumentality, or commission described in section 46(c)(3)(B).

(b) Method of making elections. A taxpayer may make the elections described in section 46(e) by filing a statement, on or before March 9, 1972, with the district director or director of the internal revenue service center with whom the taxpayer ordinarily files its income tax return. For rules in the case of taxpayers filing consolidated returns, see § 1.1502-77(a) of this Chapter (Income Tax Regulations). Such statement shall contain the following information:

(1) The name, address, and taxpayer identification number of the taxpayer,

(2) The paragraph (or paragraphs) of section 46(e) under which the taxpayer is making the election,

(3) If an election is made under the last sentence of section 46(e)(1), the name and address of all regulatory bodies which have jurisdiction over the taxpayer with respect to the section 46(e) property covered by such election and a statement setting forth the type of the public utility activity described in section 46(e)(5)(B) in which the taxpayer engages, and

(4) If an election is made under paragraph (3) of section 46(e), a statement indicating whether an election has been made by the taxpayer under section 167(1)(4)(A).

T.D. 7161, 2/16/72.

§ 1.46-8 Requirements for taxpayers electing additional one-percent investment credit (TRASOP's).

(a) Introduction. *(1) In general.* A corporation may elect under section 46(a)(2)(B) of the Code to obtain an additional investment credit for property described in section 46(a)(2)(D). This section provides rules for electing to have the provisions of section 46(a)(2)(B) apply and for implementing an employee stock ownership plan under section 301(d) of the Tax Reduction Act of 1975 ("1975 TRA"). The plan must meet the formal requirements of paragraph (d), and the operational requirements of paragraph (e), of this section. An additional credit may be obtained for the periods described in section 46(a)(2)(D). Unless otherwise indicated, statutory references in this section are to the Internal Revenue Code of 1954 as in effect prior to the amendments made by the Revenue Act of 1978.

(2) Reports. The returns required by section 6058(a) must be filed on behalf of a plan established under paragraph (c)(7) of this section, whether or not the plan is qualified under section 401(a).

(3) Cross-references. The following table indicates where in this section provisions appear relating to each provision of section 301 (d) and (f) of the 1975 TRA.

Section 301	Section 1.46-8	Subject
(d)(1)	(c)(7)(i), (c)(8)(i)	Establishing a TRASOP, in general; funding a TRASOP, in general.
(2)(A)	(c)(7)(ii)	Type of plan.
(B)	(d)(3), (e)(10)	Investment design.
(C)	(d)(1)	Plan requirements, in general.
(3)	(d)(6)	Allocation.
	(b)(8)	Compensation, definition.
(4)	(d)(7)	Nonforfeitability.
	(d)(9)	Distributions.
(5)	(d)(8)	Voting rights.
(6)	(c)	Procedures for additional credit.
(7)(A)	(c)(7)(ii)	Taxability, non-401(a) TRASOP.
(B)	(e)(3)	Allocations under 401(a).
(C)	(e)(3)	Section 410 and section 415 requirements.
(8)	(e)(9)	Reductions of investment credit.
(9)(A)	(b)(4)	Employer securities, definition.
	(e)(10), (f)	Employer securities, requirements.
(B)	(b)(7)	Value, definition.
(10)	(a)(2)	Reporting requirements.
(11)	(h)	Failure to comply.
(12)	(c)(10)	Deductibility.
(13)	(e)(6) and (7)	Reimbursement for expenses.
(14)	(c)(8)(v) and (d)(7)(i)	Contingent contributions.
(f)	(d)(7), (e)(8)(vii), (f)	Withdrawals of TRASOP securities.

(b) Definitions. When used in this section, the terms listed below have the indicated meanings:

(1) TRASOP. A "TRASOP" is an employee stock ownership plan that meets the requirements of section 301(d) of

the 1975 TRA. See § 1.46-7. It is a type of plan described in paragraph (d)(1) of this section and may, but need not, be an ESOP under § 54.4975-11 of this chapter (Pension Excise Tax Regulations). See § 1.46-8(d)(5) concerning use of TRASOP assets as collateral for debts and expenses of the plan.

(2) Additional credit. An "additional credit" is the additional one-percent investment credit under section 46(a)(2)(B)(i).

(3) Employer. An "employer" is a corporation that establishes a TRASOP.

(4) Employer securities. (i) In general. "Employer securities" are common stock, and securities convertible into common stock, of the employer or of a corporation that is a member of a controlled group of corporations including the employer. Employer securities must meet the requirements of paragraph (g) of this section. Membership in a controlled group for purposes of this section is determined under section 414(b) of the Code.

(ii) Pre-1977 employer securities. In addition, employer securities acquired by a TRASOP before January 1, 1977, include common stock, and securities convertible into common stock, of a corporation in control of the employer within the meaning of section 368(c).

(iii) Caution. An employer security under this section is not necessarily a qualifying employer security as defined in section 407(d)(5) of the Employee Retirement Income Security Act of 1974 (ERISA) or section 4975(e)(8). Moreover, sections 406, 407, and 408 of ERISA in certain cases limit the acquisition and disposition of qualifying employer securities as defined in section 407(d)(5) of ERISA.

(5) TRASOP securities. "TRASOP securities" are employer securities that—

(i) Are transferred to a TRASOP, or acquired with cash transferred to a TRASOP, to obtain an additional credit, and

(ii) Except as provided under paragraph (g)(4) and (5) of this section, or as required by applicable law, are subject to no other put, call, or other option, or buy-sell or similar arrangement while held by the plan.

(6) Publicly traded. The term "publicly traded" has the meaning specified in § 54.4975-7(b)(1)(iv) of this chapter.

(7) Value. (i) In general. With respect to the transfer of TRASOP securities by a corporation to a TRASOP or the acquisition of TRASOP securities with cash transferred by a corporation to a TRASOP, "value" means fair market value determined in good faith and based on all relevant factors as of the date of transfer or acquisition of the TRASOP securities. If the plan acquires TRASOP securities from other than a disqualified person within the meaning of section 4975(e)(2), a good faith determination of value includes a determination of fair market value based on an appraisal independently arrived at by a person who customarily makes such appraisals and who is independent of any person from whom the TRASOP securities are acquired.

(ii) Twenty-day average rule. A special 20-day average valuation rule applies to certain publicly traded securities transferred by a corporation to a TRASOP. It does not apply to securities acquired with cash transferred by a corporation to a TRASOP. Under the special rule, the term "value" refers to an average of daily closing prices for a security, as reported on any national securities exchange or as quoted on any system sponsored by a national securities association, over the 20 consecutive trading days immediately preceding the applicable last day described in paragraph (c)(8)(i) of this section. The average is based on the closing prices for each day when the security is in fact traded during the 20-day period. However, the special rule does not apply unless the security is in fact traded for at least 10 of the 20 days.

(iii) 20-day average transitional exception. If a TRASOP security is transferred before March 20, 1979, the plan may value the security on the basis of the 20 consecutive trading days preceding the date on which the security is transferred or the date as of which the security is allocated to a participant's account.

(8) Compensation. "Compensation" means "participant's compensation" under section 415(c)(3) and § 1.415-2(d). However, except for purposes of applying section 415, compensation must be determined for a plan year, not a limitation year.

(c) Procedures for additional credit. *(1) Applicable year.* (i) General rule. With respect to a qualified investment, the "applicable year" of a corporation is generally the taxable year in which the investment is made. For purposes of this section, an investment is made either in a year when section 38 property is placed in service or in a year when qualified progress expenditures are incurred.

(ii) Carryover option. A corporation may determine the applicable years for qualified investments made in any taxable year beginning after December 31, 1976, under the following method: The first applicable year with respect to the additional credit for a given year's qualified investment is the year the qualified investment is made or, if later, the first taxable year for which any additional credit is allowable if claimed for that qualified investment. If there is an investment credit carryover from the first applicable year, each taxable year to which any part of the additional credit for that qualified investment is carried over is also an applicable year. If the carryover treatment is elected for the additional credit attributable to a year's qualified investment, all applicable years for the additional credit attributable to that investment must be determined under the carryover option.

(iii) Increased credit. A taxable year in which a corporation's additional credit is increased because of a redetermination is also an applicable year. See paragraph (c)(9)(iv) of this section.

(iv) Illustration. To illustrate the application of paragraph (c)(1)(i) and (ii) of this section, assume that a calendar-year corporation makes a qualified investment in 1977 and that 1977 is an unused credit year described in section 46(b)(1). If the general rule is applied, 1977 is an applicable year. However, because 1977 is an unused credit year (at least with respect to the additional credit), if the corporation does not elect to treat 1977 as an applicable year but carries over its entire additional credit for 1977 to 1978 and uses it in 1978, then 1978 is an applicable year. If part of the additional credit is carried over further to 1979, the year 1979 is also an applicable year.

(v) Change in method. The choice between the general rule and carryover option methods of determining the additional credit attributable to applicable years is made with respect to each year's qualified investment, and does not bind the corporation with respect to selection of methods for the additional credit attributable to other years' qualified investment. A failure to comply does not occur merely because a corporation elects to apply either method for the additional credit attributable to separate years' qualified investment.

(2) Time and manner of electing. A corporation with a qualified investment must elect to be eligible for an additional credit by attaching a statement of election—

(i) To its income tax return, filed on or before the due date including extensions of time, for a taxable year not later than its first applicable year with respect to a qualified investment, or

(ii) In the case of a return filed before December 31, 1975, to an amended return filed on or before December 31, 1975.

(3) Statement of election. The statement of election must contain the name and taxpayer identification number of the corporation. Also, it must declare in the following words, or in words having substantially the same meaning, that:

(i) The corporation elects to have section 46(a)(2)(B)(i) of the Internal Revenue Code of 1954 apply; and

(ii) The corporation agrees to implement (or continue to implement, as appropriate) a TRASOP and to claim the additional credit as required by § 1.46-8 of the Income Tax Regulations.

(4) Separate election. A separate election must be made for each taxable year's qualified investment to obtain an additional credit for that qualified investment. If a corporation does not make a timely election to obtain an additional credit for a taxable year, it may not subsequently make the election on an amended return or otherwise.

(5) No partial election. An election to obtain an additional credit applies to a corporation's entire qualified investment for a taxable year. Thus, a corporation may not elect to obtain a partial additional credit for any year's qualified investment. However, the partial disallowance of an additional credit will not result in an election being treated as a partial election. Also, an election by a member of a controlled group of corporations that applies only to the electing member's qualified investment is not a partial election. See § 1.46-8(h)(9) with respect to transitional rules for elections made before January 19, 1979.

(6) No revocation of election. After the time for electing the additional credit has expired for a taxable year, a corporation may not revoke its election for that year.

(7) Establishing a TRASOP. (i) In general. A corporation electing to obtain an additional credit must establish a TRASOP with accompanying trust on or before the last day for making the election regardless of when in fact the election is made. A TRASOP is considered to be in existence on a particular date if it meets the requirements of § 1.410(a)-2(c)(1). A new plan need not be established if an existing plan qualifies as a TRASOP, or is amended to meet the requirements of this section, on or before the last day for making the election. The requirements of this section are not satisfied merely by establishing and crediting a separate "TRASOP" account on the corporation's books.

(ii) Type of plan. A TRASOP need not meet the requirements of section 401(a). However, it must be a stock bonus plan, a combination stock bonus plan and money purchase pension plan, or a profit-sharing plan under § 1.401-1(b)(1) of this chapter. See section 301(d)(7)(A) of the 1975 TRA for the tax consequences relating to a TRASOP that does not meet the requirements of section 401(a). See also Title I of ERISA for additional provisions applicable to a TRASOP as an employee pension benefit plan under section 3(2) of ERISA.

(8) Funding a TRASOP. (i) In general. A corporation electing to obtain an additional credit must fund its TRASOP by transferring TRASOP securities or cash to it no later than 30 days after the applicable last day. That day is the last day for electing the additional credit, irrespective of when the election is actually made. However, in the case of an investment credit that was carried over and claimed in a subsequent applicable year by reason of paragraph (c)(1)(ii) of this section, that day is the last day (including extensions) for filing its income tax return for the subsequent applicable year. TRASOP securities may be transferred to a plan at any time during the applicable year, but not before the first day of an applicable year. If TRASOP securities are transferred to the plan within the permissible time period after the close of the applicable year, they are treated as transferred during that applicable year first until all TRASOP securities required by this paragraph (c) for that applicable year are transferred to, and taken into account under, the TRASOP. Thus, for example, assume that on a return filed on September 17, 1979 (with extensions, the last day for filing a return for 1978), a calendar-year corporation claims an additional credit of $5,000 for 1978, an applicable year under the TRASOP. No contributions were made in 1978 on account of the 1978 credit, but TRASOP securities with a value of $6,000 were contributed in 1979. The corporation also expects to be able to claim an additional credit of $10,000 for 1979. TRASOP securities transferred between January 1, 1979, and October 17, 1979, must be taken into account under the plan for 1978 before they are taken into account for 1979. Accordingly, securities having a value of $5,000 are applied against the obligation for 1978, and $1,000 of the contribution is retained to be applied to the eventual obligation for 1979.

(ii) Cash transfers. A corporation may transfer cash to the TRASOP instead of TRASOP securities only if the TRASOP uses the cash to acquire TRASOP securities no later than 30 days after the time for funding the TRASOP.

(iii) Valuation. The value of the TRASOP securities for an applicable year must equal one percent of the corporation's qualified investment for that year. However, if paragraph (c)(1)(ii) of this section is followed by a corporation, the value of TRASOP securities for an applicable year must equal the amount of additional credit claimed for that year.

(iv) Cash reserve. The value of TRASOP securities acquired with cash transferred by a corporation may be reduced by two items. The first item is an amount not more than the value of fractional shares allocable to participants entitled to receive an immediate distribution at the time of the transfer. The second item is start-up expenses and administrative expenses to the extent permitted under section 301(d)(13) of the 1975 TRA and paragraph (e)(6) and (7) of this section.

(v) Conditional funding. The funding of a TRASOP may be conditional if the TRASOP satisfies the provisions of section 301(d)(14) of the 1975 TRA. For purposes of section 301(d)(14), an investment credit is considered to be allowed on the date the election for the applicable year is made under paragraph (c)(2) of this section.

(vi) Certain benefit offset mechanisms. A TRASOP will be deemed to be not funded to the extent that TRASOP securities are used to offset benefits under a defined benefit plan.

(9) Claiming additional credit. (i) In general. Section 46(a)(3) subjects the amount of investment credit earned with respect to a taxpayer's qualified investment for a taxable year to a limitation based on the corporation's tax liability.

(ii) Unused credit year. Section 46(a)(1) provides a first-in-first-out rule for the investment credit in a taxable year. Section 46(b)(1) provides for the carryback and carryover of unused credits. If less than all of a taxpayer's credit earned for a taxable year is allowable, the 10-percent credit determined under section 46(a)(2)(A) earned for a particular year is allowed first. Any portion of the additional credit for a taxable year that is not allowable may be carried back or carried over to the extent permitted by section 46(b)(1). However, an additional credit which is allowed for a taxable year is not reduced by a carryback to that year of an unused credit from a succeeding taxable year.

(iii) Example. Paragraph (c)(9)(ii) of this section is illustrated by the following example:

Example. A calendar-year corporation begins operation and establishes a TRASOP in 1975. The facts and treatment relating to the corporation's qualified investments and investment tax credits for 1975 and 1976 are as follows:

	1975	1976
Facts:		
1. Qualified investment	$500,000	$500,000
2. Credits earned:		
a. 10% credit	50,000	50,000
b. Additional credit	5,000	5,000
c. Carryover of additional credit from prior year, line 5		3,000
3. Sec. 46(a)(3) limitation	52,000	47,000
Treatment of credits:		
4. Credits allowed:		
a. Carryover of additional credit		3,000
b. Current 10% credit	50,000	44,000
c. Current additional credit	2,000	0
5. Unused credits:		
a. 10% credit	0	6,000
b. Additional credit	3,000	5,000

Thus, in 1975 the section 46(a)(3) limitation ($52,000) is applied first to allow all of the 10-percent investment credit ($50,000). Accordingly only $2,000 of the additional credit earned is allowed in 1975 and $3,000 of the additional credit is carried forward to 1976. In 1976, section 46(a)(1) requires that this $3,000 of additional credit is allowed first, and then only $44,000 of the 10-percent credit earned in 1976 is allowed since the section 46(a)(3) limitation for that year is $47,000. The unused credits from 1976 cannot be carried back since 1975, the only prior year, is an unused credit year.

(iv) Redeterminations increasing credit. If a corporation's allowable additional credit is increased because of a redetermination, the increase is treated as if it were an unused credit carryover for purposes of paragraphs (c)(1)(ii) and (c)(8)(i) of this section. For purposes of this subdivision (iv), the date of the increase is determined under paragraph (e)(9)(iii) of this section as if it were the date of a reduction. Thus, for example, assume that a calendar-year corporation claims an additional credit of $100,000 in 1978 because of a qualified investment in that year. In 1980, the additional credit attributable to 1978 qualified investment is redetermined to be $110,000. With respect to the 1978 qualified investment, 1980 is also an applicable year to the extent of $10,000. The increased credit is reflected on the employer's return for 1980. The corporation must fund the TRASOP with this $10,000 under paragraph (c)(8) of this section.

(v) Redeterminations increasing tax liability. If a corporation's tax liability for a year is increased such that an additional credit carried forward and claimed in a later year is allowable in the earlier year, the claim of the additional credit will be considered timely if it was otherwise timely under this section. Thus, for example, assume that a calendar-year corporation makes qualified investment of $5,000,000 in 1978 but, based on its income tax liability, is unable to use any of the credit until 1979, when the entire $50,000 additional credit can be used. The corporation adopts the TRASOP, elects the full $50,000 credit and funds in a timely manner for tax year 1979. However, as a result of a 1981 redetermination of the 1978 tax liability, the corporation is able to use $30,000 of the additional credit in 1978 and the remaining $20,000 in 1979. The allowable credit for 1978 is increased by $30,000 and the increase is treated as an unused credit carryover, for which the year of redetermination, 1981, is the applicable year. Assuming that no other credits are available, the 1979 credit is reduced from $50,000 to $20,000, and this reduction is taken into account in the redetermination year by offsetting the reduction against amounts due the plan or by deducting the amount of the reduction. The adoption of the TRASOP for 1979, rather than 1978, is considered timely.

(10) Deductions at expiration of carryover period. Under paragraph (c)(1)(i) of this section, a corporation that uses no additional credit in the year of a qualified investment may nonetheless treat the year in which the qualified investment is made as the first applicable year. If the carryover period under section 46(b)(1)(B) expires before the corporation uses the entire additional credit with respect to the qualified investment, contributions attributable to the unused credit are deductible, subject to the limitations of section 404(a), as if made in the taxable year when the carryover period expires. The amount deductible is the dollar amount of the unused credit irrespective of the current value of the securities contributed with respect to the credit.

(d) Formal plan requirements. *(1) In general.* To be a TRASOP, a plan must meet the formal requirements of this paragraph (d).

(2) Plan year. To be a TRASOP, a plan must specify a plan year that begins with or within the corporation's taxable year.

(3) Designed to invest primarily in employer securities. To be a TRASOP, a plan must state that it is designed to invest primarily in employer securities. A TRASOP intended to qualify as an ESOP under § 54.4975-11 must state that it is designed to invest primarily in employer securities. See paragraph (e)(10) of this section concerning the requirement that a plan invest in employer securities on an ongoing basis.

(4) Separate accounting. To be a TRASOP, a plan must state that TRASOP securities are to be accounted for separately from any other contributions to the plan.

(5) Debts and expenses of the TRASOP. To be a TRASOP, a plan must state that TRASOP securities cannot be used to satisfy a loan made to the TRASOP or be used as collateral for a loan made to a TRASOP. However, if the plan so provides, to the extent permitted under section 301(d)(13) of the 1975 TRA and paragraph (e)(6) and (7) of this section, certain amounts may be used for the TRASOP's start-up expenses and administrative expenses.

(6) Allocation of TRASOP securities. (i) General rules. To be a TRASOP, a plan must provide for the allocation of TRASOP securities under section 301(d)(3) of the 1975 TRA and this subparagraph (6).

(ii) Timing. TRASOP securities are allocated as of the last day of the plan year beginning with or within the appropriate applicable year.

(iii) Participants. Each employee who is a participant at any time during the plan year for which allocation is made must receive an allocation as of the end of that year even though not then employed by the employer. However, to receive allocations, employees must satisfy the minimum participation requirements of the plan (for example, 1,000 hours of service).

(iv) Compensation considered. Under section 301(d)(3) of the 1975 TRA, allocations must be based on the proportion that each participant's compensation bears to all participants' compensation. Compensation in excess of $100,000 must be disregarded in making these allocations. A plan may have a lower stated ceiling on compensation (from $0 to $100,000) and if the plan has such a lower ceiling, compensation in excess of this ceiling must likewise be disregarded. Also, allocations must be based on a participant's compensation while actually employed, not just while actually participating, in the plan year.

(v) Section 415 priority rule; transitional rule. For purposes of section 415, this subdivision (v) applies only to limitation years beginning after November 30, 1982. If a TRASOP security is not allocated to a participant's account for a plan year because of section 415 and section 301(d)(3) of the 1975 TRA, no other amount may be allocated for that participant under any defined contribution plan of the same employer after the actual allocation date for that TRASOP plan year, until all unallocated TRASOP securities have been allocated as provided in paragraph (d)(6)(vi) and (vii) of this section. This subdivision (v) applies to a TRASOP when, under section 415(f)(1)(B), the TRASOP is treated along with an employer's other defined contribution plans as one plan for purposes of section 415.

(vi) Unallocated amounts. Under section 301(d)(3) of the 1975 TRA, TRASOP securities unallocated for a plan year to participants' accounts because of section 415 must be allocated proportionately to the accounts of other participants until the addition to the account of each participant reaches the limits of section 415.

(vii) Suspense account. If, after these allocations, TRASOP securities remain unallocated, they must be held in an unallocated suspense account under the TRASOP. Any income produced by these securities must also be held in the account. A plan with such an account will not fail to qualify under section 401(a) merely because of the account. In each successive TRASOP plan year (whether or not an applicable year), the unallocated assets are released from this account for allocation on a first-in-first-out basis. They are then allocated to the participants' accounts proportionately under paragraph (d)(6)(i)–(vi) of this section for each later year until no TRASOP securities remain unallocated. Value for this allocation is determined under paragraph (b)(7) of this section as of the date of transfer from the suspense account or, if the special 20-day average rule applies, the value is determined on the basis of the 20 consecutive trading days immediately preceding the date of transfer from the suspense account.

(viii) Escrow account. A TRASOP may provide for the establishment of an escrow account instead of a suspense account. The escrow account must satisfy paragraph (d)(6)(vii) of this section. The beneficiary of the escrow account is to be the TRASOP. The corporation may establish the escrow account and contribute stock or cash to it. In such a case, the escrow agent must transfer assets to the plan each year equal to the amount to be allocated proportionately under paragraph (d)(6)(i)–(vi) of this section. Assets held in an escrow account are plan assets.

(ix) Treatment of certain plan terminations. To be a TRASOP, a plan must provide that, if a plan terminates because the corporation ceases to exist, unallocated amounts described in paragraph (d)(6)(vi) of this section must be allocated to the extent possible under section 415 for the year of termination. The remaining unallocated amounts must then be withdrawn. These unallocated amounts are treated as recaptured under all the rules of paragraph (e)(9)(vii) of this section except its last sentence. See paragraph (d)(9)(i) of this section concerning distributions of allocated TRASOP securities.

(x) No integration. No TRASOP may be integrated, directly or indirectly, with contributions or benefits under Title II of the Social Security Act or any other state or federal law.

(xi) Fractional securities. Participants' accounts are to be allocated fractional securities or fractional rights to securities.

(xii) Accounting for amounts withheld by employer or paid by plan as start-up or administrative expenses. An employer may withhold certain start-up and administrative expenses from TRASOP securities due the plan. Also, a plan may reduce amounts to be allocated to the extent that certain plan assets are used to reimburse the employer, for example for salaries of employees providing services to the plan, or to pay fees directly to independent contractors for expenses. These expenses do not reduce the amount of additional credit claimed and are not allowable as expenses in computing taxable income. Additional rules concerning these expenses are in paragraph (e)(6) and (7) of this section.

(7) Nonforfeitability. To be a TRASOP, a plan must state that each participant has a nonforfeitable right to allocated TRASOP securities. For purposes of this section, forfeitures described in section 411(a)(3) are not permitted. However, amounts shall not fail to be considered to be nonforfeitable if the plan provides for their return to the corporation—

(i) In the case of conditional contributions, under section 301(d)(14) of the 1975 TRA and paragraph (c)(8)(v) of this section, and

(ii) In the case of investment credit recapture or an event deemed to be a recapture, under section 301(f) of the 1975 TRA and paragraph (f) of this section.

(8) Voting rights. (i) Provision for passthrough. To be a TRASOP, a plan must state that each participant is entitled to direct a designated fiduciary how to exercise any voting rights on TRASOP securities allocated to the account of the participant. The plan need not permit participants to direct the voting of unallocated TRASOP or other securities held by the trust. It may authorize the designated fiduciary to exercise voting rights for unallocated securities.

(ii) Notification by the employer. To be a TRASOP, the plan must obligate the corporation to furnish the designated fiduciary and participants with notices and information statements when voting rights are to be exercised. The time and manner for furnishing participants with a notice or information statement must comply with both applicable law and the corporation's charter and bylaws as generally applicable to security holders. In general, the content of the statement must be the same for plan participants as for other security holders.

(iii) Fractional securities. To be a TRASOP, the plan must allow the participants to vote any allocated fractional securities or fractional rights to securities. This requirement is met if the designated fiduciary votes the combined fractional securities or rights to the extent possible to reflect the direction of the voting participants.

(iv) Unexercised voting rights. To be a TRASOP, the plan may not permit the designated fiduciary to exercise voting rights which a participant fails to exercise. However, the plan may permit the solicitation and exercise of participants' voting rights by management and others under a proxy provision applicable to all security holders.

(9) Distributions. (i) In general. To be a TRASOP, a plan must permit the distribution of allocated TRASOP securities only as provided under section 301(d)(4) of the 1975 TRA. Also, under § 1.401-1(b)(1)(i) of this chapter, to the extent that a TRASOP is a money purchase pension plan, it can only provide for a distribution in the case of separation from service, death, or disability. No TRASOP may provide for the distribution of TRASOP securities upon plan termination within the 84-month holding period. For purposes of section 301(d)(4) of the 1975 TRA, the 84-month holding period begins on the date as of which TRASOP securities are allocated.

(ii) Certain fractional securities. A stock bonus TRASOP may distribute cash instead of fractional securities.

(e) Operational plan requirements. *(1) General rule.* To be a TRASOP, a plan in operation must meet the requirements of this paragraph (e). However, the provisions under paragraph (e)(8) of this section apply only to TRASOPs qualified under section 401(a).

(2) Compliance with plan provisions. To be a TRASOP, a plan must operate in compliance with its provisions. Failure to operate in compliance with plan provisions constitutes an operational failure to comply. See paragraph (h)(5)(iii) of this section.

(3) Compliance with certain Code provisions. To be a TRASOP, a plan must meet the requirements of section 301(d)(7) of the 1975 TRA. Thus, whether or not it is qualified under section 401(a), a TRASOP must meet the requirements of section 401(a) with respect to allocations, section 410 with respect to participation, and section 415 with respect to limitations on contributions and benefits. However, these requirements are modified by paragraph (d)(6) of this section, relating to allocations and section 415.

(4) Employee contributions. Under a TRASOP, the participants' receipt of benefits attributable to TRASOP securities contributed for the additional credit (but not the extra additional credit) must not depend on contributions by participants. If a corporation has a plan in existence which requires employee contributions, a portion of the plan may be a TRASOP if employee contributions are not required with respect to that portion of the plan.

(5) Controlled group of corporations, etc. Whether or not a TRASOP is qualified under section 401(a), all employees who by reason of section 414 (b) and (c) are treated as employees of an electing corporation are treated as employed by the corporation in determining whether the plan satisfies the requirements of sections 301(d)(7)(B) and (C) of the 1975 TRA. A member of a controlled group under paragraph (b)(4)(i) of this section with a qualified investment but with no actual employees may obtain an additional credit even though the only participants in the corporation's TRASOP are actually employed by another member of the controlled group.

(6) Start-up expenses. (i) In general. For purposes of this section, the term "start-up expense" means any ordinary and necessary amount of a nonrecurring nature paid or incurred by the corporation or by the plan in connection with the establishment of a TRASOP under paragraph (c)(7) of this section. Thus, for example, start-up expenses may include expenses relating to: the drafting or amending of plan documents to establish a TRASOP under section 301(d) or (e) of the 1975 TRA, the seeking of agency approval for these documents and related transactions, the obtaining of shareholder approval for establishing a TRASOP, and the registering of securities for initial funding of a TRASOP.

(ii) Treatment of start-up expenses. Start-up expenses may be withheld by the employer from amounts that would otherwise be due the plan under paragraph (c)(8) of this section, to the extent that these amounts are known by the employer when funding first occurs for an applicable year. To the extent that these amounts are not withheld by the employer, the plan may pay remaining amounts from plan assets within a reasonable time after the amounts are known by the plan.

(iii) Ceiling on start-up expenses. Reimbursement for start-up expenses is limited to a ceiling. This ceiling is the sum of 10 percent of the first $100,000 that an employer is first required to transfer under paragraph (c)(8) of this section for an applicable year and 5 percent of that amount in excess of $100,000. If this first year is an unused credit year from which there is a carryover, amounts required to be transferred in subsequent years for claiming carryovers from this first year are considered in determining this ceiling. Thus, for example, assume that a calendar-year corporation first earns an additional credit in 1977 of $9,000 and that $3,000 of this amount is claimed on the income tax return for 1977, for 1978 and for 1979. The corporation's ceiling on start-up expenses is $300 when its 1977 return is filed. The total ceiling increases to $600 when its 1978 return is filed and to $900 when its 1979 return is filed, with the claiming of an additional $3,000 credit for each of the three years.

(iv) Special rule for taxable years ending before January 1, 1977. Special treatment is available for expenses paid or incurred before January 1, 1977, that were not taken into account in the manner provided by section 301(d)(13) of the 1975 TRA. These expenses may be withdrawn under paragraph (e)(9)(vii) of this section in the same manner as reductions in the corporation's additional credit caused by a recapture. This withdrawal may only be made during the first taxable year ending after March 20, 1979. It is subject to the ceiling of section 301(d)(13) of the 1975 TRA. Expenses previously deducted by a corporation must be reduced on a timely-filed amended return by the amount of this withdrawal.

(7) Administrative expenses. (i) In general. For purposes of this section, the term "administrative expense" means any amount, other than a start-up expense, paid or incurred by the corporation or by the plan that is ordinary and necessary in maintaining the TRASOP. Thus, for example, administrative expenses may include expenses relating to: compensating plan fiduciaries and administrators, leasing office space and equipment, reproducing and mailing information to participants and beneficiaries, and filing reports, returns, and amendments relating to a TRASOP. Paragraph (e)(6)(ii) and (iv), relating to treatment of start-up expenses and to a special rule for taxable years ending before January 1, 1977, also applies to administrative expenses.

(ii) Ceiling on administrative expenses. Reimbursement for administrative expenses under paragraph (e)(6)(ii) of this section is limited to the smaller of two amounts for each plan year. The first amount is $100,000. The second amount is the sum of 10 percent of the first $100,000 of dividend income paid with respect to TRASOP securities held by the plan during the plan year ending with or within the corporation's taxable year and 5 percent of any such dividend income in excess of $100,000.

(8) TRASOP qualification under section 401(a). (i) Permanence. A TRASOP is not required to be a qualified plan under section 401(a). However, to meet the requirements of section 401(a), a TRASOP must be a permanent plan, as described in § 1.401-1(b)(2) of this chapter. Under section 401(a)(21), a plan will not fail to be considered permanent merely because the amount of employer contributions under the plan is determined solely by reference to the amount of additional credit allowable under this section. Thus, for example, it will not fail to be considered permanent merely because employer contributions are not made for a year for which an additional credit is not available by reason of no qualified investment for which an additional credit can be obtained. Section 401(a)(21) applies only to the extent the TRASOP is funded with TRASOP securities and cash in lieu of TRASOP securities.

(ii) Partial discontinuance of contributions. A plan that meets the requirements of section 401(a) may receive contributions of TRASOP securities as well as other contributions. If the other contributions continue on a permanent basis, the plan's qualification under section 401(a) will not be adversely affected merely because TRASOP securities cease to be contributed to it. The discontinuance of TRASOP contributions does not alter the requirement that past TRASOP contributions remain invested in employer securities. See paragraph (e)(10) of this section.

(iii) Income distribution. Income paid with respect to employer securities acquired by a TRASOP may be distributed at any time after receipt by the plan to participants on whose behalf such securities have been allocated without adversely affecting the qualified status of the plan under section 401(a). (See the last sentence of section 803(h), Tax Reform Act of 1976.) However, under a TRASOP that is a stock bonus or profit-sharing plan, income held by the plan for a 2-year period or longer must be distributed under rules generally applicable to stock bonus and profit-sharing plans qualified under section 401(a). Income distributed by a TRASOP is not subject to the partial exclusion of dividends provided in section 116, whether or not the income is held by the plan for two or more years.

(9) Reductions in investment credit. (i) General rule. Certain reductions in a corporation's investment credit result from either a recapture under section 47 of the corporation's investment credit or a redetermination of the allowable credit. If these reductions are taken into account under a TRASOP, the plan may only use one or more of the methods described in paragraph (e)(9), (v), (vi), and (vii) of this section for taking into account these reductions. Thus, for example, more than one method is permitted upon a recapture with respect to a qualified investment made in a particular year. However, the method described in paragraph (e)(9)(vii) of this section applies only to a recapture and not to a redetermination.

(ii) Ratable reduction. A reduction is allocated ratably between the 10-percent credit and the additional credit. Thus, for example, if a calendar-year corporation claims a $33,000 investment credit for 1976, including $3,000 additional credit, and $11,000 of the total credit is recaptured in 1978, the $3,000 additional credit is reduced by $1,000. This subdivision (ii) does not apply to a reduction solely of the additional credit as could occur, for example, in the case of a redetermination caused by a mathematical error in computing the additional credit or in the case of a recapture caused by a bad faith failure to comply under paragraph (h) of this section.

(iii) Date of reduction. A reduction in investment credit occurs under this paragraph (e)(9) on the earliest of these dates: (A) The date an income tax return (or an amended return) is filed reflecting the reduction; (B) the date a judicial determination affecting the amount of the reduction becomes final; and (C) the date specified in a closing agreement made under section 7121 that is approved by the Commissioner. For purposes of this subdivision (iii), a judicial determination becomes final at the time prescribed in § 1.547-2(b)(1)(ii) or (iii), relating to personal holding company tax.

(iv) Year for taking reduction into account. A reduction in investment credit must be taken into account in the earliest year or years possible under the applicable method beginning no later than the year in which the date of the reduction falls.

(v) Decrease future contributions. The reduction may be taken into account as a decrease in the value of TRASOP securities to be transferred to the plan. The amount of the decrease is equal to the dollar amount of the reduction.

(vi) Deduct under section 404. On the date of the reduction, the amount of the reduction may be treated as an amount paid to the TRASOP for purposes of, and as a deduction to the extent allowed under, section 404.

(vii) Withdraw TRASOP securities. If an additional credit allowed for a taxable year is recaptured, the corporation may withdraw from the plan TRASOP securities transferred to, or acquired by, the plan for claiming that year's credit. The withdrawal must only be from assets segregated under paragraph (f)(2) of this section and must be first from assets accounted for in an unallocated suspense account for the particular year. The amount of assets actually withdrawn bears the same proportion to the amount of assets subject to withdrawal as the amount of additional credit recaptured bears to the amount of additional credit claimed. Thus, for example, if the assets subject to withdrawal consist of 300 shares of one class of employer stock and one-third of the additional credit is recaptured, 100 shares of the stock are withdrawn. However, if the current value of the assets subject to withdrawal exceeds the dollar amount of the additional credit claimed, assets may be withdrawn only to the extent that their current value does not exceed the dollar amount of the recaptured portion of the additional credit. Thus, for example, if the 300 segregated shares in the prior example have a current value of $9,000 and the dollar value of the additional credit claimed is $4,500, when one-third of the additional credit is recaptured, only 50 shares, not 100 shares, are withdrawn. Current value is determined under paragraph (b)(7) of this section as of the withdrawal date or, if the special 20-day average rule is applied, it is based on the 20 consecutive trading days immediately preceding the withdrawal date. Withdrawals from an individual's account for the year with respect to which recapture occurs must bear the same ratio to the total amount withdrawn for that year as the individual's TRASOP account balance for that year bears to the total TRASOP account balances for that year. In the case of a TRASOP security acquired after March 20, 1979, the corporation may not withdraw it unless the plan meets the requirements of paragraph (d)(7)(ii) of this section when the plan acquires the TRASOP security.

(viii) Prior distribution rule. If a TRASOP distributes an amount allocated with respect to an investment credit for a taxable year and the credit for that year is later recaptured, withdrawals may not reduce participants' accounts below the level to which they would have been reduced had the prior distribution not occurred. Recaptured amounts above this level may only be deducted under paragraph (e)(9)(vi) of this section. They may not be used to decrease future contributions under paragraph (e)(9)(v).

(ix) *Illustration.* The operation of paragraph (e)(9)(viii) of this section is illustrated as follows:

Example. For 1977, a calendar-year corporation claims an additional credit of $10,000. The corporation's TRASOP meets the requirements of section 301(f) of the 1975 TRA. Each of 10 participants under the plan for that year receives an equal allocation of 10 shares valued at $1,000. In 1978, one participant terminates employment and receives a distribution of 10 shares. In 1979, a recapture reduces the 1977 additional credit by $2,000. The value of employer securities has not changed from the allocation date. If the 10 shares had not been distributed, 20 shares would be available for withdrawal, 2 shares from each participant's account. Since 9 participants remain from 1977, only 18 shares are available for withdrawal (2 shares × 9 remaining participants). If these 18 shares are withdrawn, the corporation may take into account 2 shares by deducting their value to the extent permitted under paragraph (e)(9)(vi) of this section.

(10) Continued investment in employer securities. The requirement that a plan be designed to invest primarily in employer securities is a continuing obligation. Therefore, a transaction changing the status of a corporation as an employer may require the conversion of certain plan assets into other securities. See paragraphs (d)(9) and (g)(6) of this section. In general, cash or other assets derived from the disposition of employer securities must be reinvested in employer securities not later than the 90th day following the date of disposition. However, the Commissioner may grant an extension of the period for reinvestment in employer securities depending on the facts and circumstances of each case.

(f) Section 301(f) withdrawals. *(1) In general.* No assets may be withdrawn by a corporation under section 301(f) of the 1975 TRA unless the assets are either TRASOP securities or plan assets into which TRASOP securities have been converted ("withdrawal assets"). See paragraph (e)(10) concerning restrictions on investment of TRASOP assets in assets other than employer securities. Withdrawal assets must meet the segregated accounting requirements of this paragraph. The physical segregation of assets is not required.

(2) Segregated accounting. The segregated accounting requirements are that—

(i) Withdrawal assets must be segregated from other plan assets on a taxable-year-by-taxable-year basis; and

(ii) Separate accounts must be maintained on a taxable-year-by-taxable-year basis for each participant on whose behalf withdrawal assets are allocated.

(3) Aggregate plan year accounting. Withdrawal assets for taxable years beginning before October 4, 1976, also meet the segregated accounting requirements if they are aggregated and accounted for in one separate account apart from withdrawal assets in separate accounts for later taxable years.

(g) Requirements for employer securities. *(1) General rules.* The term "employer security" does not include stock rights, warrants and options. An employer security that is not common stock must at all times be immediately convertible into common stock that is an employer security at a conversion price which is no greater than the fair market value of that common stock at the time the plan acquires the security.

(2) Common stock. (i) In general. To be an employer security, common stock must meet certain voting power and dividend right requirements. For purposes of this paragraph (g), stock held by the TRASOP is not treated as outstanding.

(ii) Dividend right limitations. If dividend rights are subject to a limitation, then stock representing at least 50 percent of the fair market value of the employer's outstanding common stock at the time the common stock is transferred to or purchased by the TRASOP must be subject to the same limitation. However, common stock that satisfies paragraph (g)(3)(ii) of this section is not subject to this subdivision (ii).

(3) Voting power and dividend rights. To be an employer security, common stock must have voting power and dividend rights which, when taken together, are "no less favorable" than the voting power and dividend rights of any other common stock issued by the employer. Common stock which meets one of the following tests is "no less favorable".

(i) Ten-percent shareholder test. The stock is part of, or identical to, a class of outstanding stock of which at least 50 percent is not owned by 10-percent shareholders. For this purpose, a 10-percent shareholder is one who owns at least 10 percent of the outstanding shares in a class, including shares constructively owned under section 318.

(ii) Substantial proportionality test. More than one class of common stock is outstanding and an identical percentage of shares from each class is transferred to the TRASOP.

(iii) Voting power test. The stock is part of, or identical to, the existing class of stock having the greatest number of votes per unit of fair market value. For example, assume there are only two classes of common stock, Class A and Class B. Their fair market values per share are $1 and $.50, respectively, and the owner of each share of each class is entitled to one vote per share. Thus, Class B has two votes per $1 and Class A has one vote per $1. Accordingly, the Class B stock has the greatest number of votes per unit of fair market value.

(4) Right of first refusal. TRASOP securities may, but need not, be subject to a right of first refusal. However, whether or not the plan is an ESOP, any such right must meet the requirements of § 54.4975-7(b)(9) of this chapter.

(5) Put option. A TRASOP security that is transferred to a TRASOP after September 30, 1976, must be subject to a put option if it is not publicly traded when distributed or if it is subject to a trading limitation when distributed. The provisions of § 54.4975-7(b)(10)–(12) and § 54.4975-11(a)(3) of this chapter apply to such securities whether or not the plan is an ESOP.

(6) Change of employer security status. In general, a transaction changing the status of a corporation as an employer, or as a member of a controlled group of corporations including the employer, adversely affects the status as employer securities of common stock and securities held by a plan ("old employer securities"). However, to the extent that the transaction causing the change in status of the old employer securities does not result in a recapture under section 47 of any investment credit underlying the transfer to, or acquisition by, the plan of the old employer securities, common stock and securities ("new employer securities") substituted for old employer securities are treated as if they were the old employer securities if—

(i) The plan is not terminated,

(ii) The old employer securities and the new employer securities are of equal value at the time of the transaction changing the status of the old employer securities, and

(iii) The new employer securities otherwise meet the requirements of this section.

(h) Failure to comply. *(1) General rule.* (i) Effect of failure. If a corporation elects under paragraph (c)(2)–(5) of this section to obtain an additional credit and fails to comply with respect to that credit at any time, it is liable to the United States for a civil penalty equal to the amount involved in the failure to comply. If the corporation fails to comply with respect to an additional credit during the 84-month period described in section 301(d)(4) of the 1975 TRA, the credit is also recaptured. A separate failure to comply occurs for each taxable year in which a failure continues to exist.

(ii) Illustration of continuing failure's effect. Assume that in 1975 an additional credit is allowed and a failure to comply occurs in 1975 with respect to that credit. Assume also that in 1976 the 1975 failure continues uncorrected, another additional credit is allowed, and a failure to comply occurs with respect to the 1976 credit. Under these circumstances, on the last day of 1976 three separate failures to comply exist: (A) The 1975 failure with respect to the 1975 credit, (B) the 1976 failure with respect to the 1975 credit, and (C) the 1976 failure with respect to the 1976 credit.

(2) Assessment and collection. The civil penalty must be assessed and collected in the same manner in which a deficiency in the payment of federal income tax is assessed and collected.

(3) Exception. If a failure to comply is corrected within the correction period described in paragraph (h)(5) of this section—

(i) The corporation is not liable for a civil penalty; and

(ii) If the corporation establishes that at the time of the failure a good faith effort to comply was made, its additional credit is not disallowed.

(4) Failure to comply (penalty classifications). (i) In general. An electing corporation fails to comply if a defect described in paragraph (h)(4)(ii)–(iv) of this section occurs with respect to an additional credit allowed for a particular taxable year. The characterization of the defect in this subparagraph (4) determines the amount involved under paragraph (h)(8) of this section for the purpose of assessing the civil penalty.

(ii) Funding defect. A funding defect occurs if a corporation or its TRASOP fails to satisfy the requirements of paragraph (c)(8) or (9) of this section, relating to funding a TRASOP and claiming an additional credit.

(iii) Special operational defect. A special operational defect occurs if a TRASOP fails in operation to satisfy the requirements described in paragraph (d)(5)–(9) of this section, relating to debts and expenses of a TRASOP, allocation of TRASOP securities, nonforfeitability, voting rights, and distributions, or paragraph (e)(3) of this section, relating to compliance with certain Code provisions.

(iv) De minimis defect. A de minimis defect occurs if a corporation or its TRASOP fails to satisfy any requirement of this section other than those enumerated either in paragraph (h)(4)(ii) and (iii) of this section or in paragraphs (a)(2) and (c)(2)–(5) of this section. A failure to comply under this subdivision (iv) may be formal or operational in nature.

(5) Failure to comply (correction rules classifications). (i) In general. If for an electing corporation a defect described in paragraph (h)(4) of this section occurs, the procedure for correcting the failure to comply depends upon whether the failure is classified as a "formal" failure or an "operational" failure under this subparagraph (5).

(ii) Formal failure to comply. Formal failures are corrected by retroactive amendment. If a formal plan requirement is not met, the plan must be retroactively amended by no later than the expiration of the correction period under paragraph (h)(6) of this section. A plan fails to meet a formal plan requirement of paragraph (d) of this section if, for example, it does not state, as required by paragraph (d)(3) of this section, that it is designed to invest primarily in employer securities.

(iii) Operational failure to comply. Operational failures are corrected by undoing the defective transaction and by making the plan and the participants whole. If the value of TRASOP securities transferred to the TRASOP is less than the amount of the additional credit, the corporation must make up any resulting funding deficiency within the correction period. This is done, for example, by contributing additional TRASOP securities plus an amount equal to the dividends or interest that would have been paid between the time that the TRASOP securities should have been transferred and the actual time for the transfer. The contribution of additional TRASOP securities is based on their value under paragraph (b)(7) of this section as of the date by which they were required to be transferred to the plan. An electing corporation fails to meet an obligation undertaken under this section if, for example, it fails to comply with paragraph (c)(8) of this section.

(6) Correction period. (i) In general. For purposes of this paragraph (h), the "correction period" begins when the failure to comply occurs and ends 90 days after receipt by the corporation of a notice of deficiency under section 6212 with respect to the civil penalty and the investment credit.

(ii) Extensions of correction period. Extensions of the correction period are determined under § 53.4941(e)-1(d)(2)(i), (ii), and (iv) of this chapter (Foundation Excise Tax Regulations). For this purpose, a failure to comply is treated as an act of self-dealing, the corporation is treated as a foundation, and a civil penalty is treated as a tax under section 4941(a)(1).

(7) Good faith. The corporation has the burden of establishing under paragraph (h)(3)(ii) of this section that it made a good faith effort to comply. For example, if a corporation shows that it has made a good faith effort to establish the fair market value of the employer securities transferred to the TRASOP, it may be entitled to the additional credit even if, on later examination of the return, it is determined that more securities should have been transferred. For purposes of this paragraph (h)(7), reasonable reliance on Technical Information Release 1413 (1975-50 I.R.B. 16), questions and answers relating to ESOP's, is a good faith effort to comply.

(8) Amount involved. (i) In general. The amount involved in a failure to comply is an amount described in this subparagraph (8). A maximum amount and a minimum amount are determined with respect to an additional credit allowed for a particular taxable year.

(ii) Maximum amount involved. Notwithstanding any other rule in this paragraph (h), all amounts involved with respect to an additional credit allowed for a particular taxable year may not exceed the amount of that credit.

(iii) Minimum amount involved. The minimum amount is ½ of one percent of the additional credit times the number of full months, or parts of full months, during which the failure to comply exists. "Full month" has the meaning assigned in § 1.1250-1(d)(4) (realty depreciation recapture).

(iv) Funding amount involved. The amount involved for a funding defect is the greater of the minimum amount involved or the amount required to place the plan in the position it would have been in if no funding defect had occurred.

(v) Special operational amount involved. The amount involved for a special operational defect is the maximum amount involved.

(vi) De minimis amount involved. The amount involved for a de minimis defect is the minimum amount involved.

(9) Certain permissible actions. (i) Elections prior to January 19, 1979. A corporation does not fail to comply (within the meaning of this paragraph (h)) merely because it revokes an election made prior to January 19, 1979, under the general rule described in paragraph (c)(1)(i) of this section and with respect to which no additional credit was claimed in the taxable year for which the election was made. Such a revocation is permitted irrespective of whether the carryover option described in paragraph (c)(1)(ii) is elected with respect to qualified investment made in a year for which a general rule election is revoked.

(ii) Pro rata use of credit. A corporation does not fail to comply merely because, for an applicable year ending prior to January 19, 1979, it provides for pro rata use of the regular 10-percent credit and the 1-percent additional credit to the extent that less than all of a taxpayer's credit earned for a taxable year is allowable.

(iii) Transitional rule. The Commissioner, based on the particular facts and circumstances of individual cases, may determine that a good faith failure to comply before January 19, 1979, with a final or temporary rule adopted under this section on or after that date does not require retroactive correction under paragraph (h)(5)(ii) of this section.

T.D. 7590, 1/15/79, amend T.D. 7856, 12/3/82.

§ 1.46-9 Requirements for taxpayers electing an extra one-half percent additional investment credit.

(a) Introduction. *(1) In general.* A corporation that qualifies for an additional credit under § 1.46-8 may elect under section 46(a)(2)(B)(ii) of the Code to obtain an extra one-half percent additional investment credit for property described in section 46(a)(2)(D). Paragraph (c) of this section provides additional procedures for electing this extra credit. This section also provides rules for implementing an employee stock ownership plan that meets the requirements of sections 301(d) and (e) of the Tax Reduction Act of 1975 ("1975 TRA"). The plan must meet the additional formal requirements of paragraph (d), and the additional operational requirements of paragraph (e) of this section. Unless otherwise indicated, statutory references in this section are to the Internal Revenue Code of 1954, as applicable for the year in which a qualified investment is made.

(2) Applicability of one-percent TRASOP provisions. Subject to the exceptions and additional rules of this section, the provisions of § 1.46-8 apply to an election made, and to a plan implemented, under this section. However, this section does not change the requirements of § 1.46-8 for purposes of obtaining an additional one-percent credit.

(3) Effective date. This section applies only to taxable years beginning after December 31, 1976. See section 803(j)(2)(A) of the Tax Reform Act of 1976.

(b) Definitions. *(1) One-percent terms.* When used in this section, the terms listed below have the same meanings as in § 1.46-8(b):

(i) TRASOP. See § 1.46-8(b)(1).

(ii) Employer. See § 1.46-8(b)(3).

(iii) Employer securities. See § 1.46-8(b)(4).

(iv) TRASOP securities. See § 1.46-8(b)(5).

(v) Publicly traded. See § 1.46-8(b)(6).

(vi) Value. See § 1.46-8(b)(7).

(vii) Compensation. See § 1.46-8(b)(8).

(2) Additional credit. An "additional credit" or "extra additional credit" is the extra one-half percent additional investment credit under section 46(a)(2)(B)(ii)—

(i) For purposes of applying this section, and

(ii) When the context requires, for purposes of applying § 1.46-8 to this extra credit.

(3) Matching employee contribution. A "matching employee contribution" is a contribution that meets the requirements of paragraph (f) of this section.

(4) Basic amount. A "basic amount" is a matching employee contribution which is equal to the maximum credit multiplied by a fraction. The numerator of this fraction is a participant's compensation for the plan year. (See § 1.46-9(f)(3)(ii), concerning disregarded compensation.) The denominator is the aggregate of all participants' compensation for the plan year. The "maximum credit" is the estimated value of all employer contributions under paragraph (c)(4)(i) of this section for the applicable year, determined as if the maximum possible matching employee contributions were made.

(5) Supplemental contribution. A "supplemental contribution" is a matching employee contribution made in addition to a basic amount.

(c) Special procedures for extra additional credit. *(1) Statement of election.* A corporation's statement of election described in § 1.46-8(c)(3) must contain the name and taxpayer identification number of the corporation. Also, it must declare in the following words, or in words having substantially the same meaning, that:

(i) The corporation elects to have section 46(a)(2)(B)(i) and (ii) of the Internal Revenue Code of 1954 apply; and

(ii) The corporation agrees to implement (or continue to implement, as appropriate) a TRASOP and to claim the additional credit as required by § 1.46-8 and § 1.46-9 of the Income Tax Regulations.

(2) Separate election. A separate election must be made for each year's qualified investment to obtain the extra additional credit for the qualified investment. If a corporation does not make a timely election to obtain an extra additional credit for a taxable year, it may not subsequently make the election on an amended return or otherwise.

(3) No partial election. To reduce administrative costs, a plan may establish a ceiling on matching employee contributions. Thus, for example, it may provide for the contribution of only a basic amount without supplemental contributions under paragraph (f)(2)(iv) of this section. Such a ceiling that in effect limits the additional credit to less than one-half percent of the qualified investment is not a partial election prohibited by § 1.46-8(c)(5).

(4) Funding a TRASOP. (i) Employer contributions. The carryover option under § 1.46-8(c)(1)(ii) is available for both the one-percent and one-half percent additional credits or for the one-half percent additional credit alone. In applying § 1.46-8(c)(8)(iii), the value of TRASOP securities, other than those acquired with matching employee contributions, for an applicable year must equal one-half percent of the corporation's qualified investment for that year or, if less, the amount of matching employee contributions received (including pledges, where permitted by the plan) by the time the election for that year is made. However, if a corporation exercises the carryover option in § 1.46-8(c)(1)(ii), the value of these TRASOP securities for an applicable year must equal the amount of additional credit claimed for that year determined after being reduced, if necessary, to equal contributions received (including pledges, if permitted) by the time the credit is claimed for that year. The value of these TRASOP securities, but not the amount of credit claimed, is further reduced to the extent that the employer withholds TRASOP securities to take into account start-up and administrative expenses under paragraph (e)(1) of this section or an investment tax credit reduction under paragraph (e)(2) of this section.

(ii) Employee contributions. Paragraph (f)(4) of this section, but not § 1.46-8(c)(8)(i)–(iii), applies to TRASOP securities acquired with matching employee contributions.

(5) Claiming additional credit. In applying § 1.46-8(c)(9)(ii), if less than all of a corporation's credit earned for a taxable year is allowed, the extra additional credit under this section for that year is allowed last.

(d) Additional formal plan requirements. *(1) Contributions by employees.* (i) In general. The plan must contain statements relating to matching employee contributions as required under paragraph (f) of this section.

(ii) Aggregate floor. A plan may provide for the return of all matching employee contributions for a year if the aggregate amount of such contributions is not at least equal to an amount stated in the plan. See also § 1.46-9(f)(3)(iv).

(2) Separate accounting. The plan must state that employer contributions and matching employee contributions respectively described in paragraph (c)(4)(i) and (ii) of this section are accounted for separately from each other as well as from other contributions, including those described in § 1.46-8(c)(8).

(3) Allocation of TRASOP securities contributed by employer. The plan must provide for the allocation under section 301(e)(5) of the 1975 TRA and this subparagraph (3) of TRASOP securities contributed by the employer. These allocations reflect a ratable reduction for TRASOP securities withheld by the employer under paragraph (c)(4)(i) of this section. TRASOP securities so allocated are deemed to be allocated under section 301(d) of the 1975 TRA. In applying § 1.46-8(d)(6) to this section, only subdivisions (ii), (iv), (ix), (x), (xi) and (xii) thereof apply to allocations under this section.

(4) Effect of section 415. In applying the limitations of section 415 to limitation years beginning after January 19, 1979, allocations of TRASOP securities are considered in the following order: first, allocations under § 1.46-8; second, allocations under this section. See § 1.46-8(d)(6)(v) concerning the allocation of amounts under any other defined contribution plan. No suspense or escrow account may be maintained to hold contributions under this section that are unallocated because of section 415. Thus, section 415 in effect limits the availability of an extra additional credit in a particular year. However, if the plan so provides, a potential extra additional credit is treated as an investment credit carryover under the carryover option described in § 1.46-8(c)(1)(ii) to the extent that it is not used in a particular year because of section 415.

(5) Nonforfeitability. Employer contributions are also not considered to be forfeitable under § 1.46-8(d)(7) merely because the plan provides for their return to the corporation in an amount equal to the excess of employer contributions under this section over matching employee contributions or in the case of discriminatory operation under paragraph (f)(3) of this section. See paragraph (f)(3)(iv).

(6) Distributions. Notwithstanding § 1.46-8(d)(9)(i), a plan may not distribute from a participant's employer contribution account cash or employer securities attributable to unpaid pledges of the participant.

(e) Additional operational plan requirements. *(1) Start-up and administrative expenses.* (i) In general. The expense of establishing plan features relating to the extra additional credit is a start-up expense. The expense of collecting matching employee contributions is an administrative expense.

(ii) Payment. Under § 1.46-8(e)(6) and (7), an employee may withhold or a plan may use, to the extent not withheld, TRASOP securities for start-up and administrative expense payments. However, withdrawals must be either limited to employer contributions under § 1.46-8(c)(8) or reasonably apportioned between these employer contributions and contributions under paragraph (c)(4)(i) of this section. An example of reasonable apportionment is earmarking expenses attributable to each of the additional credits and allocating any remaining non-earmarked expenses on either a 2:1 or 1:1 ratio between the additional credits. Another example is simply apportioning expenses between the additional credits on a 2:1 or 1:1 ratio basis without earmarking. However, if one-percent and one-half percent start-up expenses are attributable to different qualified investments, withdrawals for one-half percent expenses are limited to employer contributions under paragraph (c)(4)(i) of this section.

(iii) Ceiling. In determining the ceiling on start-up expenses under § 1.46-8(e)(6)(iii), only employer contributions under § 1.46-8(c)(8) and paragraph (c)(4)(i) of this section are considered. In determining the ceiling on administrative expenses under § 1.46-8(e)(7)(ii), dividends on all TRASOP securities, including those acquired with matching employee contributions, are considered.

(2) Redeterminations and recaptures. A reduction in investment credit because of a redetermination or recapture is allocated ratably under the principles of § 1.46-8(e)(9)(ii) among the 10-percent credit, the one-percent credit, and the one-half percent credit for a particular year. However, as illustrated in § 1.46-8(e)(9)(ii), this subparagraph (3) does not apply to a redetermination solely of one or both of the additional credits.

(3) Withdrawal asset segregation. The segregated accounting provisions of § 1.46-8(f) apply independently to withdrawal assets attributable to TRASOP securities under § 1.46-8 and to TRASOP securities under this section.

(f) Matching employee contributions. *(1) Designation by employee.* The plan must state that each employee on whose behalf an allocation is made under § 1.46-8(d)(6) for an applicable year is eligible to designate and contribute an amount to the TRASOP for that year as a matching employee contribution.

(2) Form and timing of contribution. (i) Cash. A participant may contribute in a manner provide under the plan a designated amount in cash directly to the plan or indirectly by the employer's withholding from amounts otherwise due the participant. The full amount, or pledge in lieu of an amount, for an applicable year must be contributed by the applicable last day described in § 1.46-8(c)(8)(i).

(ii) Optional pledges in lieu of cash. The plan need not permit a pledge. However, when permitted by the plan, an irrevocable written pledge made in good faith by a participant is treated as a matching employee contribution of cash, whether or not the pledge is in fact contractually binding. The pledge must be to contribute, by no later than a time specified in the TRASOP, a designated amount in cash directly to the plan or indirectly by authorizing the employer to withhold from compensation otherwise due a participant. The specified time may not be later than 24 months after the close of the applicable year for which the amount is treated as a matching employee contribution.

(iii) Transitional rule. A plan may provide for the receipt of employee pledges at any time before the later of the applicable last day or January 15, 1980. If the last day for receipt of pledges for an applicable year is January 15, 1980, the one-half percent TRASOP credit for the applicable year may be elected on an amended return filed not later than that date, and employer contributions for the applicable year must be made by that date. A plan may provide that pledges which otherwise would have been payable on or before December 31, 1979 may be paid on or before January 15, 1980.

(iv) Basic and supplemental contributions. A plan formula may limit a matching employee contribution to a basic amount. It may also permit matching employee contributions of supplemental amounts to the extent that total basic amount contributions do not equal the amount of the additional credit claimed under this section. Employees may make supplemental contributions covering unpaid pledges only after the employer has disclosed the value of securities and income attributable to the unpaid pledge.

(3) Prohibited discrimination. (i) General rule. Matching employee contributions must be based on a formula stated in the plan that does not result in prohibited discrimination under section 401(a)(4) either in form or in operation. Thus, for example, a flat dollar amount required as a matching employee contribution to qualify for employer-provided benefits under this section may not be too high for lower paid employees to contribute under the plan. Further, lower paid employees must participate to such an extent that allocations under this section do not result in prohibited discrimination

(ii) Compensation disregarded. Compensation disregarded in allocations under § 1.46-8(d)(6)(iv) is disregarded under this paragraph and for purposes of determining basic amounts as defined in paragraph (b)(4) of this section.

(iii) Former employees. A TRASOP must give all participants a reasonable opportunity to make matching employee contributions. However, neither a former employee who is a participant at the end of the plan year by reason of § 1.46-8(d)(6)(iii), nor the estate of a deceased employee, need have the same options as are available to other participants. Thus, for example, a former employee may be limited to cash contributions even though other participants are permitted to make pledges. Also, if former employees of estates of deceased employees fail to make matching employee contributions, they are not considered in determining whether or not a TRASOP is discriminatory.

(iv) Return of contributions. A plan may provide for the return of employee and employer contributions for a year to the extent that plan operation would otherwise result in prohibited discrimination.

(4) Investment in employer securities. (i) General rule. Matching employee contributions must be invested in TRASOP securities no later than 30 days after the time for funding a TRASOP under § 1.46-8(c)(8)(ii) or, if later, the time specified under the special rule for pledges.

(ii) Special rule for pledges. Cash contributed to pay a pledge permitted by paragraph (f)(2)(ii) of this section must be invested in employer securities so that the cash is not held more than 3 months. The 3-month period includes the period, if any, that the cash is held by the employer.

(5) Reduction of matching employee contribution. (i) In general. Matching employee contributions must be reduced in three cases. First, they are reduced to the extent that there are no corresponding employer contributions described in paragraph (c)(4)(i) of this section. This occurs, for example, when the aggregate of the basic amounts of matching employee contributions exceeds the allowable credit. Second, they are reduced to the extent that corresponding employer contributions matching them under paragraph (c)(4)(i) of this section are withdrawn under section 301(f) of the 1975 TRA. Third, they are reduced by the amount of any pledge unpaid at the time specified in paragraph (f)(2)(ii) of this section.

(ii) Apportioning reductions. Generally, the account of each contributor under this section for an applicable year is reduced by a percentage of the account. This percentage equals the total reduction of all matching employee contributions for that year divided by the total, before the reduction, of all matching employee contributions. However, if a reduction is directly attributable to a particular contributor, only that contributor's account is reduced. A reduction is directly attributable to a particular contributor when, for example, the limits of section 415 prohibit a full allocation of employer contributions equal to the contributor's matching employee contribution for an applicable year or when a contributor fails to pay a pledge. A reduction may not yield a negative balance in a participant's account.

(iii) Disposing of reductions. If a participant's matching employee contribution is reduced, the amount of the reduction must either be treated as a voluntary contribution or returned to the participant by the later of two dates. The first date is 30 days after the time for investing in TRASOP securities under paragraph (f)(4) of this section. The second date is the 30th day after the date on which the withdrawal of employer contributions occurs that causes the reduction. It may be treated as a voluntary contribution only if, as stated in the plan, the participant so indicates in writing when making the matching employee contribution.

(iv) Supplemental contributions covering unpaid pledges. Notwithstanding the timing requirements of paragraph (f)(2) of this section, supplemental contributions covering unpaid pledges must be made no later than 60 days after accounting for the corresponding reduction under paragraph (f)(5)(ii) of this section.

(v) Effect of reduction on credit. For the purpose of applying section 415 to an additional allocation to the account of a participant attributable to a supplemental contribution covering an unpaid pledge, the contribution is treated as an annual addition to the supplemental contributor's account in the applicable year for which the reduction occurred. An amount in excess of the contribution may be allocated in equal amounts for each year from the applicable year to the year of the reduction. The employer's credit is reduced only to the extent that a proportionate transfer of assets is not made from the account of the participant to whom the reduction is attributable to the accounts of supplemental contributors.

(vi) Example. The rules contained in paragraph (f)(2) and (5) of this section are illustrated by the following example:

Example. Assume that A is an employee of corporation M, a calendar year taxpayer that maintains a TRASOP. A has pledged $100 as a matching employee contribution for 1977, the first applicable year of M's TRASOP. M has transferred employer securities valued at $100 that have been allocated to A's account under the Plan. The TRASOP provides that pledges must be paid no later then 24 months after the end of the applicable year. Thus, A's $100 pledge must be paid by December 31, 1979. As of December 31, 1979, the employer securities attributable to A's pledge have a value of $90 and have produced undistributed dividend income of $13. Thus, the value of the portion of A's account attributable to the unpaid pledge is $103. After December 31, 1979, the value of this portion of A's account is disclosed to participants, and employee B chooses to pay off A's unpaid pledge, as provided in the plan, by making a $100 supplemental contribution. The full amount of the securities and dividend income attributable to the unpaid pledge are transferred from A's account to that of B as of December 31, 1979. M's credit for 1977 is not reduced. The $100 supplemental contribution is an annual addition to B's account for purposes of applying section 415 in 1979. Income attributable to the pledge in excess of the supplemental contribution, $3 ($103 – $100), may be allocated and treated as an annual addition by spreading this excess amount over the years from the applicable year to the year of the reduction (1977, 1978, 1979).

(g) Failure to comply. *(1) General rule.* If a corporation elects under § 1.46-8(c)(2)–(5) and paragraph (c)(1) of this section to obtain an additional credit, § 1.46-8(h)(1), (2), (3), (5), (6), and (7) as modified by this paragraph (g) apply.

(2) Failure to comply (penalty classifications). (i) In general. A corporation fails to comply with an extra additional credit election if a defect described in paragraph (g)(2)(ii)–(iv) of this section occurs in a taxable year.

(ii) Funding defect. A funding defect occurs under this section if a corporation or its TRASOP fails to satisfy the requirements of § 1.46-8(c)(8) or (9) or paragraph (c)(4) of this section, as they apply directly to the extra additional credit.

(iii) Special operational defect. A special operational defect occurs if a TRASOP fails in operation to satisfy the requirements described in § 1.46-8(d)(5)–(9) (except (6)(i), (iii), and (v)–(viii)) or (e)(3), or paragraph (d)(5), (6), and (e)-(3) of this section, as they apply directly to the extra additional credit.

(iv) De minimis defect. A de minimis defect occurs if a corporation or its TRASOP fails to satisfy the requirements, other than those enumerated in paragraphs (c)(1) and (2) and (g)(2)(ii) and (iii), of this section or of § 1.46-8 other than those excluded under § 1.46-8(h)(4)(iv).

(3) Amount involved. The amount involved in a failure to comply under this section is based upon the extra additional credit within the meaning of section 46(a)(2)(B)(ii).

(4) Coordination of civil penalties. The civil penalties under § 1.46-8 and this section are determined separately. In no case may the amount involved with respect to a particular failure to comply in one year exceed under both sections the full additional credit within the meaning of section 46(a)(2)(B)(i) and (ii).

T.D. 7856, 12/3/82.

---

§ 1.46-10 [Reserved]

§ 1.46-11 Commuter highway vehicles.

(a) In general. Section 46(c)(6) provides that the applicable percentage to determine qualified investment under section 46(c)(1) for a qualifying commuter highway vehicle is 100 percent. A qualifying commuter highway vehicle is a vehicle (defined in paragraph (b) of this section)—

(1) Which is acquired by the taxpayer on or after November 9, 1978,

(2) Which is placed in service by the taxpayer before January 1, 1986, and

(3) With respect to which the taxpayer makes an election under paragraph (g) of this section.

(b) Definition of commuter highway vehicle. A commuter highway vehicle is a highway vehicle that meets the following requirements:

(1) The vehicle is section 38 property in the hands of the taxpayer. The rule of section 48(d), allowing a lessor to elect to treat the lessee of new section 38 property as having acquired the property, applies to commuter highway vehicles. If the vehicle is leased and that election is made, the lessee is treated as the taxpayer under this section. However, if that election is not made, the lessor, and not the lessee, is treated as the taxpayer under this section.

(2) The vehicle must meet the seating capacity requirement of paragraph (c) of this section; and

(3) The taxpayer reasonably expects to meet the commuter use requirement of paragraph (d) of this section for at least the first 36 months after the vehicle is placed in service.

(c) Seating capacity. A commuter highway vehicle must have a seating capacity of a least 8 adults in addition to the driver's seat.

(d) Commuter use requirement. A vehicle meets the commuter use requirement only if at least 80 percent of the miles the vehicle is driven are for trips to transport the taxpayer's employees between their residences and their places of employment. A trip for this purpose includes driving the vehicle before or after employees are in the vehicle, so long as the mileage driven is necessary either to pick up or drop off passengers or to park the vehicle in its regular parking space. A trip does not include miles driven solely for maintenance or to refuel the vehicle. A trip is not considered to transport the taxpayer's employees between their residences and their places of employment unless at least one-half the seating capacity (defined in paragraph (c) of this section) is used to seat employees of the taxpayer. In no event is the driver counted as an employee of the taxpayer.

(e) Definition of employee. An employee in this section is the same as in section 3121 (d) (definition of employee for withholding purposes).

(f) Transportation between employee's residence and place of employment. An employee is transported between that employee's residence and place of employment even if that place of employment is not the same as any of the other employees transported, and even if picked up or dropped off at some central point between that residence and place of employment. An employee is not transported between that employee's residence and place of employment if the transportation is of the type for which a deduction would be allowed under § 1.162-2 were the employee providing it, such as the transportation from one work site to another after beginning work for the day.

(g) Election. A taxpayer must elect to have the vehicle treated as a qualifying commuter highway vehicle on the return for the taxable year in which the vehicle is placed in service. The election may be made only if the vehicle actually meets the commuter use requirement under paragraph (d) of this section for that taxable year. It must be made on or before the due date (including extensions) of that return. The election is effective as of that due date.

T.D. 8035, 7/18/85.

---

§ 1.47-1 Recomputation of credit allowed by section 38.

• ***Caution:*** Reg. § 1.47-1, following, was issued under Code Sec. 47 before amendment by P.L. 101-508 (11/5/90). Provisions similar to, but not identical to, the relative provisions of Code Sec. 47 before such amendment appear in current Code Sec. 50.

Caution: The Treasury has not yet amended Reg § 1.47-1 to reflect changes made by P.L. 100-647, P.L. 99-514, P.L. 99-121, P.L. 98-369, P.L. 97-248, P.L. 97-34.

(a) General rule. *(1) In general.* (i) If during the taxable year any section 38 property the basis (or cost) of which was taken into account, under paragraph (a) of § 1.46-3, in computing the taxpayer's qualified investment is disposed of, or otherwise ceases to be section 38 property or becomes public utility property (as defined in paragraph (g) of § 1.46-3) "or is a qualifying commuter highway vehicle (as defined in paragraph (a) of § 1.46-11) which undergoes a change in use (as defined in paragraph (m)(2) of this section) with respect to the taxpayer, before the close of the estimated useful life (as determined under subparagraph (2)(i) of this paragraph) which was taken into account in computing such qualified investment, then the credit earned for the credit year (as defined in subdivision (ii)(a) of this subparagraph) shall be recomputed under the principles of paragraph (a) of § 1.46-1 and paragraph (a) of § 1.46-3 substituting, in lieu of the estimated useful life of the property that was taken into account originally in computing qualified investment, the actual useful life of the property as determined under subparagraph (2)(ii) of this paragraph. There shall also be recomputed under the principles of §§ 1.46-1 and 1.46-2 the credit allowed for the credit year and for any other taxable year affected by reason of the reduction in credit earned for the credit year, giving effect to such reduction in the computation of carryovers or carrybacks of unused credit. If the recomputation described in the preceding sentence results in the aggregate in a decrease (taking into account any recomputations under this paragraph in respect of prior recapture years, as defined in subdivision (ii)(b) of this subparagraph) in the credits allowed for the credit year and for any other taxable year affected by the reduction in credit earned for the credit year, then the income tax for the recapture year shall be increased by the amount of such decrease in credits allowed. For treatment of such increase in tax, see paragraph (b) of this section. For rules relating to 'disposition' and 'cessation', see § 1.47-2. For rules relating to certain exceptions to the application of this section, see § 1.47-3. For special rules in the case of an electing small business corporation (as defined in section 1371 (b)), an estate or trust, or a partnership, see respectively, § 1.47-4, 1.47-5, or 1.47-6. For rules applicable to energy property, see paragraph (h) of this section. For special rules relating to recomputation of credit allowed by section 38 if progress expenditure property (as defined in § 1.46-5(d)) ceases to be progress expenditure property with respect to the taxpayer, see paragraph (g) of this section.

(ii) For purposes of this section and §§ 1.47-2 through 1.47-6—

(a) The term "credit year" means the taxable year in which section 38 property was taken into account in computing a taxpayer's qualified investment.

(b) The term "recapture year" means the taxable year in which section 38 property the basis (or cost) of which was taken into account in computing a taxpayer's qualified investment is disposed of, or otherwise ceases to be section 38 property or becomes public utility property with respect to the taxpayer, before the close of the estimated useful life which was taken into account in computing such qualified investment.

(c) The term "recapture determination" means a recomputation made under this paragraph.

(2) Rules for applying subparagraph (1). For purposes of subparagraph (1) of this paragraph—

(i) In determining whether section 38 property is disposed of, or otherwise ceases to be section 38 property with respect to the taxpayer, before the close of the estimated useful life which was taken into account in computing the taxpayer's qualified investment, the term "estimated useful life" means the shortest life of the useful life category within which falls the estimated useful life which was assigned to such property under paragraph (e) of § 1.46-3. Thus, section 38 property which is assigned, under paragraph (e) of § 1.46-3, an estimated useful life of 6 years shall not be treated, for purposes of subparagraph (1) of this paragraph, as having been disposed of before the close of its estimated useful life if such property is sold 5 years (that is, the shortest life of the 5 years or more but less than 7 years useful life category) after the date on which it was placed in service. Likewise, section 38 property with an estimated useful life of 15 years which is placed in service on January 1, 1972, shall not be treated as having been disposed of before the close of its estimated useful life if such property is sold at any time after January 1, 1979 (that is, 7 years or more after the date on which it was placed in service).

(ii) In determining the recomputed qualified investment with respect to property which is disposed of or otherwise ceases to be section 38 property the term "actual useful life" means, except as otherwise provided in this section and §§ 1.47-2 through 1.47-6, the period beginning with the date on which the property was placed in service by the taxpayer and ending with the date of such disposition or cessation. See paragraph (c) of this section.

(iii) In determining the recomputed qualified investment with respect to property which ceases to be section 38 property with respect to the taxpayer after August 15, 1971, or which becomes public utility property after such date, such property shall be treated as if it were property described in section 50 at the time it was placed in service (whether or not it was property described in section 50 at such time). Thus, if property was placed in service on October 15, 1968, and was assigned an estimated useful life of 4 years, there would be no increase in tax under section 47 if the property were disposed of at any time after October 14, 1971, that is, 3 years or more after the property was placed in service.

(b) Increase in income tax and reduction of investment credit carryover. *(1) Increase in tax.* Except as provided in subparagraph (2) of this paragraph, any increase in income tax under this section shall be treated as income tax imposed on the taxpayer by chapter 1 of the Code for the recapture year notwithstanding that without regard to such increase the taxpayer has no income tax liability, has a net operating loss for such taxable year, or no income tax return was otherwise required for such taxable year.

(2) Special rule. Any increase in income tax under this section shall not be treated as income tax imposed on the taxpayer by chapter 1 of the Code for purposes of determining the amount of the credits allowable to such taxpayer under—

(i) Section 33 (relating to taxes of foreign countries and possessions of United States),

(ii) Section 34 (relating to dividends received by individuals before January 1, 1965),

(iii) Section 35 (relating to partially tax-exempt interest received by individuals),

(iv) Section 37 (relating to retirement income), and

(v) Section 38 (relating to investment in certain depreciable property).

(3) Reduction in credit allowed as a result of a net operating loss carryback. (i) If a net operating loss carryback from the recapture year or from any taxable year subsequent to the recapture year reduces the amount allowed as a credit under section 38 for any taxable year up to and including the recapture year, then there shall be a new recapture determination under paragraph (a) of this section for each recapture year affected, taking into account the reduced amount of credit allowed after application of the net operating loss carryback.

(ii) Subdivision (i) of this subparagraph may be illustrated by the following examples:

Example (1). (a) X Corporation, which makes its return on the basis of a calendar year, acquired and placed in service on January 1, 1962, an item of section 38 property with a basis of $10,000 and an estimated useful life of 8 years. The amount of qualified investment with respect to such asset was $10,000. For the taxable year 1962, X Corporation's credit earned of $700 (7 percent of $10,000) was allowed under section 38 as a credit against its liability for tax of $700. In 1963 and 1964 X Corporation had no liability for tax and placed in service no section 38 property. On January 3, 1963, such item of section 38 property was sold to Y Corporation. Since the actual useful life of such item was only 1 year, there was a recapture determination under paragraph (a) of this section. The income tax imposed by chapter 1 of the Code on X Corporation for the taxable year 1963 was increased by the $700 decrease in its credit earned for the taxable year 1962 (that is, the $700 original credit earned minus zero recomputed credit earned).

(b) For the taxable year 1965, X Corporation has a net operating loss which is carried back to the taxable year 1962 and reduces its liability for tax, as defined in paragraph (c) of § 1.46-1, for such taxable year to $200. As a result of such net operating loss carryback, X Corporation's credit allowed under section 38 for the taxable year 1962 is limited to $200 and the excess of $500 ($700 credit earned minus $200 limitation based on amount of tax) is an investment credit carryover to the taxable year 1963.

(c) For 1965, there is a recapture determination under subdivision (i) of this subparagraph for the 1963 recapture year. The $700 increase in the income tax imposed on X Corporation for the taxable year 1963 is redetermined to be $200 (that is, the $200 credit allowed after taking into account the 1965 net operating loss minus zero credit which would have been allowed taking into account the 1963 recapture determination). In addition, X Corporation's $500 investment credit carryover to the taxable year 1963 is reduced by $500 ($700 minus $200) to zero and X Corporation is entitled to a $500 refund of the tax paid as a result of the 1963 determination.

Example (2). (a) X Corporation, which makes its returns on the basis of a calendar year, acquired and placed in service on January 1, 1962, an item of section 38 property with a basis of $10,000 and an estimated useful life of 8 years. The amount of qualified investment with respect to such asset was $10,000. For the taxable year 1962, X Corporation's credit earned of $700 (7 percent of $10,000) was allowed under section 38 as a credit against its liability for tax of $700. In 1963 and in 1964 X Corporation had no liability for tax and placed in service no section 38 property. On January 3, 1965, such item of section 38 property is sold to Y Corporation. For the taxable year 1965, X Corporation has a net operating loss which is carried back to the taxable year 1962 and reduces its liability for tax, as defined in paragraph (c) of § 1.46-1, for such taxable year to $100.

(b) As a result of such net operating loss carryback, X Corporation's credit allowed under section 38 for the taxable year 1962 is limited to $100 and the excess of $600 ($700 credit earned minus $100 limitation based on amount of tax) is an investment credit carryover to the taxable year 1963.

(c) Since the actual useful life of the item of section 38 property sold to Y Corporation was only 3 years, there is a recapture determination under paragraph (a) of this section. X Corporation's $600 investment credit carryover to 1963 is reduced by $600 to zero. The income tax imposed by chapter 1 of the Code on X Corporation for the taxable year 1965 is increased by the $100 reduction in credit allowed by section 38 for 1962.

(4) Statement of recomputation. The taxpayer shall attach to his income tax return for the recapture year a separate statement showing in detail the computation of the increase in income tax imposed on such taxpayer by chapter 1 of the Code and the reduction in any investment credit carryovers.

(c) Date placed in service and date of disposition or cessation. *(1) General rule.* For purposes of this section and §§ 1.47-2 through 1.47-6, in determining the actual useful life of section 38 property—

(i) Such property shall be treated as placed in service on the first day of the month in which such property is placed in service. The month in which property is placed in service shall be determined under the principles of paragraph (d) of § 1.46-3.

(ii) If during the taxable year such property ceases to be section 38 property with respect to the taxpayer—

(a) As a result of the occurrence of an event on a specific date (for example, a sale, transfer, retirement or other disposition), such cessation shall be treated as having occurred on the actual date of such event.

(b) For any reason other than the occurrence of an event on a specific date (for example, because such property is used predominantly in connection with the furnishing of lodging during such taxable year), such cessation shall be treated as having occurred on the first day of such taxable year.

(2) Special rule. Notwithstanding subparagraph (1) of this paragraph, if a taxpayer uses an averaging convention (see § 1.167 (a)-10) in computing depreciation with respect to section 38 property, then, for purposes of this section and §§ 1.47-2 through 1.47-6, he may use the assumed dates of additions and retirements in determining the actual useful life of such property provided such assumed dates are used consistently for purposes of subpart B of part IV of subchapter A of chapter 1 of the Code with respect to all section 38 property for which such convention is used for purposes of depreciation. This subparagraph shall not apply in any case where from all the facts and circumstances it appears that the use of such assumed dates results in a substantial distortion of the investment credit allowed by section 38. Thus, for example, if the taxpayer computes depreciation under a convention under which the average of the beginning and ending balances of the asset account for the taxable year are taken into account, he may use July 1 as the assumed date of all additions and retirements to such account. Similarly, if the taxpayer computes depreciation under a convention under which the average of the beginning and ending balances of the asset account for each month is taken into account, he may use the date determined by reference to the weighted average of the monthly averages as the assumed date of all additions and retirements to such account.

(3) Example. This paragraph may be illustrated by the following example:

Example. Assume that section 38 property is placed in service (within the meaning of paragraph (d) of § 1.46-3) on December 1, 1965 (thus, the credit is treated as being earned in 1965) but under the taxpayer's depreciation practice the period for depreciation with respect to such property begins on January 1, 1966, and that the property is actually retired on December 2, 1970. Under the general rule of subparagraph (1) of this paragraph, the property is treated as placed in service on December 1, 1965, and as ceasing to be section 38 property with respect to the taxpayer on December 2, 1970, even though under the taxpayer's depreciation practice the period for depreciation with respect to such property begins on January 1, 1966, and terminates on January 1, 1971. However, under the special rule of subparagraph (2) of this paragraph the taxpayer may determine the actual useful life of the property by reference to the assumed dates of January 1, 1966, and January 1, 1971.

(d) Examples. Paragraphs (a) through (c) of this section may be illustrated by the following examples:

Example (1). (i) X Corporation, which makes its returns on the basis of the calendar year, acquired and placed in service on January 1, 1962, three items of section 38 property each with a basis of $12,000 and an estimated useful life of 15 years. The amount of qualified investment with respect to each such asset was $12,000. For the taxable year 1962, X Corporation's credit earned of $2,520 was allowed under section 38 as a credit against its liability for tax of $4,000. On December 2, 1965, one of the items of section 38 property is sold to Y Corporation.

(ii) The actual useful life of the item of property which is sold on December 2, 1965, is three years and eleven months. The recomputed qualified investment with respect to such item of property is zero ($12,000 basis multiplied by zero applicable percentage) and X Corporation's recomputed credit earned for the taxable year 1962 is $1,680 (7 percent of $24,000). The income tax imposed by chapter 1 of the Code on X Corporation for the taxable year 1965 is increased by the $840 decrease in its credit earned for the taxable year 1962 (that is, $2,520 original credit earned minus $1,680 recomputed credit earned).

Example (2). (i) The facts are the same as in example (1) and in addition on December 2, 1966, a second item of section 38 property placed in service in the taxable year 1962 is sold to Y Corporation.

(ii) The actual useful life of the item of property which is sold on December 2, 1966, is four years and eleven months. The recomputed qualified investment with respect to such item of property is $4,000 ($12,000 basis multiplied by 33⅓ percent applicable percentage) and X Corporation's recomputed credit earned for the taxable year 1962 is $1,120 (7 percent of $16,000). The income tax imposed by chapter 1 of the Code on X Corporation for the taxable year 1966 is increased by $560 (that is, $1,400 ($2,520 original credit earned minus $1,120 recomputed credit earned) reduced by the $840 increase in tax for 1965).

Example (3). (i) The facts are the same as in example (1) except that for the taxable year 1962 X Corporation's liability for tax under section 46(a)(3) is only $1,520. Therefore, for such taxable year X Corporation's credit allowed under section 38 is limited to $1,520 and the excess of $1,000 ($2,520 credit earned minus $1,520 limitation based on amount of tax) is an unused credit. Of such $1,000 unused credit, $100 is allowed as a credit under section 38 for the taxable year 1963, $100 is allowed for 1964, and $800 is carried to the taxable year 1965.

(ii) The actual useful life of the item of property which is sold on December 2, 1965, is three years and eleven months. The recomputed qualified investment with respect to such item of property is zero ($12,000 basis multiplied by zero applicable percentage) and X Corporation's recomputed credit earned for the taxable year 1962 is $1,680 (7 percent of $24,000). If such $1,680 recomputed credit earned had been taken into account in place of the $2,520 original credit earned, X's credit allowed for 1962 would have been $1,520, and of the $160 unused credit from 1962 $100 would have been allowed as a credit under section 38 for 1963, and $60 would have been allowed for 1964. X Corporation's $800 investment credit carryover to the taxable year 1965 is reduced by $800 to zero. The income tax imposed by chapter 1 of the Code on X Corporation for the taxable year 1965 is increased by $40 (that is, the aggregate reduction in the credits allowed by section 38 for 1962, 1963, and 1964).

Example (4). (i) X Corporation, which makes its returns on the basis of the calendar year, acquired and placed in service on November 1, 1962, an item of section 38 property with a basis of $12,000 and an estimated useful life of 10 years. The amount of qualified investment with respect to such property was $12,000. For the taxable year 1962, X Corporation's credit earned of $840 was allowed under section 38 as a credit against its liability for tax of $840. For each of the taxable years 1963 and 1964 X Corporation's liability for tax was zero and its credit earned was $400; therefore, for each of such years its unused credit was $400. For the taxable year 1965 its liability for tax was $200 and its credit earned was zero; therefore $200 of the $400 unused credit from 1963 was allowed as credit for 1965 and $600 ($200 from 1963 and $400 from 1964) is an investment credit carryover to 1966. On February 2, 1966, such item of section 38 property is sold to Y Corporation.

(ii) The actual useful life of such item of property is three years and three months. The recomputed qualified investment with respect to such property is zero ($12,000 basis multiplied by zero) and X Corporation's recomputed credit earned for the taxable year 1962 is zero. If such zero recomputed credit earned had been taken into account in place of the $840 original credit earned, the entire $400 unused credit from 1963 (including the $200 portion which was originally allowed as a credit for 1965) and the $400 unused credit from 1964 would have been allowed as investment credit carrybacks against X Corporation's liability for tax of $840 for 1962. (See § 1.46-2 for rules relating to the carryback of unused credits.)

(iii) Therefore, the $600 carryover from 1963 and 1964 to 1966 is eliminated and the income tax imposed by chapter 1 of the Code on X Corporation for the taxable year 1966 is increased by the $240 aggregate reduction in the credits allowed by section 38 for the taxable years 1962 and 1965 (that is, $1,040 credit allowed minus $800 which would have been allowed).

Example (5). (i) X Corporation, which makes its returns on the basis of the calendar year, acquired and placed in service on November 1, 1962, an item of section 38 property with a basis of $10,000 and an estimated useful life of 8 years. The amount of qualified investment with respect to such asset was $10,000. For the taxable year 1962, X Corporation's credit earned of $700 was allowed as a credit against its liability for tax. For each of the taxable years 1963, 1964, and 1965 X had no taxable income. On July 3, 1966, the item of section 38 property is sold to Y Corporation. For the taxable year 1966 X Corporation has a net operating loss of $3,000.

(ii) The actual useful life of the item of property is three years and eight months. The recomputed qualified investment with respect to such item of property is zero and X Corporation's recomputed credit earned for the taxable year 1962 is zero. Notwithstanding the $3,000 net operating loss for the taxable year 1966, the income tax imposed by chapter 1 of the Code on X Corporation for such year is $700 (that is, the decrease in its credit earned for the taxable year 1962).

(e) Identification of property. *(1) General rule.* (i) Record requirements. In general, the taxpayer must maintain records from which he can establish, with respect to each item of section 38 property, the following facts:

(a) The date the property is disposed of or otherwise ceases to be section 38 property,

(b) The estimated useful life which was assigned to the property under paragraph (e) of § 1.46-3,

(c) The month and the taxable year in which the property was placed in service, and

(d) The basis (or cost), actually or reasonably determined, of the property.

(ii) Recapture determination. For purposes of determining whether section 38 property is disposed of, or otherwise ceases to be section 38 property with respect to the taxpayer, before the close of its estimated useful life, and for purposes of determining recomputed qualified investment, the taxpayer must establish from his records the facts required by subdivision (i) of this subparagraph.

(iii) Examples. If the taxpayer fails to maintain records from which he can establish the facts required by subdivision (i) of this subparagraph, then this section shall be applied to the taxpayer in the manner indicated in the following examples:

Example (1). Corporation X, organized on January 1, 1964, files its income tax return on the basis of a calendar year. During the years 1964 and 1965, X places in service several items of machinery to which it assigns estimated useful lives of 8 years. X places the items of machinery in a composite account for purposes of computing depreciation. When X's 1966 return is being audited, X is unable to establish whether the items placed in service in 1964 and 1965 were still on hand at the end of 1966. Therefore, for purposes of paragraph (a) of this section, X is treated as having disposed of, in 1966, all of the items of machinery placed in service in 1964 and 1965.

Example (2). Corporation Y, organized on January 1, 1960, files its income tax return on the basis of a calendar year. During each of the years 1960 through 1965, Y places in service four items of machinery to each of which it assigns an estimated useful life of 8 years for depreciation purposes (and for purposes of computing qualified investment for relevant years). Y places the items of machinery in a composite account for purposes of computing depreciation (and for purposes of computing qualified investment for relevant years). When Y's 1965 return is being audited, Y can establish that it retired during 1965 only six items of this machinery. However, Y cannot establish the date on which these six items were placed in service, nor can Y establish that the items placed in service in 1963 or 1964 are still on hand as of the end of 1965. No previous recapture has taken place with respect to any of the items placed in service in 1963 or 1964. Assuming that paragraph (e)(2) and (3) of this section is not applicable, Y is treated, for purposes of paragraph (a) of this section, as having disposed of, in 1965, the four items placed in service in 1964, the most recent year before 1965 in which such property was placed in service, and two items from 1963, the next most recent year.

Example (3). The facts are the same as in example (2) except that when Y's 1966 return is being audited, Y can establish from its records that all four items placed in service in 1965 are still on hand and that only three items were retired in 1966. For purposes of paragraph (a) of this section, Y is treated as having disposed of, in 1966, the two remaining items of machinery placed in service in 1963, and one of the items placed in service in 1962.

(2) Treatment of "mass assets". (i) If, in the case of mass assets (as defined in subparagraph (4) of this paragraph), it is impracticable for the taxpayer to maintain records from which he can establish with respect to each item of section 38 property the facts required by subparagraph (1) of this paragraph, and if he adopts other reasonable recordkeeping practices, consonant with good accounting and engineering practices, and consistent with his prior recordkeeping practices, then he may substitute data from an appropriate mortality dispersion table. An appropriate mortality dispersion table must be based on an acceptable sampling of the taxpayer's actual experience or other acceptable statistical or engineering techniques. In lieu of such mortality dispersion table, the taxpayer may use a standard mortality dispersion table prescribed by the Commissioner. If the taxpayer uses such standard mortality dispersion table for any taxable year, it must be used for all subsequent taxable years unless the taxpayer obtains the consent of the Commissioner to change. If mass assets are placed in a multiple asset account and if the depreciation rate for such account is based on the maximum expected life of the longest lived asset in such account, in applying a mortality dispersion table (including a standard

mortality dispersion table) the average expected useful life of the mass assets in such account must be used.

(ii) Subdivision (i) of this subparagraph shall not apply with respect to assets placed in service in a taxable year ending on or after June 30, 1967, and beginning before January 1, 1971, or with respect to assets placed in service for a taxable year beginning after December 31, 1970, for which the taxpayer has not made the election provided by section 167(m), unless the estimated useful lives which were assigned to such assets for purposes of determining qualified investment—

(a) Were separate lives based on the estimated range of years taken into account in establishing the average useful life of assets similar in kind under paragraph (e)(3)(ii)*(b)* of § 1.46-3, and

(b) Were determined by use of a mortality dispersion table (including a standard mortality dispersion table).

(iii) Any standard mortality dispersion table prescribed by the Commissioner shall be based on average useful life categories and with respect to each category shall contain five columns, the first four of which shall state the percentage of property assumed to have a useful life of—

Column (1): Less than 4 years,

Column (2): 4 years or more but less than 6 years,

Column (3): 6 years or more but less than 8 years, and

Column (4): 8 years or more.

The fifth column shall show the total qualified investment as a percentage and shall be used in connection with the determination to be made under § 1.46-3(e)(3)(iii). In the case of a table which is to apply to property which is described in section 50 or to property which is treated as property described in section 50 under paragraph (a)(2)(iii) of this section, this subdivision shall be applied by substituting "3 years" for "4 years", "5 years" for "6 years", and "7 years" for "8 years".

(iv) Whenever the standard mortality dispersion table is used for a taxable year under subdivision (i) of this subparagraph (whether or not such table was used in determining qualified investment), the percentage of property shown in column (1) of the table shall (for purposes of section 47, this section, and §§ 1.47-2 through 1.47-6) be deemed to have been disposed of on the day before the expiration of the 4-year period beginning on the date on which it was considered as placed in service under § 1.47-1(c); the percentage of property shown in column (2) of the table shall be deemed to have been disposed of on the day before the expiration of the 6-year period beginning on the date on which it was so considered as placed in service; and the percentage of property shown in column (3) shall be deemed to have been disposed of on the day before the expiration of the 8-year period beginning on the date on which it was so considered as placed in service. In applying this subdivision for purposes of recomputing qualified investment, the proper average useful life category shall be used whether or not such category was used in determining qualified investment. In the case of property which is described in section 50 or property which is treated as property described in section 50 under paragraph (a)(2)(iii) of this section (other than property the qualified investment with respect to which was determined by use of the standard or an appropriate mortality dispersion table), this subdivision shall be applied by substituting "3-year period" for "4-year period", "5-year period" for "6-year period", and "7-year period" for "8-year period".

(v) In lieu of using subdivision (iv) of this subparagraph for purposes of recomputing qualified investment, a taxpayer may, for the first recapture year (as defined in paragraph (a)(1)(ii) (b) of this section) to which such subdivision (iv) would otherwise apply with respect to any mass asset account, recompute qualified investment on the basis of the difference between (a) the proper total qualified investment based on the percentage shown in column (5) of the table, and *(b)* the total qualified investment actually claimed by the taxpayer for the year in which the property was placed in service.

Example. Assume that the taxpayer places in service during 1963 mass assets costing him $100,000, that he places these assets in a multiple asset account for which he properly claims a useful life of 6 years and a qualified investment of $66,667 (⅔ × $100,000), and that he is allowed an investment credit of $4,667.67. When the taxpayer's 1967 return is being audited he is unable to establish that any of the mass assets placed in service in 1963 were still on hand at the end of 1967.

The taxpayer elects to use the standard mortality dispersion table prescribed by the Commissioner to determine the amount of recapture with respect to these mass assets. Assume that the table prescribed by the Commissioner shows with respect to mass assets with an average useful life of 6 years the following:

Percent of property assumed to have a useful life of—				
Less than 4 years (1)	4 years or more, but less than 6 years (2)	6 years or more, but less than 8 years (3)	8 years or more (4)	Total qualified investment (percent) (5)
15.87	34.13	34.13	15.87	50.00

(a) Under these circumstances 15.87 percent of the mass assets placed in service in 1963 are deemed to have been disposed of during 1967. With respect to these assets, the amount of qualified investment for 1963 was $10,580 ($15,870 × ⅔) and the amount of credit earned was $740.60 (7 percent of $10,580), whereas the recomputed qualified investment is zero and the recomputed credit earned is zero. Thus, the tax imposed by chapter 1 of the Code for 1967 is increased by $740.60.

(b) No recapture determination is required for 1968 since no assets are deemed to have been disposed of in that year. During 1969, 34.13 percent of the mass assets placed in service in 1963 are deemed to have been disposed of. With respect to these assets, the amount of qualified investment for 1963 was $22,753.34 ($34,130 × ⅔) and the amount of credit earned was $1,592.73 (7 percent of $22,753.34), whereas the recomputed qualified investment is $11,376.67 ($34,130 × ⅓) and the recomputed credit earned is $796.37 (7 percent of $11,376.67). Thus, the tax imposed by chapter 1 of the Code for 1969 is increased by $796.36 ($1,592.73 minus $796.37).

(c) If the taxpayer chooses to recompute qualified investment by using the method provided in subdivision (v) of this subparagraph, the increase in tax for 1967 (the first recapture year) would be $1,167.67, i.e., the original credit earned, $4,667.67, minus the recomputed credit earned, $3,500 (50 percent, the percentage shown in column (5), of $100,000 multiplied by 7 percent). As long as the same average useful life category reflects the taxpayer's experience for subsequent years, no recapture determination will be required for any future year, except as provided by subparagraph (3)(iv) of this paragraph.

(vi) Subdivision (i) of this subparagraph shall not apply with respect to section 38 property to which an election under section 167(m) applies unless the taxpayer assigns actual retirements of such section 38 property for all taxable years to the same vintage account for purposes of section 47 and for purposes of computing the allowance for depreciation under section 167. The assignment of actual retirements of section 38 property for a taxable year to particular vintage accounts may be made on the basis of an appropriate mortality dispersion table (based on an acceptable sampling of the taxpayer's actual experience or other statistical or engineering techniques) or on the basis of a standard mortality dispersion table prescribed by the Commissioner. If the taxpayer assigns actual retirements for any taxable year to particular vintage accounts on the basis of such standard mortality dispersion table, actual retirements for all subsequent taxable years must be assigned to particular vintage accounts on the basis of such table. Actual retirements of section 38 property for a taxable year shall be assigned to particular vintage accounts by—

(a) Determining the expected retirements for such taxable year from each vintage account containing such section 38 property, and

(b) Ratably allocating such actual retirements to each vintage account containing such section 38 property.

However, the unadjusted basis of retired assets assigned to any particular vintage account shall not exceed the unadjusted basis of the property contained in such account.

(3) Special rules. (i) Taxpayers who properly determine estimated useful lives under § 1.46-3(e)(3)(ii)(b) or (iii) may treat such assets as having been disposed of or having ceased to be section 38 assets in the order of the estimated useful lives that were assigned to such assets. Thus, the asset that is first disposed of or first ceases to be section 38 property may be treated as the asset to which there was assigned the shortest estimated useful life; the next asset disposed of or ceasing to be section 38 property may be treated as the asset to which there was assigned the second shortest life, etc.

(ii) In the case of taxpayers who use the rule of subdivision (i) of this subparagraph with respect to mass assets for which the estimated useful life was determined under § 1.46-3(e)(3)(iii), if the dispersion shown by the mortality dispersion table effective for a taxable year subsequent to the credit year is the same as the dispersion shown by the mortality table that was effective for the credit year (for example, if the same average useful life on the standard mortality dispersion table reflects the taxpayer's experience for both such years, no recapture determination is required for such subsequent taxable year.

(iii) Notwithstanding subdivision (i) of this subparagraph, taxpayers who, for purposes of determining qualified investment, do not use a mortality dispersion table with respect to certain section 38 assets similar in kind but who consistently assign under paragraph (e)(3)(ii)(b) of § 1.46-3 to such assets separate lives based on the estimated range of years taken into consideration in establishing the average useful life of such assets, may select the order in which such assets shall be considered as having been disposed of, regardless of the taxable years in which such assets were placed in service. If a taxpayer uses the method provided in this subdivision to determine that any asset is considered as having been disposed of, then, in addition to complying with the record requirements of subparagraph (1)(i) of this paragraph, such taxpayer must maintain records from which he can establish to the satisfaction of the district director that such asset has not previously been considered as having been disposed of. In addition, if, for any taxable year, a taxpayer uses the method provided in this subdivision for any asset, he must use for such year and for each subsequent taxable year (unless he obtains the district director's consent to change) with respect to all assets similar in kind to such asset—

(a) The method of determining estimated useful lives described in paragraph (e)(3)(ii)(b) of § 1.46-3, and

(b) The method he has selected under this subdivision for determining the order in which such assets are considered as having been disposed of.

A request by a taxpayer to obtain the district director's consent to change a system or method described in this subdivision with respect to assets similar in kind must be submitted to the district director on or before the last day of the taxable year with respect to which the change is sought.

(iv) Notwithstanding subdivisions (i), (ii), and (iii) of this subparagraph, there shall be taken into account separately any abnormal retirement of section 38 property of substantial value for which the estimated useful life was determined under § 1.46-3(e)(3)(ii)(b) or (iii). For definition of abnormal retirement, see paragraph (b) of § 1.167(a)-8.

(4) Reserved.

(5) Example. This paragraph may be illustrated by the following example:

Example. (i) Taxpayer A uses numerous small returnable containers in his business. It is impracticable for A to keep individual detailed records with respect to such containers which are mass assets. In 1965, A places in service 10 million containers purchased for $1 million, and reasonably determines that each of such containers has a basis of 10 cents. A places such containers in a multiple asset account to which is assigned a 5-year average useful life for purposes of computing depreciation. A has conducted an appropriate mortality study which shows that the containers have the following estimated useful lives:

Percent of assets	Useful life (years)
10	3
20	4
40	5
20	6
10	7

A assigns separate lives to such assets based on the estimated range of years taken into account in establishing the average useful life of such containers. The qualified investment with respect to such containers is $400,000 computed as follows:

Useful life	Basis	Applicable percentage	Qualified investment
4	$200,000	33⅓	$ 66,666
5	400,000	33⅓	133,334
6	200,000	66⅔	133,334
7	100,000	66⅔	66,666
			$400,000

A's credit earned for 1965 of $28,000 (7 percent times $400,000) is allowed as a credit under section 38 against A's liability for tax of $2 million. (For purposes of this example the computations of investment credit and recapture with respect to containers placed in service in years other than 1965 are omitted.) The mortality studies effective for 1966 and 1967 show that none of the containers placed in service in 1965 was retired.

(ii) A's mortality study effective with respect to 1968 shows that the containers are being retired as follows:

Percent of assets	Useful life (Years)
30	3
20	4
30	5
10	6
10	7

Thus, the 1968 study shows that 30 percent of the 10 million containers placed in service in 1965 were retired in 1968. Under the rule of subparagraph (3)(i) of this paragraph, the 3 million containers are treated as consisting of the 1 million containers to which was assigned a 3-year useful life and the 2 million containers to which was assigned a 4-year useful life. Taking into account only the fact that 30 percent of the containers placed in service in 1965 had an actual life of less than 4 years, A's recomputed qualified investment for 1965 is $333,333 and his recomputed credit earned is $23,333. A's income tax for 1968 is increased by $4,667 ($28,000 original credit earned minus $23,333 recomputed credit earned).

(iii) The mortality study effective for 1969 shows the same results as the mortality (an actual life of 4 years). Under the rule of subparagraph (3)(i) of this paragraph such 2 million containers are treated as having been among 4 million containers to which were assigned a 5-year useful life. Therefore, no recapture determination is required for 1969.

(iv) The mortality study effective for 1970 shows the same results as the mortality study effective for 1968. Thus, it shows that 3 million containers were retired in 1970 (an actual life of 5 years). Under the rule of subparagraph (3)(i) of this paragraph, the 3 million are treated as having been assigned useful lives as follows: 2 million as having been assigned a useful life of 5 years, and 1 million as having been assigned a useful life of 6 years. Taking into account only the fact that 10 percent of the containers placed in service in 1965 had an actual life of 5 years rather than the 6 years estimated useful life assigned to them, A's recomputed qualified investment is $300,000 and A's credit earned for 1965 is $21,000. Thus, taking into account the 1968 recapture determination, A's income tax for 1970 is increased by $2,333.

(f) Public utility property. *(1) Recomputed qualified investment.* In recomputing qualified investment with respect to section 38 property which becomes public utility property (as defined in paragraph (g) of § 1.46-3)—

(i) If such property becomes public utility property less than 3 years from the date on which it was placed in service, then such property shall be treated as public utility property for its entire useful life.

(ii) If such property becomes public utility property 3 years or more but less than 5 years from the date on which it was placed in service, then such property shall be treated as section 38 property which is not public utility property for the first 3 years of its estimated useful life and as public utility property for the remaining period of its estimated useful life.

(iii) If such property becomes public utility property 5 years or more but less than 7 years from the date on which it was placed in service, then such property shall be treated as section 38 property which is not public utility property for the first 5 years of its estimated useful life and as public utility property for the remaining period of its estimated useful life.

If property becomes public utility property before August 16, 1971, this subparagraph shall be applied by substituting "4 years" for "3 years", "6 years" for "5 years", and "8 years" for "7 years".

(2) Examples. Subparagraph (1) of this paragraph may be illustrated by the following examples:

Example (1). (i) X Corporation, which makes its returns on the basis of the calendar year, acquired and placed in service on January 1, 1969, an item of section 38 property with a basis of $12,000 and an estimated useful life of 8 years. The amount of qualified investment with respect to such property was $12,000. For the taxable year 1969, X Corporation's credit earned was $840 (7 percent of $12,000) and for such taxable year X Corporation was allowed under section 38 a credit of $840 against its liability for tax. During the taxable year 1972 such property becomes public utility property (as defined in paragraph (g) of § 1.46-3) with respect to X Corporation.

(ii) Such item of section 38 property is treated as section 38 property which is not public utility property for the first 3 years of its 8-year estimated useful life and is treated as public utility property for the remaining 5 years. The recomputed qualified investment with respect to such item of section 38 property is $7,428, computed as follows:

$12,000 basis × 33⅓ percent applicable percentage	$4,000
$12,000 basis × 3/7 × 66⅔ percent applicable percentage	3,428
Total recomputed qualified investment	$7,428

X Corporation's recomputed credit earned for the taxable year 1969 is $520 (7 percent of $7,428). The income tax imposed by chapter 1 of the Code on X Corporation for the taxable year 1972 is increased by the $320 decrease in its credit earned for the taxable year 1972 (that is, $840 original credit earned minus $520 recomputed credit earned).

Example (2). (i) The facts are the same as in example (1) and in addition the item of section 38 property which became public utility property in 1972 is sold to Y Corporation on January 2, 1975.

(ii) The actual useful life of such item of property is 6 years. For the first 3 years of its 8 year estimated useful life such item is treated as section 38 property which is not public utility property and for the remaining 3 years is treated as public utility property. The recomputed qualified investment with respect to such item of property is $5,714, computed as follows:

$12,000 basis × 33⅓ percent applicable percentage	$4,000
$12,000 basis × 3/7 × 33⅓ percent applicable percentage	1,714
Total recomputed qualified investment	$5,714

X Corporation's recomputed credit earned for the taxable year 1969 is $400 (7 percent of $5,714). The income tax imposed by chapter 1 of the Code on X Corporation for the taxable year 1975 is increased by $120 (that is, $440 ($840 original credit earned minus $400 recomputed credit earned) minus $320 increase in tax for 1969).

(g) Special rules for progress expenditure property. Under section 47(a)(3), a recapture determination is required if property ceases to be progress expenditure property (as defined in § 1.46-5(d)). Property ceases to be progress expenditure property if it is sold or otherwise disposed of before it is placed in service. For example, cancellation of the contract for progress expenditure property or abandonment of the project by the taxpayer will be considered a "disposition" within the meaning of § 1.47-2. A cessation occurs if progress expenditure property ceases to be property that will be section 38 property with a useful life of 7 years or more when placed in service. In general, a sale and leaseback is treated as a cessation. However, see paragraph (g)(2) of § 1.47-3 for special rules for certain sale and leaseback transactions. Recapture determinations for progress expenditure property are to be made in a way similar to that provided under §§ 1.47-1 through 1.47-6. Reduction of qualified investment must begin with the most recent credit year (*i.e.*, the most recent taxable year the property is taken into account in computing qualified investment under §§ 1.46-3 or 1.46-5).

(h) Special rules for energy property. *(1) In general.* A recapture determination is required for the investment credit attributable to the energy percentage (energy credit) if property is (i) disposed of or (ii) otherwise ceases to be energy property (as defined in section 48(l)) with regard to the taxpayer before the close of the estimated useful life (as determined under paragraph (a)(2)(i) of this section) which was taken into account in computing qualified investment.

(2) Dispositions. The term "disposition" is described in § 1.47-2(a)(1). A transfer of energy property that is a "disposition" requiring a recapture determination for the investment credit attributable to the regular percentage (regular credit) and the ESOP percentage (ESOP credit) will also be a "disposition" requiring a recapture determination for the energy credit.

(3) Cessation. (i) The term "cessation" is described in § 1.47-2(a)(2). For energy property, a cessation occurs during a taxable year if, by reason of a change in use or otherwise, the property would not have qualified for an energy credit if placed in service during that year. A change in use will not require a recapture determination for the regular or ESOP credit unless, by reason of the change, the property would not have qualified for the regular or ESOP credit if placed in service during that year.

(ii) A qualified intercity bus described in § 1.48-9(q) must meet the predominant use test (of § 1.48-9(q)(7)) for the remainder of the taxable year from the date it is placed in service and for each taxable year thereafter. A cessation occurs in any taxable year in which the bus is no longer a qualifying bus under § 1.48-9(q)(6). A qualified intercity bus does not cease to be energy property for a taxable year subsequent to the one in which it was placed in service by reason of a decrease in operating capacity (see § 1.48-9(q)(9)) for that year compared to any prior taxable year.

(4) Recordkeeping requirement. For recordkeeping requirements with respect to dispositions or cessations, the rules of paragraph (e)(1) of this section apply. For example, the taxpayer must maintain records for each recycling facility indicating the percentage of virgin materials used each year. See, § 1.48-9(g)(5)(ii).

(5) Examples. The following examples illustrate this paragraph (h).

Example (1). (a) In 1980, corporation X, a calendar year, taxpayer, acquires and places in service a computer that will perform solely energy conserving functions in connection with an existing industrial process. Assume the computer has a 10 year useful life and qualifies for both the regular and energy credits. In 1981, a change is made in the industrial process (within the meaning of § 1.48-9(l)(2)). However, for 1981 the computer continues to perform solely energy conserving functions. In 1982, the computer ceases to perform energy conserving functions and begins to perform a production related function.

(b) For 1981, a recapture determination is not required. For 1982, the entire energy credit must be recaptured, although none of the regular credit is recaptured. If in 1989 the computer first ceased to perform an energy conserving function, no part of the energy credit would be recaptured.

Example (2). Assume the same facts and conclusion as in example (1). Assume further that X sells the computer in 1985. A recapture determination is required for the regular credit.

Example (3). In 1981, corporation Y, a calendar year taxpayer, acquires and places in service recycling equipment. Assume the equipment has a 7-year useful life and qualifies for both the regular credit and energy credit. During the course of 1982, more than 10 percent of the material recycled is virgin material. The energy credit is recaptured in its entirety, although none of the regular credits is recaptured. See § 1.48-9(g)(5)(B)(ii).

Example (4). In 1980, corporation Z, a calendar year taxpayer, acquires and places in service a boiler the primary fuel for which is an alternate substance. The boiler has a 7-year useful life. Assume the boiler is a structural component of a building within the meaning of § 1.48-1(e)(2). Assume further that the boiler is not a part of a qualified rehabilitated building (as defined in section 48(g)(1)) or a single purpose agricultural or horticultural structure (as defined in section 48(p)). Z is allowed only an energy credit since the boiler is a structural component of a building. In 1984, Z modifies the boiler to use oil as the primary fuel. A recapture determination is required for the energy credit. See § 1.48-9(c)(3).

(i) [Reserved]

(j) [Reserved]

(k) [Reserved]

(l) [Reserved]

(m) Commuter highway vehicles. *(1) Recomputed qualified investment.* (i) If a qualifying commuter highway vehicle (as defined in § 1.46-11(a) undergoes a change in use but does not cease to be section 38 property, qualified investment for that vehicle is recomputed as if the vehicle was section 38 property which is not a qualifying commuter highway vehicle for its entire useful life.

(ii) The following example illustrates this paragraph (m)(1).

Example. X Corporation, a calendar year taxpayer, acquired and placed in service on January 1, 1982, a qualifying commuter highway vehicle with a basis of $10,000 and which qualified as three year recovery property under section 168(c)(2)(A)(i). The amount of qualified investment for the vehicle under section 46(c)(1) and (6) is $10,000. For the taxable year 1982, X Corporation's credit earned was $1,000 (10 percent of $10,000) and X Corporation was allowed under section 38 a $1,000 credit against its 1982 tax liability. During the taxable year 1984, the vehicle undergoes a change in use but does not cease to be section 38 property. The vehicle is treated as section 38 property which is not a qualifying commuter highway vehicle for its entire useful life. The recomputed qualified investment for the vehicle is $6,000 (60 percent of $10,000) and X Corporation's recomputed credit earned is $600 (10 percent of $6,000). The income tax imposed by chapter 1 of the Code on X Corporation for 1984 is increased by the $400 decrease in its credit earned for 1982 ($1,000 – $600).

(2) Change in use. (i) A qualifying commuter highway vehicle undergoes a change in use if the vehicle does not meet the commuter use requirement (as defined in § 1.46-11(d)) for each computation period.

(ii) Each of the following is a computation period:

(A) The period beginning on the date the vehicle was placed in service and ending on the last day of the taxpayer's taxable year in which the vehicle was placed in service;

(B) Each of the taxpayer's taxable years beginning after the date the vehicle was placed in service and ending before the end of the first 36 months after the vehicle was placed in service; and

(C) The period ending at the end of the first 36 months after the vehicle was placed in service and beginning on the first day of the taxpayer's taxable year in which the end of those first 36 months falls.

(iii) The following example illustrates this paragraph (m)(2).

Example. (a) Z Corporation, a calendar year taxpayer, acquired and placed in service a qualifying commuter highway vehicle on January 15, 1979. Z Corporation used the vehicle as set forth in the following table:

Taxable year ending	Total miles	Commuter miles	Ratio
1979	10,000	9,000	90
1980	10,000	8,000	80
1981	10,000	8,000	80
1982(1-14)	1,000	100	10

(b) The first computation period begins on the date the vehicle is placed in service, in this example 1-15-79, and ends 12-31-79. In that computation period, the ratio of commuter miles to total miles is .90 (9,000 miles ÷ 10,000 miles). Therefore, the vehicle meets the commuter use requirement for that period and has not undergone a change in use. Similar calculations for the computation periods 1-1-80 to 12-31-80 and 1-1-81 to 12-31-81 produce the same result.

(c) As of the computation period beginning 1-1-82 and ending 1-14-82, the ratio of commuter use to total mileage is .10 (100 miles vehicle does not meet the commuter use requirement for the period and the vehicle has undergone a change in use.

T.D. 6931, 10/9/67, amend T.D. 7203, 8/24/72, T.D. 7765, 1/19/81, T.D. 7982, 10/5/84, T.D. 8035, 7/18/85, T.D. 8183, 3/1/88.

PAR. 3. Section 1.47-1 is amended as follows:

1. The heading of paragraph (a)(1) is revised to read as follows: *"Property which is not recovery property within the meaning of section 168."*

2. The first sentence of paragraph (a)(1)(i) is amended by adding the language "which is not recovery property within the meaning of section 168 (see paragraph (a)(3) of this section for special rules for recovery property within the meaning of section 168)" after the phrase "section 38 property" and before the phrase "the basis (or cost)".

3. The last sentence of paragraph (a)(1)(i) is amended by removing the language "paragraph (h)" and adding in its place the language "paragraph (l)".

4. Paragraph (a) is amended by adding a new paragraph (a)(3) to read "(3) *Special rules for recovery property within the meaning of section 168.* [Reserved]."

5. Paragraphs (f), (g) and (h) are redesignated (j), (k), and (l), respectively.

6. Paragraph (e) is amended by—

a. Redesignating paragraphs (e)(2) through (e)(5) as paragraphs (f)(1) thorugh (f)(4);

b. Removing the heading for paragraph (e)(1), and redesignating paragraphs (e)(1), (i), (ii), and (iii) as paragraphs (e)(1), (2), and (3), respectively;

c. Revising redesignated paragraphs (e)(1) and (2)(2), and the introductory text of redesignated paragraph (e)(3), to read as follows:

7. Paragraph (i) is added and reserved.

8. A new heading is added to redesignated paragraph (f), and the heading for redesignated paragraph (f)(1) is revised, to read as follows: "(f) *Treatment of mass assets placed in service in taxable years beginning before [30 days after publication of this treasury decision in the "Federal Register"]* —(1) In general.".

9. Paragraph (f)(1)(i), as redesignated, is amended by removing the language "in the case of mass assets (as defined in subparagraph (4) of this paragraph)" from the first sentence and adding in its place the language "for mass assets (as defined in paragraph (f)(3) of this section) placed in service in taxable years beginning before [30 days after publication of this Treasury Decision in the FEDERAL REGISTER]" and by removing the language "facts required by subparagraph (1) of this paragraph," from the first sentence and adding in its place the language "facts required by paragraph (e) of this section,".

10. Paragraph (f)(1)(ii)(a), as redesignated, is amended by removing the language "(e)(3)(ii)(b)" and adding in its place the language "(j)(3)(ii)(b)".

11. Paragraph (f)(1)(iii), as redesignated, is amended by removing the language "§ 1.46-3(e)(3)(iii)" and adding in its place the language "§ 1.46-3(j)(3)(iii)".

12. In redesignated paragraph (f)(1)(v), paragraph (c) of the example is amended by removing the language "(3)(iv)" from the last sentence and adding in its place the language "(2)(iv)".

13. Paragraph (f)(2)(i), as redesignated, is amended by removing, in the first sentence, the language "§ 1.46-3(e)(3)(ii)(b) or (iii)" and adding in its place the language "§ 1.46-3(j)(3)(ii)(b) or (iii)".

14. Paragraph (f)(2)(ii), as redesignated, is amended by removing, in the first sentence, the language "§ 1.46-3(e)(3)(iii)" and adding in its place the language "1.46-3(j)(3)(iii)".

15. Paragraph (f)(2)(iii), as redesignated, is amended by removing from the first sentence in the introductory text and from paragraph (f)(2)(iii)(a) the language "(e)(3)(ii)(b)" and adding in its place the language "(j)(3)(ii)(b)", and by removing from the second sentence of the introductory text the

language "subparagraph (1)(i) of this paragraph" and adding in its place the language "paragraph (e)(1) of this section".

16. Paragraph (f)(2)(iv) is amended by removing the language "§ 1.46-3(e)(3)(ii)(b) or (iii)" and adding in its place the language "§ 1.46-3(j)(3)(ii)(b) or (iii)".

17. Paragraph (f)(3), as redesignated, is amended by removing in the first sentence the language "(e)(3)(iii)" and adding in its place the language "(j)(3)(iii)".

18. Paragraphs (f)(4)(ii), (iii), and (iv), as redesignated, are amended by removing the language "(3)(i)" and adding in its place the language "(2)(i)".

19. New paragraphs (g) and (h) are added to read as follows:

20. Paragraph (l)(4), as redesignated, is amended by removing "paragraph (e)(1) of this section" from the first sentence and inserting in its place "paragraph (e) of this section".

21. Paragraph (l)(5), as redesignated, is amended by removing "(h)" from the first sentence and inserting in its place "(l)"

Proposed § 1.47-1 Recomputation of credit allowed by section 38. [*For Preamble, see ¶ 151,041*]

* * * * *

(e) Identification of property. *(1) Record requirements.* In general, the taxpayer must maintain records from which he can establish, with respect to each item of section 38 property, the following facts:

(i) The date the property is disposed of or otherwise ceases to be section 38 property,

(ii) The estimated useful life or recovery period in the case of recovery property (within the meaning of section 168) which was assigned to the property under paragraph (e) of § 1.46-3,

(iii) The month and the taxable year in which the property was placed in service and,

(iv) The basis (or cost), actually or reasonably determined, of the property.

(2) Recapture determination. For purposes of determining whether section 38 property is disposed of, or otherwise ceases to be section 38 property with respect to the taxpayer, before the close of its estimated useful life or recovery period in the case of recovery property (within the meaning of section 168), and for purposes of determining recomputed qualified investment, the taxpayer must establish from his records the facts required by paragraph (e)(1) of this section.

(3) Examples. If the taxpayer fails to maintain records from which he can establish the facts required by paragraph (e)(1) of this section, then this section shall be applied to the taxpayer in the manner indicated in the following examples:

* * * * *

(g) Treatment of mass assets which are not recovery property for taxable years beginning on or after [30 days after publication of this Treasury Decision in the Federal Register]. *(1) In general.* (i) For mass assets which are not recovery property within the meaning of section 168 and are placed in service in taxable years beginning on or after [30 days after publication of this Treasury Decision in the Federal Register] the taxpayer may use its own mortality dispersion table or a standard mortality dispersion table prescribed by the Commissioner to recompute qualified investment for mass assets (as defined in paragraph (g)(2) of this section). The taxpayer must then use whichever table was chosen to determine the number of assets expected to be retired each year after the assets are placed in service. Recapture determinations must be made at the end of each taxable year in which assets are expected to be retired before the end of the useful life used to determine qualified investment. Taxpayers may rely on the table and, in general, do not need to account for actual retirements.

(ii) If the taxpayer uses its own mortality dispersion table, the table must be based on an acceptable survey of the taxpayer's actual experience and on appropriate statistical methods. The survey of the taxpayer's actual experience must be based on a sample of not less than 250 items. The taxpayer must maintain records showing the historical data used to develop the table. If the taxpayer does not maintain adequate records, the standard mortality dispersion table will be used to recompute qualified investment. The taxpayer may not use its own table for assets placed in service in a taxable year, unless the table was prepared before the beginning of that year. For example, assume a calendar year taxpayer completes preparation of its own table on July 1, 1979. It may use the table for assets placed in service in 1980, but not for assets placed in service in 1979.

(iii) A taxpayer may use the standard mortality dispersion table for one mass asset account and its own table for a different mass asset account. However, if the taxpayer applies a table to a mass asset account in any taxable year, the taxpayer must treat a subsequent change to another table for that account as a change of accounting methods under section 446(e) and obtain consent of the Commissioner.

(2) Definition of mass assets. The term "mass assets" means a mass or group of individual items of section 38 property (i) not necessarily homogeneous, (ii) each of which is minor in value relative to the total value of such mass or group, (iii) numerous in quantity, (iv) usually accounted for only on a total dollar or quantity basis, (v) with respect to which separate identification is impracticable, (vi) with the same useful life (in the case of recovery property, with the same present class life and recovery period) and (vii) placed in service in the same taxable year.

(3) Grouping of mass assets. In general, items in a mass asset account need not be of a similar type although they must have the same useful life. See paragraph (e) of § 1.46-3 for rules for assigning useful lives to mass assets. For example, hammers and saws with useful lives of 4 years may be put in the same account. Hammers with useful lives of 5 years, however, may not be put in an account with hammers with useful lives of 4 years. However, if a taxpayer uses its own mortality dispersion table, all assets in an account must have approximately the same basis or cost. All mass assets in an account must be treated as placed in service (within the meaning of § 1.46-3(d)) on the same date. Taxpayers must use appropriate averaging conventions to determine the date mass assets are placed in service. See paragraph (c)(2) of this section, paragraph (b) of § 1.167(a)-10 for property not subject to an election under section 167(m), and paragraph (c)(2) of § 1.167(a)-11 for property subject to an election under section 167(m).

(4) Useful life. The useful life of mass assets used in computing the allowance for depreciation must be used in applying the taxpayer's mortality dispersion table or the standard mortality dispersion table. See paragraph (e) of § 1.46-3 for rules for assigning useful lives to mass assets. For example, if the taxpayer computes the depreciable life of mass assets under section 167(m), it must use the same depreciable life in applying the standard mortality dispersion table.

(5) *Standard mortality dispersion table.* (i) The standard mortality dispersion table prescribed by the Commissioner and set forth below is based on whole- and half-year average useful life categories. Each category contains 30 columns. Each column shows the percentage of basis or cost in a mass asset account expected to be retired in each of the first 30 years after the property is placed in service. The table is set forth below:

STANDARD MORTALITY DISPERSION TABLE PERCENTAGE OF BASIS OR COST OF MASS ASSET ACCOUNT CONSIDERED DISPOSED OF EACH 12-MONTH PERIOD AFTER THE ACCOUNT IS PLACED IN SERVICE

Average Useful Life (Years)	1st (1)	2nd (2)	3rd (3)	4th (4)	5th (5)	6th (6)	7th (7)	8th (8)	9th (9)	10th (10)
3	2.28	13.59	34.13	34.13	13.59	2.28	—	—	—	—
3.5	1.62	8.23	23.51	33.28	23.51	8.23	1.62	—	—	—
4	1.22	5.46	15.98	27.34	27.34	15.98	5.46	1.22	—	—
4.5	.99	3.76	11.12	21.20	25.86	21.20	11.12	3.76	.99	—
5	.82	2.77	7.92	15.91	22.58	22.58	15.91	7.92	2.77	.82
5.5	.71	2.10	5.88	11.92	18.75	21.28	18.75	11.92	5.88	2.10
6	.62	1.66	4.40	9.19	14.98	19.15	19.15	14.98	9.19	4.40
6.5	.55	1.33	3.38	7.25	12.00	16.39	18.20	16.39	12.00	7.25
7	.51	1.11	2.74	5.49	9.64	13.87	16.64	16.64	13.87	9.64
7.5	.47	.92	2.20	4.49	7.79	11.55	14.65	15.86	14.65	11.55
8	.44	.78	1.85	3.61	6.46	9.52	12.91	14.43	14.43	12.91
8.5	.40	.70	1.52	2.97	5.16	8.19	10.87	13.05	14.28	13.05
9	.38	.61	1.29	2.47	4.43	6.69	9.27	11.93	12.93	12.93
9.5	.37	.52	1.13	2.07	3.69	5.57	8.13	10.44	11.72	12.72
10	.35	.47	.97	1.80	3.09	4.83	6.90	9.01	10.79	11.79
11	.32	.39	.75	1.35	2.24	3.64	5.10	6.82	8.51	10.24
12	.30	.32	.60	1.06	1.73	2.67	3.88	5.31	6.79	8.19
13	.28	.27	.49	.84	1.34	2.04	3.12	4.13	5.37	6.63
14	.27	.24	.40	.71	1.06	1.68	2.32	3.17	4.38	5.26
15	.26	.21	.35	.57	.89	1.31	1.89	2.60	3.43	4.36
16	.25	.18	.29	.49	.75	1.10	1.48	2.13	2.83	3.38
17	.24	.16	.28	.42	.60	.92	1.30	1.67	2.34	2.82
18	.23	.15	.24	.37	.51	.78	1.08	1.39	1.93	2.50
19	.23	.14	.20	.32	.47	.66	.92	1.15	1.61	2.08
20	.22	.13	.19	.28	.40	.57	.77	1.03	1.36	1.73
25	.20	.09	.12	.18	.23	.31	.41	.53	.67	.85
30	.19	.07	.09	.12	.15	.20	.25	.32	.40	.49

Average Useful Life (Years)	11th (11)	12th (12)	13th (13)	14th (14)	15th (15)	16th (16)	17th (17)	18th (18)	19th (19)	20th (20)
3	—	—	—	—	—	—	—	—	—	—
3.5	—	—	—	—	—	—	—	—	—	—
4	—	—	—	—	—	—	—	—	—	—
4.5	—	—	—	—	—	—	—	—	—	—
5	—	—	—	—	—	—	—	—	—	—
5.5	.71	—	—	—	—	—	—	—	—	—
6	1.66	.62	—	—	—	—	—	—	—	—
6.5	3.38	1.33	.55	—	—	—	—	—	—	—
7	5.49	2.74	1.11	.51	—	—	—	—	—	—
7.5	7.70	4.49	2.20	.92	.47	—	—	—	—	—
8	9.52	6.46	3.61	1.85	.78	.44	—	—	—	—
8.5	10.87	8.19	5.16	2.97	1.52	70	.40	—	—	—
9	11.93	9.27	6.69	4.43	2.47	1.29	.61	.38	—	—
9.5	11.72	10.44	8.13	5.57	3.69	2.07	1.13	.52	.37	—
10	11.79	10.79	9.01	6.90	4.83	3.09	1.80	.97	.47	.35
11	10.64	10.64	10.24	8.51	6.82	5.10	3.64	2.24	1.35	.75
12	9.28	9.87	9.87	9.28	8.19	6.79	5.31	3.88	2.67	1.73
13	7.77	8.62	9.10	9.10	8.62	7.77	6.63	5.37	4.13	3.12
14	6.62	7.25	8.32	8.32	8.32	8.32	7.25	6.62	5.26	4.38
15	5.32	6.23	7.04	7.61	7.93	7.93	7.61	7.04	6.23	5.32
16	4.22	5.30	6.11	6.80	6.89	7.54	7.54	6.89	6.80	6.11
17	3.71	4.48	4.94	5.93	6.51	6.54	7.14	7.14	6.54	6.51
18	3.12	3.57	4.46	4.81	5.71	6.19	6.21	6.75	6.75	6.21

19	2.60	2.97	3.76	4.37	4.96	5.48	5.53	6.19	6.36	6.36
20	2.17	2.66	3.18	3.72	4.25	4.76	5.22	5.57	5.83	5.96
25	1.06	1.29	1.55	1.85	2.18	2.50	2.84	3.19	3.54	3.84
30	.59	.72	.87	1.02	1.20	1.40	1.60	1.83	2.06	2.30

BILLING CODE 4830-01-C

Average Useful Life Years	21st (21)	22nd (22)	23rd (23)	24th (24)	25th (25)	26th (26)	27th (27)	28th (28)	29th (29)	30th (30)
3	—	—	—	—	—	—	—	—	—	—
3.5	—	—	—	—	—	—	—	—	—	—
4	—	—	—	—	—	—	—	—	—	—
4.5	—	—	—	—	—	—	—	—	—	—
5	—	—	—	—	—	—	—	—	—	—
5.5	—	—	—	—	—	—	—	—	—	—
6	—	—	—	—	—	—	—	—	—	—
6.5	—	—	—	—	—	—	—	—	—	—
7	—	—	—	—	—	—	—	—	—	—
7.5	—	—	—	—	—	—	—	—	—	—
8	—	—	—	—	—	—	—	—	—	—
8.5	—	—	—	—	—	—	—	—	—	—
9	—	—	—	—	—	—	—	—	—	—
9.5	—	—	—	—	—	—	—	—	—	—
10	—	—	—	—	—	—	—	—	—	—
11	.39	.32	—	—	—	—	—	—	—	—
12	1.06	.60	.32	.30	—	—	—	—	—	—
13	2.04	1.34	.84	.49	.27	.28	—	—	—	—
14	3.17	2.32	1.68	1.06	.71	.40	.24	.27	—	—
15	4.36	3.43	2.60	1.89	1.31	.89	.57	.35	.21	.26
16	5.30	4.22	3.63	2.83	2.13	1.48	1.10	.75	.49	.29
17	5.93	4.94	4.48	3.71	2.82	2.34	1.67	1.30	.92	.60
18	6.19	5.71	4.81	4.46	3.57	3.12	2.50	1.93	1.39	1.08
19	6.19	5.53	5.48	4.96	4.37	3.76	2.97	2.60	2.08	1.61
20	5.96	5.83	5.57	5.22	4.76	4.25	3.72	3.18	2.66	2.17
25	4.13	4.38	4.58	4.70	4.78	4.78	4.70	4.58	4.38	4.13
30	2.54	2.78	3.01	3.23	3.42	3.61	3.75	3.86	3.95	3.98

$$\left(Y = \frac{N}{\sigma\sqrt{2\pi}}\right) \times \left(e^{z}\right)$$

The symbols in the equation are as follows:

N = the number of mass assets in the group

σ = the standard deviation of the normal distribution

π = the constant 3.14159

$$z = \frac{-\frac{1}{2}(X - \bar{X})^2}{2}$$

e = the constant 2.71828

x = an independent variable

X̄ = mean or average of the mass assets in the group (average useful life)

(x − X̄) = the deviation of x from the mean or average of the mass assets in the group

σ2 = the variance of x

(ii) The range of expected useful lives is assumed to extend from the time of acquisition (1 × 3 Standard Deviations) to double the average useful life (3 Standard Deviations). Practically all cases (99.73 percent) fall within the (− 3 Standard Deviation range under the assumption of a normal probability distribution. The first year mortality figures shown in the table for assets with a long average useful life are greater than those shown for one or more of the succeeding years. In addition, the last year mortality figures shown in the table for assets with a long average useful life are greater than those shown for one or more of the preceding years. The reason is that the tails (beginning and ending years) of the distribution have been adjusted so that 100 percent of the assets (and not 99.73 percent) are included within the range of useful lives.

(6) *Recapture determinations.* A recapture determination must be made at the end of each taxable year in which assets are expected to be retired before the end of the useful life used to determine qualified investment. The percentage of basis or cost in a mass asset account expected to be retired under the taxpayer's mortality dispersion table or under a standard mortality dispersion table will be considered disposed of ratably over the year. The taxpayer is not required to account for actual retirements other than abnormal or extra-ordinary retirements. See paragraph (b) of § 1.67(a)-8 for definitions of abnormal retirements of non-recovery property that is not subject to an election under section 167 (m). See paragraph (d)(3)(ii) of § 1.167 (a)-11 for definitions of extraordinary retirements of nonrecovery property subject to an election under section 167 (m).

(7) Example. Paragraph (g)(6) of this section may be illustrated by the following example.

Example. (i) A calendar year taxpayer placed 1000 assets which are not recovery property in service in 1984. Taxpayer established a single mass asset account for these assets. Under the taxpayer's averaging convention the taxpayer uses July 1 as the assumed date of all additions to mas asset accounts. The assets have estimated useful lives of 3 years. The unadjusted basis in the account is $10,000.

(ii) The standard mortality dispersion table indicates that 2.28% of basis will be considered retired in the first year, 13.59% more will be considered retired in the second year, and 34.13% will be considered retired in the third year. The remaining 50% of basis will be in service for 3 years or more.

(iii) For 1984, no credit is allowed for 1.14% of the basis in the account, because 1984 is the taxable year the assets were placed in service. The standard mortality dispersion table indicates that 2.28% of basis is expected to be retired in the first year after the assets were placed in service. Since the assets were not considered placed in service until July 1, only 50 percent, or a 6-month ratable portion, of the 2.28% of basis is considered disposed of in 1984. The remaining 1.14% will be considered disposed of over the first half of 1985. Qualified investment for the remaining 98.86% is $3,295., which is 33⅓ percent of the basis attributable to that portion of the account.

(iv) For 1985, credit for 7.94% of the basis placed in service has to be recaptured. Of the 2.28% indicated by the standard mortality dispersion table to be disposed, of in the first year, 1.14%, or a 6-month ratable portion, will be considered disposed of in the first half of 1985. Of the 113.59% indicated by the table to be disposed of in the second year, 6.8%, or a 6-month ratable portion, will be considered disposed of in the second half of 1985. Removing the qualified investment with respect to 7.94% of the account from the $9886. for which the credit was allowed in year 1 results in a qualified investment of $3030.36 (33⅓% of $9092). Thus, the credit allowed is $303.04, as compared to a $329.50 credit "allowable" for the full basis placed in the account. The decrease in allowable credit and, therefore, the amount recaptured is $26.46.

(v) For 1986, credit for 23.87% of the basis placed in service has to be recaptured. Of the 13.59% indicated by the standard mortality dispersion table to be disposed of in the second year, 6.8% or a 6-month ratable portion, will be considered disposed of in the first half of 1986. Of the 34.13% indicated by the table to be disposed of in the third year, 17.07% or a 6-month ratable portion, will be considered disposed of in the second half of 1986. Removing the qualified investment with respect to 23.87% of the account from the $9886. for which the credit was allowed in year 1 results in a qualified investment of $2499.42 (33⅓ of $7499.). Thus, the credit allowed is $249.94, as compared to a $329.50 credit "allowable" for the full basis placed in the account. The decrease in allowable credit and, therefore, the amount recaptured is $79.56.

(vi) For 1987, credit for 17.07% of the basis placed in service has to be recaptured. Of the 34.13% indicated by the standard mortality dispersion table to be disposed of in the third year, 17.07%, or a 6-month ratable portion, will be considered disposed of in the first half of 1987. Removing the qualified investment with respect to 17.07% of the account from the $9886. for which the credit was allowed in year 1 results in a qualified investment of $2726.06 (33⅓ of $8179.). Thus, the credit allowed is $272.61, as compared to a $329.50 credit "allowable" for the full basis placed in the account. The decrease in allowable credit and, therefore, the amount recaptured is $56.89.

(vii) None of the credit is recaptured for the percent of basis disposed of after June 30, 1987.

(h) Treatment of mass assets which are recovery property within the meaning of section 168. *(1) In general.* (i) For mass assets (as defined in paragraph (g)(2) of this section) which are recovery property within the meaning of section 168, the taxpayer must determine dispositions of assets from a mass asset account by the use of an appropriate mortality dispersion table. Such table must be used to determine the number of assets expected to be retired each year after the assets are placed in service. Recapture determinations must be made at the end of each taxable year in which assets are expected to be retired before the end of the recapture period (as defined in subsection (a)(5)(E)(ii) of section 47).

(ii) The taxpayer may use its own mortality dispersion table prescribed by the Commissioner. The taxpayer's own mortality dispersion table or a standard mortality dispersion table must be based on an acceptable survey of the taxpayer's actual experience and on appropriate statistical methods. The survey of the taxpayer's actual experience must be based on a sample of not less than 250 items. The taxpayer must maintain records showing the historical data used to develop the table. If the taxpayer does not maintain adequate records, the standard mortality dispersion table will be used to determine dispositions of assets from a mass account. The taxpayer may not use its own table for assets placed in service in a taxable year unless the table was prepared before the beginning of that year. For example, assume a calendar year taxpayer completes preparation of its own table on July 1, 1981. It may use the table for assets placed in service in 1982, but not for assets placed in service in 1981.

(iii) A taxpayer may use the standard mortality dispersion table for one mass asset account and its own table for a different mass asset account. However, if the taxpayer applies to a mass asset account in any taxable year, the taxpayer must treat a subsequent change to another table for that account as a change of accounting methods under section 446(e) and obtain consent of the Commissioner.

(2) Grouping of mass assets. In general, all items in a mass asset account must have the same present class life (as defined in § 1.167(a)-11(b)(4)) and the same recovery period but need not be of a similar type. However, if a taxpayer uses its own mortality dispersion table, all assets in an account must have approximately the same cost. For purposes of applying a mortality dispersion table, all assets placed in service during a taxable year will be considered to be placed in service on the first day of the second half of the taxable year.

(3) Present class life. The present class life of the assets placed in a mass asset account must be used in applying either the taxpayer's mortality dispersion table or the standard mortality dispersion table, notwithstanding the fact that the appropriate recovery period is used in computing the tax credit.

(4) Standard mortality dispersion table. The standard mortality dispersion table prescribed by the Commissioner for purposes of this paragraph is set forth below.

STANDARD MORTALITY DISPERSION TABLE PERCENTAGE OF BASIS OR COST OF MASS ASSET ACCOUNT CONSIDERED DISPOSED OF EACH 12-MONTH PERIOD AFTER THE ACCOUNT IS PLACED IN SERVICE

Present Class Life	1st (1)	2nd (2)	3rd (3)	4th (4)	5th (5)	6th (6)	7th (7)	8th (8)	9th (9)	10th (10)
2.5	3.59	23.84	45.14	23.84	3.59	—	—	—	—	—
3	2.28	13.59	34.13	34.13	13.59	2.28	—	—	—	—
3.5	1.62	8.23	23.51	33.28	23.51	8.23	1.62	—	—	—
4	1.22	5.46	15.98	27.34	27.34	15.98	5.46	1.22	—	—
5	.82	2.77	7.92	15.91	22.58	22.58	15.91	7.92	2.77	.82
6	.62	1.66	4.40	9.19	14.98	19.15	19.15	14.98	9.19	4.40
6.5	.55	1.33	3.38	7.25	12.00	16.39	18.20	16.39	12.00	7.25
7	.51	1.11	2.74	5.49	9.64	13.87	16.64	16.64	13.87	9.64
7.5	.47	.92	2.20	4.49	7.79	11.55	14.65	15.86	14.65	11.55
8	.44	.78	1.85	3.61	6.46	9.52	12.91	14.43	14.43	12.91
8.5	.40	.70	1.52	2.97	5.16	8.19	10.87	13.05	14.28	13.05
9	.38	.61	1.29	2.47	4.43	6.69	9.27	11.93	12.93	12.93
9.5	.37	.52	1.13	2.07	3.69	5.57	8.13	10.44	11.72	12.72
10 and 10.5	.35	.47	.97	1.80	3.09	4.83	6.90	9.01	10.79	11.79
11 and 11.5	.32	.39	.75	1.35	2.24	3.64	5.10	6.82	8.51	10.24
12 and 12.5	.30	.32	.60	1.06	1.73	2.67	3.88	5.31	6.79	8.19
13 and 13.5	.28	.27	.49	.84	1.34	2.04	3.12	4.13	5.37	6.63
14	.27	.24	.40	.71	1.06	1.68	2.32	3.17	4.38	5.26
15	.26	.21	.35	.57	.89	1.31	1.89	2.60	3.43	4.36
16 and 16.5	.25	.18	.29	.49	.75	1.10	1.48	2.13	2.83	3.38
17	.24	.16	.28	.42	.60	.92	1.30	1.67	2.34	2.82
18	.23	.15	.24	.37	.51	.78	1.08	1.39	1.93	2.50
19	.23	.14	.20	.32	.47	.66	.92	1.15	1.61	2.08
20-24	.22	.13	.19	.28	.40	.57	.77	1.03	1.36	1.73
25-29	.20	.09	.12	.18	.23	.31	.41	.53	.67	.85
30-50	.19	.07	.09	.12	.15	.20	.25	.32	.40	.49

Present Class Life	11th (11)	12th (12)	13th (13)	14th (14)	15th (15)	16th (16)	17th (17)	18th (18)	19th (19)	20th (20)
2.5	—	—	—	—	—	—	—	—	—	—
3	—	—	—	—	—	—	—	—	—	—
3.5	—	—	—	—	—	—	—	—	—	—
4	—	—	—	—	—	—	—	—	—	—
5	—	—	—	—	—	—	—	—	—	—
6	1.66	.62	—	—	—	—	—	—	—	—
6.5	3.38	1.33	.55	—	—	—	—	—	—	—
7	5.49	2.74	1.11	.51	—	—	—	—	—	—
7.5	7.70	4.49	2.20	.92	.47	—	—	—	—	—
8	9.52	6.46	3.61	1.85	.78	.44	—	—	—	—
8.5	10.87	8.19	5.16	2.97	1.52	.70	.40	—	—	—
9	11.93	9.27	6.69	4.43	2.47	1.29	.61	.38	—	
Life	(11)	(12)	(13)	(14)	(15)	(16)	(17)	(18)	(19)	(20)
9.5	11.72	10.44	8.13	5.57	3.69	2.07	1.13	.52	.37	—
10 and 10.5	11.79	10.79	9.01	6.90	4.83	3.09	1.80	.97	.47	.35
11 and 11.5	10.64	10.64	10.24	8.51	6.82	5.10	3.64	2.24	1.35	.75
12 and 12.5	9.28	9.87	9.87	9.28	8.19	6.79	5.31	3.88	2.67	1.73
13 and 13.5	7.77	8.62	9.10	9.10	8.62	7.77	6.63	5.37	4.13	3.12
14	6.62	7.25	8.32	8.32	8.32	8.32	7.25	6.62	5.26	4.38
15	5.32	6.23	7.04	7.61	7.93	7.93	7.61	7.04	6.23	5.32
16 and 16.5	4.22	5.30	6.11	6.80	6.89	7.54	7.54	6.89	6.80	6.11
17	3.71	4.48	4.94	5.93	6.51	6.54	7.14	7.14	6.54	6.51
18	3.12	3.57	4.46	4.81	5.71	6.19	6.21	6.75	6.75	6.21
19	2.60	2.97	3.76	4.37	4.96	5.48	5.53	6.19	6.36	6.36
20-24	2.17	2.66	3.18	3.72	4.25	4.76	5.22	5.57	5.83	5.96
25-29	1.06	1.29	1.55	1.85	2.18	2.50	2.84	3.19	3.54	3.84
30-50	.59	.72	.87	1.02	1.20	1.40	1.60	1.83	2.06	2.30

Billing Code 4630-01-C Present Class Life	21st (21)	22nd (22)	23rd (23)	24th (24)	25th (25)	26th (26)	27th (27)	28th (28)	29th (29)	30th (30)
2.5	—	—	—	—	—	—	—	—	—	—
3	—	—	—	—	—	—	—	—	—	—
3.5	—	—	—	—	—	—	—	—	—	—
4	—	—	—	—	—	—	—	—	—	—
5	—	—	—	—	—	—	—	—	—	—
6	—	—	—	—	—	—	—	—	—	—
6.5	—	—	—	—	—	—	—	—	—	—
7	—	—	—	—	—	—	—	—	—	—
7.5	—	—	—	—	—	—	—	—	—	—
8	—	—	—	—	—	—	—	—	—	—
8.5	—	—	—	—	—	—	—	—	—	—
9	—	—	—	—	—	—	—	—	—	—
9.5	—	—	—	—	—	—	—	—	—	—
10 and 10.5	—	—	—	—	—	—	—	—	—	—
11 and 11.5	.39	.32	—	—	—	—	—	—	—	—
12 and 12.5	1.06	.60	.32	.30	—	—	—	—	—	—
13 and 13.5	2.04	1.34	.84	.49	.27	.28	—	—	—	—
14	3.17	2.32	1.68	1.06	.71	.40	.24	.27	—	—
15	4.36	3.43	2.60	1.89	1.31	.89	.57	.35	.21	.26
16 and 16.5	5.30	4.22	3.63	2.83	2.13	1.48	1.10	.75	.49	.29
17	5.93	4.94	4.48	3.71	2.82	2.34	1.67	1.30	.92	.60
18	6.19	5.71	4.81	4.46	3.57	3.12	2.50	1.93	1.39	1.08
19	6.19	5.53	5.48	4.96	4.37	3.76	2.97	2.60	2.08	1.61
20-24	5.96	5.83	5.57	5.22	4.76	4.25	3.72	3.18	2.66	2.17
25-29	4.13	4.38	4.58	4.70	4.78	4.78	4.70	4.58	4.38	4.13
30-50	2.54	2.78	3.01	3.23	3.42	3.61	3.75	3.86	3.95	3.98

(5) Recapture determinations. A recapture determination must be made at the end of each taxable year in which assets are expected to be retired before the end of the recapture period. The percentage of basis or cost in a mass asset account expected to be retired under the taxpayer's mortality dispersion table or under a standard mortality dispersion table will be considered disposed of ratably over the taxable year. The taxpayer is not required to account for actual retirements. The concept of abnormal or extraordinary retirements does not apply to recovery property. See paragraph (l)(1) of § 1.168-2.

(6) Example. Paragraph (h)(5) of this section may be illustrated by the following example.

Example. (i) A calendar year taxpayer placed 1000 assets which are recovery property in service in 1981. Taxpayer established a single mass asset account for these assets. July 1 is the assumed date of all additions to mass asset accounts. Each asset is 3 year recovery property and has a present class life of 4 years. The unadjusted basis in the account is $10,000.

(ii) By applying the 4 year present class life, the standard mortality dispersion table indicates that 1.22% of basis would be considered retired in the first year, 5.46% more would be considered retired in the second year, and 15.98% more would be considered retired in the third year. The remaining 77.34% of basis will be in service longer than the 3 year recapture period.

(iii) For 1981, no credit was allowed for .61% of the basis in the account, because 1981 was the taxable year the assets were placed in service. The standard mortality dispersion table indicates that 1.22% of basis was expected to be retired in the first year after the assets were placed in service. Since the assets were not considered placed in service until July 1, only 50 percent, or a 6-month ratable portion of the 1.22% of basis was considered disposed of in 1981. The remaining .61% was considered disposed of over the first half of 1982. Qualified investment for the remaining 99.39% is $5963.40, which is 60 percent of the basis attributable to that portion of the account.

(iv) For 1982, credit for 3.34% of the basis placed in service was recaptured. Of the 1.22% indicated by the standard mortality dispersion table to be disposed of in the first year, .61%, or a 6-month ratable portion, was considered disposed of in the first half of 1982. Of the 5.46% indicated by the table to be disposed of in the second year, 2.73%, or a 6-month ratable portion, was considered disposed of in the second half of 1982. Removing the qualified investment with respect to 3.34% of the account from the $9939. for which the credit was allowed in year 1 results in a qualified investment of $5763. (60% of $96050.). Thus, the credit allowed was $576.30 as compared to a $596.34. credit "allowable" for the full basis placed in the account. The decrease in allowable credit was therefore $20.04, $3.66 of which is recaptured at 100% and $16.38 of which is recaptured at 66% (see paragraph (h)(6)(viii) of this section). The amount recaptured was therefore $14.47.

(v) For 1983, credit for 10.72% of the basis placed in service must be recaptured. Of the 5.46% indicated by the standard mortality dispersion table to be disposed of in the second year, 2.73%, or a 6-month ratable portion, will be considered disposed of in the first half of 1983. Of the 15.98% indicated by the table to be disposed of in the third year, 7.99%, or a 6-month ratable portion, will be considered disposed of in the second half of 1983. Removing the qualified investment with respect to 10.72% of the account from the $9939. for which the credit was allowed in year 1 results in a qualified investment of $5320.20 (60% of $8867.). Thus, the credit allowable is $532.02, as compared to a $596.34 credit "allowable" for the full basis placed in the account. The decrease in allowable credit is therefore 64.32, $16.38 of which is recaptured at 66% and $47.94 of which is recaptured at 33%. The amount recaptured is therefore $26.63.

(vi) For 1984 credit for 7.99% of the basis placed in service must be recaptured. Of the 15.98% indicated by the standard mortality dispersion table to be disposed of in the third year, 7.99% or a 6-month ratable portion, will be considered disposed of in the first half of 1984. Removing the qualified investment with respect to 7.99% of the account from the $9939. for which the credit was allowed in year 1 results in a qualified investment of $5484. (60% of $9140.). Thus, the credit allowable is $548.40, as compared to a $596.34 credit "allowable" for the full basis placed in the account. The decrease in allowable credit is therefore $47.94, 33% of which is recaptured ($15.82).

(vii) None of the credit is recaptured for the percent of basis disposed of after June 30, 1984.

(viii) The amount of the decrease in allowable credit attributable to the first half of a taxable year is determined by multiplying the decrease in allowable credit for the entire taxable year by a fraction, the numerator of which is the percent of basis disposed of in the first half of the taxable year and the denominator of which is the entire percent of basis disposed of in the taxable year. The amount of the decrease in allowable credit attributable to the second half of a taxable year is determined by applying the formula above, except the numerator of the fraction will be the percent of basis disposed of in the second half of the taxable year.

(7) Effective date. The rules in this paragraph (h) apply to all recovery property placed in service on or after January 1, 1981.

* * * * *

§ 1.47-2 "Disposition" and "cessation".

• ***Caution:*** Reg. § 1.47-2, following, was issued under Code Sec. 47 before amendment by P.L. 101-508 (11/5/90). Provisions similar to, but not identical to, the relative provisions of Code Sec. 47 before such amendment appear in current Code Sec. 50.

Caution: The Treasury has not yet amended Reg § 1.47-2 to reflect changes made by P.L. 100-647, P.L. 99-514, P.L. 99-121, P.L. 98-443, P.L. 98-369, P.L. 97-248, P.L. 97-34, P.L. 91-676.

(a) General rule. *(1) "Disposition".* For purposes of this section and § 1.47-1 and §§ 1.47-3 through 1.47-6, the term "disposition" includes a sale in a sale-and-leaseback transaction, a transfer upon the foreclosure of a security interest and a gift, but such term does not include a mere transfer of title to a creditor upon creation of a security interest. See paragraph (g) of § 1.47-3 for treatment of certain sale-and-leaseback transactions.

(2) "Cessation". (i) A determination of whether section 38 property ceases to be section 38 property with respect to the taxpayer must be made for each taxable year subsequent to the credit year. Thus, in each such taxable year the taxpayer must determine, as if such property were placed in service in such taxable year, whether such property would qualify as section 38 property (within the meaning of § 1.48-1) in the hands of the taxpayer for such taxable year.

(ii) Section 38 property does not cease to be section 38 property with respect to the taxpayer in any taxable year subsequent to the credit year merely because under the taxpayer's depreciation practice no deduction for depreciation with respect to such property is allowable to the taxpayer for the taxable year, provided that the property continues to be used in the taxpayer's trade or business (or in the production of income) and otherwise qualifies as section 38 property with respect to the taxpayer.

(iii) This subparagraph may be illustrated by the following examples:

Example (1). A, an individual who makes his returns on the basis of the calendar year, on January 1, 1962, acquired and placed in service in his trade or business an item of section 38 property with an estimated useful life of eight years. On January 1, 1965, A removes the item of section 38 property from use in his trade or business by converting such item to personal use. Therefore no deduction for depreciation with respect to such item of property is allowable to A for the taxable year 1965. On January 1, 1965, such item of property ceases to be section 38 property with respect to A.

Example (2). On January 1, 1965, A placed in service an item of section 38 property with a basis of $10,000 and an estimated useful life of 4 years. A depreciates such item, which has a salvage value of $2,000 (after taking into account section 167(f)), on the declining balance method at a rate of 50 percent (that is, twice the straight line rate of 25 percent). With respect to such item, A is allowed deductions for depreciation of $5,000 for 1965, $2,500 for 1966, and $500 for 1967. A is not allowed a deduction for depreciation for 1968 although he continues to use such item in his trade or business. Such item does not cease to be section 38 property with respect to A in 1968.

(b) Leased property. *(1) In general.* For purposes of paragraph (a) of § 1.47-1, generally the mere leasing of section 38 property by a lessor who took the basis of such property into account in computing his qualified investment for the credit year shall not be considered to be a disposition. However, in a case where a lease is treated as a sale for income tax purposes such transaction is considered to be a disposition. Leased section 38 property ceases to be section 38 property with respect to the lessor if, in any taxable year subsequent to the credit year, such property would not qualify as section 38 property (as defined in § 1.48-1) in the hands of the lessor, the lessee, or any sublessee. Thus, if, in a taxable year subsequent to the credit year, a lessee uses the property predominantly outside the United States, such property shall be considered to have ceased to be section 38 property with respect to the lessor.

(2) Where lessor elects to treat lessee as purchaser. For purposes of paragraph (a) of § 1.47-1, if, under § 1.48-4, the lessor of new section 38 property made a valid election to treat the lessee as having purchased such property for purposes of the credit allowed by section 38, the following rules apply in determining whether such property is disposed of, or otherwise ceases to be section 38 property with respect to the lessee:

(i) Generally, a mere disposition by the lessor of property subject to a lease shall not be considered to be a disposition by the lessee.

(ii) If the lessor makes a disposition of property subject to a lease to a person who may not, under § 1.48-4, make a valid election to treat the lessee as having purchased such property for purposes of the credit allowed by section 38 (such as a person described in paragraph (a)(5) of § 1.48-4), such property shall be considered to have ceased to be section 38 property with respect to the lessee on the date of such disposition.

(iii) If a lease is terminated and the property is transferred by the lessee to the lessor or to any other person, such transfer shall be considered to be a disposition by the lessee.

(iv) If the lessee actually purchases such property in the credit year or in a taxable year subsequent to the credit year, such purchase shall not be considered to be a disposition.

(v) The property ceases to be section 38 property with respect to the lessee if in any taxable year subsequent to the credit year such property would not qualify as section 38 property (as defined in § 1.48-1) in the hands of the lessor, the lessee, or any sublessee. Thus, for example, if, in a taxable year subsequent to the credit year, a sublessee uses the property predominantly outside the United States, the property ceases to be section 38 property with respect to the lessee.

(c) Reduction in basis of section 38 property. *(1) General rule.* If, in the credit year or in any taxable year subsequent to the credit year, the basis (or cost) of section 38 property is reduced, for example, as a result of a refund of part of the cost of the property, then such section 38 property shall be treated as having ceased to be section 38 property with respect to the taxpayer to the extent of the amount of such reduction in basis (or cost) on the date the refund which results in such reduction in basis (or cost) is received or accrued, except that for purposes of § 1.47-1(a) the actual useful life of the property treated as having ceased to be section 38 property shall be considered to be less than 3 years.

(2) Example. Subparagraph (1) of this paragraph may be illustrated by the following example:

Example. (i) On January 1, 1962, A, a cash basis taxpayer, acquired from X Cooperative an item of section 38 property with a basis of $100 and an estimated useful life of 10 years which he placed in service on such date. The amount of qualified investment with respect to such asset was $100. For the taxable year 1962 A was allowed under section 38 a credit of $7 against his liability for tax. On June 1, 1963, A receives a $10 patronage dividend from X Cooperative with respect to such asset. Under paragraph (c)(2)(i) of § 1.1385-1, the basis of the asset in A's hands is reduced by $10.

(ii) Under subparagraph (1) of this paragraph, on June 1, 1963, the item of section 38 property ceases to be section 38 property with respect to A to the extent of $10 of the original $100 basis.

(d) Retirements. A retirement of section 38 property, including a normal retirement (as defined in paragraph (b) of § 1.167(a)-8, relating to definition of normal and abnormal retirements), whether from a single asset account or a multiple asset account, and an abandonment, are dispositions for purposes of paragraph (a) of § 1.47-1.

(e) Conversion of section 38 property to personal use. *(1)* If, for any taxable year subsequent to the credit year—

(i) A deduction for depreciation is allowable to the taxpayer with respect to only a part of section 38 property because such property is partially devoted to personal use, and

(ii) The part of the property (expressed as a percentage of its total basis (or cost) with respect to which a deduction for depreciation is allowable for such taxable year is less than the part of the property with respect to which a deduction for depreciation was allowable in the credit year, then such property shall be considered as having ceased to be section 38 property with respect to the taxpayer to such extent. Further, property ceases to be section 38 property with respect to the taxpayer to the extent that a deduction for depreciation thereon is disallowed under section 274 (relating to disallowance of certain entertainment, etc., expenses).

(2) Examples. Subparagraph (1) of this paragraph may be illustrated by the following examples:

Example (1). (i) A, a calendar-year taxpayer, acquired and placed in service on January 1, 1962, an automobile with a basis of $2,400 and an estimated useful life of four years. In the taxable year 1962 the automobile was used by A 80 percent of the time in his trade or business and was used 20 percent of the time for personal purposes. Thus, for the taxable year 1962 only 80 percent of the basis of the automobile qualified as section 38 property since a deduction for depreciation was allowable to A only with respect to 80 percent of the basis of the automobile. In the taxable year 1963 the automobile is used by A only 60 percent of the time in his trade or business. Thus, for the taxable year 1963 a deduction for depreciation is allowable to A only with respect to 60 percent of the basis of the automobile.

(ii) Under subparagraph (1) of this paragraph, on January 1, 1963, the automobile ceases to be section 38 property with respect to A to the extent of 20 percent (80 percent minus 60 percent) of the $2,400 basis of the automobile.

Example (2). (i) The facts are the same as in example (1) and in addition for the taxable year 1964 a deduction for depreciation is allowable to A only with respect to 40 percent of the basis of the property.

(ii) Under subparagraph (1) of this paragraph, on January 1, 1964, the automobile ceases to be section 38 property with respect to A to the extent of 20 percent (60 percent minus 40 percent) of the $2,400 basis of the automobile.

T.D. 6931, 10/9/67, amend T.D. 7203, 8/24/72.

§ 1.47-3 Exceptions to the application of § 1.47-1.

• ***Caution:*** Reg. § 1.47-3, following, was issued under Code Sec. 47 before amendment by P.L. 101-508 (11/5/90). Provisions similar to, but not identical to, the relative provisions of Code Sec. 47 before such amendment appear in current Code Sec. 50.

Caution: The Treasury has not yet amended Reg § 1.47-3 to reflect changes made by P.L. 98-369, P.L. 97-248, P.L. 97-34.

(a) In general. Notwithstanding the provisions of § 1.47-2, relating to "disposition" and "cessation," paragraph (a) of § 1.47-1 shall not apply if paragraph (b) of this section (relating to transfers by reason of death), paragraph (c) of this section (relating to property destroyed by casualty), paragraph (d) of this section (relating to reselection of used section 38 property), paragraph (e) of this section (relating to transactions to which section 381(a) applies), paragraph (f) of this section (relating to mere change in form of conducting a trade or business), paragraph (g) of this section (relating to sale-and-lease-back transactions), or paragraph (h) of this section (relating to certain property replaced after Apr. 18, 1969) applies with respect to such disposition or cessation.

(b) Transfers by reason of death. *(1) General rule.* Notwithstanding the provisions of § 1.47-2, relating to "disposition" and "cessation," paragraph (a) of § 1.47-1 shall not apply to a transfer of section 38 property by reason of the death of the taxpayer. Thus, for example, with respect to section 38 property held in joint tenancy, paragraph (a) of § 1.47-1 shall not apply to the transfer of the deceased taxpayer's interest to the surviving joint tenant. If, under § 1.48-4, the lessor of new section 38 property made a valid election to treat the lessee as having purchased such property for purposes of the credit allowed by section 38, paragraph (a) of § 1.47-1 does not apply if, by reason of the death of the lessee, there is a termination of the lease and transfer of the leased property to the lessor, or there is an assignment of the lease and transfer of the leased property to another person. Moreover, paragraph (a) of § 1.47-1 does not apply to the transfer of a partner's interest in a partnership, a beneficiary's interest in an estate or trust, or shares of stock of a shareholder of an electing small business corporation (as defined in section 1371(b)) by reason of the death of such partner, beneficiary, or shareholder. Paragraph (a) of § 1.47-1 applies to a gift by a taxpayer prior to his death even if the value of such gift is included in his gross estate for estate tax purposes (such as, a gift in contemplation of death under section 2035). The effect of this subparagraph is that any section 38 property held by a taxpayer at the time of his death is deemed to have been held by him for its entire estimated useful life.

(2) Examples. Subparagraph (1) of this paragraph may be illustrated by the following examples:

Example (1). (i) A, an individual, acquired and placed in service on January 1, 1962, an item of section 38 property with a basis of $10,000 and an estimated useful life of eight years. On April 28, 1963, A dies and, as a result of A's death, his interest in such item of section 38 property is transferred to a testamentary trust pursuant to A's will, and on February 1, 1967, the trust is terminated and the item of section 38 property is transferred to the beneficiaries of the trust.

(ii) Under subparagraph (1) of this paragraph, paragraph (a) of § 1.47-1 does not apply to the transfer as a result of A's death, of his interest in such item of section 38 property to the testamentary trust. Moreover, paragraph (a) of § 1.47-1 does not apply to the February 1, 1967, transfer of such item of section 38 property by the trust to its beneficiaries.

Example (2). (i) X Corporation, an electing small business corporation (as defined in section 1371(b)) which makes its returns on the basis of a calendar year, acquired and placed in service during 1962 an item of section 38 property. On December 31, 1962, X Corporation had 10 shares of stock outstanding which were owned as follows: A owned eight shares and B owned two shares. On December 31, 1962, 80 percent of the basis of the item of section 38 property was apportioned to A and 20 percent to B. On June 1, 1964 A dies and, as a result of A's death, his eight shares of stock in X Corporation are transferred to his wife. On July 10, 1965, X Corporation sells the item of section 38 property to Y Corporation.

(ii) Under subparagraph (1) of this paragraph, paragraph (a) of § 1.47-1 does not apply to the transfer, as a result of A's death, of his eight shares of stock in X Corporation to his wife. Moreover, with respect to the July 10, 1965, sale paragraph (a) of § 1.47-1 applies only to the 20 percent of the basis of the item of section 38 property which was apportioned to B.

(c) Property destroyed by casualty. *(1) Dispositions after April 18, 1969.* Notwithstanding the provisions of § 1.47-2, relating to "disposition" and "cessation," paragraph (a) of § 1.47-1 shall not apply to property which, after April 18, 1969, and before August 16, 1971, is disposed of or otherwise ceases to be section 38 property with respect to the taxpayer on account of its destruction or damage by fire, storm, shipwreck or other casualty, or by reason of its theft.

(2) Dispositions before April 19, 1969. (i) In the case of property which, before April 19, 1969, is disposed of or otherwise ceases to be section 38 property with respect to the taxpayer on account of its destruction or damage by fire, storm, shipwreck or other casualty, or by reason of its theft, paragraph (a) of § 1.47-1 shall apply except to the extent provided in subdivisions (ii) and (iii) of this subparagraph.

(ii) Paragraph (a) of § 1.47-1 shall not apply if—

(a) Section 38 property is placed in service by the taxpayer to replace (within the meaning of paragraph (h) of § 1.46-3) the destroyed, damaged, or stolen property, and

(b) The basis (or cost) of the section 38 property which is placed in service by the taxpayer to replace the destroyed, damaged, or stolen property is reduced under paragraph (h) of § 1.46-3.

(iii) If property which would be section 38 property but for section 49 is placed in service by the taxpayer to replace the destroyed, damaged, or stolen property, then the provisions of paragraph (h) of this section (other than the requirement that the replacement take place within 6 months after the disposition) shall apply.

(3) Examples. The provisions of subparagraph (2)(ii) of this paragraph may be illustrated by the following examples:

Example (1). (i) A acquired and placed in service on January 1, 1962, machine No. 1 which qualified as section 38 property with a basis of $30,000 and an estimated useful life of 6 years. The amount of qualified investment with respect to such machine was $20,000. For the taxable year 1962 A's credit earned of $1,400 was allowed under section 38 as a credit against its liability for tax. On January 1, 1963, machine No. 1 is completely destroyed by fire. On January 1, 1963, the adjusted basis of machine No. 1 in A's hands is $24,500. A receives $23,000 in insurance proceeds as compensation for the destroyed machine, and on February 15, 1964, A acquires and places in service machine No. 2, which qualifies as section 38 property, with a basis of $41,000 and an estimated useful life of 6 years to replace machine No. 1.

(ii) Under subparagraph (1) of this paragraph, paragraph (a) of § 1.47-1 does not apply with respect to machine No. 1 since machine No. 2 is placed in service to replace machine No. 1 and the $41,000 basis of machine No. 2 is reduced, under paragraph (h) of § 1.46-3, by $23,000. (See example (1) of paragraph (h)(3) of § 1.46-3.)

Example (2). (i) The facts are the same as in example (1) except that A receives only $19,000 in insurance proceeds as compensation for the destroyed machine.

(ii) Although machine No. 2 is placed in service to replace machine No. 1, subparagraph (1) of this paragraph does not apply with respect to machine No. 1 since the basis of machine No. 2 is not reduced under paragraph (h) of §

1.46-3. Paragraph (a) of § 1.47-1 applies with respect to the January 1, 1963, destruction of machine No. 1. The actual useful life of machine No. 1 is 1 year. The recomputed qualified investment with respect to such machine is zero ($30,000 basis multiplied by zero applicable percentage) and A's recomputed credit earned for the taxable year 1962 is zero. The income tax imposed by chapter 1 of the Code on A for the taxable year 1963 is increased by $1,400.

(d) Reselection of used section 38 property. *(1) Reselection.* If—

(i) Used section 38 property (as defined in § 1.48-3) the cost of which was taken into account in computing the taxpayer's qualified investment is disposed of, or otherwise ceases to be section 38 property with respect to the taxpayer, before the close of the estimated useful life which was taken into account in computing such qualified investment, and

(ii) For the taxable year in which the property described in subdivision (i) of this subparagraph was placed in service, the sum of (a) the cost of used section 38 property placed in service by the taxpayer, and *(b)* the cost of used section 38 property apportioned to such taxpayer exceed $50,000,

then such taxpayer may treat the cost of any used section 38 property (regardless of its estimated useful life) which was not originally selected, under paragraph (c)(4) of § 1.48-3, to be taken into account in computing qualified investment for such taxable year (or previously reselected under this subparagraph) as having been selected (in accordance with the principles of paragraph (c)(4)(ii) of § 1.48-3) in place of the cost of the used section 38 property described in subdivision (i) of this subparagraph. Hereinafter such reselected property is referred to as "newly selected used section 38 property". For purposes of this subparagraph, the cost of used section 38 property apportioned to a taxpayer means the sum of the cost of used section 38 property apportioned to him by a trust, estate, or electing small business corporation (as defined in section 1371(b)), and his share of the cost of partnership used section 38 property, with respect to the taxable year of such trust, estate, corporation or partnership ending with or within such taxpayer's taxable year. In the case of a taxpayer to whom paragraph (c)(2) of § 1.48-3 applied for the taxable year in which the property described in subdivision (i) of this subparagraph was placed in service, a $25,000 amount shall be substituted for the $50,000 amount referred to in subdivision (ii)*(b)* of this subparagraph, and in the case of a member of an affiliated group (as defined in subparagraph (6) of § 1.48-3(e)) the amount apportioned to such member under paragraph (e) of § 1.48-3 shall be substituted for such $50,000 amount.

(2) Application of paragraph (a) of § 1.47-1. (i) If a taxpayer treats, under subparagraph (1) of this paragraph, the cost of any used section 38 property which was not originally selected as having been selected in place of the cost of used section 38 property described in subparagraph (1)(i) of this paragraph, then, notwithstanding the provisions of § 1.47-2 (relating to "disposition" and "cessation"), paragraph (a) of § 1.47-1 shall not apply to the property described in subparagraph (1)(i) of this paragraph to the extent of the cost of the newly selected used section 38 property.

(ii) If the cost of the used section 38 property described in subparagraph (1)(i) of this paragraph exceeds the cost of the newly selected used section 38 property, then the property described in subparagraph (1)(i) of this paragraph shall cease to be section 38 property with respect to the taxpayer to the extent of such excess.

(iii) If the newly selected used section 38 property is disposed of, or otherwise ceases to be section 38 property with respect to the taxpayer, before the close of the estimated useful life of the property described in subparagraph (1)(i) of this paragraph, then, unless he reselects other used section 38 property, paragraph (a) of § 1.47-1 shall apply with respect to such newly selected used section 38 property. For purposes of recomputing qualified investment with respect to such newly selected used section 38 property the actual useful life shall be deemed to be the period beginning with the date on which the property described in subparagraph (1)(i) of this paragraph was placed in service by the taxpayer and ending with the date of the disposition or cessation with respect to such newly selected used section 38 property. See paragraph (c) of § 1.47-1, relating to date placed in service and date of disposition or cessation.

(3) Information requirement. (i) If in any taxable year this paragraph applies to a taxpayer, such taxpayer shall attach to his income tax return for such taxable year a statement containing the information required by subdivision (ii) of this subparagraph.

(ii) The statement referred to in subdivision (i) of this subparagraph shall contain the following information:

(a) The taxpayer's name, address and taxpayer account number; and

(b) With respect to the originally selected used section 38 property and the newly selected used section 38 property, the month and year placed in service, cost, and estimated useful life.

(4) Examples. This paragraph may be illustrated by the following examples:

Example (1). (i) X Corporation purchased and placed in service on January 1, 1962, machines No. 1 and 2, which qualified as used section 38 property, each with a cost of $50,000 and an estimated useful life of eight years. The aggregate cost of used section 38 property taken into account by X Corporation in computing its qualified investment for the taxable year 1962 could not exceed $50,000; therefore, under paragraph (c)(4) of § 1.48-3, X selected the $50,000 cost of machine No. 1 to be taken into account in computing its qualified investment for the taxable year 1962. The qualified investment with respect to machine No. 1 was $50,000. For the taxable year 1962 X's credit earned of $3,500 was allowed under section 38 as a credit against its liability for tax. On January 2, 1965, X Corporation sells machine No. 1 to Y Corporation.

(ii) Under subparagraph (1) of this paragraph, X Corporation treats the $50,000 cost of machine No. 2 as having been selected to be taken into account in computing its qualified investment for the taxable year 1962 in place of the $50,000 cost of machine No. 1. Therefore, under subparagraph (2)(i) of this paragraph, paragraph (a) of § 1.47-1 does not apply to the January 2, 1965, disposition of machine No. 1.

Example (2). (i) The facts are the same as in example (1) and in addition X Corporation, on December 2, 1966, sells machine No. 2 to Z Corporation.

(ii) Under subparagraph (2)(iii) of this paragraph, paragraph (a) of § 1.47-1 applies with respect to the December 2, 1966, disposition of machine No. 2. The actual useful life of machine No. 2 is four years and eleven months (that is, the period beginning on January 1, 1962, and ending on December 2, 1966). The recomputed qualified investment with respect to machine No. 2 is $16,667 ($50,000 cost multiplied by 33⅓ percent applicable percentage) and X Corporation's recomputed credit earned for the taxable year 1962 is

$1,167. The income tax imposed by chapter 1 of the Code on X Corporation for the taxable year 1966 is increased by the $2,333 decrease in its credit earned for the taxable year 1962 (that is, $3,500 original credit earned minus $1,167 recomputed credit earned).

Example (3). (i) The facts are the same as in example (1) except that machine No. 2 had a cost of $30,000.

(ii) Under subparagraph (1) of this paragraph, X Corporation treats the $30,000 cost of machine No. 2 as having been selected to be taken into account in computing its qualified investment for the taxable year 1962 in place of the $50,000 cost of machine No. 1. Therefore, under subparagraph (2)(i) of this paragraph, paragraph (a) of § 1.47-1 does not apply to the January 2, 1965, disposition of machine No. 1 to the extent of $30,000 of the $50,000 cost of machine No. 1. However, under subparagraph (2)(ii) of this paragraph, paragraph (a) of § 1.47-1 applies to the January 2, 1965, disposition of machine No. 1 to the extent of $20,000 (that is, $50,000 cost of machine No. 1 minus $30,000 cost of machine No. 2). The actual useful life of such $20,000 portion of machine No. 1 is three years (that is, the period beginning on January 1, 1962, and ending on January 2, 1965). The recomputed qualified investment with respect to the $20,000 portion of the cost of machine No. 1 is zero ($20,000 portion of the cost multiplied by zero applicable percentage) and X Corporation's recomputed credit earned for the taxable year 1962 is $2,100 (7 percent of $30,000). The income tax imposed by chapter 1 of the Code on X Corporation for the taxable year 1965 is increased by the $1,400 decrease in its credit earned for the taxable year 1962 (that is, $3,500 original credit earned minus $2,100 recomputed credit earned).

(e) Transactions to which section 381(a) applies. *(1) General rule.* Notwithstanding the provisions of § 1.47-2, relating to "disposition" and "cessation", paragraph (a) of § 1.47-1 shall not apply to a disposition of section 38 property in a transaction to which section 381(a) (relating to carryovers in certain corporate acquisitions) applies. If the section 38 property described in the preceding sentence is disposed of, or otherwise ceases to be section 38 property with respect to the acquiring corporation, before the close of the estimated useful life which was taken into account in computing the transferor corporation's qualified investment, then paragraph (a) of § 1.47-1 shall apply to the acquiring corporation with respect to such section 38 property. For purposes of recomputing qualified investment with respect to such property its actual useful life shall be the period beginning with the date on which it was placed in service by the transferor corporation and ending with the date of the disposition by, or cessation with respect to, the acquiring corporation.

(2) Examples. This paragraph may be illustrated by the following examples:

Example (1). (i) X Corporation, a wholly owned subsidiary of Y Corporation, acquired and placed in service on January 1, 1962, an item of section 38 property with a basis of $12,000 and an estimated useful life of eight years. Both X and Y make their returns on the basis of a calendar year. The qualified investment with respect to such item was $12,000. For the taxable year 1962 X Corporation's credit earned of $840 was allowed under section 38 as a credit against its liability for tax. On January 15, 1967, X Corporation is liquidated under section 332 and all of its properties, including the item of section 38 property, are transferred to Y Corporation. The bases of the properties in the hands of Y Corporation are determined under section 334(b)(1).

(ii) Under subparagraph (1) of this paragraph, paragraph (a) of § 1.47-1 does not apply to the January 15, 1967, transfer to Y Corporation.

Example (2). (i) The facts are the same as in example (1) and in addition on February 2, 1968, Y Corporation sells the item of section 38 property to Z Corporation.

(ii) Under subparagraph (1) of this paragraph, paragraph (a) of § 1.47-1 does not apply to the January 15, 1967, transfer to Y Corporation. However, paragraph (a) of § 1.47 applies to the February 2, 1968, sale of the property by Y Corporation. The actual useful life of the property is six years and one month (that is, the period beginning on January 1, 1962, and ending on February 2, 1968).

(f) Mere change in form of conducting a trade or business. *(1) General rule.* (i) Notwithstanding the provisions of § 1.47-2, relating to "disposition" and "cessation", paragraph (a) of § 1.47-1 shall not apply to section 38 property which is disposed of, or otherwise ceases to be section 38 property with respect to the taxpayer, before the close of the estimated useful life which was taken into account in computing the taxpayer's qualified investment by reason of a mere change in the form of conducting the trade or business in which such section 38 property is used provided that the conditions set forth in subdivision (ii) of this subparagraph are satisfied.

(ii) The conditions referred to in subdivision (i) of this subparagraph are as follows:

(a) The section 38 property described in subdivision (i) of this subparagraph is retained as section 38 property in the same trade or business,

(b) The transferor (or in a case where the transferor is a partnership, estate, trust, or electing small business corporation, the partner, beneficiary, or shareholder) of such section 38 property retains a substantial interest in such trade or business,

(c) Substantially all the assets (whether or not section 38 property) necessary to operate such trade or business are transferred to the transferee to whom such section 38 property is transferred, and

(d) The basis of such section 38 property in the hands of the transferee is determined in whole or in part by reference to the basis of section 38 property in the hands of the transferor. This subparagraph shall not apply to the transfer of section 38 property if paragraph (e) of this section, relating to transactions to which section 381 applies, applies with respect to such transfer.

(2) Substantial interest. For purposes of this paragraph, a transferor (or in a case where the transferor is a partnership, estate, trust, or electing small business corporation, the partner, beneficiary, or shareholder) shall be considered as having retained a substantial interest in the trade or business only if, after the change in form, his interest in such trade or business—

(i) Is substantial in relation to the total interest of all persons, or

(ii) Is equal to or greater than his interest prior to the change in form.

Thus, where a taxpayer owns a 5-percent interest in a partnership, and, after the incorporation of that partnership, the taxpayer retains at least a 5-percent interest in the corporation, the taxpayer will be considered as having retained a substantial interest in the trade or business as of the date of the change in form.

(3) Property held for the production of income. Subparagraph (1)(i) of this paragraph applies to section 38 property held for the production of income (within the meaning of section 167(a)(2)) as well as to section 38 property used in a trade or business.

(4) Leased property. In a case where a lessor of a new section 38 property made a valid election, under § 1.48-4, to treat the lessee as having purchased such property for purposes of the credit allowed by section 38, in determining whether subparagraph (1)(i) of this paragraph applies to an assignment of the lease and transfer of possession of such property, the condition contained in subparagraph (1)(ii)(d) of this paragraph is not applicable.

(5) Disposition or cessation. (i) If section 38 property described in subparagraph (1)(i) of this paragraph is disposed of by the transferee, or otherwise ceases to be section 38 property with respect to the transferee, before the close of the estimated useful life which was taken into account in computing the qualified investment of the transferor (or in a case where the transferor is a partnership, estate, trust, or electing small business corporation, the qualified investment of the partners, beneficiaries, or shareholders) then under paragraph (a) of § 1.47-1 such property ceases to be section 38 property with respect to the transferor (or such partners, beneficiaries, or shareholders), and a recapture determination shall be made with respect to such property. For purposes of recomputing qualified investment with respect to such property, the actual useful life shall be the period beginning with the date on which it was placed in service by the transferor and ending with the date of the disposition by, or cessation with respect to, the transferee.

(ii) If in any taxable year the transferor (or in a case where the transferor is a partnership, estate, trust, or electing small business corporation, the partner, beneficiary, or shareholder) of the section 38 property described in subparagraph (1)(i) of this paragraph does not retain a substantial interest in the trade or business directly or indirectly (through ownership in other entities provided that such other entities' bases in such interest are determined in whole or in part by reference to the basis of such interest in the hands of the transferor) then, under paragraph (a) of § 1.47-1, such property ceases to be section 38 property with respect to the transferor and he (or the partner, beneficiary, or shareholder) shall make a recapture determination. For purposes of recomputing qualified investment with respect to property described in this subdivision, its actual useful life shall be the period beginning with the date on which it was placed in service by the transferor and ending with the first date on which the transferor (or the partner, beneficiary, or shareholder) does not retain a substantial interest in the trade or business. Any taxpayer who seeks to establish his interest in a trade or business under the rule of this subdivision shall maintain adequate records to demonstrate his indirect interest in such trade or business after any such transfer or transfers.

(iii) In making a recapture determination under this subparagraph there shall be taken into account any prior recapture determinations with respect to the transferor in connection with the same property.

(iv) Notwithstanding subparagraph (1) of this paragraph and subdivision (ii) of this subparagraph in the case of a mere change in the form of a trade or business, if the interest of a taxpayer in the trade or business is reduced but such taxpayer has retained a substantial interest in such trade or business, paragraph (a)(2) of § 1.47-4 (relating to electing small business corporations), paragraph (a)(2) of § 1.47-5 (relating to estates or trusts) or paragraph (a)(2) of § 1.47-6 (relating to partnerships) shall apply, as the case may be.

(6) Examples. This paragraph may be illustrated by the following examples in each of which it is assumed that the transfer satisfies the conditions of subparagraph (1)(ii) (a), (c), and (d) of this paragraph.

Example (1). (i) On January 1, 1962, A, an individual, acquired and placed in service in his sole proprietorship an item of section 38 property with a basis of $12,000 and an estimated useful life of eight years. The qualified investment with respect to such item was $12,000. For the taxable year 1962 A's credit earned of $840 was allowed under section 38 as a credit against his liability for tax. On March 15, 1963, A transfer all of the assets used in his sole proprietorship to X Corporation, a newly formed corporation, in exchange for 45 percent of the stock of X Corporation.

(ii) Under subparagraph (1)(i) of this paragraph, paragraph (a) of § 1.47-1 does not apply to the March 15, 1963, transfer to X Corporation.

Example (2). (i) The facts are the same as in example (1) and in addition on February 2, 1964, X Corporation sells the item of section 38 property to Y Corporation.

(ii) Under subparagraph (1)(i) of this paragraph, paragraph (a) of § 1.47-1 does not apply to the March 15, 1963, transfer to X Corporation. However, under subparagraph (5)(i) of this paragraph, paragraph (a) of § 1.47-1 applies to the February 2, 1964, sale of the item of section 38 property by X Corporation to Y Corporation. The actual useful life of the property is two years and one month (that is, the period beginning on January 1, 1962, and ending on February 2, 1964). The recomputed qualified investment with respect to such property is zero ($12,000 basis multiplied by zero applicable percentage) and A's recomputed credit earned for the taxable year 1962 is zero. The income tax imposed by chapter 1 of the Code on A for 1964 is increased by the $840 decrease in his credit earned for the taxable year 1962 (that is, $840 credit earned minus zero recomputed credit earned).

Example (3). (i) On January 1, 1962, partnership ABC, which makes its returns on the basis of a calendar year, acquired and placed in service on item of section 38 property with a basis of $20,000 and an estimated useful life of eight years. Partnership ABC has 10 partners who make their returns on the basis of a calendar year and share partnership profits equally. Each partner's share of the basis of such item of section 38 property is 10 percent, that is, $2,000. On March 15, 1963, partnership ABC transfers all of the assets used in its trade or business to the X Corporation, a newly formed corporation, in exchange for all of the stock of X Corporation and immediately thereafter transfers 10 percent of such stock to each of the 10 partners.

(ii) Under subparagraph (1)(i) of this paragraph, paragraph (a) of § 1.47-1 does not apply to the March 15, 1963 transfer by the ABC Partnership to X Corporation.

Example (4). (i) The facts are the same as in example (3) except that partnership ABC transfers 10 percent of the stock in X Corporation to each of 8 partners, 20 percent to partner A, and cash to partner B.

(ii) Under subparagraph (1)(i) of this paragraph, with respect to all of the partners (including partner A) except partner B, paragraph (a) of § 1.47-1 does not apply to the March 15, 1963, transfer by the ABC Partnership to X Corporation. Paragraph (a) of § 1.47-1 applies with respect to partner B's $2,000 share of the item of section 38 property. See paragraph (a)(1) of § 1.47-6.

Example (5). (i) X Corporation operates a manufacturing business and a separate personal service business. On January 1, 1962, X acquired and placed in service a truck, which qualified as section 38 property, in its manufacturing business. The truck had a basis of $10,000 and an estimated useful life of 8 years. On February 10, 1965, X transfers all the assets used in its manufacturing business to Partnership XY in exchange for a 50-percent interest in such partnership.

(ii) Under subparagraph (1)(i) of this paragraph, paragraph (a) of § 1.47-1 does not apply to the February 10, 1965, transfer to Partnership XY.

(g) Sale-and-leaseback transactions. *(1) In general.* Notwithstanding the provisions of § 1.47-2, relating to "disposition" and "cessation", paragraph (a) of § 1.47-1 shall not apply where section 38 property is disposed of and as part of the same transaction is leased back to the vendor even though gain or loss is recognized to the vendor-lessee and the property ceases to be subject to depreciation in his hands. If paragraph (a) of § 1.47-1 applies with respect to such property subsequent to the transaction, the actual useful life shall begin with the date on which such property was first placed in service by the vendor-lessee as owner.

(2) Special rule for progress expenditure property. The sale and leaseback (or agreement or contract to leaseback) of progress expenditure property (including any contract rights to the property), in general, will be treated as a cessation described in section 47(a)(3)(A) with respect to the seller-lessee. However, a sale and leaseback (or agreement or contract to leaseback) will not be treated as a cessation to the extent qualified investment passed through to the lessee under section 48(d) in the year the property is placed in service equals or exceeds qualified progress expenditures for the property taken into account by the lessee. If a sale-leaseback transaction is treated as a cessation, qualified investment must be reduced and the credit recomputed, beginning with the most recent credit year (*i.e.,* the most recent year property is taken into account in computing qualified investment under § 1.46-3 or 1.46-5). The amount of the reduction is the amount, if any, by which qualified progress expenditures taken into account by the lessee in all prior years exceeds qualified investment passed through to the lessee under section 48(d). This paragraph (g)(2) does not apply to any progress expenditure property that has been placed in service by a vendor-lessee (as described in paragraph (g)(1) of this section) prior to a sale-leaseback of that property in a transaction described in paragraph (g)(1) of this section.

(h) Certain property replaced after April 18, 1969. *(1) In general.* (i) If section 38 property is disposed of and property which is, for purposes of section 1033 and the regulations thereunder, similar or related in service or use to the property disposed of and which would be section 38 property but for the application of section 49 is placed in service to replace the property disposed of, the increase in income tax and adjustment of investment credit carryovers and carrybacks resulting from the recomputation under paragraph (a) of § 1.47-1 shall be reduced (but not below zero) by the credit that would be allowed for the qualified investment of the replacement property (determined as if such property were section 38 property). The preceding sentence shall not apply unless the replacement takes place within 6 months after the disposition. If property otherwise qualifies as replacement property, it is immaterial that it is placed in service (for example, to undergo testing) before the replaced property is disposed of. The assignment by the taxpayer in his return of an estimated useful life to the replacement property in computing its qualified investment will be considered a representation by the taxpayer that he expects to retain the replacement property for its entire estimated useful life. If such property is disposed of before the end of such life, then the circumstances surrounding the replacement will be examined to determine whether the taxpayer's representation was in good faith and, if appropriate, the qualified investment of the replacement property will be recomputed for the year of replacement using the actual useful life of such property.

(ii) The provisions of subdivision (i) of this subparagraph may be illustrated by the following example:

Example. On January 1, 1967, A, a calendar year taxpayer, acquired and placed in service a new machine with a basis of $100 and an estimated useful life of 8 years. A's qualified investment was $100 and his credit earned was $7, which was allowed as a credit against tax for 1967. On January 15, 1971, A disposed of the machine and replaced it with a similar new machine costing $75 and having an estimated useful life of 8 years. The new machine would be section 38 property but for section 49. Since the actual useful life of the original machine was at least 4 but less than 6 years, the recomputed qualified investment of the machine is $33.33 (33⅓ percent of $100) and under paragraph (a) of § 1.47-1 the amount of recapture tax would be $4.67 ($7, the original credit earned, minus $2.33, the recomputed credit earned). However, under the provisions of this paragraph, the recapture tax is reduced (but not below zero) by the credit that would be allowed for the replacement property (determined as if such property were section 38 property). Under these facts the recapture tax is zero ($4.67, the recapture tax with respect to the original machine, minus $5.25, the credit that would be allowed on the new machine).

(2) Leased property. Property disposed of may be replaced with property leased from another, provided (i) an election with respect to the newly leased property could be made under section 48(d) but for section 49, and (ii) lessee obtains the lessor's written statement that he will not claim such property as replacement property under this paragraph. The statement of the lessor shall contain the information specified in subdivisions (i) through (vii) of § 1.48-4(f)(1) and the statement (or a copy thereof) shall be retained in the records of the lessor and the lessee for a period of at least 3 years after the property is transferred to the lessee.

T.D. 6931, 10/9/67, amend T.D. 7126, 6/9/71, T.D. 7203, 8/24/72, T.D. 8183, 3/1/88.

§ 1.47-4 Electing small business corporation.

Caution: The Treasury has not yet amended Reg § 1.47-4 to reflect changes made by P.L. 98-369, P.L. 97-354, P.L. 97-248, P.L. 97-34.

(a) In general. *(1) Disposition or cessation in hands of corporation.* If an electing small business corporation (as defined in section 1371(b)) or a former electing small business corporation disposes of any section 38 property (or if any section 38 property otherwise ceases to be section 38 property in the hands of the corporation) before the close of the estimated useful life which was taken into account in computing qualified investment with respect to such property, a recapture determination shall be made with respect to each shareholder who is treated, under § 1.48-5, as a taxpayer with respect to such property. Each such recapture determination shall be made with respect to the pro rata share of the basis (or cost) of such property taken into account by such shareholder in computing his qualified investment. For purposes of each such recapture determination the actual useful life of such property shall be the period beginning with the date on which it was placed in service by the electing small business corporation and ending with the date of the disposition or cessation. In making a recapture determination under this subparagraph there shall be taken into account any prior recapture determinations made with respect to the shareholder in connection with the same property. For definition of "recapture determination" see paragraph (a)(1) of § 1.47-1.

(2) Disposition of shareholder's interest. (i) If—

(a) The basis (or cost) of section 38 property is apportioned, under § 1.48-5, to a shareholder of an electing small business corporation who takes such basis (or cost) into account in computing his qualified investment, and

(b) After the end of the shareholder's taxable year in which such apportionment was taken into account and before the close of the estimated useful life of the property, such shareholder's proportionate stock interest in such corporation is reduced (for example, by a sale or redemption, or by the issuance of additional shares) below the percentage specified in subdivision (ii) of this subparagraph,

then, on the date of such reduction such section 38 property ceases to be section 38 property with respect to such shareholder to the extent of the actual reduction in such shareholder's proportionate stock interest. (For example, if $100 of the basis of section 38 property was apportioned to a shareholder and if his proportionate stock interest is reduced from 60 percent to 30 percent (that is, 50 percent of his original interest), then such property shall be treated as having ceased to be section 38 property to the extent of $50.) Accordingly, a recapture determination shall be made with respect to such shareholder. For purposes of such recapture determination the actual useful life of such property shall be the period beginning with the date on which it was placed in service by the electing small business corporation and ending with the date on which it is treated as having ceased to be section 38 property with respect to the shareholder. In making a recapture determination under this subparagraph there shall be taken into account any prior recapture determination made with respect to the shareholder in connection with the same property.

(ii) The percentage referred to in subdivision (i)(b) of this subparagraph is 66⅔ percent of the shareholder's proportionate stock interest in the corporation on the date of the apportionment under § 1.48-5. However, once property has been treated under this subparagraph as having ceased to be section 38 property to any extent the percentage referred to shall be 33⅓ percent of the shareholder's proportionate stock interest in the corporation on the date of apportionment under § 1.48-5.

(iii) In determining a shareholder's proportionate stock interest in a former electing small business corporation for purposes of this subparagraph, the shareholder shall be considered to own stock in such corporation which he owns directly or indirectly (through ownership in other entities provided such other entities' bases in such stock are determined in whole or in part by reference to the basis of such stock in the hands of the transferor. For example, if A, who owns all of the 100 shares of the outstanding stock of corporation X, a corporation which was formerly an electing small business corporation, transfers on November 1, 1966, 70 shares of X stock to corporation Y in exchange for 90 percent of the stock of Y in a transaction to which section 351 applies, then, for purposes of subdivision (i) of this subparagraph, A shall be considered to own 93 percent of the stock of X, 30 percent directly and 63 percent indirectly (i.e., 90 percent of 70). Any taxpayer who seeks to establish his interest in the stock of a former electing small business corporation under the rule of this subdivision shall maintain adequate records to demonstrate his indirect interest in the corporation after any such transfer or transfers.

(b) Election of a small business corporation under section 1372. *(1) General rule.* If a corporation makes a valid election under section 1372 to be an electing small business corporation (as defined in section 1371(b)), then on the last day of the taxable year immediately preceding the first taxable year for which such election is effective, any section 38 property the basis (or cost) of which was taken into account in computing the corporation's qualified investment in taxable years prior to the first taxable year for which the election is effective (and which has not been disposed of or otherwise ceased to be section 38 property with respect to the corporation prior to such last day) shall be considered as having ceased to be section 38 property with respect to such corporation and § 1.47-1 shall apply. However, if the corporation and each of the persons who are shareholders of the corporation on the first day of the first taxable year for which the election under section 1372 is to be effective, or on the date of such election, whichever is later, execute the agreement specified in subparagraph (2) of this paragraph, § 1.47-1 shall not apply to any such section 38 property by reason of the election by the corporation under section 1372.

(2) Agreement of shareholders and corporation. (i) The agreement referred to in subparagraph (1) of this paragraph shall be signed by the shareholders and the corporation, and shall recite that, in the event the section 38 property described in subparagraph (1) of this paragraph is later disposed of by, or ceases to be section 38 property with respect to, the corporation during a taxable year of the corporation for which the election under section 1372 is effective, each such signer agrees *(a)* to notify the district director of such disposition or cessation, and *(b)* to be jointly and severally liable to pay to the district director an amount equal to the increase in tax provided by section 47. The amount of such increase shall be determined as if such property had ceased to be section 38 property as of the last day of the taxable year immediately preceding the first taxable year for which the election under section 1372 is effective, except that the actual useful life (within the meaning of paragraph (a) of § 1.47-1) of the property shall be considered to have ended on the date of the actual disposition by, or cessation in the hands of, the electing small business corporation.

(ii) The agreement shall set forth the name, address, and taxpayer account number of each party and the internal revenue district in which each such party files his or its income tax return for the taxable year which includes the last day of the corporation's taxable year immediately preceding the first taxable year for which the election under section 1372 is effective. The agreement may be signed on behalf of the corporation by any person who is duly authorized. The agreement shall be filed with the district director with whom the corporation files its income tax return for its taxable year immediately preceding the first taxable year for which the election under section 1372 is effective and shall be filed on or before the due date (including extensions of time) of such return. However, if the due date (including extensions of time) of such income tax return is on or before September 1, 1967, the agreement may be filed on or before December 31, 1967. For purposes of the two preceding sentences, the district director may, if good cause is shown, permit the agreement to be filed on a later date.

(c) Examples. This section may be illustrated by the following examples in each of which it is assumed that X Corporation, an electing small business corporation which makes its returns on the basis of the calendar year, acquired and placed in service on June 1, 1962, three items of section 38 property. The basis and estimated useful life of each item of section 38 property are as follows:

Asset No.	Basis	Estimated useful life
		Years
1	$30,000	4
2	30,000	6
3	30,000	8

On December 31, 1962, X Corporation had 20 shares of stock outstanding which were owned equally by A and B who make their returns on the basis of a calendar year. Under § 1.48-5, the total bases of section 38 properties was apportioned to the shareholders of X Corporation as follows:

	Useful life category		
	4 to 6 years	6 to 8 years	8 years or more
Total bases	$20,000	$30,000	$30,000
Shareholder A (10/20)	15,000	15,000	15,000
Shareholder B (10/20)	15,000	15,000	15,000

Assuming that during 1962 shareholders A and B did not place in service any section 38 property and that they did not own any interests in other electing small business corporations, partnerships, estates, or trusts, the qualified investment of each shareholder is $30,000, computed as follows:

Basis	Applicable percentage	Qualified investment
$15,000	33⅓	$ 5,000
$15,000	66⅔	10,000
$15,000	100	15,000
		30,000

For the taxable year 1962, each shareholder's credit earned of $2,100 (7 percent of $30,000) was allowed under section 38 as a credit against his liability for tax.

Example (1). (i) On December 2, 1965, X Corporation sells asset No. 3 to Y Corporation.

(ii) The actual useful life of asset No. 3 is three years and six months. The recomputed qualified investment with respect to each shareholder's share of the basis of asset No. 3 is zero ($15,000 share of basis multiplied by zero applicable percentage) and for the taxable year 1962 each shareholder's recomputed credit earned is $1,050 (7 percent of $15,000). The income tax imposed by chapter 1 of the Code on each of the shareholders for the taxable year 1965 is increased by the $1,050 decrease in his credit earned for the taxable year 1962 (that is, $2,100 original credit earned minus $1,050 recomputed credit earned).

Example (2). (i) On December 3, 1964, shareholder A sells 5 of his 10 shares of stock in X Corporation to C, and on December 3, 1965, A sells his remaining 5 shares of stock to D. In addition, on January 2, 1966, X Corporation sells asset No. 3 to Y Corporation.

(ii) Under paragraph (a)(2) of this section, on December 3, 1964, 50 percent of the share of the basis of each of the three items of section 38 property ceases to be section 38 property with respect to shareholder A since immediately after the December 3, 1964, sale A's proportionated stock interest in X Corporation is reduced to 50 percent of the proportionate stock interest in X Corporation which he held on December 31, 1962. The actual useful life of the share of the bases of the section 38 properties which cease to be section 38 property with respect to A is two years and six months (that is, the period beginning with June 1, 1962, and ending with December 3, 1964). A's recomputed qualified investment with respect to such properties is $15,000, computed as follows:

Basis	Applicable percentage	Recomputed qualified investment
$7,500	33⅓	$ 2,500
$7,500	66⅔	5,000
$7,500	100	7,500
		$15,000

For the taxable year 1962 shareholder A's recomputed credit earned is $1,050 (7 percent of $15,000). The income tax imposed by chapter 1 of the Code on shareholder A for the taxable year 1964 is increased by the $1,050 decrease in his credit earned for the taxable year 1962 (that is, $2,100 original credit earned minus $1,050 recomputed credit earned).

(iii) Under paragraph (a)(2) of this section, on December 3, 1965, the remaining 50 percent of the share of the basis of each of the three items of section 38 property ceases to be section 38 property with respect to shareholder A since immediately after the December 3, 1965, sale A's proportionate stock interest in X Corporation is reduced to zero. The actual useful life of the share of the bases of the section 38 properties which cease to be section 38 property with respect to A is three years and six months (that is, the period beginning with June 1, 1962, and ending with December 3, 1965). A's recomputed qualified investment with respect to such properties is zero. For the taxable year 1962 shareholder A's recomputed credit earned is zero. The income tax imposed by chapter 1 of the Code on shareholder A for the taxable year 1965 is increased by $1,050 (that is, $2,100 ($2,100 original credit earned minus zero recomputed credit earned) reduced by the $1,050 increase in tax for 1964).

(iv) The actual useful life of asset No. 3 which was sold on January 2, 1966, is three years and seven months. The recomputed qualified investment with respect to B's share of the basis of asset No. 3 is zero ($15,000 share of basis multiplied by zero applicable percentage) and for the taxable year 1962, B's recomputed credit earned is $1,050 (7 percent of $15,000). The income tax imposed by chapter 1 of the Code on shareholder B for the taxable year 1966 is increased by the $1,050 decrease in his credit earned for the taxable year 1962 ($2,100 original credit earned minus $1,050 recomputed credit earned). The sale of asset No. 3 on January 2, 1966, by X Corporation has no effect on A.

(d) Termination or revocation of an election under section 1372. Section 38 property shall not be considered to be disposed of or to have ceased to be section 38 property solely by reason of a termination or revocation of a corporation's election under section 1372.

T.D. 6931, 10/9/67.

§ 1.47-5 Estates and trusts.

• ***Caution:*** Reg. § 1.47-5, following, was issued under Code Sec. 47 before amendment by P.L. 101-508 (11/5/90). Provisions similar to, but not identical to, the relative provisions of Code Sec. 47 before such amendment appear in current Code Sec. 50.

Caution: The Treasury has not yet amended Reg § 1.47-5 to reflect changes made by P.L. 98-369, P.L. 97-354, P.L. 97-248, P.L. 97-34.

(a) In general. *(1) Disposition or cessation in hands of estate or trust.* If an estate or trust disposes of any section 38 property (or if any section 38 property otherwise ceases to be section 38 property in the hands of the estate or trust) before the close of the estimated useful life which was taken into account in computing qualified investment with respect to such property, a recapture determination shall be made with respect to the estate or trust, and each beneficiary who is treated, under § 1.48-6, as a taxpayer with respect to such property. Each such recapture determination shall be made with respect to the share of the basis (or cost) of such property taken into account by such estate or trust and such beneficiary in computing its or his qualified investment. For purposes of each such recapture determination the actual useful life of such property shall be the period beginning with the date on which it was placed in service by the estate or trust and ending with the date of the disposition or cessation. In making a recapture determination under this subparagraph with respect to a taxpayer there shall be taken into account any prior recapture determinations made with respect to such taxpayer in connection with the same property. For definition of "recapture determination" see paragraph (a)(1) of § 1.47-1.

(2) Disposition of interest. (i) If—

(a) The basis (or cost) of section 38 property is apportioned, under § 1.48-6, to an estate or trust which, or to a beneficiary of an estate or trust who, takes such basis (or cost) into account in computing his qualified investment, and

(b) After the date on which such section 38 property was placed in service by the estate or trust and before the close of the estimated useful life of the property, such estate's trust's, or such beneficiary's proportionate interest in the income of the estate or trust is reduced (for example, by a sale, or by the terms of the estate or trust instrument) below the percentage specified in subdivision (ii) of this subparagraph,

then, on the date of such reduction, such section 38 property ceases to be section 38 property with respect to such estate, trust, or beneficiary to the extent of the actual reduction in such estate's, trust's, or beneficiary's proportionate interest in the income of the estate or trust. (For example, if $100 of the basis of section 38 property was apportioned to a beneficiary and if his proportionate interest in the income of the estate or trust is reduced from 60 percent to 30 percent (that is, 50 percent of his original interest), then such property shall be treated as having ceased to be section 38 property to the extent of $50). Accordingly, a recapture determination shall be made with respect to such estate, trust, or beneficiary. For purposes of such recapture determination the actual useful life of such property shall be the period beginning with the date on which it was placed in service by the estate or trust and ending with the date on which it is treated as having ceased to be section 38 property with respect to the estate, trust, or beneficiary. In making a recapture determination under this subparagraph there shall be taken into account any prior recapture determination made with respect to the estate, trust, or beneficiary in connection with the same property.

(ii) The percentage referred to in subdivision (i) (b) of this subparagraph is 66⅔ percent of the estate's, trust's, or beneficiary's proportionate interest in the income of the estate or trust for the taxable year of the apportionment under § 1.48-6. However, once property has been treated under this subparagraph as having ceased to be section 38 property to any extent the percentage referred to shall be 33⅓ percent of the estate's, trust's, or beneficiary's proportionate interest in the income of the estate or trust for the taxable year of the apportionment under § 1.48-6.

(iii) In determining a beneficiary's proportionate interest in the income of an estate or trust for purposes of this subparagraph, the beneficiary shall be considered to own any interest in such an estate or trust which he owns directly or indirectly (through ownership in other entities provided such other entities' bases in such interest are determined in whole or in part by reference to the basis of such interest in the hands of the beneficiary). For example, if A, whose proportionate interest in the income of trust X is 30 percent, transfers all of such interest to corporation Y in exchange for all of the stock of Y in a transaction to which section 351 applies, then, for purposes of subdivision (i) of this subparagraph, A shall be considered to own a 30-percent interest in trust X. Any taxpayer who seeks to establish his interest in an estate or trust under the rule of this subdivision shall maintain adequate records to demonstrate his indirect interest in the estate or trust after any such transfer or transfers.

(b) Examples. Paragraph (a) of this section may be illustrated by the following examples in each of which it is assumed that XYZ Trust, which makes its returns on the basis of the calendar year, acquired and placed in service on June 1, 1962, three items of section 38 property. The basis and estimated useful life of each item of section 38 property are as follows:

Asset No.	Basis	Estimated useful life
1	$30,000	4
2	30,000	6
3	30,000	8

For the taxable year 1962 the income of XYZ Trust is $20,000, which is allocable equally to XYZ Trust and beneficiary A. Beneficiary A makes his returns on the basis of a calendar year. Under § 1.48-6, the total bases of the section 38 properties was apportioned to XYZ Trust and beneficiary A as follows:

		Useful life category		
		4 to 6 years	6 to 8 years	8 years or more
Total bases		$30,000	$30,000	$30,000
	($10,000)	15,000	15,000	15,000
XYZ Trust	($20,000)			
Beneficiary A	($10,000)	15,000	15,000	15,000
	($20,000)			

Assuming that during 1962 beneficiary A did not place in service any section 38 property and that he did not own any interests in other estates, trusts, electing small business corporations, or partnerships, the qualified investment of XYZ Trust and of beneficiary A is $30,000 each, computed as follows:

Basis	Applicable percentage	Qualified investment
$15,000	33⅓	$ 5,000
$15,000	66⅔	10,000
$15,000	100	15,000
		$30,000

For the taxable year 1962, XYZ Trust and beneficiary A each had a credit earned of $2,100 (7 percent of $30,000). Each such credit earned was allowed under section 38 as a credit against the liability for tax.

Example (1). (i) On December 2, 1965, XYZ Trust sells asset No. 3 to X Corporation.

(ii) The actual useful life of asset No. 3 is three years and six months. The recomputed qualified investment with respect to XYZ Trust's and beneficiary A's share of the basis of asset No. 3 is zero ($15,000 share of basis multiplied by zero applicable percentage) and for the taxable year 1962, XYZ Trust's and beneficiary A's recomputed credit earned is $1,050 (7 percent of $15,000). The income tax imposed by chapter 1 of the Code on XYZ Trust and on beneficiary A for the taxable year 1965 is increased by the $1,050 decrease in his credit earned for the taxable year 1962 (that is, $2,100 original credit earned minus $1,050 recomputed credit earned).

Example (2). (i) On December 3, 1964, beneficiary A sells 50 percent of his interest in the income of XYZ Trust to B, and on December 3, 1965, A sells his remaining 50 percent interest to C. In addition, on January 2, 1966, XYZ Trust sells asset No. 3 to Y Corporation.

(ii) Under paragraph (a)(2) of this section, on December 3, 1964, 50 percent of the basis of each of the three items of section 38 property ceases to be section 38 property with respect to beneficiary A since immediately after the December 3, 1964 sale A's proportionate interest in the income of XYZ Trust is reduced to 50 percent of his proportionate interest in the income of XYZ Trust for the taxable year 1962. The actual useful life of the share of the bases of the section 38 properties which cease to be section 38 property with respect to A is two years and six months (that is, the period beginning with June 1, 1962, and ending with December 3, 1964). Beneficiary A's recomputed qualified investment with respect to such properties is $15,000, computed as follows:

Basis	Applicable percentage	Qualified investment
$7,500	33⅓	$ 2,500
$7,500	66⅔	5,000
$7,500	100	7,500
		$15,000

For the taxable year 1962 beneficiary A's recomputed credit earned is $1,050 (7 percent of $15,000). The income tax imposed by chapter 1 of the Code on beneficiary A for the taxable year 1964 is increased by the $1,050 decrease in his credit earned for the taxable year 1962 (that is, $2,100 original credit earned minus $1,050 recomputed credit earned).

(iii) Under paragraph (a)(2) of this section, on December 3, 1965, the remaining 50 percent of the share of the basis of each of the three items of section 38 property ceases to be section 38 property with respect to beneficiary A since immediately after the December 3, 1965, sale A's proportionate interest in the income of XYZ Trust is reduced to zero. The actual useful life of the share of the basis of the section 38 properties which cease to be section 38 property with respect to A is three years and six months (that is, the period beginning with June 1, 1962, and ending with December 3, 1965). A's recomputed qualified investment with respect to such properties is zero. For the taxable year 1962 beneficiary A's recomputed credit earned is zero. The income tax imposed by chapter 1 of the Code on beneficiary A for the taxable year 1965 is increased by $1,050 (that is, $2,100 ($2,100 original credit earned minus zero recomputed credit earned) reduced by the $1,050 increase in tax for 1964).

(iv) The actual useful life of asset No. 3 which was sold on January 2, 1966, is three years and seven months. The recomputed qualified investment with respect to XYZ Trust's share of the basis of asset No. 3 is zero ($15,000 share of basis multiplied by zero applicable percentage) and for the taxable year 1962, XYZ Trust's recomputed credit earned is $1,050 (7 percent of $15,000). The income tax imposed by chapter 1 of the Code on XYZ Trust for the taxable year 1966 is increased by the $1,050 decrease in its credit earned for the taxable year 1962 ($2,100 original credit earned minus $1,050 recomputed credit earned). The sale of asset No. 3 on January 2, 1966, has no effect on A.

T.D. 6931, 10/9/67.

§ 1.47-6 Partnerships.

• ***Caution:*** Reg. § 1.47-6, following, was issued under Code Sec. 47 before amendment by P.L. 101-508 (11/5/90). Provisions similar to, but not identical to, the relative provisions of Code Sec. 47 before such amendment appear in current Code Sec. 50.

Caution: The Treasury has not yet amended Reg § 1.47-6 to reflect changes made by P.L. 98-369, P.L. 97-248, P.L. 97-34.

(a) In general. *(1) Disposition or cessation in hands of partnership.* If a partnership disposes of any partnership section 38 property (or if any partnership section 38 property otherwise ceases to be section 38 property in the hands of the partnership) before the close of the estimated useful life which was taken into account in computing qualified investment with respect to such property, a recapture determination shall be made with respect to each partner who is treated, under paragraph (f) of § 1.46-3, as a taxpayer with respect to such property. Each such recapture determination shall be made with respect to the share of the basis (or cost) of such property taken into account by such partner in computing his qualified investment. For purposes of each such recapture determination the actual useful life of such property shall be the period beginning with the date on which it was placed in service by the partnership and ending with the date of the disposition or cessation. In making a recapture determination under this subparagraph there shall be taken into account any prior recapture determinations made with respect to the partner in connection with the same property.

For definition of "recapture determination" see paragraph (a)(1) of § 1.47-1.

(2) Disposition of partner's interest. (i) If—

(a) The basis (or cost) of partnership section 38 property is taken into account by a partner in computing his qualified investment, and

(b) After the date on which such partnership section 38 property was placed in service by the partnership and before the close of the estimated useful life of the property, such partner's proportionate interest in the general profits of the partnership (or in the particular item of property) is reduced (for example, by a sale, by a change in the partnership agreement, or by the admission of a new partner) below the percentage specified in subdivision (ii) of this subparagraph, then, on the date of such reduction such partnership section 38 property ceases to be section 38 property with respect to such partner to the extent of the actual reduction in such partner's proportionate interest in the general profits of the partnership (or in the particular item of property). (For example, if $100 of the basis of section 38 property was taken into account by a partner and if his proportionate interest in the general profits of the partnership is reduced from 60 percent to 30 percent (that is, 50 percent of his original interest), then such property shall be treated as having ceased to be section 38 property to the extent of $50.) Accordingly, a recapture determination shall be made with respect to such partner. For purposes of such recapture determination the actual useful life of such property shall be the period beginning with the date on which it was placed in service by the partnership and ending with the date on which it is treated as having ceased to be section 38 property with respect to the partner. In making a recapture determination under this subparagraph there shall be taken into account any prior recapture determination made with respect to the partner in connection with the same property.

(ii) The percentage referred to in subdivision (i) (b) of this subparagraph is 66⅔ percent of the partner's proportionate interest in the general profits of the partnership (or in the particular item of property) for the year in which such property was placed in service. However, once property has been treated under this subparagraph as having ceased to be section 38 property to any extent the percentage referred to shall be 33⅓ percent of the partner's proportionate interest in the general profits of the partnership (or in the particular item of property) for the year in which such property was placed in service.

(iii) In determining a partner's proportionate interest in the general profits of a partnership for purposes of this subparagraph, the partner shall be considered to own any interest in such a partnership which he owns directly or indirectly (through ownership in other entities provided the other entities' bases in such interest are determined in whole or in part by reference to the basis of such interest in the hands of the partner). For example, if A, whose proportionate interest in the general profits of partnership X is 20 percent, transfers all of such interest to corporation Y in exchange for all of the stock of Y in a transaction to which section 351 applies, then, for purposes of subdivision (i) of this subparagraph, A shall be considered to own a 20-percent interest in partnership X. Any taxpayer who seeks to establish his interest in a partnership under the rule of this subdivision shall maintain adequate records to demonstrate his indirect interest in the partnership after any such transfer or transfers.

(b) Examples. Paragraph (a) of this section may be illustrated by the following examples in each of which it is assumed that ABC Partnership, which makes its returns on the basis of the calendar year, acquired and placed in service on June 1, 1962, three items of section 38 property. The basis and estimated useful life of each item of section 38 property are as follows:

Asset No.	Basis	Estimated useful life
		Years
1	$30,000	4
2	30,000	6
3	30,000	8

Partners A and B, who make their returns on the basis of a calendar year, share the profits and losses of ABC Partnership equally. Under paragraph (f)(2) of § 1.46-3, each partner's share of the basis of the partnership section 38 property is as follows:

Asset No.	Estimated useful life	Basis	Partners share of basis: A 50 percent	Partners share of basis: B 50 percent
1	4	$30,000	$15,000	$15,000
2	6	30,000	15,000	15,000
3	8	30,000	15,000	15,000

Assuming that during 1962 partners A and B did not place in service any section 38 property and that they did not own any interest in other partnerships, electing small business corporations, estates, or trusts, the qualified investment of each partner is $30,000, computed as follows:

Partnership asset number	Share of basis	Applicable percentage	Qualified investment
1	$15,000	33⅓	$ 5,000
2	15,000	66⅔	10,000
3	15,000	100	15,000
			$30,000

For the taxable year 1962, each partner's credit earned of $2,100 (7 percent of $30,000) was allowed under section 38 as a credit against his liability for tax.

Example (1). (i) On December 2, 1965, ABC Partnership sells asset No. 3 to X Corporation.

(ii) The actual useful life of asset No. 3 is three years and six months. The recomputed qualified investment with respect to each partner's share of the basis of asset No. 3 is zero ($15,000 share of basis multiplied by zero applicable percentage) and for the taxable year 1962, each partner's recomputed credit earned is $1,050 (7 percent of $15,000). The income tax imposed by chapter 1 of the Code on each of the partners for the taxable year 1965 is increased by the $1,050 decrease in his credit earned for the taxable year 1962 (that is, $2,100 original credit earned minus $1,050 recomputed credit earned).

Example (2). (i) On December 3, 1964, partner A sells one-half of his 50 percent interest in ABC Partnership to C, and on December 3, 1965, A sells the remaining one-half of his interest to D. In addition, on January 2, 1966, ABC Partnership sells asset No. 3 to X Corporation.

(ii) Under paragraph (a)(2) of this section, on December 3, 1964, 50 percent of the basis of each of the three items of section 38 property ceases to be section 38 property with respect to partner A since immediately after the December 3, 1964, sale A's proportionate interest in the general profits of ABC Partnership is reduced to 50 percent of his proportionate interest in the general profits of ABC Partnership for 1962. The actual useful life of the share of the basis of each of the section 38 properties which cease to be section 38 property with respect to A is two years and six months (that is, the period beginning with June 1, 1962, and ending with December 3, 1964). Partner A's recomputed qualified investment with respect to such property is $15,000, computed as follows:

Partnership asset No.	Share of basis	Applicable percentage	Qualified investment
1	$ 7,500	33⅓	$ 2,500
2	7,500	66⅔	5,000
3	7,500	100	7,500
			$15,000

For the taxable year 1962 partner A's recomputed credit earned is $1,050 (7 percent of $15,000). The income tax imposed by chapter 1 of the Code on partner A for the taxable year 1964 is increased by the $1,050 decrease in his credit earned for the taxable year 1962 (that is, $2,100 original credit earned minus $1,050 recomputed credit earned).

(iii) Under paragraph (a)(2) of this section, on December 3, 1965, the remaining 50 percent of the share of the basis of each of the three items of section 38 property ceases to be section 38 property with respect to partner A since immediately after the December 3, 1965, sale A's proportionate interest in the general profits of ABC Partnership is reduced to zero. The actual useful life of the share of the bases of the section 38 properties which cease to be section 38 property with respect to A is three years and six months (that is, the period beginning with June 1, 1962, and ending with December 3, 1965). A's recomputed qualified investment with respect to such properties is zero. For the taxable year 1962 partner A's recomputed credit earned is zero. The income tax imposed by chapter 1 of the Code on partner A for the taxable year 1965 is increased by $1,050 (that is, $2,100 ($2,100 original credit earned minus zero recomputed credit earned) reduced by the $1,050 increase in tax for 1964).

(iv) The actual useful life of asset No. 3 which was sold on January 2, 1966, is three years and seven months. The recomputed qualified investment with respect to partner B's share of the basis of asset No. 3 is zero ($15,000 share of basis multiplied by zero applicable percentage) and for the taxable year 1962, partner B's recomputed credit earned is $1,050 (7 percent of $15,000). The income tax imposed by chapter 1 of the Code on partner B for the taxable year 1966 is increased by the $1,050 decrease in his credit earned for the taxable year 1962 ($2,100 original credit earned minus $1,050 recomputed credit earned). The sale of asset No. 3 on January 2, 1966, has no effect on A.

T.D. 6931, 10/9/67.

§ 1.48-1 Definition of section 38 property.

(a) In general. Property which qualifies for the credit allowed by section 38 is known as "section 38 property". Except as otherwise provided in this section, the term "section 38 property" means property (1) with respect to which depreciation (or amortization in lieu of depreciation) is allowable to the taxpayer, (2) which has an estimated useful life of 3 years or more (determined as of the time such property is placed in service), and (3) which is (i) tangible personal property, (ii) other tangible property (not including a building and its structural components) but only if such other property is used as an integral part of manufacturing, production, or extraction, or an an integral part of furnishing transportation, communications, electrical energy, gas, water or sewage disposal services by a person engaged in a trade or business of furnishing any such service, or is a research or storage facility used in connection with any of the foregoing activities, (iii) an elevator or escalator which satisfies the conditions of section 48(a)(1)(C), or (iv) in the case of a qualified rehabilitated building, that portion of the basis which is attributable to qualified rehabilitation expenditures. The determination of whether property qualifies as section 38 property in the hands of the taxpayer for purposes of the credit allowed by section 38 must be made with respect to the first taxable year in which such property is placed in service by the taxpayer. See paragraph (d) of § 1.46-3. For the meaning of "estimated useful life", see paragraph (c) of § 1.46-3. In the case of property which is not described in section 50, this paragraph shall be applied by substituting "4 years" for "3 years".

(b) Depreciation allowable. *(1)* Property (with the exception of property described in section 48(a)(1)(F) and paragraph (p) of this section) is not section 38 property unless a deduction for depreciation (or amortization in lieu of depreciation) with respect to such property is allowable to the taxpayer for the taxable year. A deduction for depreciation is allowable if the property is of a character subject to the allowance for depreciation under section 167 and the basis (or cost) of the property is recovered through a method of depreciation, including, for example, the unit of production method and the retirement method as well as methods of depreciation which measure the life of the property in terms of years. If property is placed in service (within the meaning of paragraph (d) of § 1.46-3) in a trade or business (or in the production of income), but under the taxpayer's depreciation practice the period for depreciation with respect to such property begins in a taxable year subsequent to the taxable year in which such property is placed in service, then a deduction for depreciation shall be treated as allowable with respect to such property in the earlier taxable year (or years). Thus, for example, if a machine is placed in service in a trade or business in 1963, but the period for depreciation with respect to such machine begins in 1964, because the taxpayer uses an averaging convention (see § 1.167(a)-10) in computing depreciation, then, for purposes of determining whether the machine qualifies as section 38 property, a deduction for depreciation shall be treated as allowable in 1963.

(2) If, for the taxable year in which property is placed in service, a deduction for depreciation is allowable to the taxpayer only with respect to a part of such property, then only the proportionate part of the property with respect to which such deduction is allowable qualifies as section 38 property for the purpose of determining the amount of credit allowable under section 38. Thus, for example, if property is used 80 percent of the time in a trade or business and is used 20 percent of the time for personal purposes, only 80 percent of the basis (or cost) of such property qualifies as section 38 property. Further, property does not qualify to the extent that a deduction for depreciation thereon is disallowed under section 274 (relating to disallowance of certain entertainment, etc., expenses).

(3) If the cost of property is not recovered through a method of depreciation but through a deduction of the full cost in one taxable year, for purposes of subparagraph (1) of

this paragraph a deduction for depreciation with respect to such property is not allowable to the taxpayer. However, if an adjustment with respect to the income tax return for such taxable year requires the cost of such property to be recovered through a method of depreciation, a deduction for depreciation will be considered as allowable to the taxpayer.

(4) If depreciation sustained on property is not an allowable deduction for the taxable year but is added to the basis of property being constructed, reconstructed, or erected by the taxpayer, for purposes of subparagraph (1) of this paragraph a deduction for depreciation shall be treated as allowable for the taxable year with respect to the property on which depreciation is sustained. Thus, if $1,000 of depreciation sustained with respect to property no. 1, which is placed in service in 1964 by taxpayer A, is not allowable to A as a deduction for 1964 but is added to the basis of property being constructed by A (property no. 2), for purposes of subparagraph (1) of this paragraph a deduction for depreciation shall be treated as allowable to A for 1964 with respect to property no. 1. However, the $1,000 amount is not included in the basis of property no. 2 for purposes of determining A's qualified investment with respect to property no. 2. See paragraph (c)(1) of § 1.46-3.

(c) Definition of tangible personal property. If property is tangible personal property it may qualify as section 38 property irrespective of whether it is used as an integral part of an activity (or constitutes a research or storage facility used in connection with such activity) specified in paragraph (a) of this section. Local law shall not be controlling for purposes of determining whether property is or is not "tangible" or "personal". Thus, the fact that under local law property is held to be personal property or tangible property shall not be controlling. Conversely, property may be personal property for purposes of the investment credit even though under local law the property is considered to be a fixture and therefore real property. For purposes of this section, the term "tangible personal property" means any tangible property except land and improvements thereto, such as buildings or other inherently permanent structures (including items which are structural components of such buildings or structures). Thus, buildings, swimming pools, paved parking areas, wharves and docks, bridges, and fences are not tangible personal property. Tangible personal property includes all property (other than structural components) which is contained in or attached to a building. Thus, such property as production machinery, printing presses, transportation and office equipment, refrigerators, grocery counters, testing equipment, display racks and shelves, and neon and other signs, which is contained in or attached to a building constitutes tangible personal property for purposes of the credit allowed by section 38. Further, all property which is in the nature of machinery (other than structural components of a building or other inherently permanent structure) shall be considered tangible personal property even though located outside a building. Thus, for example, a gasoline pump, hydraulic car lift, or automatic vending machine, although annexed to the ground, shall be considered tangible personal property.

(d) Other tangible property. *(1) In general.* In addition to tangible personal property, any other tangible property (but not including a building and its structural components) used as an integral part of manufacturing, production, or extraction, or as an integral part of furnishing transportation, communications, electrical energy, gas, water, or sewage disposal services by a person engaged in a trade or business of furnishing any such service, or which constitutes a research or storage facility used in connection with any of the foregoing activities, may qualify as section 38 property.

(2) Manufacturing, production, and extraction. For purposes of the credit allowed by section 38, the terms "manufacturing", "production", and "extraction" include the construction, reconstruction, or making of property out of scrap, salvage, or junk material, as well as from new or raw material, by processing, manipulating, refining, or changing the form of an article, or by combining or assembling two or more articles, and include the cultivation of the soil, the raising of livestock, and the mining of minerals. Thus, section 38 property would include, for example, property used as an integral part of the extracting, processing, or refining of metallic and nonmetallic minerals, including oil, gas, rock, marble, or slate; the construction of roads, bridges, or housing; the processing of meat, fish or other foodstuffs; the cultivation of orchards, gardens, or nurseries; the operation of sawmills, the production of lumber, lumber products or other building materials; the fabrication or treatment of textiles, paper, leather goods, or glass; and the rebuilding, as distinguished from the mere repairing, of machinery.

(3) Transportation and communications businesses. Examples of transportation businesses include railroads, airlines, bus companies, shipping or trucking companies, and oil pipeline companies. Examples of communications businesses include telephone or telegraph companies and radio or television broadcasting companies.

(4) Integral part. In order to qualify for the credit, property (other than tangible personal property and research or storage facilities used in connection with any of the activities specified in subparagraph (1) of this paragraph) must be used as an integral part of one or more of the activities specified in subparagraph (1) of this paragraph. Property such as pavements, parking areas, inherently permanent advertising displays or inherently permanent outdoor lighting facilities, or swimming pools, although used in the operation of a business, ordinarily is not used as an integral part of any of such specified activities. Property is used as an integral part of one of the specified activities if it is used directly in the activity and is essential to the completeness of the activity. Thus, for example, in determining whether property is used as an integral part of manufacturing, all properties used by the taxpayer in acquiring or transporting raw materials or supplies to the point where the actual processing commences (such as docks, railroad tracks and bridges), or in processing raw materials into the taxpayer's final product, would be considered as property used as an integral part of manufacturing. Specific examples of property which normally would be used as an integral part of one of the specified activities are blast furnaces, oil and gas pipelines, railroad tracks and signals, telephone poles, broadcasting towers, oil derricks, and fences used to confine livestock. Property shall be considered used as an integral part of one of the specified activities if so used either by the owner of the property or by the lessee of the property.

(5) Research or storage facilities. (i) If property (other than a building and its structural components) constitutes a research or storage facility and if it is used in connection with an activity specified in subparagraph (1) of this paragraph, such property may qualify as section 38 property even though it is not used as an integral part of such activity. Examples of research facilities include wind tunnels and test stands. Examples of storage facilities include oil and gas storage tanks and grain storage bins. Although a research or storage facility must be used in connection with, for exam-

ple, a manufacturing process, the taxpayer-owner of such facility need not be engaged in the manufacturing process.

(ii) In the case of property described in section 50, property will constitute a storage facility only if the facility is used principally for the bulk storage of fungible commodities. Bulk storage means the storage of a commodity in a large mass prior to its consumption or utilization. Thus, if a facility is used to store oranges that have been sorted and boxed, it is not used for bulk storage.

(e) Definition of building and structural components. *(1)* Generally, buildings and structural components thereof do not qualify as section 38 property. See, however, section 48(a)(1)(E) and (g), and § 1.48-11 (relating to investment credit for qualified rehabilitated building). The term "building" generally means any structure or edifice enclosing a space within its walls, and usually covered by a roof, the purpose of which is, for example, to provide shelter or housing, or to provide working, office, parking, display, or sales space. The term includes, for example, structures such as apartment houses, factory and office buildings, warehouses, barns, garages, railway or bus stations, and stores. Such term includes any such structure constructed by, or for, a lessee even if such structure must be removed, or ownership of such structure reverts to the lessor, at the termination of the lease. Such term does not include (i) a structure which is essentially an item of machinery or equipment, or (ii) a structure which houses property used as an integral part of an activity specified in section 48(a)(1)(B)(i) if the use of the structure is so closely related to the use of such property that the structure clearly can be expected to be replaced when the property it initially houses is replaced. Factors which indicate that a structure is closely related to the use of the property it houses include the fact that the structure is specifically designated to provide for the stress and other demands of such property and the fact that the structure could not be economically used for other purposes. Thus, the term "building" does not include such structures as oil and gas storage tanks, grain storage bins, silos, fractionating towers, blast furnaces, basic oxygen furnaces, coke ovens, brick kilns, and coal tipples.

(2) The term "structural components" includes such parts of a building as walls, partitions, floors, and ceilings, as well as any permanent coverings therefor such as paneling or tiling; windows and doors; all components (whether in, on, or adjacent to the building) of a central air conditioning or heating system, including motors, compressors, pipes and ducts; plumbing and plumbing fixtures, such as sinks and bathtubs; electric wiring and lighting fixtures; chimneys; stairs, escalators, and elevators, including all components thereof; sprinkler systems; fire escapes; and other components relating to the operation or maintenance of a building. However, the term "structural components" does not include machinery the sole justification for the installation of which is the fact that such machinery is required to meet temperature or humidity requirements which are essential for the operation of other machinery or the processing of materials or foodstuffs. Machinery may meet the "sole justification" test provided by the preceding sentence even though it incidentally provides for the comfort of employees, or serves, to an insubstantial degree, areas where such temperature or humidity requirements are not essential. For example, an air conditioning and humidification system installed in a textile plant in order to maintain the temperature or humidity within a narrow optimum range which is critical in processing particular types of yarn or cloth is not included within the term "structural components." For special rules, with respect to an elevator or escalator, the construction, reconstruction, or erection of which is completed by the taxpayer after June 30, 1963, or which is acquired after June 30, 1963 and the original use of which commences with the taxpayer and commences after such date, see section 48(a)(1)(C) and paragraph (m) of this section.

(f) Intangible property. Intangible property, such as patents, copyrights, and subscription lists, does not qualify as section 38 property. The cost of intangible property, in the case of a patent or copyright, includes all costs of purchasing or producing the item patented or copyrighted. Thus, in the case of a motion picture or television film or tape, the cost of the intangible property includes manuscript and screenplay costs, the cost of wardrobe and set design, the salaries of cameramen, actors, directors, etc., and all other costs properly includible in the basis of such film or tape. In the case of a book, the cost of the intangible property includes all costs of producing the original copyrighted manuscript, including the cost of illustration, research, and clerical and stenographic help. However, if tangible depreciable property is used in the production of such intangible property, see paragraph (b)(4) of this section.

(g) Property used outside the United States. *(1) General rule.* (i) Except as provided in subparagraph (2) of this paragraph, the term "section 38 property" does not include property which is used predominantly outside the United States (as defined in section 7701(a)(9)) during the taxable year. The determination of whether property is used predominantly outside the United States during the taxable year shall be made by comparing the period of time in such year during which the property is physically located outside the United States with the period of time in such year during which the property is physically located within the United States. If the property is physically located outside the United States during more than 50 percent of the taxable year, such property shall be considered used predominantly outside the United States during that year. If property is placed in service after the first day of the taxable year, the determination of whether such property is physically located outside the United States during more than 50 percent of the taxable year shall be made with respect to the period beginning on the date on which the property is placed in service and ending on the last day of such taxable year.

(ii) Since the determination of whether a credit is allowable to the taxpayer with respect to any property may be made only with respect to the taxable year in which the property is placed in service by the taxpayer, property used predominantly outside the United States during the taxable year in which it is placed in service cannot qualify as section 38 property with respect to such taxpayer, regardless of the fact that the property is permanently returned to the United States in a later year. Furthermore, if property is used predominantly in the United States in the year in which it is placed in service by the taxpayer, and a credit under section 38 is allowed with respect to such property, but such property is thereafter in any one year used predominantly outside the United States, such property ceases to be section 38 property with respect to the taxpayer and is subject to the application of section 47.

(iii) This subparagraph applies whether property is used predominantly outside the United States by the owner of the property, or by the lessee of the property. If property is leased and if the lessor makes a valid election under § 1.48-4 to treat the lessee as having purchased such property for purposes of the credit allowed by section 38, the determination of whether such property is physically located outside the

United States during more than 50 percent of the taxable year shall be made with respect to the taxable year of the lessee; however, if the lessor does not make such an election, such determination shall be made with respect to the taxable year of the lessor.

(2) Exceptions. The provisions of subparagraph (1) of this paragraph do not apply to—

(i) Any aircraft which is registered by the Administrator of the Federal Aviation Agency, and which (a) is operated, whether on a scheduled or non-scheduled basis, to and from the United States, or (b) is placed in service by the taxpayer during a taxable year ending after March 9, 1967, and is operated under contract with the United States: Provided, That use of the aircraft under the contract constitutes its principal use outside the United States during the taxable year. The term "to and from the United States" is not intended to exclude an aircraft which makes flights from one point in a foreign country to another such point, as long as such aircraft returns to the United States with some degree of frequency;

(ii) Rolling stock, of a domestic railroad corporation subject to part I of the Interstate Commerce Act, which is used within and without the United States. For purposes of this subparagraph, the term "rolling stock" means locomotives, freight and passenger train cars, floating equipment, and miscellaneous transportation equipment on wheels, the expenditures for which are chargeable (or, in the case of leased property, would be chargeable) to the equipment investment accounts in the uniform system of accounts for railroad companies prescribed by the Interstate Commerce Commission;

(iii) Any vessel documented under the laws of the United States which is operated in the foreign or domestic commerce of the United States. A vessel is documented under the laws of the United States if it is registered, enrolled, or licensed under the laws of the United States by the Commandant, U.S. Coast Guard. Vessels operated in the foreign or domestic commerce of the United States include those documented for use in foreign trade, coastwise trade, or fisheries;

(iv) Any motor vehicle of a United States person (as defined in section 7701(a)(30)) which is operated to and from the United States with some degree of frequency;

(v) Any container of a United States person which is used in the transportation of property to and from the United States;

(vi) Any property (other than a vessel or an aircraft) of a U.S. person which is used for the purpose of exploring for, developing, removing, or transporting resources from the outer Continental Shelf (within the meaning of section 2 of the Outer Continental Shelf Lands Act, as amended and supplemented; 43 U.S.C., sec. 1331). Thus for example, offshore drilling equipment may be section 38 property;

(vii) Any property placed in service after December 31, 1965 which (a) is owned by a domestic corporation (other than a corporation entitled to the benefits of section 931 or 934(b)) or by a United States citizen (other than a citizen entitled to the benefits of section 931, 932, 933, or 934(c)), and (b) is used predominantly in a possession of the United States during the taxable year by such a corporation or such a citizen, or by a corporation created or organized in, or under the law of, a possession of the United States. Thus, property placed in service after December 31, 1965, which is owned by a domestic corporation not entitled to the benefits of section 931 or 934(b), which is leased to a corporation organized under the laws of a U.S. possession, and which is used by such lessee predominantly in a possession of the United States may qualify as section 38 property. However, property which is owned by a corporation not entitled to the benefits of section 931 or 934(b) but which is leased to a domestic corporation entitled to such benefits would not qualify as section 38 property. The determination of whether property is used predominantly in a possession of the United States during the taxable year shall be made under principles similar to those described in subparagraph (1) of this paragraph. For example, if a machine is placed in service in a possession of the United States on July 1, 1966, by a calendar year taxpayer and if it is physically located in such a possession during more than 50 percent of the period beginning on July 1, 1966 and ending on December 31, 1966, then such machine shall be considered used predominantly in a possession of the United States during the taxable year 1966;

(viii) Any communications satellite (as defined in section 103(3) of the Communications Satellite Act of 1962, 47 U.S.C., sec. 702(3)), or any interest therein, of a U.S. person;

(ix) Any cable which is property described in section 50, or any interest therein, of a domestic corporation engaged in furnishing telephone service to which section 46(c)(3)(B)(iii) applies (or of a wholly owned domestic subsidiary of such corporation), if such cable is part of a submarine cable system which constitutes part of a communications link exclusively between the United States and one or more foreign countries; and

(x) Any property described in section 50 (other than a vessel or an aircraft) of a U.S. person which is used in international or territorial waters for the purpose of exploring for, developing, removing, or transporting resources from ocean waters or deposits under such waters.

(h) Property used for lodging. *(1) In general.* (i) Except as provided in subparagraph (2) of this paragraph, the term "section 38 property" does not include property which is used predominantly to furnish lodging or is used predominantly in connection with the furnishing of lodging during the taxable year. Property used in the living quarters of a lodging facility, including beds and other furniture, refrigerators, ranges, and other equipment, shall be considered as used predominantly to furnish lodging. The term "lodging facility" includes an apartment house, hotel, motel, dormitory, or any other facility (or part of a facility) where sleeping accommodations are provided and let, except that such term does not include a facility used primarily as a means of transportation (such as an aircraft, vessel, or a railroad car) or used primarily to provide medical or convalescent services, even though sleeping accommodations are provided.

(ii) Property which is used predominantly in the operation of a lodging facility or in serving tenants shall be considered used in connection with the furnishing of lodging, whether furnished by the owner of the lodging facility or another person. Thus, for example, lobby furniture, office equipment, and laundry and swimming pool facilities used in the operation of an apartment house or in serving tenants would be considered used predominantly in connection with the furnishing of lodging. However, property which is used in furnishing, to the management of a lodging facility or its tenants, electrical energy, water, sewage disposal services, gas, telephone service, or other similar services shall not be treated as property used in connection with the furnishing of lodging. Thus, such items as gas and electric meters, telephone poles and lines, telephone station and switchboard equipment, and water and gas mains, furnished by a public utility would not be considered as property used in connection with the furnishing of lodging.

(iii) Notwithstanding any other provision of this paragraph (h), in the case of a qualified rehabilitated building (within the meaning of section 48(g)(1) and § 1.48-12(b)), expenditures for property resulting in basis described in section 48(a)(1)(E) shall not be treated as section 38 property to the extent that such property is attributable to a portion of the building that is used for lodging or in connection with lodging. For example, if expenditures are incurred to rehabilitate a five story qualified rehabilitated building, three floors of which are used for apartments and two floors of which are used as commercial office space, the portion of the basis of the building attributable to qualified rehabilitated expenditures attributable to the commercial part of the building shall not be considered to be expenditures for property, or in connection with property, used predominantly for lodging. Allocation of expenditures between the two portions of the building are to be made using the principles contained in § 1.48-12(c)(10)(ii).

(2) Exceptions. (i) Nonlodging commercial facility. A nonlodging commercial facility which is available to persons not using the lodging facility on the same basis as it is available to the tenants of the lodging facility shall not be treated as property which is used predominantly to furnish lodging or predominantly in connection with the furnishing of lodging. Examples of nonlodging commercial facilities include restaurants, drug stores, grocery stores, and vending machines located in a lodging facility.

(ii) Property used by a hotel or motel. Property used by a hotel, motel, inn, or other similar establishment, in connection with the trade or business of furnishing lodging shall not be considered as property which is used predominantly to furnish lodging or predominantly in connection with the furnishing of lodging, provided that the predominant portion of the living accommodations in the hotel, motel, etc., is used by transients during the taxable year. For purposes of the preceding sentence, the term "predominant portion" means "more than one-half". Thus, if more than one-half of the living quarters of a hotel, motel, inn, or other similar establishment is used during the taxable year to accommodate tenants on a transient basis, none of the property used by such hotel, motel, etc., in the trade or business of furnishing lodging shall be considered as property which is used predominantly to furnish lodging or predominantly in connection with the furnishing of lodging. Accommodations shall be considered used on a transient basis if the rental period is normally less than 30 days.

(iii) Coin-operated machines. In the case of property which is described in section 50, coin-operated vending machines and coin-operated washing machines and dryers shall not be considered as property which is used predominantly to furnish lodging or predominantly in connection with the furnishing of lodging.

(iv) Certified historic structures. For purposes of this paragraph (h), regardless of the actual use of a certified historic structure, that portion of the basis of such certified historic structure which is attributable to qualified rehabilitation expenditures (as defined in § 1.48-12(c)) shall not be considered as property which is either used predominantly to furnish lodging or predominantly in connection with the furnishing of lodging. Accordingly, such portion of the basis may qualify as section 38 property. (For the definition of "certified historic structure," see section 48(g)(3) and § 1.48-12(d).)

(i) Reserved

(j) Property used by certain tax-exempt organizations. The term "section 38 property" does not include property used by an organization (other than a cooperative described in section 521) which is exempt from the tax imposed by chapter 1 of the Code unless such property is used predominantly in an unrelated trade or business the income of which is subject to tax under section 511. If such property is debt-financed property as defined in section 514(b), the basis or cost of such property for purposes of computing qualified investment under section 46(c) shall include only that percentage of the basis or cost which is the same percentage as is used under section 514(a), for the year the property is placed in service, in computing the amount of gross income to be taken into account during such taxable year with respect to such property. The term "property used by an organization" means (1) property owned by the organization (whether or not leased to another person), and (2) property leased to the organization. Thus, for example, a data processing or copying machine which is leased to an organization exempt from tax would be considered as property used by such organization. Property (unless used predominantly in an unrelated trade or business) leased by another person to an organization exempt from tax or leased by such an organization to another person is not section 38 property to either the lessor or the lessee, and in either case the lessor may not elect under § 1.48-4 to treat the lessee of such property as having purchased such property for purposes of the credit allowed by section 38. This paragraph shall not apply to property leased on a casual or short-term basis to an organization exempt from tax.

(k) Property used by governmental units. The term "section 38 property" does not include property used by the United States, any State (including the District of Columbia) or political subdivision thereof, any international organization (as defined in section 7701(a)(18)) other than the International Telecommunications Satellite Consortium or any successor organization, or any agency or instrumentality of the United States, of any State or political subdivision thereof, or of any such international organization. The term "property" used by the United States, etc. means (1) property owned by any such governmental unit (whether or not leased to another person), and (2) property leased to any such governmental unit. Thus, for example, a data processing or copying machine which is leased to any such governmental unit would be considered as property used by such governmental unit. Property leased by another person to any such governmental unit or leased by such governmental unit to another person is not section 38 property to either the lessor or the lessee, and in either case the lessor may not elect under § 1.48-4 to treat the lessee of such property as having purchased such property for purposes of the credit allowed by section 38. This paragraph shall not apply to property leased on a casual or short-term basis to any such governmental unit.

(l) Reserved.

(m) Elevators and escalators. *(1) In general.* Under section 48(a)(1)(C), an elevator or escalator qualifies as section 38 property if—

(i) The construction, reconstruction, or erection of the elevator or escalator is completed by the taxpayer after June 30, 1963, or

(ii) The elevator or escalator is acquired after June 30, 1963, and the original use of such elevator or escalator commences with the taxpayer and commences after such date.

In the case of construction, reconstruction, or erection of an elevator or escalator commenced before January 1, 1962, and completed after June 30, 1963, there shall be taken into account in determining the qualified investment under section 46(c) only that portion of the basis which is properly attributable to construction, reconstruction, or erection after December 31, 1961. Further, if the construction, reconstruction, or erection of such property is commenced after December 31, 1961, and is completed after June 30, 1963, the entire basis of the elevator or escalator shall be taken into account in determining qualified investment under section 46(c). Also, if an elevator or escalator is reconstructed by the taxpayer after June 30, 1963, the basis attributable to such reconstruction may be taken into account in determining the qualified investment under section 46(c), irrespective of the fact that the original construction or erection of such elevator or escalator may have occurred before January 1, 1962. Paragraph (b) of § 1.48-2 shall be applied in determining the date of acquisition, original use, and basis attributable to construction, reconstruction, or erection.

(2) Definition of elevators and escalators. For purposes of this section the term "elevator" means a cage or platform and its hoisting machinery for conveying persons or freight to or from different levels and functionally related equipment which is essential to its operation. The term includes, for example, guide rails and cables, motors and controllers, control panels and landing buttons, and elevator gates and doors, which are essential to the operation of the elevator. The term "elevator" does not, however, include a structure which is considered a building for purposes of the investment credit. The term "escalator" means a moving staircase and functionally related equipment which is essential to its operation. For purposes of determining qualified investment under section 46(c) and § 1.46-3, the basis of an elevator or escalator does not include the cost of any structural alterations to the building, such as the cost of constructing a shaft or of making alterations to the floor, walls, or ceiling, even though such alterations may be necessary in order to install or modernize the elevator or escalator.

(3) Examples. The provisions of this paragraph may be illustrated by the following examples:

Example (1). If an elevator with a total basis of $100,000 is completed after June 30, 1963, and the portion attributable to construction by the taxpayer after December 31, 1961, is determined by engineering estimates or by cost accounting records to be $30,000, only the $30,000 portion may be taken into account as an investment in new section 38 property in computing qualified investment.

Example (2). If construction of an elevator with a total basis of $90,000 is commenced by the taxpayer after December 31, 1961, and is completed after June 30, 1963, the entire basis of $90,000 may be taken into account as an investment in new section 38 property.

Example (3). The facts are the same as in example (2) except that construction of the elevator was completed before June 30, 1963. The elevator is not considered to be section 38 property.

Example (4). In 1964, a taxpayer reconditions an elevator, which had been constructed and placed in service in 1962 and which had an adjusted basis in 1964 of $75,000. The cost of reconditioning amounts to an additional $50,000. The basis of the elevator which may be taken into account in computing qualified investment in section 38 property is $50,000, irrespective of whether the taxpayer contracts to have it reconditioned or reconditions it himself, and irrespective of whether the materials used in the process are new in use.

(n) Amortized property. Any property with respect to which an election under 167(k), 169, 184, 187, or 188 applies shall not be treated as section 38 property. In the case of any property to which section 169 applies, the preceding sentence shall apply only to so much of the adjusted basis of the property as (after the application of section 169(f)) constitutes the amortizable basis for purposes of section 169. This paragraph shall not apply to property with respect to which an election under section 167(k), 184, 187, or 188 applies such property is described in section 50.

(o) Reserved.

(p) Qualified timber property. *(1)* Qualified timber property (within the meaning of section 194(c)(1)) shall be treated as section 38 property to the extent of the portion of the basis of such property which is the amortizable basis (as defined in § 1.194-3(b)) acquired during the taxable year and taken into account under section 194 (after applying the limitation of section 194(b)(1)). Such amortizable basis shall qualify as section 38 property whether or not an election is made under section 194. However, any portion of such amortizable basis which is attributable to property which otherwise qualifies as section 38 property shall not be treated as section 38 property under section 48(a)(1)(F) and this paragraph. For example, amortizable basis attributable to depreciation on equipment would not qualify as section 38 property under this paragraph if such equipment qualifies as section 38 property under sections 48(a)(1)(A) or (B). In determining the portion of amortizable basis which qualifies as section 38 property under this paragraph, the reduction in amortizable basis to account for depreciation sustained with respect to property used in the reforestation process (which otherwise qualifies as section 38 property) shall be applied before the $10,000 limitation on eligible costs under section 194(b)(1). For example, if in a taxable year a taxpayer incurs qualifying reforestation cost resulting in $12,000 of amortizable basis with respect to property for which an election is in effect, and $2,000 of these costs are attributable to depreciation of the taxpayer's equipment, such $12,000 would first be reduced by the $2,000 of depreciation, and the $10,000 limitation under section 194(b)(1) would be applied following such reduction.

(2) If a taxpayer makes an election to amortize reforestation expenditures under section 194, and allocates the $10,000 limitation among more than one property under § 1.194-2(b)(2), then such allocation shall apply for purposes of determining the amortizable basis that qualifies as section 38 property under paragraph (p)(1) of this section. If no election is made under section 194, the taxpayer may select the manner in which the $10,000 limitation is to be allocated among the qualified timber properties.

T.D. 6731, 5/7/64, amend T.D. 6838, 7/19/65, T.D. 6858, 6/20/68, T.D. 6971, 9/11/68, T.D. 7203, 8/24/72, T.D. 7229, 12/20/72, T.D. 7927, 12/15/83, T.D. 8031, 6/18/85, T.D. 8233, 10/7/88, T.D. 8474, 4/26/93.

---

§ 1.48-2 New section 38 property.

Caution: The Treasury has not yet amended Reg § 1.48-2 to reflect changes made by P.L. 101-508, P.L. 99-514, P.L. 98-369, P.L. 97-248.

(a) In general. Section 48(b) defines "new section 38 property" as section 38 property—

(1) The construction, reconstruction, or erection of which is completed by the taxpayer after December 31, 1961, or

(2) Which is acquired by the taxpayer after December 31, 1961, provided that the original use of such property commences with the taxpayer and commences after such date.

In the case of construction, reconstruction, or erection of such property commenced before January 1, 1962, and completed after December 31, 1961, there shall be taken into account as the basis of new section 38 property in determining qualified investment only that portion of the basis which is properly attributable to construction, reconstruction, or erection after December 31, 1961. See § 1.48-1 for the definition of section 38 property.

(b) Special rules for determining date of acquisition, original use, and basis attributable to construction, reconstruction, or erection. For purposes of paragraph (a) of this section, the principles set forth in paragraph (a)(1) and (2) of § 1.167(c)-1 shall be applied. Thus, for example the following rules are applicable:

(1) Property is considered as constructed, reconstructed, or erected by the taxpayer if the work is done for him in accordance with his specifications.

(2) The portion of the basis of property attributable to construction, reconstruction, or erection after December 31, 1961, consists of all costs of construction, reconstruction, or erection allocable to the period after December 31, 1961, including the cost or other basis of materials entering into such work (but not including, in the case of reconstruction of property, the adjusted basis of the reconstructed property as of the time such reconstruction is commenced).

(3) It is not necessary that materials entering into construction, reconstruction, or erection be acquired after December 31, 1961, or that they be new in use.

(4) If construction or erection by the taxpayer began after December 31, 1961, the entire cost or other basis of such construction or erection may be taken into account as the basis of new section 38 property.

(5) Construction, reconstruction, or erection by the taxpayer begins when physical work is started on such construction, reconstruction, or erection.

(6) Property shall be deemed to be acquired when reduced to physical possession, or control.

(7) The term "original use" means the first use to which the property is put, whether or not such use corresponds to the use of such property by the taxpayer. For example, a reconditioned or rebuilt machine acquired by the taxpayer will not be treated as being put to original use by the taxpayer. The question of whether property is reconditioned or rebuilt property is a question of fact. Property will not be treated as reconditioned or rebuilt merely because it contains some used parts. If the cost of reconstruction may properly either be capitalized and recovered through depreciation or charged against the depreciation reserve, such cost may be taken into account as the basis of new section 38 property even though it is charged against the depreciation reserve.

(c) Examples. This section may be illustrated by the following examples:

Example (1). If a machine with a total cost of $100,000 is completed after December 31, 1961, and the portion attributable to construction by the taxpayer after December 31, 1961, is determined by engineering estimates or by cost accounting records to be $30,000, the $30,000 amount shall be taken into account by the taxpayer in computing qualified investment in new section 38 property.

Example (2). In 1965, a taxpayer reconditions a machine, which he constructed and placed in service in 1962 and which has an adjusted basis in 1965 of $10,000. The cost of reconditioning amounts to an additional $20,000. The basis of the machine which shall be taken into account in computing qualified investment in new section 38 property for 1965 is $20,000, whether he contracts to have it reconditioned or reconditions it himself, and irrespective of whether the materials used for reconditioning are new in use.

Example (3). In 1961, a taxpayer pays the entire purchase price of $10,000 for section 38 property to be delivered in 1962. In 1962 he takes possession of the property and commences the original use of the asset in that year. The $10,000 amount shall be taken into account in computing qualified investment in new section 38 property for 1962.

Example (4). A taxpayer, instead of reconditioning his old machine, buys a "factory reconditioned" or "rebuilt" machine in 1962 to replace it. The reconditioned or rebuilt machine is not new section 38 property since such taxpayer is not the first user of the machine. See, however, § 1.48-3 (relating to used section 38 property).

Example (5). In 1962, a taxpayer buys from X for $20,000 an item of section 38 property which has been previously used by X. The taxpayer in 1962 makes an expenditure on the property of $5,000 of the type that must be capitalized. Regardless of whether the $5,000 is added to the basis of such property or is capitalized in a separate account, such amount shall be taken into account by the taxpayer in computing qualified investment in new section 38 property for 1962. No part of the $20,000 purchase price may be taken into account for such purpose. See, however, § 1.48-3 (relating to used section 38 property).

(d) Special rule for qualified rehabilitated buildings. Notwithstanding the rules in paragraphs (a) through (c) of this section, that portion of the basis of a qualified rehabilitated building attributable to qualified rehabilitation expenditures is treated as new section 38 property. See section 48(a)(1)(E) and (g), and § 1.48-11.

T.D. 6731, 5/7/64, amend T.D. 8031, 6/18/85.

§ 1.48-3 Used section 38 property.

Caution: The Treasury has not yet amended Reg § 1.48-3 to reflect changes made by P.L. 98-369, P.L. 97-34, P.L. 96-223, P.L. 96-222, P.L. 95-600, P.L. 94-455, P.L. 94-12.

(a) In general. *(1)* Section 48(c) provides that "used section 38 property" means section 38 property acquired by purchase after December 31, 1961, which is not "new section 38 property". See §§ 1.48-1 and 1.48-2, respectively, for definitions of section 38 property and new section 38 property. In determining whether property is acquired by purchase, the provisions of paragraph (c)(1) of § 1.179-3 shall apply, except that (i) "1961" shall be substituted for "1957", and (ii) the definition of "component member" of a controlled group of corporations in paragraph (d)(4) of this section shall be substituted for the definition of such term in paragraph (e) of § 1.179-3.

(2) (i) Property shall not qualify as used section 38 property if, after its acquisition by the taxpayer, it is used by (a) a person who used such property before such acquisition, or (b) a person who bears a relationship described in section 179(d)(2) (A) or (B) to a person who used such property before such acquisition. Thus, for example, if property is used by a person and is later sold by him under a sale and lease-back arrangement, such property in the hands of the purchaser-lessor is not used section 38 property because the

property, after its acquisition, is being used by the same person who used it before its acquisition. Similarly, where a lessee has been leasing property and subsequently purchases it (whether or not the lease contains an option to purchase), such property is not used section 38 property with respect to the purchaser because the property is being used by the same person who used it before its acquisition. In addition, if property owned by a lessor is sold subject to the lease, or is sold upon the termination of the lease, the property will not qualify as used section 38 property with respect to the purchaser if, after the purchase, the property is used by a person who used the property as a lessee before the purchase.

(ii) For purposes of applying subdivision (i) of this subparagraph, property shall not be considered as used by a person before its acquisition if such property was used only on a casual basis by such person.

(iii) In determining whether a person bears a relationship described in section 179(d)(2) (A) or (B) to a person who used property before its acquisition by the taxpayer, the provisions of paragraph (c)(1) (i) and (ii) of § 1.179-3 shall apply, except that the definition of "component member" of a controlled group of corporations in paragraph (d)(4) of this section shall be substituted for the definition of such term in paragraph (e) of § 1.179-3.

(3) The provisions of this paragraph may be illustrated by the following examples:

Example (1). Corporation P acquires properties 1 and 2 in 1960 and uses them in its trade or business until 1962. In 1962, corporation P sells such properties to corporation Y, which leases back property 1 to corporation P and leases property 2 to corporation S, a wholly owned subsidiary of corporation P. Property 1 is not used section 38 property in the hands of corporation Y because, after its acquisition by corporation Y, it is used by a person (corporation P) who used it prior to such acquisition. Property 2 is not used section 38 property because, after its acquisition by corporation Y, it is used by a person (corporation S) who is related, within the meaning of section 179(d)(2)(B), to a person (corporation P) who used it before such acquisition.

Example (2). In 1962, corporation L leases property from corporation M. In 1964, corporation L acquires the property that it previously had been leasing. The property acquired by corporation L is not used section 38 property because such property is used after such acquisition by the same person (corporation L) who used the property before its acquisition (corporation L).

Example (3). Corporation X buys property in 1962 and leases such property to corporation Y. Corporation X in 1965 sells the property to A subject to the lease. The property acquired by A is not used section 38 property if such property continues to be used by corporation Y, because corporation Y used the property before its acquisition by A.

Example (4). A owns a bulldozer which he rents out to a number of different users, including B. In 1962, B used the bulldozer from February 16 to March 12 and again on October 15 and 16. B purchases the bulldozer from A on December 1, 1962. The prior use of the property by B does not disqualify such property as used section 38 property to B, because he used such property only on a casual basis prior to its purchase.

(b) Cost. *(1)* The cost of used section 38 property is equal to the basis of such property, but does not include so much of such basis as is determined by reference to the adjusted basis of other property (whether or not section 38 property) held at any time by the taxpayer acquiring such used section 38 property.

(2) If property (whether or not section 38 property) is disposed of by the taxpayer (other than by reason of its destruction or damage by fire, storm, shipwreck, or other casualty, or its theft) and used section 38 property similar or related in service or use is acquired as a replacement therefor in a transaction in which the basis of the replacement property is not determined by reference to the adjusted basis of the property replaced, then the cost of the used section 38 property so acquired shall be its basis reduced by the adjusted basis of the property replaced. The preceding sentence shall apply only if the taxpayer acquires (or enters into a contract to acquire) the replacement property within a period of 60 days before or after the date of the disposition.

(3) Notwithstanding subparagraphs (1) and (2) of this paragraph, the cost of used section 38 property shall not be reduced with respect to the adjusted basis of any property disposed of if, by reason of section 47, such disposition resulted in an increase of tax or a reduction of investment credit carrybacks or carryovers described in section 46(b).

(4) The provisions of this paragraph may be illustrated by the following examples:

Example (1). In 1972, A acquires machine 2 (an item of used section 38 property which has a sales price of $5,600) by trading in machine 1 (an item of section 38 property acquired in 1962), and by paying an additional $4,000 cash. The adjusted basis of machine 1 is $1,600. Under the provisions of sections 1012 and 1031(d), the basis of machine 2 is $5,600 ($1,600 adjusted basis of machine 1 plus cash expended of $4,000). The cost of machine 2 which may be taken into account in computing qualified investment for 1972 is $4,000 (basis of $5,600 less $1,600 adjusted basis of machine 1).

Example (2). The facts are the same as in example (1) except that machine 2 has a sales price of $6,000. The trade-in allowance on machine 1 is $2,000. The result is the same as in example (1), that is, the basis of machine 2 is $5,600 ($1,600 plus $4,000); therefore, the cost of machine 2 which may be taken into account in computing qualified investment for 1972 is $4,000 (basis of $5,600 less $1,600 adjusted basis of machine 1).

Example (3). On September 18, 1962, B sells truck 1, which he acquired in 1961 and which has an adjusted basis in his hands of $1,200. On October 15, 1962, he purchases for $2,000 truck 2 (an item of used section 38 property) as a replacement therefor. The cost of truck 2 which may be taken into account in computing qualified investment is $800 ($2,000 less $1,200).

Example (4). In 1962, C acquires property 1, an item of new section 38 property with a basis of $12,000 and a useful life of eight years or more. He is allowed a credit under section 38 of $840 (7 percent of $12,000) with respect to such property. In 1968, C acquires property 2 (an item of used section 38 property) by trading in property 1 and by paying an additional amount in cash. Section 47(a) applies to the disposition of property 1 and C's tax liability for 1968 is increased by $280. Since the application of section 47(a) results in an increase in tax, for purposes of computing qualified investment the cost of property 2 is not reduced by any part of the adjusted basis of the property traded in.

(c) Dollar limitation. *(1) In general.* Section 48(c)(2) provides that the aggregate cost of used section 38 property which may be taken into account for any taxable year in computing qualified investment under section 46(c)(1)(B) shall not exceed $50,000. If the total cost of used section 38 property exceeds $50,000, there must be selected, in the manner provided in subparagraph (4) of this paragraph, the particular items of used section 38 property the cost of which is to be taken into account in computing qualified investment. The cost of used section 38 property that may be taken into account by a person in applying the $50,000 limitation for any taxable year includes not only the cost of used section 38 property placed in service by such person during such taxable year, but also the cost of used section 38 property apportioned to such person. For purposes of this section, the cost of used section 38 property apportioned to any person means the cost of such property apportioned to him by a trust, estate, or electing small business corporation (as defined in section 1371(b)), and his share of the cost of partnership used section 38 property, with respect to the taxable year of such trust, estate, corporation or partnership ending with or within such person's taxable year. Thus, if an individual places in service during his taxable year used section 38 property with a cost of $25,000, if the cost of used section 38 property apportioned to him by an electing small business corporation for such year is $30,000, and if his share for such year of the cost of used section 38 property placed in service by a partnership is $20,000, he may select from the used section 38 property with a total cost of $75,000 the particular used section 38 property with cost of which he wishes to take into account. No part of the excess of $25,000 ($75,000 cost minus $50,000 annual limitation) may be taken into account in any other taxable year. For determining the amount of the cost to be apportioned by an electing small business corporation, see paragraph (a)(2) of § 1.48-5; in the case of estates and trusts, see paragraph (a)(2) of § 1.48-6. See paragraph (e) of this section for application of $50,000 limitation in the case of affiliated groups.

(2) Married individuals filing separate returns. In the case of a husband or wife who files a separate return, the aggregate cost of used section 38 property which may be taken into account for the taxable year to which such return relates cannot exceed $25,000. The preceding sentence shall not apply, however, unless the taxpayer's spouse places in service (or is apportioned the cost of) used section 38 property for the taxable year of such spouse which ends with or within the taxpayer's taxable year. Thus, if a husband and wife who file separate returns on a calendar year basis both place in service used section 38 property during the taxable year, the maximum cost of used section 38 property which may be taken into account by each is $25,000. However, in such case, if only one spouse places in service (or is apportioned the cost of) used section 38 property during the taxable year, such spouse may take into account a maximum of $50,000 for such year. The determination of whether an individual is married shall be made under the principles of section 143 and the regulations thereunder.

(3) Partnerships. In the case of a partnership, the aggregate cost of used section 38 property placed in service by the partnership (or apportioned to the partnership) which may be taken into account by the partners with respect to any taxable year of the partnership may not exceed $50,000. If such aggregate cost exceeds $50,000, the partnership must make a selection in the manner provided in subparagraph (4) of this paragraph. The $50,000 limitation applies to each partner, as well as to the partnership.

(4) Selection of $50,000 cost. (i) If the sum of (a) the cost of used section 38 property placed in service during the taxable year by person, (b) such person's share of the cost of partnership used section 38 property placed in service during the taxable year of a partnership ending with or within such person's taxable year, and (c) the cost of used section 38 property apportioned to such person for such taxable year by an electing small business corporation, estate, or trust, exceeds $50,000, such person must make a selection for such taxable year in the manner provided in subdivision (ii) of this subparagraph.

(ii) For purposes of computing qualified investment (or, in the case of a partnership, electing small business corporation, estate, or trust, for purposes of selecting used section 38 property the cost of which may be taken into account by the partners, shareholders, or estate or trust and its beneficiaries) any person to whom subdivision (i) of this subparagraph applies must select a total cost of $50,000 from (a) the cost of specific used section 38 property placed in service by such person, (b) such person's share of the cost of specific used section 38 property placed in service by a partnership, and (c) the cost of used section 38 property apportioned to such person by an electing small business corporation, estate, or trust. When a particular property is selected, the entire cost (or entire share of cost of a particular property in the case of partnership property) of such property must be taken into account unless, as a result of the selection of such particular property, the $50,000 limitation is exceeded. Likewise, in the case of an apportionment from an electing small business corporation, estate, or trust, when the cost in a particular useful life category is selected, the entire cost in such category must be taken into account unless, as a result of the selection of such cost, the $50,000 limitation is exceeded. Thus, if a person places in service during the taxable year three items of used section 38 property, each with a cost of $20,000, he must select the entire cost of two of the items and only $10,000 of the cost of the third item; he may not select a portion of the cost of each of the three items. The selection by any person shall be made by taking the cost of used section 38 property into account in computing qualified investment (or in selecting the used section 38 property the cost of which may be taken into account by the partners, etc.), and if such property was placed in service by such person, he must maintain records which permit specific identification of any item of used section 38 property selected.

(5) Examples. The provisions of this paragraph may be illustrated by the following examples:

Example (1). H, who operates a sole proprietorship, purchases and places in service in 1963 used section 38 property with a cost of $60,000. His spouse, W, is a shareholder in an electing small business corporation which purchases and places in service during its fiscal year ending June 30, 1963, used section 38 property with a cost of $50,000. Both spouses file separate returns on a calendar year basis. W, as a 60 percent shareholder on the last day of the taxable year of the corporation, is apportioned $30,000 (60 percent of $50,000) of the cost of the used section 38 property placed in service by the corporation. The cost of used section 38 property that may be taken into account by H on his separate return is $25,000. The cost of used section 38 property that may be taken into account by W on her separate return is $25,000. On the other hand, if the corporation had made no investment in used section 38 property, H could take $50,000 of the $60,000 cost into account.

Example (2). Partners X, Y, and Z share the profits and losses of partnership XYZ in the ratio of 50 percent, 30 percent, and 20 percent, respectively. The partnership and each partner make returns on the basis of the calendar year. Each partner also operates a sole proprietorship. In 1963, the partnership and the partners purchase and place in service the following used section 38 property:

Property	Estimated useful life	Cost
Partnership XYZ		
Property No. 1	9 years..................	$10,000
Property No. 2	7 years..................	50,000
Property No. 3	7 years..................	50,000
Property No. 4	5 years..................	30,000
Partner X		
Property No. 5	6 years..................	30,000
Partner Y		
Property No. 6	10 years.................	60,000
Partner Z		
Property No. 7	4 years..................	36,000

(i) Selection by partnership. In accordance with subparagraph (4)(ii) of this paragraph, the partnership selects property No. 1 and $40,000 of the cost of property No. 2 to be taken into account. Therefore, each partner's share of cost of the property selected by the partnership is as follows:

Property No.	Estimated useful life	Selected cost	Partner's share of cost X(50%)	Y(30%)	Z(20%)
1..........	9 years..........	$10,000	$ 5,000	$ 3,000	$ 2,000
2..........	7 years..........	40,000	20,000	12,000	8,000
Total		50,000	25,000	15,000	10,000

(ii) Selection by partners. In accordance with subparagraph (4)(ii) of this paragraph, the partners make the following selections: Partner X selects property No. 5 ($30,000), his share of the cost of property No. 1 ($5,000), and $15,000 of his share of the cost of property No. 2. Partner Y selects $50,000 of the cost of property No. 6, and no part of his share of the cost of partnership property. Partner Z, having an aggregate cost of used section 38 property of only $46,000 (partnership property of $10,000 and individually owned property of $36,000), takes into account the entire $46,000.

(iii) Qualified investment of partner X. X's total qualified investment in used section 38 property for 1963 is $35,000, computed as follows:

Property No.	Estimated useful life	Selected cost	Applicable percentage	Qualified investment
1	9 years	$ 5,000	100	$ 5,000
2	7 years	15,000	66⅔	10,000
5	6 years	30,000	66⅔	20,000
Total		50,000		35,000

(iv) Qualified investment of partner Y. Y's total qualified investment in used section 38 property for 1963 is $50,000 (100 percent of $50,000) since he selected $50,000 of the cost of property No. 6 which has a useful life of 8 years or more.

(v) Qualified investment of partner Z. Z's total qualified investment in used section 38 property for 1963 is $19,333, computed as follows:

Property No.	Estimated useful life	Selected cost	Applicable percentage	Qualified investment
1	9 years	$ 2,000	100	$ 2,000
2	7 years	8,000	66⅔	5,333
7	4 years	36,000	33⅓	12,000
Total		46,000		19,333

(d) Dollar limitation for component members of a controlled group. *(1) In general.* (i) Section 48(c)(2)(C) provides that the $50,000 limitation on the cost of used section 38 property which may be taken into account for any taxable year shall, in the case of component members of a controlled group (as defined in subparagraph (4) of this paragraph) on a particular December 31, be reduced for each such member by apportioning the $50,000 amount among such component members for their taxable years that include such December 31 in accordance with their respective amounts of used section 38 property which may be taken into account, that is, in accordance with the total cost of used section 38 property placed in service by each such member during its taxable year (without regard to the $50,000 limitation or the applicable percentages to be applied in computing qualified investment).

(ii) Except as otherwise provided in this paragraph, the $50,000 amount shall be apportioned among those corporations which are component members of the controlled group on a December 31. For the taxable year of each such member which includes such December 31, the cost of used section 38 property taken into account in computing qualified investment under section 46(c)(1)(B) shall not exceed the amount which bears the same ratio to $50,000 as the cost of used section 38 property placed in service by such member for such taxable year bears to the total cost of used section 38 property placed in service by all component members of the controlled group for their taxable years which include such December 31.

(iii) If a component member of the group makes its income tax return on the basis of a 52-53-week taxable year, the principles of section 441(f)(2)(A)(ii) and § 1.441-2 apply in determining the last day of such a taxable year.

(2) Statement by the "filing member". For purposes of this paragraph, the term "filing member" with respect to a particular December 31 means the member (or members) of a controlled group which has, among those members of the group which are apportioned part of the $50,000 amount for their taxable years which include such December 31, the taxable year including such December 31 which ends on the earliest date. The filing member of the group shall attach to its income tax return a statement containing the name, address, and employer identification number of each component member of the controlled group on such December 31 and a schedule showing the computation of the apportionment of the $50,000 amount among the component members of the group. Each such other member shall retain as part of its records a copy of the statement containing the apportionment schedule. Except as otherwise provided in subparagraph (3)(ii) of this paragraph, each member which is apportioned part of the $50,000 amount shall take such

apportioned amount into account in filing its return for its taxable year which includes such December 31.

(3) Estimate of used section 38 property to be placed in service. (i) For purposes of subparagraphs (1) and (2) of this paragraph, if on the date (including extensions of time) for filing the income tax return of the filing member of the group with respect to a particular December 31, the total cost of used section 38 property actually placed in service by any component member of the group during such member's taxable year that includes such December 31 is not known then such member shall estimate such cost. The estimate shall be made on the basis of the facts and circumstances known as of the time of the estimate. Any such estimate shall also be used in determining the total cost of used section 38 property placed in service by all component members for their taxable years including such December 31.

(ii) If an estimate is used by any component member of a controlled group pursuant to subdivision (i) of this subparagraph, each member may later file an original or amended return in which the apportionment of the $50,000 amount is based upon the cost of used section 38 property actually placed in service by all component members of the group during their taxable year which includes such December 31. Such amended apportionment shall be made only if each component member of the group whose limitation would be changed files an original or amended return which reflects the amended apportionment based upon the cost of the used section 38 property actually placed in service by component members of the group. In such case, the new statement reflecting the amended apportionment shall be attached to the amended return of the filing member of the group, and a copy of such statement shall be retained by each such member pursuant to the requirements of subparagraph (2) of this paragraph.

(4) Definitions of controlled group of corporations and component member of controlled group. For purposes of this section, the terms "controlled group of corporations" and "component member" of a controlled group of corporations shall have the same meaning assigned to those terms in section 1563(a) and (b), except that the phrase "more than 50 percent" shall be substituted for the phrase "at least 80 percent" each place it appears in section 1563(a)(1). For purposes of applying § 1.1563-1(b)(2)(ii)(c), an electing small business corporation shall be treated as an excluded member whether or not it is subject to the tax imposed by section 1378.

(5) Members of controlled group filing a consolidated return. For the purpose of apportioning the $50,000 amount in the case of component members of a controlled group which join in filing a consolidated return, all such members shall be treated as though they were a single component member of the controlled group. Thus, in determining the limitation on the cost of used section 38 property which may be taken into account by the group filing the consolidated return, the apportionment provided in subparagraph (1)(ii) of this paragraph shall be made by using the aggregate cost of such property placed in service by all members of the group filing the consolidated return. If all component members of the controlled group join in filing a consolidated return, the group may select the items to be taken into account to the extent of an aggregate cost of $50,000; if some component members of the controlled group do not join in filing the consolidated return, then the members of the group which join in filing the consolidated return may select the items to be taken into account to the extent of the amount apportioned to such members under subparagraph (1)(ii) of this paragraph.

(6) Examples. This paragraph may be illustrated by the following examples:

Example (1). (i) On December 31, 1970, corporations M, N, and O are component members of the same controlled group. The taxable years of M, N, and O end, respectively, on January 31, March 31, and April 30. During the respective taxable years of each corporation which include December 31, 1970, M places in service no used section 38 property, and N and O place in service used section 38 property with respective costs of $100,000 and $150,000. N is the "filing member" of the group since N, among the members (N and O) which are apportioned part of the $50,000 amount for their taxable years which include such December 31, has the taxable year ending on the earliest date.

(ii) The cost of used section 38 property taken into account by N for its taxable year ending March 31, 1971, may not exceed $20,000, that is, an amount which bears the same ratio to $50,000 as the cost of used section 38 property placed in service by N for its taxable year ($100,000) bears to the total cost of used section 38 property placed in service by all component members of the controlled group (M, N, and O) for their taxable years which include December 31, 1970 ($250,000). Similarly, the cost of used section 38 property taken into account by O for its taxable year ending April 30, 1971, may not exceed $30,000.

Example (2). (i) On December 31, 1971, corporations S and T are component members of the same controlled group. The taxable years of corporations S and T end, respectively, on January 31 and June 30. On April 15, 1972, S files an income tax return for its taxable year ending January 31, 1972, during which year it places in service used section 38 property costing $100,000. T estimates that it will place in service used section 38 property costing $150,000 during its taxable year ending June 30, 1972.

(ii) S, the "filing member" of the group, must file an apportionment schedule under which it may take into account as the cost of used section 38 property an amount not in excess of $20,000 ($100,000/$250,000 × $50,000). If T actually places in service during its taxable year used section 38 property costing more or less than $150,000, its income tax return for its taxable year ending June 30, 1972, may reflect the amended apportionment of the $50,000 limitation based upon the cost of used section 38 property actually placed in service by the group, provided that S attaches a new apportionment schedule to an amended return to reflect the amended apportionment. For example, if T places in service used section 38 property costing $200,000, the cost of used section 38 property taken into account by S and T for their respective taxable years could not exceed $16,667 ($100,000/$300,000 × $50,000) and $33,333 ($200,000/$300,000 × $50,000), respectively, under an amended apportionment.

T.D. 6731, 5/7/64, amend T.D. 6931, 10/9/67, T.D. 7181, 4/24/72, T.D. 7820, 6/9/82, T.D. 8996, 5/16/2002.

Proposed § 1.48-3 [*For Preamble, see ¶ 152,177*]

§ 1.48-4 Election of lessor of new section 38 property to treat lessee as purchaser.

• ***Caution:*** Reg. § 1.48-4, following, was issued under Code Sec. 48 before amendment by P.L.

101-508 (11/5/90). The relative provisions of Code Sec. 48 before such amendment were adopted by reference in current Code Sec. 50.

Caution: The Treasury has not yet amended Reg § 1.48-4 to reflect changes made by P.L. 104-188, P.L. 101-508, P.L. 99-514, P.L. 98-369, P.L. 97-248, P.L. 97-34.

(a) In general. *(1) Lessee treated as purchaser.* Under section 48(d), a lessor of property may elect to treat the lessee of such property as having purchased such property (or, in the case of short-term lease property described in subparagraph (2) of this paragraph, a portion of such property) for purposes of the credit allowed by section 38 if the following conditions are satisfied:

(i) The property must be "section 38 property" in the hands of the lessor; that is, it must be property with respect to which depreciation (or amortization in lieu of depreciation) is allowable to the lessor, it must have a useful life of 3 years (4 years in the case of property which is not described in section 50) or more in his hands, and in every other respect it must meet the requirements of § 1.48-1. Thus, for example, property leased by a municipality to a taxpayer for use in what is commonly known as an "industrial park" is not eligible for the election since under paragraph (k) of § 1.48-1, property used by a governmental unit is not section 38 property. In addition, property used by the lessee predominantly outside the United States is not eligible for the election since, under paragraph (g) of § 1.48-1, such property is not section 38 property. For purposes of this subdivision, if the lessor is an estate or trust, depreciation (or amortization in lieu of depreciation) will be considered allowable to the estate or trust even if it is apportioned to the beneficiaries or other persons.

(ii) The property must be "new section 38 property" (within the meaning of § 1.48-2) in the hands of the lessor, and the original use of such property must commence with the lessor. See paragraph (b) of this section for the application of the rules relating to "original use" in the case of leased property.

(iii) The property would constitute "new section 38 property" to the lessee if such lessee had actually purchased the property. Thus, the election is not available if the lessee is not the original user of the property. See paragraph (b) of this section for the application of the rules relating to "original use" in the case of leased property. See paragraph (d) of this section for the determination of the estimated useful life of leased property in the hands of the lessee.

(iv) A statement of election to treat the lessee as a purchaser has been filed in the manner and within the time provided in paragraph (f) or (g) of this section.

(v) The lessor is not a person referred to in section 46(d)(1), that is, a mutual savings bank, cooperative bank, or domestic building and loan association to which section 593 applies; a regulated investment company or real estate investment trust subject to taxation under subchapter M, chapter 1 of the Code; or a cooperative organization described in section 1381(a).

The election may be made on a property-by-property basis or a general election may be made with respect to each taxable year of a particular lessee. If the conditions of this subparagraph have been met, the lessee shall be treated as though he were the actual owner of all or a portion of the property for purposes of the credit allowed by section 38. Thus, the lessee shall be entitled to a credit allowed by section 38 with respect to such property for the taxable year in which he places such property in service, and the lessor shall not be entitled to a credit allowed by section 38 with respect to such property unless the property is short-term lease property (as defined in subparagraph (2) of this paragraph). Moreover, if the leased property is disposed of, or if it otherwise ceases to be section 38 property, the property will be subject to the provisions of section 47 (relating to early dispositions, etc.).

(2) Short-term lease property. For purposes of this section, the term "short-term lease property" means property which—

(i) Is new section 38 property;

(ii) Has a class life (determined under section 167(m)) in excess of 14 years;

(iii) Is leased under a lease entered into after November 8, 1971, for a period which is less than 80 percent of the class life of such property; and

(iv) Is not leased subject to a net lease within the meaning of section 57(c)(1)(B) and the regulations thereunder.

The class life of property shall be determined under section 167(m) and the regulations prescribed in connection with that section, except that such class life shall be determined without regard to any variance from the class life permitted under such section. If a class life has not been prescribed for property under section 167(m) on the date such property is leased, the class life of the property shall be the estimated useful life used to compute the allowance for depreciation with respect to such property under section 167. For purposes of subdivision (iii) of this subparagraph, the period for which a lease is entered into shall be determined without regard to any option on the part of the lessee to extend or renew such lease, and without regard to any option on the part of the lessee to cancel the lease after a specified period if under the terms of such lease, such a cancellation would result in the imposition of a substantial penalty upon the lessee. Generally, a penalty equal to 25 percent of the total remaining rental payments due under the lease will be regarded as substantial.

(b) Original use. For purposes of this section only, the lessor and the lessee may both be considered as the original users of an item of leased property. The determination of whether the lessor qualifies as the original user of leased property shall be made under paragraph (b)(7) of § 1.48-2. The determination of whether the lessee qualifies as the original user of leased property shall be made, under paragraph (b)(7) of § 1.48-2, as if the lessee actually purchased the property. Thus, the lessee would not be considered the original user of the property if it has been previously used by the lessor or another person, or if it is reconstructed, rebuilt, or reconditioned property. However, the lessee would be considered the original user if he is the first person to use the property for its intended function. Thus, the fact that the lessor may have, for example, tested, stored, or attempted to lease the property to other persons will not preclude the lessee from being considered the original user.

(c) Qualified investment. *(1) In general.* If a valid election is made under this section, the amount of qualified investment under section 46(c) with respect to the leased property shall be determined under this paragraph and paragraphs (d) and (e) of this section.

(2) Nonshort-term lease property. In the case of property which is not short-term lease property, the lessee is treated

as having acquired the entire property for an amount equal to—

(i) The fair market value of such property on the date possession is transferred to the lessee, or

(ii) If the property is leased by a component member of a controlled group to another component member of the same controlled group (within the meaning of paragraph (f)(4) of § 1.46-1) on the date possession of the property is transferred to the lessee, the basis of the property in the hands of the lessor.

(3) Short-term lease property. (i) In the case of short-term lease property, the lessee is treated as having acquired a portion of such property. The amount for which the lessee is treated as having acquired such portion is an amount equal to a fraction, the numerator of which is the term of the lease and the denominator of which is the class life of the property leased, of the amount for which the lessee would be treated as having acquired the property under subparagraph (2) of this paragraph if the property were not short-term lease property.

(ii) In the case of short-term lease property, the qualified investment of the lessor is an amount equal to his qualified investment in such property determined under section 46(c) multiplied by a fraction, the numerator of which is the class life of the property leased minus the term of the lease and the denominator of which is the class life of such property.

(4) Example. The provisions of this paragraph may be illustrated by the following example:

Example. (a) On December 1, 1971, X corporation completed construction of an item of new section 38 property with a basis of $10,000. Under section 167(m), the property has a class life of 16 years. On December 1, 1971, X leases the property to individual A for 4 years and A immediately places the property in service. The lease is not a net lease within the meaning of section 57(c)(1)(B). On the date of the lease, the fair market value of the property is $12,000. The property would qualify as new section 38 property in A's hands if it had been purchased by A. Under this section, the property is short-term lease property. X makes the election under this section to treat A as having acquired a portion of the property.

(b) A is treated as having acquired from X a portion of the property for $3,000 (the fair market value of the property, $12,000, multiplied by a fraction, 4/16, the numerator of which is the term of the lease and the denominator of which is the class life of the leased property). Since under paragraph (d) of this section the useful life of such property in the hands of A is the same as the useful life of such property in the hands of X, and such useful life is at least 7 years, A's qualified investment with respect to the property is $3,000.

(c) The qualified investment of X is $7,500 (the qualified investment of X under section 46(c), $10,000, multiplied by a fraction, 12/16, the numerator of which is the class life of the leased property, 16, minus the term of the lease, 4, and the denominator of which is the class life of the property).

(d) Estimated useful life of leased property. The estimated useful life to the lessee of property subject to the election shall be deemed to be the estimated useful life in the hands of the lessor for purposes of computing depreciation, regardless of the term of the lease. The lessor shall determine the estimated useful life of each leased property on an individual basis even though multiple asset accounts are used. However, in the case of assets similar in kind contained in a multiple asset account, the lessor shall assign to each of such assets the average useful life of such assets used in computing depreciation. Thus, for example, if during a taxable year a lessor leases 10 similar trucks with an average estimated useful life for depreciation purposes of 6 years, based on an estimated range of 5 to 7 years, he must assign a useful life of 6 years to each of the 10 trucks.

(e) Lessor itself a lessee. *(1) In general.* If the lessee of property is treated, under this section, as having purchased all or a portion of such property and if such lessee leases such property to a sublessee, the qualified investment with respect to such property in the hands of the sublessee shall be determined under paragraphs (c) and (d) of this section as if the original lessor had leased the property directly to the sublessee for the term of the sublessee's lease on the date possession of the property is transferred to the sublessee. For this purpose, property which is short-term lease property in the hands of the lessee shall be treated as short-term lease property in the hands of the sublessee regardless of whether such property is leased to the sublessee subject to a net lease (within the meaning of section 57(c)(1)(B)). In the case of property which is short-term lease property in the hands of the sublessee, the amount for which the lessee is treated as having acquired such property under paragraph (c) of this section shall be reduced by an amount equal to such amount multiplied by a fraction, the numerator of which is the term of the lease of the sublessee and the denominator of which is the term of the lease of the lessee.

(2) Example. The provisions of this paragraph may be illustrated by the following example:

Example. (a) On December 1, 1971, corporation X completes construction of a machine at a cost of $10,000. The machine has a class life under section 167(m) of 20 years. On December 1, 1971, X leases the machine to corporation Y for 12 years, and Y immediately subleases the machine to individual A for 8 years. X and Y are component members of the same controlled group. The lease between X and Y is not a net lease within the meaning of section 57(c)(1)(B). The fair market value of the property on December 1, 1971, is $16,000. Both X and Y make valid elections under this section.

(b) The property is short-term lease property and this paragraph applies.

(c) The qualified investment of A is $6,400. Such amount is determined by multiplying $16,000, the amount for which A would be treated under paragraph (c)(2) of this section as having acquired the property if it were not short-term lease property, by 8/20.

(d) The qualified investment of Y is $2,000. Such amount is determined by multiplying $10,000, the amount for which Y would be treated under paragraph (c)(2) of this section as having acquired the property if it were not short-term lease property, by 12/20, and by reducing the amount so determined ($6,000) by 8/12 of such amount ($4,000) to $2,000.

(e) The qualified investment of X is $4,000. Such amount is determined by multiplying the amount of X's qualified investment determined under section 46(c) without regard to this section ($10,000) by 8/20.

(f) Property-by-property election. *(1) Manner of making election.* The election of a lessor with respect to a particular property (or properties) shall be made by filing a statement with the lessee, signed by the lessor and including the written consent of the lessee, containing the following information:

(i) The name, address, and taxpayer account number of the lessor and the lessee;

(ii) The district director's office with which the income tax returns of the lessor and the lessee are filed;

(iii) A description of each property with respect to which the election is being made;

(iv) The date on which possession of the property (or properties) is transferred to the lessee;

(v) The estimated useful life category of the property (or properties) in the hands of the lessor, that is, 3 years or more but less than 5 years, 5 years or more but less than 7 years, or 7 years or more;

(vi) The amount for which the lessee (or sublessee) is treated as having acquired the leased property under paragraph (c)(2) or (3) of this section; and

(vii) If the lessor is itself a lessee, the name, address, and taxpayer account number of the original lessor, and the district director's office with which the income tax return of such original lessor is filed.

(2) Time for making election. The statement referred to in subparagraph (1) of this paragraph shall be filed with the lessee on or before the due date (including any extensions of time) of the lessee's return for the lessee's taxable year during which possession of the property is transferred to the lessee, except that if such taxable year ends after March 31, 1971, and before December 11, 1971, the statement shall be filed with the lessee on or before the due date (including any extensions of time) of the lessee's return for such taxable year, or on or before October 24, 1972, whichever is later.

(3) Election is irrevocable. An election under this paragraph shall be irrevocable as of the time the statement referred to in subparagraph (1) of this paragraph is filed with the lessee.

(g) General election. *(1) In general.* In lieu of making elections on a property-by-property basis in the manner and time prescribed in paragraph (f) of this section, a lessor may, with respect to a particular taxable year of a particular lessee, make a general election to treat such lessee as having purchased all properties possession of which is transferred under lease by the lessor to the lessee during such taxable year of the lessee.

(2) Manner and the time for making general election. The general election of a lessor with respect to a taxable year of a lessee shall be made by filing a statement with the lessee, signed by the lessor and including the written consent of the lessee, on or before the due date (including any extensions of time) of the lessee's return for such taxable year, except that if such taxable year ends after March 31, 1971, and before December 11, 1971, the statement shall be filed with the lessee on or before the due date (including any extensions of time) of the lessee's return for such taxable year, or on or before October 24, 1972, whichever is later. Such statement of general election shall contain:

(i) The name, address, and taxpayer account number of the lessor and the lessee;

(ii) The taxable year of the lessee with respect to which such general election is made;

(iii) The district director's office with which the income tax returns of the lessor and the lessee are filed;

(iv) If the lessor is itself a lessee, the name, address, and taxpayer account number of the original lessor, and the district director's office with which the income tax return of such original lessor is filed.

(3) Election is irrevocable. A general election under this paragraph shall be irrevocable as of the time the statement referred to in subparagraph (2) of this paragraph is filed with the lessee and shall be binding on the lessor and the lessee for the entire taxable year of the lessee with respect to which such general election is made.

(4) Information requirement. If a lessor, with respect to a taxable year of the lessee, makes a general election under this paragraph, such lessor shall provide such lessee, on or before the date required for filing the statement under subparagraph (2) of this paragraph, with a statement (or statements) containing the information required by paragraph (f)(1)(iii), (iv), (v), and (vi) of this section with respect to all properties possession of which is transferred under lease by the lessor to the lessee during such taxable year.

(h) Signature. The statement referred to in paragraph (f)(1) or (g)(2) of this section shall not be valid unless signed by both the lessor and the lessee. The signature of the lessee shall constitute the consent of the lessee to the election. The statement shall be signed by the taxpayer or a duly authorized agent of the taxpayer. For purposes of this section, a facsimile signature may be used in lieu of a signature manually executed and, if used, shall be as binding as a signature manually executed.

(i) [Reserved]

(j) Record requirements. The lessor and the lessee shall keep as a part of their records the statement referred to in paragraph (f)(1), or the statements referred to in paragraphs (g)(2) and (g)(4), of this section. The lessor shall attach to his income tax return a summary statement of all property leased during his taxable year with respect to which an election is made. In the case of a taxable year ending after March 31, 1971, and before December 11, 1971, a summary statement may be filed on or before the due date (including any extensions of time) of the return or on or before October 24, 1972, whichever is later, with the Internal Revenue Service Center with which the return has been filed. Such summary statement shall contain the following information: (1) The name, address, and taxpayer account number of the lessor; and (2) in numerical account number order, each lessee's account number, name, and address, the estimated useful life category of the property (or, if applicable, the estimated useful life expressed in years), and the basis or fair market value of the property, whichever is applicable.

(k) Adjustment of rental deductions. *(1) In general.* The rules of this paragraph apply only to section 38 property placed in service before January 1, 1964, and with respect to any such property only for taxable years of a lessee beginning before January 1, 1964. If a lessor makes a valid election under this section with respect to property placed in service by the lessee before January 1, 1964, section 48(g) and § 1.48-7 (relating to adjustments to basis of property) shall not apply to the lessor with respect to such property. Thus, the lessor is not required to reduce under section 48(g)(1) the basis of such property. However, if such an election is made, the deductions otherwise allowable under section 162 to the lessee for amounts paid or accrued to the lessor under the lease shall be adjusted in the manner provided in this paragraph. For special adjustment for taxable years beginning after December 31, 1963, see paragraph (m) of this section.

(2) Decrease in rental deduction. (i) The deductions otherwise allowable under section 162 to the lessee for amounts paid or accrued to the lessor under the lease with respect to leased property placed in service before January 1, 1964, shall be decreased under subdivision (ii) or (iii) of this subparagraph, whichever is applicable, by an amount deter-

mined by reference to the credit earned on the leased property. The "credit earned" on the leased property is determined by multiplying the qualified investment (as defined in section 46(c)) with respect to such property by 7 percent. Thus, the credit earned (and the decrease in deductions) is determined without regard to the limitation based on tax which, under section 46(a)(2), may limit the amount of the credit the lessee may take into account in any one year.

(ii) If, in the case of property placed in service before January 1, 1964, the lessor, under paragraph (f)(1)(v) of this section, supplies the lessee with the useful life of such property expressed in years, then for each taxable year beginning before January 1, 1964, any part of which falls within a period beginning with the month in which the leased property is placed in service by the lessee and ending with the close of the estimated useful life of such property (as determined under paragraph (d) of this section), the lessee shall decrease the deduction otherwise allowable under section 162 for each such taxable year with respect to such property. The decrease for each such taxable year shall be equal to (a) the credit earned, divided by (b) the estimated useful life of the property (expressed in months), multiplied by (c) the number of calendar months in which the leased property was held by the lessee during such taxable year. Thus, if leased property with a basis of $27,000 in the hands of a calendar-year lessee, and with an estimated useful life of 10 years, is placed in service by the lessee on July 15, 1963, the lessee must decrease his section 162 deduction with respect to the leased property for the taxable year 1963 by $94.50 ($1,890 credit earned, divided by 120, multiplied by 6).

(iii) If, in the case of property placed in service before January 1, 1964, the lessor, under paragraph (f)(1)(v) of this section, supplies the lessee with the useful life category of such property, then for each taxable year beginning before January 1, 1964, during a period equal to the shortest life of the useful life category used by the lessee in computing qualified investment under section 46(c) with respect to the leased property, the lessee shall decrease the deduction otherwise allowable under section 162 for such taxable year with respect to such property. The decrease for each such taxable year shall be equal to the credit earned divided by such shortest life, that is, 4, 6, or 8. Such decreases shall begin with the taxable year during which the lessee places the property in service. Thus, if leased property with a basis of $30,000 to the lessee, and an estimated useful life falling within the 4 years or more but less than 6 years useful life category, is placed in service by the lessee within the lessee's taxable year ending December 31, 1962, the lessee must decrease his section 162 deduction with respect to the leased property for each of the taxable years 1962 and 1963 by $175 ($700 credit earned divided by 4).

(iv) To the extent that a required decrease, under subdivision (ii) or (iii) of this subparagraph, is not taken into account for any taxable year beginning before January 1, 1964, because the deduction otherwise allowable under section 162 for such taxable year with respect to the leased property is less than the required decrease for such taxable year, then the balance of the required decrease not taken into account for such taxable year shall decrease the amount otherwise allowable as a deduction under section 162 with respect to such property for the next succeeding taxable year (or years) beginning before January 1, 1964, if any, for which a deduction is allowable with respect to such property. Thus, if the required decrease with respect to leased property is $200 for 1962 but the lessee's deduction otherwise allowable under section 162 for such taxable year with respect to such property is only $50, the balance of $150 must be applied in 1963 to decrease the deduction otherwise allowable to the lessee with respect to the leased property for such taxable year.

(v) See paragraph (b) of § 1.48-7 for reduction of basis in the case of an actual purchase of leased property by a lessee (in a taxable year of such lessee beginning before January 1, 1964) who has been treated as a purchaser of such property under this section.

(3) Increase in rental deductions on account of early disposition, etc. (i) If, as a result of an early disposition, etc., in a taxable year beginning before January 1, 1964, with respect to leased property placed in service before such date, the lessee's tax is increased under section 47(a)(1) or (2), or an adjustment in a carryback or carryover is made under section 47(a)(3) by reduction of an unused credit, the rental deductions (if any) otherwise allowable under section 162 to such lessee for amounts paid or accrued to the lessor under the lease with respect to such property shall be increased in an amount equal to the total decreases previously made in the lessee's rental deductions under subparagraph (2) of this paragraph.

(ii) Except as provided in subdivision (iii) of this subparagraph, the increase in rental deductions described in subdivision (i) of this subparagraph shall be taken into account as an increase in rental deductions otherwise allowable under section 162 for the taxable year in which the early disposition, etc., occurred.

(iii) If, after the event which caused section 47(a)(1), (2), or (3) to apply, the lessee continues the use of the property in a trade or business or in the production of income, the increase in rental deductions described in subdivision (i) of this subparagraph shall be taken into account ratably over the remaining portion of the useful life of the property which was used in making the decreases in rental deductions with respect to the property under subparagraph (2) of this paragraph.

(iv) If subdivision (iii) of this subparagraph applies, and if, prior to the expiration of the useful life of the property used in making the decreases in rental deductions, the lease is terminated other than by actual purchase of the property by the lessee, any increase in rental deductions not previously taken into account shall be taken into account as an increase in rental deductions for the taxable year in which the lease is terminated. In the case of an actual purchase of the property by the lessee, see paragraph (e) of § 1.48-7.

(l) Examples. The provisions of this section may be illustrated by the following examples:

Example (1). X Corporation is engaged in the business of manufacturing and leasing new and reconstructed equipment which in its hands has an estimated useful life of 12 years. After December 31, 1961, X Corporation constructs machine no. 1 at a cost of $20,000 and reconstructs machine no. 2 at a cost of $5,000. On February 15, 1962, Y Corporation, a calendar-year taxpayer, leases both machines from X Corporation and places them in service. The fair market value of machine no. 1 on the date on which possession is transferred to Y is $25,200. Machine no. 1 would qualify as new section 38 property in Y's hands if it had been purchased by Y. If X elects to treat Y as the purchaser of machine no. 1, under paragraph (c)(2)(ii) of this section such machine will have a basis of $25,200 in Y's hands. Under paragraph (f)(1)(v) of this section, X supplies Y with an estimated useful life of 12 years (expressed in years rather than useful life category) with respect to machine no. 1 for purposes of determining Y's qualified investment. Y's credit earned with respect to the property is $1,764 (7 percent of $25,200). Under paragraph (k)(2)(ii) of this section, Y's deduction attributable to the leased property for 1962 will be decreased by $134.75 (credit earned of $1,764, divided by 144, multiplied by 11), and for 1963 such deduction will be decreased by $147 ($1,764, divided by 144, multiplied by 12). The election is not available with respect to machine no. 2 since a reconstructed machine would not constitute new section 38 property if Y had purchased it. In such case, while X cannot make the election to treat Y as a purchaser, X would be entitled to a credit under section 38 based on its expenditure of $5,000 as an investment in new section 38 property, since such amount represents cost of reconstruction after December 31, 1961.

Example (2). Assume the same facts as in example (1) except that under paragraph (f)(1)(v) of this section, X supplies Y with an estimated useful life category of 8 years or more (rather than an estimated useful life expressed in years) with respect to machine no. 1 for purposes of determining Y's qualified investment. Under paragraph (k)(2)(iii) of this section, Y's deduction attributable to the leased property will be decreased by $220.50 (credit earned of $1,764, divided by 8) for each of its taxable years 1962 and 1963.

Example (3). Assume the same facts as in example (1) except that the lessee disposes of his interest in the lease on January 1, 1963, and that there is an increase in Y's tax for 1963 under section 47(a)(1) in the amount of $1,764. Under paragraph (k)(2) of this section, Y's deductions attributable to the leased property are decreased only in 1962, and the amount of such decrease is $134.75. In 1963 there shall be an increase of $134.75 in the deductions otherwise allowable under section 162 for such taxable year with respect to the leased property.

Example (4). Assume the same facts as in example (1) except that during the year 1963 the property was used by Y predominantly outside the United States within the meaning of paragraph (g) of § 1.48-1, and thereafter was used in Y's trade or business. Under paragraph (k)(3) of this section, the increase of $134.75 described in example (3) is taken into account ratably as an increase in rental deductions otherwise allowable under section 162 in the amount of $12.25 ($134.75 divided by 11 years) for 1963 and each of the 10 succeeding years.

(m) Increase in rental deductions on account of section 203(a)(2)(B) of the Revenue Act of 1964. *(1) In general.* (i) Under section 203(a)(2)(B) of the Revenue Act of 1964, if, for any taxable year of a lessee beginning before January 1, 1964, the rental deductions otherwise allowable under section 162 to such lessee for amounts paid or accrued to the lessor under the lease with respect to leased property placed in service before January 1, 1964, were decreased under paragraph (k)(2) of this section, such rental deductions shall be increased.

(ii) The increase in rental deductions described in subdivision (i) of this subparagraph shall be in an amount equal to the total decreases in the lessee's rental deductions previously made under paragraph (k)(2) of this section less any increases in rental deductions made under paragraph (k)(3) of this section.

(iii) Except as provided in subdivision (iv) of this subparagraph, the increase in rental deductions described in subdivision (i) of this subparagraph shall be taken into account ratably over the remaining portion of the useful life of the property commencing with the first day of the first taxable year beginning after December 31, 1963. For this purpose, the useful life of the property shall be the useful life used in making the decreases in rental deductions with respect to the property under paragraph (k)(2) of this section.

(iv) If the lease is terminated other than by the lessee's actual purchase of the property during a taxable year beginning after December 31, 1963, and before the end of the remaining useful life of the property used in making the decreases in rental deductions, the amount of the increase in rental deductions described in subdivision (i) of this subparagraph and not previously taken into account shall be allowed as a deduction for the taxable year in which such termination occurs.

(v) The rental deductions with respect to any section 38 property are not to be increased under this paragraph if the lessee dies in a taxable year beginning before January 1, 1964.

(vi) The increase in rental deductions described in subdivision (i) of this subparagraph shall ordinarily be taken into account by the lessee treated as the purchaser, that is, the lessee entitled to the credit. However, if the property under the lease is transferred by the lessee to a successor lessee in a transaction described in section 47(b) (other than a transfer by reason of death) under which the successor lessee assumes the lessee's obligations under the lease, such increase in rental deductions shall be taken into account by the successor lessee in the manner prescribed in this paragraph.

(2) Examples. The operation of this paragraph may be illustrated by the following examples:

Example (1). (a) X Corporation acquired on January 1, 1962, an item of new section 38 property with a basis of $24,000 and with a useful life to the lessor of 10 years. Y Corporation, which makes its returns on the basis of a calendar year, leased such property from X Corporation and placed it in service on January 2, 1962. Under this section, X Corporation made a valid election to treat Y Corporation as having purchased such property for purposes of the credit allowed by section 38 and supplied the lessee with information that the property had a useful life of 10 years. The amount of the credit earned with respect to such property was $1,680 (7 percent of $24,000). For each of the taxable years 1962 and 1963, Y Corporation decreased under paragraph (k)(2) of this section, its deductions otherwise allowable under section 162 with respect to such property by $168 ($1,680 multiplied by 12/120).

(b) For each of the taxable years 1964 through 1971, Y Corporation increases its deductions otherwise allowable under section 162 for amounts paid to X Corporation under the lease by $42 ($336 (that is, $168 multiplied by 2) divided by the remaining useful life of 8 years).

Example (2). (a) The facts are the same as in example (1) except that the lease is terminated on January 3, 1965.

(b) For the taxable year 1964, Y Corporation increases its deductions otherwise allowable under section 162 by $42.

(c) For the taxable year 1965, Y Corporation increases its deductions otherwise allowable under section 162 for the portion of the increase which had not been taken into account as of the time of the termination of the lease. Thus, the amount of such increase for the taxable year 1965 is $294 ($336 minus $42).

T.D. 6731, 5/7/64, amend T.D. 6838, 7/19/65, T.D. 6953, 4/22/68, T.D. 7181, 4/24/72, T.D. 7203, 8/24/72.

PAR. 2. Section 1.48-4 is amended by adding new paragraphs (n), (o), and (p) to read as follows:

Proposed § 1.48-4 Election of lessor of new section 38 property to treat lessee as purchaser. [*For Preamble, see ¶ 151,105*]

* * * * *

(n) Adjustment to lessee's income. *(1) In general.* If a lessor of new section 38 property makes a valid election under section 48(d) with respect to such property, section 48(d) (except paragraph (4) thereof) and § 1.48-7 (except paragraphs (l) and (m) thereof) shall not apply. Thus, the lessor is not required under section 48(q) to reduce the basis of such property. However, if such an election is made, the lessee shall include ratably in gross income, over the shortest recovery period which could be applicable under section 168 with respect to the property, an amount equal to 50 percent of the amount of the credit allowable under section 38 with respect to such property. For purposes of this paragraph (n), the amount of the credit allowable is determined by multiplying the qualified investment (as defined in section 46(c)) with respect to such property by the percentage specified in section 46(a) (section 46(a)(2) in the case of taxable years beginning on or before December 31, 1983) for such property, without regard to the limitation based on tax which, under section 38(c) (section 46(a)(3) in the case of taxable years beginning on or before December 31, 1983), may limit the amount of credit the lessee may take into account in any one year.

(2) Adjustments as a result of an early disposition, etc. (i) Except as provided in paragraph (n)(2)(iii) of this section, if section 47 requires an increase in the lessee's tax or a reduction in the carryback or carryover of an unused credit as a result of an early disposition, etc., of leased property for which an election had been made under section 48(d), the lessee's gross income shall be reduced by an amount equal to the excess (if any) of the total increases in gross income previously made under paragraph (n)(1) of this section over 50 percent of the portion of the credit that is not recaptured for the taxable year in which the early disposition, etc., occurred.

(ii) If the total increases in gross income of the lessee previously made under paragraph (n)(1) of this section are less than 50 percent of the credit that is not recaptured for the taxable year in which the early disposition, etc., occurred, the lessee shall include the difference in income in the year of disposition.

(iii) If, after the event which caused section 47 to apply, the lessee continues the use of the property in a trade or business or in the production of income, the amount described in paragraph (n)(2)(i) or (ii) of this section shall be taken into account ratably over the remaining portion of the recovery period described in paragraph (n)(1) of this section.

(iv) If paragraph (n)(2)(iii) of this section applies, and if, prior to the expiration of the recovery period described in paragraph (n)(1) of this section, the lease is terminated other than by purchase of the property by the lessee, any deduction allowable or inclusion necessitated under this paragraph not previously taken into account shall be taken into account for the taxable year in which the lease is terminated. In the case of a purchase of the property by the lessee, see paragraph (b) of § 1.48-7.

(3) Effective dates. The effective dates described in paragraph (m) of § 1.48-7 (relating to adjustment to basis) shall apply to this paragraph.

(4) Examples. The provisions of this paragraph may be illustrated by the following examples:

Example (1). Corporation X is engaged in the business of manufacturing and leasing new equipment. X constructs a machine at a cost of $20,000, which Corporation Y, a calendar year taxpayer, leases from X and places in service on July 1, 1983. The machine is 5-year recovery property. The fair market value of the machine on the date possession is transferred to Y is $25,000. If X elects to treat Y as the purchaser of the machine under this section, Y's investment credit determined under section 46(a) for 1983 is $2,500 (10 percent of $25,000). Under paragraph (n) of this section, Y's increase in gross income for each of the five years beginning with 1983 will be $250 ($1,250/5-year recovery period).

Example (2). The facts are the same as in example (1) except that Y disposes of its interest in the lease on January 1, 1985, and that there is an increase in Y's tax for 1985 under section 47(a)(1) in the amount of $2,000 (80 percent of $2,500). The amount of $250 (fifty percent of the unrecaptured credit) is compared to the amount previously included in income, $500 ($250 in 1983 + $250 in 1984), to determine whether Y is entitled to a reduction in income as a result of a possible over-inclusion in income under paragraph (n)(1) of this section. In this case, Y has over-included $250 ($500 − $250) and, as a result, will decrease its gross income in the year of disposition by $250.

Example (3). A lessor elects under section 48(d) to treat a lessee as making qualified rehabilitation expenditures with respect to a qualified rehabilitated building in the amount of $100,000. The property subject to such expenditures is placed in service on March 1, 1984, generating an investment tax credit of $15,000 ($100,000 × 15%) and potential income inclusions of $1,000 a year for 15 years. Assuming the lessee is a calendar year taxpayer, if the property were to be disposed of on June 1, 1985, the lessee would be entitled to a credit that is not recaptured of $3,000 ($15,000 × 20%) but would have included only $1,000 in income for 1984. In this case the lessee has under-included $2,000 ($3,000 − $1,000) and will increase gross income by such amount in the year of disposition (i.e., 1985).

(o) Special rule for qualified rehabilitated buildings. In the case of a credit determined under section 46(a) (section 46(a)(2) in the case of taxable years beginning on or before December 31, 1983) for any qualified rehabilitation expenditure in connection with a qualified rehabilitated building other than a certified historic structure, paragraph (n) of this section shall be applied by substituting the phrase "100 percent of" for the phrase "50 percent of".

(p) Lessee's election for a reduction in credit in lieu of adjustment to lessee's income. *(1) In general.* An election may be made by the lessee not to have the rules of paragraph (n) of this section apply with respect to so much of the credit determined under section 46(a) (section 46(a)(2) in the case of taxable years beginning on or before December 31, 1983) as is attributable to the regular percentage. The election is made on a property-by-property basis. In the case of such an election, the amount of the investment credit with respect to the regular percentage shall be determined under paragraph (p)(2) of this section. A separate election must be made for each taxable year in which the reduced regular credit is elected. In the case of a partnership, S corporation, trust, or estate, the election shall be made by the partnership, S corporation, trust, or estate.

(2) Reduction in credit. In the case of any property for which an election under this paragraph has been made, the investment credit shall be determined as follows:

(i) The regular percentage shall be—

(A) 8 percent in the case of recovery property other than 3-year recovery property (RRB replacement property under section 168(f)(3)(B) shall be treated as property which is other than 3-year property), or

(B) 4 percent in the case of recovery property which is 3-year property.

(ii) For purposes of applying the regular percentage in paragraph (p)(2)(i) of this section, the applicable percentage under subsection (c) or (d) of section 46 shall be deemed to be 100 percent.

(3) Time and manner of making the election. The election specified in paragraph (p)(1) of this section shall be made by attaching a statement to the first income tax return for the taxable year for which the election is made (whether or not the return is timely) or to an amended return filed within the time prescribed by law (including extensions) for filing the return for such taxable year. For purposes of this paragraph (p), the term "income tax return for the taxable year for which the election is made" with respect to any property is the tax return for the taxable year in which such property is placed in service, or in the case of property to which an election under section 46(d) (relating to qualified progress expenditures) applies, the appropriate return is the return for the first taxable year which includes a period after December 31, 1982, for which qualified progress expenditures were taken into account with respect to such property. Except as otherwise provided in the return or instructions accompanying the return for the taxable year, the statement shall—

(i) Contain the name, address, and taxpayer identification number of the electing lessee,

(ii) Identify the election by indicating that the election is being made under sections 48(d)(5)(A) and 48(q)(4) of the Code,

(iii) Specify that the election is being made by the lessee of new section 38 property where the lessor of such property has made a valid election under section 48(d) to treat such lessee as the purchaser of the property for purposes of the section 38 credit, and

(iv) Specify the property to which the election is to apply. The election to claim a reduced credit in lieu of increasing gross income is revocable only with the consent of the Commissioner.

(4) Revocation. Any election under section 48(q)(4), and any specification contained in such election, may be revoked only with the consent of the Commissioner. Such consent will be granted only in extraordinary circumstances. Requests for consent must be filed with the Commissioner of Internal Revenue, Washington, DC 20224. The request shall include the name, address, and taxpayer identification number of the lessee and shall be signed by the taxpayer or his duly authorized representative. The request shall set forth the following information:

(i) The taxable year for which the election was made.

(ii) The Code sections applicable to the revocation (sections 48(d)(5)(A) and 48(q)(4)),

(iii) The property subject to the election for which the renovation is requested, and

(iv) The reasons why the revocation is sought.

§ 1.48-5 Electing small business corporations.

Caution: The Treasury has not yet amended Reg § 1.48-5 to reflect changes made by P.L. 98-369, P.L. 97-354, P.L. 97-34.

(a) In general. *(1)* In the case of an electing small business corporation (as defined in section 1371(b)), the basis of "new section 38 property" and the cost of "used section 38 property" placed in service during the taxable year shall be apportioned pro rata among the persons who are shareholders of such corporation on the last day of such corporation's taxable year. Section 38 property shall not (by reason of such apportionment) lose its character as new section 38 property or used section 38 property, as the case may be. The estimated useful life of such property in the hands of a shareholder shall be deemed to be the estimated useful life of such property in the hands of the electing small business corporation. The bases of all new section 38 properties which have a useful life falling within a particular useful life category shall be aggregated; likewise, the cost of all used section 38 properties which have a useful life falling within a particular useful life category shall be aggregated. The total bases of new section 38 properties within each useful life category and the total cost of used section 38 properties within each useful life category shall be apportioned separately. The useful life categories are: (i) 3 years or more but less than 5 years; (ii) 5 years or more but less than 7 years; and (iii) 7 years or more. There shall be apportioned to each person who is a shareholder of the electing small business corporation on the last day of the taxable year of such corporation, for his taxable year in which or with which the taxable year of such corporation ends, his pro rata share of the total bases of new section 38 properties within each useful life category, and his pro rata share of the total cost of used section 38 properties within each useful life category. In determining who are shareholders of an electing small business corporation on the last day of its taxable year, the rules of paragraph (d)(1) of § 1.137-1 and of paragraph (a)(2) of § 1.1373-1 shall apply.

(2) The total cost of used section 38 property that may be apportioned by an electing small business corporation to its shareholders for any taxable year of such corporation shall not exceed $50,000. If the total cost of used section 38 property placed in service during the taxable year by the electing small business corporation exceeds $50,000 such corporation must select, under paragraph (c)(4) of § 1.48-3, the used section 38 property the cost of which is to be apportioned to its shareholders.

(3) A shareholder to whom the basis (or cost) of section 38 property is apportioned shall, for purposes of the credit allowed by section 38, be treated as the taxpayer with respect to such property. Thus, the total cost of used section 38 property apportioned to him by the electing small business corporation must be taken into account as cost of used section 38 property in determining whether the $50,000 limitation on the cost of used section 38 property which may be taken into account by the shareholder in computing qualified investment for any taxable year is exceeded. If a shareholder takes into account in determining his qualified investment any portion of the basis (or cost) of section 38 property placed in service by an electing small business corporation and if such property subsequently is disposed of or otherwise ceases to be section 38 property in the hands of the corporation, such shareholder shall be subject to the provisions of section 47. See § 1.47-4.

(b) Summary statement. An electing small business corporation shall attach to its return a statement showing the apportionment to each shareholder of the total bases of new, and the total cost of used, section 38 properties within each useful life category.

(c) **Example.** This section may be illustrated by the following example:

Useful life category	New—4 to 6 years	New—8 years or more	Used—6 to 8 years	Used—8 years or more
Total bases or total cost	$60,000	$30,000	$24,000	$12,000
Shareholder A (3/10)	18,000	9,000	7,200	3,600
Shareholder B (2/10)	12,000	6,000	4,800	2,400
Shareholder C (5/10)	30,000	15,000	12,000	6,000

Assume that shareholders A, B and C did not place in service during their taxable years in which falls December 31, 1962 (the last day of X Corporation's taxable year) any section 38 property and that such shareholders did not own any interests in other electing small business corporations, partnerships, estates, or trusts. Under section 46(c), the qualified investment of shareholder A is $23,400, of shareholder B is $15,600, and of shareholder C is $39,000, computed as follows:

Shareholder A

Basis (or cost)	Applicable percentage	Qualified investment
$18,000 (new)	33⅓	$ 6,000
$9,000 (new)	100	9,000
$7,200 (used)	66⅔	4,800
$3,600 (used)	100	3,600
Total		23,400

Example. (1) X Corporation, an electing small business corporation which makes its return on the basis of the calendar year, acquires and places in service on June 1, 1962, three new assets which qualify as new section 38 property and three used assets which qualify as used section 38 property. The basis of each new, and the cost of each used, section 38 property and the estimated useful life of each property are as follows:

Asset No.	Basis (or cost)	Estimated useful life
1 (new)	$30,000	4 years.
2 (new)	30,000	4 years.
3 (new)	30,000	8 years.
4 (used)	12,000	6 years.
5 (used)	12,000	6 years.
6 (used)	12,000	8 years.

On December 31, 1962, X Corporation has 10 shares of stock outstanding which are owned as follows: A owns 3 shares, B owns 2 shares, and C owns 5 shares.

(2) Under this section, the total bases of the new, and the total cost of the used, section 38 properties are apportioned to the shareholders of X Corporation as follows:

Shareholder B

$12,000 (new)	33⅓	$ 4,000
$6,000 (new)	100	6,000
$4,800 (used)	66⅔	3,200
$2,400 (used)	100	2,400
Total		15,600

T.D. 6731, 5/7/64, amend T.D. 6931, 10/9/67, T.D. 7203, 8/24/72.

§ 1.48-6 Estates and trusts.

• ***Caution:*** Reg. § 1.48-6, following, was issued under Code Sec. 48 before amendment by P.L. 101-508 (11/5/90). The relative provisions of Code Sec. 48 before such amendment were adopted by reference in current Code Sec. 50.

Caution: The Treasury has not yet amended Reg § 1.48-6 to reflect changes made by P.L. 98-369, P.L. 97-248, P.L. 97-34, P.L. 94-12.

(a) **In general.** *(1)* In the case of an estate or trust, the basis of "new section 38 property" and the cost of "used section 38 property" placed in service during the taxable year shall be apportioned among the estate or trust and its beneficiaries on the basis of the income of such estate or trust allocable to each. Section 38 property shall not (by reason of such apportionment) lose its character as new section 38 property or used section 38 property, as the case may be. The estimated useful life of such property in the hands of a beneficiary shall be deemed to be the estimated useful life of such property in the hands of the estate or trust. The bases of all new section 38 properties which have a useful life falling within a particular useful life category shall be aggregated; likewise, the cost of all used section 38 properties which have a useful life falling within a particular useful life category shall be aggregated. The total bases of new section 38 properties within each useful life category and the total cost of used section 38 properties within each useful life category shall be apportioned separately. The useful life categories are (i) 3 years or more but less than 5 years; (ii) 5 years or more but less than 7 years; and (iii) 7 years or more. There shall be apportioned to the estate or trust for its taxable year, and to each beneficiary of such estate or trust for his taxable year in which or with which the taxable year of such estate or trust ends, his share (as determined under paragraph (b) of this section) of the total bases of new section 38 properties within each useful life category, and his share of the total cost of used section 38 properties within each useful life category.

(2) The total cost of used section 38 property that may be apportioned among an estate or trust and its beneficiaries for any taxable year of such estate or trust shall not exceed $50,000. If the total cost of used section 38 property placed in service during the taxable year by the estate or trust exceeds $50,000, such estate or trust must select, under paragraph (c)(4) of § 1.48-3, the used section 38 property the

cost of which is to be apportioned among such estate or trust and its beneficiaries.

(3) A beneficiary to whom the basis (or cost) of section 38 property is apportioned shall, for purposes of the credit allowed by section 38, be treated as the taxpayer with respect to such property. Thus, the total cost of used section 38 property apportioned to him by the estate or trust must be taken into account as cost of used section 38 property in determining whether the $50,000 limitation on the cost of used property which may be taken into account by the beneficiary in computing qualified investment for any taxable year is exceeded. If a beneficiary takes into account in determining his qualified investment any portion of the basis (or cost) of section 38 property placed in service by an estate or trust and if such property subsequently is disposed of or otherwise ceases to be section 38 property in the hands of the estate or trust, such beneficiary shall be subject to the provisions of section 47. See § 1.47-5.

(4) For purposes of this section, the term "beneficiary" includes heir, legatee, and devisee.

(5) If during the taxable year of an estate or trust a beneficiary's interest in the income of such estate or trust terminates, the basis (or cost) of section 38 property placed in service by such estate or trust after such termination shall not be apportioned to such beneficiary.

(b) Share. A trust's, estate's, or beneficiary's share of the total bases of new section 38 properties and the total cost of used section 38 properties, within a useful life category shall be—

(1) The total bases of new (or the total cost of used) section 38 properties which have a useful life falling within such useful life category placed in service in the taxable year of the estate or trust, multiplied by

(2) The amount of income allocable to such estate or trust or to such beneficiary for such taxable year, divided by

(3) The sum of the amounts of income allocable to such estate or trust and all its beneficiaries taken into account under subparagraph (2) of this paragraph.

(c) Limitation based on amount of tax. In the case of an estate or trust, the $25,000 amount specified in section 46(a)(2), relating to limitation based on amount of tax, shall be reduced for the taxable year to—

(1) $25,000, multiplied by

(2) The qualified investment with respect to the total bases of new section 38 properties plus the qualified investment with respect to the total cost of used section 38 properties, apportioned to such estate or trust under paragraph (a) of this section, divided by

(3) The qualified investment with respect to the total bases of all new section 38 properties plus the qualified investment with respect to the total cost of all used section 38 properties, apportioned among such estate or trust and its beneficiaries.

For purposes of subparagraph (3) of this paragraph, cost of used section 38 property shall not be considered as apportioned to any beneficiary to the extent that such cost is not taken into account by such beneficiary in computing qualified investment in used section 38 property.

(d) Summary statement. An estate or trust shall attach to its return a statement showing the apportionment to such estate or trust and to each beneficiary of the total bases of new, and the total cost of used, section 38 properties within each useful life category.

(e) Example. This section may be illustrated by the following example:

Example. (1) XYZ Trust, which makes its return on the basis of the calendar year, acquires and places in service on June 1, 1962, three new assets which qualify as new section 38 property and three used assets which qualify as used section 38 property. The basis of the new, and the cost of the used, section 38 property and the estimated useful life of each property are as follows:

Asset No.	Basis (or cost)	Estimated useful life
1 (new)	$30,000	4 years.
2 (new)	30,000	4 years.
3 (new)	30,000	8 years.
4 (used)	12,000	6 years.
5 (used)	12,000	6 years.
6 (used)	12,000	8 years.

For the taxable year 1962 the income of XYZ Trust is $20,000 which is allocable as follows: $10,000 to XYZ Trust, $6,000 to beneficiary A, and $4,000 to beneficiary B. Beneficiaries A and B make their returns on the basis of a calendar year.

(2) Under this section, the total bases of the new, and the total cost of the used, section 38 properties are apportioned to XYZ Trust and its beneficiaries as follows:

Useful life category	New—4 to 6 years	New—8 years or more	Used—6 to 8 years	Used—8 years or more
Total bases or total cost	$60,000	$30,000	$24,000	$12,000
XYZ Trust $\left(\frac{\$10,000}{20,000}\right)$	30,000	15,000	12,000	6,000
Beneficiary A $\left(\frac{\$6,000}{20,000}\right)$	18,000	9,000	7,200	3,600
Beneficiary B $\left(\frac{\$4,000}{20,000}\right)$	12,000	6,000	4,800	2,400

Assume that beneficiary A placed in service during his taxable year 1962 new section 38 property with a basis of $10,000 and an estimated useful life of 8 years. Also, assume that beneficiary B did not place in service during his taxable year 1962 any section 38 property and that beneficiaries A and B did not own any interests in other trusts, estates, partnerships, or electing small business corporations. Under section 46(c), the qualified investment of XYZ Trust is $39,000, of beneficiary A is $33,400, and of beneficiary B is $15,600, computed as follows:

XYZ Trust

Basis (or cost)	Applicable percentage	Qualified investment
$30,000 (new)	33⅓	$10,000
$15,000 (new)	100	15,000
$12,000 (used)	66⅔	8,000
$6,000 (used)	100	6,000
Total		39,000

Beneficiary A

Basis (or cost)	Applicable percentage	Qualified investment
$18,000 (new)	33⅓	$ 6,000
$9,000 (new)	100	9,000
$7,200 (used)	66⅔	4,800
$3,600 (used)	100	3,600
		23,400
$10,000 (new)	100	10,000
Total		33,400

Beneficiary B

Basis (or cost)	Applicable percentage	Qualified investment
$12,000 (new)	33⅓	$ 4,000
$6,000 (new)	100	6,000
$4,800 (used)	66⅔	3,200
$2,400 (used)	100	2,400
Total		15,600

(3) In the case of XYZ Trust, the $25,000 amount specified in section 46(a)(2) is reduced to $12,500, computed as follows: (i) $25,000, multiplied by (ii) $39,000 (qualified investment apportioned to the trust), divided by (iii) $78,000 (total qualified investment apportioned among such trust ($39,000), beneficiary A ($23,400), and beneficiary B ($15,600)).

T.D. 6731, 5/7/64, amend T.D. 6931, 10/9/67, T.D. 6958, 6/20/68, T.D. 7203, 8/24/72.

§ 1.48-9 Definition of energy property.

Caution: The Treasury has not yet amended Reg § 1.48-9 to reflect changes made by P.L. 98-369, P.L. 97-34.

(a) General rule. *(1) In general.* Under section 48(l)(2), energy property means property that is described in at least one of 6 categories of energy property and that meets the other requirements of this section. If property is described in more than one of these categories, or is described more than once in a single category, only a single energy investment credit is allowed. In that case, the energy investment credit will be allowed under the category the taxpayer chooses by indicating the chosen category on Form 3468, Schedule B. The 6 categories of energy property are:

(i) alternative energy property,

(ii) solar or wind energy property,

(iii) specially defined energy property,

(iv) recycling equipment,

(v) shale oil equipment, and

(vi) equipment for producing natural gas from geopressured brine.

(2) Depreciable property with 3-year useful life. Property is not energy property unless depreciation (or amortization in lieu of depreciation) is allowable and the property has an estimated useful life (determined at the time when the property is placed in service) of 3 years or more.

(3) Effective date rules. To be energy property—

(i) If property is constructed, reconstructed or erected by the taxpayer, the construction, reconstruction, or erection must be completed after September 30, 1978, or

(ii) If the property is acquired, the original use of the property must (A) commence with the taxpayer and (B) commence after September 30, 1978, and before January 1, 1983.

For transitional rules, see section 48(m).

(4) Cross references. (i) To determine if depreciation (or amortization in lieu of depreciation) is allowable for property, see § 1.48-1(b).

(ii) For the meaning of "estimated useful life", see § 1.46-3(e)(7).

(iii) The meaning of "acquired", "original use", "construction", "reconstruction", and "erection" is determined under the principles of § 1.48-2(b).

(iv) For the definition of energy investment credit (energy credit), see section 48(o)(2).

(v) For special rules relating to public utility property, see paragraph (n) of this section.

(b) Relationship to section 38 property. *(1) In general.* (i) Energy property is treated under section 48(l)(1) as meeting the general requirements for section 38 property set forth in section 48(a)(1). For example, structural components of a building may qualify for the energy credit. In addition, the exclusion from section 38 property under section 48(a)(3) (lodging limitation) does not apply to energy property. For purposes of the energy credit, energy property is treated as section 38 property solely by reason of section 48(l)(1). For example, if property ceases to be energy property, it ceases to be section 38 property for all purposes relating to the energy credit and, thus, if subject to recapture under section 47. See § 1.47-1(h).

(ii) See the effective date rules under paragraph (a)(3) of this section for limitations on the eligibility of property as energy property.

(iii) Section 48(l)(1) does not affect the character of property under sections of the Code outside the investment credit provisions. For example, structural components of a building that are treated as section 38 property under section 48(l)(1) remain section 1250 property and are not section 1245 property.

(2) Other section 48 rules apply. (i) In general, section 48(a) otherwise applies in determining if energy property is section 38 property. Thus, energy property excluded from the definition of section 38 property under section 48(a) (except by reason of section 48(a)(1) or (a)(3)) is not eligible for the energy credit. For example, energy property used predominantly outside the United States (section 48(a)(2)) or used by tax exempt organizations (section 48(a)(4)), in general, is not treated as section 38 property for any purpose and thus, is not eligible for the energy credit.

(ii) Other rules of section 48, such as those for leased property under section 48(d), also apply to energy property.

(3) Regular credit denied for certain energy property. In computing the amount of credit under section 46(a)(2), the regular percentage does not apply to any energy property

which, but for section 48(l)(1), would not be section 38 property. See section 46(a)(2)(D). For example, energy property used for lodging (section 48(a)(3)) and, in general, structural components of a building (section 48(a)(1)(B)) re not eligible for the regular credit even though they may be eligible for the energy credit. However, a structural component of a qualified rehabilitated building (as defined in section 48(g)(1)) or a single purpose agricultural or horticultural structure (as defined in section 48(p)) may qualify for the regular credit without regard to section 48(l)(1).

(c) Alternative energy property. *(1) In general.* Alternative energy property means property described in paragraph (c)(3) through (10) of this section. In general alternative energy property includes certain property that uses an alternate substance as a fuel or feedstock or converts an alternate substance to a synthetic fuel and certain associated equipment.

(2) Alternate substance. (i) An alternate substance is any substance or combination of substances other than an oil or gas substance. Alternate substances include coal, wood, and agricultural, industrial, and municipal wastes or by-products. Alternate substances do not include synthetic fuels or other products that are produced from an alternate substance and that have undergone a chemical change as described in paragraph (c)(5)(ii) of this section. For example, methane produced from landfills is not an alternate substance; rather it is a synthetic fuel produced from an alternate substance. However, preparing an alternate substance for use as a fuel or feedstock or for conversion into a fuel does not create a new product if no chemical change occurs. For example, pelletizing, drying, compacting, and liquefying do not result in a new product if no chemical change occurs.

(ii) The term "oil or gas substance" means—

(A) oil or gas and

(B) any primary product of oil or gas

(iii) For the definition of primary product of oil or gas, see § 1.993-3(g)(3)(i), (ii), and (vi). Thus, petrochemicals are not primary products of oil or gas.

(3) Boiler. (i) A boiler that uses an alternate substance as its primary fuel is alternative energy property.

(ii) A boiler is a device for producing vapor from a liquid. Boilers, in general, have a burner in which fuel is burned. A boiler includes a fire box, boiler tubes, the containment shell, pumps, pressure and operating controls, and safety equipment, but not pollution control equipment (as defined in paragraph (c)(8) of this section).

(iii) A "primary fuel" is a fuel comprising more than 50 percent of the fuel requirement of an item of equipment, measured in terms of Btu's for the remainder of the taxable year from the date the equipment is placed in service and for each taxable year thereafter. Electricity and waste heat are not fuels. For example, electric boilers do not qualify as alternative energy property even if the electricity is derived from an alternate substance.

(4) Burners. (i) A burner for a combustor other than a burner described in paragraph (c)(3)(ii) of this section is alternative energy property if the burner uses an alternate substance as its primary fuel (as defined in paragraph (c)(3)(iii) of this section).

(ii) A burner is the part of a combustor that produces a flame. A combustor is a process heater which includes ovens, kilns, and furnaces.

(iii) A burner includes equipment (such as conveyors, flame control devices, and safety monitoring devices) located at the site of the burner and necessary to bring the alternate substance to the burner.

(5) Synthetic fuel production equipment. (i) Equipment (synthetic fuel equipment) that converts an alternate substance into a synthetic solid, liquid, or gaseous fuel (other than coke or coke gas) is alternative energy property. Synthetic fuel production equipment does not include equipment, such as an oxygen plant, that is not directly involved in the treatment of an alternate substance, but produces a substance that is, like the alternate substance, a basic feedstock or catalyst used in the conversion process. Equipment is not eligible if it is used beyond the point at which a substance usable as a fuel has been produced. Equipment is eligible only to the extent of the equipment's cost or basis allocable to the annual production of substances used as a fuel or used in the production of a fuel. For example, assume for the taxable year that 50 percent of the output of equipment is used to produce alcohol for production of whiskey and 50 percent is used to produce alcohol for use in a fuel mixture, such as gasohol. The alcohol production equipment qualifies as synthetic fuel equipment but only to the extent of one-half of its cost or basis. If, in a later taxable year, the equipment is used exclusively to produce whiskey, all of the equipment ceases to be synthetic fuel equipment.

(ii) A fuel is a material that produces usable heat upon combustion. To be "synthetic", the fuel either must differ significantly in chemical composition, as opposed to physical composition, from the alternate substance used to produce it or, in the case of solid fuel produced from biomass, the chemical change must consist of defiberization. Examples of synthetic fuels include alcohol derived from coal, peat, and vegetative matter, such as wood and corn, and methane from landfills.

(iii) Synthetic fuel equipment includes coal gasification equipment, coal liquefaction equipment, equipment for recovering methane from landfill, and equipment that converts biomass to a synthetic fuel.

(iv) Synthetic fuel equipment does not include equipment that merely mixes an alternate substance with another substance. For example, synthetic fuel equipment includes neither equipment that mixes coal and water to produce a slurry nor equipment that mixes alcohol and gasoline to produce gasohol. Equipment used to produce coke or coke gas, such as coke ovens, is also ineligible.

(6) Modification equipment. (i) Alternative energy property includes equipment (modification equipment) designed to modify existing equipment. For the definition of "existing," see paragraph (l)(1)(i) of this section. To be eligible, the modification must result in a substitution for the remainder of the taxable year from the date the equipment is placed in service and for each taxable year thereafter of the items in paragraph (c)(6)(ii)(A) or (B) of this section for all or a portion of the oil or gas substance used as a fuel or feedstock. As a result of the modification, the substituted alternate substance must comprise at least 25 percent of the fuel or feedstock (determined on the basis of Btu equivalency). If the modification also increases the capacity of the equipment, only the incremental cost (as defined in paragraph (k) of this section) of the equipment qualifies.

(ii) The substitutes for an oil or gas substance are—

(A) An alternate substance or

(B) A mixture of oil and an alternate substance.

(iii) Modification equipment does not include replacements or a boiler of burner. If the boiler or burner is replaced, the items must be described in paragraph (c)(3) or

(4) of this section to qualify as alternative energy property. Modification may include, however, replacements of components of a boiler or burner, such as a heat exchanger.

(iv) The following examples illustrate this paragraph (c)(6).

Example (1). On January 1, 1980, corporation X is using oil to fuel its boiler. On June 1, 1980, X modifies the boiler to permit substitution of a coal and oil mixture for 40 percent of X's oil fuel needs. The mixture consists 75 percent of oil and 25 percent of coal. The equipment modifying the boiler does not qualify as modification equipment because the alternate substance comprises only 10 percent of the fuel.

Example (2). Assume the same facts as in example (1) except 75 percent of the mixture is coal. The equipment modifying the boiler qualifies.

Example (3). Assume the same facts as in example (2) except, instead of substituting an oil and coal mixture for 40 percent of X's oil fuel needs, X uses the modification to expand the boiler's fuel capacity by 40 percent using the mixture as additional fuel. The additional fuel mixture comprises only 28 percent of X's total fuel needs. Thus, even though 75 percent of the additional fuel mixture is an alternate substance, the boiler does not qualify as modification equipment because the alternate substance comprises only 21 percent of the total fuel.

(7) Equipment using coal as feedstock. Equipment that uses coal (including lignite) to produce a feedstock for the manufacture of chemicals, such as petrochemicals, or other products is alternative energy property. Equipment is not eligible if it is not directly involved in the treatment of coal or a coal product, but produces a substance that is, like coal, a basic feedstock or catalyst used in the coal conversion process. Equipment is not eligible if it is used beyond the point at which the first product marketable as a feedstock has been produced. Equipment used to produce coke or coke gas, such as coke ovens, is ineligible.

(8) Pollution control equipment. (i) Pollution control equipment is alternative energy property. Eligible equipment is limited to property or equipment to the extent it qualifies as a pollution control facility under section 103(b)(4)(F) and the regulations thereunder except that, if control of pollution is not the only significant purpose (within the meaning of those regulations), only the incremental cost (as defined in paragraph (k) of this section) of the equipment qualifies. However, if a Treasury decision changes the regulations under section 103(b)(4)(F) and, thus, the rules reflected in this subdivision (i), the rules as changed will apply as of the effective date of the Treasury decision.

(ii) To be eligible, the equipment must be required by a Federal, State, or local government regulation to be installed on, or used in connection with, eligible alternative energy property (as defined in paragraph (c)(8)(v) of this section).

(iii) Under section 48(l)(3)(D) equipment is not eligible if required by a Federal, State, or local government regulation in effect on October 1, 1978, to be installed on, or in connection with, property using coal (including lignite) as of October 1, 1978.

(iv) Under this subparagraph (8), pollution control equipment is required by regulation if it would be necessary to install the equipment to satisfy the requirements of any applicable law, including nuisance law. The pollution control equipment need not be specifically identified in the applicable law. If several different types of equipment may be used to comply with the applicable law, each type of equipment is considered necessary to satisfy the requirements of the law. An order permitting a taxpayer to delay compliance with any applicable law is disregarded.

(v) Under this subparagraph (8) "eligible alternative energy property" is energy property (as defined in section 48(l)(2)) described in paragraph (c)(3) through (7) of this section. If equipment otherwise qualifying as pollution control equipment is installed on, or used in connection with, both eligible alternative energy property and property other than eligible alternative energy property, only the incremental cost (as defined in paragraph (k) of this section) of the equipment qualifies.

(vi) Examples. The following examples illustrate this subparagraph (8). Assume that the property or equipment in the examples are described in § 1.103-8(g)(2)(ii) and that their only purpose is control of pollution.

Example (1). On October 1, 1978, corporation X acquires and places in service in State A a paper mill. The facility includes a boiler the primary fuel for which is wood chips. The facility includes equipment necessary to comply with pollution control standards in effect on October 1, 1978 in State A. This equipment qualifies as pollution control equipment.

Example (2). On October 1, 1978, corporation Y was burning coal at its facility in State B. The emissions from the facility exceeded State air pollution control requirements in effect on October 1, 1978. On January 1, 1979, X installed cyclone separators to comply with the State pollution control requirements. The cyclone separators do not qualify as pollution control equipment.

Example (3). Assume the same facts as in example (2) except that Y installs a baghouse instead of cyclone separators to meet more stringent standards that take effect on December 31, 1978. The baghouse qualifies as pollution control equipment because the baghouse was not necessary to meet the standards in effect on October 1, 1978.

Example (4). On October 1, 1978, corporation Z is burning coal at its facility in State C. The emissions from that facility exceed State air pollution control standards in effect on October 1, 1978. C orders Z to install cyclone separators before January 1, 1979. However, C allows Z to operate its facility until January 1, 1979, under less stringent interim standards applicable only to Z. The separators do not qualify as pollution control equipment. The delayed compliance order is disregarded.

(9) Handling and preparation equipment. (i) Alternative energy property includes equipment (handling and preparation equipment) used for unloading, transfer, storage, reclaiming from storage, or preparation of an alternate substance for use in eligible alternative energy property (as defined in paragraph (c)(9)(ii) of this section). Handling and preparation equipment must be located at the site the alternate substance is used as a fuel or feedstock. For example, equipment used to screen and prepare coal for use at a power plant qualifies if located at the plant. However, similar equipment located at the coal mine would not qualify.

(ii) Under this subparagraph (9), "eligible alternative energy property" is energy property (as defined in section 48(l)(2)) described in paragraph (c)(3) through (8) of this section. If equipment otherwise qualifying as handling and preparation equipment is installed on, or used in connection with, property other than eligible alternative energy property, only the incremental cost (as defined in paragraph (k) of this section) of the equipment qualifies.

(iii) The term "preparation" includes washing, crushing, drying, compacting, and weighing of an alternate substance.

Handling and preparation equipment also includes equipment for shredding, chopping, pulverizing, or screening agricultural or forestry byproducts at the site of use.

(iv) Handling and preparation equipment does not include equipment, such as coal slurry pipelines and railroad cars, that transports a fuel or a feedstock to the site of its use.

(10) Geothermal equipment. (i) Alternative energy property includes equipment (geothermal equipment) that produces, distributes, or uses energy derived from a geothermal deposit (as defined in § 1.44C-2(h)).

(ii) In general, production equipment includes equipment necessary to bring geothermal energy from the subterranean deposit to the surface, including well-head and downhole equipment (such as screening or slotting liners, tubing, downhole pumps, and associated equipment). Reinjection wells required for production also may qualify. Production does not include exploration and development.

(iii) Distribution equipment includes equipment that transports geothermal steam or hot water from a geothermal deposit to the site of ultimate use. If geothermal energy is used to generate electricity, distribution equipment includes equipment that transports hot water from the geothermal deposit to a power plant. Distribution equipment also includes components of a heating system, such as pipes and ductwork that distribute within a building the energy derived from the geothermal deposit.

(iv) Geothermal equipment includes equipment that uses energy derived both from a geothermal deposit and from sources other than a geothermal deposit (dual use equipment). Such equipment, however, is geothermal equipment (A) only if its use of energy from sources other than a geothermal deposit does not exceed 25 percent of its total energy input in an annual measuring period and (B) only to the extent of its basis or cost allocable to its use of energy from a geothermal deposit during an annual measuring period. An "annual measuring period" for an item of dual use equipment is the 365 day period beginning with the day it is placed in service or a 365 day period beginning the day after the last day of the immediately preceding annual measuring period. The allocation of energy use required for purposes of paragraph (c)(10)(iv)(A) and (B) of this section may be made by comparing, on a Btu basis, energy input to dual use equipment from the geothermal deposit with energy input from other sources. However, the Commissioner may accept any other method that, in his opinion, accurately establishes the relative annual use by dual use equipment of energy derived from a geothermal deposit and energy derived from other sources.

(v) The existence of a backup system designed for use only in the event of a failure in the system providing energy derived from a geothermal deposit will not disqualify any other equipment. If geothermal energy is used to generate electricity, equipment using geothermal energy includes the electrical generating equipment, such as turbines and generators. However, geothermal equipment does not include any electrical transmission equipment, such as transmission lines and towers, or any equipment beyond the electrical transmission stage, such as transformers and distribution lines.

(vi) Examples. The following examples illustrate this subparagraph (10):

Example (1). On October 1, 1979, corporation X, a calendar year taxpayer, places in service a system which heats its office building by circulating hot water heated by energy derived from a geothermal deposit through the building. Geothermal equipment includes the circulation system, including the pumps and pipes which circulate the hot water through the building.

Example (2). The facts are the same as in Example (1), except that corporation X also places in service a boiler to produce hot water for heating the building exclusively in the event of a failure of the geothermal equipment. Such a boiler is not geothermal equipment, but the existence of such a backup system does not serve to disqualify property eligible in Example (1).

Example (3). The facts are the same as in Example (1), except that the water heated by energy derived from a geothermal deposit is not hot enough to provide sufficient heat for the building. Therefore, the system includes an electric boiler in which the water is heated before being circulated in the heating system. Assume that, on a Btu basis, eighty percent of the total energy input to the circulating system during the 365 day period beginning on October 1, 1979, is energy derived from a geothermal deposit. The boiler is not geothermal equipment. For the 1979 taxable year, eighty percent of the circulating system is geothermal equipment because eighty percent of its basis or cost is allocable to use of energy from a geothermal deposit. If, in a subsequent taxable year, the basis or cost allocable to use of energy from a geothermal deposit falls below eighty percent, recapture may be required under section 47 and § 1.47-1(h). Thus, if, on a Btu basis, only 70 percent of the total energy input to the circulating system for the 365 day period beginning October 1, 1980, is energy derived from a geothermal deposit, then there will be complete recapture of the credit during the 1980 taxable year. If, however, for that 365 day period, the portion of the total energy input that is derived from a geothermal deposit is less than 80 percent but greater than or equal to 75 percent, then only a proportional amount of credit will be recaptured during the 1980 taxable year. No additional credit is allowable in a subsequent taxable year, however, if the portion of the basis or cost allocable to use of energy from a geothermal deposit increases above what it was for a previous taxable year (see § 1.46-3(d)(4)(i)).

Example (4). Corporation Y acquires a commercial vegetable dehydration system in 1981. The system operates by placing fresh vegetables on a conveyor belt and moving them through a dryer. The conveyor belt is powered by electricity. The dryer uses solely energy derived from a geothermal deposit. The dryer is geothermal equipment while the equipment powered by electricity does not qualify.

(d) Solar energy property. *(1) In general.* Energy property includes solar energy property. The term "solar energy property" includes equipment and materials (and parts related to the functioning of such equipment) that use solar energy directly to (i) generate electricity, (ii) heat or cool a building or structure, or (iii) provide hot water for use within a building or structure. Generally, those functions are accomplished through the use of equipment such as collectors (to absorb sunlight and create hot liquids or air), storage tanks (to store hot liquids), rockbeds (to store hot air), thermostats (to activate pumps or fans which circulate the hot liquids or air), and heat exchangers (to utilize hot liquids or air to create hot air or water). Property that uses, as an energy source, fuel or energy derived indirectly from solar energy, such as ocean thermal energy, fossil fuel, or wood, is not considered solar energy property.

(2) Passive solar excluded. (i) Solar energy property excludes the materials and components of "passive solar systems," even if combined with "active solar systems."

(ii) An active solar system is based on the use of mechanically forced energy transfer, such as the use of fans or pumps to circulate solar generated energy.

(iii) A passive system is based on the use of conductive, convective, or radiant energy transfer. Passive solar property includes greenhouses, solariums, roof ponds, glazing, and mass or water trombe walls.

(3) Electric generation equipment. Solar energy property includes equipment that uses solar energy to generate electricity, and includes storage devices, power conditioning equipment, transfer equipment, and parts related to the functioning of those items. In general, this process involves the transformation of sunlight into electricity through the use of such devices as solar cells or other collectors. However, solar energy property used to generate electricity includes only equipment up to (but not including) the stage that transmits or uses electricity.

(4) Pipes and ducts. Pipes and ducts that are used exclusively to carry energy derived from solar energy are solar energy property. Pipes and ducts that are used to carry both energy derived from solar energy and energy derived from other sources are solar energy property (i) only if their use of energy other than solar energy does not exceed 25 percent of their total energy input in an annual measuring period and (ii) only to the extent of their basis or cost allocable to their use of solar energy during an annual measuring period. (See paragraph (d)(6) of this section for the definition of "annual measuring period" and for rules relating to the method of allocation.)

(5) Specially adapted equipment. Equipment that uses solar energy beyond the distribution stage is eligible only if specially adapted to use solar energy.

(6) Auxiliary equipment. Solar energy property does not include equipment (auxiliary equipment), such as furnaces and hot water heaters, that use a source of power other than solar or wind energy to provide usable energy. Solar energy property does include equipment, such as ducts and hot water tanks, which is utilized by both auxiliary equipment and solar energy equipment (dual use equipment). Such equipment is solar energy property (i) only if its use of energy from sources other than solar energy does not exceed 25 percent of its total energy input in an annual measuring period and (ii) only to the extent of its basis of cost allocable to its use of solar or wind energy during an annual measuring period. An "annual measuring period" for an item of dual use equipment is the 365 day period beginning with the day it is placed in service or a 365 day period beginning the day after the last day of the immediately preceding annual measuring period. The allocation of energy use required for purposes of paragraph (d)(6)(i) and (ii) of this section may be made by comparing, on a Btu basis, energy input to dual use equipment from solar energy with energy input from other sources. However, the Commissioner may accept any other method that, in his opinion, accurately establishes the relative annual use by dual use equipment of solar energy and energy derived from other sources.

(7) Solar process heat equipment. Solar energy property does not include equipment that uses solar energy to generate steam at high temperatures for use in industrial or commercial processes (solar process heat).

(8) Example. The following example illustrates this paragraph (d).

Example. (a) In 1979, corporation X, a calendar year taxpayer, constructs an apartment building and purchases equipment to convert solar energy into heat for the building. Corporation X also installs an oil-fired water heater and other equipment to provide a backup source of heat when the solar energy equipment cannot meet the energy needs of the building. For purposes of this example, all equipment is placed in service on October 1, 1979. On a Btu basis, eighty percent of the total energy input to the dual use equipment during the 365 day period beginning October 1, 1979, is from solar energy.

(b) The items purchased, in addition to the water heater, include a roof solar collector, a heat exchanger, a hot water tank, a control component, pumps, pipes, fan-coil units, and valves. Assume the fan-coil units could be used with energy derived from an oil or gas substance without significant modification. All items are depreciable and have a useful life of three years or more. The use of the equipment to heat the building is the first use to which the equipment has been put.

(c) Water is pumped from the basement through pipes to the roof solar collector. Heated water returns through pipes to a heat exchanger which transfers heat to the water in the hot water tank.

(d) The hot water tank and the oil-fired water heater utilize the same distribution pipe. Pumps and valves at the points of connection between the hot water tank, the oil-fired water heater, and the distribution pipe regulate the auxiliary energy supply use. They also prevent the oil-fired water heater from heating water in the hot water tank.

(e) An integrated control component determines whether hot water from the hot water tank or from the oil-fired water heater is distributed to fan-coil units located throughout the building.

(f) The roof solar collector is solar energy property. the pump that moves the water to the roof collector and the pipes between the roof collector and the hot water tank qualify because they are solely related to transporting solar heated water. The hot water tank qualifies because it stores water heated solely by solar radiation. The heat exchanger also qualifies.

(g) The oil-fired water heater does not qualify as solar energy property because it is auxiliary equipment.

(h)

(i) Because the distribution pipe, the control component, and the pumps and valves serve the oil-fired water heater as well as the solar energy equipment; they qualify only to the extent of eighty percent of their cost or basis, the portion allocable to use of solar energy. If, in a subsequent taxable year, the basis or cost allocable to their use of solar energy falls below eighty percent, recapture may be required under section 47 and § 1.47-1(h). Thus, if, on a Btu basis, only 70 percent of the total energy input to that equipment for the 365 day period beginning October 1, 1980, is from solar energy, then there will be complete recapture of the credit during the 1980 taxable year. If, however, for that 365 day period, the portion of that equipment's total energy input that is from solar energy is less than 80 percent but greater than or equal to 75 percent, then only a proportional amount of credit will be recaptured during the 1908 taxable year. No additional credit is allowable for the equipment in a subsequent taxable year, however, if the portion of its basis or cost allocable to use of solar energy increases above what it was for a previous taxable year (see § 1.46-3(d)(4)(i)).

(ii) The fan-coil units do not qualify as solar energy property because they are not specially adapted to use energy derived from solar energy.

(e) Wind energy property. *(1) In general.* Energy property includes wind energy property. Wind energy property is equipment (and parts related to the functioning of that equipment) that performs a function described in paragraph (e)(2) of this section. In general, wind energy property consists of a windmill, wind-driven generator, storage devices, power conditioning equipment, transfer equipment, and parts related to the functioning of those items. Wind energy property does not include equipment that transmits or uses electricity derived from wind energy. In addition, limitations apply similar to those set forth in paragraph (d)(5), (6), and (8) of this section. For example, if equipment is used by both auxiliary equipment and wind energy equipment, such equipment is wind energy property only if its use of energy other than wind energy does not exceed 25 percent of its total energy input in an annual measuring period and only to the extent of its basis or cost allocable to its use of wind energy during an annual measuring period.

(2) Eligible functions. Wind energy property is limited to equipment (and parts related to the functioning of that equipment) that—

(i) Uses wind energy to heat or cool, or provide hot water for use in, a building or structure, or

(ii) Uses wind energy to generate electricity (but not mechanical forms of energy).

(f) Specially defined energy property. *(1) In general.* Specially defined energy property means only those items described in paragraph (f)(4) through (14) of this section that meet the requirements of paragraph (f)(2) of this section. The items described in paragraph (f)(4) through (14) of this section also consist of related equipment, such as fans, pumps, ductwork, piping, and controls, the installation of which is necessary for the specified item to reduce the energy consumed or heat wasted by the process.

(2) General requirements. To be eligible, each item described in paragraph (f)(4) through (14) of this section must be installed in connection with an existing industrial or commercial facility. In addition, the principal purpose of each of those items must be reduction of energy consumed or heat wasted in any existing industrial or commercial process. See section 48(l)(10) and paragraph (l) of this section. If an item performs more than one function, only the incremental cost (as defined in paragraph (k) of this section) of the equipment qualifies.

(3) Industrial or commercial process. (i) A process is a means or method of producing a desired result by chemical, physical, or mechanical action. For example, equipment installed in connection with retail sales, general office use, and residential use are not used in a process within the meaning of this paragraph (f)(3).

(ii) An industrial process includes agricultural processes and thermal processes relating to production or manufacture, such as those involving boilers and furnaces.

(iii) A commercial process includes laundering and food preparation.

(iv) More than one process may be conducted in a single facility. The fact that several processes involved in the production of a product are integrated does not cause such integrated processes to be treated as one process. For example, in a food canning facility, producing prepared food from fresh vegetables is not one process but rather an integration of several processes including washing, cooking and canning.

(v) The following example illustrates this paragraph (f)(3).

Example. Corporation X, an advertising agency, acquires an automatic energy control system designed to reduce energy consumed by heating and cooling its office building. Although the use of an office for X's business is a commercial activity, heating or cooling an office is not an industrial or commercial process. The automatic energy control system does not qualify because it does not reduce energy consumed in an industrial or commercial process.

(4) Recuperators. Recuperators recover energy, usually in the form of waste heat from combustion exhaust gases, hot exiting product, or product cooling air, that is used to heat incoming combustion air, raw materials, or fuel. Recuperators are configurations of equipment consisting in part of fixed heat transfer surfaces between two gas flows, and include related baffles, dividers, entrance flanges, transition sections, and shells or cases enclosing the other components of the recuperator. In general, a fixed heat transfer surface absorbs heat from a gas or liquid flow or dissipates heat to the gas or liquid flow.

(5) Heat wheels. Heat wheels recover energy, usually in the form of waste heat, from exhaust gases to preheat incoming gases. Heat wheels are items of equipment consisting in part of regenerators (which rotate between two gas flows) and related drive components, wiper seals, entrance flanges, and transition sections.

(6) Regenerators. Regenerators are devices, such as clinker columns or chains, that recover energy by efficiently storing heat while exposed to high temperature gases and releasing heat while exposed to low temperature gases, fluids, or solids.

(7) Heat exchangers. Heat exchangers recover energy, usually in the form of waste heat, from high temperature gases, liquids, or solids for transfer to low temperature gases, liquids, or solids. Heat exchangers consist in part of fixed heat transfer surfaces (described in paragraph (f)(4) of this section) separating two media. Heat exchange equipment does not include fluidized bed combustion equipment.

(8) Waste heat boilers. Waste heat boilers use waste heat, usually in the form of combustion exhaust gases, as a substantial source of energy. A substantial source of energy is one that comprises more than 20 percent of the energy requirement on the basis of Btu's during the course of each taxable year (including the start-up year).

(9) Heat pipes. Heat pipes recover energy, usually in the form of waste heat, from high temperature fluids to heat low temperature fluids. A heat pipe consists in part of sealed heat transfer chambers and a capillary structure. In general, the heat transfer chambers alternatively vaporize and condense a working fluid as it passes from one end of the chamber to the other.

(10) Automatic energy control systems. Automatic energy control systems automatically reduce energy consumed in an industrial or commercial process for such purposes as environmental space conditioning (i.e., lighting, heating, cooling or ventilating, etc.). Automatic energy control systems include, for example, automatic equipment settings controls, load shedding devices, and relay devices used as part of such system. Property such as computer hardware installed as a part of the energy control system also qualifies, but only to the extent of its incremental cost (as defined in paragraph (k) of this section).

(11) Turbulators. Turbulators increase the rate of transfer of heat from combustion gases to heat exchange surfaces by increasing the turbulence in the gases. A turbulator is a baffle placed in a boiler firetube or in a heat exchange tube in

industrial process equipment to deflect gases to the heat transfer surface.

(12) Preheaters. Preheaters recover energy, usually in the form of waste heat, from either combustion exhaust gases or steam, to preheat incoming combustion air or boiler feedwater. A preheater consists in part of fixed heat transfer surfaces (described in paragraph (f)(4) of this section) separating two fluids.

(13) Combustible gas recovery systems. Combustible gas recovery systems are items of equipment used to recover unburned fuel from combustion exhaust gases.

(14) Economizers. Economizers are configurations of equipment used to reduce energy demand or recover energy from combustion exhaust gases and other high temperature sources to preheat boiler feedwater.

(15) Other property added by the Secretary. [Reserved]

(g) Recycling equipment. *(1) In general.* Recycling equipment is equipment used exclusively to sort and prepare, or recycle, solid waste (other than animal waste) to recover usable raw materials ("recovery equipment"), or to convert solid waste (including animal waste) into fuel or other useful forms of energy ("conversion equipment"). Recycling equipment may include certain other onsite related equipment.

(2) Recovery equipment. Recovery equipment includes equipment that—

(i) Separates solid waste from a mixture of waste,

(ii) Applies a thermal, mechanical, or chemical treatment to solid waste to ensure the waste will properly respond to recycling, or

(iii) Recycles solid waste to recover usable raw materials, but not beyond occurrence of the first of the following:

(A) The point at which a material has been created that can be used in beginning the fabrication of an end-product in the same way as materials from a virgin substance. Examples are the fiber stage in textile recycling, the newsprint or paperboard stage in paper recycling, and the ingot stage for other metals (other than iron and steel). In the case of recycling iron or steel, recycling equipment does not include any equipment used to reduce solid waste to a molten state or any process thereafter.

(B) The point at which the material is a marketable product (i.e., has a value other than for recycling) even if the material is not marketed by the taxpayer at that point.

(3) Conversion equipment. Conversion equipment includes equipment that converts solid waste into a fuel or other usable energy, but not beyond the point at which a fuel, steam, electricity, hot water, or other useful form of energy has been created. Thus, combustors, boilers, and similar equipment may be eligible if used for a conversion process, but steam and heat distribution systems between the combustor or boiler and the point of use are not eligible.

(4) On-site related equipment. Recycling equipment also includes onsite loading and transportation equipment, such as conveyors, integrally related to other recycling equipment. This equipment may include equipment to load solid waste into a sorting or preparation machine and also a conveyor belt system that transports solid waste from preparation equipment to other equipment in the recycling process.

(5) Solid waste. (i) The term "solid waste" has the same meaning as in § 1.103-8(f)(2)(ii)(b), subject to the following exceptions and the other rules of this subparagraph (5):

(A) The date the equipment is placed in service is substituted in the first sentence of § 1.103-8(f)(2)(ii)(b) for the date of issue of the obligations, and

(B) Material that has a market value at the place it is located only by reason of its value for recycling is not considered to have a market value.

(ii) Solid waste may include a nominal amount of virgin materials, liquids, or gases, not to exceed 10 percent. If more than 10 percent of the material recycled during the course of any taxable year (including the "start up" year) consists of virgin material, liquids, or gases, the equipment ceases to be energy property and is subject to recapture under section 47. The determination of the portion of virgin material, liquids, or gases used is based on volume, weight, or Btu's whichever is appropriate.

(6) Ineligible equipment. Transportation equipment, such as trucks, that transfer solid waste between geographically separated sites (e.g., the collection point and the recycling point) is not eligible. Steam and heat distribution systems are also ineligible.

(7) Increased recycling capacity. If the equipment both replaces recycling capacity and increases that capacity at a particular site, only the incremental cost (as defined in paragraph (k) of this section) of increasing the capacity qualifies. Recycling capacity is determined by the ability to produce a product not previously produced by the taxpayer, or more of an existing product, in a way that does not lower overall production.

(8) Examples. The following examples illustrate this paragraph (g).

Example (1). Corporation W recycles aluminum scrap metal. W owns a junk yard where it collects and crushes the metal into compact units. W's trucks bring the scrap metal from the junk yard to its main plant located 3 miles away. W's furnace equipment at the main plant reduces the scrap to the molten state and W's rolling equipment rolls the aluminum into sheets. The furnace qualifies, but for two separate reasons the rolling equipment does not qualify. First, the molten aluminum would be a marketable product if reduced to ingots prior to rolling. It is not necessary that W actually reduce the molten aluminum to ingots. Second, the molten aluminum could be used in the same way as virgin material.

Example (2). Corporation X manufactures newsprint using wood chips discarded during X's lumber operations. Assume X could sell the wood chips to other companies located a short distance from X's mill for use as a fuel. None of the equipment used to manufacture the newsprint qualifies.

Example (3). Assume the same facts as in example (2) except X uses old newspapers which have no value except for recycling in the area where X's mill is located. The equipment qualifies.

Example (4). Corporation Y recycles municipal waste. Assume the municipal waste is "solid waste" under paragraph (g)(5) of this section. During the first taxable year Y operates the equipment, Y uses 8,500 pounds of municipal waste and 1,500 pounds of virgin material and liquids. No energy credit is allowed for the equipment.

Example (5). Corporation Z owns a waste recovery facility. The corrugated paper portion of the waste stream is picked off a conveyor as it enters the facility. The corrugated paper is baled and sold as a secondary paper product. Z acquires shredding and air-classification equipment. Corrugated paper that is not removed from the conveyor belt enters the new equipment for production as a fuel. Z increases the input of corrugated paper so that the same amount of corrugated paper is removed from the conveyor to be baled. The excess paper that is not removed for baling enters the shredding and air-classification equipment. The new equipment qualifies.

(h) Shale oil equipment. *(1) In general.* Shale oil equipment used in mining or either surface or in situ processing qualifies as energy property. Shale oil equipment means equipment used exclusively to mine, or produce or extract oil from, shale rock.

(2) Eligible processes. In general, processing equipment qualifies if used in or after the mining stage and up through the retorting process. Thus, eligible processes include crushing, loading into the retort, and retorting, but not hydrogenation, refining, or any process subsequent to retorting. However, with respect to in situ processing, eligible processes include creating the underground cavity.

(3) Eligible equipment. Shale oil equipment includes—

(i) Heading jumbos, bulldozers, and scaling and bolting rigs used to create an underground cavity for in situ processing,

(ii) On-site water supply and treatment equipment and handling equipment for spent shale.

(iii) Crushing and screening plant equipment, such as hoppers, feeders, vibrating screens, and conveyors,

(iv) Briquetting plant equipment, such as hammer mills and vibratory pan feeders, and

(v) Retort equipment, including direct cooling and condensing equipment.

(i) [Reserved]

(j) Natural gas from geopressured brine. Equipment used exclusively to extract natural gas from geopressured brine described in section 613A(b)(3)(C)(i) is energy property. Eligible equipment includes equipment used to separate the gas from saline water and remove other impurities from the gas. Equipment is eligible only up to the point the gas may be introduced into a pipeline.

(k) Incremental cost. The term "incremental cost" means the excess of the total cost of equipment over the amount that would have been expended for the equipment if the equipment were not used for a qualifying purpose. For example, assume equipment costing $100 performs a pollution control function and another function. Assuming it would cost $60 solely to perform the nonqualifying function, the incremental cost would be $40.

(l) Existing. *(1) In general.* for purposes of section 48(l), the term "existing" means—

(i) When used in connection with a facility or equipment, 50 percent or more of the basis of that facility or equipment is attributable to construction, reconstruction, or erection before October 1, 1978, or

(ii) When used in connection with an industrial or commercial process, that process was carried on in the facility as of October 1, 1978.

(2) Industrial or commercial process. (i) A process will be considered the same as the process carried on in the facility as of October 1, 1978, unless and until capitalizable expenditures are paid or incurred for modification of the process. The expenditures need not be capitalized in fact; it is sufficient if the taxpayer has an option or may elect to capitalize. In general, the date of change will be the date the expenditures are properly chargeable to capital account. If the taxpayer properly elects to expense a capitalizable expenditure, the date of change will be the date the expenditure could have been properly chargeable to capital account if the expenditure had been capitalized. Recapture will not occur by reason of a change in a process unless the process change also changes the use of the equipment. See example (1) of § 1.47-1(h)(5).

(m) Quality and performance standards. *(1) In general.* Energy property must meet quality and performance standards, if any, that have been prescribed by the Secretary (after consultation with the Secretary of Energy) and are in effect at the time of acquisition.

(2) Time of acquisition. Under this paragraph (m) the time of acquisition is—

(i) The date the taxpayer enters into a binding contract to acquire the property or

(ii) For property constructed, reconstructed, or erected by the taxpayer, (A) the earlier of the date it begins construction, reconstruction, or erection of the property, or (B) the date the taxpayer and another person enter into a binding contract requiring each to construct, reconstruct, or erect property and place the property in service for an agreed upon use. See example under paragraph (m)(4) of this section.

(3) Binding contract. Under this paragraph (m), a binding contract to construct, reconstruct, or erect property, or to acquire property, is a contract that is binding at all times on the taxpayer under applicable State or local law. A binding contract to construct, reconstruct, or erect property or to acquire property, does not include a contract for preparation of architect's sketches, blueprints, or performance of any other activity not involving the beginning of physical work.

(4) Example. The following example illustrates this paragraph (m).

Example. Corporation X owns a junk yard. Corporation Y manufactures recycling equipment and operates several recycling facilities. On January 1, 1979, X and Y enter into a written contract that is binding on both parties on that date and at all times thereafter. Under the contract's terms X will supply scrap metals to Y and Y agrees in return to build a recycling facility on land adjacent to the junk yard. Y will own and operate the facility using the scrap metal supplied by X. Y may treat the agreement as a binding contract under paragraph (m)(2) and (3) of this section.

(n) Public utility property. *(1) Inclusions.* Public utility property is included in both of the following categories of energy property:

(i) Shale oil equipment and

(ii) Equipment for producing natural gas from geopressured brine.

(2) Exclusions. Public utility property is excluded from each of the following categories of energy property:

(i) Alternative energy property,

(ii) Specially defined energy property,

(iii) Solar or wind energy property, and

(iv) Recycling equipment.

(3) Public utility property. The term "public utility property" has the meaning given in section 46(f)(5).

(o) [Reserved]

(p) [Reserved]

(q) Qualified intercity buses. *(1) In general.* This paragraph (q) prescribes rules and definitions for purposes of section 48(l)(2)(A)(ix) and (16). Energy property includes qualified intercity buses of an eligible taxpayer, but only to the extent of the increase in the taxpayer's total operating seating capacity (operating capacity) under paragraphs (q)(9), (10), and (11) of this section. For application of recapture rules see § 1.47-1(h)(3)(ii).

(2) Eligible taxpayer. A taxpayer is an eligible taxpayer only if it is determined to be both—

(i) A common carrier regulated by the Interstate Commerce Commission or an appropriate State agency and

(ii) Engaged in the trade or business of furnishing intercity transportation by bus.

(3) Common carrier. The taxpayer is a common carrier only if the taxpayer holds itself out to the general public as providing passenger bus transportation for compensation over regular or irregular routes, or both.

(4) Appropriate State agency. A State agency is appropriate only if it has both—

(i) Power to regulate intrastate transportation provided by a motor carrier, within the meaning of section 10521(b)(1) of the Revised Interstate Commerce Act (49 U.S.C. 10521(b)(1)), and

(ii) Power to initiate an exemption proceeding under section 1025(b) of that Act (49 U.S.C. 10521(b)).

(5) Intercity transportation. Intercity transportation means intercity passenger transportation or intercity passenger charter service. Intercity transportation does not include transportation provided entirely within a municipality, contiguous municipalities, or within a zone that is adjacent to, and commercially a part of, the municipality or municipalities (within the meaning of section 10526(b)(1) of the Revised Interstate Commerce Act (49 U.S.C. 10526(b)(1)). See 49 CFR Part 1048 (regulations defining commercial zones under that statute).

(6) Definition of qualified intercity bus. A qualified intercity bus (qualifying bus) is an automobile bus—

(i) The chassis and body of which are exempt (under section 4063(a)(6)) from the 10-percent excise tax generally imposed under section 4061(a) on trucks and buses.

(ii) With a seating capacity of at least 36 passengers (in addition to the driver).

(iii) With one or more baggage compartments, in an area separated from the passenger area, with an aggregate capacity of at least 200 cubic feet, and

(iv) Which meets the predominant use test.

(7) Predominant use test. (i) A bus meets the predominant use test for a taxable year only if it meets the following conditions:

(A) It is used on a full-time basis during the taxable year, and

(B) At least 70 percent of the total miles driven are driven while furnishing intercity transportation.

(ii) A bus driven from the end point of one trip to the beginning point of another trip ("deadheading"), both of which furnish intercity transportation of passengers, will be considered to have been driven while furnishing intercity transportation of passengers, even if no passengers are carried.

(iii) A bus is considered used on a full-time basis in a taxable year if it was driven 10,000 miles in that year. If available, the best evidence of annual mileage is the difference odometer readings at the beginning and end of each taxable year. If the bus was placed in service during the taxable year, or for a short taxable year described in section 441(b)(3), that 10,000 mile figure is prorated on a daily basis.

(iv) If a qualifying bus fails to meet the predominant use test in a taxable year, a cessation occurs in that taxable year. See § 1.47-1(h)(3)(ii).

(v) The following examples illustrate this paragraph (g)(7):

Example (1). X, a bus company, used a bus for trips between city M and city N, a distance of 100 miles. These trips qualify as furnishing intercity transportation. During the taxable year, 300 round trips were run carrying passengers both ways and 75 trips were run carrying passengers from city M to city N immediately after each of which the bus was returned to city M for the next trip. The bus was also driven 20,000 miles to furnish passenger service which was local transportation. During the taxable year, the bus was driven a total of 100,000 miles. X makes the following calculations to determine if it met the predominant use test for the taxable year.

1. Total miles driven	100,000
2. Intercity miles driven:	
a. Passenger round trips (100 × 2 × 300)	60,000
b. Passenger one-way (75 × 100)	7,500
c. Non-passenger return trips (75 × 100)	7,500
3. Total intercity passenger miles (sum of lines 2a, b, and c)	75,000
4. 79% of line 1	70,000

Since line 1 is not less than 10,000 miles, the full-time use requirement is met. Since line 3 is greater than line 4, the 70 percent intercity mileage test is met. Thus, for the taxable year, the bus meets the predominant use test in paragraph (q)(7)(i) of this section.

Example (2). The facts are the same as in example (1), except that the bus was placed in service on the last day of the taxable year. The bus was used only to run one round trip, carrying passengers, between cities M and N. 10,000 miles X one day ÷ 365 days = 27.4 miles. Because, for the one day of the taxable year that the bus was in service, the bus was driven more than 27.4 miles, and all these miles were driven to furnish intercity transportation, it met the predominant use test for the taxable year.

(8) Leased buses. (i) A bus which is leased is energy property only if it meets the requirements of paragraph (q)(6)(i), (ii), and (iii) of this section, the lessee is an eligible taxpayer, and the bus meets the predominant use test in the hands of the lessee. If a leased bus is energy property, the energy credit is available only to the lessee unless paragraph (q)(8)(ii) of this section applies. The lessor must elect under section 48(d) for the lessee to claim the energy credit.

(ii) If a leased bus is energy property and, on or before October 9, 1984, either (A) the lessor and lessee enter into a lease and the lessee places the bus in service, or (B) the bus is not placed in service but the lessor and lessee enter into a binding contract under which the amount of the lease payments cannot be modified, then the energy credit is available to the lessor even if the lessor is not an eligible taxpayer.

(iii) Notwithstanding § 1.47-2(b)(1) (relating to the effect of a disposition by the lessee on the credit claimed by the lessor), if, by reason of a lease or the termination of a lease, a bus is used in a taxable year subsequent to the credit year by a person other than the one whose increase in operating capacity determined the amount of qualified investment for the energy credit, a disposition of the bus under § 1.47-1(h)(2) results. However, if the energy credit for a bus was earned in a taxable year and a lease of the bus which qualifies under section 168(f)(8) (safe-harbor lease) is entered into in a subsequent taxable year, the safe-harbor lease is not a disposition of the bus and the lessee under that lease is treated as the lessee for purposes of this paragraph (q)(8). For the requirement to file an amended return if the energy credit was allowed in a prior taxable year, see § 5c.168(f)(8)-6(b)(2)(ii) (Temporary Income Tax Regulations under the Economic Recovery Tax Act of 1981). For the rule for determining whose operating capacity determines qualified investment for the energy credit, see paragraph (q)(9)(ii) of this section. For the rule for leases to related taxpayers, see paragraph (q)(10)(ii) of this section.

(9) Operating capacity. (i) Qualified investment for a qualifying bus is taken into account for the energy credit only to the extent the bus increases the taxpayer's operating capacity. To increase operating capacity, a bus must be counted in operating capacity. The increase in a taxpayer's operating capacity is the excess of the taxpayer's operating capacity for the current taxable year over its operating capacity for the immediately preceding taxable year. Related taxpayers determine operating capacity on a group basis under paragraph (q)(10) of this section.

(ii) Operating capacity for a particular taxable year is determined by adding together the seating capacities of all intercity buses used by the taxpayer in that year and still owned by the taxpayer at the end of that year. An intercity bus is a bus which meets the chassis and body test and the predominant use test in paragraph (q)(6) of this section whether or not the bus is still in use at the end of the taxable year. In the case of a leased bus to which paragraph (q)(8) of this section applies, the lessee's operating capacity determines qualified investment for the energy credit.

(iii) The qualified investment for the energy credit for a qualifying bus is the bus's qualified investment for the regular credit multiplied by a fraction. The numerator of the fraction is the increase in the taxpayer's operating capacity for the taxable year. The denominator is the added operating capacity for the taxable year. Added operating capacity for the taxable year is determined for a taxpayer by adding together the seating capacities of the taxpayer's intercity buses included in operating capacity for the taxable year which were not included in operating capacity for the immediately preceding taxable year.

(iv) In the case of a partnership, each partner's qualified investment for the energy credit for a qualifying bus is the partner's qualified investment for the regular credit (determined under § 1.46-3(f) multiplied by the fraction referred to in paragraph (q)(9)(iii) of this section for the partnership, as determined for the partnership taxable year in which the bus is placed in service.

(v) The following example illustrates this paragraph (q)(9):

Example. Corporation Y is a calendar year bus company that is an eligible taxpayer under paragraph (q)(2) of this section. Based upon the facts as set forth in the following table, Y makes the following calculations to determine the energy credit earned in 1981:

1. 1980 operating capacity determined as of 12/31/80:	
a. 5 intercity buses × 50 seats each	250
b. Total 1980 operating capacity	250
2. 1981 operating capacity determined as of 12/31/81:	
a. 2 1980 buses used on a full-time basis in 1981	100
b. 1981 added capacity:	
i. Qualifying buses:	
Bus 1	45
Bus 2	55
Bus 3	50
ii. Intercity bus not a qualifying bus	50
iii. Total 1981 added capacity	200
c. Total 1981 operating capacity	300
3. 1981 increase in operating capacity (line 2c – line 1b)	50
4. Fraction for determining qualified investment attributable to increase in capacity (line 3 ÷ line 2(b)(iii))	¼

Accordingly, the energy credit earned in 1981 for each of the qualifying buses is determined as follows:

Qualified Investment for the regular credit	× Line 4	× Energy percentage	= Energy credit earned
Bus 1: $15,000	¼	10	$ 375
Bus 2: $20,000	¼	10	500
Bus 3: $25,000	¼	10	625
Total energy credit earned in 1981			1,500

(10) Related taxpayers. (i) Related taxpayers are treated as one taxpayer in determining the increase in operating capacity under paragraph (q)(9)(ii) of this section and in determining the qualified investment in qualified intercity buses for the energy credit under paragraph (q)(9)(iii) of this section. Related taxpayers are members of a group of trades or businesses that are under common control (as defined in § 1.52-1(b)).

(ii) Related taxpayers make all computations relating to operating capacity on a group basis. Also, the determination of whether a bus meets the predominant use test is made on a group basis by aggregating bus usage by each member of the group. For example, if a bus is acquired by one member and used by that member for part of a taxable year and used by other members for the remainder, the combined usage is aggregated in determining whether the predominant use test is met. In addition, all related taxpayers are treated as one person in applying paragraph (q)(8) of this section (relating to leasing).

(iii) The energy credit earned for a qualifying bus is allocated to the member which acquired (or is a lessee treated under section 48(d) as having acquired) the bus whether or not that member had a separate increase in operating capacity for the taxable year.

(iv) Each member must make its own computation of the group's increase in operating capacity for the period comprising its taxable year. A member will make this computation as of the end of its taxable year ignoring different taxable years of other members. For the period comprising its taxable year, the member makes all calculations relating to group operating capacity, including the determination of full-time use by other members.

(v) Each member determines the composition of the group as of the end of that member's taxable year. For example, if X uses the calendar year and makes its computation as of December 31, 1981, and Y is a member of X's group at that time, Y's operating capacity determined as of the end of X's immediately preceding taxable year (December 31, 1980) is taken into account by X for 1980 even if Y was not a member of the group for any day prior to December 31, 1981.

(vi) The following example illustrates this paragraph (q)(10):

Example. (a) Corporations X and Y are related taxpayers. In this example, each bus is a qualifying bus with a seating capacity of 50. Each bus owned at the close of either X's or Y's taxable year was used on a full-time basis for the relevant period corresponding to X's or Y's taxable year. Other facts are set forth in the following table:

	X	Y
Taxable year ends	Dec. 31	June 30.
Operating capacity for 1979.	5 buses..........	10 buses.
Buses added	3 buses Mar. 1, 1980.	3 buses May 15, 1981.
Buses sold	2 buses Mar. 31, 1981.	2 buses Sept. 30, 1980.
Cost of each added bus.	$40,000	$60,000.

(b) X makes the following calculations to determine the energy credit earned for calendar year 1980.

1. 1979 operating capacity determined as of 12/31/79:
   a. Attributable to X (5 buses × 50 seats) 250
   b. Attributable to Y (10 buses × 50 seats) 500
   c. Total 1979 operating capacity 750
2. 1980 operating capacity determined as of 12/31/80:
   a. X's 5 and Y's 8 1979 buses used on a full-time basis in 1980 and still owned on 12/31/80 650
   b. 1980 added capacity (X's 3 buses × 50 seats)... 150
   c. Total 1980 operating capacity 800
3. 1980 increase in operating capacity (line 2c – line 1c)... 50
4. Fraction in paragraph (q)(9)(iii) of this section (line 3 ÷ line 2b) .... ⅓

Accordingly, X earned an energy credit of $4,000 in 1980 ($40,000 × ⅓ × 10% × 3 buses).

(c) Since in calendar year 1981 X placed no qualifying buses in service, X earned no energy credit in 1981.

(d) Since in the taxable year 7/1/79–6/30/80 Y placed no qualifying buses in service, Y earned no energy credit in that taxable year.

(e) Y makes the following calculations to determine the energy credit earned in the taxable year 7/1/80–6/30/81.

1. Operating capacity for the taxable year ending 6/30/80 determined as of the close of that year:....
   a. Attributable to X (8 buses × 50 seats) 400
   b. Attributable to Y (10 buses X 50 seats)........ 500
   c. total operating capacity for that year 900
2. Operating capacity for the taxable year ending 6/30/81 determined as of the close of that year:....
   a. X's 6 and Y's 8 buses from prior taxable year used on a full-time basis during current taxable year and still owned on 6/30/81 700
   b. Capacity added during current taxable year (Y's 3 buses × 50 seats)........................... 150
   c. Total operating capacity for that year.......... 850
3. Increase in operating capacity for taxable year ending 6/30/81 (line 2c – line 1c) 50

As determined for Y's taxable year ending 6/30/81 the group experienced a decrease in operating capacity. Thus, no energy credit is available for the buses Y placed in service in its taxable year ending 6/30/81.

(11) Section 381(a) transactions. (i) In the case of a transaction described in section 381(a), the operating capacity of each transferor or distributor corporation, determined as of the date of distribution or transfer (within the meaning of § 1.381(b)-1(b)), shall reduce the operating capacity of the acquiring corporation (determined without this paragraph (q)(11)) for its first taxable year ending on or after that date for purposes of determining the acquiring corporation's energy credit for that year. This paragraph (q)(11) shall not apply to any case to which paragraph (q)(10) of this section (dealing with related taxpayers) applies.

(ii) The following example illustrates this paragraph (q)(11):

Example. X and Y are unrelated corporations which use the calendar year. For 1981, each has an operating capacity of 250 seats (5 buses × 50 seats). X merges into Y on January 1, 1982. On May 1, 1982, Y retires and sells two buses and acquires four 50-seat qualifying buses at a cost of $40,000 each. All buses owned by Y on December 31, 1982, are included in operating capacity. Y makes the following calculations to determine the energy credit earned in taxable year 1982.

1. Y's 1981 operating capacity determined as of 12/31/81 250
2. 1982 operating capacity determined as of 12/31/82 without this paragraph (q)(11):........
   a. X's 5 buses plus Y's 5 1981 buses less 2 retired buses (8 buses × 50 seats) 400
   b. 1982 added capacity (4 buses × 50 seats).... 200
   c. Total 600
3. Operating capacity of transferor (X) on 1/1/82 .. 250
4. Y's 1982 operating capacity (line 2c – line 3)... 350
5. 1982 increase in operating capacity (line 4 – line 1) 100
6. Fraction in paragraph (q)(9)(iii) of this section (line 5 ÷ line 2b)........................ 1/2
7. Energy credit earned in 1982 ($40,000 × ½ 10% × 4 buses) $8,000

T.D. 7762, 1/19/81, amend T.D. 7982, 10/5/84, T.D. 8014, 3/25/85, T.D. 8147, 7/20/87.

PAR. 4. Section 1.48-9 is amended as follows:

1. Paragraph (a)(4)(ii) is amended by removing "§ 1.46-3(e)(7)" and inserting in its place "§ 1.46-3(e)".

2. Paragraph (b)(1)(i) is amended by removing "§ 1.47-1(h)" from the last sentence and inserting in its place "§ 1.47-1(l)"

3. Paragraph (l)(2) is amended by removing "§ 1.47-1(h)(5)" from the last sentence and inserting in its place "§ 1.47-1(l)(5)"

4. Paragraph (q)(1) is amended by removing "(h)(3)(ii)" from the last sentence and inserting in its place "(l)(3)(ii)"

5. Paragraph (q)(7)(iv) is amended by removing "(h)(3)(ii)" from the last sentence and inserting in its place "(l)(3)(ii)".

Proposed § 1.48-9 Definition of energy property [Amended]. [*For Preamble, see ¶ 151,041*]

Section 1.48-9 is amended by adding a new paragraph (o) to read as follows:

Proposed § 1.48-9 Definition of energy property. [*For Preamble, see ¶ 150,725*]

* * * * *

(o) Energy property financed by subsidized energy financing or industrial development bonds. *(1) In general.* (i) This paragraph (o) prescribes rules—

(A) for reducing the qualified investment for purposes of the energy credit. See section 48(l)(11) as amended by section 223(c)(1) of the Crude Oil Windfall Profit Tax Act of 1980 (Pub. L. 96-223) and paragraph (o)(2) of this section.

(B) For reducing the energy credit percentage. See section 48(l)(11) as amended by section 221(b)(2) of that Act and paragraph (o)(6) of this section.

(ii) For effective dates, see paragraph (o)(8) of this section.

(2) General rule. For purposes of the energy credit, qualified investment in any energy property (determined without this paragraph (o)) is reduced by the amount of subsidized borrowed funds used to finance in whole or in part the energy property. Funds borrowed are subsidized if they are directly or indirectly attributable to the proceeds of exempt IDB's or subsidized energy financing.

(3) Exempt IDB defined. For purposes of this paragraph (c), an exempt IDB is an industrial development bond (within the meaning of section 103(b)(2)) with respect to which the interest paid is excluded from gross income under section 103.

(4) Subsidized energy financing. (i) Funds are attributable to subsidized energy financing if the source of the funds for financing (other than exempt IDB's) is provided directly or indirectly (such as in association with, or through the facilities of, a bank or other lender) by, or through, a government agency under a program a principal purpose of which is to provide (or assist in providing) financing for projects designed to conserve or produce energy. For purposes of this paragraph (o), a government agency is a State or local governmental unit referred to in § 1.103-1(a) or the Federal government.

(ii) Subsidized energy financing does not include a grant includible in gross income under section 61, a nontaxable government grant, or a credit against State or local taxes. Loan guarantees, price guarantees, purchase commitments, price support loans, and similar arrangements are not considered subsidized energy financing unless the arrangement is essentially subsidized borrowing under paragraph (o)(4)(i) of this section.

(iii) The following examples illustrate this paragraph (o)(4).

Example (1). A law in State A requires, as part of its State-wide energy program, that public utilities in the State provide low-interest loans to business enterprises for the purchase of energy property. The utilities are able to make these low-interest loans available to the enterprises by charging a 2 percent surcharge on each utility service bill. The funds from the surcharge are kept separate in an escrow account. This type of low interest loan is not subsidized energy financing and will not reduce the qualified investment of any energy property purchased with these funds.

Example (2). Assume the same facts as in example (1) except that, in lieu of the surcharge, the utilities receive money from the State for the express purpose of providing energy loans. Any low-interest loans made from these funds will be considered subsidized energy financing.

Example (3). State B allows a tax credit to a financial institution which makes low interest loans to corporations for the purpose of acquiring energy devices. The financial institution receives a credit each year in the amount of the excess of the interest that would have been paid at market rates and the actual interest paid on such loans. The State B tax credit arrangement is an interest subsidy. Thus, any low-interest loans pursuant to this credit arrangement is considered subsidized energy financing.

Example (4). State C wishes to encourage the production of synthetic fuels. As an inducement to Corporation X to build a synthetic fuel production plant, C enters into a contract with X guaranteeing X a certain price for the first 1,000 barrels of daily production. Before the plant is operational and pursuant to the price guarantee commitment, X receives an interest free advance of $10,000. Since the advance of funds is essentially a subsidized energy loan, it is considered to be subsidized energy financing.

(5) Allocation of proceeds. (i) For purposes of the general rule, this paragraph (o)(5) sets forth the manner of determining the amount of subsidized borrowed funds that are considered used to finance energy property.

(ii) If borrowings attributable to subsidized energy financing are used to finance a facility, the entire amount of the borrowings are considered used to finance the energy property included in that facility and thus is applied directly to reduce the qualified investment in the energy property.

(iii) (A) If borrowings attributable to the proceeds of exempt IDB's are used to finance a facility, the borrowings reduce the qualified investment in that energy property. The amount of those borrowings considered used to finance energy property included in that facility equals to the amount of the borrowings multiplied by a fraction. The numerator of the fraction is the qualified investment in the energy property before the reduction and the denominator is the total cost of that facility.

(B) If borrowings are attributable to the proceeds of exempt IDB's the exempt status of which is derived solely under section 103(b)(4), and the proceeds of such borrowings are used solely to finance the type of property or facility described in section 103(b)(4) from which the issue derives its tax-exempt status, then the facility referred to in paragraph (o)(5)(iii)(A) of this section is the property or facility from which the issue derives its tax-exempt status.

(iv) If both borrowings attributable to subsidized energy financing and borrowings attributable to exempt IDB financing are used to finance a facility, the total amount of subsidized energy financing is first applied directly to reduce the qualified investment (determined without this subdivision (iv)) in the energy property included in the facility. Then, paragraph (o)(5)(iii) of this section is applied to the exempt IDB financing by reducing both the numerator and the denominator of the fraction by the same total amount.

(v) The following examples illustrate this paragraph (o)(5).

Example (1). In 1983, Corporation X builds a facility costing $10,000. The facility includes energy property having a useful life of 7 years and the qualified investment (before reduction) is $8,000. X receives in 1983 a $6,000 energy loan from the Department of Energy for this facility at a subsidized rate of interest. The qualified investment for the energy property is reduced by $6,000 to $2,000. See paragraph (o)(5)(ii) of this section.

Example (2). Assume the same facts as in example (1) except that the $6,000 is borrowed from a fund established by a local government unit from the proceeds of exempt IDB's. The qualified investment in the energy property is reduced by $4,800 (i.e., $6,000 × $8,000/$10,000). Thus, the qualified investment is reduced from $8,000 to $3,200. See paragraph (o)(5)(iii)(A) of this section.

Example (3). Assume the same facts as in example (1) except that the total $6,000 borrowed to finance the property is from two sources. $2,000 is a subsidized energy loan and $4,000 is attributable to the proceeds of exempt IDB's. First, the qualified investment in the energy property of $8,000 is reduced by the subsidized energy loan of $2,000 to $6,000. For purposes of allocating the proceeds from exempt IDB's, the numerator and denominator of the fraction in example (2) are both reduced by this $2,000 from $8,000/$10,000 to $6,000/$8,000. Thus, the amount attributed to the proceeds of exempt IDB's is $3,000 (i.e., $4,000 × $6,000/$8,000), and the qualified investment for the energy property is $3,000, i.e., $6,000−$3,000. See paragraph (o)(5)(iv) of this section.

Example (4). (a) In 1983, Corporation Y constructs a coal gasification project having an estimated useful life of 20 years and consisting of a gasifier and air pollution control equipment. The total cost of the project is $60 million, allocable to various types of property as follows:

($000,000 omitted)

	Gasifier	Pollution control equipment
Energy property	$30	$10
Other	10	10
	40	20

(b) Y finances construction of the project with subsidized financing ($10 million) and conventional financing ($36 million). Y also receives proceeds of $14 million from an issue of exempt IDB's, the exempt status of which is derived solely under section 103(b)(4)(F). Y uses the proceeds of the exempt IDB's solely to provide the pollution control equipment.

(c) Qualified investment for the energy credit is determined as follows:

	Energy property	
	Gasifier	Pollution control equipment
1. Cost	$30	$10
2. Allocation of subsidized energy financing ($10) to energy property:		
(a) $10 × 30/40	7.5	
(b) $10 × 10/40		2.5
3. Remainder after applying paragraph (o)(5)(ii) of this section	$22.5	$7.5
4. Allocation of proceeds ($14) of IDB exempt solely under section 103(b)(4):		
(a) Fraction of cost of pollution control equipment that is energy property		10/20
(b) Reduce numerator and denominator of fraction by line 2(b)		7.5/17.5
(c) Multiply by proceeds		$14
(d) Allocated proceeds (line (b) × (c))		$6
5. Qualified investment for energy credit after applying paragraph (o)(5)(i)-(iv) of this section (line 3-line 4(d))	$22.5	$1.5

(6) One-half exempt IDB rule for certain periods. For periods beginning on or after October 1, 1978, to which the general rule of paragraph (o)(2) of this section does not apply, the energy percentage for property is one-half of the energy percentage determined under section 46(a)(2)(C) if any funds borrowed to finance the facility of which the energy property is a part are directly or indirectly attributable to the proceeds of exempt IDB's. For explanation of the effective date of this paragraph (o)(6), see paragraph (o)(8) of this section.

(7) Add-on equipment rule. (i) Energy property is not considered to be financed with subsidized borrowings solely because it is installed in an existing facility which has been previously so financed.

(ii) The facts and circumstances determine if energy property installed in connection with existing property is a separate unit or installed pursuant to a design, plan, or as a component of a larger property (such as a project or facility).

(iii) The following example illustrates this paragraph (o)(7).

Example. In 1981, Corporation X finances its energy facility with the proceeds of exempt IDB's. The facility meets all air pollution laws and regulations in existence, or anticipated, when it is placed in service. In 1982, a new State regulation requires the installation of additional air pollution control equipment which is alternative energy property under section 48(f)(3)(A)(vi). X receives subsidized energy financing and installs the added equipment pursuant to the new regulation. The added air pollution control equipment is a separate unit. Therefore, the subsidized energy loan for the facility is not imputed to the qualified investment in this new separate unit.

(8) Effective dates. (i) The general rule in paragraph (o)(2) of this section applies to early application property for periods after December 31, 1979. Early application property is defined in paragraph (o)(9) of this section. For other property, it applies to periods after December 31, 1982.

(ii) Notwithstanding paragraph (o)(8)(i) of this section, funds attributable under paragraph (o)(4) of this section to subsidized energy financing made before January 1, 1980, shall not be taken into account for purposes of reducing qualified investment under the general rule of paragraph (o)(2) of this section. See section 223(c)(2)(D) of Pub. L. 96-223. Subsidized energy financing is considered made before January 1, 1980, if it meets the requirements of § 1.167(j)-4(c) (applied without reference to any dates therein).

(iii) The one-half-exempt IDB rule in paragraph (o)(6) of this section applied for periods beginning after October 1, 1978, to which the general rule of paragraph (o)(2) of this section does not apply.

(iv) For purposes of this subparagraph (8), whether qualified investment (without any reduction under this paragraph (o)) falls within a period is determined under section 48(m). If under section 48(m) this qualified investment for energy property is allocable to more than one period, the portion of subsidized borrowings used to finance the property (as determined under paragraph (o)(5) of this section) is ratably apportioned to this qualified investment for each period in proportion to this qualified investment for each period.

(v) The following examples illustrate this paragraph (o)(8).

Example (1). (a) Corporation Z begins building on February 1, 1980, a facility costing $100,000, $75,000 of which is solar energy property which generates electricity. The energy property has a useful life of seven years. The facility is completed in 1983. Z spent $45,000 for the energy property for the period ending on December 31, 1982, and $30,000 for periods after that date. In connection with this facility, Z receives a loan of $10,000 attributable to subsidized energy financing made in January 1980.

(b) The subsidized energy financing is allocated between the two periods in proportion to the amount of basis of energy property attributable to each period. Thus, $6,000 of the subsidized financing is allocated to the period before 1983 (i.e., $10,000 × $45,000/$75,000) and $4,000 is allocated to the period after 1982 (i.e., $10,000 × $30,000/$75,000). See paragraph (o)(8)(iv) of this section.

(c) The $6,000 of subsidized energy financing attributable to the period before 1983 does not reduce qualified investment in energy property (other than early application property) because the general rule in paragraph (o)(2) of this section does not apply. However, the qualified investment of $30,000 for the period after 1982 is reduced by $4,000 to $26,000.

Example (2). Assume the same facts as in example (1) except that the energy property is early application property. The general rule in paragraph (o)(2) of this section applies and the total amount of subsidized energy financing ($10,000) is subtracted from the total qualified investment. Thus, the qualified investment for the energy credit is reduced from $75,000 to $65,000.

Example (3). (a) Assume the same facts as in example (1) except that the $10,000 loan was attributable to the proceeds of exempt IDB financing. Exempt IDB financing allocated to pre-1983 periods does not reduce the qualified investment. Instead, the energy percentage is reduced by one-half from 15 percent to 7½ percent and applied against the qualified investment allocable to such periods, i.e., $45,000. See section 46(a)(2)(C).

(b) The amount of exempt IDB financing attributable to qualified investment in energy property is $7,500 (i.e., $10,000 × $75,000/$100,000). The portion of that amount attributable to periods after 1982 is $3,000 (i.e., $7,500 × $30,000/$75,000). Accordingly, the qualified investment for the energy property attributable to periods after 1982 is reduced from $30,000 by $3,000 to $27,000. See paragraph (o)(8)(iv) of this section.

Example (4). Assume the same facts in example (3) except that the energy property is early application property. The general rule in paragraph (o)(2) of this section applies to the entire energy property, and the total amount of the proceeds of exempt IDB's is multiplied by the fraction in paragraph (o)(5)(iii) of this section. Thus, the qualified investment of $75,000 is reduced by $7,500 (i.e., $10,000 × $75,000/$100,000) by $67,500.

(9) Early application property. (i) Early application property is—

(A) Qualified hydroelectric generating property (described in section 48(l)(2)(A)(vii)),

(B) Cogeneration equipment (described in section 48(l)(2)(A)(viii)),

(C) Qualified intercity buses (described in section 48(l)(2)(A)(ix)),

(D) Ocean thermal property (described in section 48(l)(3)(A)(ix)), or

(E) Expanded energy property.

(ii) Expanded energy property is—

(A) Property that is included for the first time as alternative energy property under clause (iii) or (v) of section 48 (l)(3)(A) by reason of the amendments thereto by section 222(b)(1) and (2) of the Crude Oil Windfall Profit Tax Act of 1980 (Pub. L. 96-223, 94 Stat. 229),

(B) Solar or wind energy property that provides solar process heat referred to in section 48(l)(4)(C),

(C) Modifications to alumina electrolyte cells referred to in section 48(l)(5)(L), and

(D) Property described in the last sentence of section 48(l)(3)(A) (relating to storage equipment for refuse-derived fuel).

§ 1.48-10 Single purpose agricultural or horticultural structures.

(a) In general. *(1) Scope.* Under section 48(a)(1)(D), "section 38 property" includes single purpose agricultural and horticultural structures, as defined in section 48(p) and paragraphs (b) and (c) of this section. These structures are subject to a special rule for recapture of the credit. See paragraph (g) of this section. For the relation of this section to section 48(a)(1)(B) (other tangible property) and to sections 1245 and 1250 (depreciation recapture), see paragraph (h) of this section.

(2) Effective date. The provisions of section 48(a)(1)(D) and this section apply to open taxable years ending after August 15, 1971.

(b) Definition of single purpose agricultural structure *(1) In general.* Under section 48(p)(2), a single purpose agricultural structure is any structure or enclosure that meets all of the following requirements:

(i) It is specifically designed and constructed for permissible purposes (as defined in paragraph (b)(2) of this section). See paragraph (d) of this section for the rule regarding "specifically designed and constructed".

(ii) It is specifically used exclusively for those permissible purposes. See paragraph (e) of this section for the rules regarding "specifically used".

(iii) It houses equipment necessary to house, raise, and feed livestock and their produce. See paragraph (b)(3) and (4) of this section.

(2) Permissible purposes. The following are the only permissible purposes for a single purpose agricultural structure:

(i) Housing, raising, and feeding a particular type of livestock and, at the taxpayer's option, its produce. The term "housing, raising, and feeding" includes the full range of livestock breeding and raising activities, including ancillary post-production activities (as defined in paragraph (f) of this section). Thus, for example, use of a structure for breeding livestock, or for producing eggs or livestock, is permitted. The structure may also be used for storing feed or machinery, but more than strictly incidental use for these purposes will disqualify the structure. See paragraph (e)(1) of this section. For the special rule concerning the permissible purposes for a milking parlor, see paragraph (b)(2)(iii) of this section.

(ii) Housing required equipment (including any replacements) as defined in paragraph (b)(4) of this section.

(iii) If the structure is a dairy facility, it will qualify if it is used for: (A) activities consisting of the production of milk or of the production of milk and the housing, raising, or feeding dairy cattle, and (B) housing equipment (including any replacements) necessary for these activities. The term "housing, raising, or feeding" includes the full range of dairy cattle breeding and raising activities including ancillary post-production activities (as defined in paragraph (f) of this section). The structure may also be used for storing feed or machinery, but, more than incidental use for these purposes will disqualify the structure. See paragraph (e)(1) of this section.

(3) Livestock; particular type of livestock. (i) Livestock. Livestock qualifying as "section 38 property" under § 1.48-1(l) constitutes livestock for purposes of this section. Thus, for example, horses are not livestock for purposes of this section since they do not qualify as "section 38 property" under § 1.48-1(l). Under section 48(p)(6) poultry constitutes livestock for purposes of section 48(a)(1)(D). The term "livestock" includes the offspring of livestock. "Livestock" is distinguished from the produce of livestock, such as milk and eggs held for sale. For purposes of this section, eggs held for hatching and newborn livestock are considered livestock. A structure used solely to house produce of livestock or equipment necessary to house produce of livestock will not qualify as a single purpose agricultural structure. Thus, for example, a dairy facility used solely for storing milk will not qualify.

(ii) Particular type of livestock. A structure qualifies as a single purpose agricultural structure only if it is specifically designed, constructed, and used exclusively for permissible purposes with respect to one particular type of livestock. For purposes of this section, each species is a different type except that all species of poultry are considered to be of a single type. Thus, for example, a structure specifically designed and constructed as a single purpose hog-raising facility will not qualify if it is used to raise dairy cows, but a structure specifically designed, constructed, and used to raise poultry may house, raise, and feed both chickens and turkeys.

(4) Required equipment rule. (i) A single purpose agricultural structure must also house equipment necessary to house, raise, and feed the livestock ("required equipment"). Required equipment must be an integral part of the structure, and includes, but is not limited to, equipment necessary to contain the livestock, to provide them with water or feed, and to control the temperature, lighting, and humidity of the interior of the structure. For purposes of this section, equipment is an integral part of the structure if it is physically attached to or a part of the structure. The useful life of the structure, however, need not be contemporaneous with the life of the equipment it houses. A structure without required equipment is not a single purpose agricultural structure.

(ii) A single purpose agricultural structure may, but is not required to, house equipment (for example, loading chutes) necessary to the conduct of ancillary post-production activities as defined in paragraph (f) of this section.

(5) Livestock structure. In section 48(p)(2), the terms "single purpose livestock structure" and "single purpose agricultural structure" are interchangeable.

(c) Definition of single purpose horticultural structure *(1) In general.* Under section 48(p)(3), a single purpose horticultural structure is any structure that meets both of the following requirements:

(i) It is a greenhouse or other structure specifically designed and constructed for permissible purposes (as defined in paragraph (c)(2) of this section). See paragraph (d) of this section for the rule regarding "specifically designed and constructed."

(ii) It is specifically used exclusively for those permissible purposes. See paragraph (e) of this section for the rules regarding "specifically used."

(2) Permissible purposes. The following are the only permissible purposes for a single purpose horticultural structure:

(i) The commercial production of plants (including plant products such as flowers, vegetables, or fruit) in a greenhouse.

(ii) The commercial production of mushrooms.

(iii) A single purpose horticultural structure also may, but is not required to, house equipment necessary to carry out these permissible purposes listed in paragraph (c)(2)(i) and (ii) of this section.

(3) Ancillary post-production activities. The terms "commercial production of plants" and "commercial production of mushrooms" include ancillary post-production activities (as defined in paragraph (f) of this section).

(d) Specifically designed and constructed. A structure is specifically designed and constructed if it is not economic to design and construct the structure for the intended qualifying purpose and then use the structure for a different purpose. For example, if a hog raising structure is designed and constructed in accordance with a standard set of plans for such a structure provided by the Department of Agriculture, it would not be economic to use the structure for purposes other than hog raising.

(e) Specifically used. There are two aspects of the specific use requirement—exclusive use and actual use.

(1) Exclusive use. (i) A structure qualifies as a single purpose agricultural or horticultural structure only if it is used exclusively for the permitted purposes by reason of which it qualified for the credit. Thus—

(A) The structure may not be used for any nonpermissible purposes (for example, processing, marketing, or more than incidental use for storing feed or equipment) and

(B) It may not be put to any use other than the specific use by reason of which it qualifies for the credit.

(ii) For purposes of this section, the term "incidental use" means a use which is both related and subordinate to the qualifying purpose. Thus, for example, if feed is stored in an agricultural structure which will be used for raising hogs, the feed must be used only for the hogs in order to be related to the qualifying purpose. In determining whether use of the structure for feed storage is subordinate to the qualifying purpose, all of the facts and circumstances must be considered, including, with respect to feed storage, the following:

(A) Type of animal involved;

(B) Number of, and consumption rate for, each animal;

(C) Climate of area;

(D) Total volume of storage area; and

(E) Percentage of structure's total volume devoted to storage.

(iii) It will be presumed that the storage function is not subordinate to the qualifying purpose of the structure if more than one-third of the structure's total usable volume is devoted to storage. This presumption may be rebutted with clear and convincing evidence.

(iv) A structure may fail the exclusive use test if either of the requirements of paragraph (e)(1)(i) of this section is not met. Thus, for example, a horticultural structure that contains an area for processing plants or plant products will fail the exclusive use test because there is a nonpermissible use. An agricultural structure that is used to house more than one particular type of livestock fails the exclusive use test for the same reason. A change in the use of an agricultural structure from one species of livestock to another will cause the structure to fail the exclusive use test when the change occurs. Thus, for example, a hog-raising facility which qualified for the credit when it was placed in service cannot later be modified and used for producing broiler chickens even if the structure would have qualified for the credit if it had been originally designed, constructed, and used exclusively for producing broiler chickens.

(2) Actual use. (i) A single purpose agricultural or horticultural structure also must actually be used for the permissible purpose by reason of which it qualifies for the credit. "Actual use" means "placed in service" (as defined in § 1.46-3(d)). Mere vacancy, on a temporary basis, will not disqualify the structure. Thus, for example, a structure that is designed and constructed as a hog-raising structure will not qualify if it is never placed in service for raising hogs. However, a turkey-raising facility will not be disqualified if the turkeys are all sent to a packing plant in November and the structure remains vacant until the next spring when newly hatched turkeys are placed in the structure to be raised.

(ii) For purposes of this section, "vacancy on a temporary basis" includes temporary vacancy caused by market fluctuations or other economic considerations and vacancy on a seasonal basis.

(f) Work space; ancillary post-production activities *(1) Permissible work space.* Under section 48(p)(4), a single purpose agricultural or horticultural structure may contain work space only if it is used for—

(i) Stocking, caring for, or collecting livestock, plants, or mushrooms,

(ii) Maintenance of the structure, or

(iii) Maintenance or replacement of the equipment or stock enclosed by or contained in the structure. Thus, for example, an eligible structure may not contain space devoted to processing or marketing or other nonpermissible purposes.

(2) Ancillary post-production activities. The term "stocking, caring for, or collecting" the livestock, plants, or mushrooms includes ancillary post-production activities. These activities, therefore, constitute permissible purposes when carried on in conjunction with other permissible purposes, and a qualifying structure may contain work space devoted to such activities. Ancillary post-production activities include gathering, sorting, and loading livestock, plants, and mushrooms and packing unprocessed plants, mushrooms, and the live offspring and unprocessed produce of the livestock. Ancillary post-production activities do not include processing activities, such as slaughtering or packing meat, nor do they include marketing activities.

(g) Special rule for recapture under section 47. Under section 48(p)(5), if a structure which qualifies for the credit under this section becomes ineligible because it ceases to be held for the specific use by reason of which it qualified (or it is used for other than that qualifying use) before the end of the applicable estimated useful life or period specified in section 47(a), then the investment credit previously allowed with respect to the structure may be partially or entirely recaptured under section 47. Unlike other property to which section 47 applies, single purpose structures may not be converted from one permissible use to another without recapture. See subparagraph (e)(2) of this section.

(h) Relationship to other sections *(1) Relation to section 48(a)(1)(B).* All structures satisfying the requirements of section 48(a)(1)(B) and (a)(1)(D) will be considered to qualify under either provision.

(2) Relationship to sections 1245 and 1250. For purposes of depreciation recapture, property to which section 48(a)(1)(D) applies is section 1245 property, except that property placed in service prior to January 1, 1981, may, at the option of the taxpayer, be treated as section 1250 property if depreciation deductions allowed were not under one of the methods authorized only for section 1245 property.

(i) [Reserved]

(j) Examples. The provisions of this section may be illustrated by the following examples:

Example (1). A constructs a rectangular structure for use as an egg-producing facility. The structure has no windows. The walls and roof are made of corrugated steel and there is a door which is 4 feet wide and 8 feet tall at each end of the structure. At the end of each wall are louvered openings approximately 4 feet high and 8 feet long. These openings house thermostatically controlled fans. In the center of the walls are manually operated fresh-air openings. Corrugated steel "curtains" hang from the top of the openings so that the openings can be completely closed in cold weather, but the curtains can be propped open to admit fresh air. The building is well insulated. A has reinforced the roof with extra trusses and rafters and reinforced the building with extra wall studs. Two rows of cages are suspended from the rafters by thin steel girders and wires. The floor of the structure is a sloping concrete slab pierced with long troughs which run the length of the structure beneath the cages. The troughs are used for collection and disposal of chicken wastes. When this structure is placed in service it will qualify for an investment credit under this section.

Example (2). B constructs a greenhouse for the commercial production of plants. The greenhouse is a rectangular structure with translucent fiberglass walls and roof. The structure is equipped with an automatic temperature and humidity control system. Pipes were installed to carry water and liquid fertilizer to the plants and to release minute amounts of carbon dioxide into the air. When the structure was originally placed in service B used the entire structure for growing flowers commercially. In September 1978, B began to use the structure for growing tomatoes. Because of the success of the venture, in January 1979, B began to use the entire structure for growing tomatoes. In February 1980, B set up a small counter with a cash register at one end of the structure so that workers could sell tomatoes to customers at the greenhouse. Until February 1980, the structure would qualify for the credit under this section. The change in use from growing flowers to growing tomatoes will not affect the eligibility of the structure. Once the cash register is installed, however, the structure fails to meet both the exclusive use test of paragraph (e)(1) of this section and the work space rule of paragraph (f) of this section since a single purpose structure may not be used for marketing activities.

Example (3). C purchases a prefabricated structure and makes modifications so that the structure will meet C's requirements. C adds gates and constructs a partition which divides the structure into two parts. One part of the structure constitutes less than one-third of the total usable volume of the structure and is used to house feeder cattle while they are fed with hay. This part of the structure has a sloping concrete floor. The other part of the structure constitutes more than two-thirds of the total usable volume of the structure and is used to store the hay used to feed the cattle. This structure will not qualify for the credit since it fails the required equipment test. The structure does not contain equipment which is an integral part of the structure. This structure also fails the "specifically designed and constructed" test of paragraph (d) of this section since it would be economic to use the structure for purposes other than housing, raising, and feeding cattle (such as a general purpose barn, for example). Finally, the structure fails the incidental use test of paragraph (e) of this section because the storage function is presumptively not subordinate to the qualifying purpose since more than two-thirds of the structure's total usable volume is devoted to storage and none of the facts will serve to rebut the presumption.

T.D. 7900, 7/18/83.

---

§ 1.48-11 Qualified rehabilitated building; expenditures incurred before January 1, 1982.

Caution: The Treasury has not yet amended Reg § 1.48-11 to reflect changes made by P.L. 98-369, P.L. 97-34.

(a) In general. Under section 48(a)(1)(E), that portion of the basis of a qualified rehabilitated building which is attributable to qualified rehabilitation expenditures qualifies as section 38 property. In general, property which is treated as section 38 property by reason of section 48(a)(1)(E) is treated as new section 38 property and therefore is not subject to the used property limitation. See § 1.48-2(d). Section 48(g)(1) and paragraph (b) of this section define the term "qualified rehabilitated building". Section 48(g)(2) and paragraph (c) of this section define the term "qualified rehabilitation expenditure". Paragraph (d) of this section provides guidance for coordination of these provisions with other sections of the Code.

(b) Definition of qualified rehabilitated building. *(1) In general.* The term "qualified rehabilitated building" means any building and its structural components—

(i) Which has been rehabilitated (within the meaning of paragraph (b)(3) of this section),

(ii) Which was placed in service (within the meaning of § 1.46-3(d)) by any person at any time before the beginning of the rehabilitation,

(iii) 75 percent or more of the existing external walls of which are retained in place as external walls (within the meaning of paragraph (b)(4) of this section) in the rehabilitation process, and

(iv) Which meets the twenty-year requirement in paragraph (b)(2) of this section.

In addition, a major portion of a building may be treated as a separate building for purposes of this paragraph if the requirement of paragraph (b)(5) of this section are met.

(2) Twenty-year requirement. (i) In general. A building is considered a qualified rehabilitated building only if a period of at least 20 years has elapsed between the date physical work on the rehabilitation of the building began, and the later of—

(A) The date the building was first placed in service (see § 1.46-3(d)) by any person as a building, or

(B) The date the building was placed in service by any taxpayer in connection with a prior rehabilitation with respect to which a credit was allowed by reason of section 48(a)(1)(E).

(ii) Vacant periods. The 20-year period includes periods during which a building was vacant or devoted to a personal use and is computed without regard to the number of owners or the identity of owners during the period.

(iii) Physical work on a rehabilitation. For purposes of this section, "physical work on a rehabilitation" begins when actual construction begins. The term "physical work on a rehabilitation" does not include preliminary activities such as planning, designing, securing financing, exploring, researching, developing plans and specifications, or stabilizing a building to prevent deterioration (e.g., placing boards over broken windows).

(iv) Special rule. If a part of a building meets the twenty-years requirement in subdivision (i) of this subparagraph and a part (for example, an addition) does not, a rehabilitation of that part that meets the requirement may qualify for a credit only if that part constitutes a major portion (as defined in paragraph (b)(5) of this section) of the building.

(3) Rehabilitation. (i) In general. For purposes of this paragraph, rehabilitation includes renovation, restoration, or reconstruction. However, the term "rehabilitation" does not include enlargement (within the meaning of paragraph (c)(7)(ii) of this section), new construction, or the completion of new construction after a building has been placed in service. For purposes of this paragraph (b)(3), whether expenditures are attributable to the rehabilitation of an existing building, or to new construction, is determined upon all the facts and circumstances.

(ii) Substantial rehabilitation. For a building to be considered rehabilitated, the rehabilitation must be substantial. Whether a rehabilitation is substantial is determined upon the basis of all the facts and circumstances. In general, to be substantial, the rehabilitation must do one of the following:

(A) materially extend the useful life of the building;

(B) significantly upgrade its usefulness (for either the same or a new use); or

(C) preserve it in a way that significantly improves its condition or enhances its historic value.

A substantial rehabilitation may vary in degree from gutting and extensive reconstruction of a building's major structural components to the cure of a substantial accumulation of major disrepairs. It may also include renovation, alteration, or remodeling for the conversion of a structurally sound building to a design and condition required for a new use. Cosmetic improvements alone, however, do not qualify as a substantial rehabilitation.

(iii) Aggregation of rehabilitation. In the case where qualified rehabilitation expenditures are incurred with respect to a rehabilitation of a building by more than one person (e.g., a lessor and a lessee, several lessees, or several condominium owners), the substantial rehabilitation requirement in this paragraph (b)(3) shall be applied by aggregating all the rehabilitation work done by such persons.

(iv) Special rule by qualified rehabilitation expenditures treated as incurred by the taxpayer. In the case where qualified rehabilitation expenditures are treated as having been incurred by a taxpayer because of the application of paragraph (c)(3)(ii) of this section, the substantial rehabilitation test in paragraph (b)(3)(ii) of this section will be applied by aggregating the rehabilitation work done by the transferor and the transferee.

(v) Examples. The provisions of this subparagraph (3) may be illustrated by the following examples:

Example (1). Taxpayer A is the owner of a 30-year old building. The building is air conditioned by means of window air conditioning units. A replaces the window units with a central air conditioning system and no other rehabilitation is performed by A. The expenditures incurred by A did not materially extend the building's useful life, significantly upgrade its usefulness, or preserve it in a manner that significantly improves its condition or enhances its historic value. Although expenditures for replacement of window units with a central air conditioning system may constitute qualified expenditures as part of an overall rehabilitation, alone they do not qualify as a substantial rehabilitation and the building is not considered rehabilitated within the meaning of this subparagraph.

Example (2). Taxpayer B is the owner of a 10 story office building that is 35 years old. The building is in substantial disrepair and in order to modernize it as an office building B installs new plumbing, electrical wiring, and heating and air conditioning systems. In addition, the layout of each floor is changed by means of tearing down many existing interior walls and partitions and building new walls, partitions, and doors. Old plaster is removed from many walls and replaced by new wall covering. New windows and new flooring are installed throughout the building. The improvements made by B materially extend the useful life of the building and significantly upgrade its usefulness. The building is considered rehabilitated within the meaning of the facts and circumstances test in this subparagraph.

Example (3). Taxpayer C is the owner of a 100-year old building that has substantial historic character, although the building is not a certified historic structure (as defined in section 191(d)(1) and the regulations thereunder). C uncovers and restores the original woodwork, wall coverings and moldings throughout the building. The windows and doors are replaced with replicas of the original. The improvements made by C significantly preserve the building and significantly enhance its historic value. Thus, the building is considered rehabilitated within the meaning of this subparagraph.

(4) Retention of 75 percent of external walls. (i) In general. A building meets the requirements set forth in paragraph (b)(1)(iii) only if 75 percent or more of the existing external walls (as measured by the total area of the existing external walls) are retained in place as external walls in the rehabilitation process. For this purpose, the area of existing external walls includes the area of windows and doors.

(ii) External wall. For purposes of this paragraph (b)(4), a wall includes both the supporting elements of the wall and the nonsupporting elements (e.g., a curtain) of the wall. Except as otherwise provided in this paragraph (b)(4), the term "external wall" includes any wall that has one face exposed to the weather, earth, or an abutting wall erected on an adjacent property. An external wall also includes a shared wall (i.e., a single wall shared with an adjacent building), generally referred to as a "party wall" .

(iii) Alternative rule. Notwithstanding the definition of external wall contained in paragraph (b)(4)(ii) of this section, in any case in which the building being rehabilitated would fail to meet the requirements of a qualified rehabilitation building if the definition of external wall in paragraph (b)(4)(ii) of this section were used, then the term "external wall" shall be defined as a wall, including its supporting elements, with one face exposed to the weather or earth, and a common wall shall not be treated as an external wall.

(iv) Retained in place. An existing external wall is retained in place if the supporting elements of the wall are retained in place. An existing external wall is not retained in place if the supporting elements of the wall are replaced by new supporting elements. An external wall is retained in place, however, if the supporting elements are reinforced in the rehabilitation, provided that such supporting elements of the external wall are retained in place. An external wall is retained in place even though it is covered (e.g., with new siding). Moreover, the existing curtain may be replaced with a new curtain provided that the structural framework that provides for the support of the existing curtain is retained in place. An external wall is retained in place notwithstanding that the existing doors and windows in the wall are modified, eliminated, or replaced. A wall may be disassembled and reassembled so long as the same supporting elements are used when the wall is reassembled. Thus, for example, in the case of the brick wall, the wall is considered retained in place even though the original bricks are removed (for cleaning, etc.) and put back to form the wall.

(v) Retention as an external wall. For purposes of meeting the 75 percent requirement of this subparagraph (4), an existing external wall must be retained in place as an external wall. If an addition is made that results in an existing external wall being converted into an internal wall, the wall is not retained in place as an external wall.

(vi) Special rule. Solely for the purpose of meeting the 75 percent requirement of this subparagraph (4), the walls of an uncovered internal shaft designed solely to bring light or air into the center of a building which are completely surrounded by external walls of the building and which enclose space not designated for occupancy or other use by people (other than for maintenance or emergency) are not considered external walls. Thus, a wall of a light well in the center of an office building is not an external wall. However, walls surrounding an uncovered courtyard which is usable by the building's occupants, (e.g., at lunch time) are external walls.

(vii) Examples. The provisions of this subparagraph (4) may be illustrated by the following examples:

Example (1). Taxpayer A rehabilitated a building all of the walls of which consisted of wood siding attached to gypsum board sheets (which covered the studs). A covered the existing wood siding with aluminum siding in a part of a rehabilitation that otherwise qualified under this subparagraph. A satisfied the requirement that 75 percent of the existing external walls must be retained in place as external walls.

Example (2). Taxpayer B rehabilitated a building the external walls of which had a masonry curtain. The masonry on the wall face was replaced with a glass curtain. The steel beam and girders supporting the existing curtain were retained in place. B satisfied the requirement that 75 percent of the existing external walls must be retained in place as external walls.

Example (3). Taxpayer C rehabilitated a building which has two external walls measuring 75' × 20' and two other external walls measuring 100' × 20'. C tore down one of the larger walls, including its supporting elements, which accounted for more than 25% of the building's external walls and constructed a new wall. C has not satisfied the requirement that 75 percent of the existing external walls must be retained in place as external walls.

Example (4). The facts are the same as in example 3, except C does not tear down any walls, but makes an addition that results in one of the smaller walls becoming an internal wall. In addition, C enlarged 8 of the existing windows on the larger walls, increasing them from a size of 3' × 4' to 6' than 25 percent of the total wall area, C has satisfied the requirement that 75 percent of the existing external walls must be retained in place as external walls in the rehabilitation process. The enlargement of the existing windows on the larger wall does not change the result.

(5) Major portion treated as separate building. (i) In general. Where there is a separate rehabilitation of a major portion of a building, such major portion shall be treated as a separate building. Thus, such major portion may qualify as a qualified rehabilitated building if the requirements of this paragraph are met with respect to such major portion. Expenditures for property that services both a major portion of a building and another portion must be specifically allocated to each portion to the extent possible. If it is not possible to make such an allocation, the expenditures must be allocated to each portion on some reasonable basis. What constitutes a reasonable basis for an allocation depends on factors such as the type of improvement and how the improvement relates functionally to the building. For example, in the case of expenditures for an air-conditioning system or a roof, a reasonable basis for allocating the expenditures would be the volume of the major portion served by the improvement relative to the volume of the other portion of the building served by the improvement.

(ii) Major portion defined. Whether a part of a building constitutes a major portion of the building is determined upon the basis of all the facts and circumstances. A major portion must generally consist of clearly identifiable parts of a building (e.g., a wing of a building or the first 5 stories of a 7 story building). The following factors shall be taken into account:

(A) Whether the portion comprises an entire leasehold interest or an entire ownership (e.g., condominium) interest;

(B) Whether the portion (as measured by volume) is sufficiently large that it would be reasonable to treat it as a separate building; and

(C) Whether the portion is functionally different from other parts of the building.

(6) Special rule for rehabilitation done in phases. If rehabilitation which is not continuous is determined under this subparagraph to be a single rehabilitation done in phases, the requirements of this paragraph (b) are to be applied with respect to the overall rehabilitation and not merely to a phase of the rehabilitation. In such case, a phase of a single overall rehabilitation will not be considered as "prior rehabilitation" for purposes of subparagraph (2)(i)(B) of this paragraph (b). Whether rehabilitation which is not continuous is a single rehabilitation that is done in phases is determined on the basis of all the facts and circumstances. Generally, however, to constitute a single rehabilitation that is done in phases, there must exist, prior to the time any rehabilitation work is commenced, a set of written plans describing generally all phases of the rehabilitation of the building and a reasonable expectation that all phases of the rehabilitation will be completed. Such written plans are not required to contain detailed working drawings or detailed specifications of the material to be used. In addition, the period between the time that physical work on the first phase of the overall rehabilitation begins and physical work on the last phase of the overall rehabilitation begins must be reasonable. In determining whether the rehabilitation is completed within a reasonable time, the fact that a building is occupied during the rehabilitation, the necessity of acquiring a lease (of additional portions of the building), and unforeseen delays shall be taken into account. Other factors that are relevant in determining whether rehabilitation is a single rehabilitation include the length of time between each phase of rehabilitation activities and the extent of rehabilitation activity in each phase.

(7) Special rule for adjoining buildings that are combined. For purposes of this paragraph (b), if as part of a rehabilitation process two or more adjoining buildings are combined and placed in service as a single building after the rehabilitation process, then all of the requirements of a qualified rehabilitated building in section 48(g)(1) and this section may be applied to the constituent adjoining buildings in the aggregate. Any party walls or abutting walls between the constituent buildings that would otherwise be treated as external walls (within the meaning of paragraph (b)(4)(ii) of this section) would not be treated as external walls of the building; the substantial rehabilitation test in paragraph (b)(3)(ii) of this section would be applied to the aggregate rehabilitation work with respect to all of the constituent buildings.

(c) Definition of qualified rehabilitation expenditures. *(1) In general.* Except as provided in subparagraph (2) of this paragraph, the term "qualified rehabilitation expenditure" means any amount—

(i) Properly chargeable to capital account (as described in subparagraph (2) of this paragraph),

(ii) Incurred after October 31, 1978, for depreciable or amortizable property (or additions or improvements to property) with a useful life of five years or more, and

(iii) Made in connection with the rehabilitation of a qualified rehabilitated building.

(2) Chargeable to capital account. For purposes of paragraph (c)(1)(i) of this section, amounts paid or incurred are chargeable to capital account if under the taxpayer's method of accounting they are property includible in computing basis under § 1.46-3. Amounts treated as an expense and deducted in the year they are paid or incurred are not chargeable to capital account.

(3) Incurred by the taxpayer. (i) In general. Generally, to qualify for a credit under section 48(a)(1)(E), qualified rehabilitation expenditures must be incurred by the taxpayer after October 31, 1978. An expenditure is incurred for purposes of this paragraph on the date such expenditure would be considered incurred under the accrual method of accounting, regardless of the method of accounting used by the taxpayer with respect to other items of income and expense. If qualified rehabilitation expenditures are treated as having been incurred by a taxpayer under paragraph (c)(3)(ii)) of this section, the taxpayer shall be treated as having incurred the expenditures on the date such expenditures were incurred by the transferor.

(ii) Qualified rehabilitation expenditures treated as incurred by the taxpayer.

(A) Where rehabilitation expenditures are incurred with respect to a building by a person (or persons) other than the taxpayer and the taxpayer acquires the building, or a portion of the building to which the expenditures are allocable, the taxpayer acquiring such property will be treated as having incurred the rehabilitation expenditures actually incurred by the transferor (or treated as incurred by the transferor under this paragraph (c)(3)(ii)) with respect to the acquired property, provided that—

(1) The building, or the portion of the building, acquired by the taxpayer was not used after the rehabilitation expenditures were incurred and prior to the date of acquisition by the taxpayer, and

(2) No credit with respect to such qualified rehabilitation expenditures is claimed by anyone other than the taxpayer acquiring the property.

For purposes of this paragraph (c)(3)(ii), use shall mean actual use, whether personal or business.

(B) The amount of qualified rehabilitation expenditures treated as incurred by the taxpayer under this paragraph is the lesser of—

(1) The qualified rehabilitation expenditures incurred before the date on which the taxpayer acquired the building (or portion thereof), to which the expenditures are attributable, or

(2) That portion of the taxpayer's cost or other basis for the property which is attributable to the qualified rehabilitation expenditures described in paragraph (c)(3)(B)(1) of this section incurred before such date.

For purposes of paragraph (c)(6)(ii) of this section, the amount of rehabilitation expenditures treated as incurred by the taxpayer under this paragraph (c)(3)(ii) shall not be considered to be part of the cost of acquiring a building or any interest in the building. The portion of the cost of acquiring a building (or an interest therein) which is not treated under this paragraph as qualified rehabilitation expenditures incurred by the taxpayer is not eligible for a rehabilitation investment credit. See paragraph (c)(6)(ii) of this section.

(C) See paragraph (b)(2)(iv) of this section for rules concerning the application of the substantial rehabilitation test to expenditures treated as incurred by the taxpayer.

(iii) Examples. The provisions of this subparagraph may be illustrated by the following examples:

Example (1). In 1978, taxpayer A, a cash basis taxpayer, commenced the rehabilitation of a 30-year old building. In June 1978, A signed contract with a plumbing contractor for replacement of the plumbing in the building. A agreed to pay the contractor as soon as the work was completed. The work was completed in September 1978, but A did not pay the amount due until November 1, 1978. The expenditures for the plumbing are not qualified rehabilitation expenditures because they were not incurred after October 31, 1978.

Example (2). B incurred qualified rehabilitation expenditures of $300,000 with respect to an existing building between January 1, 1980, and May 15, 1980, and then sold the building to C on June 1, 1980. If the property attributable to the expenditures was not placed in service by A during the period from January 1, 1980, to June 1, 1980, C will be treated as having incurred the expenditures.

(4) Incurred for 5-year property. An expenditure is incurred for depreciable or amortizable property if the amount of the expenditure is added to the basis of property which is depreciable or amortizable under section 167. The determination of whether property has a useful life of five years or more is made by applying the principles of § 1.46-3(e). In the case of expenditures for property made by a lessee, see sections 167 and 178 and the regulations thereunder for rules relating to whether improvements made to leased property are depreciable or amortizable.

(5) Made in connection with the rehabilitation of a qualified rehabilitated building. Expenditures attributable to work done to facilities related to a building (e.g., sidewalk, parking lot, landscaping) are not considered made in connection with a rehabilitation of a qualified rehabilitated building.

(6) Certain expenditures excluded from qualified rehabilitation expenditures. The term "qualified rehabilitation expenditures" does not include the following expenditures:

(i) An expenditure for property which is "section 38 property" (determined without regard to section 48(a)(1)(E) and (l)).

(ii) The cost of acquiring a building or any interest in a building (including a leasehold interest) except as provided in paragraph (c)(3)(ii) of this section.

(iii) An expenditure attributable to enlargement of a building (as defined in paragraph (c)(7) of this section).

(iv) An expenditure attributable to rehabilitation of a certified historic structure (as defined in section 191(d)(1) and the regulations thereunder), unless the rehabilitation is a certified rehabilitation (as defined in paragraph (c)(8) of this section).

(7) Expenditures for enlargement distinguished. (i) In general. Expenditures attributable to an enlargement of an existing building do not qualify as qualified rehabilitated expenditures. A building is enlarged to the extent that the total volume of the building is increased. An increase in floor space resulting from interior remodeling is not considered an enlargement. Generally, the total volume of a building is equal to the product of the floor area of the base of the building and the height from the underside of the lowest floor (including the basement) to the average height of the finished roof (as it exists or existed). For this purpose, floor area is measured from the exterior faces of external walls (other than shared walls that are external walls) and from the centerline of shared walls that are external walls. In addition, a building is enlarged to the extent of any construction outside the exterior faces of the existing external wall of the building.

(ii) Rehabilitation which includes enlargement. If expenditures for property only partially qualify as qualified rehabilitation expenditures because some of the expenditures are also attributable to the enlargement of the building, the expenditures must be apportioned between the original portion of the building and the enlargement. This allocation should be made using the principles contained in paragraph (b)(5)(i) of this section.

(8) Certified rehabilitation. (i) In general. For the purpose of this paragraph (c) of this section, the term "certified rehabilitation" means any rehabilitation of a certified historic building in a registered historic district which the Secretary of the Interior has certified to the Secretary as being consistent with the historic character of such building or the district in which such building is located.

(ii) Revoked or invalidated certifications. If the Department of Interior revokes or otherwise invalidates a certification after it has been provided to a taxpayer, the decertified property will cease to be section 38 property described in section 48(a)(1)(e). Such cessation shall be effective as of the date the activity giving rise to the revocation or invalidation occurred. See section 47 for the rules applicable to property that ceases to be section 38 property.

(d) Coordination with other provisions of the Code. *(1) Credit by lessees.* (i) Rehabilitation performed by lessor. A lessee may take the credit for rehabilitation performed by the lessor if the requirements of this section and section 48(d) are satisfied. For purposes of applying section 48(d), the fair market value of section 38 property described in section 48(a)(1)(E) shall be equal to that portion of the lessor's basis in a qualified rehabilitated building that is attributable to qualified rehabilitation expenditures.

(ii) Rehabilitation performed by lessee. A lessee may take the credit for rehabilitation performed by the lessee, provided that the property (or improvements or additions to property) for which the rehabilitation expenditures are made is depreciable (or amortizable) by the lessee (see sections

167 and 178, and the regulations thereunder) and the requirements of this section are satisfied.

(2) When credit may be claimed. The investment credit for qualified rehabilitation expenditures is allowed generally in the taxable year in which the property to which the rehabilitation expenditures is attributable is placed in service, provided the building is a qualified rehabilitated building for the taxable year. See § 1.46-3(d). Under certain circumstances, however, the credit may be available prior to the date the property is placed in service. See section 46(d) and § 1.46-5 (relating to qualified progress expenditures).

(3) Recapture. If property described in section 48(a)(1)(E) is disposed of by the taxpayer, or otherwise ceases to be "section 38 property," recapture may result under section 47. Property will cease to be section 38 property, and therefore recapture may occur under section 47, in any case where the Department of Interior revokes or otherwise invalidates a certification of rehabilitation (see section 48(g)(2)(C)) after the property is placed in service because, for example, the taxpayer made modifications to the building inconsistent with Department of Interior standards.

(e) Effective date. *(1) General rule.* Except as provided in paragraph (e)(2) of this section, this § 1.48-11 shall not apply to expenditures incurred after December 31, 1981.

(2) Transitional rule. This § 1.48-11 shall continue to apply to expenditures incurred after December 31, 1981, for the rehabilitation of a building if—

(i) The physical work on the rehabilitation began before January 1, 1982, and

(ii) The building does not meet the requirements of section 48(g)(1) of the Code as amended by the Economic Recovery Tax Act of 1981.

T.D. 8031, 6/18/85.

---

§ 1.48-12 Qualified rehabilitated building; expenditures incurred after December 31, 1981.

Caution: The Treasury has not yet amended Reg § 1.48-12 to reflect changes made by P.L. 101-508.

(a) General rule. *(1) In general.* Under section 48(a)(1)(E), the portion of the basis of a qualified rehabilitated building that is attributable to qualified rehabilitation expenditures (within the meaning of section 48(g) and this section) is section 38 property. Property that is section 38 property by reason of section 48(a)(1)(E) is treated as new section 38 property and, therefore, is not subject to the used property limitation in section 48(c). Section 48(g)(1) and paragraph (b) of this section define the term "qualified rehabilitated building." Section 48(g)(2) and paragraph (c) of this section define the term "qualified rehabilitation expenditure." Section 48(g)(2)(B)(iv) and (3) and paragraph (d) of this section describe the rules applicable to "certified historic structures." Section 48(q) and paragraph (e) of this section provide rules concerning an adjustment to the basis of the rehabilitated building. Paragraph (f) of this section provides guidance for coordination of these provisions with other sections of the Code, including rules for determining when the rehabilitation credit may be claimed.

(2) Effective dates and transition rules. (i) In general. Except as otherwise provided in this paragraph (a)(2)(i), this section applies to expenditures incurred after December 31, 1981, in connection with the rehabilitation of a qualified rehabilitated building. (See paragraph (c)(3)(i) of this section for rules concerning the determination of when an expenditure is incurred.) If, however, physical work on the rehabilitation began before January 1, 1982, and the building does not meet the requirements of paragraph (b) of this section, the rules in § 1.48-11 shall apply to the expenditures incurred after December 31, 1981, in connection with such rehabilitation. (See paragraph (b)(6)(i) of this section for rules determining when physical work on a rehabilitation begins.) The last sentence of paragraph (c)(8)(i) of this section applies to qualified rehabilitation expenditures that are qualified property under section 168(k)(2) or qualified New York Liberty Zone property under section 1400L(b) acquired by a taxpayer after September 10, 2001, and to qualified rehabilitation expenditures that are 50 percent bonus depreciation property under section 168(k)(4) acquired by a taxpayer after May 5, 2003.

(ii) Transition rules concerning ACRS lives. (A) For property placed in service before March 16, 1984, and any property subject to the exception set forth in section 111(g)(2) of Pub. L. 98-369 (Deficit Reduction Act of 1984), the references to "19 years" in paragraph (c)(4)(ii) and (7)(v) shall be replaced with "15 years" and the reference to "19-year real property" in paragraph (c)(4)(ii) shall be replaced with "15-year real property."

(B) Except as otherwise provided in paragraph (a)(2)(ii)(A) of this section, for property placed in service before May 9, 1985, and any property subject to the exception set forth in section 105(b)(2) and (5) of Pub. L. 99-121 (99 Stat. 501, 511), the reference to "19 years" in paragraph (c)(4)(ii) and (7)(v) shall be replaced with "18 years" and the references to "19-years real property" in paragraph (c)(4)(ii) shall be replaced with "18-year real property."

(iii) Transition rule concerning external wall definition. Notwithstanding the definition of external wall contained in paragraph (b)(3)(ii) of this section, in any case in which the written plans and specifications for a rehabilitation were substantially completed on or before June 28, 1985, and the building being rehabilitated would fail to meet the requirement of paragraph (b)(1)(iii) of this section if the definition of external wall in paragraph (b)(3)(ii) of this section were used, the term "external wall" shall be defined as a wall, including its supporting elements, with one face exposed to the weather or earth, and a common wall shall not be treated as an external wall. See paragraph (b)(2)(v) of this section for the definition of written plans and specifications.

(iv) Transition rules concerning amendments made by the Tax Reform Act of 1986. (A) In general. Except as otherwise provided in section 251(d) of the Tax Reform Act of 1986 and this paragraph (a)(2)(iv), the amendments made by section 251 of the Tax Reform Act of 1986 shall apply to property placed in service after December 31, 1986, in taxable years ending after that date, regardless of when the rehabilitation expenditures attributable to such property were incurred. If property attributable to qualified rehabilitation expenditures is incurred with respect to a rehabilitation to a building placed in service in segments or phases and some segments are placed in service before January 1, 1987, and the remaining segments are placed in service after December 31, 1986, the amendments under the Tax Reform Act would not apply to the property placed in service before January 1, 1987, but would apply to the segments placed in service after December 31, 1986, unless one of the transition rules in paragraph (a)(2)(iv)(B) or (C) of this section applies.

(B) General transition rule. The amendments made by sections 251 and 201 of the Tax Reform Act of 1986 shall not apply to property that qualifies under section 251(d)(2), (3), or (4) of the Tax Reform Act of 1986. Property qualifies for the general transition rule in section 251(d)(2) of the Act if such property is placed in service before January 1, 1994, and if such property is placed in service as part of —

(1) A rehabilitation that was completed pursuant to a written contract that was binding on March 1, 1986, or

(2) A rehabilitation incurred in connection with property (including any leasehold interest) acquired before March 2, 1986, or acquired on or after such date pursuant to a written contract that was binding on March 1, 1986, if—

(i) Parts 1 and 2 of the Historic Preservation Certificate Application were filed with the Department of the Interior (or its designee) before March 2, 1986, or

(ii) The lesser of $1,000,000 or 5 percent of the cost of the rehabilitation is incurred before March 2, 1986, or is required to be incurred pursuant to a written contract which was binding on March 1, 1986.

(C) Specific rehabilitations. See section 251(d)(3) and (4) of the Tax Reform Act of 1986 for additional rehabilitations that are exempted from the amendments made by sections 251 and 201 of the Tax Reform Act of 1986.

(b) Definition of qualified rehabilitated building. *(1) In general.* The term "qualified rehabilitated building" means any building and its structural components—

(i) That has been substantially rehabilitated (within the meaning of paragraph (b)(2) of this section) for the taxable year.

(ii) That was placed in service (within the meaning of § 1.46-3(d)) as a building by any person before the beginning of the rehabilitation, and

(iii) That meets the applicable existing external wall retention test or the existing external wall and internal structural framework retention test in accordance with paragraph (b)(3) of this section.

The requirement in paragraph (b)(1)(iii) of this section does not apply to a certified historic structure. See paragraph (b)(4) and (5) of this section for additional requirements related to the definition of a qualified rehabilitated building.

(2) Substantially rehabilitated building. (i) Substantial rehabilitation test. A building shall be treated as having been substantially rehabilitated for a taxable year only if the qualified rehabilitation expenditures (as defined in paragraph (c) of this section) incurred during any 24-month period selected by the taxpayer ending with or within the taxable year exceed the greater of—

(A) The adjusted basis of the building (and its structural components), or

(B) $5,000.

(ii) Date to determine adjusted basis of the building. (A) In general. The adjusted basis of the building (and its structural components) shall be determined as of the beginning of the first day of the 24-month period selected by the taxpayer or the first day of the taxpayer's holding period of the building (within the meaning of section 1250(e)), whichever is later. For purposes of determining the holding period under section 1250(e), any reconstruction that is part of the rehabilitation shall be disregarded.

(B) Special rules. In the event that a building is not owned by the taxpayer, the adjusted basis of the building shall be determined as of the date that would have been used if the owner had been the taxpayer. The adjusted basis of a building that is being rehabilitated by a taxpayer other than the owner shall thus be determined as of the beginning of the first day of the 24-month period selected by the taxpayer or the first day of the owner's holding period, whichever is later. Therefore, if a building that is being rehabilitated by a lessee is sold subject to the lease prior to the date that the lessee has substantially rehabilitated the building, the lessee's adjusted basis is determined as of the beginning of the first day of the new lessor's holding period or the beginning of the first day of the 24-month period selected by the lessee (the taxpayer), whichever is later. If, therefore, the first day of the new lessor's holding period were later than the first day of the 24-month period selected by the lessee (the taxpayer), the lessee's adjusted basis for purposes of the substantial rehabilitation test would be the same as the adjusted basis of the new lessor as determined under paragraph (b)(2)(vii) of this section. If a building is sold after the date that a lessee has substantially rehabilitated the building with respect to the original lessor's adjusted basis, however, the lessee's basis may be determined as of the first day of the 24-month period selected by the lessee or the first day of the original lessor's holding period, whichever is later, and the transfer of the building will not affect the adjusted basis for purposes of the substantial rehabilitation test. The preceding sentence shall not apply, however, if the building is sold to the lessee or a related party within the meaning of section 267(b) or section 707(b)(1).

(iii) Adjusted basis of the building. (A) In general. The term "adjusted basis of the building" means the aggregate adjusted basis (within the meaning of section 1011(a)) in the building (and its structural components) of all the parties who have an interest in the building.

(B) Special rules. In the case of a building that is leased to one or more tenants in whole or in part, the adjusted basis of the building is determined by adding the adjusted basis of the owner (lessor) in the building to the adjusted basis of the lessee (or lessees) in the leasehold and any leasehold improvements that are structural components of the building. Similarly, in the case of a building that is divided into condominium units, the adjusted basis of the building means the aggregate adjusted basis of all of the respective condominium owners (including the basis of any lessee in the leasehold and leasehold improvements) in the building (and its structural components). If the adjusted basis of a building would be determined in whole or in part by reference to the adjusted basis of a person or persons other than the taxpayer (e.g., a rehabilitation by a lessee) and the taxpayer is unable to obtain the required information, the taxpayer must establish by clear and convincing evidence that the adjusted basis of such person or persons in the building on the date specified in paragraph (b)(2)(ii) of this section is an amount that is less than the amount of qualified rehabilitation expenditures incurred by the taxpayer. If no such amount can be so established, the adjusted basis of the building will be deemed to be the fair market value of the building on the relevant date. For purposes of determining the adjusted basis of a building, the portion of the adjusted basis of a building that is allocable to an addition (within the meaning of paragraph (b)(4)(ii) of this section) to the building that does not meet the age requirement in paragraph (b)(4)(i) of this section shall be disregarded. (See paragraph (b)(2)(vii) of this section for the rule applicable to the determination of the adjusted basis of a building when qualified rehabilitation expenditures are treated as incurred by the taxpayer.)

(iv) Rehabilitation. Rehabilitation includes renovation, restoration, or reconstruction of a building, but does not include an enlargement (within the meaning of paragraph (c)(10) of this section) of new construction. The determination of whether expenditures are attributable to the rehabilitation of an existing building or to new construction shall be based upon all the facts and circumstances.

(v) Special rule for phased rehabilitation. In the case of any rehabilitation that may reasonably be expected to be completed in phases set forth in written architectural plans and specifications completed before the physical work on the rehabilitation begins, paragraphs (b)(2)(i), (ii), and (vii) of this section shall be applied by substituting "60-month period" for "24-month period." A rehabilitation may reasonably be expected to be completed in phases if it consists of two or more distinct stages of development. The determination of whether a rehabilitation consists of distinct stages and therefore may reasonably be expected to be completed in phases shall be made on the basis of all the relevant facts and circumstances in existence before physical work on the rehabilitation begins. For purposes of this paragraph and paragraph (a)(2)(iii) of this section, written plans that describe generally all phases of the rehabilitation process shall be treated as written architectural plans and specifications. Such written plans are not required to contain detailed working drawings or detailed specifications of the materials to be used. In addition, the taxpayer may include a description of work to be done by lessees in the written plans. For example, where the owner of a vacant four story building plans to rehabilitate two floors of the building and plans to require, as a condition of any lease, that tenants of the other two floors must rehabilitate those floors, the requirements of this paragraph (b)(2)(v) shall be met if the owner provides written plans for the rehabilitation work to be done by the owner and a description of the rehabilitation work that the tenants will be required to complete. The work required of the tenants may be described in the written plans in terms of minimum specifications (e.g., as to lighting, wiring, materials, appearance) that must be met by such tenants. See paragraph (b)(6)(i) of this section for the definition of physical work on a rehabilitation.

(vi) Treatment of expenses incurred by persons who have an interest in the building. For purposes of the substantial rehabilitation test in paragraph (b)(2)(i) of this section, the taxpayer may take into account qualified rehabilitation expenditures incurred during the same rehabilitation process by any other person who has an interest in the building. Thus, for example, to determine whether a building has been substantially rehabilitated, a lessee may include the expenditures of the lessor and of other lessees; a condominium owner may include the expenditures incurred by other condominium owners; and an owner may include the expenditures of the lessees.

(vii) Special rules when qualified rehabilitation expenditures are treated as incurred by the taxpayer. In the case where qualified rehabilitation expenditures are treated as having been incurred by a taxpayer under paragraph (c)(3)(ii) of this section, the transferee shall be treated as having incurred the expenditures incurred by the transferor on the date that the transferor incurred the expenditures with the meaning of paragraph (c)(3)(i) of this section. For purposes of the substantial rehabilitation test in paragraph (b)(2)(i) of this section, the transferee's adjusted basis in the building shall be determined as of the beginning of the first day of a 24-month period, or the first day of the transferee's holding period, whichever is later, as provided in paragraph (b)(2)(ii) of this section. The transferee's basis as of the first day of the transferee's holding period for purposes of the substantial rehabilitation test in paragraph (b)(2)(i) of this section, however, shall be considered to be equal to the transferee's basis in the building on such date less—

(A) The amount of any qualified rehabilitation expenditures incurred (or treated as having been incurred) by the transferor during the 24-month period that are treated as having been incurred by the transferee under paragraph (c)(3)(ii) of this section, and

(B) The amount of qualified rehabilitation expenditures incurred before the transfer and during the 24-month period by any other person who has an interest in the building (e.g., a lessee of the transferor). The preceding sentence shall not apply, however, unless the transferee's basis in the building is determined with reference to (1) the transferee's cost of the building (including the rehabilitation expenditures), (2) the transferor's basis in the building (where such basis includes the amount of the expenditures), or (3) any other amount that includes the cost of the rehabilitation expenditures. In the event that the transferee's basis is determined with reference to an amount not described above (e.g., transferee's basis in one building is determined with reference to the transferee's basis in another building under section 1031(d)), the amount of the expenditures incurred by the transferor and treated as having been incurred by the transferee are not deducted from the transferee's basis for purposes of the substantial rehabilitation test. If a transferee's basis is determined under section 1014, any expenditures incurred by the decedent within the measuring period that are treated as having been incurred by the transferee under paragraph (c)(3)(ii) of this section shall decrease the transferee's basis for purposes of the substantial rehabilitation test.

(viii) Statement of adjusted basis, measuring period, and qualified rehabilitation expenditures. In the case of any tax return filed after August 27, 1985, on which an investment tax credit for property, described in section 48(a)(1)(E) is claimed, the taxpayer shall indicate by way of a marginal notation on, or a supplemental statement attached to, Form 3468—

(A) The beginning and ending dates for the measuring period selected by the taxpayer under section 48(g)(1)(C)(i) and paragraph (b)(2) of this section,

(B) The adjusted basis of the building (within the meaning of paragraph (b)(2)(iii) or (vii) of this section) as of the beginning of such measuring period, and

(C) The amount of qualified rehabilitation expenditures incurred, and treated as incurred, respectively, during such measuring period. Furthermore, for returns filed after August 27, 1985, if the adjusted basis of the building for purposes of the substantial rehabilitation test is determined in whole or in part by reference to the adjusted basis of a person, or persons, other than the taxpayer (e.g., a rehabilitation by a lessee), the taxpayer must attach to the Form 3468 filed with the tax return on which the credit is claimed a statement addressed to the District Director, signed by such third party, that states the first day of the third party's holding period and the amount of the adjusted basis of such third party in the building at the beginning of the measuring period or the first day of the holding period, whichever is later. If the taxpayer is unable to obtain the required information, that fact should be indicated and the taxpayer should state the manner in which the adjusted basis was determined and, if different, the fair market value of the building on the relevant date.

(ix) Partnerships and S corporations. If a building is owned by a partnership (i.e., the building is partnership property) or an S corporation, the substantial rehabilitation test shall be determined at the entity level. Thus, the entity shall compare the amount of qualified rehabilitation expenditures incurred during the measuring period against its basis in the building at the beginning of its holding period or the beginning of its measuring period, whichever is later. (See section 1223(2) for rules concerning the determination of a partnership's holding period in the case of a contribution of property to the partnership meeting the requirements of section 721.) The adjusted basis of the building to a partnership shall be determined by taking into account any adjustments to the basis of the building made under section 743 and section 734. Any adjustments to the building's basis that are made under section 743 or section 734 after the beginning of the partnership's holding period, but before the end of the measuring period, shall be deemed for purposes of the substantial rehabilitation test to have been made on the first day of the partnership's holding period. However, in such case, the partnership's basis in the building shall be reduced by the amount of qualified rehabilitation expenditures incurred by the partnership. In the case of any tax return filed after January 9, 1989 on which a credit is claimed by a partner or a shareholder of an S corporation for rehabilitation expenditures incurred by a partnership or an S corporation, the partner or shareholder shall indicate on the Form 3468 on which the credit is claimed the name, address, and identification number of the partnership or S corporation that incurred the rehabilitation expenditures, and the partnership or S corporation shall, by way of a marginal notation on or a supplemental statement attached to the entity's return, provide the information required by paragraph (b)(2)(viii) of this section.

(x) Examples. The following examples illustrate the application of the substantial rehabilitation test in this paragraph (b)(2):

Example (1). Assume that A, a calendar year taxpayer, purchases a building for $140,000 on January 1, 1982, incurs qualified rehabilitation expenditures in the amount of $48,000 (at the rate of $4,000 per month) in 1982, $100,000 in 1983, and $20,000 (at the rate of $2,000 per month) in the first ten months of 1984, and places the rehabilitated building in service on October 31, 1984. Assume that A did not have written architectural plans and specifications describing a phased rehabilitation within the meaning of paragraph (b)(2)(v) of this section in existence prior to the beginning of physical work on the rehabilitation. For purposes of the substantial rehabilitation test in paragraph (b)(2) of this section, A may select any 24-consecutive-month measuring period that ends in 1984, the taxable year in which the rehabilitated building was placed in service. Assume that on A's 1984 return, A selects a measuring period beginning on February 1, 1982, and ending on January 31, 1984, and specifies that A's basis in the building (within the meaning of section 1011(a)) was $144,000 on February 1, 1982 ($140,000 + $4,000). (The $4,000 of rehabilitation expenditures incurred during January 1982 are included in A's basis under section 1011 even though such property has not been placed in service.) The amount of qualified rehabilitation expenditures incurred during the measuring period was $146,000 ($44,000 from February 1 to December 31, 1982, plus $100,000 in 1983, plus $2,000 in January 1984). The building shall be treated as "substantially rehabilitated" within the meaning of this paragraph (b)(2) for A's 1984 taxable year because the $146,000 of expenditures incurred by A during the measuring period exceeded A's adjusted basis of $144,000 at the beginning of the period. If the other requirements of section 48(g)(1) and this paragraph are met, the building is treated as a qualified rehabilitated building, and A can treat as qualified rehabilitation expenditures the amount of $168,000 (i.e., $146,000 of expenditures incurred during the measuring period, $4,000 of expenditures incurred prior to the beginning of the measuring period as part of the rehabilitation process, and $18,000 of expenditures incurred after the measuring period during the taxable year within which the measuring period ends (See paragraph (c)(6) of this section.)). The result would generally be the same if the property attributable to the rehabilitation expenditures was placed in service as the expenditures were incurred, but A would have $148,000 of qualified rehabilitation expenditures for 1983 and $20,000 of qualified rehabilitation expenditures for 1984. (See paragraph (f)(2) of this section).

Example (2). Assume the same facts as in example (1), except that additional rehabilitation expenditures are incurred after the portion of the basis of the building attributable to qualified rehabilitation expenditures was placed in service on October 31, 1984. Such expenditures are incurred through the end of 1984 and in 1985 when the portion of the basis attributable to the additional expenditures is placed in service. The fact that the building qualified as a substantially rehabilitated building for A's 1984 taxable year has no effect on whether the building is a qualified rehabilitated building for property placed in service in A's 1985 taxable year. In order to determine whether the building is a qualified rehabilitated building for A's 1985 taxable year, A must select a measuring period that ends in 1985 and compare the expenditures incurred within that period with the adjusted basis as of the beginning of the period. Solely for the purpose of determining whether the building was substantially rehabilitated for A's 1985 taxable year, expenditures incurred during 1983 and 1984, even though considered in determining whether the building was substantially rehabilitated in 1984, may also be used to determine whether the building was substantially rehabilitated for A's 1985 taxable year, provided the expenditures were incurred during any 24-month measuring period selected by A that ends in 1985.

Example (3). (i) Assume the B purchases a building for $100,000 on January 1, 1982, and leases the building to C who rehabilitates the building. Assume that C, a calendar year taxpayer, places the property with respect to which rehabilitation expenditures were made in service in 1982 and selects December 31, 1982, as the end of the measuring period for purposes of the substantial rehabilitation test. The beginning of the measuring period is January 2, 1982, the beginning of B's holding period under section 1250(e), and the adjusted basis of the building is $100,000. Accordingly, if C incurred more than $100,000 of qualified rehabilitation expenditures during 1982, the building would be substantially rehabilitated within the meaning of paragraph (b)(2)(i) of this section.

(ii) Assume the facts of example (3)(i), except that after C begins physical work on the rehabilitation, but before C incurs $100,000 of expenditures, D acquires the building, subject to C's lease, from B for $200,000. D's holding period under section 1250(e) begins on the day after D acquired the building, and C's adjusted basis for purposes of the substantial rehabilitation test is $200,000, less the the amount of expenditures incurred by C before the transfer. (See paragraph (b)(2)(ii) and (vii) of this section.) Accordingly, if C incurred more than $200,000 (less the amount of expenditures incurred prior to the transfer) of qualified rehabilitation expenditures during 1982, the building would be substantially rehabilitated within the meaning of paragraph (b)(2) of this section. Under paragraph (b)(2)(ii)(B) of this section, however, C's adjusted basis for purposes of the substantial rehabilitation test would be $100,000 if C had substantially rehabilitated the building (i.e., incurred more than $100,000 in rehabilitation expenditures) prior to B's sale to D.

Example (4). E owns a building with a basis of $10,000 and E incurs $5,000 of rehabilitation expenditures. Before completing the rehabilitation project, E sells the building to F for $30,000. Assume that F is treated under paragraph (c)(3)(ii) of this section as having incurred the $5,000 of rehabilitation expenditures actually incurred by E. Because F's basis in the building is determined under section 1011 with reference to F's $30,000 cost of the building (which includes the property attributable to E's rehabilitation expenditures), F's basis for purposes of the substantial rehabilitation test is $25,000 ($80,000 cost basis less $5,000 rehabilitation expenditures treated as if incurred by F). (See paragraph (b)(2)(vii) of this section.) F would thus be required to incur more than $20,000 of rehabilitation expenditures (in addition to the $5,000 incurred by E and treated as having been incurred by F) during a measuring period selected by F to satisfy the substantial rehabilitation test.

Example (5). G owns Building I with a basis of $10,000 and a fair market value of $20,000. H owns Building II with a basis of $5,000 and a fair market value of $20,000, with respect to which H has incurred $1,000 of rehabilitation expenditures. G and H exchange their buildings in a transaction that qualifies for nonrecognition treatment under section 1031. Assume that G is treated under paragraph (c)(3)(ii) of this section as having incurred $1,000 of rehabilitation expenditures. G's basis in Building II, computed under section 1031(d), is $10,000. G's basis in Building II is not determined with reference to (A) the cost of Building II, (B) H's basis in Building II (including the cost of the rehabilitation expenditures) or (C) any other amount that includes the cost of expenditures, but is instead determined with reference to G's basis in other property (Building I). Therefore, G's basis in Building II for purposes of the substantial rehabilitation test is not reduced by the $1,000 of rehabilitation expenditures treated as if incurred by G. (See paragraph (b)(2)(vii) of this section.) Accordingly, G's basis in Building II for purposes of the substantial rehabilitation test is $10,000, and G must incur additional rehabilitation expenditures in excess of $9,000 within a measuring period selected by G to satisfy the test.

(3) Retention of existing external walls and internal structural framework. (i) In general. (A) Property placed in service after December 31, 1986. Except in the case of property that qualifies for the transition rules in paragraph (a)(2)(iv)(B) and (C) of this section, in the case of property that is placed in service after December 31, 1986, a building (other than a certified historic structure) meets the requirement in paragraph (b)(1)(iii) of this section only if in the rehabilitation process—

(1) 50 percent or more of the existing external walls of such building are retained in place as external walls;

(2) 75 percent or more of the existing external walls of such building are retained in place as internal or external walls, and

(3) 75 percent or more of the internal structural framework of such building (as defined in paragraph (b)(3)(iii) of this section) is retained in place.

(B) Expenditures incurred before January 1, 1984, for property placed in service before January 1, 1987. With respect to rehabilitation expenditures incurred before January 1, 1984, for property that is either placed in service before January 1, 1987, or that qualifies for the transition rules in paragraph (a)(2)(iv)(B) or (C) of this section, a building meets the requirement in paragraph (b)(1)(iii) of this section only if 75 percent or more of the existing external walls of the building are retained in place as external walls in the rehabilitation process. If an addition to a building is not treated as part of a qualified rehabilitated building because it does not meet the 30-year requirement in paragraph (b)(4)(i)(B) of this section, then the external walls of such addition shall not be considered to be existing external walls of the building for purposes of section 48(g)(1)(A)(iii) (as in effect prior to enactment of the Tax Reform Act of 1986), and this section.

(C) Expenditures incurred after December 31, 1983, for property placed in service before January 1, 1987. With respect to expenditures incurred after December 31, 1983, for property that is either placed in service before January 1, 1987, or that qualifies for the transition rules in paragraph (a)(2)(iv)(B) or (C) of this section, the requirement of paragraph (b)(1)(iii) of this section is satisfied only if in the rehabilitation process either the existing external wall retention requirement in paragraph (b)(3)(i)(B) of this section is satisfied, or:

(1) 50 percent or more of the existing external walls of the building are retained in place as external walls,

(2) 75 percent or more of the existing external walls are retained in place as internal or external walls, and

(3) 75 percent or more of the existing internal structural framework of such building is retained in place.

(D) Area of external walls and internal structural framework. The determinations required by paragraph (b)(3)(i)(A), (B), and (C) of this section shall be based upon the area of the external walls or internal structural framework that is retained in place compared to the total area of each prior to the rehabilitation. The area of the existing external walls and internal structural framework of a building shall be determined prior to any destruction, modification, or construction of external walls or internal structural framework that is undertaken by any party in anticipation of the rehabilitation.

(ii) Definition of external wall. For purposes of this paragraph (b), a wall includes both the supporting elements of the wall and the nonsupporting elements, (e.g., a curtain, windows or doors) of the wall. Except as otherwise provided in this paragraph (b)(3), the term "external wall" includes any wall that has one face exposed to the weather, earth, or an abutting wall of an adjacent building. The term "external wall" also includes a shared wall (i.e., a single wall shared with an adjacent building), generally referred to as a "party wall," provided that the shared wall has no windows or doors in any portion of the wall that does not have one face exposed to the weather, earth, or an abutting wall. In general, the term "external wall" includes only those external walls that form part of the outline or perimeter of the building or that surround an uncovered courtyard. Therefore, the walls of an uncovered internal shaft, designed solely to bring light or air into the center of a building, which are completely surrounded by external walls of the building and which enclose space not designated for occupancy or other use by people (other than for maintenance or emergency), are not considered external walls. Thus, for example, a wall of a light well in the center of a building is not an external wall. However, walls surrounding an outdoor space which is usable by people, such as a courtyard, are external walls.

(iii) Definition of internal structural framework. For purposes of this section, the term "internal structural framework" includes all load-bearing internal walls and any other internal structural supports, including the columns, girders, beams, trusses, spandrels, and all other members that are essential to the stability of the building.

(iv) Retained in place. An existing external wall is retained in place if the supporting elements of the wall are retained in place. An existing external wall is not retained in place if the supporting elements of the wall are replaced by new supporting elements. An external wall is retained in place, however, if the supporting elements are reinforced in the rehabilitation, provided that such supporting elements of the external wall are retained in place. An external wall also is retained in place if it is covered (e.g., with new siding). Moreover, an external wall is retained in place if the existing curtain is replaced with a new curtain, provided that the structural framework that provides for the support of the existing curtain is retained in place. An external wall is retained in place notwithstanding that the existing doors and windows in the wall are modified, eliminated, or replaced. An external wall is retained in place if the wall is disassembled and reassembled, provided the same supporting elements are used when the wall is reassembled and the configuration of the external walls of the building after the rehabilitation is the same as it was before the rehabilitation process commenced. Thus, for example, a brick wall is considered retained in place even though the original bricks are removed (for cleaning, etc.) and replaced to form the wall. The principles of this paragraph (b)(3)(iv) shall also apply to determine whether internal structural framework of the building is retained in place.

(v) Effect of additions. If an existing external wall is converted into an internal wall (i.e., a wall that is not an external wall), the wall is not retained in place as an external wall for purposes of this section.

(vi) Examples. The provisions of this paragraph (b)(3) may be illustrated by the following examples:

Example (1). Taxpayer A rehabilitated a building all of the walls of which consisted of wood siding attached to gypsum board sheets (which covered the supporting elements of the wall, i.e., studs). A covered the existing wood siding with aluminum siding as part of a rehabilitation that otherwise qualified under this subparagraph. The addition of the aluminum siding does not affect the status of the existing external walls as external walls and they would be considered to have been retained in place.

Example (2). Taxpayer B rehabilitated a building, the external walls of which had a masonry curtain. The masonry on the wall face was replaced with a glass curtain. The steel beam and girders supporting the existing masonry curtain were retained in place. The walls of the building are considered to be retained in place as external walls, notwithstanding the replacement of the curtain.

Example (3). Taxpayer C rehabilitated a building that has two external walls measuring 75' x 20' and two other external walls measuring 100' x 20' C demolished one of the larger walls, including its supporting elements and constructed a new wall. Because one of the larger walls represents more than 25 percent of the area of the building's external walls, C has not satisfied the requirements that 75 percent of the existing external walls must be retained in place as either internal or external walls. If however, C had not demolished the wall, but had converted it into an internal wall (e.g., by building a new external wall), the building would satisfy the external wall requirements.

Example (4). The facts are the same as in example (3), except that C does not tear down any walls, but builds an addition that results in one of the smaller walls becoming an internal wall. In addition, C enlarged 8 of the existing windows on one of the larger walls, increasing them from a size of 3' × 4' to 6' × 8' Since the smaller wall accounts for less than 25 percent of the total wall area, C has satisfied the requirement that 75 percent of the existing external walls must be retained in place as external walls in the rehabilitation process. The enlargement of the existing windows on the larger wall does not affect its status as an external wall.

Example (5). Taxpayer D rehabilitated a building that was in the center of a row of three buildings. The building being rehabilitated by D shares its side walls with the buildings on either side. The shared walls measure 100' × 20' and the rear and front walls measure 75' × 20' As part of a rehabilitation, D tears down and replaces the front wall. Because the shared walls as well as the front and back walls are considered external walls and the front wall accounts for less than 25 percent of the total external wall area (including the shared walls), D has satisfied the requirement that 75 percent of the existing external walls must be retained in place as external walls in the rehabilitation process.

(4) Age requirement. (i) In general. (A) Property placed in service after December 31, 1986. Except in the case of property that qualifies for the transition rules in paragraph (a)(2)(iv)(B) or (C) of this section, a building other than a certified historic structure shall not be considered a qualified rehabilitated building unless the building was first placed in service (within the meaning of § 1.46-3(d)) before January 1, 1936.

(B) Property placed in service before January 1, 1987, and property qualifying under a transition rule. In the case of property placed in service before January 1, 1987, and property that qualifies under the transition rules in paragraph (a)(2)(iv)(B) or (C) of this section, a building other than a certified historic structure is considered a qualified rehabilitated building only if a period of at least 30 years has elapsed between the date physical work on the rehabilitation of the building began and the date the building was first placed in service (within the meaning of § 1.46-3(d)) as a building by any person.

(ii) Additions. A building that was first placed in service before 1936 in the case described in paragraph (b)(4)(i)(A) of this section, or at least 30 years before physical work on the rehabilitation began in the case described in paragraph (b)(4)(i)(B) of this section, will not be disqualified because additions to such building have been added since 1936 in the case described in paragraph (b)(4)(i)(A) of this section, or are less than 30 years old in the case described in paragraph (b)(4)(i)(B). Such additions, however, shall not be treated as part of the qualified rehabilitated building. The term "addition" means any construction that resulted in any portion of an external wall becoming an internal wall, that resulted in an increase in the height of the building, or that increased the volume of the building.

(iii) Vacant periods. The determinations required by paragraph (b)(4)(i) of this section include periods during which a building was vacant or devoted to a personal use and is computed without regard to the number of owners or the identify of owners during the period.

(5) Location at which the rehabilitation occurs. A building, other than a certified historic structure is not a qualified rehabilitated building unless it has been located where it is rehabilitated since before 1936 in the case described in paragraph (b)(4)(i)(A) of this section. Similarly, in the case described in paragraph (b)(4)(i)(B) of this section, a building, other than a certified historic structure, is not a qualified rehabilitation building unless it has been located where it is rehabilitated for the thirty-year period immediately preceding

the date physical work on the rehabilitation began in the case of a "30-year building" or the forty-year period immediately preceding the date physical work on the rehabilitation began in the case of a "40-year building." (See § 1.46-1(q)(1)(iii) for the definitions of "30-year building" and "40-year building.")

(6) Definition and special rule. (i) Physical work on a rehabilitation. For purposes of this section, "physical work on a rehabilitation" begins when actual construction, or destruction in preparation for construction, begins. The term "physical work on a rehabilitation," however, does not include preliminary activities such as planning, designing, securing financing, exploring, researching, developing plans and specifications, or stabilizing a building to prevent deterioration (e.g., placing boards over broken windows).

(ii) Special rule for adjoining buildings that are combined. For purposes of this paragraph (b), if as part of a rehabilitation process two or more adjoining buildings are combined and placed in service as a single building after the rehabilitation process, then, at the election of the taxpayer, all of the requirements for a qualified rehabilitated building in section 48(g)(1) and this section may be applied to the constituent adjoining buildings in the aggregate. For example, if such requirements are applied in the aggregate, any shared walls or abutting walls between the constituent buildings that would otherwise be treated as external walls (within the meaning of paragraph (b)(3) of this section) would not be treated as external walls of the building, and the substantial rehabilitation test in paragraph (b)(2) of this section would be applied to the aggregate expenditures with respect to all of the constituent buildings and to the aggregate adjusted basis of all of the constituent buildings. A taxpayer shall elect the special rule of this paragraph (b)(6)(ii) for adjoining buildings by indicating by way of a marginal notation on, or a supplemental statement attached to, the Form 3468 on which a credit is first claimed for qualified rehabilitation expenditures with respect to such buildings that such buildings are a single qualified rehabilitated building because of the application of the special rule in this paragraph (b)(6)(ii).

(c) Definition of qualified rehabilitation expenditures. *(1) In general.* Except as otherwise provided in paragraph (c)(7) of this section, the term "qualified rehabilitation expenditure" means any amount that is—

(i) Properly chargeable to capital account (as described in paragraph (c)(2) of this section),

(ii) Incurred by the taxpayer after December 31, 1981 (as described in paragraph (c)(3) of this section),

(iii) For property for which depreciation is allowable under section 168 and which is real property described in paragraph (c)(4) of this section, and

(iv) Made in connection with the rehabilitation of a qualified rehabilitated building (as described in paragraph (c)(5) of this section).

(2) Chargeable to capital account. For purposes of paragraph (c)(1) of this section, amounts are chargeable to capital account if they are properly includible in computing basis of real property under § 1.46-3(c). Amounts treated as an expense and deducted in the year they are paid or incurred or amounts that are otherwise not added to the basis of real property described in paragraph (c)(4) of this section do not qualify. For purposes of this paragraph (c), amounts incurred for architectural and engineering fees, site survey fees, legal expenses, insurance premiums, development fees, and other construction related costs, satisfy the requirement of this paragraph (c)(2) if they are added to the basis of real property that is described in paragraph (c)(4) of this section. Construction period interest and taxes that are amortized under section 189 (as in effect prior to its repeal by the Tax Reform Act of 1986) do not satisfy the requirement of this paragraph (c)(2). If, however, such interest and taxes are treated by the taxpayer as chargeable to capital account with respect to property described in paragraph (c)(4) of this section, they shall be treated in the same manner as other costs described in this paragraph (c)(2). Any construction period interest or taxes or other fees or costs incurred in connection with the acquisition of a building, any interest in a building, or land, are subject to paragraph (c)(7)(ii) of this section. See paragraph (c)(9) of this section for additional rules concerning interest.

(3) Incurred by the taxpayer. (i) In general. Qualified rehabilitation expenditures are incurred by the taxpayer for purposes of this section on the date such expenditures would be considered incurred under an accrual method of accounting, regardless of the method of accounting used by the taxpayer with respect to other items of income and expense. If qualified rehabilitation expenditures are treated as having been incurred by a taxpayer under paragraph (c)(3)(ii) of this section, the taxpayer shall be treated as having incurred the expenditures on the date such expenditures were incurred by the transferor.

(ii) Qualified rehabilitation expenditures treated as incurred by the taxpayer. (A) Where rehabilitation expenditures are incurred with respect to a building by a person (or persons) other than the taxpayer and the taxpayer subsequently acquires the building, or a portion of the building to which some or all of the expenditures are allocable (e.g., a condominium unit to which rehabilitation expenditures have been allocated), the taxpayer acquiring such property shall be treated as having incurred the rehabilitation expenditures actually incurred by the transferor (or treated as incurred by the transferor under this paragraph (c)(3)(ii)) allocable to the acquired property, provided that—

(1) The building, or the portion of the building, acquired by the taxpayer was not used (or, if later, was not placed in service (as defined in paragraph (f)(2) of this section)) after the rehabilitation expenditures were incurred and prior to the date of acquisition, and

(2) No credit with respect to such qualified rehabilitation expenditures is claimed by anyone other than the taxpayer acquiring the property. For purposes of this paragraph (c)(3)(ii), use shall mean actual use, whether personal or business. In the case of a building that is divided into condominium units, expenditures attributable to the common elements shall be allocable to the individual condominium units in accordance with the principles of paragraph (c)(10)(ii) of this section. Furthermore, for purpose of this paragraph (c)(3)(ii), a condominium unit's share of the common elements shall not be considered to have been used (or placed in service) prior to the time that the particular condominium unit is used.

(B) The amount of rehabilitation expenditures described in paragraph (c)(3)(ii)(A) of this section treated as incurred by the taxpayer under this paragraph shall be the lesser of—

(1) The amount of rehabilitation expenditures incurred before the date on which the taxpayer acquired the building (or portion thereof) to which the rehabilitation expenditures are attributable, or

(2) The portion of the taxpayer's cost or other basis for the property that is properly allocable to the property result-

ing from the rehabilitation expenditures described in paragraph (c)(3)(ii)(B)(1) of this section.

(C) For purposes of this paragraph (c)(3)(ii), the amount of rehabilitation expenditures treated as incurred by the taxpayer under this paragraph (c) shall not be treated as costs for the acquisition of a building. The portion of the cost of acquiring a building (or an interest therein) that is not treated under this paragraph as qualified rehabilitation expenditures incurred by the taxpayer is not treated as section 38 property in the hands of the acquiring taxpayer. (See paragraph (c)(7)(ii) of this section.) (See paragraph (b)(2)(vii) for rules concerning the application of the substantial rehabilitation test when expenditures are treated as incurred by the taxpayer.)

(iii) Examples. The provisions of this paragraph (c) may be illustrated by the following examples:

Example (1). In 1981, A, a taxpayer using the cash receipts and disbursements method of accounting, commenced the rehabilitation of a 30-year old building. In June 1981, A signed a contract with a plumbing contractor for replacement of the plumbing in the building. A agreed to pay the contractor as soon as the work was completed. The work was completed in December 1981, but A did not pay the amount due until January 15, 1982. The expenditures for the plumbing are not qualified rehabilitation expenditures (within the meaning of this paragraph (c)) because they were not incurred under an accrual method of accounting after December 31, 1981.

Example (2). B incurred qualified rehabilitation expenditures of $300,000 with respect to an existing building between January 1, 1982, and May 15, 1982, and then sold the building to C on June 1, 1982. The portion of the building to which the expenditures were allocable was not used by B or any other person during the period from January 1, 1982, to June 1, 1982, and neither B nor any other person claimed the credit. Consequently, C will be treated as having incurred the expenditures on the dates that B incurred the expenditures.

Example (3). D, a taxpayer using the cash receipts and disbursements method of accounting, begins the rehabilitation of a building on January 11, 1982. Prior to May 1, 1982, D makes rehabilitation expenditures of $16,000. On May 3, 1982, D sells the building, the land, and the property attributable to the rehabilitation expenditures to E for $35,000. The purchase price is properly allocable as follows:

Land	$ 5,000
Existing building	11,000
Property attributable to rehabilitation expenditures	19,000
Total purchase price	35,000

The property attributable to the rehabilitation expenditures is placed in service by E on September 5, 1982. E may treat a portion of the $35,000 purchase price as rehabilitation expenditures paid or incurred by him. Since the rehabilitation expenditures paid by D ($16,000) are less than the portion of the purchase price properly allocable to property attributable to these expenditures ($19,000), E may treat only $16,000 as rehabilitation expenditures paid or incurred by him. The excess of the purchase price allocable to rehabilitation expenditures ($19,000) over the rehabilitation expenditures paid by D ($16,000), or $3,000, is treated as the cost of acquiring an interest in the building and is not a qualified rehabilitation expenditure treated as incurred by E.

Example (4). The facts are the same as in example (3), except that the purchase price properly allocable to the property attributable to rehabilitation expenditures is $15,000. Under these circumstances, E may treat only $15,000 of D's $16,000 expenditures as rehabilitation expenditures paid by D. The excess of the rehabilitation expenditures paid by D ($16,000) over the purchase price allocable to rehabilitation expenditures ($15,000), or $1,000, is treated as the cost of acquiring an interest in the building and is not a qualified rehabilitation expenditure treated as incurred by E.

(4) Incurred for depreciable real property. (i) Property placed in service after December 31, 1986. Except as otherwise provided in paragraph (c)(4)(ii) of this section (relating to certain property that qualifies under a transition rule), in the case of property placed in service after December 31, 1986, an expenditure is incurred for depreciable real property for purposes of paragraph (c)(1)(iii) of this section, only if it is added to the depreciable basis of depreciable property which is—

(A) Nonresidential real property.

(B) Residential rental property.

(C) Real property which has a class life of more than 12.5 years, or

(D) An addition or improvement to property described in paragraph (c)(4)(i)(A), (B); or (C) of this section.

For purposes of this paragraph (c)(4)(i), the terms "nonresidential real property", "residential rental property", and "class life" have the respective meanings given to such terms by section 168 and the regulations thereunder.

(ii) Property placed in service before January 1, 1987, and property that qualifies under a transition rule. In the case of property placed in service before January 1, 1987, and property placed in service after December 31, 1986, that qualifies for the transition rules in paragraph (a)(2)(iv)(B) or (C) of this section, an expenditure attributable to such property shall be a qualified rehabilitation expenditure only if such expenditure is incurred for property that is real property (or additions or improvements to real property) with a recovery period (within the meaning of section 168 as in effect prior to its amendment by the Tax Reform Act of 1986) of 19 years (15 years for low-income housing) and if the other requirements of this paragraph (c) are met. For purposes of this section, an expenditure is incurred for recovery property having a recovery period of 19 years only if the amount of the expenditure is added to the basis of property which is 19- year real property or 15-year real property in the case of low-income housing. For purposes of this section, the term "low-income housing" has the meaning given such term by section 168(c)(2)(F) (as in effect prior to the amendments made by the Tax Reform Act of 1986).

(5) Made in connection with the rehabilitation of a qualified rehabilitated building. In order for an expenditure to be a qualified rehabilitation expenditure, such expenditure must be incurred in connection with a rehabilitation (as defined in paragraph (b)(2)(iv) of this section) of a qualified rehabilitated building. Expenditures attributable to work done to facilities related to a building (e.g., sidewalk, parking lot, landscaping) are not considered made in connection with the rehabilitation of a qualified rehabilitated building.

(6) When expenditures may be incurred. An expenditure is a qualified rehabilitation expenditure only if the building with respect to which the expenditures are incurred is substantially rehabilitated (within the meaning of paragraph (b)(2) of this section) for the taxable year in which the property attributable to the expenditures is placed in service (i.e., the building is substantially rehabilitated during a measuring period ending with or within the taxable year in which a

credit is claimed). (See paragraph (f)(2) of this section for rules relating to when property is placed in service.) Once the substantial rehabilitation test is met for a taxable year, the amount of qualified rehabilitation expenditures upon which a credit can be claimed for the taxable year is limited to expenditures incurred:

(i) Before the beginning of a measuring period during which the building was substantially rehabilitated that ends with or within the taxable year, provided that the expenditures were incurred in connection with the rehabilitation process that resulted in the substantial rehabilitation of the building;

(ii) Within a measuring period during which the building was substantially rehabilitated that ends with or within the taxable year, and

(iii) After the end of a measuring period during which the building was substantially rehabilitated but prior to the end of the taxable year with or within which the measuring period ends.

(7) Certain expenditures excluded from qualified rehabilitation expenditures. The term "qualified rehabilitation expenditures" does not include the following expenditures:

(i) Except as otherwise provided in paragraph (c)(8) of this section, any expenditure with respect to which the taxpayer does not use the straight line method over a recovery period determined under section 168(c) and (g).

(ii) The cost of acquiring a building, any interest in a building (including a leasehold interest), or land, except as provided in paragraph (c)(3)(ii) of this section.

(iii) Any expenditure attributable to an enlargement of a building (within the meaning of paragraph (c)(10) of this section).

(iv) Any expenditure attributable to the rehabilitation of a certified historic structure or a building located in a registered historic district, unless the rehabilitation is a certified rehabilitation. (See paragraph (d) of this section which contains definitions and special rules applicable to rehabilitations of certified historic structures and buildings located in registered historic districts.)

(v) Any expenditure of a lessee of a building or a portion of a building, if, on the date the rehabilitation is completed with respect to property placed in service by such lessee, the remaining term of the lease (determined without regard to any renewal period) is less than the recovery period determined under section 168(c) (or 19 years in the case of property placed in service before January 1, 1987, and property placed in service that qualifies under the transition rules in paragraph (a)(2)(iv)(B) or (C) of this section).

(vi) Any expenditure allocable to that portion of a building which is (or may reasonably be expected to be) tax-exempt use property (within the meaning of section 168 and the regulations thereunder), except that the exclusion in this paragraph (c)(7)(vi) shall not apply for purposes of determining whether the building is a substantially rehabilitated building under paragraph (b)(2) of this section.

(8) Requirement to use straight line depreciation. (i) Property placed in service after December 31, 1986. The requirement in section 48(g)(2)(B)(i) and paragraph (c)(7)(i) of this section to use straight line cost recovery does not apply to any expenditure to the extent that the alternative depreciation system of section 168(g) applies to such expenditure by reason of section 168(g)(1)(B) or (C). In addition, the requirement in section 48(g)(2)(B)(i) and paragraph (c)(7)(i) of this section applies only to the depreciation of the portion of the basis of a qualified rehabilitated building that is attributable to qualified rehabilitation expenditures. However, see § 1.168(k)-1(f)(10) if the qualified rehabilitation expenditures are qualified property or 50-percent bonus depreciation property under section 168(k) and see § 1.1400L(b)-1(f)(9) if the qualified rehabilitation expenditures are qualified New York Liberty Zone property under section 1400L(b).

(ii) Property placed in service before January 1, 1987, and property placed in service after December 31, 1986, that qualifies for a transition rule. In the case of expenditures attributable to property placed in service before January 1, 1987, and property that qualifies for the transition rules in paragraph (a)(2)(iv)(B) or (C) of this section, the term "qualified rehabilitation expenditure" does not include an expenditure with respect to which an election was not made under section 168(b)(3) as in effect prior to its amendment by the Tax Reform Act of 1986, to use the straight line method of depreciation. In such case, the requirement that an election be made to use straight line cost recovery applies only to the cost recovery of the portion of the basis of a qualified rehabilitated building that is attributable to qualified rehabilitation expenditures. See section 168(f)(1), as in effect prior to its amendment by the Tax Reform Act of 1986, for rules relating to the use of different methods of cost recovery for different components of a building. In addition, such requirement shall not apply to any expenditure to the extent that section 168(f)(12) or (j), as in effect prior to the amendments made by the Tax Reform Act of 1986, applied to such expenditure.

(9) Cost of acquisition. For purposes of paragraph (c)(7)(ii) of this section, cost of acquisition includes any interest incurred on indebtedness the proceeds of which are attributable to the acquisition of a building, an interest in a building, or land open which a building exists. Interest incurred on a construction loan the proceeds of which are used for qualified rehabilitation expenditures, however, is not treated as a cost of acquisition.

(10) Enlargement defined. (i) In general. A building is enlarged to the extent that the total volume of the building is increased. An increase in floor space resulting from interior remodeling is not considered an enlargement. The total volume of a building is generally equal to the product of the floor area of the base of the building and the height from the underside of the lowest floor (including the basement) to the average height of the finished roof (as it exists or existed). For this purpose, floor area is measured from the exterior faces of external walls (other than shared walls that are external walls) and from the centerline of shared walls that are external walls.

(ii) Rehabilitation that includes enlargement. If expenditures for property only partially qualify as qualified rehabilitation expenditures because some of the expenditures are attributable to the enlargement of the building, the expenditures must be apportioned between the original portion of the building and the enlargement. The expenditures must be specifically allocated between the original portion of the building and the enlargement to the extent possible. If it is not possible to make a specific allocation of the expenditures, the expenditures must be allocated to each portion on some reasonable basis. The determination of a reasonable basis for an allocation depends on factors such as the type of improvement and how the improvement relates functionally to the building. For example, in the case of expenditures for an air-conditioning system or a roof, a reasonable basis for allocating the expenditures among the two portions generally would be the volume of the building, excluding the enlargement, served by the air-conditioning system or the roof relative to the volume of the enlargement served by the improvement.

(d) Rules applicable to rehabilitations of certified historic structures *(1) Definition of certified historic structure.* The term "certified historic structure" means any building (and its structural components) that is—

(i) Listed in the National Register of Historic Places ("National Register"); or

(ii) Located in a registered historic district and certified by the Secretary of the Interior to the Internal Revenue Service as being of historic significance to the district.

For purposes of this section, a building shall be considered to be a certified historic structure at the time it is placed in service if the taxpayer reasonably believes on that date the building will be determined to be a certified historic structure and has requested on or before that date a determination from the Department of Interior that such building is a certified historic structure within the meaning of this paragraph (d)(1)(i) or (ii) and the Department of Interior later determines that the building is a certified historic structure.

(2) Definition of registered historic district. The term "registered historic district" means any district that is—

(i) Listed in the National Register, or

(ii) (A) Designated under a statute of the appropriate State or local government that has been certified by the Secretary of the Interior to the Internal Revenue Service as containing criteria that will substantially achieve the purpose of preserving and rehabilitating buildings of historic significance to the district, and

(B) certified by the Secretary of the Interior as meeting substantially all of the requirements for the listing of districts in the National Register.

(3) Definition of certified rehabilitation. The term "certified rehabilitation" means any rehabilitation of a certified historic structure that the Secretary of the Interior has certified to the Internal Revenue Service as being consistent with the historic character of the building and, where applicable, the district in which such building is located. The determination of the scope of a rehabilitation shall be made on the basis of all the facts and circumstances surrounding the rehabilitation and shall not be made solely on the basis of ownership. The Secretary of the Interior shall take all of the rehabilitation work performed as part of a single rehabilitation, including any post-certification work, into account in determining whether the rehabilitation complies with the Department of Interior standards for rehabilitation and whether the certification should be granted, revoked, or otherwise invalidated.

(4) Revoked or invalidated certification. If the Department of Interior revokes or otherwise invalidates a certification after it has been issued to a taxpayer, the basis attributable to rehabilitation of the decertified property shall cease to be section 38 property described in section 48(a)(1)(E). Such cessation shall be effective as of the date the activity giving rise to the revocation or invalidation commenced. See section 47 for the rules applicable to property that ceases to be section 38 property.

(5) Special rule for certain buildings located in registered historic districts. The exclusion in paragraph (c)(7)(iv) of this section does not apply to a building in a registered historic district if—

(i) Such building was not a certified historic structure during the rehabilitation process; and

(ii) The Secretary of the Interior certified to the Internal Revenue Service that such building was not of historic significance to the district. In general, the certification referred to in paragraph (d)(5)(ii) of this section must be requested by the taxpayer prior to the time that physical work on the rehabilitation began. If, however, the certification referred to in paragraph (d)(5)(ii) of this section is requested by the taxpayer after physical work on the rehabilitation of the building has begun, the taxpayer must certify to the Internal Revenue Service that, prior to the date that physical work on the rehabilitation began, the taxpayer in good faith was not aware of the requirement of paragraph (d)(5)(ii) of this section. The certification referred to in the previous sentence must be attached to the Form 3468 filed with the tax return for the year in which the credit is claimed.

(6) Special rule for certain rehabilitations begun before an area is designated as a registered historic district. In general, the exclusion from the definition of qualified rehabilitation expenditure in paragraph (c)(7)(iv) of this section applies to any rehabilitation expenditures that are incurred after a building becomes a certified historic structure within the meaning of section 48(g)(3)(A) and paragraph (d)(1) of this section or the area in which a building is located becomes a registered historic district within the meaning of section 46(g)(3)(B) and paragraph (d)(2) of this section. Rehabilitation expenditures incurred prior to such date, however, are not disqualified. In addition, rehabilitation expenditures made after the date the area in which a building is located becomes a registered historic district shall not be disqualified under paragraph (c)(7)(iv) of this section in any case in which physical work on the rehabilitation of a building begins prior to the date the taxpayer knows or has reason to know of an intention to nominate the area in which such building is located as a registered historic district. For purposes of this paragraph (d)(8), the taxpayer knows or has reason to know of such an intention if there is (A) a communication (written or oral) to the owner of any building within the district from the Department of the Interior, or any agency or instrumentality of the appropriate state or local government (or a designee of such agency or instrumentality) that the district in which the building is located is being considered for designation as a registered historic district, (B) a legal notice of such consideration published in a newspaper, or (C) a public meeting held to discuss such consideration. In order to take advantage of the special rule of this paragraph (d)(6), the taxpayer must attach to the Form 3468 filed for the taxable year in which the credit is claimed a statement that the taxpayer in good faith did not know, or have reason to know, of an intention to nominate the area in which the building is located as a registered historic district.

(7) Notice of certification. (i) In general. Except as otherwise provided in paragraph (d)(7)(ii) of this section, a taxpayer claiming the credit for rehabilitation of a certified historic structure (within the meaning of section 48(g)(3) and paragraph (d)(1) of this section) must attach to the Form 3468 filed with the tax return for the taxable year in which the credit is claimed a copy of the final certification of completed work by the Secretary of the Interior, and for returns filed after January 9, 1989, evidence that the building is a certified historic structure.

(ii) Late certification. If the final certification of completed work has not been issued by the Secretary of the Interior at the time the tax return is filed for a year in which the credit is claimed, a copy of the first page of the Historic Preservation Certification Application—Part 2—Description of Rehabilitation (NPS Form 10-168a), with an indication that it has been received by the Department of the Interior or its designate, together with proof that the building is a certified historic structure (or that such status has been requested) must be attached to the Form 3468 filed with the return. A notice from the Department of the Interior or the State Historic Preservation Officer, stating that the nomination or application has been received, or a date-stamped nomination or application shall be sufficient indication that the nomination or application has been received. The building need not be either listed in the National Register or be determined to be of historic significance to a registered historic district at the time the return is filed for the year in which the credit is claimed. (See paragraph (d)(1) of this section.) The taxpayer must submit a copy of the final certification as an attachment to Form 3468 with the first income tax return filed after the receipt by the taxpayer of the certification. If the final certification is denied by the Department of Interior, the credit will be disallowed for any taxable year in which it was claimed. If the taxpayer fails to receive final certification of completed work prior to the date that is 30 months after the date that the taxpayer filed the tax return on which the credit was claimed, the taxpayer must submit a written statement to the District Director stating such fact prior to the last day of the 30th month, and the taxpayer shall be requested to consent to an agreement under section 6501(c)(4) extending the period of assessment for any tax relating to the time for which the credit was claimed. The procedure permitted by the preceding sentence shall be used whenever the entire rehabilitation project is not fully completed by the date that is 30 months after the taxpayer filed the tax return upon which the credit was claimed (e.g. a phased rehabilitation) and the Secretary of the Interior has thus not yet certified the rehabilitation.

(iii) Effective dates. Paragraph (d)(7)(i) of this section applies to returns for taxable years beginning before January 1, 2002. The requirement in the fourth sentence of paragraph (d)(7)(ii) of this section applies only if the first income tax return filed after receipt by the taxpayer of the certification is for a taxable year beginning before January 1, 2002. For rules applicable to returns for taxable years beginning after December 31, 2001, see paragraph (d)(7)(iv) of this section.

(iv) Returns for taxable years beginning after December 31, 2001— (A) In general. Except as otherwise provided in paragraph (d)(7)(ii) of this section and this paragraph (d)(7)(iv), a taxpayer claiming the credit for rehabilitation of a certified historic structure (within the meaning of section 47(c)(3) and paragraph (d)(1) of this section) for a taxable year beginning after December 31, 2001, must provide with the return for the taxable year in which the credit is claimed, the NPS project number assigned by, and the date of the final certification of completed work received from, the Secretary of the Interior. If a credit (including a credit for a taxable year beginning before January 1, 2002) is claimed under the late certification procedures of paragraph (d)(7)(ii) of this section and the first income tax return filed by the taxpayer after receipt of the certification is for a taxable year beginning after December 31, 2001, the taxpayer must provide the NPS project number assigned by, and the date of the final certification of completed work received from, the Secretary of the Interior with that return.

(B) Reporting and recordkeeping requirements. The information required under paragraph (d)(7)(iv)(A) of this section must be provided on Form 3468 (or its successor) filed with the taxpayer's return. In addition, the taxpayer must retain a copy of the final certification of completed work for as long as its contents may become material in the administration of any internal revenue law.

(C) Passthrough entities. In the case of a credit for qualified rehabilitation expenditures of a partnership, S corporation, estate, or trust, the requirements of this paragraph (d)(7)(iv) apply only to the entity. Each partner, shareholder or beneficiary claiming a credit for such qualified rehabilitation expenditures from a passthrough entity must, however, provide the employer identification number of the entity on Form 3468 (or its successor).

(e) Adjustment to basis. *(1) General rule.* Except as otherwise provided by this paragraph (e), if a credit is allowed with respect to property attributable to qualified rehabilitation expenditures incurred in connection with the rehabilitation of a qualified rehabilitated building, the increase in the basis of the rehabilitated property that would otherwise result from the qualified rehabilitation expenditures must be reduced by the amount of the credit allowed. See section 48(q) and the regulations there under for other rules concerning adjustments to basis in the case of section 38 property.

(2) Special rule for certain property relating to certified historic structures. If a rehabilitation investment credit is allowed with respect to property that is placed in service before January 1, 1987, or property that qualifies for the transition rules in paragraph (a)(2)(iv)(B) or (C) of this section, and such property is attributable to qualified rehabilitation expenditures incurred in connection with the rehabilitation of a certified historic structure, the increase in the basis of the rehabilitated property that would otherwise result from the qualified rehabilitation expenditures must be reduced by one-half of the amount of the credit allowed.

(3) Recapture of rehabilitation investment credit. If during any taxable year there is a recapture amount determined with respect to any credit that resulted in a basis adjustment under paragraph (e)(1) or (2) of this section, the basis of such building (immediately before the event resulting in such recapture) shall be increased by an amount equal to such recapture amount. For purposes of the preceding sentence, the term "recapture amount" means any increase in tax (or adjustment in carrybacks or carryovers) determined under section 47(a)(5).

(f) Coordination with other provisions of the Code. *(1) Credit claimed by lessee for rehabilitation performed by lessor.* A lessee may take the credit for rehabilitation performed by the lessor if the requirements of this section and section 48(d) are satisfied. For purposes of applying section 48(d), the fair market value of section 38 property described in section 48(a)(1)(E) shall be limited to that portion of the lessor's basis in the qualified rehabilitated building that is attributable to qualified rehabilitation expenditures. In the case of a portion of a building that is divided into more than one leasehold interest, the qualified rehabilitation expenditures attributable to the common elements shall be allocated to the individual leasehold interests in accordance with the principles of paragraph (c)(10)(ii) of this section. Furthermore, a leasehold interest's share of the common elements shall not be considered to have been placed in service prior to the time that the particular leasehold interest is placed in service.

(2) When the credit may be claimed. (i) In general. The investment credit for qualified rehabilitation expenditures is generally allowed in the taxable year in which the property attributable to the expenditure is placed in service, provided the building is a qualified rehabilitated building for the taxable year. See paragraph (b) of this section and section 46(c) and § 1.46-3(d). Under certain circumstances, however, the credit may be available prior to the date the property is

placed in service. See section 46(d) and § 1.46-5 (relating to qualified progress expenditures). Solely for purposes of section 46(c), property attributable to qualified rehabilitation expenditures will not be treated as placed in service until the building with respect to which the expenditures are made meets the definition of a qualified rehabilitated building (as defined in section 48(g)(1) and paragraph (b) of this section) for the taxable year. Accordingly, in the first taxable year for which the building becomes a qualified rehabilitated building, the property described in section 48(a)(1)(E) attributable to expenditures described in paragraph (c) of this section shall be considered to be placed in service, if such property was considered placed in service under section 46(c) and the regulations thereunder without regard to this paragraph (f)(2)(i) in that taxable year or a prior taxable year. For purposes of the preceding sentence, the requirement of section 48(g)(1)(A)(iii) and paragraph (b)(3) of this section relating to the definition of a qualified rehabilitated building shall be deemed to be met if the taxpayer reasonably expects that no rehabilitation work undertaken during the remainder of the rehabilitation process will result in a failure to satisfy the requirements of paragraph (b)(3) of this section. If the requirements of paragraph (b)(3) are not satisfied, however, the credit shall be disallowed for the taxable year in which it was claimed. If a taxpayer fails to complete physical work on the rehabilitation prior to the date that is 30 months after the date that the taxpayer filed a tax return on which the credit is claimed, the taxpayer must submit a written statement to the District Director stating such fact prior to the last day of the 30th month, and shall be requested to consent to an agreement under section 6501(c)(4) extending the period of assessment for any tax relating to the item for which the credit was claimed.

(ii) Section 38 property described in section 48(a)(1)(E). In the case of section 38 property described in section 48(a)(1)(E), the section 38 property is not the building. Instead, the section 38 property is the portion of the basis of the building that is attributable to qualified rehabilitation expenditures. Therefore, for example, for purposes of the determination of when such section 38 property is placed in service, a determination must be made regarding when property attributable to the portion of the basis of the building attributable to qualified rehabilitation expenditures is placed in service. The issue of when the building is placed in service is thus not relevant. In fact, under this test, the building itself may never have been taken out of service during the rehabilitation process. If the building is rehabilitated over several years in stages (e.g., by floors), section 38 property attributable to qualified rehabilitation expenditures to a qualified rehabilitated building placed in service in each taxable year shall, generally, be treated as a separate item of section 38 property.

(iii) Example. The application of this paragraph (f)(2) may be illustrated by the following example:

Example. Assume that A, a calendar year taxpayer, purchases a four-story building on January 1, 1983, for $100,000, and incurs $10,000 of qualified rehabilitation expenditures in 1983 to rehabilitate floor one, $50,000 of qualified rehabilitation expenditures in 1984 to rehabilitate floor two, $70,000 of qualified rehabilitation expenditures in 1985 to rehabilitate floor three, and $60,000 of qualified rehabilitation expenditures in 1986 to rehabilitate floor four. Assume further that A places the property attributable to these expenditures in service on the last day of the year in which the respective expenditures were incurred and that the building is never taken out of service since as each floor is rehabilitated, the other three floors are occupied by tenants. Under the rule in this paragraph (f)(2), the portion of the basis of the building that is attributable to qualified rehabilitation expenditures incurred with respect to floor one and two are deemed to be placed in service in 1985, because that is the first year that the substantial rehabilitation test described in paragraph (b) of this section is met ($120,000 of expenditures incurred by A during a measuring period ending on December 31, 1985 is greater than the $110,000 basis at the beginning of the period). Assume that as of December 31, 1985, at least 75 percent of the external walls of the building have been retained during the rehabilitation process and that A has a reasonable expectation that no work during the remainder of the rehabilitation process will result in less than 75 percent of the external walls being retained. A may claim a credit for A's 1985 taxable year on $130,000 of qualified rehabilitation expenditures ($10,000 in 1983, $50,000 in 1984, and $70,000 in 1985). (See paragraph (c)(6) of this section for rules applicable to when qualified expenditures may be incurred. In addition, see section 46(d) and § 1.46-5 for rules relating to qualified progress expenditures.) The fact that the building was a qualified rehabilitated building for A's 1985 taxable year, however, has no effect on whether the building is a qualified rehabilitated building for A's 1986 taxable year. In order to determine whether A is entitled to claim a credit on A's 1986 return for the $60,000 of qualified rehabilitation expenditures incurred in 1986, A must select a measuring period ending in 1986 and must determine whether the building is a qualified rehabilitated building for that year. Solely for purposes of determining whether the building was substantially rehabilitated, expenditures incurred in 1984 and 1985, even though considered in determining whether the building was substantially rehabilitated for A's 1985 taxable year, may be used in addition to the expenditures incurred in 1986 to determine whether the building was substantially rehabilitated for A's 1986 taxable year, provided the expenditures were incurred during any measuring period selected by A that ends in 1986.

(3) Coordination with section 47. If property described in section 48(a)(1)(E) is disposed of by the taxpayer, or otherwise ceases to be "section 38 property," section 47 may apply. Property will cease to be section 38 property, and therefore section 47 may apply, in any case in which the Department of Interior revokes or otherwise invalidates a certification of rehabilitation after the property is placed in service or a building (other than a certified historic structure) is moved from the place where it is rehabilitated after the property is placed in service. If, for example, the taxpayer made modifications to the building inconsistent with Department of Interior standards, the Secretary of the Interior might revoke the certification. In addition, if all or a portion of a substantially rehabilitated building becomes tax-exempt use property (see paragraph (c)(7)(vi) of this section) for the first time within five years after the credit is claimed, the credit will be recaptured under section 47 at that time as if the building or portion of the building which becomes tax-exempt use property had then been sold.

T.D. 8233, 10/7/88, amend T.D. 8989, 4/23/2002, T.D. 9040, 1/30/2003, T.D. 9283, 8/28/2006.

§ 1.50-1 Restoration of credit.

Caution: The Treasury has not yet amended Reg § 1.50-1 to reflect changes made by P.L. 95-600.

(a) In general. Section 49(a) (relating to termination of credit) does not apply to property—

(1) The construction, reconstruction, or erection of which by the taxpayer—

(i) Is completed after August 15, 1971, or

(ii) Is begun after March 31, 1971, or

(2) Which is acquired by the taxpayer—

(i) After August 15, 1971, or

(ii) After March 31, 1971, and before August 16, 1971, pursuant to an order which the taxpayer establishes was placed after March 31, 1971.

(b) Transitional rule. In the case of property (other than pretermination property) the construction, reconstruction, or erection of which by the taxpayer is begun before April 1, 1971, and completed after August 15, 1971, there shall be taken into account as the basis of new section 38 property in determining qualified investment only that portion of the basis which is properly attributable to construction, reconstruction, or erection after August 15, 1971.

(c) Principles to be applied. The principles of § 1.48-2(b) and (c) shall be applied in determining when property is acquired and in in determining that portion of the basis of property properly attributable to construction, reconstruction, or erection after August 15, 1971.

T.D. 7203, 8/24/72.

§ 1.51-1 Amount of credit.

Caution: The Treasury has not yet amended Reg § 1.51-1 to reflect changes made by P.L. 110-245, P.L. 110-28, P.L. 109-432, P.L. 109-73, P.L. 108-311, P.L. 107-147, P.L. 106-554, P.L. 106-170, P.L. 105-277, P.L. 105-34, P.L. 104-188, P.L. 103-66, P.L. 101-508, P.L. 101-239, P.L. 100-647, P.L. 100-485, P.L. 100-203, P.L. 99-514, P.L. 98-369.

(a) Determination of amount. *(1) General rule.* Except as provided in paragraph (a)(2) of this section, the amount of the targeted jobs credit for purposes of section 38 (formerly designated section 44B) for the taxable year equals 50 percent of the qualified first-year wages (minus any qualified first-year wages paid to individuals while such individuals are qualified summer youth employees) plus 25 percent of the qualified second-year wages.

(2) Special rule for employment of qualified summer youth employees. In the case of an employer who pays or incurs qualified wages after April 30, 1983, to a qualified summer youth employee beginning work for the employer after such date, the amount of the targeted jobs credit for the taxable year is equal to the amount determined under paragraph (a)(1) of this section plus an amount equal to 85 percent of the first $3,000 of qualified wages paid to each qualified summer youth employee during the taxable year. Such wages must be attributable to services tendered by the qualified summer youth employee during any 90-day period beginning on or after May 1 and ending on or before September 15.

(3) Limitation. See section 38(c) for rules limiting the amount of the credit to a percentage of the amount of the taxpayer's net tax liability.

(b) Definitions. *(1) Qualified wages.* The term "qualified wages" means wages (as defined in paragraph (b)(4)) paid or incurred by the employer during the taxable year to individuals who are members of a targeted group (within the meaning of section 51(d)).

(2) Qualified first-year wages. (i) General rule. Except in the case of qualified summer youth employees, the term "qualified first-year wages" means the first $6,000 of wages (as defined in paragraph (b)(4) of this section) attributable to service rendered by a member of a targeted group during the 1-year period beginning with the day the individual first begins work for the employer. In the case of a vocational rehabilitation referral (as defined in section 51(d)(2)) who begins work for the employer before July 19, 1984, the one-year period begins with the day the individual begins work for the employer on or after the beginning of such individual's rehabilitation plan. However, with the exception of vocational rehabilitation referrals for whom the employer claimed a credit under section 44B (as in effect prior to enactment of the Revenue Act of 1978) for a taxable year beginning before January 1, 1979, members of a targeted group who are first hired after September 26, 1978, and before January 1, 1979, will be treated as if they first began work for the employer on January 1, 1979. The date on which the wages are paid is not determinative of whether the wages are first-year wages; rather, the wages must be attributed to the period during which the work was performed. See paragraph (f)(1) of this section for an additional limitation on the term "qualified first-year wages". (See examples (1), (2), (3), (4), (5), and (6) in paragraph (j) of this section for examples illustrating the application of the rules in this paragraph (b)(2)).

(ii) Special rule for qualified summer youth employees. In the case of a qualified summer youth employee, qualified first-year wages for purposes of the 85 percent credit referred to in paragraph (a)(2) of this section include only wages attributable to services rendered by a qualified summer youth employee during any 90-day period beginning on or after May 1 and ending on or before September 15. If the individual is retained by the employer after the 90-day period and recertified as a member of another targeted group, the term "qualified first-year wages" for purposes of the 50 percent credit described by section 51(a)(1) has the meaning assigned that term in paragraph (b)(2)(i) of this section except that the $6,000 limitation for qualified first-year wages shall be reduced by wages up to, but not more than, $3,000 attributable to services rendered during the 90-day period.

(3) Qualified second-year wages. The term "qualified second-year wages" means the first $6,000 of wages attributable to services rendered by a member of a targeted group, other than a qualified summer youth employee, during the 1-year period beginning on the day after the last day of the period for qualified first-year wages. The date on which the wages are paid is not determinative of whether the wages are second-year wages; rather, the wages must be attributed to the period during which the work was performed.

(4) Wages. (i) General rule. Except as otherwise provided in paragraph (b)(4)(ii) and (iii) of this section, the term "wages" shall only include amounts paid or incurred after December 31, 1978, for taxable years ending after December 31, 1978. For purposes of this section, the term "wages" has the meaning assigned such term by section 3306(b) (determined without regard to any dollar limitation contained in such subsection).

(ii) Special rules. In the case of agricultural labor or railway labor, the term "wages" means unemployment insurance wages within the meaning of subparagraph (A) or (B) of section 51(h)(1). The term "wages" shall not include any amounts paid or incurred by an employer for any pay period to any individual for whom the employer receives federally funded payments for on-the-job training for such individual for such pay period. (See example (7) in paragraph (j) of this section.) The amount of wages which would otherwise be qualified wages under this section with respect to an individual for a taxable year shall be reduced by an amount equal to the amount of payments made to the employer (however utilized by such employer) with respect to such individual for such taxable year under a program established under section 414 of the Social Security Act. In addition, the term "wages" shall not include any amount paid or incurred by the employer in a taxable year beginning before January 1, 1982, to an individual with respect to whom the employer claims a credit under section 40 (relating to expenses of work incentive programs). For youths participating in a qualified cooperative education program:

(A) Section 3306(c)(10)(C) (relating to the definition of employment for certain students) does not apply in determining wages under this section; and

(B) The term "wages" shall include only those amounts paid or incurred by the employer that are attributable to services rendered by the individual while he or she meets the conditions specified in section 51(d)(8)(A). For purposes of the preceding sentence, an employee who met the requirement in section 51(d)(8)(A)(iv), dealing with economically disadvantaged status, when hired, shall be deemed to continuously meet the requirement in section 51(d)(8)(A)(iv) during the time the employee is in the cooperative education program. See also paragraph (e) of this section for rules relating to the exclusion of wages paid to certain individuals.

(iii) Termination. The term "wages" shall not include any amount paid or incurred to an individual who begins work for the employer after December 31, 1985.

(5) Special rule for eligible work incentive employees. In the case of an eligible work incentive employee (as defined in § 1.51-1(c)(4)), this paragraph (b) shall be applied for taxable years beginning after December 31, 1981, as if such employee had been a member of a targeted group for taxable years beginning before January 1, 1982. (See example (8) in paragraph (j) of this section.)

(c) Members of targeted groups. *(1) In general.* An individual is a member of a targeted group if the individual is certified as (i) a vocational rehabilitation referral, (ii) an economically disadvantaged youth, (iii) an economically disadvantaged Vietnam-era veteran, (iv) an SSI recipient, (v) a general assistance recipient, (vi) a youth participating in a cooperative education program, (vii) an economically disadvantaged ex-convict, (viii) an eligible work incentive employee, (ix) a qualified summer youth employee, or (x) an involuntarily terminated CETA employee. Except as provided below, see section 51(d) of this section for a definition of these groups. See paragraph (d) of this section for rules concerning the certification of individuals as members of one of these targeted groups.

(2) Youths participating in a qualified cooperative education Program. (i) Student requirements. For an individual to qualify as a youth participating in a qualified cooperative education program, the individual must meet each of the following conditions (A) through (D)—

(A) The youth must have attained the age of 16 but not 20. (An individual reaching 19 will be treated as a youth participating in a qualified cooperative education program only for wages paid or incurred after November 26, 1979.)

(B) The youth must not have graduated from a high school or vocational school.

(C) The youth must be enrolled in and actively pursuing a qualified cooperative education program (as defined in paragraph (c)(2)(iii) of this section).

(D) With respect to wages paid or incurred after December 31, 1981, the youth must be a member of an economically disadvantaged family when initially hired.

(ii) Economically disadvantaged family. See section 51(d)(11) for the rules relating to the determination of whether an individual is a member of an economically disadvantaged family.

(iii) Qualified cooperative education program. The term "qualified cooperative education program" means a program of vocational education for individuals who (through written cooperative arrangements between a qualified school and one or more employers) receive instruction (including required academic instruction) by alternation of study in school with a job in any occupational field (but only if these two experiences are planned by the school and employer so that each contributes to the student's education and employability). See section 51(d)(8)(C) for the definition of a "qualified school." For purposes of this paragraph, the term "program of vocational education" means an organized educational program which is directly related to the preparation of individuals for employment, or for additional preparation for a career requiring other than a baccalaureate or advanced degree. An "organized educational program" means only instruction related to the occupation or occupations for which the students are in training or instruction necessary for students to benefit from such training. The student's employment contributes to his or her education and employability only if it is related to the occupation, or a cluster of closely related occupations, for which the student is in training in school. However, the student's employment need not be directly related to or in the same technical field as the training the student receives in school. For example, a student studying carpentry does not have to work as a carpenter for the program to constitute a "qualified cooperative education program." The program will qualify if, for example, the student works at a hardware store because the student's work would familiarize the student with the materials and tools used by carpenters. The program would not qualify, however, if the student works at a restaurant and generally performs tasks in such employment not related to carpentry.

(iv) Actively pursuing. For purposes of this paragraph (c)(2), a youth will not be considered to be "actively pursuing" a school's qualified cooperative education program (within the meaning of paragraph (c)(2)(iii) of this section) during summer vacation unless that school program continues during the summer vacation. Whether the school program continues during the summer vacation will be determined by examining the written agreement between the school and the employer. Thus, if a written agreement specifically covers the summer vacation period and provides for a significant degree of involvement by school personnel to provide supervision for the students in the program during that period, the school program will be considered to continue during the summer, regardless of whether classes are held during the vacation period.

(3) General assistance recipients. In order for an individual to qualify as a general assistance recipient, the individual, or another member of the assistance unit (within the meaning of 45 CFR 205.40(a)(1)) that the individual is a member of, must receive assistance for a period of not less than 30 days ending within the preemployment period (as defined in section 51(d)(13)) from a qualified general assistance program. A qualified general assistance program is a program of a State or a political subdivision of a State that the Secretary (after consultation with the Secretary of Health and Human Services) has designated as providing general

assistance (or similar assistance) which is based on need and consists of money payments or voucher or scrip. For purposes of the preceding sentences, a program qualifying as a general assistance program by reason of non-cash assistance (i.e., voucher or scrip) shall be so treated only with respect to amounts paid or incurred after July 1, 1982, to individuals beginning work for the employer after such date. For purposes of this subparagraph, the term "money" means cash or an instrument convertible into cash (e.g., a check).

(4) Eligible work incentive employees. An eligible work incentive employee means an individual who has been certified by the designated local agency (as defined in paragraph (d)(10) of this section) as—

(i) Being eligible for financial assistance under part A of title IV of the Social Security Act and as having continuously received such financial assistance during the 90-day period which immediately precedes the date on which such individual is hired by the employer, or

(ii) Having been placed in employment under a work incentive program established under section 432(b)(1) or 445 of the Social Security Act.

The provisions of this paragraph (c)(4) are effective with respect to taxable years of the employer beginning after December 31, 1981. (See paragraph (b)(5) of this section for a special rule relating to eligible work incentive employees.)

(5) Involuntarily terminated CETA employees. (i) In general. An involuntarily terminated CETA employee is an individual who first began work for an employer after August 13, 1981, in taxable years of the employer ending after August 13, 1981, and is certified by the designated local agency (as defined in paragraph (d)(10) of this section) as having been involuntarily terminated after December 31, 1980, from employment financed in whole, or in part, under a program under part D of title II or title VI of the Comprehensive Employment and Training Act.

(ii) Termination. Section 51(d)(10) and this paragraph (c)(5) shall not apply to any individual who begins work for the employer after December 31, 1982.

(d) Certification. *(1) General rule.* Except as otherwise provided in this paragraph, an individual shall not be treated as a member of a targeted group unless, on or before the day on which such individual begins work for the employer, the employer has received, or has requested in writing, a certification that the individual is a member of a targeted group from the designated local agency (as defined in paragraph (d)(10) of this section). In addition, the employer must receive a certification before the targeted jobs credit can be claimed. However, with respect to individuals who began work for the employer on or before May 11, 1982, the certification will be timely only if requested or received before the day the individual began work for the employer. In the case of a request in writing mailed via the United States Postal Service, the request shall be deemed to be made on the date of the postmark stamped on the cover in which such request was mailed to the designated local agency provided the request is mailed in accordance with the mailing requirements in § 301.7502-1(c) and delivered in accordance with the delivery requirements in § 301.7502-1(d). In the case of a deadline that but for this sentence would fall on a Saturday, Sunday, or a legal holiday, the deadline for making a timely request in writing for a certification or receiving a timely certification shall be the next succeeding day which is not a Saturday, Sunday, or legal holiday. (See section 7503 for the definition of "legal holiday.") See paragraph (d)(2) of this section for transitional rules applicable to certain employees who began work for the employer before September 26, 1981. See paragraph (d)(3) of this section for special rules applicable to cooperative education students and paragraph (d)(4) of this section for special rules applicable to eligible work incentive employees.

(2) Timeliness of certification in the case of an individual to whom a written preliminary eligibility determination has been issued. If on or before the day on which an individual begins work for the employer, such individual has received from a designated local agency (or other agency or organization designated pursuant to a written agreement with such designated local agency) a written preliminary determination that such individual is a member of a targeted group, then such individual may be treated as a member of a targeted group if on or before the fifth day after the day such individual begins work for the employer such employer receives, or requests in writing, from the designated local agency a certification that such individual is a member of a targeted group. This paragraph (d)(2) only applies to individuals who begin work for the employer after July 18, 1984.

(3) Transitional rules for certain employees who began work for the employer on or before September 26, 1981. In the case of an individual, other than a cooperative education student, who began work for the employer before June 29, 1981, the employer must either receive, or request in writing, a certification before July 23, 1981. In the case of an individual, other than a cooperative education student, who began work for the employer after June 28, 1981, and on or before September 26, 1981, the employer must either receive, or request in writing, a certification before September 26, 1981.

(4) Cooperative education students. In the case of cooperative education students, the school administering the cooperative education program must issue the certification. Form 6199 is provided for this purpose. If the student begins work for the employer after September 26, 1981, see the general rule in § 1.51-1(d)(1) for the date when this certification must be received or requested. If the student begins work for the employer on or before September 26, 1981, the employer must receive the certification or request it in writing before September 26, 1981. In order for an employer to claim a credit on wages paid or incurred to a cooperative education student after December 31, 1981, the employer must receive or request in writing a determination that the student is a member of an economically disadvantaged family. A request for economic eligibility determination for a cooperative education student must be made in writing by the employer to the participating school. If the student begins work for the employer on or before September 26, 1981, the employer must receive or request in writing such determination before September 26, 1981. However, a request in writing on or after August 13, 1981, to a participating school for certification will be deemed to include a request for an economic eligibility determination. In addition, any certification issued by a school after August 13, 1981, will be deemed to be issued in response to a request for certification which includes a request for an economic eligibility determination. The rule in the preceding sentence does not eliminate the requirement that the employer receive a certification that includes an economic eligibility determination in order to claim a credit for wages paid or incurred after December 31, 1981. If a certification issued by a school after August 13, 1984, does not contain an economic eligibility determination and the employer wishes to claim a credit for wages paid or incurred after December 31, 1981, the employer must receive a com-

pleted certification before the date on which the credit is claimed.

(5) Eligible work incentive employees. In the case of eligible work incentive employees, the employer must either receive, or request in writing, a certification within the time requirements of paragraph (d)(1),(2), or (3) of this section, whichever is applicable. Before October 12, 1981 (the date the Economic Recovery Tax Act of 1981 codified the State employment security agency as the designated local agency for certifying targeted groups), a certificate may be received or requested in writing from either the designated local agency (as defined in paragraph (d)(10) of this section) or the office or agency that properly issued certifications under former section 50B(h)(1) (relating to the work incentive credit).

(6) Certifications that are not timely. Any certification that is not timely received or requested by the employer in accordance with the rules of this paragraph will be treated as invalid. Thus, the employer will not be allowed to claim a credit under section 51 with respect to any wages paid or incurred to an employee whose certification or request for certification is not timely. A timely request for certification does not eliminate the need for the employer to receive a certification before claiming the credit. In the case of a request for certification that was denied, resubmitted, and then approved, the timeliness of the request shall be determined by the timeliness of the first request.

(7) Incorrect certification. (i) In general. Except as otherwise provided in paragraph (d)(7)(ii) of this section, if an individual has been certified as a member of a targeted group, and such certification is based on false information provided by such individual, the certification shall be revoked and wages paid by the employer after the date on which notice of revocation is received by the employer shall not be treated as qualified wages. For purposes of this paragraph, a certification will be revoked only if the individual would not have been certified had correct information been provided to the issuer of the certification. Thus, false information that is not material to an individual's eligibility as a member of a targeted group will not invalidate an otherwise valid certification.

(ii) Employer's knowledge that the certification was incorrect. In the case of an employer who knew, or had reason to know, at the time of certification that the information provided to the designated local agency was false, none of the wages paid by such employer to an individual to whom an incorrect certification has been issued will be qualified wages.

(8) Certifications issued to certain rehires. This paragraph (d)(8) applies in the case of an employee who first began work for the employer before August 13, 1981, and was dismissed and rehired by the employer. A certification received or requested by an employer with respect to such an employee will be considered timely only if there was a valid business reason, unrelated to the availability of the credit, for the dismissal and rehire and if the employer did not dismiss and then rehire the employee in order to meet the timing requirement with respect to certification. An individual who is dismissed and then rehired for the purpose described in the preceding sentence will be considered for purposes of section 51(d)(16) and this paragraph to have been continuously employed by the employer during the time between the dismissal and the rehire. Whether the employer was motivated by reason of the certification rules in section 51(d)(16) and this paragraph to dismiss and then rehire an employee is a question of fact to be determined from all the circumstances surrounding the dismissal and rehire. (See paragraph (e)(2) of this section for a separate rule disallowing the credit in the case of nonqualifying rehires.)

(9) Individuals who continue to be employed by the same employer but as a member of another targeted group. This paragraph (d)(9) applies in the case of an employee who continues to be employed by the same employer but no longer qualifies as a member of the targeted group for which such employee was first certified (e.g., the employee was originally certified as a qualified summer youth employee with respect to a ninety-day period between May 1 and September 15, but such ninety-day period has ended). In such case, the employer may request a certification that the employee is a member of another targeted group, and if any wages paid to such individual are qualified first-year wages or qualified second-year wages, the employer may be entitled to a targeted jobs credit with respect to such wages. The second certification will not be invalid merely because it was requested or received after the individual began work for the employer; only the first certification (for example, the certification with respect to an individual hired first as a qualified summer youth employee) must meet the requirement of section 51(d)(16) that a certification must be requested or received by an employer on or before the day on which the individual begins work for the employer. In the case of a former qualified summer youth employee or a youth participating in a qualified cooperative education program who is recertified as an economically disadvantaged youth, the term "hiring date" in section 51(d)(3)(B) does not mean the day the individual is hired by the employer but means the day the individual is certified as a member of the new targeted group. Accordingly, the age requirement of section 51(d)(3)(B) shall be applied as of the day the individual is certified as a member of the second targeted group. In addition, see section 51(d)(11) for rules concerning the viability of the original economic eligibility determination.

(10) Certification where a trade or business has been transferred to a new employer. In the case of a transfer of a trade or business in which an individual who is a member of a targeted group is retained as an employee in the trade or business, the certification obtained for such employee by the transferor-employer will apply with respect to the transferee-employer.

(11) Designated local agency. (i) In general. For the period before October 12, 1981, the term "designated local agency" means the agency for any locality designated jointly by the Secretary and the Secretary of Labor to perform certifications of employees for employers in that locality. On or after October 12, 1981, the term "designated local agency" means a State employment security agency established in accordance with the Act of June 6, 1933, as amended (29 U.S.C. 49-49n).

(ii) Jurisdiction. The designated local agency is the agency that has, pursuant to its charter, jurisdiction over the individual that is sought to be certified. Thus, any certification that is issued with respect to an individual that is sought to be certified. Thus, any certification that is issued with respect to an individual who is not within the jurisdiction of the designated local agency that issued the certification will be invalid. Notwithstanding any other provision of this section, a request in writing for certification to the appropriate designated local agency that is made before January 23, 1984, will be considered to be timely if it is made after an otherwise timely request in writing for certification was made to a designated local agency that does not have jurisdiction over the individual sought to be certified.

(e) Certain ineligible individuals. *(1) Related individuals.* For purposes of section 51(a), "qualified wages" does not include any amounts paid or incurred by a taxpayer to any of the following individuals:

(i) An individual who is related (within the meaning of any of paragraphs (1) through (8) of section 152 (a)) to the taxpayer;

(ii) An individual who is a dependent (within the meaning of section 152(a)(9)) of the taxpayer;

(iii) An individual who is related (within the meaning of any of paragraphs (1) through (8) of section 152(a)) to a shareholder who owns (within the meaning of section 267(c)) more than 50 percent in value of the outstanding stock of the taxpayer, if the taxpayer is a corporation;

(iv) An individual who is a dependent (within the meaning of section 152(a)(9)) of a shareholder described in paragraph (e)(1)(iii) of this section;

(v) An individual who is a grantor, beneficiary or fiduciary of the taxpayer, if the taxpayer is an estate or trust;

(vi) An individual who is a dependent (within the meaning of section 152(a)(9)) of an individual described in paragraph (e)(1)(v) of this section; or

(vii) An individual who is related (within the meaning of any of paragraphs (1) through (8) of section 152(a)) to an individual described in paragraph (e)(1)(v) of this section.

(2) Nonqualifying rehires. For purposes of section 51(a), "qualified wages" does not include wages paid to an employee who had been employed by the employer prior to the current hiring date of the employee if at any time during such prior employment the employee was not a member of a targeted group. The preceding sentence shall not apply to an employee who was previously timely certified as a member of a targeted group with respect to the same employer. An employee shall be treated as not having been a member of a targeted group if the certification requirements of section 51(d)(16) were not met. (See example (8) in paragraph (j) of this section.)

(3) Effective date. The provisions of this paragraph (e) are effective with respect to employees first beginning work for an employer after August 13, 1981.

(f) Limitations. *(1) Limitation on qualified first-year wages.* With respect to taxable years beginning before January 1, 1982, the amount of the qualified first-year wages which may be taken into account for purposes of the targeted jobs credit for any taxable year shall not exceed 30 percent of the aggregate unemployment insurance wages paid by the employer during the calendar year ending in such taxable year. In the case of a group of trades or businesses under common control (as defined in § 1.52-1(b)), the qualified first-year wages cannot exceed 30 percent of the aggregate unemployment insurance wages paid to all employees of that group of trades or businesses under common control during the calendar year ending in such taxable year. For this purpose, the term "unemployment insurance wages" has the same meaning given to the term "wages" as defined in § 1.51-1(b)(4). In this case of agricultural or railway labor, see section 51(h)(1) for the applicable definition of unemployment insurance wages. (See examples (13) and (14) in paragraph (j) of this section.)

(2) Remuneration must be for trade or business employment. Remuneration paid by an employer to an employee during any taxable year shall be taken into account only if more than one-half of the remuneration paid by the employer to an employee is for services in a trade or business of the employer. This determination shall be made by each employer without regard to section 52(a) or (b). Accordingly, employees of corporations that are members of a controlled group or employees of partnerships, proprietorships, and other trades or businesses (whether or not incorporated) which are under common control will be treated as being employed by each separate employer for this purpose. For this purpose, the term "year" means the taxable year of the employer. (See example (15) in paragraph (j) of this section.)

(g) Election not to claim the targeted jobs credit. The election under section 51(j) (as amended by section 474(p) of the Tax Reform Act of 1984) not to claim the targeted jobs credit is available for taxable years beginning after December 31, 1983, and shall be made for the taxable year in which such credit is available by not claiming such credit on an original return or amended return at any time before the expiration of the 3-year period beginning on the last date prescribed by law for filing the return for the taxable year (determined without regard to extensions). The election may be revoked within the 3-year period by filing an amended return on which the credit is claimed.

(h) Treatment of successor-employers. In the case of a successor-employer referred to in section 3306(b)(1), the determination of the amount of credit under this section with respect to wages paid by such successor-employer shall be made in the same manner as if such wages were paid by the predecessor-employer referred to in such section. Thus, the 1-year period referred to in § 1.51-1(b)(2)(i) will be considered to begin with the day the employee first began work for the transferor-employer, and the amount of qualified first-year wages and qualified second-year wages paid or incurred with respect to the employee must be reduced by the amount of any such wages paid or incurred by the transferor-employer. (See examples (10) and (11) in paragraph (j) of this section.) Also, see paragraph (d)(10) of this section for rules concerning the viability of the employee's certification.

(i) Treatment of employees performing services for other persons. No credit shall be determined under this section with respect to remuneration paid by an employer to an employee for services performed by such employee for another person unless the amount reasonably expected to be received by the employer for such services from such other person exceeds the remuneration paid by the employer to such employee for such services.

(j) Examples. The application of this section may be illustrated by the following examples which, except as otherwise stated, assume that the limitations imposed by §§ 1.51-1(f)(2) and 1.53-3 are inapplicable:

Example (1). Corporation M is a calendar year, cash receipts and disbursements method taxpayer. A, an economically disadvantaged youth, first began work for Corporation M on October 1, 1978. Qualified first-year wages with respect to A are wages attributable to the period beginning on January 1, 1979 (since A was first hired after September 26, 1978, he is treated as having begun work on January 1, 1979) and ending on December 31, 1979. In the 1979 taxable year, Corporation M pays A $5,000 of qualified first-year wages attributable to services performed in 1979. Corporation M's allowable credit is equal to $2,500 (50 percent of $5,000).

Example (2). Assume the same facts as in example (1), except that in 1980 Corporation M pays to A $100 of wages attributable to services rendered in 1979. These wages will still be considered as qualified first-year wages, but the credit may not be claimed until the 1980 taxable year.

Example (3). Corporation O is a calendar year, cash receipts and disbursements method taxpayer. C, a vocational rehabilitation referral, first began work for Corporation O on July 1, 1978. Corporation O claimed a credit under section 44B (as in effect prior to enactment of the Revenue Act of 1978) for $3,000 of wages paid to C in the 1978 taxable year. Corporation O paid C $6,000 for services performed from January 1, 1979 to June 30, 1979. The period during which qualified first-year wages are determined begins on July 1, 1978, and ends on June 30, 1979. Amounts paid before January 1, 1979, however, are not taken into consideration in determining the amount of qualified first-year wages. Accordingly, only the wages attributable to services performed from January 1, 1979, through June 30, 1979, are considered as qualified first-year wages. Corporation O's allowable credit is equal to $3,000 (50 percent of $6,000).

Example (4). I first began work for Corporation Q, a cash receipts and disbursements method taxpayer, on January 1, 1981, and was not a member of a targeted group. On March 1, 1981, I was convicted of a felony and sentenced to prison. I quit working for Corporation Q, and served the prison sentence. On November 1, 1981, I again was hired by Corporation Q and began work on that date. On the November 1, 1981 hiring date, I was an economically disadvantaged ex-convict for whom Corporation Q received a certificate. Corporation Q paid I $500 of wages for services performed from November 1, 1981, to December 31, 1981, and $6,000 of wages for services performed during 1982. The $500 of wages paid for services performed from November 1, 1981, to December 31, 1981, would be qualified first-year wages because these qualified wages were paid for services performed during the 1-year period beginning on the date I first began work for Corporation Q (January 1, 1981). The $6,000 of wages paid for services performed during 1982 would be qualified second-year wages because these qualified wages were paid for services performed during the 1-year period beginning on the day after the first 1-year period. Accordingly, Corporation Q has an allowable credit of $250 attributable to qualified first-year wages and $1,500 attributable to qualified second-year wages.

Example (5). Assume the same facts as in example (4), except that all dates are 1 year later. Thus, I first began work for Corporation Q on January 1, 1982, was convicted on March 1, 1982, and was rehired on November 1, 1982. Under these facts, Q is not entitled to take a targeted jobs credit with respect to I's wages because I is a nonqualifying rehire.

Example (6). J, an economically disadvantaged youth, first began work for Corporation R, a calendar year cash receipts and disbursements method taxpayer, on December 1, 1979. On July 1, 1980, J was laid off by Corporation R and began work for Corporation S, which is unrelated to Corporation R, on July 2, 1980. On November 1, 1980, J again began work for Corporation R and continued working for Corporation R until January 1, 1982. At the time J first began work for Corporation S, J no longer met the qualifications of an economically disadvantaged youth. Corporation S may not claim a credit for wages paid to J because J was not a member of a targeted group at the time he began work for Corporation S. Corporation R, however, may claim a credit for wages paid to J because J was a member of a targeted group when he was hired by Corporation R. Corporation R's qualified first-year wages paid to J are the wages paid for services performed by J from December 1, 1979, to July 1, 1980, and from November 1, 1980, to November 30, 1980. Corporation R's qualified second-year wages paid to J are wages paid for services performed by J from December 1, 1980, to November 30, 1981. Corporation R may not claim a credit for wages paid for services performed by J after November 30, 1981.

Example (7). K, a member of a targeted group, first began work for Corporation T on January 1, 1979. For the pay periods from January 1, 1979, to March 31, 1979, Corporation T received federally funded payments for on-the-job training for K and paid wages of $2,000 to K. During the remainder of 1979 Corporation T paid wages of $7,000 to K. Corporation T may claim a credit on $6,000 of qualified first-year wages. Amounts paid to K by Corporation T during the pay periods for which Corporation T received federally funded payments for on-the-job training for K are not considered wages for purposes of the credit. However, Corporation T may consider $6,000 of the total $7,000 of wages paid after March 31, 1979, as qualified first-year wages.

Example (8). P first began work for Corporation X on January 1, 1981, as an individual who was certified to be an eligible employee for purposes of the WIN credit provided in section 40. Corporation X paid P $6,000 of wages during its taxable year beginning on January 1, 1981, and $6,000 of wages during its taxable year beginning on January 1, 1982. X can claim a targeted jobs credit for the wages paid in 1982 if the requirements of section 51 are met. For purposes of section 51(a), P's qualified first-year wages are the wages paid from January 1, 1981, to December 31, 1981, and P's qualified second-year wages are the wages paid from January 1, 1982, to December 31, 1982. Thus, Corporation X is only entitled to claim a targeted job credit based on P's qualified second-year wages.

Example (9). (i) L, 15 years of age, first began work for Corporation U on August 1, 1979. On September 3, 1979, L began her junior year in high school and enrolled in a qualified cooperative education program that was to run for her junior and senior years. On October 1, 1979, when L turned 16, she met all the requirements of § 1.51-1(c)(2)(i) and qualified as a youth participating in a qualified cooperative education program. Corporation U is entitled to claim a credit on wages paid or incurred for services performed by L after September 30, 1979, so long as L meets the requisite requirements. L's summer vacation began on June 1, 1980. Assume that the cooperative education program L was enrolled in did not continue during the summer vacation (i.e., the written agreement between the employer and the school did not cover the summer vacation). Thus, during her summer vacation, L did not meet the requirement of actively pursuing a qualified cooperative education program. Accordingly, Corporation U may not claim a credit on wages paid for services performed by L during L's summer vacation. On September 2, 1980, L began her senior year, and again met all the requirements of § 1.51-1(c)(2)(i). She continued to meet these requirements until June 5, 1981, when she graduated from high school. Accordingly, Corporation U may claim a credit on wages paid for services performed after September 1, 1980, and before June 5, 1981.

(ii) Assume the same facts as in (i), above, except that all dates are 3 years later. Under these facts, U is not entitled to claim a targeted jobs credit with respect to any of L's wages because L has not been timely certified under section 51(d)(16) and § 1.51-1(d)(3).

Example (10). D began work for a drugstore owned by E as a sole proprietor on January 1, 1979, and was certified as a member of a targeted group with respect to E. On June 1, 1979, E sold the drugstore where D worked to F, who continued to operate the drugstore with D as an employee. D's qualification as a member of a targeted group is not required to be redetermined in order for F to qualify for the targeted jobs credit. F will take into account the certification of D's eligibility that was provided to E. F will have qualified first-year wages consisting of the first $8,000 of wages paid or incurred to D by E and F from January 1, 1979 to December 31, 1979 (reduced by any qualified wages paid or incurred by E to D from January 1, 1979, to May 31, 1979). F's qualified second-year wages will consist of the first $6,000 of wages paid or incurred to D by F from January 1, 1980, to December 31, 1980.

Example (11). G began work in a machine shop owned by H as a sole proprietor on January 1, 1979, and was certified as a member of a targeted group with respect to H. On June 1, 1980, H transferred all the assets of the machine shop to newly formed Corporation P. Corporation P retained G as an employee in the machine shop. G's qualification as a member of a targeted group is not required to be redetermined in order for P to qualify for the targeted jobs credit. H has qualified first-year wages in the amount of the first $6,000 of wages paid or incurred to G by H from January 1, 1979, to December 31, 1979. Corporation P has qualified second-year wages in the amount of the first $6,000 of wages paid or incurred to G by H and Corporation P from January 1, 1980, to December 31, 1980 (reduced by any qualified second-year wages paid by H to G).

Example (12). W operates a retail store as a sole proprietor. On June 1, 1982, W hires S after receiving a written determination from a local community organization that S meets the requirements of an economically disadvantaged youth. W does not request a certification from the State employment security agency as to S's eligibility. W is not entitled to claim a credit with respect to wages paid to S because W did not receive, or request in writing, a certification from the State employment security agency as to S's eligibility on or before the day on which S began work for W.

Example (13). Corporation V is a cash receipts and disbursements method taxpayer with a July 1 through June 30 taxable year. In the taxable year ending June 30, 1980, the aggregate unemployment insurance wages paid by V were $150,000. In calendar year 1979 the aggregate unemployment insurance wages paid by Corporation V were $110,000. Corporation V's qualified first-year wages are limited to 30 percent of the aggregate unemployment insurance wages paid by it in calendar year 1979 or $33,000 (30 percent of $110,000), even though the aggregate unemployment insurance wages paid by it in the taxable year ending June 30, 1980, were $150,000.

Example (14). Assume the same facts as in example (13), except that all dates are 3 years later. Since the limitation on qualified first-year wages does not apply to taxable years beginning after December 31, 1981. Corporation V's qualified first-year wages are $150,000.

Example (15). M operates a retail store as a sole proprietor. N and O, both members of a targeted group, first began work for M on January 1, 1979. M paid N total qualified first-year wages of $6,000 in 1979. Three thousand one hundred dollars of those wages were for services in M's retail store, and $2,900 of those wages were for services as M's maid. M paid O total qualified first-year wages of $6,000 in 1979. Three thousand dollars of those wages were for services in M's store and $3,000 of those wages were for services as M's chauffeur. M has an allowable credit of $3,000 in 1979 on all $6,000 of qualified first-year wages paid to N because more than one-half of the remuneration paid by M to N was for services in M's trade or business. M may not take into account the wages paid to O because not more than one-half of the remuneration paid by M to O was for services in M's trade or business. Accordingly, M may not claim a credit on wages paid to O.

T.D. 7921, 11/18/83, amend T.D. 8062, 11/5/85.

§ 1.52-1 Trades or businesses that are under common control.

Caution: The Treasury has not yet amended Reg § 1.52-1 to reflect changes made by P.L 105-277, P.L. 105-34, P.L. 104-188.

(a) Apportionment of jobs credit among members of a group of trades or businesses that are under common control. *(1) Targeted jobs credit.* (i) In the case of a group of trades or businesses that are under common control (within the meaning of paragraph (b) of this section) at any time during the calendar year, the amount of the targeted jobs credit (computed under section 51 as if all the organizations that are under common control are one trade or business) under section 4-1B must be apportioned among the members of the group on the basis of each member's proportionate share of the wages giving rise to such credit. If the group of trades or businesses that are under common control have different taxable years, the credit shall be computed as if all the organizations have the same taxable year as the organization for which a determination of the proportionate share of the credit is being made. For taxable years beginning before January 1, 1982, the amount of the qualified first-year wages cannot exceed 30 percent of the aggregate unemployment insurance wages paid by the group of trades or businesses under common control during the calendar year ending in the taxable year of the organization for which a determination of the proportionate share of the credit is being made. The limitations in section 53 and the regulations thereunder apply to each organization individually (although, in applying these limitations, an affiliated group of corporations electing to make a consolidated return shall be treated as one organization).

(ii) The application of the subparagraph may be illustrated by the following examples:

Example (1). (a) Corporation M and its three subsidiaries, Corporations N, O, and P, are a group of businesses that are under common control and each uses the cash receipts and disbursements method of accounting and has a calendar year taxable year. Corporations M, N, O, and P paid out the following amounts in unemployment insurance wages, qualified first-year wages and qualified second-year wages during 1980.

	Unemployment insurance wages	Qualified 1st-year wages	Qualified 2nd-year wages
Corporation:			
M	$600,000	$184,000	$ 75,000
N	300,000	85,000	90,000
O	360,000	120,000	115,000
P	24,000	24,000	0
Total	1,284,000	413,000	280,000

(b) Since Corporations M, N, O, and P are under common control, the amount of qualified first-year wages paid by the group is limited to 30 percent of the aggregate unemployment insurance wages paid by the group in the calendar year ending in the group's taxable year. Since the qualified first-year wages of $413,000 exceeds 30% of the aggregate unemployment insurance wages, the group is limited to qualified first-year wages of $385,200 (30% of $1,284,000). The amount of the targeted jobs credit attributable to qualified first-year wages is equal to $192,600 (50% of $385,200). The amount of the credit attributable to qualified second-year wages is equal to $70,000 (25% of $280,000).

(c) The credit is apportioned among Corporations M, N, O, and P on the basis of their proportionate share of the qualified first-year wages or qualified second-year wages giving rise to the credit. Each corporation's share of the credit attributable to qualified first-year wages would be computed as follows:

Corporation:		Amount of credit
M	$192,600 × $184,000/$413,000 =	$85,807.26
N	$192,600 × $85,000/$413,000 =	$39,639.23
O	$192,600 × $120,000/$413,000 =	$55,961.26
P	$192,600 × $24,000/$413,000 =	$11,192.25

Each corporation's share of the credit attributable to qualified second-year wages is computed as follows:

Corporation:		Amount of credit
M	$70,000 × $75,000/$280,000 =	$18,750
N	$70,000 × $90,000/$280,000 =	$22,500
O	$70,000 × $115,000/$280,000 =	$28,750
P	$70,000 × $0/$280,000 =	0

Example (2). Assume the facts in example (1) with these additional facts. A, a member of a targeted group, worked for more than one of the members of the controlled group in the taxable year. A first began work for Corporation M on January 1, 1980, and later worked for Corporations N and O during 1980. For services rendered by A during 1980, the following wages were paid to A: Corporation M paid A $2,500 of qualified first-year wages: Corporation N paid A $1,500 of qualified first-year wages; Corporation O paid A $3,000 of qualified first-year wages. Corporations M, N, and O paid A a total of $7,000 of wages during 1980. Only $6,000 of qualified first-year wages per year per employee may be taken into account for purposes of the credit. See § 1.51-1(d)(1). Since Corporations M, N, and O are treated as a single employer under section 52(a), the maximum $6,000 of qualified first-year wages paid A by the group must be apportioned among Corporations M, N, and O as follows:

Corporation:		Qualified 1st-year Wages
M	$6,000 × $2,500/$7,000 =	$2,142.86
N	$6,000 × $1,500/$7,000 =	$1,285.71
O	$6,000 × $3,000/$7,000 =	$2,571.43

Example (3). (a) Corporation Q and its two subsidiaries, Corporations R and S, are a group of businesses that are under common control and each uses the cash receipts and disbursements method of accounting. Corporation Q has a calendar year taxable year. Corporation R has a July 1 through June 30 taxable year. Corporation S has an October 1 through September 30 taxable year. For purposes of determining Corporation R's proportionate share of the credit, the credit is computed as if Corporations Q and S have the same taxable year as Corporation R. Accordingly, Corporation R would compute its share of the credit for its 1979–1980 taxable year as set forth below.

		Qualified wages paid from July 1, 1979, to June 30, 1980	
	Unemployment insurance wages, 1979	1st year wages	2nd year wages
Corporation:			
Q	$500,000	$150,000	$80,000
R	300,000	110,000	50,000
S	100,000	25,000	10,000
Total	900,000	285,000	140,000

(b) Since Corporations Q, R, and S are under common control, the amount of qualified first-year wages is limited to 30 percent of the aggregate unemployment insurance wages paid by the group during the calendar year ending in Corporation R's taxable year. Since the qualified first-year wages of $285,000 exceeds 30 percent of the aggregate unemployment insurance wages, the group is limited to qualified first-year wages of $270,000 (30% of $900,000). The amount of the targeted jobs credit attributable to qualified first-year wages paid by members of the group during the period of the taxpayer's taxable year is $135,000 (50% of $270,000). The amount of the credit attributable to qualified second-year wages paid or incurred by members of the group during the period of the taxpayer's taxable year is $35,000 (25% of $140,000).

(c) The credit is apportioned to Corporation R on the basis of its proportionate share of the qualified first-year wages and qualified second-year wages giving rise to the credit. Corporation R's share of the credit attributable to qualified first-year wages is $52,105.26.

$$\$135{,}000 \times \frac{\$110{,}000}{\$285{,}000}$$

$$\$35{,}000 \times \frac{\$50{,}000}{\$140{,}000}$$

Corporation R's share of the credit for its 1979–1980 taxable year is $64,605.26 ($52,105.26 + $12,500).

(2) New jobs credit. In the case of a group of trades or businesses that are under common control at any time during the calendar year, the amount of the new jobs credit (computed under section 51 as if all the organizations that are under common control are one trade or business) under section 44B (as in effect prior to enactment of the Revenue Act of 1978) must be apportioned among the members of the group on the basis of each member's proportionate contribution to the increase in unemployment insurance wages for the entire group. The limitations in section 53 (as in effect prior to enactment of the Revenue Act of 1978) and the regulations thereunder apply to each organization individually (although, in applying these limitations, an affiliated group of corporations electing to make a consolidated return shall be treated as one organization). The application of this subparagraph may be illustrated by the following example:

Example. (a) Corporation T and its three subsidiaries, U, V, and W, are a group of businesses that are under common control and each has a calendar year taxable year. Corporations T, U, V, and W have paid out the following amounts in unemployment insurance wages during 1976 and 1977:

	1976	1977	Increase in FUTA wages in 1977 over 1976
Corporation:			
T	$1,000,000	$1,015,000	+ $15,000
U	500,000	650,000	+ 150,000
V	600,000	580,000	− 20,000
W	40,000	100,000	+ 60,000
Total	2,140,000	2,345,000	205,000

(b) Since all employees of trades or, businesses that are under common control are treated as employed by a single employer, the computations in section 51 are performed as if all the organizations which are under common control are one trade or business. Consequently, the amounts of the total unemployment insurance wages of the group in 1976 (i.e., $2,140,000) and 1977 (i.e., $2,345,000) are used to determine the increase in unemployment insurance wages in 1977 over the 1976 wage base. Since the amount equal to 102 percent of the 1976 unemployment insurance wages ($2,182,800) is greater than the amount equal to 50 percent of the 1977 unemployment insurance wages ($1,172,500), the increase in unemployment insurance wages in 1977 over the 1976 wage base is $162,200 ($2,345,000 – $2,182,800). The limitations in section 51(c), (d), and (g) (as in effect prior to enactment of the Revenue Act of 1978) must also be computed as though all the organizations under common control are one trade or business. For purposes of this example, it is assumed that none of those limitations reduce the amount of increase in unemployment insurance wages. As a result, the amount of the new jobs credit allowed to the group of business is $81,100 (50% of $162,200).

(c) The credit is apportioned among Corporations T, U, and W on the basis of their proportionate contributions to the increase in unemployment insurance wages. No credit would be allowed to Corporation V because it did not contribute to the increase in the group's unemployment insurance wages. Corporation T's share of the credit would be $5,406.66 ($81,100 × ($15,000 ÷ $225,000 (i.e., $15,000 would be $54,066.67 ($81,100 × ($150,000 ÷ 225,000)), and Corporation W's share would be $21,626.67 ($81,100 × ($60,000 ÷ 225,000)).

(b) Trades or businesses that are under common control. For purposes of this section, the term "trades or businesses that under common control" means any group of trades or businesses that is either a "parent-subsidiary group under common control" as defined in paragraph (c) of this section, a "brother-sister group under common control" as defined in paragraph (d) of this section, or a "combined group under common control" as defined in paragraph (e) of this section. For purposes of this section and §§ 1.52-2 and 1.52-3, the term "organization" means a sole proprietorship, a partnership, a trust, an estate, or a corporation. An organization may be a member of only one group of trades or businesses under common control. If, without the application of this paragraph, an organization would be a member of more than one such group, that organization shall indicate in its timely filed return the group in which it is being included. If the organization does not so indicate, then the district director with audit jurisdiction of the organization's return will determine the group in which the organization is to be included.

(c) Parent-subsidiary group under common control. *(1) In general.* The term "parent-subsidiary group under common control" means one or more chains of organizations conducting trades or businesses that are connected through ownership of a controlling interest with a common parent organization if—

(i) A controlling interest in each of the organizations, except the common parent organization, is owned (directly and with the application of § 1.414(c)-4(b)(1), relating to options) by one or more of the other organizations; and

(ii) The common parent organization owns (directly and with the application of § 1.414(c)-4(b)(1), relating to options) a controlling interest in at least one of the other organizations, excluding, in computing the controlling interest, any direct ownership interest by the other organizations.

(2) Controlling interest defined. For purposes of this paragraph, the term "controlling interest" means:

(i) In the case of a corporation, ownership of stock possessing more than 50 percent of the total combined voting power of all classes of stock entitled to vote or more than 50 percent of the total value of the shares of all classes of stock of the corporation.

(ii) In the case of a trust or estate, ownership of an actuarial interest (determined under paragraph (f) of this section) of more than 50 percent of the trust or estate;

(iii) In the case of a partnership, ownership of more than 50 percent of the profit interest or capital interest of the partnership; and

(iv) In the case of a sole proprietorship, ownership of the sole proprietorship.

(d) Brother-sister group under common control. *(1) In general.* The term "brother-sister group under common control" means two or more organizations conducting trades or businesses if—

(i) The same five or fewer persons who are individuals, estates, or trusts own (directly and with the application of § 1.414(c)-4), a controlling interest of each organization; and

(ii) Taking into account the ownership of each person only to the extent that person's ownership is identical with respect to each organization, such persons are in effective control of each organization. The five or fewer persons whose ownership is considered for purposes of the controlling interest requirement for each organization must be the same persons whose ownership is considered for purposes of the effective control requirement.

(2) Controlling interest defined. For purposes of this paragraph, the term "controlling interest" means:

(i) In the case of a corporation, ownership of stock possessing at least 80 percent of the total combined voting power of all classes of stock entitled to vote or at least 80 percent of the total value of the shares of all classes of stock of the corporation;

(ii) In case of a trust or estate, ownership of an actuarial interest (determined under paragraph (f) of this section) of at least 80 percent of the trust or estate;

(iii) In the case of a partnership, ownership of at least 80 percent of the profit interest or capital interest of the partnership; and

(iv) In the case of a sole proprietorship, ownership of the sole proprietorship.

(3) Effective control defined. For purposes of this paragraph "effective control" means:

(i) In the case of a corporation, ownership of stock possessing more than 50 percent of the total combined voting power of all classes of stock entitled to vote or more than 50 percent of the total value of the shares of all classes of stock of the corporation;

(ii) In the case of a trust or estate, ownership of an actuarial interest (determined under paragraph (f) of this section) of more than 50 percent of the trust or estate;

(iii) In the case of a partnership, ownership of more than 50 percent of the profit interest or capital interest of the partnership; and

(iv) In the case of a sole proprietorship, ownership of the sole proprietorship.

(e) Combined group under common control. The term "combined group under common control" means a group of three or more organizations, in which (1) each organization is a member of either a parent-subsidiary group under common control or brother-sister group under common control, and (2) at least one organization is the common parent organization of a parent-subsidiary group under common control and also a member of a brother-sister group under common control.

(f) Actuarial interest. For purposes of this section, the actuarial interest of each beneficiary of a trust or estate shall be determined by assuming the maximum exercise of discretion by the fiduciary in favor of the beneficiary. The factor and method prescribed in § 20.2031-7 or, for certain prior periods, 20.2031-7A, of this chapter (Estate Tax Regulations) for use in ascertaining the value of an interest in property for estate tax purposes will be used to determine a beneficiary's actuarial interest.

(g) Exclusion of certain interests and stock in determining control. In determining control under this paragraph, the term "interest" and the term "stock" do not include an interest that is treated as not outstanding under § 1.414(c)-3. In addition, the term "stock" does not include treasury stock or nonvoting stock that is limited and preferred regarding dividends.

(h) Transitional rule. *(1) In general.* Paragraph (d) of this section, as amended by T.D. 8179, applies to all taxable years to which section 52(b) applies.

(2) Election. In the case of taxable years ending before March 2, 1988.

(i) If, pursuant to paragraph (b) of this section, an organization indicated in a timely filed return that it chose to be a member of a brother-sister group under common control, and it is not a member of such group because of the amendments to paragraph (d) of this section made by T.D. 8179 such organization may make the choice described in paragraph (b) of this section by filing an amended return on or before September 2, 1988 if such organization would otherwise still be a member of more than one group of trades or businesses under common control, and

(ii) If an organization

(A) Is a member of a brother-sister group of trades or businesses under common control under § 1.52-1(d)(1) as in effect before amendment by T.D. 8179 ("old group"), for such taxable year and

(B) Is not such a member for such taxable year because of the amendments made by such Treasury decision. Such organization (whether or not a corporation) nevertheless will be treated as a member of such old group if all the organizations (whether or not corporations) that are members of the old group meet all the requirements of § 1.1563-1(d)(3) with respect to such taxable year.

T.D. 7553, 7/20/78, amend T.D. 7921, 11/18/83, T.D. 7955, 5/10/84, T.D. 8179, 3/1/88, T.D. 8540, 6/9/94.

§ 1.52-2 Adjustments for acquisitions and dispositions.

Caution: The Treasury has not yet amended Reg § 1.52-2 to reflect changes made by P.L. 105-277, P.L. 105-34, P.L. 104-188, P.L. 101-508, P.L. 98-369, P.L. 95-600.

(a) General rule. The provisions in this section only apply to the computation of the new jobs credit. If, after December 31, 1975, an employer acquires the major portion of a trade or business or the major portion of a separate unit of a trade or business, then, for purposes of computing the new jobs credit for any calendar year ending after the acquisition, both the amount of unemployment insurance wages and the amount of total wages considered to have been paid by the acquiring employer, for both the year in which the acquisition occurred and the preceding year, must be increased, respectively, by the amount of unemployment insurance wages and the amount of total wages paid by the predecessor employer that are attributable to the acquired portion of the trade or business or separate unit. If the predecessor employer informs the acquiring employer in writing of the amount of unemployment insurance wages and the amount of total wages attributable to the acquired portion of the trade or business that have been paid during the periods preceding the acquisition, then, for purposes of computing the credit for any calendar year ending after the acquisition the amount of unemployment insurance wages and the amount of total wages considered paid by the predecessor employer shall be decreased by those amounts. Regardless of whether the predecessor employer so informs the acquiring employer, the predecessor employer shall not be allowed a credit for the amount of any increase in the employment insurance wages or the total wages in the calendar year of the acquisition attributable to the acquired portion of the trade or business over the amount of such wages in the calendar year preceding the acquisition.

(b) Meaning of terms. *(1) Acquisition.* (i) For the purposes of this section, the term "acquisition" includes a lease agreement if the effect of the lease is to transfer the major portion of the trade or business or of a separate unit of the trade or business for the period of the lease. For instance, if one company leases a factory (including equipment) to another company for a 2-year period, the employees are retained by the second company, and the factory is used for the same general purposes as before, then for purposes of this section the lessee has acquired the lessor's trade or business for the period of the lease.

(ii) Neither the major portion of a trade or business nor the major portion of a separate unit of a trade or business is acquired merely by acquiring physical assets. The acquisition must transfer a viable trade or business.

(iii) Subdivision (ii) of this subparagraph may be illustrated by the following examples:

Example (1). R Co., a restaurant, sells its building and all its restaurant equipment to S Co. and moves into a larger, more modern building across the street. R Co. purchases new equipment, retains its name and continues to operate as a restaurant. S Co. opens a new restaurant in the old R Co. building. S Co. has merely acquired the old R Co. assets; it has not acquired any portion of R Co.'s business.

Example (2). The facts are the same as in Example (1), except that R Co. also sells its name and goodwill to S Co. and ceases to operate a restaurant business. S Co. operates its restaurant using the old R Co. name. In this situation, S Co. has acquired R Co.'s business.

(2) Separate unit. (i) A separate unit is a segment of a trade or business capable of operating as a self-sustaining enterprise with minor adjustments. The allocation of a portion of the goodwill of a trade or business to one of its segments is a strong indication that that segment is a separate unit.

(ii) The following examples are illustrations of the acquisition of a separate unit of a trade or business:

Example (1). The M Corp., which has been engaged in the sale and repair of boats, leases the repair shop building and all the property used in its boat repair operations to the N Co. for four years and gives the N Co. a covenant not to compete in the boat repair business for the period of the lease. The N Co. is considered to have acquired a separate unit of M Corp.'s business for the period of the lease.

Example (2). (a) The P CO. is engaged in the operation of a chain of department stores. There are eight divisions, each division is located in a different metropolitan area of the country, and each division operates under a different name. Although certain buying and merchandising functions are centralized, each division's day-to-day operations are independent of the others. The Q Corp. acquires all of the physical and intangible assets of one of the divisions, including the division's name. Other than making those minor adjustments necessary to give the division buying and merchandising departments, the Q Corp. allows the division to continue doing business in the same manner as it had been operating prior to the acquisition. The Q Corp. has acquired a separate unit of the P Co.'s business.

(b) The facts are the same as in (a) above, except that Q Corporation buys the division merely to obtain its store locations. Before the Q Corporation takes over, the division liquidates its inventory in a going-out-of-business sale. The Q Corporation has merely acquired assets in this transaction, not a separate unit of P Company's business.

Example (3). The R Company processes and distributes meat products. Both the processing division and the distributorship are self-sustaining, profitable operations. The acquisition of either the meat processing division or the distributorship would be an acquisition of a separate unit of the R Company's business.

Example (4). The S Corporation is engaged in the manufacture and sale of steel and steel products. S Corporation also owns a coal mine, which it operates for the sole purpose of supplying its coal requirements for its steel manufacturing operations. The acquisition of the coal mine would be an acquisition of a separate unit of the S company's business.

Example (5). The T Company, which is engaged in the business of operating a chain of drug stores, sells its only downtown drug store to the V Company and agrees not to open another T Company store in the downtown area for five years. Included in the purchase price is an amount that is charged for the goodwill of the store location. The V Company has acquired a separate unit of the T Company's business.

Example (6). The W Company, which is engaged in the business of operating a chain of drug stores sells one of its stores to the X Company, but continues to operate another drug store three blocks away. The X Company opens the store doing business under its own name. The X Company has not acquired a separate unit of the W Company's business.

Example (7). (a) The Y Corporation, which is engaged in the manufacture of mattresses, sells one of its three factories to the Z Company. At the time of the sale, the factory is capable of profitably manufacturing mattresses on its own. Z Company has acquired a separate unit of the Y Corporation.

(b) The facts are the same as in (a) above, except that a profitable manufacturing operation cannot be conducted in the factory standing on its own. Z Company has not acquired a separate unit of the Y Corporation.

Example (8). The O Construction Company is owned by A, B, and C, who are unrelated individuals. It owns equipment valued at 1.5 million dollars and construction contracts valued at 6 million dollars. A, wishing to start his own company, exchanges his interest in O Company for 2 million dollars of contracts and a sufficient amount of equipment to enable him to begin business immediately. A has acquired a separate unit of the O Company's business.

(3) Major portion. All the facts and circumstances surrounding the transaction shall be taken into account in determining what constitutes a major portion of a trade or business (or separate unit). Factors to be considered include:

(i) The fair market value of the assets in the portion relative to the fair market value of the other assets of the trade or business (or separate unit);

(ii) The proportion of goodwill attributable to the portion of the trade or business (or separate unit);

(iii) The proportion of the number of employees of the trade or business (or separate unit) attributable to the portion in the periods immediately preceding the transaction; and

(iv) The proportion of the sales or gross receipts, net income, and budget of the trade or business (or separate unit) attributable to the portion.

T.D. 7553, 7/20/78, amend T.D. 7921, 11/18/83.

§ 1.52-3 Limitation with respect to certain persons.

Caution: The Treasury has not yet amended Reg § 1.52-3 to reflect changes made by P.L. 105-277, P.L. 105-34, P.L. 104-188, P.L. 101-508, P.L. 98-369.

(a) Mutual savings institutions. In the case of an organization to which section 593 applies (that is, a mutual savings bank, a cooperative bank or a domestic building and loan association), the amount of the targeted jobs credit (new jobs credit in the case of wages paid before 1979) allowable under section 44B shall be 50 percent of the amount otherwise determined under section 51, or, in the case of an organization under common control, under § 1.52-1 (a) and (b).

(b) Regulated investment companies and real estate investment trusts. In the case of a regulated investment company or a real estate investment trust subject to taxation under subchapter M, chapter 1 of the Code, the amount of the targeted jobs credit (new jobs credit in the case of wages paid before 1979) allowable under section 44B shall be reduced to the company's or trust's ratable share of the credit. The ratable share shall be determined in accordance with rules similar to the rules provided in section 46(e)(2)(B) and the regulations thereunder. For purposes of computing the ratable share, the reduction of the deduction for wage or salary expenses under § 1.280C-1 shall not be taken into account.

(c) Cooperatives. *(1) Taxable years ending after October 31, 1978.* For taxable years ending after October 31, 1978, in the case of a cooperative organization described in section 1381(a), rules similar to rules provided in section 46(h) and the regulations thereunder shall apply in determining the distribution of the amount of the targeted jobs credit (new jobs credit in the case of wages paid before 1979) allowable to the cooperative organization and its patrons under section 44B.

(2) Taxable years ending before November 1, 1978. For taxable years ending before November 1, 1978, in the case of a cooperative organization described in section 1381(a), the amount of new jobs credit allowable under section 44B shall be reduced to the cooperative's ratable share of the credit. The ratable share shall be the ratio which the taxable income of the cooperative for the taxable year bears to its taxable income increased by the amount of the deductions allowed under section 1382(b) and (c). For purposes of computing the ratable share, the reduction of the deduction for wage or salary expenses under § 1.280C-1 shall not be taken into account.

T.D. 7921, 11/18/83.

§ 1.53-1 Limitation based on amount of tax.

(a) General rule. *(1) Targeted jobs credit.* For taxable years beginning after December 31, 1978, the amount of the targeted jobs credit allowed by section 44B (as amended by the Revenue Act of 1978) shall not exceed 90 percent of the tax imposed by chapter 1, reduced by the credits enumerated in section 53(a).

(2) New jobs credit. For taxable years beginning before January 1, 1979, the amount of the new jobs credit allowed by section 44B (as in effect prior to enactment of the Revenue Act of 1978) shall not exceed the tax imposed by chapter 1, reduced by the credits enumerated in section 53(a).

(b) Special rule for 1978–79 fiscal year. In the case of a taxable year beginning before January 1, 1979, and ending after that date, the sum of the targeted jobs credit (determined without regard to the tax liability limitation in paragraph (a)(1) of this section) and the new jobs credit (determined without regard to the tax liability limitation in (a)(2) of this section) shall not exceed the tax imposed by chapter 1, reduced by the credits enumerated in section 53(a).

T.D. 7921, 11/18/83.

§ 1.53-2 Carryback and carryover of unused credit.

(a) Allowance of unused credit as a carryback or carryover. *(1) In general.* Section 53(b) (formerly designated as section 53(c) for taxable years beginning before 1979) provides for carrybacks and carryovers of unused targeted jobs credit (new jobs credit in the case of wages paid before 1979). An unused credit is the excess of the credit determined under section 51 for the taxable year over the limitation provided by § 1.53-1 for such taxable year. Subject to the limitations contained in paragraph (b) of this section and paragraph (f) of § 1.53-3, an unused credit shall be added to the amount allowable as a credit under section 44B for the years to which an unused credit can be carried. The year with respect to which an unused credit arises shall be referred to in this section as the "unused credit year."

(2) Taxable years to which unused credit may be carried. An unused targeted jobs credit (new jobs credit in the case of wages paid before 1979) shall be a new employee credit carryback to each of the 3 taxable years preceding the unused credit year and a new employee credit carryover to each of the 15 taxable years succeeding the unused credit year. An unused credit must be carried first to the earliest of the taxable years to which it may be carried, and then to each of the other taxable years (in order of time) to the extent that the unused credit may not be added (because of the limitation contained in paragraph (b) of this section) to the amount allowable as a credit under section 44B for a prior taxable year.

(b) Limitations on allowance of unused credit. *(1) In general.* The amount of the unused targeted jobs credit (new jobs credit in the case of wages paid before 1979) from any particular unused credit year which may be added under section 53(b)(1) (section 53(c)(1) in the case of a new jobs credit) to the amount allowable as a credit under section 44B for any of the preceding or succeeding taxable years to which such credit may be carried shall not exceed the amount by which the limitation in § 1.53-1 for such preceding or succeeding taxable year exceeds the sum of (i) the credit allowable under section 44B for such preceding or succeeding taxable year, and (ii) other unused credits carried to such preceding or succeeding taxable year which are attributable to unused credit years prior to the particular unused credit year. Thus, in determining the amount, if any, of an unused credit from a particular unused credit year which shall be added to the amount allowable as a credit for any preceding or succeeding taxable year, the credit earned for such preceding or succeeding taxable year, plus any unused credits originating in taxable years prior to the particular unused credit year, shall first be applied against the limitation based on amount of tax for such preceding or succeeding taxable year. To the extent the limitation based on amount of tax for the preceding or succeeding year exceeds the sum of the credit earned for such year and other unused credits attributable to years prior to the particular unused credit year, the unused credit from the particular unused credit year shall be added to the amount allowable as a credit under section 44B for such preceding or succeeding year. If any portion of the unused credit is a carryback to a taxable year beginning before January 1, 1977, section 44B shall be deemed to have been in effect for such taxable year for purposes of allowing such carryback as a credit under section 44B. To the extent that an unused credit cannot be added for a particular preceding or succeeding taxable year because of the limitation contained in this paragraph, such unused credit shall be available as a carryback or carryover to the next succeeding taxable year to which it may be carried.

(2) Special rules for an electing small business corporation. An unused targeted jobs credit (new jobs credit in the case of wages paid before 1979) under section 44B of a corporation which arises in an unused credit year for which the corporation is not an electing small business corporation (as defined in section 1371(b)) and which is a carryback or carryover to a taxable year for which the corporation is an electing small business corporation shall not be added to the amount allowable as a credit under section 44B to the shareholders of such corporation for any taxable year. However, a taxable year for which the corporation is an electing small business corporation shall be counted as a taxable year for purposes of determining the taxable years to which such unused credit may be carried.

(3) Corporate acquisitions. For the carryover of unused credits under section 44B in the case of certain corporate acquisitions, see section 381(c)(26) and § 1.381(c)(26)-1.

(4) Examples. This paragraph may be illustrated by the following examples.

Example (1). In 1978, A a calendar year taxpayer, had an unused new jobs credit of $2,000. In 1979, A has a targeted jobs credit of $2,000 and a tax liability imposed by chapter 1 of the Code of $4,000 after all credits listed in section 53(a) have been taken into account. The amount of A's targeted jobs credit allowable under section 44B for 1979 is 90 percent of A's tax liability. The amount of the new jobs credit that may be carried to 1979 is limited to $1,600 ($3,600 [90% of $4,000] – $2,000).

Example (2). In 1979, B, a calendar year taxpayer, has a tax liability imposed by chapter 1 of the Code of $10,000 after all credits listed in section 53(a) have been taken. B's targeted jobs credit for that taxable year is limited to 90 percent of his income tax liability or $9,000. B had a $15,000 targeted jobs credit in 1979 resulting in an unused targeted jobs credit of $5,000 for that year. In 1976 and 1977 B had tax liabilities imposed by chapter 1 of the Code of $3,000 and $4,000 respectively after all credits listed in section 53(a) had been taken. For purposes of carrying back an unused targeted jobs credit to a taxable year beginning before January 1, 1977, section 44B as amended by the Revenue Act of 1978 is deemed to have been in effect for such taxable year. Accordingly, the applicable tax liability limitation for 1976 would be governed by section 53(a) (as amended by the Revenue Act of 1978) which limits the amount of targeted jobs credit allowed to 90 percent of the tax imposed by chapter 1 of the Code after all credits listed in section 53(a) have been taken. B may carry back $2,700 (90% of $3,000) of the 1979 unused targeted jobs credit to 1976. B may carry back $4,000 of the unused targeted jobs credit to 1977 because section 53(a) as it applied to the 1977 taxable year limited the amount of the credit to 100 percent of the taxpayer's tax liability imposed by chapter 1 of the Code after all credits listed in section 53(a) had been taken.

T.D. 7921, 11/18/83.

---

§ 1.53-3 Separate rule for pass-through of jobs credit.

(a) In general. Under section 53(b), in the case of a new jobs credit or targeted jobs credit earned under section 44B by a partnership, estate or trust, or subchapter S corporation, the amount of the credit that may be taken into account by a partner, beneficiary, or shareholder may not exceed a limitation under section 53(b) separately computed with respect to the partner's, beneficiary's, or shareholder's interest in the entity. A credit is subject to the limitation of section 53(b) with respect to a partner, beneficiary, or shareholder if it is earned by a partnership, estate or trust, or subchapter S corporation in a taxable year ending within, or ending before, a taxable year beginning before January 1, 1979 of the partner, beneficiary, or shareholder. See paragraph (f) of this section for rules on carryback or carryover of a credit subject to separate limitation. This section prescribes rules, under the authority of section 44B(b), relating to the computation of the separate limitation. For purposes of this section, references to section 53(a) and (b) are to that section as it existed before it was amended by the Revenue Act of 1978. This paragraph may be illustrated by the following examples:

Example (1). A, a calendar year taxpayer, is a partner in P, a calendar year partnership. A's pro rata portion of the credit earned by P in 1978 is $200. The $200 credit to be claimed on A's 1978 return is subject to the separate limitation in section 53(b) because the limitation applies to taxable years of the taxpayer beginning before January 1, 1979.

Example (2). B, a calendar year taxpayer, is a shareholder in Corporation M, a subchapter S corporation with a July to June fiscal year. B's pro rata portion of the credit earned by Corporation M in its taxable year beginning in 1978 is $100. The $100 credit to be claimed on B's 1979 return is not subject to the separate limitation requirement of section 53(b) because the limitation only applies to taxable years of the taxpayer beginning before 1979, notwithstanding the credit was earned by Corporation M before 1979.

(b) Application of credit earned. A credit earned under section 44B by a partnership, estate or trust, or subchapter S corporation shall be applied by a partner, beneficiary, or shareholder, to the extent allowed under section 53(b), before applying any other credit earned under section 44B. For example, if an individual has a new jobs credit from a proprietorship of $2,000 and from a partnership (after applying section 53(b)) of $1,800, but the credit must be limited under section 53(a) to $3,000, the entire $1,800 credit from the partnership would be applied before any part of the $2,000 amount is applied.

(c) Amount of separate limitation. The amount of the separate limitation is equal to the partner's, beneficiary's, or shareholder's limitation under section 53(a) for the taxable year multiplied by a fraction. The numerator of the fraction is the portion of the taxpayer's taxable income for the year attributable to the taxpayer's interest in the entity. The denominator of the fraction is the taxpayer's total taxable income for the year reduced by the zero bracket amount, if any.

(d) Portion of taxable income attributable to an interest in a partnership, estate or trust, or subchapter S corporation. *(1) General rule.* The portion of a taxpayer's taxable income attributable to an interest in a partnership, estate or trust, or subchapter S corporation is the amount of income from the entity that taxpayer is required to include in gross income, reduced by—

(i) The amount of the deductions allowed to the taxpayer that are attributable to the taxpayer's interest in the entity; and

(ii) A proportionate share of the deductions allowed to the taxpayer not attributable to a specific activity (as defined in paragraph (e)).

If a deduction comprises both an item that is attributable to the taxpayer's interest in the entity and an item or items that are not attributable to the interest in the entity, and if the deduction is limited by a provision of the Code (such as section 170(b), relating to limitations on charitable contributions), the deduction must be prorated among the items taken into account in computing the deduction. For example, if an individual makes a charitable contribution of $5,000 and his distributive share of a partnership includes $2,000 in charitable contributions made by the partnership, and if the charitable contribution deduction is limited to $3,500 under section 170(b), then the portion of the deduction allowed to the taxpayer that is not attributable to a specific activity is $2,500 ($3,500 × ($5,000 ÷ $7,000)) and the portion of the deduction allowed to the taxpayer that is attributable to the interest in the partnership is $1,000 ($3,500 × ($2,000 ÷ $7,000)).

(2) Deductions attributable to an interest in an entity. Examples of deductions that are attributable to the taxpayer's interest in an entity include (but are not limited to) a deduction under section 1202 attributable to a net capital gain passed through the entity, and a deduction attributable to a deductible item (such as a charitable contribution) that has been passed through the entity.

(3) Computation of the proportionate share of deductions not attributable to a specific activity. The proportionate share of a deduction of the taxpayer not attributable to a specific activity is obtained by multiplying the amount of the deduction by a fraction. The numerator of the fraction is the income from the entity that the taxpayer is required to include in gross income, reduced by the amount of the deductions of the taxpayer that are attributable to the taxpayer's interest in the entity. The denominator is the taxpayer's gross income reduced by the amount of all the deductions attributable to specific activities.

(4) Examples. The method of determining the amount of taxable income attributable to an interest in a partnership, estate or trust, or subchapter S corporation is illustrated by the following examples:

Example (1). (a) A, a single individual, is a shareholder in S Corporation, a subchapter S corporation. A is required to include the following amounts from S corporation is his gross income:

Salary	$3,000
Undistributed taxable income:	
Ordinary income	8,000
Net capital gain	2,000
Total	10,000
Total	13,000
A has income from other activities:	
Ordinary income	6,000
Net capital gain	4,000
Total	10,000

(b) In order to determine the taxable income attributable to A's interest in S Corporation, it is necessary to reduce the amount of income from S Corporation that A is required to include in gross income by the amount of A's deductions attributable to the interest in S Corporation and by a proportionate share of A's deductions not attributable to a specific activity. These computations are made in paragraph (c) of this example. However, before the computation reducing A's income by a proportionate share of the deductions not attributable to a specific activity can be made, the ratio described in subparagraph (3) of this paragraph (d) must be determined. The numerator of the ratio (the amount of income from S Corporation that A is required to include in gross income, reduced by the amount of the deductions attributable to A's interest in S Corporation) is obtained in paragraph (c) of this example in the process of computing A's taxable income attributable to the interest in S Corporation. The determination of the denominator (A's gross income reduced by the amount of all deductions attributable to specific activities), however, requires a separate computation, which follows:

Gross income:	
Income from S Corporation	$13,000
Income from other sources	10,000
Total	23,000
Less: Deductions attributable to specific activities:	
Section 1202 deduction (50 pct. of $6,000)	3,000
A's gross income reduced by the amount of the deductions attributable to specific activities (denominator of the ratio for determining the proportionate share of deductions not attributable to a specific activity)	20,000

(c) Computation of the amount of A's taxable income attributable to the interest in S Corporation:

Income from S Corporation that A is required to include in gross income:	
Ordinary income	$11,000
Net capital gain	2,000
Total	13,000
Less: Deductions of the taxpayer attributable to the interest in S Corporation:	
Section 1202 deduction (50 pct. of $2,000)	1,000
(Numerator of the ratio for determining the proportionate share of deductions not attributable to a specific activity)	12,000
Less: Proportionate share of the deductions of the taxpayer not attributable to a specific activity:	
Personal exemption deduction ($750 × $12,000/$20,000)	450
Zero bracket amount ($2,200 × $12,000/$20,000)	1,320
Total	1,770
Portion of A's taxable income attributable to interest in S Corporation	10,230

Example (2). (a) C, a married individual with two children, is a partner in the CD Company. C's distributive share of the CD Company consists of the following:

Ordinary income (other than guaranteed payment)	$38,420
Guaranteed payment	20,000
Net long-term capital gain	6,000
Net short-term capital loss	2,000
Dividends qualifying for exclusion	100
Charitable contributions	500

C also has items of income from other sources and deductions, as follows:

Ordinary income	$21,680
Short-term capital gain	2,000
Dividends qualifying for exclusion	400
Deductions:	
Deductible medical expenses	16,000
Charitable contributions	4,000
Alimony	18,000
Interest and taxes on home	8,000
Loss relating to another specific activity	4,000

(b) In order to determine C's taxable income attributable to the interest in the partnership, it is necessary to reduce the amount of income from the partnership that C is required to include in gross income by the amount of C's deductions attributable to the interest in the partnership and by a proportionate share of C's deductions not attributable to a specific activity. These computations are made in paragraph (c) of this example. However, before the computation reducing C's income by a proportionate share of the deductions not attributable to a specific activity can be made, the ratio described in paragraph (d)(3) of this section must be determined. The numerator of the ratio is determined in paragraph (c) of this example in the process of computing C's taxable income attributable to the interest in the partnership. The denominator, however, requires a separate computation, reducing C's gross income by the amount of all deductions attributable to specific activities. This computation is as follows:

Gross income: Income from the partnership:	
Ordinary income	$58,420
Net long-term capital gain	6,000
Dividends	100
Less: Proportionate share of dividend exclusion ($100 × $100/$500)	20
	80
	64,500
Income from other sources:	
Ordinary income	21,680
Net short-term capital gain	2,000
Dividends	400
Less: Proportionate share of dividend exclusion ($100 × $400/$500)	80
	320
	24,000
	88,500
Less: Deductions attributable to specific activities:	
Net short-term capital loss passed through the partnership	2,000
Loss related to another specific activity	4,000
Section 1202 deduction attributable to the interest in the partnership	2,000
Charitable contribution deduction passed through the partnership	500
	8,500
C's gross income, reduced by the amount of the deductions attributable to specific activities (denominator of the ratio for determining the proportionate share of deductions not attributable to a specific activity)	80,000

(c) Computation of the amount of C's taxable income attributable to the interest in the partnership:

Distributive share of ordinary income (other than guaranteed payments)	$38,420
Guaranteed payment	20,000
Distributive share of dividends less share of exclusion	80
Distributive share of net long-term capital gain	6,000
	64,500
Less: Deductions of the partner attributable to the interest in the partnership:	
Section 1202 deduction (50 pct of $4,000)	2,000
Charitable contribution passed through the partnership	500
Net short-term capital loss passed through the partnership	2,000
	4,500
(Numerator of the ratio for determining the proportionate share of deductions not attributable to a specific activity)	60,000
Less: Proportionate share of the deductions of the partner not attributable to a specific activity:	
Section 1202 deduction ($1,000 × $60,000/$80,000)	750
Deductible medical expenses (16,000 × $60,000/$80,000)	12,000
Charitable contributions ($4,000 × $60,000/$80,000)	3,000
Alimony ($18,000 × $60,000/$80,000)	13,500
Interest and taxes on home ($8,000 × $60,000/$80,000	6,000
Personal exemption deduction ($3,000 × $60,000/$80,000)	2,250
Total	37,500
Portion of C's taxable income attributable to the interest in the partnership	22,500

C has a deduction under section 1202 of $3,000. Of that deduction, $2,000 is attributable directly to C's interest in the partnership (50 percent of the net capital gain that would result from offsetting the $6,000 net long-term capital gain and the $2,000 net short-term capital loss that are attributable to C's interest in the partnership). Since the remaining $1,000 deduction under section 1202 cannot be attributed directly to either C's income from the partnership or any other specific activity, it must be treated as a deduction not attributable to a specific activity.

(e) Deductions not attributable to a specific activity. *(1) "Specific activity" defined.* A "specific activity" means a course of continuous conduct involving a particular line of endeavor, whether or not the activity is carried on for profit. Examples of a specific activity are:

(i) A trade or business carried on by the taxpayer;

(ii) A trade or business carried on by an entity in which the taxpayer has an interest;

(iii) An activity with respect to which the taxpayer is entitled to a deduction under section 212;

(iv) The operation of a farm as a hobby.

(2) Types of deductions not attributable to a specific activity. Examples of deductions not attributable to a specific activity include charitable contributions made by the partner, beneficiary, or shareholder; medical expenses; alimony; interest on personal debts of the partner, beneficiary, or shareholder; and real estate taxes on the personal residence of the partner, beneficiary, or shareholder. For purposes of this section, in cases in which deductions are not itemized, the zero bracket amount is considered to be a deduction not attributable to a specific activity.

(f) Carryback or carryover of credit subject to separate limitations. A credit subject to the separate limitation under section 53(b) that is carried back or carried over to a taxable year beginning before January 1, 1979, is also subject to the separate limitation in the carryback or carryover year. For purposes of the preceding sentence, a credit that is earned by a partnership, a trust, or estate, or a subchapter S corporation in a taxable year of such entity ending within, or after, the taxable year of a partner beneficiary or shareholder beginning after December 31, 1978, will not be subject to the separate limitation in section 53(b) with respect to such partner, beneficiary, or shareholder. The taxpayer to whom the credit has been passed through shall not be prevented from applying the unused portion in a carryback or carryover year merely because the entity that earned the credit changes its form of conducting business if the nature of its trade or business essentially remains the same. The computation of the separate limitation in such a case shall reflect the income attributable to the taxpayer's interest in the entity in its revised form. Thus, a shareholder carrying over a credit from a subchapter S corporation may include dividends declared by that corporation after the subchapter S election had been terminated as income attributable to that person's interest in the entity. Similarly, if a partnership incorporates in a carryover year, any income attributable to an interest in the corporation will be regarded, for purposes of computing the separate limitation under section 53(b), as income attributable to an interest in the entity. This paragraph may be illustrated by the following examples:

Example (1). A, a calendar year taxpayer, is a shareholder in Corporation M, a subchapter S corporation. In 1977, A's pro rata share of the new jobs credit earned by Corporation M was $10,000. A could only use $2,000 of the credit in 1977 because of the separate limitation under section 53(b). In 1978, A carries the unused credit over from 1977. The carryover credit is subject to the separate limitation under section 53(b).

Example (2). Assume the same facts as in example (1) except that the unused credit is carried over to 1979. The carryover credit is not subject to the separate limitation under section 53(b) because that limitation does not apply to taxable years of a taxpayer beginning after December 31, 1978.

Example (3). B, a calendar year taxpayer, is a shareholder in Corporation W, a subchapter S corporation. In 1979, B's pro rata share of the targeted jobs credit covered by Corporation W was $5,000 but B could only use $3,000 of the credit in 1979. B carries back the unused credit to 1978. The carryback credit is not subject to the separate limitation under section 53(b).

T.D. 7560, 8/22/78, amend T.D. 7921, 11/18/83.

§ 1.55-1 Alternative minimum taxable income.

Caution: The Treasury has not yet amended Reg § 1.55-1 to reflect changes made by P.L. 108-27, P.L. 105-206.

(a) General rule for computing alternative minimum taxable income. Except as otherwise provided by statute, regulations, or other published guidance issued by the Commissioner, all Internal Revenue Code provisions that apply in determining the regular taxable income of a taxpayer also apply in determining the alternative minimum taxable income of the taxpayer.

(b) Items based on adjusted gross income or modified adjusted gross income. In determining the alternative minimum taxable income of a taxpayer other than a corporation, all references to the taxpayer's adjusted gross income or modified adjusted gross income in determining the amount of items of income, exclusion, or deduction must be treated as references to the taxpayer's adjusted gross income or modified adjusted gross income as determined for regular tax purposes.

(c) Effective date. These regulations are effective for taxable years beginning after December 31, 1993.

T.D. 8569, 11/23/94.

§ 1.56-0 Table of contents to § 1.56-1, adjustment for book income of corporations.

(a) Computation of the book income adjustment.

(1) In general.

(2) Taxpayers subject to the book income adjustment.

(3) Consolidated returns.

(4) Examples.

(b) Adjusted net book income.

(1) In general.

(2) Net book income.

(i) In general.

(ii) Measures of net book income.

(iii) Tax-free transactions and tax-free income.

(iv) Treatment of dividends and other amounts.

(3) Additional rules for consolidated groups.

(i) consolidated adjusted net book income.

(ii) Consolidated net book income.

(iii) Consolidated pre-adjustment alternative minimum taxable income.

(iv) Cross references.

(4) Computation of adjusted net book income when taxable year and financial accounting year differ.

(i) In general.

(ii) Estimating adjusted net book income.

(iii) Election to compute adjusted net book income based on the financial statement for the year ending within the taxable year.

(A) In general.

(B) Time of making election.

(C) Eligibility to make and manner of making election.

(D) Election or revocation of election made on an amended return.

(iv) Quarterly statement filed with the Securities and Exchange Commission (SEC).

(5) Computation of net book income using current earnings and profits.

(i) In general.

(ii) Current earnings and profits of a consolidated group.

(6) Additional rules for computation of net book income of a foreign corporate taxpayer.

(i) Adjusted net book income of a foreign taxpayer.

(ii) Effectively connected net book income of a foreign taxpayer.

(A) In general.

(B) Certain exempt amounts.

(iii) Computation of net book income of a foreign taxpayer using current earnings and profits.

(7) Examples.

(c) Applicable financial statement.

(1) In general.

(i) Statement required to be filed with the Securities and Exchange Commission (SEC).

(ii) Certified audited financial statement.

(iii) Financial statement provided to a government regulator.

(iv) Other financial statements.

(v) Required use of current earnings and profits.

(2) Election to treat net book income as equal to current earnings and profits for the taxable year.

(i) In general.

(ii) Time of making election.

(iii) Eligibility to make and manner of making election.

(iv) Election by common parent of consolidated group.

(v) Election or revocation of election made on an amended return.

(3) Priority among statements.

(i) In general.

(ii) Special priority rules for use of certified audited financial statements and other financial statements.

(iii) Priority among financial statements provided to a government regulator.

(iv) Statements of equal priority.

(A) In general.

(B) Exceptions to the general rule in paragraph (c)(3)(iv)(A).

(4) Use of financial statement for a substantial non-tax purpose.

(5) Special rules.

(i) Applicable financial statement of related corporations.

(A) Applicable financial statement of a consolidated group.

(B) Special rule for statements of equal priority.

(C) Special rule for related corporations.

(D) Anti-abuse rule.

(ii) Applicable financial statement of foreign corporation with a United States trade or business.

(A) In general.

(B) Special rules for applicable financial statement of a trade or business of a foreign taxpayer.

(C) Special rule for statements of equal priority.

(D) Anti-abuse rule.

(iii) Supplement or amendment to an applicable financial statement.

(A) Excluding a restatement of net book income.

(B) Restatement of net book income.

(6) Examples.

(d) Adjustments to net book income.

(1) In general.

(2) Definitions.

(i) Historic practice.

(ii) Accounting literature.

(3) Adjustments for certain taxes.

(i) In general.

(ii) Exception for certain foreign taxes.

(iii) Certain valuation adjustments.

(iv) Examples.

(4) Adjustments to prevent omission or duplication.

(i) In general.

(ii) Special rule for depreciating an asset below is cost.

(iii) Consolidated group using current earnings and profits.

(iv) Restatement of a prior year's applicable financial statement.

(A) In general.

(B) Reconciliation of owner's equity in applicable financial statements.

(B) Use of different priority applicable financial statements in consecutive taxable years.

(D) First successor year defined.

(E) Exceptions.

(v) Adjustment for items previously taxed as subpart F income.

(vi) Adjustment for pooling of interests.

(vii) Adjustment for certain deferred foreign taxes.

(viii) Examples.

(5) Adjustments resulting from disclosure.

(i) Adjustment for footnote disclosure or other supplementary information.

(A) In general.

(B) Disclosures not specifically authorized in the accounting literature.

(ii) Equity adjustments.

(A) In general.

(B) Definition of equity adjustment.

(iii) Amount disclosed in an accountant's opinion.

(iv) Accounting method changes that result in cumulative adjustments to the current year's applicable financial statement.

(A) In general.

(B) Exception.

(v) Examples.

(6) Adjustments applicable to related corporations.

(i) Consolidated returns.

(A) In general.

(B) Corporations included in the consolidated Federal income tax return but excluded from the applicable financial statement.

(C) Corporations included in the applicable financial statement but excluded from the consolidated tax return.

(ii) Adjustment under the principles of section 482.

(iii) Adjustment for dividends received from section 936 corporations.

(A) In general.

(B) Treatment as foreign taxes.

(C) Treatment of taxes imposed on section 936 corporations.

(iv) Adjustment to net book income on sale of certain investments.

(v) Examples.

(7) Adjustments for foreign taxpayers with a United States trade or business.

(i) In general.

(ii) Example.

(8) Adjustment for corporations subject to subchapter F.

(e) Special rules.

(1) Cooperatives.

(2) Alaska Native Corporations.

(3) Insurance companies.

(4) Estimating the net book income adjustment for purposes of estimated tax liability.

(5) Effective/applicability date.

T.D. 8138, 4/23/87, amend T.D. 8197, 4/22/88, T.D. 8307, 8/16/90, T.D. 9347, 8/6/2007.

---

§ 1.56-1 Adjustment for the book income of corporations.

Caution: The Treasury has not yet amended Reg § 1.56-1 to reflect changes made by P.L. 104-88.

(a) Computation of the book income adjustment. *(1) In general.* For taxable years beginning in 1987, 1988, and 1989, the alternative minimum taxable income of any taxpayer is increased by the book income adjustment described in this paragraph (a)(1). The book income adjustment is 50 percent of the excess, if any, of—

(i) The adjusted net book income (as defined in paragraph (b) of this section) of the taxpayer, over

(ii) The pre-adjustment alternative minimum taxable income for the taxable year.

For purposes of this section, pre-adjustment alternative minimum taxable income is alternative minimum taxable income, determined without regard to the book income adjustment or the alternative tax net operating loss determined under section 56(a)(4). See paragraph (a)(4) of this section for examples relating to the computation of the income adjustment.

(2) Taxpayers subject to the book income adjustment. The book income adjustment is applicable to any corporate taxpayer that is not an S corporation, regulated investment company (RIC), real estate investment trust (REIT), or real estate mortgage investment company (REMIC).

(3) Consolidated returns. In the case of a taxpayer that is a consolidated group, the book income adjustment equals 50 percent of the amount, if any, by which its consolidated adjusted net book income (as defined in paragraph (b)(3)(i) of this section) exceeds its consolidated pre-adjustment alternative minimum taxable income (as defined in paragraph (b)(3)(iii) of this section). See paragraph (a)(4), Example (4) of this section. For purposes of this section, with respect to any taxable year the term "consolidated group" has the same meaning as in § 1.1502-1T. See paragraph (d)(6) of this section for rules relating to adjustments attributable to related corporations.

(4) Examples. The provisions of this paragraph may be illustrated by the following examples.

Example (1). Corporation A has adjusted net book income of $200 and pre-adjustment alternative minimum taxable income of $100. A must increase its pre-adjustment alternative minimum taxable income by $50 (($200-$100) × .50).

Example (2). Corporation B has adjusted net book income of $200 and pre-adjustment alternative minimum taxable income of $300. B does not have a book income adjustment for the taxable year because its adjusted net book income does not exceed its pre-adjustment alternative minimum taxable income.

Example (3). Corporation C has adjusted net book income of negative $200 and pre-adjustment alternative minimum taxable income of negative $300. C must increase its pre-adjustment alternative minimum taxable income by $50 ((– $200 – (– $300)) × .50). Thus, C's alternative minimum taxable income determined after the book income adjustment, but without regard to the alternative tax net operating loss, is negative $250 (– $300 + $50).

Example (4). Corporations D and E are a consolidated group for tax purposes. D and E do not have a consolidated financial statement. On their separate financial statements D and E have adjusted net book income of $100 and $50 respectively, and pre-adjustment alternative minimum taxable income of $50 and $80 respectively. Assuming there are no intercompany transactions, DE's consolidated adjusted net book income (as defined in paragraph (b)(3)(i) of this section) is $150 and its consolidated pre-adjustment alternative minimum taxable income (as defined in paragraph (b)(3)(iii) of this section) is $130. DE must increase its consolidated pre-adjustment alternative minimum taxable income by $10 (($150 – $130) × .50).

(b) Adjusted net book income. *(1) In general.* "Adjusted net book income" means the net book income (as defined in paragraph (b)(2) of this section) adjusted as provided in paragraph (d) of this section. Except as provided in paragraph (d) of this section, a taxpayer may not make any adjustments to net book income.

(2) Net book income. (i) In general. "Net book income" means the income or loss for a taxpayer reported in the taxpayer's applicable financial statement (as defined in paragraph (c) of this section). Net book income must take into account all items of income, expense, gain and loss of the taxable year, including extraordinary items, income or loss from discontinued operations, and cumulative adjustments resulting from accounting method changes. Net book income is not reduced by any distributions to shareholders. See paragraph (b)(5)(i) of this section for a similar rule for corporations using current earnings and profits to compute net book income.

(ii) Measures of net book income. Except as described in paragraph (b)(5) of this section, net book income is disclosed on the income statement included in a taxpayer's applicable financial statement. Such income statement must reconcile with the balance sheet, if any, that is included in the applicable financial statement and must be used in computing changes in owner's equity reflected in the applicable financial statement. See paragraph (c) of this section for the definition of an applicable financial statement.

(iii) Tax-free transactions and tax-free income. Net book income includes income or loss that is reported on a taxpayer's applicable financial statement regardless of whether such income or loss is recognized, realized or otherwise taken into account for other Federal income tax purposes. See paragraph (b)(7), Examples (1), (2) and (3) of this section.

(iv) Treatment of dividends and other amounts. The adjusted net book income of a taxpayer shall include the earnings of other corporations not filing a consolidated Federal income tax return with the taxpayer only to the extent that amounts are required to be included in the taxpayer's gross income under chapter 1 of the Code with respect to the earnings of such other corporation (e.g., dividends received from such corporation and amounts included under subpart A). See paragraph (b)(7), Examples (4) and (5) of this section.

(3) Additional rules for consolidated groups. (i) Consolidated adjusted net book income. "Consolidated adjusted net book income" means the consolidated net book income (as defined in paragraph (b)(3)(ii) of this section), after taking into account the adjustments under the rules of paragraph (d) of this section.

(ii) Consolidated net book income. Consolidated net book income is the income or loss of a consolidated group as reported on its applicable financial statement as defined in paragraph (c)(5) of this section.

(iii) Consolidated pre-adjustment alternative minimum taxable income. Consolidated pre-adjustment alternative minimum taxable income is the taxable income of the consolidated group for the taxable year, determined with the adjustments provided in sections 56 and 58 (except for the book income adjustment and the alternative tax net operating loss determined under section 56(a)(4)) and increased by the preference items described in section 57.

(iv) Cross references. See paragraph (c)(5) of this section for rules relating to the applicable financial statement of related corporations and paragraph (d)(6) of this section for rules relating to adjustments attributable to related corporations.

(4) Computation of adjusted net book income when taxable year and financial accounting year differ. (i) In general. If a taxpayer's applicable financial statement is prepared on the basis of a financial accounting year that differs from the year that the taxpayer uses for filing its Federal income tax return, adjusted net book income must be computed either—

(A) By including a pro rata portion of the adjusted net book income for each financial accounting year that includes any part of the taxpayer's taxable year (see paragraph (b)(7), Example (6) of this section), or

(B) In accordance with the election described in paragraph (b)(4)(iii) of this section.

(ii) Estimating adjusted net book income. If a taxpayer is using the pro rata approach described in paragraph (b)(4)(i)(A) of this section and an applicable financial statement for part of the taxpayer's taxable year is not available when the taxpayer files its Federal income tax return, the taxpayer must make a reasonable estimate of adjusted net book income for the pro rata portion of the taxable year. If the actual pro rata portion of adjusted net book income that results from the taxpayer's applicable financial statement for the financial accounting year exceeds the estimate of adjusted net book income used on the original tax return and results in additional tax liability, the taxpayer must file an amended Federal income tax return reflecting such additional liability. The amended return must be filed within 90 days of the date the previously unavailable applicable financial statement is available.

(iii) Election to compute adjusted net book income based on the financial statement for the year ending within the taxable year. (A) In general. If a taxpayer's accounting year ends five or more months after the end of its taxable year, the taxpayer may elect to compute adjusted net book income based on the net book income reported on the applicable financial statement prepared for the financial accounting year ending within the taxpayer's taxable year. See paragraph (b)(7), Examples (7) and (8) of this section. For purposes of this paragraph (b)(4)(iii)(A), if a taxpayer uses a 52-53 week year for financial accounting or Federal income tax purposes, the last day of such year shall be deemed to occur on the last day of the calendar month ending closest to the end of such year.

(B) Time of making election. An election under this paragraph (b)(4)(iii) is made by attaching the statement described in paragraph (b)(4)(iii)(C) of this section to the taxpayer's Federal income tax return for the first taxable year in which the taxpayer is eligible to make the election. An election under this paragraph (b)(4)(iii) that is made prior to the first taxable year in which the taxpayer is eligible to make the election (as determined under paragraph (b)(4)(iii)(C) of this section) is valid unless revoked pursuant to paragraph (b)(4)(iii)(D) of this section.

(C) Eligibility to make and manner of making election. A taxpayer is eligible to make the election specified in paragraph (b)(4)(iii)(A) of this section in the first taxable year beginning after 1986 in which—

(1) The taxpayer has an accounting year ending five or more months after the end of its taxable year,

(2) The use of the pro rata approach described in paragraph (b)(4)(i)(A) of this section produces an excess of adjusted net book income over pre-adjustment alternative minimum taxable income, as defined in paragraph (a)(1) of this section, and

(3) The taxpayer has an excess of tentative minimum tax over regular tax for the taxable year, as defined in section 55(a), or is liable for the environmental tax imposed by section 59A.

Thus, a taxpayer is not required to evaluate the merits of an election to compute its adjusted net book income based on the applicable financial statement prepared for the financial accounting year ending within the taxpayer's taxable year unless the taxpayer, when using the pro rata approach described in paragraph (b)(4)(i)(A) of this section, either has an excess of tentative minimum tax over its regular tax or is liable for the environmental tax imposed by section 59A. The election statement must set forth the electing taxpayer's name, address, taxpayer identification number, taxable year and financial accounting year. An election under this paragraph (b)(4)(iii) will apply for the taxable year when initially made and for all subsequent years until revoked with the consent of the District Director.

(D) Election or revocation of election made on an amended return. An election under paragraph (b)(4)(iii) of this section may be made by attaching the statement described in paragraph (b)(4)(iii)(C) to an amended return for the first taxable year in which the taxpayer is eligible to make the election. An election under paragraph (b)(4)(iii) of this section that was made prior to the first taxable year in which the taxpayer was eligible to make the election, as determined under paragraph (b)(4)(iii)(C) of this section, may be revoked by filing an amended return for the taxable year in which the election was initially made. However, an election made or revoked on an amended return under paragraph (b)(4)(iii) of this section will be allowed only if the amended return is filed no later than December 14, 1990.

(iv) Quarterly statement filed with the Securities and Exchange Commission (SEC). A taxpayer with different financial accounting and taxable years that is required to file both annual and quarterly financial statements with the SEC may not aggregate quarterly statements filed with the SEC in order to obtain a statement covering the taxpayer's taxable year. See paragraph (b)(7), Example (9) of this section. See paragraph (c)(3)(iv)(B)(1) of this section for priority rules relating to statements required to be filed with the SEC.

(5) Computation of net book income using current earnings and profits. (i) In general. If a taxpayer does not have an applicable financial statement, or only has a statement described in paragraph (c)(1)(iv) of this section and makes the election described in paragraph (c)(2) of this section, net book income for purposes of this section is equal to the taxpayer's current earnings and profits for its taxable year. Generally, a taxpayer's current earnings and profits is computed under the rules of section 312 and the regulations thereunder. Current earnings and profits therefore is reduced by Federal income tax expense and any foreign tax expense for foreign taxes eligible for the foreign tax credit under section 27 of the Code. Current earnings and profits is then adjusted as described in paragraph (d) of this section to arrive at adjusted net book income. No adjustment is made under paragraph (d) of this section, however, for any adjustment that is already reflected in current earnings and profits. See paragraph (d)(3) of this section for adjustments to net book income with respect to certain taxes. For purposes of this section, current earnings and profits is not reduced by any distribution to shareholders. See paragraph (d)(3)(iv), Example (5) of this section.

(ii) Current earnings and profits of a consolidated group. For purposes of this paragraph (b)(5), the current earnings and profits of a consolidated group is the aggregate of the current earnings and profits of each member of the group, as determined pursuant to paragraph (d)(4)(iii) of this section.

(6) Additional rules for computation of net book income of a foreign corporate taxpayer. (i) Adjusted net book income of a foreign taxpayer. Adjusted net book income of a foreign corporate taxpayer ("foreign taxpayer") means the effectively connected net book income (as defined in paragraph (b)(6)(ii) of this section) of the foreign taxpayer, after taking into account the adjustments under the rules of paragraph (d) of this section.

(ii) Effectively connected net book income of a foreign taxpayer. (A) In general. Effectively connected net book income of a foreign taxpayer is the income or loss reported in its applicable financial statement (as defined in paragraph (c)(5)(ii) of this section), but only to the extent that such amount is attributable to items of income or loss that would be treated as effectively connected with the conduct of a trade or business in the United States by the foreign taxpayer as determined under either the principles of section 864(c) and the regulations thereunder, or any other applicable provision of the Internal Revenue Code of 1986. Thus, if for tax purposes an item of income or loss is treated as effectively connected with the conduct of a trade or business in the United States, then the income or loss reported on the foreign taxpayer's applicable financial statement attributable to such item is effectively connected net book income. See paragraph (b)(7), Examples (11), (12) and (13) of this section.

(B) Certain exempt amounts. Effectively connected net book income does not include any amount attributable to an item that is exempt from United States taxation under sections 883, 892, 894 or 895 of the Internal Revenue Code of 1986. See paragraph (b)(7), Examples (14) and (15) of this section.

(iii) Computation of net book income of a foreign taxpayer using current earnings and profits. If a foreign taxpayer does not have an applicable financial statement or only has a statement described in paragraph (c)(1)(iv) of this section and makes the election described in paragraph (c)(2) of this section, net book income for purposes of this section is equal to the foreign taxpayer's current earnings and profits that are attributable to income or loss that is effectively connected (or treated as effectively connected) with the conduct of a trade or business in the United States. Effectively connected current earnings and profits are computed under the rules of section 884(d) and the regulations thereunder, relating to effectively connected earnings and profits for purposes of computing the branch profits tax, but without regard to the exceptions set forth under section 884(d)(2)(B) through (E). For purposes of this section, effectively connected current earnings and profits are not reduced by any remittances or distributions. Effectively connected current earnings and profits takes into account Federal income tax expense and any foreign tax expense; however, see paragraph (d)(3) of this section for adjustments to net book income with respect to certain taxes.

(7) Examples. The provisions of this paragraph may be illustrated by the following examples.

Example (1). Corporation A owns 100 percent of corporation B and the AB affiliated group files a consolidated Federal income tax return. AB uses a calendar year for both financial accounting and tax purposes. During 1987, A transfers all of its stock in B for stock on an acquiring corporation in a transaction described in section 368(a)(1)(B). Although AB recognizes no taxable gain on the transfer pursuant to section 354, gain from the transfer is reported on AB's 1987 applicable financial statement. Pursuant to paragraph (b)(2)(iii) of this section, AB's net book income includes the book gain attributable to the transfer.

Example (2). Corporation C uses a calendar year for both financial accounting and tax purposes. C adopted a plan of liquidation prior to August 1, 1986. On June 1, 1987, C makes a bulk sale of all of its assets subject to liabilities and completely liquidates. Pursuant to section 633(c) of the Tax Reform Act of 1986 (the Act), section 337, as in effect prior to its amendment by the Act, applies. Thus, C will generally not recognize taxable gain upon the bulk sale. However, C's applicable financial statement for the period January 1, 1987 through June 1, 1987, reports net book income of $500, $400 of which is attributable to the bulk sale of assets on June 1, 1987. Pursuant to paragraph (b)(2)(iii) of this section, C's net book income includes the amount attributable to the bulk sale. Thus, assuming C has no other adjustments to net book income, its adjusted net book income for the period January 1, 1987 through June 1, 1987, is $500.

Example (3). Corporation Z has a large inventory of marketable securities. On its applicable financial statement, Z marks these securities to market, i.e., as they appreciate in value, Z restates their value on its balance sheet to their fair market value, and increases the income on its income statement by that amount. Pursuant to paragraph (b)(2)(iii) of this section, the adjusted net book income of Z includes the income from the valuation adjustment.

Example (4). Corporation D owns 100 percent of E, a controlled foreign corporation as defined in section 957. Both D and E use a calendar year for financial accounting and tax purposes. D's applicable financial statement includes

E. Pursuant to section 951, D includes $100 of E's subpart F income in its gross income for 1987. Although D's applicable financial statement is adjusted to eliminate E's income, pursuant to paragraph (b)(2)(iv) of this section, D's adjusted net book income for 1987 includes the $100 of gross income included under section 951.

Example (5). Corporation F owns 20 percent of G, a foreign corporation. Both F and G use a calendar year for financial accounting and tax purposes. During 1987, G pays F a $100 dividend. F's applicable financial statement accounts for F's investment in G by the equity method. F is eligible for a deemed paid foreign tax credit of $30 with respect to the dividend from G and must include the $130 in gross income pursuant to section 78 of the Code. Although F's applicable financial statement is adjusted to eliminate F's income from G under the equity method, pursuant to paragraph (b)(2)(iv) of this section, F's adjusted net book income for 1987 includes the $130 of gross income recognized with respect to the dividend from G.

Example (6). Corporation H files its Federal income tax return on a calendar year basis. However, its applicable financial statement is based on a fiscal year ending June 30. H does not make the election described in paragraph (b)(4)(iii) of this section. Pursuant to paragraph (b)(4)(i) of this section, H's adjusted net book income for calendar year 1987 is computed by adding 50 percent of adjusted net book income from the applicable financial statement for the year ending June 30, 1987 and 50 percent of adjusted net book income from the applicable financial statement for the year ending June 30, 1988.

Example (7). Corporation J files its Federal income tax returns for 1987, 1988, and 1989 on a calendar year basis. However, its applicable financial statement is based on a year ending May 31. Pursuant to paragraph (b)(4)(iii) of this section, J elects in 1987 to compute its adjusted net book income by using the applicable financial statement for the fiscal year ending May 31, 1987. Unless the District Director consents to revocation of the election, for calendar year 1988 or 1989, J's adjusted net book income for 1988 and 1989 is determined from its applicable financial statements for the years ending May 31, 1988 and May 31, 1989, respectively.

Example (8). The facts are the same as in Example (7), except that J's applicable financial statement is based on a year ending April 30. Since April 30, is less than 5 months after December 31, the end of J's taxable year, J is not permitted to make the election described in paragraph (b)(4)(iii) of this section.

Example (9). The facts are the same as in Example (8), except H files quarterly and annual financial statements with the Securities and Exchange Commission (SEC). The fourth quarter statement is included as a footnote to the annual statement that it files with the SEC. Pursuant to paragraph (b)(4)(iv) of this section, H may not determine its net book income by aggregating its four quarterly statements for 1987. Thus, H's net book income is computed as described in Example (8).

Example (10). Corporation I is a United States corporation with a 100 percent owned subsidiary, J, a foreign sales corporation (FSC). I uses a calendar year for both financial accounting and tax purposes. Income from J is consolidated in I's applicable financial statement. I and J do not file a consolidated tax return. In 1987, J pays a dividend to I of $100 out of J's earnings and profits. For purposes of this example, it is assumed that the distribution is made out of the profits attributable solely to foreign trade income determined through use of the administrative pricing rules of section 925(a)(1) and (2). Accordingly, the distribution is eligible for the 100 percent dividends received deduction under section 245(c). Although I's applicable financial statement is adjusted to eliminate income or loss attributable to J, the entire amount of the dividend distribution must be included in I's adjusted net book income pursuant to paragraph (b)(2)(iv) of this section.

Example (11). Corporation K is a foreign corporation incorporated under the laws of country X. K uses a calendar year for both financial accounting and tax purposes. In 1987, K actively conducts a real estate business, L, in the United States. The financial statement that is used as K's applicable financial statement (as determined under paragraph (c)(5)(ii) of this section) discloses total net income of $150. Of this amount, $100 is attributable to L's real estate business and $50 is attributable to dividends paid to L from its investment in certain securities. The securities investment is not connected with L's real estate business. Under the rules of section 864, only $100 is effectively connected to the conduct of a trade or business in the United States. Thus, K's effectively connected net book income for 1987 equals $100.

Example (12). Assume the same facts as in Example (11) except that K's applicable financial statement also discloses $75 attributable to investment real property located in the United States, so that the net income amount reported on the financial statement equals $225. The $75 of income is not effectively connected with the conduct of a trade or business in the United States. K, for regular tax purposes, makes an election under section 882(d) to treat this income as effectively connected with the conduct of a trade or business in the United States. As a result, K's effectively connected net book income for 1987 equals $175 ($100 + $75).

Example (13). Corporation M is a foreign corporation that actively conducts a manufacturing business, N, in the United States. M is a calendar year taxpayer for both financial accounting and tax purposes. In 1987, the financial statement that is used as M's applicable financial statement (as determined under paragraph (c)(5)(ii) of this section) reflects an anticipated loss from the sale of a division of N. For Federal income tax purposes the loss is not recognized in 1987, but rather is recognized in 1988 when M sells the division. In determining M's effectively connected net book income for 1987, the anticipated loss reported on M's 1987 applicable financial statement is taken into account because the reported loss is effectively connected to the conduct of a trade or business in the United States under the principles of section 864.

Example (14). Corporation O is a foreign corporation that is engaged in the international shipping business. O is incorporated under the laws of X. O is a calendar year taxpayer for both financial accounting and tax purposes. In 1987, O actively conducts a shipping business, P, within the United States. The statement that is used in 1987 as O's applicable financial statement (as determined under paragraph (c)(5)(ii) of this section) discloses income of $100 that is attributable to P's operation of ships in international traffic. Under section 864, $50 is effectively connected with the conduct of a trade or business in the United States. However, the United States income tax treaty with X exempts from United States income tax any income derived by a resident of X from the operation of ships in international traffic. Thus, pursuant to paragraph (b)(6)(ii)(B) of this section, no amount of P's income is includible in O's effectively connected net book income.

Example (15). Assume the same facts as in Example (14) except that there is no United States income tax treaty with

X. However, X by statute exempts United States citizens and United States corporations from tax imposed by X on gross income derived from the operation of a ship or ships in international traffic. Under section 883(a), P's income of $50 that is effectively connected with the conduct of a trade or business in the United States is exempt from United States taxation. Thus, pursuant to paragraph (b)(6)(ii)(B) of this section, no amount of P's income is includible in O's effectively connected net book income.

(c) Applicable financial statement. *(1) In general.* A taxpayer's applicable financial statement is the statement described in this paragraph (c)(1) that has the highest priority, as determined under paragraph (c)(3) of this section. Generally, an applicable financial statement includes an income statement, a balance sheet (listing assets, liabilities, and owner's equity including changes thereto), and other appropriate information. An income statement alone may constitute an applicable financial statement for purposes of this section if the other materials described in this paragraph are not prepared or used by the taxpayer. However, an income statement that does not reconcile with financial materials otherwise issued will not qualify as an applicable financial statement. For purposes of determining the book income adjustment, the following may be considered applicable financial statements (subject to the rules relating to priority among statements under paragraph (c)(3) of this section)—

(i) Statement required to be filed with the Securities and Exchange Commission (SEC). A financial statement that is required to be filed with the Securities and Exchange Commission.

(ii) Certified audited financial statement. A certified audited financial statement that is used for credit purposes, for reporting to shareholders or for any other substantial non-tax purpose. Such a statement must be accompanied by the report of an independent (as defined in the American Institute of Certified Public Accountants Professional Standards, Code of Professional Conduct, Rule 101 and its interpretations and rulings) Certified Public Accountant or, in the case of a foreign corporation, a similarly qualified and independent professional who is licensed in any foreign country. A financial statement is "certified audited" for purposes of this section if it is—

(A) Certified to be fairly presented (an unqualified or "clean" opinion),

(B) Subject to a qualified opinion that such financial statement is fairly presented subject to a concern about a contingency (a qualified "subject to" opinion),

(C) Subject to a qualified opinion that such financial statement is fairly presented, except for a method of accounting with which the accountant disagrees (a qualified "except for" opinion), or

(D) Subject to an adverse opinion, but only if the accountant discloses the amount of the disagreement with the statement.

Any other statement or report, such as a review statement or a compilation report that is not subject to a full audit is not a certified audited statement. See paragraph (c)(3)(iv)(B)(2) of this section for a special rule for a statement accompanied by a review report when there are statements of equal priority. See also paragraph (d)(5)(iii) of this section for rules relating to adjustments for information disclosed in an accountant's opinion to a certified audited statement.

(iii) Financial statement provided to a government regulator. A financial statement that is required to be provided to the Federal government or any agency thereof (other than the Securities and Exchange Commission), a state government or any agency thereof, or a political subdivision of a state or any agency thereof. An income tax return, franchise tax return or other tax return prepared for the purpose of determining any tax liability that is filed with a Federal, state or local government or agency cannot be an applicable financial statement.

(iv) Other financial statements. A financial statement that is used for credit purposes, for reporting to shareholders, or for any other substantial non-tax purpose, even though such financial statement is not described in paragraphs (c)(1)(i) through (c)(1)(iii) of this section.

(v) Required use of current earnings and profits. If a taxpayer does not have a financial statement described in paragraphs (c)(1)(i) through (c)(1)(iv) of this section, the taxpayer does not have an applicable financial statement. In that case, net book income for the taxable year will be treated as being equal to the taxpayer's current earnings and profits for the taxable year. See paragraph (b)(5) of this section for rules relating to the computation of current earnings and profits for the taxable year. See paragraph (c)(4) of this section for rules relating to use of a financial statement for a substantial non-tax purpose.

(2) Election to treat net book income as equal to current earnings and profits for the taxable year. (i) In general. If a taxpayer's only financial statement is a statement described in paragraph (c)(1)(iv) of this section, the taxpayer may elect to treat net book income as equal to the taxpayer's current earnings and profits for all taxable years in which the taxpayer is eligible to make the election.

(ii) Time of making election. An election under this paragraph (c)(2) is made by attaching the statement described in paragraph (c)(2)(iii) of this section to the taxpayer's Federal income tax return for the first taxable year the taxpayer is eligible to make the election. An election under this paragraph (c)(2), which is made prior to the first taxable year in which the taxpayer is eligible to make the election, as determined under paragraph (c)(2)(iii) of this section, is valid unless revoked pursuant to paragraph (c)(2)(iv) of this section.

(iii) Eligibility to make and manner of making election. A taxpayer is eligible to make the election in the first taxable year in which—

(A) The taxpayer has an applicable financial statement described in paragraph (c)(1)(iv) of this section;

(B) The use of this applicable financial statement produces an excess of adjusted net book income over preadjustment alternative minimum taxable income, as defined in paragraph (a)(1) of this section, and

(C) The taxpayer has, as determined under section 55(a), an excess of tentative minimum tax over regular tax for the taxable year, or is liable for the environmental tax imposed by section 59A.

Thus, a taxpayer is not required to evaluate the merits of an election to use its current earnings and profits as its net book income unless the taxpayer, when using an applicable financial statement described in paragraph (c)(1)(iv) of this section, has an excess of tentative minimum tax over its regular tax or is liable for the environmental tax imposed by section 59A. The election statement must set forth the electing taxpayer's name, address and taxpayer identification number, state that the election is being made under the provisions of section 56(f)(3)(B), and state that the only financial statement of the taxpayer is a financial statement described in paragraph (c)(1)(iv) of this section. An election under this paragraph (c)(2) is effective for every taxable year in which the taxpayer does not have a financial statement described in paragraphs (c)(1)(i) through (c)(1)(iii) of this section and may be revoked only with the consent of the District Director. See paragraph (c)(6), Example (1) of this section.

(iv) Election or revocation of election made on an amended return. An election under paragraph (c)(2) of this section may be made by attaching the statement described in paragraph (c)(2)(iii) to an amended return for the first taxable year in which the taxpayer is eligible to make the election. An election under paragraph (c)(2) of this section that was made prior to the first taxable year in which the taxpayer was eligible to make the election, as determined under paragraph (c)(2)(iii) of this section, may be revoked by filing an amended return for the taxable year in which the election was initially made. However, an election made or revoked on an amended return will be allowed only if the amended return is filed no later than December 14, 1990.

(v) Election by common parent of consolidated group. The election by the common parent of a consolidated group to treat net book income as equal to current earnings and profits shall bind all members of the group. This rule shall not apply in the case of any taxpayer that first, has made the election on a return filed before August 16, 1990, second, applied the election only to those members of the group that are themselves eligible to make the election, and third, properly consolidated the adjusted net book income of the group. In order to change its election to apply to all members of the group, a taxpayer must attach a statement to an amended return for the first taxable year the taxpayer is eligible to make the election. However, an election made on an amended return under this paragraph (c)(2)(iv) will be allowed only if the amended return is filed no later than December 14, 1990. See paragraph (b)(5)(ii) of this section regarding the current earnings and profits of a consolidated group. See paragraph (d)(4)(iii) of this section for adjustments that apply when a consolidated group uses current earnings and profits to compute its net book income.

(3) Priority among statements. (i) In general. If a taxpayer has more than one financial statement described in paragraph (c)(1)(i) through (c)(1)(iv) of this section, the taxpayer's applicable financial statement is the statement with the highest priority. Priority is determined in the following order—

(A) A financial statement described in paragraph (c)(1)(i) of this section.

(B) A certified audited statement described in paragraph (c)(1)(ii) of this section.

(C) A financial statement required to be provided to a Federal or other government regulator described in paragraph (c)(1)(iii) of this section.

(D) Any other financial statement described in paragraph (c)(1)(iv) of this section.

For example, corporation A, which uses a calendar year for both financial accounting and tax purposes, prepares a financial statement for calendar year 1987 that is provided to a state regulator and an unaudited financial statement that is provided to A's creditors. The statement provided to the state regulator is A's financial statement with the highest priority and thus is A's applicable financial statement.

(ii) Special priority rules for use of certified audited financial statements and other financial statements. In the case of financial statements described in paragraphs (c)(1)(ii) and (c)(1)(iv) of this section, within each of these categories the taxpayer's applicable financial statement is determined according to the following priority—

(A) A statement used for credit purposes,

(B) A statement used for disclosure to shareholders, and

(C) Any other statement used for other substantial non-tax purposes.

For example, corporation B uses a calendar year for both financial accounting and tax purposes. B prepares a financial statement for calendar year 1987 that it uses for credit purposes and prepares another financial statement for calendar year 1987 that it uses for disclosure to shareholders. Both financial statements are unaudited. The statement used for credit purposes is B's financial statement with the highest priority and thus is B's applicable financial statement.

(iii) Priority among financial statements provided to a government regulator. In the case of two or more financial statements described in paragraph (c)(1)(iii) of this section (relating to financial statements required to be provided to a Federal or other governmental regulator) that are of equal priority, the taxpayer's applicable financial statement is determined according to the following priority—

(A) A statement required to be provided to the Federal government or any of its agencies,

(B) A statement required to be provided to a State government or any of its agencies, and

(C) A statement required to be provided to any subdivision of a state or any agency of a subdivision.

(iv) Statements of equal priority. (A) In general. Except as provided in paragraph (c)(3)(iv)(B) and paragraph (c)(5)(i)(B) of this section, if a taxpayer has two or more financial statements of equal priority (determined under paragraphs (c)(3)(i), (c)(3)(ii) and (c)(3)(iii) of this section), the taxpayer's applicable financial statement is the statement that results in the greatest amount of adjusted net book income.

(B) Exceptions to the general rule in paragraph (c)(3)(iv)(A). (1) In the case of two or more financial statements described in paragraph (c)(1)(i) of this section (relating to financial statements required to be filed with the SEC) that are of equal priority, a certified audited financial statement has a higher priority than an unaudited financial statement.

(2) In the case of two or more financial statements described in paragraph (c)(1)(iv) of this section (relating to other financial statements) that are of equal priority, a financial statement accompanied by an auditor's "review report" has a higher priority than another financial statement of otherwise equal priority. For purposes of this section, an auditor's review report is defined in the American Institute of Certified Public Accountant Professional Standards, AR section 100.32. See paragraph (c)(6), Examples (2) and (3) of this section.

(4) Use of financial statement for a substantial non-tax purpose. In order to be an applicable financial statement for purposes of computing the book income adjustment, a financial statement described in paragraph (c)(1)(ii) or (c)(1)(iv) must be used by the taxpayer for credit purposes, for disclosure to shareholders, or for any other substantial non-tax purpose. A financial statement is used by a taxpayer if the taxpayer reasonably anticipates that users of the statement will rely on it for non-tax purposes. Thus, a financial statement used for the purpose of computing the book income adjustment is not an applicable financial statement even if it is provided to shareholders or creditors, unless the taxpayer reasonably anticipates that users of the statement will rely on it for non-tax purposes. See paragraph (c)(6), Examples (4), (5), (19) and (20) of this section.

(5) Special rules. (i) Applicable financial statement of related corporations. (A) Applicable financial statement of a consolidated group. The applicable financial statement of a consolidated group (as defined in paragraph (a)(3) of this section) is the financial statement of the common parent (within the meaning of section 1504(a)(1)) of the consolidated group that has the highest priority under the rules of paragraphs (c)(3)(i), (c)(3)(ii) and (c)(5)(i)(B) of this section. See paragraph (d)(6)(i) of this section for rules relating to adjustments to net book income of a consolidated group. See paragraph (c)(6), Example (7) of this section. See paragraph (c)(2)(iv) of this section for rules relating to the election by the common parent of a consolidated group to use current earnings and profits to compute net book income.

(B) Special rule for statements of equal priority. If a consolidated group has two or more financial statements of equal priority (determined under paragraphs (c)(3)(i) and (c)(3)(ii) of this section and this paragraph (c)(5)), the consolidated group's applicable financial statement is determined under either paragraph (c)(5)(i)(B)(1) or (2), whichever is applicable.

(1) Two or more financial statements reporting on the same corporations. If two or more financial statements of equal priority report on the same corporations, the consolidated group's applicable financial statement is determined under the rules of paragraph (c)(3)(iv) of this section. Thus, the financial statement that results in the greatest consolidated adjusted net book income is the consolidated group's applicable financial statement.

(2) Two or more financial statements reporting on different corporations. If two or more financial statements of equal priority report on different corporations, the consolidated group's applicable financial statement is—

(i) The statement that reflects the greatest amount of gross receipts attributable to members of the consolidated group, or

(ii) The statement that reflects the greatest amount of gross receipts (including gross receipts attributable to corporations that are not members of the consolidated group), but only if the consolidated group has financial statements of equal priority after applying the rules of paragraph (c)(5)(i)(B)(2)(i).

If after applying the rules of paragraphs (c)(5)(i)(B)(2)(i) and (ii) of this section, the consolidated group still has financial statements of equal priority, the rules of paragraph (c)(3)(iv) of this section apply. See paragraph (c)(6), Examples (7) and (8) of this section.

(C) Special rule for related corporations. If any portion of the net book income of a corporation (the "first corporation") is included on the applicable financial statement of a second corporation, but the first and second corporations are not members of the same consolidated group, the applicable financial statement of the second corporation is disregarded when determining the applicable financial statement of the first corporation. Thus, the applicable financial statement of the first corporation is the financial statement of highest priority determined under the rules of paragraph (c)(3) of this section without regard to the financial statement of the second corporation. Pursuant to paragraph (c)(1)(iv) of this section, if a separate financial statement is not prepared by the first corporation, the rules of paragraph (b)(5) (relating to current earnings and profits) apply. See paragraph (c)(6), Examples (9) and (10) of this section.

(D) Anti-abuse rule. The special rules of this paragraph (c)(5)(i) will not apply if the taxpayer rearranges its corporate structure or modifies its financial reporting and the principal purpose of such action is to use the special rules of this paragraph (c)(5)(i) to reduce the amount of the book income adjustment. In such cases, the District Director may, based upon all the facts and circumstances, determine the taxpayer's applicable financial statement. See paragraph (c)(6), Examples (13) and (14) of this section.

(ii) Applicable financial statement of a foreign corporation with a United States trade or business. (A) In general. The applicable financial statement of a foreign taxpayer conducting one or more trades or businesses in the United States is the financial statement prepared by any such trade or business (or attributable to more than one such trades or businesses) that has the highest priority as determined under paragraph (c)(3) of this section. See paragraph (c)(6), Example (15) of this section.

(B) Special rules for applicable financial statement of a trade or business of a foreign taxpayer. (1) Financial statement prepared under foreign generally accepted accounting principles. Subject to the rules of this section, a financial statement prepared by a United States trade or business using generally accepted accounting principles of a foreign country may be an applicable financial statement under this paragraph (c). See paragraph (c)(6), Example (16) of this section.

(2) Financial statement denominated in United States dollars. Except as provided in paragraph (c)(5)(ii)(D) of this section, the financial statement of a United States trade or business must be denominated in United States dollars in order to be considered the applicable financial statement of the foreign taxpayer under this paragraph (c). See paragraph (c)(6), Example (17) of this section.

(C) Special rule for statements of equal priority. If a foreign taxpayer has two or more financial statements of equal priority (determined under paragraphs (c)(3)(i) and (c)(3)(ii) of this section and this paragraph (c)(5)(ii)), the foreign taxpayer's applicable financial statement is determined under either paragraph (c)(5)(ii)(C)(1) or (2) of this section, whichever is applicable.

(1) Two or more financial statements reporting on the same trades or businesses. If two or more financial statements of equal priority report on the same United States trades or businesses, the applicable financial statement of the foreign taxpayer is determined under the rule of paragraph (c)(3)(iv) of this section. In applying this rule, adjusted net book income (as defined under paragraph (b)(6) of this section) shall be used. Thus, the financial statement that results in the greatest amount of adjusted net book income is the foreign taxpayer's applicable financial statement.

(2) Two or more financial statements reporting on different trades or businesses. If two or more financial statements of equal priority report on different United States trades or businesses, the foreign taxpayer's applicable financial statement is—

(i) The financial statement that reflects the greatest amount of gross receipts attributable to United States trades or businesses, or

(ii) If after applying the rules of paragraph (c)(5)(ii)(C)(2)(i) of this section, the foreign taxpayer still has financial statements of equal priority, the financial statement determined under the rules of paragraph (c)(3)(iv) of this section (using effectively connected adjusted net book income).

See paragraph (c)(6), Example (18) of this section.

(D) Anti-abuse rules. The special rules of this paragraph (c)(5)(ii) will not apply if a trade or business conducted in the United States by a foreign taxpayer modifies its financial reporting and the principal purpose of such action is to reduce the amount of the book income adjustment. In such cases, the District Director may, based upon all the facts and circumstances, determine the taxpayer's applicable financial statement. See paragraph (c)(6), Example (21), of this section.

(iii) Supplement or amendment to an applicable financial statement. (A) Excluding a restatement of net book income. An applicable financial statement includes any supplement or amendment thereto (excluding a restatement of net book income) for the taxable year that is prepared and used for a substantial non-tax purpose (within the meaning of paragraph (c)(4) of this section) prior to the date the taxpayer's Federal income tax return for the taxable year would be due if the time for filing were extended under section 6081. For example, a calendar year taxpayer's applicable financial statement includes any supplement or amendment prepared and used prior to September 15 of the year immediately following its taxable year. If a taxpayer files its Federal income tax return before the issuance of a supplement or amendment to the applicable financial statement and before the extended due date for filing under section 6081, the taxpayer must file an amended Federal income tax return reporting any additional tax that results from treating the supplement or amendment as part of the applicable financial statement. A supplement or amendment (excluding restatements of net book income) to an applicable financial statement after the date specified in section 6081 is disregarded for purposes of the book income adjustment.

(B) Restatement of net book income. If a taxpayer restates net book income in what otherwise would have been its applicable financial statement (its "original financial statement"), referred to in this section as a "restatement of net book income," prior to the date that the taxpayer's Federal income tax return for such taxable year would be due if the time for filing were extended under section 6081, then—

(1) If the financial statement that includes the restated net book income is of a higher priority than the original financial statement, the restated financial statement is the taxpayer's applicable financial statement.

(2) If the financial statement that includes the restated net book income is of equal priority to the original financial statement and—

(i) The restatement is attributable to an error (as described in Accounting Principles Board Opinion No. 20, paragraph 13), the restated financial statement is the taxpayer's applicable financial statement, or

(ii) The restatement is not attributable to an error, the original and restated financial statements will be considered of equal priority, and paragraph (c)(3)(iv) will apply. Thus, the taxpayer's applicable financial statement is the financial statement that results in the greatest amount of adjusted net book income.

See paragraph (d)(4)(iv) of this section for rules that apply to restatements occurring after the due date (including the extension under section 6081) of the return for the taxable year to which the applicable financial statement relates. See paragraph (c)(6), Examples (11) and (12) of this section.

(6) Examples. The provisions of this paragraph may be illustrated by the following examples.

Example (1). In 1987, Corporation A only has a financial statement described in paragraph (c)(1)(iv) of this section and elects to treat net book income as equal to its current earnings and profits. In 1988, A has a certified audited financial statement (as described in paragraph (c)(1)(ii) of this section). In 1989, A only has a statement described in paragraph (c)(1)(iv) of this section. In 1988, A's certified audited financial statement is its applicable financial statement. However, in 1989, A is bound by the election it made in 1987 (unless revoked with the consent of the District Director) and must treat net book income as equal to its current earnings and profits.

Example (2). Corporation B prepares two unaudited financial statements. Both statements are distributed to creditors and are used for substantial non-tax purposes. The first financial statement is accompanied by an auditor's review report while the second statement has no auditor's review report. B has no other financial statement. Pursuant to paragraph (c)(3)(iv)(B)(2) of this section, the financial statement accompanied by the auditor's review report is B's applicable financial statement.

Example (3). Assume the same facts as in Example (2), except the financial statement accompanied by an auditor's review report is distributed to shareholders while the other statement is distributed to creditors, and both statements are used for substantial non-tax purposes. Pursuant to paragraph (c)(3)(ii) of this section, B's applicable financial statement is the statement distributed to its creditors. Paragraph (c)(3)(iv)(B)(2) of this section does not apply because the two statements are not of equal priority after applying paragraphs (c)(3)(i) and (ii) of this section.

Example (4). Corporation C is a closely held corporation with two shareholders. Both shareholders participate in the business on a day-to-day basis and are aware of the financial status of the business. C prepares a financial statement that is used by C's two shareholders to calculate bonuses. The financial statement prepared by C is used for a substantial non-tax purpose.

Example (5). Corporation D prepares a financial statement that it only sends to banks with which D is neither currently doing business nor negotiating. D does not reasonably anticipate that the financial statement will be relied on by the banks for any non-tax purpose, and therefore, for purposes of computing net book income, the financial statement is not used for a substantial non-tax purpose. The result would be the same if D sent the statement to a bank whose only relationship to D is that it holds a mortgage on D's property and D's rights and obligations under the mortgage are not affected by changes in its financial condition. The result would also be the same if D sent the statement to a bank with which D is doing business, and the statement is not reasonably expected to come to the attention of the bank's employees who are responsible for D's account.

Example (6). Corporation E and its subsidiaries, F and G are a consolidated group. Certified audited financial statements are prepared by EF and by FG. Both statements are used for substantial non-tax purposes. Pursuant to paragraph (c)(5)(i)(A) of this section, the financial statement that is prepared by EF is the applicable financial statement of the consolidated group. However, pursuant to paragraph (d)(6)(i)(B) of this section, an adjustment will be required to include the adjusted net book income attributable to G. The result would be the same even if the financial statement prepared by FG is of higher priority (under the rules of paragraph (c)(3) of this section) than the statement prepared by E and F.

Example (7). Corporation H and its subsidiaries I, J and K are a consolidated group. Certified audited financial statements are prepared by H and I and by H, J and K. Both statements are used for substantial non-tax purposes. The financial statement prepared by H, J, and K includes the greater amount of gross receipts attributable to members of the consolidated group and thus, pursuant to paragraph (c)(5)(i)(B)(2)(i) of this section, it is the consolidated group's applicable financial statement.

Example (8). Corporation L and its subsidiary M are a consolidated group. Corporation L also owns 100 percent of N, a foreign corporation that is not part of the consolidated group. A certified audited financial statement prepared by L, M and N discloses gross receipts of $200, of which $150 is attributable to L and M, and a separate certified audited financial statement prepared by L and M discloses gross receipts of $150. Both statements are used for substantial non-tax purposes. Pursuant to paragraph (c)(5)(i)(B) of this section, the consolidated group's applicable financial statement is the statement prepared by L, M and N.

Example (9). Corporation O is 60 percent owned by corporation P and 40 percent owned by corporation Q. Both P and Q prepare financial statements that are required to be filed with the SEC reflecting their respective interests in O. O also separately prepares a certified audited financial statement, or uses a summary of its books and records for credit purposes. Under paragraph (c)(5)(i)(C), O's separate statement is its applicable financial statement.

Example (10). Assume the same facts as in Example (9) except that O does not prepare a separate financial statement or a summary of its books and records for credit purposes. Pursuant to paragraph (c)(5)(i)(C) of this section, O must treat its net book income as equal to its current earnings and profits.

Example (11). Corporation R uses a calendar year for both financial accounting and tax purposes. Initially, R issues its calendar year 1987 financial statement on March 1, 1988. R's adjusted net book income resulting from this statement is $80. This would be R's applicable financial statement for 1987, but for the restatement described in the next sentence. On September 1, 1988, R restates its 1987 financial statement to correct an error (as described in Accounting Principles Board Opinion No. 20, paragraph 13). The restated financial statement is of the same priority as the initial financial statement. The restatement results in adjusted net book income for calendar year 1987 of $50. Pursuant to paragraph (c)(5)(iii)(B)(2)(i) of this section, the restated financial statement is treated as R's 1987 applicable financial statement.

Example (12). Assume the same facts as in Example (11), except that R restates its financial statement in order to reflect a change in accounting method. Since the restatement does not result from an error, paragraph (c)(5)(iii)(B)(2)(i) of this section does not apply. Pursuant to paragraph (c)(5)(iii)(B)(2)(ii) of this section, R's 1987 applicable financial statement is the financial statement for 1987 that results in the greater amount of adjusted net book income. Thus, R's March 1, 1988 financial statement is treated as its 1987 applicable financial statement.

Example (13). Corporation S, which is not a member of an affiliated group, uses a calendar year for both financial accounting and tax purposes. S's 1987 applicable financial statement is a certified audited financial statement. On January 1, 1988, S transfers all of its assets subject to liabilities to T, a newly created subsidiary that is 100 percent owned by S. The principal purpose of the transfer is to use the special rules of paragraph (c)(5)(i) of this section to reduce the adjusted net book income of S. For calendar year 1988, T prepares and uses a certified audited financial statement. Since S's only asset is its investment in T, S does not prepare a financial statement for calendar year 1988. In addition, since S is only a holding company, T's 1988 certified audited financial statement reports the same net book income that would have been reported on a consolidated ST financial statement. If paragraph (c)(5)(i)(D) of this section does not apply, ST's 1988 applicable financial statement is the financial statement of S (the parent of the consolidated group) with the highest priority. Under paragraph (c)(1) of this section, since S does not have a financial statement in 1988, the net book income of the ST consolidated group is ordinarily deemed to equal the aggregate earnings and profits of the members of the consolidated group. However, given these facts, the District Director may determine that the 1988 certified audited financial statement of T is the 1988 applicable financial statement of the ST consolidated group.

Example (14). The facts are the same as in Example 13, except that S has owned 100 percent of T for several years prior to calendar year 1987. In addition, prior to 1987, ST prepared a consolidated certified audited financial statement. For calendar year 1987, ST does not prepare a consolidated certified audited financial statement. Instead, T prepares and uses a certified audited financial statement while S does not prepare a financial statement. The principal purpose of the change in financial reporting is to use the special rules of paragraph (c)(5)(i) of this section to reduce the adjusted net book income of the ST consolidated group. Given these facts, the District Director may determine that the 1987 certified audited financial statement of T is the 1987 applicable financial statement of the ST consolidated group.

Example (15). Corporation U is a foreign corporation incorporated in A. U is a calendar year taxpayer for both financial accounting and tax purposes. U actively conducts three real estate businesses, X, Y and Z, in the United States. In 1987, X prepares a certified audited financial statement that it provides to its United States creditor. In addition, in 1987, X, Y and Z each prepare unaudited financial statements that they provide to U for incorporation in U's worldwide financial statement. Under paragraph (c)(5)(ii)(A) of this section, U's applicable financial statement is the certified audited financial statement prepared by X. However, pursuant to paragraph (d)(7) of this section, an adjustment is required to include any of U's effectively connected net book income that is not included in X's certified audited financial statement (i.e., the effectively connected net book income attributable to Y and Z).

Example (16). Corporation A is a foreign corporation incorporated in Z. A is a calendar year taxpayer for both financial accounting and tax purposes. A actively conducts a real estate business, B, in the United States. B prepares a certified audited financial statement for 1987 using the accounting principles of Z that it provides to A for incorporation into A's worldwide financial statement. In addition, B prepares a review statement for 1987 using United States generally accepted accounting principles that it provides to its United States creditors. Both the certified statement and the review statement are denominated in United States dollars. Under paragraphs (c)(5)(ii)(A) and (c)(5)(ii)(B)(1) of this section, the financial statement prepared under the accounting principles of Z is the applicable financial statement.

Example (17). Assume the same facts as in Example (16) except that amounts are reported on B's certified audited financial statement in the currency of Z and amounts are reported on B's review statement in United States dollars. Since the review statement is denominated in United States dollars, under paragraph (c)(5)(ii)(B)(2) of this section, it is the applicable financial statement.

Example (18). Corporation C is a foreign corporation incorporated in Z. C is a calendar year taxpayer for both financial accounting and tax purposes. C actively conducts two real estate businesses, D and E, in the United States. D and E each separately prepare a certified audited financial statement for 1987 that they provide to their United States creditors. D's financial statement reports gross receipts of $100. E's financial statement reports gross receipts of $200. Under paragraph (c)(5)(ii)(C)(2) of this section, E's certified audited financial statement is the applicable financial statement and must be adjusted under the rules of paragraph (d)(7) of this section to include effectively connected book income attributable to D.

Example (19). F is a foreign corporation incorporated in X. F is a calendar year taxpayer for both financial accounting and tax purposes. F actively conducts a banking business, G, in the United States. G has been engaged in business in the United States since 1977. For the years 1977 through 1986, G did not prepare a separate financial statement. However, each year G provided F with its books, records and other raw financial data. F used this data in preparing its worldwide financial statement. G provides F with its 1987 books and records on January 5, 1988, in accordance with its historic practice. On February 15, 1988, G prepares an unaudited financial statement for calendar year 1987 that it provides to F. The principal purpose of creating this financial statement is to reduce net book income. Under these facts, the financial statement provided by G is not intended to be reasonably relied upon by F in preparing its worldwide financial statement. Therefore, for purposes of computing net book income, G's financial statement has not been used for a substantial non-tax purpose.

Example (20). Assume the same facts as in Example (19) except that for purposes of preparing F's 1987 worldwide financial statement, G does not provide F with any raw financial data, and G only provides F with an audited financial statement that is prepared for a substantial non-tax purpose. Under these facts, the financial statement provided by G is intended to be relied upon by F in preparing its worldwide financial statement. Therefore, for purposes of computing net book income, G's financial statement has been used for a substantial non-tax purpose.

Example (21). Corporation H is a foreign corporation incorporated in I. H is a calendar year taxpayer for both financial accounting and tax purposes. H actively conducts a real estate business, J, in the United States. For the years 1976 through 1986, J prepared a certified audited financial statement using United States dollars that it provided to H. In 1987, J prepares a certified audited financial statement using the currency of I. The principal purpose of the modification of J's financial reporting is to reduce the amount of the book income adjustment. Given these facts, the District Director may determine that J's 1987 certified audited financial statement prepared in the currency of I is J's applicable financial statement for 1987, and such statement must be converted into United States dollars based upon the translation used to prepare the certified audited financial statement in the currency of I. Accordingly, the effectively connected net book income of J for 1987 is the effectively connected net book income reported on the financial statement that has been converted into United States dollars.

(d) Adjustments to net book income. *(1) In general.* Adjusted net book income is computed by making the adjustments described in this paragraph (d) to net book income (as defined in paragraph (b)(2) of this section). No adjustment may be made to net book income except as provided in this paragraph (d).

(2) Definitions. (i) Historic practice. For purposes of this paragraph (d), historic practice is defined as an accounting practice that—

(A) Was used consistently by the taxpayer for each of the 2 years immediately preceding its first taxable year beginning after 1986, and

(B) Was used on the financial statement that would have been the taxpayer's applicable financial statement (as determined under paragraph (c) of this section) for each of the 2 years immediately preceding its first taxable year beginning after 1986 if section 56(f), as amended by the Tax Reform Act of 1986, had been in effect.

Thus, in order for a calendar year corporation to have an historic practice in 1987, the corporation must have used the accounting practice in its 1985 and 1986 financial statements. However, to be treated as used for purposes of this paragraph, an accounting practice must have been used prior to April 23, 1987. For example, an accounting practice that is first used after April 23, 1987, in a restatement of a taxpayer's 1985 and 1986 financial statements is not the taxpayer's historic practice.

(ii) Accounting literature. For purposes of this paragraph (d), the term "accounting literature" means—

(A) Generally accepted accounting principles (GAAP) as defined in the American Institute of Certified Public Accountants Professional Standards, AU § 411.05, paragraphs (a) through (c), and

(B) Pronouncements by the SEC including, but not limited to, Regulations S-X, SEC Financial Reporting Releases, and SEC Staff Accounting Bulletins, that are effective for the accounting period covered by the applicable financial statement.

(3) Adjustments for certain taxes. (i) In general. Net book income for purposes of this paragraph (d) must be adjusted to disregard (for example, by adding back) any Federal income taxes or income, war profits, or excess profits taxes imposed by any foreign country or possession of the United States that are directly or indirectly taken into account on the taxpayer's applicable financial statement. No adjustment is made for taxes not described in the preceding sentence. Taxes directly or indirectly taken into account consist of the taxpayer's total income tax expense that includes both current and deferred income tax expense. In addition, items of income and expense, including extraordinary items that are stated net of tax, must be adjusted to disregard the taxes described in this paragraph (d)(3)(i). See paragraph (d)(4)(vii) of this section for an adjustment for certain deferred foreign taxes.

(ii) Exception for certain foreign taxes. Net book income is not adjusted to disregard taxes imposed by a foreign country or possession of the United States if the taxpayer does not choose to take the benefits of section 901 (relating to the foreign tax credit) with respect to these taxes for the taxable year. The rule in the preceding sentence only applies to the amount of taxes the taxpayer deducts in the current taxable year under section 164(a). See paragraph (d)(3)(iv), Example (4) of this section. Net book income also is not adjusted to disregard foreign taxes that cannot be claimed as a credit (other than by virtue of a foreign tax credit limitation). Thus, a taxpayer does not add back to net book income any taxes it is not allowed to claim as a credit against its United States income tax liability because of section 245(a)(8), 901(j), 907(b) or 968 of the Code.

(iii) Certain valuation adjustments. Income tax expense under paragraph (d)(3)(i) of this section does not include valuation adjustments such as the valuation adjustments related to purchase accounting described in Accounting Principles Board (APB) Opinion No. 16, paragraph 89. However, income tax expense does include the tax associated with any gain or loss on the sale or other disposition of any asset the basis of which was adjusted under paragraph 89 of Opinion 16. See paragraph (d)(3)(iv), Example (6) of this section.

(iv) Examples. The provisions of this paragraph may be illustrated by the following examples:

Example (1). Corporation A has $120 of net book income. In calculating net book income, A has deducted $20 of state income tax expense and $60 of Federal income tax expense. Assuming there are no other adjustments to net book income, A's adjusted net book income is $180 ($120 of net book income + $60 of Federal income tax expense). Pursuant to paragraph (d)(3)(i) of this section, no adjustment is made for the state income tax expense.

Example (2). Assume the same facts as in Example (1), except that A also has a net extraordinary item of $40. Thus, A has net book income of $160 ($120 + $40). The $40 net extraordinary item is composed of a $70 gross extraordinary item less $30 of Federal income tax expense. Assuming there are no other adjustments to net book income, A's adjusted net book income is $250 ($160 of net book income + $60 of Federal income tax expense on book income other than the extraordinary item + $30 of Federal income tax expense on the extraordinary item).

Example (3). Assume the same facts as in Example (1), except that in calculating A's $120 of net book income, A has $50 of Federal income tax expense and $10 of foreign income tax expense. The $10 of foreign income tax expense results from a foreign branch and is composed of $7 of current foreign income tax expense and $3 of deferred foreign income tax expense. A chooses to take the benefits of the foreign tax credit under section 901 for the current taxable year. Assuming there are no other adjustments to net book income, A's adjusted net book income is $180 ($120 of net book income + $50 of Federal income tax expense + $10 of foreign income tax expense).

Example (4). Assume the same facts as in Example (3), except that A does not choose to take the benefits of the foreign tax credit in the current taxable year and instead deducts the $7 of current foreign income tax paid. Pursuant to paragraph (d)(3)(ii) of this section, net book income is not adjusted for the $7 of current foreign income tax expense. However, net book income is adjusted for the $3 of deferred foreign income tax expense. Thus, assuming there are no other adjustments to net book income, D's adjusted net book income is $173 ($120 of net book income + $50 of Federal income tax expense + $3 of deferred foreign income tax expenses).

Example (5). In 1987, corporation B only has a financial statement described in paragraph (c)(1)(iv) of this section. B elects pursuant to paragraph (c)(2) of this section to treat net book income as equal to its current earnings and profits. B's current earnings and profits in 1987 is $60, after reduction for $40 of Federal income tax (see paragraph (b)(5)(i) of this section). Pursuant to paragraph (d)(3) of this section, B must make a $40 adjustment to net book income. Thus, assuming no other adjustments to net book income, B's 1987 adjusted net book income is $100 ($60 of net book income + $40 adjustment for Federal income taxes).

Example (6). Corporation A acquires assets from corporation B in a transaction where the tax basis of B's assets will carry over to A. For financial accounting purposes, A will account for the acquisition in accordance with Accounting Principles Board (APB) Opinion No. 16. One of the assets acquired from B has an appraised value of $10,000. However, because the tax basis of B's assets will carry over to A, A's tax basis in the asset is only $7,000. Given these facts, APB Opinion No. 16, paragraph 89 requires that the asset be recorded at $10,000 less the tax effect of the difference between the appraised value and the tax basis. Assuming a 30 percent tax rate for A, the asset would be recorded at $9,100 ($10,000 appraised value − ($3,000 difference between the appraised value and the tax basis × 30 percent)). If A sells the asset for $10,000, A will recognize a book gain of $900 with respect to the sale (assuming the asset is not amortized for book purposes). However, A will also have income tax expense of $900 (($10,000 sales proceeds − $7,000 tax basis) × 30 percent) with respect to the sale. Thus, A will have no net book income from the sale. Pursuant to paragraph (d)(3)(iii) of this section, A's income tax expense includes the $900 of income tax expense attributable to the effects of the valuation adjustment made in accordance with APB Opinion No. 16, paragraph 89. As a result, A's adjusted net book income with respect to its asset sale is $900 ($0 of net book income + $900 adjustment for income tax expense).

(4) Adjustments to prevent omission or duplication. (i) In general. In order to prevent omissions or duplications, net book income must be adjusted for the items described in paragraph (d)(4)(ii) through (d)(4)(vii) of this section and for such other items as approved or required by the Commissioner in published guidance. Except as provided in this paragraph (d), a taxpayer may not adjust net book income to prevent omission or duplication of items. See paragraph (d)(4)(viii), Example (1) of this section.

(ii) Special rule for depreciating an asset below its cost. Net book income must be adjusted to exclude depreciation or amortization expense to the extent such expense exceeds the asset's financial accounting historical cost ("excess depreciation"). However, no adjustment is required if excess depreciation has been the taxpayer's historic practice (as defined in paragraph (d)(2)(i) of this section) or if the excess depreciation is properly attributable to negative salvage value (i.e., where the cost of removal or cleanup exceeds the salvage value).

(iii) Consolidated group using current earnings and profits. In the case of a consolidated group that uses its aggregate current earnings and profits as net book income (as determined under the rules of paragraph (b)(5)(ii) of this section), the current earnings and profits of the group is the aggregate of the current earnings and profits of each member of the group. In determining aggregate current earnings and profits, the adjustments described in § 1.1502-33 apply except for the adjustments for intercompany distributions with respect to stock and obligations or members of the group described in § 1.1502-33(c)(1) and the investment adjustment described in § 1.1502-33(c)(4)(ii)(a).

(iv) Restatement of a prior year's applicable financial statement. (A) In general. If a taxpayer restates an applicable financial statement and as a result, the net book income for a taxable year is restated after the last date that the taxpayer could have filed its Federal income tax return for such taxable year (if it had obtained an extension of time under section 6081 of the Code), net book income for the first successor year (as defined in paragraph (d)(4)(iv)(D) of this section) must be adjusted by that part of the cumulative effect of the restatement on net book income attributable to taxable years beginning after 1986. To the extent that the cumulative effect of the restatement on net book income includes a tax component, paragraph (d)(3) of this section may apply. See paragraph (c)(5)(iii) of this section for rules relating to the restatement of an applicable financial statement prior to the date the taxpayer's return for the taxable year would be due if the time for filing the return is extended.

(B) Reconciliation of owner's equity in applicable financial statements. If—

(1) The beginning balance of owner's equity on the taxpayer's applicable financial statement for the current taxable year is different than the ending balance of owner's equity on the taxpayer's applicable financial statement for the preceding taxable year, and

(2) The taxpayer is not otherwise subject to the restatement rules in paragraph (d)(4)(iv)(A) of this section, the taxpayer will be deemed to have restated its applicable financial statement for the preceding year and paragraph (d)(4)(iv)(A) of this section will apply.

(C) Use of different priority applicable financial statements in consecutive taxable years. If the priority of a taxpayer's applicable financial statement (as determined under the rules of paragraph (c)(3) of this section) for the current taxable year is different than the priority of the taxpayer's applicable financial statement for the preceding taxable year, the taxpayer shall be required to adjust net book income to the extent required under the rules of either paragraph (d)(4)(iv)(A) or (B) of this section.

(D) First successor year defined. The "first successor year" is the first taxable year for which the taxpayer could have timely filed a return if it had obtained an extension of time under section 6081 of the Code after the restatement occurs. For example, if a calendar year corporation restates and uses its 1987 applicable financial statement between September 16, 1988 and September 15, 1989, any adjustment resulting from the restatement will be made in the taxpayer's 1988 Federal income tax return. If the restatement occurs prior to September 15, 1988, the rules of paragraph (c)(5)(iii) of this section will apply.

(E) Exceptions. (1) No adjustment is made under paragraph (d)(4)(iv)(A) of this section for a restatement prepared in accordance with APB Opinion No. 16, paragraph 53, requiring restatements of financial statements to reflect the combined operation of corporations combined in a pooling transaction.

(2) In order to prevent duplication of an adjustment, an adjustment otherwise required under paragraph (d)(4)(iv)(A) of this section may be decreased to take into account an adjustment previously made under the disclosure rules described in paragraph (d)(5) of the section. See paragraph (d)(4)(viii), Example (3) of this section.

(v) Adjustment for items previously taxed as subpart F income. Net book income does not include any item excluded from regular taxable income under section 959 if the item was included in adjusted net book income in a prior taxable year under the provisions of paragraph (b)(2)(iv) of this section and due to section 951. A taxpayer may not adjust net book income under this paragraph (d)(4)(v) to the extent any portion of the subpart F income was recognized during taxable years beginning before 1987. See example (5) of paragraph (d)(4)(viii) of this section.

(vi) Adjustment for poolings of interests. In a business combination accounted for as a pooling of interests under paragraph 50 of APB Opinion 16, net book income does not include the income of a separate corporation for that part of the taxable year preceding the combination of that corporation with the taxpayer, to the extent the separate corporation included this income in its net book income for the taxable year preceding the business combination. A taxpayer may not adjust net book income under this paragraph (d)(4)(vi) to the extent the separate corporation's income is attributable to taxable years beginning before 1987.

(vii) Adjustment for certain deferred foreign taxes. In the case of deferred foreign taxes that were previously added back to net book income in accordance with paragraph (d)(3) of this section, a deduction is allowed in computing adjusted net book income for the taxable year in which the deferred foreign taxes are deducted under section 164(a). A taxpayer may not adjust net book income under this paragraph (d)(4)(vii) to the extent the foreign taxes were deferred during taxable years beginning before 1987.

(viii) Examples. The provisions of this paragraph may be illustrated by the following examples.

Example (1). Corporation A uses a calendar year for both financial accounting and tax purposes. In 1986, A's financial statement included a $100 financial accounting loss for a plant shutdown. A could not deduct the loss on its 1986 Federal income tax return. In 1987, A deducts the loss from the 1986 plant shutdown in its 1987 Federal income tax return. As a result, A's 1987 adjusted net book income exceeds its 1987 pre-adjustment alternative minimum taxable income by $100 (an amount equal to the deduction for the 1986 plant shutdown). Pursuant to paragraph (d)(4)(i) of this section, A cannot make an adjustment to net book income.

Example (2). Corporation B uses a calendar year for both financial accounting and tax purposes. B issues its calendar year 1987 applicable financial statement on March 1, 1988. The applicable financial statement reports net book income for the calendar years 1985 through 1987 of $50, $70, and $80, respectively. On March 1, 1989 when it issues its calendar year 1988 applicable financial statement, B restates its 1985, 1986 and 1987 applicable financial statements. The restatement results from a change in accounting method that is made during calendar year 1988. After restatement, B's net book income for 1985, 1986, and 1987 is $60, $80, and $90, respectively. Based upon these facts, the cumulative effect of the restatement on B's net book income for years prior to 1988 is $30. However, since $20 of the cumulative effective is attributable to years beginning before 1987, B's 1988 net book income is increased by only $10 ($30 – $20). If the cumulative effect includes a tax adjustment, see paragraph (d)(3) of this section

Example (3). Assume the same facts for Corporation B as in Example (2), except that B's 1987 net book income of $80 is increased by $10 for purposes of B's 1987 Federal income tax return. The $10 adjustment is made pursuant to paragraph (d)(5)(iii) of this section relating to disclosure in the accountant's opinion. Specifically, the accountant's opinion on B's 1987 applicable financial statement disclosed that if D had used a certain accounting method, B's 1987 net book income would have been $90 rather than $80. The restatement of B's 1987 applicable financial statement on March 1, 1989 results entirely from B changing to the accounting method referred to in the 1987 accountant's opinion. Pursuant to paragraph (d)(4)(iv)(E)(2) of this section, no adjustment is made to B's 1988 net book income as a result of the restatement of B's 1987 applicable financial statement.

Example (4). Assume the same facts as in Example (1), except that when A issues its 1987 applicable financial statement it also restates the net book income reported on its 1986 financial statement to exclude the $100 loss attributable to the plant shutdown. Furthermore, the $100 loss from the plant shutdown is included in A's 1987 net book income as reported on its 1987 applicable financial statement. Pursuant to paragraph (d)(4) of this section, no adjustment is made to A's 1987 net book income as a result of the restatement of A's 1986 net book income.

Example (5). Corporation D is a domestic corporation. D owns ten percent of the issued and outstanding stock of corporation F, a foreign corporation. D and F file separate financial statements and federal income tax returns, both on a calendar-year basis. F is a controlled foreign corporation as defined in section 957. In 1987, D includes ten percent of F's subpart F income in its income under section 951. F makes no actual distributions to D in that year, and D's applicable financial statement includes the earnings of F only when actual distributions are made. See paragraph (d)(6)(i)(A) of this section. In 1987, D must adjust its net book income under paragraph (b)(2)(iv) of this section to include ten percent of F's subpart F income. In 1988, F makes an actual distribution to D which qualifies for the exclusion of section 959. D includes this actual distribution as income on its applicable financial statement for 1987. Pursuant to paragraph (d)(4)(v) of this section, D must adjust its net book income for 1988 to exclude the actual distribution from F.

(5) Adjustments resulting from disclosure. (i) Adjustment for footnote disclosure or other supplementary information. (A) In general. Except as described in this paragraph (d)(5)(i), net book income must be increased by any amount disclosed in a footnote or other supplementary information to the applicable financial statement if the disclosure supports a calculation of a net book income amount that would be greater than the net book income reported on the taxpayer's applicable financial statement. However, net book income will not be increased if the disclosure—

(1) Is specifically authorized by the accounting literature described in paragraph (d)(2)(ii) of this section, or

(2) Is in accordance with the taxpayer's historic practice as defined in paragraph (d)(2)(i) of this section.

See paragraph (d)(5)(v), Examples (1) and (2) of this section.

(B) Disclosures not specifically authorized in the accounting literature. The following footnote or other supplementary disclosure will not be considered specifically authorized in the accounting literature—

(1) Disclosure of what the taxpayer's net book income would have if GAAP had been used in preparing the applicable financial statement instead of tax accounting rules (or disclosure of the adjustment necessary to determine net book income on a GAAP basis), and

(2) Disclosure of what the taxpayer's net book income would have been if the accrual method had been used in preparing the applicable financial statement instead of the cash method (or disclosure of the adjustment necessary to determine net book income on the accrual method).

(ii) Equity adjustments. (A) In general. Except as described in this paragraph (d)(5)(ii), net book income must be increased by the amount of any equity adjustment (as defined in paragraph (d)(5)(ii)(B) of this section) included in the applicable financial statement if the equity adjustment increases owner's equity as reported on the taxpayer's applicable financial statement and the increase is attributable to the taxpayer or a member of the taxpayer's consolidated group. However, net book income will not be increased if the equity adjustment—

(1) Is specifically authorized by the accounting literature described in paragraph (d)(2)(ii) of this section, or

(2) Is in accordance with the taxpayer's historic practice as defined in paragraph (d)(2)(i) of this section.

See paragraph (d)(5)(v), Examples (3) and (4) of this section.

(B) Definition of equity adjustment. An equity adjustment is any reconciling item between beginning and ending owner's equity as reported on the taxpayer's applicable financial statement for the current taxable year. However, if properly accounted for, the following reconciling items are not considered equity adjustments and do not require adjustment under paragraph (d)(5)(ii)(A) of this section—

(1) Net book income,

(2) Non-liquidating dividend distributions, and

(3) Contributions to capital.

(iii) Amounts disclosed in an accountant's opinion. Net book income must be increased by the amount of any item disclosed in the accountant's opinion (as described in paragraphs (c)(1)(ii)(C) and (c)(1)(ii)(D) of this section) if the disclosure supports a calculation of a net book income amount that would be greater than the net book income reported on the taxpayer's applicable financial statement. However, net book income will not be increased if the disclosure is in accordance with the taxpayer's historic practice, as defined in paragraph (d)(2)(i) of this section.

(iv) Accounting method changes that result in cumulative adjustments to the current year's applicable financial statement. (A) In general. If net book income for the current taxable year includes a cumulative adjustment attributable to an accounting method change and the amount of the cumulative adjustment may be determined upon review of the applicable financial statement (including footnotes) or other supplementary disclosure, net book income for the current taxable year shall be adjusted to exclude that portion of the cumulative adjustment attributable to taxable years beginning before 1987. To the extent the cumulative adjustment is reported net of a tax, paragraph (d)(3) of this section may apply. See paragraph (d)(5)(V), Example (5) of this section. If an accounting method change results in a restatement of an applicable financial statement, paragraphs (c)(5)(iii) or (d)(4)(iv)(A) of this section may apply.

(B) Exception. In order to prevent duplication of an adjustment, the adjustment required under paragraph (d)(5)(iv)(A) of this section may be decreased to take into account any adjustment for the accounting method change previously made under the rules described in paragraph (d)(5) of this section (relating to adjustments resulting from disclosure).

(v) Examples. The provisions of this paragraph may be illustrated by the following examples.

Example (1). Corporation A uses a calendar year for both financial accounting and tax purposes. For calendar years 1984 through 1986, A used the cash method of accounting on its financial statement and disclosed in a footnote the net income or loss that would have resulted if the accrual method of accounting had been used. A's 1987 net book income, as reported on its 1987 applicable financial statement, is $100 and is calculated on the cash method of accounting. In addition, a footnote in A's 1987 applicable financial statement states that A's 1987 net book income would have been $30 greater had the accrual method of accounting been used. Pursuant to paragraph (d)(5)(i)(B)(2) of this section, A's 1987 footnote disclosure is not considered specifically authorized by the accounting literature. However, since A made such disclosure for calendar years 1985 and 1986, the 1987 disclosure is in accordance with A's historic practice, as defined in paragraph (d)(2)(i) of this section. Since A satisfies the exception described in paragraph (d)(5)(i)(A)(2) of this section, no adjustment is made to A's 1987 net book income for the footnote disclosure.

Example (2). Assume the same facts for corporation B as in Example (1), except that B's 1985 and 1986 financial statements did not disclose the amount of income or loss that would result if the accrual method of accounting (rather than the cash method of accounting) were used. Since B does not satisfy either of the exceptions described in paragraph (d)(5)(i)(A) of this section, B's 1987 adjusted net book income is $130 ($100 of net book income plus $30 adjustment for footnote disclosure).

Example (3). Corporation C uses a calendar year for both financial accounting and tax purposes. C's 1987 net book income, as reported on its 1987 applicable financial statement, is $200. However, as specifically authorized in FASB Statement of Standards No. 52, C's 1987 applicable financial statement also includes a $50 equity adjustment (as defined in paragraph (d)(5)(ii)(B) of this section) for foreign currency translation gains. Since the equity adjustment is specifically authorized in the accounting literature, C satisfies the exception described in paragraph (d)(5)(ii)(A)(1) of this section, and no adjustment is made to C's 1987 net book income for the $50 equity adjustment.

Example (4). Assume the same facts for corporation D as in Example (3), except that D's equity adjustment is for foreign currency transaction gains instead of foreign currency translation gains. Pursuant to FASB Statement of Financial Accounting Standards No. 52, foreign currency transaction gains (as compared with foreign currency translation gains) are included in the income statement rather than in equity. In addition, in 1985 and 1986, D included foreign currency transaction gains in its income statement. Since D does not satisfy either of the exceptions described in paragraph (d)(5)(ii)(A) of this section, D's 1987 adjusted net book income is $250 ($200 of net book income plus $50 equity adjustment).

Example (5). Corporation E uses a calendar year for both financial accounting and tax purposes. E's net book income for 1988 is $100. The $100 of net book income includes $30 of financial accounting loss attributable to a cumulative adjustment as of January 1, 1988, resulting from a change in E's accounting method. The $30 cumulative loss is disclosed in E's 1988 applicable financial statement. If E had made the accounting method change in calendar year 1987, the cumulative loss as of January 1, 1987 would have been $20. Based upon the above facts, E must increase net book income by $20 to disregard that portion of the cumulative adjustment attributable to years beginning before 1987. Thus, assuming no other adjustments to net book income, E's adjusted net book income for 1988 is $120 ($100 plus $20).

(6). Adjustments applicable to related corporations. (i) Consolidated returns. (A) In general. Pursuant to paragraphs (a)(3) and (b)(3) of this section, the book income adjustment with respect to a consolidated group (as described under paragraph (a)(3) of this section) is computed based on the consolidated adjusted net book income (as defined in paragraph (b)(3)(i) of this section). In the case of any corporation that is not included in the consolidated group, consolidated adjusted net book income of the consolidated group shall include only the sum of the dividends received from such other corporation and other amounts includible in gross income under this chapter with respect to the earnings of such other corporation. See paragraph (d)(6)(v), Example (4) of this section.

(B) Corporations included in the consolidated Federal income tax return but excluded from the applicable financial statement. (1) In general. Consolidated net book income reported on the applicable financial statement (as determined under paragraph (c)(5) of this section) shall be adjusted to include net book income attributable to a corporation that is included in the consolidated group but is not included in the applicable financial statement. Net book income for the corporation not included in the applicable financial statement of the consolidated group is the net book income reported on such corporation's applicable financial statement (determined under the rules of paragraph (c) of this section and adjusted under the rules of this paragraph (d)). The adjusted net book income of such corporation must be consolidated with the adjusted net book income of other members of the consolidated group and appropriate adjustments, including consolidating elimination entries, must be made.

(2) Adjustments to net book income for minority interests. Consolidated net book income must be adjusted to include income or loss allocated to minority interests in members of the consolidated group. Failure to include income or loss allocated to minority interests shall be treated as an omission of net book income. See paragraph (d)(6)(v), Example (1) of this section.

(3) Corporations included in the consolidated group that are accounted for under the equity method of accounting. No adjustment is required to consolidated net book income for income or loss of a member of the consolidated group that is reported in the applicable financial statement under the equity method of accounting (as described in APB Opinion No. 18, paragraph (6)). However, consolidated adjusted net book income (as defined in paragraph (b)(3)(i) of this section) must include 100 percent of the net book income attributable to such member. See paragraph (d)(6)(i)(B)(2) of this section. For example, if consolidated net book income (as defined in paragraph (b)(3)(ii) of this section) only includes 85 percent of the equity income attributable to a member of the consolidated group, an adjustment will be required to include the 15 percent of equity income excluded from consolidated net book income. In addition, to the extent the equity income reflects an adjustment for tax expense or benefit, paragraph (d)(3) may apply. See paragraph (d)(6)(v), Examples (2) and (3) of this section.

(C) Corporations included in the applicable financial statement but excluded from the consolidated tax return. Net book income or consolidated net book income must be adjusted to eliminate the income or loss of a corporation that is included in the applicable financial statement, but is not included in the consolidated group. When net book income attributable to a corporation that is not a member of the consolidated group is removed from the computation of net book income in the applicable financial statement, consolidating elimination entries attributable to the excluded member must also be removed.

(ii) Adjustment under the principles of section 482. In order to fairly allocate items relating to intercompany transactions between corporations that are owned or controlled directly or indirectly by the same interests but are not members of a consolidated group, adjustments must be made to the net book income reported on the applicable financial statement of each corporation under the principles of section 482 and the regulations thereunder (relating to allocation of income and deductions among related taxpayers). For example, assume corporation A owns 100 percent of F, a foreign subsidiary, but A and F are not members of a consolidated group. However, A and F prepare a consolidated financial statement. In adjusting A's applicable financial statement to eliminate the net book income attributable to F, A must apply the principles of section 482. If a corporation fails to make appropriate adjustments to its applicable financial statement under the rules of this paragraph (d)(6)(ii), the District Director may make such adjustments under the principles of section 482 and the regulations thereunder.

(iii) Adjustment for dividends received from section 936 corporations. (A) In general. Any dividend received from a corporation eligible for the credit provided by section 936 (relating to the possession tax credit) shall be included in adjusted net book income. For example, assume corporation A owns 100 percent of B, a section 936 corporation, and B pays a $100 dividend to A. Furthermore, assume that of the $100 dividend, $15 of withholding tax is paid to a possession of the United States, so that A only receives $85 from the dividend. Given these facts, A's adjusted net book income includes $100 with respect to the dividend from B.

(B) Treatment as foreign taxes. Fifty percent of any withholding tax paid to a possession of the United States with respect to dividends referred to in paragraph (d)(6)(iii)(A) of this section may be treated for purposes of the alternative minimum foreign tax credit as a tax paid to a foreign country by the corporation receiving the dividend. However, if the aggregate of these dividends exceeds the excess referred to in paragraph (a)(1) of this section, the amount treated as a tax paid to the foreign country shall not exceed 50 percent of the aggregate amount of the tax withheld multiplied by a fraction.

(1) The numerator of which is the excess referred to in paragraph (a)(1) of this section; and

(2) The denominator numerator of which is the aggregate amount of these dividends.

(C) Treatment of taxes imposed on section 936 corporations. Taxes paid by any corporation eligible for the credit provided under section 936 shall be treated as a withholding tax paid with respect to any dividend paid by such corporation, and thus subject to the rules of this paragraph (d)(6)(iii), but only to the extent such taxes would be treated as paid by the corporation receiving the dividend under rules similar to the rules of section 902.

(iv) Adjustment to net book income on sale of certain investments. If a taxpayer accounts for an investment under any method equivalent to the equity method of accounting (as described in APB Opinion No. 18, paragraph 6) and pursuant to paragraphs (b)(2)(iv) or (d)(6)(i) of this section the taxpayer excludes net book income attributable to that investment, the taxpayer must adjust its net book income in the year the investment is sold (or partially sold). The adjustment equals the amount of net book income previously excluded under paragraphs (b)(2)(iv) or (d)(6)(i)(A) of this section). See paragraph (d)(6)(v), Example (4) of this section.

(v) Examples. The provisions of this paragraph may be illustrated by the following examples.

Example (1). Corporation A and its 100 percent owned subsidiary B and its 90 percent owned subsidiary C are a consolidated group. A also owns 100 percent of D, a foreign corporation. ABC's applicable financial statement is a certified audited financial statement that includes A, B, C and D. The net book income reported on the statement excludes $10 of C's net book income that is attributable to the 10 percent minority interest in C held outside of the consolidated group. Pursuant to paragraph (d)(6)(i)(B)(2) of this section, net book income of the consolidated group must be adjusted to include the $10 of net book income attributable to the minority interest in C. In addition, pursuant to paragraph (d)(6)(i)(C) of this section, net book income shown on the applicable financial statement must be adjusted to eliminate the net book income attributable to D.

Example (2). Corporation E owns 100 percent of F, a finance subsidiary, and EF are a consolidated group. Since F is a finance subsidiary E's applicable financial statement accounts for F under the equity method of accounting. F also prepares a separate financial statement that is of equal or higher priority than E's applicable financial statement. In 1987, E's applicable financial statement includes $60 of equity income from F. The $60 of equity income reflects a reduction for $40 of Federal income tax expense. Thus, E's equity income from F prior to the reduction for Federal income tax expense, is $100 ($60 + $40). Since E's applicable financial statement includes E's equity income in F, F's separate financial statement is not relevant for determining the adjusted net book income of the EF consolidated group. However, pursuant to paragraphs (d)(3) and (d)(6)(i)(B)(3) of this section, E is required to adjust its equity income in F by the $40 of Federal income tax expense attributable to F. Thus, assuming there are no other adjustments, E's adjusted net book income with respect to F is $100.

Example (3). The facts are the same as Example (2), except that E reports its equity income in F without reduction for F's Federal income tax expense. The $40 of Federal income tax expense attributable to F is combined with E's Federal income tax expense. Assuming no other adjustments, E's adjusted net book income with respect to F is $100. Thus, E's adjusted net book income with respect to F will be the same regardless of whether E's equity income in F is reported before or after taxes.

Example (4). A, a domestic corporation, uses a calendar year for both financial accounting and tax purposes. On January 1, 1987, A purchases 100 percent of F, a foreign corporation, for $100. F does not file a Federal income tax return and A does not recognize any taxable income with respect to F under section 951 (relating to controlled foreign corporations). In its applicable financial statement, A accounts for its investment in F under the equity method of accounting. Thus, A's initial investment in F is $100. During calendar year 1987, F has $50 of net book income but makes no dividend payments to A. Under the equity method of accounting, A's net book income includes the $50 of net book income attributable to A's net book investment in F. Thus, A's investment in F is increased to $150. Pursuant to paragraph (d)(6)(i)(C) of this section, A's net book income is adjusted to eliminate the $50 of net book income attributable to F. On January 1, 1988, A sells F for $150. Since A's investment in F under the equity method of accounting is $150, A's net book income for 1988 will not include any gain on the sale of F. However, pursuant to paragraph (d)(6)(iv), A's 1988 net book income must be increased by $50, the amount of net book income previously eliminated with respect to A's investment in F. The result would be the same if instead of accounting for its investment in F under the equity method of accounting, A and F prepare a consolidated financial statement.

(7) Adjustments for foreign taxpayers with a United States trade or business. (i) In general. Pursuant to paragraph (b)(6) of this section, the book income adjustment with respect to a foreign taxpayer with a United States trade or business is computed based on the effectively connected net book income of the foreign taxpayer (as defined in paragraph (b)(6)(ii) of this section). The net book income amount reported on the applicable financial statement of the foreign taxpayer (as determined under paragraph (c)(5)(ii) of this section) must be adjusted to—

(A) Include effectively connected net book income attributable to a trade or business conducted in the United States by the foreign taxpayer that is not reported on the applicable financial statement. Such amounts shall be determined from a financial statement (determined under paragraph (c) of this section and adjusted under the rules of this paragraph (d)) that would have qualified as an applicable financial statement of such excluded trade or business or upon effectively connected earnings and profits (if the rules of section (b)(6)(iii) of this section apply), and

(B) Exclude any amount reported on such applicable financial statement that does not qualify as effectively connected net book income.

See the example in paragraph (d)(7)(ii) of this section.

(ii) Example. The provisions of this paragraph may be illustrated by the following example.

Example. Foreign corporation A, a calendar year taxpayer for financial accounting and tax purposes, is incorporated in X. A actively conducts two real estate businesses, B and C, in the United States. B prepares a certified audited financial statement that it provides to its United States creditor. C does not prepare a financial statement. The certified audited financial statement prepared by B is treated as A's applicable financial statement under paragraph (c)(5)(ii) of this section. B's certified audited financial statement, in addition to amounts related to the conduct of its real estate business, also reports income received from its investment in United States securities, unrelated to its conduct of business in the United States that does not qualify as effectively connected net book income. In order to determine A's effectively connected net book income from the net book income reported on the applicable financial statement, such statement must be adjusted to exclude amounts attributable to the securities. In addition, book income or loss attributable to C, to the extent effectively connected to its business in the United States, must be included in the effectively connected net book income reported on B's financial statement. Since C does not have a financial statement, C's effectively connected net book income is determined by computing its effectively connected earnings and profits under paragraph (b)(6)(iii) of this section.

(8) Adjustment for corporations subject to subchapter F. A corporation subject to tax under subchapter F of chapter 1 of the Code shall adjust its book income to exclude all items of income, loss or expense other than those relating to the calculation of unrelated business taxable income for purposes of section 512(a).

(e) Special rules. *(1) Cooperatives.* For purposes of computing the book income adjustment, net book income of a cooperative to which section 1381 applies is reduced by patronage dividends and per-unit retain allocations under section 1382(b) that are paid by the cooperative to the extent such amounts are deductible for regular income tax and general alternative minimum tax purposes under section 1382, and not otherwise taken into account in determining adjusted net book income.

(2) Alaska Native Corporations. In computing the net book income of an Alaska Native Corporation, cost recovery and depletion are computed using the asset basis determined under section 21(c) of the Alaska Native Claims Settlement Act (43 U.S.C. 1620(c)). In addition, net book income is reduced by expenses payable under either section 7(i) or section 7(j) of the Alaska Native Claims Settlement Act (43 U.S.C. 1606(i) and (j)) only when deductions for such expenses are allowed for tax purposes.

(3) Insurance companies. In the case of an insurance company whose applicable financial statement is a statement describing in paragraph (c)(1)(iii) of this section (relating to statements provided to a government regulator), net book income for purposes of the book income adjustment is the net income or loss from operations, after reduction for dividends paid to policyholders, but without reduction for Federal income taxes.

(4) Estimating the book income adjustment for purposes of the estimated tax liability. See § 1.6655-7, as contained in 26 CFR part 1 revised as of April 1, 2007, for special rules for estimating the corporate alternative minimum tax book income adjustment under the annualization exception.

(5) Effective/applicability date. Paragraph (e)(4) of this section is applicable for taxable years beginning after September 6, 2007.

T.D. 8138, 4/23/87, amend T.D. 8197, 4/27/88, T.D. 8307, 8/16/90, T.D. 9347, 8/6/2007.

§ 1.56(g)-0 Table of contents.

This section lists the paragraphs contained in § 1.56(g)-1.

§ 1.56(g)-1 Adjusted current earnings.

(a) Adjustment for adjusted current earnings.

(1) Positive adjustment.

(2) Negative adjustment.

(i) In general.

(ii) Limitation on negative adjustments.

(iii) Example.

(3) Negative amounts.

(4) Taxpayers subject to adjustment for adjusted current earnings.

(5) General rule for applying Internal Revenue Code provisions in determining adjusted current earnings.

(i) In general.

(ii) Example.

(6) Definitions.

(i) Pre-adjustment alternative minimum taxable income.

(ii) Adjusted current earnings.

(iii) Earnings and profits.

(7) Application to foreign corporations.

(b) Depreciation allowed.

(1) Property placed in service after 1989.

(2) Property subject to new ACRS.

(i) In general.

(ii) Rules for computing the depreciation deduction.

(iii) Example.

(3) Property subject to original ACRS.
(i) In general.
(ii) Rules for computing the depreciation deduction.
(iii) Example.
(4) Special rule for certain section 168(f) property.
(5) Certain property not subject to ACRS.
(c) Inclusion in adjusted current earnings of items included in earnings and profits.
(1) In general.
(2) Certain amounts not taken into account in determining whether an item is permanently excluded.
(3) Allowance of offsetting deductions.
(4) Special rules.
(i) Income from the discharge of indebtedness.
(ii) Federal income tax refunds.
(iii) Income earned on behalf of states and municipalities.
(5) Treatment of life insurance contracts.
(i) In general.
(ii) Inclusion of inside buildup.
(iii) Calculation of income on the contract.
(iv) Treatment of distributions under the life insurance contract.
(v) Treatment of death benefits.
(vi) Other rules.
(A) Term life insurance contracts without net surrender values.
(B) Life insurance contracts involving divided ownership.
(vii) Examples.
(6) Partial list of income items excluded from gross income but included in earnings and profits.
(7) Partial list of items excluded from both pre-adjustment alternative minimum taxable income and adjusted current earnings.
(d) Disallowance of items not deductible in computing earnings and profits.
(1) In general.
(2) Deductions for certain dividends received.
(i) Certain amounts deducted under sections 243 and 245.
(ii) Special rules.
(A) Dividends received from a foreign sales corporation.
(B) Dividends received from a section 936 corporation.
(iii) Special rule for certain dividends received by certain cooperatives.
(3) Partial list of items not deductible in computing earnings and profits.
(4) Partial list of items deductible for purposes of computing both pre-adjustment alternative minimum taxable income and adjusted current earnings.
(e) Treatment of income items included, and deduction items not allowed, in computing pre-adjustment alternative minimum taxable income.
(f) Certain other earnings and profits adjustments.
(1) Intangible drilling costs.
(2) Certain amortization provisions do not apply.
(3) LIFO recapture adjustment.
(i) In general.
(ii) Beginning LIFO and FIFO inventory.
(iii) Definitions.
(A) LIFO recapture amount.
(1) Definition.
(2) Assets included.
(B) FIFO method.
(C) LIFO method.
(D) Inventory amounts.
(iv) Exchanges under sections 351 and 721.
(v) Examples.
(vi) Effective date.
(4) Installment sales.
(i) In general.
(ii) Exception for prior dispositions.
(iii) Special rules for obligations to which section 453A applies.
(A) In general.
(B) Limitation on application of installment method.
(C) Treatment of the ineligible portion.
(D) Treatment of the eligible portion.
(E) Coordination with the pledge rule.
(F) Example.
(g) Disallowance of loss on exchange of debt pools. [Reserved].
(h) Policy acquisition expenses of life insurance companies.
(1) In general.
(2) Reasonably estimated life.
(3) Reasonable allowance for amortization.
(4) Safe harbor for public financial statements.
(i) [Reserved].
(j) Depletion.
(k) Treatment of certain ownership changes.
(1) In general.
(2) Definition of ownership change.
(3) Determination of net unrealized built-in loss immediately before an ownership change.
(4) Example.
(l) [Reserved].
(m) Adjusted current earnings of a foreign corporation.
(1) In general.
(2) Definitions.
(i) Effectively connected pre-adjustment alternative minimum taxable income.
(ii) Effectively connected adjusted current earnings.
(3) Rules to determine effectively connected pre-adjustment alternative minimum taxable income and effectively connected adjusted current earnings.
(4) Certain exempt amounts.
(n) Adjustment for adjusted current earnings of consolidated groups.
(1) Positive adjustments.
(2) Negative adjustments.
(i) In general.
(ii) Limitation on negative adjustments.
(3) Definitions.

(i) Consolidated pre-adjustment alternative minimum taxable income.

(ii) Consolidated adjusted current earnings.

(4) Example.

(o) [Reserved].

(p) Effective dates for corporate partners in partnerships.

(1) In general.

(2) Application of effective dates.

(3) Example.

(q) Treatment of distributions of property to shareholders.

(1) In general.

(2) Examples.

(r) Elections to use simplified inventory methods to compute alternative minimum tax.

(1) In general.

(2) Effect of election.

(i) Inventories.

(ii) Modifications required.

(A) In general.

(B) Negative modifications allowed.

(iii) LIFO recapture adjustment.

(3) Time and manner of making election.

(i) Prospective election.

(ii) Retroactive election.

(iii) Taxpayers under examination.

(A) In general.

(1) Year of change under examination.

(2) Other open years under examination.

(B) Statement required.

(C) Year of change.

(D) Treatment of additional tax liability.

(iv) Election as method of accounting.

(v) Untimely election to use simplified inventory method.

(4) Example.

(5) Election to use alternative minimum tax inventories to compute adjusted current earnings.

(s) Adjustment for alternative tax energy preference deduction.

(1) In general.

(2) Example.

T.D. 8340, 3/14/91, amend T.D. 8454, 12/18/92.

§ 1.56(g)-1 Adjusted current earnings.

Caution: The Treasury has not yet amended Reg § 1.56(g)-1 to reflect changes made by P.L. 108-357, P.L. 107-147, P.L. 104-188, P.L. 103-66.

(a) Adjustment for adjusted current earnings. *(1) Positive adjustment.* For taxable years beginning after December 31, 1989, the alternative minimum taxable income of any taxpayer described in paragraph (a)(4) of this section is increased by the adjustment for adjusted current earnings. The adjustment for adjusted current earnings is 75 percent of the excess, if any, of—

(i) The adjusted current earnings (as defined in paragraph (a) (6)(ii) of this section) of the taxpayer for the taxable year over.

(ii) The pre-adjustment alternative minimum taxable income (as defined in paragraph (a)(6)(i) of this section) of the taxpayer for the taxable year.

(2) Negative adjustment. (i) In general. For taxable years beginning after December 31, 1989, the alternative minimum taxable income of any taxpayer is decreased, subject to the limitation of paragraph (a)(2)(ii) of this section, by 75 percent of the excess, if any, of pre-adjustment alternative minimum taxable income (as defined in paragraph (a)(6)(i) of this section), over adjusted current earnings (as defined in paragraph (a)(6)(ii) of this section).

(ii) Limitation on negative adjustments. The amount of the negative adjustment for any taxable year is limited to the excess, if any, of—

(A) The aggregate increases in alternative minimum taxable income in prior years under paragraph (a)(1) of this section over

(B) The aggregate decreases in alternative minimum taxable income in prior years under this paragraph (a)(2).

Any excess of pre-adjustment alternative minimum taxable income over adjusted current earnings that is not allowed as a negative adjustment for the taxable year because of the limitation in this paragraph (a)(2)(ii) is not applied to reduce any positive adjustment in any other taxable year.

(iii) Example. The following, example illustrates the provisions of this paragraph (a)(2):

(A) Corporation P is a calendar-year taxpayer and has pre-adjustment alternative minimum taxable income and adjusted current earnings in the following amounts for 1990 through 1993:

Year	Preadjustment alternative minimum taxable income	Adjusted current earnings
1990	$800,000	$700,000
1991	600,000	900,000
1992	500,000	400,000
1993	500,000	100,000

(B) Under these facts, corporation P has the following positive and negative adjustments for adjusted current earnings:

Year	Negative adjustment	Positive adjustment
1990	0	0
1991	0	$225,000
1992	75,000	0
1993	150,000	0

(C) In 1990, P has a potential negative adjustment (before the cumulative limitation) of $75,000 (75 percent of the $100,000 excess of pre-adjustment alternative minimum taxable income over adjusted current earnings). Nonetheless, P is not permitted a negative adjustment because P had no prior increases in its alternative minimum taxable income due to an adjustment for adjusted current earnings.

(D) In 1991, P has a positive adjustment of $225,000 (75 percent of the $300,000 excess of adjusted current earnings over pre-adjustment alternative minimum taxable income). P is not allowed to use the prior year's excess of pre-adjustment alternative minimum taxable income over adjusted current earnings to reduce its 1991 positive adjustment.

(E) In 1992, P is permitted a negative adjustment of $75,000, the full amount of 75 percent of the $100,000 excess of pre-adjustment alternative minimum taxable income over adjusted current earnings for the taxable year. This is because P's prior cumulative increases in alternative minimum taxable income due to the positive adjustments for adjusted current earnings exceed the negative adjustment for the year.

(F) In 1993, P has a potential negative adjustment (before the cumulative limitation) of $300,000 (75 percent of the $400,000 excess of pre-adjustment alternative minimum taxable income over adjusted current earnings). P's net cumulative increases in alternative minimum taxable income due to the adjustment for adjusted current earnings are $150,000 ($225,000 increase in 1991, less $75,000 decrease in 1992). Thus, P's negative adjustment in 1993 is limited to $150,000 P may not use the remaining portion ($150,000) of the negative adjustment for 1993 to reduce positive adjustments in other taxable years.

(3) Negative amounts. In determining whether an excess exists under paragraph (a)(1) or (a)(2) of this section, a positive amount exceeds a negative amount by the sum of the absolute numbers, and a smaller negative amount exceeds a larger negative amount by the difference between the absolute numbers. Thus, for example, a positive amount of adjusted current earnings of $30 exceeds a negative amount (or loss) of pre-adjustment AMTI of $10 by the sum of the absolute numbers, or $40 (30 + 10). Accordingly, the adjustment for adjusted current earnings would be 75 percent of $40, or $30. In contrast, a negative amount of adjusted current earnings of $10 exceeds a negative amount (or loss) of pre-adjustment alternative minimum taxable income of $30 by the difference between the absolute numbers, or $20 (30 – 10). Accordingly, the adjustment for adjusted current earnings would be 75 percent of $20, or $15.

(4) Taxpayers subject to adjustment for adjusted current earnings. The adjustment for adjusted current earnings applies to any corporation other than—

(i) An S corporation as defined in section 1361,

(ii) A regulated investment company as defined in section 851,

(iii) A real estate investment trust as defined in section 856, or

(iv) A real estate mortgage investment conduit as defined in section 860A.

(5) General rule for applying Internal Revenue Code provisions in determining adjusted current earnings. (i) In general. Except as otherwise provided by regulations or other guidance issued by the Internal Revenue Service, all Internal Revenue Code provisions that apply in determining the regular taxable income of a taxpayer also apply in determining adjusted current earnings. For example, the rules of part V of subchapter P (relating to original issue discount and similar matters) of the Code apply in determining the amount (and the timing) of any interest income included in adjusted current earnings under this section. In applying Code provisions, however, the adjustments of section 56(g) and this section are also taken into account. For example, in applying the capitalization provisions of section 263A, the amount of depreciation to be capitalized is based on the amount of depreciation allowed in computing adjusted current earnings.

(ii) Example. The following example illustrates the provisions of this paragraph (a)(5):

(A) Corporation N is a calendar year manufacturer of golf clubs. N places new manufacturing equipment in service in 1990. The regular tax depreciation allowable for this equipment is $80,000; the pre-adjustment alternative minimum taxable income depreciation is $60,000; and the adjusted current earnings depreciation is $40,000. All of the golf clubs N produces in 1990 are unsold and are in ending inventory.

(B) Pursuant to section 263A and § 1.263A-1(e)(3)(ii)(I), N must capitalize the depreciation allowed for the year for the new manufacturing equipment in the ending inventory of golf clubs. Thus, when N sells the golf clubs (or is deemed to have sold them under its normal method of accounting), the cost of goods sold attributable to the capitalized depreciation will be $80,000 in computing regular taxable income; $60,000 in computing pre-adjustment alternative minimum taxable income; and $40,000 in computing adjusted current earnings.

(6) Definitions. The following terms have the following meanings for purpose of this section.

(i) Pre-adjustment alternative minimum taxable income is the alternative minimum taxable income of the taxpayer for the taxable year, determined under section 55(b)(2), but without the adjustment for adjusted current earnings under section 56(g) and this section, without the alternative tax net operating loss deduction under section 56(a)(4), and without the alternative tax energy preference deduction under section 56(h).

(ii) Adjusted current earnings. Adjusted current earnings is the pre-adjustment alternative minimum taxable income of the taxpayer for the taxable year, adjusted as provided in section 56(g) and this section. To the extent an amount is included (or deducted) in computing pre-adjustment alternative minimum taxable income for the taxable year (whether because an adjustment is made under section 56 or 58, because of a tax preference item under section 57, or because the item is reflected in taxable income), that amount is not again included (or deducted) in computing adjusted current earnings for the taxable year.

(iii) Earnings and profits. Earnings and profits means current earnings and profits within the meaning of section 316(a)(2), that is, earnings and profits for the taxable year computed as of the close of the taxable year of the corporation without diminution by reason of any distributions made during the taxable year.

(7) Application to foreign corporations. See paragraph (m) of this section for rules relating to the application of this section to foreign corporations.

(b) Depreciation allowed. The depreciation deduction allowed in computing adjusted current earnings is determined under the rules of this paragraph (b). Generally, the rules for computing the adjusted current earnings depreciation deduction differ depending on the taxable year in which the property is placed in service and the method used in computing the depreciation deduction for taxable income purposes. See § 1.168(i)-1(k) for an election to use general asset accounts.

(1) Property placed in service after 1989. The depreciation deduction for property placed in service in a taxable year beginning after December 31, 1989, is the amount determined by using the alternative depreciation system of section 168(g). This paragraph (b)(1) does not apply to property to which paragraph (b)(4) of this section applies (relating to certain property described in sections 168(f)(1) through (f)(4)).

(2) Property subject to new ACRS. (i) In general. This paragraph (b)(2) provides the rules for computing the depreciation deduction for property to which the amendments made by section 201 of the Tax Reform Act of 1986 (new ACRS) apply (generally property placed in service after December 31, 1986), and that is placed in service in a taxable year beginning before January 1, 1990. This paragraph (b)(2) does not apply to property described in paragraph (b)(4) of this section (relating to certain property described in sections 168(f)(1) through (f)(4)) or to property described in paragraph (b)(5)(i) of this section (relating to certain churning transactions described in section 168(f)(5)).

(ii) Rules for computing the depreciation deduction. The depreciation deduction for property described in this paragraph (b)(2) is the amount determined by using—

(A) The adjusted basis of the property as determined in computing alternative minimum taxable income as of the close of the last taxable year beginning before January 1, 1990,

(B) The straight-line method, and

(C) The recovery period that consists of the remainder of the recovery period applicable to the property under the alternative depreciation system of section 168(g).

Thus, the recovery period begins on the first day of the first taxable year beginning after December 31, 1989, and ends on the last day of the recovery period that would have applied had the recovery period for the property originally been determined under section 168(g). In determining the recovery period that would have applied, the property is deemed placed in service on the date it was considered placed in service under the depreciation convention that would have applied to the property under section 168(d).

(iii) Example. The following example illustrates the provisions of this paragraph (b)(2).

Example. Corporation X, a calendar-year taxpayer, purchases and places in service on August 1, 1987, computer-based telephone central office switching equipment. This is the only item of depreciable property X places in service during 1987. Thus, the applicable convention under section 168(d) is the half-year convention. As of December 31, 1989, the adjusted basis of the property used in computing alternative minimum taxable income is $42,000. The recovery period that would have applied to the property under section 168(g)(2) is 9.5 years (from July 1, 1987 to December 31, 1996). Thus, the recovery period for computing adjusted current earnings under section 56(g)(4)(A)(ii) and this paragraph (b)(2) begins on January 1, 1990, and ends on December 31, 1996. X's 1990 depreciation deduction for computing adjusted current earnings is $6,000, determined under the straight-line method by dividing $42,000 (adjusted basis) by 7 (recovery period).

(3) Property subject to original ACRS. (i) In general. This paragraph (b)(3) provides the rules for computing the depreciation deduction for property to which section 168 as in effect on the day before the date of enactment of the Tax Reform Act of 1986 (original ACRS) applies and that is placed in service in a taxable year beginning before January 1, 1990 (generally property that was placed in service after December 31, 1980 and before January 1, 1987). In determining whether original ACRS applies to property, the fact that the unadjusted basis of the property is reduced or eliminated under section 168(d)(4)(A)(i) of original ACRS is not taken into account. This paragraph (b)(3) does not apply to property described in paragraph (b)(4) or (b)(5)(i) of this section (relating to certain section 168(f) property).

(ii) Rules for computing the depreciation deduction. The depreciation deduction for property described in this paragraph (b)(3) is the amount determined by using—

(A) The adjusted basis of the property as determined in computing taxable income as of the close of the last taxable year beginning before January 1, 1990,

(B) The straight-line method, and

(C) The recovery period that consists of the remainder of the recovery period applicable to the property under the alternative depreciation system of section 168(g). Thus, the recovery period begins on the first day of the first taxable year beginning after December 31, 1989, and ends on the last day of the recovery period that would have applied had the recovery period for the property originally been determined under section 168(g)(2). In determining the recovery period that would have applied, the property is deemed placed in service one the date it was considered placed in service under the depreciation convention that would have applied to the property under section 168(d) (without regard to section 168(d)(3)).

(iii) Example. The following example illustrates the provisions of this paragraph (b)(3).

Example. Corporation Y, a calendar-year taxpayer, purchases and places in service on December 1, 1986, computer-based telephone central office switching equipment. The depreciation convention that would have applied to this property under section 168(d) (without regard to section 168(d)(3)) is the half-year convention. As of December 31, 1989, the adjusted basis of the property used in computing taxable income is $21,000. The recovery period for the property under section 168(g)(2) is 9.5 years (from July 1, 1986 to December 31, 1995). Thus, the recovery period for computing adjusted current earnings under section 56(g)(4)(A)(iii) and this paragraph (b)(3) begins on January 1, 1990, and ends on December 31, 1995. Y's 1990 depreciation deduction for computing adjusted current earnings is $3,500, determined under the straight-line method by dividing $21,000 (adjusted basis) by 6 (recovery period).

(4) Special rule for certain section 168(f) property. The depreciation or amortization deduction for property described in section 168(f)(1) through (4) is determined in the same manner as used in computing taxable income, without regard to when the property is placed in service.

(5) Certain property not subject to ACRS. The depreciation or amortization deduction for property not described in paragraphs (b)(1) through (4) of this section is determined in the same manner as used in computing taxable income. Thus, this paragraph (b)(5) applies to—

(i) Property placed in service after December 31, 1980, in a taxable year beginning before January 1, 1990, and that is excluded from the application of original ACRS or new ACRS by section 168(e)(4) of original ACRS or section 168(f)(5)(A)(i) of new ACRS, and

(ii) Property placed in service before January 1, 1981.

(c) Inclusion in adjusted current earnings of items included in earnings and profits. *(1) In general.* Except as otherwise provided in paragraph (c)(4) of this section, adjusted current earnings includes all income items that are permanently excluded from (i.e., not taken into account in determining) pre-adjustment alternative minimum taxable income but that are taken into account in determining earnings and profits. An income item is considered taken into account in determining pre-adjustment alternative minimum taxable income without regard to the timing of its inclusion. Thus, this paragraph (c)(1) does not apply to any income item that is, has been, or will be included in pre-adjustment alternative minimum taxable income. For example, a taxpayer eligible to use the completed contract method of accounting for long-term construction contracts does not take income (or expenses) into account in determining pre-adjustment alternative minimum taxable income for taxable years before the, taxable year the contract is completed. The taxpayer is required under section 312(n)(6) to include income (and expenses) in earnings and profits throughout the term of the contract under the percentage of completion method. This paragraph (c)(1) does not require the income on the contract to be included in adjusted current earnings, however, because the income will be taken into account in the taxable year the contract is completed and therefore is considered to be taken into account in determining pre-adjustment alternative minimum taxable income.

(2) Certain amounts not taken into account in determining whether an item is permanently excluded. The fact that proceeds from an income item may eventually be reflected in pre-adjustment alternative minimum taxable income of another taxpayer on the liquidation or disposal of a business, or similar circumstances, is not taken into account in determining whether the item is permanently excluded from pre-adjustment alternative minimum taxable income. Thus, for example, a corporation's adjusted current earnings include interest excluded from pre-adjustment alternative minimum taxable income under section 103 even though the interest might eventually be reflected in the pre-adjustment alternative minimum taxable income of a corporate shareholder as gain on the liquidation of the corporation.

(3) Allowance of offsetting deductions. In determining adjusted current earnings under this paragraph (c), a deduction is allowed for all items that relate to income required to be included in adjusted current earnings under this paragraph (c) and that would be deductible in computing pre-adjustment alternative minimum taxable income if the income items to which the items of deduction relate were included in pre-adjustment alternative minimum taxable income for any taxable year. For example, deductions disallowed under section 265(a)(2) for the costs of carrying tax-exempt obligations, the interest on which is excluded from pre-adjustment alternative minimum taxable income under section 103 but is included in adjusted current earnings under this paragraph (c), are generally allowed as deductions in computing adjusted current earnings. Amounts deductible under this paragraph (c)(3) are taken into account using the taxpayer's method of accounting and are subject to any provisions or limitations of the Code that would have applied if the amounts had been deductible in determining pre-adjustment alternative minimum taxable income. For example, section 267(a)(2) may affect the timing of a deduction otherwise disallowed under section 265(a)(2).

(4) Special rules. Adjusted current earnings does not include the following amounts.

(i) Income from the discharge of indebtedness. Amounts that are excluded from gross income under section 108 of the Internal Revenue Code of 1986 or any corresponding provision of prior law (including the Bankruptcy Tax Act of 1980, case law, income tax regulations and administrative pronouncements).

(ii) Federal income tax refunds. Refunds of federal income taxes.

(iii) Income earned on behalf of states and municipalities. Amounts that are excluded from gross income under section 115.

(5) Treatment of life insurance contracts. (i) In general. This paragraph (c)(5) addresses the treatment of life insurance contracts in determining adjusted current earnings. These rules apply to life insurance contracts as defined in section 7702. Generally, death benefits under a life insurance contract are included in adjusted current earnings, and all other distributions (including surrenders) are taxed in accordance with the principles of section 72(e), taking into account the taxpayer's basis in the contract for purposes of adjusted current earnings. If the adjusted basis in the contract for purposes of adjusted current earnings exceeds the amount of death benefits received or the amount received when the contract is surrendered (increased by the amount of any outstanding policy loan), the resulting loss is allowed as a deduction under paragraph (c)(3) of this section in computing adjusted current earnings for the taxable year. In addition, undistributed income on the contract is included in adjusted current earnings as provided in paragraph (c)(5)(ii) of this section. Paragraph (c)(5)(vi)(A) of this section provides special rules for term insurance that has no net surrender value.

(ii) Inclusion of inside buildup. Income on a life insurance contract with respect to a taxable year (or any shorter period either ending or beginning with the date of a distribution from the contract) is included in adjusted current earnings for the taxable year. Thus, income on the contract is calculated from the beginning of a taxable year to the date of any distribution, from immediately after any distribution to the date of the next distribution, and from the last distribution during the taxable year through the end of the taxable year. Income on a life insurance contract is not included in adjusted current earnings for any taxable year in which the insured dies or the contract is completely surrendered for its entire net surrender value. Solely for purposes of computing adjusted current earnings, the taxpayer's adjusted basis in the contract (as determined under section 72(e)(6)) is increased to reflect any positive income on the contract included in adjusted current earnings under this paragraph (c)(5)(ii). The manner in which the income on the contract is determined for adjusted current earnings purposes is prescribed in paragraph (c)(5)(iii) of this section. If the income on the contract determined under paragraph (c)(5)(iii) of this section is a negative amount, income on the contract is not included in adjusted current earnings and no deduction from adjusted current earnings is allowed for the negative amount.

(iii) Calculation of income on the contract. For purposes of determining adjusted current earnings, the income on a life insurance contract for any period, including a taxable year, is the excess, if any, of—

(A) The sum of the contract's net surrender value (as defined in section 7702(f)(2)(B)) at the end of the period, and any distributions under the contract during the period that, in accordance with the principles of section 72(e), are not taxed because they represent recoveries of the taxpayer's basis in the contract for adjusted current earnings, over

(B) The sum of the contract's net surrender value at the end of the preceding period, and any premiums paid under the contract during the period.

(iv) Treatment of distributions under the life insurance contract. Any distribution under a life insurance contract (whether a partial withdrawal or an amount received on complete surrender of the contract) is included in adjusted current earnings in accordance with the principles of section

72(e), taking into account the taxpayer's basis in the contract for purposes of computing adjusted current earnings. The taxpayer's basis in the contract is equal to the basis at the end of the immediately preceding period plus any premiums paid before the distribution. The taxpayer's basis in the contract for purposes of adjusted current earnings is reduced, in accordance with the principles of section 72(e), to the extent that the distribution is not included in adjusted current earnings because it represents a recovery of that basis.

(v) Treatment of death benefits. The excess of the contractual death benefit of a life insurance contract over the taxpayer's adjusted basis in the contract for purposes of computing adjusted current earnings at the time of the insured's death is included in adjusted current earnings as provided by paragraph (c)(6)(i) of this section. The amount of the death benefit that is taken into account for adjusted current earnings includes the amount of any outstanding policy loan treated as forgiven or discharged by the insurance company upon the death of the insured.

(vi) Other rules. (A) Term life insurance contract without net surrender values. Except as provided in this paragraph (c)(5)(vi), the requirements of paragraph (c)(5) of this section do not apply to term life insurance contracts that provide no net surrender value. Adjusted current earnings are reduced by any premiums paid under such a contract that are allocable to the taxable year. Any premiums paid that are not allocable to the taxable year must be included in the basis of the contract. The death benefit under such a term insurance contract is included in adjusted current earnings as provided by paragraph (c)(5)(v) of this section.

(B) Life insurance contracts involving divided ownership. If the ownership of a life insurance contract is divided between different persons (for example, a split-dollar arrangement), the requirements of paragraph (c)(5) of this section apply to the separate ownership interests as though each interest were a separate contract.

(vii) Examples. The following examples illustrate the provisions of this paragraph (c)(5).

Example (1). (i) On January 1, 1987, corporation X, a calendar year taxpayer, purchased a flexible premium life insurance contract with a death benefit of $100,000 and planned annual gross premiums of $2,200 payable on January 1 of each year. The net surrender value of the contract at the end of 1987 and subsequent years, together with the cumulative premiums for the contract at the end of each year, are set forth in the following table:

Year	Cumulative premiums paid	Year-end net surrender value
1987	$2,200	$2,420
1988	4,400	5,082
1989	6,600	8,010
1990	8,800	11,231
1991	11,000	14,774

(ii) Under paragraph (c)(5)(ii) of this section, X must include $1,021 in adjusted current earnings for 1990. The inclusion is computed by subtracting from the net surrender value of the contract at the end of the taxable year ($11,231) the sum of the net surrender value of the contract at the end of the preceding taxable year ($8,010) plus the premiums paid during the taxable year ($2,200). See paragraph (c)(5)(iii) of this section. For purposes of determining adjusted current earnings, X's adjusted basis in the contract would be increased at the end of 1990 from $8,800 to $9,821 to reflect the $1,021 inclusion. See paragraph (c)(5)(ii) of this section. The income under the contract attributable to taxable years prior to 1990 does not increase X's adjusted basis in the contract.

(iii) For 1991, the income on the contract included in adjusted current earnings is determined in the same manner as the preceding year, and there is a corresponding increase in X's adjusted basis in the contract. Thus, for 1991, the income on the contract is $1,343, which is determined by subtracting from the net surrender value of the contract at the end of the taxable year ($14,774) the sum of the net surrender value at the end of the preceding taxable year ($11,231) plus the premiums paid during the taxable year ($2,200). At the end of 1991, X's adjusted basis in the contract for adjusted current earnings is $13,364, which reflects the basis of the contract at the beginning of 1991, increased by the premium paid during the year ($2,200) and the income on the contract that has been included in adjusted current earnings for the taxable year ($1,343).

Example (2). The facts are the same as in example 1, except that, after the payment of the premium for 1991, the insured dies and X receives the $100,000 death benefit under the contract. Under paragraph (c)(5)(ii) of this section, no amount is included in adjusted current earnings for income on the contract for the taxable year in which the insured dies. Instead, under paragraph (c)(5)(v) of this section, X must include the adjusted current earnings for 1991 the excess of the death benefit ($100,000) over the adjusted basis in the contract for purposes of computing adjusted current earnings at the time of the insured's death ($12,021), which equals X's adjusted basis in the contract at the end of 1990 ($9,821), increased by X's premium payment for 1991 ($2,200).

Example (3). (i) The facts are the same as in example 1, except that in addition to making the $2,200 planned premium payment for 1992, X receives a $16,200 distribution under the contract on February 1, 1992, leaving a net surrender value of $915 immediately following the distribution. On March 1, 1992, X pays an additional premium of $5,000 under the contract. The net surrender value of the contract at the end of 1992 is $6,417.

(ii) Treatment of the distribution. Under paragraph (c)(5)(iv) of this section, the $16,200 distribution in 1992 is included in adjusted current earnings as an amount taxable in accordance with the principles of section 72(e) to the extent that the distribution ($16,200) exceeds X's adjusted basis for adjusted current earnings, as determined at the end of the immediately preceding period, and including premiums paid through the period ending on the date of the distribution ($15,564). Thus, X must include $636 in adjusted current earnings for 1992 as an amount taxable in accordance with the principles of section 72(e).

(iii) Determination of the income on the contract. Under paragraph (c)(5)(iii) of this section for 1992, the income on the contract must be separately determined for the period beginning with the first day of the taxable year to the date of the distribution and for the period beginning immediately after the distribution to the end of the taxable year, using the contract's net surrender values at the beginning and end of each of these periods. The income on the contract for the period beginning on January 1, 1992 and ending on February 1, 1992 (the date of the distribution) is equal to the excess, if any, of (A) the sum of the net surrender value at the end of the period ($915) and the amount of the distribution that is allocable to X's basis in the contract for adjusted current earnings ($15,564), over (B) the sum of the net surrender value at the end of the preceding taxable year ($14,774) plus any premiums paid on the contract during the period ($2,200). Because the net result of this computation is a negative amount (($915 + $15,564) – ($14,774 + $2,200) = – 495), no income on the contract for the period ending with the date of the distribution is included in adjusted current earnings for 1992.

(iv) Under paragraph (c)(5)(ii), X must also determine the income on the contract for the period beginning immediately after the distribution through the end of the taxable year. The income on the contract for this period is $502, which is equal to the excess of the net surrender value at the end of the taxable year ($6,417) over the sum of the net surrender value at the end of the preceding period ($915), plus any premiums paid during the period ($5,000). At the end of 1992, X's adjusted basis in the contract for adjusted current earnings is $5,502, determined by adding the income on the contract ($502) and the premiums paid during the period ($5,000) to the basis at the end of the preceding period ($0).

(v) Thus, X must include a total of $1,138 ($636 + 502) in adjusted current earnings for 1992. This inclusion reflects both the undistributed income on the contract for the taxable year plus the amount of income from distributions under the contract that is taxed in accordance with the principles of section 72(e) using X's adjusted basis in the contract for adjusted current earnings.

(6) Partial list of income items excluded from gross income but included in earnings and profits. The following is a partial list of items that are permanently excluded from pre-adjustment alternative minimum taxable income but that are included in earnings and profits, and are therefore included in adjusted current earnings under this paragraph (c).

(i) Proceeds of life insurance contracts that are excluded under section 101, to the extent provided in paragraph (c)(5)(v) or (c)(5)(vi) of this section.

(ii) Interest that is excluded under section 103.

(iii) Amounts received as compensation for injuries or sickness that are excluded under section 104.

(iv) Income taxes of a lessor of property that are paid by a lessee and are excluded under section 110.

(v) Income attributable to the recovery of an item deducted in computing earnings and profits in a prior year that is excluded under section 111.

(vi) Amounts received as proceeds from sports programs that are excluded under section 114.

(vii) Cost-sharing payments that are excluded under section 126, to the extent section 126(e) does not apply.

(viii) Interest on loans used to acquire employer securities that is excluded under section 133.

(ix) Financial assistance that is excluded under section 597.

(x) Amounts that are excluded from pre-adjustment alternative minimum taxable income as a result of an election under section 831(b) (allowing certain insurance companies to compute their pre-adjustment alternative minimum taxable income using only their investment income).

Items described in paragraph (c)(1) of this section must be included in earnings and profits (and therefore in adjusted current earnings) even if they are not identified in this paragraph (c)(6). The Commissioner may identify additional items described in paragraph (c)(1) in other published guidance.

(7) Partial list of items excluded from both pre-adjustment alternative minimum taxable income and adjusted current earnings. The following is a partial list of items that are excluded from both pre-adjustment alternative minimum taxable income and adjusted current earnings, and for which no adjustment is allowed under this section.

(i) The value of improvements made by a lessee to a lessor's property that is excluded from the lessor's income under section 109.

(ii) contributions to the capital of a corporation by a nonshareholder that are excluded from the corporation's income under section 118.

The Commissioner may identify additional items described in this paragraph (c)(7) in other published guidance.

(d) Disallowance of items not deductible in computing earnings and profits. *(1) In general.* Except as otherwise provided in this paragraph (d), no deduction is allowed in computing adjusted current earnings for any items that are not taken into account in determining earnings and profits for any taxable year, even if the items are taken into account in determining pre-adjustment alternative minimum taxable income. These items therefore increase adjusted current earnings to the extent they are deducted in computing pre-adjustment alternative minimum taxable income. An item of deduction is considered taken into account without regard to the timing of its deductibility in computing earnings and profits. Thus, to the extent an item is, has been, or will be deducted for purposes of determining earnings and profits, it does not increase adjusted current earnings in the taxable year in which it is deducted for purposes of determining pre-adjustment alternative minimum taxable income. For example, a deduction allowed (in determining preadjustment alternative minimum taxable income) under section 196 for unused research credits allowable under section 41 is taken into account in computing earnings and profits because the costs that gave rise to the credit were deductible in computing earnings and profits when incurred. Therefore, the deduction does not increase adjusted current earnings. As a further example, payments by a United States parent corporation with respect to employees of certain foreign subsidiaries, which are deductible under section 176, are considered contributions to the capital of the foreign subsidiary for purposes of computing earnings and profits. Although the payments are not deductible in computing the earnings and profits of the United States parent corporation in the year incurred, the payments do increase the parent's basis in its stock in the foreign subsidiary. This basis increase will reduce any gain the parent may later realize for purposes of computing earnings and profits on the disposition of the stock of the foreign subsidiary. Therefore, the amount of the payment by the parent is considered taken into account in computing the earnings and profits of the parent and does not increase adjusted current earnings. Thus, only deduction items that are never taken into account in computing earnings and profits are disallowed in computing adjusted current earnings under this paragraph (d).

(2) Deductions for certain dividends received. (i) Certain amounts deducted under sections 243 and 245. Paragraph (d)(1) of this section does not apply to, and adjusted current earnings therefore are not increased by, amounts deducted under sections 243 and 245 that qualify as 100-percent deductible dividends under sections 243(a), 245(b) or 245(c), or to any dividend received from a 20-percent owned corpo-

ration (as defined in section 243(c)(2)), to the extent that the dividend giving rise to the deductions is attributable to earnings of the paying corporation that are subject to federal income tax. Earnings are considered subject to federal income tax return (that is filed or, if not, that should be filed) of an entity subject to United States taxation, even if there is no resulting United States tax liability (e.g., because of net operating losses or tax credits, other than the credit provided for in section 936).

(ii) Special rules. (A) Dividends received from a foreign sales corporation. The portion of a dividend received from a foreign sales corporation (FSC) that is classified as a 100-percent deductible dividend attributable to earnings of the FSC subject to federal income tax is that portion of the dividend distributed out of earnings and profits of the FSC attributable to non-exempt foreign trade income determined under either of the administrative pricing methods of section 925(a)(1) or (2), and to non-exempt foreign trade income determined under section 925(a)(3) that is effectively connected with the conduct of a trade or business in the United States (determined without regard to section 921). If the FSC is a 20-percent owned corporation (as defined in section 243(c)(2)), an additional portion of that dividend is classified as being attributable to earnings of the FSC subject to federal income tax to the extent that the dividend is distributed out of earnings and profits of the FSC attributable to effectively connected income (as defined in section 245(c)(4)(B)). A FSC is defined in section 922 and, for purposes of this paragraph, includes a small FSC and a former FSC. The ordering rules for distributions from a FSC set forth in § 1.926(a)-1T(b)(1) apply to determine the classification of earnings and profits out of which a distribution has been made.

(B) Dividends received from a section 936 corporation. In the case of a dividend received from a corporation eligible for the credit provided by section 936, only that part of the dividend that is attributable to income that is not eligible for the credit is attributable to earnings of the paying corporation that are subject to federal income tax. Dividends are deemed to be distributed first out of earnings and profits for the current taxable year of the section 936 corporation, to the extent thereof, and then out of the most recently accumulated earnings and profits, under the principles of section 316. With respect to a distribution of less than all of the earnings and profits for the current or any prior taxable year, the amount of the distribution attributable to income not eligible for the section 936 credit is determined on a pro rata basis. For example, assume that a section 936 corporation earns $100 of income in its current taxable year, $10 of which is not eligible for the credit under section 936. If the section 936 corporation makes a distribution of $50 during that year, $5 of that distribution ($10 of income not eligible for the section 936 credit divided by $100 of income, times $50 distributed) is deemed to be attributable to earnings of the paying corporation that are subject to federal income tax.

(iii) Special rule for certain dividends received by certain cooperatives. Paragraph (d)(1) of this section does not apply to, and adjusted current earnings do not include, any dividend received by any organization to which part I of subchapter T of the Code applies and that is engaged in the marketing of agricultural or horticultural products, if the dividend is paid by a FSC and is allowable as a deduction under section 245(c).

(3) Partial list of items not deductible in computing earnings and profits. The following is a partial list of items that are not taken into account in computing earnings and profits and thus are not deductible in computing adjusted current earnings.

(i) Unrecovered losses attributable to certain damages that are deductible under section 186, to the extent those damages were previously deducted in computing earnings and profits.

(ii) The deduction for small life insurance companies allowed under section 806.

(iii) Dividends deductible under the following sections of the Code:

(A) Dividends received by corporations that are deductible under section 243, to the extent paragraph (d)(2)(i) of this section does not apply.

(B) Dividends received on certain preferred stock that are deductible under section 244.

(C) Dividends received from certain foreign corporations that are deductible under section 245, to the extent neither paragraph (d)(2)(i) nor (d)(2)(iii) of this section applies.

(D) Dividends paid on certain preferred stock of public utilities that are deductible under section 247.

(E) Dividends paid to an employee stock ownership plan that are deductible under section 404(k).

(F) Non-patronage dividends that are paid and deductible under section 1382(c)(1).

Items described in paragraph (d)(1) of this section are not taken into account in computing earnings and profits (and thus are not deductible in computing adjusted current earnings) even if they are not identified in this paragraph (d)(3). The Commissioner may identify additional items described in paragraph (d)(1) of this section in other published guidance.

(4) Partial list of items deductible for purposes of computing both pre-adjustment alternative minimum taxable income and adjusted current earnings. The following is a partial list of items that are deductible for purposes of computing both pre-adjustment alternative minimum taxable income and adjusted current earnings, and for which no adjustment is allowed under this section.

(i) Payments by a United States corporation with respect to employees of certain foreign corporations that are deductible under section 176.

(ii) Dividends paid on deposits by thrift institutions that are deductible under section 591.

(iii) Life insurance policyholder dividends that are deductible under section 808.

(iv) Dividends paid by cooperatives that are deductible under sections 1382(b) or 1382(c)(2) and that are not paid with respect to stock.

The Commissioner may identify additional items described in this paragraph (d)(4) in other published guidance.

(e) Treatment of income items included, and deduction items not allowed, in computing pre-adjustment alternative minimum taxable income. Adjusted current earnings includes any income item that is included in pre-adjustment alternative minimum taxable income, even if that income item is not included in earnings and profits for the taxable year. Except as specifically provided in paragraph (c)(3) or (c)(5) of this section, no deduction is allowed for an item in computing adjusted current earnings if the item is not deductible in computing pre-adjustment alternative minimum taxable income for the taxable year, even if the item is deductible in computing earnings and profits for the year. Thus, for example, capital losses in excess of capital gains for the taxable year are not deductible in computing adjusted current earnings for the taxable year.

(f) Certain other earnings and profits adjustments. *(1) Intangible drilling costs.* For purposes of computing adjusted current earnings, the amount allowable as a deduction for intangible drilling costs (as defined in section 263(c)) for amounts paid or incurred in taxable years beginning after December 31, 1989, is determined as provided in section 312(n)(2)(A). See section 56(h) for an additional adjustment to alternative minimum taxable income based on energy preferences for taxable years beginning after 1990.

(2) Certain amortization provisions do not apply. For purposes of computing adjusted current earnings, sections 173 (relating to circulation expenditures) and 248 (relating to organizational expenditures) do not apply to amounts paid or incurred in taxable years beginning after December 31, 1989. If an election is made under section 59(e) to amortize circulation expenditures described in section 173 over a three-year period, the expenditures to which the election applies are deducted ratably over the three-year period for purposes of computing taxable income, pre-adjustment alternative minimum taxable income, and adjusted current earnings.

(3) LIFO recapture adjustment. (i) In general. Adjusted current earnings are generally increased or decreased by the increase or decrease in the taxpayer's LIFO recapture amount (as defined in paragraph (f)(3)(iii)(A) of this section) as of the close of each taxable year.

(ii) Beginning LIFO and FIFO inventory. For purposes of computing the increase or decrease in the LIFO recapture amount, the beginning LIFO and FIFO inventory amounts for the first taxable year beginning after December 31, 1989, are—

(A) The ending LIFO inventory amount used in computing pre-adjustment alternative minimum taxable income for the last year beginning before January 1, 1990; and

(B) The ending FIFO inventory amount for the last year beginning before January 1, 1990, computed with the adjustments described in section 56 (other than the adjustment described in section 56(g)) and section 58, the items of tax preference described in section 57 and using the methods used in computing pre-adjustment alternative minimum taxable income.

(iii) Definitions. (A) LIFO recapture amount. (1) Definition. The taxpayer's LIFO recapture amount is the excess, if any, of—

(i) the inventory amount of its assets under the FIFO method, computed using the rules of this section; over

(ii) the inventory amount of its assets under the LIFO method, computed using the rules of this section.

(2) Assets included. Only the assets for which the taxpayer uses the LIFO method to compute pre-adjustment alternative minimum taxable income are taken into account in determining the LIFO recapture amount.

(B) FIFO Method. For purposes of this paragraph, the FIFO method is the first in, first out method described in section 471, determined by using—

(1) The retail method if that is the method the taxpayer uses in computing pre-adjustment alternative minimum taxable income; or

(2) The lower of cost or market method for all other taxpayers.

(C) LIFO method. The LIFO method is the last in, first out method authorized by section 472.

(D) Inventory amounts. Except as otherwise provided, inventory amounts are computed using the methods used in computing pre-adjustment alternative minimum taxable income. To the extent inventory is treated as produced or acquired during taxable years beginning after December 31, 1989, the inventory amount is determined with the adjustments described in sections 56 and 58 and the items of tax preference described in section 57. Thus, for example, the amount of depreciation to be capitalized under section 263A with respect to inventory produced in taxable years beginning after December 31, 1989, is based on the depreciation allowed under the rules of paragraph (b) of this section. See paragraph (a)(5) of this section.

(iv) Exchanges under sections 351 and 721. For purposes of this section, any decrease in a transferor's LIFO recapture amount that occurs as a result of a transfer of inventories in an exchange to which section 351 or section 721 applies cannot be used to decrease the adjusted current earnings of the transferor. A decrease that is disallowed under the preceding sentence is instead carried over to reduce any LIFO recapture adjustment that the transferee (or its corporate partners, if section 721 applies) would otherwise make (in the absence of this paragraph (f)(3)(iv)) solely by reason of its carryover basis in inventories received in the section 351 or section 721 exchange. Nothing in this paragraph (f)(3)(iv), however, alters the computation of the LIFO recapture amount of the transferor or transferee as of the close of any taxable year.

(v) Examples. The following examples illustrate the provisions of this paragraph (f)(3).

Example (1). M Corporation, a calendar-year taxpayer, uses the LIFO method of accounting for its inventory for purposes of computing pre-adjustment alternative minimum taxable income. M's ending LIFO inventory for all of its pools for purposes of computing pre-adjustment alternative minimum taxable income on December 31, 1989, is $300. M computes a $500 FIFO inventory amount on that date, after applying the provisions of section 263A along with the adjustments and preferences required in computing pre-adjustment alternative minimum taxable income. M's FIFO and LIFO ending inventory amounts at the close of its taxable years, its LIFO reserves, and its adjustment under this paragraph (f)(3), are as follows:

	1989	1990	1991	1992
Ending inventory				
A. FIFO	$500[1]	$360	$560	$600
B. LIFO	300[2]	180	320	440
LIFO recapture amount				
A − B	$200	$180	$240	$160
Change in LIFO recapture amount and adjustment under paragraph (f)(3)	—	$(20)	$ 60	$(80)

[1] Beginning FIFO inventory amount under paragraph (f)(3)(ii).
[2] Beginning LIFO inventory amount under paragraph (f)(3)(ii).

Example (2). (A) X Corporation, a calendar-year taxpayer, uses the LIFO method for purposes of computing pre-adjustment alternative minimum taxable income. X's LIFO recapture amount is $300 as of December 31, 1992, and is $200 as of December 31, 1993. Immediately prior to calculating its LIFO recapture amount as of December 31, 1993, X transfers inventory with an adjusted current earnings (ACE) basis of $500 to Y Corporation in an exchange to which section 351 applies. X determines that the $100 decrease in its

LIFO recapture amount occurred as a result of its transfer of inventories to Y in the section 351 exchange. Thus, under paragraph (f)(3)(iv) of this section, X cannot decrease its adjusted current earnings by that amount. In computing its 1994 LIFO recapture adjustment, X will use $200 as its LIFO recapture amount as of December 31, 1993, even though it was not entitled to reduce adjusted current earnings by the $100 decrease in its LIFO recapture amount in 1993.

(B) For purposes of computing its ACE, Y takes a $500 carryover basis in the inventories received from X. If Y, a newly-formed calendar-year taxpayer, engages in no other inventory transactions in 1993 and adopts the LIFO inventory method on its 1993 tax return, it will have a LIFO recapture amount of $0 as of December 31, 1993 (because its FIFO inventory amount and its LIFO inventory amount are both $500). Assume that at December 31, 1994, Y has a LIFO recapture amount of $200 ($1,000 FIFO inventory amount − $800 LIFO inventory amount). Under paragraph (f)(3)(i) of this section, Y computes a LIFO recapture adjustment for 1994 of $200 ($200 − $0). If any portion of Y's $200 LIFO recapture adjustment occurs solely by reason of its carryover basis in the inventories it received from X, Y reduces its $200 LIFO recapture adjustment by that portion under paragraph (f)(3)(iv). In any event, however, Y will use its $200 LIFO recapture amount as of December 31, 1994, in computing its 1995 LIFO recapture adjustment.

(vi) Effective date. Paragraph (f)(3) is effective for taxable years beginning after December 18, 1992. A taxpayer may choose to apply this paragraph, however, to all taxable years beginning after December 31, 1989.

(4) Installment sales. (i) In general. Adjusted current earnings are computed without regard to the installment method, except as provided in this paragraph (f)(4).

(ii) Exception for prior dispositions. Paragraph (f)(4)(i) of this section does not apply to any disposition in a taxable year beginning before January 1, 1990, that is taken into account under the installment method for purposes of computing pre-adjustment alternative minimum taxable income. Thus, for any disposition in a taxable year beginning before January 1, 1990, the installment method applies in computing adjusted current earnings for taxable years beginning after December 31, 1989, to the same extent it applies in determining pre-adjustment alternative minimum taxable income for the taxable year.

(iii) Special rules for obligations to which section 453A applies. (A) In general. The following special rules apply to any installment sale occurring in a taxable year beginning after December 31, 1989, that results in an installment obligation to which section 453A(a)(1) applies and with respect to which preadjustment alternative minimum taxable income is determined under the installment method. As explained in paragraph (f)(4)(iii)(B) of this section, for purposes of computing adjusted current earnings, a portion of the contract price is eligible for the installment method, and the remainder of the contract price is not eligible for the installment method. Payments under the obligation are allocated pro-rata between the two accounting methods.

(B) Limitation on application of installment method. Only a portion of the contract price of an installment sale described in paragraph (f)(4)(iii)(A) of this section is eligible to be accounted for under the installment method for purposes of computing adjusted current earnings. The portion eligible for the installment method is equal to the total contract price of the sale multiplied by the applicable percentage (as determined under section 453A(c)(4)) for the taxable year of the sale. The remainder of the contract price is not eligible to be accounted for under the installment method for purposes of computing adjusted current earnings. The gross profit ratio is determined without regard to this bifurcated treatment of the sale.

(C) Treatment of the ineligible portion. The gain on the sale that is taken into account in the taxable year of the sale for purposes of computing adjusted current earnings is equal to the gross profit ratio multiplied by the entire portion of the contract price that is ineligible for the installment method.

(D) Treatment of the eligible portion. For purposes of calculating adjusted current earnings, the amount of gain recognized in a taxable year on the portion of the contract price that is eligible for the installment method is equal to—

(1) The amount of payments received during the taxable year, multiplied by

(2) The applicable percentage for the taxable year of the sale, multiplied by

(3) The gross profit ratio.

(E) Coordination with the pledge rule. For purposes of determining the amount of payments received during the taxable year under paragraph (f)(4)(iii)(D), the rules of section 453A(d) (relating to the treatment of certain pledge proceeds as payments) apply. This includes the rules under section 453A(d)(3) that relate to treating later payments as receipts of amounts on which tax has already been paid.

(F) Example. The following example illustrates the provisions of this paragraph (f)(4)(iii):

(1) On January 1, 1990, corporation A, a calendar-year taxpayer, sells a building with an adjusted basis for purposes of computing adjusted current earnings of $10 million, for $5 million and an installment obligation bearing adequate stated interest with a principal amount of $20 million. The installment obligation calls for 4 annual payments of $5 million on January 1 of 1991, 1992, 1993, and 1994. A does not elect out of the installment method, and disposes of no other property under the installment method during 1990. No gain with respect to the sale is recaptured pursuant to section 1250.

(2) The gross profit percentage for purposes of computing adjusted current earnings on the sale is 60 percent, computed as follows: gross profit of $15 million ($25 million contract price less $10 million adjusted basis) divided by $25 million contract price. The applicable percentage on the sale is 75 percent, computed as follows: $15 million ($20 million of installment obligations arising during and outstanding at the end of 1990 less $5 million) divided by $20 million of installment obligations arising during and outstanding at the end of 1990. See section 453A(c)(4). The portion of the contract price eligible for accounting under the installment method for purposes of computing adjusted current earnings is $18.75 million, or $25 million total contract price times applicable percentage of 75 percent. The portion of the contract price ineligible for the installment method is $6.25 million, or $25 million less $18.75 million.

(3) In computing adjusted current earnings for 1990, A must include $3.75 million of the gain on the sale. This amount is equal to the portion of the contract price that is ineligible for the installment method times the gross profit ratio, or $6.25 million times 60 percent. A must also include $2.25 million of gain from the $5 million payment received in 1990. This amount is computed as follows: the eligible portion of the payment, $3.75 million ($5 million payment

times the applicable percentage of 75 percent), times the gross profit ratio of 60 percent. Thus, the total amount of gain from the sale that A must include in adjusted current earnings for 1990 is $6 million ($3.75 million of gain from the portion of the contract price that is not eligible for the installment method, plus $2.25 million of gain from the 1990 payment).

(4) A does not pledge or otherwise accelerate payments on the note in any other taxable year. In computing adjusted current earnings for 1991, 1992, 1993, and 1994, A therefore includes $2.25 million of gain on the installment sale, computed as follows: $5 million payment times the applicable percentage of 75 percent, times the gross profit ratio of 60 percent.

(g) disallowance of loss on exchange of debt pools. [Reserved]

(h) Policy acquisition expenses of life insurance companies. *(1) In general.* This paragraph (h) addresses the treatment of policy acquisition expenses of life insurance companies in determining adjusted current earnings. Policy acquisition expenses are those expenses that, under generally accepted accounting principles in effect at the time the expenses are incurred, are considered to vary with and to be primarily related to the acquisition of new and renewal insurance policies. Generally, these acquisition expenses must be capitalized and amortized for purposes of adjusted current earnings over the reasonably estimated life of the acquired policy, using a method that provides à reasonable allowance for amortization. This method of amortization is treated as if it applied to all taxable years in determining the amount of policy acquisition expenses deducted for adjusted current earnings. The rules in this paragraph (h) apply to any life insurance company, as defined in section 816(a).

(2) Reasonably estimated life. The reasonably estimated life of an acquired policy is determined based on the facts with respect to each policy (such as the age, sex and health of the insured), and the company's experience (such as mortality, lapse rate and renewals) with similar policies. A company may treat as the reasonably estimated life of an acquired policy the period for amortizing expenses of the acquired policy that would be required by the Financial Accounting Standards Board (FASB) at the time the acquisition expenses are incurred. If the FASB has not established such a period, the period for amortizing acquisition expense of an acquired policy under guidelines issued by the American Institute of Certified Public Accountants in effect at the time the acquisition expenses are incurred may be treated as the reasonably estimated life of the acquired policy.

(3) Reasonable allowance for amortization. For purposes of determining a reasonable allowance for amortization, a company may use a method that amortizes acquisition expenses in the same proportion that gross premiums and gross investment income for the taxable year bear to total anticipated receipts of gross premiums (including anticipated renewal premiums) and gross investment income to be realized over the reasonably estimated life of the policy.

(4) Safe harbor far public financial statements. Any company that is required to file with the Securities and Exchange Commission (SEC) a financial statement with respect to the taxable year will be treated as having complied with paragraph (h)(1) of this section if it accounts for acquisition expenses for adjusted current earnings purposes in the same manner as it accounts for those expenses on its financial statements filed with the SEC.

(i) [Reserved]

(j) Depletion. For purposes of computing adjusted current earnings, the allowance for depletion with respect to any property placed in service in a taxable year beginning after December 31, 1989 is determined under the cost depletion method of section 611.

(k) Treatment of certain ownership changes. *(1) In general.* In the case of any corporation that has an ownership change as defined in paragraph (k)(2) of this section in a taxable year beginning after December 31, 1989, and that also has a net unrealized built-in loss (as defined in paragraph (k)(3) of this section) immediately before the ownership change, the adjusted basis of each asset of the corporation for purposes of computing adjusted current earnings following the ownership change shall be its proportionate share (determined on the basis of the respective fair market values of each asset) of the fair market value of the assets of the corporation immediately before the ownership change. The rules of § 1.338(b)-6(b), if otherwise applicable to the transaction, are applied in making this allocation of basis. If such rules apply, the limitations of §§ 1.338(b)-6(c)(1) and (2) also apply in allocating basis under this paragraph (k)(1).

(2) Definition of ownership change. A corporation has an ownership change for purposes of section 56(g)(4)(G)(i) and this paragraph (k) if there is an ownership change under section 382(g) for purposes of computing the corporation's amount of taxable income that may be offset by pre-change losses or the regular tax liability that may be offset by pre-change credits. See § 1.382-2T for rules to determine whether a corporation has an ownership change. Accordingly, in order for an ownership change to occur for purposes of this paragraph (k), a corporation must be a loss corporation as defined in § 1.382-2(a)(1). In determining whether the corporation is a loss corporation, the determination of whether there is a net unrealized built-in loss is made by using the aggregate adjusted basis of the assets of the corporation used in computing taxable income. The aggregate adjusted basis of the corporation's assets for purposes of computing adjusted current earnings is not relevant in determining whether the corporation is a loss corporation. See part (iv) of the example in paragraph (k)(4) of this section.

(3) Determination of net unrealized built-in loss immediately before an ownership change. In order to determine whether it has a net unrealized built-in loss for purposes of section 56(g)(4)(G)(ii) and paragraph (k)(1) of this section, a corporation that has an ownership change as defined in paragraph (k)(2) of this section must use the aggregate adjusted basis of its assets that it uses in computing its adjusted current earnings. The rules of section 382 (including sections 382(h)(3)(B)(i) and 382(h)(8)) otherwise apply in determining whether the corporation has a net unrealized built-in loss.

(4) Example. The following example illustrates the provisions of this paragraph (k):

(i) Individual A has owned all the issued and outstanding stock of corporation L for the past 5 years. A sells all of his stock in L to unrelated individual B. On the date of the sale, L owns the following assets (all numbers are in millions):

Asset	Adjusted basis for computing taxable income	Adjusted basis for computing adjusted current earnings	Fair market value
x	$ 45	$ 50	$ 50

y	55	60	30
z	10	10	20
	$110	$120	$100

For purposes of computing taxable income, L has a $500 million net operating loss carryforward to the taxable year in which the sale occurs. Therefore, L is a loss corporation. As a result of the transfer of shares of L from A to B, L has had an ownership change.

(ii) L has no net unrealized built-in loss for purposes of computing taxable income because the amount by which the aggregate adjusted basis of its assets for that purpose exceeds their fair market value is $10 million, which is less than 15 percent of their fair market value and is not greater than $10 million. See section 381(h)(3)(B)(i). L, however, does have a net unrealized built-in loss for purposes of computing adjusted current earnings because the aggregate adjusted basis of its assets for the purpose exceeds their fair market value by $20 million, and that amount is greater than $10 million.

(iii) Under paragraph (k)(1) of this section, L must restate the adjusted basis of its assets for purposes of computing adjusted current earnings to their fair market values, as follows (all numbers are in millions):

Asset	New Adjusted basis
x	$50
y	30
z	20

L must use these new adjusted bases for all purposes in determining adjusted current earnings, including computing depreciation and any gain or loss on disposition.

(iv) If L did not have the net operating loss carryforward, and had no other loss or credit carryovers or other attributes described in § 1.382-2(a)(1) for purposes of computing the amount of its taxable income that may be offset by prechange losses or its regular tax liability that may be offset by pre-change credits, it would not have been a loss corporation on the date of the sale and therefore would not be treated as having had an ownership change for purposes of computing adjusted current earnings. This would be true even though L had a net unrealized built-in loss for purposes of computing adjusted current earnings. Therefore, this paragraph (k) would not have applied.

(l) [Reserved]

(m) Adjusted current earnings of a foreign corporation. *(1) In general.* The alternative minimum taxable income of a foreign corporation is increased by 75 percent of the excess of—

(i) Its effectively connected adjusted current earnings for the taxable year; over

(ii) Its effectively connected pre-adjustment alternative minimum taxable income for the taxable year.

(2) Definitions. (i) Effectively connected pre-adjustment alternative minimum taxable income. Effectively connected pre-adjustment alternative minimum taxable income is the effectively connected taxable income of the foreign corporation for the taxable year, determined with the adjustments under sections 56 and 58 (except for the adjustment for adjusted current earnings, the alternative tax net operating loss and the alternative tax energy preference deduction) and increased by the tax preference items of section 57, but taking into account only items of income of the foreign corporation that are effectively connected (or treated as effectively connected) with the conduct of a trade or business in the United States, and any expense, loss or deduction that is properly allocated and apportioned to that income.

(ii) Effectively connected adjusted current earnings. Effectively connected adjusted current earnings is the effectively connected pre-adjustment alternative minimum taxable income of the foreign corporation for the taxable year, adjusted under section 56(g) and this section, but taking into account only items of income of the foreign corporation that are effectively connected (or treated as effectively connected) with the conduct of a trade or business in the United States, and any expense, loss or deduction that is properly allocated and apportioned to that income.

(3) Rules to determine effectively connected pre-adjustment alternative minimum taxable income and effectively connected adjusted current earnings. The principles of section 864(c) (and the regulations thereunder) and any other applicable provision of the Internal Revenue Code apply to determine whether items of income of the foreign corporation are effectively connected (or treated as effectively connected) with the conduct of a trade or business in the United States, and whether any expense, loss or deduction is properly allocated and apportioned to that income.

(4) Certain exempt amounts. Effectively connected adjusted current earnings and effectively connected pre-adjustment alternative minimum taxable income do not include any item of income, or any expense, loss or deduction that is properly allocated and apportioned to income that is exempt from United States taxation under section 883 or an applicable income tax treaty. See section 894.

(n) Adjustment for adjusted current earnings of consolidated groups. *(1) Positive adjustments.* For taxable years beginning after December 31, 1989, the alternative minimum taxable income of a consolidated group (as defined in § 1.1502-1T) is increased by 75 percent of the excess, if any, of—

(i) The consolidated adjusted current earnings for the taxable year, over

(ii) The consolidated pre-adjustment alternative minimum taxable income for the taxable year.

(2) Negative adjustments. (i) In general. The alternative minimum taxable income of a consolidated group is decreased, subject to the limitation of paragraph (n)(2)(ii) of this section, by 75 percent of the excess, if any, of the consolidated pre-adjustment alternative minimum taxable income over consolidated adjusted current earnings.

(ii) Limitation on negative adjustments. The amount of the negative adjustment for any taxable year shall be limited to the excess, if any, of—

(A) The aggregate increases in the alternative minimum taxable income of the group in prior years under this section, over

(B) The aggregate decreases in the alternative minimum taxable income of the group in prior years under this section.

(3) Definitions. (i) Consolidated pre-adjustment alternative minimum taxable income. Consolidated pre-adjustment alternative minimum taxable income is the consolidated taxable income (as defined in § 1.1502-11) of a consolidated group for the taxable year, determined with the adjustments provided in sections 56 and 58 (except for the adjustment for adjusted current earnings and the alternative tax net operat-

ing loss determined under section 56(a)(4)) and increased by the preference items described in section 57.

(ii) Consolidated adjusted current earnings. The consolidated adjusted current earnings of a consolidated group is the consolidated pre-adjustment alternative minimum taxable income of the consolidated group for the taxable year, adjusted as provided in section 56(g) and this section.

(4) Example. The following example illustrates the provisions of this paragraph (n):

(i) P is the common parent of a consolidated group. In 1990, the group has consolidated pre-adjustment alternative minimum taxable income of $1,400,000 and consolidated adjusted current earnings of $1,600,000. Thus, the group has a consolidated adjustment for adjusted current earnings for 1990 of $150,000 (75 percent of the $200,000 excess of consolidated adjusted current earnings over consolidated pre-adjustment alternative minimum taxable income), and alternative minimum taxable income of $1,550,000 ($1,400,000 plus $150,000).

(ii) In 1991, the group has consolidated pre-adjustment alternative minimum taxable income of $1,500,000 and consolidated adjusted current earnings of $1,100,000. Thus, the group can reduce its alternative minimum taxable income by $150,000. The potential negative adjustment of $300,000 (75 percent of the $400,000 excess of consolidated pre-adjustment alternative minimum taxable income over consolidated adjusted current earnings) is limited to the $150,000 consolidated adjustment for adjusted current earnings taken into account in 1990.

(o) [Reserved]

(p) Effective dates for corporate partners in partnerships. *(1) In general.* The provisions of this section apply to a corporate partner's distributive share of items of income and expense from a partnership for any taxable year of the partnership ending within or with any taxable year of the corporate partner beginning after December 31, 1989.

(2) Application of effective dates. Solely for purposes of the effective date provisions of this section, a partnership event (such as placing property in service, paying or incurring a cost, or closing an installment sale) is deemed to occur on the last day of the partnership's taxable year.

(3) Example. The following example illustrates the provisions of this paragraph (p):

(i) X is a calendar-year corporation that is a partner in P, an accrual-basis partnership with a taxable year ending March 31. During P's taxable year ending March 31, 1990, P earned ratably throughout the year interest income on tax-exempt obligations. In addition, P incurred intangible drilling costs in November 1989 and in February 1990.

(ii) X's adjusted current earnings for 1990 includes X's distributive share of the interest on the tax-exempt obligations earned by P for its taxable year ending March 31, 1990. This is true even though P earned a portion of the interest prior to January 1, 1990.

(iii) For purposes of computing X's adjusted current earnings for 1990, the adjustment provided in paragraph (f)(1) of this section applies to X's distributive share of P's November 1989 and February 1990 intangible drilling costs.

(q) Treatment of distributions of property to shareholders. *(1) In general.* If a distribution of an item of property by a corporation with respect to its stock gives rise to more than one adjustment to earnings and profits under section 312, all of the adjustments with respect to that item of property (including the adjustment described in section 312(c) with respect to liabilities to which the item is subject or which are assumed in connection with the distribution) are combined for purposes of determining the corporation's adjusted current earnings for the taxable year. If the amount included in pre-adjustment alternative minimum taxable income with respect to a distribution of an item of property exceeds the net increase in earnings and profits caused by the distribution, pre-adjustment alternative minimum taxable income is not reduced in computing adjusted current earnings. If the net increase in earnings and profits caused by a distribution of an item of property exceeds the amount included in pre-adjustment alternative minimum taxable income with respect to the distribution, that excess is added to pre-adjustment alternative minimum taxable income in computing adjusted current earnings.

(2) Examples. The following examples illustrate the provisions of this paragraph (q).

(i) Example 1. K corporation distributes property with a fair market value of $150 and an adjusted basis of $100. The adjusted basis is the same for purposes of computing taxable income, pre-adjustment alternative minimum taxable income, adjusted current earnings, and earnings and profits. Under section 312(a)(3), as modified by section 312(b)(2), K decreases its earnings and profits by the fair market value of the property, or $150. Under section 312(b)(1), K increases its earnings and profits by the excess of the fair market value of the property over its adjusted basis, or $50. As a result of the distribution, there is a net decrease in K's earnings and profits of $100. K recognizes $50 of gain under section 311(b) as a result of the distribution as if K sold the property for $150. K thus has no amount permanently excluded from pre-adjustment alternative minimum taxable income that is taken into account in determining current earnings and profits, and thus has no adjustment under paragraph (c)(1) of this section.

(ii) Example 2. The facts are the same as in example 1, except that the distribution shareholder assumes a $190 liability in connection with the distribution. Under section 312(c)(1), K must adjust the adjustments to its earnings and profits under section 312(a) and (b) to account for the liability the shareholder assumes. K adjusts the $100 net decrease in its earnings and profits to reflect the $190 liability, resulting in an increase in its earnings and profits of $90. Because section 311(b)(2) makes the rules of section 336(b) apply, the fair market value of the property is not less than the amount of the liability, or $190. K therefore is treated as if it sold the property for $190, recognizing $90 of gain. K thus has no amount permanently excluded from pre-adjustment alternative minimum taxable income that is taken into account in determining current earnings and profits, and thus has no adjustment under paragraph (c)(1) of this section.

(r) Elections to use simplified inventory methods to compute alternative minimum tax. *(1) In general.* If a taxpayer makes an election under this paragraph (r) (and does not make the election in paragraph (r)(5) of this section), the rules of paragraph (r)(2) of this section apply in computing the taxpayer's pre-adjustment alternative minimum taxable income and adjusted current earnings.

(2) Effect of election. (i) Inventories. The taxpayer's inventory amounts as determined for purposes of computing taxable income are used for purposes of computing pre-adjustment alternative minimum taxable income and adjusted current earnings. Subject to the further modification described in paragraph (r)(2)(ii) of this section, the taxpayer's cost of sales as determined for purposes of computing taxable income is also used for purposes of computing pre-ad-

justment alternative minimum taxable income and adjusted current earnings.

(ii) Modifications required. (A) In general. If a taxpayer makes an election under this paragraph (r), pre-adjustment alternative minimum taxable income and adjusted current earnings are computed with the modifications described in this paragraph. The items of adjustment under sections 56 and 58 and the items of tax preference under section 57 are computed without regard to the portion of those adjustments and preferences which, but for the election described in this paragraph, would have been capitalized in ending inventory. For example, pre-adjustment alternative minimum taxable income is increased by the excess of the depreciation allowable for the taxable year under section 168 for purposes of computing taxable income (determined without regard to section 263A) over the depreciation allowable for the taxable year under section 56(a)(1) and section 57 for purposes of computing pre-adjustment alternative minimum taxable income (determined without regard to section 263A). Similarly, adjusted current earnings is further increased by the excess of the depreciation allowable for the taxable year under section 56(a)(1) and section 57 for purposes of computing pre-adjustment alternative minimum taxable income (determined without regard to section 263A) over the depreciation allowable for the taxable year under section 56(g)(4)(A) for purposes of computing adjusted current earnings (determined without regard to section 263A). Thus, the modifications described in the preceding sentence do not duplicate amounts that are taken into account in computing pre-adjustment alternative minimum taxable income. See paragraph (a)(6)(ii) of this section.

(B) Negative modifications allowed. An election under this paragraph(r) does not affect the taxpayer's ability to make negative adjustments. Thus, if an election is made under this paragraph (r) and the amount of any adjustment under section 56 or 58, determined after modification under paragraph (r)(2)(ii)(A) of this section, is a negative amount, then this amount reduces pre-adjustment alternative minimum taxable income or adjusted current earnings. However, no negative adjustment under this paragraph (r)(2)(ii)(B) is allowed for the items of tax preference under section 57.

(iii) LIFO recapture adjustment. If a taxpayer makes an election under this paragraph (r) and uses the LIFO method for some assets, for purposes of computing the LIFO recapture adjustment under paragraph (f)(3) of this section for taxable years beginning after December 31, 1989—

(A) The LIFO inventory amount as determined for purposes of computing taxable income is used in lieu of the LIFO inventory amount as determined under paragraph (f)(3)(iii) of this section;

(B) The FIFO inventory amount is computed without regard to the adjustments under sections 56 (including the adjustments of section 56(g)(4)) and 58 and the items of tax preference of section 57; and

(C) The beginning LIFO and FIFO inventory amounts under paragraph (f)(3)(ii) of this section are the ending LIFO inventory amount as determined for purposes of computing taxable income and the ending FIFO inventory amount computed without regard to the adjustments under sections 56 (including the adjustments of section 56(g)(4)) and 58 and the items of tax preference of section 57 for the last taxable year beginning before January 1, 1990.

(3) Time and manner of making election. (i) Prospective election. (A) A prospective election under this paragraph (r) may be made by any taxpayer—

(1) That has computed pre-adjustment alternative minimum taxable income and adjusted current earnings for all prior taxable years in accordance with the method described in this paragraph (r); or

(2) That has not computed pre-adjustment alternative minimum taxable income and adjusted current earnings for all prior tax years in accordance with the method described in this paragraph (r), but for which the use of the method described in this paragraph (r) for all prior taxable years would not have changed the taxpayer's tax liability (as shown on returns filed as of the date the election is made) for any prior taxable year for which the period of limitations under section 6501 (a) has not expired (as of the date the election is made).

(B) A prospective election under this paragraph (r) may only be made by attaching a statement to the taxpayer's timely filed (including extensions) original Federal income tax return for any taxable year that is no later than its first taxable year to which this paragraph (r) applies and in which the taxpayer's tentative minimum tax (computed under the provisions of this paragraph (r)) exceeds its regular tax. However, in the case of a taxpayer described in paragraph (r)(3)(i)(A)(1) of this section that had tentative minimum tax in excess of its regular tax for any prior taxable year, the election may only be made by attaching a statement to its timely filed (including extensions) original Federal income tax return for the first taxable year ending after December 18, 1992. The statement must—

(1) Give the name, address and employer identification number of the taxpayer; and

(2) Identify the election as made under this paragraph (r).

(C) The determination of whether a taxpayer is described in paragraph (r)(3)(i)(A)(2) of this section is to be made as of the time the taxpayer makes a prospective election in accordance with the procedures in paragraph (r)(3)(i)(B) of this section.

(D) Any taxpayer described in paragraph (r)(3)(i)(A)(2) of this section that makes a prospective election will be deemed to have used the method described in this paragraph (r) in computing pre-adjustment alternative minimum taxable income and adjusted current earnings for all prior taxable years.

(ii) Retroactive election. (A) A retroactive election under this paragraph (r) may be made by any taxpayer not described in paragraph (r)(3)(i)(A)(1) or (2) of this section. Except as provided in paragraph (r)(3)(iii) of this section, a retroactive election may only be made by attaching a statement to the taxpayer's amended Federal income tax return for the earliest taxable year for which the period of limitations under section 6501(a) has not expired and which begins after December 31, 1986. The amended return to which the election under this paragraph (r)(3)(ii) is attached must be filed no later than June 19, 1993.

(B) The amended return must contain the statement described in paragraph (r)(3)(i)(B) of this section. In addition, the statement must contain a representation that the taxpayer will modify its pre-adjustment alternative minimum taxable income and adjusted current earnings for all open taxable years in accordance with paragraph (r)(2) of this section. Upon this change in method of accounting, the taxpayer must include the entire adjustment required under section 481(a), if any, in pre-adjustment alternative minimum taxable income and adjusted current earnings on the amended return for the year of the election. The taxpayer must also reflect the method of accounting described in paragraph (r)(2) of this section on amended returns filed for all taxable years after the year of the election for which returns were originally filed before making the election (and for which the period of limitations under section 6501(a) has not expired).

(C) Provided a taxpayer meets the requirements of this paragraph (r), any change in method of accounting arising as a result of making a retroactive election will be treated as made with the advance consent of the Commissioner.

(D) Any retroactive election under this paragraph (r) that is made without filing amended returns required under this paragraph (r)(3)(ii) shall constitute a change in method of accounting made without the consent of the Commissioner.

(iii) Taxpayers under examination. (A) In general. A taxpayer that wishes to make a retroactive election under section (r)(3)(ii) of this section may use the procedures in paragraph (r)(3)(iii)(A)(1) or (2) in lieu of filing an amended return for any taxable year that is under examination by the Internal Revenue Service.

(1) Year of change under examination. If the year of the change is under examination at the time the taxpayer timely makes the election, the taxpayer may (in lieu of filing an amended return for the year of the change) furnish the written statement described in paragraph (r)(3)(iii)(B) of this section to the revenue agent responsible for examining the taxpayer's return no later than June 19, 1993. It is the taxpayer's responsibility to make a timely election either by furnishing the statement to the revenue agent or by filing amended returns by June 19, 1993.

(2) Other open years under examination. If any other year for which the taxpayer must modify its pre-adjustment alternative minimum taxable income and adjusted current earnings (see paragraph (r)(3)(ii)(B) of this section) is examined, the taxpayer may (in lieu of filing an amended return) furnish the amount of the conforming adjustment to the revenue agent responsible for examining the taxpayer's return. It is the taxpayer's responsibility to timely modify its pre-adjustment alternative minimum taxable income and adjusted current earnings for each year other than the year of change, either by furnishing the amount of the adjustment to the revenue agent or by filing amended returns.

(B) Statement required. The statement required under paragraph (r)(3)(iii)(A)(1) of this section must include all of the items required under paragraph (r)(3)(ii)(B) of this section, as well as—

(1) The caption "Election to use regular tax inventories for AMT purposes;"

(2) A description of the nature and amount of all items that would result in adjustments and that the taxpayer would have reported if the taxpayer had used the method described in this paragraph (r) for all prior taxable years for which the period of limitations under section 6501(a) has not expired and which begin after December 31, 1986; and

(3) The following declaration signed by the person authorized to sign the return for the taxpayer: "Under penalties of perjury, I declare that I have examined this written statement, and to the best of my knowledge and belief this written statement is true, correct, and complete."

(C) Year of change. The year of change is the earliest taxable year for which the period of limitations under section 6501(a) has not expired at the time the statement is submitted to the appropriate revenue agent and that begins after December 31, 1986. Thus, the adjustments required to be included on the statement must include any adjustment under section 481(a) determined as if the method described in this paragraph (r) had been used in all taxable years prior to the year of change that began after December 31, 1986.

(D) Treatment of additional tax liability. Any additional tax liability that results from the adjustments identified in the written statement described in paragraph (r)(3)(iii)(B) of this section is treated as an additional amount of tax shown on an amended return.

(iv) Election as method of accounting. The elections provided in paragraphs (r)(3)(i) and (ii) of this section constitute either adoptions of, or changes in, methods of accounting. These elections, once made, may be revoked only with the consent of the Commissioner in accordance with the rules of section 446(e) and § 1.446-1(e).

(v) Untimely election to use simplified inventory method. If a taxpayer makes an election described in this paragraph (r) after the times set forth in paragraph (r)(3)(i) or (ii) of this section, the taxpayer must comply with the requirements of § 1.446-1(e)(3) in order to secure the consent of the Commissioner to change to the method of accounting prescribed in this paragraph (r). The taxpayer generally will be subject to terms and conditions designed to place the taxpayer in a position no more favorable than a taxpayer that timely complied with paragraph (r)(3)(i) or (ii) of this section, whichever is applicable.

(4) Example. The following example illustrates the provisions of this paragraph (r).

Example. (i) Corporation L is a calendar year manufacturer of baseball bats and uses the LIFO method of accounting for inventories. During 1987, 1988, and 1989, L's cost of goods sold in computing taxable income was as follows:

	1987	1988	1989
Beginning LIFO inventory	$3,000	$4,000	$5,000
Purchases and other costs	9,000	9,000	9,000
Ending LIFO inventory	(4,000)	(5,000)	(6,000)
Cost of goods sold	$8,000	$8,000	$8,000

(ii) L has no preferences under section 57 during 1987, 1988 and 1989. L's sole adjustment in computing alternative minimum tax during 1987, 1988, and 1989 was the depreciation adjustment under section 56(a)(1). Depreciation determined for both production and non-production assets under section 168 and under section 56(a)(1) during 1987, 1988, and 1989 was as follows:

	1987	1988	1989
Section 168 depreciation	$1,800	$1,800	$1,800
Section 56(a)(1) depreciation	(900)	(900)	(900)
Depreciation difference	$ 900	$ 900	$ 900
Portion of difference capitalized in the increase in inventory	(100)	(100)	(100)
Adjustment required under section 56(a)(1)	$ 800	$ 800	$ 800

(iii) In computing taxable income, a portion of each year's section 168 depreciation attributable to production assets is deducted currently and a portion is capitalized into the increase in ending inventory. For 1987, 1988, and 1989, L computed alternative minimum tax by deducting the cost of goods sold which was reflected in taxable income ($8,000) in accordance with paragraph (r)(2)(i) of this section. For 1987, 1988, and 1989, L also modified its adjustments under sections 56 and 58 and its preferences under section 57 to disregard the portion of any adjustment or preference that was capitalized in inventory. Thus, under section 56(a)(1), L increased alternative minimum taxable income during each year by $900.

(iv) L is eligible to make the election under paragraph (r)(1) of this section in accordance with paragraph (r)(3)(i) of this section (a prospective election).

(v) L must compute its LIFO recapture adjustment for each year by reference to—

(A) The FIFO inventory amount after applying the provisions of section 263A but before applying the adjustments of sections 56 and 58 and the items of preference in section 57; and

(B) The LIFO inventory amount used in computing taxable income.

(5) Election to use alternative minimum tax inventories to compute adjusted current earnings. A taxpayer may elect under this paragraph (r)(5) to use the inventory amounts used to compute pre-adjustment alternative minimum taxable income in computing its adjusted current earnings. Rules similar to those of paragraphs (r)(2) and (r)(3) of this section apply for purposes of this election.

(s) Adjustment for alternative tax energy preference deduction. *(1) In general.* For purposes of computing adjusted current earnings, any taxpayer claiming a deduction under section 56(h) must properly decrease basis by the portion of the deduction allowed under section 56(h) which is attributable to adjustments under section 56(g)(4). In taxable years following the taxable year in which the section 56(h) deduction is claimed, basis recovery (including amortization, depletion, and gain on sale) must properly take into account this basis reduction.

(2) Example. The following example illustrates the provisions of this paragraph (s):

Example. Corporation A, a calendar year taxpayer, incurs $100 of intangible drilling costs on January 1, 1994 and as a result of these intangible drilling costs A claims a deduction under section 56(h) of $40. Assume that $20 of A's deduction under section 56(h) is attributable to the adjustment under paragraph (f)(1) of this section. A must reduce by $20 the amount of intangible drilling costs to be amortized under paragraph (f)(1) of this section in 1995 through 1998 (the balance of the 60 month amortization period).

T.D. 8340, 3/14/91, amend T.D. 8352, 6/26/91, T.D. 8454, 12/18/92, T.D. 8482, 8/6/93, T.D. 8566, 10/7/94, T.D. 8858, 1/5/2000, T.D. 8940, 2/12/2001.

PAR. 2. Section 1.56(g)-1 is amended by revising paragraph (n) to read as follows:

Proposed § 1.56(g)-1 Adjusted current earnings. [*For Preamble, see ¶ 151,475*]

* * * * *

(n) Adjustment for adjusted current earnings of consolidated groups. For consolidated return years for which the due date of the income tax return (without regard to extensions) is on or after [the date that is sixty days after final regulations are filed with the FEDERAL REGISTER], the rules of § 1.1502-55(b)(3) apply in computing the adjustment for adjusted current earnings of a consolidated group.

* * * * *

§ 1.56A-1 Imposition of tax.

Caution: The Treasury has not yet amended Reg § 1.56A-1 to reflect changes made by P.L. 99-514.

(a) In general. Section 56(a) imposes an income tax on the items of tax preference (as defined in § 1.57-1) of all persons other than persons specifically exempt from the taxes imposed by chapter 1. The items of tax preference represent income of a person which either is not subject to current taxation by reason of temporary exclusion (such as stock options) or by reason of an acceleration of deductions (such as accelerated depreciation) or is sheltered from full taxation by reason of certain deductions (such as percentage depletion) or by reason of a special rate of tax (such as the rate of tax on corporate capital gains). The tax imposed by section 56 is in addition to the other taxes imposed by chapter 1.

(b) Computation of tax. The amount of such tax is 10 percent of the excess (referred to herein as "the minimum tax base") of—

(1) The sum of the taxpayer's items of tax preference for such year in excess of the taxpayer's minimum tax exemption (determined under § 1.58-1) for such year, over

(2) The sum of:

(i) The taxes imposed for such year under chapter 1 other than the taxes imposed by section 56 (relating to minimum tax for tax preferences), by section 531 (relating to accumulated earnings tax), or by section 541 (relating to personal holding company tax), reduced by the sum of the credits allowable under—

(a) Section 33 (relating to taxes of foreign countries and possessions of the United States),

(b) Section 37 (relating to retirement income),

(c) Section 38 (relating to investment credit),

(d) Section 40 (relating to expenses of work incentive programs), and

(e) Section 41 (relating to contributions to candidates for public office, and

(ii) The tax carryovers to such taxable year (as described in § 1.56A-5).

(c) Special rule. For purposes of paragraph (b) of this section where for any taxable year in which a tax is imposed under section 667 (relating to treatment of amounts deemed distributed by a trust in preceding years), that portion of the section 667 tax representing an increase in an earlier year's chapter 1 taxes (as recomputed), which taxes are allowed as a reduction in any such earlier year's minimum tax base, is not allowable as a reduction in the minimum tax base for the current taxable year. The remaining portion of the section 667 tax, representing the taxes imposed by section 56, section 531, and section 541, is not allowable as a reduction in the minimum tax base for any taxable year. Similarly, taxes imposed under section 614(c)(4) (relating to increase in tax with respect to aggregation of certain mineral interests) or under section 1351(d) (relating to recoveries of foreign expropriation losses) for any taxable year are not allowed as a reduction in the minimum tax base for such taxable year to the extent they represent chapter 1 taxes which are allowed as a reduction in a minimum tax base for an earlier taxable year for purposes of the computations under section 614(c)(4) or section 1351(d) or to the extent they represent an increase in the tax imposed by section 56, section 531, or section 541 in an earlier taxable year.

T.D. 7564, 9/11/78, amend T.D. 8138, 4/23/87.

§ 1.56A-2 Deferral of tax liability in case of certain net operating losses.

Caution: The Treasury has not yet amended Reg § 1.56A-2 to reflect changes made by P.L. 99-514.

(a) In general. Section 56(b) provides for the deferral of liability for the minimum tax where, for the taxable year, the taxpayer has—

(1) A net operating loss for such taxable year any portion of which (under sec. 172) remains as a net operating loss carryover to a succeeding taxable year, and

(2) Items of tax preference in excess of the minimum tax exemptions (hereinafter referred to as "excess tax preferences").

In such a case, an amount of tax equal to the lesser of the tax imposed under section 56(a) (after allowance of the retirement income credit to the extent that such credit cannot be used against the other taxes imposed by chapter 1) or 10 percent of the amount of the net operating loss carryover described in subparagraph (1) of this paragraph is deferred. Such amount is not treated as tax imposed in such taxable year, but is treated as tax imposed in the succeeding taxable year or years in which the net operating loss is used as provided in paragraphs (b) and (c) of this section. Deferral will result in the above case regardless of the character of the tax preference items. Thus, for example, if the taxpayer has $1,030,000 of items of tax preference, including the stock option item of tax preference, and a $750,000 net operating loss available for carryover to subsequent taxable years, the amount of tax imposed for the taxable year under section 56(a) is $100,000 and $75,000 is deferred by application of section 56(b). Therefore, only $25,000 is treated as tax imposed for the taxable year. The provisions of this section are applicable in the case of a net operating loss or comparable item such as an operations loss under section 812 and an unused loss as defined in section 825(b).

(b) Year of liability. In any taxable year in which any portion of a net operating loss carryover attributable to the amount of excess tax preferences reduces taxable income (in the form of a net operating loss deduction), section 56(b)(2) treats as tax liability imposed in such taxable year an amount equal to 10 percent of such reduction. For this purpose, the portion of such net operating loss which is considered attributable to the amount of excess tax preferences is an amount equal to the lesser of such excess or the amount of the net operating loss carryover described in paragraph (a)(1) of this section. In no case, however, shall the total amount of tax imposed by reason of section 56(b) in subsequent years exceed the amount of the tax that was deferred in the loss year.

(c) Priority of reduction. *(1)* If a portion of a net operating loss is attributable to an amount of excess tax preferences, such portion is considered to reduce taxable income in succeeding taxable years only after the other portion (if any) of such net operating loss is used to reduce taxable income. Accordingly, if the amount of a net operating loss which may be carried to succeeding taxable years is reduced because of a modification required to be made pursuant to section 172(b)(2), such reduction is to be considered to be first from that portion of the net operating loss that is attributable to excess tax preferences. If a portion of a net operating loss carryover which is attributable to an amount of excess tax preferences is not used to reduce taxable income in any succeeding taxable year, no minimum tax will be imposed with respect to such portion.

(2) In the case of taxpayers with deductions attributable to foreign sources which are suspense preferences (as defined in paragraphs (c)(1)(ii) and (2)(ii) of § 1.58-7), the amount of such deductions is not included in the portion of the net operating loss not attributable to excess tax preferences. The portion of the net operating loss attributable to excess tax preferences is increased by the amount of suspense preferences which are, in accordance with the provisions of § 1.58-7(c), converted to actual items of tax preference (and not used against the minimum tax exemption of the loss year) in subsequent taxable years. The other portion of the net operating loss is increased by the amount of suspense preferences which reduce taxable income in subsequent taxable years but are not converted to actual items of tax preference (or are so converted but used against the minimum tax exemption of the loss year). See § 1.58-7(c)(1)(iii) example (4).

(d) Multiple net operating loss carryovers. In determining whether a net operating loss is used to reduce taxable income in a taxable year to which two or more net operating losses are carried, the ordering rules of section 172(b) and the regulations thereunder are to be applied. Thus, for example, the portion of a net operating loss carried over from an earlier taxable year which is attributable to an amount of excess tax preference is used to reduce taxable income in the carryover year before any portion of any other net operating loss carried over or back from a taxable year subsequent to the earlier taxable year.

(e) Examples. The application of this section may be illustrated by the following examples:

Example (1). In 1970, A, a calendar year taxpayer, who is a single individual, has $180,000 of items of tax preference, a $150,000 net operating loss of which $100,000 may be carried forward, and no tax liability under chapter 1 without regard to the minimum tax. His minimum tax computed under section 56(a) is $15,000 (10 percent times ($180,000 minus $30,000)). Under section 56(b)(1) an amount equal to the lesser of the amount determined under section 56(a) ($15,000) or 10 percent of the net operating loss which may be carried forward ($10,000) is treated as a deferred liability. Thus, his minimum tax liability for 1970 is $5,000 ($15,000 minimum tax under section 56(a) minus $10,000 deferred tax liability under section 56(b)). If, in 1971, he has $80,000 of taxable income before the deduction for the 1970 net operating loss, his minimum tax liability is $8,000 (10 percent of the amount by which the net operating loss carryforward from 1970 reduces taxable income) plus any minimum tax liability resulting from items of tax preference arising in 1971. If, by reason of the modifications provided by section 172(b)(2), no portion of the 1970 net operating loss remains as a carryover from 1971, no further minimum tax liability will result from the items of tax preference arising in 1970.

Example (2). In 1970, A, a calendar year taxpayer who is a single individual, has $90,000 of items of tax preference, a $100,000 net operating loss available for carryover to future taxable years, no net operating loss carryovers from prior taxable years, and no tax liability under chapter 1 without regard to the minimum tax. His minimum tax computed under section 56(a) is $6,000 (10 percent times ($90,000 minus $30,000)). Under section 56(b)(1) an amount equal to the lesser of the amount determined under section 56(a) ($6,000) or 10 percent of the net operating loss subject to carryforward ($10,000) is treated as a deferred liability. Thus, A owes no minimum tax in 1970 and the entire

$6,000 of minimum tax liability is deferred. Under section 56(b)(2), the portion of the net operating loss attributable to the excess tax preferences described in section 56(b)(1)(B) is $60,000.

(a) In 1971, A has $25,000 of taxable income before the deduction for the 1970 net operating loss. Thus, in 1971, A has no minimum tax liability attributable to the items of tax preference arising in 1970 since, by application of section 56(b)(3), the portion of the 1970 net operating loss carryforward not attributable to the excess described in section 56(b)(1)(B), or $40,000, is considered applied against taxable income before the remaining portion.

(b) In 1972, A has $50,000 of taxable income before the deduction for the remaining 1970 net operating loss. Thus, the first $15,000 of reduction in taxable income is considered as from the portion of the 1970 net operating loss carryforward not attributable to the excess tax preferences described in section 56(b)(1)(B) and the remaining $35,000 of reduction in taxable income is considered attributable to such excess. A's 1972 minimum tax attributable to items of tax preference arising in 1970 is, therefore, $3,500 (10 percent times $35,000).

(c) In 1973, A has $80,000 of taxable income before the deduction for the 1970 net operating loss. The remaining $25,000 of the 1970 net operating loss carryforward is used to reduce taxable income in 1973. Thus, A's 1973 minimum tax liability attributable to items of tax preference arising in 1970 is $2,500 (10 percent times $25,000).

Example (3). In 1971, M Corporation, a Western Hemisphere trade corporation (as defined in sec. 921), reporting on a calendar year basis has $20,000 of taxable income after all deductions including the Western Hemisphere trade deduction allowable under section 922 in the amount of $30,000. In 1970, M Corporation had a net operating loss of $100,000 all of which was available for carryover to 1971 and $60,000 of which was attributable to excess tax preferences. In computing the amount of the 1970 net operating loss carried over to 1972 pursuant to section 172(b), the 1971 Western Hemisphere trade corporation deduction is not taken into account. Thus, M Corporation's recomputed income under section 172(b) is $50,000 ($20,000 taxable income plus $30,000 Western Hemisphere trade corporation deduction). Pursuant to paragraph (c)(1) of this section, $20,000 of the $40,000 portion of the 1970 net operating loss not attributable to excess tax preferences is considered to reduce taxable income in 1971 and $30,000 of the $60,000 portion of the 1970 net operating loss attributable to excess tax preferences is considered reduced pursuant to section 172(b)(2). Thus, M Corporation has no 1971 minimum tax attributable to items of tax preference arising in 1970. Of the $50,000 remaining of the 1970 net operating loss, $30,000 is attributable to excess tax preference.

Example (4). In 1972, A, a calendar year taxpayer who is a single individual, has $25,000 of taxable income resulting from $50,000 of net long-term capital gains. In 1971, A had a net operating loss of $100,000 all of which is available to carryover to 1972 and $60,000 of which is attributable to excess tax preferences. By application of section 172(b) only $50,000 of the 1971 net operating loss is carried over to 1973. Pursuant to paragraph (c) of this section, $25,000 of the $40,000 portion of the 1971 net operating loss not attributable to excess tax preferences is considered to reduce taxable income in 1972. Of the $50,000 remaining of the 1971 net operating loss, $15,000 is not attributable to excess tax preferences and $35,000 is attributable to excess tax preferences. Thus, the $25,000 section 1202 deduction, in effect, reduces the portion of the 1971 net operating loss attributable to excess tax preferences. Because a net operating loss carryover is reduced to the extent of any section 1202 deduction, section 1202 deductions do not normally produce a tax benefit in such circumstances and, pursuant to § 1.57-4, would not be treated as items of tax preference. However, in this case, to the extent the portion of the 1971 net operating loss carryover attributable to excess tax preferences is reduced by reason of the section 1202 deduction, such deduction does result in a tax benefit to the taxpayer and is, therefore, treated as an item of tax preference in 1971. See § 1.57-4(b)(2).

T.D. 7564, 9/11/78, amend T.D. 8138, 4/23/87.

§ 1.56A-3 Effective date.

Caution: The Treasury has not yet amended Reg § 1.56A-3 to reflect changes made by P.L. 99-514.

(a) In general. The minimum tax is effective for taxable years ending after December 31, 1969.

(b) Taxable year beginning in 1969 and ending in 1970. In the case of a taxable year beginning in 1969 and ending in 1970, the amount of the minimum tax shall be an amount equal to the amount determined under section 56 multiplied by the following fraction:

Number of days in the taxable year ending after December 31, 1969 ÷ Number of days in the entire taxable year.

Where, by reason of section 56(b) and § 1.56A-2, tax initially imposed in a 1969-70 fiscal year is deferred until a subsequent taxable year or years, the amount of such tax liability in any subsequent taxable year is determined by application of the above fraction. Section 21, relating to computation of tax in years where there is a change in rates, is not applicable to the initial imposition of the minimum tax for tax preferences. The applications of this paragraph may be illustrated by the following example:

Example. The taxpayer uses a June 30 fiscal year. For fiscal 1969-70 the taxpayer has $180,000 of items of tax preference and a $50,000 net operating loss. In fiscal year 1970-71, the taxpayer uses the full net operating loss carryover from 1969-70 to reduce his taxable income by $50,000. Thus, without regard to the proration rules applicable under this section, the taxpayer's minimum tax liability for items of tax preference arising in 1969-70 is $15,000, i.e., 10 percent × ($180,000 − $30,000), of which $5,000, i.e., 10 percent × $50,000, is deferred until 1970-71 under the principles of section 56(b) and section 1.56A-2. By application of the above formula the taxpayer's actual minimum tax liability is $4,958.90 in 1969-70 and $2,479.45 in 1970-71 determined as follows:

1969-70: 181/365 × $10,000

1970-71: 181/365 × $5,000

T.D. 7564, 9/11/78, amend T.D. 8138, 4/23/87.

§ 1.56A-4 Certain taxpayers.

Caution: The Treasury has not yet amended Reg § 1.56A-4 to reflect changes made by P.L. 99-514.

For application of the minimum tax in the case of estates and trusts, electing small business corporations, common trust funds, regulated investment companies, real estate investment trusts, and partnerships, see §§ 1.58-2 through 1.58-6.

T.D. 7564, 9/11/78, amend T.D. 8138, 4/23/87.

§ 1.56A-5 Tax carryovers.

Caution: The Treasury has not yet amended Reg § 1.56A-5 to reflect changes made by P.L. 99-514.

(a) In general. Section 56(c) provides a 7-year carryover of the excess of the taxes described in paragraph (1) of such section imposed during the taxable year over the items of tax preference described in paragraph (2) of such section for such taxable year for the purpose of reducing the amount subject to tax under section 56(a) in subsequent taxable years.

(b) Computation of amount of carryover. The amount of tax carryover described in section 50(c) is the excess (if any) of—

(1) The taxes imposed for the taxable year under chapter 1 other than taxes imposed by section 56 (relating to minimum tax for tax preferences), by section 531 (relating to accumulated earnings tax), or by section 541 (relating to personal holding company tax), reduced by the sum of the credits allowable under—

(i) Section 33 (relating to taxes of foreign countries and possessions of the United States),

(ii) Section 37 (relating to retirement income,

(iii) Section 38 (relating to investment credit),

(iv) Section 40 (relating to expenses of work incentive programs), and

(v) Section 41 (relating to contributions to candidates for public office), over

(2) The sum of the taxpayer's items of tax preference for such year in excess of the taxpayer's minimum tax exemption (determined under § 1.58-1) for such year.

For purposes of section 56(c) and this section, taxes imposed in a taxable year ending on or before December 31, 1969, are not included in the taxes described in subparagraph (1) of this paragraph. In addition, the rules of paragraph (c) of § 1.56A-1 are applicable in determining the taxable year for which taxes are imposed under chapter 1 for purposes of paragraph (a)(1) of this section.

(c) Operation of carryover. Tax carryovers attributable to the taxable year shall be carried over to each of the 7 succeeding taxable years as follows:

(1) To the first such succeeding taxable year to reduce in the manner described in paragraph (d) of this section the amount subject to tax under section 56(a) for such first succeeding taxable year and

(2) To the extent such amount is not used as a reduction in the amount subject to tax under section 56(a) for such taxable year, such amount (if any) is carried over to each of the succeeding 6 taxable years but only to the extent such amount is not used to reduce the amount subject to tax under section 56(a) in taxable years intervening between the taxable year to which such amount is attributable and the taxable year to which such amount may otherwise be carried over.

(d) Priority of reduction. Where tax carryovers attributable to two or more taxable years are carried over to a subsequent taxable year such amounts attributable to the earliest taxable year shall be used to reduce the amount subject to tax under section 56(a) for such subsequent taxable year before any such amounts attributable to a later taxable year.

(e) Special rules. *(1) Periods of less than 12 months.* A fractional part of a year which is a taxable year under section 441(b) or 7701(a)(23) is a taxable year for purposes of section 56(c) and this section.

(2) Electing small business corporations. A taxable year for which a corporation is an electing small business corporation (as defined in section 1371(b)) shall be counted as a taxable year for purposes of determining the taxable years to which amounts which are available as a carryover under paragraph (a) of this section may be carried whether or not such carryovers arose in a year in which an election was in effect.

(3) Husband and wife. (i) From joint to separate return. If a joint return is filed by a husband and wife in a taxable year or years to which a tax carryover is attributable but separate returns are filed in any subsequent taxable year to which such carryover may be carried over to reduce the amount subject to tax under section 56(a), such carryover described in paragraph (b) of this section shall be allocated between husband and wife for purposes of reducing the amount subject to tax under section 56(a) for such subsequent taxable year in accordance with the principles of § 1.172-7(d).

(ii) From separate to joint return. If separate returns are filed by a husband and wife in a taxable year or years in which a tax carryover is attributable but a joint return is filed in any subsequent taxable year to which such carryover may be carried over to reduce the amount subject to tax under section 56(a), such carryover shall be aggregated for purposes of reducing the amount subject to tax under section 56(a), for such subsequent taxable year.

(4) Estates and trusts. In the case of the termination of an estate or trust, tax carryovers attributable to the estate or trust shall not be allowed to the beneficiaries succeeding to the property of the estate or trust.

(5) Corporate acquisitions. In the case of a transaction to which section 381(a) applies, the acquiring corporation shall succeed to and take into account, as of the close of the date transfer the tax carryovers attributable to the distributor or distribution or transferor corporation. The portion of such carryovers which may be taken into account under paragraph (b)(2)(ii) of § 1.56A-1 for any taxable year shall not exceed the excess of (i) the sum of the items of tax preference for such year resulting from the continuation of the business in which the distributor or transferor corporation was engaged at the time of such transaction and the items of tax preference not related to the continuation of such business which are directly attributable to the assets acquired from the distributor or transferor corporation over/(ii) an amount which bears the same ratio to the acquiring corporation's minimum tax exemption for such year as the items of tax preference described in subdivision (i) of this subparagraph bears to all of the acquiring corporation's items of tax preference for such year. This item shall be taken into account by the acquiring corporation subject to the rules in section 381(b) and the regulations thereunder.

(f) Suspense preferences. Where an item of tax preference which is a suspense preference (as defined in § 1.58-7) arises in a taxable year in which tax carryovers may be used to reduce the minimum tax base (or in which such carryovers arise the minimum tax liability for that year and the tax carryovers to subsequent taxable years shall be recomputed upon the conversion of the suspense preference in a subsequent year. In lieu of the above, in all cases, since there is no difference in tax consequence, the recomputation may be accomplished by recomputing the minimum tax liability of the taxable year in which the suspense preference arose without reduction of the minimum tax base for the tax carryovers which have been used as a reduction in the minimum tax base in intervening taxable years. If such method is used, the minimum tax liability of the intervening year is not recomputed and any tax carryovers carried from the taxable year in which the suspense preference arose which remain as a carryover in the year of conversion are reduced, in the priority provided in paragraph (d) of this section, to the extent used to reduce an increase in the minimum tax base for the earlier year resulting from the conversion of the suspense preference.

(g) Taxes imposed in a taxable year beginning in 1969 and ending in 1970. In the case of a taxable year beginning in 1969 and ending in 1970 the amount of the carryover determined under paragraph (b) of this section is reduced to an amount equal to the amount of such carryover (without regard to this paragraph) multiplied by the following fraction:

Number of days in taxable year ending after December 31, 1969 ÷ Number of days in the entire taxable year.

(h) Examples. The provisions of this section may be illustrated by the following examples:

Example (1). A is a single individual who uses a June 30 fiscal year. For fiscal 1968-1969, A had income tax liability under chapter 1 in the amount of $100,000. For fiscal 1969-1970, A had items of tax preference in the amount of $212,500 and income tax liability under chapter 1 (other than taxes imposed under sections 56, 531, and 541) of $365,000.

(a) The chapter 1 tax attributable to fiscal 1968-1969 is not available as a carryover under section 56(c) to reduce the amount subject to tax under section 56(a) since this tax arose in a taxable year ending on or before December 31, 1969.

(b) A portion of the excess of chapter 1 tax over the amount subject to tax under section 56(a) attributable to fiscal year 1969-1970 is available as a carryover as provided in section 56(c) to reduce the amount subject to tax under section 56(a). The amount of this carryover is $91,000 computed as follows:

1. Carryover under paragraph (b) of this section:	
Chapter 1 taxes	$365,000
Items of tax preference in excess of exemption	182,500
Total	182,500
2. Reduction pursuant to paragraph (g) of this section:	
$^{182}/_{365}$ × $182,500 = $91,000	

Example (2). A is a calendar year taxpayer who is a single individual. In 1972, A had chapter 1 income tax liability (other than taxes imposed under sections 56, 531, and 541) of $200,000 and $50,000 of items of tax preference. In 1973, A had chapter 1 income tax liability (other than taxes imposed under sections 56, 531, and 541) of $120,000 and $40,000 of items of tax preference. In 1974, A had $400,000 of items of tax preference and no liability for tax under chapter 1 other than under section 56(a). Under section 56(c), the excess of the taxes described in paragraph (1) of that section arising in an earlier taxable year not used to reduce the amount subject to tax under section 56(a) for such taxable year can be carried over as provided in section 56(c) to reduce the amount subject to tax under section 56(a).

(a) The amount of the carryover from 1972 is $180,000 computed as follows:

Carryover under paragraph (b) of this section:	
Chapter 1 taxes	$200,000
Items of tax preference in excess of exemption	20,000
Total	180,000

(b) The amount of the carryover from 1973 is $110,000 computed as follows:

Carryover under paragraph (b) of this section:	
Chapter 1 taxes	$120,000
Items of tax preference in excess of exemption	10,000
Total	110,000

(c) For 1974, the excess of taxes in the preceding taxable years is used to reduce the amount subject to tax under section 56(a). The amount of carryover attributable to excess taxes arising in 1972 is used before such excess arising in 1973. The amount of tax under section 56(a) is $8,000 computed as follows:

1974 tax preferences	$400,000
Less exemption	30,000
	370,000
Less 1972 carryover	180,000
	190,000
Less 1973 carryover	110,000
1974 minimum tax base	80,000
1974 minimum tax ($80,000 × 10%)	8,000

Example (3). The facts are the same as in example (2) except that in 1974 A had $300,000 of items of tax preference. The amount of the carryover for taxable years after 1974 is computed as follows:

1974 tax preferences	$300,000
Less exemption	30,000
	270,000
Less 1972 carryover	180,000
	90,000
Less 1973 carryover	90,000
Minimum tax base	0
1973 carryover	110,000
Amount used in 1974	90,000
Amount available for taxable years after 1974	20,000

The $20,000 remaining of the 1973 carryover is available to reduce the amount subject to tax under section 56(a) in 1975 or other future taxable years as provided in section 56(c).

Example (4). M Corporation is a calendar year taxpayer. N Corporation uses a June 30 fiscal year. For the fiscal year 1970-1971, N Corporation had excess chapter 1 tax liability as described in paragraph (a) of this section in the amount of $75,000. On January 1, 1972, M Corporation acquired N Corporation in a reorganization described in section 368(a)(1)(A). N Corporation does not use any of such excess chapter 1 tax liability to reduce the amount subject to tax under section 56(a) for the short taxable year beginning on July 1, 1971, and ending on December 31, 1971. Thus, the excess chapter 1 tax liability is available to M Corporation as a carryover under paragraph (a) of this section to reduce the amount subject to tax for the next 6 succeeding taxable years beginning with taxable year 1972 as provided in this section. In applying the carryover to 1972 and succeeding taxable years, the carryover of N Corporation subject to the limitation of § 1.56A-5(e)(4) is combined with any carryovers originating with M Corporation in 1970.

T.D. 7564, 9/11/78, amend T.D. 8138, 4/23/87.

§ 12.8 Elections with respect to net leases of real property.

Caution: The Treasury has not yet amended Reg § 12.8 to reflect changes made by P.L. 99-514.

(a) In general. The elections described in this section are available for determining whether real property held by the taxpayer is subject to a net lease for purposes of section 57 (relating to items of tax preference for purposes of the minimum tax for tax preferences) or 163(d) (relating to limitation on interest on investment indebtedness). Under sections 57(c)(1)(A) and 163(d)(4)(A)(i), property will be considered to be subject to a net lease for a taxable year where the sum of the deductions of the lessor with respect to the property for the taxable year allowable solely by reason of section 162 (other than rents and reimbursed amounts with respect to the property) is less than 15 percent of the gross income from rents produced by the property (hereinafter referred to as the "expense test"). Under sections 57(c)(2) and 163(d)(7)(A), where a parcel of real property of the taxpayer is leased under two or more leases, the taxpayer may elect to apply the expense test set forth in sections 57(c)(1)(A) and 163(d)(4)(A)(i) by treating all leased portions of such property as subject to a single lease. Under sections 57(c)(3) and 163(d)(7)(B), at the election of the taxpayer, the expense test set forth in sections 57(c)(1)(A) and 163(d)(4)(A)(i) shall not apply with respect to real property of the taxpayer which has been in use for more than 5 years.

(b) Election with respect to multiple leases of single parcel of real property. If a parcel of real property of the taxpayer is leased under two or more leases, the expense test referred to in paragraph (a) of this section shall, at the election of the taxpayer, be applied by treating all leased portions of such property as subject to a single lease. For purposes of this paragraph, the term "parcel of real property" includes adjacent properties each of which is subject to lease.

(c) Election with respect to real property in use for more than 5 years. At the election of the taxpayer, the expense test referred to in paragraph (a) of this section shall not apply with respect to real property of the taxpayer which has been in use for more than 5 years. For this purpose, real property is in use only during the period that such property is both owned and used for commercial purposes by the taxpayer. If an improvement to the property was made during the time such property was owned by the taxpayer, and if, as a result of such improvement, the adjusted basis of such property was increased by 50 percent or more, use of such property for commercial purposes shall be deemed to have commenced for purposes of this paragraph as of the date such improvement was completed. An election under this paragraph shall apply to all real property of the taxpayer which has been in use for more than 5 years.

(d) Procedure for making election. *(1) Time and scope of election.* An election under paragraph (b) or (c) of this section shall be made for each taxable year to which such election is to apply. The election must be made before the later of (i) the time prescribed by law for filing the taxpayer's return for the taxable year for which the election is made (determined with regard to any extension of time) or (ii) August 31, 1973, but the election may not be made after the expiration of the time prescribed by law for the filing of a claim for credit or refund of tax with respect to the taxable year for which the election is to apply.

(2) Manner of making election. Except as provided in the following sentence, an election by the taxpayer with respect to a taxable year shall be made by a statement containing the information described in paragraph (d)(3) of this section which is—

(i) Attached to the taxpayer's return or amended return for such taxable year,

(ii) Attached to a timely filed claim by the taxpayer for credit or refund of tax for such taxable year, or

(iii) Filed by the taxpayer with the director of the Internal Revenue Service Center where the return for such taxable year was filed.

In the case of a taxable year ending before July 1, 1973, no formal statement of election is necessary if the taxpayer's return took into account an election under paragraph (b) or (c) of this section; the taxpayer will be considered to have made an election in accordance with the manner in which leases with respect to parcels of real property described in paragraph (b) of this section, or leases of property which has been in use for more than 5 years as described in paragraph (c) of this section, are treated in the return.

(3) Statement. The statement described in paragraph (d)(2) of this section shall contain the following information:

(i) The name, address, and taxpayer identification number of the taxpayer;

(ii) The taxable year to which the election is to apply if the statement is not attached to the return or a claim for credit or refund;

(iii) A description of any leases which are to be treated as a single lease; and

(iv) A description of any real property in use for more than 5 years to which the expense test is not to apply.

(4) Revocation of election. An election made pursuant to this paragraph may be revoked within the time prescribed in paragraph (d)(1) of this section for making an election and may not be revoked thereafter. Any such revocation shall be made in the manner prescribed by paragraph (d)(2) of this section for the making of an election.

(e) Election by members of partnership. Under section 703(b) (as amended by section 304(c) of the Revenue Act of 1971), any election under section 57(c) of 163(d)(7) with respect to property held by a partnership shall be made by each partner separately, rather than by the partnership. If an election made by a taxpayer under paragraph (b) of this section applies in whole or in part to property held by a partnership, the taxpayer shall, in applying the expense test referred to in paragraph (a) of this section, take into account his distributive share of the deductions of the partnership with respect to the property for the taxable year allowable solely by reason of section 162 (other than rents and reimbursed amounts with respect to the property) and also his distributive share of the partnership's rental income from such property for the taxable year.

T.D. 7271, 4/11/73.

§ 1.57-0 Scope.

Caution: The Treasury has not yet amended Reg § 1.57-0 to reflect changes made by P.L. 105-34, P.L. 103-66, P.L. 99-514.

For purposes of the minimum tax for tax preferences (subtitle A, ch. I, pt. VI), the items of tax preference are:

(a) Excess investment interest,

(b) The excess of accelerated depreciation on section 1250 property over straight line depreciation,

(c) The excess of accelerated depreciation on section 1245 property subject to a net lease over straight line depreciation,

(d) The excess of the amortization deduction for certified pollution control facilities over the depreciation otherwise allowable,

(e) The excess of the amortization deduction for railroad rolling stock over the depreciation otherwise allowable,

(f) The excess of the fair market value of a share of stock received pursuant to a qualified or restricted stock option over the exercise price,

(g) The excess of the addition to the reserve for losses on bad debts of financial institutions over the amount which have been allowable based on actual experience,

(h) The excess of the percentage depletion deduction over the adjusted basis of the property, and

(i) The capital gains deduction allowable under section 1202 or an equivalent amount in the case of corporations.

Accelerated depreciation on section 1245 property subject to a net lease and excess investment interest are not items of tax preference in the case of a corporation, other than a personal holding company (as defined in section 542) and an electing small business corporation (as defined in section 1371(b)). In addition, excess investment interest is an item of tax preference only for taxable years beginning before January 1, 1972. Rules for the determination of the items of tax preference are contained in §§ 1.57-1 through 1.57-5. Generally, in the case of a nonresident alien or foreign corporation, the application of §§ 1.57-1 through 1.57-5 will be limited to cases in which the taxpayer has income effectively connected with the conduct of a trade or business within the United States. Special rules for the treatment of items of tax preference in the case of certain entities and the treatment of items of tax preference relating to income from sources outside the United States are provided in section 58 and in §§ 1.58-1 through 1.58-8.

T.D. 7564, 9/11/78.

§ 1.57-1 Items of tax preference defined.

Caution: The Treasury has not yet amended Reg § 1.57-1 to reflect changes made by P.L. 105-206, P.L. 105-34, P.L. 104-188, P.L. 103-66, P.L. 99-514.

(a) [Reserved]

(b) Accelerated depreciation on section 1250 property. *(1) In general.* Section 57(a)(2) provides that, with respect to each item of section 1250 property (as defined in section 1250(c)), there is to be included as an item of tax preference the amount by which the deduction allowable for the taxable year for depreciation or amortization exceeds the deduction which would have been allowable for the taxable year if the taxpayer had depreciated the property under the straight line method for each year of its useful life for which the taxpayer has held the property. The determination of the excess under section 57(a)(2) is made with respect to each separate item of section 1250 property. Accordingly, where the amount of depreciation which would have been allowable with respect to one item of section 1250 property if the taxpayer had originally used the straight line method exceeds the allowable depreciation or amortization with respect to such property, such excess may not be used to reduce the amount of the item of tax preference resulting from another item of section 1250 property.

(2) Separate items of section 1250 property. The determination of what constitutes a separate item of section 1250 property is to be made on the facts and circumstances of each individual case. In general, each building (or component thereof, if the taxpayer uses the component method of computing depreciation) is a separate item of section 1250 property. However, for purposes of this section, assets placed in a group, classified, or composite account are to be treated as a single item by a taxpayer, provided that such account contains only property placed in service during a single taxable year. In addition, two or more items may be treated as one item of section 1250 property for purposes of this paragraph where, with respect to each such item: (i) The period for which depreciation is taken begins on the same date, (ii) the same estimated useful life has continually been used for purposes of taking depreciation or amortization, and (iii) the same method (and rate) of depreciation or amortization has continually been used. For example, assume a taxpayer constructed a 40-unit rental townhouse development and began taking declining balance depreciation on all 40 units as of January 1, 1970, at a uniform rate and has consistently taken depreciation on all 40 units on this same basis. Although each townhouse is a separate item of section 1250 property, all 40 townhouses may be treated as one item of section 1250 property for purposes of the minimum tax since the conditions of subdivisions (i), (ii), and (iii) of this subparagraph are met. This would be true even if the 40 townhouses comprised two 20-unit developments located apart from each other. However, if the taxpayer constructed an additional development or new section on the existing development for which he began taking depreciation on July 1, 1970, at a uniform rate for all the additional units, the additional units and the original units may not be treated as one item of section 1250 property since the condition of subdivision (i) of this subparagraph is not met. Where a portion of an item of section 1250 property has been depreciated or amortized under a method (or rate) which is different from the method (or rate) under which the other portion or portions of such item have been depreciated or amortized, such portion is considered a separate item of section 1250 property for purposes of this paragraph.

(3) Allowable depreciation or amortization. The phrase "deduction allowable for the taxable year for exhaustion, wear and tear, obsolescence, or amortization" and references in this paragraph to "allowable depreciation or amortization" include deductions allowable for the taxable year under sections 162, 167, 212, or 611 for the depreciation or amortization of section 1250 property. Such phrase does not include depreciation allowable in the year in which the section 1250 property is disposed of. For the determination of "allowable depreciation or amortization" for taxable years in which the taxpayer has taken no deduction, see § 1.1016-3(a)(2).

(4) Straight line depreciation. (i) For purposes of computing the depreciation which would have been allowable for the taxable year if the taxpayer had depreciated the property under the straight line method for each taxable year of its useful life, the taxpayer must use the same useful life and salvage value as was used for the first taxable year in which the taxpayer depreciated or amortized the property (subject to redeterminations made pursuant to § 1.167(a)-1 (b) and (c)). If, however, for any taxable year, no useful life was used under the method of depreciation or amortization used or an artificial period was used, such as, for example, by application of section 167(k), or salvage value was not taken

into account in determining the annual allowances, such as, for example, under the declining balance method, then, for purposes of computing the depreciation which would have been allowable under the straight line method for the taxable year—

(a) There is to be used the useful life and salvage value which would have been proper if depreciation had actually been determined under the straight line method (without reference to an artificial life) throughout the period the property was held, and

(b) Such useful life and such salvage value is to be determined by taking into account for each taxable year the same facts and circumstances as would have been taken into account if the taxpayer had used such method throughout the period the property was held.

If an election under § 1.167(a)-11(f), § 1.167(a)-12(e), or § 1.167(a)-12(f) is applicable to the property, the salvage value of the property shall be determined in accordance with such election, and the asset depreciation period (or asset guideline period) applicable to the property pursuant to such election shall be considered to be the useful life of the property for the purposes of this section.

(ii) Where the taxpayer acquires property in a transaction to which section 381(a) applies or from another member of an affiliated group during a consolidated return year and an "accelerated" method of depreciation as described in section 167(b)(2), (3), or (4) or section 167(j)(1)(B) or (C) is permitted (see § 1.381(c)(6)-1 and § 1.1502-12(g)), the depreciation which would have been allowable under the straight line method is determined as if the property had been depreciated under the straight line method since depreciation was first taken on the property by the transferor of such property. In such cases, references in this paragraph to the period for which the property is held or useful life of the property are treated as including the period beginning with the commencement of the original use of the property.

(iii) For purposes of section 57(a)(2), the straight line method includes the method of depreciation described in § 1.167(b)-1 or any other method which provides for a uniform proration of the cost or other basis (less salvage value) of the property over the estimated useful life of the property to the taxpayer (in terms of years, hours of use, or other similar time units) or estimated number of units to be produced over the life of the property to the taxpayer. If a method other than the method described in § 1.167(b)-1 is used, the estimated useful life or estimated units of production shall be determined in a manner consistent with subdivision (i) of this subparagraph.

(iv) In the case of property constructed by or improvements made by a lessee, the useful life is to be determined in accordance with § 1.167(a)-4.

(5) Application for partial period. If an item is section 1250 property for less than the entire taxable year, the allowable depreciation or amortization includes only the depreciation or amortization for that portion of the taxable year during which the item is section 1250 property and the amount of the depreciation which would have been allowable under the straight line method is determined only with regard to such portion of the taxable year.

(6) No section 1250 and basis adjustment. No adjustment is to be made as a result of the minimum tax either to the basis of section 1250 property or with respect to computations under section 1250.

(7) Example. The principles of this paragraph may be illustrated by the following example:

Example. The taxpayer's only item of section 1250 property is an office building with respect to which operations were commenced on January 1, 1971. The taxpayer depreciates the component parts of the building on the declining balance method. The useful life and costs of the component parts for depreciation purposes are as follows:

Asset	Useful life	Cost	Salvage value
Building shell	50	$100,000	$50,000
Partitions and walls	10	40,000	
Ceilings	10	20,000	
Electrical system	25	40,000	2,500
Heating and air-conditioning system	25	60,000	2,500

For purposes of computing the item of tax preference under this paragraph for the taxpayer, the partitions, walls, and ceilings may be grouped together and the electrical, heating, and air-conditioning systems may be grouped together since the period for which depreciation is taken began with respect to the assets within these two groups on the same date and the assets within each group have continually had the same useful life and have continually been depreciated under the same method (and rate).

(a) The taxpayer's 1971 item of tax preference under this paragraph would be determined as follows:

(1) Item of 1250 property	(2) Declining balance depreciation	(3) Straight line depreciation	(4) Excess of (2) over (3)
1. Shell	$12,000	$ 7,000	$5,000
2. Partitions, walls, ceilings	9,000	6,000	3,000
3. Electrical, heating and air-conditioning systems	6,000	3,800	2,200
1971 preference			10,200

(b) Assuming the above facts are the same for 1974, the taxpayer's 1974 item of tax preference under this paragraph would be determined as follows:

(1) Item of 1250 property	(2) Declining balance depreciation	(3) Straight line depreciation	(4) Excess of (2) over (3)
1. Shell	$10,952	$ 7,000	$3,952
2. Partitions, walls, ceilings	5,529	8,000	None
3. Electrical, heating and air-conditioning systems	4,983	3,800	1,183
1974 preference			5,135

(c) Accelerated depreciation on section 1245 property subject to a net lease. *(1) In general.* Section 57(a)(3) provides that, with respect to each item of section 1245 property (as defined in section 1245(a)(3)) which is the subject of a net lease for the taxable year, there is to be included as an item of tax preference the amount by which the deduction allowable for the taxable year for depreciation or amortization exceeds the deduction which would have been allowable for the taxable year if the taxpayer had depreciated the property under the straight line method for each year of its useful life for which the taxpayer has held the property. Except as provided in paragraph (b)(1)(ii) of this section, the determination of the excess under section 57(a)(3) is made with respect to each separate item of section 1245 property. Accordingly, where the amount of depreciation which would have been allowable with respect to one item of section 1245 property if the taxpayer had originally used the straight line method exceeds the allowable depreciation or amortization with respect to such property, such excess may not be used to reduce the amount of the item of tax preference resulting from another item of section 1245 property.

(2) Separate items of property. The determination of what constitutes a separate item of section 1245 property must be made on the facts and circumstances of each individual case. Such determination shall be made in a manner consistent with the principles expressed in paragraph (b)(2) of this section.

(3) Allowable depreciation or amortization. The phrase "deduction allowable for the taxable year for exhaustion, wear and tear, obsolescence, or amortization" and references in this paragraph to "allowable depreciation or amortization" include deductions allowable for the taxable year under sections 162, 167 (including depreciation allowable under section 167 by reason of section 179), 169, 184, 185, 212, or 611 for the depreciation or amortization of section 1245 property. Such phrase does not include depreciation allowable in the year in which the section 1245 property is disposed of. Amortization of certified pollution control facilities under section 169, and amortization of railroad rolling stock under section 184 are not to be treated as amortization for purposes of section 57(a)(3) to the extent such amounts are treated as an item of tax preference under section 57(a) (4) or (5) (see paragraphs (d) and (e) of this section). For the determination of "allowable depreciation or amortization" for taxable years in which the taxpayer has taken no deduction, see § 1.1016-3(a)(2).

(4) Straight line method of depreciation. The determination of the depreciation which would have been allowable under the straight line method shall be made in a manner consistent with paragraph (b)(4) of this section. Such amount shall include any amount allowable under section 167 by reason of section 179 (relating to additional first-year depreciation for small business).

(5) Application for partial period. If an item is section 1245 property for less than the entire taxable year or subject to a net lease for less than the entire taxable year the allowable depreciation or amortization includes only the depreciation or amortization for that portion of the taxable year during which the item was both section 1245 property and subject to a net lease and the amount of the depreciation which would have been allowable under the straight line method is to be determined only with regard to such portion of the taxable year.

(6) Net lease. Section 57(a)(3) applies only if the section 1245 property is the subject of a net lease for all or part of the taxable year. See § 1.57-3 for the determination of when an item is considered the subject of a net lease.

(7) No section 1245 and basis adjustment. No adjustment is to be made as a result of the minimum tax either to the basis of section 1245 property or with respect to computations under section 1245.

(8) Nonapplicability to corporations. Section 57(a)(3) does not apply to a corporation other than an electing small business corporation (as defined in section 1371(b)) and a personal holding company (as defined in section 542).

(d) Amortization of certified pollution control facilities. *(1) In general.* Section 57(a)(4) provides that, with respect to each certified pollution control facility for which an election is in effect under section 169, there is to be included as an item of tax preference the amount by which the deduction allowable for the taxable year under such section exceeds the depreciation deduction which would otherwise be allowable under section 167. The determination under section 57(a)(4) is made with respect to each separate certified pollution control facility. Accordingly, where the amount of the depreciation deduction which would otherwise be allowable under section 167 with respect to one facility exceeds the allowable amortization deduction under section 169 with respect to such facility, such excess may not be used to offset an item of tax preference resulting from another facility.

(2) Separate facilities. The determination of what constitutes a separate facility must be made on the facts and circumstances of each individual case. Generally, each facility with respect to which a separate election is in effect under section 169 shall be treated as a separate facility for purposes of this paragraph. However, if the depreciation or amortization which would have been allowable without regard to section 169 with respect to any part of a facility is based on a different useful life, date placed in service, or method of depreciation or amortization from the other part or parts of such facility, such part is considered a separate facility for purposes of this paragraph. For example, if a building constitutes a certified pollution control facility and various component parts of the building have different useful lives, each group of component parts with the same useful life would be treated as a separate facility for purposes of this paragraph. Two or more facilities may be treated as one facility for purposes of this paragraph where, with respect to each such facility: (i) the initial amortization under section 169 commences on the same date, (ii) the facility is placed

in service on the same date, (iii) the estimated useful life which would be the basis for depreciation or amortization other than under section 169 has continually been the same, and (iv) the method of depreciation or amortization which could have been used without regard to section 169 could have continually been the same.

(3) Amount allowable under section 169. For purposes of the determination of the amount of the deduction allowable under section 169, see section 169 and the regulations thereunder. Such amount, however, does not include amortization allowable in the year in which the pollution control facility is disposed of.

(4) Otherwise allowable deduction. (i) The determination of the amount of the depreciation deduction otherwise allowable under section 167 is made as if the taxpayer had depreciated the property under section 167 for each year of its useful life for which the property has been held. This amount may be determined under § 1.167(a)-(11)(c) if the property is eligible property (as defined in § 1.167(a)-11(b)(2)) and, during the taxable year in which the property was first placed in service, the taxpayer—

(a) Has made an election under § 1.167(a)-11(f) with respect to eligible property first placed in service in such taxable year, or

(b) Has placed no eligible property in service other than property described in § 1.167(a)-11(b)(5)(iii), (iv), or (v).

The amount determined pursuant to the preceding sentence shall be determined as if the taxpayer had depreciated the property in accordance with § 1.167(a)-11 for all years to which such section applies and during which the taxpayer held the property. This amount may be determined under § 1.167(a)-12(a)(5) if the property is qualified property (as defined in § 1.167(a)-12(a)(3) and the taxpayer has made an election with respect to such property under § 1.167(a)-12(e). If the taxpayer has made an election under § 1.167(a)-12(f)(1) for a taxable year ending before January 1, 1971, this amount shall be determined for such year in accordance with such election. For purposes of this determination, any method selected by the taxpayer which would have been permissible under section 167 for such taxable year, including accelerated methods, may be used. Any additional amount which would have been allowable by reason of section 179 (relating to additional first-year depreciation for small business) may be included provided such amount is reflected in the determination made under this paragraph in subsequent years.

(ii) If a deduction for depreciation has not been taken by the taxpayer in any taxable year under section 167 with respect to the facility—

(a) There is to be used the useful life and salvage value which would have been proper under section 167.

(b) Such useful life and salvage value is determined by taking into account for each taxable year the same facts and circumstances as would have been taken into account if the taxpayer had used such method throughout the period the property has been held, and

(c) The date the property is placed in service is, for purposes of this section, deemed to be the first day of the first month for which the amortization deduction is taken with respect to the facility under section 169.

If, prior to the date amortization begins under section 169, a deduction for depreciation has been taken by the taxpayer in any taxable year under section 167 with respect to the facility, the useful life, salvage value, etc., used for that purpose is deemed to be the appropriate useful life, salvage value, etc., for purposes of this paragraph, with such adjustments as are appropriate in light of the facts and circumstances which would have been taken into account since the time the last such depreciation deduction was taken, unless it is established by clear and convincing evidence that some other useful life, salvage value, or date the property is placed in service is more appropriate.

(iii) For purposes of section 57(a)(4) and this paragraph, if the deduction for amortization or depreciation which would have been allowable had no election been made under section 169 would have been—

(a) An amortization deduction based on the term of a leasehold or

(b) A depreciation deduction determined by reference to section 611, such deduction is to be deemed to be a deduction allowable under section 167.

(iv) If a facility is subject to amortization under section 169 for less than the entire taxable year, the otherwise allowable depreciation deduction under section 167 shall be determined only with regard to that portion of the taxable year during which the election under section 169 is in effect.

(v) If less than the entire adjusted basis of a facility is subject to amortization under section 169, the otherwise allowable depreciation deduction under section 167 shall be determined only with regard to that portion of the adjusted basis subject to amortization under section 169.

(5) No section 1245 and basis adjustment. No adjustment is to be made as a result of the minimum tax either to the basis of a certified pollution control facility or with respect to computation under sections 1245.

(6) Relationship to section 57(a)(3). See paragraph (c)(3) with respect to an adjustment in the amount treated as amortization under that provision where both paragraphs (3) and (4) of section 57(a) are applicable to the same item of property.

(7) Example. The principles of this paragraph may be illustrated by the following example:

Example. A calendar year taxpayer has a certified pollution control facility on which an election is in effect under section 169 commencing with January 1, 1971. No part of the facility is section 1250 property. The original basis of the facility is $100,000 of which $75,000 constitutes amortizable basis. The useful life of the facility is 20 years. The taxpayer depreciates the $25,000 portion of the facility which is not amortizable basis under the double declining method and began taking depreciation on January 1, 1971.

(a) The taxpayer's 1971 item of tax preference under this paragraph would be determined as follows:

1. Amortization deduction	$15,000
2. Depreciation deduction on amortizable basis (double declining method)	7,500
1971 preference (excess of 1 over 2)	7,500

(b) If the taxpayer terminated his election under section 169 in 1972 effective as of July 1, 1972, the taxpayer's 1972 item of tax preference would be determined as follows:

1. Amortization deduction	$7,500
2. Depreciation deduction on amortizable basis:	
Full year ($75,000 (original basis) less $7,500 ("depreciation" to 1-1-72) equals adjusted basis of $67,500; multiplied by 0.10 (double declining rate))	6,750
Portion of full year's depreciation attributable to amortization period (one-half)	3,375
1972 preference (excess of 1 over 2)	4,125

(e) Amortization of railroad rolling stock. *(1) In general.* Section 57(a)(5) provides that, with respect to each unit of railroad rolling stock for which an election is in effect under section 184, there is to be included as an item of tax preference the amount by which the deduction allowable for the taxable year under such section exceeds the depreciation deduction which would otherwise be allowable under section 167. The determination under section 57(a)(5) is made with respect to each separate unit of rolling stock. Accordingly, where the amount of the depreciation deduction which would otherwise be allowable under section 167 with respect to one unit exceeds the allowable amortization deduction under section 184 with respect to such unit, such excess may not be used to offset an item of tax preference resulting from another unit.

(2) Separate units of rolling stock. The determination of what constitutes a separate unit of rolling stock must be made on the facts and circumstances of each individual case. Such determination shall be made in a manner consistent with the manner in which the comparable determination is made with respect to separate certified pollution control facilities under paragraph (d)(2) of this section.

(3) Amount allowable under section 184. For purposes of the determination of the amount of the deduction allowable under section 184, see section 184. Such amount, however, does not include amortization allowable in the year in which the rolling stock is disposed of.

(4) Otherwise allowable deduction. The determination of the amount of the depreciation deduction otherwise allowable under section 167 is to be made in a manner consistent with the manner in which the comparable deduction with respect to certified pollution control facilities is determined under paragraph (d)(4) of this section.

(5) No section 1245 or basis adjustment. No adjustment is to be made as a result of the minimum tax either to the basis of a unit of railroad rolling stock or with respect to computations under section 1245.

(6) Relationship to section 57(a)(3). See paragraph (c)(3) of this section with respect to an adjustment in the amount treated as amortization under that provision where both paragraphs (3) and (5) of section 57(a) are applicable to the same item.

(f) Stock options. *(1) In general.* Section 57(a)(6) provides that with respect to each transfer of a share of stock pursuant to the exercise of a qualified stock option or a restricted stock option, there shall be included by the transferee as an item of tax preference the amount by which the fair market value of the share at the time of exercise exceeds the option price. The stock option item of tax preference is subject to tax under section 56(a) in the taxable year of the transferee in which the transfer is made.

(2) Definitions. See generally § 1.421-7(e), (f), and (g) for the definitions of "option price," "exercise," and "transfer," respectively; however, in the case of a transfer of a share of stock pursuant to the exercise of a qualified stock option or a restricted stock option after the death of an employee by the estate of the decedent (or by a person who acquired the right to exercise such option by bequest or inheritance or by reason of the death of the decedent), the term "option price" shall, for purposes of this paragraph, include both the consideration paid by the estate (or such person) for such share of stock and so much of the basis of the option as is attributable to such share of stock. For the definition of a qualified stock option see section 422(b) and § 1.422-2. For the definition of a restricted stock option see section 424(b) and § 1.424-2. The definitions and special rules contained in section 425 and the regulations thereunder are applicable to this paragraph.

(3) Fair market value. In accordance with the principles of section 83(a)(1), the fair market value of a share of stock received pursuant to he exercise of a qualified or restricted stock option is to be determined without regard to restrictions (other than non-lapse restrictions within the meaning of § 1.83-3(h)). Notwithstanding any valuation date given in section 83(a)(1), for purposes of this section, fair market value is determined as of the date the option is exercised.

(4) Foreign source options. In the case of an option attributable to sources within any foreign country or possession, see section 58(g) and § 1.58-8.

(5) Inapplicability in certain cases. (i) Section 57(a)(6) is inapplicable if during the same taxable year in which stock is transferred pursuant to the exercise of an option, the transferee makes a disposition (within the meaning of section 425(c)) of such stock. In the case of a nonresident alien, section 57(a)(6) is inapplicable to the extent the stock option is attributable (in accordance with the principles of sections 861 through 863 and the regulations thereunder) to sources without the United States.

(ii) Section 57(a)(6) is inapplicable if section 421(a) does not apply to the transfer because of employment requirements of section 422(a)(2) or section 424(a)(2).

(6) Proportionate applicability. Where, by reason of section 422(b)(7) and (c)(3) (relating to percentage ownership limitations), only a portion of a transfer qualifies for application of section 421, the fair market value and option price shall be determined only with regard to that portion of the transfer which so qualifies.

(7) No basis adjustment. No adjustment shall be made to the basis of the stock received pursuant to the exercise of a qualified or restricted stock option as a result of the minimum tax.

(g) Reserves for losses on bad debts of financial institutions. *(1) In general.* Section 57(a)(7) provides that, in the case of a financial institution to which sections 585 or 593 (both relating to reserves for losses on loans) applies, there shall be included as an item of tax preference the amount by which the deduction allowable for the taxable year for a reasonable addition to a reserve for bad debts exceeds the amount that would have been allowable had the institution maintained its bad debt reserve for all taxable years on the basis of the institution's actual experience.

(2) Taxpayers covered. Section 57(a)(7) applies only to an institution (or organization) to which section 585 or 593 applies. See sections 585(a) and 593(a) and the regulations thereunder for a description of those institutions.

(3) Allowable deduction. For purposes of this paragraph, the amount of the deduction allowable for the taxable year for a reasonable addition to a reserve for bad debts is the amount of the deduction allowed under section 166(c) by reference to sections 585 or 593.

(4) Actual experience. (i) For purposes of this paragraph, the determination of the amount which would have been allowable had the institution maintained its reserve for bad debts on the basis of actual experience is the amount determined under section 585(b)(3)(A) and the regulations thereunder. For this purpose, the beginning balance for the first taxable year ending in 1970 is the amount which bears the same ratio to loans outstanding at the beginning of the taxable year as (a) the total bad debts sustained during the 5 preceding taxable years, adjusted for recoveries of bad debts during such period, bears to (b) the sum of the loans outstanding at the close of such 5 taxable years. The taxpayer may, however, select a more appropriate balance based on its actual experience during a shorter period subject to the approval of the district director upon examination of the return provided there are unusual circumstances which indicate that such period is more indicative of the taxpayer's actual loss experience. Any such selection and approval shall be made in a manner consistent with the selection and approval of a bad debt reserve method under § 1.166-1(b). In the case of an institution which has been in existence for less than 5 taxable years as of the beginning of the first taxable year ending in 1970, the above formula for determining the beginning balance is applied by substituting the number of taxable years for which the institution has been in existence as of the beginning of the taxable year for "5" each time it appears. If any taxable year utilized in the above formula for determining the beginning balance is a short taxable year the amount of the bad debts, adjusted for recoveries, for such taxable year is modified by dividing such amount by the number of days in the taxable year and multiplying the resulting amount by 365. The beginning balance for any subsequent taxable year is the amount of the beginning balance of the preceding taxable year, decreased by bad debt losses during such year, increased by recoveries of bad debts during such year and increased by the lower of the maximum amount determined under section 585(b)(3)(A) for such year or the amount of the deduction allowed for such year. The application of this subdivision (i) may be illustrated by the following example:

Example. The Y Bank, a calendar year taxpayer, uses the reserve method of accounting for bad debts. On December 31, 1969, Y determines the balance of its reserve for bad debts to be $70,000 under the percentage method. On the same date Y's 5-year moving average is $52,000. Y incurs net bad debt losses (bad debt losses less recoveries of bad debts) of $3,000 for each of the years 1970, 1971, and 1972, which it charges to its reserve for bad debts. Y's 6-year moving averages computed under section 585(b)(3)(A) at the close of 1970, 1971, and 1972 are $50,000, $49,000, and $51,000, respectively. Y's preference items are computed as follows based upon additional facts assumed:

	1970	1971	1972
1. Bad debt reserve—percentage method:			
(a) Balance beginning of year (closing balance prior year)	$70,000	$70,000	$68,000
(b) Net bad debts charged to reserve	3,000	3,000	3,000
(c) Subtotal	67,000	67,000	65,000
(d) Deduction allowed	3,000	1,000	4,000
(e) Balance end of year	70,000	68,000	69,000
2. Bad debt reserve—"actual experience":			
(a) Beginning balance (for 1970, 5-year moving average; for other years, closing balance prior year)	52,000	50,000	48,000
(b) Net bad debts charged to reserve	3,000	3,000	3,000
(c) Subtotal	49,000	47,000	45,000
(d) Maximum amount under section 585(b)(3)(A) (6-year moving average minus (c))	1,000	2,000	6,000
(e) Deduction allowed (line 1(d))	3,000	1,000	4,000
(f) Lower of (d) or (e)	1,000	1,000	4,000
(g) Closing balance (line (c) + (f))	50,000	48,000	49,000
3. Preference item under section 57(a)(7):			
(a) Deduction allowed	3,000	1,000	4,000
(b) Maximum amount under section 585(b)(3)(A)	1,000	2,000	6,000
(c) Preference item (excess of (a) over (b))	2,000	0	0

(ii) In the case of a new institution whose first taxable year ends after 1969, its beginning balance for its reserve for bad debts, for purposes of this paragraph, is zero and its reasonable addition to the reserve for such taxable year is determined on the basis of the actual experience of similar institutions located in the area served by the taxpayer.

(h) Depletion. *(1) In general.* Section 57(a)(8) provides that with respect to each property (as defined in section 614), there is to be included as an item of tax preference the amount by which the deduction allowable for the taxable year under section 611 for depletion for the property exceeds the adjusted basis of the property at the end of the taxable year (determined without regard to the depletion deduction for that taxable year). The determination under section 57(a)(8) is made with respect to each separate property. Thus, for example, if one mineral property has an adjusted basis remaining at the end of the taxable year, such basis may not be used to reduce the amount of an item of tax preference resulting from another mineral property.

(2) Allowable depletion. For the determination of the amount of the deduction for depletion allowable for the taxable year see section 611 and the regulations thereunder.

(3) Adjusted basis. For the determination of the adjusted basis of the property at the end of the taxable year see section 1016 and the regulations thereunder.

(4) No basis adjustment. No adjustment is to be made to the basis of property subject to depletion as a result of the minimum tax.

(i) Capital gains. *(1) Taxpayers other than corporations.* Section 57(a)(9)(A) provides that, in the case of a taxpayer other than a corporation, there is to be included as an item of tax preference one-half of the amount by which the taxpayer's net long-term capital gain for the taxable year exceeds the taxpayer's net short-term capital loss for the taxable year. For this purpose, for taxable years beginning after December 31, 1971, the taxpayer's net long-term capital gain does not include an amount equal to the deduction allowable under section 163 (relating to interest expense) by reason of subsection (d)(1)(C) of that section, and the excess described in the preceding sentence is reduced by an amount equal to the reduction of disallowed interest expense by reason of section 163(d)(2)(B). Furthermore, the net long-term capital gain of an estate or trust does not include capital gains described in section 642(c)(4). Included in the computation of the taxpayer's capital gains item of tax preference are amounts reportable by the taxpayer as distributive shares of gain or loss from partnerships, estates or trusts, electing small business corporations, common trust funds, etc. See section 58 and the regulations thereunder with respect to the above entities.

Example. For 1971, A, a calendar year individual taxpayer, recognized $50,000 from the sale of securities held for more than 6 months. In addition, A received a $15,000 dividend from X Fund, a regulated investment company, $12,000 of which was designated as a capital gain dividend by the company pursuant to section 852(b)(3)(C). The AB partnership reçognized a gain of $20,000 from the sale of section 1231 property held by the partnership. The AB partnership agreement provides that A is entitled to 50 percent of the income and gains of the partnership. A had net short-term capital loss for the year of $10,000. A's 1971 capital gains item of tax preference is computed as follows:

Capital gain recognized from securities	$ 50,000
Capital gain dividend from regulated investment company	12,000
Distributive share of partnership capital gain	10,000
Total net long-term capital gain	72,000
Less: net short-term capital loss	(10,000)
Excess of net long-term capital gain over net short-term capital loss	62,000
One-half of above excess	31,000

(2) Corporations. (i) Section 57(a)(9)(B) provides that in the case of corporations there is to be included as an item of tax preference with respect to a corporation's net section 1201 gain an amount equal to the product obtained by multiplying the excess of the net long-term capital gain over the net short-term capital loss by a fraction. The numerator of this fraction is the sum of the normal tax rate and the surtax rate under section 11 minus the alternative tax rate under section 1201(a) for the taxable year, and the denominator of the fraction is the sum of the normal tax rate and the surtax rate under section 11 for the taxable year. Included in the above computation are amounts reportable by the taxpayer as distributive shares of gain or loss from partnerships, estates or trusts, common trust funds, etc. In certain cases the amount of the net section 1201 gain which results in preferential treatment will be less than the amount determined by application of the statutory formula. Therefore, in lieu of the statutory formula, the capital gains item of tax preference for corporations may in all cases be determined by dividing—

(a) The amount of tax which would have been imposed under section 11 if section 1201(a) did not apply minus—

(b) The amount of the taxes actually imposed by the sum of the normal tax rate plus the surtax rate under section 11. In case of foreign source capital gains and losses which are not taken into account pursuant to sections 58(g)(2)(B) and 1.58-8, the amount determined in the preceding sentence shall be multiplied by a fraction the numerator of which is the corporation's net section 1201 gain without regard to such gains and losses which are not taken into account and the denominator of which is the corporation's net section 1201 gain. The computation of the corporate capital gains item of tax preference may be illustrated by the following examples:

Example (1). For 1971, A, a calendar year corporate taxpayer, has ordinary income of $10,000 and net section 1201 gain of $50,000, none of which is subsection (d) gain (as defined in sec. 1201(d)) and none of which is attributable to foreign sources. A's 1971 capital gain item of tax preference may be computed as follows:

1. Tax under section 11:		
Normal tax (0.22 × $60,000)		$13,200
Surtax (0.26 × $35,000)		9,100
		22,300
2. Tax under section 1201(a) Normal tax on ordinary income (0.22 × $10,000)	22,000	
Tax on net section 1201 gain (0.30 × $50,000)	15,000	17,200
3. Excess		5,100
4. Normal tax rate plus surtax rate		.48
5. Capital gains preference (line 3 divided by line 4)		10,625

Example (2). For 1971, A, a calendar year corporate taxpayer, has a loss from operations of $30,000 and net section 1201 gain of $150,000, none of which is subsection (d) gain (as defined in sec. 1201(d)) and none of which is attributable to foreign sources. A's 1971 capital gain item of tax preference may be computed as follows:

1. Tax under section 11:		
Normal tax (0.22 × $120,000)		$26,400
Surtax (0.26 × $95,000)		24,700
		51,100
2. Tax under section 1201(a) Normal tax on ordinary income	None	
Tax on net section 1201 gain (0.30 × $150,000)	45,000	45,000
3. Excess		6,100
4. Normal tax rate plus surtax rate		.48
5. Capital gains preference (line 3 divided by line 4)		12,708

(ii) In the case of organizations subject to the tax imposed by section 511(a), mutual savings banks conducting a life insurance business (see sec. 594), life insurance companies (as defined in sec. 801), mutual insurance companies to which part II of subchapter L applies, insurance companies to which part III of subchapter L applies, regulated investment companies subject to tax under part I of subchapter M, real estate investment trusts subject to tax under part II of subchapter M, or any other corporation not subject to the taxes imposed by sections 11 and 1201(a), the capital gains item of tax preference may be computed in accordance with subdivision (i) of this subparagraph except that, in lieu of references to section 11, there is to be substituted the section which imposes the tax comparable to the tax imposed by section 11 and, in lieu of references to section 1201(a), there is to be substituted the section which imposes the alternative or special tax applicable to the capital gains of such corporation.

(iii) For purposes of this paragraph, where the net section 1201 gain is not in any event subject to the tax comparable to the normal tax and the surtax under section 11, such as in the case of regulated investment companies subject to tax under subchapter M, such comparable tax shall be computed as if it were applicable to net section 1201 gain to the extent such gain is subject to the tax comparable to the alternative tax under section 1201(a). Thus, in the case of a regulated investment company subject to tax under subchapter M, the tax comparable to the normal tax and the surtax would be the tax computed under section 852(b)(1) determined as if the amount subject to tax under section 852(b)(3) were included in investment company taxable income. The principles of this subdivision (iii) may be illustrated by the following example:

Example. M, a calendar year regulated investment company, in 1971, has investment company taxable income (subject to tax under sec. 852(b)(1)) of $125,000 and net long-term capital gain of $800,000. M company has no net short-term capital loss but has a deduction for dividends paid (determined with reference to capital gains only) of $700,000, M's 1971 capital gains item of tax preference is computed as follows:

1. Section 852(b)(1) tax computed as if it were applicable to all income including capital gains:			
Amount subject to section 852(b)(1)		$125,000	
Net section 1201 gain	$800,000		
Less: Dividends paid deduction	700,000		
Net section 1201 gain subject to tax at the company level		100,000	
		225,000	
Normal tax (0.22 × $225,000)			$49,500
Surtax (0.26 × 200,000)			52,000
			101,500
2. Tax comparable to section 1201(a) tax section 852(b)(1) tax:			
Normal tax (0.22 × 125,000)	$ 27,500		
Surtax (0.26 × 100,000)	26,000	$ 53,500	
Section 852(b)(3) tax (0.30 × 100,000)		30,000	
			$83,500
3. Excess	18,000		
4. Normal tax rate plus surtax rate	.48		
5. Capital gains preference (line 3 divided by line 4)	37,500		

(iv) For the computation of the capital gains item of tax preference in the case of an electing small business corporation (as defined in sec. 1371(b)), see section 1.58-4(c).

(3) Nonresident aliens, foreign corporations. In the case of a nonresident alien individual or foreign corporation, there shall be included in computing the capital gains item of tax preference under section 57(a)(9) only those capital gains and losses included in the computation of income effectively connected with the conduct of a trade or business within the United States as provided in section 871(b) or 882.

T.D. 7564, 9/11/78.

§ 1.57-4 Limitation on amounts treated as items of tax preference for taxable years beginning before January 1, 1976.

(a) In general. If in any taxable year beginning before January 1, 1976, a taxpayer has deductions in excess of gross income and all or a part of any item of tax preference described in § 1.57-1 results in no tax benefit due to modifications required under section 172(c) or section 172(b)(2) in computing the amount of the net operating loss or the net operating loss to be carried to a succeeding taxable year, then, for purposes of section 56(a)(1), the sum of the items of tax preference determined under section 57(a) (and § 1.57-1) is to be limited as provided in paragraph (b) of this section.

(b) Limitation. The sum of the items of tax preference, for purposes of section 56(a)(1) and § 1.56A-1(a), is limited to an amount determined under subparagraphs (1) and (2) of this paragraph.

(1) Loss year. If the taxpayer has no taxable income for the taxable year without regard to the net operating loss deduction, the amount of the limitation is equal to--

(i) In cases where the taxpayer does not have a net operating loss for the taxable year, the amount of the recomputed income (as defined in paragraph (c) of this section) or

(ii) In cases where the taxpayer has a net operating loss for the taxable year, the amount of the net operating loss (expressed as a positive amount) increased by the recomputed income or decreased by the recomputed loss for the taxable year (as defined in paragraph (c) of this section, plus the amount of the taxpayer's stock option item of tax preference (as described in § 1.57-1(f)).

(2) Loss carryover and carryback years. Except in cases to which subparagraph (1)(ii) of this paragraph applies, if, in any taxable year to which a net operating loss is carried, a capital gains deduction is disallowed under section 172(b)(2) in computing the amount of such net operating loss which may be carried to succeeding taxable years, the amount of the limitation is equal to the amount, if any, by which the sum of the items of tax preference (computed with regard to subparagraph (1)(i) of this paragraph) exceeds the lesser of--

(i) The amount by which such loss is reduced because of a disallowance of the capital gains deduction in such taxable year, or

(ii) The capital gains deduction.

The amount determined pursuant to the preceding sentence shall be increased by the amount, if any, that such reduction is attributable to that portion of such a net operating loss described in section 56(b)(1)(B) and § 1.56A-2(a)(2) (relating to excess tax preferences).

(c) Recomputed income or loss. For purposes of this section, the phrase "recomputed income or loss" means the taxable income or net operating loss for the taxable year computed without regard to the amounts described in § 1.57-1 except paragraph (i)(2) of that section (relating to corporate capital gains) and without regard to the net operating loss deduction. For this purpose, the reference to the amounts described in § 1.57-1 is a reference to that portion of the deduction allowable in computing taxable income under the appropriate section equal to the amount which is determined in each paragraph of § 1.57-1. For example, the amount described in § 1.57-1(h) (relating to excess of percentage depletion over basis) is that portion of the deduction allowable for depletion under section 611 which is equal to the amount determined under § 1.57-1(h). For purposes of this paragraph, the amount described in § 1.57-1(i)(1) (relating to capital gains) is to be considered as the amount of the deduction allowable for the taxable year under section 1202.

(d) Determination of preferences reduced. When, pursuant to paragraph (b)(1) of this section, the sum of the items of tax preference (determined without regard to this section) are reduced, such reduction is first considered to be from the capital gains item of tax preference (described in § 1.57-1(i)(1)) and each item of tax preference relating to a deduction disallowed in computing the net operating loss pursuant to section 172(d), pro rata. The balance of the reduction, if any, is considered to be from the remaining items of tax preference, pro rata. For purposes of this subparagraph, deductions not attributable to the taxpayer's trade or business which do not relate to items of tax preference are considered as being applied in reducing gross income not derived from such trade or business before such deductions which do relate to items of tax preferences.

(e) Examples. The principles of this section may be illustrated by the following examples in each of which the deduction for the personal exemption is disregarded and the taxpayer is an individual who is a calendar year taxpayer.

Example (1). The taxpayer has the following items of income and deduction for 1970:

Gross income (all business income)	$120,000
Deductions:	
Nonbusiness deductions	30,000
Items of tax preference (excess accelerated depreciation on real property held in taxpayer's business)	80,000
Other business deductions	50,000

Based on the above figures, the taxpayer has a net operating loss of $10,000 (business deductions of $130,000 less business income of $120,000, the nonbusiness deductions having been disallowed by reason of section 172(d)(4)). The limitation on the amount treated as items of tax preference is computed as follows:

Tax preferences			$80,000
Net operating loss		$10,000	
Recomputed income or loss:			
Gross income	$120,000		
Deductions other than tax preference items	80,000		
Recomputed income		40,000	
Sum of net operating loss and recomputed income		50,000	
Stock options preference		0	
Limitation		50,000	

Thus, the minimum tax computed under section 56(a) would be 10 percent of $20,000 (items of tax preference of $50,000 less the minimum tax exemption of $30,000), $1,000 of which would be deferred tax liability pursuant to section 56(b).

Example (2). Assume the same facts as in example 1 except that the other business deductions are $130,000, resulting in a net operating loss of $90,000. The limitation on the amount treated as items of tax preference is computed as follows:

Tax preferences			$80,000
Net operating loss		$90,000	
Recomputed income or loss:			
Gross income	$120,000		
Deductions other than tax preference items	160,000		
	(40,000)		
Disallowance of nonbusiness deductions under sec 172(d)	30,000		
Recomputed loss		10,000	
Net operating loss less recomputed loss		80,000	
Stock options preference		0	

Limitation	80,000

Thus, the minimum tax computed under section 56(a) would be 10 percent of $50,000 (items of tax preference of $80,000 less the minimum tax exemption of $30,000), all of which will be deferred tax liability pursuant to section 56(b).

Example (2). The taxpayer has the following items of income and deduction for 1970:

Gross income (all from business):		
Ordinary		$ 50,000
Net section 1201 gains		120,000
Deductions:		
Items of tax preference:		
Excess amortization of certified pollution control facilities	$ 45,000	
Capital gains deduction	60,000	105,000
Other business deductions		75,000

In addition, the taxpayer has a $55,000 item of tax preference resulting from qualified stock options. Based on the above figures, the taxpayer has no taxable income and no net operating loss as the capital gains deduction is disallowed in determining the net operating loss pursuant to section 172(d). The limitation on the amount treated as items of tax preference is computed as follows:

Tax preferences			$160,000
Net operating loss		0	
Recomputed income or loss:			
Gross income	$170,000		
Deductions other than tax preference items	75,000		
Recomputed income		$95,000	
Plus: Stock options preference		55,000	
Limitation			150,000

Thus, the minimum tax computed under section 56 would be 10 percent of $120,000 (items of tax preference of $150,000 less the minimum tax exemption of $30,000).

Example (4). Assume the same facts as in example (3) except that the taxpayer has a net operating loss carryover from 1969 of $80,000. The taxpayer has $160,000 of tax preferences which are limited to $150,000 pursuant to § 1.57-4(b)(1). In order to determine the amount of the 1969 net operating loss which remains as a carryover to 1971, the 1970 taxable income is redetermined in accordance with section 172(b)(2) and the regulations thereunder, as follows:

Gross income--1970	$170,000	
Deductions:		
Capital gains deduction disallowed business deductions	$120,000	120,000
Taxable income for section 172(b)(2)		50,000

Thus, the 1969 net operating loss which remains as a carryover to 1971 is $30,000. Pursuant to paragraph (b)(2) of this section, the limitation on the amount treated as items of tax preference is computed as follows:

Items of tax preference computed with regard to § 157-4(b)(1) (per example (3))	$150,000
Less: Lesser of capital gains deduction ($60,000) or amount of reduction in carryover due to its disallowance ($50,000)	50,000
Limitation	100,000

Thus, the minimum tax computed under section 56 would be 10 percent of $70,000 (items of tax preference of $100,000 less the minimum tax exemption of $30,000).

Example (5). The taxpayer has the following items of income and deduction for the taxable year 1970 without regard to any net operating loss deduction:

Gross income (all from business):		
Ordinary	$50,000	
Net section 1201 gain	40,000	
		$90,000
Deductions:		
Capital gains deduction	20,000	
Medical expenses ($4,100 actually paid but allowable only to the extent in excess of 3 percent of adjusted gross income of $70,000)	2,000	
Other itemized deductions	40,000	
		62,000
Taxable income (before net operating loss deduction)		28,000

In addition, the taxpayer has an item of tax preference of $35,000 resulting from qualified stock options. In 1973, the taxpayer has a net operating loss of $60,000 (no portion of which is attributable to excess tax preferences pursuant to § 1.56A-2) which is carried back to 1970 resulting in no taxable income in 1970. In order to determine the amount of the 1973 net operating loss which remains as a carryover to 1971, the 1970 taxable income is redetermined, in accordance with section 172(b)(2) and the regulations thereunder, as follows:

Gross income		$90,000
Deductions:		
Capital gains deduction disallowed		
Medical expenses ($4,100 actually paid but allowable only to the extent in excess of 3 percent of adjusted gross income of $90,000)	$ 1,400	
Other itemized deductions	40,000	
		$41,400
Taxable income for section 172(b)(2)		48,600

The limitation on the amount treated as items of tax preference is computed as follows:

Items of tax preference:	
Capital gains	$20,000
Stock options	35,000
	55,000
Less:	
Lesser of capital gains deduction ($20,000) or amount of reduction in carryover due to its disallowance ($20,600)	(20,000)
Limitation	35,000

Thus, the minimum tax for 1970 under section 56 would be 10 percent of $5,000 (items of tax preference of $35,000 less the minimum tax exemption of $30,000).

Example (6). Assume the same facts as in example (5) except that the 1973 net operating loss was $45,000. In this case, the $20,600 increase in the 1970 taxable income as redetermined, results in a decrease of $17,000 (i.e., the remaining 1973 net operating loss after an initial decrease of $28,000 resulting from the 1970 taxable income before redetermination). The limitation on the amount treated as items of tax preference is computed as follows:

Items of tax preference computed without regard to this section	$55,000
Less: Lesser of capital gains deduction ($20,000) or amount of reduction in carryover due to its disallowance ($17,000)	(17,000)
Limitation	38,000

Thus, the minimum tax for 1970 under section 56 would be 10 percent of $8,000 (items of tax preference of $38,000 less the minimum tax exemption of $30,000).

Example (7). The taxpayer has the following items of income and deduction for 1973 without regard to any net operating loss deduction:

Gross income (all from business):		
Ordinary	$100,000	
Net section 1201 gains	120,000	
		$220,000
Deductions:		
Items of tax preference:		
Excess amortization of certified pollution control facilities	45,000	
Capital gains deduction	60,000	
	105,000	
Other business deductions	75,000	
		$180,000
Taxable income (before net operating loss deduction)		40,000

In 1972, the taxpayer had a net operating loss of $70,000 which is carried forward to 1973; $20,000 of this net operating loss is attributable to excess tax preferences. In order to determine the amount of the 1972 net operating loss which remains as a carryover to 1974, the 1973 taxable income is redetermined, in accordance with section 172(b)(2) and the regulations thereunder, as follows:

Gross income	$220,000
Deductions:	
Capital gains deduction	Disallowed
Business deductions	120,000
Taxable income per section 172(b)(2)	100,000

In this case, the $60,000 increase in the 1972 taxable income as redetermined and the $30,000 decrease in the amount of the 1973 net operating loss remaining as a carryover to 1974 (i.e., the remaining 1972 net operating loss after an initial decrease of $40,000 resulting from the 1973 taxable income before redetermination) is entirely attributable to the disallowance of the capital gains deduction. The limitation on the amount treated as items of tax preference is computed as follows:

Items of tax preference computed without regard to this section:	
Capital gains	$ 60,000
Excess amortization of certified pollution control facilities	45,000
	105,000
Less: Lesser of capital gains deduction (60,000) or amount of reduction in carryover due to its disallowance ($30,000)	(30,000)
	75,000
Plus: Amount of reduction of carryover (due to disallowance of capital gains deduction) attributable to excess tax preferences	20,000
Limitation	95,000

T.D. 7564, 9/11/78, amend T.D. 8138, 4/23/87.

§ 1.57-5 Records to be kept.

Caution: The Treasury has not yet amended Reg § 1.57-5 to reflect changes made by P.L. 99-514.

(a) In general. The taxpayer shall have available permanent records of all the facts necessary to determine with reasonable accuracy the amounts described in § 1.57-1. Such records shall include:

(1) In the case of amounts described in paragraph (a) of § 1.57-1: the amount and nature of indebtedness outstanding for the taxable year and the date or dates on which each such indebtedness was incurred or renewed in any form; the amount expended for property held for investment during any taxable year during which such indebtedness was incurred or renewed; and the manner in which it was determined that property was or was not held for investment.

(2) In the case of amounts described in paragraphs (b), (c), (d), (e), and (h) of § 1.57-1:

(i) The dates, and manner in which, the property was acquired and placed in service,

(ii) The taxpayer's basis on the date the property was acquired and the manner in which the basis was determined,

(iii) An estimate of the useful life (in terms of months, hours of use, etc., whichever is appropriate) of the property on the date placed in service or an estimate of the number of units to be produced by the property on the date the property is placed in service, whichever is appropriate, and the manner in which such estimate was determined,

(iv) The amount and date of all adjustments by the taxpayer to the basis of the property and an explanation of the nature of such adjustments, and

(v) In the case of property which has an adjusted basis reflecting adjustments taken by another taxpayer with respect to the property or taken by the taxpayer with respect to other property, the information described in subdivisions (i) through (iv) above, with respect to such other property or other taxpayer.

(3) In the case of amounts described in paragraph (f) of § 1.57-1, the fair market value of the shares of stock at the

date of exercise of the option and the option price and the manner in which each was determined.

(4) In the case of amounts described in paragraph (g) of § 1.57-1, the amount of debts written off and the amount of the loans outstanding for the taxable year and the 5 preceding taxable years or such shorter or longer period as is appropriate.

(b) Net operating losses. The taxpayer shall have available permanent records for the first taxable year in which a portion of a net operating loss was attributable to items of tax preference (within the meaning of § 1.56A-2(b)) and each succeeding taxable year in which there is a net operating loss or a net operating loss carryover a portion of which is so attributable. Such records shall include all the facts necessary to determine with reasonable accuracy the amount of deferred tax liability under section 56, including the amount of the net operating loss in each taxable year in which there are items of tax preference in excess of the minimum tax exemption (as determined under § 1.58-1), the amount of the items of tax preference for each such taxable year, the amount by which each such net operating loss reduces taxable income in any taxable year, and the amount by which each such net operating loss is reduced in any taxable year.

T.D. 7564, 9/11/78, amend T.D. 8138, 4/23/87.

---

§ 7.57(d)-1 Election with respect to straight line recovery of intangibles.

Caution: The Treasury has not yet amended Reg § 7.57(d)-1 to reflect changes made by P.L. 99-514.

(a) Purpose. This section prescribes rules for making the election permitted under section 57(d)(2), as added by the Tax Reform Act of 1976. Under this election taxpayers may use cost depletion to compute straight line recovery of intangibles.

(b) Election. The election under section 57(d) is subject to the following rules:

(1) The election is made within the time prescribed by law (including extensions thereof) for filing the return for the taxable year in which the intangible drilling costs are paid or incurred or, if later, by July 25, 1978.

(2) The election is made separately for each well. Thus, a taxpayer may make the election for only some of his or her wells.

(3) The election is made by using, for the well or wells to which the election applies, cost depletion to compute straight line recovery of intangibles for purposes of determining the amount of the preference under section 57(a)(11).

(4) The election may be made whether or not the taxpayer uses cost depletion in computing taxable income.

(5) The election is made by a partnership rather than by each partner.

(c) Computation of cost depletion. For purposes of computing straight line recovery of intangibles through cost depletion, both depletable and depreciable intangible drilling and development costs for the taxable year are taken into account. They are treated as if capitalized, added to basis, and recovered under § 1.611-2(a). Costs paid or incurred in other taxable years are not taken into account.

T.D. 7541, 4/25/78.

---

§ 1.58-1 Minimum tax exemption.

Caution: The Treasury has not yet amended Reg § 1.58-1 to reflect changes made by P.L. 110-166, P.L. 99-514.

(a) In general. For purposes of the minimum tax for tax preferences (subtitle A, chapter 1A, part VI), the minimum tax exemption is $30,000 except as otherwise provided in this section.

(b) Husband and wife. In the case of a married individual filing a separate return, section 58(a) provides that the minimum tax exemption is $15,000. This rule applies without regard to whether the married individual is living together with or apart from his spouse and without regard to whether or not his spouse has any items of tax preference.

(c) Members of controlled groups. *(1) Amount of exemption.* (i) General rule. Under section 58(b), if a corporation is a component member of a controlled group of corporations on December 31 (as defined in section 1563(a) and (b) and the regulations thereunder), the minimum tax exemption for such taxable year which includes such December 31 is an amount equal to—

(a) $30,000 divided by the number of corporations which are component members of such group on December 31, or

(b) If an apportionment plan is adopted under subparagraph (3) of this paragraph, such portion of the $30,000 as is apportioned to such member in accordance with such plan.

(ii) Consolidated returns. The minimum tax exemption of a controlled group all of whose component members join in the filing of a consolidated return is $30,000. If there are component members of the controlled group which do not join in the filing of a consolidated return, and there is no apportionment plan effective under subparagraph (3) of this paragraph apportioning the $30,000 among the component members filing the consolidated return and the other component members of the controlled group, each component member of the controlled group (including each component member which joins in filing the consolidated return) is treated as a separate corporation for purposes of equally apportioning the $30,000 amount under subdivision (i)(a) of this subparagraph. In such case, the minimum tax exemption of the corporations filing the consolidated return is the sum of the amounts apportioned to each component member which joins in the filing of the consolidated return.

(2) Certain short taxable years. If the return of a corporation is for a short period which does not include a December 31, and such corporation is a component member of a controlled group of corporations with respect to such short period, the minimum tax exemption of such corporation for such short period is an amount equal to $30,000 divided by the number of corporations which are component members of such group on the last day of such short period. The minimum tax exemption so determined is also subject to the rules of section 443(d) (relating to reduction in the amount of the exemption for short periods) and the regulations thereunder. For purposes of this subparagraph, the term "short period" does not include any period if the income for such period is required to be included in a consolidated return under § 1.1502-76(b). The determination of whether a corporation is a component member of a controlled group of corporations on the last day of a short period is made by applying the definition of "component member" contained in section 1563(b) and § 1.1563-1 as if the last day of such short period were a December 31.

(3) Apportionment of minimum tax exemption. (i) Apportionment plan. (a) In general. In the case of corporations

which are component members of a controlled group of corporations on a December 31, a single minimum tax exemption may be apportioned among such members if all such members consent, in the manner provided in subdivision (ii) of this subparagraph, to an apportionment plan with respect to such December 31. Such plan must provide for the apportionment of a fixed dollar amount to one or more of such members, but in no event may the sum of the amount so apportioned exceed $30,000. An apportionment plan is not considered as adopted with respect to a particular December 31 until each component member which is required to consent to the plan under subdivision (ii)(a) of this subparagraph files the original of a statement described in such subdivision (or, the original of a statement incorporating its consent is filed on its behalf). In the case of a return filed before a plan is adopted, the minimum tax exemption for purposes of such return is to be equally apportioned in accordance with subparagraph (1) of this paragraph. If a valid apportionment plan is adopted after the return is filed and within the time prescribed in (b) of this subdivision (i), such return must be amended (or a claim for refund should be made) to reflect the change from equal apportionment.

(b) Time for adopting plan. A controlled group may adopt an apportionment plan with respect to a particular December 31 only if, at the time such plan is sought to be adopted, there is at least 1 year remaining in the statutory period (including any extensions thereof) for the assessment of the deficiency against any corporation the tax liability of which would be increased by the adoption of such plan. If there is less than 1 year remaining with respect to any such corporation, the district director or the director of the service center with whom such corporation files its income tax return will ordinarily, upon request, enter into an agreement to extend such statutory period for the limited purpose of assessing any deficiency against such corporation attributable to the adoption of such apportionment plan.

(c) Years for which effective. (1) The amount apportioned to a component member of a controlled group of corporations in an apportionment plan adopted with respect to a particular December 31 constitutes such member's minimum tax exemption for its taxable year including the particular December 31, and for all taxable years including succeeding December 31's, unless the apportionment plan is amended in accordance with subdivision (iii) of this subparagraph or is terminated under (c) (2) of this subdivision (i). Thus, the apportionment plan (including any amendments thereof) has a continuing effect and need not be renewed annually.

(2) If an apportionment plan is adopted with respect to a particular December 31, such plan terminates with respect to a succeeding December 31, if: the controlled group goes out of existence with respect to such succeeding December 31 within the meaning of paragraph (b) of § 1.1562-5, any corporation which was a component member of such group on the particular December 31 is not a component member of such group on such succeeding December 31, or any corporation which was not a component member of such group on the particular December 31 is a component member of such group on such succeeding December 31. An apportionment plan, once terminated with respect to a December 31, is no longer effective. Accordingly, unless a new apportionment plan is adopted, the minimum tax exemption of the component members of the controlled group for their taxable years which include such December 31 and all December 31's thereafter will be determined under subparagraph (1) of this paragraph.

(3) If an apportionment plan is terminated with respect to a particular December 31 by reason of the addition or withdrawal of a component member, each corporation which is a component member of the controlled group on such particular December 31 must, on or before the date it files its income tax return for the taxable year which includes such particular December 31, notify the district director or the director of the service center with whom it files such return to such termination. If an apportionment plan is terminated with respect to a particular December 31 by reason of the controlled group going out of existence, each corporation which was a component member of the controlled group on the preceding December 31 must, on or before the date it files its income tax return for the taxable year which includes such particular December 31, notify the district director or the director of the service center with whom it files such return to such termination.

(ii) Consents to plan. (a) General rule. (1) The consent of a component member (other than a wholly-owned subsidiary) to an apportionment plan with respect to a particular December 31 is to be made by means of a statement, signed by any person who is duly authorized to act on behalf of the consenting member, stating that such member consents to the apportionment plan with respect to such December 31. The statement must set forth the name, address, taxpayer identification number, and taxable year of the consenting component member, the amount apportioned to such member under the plan, and the internal revenue district or service center where the original of the statement is to be filed. The consent of more than one component member may be incorporated in a single statement. The original of a statement of consent is to be filed with he district director or the director of the service center with whom the component member of the group on such December 31 which has the taxable year ending first on or after such date filed its return for such taxable year. If two or more component members have the same such taxable year, a statement of consent may be filed with the district director or the director of the service center with whom the return for any such taxable year is filed. The original of a statement of consent is to have attached thereto information (referred to in this subdivision as "group identification") setting forth the name, address, taxpayer identification number, and taxable year of each component member of the controlled group on such December 31 (including wholly-owned subsidiaries) and the amount apportioned to each such member under the plan. If more than one original statement is filed, a statement may incorporate the group identification by reference to the name, address, taxpayer identification number, and taxable year of the component member of the group which has attached such group identification to the original of its statement.

(2) Each component member of the group on such December 31 (other than wholly-owned subsidiaries) must attach a copy of its consent (or a copy of the statement incorporating its consent) to the income tax return, amended return, or claim for refund filed with its district director or director of the service center for the taxable year including such date. Such copy must either have attached thereto information on group identification or must incorporate such information by reference to the name, address, taxpayer identification number, and taxable year of the component member of the group which has attached such information to its income tax return, amended return, or claim for refund filed with the same district director or director of the service center for the taxable year including such date.

(b) Wholly-owned subsidiaries. (1) Each component member of a controlled group which is a wholly-owned subsidiary of such group with respect to a December 31 is deemed to consent to an apportionment plan with respect to such December 31, provided each component member of the group which is not a wholly-owned subsidiary consents to the plan. For purposes of this paragraph, a component member of a controlled group is considered to be a wholly-owned subsidiary of the group with respect to a December 31, if, on each day preceding such date and during its taxable year which includes such date, all of its stock is owned directly by one or more corporations which are component members of the group on such December 31.

(2) Each wholly-owned subsidiary of a controlled group with respect to a December 31 must attach a statement containing the information which is required to be set forth in a statement of consent to an apportionment plan with respect to such December 31 to the income tax return, amended return, or claim for refund filed with its district director or director of the service center for the taxable year which includes such date. Such statement must either have attached thereto information on group identification or incorporate such information by reference to the name, address, taxpayer identification number, and taxable year of a component member of the group which has attached such information to its income tax return, amended return, or claim for refund filed with the same district director or director of the service center for the taxable year including such date.

(iii) Amendment of plan. An apportionment plan adopted with respect to a December 31 by a controlled group of corporations may be amended with respect to such December 31 or with respect to any succeeding December 31 for which the plan is effective under subdivision (i)(c) of this subparagraph. An apportionment plan must be amended with respect to a particular December 31 and the amendments to the plan are effective only if adopted in accordance with the rules prescribed in this paragraph for the adoption of an original plan with respect to such December 31.

(iv) Component members filing consolidated return. If the component members of a controlled group of corporations on a December 31 include corporations which join the filing of a consolidated return, the corporations filing the consolidated return are treated as a single component member for purposes of this subparagraph. Thus, for example, only one consent executed by the common parent to an apportionment plan filed pursuant to this section is required on behalf of the component members filing the consolidated return.

(d) Estates and trusts. Section 58(c)(2) provides that, in the case of an estate or trust, the minimum tax exemption applicable to such estate or trust is an amount which bears the same ratio to $30,000 as the portion of the sum of the items of tax preference apportioned to the estate or trust bears to the full sum before apportionment. For example, if one-third of the sum of the items of tax preference of a trust are subject to tax at the trust level after apportionment under section 58(c)(1) and § 1.58-3, the trust's minimum tax exemption is $10,000. See § 1.58-3 for rules with respect to the apportionment of items of tax preference of an estate or trust.

(e) Short taxable year. See section 443(d) and § 1.443-1(d) with respect to reduction in the amount of the minimum tax exemption in the case of a short taxable year.

T.D. 7564, 9/11/78.

§ 1.58-2 General rules for conduit entities; partnerships and partners.

Caution: The Treasury has not yet amended Reg § 1.58-2 to reflect changes made by P.L. 104-188, P.L. 99-514.

(a) General rules for conduit entities. Sections 1.58-3 through 1.58-6 provide rules under which items of tax preference of an estate, trust, electing small business corporation, common trust fund, regulated investment company, or real estate investment trust (referred to in this paragraph as the "conduit entity") are treated as items of tax preference of the beneficiaries, shareholders, participants, etc. (referred to in this paragraph as the "distributees"). Where an item of tax preference of a conduit entity is so apportioned to a distributee, the item of tax preference retains its character in the hands of the distributee and is adjusted to reflect: (1) The separate items of income and deduction of the distributee and (2) the tax status of the distributee as an individual, corporation, etc. For example, if a trust has $100,000 of capital gains for the taxable year, all of which are distributed to A, an individual, the item of tax preference apportioned to A under section 57(a)(9) (and § 1.57-1(i)(1) is $50,000. If, however, A had a net capital loss for the taxable year of $60,000 without regard to the distribution from the trust, the trust tax preference would be adjusted in the hands of A to reflect the separate items of income and deduction passed through to the distributee, or, in this case, to reflect the net section 1201 gain to A of $40,000. Thus, A's capital gains items of tax preference would be $20,000. By application of this rule, A, in effect, treats capital gains distributed to him from the trust the same as his other capital gains in computing his capital gains item of tax preference. If A had been a corporation, the trust tax preference would be adjusted both to reflect the capital loss and to reflect A's tax status by recomputing the capital gains item of tax preference (after adjustment for the capital loss) under section 57(a)(9)(B) and § 1.57-1(i)(2). Similarly, if depreciation on section 1245 property subject to a net lease (as defined in section 57(a)(3) and § 1.57-1(c)) is apportioned from a conduit entity to a corporation (other than a personal holding company or electing small business corporation), the amount so apportioned to the corporation is not treated as an item of tax preference to such corporation since such item is not an item of tax preference in the case of a corporation (other than a personal holding company or an electing small business corporation).

(b) Partnerships and partners. *(1)* Section 701 provides that a partnership as such is not subject to the income tax imposed by chapter 1. Thus, a partnership as such is not subject to the minimum tax for tax preferences. Section 702 provides that, in determining his income tax, each partner is to take into account separately his distributive share of certain items of income, deductions, etc. of the partnership and other items of income, gain, loss, deduction, or credit of the partnership to the extent provided by regulations prescribed by the Secretary or his delegate. Accordingly, each partner, in computing his items of tax preference, must take into account separately those items of income and deduction of the partnership which enter into the computation of the items of tax preference in accordance with subparagraph (2) of this paragraph.

(2) Pursuant to section 702, each partner must, solely for purposes of the minimum tax for tax preferences (to the extent not otherwise required to be taken into account separately under section 702 and the regulations thereunder), take into account separately in the manner provided in sub-chapter K and the regulations thereunder those items of income

and deduction of the partnership which enter into the computation of the items of tax preference specified in section 57 and the regulations thereunder. A partner must, for this purpose, take into account separately his distributive share of:

(i) Investment interest expense (as defined in section 57(b)(2)(D) determined at the partnership level;

(ii) Investment income (as defined in section 57(b)(2)(B) determined at the partnership level;

(iii) Investment expenses (as defined in section 57(b)(2)(C)) determined at the partnership level;

(iv) With respect to each section 1250 property (as defined in section 1250(c)), the amount of the deduction allowable for the taxable year for exhaustion, wear and tear, obsolescence, or amortization and the deduction which would have been allowable for the taxable year had the property been depreciated under the straight line method each taxable year of its useful life (determined without regard to section 167(k)) for which the partnership has held the property;

(v) With respect to each item of section 1245 property (as defined in section 1245(a)(3)) which is subject to a net lease, the amount of the deduction allowable for exhaustion, wear and tear, obsolescence, or amortization and the deduction which would have been allowable for the taxable year had the property been depreciated under the straight line method for each taxable year of its useful life for which the partnership has held the property;

(vi) With respect to each certified pollution control facility for which an election is in effect under section 169, the amount of the deduction allowable for the taxable year under such section and the deduction which would have been allowable under section 167 had no election been in effect under section 169;

(vii) With respect to each unit of railroad rolling stock for which an election is in effect under section 184, the amount of the deduction allowable for the taxable year under such section and the deduction which would have been allowable under section 167 had no election been in effect under section 184;

(viii) In the case of a partnership which is a financial institution to which section 585 or 593 applies, the amount of the deduction allowable for the taxable year for a reasonable addition to a reserve for bad debts and the amount of the deduction that would have been allowable for the taxable year had the institution maintained its bad debt reserve for all taxable years on the basis of actual experience; and

(ix) With respect to each mineral property, the deduction for depletion allowable under section 611 for the taxable year and the adjusted basis of the property at the end of the taxable year (determined without regard to the depreciation deduction for the taxable year).

If, pursuant to section 743 (relating to optional adjustment to basis), the basis of partnership property is adjusted with respect to a transferee partner due to an election being in effect under section 754 (relating to manner of electing optional adjustment), items representing amortization, depreciation, depletion, gain or loss, and the adjusted basis of property subject to depletion, described above, shall be adjusted to reflect the basis adjustment under section 743.

(3) The minimum tax is effective for taxable years ending after December 31, 1969. Thus, subparagraph (2) of this paragraph is inapplicable in the case of items of income or deduction paid or accrued in a partnership's taxable year ending on or before December 31, 1969.

T.D. 7564, 9/11/78.

---

§ 1.58-3 Estates and trusts.

Caution: The Treasury has not yet amended Reg § 1.58-3 to reflect changes made by P.L. 99-514.

(a) In general. *(1)* Section 58(c)(1) provides that the sum of the items of tax preference of an estate or trust shall be apportioned between the estate or trust and the beneficiary on the basis of the income of the estate or trust allocable to each. Income for this purpose is the income received or accrued by the trust or estate which is not subject to current taxation either in the hands of the trust or estate or the beneficiary by reason of an item of tax preference. The character of the amounts distributed is determined under section 652(b) or 662(b) and the regulations thereunder.

(2) Additional computations required by reason of excess distributions are to be made in accordance with the principles of sections 665-669 and the regulations thereunder.

(3) In the case of a charitable remainder annuity trust (as defined in section 664(d)(1) and § 1.664-2) or a charitable remainder unitrust (as defined in section 664(d)(2) and § 1.664-3), the determination of the income not subject to current taxation by reason of an item of tax preference is to be made as if such trust were generally subject to taxation. Where income of such a trust is not subject to current taxation in accordance with this section and is distributed to a beneficiary in a taxable year subsequent to the taxable year in which the trust received or accrued such income, the items of tax preference relating to such income are apportioned to the beneficiary in such subsequent year (without credit for minimum tax paid by the trust with respect to items of tax preference which are subject to the minimum tax by reason of section 664(c)).

(4) Items of tax preference apportioned to a beneficiary pursuant to this section are to be taken into account by the beneficiary in his taxable year within or with which ends the taxable year of the estate or trust during which it has such items of tax preference.

(5) Where a trust or estate has items of income or deduction which enter into the computation of the excess investment interest item of tax preference, but such items do not result in an item of tax preference at the trust or estate level, each beneficiary must take into account, in computing his excess investment interest, the portion of such items distributed to him. The determination of the portion of such items distributed to each beneficiary is made in accordance with the character rules of section 652(b) or section 662(b) and the regulations thereunder.

(6) Where, pursuant to subpart E of part 1 of subchapter J (sections 671-678), the grantor of a trust or another person is treated as the owner of any portion of the trust, there shall be included in computing the items of tax preference of such person those items of income, deductions, and credits against tax of the trust which are attributable to that portion of the trust to the extent such items are taken into account under section 671 and the regulations thereunder. Any remaining portion of the trust is subject to the provisions of this section.

(b) Examples. The principles of this section may be illustrated by the following examples in each of which it is assumed that none of the distributions are accumulation distributions (see sections 665-669 and the regulations thereunder):

Example (1). Trust A, with one income beneficiary, has the following items of income and deduction without regard to the deduction for distributions:

Income:	
Business income	$200,000
Investment income	20,000
	220,000
Deductions:	
Business deductions (nonpreference)	100,000
Investment interest expense	80,000
	180,000

Based on the above figures, the trust has $100,000 of taxable income without regard to items which enter into the computation of excess investment interest and the deduction for distributions. The trust also has $60,000 of excess investment interests, resulting in $40,000 of distributable net income. Thus, $60,000 of the $100,000 of noninvestment income is not subject to current taxation by reason of the excess investment interest.

(a) If $40,000 is distributed to the beneficiary, the beneficiary will normally be subject to tax on the full amount received and the "sheltered" portion of the income will remain at the trust level. Thus, none of the excess investment interest item of tax preference is apportioned to the beneficiary.

(b) If the beneficiary receives $65,000 from the trust, the beneficiary is still subject to tax on only $40,000 (the amount of the distributable net income) and thus, is considered to have received $25,000 of business income "sheltered" by excess investment interest. Thus, $25,000 of the $60,000 of excess investment interest of the trust is apportioned to the beneficiary.

Example (2). Trust B has $150,000 of net section 1201 gain.

(a) If none of the gain is distributed to the beneficiaries, none of the capital gains item of tax preference is apportioned to the beneficiaries.

(b) If all or a part of the gain is distributed to the beneficiaries, a proportionate part of the capital gains item of tax preference is apportioned to the beneficiaries. If any of the beneficiaries are corporations the capital gains item of tax preference is adjusted in the hands of the corporations as provided in § 1.58-2(a).

Example (3). Trust C has taxable income of $200,000 computed without regard to depreciation on section 1250 property and the deduction for distributions. The depreciation on section 1250 property held by the trust is $160,000. The trust instrument provides for income to be retained by the trust in an amount equal to the depreciation on the property determined under the straight line method (which method has been used for this purpose for the entire period the trust has held the property) which, in this case is equal to $100,000. The $60,000 excess of the accelerated depreciation of $160,000 over the straight line amount which would have resulted had the property been depreciated under that method for the entire period for which the trust has held the property is an item of tax preference pursuant to section 57(a)(2). Of the remaining $100,000 of net income of the trust (after the reserve for depreciation), 80 percent is distributed to the beneficiaries. Pursuant to sections 167(h) and 642(e), 80 percent of the remaining $60,000 of depreciation deduction (or $48,000) is taken as a deduction directly by the beneficiaries and "shelters" the income received by the beneficiaries. Thus, the full $48,000 deduction taken by the beneficiaries is "excess accelerated depreciation" on section 1250 property and is an item of tax preference in the hands of the beneficiaries. None of the remaining $12,000 of "excess accelerated depreciation" is apportioned to the beneficiaries since this amount "shelters" income retained at the trust level.

Example (4). G creates a trust the ordinary income of which is payable to his adult son. Ten years from the date of the transfer, corpus is to revert to G. G retains no other right or power which would cause him to be treated as an owner under subpart E of part 1 of subchapter J (section 671 and following). Under the terms of the trust instrument and applicable local law capital gains must be applied to corpus. During the taxable year 1970 the trust has $200,000 income from dividends and interest and a net long-term capital gain of $100,000. Since the capital gain is held or accumulated for future distribution to G, he is treated under section 677(a)(2) as an owner of a portion of the trust to which the gain is attributable. Therefore, he must include the capital gain in the computation of his taxable income in 1970 and the capital gain item of tax preference is treated as being directly received by G. Accordingly, no adjustment is made to the trust's minimum tax exemption by reason of the capital gain.

Example (5). For its taxable year 1971 the trust referred to in example (4) has taxable income of $200,000 computed without regard to depreciation on section 1250 property and the deduction for distributions. The depreciation on section 1250 property held by the trust is $160,000. The trust instrument provides for income to be retained by the trust in an amount equal to the depreciation on the property determined for purposes of the Federal income tax. If the property had been depreciated under the straight line method for the entire period for which the trust held the property the resulting depreciation deduction would have been $100,000. The $60,000 excess is, therefore, an item of tax preference pursuant to section 57(a)(2) and § 1.57-1(d). Since this amount of "income" is held or accumulated for future distributions to G, he is treated under section 677(a)(2) as an owner of a portion of the trust to which such income is attributable. Therefore, section 671 requires that in computing the tax liability of the grantor the income, deductions, and credits against tax of the trust which are attributable to such portion shall be taken into account. Thus, the grantor has received $160,000 of income and is entitled to a depreciation deduction in the same amount. The $60,000 item of tax preference resulting from the excess depreciation is treated as being directly received by G as he has directly received the income sheltered by that preference. Accordingly, no adjustment is made to the trust's minimum tax exemption by reason of such depreciation.

T.D. 7564, 9/11/78.

§ 1.58-3T Treatment of non-alternative tax itemized deductions by trusts and estates and their beneficiaries in taxable years beginning after December 31, 1982.

Caution: The Treasury has not yet amended Reg § 1.58-3T to reflect changes made by P.L. 99-514.

For purposes of section 58(c), in taxable years beginning after December 31, 1982, itemized deductions of a trust or estate which are not alternative tax itemized deductions (as defined in section 55(e)(1)), shall be treated as items of tax preference and apportioned between trusts and their beneficiaries, and estates and their beneficiaries.

T.D. 8083, 4/22/86.

§ 1.58-4 Electing small business corporations.

Caution: The Treasury has not yet amended Reg § 1.58-4 to reflect changes made by P.L. 99-514.

(a) In general. Section 58(d)(1) provides rules for the apportionment of the items of tax preference of an electing small business corporation among the shareholders of such corporation. Section 58(d)(2) provides rules for the imposition of the minimum tax on an electing small business corporation with respect to certain capital gains. For purposes of section 58(d) and this section, the items of tax preference are computed at the corporate level as if section 57 generally applied to the corporation. However, the items of tax preference so computed are treated as items of tax preference of the shareholders of such corporation and not as items of tax preference of such corporation (except as provided in paragraph (c) of this section). The items of tax preference specified in section 57(a)(1) and § 1.57-1(a) (excess investment interest) and section 57(a)(3) and § 1.57-1(c) (accelerated depreciation on section 1245 property subject to a net lease), while generally inapplicable to corporations, are included as items of tax preference in the case of an electing small business corporation.

(b) Apportionment to shareholders. *(1)* The items of tax preference of an electing small business corporation, other than the capital gains item of tax preference described in paragraph (c) of this section, are apportioned pro rata among the shareholders of such corporation in a manner consistent with section 1374(c)(1). Thus, with respect to the items of tax preference of the electing small business corporation, there is to be treated as items of tax preference of each shareholder a pro rata share of such items computed as follows:

(i) Divide the total amount of such items of tax preference of the corporation by the number of days in the taxable year of the corporation, thus determining the daily amount of such items of tax preference.

(ii) Determine for each day the shareholder's portion of the daily amount of each such item of tax preference by applying to such amount the ratio which the stock owned by the shareholder on that day bears to the total stock outstanding on that day.

(iii) Total the shareholder's daily portions of each such item of tax preference of the corporation for it taxable year.

Amounts taken into account by shareholders in accordance with this paragraph are considered to consist of a pro rata share of each item of tax preference of the corporation. Thus, for example, if the corporation has $50,000 of excess investment interest and $150,000 of excess accelerated depreciation on section 1250 property and a shareholder, in accordance with this paragraph, takes into account $60,000 of the total $200,000 of tax preference items of the corporation, one-fourth ($50,000 ÷ $200,000) of the $60,000, or $15,000, taken into account by the shareholder is considered excess investment interest and three-fourths of the $60,000, or $45,000, is considered excess accelerated depreciation on section 1250 property.

(2) Items of tax preference apportioned to a shareholder pursuant to subparagraph (1) of this paragraph are taken into account by the shareholder for the shareholder's taxable year in which or with which the taxable year of the corporation ends, except that, in the case of the death of a shareholder during any taxable year of the corporation (during which the corporation is an electing small business corporation), the items of tax preference of the corporation for such taxable year are taken into account for the final taxable year of the shareholder.

(c) Capital gains. *(1)* Capital gains of an electing small business corporation, other than those capital gains subject to tax under section 1378, do not result in an item of tax preference at the corporate level since, in applying the formula specified in sections 57(a)(9)(B) and 1.57-1(i)(2), the rate of tax on capital gains (and the resulting tax) at the corporate level is zero. Under section 1375(a) shareholders of an electing small business corporation take into account the capital gains of the corporation (including capital gains subject to tax under sec. 1378). Therefore, the computation of the capital gains item of tax preference at the shareholder level, with respect to such capital gains, is taken into account automatically by operation of sections 57(a)(9) and 1.57-1(i). To avoid double inclusion of the capital gains subject to tax under section 1378, the capital gains item of tax preference which results at the corporate level by reason of section 58(d)(2) is not treated under section 58(d)(1) as an item of tax preference of the shareholders of the corporation.

(2) The capital gains item of tax preference of an electing small business corporation subject to the tax imposed by section 1378 is the excess of the amount of tax computed under section 1378(b)(2) over the sum of—

(i) The amount of tax that would be computed under section 1378(b)(2) if the following amount were excluded:

(a) That portion of the net section 1201 gain of the corporation described in section 1378(b)(1), or

(b) If section 1378(c)(3) applies, that portion of the net section 1201 gain attributable to the property described in section 1378(c)(3), and

(ii) The amount of tax imposed under section 1378 divided by the sum of the normal tax rate and the surtax rate under section 11 for the taxable year.

(3) The principles of this paragraph may be illustrated by the following example.

Example. Corporation X is a calendar year taxpayer and an electing small business corporation. For its taxable year 1971 the corporation has net section 1201 gain of $650,000 and taxable income of $800,000 (including the net section 1201 gain). Although X's election under section 1372(a) has been in effect for its three immediately preceding taxable years, X is subject to the tax imposed by section 1378 for 1971 since it has net section 1201 gain (in the amount of $200,000) attributable to property with a substituted basis. The tax computed under section 1378(b)(1) is $187,500 (30 percent of ($650,000 minus $25,000)) and under section 1378(b)(2) is $377,500 (22 percent of $800,000 plus 26 percent of $775,000). By reason of the limitation imposed by section 1378(c) the tax actually imposed by section 1378 is $60,000 (30 percent of $200,000, the net section 1201 gain). The tax computed under section 1378(b)(2) with the modification required under subparagraph (2)(i) of this paragraph is $281,500 (22 percent of $600,000 plus 26 percent of $576,000). Thus, the 1971 capital gains item of tax preference X is $75,000 computed as follows:

1. Tax computed under 1378(b)(2)	$377,500
2. Tax computed under 1378(b)(2) with modification	281,500
3. Excess	96,000
4. Tax actually imposed under 1378	60,000
5. Difference	36,000
6. Normal tax rate plus surtax rate	.48
7. Tax preference (line 5 divided by line 6)	$ 75,000

In addition each shareholder of X will take into account his distributive share of the $650,000 of net section 1201 gain of X less the taxes paid by X under sections 56 and 1378 on the gain.

T.D. 7564, 9/11/78.

§ 1.58-5 Common trust funds.

Caution: The Treasury has not yet amended Reg § 1.58-5 to reflect changes made by P.L. 99-514.

Section 58(e) provides that each participant in a common trust fund (as defined in sec. 584 and the regulations thereunder) is to treat as items of tax preference his proportionate share of the items of tax preference of the fund computed as if the fund were an individual subject to the minimum tax. The participant's proportionate share of the items of tax preference of the fund is determined as if the participant has realized, or incurred, his pro rata share of items of income, gain, loss, or deduction of the fund directly from the source from which realized or incurred by the fund. The participant's pro rata share of such items is determined in a manner consistent with section 1.584-2(c). Items of tax preference apportioned to a participant pursuant to this paragraph are taken into account by the participant for the participant's taxable year in which or with which the taxable year of the trust ends.

T.D. 7564, 9/11/78.

§ 1.58-6 Regulated investment companies; real estate investment trusts.

Caution: The Treasury has not yet amended Reg § 1.58-6 to reflect changes made by P.L. 99-514.

(a) In general. Section 58(f) provides rules with respect to the determination of the items of tax preference of regulated investment companies (as defined in sec. 851) and their shareholders and real estate investment trusts (as defined in sec. 856) and their shareholders, or holders of beneficial interest. In general, the items of tax preference of such companies and such trusts are determined at the company or trust level and the items of tax preference so determined (other than the capital gains item of tax preference (secs. 57(a)(9) and 1.57-1(i)) and, in the case of a real estate investment trust, accelerated depreciation on section 1250 property (secs. 57(a)(2) and 1.57-1(b)) are treated as items of tax preference of the shareholders, or holders of beneficial interest, in the same proportion that the dividends (other than capital gains dividends) paid to each such shareholder, or holder of beneficial interest, bear to the taxable income of such company or such trust determined without regard to the deduction for dividends paid. In no case, however, is such proportion to be considered in excess of 100 percent. For example, if a regulated investment company has items of tax preference of $500,000 for the taxable year, none of which resulted from capital gains, and distributes dividends in an amount equal to 90 percent of its taxable income, each shareholder treats his share of 90 percent of the company's items of tax preference, or (a proportionate share of) $450,000, as items of tax preference of the shareholder. The remaining $50,000 constitutes items of tax preference of the company. Amounts treated under this paragraph as items of tax preference of the shareholders, or holders of beneficial interest, are deemed to be derived proportionately from each item of tax preference of the company or trust, other than the capital gains item of tax preference and, in the case of a real estate investment trust, accelerated depreciation on section 1250 property. Such amounts are taken into account by the shareholders, or holders of beneficial interest, in the same taxable year in which the dividends on which the apportionment is based are includible in income. The minimum tax exemption of the trust or company shall not be reduced because a portion of the trust's or company's items of tax preference are allocated to the shareholders or holders of beneficial interests.

(b) Capital gains. Section 58(g)(1) provides that a regulated investment company or real estate investment trust does not treat as an item of tax preference the capital gains item of tax preference under section 57(a)(9) (and sec. 1.57-1(i)) to the extent that such item is attributable to amounts taken into income by the shareholders of such company under section 852(b)(3) or by the shareholders or holders of beneficial interest of such trust under section 857(b)(3). Thus, such a company or trust computes its capital gains item of tax preference on the basis of its net section 1201 gain less the sum of (1) the capital gains dividend (as defined in sec. 852(b)(3)(C) or sec. 857(b)(3)(C)) for the taxable year of the company or trust plus (2), in the case of a regulated investment company, that portion of the undistributed capital gains designated, pursuant to section 852(b)(3)(D) and the regulations thereunder, by the company to be includible in the shareholder's return as long-term capital gains for the shareholder's taxable year in which the last day of the company's taxable years falls. Amounts treated under section 852(b)(3) or 857(b)(3) as long-term capital gains of shareholders, or holders of beneficial interest, are automatically included, pursuant to sections 57(a)(9) and 1.57-1(i), in the computation of the capital gains item of tax preference of the shareholders, or holders of beneficial interest.

(c) Accelerated depreciation on section 1250 property. In the case of a real estate investment trust, all of the items of tax preference resulting from accelerated depreciation on section 1250 property held by the trust (section 57(a)(2) and § 1.57-1(b)) are treated as items of tax preference of the trust, and, thus, none are treated as items of tax preference of the shareholder, or holder of beneficial interest.

T.D. 7564, 9/11/78.

§ 1.58-7 Tax preferences attributable to foreign sources; preferences other than capital gains and stock options.

Caution: The Treasury has not yet amended Reg § 1.58-7 to reflect changes made by P.L. 99-514.

(a) In general. Section 58(g)(1) provides that except in the case of the stock options item of tax preference (section 57(a)(6) and § 1.57-1(f)) and the capital gains item of tax preference (section 57(a)(9) and § 1.57-1(i)), items of tax preference which are attributable to sources within any foreign country or possession of the United States shall, for purposes of section 56, be taken into account only to the extent that such items reduce the tax imposed by chapter 1 (other than the minimum tax under section 56) on income derived from sources within the United States. Items of tax preference from sources within any foreign country or possession of the United States reduce the chapter 1 tax on income from sources within the United States to the extent the deduction relating to such preferences, in combination with other foreign deductions, exceed the income from such sources and, in effect, offset income from sources within the United States. Items of tax preference, for this purpose, are determined after application of § 1.57-4 (relating to limitation on amounts treated as items of tax preference). In the case of a taxpayer who deducted foreign taxes under section 164 for a taxable year, the provisions of this section shall be applied) without regard to section 275(a)(4)) as if he had elected the overall foreign tax credit limitation under section 904(a)(2) for such year.

(b) Preferences attributable to foreign sources. *(1) Preferences other than excess investment interest.* Except in the case of excess investment interest (see subparagraph (2) of this paragraph), an item tax preference to which this section applies is attributable to sources within a foreign country or possession of the United States to the extent such item is attributable to a deduction properly allocable or apportionable to an item or class of gross income from sources within a foreign country or possession of the United States under the principles of section 862(b), or section 863, and the regulations thereunder. Where, in the case of income partly from sources within the United States and partly from sources within a foreign country or possession of the United States, taxable income is computed before apportionment to domestic and foreign sources, and is then apportioned by processes or formulas of general apportionment (pursuant to section 863(b) and the regulations thereunder), deductions attributable to such taxable income are considered to be proportionately from sources within the United States and within the foreign country or possession of the United States on the same basis as taxable income.

(2) Excess investment interest. (i) Per-country limitation. (a) In the case of a taxpayer on the per-country foreign tax credit limitation under section 904(a) for the taxable year, excess investment interest (as defined in section 57(b)(1)), and the resulting item of tax preference, is attributable to sources within a foreign country or a possession of the United States to the extent that investment interest expense attributable to income from sources within such foreign country or possession of the United States exceeds the net investment income from sources within such foreign country or such possession. For this purpose, net investment income from within a foreign country or possession of the United States is the excess (if any) of the investment income from sources within such country or possession over the investment expenses attributable to income from sources within such country or such possession. For the definition of investment interest expense see section 57(b)(2)(D); for the definition of investment income see section 57(b)(2)(B); for the definition of investment expense see section 57(b)(2)(C).

(b) If the taxpayer's excess investment interest computed on a worldwide basis is less than the taxpayer's total separately determined excess investment interest (as defined in this subdivision (b)), the amount of the taxpayer's excess investment interest from each foreign country or possession is the amount which bears the same relationship to the taxpayer's excess investment interest from each such country or possession, determined without regard to this subdivision (b), as the taxpayer's worldwide excess investment interest bears to the taxpayer's total separately determined excess investment interest. For purposes of this subdivision (b), the taxpayer's total separately determined excess investment interest is the sum of the total excess investment interest determined without regard to this subdivision (b) plus the taxpayer's excess investment interest from sources within the United States determined in a manner consistent with (a) of this subdivision (i).

(ii) Overall limitation. In the case of a taxpayer who has elected the overall foreign tax credit limitation under section 904(a)(2) for the taxable year, excess investment interest (as defined in section 57(b)(1)), and the resulting item of tax preference, is attributable to sources within any foreign country or possession of the United States to the extent that investment interest expense attributable to income from such sources exceeds the sum of (a) the net investment income from such sources plus (b) the excess, if any, of net investment income from sources within the United States over investment interest expense attributable to sources within the United States. For this purpose, net investment income from sources within any foreign country or possession of the United States is the excess (if any) of the investment income from all such sources over the investment expenses attributable to income from such sources. For the definition of investment interest expense see section 57(b)(2)(D) for the definition of investment income see section 57(b)(2)(B); for the definition of investment expense see section 57(b)(2)(C).

(iii) Allocation of expenses. The determination of the investment interest expense and investment expenses attributable to a foreign country or possession of the United States is made in a manner consistent with subparagraph (1) of this paragraph.

(iv) Attribution of certain interest deductions to foreign sources. Where net investment income from sources within any foreign country or possession has the effect of offsetting investment interest expense attributable to income from sources within the United States, the deductions for the investment interest expense so offset are, for purposes of § 1.58-7(c) (relating to reduction in taxes on United States source income), treated as deductions attributable to income from sources within the foreign country or possession from which such net investment income is derived. Such an offset will occur where there is an excess of investment interest expense attributable to income from sources within the United States over net investment income from such sources and (a) in the case of a taxpayer on the per-country foreign tax credit limitation, an excess of net investment income from sources within a foreign country or possession of the United States over investment interest expense from within such foreign country or possession, or (b) in the case of a taxpayer who has elected the overall foreign tax credit limitation, there is an excess of net investment income from sources within foreign countries or possessions of the United States over investment interest expense attributable to income from within such sources.

(v) Separate limitation on interest income. Where a taxpayer has income described in section 904(f)(2) (relating to interest income subject to the separate foreign tax credit limitation) or expenses attributable to such income, the determination of the excess investment interest resulting therefrom must be determined separately with respect to such income and the expenses properly allocable or apportionable thereto in the same manner as such determination is made in the case of a taxpayer on the per-country foreign tax credit limitation for the taxable year (see subdivision (i) of this subparagraph).

(vi) Examples. The principles of this subparagraph may be illustrated by the following examples in each of which the taxpayer is an individual and a citizen of the United States:

Example (1). The taxpayer's only items of income and deduction relating to excess investment interest are as follows:

	United States	France	Germany	Total
Investment income from sources within	$ 150,000	$120,000	$180,000	$450,000
Investment expenses relating to income from sources within	(100,000)	(90,000)	(120,000)	(310,000)
Net investment income	50,000	30,000	60,000	140,000
Investment interest expense relating to income from sources within	(110,000)	(70,000)	(50,000)	(230,000)
(Excess) of investment interest expense over net investment income	(60,000)	(40,000)	10,000*	(90,000)

* Excess of net investment income over investment interest expense.

(a) If the taxpayer has elected the overall foreign tax credit limitation, his excess investment interest from sources within any foreign countries or possessions of the United States determined under subdivision (ii) of this subparagraph is computed as follows:

Investment interest:			
French	($ 70,000)		
German	(50,000)	($ 120,000)	
Net investment income:			
Investment income:			
French	120,000		
German	180,000	$ 300,000	
Less:			
Investment expenses			
French	(90,000)		
German	(120,000)	(210,000)	90,000
Excess of U.S. net income over investment interest expenses:			
Total foreign excess investment interest			(30,000)

(b) If the taxpayer is on the per-country foreign tax credit limitation, his excess investment interest from France and Germany determined under subdivision (i) (a) of this subparagraph is $40,000 and zero, respectively. Since the taxpayer's worldwide excess investment interest ($90,000) is less than his total separately determined excess investment interest ($60,000 (United States) plus $40,000 (French) plus zero (German), or $100,000), the limitation in subdivision (i)(b) of this subparagraph applies and the excess investment interest attributable to France is limited as follows: Total worldwide excess ($90,000)/Total separately determined excess ($100,000) × French excess ($40,000) = $36,000

The taxpayer's total excess investment interest attributable to sources within any foreign country or possession of the United States is, thus, $36,000 ($36,000 (French) plus zero (German)). The taxpayer's excess investment interest attributable to sources within the United States is $54,000 ($90,000/$100,000 × $60,000).

Since, in making the latter determination, $6,000 of the $60,000 of U.S. investment interest expense in excess of U.S. net investment income is, in effect, offset by German net investment income, for purposes of § 1.58-7(c), $6,000 of interest deductions attributable to income from sources within the United States are, pursuant to subdivision (iv) of this subparagraph, treated as deductions attributable to income from sources within Germany.

Example (2). Assume the same facts as in example (1) except that the items of income and deduction in Germany and the United States are reversed. The worldwide excess investment interest, thus, remains $90,000 and the items of income and deduction relating to excess investment interest are as follows:

	United States	France	Germany	Total
Investment income from sources within	$180,000	$120,000	$150,000	$450,000
Investment expenses relating to income from sources within	(120,000)	(90,000)	(100,000)	(310,000)
Net investment income	60,000	30,000	50,000	140,000
Investment interest expense relating to income from sources within	(50,000)	(70,000)	(110,000)	(230,000)
(Excess) of investment interest expense over net investment income	10,000	(40,000)	(60,000)	(90,000)

(a) If the taxpayer has elected the overall limitation, his excess investment interest from sources within any foreign countries or possessions of the United States determined under subdivision (ii) of this subparagraph is determined as follows:

Foreign investment interest:			
French	($ 70,000)		
German	(110,000)		($ 180,000)
Foreign net investment income:			
French	120,000		
German	150,000	$ 270,000	
Less:			
Investment expenses			
French	(90,000)		
German	(100,000)	(190,000)	80,000
Excess of U.S. net investment income over U.S. investment interest expense			10,000
Excess investment interest attributable to foreign sources			(90,000)

(b) If the taxpayer has not elected the overall foreign tax credit limitation, his excess investment interest from France and Germany determined under subdivision (i) of this subparagraph (without regard to the limitation to worldwide excess investment interest) is $40,000 and $60,000 respectively, and his total separately determined excess investment interest is, thus, $10,000. Since the total separately determined excess would exceed the worldwide excess, the limitation to the worldwide excess in subdivision (i) applies and the excess investment interest is determined as follows:

France:

France:

$90,000/$100,000 × $40,000 = $36,000

Germany:

$90,000/$100,000 × $60,000 = $54,000

Total excess investment interest attributable to sources within any foreign countries and possessions—$90,000.

Example (3). Assume the same facts as in example (1) except that the taxpayer, in addition has investment income, investment expenses, and investment interest subject to the separate limitation under section 904(f).

(a) If the taxpayer has elected the overall foreign tax credit limitation, his excess investment interest from sources within any foreign countries or possessions of the United States determined under subdivision (ii) of this subparagraph is the same as in (a) of example (1) of this subdivision (vi). He then treats such amount as separately determined excess investment interest attributable to a single foreign country as determined under subdivision (i) of this subparagraph and proceeds as in (b) of example (1) of this subdivision (vi) treating items of income and deduction subject to section 904(f) and from each separate foreign country or possession separately in making the additional determinations under subdivisions (i) and (iv) of this subparagraph.

(b) If the taxpayer has not elected the overall foreign tax credit limitation, his excess investment interest from sources within any foreign country or possession of the United States would be determined in the same manner as in (b) of example (1) treating items of income and deduction which are subject to section 904(f) and from each separate foreign country or possession separately in making the determinations under subdivisions (i) and (iv) of this subparagraph.

(c) Reduction in taxes on United States source income. *(1) Overall limitation.* (i) In general. If a taxpayer is on the overall foreign tax credit limitation under section 904(a)(2), the items of tax preference determined to be attributable to foreign sources under paragraph (b) of this section reduce the tax imposed by chapter 1 (other than the minimum tax imposed under section 56) on income from sources within the United States for the taxable year to the extent of the smallest of the following three amounts:

(a) Items of tax preference (other than stock options and capital gains) attributable to sources within a foreign country or possession of the United States,

(b) The excess (if any) of the total deductions properly allocable or apportionable to items or classes of gross income from sources within foreign countries and possessions of the United States over the gross income from such sources, or

(c) Taxable income from sources within the United States. See § 1.58-7(b)(2)(iv) with respect to the attribution of certain interest deductions to foreign sources in cases involving the excess investment interest item of tax preference.

(ii) Net operating loss. Where there is an overall net operating loss for the taxable year, to the extent that the lesser of the amounts determined under (a) or (b) of subdivision (i) of this subparagraph exceeds the taxpayer's taxable income from sources within the United States (and, therefore do not offset taxable income from sources within the United States for the taxable year) the amount of such excess is treated as "suspense preferences." Suspense preferences are converted to actual items of tax preference, arising in the loss year and subject to the provisions of section 56, as the net operating loss is used in other taxable years, in the form of a net operating loss deduction under section 172, to offset taxable income from sources within the United States. Suspense preferences which, in other taxable years, reduce taxable income from sources within any foreign country or possession of the United States lose their character as suspense preferences and, thus, are never converted into actual items of tax preference. The amount of the suspense preferences which are converted into actual items of tax preference is equal to that portion of the net operating loss attributable to the suspense preferences which offset taxable income from sources within the United States in taxable years other than the loss year. The determination of the component parts of the net operating loss and the determination of the amount by which the portion of the net operating loss attributable to suspense preferences offsets taxable income from sources within the United States is made on a year-by-year basis in the same order a the net operating loss is used in accordance with section 172(b). Such determination is made by applying deductions attributable to U.S. source income first against such income and deductions attributable to foreign source income first against such foreign source income and in accordance with the following principles:

(a) Deductions attributable to items or classes of gross income from sources within the United States offset taxable income from sources within the United States before any remaining portion of the net operating loss;

(b) Deductions attributable to items or classes of gross income from sources within foreign countries or possessions of the United States offset taxable income from such sources before any remaining portion of the net operating loss;

(c) Deductions described in (b) of the subdivision (ii) which are not suspense preferences (referred to in this subparagraph as "other foreign deductions") offset taxable income from sources within foreign countries and possessions of the United States before suspense preferences; and

(d) Suspense preferences offset taxable income from sources within the United States before other foreign deductions.

For purposes of the above computations, taxable income is computed with the modifications specified in section 172(b)(2) or section 172(c), whichever is applicable. However, the amount of suspense preferences which are converted into actual items of tax preference in accordance with the above principles is reduced to the extent suspense preferences offset increases in taxable income from sources within the United States due to the modifications specified in section 172(b)(2) or section 172(c). For this purpose, suspense preferences are considered to offset an increase in taxable income due to the section 172(b)(2) modifications only after reducing taxable income computed before the section 172(b)(2) or section 172(c) modifications.

(iii) Examples. The principles of this subparagraph may be illustrated by the following examples. In each example the taxpayer is an individual citizen of the United States and has elected the overall foreign tax credit limitation. Personal deductions and exemptions are disregarded for purposes of these examples.

Example (1). In 1974, the taxpayer has the following items of income and deduction:

United States taxable income:			
Gross income		$750,000	
Deductions		(250,000)	$500,000
Foreign source loss:			
Gross income		200,000	
Deductions:			
Preference items (excess of percentage depletion over basis)	$550,000		
Other	50,000	(600,000)	(400,000)
Overall taxable income			100,000

Pursuant to subdivision (i) of this subparagraph the smallest of (a) the items of tax preference attributable to the foreign sources ($550,000), (b) the foreign source loss ($400,000), or (c) the taxable income from sources within the United States ($500,000) reduces the tax imposed by chapter 1 (other than the minimum tax) on income from sources within the United States. Thus, $400,000 of the $550,000 of excess depletion is treated as an item of tax preference in 1974 subject to the minimum tax.

Example (2). Assume the same facts as in example (1) except that the gross income from sources within the United States is $350,000 resulting in U.S. taxable income of $100,000 and an overall net operating loss of $300,000. Pursuant to subdivision (i) of this subparagraph, $100,000 of the $550,000 excess depletion would be treated as an item of tax preference in 1974 subject to the minimum tax. In addition, pursuant to subdivision (ii) of this subparagraph, the excess of the items of tax preference from foreign sources ($550,000) or the foreign source loss ($400,000), whichever is less, over the U.S. taxable income ($100,000), or, in this example, $300,000, is treated as suspense preferences.

(a) If, in 1971, the taxpayer's total items of income and deduction result in $350,000 of taxable income all of which is from sources within the United States, the entire $300,000 net operating loss, all of which is attributable to suspense preferences, is used to offset U.S. taxable income. Accordingly, the full $300,000 of suspense preferences are converted into actual items of tax preference arising in 1974 and are subject to tax under section 56.

(b) If the $350,000 in 1971 is modified taxable income resulting from the denial of a section 1202 capital gains deduction of $175,000 by reason of section 172(b)(2), the $300,000, otherwise treated as actual items of tax preference, is reduced by $125,000, i.e., the extent to which the suspense preferences offset U.S. taxable income attributable to the increase in taxable income resulting from the denial of the section 1202 deduction.

Example (3). In 1974, the taxpayer has the following items of income and deduction:

United States loss:			
Gross income		$75,000	
Deductions		(225,000)	$150,000
Foreign loss:			
Gross income		400,000	
Deductions:			
Preference items (excess of accelerated depreciation on sec. 1250 property over straight-line amount)	$200,000		
Other	550,000	(750,000)	(350,000)
Overall net operating loss			(500,000)

Since the nonpreference deductions reduce the foreign source income before the preference portion, the $350,000 foreign source loss consists of $200,000 of suspense preferences and $150,000 of other deductions. In 1971, 1972, and 1973 the taxpayer had taxable income from sources within the United States of $100,000, $200,000, and $300,000, respectively and taxable income from sources within foreign countries of $80,000 each year. Of the $200,000 of suspense preferences, $150,000 are converted into actual items of tax preference, subject to the minimum tax in 1974, determined as follows:

[In thousands of dollars]

Year—Explanation	Taxable income			Foreign deductions	
	U.S. source	Foreign source	U.S. deductions	Suspense preferences	Other
1971 End of year balance before section 58(g) computations	100	80	150	200	150
1. U.S. deductions against U.S. income	(100)		(100)		
2. Other foreign deductions against foreign income		(80)			(80)
1972 End of year balance before section 58(g) computations	200	80	50	200	70
1. U.S. deductions against U.S. income	(50)		(50)		
2. Other foreign deductions against foreign income		(70)			(70)
3. Suspense preferences against foreign income		(10)		(10)	
4. Suspense preferences against U.S. income	(150)*			(150)*	
1973 End of year balance before section 58(g) computations	300	80		40	
1. U.S. deductions against U.S. income	Not applicable.				
2. Other foreign deductions against foreign income	Not applicable.				
3. Suspense preference against foreign income		(40)		(40)	
4. Suspense preferences against U.S. income	Not applicable.				
Balances	300	40			

* Suspense preferences converted to actual items of tax preference.

Example (4). In 1970, the taxpayer's total items of income and deduction, all of which are attributable to foreign sources, are as follows:

Foreign loss:		
Gross income		$400,000
Deductions:		
Preferences (excess of accelerated depreciation on section 1250 property over straight-line)	$200,000	
Net operating loss		350,000

Pursuant to subdivision (i) of this subparagraph, none of the preferences attributable to foreign sources reduce the tax imposed by chapter 1 (other than the minimum tax) on taxable income from sources within the United States. Pursuant to subdivision (ii) of this subparagraph, the $200,000 portion of the net operating loss resulting from the excess accelerated depreciation constitutes suspense preferences. No part of the net operating loss that is carried back to previous years is reduced in such previous years. In 1971 and 1972, the taxpayer's income (before the net operating loss deduction) consists of the following:

1971 taxable income:	
United States	$160,000
Foreign	70,000
Total	230,000
1972 taxable income:	
United States	25,000
Foreign	105,000
Total	130,000

(a) In 1971, the conversion of suspense preferences into actual items of tax preference under section 58(g) (and this paragraph) and the imposition of the minimum tax on 1970 items of tax preference under section 56(b) and (§ 1.56A-2) are determined as follows:

1970 Net Operating Loss

[In thousands of dollars]

	U.S. taxable income	Foreign taxable income	U.S. deductions	Suspense preferences	Other foreign deductions
Total	$160	$70		$200	$150
1. U.S. deductions against U.S. income			Not applicable		
2. Other foreign deductions against foreign income	—	70			(70)
3. Suspense preference against foreign income			Not applicable		
4. Suspense preference against U.S. income	(160)*			(160)	
Balance to 1972				40	80

* Suspense preferences converted into actual items of tax preference.

Imposition of minimum tax on 1970 items of tax preference:

1970 Net Operating Loss

	[In thousands of dollars]				
	1971 taxable income	Nonpreference portion	Preference portion	Suspense portion	
Total	$230	$150	___	$ 200	
1. 1971 conversion of suspense preferences pursuant to sec. 58(g)			30[1]	$ 130	(160)
Adjusted NOL			180	130	40
2. Nonpreference portion against taxable income		(180)	(180)		
3. Preference portion against taxable income	___	(50)[2]	___	(50)	___
Balance to 1972				80	40

[1] Represents the 1970 minimum tax exemption.
[2] Imposition of 1970 minimum tax (10 pct × $50,000 = $5,000).

(b) In 1972, the conversion of suspense preferences into actual items of tax preferences under section 58(g) (and this paragraph) and the imposition of the minimum tax on 1970 items of tax preference under section 56(b) (and § 1.56A-2) are determined as follows: Conversion of suspense preferences:

1970 Net Operating Loss

	[In thousands of dollars]				
	U.S. taxable income	Foreign taxable income	U.S. deductions	Suspense preferences	Other foreign deduction
Total	$25	$105	—	$40	$80
1. U.S. deduction against U.S. income			Not applicable		
2. Other foreign deductions against foreign income		(80)			(80)
3. Suspense preferences against foreign income		(25)		(25)	
4. Suspense preference against U.S. income	(15)[1]	___	___	(15)	___
Balance	10				

[1] Suspense preferences converted into actual items of tax preference.

Imposition of minimum tax on 1970 items of tax preference:

1970 Net Operating Loss

	[In thousands of dollars]			
	1972 taxable income	Nonpreference portion	Preference portion	Suspense portion
Total	$130	___	$80	$40
1. 1972 conversion of suspense preferences pursuant to sec. 58(g)		$25	15	(40)
Adjusted NOL		25	95	
2. Nonpreference portion against taxable income	(25)	(25)		
3. Preference portion against taxable income	(95)[1]	___	(95)	___
Balance	10			

[1] Imposition of 1970 minimum tax (10 pct × $95,000 = $9,500).

(2) Per-country limitation. (i) In general. If a taxpayer is on the per-country foreign tax credit limitation for the taxable year, the amount by which the items of tax preference to which this section applies reduce the tax imposed by chapter 1 (other than the minimum tax under section 56) on income from sources within the United States is determined separately with respect to each foreign country or possession of the United States.

Such determination is made in a manner consistent with subparagraph (1) of this paragraph as modified in subdivision (ii) of this subparagraph. In applying subparagraph (1)(i) of this paragraph to a taxpayer on the per-country limitation, if the total potential preference amounts (as defined in this subdivision (i)) exceed the taxpayer's taxable income from sources within the United States, then, for purposes of subparagraph (1)(i)(c) of this paragraph (relating to the U.S. taxable income limitation on the amount treated as a reduction of U.S. taxable income), the taxable income from sources within the United States which is reduced by potential preference amounts with respect to each foreign country or possession is an amount which bears the same relationship to such income as the potential preference amount with respect to such foreign country or possession bears to the total of the potential preference amounts with respect to all foreign countries and possessions. For purposes of this subparagraph, the potential preference amount with respect to a foreign country or possession is the lesser of the amount of foreign source preference (described in subparagraph (1)(i)(a) of this paragraph) attributable to such country or possession or the amount of foreign source loss (described in subparagraph (1)(i)(b) of this paragraph) attributable to such country or possession.

(ii) Net operating loss. Where there is an overall net operating loss for the taxable year and the total of the potential preference amounts with respect to all foreign countries and possessions exceeds the taxpayer's taxable income from sources within the United States, the amount of such excess is treated as "suspense preferences". The suspense preferences are converted into actual items of tax preference, arising in the loss year and subject to the provisions of section 56, as the net operating loss is used in other taxable years, in the form of a net operating loss deduction under section 172, to offset taxable income from sources within the United States. Suspense preferences attributable to a foreign country or possession which, in other taxable years, reduce taxable income from sources within such country or possession or offset taxable income from sources within any other foreign country or possession loose their character as suspense preferences and, thus, are never converted into actual items of tax preference. The amount of the suspense preferences which are converted into actual items of tax preference is equal to that portion of the net operating loss attributable to the suspense preferences which offsets taxable income from sources within the United States in taxable years other than the loss year. The determination of the component parts of the net operating loss and the determination of the amount by which the portion of the net operating loss attributable to the suspense preferences offsets taxable income from sources within the United States is made on a year-by-year basis in the same order as the net operating loss is used in accordance with section 172(b).

Such determination is made by applying deductions attributable to United States source income first against such income and applying deductions attributable to income from sources within a foreign country or possession of the United States first against income from sources within such country or possession and in accordance with the following principles:

(a) Deductions attributable to items or classes of gross income from sources within the United States offset taxable income from sources within the United States before any remaining deductions;

(b) Deductions attributable to items or classes of gross income from sources within any foreign country or possession of the United States which are not suspense preferences (referred to in this paragraph as "other foreign deductions") offset taxable income from sources within such country or possession before any remaining deductions;

(c) Suspense preferences attributable to items or classes of gross income from sources within a foreign country or possession offset any remaining taxable income from sources within such foreign country or possession after application of (b) of this subdivision (ii) before any remaining deductions;

(d) Suspense preferences from each foreign country and possession (remaining after application of (c) of this subdivision (ii)) offset taxable income from sources within the United States (remaining after application of (a) of this subdivision (ii)) before other foreign deductions pro rata on the basis of the total of such suspense preferences;

(e) Other foreign deductions from each foreign country and possession (remaining after application of (b) of this subdivision (ii)) offset taxable income from sources within the United States (remaining after application (a) and (b) of this subdivision (ii)) pro rata on the basis of the total of such other foreign deductions;

(f) Deductions attributable to income from sources within the United States (remaining after application of (a) of this subdivision (ii)) offset taxable income from sources within any foreign country or possession before any foreign deductions;

(g) Other foreign deductions from each foreign country and possession (remaining after application of (b) and (e) of this subdivision (ii)) offset taxable income from sources within any other foreign countries or possessions (remaining after application of (f) of this subdivision (ii)) pro rata on the basis of the total of such other foreign deductions; and

(h) Suspense preferences (remaining after the application of (c) and (d) of this subdivision (ii)) offset taxable income from sources within any foreign country or possession (remaining after the application of (f) and (g) of this subdivision (ii)) pro rata on the basis of the total of such suspense preferences.

For purposes of the above computations, taxable income is computed with the modifications specified in section 172(b)(2) or section 172(c), whichever is applicable. However, the amount of suspense preferences which are converted into actual items of tax preference in accordance with the above principles is reduced to the extent the suspense preferences offset increases in taxable income from sources within the United States due to the modifications specified in section 172(b)(2) or section 172(c). For this purpose, suspense preferences are considered to offset an increase in taxable income due to section 172(b)(2) or section 172(c) modifications only after reducing taxable income computed before such modifications.

(iii) Examples. The principles of this subparagraph may be illustrated by the following examples in each of which the per-country foreign tax credit limitation is applicable. For purposes of these examples, personal deductions and exemptions are disregarded.

Example (1). The taxpayer has the following items of income and deduction for the taxable year 1971:

	United States	France	Germany	United Kingdom
Gross income	$180,000	$165,000	$50,000	$75,000
Deductions:				
Preference				(45,000)
Other	(120,000)	(125,000)	(80,000)	(100,000)
Taxable income (or loss)	60,000	40,000	(30,000)	(70,000)

(a) Pursuant to subdivision (i) of this subparagraph, the potential preference amount in the case of the United Kingdom is the lesser of the preferences attributable to the United Kingdom ($45,000) or the excess of deductions over gross income from sources within the United Kingdom ($70,000) and the potential preference amounts in the case of France and Germany are zero in both cases since the preferences attributable to both countries are zero. Since the total potential preference amounts ($45,000) is less than the taxable income from sources within the United States ($60,000), no modification of U.S. taxable income is required. Thus, the amount by which the U.K. preferences reduce the tax on taxable income from sources within the United States, determined in a manner consistent with subparagraph (1)(i) of this paragraph, is the smallest of (1) the items of tax preference attributable to the United Kingdom ($45,000), (2) the excess of deductions over gross income attributable to the United Kingdom ($70,000), or (3) taxable income from sources within the United States ($60,000). The full $45,000 of U.K. preference items are, therefore, taken into account as items of tax preference in 1971 and subject to the minimum tax. Since there is no net operating loss, subdivision (ii) of this subparagraph does not apply.

(b) If the French taxable income is $15,000 instead of $40,000, a $25,000 net operating loss (on a worldwide basis) results. The determination of the foreign preference items taken into account pursuant to subdivision (i) of this subparagraph is the same as in (a) of this example. Subdivision (ii) of this subparagraph again does not apply since the total potential preference amounts ($45,000) is less than the U.S. taxable income ($60,000).

Example (2). For the taxable year 1972, the taxpayer has a net operating loss of $35,000 consisting of the following items of income and deduction:

	United States	France	Germany	United Kingdom	Belgium
Gross income	$250,000	$50,000	$60,000	$5,000	$45,000
Deductions:					
Preferences		(35,000)	(70,000)	(95,000)	
Other	(100,000)	(75,000)	(30,000)		(40,000)
Taxable income (or loss)	150,000	(60,000)	(40,000)	(90,000)	5,000

(a) Pursuant to subdivision (i) of this subparagraph the potential preference amount with respect to each country is the lesser of the amount shown as preferences with respect to such country or the amount of the loss from such country. Thus, the potential preference amounts in this case are:

France	$35,000
Germany	40,000
United Kingdom	90,000
Belgium	0
Total	165,000

Since the total of the potential preference amounts exceeds the U.S. taxable income, in applying the principles of subparagraph (1)(i) of this paragraph, U.S. taxable income which is reduced by potential preference amounts with respect to each country is a pro-rata amount based on the total potential preference amounts as follows:

France (35,000/165,000 × $150,000)
Germany (40,000/165,000 × $150,000) – $36,364
United Kingdom (90,000/165,000 × $150,000) – $81,818
Belgium (0/165,000 × $150,000) – $0
Total—$150,000

The amount by which the foreign preference items offset U.S. taxable income pursuant to subdivision (i) of this subparagraph is then determined as follows:

	(a) Preferences	(b) Loss	(c) U.S. taxable income	(d) Smallest of (a), (b), or (c)
France	$35,000	$60,000	$81,818	$31,818
Germany	70,000	40,000	36,364	36,364
United Kingdom	95,000	90,000	81,818	81,818
Belgium				
Total				150,000

Thus, $150,000 of the total foreign preference items will be taken into account pursuant to subdivision (i) of this subparagraph as items of tax preference in 1972 and subject to the provisions of section 56.

(b) Pursuant to subdivision (ii) of this subparagraph, the 1972 net operating loss of $35,000 will consist of suspense preferences of $15,000 and other foreign deductions of $20,000 attributable to each foreign country as shown below and determined as follows:

Explanation	Deductions						
	United States	France Preferences	France Other	Germany Preferences	Germany Other	United Kingdom preferences	Belgium other
	$100,000	$35,000	$75,000	$70,000	$30,000	$95,000	$40,000
1. U.S. deductions against U.S. income ($250,000)	(100,000)						
2. Other foreign deductions against foreign income (per-country)[1]			(50,000)		(30,000)		(40,000)
3. Suspense preferences against remaining foreign income (per-country)				(30,000)			(5,000)
4. Suspense preferences against remaining U.S. income:							
France (35,000/165,000 × $150,000)		(31,818)					
Germany (40,000/165,000 × $150,000)				(36,364)			
U.K. (90,000/165,000 × $150,000)						(81,818)	
5. Other foreign deductions against remaining U.S. income (0)				Not applicable.			
6. U.S. deductions against other foreign income				Not applicable.			
7. Other foreign deductions against remaining foreign income ($5,000)			(5,000)				
8. Suspense preferences against remaining foreign income (0):				Not applicable.			
Balance (components of NOL)		3,182	20,000	3,636		8,182	

[1] Foreign income amounts before step 2 are: France—$50,000; Germany—$60,000; United Kingdom—$5,000; Belgium—$45,000.

Example (3). In 1973, the taxpayer has taxable income (computed without regard to the net operating loss deduction) from the following sources and in the following amounts:

United States	France	Germany	United Kingdom
$100,000	$60,000	$20,000	$30,000

In addition, the taxpayer has a net operating loss deduction of $235,000 resulting from a 1972 net operating loss consisting of the following amounts:

Deductions attributable to income from sources within the United States	$25,000
Suspense preferences attributable to income from sources within France	$75,000
Deductions other than suspense preferences attributable to income from sources within France	$85,000
Deductions other than suspense preferences attributable to sources within the Netherlands	$50,000

(a) Pursuant to subdivision (ii) of this subparagraph, the converted suspense preferences and the remaining portions of the 1972 net operating loss carried over to 1974 are computed as follows:

[In thousands of dollars]

	1973 income				1972 net operating loss			
	United States	France	Germany	United Kingdom	United States	French suspense preferences	French other deductions	Dutch other deductions
	100	60	20	30	25	75	85	50
U.S. deductions against U.S. income	(25)				(25)			
Other foreign deductions against foreign income (per-country)		(60)					(60)	
Suspense preferences against remaining foreign income (per-country)				Not applicable.				
Suspense preferences against remaining U.S. income	(75[1])					(75)		
Other foreign deductions against remaining U.S. income				Not applicable.				
U.S. deductions against remaining foreign income				Not applicable.				
Other foreign deductions against remaining foreign income:								
French (25,000/75,000 × $50,000)			(16.7)				(16.7)	
Dutch (50,000/75,000 × $50,000)			(33.3)					(33.3)
Suspense preferences against remaining foreign income				Not applicable.				
Balance (1972 carryover to 1974)							8.3	16.7

[1] Suspense preferences converted to actual items of tax preference.

(b) If, in 1972, there had been no items of tax preference without regard to the suspense preferences, the conversion of the suspense preferences in 1973 would result in a 1972 minimum tax liability under section 56(a) of $4,500 (10 percent × ($75,000 − $30,000)), all of which would have been deferred by reason of section 56(b). Further, by application of section 56(b) and § 1.56A-2, $20,000 of the $45,000 preference portion of the 1972 net operating loss would be treated as having reduced taxable income in 1973 resulting in the imposition in 1973 of $2,000 of the deferred 1972 minimum tax liability.

(3) Separate limitation under section 904(f). In the case of a taxpayer subject to the separate limitation on interest income under section 904(f), the provisions of this paragraph shall be applied in the same manner as in subparagraph (2) of this paragraph. If the taxpayer has elected the overall foreign tax credit limitation, subparagraph (2) of this paragraph shall be applied as if all income from sources within any foreign countries or possessions of the United States and deductions relating to income from such sources other than income or deductions subject to the separate limitation under section 904(f) were from a single foreign country.

(4) Carryover of excess taxes. For rules relating to carryover of excess taxes described in paragraph (1) of section 56(c) when suspense preferences are converted to actual items of tax preference, see § 1.56A-5(f).

(5) Character of amounts. Where the amounts from sources within a foreign country or possession of the United States (or all such countries or possessions in the case of a taxpayer who has elected the overall foreign tax credit limitation) which are treated as reducing chapter 1 tax on income from sources within the United States or as suspense preferences are less than the total items of tax preference described in subparagraph (1)(i)(a) of this paragraph attributable to such sources, the amounts so treated are considered derived proportionately from each such item of tax preference.

T.D. 7564, 9/11/78, amend T.D. 8138, 4/23/87.

§ 1.58-8 Capital gains and stock options.

Caution: The Treasury has not yet amended Reg § 1.58-8 to reflect changes made by P.L. 99-514.

(a) In general. Section 58(g)(2) provides that the items of tax preference specified in section 57(a)(6), and § 1.57-1(b) (stock options), and section 57(a)(9), and § 1.57-1(i) (capital gains), which are attributable to sources within any foreign country or possession of the United States shall not be taken into account as items of tax preference if, under the tax laws of such country or possession, preferential treatment is not accorded:

(1) In the case of stock options, to the gain, profit, or other income realized from the transfer of shares of stock pursuant to the exercise of an option which is under United States tax law a qualified or restricted stock option (under section 422 or section 424); and

(2) In the case of capital gains, to gain from the sale or exchange of capital assets (or property treated as capital assets under United States tax law).

Where capital gains are not accorded preferential treatment within a foreign country, capital losses as well as capital gains from such country are not taken into account for purposes of the minimum tax.

(b) Source of capital gains and stock options. Generally, in determining whether the capital gain or stock option item of tax preference is attributable to sources within any foreign country or possession of the United States, the principles of sections 861–863 and the regulations thereunder are applied. Thus, the stock option item of tax preference, representing compensation for personal services, is attributable, in accordance with § 1.861-4, to sources within the country in which the personal services were performed. Where the capital gain item of tax preference represents gain from the purchase and sale of personal property, such gain is attributable, in accordance with § 1.861-7, entirely to sources within the country in which the property is sold. In accordance with paragraph (c) of § 1.861-7, in any case in which the sales transactions is arranged in a particular manner for the primary purpose of tax avoidance, all factors of the transaction, such as negotiations, the execution of the agreement, the location of the property, and the place of payment, will be considered, and the sale will be treated as having been consummated at the place where the substance of the sale occurred.

(c) Preferential treatment. For purposes of this section, gain, profit, or other income is accorded preferential treatment by a foreign country or possession of the United States if (1) recognition of the income, for foreign tax purposes, is deferred beyond the taxpayer's taxable year or comparable period for foreign tax purposes which coincides with the taxpayer's U.S. taxable year in cases where other items of profit, gain, or other income may not be deferred; (2) it is subject to tax at a lower effective rate (including no rate of tax) than other items of profit, gain, or other income, by means of a special rate of tax, artificial deductions, exemptions, exclusions, or similar reductions in the amount subject to tax; (3) it is subject to no significant amount of tax; or (4) the laws of the foreign country or possession by any other method provide tax treatment for such profit, gain, or other income more beneficial than the tax treatment otherwise accorded income by such country or possession. For the purpose of the preceding sentence, gain, profit, or other income is subject to no significant amount of tax if the amount of taxes imposed by the foreign country or possession of the United States is equal to less than 2.5 percent of the gross amount of such income.

(d) Examples. The principles of this section may be illustrated by the following examples:

Example (1). The Bahamas imposes no income tax on individuals or corporations, whether resident or nonresident. Since capital gains are subject to no tax in the Bahamas, capital gains are considered to be accorded preferential treatment and will be taken into account for purposes of the minimum tax.

Example (2). In France, except in certain cases involving the sale of large blocks of stock, a nonresident individual is not subject to tax on isolated capital gains transactions. Since such capital gains are not subject to tax in France, they are considered to be accorded preferential treatment irrespective of the treatment accorded other capital gains in France and such gains will be taken into account for purposes of the minimum tax.

Example (3). In Germany, in the case of the sale within 1 taxable year of 1 percent or more of the shares of a corporation in which an individual taxpayer is regarded as holding a substantial interest, the gains on the sale of the large block of stock will be taxed as extraordinary income at one-half the ordinary income tax rate. Since these gains are taxed as a reduced rate of tax in comparison to other income, they are considered to be accorded preferential treatment and will be taken into account for purposes of the minimum tax.

Example (4). In Belgium, gains derived by an individual in the course of regular speculative transactions are taxed as ordinary income, but with an upper limit of 30 percent. Rates of tax on individuals in Belgium range from approximately 30 percent to approximately 60 percent. Since the gains on speculative transactions are taxed at a maximum rate which is more beneficial then the rates accorded to other income, such gains are considered to be accorded preferential treatment and will be taken into account for purposes of the minimum tax.

Example (5). In France, gains derived by a company on the sale of fixed assets held for less than 2 years are treated as short-term gains. The excess of short-term gains in any fiscal year is taxed at the full company tax rate of 50 percent. However, this tax may be paid in equal portions over the 5 years immediately following the realization of such short-term gains. Since recognition of the short-term gains for tax purposes is subject to deferral over a 5-year period, such gains are considered to be accorded preferential treatment and will be taken into account for purposes of the minimum tax.

Example (6). Also in France, in the case of the sale or exchange by a company of depreciable assets and nondepreciable asset owned for at least 2 years, the excess of long-term capital gains over long-term capital losses in a fiscal year is subject to an immediate tax at the reduced rate of 10 percent. Such excess, reduced by the 10-percent tax, is carried in a special reserve account on the taxpayer's books. If the excess is reinvested in other fixed asset within a stated period, no further tax is due. If the amounts in the special reserve are distributed, they will be treated as ordinary income for the fiscal year in which the distribution is made. Since such gains (other than those distributed in the same fiscal year they are realized) are subject to deferral or a reduced rate of tax, they are (except to the extent distributed in the year of realization) considered to be accorded preferential treatment and are taken into account for purposes of the minimum tax.

Example (7). In Sweden, in the case of gains derived by an individual on the sale of shares or bonds held for 5 years or less, 25 percent of the gains are taxed if the holding period is 4 to 5 years, 50 percent of the gain is taxed if the holding period is 3 to 4 years, and 75 percent of the gain is taxed if the holding period is 2 to 3 years. The gain is fully taxable at ordinary income rates if held for less than 2 years. Thus, gains on shares or bonds held for 2 years or more are considered accorded preferential treatment in Sweden since they are either subject to exemption or treatment comparable to the U.S. capital gains deduction and are taxed at a reduced rate. Thus, such gains are taken into account for purposes of the minimum tax.

Example (8). Pursuant to Article XIV of the United States-United Kingdom Income Tax Convention, a resident of the United States is exempt from United Kingdom tax on most capital gains. Since such capital gains are exempt from United Kingdom taxation, they are considered to be accorded preferential treatment and are taken into account for purposes of the minimum tax.

Example (9). An individual resident of the United States, is desirous of selling his stock in a corporation listed on the New York Stock Exchange. He requests the stock certificates from his broker in the United States, travels to a foreign country, delivers the certificates to a broker in that country, and has the foreign broker execute the sale which takes place on the New York Stock Exchange. Since the sale was consummated in the United States, pursuant to paragraph (b) of this section and § 1.861-7, the resulting capital gain item of tax preference is attributable to sources within the United States.

Example (10). Two individuals, both residing in the United States, negotiate and reach agreement in New York City for the sale of stock of a closed corporation. Prior to the transfer of the stock, in order to avoid imposition of the minimum tax, both individuals travel to a foreign country which does not accord preferential treatment to capital gains, but imposes a 5-percent rate of income tax which would be fully creditable against U.S. tax under sections 901 and 904 if the capital gains were sourced in that country. The stock is actually transferred and consideration paid in the foreign country. Since the primary purpose of consummating the sale in the foreign country was the avoidance of tax, pursuant to paragraph (b) of this section, and § 1.861-7(c), the resulting capital gain item of tax preference will be considered attributable to sources within the country in which the substance of sale took place or, in this case, the United States.

T.D. 7564, 9/11/78.

§ 1.58-9 Application of the tax benefit rule to the minimum tax for taxable years beginning prior to 1987.

(a) In general. For purposes of computing the minimum tax liability imposed under section 56 of the Internal Revenue Code of 1954 (Code), taxpayers are not liable for minimum tax on tax preference items that do not reduce the taxpayer's tax liability under subtitle A of the Code for the taxable year. In general, tax preference items that do not reduce tax liability under subtitle A for the taxable year are those from which no current tax benefit is derived because available credits would have reduced or eliminated the taxpayer's regular tax liability if the preference items had not been allowed in computing taxable income. However, any credits that, because of such preference items, are not needed for use against regular tax ("freed-up credits"), are required to be reduced under the rules of paragraph (c) of this section. For purposes of this section, a taxpayer's regular tax is the Federal income tax liability under subchapter A of chapter 1 of the Code, not including the minimum tax imposed by section 56. Unless otherwise noted, all references to Internal Revenue Code sections refer to the Internal Revenue Code of 1954.

(b) Effective date. The rules of this section are effective May 5, 1992, but only as they affect tax preference items that arise in taxable years beginning after December 31, 1976, and before January 1, 1987.

(c) Adjustment of carryover credits. *(1) In general.* A taxpayer's freed-up credits must be reduced by the additional minimum tax that would have been imposed if a current tax benefit had been derived from preference items that did not actually produce a current tax benefit. The amount of this reduction shall be calculated in the following manner—

(i) Determine the amount of freed-up credits;

(ii) Determine the amount of tax preference items (if any) from which a current tax benefit was derived for the taxable year ("beneficial preferences"), and the amount of preferences from which no current tax benefit was derived for the taxable year ("non-beneficial preferences"); and

(iii) Determine the portion of the total minimum tax on all tax preference items for the taxable year that is attributable to the non-beneficial preferences.

The freed-up credits are then reduced by an amount equal to such portion of the minimum tax.

(2) Determine freed-up credits. (i) To determine the freed-up credits for the taxable year, first determine the regular tax that would have been imposed for the taxable year if preference items had not been allowed in computing taxable income ("non-preference regular tax"). In the case of a taxpayer with the capital gain preference described in section 57(a)(9)(B), non-preference regular tax is computed without regard to section 1201 and without adding the section 57(a)(9)(B) preference amount to taxable income. Second, compute the amount of credits that would have been allowed to reduce the non-preference regular tax. The credits available to reduce non-preference regular tax shall include any freed-up credits from other taxable years, as reduced under paragraph (c)(5) of this section, that are carried to the current taxable year. Third, subtract the amount of credits that were actually allowed to reduce the regular tax for such taxable year from the amount of credits that would have been allowed to reduce non-preference regular tax. The result is the amount of the freed-up credits.

(ii) The following examples illustrate the determination of freed-up credits. The first two examples assume that the foreign tax credits being used do not exceed the limitation under section 904.

Example (1). In 1982 Corporation B has $17.6 million dollars in foreign tax credits available for the taxable year. If preference items were not allowed in determining regular tax, the regular tax would have been $10.2 million and foreign tax credits used to reduce regular tax would have been $10.2 million. Because of tax preference items, however, B's regular tax is $6.3 million and the amount of foreign tax credits actually used to reduce the regular tax is $6.3 million. The amount of freed-up foreign tax credits is $3.9 million ($10.2 million minus $6.3 million).

Example (2). Assume the same facts as in Example 1 of paragraph (c)(2)(ii) of this section except that Corporation B has $7.2 million dollars in foreign tax credits. If preference items were not allowed, the non-preference regular tax would have been $10.2 million and the foreign tax credits used to reduce the regular tax would have been $7.2 million. Because of tax preference items, however, B's regular tax is $6.3 million, and the amount of foreign tax credits actually used to reduce the regular tax is $6.3 million. The amount of freed-up foreign tax credits is $.9 million ($7.2 million minus $6.3 million).

Example (3). In 1983 Corporation C has $500,000 of investment tax credits available. If preference items were not allowed, non-preference regular tax would have been $690,000 and all $500,000 of investment tax credits would have been allowed to reduce non-preference regular tax liability. Because of tax preferences, however, C's actual regular tax is $439,750. As a result of the limitation under section 38(c), only $377,537 of the investment tax credits are allowed to reduce the actual regular tax. Freed-up credits are $122,463 ($500,000 minus $377,537).

Example (4). In 1984 Corporation B has ordinary income of $20,000 and net section 1201 gain of $300,000, none of which is attributable to foreign sources. B has no other items of tax preference in 1984. B's non-preference regular tax for 1984 is $126,950, the amount of tax that would be imposed without regard to section 1201.

(3) Determination of beneficial and non-beneficial preferences. (i) In general. The amount of tax preferences from which a current tax benefit is derived ("beneficial preferences") and the amount from which no current tax benefit is derived ("non-beneficial preferences") for the taxable year are determined as set forth below.

(ii) Regular tax liability is the same regardless of preference items. (A) If the taxpayer's tax liability (after credits) would be the same regardless of whether preference items were allowed to reduce taxable income, then all of the taxpayer's preference items are non-beneficial preference items.

(B) The following example illustrates the rule set forth in paragraph (c)(3)(ii)(A) of this section. This example assumes that foreign tax credits being used do not exceed the limitation under section 904.

Example. (i) In 1982 Corporation B has $17.6 million dollars in foreign tax credits available for the taxable year. If preference items were not allowed in determining regular tax, the regular tax would have been $10.2 million and foreign tax credits used to reduce regular tax would have been $10.2 million. Because of tax preference items, however, B's regular tax is $6.3 million and the amount of foreign tax credits actually used to reduce the regular tax is $6.3 million. The amount of freed-up foreign tax credits is $3.9 million ($10.2 million minus $6.3 million).

(ii) The total amount of B's tax preference items is $8.4 million. B's non-preference regular tax is $10.2 million and, reduced by foreign tax credits, is zero. B's actual regular tax is $6.3 million and, reduced by foreign tax credits, is zero. Since the amount of credits that would have been allowed to offset the non-preference regular tax would have reduced such tax to an amount ($0) equal to the actual regular tax liability ($0), B received a tax benefit from none of the $8.4 million of tax preferences and therefore all of these preferences are non-beneficial preferences.

(iii) Regular tax liability differs because of preference items. If tax liability (after credits) is less because preference items are allowed to reduce taxable income, then some of these preference items have provided a current tax benefit. In such cases, the amount of beneficial and non-beneficial preferences are determined as follows:

(A) Non-beneficial preferences.

(1) The non-beneficial preferences are determined by converting the freed-up credits for such taxable year into an amount of taxable income. To make this conversion, freed-up credits are "grossed up" (i.e., divided by the regular tax marginal rate at which such credits would have offset non-preference regular tax) to determine the amount of tax preferences that freed up such credits. For purposes of this calculation, the 5-percent addition to tax provided by section 11(b) shall be included in determining the marginal rate. The aggregate of these grossed-up amounts is the total amount of non-beneficial preferences for the taxable year.

(2) The freed-up credits shall be grossed up beginning at the lowest marginal tax rate that would have applied to the additional taxable income arising if tax preferences were not allowed. Thus, the marginal tax rates at which the actual regular tax was imposed shall not be taken into account in grossing up freed-up credits, even if all or a portion of such tax is not offset by credits because of limitations on the allowance of such credits (such as the section 904 limit on foreign tax credits or the section 38(c) limit on investment tax credits). For example, if the first dollar of additional non-preference taxable income would have been taxed at a rate of 46 percent, then freed-up credits shall be grossed up at 46 percent, even if regular tax imposed on taxable income at a 40-percent rate was not offset by credits because of the limitations on investment tax credits under section 38(c). See Examples 1 and 2 in paragraph (d) of this section for illus-

trations of the gross up of freed-up credits in cases where limitations apply to the amount of credit allowed to offset actual regular tax.

(3) The following example illustrates the gross up of freed-up credits to determine non-beneficial preferences. This example assumes that foreign tax credits being used do not exceed the limitation under section 904.

Example. (i) Corporation L has the following items for the 1985 taxable year:

Actual taxable income		$90,000
Regular tax		21,750
Available credits:		
Foreign tax credits for 1985	$15,000	
Foreign tax credits carried forward from 1984	25,000	
Investment tax credits carried forward from 1984	20,000	
		60,000
Credit allowed to offset actual regular tax:		
Foreign tax credits for 1985	$15,000	
Foreign tax credits carried forward from 1984	6,750	
		21,750
Actual regular tax liability		-0-
Preferences		110,000
Taxable income for 1985 determined as though preferences were not allowed		200,000
Non-preference regular tax		71,750
Credits allowed to offset non-preference regular tax:		
Foreign tax credits for 1985	$15,000	
Foreign tax credits carried forward from 1984	25,000	
Investment tax credits carried forward from 1984	20,000	
		60,000
Non-preference regular tax liability		11,750

(ii) The freed-up credits for 1985 are $38,250 ($60,000 minus $21,750). The non-preference regular tax of $71,750 is determined by applying the regular tax rates set forth in section 11(b) to the $200,000 of taxable income as follows:

Taxable Income		Rate		Tax
$ 25,000	×	.15	=	$ 3,750
25,000	×	.18	=	4,500
25,000	×	.30	=	7,500
25,000	×	.40	=	10,000
100,000	×	.46	=	46,000
$200,000				$71,750

(iii) Thus, for purposes of determining the non-beneficial preferences, freed-up credits are grossed up as follows: The credits allowed against the regular tax and the freed-up credits are treated as offsetting non-preference regular tax in the same order as such credits would have been allowed to offset such tax, beginning at the lowest marginal tax rate. The freed-up credits are grossed up beginning at the lowest marginal tax rate at which additional taxable income would have been taxed if preferences were not allowed. Thus, in this example freed-up credits are grossed up beginning at 40 percent, and the amount of L's non-beneficial preferences for the 1985 taxable year is $84,456.

Type	Credit allowed against regular tax	Freed-up Credit	Divided by tax Rate		Non-beneficial preferences
FTC (85)	$ 3,750		.15		
	4,500		.18		
	6,750		.30		
FTC (84)	750		.30		
	6,000		.40		
		$ 4,000	.40	=	$10,000
		14,250	.46	=	30,978
ITC (84)		20,000	.46	=	43,478
	$21,750	$38,250			$84,456

Foreign tax credit = FTC (year)
Investment tax credit = ITC (year)

(B [sic C]) Beneficial preferences. The amount of beneficial preferences for the taxable year is computed by subtracting the non-beneficial preferences for the taxable year from the total amount of tax preferences for such year. This rule may be illustrated by the following example:

Example. Assume the same facts as in the Example in paragraph (c)(3)(iii)(A)(3) of this section. The amount of L's beneficial preferences for 1985 is $25,544 (total preferences of $110,000, minus non-beneficial preferences of $84,456).

(4) Determine the minimum tax attributable to non-beneficial preferences. (i) The portion of the minimum tax that is attributable to the non-beneficial preferences is computed as follows—

(A) Compute the minimum tax that would be imposed on all tax preference items for the taxable year if all of the preferences had produced a tax benefit.

(B) Compute the minimum tax that would be imposed on the beneficial preferences if these were the taxpayer's only preferences. (This is the amount of minimum tax actually imposed for the taxable year.)

(C) Subtract the amount computed in paragraph (c)(4)(i)(B) of this section from the amount computed in paragraph (c)(4)(i)(A) of this section. The result is the minimum tax attributable to the non-beneficial preferences for the taxable year. This amount is sometimes referred to hereinafter as the "credit reduction amount".

(ii) The following examples illustrate determination of the credit reduction amount. These examples assume that foreign tax credits being used do not exceed the limitation under section 904.

Example (1). (i) In 1982 Corporation B has $17.6 million dollars in foreign tax credits available for the taxable year. If preference items were not allowed in determining regular tax, the regular tax would have been $10.2 million and foreign tax credits used to reduce regular tax would have been $10.2 million. Because of tax preference items, however, B's regular tax is $6.3 million and the amount of foreign tax credits actually used to reduce the regular tax is $6.3 million. The amount of freed-up foreign tax credits is $3.9 million ($10.2 million minus $6.3 million).

(ii) The total amount of B's tax preference items is $8.4 million. B's non-preference regular tax is $10.2 million and, reduced by foreign tax credits, is zero. B's actual regular tax is $6.3 million and, reduced by foreign tax credits, is zero. Since the amount of credits that would have been allowed to offset the non-preference regular tax would have reduced such tax to an amount ($0) equal to the actual regular tax liability ($0), B received a tax benefit from none of the $8.4 million of tax preferences and therefore all of these preferences are non-beneficial preferences.

(iii) Since B has $8.4 million in total preference items and no regular tax liability, the minimum tax on that amount would be $1,258,500 (($8.4 million minus $10,000) multiplied by .15). None of the preference items is a beneficial preference. Thus, the minimum tax attributable to non-beneficial preferences (and therefore, the credit reduction amount) is $1,258,500.

Example (2). (i) Corporation L has the following items for the 1985 taxable year:

Actual taxable income		$ 90,000
Regular tax		21,750
Available credits:		
Foreign tax credits for 1985	$15,000	
Foreign tax credits carried forward from 1984	25,000	
Investment tax credits carried forward from 1984	20,000	
		$ 60,000
Credit allowed to offset actual regular tax:		
Foreign tax credits for 1985	$15,000	
Foreign tax credits carried forward from 1984	6,750	
		$ 21,750
Actual regular tax liability		-0-
Preferences		110,000
Taxable income for 1985 determined as though preferences were not allowed		200,000
Non-preference regular tax		71,750
Credits allowed to offset non-preference regular tax:		
Foreign tax credits for 1985	$15,000	
Foreign tax credits carried forward from 1984	25,000	
Investment tax credits carried forward from 1984	20,000	
		$ 60,000
Non-preference regular tax liability		11,750

(ii) The freed-up credits for 1985 are $38,250 ($60,000 minus $21,750). The non-preference regular tax is $71,750. The amount of L's non-beneficial preferences for the 1985 taxable year is $84,456.

(iii) The minimum tax on L's total preference items of $110,000 would be $15,000 (($110,000 minus $10,000) multiplied by .15). Since the amount of non-beneficial preferences is $84,456, the amount of L's beneficial preferences for 1985 is $25,544 ($110,000 minus $84,456). The minimum tax on L's beneficial preferences of $25,544 is $2,332 (($25,544 minus $10,000) multiplied by .15). (This is the amount of minimum tax imposed for 1985.) The minimum tax attributable to non-beneficial preference items (and therefore, the credit reduction amount) is $12,668 ($15,000 minus $2,332).

(5) Reduction of freed-up credits. (i) In general. The freed-up credits are reduced by an amount equal to the minimum tax attributable to the non-beneficial preferences ("credit reduction amount"). If the taxpayer has only one type of freed-up credit (i.e., only investment tax credit or only foreign tax credit) and that credit was earned in only one year (the current year or a carryover year), then the credit is reduced by the credit reduction amount. This rule may illustrated by the following example. This example assumes that foreign tax credits being used do not exceed the limitation under section 904.

Example. (i) In 1982 Corporation B has $17.6 million dollars in foreign tax credits available for the taxable year. If preference items were not allowed in determining regular tax, the regular tax would have been $10.2 million and foreign tax credits used to reduce regular tax would have been $10.2 million. Because of tax preference items, however, B's regular tax is $6.3 million and the amount of foreign tax credits actually used to reduce the regular tax is $6.3 million. The amount of freed-up foreign tax credits is $3.9 million ($10.2 million minus $6.3 million).

(ii) The total amount of B's tax preference items is $8.4 million. B's non-preference regular tax is $10.2 million and, reduced by foreign tax credits, is zero. B's actual regular tax is $6.3 million and, reduced by foreign tax credits, is zero. Since the amount of credits that would have been allowed to offset the non-preference regular tax would have reduced such tax to an amount ($0) equal to the actual regular tax liability ($0), B received a tax benefit from none of the $8.4 million of tax preferences and therefore all of these preferences are non-beneficial preferences.

(iii) Since B has $8.4 million in total preference items and no regular tax liability, the minimum tax on that amount would be $1,258,500 (($8.4 million minus $10,000) multiplied by .15). None of the preference items is a beneficial preference. Thus, the minimum tax attributable to non-beneficial preferences (and therefore, the credit reduction amount) is $1,258,500.

(iv) All of the $3.9 million of freed-up credits are foreign tax credits that arise in the same year and that otherwise would be carried forward. Since the entire amount of B's tax preferences are non-beneficial preferences, the minimum tax of $1,258,500 that would be imposed on the total tax preferences is the credit reduction amount. Thus, B's $3.9 million of freed-up foreign tax credits is reduced by $1,258,500. The foreign tax credit carryforward from 1982 is $10,041,500. This amount is the sum of $2,641,500 (the freed-up foreign tax credit of $3,900,000, reduced by the credit reduction amount of $1,258,500), plus $7.4 million (the foreign tax credit that would have been carried over even if tax preference items had not been allowed).

However, if the taxpayer has more than one type of freed-up credit, or the taxpayer's freed-up credits are from more than one taxable year, then the credit reduction amount must be allocated under the exact method described in paragraph (c)(5)(ii) of this section, unless an election is made under paragraph (c)(5)(iii) of this section to use the simplified method.

(ii) Exact method. For each type of freed-up credits and for each taxable year within such type from which any such credits are earned, the amount of credit reduction shall be equal to the amount of minimum tax attributable to the non-beneficial preferences that freed up the credits for that type and taxable year. The amount of the credit reduction is computed by multiplying the amount of non-beneficial preferences which freed up credits for each type and taxable year by the minimum tax rate. For purposes of this computation, if the amount of the taxpayer's minimum tax exemption for the taxable year (as determined under section 56(a)) exceeds the amount of the taxpayer's beneficial preferences, such excess exemption shall reduce the amount of non-beneficial preferences to be multiplied by the minimum tax rate. The non-beneficial preferences shall be reduced by any such excess exemption in the same order in which the credits that were freed up by such preferences would have been allowed to offset tax. Thus, for example, any excess exemption shall first reduce non-beneficial preferences that freed up foreign tax credits. Any such excess exemption remaining after reducing non-beneficial preferences that freed up foreign tax credits to zero would then be used to reduce the non-beneficial preferences that freed up investment tax credits.

(iii) Simplified method. (A) Description of method. In lieu of the exact credit reduction method described in paragraph (c)(5)(ii) of this section, taxpayers may elect to use the simplified credit reduction method. Under the simplified credit reduction method, the amount of freed-up credits for each type of credit and for each taxable year in which such credit is earned is multiplied by a fraction. The numerator of the fraction is the total credit reduction amount as determined in paragraph (c)(4)(i)(C) of this section. The denominator is the total amount of freed-up credits as determined in paragraph (c)(2)(i) of this section. The product of this multiplication is the amount of credit reduction for each type and taxable year of freed-up credit.

(B) Election to use simplified method. A taxpayer may elect to use the simplified credit reduction method for all taxable years to which this section applies by attaching a statement indicating such an election on the amended Federal income tax return or returns applying the adjustments of this section. If an election is made for any taxable year, it must be made for all taxable years. Once an election has been made, it can be revoked only with the permission of the Commissioner. Similarly, once returns have been filed applying the exact credit reduction method, an election to apply the simplified method can be made only with the consent of the Commissioner.

(iv) Effect of credit reduction on credit carryovers. Under both the exact method and the simplified method, the determination of credit carryovers to other taxable years is made on the basis of freed-up credits remaining after such reduction, plus any other unused credits. Thus, an amount of freed-up credits that is equal to the credit reduction amount shall not be allowed to reduce tax liability in any taxable year. Such disallowance is without regard to whether such credits would otherwise be allowed as a carryover. The freed-up credits, as reduced under this paragraph (c)(5), shall be carried over or carried back in applying this section in a carryover or carryback year. No minimum tax liability shall be due with respect to the non-beneficial preferences for any taxable year.

(v) Examples. The following examples illustrate reduction of freed-up credits.

Example (1). (i) Corporation L has the following items for the 1985 taxable year:

Actual taxable income		$ 90,000
Regular tax		21,750
Available credits:		
Foreign tax credits for 1985	$15,000	
Foreign tax credits carried forward from 1984	25,000	
Investment tax credits carried forward from 1984	20,000	
		$ 60,000
Credit allowed to offset actual regular tax:		
Foreign tax credits for 1985	$15,000	
Foreign tax credits carried forward from 1984	6,750	
		$ 21,750
Actual regular tax liability		-0-
Preferences		110,000
Taxable income for 1985 determined as though preferences were not allowed		200,000
Non-preference regular tax		71,750
Credits allowed to offset non-preference regular tax:		
Foreign tax credits for 1985	$15,000	
Foreign tax credits carried forward from 1984	25,000	
Investment tax credits carried forward from 1984	20,000	
		$ 60,000
Non-preference regular tax liability		11,750

(ii) The freed-up credits for 1985 are $38,250 ($60,000 minus $21,750). The non-preference regular tax is $71,750. The amount of L's non-beneficial preferences for the 1985 taxable year is $84,456.

(iii) The credit reduction amount for 1985 is $12,668, the amount of minimum tax attributable to L's non-beneficial preferences. This amount is allocated to reduce each category of freed-up credit and to each year from which such credit is carried over. L's $38,250 of freed-up credits consists of $18,250 of foreign tax credits carried forward from 1984, which were freed up by $40,978 of non-beneficial preferences, and $20,000 of investment tax credits carried forward from 1984, which were freed up by $43,478 of non-beneficial preferences.

(iv) The apportionment of this credit reduction amount to each category of freed-up credit and each taxable year from which such credits are carried over is determined as follows under the exact credit reduction method:

(A) Foreign tax credits carried forward from 1984:

Non-beneficial preferences that freed up 1984 FTC		Credit reduction of 1984 FTC
$40,978	× .15 =	$6,146

(B) Investment tax credits carried forward from 1984:

Non-beneficial preferences that freed up 1984 ITC		Credit reduction of 1984 ITC
$43,478	× .15 =	$6,522

Thus, the foreign tax credits from 1984 that are carried forward to 1986 are $12,104 ($18,250 minus $6,146). The investment tax credits from 1984 that are carried forward to 1986 are $13,478 ($20,000 minus $6,522).

(v) The reduction of the freed-up credit under the simplified credit reduction method is as follows:

(A) Foreign tax credit carried forward from 1984:

$$\text{Freed-up foreign tax credits from 1984} \times \frac{\text{Credit reduction amount}}{\text{Total freed-up credit}}$$

= Credit reduction allocated to freed-up foreign tax credits carried forward from 1984

$$\$18{,}250 \times \frac{\$12{,}668}{\$38{,}250} = \$6{,}044$$

(B) Investment tax credits carried forward from 1984:

$$\text{Freed-up investment tax Credits from 1984} \times \frac{\text{Credit reduction amount}}{\text{Total freed-up credit}}$$

= Credit reduction allocated to freed-up foreign tax credits carried forward from 1984

$$\$20{,}000 \times \frac{\$12{,}668}{\$38{,}250} = \$6{,}624$$

Thus, under the simplified credit reduction method, L has $12,206 of foreign tax credits for 1984 ($18,250 minus $6,044) that are carried forward to 1986, and $13,376 of investment tax credits for 1984 ($20,000 minus $6,624) that are carried forward to 1986.

Example (2). Assume the same facts as in Example 1 of this paragraph (c)(5)(v), except that the foreign tax credits available for use in 1985 include $10,750 in credits carried forward from 1980 and $14,250 in credits carried forward from 1984, rather than $25,000 carried forward from 1984. Thus, $4,000 of the freed-up foreign tax credit is carried over from 1980. The other $14,250 of freed-up foreign tax credit is carried over from 1984. The non-beneficial preferences that freed up the 1980 foreign tax credit are $10,000. The non-beneficial preferences that freed up the 1984 foreign tax credit are $30,978. Under the exact credit reduction method, the credit reduction amounts for each of these credits are determined as follows:

(i) Foreign tax credit carried forward from 1980:

$10,000 × .15 = $1,500

(ii) Foreign tax credit carried forward from 1984:

$30,978 × .15 = $4,646

Thus, the foreign tax credit from 1984 that is carried forward to 1986 is $9,604 ($14,250 minus $4,646). Since the foreign tax credit from 1980 expires after 1985, none of that credit is carried forward to 1986.

(d) Examples. The following examples are comprehensive illustrations of the adjustments described in paragraph (c) of this section:

Example (1). (i) This example illustrates the operation of the credit reduction adjustment when the amount of foreign tax credit allowed is subject to the overall limitation under section 904. For purposes of this example, assume that Corporation X has the following items for the 1984 taxable year:

Taxable income (determined as though preferences were not allowed)	$140,000
From foreign sources	70,000
Foreign tax credits from 1984	5,000
Foreign tax credits from 1983	7,000
Actual taxable income	50,000
From foreign sources	25,000

(ii) The credit reduction adjustment and minimum tax liability for the taxable year are determined as follows:

1. Taxable income (determined as though preferences were not allowed) $140,000
2. Tax preferences for 1984 90,000
3. Taxable income (line 1 minus line 2) 50,000
4. Regular tax on line 3 amount (actual regular tax) before credits:
   $25,000 × .15 = $3,750
   25,000 × .18 = 4,500 8,250
5. Foreign tax credits allowed against regular tax (limited to 50% of actual regular tax under sec. 904) - 1984 foreign tax credits.......... 4,125
6. Regular tax after credits 4,125
   (line 4 minus line 5)
7. Regular tax on line 1 amount (non-preference regular tax) before credits:
   $25,000 × .15 = $3,750
   25,000 × .18 = 4,500
   25,000 × .3 = 7,500
   25,000 × .4 = 10,000
   40,000 × .46 = 18,400 44,150
8. Foreign tax credits allowed against non-preference regular tax:
   $5,000 (1984 foreign tax credits)
   7,000 (1983 foreign tax credits) .. 12,000
   (the allowed credits do not exceed the section 904 limitation of $22,075) ...
9. Non-preference regular tax after credits (line 7 minus line 8) 32,150
10. Freed-up credits (line 8 minus line 5):

1984 foreign tax credits ...	$5,000	
	(4,125)	
		$ 875
1983 foreign tax credits ...	$7,000	
	- 0 -	
		7,000
Total..........		$7,875

11. Non-beneficial preferences are computed as set forth in the table below. Under this computation, non-beneficial preferences are considered to free up credits that would have offset non-preference regular tax beginning at the lowest tax rates at which income that was offset by tax preferences otherwise would have been subject to regular tax. In this case, income that was offset by tax preferences would have been taxed beginning at the 30 percent marginal tax rate.

Type	Freed-up Credit	Divided by tax Rate	Non-beneficial preferences
FTC (84)	$ 875	.30	$ 2,917
FTC (83)	6,625	.30	22,083
	375	.40	938
	$7,875		$25,938
Total non-beneficial preferences			25,938

12. Beneficial preferences (line 2 minus line 11) ... 64,062
13. Minimum tax on total tax preferences ((line 2 minus the greater of line 6 or $10,000) × .15) ... 12,000
14. Minimum tax on beneficial preferences ((line 12 minus the greater of line 6 or $10,000) × .15) ... 8,109
15. Credit reduction amount (line 13 minus line 14) ... 3,891
16. Reduction of freed-up credits under the exact method (subtotals of line 11 multiplied by .15):
  (a) 1984 foreign tax credits:
    $2,917 × .15 = $438
  (b) 1983 foreign tax credits:
    ($22,083 + $938) × .15 = $3,453
  (c) Total credit reduction ... 3,891

Note: If X had elected to use the simplified credit reduction method, the amount of credit reduction would be determined by multiplying the amount of freed-up credit in each category and taxable year by the following ratio:

credit reduction amount	= $3,891 = .494
total freed-up credit	= $7,875

17. Freed-up credits after reduction under the exact method (line 10 subtotal minus line 16 subtotals):
(a) 1984 foreign tax credits ($875 minus $438) 437
(b) 1983 foreign tax credits ($7,000 minus $3,453) .. 3,547

Thus, assuming that Corporation X did not elect to use the simplified method, Corporation X will carryover $437 of 1984 foreign tax credits to 1985 and $3,547 of 1983 foreign tax credits to 1985. Had Corporation X elected to use the simplified method, freed-up credits after reduction would be as follows:

(a) 1984 foreign tax credits ($875 minus $433) 442
(b) 1983 foreign tax credits ($7,000 minus $3,458) .. 3,542

Example (2). (i) Corporation X has the following items for its 1985 taxable year:

Taxable income (determined as though preferences were not allowed	$1,500,000
1984 investment tax credits	400,000
1985 investment tax credits	100,000
Actual taxable income	1,000,000

(ii) The credit reduction and minimum tax of X for 1985 are determined as follows:

1. Taxable income determined as though preferences were not allowed ... $1,500,000
2. Tax preferences for 1985 ... 500,000
3. Taxable income (line 1 minus line 2) ... 1,000,000
4. Regular tax on line 3 amount (actual regular tax) before credits:
  $25,000 × .15 = $3,750
  25,000 × .18 = 4,500
  25,000 × .30 = 7,500
  25,000 × .40 = 10,000
  900,000 × .46 = 414,000 ... 439,750
5. Investment tax credits allowed (limited under section 38 (c) to $25,000 of net tax liability, plus 85 percent of net tax liability in excess of $25,000 ... 377,537
6. Regular tax after credits (line 4 minus line 5) ... 62,212
7. Regular tax on line 1 amount (non-preference regular tax) before credits:
  $25,000 × .15 = $3,750
  25,000 × .18 = 4,500
  25,000 × .30 = 7,500
  25,000 × .40 = 10,000
  900,000 × .46 = 414,000
  405,000 × .51 = 206,550
  95,000 × .46 = 43,700 ... 690,000
8. Investment tax credits allowed against non-preference regular tax ... 500,000
9. Non-preference regular tax after credits (line 7 minus line 8) ... 190,000
10. Freed-up credits (line 8 minus line 5):

1984 investment tax credit	$400,000	
	(377,537)	
		22,463
1985 investment tax credit	$100,000	
	- 0 -	
		100,000
Total ...		$ 122,463

11. Non-beneficial preferences are computed as set forth in the table below. Under this computation, non-beneficial preferences are considered to free up credits that would have offset non-preference regular tax beginning at the lowest tax rates at which income that was offset by tax preferences otherwise would have been subject to regular tax. In this case, income that was offset by tax preferences would have been taxed beginning at the 51 percent marginal tax rate. Although some of the income offset by preferences would be taxed at the 46 percent marginal rate (because taxable income in excess of $1,405,000 is not subject to the 5 percent addition to tax on taxable income in excess of $1 million), the 51 percent marginal rate is taken into account first.

Type	Freed-up Credit	Divided by tax Rate	Non-beneficial preferences
ITC (84)	$ 22,463	.51	$ 44,045
IRTC (85)	100,000	.51	196,078
	$122,463		$240,123
Total non-beneficial preferences			240,123

12. Beneficial preferences (line 2 minus line 11) .. 259,877
13. Minimum tax on total tax preferences ((line 2 minus the greater of line 6 or $10,000) × .15) .. 65,668
14. Minimum tax on beneficial preferences ((line 12 minus the greater of line 6 or $10,000) × .15) ... 29,650
15. Credit reduction amount (line 13 minus line 14) ... 36,018
16. Reduction of freed-up credits under the exact method (subtotals of line 11 multiplied by .15):
  (a) 1984 foreign tax credits:
    $44,045 × .15 = $6,607
  (b) 1985 investment tax credits:
    $196,078 × .15 = $29,411
  (c) Total credit reduction ... 36,018
17. Freed-up credits after reduction (assuming that Corporation X does not elect the simplified method):
  (a) 1984 foreign tax credits ($22,463 minus $6,607) ... 15,856
  (b) 1985 investment tax credit ($100,000 minus $29,411) ... 70,589

(e) Miscellaneous rules. *(1) Investment credit recapture.* If during any taxable year property to which section 47 applies is disposed of, then for purposes of determining any increase in tax under section 47 for such year, the amount of any reduction under this section of freed-up section 38 credit which was earned in the year the property was placed in service shall be treated as a credit that was allowed in a prior taxable year.

Example. Corporation D places property in service in 1983 that generates investment tax credits of $10,000. D earns no other investment tax credits in 1983. None of the investment tax credits are used to reduce tax liability in 1983 or any prior years. In 1984, D uses $1,000 of this credit to reduce regular tax liability. In addition, D has items of tax preference in 1984. However, under section 58(h), D is not liable for minimum tax on any of these preference items because none of these preference items produces a tax benefit in 1984. As a result, an adjustment is made under the provisions of § 1.58-9 and the investment tax credit carryforward from 1983 is reduced by $4,000. Thus, D has an investment tax credit carryforward of $5,000 that is attributable to the property placed in service in 1983. In 1986, the property is disposed of and the investment tax credits earned in 1983 are recomputed as required under section 47. This recomputation results in a reduction of $6,000 of the investment tax credits earned in 1983. D must now adjust its 1983 investment tax credit carryforward under section 47(a)(6) by reducing this carryforward to zero. In addition, D has an additional tax liability of $1,000 for 1986.

(2) Period of limitations; adjustments to tax liability. The adjustments described in this section shall, in general, apply for purposes of assessing deficiencies or claiming refunds of tax for any taxable year for which the tax liability is affected by the adjustments of this section, provided that the period of limitations under section 6501 has not expired for such taxable year. Therefore, these adjustments generally apply for purposes of assessing deficiencies and refunding any overpayment of tax for all years for which the period of limitations has not expired regardless of whether the period of limitations has expired for the taxable year in which the non-beneficial preferences arose. However, the adjustments of this section do not apply to reduce otherwise allowable credits that were freed up by such non-beneficial preferences where:

(i) The taxpayer paid minimum tax on all tax preference items arising in the taxable year in which the non-beneficial preferences arose;

(ii) The taxpayer has not made a claim for a credit or refund for such minimum tax; and

(iii) The period of limitations for claiming a credit or refund under section 6511 has expired for such taxable year.

(A) Further, if—

(1) the taxpayer never paid minimum tax attributable to non-beneficial preferences;

(2) credits that were freed up by such preferences were used to reduce tax liability for a taxable year for which the period of limitations has expired; and

(3) credits so used exceed the amount of credits that would have been available if the credit reduction required under this section with respect to such preferences had been made,

(B) Then, the taxpayer shall be liable for the minimum tax equal to the amount of credits so used, provided the period of limitations has not expired for the taxable year in which preferences arose.

(3) Claims for credit or refund. A taxpayer may claim a credit or refund of minimum tax that was paid on non-beneficial preferences. However, such a claim for a credit or refund shall be disallowed to the extent that the taxpayer has reduced tax liability in a taxable year for which the period of limitations has expired by using freed-up credits in excess of the amount that would have been available if the credit reduction required under this section had been made. Such claim must be made by filing an amended return for the taxable year for which such minimum tax was paid. Further, if a claim for credit or refund is filed, amended returns must also be filed for any taxable year for which tax liability would be affected as a result of the reduction, under this section, of credits freed up by such non-beneficial preferences. See section 6511 and the regulations thereunder regarding the period of limitations for claiming a credit or refund.

(4) Carryovers of foreign tax credit to taxable years after 1986. In the case of foreign tax credit carryforwards to taxable years beginning after December 31, 1986, reductions in such credits required under this section shall apply for purposes of computing the alternative minimum tax foreign tax credit under section 59(a) of the Internal Revenue Code of 1986 as well as for purposes of computing the foreign tax credit for regular tax purposes.

(5) Credit carrybacks. If credit carrybacks increase the amount of credits for a taxable year, the adjustments described in this section shall be recomputed taking into account the additional credits. This rule may be illustrated by the following examples:

Example (1). (i) In 1981 corporation D has actual taxable income of $72,500 and regular tax before credits of $15,000. In computing actual regular taxable income, D made use of $36,739 of tax preference items, so that D's taxable income determined as though preference were not allowed would be $109,239. D's non-preference regular tax before credits is $30,000. D earns $25,000 of foreign tax credits in 1981, none of which exceed the limitation under section 904 determined using either actual regular taxable income or the non-preference taxable income. These credits reduce actual regular tax to zero ($0) and would have reduced non-preference regular tax to $5,000 ($30,000 minus $25,000). Thus, D has freed-up foreign tax credits from 1981 of $10,000 ($25,000 minus $15,000). Pursuant to the adjustments required under this section, D determines that its credit reduction amount is $3,843 and reduces its freed-up credit (and its credit carryover) from 1981 to $6,157 ($10,000 minus $3,843). D also pays minimum tax of $167 on $11,114 of beneficial preferences (($11,114 minus $10,000) multiplied by .15).

(ii) In 1982 D earns additional foreign tax credits. After application of the foreign tax credit carryback rules, D would have $5,000 of 1982 foreign tax credits available for use in 1981. D must recalculate the adjustments required under this section by treating $5,000 of foreign tax credit from 1982 as carried back and (assuming that these credits do not exceed the limitation under section 904) used to reduce non-preference regular tax liability in 1981 to zero ($0). That is, $5,000 of the foreign tax credits earned in 1982 are treated as credits freed up because of D's tax preference items in 1981. Pursuant to the rules set forth herein, D must take into account the foreign tax credits from both 1981 and 1982 in determining to what extent a tax benefit was derived from the preference items used to determine actual regular tax liability in 1981 and in computing the credit reduction amount. When the $5,000 of foreign tax credits from 1982 are considered, all preferences become non-beneficial preferences, and the credit reduction amount is $4,010. Assuming that D elects the simplified method, the 1981 freed-up credits and the 1982 freed-up credits will each be reduced by the following percentage:

$$\frac{\$4{,}010 \text{ (credit reduction amount)}}{\$15{,}000 \text{ (total freed up credits)}} = .2673$$

The 1981 freed-up foreign tax credits of $10,000 are thus reduced by $2,673 ($10,000 multiplied by .2673), to $7,327 and the 1982 freed-up foreign tax credits of $5,000 are reduced by $1,334 ($5,000 multiplied by .2673) to $3,666. D also files a claim for credit or refund of the $167 of minimum tax paid in 1981.

Example (2). In 1985 corporation E's non-preference regular taxable income was $25,000. E had no available credits. It paid zero in regular tax, however, because of $25,000 in preference items. E paid $2,250 of minimum tax on these preferences (($25,000 minus $10,000) multiplied by .15). In 1986, E has additional investment tax credits. After application of the investment tax credit carryback rules, E would have $1,000 investment tax credit from 1986 available for use in 1985. E must recompute the adjustments required under this section by treating $1,000 of these 1986 investment tax credits as carried back and used to reduce non-preference regular tax liability for 1985. Pursuant to the rules of this section, all of these $1,000 of credits are freed-up credits. Non-beneficial preferences are $6,667 ($1,000 grossed up at a 15 percent regular tax rate). Beneficial preferences are $18,333 ($25,000 minus $6,667). Minimum tax on all preferences would be $2,250 (($25,000 minus $10,000) multiplied by .15); minimum tax on beneficial preferences would be $1,250 (($18,333 minus $10,000) multiplied by .15) Minimum tax attributable to the non-beneficial preferences is thus $1,000 ($2,250 minus $1,250), which is the credit reduction amount. E thus reduces the $1,000 of credits carried back to 1985 to zero. Under the rules of this section, the amount of minimum tax due for 1985 is redetermined. It is equal to the minimum tax on beneficial preferences, which, as described above, is $1,250. Because E paid minimum tax of $2,250 in 1985, E files a claim for credit or refund for $1,000 of the minimum tax paid in 1985.

(f) Treatment of net operating losses. [Reserved]

T.D. 8416, 5/4/92.

§ 1.59-1 Optional 10-year writeoff of certain tax preferences.

(a) In general. Section 59(e) allows any qualified expenditure to which an election under section 59(e) applies to be deducted ratably over the 10-year period (3-year period in the case of circulation expenditures described in section 173) beginning with the taxable year in which the expenditure was made (or, in the case of intangible drilling and development costs deductible under section 263(c), over the 60-month period beginning with the month in which the expenditure was paid or incurred).

(b) Election. *(1) Time and manner of election.* An election under section 59(e) shall only be made by attaching a statement to the taxpayer's income tax return (or amended return) for the taxable year in which the amortization of the qualified expenditures subject to the section 59(e) election begins. The statement must be filed no later than the date prescribed by law for filing the taxpayer's original income tax return (including any extensions of time) for the taxable year in which the amortization of the qualified expenditures subject to the section 59(e) election begins. Additionally, the statement must include the following information—

(i) The taxpayer's name, address, and taxpayer identification number; and

(ii) The type and amount of qualified expenditures identified in section 59(e)(2) that the taxpayer elects to deduct ratably over the applicable period described in section 59(e)(1).

(2) Elected amount. A taxpayer may make an election under section 59(e) with respect to any portion of any qualified expenditure paid or incurred by the taxpayer in the taxable year to which the election applies. An election under section 59(e) must be for a specific dollar amount and the amount subject to an election under section 59(e) may not be made by reference to a formula. The amount elected under section 59(e) is properly chargeable to a capital account under section 1016(a)(20), relating to adjustments to basis of property.

(c) Revocation. *(1) In general.* An election under section 59(e) may be revoked only with the consent of the Commissioner. Such consent will only be granted in rare and unusual circumstances. The revocation, if granted, will be effective in the first taxable year in which the section 59(e) election was applicable. However, if the period of limitations for the first taxable year the section 59(e) election was applicable has expired, the revocation, if granted, will be effective in the earliest taxable year for which the period of limitations has not expired.

(2) Time and manner for requesting consent. A taxpayer requesting the Commissioner's consent to revoke a section 59(e) election must submit the request prior to the end of the taxable year the applicable amortization period described in section 59(e)(1) ends. The application for consent to revoke the election must be submitted to the Internal Revenue Service in the form of a letter ruling request.

(3) Information to be provided. A request to revoke a section 59(e) election must contain all of the information necessary to demonstrate the rare and unusual circumstances that would justify granting revocation.

(4) Treatment of unamortized costs. The unamortized balance of the qualified expenditures subject to the revoked section 59(e) election as of the first day of the taxable year the revocation is effective is deductible in the year the revocation is effective (subject to the requirements of any other provision under the Code, regulations, or any other published guidance) and the taxpayer will be required to amend any federal income tax returns affected by the revocation.

(d) Effective date. These regulations apply to a section 59(e) election made for a taxable year ending, or a request to revoke a section 59(e) election submitted, on or after December 22, 2004.

T.D. 9168, 12/21/2004.

§ 1.61-1 Gross income.

(a) General definition. Gross income means all income from whatever source derived, unless excluded by law. Gross income includes income realized in any form, whether in money, property, or services. Income may be realized, therefore, in the form of services, meals, accommodations, stock, or other property, as well as in cash. Section 61 lists the more common items of gross income for purposes of illustration. For purposes of further illustration, § 1.61-14 mentions several miscellaneous items of gross income not listed specifically in section 61. Gross income, however, is not limited to the items so enumerated.

(b) Cross references. Cross references to other provisions of the Code are to be found throughout the regulations under section 61. The purpose of these cross references is to direct attention to the more common items which are included in or excluded from gross income entirely, or treated in some special manner. To the extent that another section of the Code or of the regulations thereunder, provides specific treatment for any item of income, such other provision shall apply notwithstanding section 61 and the regulations thereunder. The cross references do not cover all possible items.

(1) For examples of items specifically included in gross income, see part II (section 71 and following), subchapter B, chapter 1 of the Code.

(2) For examples of items specifically excluded from gross income, see part III (section 101 and following), subchapter B, chapter 1 of the Code.

(3) For general rules as to the taxable year for which an item is to be included in gross income, see section 451 and the regulations thereunder.

T.D. 6272, 11/25/57.

§ 1.61-2 Compensation for services, including fees, commissions, and similar items.

(a) In general. *(1)* Wages, salaries, commissions paid salesmen, compensation for services on the basis of a percentage of profits, commissions on insurance premiums, tips, bonuses (including Christmas bonuses), termination or severance pay, rewards, jury fees, marriage fees and other contributions received by a clergyman for services, pay of persons in the military or naval forces of the United States, retired pay of employees, pensions, and retirement allowances are income to the recipients unless excluded by law. Several special rules apply to members of the Armed Forces, National Oceanic and Atmospheric Administration, and Public Health Service of the United States; see paragraph (b) of this section.

(2) The Code provides special rules including the following items in gross income:

(i) Distributions from employees' trusts, see sections 72, 402, and 403, and the regulations thereunder;

(ii) Compensation for child's services (in child's gross income), see section 73 and the regulations thereunder;

(iii) Prizes and awards, see section 74 and the regulations thereunder.

(3) Similarly, the Code provides special rules excluding the following items from gross income in whole or in part:

(i) Gifts, see section 102 and the regulations thereunder;

(ii) Compensation for injuries or sickness, see section 104 and the regulations thereunder;

(iii) Amounts received under accident and health plans, see section 105 and the regulations thereunder;

(iv) Scholarship and fellowship grants, see section 117 and the regulations thereunder;

(v) Miscellaneous items, see section 122.

(b) Members of the Armed Forces, National Oceanic and Atmospheric Administration, and Public Health Service. *(1)* Subsistence and uniform allowances granted commissioned officers, chief warrant officers, warrant officers, and enlisted personnel of the Armed Forces, National Oceanic and Atmospheric Administration, and Public Health Service of the United States, and amounts received by them as commutation of quarters, are excluded from gross income. Similarly, the value of quarters or subsistence furnished to such persons is excluded from gross income.

(2) For purposes of this section, quarters or subsistence includes the following allowances for expenses incurred after December 31, 1993, by members of the Armed Forces, members of the commissioned corps of the National Oceanic and Atmospheric Administration, and members of the commissioned corps of the Public Health Service, to the extent that the allowances are not otherwise excluded from gross income under another provision of the Internal Revenue Code: a dislocation allowance, authorized by 37 U.S.C. 407; a temporary lodging allowance, authorized by 37 U.S.C. 405; a temporary lodging expense, authorized by 37 U.S.C. 404a; and a move-in housing allowance, authorized by 37 U.S.C. 405. No deduction is allowed under this chapter for any expenses reimbursed by such excluded allowances. For the exclusion from gross income of—

(i) Disability pensions, see section 104(a)(4) and the regulations thereunder;

(ii) Miscellaneous items, see section 122.

(3) The per diem or actual expense allowance, the monetary allowance in lieu of transportation, and the mileage allowance received by members of the Armed Forces, National Oceanic and Atmospheric Administration, and the Public Health Service, while in a travel status or on temporary duty away from their permanent stations, are included in their gross income except to the extent excluded under the accountable plan provisions of § 1.62-2.

(c) Payment to charitable, etc., organization on behalf of person rendering services. The value of services is not includible in gross income when such services are rendered directly and gratuitously to an organization described in section 170(c). Where, however, pursuant to an agreement or understanding, services are rendered to a person for the benefit of an organization described in section 170(c) and an amount for such services is paid to such organization by the person to whom the services are rendered, the amount so paid constitutes income to the person performing the services.

(d) Compensation paid other than in cash. *(1) In general.* Except as otherwise provided in paragraph (d)(6)(i) of this section (relating to certain property transferred after June 30, 1969), if services are paid for in property, the fair market value of the property taken in payment must be included in income as compensation. If services are paid for in exchange for other services, the fair market value of such other services taken in payment must be included in income as compensation. If the services are rendered at a stipulated price, such price will be presumed to be the fair market value of the compensation received in the absence of evidence to the contrary. For special rules relating to certain options received as compensation, see §§ 1.61-15, 1.83-7, and section 421 and the regulations thereunder. For special rules relating to premiums paid by an employer for an annuity contract which is not subject to section 403(a), see section 403(c) and the regulations thereunder and § 1.83-8(a). For special rules relating to contributions made to an employees' trust which is not exempt under section 501, see section 402(b) and the regulations thereunder and § 1.83-8(a).

(2) Property transferred to employee or independent contractor. (i) Except as otherwise provided in section 421 and the regulations thereunder and § 1.61-15 (relating to stock options), and paragraph (d)(6)(i) of this section, if property is transferred by an employer to an employee or if property is transferred to an independent contractor, as compensation for services, for an amount less than its fair market value, then regardless of whether the transfer is in the form of a

sale or exchange, the difference between the amount paid for the property and the amount of its fair market value at the time of the transfer is compensation and shall be included in the gross income of the employee or independent contractor. In computing the gain or loss from the subsequent sale of such property, its basis shall be the amount paid for the property increased by the amount of such difference included in gross income.

(ii) (A) Cost of life insurance on the life of the employee. Generally, life insurance premiums paid by an employer on the life of his employee where the proceeds of such insurance are payable to the beneficiary of such employee are part of the gross income of the employee. For example, if an employee or independent contractor is the owner (as defined in § 1.61-22(c)(1)) of a life insurance contract and the payments with regard to such contract are not split-dollar loans under § 1.7872-15(b)(1), the employee or independent contractor must include in income the amount of any such payments by the employer or service recipient with respect to such contract during any year to the extent that the employee's or independent contractor's rights to the life insurance contract are substantially vested (within the meaning of § 1.83-3(b)). This result is the same regardless of whether the employee or independent contractor has at all times been the owner of the life insurance contract or the contract previously has been owned by the employer or service recipient as part of a split-dollar life insurance arrangement (as defined in § 1.61-22(b)(1) or (2)) and was transferred by the employer or service recipient to the employee or independent contractor under § 1.61-22(g). However, the amount includible in the employee's gross income is determined with regard to the provisions of section 403 and the regulations thereunder in the case of an individual contract issued after December 31, 1962, or a group contract, which provides incidental life insurance protection and which satisfies the requirements of section 401(g) and § 1.401-9, relating to the nontransferability of annuity contracts. For the special rules relating to the includibility in an employee's gross income of an amount equal to the cost of certain group-term life insurance on the employee's life which is carried directly or indirectly by his employer, see section 79 and the regulations thereunder. For special rules relating to the exclusion of contributions by an employer to accident and health plans for the employee, see section 106 and the regulations thereunder.

(B) Cost of group-term life insurance on the life of an individual other than an employee. The cost (determined under paragraph (d)(2) of § 1.79-3) of group-term life insurance on the life of an individual other than an employee (such as the spouse or dependent of the employee) provided in connection with the performance of services by the employee is includible in the gross income of the employee.

(3) Meals and living quarters. The value of living quarters or meals which an employee receives in addition to his salary constitutes gross income unless they are furnished for the convenience of the employer and meet the conditions specified in section 119 and the regulations thereunder. For the treatment of rental value of parsonages or rental allowance paid to ministers, see section 107 and the regulations thereunder; for the treatment of statutory subsistence allowances received by police, see section 120 and the regulations thereunder.

(4) Stock and notes transferred to employee or independent contractor. Except as otherwise provided by section 421 and the regulations thereunder and § 1.61-15 (relating to stock options), and paragraph (d)(6)(i) of this section, if a corporation transfers its own stock to an employee or independent contractor as compensation for services, the fair market value of the stock at the time of transfer shall be included in the gross income of the employee or independent contractor. Notes or other evidences of indebtedness received in payment for services constitute income in the amount of their fair market value at the time of the transfer. A taxpayer receiving as compensation a note regarded as good for its face value at maturity, but not bearing interest, shall treat as income as of the time of receipt its fair discounted value computed at the prevailing rate. As payments are received on such a note, there shall be included in income that portion of each payment which represents the proportionate part of the discount originally taken on the entire note.

(5) Property transferred on or before June 30, 1969, subject to restrictions. Notwithstanding paragraph (d) (1), (2), or (4) of this section, if any property is transferred after September 24, 1959, by an employer to an employee or independent contractor as compensation for services, and such property is subject to a restriction which has a significant effect on its value at the time of transfer, the rules of § 1.421-6(d)(2) shall apply in determining the time and the amount of compensation to be included in the gross income of the employee or independent contractor. This (5) is also applicable to transfers subject to a restriction which has a significant effect on its value at the time of transfer and to which § 1.83-8(b) (relating to transitional rules with respect to transfers of restricted property) applies. For special rules relating to options to purchase stock or other property which are issued as compensation for services, see § 1.61-15 and section 421 and the regulations thereunder.

(6) Certain property transferred, premiums paid, and contributions made in connection with the performance of services after June 30, 1969. (i) Exception. Paragraph (d)(1), (2), (4), and (5) of this section and § 1.61-15 do not apply to the transfer of property (as defined in § 1.83-3(e)) after June 30, 1969, unless § 1.83-8 (relating to the applicability of section 83 and transitional rules) applies. If section 83 applies to a transfer of property, and the property is not subject to a restriction that has a significant effect on the fair market value of such property, then the rules contained in paragraph (d)(1), (2), and (4) of this section and § 1.61-15 shall also apply to such transfer to the extent such rules are not inconsistent with section 83.

(ii) Cross references. For rules relating to premiums paid by an employer for an annuity contract which is not subject to section 403(a), see section 403(c) and the regulations thereunder. For rules relating to contributions made to an employees' trust which is not exempt under section 501(a), see section 402(b) and the regulations thereunder.

T.D. 6272, 11/25/57, amend T.D. 6416, 9/24/59, T.D. 6696, 12/11/63, T.D. 6856, 10/19/65, T.D. 6888, 7/6/66, T.D. 7554, 7/21/78, T.D. 7623, 5/14/79, T.D. 8256, 7/6/89, T.D. 8607, 8/4/95, T.D. 9092, 9/11/2003.

---

§ 1.61-2T Taxation of fringe benefits —1985 through 1988 (temporary).

(a) Fringe benefits. *(1) In general.* Section 61(a)(1) provides that, except as otherwise provided in subtitle A, gross income includes compensation for services, including fees, commissions, fringe benefits, and similar items. Examples of fringe benefits include: an employer-provided automobile, a flight on an employer-provided aircraft, an employer-provided free or discounted commercial airline flight, an employer-provided vacation, an employer-provided discount on property or services, an employer-provided membership in a country club or other social club, and an employer-provided ticket to an entertainment or sporting event.

(2) Fringe benefits excluded from income. To the extent that a particular fringe benefit is specifically excluded from gross income pursuant to another section of subtitle A, that section shall govern the treatment of that fringe benefit. Thus, if the requirements of the governing section are satisfied, the fringe benefits may be excludable from gross income. Examples of excludable fringe benefits are qualified tuition reductions provided to an employee (section 117(d)); meals and lodging furnished to an employee for the convenience of the employer (section 119); and benefits provided under a dependent care assistance program (section 129). Similarly, the value of the use by an employee of an employer-provided vehicle or a flight provided to an employee on an employer-provided aircraft may be excludable from income under section 105 (because, for example, the transportation is provided for medical reasons) if and to the extent that the requirements of that section are satisfied. Section 61 and the regulations thereunder shall apply, however, to the extent that they are not inconsistent with such other section. For example, many fringe benefits specifically addressed in other sections of subtitle A are excluded from gross income only to the extent that they do not exceed specific dollar or percentage limits, or only if certain other requirements are met. If the limits are exceeded or the requirements are not met, some or all of the fringe benefit may be includible in gross income. See paragraph (b)(3) of this section.

(3) Compensation for services. A fringe benefit provided in connection with the performance of services shall be considered to have been provided as compensation for services. Refraining from the performance of services (such as pursuant to a covenant not to compete) is deemed to be the performance of services for purposes of this section.

(4) Recipient of a fringe benefit. (i) Definition. A fringe benefit is included in the income of the "recipient" of the fringe benefit. The recipient of a fringe benefit is the person performing the services in connection with which the fringe benefit is provided. Thus, a person may be considered to be a recipient, even though that person did not actually receive the fringe benefit. For example, a fringe benefit provided to any person in connection with the performance of services by another person is considered to have been provided to the person who performs the services and not the person who receives the fringe benefit. In addition, if a fringe benefit is provided to a person, but taxable to a second person as the recipient, such benefit is referred to as provided to the second person and use by the first person is considered use by the second person. For example, provision of an automobile to an employee's spouse by the employer is taxable to the employee as the recipient. The automobile is referred to as available to the employee and use by the employee's spouse is considered use by the employee.

(ii) Recipient may be other than an employee. The recipient of a fringe benefit need not be an employee of the provider of the fringe benefit, but may be a partner, director, or an independent contractor. For convenience, the term "employee" includes a reference to any recipient of a fringe benefit, unless otherwise specifically provided in this section.

(5) Provider of a fringe benefit. The "provider" of a fringe benefit is that person for whom the services are performed, regardless of whether that person actually provides the fringe benefit to the recipient. The provider of a fringe benefit need not be the employer of the recipient of the fringe benefit, but may be, for example, a client or customer of an independent contractor. For convenience, the term "employer" includes a reference to any provider of a fringe benefit, unless otherwise specifically provided in this section.

(6) Effective date. This section is effective from January 1, 1985, to December 31, 1988, with respect to fringe benefits furnished before January 1, 1989. No inference may be drawn from the promulgation or terms of this section concerning the application of law in effect prior to January 1, 1985.

(b) Valuation of fringe benefits. *(1) In general.* An employee must include in gross income the amount by which the fair market value of the fringe benefit exceeds the sum of (i) the amount, if any, paid for the benefit, and (ii) the amount, if any, specifically excluded from gross income by some other section of subtitle A. Therefore, for example, if the employee pays fair market value for what is received, no amount is includible in the gross income of the employee.

(2) Fair market value. In general, fair market value is determined on the basis of all the facts and circumstances. Specifically, the fair market value of a fringe benefit is that amount a hypothetical person would have to pay a hypothetical third party to obtain (i.e., purchase or lease) the particular fringe benefit. Thus, for example, the effect of any special relationship that may exist between the employer and the employee must be disregarded. This also means that an employee's subjective perception of the value of a fringe benefit is not relevant to the determination of a fringe benefit's fair market value. In addition, the cost incurred by the employer is not determinative of the fair market value of the fringe benefit. For special rules relating to the valuation of certain fringe benefits, see paragraph (c) of this section.

(3) Exclusion from income based on cost. If a statutory exclusion phrased in terms of cost applies to the provision of a fringe benefit, section 61 does not require the inclusion in the recipient's gross income of the difference between the fair market value and the excludable cost of that fringe benefit. For example, section 129 provides an exclusion from an employee's gross income for amounts paid or incurred by an employer to provide dependent care assistance to employees. Even if the fair market value of the dependent care assistance exceeds the employer's cost, the excess is not subject to inclusion under section 61 and this section. If the statutory cost exclusion is a limited amount, however, then the fair market value of the fringe benefit attributable to any excess cost is subject to inclusion.

(4) Fair market value of the availability of an employer-provided vehicle. If the vehicle special valuation rules of paragraphs (d), (e), or (f) of this section are not used by a taxpayer entitled to use such rules, the value of the availability of an employer-provided vehicle is determined under the general valuation principles set forth in this section. In general, such valuation must be determined by reference to the cost to a hypothetical person of leasing from a hypothetical third party the same or comparable vehicle on the same or comparable terms in the geographic area in which the vehicle is available for use. Unless the employee can substantiate that the same or comparable vehicle could have been leased on a cents-per-mile basis, the value of the availability of the vehicle cannot be determined by reference to a cents-per-mile rate applied to the number of miles the vehicle is driven. An example of a comparable lease term is the amount of time that the vehicle is available to the employee for use, e.g., a one-year period.

(5) Fair market value of a flight on an employer-provided aircraft. If the non-commercial flight special valuation rule of paragraph (g) of this section is not used (or is not properly used) by a taxpayer entitled to use such rule, the value of a flight on an employer-provided aircraft is determined under the general valuation principles set forth in this section. An example of how the general valuation principles would apply is that if an employee whose flight is primarily personal controls the use of an aircraft with respect to such flight, such flight is valued by reference to how much it would cost a hypothetical person to charter the same or comparable aircraft for the same or comparable flight. The cost to charter the aircraft must be allocated among all employees on board the aircraft based on all the facts and circumstances, including which employee or employees controlled the use of the aircraft. Notwithstanding the allocation required by the preceding sentence, no additional amount shall be included in the income of any employee whose flight is properly valued under the special valuation rule of paragraph (g) of this section.

(c) Special valuation rules. *(1) In general.* Paragraphs (d) through (j) of this section provide special valuation rules that may be used under certain circumstances for certain commonly provided fringe benefits. Paragraph (d) provides a lease valuation rule relating to employer-provided automobiles. Paragraph (e) provides a cents-per-mile valuation rule relating to employer-provided vehicles. Paragraph (f) provides a commuting valuation rule relating to employer-provided vehicles. Paragraph (g) provides a flight valuation rule relating to flights on employer-provided aircraft. Paragraph (h) provides a flight valuation rule relating to flights on commercial airlines. Paragraph (i) is reserved. Paragraph (j) provides a meal valuation rule relating to employer-operated eating facilities for employees. For general rules relating to the valuation of fringe benefits not eligible for valuation under the special valuation rules, see paragraph (b) of this section.

(2) Use of the special valuation rules. (i) In general. The special valuation rules may be used for income, employment tax, and reporting purposes. Use of any of the special valuation rules is optional. An employer need not use the same vehicle special valuation rule for all vehicles provided to all employees. For example, an employer may use the automobile lease valuation rule for automobiles provided to some employees, and the commuting and vehicle cents-per-mile valuation rules for automobiles provided to other employees. Except as otherwise provided, however, if either the commercial flight valuation rule or the noncommercial flight valuation rule is used, such rule must be used by an employer to value all flights taken by employees in a calendar year. Effective January 1, 1986, if an employer uses one of the special rules to value the benefit provided to an employee, the employee may not use another special rule to value that benefit. The employee may, however, use general valuation rules based on facts and circumstances (see paragraph (b) of this section). Effective January 1, 1986, an employee may only use a special valuation rule if the employer uses the rule. If a special rule is used, it must be used for all purposes. If an employer properly uses a special rule and the employee uses the special rule, the employee must include in gross income the amount determined by the employer under the special rule less any amount reimbursed by the employee to the employer. The employer and the employee may use the special rules to determine the amount of the reimbursement due the employer by the employee. If an employer properly uses a special rule and properly determines the amount of an employee's working condition fringe under section 132 and § 1.132-1T (under the general rule or under a special rule), and the employee uses the special valuation rule, the employee must include in gross income the amount determined by the employer less any amount reimbursed by the employee to the employer.

(ii) Transitional rules. (A) Use of vehicle special valuation rules for 1985 and 1986. For purposes of valuing the use or availability of a vehicle, the consistency rules provided in paragraphs (d)(6) and (e)(5) of this section (relating to the automobile lease valuation rule and the vehicle cents-per-mile valuation rule, respectively) apply for 1987 and thereafter. Therefore, for 1985 and 1986 an employer (and employee, subject to paragraph (c)(2)(i) of this section) may use any applicable special valuation rule (or no special valuation rule) to value the use or availability of a vehicle, subject to paragraph (c)(2)(ii)(B) of this section.

(B) Consistency Rules for 1985 and 1986. If an employer uses the automobile lease valuation rule of paragraph (d) of this section in 1985 or 1986 with respect to an automobile, such rule must be used for the entire calendar year with respect to the automobile except for any period during which the commuting valuation rule of paragraph (f) of this section is properly used. If an employer uses the vehicle cents-per-mile valuation rule of paragraph (e) of this section in 1985 or 1986 with respect to a vehicle, such rule must be used for the entire calendar year with respect to the vehicle except for any period during which the commuting valuation rule of paragraph (f) of this section is properly used. The rules of this paragraph (c)(2)(ii)(B) also apply to employees using the special valuation rules of paragraphs (d) or (e) of this section.

(C) Employee's use of special valuation rules for 1985. An employee may use a special valuation rule (other than the rule in paragraph (e) of this section relating to the vehicle cents-per-mile valuation rule) during 1985 even if the employer does not use the same special valuation rule during 1985. An employee's use of a special valuation rule in 1986 and thereafter must be consistent with his employer's use of the rule as required under paragraph (c)(2)(i) of this section.

(D) Examples. The following examples illustrate the rules of paragraph (c)(2)(ii) of this section:

Example (1). Assume that an employer properly uses the automobile lease valuation rule in 1985. The employer may use the vehicle cents-per-mile valuation rule in 1986 if the requirements of the vehicle cents-per-mile valuation rule are satisfied.

Example (2). Assume that an employer does not use a special valuation rule to value the availability of an automobile in 1985. The employer may use any of the special valuation rules in 1986 if the requirements of the rule chosen are satisfied. The same applies for 1987.

Example (3). Assume that an employer properly uses the vehicle cents-per-mile valuation rule in 1985. The employer may continue to use the rule or use any of the other special valuation rules to value the benefit provided in 1986 if the requirements of the rule chosen are satisfied. Alternatively, the employer may use none of the special valuation rules in 1986 but use any of the rules in 1987 if the requirements of the rule chosen are satisfied.

Example (4). Assume that an employee properly uses the automobile lease valuation rule in 1985. In 1986 and thereafter the employee may use a special valuation rule only if the employee's employer uses the same special valuation rule.

The employee may use general valuation principles to value the benefit provided in 1986 and thereafter.

(3) Election to use the special valuation rules. A particular special valuation rule is deemed to have been elected by the employer (and, if applicable, by the employee), if the employer (and, if applicable, the employee) determines the value of the fringe benefit provided by applying the special valuation rule and treats such value as the fair market value of the fringe benefit for income, employment tax, and reporting purposes. Neither the employer nor the employee is required to notify the Internal Revenue Service of the election.

(4) Application of section 414 to employers. For purposes of paragraphs (c) through (j) of this section, except as otherwise provided therein, the term "employer" includes all entities required to be treated as a single employer under section 414(b), (c), or (m).

(5) Valuation formulas contained in the special valuation rules. The valuation formulas contained in the special valuation rules are provided only for use in connection with such rules. Thus, when a special valuation rule is properly applied to a fringe benefit, the Commissioner will accept the value calculated pursuant to the rule as the fair market value of that fringe benefit. However, when a special valuation rule is not properly applied to a fringe benefit (see, for example, paragraph (g)(11) of this section), or when a special valuation rule is not used to value a fringe benefit by a taxpayer entitled to use the rule, the fair market value of that fringe benefit may not be determined by reference to any value calculated under any special valuation rule. Under the circumstances described in the preceding sentence, the fair market value of the fringe benefit must be determined pursuant to paragraph (b) of this section.

(6) Modification of the special valuation rules. The Commissioner may, if he deems it necessary, add, delete, or modify the special valuation rules, including the valuation formulas contained herein, on a prospective basis.

(7) Special accounting period. If the employer is using the special accounting rule provided in Announcement 85-113 (1985-31 I.R.B., August 5, 1985) (relating to the reporting of and withholding on the value of noncash fringe benefits), benefits which are deemed provided in a subsequent calendar year pursuant to such rule are considered as provided in such subsequent calendar year for purposes of the special valuation rules. Thus, if a particular special valuation rule is in effect for a calendar year, it applies to benefits deemed provided during such calendar year under the special accounting rule.

(d) Automobile lease valuation rule. *(1) In general.* (i) Annual Lease Value. Under the special valuation rule of this paragraph (d), if an employer provides an employee with an automobile that is available to the employee for an entire calendar year, the value of the benefit provided is the Annual Lease Value (determined under paragraph (d)(2) of this section) of that automobile. Except as otherwise provided, for an automobile that is available to an employee for less than an entire calendar year, the value of the benefit provided is either a pro-rated Annual Lease Value or the Daily Lease Value (as defined in paragraph (d)(4) of this section), whichever is applicable. Absent any statutory exclusion relating to the employer-provided automobile (see, for example, section 132(a)(3) and § 1.132-5T (b)), the amount of the Annual Lease Value (or a pro-rated Annual Lease Value or the Daily Lease Value, as applicable) is included in the gross income of the employee.

(ii) Definition of automobile. For purposes of this paragraph (d), the term "automobile" means any four-wheeled vehicle manufactured primarily for use on public streets, roads, and highways.

(2) Calculation of Annual Lease Value. (i) In general. The Annual Lease Value of a particular automobile is calculated as follows:

(A) Determine the fair market value of the automobile as of the first date on which the automobile is made available to any employee of the employer for personal use. For an automobile first made available to any employee for personal use prior to January 1, 1985, determine the fair market value as of January 1, 1985. For rules relating to determination of the fair market value of an automobile for purposes of this paragraph (d), see paragraph (d)(5) of this section.

(B) Select the dollar range in column 1 of the Annual Lease Value Table, set forth in paragraph (d)(2)(iii) of this section, corresponding to the fair market value of the automobile. Except as otherwise provided in paragraphs (d)(2)(iv) and (v) of this section, the Annual Lease Value for each year of availability of the automobile is the corresponding amount in column 2 of the Table.

(ii) Use by employee only in 1985. If the employee, but not the employer, is using the special rule of this paragraph (d), the employee may calculate the Annual Lease Value in the same manner as described in paragraph (d)(2)(i)(A) of this section, except that the fair market value of the automobile is determined as of the first date on which the automobile is made available to the employee for personal use or, for an automobile made available to the employee for personal use prior to January 1, 1985, by determining the fair market value as of January 1, 1985. If the employer is also using the special rule of this paragraph (d), however, then the employee to whom the automobile is made available must use the special rule, if at all, by using the Annual Lease Value calculated by the employer. The rules of this paragraph (d)(2)(ii) apply only for 1985.

(iii) Annual Lease Value Table.

Automobile fair market value (1)	Annual Lease Value (2)
$0 to 999	$600
1,000 to 1,999	850
2,000 to 2,999	1,100
3,000 to 3,999	1,350
4,000 to 4,999	1,600
5,000 to 5,999	1,850
6,000 to 6,999	2,100
7,000 to 7,999	2,350
8,000 to 8,999	2,600
9,000 to 9,999	2,850
10,000 to 10,999	3,100
11,000 to 11,999	3,350
12,000 to 12,999	3,600
13,000 to 13,999	3,850
14,000 to 14,999	4,100
15,000 to 15,999	4,350
16,000 to 16,999	4,600
17,000 to 17,999	4,850
18,000 to 18,999	5,100
19,000 to 19,999	5,350
20,000 to 20,999	5,600
21,000 to 21,999	5,850

22,000 to 22,999	6,100
23,000 to 23,999	6,350
24,000 to 24,999	6,600
25,000 to 25,999	6,850
26,000 to 27,999	7,250
28,000 to 29,999	7,750
30,000 to 31,999	8,250
32,000 to 33,999	8,750
34,000 to 35,999	9,250
36,000 to 37,999	9,750
38,000 to 39,999	10,250
40,000 to 41,999	10,750
42,000 to 43,999	11,250
44,000 to 45,999	11,750
46,000 to 47,999	12,250
48,000 to 49,999	12,750
50,000 to 51,999	13,250
52,000 to 53,999	13,750
54,000 to 55,999	14,250
56,000 to 57,999	14,750
58,000 to 59,999	15,250

For vehicles having a fair market value in excess of $59,999, the Annual Lease Value is equal to: (.25 × the fair market value of the automobile) + $500.

(iv) Recalculation of Annual Lease Value. The Annual Lease Values determined under the rules of this paragraph (d) are based on a four-year lease term. Therefore, except as otherwise provided in paragraph (d)(2)(v) of this section, the Annual Lease Value calculated by applying paragraph (d)(2)(i) or (ii) of this section shall remain in effect for the period that begins with the first date the special valuation rule of paragraph (d) of this section is applied by the employer to the automobile and ends on December 31 of the fourth full calendar year following that date. The Annual Lease Value for each subsequent four-year period is calculated by determining the fair market value of the automobile as of the January 1 following the period described in the previous sentence and selecting the amount in column 2 of the Annual Lease Value Table corresponding to the appropriate dollar range in column 1 of the Table. If, however, the employer is using the special accounting rule provided in Announcement 85-113 (1985-31 I.R.B., August 5, 1985) (relating to the reporting of and withholding on the value of noncash fringe benefits), the employer may calculate the Annual Lease Value for each subsequent four-year period as of the beginning of the special accounting period that begins immediately prior to the January 1 described in the previous sentence. For example, assume that pursuant to Announcement 85-113, an employer uses the special accounting rule. Assume further that beginning on November 1, 1985, the special accounting period is November 1 to October 31 and that the employer elects to use the special valuation rule of this paragraph (d) as of January 1, 1985. The employer may recalculate the Annual Lease Value as of November 1, 1988, rather than as of January 1, 1989.

(v) Transfer of the automobile to another employee. Unless the primary purpose of the transfer is to reduce Federal taxes, if an employer transfers an automobile from one employee to another employee, the employer may recalculate the Annual Lease Value based on the fair market value of the automobile as of January 1 of the year of transfer. If, however, the employer is using the special accounting rule provided in Announcement 85-113 (1985-31 I.R. B., August 5, 1985) (relating to the reporting of and withholding on the value of noncash fringe benefits), the employer may recalculate the Annual Lease Value based on the fair market value of the automobile as of the beginning of the special accounting period in which the transfer occurs. If the employer does not recalculate the Annual Lease Value, and the employee to whom the automobile is transferred uses the special valuation rule, the employee may not recalculate the Annual Lease Value.

(3) Services included in, or excluded from, the Annual Lease Value Table. (i) Maintenance and insurance included. The Annual Lease Values contained in the Annual Lease Value Table include the fair market value of maintenance of, and insurance for, the automobile. Neither an employer nor an employee may reduce the Annual Lease Value by the fair market value of any service included in the Annual Lease Value that is not provided by the employer, such as reducing the Annual Lease Value by the fair market value of a maintenance service contract or insurance. An employer or employee may take into account the services actually provided with respect to the automobile by valuing the availability of the automobile under the general valuation rules of paragraph (b) of this section.

(ii) Fuel excluded. (A) In general. The Annual Lease Values do not include the fair market value of fuel provided by the employer, regardless of whether fuel is provided in kind or its cost is reimbursed by or charged to the employer.

(B) Valuation of fuel provided in kind. The provision of fuel in kind may be valued at fair market value based on all the facts and circumstances or, in the alternative, it may be valued at 5.5 cents per mile for all miles driven by the employee. However, the provision of fuel in kind may not be valued at 5.5 cents per mile for miles driven outside the United States, Canada, and Mexico. For purposes of this section, the United States includes the United States and its territories.

(C) Valuation of fuel where cost reimbursed by or charged to employer. The fair market value of fuel, the cost of which is reimbursed by or charged to an employer, is generally the amount of the actual reimbursement or the amount charged, provided the purchase of the fuel is at arm's length. If an employer with a fleet of at least 20 automobiles that meet the requirements of paragraph (d)(5)(v)(C) of this section reimburses employees for the cost of fuel or allows employees to charge the employer for the cost of the fuel, however, the fair market value of fuel provided to those automobiles may be determined by reference to the employer's fleet-average cents-per-mile fuel cost. The fleet-average cents-per-mile fuel cost is equal to the fleet-average per-gallon fuel cost divided by the fleet-average miles-per-gallon rate. The averages described in the preceding sentence must be determined by averaging the per-gallon fuel costs and miles-per-gallon rates of a representative sample of the automobiles in the fleet equal to the greater of ten percent of the automobiles in the fleet or 20 automobiles for a representative period, such as a two month period.

(iii) All other services excluded. The fair market value of any service not specifically identified in paragraph (d)(3)(i) of this section that is provided by the employer with respect to an automobile (such as the services of a chauffeur) must be added to the Annual Lease Value of the automobile in determining the fair market value of the benefit provided.

(4) Availability of an automobile for less than an entire calendar year. (i) Pro-rated Annual Lease Value used for continuous availability of 30 or more days. Except as otherwise provided in paragraph (d)(4)(iv) of this section, for periods of continuous availability of 30 or more days, but less than an entire calendar year, the value of the availability of

the employer-provided automobile is the pro-rated Annual Lease Value. The pro-rated Annual Lease Value is calculated by multiplying the applicable Annual Lease Value by a fraction, the numerator of which is the number of days of availability and the denominator of which is 365.

(ii) Daily Lease Value used for continuous availability of less than 30 days. Except as otherwise provided in paragraph (d)(4)(iii) of this section, for periods of continuous availability of one or more but less than 30 days, the value of the availability of the employer-provided automobile is the Daily Lease Value. The Daily Lease Value is calculated by multiplying the applicable Annual Lease Value by a fraction, the numerator of which is four times the number of days of availability and the denominator of which is 365.

(iii) Election to treat all periods as periods of at least 30 days. A pro-rated Annual Lease Value may be applied with respect to a period of continuous availability of less than 30 days, by treating the automobile as if it had been available for 30 days, if to do so would result in a lower valuation than applying the Daily Lease Value to the shorter period of actual availability.

(iv) Periods of unavailability. (A) General rule. In general, a pro-rated Annual Lease Value (as provided in paragraph (d)(4)(i) of this section) is used to value the availability of an employer-provided automobile when the automobile is available to an employee for a period of continuous availability of at least 30 days but less than the entire calendar year. Neither an employer nor an employee may use a pro-rated Annual Lease Value when the reduction of Federal taxes is the primary reason the automobile is unavailable to an employee during the calendar year.

(B) Unavailability for personal reasons of the employee. If an automobile is unavailable to an employee because of personal reasons of the employee, such as while the employee is on vacation, a pro-rated Annual Lease Value may not be used. For example, assume an automobile is available to an employee during the first five months of the year and during the last five months of the year. Assume further that the period of unavailability occurs because the employee is on vacation. The Annual Lease Value, if it is applied, must be applied with respect to the entire 12 month period. The Annual Lease Value may not be pro-rated to take into account the two-month period of unavailability.

(5) Fair market value. (i) In general. For purposes of determining the Annual Lease Value of an automobile under the Annual Lease Value Table, the fair market value of an automobile is that amount a hypothetical person would have to pay a hypothetical third party to purchase the particular automobile provided. Thus, for example, any special relationship that may exist between the employee and the employer must be disregarded. Also, the employee's subjective perception of the value of the automobile is not relevant to the determination of the automobile's fair market value. In addition, except as provided in paragraph (d)(5)(ii) of this section, the cost incurred by the employer of either purchasing or leasing the automobile is not determinative of the fair market value of the automobile.

(ii) Safe-harbor valuation rule. For purposes of calculating the Annual Lease Value of an automobile under this paragraph (d), the safe-harbor value of the automobile may be used as the fair market value of the automobile. For an automobile owned by the employer, the safe-harbor value of the automobile is the employer's cost of purchasing the automobile, provided the purchase is made at arm's length. For an automobile leased by the employer, the safe-harbor value of the automobile is the value determined under paragraph (d)(5)(iii) of this section.

(iii) Use of nationally recognized pricing guides. The fair market value of an automobile that is (A) provided to an employee prior to January 1, 1985, (B) being revalued pursuant to paragraphs (d)(2)(iv) or (v) of this section, or (C) is a leased automobile being valued pursuant to paragraph (d)(5)(ii) of this section, may be determined by using the retail value of such automobile as reported in a nationally recognized publication that regularly reports new or used automobile retail values, whichever is applicable. The values contained in (and obtained from) the publication must be reasonable with respect to the automobile being valued.

(iv) Fair market value of special equipment. (A) Certain equipment excluded. The fair market value of an automobile does not include the fair market value of any telephone or any specialized equipment that is added to or carried in the automobile if the presence of such equipment is necessitated by, and attributable to, the business needs of the employer.

(B) Use of specialized equipment outside of employer's business. The value of specialized equipment must be included, however, if the employee to whom the automobile is available uses the specialized equipment in a trade or business of the employee other than the employee's trade or business of being an employee of the employer.

(C) Equipment susceptible to personal use. The exclusion rule provided in this paragraph (d)(5)(iv) does not apply to specialized equipment susceptible to personal use.

(v) Fleet-average valuation rule. (A) In general. An employer with a fleet of 20 or more automobiles may use a fleet-average value for purposes of calculating the Annual Lease Values of the automobiles in the fleet. The fleet-average value is the average of the fair market values of each automobile in the fleet. The fair market value of each automobile in the fleet shall be determined, pursuant to the rules of paragraphs (d)(5)(i) through (iv) of this section, as of the later of January 1, 1985, or the first date on which the automobile is made available to any employee of the employer for personal use.

(B) Period for use of rule. The fleet-average valuation rule of this paragraph (d)(5)(v) may be used by an employer as of January 1 of any calendar year following the calendar year in which the employer acquires a fleet of 20 or more automobiles. The Annual Lease Value calculated for the automobiles in the fleet, based on the fleet-average value, shall remain in effect for the period that begins with the first January 1 the fleet-average valuation rule of this paragraph (d)(5)(v) is applied by the employer to the automobiles in the fleet and ends on December 31 of the subsequent calendar year. The Annual Lease Value for each subsequent two year period is calculated by determining the fleet-average value of the automobiles in the fleet as of the first January 1 of such period. An employer may cease using the fleet-average valuation rule as of any January 1. The fleet-average valuation rule does not apply as of January 1 of the year in which the number of automobiles in the employer's fleet declines to fewer than 20. If, however, the employer is using the special accounting rule provided in Announcement 85-113 (I.R.B. No. 31, August 5, 1985), the employer may apply the rules of this paragraph (d)(5)(v)(B) on the basis of the special accounting period rather than the calendar year. (This is accomplished by substituting (1) the beginning of the special accounting period that begins immediately prior to the January 1 described in this paragraph (d)(5)(v)(B) for January 1 wherever it appears in this paragraph (d)(5)(v)(B) and (2) the end of such accounting period for December 31.) The revaluation rules of paragraph (d)(2)(iv) and (v) of this section do not apply to automobiles valued under this paragraph (d)(5)(v).

(C) Limitations on use of fleet-average rule. The rule provided in this paragraph (d)(5)(v) may not be used for any automobile whose fair market value (determined pursuant to paragraphs (d)(5)(i) through (iv) of this section as of either the first date on which the automobile is made available to any employee of the employer for personal use or, if later, January 1, 1985) exceeds $16,500. In addition, the rule provided in this paragraph (d)(5)(v) may only be used for automobiles that the employer reasonably expects will regularly be used in the employer's trade or business. Infrequent use of the vehicle, such as for trips to the airport or between the employer's multiple business premises, does not constitute regular use of the vehicle in the employer's trade or business.

(D) Additional automobiles added to the fleet. If the rule provided in this paragraph (d)(5)(v) is used by an employer, it must be used for every automobile included in or added to the fleet that meets the requirements of paragraph (d)(5)(v)(C) of this section. The fleet-average value in effect at the time an automobile is added to the fleet is treated as the fair market value of the automobile for purposes of determining the Annual Lease Value of the automobile until the fleet-average value changes pursuant to paragraph (d)(5)(v)(B) of this section.

(E) Use of the fleet-average rule by employees. An employee can only use the fleet-average value if it is used by the employer. If an employer uses the fleet-average value, and the employee uses the special valuation rule of paragraph (d) of this section, the employee must use the fleet-average value.

(6) Consistency rules. (i) Use of the automobile lease valuation rule by an employer. Except as provided in paragraph (d)(5)(v)(B) of this section, an employer may adopt the automobile lease valuation rule of this paragraph (d) for an automobile only if the rule is adopted with respect to the later of the period that begins on January 1, 1987, or the first period in which the automobile is made available to an employee of the employer for personal use or, if the commuting valuation rule of paragraph (f) of this section is used when the automobile is first made available to an employee of the employer for personal use, the first period in which the commuting valuation rule is not used.

(ii) An employer must use the automobile lease valuation rule for all subsequent periods. Once the automobile lease valuation rule has been adopted for an automobile by an employer, the rule must be used by the employer for all subsequent periods in which the employer makes the automobile available to any employee, except that the employer may, for any period during which use of the automobile qualifies for the commuting valuation rule of paragraph (f) of this section, use the commuting valuation rule with respect to the automobile.

(iii) Use of the automobile lease valuation rule by an employee. Except as provided in paragraph (c)(2)(ii)(C) of this section, an employee may adopt the automobile lease valuation rule for an automobile only if the rule is adopted (A) by the employer and (B) with respect to the first period in which the automobile for which the employer (consistent with paragraph (d)(6)(i) of this section) adopted the rule is made available to that employee for personal use, or, if the commuting valuation rule of paragraph (f) of this section is used when the automobile is first made available to that employee for personal use, the first period in which the commuting valuation rule is not used.

(iv) An employee must use the automobile lease valuation rule for all subsequent periods. Once the automobile lease valuation rule has been adopted for an automobile by an employee, the rule must be used by the employee for all subsequent periods in which the automobile for which the rule is used is available to the employee, except that the employee may, for any period during which use of the automobile qualifies for use of the commuting valuation rule of paragraph (f) of this section and for which the employer uses the rule, use the commuting valuation rule with respect to the automobile.

(v) Replacement automobiles. Notwithstanding anything in this paragraph (d)(6) to the contrary, if the automobile lease valuation rule is used by an employer, or by an employer and an employee, with respect to a particular automobile, and a replacement automobile is provided to the employee for the primary purpose of reducing Federal taxes, then the employer, or the employer and the employee, using the rule must continue to use the rule with respect to the replacement automobile.

(e) Vehicle cents-per-mile valuation rule. *(1) In general.* (i) General rule. Under the vehicle cents-per-mile valuation rule of this paragraph (e), if an employer provides an employee with the use of a vehicle that (A) the employer reasonably expects will be regularly used in the employer's trade or business throughout the calendar year (or such shorter period as the vehicle may be owned or leased by the employer) or (B) satisfies the requirements of paragraph (e)(1)(ii) of this section, the value of the benefit provided in the calendar year is the standard mileage rate provided in the applicable Revenue Ruling or Revenue Procedure ("cents-per-mile rate") multiplied by the total number of miles the vehicle is driven by the employee for personal purposes. For 1985, the standard mileage rate is 21 cents per mile for the first 15,000 miles and 11 cents per mile for all miles over 15,000. See Rev. Proc. 85-49. The standard mileage rate must be applied to personal miles independent of business miles. Thus, for example, if an employee drives 20,000 personal miles and 35,000 business miles in 1985, the value of the personal use of the vehicle is $3,700 (15,000 × $.21 + 5,000 × $.11). For purposes of this section, the use of a vehicle for personal purposes is any use of the vehicle other than use in the employee's trade or business of being an employee of the employer. Infrequent use of the vehicle, such as for trips to the airport or between the employer's multiple business premises, does not constitute regular use of the vehicle in the employer's trade or business.

(ii) Mileage rule. A vehicle satisfies the requirements of this paragraph (e)(1)(ii) in a calendar year if (A) it is actually driven at least 10,000 miles in that year, and (B) use of the vehicle during the year is primarily by employees. For example, if a vehicle is used by only one employee during the year and that employee drives a vehicle at least 10,000 miles in a calendar year, such vehicle satisfies the requirements of this paragraph (e)(1)(ii) even if all miles driven by the employee are personal. The requirements of this paragraph (e)(1)(ii), however, will not be satisfied if during the year the vehicle is transferred among employees in such a way which enables an employee whose use was at a rate significantly less than 10,000 miles per year to meet the 10,000 mile threshold. Assume that an employee uses a vehicle for the first six months of the year and drives 2,000 miles, and that vehicle is then used by other employees who drive the vehicle 8,000 miles in the last six months of the year. Because the rate at which miles were driven in the first six months of the year would result in only 4,000 miles being driven in the year, and because the first employee did not use the vehicle during the last six months of the year, the requirements of this paragraph (e)(1)(ii) are not satisfied. The requirement of paragraph (e)(1)(ii)(B) of this section is deemed satisfied if employees use the vehicle on a consistent basis for commuting. If the employer does not own or lease the vehicle during a portion of the year, the 10,000 mile threshold is to be reduced proportionately to reflect the periods when the employer owned or leased the vehicle. For purposes of this paragraph (e)(1)(ii), use of the vehicle by an individual (other than the employee) whose use would be taxed to the employee is not considered use by the employee.

(iii) Limitation on use of the vehicle cents-per-mile valuation rule. The value of the use of an automobile (as defined in paragraph (d)(1)(ii) of this section) may not be determined under the vehicle cents-per-mile valuation rule of this paragraph (e) if the fair market value of the automobile (determined pursuant to paragraphs (d)(5)(i) through (iv) of this section as of the later of January 1, 1985, or the first date on which the automobile is made available to any employee of the employer for personal use) exceeds the sum of the maximum recovery deductions allowable under section 280F (a)(2) for the first three taxable years in the recovery period for an automobile first placed in service during that calendar year. For 1985, that value is $12,800.

(2) Definition of vehicle. For purposes of this paragraph (e), the term "vehicle" means any motorized wheeled vehicle manufactured primarily for use on public streets, roads, and highways. The term "vehicle" includes an automobile as defined in paragraph (d)(1)(ii) of this section.

(3) Services included in, or excluded from, the cents-per-mile rate. (i) Maintenance and insurance included. The cents-per-mile rate includes the fair market value of maintenance of, and insurance for, the vehicle. An employer may not reduce the cents-per-mile rate by the fair market value of any service included in the cents-per-mile rate but not provided by the employer. An employer or employee may take into account the services provided with respect to the automobile by valuing the availability of the automobile under the general valuation rules of paragraph (b) of this section.

(ii) Fuel provided by the employer. (A) Miles driven in the United States, Canada, and Mexico. With respect to miles driven in the United States, Canada, and Mexico, the cents-per-mile rate includes the fair market value of fuel provided by the employer. If fuel is not provided by the employer, the cents-per-mile rate may be reduced by no more than 5.5 cents or the amount specified in any applicable Revenue Ruling or Revenue Procedure. For purposes of this section, the United States includes the United States and its territories.

(B) Miles driven outside the United States, Canada, and Mexico. With respect to miles driven outside the United States, Canada, and Mexico, the fair market value of fuel provided by the employer is not reflected in the cents-per-mile rate. Accordingly, the cents-per-mile rate may be reduced but by no more than 5.5 cents or the amount specified in any applicable Revenue Ruling or Revenue Procedure. If the employer provides the fuel in kind, it must be valued based on all the facts and circumstances. If the employer reimburses the employee for the cost of fuel or allows the employee to charge the employer for the cost of fuel, the fair market value of the fuel is generally the amount of the actual reimbursement or the amount charged, provided the purchase of fuel is at arm's length.

(4) Valuation of personal use only. The vehicle cents-per-mile valuation rule of this paragraph (e) may only be used to value the miles driven for personal purposes. Thus, the employer must include an amount in an employee's income with respect to the use of a vehicle that is equal to the product of the number of personal miles driven by the employee and the appropriate cents-per-mile rate. The employer may not include in income a greater or lesser amount; for example, the employer may not include in income 100 percent (all business and personal miles) of the value of the use of the vehicle. The term "personal miles" means all miles driven by the employee except miles driven by the employee in the employee's trade or business of being an employee of the employer.

(5) Consistency rules. (i) Use of the vehicle cents-per-mile valuation rule by an employer. An employer must adopt the vehicle cents-per-mile valuation rule of this paragraph (e) for a vehicle by the later of the period that begins on January 1, 1987, or the first period in which the vehicle is used by an employee of the employer for personal use or, if the commuting valuation rule of paragraph (f) of this section is used when the vehicle is first used by an employee of the employer for personal use, the first period in which the commuting valuation rule is not used.

(ii) An employer must use the vehicle cents-per-mile valuation rule for all subsequent periods. Once the vehicle cents-per-mile valuation rule has been adopted for a vehicle by an employer, the rule must be used by the employer for all subsequent periods in which the vehicle qualifies for use of the rule, except that (A) the employer may, for any period during which use of the vehicle qualifies for the commuting valuation rule of paragraph (f) of this section, use the commuting valuation rule with respect to the vehicle, and (B) if the employer elects to use the automobile lease valuation rule of paragraph (d) of this section for a period in which the vehicle does not qualify for use of the vehicle cents-per-mile valuation rule, then the employer must comply with the requirements of paragraph (d)(6) of this section. If the vehicle fails to qualify for use of the vehicle cents-per-mile valuation rule during a subsequent period, the employer may adopt for such subsequent period and thereafter any other special valuation rule for which the vehicle then qualifies. For purposes of paragraph (d)(6) of this section, the first day on which an automobile with respect to which the vehicle cents-per-mile rule had been used fails to qualify for use of the vehicle cents-per-mile valuation rule may be deemed to be the first day on which the automobile is available to an employee of the employer for personal use.

(iii) Use of the vehicle cents-per-mile valuation rule by an employee. An employee may adopt the vehicle cents-per-mile valuation rule for a vehicle only if the rule is adopted (A) by the employer and (B) with respect to the first period in which the vehicle for which the employer (consistent with paragraph (e)(5)(i) of this section) adopted the rule is available to that employee for personal use or, if the commuting valuation rule of paragraph (f) of this section is used by both the employer and the employee when the vehicle is first used by an employee for personal use, the first period in which the commuting valuation rule is not used.

(iv) An employee must use the vehicle cents-per-mile valuation rule for all subsequent periods. Once the vehicle cents-per-mile valuation rule has been adopted for a vehicle by an employee, the rule must be used by the employee for all subsequent periods of personal use of the vehicle by the employee for which the rule is used by the employer, except that the employee may, for any period during which use of the vehicle qualifies for use of the commuting valuation rule of paragraph (f) of this section and for which such rule is used by the employer, use the commuting valuation rule with respect to the vehicle.

(v) Replacement vehicles. Notwithstanding anything in this paragraph (e)(5) to the contrary, if the vehicle cents-per-mile valuation rule is used by an employer, or by an employer and an employee, with respect to a particular vehicle, and a replacement vehicle is provided to the employee for the primary purpose of reducing Federal taxes, then the employer, or the employer and the employee, using the rule must continue to use the rule with respect to the replacement vehicle if the replacement vehicle qualifies for use of the rule.

(f) Commuting valuation rule. *(1) In general.* Under the commuting valuation rule of this paragraph (f), the value of the commuting use of an employer-provided vehicle may be determined pursuant to paragraph (f)(3) of this section if the following criteria are met by the employer and employees with respect to the vehicle:

(i) The vehicle is owned or leased by the employer and is provided to one or more employees for use in connection with the employer's trade or business and is used in the employer's trade or business;

(ii) For bona fide noncompensatory business reasons, the employer requires the employee to commute to and/or from work in the vehicle;

(iii) The employer has established a written policy under which the employee may not use the vehicle for personal purposes, other than for commuting or de minimis personal use (such as a stop for a personal errand on the way between a business delivery and the employee's home);

(iv) Except for de minimis personal use, the employee does not use the vehicle for any personal purpose other than commuting; and

(v) The employee required to use the vehicle for commuting is not a control employee of the employer (as defined in paragraphs (f)(5) and (6) of this section).

If the vehicle is a chauffeur-driven vehicle, the commuting valuation rule of this paragraph (f) may not be used to value the commuting use of any passenger who commutes in the vehicle. The rule may be used, however, to value the commuting use of the chauffeur. Personal use of a vehicle is all use of the vehicle by the employee that is not use in the employee's trade or business of being an employee of the employer.

(2) Special rules. Notwithstanding anything in paragraph (f)(1) of this section to the contrary, the following special rules apply—

(i) Written policy not required in 1985. The policy described in paragraph (f)(1)(iii) of this section prohibiting personal use need not be written with respect to the commuting use which occurs prior to January 1, 1986;

(ii) Commuting use during 1985. For commuting use that occurs after December 31, 1984, but before January 1, 1986, the restrictions of paragraph (f)(1)(v) of this section shall be applied by substituting "an employee who is an officer or a five-percent owner of the employer" in lieu of "a control employee". For purposes of determining who is a five-percent owner, any individual who owns (or is considered as owning) five or more percent of the fair market value of an entity (the "owned entity") is considered a five-percent owner of all entities that would be aggregated with the owned entity under the rules of section 414(b), (c), or (m). An employee who is an officer of an employer shall be treated as an officer of all entities treated as a single employer pursuant to section 414(b), (c), or (m). The definitions provided in paragraphs (f)(5)(i) and (f)(6) of this section may be used to define an officer; and

(iii) Control employee exception. If the vehicle in which the employee is required to commute is not an automobile as defined in paragraph (d)(1)(ii) of this section, the restrictions of paragraph (f)(1)(v) of this section do not apply.

(3) Commuting value. (i) $1.50 per one-way commute. If the requirements of this paragraph (f) are satisfied, the value of the commuting use of an employer-provided vehicle is $1.50 per one-way commute (e.g., from home to work or from work to home).

(ii) Value per employee. If there is more than one employee who commutes in the vehicle, such as in the case of an employer-sponsored car pool, the amount includible in the income of each employee is $1.50 per one-way commute. Thus, the amount includible for each round-trip commute is $3.00 per employee.

(4) Definition of vehicle. For purposes of this paragraph (f), the term "vehicle" means any motorized wheeled vehicle manufactured primarily for use on public streets, roads, and highways. The term "vehicle" includes an automobile as defined in paragraph (d)(1)(ii) of this section.

(5) Control employee defined—Non-government employer. For purposes of this paragraph (f), a control employee of a non-government employer is any employee—

(i) Who is a Board-or shareholder-appointed, confirmed, or elected officer of the employer,

(ii) Who is a director of the employer, or

(iii) Who owns a one-percent or greater equity, capital, or profits interest in the employer.

For purposes of determining who is a one-percent owner under paragraph (f)(5)(iii) of this section, any individual who owns (or is considered as owning under section 318(a) or principles similar to section 318(a) for entities other than corporations) one percent or more of the fair market value of an entity (the "owned entity") is considered a one-percent owner of all entities which would be aggregated with the owned entity under the rules of section 414(b), (c), or (m). An employee who is an officer of an employer shall be treated as an officer of all entities treated as a single employer pursuant to section 414(b), (c) or (m).

(6) Control employee defined—Government employer. For purposes of this paragraph (f), a control employee of a government employer is any—

(i) Elected official,

(ii) Federal employee who is appointed by the President and confirmed by the Senate. In the case of commissioned officers of the United States Armed Forces, an officer is any individual with the rank of brigadier general or above or the rank of rear admiral (lower half) or above; or

(iii) State or local executive officer comparable to the individuals described in paragraph (f)(6)(i) and (ii) of this section. For purposes of this paragraph (f), the term "government" includes any Federal, state, or local governmental unit, and any agency or instrumentality thereof.

(g) Non-commercial flight valuation rule. *(1) In general.* Under the non-commercial flight valuation rule of this paragraph (g), if an employee is provided with a flight on an employer-provided aircraft, the value of the flight is calculated using the aircraft valuation formula provided in paragraph (g)(5) of this section. Except as otherwise provided, for purposes of this paragraph (g), a flight provided to a person whose flight would be taxable to an employee as the recipient is referred to as provided to the employee, and a flight taken by such person is considered a flight taken by the employee.

(2) Eligible flights and eligible aircraft. The valuation rule of this paragraph (g) may be used to value flights on all employer-provided aircraft, including helicopters. The valuation rule of this paragraph (g) may be used to value international as well as domestic flights. The valuation rule of this paragraph (g) may not be used to value a flight on any commercial aircraft on which air transportation is sold to the public on a per-seat basis. For a special valuation rule relating to certain flights on commercial aircraft, see paragraph (h) of this section.

(3) Definition of a flight. (i) General rule. Except as otherwise provided in paragraph (g)(3)(iii) of this section (relating to intermediate stops), for purposes of this paragraph (g), an individual's flight is the distance (in statute miles) between the place at which the individual boards the aircraft and the place at which the individual deplanes.

(ii) Valuation of each flight. Under the valuation rule of this paragraph (g), value is determined separately for each flight. Thus, a round-trip is comprised of at least two flights. For example, an employee who takes a personal trip on an employer-provided aircraft from New York, New York to Denver, Colorado, Denver to Los Angeles, California, and Los Angeles to New York has taken three flights and must apply the aircraft valuation formula separately to each flight. The value of a flight must be determined on a passenger-by-passenger basis. For example, if an individual accompanies an employee and the flight taken by the individual would be taxed to the employee, the employee would be taxed on the special rule value of the flight by the employee and by the individual.

(iii) Intermediate stop. If the primary purpose of a landing is necessitated by weather conditions, by an emergency, for purposes of refueling or obtaining other services relating to the aircraft, or for purposes of the employer's business unrelated to the employee whose flight is being valued ("an intermediate stop"), the distance between the place at which the trip originates and the place at which the intermediate stop occurs is not considered a flight. For example, assume that an employee's trip originates in St. Louis, Missouri, on route to Seattle, Washington, but, because of weather conditions, the aircraft lands in Denver, Colorado, and the employee stays in Denver overnight. Assume further that the next day the aircraft flies to Seattle where the employee deplanes. The employee's flight is the distance between the airport in St. Louis and the airport in Seattle. Assume that a trip originates in New York, New York, with five passengers and makes an intermediate stop in Chicago, Illinois, before going on to Los Angeles, California. If one of the five passengers deplanes in Chicago, the distance of that passenger's flight would be the distance between the airport in New York and the airport in Chicago. The intermediate stop is disregarded when measuring the flights taken by each of the other passengers. Their flights would be the distance between the airport in New York and the airport in Los Angeles.

(4) Personal and non-personal flights. (i) In general. The valuation rule of this paragraph (g) applies to personal flights on employer-provided aircraft. A personal flight is one the value of which is not excludable under another section of subtitle A, such as under section 132(d) (relating to a working condition fringe). However, solely for purposes of paragraphs (g)(4)(ii) and (g)(4)(iii) of this section, references to personal flights do not include flights a portion of which would not be excludable by reason of section 274(c).

(ii) Trip primarily for employer's business. If an employee combines, in one trip, personal and business flights on an employer-provided aircraft and the employee's trip is primarily for the employer's business (see § 1.162-2(b)(2)), the employee must include in income the excess of the value of all the flights that comprise the trip over the value of the flights that would have been taken had there been no personal flights but only business flights. For example, assume that an employee flies on an employer-provided aircraft from Chicago, Illinois to Miami, Florida, for the employer's business and that from Miami the employee flies on the employer-provided aircraft to Orlando, Florida, for personal purposes and then flies back to Chicago. Assume further that the primary purpose of the trip is for the employer's business. The amount includible in income is the excess of the value of the three flights (Chicago to Miami, Miami to Orlando, and Orlando to Chicago), over the value of the flights that would have been taken had there been no personal flights but only business flights (Chicago to Miami and Miami to Chicago).

(iii) Primarily personal trip. If an employee combines, in one trip, personal and business flights on an employer-provided aircraft and the employee's trip is primarily personal (see § 1.162-2(b)(2)), the amount includible in the employee's income is the value of the personal flights that would have been taken had there been no business flights but only personal flights. For example, assume that an employee flies on an employer-provided aircraft from San Francisco, California, to Los Angeles, California, for the employer's business and that from Los Angeles the employee flies on an employer-provided aircraft to Palm Springs, California, primarily for personal reasons and then flies back to San Francisco. Assume further that the primary purpose of the trip is personal. The amount includible in the employee's income is the value of personal flights that would have been taken had there been no business flights but only personal flights (San Francisco to Palm Springs and Palm Springs to San Francisco).

(iv) Application of section 274(c). The value of employer-provided travel outside the United States away from home may not be excluded from the employee's gross income as a working condition fringe, by either the employer or the employee, to the extent not deductible by reason of section 274(c). The valuation rule of this paragraph (g) applies to that portion of the value of any flight not excludable by reason of section 274(c). Such value must be included in income in addition to the amounts determined under paragraphs (g)(4)(ii) and (g)(4)(iii) of this section.

(v) Flight by individuals who are not personal guests. If an individual who is not an employee of the employer providing the aircraft is on a flight, and the individual is not the personal guest of any employee, the flight by the individual is not taxable to any employee of the employer providing the aircraft. The rule in the preceding sentence applies where the individual is provided the flight by the employer for non-compensatory business reasons of the employer. For example, assume that G, an employee of company Y, accompanies A, an employee of company X, on company X's aircraft for the purpose of inspecting land under consideration for purchase by company X from company Y. The flight by G is not taxable to A.

(5) Aircraft valuation formula. Under the valuation rule of this paragraph (g), the value of a flight is determined by multiplying the base aircraft valuation formula for the period during which the flight was taken by the appropriate aircraft multiple (as provided in paragraph (g)(7) of this section) and then adding the applicable terminal charge. The base aircraft valuation formula (also known as the Standard Industry Fare Level formula or SIFL) in effect on June 30, 1985, is as follows: ($.1402 per mile for the first 500 miles, $.1069 per mile for miles between 501 and 1500, and $.1028 per mile for miles over 1500). The terminal charge in effect on June 30, 1985, is $25.62. The SIFL cents-per-mile rates in the formula and the terminal charge are calculated by the Department of Transportation and are revised semi-annually.

(6) SIFL formula in effect for a particular flight. For purposes of this paragraph (g), in determining the value of a particular flight during the first six months of a calendar year, the SIFL formula (and terminal charge) in effect on December 31 of the preceding year applies, and in determining the value of a particular flight during the last six months of a calendar year, the SIFL formula (and terminal charge) in effect on June 30 of that year applies. The following is the SIFL formula in effect on December 31, 1984: ($.1480 per mile for the first 500 miles, $.1128 per mile for miles between 501 and 1500, and $.1085 per mile for miles over 1500. The terminal charge in effect on December 31, 1984, is $27.05.

(7) Aircraft multiples. (i) In general. The aircraft multiples are based on the maximum certified takeoff weight of the aircraft. For purposes of applying the aircraft valuation formula described in paragraph (g)(5) of this section, the aircraft multiples are as follows:

Maximum certified takeoff weight of the aircraft	Aircraft multiple for a—	
	Control employee	Non-control employee
6,000 lbs. or less	62.5	15.6
6,001 to 10,000 lbs.	125.0	23.4
10,001 to 25,000 lbs.	300.0	31.3
25,001 lbs. or more	400.0	31.3

(ii) Flights treated as provided to a control employee. Except as provided in paragraph (g)(10) of this section, any flight provided to an individual whose flight would be taxable to a control employee (as defined in paragraph (g)(8) and (9) of this section) as the recipient shall be valued as if such flight had been provided to that control employee. For example, assume that the chief executive officer of an employer, his spouse, and his two children fly on an employer-provided aircraft for personal purposes. Assume further that the maximum certified takeoff weight of the aircraft is 12,000 lbs. The amount includible in the employee's income is 4 × (300 percent × base aircraft valuation formula) plus the applicable terminal charge.

(8) Control employee defined—Nongovernment employer. For purposes of this paragraph (g), a control employee of a non-government employer is any employee—

(i) Who is a Board- or shareholder-appointed, confirmed, or elected officer of the employer, limited to the lesser of (A) one-percent of all employees (increased to the next highest integer, if not an integer) or (B) ten employees;

(ii) Whose compensation equals or exceeds the compensation of the top one percent most highly-paid employees of the employer (increased to the next highest integer, if not an integer) limited to a maximum of 25 employees;

(iii) Who owns a ten-percent or greater equity, capital or profits interest in the employer; or

(iv) Who is a director of the employer. For purposes of this paragraph (g), any employee who is a family member (within the meaning of section 267(c)(4)) of a control employee is also a control employee. Pursuant to this paragraph (g)(8), an employee may be a control employee under more than one of the requirements listed in paragraphs (g)(8)(i) through (iv) of this section. For example, an employee may be both an officer under paragraph (g)(8)(i) of this section and a highly-paid employee under paragraph (g)(8)(ii) of this section. In this case, for purposes of the officer limitation rule of paragraph (g)(8)(i) of this section and the highly-paid employee limitation rule of paragraph (g)(8)(ii) of this section, the employee would be counted as reducing both such limitation rules. In no event shall an employee whose compensation is less than $50,000 be a control employee under paragraph (g)(8)(ii) of this section. For purposes of determining who is a ten-percent owner under paragraph (g)(8)(iii) of this section, any individual who owns (or is considered as owning under section 318(a) or principles similar to section 318(a) for entities other than corporations) ten percent or more of the fair market value of an entity (the "owned entity") is considered a ten-percent owner of all entities which would be aggregated with the owned entity under the rules of section 414(b), (c), or (m). For purposes of determining who is an officer under paragraph (g)(8)(i) of this section, notwithstanding anything in this section to the contrary, if the employer would be aggregated with other employers under the rules of section 414(b), (c), or (m), the officer definition and the limitations are applied to each separate employer rather than to the aggregated employer. If applicable, the officer limitation rule of paragraph (g)(8)(i) of this section is applied to employees in descending order of their compensation. Thus, if an employer has 11 board-appointed officers, the employee with the least compensation of those officers would not be an officer under paragraph (g)(8)(i) of this section. For purposes of this paragraph (g), the term "compensation" means the amount reported on a Form W-2 as income for the prior calendar year. Compensation includes all amounts received from all entities treated as a single employer under section 414(b), (c), or (m).

(9) Control employee defined—Government. For purposes of this paragraph (g), a control employee of a government employer is any—

(i) Elected official;

(ii) Federal employee who is appointed by the President and confirmed by the Senate. In the case of commissioned officers of the United States Armed Forces, an officer is any individual with the rank of brigadier general or above or the the rank of rear admiral (lower half) or above; or

(iii) State or local executive officer comparable to the individuals in paragraph (g)(9)(i) and (ii) of this section.

For purposes of this paragraph (g), the term "government" includes any Federal, state, or local government unit, and any agency or instrumentality thereof.

(10) Seating capacity rule. (i) In general. Where 50 percent or more of the regular passenger seating capacity of an aircraft (as used by the employer) is occupied by individuals whose flights are primarily for the employer's business (and whose flights are excludable from income under section

132(d)), the value of a flight on that aircraft by any employee who is not flying primarily for the employer's business (or who is flying primarily for the employer's business but the value of whose flight is not excludable under section 132(d) by reason of section 274(c)) is deemed to be zero. See § 1.132-5T which limits the exclusion under section 132(d) to situations where the employee receives the flight in connection with the performance of services for the employer providing the aircraft. For purposes of this paragraph (g)(10), the term "employee" includes only employees and partners of the employer providing the aircraft and does not include independent contractors and directors of the employer. For purposes of this paragraph (g)(10), the second sentence of paragraph (g)(1) of this section will not apply. Instead, a flight taken by an individual who is either treated as an employee pursuant to section 132(f)(1) or whose flight is treated as a flight taken by an employee pursuant to section 132(f)(2) is considered a flight taken by an employee. If (A) a flight is considered taken by an individual other than an employee (as defined in this paragraph (g)(10)), (B) the value of that individual's flight is not excludable under section 132(d), and (C) the seating capacity rule of this paragraph (g)(10) otherwise applies, then the value of the flight provided to such an individual is the value of a flight provided to a non-control employee (even if the individual who would be taxed on the value of such individual's flight is a control employee).

(ii) Application of 50-percent test to multiple flights. The seating capacity rule of this paragraph (g)(10) must be met both at the time the individual whose flight is being valued boards the aircraft and at the time the individual deplanes. For example, assume that employee A boards an employer-provided aircraft for personal purposes in New York, New York, and that at that time 80 percent of the regular passenger seating capacity of the aircraft is occupied by individuals whose flights are primarily for the employer's business (and whose flights are excludable from income under section 132(d)) ("the business passengers"). If the aircraft flies directly to Hartford, Connecticut where all of the passengers, including A, deplane, the requirements of the seating capacity rule of this paragraph (g)(10) have been satisfied. If instead, some of the passengers, including A, remain on the aircraft in Hartford and the aircraft continues on to Boston, Massachusetts, where they all deplane, the requirements of the seating capacity rule of this paragraph (g)(10) will not be satisfied unless at least 50 percent of the seats comprising the aircraft's regular passenger seating capacity were occupied by the business passengers at the time A deplanes in Boston.

(iii) Regular passenger seating capacity. The regular passenger seating capacity of an aircraft is the maximum number of seats that have at any time been on the aircraft (while owned or leased by the employer). Except to the extent excluded pursuant to paragraph (g)(10)(v) of this section, regular seating capacity includes all seats which may be occupied by members of the flight crew. It is irrelevant that on a particular flight, less than the maximum number of seats are available for use, because, for example, some of the seats are removed. When determining the maximum number of seats, those seats that cannot at any time be legally used during takeoff and are not any time used during takeoff are not counted.

(iv) Examples. The rules of paragraph (g)(10)(iii) of this section are illustrated by the following examples:

Example (1). Employer A and employer B order the same aircraft, except that A orders it with 10 seats and B orders it with eight seats. A always uses its aircraft as a 10-seat aircraft; B always uses its aircraft as an eight-seat aircraft. The regular passenger seating capacity of A's aircraft is 10 and of B's aircraft is eight.

Example (2). Assume the same facts as in example (1), except that whenever A's chief executive officer and spouse use the aircraft eight seats are removed. Even if substantially all of the use of the aircraft is by the chief executive officer and spouse the regular passenger seating capacity of the aircraft is 10.

Example (3). Assume the same facts as in example (1), except that whenever more than eight people want to fly in B's aircraft, two extra seats are added. Even if substantially all of the use of the aircraft occurs with eight seats, the regular passenger seating capacity of the aircraft is 10.

(v) Seats occupied by flight crew. When determining the regular passenger seating capacity of an aircraft, any seat occupied by a member of the flight crew (whether or not such individual is an employee of the employer providing the aircraft) shall not be counted, unless the purpose of the flight by such individual is not primarily to serve as a member of the flight crew. If the seat occupied by a member of the flight crew is not counted as a passenger seat pursuant to the previous sentence, such member of the flight crew is disregarded in applying the 50 percent test described in the first sentence of paragraph (g)(10)(i) of this section. For example, assume that, prior to application of this paragraph (g)(10)(v), the regular passenger seating capacity of an aircraft is two seats. Assume further that an employee pilots the aircraft and that the employee's flight is not primarily for the employer's business. If the employee's spouse occupies the other seat for personal purposes, the seating capacity rule is not met and the value of both flights must be included in the employee's income. If, however, the employee's flight were primarily for the employer's business (unrelated to serving as a member of the flight crew), then the seating capacity rule is met and the value of the flight for the employee's spouse is deemed to be zero. If the employee's flight were primarily to serve as a member of the flight crew, then the seating capacity rule is not met and the value of a flight by any passenger for primarily personal reasons is not deemed to be zero.

(11) Erroneous use of the non-commercial flight valuation rule. (i) In general. If the non-commercial flight valuation rule of this paragraph (g) is used by an employer or a control employee, as the case may be, on a return as originally filed, on the grounds that either the control employee is not in fact a control employee, or that the aircraft is within a specific weight classification, and either position is subsequently determined to be erroneous, the valuation rule of this paragraph (g) (including paragraph (g)(13) of this section) is not available to value the flight taken by that control employee by the person or persons taking the erroneous position. With respect to the weight classifications, the previous sentence does not apply if the position taken is that the weight of the aircraft is greater than it is subsequently determined to be. If, with respect to a flight by a control employee, the seating capacity rule of paragraph (g)(10) of this section is used by an employer or the control employee, as the case may be, on a return as originally filed, and it is subsequently determined that the requirements of paragraph (g)(10) of this section were not met, the valuation rule of this paragraph (g) (including paragraph (g)(13) of this section) is not available to value the flight taken by that control employee by the person or persons taking the erroneous position.

(ii) Value of flight excluded as a working condition fringe. If either an employer or an employee, on a return as originally filed, excludes from the employee's income or wages the value of a flight on the grounds that the flight was excludable as a working condition fringe under section 132, and that position is subsequently determined to be erroneous, the valuation rule of this paragraph (g) (including paragraph (g)(13) of this section) is not available to value the flight taken by that employee by the person or persons taking the erroneous position.

(12) Consistency rules. (i) Use by the employer. Except as otherwise provided in paragraphs (g)(11) and (g)(13)(iv) of this section, if the non-commercial flight valuation rule of this paragraph (g) is used by an employer to value flights provided in a calendar year, the rule must be used to value all flights provided in the calendar year.

(ii) Use by the employee. Except as otherwise provided in paragraphs (g)(11) and (g)(13)(iv) of this section, if the non-commercial flight valuation rule of this paragraph (g) is used by an employee to value a flight taken in a calendar year, the rule must be used to value all flights taken in the calendar year.

(13) Transitional valuation rule. (i) In general. If the value of a flight determined under this paragraph (g)(13) is lower than the value of the flight otherwise determined under paragraph (g) of this section, the value of the flight is the lower amount. The transitional valuation rule of this paragraph (g)(13) is available only for flights provided after December 31, 1984, and before January 1, 1986.

(ii) Transitional valuation rule aircraft multiples. The appropriate aircraft multiples under the transitional valuation rule are as follows:

(A) 125 percent of the base aircraft valuation formula, plus the applicable terminal charge, for any flight by any employee who is not a key employee (as defined in paragraph (g)(13)(iii) of this section).

(B) 125 percent of the base aircraft valuation formula, plus the applicable terminal charge, for a flight by a key employee if there is a primary business purpose for the trip by the aircraft. For purposes of this paragraph (g)(13)(ii)(B), entertaining an employee or other individual is not a business purpose.

(C) 600 percent of the base aircraft valuation formula, plus the applicable terminal charge, for a flight by a key employee if there is no primary business purpose for the trip by the aircraft. Where there is no business purpose for the trip by the aircraft, the alternative valuation rule may not be used to value a flight by a key employee. For purposes of this section, compensating an employee is not a business purpose.

(iii) Key employee defined. A "key employee" is any employee who is a five-percent owner or an officer of the employer, or who, with respect to a particular trip by the aircraft, controls the use of the aircraft. For purposes of determining who is a five-percent owner, any individual who owns (or is considered as owning) five or more percent of the fair market value of an entity (the "owned entity") is considered a five-percent owner of all entities that would be aggregated with the owned entity under the rules of section 414(b), (c), or (m).

(iv) Erroneous use of transitional valuation rule. If the transitional valuation rule is used by an employer or a key employee, as the case may be, on a return as originally filed, on the grounds that—

(A) The key employee is not in fact a key employee,

(B) An aircraft trip had a primary business purpose, or

(C) An aircraft trip had some business purpose, and such position is subsequently determined to be erroneous, neither the transitional valuation rule nor the non-commercial flight valuation rule of this paragraph (g) is available to value such flight taken by that key employee by the person or persons taking the erroneous position.

(h) Commercial flight valuation rule. *(1) In general.* Under the commercial flight valuation rule of this paragraph (h), the value of a space-available flight (as defined in paragraph (h)(2) of this section) on a commercial aircraft is 25 percent of the actual carrier's highest unrestricted coach fare in effect for the particular flight taken.

(2) Space-available flight. The commercial flight valuation rule of this paragraph (h) is available to value a space-available flight. The term "space-available flight" means a flight on a commercial aircraft (i) for which the airline (the actual carrier) incurs no substantial additional cost (including forgone revenue) determined without regard to any amount paid for the flight and (ii) which is subject to the same types of restrictions customarily associated with flying on an employee "standby" or "space-available" basis. A flight may be a space-available flight even if the airline that is the actual carrier is not the employer of the employee.

(3) Commercial aircraft. If the actual carrier does not offer, in the ordinary course of its business, air transportation to customers on a per-seat basis, the commercial flight valuation rule of this paragraph (h) is not available. Thus, if, in the ordinary course of its line of business, the employer only offers air transportation to customers on a charter basis, the commercial flight valuation rule of this paragraph (h) may not be used to value a space-available flight on the employer's aircraft. Similarly, if, in the ordinary course of its line of business, an employer only offers air transportation to customers for the transport of cargo, the commercial flight valuation rule of this paragraph (h) may not be used to value a space-available flight on the employer's aircraft.

(4) Timing of inclusion. The date that the flight is taken is the relevant date for purposes of applying section 61(a)(1) and this section to a space-available flight on a commercial aircraft. The date of purchase or issuance of a pass or ticket is not relevant. Thus, this section applies to a flight taken on or after January 1, 1985, regardless of the date on which the pass or ticket for the flight was purchased or issued.

(5) Consistency rules. (i) Use by employer. If the commercial flight valuation rule of this paragraph (h) is used by an employer to value flights provided in a calendar year, the rule must be used to value all flights provided in the calendar year.

(ii) Use by employee. If the commercial flight valuation rule of this paragraph (h) is used by an employee to value a flight taken in a calendar year, the rule must be used to value all flights taken by such employee in the calendar year.

(i) [Reserved]

(j) Valuation of meals provided at an employer-operated eating facility for employees. *(1) In general.* The valuation rule of this paragraph (j) may be used to value a meal provided at an employer-operated eating facility for employees (as defined in § 1.132-7T). For rules relating to an exclusion for the value of meals provided at an employer-operated eating facility for employees, see § 1.132-7T.

(2) Valuation formula. (i) In general. The value of all meals provided at an employer-operated eating facility for employees during a calendar year is 150 percent of the direct operating costs of the eating facility ("total meal value"). For purposes of this paragraph (j), the definition of direct operating costs provided in § 1.132-7T applies. The taxable value of meals provided at an eating facility may be determined in two ways. The "individual meal subsidy" may be treated as the taxable value of a meal provided at the eating facility (see paragraph (j)(2)(ii) of this section). Alternatively, the employer may allocate the "total meal subsidy" among employees (see paragraph (j)(2)(iii) of this section).

(ii) "Individual meal subsidy" defined. The "individual meal subsidy" is determined by multiplying the price charged for a particular meal by a fraction, the numerator of which is the total meal value and the denominator of which is the gross receipts of the eating facility, and then subtracting the amount paid for the meal. The taxable value of meals provided to a particular employee during a calendar year, therefore, is the sum of the individual meal subsidies provided to the employee during the calendar year.

(iii) Allocation of "total meal subsidy." Instead of using the individual meal value method, the employer may allocate the "total meal subsidy" (total meal value less the gross receipts of the facility) among employees in any manner reasonable under the circumstances.

T.D. 8004, 1/2/85, amend T.D. 8009, 2/15/85, T.D. 8061, 11/1/85, T.D. 8063, 12/18/85, T.D. 8256, 7/5/89, T.D. 8457, 12/29/92.

§ 1.61-3 Gross income derived from business.

(a) In general. In a manufacturing, merchandising, or mining business, "gross income" means the total sales, less the cost of goods sold, plus any income from investments and from incidental or outside operations or sources. Gross income is determined without subtraction of depletion allowances based on a percentage of income to the extent that it exceeds cost depletion which may be required to be included in the amount of inventoriable costs as provided in § 1.471-11 and without subtraction of selling expenses, losses or other items not ordinarily used in computing costs of goods sold or amounts which are of a type for which a deduction would be disallowed under section 162(c), (f), or (g) in the case of a business expense. The cost of goods sold should be determined in accordance with the method of accounting consistently used by the taxpayer. Thus, for example, an amount cannot be taken into account in the computation of cost of goods sold any earlier than the taxable year in which economic performance occurs with respect to the amount (see § 1.446-1(c)(1)(ii)).

(b) State contracts. The profit from a contract with a State or political subdivision thereof must be included in gross income. If warrants are issued by a city, town, or other political subdivision of a State, and are accepted by the contractor in payment for public work done, the fair market value of such warrants should be returned as income. If, upon conversion of the warrants into cash, the contractor does not receive and cannot recover the full value of the warrants so returned, he may deduct any loss sustained from his gross income for the year in which the warrants are so converted. If, however, he realizes more than the value of the warrants so returned, he must include the excess in his gross income for the year in which realized.

T.D. 6272, 11/25/57, amend T.D. 7207, 10/3/72, T.D. 7285, 9/14/73, T.D. 8408, 4/9/92.

§ 1.61-4 Gross income of farmers.

Caution: The Treasury has not yet amended Reg § 1.61-4 to reflect changes made by P.L. 110-246.

(a) Farmers using the cash method of accounting. A farmer using the cash receipts and disbursements method of accounting shall include in his gross income for the taxable year—

(1) The amount of cash and the value of merchandise or other property received during the taxable year from the sale of livestock and produce which he raised,

(2) The profits from the sale of any livestock or other items which were purchased,

(3) All amounts received from breeding fees, fees from rent of teams, machinery, or land, and other incidental farm income,

(4) All subsidy and conservation payments received which must be considered as income, and

(5) Gross income from all other sources.

The profit from the sale of livestock or other items which were purchased is to be ascertained by deducting the cost from the sales price in the year in which the sale occurs, except that in the case of the sale of purchased animals held for draft, breeding, or dairy purposes, the profits shall be the amount of any excess of the sales price over the amount representing the difference between the cost and the depreciation allowed or allowable (determined in accordance with the rules applicable under section 1016(a) and the regulations thereunder). However, see section 162 and the regulations thereunder with respect to the computation of taxable income on other than the crop method where the cost of seeds or young plants purchased for further development and cultivation prior to sale is involved. Crop shares (whether or not considered rent under State law) shall be included in gross income as of the year in which the crop shares are reduced to money or the equivalent of money. See section 263A for rules regarding costs that are required to be capitalized.

(b) Farmers using an accrual method of accounting. A farmer using an accrual method of accounting must use inventories to determine his gross income. His gross income on an accrual method is determined by adding the total of the items described in subparagraphs (1) through (5) of this paragraph and subtracting therefrom the total of the items described in subparagraphs (6) and (7) of this paragraph. These items are as follows:

(1) The sales price of all livestock and other products held for sale and sold during the year;

(2) The inventory value of livestock and products on hand and not sold at the end of the year;

(3) All miscellaneous items of income. such as breeding fees, fees from the rent of teams, machinery, or land, or other incidental farm income;

(4) Any subsidy or conservation payments which must be considered as income;

(5) Gross income from all other sources;

(6) The inventory value of the livestock and products on hand and not sold at the beginning of the year; and

(7) The cost of any livestock or products purchased during the year (except livestock held for draft, dairy, or breeding purposes, unless included in inventory).

All livestock raised or purchased for sale shall be added in the inventory at their proper valuation determined in accordance with the method authorized and adopted for the purpose. Livestock acquired for draft, breeding, or dairy purposes and not for sale may be included in the inventory (see subparagraphs (2), (6), and (7) of this paragraph) instead of being treated as capital assets subject to depreciation, provided such practice is followed consistently from year to year by the taxpayer. When any livestock included in an inventory are sold, their cost must not be taken as an additional deduction in computing taxable income, because such deduction is reflected in the inventory. See the regulations under section 471. See section 263A for rules regarding costs that are required to be capitalized. Crop shares (whether or not considered rent under State law) shall be included in gross income as of the year in which the crop shares are reduced to money or the equivalent of money.

(c) Special rules for certain receipts. In the case of the sale of machinery, farm equipment, or any other property (except stock in trade of the taxpayer, or property of a kind which would properly be included in the inventory of the taxpayer if on hand at the close of the taxable year, or property held by the taxpayer primarily for sale to customers in the ordinary course of his trade or business), any excess of the proceeds of the sale over the adjusted basis of such property shall be included in the taxpayer's gross income for the taxable year in which such sale is made. See, however, section 453 and the regulations thereunder for special rules relating to certain installment sales. If farm produce is exchanged for merchandise, groceries, or the like, the market value of the article received in exchange is to be included in gross income. Proceeds of insurance, such as hail or fire insurance on growing crops, should be included in gross income to the extent of the amount received in cash or its equivalent for the crop injured or destroyed. See section 451(d) for special rule relating to election to include crop insurance proceeds in income for taxable year following taxable year of destruction. For taxable years beginning after July 12, 1972, where a farmer is engaged in producing crops and the process of gathering and disposing of such crops is not completed within the taxable year in which such crops are planted, the income therefrom may, with the consent of the Commissioner (see section 446 and the regulations thereunder), be computed upon the crop method. For taxable years beginning on or before July 12, 1972, where a farmer is engaged in producing crops which take more than a year from the time of planting to the time of gathering and disposing, the income therefrom may, with the consent of the Commissioner (see section 446 and the regulations thereunder), be computed upon the crop method. In any case in which the crop method is used, the entire cost of producing the crop must be taken as a deduction for the year in which the gross income from the crop is realized, and not earlier.

(d) Definition of "farm". As used in this section, the term "farm" embraces the farm in the ordinarily accepted sense, and includes stock, dairy, poultry, fruit, and truck farms; also plantations, ranches, and all land used for farming operations. All individuals, partnerships, or corporations that cultivate, operate, or manage farms for gain or profit, either as owners or tenants, are designated as farmers. For more detailed rules with respect to the determination of whether or not an individual is engaged in farming, see § 1.175-3. For rules applicable to persons cultivating or operating a farm for recreation or pleasure, see sections 162 and 165, and the regulations thereunder.

(e) Cross references. *(1)* For election to include Commodity Credit Corporation loans as income, see section 77 and regulations thereunder.

(2) For definition of gross income derived from farming for purposes of limiting deductibility of soil and water conservation expenditures, see section 175 and regulations thereunder.

(3) For definition of gross income from farming in connection with declarations of estimated income tax, see section 6073 and regulations thereunder.

T.D. 6272, 11/25/57, amend T.D. 7198, 7/12/72, T.D. 8729, 8/21/97.

---

§ 1.61-5 Allocations by cooperative associations; per-unit retain certificates— tax treatment as to cooperatives and patrons.

(a) In general. Amounts allocated on the basis of the business done with or for a patron by a cooperative association, whether or not entitled to tax treatment under section 522, in cash, merchandise, capital stock, revolving fund certificates, retain certificates, certificates of indebtedness, letters of advice or in some other manner disclosing to the patron the dollar amount allocated, shall be included in the computation of the gross income of such patron for the taxable year in which received to the extent prescribed in paragraph (b) of this section, regardless of whether the allocation is deemed, for the purpose of section 522, to be made at the close of a preceding taxable year of the cooperative association. The determination of the extent of taxability of such amounts is in no way dependent upon the method of accounting employed by the patron or upon the method, cash, accrual, or otherwise, upon which the taxable income of such patron is computed.

(b) Extent of taxability. *(1)* Amounts allocated to a patron on a patronage basis by a cooperative association with respect to products marketed for such patron, or with respect to supplies, equipment, or services, the cost of which was deductible by the patron under section 162 or section 212, shall be included in the computation of the gross income of such patron, as ordinary income, to the following extent:

(i) If the allocation is in cash, the amount of cash received.

(ii) If the allocation is in merchandise, the amount of the fair market value of such merchandise at the time of receipt by the patron.

(iii) If the allocation is in the form of revolving fund certificates, retain certificates, certificates of indebtedness, letters of advice, or similar documents, the amount of the fair market value of such document at the time of its receipt by the patron. For purposes of this subdivision, any document containing an unconditional promise to pay a fixed sum of money on demand or at a fixed or determinable time shall be considered to have a fair market value at the time of its receipt by the patron, unless it is clearly established to the contrary. However, for purposes of this subdivision, any document which is payable only in the discretion of the cooperative association, or which is otherwise subject to conditions beyond the control of the patron, shall be considered not to have any fair market value at the time of its receipt by the patron, unless it is clearly established to the contrary.

(iv) If the allocation is in the form of capital stock, the amount of the fair market value, if any, of such capital stock at the time of its receipt by the patron.

(2) If any allocation to which subparagraph (1) of this paragraph applies is received in the form of a document of the type described in subparagraph (1)(iii) or (iv) of this paragraph and is redeemed in full or in part or is otherwise dis-

posed of, there shall be included in the computation of the gross income of the patron, as ordinary income, in the year of redemption or other disposition, the excess of the amount realized on the redemption or other disposition over the amount previously included in the computation of gross income under such subparagraph.

(3) (i) Amounts which are allocated on a patronage basis by a cooperative association with respect to supplies, equipment, or services, the cost of which was not deductible by the patron under section 162 or section 212, are not includible in the computation of the gross income of such patron. However, in the case of such amounts which are allocated with respect to capital assets (as defined in section 1221) or property used in the trade or business within the meaning of section 1231, such amounts shall, to the extent set forth in subparagraph (1) of this paragraph, be taken into account by such patron in determining the cost of the property to which the allocation relates. Notwithstanding the preceding sentence, to the extent that such amounts are in excess of the unrecovered cost of such property, and to the extent that such amounts relate to such property which the patron no longer owns, they shall be included in the computation of the gross income of such patron.

(ii) If any patronage dividend is allocated to the patron in the form of a document of the type described in subparagraph (1)(iii) or (iv) of this paragraph, and if such allocation is with respect to capital assets (as defined in section 1221) or property used in the trade or business within the meaning of section 1231, any amount realized on the redemption or other disposition of such document which is in excess of the amount which was taken into account upon the receipt of the document by the patron shall be taken into account by such patron in the year of redemption or other disposition as an adjustment to basis or as an inclusion in the computation of gross income, as the case may be.

(iii) Any adjustment to basis in respect of an amount to which subdivision (i) or (ii) of this subparagraph applies shall be made as of the first day of the taxable year in which such amount is received.

(iv) The application of the provisions of this subparagraph may be illustrated by the following examples:

Example (1). On July 1, 1959, P, a patron of a cooperative association, purchases a tractor for use in his farming business from such association for $2,200. The tractor has an estimated useful life of five years and an estimated salvage value of $200. P files his income tax returns on a calendar year basis and claims depreciation on the tractor for the year 1959 of $200 pursuant to his use of the straight-line method at the rate of $400 per year. On July 1, 1960, the cooperative association allocates to P with respect to his purchase of the tractor a dividend of $300 in cash. P will reduce his depreciation allowance with respect to the tractor for 1960 (and subsequent taxable years) to $333.33, determined as follows:

Cost of tractor, July 1, 1959		$2,200
Less:		
Depreciation for 1959 (6 mos.)	$200	
Adjustment as of Jan. 1, 1960, for cash patronage dividend	300	
Salvage value	200	
		700
Basis for depreciation for the remaining 4½ years of estimated life		1,500
Basis for depreciation divided by the 4½ years of remaining life		333.33

Example (2). Assume the same facts as in example (1), except that on July 1, 1960, the cooperative association allocates a dividend to P with respect to his purchase of the tractor in the form of a revolving fund certificate having a face amount of $300. The certificate is redeemable in cash at the discretion of the directors of the association and is subject to diminution by any future losses of the association, and has no fair market value when received by P. Since the certificate had no fair market value when received by P, no amount with respect to such certificate was taken into account by him in the year 1960. In 1965, P receives $300 cash from the association in full redemption of the certificate. Prior to 1965, he had recovered through depreciation $2,000 of the cost of the tractor, leaving an unrecovered cost of $200 (the salvage value). For the year 1965, the redemption proceeds of $300 are applied against the unrecovered cost of $200, reducing the basis to zero, and the balance of the redemption proceeds, $100, is includible in the computation of P's gross income.

Example (3). Assume the same facts as in example (2), except that the certificate is redeemed in full on July 1, 1962. The full $300 received on redemption of the certificate will be applied against the unrecovered cost of the tractor as of January 1, 1962, computed as follows:

Cost of tractor, July 1, 1959		$2,200
Less:		
Depreciation for 1959 (6 mos.)	$200	
Depreciation for 1960	400	
Depreciation for 1961	400	
		1,000
Unrecovered cost on Jan. 1, 1962		1,200
Adjustment as of Jan. 1, 1962, for proceeds of the redemption of the revolving fund certificate		300
Unrecovered cost on Jan. 1, 1962, after adjustment		$ 900
Less: Salvage value		200
Basis for depreciation on Jan. 1, 1962		700
If P uses the tractor in his business until June 30, 1964, he would be entitled to the following depreciation allowances with respect to the the tractor:		
For 1962	$280	
For 1963	280	
For 1964 (6 mos.)	140	700
Balance to be depreciated		0

Example (4). Assume the same facts as in example (3), except that P sells the tractor in 1961. The entire $300 received in 1962 in redemption of the revolving fund certificate is includible in the computation of P's gross income for the year 1962.

(c) Special rule. If, for any taxable year ending before December 3, 1959, a taxpayer treated any patronage dividend received in the form of a document described in paragraph (b)(1)(iii) or (iv) of this section in accordance with the regulations then applicable (whether such dividend is subject to paragraph (b)(1) or (3) of this section), such taxpayer is not required to change the treatment of such patronage dividends for any such prior taxable year. On the other hand, the taxpayer may, if he so desires, amend his income tax returns to treat the receipt of such patronage dividend in accordance with the provisions of this section, but no provision in this paragraph shall be construed as extending the period of limitations within which a claim for credit or refund may be filed under section 6511.

(d) Per-unit retain certificates; tax treatment of cooperative associations; distribution and reinvestment alternative. *(1)* (i) In the case of a taxable year to which this paragraph applies to a cooperative association, such association shall, in computing the amount paid or returned to a patron with respect to products marketed for such patron, take into account the stated dollar amount of any per-unit retain certificate (as defined in paragraph (g) of this section)—

(a) Which is issued during the payment period for such year (as defined in subparagraph (3) of this paragraph) with respect to such products.

(b) With respect to which the patron is a qualifying patron (as defined in subparagraph (2) of this paragraph), and

(c) Which clearly states the fact that the patron has agreed to treat the stated dollar amount thereof as representing a cash distribution to him which he has reinvested in the cooperative association.

(ii) No amount shall be taken into account by a cooperative association by reason of the issuance of a per-unit retain certificate to a patron who was not a qualifying patron with respect to such certificate. However, any amount paid in redemption of a per-unit retain certificate which was issued to a patron who was not a qualifying patron with respect to such certificate shall be taken into account by the cooperative in the year of redemption, as an amount paid or returned to such patron with respect to products marketed for him. This subdivision shall apply only to per-unit retain certificates issued with respect to taxable years of the cooperative association to which this paragraph applied to the association (that is, taxable years with respect to which per-unit retain certificates were issued to one or more patrons who are qualifying patrons.

(2) (i) A patron shall be considered to be a "qualifying patron" with respect to a per-unit retain certificate if there is in effect an agreement between the cooperative association and such patron which clearly provides that such patron agrees to treat the stated dollar amounts of all per-unit retain certificates issued to him by the association as representing cash distributions which he has constructively received and which he has, of his own choice, reinvested in the cooperative association. Such an agreement may be included in a by-law of the cooperative which is adopted prior to the time the products to which the per-unit retain certificates relate are marketed. However, except where there is in effect a "written agreement" described in subdivision (ii) of this subparagraph, a patron shall not be considered to be a "qualifying patron" with respect to a per-unit retain certificate if it has been established by a determination of the Tax Court of the United States, or any other court of competent jurisdiction, which has become final, that the stated dollar amount of such certificate, or of a similar certificate issued under similar circumstances to such patron or any other patron by the cooperative association, is not required to be included (as ordinary income) in the gross income of such patron, or such other patron, for the taxable year of the patron in which received.

(ii) The "written agreement" referred to in subdivision (i) of this subparagraph is an agreement in writing, signed by the patron, on file with the cooperative association, and revocable as provided in this subdivision. Unless such an agreement specifically provides to the contrary, it shall be effective for per-unit retain certificates issued with respect to the taxable year of the cooperative association in which the agreement is received by the association, and unless revoked, for per-unit retain certificates issued with respect to all subsequent taxable years. A "written agreement" must be revocable by the patron at any time after the close of the taxable year in which it is made. To be effective, a revocation must be in writing, signed by the patron, and furnished to the cooperative association. A revocation shall be effective only for per-unit retain certificates issued with respect to taxable years of the cooperative association following the taxable year in which it is furnished to the association. Notwithstanding the preceding sentence, a revocation shall not be effective for per-unit retain certificates issued with respect to products marketed for the patron under a pooling arrangement in which such patron participated before such revocation. The following is an example of an agreement which would meet the requirements of this subparagraph:

I agree that, for purposes of determining the amount I have received from this cooperative in payment for my goods, I shall treat the face amount of any per-unit retain certificates issued to me on and after .... as representing a cash distribution which I have constructively received and which I have reinvested in the cooperative.

....
(Signed)

(3) For purposes of this paragraph and paragraph (e) of this section, the payment period for any taxable year of the cooperative is the period beginning with the first day of such taxable year and ending with the 15th day of the 9th month following the close of such year.

(4) This paragraph shall apply to any taxable year of a cooperative association if, with respect to such taxable year, the association has issued per-unit retain certificates to one or more of its patrons who are qualifying patrons with respect to such certificates within the meaning of subparagraph (2) of this paragraph.

(e) Tax treatment of cooperative association; taxable years for which paragraph (d) does not apply. *(1)* In the case of a taxable year to which paragraph (d) of this section does not apply to a cooperative association, such association shall, in computing the amount paid or returned to a patron with respect to products marketed for such patron, take into account the fair market value (at the time of issue) of any per-unit retain certificates which are issued by the association with respect to such products during the payment period for such taxable year.

(2) An amount paid in redemption of a per-unit retain certificate issued with respect to a taxable year of the cooperative association for which paragraph (d) of this section did not apply to the association, shall, to the extent such amount exceeds the fair market value of the certificate at the time of its issue, be taken into account by the association in the year of redemption, as an amount paid or returned to a patron with respect to products marketed for such patron.

(3) For purposes of this paragraph and paragraph (f)(2) of this section, any per-unit retain certificate containing an unconditional promise to pay a fixed sum of money on demand or at a fixed or determinable time shall be considered to have a fair market value at the time of its issue, unless it is clearly established to the contrary. On the other hand, any per-unit retain certificate (other than capital stock) which is redeemable only in the discretion of the cooperative association, or which is otherwise subject to conditions beyond the control of the patron, shall be considered not to have any fair market value at the time of its issue, unless it is clearly established to the contrary.

(f) Tax treatment of patron. *(1)* The following rules apply for purposes of computing the amount includible in gross income with respect to a per-unit retain certificate which was issued to a patron by a cooperative association with respect to a taxable year of such association for which paragraph (d) of this section applies.

(i) If the patron is a qualifying patron with respect to such certificate (within the meaning of paragraph (d)(2) of this section), he shall, in accordance with his agreement, include (as ordinary income) the stated dollar amount of the certificate in gross income for his taxable year in which the certificate is received by him.

(ii) If the patron is not a qualifying patron with respect to such certificate, no amount is includible in gross income on the receipt of the certificate; however, any gain on the redemption, sale, or other disposition of such certificate shall, to the extent of the stated dollar amount thereof, be considered as gain from the sale or exchange of property which is not a capital asset.

(2) The amount of the fair market value of a per-unit retain certificate which is issued to a patron by a cooperative association with respect to a taxable year of the association for which paragraph (d) of this section does not apply shall be included, as ordinary income, in the gross income of the patron for the taxable year in which the certificate is received. Any gain on the redemption, sale, or other disposition of such a per-unit retain certificate shall, to the extent its stated dollar amount exceeds its fair market value at the time of issue, be treated as gain on the redemption, sale, or other disposition of property which is not a capital asset.

(g) "Per-unit retain certificate" defined. For purposes of paragraphs (d), (e), and (f), of this section, the term "per-unit retain certificate" means any capital stock, revolving fund certificate, retain certificate, certificate of indebtedness, letter of advice, or other written notice—

(1) Which is issued to a patron with respect to products marketed for such patron;

(2) Which discloses to the patron the stated dollar amount allocated to him on the books of the cooperative association; and

(3) The stated dollar amount of which is fixed without reference to net earnings.

(h) Effective date. This section shall not apply to any amount the tax treatment of which is prescribed in section 1385 and § 1.1385-1. Paragraphs (d), (e), and (f) of this section shall apply to per-unit retain certificates as defined in paragraph (g) of this section issued by a cooperative association during taxable years of the association beginning after April 30, 1966, with respect to products marketed for patrons during such years.

T.D. 6272, 11/25/57, amend T.D. 6428, 12/2/59, T.D. 6643, 4/1/63, T.D. 6855, 10/14/65.

---

§ 1.61-6 Gains derived from dealings in property.

Caution: The Treasury has not yet amended Reg § 1.61-6 to reflect changes made by P.L. 98-369, P.L. 88-272.

(a) In general. Gain realized on the sale or exchange of property is included in gross income, unless excluded by law. For this purpose property includes tangible items, such as a building, and intangible items, such as good will. Generally, the gain is the excess of the amount realized over the unrecovered cost or other basis for the property sold or exchanged. The specific rules for computing the amount of gain or loss are contained in section 1001 and the regulations thereunder. When a part of a larger property is sold, the cost or other basis of the entire property shall be equitably apportioned among the several parts, and the gain realized or loss sustained on the part of the entire property sold is the difference between the selling price and the cost or other basis allocated to such part. The sale of each part is treated as a separate transaction and gain or loss shall be computed separately on each part. Thus, gain or loss shall be determined at the time of sale of each part and not deferred until the entire property has been disposed of. This rule may be illustrated by the following examples:

Example (1). A, a dealer in real estate, acquires a 10-acre tract for $10,000, which he divides into 20 lots. The $10,000 cost must be equitably apportioned among the lots so that on the sale of each A can determine his taxable gain or deductible loss.

Example (2). B purchases for $25,000 property consisting of a used car lot and adjoining filling station. At the time, the fair market value of the filling station is $15,000 and the fair market value of the used car lot is $10,000. Five years later B sells the filling station for $20,000 at a time when $2,000 has been properly allowed as depreciation thereon. B's gain on this sale is $7,000, since $7,000 is the amount by which the selling price of the filling station exceeds the portion of the cost equitably allocable to the filling station at the time of purchase reduced by the depreciation properly allowed.

(b) Nontaxable exchanges. Certain realized gains or losses on the sale or exchange of property are not "recognized", that is, are not included in or deducted from gross income at the time the transaction occurs. Gain or loss from such sales or exchanges is generally recognized at some later time. Examples of such sales or exchanges are the following:

(1) Certain formations, reorganizations, and liquidations of corporations, see sections 331, 333, 337, 351, 354, 355, and 361;

(2) Certain formations and distributions of partnerships, see sections 721 and 731;

(3) Exchange of certain property held for productive use or investment for property of like kind, see section 1031;

(4) A corporation's exchange of its stock for property, see section 1032;

(5) Certain involuntary conversions of property if replaced, see section 1033;

(6) Sale or exchange of residence if replaced, see section 1034;

(7) Certain exchanges of insurance policies and annuity contracts, see section 1035; and

(8) Certain exchanges of stock for stock in the same corporation, see section 1036.

(c) Character of recognized gain. Under subchapter P, chapter 1 of the Code, relating to capital gains and losses, certain gains derived from dealings in property are treated specially, and under certain circumstances the maximum rate of tax on such gains is 25 percent, as provided in section 1201. Generally, the property subject to this treatment is a "capital asset", or treated as a "capital asset". For definition of such assets, see sections 1221 and 1231, and the regulations thereunder. For some of the rules either granting or denying this special treatment, see the following sections and the regulations thereunder:

(1) Transactions between partner and partnership, section 707;

(2) Sale or exchange of property used in the trade or business and involuntary conversions, section 1231;

(3) Payment of bonds and other evidences of indebtedness, section 1232;

(4) Gains and losses from short sales, section 1233;

(5) Options to buy or sell, section 1234;

(6) Sale or exchange of patents, section 1235;

(7) Securities sold by dealers in securities, section 1236;

(8) Real property subdivided for sale, section 1237;

(9) Amortization in excess of depreciation, section 1238;

(10) Gain from sale of certain property between spouses or between an individual and a controlled corporation, section 1239;

(11) Taxability to employee of termination payments, section 1240.

T.D. 6272, 11/25/57.

PAR. 2. Paragraph (c)(3) of § 1.61-6 is revised to read as follows:

Proposed § 1.61-6 Gains derived from dealings in property. [*For Preamble, see ¶ 151,065*]

• ***Caution:*** Prop reg § 1.482-2 was finalized by T.D. 8204, 5/20/88. Prop regs §§ 1.163-7, 1.446-2, 1.483-1 through -5, 1.1001-1, 1.1012-1, 1.1271 through -3, 1.1272-1, 1.1273-1, 1.1273-2, 1.1274-1 throught -7, 1.1274A-1, 1.1275-1 through -3, and 1.1275-5 were withdrawn by the Treasury on 12/22/92, 57 Fed. Reg. 67050. Prop reg § 1.1275-4 was superseded by the Treasury on 12/16/94, Fed. Reg. 59, 64884, which was finalized by T.D. 8674, 6/11/96.

* * * * *

(c) Character of recognized gain. * * *

(3) Amounts received on retirement or sale or exchange of debt instruments, section 1271;

* * * * *

§ 1.61-7 Interest.

(a) In general. As a general rule, interest received by or credited to the taxpayer constitutes gross income and is fully taxable. Interest income includes interest on savings or other bank deposits; interest on coupon bonds; interest on an open account, a promissory note, a mortgage, or a corporate bond or debenture; the interest portion of a condemnation award; usurious interest (unless by State law it is automatically converted to a payment on the principal); interest on legacies; interest on life insurance proceeds held under an agreement to pay interest thereon; and interest on refunds of Federal taxes. For rules determining the taxable year in which interest, including interest accrued or constructively received, is included in gross income, see section 451 and the regulations thereunder. For the inclusion of interest in income for the purpose of the retirement income credit, see section 37 and the regulations thereunder. For credit of tax withheld at source on interest on taxfree covenant bonds, see section 32 and the regulations thereunder. For rules relating to interest on certain deferred payments, see section 483 and the regulations thereunder.

(b) Interest on Government obligations. *(1) Wholly tax-exempt interest.* Interest upon the obligations of a State, Territory, or a possession of the United States, or any political subdivision of any of the foregoing, or of the District of Columbia, is wholly exempt from tax. Interest on certain United States obligations issued before March 1, 1941, is exempt from tax to the extent provided in the acts of Congress authorizing the various issues. See section 103 and the regulations thereunder.

(2) Partially tax-exempt interest. Interest earned on certain United States obligations is partly tax exempt and partly taxable. For example, the interest on United States Treasury bonds issued before March 1, 1941, to the extent that the principal of such bonds exceeds $5,000, is exempt from normal tax but is subject to surtax. See sections 35 and 103, and the regulations thereunder.

(3) Fully taxable interest. In general, interest on United States obligations issued on or after March 1, 1941, and obligations issued by any agency or instrumentality of the United States after that date, is fully taxable; but see section 103 and the regulations thereunder. A taxpayer using the cash receipts and disbursements method of accounting who owns United States savings bonds issued at a discount has an election as to when he will report the interest; see section 454 and the regulations thereunder.

(c) Obligations bought at a discount; bonds bought when interest defaulted or accrued. When notes, bonds, or other certificates of indebtedness are issued by a corporation or the Government at a discount and are later redeemed by the debtor at the face amount, the original discount is interest, except as otherwise provided by law. See also paragraph (b) of this section for the rules relating to Government bonds. If a taxpayer purchases bonds when interest has been defaulted or when the interest has accrued but has not been paid, any interest which is in arrears but has accrued at the time of purchase is not income and is not taxable as interest if subsequently paid. Such payments are returns of capital which reduce the remaining cost basis. Interest which accrues after the date of purchase, however, is taxable interest income for the year in which received or accrued (depending on the method of accounting used by the taxpayer).

(d) Bonds sold between interest dates; amounts received in excess of original issue discount; interest on life insurance. When bonds are sold between interest dates, part of the sales price represents interest accrued to the date of the sale and must be reported as interest income. Amounts received in excess of the original issue discount upon the retirement or sale of a bond or other evidence of indebtedness may under some circumstances constitute capital gain instead of ordinary income. See section 1232 and the regulations thereunder. Interest payments on amounts payable as employees' death benefits (whether or not section 101(b) applies thereto) and on the proceeds of life insurance policies payable by reason of the insured's death constitute gross income under some circumstances. See section 101 and the regulations thereunder for details. Where accrued interest on unwithdrawn insurance policy dividends is credited annually and is subject to withdrawal annually by the taxpayer, such interest credits constitute gross income to such taxpayer as of the year of credit. However, if under the terms of the insurance policy the interest on unwithdrawn policy dividends is subject to withdrawal only on the anniversary date of the policy (or some other date specified therein), then such interest shall constitute gross income to the taxpayer for the taxable year in which such anniversary date (or other specified date) falls.

T.D. 6272, 11/25/57, amend T.D. 6723, 4/20/64, T.D. 6873, 1/24/66.

PAR. 3. In paragraph (d) of § 1.61-7, the third sentence is amended by removing the phrase "section 1232" and adding in its place the phrase "section 1271".

Proposed § 1.61-7 [Amended] [*For Preamble, see ¶ 151,065*]

• ***Caution:*** Prop reg § 1.482-2 was finalized by T.D. 8204, 5/20/88. Prop regs §§ 1.163-7, 1.446-2, 1.483-1 through -5, 1.1001-1, 1.1012-1, 1.1271 through -3, 1.1272-1, 1.1273-1, 1.1273-2, 1.1274-1 throught -7, 1.1274A-1, 1.1275-1 through -3, and 1.1275-5 were withdrawn by the Treasury on 12/22/92, 57 Fed. Reg. 67050. Prop reg § 1.1275-4 was superseded by the Treasury on 12/16/94, Fed. Reg. 59, 64884, which was finalized by T.D. 8674, 6/11/96.

§ 1.61-8 Rents and royalties.

(a) In general. Gross income includes rentals received or accrued for the occupancy of real estate or the use of personal property. For the inclusion of rents in income for the purpose of the retirement income credit, see section 37 and the regulations thereunder. Gross income includes royalties. Royalties may be received from books, stories, plays, copyrights, trademarks, formulas, patents, and from the exploitation of natural resources, such as coal, gas, oil, copper, or timber. Payments received as a result of the transfer of patent rights may under some circumstances constitute capital gain instead of ordinary income. See section 1235 and the regulations thereunder. For special rules for certain income from natural resources, see subchapter I (section 611 and following), chapter 1 of the Code, and the regulations thereunder.

(b) Advance rentals; cancellation payments. Except as provided in section 467 and the regulations thereunder, and except as otherwise provided by the Commissioner in published guidance (see § 601.601(d)(2) of this chapter), gross income includes advance rentals, which must be included in income for the year of receipt regardless of the period covered or the method of accounting employed by the taxpayer. An amount received by a lessor from a lessee for cancelling a lease constitutes gross income for the year in which it is received, since it is essentially a substitute for rental payments. As to amounts received by a lessee for the cancellation of a lease, see section 1241 and the regulations thereunder.

(c) Expenditures by lessee. As a general rule, if a lessee pays any of the expenses of his lessor such payments are additional rental income of the lessor. If a lessee places improvements on real estate which constitute, in whole or in part, a substitute for rent, such improvements constitute rental income to the lessor. Whether or not improvements made by a lessee result in rental income to the lessor in a particular case depends upon the intention of the parties, which may be indicated either by the terms of the lease or by the surrounding circumstances. For the exclusion from gross income of income (other than rent) derived by a lessor of real property on the termination of a lease, representing the value of such property attributable to buildings erected or other improvements made by a lessee, see section 109 and the regulations thereunder. For the exclusion from gross income of a lessor corporation of certain of its income taxes on rental income paid by a lessee corporation under a lease entered into before January 1, 1954, see section 110 and the regulations thereunder.

T.D. 6272, 11/25/57, amend T.D. 8820, 5/17/99, T.D. 9135, 7/7/2004.

PAR. 2. In § 1.61-8, the first sentence of paragraph (b) is revised to read as follows:

Proposed § 1.61-8 Rents and royalties. [*For Preamble, see ¶ 152,347*]

* * * * *

(b) * * * Except as provided in section 467 and the regulations thereunder, and except as otherwise provided by the Commissioner in published guidance (see § 601.601(d)(2) of this chapter), gross income includes advance rentals, which must be included in income for the year of receipt regardless of the period covered or the method of accounting employed by the taxpayer. * * *

* * * * *

§ 1.61-9 Dividends.

(a) In general. Except as otherwise specifically provided, dividends are included in gross income under sections 61 and 301. For the principal rules with respect to dividends includible in gross income, see section 316 and the regulations thereunder. As to distributions made or deemed to be made by regulated investment companies, see sections 851 through 855, and the regulations thereunder. As to distributions made by real estate investment trusts, see sections 856 through 858, and the regulations thereunder. See section 116 for the exclusion from gross income of $100 ($50 for dividends received in taxable years beginning before January 1, 1964) of dividends received by an individual, except those from certain corporations. Furthermore, dividends may give rise to a credit against tax under section 34, relating to dividends received by individuals (for dividends received on or before December 31, 1964), and under section 37, relating to retirement income.

(b) Dividends in kind; stock dividends; stock redemptions. Gross income includes dividends in property other than cash, as well as cash dividends. For amounts to be included in gross income when distributions of property are made, see section 301 and the regulations thereunder. A distribution of stock, or rights to acquire stock, in the corporation making the distribution is not a dividend except under the circumstances described in section 305(b). However, the term "dividend" includes a distribution of stock, or rights to acquire stock, in a corporation other than the corporation making the distribution. For determining when distributions in complete liquidation shall be treated as dividends, see section 333 and the regulations thereunder. For rules determining when amounts received in exchanges under section 354 or exchanges and distributions under section 355 shall be treated as dividends, see section 356 and the regulations thereunder.

(c) Dividends on stock sold. When stock is sold, and a dividend is both declared and paid after the sale, such dividend is not gross income to the seller. When stock is sold after the declaration of a dividend and after the date as of which the seller becomes entitled to the dividend, the dividend ordinarily is income to the seller. When stock is sold between the time of declaration and the time of payment of the dividend, and the sale takes place at such time that the purchaser becomes entitled to the dividend, the dividend ordinarily is income to him. The fact that the purchaser may have included the amount of the dividend in his purchase price in contemplation of receiving the dividend does not exempt him from tax. Nor can the purchaser deduct the added amount he advanced to the seller in anticipation of the dividend. That added amount is merely part of the purchase price of the stock. In some cases, however, the purchaser may be considered to be the recipient of the dividend even though he has not received the legal title to the stock itself and does not himself receive the dividend. For example, if the seller retains the legal title to the stock as trustee solely for the purpose of securing the payment of the purchase price, with the understanding that he is to apply the dividends received from time to time in reduction of the purchase price, the dividends are considered to be income to the purchaser.

T.D. 6272, 11/25/57, amend T.D. 6598, 4/25/62, T.D. 6777, 12/15/64.

§ 1.61-10 Alimony and separate maintenance payments; annuities; income from life insurance and endowment contracts.

(a) In general. Alimony and separate maintenance payments, annuities, and income from life insurance and endowment contracts in general constitute gross income, unless excluded by law. Annuities paid by religious, charitable, and educational corporations are generally taxable to the same extent as other annuities. An annuity charged upon devised land is taxable to the donee-annuitant to the extent that it becomes payable out of the rents or other income of the land, whether or not it is a charge upon the income of the land.

(b) Cross references. For the detailed rules relating to—

(1) Alimony and separate maintenance payments, see section 71 and the regulations thereunder;

(2) Annuities, certain proceeds of endowment and life insurance contracts, see section 72 and the regulations thereunder;

(3) Life insurance proceeds paid by reason of death of insured, employees' death benefits, see section 101 and the regulations thereunder;

(4) Annuities paid by employees' trusts, see section 402 and the regulations thereunder;

(5) Annuities purchased for employee by employer, see section 403 and the regulations thereunder.

T.D. 6272, 11/25/57.

§ 1.61-11 Pensions.

(a) In general. Pensions and retirement allowances paid either by the Government or by private persons constitute gross income unless excluded by law. Usually, where the taxpayer did not contribute to the cost of a pension and was not taxable on his employer's contributions, the full amount of the pension is to be included in his gross income. But see sections 72, 402, and 403, and the regulations thereunder. When amounts are received from other types of pensions, a portion of the payment may be excluded from gross income. Under some circumstances, amounts distributed from a pension plan in excess of the employee's contributions may constitute long-term capital gain, rather than ordinary income.

(b) Cross references. For the inclusion of pensions in income for the purpose of the retirement income credit, see section 37 and the regulations thereunder. Detailed rules concerning the extent to which pensions and retirement allowances are to be included in or excluded from gross income are contained in other sections of the Code and the regulations thereunder. Amounts received as pensions or annuities under the Social Security Act (42 U.S.C. ch. 7) or the Railroad Retirement Act (45 U.S.C. ch. 9) are excluded from gross income. For other partial and total exclusions from gross income, see the following:

(1) Annuities in general, section 72 and the regulations thereunder;

(2) Employees, annuities, sections 402 and 403 and the regulations thereunder;

(3) References to other acts of Congress exempting veterans' pensions and railroad retirement annuities and pensions, section 122.

T.D. 6272, 11/25/57, amend T.D. 6856, 10/19/65.

§ 1.61-12 Income from discharge of indebtedness.

(a) In general. The discharge of indebtedness, in whole or in part, may result in the realization of income. If, for example, an individual performs services for a creditor, who in consideration thereof cancels the debt, the debtor realizes income in the amount of the debt as compensation for his services. A taxpayer may realize income by the payment or purchase of his obligations at less than their face value. In general, if a shareholder in a corporation which is indebted to him gratuitously forgives the debt, the transaction amounts to a contribution to the capital of the corporation to the extent of the principal of the debt.

(b) Proceedings under Bankruptcy Act. *(1)* Income is not realized by a taxpayer by virtue of the discharge, under section 14 of the Bankruptcy Act (11 U.S.C. 32), of his indebtedness as the result of an adjudication in bankruptcy, or by virtue of an agreement among his creditors not consummated under any provision of the Bankruptcy Act, if immediately thereafter the taxpayer's liabilities exceed the value of his assets. Furthermore, unless one of the principal purposes of seeking a confirmation under the Bankruptcy Act is the avoidance of income tax, income is not realized by a taxpayer in the case of a cancellation or reduction of his indebtedness under—

(i) A plan of corporate reorganization confirmed under Chapter X of the Bankruptcy Act (11 U.S.C., ch. 10);

(ii) An "arrangement" or a "real property arrangement" confirmed under Chapter XI or XII, respectively, of the Bankruptcy Act (11 U.S.C., ch. 11, 12); or

(iii) A "wage earner's plan" confirmed under Chapter XIII of the Bankruptcy Act (11 U.S.C., ch. 13).

(2) For adjustment of basis of certain property in the case of cancellation or reduction of indebtedness resulting from a proceeding under the Bankruptcy Act, see the regulations under section 1016.

(c) Issuance and repurchase of debt instruments. *(1) Issuance.* An issuer does not realize gain or loss upon the issuance of a debt instrument. For rules relating to an issuer's interest deduction for a debt instrument issued with bond issuance premium, see § 1.163-13.

(2) Repurchase. (i) In general. An issuer does not realize gain or loss upon the repurchase of a debt instrument. However, if a debt instrument provides for payments denominated in, or determined by reference to, a nonfunctional currency, an issuer may realize a currency gain or loss upon the repurchase of the instrument. See section 988 and the regulations thereunder. For purposes of this paragraph (c)(2), the

term *repurchase* includes the retirement of a debt instrument, the conversion of a debt instrument into stock of the issuer, and the exchange (including an exchange under section 1001) of a newly issued debt instrument for an existing debt instrument.

(ii) Repurchase at a discount. An issuer realizes income from the discharge of indebtedness upon the repurchase of a debt instrument for an amount less than its adjusted issue price (within the meaning of § 1.1275-1(b)). The amount of discharge of indebtedness income is equal to the excess of the adjusted issue price over the repurchase price. See section 108 and the regulations thereunder for additional rules relating to income from discharge of indebtedness. For example, to determine the repurchase price of a debt instrument that is repurchased through the issuance of a new debt instrument, see section 108(e)(10).

(iii) Repurchase at a premium. An issuer may be entitled to a repurchase premium deduction upon the repurchase of a debt instrument for an amount greater than its adjusted issue price (within the meaning of § 1.1275-1(b)). See § 1.163-7(c) for the treatment of repurchase premium.

(iv) Effective date. This paragraph (c)(2) applies to debt instruments repurchased on or after March 2, 1998.

(d) Cross references. For exclusion from gross income of—

(1) Income from discharge of indebtedness in certain cases, see sections 108 and 1017, and regulations thereunder;

(2) Forgiveness of Government payments to encourage exploration, development, and mining for defense purposes, see section 621 and regulations thereunder.

(e) Cross reference. For rules relating to the treatment of liabilities on the sale or other disposition of encumbered property, see § 1.1001-2.

T.D. 6272, 11/25/57, amend T.D. 6653, 5/22/63, T.D. 6984, 12/23/68, T.D. 7741, 12/11/80, T.D. 8746, 12/30/97.

§ 1.61-13 Distributive share of partnership gross income; income in respect of a decedent; income from an interest in an estate or trust.

(a) In general. A partner's distributive share of partnership gross income (under section 702(c)) constitutes gross income to him. Income in respect of a decedent (under section 691) constitutes gross income to the recipient. Income from an interest in an estate or trust constitutes gross income under the detailed rules of part I (section 641 and following), subchapter J, chapter 1 of the Code. In many cases, these sections also determine who is to include in his gross income the income from an estate or trust.

(b) Creation of sinking fund by corporation. If a corporation, for the sole purpose of securing the payment of its bonds or other indebtedness, places property in trust or sets aside certain amounts in a sinking fund under the control of a trustee who may be authorized to invest and reinvest such sums from time to time, the property or fund thus set aside by the corporation and held by the trustee is an asset of the corporation, and any gain arising therefrom is income of the corporation and shall be included as such in its gross income.

T.D. 6272, 11/25/57.

§ 1.61-14 Miscellaneous items of gross income.

(a) In general. In addition to the items enumerated in section 61(a), there are many other kinds of gross income. For example, punitive damages such as treble damages under the antitrust laws and exemplary damages for fraud are gross income. Another person's payment of the taxpayer's income taxes constitutes gross income to the taxpayer unless excluded by law. Illegal gains constitute gross income. Treasure trove, to the extent of its value in United States currency, constitutes gross income for the taxable year in which it is reduced to undisputed possession.

(b) Cross references. *(1)* Prizes and awards, see section 74 and regulations thereunder;

(2) Damages for personal injury or sickness, see section 104 and the regulations thereunder;

(3) Income taxes paid by lessee corporation, see section 110 and regulations thereunder;

(4) Scholarships and fellowship grants, see section 117 and regulations thereunder;

(5) Miscellaneous exemptions under other acts of Congress, see section 122;

(6) Tax-free covenant bonds, see section 1451 and regulations thereunder.

(7) Notional principal contracts, see § 1.446-3.

T.D. 6272, 11/25/57, amend T.D. 6856, 10/19/65, T.D. 8491, 10/8/93.

§ 1.61-15 Options received as payment of income.

(a) In general. Except as otherwise provided in § 1.61-2(d)(6)(i) (relating to certain restricted property transferred after June 30, 1969), if any person receives an option in payment of an amount constituting compensation of such person (or any other person), such option is subject to the rules contained in § 1.421-6 for purposes of determining when income is realized in connection with such option and the amount of such income. In this regard, the rules of § 1.421-6 apply to an option received in payment of an amount constituting compensation regardless of the form of the transaction. Thus, the rules of § 1.421-6 apply to an option transferred for less than its fair market value in a transaction taking the form of a sale or exchange if the difference between the amount paid for the option and its fair market value at the time of transfer is the payment of an amount constituting compensation of the transferee or any other person. This section, for example, makes the rules of § 1.421-6 applicable to options granted in whole or partial payment for services of an independent contractor. If an amount of money or property is paid for an option to which this paragraph applies, then the amount paid shall be part of the basis of such option.

(b) Options to which paragraph (a) does not apply. *(1)* Paragraph (a) of this section does not apply to:

(i) An option which is subject to the rules contained in section 421; and

(ii) An option which is not granted as the payment of an amount constituting compensation, such as an option which is acquired solely as an investment (including an option which is part of an investment unit described in paragraph (b) of § 1.1232-3). For rules relating to the taxation of options described in this subdivision, see section 1234 and the regulations thereunder.

(2) If a person acquires an option which is not subject to the rules contained in section 421, and if such option has a

readily ascertainable fair market value, such person may establish that such option was not acquired as payment of an amount constituting compensation by showing that the amount of money or its equivalent paid for the option equaled the readily ascertainable fair market value of the option. If a person acquires an option which is not subject to the rules contained in section 421, and if such option does not have a readily ascertainable fair market value, then to establish that such option was not acquired as payment of an amount constituting compensation, such person must show that, from an examination of all the surrounding circumstances, there was no reason for the option to have been granted as the payment of an amount constituting compensation. For example, such person must show that neither rendered nor was obligated to render substantial services in consideration for the granting of the option. In determining whether an option, such as an option acquired in connection with an obligation as part of an investment unit, has been granted as compensation for services, the ordinary services performed by an investor in his own self-interest in connection with his investing activities will not be treated as the consideration for the grant of the option. For example, if a small business investment company takes an active part in the management of its debtor small business company, the rendering of such management services will not be treated as the consideration for the granting of the option, provided such services are rendered for an independent consideration, or are merely protective of the small business investment company's investment in the borrower. See paragraph (c) of § 1.421-6 for the meaning of the term "readily ascertainable fair market value."

(c) Statement required in connection with certain options. *(1)* Any person acquiring any option to purchase securities (other than an option described in subparagraph (2) of this paragraph) shall attach a statement to his income tax return for the taxable year in which the option was acquired. For the definition of the term "securities", see section 165(g)(2).

(2) The statement otherwise required by subparagraph (1) of this paragraph shall not be required with respect to the following options:

(i) Options subject to the rules contained in section 305(a) or section 421;

(ii) Options acquired as part of an investment until consisting of an option and a debenture, note, or other similar obligation—

(a) If such unit is acquired as part of a public offering and the amount of money or its equivalent paid for such unit is not less than the public offering price, or

(b) If such unit is actively traded on an established market and the amount of money or its equivalent paid for such unit is not less than the price paid for such unit in contemporaneous purchases of such unit by persons independent of both the seller and the taxpayer;

(iii) Options acquired as part of a public offering, if the amount of money or its equivalent paid for such options is not less than the public offering price; and

(iv) Options which are actively traded on an established market and which are acquired for money or its equivalent at a price not less than the price paid for such options in contemporaneous purchases of such options by persons independent of both the seller and the taxpayer.

(3) The statement required by subparagraph (1) of this paragraph shall contain the following information:

(i) Name and address of the taxpayer;

(ii) Description of the securities subject to the option (including number of shares of stock);

(iii) Period during which the option is exercisable;

(iv) Whether the option had a readily ascertainable fair market value at date of grant; and

(v) Whether the option is subject to paragraph (a) of this section.

(4) If the statement required by subparagraph (1) of this paragraph indicates either that the option is not subject to paragraph (a) of this section, or that the option is subject to paragraph (a) of this section but that such option had a readily ascertainable fair market value at date of grant, then such statement shall contain the following additional information:

(i) Option price;

(ii) Value at date of grant of securities subject to the option;

(iii) Restrictions (if any) on exercise or transfer of option;

(iv) Restrictions (if any) on transfer of securities subject to the option;

(v) Value of the option (if readily ascertainable);

(vi) How value of option was determined;

(vii) Amount of money (or its equivalent) paid for the option;

(viii) Person from whom the option was acquired;

(ix) A concise description of the circumstances surrounding the acquisition of the option and any other factors relied upon by the taxpayer to establish that the option is not subject to paragraph (a) of this section, or, if the option is treated by the taxpayer as subject to paragraph (a) of this section, that the option had a readily ascertainable fair market value at date of grant.

(d) Effective date. This section shall apply to options granted after July 11, 1963, other than options required to be granted pursuant to the terms of a written contract entered into on or before such date.

T.D. 6696, 12/11/63, amend T.D. 6706, 3/2/64, T.D. 6984, 12/23/68, T.D. 7554, 7/21/78.

Proposed amendments to the regulations. —26 CFR Part 1 is amended by adding a new § 1.61-16 immediately after § 1.61-15. The new section reads as follows:

Proposed § 1.61-16 Amounts payments of which are deferred under certain compensation reduction plans or arrangements. [*For Preamble, see ¶ 150,305*]

Caution: The Treasury has not yet amended Reg § 1.61-16 to reflect changes made by P.L. 98-369, P.L. 95-600.

(a) In general. Except as otherwise provided in paragraph (b) of this section, if under a plan or arrangement (other than a plan or arrangement described in sections 401(a), 403(a), or (b), or 405(a)) payment of an amount of a taxpayer's basic or regular compensation fixed by contract, statute, or otherwise (or supplements to such compensation, such as bonuses, or increases in such compensation) is, at the taxpayer's individual option, deferred to a taxable year later than that in which such amount would have been payable but for his exercise of such option, the amount shall be treated as received by the taxpayer in such earlier taxable year. For purposes of this paragraph, it is immaterial that the taxpayer's rights in the amount payment of which is so deferred become forfeitable by reason of his exercise of the option to defer payment.

(b) Exception. Paragraph (a) of this section shall not apply to an amount payment of which is deferred as described in paragraph (a) under a plan or arrangement in existence on February 3, 1978 if such amount would have been payable, but for the taxpayer's exercise of the option, at any time prior to [date 30 days following publication of this section as a Treasury decision]. For purposes of this paragraph, a plan or arrangement in existence on February 3, 1978 which is significantly amended after such date will be treated as a new plan as of the date of such amendment. Examples of significant amendments would be extension of coverage to an additional class of taxpayers or an increase in the maximum percentage of compensation subject to the taxpayer's option.

§ 1.61-21 Taxation of fringe benefits.

Caution: The Treasury has not yet amended Reg § 1.61-21 to reflect changes made by P.L. 104-188.

(a) Fringe benefits. *(1) In general.* Section 61(a)(1) provides that, except as otherwise provided in subtitle A of the Internal Revenue Code of 1986, gross income includes compensation for services, including fees, commissions, fringe benefits, and similar items. For an outline of the regulations under this section relating to fringe benefits, see paragraph (a)(7) of this section. Examples of fringe benefits include: an employer-provided automobile, a flight on an employer-provided aircraft, an employer-provided free or discounted commercial airline flight, an employer-provided vacation, an employer-provided discount on property or services, an employer-provided membership in a country club or other social club, and an employer-provided ticket to an entertainment or sporting event.

(2) Fringe benefits excluded from income. To the extent that a particular fringe benefit is specifically excluded from gross income pursuant to another section of subtitle A of the Internal Revenue Code of 1986, that section shall govern the treatment of that fringe benefit. Thus, if the requirements of the governing section are satisfied, the fringe benefits may be excludable from gross income. Examples of excludable fringe benefits include qualified tuition reductions provided to an employee (section 117(d)); meals or lodging furnished to an employee for the convenience of the employer (section 119); benefits provided under a dependent care assistance program (section 129); and no-additional-cost services, qualified employee discounts, working condition fringes, and de minimis fringes (section 132). Similarly, the value of the use by an employee of an employer-provided vehicle or a flight provided to an employee on an employer-provided aircraft may be excludable from income under section 105 (because, for example, the transportation is provided for medical reasons) if and to the extent that the requirements of that section are satisfied. Section 134 excludes from gross income "qualified military benefits." An example of a benefit that is not a qualified military benefit is the personal use of an employer-provided vehicle. The fact that another section of subtitle A of the Internal Revenue Code addresses the taxation of a particular fringe benefit will not preclude section 61 and the regulations thereunder from applying, to the extent that they are not inconsistent with such other section. For example, many fringe benefits specifically addressed in other sections of subtitle A of the Internal Revenue Code are excluded from gross income only to the extent that they do not exceed specific dollar or percentage limits, or only if certain other requirements are met. If the limits are exceeded or the requirements are not met, some or all of the fringe benefit may be includible in gross income pursuant to section 61. See paragraph (b)(3) of this section.

(3) Compensation for services. A fringe benefit provided in connection with the performance of services shall be considered to have been provided as compensation for such services. Refraining from the performance of services (such as pursuant to a covenant not to compete) is deemed to be the performance of services for purposes of this section.

(4) Person to whom fringe benefit is taxable. (i) In general. A taxable fringe benefit is included in the income of the person performing the services in connection with which the fringe benefit is furnished. Thus, a fringe benefit may be taxable to a person even though that person did not actually receive the fringe benefit. If a fringe benefit is furnished to someone other than the service provider such benefit is considered in this section as furnished to the service provider, and use by the other person is considered use by the service provider. For example, the provision of an automobile by an employer to an employee's spouse in connection with the performance of services by the employee is taxable to the employee. The automobile is considered available to the employee and use by the employee's spouse is considered use by the employee.

(ii) All persons to whom benefits are taxable referred to as employees. The person to whom a fringe benefit is taxable need not be an employee of the provider of the fringe benefit, but may be, for example, a partner, director, or an independent contractor. For convenience, the term "employee" includes any person performing services in connection with which a fringe benefit is furnished, unless otherwise specifically provided in this section.

(5) Provider of a fringe benefit referred to as an employer. The "provider" of a fringe benefit is that person for whom the services are performed, regardless of whether that person actually provides the fringe benefit to the recipient. The provider of a fringe benefit need not be the employer of the recipient of the fringe benefit, but may be, for example, a client or customer of the employer or of an independent contractor. For convenience, the term "employer" includes any provider of a fringe benefit in connection with payment for the performance of services, unless otherwise specifically provided in this section.

(6) Effective date. Except as otherwise provided, this section is effective as of January 1, 1989 with respect to fringe benefits provided after December 31, 1988. See § 1.61-2T for rules in effect from January 1, 1985, to December 31, 1988.

(7) Outline of this section. The following is an outline of the regulations in this section relating to fringe benefits:

§ 1.61-21(a) Fringe benefits.

(1) In general.

(2) Fringe benefits excluded from income.

(3) Compensation for services.

(4) Person to whom fringe benefit is taxable.

(5) Provider of a fringe benefit referred to as an employer.

(6) Effective date.

(7) Outline of this section.

§ 1.61-21(b) Valuation of fringe benefits

(1) In general.

(2) Fair market value.

(3) Exclusion from income based on cost.

(4) Fair market value of the availability of an employer-provided vehicle.

(5) Fair market value of chauffeur services.

(6) Fair market value of a flight on an employer-provided piloted aircraft.

(7) Fair market value of the use of an employer-provided aircraft for which the employer does not furnish a pilot.

§ 1.61-21(c) Special valuation rules.

(1) In general.

(2) Use of the special valuation rules.

(3) Additional rules for using special valuation.

(4) Application of section 414 to employers.

(5) Valuation formulae contained in the special valuation rules.

(6) Modification of the special valuation rules.

(7) Special accounting rule.

§ 1.61-21(d) Automobile lease valuation rule.

(1) In general.

(2) Calculation of Annual Lease Value.

(3) Services included in, or excluded from, the Annual Lease Value Table.

(4) Availability of an automobile for less than an entire calendar year.

(5) Fair market value.

(6) Special rules for continuous availability of certain automobiles.

(7) Consistency rules.

§ 1.61-21(e) Vehicle cents-per-mile valuation rule.

(1) In general.

(2) Definition of vehicle.

(3) Services included in, or excluded from, the cents-per-mile rate.

(4) Valuation of personal use only.

(5) Consistency rules.

§ 1.61-21(f) Commuting valuation rule.

(1) In general.

(2) Special rules.

(3) Commuting value.

(4) Definition of vehicle.

(5) Control employee defined—Non-government employer.

(6) Control employee defined—Government employer.

(7) "Compensation" defined.

§ 1.61-21(g) Non-commercial flight valuation rule.

(1) In general.

(2) Eligible flights and eligible aircraft.

(3) Definition of a flight.

(4) Personal and non-personal flights.

(5) Aircraft valuation formula.

(6) Discretion to provide new formula.

(7) Aircraft multiples.

(8) Control employee defined—Non-government employer.

(9) Control employee defined—Government employer.

(10) "Compensation" defined.

(11) Treatment of former employees.

(12) Seating capacity rule.

(13) Erroneous use of the non-commercial flight valuation rule.

(14) Consistency rules.

§ 1.61-21(h) Commercial flight valuation rule.

(1) In general.

(2) Space-available flight.

(3) Commercial aircraft.

(4) Timing of inclusion.

(5) Consistency rules.

§ 1.61-21(i) [Reserved]

§ 1.61-21(j) Valuation of meals provided at an employer-operated eating facility for employees.

(1) In general.

(2) Valuation formula.

§ 1.61-21(k) Commuting valuation rule for certain employees

(1) In general.

(2) Trip-by-trip basis.

(3) Commuting value.

(4) Definition of employer-provided transportation.

(5) Unsafe conditions.

(6) Qualified employee defined.

(7) Examples.

(8) Effective date.

(b) Valuation of fringe benefits. *(1) In general.* An employee must include in gross income the amount by which the fair market value of the fringe benefit exceeds the sum of—

(i) The amount, if any, paid for the benefit by or on behalf of the recipient, and

(ii) The amount, if any, specifically excluded from gross income by some other section of subtitle A of the Internal Revenue Code of 1986.

Therefore, for example, if the employee pays fair market value for what is received, no amount is includible in the gross income of the employee. In general, the determination of the fair market value of a fringe benefit must be made before subtracting out the amount, if any, paid for the benefit and the amount, if any, specifically excluded from gross income by another section of subtitle A. See paragraphs (d)(2)(ii) and (e)(1)(iii) of this section.

(2) Fair market value. In general, fair market value is determined on the basis of all the facts and circumstances. Specifically, the fair market value of a fringe benefit is the amount that an individual would have to pay for the particular fringe benefit in an arm's-length transaction. Thus, for example the effect of any special relationship that may exist between the employer and the employee must be disregarded. Similarly, an employee's subjective perception of the value of a fringe benefit is not relevant to the determination of the fringe benefit's fair market value nor is the cost incurred by the employer determinative of its fair market value. For special rules relating to the valuation of certain fringe benefits, see paragraph (c) of this section.

(3) Exclusion from income based on cost. If a statutory exclusion phrased in terms of cost applies to the provision of a fringe benefit, section 61 does not require the inclusion in the recipient's gross income of the difference between the fair market value and the excludable cost of that fringe bene-

fit. For example, section 129 provides an exclusion from an employee's gross income for amounts contributed by an employer to a dependent care assistance program for employees. Even if the fair market value of the dependent care assistance exceeds the employer's cost, the excess is not subject to inclusion under section 61 and this section. However, if the statutory cost exclusion is a limited amount, the fair market value of the fringe benefit attributable to any excess cost is subject to inclusion. This would be the case, for example, where an employer pays or incurs a cost of more than $5,000 to provide dependent care assistance to an employee.

(4) Fair market value of the availability of an employer-provided vehicle. (i) In general. If the vehicle special valuation rules of paragraphs (d), (e), or (f) of this section do not apply with respect to an employer-provided vehicle, the value of the availability of that vehicle is determined under the general valuation principles set forth in this section. In general, that value equals the amount that an individual would have to pay in an arm's-length transaction to lease the same or comparable vehicle on the same or comparable conditions in the geographic area in which the vehicle is available for use. An example of a comparable condition is the amount of time that the vehicle is available to the employee for use, e.g., a one-year period. Unless the employee can substantiate that the same or comparable vehicle could have been leased on a cents-per-mile basis, the value of the availability of the vehicle cannot be computed by applying a cents-per-mile rate to the number of miles the vehicle is driven.

(ii) Certain equipment excluded. The fair market value of a vehicle does not include the fair market value of any specialized equipment not susceptible to personal use or any telephone that is added to or carried in the vehicle, provided that the presence of that equipment or telephone is necessitated by, and attributable to, the business needs of the employer. However, the value of specialized equipment must be included, if the employee to whom the vehicle is available uses the specialized equipment in a trade or business of the employee other than the employee's trade or business of being an employee of the employer.

(5) Fair market value of chauffeur services. (i) Determination of value. (A) In general. The fair market value of chauffeur services provided to the employee by the employer is the amount that an individual would have to pay in an arm's-length transaction to obtain the same or comparable chauffeur services in the geographic area for the period in which the services are provided. In determining the applicable fair market value, the amount of time, if any, the chauffeur remains on-call to perform chauffeur services must be included. For example, assume that A an employee of corporation M, needs a chauffeur to be on-call to provide services to A during a twenty-four hour period. If during that twenty-four hour period, the chauffeur actually drives A for only six hours, the fair market value of the chauffeur services would have to be the value of having a chauffeur on-call for a twenty-four hour period. The cost of taxi fare or limousine service for the six hours the chauffeur actually drove A would not be an accurate measure of the fair market value of chauffeur services provided to A. Moreover, all other aspects of the chauffeur's services (including any special qualifications of the chauffeur (e.g., training in evasive driving skills) or the ability of the employee to choose the particular chauffeur) must be taken into consideration.

(B) Alternative valuation with reference to compensation paid. Alternatively, the fair market value of the chauffeur services may be determined by reference to the compensation (as defined in paragraph (b)(5)(ii)) received by the chauffeur from the employer.

(C) Separate valuation for chauffeur services. The value of chauffeur services is determined separately from the value of the availability of an employer-provided vehicle.

(ii) Definition of compensation. (A) In general. For purposes of this paragraph (b)(5)(ii), the term "compensation" means compensation as defined in section 414(q)(7) and the fair market value of nontaxable lodging (if any) provided by the employer to the chauffeur in the current year.

(B) Adjustments to compensation. For purposes of this paragraph (b)(5)(ii), a chauffeur's compensation is reduced proportionately to reflect the amount of time during which the chauffeur performs substantial services for the employer other than as a chauffeur and is not on-call as a chauffeur. For example, assume a chauffeur is paid $25,000 a year for working a ten-hour day, five days a week and also receives $5,000 in nontaxable lodging. Further assume that during four hours of each day, the chauffeur is not on-call to perform services as a chauffeur because that individual is performing secretarial functions for the employer. Then, for purposes of determining the fair market value of this chauffeur's services, the employer may reduce the chauffeur's compensation by 4/10 or $12,000 (.4 × ($25,000 + $5,000) = $12,000). Therefore, in this example, the fair market value of the chauffeur's services is $18,000 ($30,000 − $12,000). However, for purposes of this paragraph (b)(5)(ii), a chauffeur's compensation is not to be reduced by any amounts paid to the chauffeur for time spent "on-call," even though the chauffeur actually performs other services for the employer during such time. For purposes of this paragraph (b)(5)(ii), a determination that a chauffeur is performing substantial services for the employer other than as a chauffeur is based upon the facts and circumstances of each situation. An employee will be deemed to be performing substantial services for the employer other than as a chauffeur if a certain portion of each working day is regularly spent performing other services for the employer.

(iii) Calculation of chauffeur services for personal purposes of the employee. The fair market value of chauffeur services provided to the employee for personal purposes may be determined by multiplying the fair market value of chauffeur services, as determined pursuant to paragraph (b)(5)(i)(A) or (B) of this section, by a fraction, the numerator of which is equal to the sum of the hours spent by the chauffeur actually providing personal driving services to the employee and the hours spent by the chauffeur in "personal on-call time," and the denominator of which is equal to all hours the chauffeur spends in driving services of any kind paid for by the employer, including all hours that are "on-call."

(iv) Definition of on-call time. For purposes of this paragraph, the term "on-call time" means the total amount of time that the chauffeur is not engaged in the actual performance of driving services, but during which time the chauffeur is available to perform such services. With respect to a round-trip, time spent by a chauffeur waiting for an employee to make a return trip is generally not treated as on-call time; rather such time is treated as part of the round-trip.

(v) Definition of personal on-call time. For purposes of this paragraph, the term "personal on-call time" means the amount of time outside the employee's normal working hours for the employer when the chauffeur is available to the employee to perform driving services.

(vi) Presumptions. (A) An employee's normal working hours will be presumed to consist of a ten hour period during which the employee usually conducts business activities for that employer.

(B) It will be presumed that if the chauffeur is on-call to provide driving services to an employee during the employee's normal working hours, then that on-call time will be performed for business purposes.

(C) Similarly, if the chauffeur is on-call to perform driving services to an employee after normal working hours, then that on-call time will be presumed to be "personal on-call time."

(D) The presumptions set out in paragraph (b)(5)(vi)(A), (B), and (C) of this section may be rebutted. For example, an employee may demonstrate by adequate substantiation that his or her normal working hours consist of more than ten hours. Furthermore, if the employee keeps adequate records and is able to substantiate that some portion of the driving services performed by the chauffeur after normal working hours is attributable to business purposes, then personal on-call time may be reduced by an amount equal to such personal on-call time multiplied by a fraction, the numerator of which is equal to the time spent by the chauffeur after normal working hours driving the employee for business purposes, and the denominator of which is equal to the total time spent by the chauffeur driving the employee after normal working hours for all purposes.

(vii) Examples. The rules of this paragraph (b)(5) may be illustrated by the following examples:

Example (1). An employer makes available to employee A an automobile and a full-time chauffeur B (who performs no other services for A's employer) for an entire calendar year. Assume that the automobile lease valuation rule of paragraph (d) of this section is used and that the Annual Lease Value of the automobile is $9,250. Assume further that B's compensation for the year is $12,000 (as defined in section 414(q)(7)) and that B is furnished lodging with a value of $3,000 that is excludable from B's gross income. The maximum amount subject to inclusion in A's gross income for use of the automobile and chauffeur is therefore $24,250 ($12,000 + $3,000 + $9,250). If 70 percent of the miles placed on the automobile during the year are for A's employer's business, then $6,475 is excludable from A's gross income with respect to the automobile as a working condition fringe ($9,250 × .70). Thus, $2,775 is includible in A's gross income with respect to the automobile ($9,250 – $6,475). With respect to the chauffeur, if 20 percent of the chauffeur's time is spent actually driving A or being on-call to drive A for personal purposes; then $3,000 is includible in A's income (.20 × $15,000). Eighty percent of $15,000, or $12,000, is excluded from A's income as a working condition fringe.

Example (2). Assume the same facts as in example (1) except that in addition to providing chauffeur services, B is responsible for performing substantial non-chauffeur-related duties (such as clerical or secretarial functions) during which time B is not "on-call" as a chauffeur. If B spends only 75 percent of the time performing chauffeur services, then the maximum amount subject to inclusion in A's gross income for use of the automobile and chauffeur is $20,500 (($15,000 × .75) + $9,250). If B is actually driving A for personal purposes or is on-call to drive A for personal purposes for 20 percent of the time during which B is available to provide chauffeur services, then $2,250 is includible in A's gross income (.20 × $11,250). The income inclusion with respect to the automobile is the same as in example (1).

Example (3). Assume the same facts as in example (2) except that while B is performing non-chauffeur-related duties, B is on call as A's chauffeur. No part of B's compensation is excluded when determining the value of the benefit provided to A. Thus, as in example (1), $3,000 is includible in A's gross income with respect to the chauffeur.

(6) Fair market value of a flight on an employer-provided piloted aircraft. (i) In general. If the non-commercial flight special valuation rule of paragraph (g) of this section does not apply, the value of a flight on an employer-provided piloted aircraft is determined under the general valuation principles set forth in this paragraph.

(ii) Value of flight. If an employee takes a flight on an employer-provided piloted aircraft and that employee's flight is primarily personal (see § 1.162-2(b)(2)), the value of the flight is equal to the amount that an individual would have to pay in an arm's-length transaction to charter the same or a comparable piloted aircraft for that period for the same or a comparable flight. A flight taken under these circumstances may not be valued by reference to the cost of commercial airfare for the same or a comparable flight. The cost to charter the aircraft must be allocated among all employees on board the aircraft based on all the facts and circumstances unless one or more of the employees controlled the use of the aircraft. Where one or more employees control the use of the aircraft, the value of the flight shall be allocated solely among such controlling employees, unless a written agreement among all the employees on the flight otherwise allocates the value of such flight. Notwithstanding the allocation required by the preceding sentence, no additional amount shall be included in the income of any employee whose flight is properly valued under the special valuation rule of paragraph (g) of this section. For purposes of this paragraph (b)(6), "control" means the ability of the employee to determine the route, departure time and destination of the flight. The rules provided in paragraph (g)(3) of this section will be used for purposes of this section in defining a flight. Notwithstanding the allocation required by the preceding sentence, no additional amount shall be included in the income of an employee for that portion of any such flight which is excludible from income pursuant to section 132(d) or § 1.132-5 as a working condition fringe.

(iii) Examples. The rules of paragraph (b)(6) of this section may be illustrated by the following examples:

Example (1). An employer makes available to employees A and B a piloted aircraft in New York, New York. A wants to go to Los Angeles, California for personal purposes. B needs to go to Chicago, Illinois for business purposes, and then wants to go to Los Angeles, California for personal purposes. Therefore, the aircraft first flies to Chicago, and B deplanes and then boards the plane again. The aircraft then flies to Los Angeles, California where A and B deplane. The value of the flight to employee A will be no more than the amount that an individual would have to pay in an arm's length transaction to charter the same or a comparable piloted aircraft for the same or comparable flight from New York City to Los Angeles. No amount will be imputed to employee A for the stop at Chicago. As to employee B, the value of the personal flight will be no more than the value of the flight from Chicago to Los Angeles. Pursuant to the rules set forth in § 1.132-5(k), the flight from New York to Chicago will not be included in employee B's income since that flight was taken solely for business purposes. The charter cost must be allocated between A and B, since both employees controlled portions of the flight. Assume that the employer allocates according to the relative value of each employee's flight. If the charter value of A's flight from New York City to Los Angeles is $1,000 and the value of B's flight from Chicago to Los Angeles is $600 and the value of the actual flight from New York to Chicago to Los Angeles is $1200, then the amount to be allocated to employee A is $750 ($1000/($1000 + $600) × $1200) and the amount to be allocated to employee B is $450 ($600/($1000 + $600) × $1200).

Example (2). Assume the same facts as in example (1), except that employee A also deplanes at Chicago, Illinois, but for personal purposes. The value of the flight to employee A then becomes the value of a flight from New York to Chicago to Los Angeles, i.e., $1200. Therefore, the amount to be allocated to employee A is $800 ($1200/($1200 + $600) × $1200) and the amount to be allocated to employee B is $400 ($600/($1200 + $600) × $1200).

(7) Fair market value of the use of an employer-provided aircraft for which the employer does not furnish a pilot. (i) In general. If the non-commercial flight special valuation rule of paragraph (g) of this section does not apply and if an employer provides an employee with the use of an aircraft without a pilot, the value of the use of the employer-provided aircraft is determined under the general valuation principles set forth in this paragraph (b)(7).

(ii) Value of flight. In general, if an employee takes a flight on an employer-provided aircraft for which the employer does not furnish a pilot, the value of that flight is equal to the amount that an individual would have to pay in an arm's-length transaction to lease the same or comparable aircraft on the same or comparable terms for the same period in the geographic area in which the aircraft is used. For example, if an employer makes its aircraft available to an employee who will pilot the aircraft for a two-hour flight, the value of the use of the aircraft is the amount that an individual would have to pay in an arm's-length transaction to rent a comparable aircraft for that period in the geographic area in which the aircraft is used. As another example, assume that an employee uses an employer-provided aircraft to commute between home and work. The value of the use of the aircraft is the amount that an individual would have to pay in an arm's-length transaction to rent a comparable aircraft for commuting in the geographic area in which the aircraft is used. If the availability of the flight is of benefit to more than one employee, than such value shall be allocated among such employees on the basis of the relevant facts and circumstances.

(c) Special valuation rules. *(1) In general.* Paragraphs (d) through (k) of this section provide special valuation rules that may be used under certain circumstances for certain commonly provided fringe benefits. For general rules relating to the valuation of fringe benefits not eligible for valuation under the special valuation rules or fringe benefits with respect to which the special valuation rules are not used, see paragraph (b) of this section.

(2) Use of the special valuation rules. (i) For benefits provided before January 1, 1993. The special valuation rules may be used for income tax, employment tax, and reporting purposes. The employer has the option to use any of the special valuation rules. However, an employee may only use a special valuation rule if the employer uses the rule. Moreover, an employee may only use the special rule that the employer uses to value the benefit provided; the employee may not use another special rule to value that benefit. The employee may always use general valuation rules based on facts and circumstances (see paragraph (b) of this section) even if the employer uses a special rule. If a special rule is used, it must be used for all purposes. If an employer properly uses a special rule and the employee uses the special rule, the employee must include in gross income the amount determined by the employer under the special rule reduced by the sum of—

(A) Any amount reimbursed by the employee to the employer, and

(B) Any amount excludable from income under another section of subtitle A of the Internal Revenue Code of 1986.

If an employer properly uses a special rule and properly determines the amount of an employee's working condition fringe under section 132 and § 1.132-5 (under the general rule or under a special rule), and the employee uses the special valuation rule, the employee must include in gross income the amount determined by the employer less any amount reimbursed by the employee to the employer. The employer and employee may use the special rules to determine the amount of the reimbursement due the employer by the employee. Thus, if an employee reimburses an employer for the value of a benefit as determined under a special valuation rule, no amount is includible in the employee's gross income with respect to the benefit. The provisions of this paragraph are effective for benefits provided before January 1, 1993.

(ii) For benefits provided after December 31, 1992. The special valuation rules may be used for income tax, employment tax, and reporting purposes. The employer has the option to use any of the special valuation rules. An employee may use a special valuation rule only if the employer uses that rule or the employer does not meet the condition of paragraph (c)(3)(ii)(A) of this section, but one of the other conditions of paragraph (c)(3)(ii) of this section is met. The employee may always use general valuation rules based on facts and circumstances (see paragraph (b) of this section) even if the employer uses a special rule. If a special rule is used, it must be used for all purposes. If an employer properly uses a special rule and the employee uses the special rule, the employee must include in gross income the amount determined by the employer under the special rule reduced by the sum of—

(A) Any amount reimbursed by the employee to the employer; and

(B) Any amount excludable from income under another section of subtitle A of the Internal Revenue Code of 1986. If an employer properly uses a special rule and properly determines the amount of an employee's working condition fringe under section 132 and § 1.132-5 (under the general rule or under a special rule), and the employee uses the special valuation rule, the employee must include in gross income the amount determined by the employer less any amount reimbursed by the employee to the employer. The employer and employee may use the special rules to determine the amount of the reimbursement due the employer by the employee. Thus, if an employee reimburses an employer for the value of a benefit as determined under a special valuation rule, no amount is includible in the employee's gross income with respect to the benefit. The provisions of this paragraph are effective for benefits provided after December 31, 1992.

(iii) Vehicle special valuation rules. (A) Vehicle by vehicle basis. Except as provided in paragraphs (d)(7)(v) and (e)(5)(v) of this section, the vehicle special valuation rules of paragraphs (d), (e), and (f) of this section apply on a vehicle by vehicle basis. An employer need not use the same vehicle special valuation rule for all vehicles provided to all employees. For example, an employer may use the automobile lease valuation rule for automobiles provided to some employees, and the commuting and vehicle cents-per-mile valuation rules for automobiles provided to other employees. For purposes of valuing the use or availability of a vehicle, the consistency rules provided in paragraphs (d)(7) and (e)(5) of this section (relating to the automobile lease valuation rule and the vehicle cents-per-mile valuation rule, respectively) apply.

(B) Shared vehicle usage. If an employer provides a vehicle to employees for use by more than one employee at the same time, such as with an employer-sponsored vehicle commuting pool, the employer may use any of the special valuation rules that may be applicable to value the use of the vehicle by the employees. The employer must use the same special valuation rule to value the use of the vehicle by each employee who shares such use. The employer must allocate the value of the use of the vehicle based on the relevant facts and circumstances among the employees who share use of the vehicle. For example, assume that an employer provides an automobile to four of its employees and that the employees use the automobile in an employer-sponsored vehicle commuting pool. Assume further that the employer uses the automobile lease valuation rule of paragraph (d) of this section and that the Annual Lease Value of the automobile is $5,000.

The employer must treat $5,000 as the value of the availability of the automobile to the employees, and must apportion the $5,000 value among the employees who share the use of the automobile based on the relevant facts and circumstances. Each employee's share of the value of the availability of the automobile is then to be reduced by the amount, if any, of each employee's working condition fringe exclusion and the amount reimbursed by the employee to the employer.

(iv) Commercial and noncommercial flight valuation rules. Except as otherwise provided, if either the commercial flight valuation rule or the non-commercial flight valuation rule is used, that rule must be used by an employer to value all eligible flights taken by all employees in a calendar year. See paragraph (g)(14) of this section for the applicable consistency rules.

(3) Additional rules for using special valuation. (i) Election to use special valuation rules for benefits provided before January 1, 1993. A particular special valuation rule is deemed to have been elected by the employer (and, if applicable, by the employee), if the employer (and, if applicable, the employee) determines the value of the fringe benefit provided by applying the special valuation rule and treats that value as the fair market value of the fringe benefit for income, employment tax, and reporting purposes. Neither the employer nor the employee must notify the Internal Revenue Service of the election. The provisions of this paragraph are effective for benefits provided before January 1, 1993.

(ii) Conditions on the use of special valuation rules for benefits provided after December 31, 1992. Neither the employer nor the employee may use a special valuation rule to value a benefit provided after December 31, 1992, unless one of the following conditions is satisfied—

(A) The employer treats the value of the benefit as wages for reporting purposes within the time for filing the returns for the taxable year (including extensions) in which the benefit is provided;

(B) The employee includes the value of the benefit in income within the time for filing the returns for the taxable year (including extensions) in which the benefit is provided;

(C) The employee is not a control employee as defined in paragraphs (f)(5) and (f)(6) of this section; or

(D) The employer demonstrates a good faith effort to treat the benefit correctly for reporting purposes.

(4) Application of section 414 to employers. For purposes of paragraphs (c) through (k) of this section, except as otherwise provided therein, the term "employer" includes all entities required to be treated as a single employer under section 414(b), (c), (m), or (o).

(5) Valuation formulae contained in the special valuation rules. The valuation formulae contained in the special valuation rules are provided only for use in connection with those rules. Thus, when a special valuation rule is properly applied to a fringe benefit, the Commissioner will accept the value calculated pursuant to the rule as the fair market value of that fringe benefit. However, when a special valuation rule is not properly applied to a fringe benefit (see, for example, paragraph (g)(13) of this section), or when a special valuation rule is used to value a fringe benefit by a taxpayer not entitled to use the rule, the fair market value of that fringe benefit may not be determined by reference to any value calculated under any special valuation rule. Under the circumstances described in the preceding sentence, the fair market value of the fringe benefit must be determined pursuant to the general valuation rules of paragraph (b) of this section.

(6) Modification of the special valuation rules. The Commissioner may, to the extent necessary for tax administration, add, delete, or modify any special valuation rule, including the valuation formulae contained herein, on a prospective basis by regulation, revenue ruling or revenue procedure.

(7) Special accounting rule. If the employer is using the special accounting rule provided in Announcement 85-113 (1985-31 I.R.B. 31, August 5, 1985) (see § 601.601(d)(2)(ii)(b) of this chapter) (relating to the reporting of and withholding on the value of noncash fringe benefits), benefits which are deemed provided in a subsequent calendar year pursuant to that rule are considered as provided in that subsequent calendar year for purposes of the special valuation rules. Thus, if a particular special valuation rule is in effect for a calendar year, it applies to benefits deemed provided during that calendar year under the special accounting rule.

(d) Automobile lease valuation rule. *(1) In general.* (i) Annual lease value. Under the special valuation rule of this paragraph (d), if an employer provides an employee with an automobile that is available to the employee for an entire calendar year, the value of the benefit provided is the Annual Lease Value (determined under paragraph (d)(2) of this section) of that automobile. Except as otherwise provided, for an automobile that is available to an employee for less than an entire calendar year, the value of the benefit provided is either a pro-rated Annual Lease Value or the Daily Lease Value (both as defined in paragraph (d)(4) of this section), whichever is applicable. Absent any statutory exclusion relating to the employer-provided automobile (see, for example, section 132(a)(3) and § 1.132-5(b)), the amount of the Annual Lease Value (or a pro-rated Annual Lease Value or the Daily Lease Value, as applicable) is included in the gross income of the employee.

(ii) Definition of automobile. For purposes of this paragraph (d), the term "automobile" means any four-wheeled vehicle manufactured primarily for use on public streets, roads, and highways.

(2) Calculation of annual lease value. (i) In general. The Annual Lease Value of a particular automobile is calculated as follows:

(A) Determine the fair market value of the automobile as of the first date on which the automobile is made available to any employee of the employer for personal use. For an automobile first made available to any employee for personal use prior to January 1, 1985, determine the fair market value as of January 1 of the first year the special valuation rule of this paragraph (d) is used with respect to the automobile. For rules relating to determination of the fair market value of an automobile for purposes of this paragraph (d), see paragraph (d)(5) of this section.

(B) Select the dollar range in column 1 of the Annual Lease Value Table, set forth in paragraph (d)(2)(iii) of this section corresponding to the fair market value of the automobile. Except as otherwise provided in paragraphs (d)(2)(iv) and (v) of this section, the Annual Lease Value for each year of availability of the automobile is the corresponding amount in column 2 of the Table.

(ii) Calculation of annual lease value of automobile owned or leased by both an employer and an employee. (A) Purchased automobiles. Notwithstanding anything in this section to the contrary, if an employee contributes an amount toward the purchase price of an automobile in return for a percentage ownership interest in the automobile, the Annual Lease Value or the Daily Lease Value, whichever is applicable, is determined by reducing the fair market value of the employer-provided automobile by the lesser of—

(1) The amount contributed, or

(2) An amount equal to the employee's percentage ownership interest multiplied by the unreduced fair market value of the automobile.

If the automobile is subsequently revalued, the revalued amount (determined without regard to this paragraph (d)(2)(ii)(A)) is reduced by an amount which is equal to the employee's percentage ownership interest in the vehicle). If the employee does not receive an ownership interest in the employer-provided automobile then the Annual Lease Value or the Daily Lease Value, whichever is applicable, is determined without regard to any amount contributed. For purposes of this paragraph (d)(2)(ii)(A), an employee's ownership interest in an automobile will not be recognized unless it is reflected in the title of the automobile. An ownership interest reflected in the title of an automobile will not be recognized if under the facts and circumstances the title does not reflect the benefits and burdens of ownership.

(B) Leased automobiles. Notwithstanding anything in this section to the contrary, if an employee contributes an amount toward the cost to lease an automobile in return for a percentage interest in the automobile lease, the Annual Lease Value or the Daily Lease Value, whichever is applicable, is determined by reducing the fair market value of the employer-provided automobile by the amount specified in the following sentence. The amount specified in this sentence is the unreduced fair market value of vehicle multiplied by the lesser of—

(1) The employee's percentage interest in the lease, or

(2) A fraction, the numerator of which is the amount contributed and the denominator of which is the entire lease cost.

If the automobile is subsequently revalued, the revalued amount (determined without regard to this paragraph (d)(2)(ii)(B)) is reduced by an amount which is equal to the employee's percentage interest in the lease) multiplied by the revalued amount. If the employee does not receive an interest in the automobile lease, then the Annual Lease Value or the Daily Lease Value, whichever is applicable, is determined without regard to any amount contributed. For purposes of this paragraph (d)(2)(ii)(B), an employee's interest in an automobile lease will not be recognized unless the employee is a named co-lessee on the lease. An interest in a lease will not be recognized if under the facts and circumstances the lease does not reflect the true obligations of the lessees.

(C) Example. The rules of paragraph (d)(2)(ii)(A) and (B) of this section are illustrated by the following example:

Example. Assume that an employer pays $15,000 and an employee pays $5,000 toward the purchase of an automobile. Assume further that the employee receives a 25 percent interest in the automobile and is named as a co-owner on the title to the automobile. Under the rule of paragraph (d)(2)(ii)(A) of this section, the Annual Lease Value of the automobile is determined by reducing the fair market value of the automobile ($20,000) by the $5,000 employee contribution. Thus, the Annual Lease Value of the automobile under the table in paragraph (d)(2)(iii) of this section is $4,350. If the employee in this example does not receive an ownership interest in the automobile and is provided the use of the automobile for two years, the Annual Lease Value would be determined without regard to the $5,000 employee contribution. Thus, the Annual Lease Value would be $5,600. The $5,000 employee contribution would reduce the amount includible in the employee's income after taking into account the amount, if any, excluded from income under another provision of subtitle A the Internal Revenue Code, such as the working condition fringe exclusion. Thus, if the employee places 50 percent of the mileage on the automobile for the employer's business each year, then the amount includible in the employee's income in the first year would be ($5,600 – 2,800 – 2,800), or $0, the amount includible in the employee's income in the second year would be ($5,600 – 2,800 – 2,200 ($5,000 – 2,800)) or $600 and the amount includible in the third year would be ($5,600 – 2,800) or $2,800 since the employee's contribution has been completely used in the first two years.

(iii) Annual lease value table.

Automobile fair market value (1)	Annual Lease Value (2)
$0 to 999	$600
1,000 to 1,999	850
2,000 to 2,999	1,100
3,000 to 3,999	1,350
4,000 to 4,999	1,600
5,000 to 5,999	1,850
6,000 to 6,999	2,100
7,000 to 7,999	2,350
8,000 to 8,999	2,600
9,000 to 9,999	2,850
10,000 to 10,999	3,100
11,000 to 11,999	3,350
12,000 to 12,999	3,600
13,000 to 13,999	3,850
14,000 to 14,999	4,100

15,000 to 15,999	4,350
16,000 to 16,999	4,600
17,000 to 17,999	4,850
18,000 to 18,999	5,100
19,000 to 19,999	5,350
20,000 to 20,999	5,600
21,000 to 21,999	5,850
22,000 to 22,999	6,100
23,000 to 23,999	6,350
24,000 to 24,999	6,600
25,000 to 25,999	6,850
26,000 to 27,999	7,250
28,000 to 29,999	7,750
30,000 to 31,999	8,250
32,000 to 33,999	8,750
34,000 to 35,999	9,250
36,000 to 37,999	9,750
38,000 to 39,999	10,250
40,000 to 41,999	10,750
42,000 to 43,999	11,250
44,000 to 45,999	11,750
46,000 to 47,999	12,250
48,000 to 49,999	12,750
50,000 to 51,999	13,250
52,000 to 53,999	13,750
54,000 to 55,999	14,250
56,000 to 57,999	14,750
58,000 to 59,999	15,250

For vehicles having a fair market value in excess of $59,999, the Annual Lease Value is equal to: (.25 × the fair market value of the automobile) + $500.

(iv) Recalculation of annual lease value. The Annual Lease Values determined under the rules of this paragraph (d) are base on four-year lease terms. Therefore, except as otherwise provided in paragraph (d)(2)(v) of this section, the Annual Lease Value calculated by applying paragraph (d)(2)(i) or (ii) of this section shall remain in effect for the period that begins with the first date the special valuation rule of paragraph (d) of this section is applied by the employer to the automobile and ends on December 31 of the fourth full calendar year following that date. The Annual Lease Value for each subsequent four-year period is calculated by determining the fair market value of the automobile as of the first January 1 following the period described in the previous sentence and selecting the amount in column 2 of the Annual Lease Value Table corresponding to the appropriate dollar range in column 1 of the Table. If, however, the employer is using the special accounting rule provided in Announcement 85-113 (1985-31 I.R.B. 31, August 5, 1985) (relating to the reporting of and withholding on the value of noncash fringe benefits), the employer may calculate the Annual Lease Value for each subsequent four-year period as of the beginning of the special accounting period that begins immediately prior to the January 1 described in the previous sentence. For example, assume that pursuant to Announcement 85-113, an employer uses the special accounting rule. Assume further that beginning on November 1, 1988, the special accounting period is November 1 to October 31 and that the employer elects to use the special valuation rule of this paragraph (d) as of January 1, 1989. The employer may recalculate the Annual Lease Value as of November 1, 1992, rather than as of January 1, 1993.

(v) Transfer of the automobile to another employee. Unless the primary purpose of the transfer is to reduce Federal taxes, an employer transfers the use of an automobile from one employee to another employee, the employer may recalculate the Annual Lease Value based on the fair market value of the automobile as of January 1 of the calendar year of transfer. If, however, the employer is using the special accounting rule provided in Announcement 85-113 (1985-31 I.R.B. 31, August 5, 1985) (relating to the reporting of and withholding on the value of noncash fringe benefits), the employer may recalculate the Annual Lease Value based on the fair market value of the automobile as of the beginning of the special accounting period in which the transfer occurs. If the employer does not recalculate the Annual Lease Value, and the employee to whom the automobile is transferred uses the special valuation rule, the employee may not recalculate the Annual Lease Value.

(3) Services included in, or excluded from, the annual lease value table. (i) Maintenance and insurance included. The Annual Lease Values contained in the Annual Lease Value Table include the fair market value of maintenance of, and insurance for, the automobile. Neither an employer nor an employee may reduce the Annual Lease Value by the fair market value of any service included in the Annual Lease Value that is not provided by the employer, such as reducing the Annual Lease Value by the fair market value of a maintenance service contract or insurance. An employer or employee who wishes to take into account only the services actually provided with respect to an automobile may value the availability of the automobile under the general valuation rules of paragraph (b) of this section.

(ii) Fuel excluded. (A) In general. The Annual Lease Values do not include the fair market value of fuel provided by the employer, whether fuel is provided in kind or its cost is reimbursed by or charged to the employer. Thus, if an employer provides fuel, the fuel must be valued separately for inclusion income.

(B) Valuation of fuel provided in kind. The provision of fuel in kind may be valued at fair market value based on all the facts and circumstances or, in the alternative, it may be valued at 5.5 cents per mile for all miles driven by the employee. However, the provision of fuel in kind may not be valued at 5.5 cents per mile for miles driven outside the United States, Canada or Mexico. For purposes of this section, the United States includes the United States, its possessions and its territories.

(C) Valuation of fuel where cost reimbursed by or charged to an employer. The fair market value of fuel, the cost of which is reimbursed by or charged to an employer, is generally the amount of the actual reimbursement or the amount charged, provided the purchase of the fuel is at arm's-length.

(D) Fleet-average cents-per-mile fuel cost. If an employee with a fleet of at least 20 automobiles that meets the requirements of paragraph (d)(5)(v)(D) of this section reimburses employees for the cost of fuel or allows employees to charge the employer for the cost of fuel, the fair market value fuel provided to those automobiles may be determined by reference to the employer's fleet-average cents-per-mile fuel cost. The fleet-average cents-per-mile fuel cost is equal to the fleet-average per-gallon fuel cost divided by the fleet-average miles-per-gallon rate. The averages described in the preceding sentence must be determined by averaging the per-gallon fuel costs and miles-per-gallon rates of a representative sample of the automobiles in the fleet equal to the greater of ten percent of the automobiles in the fleet or 20 automobiles for a representative period, such as a two-month period. In lieu of determining the fleet-average cents-per-mile fuel cost, if an employer is using the fleet-average valuation rule of paragraph (d)(5)(v) of this section and if determining the amount of the actual reimbursement or the amount charged for the purchase of fuel would impose unreasonable administrative burdens on the employer, the provision of fuel may be valued under the rule provided in paragraph (d)(3)(ii)(B) of this section.

(iii) Treatment of other services. The fair market value of any service not specifically identified in paragraph (d)(3)(i) of this section that is provided by the employer with respect to an automobile (other than the services of a chauffeur) must be added to the Annual Lease Value of the automobile in determining the fair market value of the benefit provided. See paragraph (b)(5) of this section for rules relating to the valuation of chauffeur services.

(4) Availability of an automobile for less than an entire calendar year. (i) Pro-rated annual lease value used for continuous availability of at least 30 days. (A) In general. Except as otherwise provided in paragraph (d)(4)(iv) of this section, for periods of continuous availability of at least 30 days, but less than an entire calendar year, the value of the availability of an automobile provided by an employer electing to use the automobile lease valuation rule of this paragraph (d) is the pro-rated Annual Lease Value. The pro-rated Annual Lease Value is calculated by multiplying the applicable Annual Lease Value by a fraction, the numerator of which is the number of days of availability and the denominator of which is 365.

(B) Special rule for continuous availability of at least 30 days that straddles two reporting years. If an employee is provided with the continuous availability of an automobile for at least 30 days, but the continuous period straddles two calendar years (or two special accounting periods if the special accounting rule of Announcement 85-113 (1985-31 I.R.B. 31, August 5, 1985) (relating to the reporting of and withholding on noncash fringe benefits) is used), the prorated Annual Lease Value, rather than the Daily Lease Value, may be applied with respect to such period of continuous availability.

(ii) Daily lease value used for continuous availability of less than 30 days. Except as otherwise provided in paragraph (d)(4)(iii) of this section, for periods of continuous availability of one or more but less than 30 days, the value of the availability of the employer-provided automobile is the Daily Lease Value. The Daily Lease Value is calculated by multiplying the applicable Annual Lease Value by a fraction, the numerator of which is four times the number of days of availability and the denominator of which is 365.

(iii) Election to treat all periods as periods of at least 30 days. The value of the availability of an employer-provided automobile for a period of continuous availability of less than 30 days may be determined by applying the pro-rated Annual Lease Value by treating the automobile as if it had been available for 30 days, if doing so would result in a lower valuation than applying the Daily Lease Value to the shorter period of actual availability.

(iv) Periods of unavailability. (A) General rule. In general, a pro-rated Annual Lease Value (as provided in paragraph (d)(4)(i) of this section) is used to value the availability of an employer-provided automobile when the automobile is available to an employee for a continuous period of at least 30 days but less than the entire calendar year. Neither an employer nor an employee, however, may use a pro-rated Annual Lease Value when the reduction of Federal taxes is the primary reason the automobile is unavailable to an employee at certain times during the calendar year.

(B) Unavailability for personal reasons of the employee. If an automobile is unavailable to an employee because of personal reasons of the employee, such as while the employee is on vacation, a pro-rated Annual Lease Value, if used, must not take into account such periods of unavailability. For example, assume that an automobile is available to an employee during the first five months of the year and during the last five months of the year. Assume further that the period of unavailability occurs because the employee is on vacation. The Annual Lease Value, if it is applied, must be applied with respect to the entire 12-month period. The Annual Lease Value may not be pro-rated to take into account the two-month period of unavailability.

(5) Fair market value. (i) In general. For purposes of determining the Annual Lease Value of an automobile under the Annual Lease Value Table, the fair market value of an automobile is the amount that an individual would have to pay in an arm's-length transaction to purchase the particular automobile in the jurisdiction in which the vehicle is purchased or leased. That amount includes all amounts attributable to the purchase of an automobile such as sales tax and title fees as well as the purchase price of the automobile. Any special relationship that may exist between the employee and the employer must be disregarded. Also, the employee's subjective perception of the value of the automobile is not relevant to the determination of the automobile's fair market value, and, except as provided in paragraph (d)(5)(ii) of this section, the cost incurred by the employer in connection with the purchase or lease of the automobile is not determinative of the fair market value of the automobile.

(ii) Safe-harbor valuation rule. (A) General rule. For purposes of calculating the Annual Lease Value of an automobile under this paragraph (d), the safe-harbor value of the automobile may be as the fair market value of the automobile.

(B) Automobiles owned by the employer. For an automobile owned by the employer, the safe-harbor value of the automobile is the employer's cost of purchasing the automobile (including sale tax, title, and other expenses attributable to such purchase), provided the purchase is made at arm's-length. Notwithstanding the preceding sentence, the safe-harbor value of this paragraph (d)(5)(ii)(B) is not available with respect to an automobile manufactured by the employer. Thus, for example, if one entity manufactures an automobile and sells it to an entity with which is aggregated pursuant to paragraph (c)(4) of this section, this paragraph (d)(5)(ii)(B) does not apply to value the automobile by the aggregated employer. In this case, value must be determined under paragraph (d)(5)(i) of this section.

(C) Automobiles leased by the employer. For an automobile leased but not manufactured by the employer, the safe-harbor value of the automobile is either the manufacturer's suggested retail price of the automobile less eight percent (including sales tax, title, and other expenses attributable to such purchase), or the value determined under paragraph (d)(5)(iii) of this section.

(iii) Use of nationally recognized pricing sources. The fair market value of an automobile that is—

(A) Provided to an employee prior to January 1, 1985,

(B) Being revalued pursuant to paragraphs (d)(2)(iv) or (v) of this section, or

(C) A leased automobile being valued pursuant to paragraph (d)(5)(ii) of this section, may be determined by reference to the retail value of such automobile as reported by a nationally recognized pricing source that regularly reports new or used automobile retail values, whichever is applicable. That retail value must be reasonable with respect to the automobile being valued. Pricing sources consist of publications and electronic data bases.

(iv) Fair market value of special equipment. When determining the fair market value of an automobile, the employer may exclude the fair market value of any specialized equipment or telephone that is added to or carried in the automobile provided that the presence of that equipment or telephone is necessitated by, and attributable to, the business needs of the employer. The value of the specialized equipment must be included if the employee to whom the automobile is available uses the specialized equipment in a trade or business of the employee other than the employee's trade or business of being an employee of the employer.

(v) Fleet-average valuation rule. (A) In general. An employer with a fleet of 20 or more automobiles meeting the requirements of this paragraph (d)(5)(v) (including the business-use and fair market value conditions of paragraph (d)(5)(v)(D) of this section) may use a fleet-average value for purposes of calculating the Annual Lease Values of the automobile in the fleet. The fleet-average value is the average of the fair market values of all automobiles in the fleet. The fair market value of each automobile in the fleet shall be determined, pursuant to the rules of paragraphs (d)(5)(i) through (iv) of this section, as of the date described in paragraph (d)(2)(i)(A) of this section.

(B) Period for use of rule. The fleet-average valuation rule of this paragraph (d)(5)(v) may be used by an employer as of January 1 of any calendar year following the calendar year in which the employer acquires a sufficient number of automobiles to total a fleet of 20 or more automobiles. The Annual Lease Value calculated for the automobiles in the fleet, based on the fleet-average value, shall remain in effect for the period that begins with the first January 1 the fleet-average valuation rule of this paragraph (d)(5)(v) is applied by the employer to the automobiles in the fleet and ends on December 31 of the subsequent calendar year. The Annual Lease Value for each subsequent two-year period is calculated by determining the fleet-average value of the automobiles in the fleet as of the first January 1 of such period. An employer may cease using the fleet-average valuation rule as of any January 1. If, however, the employer is using the special accounting rule provided in Announcement 85-113 (1985-31 I.R.B. 31, August 5, 1985) (relating to the reporting of and withholding on noncash fringe benefits), the employer may apply the rules of this paragraph (d)(5)(v)(B) on the basis of the special accounting period rather than the calendar year. (This is accomplished by substituting *(1)* the beginning of the special accounting period that begins immediately prior to the January 1 described in this paragraph (d)(5)(v)(B) for January 1 wherever it appears in this paragraph (d)(5)(v)(B) and (2) the end of such accounting period for December 31.) If the number of qualifying automobiles in the employer's fleet declines to fewer than 20 for more than 50 percent of the days in a year, then the fleet-average valuation rule does not apply as of January 1 of such year. In this case, the Annual Lease Value must be determined separately for each remaining automobile. The revaluation rules of paragraph (d)(2)(iv) and (v) of this section do not apply to automobiles valued under this paragraph (d)(5)(v).

(C) Automobiles included in the fleet. An employer may include in a fleet any automobile that meets the requirements of this paragraph (d)(5)(v) and is available to any employee of the employer for personal use. An employer may include in the fleet only automobiles the availability of which is valued under the automobile lease valuation rule of this paragraph (d). An employer need not include in the fleet all automobiles valued under the automobile lease valuation rule. An employer may have more than one fleet for purposes of the fleet-average rule of this paragraph (d)(5)(v). For example, an employer may group automobiles in a fleet according to their physical type or use.

(D) Limitations on use of fleet-average rule. The rule provided in this paragraph (d)(5)(v) may not be used for any automobile the fair market value of which (determined pursuant to paragraphs (d)(5)(i) through (iv) of this section as of either the first date on which the automobile is made available to any employee of the employer for personal use or, if later, January 1, 1985) exceeds $16,500. The fair market value limitation of $16,500 shall be adjusted pursuant to section 280F(d)(7) of the Internal Revenue Code of 1986. The first such adjustment shall be for calendar year 1989 (substitute October 1986 for October 1987 in applying the formula). In addition, the rule provided in this paragraph (d)(5)(v) may only be used for automobiles that the employer reasonably expects will regularly be used in the employer's trade or business. For rules concerning when an automobile is regularly used in the employer's business, see paragraph (e)(1)(iv) of this section.

(E) Additional automobiles added to the fleet. The fleet-average value in effect at the time an automobile is added to a fleet is treated as the fair market value of the additional automobile for purposes of determining the Annual Lease Value of the automobile until the fleet-average value changes pursuant to paragraph (d)(5)(v)(B) of this section.

(F) Use of the fleet-average rule by employees. An employee may only use the fleet-average rule if it is used by the employer. If an employer uses the fleet-average rule, and the employee uses the special valuation rule of paragraph (d) of this section, the employee must use the fleet-average value determined by the employer.

(6) Special rules for continuous availability of certain automobiles. (i) Fleet automobiles. If an employer is using the fleet-average valuation rule of paragraph (d)(5)(v) of this section and the employer provides an employee with the continuous availability of an automobile from the same fleet during a period (though not necessarily the same fleet automobile for the entire period), the employee is treated as having the use of a single fleet automobile for the entire period, e.g., an entire calendar year. Thus, when applying the automobile lease valuation rule of this paragraph (d), the employer may treat the fleet-average value as the fair market value of the automobile deemed available to the employee for the period for purposes of calculating the Annual Lease Value (or pro-rated Annual Lease Value or Daily Lease Value, whichever is applicable) of the automobile. If an employer provides an employee with the continuous availability of more than one fleet automobile during a period, the employer may treat the fleet-average value as the fair market value of each automobile provided to the employee provided that the rules of paragraph (d)(5)(v)(D) of this section are satisfied.

(ii) Demonstration automobiles. (A) In general. If an automobile dealership provides an employee with the continuous availability of a demonstration automobile (as defined in § 1.132-5(o)(3)) during a period (though not necessarily the same demonstration automobile for the entire period), the employee is treated as having the use of a single demonstration automobile for the entire period, e.g., an entire calendar year. If an employer provides an employee with the continuous availability of more than one demonstration automobile during a period, the employer may treat the value determined under paragraph (d)(6)(ii)(B) of this section as the fair market value of each automobile provided to the employee. For rules relating to the treatment as a working condition fringe of the qualified automobile demonstration use of a demonstration automobile by a full-time automobile salesman, see § 1.132-5(o).

(B) Determining the fair market value of a demonstration automobile. When applying the automobile lease valuation rule of this paragraph (d), the employer may treat the average of the fair market values of the demonstration automobiles which are available to an employee and held in the dealership's inventory during the calendar year as the fair market value of the demonstration automobile deemed available to the employee for the period for purposes of calculating the Annual Lease Value of the automobile. If under the facts and circumstances it is inappropriate to take into account, with respect to an employee, certain models of demonstration automobiles, the value of the benefit is determined without reference to the fair market values of such models. For example, assume that an employee has the continuous availability for an entire calendar year of one demonstration automobile, although not the same one for the entire year. Assume further that the fair market values of the automobiles in the dealership's inventory during the year range from $8,000 to $20,000. If there is not a substantial period (such as three months) during the year when the employee uses demonstration automobiles valued at less than $16,000, then those automobiles are not considered in determining the value of the benefit provided to the employee. In this case, the average of the fair market values of the demonstration automobiles in the dealership's inventory valued at $16,000 or more is treated as the fair market value of the automobile deemed available to the employee for the calendar year for purposes of calculating the Annual Lease Value of the automobile.

(7) Consistency rules. (i) Use of the automobile lease valuation rule by an employer. Except as provided in paragraph (d)(5)(v)(B) of this section, an employer may adopt the automobile lease valuation rule of this paragraph (d) for an automobile only if the rule is adopted to take effect by the later of—

(A) January 1, 1989, or

(B) The first day on which the automobile is made available to an employee of the employer for personal use (or, if the commuting valuation rule of paragraph (f) of this section is used when the automobile is first made available to an employee of the employer for personal use, the first day on which the commuting valuation rule is not used).

(ii) An employer must use the automobile lease valuation rule for all subsequent years. Once the automobile lease valuation rule has been adopted for an automobile by an employer, the rule must be used by the employer for all subsequent years in which the employer makes the automobile available to any employee, except that the employer may, for any year during which (or for any employee for whom) use of the automobile qualifies for the commuting valuation rule of paragraph (f) of this section, use the commuting valuation rule with respect to the automobile.

(iii) Use of the automobile lease valuation rule by an employee. An employee may adopt the automobile lease valuation rule for an automobile only if the rule is adopted—

(A) By the employer, and

(B) Beginning with the first day on which the automobile for which the employer (consistent with paragraph (d)(7)(i) of this section) adopted the rule is made available to that employee for personal use (or, if the commuting valuation rule of paragraph (f) of this section is used when the automobile is first made available to that employee for personal use, the first day on which the commuting valuation rule is not used).

(iv) An employee must use the automobile lease valuation rule for all subsequent years. Once the automobile lease valuation rule has been adopted for an automobile by an employee, the rule must be used by the employee for all subsequent years in which the automobile for which the rule is used is available to the employee. However, the employee may, for any year during which use of the automobile qualifies for use of the commuting valuation rule of paragraph (f) of this section and for which the employer uses such rule, use the commuting valuation rule with respect to the automobile.

(v) Replacement automobiles. Notwithstanding anything in this paragraph (d)(7) to the contrary, if the automobile lease valuation rule is used by an employer, or by an employer and an employee, with respect to a particular automobile, and a replacement automobile is provided to the employee for the primary purpose of reducing Federal taxes, then the employer, or the employer and the employee, using the rule must continue to use the rule with respect to the replacement automobile.

(e) Vehicle cents-per mile valuation rule. *(1) In general.* (i) General rule. Under the vehicle cents-per-mile valuation rule of this paragraph (e), if an employer provides an employee with the use of a vehicle that—

(A) The employer reasonably expects will be regularly used in the employer's trade or business throughout the calendar year (or such shorter period as the vehicle may be owned or leased by the employer), or

(B) Satisfies the requirements of paragraph (e)(1)(ii) of this section, the value of the benefit provided in the calendar year is the standard mileage rate provided in the applicable Revenue Ruling or Revenue Procedure ("cents-per-mile rate") multiplied by the total number of miles the vehicle is driven by the employee for personal purposes. The cents-per-mile rate is to be applied prospectively from the first day of the taxable year following the date of publication of the applicable Revenue Ruling or Revenue Procedure. An employee who uses an employer-provided vehicle, in whole or in part, for a trade or business other than the employer's trade or business, may take a deduction for such business use based upon the vehicle cents-per-mile rule as long as such deduction is at the same standard mileage rate as that used in calculating the employee's income inclusion. The standard mileage rate must be applied to personal miles independent of business miles. Thus, for example, if the standard mileage rate were 24 cents per mile for the first 15,000 miles and 11 cents per mile for all miles over 15,000 and an employee drives 20,000 personal miles and 45,000 business miles in a year, the value of the personal use of the vehicle is $4,150 ((15,000 × $.24) (5,000 × $.11)). For purposes of this section, the use of a vehicle for personal purposes is any use of the vehicle other than use in the employee's trade or business of being an employee of the employer.

(ii) Mileage rule. A vehicle satisfies the requirements of this paragraph (e)(1)(ii) for a calendar year if—

(A) It is actually driven at least 10,000 miles in that year; and

(B) Use of the vehicle during the year is primarily by employees.

For example, if a vehicle is used by only one employee during the calendar year and that employee drives the vehicle at least 10,000 miles during the year, the vehicle satisfies the requirements of this paragraph (e)(1)(ii) even if all miles driven by the employee are personal. A vehicle is considered used during the year primarily by employees in accordance with the requirement of paragraph (e)(1)(ii)(B) of this section if employees use the vehicle on a consistent basis for commuting. If the employer does not own or lease the vehicle during a portion of the year, the 10,000 mile threshold is to be reduced proportionately to reflect the periods when the employer did not own or lease the vehicle. For purposes of this paragraph (e)(1)(ii), use of the vehicle by an individual (other than the employee) whose use would be taxed to the employee is not considered use by the employee.

(iii) Limitation on use of the vehicle cents-per-mile valuation rule. (A) In general. Except as otherwise provided in the last sentence of this paragraph (e)(1)(iii)(A), the value of the use of an automobile (as defined in paragraph (d)(1)(ii) of this section) may not be determined under the vehicle cents-per-mile valuation rule of this paragraph (e) for a calendar year if the fair market value of the automobile (determined pursuant to paragraphs (d)(5)(i) through (iv) of this section as of the later of January 1, 1985, or the first date on which the automobile is made available to any employee of the employer for personal use) exceeds the sum of the maximum recovery deductions allowable under section 280F(a)(2) for a five-year period for an automobile first placed in service during that calendar year (whether or not the automobile is actually placed in service during that year) as adjusted by section 280F(d)(7). With respect to a vehicle placed in service prior to January 1, 1989, the limitation on value will be not less than $12,800. With respect to a vehicle placed in service in or after 1989, the limitation on value is $12,800 as adjusted by section 280F(d)(7).

(B) Application of limitation with respect to a vehicle owned by both an employer and an employee. If an employee contributes an amount towards the purchase price of a vehicle in return for a percentage ownership interest in the vehicle, for purposes of determining whether the limitation of this paragraph (e)(1)(iii) applies, the fair market value of the vehicle is reduced by the lesser of—

(1) The amount contributed, or

(2) An amount equal to the employee's percentage ownership interest multiplied by the unreduced fair market value of the vehicle.

If the employee does not receive an ownership interest in the employer-provided vehicle, then the fair market value of the vehicle is determined without regard to any amount contributed. For purposes of this paragraph (e)(1)(iii)(B), an employee's ownership interest in a vehicle will not be recognized unless it is reflected in the title of the vehicle. An ownership interest reflected in the title of a vehicle will not be recognized if under the facts and circumstances the title does not reflect the benefits and burdens of ownership.

(C) Application of limitation with respect to a vehicle leased by both an employer and employee. If an employee contributes an amount toward the cost to lease a vehicle in return for a percentage interest in the vehicle lease, for purposes of determining whether the limitation of this paragraph (e)(1)(iii) applies, the fair market value of the vehicle is reduced by the amount specified in the following sentence. The amount specified in this sentence is the unreduced fair market value of a vehicle multiplied by the lesser of—

(1) The employee's percentage interest in the lease, or

(2) A fraction, the numerator of which is the amount contributed and the denominator of which is the entire lease cost. If the employee does not receive an interest in the vehicle lease, then the fair market value is determined without regard to any amount contributed. For purposes of this paragraph (e)(1)(iii)(C), an employee's interest in a vehicle lease will not be recognized unless the employee is a named colessee on the lease. An interest in a ease will not be recognized if under the facts and circumstances, the lease does not reflect the true obligations of the lessees.

(iv) Regular use in an employer's trade or business. Whether a vehicle is regularly used in an employer's trade or business is determined on the basis of all facts and circumstances. A vehicle is considered regularly used in an employer's trade or business for purposes of paragraph (e)(1)(i)(A) of this section if one of the following safe harbor conditions is satisfied:

(A) At least 50 percent of the vehicle's total annual mileage is for the employer's business; or

(B) The vehicle is generally used each workday to transport at least three employees of the employer to and from work in an employer-sponsored commuting vehicle pool. Infrequent business use of the vehicle, such as for occasional trips to the airport or between the employer's multiple business premises, does not constitute regular use of the vehicle in the employer's trade or business.

(v) Application of rule to shared usage. If an employer regularly provides a vehicle to employees for use by more than one employee at the same time, such as with an employer-sponsored vehicle commuting pool, the employer may use the vehicle cents-per-mile valuation rule to value the use of the vehicle by each employee who shares such use. See § 1.61-21(c)(2)(ii)(B) for provisions relating to the allocation of the value of an automobile to more than one employee.

(2) Definition of vehicle. For purposes of this paragraph (e), the term "vehicle" means any motorized wheeled vehicle manufactured primarily for use on public streets, roads, and highways. The term "vehicle" includes an automobile as defined in paragraph (d)(1)(ii) of this section.

(3) Services included in, or excluded from, the cents-per-mile rate. (i) Maintenance and insurance included. The cents-per-mile rate includes the fair market value of maintenance of, and insurance for, the vehicle. The cents-per-mile rate may not be reduced by the fair market value of any service included in the cents-per-mile rate but not provided by the employer. An employer or employee who wishes to take into account only the particular services provided with respect to a vehicle may value the availability of the vehicle under the general valuation rules of paragraph (b) of this section.

(ii) Fuel provided by the employer. (A) Miles driven in the United States, Canada, or Mexico. With respect to miles driven in the United States, Canada, or Mexico, the cents-per-mile rate includes the fair market value of fuel provided by the employer. If fuel is not provided by the employer, the cents-per-mile rate may be reduced by no more than 5.5 cents or the amount specified in any applicable Revenue Ruling or Revenue Procedure. For purposes of this section, the United States includes the United States, its possessions and its territories.

(B) Miles driven outside the United States, Canada, or Mexico. With respect to miles driven outside the United States, Canada, or Mexico, the fair market value of fuel provided by the employer is not reflected in the cents-per-mile rate. Accordingly, the cents-per-mile rate may be reduced but by no more than 5.5 cents or the amount specified in any applicable Revenue Ruling or Revenue Procedure. If the employer provides the fuel in kind, it must be valued based on all the facts and circumstances. If the employer reimburses the employee for the cost of fuel or allows the employee to charge the employer for the cost of fuel, the fair market value of the fuel is generally the amount of the actual reimbursement or the amount charged, provided the purchase of fuel is at arm's length.

(iii) Treatment of other services. The fair market value of any service not specifically identified in paragraph (e)(3)(i) of this section that is provided by the employer with respect to a vehicle is not reflected in the cents-per-mile rate. See paragraph (b)(5) of this section for rules relating to valuation of chauffeur services.

(4) Valuation of personal use only. The vehicle cents-per-mile valuation rule of this paragraph (e) may only be used to value the miles driven for personal purposes. Thus, the employer must include an amount in an employee's income with respect to the use of a vehicle that is equal to the product of the number of personal miles driven by the employee and the appropriate cents-per-mile rate. The term "personal miles" means all miles for which the employee used the automobile except miles driven in the employee's trade or business of being an employee of the employer. Unless additional services are provided with respect to the vehicle (see paragraph (e)(3)(iii) of this section), the employer may not include in income a greater amount; for example, the employer may not include in income 100 percent (all business and personal miles) of the value of the use of the vehicle.

(5) Consistency rules. (i) Use of the vehicle cents-per-mile valuation rule by an employer. An employer must adopt the vehicle cents-per-mile valuation rule of this paragraph (e) for a vehicle to take effect by the later of—

(A) January 1, 1989, or

(B) The first day on which the vehicle is used by an employee of the employer for personal use (or, if the commuting valuation rule of paragraph (f) of this section is used when the vehicle is first used by an employee of the employer for personal use, the first day on which the commuting valuation rule is not used).

(ii) An employer must use the vehicle cents-per-mile valuation rule for all subsequent years. Once the vehicle cents-per-mile valuation rule has been adopted for a vehicle by an employer, the rule must be used by the employer for all subsequent years in which the vehicle qualifies for use of the rule, except that the employer may, for any year during which use of the vehicle qualifies for the commuting valuation rule of paragraph (f) of this section, use the commuting valuation rule with respect to the vehicle. If the vehicle fails to qualify for use of the vehicle cents-per-mile valuation rule during a subsequent year, the employer may adopt for such subsequent year and thereafter any other special valuation rule for which the vehicle then qualifies. If the employer elects to use the automobile lease valuation rule of paragraph (d) of this section for a period in which the automobile does not qualify for use of the vehicle cents-per-mile valuation rule, then the employer must comply with the requirements of paragraph (d)(7) of this section. For purposes of paragraph (d)(7) of this section, the first day on which the automobile with respect to which the vehicle cents-per-mile rule had been used fails to qualify for use of the vehicle cents-per-mile valuation rule may be deemed to be the first day on which the automobile is available to an employee of the employer for personal use.

(iii) Use of the vehicle cents-per-mile valuation rule by an employee. An employee may adopt the vehicle cents-per-mile valuation rule for a vehicle only if the rule is adopted—

(A) By the employer, and

(B) Beginning with respect to the first day on which the vehicle for which the employer (consistent with paragraph (e)(5)(i) of this section) adopted the rule is available to that employee for personal use (or, if the commuting valuation rule of paragraph (f) of this section is used when the vehicle is first used by an employee for personal use, the first day on which the commuting valuation rule is not used).

(iv) An employee must use the vehicle cents-per-mile valuation rule for all subsequent years. Once the vehicle cents-per-mile valuation rule has been adopted for a vehicle by an employee, the rule must be used by the employee for all subsequent years of personal use of the vehicle by the employee for which the rule is used by the employer. However, see paragraph (f) of this section for rules relating to the use of the commuting valuation rule for a subsequent year.

(v) Replacement vehicles. Notwithstanding anything in this paragraph (e)(5) to the contrary, if the vehicle cents-per-mile valuation rule is used by an employer, or by an employer and an employee, with respect to a particular vehicle, and a replacement vehicle is provided to the employee for the primary purpose of reducing Federal taxes, then the employer, or the employer and the employee, using the rule must continue to use the rule with respect to the replacement vehicle if the replacement vehicle qualifies for use of the rule.

(f) Commuting valuation rule. *(1) In general.* Under the commuting valuation rule of this paragraph (f), the value of the commuting use of an employer-provided vehicle may be determined pursuant to paragraph (f)(3) of this section if the following criteria are met by the employer and employees with respect to the vehicle:

(i) The vehicle is owned or leased by the employer and is provided to one or more employees for use in connection with the employer's trade or business and is used in the employer's trade or business;

(ii) For bona fide noncompensatory business reasons, the employer requires the employee to commute to and/or from work in the vehicle;

(iii) The employer has established a written policy under which neither the employee, nor any individual whose use would be taxable to the employee, may use vehicle for personal purposes, other than for commuting or de minimis personal use (such as a stop for a personal errand on the way between a business delivery and the employee's home);

(iv) Except for de minimis personal use, the employee does not use the vehicle for any personal purpose other than commuting; and

(v) The employee required to use the vehicle for commuting is not a control employee of the employer (as defined in paragraphs (f)(5) and (6) of this section).

Personal use of a vehicle is all use of the vehicle by an employee that is not use in the employee's trade or business of being an employee of the employer. An employer-provided vehicle that is generally used each workday to transport at least three employees of the employer to and from work in an employer-sponsored commuting vehicle pool is deemed to meet the requirements of paragraphs (f)(1)(i) and (ii) of this section.

(2) Special rules. Notwithstanding anything in paragraph (f)(1) of this section to the contrary, the following special rules apply—

(i) Chauffeur-driven vehicles. If a vehicle is chauffeur-driven, the commuting valuation rule of this paragraph (f) may not be used to value the commuting use of any person (other than the chauffeur) who rides in the vehicle. (See paragraphs (d) and (e) of this section for other vehicle special valuation rules.) The special rule of this paragraph (f) may be used to value the commuting-only use of the vehicle by the chauffeur if the conditions of paragraph (f)(1) of this section are satisfied. For purposes of this paragraph (f)(2), an individual will not be considered a chauffeur if he or she performs non-driving services for the employer, is not available to perform driving services while performing such other services and whose only driving services consist of driving a vehicle used for commuting by other employees of the employer.

(ii) Control employee exception. If the vehicle in which the employee is required to commute is not an automobile as defined in paragraph (d)(1)(ii) of this section, the restriction of paragraph (f)(1)(v) of this section (relating to control employees) does not apply.

(3) Commuting value. (i) $1.50 Per one-way commute. If the requirements of this paragraph (f) are satisfied, the value of the commuting use of an employer-provided vehicle is $1.50 per one-way commute (e.g., from home to work or from work to home). The value provided in this paragraph (f)(3) includes the value of any goods or services directly related to the vehicle (e.g., fuel).

(ii) Value per employee. If there is more than one employee who commutes in the vehicle, such as in the case of an employer-sponsored commuting vehicle pool, the amount includible in the income of each employee is $1.50 per one-way commute. Thus, the amount includible for each round-trip commute is $3.00 per employee. See paragraphs (d)(7)(vi) and (e)(5)(vi) of this section for use of the automobile lease valuation and vehicle cents-per-mile valuation special rules for valuing the use or availability of the vehicle in the case of an employer-sponsored vehicle or automobile commuting pool.

(4) Definition of vehicle. For purposes of this paragraph (f), the term "vehicle" means any motorized wheeled vehicle manufactured primarily for use on public streets, roads, and highways. The term "vehicle" includes an automobile as defined in paragraph (d)(1)(ii) of this section.

(5) Control employee defined. Non-government employer. For purposes of this paragraph (f), a control employee of a non-government employer is any employee—

(i) Who is a Board- or shareholder-appointed, confirmed, or elected officer of the employer whose compensation equals or exceeds $50,000,

(ii) Who is a director of the employer,

(iii) Whose compensation equals or exceeds $100,000, or

(iv) Who owns a one-percent or greater equity, capital, or profits interest in the employer.

For purposes of determining who is a one-percent owner under paragraph (f)(5)(iv) of this section, any individual who owns (or is considered as owning under section 318(a) or principles similar to section 318(a) for entities other than corporations) one percent or more of the fair market value of an entity (the "owned entity") is considered a one-percent owner of all entities which would be aggregated with the owned entity under the rules of section 414(b), (c), (m), or (o). For purposes of determining who is an officer or director with respect to an employer under this paragraph (f)(5), notwithstanding anything in this section to the contrary, if an entity would be aggregated with other entities under the rules of section 414(b), (c), (m), or (o), the officer definition (but not the compensation requirement) and the director definition apply to each such separate entity rather than to the aggregated employer. An employee who is an officer r a director of an entity (the "first entity") shall be treated as an officer or a director of all entities aggregated with the first entity under the rules of section 414(b), (c), (m), or (o). Instead of applying the control employee definition of this paragraph (f)(5), an employer may treat all, and only, employees who are "highly compensated" employees (as defined in § 1.132-8(g)) as control employees for purposes of this paragraph (f).

(6) Control employee defined—Government employer. For purposes of this paragraph (f), a control employee of a government employer is any—

(i) Elected official, or

(ii) Employee whose compensation equals or exceeds the compensation paid to a Federal Government employee holding a position at Executive Level V, determined under Chapter 11 of title 2, United States Code, as adjusted by section 5318 of Title 5 United States Code.

For purposes of this paragraph (f), the term "government" includes any Federal, state or local governmental unit, and any agency or instrumentality thereof. Instead of applying the control employee definition of paragraph (f)(6), an employer may treat all and only employees who are "highly compensated" employees (as defined in § 1.132-8 (f)) as control employees for purposes of this paragraph (f).

(7) "Compensation" defined. For purposes of this paragraph (f), the term "compensation" has the same meaning as in section 414(q)(7). Compensation includes all amounts received from all entities treated as a single employer under section 414(b), (c), (m), or (o). Levels of compensation shall be adjusted at the same time and in the same manner as provided in section 415(d). The first such adjustment shall be for calendar year 1988.

(g) Non-commercial flight valuation rule. *(1) In general.* Under the non-commercial flight valuation rule of this paragraph (g), except as provided in paragraph (g)(12) of this section, if an employee is provided with a flight on an employer-provided aircraft, the value of the flight is calculated using the aircraft valuation formula of paragraph (g)(5) of this section. For purposes of this paragraph (g), the value of a flight on an employer-provided aircraft by an individual who is less than two years old is deemed to be zero. See paragraph (b)(1) of this section for rules relating to the amount includible in income when an employee reimburses the employee's employer for all or part of the fair market value of the benefit provided.

(2) Eligible flights and eligible aircraft. The valuation rule of this paragraph (g) may be used to value flights on all employer-provided aircraft, including helicopters. The valuation rule of this paragraph (g) may be used to value international as well as domestic flights. The valuation rule of this paragraph (g) may not be used to value a flight on any commercial aircraft on which air transportation is sold to the public on a per-seat basis. For a special valuation rule relating to certain flights on commercial aircraft, see paragraph (h) of this section.

(3) Definition of a flight. (i) General rule. Except as otherwise provided in paragraph (g)(3)(iii) of this section (relating to intermediate stops), for purposes of this paragraph (g), a flight is the distance (in statute miles, i.e., 5,280 feet per statute mile) between the place at which the individual

boards the aircraft and the place at which the individual deplanes.

(ii) Valuation of each flight. Under the valuation rule of this paragraph (g), value is determined separately for each flight. Thus, a round-trip is comprised of at least two flights. For example, an employee who takes a personal trip on an employer-provided aircraft from New York City to Denver, then Denver to Los Angeles, and finally Los Angeles to New York City has taken three flights and must apply the aircraft valuation formula separately to each flight. The value of a flight must be determined on a passenger-by-passenger basis. For example, if an individual accompanies an employee and the flight taken by the individual would be taxed to the employee, the employee would be taxed on the special rule value of the flight by the employee and the flight by the individual.

(iii) Intermediate stop. If a landing is necessitated by weather conditions, by an emergency, for purposes of refueling or obtaining other services relating to the aircraft, or for any other purpose unrelated to the personal purposes of the employee whose flight is being valued, that landing is an intermediate stop. Additional mileage attributable to an intermediate stop is not considered when determining the distance of an employee's flight.

(iv) Examples. The rules of paragraph (g)(3)(iii) of this section may be illustrated by the following examples:

Example (1). Assume that an employee's trip originates in St. Louis, Missouri, with Seattle, Washington as its destination, but, because of weather conditions, the aircraft lands in Denver, Colorado, and the employee stays in Denver overnight. Assume further that the next day the aircraft flies to Seattle where the employee deplanes. The employee's flight is the distance between the airport in St. Louis and the airport in Seattle.

Example (2). Assume that a trip originates in New York, New York, with five passengers and that the aircraft makes a stop in Chicago, Illinois, so that one of the passengers can deplane for a purpose unrelated to the personal purposes of the other passengers whose flights are being valued. The aircraft then goes on to Los Angeles, California, where the other four passengers will deplane. The flight of the passenger who deplaned in Chicago is the distance between the airport in New York and the airport in Chicago. The stop in Chicago is disregarded as an intermediate stop, however, when measuring the flights taken by each of the other four passengers. Their flights would be the distance between the airport in New York and the airport in Los Angeles.

(4) Personal and non-personal flights. (i) In general. The valuation rule of this paragraph (g) applies to personal flights on employer-provided aircraft. A personal flight is one the value of which is not excludable under another section of subtitle A of the Internal Revenue Code of 1986, such as under section 132(d) (relating to a working condition fringe). However, solely for purposes of paragraphs (g)(4)(I) and (g)(4)(iii) of this section, references to personal flights do not include flights a portion of which would not be excludable from income by reason of section 274(c).

(ii) Trip primarily for employer's business. If an employee combines, in one trip, personal and business flights on an employer- provided aircraft and the employee's trip is primarily for the employer's business (see § 1.162-2(b)(2)), the employee must include in income the excess of the value of all the flights that comprise the trip over the value of the flights that would have been taken had there been no personal flights but only business flights. For example, assume that an employee flies on an employer-provided aircraft from Chicago, Illinois, to Miami, Florida, for the employer's business and that from Miami the employee flies on the employer-provided aircraft to Orlando, Florida, for personal purposes and then flies back to Chicago. Assume further that the primary purpose of the trip is for the employer's business. The amount includible in income is the excess of the value of the three flights (Chicago to Miami, Miami to Orlando, and Orlando to Chicago), over the value of the flights that would have been taken had there been no personal flights but only business flights (Chicago to Miami and Miami to Chicago).

(iii) Primarily personal trip. If an employee combines, in one trip, personal and business flights on an employer-provided aircraft and the employee's trip is primarily personal (see § 1.162-2(b)(2)), the amount includible in the employee's income is the value of the personal flights that would have been taken had there been no business flights but only personal flights. For example, assume that an employee flies on an employer-provided aircraft from San Francisco, California, to Los Angeles, California, for the employer's business and that from Los Angeles the employee flies on an employer-provided aircraft to Palm Springs, California, primarily for personal reasons and then flies back to San Francisco. Assume further that the primary purpose of the trip is personal. The amount includible in the employee's income is the value of personal flights that would have been taken had there been no business flights but only personal flights (San Francisco to Palm Springs and Palm Springs to San Francisco).

(iv) Application of section 274(c). The value of employer-provided travel outside the United States away from home may not be excluded from the employee's gross income as a working condition fringe, by either the employer or the employee, to the extent not deductible by reason of section 274(c). The valuation rule of this paragraph (g) applies to that portion of the value of any flight not excludable by reason of section 274(c). Such value is includible in income in addition to the amounts determined under paragraphs (g)(4)(ii) and (g)(4)(iii) of this section.

(v) Flights by individuals who are not personal guests. If an individual who is not an employee of the employer providing the aircraft is on a flight, and the individual is not the personal guest of any employee of the employer, the flight by the individual is not taxable to any employee of the employer providing the aircraft. The rule in the preceding sentence applies where the individual is provided the flight by the employer for noncompensatory business reasons of the employer. For example, assume that G, an employee of company Y, accompanies A, an employee of company X, on company X's aircraft for the purpose of inspecting land under consideration for purchase by company X from company Y. The flight by G is not taxable to A. No inference may be drawn from this paragraph (g)(4)(v) concerning the taxation of a flight provided to an individual who is neither an employee of the employer nor a personal guest of any employee of the employer.

(5) Aircraft valuation formula. Under the valuation rule of this paragraph (g), the value of a flight is determined under the base aircraft valuation formula (also known as the Standard Industry Fare Level formula or SIFL) by multiplying the SIFL cents-per-mile rates applicable for the period during which the flight was taken by the appropriate aircraft multiple (as provided in paragraph (g)(7) of this section) and then adding the applicable terminal charge. The SIFL cents-per-mile rates in the formula and the terminal charge are cal-

culated by the Department of Transportation and are revised semi-annually. The base aircraft valuation formula in effect from January 1, 1989 through June 30, 1989, is as follows: a terminal charge of $26.48 plus ($.1449 per mile for the first 500 miles, $.1105 per mile for miles between 501 and 1500, and $.1062 per mile for miles over 1500). For example, if a flight taken on January 15, 1989, by a non-control employee on an employer-provided aircraft with a maximum certified takeoff weight of 26,000 lbs. is 2,000 miles long, the value of the flight determined under this paragraph (g)(5) is $100.36 ((.313 × (($.1449 × 500) + ($.1105 × 1,000) + ($.1062 × 500))) + $26.48). The aircraft valuation formula applies separately to each flight being valued under this paragraph (g). Therefore, the number of miles an employee has flown on employer-provided aircraft flights prior to the flight being valued does not affect the determination of the value of the flight.

(6) Discretion to provide new formula. The Commissioner may prescribe a different base aircraft valuation formula by regulation, Revenue Ruling or Revenue Procedure in the event that the calculation of the Standard Industry Fare Level is discontinued.

(7) Aircraft multiples. (i) In general. The aircraft multiples are based on the maximum certified takeoff weight of the aircraft. When applying the aircraft valuation formula to a flight, the appropriate aircraft multiple is multiplied by the product of the applicable SIFL cents-per-mile rates multiplied by the number of miles in the flight and then the terminal charge is added to the product. For purposes of applying the aircraft valuation formula described in paragraph (g)(5) of this section, the aircraft multiples are as follows:

Maximum Certified Takeoff Weight of the Aircraft	Aircraft multiple for a Control Employee	Aircraft multiple for a Non-Control Employee
6,000 lbs. or less	62.5 percent	15.6 percent
6,001-10,000 lbs.	125 percent	23.4 percent
10,001-25,000 lbs.	300 percent	31.3 percent
25,001 lbs. or more	400 percent	31.3 percent

(ii) Flights treated as provided to a control employee. Except as provided in paragraph (g)(12) of this section, any flight provided to an individual whose flight would be taxable to a control employee (as defined in paragraphs (g)(8) and (9) of this section) as the recipient shall be valued as if such flight had been provided to that control employee. For example, assume that the chief executive officer of an employer, his spouse, and his two children fly on an employer-provided aircraft for personal purposes. Assume further that the maximum certified takeoff weight of the aircraft is 12,000 lbs. The amount includible in the employee's income is 4 × ((300 percent × the applicable SIFL cents-per-mile rates provided in paragraph (g)(5) of this section multiplied by the number of miles in the flight) plus the applicable terminal charge).

(8) Control employee defined—Non-government employer. (i) Definition. For purposes of this paragraph (g), a control employee of a non-government employer is any employee—

(A) Who is a Board- or shareholder-appointed, confirmed, or elected officer of the employer, limited to the lesser of—

(1) One percent of all employees (increased to the next highest integer, if not an integer) or

(2) Ten employees;

(B) Who is among the top one percent most highly-paid employees of the employer (increased to the next highest integer, if not an integer) limited to a maximum of 50;

(C) Who owns a five-percent or greater equity, capital, or profits interest in the employer; or

(D) Who is a director of the employer.

(ii) Special rules for control employee definition. (A) In general. For purposes of this paragraph (g), any employee who is a family member (within the meaning of section 267(c)(4)) of a control employee is also a control employee. For purposes of paragraph (g)(8)(i)(B) of this section, the term "employee" does not include any individual unless such individual is a common-law employee, partner, or one-percent or greater shareholder of the employer. Pursuant to this paragraph (g)(8), an employee may be a control employee under more than one of the requirements listed in paragraphs (g)(8)(i)(A) through (D) of this section. For example, an employee may be both an officer under paragraph (g)(8)(i)(A) of this section and a highly-paid employee under paragraph (g)(8)(i)(B) of this section. In this case, for purposes of the officer limitation rule of paragraph (g)(8)(i)(A) of this section and the highly-paid employee limitation rule of paragraph (g)(8)(i)(B) of this section, the employee would be counted in applying both limitations. For purposes of determining the one-percent limitation under paragraphs (g)(8)(i)(A) and (B) of this section, an employer shall exclude from consideration employees described in § 1.132-8(b)(3). Instead of applying the control employee definition of this paragraph (g)(8), an employer may treat all (and only) employees who are "highly compensated" employees (as defined in § 1.132-8(f)) as control employees for purposes of this paragraph (g).

(B) Special rules for officers, owners, and highly-paid control employees. In no event shall an employee whose compensation is less than $50,000 be a control employee under paragraph (g)(8)(i)(A) or (B) of this section. For purposes of determining who is a five-percent (or one-percent) owner under this paragraph (g)(8), any individual who owns (or is considered as owning under section 318(a) or principles similar to section 318(a) for entities other than corporations) five percent (or one-percent) or more of the fair market value of an entity (the "owned entity") is considered a five-percent (or one-percent) owner of all entities which would be aggregated with the owned entity under the rules of section 414(b), (c), (m), or (o). For purposes of determining who is an officer or director with respect to an employer under this paragraph (g)(8), notwithstanding anything in this section to the contrary, if the employer would be aggregated with other employers under the rules of section 414(b), (c), (m), or (o), the officer definition and the limitations and the director definition are applied to each such separate employer rather than to the aggregated employer. An employee who is an officer or director of one employer (the "first employer") shall not be counted as an officer or a director of an other employer aggregated with the first employer under the rules of section 414(b), (c), or (m). If applicable, the officer limitation rule of paragraph (g)(8)(i)(A) of this section is applied to employees in descending order of their compensation. Thus, if an employer has 11 board-appointed officers and the limit imposed under paragraph (g)(8)(i)(A) of this section is 10 officers, the employee with the least compensation of those officers would not be a control employee under paragraph (g)(8)(i)(A) of this section.

(9) Control employee defined—Government employer. For purposes of this paragraph (g), a control employee of a government employer is any—

(i) Elected official, or

(ii) Employee whose compensation equals or exceeds the compensation paid to a Federal Government employee holding a position at Executive Level V, determined under Chapter 11 of title 2, United States Code, as adjusted by section 5318 of title 5 United States Code.

For purposes of paragraph (f), the term "government" includes any Federal, state or local governmental unit, and any agency or instrumentality thereof. Instead of applying the control employee definition of paragraph (f)(6), an employer may treat all and only employees who are "highly compensated" employees (as defined in § 1.132-8(f)) as control employees for purposes of this paragraph (f).

(10) "Compensation" defined. For purposes of this paragraph (g), the term "compensation" has the same meaning as in section 414(q)(7). Compensation includes all amounts received from all entities treated as a single employer under section 414(b), (c), (m), or (o). Levels of compensation shall be adjusted at the same time and in the same manner as provided in section 415(d). The first such adjustment was for calendar year 1988.

(11) Treatment of former employees. For purposes of this paragraph (g), an employee who was a control employee of the employer (as defined in this paragraph (g)) at any time after reaching age 55, or within three years of separation from the service of the employer, is a control employee with respect to flights taken after separation from the service of the employer. An individual who is treated as a control employee under this paragraph (g)(11) is not counted when determining the limitation of paragraph (g)(8)(i)(A) and (B) of this section. Thus, the total number of individuals treated as control employees under such paragraphs may exceed the limitations of such paragraphs to the extent that this paragraph (g)(11) applies.

(12) Seating capacity rule. (i) In general. (A) General rule. Where 50 percent or more of the regular passenger seating capacity of an aircraft (as used by the employer) is occupied by individuals whose flights are primarily for the employer's business (and whose flights are excludable from income under section 132(d)), the value of a flight on that aircraft by any employee who is not flying primarily for the employer's business (or who is flying primarily for the employer's business but the value of whose flight is not excludable under section 132(d) by reason of section 274(c)) is deemed to be zero. See § 1.132-5 which limits the working condition fringe exclusion under section 132(d) to situations where the employee receives the flight in connection with the performance of services for the employer providing the aircraft.

(B) Special rules. (1) Definition of "employee." For purposes of this paragraph (g)(12), the term "employee" includes only employees of the employer, including a partner of a partnership, providing the aircraft and does not include independent contractors and directors of the employer. A flight taken by an individual other than an "employee" as defined in the preceding sentence is considered a flight taken by an employee for purposes of this paragraph (g)(12) only if that individual is treated as an employee pursuant to section 132(f)(1) or that individual's flight is treated as a flight taken by an employee pursuant to section 132(f)(2). If—

(i) A flight by an individual is not considered a flight taken by an employee (as defined in this paragraph (g)(12)(i)),

(ii) The value of that individual's flight is not excludable under section 132(d), and

(iii) The seating capacity rule of this paragraph (g)(12) otherwise applies,

then the value of the flight provided to such an individual is the value of a flight provided to a non-control employee pursuant to paragraph (g)(5) of this section (even if the individual who would be taxed on the value of the flight is a control employee)

(2) Example. The special rules of paragraph (g)(12)(i)(B)(1) of this section are illustrated by the following example

Example. Assume that 60 percent of the regular passenger seating capacity of an employer's aircraft is occupied by individuals whose flights are primarily for the employer's business and are excludable from income under section 132(d). A control employee, his spouse, and his dependent child fly on the employer's aircraft for primarily personal reasons, the value of the three flights is deemed to be zero. If, however, the control employee's cousin were provided a flight on the employer's aircraft, the value of the flight taken by the cousin is determined by applying the aircraft valuation formula of paragraph (g)(5) of this section (including the terminal charge) and the non-control employee aircraft multiples of paragraph (g)(7) of this section.

(ii) Application of 50-percent test to multiple flights. The seating capacity rule of this paragraph (g)(12) must be met both at the time the individual whose flight is being valued boards the aircraft and at the time the individual deplanes. For example, assume that employee A boards an employer-provided aircraft for personal purposes in New York, New York, and that at that time 80 percent of the regular passenger seating capacity of the aircraft is occupied by individuals whose flights are primarily for the employer's business (and whose flights are excludable from income under section 132(d)) ("the business passengers"). If the aircraft flies directly to Hartford, Connecticut where all of the passengers, including A, deplane, the requirements of the seating capacity rule of this paragraph (g)(12) have been satisfied. If instead, some of the passengers, including A, remain on the aircraft in Hartford and the aircraft continues on to Boston, Massachusetts, where they all deplane, the requirements of the seating capacity rule of this paragraph (g)(12) will not be satisfied with respect to A's flight from New York to Boston unless at least 50 percent of the seats comprising the aircraft's regular passenger seating capacity were occupied by the business passengers at the time A deplanes in Boston.

(iii) Regular passenger seating capacity. (A) General rule. Except as otherwise provided, the regular passenger seating capacity of an aircraft is the maximum number of seats that have at any time on or prior to the date of the flight been on the aircraft (while owned or leased by the employer). Except to the extent excluded pursuant to paragraph (g)(12)(v) of this section, regular seating capacity includes all seats which may be occupied by members of the flight crew. It is irrelevant that, on a particular flight, less than the maximum number of seats are available for use because, for example, some of the seats are removed.

(B) Special rules. When determining the maximum number of seats that have at any time on or prior to the date of the flight been on the aircraft (while owned or leased by the employer), seats that could not at any time be legally used during takeoff and have not at any time been used during takeoff are not counted. As of the date an employer permanently reduces the seating capacity of an aircraft, the regular passenger seating capacity is the reduced number of seats on the aircraft. The previous sentence shall not apply if at any time within 24 months after such reduction any seats are added in the aircraft. Unless the conditions of this paragraph (g)(12)(iii)(B) are satisfied, jumpseats and removable seats used solely for purposes of flight crew training are counted for purposes of the seating capacity rule of this paragraph (g)(12).

(iv) Examples. The rules of paragraph (g)(12)(iii) of this section are illustrated by the following examples:

Example (1). Employer A and employer B order the same aircraft, except that A orders it with 10 seats and B orders it with eight seats. A always uses its aircraft as a 10-seat aircraft; B always uses its aircraft as an eight-seat aircraft. The regular passenger seating capacity of A's aircraft is 10 and of B's aircraft is eight.

Example (2). Assume the same facts as in example (1), except that whenever A's chief executive officer and spouse use the aircraft eight seats are removed. Even if substantially all of the use of the aircraft is by the chief executive officer and spouse, the regular passenger seating capacity of the aircraft is 10.

Example (3). Assume the same facts as in example (1), except that whenever more than eight people want to fly in B's aircraft, two extra seats are added. Even if substantially all of the use of the aircraft occurs with eight seats, the regular passenger seating capacity of the aircraft is 10.

Example (4). Employer C purchases an aircraft with 12 seats. Three months later C remodels the interior of the aircraft and permanently removes four of the seats. Upon completion of the remodeling, the regular passenger seating capacity of the aircraft is eight. If, however, any seats are added within 24 months after the remodeling, the regular seating capacity of the aircraft is treated as 12 throughout the entire period.

(v) Seats occupied by flight crew. When determining the regular passenger seating capacity of an aircraft, any seat occupied by a member of the flight crew (whether or not such individual is an employee of the employer providing the aircraft) shall not be counted, unless the purpose of the flight by such individual is not primarily to serve as a member of the flight crew. If the seat occupied by a member of the flight crew is not counted as a passenger seat pursuant to the previous sentence, such member of the flight crew is disregarded in applying the 50-percent test described in the first sentence of paragraph (g)(12)(i) of this section. For example, assume that prior to application of this paragraph (g)(12)(v) the regular passenger seating capacity of an aircraft is one. Assume further that an employee pilots the aircraft and that the employee's flight is no primarily for the employer's business. If the employee's spouse occupies the other seat for personal purposes, the seating capacity rule is not met and the value of both flights must be included in the employee's income. If, however, the employee's flight were primarily for the employer's business (unrelated to serving as a member of the flight crew), then the seating capacity rule is met and the value of the flight for the employee's spouse is deemed to be zero. If the employee's flight were primarily to serve as a member of the flight crew, then the seating capacity rule is not met and the value of a flight by any passenger for primarily personal reasons is not deemed to be zero.

(13) Erroneous use of the non-commercial flight valuation rule. (i) Certain errors in the case of a flight by a control employee. If—

(A) The non-commercial flight valuation rule of this paragraph (g) is applied by an employer or a control employee, as the case may be, on a return as originally filed or on an amended return on the grounds that either—

(*1*) The control employee is not in fact a control employee or

(*2*) The aircraft is within a specific weight classification, and

(B) Either position is subsequently determined to be erroneous,

the valuation rule of this paragraph (g) is not available to value the flight taken by that control employee by the person or persons taking the erroneous position. With respect to the weight classifications, the previous sentence does not apply if the position taken is that the weight of the aircraft is greater than it is subsequently determined to be. If, with respect to a flight by a control employee, the seating capacity rule of paragraph (g)(12) of this section is used by an employer or the control employee, as the case may be, on a return as originally filed or on an amended return, the valuation rule of this paragraph (g) is not available to value the flight taken by that control employee by the person or persons taking the erroneous position.

(ii) Value of flight excluded as a working condition fringe. If either an employer or an employee, on a return as originally filed or on an amended return, excludes from the employee's income or wages all or any part of the value of a flight on the grounds that the flight was excludable as a working condition fringe under section 132, and that position is subsequently determined to be erroneous, the valuation rule of this paragraph (g) is not available to value the flight taken by that employee by the person or persons taking the erroneous position. Instead, the general valuation rules of paragraph (b)(5) and (6) of this section apply.

(14) Consistency rules. (i) Use by the employer. Except as otherwise provided in paragraph (g)(13) of this section or section 1.132-5(m)(4), if the non-commercial flight valuation rule of this paragraph (g) is used by an employer to value any flight provided to an employee in a calendar year, the rule must be used to value all flights provided to all employees in the calendar year.

(ii) Use by the employee. Except as otherwise provided in paragraph (g)(13) of this section or § 1.132-5(m)(4), if the non-commercial flight valuation rule of this paragraph (g) is used by an employee to value a flight provided by an employer in a calendar year, the rule must be used to value all flights provided to the employee by that employer in the calendar year.

(h) Commercial flight valuation rule. *(1) In general.* Under the commercial flight valuation rule of this paragraph (h), the value of a space-available flight (as defined in paragraph (h)(2) of this section) on a commercial aircraft is 25 percent of the actual carrier's highest unrestricted coach fare in effect for the particular flight taken. The rule of this paragraph (h) is available only to an individual described in § 1.132-1(b)(1).

(2) Space-available flight. The commercial flight valuation rule of this paragraph (h) is available to value a space-available flight. The term "space-available flight" means a flight on a commercial aircraft—

(i) Which is subject to the same types of restrictions customarily associated with flying on an employee "stand-by" or "space-available" basis, and

(ii) Which meets the definition of a no-additional-cost service under section 132(b), except that the flight is provided to an individual other than the employee or an individual treated as the employee under section 132(f). Thus, a flight is not a space-available flight if the employer guarantees the employee a seat on the flight or if the nondiscrimination requirements of section 132(h)(1) and § 1.132-8 are not satisfied. A flight may be a space-available flight even if the airline that is the actual carrier is not the employer of the employee.

(3) Commercial aircraft. If the actual carrier does not offer, in the ordinary course of its business, air transportation to customers on a per-seat basis, the commercial flight valuation rule of this paragraph (h) is not available. Thus, if, in the ordinary course of its line of business, the employer only offers air transportation to customers on a charter basis, the commercial flight valuation rule of this paragraph (h) may not be used to value a space-available flight on the employer's aircraft. If the commercial flight valuation rule is not available, the flight may be valued under the non-commercial flight valuation rule of paragraph (g) of this section.

(4) Timing of inclusion. The date that the flight is taken is the relevant date for purposes of applying section 61(a)(1) and this section to a space-available flight on a commercial aircraft. The date of purchase or issuance of a pass or ticket is not relevant. Thus, this section applies to a flight taken on or after January 1, 1989, regardless of the date on which the pass or ticket for the flight was purchased or issued.

(5) Consistency rules. (i) Use by employer. If the commercial flight valuation rule of this paragraph (h) is used by an employer to value any flight provided in a calendar year, the rule must be used to value all flights eligible for use of the rule provided in the calendar year.

(ii) Use by employer. If the commercial flight valuation rule of this paragraph (h) is used by an employee to value a flight provided by an employer in a calendar year, the rule must be used to value all flights provided by that employer eligible for use of the rule taken by such employee in the calendar year.

(i) [Reserved]

(j) Valuation of meals provided at an employer-operated eating facility for employees. *(1) In general.* The valuation rule of this paragraph (j) may be used to value a meal provided at an employer-operated eating facility for employees (as defined in § 1.132-7). For rules relating to an exclusion for the value of meals provided at an employer-operated eating facility for employees, see section 132(e)(2) and § 1.132-7.

(2) Valuation formula. (i) In general. The value of all meals provided at an employer-operated eating facility for employees during a calendar year ("total meal value") is 150 percent of the direct operating costs of the eating facility determined separately with respect to such eating facility whether or not the direct operating costs test is applied separately to such eating facility under § 1.132-7(b)(2). For purposes of this paragraph (j), the definition of direct operating costs provided in § 1.132-7(b) and the adjustments specified in § 1.132-7(a)(2) apply. The taxable value of meals provided at an eating facility may be determined in two ways. The "individual meal subsidy" may be treated as the taxable value of a meal provided at the eating facility (see paragraph (j)(2)(ii) of this section) to a particular employee. Alternatively, the employer may allocate the "total meal subsidy" among employees (see paragraph (j)(2)(iii) of this section).

(ii) "Individual meal subsidy" defined. The "individual meal subsidy" is determined by multiplying the amount paid by the employee for a particular meal by a fraction, the numerator of which is the total meal value and the denominator of which is the gross receipts of the eating facility for the calendar year and then subtracting the amount paid by the employee for the meal. The taxable value of meals provided to a particular employee during a calendar year, therefore, is the sum of the individual meal subsidies provided to the employee during the calendar year. This rule is available only if there is a charge for each meal selection and if each employee is charged the same price for any given meal selection.

(iii) Allocation of "total meal subsidy." Instead of using the individual meal subsidy method provided in paragraph (j)(2)(ii) of this section, the employer may allocate the "total meal subsidy" (total meal value less the gross receipts of the facility) among employees in any manner reasonable under the circumstances. It will be presumed reasonable for an employer to allocate the total meal subsidy on a per-employee basis if the employer has information that would substantiate to the satisfaction of the Commissioner that each employee was provided approximately the same number of meals at the facility.

(k) Commuting valuation rule for certain employees. *(1) In general.* Under the rule of this paragraph (k), the value of the commuting use of employer-provided transportation may be determined under paragraph (k)(3) of this section if the following criteria are met by the employer and employee with respect to the transportation:

(i) The transportation is provided, solely because of unsafe conditions, to an employee who would ordinarily walk or use public transportation for commuting to or from work;

(ii) The employer has established a written policy (e.g., in the employer's personnel manual) under which the transportation is not provided for the employee's personal purposes other than for commuting due to unsafe conditions and the employer's practice in fact corresponds with the policy;

(iii) The transportation is not used for personal purposes other than commuting due to unsafe conditions; and

(iv) The employee receiving the employer-provided transportation is a qualified employee of the employer (as defined in paragraph (k)(6) of this section).

(2) Trip-by-trip basis. The special valuation rule of this paragraph (k) applies on a trip-by-trip basis. If an employer and employee fail to meet the criteria of paragraph (k)(1) of this section with respect to any trip, the value of the transportation for that trip is not determined under paragraph (k)(3) of this section and the amount includible in the employee's income is determined by reference to the fair market value of the transportation.

(3) Commuting value. (i) $1.50 per one-way commute. If the requirements of this paragraph (k) are satisfied, the value of the commuting use of the employer-provided transportation is $1.50 per one-way commute (i.e., from home to work or from work to home).

(ii) Value per employee. If transportation is provided to more than one qualified employee at the same time, the amount includible in the income of each employee is $1.50 per one-way commute.

(4) Definition of employer-provided transportation. For purposes of this paragraph (k), "employer-provided transpor-

tation" means transportation by vehicle (as defined in paragraph (f)(4) of this section) that is purchased by the employer (or that is purchased by the employee and reimbursed by the employer) from a party that is not related to the employer for the purpose of transporting a qualified employee to or from work. Reimbursements made by an employer to an employee to cover the cost of purchasing transportation (e.g., hiring cabs) must be made under a bona fide reimbursement arrangement.

(5) Unsafe conditions. Unsafe conditions exist if a reasonable person would, under the facts and circumstances, consider it unsafe for the employee to walk to or from home, or to walk to or use public transportation at the time of day the employee must commute. One of the factors indicating whether it is unsafe is the history of crime in the geographic area surrounding the employee's workplace or residence at the time of day the employee must commute.

(6) Qualified employee defined. (i) In general. For purposes of this paragraph (k), a qualified employee is one who meets the following requirements with respect to the employer:

(A) The employee performs services during the current year, is paid on an hourly basis, is not claimed under section 213(a)(1) of the Fair Labor Standards Act of 1938 (as amended), 29 U.S.C. 201-219 (FLSA), to be exempt from the minimum wage and maximum hour provisions of the FLSA, and is within a classification with respect to which the employer actually pays, or has specified in writing that it will pay, compensation for overtime equal to or exceeding one and one-half times the regular rate as provided by section 207 of the FLSA; and

(B) The employee does not receive compensation from the employer in excess of the amount permitted by section 414(q)(1)(C) of the Code.

(ii) "Compensation" and "paid on an hourly basis" defined. For purposes of this paragraph (k), "compensation" has the same meaning as in section 414(q)(7). Compensation includes all amounts received from all entities treated as a single employer under section 414(b), (c), (m), or (o). Levels of compensation shall be adjusted at the same time and in the same manner as provided in section 415(d). If an employee's compensation is stated on an annual basis, the employer is treated as "paid on an hourly basis" for purposes of this paragraph (k) as long as the employee is not claimed to be exempt from the minimum wage and maximum hour provisions of the FLSA and is paid overtime wages either equal to or exceeding one and one-half the employee's regular hourly rate of pay.

(iii) FLSA compliance required. An employee will not be considered a qualified employee for purposes of this paragraph (k), unless the employer is in compliance with the recordkeeping requirements concerning that employee's wages, hours, and other conditions and practices of employment as provided in section 211(c) of the FLSA and 29 CFR part 516.

(iv) Issues arising under the FLSA. If questions arise concerning an employee's classification under the FLSA, the pronouncements and rulings of the Administrator of the Wage and Hour Division, Department of Labor are determinative.

(v) Non-qualified employees. If an employee is not a qualified employee within the meaning of this paragraph (k)(6), no portion of the value of the commuting use of employer-provided transportation is excluded under this paragraph (k).

(7) Examples. This paragraph (k) is illustrated by the following examples:

Example (1). A and B are word-processing clerks employed by Y, an accounting firm in a large metropolitan area, and both are qualified employees under paragraph (k)(6) of this section. The normal working hours for A and B are from 11:00 p.m. until 7:00 a.m. and public transportation, the only means of transportation available to A or B, would be considered unsafe by a reasonable person at the time they are required to commute from home to work. In response, Y hires a car service to pick up A and B at their homes each evening for purposes of transporting them to work. The amount includible in the income of both A and B is $1.50 for the one-way commute from home to work.

Example (2). Assume the same facts as in Example 1, except that Y also hires a car service to return A and B to their homes each morning at the conclusion of their shifts and public transportation would not be considered unsafe by a reasonable person at the time of day A and B commute to their homes. The value of the commute from work to home is includible in the income of both A and B by reference to fair market value since unsafe conditions do not exist for that trip.

Example (3). C is an associate for Z, a law firm in a metropolitan area. The normal working hours for C's law firm are from 9 a.m. until 6 p.m., but C's ordinary office hours are from 10 a.m. until 8 p.m. Public transportation, the only means of transportation available to C at the time C commutes from work to home during the evening, would be considered unsafe by a reasonable person. In response, Z hires a car service to take C home each evening. C does not receive annual compensation from Z in excess of the amount permitted by section 414(q)(1)(C) of the Code. However, C is treated as an employee exempt from the provisions of the FLSA and, accordingly, is not paid overtime wages. Therefore, C is not a qualified employee within the meaning of paragraph (k)(6) of this section. The value of the commute from work to home is includible in C's income by reference to fair market value.

(8) Effective date. This paragraph (k) applies to employer-provided transportation provided to a qualified employee on or after July 1, 1991.

T.D. 8256, 7/6/89, amend T.D. 8389, 1/15/92, T.D. 8457, 12/29/92.

PAR. 2. Section 1.61-21(d) is amended by revising paragraphs (d)(3)(ii)(A), (B), and (D) as follows:

Proposed § 1.61-21 Taxation of fringe benefits. [*For Preamble, see ¶ 151,421*]

* * * * *

(d) * * *

(3) * * *

(ii) Fuel excluded. (A) In general. The Annual Lease Values do not include the fair market value of fuel provided by the employer, whether fuel is provided in kind or its cost is reimbursed by or charged to the employer. Thus, if an employer provides fuel for the employee's personal use, the fuel must be valued separately for inclusion in income.

(B) Valuation of fuel provided in kind. Fuel provided in kind may be valued at fair market value based on all the facts and circumstances or, in the alternative, may be valued at 5.5 cents per mile for all miles driven by the employee in calendar years 1989 through 1992. For subsequent calendar years, the applicable cents-per-mile rate is the amount specified in the annual Revenue Procedure concerning the optional standard mileage rates used in computing deductible costs of operating a passenger automobile for business. However, fuel provided in kind may not be valued at the alternative cents-per-mile rate for miles driven outside the United States, Canada, or Mexico. * * *

(D) Additional methods available to employers with fleets of at least 20 automobiles. (1) Fleet-average cents-per-mile fuel cost. If an employer with a fleet of at least 20 automobiles (regardless of whether the requirements of paragraph (d)(5)(v)(D) of this section are met) reimburses employees for the cost of fuel or allows employees to charge the employer for the cost of fuel, the fair market value of fuel provided to those automobiles may be determined by reference to the employer's fleet-average cents-per-mile fuel cost. The fleet-average cents-per-mile fuel cost is equal to the fleet-average per-gallon fuel cost divided by the fleet-average miles-per-gallon rate. The averages described in the preceding sentence must be determined by averaging the per-gallon fuel costs and miles-per-gallon rates of a representative sample of the automobiles in the fleet equal to the greater of ten percent of the automobiles in the fleet or 20 automobiles for a representative period, such as a two-month period.

(2) Alternative cents-per-mile method. In lieu of determining the fleet-average cents-per-mile fuel cost under paragraph (d)(3)(ii)(D)(1) of this section, an employer with a fleet of at least 20 automobiles may value the fuel provided for these automobiles by reference to the cents-per-mile rate set forth in paragraph (d)(3)(ii)(B) of this section (regardless of whether the requirements of paragraph (d)(5)(v)(D) of this section are met).

* * * * *

PAR. 2. Section 1.61-21 is amended by revising paragraph (g)(14)(i) and (ii) and adding paragraph (g)(14)(iii) to read as follows:

Proposed § 1.61-21 Taxation of fringe benefits. [*For Preamble, see ¶ 152,867*]

* * * * *

(g) * * *

(14) * * *

(i) Use by employer. Except as otherwise provided in paragraph (g)(13) or paragraph (g)(14)(iii) of this section or in § 1.132-5(m)(4), if the non-commercial flight valuation rule of this paragraph (g) is used by an employer to value any flight provided in a calendar year, the rule must be used to value all flights provided to all employees in the calendar year.

(ii) Use by employee. Except as otherwise provided in paragraph (g)(13) or (g)(14)(iii) of this section or in § 1.132-5(m)(4), if the non-commercial flight valuation rule of this paragraph (g) is used by an employee to value a flight provided by an employer in a calendar year, the rule must be used to value all flights provided to the employee by that employer in the calendar year.

(iii) Exception for entertainment flights provided to specified individuals after October 22, 2004. Notwithstanding the provisions of paragraph (g)(14)(i) of this section, an employer may use the general valuation rules of § 1.61-21(b) to value the entertainment use of an aircraft by a specified individual. An employer who uses the general valuation rules of § 1.61-21(b) to value any entertainment use of an aircraft by a specified individual in a calendar year must use the general valuation rules of § 1.61-21(b) to value all entertainment use of aircraft provided to all specified individuals during that calendar year.

(A) Specified individuals defined. For purposes of paragraph (g)(14)(iii) of this section, specified individual is defined in section 274(e)(2)(B) and § 1.274-9(b).

(B) Entertainment defined. For purposes of paragraph (g)(14)(iii) of this section, entertainment is defined in § 1.274-2(b)(1).

* * * * *

§ 1.61-22 Taxation of split-dollar life insurance arrangements.

(a) Scope. *(1) In general.* This section provides rules for the taxation of a split-dollar life insurance arrangement for purposes of the income tax, the gift tax, the Federal Insurance Contributions Act (FICA), the Federal Unemployment Tax Act (FUTA), the Railroad Retirement Tax Act (RRTA), and the Self-Employment Contributions Act of 1954 (SECA). For the Collection of Income Tax at Source on Wages, this section also provides rules for the taxation of a split-dollar life insurance arrangement, other than a payment under a split-dollar life insurance arrangement that is a split-dollar loan under § 1.7872-15(b)(1). A split-dollar life insurance arrangement (as defined in paragraph (b) of this section) is subject to the rules of paragraphs (d) through (g) of this section, § 1.7872-15, or general tax rules. For rules to determine which rules apply to a split-dollar life insurance arrangement, see paragraph (b)(3) of this section.

(2) Overview. Paragraph (b) of this section defines a split-dollar life insurance arrangement and provides rules to determine whether an arrangement is subject to the rules of paragraphs (d) through (g) of this section, § 1.7872-15, or general tax rules. Paragraph (c) of this section defines certain other terms. Paragraph (d) of this section sets forth rules for the taxation of economic benefits provided under a split-dollar life insurance arrangement. Paragraph (e) of this section sets forth rules for the taxation of amounts received under a life insurance contract that is part of a split-dollar life insurance arrangement. Paragraph (f) of this section provides rules for additional tax consequences of a split-dollar life insurance arrangement, including the treatment of death benefit proceeds. Paragraph (g) of this section provides rules for the transfer of a life insurance contract (or an undivided interest in the contract) that is part of a split-dollar life insurance arrangement. Paragraph (h) of this section provides examples illustrating the application of this section. Paragraph (j) of this section provides the effective date of this section.

(b) Split-dollar life insurance arrangement. *(1) In general.* A split-dollar life insurance arrangement is any arrangement between an owner and a non-owner of a life insurance contract that satisfies the following criteria—

(i) Either party to the arrangement pays, directly or indirectly, all or any portion of the premiums on the life insurance contract, including a payment by means of a loan to the other party that is secured by the life insurance contract;

(ii) At least one of the parties to the arrangement paying premiums under paragraph (b)(1)(i) of this section is entitled to recover (either conditionally or unconditionally) all or any portion of those premiums and such recovery is to be made from, or is secured by, the proceeds of the life insurance contract; and

(iii) The arrangement is not part of a group-term life insurance plan described in section 79 unless the group-term life insurance plan provides permanent benefits to employees (as defined in § 1.79-0).

(2) Special rule. (i) In general. Any arrangement between an owner and a non-owner of a life insurance contract is treated as a split-dollar life insurance arrangement (regardless of whether the criteria of paragraph (b)(1) of this section are satisfied) if the arrangement is described in paragraph (b)(2)(ii) or (iii) of this section.

(ii) Compensatory arrangements. An arrangement is described in this paragraph (b)(2)(ii) if the following criteria are satisfied—

(A) The arrangement is entered into in connection with the performance of services and is not part of a group-term life insurance plan described in section 79;

(B) The employer or service recipient pays, directly or indirectly, all or any portion of the premiums; and

(C) Either—

(*1*) The beneficiary of all or any portion of the death benefit is designated by the employee or service provider or is any person whom the employee or service provider would reasonably be expected to designate as the beneficiary; or

(*2*) The employee or service provider has any interest in the policy cash value of the life insurance contract.

(iii) Shareholder arrangements. An arrangement is described in this paragraph (b)(2)(iii) if the following criteria are satisfied—

(A) The arrangement is entered into between a corporation and another person in that person's capacity as a shareholder in the corporation;

(B) The corporation pays, directly or indirectly, all or any portion of the premiums; and

(C) Either—

(*1*) The beneficiary of all or any portion of the death benefit is designated by the shareholder or is any person whom the shareholder would reasonably be expected to designate as the beneficiary; or

(*2*) The shareholder has any interest in the policy cash value of the life insurance contract.

(3) Determination of whether this section or § 1.7872-15 applies to a split-dollar life insurance arrangement. (i) Split-dollar life insurance arrangements involving split-dollar loans under § 1.7872-15. Except as provided in paragraph (b)(3)(ii) of this section, paragraphs (d) through (g) of this section do not apply to any split-dollar loan as defined in § 1.7872-15(b)(1). Section 1.7872-15 applies to any such loan. See paragraph (b)(5) of this section for the treatment of a payment made by a non-owner under a split-dollar life insurance arrangement if the payment is not a split-dollar loan.

(ii) Exceptions. Paragraphs (d) through (g) of this section apply (and § 1.7872-15 does not apply) to any split-dollar life insurance arrangement if—

(A) The arrangement is entered into in connection with the performance of services, and the employer or service recipient is the owner of the life insurance contract (or is treated as the owner of the contract under paragraph (c)(1)(ii)(A)(*1*) of this section); or

(B) The arrangement is entered into between a donor and a donee (for example, a life insurance trust) and the donor is the owner of the life insurance contract (or is treated as the owner of the contract under paragraph (c)(1)(ii)(A)(*2*) of this section).

(4) Consistency requirement. A split-dollar life insurance arrangement described in paragraph (b)(1) or (2) of this section must be treated in the same manner by the owner and the non-owner of the life insurance contract under either the rules of this section or § 1.7872-15. In addition, the owner and non-owner must fully account for all amounts under the arrangement under paragraph (b)(5) of this section, paragraphs (d) through (g) of this section, or § 1.7872-15.

(5) Non-owner payments that are not split-dollar loans. If a non-owner of a life insurance contract makes premium payments (directly or indirectly) under a split-dollar life insurance arrangement, and the payments are neither split-dollar loans nor consideration for economic benefits described in paragraph (d) of this section, then neither the rules of paragraphs (d) through (g) of this section nor the rules in § 1.7872-15 apply to such payments. Instead, general income tax, employment tax, self-employment tax, and gift tax principles apply to the premium payments. See, for example, § 1.61-2(d)(2)(ii)(A).

(6) Waiver, cancellation, or forgiveness. If a repayment obligation described in § 1.7872-15(a)(2) is waived, cancelled, or forgiven at any time, then the parties must take the amount waived, cancelled, or forgiven into account in accordance with the relationships between the parties (for example, as compensation in the case of an employee-employer relationship).

(7) Change in the owner. If payments made by a non-owner to an owner were treated as split-dollar loans under § 1.7872-15 and the split-dollar life insurance arrangement is modified such that, after the modification, the non-owner is the owner (within the meaning of paragraph (c)(1) of this section) of the life insurance contract under the arrangement, paragraphs (d) through (g) of this section apply to the split-dollar life insurance arrangement from the date of the modification. The payments made (both before and after the modification) are not treated as split-dollar loans under § 1.7872-15 on or after the date of the modification. The non-owner of the life insurance contract under the modified split-dollar life insurance arrangement must fully take into account all economic benefits provided under the arrangement under paragraph (d) of this section on or after the date of the modification. For the treatment of a transfer of the contract when the unmodified arrangement is governed by paragraphs (d) through (g) of this section, see paragraph (g) of this section.

(c) Definitions. The following definitions apply for purposes of this section:

(1) Owner. (i) In general. With respect to a life insurance contract, the person named as the policy owner of such contract generally is the owner of such contract. If two or more persons are named as policy owners of a life insurance contract and each person has, at all times, all the incidents of ownership with respect to an undivided interest in the contract, each person is treated as the owner of a separate contract to the extent of such person's undivided interest. If two or more persons are named as policy owners of a life insurance contract but each person does not have, at all times, all the incidents of ownership with respect to an undivided interest in the contract, the person who is the first-named policy owner is treated as the owner of the entire contract.

(ii) Special rule for certain arrangements. (A) In general. Notwithstanding paragraph (c)(1)(i) of this section—

(*1*) An employer or service recipient is treated as the owner of a life insurance contract under a split-dollar life insurance arrangement that is entered into in connection with the performance of services if, at all times, the only economic benefit that will be provided under the arrangement is current life insurance protection as described in paragraph (d)(3) of this section; and

(2) A donor is treated as the owner of a life insurance contract under a split-dollar life insurance arrangement that is entered into between a donor and a donee (for example, a life insurance trust) if, at all times, the only economic benefit that will be provided under the arrangement is current life insurance protection as described in paragraph (d)(3) of this section.

(B) Modifications. If an arrangement described in paragraph (c)(1)(ii)(A) of this section is modified such that the arrangement is no longer described in paragraph (c)(1)(ii)(A) of this section, the following rules apply:

(1) If, immediately after such modification, the employer, service recipient, or donor is the owner of the life insurance contract under the split-dollar life insurance arrangement (determined without regard to paragraph (c)(1)(ii)(A) of this section), the employer, service recipient, or donor continues to be treated as the owner of the life insurance contract.

(2) If, immediately after such modification, the employer, service recipient, or donor is not the owner of the life insurance contract under the split-dollar life insurance arrangement (determined without regard to paragraph (c)(1)(ii)(A) of this section), the employer, service recipient, or donor is treated as having made a transfer of the entire life insurance contract to the employee, service provider, or donee under the rules of paragraph (g) of this section as of the date of such modification.

(3) For purposes of this paragraph (c)(1)(ii)(B), entering into a successor split-dollar life insurance arrangement that has the effect of providing any economic benefit in addition to that described in paragraph (d)(3) of this section is treated as a modification of the prior split-dollar life insurance arrangement.

(iii) Attribution rules for compensatory arrangements. For purposes of this section, if a split-dollar life insurance arrangement is entered into in connection with the performance of services, the employer or service recipient is treated as the owner of the life insurance contract if the owner (within the meaning of paragraph (c)(1)(i) of this section) of the life insurance contract under the split-dollar life insurance arrangement is—

(A) A trust described in section 402(b);

(B) A trust that is treated as owned (within the meaning of sections 671 through 677) by the employer or the service recipient;

(C) A welfare benefit fund within the meaning of section 419(e)(1); or

(D) A member of the employer or service recipient's controlled group (within the meaning of section 414(b)) or a trade or business that is under common control with the employer or service recipient (within the meaning of section 414(c)).

(iv) Life insurance contracts owned by partnerships. [Reserved]

(2) Non-owner. (i) Definition. With respect to a life insurance contract, a non-owner is any person (other than the owner of such contract under paragraph (c)(1) of this section) that has any direct or indirect interest in such contract (but not including a life insurance company acting only in its capacity as the issuer of a life insurance contract).

(ii) Example. The following example illustrates the provisions of this paragraph (c)(2):

Example. (i) On January 1, 2009, Employer R and Trust T, an irrevocable life insurance trust that is not treated under sections 671 through 677 as owned by a grantor or other person, enter into a split-dollar life insurance arrangement in connection with the performance of services under which R will pay all the premiums on the life insurance contract until the termination of the arrangement or the death of E, an employee of R. C, the beneficiary of T, is E's child. R is the owner of the contract under paragraph (c)(1)(i) of this section. E is the insured under the life insurance contract. Upon termination of the arrangement or E's death, R is entitled to receive the lesser of the aggregate premiums or the policy cash value of the contract and T will be entitled to receive any remaining amounts. Under the terms of the arrangement and applicable state law, the policy cash value is fully accessible by R and R's creditors but T has the right to borrow or withdraw at any time the portion of the policy cash value exceeding the amount payable to R.

(ii) Because E and T each have an indirect interest in the life insurance contract that is part of the split-dollar life insurance arrangement, each is a non-owner under paragraph (c)(2)(i) of this section. E and T each are provided economic benefits described in paragraph (d)(2) of this section pursuant to the split-dollar life insurance arrangement. Economic benefits are provided by owner R to E as a payment of compensation, and separately provided by E to T as a gift.

(3) Transfer of entire contract or undivided interest therein. A transfer of the ownership of a life insurance contract (or an undivided interest in such contract) that is part of a split-dollar life insurance arrangement occurs on the date that a non-owner becomes the owner (within the meaning of paragraph (c)(1) of this section) of the entire contract or of an undivided interest in the contract.

(4) Undivided interest. An undivided interest in a life insurance contract consists of an identical fractional or percentage interest or share in each right, benefit, and obligation with respect to the contract. In the case of any arrangement purporting to create undivided interests where, in substance, the rights, benefits or obligations are shared to any extent among the holders of such interests, the arrangement will be treated as a split-dollar life insurance arrangement.

(5) Employment tax. The term employment tax means any tax imposed by, or collected under, the Federal Insurance Contributions Act (FICA), the Federal Unemployment Tax Act (FUTA), the Railroad Retirement Tax Act (RRTA), and the Collection of Income Tax at Source on Wages.

(6) Self-employment tax. The term self-employment tax means the tax imposed by the Self-Employment Contributions Act of 1954 (SECA).

(d) Economic benefits provided under a split-dollar life insurance arrangement. *(1) In general.* In the case of a split-dollar life insurance arrangement subject to the rules of paragraphs (d) through (g) of this section, economic benefits are treated as being provided to the non-owner of the life insurance contract. The non-owner (and the owner for gift and employment tax purposes) must take into account the full value of all economic benefits described in paragraph (d)(2) of this section, reduced by the consideration paid directly or indirectly by the non-owner to the owner for those economic benefits. Depending on the relationship between the owner and the non-owner, the economic benefits may constitute a payment of compensation, a distribution under section 301, a contribution to capital, a gift, or a transfer having a different tax character. Further, depending on the relationship between or among a non-owner and one or more other persons (including a non-owner or non-owners), the economic benefits may be treated as provided from the owner to the non-owner and as separately provided from the non-owner to such other person or persons (for example, as a payment of compensation from an employer to an employee and as a gift from the employee to the employee's child).

(2) Value of economic benefits. The value of the economic benefits provided to a non-owner for a taxable year under the arrangement equals—

(i) The cost of current life insurance protection provided to the non-owner as determined under paragraph (d)(3) of this section;

(ii) The amount of policy cash value to which the non-owner has current access within the meaning of paragraph (d)(4)(ii) of this section (to the extent that such amount was not actually taken into account for a prior taxable year); and

(iii) The value of any economic benefits not described in paragraph (d)(2)(i) or (ii) of this section provided to the non-owner (to the extent not actually taken into account for a prior taxable year).

(3) Current life insurance protection. (i) Amount of current life insurance protection. In the case of a split-dollar life insurance arrangement described in paragraph (d)(1) of this section, the amount of the current life insurance protection provided to the non-owner for a taxable year (or any portion thereof in the case of the first year or the last year of the arrangement) equals the excess of the death benefit of the life insurance contract (including paid-up additions thereto) over the total amount payable to the owner (including any outstanding policy loans that offset amounts otherwise payable to the owner) under the split-dollar life insurance arrangement, less the portion of the policy cash value actually taken into account under paragraph (d)(1) of this section or paid for by the non-owner under paragraph (d)(1) of this section for the current taxable year or any prior taxable year.

(ii) Cost of current life insurance protection. The cost of current life insurance protection provided to the non-owner for any year (or any portion thereof in the case of the first year or the last year of the arrangement) equals the amount of the current life insurance protection provided to the non-owner (determined under paragraph (d)(3)(i) of this section) multiplied by the life insurance premium factor designated or permitted in guidance published in the Internal Revenue Bulletin (see § 601.601(d)(2)(ii) of this chapter).

(4) Policy cash value. (i) In general. For purposes of this paragraph (d), policy cash value is determined disregarding surrender charges or other similar charges or reductions. Policy cash value includes policy cash value attributable to paid-up additions.

(ii) Current access. For purposes of this paragraph (d), a non-owner has current access to that portion of the policy cash value—

(A) To which, under the arrangement, the non-owner has a current or future right; and

(B) That currently is directly or indirectly accessible by the non-owner, inaccessible to the owner, or inaccessible to the owner's general creditors.

(5) Valuation date. (i) General rules. For purposes of this paragraph (d), the amount of the current life insurance protection and the policy cash value shall be determined on the same valuation date. The valuation date is the last day of the non-owner's taxable year, unless the owner and non-owner agree to instead use the policy anniversary date as the valuation date. Notwithstanding the previous sentence, if the split-dollar life insurance arrangement terminates during the taxable year of the non-owner, the value of such economic benefits is determined on the day that the arrangement terminates.

(ii) Consistency requirement. The owner and non-owner of the split-dollar life insurance arrangement must use the same valuation date. In addition, the same valuation date must be used for all years prior to termination of the split-dollar life insurance arrangement unless the parties receive consent of the Commissioner to change the valuation date.

(iii) Artifice or device. Notwithstanding paragraph (d)(5)(i) of this section, if any artifice or device is used to understate the amount of any economic benefit on the valuation date in paragraph (d)(5)(i) of this section, then, for purposes of this paragraph (d), the date on which the amount of the economic benefit is determined is the date on which the amount of the economic benefit is greatest during that taxable year.

(iv) Special rule for certain taxes. For purposes of employment tax (as defined in paragraph (c)(5) of this section), self-employment tax (as defined in paragraph (c)(6) of this section), and sections 6654 and 6655 (relating to the failure to pay estimated income tax), the portions of the current life insurance protection and the policy cash value that are treated as provided by the owner to the non-owner shall be treated as so provided on the last day of the taxable year of the non-owner. Notwithstanding the previous sentence, if the split-dollar life insurance arrangement terminates during the taxable year of the non-owner, such portions of the current life insurance protection and the policy cash value shall be treated as so provided on the day that the arrangement terminates.

(6) Examples. The following examples illustrate the rules of this paragraph (d). Except as otherwise provided, both examples assume the following facts: employer (R) is the owner (as defined in paragraph (c)(1)(i) of this section) and employee (E) is the non-owner (as defined in paragraph (c)(2)(i) of this section) of a life insurance contract that is part of a split-dollar life insurance arrangement that is subject to the provisions of paragraphs (d) through (g) of this section; the contract is a life insurance contract as defined in section 7702 and not a modified endowment contract as defined in section 7702A; R does not withdraw or obtain a loan of any portion of the policy cash value and does not surrender any portion of the life insurance contract; the compensation paid to E is reasonable; E is not provided any economic benefits described in paragraph (d)(2)(iii) of this section; E does not make any premium payments; E's taxable year is the calendar year; the value of the economic benefits is determined on the last day of E's taxable year; and E reports on E's Federal income tax return for each year that the split-dollar life insurance arrangement is in effect the amount of income required to be reported under paragraph (d) of this section. The examples are as follows:

Example (1). (i) Facts. On January 1 of year 1, R and E enter into the split-dollar life insurance arrangement. Under the arrangement, R pays all of the premiums on the life insurance contract until the termination of the arrangement or E's death. The arrangement provides that upon termination of the arrangement or E's death, R is entitled to receive the lesser of the aggregate premiums paid or the policy cash value of the contract and E is entitled to receive any remaining amounts. Under the terms of the arrangement and applicable state law, the policy cash value is fully accessible by R and R's creditors but E has the right to borrow or withdraw at any time the portion of the policy cash value exceeding the amount payable to R. To fund the arrangement, R purchases a life insurance contract with constant death benefit protection equal to $1,500,000. R makes premium payments on the life insurance contract of $60,000 in each of years 1, 2, and 3. The policy cash value equals $55,000 as of December 31 of year 1, $140,000 as of December 31 of year 2, and $240,000 as of December 31 of year 3.

(ii) Analysis. Under the terms of the split-dollar life insurance arrangement, E has the right for year 1 and all subsequent years to borrow or withdraw the portion of the policy cash value exceeding the amount payable to R. Thus, under paragraph (d)(4)(ii) of this section, E has current access to such portion of the policy cash value for each year that the arrangement is in effect. In addition, because R pays all of the premiums on the life insurance contract, R provides to E all of the economic benefits that E receives under the arrangement. Therefore, under paragraph (d)(1) of this section, E includes in gross income the value of all economic benefits described in paragraphs (d)(2)(i) and (ii) of this section provided to E under the arrangement.

(iii) Results for year 1. For year 1, E is provided, under paragraph (d)(2)(ii) of this section, $0 of policy cash value (excess of $55,000 policy cash value determined as of December 31 of year 1 over $55,000 payable to R). For year 1, E is also provided, under paragraph (d)(2)(i) of this section, current life insurance protection of $1,445,000 ($1,500,000 minus $55,000 payable to R). Thus, E includes in gross income for year 1 the cost of $1,445,000 of current life insurance protection.

(iv) Results for year 2. For year 2, E is provided, under paragraph (d)(2)(ii) of this section, $20,000 of policy cash value ($140,000 policy cash value determined as of December 31 of year 2 minus $120,000 payable to R). For year 2, E is also provided, under paragraph (d)(2)(i) of this section, current life insurance protection of $1,360,000 ($1,500,000 minus the sum of $120,000 payable to R and the aggregate of $20,000 of policy cash value that E actually includes in income on E's year 1 and year 2 federal income tax returns). Thus, E includes in gross income for year 2 the sum of $20,000 of policy cash value and the cost of $1,360,000 of current life insurance protection.

(v) Results for year 3. For year 3, E is provided, under paragraph (d)(2)(ii) of this section, $40,000 of policy cash value ($240,000 policy cash value determined as of December 31 of year 3 minus the sum of $180,000 payable to R and $20,000 of aggregate policy cash value that E actually included in gross income on E's year 1 and year 2 federal income tax returns). For year 3, E is also provided, under paragraph (d)(2)(i) of this section, current life insurance protection of $1,260,000 ($1,500,000 minus the sum of $180,000 payable to R and $60,000 of aggregate policy cash value that E actually includes in gross income on E's year 1, year 2, and year 3 federal income tax returns). Thus, E includes in gross income for year 3 the sum of $40,000 of policy cash value and the cost of $1,260,000 of current life insurance protection.

Example (2). (i) Facts. The facts are the same as in Example 1 except that E cannot directly or indirectly access any portion of the policy cash value, but the terms of the split-dollar life insurance arrangement or applicable state law provide that the policy cash value in excess of the amount payable to R is inaccessible to R's general creditors.

(ii) Analysis. Under the terms of the split-dollar life insurance arrangement or applicable state law, the portion of the policy cash value exceeding the amount payable to R is inaccessible to R's general creditors and E has a current or future right to that portion of the cash value. Thus, under paragraph (d)(4)(ii) of this section, E has current access to such portion of the policy cash value for each year that the arrangement is in effect. In addition, because R pays all of the premiums on the life insurance contract, R provides to E all of the economic benefits that E receives under the arrangement. Therefore, under paragraph (d)(1) of this section, E includes in gross income the value of all economic benefits described in paragraphs (d)(2)(i) and (ii) of this section provided to E under the arrangement.

(iii) Results for years 1, 2 and 3. The results for this example are the same as the results in Example 1.

(e) Amounts received under the contract. *(1) In general.* Except as otherwise provided in paragraph (f)(3) of this section, any amount received under a life insurance contract that is part of a split-dollar life insurance arrangement subject to the rules of paragraphs (d) through (g) of this section (including, but not limited to, a policy owner dividend, proceeds of a specified policy loan described in paragraph (e)(2) of this section, or the proceeds of a withdrawal from or partial surrender of the life insurance contract) is treated, to the extent provided directly or indirectly to a non-owner of the life insurance contract, as though such amount had been paid to the owner of the life insurance contract and then paid by the owner to the non-owner. The amount received is taxable to the owner in accordance with the rules of section 72. The non-owner (and the owner for gift tax and employment tax purposes) must take the amount described in paragraph (e)(3) of this section into account as a payment of compensation, a distribution under section 301, a contribution to capital, a gift, or other transfer depending on the relationship between the owner and the non-owner.

(2) Specified policy loan. A policy loan is a specified policy loan to the extent—

(i) The proceeds of the loan are distributed directly from the insurance company to the non-owner;

(ii) A reasonable person would not expect that the loan will be repaid by the non-owner; or

(iii) The non-owner's obligation to repay the loan to the owner is satisfied or is capable of being satisfied upon repayment by either party to the insurance company.

(3) Amount required to be taken into account. With respect to a non-owner (and the owner for gift tax and employment tax purposes), the amount described in this paragraph (e)(3) is equal to the excess of—

(i) The amount treated as received by the owner under paragraph (e)(1) of this section; over

(ii) The amount of all economic benefits described in paragraphs (d)(2)(ii) and (iii) of this section actually taken into account by the non-owner (and the owner for gift tax and employment tax purposes) plus any consideration described in paragraph (d)(1) of this section paid by the non-owner for such economic benefits described in paragraphs (d)(2)(ii) and (iii) of this section. The amount determined under the preceding sentence applies only to the extent that neither this paragraph (e)(3)(ii) nor paragraph (g)(1)(ii) of this section previously has applied to such economic benefits.

(f) Other tax consequences. *(1) Introduction.* In the case of a split-dollar life insurance arrangement subject to the rules of paragraphs (d) through (g) of this section, this paragraph (f) sets forth other tax consequences to the owner and non-owner of a life insurance contract that is part of the arrangement for the period prior to the transfer (as defined in paragraph (c)(3) of this section) of the contract (or an undivided interest therein) from the owner to the non-owner. See paragraph (g) of this section and § 1.83-6(a)(5) for tax consequences upon the transfer of the contract (or an undivided interest therein).

(2) Investment in the contract. (i) To the non-owner. A non-owner does not receive any investment in the contract under section 72(e)(6) with respect to a life insurance contract that is part of a split-dollar life insurance arrangement subject to the rules of paragraphs (d) through (g) of this section.

(ii) To owner. Any premium paid by an owner under a split-dollar life insurance arrangement subject to the rules of paragraphs (d) through (g) of this section is included in the owner's investment in the contract under section 72(e)(6). No premium or amount described in paragraph (d) of this section is deductible by the owner (except as otherwise provided in § 1.83-6(a)(5)). Any amount paid by a non-owner, directly or indirectly, to the owner of the life insurance contract for current life insurance protection or for any other economic benefit under the life insurance contract is included in the owner's gross income and is included in the owner's investment in the life insurance contract for purposes of section 72(e)(6) (but only to the extent not otherwise so included by reason of having been paid by the owner as a premium or other consideration for the contract).

(3) Treatment of death benefit proceeds. (i) Death benefit proceeds to beneficiary (other than the owner). Any amount paid to a beneficiary (other than the owner) by reason of the death of the insured is excluded from gross income by such beneficiary under section 101(a) as an amount received under a life insurance contract to the extent such amount is allocable to current life insurance protection provided to the non-owner pursuant to the split-dollar life insurance arrangement, the cost of which was paid by the non-owner, or the value of which the non-owner actually took into account pursuant to paragraph (d)(1) of this section.

(ii) Death benefit proceeds to owner as beneficiary. Any amount paid or payable to an owner in its capacity as a beneficiary by reason of the death of the insured is excluded from gross income of the owner under section 101(a) as an amount received under a life insurance contract to the extent such amount is not allocable to current life insurance protection provided to the non-owner pursuant to the split-dollar life insurance arrangement, the cost of which was paid by the non-owner, or the value of which the non-owner actually took into account pursuant to paragraph (d)(1) of this section.

(iii) Transfers of death benefit proceeds. Death benefit proceeds paid to a party to a split-dollar life insurance arrangement (or the estate or beneficiary of that party) that are not excludable from that party's income under section 101(a) to the extent provided in paragraph (f)(3)(i) or (ii) of this section, are treated as transferred to that party in a separate transaction. The death benefit proceeds treated as so transferred will be taxed in a manner similar to other transfers. For example, if death benefit proceeds paid to an employee, the employee's estate, or the employee's beneficiary are not excludable from the employee's gross income under section 101(a) to the extent provided in paragraph (f)(3)(i) of this section, then such payment is treated as a payment of compensation by the employer to the employee.

(g) Transfer of entire contract or undivided interest therein. *(1) In general.* Upon a transfer within the meaning of paragraph (c)(3) of this section of a life insurance contract (or an undivided interest therein) to a non-owner (transferee), the transferee (and the owner (transferor) for gift tax and employment tax purposes) takes into account the excess of the fair market value of the life insurance contract (or the undivided interest therein) transferred to the transferee at that time over the sum of—

(i) The amount the transferee pays to the transferor to obtain the contract (or the undivided interest therein); and

(ii) The amount of all economic benefits described in paragraph (d)(2)(ii) and (iii) of this section actually taken into account by the transferee (and the transferor for gift tax and employment tax purposes), plus any consideration described in paragraph (d)(1) of this section paid by the transferee for such economic benefits described in paragraphs (d)(2)(ii) and (iii) of this section. The amount determined under the preceding sentence applies only to the extent that neither this paragraph (g)(1)(ii) nor paragraph (e)(3)(ii) of this section previously has applied to such economic benefits.

(2) Determination of fair market value. For purposes of paragraph (g)(1) of this section, the fair market value of a life insurance contract is the policy cash value and the value of all other rights under such contract (including any supplemental agreements thereto and whether or not guaranteed), other than the value of current life insurance protection. Notwithstanding the preceding sentence, the fair market value of a life insurance contract for gift tax purposes is determined under § 25.2512-6(a) of this chapter.

(3) Exception for certain transfers in connection with the performance of services. To the extent the ownership of a life insurance contract (or undivided interest in such contract) is transferred in connection with the performance of services, paragraph (g)(1) of this section does not apply until such contract (or undivided interest in such contract) is taxable under section 83. For purposes of paragraph (g)(1) of this section, fair market value is determined disregarding any lapse restrictions and at the time the transfer of such contract (or undivided interest in such contract) is taxable under section 83.

(4) Treatment of non-owner after transfer. (i) In general. After a transfer of an entire life insurance contract (except when such transfer is in connection with the performance of services and the transfer is not yet taxable under section 83), the person who previously had been the non-owner is treated as the owner of such contract for all purposes, including for purposes of paragraph (b) of this section and for purposes of § 1.61-2(d)(2)(ii)(A). After the transfer of an undivided interest in a life insurance contract (or, if later, at the time such transfer is taxable under section 83), the person who previously had been the non-owner is treated as the owner of a separate contract consisting of that interest for all purposes, including for purposes of paragraph (b) of this section and for purposes of § 1.61-2(d)(2)(ii)(A).

(ii) Investment in the contract after transfer. (A) In general. The amount treated as consideration paid to acquire the contract under section 72(g)(1), in order to determine the aggregate premiums paid by the transferee for purposes of section 72(e)(6)(A) after the transfer (or, if later, at the time such transfer is taxable under section 83), equals the greater of the fair market value of the contract or the sum of the amounts determined under paragraphs (g)(1)(i) and (ii) of this section.

(B) Transfers between a donor and a donee. In the case of a transfer of a contract between a donor and a donee, the amount treated as consideration paid by the transferee to acquire the contract under section 72(g)(1), in order to determine the aggregate premiums paid by the transferee for purposes of section 72(e)(6)(A) after the transfer, equals the sum of the amounts determined under paragraphs (g)(1)(i) and (ii) of this section except that—

(1) The amount determined under paragraph (g)(1)(i) of this section includes the aggregate of premiums or other consideration paid or deemed to have been paid by the transferor; and

(2) The amount of all economic benefits determined under paragraph (g)(1)(ii) of this section actually taken into account by the transferee does not include such benefits to the extent such benefits were excludable from the transferee's gross income at the time of receipt.

(C) Transfers of an undivided interest in a contract. If a portion of a contract is transferred to the transferee, then the amount to be included as consideration paid to acquire the contract is determined by multiplying the amount determined under paragraph (g)(4)(ii)(A) of this section (as modified by paragraph (g)(4)(ii)(B) of this section, if the transfer is between a donor and a donee) by a fraction, the numerator of which is the fair market value of the portion transferred and the denominator of which is the fair market value of the entire contract.

(D) Example. The following example illustrates the rules of this paragraph (g)(4)(ii):

Example. (i) In year 1, donor D and donee E enter into a split-dollar life insurance arrangement as defined in paragraph (b)(1) of this section. D is the owner of the life insurance contract under paragraph (c)(1) of this section. The life insurance contract is not a modified endowment contract as defined in section 7702A. In year 5, D gratuitously transfers the contract, within the meaning of paragraph (c)(3) of this section, to E. At the time of the transfer, the fair market value of the contract is $200,000 and D had paid $50,000 in premiums under the arrangement. In addition, by the time of the transfer, E had current access to $80,000 of policy cash value which was excludable from E's gross income under section 102.

(ii) E's investment in the contract is $50,000, consisting of the $50,000 of premiums paid by D. The $80,000 of policy cash value to which E had current access is not included in E's investment in the contract because such amount was excludable from E's gross income when E had current access to that policy cash value.

(iii) No investment in the contract for current life insurance protection. Except as provided in paragraph (g)(4)(ii)(B) of this section, no amount allocable to current life insurance protection provided to the transferee (the cost of which was paid by the transferee or the value of which was provided to the transferee) is treated as consideration paid to acquire the contract under section 72(g)(1) to determine the aggregate premiums paid by the transferee for purposes of determining the transferee's investment in the contract under section 72(e) after the transfer.

(h) Examples. The following examples illustrate the rules of this section. Except as otherwise provided, each of the examples assumes that the employer (R) is the owner (as defined in paragraph (c)(1) of this section) of a life insurance contract that is part of a split-dollar life insurance arrangement subject to the rules of paragraphs (d) through (g) of this section, that the employee (E) is not provided any economic benefits described in paragraph (d)(2)(iii) of this section, that the life insurance contract is not a modified endowment contract under section 7702A, that the compensation paid to E is reasonable, and that E makes no premium payments. The examples are as follows:

Example (1). (i) In year 1, R purchases a life insurance contract on the life of E. R is named as the policy owner of the contract. R and E enter into an arrangement under which R will pay all the premiums on the life insurance contract until the termination of the arrangement or E's death. Upon termination of the arrangement or E's death, R is entitled to receive the greater of the aggregate premiums or the policy cash value of the contract. The balance of the death benefit will be paid to a beneficiary designated by E.

(ii) Because R is designated as the policy owner of the contract, R is the owner of the contract under paragraph (c)(1)(i) of this section. In addition, R would be treated as the owner of the contract regardless of whether R were designated as the policy owner under paragraph (c)(1)(i) of this section because the split-dollar life insurance arrangement is described in paragraph (c)(1)(ii)(A)(1) of this section. E is a non-owner of the contract. Under the arrangement between R and E, a portion of the death benefit is payable to a beneficiary designated by E. The arrangement is a split-dollar life insurance arrangement under paragraph (b)(1) or (2) of this section. Because R pays all the premiums on the life insurance contract, R provides to E the entire amount of the current life insurance protection E receives under the arrangement. Therefore, for each year that the split-dollar life insurance arrangement is in effect, E must include in gross income under paragraph (d)(1) of this section the value of current life insurance protection described in paragraph (d)(2)(i) of this section provided to E in each year.

Example (2). (i) The facts are the same as in Example 1 except that, upon termination of the arrangement or E's death, R is entitled to receive the lesser of the aggregate premiums or the policy cash value of the contract. Under the terms of the arrangement and applicable state law, the policy cash value is fully accessible by R and R's creditors but E has the right to borrow or withdraw at any time the portion of the policy cash value exceeding the amount payable to R.

(ii) Because R is designated as the policy owner, R is the owner of the contract under paragraph (c)(1)(i) of this section. E is a non-owner of the contract. For each year that the split-dollar life insurance arrangement is in effect, E has the right to borrow or withdraw at any time the portion of the policy cash value exceeding the amount payable to R. Thus, under paragraph (d)(4)(ii) of this section, E has current access to such portion of the policy cash value for each year that the arrangement is in effect. In addition, because R pays all the premiums on the life insurance contract, R provides to E all the economic benefits that E receives under the arrangement. Therefore, for each year that the split-dollar life insurance arrangement is in effect, E must include in gross income under paragraph (d)(1) of this section, the value of all economic benefits described in paragraph (d)(2)(i) and (ii) of this section provided to E in each year.

Example (3). (i) The facts are the same as in Example 1 except that in year 5, R and E modify the split-dollar life insurance arrangement to provide that, upon termination of the arrangement or E's death, R is entitled to receive the greater of the aggregate premiums or one-half the policy cash value of the contract. Under the terms of the modified arrangement and applicable state law, the policy cash value is fully accessible by R and R's creditors but E has the right to borrow or withdraw at any time the portion of the policy cash value exceeding the amount payable to R.

(ii) For each year that the split-dollar life insurance arrangement is in effect, E must include in gross income under paragraph (d)(1) of this section the value of the economic benefits described in paragraph (d)(2)(i) of this section provided to E under the arrangement during that year. In year 5 (and subsequent years), E has the right to borrow or withdraw at any time the portion of the policy cash value exceeding the amount payable to R. Thus, under paragraph (d)(4)(ii) of this section, E has current access to such portion of the policy cash value. Thus, in year 5 (and each subsequent year), E must also include in gross income under paragraph (d)(1) of this section the value of the economic benefits described in paragraph (d)(2)(ii) of this section provided to E in each year.

(iii) The arrangement is not described in paragraph (c)(1)(ii)(A)(1) of this section after it is modified in year 5. Because R is the designated owner of the life insurance contract, R continues to be treated as the owner of the contract under paragraph (c)(1)(ii)(B)(1) of this section after the arrangement is modified. In addition, because the modification made by R and E in year 5 does not involve the transfer (within the meaning of paragraph (c)(3) of this section) of an undivided interest in the life insurance contract from R to E, the modification is not a transfer for purposes of paragraph (g) of this section.

Example (4). (i) The facts are the same as in Example 2 except that in year 7, R and E modify the split-dollar life insurance arrangement to provide that, upon termination of the arrangement or E's death, R will be paid the lesser of 80 percent of the aggregate premiums or the policy cash value of the contract. Under the terms of the modified arrangement and applicable state law, the policy cash value is fully accessible by R and R's creditors but E has the right to borrow or withdraw at any time the portion of the policy cash value exceeding the lesser of 80 percent of the aggregate premiums paid by R or the policy cash value of the contract.

(ii) Commencing in year 7 (and in each subsequent year), E must include in gross income the economic benefits described in paragraph (d)(2)(ii) of this section as provided in this Example 4(ii) rather than as provided in Example 2(ii). Thus, in year 7 (and in each subsequent year) E must include in gross income under paragraph (d) of this section, the excess of the policy cash value over the lesser of 80 percent of the aggregate premiums paid by R or the policy cash value of the contract (to the extent E did not actually include such amounts in gross income for a prior taxable year). In addition, in year 7 (and each subsequent year) E must also include in gross income the value of the economic benefits described in paragraph (d)(2)(i) of this section provided to E under the arrangement in each such year.

Example (5). (i) The facts are the same as in Example 3 except that in year 7, E is designated as the policy owner. At that time, E's rights to the contract are substantially vested as defined in § 1.83-3(b).

(ii) In year 7, R is treated as having made a transfer (within the meaning of paragraph (c)(3) of this section) of the life insurance contract to E. E must include in gross income the amount determined under paragraph (g)(1) of this section.

(iii) After the transfer of the contract to E, E is the owner of the contract and any premium payments by R will be included in E's income under paragraph (b)(5) of this section and § 1.61-2(d)(2)(ii)(A) (unless R's payments are split-dollar loans as defined in § 1.7872-15(b)(1)).

Example (6). (i) In year 1, E and R enter into a split-dollar life insurance arrangement as defined in paragraph (b)(2) of this section. Under the arrangement, R is required to make annual premium payments of $10,000 and E is required to make annual premium payments of $500. In year 5, a $500 policy owner dividend payable to E is declared by the insurance company. E directs the insurance company to use the $500 as E's premium payment for year 5.

(ii) For each year the arrangement is in effect, E must include in gross income the value of the economic benefits provided during the year, as required by paragraph (d)(2) of this section, over the $500 premium payments paid by E. In year 5, E must also include in gross income as compensation the excess, if any, of the $500 distributed to E from the proceeds of the policy owner dividend over the amount determined under paragraph (e)(3)(ii) of this section.

(iii) R must include in income the premiums paid by E during the years the split-dollar life insurance arrangement is in effect, including the $500 of the premium E paid in year 5 with proceeds of the policy owner dividend. R's investment in the contract is increased in an amount equal to the premiums paid by E, including the $500 of the premium paid by E in year 5 from the proceeds of the policy owner dividend. In year 5, R is treated as receiving a $500 distribution under the contract, which is taxed pursuant to section 72.

Example (7). (i) The facts are the same as in Example 2 except that in year 10, E withdraws $100,000 from the cash value of the contract.

(ii) In year 10, R is treated as receiving a $100,000 distribution from the insurance company. This amount is treated as an amount received by R under the contract and taxed pursuant to section 72. This amount reduces R's investment in the contract under section 72(e). R is treated as paying the $100,000 to E as cash compensation, and E must include that amount in gross income less any amounts determined under paragraph (e)(3)(ii) of this section.

Example (8). (i) The facts are the same as in Example 7 except E receives the proceeds of a $100,000 specified policy loan directly from the insurance company.

(ii) The transfer of the proceeds of the specified policy loan to E is treated as a loan by the insurance company to R. Under the rules of section 72(e), the $100,000 loan is not included in R's income and does not reduce R's investment in the contract. R is treated as paying the $100,000 of loan proceeds to E as cash compensation. E must include that amount in gross income less any amounts determined under paragraph (e)(3)(ii) of this section.

(i) [Reserved]

(j) Effective date. *(1) General rule.* (i) In general. This section applies to any split-dollar life insurance arrangement (as defined in paragraph (b)(1) or (2) of this section) entered into after September 17, 2003.

(ii) Determination of when an arrangement is entered into. For purposes of paragraph (j) of this section, a split-dollar life insurance arrangement is entered into on the latest of the following dates:

(A) The date on which the life insurance contract under the arrangement is issued;

(B) The effective date of the life insurance contract under the arrangement;

(C) The date on which the first premium on the life insurance contract under the arrangement is paid;

(D) The date on which the parties to the arrangement enter into an agreement with regard to the policy; or

(E) The date on which the arrangement satisfies the definition of a split-dollar life insurance arrangement (as defined in paragraph (b)(1) or (2) of this section).

(2) Modified arrangements treated as new arrangements. (i) In general. For purposes of paragraph (j)(1) of this section, if an arrangement entered into on or before September 17, 2003 is materially modified after September 17, 2003, the arrangement is treated as a new arrangement entered into on the date of the modification.

(ii) Non-material modifications. The following is a non-exclusive list of changes that are not material modifications under paragraph (j)(2)(i) of this section (either alone or in conjunction with other changes listed in paragraphs (j)(2)(ii)(A) through (I) of this section)—

(A) A change solely in the mode of premium payment (for example, a change from monthly to quarterly premiums);

(B) A change solely in the beneficiary of the life insurance contract, unless the beneficiary is a party to the arrangement;

(C) A change solely in the interest rate payable under the life insurance contract on a policy loan;

(D) A change solely necessary to preserve the status of the life insurance contract under section 7702;

(E) A change solely to the ministerial provisions of the life insurance contract (for example, a change in the address to send payment);

(F) A change made solely under the terms of any agreement (other than the life insurance contract) that is a part of the split-dollar life insurance arrangement if the change is non-discretionary by the parties and is made pursuant to a binding commitment (whether set forth in the agreement or otherwise) in effect on or before September 17, 2003;

(G) A change solely in the owner of the life insurance contract as a result of a transaction to which section 381(a) applies and in which substantially all of the former owner's assets are transferred to the new owner of the policy;

(H) A change to the policy solely if such change is required by a court or a state insurance commissioner as a result of the insolvency of the insurance company that issued the policy; or

(I) A change solely in the insurance company that administers the policy as a result of an assumption reinsurance transaction between the issuing insurance company and the new insurance company to which the owner and the non-owner were not a party.

(iii) Delegation to Commissioner. The Commissioner, in revenue rulings, notices, and other guidance published in the Internal Revenue Bulletin, may provide additional guidance with respect to other modifications that are not material for purposes of paragraph (j)(2)(i) of this section. See § 601.601(d)(2)(ii) of this chapter.

T.D. 9092, 9/11/2003.

---

§ 1.62-1 Adjusted gross income.

Caution: The Treasury has not yet amended Reg § 1.62-1 to reflect changes made by P.L. 108-311, P.L. 108-173.

(a) [Reserved]

(b) [Reserved]

(c) Deductions allowable in computing adjusted gross income. The deductions specified in section 62(a) for purposes of computing adjusted gross income are—

(1) Deductions set forth in § 1.62-1T(c); and

(2) Deductions allowable under part VI, subchapter B, chapter 1 of the Internal Revenue Code, (section 161 and following) that consist of expenses paid or incurred by the taxpayer in connection with the performance of services as an employee under a reimbursement or other expense allowance arrangement (as defined in § 1.62-2) with his or her employer. For the rules pertaining to expenses paid or incurred in taxable years beginning before January 1, 1989, see paragraphs (c)(2) and (f) (see § 1.62-1T(c)(2) and (f) (as amended in 26 CFR part 1 §§ 1.61 to 1.169) revised April 1, 1992).

(d) through **(h) [Reserved]**

(i) Effective date. Paragraph (c) of this section is effective for taxable years beginning on or after January 1, 1989.

T.D. 8451, 12/4/92.

PARAGRAPH 1. Section 1.62-1 is amended by revising paragraph (c)(13) to read as follows:

Proposed § 1.62-1 Adjusted gross income. [*For Preamble, see ¶ 150,703*]

* * * * *

(c) * * *

(13) Deductions allowed by sections 219 and 220 for contributions to an individual retirement account described in section 408(a), for an individual retirement annuity described in section 408(b), or for a retirement bond described in section 409;

§ 1.62-1T Adjusted gross income (temporary).

Caution: The Treasury has not yet amended Reg § 1.62-1T to reflect changes made by P.L. 108-357, P.L. 107-173, P.L. 107-147, P.L. 105-34, P.L. 103-66, P.L. 100-647.

(a) Basis for determining the amount of certain deductions. The term "adjusted gross income" means the gross income computed under section 61 minus such of the deductions allowed by chapter 1 of the Code as are specified in section 62(a). Adjusted gross income is used as the basis for determining the following:

(1) The limitation on the amount of miscellaneous itemized deductions (under section 67),

(2) The limitation on the amount of the deduction for casualty losses (under section 165(h)(2)),

(3) The limitation on the amount of the deduction for charitable contributions (under section 170(b)(1)),

(4) The limitation on the amount of the deduction for medical and dental expenses (under section 213),

(5) The limitation on the amount of the deduction for qualified retirement contributions for active participants in certain pension plans (under section 219(g)), and

(6) The phase-out of the exemption from the disallowance of passive activity losses and credits (under section 469(i)(3)).

(b) Double deduction not permitted. Section 62(a) merely specifies which of the deductions provided in chapter

1 of the Code shall be allowed in computing adjusted gross income. It does not create any new deductions. The fact that a particular item may be described in more than one of the paragraphs under section 62(a) does not permit the item to be deducted twice in computing adjusted gross income or taxable income.

(c) Deductions allowable in computing adjusted gross income. The deductions specified in section 62(a) for purposes of computing adjusted gross income are:

(1) Deductions allowable under chapter 1 of the Code (other than by part VII (section 211 and following), subchapter B of such chapter) that are attributable to a trade or business carried on by the taxpayer not consisting of services performed as an employee;

(2) Reserved.

(3) For taxable years beginning after December 31, 1986, deductions allowable under section 162 that consist of expenses paid or incurred by a qualified performing artist (as defined in section 62(b)) in connection with the performance by him or her of services in the performing arts as an employee;

(4) Deductions allowable under part VI as losses from the sale or exchange of property;

(5) Deductions allowable under part VI, section 212, or section 611 that are attributable to property held for the production of rents or royalties;

(6) Deductions for depreciation or depletion allowable under sections 167 or 611 to a life tenant of property or to an income beneficiary of property held in trust or to an heir, legatee, or devisee of an estate;

(7) Deductions allowed by section 404 for contributions on behalf of a self-employed individual;

(8) Deductions allowed by section 219 for contributions to an individual retirement account described in section 408(a), or for an individual retirement annuity described in section 408(b);

(9) Deductions allowed by section 402(e)(3) with respect to a lump-sum distribution;

(10) For taxable years beginning after December 31, 1972, deductions allowed by section 165 for losses incurred in any transaction entered into for profit though not connected with a trade or business, to the extent that such losses include amounts forfeited to a bank, mutual savings bank, savings and loan association, building and loan association, cooperative bank or homestead association as a penalty for premature withdrawal of funds from a time savings account, certificate of deposit, or similar class of deposit;

(11) For taxable years beginning after December 31, 1976, deductions for alimony and separate maintenance payments allowed by section 215;

(12) Deductions allowed by section 194 for the amortization of reforestation expenditures; and

(13) Deductions allowed by section 165 for the repayment (made in a taxable year beginning after December 28, 1980) to a trust described in paragraph (9) or (17) of section 501(c) of supplemental unemployment compensation benefits received from such trust if such repayment is required because of the receipt of trade readjustment allowances under section 231 or 232 of the Trade Act of 1974 (19 U.S.C. 2291 and 2292).

(d) Expenses directly related to a trade or business. For the purpose of the deductions specified in section 62, the performance of personal services as an employee does not constitute the carrying on of a trade or business, except as otherwise expressly provided. The practice of a profession, not as an employee, is considered the conduct of a trade or business within the meaning of such section. To be deductible for the purposes of determining adjusted gross income, expenses must be those directly, and not those merely remotely, connected with the conduct of a trade or business. For example, taxes are deductible in arriving at adjusted gross income only if they constitute expenditures directly attributable to a trade or business or to property from which rents or royalties are derived. Thus, property taxes paid or incurred on real property used in a trade or business are deductible, but state taxes on net income are not deductible even though the taxpayer's income is derived from the conduct of a trade or business.

(e) Reimbursed and unreimbursed employee expenses. *(1) In general.* Expenses paid or incurred by an employee that are deductible from gross income under part VI in computing taxable income (determined without regard to section 67) and for which the employee is reimbursed by the employer, its agent, or third party (for whom the employee performs a benefit as an employee of the employer) under an express agreement for reimbursement or pursuant to an *express* expense allowance arrangement may be deducted from gross income in computing adjusted gross income. Except as provided in paragraphs (e)(2) and (e)(4) of this section, for taxable years beginning after December 31, 1986, if the amount of a reimbursement made by an employer, its agent, or third party to an employee is less than the total amount of the business expenses paid or incurred by the employee, the determination of to which of the employee's business expenses the reimbursement applies and the amount of each expense that is covered by the reimbursement is made on the basis of all of the facts and circumstances of the particular case.

(2) Facts and circumstances unclear on business expenses for meals and entertainment. If—

(i) The facts and circumstances do not make clear—

(A) That a reimbursement does not apply to business expenses for meals or entertainment, or

(B) The amount of business expenses for meals or entertainment that is covered by the reimbursement, and

(ii) The employee pays or incurs business expenses for meals or entertainment,

the amount of the reimbursement that applies to such expenses (or portion thereof with respect to which the facts and circumstances are unclear) shall be determined by multiplying the amount of the employee's business expenses for meals and entertainment (or portion thereof with respect to which the facts and circumstances are unclear) by a fraction, the numerator of which is the total amount of the reimbursement (or portion thereof with respect to which the facts and circumstances are unclear) and the denominator of which is the aggregate amount of all the business expenses of the employee (or portion thereof with respect to which the facts and circumstances are unclear).

(3) Deductibility of unreimbursed expenses. The amount of expenses that is determined not to be reimbursed pursuant to paragraph (e)(1) or (2) of this section is deductible from adjusted gross income in determining the employee's taxable income subject to the limitations applicable to such expenses (e.g., the 2-percent floor of section 67 and the 80-percent limitation on meal and entertainment expenses provided for in section 274(n)).

(4) Unreimbursed expenses of State legislators. For taxable years beginning after December 31, 1986, any portion of the amount allowed as a deduction to State legislators pursuant to section 162(h)(1)(B) that is not reimbursed by the State or a third party shall be allocated between lodging and meals in the same ratio as the amounts allowable for lodging and meals under the Federal per diem applicable to the legislator's State capital at the end of the legislator's taxable year (see Appendix 1-A of the Federal Travel Regulations (FTR), which as of March 28, 1988, are contained in GSA Bulletin FPMR A-40, Supplement 20). For purposes of this paragraph (e)(4), the amount allowable for meals under the Federal per diem shall be the amount of the Federal per diem allowable for meals and incidental expenses reduced by $2 per legislative day (or other amount allocated to incidental expenses in 1-7.5(a)(2) of the FTR). The unreimbursed portion of each type of expense is deductible from adjusted gross income in determining the State legislator's taxable income subject to the limitations applicable to such expenses. For example, the unreimbursed portion allocable to meals shall be reduced by 20 percent pursuant to section 274(n) before being subjected to the 2-percent floor of section 67 for purposes of computing the taxable income of a State legislator. See § 1.67-1T(a)(2).

(5) Expenses paid directly by an employer, its agent, or third party. In the case of an employer, its agent, or a third party who provides property or services to an employee or who pays an employee's expenses directly instead of reimbursing the employee, see section 132 and the regulations thereunder for the income tax treatment of such expenses.

(6) Examples. The provisions of this paragraph (e) may be illustrated by the following examples:

Example (1). During 1987, A, an employee, while on business trips away from home pays $300 for travel fares, $200 for lodging and $100 for meals. In addition, A pays $50 for business meals in the area of his place of employment ("local meals"), $250 for continuing education courses, and $100 for business-related entertainment (other than meals). The total amount of the reimbursements received by A for his employee expenses from his employer is $750, and it is assumed that A's expenses meet the deductibility requirements of sections 162 and 274. A includes the amount of the reimbursement in his gross income. A's employer designates the reimbursement to cover in full A's expenses for travel fares, lodging, and meals while away from home, local meals, and entertainment, and no facts or circumstances indicate a contrary intention of the employer. Because the facts and circumstances make clear the amount of A's business expenses for meals and entertainment that is covered by the reimbursement, the reimbursement will be allocated to these expenses. In determining his adjusted gross income under section 62, A may deduct the full amount of the reimbursement for travel fares, lodging, and meals while away from home, local meals, and entertainment. In determining his taxable income under section 63, A may deduct his expenses for continuing education courses to the extent allowable by sections 67 and 162.

Example (2). Assume the facts are the same as in example (1) except that the facts and circumstances make clear that the reimbursement covers all types of deductible expenses but they do not make clear the amount of each type of expense that is covered by the reimbursement. The amount of the reimbursement that is allocated to A's business expenses for meals and entertainment is $187.50. This amount is determined by multiplying the total amount of A's business expenses for meals and entertainment ($250) by the ratio of A's total reimbursement to A's total business expenses ($750/$1,000). The remaining amount of the reimbursement, $562.50 ($750 – $187.50), is allocated to A's business expenses other than meal and entertainment expenses. Therefore, in determining his adjusted gross income under section 62, A may deduct $750 for reimbursed business expenses (including meals and entertainment). In determining his taxable income under section 63, A may deduct (subject to the limitations and conditions of sections 67, 162, and 274) the unreimbursed portion of his expenses for meals and entertainment ($62.50 ($250 – $187.50), and other employee business expenses ($187.50 ($750 – $562.50)).

Example (3). Assume the facts are the same as in example (1) except that the amount of the reimbursement is $500. Assume further that the facts and circumstances make clear that the reimbursement covers $100 of expenses for meals and that the remaining $400 of the reimbursement covers all types of deductible expenses (including any expenses for meals in excess of the $100 already designated) other than expenses for entertainment. The amount of the reimbursement that is allocated to A's business expenses for meals and entertainment is $125. This amount is equal to the sum of the amount of the reimbursement that clearly applies to meals ($100) and the amount of the reimbursement with respect to which the facts are unclear that is allocated to meals ($25). The latter amount is determined by multiplying the total amount of A's business expenses for meals and entertainment with respect to which the facts are unclear ($50) by the ratio of A's total reimbursement with respect to which the facts are unclear to A's total business expenses with respect to which the facts are unclear ($400/$800). The remaining amount of the reimbursement, $375 ($500 – $125) is allocated to A's business expenses other than meals and entertainment. Therefore, in determining his adjusted gross income under section 62, A may deduct $500 for reimbursed business expenses (including meals). In determining his taxable income under section 63, A may deduct (subject to the limitations and conditions of sections 67, 162, and 274) the unreimbursed portion of his expenses for meals ($25 ($150 – $125)), entertainment ($100), and other employee business expenses ($375 ($750 – $375)).

Example (4). During 1987 B, a research scientist, is employed by Corporation X. B gives a speech before members of Association Y, a professional organization of scientists, describing her most recent research findings. Pursuant to a reimbursement arrangement, Y reimburses B for the full amount of her travel fares to the site of the speech and for the full amount of her expenses for lodging and meals while there. B includes the amount of the reimbursement in her gross income. B may deduct the full amount of her travel expenses pursuant to section 62(a)(2)(A) in computing her adjusted gross income.

(f) [Reserved]

(g) Moving expenses. For taxable years beginning after December 31, 1986, a taxpayer described in section 217(a) shall not take into account the deduction described in section 217 relating to moving expenses in computing adjusted gross income under section 62 even if the taxpayer is reimbursed for his or her moving expenses. Such a taxpayer shall include the amount of any reimbursement for moving expenses in income pursuant to section 82. The deduction described in section 217 shall be taken into account in computing the taxable income of the taxpayer under section 63. Pursuant to section 67(b)(6), the 2-percent floor described in section 67(a) does not apply to moving expenses.

(h) Cross-reference. See 26 CFR 1.62-1 (Rev. as of April 1, 1986) with respect to pre-1987 deductions for travel, meal, lodging, transportation, and other trade or business expenses of an employee, reimbursed expenses of an employee, expenses of an outside salesperson, long-term capital gains, contributions described in section 405(c) to a bond purchase plan on behalf of a self-employed individual, moving expenses, amounts not received as benefits pursuant to section 1379(b)(3), and retirement bonds described in section 409 (allowed by section 219).

T.D. 8189, 3/25/88, amend T.D. 8276, 12/7/89, T.D. 8324, 12/14/90, T.D. 8451, 12/4/92.

§ 1.62-2 Reimbursements and other expense allowance arrangements.

Caution: The Treasury has not yet amended Reg § 1.62-2 to reflect changes made by P.L. 105-34.

(a) Table of contents. The contents of this section are as follows:

(a) Table of contents.
(b) Scope.
(c) Reimbursement or other expense allowance arrangement.
(1) Defined.
(2) Accountable plans.
(i) In general.
(ii) Special rule for failure to return excess.
(3) Nonaccountable plans.
(i) In general.
(ii) Special rule for failure to return excess.
(4) Treatment of payments under accountable plans.
(5) Treatment of payments under nonaccountable plans.
(d) Business connection.
(1) In general.
(2) Other bona fide expenses.
(3) Reimbursement requirement.
(i) In general.
(ii) Per diem allowances.
(e) Substantiation
(1) In general.
(2) Expenses governed by section 274(d).
(3) Expenses not governed by section 274(d).
(f) Returning amounts in excess of expenses.
(1) In general.
(2) Per diem or mileage allowances.
(g) Reasonable period.
(1) In general.
(2) Safe harbors.
(i) Fixed date method.
(ii) Periodic payment method.
(3) Pattern of overreimbursements.
(h) Withholding and payment of employment taxes.
(1) When excluded from wages.
(2) When included in wages.
(i) Accountable plans.
(A) General rule.
(B) Per diem or mileage allowances.
(1) In general.
(2) Reimbursements.
(3) Advances.
(4) Special rules.
(ii) Nonaccountable plans.
(i) Application.
(j) Examples.
(k) Anti-abuse provision.
(l) Cross references.
(m) Effective dates.

(b) Scope. For purposes of determining "adjusted gross income," section 62(a)(2)(A) allows an employee a deduction for expenses allowed by part VI (section 161 and following), subchapter B, chapter 1 of the Code, paid by the employee, in connection with the performance of services as an employee of the employer, under a reimbursement or other expense allowance arrangement with a payor (the employer, its agent, or a third party). Section 62(c) provides that an arrangement will not be treated as a reimbursement or other expense allowance arrangement for purposes of section 62(a)(2)(A) if—

(1) Such arrangement does not require the employee to substantiate the expenses covered by the arrangement to the payor, or

(2) Such arrangement provides the employee the right to retain any amount in excess of the substantiated expenses covered under the arrangement. This section prescribes rules relating to the requirements of section 62(c).

(c) Reimbursement or other expense allowance arrangement. *(1) Defined.* For purposes of §§ 1.62-1, 1.62-1T, and 1.62-2, the phrase "reimbursement or other expense allowance arrangement" means an arrangement that meets the requirements of paragraphs (d) (business connection, (e) (substantiation), and (f) (returning amounts in excess of expenses) of this section. A payor may have more than one arrangement with respect to a particular employee, depending on the facts and circumstances. See paragraph (d)(2) of this section (payor treated as having two arrangements under certain circumstances).

(2) Accountable plans. (i) In general. Except as provided in paragraph (c)(2)(ii) of this section, if an arrangement meets the requirements of paragraphs (d), (e), and (f) of this section, all amounts paid under the arrangement are treated as paid under an "accountable plan."

(ii) Special rule for failure to return excess. If an arrangement meets the requirements of paragraphs (d), (e), and (f) of this section, but the employee fails to return, within a reasonable period of time, any amount in excess of the amount of the expenses substantiated in accordance with paragraph (e) of this section, only the amounts paid under the arrangement that are not in excess of the substantiated expenses are treated as paid under an accountable plan.

(3) Nonaccountable plans. (i) In general. If an arrangement does not satisfy one or more of the requirements of paragraphs (d), (e), or (f) of this section, all amounts paid under the arrangement are treated as paid under a "nonaccountable plan." If a payor provides a nonaccountable plan, an employee who receives payments under the plan cannot compel the payor to treat the payments as paid under an accountable plan by voluntarily substantiating the expenses and returning any excess to the payor.

(ii) Special rule for failure to return excess. If an arrangement meets the requirements of paragraphs (d), (e), and (f) of this section, but the employee fails to return, within a reasonable period of time, any amount in excess of the amount of the expenses substantiated in accordance with paragraph (e) of this section, the amounts paid under the arrangement that are in excess of the substantiated expenses are treated as paid under a nonaccountable plan.

(4) Treatment of payments under accountable plans. Amounts treated as paid under an accountable plan are excluded from the employee's gross income, are not reported as wages or other compensation on the employee's Form W-2, and are exempt from the withholding and payment of employment taxes (Federal Insurance Contributions Act (FICA), Federal Unemployment Tax Act (FUTA), Railroad Retirement Tax Act (RRTA), Railroad Unemployment Repayment Tax (RURT), and income tax.) See paragraph (1) of this section for cross references.

(5) Treatment of payments under nonaccountable plans. Amounts treated as paid under a nonaccountable plan are included in the employee's gross income, must be reported as wages or other compensation on the employee's Form W-2, and are subject to withholding and payment of employment taxes (FICA, FUTA, RRTA, RURT, and income tax). See paragraph (h) of this section. Expenses attributable to amounts included in the employee's gross income may be deducted, provided the employee can substantiate the full amount of his or her expenses (i.e., the amount of the expenses, if any, the reimbursement for which is treated as paid under an accountable plan as well as those for which the employee is claiming the deduction) in accordance with §§ 1.274-5T and 1.274(d)-1 or § 1.162-17, but only as a miscellaneous itemized deduction subject to the limitations applicable to such expenses (e.g., the 80-percent limitation on meal and entertainment expenses provided in section 274(n) and the 2-percent floor provided in section 67).

(d) Business connection. *(1) In general.* Except as provided in paragraphs (d)(2) and (d)(3) of this section, an arrangement meets the requirements of this paragraph (d) if it provides advances, allowances (including per diem allowances, allowances only for meals and incidental expenses, and mileage allowances), or reimbursements only for business expenses that are allowable as deductions by part VI (section 161 and the following), subchapter B, chapter 1 of the Code, and that are paid or incurred by the employee in connection with the performance of services as an employee of the employer. The payment may be actually received from the employer, its agent, or a third party for whom the employee performs a service as an employee of the employer, and may include amounts charged directly or indirectly to the payor through credit card systems or otherwise. In addition, if both wages and the reimbursement or other expense allowance are combined in a single payment, the reimbursement or other expense allowance must be identified either by making a separate payment or by specifically identifying the amount of the reimbursement or other expense allowance.

(2) Other bona fide expenses. If an arrangement provides advances, allowances, or reimbursements for business expenses described in paragraph (d)(1) of this section (i.e., deductible employee business expenses) and for other bona fide expenses related to the employer's business (e.g., travel that is not away from home) that are not deductible under part VI (section 161 and the following), subchapter B, chapter 1 of the Code, the payor is treated as maintaining two arrangements. The portion of the arrangement that provides payments for the deductible employee business expenses is treated as one arrangement that satisfies this paragraph (d). The portion of the arrangement that provides payments for the nondeductible employee expenses is treated as a second arrangement that does not satisfy this paragraph (d) and all amounts paid under this second arrangement will be treated as paid under a nonaccountable plan. See paragraphs (c)(5) and (h) of this section.

(3) Reimbursement requirement. (i) In general. If a payor arranges to pay an amount to an employee regardless of whether the employee incurs (or is reasonably expected to incur) business expenses of a type described in paragraph (d)(1) or (d)(2) of this section, the arrangement does not satisfy this paragraph (d) and all amounts paid under the arrangement are treated as paid under a nonaccountable plan. See paragraphs (c)(5) and (h) of this section.

(ii) Per diem allowances. An arrangement providing a per diem allowance for travel expenses of a type described in paragraph (d)(1) or (d)(2) of this section that is computed on a basis similar to that used in computing the employee's wages or other compensation (e.g., the number of hours worked, miles traveled, or pieces produced) meets the requirements of this paragraph (d) only if, on December 12, 1989, the per diem allowance was identified by the payor either by making a separate payment or by specifically identifying the amount of the per diem allowance, or a per diem allowance computed on that basis was commonly used in the industry in which the employee is employed. See section 274(d) and § 1.274(d)-1. A per diem allowance described in this paragraph (d)(3)(ii) may be adjusted in a manner that reasonably reflects actual increases in employee business expenses occurring after December 12, 1989.

(e) Substantiation. *(1) In general.* An arrangement meets the requirements of this paragraph (e) if it requires each business expense to be substantiated to the payor in accordance with paragraph (e)(2) or (e)(3) of this section, whichever is applicable, within a reasonable period of time. See § 1.274-5T or § 1.162-17.

(2) Expenses governed by section 274(d). Expenses governed by section 274(d). An arrangement that reimburses travel, entertainment, use of a passenger automobile or other listed property, or other business expenses governed by section 274(d) meets the requirements of this paragraph (e)(2) if information sufficient to satisfy the substantiation requirements of section 274(d) and the regulations thereunder is submitted to the payor. See § 1.274-5. Under section 274(d), information sufficient to substantiate the requisite elements of each expenditure or use must be submitted to the payor. For example, with respect to travel away from home, § 1.274-5(b)(2) requires that information sufficient to substantiate the amount, time, place, and business purpose of the expense must be submitted to the payor. Similarly, with respect to use of a passenger automobile or other listed property, § 1.274-5(b)(6) requires that information sufficient to substantiate the amount, time, use, and business purpose of the expense must be submitted to the payor. See § 1.274-5(g) and (j), which grant the Commissioner the authority to establish optional methods of substantiating certain expenses. Substantiation of the amount of a business expense in accordance with rules prescribed pursuant to the authority granted by § 1.274-5(g) or (j) will be treated as substantiation of the amount of such expense for purposes of this section.

(3) Expenses not governed by section 274(d). An arrangement that reimburses business expenses not governed by section 274(d) meets the requirements of this paragraph (e)(3) if information is submitted to the payor sufficient to enable the payor to identify the specific nature of each expense and to conclude that the expense is attributable to the payor's busi-

ness activities. Therefore, each of the elements of an expenditure or use must be substantiated to the payor. It is not sufficient if an employee merely aggregates expenses into broad categories (such as "travel") or reports individual expenses through the use of vague, nondescriptive terms (such as "miscellaneous business expenses"). See § 1.162-17(b).

(f) Returning amounts in excess of expenses. *(1) In general.* Except as provided in paragraph (f)(2) of this section, an arrangement meets the requirements of this paragraph (f) if it requires the employee to return to the payor within a reasonable period of time may amount paid under the arrangement in excess of the expenses substantiated in accordance with paragraph (e) of this section. The determination of whether an arrangement requires an employee to return amounts in excess of substantiated expenses will depend on the facts and circumstances. An arrangement whereby money is advanced to an employee to defray expenses will be treated as satisfying the requirements of this paragraph (f) only if the amount of money advanced is reasonably calculated not to exceed the amount of anticipated expenditures, the advance of money is made on a day within a reasonable period of the day that the anticipated expenditures are paid or incurred, and any amounts in excess of the expenses substantiated in accordance with paragraph (e) of this section are required to be returned to the payor within a reasonable period of time after the advance is received.

(2) Per diem or mileage allowances. The Commissioner may, in his discretion, prescribe rules in pronouncements of general applicability under which a reimbursement or other expense allowance arrangement that provides per diem allowances providing for ordinary and necessary expenses of traveling away from home (exclusive of transportation costs to and from destination) or mileage allowances providing for ordinary and necessary expenses of local travel and transportation while traveling away from home will be treated as satisfying the requirements of this paragraph (f), even though the arrangement does not require the employee to return the portion of such an allowance that relates to the days or miles of travel substantiated and that exceeds the amount of the employee's expenses deemed substantiated pursuant to rules prescribed under section 274(d), provided the allowance is paid at a rate for each day or mile of travel that is reasonably calculated not to exceed the amount of the employee's expenses or anticipated expenses and the employee is required to return to the payor within a reasonable period of time any portion of such allowance which relates to days or miles of travel not substantiated in accordance with paragraph (e) of this section.

(g) Reasonable period. *(1) In general.* The determination of a reasonable period of time will depend on the facts and circumstances.

(2) Safe harbors. (i) Fixed date method. An advance made within 30 days of when an expense is paid or incurred, an expense substantiated to the payor within 60 days after it is paid or incurred, or an amount returned to the payor within 120 days after an expense is paid or incurred will be treated as having occurred within a reasonable period of time.

(ii) Periodic statement method. If a payor provides employees with periodic statements (no less frequently than quarterly) stating the amount, if any, paid under the arrangement in excess of the expenses the employee has substantiated in accordance with paragraph (e) of this section, and requesting the employee to substantiate any additional business expenses that have not yet been substantiated (whether or not such expenses relate to the expenses with respect to which the original advance was paid) and/or to return any amounts remaining unsubstantiated within 120 days of the statement, an expense substantiated or an amount returned within that period will be treated as being substantiated or returned within a reasonable period of time.

(3) Pattern of overreimbursements. If, under a reimbursement or other expense allowance arrangement, a payor has a plan or practice to provide amounts to employees in excess of expenses substantiated in accordance with paragraph (e) of this section and to avoid reporting and withholding on such amounts, the payor may not use either of the safe harbors provided in paragraph (g)(2) of this section for any years during which such plan or practice exists.

(h) Withholding and payment of employment taxes. *(1) When excluded from wages.* If an arrangement meets the requirements of paragraphs (d), (e), and (f) of this section, the amounts paid under the arrangement that are not in excess of the expenses substantiated in accordance with paragraph (e) of this section (i.e., the amounts treated as paid under an accountable plan) are not wages and are not subject to withholding and payment of employment taxes. If an arrangement provides advances, allowances, or reimbursements for meal and entertainment expenses and a portion of the payment is treated as paid under a nonaccountable plan under paragraph (d)(2) of this section due solely to section 274(n), then notwithstanding paragraph (h)(2)(ii) of this section, these nondeductible amounts are neither treated as gross income nor subject to withholding and payment of employment taxes.

(2) When included in wages. (i) Accountable plans. (A) General rule. Except as provided in paragraph (h)(2)(i)(B) of this section, if the expenses covered under an arrangement that meets the requirements of paragraphs (d), (e), and (f) of this section are not substantiated to the payor in accordance with paragraph (e) of this section within a reasonable period of time or if any amounts in excess of the substantiated expenses are not returned to the payor in accordance with paragraph (f) of this section within a reasonable period of time, the amount which is treated as paid under a nonaccountable plan under paragraph (c)(3)(ii) of this section is subject to withholding and payment of employment taxes no later than the first payroll period following the end of the reasonable period. A payor may treat any amount not substantiated or returned within the periods specified in paragraph (g)(2) of this section as not substantiated or returned within a reasonable period of time.

(B) Per diem or mileage allowances. (1) In general. If a payor pays a per diem or mileage allowance under an arrangement that meets the requirements of the paragraphs (d), (e), and (f) of this section, the portion, if any, of the allowance paid that relates to days or miles of travel substantiated in accordance with paragraph (e) of this section and that exceeds the amount of the employee's expenses deemed substantiated for such travel pursuant to rules prescribed under section 274(d) and § 1.274(d)-1 or § 1.274-5T(j) is treated as paid under a nonaccountable plan. See paragraph (c)(3)(ii) of this section. Because the employee is not required to return this excess portion, the reasonable period of time provisions of paragraph (g) of this section (relating to the return of excess amounts) do not apply to this excess portion.

(2) Reimbursements. Except as provided in paragraph (h)(2)(i)(B)(4) of this section, in the case of a per diem or mileage allowance paid as a reimbursement at a rate for each day or mile of travel that exceeds the amounts of the employee's expenses deemed substantiated for a day or mile of travel, the excess portion described in paragraph (h)(2)(i) of this section is subject to withholding and payment of em-

ployment taxes in the payroll period in which the payor reimburses the expenses for the days or miles of travel substantiated in accordance with paragraph (e) of this section.

(3) Advances. Except as provided in paragraph (h)(2)(i)(B)(4) of this section, in the case of a per diem or mileage allowance paid as an advance at a rate for each day or mile of travel that exceeds the amount of the employee's expenses deemed substantiated for a day or mile of travel, the excess portion described in paragraph (h)(2)(i) of this section is subject to withholding and payment of employment taxes no later than the first payroll period following the payroll period in which the expenses with respect to which the advance was paid (i.e., the days or miles of travel) are substantiated in accordance with paragraph (e) of this section. The expenses with respect to which the advance was paid must be substantiated within a reasonable period of time. See paragraph (g) of this section.

(4) Special rules. The Commissioner may, in his discretion, prescribe special rules in pronouncements of general applicability regarding the timing of withholding and payment of employment taxes on per diem and mileage allowances.

(ii) Nonaccountable plans. If an arrangement does not satisfy one or more of the requirements of paragraphs (d), (e), or (f) of this section, all amounts paid under the arrangement are wages and are subject to withholding and payment of employment taxes when paid.

(i) Application. The requirements of paragraphs (d) (business connection), (e) (substantiation), and (f) (returning amounts in excess of expenses) of this section will be applied on an employee-by-employee basis. Thus, for example, the failure by one employee to substantiate expenses under an arrangement in accordance with paragraph (e) of this section will not cause amounts paid to other employees to be treated as paid under a nonaccountable plan.

(j) Examples. The rules contained in this section may be illustrated by the following examples:

Example (1). Reimbursement requirement. Employer S pays its engineers $200 a day. On those days that an engineer travels away from on business for Employer S, Employer S designates $50 of the $200 as paid to reimburse the engineer's travel expenses. Because Employer S would pay an engineer $200 a day regardless of whether the engineer was traveling away from home, the arrangement does not satisfy the reimbursement requirement of paragraph (d)(3)(i) of this section. Thus, no part of the $50 Employer S designated as a reimbursement is treated as paid under an accountable plan. Rather, all payments under the arrangement are treated as paid under a nonaccountable plan. Employer S must report the entire $200 as wages or other compensation on the employees' Forms W-2 and must withhold and pay employment taxes on the entire $200 when paid.

Example (2). Reimbursement requirement, multiple arrangements. Airline T pays all its employees a salary. Airline T also pays an allowance under an arrangement that otherwise meets the requirements of paragraphs (d), (e), and (f) of this section to its pilots and flight attendants who travel away from their home base airports, whether or not they are "away from home." Because the allowance is paid only to those employees who incur (or are reasonably expected to incur) expenses of a type described in paragraph (d)(1) or (d)(2) of this section, the arrangement satisfies the reimbursement requirement of paragraph (d)(3)(i) of this section. Under paragraph (d)(2) of this section, Airline T is treated as maintaining two arrangements. The portion of the arrangement providing the allowances for away from home travel is treated as an accountable plan. The portion of the arrangement providing the allowances for non-away from home travel is treated as a nonaccountable plan. Airline T must report the non-away from home allowances as wages or other compensation on the employees' Forms W-2 and must withhold and pay employment taxes on these payments when paid.

Example (3). Reimbursement requirement. Corporation R pays all its salespersons a salary. Corporation R also pays a travel allowance under an arrangement that otherwise meets the requirements of paragraphs (d), (e), and (f) of this section. This allowance is paid to all salespersons, including salespersons that Corporation R knows, or has reason to know, do not travel away from their offices on Corporation R business and would not be reasonably expected to incur travel expenses. Because the allowance is not paid only to those employees who incur (or are reasonably expected to incur) expenses of a type described in paragraph (d)(1) or (d)(2) of this section, the arrangement does not satisfy the reimbursement requirement of paragraph (d)(3)(i) of this section. Thus, no part of the allowance Corporation R designated as a reimbursement is treated as paid under an accountable plan. Rather, all payments under the arrangement are treated as paid under a nonaccountable plan. Corporation R must report all payments under the arrangement as wages or other compensation on the employees' Forms W-2 and must withhold and pay employment taxes on the payments when paid.

Example (4). Separate arrangement, miscellaneous expenses. Under an arrangement that meets the requirements of paragraphs (d), (e), and (f) of this section, County U reimburses its employees for lodging and meal expenses incurred when they travel away from home on County U business. For its own convenience, County U also separately pays certain of its employees a $25 monthly allowance to cover the cost of small miscellaneous office expenses. County U does not require its employees to substantiate these miscellaneous expenses and does not require them to return the amounts by which the monthly allowance exceeds the miscellaneous expenses. The monthly allowance arrangement is a nonaccountable plan. County U must report the monthly allowances as wages or other compensation on the employees' Forms W-2 and must withhold and pay employment taxes on the monthly allowances when paid. The nonaccountable plan providing the monthly allowances is treated as separate from the accountable plan providing reimbursements for lodging and meal expenses incurred for travel away from home on County U business.

Example (5). Excessive advances. In anticipation of employee business expenses that Corporation V does not reasonably expect to exceed $400 in any quarter, Corporation V nonetheless advances $1,000 to Employee A for such expenses. Whenever Employee A substantiates an expense in accordance with paragraph (e) of this section, Corporation V provides an additional advance in an amount equal to the amount substantiated, thereby providing a continuing advance of $1,000. Because the amounts advanced under this arrangement are not reasonably calculated so as not to exceed the amount of anticipated expenditures and because the advance of money is not made on a day within a reasonable period of the day that the anticipated expenditures are paid or incurred, the arrangement is a nonaccountable plan. The arrangement fails to satisfy the requirements of paragraphs (d) (business connection) and (f) (reasonable calculation of advances) of this section. Thus, Corporation V must report the entire amount of each advance as wages or other compensation and must withhold and pay employment taxes on the entire amount of each advance when paid.

Example (6). Excess mileage advance. Under an arrangement that meets the requirements of paragraphs (d), (e), and (f) of this section, Employer W pays its employees a mileage allowance at a rate of 30 cents per mile (when the amount deemed substantiated for each mile of travel substantiated is 26 cents per mile) to cover automobile business expenses. The allowance is paid at a rate for each mile of travel that is reasonably calculated not to exceed the amount of the employee's expenses or anticipated expenses. Employer W does not require the return of the portion of the mileage allowance (4 cents) that exceeds the amount deemed substantiated for each mile of travel substantiated in accordance with paragraph (e) of this section. In June, Employer W advances Employee B $150 for 500 miles to be traveled by Employee B during the month. In July, Employee B substantiates 500 miles of business travel. The amount deemed substantiated by Employee B is $130. However, Employer W does not require Employee B to return the remaining $20 of the advance. No later than the first payroll period following the payroll period in which the business miles of travel are substantiated, Employer W must withhold and pay employment taxes on $20 (500 miles × 4 cents per mile).

Example (7). Excess per diem reimbursement. Under an arrangement that meets the requirements of paragraphs (d), (e), and (f) of this section, Employer X pays its employees a per diem allowance to cover lodging, meal, and incidental expenses incurred for travel away from home on Employer X business at a rate equal to 120 percent of the amount deemed substantiated for each day of travel to the localities to which the employees travel. Employer X does not require the employees to return the 20 percent by which the reimbursement for those expenses exceeds the amount deemed substantiated for each day of travel substantiated in accordance with paragraph (e) of this section. Employee C substantiates six days of business travel away from home: Two days in a locality for which the amount deemed substantiated is $100 a day and four days in a locality for which the amount deemed substantiated is $125 a day. Employer X reimburses Employee C $840 for the six days of travel away from home (2 × (120% × $100) + 4 × (120% × $125)), and does not require Employee C to return the excess portion ($140 excess portion = (2 days × $20 ($120 − $100) + 4 days × $25 ($150 − $125)). For the payroll period in which Employer X reimburses the expenses, Employer X must withhold and pay employment taxes on $140.

Example (8). Return Requirement. Employer Y provides expense allowances to certain of its employees to cover business expenses of a type described in paragraph (d)(1) of this section under an arrangement that requires the employees to substantiate their expenses within a reasonable period of time and to return any excess amounts within a reasonable period of time. Each time an employee returns an excess amount to Employer Y, however, Employer Y pays the employee a "bonus" equal to the amount returned by the employee. The arrangement fails to satisfy the requirements of paragraph (f) (returning amounts in excess of expenses) of this section. Thus, Employer Y must report the entire amount of the expense allowance payments as wages or other compensation and must withhold and pay employment taxes on the payments when paid. Compare example (6) (where the employee is not required to return the portion of the mileage allowance that exceeds the amount deemed substantiated for each mile of travel substantiated).

Example (9). Timely substantiation. Employer Z provides a $500 advance to Employee D for a trip away from home on Employer Z business. Employee D incurs $500 in business expenses on the trip. Employer Z uses the periodic statement method safe harbor. At the end of the quarter during which the trip occurred, Employer Z sends a quarterly statement to Employee D stating that $500 was advanced to Employee D during the quarter and that no expenses were substantiated and no excess amounts returned. The statement advises Employee D that Employee D must substantiate any additional business expenses within 120 days of the date of the statement, and must return any unsubstantiated excess within the 120-day period. Employee D fails to substantiate any expenses or to return the excess within the 120-day period. Employer Z treats the $500 as wages and withholds and pays employment taxes on the $500. After the 120-day period has expired, Employee D substantiates the $500 in travel expenses in accordance with paragraph (e) of this section. Employer Z properly reported and withheld and paid employment taxes on the $500 and no adjustments may be made. Employee D must include the $500 in gross income and may deduct the $500 of expenses as a miscellaneous itemized deduction subject to the 2-percent floor provided in section 67.

(k) Anti-abuse provision. If a payor's reimbursement or other expense allowance arrangement evidences a pattern of abuse of the rules of section 62(c) and this section, all payments made under the arrangement will be treated as made under a nonaccountable plan.

(l) Cross references. For employment tax regulations relating to reimbursement and expense allowance arrangements, see §§ 31.3121(a)-3, 31.3231(e)-(3), 31.3306(b)-2, and 31.3401(a)-4, which generally apply to payments made under reimbursement or other expense allowance arrangements received by an employee on or after July 1, 1990 with respect to expenses paid or incurred on or after July 1, 1990. For reporting requirements, see § 1.6041-3(i), which generally applies to payments made under reimbursement or other expense allowance arrangements received by an employee on or after January 1, 1989 with respect to expenses paid or incurred on or after January 1, 1989.

(m) Effective dates. This section generally applies to payments made under reimbursement or other expense allowance arrangements received by an employee in taxable years of the employee beginning on or after January 1, 1989, with respect to expenses paid or incurred in taxable years beginning on or after January 1, 1989. Paragraph (h) of this section generally applies to payments made under reimbursement or other expense allowance arrangements received by an employee on or after July 1, 1990 with respect to expenses paid or incurred on or after July 1,1990. Paragraphs (d)(3)(ii) and (h)(2)(i)(B) of this section apply to payments made under reimbursement or other expense allowance arrangements received by an employee on or after January 1, 1991 with respect to expenses paid or incurred on or after January 1, 1991. Paragraph (e)(2) of this section applies to payments made under reimbursement or other expense allowance arrangements received by an employee with respect to expenses paid or incurred after December 31, 1997.

T.D. 8324, 12/14/90, amend T.D. 8451, 12/4/92, T.D. 8666, 5/29/96, T.D. 8784, 9/30/98, T.D. 8864, 1/21/2000, T.D. 9064, 6/30/2003.

---

§ 1.63-1 Change of treatment with respect to the zero bracket amount and itemizes deductions.

Caution: The Treasury has not yet amended Reg § 1.63-1 to reflect changes made by P.L. 101-508, P.L. 100-647, P.L. 99-514.

(a) In general. An individual who files a return on which the individual itemized deductions in accordance with section 63(g) may later make a change of treatment by recomputing taxable income for the taxable year to which that return relates without itemizing deductions. Similarly, an individual who files a return on which the individual computes taxable income without itemizing deductions may later make a change of treatment by itemizing deductions in accordance with section 63(g) in recomputing taxable income for the taxable year to which that return relates.

(b) No extension of time for claiming credit or refund. A change of treatment described in paragraph (a) of this section does not extend the period of time prescribed in section 6511 within which the taxpayer may make a claim for credit or refund of tax.

(c) Special requirements if spouse filed separate return. *(1) Requirements.* If the spouse of the taxpayer filed a separate return for a taxable year corresponding to the taxable year of the taxpayer, the taxpayer may not make a change of treatment described in paragraph (a) of this section for that year unless—

(i) The spouse makes a change of treatment on the separate return consistent with the change of treatment sought by the taxpayer; and

(ii) The taxpayer and the taxpayer's spouse file a consent in writing to the assessment of any deficiency of either spouse to the extent attributable to the change of treatment, even though the assessment of the deficiency would otherwise be prevented by the operation of any law or rule of law. The consent must be filed with the district director for the district in which the taxpayer applies for the change of treatment, and the period during with a deficiency may be assessed shall be established by agreement of the spouses and the district director.

(2) Corresponding taxable year. A taxable year of one spouse corresponds to a taxable year of the other spouse if both taxable years end in the same calendar year. If the taxable year of one spouse ends with death, however, the corresponding taxable year of the surviving spouse is that in which the death occurs.

(d) Inapplicable if tax liability has been compromised. The taxpayer may not make a change of treatment described in paragraph (a) of this section for any taxable year if—

(1) The tax liability of the taxpayer for the taxable year has been compromised under section 7122; or

(2) The tax liability of the taxpayer's spouse for a taxable year corresponding to the taxable year of the taxpayer has been compromised under section 7122. See paragraph (c)(2) of this section for the determination of a corresponding taxable year.

(e) Effective date. This section applies to taxable years beginning after 1976.

T.D. 7585, 1/3/79.

§ 1.63-2 Cross reference.

For rules with respect to charitable contribution deductions for nonitemizing taxpayers, see section 63(b)(1)(C) and (i) and section 170(i) of the Internal Revenue Code of 1954.

T.D. 8002, 12/26/84.

§ 1.66-1 Treatment of community income.

(a) In general. Married individuals domiciled in a community property state who do not elect to file a joint individual Federal income tax return under section 6013 generally must report half of the total community income earned by the spouses during the taxable year except at times when one of the following exceptions applies:

(1) The spouses live apart and meet the qualifications of § 1.66-2.

(2) The Secretary denies a spouse the Federal income tax benefits resulting from community property law under § 1.66-3, because that spouse acted as if solely entitled to the income and failed to notify his or her spouse of the nature and amount of the income prior to the due date for the filing of his or her spouse's return.

(3) A requesting spouse qualifies for traditional relief from the Federal income tax liability resulting from the operation of community property law under § 1.66-4(a).

(4) A requesting spouse qualifies for equitable relief from the Federal income tax liability resulting from the operation of community property law under § 1.66-4(b).

(b) Applicability. *(1)* The rules of this section apply only to community income, as defined by state law. The rules of this section do not apply to income that is not community income. Thus, the rules of this section do not apply to income from property that was formerly community property, but in accordance with state law, has ceased to be community property, becoming, e.g., separate property or property held by joint tenancy or tenancy in common.

(2) When taxpayers report income under paragraph (a) of this section, all community income for the calendar year is treated in accordance with the rules provided by section 879(a). Unlike the other provisions under section 66, section 66(a) does not permit inclusion on an item-by-item basis.

(c) Transferee liability. The provisions of section 66 do not negate liability that arises under the operation of other laws. Therefore, a spouse who is not subject to Federal income tax on community income may nevertheless remain liable for the unpaid tax (including additions to tax, penalties, and interest) to the extent provided by Federal or state transferee liability or property laws (other than community property laws). For the rules regarding the liability of transferees, see sections 6901 through 6904 and the regulations thereunder.

T.D. 9074, 7/9/2003.

§ 1.66-2 Treatment of community income where spouses live apart.

(a) Community income of spouses domiciled in a community property state will be treated in accordance with the rules provided by section 879(a) if all of the following requirements are satisfied—

(1) The spouses are married to each other at any time during the calendar year;

(2) The spouses live apart at all times during the calendar year;

(3) The spouses do not file a joint return with each other for a taxable year beginning or ending in the calendar year;

(4) One or both spouses have earned income that is community income for the calendar year; and

(5) No portion of such earned income is transferred (directly or indirectly) between such spouses before the close of the calendar year.

(b) Living apart. For purposes of this section, living apart requires that spouses maintain separate residences. Spouses who maintain separate residences due to temporary absences are not considered to be living apart. Spouses who are not members of the same household under § 1.6015-3(b) are considered to be living apart for purposes of this section.

(c) Transferred income. For purposes of this section, transferred income does not include a de minimis amount of earned income that is transferred between the spouses. In addition, any amount of earned income transferred for the benefit of the spouses' child will not be treated as an indirect transfer to one spouse. Additionally, income transferred between spouses is presumed to be a transfer of earned income. This presumption is rebuttable.

(d) Examples. The following examples illustrate the rules of this section:

Example (1). Living apart. H and W are married, domiciled in State A, a community property state, and have lived apart the entire year of 2002. W, who is in the Army, was stationed in Korea for the entire calendar year. During their separation, W intended to return home to H, and H intended to live with W upon W's return. H and W do not file a joint return for taxable year 2002. H and W may not report their income under this section because a temporary absence due to military service is not living apart as contemplated under this section.

Example (2). Transfer of earned income—de minimis exception. H and W are married, domiciled in State B, a community property state, and have lived apart the entire year of 2002. H and W are estranged and intend to live apart indefinitely. H and W do not file a joint return for taxable year 2002. H occasionally visits W and their two children, who live with W. When H visits, he often buys gifts for the children, takes the children out to dinner, and occasionally buys groceries or gives W money to buy the children new clothes for school. Both W and H have earned income in the year 2002 that is community income under the laws of State B. H and W may report their income on separate returns under this section.

Example (3). Transfer of earned income—source of transfer. H and W are married, domiciled in State C, a community property state, and have lived apart the entire year of 2002. H and W are estranged and intend to live apart indefinitely. H and W do not file a joint return for taxable year 2002. W provides H $1,000 a month from March 2002 through August 2002 while H is working part-time and seeking full-time employment. W is not legally obligated to make the $1,000 payments. W earns $75,000 in 2002 in wage income. W also receives $10,000 in capital gains income in December 2002. H wants to report his income in accordance with this section, alleging that the $6,000 that he received from W was not from W's earned income, but from the capital gains income W received in 2002. The facts and circumstances surrounding the periodic payments to H from W do not indicate that W made the payments out of her capital gains. H and W may not report their income in accordance with this section, as the $6,000 W transferred to H is presumed to be from W's earned income, and H has not presented any facts to rebut the presumption.

T.D. 9074, 7/9/2003.

---

§ 1.66-3 Denial of the Federal income tax benefits resulting from the operation of community property law where spouse not notified.

(a) In general. The Secretary may deny the Federal income tax benefits of community property law to any spouse with respect to any item of community income if that spouse acted as if solely entitled to the income and failed to notify his or her spouse of the nature and amount of the income before the due date (including extensions) for the filing of the return of his or her spouse for the taxable year in which the item of income was derived. Whether a spouse has acted as if solely entitled to the item of income is a facts and circumstances determination. This determination focuses on whether the spouse used, or made available, the item of income for the benefit of the marital community.

(b) Effect. The item of community income will be included, in its entirety, in the gross income of the spouse to whom the Secretary denied the Federal income tax benefits resulting from community property law. The tax liability arising from the inclusion of the item of community income must be assessed in accordance with section 6212 against this spouse.

(c) Examples. The following examples illustrate the rules of this section:

Example (1). Acting as if solely entitled to income.

(i) H and W are married and are domiciled in State A, a community property state. W's Form W-2 for taxable year 2000 showed wage income of $35,000. W also received a Form 1099-INT, "Interest Income," showing $1,000 W received in taxable year 2000. W's wage income was directly deposited into H and W's joint account, from which H and W paid bills and household expenses. W did not inform H of her interest income or the Form 1099-INT, but W gave H a copy of the W-2 when she received it in January 2001. W did not use her interest income for bills or household expenses. Instead W gave her interest income to her brother, who was unemployed. Neither the separate return filed by H nor the separate return filed by W included the interest income. In 2002, the IRS audits both H and W. The Internal Revenue Service (IRS) may raise section 66(b) as to W's interest income, denying W the Federal income tax benefit resulting from community property law as to this item of income.

(ii) H and W are married and are domiciled in State B, a community property state. For taxable year 2000, H receives $45,000 in wage income that H places in a separate account. H and W maintain separate residences. H's wage income is community income under the laws of State B. That same year, W loses her job, and H pays W's mortgage and household expenses for several months while W seeks employment. Neither H nor W files a return for 2000, the taxable year for which the IRS subsequently audits them. The IRS may not raise section 66(b) and deny H the Federal income tax benefits resulting from the operation of community property law as to H's wage income of $45,000, as H has not treated this income as if H were solely entitled to it.

Example (2). Notification of nature and amount of the income. H and W are married and domiciled in State C, a community property state. H and W do not file a joint return for taxable year 2001. H's and W's earned income for 2001 is community income under the laws of State C. H receives $50,000 in wage income in 2001. In January 2002, H receives a Form W-2 that erroneously states that H earned $45,000 in taxable year 2001. H provides W a copy of H's Form W-2 in February 2002. W files for an extension prior to April 15, 2002. H receives a corrected Form W-2 reflecting wages of $50,000 in May 2002. H provides a copy of the corrected Form W-2 to W in May 2002. W files a separate return in June 2002, but reports one half of $45,000 ($22,500) of wage income that H earned. H files a separate return reporting half of $50,000 ($25,000) in wage income. The IRS audits both H and W. Even if H had acted as if solely entitled to the wage income, the IRS may not raise section 66(b) as to this income because H notified W of the nature and amount of the income prior to the due date of W's return (including extensions).

T.D. 9074, 7/9/2003.

§ 1.66-4 Request for relief from the Federal income tax liability resulting from the operation of community property law.

(a) Traditional relief. *(1) In general.* A requesting spouse will receive relief from the Federal income tax liability resulting from the operation of community property law for an item of community income if—

(i) The requesting spouse did not file a joint Federal income tax return for the taxable year for which he or she seeks relief;

(ii) The requesting spouse did not include in gross income for the taxable year an item of community income properly includible therein, which, under the rules contained in section 879(a), would be treated as the income of the nonrequesting spouse;

(iii) The requesting spouse establishes that he or she did not know of, and had no reason to know of, the item of community income; and

(iv) Taking into account all of the facts and circumstances, it is inequitable to include the item of community income in the requesting spouse's individual gross income.

(2) Knowledge or reason to know. (i) A requesting spouse had knowledge or reason to know of an item of community income if he or she either actually knew of the item of community income, or if a reasonable person in similar circumstances would have known of the item of community income. All of the facts and circumstances are considered in determining whether a requesting spouse had reason to know of an item of community income. The relevant facts and circumstances include, but are not limited to, the nature of the item of community income, the amount of the item of community income relative to other income items, the couple's financial situation, the requesting spouse's educational background and business experience, and whether the item of community income was reflected on prior years' returns (e.g., investment income omitted that was regularly reported on prior years' returns).

(ii) If the requesting spouse is aware of the source of community income or the income-producing activity, but is unaware of the specific amount of the nonrequesting spouse's community income, the requesting spouse is considered to have knowledge or reason to know of the item of community income. The requesting spouse's lack of knowledge of the specific amount of community income does not provide a basis for relief under this section.

(3) Inequitable. All of the facts and circumstances are considered in determining whether it is inequitable to hold a requesting spouse liable for a deficiency attributable to an item of community income. One relevant factor for this purpose is whether the requesting spouse benefitted, directly or indirectly, from the omitted item of community income. A benefit includes normal support, but does not include de minimis amounts. Evidence of direct or indirect benefit may consist of transfers of property or rights to property, including transfers received several years after the filing of the return. Thus, for example, if a requesting spouse receives from the nonrequesting spouse property (including life insurance proceeds) that is traceable to items of community income attributable to the nonrequesting spouse, the requesting spouse will have benefitted from those items of community income. Other factors may include, if the situation warrants, desertion, divorce or separation. Factors relevant to whether it would be inequitable to hold a requesting spouse liable, more specifically described under the applicable administrative procedure issued under section 66(c) (Revenue Procedure 2000-15 (2000-1 C.B. 447) (See § 601.601(d)(2) of this chapter), or other applicable guidance published by the Secretary), are to be considered in making a determination under this paragraph.

(b) Equitable relief. Equitable relief may be available when the four requirements of paragraph (a)(1) of this section are not satisfied, but it would be inequitable to hold the requesting spouse liable for the unpaid tax or deficiency. Factors relevant to whether it would be inequitable to hold a requesting spouse liable, more specifically described under the applicable administrative procedure issued under section 66(c) (Revenue Procedure 2000-15 (2000-1 C.B. 447), or other applicable guidance published by the Secretary), are to be considered in making a determination under this paragraph.

(c) Applicability. Traditional relief under paragraph (a) of this section applies only to deficiencies arising out of items of omitted income. Equitable relief under paragraph (b) of this section applies to any deficiency or any unpaid tax (or any portion of either). Equitable relief is available only for the portion of liabilities that were unpaid as of July 22, 1998, and for liabilities that arise after July 22, 1998.

(d) Effect of relief. When the requesting spouse qualifies for relief under paragraph (a) or (b) of this section, the IRS must assess any deficiency of the nonrequesting spouse arising from the granting of relief to the requesting spouse in accordance with section 6212.

(e) Examples. The following examples illustrate the rules of this section:

Example (1). Item-by-item approach. H and W are married, living together, and domiciled in State A (a community property state). H and W file separate returns for taxable year 2002 on April 15, 2003. H earns $56,000 in wages, and W earns $46,000 in wages, in 2002. H reports half of his wage income as shown on his Form W-2, in the amount of $28,000, and half of W's wage income as shown on her Form W-2, in the amount of $23,000. W reports half of her wage income as shown on her W-2, in the amount of $23,000, and half of H's wage income as shown on his Form W-2, in the amount of $28,000. Neither H nor W reports W's income from her sole proprietorship of $34,000 or W's investment income of $5,000 for taxable year 2002. The Internal Revenue Service (IRS) proposes deficiencies with respect to H's and W's taxable year 2002 returns due to the omission of W's income from her sole proprietorship and investments. H timely requests relief under section 66(c). Because the IRS determines that H satisfies the four requirements of the traditional relief provision of section 66(c) with respect to W's omitted investment income, the IRS grants H's request for relief as to the omitted investment income. The IRS determines that H does not satisfy the four requirements of the traditional relief provision of section 66(c) as to

W's sole proprietorship income. The IRS further determines that, under the equitable relief provision of section 66(c), it is not inequitable to hold H liable for the sole proprietorship income. Relief is applicable on an item-by-item basis. Thus, H is liable for the tax on half of his wage income in the amount of $28,000, half of W's wage income in the amount of $23,000, half of W's sole proprietorship income in the amount of $17,000, but none of W's investment income, for which H obtained relief under section 66(c). W is liable for the tax on half of H's wage income in the amount of $28,000, half of W's wage income in the amount of $23,000, half of W's sole proprietorship income in the amount of $17,000, and all of W's investment income in the amount of $5,000, because H obtained relief under section 66(c).

Example (2). Benefit. H and W are married, living together, and domiciled in State B (a community property state). Neither H nor W files a return for taxable year 2000. H earns $60,000 in 2000, which he deposits in a joint account. H and W pay the mortgage payment, household bills, and other family expenses out of the joint account. W earns $20,000 in 2000. W uses a portion of the $20,000 to make monthly loan payments on the family cars, but loses the remainder at the local racetrack. In 2002, the IRS audits H and W. H requests relief under section 66(c), stating that he did not know or have reason to know of W's additional income, as H travels extensively while W handles the family finances. Regardless of whether H had knowledge or reason to know of the source of W's income, H is not eligible for traditional relief under section 66(c) because H benefitted from W's income. H's benefit, the portion of W's income used to make monthly payments on the car loans, was more than a de minimis amount. While this benefit was not in excess of normal support, it is enough to preclude relief under the traditional relief provision of section 66(c). H may still qualify for equitable relief under section 66(c), depending on all of the facts and circumstances.

(f) Fraudulent scheme. If the Secretary establishes that a spouse transferred assets to his or her spouse as part of a fraudulent scheme, relief is not available under this section. For purposes of this section, a fraudulent scheme includes a scheme to defraud the Secretary or another third party, such as a creditor, ex-spouse, or business partner.

(g) Definitions. *(1) Requesting spouse.* A requesting spouse is an individual who does not file a joint Federal income tax return with the nonrequesting spouse for the taxable year in question, and who requests relief from the Federal income tax liability resulting from the operation of community property law under this section for the portion of the liability arising from his or her share of community income for such taxable year.

(2) Nonrequesting spouse. A nonrequesting spouse is the individual to whom the requesting spouse was married and whose income or deduction gave rise to the tax liability from which the requesting spouse seeks relief in whole or in part.

(h) Effect of prior closing agreement or offer in compromise. A requesting spouse is not entitled to relief from the Federal income tax liability resulting from the operation of community property law under section 66 for any taxable year for which the requesting spouse has entered into a closing agreement (other than an agreement pursuant to section 6224(c) relating to partnership items) with the Secretary that disposes of the same liability that is the subject of the request for relief. In addition, a requesting spouse is not entitled to relief from the Federal income tax liability resulting from the operation of community property law under section 66 for any taxable year for which the requesting spouse has entered into an offer in compromise with the Secretary. For rules relating to the effect of closing agreements and offers in compromise, see sections 7121 and 7122, and the regulations thereunder.

(i) [Reserved]

(j) Time and manner for requesting relief. *(1) Requesting relief.* To request relief from the Federal income tax liability resulting from the operation of community property law under this section, a requesting spouse must file, within the time period prescribed in paragraph (j)(2) of this section, Form 8857, "Request for Innocent Spouse Relief" (or other specified form), or other written request, signed under penalties of perjury, stating why relief is appropriate. The requesting spouse must include the nonrequesting spouse's name and taxpayer identification number in the written request. The requesting spouse must also comply with the Secretary's reasonable requests for information that will assist the Secretary in identifying and locating the nonrequesting spouse.

(2) Time period for filing a request for relief. (i) Traditional relief. The earliest time for submitting a request for relief from the Federal income tax liability resulting from the operation of community property law under paragraph (a) of this section, for an amount underreported on, or omitted from, the requesting spouse's separate return, is the date the requesting spouse receives notification of an audit or a letter or notice from the IRS stating that there may be an outstanding liability with regard to that year (as described in paragraph (j)(2)(iii) of this section). The latest time for requesting relief under paragraph (a) of this section is 6 months before the expiration of the period of limitations on assessment, including extensions, against the nonrequesting spouse for the taxable year that is the subject of the request for relief, unless the examination of the requesting spouse's return commences during that 6-month period. If the examination of the requesting spouse's return commences during that 6-month period, the latest time for requesting relief under paragraph (a) of this section is 30 days after the commencement of the examination.

(ii) Equitable relief. The earliest time for submitting a request for relief from the Federal income tax liability resulting from the operation of community property law under paragraph (b) of this section is the date the requesting spouse receives notification of an audit or a letter or notice from the IRS stating that there may be an outstanding liability with regard to that year (as described in paragraph (j)(2)(iii) of this section). A request for equitable relief from the Federal income tax liability resulting from the operation of community property law under paragraph (b) of this section for a liability that is properly reported but unpaid is properly submitted with the requesting spouse's individual Federal income tax return, or after the requesting spouse's individual Federal income tax return is filed.

(iii) Premature requests for relief. The Secretary will not consider a premature request for relief under this section. The notices or letters referenced in this paragraph (j)(2) do not include notices issued pursuant to section 6223 relating to TEFRA partnership proceedings. These notices or letters include notices of computational adjustment to a partner or partner's spouse (Notice of Income Tax Examination Changes) that reflect a computation of the liability attributable to partnership items of the partner or the partner's spouse.

(k) Nonrequesting spouse's notice and opportunity to participate in administrative proceedings. *(1) In general.*

When the Secretary receives a request for relief from the Federal income tax liability resulting from the operation of community property law under this section, the Secretary must send a notice to the nonrequesting spouse's last known address that informs the nonrequesting spouse of the requesting spouse's request for relief. The notice must provide the nonrequesting spouse with an opportunity to submit any information for consideration in determining whether to grant the requesting spouse relief from the Federal income tax liability resulting from the operation of community property law. The Secretary will share with each spouse the information submitted by the other spouse, unless the Secretary determines that the sharing of this information will impair tax administration.

(2) Information submitted. The Secretary will consider all of the information (as relevant to the particular relief provision) that the nonrequesting spouse submits in determining whether to grant relief from the Federal income tax liability resulting from the operation of community property law under this section.

T.D. 9074, 7/9/2003.

§ 1.66-5 Effective date.

Sections 1.66-1 through 1.66-4 are applicable on July 10, 2003. In addition, § 1.66-4 applies to any request for relief filed prior to July 10, 2003, for which the Internal Revenue Service has not issued a preliminary determination as of July 10, 2003.

T.D. 9074, 7/9/2003.

§ 1.67-1T 2-percent floor on miscellaneous itemized deductions (temporary).

Caution: The Treasury has not yet amended Reg § 1.67-1T to reflect changes made by P.L. 108-121, P.L. 107-16, P.L 105-277, P.L. 103-66, P.L. 100-647, P.L. 100-203.

(a) Type of expenses subject to the floor. *(1) In general.* With respect to individuals, section 67 disallows deductions for miscellaneous itemized deductions (as defined in paragraph (b) of this section) in computing taxable income (i.e., so-called "below-the-line" deductions) to the extent that such otherwise allowable deductions do not exceed 2 percent of the individual's adjusted gross income (as defined in section 62 and the regulations thereunder). Examples of expenses that, if otherwise deductible, are subject to the 2-percent floor include but are not limited to—

(i) Unreimbursed employee expenses, such as expenses for transportation, travel fares and lodging while away from home, business meals and entertainment, continuing education courses, subscriptions to professional journals, union or professional dues, professional uniforms, job hunting, and the business use of the employee's home.

(ii) Expenses for the production or collection of income for which a deduction is otherwise allowable under section 212(1) and (2), such as investment advisory fees, subscriptions to investment advisory publications, certain attorneys' fees, and the cost of safe deposit boxes,

(iii) Expenses for the determination of any tax for which a deduction is otherwise allowable under section 212(3), such as tax counsel fees and appraisal fees, and

(iv) Expenses for an activity for which a deduction is otherwise allowable under section 183.

See section 62 with respect to deductions that are allowable in computing adjusted gross income (i.e., so-called "above-the-line" deductions).

(2) Other limitations. Except as otherwise provided in paragraph (d) of this section, to the extent that any limitation or restriction is placed on the amount of a miscellaneous itemized deduction, that limitation shall apply prior to the application of the 2-percent floor. For example, in the case of an expense for food or beverages, only 80 percent of which is allowable as a deduction because of the limitations provided in section 274(n), the otherwise deductible 80 percent of the expense is treated as a miscellaneous itemized deduction and is subject to the 2-percent limitation of section 67.

(b) Definition of miscellaneous itemized deductions. For purposes of this section, the term "miscellaneous itemized deductions" means the deductions allowable from adjusted gross income in determining taxable income, as defined in section 63, other than—

(1) The standard deduction as defined in section 63(c),

(2) Any deduction allowable for impairment-related work expenses as defined in section 67(d),

(3) The deduction under section 72(b)(3) (relating to deductions if annuity payments cease before the investment is recovered),

(4) The deductions allowable under section 151 for personal exemptions,

(5) The deduction under section 163 (relating to interest),

(6) The deduction under section 164 (relating to taxes),

(7) The deduction under section 165(a) for losses described in subsection (c)(3) or (d) of section 165,

(8) The deduction under section 170 (relating to charitable contributions and gifts),

(9) The deduction under section 171 (relating to deductions for amortizable bond premiums),

(10) The deduction under section 213 (relating to medical and dental expenses),

(11) The deduction under section 216 (relating to deductions in connection with cooperative housing corporations),

(12) The deduction under section 217 (relating to moving expenses),

(13) The deduction under section 691(c) (relating to the deduction for estate taxes in the case of income in respect of the decedent),

(14) The deduction under 1341 (relating to the computation of tax if a taxpayer restores a substantial amount held under claim of right), and

(15) Any deduction allowable in connection with personal property used in a short sale.

(c) Allocation of expenses. If a taxpayer incurs expenses that relate to both a trade or business activity (within the meaning of section 162) and a production of income or tax preparation activity (within the meaning of section 212), the taxpayer shall allocate such expenses between the activities on a reasonable basis.

(d) Members of Congress. *(1) In general.* With respect to the deduction for living expenses of Members of Congress referred to in section 162(a), the 2-percent floor described in section 67 and paragraph (a) of this section shall be applied to the deduction before the application of the $3,000 limitation on deductions for living expenses referred to in section 162(a). (For purposes of this paragraph (d), the term "Member(s) of Congress" include any Delegate or Resident Commissioner.) The amount of miscellaneous itemized deductions of a Member of Congress that is disallowed pursuant to section 67 and paragraph (a) of this section shall be allocated between deductions for living expenses (within the meaning of section 162(a)) and other miscellaneous itemized deductions. The amount of deductions for living expenses of a Member of Congress that is disallowed pursuant to section 67 and paragraph (a) of this section is determined by multiplying the aggregate amount of such living expenses (determined without regard to the $3,000 limitation of section 162(a) but with regard to any other limitations) by a fraction, the numerator of which is the aggregate amount disallowed pursuant to section 67 and paragraph (a) of this section with respect to miscellaneous itemized deductions of the Member of Congress and the denominator of which is the amount of miscellaneous itemized deductions (including deductions for living expenses) of the Member of Congress (determined without regard to the $3,000 limitation of section 162(a) but without regard to any other limitations). The amount of deductions for miscellaneous itemized deductions (other than deductions for living expenses) of a Member of Congress that are disallowed pursuant to section 67 and paragraph (a) of this section is determined by multiplying the amount of miscellaneous itemized deductions (other than deductions for living expenses) of the Member of Congress (determined with regard to any limitations) by the fraction described in the preceding sentence.

(2) Example. The provisions of this paragraph (d) may be illustrated by the following example:

Example. For 1987 A, a Member of Congress, has adjusted gross income of $100,000, and miscellaneous itemized deductions of $10,750 of which $3,750 is for meals, $3,000 is for other living expenses, and $4,000 is for other miscellaneous itemized deductions (none of which is subject to any percentage limitations other than the 2-percent floor of section 67). The amount of A's business meal expenses that are disallowed under section 274(n) is $750 ($3,750 × 20%). The amount of A's miscellaneous itemized deductions that are disallowed under section 67 is $2,000 ($100,000 × 2%). The portion of the amount disallowed under section 67 that is allocated to A's living expenses is $1,200. This portion is equal to the amount of A's deductions for living expenses allowable after the application of section 274(n) and before the application of section 67 ($6,000) multiplied by the ratio of A's total miscellaneous itemized deductions disallowed under section 67 to A's total miscellaneous itemized deductions, determined without regard to the $3,000 limitation of section 162(a) ($2,000/$10,000). Thus, after application of section 274(n) and section 67, A's deduction for living expenses is $4,800 ($6,750 – $750 – $1,200). However, pursuant to section 162(a), A may deduct only $3,000 of such expenses. The amount of A's other miscellaneous itemized deductions that are disallowed under section 67 is $800 ($4,000 × $2,000/$10,000). Thus, $3,200 ($4,000 – $800) of A's miscellaneous itemized deductions (other than deductions for living expenses) are allowable after application of section 67. A's total allowable miscellaneous itemized deductions are $6,200 ($3,000 + $3,200). (e) State legislators. See § 1.62-1T(e)(4) with respect to rules regarding state legislator's expenses.

T.D. 8189, 3/25/88.

---

§ 1.67-2T Treatment of pass-through entities (Temporary).

Caution: The Treasury has not yet amended Reg § 1.67-2T to reflect changes made by P.L. 100-647, P.L. 100-203.

(a) Application of section 67. This section provides rules for the application of section 67 to partners, shareholders, beneficiaries, participants, and others with respect to their interests in pass-through entities (as defined in paragraph (g) of this section). In general, an affected investor (as defined in paragraph (h) of this section) in a pass-through entity shall separately take into account as an item of income and as an item of expense an amount equal to his or her allocable share of the affected expenses (as defined in paragraph (i) of this section) of the pass-through entity for purposes of determining his or her taxable income. Except as provided in paragraph (e)(1)(ii)(B) of this section, the expenses so taken into account shall be treated as paid or incurred by the affected investor in the same manner as paid or incurred by the pass-through entity. For rules regarding the application of section 67 to affected investors in—

(1) Partnerships, S corporations, and grantor trusts, see paragraph (b) of this section,

(2) Real estate mortgage investment conduits, see paragraph (c) of this section,

(3) Common trust funds, see paragraph (d) of this section,

(4) Nonpublicly offered regulated investment companies, see paragraph (e) of this section, and

(5) Publicly offered regulated investment companies, see paragraph (p) of this section.

(b) Partnerships, S corporations, and grantor trusts. *(1) In general.* Pursuant to section 702(a) and 1366(a) of the Code and the regulations thereunder, each partner of a partnership or shareholder of an S corporation shall take into account separately his or her distributive or pro rata share of any items of deduction of such partnership or corporation that are defined as miscellaneous itemized deductions pursuant to section 67(b). The 2-percent limitation described in section 67 does not apply to the partnership or corporation with respect to such deductions, but such deductions shall be included in the deductions of the partner or shareholder to which that limitation applies. Similarly, the limitation applies to the grantor or other person treated as the owner of a grantor trust with respect to items that are paid or incurred by a grantor trust and are treated as miscellaneous itemized deductions of the grantor or other person pursuant to subpart E, part 1, subchapter J, chapter 1 of the Code, but not to the trust itself. The 2-percent limitation applies to amounts otherwise deductible in taxable years of partners, shareholders, or grantors beginning after December 31, 1986, regardless of the taxable year of the partnership, corporation, or trust.

(2) Example. The provisions of this paragraph (b) may be illustrated by the following example:

Example. P, a partnership, incurs $1,000 in expenses to which section 212 applies during its taxable year. A, an individual, is a partner in P. A's distributive share of the expenses to which section 212 applies is $20, determined without regard to the 2-percent limitation of section 67. Pursuant to section 702(a), A must take $20 of expenses to which section 212 applies into account in determining his income tax. Pursuant to section 67, in determining his taxable income A may deduct his miscellaneous itemized deductions (including his $20 distributive share of deductions from P) to the extent the total amount exceeds 2 percent of his adjusted gross income.

(c) Real estate mortgage investment conduit. See § 1.67-3T for rules regarding the application of section 67 to holders of interests in REMICs.

(d) Common trust funds. *(1) In general.* For purposes of determining the taxable income of an affected investor that is a participant in a common trust fund—

(i) The ordinary taxable income and ordinary net loss of the common trust fund shall be computed under section 584(d)(2) without taking into account any affected expenses, and

(ii) Each affected investor shall be treated as having paid or incurred an expense described in section 212 in an amount equal to the affected investor's proportionate share of the affected expenses.

The 2-percent limitation described in section 67 applies to amounts otherwise deductible in taxable years of participants beginning after December 31, 1986, regardless of the taxable year of the common trust fund.

(2) Example. The provisions of this paragraph (d) may be illustrated by the following example:

Example. During 1987, the gross income and deductions of common trust fund C, a calendar year taxpayer, consist of the following items: (i) $50,000 of short-term capital gains; (ii) $150,000 of long-term capital gains; (iii) $1,000,000 of dividend income; (iv) $10,000 of deductions that are not affected expenses; and (v) $60,000 of deductions that are affected expenses. The proportionate share of Trust T in the income and losses of C is one percent. In computing its taxable income for 1987, T, a calendar year taxpayer, shall take into account the following items: (A) $500 of short-term capital gains (one percent of $50,000, C's short-term capital gains); (B) $1,500 of long-term capital gains (one percent of $150,000, C's long-term capital gains); (C) $9,900 of ordinary taxable income (one percent of $990,000, the excess of $100,000, C's gross income after excluding capital gains and losses, over $10,000, C's deductions that are not affected expenses); (D) $600 of expenses described in section 212 (one percent of $60,000, C's affected expenses).

(e) Nonpublicly offered regulated investment companies. *(1) In general.* For purposes of determining the taxable income of an affected investor that is a shareholder of a nonpublicly offered regulated investment company (as defined in paragraph (g)(3) of this section) during a calendar year—

(i) The current earnings and profits of the nonpublicly offered regulated investment company shall be computed without taking into account any affected RIC expenses that are allocated among affected investors, and

(ii) The affected investor shall be treated—

(A) As having received or accrued a dividend in an amount equal to the affected investor's allocable share of the affected RIC expenses of the nonpublicly offered regulated investment company for the calendar year, and

(B) As having paid or incurred an expense described in section 212 (or section 162 in the case of an affected investor that is a nonpublicly offered regulated investment company) in an amount equal to the affected investor's allocable share of the affected RIC expenses of the nonpublicly offered regulated investment company for the calendar year.

In the affected investor's taxable year with which (or within which) the calendar year with respect to which the expenses are allocated ends. An affected investor's allocable share of the affected RIC expenses is the amount allocated to that affected investor pursuant to paragraph (k) of this section.

(2) Shareholders that are not affected investors. A shareholder of a nonpublicly offered regulated investment company that is not an affected investor shall not take into account in computing its taxable income any amount of income or expense with respect to its allocable share of affected RIC expenses.

(3) Example. The provisions of this paragraph (e) may be illustrated by the following example:

Example. During calendar year 1987, nonpublicly offered regulated investment company M distributes to individual shareholder A, a calendar year taxpayer, capital gain dividends of $1,000 and other dividends of $5,000. A's allocable share of the affected RIC expenses of M is $200. In computing A's taxable income for 1987, A shall take into account the following items: (i) $1,000 of long-term capital gains (the capital gain dividends received by A); (ii) $5,200 of dividend income (the sum of the other dividends received by A and A's allocable share of the affected RIC expenses of M); and (iii) $200 of expenses described in section 212 (A's allocable share of the affected RIC expenses of M). A is allowed a deduction for miscellaneous itemized deductions (including A's $200 allocable share of the affected RIC expenses of M, which is treated as an expense described in section 212) for 1987 only to the extent the aggregate of such deductions exceeds 2 percent of A's adjusted gross income for 1987.

(f) Cross-reference. See § 1.67-1T with respect to limitations on deductions for expenses described in section 212 (including amounts treated as such expenses under this section).

(g) Pass-through entity. *(1) In general.* Except as provided in paragraph (g)(2) of this section, for purposes of section 67(c) and this section, a pass-through entity is—

(i) A trust (or any portion thereof) to which subpart E, part 1, subchapter J, chapter 1 of the Code applies,

(ii) A partnership,

(iii) An S corporation,

(iv) A common trust fund described in section 584,

(v) A nonpublicly offered regulated investment company,

(vi) A real estate mortgage investment conduit, and

(vii) Any other person—

(A) Which is not subject to the income tax imposed by subtitle A, chapter 1, or which is allowed a deduction in computing such tax for distributions to owners or beneficiaries, and

(B) The character of the income of which may affect the character of the income recognized with respect to that person by its owners or beneficiaries.

Entities that do not meet the requirements of paragraph (g)(1)(vii)(A) and (B) of this section, such as qualified pension plans, individual retirement accounts, and insurance companies holding assets in separate asset accounts to fund variable contracts defined in section 817(d), are not described in this paragraph (g)(1).

(2) Exception. For purposes of section 67(c) and this section, a pass-through entity does not include:

(i) An estate;

(ii) A trust (or any portion thereof) not described in paragraph (g)(1)(i) of this section,

(iii) A cooperative described in section 1381(a)(2), determined without regard to subparagraphs (A) and (C) thereof, or

(iv) A real estate investment trust.

(3) Nonpublicly offered regulated investment company. (i) In general. For purposes of this section, the term "nonpublicly offered regulated investment company" means a regulated investment company to which Part I of Subchapter M of the Code applies that is not a publicly offered regulated investment company.

(ii) Publicly offered regulated investment company. For purposes of this section, the term "publicly offered regulated investment company" means a regulated investment company to which Part I of Subchapter M of the Code applies the shares of which are—

(A) Continuously offered pursuant to a public offering (within the meaning of section 4 of the Securities Act of 1933, as amended (15 U.S.C. 77a to 77aa)),

(B) Regularly traded on an established securities market, or

(C) Held by or for no fewer than 500 persons at all times during the taxable year.

(h) Affected investor. *(1) In general.* For purposes of this section, the term "affected investor" means a partner, shareholder, beneficiary, participant, or other interest holder in a pass-through entity at any time during the pass-through entity's taxable year that is—

(i) An individual (other than a nonresident alien whose income with respect to his or her interest in the pass-through entity is not effectively connected with the conduct of a trade or business within the United States),

(ii) A person, including a trust or estate, that computes its taxable income in the same manner as in the case of an individual; or

(iii) A pass-through entity if one or more of its partners, shareholders, beneficiaries, participants, or other interest holders is (A) a pass-through entity or (B) a person described in paragraph (h)(1)(i) or (ii) of this section.

(2) Examples. The provisions of this paragraph (h) may be illustrated by the following examples:

Example (1). Corporation X holds shares of nonpublicly offered regulated investment company R in its capacity as a nominee or custodian for individual A, the beneficial owner of the shares. Because the owner of the shares for Federal income tax purposes is an individual, the shares are owned by an affected investor.

Example (2). Individual retirement account I owns shares of a nonpublicly offered regulated investment company. Because an individual retirement account is not a person described in paragraph (h)(1) of this section, the shares are not owned by an affected investor.

(i) Affected expenses. *(1) In general.* In general, for purposes of this section, the term "affected expenses" means expenses that, if paid or incurred by an individual, would be deductible, if at all, as miscellaneous itemized deductions as defined in section 67(b).

(2) Special rule for nonpublicly offered regulated investment companies. In the case of a nonpublicly offered regulated investment company, the term "affected expenses" means only affected RIC expenses.

(j) Affected RIC expenses. *(1) In general.* In general, for purposes of this section the term "affected RIC expenses" means the excess of—

(i) The aggregate amount of the expenses (other than expenses described in sections 62(a)(3) and 67(b) and § 1.67-1T(b)) paid or incurred in the calendar year that are allowable as a deduction in determining the investment company taxable income (without regard to section 852(b)(2)(D)) of the nonpublicly offered regulated investment company for a taxable year that begins or ends with or within the calendar year, over

(ii) The amount of expenses taken into account under paragraph (j)(1)(i) of this section that are allocable to the following items (whether paid separately or included as part of a fee paid to an investment advisor or other person for a variety of services):

(A) Registration fees;

(B) Directors' or trustees' fees;

(C) Periodic meetings of directors, trustees, or shareholders;

(D) Transfer agent fees;

(E) Legal and accounting fees (other than fees for income tax return preparation or income tax advice); and

(F) Shareholder communications required by law (e.g. the preparation and mailing of prospectuses and proxy statements).

Expenses described in paragraph (j)(1)(ii)(A) through (F) of this section do not include, for example, expenses allocable to investment advice, marketing activities, shareholder communications and other services not specifically described in paragraph (j)(1)(ii)(A) through (F) of this section, and custodian fees.

(2) Safe harbor. If a nonpublicly offered regulated investment company makes an election under this paragraph (j)(2), the affected RIC expenses for a calendar year shall be treated as equal to 40 percent of the amount determined under paragraph (j)(1)(i) of this section for that calendar year. The nonpublicly offered regulated investment company shall make the election by attaching to its income tax return for the taxable year that includes the last day of the first calendar year for which the nonpublicly offered regulated investment company makes the election a statement that it is making an election under paragraph (j)(2) of this section. An election made pursuant to this paragraph (j)(2) shall remain in effect for all subsequent calendar years unless revoked with the consent of the Commissioner.

(3) Reduction for unused RIC expenses. The amount determined under paragraph (j)(1)(i) of this section shall be reduced by the nonpublicly offered regulated investment company's net operating loss, if any, for the taxable year ending with or within the calendar year. In computing the nonpublicly offered regulated investment company's net operating loss for purposes of this section, the deduction for dividends paid shall not be allowed and any net capital gain for the taxable year shall be excluded.

(4) Exception. The affected RIC expenses of a nonpublicly offered regulated investment company will be treated as zero if the amount of its gross income for the calendar year (determined without regard to capital gain net income) is not greater than 1 percent of the sum of (i) such gross income and (ii) the amount of its interest income for the calendar year that is not includible in gross income pursuant to section 103.

(k) Allocation of expenses among nonpublicly offered regulated investment company shareholders. *(1) General rule.* A nonpublicly offered regulated investment company shall allocate to each of its affected investors that is a shareholder at any time during the calendar year, the affected investor's allocable share of the affected RIC expenses of the nonpublicly offered regulated investment company for that calendar year. (See paragraph (m) of this section for rules regarding estimates with respect to the amount of an affected investor's share of affected RIC expenses upon which certain persons can rely for certain purposes.) A nonpublicly offered regulated investment company may use any reasonable method to make the allocation. A method of allocation shall not be reasonable if—

(i) The method can be expected to have the effect, if applied to all affected RIC expenses and all shareholders (whether or not affected investors), of allocating to the shareholders an amount of affected RIC expenses that is less than the affected RIC expenses of the nonpublicly offered regulated investment company for the calendar year.

(ii) The method can be expected to have the effect of allocating a disproportionately high share of the affected RIC expenses of the nonpublicly offered regulated investment company to shareholders that are not affected investors or affected investors, the amount of whose miscellaneous itemized deductions (including their allocable share of affected RIC expenses) exceeds the 2-percent floor described in section 67, or

(iii) A principal purpose of the method of allocation is to avoid allocating affected RIC expenses to persons described in paragraph (h)(1)(i) or (ii) of this section whose miscellaneous itemized deductions (inclusive of their allocable share of affected RIC expenses) may not exceed the 2-percent floor described in seotion 67.

(2) Reasonable allocation method described. (i) In general. The allocation method described in this paragraph (k)(2) shall be treated as a reasonable allocation method. Under the method described in this paragraph, an affected investor's allocable share of the affected RIC expenses of a nonpublicly offered regulated investment company is the amount that bears the same ratio to the amount of affected RIC expenses of the nonpublicly offered regulated investment company for the calendar year as—

(A) The amount of dividends paid to the affected investor during the calendar year, bears to

(B) The sum of—

(1) The aggregate amount of dividends paid by the nonpublicly offered regulated investment company during the calendar year to all shareholders, and

(2) Any amount on which tax is imposed under section 852(b)(1) for any taxable year of the nonpublicly offered regulated investment company ending within or with the calendar year.

(ii) Exception. Paragraph (k)(2)(i) of this section does not apply if the amount of the deduction for dividends paid during the calendar year is zero.

(iii) Dividends paid. For purposes of this paragraph (k)(2)—

(A) Dividends that are treated as paid during a calendar year pursuant to section 852(b)(7) are treated as paid during that calendar year and not during the succeeding calendar year.

(B) The term "dividends paid" does not include capital gain dividends (as defined in section 852(b)(3)(C)), exempt-interest dividends (as defined in section 852(b)(5)(A)), or any amount to which section 302(a) applies.

(C) The dividends paid during a calendar year is determined without regard to section 855(a).

(3) Reasonable allocation made by District Director. If a nonpublicly offered regulated investment company does not make a reasonable allocation of affected RIC expenses to its affected investors as required by paragraph (k)(1) of this section, a reasonable allocation shall be made by the District Director of the internal revenue district in which the principal place of business or principal office or agency of the nonpublicly offered regulated investment company is located.

(4) Examples. The provisions of this paragraph (k) may be illustrated by the following examples:

Example (1). Nonpublicly offered regulated investment company M, in calculating its investment company taxable income, claims a dividends paid deduction for a portion of redemption distributions (to which section 302(a) applies) to shareholders, as well as for nonredemption distributions. M allocates affected expenses among shareholders who have received nonredemption distributions by multiplying the amount of nonredemption distributions distributed to each shareholder by a fraction, the numerator of which is the affected RIC expenses of M and the denominator of which is M's investment company taxable income, determined on a calendar year basis and without regard to deductions described in section 852(b)(2)(D). No affected RIC expenses are allocated with respect to the redemption distributions. This allocation method can be expected to have the effect of allocating among the shareholders an amount of expenses that is less than the total amount of affected RIC expenses of M. Accordingly, the allocation method is not reasonable.

Example (2). Nonpublicly offered regulated investment company N has two classes of stock, a "capital" class and an "income" class. Owners of the capital class receive the benefit of all capital appreciation on the stocks owned by N, and bear the burden of certain capital expenditures of N; owners of the income class receive the benefit of all other income of N, and bear the burden of all expenses of N that are deductible under section 162. M allocates all affected RIC expenses among shareholders of the income class shares under a method that would be reasonable if the income class were the only class of N stock. Corporations and other shareholders that are not affected investors own a higher proportion of income class shares than of capital class shares. The affected RIC expenses of N are properly allocated among the shareholders who bear the burden of those expenses. Accordingly, the allocation method does not have the effect of allocating a disproportionately high share of the affected RIC expenses of N to shareholders that are not affected investors merely because a disproportionate share of income class shares are owned by shareholders that are not affected investors. The allocation method is reasonable.

Example (3). Nonpublicly offered regulated investment company O has two classes of stock, Class A and Class B. Shares of Class A, which may be purchased without payment of a sales or brokerage commission, are charged with the expenses of a Rule 12b-1 distribution plan of O. Shares of Class B, which may be purchased only upon payment of a sales or brokerage commission, are not charged with the expenses of the Rule 12b-1 distribution plan of O. O allocates all affected RIC expenses among shareholders of Class A and Class B shares under a method that would be reasonable if Class A or Class B shares, respectively, were the only class of O stock. The affected RIC expenses attributable to the Rule 12b-1 plan are allocated to the shareholders of Class A shares. Shareholders that are not affected investors own a higher proportion of Class A shares than of Class B shares. The affected RIC expenses of O are properly allocated among the shareholders who bear the burden of those expenses. Accordingly, the allocation method does not have the effect of allocating a disproportionately high share of the affected RIC expenses of O to shareholders that are not affected investors merely because a disproportionately high share of Class A shares are owned by persons that are not affected investors. The allocation method is reasonable.

Example (4). Assume the facts are the same as in example (3) except that a portion of the affected RIC expenses attributable to the Rule 12b-1 plan are allocated to the shareholders of Class B shares, and shareholders that are not affected investors own a higher proportion of Class B shares than of Class A shares. Thus, the affected RIC expenses are not allocated among the class of shareholders that bear the burden of the expenses. Accordingly, the allocation method has the effect of allocating a disproportionate share of the affected RIC expenses of O to the shareholders of Class B shares. Because shareholders that are not affected investors own a higher proportion of Class B shares than Class A shares, the method can be expected to allocate a disproportionately high share of the affected RIC expenses of O to shareholders that are not affected investors. Accordingly, the allocation method is not reasonable.

(l) Affected RIC expenses not subject to backup withholding. The amount of dividend income that an affected investor in a nonpublicly offered regulated investment company is treated as having received or accrued under paragraph (e)(1)(ii) of this section is not subject to backup withholding under section 3406.

(m) Reliance by nominees and pass-through investors on notices. *(1) General Rule.* Persons described in paragraph (m)(3) of this section may, for the purposes described in that paragraph (m)(3), treat an affected investor's allocable share of the affected RIC expenses of a nonpublicly offered regulated investment company as being equal to an amount determined by the nonpublicly offered regulated investment company on the basis of a reasonable estimate (e.g., of allocable expenses as a percentage of dividend distributions or allocable expenses per share) that is (i) reported in writing by the nonpublicly offered regulated investment company to the person or (ii) reported in a newspaper or financial publication having a nationwide circulation (e.g., the Wall Street Journal or Standard and Poor's Weekly Dividend Record).

(2) Estimates must be reasonable. In general, for purposes of paragraph (m)(1) of this section, estimates of affected RIC expenses of a nonpublicly offered regulated investment company will be treated as reasonable only if the nonpublicly offered regulated investment company makes a reasonable effort to offset material understatements (or overstatements) of affected RIC expenses for a period by increasing (or decreasing) estimates of affected RIC expenses for a subsequent period. Understatements or overstatements of affected RIC expenses that are not material may be corrected by making offsetting adjustments in future periods, provided that understatements and overstatements are treated consistently.

(3) Application. Paragraph (m)(1) of this section shall apply to the following persons for the following purposes:

(i) A nominee who, pursuant to section 6042(a)(1)(B) and paragraph (n)(2) of this section, is required to report dividends paid by a nonpublicly offered regulated investment company to the Internal Revenue Service and to the person to whom the payment is made, for purposes of reporting to the Internal Revenue Service and the person to whom the payment is made the amount of affected RIC expenses allocated to such person.

(ii) An affected investor to whom a nominee (to which paragraph (m)(3)(i) of this section applies) reports, for purposes of calculating the affected investor's taxable income and the amount of its affected expenses.

(iii) A shareholder that is a pass-through entity, for purposes of calculating its taxable income and the amount of its affected expenses.

(n) Return of information and reporting to affected investors by a nonpublicly offered regulated investment company. *(1) In general.* (i) Return of information. A nonpublicly offered regulated investment company shall make an information return (e.g., Form 1099-DIV, Dividends and Distributions, for 1987) with respect to each affected investor to which an allocation of affected RIC expenses is required to be made pursuant to paragraph (k) of this section and for which the nonpublicly offered regulated investment company is required to make an information return to the Internal Revenue Service pursuant to section 6042 (or would be required to make such information return but for the $10 threshold described in section 6042(a)(1)(A) and (B). The nonpublicly offered regulated investment company shall make the information return for each calendar year and shall state separately on such return—

(A) The amount of affected RIC expenses required to be allocated to the affected investor for the calendar year pursuant to paragraph (k) of this section.

(B) The sum of—

(1) The aggregate amount of the dividends paid to the affected investor during the calendar year, and

(2) The amount of the affected RIC expenses required to be allocated to the affected investor for the calendar year pursuant to paragraph (k) of this section, and

(C) Such other information as may be specified by the form or its instructions.

(ii) Statement to be furnished to affected investors. A nonpublicly offered regulated investment company shall provide to each affected investor for each calendar year (whether or not the nonpublicly offered regulated investment company is required to make an information return with respect to the affected investor pursuant to section 6042), a written statement showing the following information:

(A) The information described in paragraph (n)(1)(i) of this section with respect to the affected investor;

(B) The name and address of the nonpublicly offered regulated investment company;

(C) The name and address of the affected investor; and

(D) If the nonpublicly offered regulated investment company is required to report the amount of the affected investor's allocation of affected RIC expense to the Internal Revenue Service pursuant to paragraph (n)(1)(i) of this section a statement to that effect.

(iii) Affected investor's shares held by a nominee. If an affected investor's shares in a nonpublicly offered regulated investment company are held in the name of a nominee, the nonpublicly offered regulated investment company may make the information return described in paragraph (n)(1)(i) of this section with respect to the nominee in lieu of the affected investor and may provide the written statement described in paragraph (n)(1)(ii) of this section to such nominee in lieu of the affected investor.

(2) By a nominee. (i) In general. Except as otherwise provided for in paragraph (n)(2)(iii) of this section, in any case in which a nonpublicly offered regulated investment company provides, pursuant to paragraph (n)(1)(iii) of this section, a written statement to the nominee of an affected investor for a calendar year, the nominee shall—

(A) If the nominee is required to make an information return pursuant to section 6042 (or would be required to make an information return but for the $10 threshold described in section 6042(a)(1)(A) and (B), make an information return (e.g., Form 1099-DIV, Dividends and Distributions, for 1987) for the calendar year with respect to each affected investor and state separately on such information return the information described in paragraph (n)(1)(i) of this section, and

(B) Furnish each affected investor with a written statement for the calendar year showing the information required by paragraph (n)(2)(ii) of this section (whether or not the nominee is required to make an information return with respect to the affected investor pursuant to section 6042).

(ii) Form of statement. The written statement required to be furnished for a calendar year pursuant to paragraph (n)(2)(i)(B) of this section shall show the following information:

(A) The affected investor's proportionate share of the items described in paragraph (n)(1)(i) of this section for the calendar year,

(B) The name and address of the nominee,

(C) The name and address of the affected investor, and

(D) If the nominee is required to report the affected investor's share of the allocable investment expenses to the Internal Revenue Service pursuant to paragraph (n)(2)(i)(A) of this section, a statement to that effect.

(iii) Return not required. A nominee is not required to make an information return with respect to an affected investor pursuant to paragraph (n)(2)(i)(A) of this section if the nominee is excluded from the requirements of section 6042 pursuant to § 1.6042-2(a)(1)(ii) or (iii).

(iv) Statement not required. A nominee is not required to furnish a written statement to an affected investor pursuant to paragraph (n)(2)(i)(B) of this section if the nonpublicly offered regulated investment company furnishes the written statement to the affected investor pursuant to an agreement with the nominee described in § 1.6042-2(a)(1)(iii).

(v) Special rule. Paragraph (n)(1)(i) and (ii) of this section applies to a nonpublicly offered regulated investment company that agrees with the nominee to satisfy the requirements of section 6042 as described in § 1.6042-2(a)(1)(iii) with respect to the affected investor.

(3) Time and place for furnishing returns. The returns required by paragraph (n)(1)(i) and (2)(i)(A) of this section for any calendar year shall be filed at the time and place that a return required under section 6042 is required to be filed. See § 1.6042-2(c).

(4) Time for furnishing statements. The statements required by paragraph (n)(1)(ii) and (2)(i)(B) of this section to be furnished by a nonpublicly offered regulated investment company and a nominee, respectively, to an affected investor for a calendar year shall be furnished to such affected investor on or before January 31 of the following year.

(5) Duplicative returns and statements not required. (i) Information return. The requirements of paragraph (n)(1)(i) and (2)(i)(A) of this section for the making of an information return shall be met by the timely filing of an information return pursuant to section 6042 that contains the information required by paragraph (n)(1)(i).

(ii) Written statement. The requirements of paragraph (n)(1)(ii) and (2)(i)(B) of this section for the furnishing of a written statement (including the statement required by paragraph (n)(1)(ii)(D) and (2)(ii)(D) of this section) shall be met by furnishing the affected investor a copy of the information return to which section 6042 applies (whether or not the nonpublicly offered regulated investment company or nominee is required to file an information return with respect to the affected investor pursuant to section 6042) that contains the information required by paragraph (n)(1)(ii) or (2)(ii), whichever is applicable, of this section. Nonpublicly offered regulated investment companies and nominees may use a substitute form that contains provisions substantially similar to those of the prescribed form if the nonpublicly offered regulated investment company or nominee complies with all revenue procedures relating to substitute forms in effect at the time. The statement shall be furnished either in person or in a statement mailed by first-class mail that includes adequate notice that the statement is enclosed. A statement shall be considered to be furnished to an affected investor within the meaning of this section if it is mailed to such affected investor at its last known address.

(o) Return of information by a common trust fund. With respect to each affected investor to which paragraph (d) of this section applies, the common trust fund shall state on the return it is required to make pursuant to section 6032 for its taxable year, the following information:

(1) The amount of the affected investor's proportionate share of the affected expenses for the taxable year as described in paragraph (d)(1)(ii) of this section.

(2) The amount of the affected investor's proportionate share of ordinary taxable income or ordinary net loss for the taxable year determined pursuant to paragraph (d)(1)(i) of this section, and

(3) Such other information as may be specified by the form or its instructions.

(p) Publicly offered regulated investment companies. [Reserved]

T.D. 8189, 3/25/88.

---

§ 1.67-3 Allocation of expenses by real estate mortgage investment conduits.

(a) Allocation of allocable investment expenses. [Reserved]

(b) Treatment of allocable investment expenses. [Reserved]

(c) Computation of proportionate share. [Reserved]

(d) Example. [Reserved]

(e) Allocable investment expenses not subject to backup withholding. [Reserved]

(f) Notice to pass-through interest holders. *(1) Information required.* A REMIC must provide to each pass-through interest holder to which an allocation of allocable investment expense is required to be made under § 1.67-3T(a)(1) notice of the following—

(i) If, pursuant to paragraph (f)(2)(i) or (ii) of this section, notice is provided for a calendar quarter, the aggregate amount of expenses paid or accrued during the calendar quarter for which the REMIC is allowed a deduction under section 212;

(ii) If, pursuant to paragraph (f)(2)(ii) of this section, notice is provided to a regular interest holder for a calendar year, the aggregate amount of expenses paid or accrued during each calendar quarter that the regular interest holder held the regular interest in the calendar year and for which the REMIC is allowed a deduction under section 212; and

(iii) The proportionate share of these expenses allocated to that pass-through interest holder, as determined under § 1.67-3T(c).

(2) Statement to be furnished. (i) To residual interest holder. For each calendar quarter, a REMIC must provide to each pass-through interest holder who holds a residual interest during the calendar quarter the notice required under paragraph (f)(1) of this section on Schedule Q (Form 1066), as required in § 1.860F-4(e).

(ii) To regular interest holder. For each calendar year, a single-class REMIC (as described in § 1.67-3T(a)(2)(ii)(B)) must provide to each pass-through interest holder who held a regular interest during the calendar year the notice required under paragraph (f)(1) of this section. Quarterly reporting is not required. The information required to be included in the notice may be separately stated on the statement described in § 1.6049-7(f) instead of on a separate statement provided in a separate mailing. See § 1.6049-7(f)(4). The separate statement provided in a separate mailing must be furnished to each pass-through interest holder no later than the last day of the month following the close of the calendar year.

(3) Returns to the Internal Revenue Service. (i) With respect to residual interest holders. Any REMIC required under paragraphs (f)(1) and (2)(i) of this section to furnish information to any pass-through interest holder who holds a residual interest must also furnish such information to the Internal Revenue Service as required in § 1.860F-4(e)(4).

(ii) With respect to regular interest holders. A single-class REMIC (as described in § 1.67-3T(a)(2)(ii)(B)) must make an information return on Form 1099 for each calendar year, with respect to each pass-through interest holder who holds a regular interest to which an allocation of allocable investment expenses is required to be made pursuant to § 1.67-3T(a)(1) and (2)(ii). The preceding sentence applies with respect to a holder for a calendar year only if the REMIC is required to make an information return to the Internal Revenue Service with respect to that holder for that year pursuant to section 6049 and § 1.6049-7(b)(2)(i) (or would be required to make an information return but for the $10 threshold described in section 6049(a)(1) and § 1.6049-7(b)(2)(i)). The REMIC must state on the information return—

(A) The sum of—

(1) The aggregate amounts includible in gross income as interest (as defined in § 1.6049-7(a)(1)(i) and (ii)), for the calendar year; and

(2) The sum of the amount of allocable investment expenses required to be allocated to the pass-through interest holder for each calendar quarter during the calendar year pursuant to § 1.67-3T(a); and

(B) Any other information specified by the form or its instructions.

(4) Interest held by nominees and other specified persons. (i) Pass-through interest holder's interest held by a nominee. If a pass-through interest holder's interest in a REMIC is held in the name of a nominee, the REMIC may make the information return described in paragraphs (f)(3)(i) and (ii) of this section with respect to the nominee in lieu of the pass-through interest holder and may provide the written statement described in paragraphs (f)(2)(i) and (ii) of this section to that nominee in lieu of the pass-through interest holder.

(ii) Regular interests in a single-class REMIC held by certain persons. If a person specified in § 1.6049-7(e)(4) holds a regular interest in a single-class REMIC (as described in § 1.67-3T(a)(2)(ii)(B)), then the single-class REMIC must provide the information described in paragraphs (f)(1) and (f)(3)(ii)(A) and (B) of this section to that person with the information specified in § 1.6049-7(e)(2) as required in § 1.6049-7(e).

(5) Nominee reporting. (i) In general. In any case in which a REMIC provides information pursuant to paragraph (f)(4) of this section to a nominee of a pass-through interest holder for a calendar quarter or, as provided in paragraph (f)(2)(ii) of this section, for a calendar year—

(A) The nominee must furnish each pass-through interest holder with a written statement described in paragraph (f)(2)(i) or (ii) of this section, whichever is applicable, showing the information described in paragraph (f)(1) of this section; and

(B) The nominee must make an information return on Form 1099 for each calendar year, with respect to the pass-through interest holder and state on this information return the information described in paragraphs (f)(3)(ii)(A) and (B) of this section, if—

(1) The nominee is a nominee for a pass-through interest holder who holds a regular interest in a single-class REMIC (as described in § 1.67-3T(a)(2)(ii)(B)); and

(2) The nominee is required to make an information return pursuant to section 6049 and § 1.6049-7(b)(2)(i) and (b)(2)(ii)(B) (or would be required to make an information return but for the $10 threshold described in section 6049(a)(2) and § 1.6049-7(b)(2)(i)) with respect to the pass-through interest holder.

(ii) Time for furnishing statement. The statement required by paragraph (f)(5)(i)(A) of this section to be furnished by a nominee to a pass-through interest holder for a calendar quarter or calendar year must be furnished to this holder no later than 30 days after receiving the written statement described in paragraph (f)(2)(i) or (ii) of this section from the REMIC. If, however, pursuant to paragraph (f)(2)(ii) of this section, the information is separately stated on the statement described in § 1.6049-7(f), then the information must be furnished to the pass-through interest holder in the time specified in § 1.6049-7(f)(5).

(6) Special rules. (i) Time and place for furnishing returns. The returns required by paragraphs (f)(3)(ii) and (f)(5)(i)(B) of this section for any calendar year must be filed at the time and place that a return required under section 6049 and § 1.6049-7(b)(2) is required to be filed. See § 1.6049-4(g) and § 1.6049-7(b)(2)(iv).

(ii) Duplicative returns not required. The requirements of paragraphs (f)(3)(ii) and (f)(5)(i)(B) of this section for the making of an information return are satisfied by the timely filing of an information return pursuant to section 6049 and § 1.6049-7(b)(2) that contains the information required by paragraph (f)(3)(ii) of this section.

T.D. 8431, 9/2/92.

§ 1.67-3T Allocation of expenses by real estate mortgage investment conduits (temporary).

Caution: The Treasury has not yet amended Reg § 1.67-3T to reflect changes made by P.L. 100-647, P.L. 100-203.

(a) Allocation of allocable investment expenses. *(1) In general.* A real estate mortgage investment conduit or REMIC (as defined in section 860D) shall allocate to each of its pass-through interest holders that holds an interest at any time during the calendar quarter the holder's proportionate share (as determined under paragraph (c) of this section) of the aggregate amount of allocable investment expenses of the REMIC for the calendar quarter.

(2) Pass-through interest holder. (i) In general. (A) Meaning of term. Except as provided in paragraph (a)(2)(ii) of this section, the term "pass-through interest holder" means any holder of a REMIC residual interest (as definition in section 860G(a)(2)) that is—

(1) An individual (other than a nonresident alien whose income with respect to his or her interest in the REMIC is not effectively connected with the conduct of a trade or business within the United States),

(2) A person, including a trust or estate, that computes its taxable income in the same manner as in the case of an individual, or

(3) A pass-through entity (as defined in paragraph (a)(3) of this section) if one or more of its partners, shareholders, beneficiaries, participants, or other interest holders is (i) a pass-through entity or (ii) a person described in paragraph (a)(2)(i)(A)(1) or (2) of this section.

(B) Examples. The provisions of this paragraph (a)(2)(i) may be illustrated by the following examples:

Example (1). Corporation X holds a residual interest in REMIC R in its capacity as a nominee or custodian for individual A, the beneficial owner of the interest. Because the owner of the interest for Federal income tax purposes is an individual, the interest is owned by a pass-through interest holder.

Example (2). Individual retirement account 1 holds a residual interest in a REMIC. Because an individual retirement account is not a person described in paragraph (a)(2)(i)(A) of this section, the interest is not held by a pass-through interest holder.

(ii) Single-class REMIC. (A) In general. In the case of a single-class REMIC, the term "pass-through interest holder" means any holder of either—

(1) A REMIC regular interest (as defined in section 860G(a)(1)), or

(2) A REMIC residual interest, that is described in paragraph (a)(2)(i)(A)(1), (2), or (3) of this section.

(B) Single-class REMIC. For purposes of paragraph (a)(2)(ii)(A) of this section, a single-class REMIC is either—

(1) A REMIC that would be classified as an investment trust under § 301.7701-4(c)(1) but for its qualification as a REMIC under section 860D and § 1.860D-1T, or

(2) A REMIC that—

(i) is substantially similar to an investment trust under § 301.7701-4(c)(1), and

(ii) Is structured with the principal purpose of avoiding the requirement of paragraph (a)(1) and (2)(ii)(A) of this section to allocate allocable investment expenses to pass-through interest holders that hold regular interests in the REMIC.

For purposes of this paragraph (a)(2)(ii)(B), in determining whether a REMIC would be classified as an investment trust or is substantially similar to an investment trust, all interests in the REMIC shall be treated as ownership interests in the REMIC, without regard to whether or not they would be classified as debt for Federal income tax purposes in the absence of a REMIC election.

(C) Examples. The provisions of paragraph (a)(2)(ii) of this section must be illustrated by the following examples:

Example (1). Corporation M transfers mortgages to a bank under a trust agreement as described in Example (2) of § 301.7701-4(c)(2). There are two classes of certificates. Holders of class C certificates are entitled to receive 90 percent of the payment of principal and interest on the mortgages; holders of class D certificates are entitled to receive the remaining 10 percent. The two classes of certificates are identical except that, in the event of a default on the underlying mortgages, the payment rights of class D certificates holders are subordinated to the rights of class C certificate holders. M sells the class C certificates to investors and retains the class D certificates. The trust would be classified as an investment trust under § 301.7701-4(c)(1) but for its qualification a REMIC under section 860D, the class C certificates represent regular interests in the REMIC and the class D certificates represent residual interest in the REMIC. The REMIC is a single-class REMIC within the meaning of paragraph (a)(2)(ii)(B)(1) of this section and, accordingly, holders of both the class C and class D certificates who are described in paragraph (a)(2)(i)(A)(1), (2), or (3) of this section are treated as pass-through interest holders.

Example (2). Assume that the facts are the same as in Example (1) except that M structures the REMIC to include a second regular interest represented by class E certificates. The principal purpose of M in structuring the REMIC to include class E certificates is to avoid allocating allocable investment expenses to class C certificate holders. The class E certificate holders are entitled to receive the payments otherwise due the class D certificate holders until they have been paid a stated amount of principal plus interest. The fair market value of the class E certificate is ten percent of the fair market value of the class D certificate and, therefore, less than one percent of the fair market value of the REMIC. The REMIC would not be classified as an investment trust under § 301.7701-4(c)(1) because the existence of the class E certificates is not incidental to the trust's purpose of facilitating direct investment in the assets of the trust. Nevertheless, because the fair market value of the class E certificates is de minimis, the REMIC is substantially similar to an investment trust under § 301.7701-4(c)(1). In addition, avoidance of the requirement to allocate allocable investment expenses to regular interest holders is the principal purpose of M in structuring the REMIC to include class E certificates. Therefore, the REMIC is a single-class REMIC within the meaning of paragraph (a)(2)(ii)(B)(2) of this section, and, accordingly, holders of both residual and regular interests who are described in paragraph (a)(2)(i)(A)(1), (2), or (3) of this section are treated as pass-through interest holders.

(3) Pass-through entity. (i) In general. Except as provided in paragraph (a)(3)(ii) of this section, for purposes of this section, a pass-through entity is—

(A) A trust (or any portion thereof) to which Subpart E, Part 1, Subchapter J, Chapter 1 of the Code applies.

(B) A partnership,

(C) An S corporation,

(D) A common trust fund described in section 584,

(E) A nonpublicly offered regulated investment company (as defined in paragraph (a)(5)(i) of this section),

(F) A REMIC, and

(G) Any other person—

(1) Which is not subject to income tax imposed by Subtitle A, Chapter 1, or which is allowed a deduction in computing such tax for distributions to owners or beneficiaries, and

(2) The character of the income of which may affect the character of the income recognized with respect to that person by its owners or beneficiaries.

Entities that do not meet the requirements of paragraphs (a)(3)(i)(G)(1) and (2), such as qualified pension plans, individual retirement accounts, and insurance companies holding assets in separate asset accounts to fund variable contracts defined in section 817(d), are not described in this paragraph (a)(3)(i).

(ii) Exception. For purposes of this section, a pass-through entity does not include—

(A) An estate,

(B) A trust (or any portion thereof) not described in paragraph (a)(3)(i)(A) of this section,

(C) A cooperative described without regard to subparagraphs (A) and (C) thereof, or

(D) A real estate investment trust.

(4) Allocable investment expenses. The term "allocable investment expenses" means the aggregate amount of the expenses paid or accrued in the calendar quarter for which a deduction is allowable under section 212 in determining the taxable income of the REMIC for the calendar quarter.

(5) Nonpublicly offered regulated investment company. (i) In general. For purposes of this section, the term "nonpublicly offered regulated investment company" means a regulated investment company to which Part I of Subchapter M of the Code applies that is not a publicly offered regulated investment company.

(ii) Publicly offered regulated investment company. For purposes of this section, the term "publicly offered regulated investment company" means a regulated investment company to which Part I of Subchapter M of the Code applies, the shares of which are—

(A) Continuously offered pursuant to a public offering (within the meaning of section 4 of the Securities Act of 1933, as amended (15 U.S.C. 77a to 77aa)),

(B) Regularly traded on an established securities market, or

(C) Held by or for no fewer than 500 persons at all times during the taxable year.

(b) Treatment of allocable investment expenses. *(1) By pass-through interest holders.* (i) Taxable year ending with calendar quarter. A pass-through interest holder whose taxable year is the calendar year or ends with a calendar quarter shall be treated as having—

(A) Received or accrued income, and

(B) Paid or incurred an expense described in section 212 (or section 162 in the case of a pass-through interest holder that is a regulated investment company), in an amount equal to the pass-through interest holder's proportionate share of the allocable investment expenses of the REMIC for those calendar quarters that fall within the holder's taxable year.

(ii) Taxable year not ending with calendar quarter. A pass-through interest holder whose taxable year does not end with a calendar quarter shall be treated as having—

(A) Received or accrued income, and

(B) Paid or incurred an expense described in section 212 (or section 162 in the case of a pass-through interest holder that is a regulated investment company), in an amount equal to the sum of—

(C) The pass-through interest holder's proportionate share of the allocable investment expenses of the REMIC for those calendar quarters that fall within the holder's taxable year, and

(D) For each calendar quarter that overlaps the beginning or end of the taxable year, the sum of the daily amounts of the allocable investment expenses allocated to the holder pursuant to paragraph (c)(1)(ii) of this section for the days in the quarter that fall within the holder's taxable year.

(2) Proportionate share of allocable investment expenses. For purposes of paragraph (b) of this section, a pass-through interest holder's proportionate share of the allocable investment expenses is the amount allocated to the pass-through interest holder pursuant to paragraph (a)(1) of this section.

(3) Cross-reference. See § 1.67-1T with respect to limitations on deductions for expenses described in section 212 (including amounts treated as such expenses under this section).

(4) Interest income to holders of regular interests in certain REMICs. Any amount allocated under this section to the holder of a regular interest in a single-class REMIC (as described in paragraph (a)(2)(ii)(B) of this section) shall be treated as interest income.

(5) No adjustment to basis. The basis of any holder's interest in a REMIC shall not be increased or decreased by the amount of the holder's proportionate share of allocable investment expenses.

(6) Interest holders other than pass-through interest holders. An interest holder of a REMIC that is not a pass-through interest holder shall not take into account in computing its taxable income any amount of income or expense with respect to its proportionate share of allocable investment expenses.

(c) Computation of proportionate share. *(1) In general.* For purposes of paragraph (a)(1) of this section, a REMIC shall compute a pass-through interest holder's proportionate share of the REMIC's allocable investment expenses by—

(i) Determining the daily amount of the allocable investment expenses for the calendar quarter by dividing the total amount of such expenses by the number of days in that calendar quarter.

(ii) Allocating the daily amount of the allocable investment expenses to the pass-through interest holder in proportion to its respective holdings on that day, and

(iii) Totaling the interest holder's daily amounts of allocable investment expenses for the calendar quarter.

(2) Other holders taken into account. For purposes of paragraph (c)(1)(ii) of this section, a pass-through interest holder's proportionate share of the daily amount of the allocable investment expenses is determined by taking into account all holders of residual interests in the REMIC, whether or not pass-through interest holders.

(3) Single-class REMIC. (i) Daily allocation. In lieu of the allocation specified in paragraph (c)(1)(ii) of this section, a single-class REMIC (as described in paragraph (a)(2)(ii)(B) of this section) shall allocate the daily amount of the allocable investment expenses to each pass-through interest holder

in proportion to the amount of income accruing to the holder with respect to its interest in the REMIC on that day.

(ii) Other holders taken into account. For purposes of paragraph (c)(3)(i) of this section, the amount of the allocable investment expenses that is allocated on any day to each pass-through interest holder shall be determined by multiplying the daily amount of allocable investment expenses (determined pursuant to paragraph (c)(1)(i) of this section) by a fraction, the numerator of which is equal to the amount of income that accrues (but not less than zero) to the pass-through interest holder on that day and the denominator of which is the total amount of income (as determined under paragraph (c)(3)(iii) of this section) that accrues to all regular and residual interest holders, whether or not pass-through interest holders, on that day.

(iii) Total income accruing. The total amount of income that accrues to all regular and residual interest holders is the sum of—

(A) The amount includible under section 860B in the gross income (but not less than zero) of the regular interest holders, and

(B) The amount of REMIC taxable income (but not less than zero) taken into account under section 860C by the residual interest holders.

(4) Dates of purchase and disposition. For purposes of this section, a pass-through interest holder holds an interest on the date of its purchase but not on the date of its disposition.

(d) Example. The provisions of this section may be illustrated by the following example:

Example. (i) During the calendar quarter ending March 31, 1989, REMIC X, which is not a single-class REMIC, incurs $900 of allocable investment expenses. At the beginning of the calendar quarter, X has 4 residual interest holders, who hold equal proportionate shares, and 10 regular interest holders. The residual interest holders, who hold equal proportionate shares, and 10 regular interest holders. The residual interest holders, all of whom have calendar-year taxable years, are as follows: A, an individual,

C, a C corporation that is a nominee for individual I,

S, an S corporation, and

M, a C corporation that is not a nominee.

(ii) Except for A, all of the residual interest holders hold their interests in X for the entire calendar quarter. On January 31, 1989, A sells his interest to S. Thus, for the first month of the calendar quarter, each residual interest holder holds a 25 percent interest (100%/4 interest holders) in X. For the last two months, S's holding is increased to 50 percent and A's holding is decreased to zero. The daily amount of allocable investment expenses for the calendar quarter is $10 ($900/90 days).

(iii) The amount of allocable investment expenses apportioned to the residual interest holders is as follows:

(A) $75 ($10 × 25% × 30 days) is allocated to A for the 30 days that A holds an interest in X during the calendar quarter. A includes $75 in gross income in calendar year 1989. The amount of A's expenses described in section 212 is increased by $75 in calendar year 1989. A's deduction under section 212 (including the $75 amount of the allocation) is subject to the limitations contained in section 67.

(B) $225 ($10 × 25% × 90 days) is allocated to C. Because C is a nominee for I, C does not include $225 in gross income or increase its deductible expenses by $225. Instead, I includes $225 in gross income in calendar year 1989, her taxable year. The amount of I's expenses described in section 212 is increased by $225. I's deduction under section 212 (including the $225 amount of the allocation) is subject to the limitations contained in section 67.

(C) $375 (($10 × 25% × 30 days) + ($10 × 50% × 60 days)) is allocated to S. S includes in gross income $375 of allocable investment expenses in calendar year 1989. The amount of S's expenses described in section 212 for that taxable year is increased by $375. S allocates the $375 to its shareholders in accordance with the rules described in sections 1366 and 1377 in calendar year 1989. Thus, each shareholder of S includes its pro rata share of the $375 in gross income in its taxable year in which or with which calendar year 1989 ends. The amount of each shareholder's expenses described in section 212 is increased by the amount of the shareholder's allocation for the shareholder's taxable year in which or with which calendar year 1989 ends. The shareholder's deduction under section 212 (including the allocation under this section) is subject to the limitations contained in section 67.

(D) No amount is allocated to M. However, M's interest is taken into account for purposes of determining the proportionate share of those residual interest holders to whom an allocation is required to be made.

(iv) No allocation is made to the 10 regular interest holders pursuant to paragraph (a) of this section. In addition, the interests held by these interest holders are not taken into account for purposes of determining the proportionate share of the residual interest holders to whom an allocation is required to be made.

(e) Allocable investment expenses not subject to backup withholding. The amount of allocable investment expenses required to be allocated to a pass-through interest holder pursuant to paragraph (a)(1) of this section is not subject to backup withholding under section 3406.

(f) Notice to pass-through interest holders *(1) Information required.* A REMIC must provide to each pass-through interest holder to which an allocation of allocable investment expense is required to be made under paragraph (a)(1) of this section notice of the following—

(i) If, pursuant to paragraph (f)(2)(i) or (ii) of this section, notice is provided for a calendar quarter, the aggregate amount of expenses paid or accrued during the calendar quarter for which the REMIC is allowed a deduction under section 212;

(ii) If, pursuant to paragraph (f)(2)(ii) of this section, notice is provided to a regular interest holder for a calendar year, the aggregate amount of expenses paid or accrued during each calendar quarter that the regular interest holder held the regular interest in the calendar year and for which the REMIC is allowed a deduction under section 212; and

(iii) The proportionate share of these expenses allocated to that pass-through interest holder, as determined under paragraph (c) of this section.

(2) Statement to be furnished. (i) To residual interest holder. For each calendar quarter, a REMIC shall provide to each pass-through interest holder who holds a residual interest during the calendar quarter the notice required under paragraph (f)(1) of this section on Schedule Q (Form 1066), as required in § 1.860F-4(e).

(ii) To regular interest holder. (A) In general. For each calendar year, a single-class REMIC (as described in paragraph (a)(2)(ii)(B) of this section) must provide to each pass-through interest holder who held a regular interest during the calendar year the notice required under paragraph (f)(1) of this section. Quarterly reporting is not required. The information required to be included in the notice may be separately stated on the statement described in § 1.6049-7(f) instead of on a separate statement provided in a separate mailing. See § 1.6049-7(f)(4). The separate statement provided in a separate mailing must be furnished to each pass-through interest holder no later than the last day of the month following the close of the calendar year.

(B) Special rule for 1987. The information required under paragraph (f)(2)(ii)(A) of this section for any calendar quarter of 1987 shall be mailed (or otherwise delivered) to each pass-through interest holder who holds a regular interest during that calendar quarter no later than March 28, 1988.

(3) Returns to the Internal Revenue Service. (i) With respect to residual interest holders. Any REMIC required under paragraphs (f)(1) and (2)(i) of this section to furnish information to any pass-through interest holder who holds a residual interest shall also furnish such information to the Internal Revenue Service as required in § 1.860F-4(e)(4).

(ii) With respect to regular interest holders. A single-class REMIC (as described in paragraph (a)(2)(ii)(B) of this section) shall make an information return on Form 1099 for each calendar year beginning after December 31, 1987, with respect to each pass-through interest holder who holds a regular interest to which an allocation of allocable investment expenses is required to be made pursuant to paragraphs (a)(1) and (2)(ii) of this section. The preceding sentence applies with respect to a holder for a calendar year only if the REMIC is required to make an information return to the Internal Revenue Service with respect to that holder for that year pursuant to section 6049 and § 1.6049-7(b)(2)(i) (or would be required to make an information return but for the $10 threshold described in section 6049(a)(1) and § 1.6049-7(b)(2)(i)). The REMIC shall state on the information return—

(A) The sum—

(1) The aggregate amounts includible in gross income as interest (as defined in § 1.6049-7(a)(1)(i) and (ii)), for the calendar year, and

(2) The sum of the amount of allocable investment expenses required to be allocated to the pass-through interest holder for each calendar quarter during the calendar year pursuant to paragraph (a) of this section, and

(B) Any other information specified by the form or its instructions.

(4) Interest held by nominees and other specified persons. (i) Pass-through interest holder's interest held by a nominee. If a pass-through interest holder's interest in a REMIC is held in the name of a nominee, the REMIC may make the information return described in paragraphs (f)(3)(i) and (ii) of this section with respect to the nominee in lieu of the pass-through interest holder and may provide the written statement described in paragraphs (f)(2)(i) and (ii) of this section to that nominee in lieu of the pass-through interest holder.

(ii) Regular interests in a single-class REMIC held by certain persons. For calendar quarters and calendar years after December 31, 1991, if a person specified in § 1.6049-7(e)(4) holds a regular interest in a single-class REMIC (as described in paragraph (a)(2)(ii)(B) of this section), then the single-class REMIC must provide the information described in paragraphs (f)(1) and (f)(3)(ii)(A) and (B) of this section to that person with the information specified in § 1.6049-7(e)(2) as required in § 1.6049-7(e).

(5) Nominee reporting. (i) In general. In any case in which a REMIC provides information pursuant to paragraph (f)(4) of this section to a nominee of a pass-through interest holder for a calendar quarter or, as provided in paragraph (f)(2)(ii) of this section, for a calendar year—

(A) The nominee shall furnish each pass-through interest holder with a written statement described in paragraph (f)(2)(i) or (ii) of this section, whichever is applicable, showing the information described in paragraph (f)(1) of this section, and

(B) If—

(1) The nominee is a nominee for a pass-through interest holder who holds a regular interest in a single-class REMIC (as described in paragraph (a)(2)(ii)(B) of this section), and

(2) The nominee is required to make an information return pursuant to section 6049 and § 1.6049-7(b)(2)(i) and (b)(2)(ii)(B) (or would be required to make an information return but for the $10 threshold described in section 6049(a)(2) and § 1,6049-7(b)(2)(i)) with respect to the pass-through interest holder, the nominee shall make an information return on Form 1099 for each calendar year beginning after December 31, 1987, with respect to the pass-through interest holder and state on this information return the information described in paragraph (f)(3)(ii)(A) and (B) of this section.

(ii) Time for furnishing statement. The statement required by paragraph (f)(5)(i)(A) of this section to be furnished by a nominee to a pass-through interest holder for a calendar quarter or calendar year shall be furnished to this holder no later than 30 days after receiving the written statement described in paragraph (f)(2)(i) or (ii) of this section from the REMIC. If, however, pursuant to paragraph (f)(2)(ii) of this section, the information is separately stated on the statement described in § 1.6049-7(f), then the information must be furnished to the pass-through interest holder in the time specified in § 1.6049-7(f)(5).

(6) Special rules. (i) Time and place for furnishing returns. The returns required by paragraphs (f)(3)(ii) and (f)(5)(i)(B) of this section for any calendar year shall be filed at the time and place that a return required under section 6049 and § 1.6049-7(b)(2) is required to be filed. See § 1.6049-4(g) and § 1.6049-7(b)(2)(iv).

(ii) Duplicative returns not required. The requirements of paragraphs (f)(3)(ii) and (f)(5)(i)(B) of this section for the making of an information return shall be met by the timely filing of an information return pursuant to section 6049 and § 1.6049-7(b)(2) that contains the information required by paragraph (f)(3)(ii) of this section.

T.D. 8186, 3/4/88, amend T.D. 8259, 9/6/89, T.D. 8366, 9/27/91.

PAR. 2. Section 1.67-3T is amended by revising the last sentence of paragraph (f)(2)(ii)(A) to read as follows:

Proposed § 1.67-3T Allocation of expenses by real estate mortgage investment conduits (temporary). [*For Preamble, see ¶ 151,317*]

* * * * *

(f) * * *

(2) * * *

(ii) * * *

(A) * * * The separate statement provided in a separate mailing must be furnished to each pass-through interest holder no later than the 41st day following the close of the calendar year.

*　　*　　*　　*　　*

Proposed § 1.67-3T [Amended] [*For Preamble, see ¶ 151,413*]

Proposed § 1.67-4 Costs paid or incurred by estates or non-grantor trusts. [*For Preamble, see ¶ 152,887*]

(a) In general. Section 67(e) provides an exception to the 2-percent floor on miscellaneous itemized deductions for costs that are paid or incurred in connection with the administration of an estate or a trust not described in § 1.67-2T(g)(1)(i) (a non-grantor trust) and which would not have been incurred if the property were not held in such estate or trust. To the extent that a cost incurred by an estate or non-grantor trust is unique to such an entity, that cost is not subject to the 2-percent floor on miscellaneous itemized deductions. To the extent that a cost included in the definition of miscellaneous itemized deductions and incurred by an estate or non-grantor trust is not unique to such an entity, that cost is subject to the 2-percent floor.

(b) Unique. For purposes of this section, a cost is unique to an estate or a non-grantor trust if an individual could not have incurred that cost in connection with property not held in an estate or trust. In making this determination, it is the type of product or service rendered to the estate or trust, rather than the characterization of the cost of that product or service, that is relevant. A non-exclusive list of products or services that are unique to an estate or trust includes those rendered in connection with: Fiduciary accountings; judicial or quasi-judicial filings required as part of the administration of the estate or trust; fiduciary income tax and estate tax returns; the division or distribution of income or corpus to or among beneficiaries; trust or will contest or construction; fiduciary bond premiums; and communications with beneficiaries regarding estate or trust matters. A non-exclusive list of products or services that are not unique to an estate or trust, and therefore are subject to the 2-percent floor, includes those rendered in connection with: Custody or management of property; advice on investing for total return; gift tax returns; the defense of claims by creditors of the decedent or grantor; and the purchase, sale, maintenance, repair, insurance or management of non-trade or business property.

(c) "Bundled fees." If an estate or a non-grantor trust pays a single fee, commission or other expense for both costs that are unique to estates and trusts and costs that are not, then the estate or non-grantor trust must identify the portion (if any) of the legal, accounting, investment advisory, appraisal or other fee, commission or expense that is unique to estates and trusts and is thus not subject to the 2-percent floor. The taxpayer must use any reasonable method to allocate the single fee, commission or expense between the costs unique to estates and trusts and other costs.

(d) Effective/applicability date. These regulations are proposed to be effective for payments made after the date final regulations are published in the Federal Register.

§ 1.67-4T Allocation of expenses by nongrantor trusts and estates (Temporary) [Reserved]

T.D. 8189, 3/25/88.

---

§ 1.71-1 Alimony and separate maintenance payments; income to wife or former wife.

Caution: The Treasury has not yet amended Reg § 1.71-1 to reflect changes made by P.L. 99-514, P.L. 98-369.

(a) In general. Section 71 provides rules for treatment in certain cases of payments in the nature of or in lieu of alimony or an allowance for support as between spouses who are divorced or separated. For convenience, the payee spouse will hereafter in this section be referred to as the "wife" and the spouse from whom she is divorced or separated as the "husband." See section 7701(a)(17). For rules relative to the deduction by the husband of periodic payments not attributable to transferred property, see section 215 and the regulations thereunder. For rules relative to the taxable status of income of an estate or trust in case of divorce, etc., see section 682 and the regulations thereunder.

(b) Alimony or separate maintenance payments received from the husband. *(1) Decree of divorce or separate maintenance.* (i) In the case of divorce or legal separation, paragraph (1) of section 71(a) requires the inclusion in the gross income of the wife of periodic payments (whether or not made at regular intervals) received by her after a decree of divorce or of separate maintenance. Such periodic payments must be made in discharge of a legal obligation imposed upon or incurred by the husband because of the marital or family relationship under a court order or decree divorcing or legally separating the husband and wife or a written instrument incident to the divorce status or legal separation status.

(ii) For treatment of payments attributable to property transferred (in trust or otherwise), see paragraph (c) of this section.

(2) Written separation agreement. (i) Where the husband and wife are separated and living apart and do not file a joint income tax return for the taxable year, paragraph (2) of section 71(a) requires the inclusion in the gross income of the wife of periodic payments (whether or not made at regular intervals) received by her pursuant to a written separation agreement executed after August 16, 1954. The periodic payments must be made under the terms of the written separation agreement after its execution and because of the marital or family relationship. Such payments are includible in the wife's gross income whether or not the agreement is a legally enforceable instrument. Moreover, if the wife is divorced or legally separated subsequent to the written separation agreement, payments made under such agreement continue to fall within the provisions of section 71(a)(2).

(ii) For purposes of section 71(a)(2), any written separation agreement executed on or before August 16, 1954, which is altered or modified in writing by the parties in any material respect after that date will be treated as an agreement executed after August 16, 1954, with respect to payments made after the date of alteration or modification.

(iii) For treatment of payments attributable to property transferred (in trust or otherwise), see paragraph (c) of this section.

(3) Decree for support. (i) Where the husband and wife are separated and living apart and do not file a joint income tax return for the taxable year, paragraph (3) of section 71(a) requires the inclusion in the gross income of the wife of periodic payments (whether or not made at regular intervals) received by her after August 16, 1954, from her husband under any type of court order or decree (including an interlocutory decree of divorce or a decree of alimony pendente

lite) entered after March 1, 1954, requiring the husband to make the payments for her support or maintenance. It is not necessary for the wife to be legally separated or divorced from her husband under a court order or decree; nor is it necessary for the order or decree for support to be for the purpose of enforcing a written separation agreement.

(ii) For purposes of section 71(a)(3), any decree which is altered or modified by a court order entered after March 1, 1954, will be treated as a decree entered after such date.

(4) Scope of section 71(a). Section 71(a) applies only to payments made because of the family or marital relationship in recognition of the general obligation to support which is made specific by the decree, instrument, or agreement. Thus, section 71(a) does not apply to that part of any periodic payment which is attributable to the repayment by the husband of, for example, a bona fide loan previously made to him by the wife, the satisfaction of which is specified in the decree, instrument, or agreement as a part of the general settlement between the husband and wife.

(5) Year of inclusion. Periodic payments are includible in the wife's income under section 71(a) only for the taxable year in which received by her. As to such amounts, the wife is to be treated as if she makes her income tax returns on the cash receipts and disbursements method, regardless of whether she normally makes such returns on the accrual method. However, if the periodic payments described in section 71(a) are to be made by an estate or trust, such periodic payments are to be included in the wife's taxable year in which they are includible according to the rules as to income of estates and trusts provided in sections 652, 662, and 682, whether or not such payments are made out of the income of such estates or trusts.

(6) Examples. The foregoing rules are illustrated by the following examples in which it is assumed that the husband and wife file separate income tax returns on the calendar year basis:

Example (1). W files suit for divorce from H in 1953. In consideration of W's promise to relinquish all marital rights and not to make public H's financial affairs, H agrees in writing to pay $200 a month to W during her lifetime if a final decree of divorce is granted without any provision for alimony. Accordingly, W does not request alimony and no provision for alimony is made under a final decree of divorce entered December 31, 1953. During 1954, H pays W $200 a month, pursuant to the promise. The $2,400 thus received by W is includible in her gross income under the provisions of section 71(a)(1). Under section 215, H is entitled to a deduction of $2,400 from his gross income.

Example (2). During 1945, H and W enter into an antenuptial agreement, under which, in consideration of W's relinquishment of all marital rights (including dower) in H's property, and, in order to provide for W's support and household expenses, H promises to pay W $200 a month during her lifetime. Ten years after their marriage, W sues H for divorce but does not ask for or obtain alimony because of the provision already made for her support in the antenuptial agreement. Likewise, the divorce decree is silent as to such agreement and H's obligation to support W. Section 71(a) does not apply to such a case. If, however, the decree were modified so as to refer to the antenuptial agreement, or if reference had been made to the antenuptial agreement in the court's decree or in a written instrument incident to the divorce status, section 71(a)(1) would require the inclusion in W's gross income of the payments received by her after the decree. Similarly, if a written separation agreement were executed after August 16, 1954, and incorporated the payment provisions of the antenuptial agreement, section 71(a)(2) would require the inclusion in W's income of payments received by W after W begins living apart from H, whether or not the divorce decree was subsequently entered and whether or not W was living apart from H when the separation agreement was executed, provided that such payments were made after such agreement was executed and pursuant to its terms. As to including such payments in W's income, if made by a trust created under the antenuptial agreement, regardless of whether referred to in the decree or a later instrument, or created pursuant to the written separation agreement, see section 682 and the regulations thereunder.

Example (3). H and W are separated and living apart during 1954. W sues H for support and on February 1, 1954, the court enters a decree requiring H to pay $200 a month to W for her support and maintenance. No part of the $200 a month support payments is includible in W's income under section 71(a)(3) or deductible by H under section 215. If, however, the decree had been entered after March 1, 1954, or had been altered or modified by a court order entered after March 1, 1954, the payments received by W after August 16, 1954, under the decree as altered or modified would be includible in her income under section 71(a)(3) and deductible by H under section 215.

Example (4). W sues H for divorce in 1954. On January 15, 1954, the court awards W temporary alimony of $25 a week pending the final decree. On September 1, 1954, the court grants W a divorce and awards her $200 a month permanent alimony. No part of the $25 a week temporary alimony received prior to the decree is includible in W's income under section 71(a), but the $200 a month received during the remainder of 1954 by W is includible in her income for 1954. Under section 215, H is entitled to deduct such $200 payments from his income. If, however, the decree awarding W temporary alimony had been entered after March 1, 1954, or had been altered or modified by a court order entered after March 1, 1954, temporary alimony received by her after August 16, 1954, would be includible in her income under section 71(a)(3) and deductible by H under section 215.

(c) Alimony and separate maintenance payments attributable to property. *(1)* (i) In the case of divorce or legal separation, paragraph (1) of section 71(a) requires the inclusion in the gross income of the wife of periodic payments (whether or not made at regular intervals) attributable to property transferred, in trust or otherwise, and received by her after a decree of divorce or of separate maintenance. Such property must have been transferred in discharge of a legal obligation imposed upon or incurred by the husband because of the marital or family relationship under a decree of divorce or separate maintenance or under a written instrument incident to such divorce status or legal separation status.

(ii) Where the husband and wife are separated and living apart and do not file a joint income tax return for the taxable year, paragraph (2) of section 71(a) requires the inclusion in the gross income of the wife of periodic payments (whether or not made at regular intervals) received by her which are attributable to property transferred, in trust or otherwise, under a written separation agreement executed after August 16, 1954. The property must be transferred because of the marital or family relationship. The periodic payments attributable to the property must be received by the wife after the written separation agreement is executed.

(iii) The periodic payments received by the wife attributable to property transferred under subdivisions (i) and (ii) of this subparagraph and includible in her gross income are not to be included in the gross income of the husband.

(2) The full amount of periodic payments received under the circumstances described in section 71(a)(1), (2), and (3) is required to be included in the gross income of the wife regardless of the source of such payments. Thus, it matters not that such payments are attributable to property in trust, to life insurance, endowment, or annuity contracts, or to any other interest in property, or are paid directly or indirectly by the husband from his income or capital. For example, if in order to meet an alimony or separate maintenance obligation of $500 a month the husband purchases or assigns for the benefit of his wife a commercial annuity contract paying such amount, the full $500 a month received by the wife is includible in her income, and no part of such amount is includible in the husband's income or deductible by him. See section 72(k) and the regulations thereunder. Likewise, if property is transferred by the husband, subject to an annual charge of $5,000, payable to his wife in discharge of his alimony or separate maintenance obligation under the divorce or separation decree or written instrument incident to the divorce status or legal separation status or if such property is transferred pursuant to a written separation agreement and subject to a similar annual charge, the $5,000 received annually is, under section 71(a)(1) or (2), includible in the wife's income, regardless of whether such amount is paid out of income or principal of the property.

(3) The same rule applies to periodic payments attributable to property in trust. The full amount of periodic payments to which section 71(a)(1) and (2) applies is includible in the wife's income regardless of whether such payments are made out of trust income. Such periodic payments are to be included in the wife's income under section 71(a)(1) or (2) and are to be excluded from the husband's income even though the income of the trust would otherwise be includible in his income under subpart E, part I, subchapter J, chapter 1 of the Code, relating to trust income attributable to grantors and others as substantial owners. As to periodic payments received by a wife attributable to property in trust in cases to which section 71(a)(1) or (2) does not apply because the husband's obligation is not specified in the decree or an instrument incident to the divorce status or legal separation status or the property was not transferred under a written separation agreement, see section 682 and the regulations thereunder.

(4) Section 71(a)(1) or (2) does not apply to that part of any periodic payment attributable to that portion of any interest in property transferred in discharge of the husband's obligation under the decree or instrument incident to the divorce status or legal separation status, or transferred pursuant to the written separation agreement, which interest originally belonged to the wife. It will apply, however, if she received such interest from her husband in contemplation of or as an incident to the divorce or separation without adequate and full consideration in money or money's worth, other than the release of the husband or his property from marital obligations. An example of the first rule is a case where the husband and wife transfer securities, which were owned by them jointly, in trust to pay an annuity to the wife. In this case, the full amount of that part of the annuity received by the wife attributable to the husband's interest in the securities transferred in discharge of his obligations under the decree, or instrument incident to the divorce status or legal separation status, or transferred under the written separation agreement, is taxable to her under section 71(a)(1) or (2), while that portion of the annuity attributable to the wife's interest in the securities so transferred is taxable to her only to the extent it is out of trust income as provided in part I (sections 641 and following), subchapter J, chapter 1 of the Code. If, however, the husband's transfer to his wife is made before such property is transferred in discharge of his obligation under the decree or written instrument, or pursuant to the separation agreement in an attempt to avoid the application of section 71(a)(1) or (2) to part of such payments received by his wife, such transfers will be considered as a part of the same transfer by the husband of his property in discharge of his obligation or pursuant to such agreement. In such a case, section 71(a)(1) or (2) will be applied to the full amount received by the wife. As to periodic payments received under a joint purchase of a commercial annuity contract, see section 72 and the regulations thereunder.

(d) Periodic and installment payments. *(1)* In general, installment payments discharging a part of an obligation the principal sum of which is, in terms of money or property, specified in the decree, instrument, or agreement are not considered "periodic payments" and therefore are not to be included under section 71(a) in the wife's income.

(2) An exception to the general rule stated in subparagraph (1) of this paragraph is provided, however, in cases where such principal sum, by the terms of the decree, instrument, or agreement, may be or is to be paid over a period ending more than 10 years from the date of such decree, instrument, or agreement. In such cases, the installment payment is considered a periodic payment for the purposes of section 71(a) but only to the extent that the installment payment, or sum of the installment payments, received during the wife's taxable year does not exceed 10 percent of the principal sum. This 10-percent limitation applies to installment payments made in advance but does not apply to delinquent installment payments for a prior taxable year of the wife made during her taxable year.

(3) (i) Where payments under a decree, instrument, or agreement are to be paid over a period ending 10 years or less from the date of such decree, instrument, or agreement, such payments are not installment payments discharging a part of an obligation the principal sum of which is, in terms of money or property, specified in the decree, instrument, or agreement (and are considered periodic payments for the purposes of section 71(a)) only if such payments meet the following two conditions:

(a) Such payments are subject to any one or more of the contingencies of death of either spouse, remarriage of the wife, or change in the economic status of either spouse, and

(b) Such payments are in the nature of alimony or an allowance for support.

(ii) Payments meeting the requirements of subdivision (i) are considered periodic payments for the purposes of section 71(a) regardless of whether—

(a) The contingencies described in subdivision (i) (a) of this subparagraph are set forth in the terms of the decree, instrument, or agreement, or are imposed by local law, or

(b) The aggregate amount of the payments to be made in the absence of the occurrence of the contingencies described in subdivision (i) (a) of this subparagraph is explicitly stated in the decree, instrument, or agreement or may be calculated from the face of the decree, instrument, or agreement, or

(c) The total amount which will be paid may be calculated actuarially.

(4) Where payments under a decree, instrument, or agreement are to be paid over a period ending more than ten years from the date of such decree, instrument, or agreement, but where such payments meet the conditions set forth in subparagraph (3)(i) of this paragraph, such payments are considered to be periodic payments for the purpose of section 71 without regard to the rule set forth in subparagraph (2) of this paragraph. Accordingly, the rules set forth in subparagraph (2) of this paragraph are not applicable to such payments.

(5) The rules as to periodic and installment payments are illustrated by the following examples:

Example (1). Under the terms of a written instrument, H is required to make payments to W which are in the nature of alimony, in the amount of $100 a month for nine years. The instrument provides that if H or W dies the payments are to cease. The payments are periodic.

Example (2). The facts are the same as in example (1) except that the written instrument explicitly provides that H is to pay W the sum of $10,800 in monthly payments of $100 over a period of nine years. The payments are periodic.

Example (3). Under the terms of a written instrument, H is to pay W $100 a month over a period of nine years. The monthly payments are not subject to any of the contingencies of death of H or W, remarriage of W, or change in the economic status of H or W under the terms of the written instrument or by reason of local law. The payments are not periodic.

Example (4). A divorce decree in 1954 provides that H is to pay W $20,000 each year for the next five years, beginning with the date of the decree, and then $5,000 each year for the next ten years. Assuming the wife makes her returns on the calendar year basis, each payment received in the years 1954 to 1958, inclusive, is treated as a periodic payment under section 71(a)(1), but only to the extent of 10 percent of the principal sum of $150,000. Thus, for such taxable years, only $15,000 of the $20,000 received is includible under section 71(a)(1) in the wife's income and is deductible by the husband under section 215. For the years 1959 to 1968, inclusive, the full $5,000 received each year by the wife is includible in her income and is deductible from the husband's income.

(e) Payments for support of minor children. Section 71(a) does not apply to that part of any periodic payment which, by the terms of the decree, instrument, or agreement under section 71(a), is specifically designated as a sum payable for the support of minor children of the husband. The statute prescribes the treatment in cases where an amount or portion is so fixed but the amount of any periodic payment is less than the amount of the periodic payment specified to be made. In such cases, to the extent of the amount which would be payable for the support of such children out of the originally specified periodic payment, such periodic payment is considered a payment for such support. For example, if the husband is by terms of the decree, instrument, or agreement required to pay $200 a month to his divorced wife, $100 of which is designated by the decree, instrument, or agreement to be for the support of their minor children, and the husband pays only $150 to his wife, $100 is nevertheless considered to be a payment by the husband for the support of the children. If, however, the periodic payments are received by the wife for the support and maintenance of herself and of minor children of the husband without such specific designation of the portion for the support of such children, then the whole of such amounts is includible in the income of the wife as provided in section 71(a). Except in cases of a designated amount or portion for the support of the husband's minor children, periodic payments described in section 71(a) received by the wife for herself and any other person or persons are includible in whole in the wife's income, whether or not the amount or portion for such other person or persons is designated.

T.D. 6270, 11/16/57.

---

§ 1.71-1T Alimony and separate maintenance payments (temporary).

Caution: The Treasury has not yet amended Reg § 1.71-1T to reflect changes made by P.L. 99-514.

(a) In general.

Q-1. What is the income tax treatment of alimony or separate maintenance payments?

A-1. Alimony or separate maintenance payments are, under section 71, included in the gross income of the payee spouse and, under section 215, allowed as a deduction from the gross income of the payor spouse.

Q-2. What is an alimony or separate maintenance payment?

A-2. An alimony or separate maintenance payment is any payment received by or on behalf of a spouse (which for this purpose includes a former spouse) of the payor under a divorce or separation instrument that meets all of the following requirements:

(a) The payment is in cash (see A-5).

(b) The payment is not designated as a payment which is excludible from the gross income of the payee and nondeductible by the payor (see A-8).

(c) In the case of spouses legally separated under a decree of divorce or separate maintenance, the spouses are not members of the same household at the time the payment is made (see A-9).

(d) The payor has no liability to continue to make any payment after the death of the payee (or to make any payment as a substitute for such payment) and the divorce or separation instrument states that there is no such liability (see A-10).

(e) The payment is not treated as child support (see A-15).

(f) To the extent that one or more annual payments exceed $10,000 during any of the 6-post-separation years, the payor is obligated to make annual payments in each of the 6 post-separation years (see A-19).

Q-3. In order to be treated as alimony or separate maintenance payments, must the payments be "periodic" as that term was defined prior to enactment of the Tax Reform Act of 1984 or be made in discharge of a legal obligation of the payor to support the payee arising out of a marital or family relationship?

A-3. No. The Tax Reform Act of 1984 replaces the old requirements with the requirements described in A-2 above. Thus, the requirements that alimony or separate maintenance payments be "periodic" and be made in discharge of a legal obligation to support arising out of a marital or family relationship have been eliminated.

Q-4. Are the instruments described in section 71(a) of prior law the same as divorce or separation instruments described in section 71, as amended by the Tax Reform Act of 1984?

A-4. Yes.

(b) Specific requirements.

Q-5. May alimony or separate maintenance payments be made in a form other than cash?

A-5. No. Only cash payments (including checks and money orders payable on demand) qualify as alimony or separate maintenance payments. Transfers of services or property (including a debt instrument of a third party or an annuity contract), execution of a debt instrument by the payor, or the use of property of the payor do not qualify as alimony or separate maintenance payments.

Q-6. May payments of cash to a third party on behalf of a spouse qualify as alimony or separate maintenance payments if the payments are pursuant to the terms of a divorce or separation instrument?

A-6. Yes. Assuming all other requirements are satisfied, a payment of cash by the payor spouse to a third party under the terms of the divorce or separation instrument will qualify as a payment of cash which is received "on behalf of a spouse". For example, cash payments of rent, mortgage, tax, or tuition liabilities of the payee spouse made under the terms of the divorce or separation instrument will qualify as alimony or separate maintenance payments. Any payments to maintain property owned by the payor spouse and used by the payee spouse (including mortgage payments, real estate taxes and insurance premiums) are not payments on behalf of a spouse even if those payments are made pursuant to the terms of the divorce or separation instrument. Premiums paid by the payor spouse for term or whole life insurance on the payor's life made under the terms of the divorce or separation instrument will qualify as payments on behalf of the payee spouse to the extent that the payee spouse is the owner of the policy.

Q-7. May payments of cash to a third party on behalf of a spouse qualify as alimony or separate maintenance payments if the payments are made to the third party at the written request of the payee spouse?

A-7. Yes. For example, instead of making an alimony or separate maintenance payment directly to the payee, the payor spouse may make a cash payment to a charitable organization if such payment is pursuant to the written request, consent or ratification of the payee spouse. Such request, consent or ratification must state that the parties intend the payment to be treated as an alimony or separate maintenance payment to the payee spouse subject to the rules of section 71, and must be received by the payor spouse prior to the date of filing of the payor's first return of tax for the taxable year in which the payment was made.

Q-8. How may spouses designate that payments otherwise qualifying as alimony or separate maintenance payments shall be excludible from the gross income of the payee and nondeductible by the payor?

A-8. The spouses may designate that payments otherwise qualifying as alimony or separate maintenance payments shall be nondeductible by the payor and excludible from gross income by the payee by so providing in a divorce or separation instrument (as defined in section 71(b)(2)). If the spouses have executed a written separation agreement (as described in section 71(b)(2)(B)), any writing signed by both spouses which designates otherwise qualifying alimony or separate maintenance payments as nondeductible and excludible and which refers to the written separation agreement will be treated as a written separation agreement (and thus a divorce or separation instrument) for purposes of the preceding sentence. If the spouses are subject to temporary support orders (as described in section 71(b)(2)(C)), the designation of otherwise qualifying alimony or separate payments as nondeductible and excludible must be made in the original or a subsequent temporary support order. A copy of the instrument containing the designation of payments as not alimony or separate maintenance payments must be attached to the payee's first filed return of tax (Form 1040) for each year in which the designation applies.

Q-9. What are the consequences if, at the time a payment is made, the payor and payee spouses are members of the same household?

A-9. Generally, a payment made at the time when the payor and payee spouses are members of the same household cannot qualify as an alimony or separate maintenance payment if the spouses are legally separated under a decree of divorce or of separate maintenance. For purposes of the preceding sentence, a dwelling unit formerly shared by both spouses shall not be considered two separate households even if the spouses physically separate themselves within the dwelling unit. The spouses will not be treated as members of the same household if one spouse is preparing to depart from the household of the other spouse, and does depart not more than one month after the date the payment is made. If the spouses are not legally separated under a decree of divorce or separate maintenance, a payment under a written separation agreement or a decree described in section 71(b)(2)(C) may qualify as an alimony or separate maintenance payment notwithstanding that the payor and payee are members of the same household at the time the payment is made.

Q-10. Assuming all other requirements relating to the qualification of certain payments as alimony or separate maintenance payments are met, what are the consequences if the payor spouse is required to continue to make the payments after the death of the payee spouse?

A-10. None of the payments before (or after) the death of the payee spouse qualify as alimony or separate maintenance payments.

Q-11. What are the consequences if the divorce or separation instrument fails to state that there is no liability for any period after the death of the payee spouse to continue to make any payments which would otherwise qualify as alimony or separate maintenance payments?

A-11. If the instrument fails to include such a statement, none of the payments, whether made before or after the death of the payee spouse, will qualify as alimony or separate maintenance payments.

Example (1). A is to pay B $10,000 in cash each year for a period of 10 years under a divorce or separation instrument which does not state that the payments will terminate upon the death of B. None of the payments will qualify as alimony or separate maintenance payments.

Example (2). A is to pay B $10,000 in cash each year for a period of 10 years under a divorce or separation instrument which states that the payments will terminate upon the death of B. In addition, under the instrument, A is to pay B or B's estate $20,000 in cash each year for a period of 10 years. Because the $20,000 annual payments will not terminate upon the death of B, these payments will not qualify as alimony or separate maintenance payments. However, the separate $10,000 annual payments will qualify as alimony or separate maintenance payments.

Q-12. Will a divorce or separation instrument be treated as stating that there is no liability to make payments after the death of the payee spouse if the liability to make such payments terminates pursuant to applicable local law or oral agreement?

A-12. No. Termination of the liability to make payments must be stated in the terms of the divorce or separation instrument.

Q-13. What are the consequences if the payor spouse is required to make one or more payments (in cash or property) after the death of the payee spouse as a substitute for the continuation of pre-death payments which would otherwise qualify as alimony or separate maintenance payments?

A-13. If the payor spouse is required to make any such substitute payments, none of the otherwise qualifying payments will qualify as alimony or separate maintenance payments. The divorce or separation instrument need not state, however, that there is no liability to make any such substitute payment.

Q-14. Under what circumstances will one or more payments (in cash or property) which are to occur after the death of the payee spouse be treated as a substitute for the continuation of payments which would otherwise qualify as alimony or separate maintenance payments?

A-14. To the extent that one or more payments are to begin to be made, increase in amount, or become accelerated in time as a result of the death of the payee spouse, such payments may be treated as a substitute for the continuation of payments terminating on the death of the payee spouse which would otherwise qualify as alimony or separate maintenance payments. The determination of whether or not such payments are a substitute for the continuation of payments which would otherwise qualify as alimony or separate maintenance payments, and of the amount of the otherwise qualifying alimony or separate maintenance payments for which any such payments are a substitute, will depend on all of the facts and circumstances.

Example (1). Under the terms of a divorce decree, A is obligated to make annual alimony payments to B of $30,000, terminating on the earlier of the expiration of 6 years or the death of B. B maintains custody of the minor children of A and B. The decree provides that at the death of B, if there are minor children of A and B remaining, A will be obligated to make annual payments of $10,000 to a trust, the income and corpus of which are to be used for the benefit of the children until the youngest child attains the age of majority. These facts indicate that A's liability to make annual $10,000 payments in trust for the benefit of his minor children upon the death of B is a substitute for $10,000 of the $30,000 annual payments to B. Accordingly, $10,000 of each of the $30,000 annual payments to B will not qualify as alimony or separate maintenance payments.

Example (2). Under the terms of a divorce decree, A is obligated to make annual alimony payments to B of $30,000, terminating on the earlier of the expiration of 15 years or the death of B. The divorce decree provides that if B dies before the expiration of the 15 year period, A will pay to B's estate the difference between the total amount that A would have paid had B survived, minus the amount actually paid. For example, if B dies at the end of the 10th year in which payments are made, A will pay to B's estate $150,000 ($450,000−$300,000). These facts indicate that A's liability to make a lump sum payment to B's estate upon the death of B is a substitute for the full amount of each of the annual $30,000 payments to B. Accordingly, none of the annual $30,000 payments to B will qualify as alimony or separate maintenance payments. The result would be the same if the lump sum payable at B's death were discounted by an appropriate interest factor to account for the prepayment.

(c) Child support payments.

Q-15. What are the consequences of a payment which the terms of the divorce or separation instrument fix as payable for the support of a child of the payor spouse?

A-15. A payment which under the terms of the divorce or separation instrument is fixed (or treated as fixed) as payable for the support of a child of the payor spouse does not qualify as an alimony or separate maintenance payment. Thus, such a payment is not deductible by the payor spouse or includible in the income of the payee spouse.

Q-16. When is a payment fixed (or treated as fixed) as payable for the support of a child of the payor spouse?

A-16. A payment is fixed as payable for the support of a child of the payor spouse if the divorce or separation instrument specifically designates some sum or portion (which sum or portion may fluctuate) as payable for the support of a child of the payor spouse. A payment will be treated as fixed as payable for the support of a child of the payor spouse if the payment is reduced (a) on the happening of a contingency relating to a child of the payor, or (b) at a time which can clearly be associated with such a contingency. A payment may be treated as fixed as payable for the support of a child of the payor spouse even if other separate payments specifically are designated as payable for the support of a child of the payor spouse.

Q-17. When does a contingency relate to a child of the payor?

A-17. For this purpose, a contingency relates to a child of the payor if it depends on any event relating to that child, regardless of whether such event is certain or likely to occur. Events that relate to a child of the payor include the following: the child's attaining a specified age or income level, dying, marrying, leaving school, leaving the spouse's household, or gaining employment.

Q-18. When will a payment be treated as to be reduced at a time which can clearly be associated with the happening of a contingency relating to a child of the payor?

A-18. There are two situations, described below, in which payments which would otherwise qualify as alimony or separate maintenance payments will be presumed to be reduced at a time clearly associated with the happening of a contingency relating to a child of the payor. In all other situations, reductions in payments will not be treated as clearly associated with the happening of a contingency relating to a child of the payor.

The first situation referred to above is where the payments are to be reduced not more than 6 months before or after the date the child is to attain the age of 18, 21, or local age of majority. The second situation is where the payments are to be reduced on two or more occasions which occur not more than one year before or after a different child of the payor spouse attains a certain age between the ages of 18 and 24, inclusive. The certain age referred to in the preceding sentence must be the same for each such child, but need not be a whole number of years.

The presumption in the two situations described above that payments are to be reduced at a time clearly associated with the happening of a contingency relating to a child of the payor may be rebutted (either by the Service or by taxpayers) by showing that the time at which the payments are to be reduced was determined independently of any contingencies relating to the children of the payor. The presumption in the first situation will be rebutted conclusively if the reduction is a complete cessation of alimony or separate maintenance payments during the sixth post-separation year (described in A-21) or upon the expiration of a 72-month period. The presumption may also be rebutted in other circumstances, for example, by showing that alimony payments are to be made for a period customarily provided in the local jurisdiction, such as a period equal to one-half the duration of the marriage.

Example. A and B are divorced on July 1, 1985, when their children, C (born July 15, 1970) and D (born September 23, 1972), are 14 and 12, respectively. Under the divorce decree, A is to make alimony payments to B of $2,000 per month. Such payments are to be reduced to $1,500 per month on January 1, 1991 and to $1,000 per month on January 1, 1995. On January 1, 1991, the date of the first reduction in payments, C will be 20 years 5 months and 17 days old. On January 1, 1995, the date of the second reduction in payments, D will be 22 years 3 months and 9 days old. Each of the reductions in payments is to occur not more than one year before or after a different child of A attains the age of 21 years and 4 months. (Actually, the reductions are to occur not more than one year before or after C and D attain any of the ages 21 years 3 months and 9 days through 21 years 5 months and 17 days.) Accordingly, the reductions will be presumed to clearly be associated with the happening of a contingency relating to C and D. Unless this presumption is rebutted, payments under the divorce decree equal to the sum of the reduction ($1,000 per month) will be treated as fixed for the support of the children of A and therefore will not qualify as alimony or separate maintenance payments.

(d) Excess front-loading rules.

Q-19. What are the excess front-loading rules?

A-19. The excess front-loading rules are two special rules which may apply to the extent that payments in any calendar year exceed $10,000. The first rule is a minimum term rule, which must be met in order for any annual payment, to the extent in excess of $10,000, to qualify as an alimony or separate maintenance payment (see A-2(f)). This rule requires that alimony or separate maintenance payments be called for, at a minimum, during the 6 "post-separation years". The second rule is a recapture rule which characterizes payments retrospectively by requiring a recalculation and inclusion in income by the payor and deduction by the payee of previously paid alimony or separate maintenance payment to the extent that the amount of such payments during any of the 6 "post-separation years" falls short of the amount of payments during a prior year by more than $10,000.

Q-20. Do the excess front-loading rules apply to payments to the extent that annual payments never exceed $10,000?

A-20. No. For example, A is to make a single $10,000 payment to B. Provided that the other requirements of section 71 are met, the payment will qualify as an alimony or separate maintenance payment. If A were to make a single $15,000 payment to B, $10,000 of the payment would qualify as an alimony or separate maintenance payment and $5,000 of the payment would be disqualified under the minimum term rule because payments were not to be made for the minimum period.

Q-21. Do the excess front-loading rules apply to payments received under a decree described in section 71(b)(2)(C)?

A-21. No. Payments under decrees described in section 71(b)(2)(C) are to be disregarded entirely for purposes of applying the excess front-loading rules.

Q-22. Both the minimum term rule and the recapture rule refer to 6 "post-separation years". What are the 6 "post separation years"?

A-22. The 6 "post-separation years" are the 6 consecutive calendar years beginning with the first calendar year in which the payor pays to the payee an alimony or separate maintenance payment (except a payment made under a decree described in section 71(b)(2)(C)). Each year within this period is referred to as a "post-separation year". The 6-year period need not commence with the year in which the spouses separate or divorce, or with the year in which payments under the divorce or separation instrument are made, if no payments during such year qualify as alimony or separate maintenance payments. For example, a decree for the divorce of A and B is entered in October, 1985. The decree requires A to make monthly payments to B commencing November 1, 1985, but A and B are members of the same household until February 15, 1986 (and as a result, the payments prior to January 16, 1986, do not qualify as alimony payments). For purposes of applying the excess front-loading rules to payments from A to B, the 6 calendar years 1986 through 1991 are post-separation years. If a spouse has been making payments pursuant to a divorce or separation instrument described in section 71(b)(2)(A) or (B), a modification of the instrument or the substitution of a new instrument (for example, the substitution of a divorce decree for a written separation agreement) will not result in the creation of additional post-separation years. However, if a spouse has been making payments pursuant to a divorce or separation instrument described in section 71(b)(2)(C), the 6-year period does not begin until the first calendar year in which alimony or separate maintenance payments are made under a divorce or separation instrument described in section 71(b)(2)(A) or (B).

Q-23. How does the minimum term rule operate?

A-23. The minimum term rule operates in the following manner. To the extent payments are made in excess of $10,000, a payment will qualify as an alimony or separate maintenance payment only if alimony or separate maintenance payments are to be made in each of the 6 post-separation years. For example, pursuant to a divorce decree, A is to make alimony payments to B of $20,000 in each of the 5 calendar years 1985 through 1989. A is to make no payment in 1990. Under the minimum term rule, only $10,000 will qualify as an alimony payment in each of the calendar years 1985 through 1989. If the divorce decree also required A to make a $1 payment in 1990, the minimum term rule would be satisfied and $20,000 would be treated as an alimony payment in each of the calendar years 1985 through 1989. The recapture rule would, however, apply for 1990. For purposes of determining whether alimony or separate maintenance payments are to be made in any year, the possible termination of such payments upon the happening of a contingency (other than the passage of time) which has not yet occurred is ignored (unless such contingency may cause all or a portion of the payment to be treated as a child support payment).

Q-24. How does the recapture rule operate?

A-24. The recapture rule operates in the following manner. If the amount of alimony or separate maintenance payments paid in any post-separation year (referred to as the "computation year") falls short of the amount of alimony or separate maintenance payments paid in any prior post-separation year by more than $10,000, the payor must compute an "excess amount" for the computation year. The excess amount for any computation year is the sum of excess amounts determined with respect to each prior post-separation year. The excess amount determined with respect to a prior post-separation year is the excess of (1) the amount of alimony or separate maintenance payments paid by the payor spouse during such prior post-separation year, over (2) the amount of the alimony or separate maintenance payments paid by the payor spouse during the computation year plus $10,000. For purposes of this calculation, the amount of alimony or separate maintenance payments made by the payor spouse during any post-separation year preceding the computation year is reduced by any excess amount previously determined with respect to such year. The rules set forth above may be illustrated by the following example. A makes alimony payments to B of $25,000 in 1985 and $12,000 in 1986. The excess amount with respect to 1985 that is recaptured in 1986 is $3,000 ($25,000 – ($12,000 + $10,000)). For purposes of subsequent computation years, the amount deemed paid in 1985 is $22,000. If A makes alimony payments to B of $1,000 in 1987, the excess amount that is recaptured in 1987 will be $12,000. This is the sum of an $11,000 excess amount with respect to 1985 ($22,000 – $1,000 + $10,000)) and a $1,000 excess amount with respect to 1986 ($12,000 – ($1,000 + $10,000)). If, prior to the end of 1990, payments decline further, additional recapture will occur. The payor spouse must include the excess amount in gross income for his/her taxable year beginning with or in the computation year. The payee spouse is allowed a deduction for the excess amount in computing adjusted gross income for his/her taxable year beginning with or in the computation year. However, the payee spouse must compute the excess amount by reference to the date when payments were made and not when payments were received.

Q-25. What are the exceptions to the recapture rule?

A-25. Apart from the $10,000 threshold for application of the recapture rule, there are three exceptions to the recapture rule. The first exception is for payments received under temporary support orders described in section 71(b)(2)(C) (see A-21). The second exception is for any payment made pursuant to a continuing liability over the period of the post-separation years to pay a fixed portion of the payor's income from a business or property or from compensation for employment or self-employment. The third exception is where the alimony or separate maintenance payments in any post-separation year cease by reason of the death of the payor or payee or the remarriage (as defined under applicable local law) of the payee before the close of the computation year. For example, pursuant to a divorce decree, A is to make cash payments to B of $30,000 in each of the calendar years 1985 through 1990. A makes cash payments of $30,000 in 1985 and $15,000 in 1986, in which year B remarries and A's alimony payments cease. The recapture rule does not apply for 1986 or any subsequent year. If alimony or separate maintenance payments made by A decline or cease during a post-separation year for any other reason (including a failure by the payor to make timely payments, a modification of the divorce or separation instrument, a reduction in the support needs of the payee, or a reduction in the ability of the payor to provide support) excess amounts with respect to prior post-separation years will be subject to recapture.

(e) Effective dates

Q-26. When does section 71, as amended by the Tax Reform Act of 1984, become effective?

A-26. Generally, section 71, as amended, is effective with respect to divorce or separation instruments (as defined in section 71(b)(2)) executed after December 31, 1984. If a decree of divorce or separate maintenance executed after December 31, 1984, incorporates or adopts without change the terms of the alimony or separate maintenance payments under a divorce or separation instrument executed before January 1, 1985, such decree will be treated as executed before January 1, 1985. A change in the amount of alimony or separate maintenance payments or the time period over which such payments are to continue, or the addition or deletion of any contingencies or conditions relating to such payments is a change in the terms of the alimony or separate maintenance payments. For example, in November 1984, A and B executed a written separation agreement. In February 1985, a decree of divorce is entered in substitution for the written separation agreement. The decree of divorce does not change the terms of the alimony A pays to B. The decree of divorce will be treated as executed before January 1, 1985 and hence alimony payments under the decree will be subject to the rules of section 71 prior to amendment by the Tax Reform Act of 1984. If the amount or time period of the alimony or separate maintenance payments are not specified in the pre-1985 separation agreement or if the decree of divorce changes the amount or term of such payments, the decree of divorce will not be treated as executed before January 1, 1985, and alimony payments under the decree will be subject to the rules of section 71, as amended by the Tax Reform Act of 1984.

Section 71, as amended, also applies to any divorce or separation instrument executed (or treated as executed) before January 1, 1985 that has been modified on or after January 1, 1985, if such modification expressly provides that section 71, as amended by the Tax Reform Act of 1984, shall apply to the instrument as modified. In this case, section 71, as amended, is effective with respect to payments made after the date the instrument is modified.

T.D. 7973, 8/30/84.

§ 1.71-2 Effective date; taxable years ending after March 31, 1954, subject to the Internal Revenue Code of 1939.

Caution: The Treasury has not yet amended Reg § 1.71-2 to reflect changes made by P.L. 99-514.

Pursuant to section 7851(a)(1)(C), the regulations prescribed in § 1.71-1, to the extent that they relate to payments under a written separation agreement executed after August 16, 1954, and to the extent that they relate to payments under a decree for support received after August 16, 1954, under a decree entered after March 1, 1954, shall also apply to taxable years beginning before January 1, 1954, and ending after August 16, 1954, although such years are subject to the Internal Revenue Code of 1939.

T.D. 6270, 11/15/57.

§ 1.72-1 Introduction.

Caution: The Treasury has not yet amended Reg § 1.72-1 to reflect changes made by P.L. 98-369, P.L. 97-248.

(a) General principle. Section 72 prescribes rules relating to the inclusion in gross income of amounts received under a life insurance, endowment, or annuity contract unless such amounts are specifically excluded from gross income under other provisions of chapter 1 of the Code. In general, these rules provide that amounts subject to the provisions of section 72 are includible in the gross income of the recipient except to the extent that they are considered to represent a reduction or return of premiums or other consideration paid.

(b) Amounts to be considered as a return of premiums. For the purpose of determining the extent to which amounts received represent a reduction or return of premiums or other consideration paid, the provisions of section 72 distinguish between "amounts received as an annuity" and "amounts not received as an annuity". In general, "amounts received as an annuity" are amounts which are payable at regular intervals over a period of more than one full year from the date on which they are deemed to begin, provided the total of the amounts so payable or the period for which they are to be paid can be determined as of that date. See paragraph (b)(2) and (3) of § 1.72-2. Any other amounts to which the provisions of section 72 apply are considered to be "amounts not received as an annuity". See § 1.72-11.

(c) "Amounts received as an annuity". *(1)* In the case of "amounts received as an annuity" (other than certain employees' annuities described in section 72(d) and in § 1.72-13), a proportionate part of each amount so received is considered to represent a return of premiums or other consideration paid. The proportionate part of each annuity payment which is thus excludable from gross income is determined by the ratio which the investment in the contract as of the date on which the annuity is deemed to begin bears to the expected return under the contract as of that date. See § 1.72-4.

(2) In the case of employees' annuities of the type described in section 72(d), no amount received as an annuity in a taxable year to which the Internal Revenue Code of 1954 applies is includible in the gross income of a recipient until the aggregate of all amounts received thereunder and excluded from gross income under the applicable income tax law exceeds the consideration contributed (or deemed contributed) by the employee under § 1.72-8. Thereafter, all amounts so received are includible in the gross income of the recipient. See § 1.72-13.

(d) "Amounts not received as an annuity". In the case of "amounts not received as an annuity", if such amounts are received after an annuity has begun and during its continuance, amounts so received are generally includible in the gross income of the recipient. Amounts not received as an annuity which are received at any other time are generally includible in the gross income of the recipient only to the extent that such amounts, when added to all amounts previously received under the contract which were excludable from the gross income of the recipient under the income tax law applicable at the time of receipt, exceed the premiums or other consideration paid (see § 1.72-11). However, if the aggregate of premiums or other consideration paid for the contract includes amounts for which a deduction was allowed under section 404 as contributions on behalf of an owner-employee, the amounts received under the circumstances of the preceding sentence shall be includible in gross income until the amount so included equals the amount for which the deduction was so allowed. See paragraph (b) of § 1.72-17.

(e) Classification of recipients. For the purpose of the regulations under section 72, a recipient shall be considered an "annuitant" if he receives amounts under an annuity contract during the period that the annuity payments are to continue, whether for a term certain or during the continuing life or lives of the person or persons whose lives measure the duration of such annuity. However, a recipient shall be considered a "beneficiary" rather than an "annuitant" if the amounts he receives under a contract are received after the term of the annuity for a life or lives has expired and such amounts are paid by reason of the fact that the contract guarantees that payments of some minimum amount or for some minimum period shall be made. For special rules with respect to beneficiaries, see paragraphs (a)(1)(iii) and (c) of § 1.72-11.

T.D. 6211, 11/14/56, amend T.D. 6676, 9/16/63.

§ 1.72-2 Applicability of section.

Caution: The Treasury has not yet amended Reg § 1.72-2 to reflect changes made by P.L. 101-239, P.L. 100-647, P.L. 99-514, P.L. 93-406.

(a) Contracts. *(1)* The contracts under which amounts paid will be subject to the provisions of section 72 include contracts which are considered to be life insurance, endowment, and annuity contracts in accordance with the customary practice of life insurance companies. For the purposes of section 72, however, it is immaterial whether such contracts are entered into with an insurance company. The term "endowment contract" also includes the "face-amount certificates" described in section 72(1).

(2) If two or more annuity obligations or elements to which section 72 applies are acquired for a single consideration, such as an obligation to pay an annuity to A for his life accompanied by an obligation to pay an annuity to B for his life, there being a single consideration paid for both obligations (whether paid by one or more persons in equal or different amounts, and whether paid in a single sum or otherwise), such annuity elements shall be considered to comprise a single contract for the purpose of the application of section 72 and the regulations thereunder. For rules relating to the allocation of investment in the contract in the case of annuity elements payable to two or more persons, see paragraph (b) of § 1.72-6.

(3) (i) Sections 402 and 403 provide that certain distributions by employees' trusts and certain payments under employee plans are taxable under section 72. For taxable years beginning before January 1, 1964, section 72(e)(3), as in effect before such date, does not apply to such distributions or payments. For purposes of applying section 72 to such distributions and payments (other than those described in subdivision (iii) of this subparagraph), each separate program of the employer consisting of interrelated contributions and benefits shall be considered a single contract. Therefore, all distributions or payments (other than those described in subdivision (iii) of this subparagraph) which are attributable to a separate program of interrelated contributions and benefits are considered as received under a single contract. A separate program of interrelated contributions and benefits may be financed by the purchase from an insurance company of one or more group contracts or one or more individual contracts, or may be financed partly by the purchase of contracts from an insurance company and partly through an investment fund, or may be financed completely through an investment fund. A program may be considered separate for purposes of section 72 although it is only a part of a plan which qualifies under section 401. There may be several trusts under one separate program, or several separate programs may make use of a single trust. See, however, subdivision (iii) of this subparagraph for rules relating to what constitutes a "contract" for purposes of applying section 72 to distributions commencing before October 20, 1960.

(ii) The following types of benefits, and the contributions used to provide them, are examples of separate programs of interrelated contributions and benefits:

(a) Definitely determinable retirement benefits.

(b) Definitely determinable benefits payable prior to retirement in case of disability.

(c) Life insurance.

(d) Accident and health insurance. However, retirement benefits and life insurance will be considered part of a single separate program of interrelated contributions and benefits to the extent they are provided under retirement income, endowment, or other contracts providing life insurance protection. See examples (6), (7), and (8) contained in subdivision (iv) of this subparagraph for illustrations of the principles of this subdivision. See, also, § 1.72-15 for rules relating to the taxation of amounts received under an employee plan which provides both retirement benefits and accident and health benefits.

(iii) If any amount which is taxable under section 72 by reason of section 402 or 403 is actually distributed or made available to any person under an employees' trust or plan (other than the Civil Service Retirement Act (5 U.S.C. ch. 14) before October 20, 1960, section 72 shall, notwithstanding any other provisions in this subparagraph, be applied to all the distributions with respect to such person (or his beneficiaries) under such trust or plan (whether received before or after October 20, 1960) as though such distributions were provided under a single contract. For purposes of applying section 72 to distributions to which this subdivision applies, therefore, the term "contract" shall be considered to include the entire interest of an employee in each trust or plan described in sections 402 and 403 to the extent that distributions thereunder are subject to the provisions of section 72. Section 72 shall be applied to distributions received under the Civil Service Retirement Act in the manner prescribed in subdivision (i) of this subparagraph (see example (4) in subdivision (iv) of this subparagraph).

(iv) The application of this subparagraph may be illustrated by the following examples:

Example (1). On January 1, 1961, X Corporation established a noncontributory profit-sharing plan for its employees providing that the amount standing to the account of each participant will be paid to him at the time of his retirement and also established a contributory pension plan for its employees providing for the payment to each participant of a lifetime pension after retirement. The profit-sharing plan is designed to enable the employees to participate in the profits of X Corporation; the amount of the contributions to it are determined by reference to the profits of X Corporation; and the amount of any distribution is determined by reference to the amount of contributions made on behalf of any participant and the earnings thereon. On the other hand, the pension plan is designed to provide a lifetime pension for a retired employee; the amount of the pension is to be determined by a formula set forth in the plan; and the amount of contributions to the plan is the amount necessary to provide such pensions. In view of the fact that each of these plans constitutes a separate program of interrelated contributions and benefits, the distributions from each shall be treated as received under a separate contract. If these plans had been established before October 20, 1960, then, in the case of an employee who receives a distribution under the plans before October 20, 1960, the determination as to whether that distribution and all subsequent distributions to such employee are received under a single contract or under more than one contract shall be made by applying the rules in subdivision (iii) of this subparagraph. On the other hand, in the case of an employee who does not receive any distribution under these plans before October 20, 1960, the determination as to whether distributions to him are received under a single contract or under more than one contract shall be made in accordance with the rules illustrated by this example.

Example (2). On January 1, 1961, Z Corporation established a profit-sharing plan for its employees providing that any employee may make contributions, not in excess of 6 percent of his compensation, to a trust and that the employer would make matching contributions out of profits. Under the plan, a participant may receive a periodic distribution of the amount standing in his account during any period that he is absent from work due to a personal injury or sickness. On separation from service, the participant is entitled to receive a distribution of the balance standing in his account in accordance with one of several options. One option provides for the immediate distribution of one-half of the account and for the periodic distribution of the remaining one-half of the account. In addition, any participant may, after the completion of five years of participation, withdraw any part of his account, but in the case of such a withdrawal, the participant forfeits his rights to participate in the plan for a period of two years. Thus, a participant may receive distributions before separation from service; he may receive a distribution of a lump sum upon separation from service; he may also receive periodic distributions upon separation from service. However, since it is the total amount received under all the options that is interrelated with the contributions to the plan and not the amount received under any one option, this profit-sharing plan consists of only one separate program of interrelated contributions and benefits and all distributions under the plan (regardless of the option under which received) are treated as received under one contract. However, if, instead of providing that the amount standing in an employee's account would be paid to him during any period that he is absent from work due to a personal injury or sickness, the plan provided that a portion of the amount in the employee's account would be used to purchase incidental accident and health insurance, this plan would consist of two separate programs of interrelated contributions and benefits. The accident and health insurance, and the contributions used to purchase it, would be considered as one separate program of interrelated contributions and benefits and, therefore, a separate contract; whereas, the remaining contributions and benefits would be considered another separate program of interrelated contributions and benefits and, consequently, another separate contract.

Example (3). On January 1, 1961, N Corporation established a profit-sharing plan for its employees providing that the employees may make contributions, not in excess of 6 percent of their compensation, to a trust and that N Corporation would make matching contributions out of its profits. Under the plan, the employee may elect each year to have his and the employer's contributions for such year placed in either a savings arrangement or a retirement arrangement. Such an election is irrevocable. Under the savings arrangement, contributions to such arrangement for any one year and the earnings thereon will be distributed five years later. The retirement arrangement provides that all contributions thereto and the earnings thereon will be distributed when the employee is separated from the service of N Corporation. Since the distributions under the retirement arrangement are attributable solely to the contributions made to such arrangement and are not affected in any manner by contributions or distributions under the savings arrangement or any other plan, such distributions are treated as received under a separate program of interrelated contributions and benefits. Similarly, since distributions during any year under the savings arrangement are attributable only to contributions to such arrangement made during the fifth preceding year and are not affected in any manner by any other contributions to or distributions from such arrangement or any other plan, the savings arrangement constitutes a series of separate programs of interrelated contributions and benefits. The contributions to the savings arrangement for any year and the distribution in a subsequent year based thereon constitute a separate contract for purposes of section 72.

Example (4). The Civil Service Retirement Act (5 U. S. C. ch. 14), which provides retirement benefits for participating employees, consists of a compulsory program and a voluntary program. Under the compulsory program, all participating employees are required to make certain contributions and, upon retirement, are provided retirement benefits computed on the basis of compensation and length of service. Under the voluntary program, such participating employees are permitted to make contributions in addition to those required under the compulsory program and, upon retirement, are provided additional retirement benefits computed on the basis of their voluntary contributions. Distributions received under the Act constitute distributions from two separate contracts for purposes of section 72. Distributions received under the compulsory program are considered as received under a separate program of interrelated contributions and benefits since they are computed solely under the compulsory program and are not affected by any contributions or distributions under the voluntary program or under any other plan. For similar reasons, distributions which are attributable to the voluntary contributions are considered as received under a separate program of interrelated contributions and benefits.

Example (5). On January 1, 1961, M Corporation established a contributory pension plan for its employees and created a trust to which it makes contributions to fund such plan. The plan provides that each participant will receive after age 65 a pension of 1½ percent of his compensation for each year of service performed subsequent to the establishment of such plan. In order to fund part of the benefits under the plan, the trustee purchased a group annuity contract. The remaining part of the benefits are to be paid out of a separate investment fund. This pension plan constitutes a single program of interrelated contributions and benefits and, therefore, all distributions received by an employee under the plan are considered as received under a single contract for purposes of section 72.

Example (6). On January 1, 1961, Y Corporation established a noncontributory pension plan (including incidental death benefits) for its employees and created a trust to which it makes contributions to fund such plan. The plan provides that each participant will receive after age 65 a pension of 1½ percent of his compensation for each year of service performed subsequent to the establishment of such plan. In addition, such plan provides for the payment of a death benefit if the employee dies before age 65. The trustee funded the death benefits through the purchase of a group term insurance policy and funded the retirement benefits through the purchase of a group annuity contract. Because of a subsequent change in funding from the deferred annuity method to the deposit administration method, the trustee purchased a second group annuity contract to provide the retirement benefits under the plan accruing after the effective date of the change in method of funding. Thus, retirement benefits distributed to an employee whose service with Y Corporation commenced before the effective date of the change in method of funding will be attributable to both group annuity contracts. This pension plan includes two separate programs of interrelated contributions and benefits. The death benefits, and the contributions required to provide them, are considered as one separate program of interrelated contributions and benefits; whereas, the retirement benefits, and the contributions required to provide them, are considered as another separate program of interrelated contributions and benefits. Therefore, any retirement benefits received by an employee, whether attributable to one or both of the group annuity contracts, shall be considered as received under a single contract for purposes of section 72. In determining the tax treatment of any such retirement benefits under section 72, no amount of the premiums used to purchase the group term insurance policy shall be taken into account, since such premiums, and the death benefits which they purchased, constitute a separate program of interrelated contributions and benefits.

Example (7). Assume the same facts as in example (6) except that, in lieu of funding the benefits in the manner described in that example, the trustee purchased individual retirement income contracts from an insurance company. Additional individual retirement income contracts are purchased in order to fund any increase in benefits resulting from increases in salary. Therefore, distributions to a particular employee may be attributable to a single retirement income contract or to more than one such contract. All distributions received by an employee under the pension plan, whether attributable to one or more retirement income contracts and whether made directly from the insurance company to the employee or made through the trustee, are considered as received under a single contract for purposes of section 72. For rules relating to the tax treatment of contributions and distributions under retirement income, endowment, or other life insurance contracts purchased by a trust described in section 401(a) and exempt under section 501(a), see paragraph (a)(2), (3), and (4) of § 1.402(a)-1.

Example (8). Assume the same facts as in example (6) except that, in lieu of funding the benefits in the manner described in that example, the trustee funded the death benefits and part of the retirement benefits by purchasing individual retirement income contracts from an insurance company. The remaining part of the retirement benefits (such as any increase in benefits resulting from increases in salary) are to be paid out of a separate investment fund. This pension plan includes, with respect to each participant, two separate contracts for purposes of section 72. The retirement income contract purchased by the trust for each participant is a separate program of interrelated contributions and benefits and all distributions attributable to such contract (whether made directly from the insurance company to the employee or made through the trustee) are considered as received under a single contract. For rules relating to the tax treatment of contributions and distributions under retirement income, endowment, or other life insurance contracts purchased by a trust described in section 401(a) and exempt under section 501(a), see paragraph (a)(2), (3), and (4) of § 1.402(a)-1. The remaining distributions under the plan are considered as received under another separate program of interrelated contributions and benefits.

(b) Amounts. *(1)* (i) In general, the amounts to which section 72 applies are any amounts received under the contracts described in paragraph (a)(1) of this section. However, if such amounts are specifically excluded from gross income under other provisions of chapter 1 of the Code, section 72 shall not apply for the purpose of including such amounts in gross income. For example, section 72 does not apply to amounts received under a life insurance contract if such amounts are paid by reason of the death of the insured and are excludable from gross income under section 101(a). See also sections 101(d), relating to proceeds of life insurance paid at a date later than death, and 104(a)(4), relating to compensation for injuries or sickness.

(ii) Section 72 does not exclude from gross income any amounts received under an agreement to hold an amount and pay interest thereon. See paragraph (a) of § 1.72-14. However, section 72 does apply to amounts received by a surviving annuitant under a joint and survivor annuity contract since such amounts are not considered to be paid by reason of the death of an insured. For a special deduction for the estate tax attributable to the inclusion of the value of the interest of a surviving annuitant under a joint and survivor annuity contract in the estate of the deceased primary annuitant, see section 691(d) and the regulations thereunder.

(2) Amounts subject to section 72 in accordance with subparagraph (1) of this paragraph are considered "amounts received as an annuity" only in the event that all of the following tests are met:

(i) They must be received on or after the "annuity starting date" as that term is defined in paragraph (b) of § 1.72-4;

(ii) They must be payable in periodic installments at regular intervals (whether annually, semiannually, quarterly, monthly, weekly, or otherwise) over a period of more than one full year from the annuity starting date; and

(iii) Except as indicated in subparagraph (3) of this paragraph, the total of the amounts payable must be determinable at the annuity starting date either directly from the terms of the contract or indirectly by the use of either mortality tables or compound interest computations, or both, in conjunction with such terms and in accordance with sound actuarial theory.

For the purpose of determining whether amounts subject to section 72(d) and § 1.72-13 are "amounts received as an annuity", however, the provisions of subdivision (i) of this subparagraph shall be disregarded. In addition, the term "amounts received as an annuity" does not include amounts received to which the provisions of paragraph (b) or (c) of § 1.72-11 apply, relating to dividends and certain amounts received by a beneficiary in the nature of a refund. If an amount is to be paid periodically until a fund plus interest at a fixed rate is exhausted, but further payments may be made thereafter because of earnings at a higher interest rate, the requirements of subdivision (iii) of this subparagraph are met with respect to the payments determinable at the outset by means of computations involving the fixed interest rate, but any payments received after the expiration of the period determinable by such computations shall be taxable as dividends received after the annuity starting date in accordance with paragraph (b)(2) of § 1.72-11.

(3) (i) Notwithstanding the requirement of subparagraph (2)(iii) of this paragraph, if amounts are to be received for a definite or determinable time (whether for a period certain or for a life or lives) under a contract which provides:

(a) That the amount of the periodic payments may vary in accordance with investment experience (as in certain profit-sharing plans), cost of living indices, or similar fluctuating criteria, or

(b) For specified payments the value of which may vary for income tax purposes, such as in the case of any annuity payable in foreign currency, each such payment received shall be considered as an amount received as an annuity only to the extent that it does not exceed the amount computed by dividing the investment in the contract, as adjusted for any refund feature, by the number of periodic payments anticipated during the time that the periodic payments are to be made. If payments are to be made more frequently than annually, the amount so computed shall be multiplied by the number of periodic payments to be made during the taxable year for the purpose of determining the total amount which may be considered received as an annuity during such year. To this extent, the payments received shall be considered to represent a return of premium or other consideration paid and shall be excludable from gross income in the taxable year in which received. See paragraph (d)(2) and (3) of § 1.72-4. To the extent that the payments received under the contract during the taxable year exceed the total amount thus considered to be received as an annuity during such year, they shall be considered to be amounts not received as an annuity and shall be included in the gross income of the recipient. See section 72(e) and paragraph (b)(2) of § 1.72-11.

(ii) For purposes of subdivision (i) of this subparagraph, the number of periodic payments anticipated during the time payments are to be made shall be determined by multiplying the number of payments to be made each year (a) by the number of years payments are to be made, or (b) if payments are to be made for a life or lives, by the multiple found by the use of the appropriate tables contained in § 1.72-9, as adjusted in accordance with the table in paragraph (a)(2) of § 1.72-5.

(iii) For an example of the computation to be made in accordance with this subparagraph and a special election which may be made in a taxable year subsequent to a taxable year in which the total payments received under a contract described in this subparagraph are less than the total of the amounts excludable from gross income in such year under subdivision (i) of this subparagraph, see paragraph (d)(3) of § 1.72-4.

T.D. 6211, 11/14/56, amend T.D. 6497, 10/19/60, T.D. 6885, 6/1/66.

---

§ 1.72-3 Excludable amounts not income.

In general, amounts received under contracts described in paragraph (a)(1) of § 1.72-2 are not to be included in the income of the recipient to the extent that such amounts are excludable from gross income as the result of the application of section 72 and the regulations thereunder.

T.D. 6211, 11/14/56.

---

§ 1.72-4 Exclusion ratio.

Caution: The Treasury has not yet amended Reg § 1.72-4 to reflect changes made by P.L. 99-514.

(a) General rule. *(1)* (i) To determine the proportionate part of the total amount received each year as an annuity which is excludable from the gross income of a recipient in the taxable year of receipt (other than amounts received under (a) certain employee annuities described in section 72(d) and § 1.72-13, or (b) certain annuities described in section 72(o) and § 1.122-1), an exclusion ratio is to be determined for each contract. In general, this ratio is determined by dividing the investment in the contract as found under § 1.72-6 by the expected return under such contract as found under § 1.72-5. Where a single consideration is given for a particular contract which provides for two or more annuity elements, an exclusion ratio shall be determined for the contract as a whole by dividing the investment in such contract by the aggregate of the expected returns under all the annuity elements provided thereunder. However, where the provisions of paragraph (b)(3) of § 1.72-2 apply to payments received under such a contract, see paragraph (b)(3) of § 1.72-6. In the case of a contract to which § 1.72-6(d) (relating to contracts in which amounts were invested both before July 1, 1986, and after June 30, 1986) applies, the exclusion ratio for purposes of this paragraph (a) is determined in accordance with § 1.72-6(d) and, in particular, § 1.72-6(d)(5)(i).

(ii) The exclusion ratio for the particular contract is then applied to the total amount received as an annuity during the taxable year by each recipient. See, however, paragraph (e)(3) of § 1.72-5. Any excess of the total amount received as an annuity during the taxable year over the amount determined by the application of the exclusion ratio to such total amount shall be included in the gross income of the recipient for the taxable year of receipt.

(2) The principles of subparagraph (1) may be illustrated by the following example:

Example. Taxpayer A purchased an annuity contract providing for payments of $100 per month for a consideration of $12,650. Assuming that the expected return under this contract is $16,000 the exclusion ratio to be used by A is $12,650 ÷ 16,000; or 79.1 percent (79.06 rounded to the nearest tenth). If 12 such monthly payments are received by A during his taxable year, the total amount he may exclude from his gross income in such year is $949.20 ($1,200 × 79.1 percent). The balance of $250.80 ($1,200 less $949.20) is the amount to be included in gross income. If A instead received only five such payments during the year, he should exclude $395.50 (500 × 79.1 percent) of the total amounts received.

For examples of the computation of the exclusion ratio in cases where two annuity elements are acquired for a single consideration, see paragraph (b)(1) of § 1.72-6.

(3) The exclusion ratio shall be applied only to amounts received as an annuity within the meaning of that term under paragraph (b)(2) and (3) of § 1.72-2. Where the periodic payments increase in amount after the annuity starting date in a manner not provided by the terms of the contract at such date, the portion of such payments representing the increase is not an amount received as an annuity. For the treatment of amounts not received as an annuity, see section 72(e) and § 1.72-11. For special rules where paragraph (b)(3) of § 1.72-2 applies to amounts received, see paragraph (d)(3) of this section.

(4) After an exclusion ratio has been determined for a particular contract, it shall be applied to any amounts received as an annuity thereunder unless or until one of the following occurs:

(i) The contract is assigned or transferred for a valuable consideration (see section 72(g) and paragraph (a) of § 1.72-10);

(ii) The contract matures or is surrendered, redeemed, or discharged in accordance with the provisions of paragraph (c) or (d) of § 1.72-11;

(iii) The contract is exchanged (or is considered to have been exchanged) in a manner described in paragraph (e) of § 1.72-11.

(b) Annuity starting date. *(1)* Except as provided in subparagraph (2) of this paragraph, the annuity starting date is the first day of the first period for which an amount is received as an annuity, except that if such date was before January 1, 1954, then the annuity starting date is January 1, 1954. The first day of the first period for which an amount is received as an annuity shall be whichever of the following is the later:

(i) The date upon which the obligations under the contract became fixed, or

(ii) The first day of the period (year, half-year, quarter, month, or otherwise, depending on whether payments are to be made annually, semiannually, quarterly, monthly, or otherwise) which ends on the date of the first annuity payment.

(2) Notwithstanding the provisions of paragraph (b)(1) of this section; the annuity starting date shall be determined in accordance with whichever of the following provisions is appropriate:

(i) In the case of a joint and survivor annuity contract described in section 72(i) and paragraph (b)(3) of § 1.72-5, the annuity starting date is January 1, 1954, or the first day of the first period for which an amount is received as an annuity by the surviving annuitant, whichever is the later;

(ii) In the case of the transfer of an annuity contract for a valuable consideration, as described in section 72(g) and paragraph (a) of § 1.72-10, the annuity starting date shall be January 1, 1954, or the first day of the first period for which the transferee received an amount as an annuity, whichever is the later; and

(iii) If the provisions of paragraph (e) of § 1.72-11 apply to an exchange of one contract for another, or to a transaction deemed to be such an exchange, the annuity starting date of the contract received (or deemed received) in exchange shall be January 1, 1954, or the first day of the first period for which an amount is received as an annuity under such contract, whichever is the later; and

(iv) In the case of an employee who has retired from work because of personal injuries or sickness, and who is receiving amounts under a plan that is a wage continuation plan under section 105(d) and § 1.105-4, the annuity starting date shall be the date the employee reaches mandatory retirement age, as defined in § 1.105-4(a)(3)(i)(B). (See, also §§ 1.72-15 and 1.105-6 for transitional and other special rules.)

(c) Fiscal year taxpayers. Fiscal year taxpayers receiving amounts as annuities in a taxable year to which the Internal Revenue Code of 1954 applies shall determine the annuity starting date in accordance with section 72(c)(4) and this section. The annuity starting date for fiscal year taxpayers receiving amounts as an annuity in a taxable year to which the Internal Revenue Code of 1939 applies shall be January 1, 1954, except where the first day of the first period for which an amount is received by such a taxpayer as an annuity is subsequent thereto and before the end of a fiscal year to which the Internal Revenue Code of 1939 applied. In such case, the latter date shall be the annuity starting date. In all cases where a fiscal year taxpayer received an amount as an annuity in a taxable year to which the Internal Revenue Code of 1939 applied and subsequent to the annuity starting date determined in accordance with the provisions of this paragraph, such amount shall be disregarded for the purposes of section 72 and the regulations thereunder.

(d) Exceptions to the general rule. *(1)* Where the provisions of section 72 would otherwise require an exclusion ratio to be determined, but the investment in the contract (determined under § 1.72-6) is an amount of zero or less, no exclusion ratio shall be determined and all amounts received under such a contract shall be includible in the gross income of the recipient for the purposes of section 72.

(2) Where the investment in the contract is equal to or greater than the total expected return under such contract

found under § 1.72-5, the exclusion ratio shall be considered to be 100 percent and all amounts received as an annuity under such contract shall be excludable from the recipient's gross income. See, for example, paragraph (f)(1) of § 1.72-5. In the case of a contract to which § 1.72-6(d) (relating to contracts in which amounts were invested both before July 1, 1986, and after June 30, 1986) applies, this paragraph (d)(2) is applied in the manner prescribed in § 1.72-6(d) and, in particular, § 1.72-6(d)(5)(ii).

(3) (i) If a contract provides for payments to be made to a taxpayer in the manner described in paragraph (b)(3) of § 1.72-2, the investment in the contract shall be considered to be equal to the expected return under such contract and the resulting exclusion ratio (100%) shall be applied to all amounts received as an annuity under such contract. For any taxable year, payments received under such a contract shall be considered to be amounts received as an annuity only to the extent that they do not exceed the portion of the investment in the contract which is properly allocable to that year and hence excludable from gross income as a return of premiums or other consideration paid for the contract. The portion of the investment in the contract which is properly allocable to any taxable year shall be determined by dividing the investment in the contract (adjusted for any refund feature in the manner described in paragraph (d) of § 1.72-7) by the applicable multiple (whether for a term certain, life, or lives) which would otherwise be used in determining the expected return for such a contract under § 1.72-5. The multiple shall be adjusted in accordance with the provisions of the table in paragraph (a)(2) of § 1.72-5, if any adjustment is necessary, before making the above computation. If payments are to be made more frequently than annually and the number of payments to be made in the taxable year in which the annuity begins are less than the number of payments to be made each year thereafter, the amounts considered received as an annuity (as otherwise determined under this subdivision) shall not exceed, for such taxable year (including a short taxable year), an amount which bears the same ratio to the portion of the investment in the contract considered allocable to each taxable year as the number of payments to be made in the first year bears to the number of payments to be made in each succeeding year. Thus, if payments are to be made monthly, only seven payments will be made in the first taxable year, and the portion of the investment in the contract allocable to a full year of payments is $600, the amounts considered received as an annuity in the first taxable year cannot exceed $350 ($600 × 7/12). See subdivision (iii) of this subparagraph for an example illustrating the determination of the portion of the investment in the contract allocable to one taxable year of the taxpayer.

(ii) If subdivision (i) of this subparagraph applies to amounts received by a taxpayer and the total amount of payments he receives in a taxable year is less than the total amount excludable for such year under subdivision (i) of this subparagraph, the taxpayer may elect, in a succeeding taxable year in which he receives another payment, to redetermine the amounts to be received as an annuity during the current and succeeding taxable years. This shall be computed in accordance with the provisions of subdivision (i) of this subparagraph except that:

(a) The difference between the portion of the investment in the contract allocable to a taxable year, as found in accordance with subdivision (i) of this subparagraph, and the total payments actually received in the taxable year prior to the election shall be divided by the applicable life expectancy of the annuitant (or annuitants), found in accordance with the appropriate table in § 1.72-9 (and adjusted in accordance with paragraph (a)(2) of § 1.72-5), or by the remaining term of a term certain annuity, computed as of the first day of the first period for which an amount is received as an annuity in the taxable year of the election; and

(b) The amount determined under (a) of this subdivision shall be added to the portion of the investment in the contract allocable to each taxable year (as otherwise found). To the extent that the total periodic payments received under the contract in the taxable year of the election or any succeeding taxable year does not equal this total sum, such payments shall be excludable from the gross income of the recipient. To the extent such payments exceed the sum so found, they shall be fully includible in the recipient's gross income. See subdivision (iii) of this subparagraph for an example illustrating the redetermination of amounts to be received as an annuity and subdivision (iv) of this subparagraph for the method of making the election provided by this subdivision.

(iii) The application of the principles of paragraph (d)(3) (i) and (ii) of this section may be illustrated by the following example:

Example. Taxpayer A, a 64 year old male, files his return on a calendar year basis and has a life expectancy of 15.6 years on June 30, 1954, the annuity starting date of a contract to which § 1.72-2(b)(3) applies and which he purchased for $20,000. The contract provides for variable annual payments for his life. He receives a payment of $1,000 on June 30, 1955, but receives no other payment until June 30, 1957. He excludes the $1,000 payment from his gross income for the year 1955 since this amount is less than $1,324.50, the amount determined by dividing his investment in the contract ($20,000) by his life expectancy adjusted for annual payments, 15.1 (15.6 – 0.5), as of the original annuity starting date. Taxpayer A may elect, in his return for the taxable year 1957, to redetermine amounts to be received as an annuity under his contract as of June 30, 1956. For the purpose of determining the extent to which amounts received in 1957 or thereafter shall be considered amounts received as an annuity (to which a 100 percent exclusion ratio shall apply) he shall add $118.63 to the $1,324.50 originally determined to be receivable as an annuity under the contract, making a total of $1,443.13. This is determined by dividing the difference between what was excludable in 1955 and 1956, $2,649 (2 × $1,324.50) and what he actually received in those years ($1,000) by his life expectancy adjusted for annual payments, 13.9 (14.4 – 0.5), as of his age at his nearest birthday (66) on the first day of the first period for which he received an amount as an annuity in the taxable year of election (June 30, 1956). The result, $1,443.13, is excludable in that year and each year thereafter as an amount received as an annuity to which the 100% exclusion ratio applies. It will be noted that in this example the taxpayer received amounts less than the excludable amounts in two successive years and deferred making his election until the third year, and thus was able to accumulate the portion of the investment in the contract allocable to each taxable year to the extent he failed to receive such portion in both years. Assuming that he received $1,500 in the taxable year of his election, he would include $56.87 in his gross income and exclude $1,443.13 therefrom for that year.

(iv) If the taxpayer chooses to make the election described in subdivision (ii) of this subparagraph, he shall file with his return a statement that he elects to make a redetermination of the amounts excludable from gross income under his annuity contract in accordance with the provisions of paragraph (d)(3) of § 1.72-4. This statement shall also contain the following information:

(a) The original annuity starting date and his age on that date,

(b) The date of the first day of the first period for which he received an amount in the current taxable year,

(c) The investment in the contract originally determined (as adjusted for any refund feature), and

(d) The aggregate of all amounts received under the contract between the date indicated in (a) of this subdivision and the day after the date indicated in (b) of this subdivision to the extent such amounts were excludable from gross income.

He shall include in gross income any amounts received during the taxable year for which the return is made in accordance with the redetermination made under this subparagraph.

(v) In the case of a contract to which § 1.72-6(d) (relating to contracts in which amounts were invested both before July 1, 1986, and after June 30, 1986) applies, this paragraph (d)(3) is applied in the manner prescribed in § 1.72-6(d) and, in particular, § 1.72-6(d)(5)(iii). This application may be illustrated by the following example:

Example. B, a male calendar year taxpayer, purchases a contract which provides for variable annual payments for life and to which § 1.72-2(b)(3) applies. The annuity starting date of the contract is June 30, 1990, when B is 64 years old. B receives a payment of $1,000 on June 30, 1991, but receives no other payment until June 30, 1993. B's total investment in the contract is $25,000. B's pre-July 1986 investment in the contract is $12,000. If B makes the election described in § 1.72-6(d)(6), separate computations are required to determine the amounts received as an annuity and excludable from gross income with respect to the pre-July 1986 investment in the contract and the post-June 1986 investment in the contract. In the separate computations, B first determines the applicable portions of the total payment received which are allocable to the pre-July 1986 investment in the contract and the post-June 1986 investment in the contract. The portion of the payment received allocable to the pre-July 1986 investment in the contract is $480 ($12,000/$25,000 × $1,000). The portion of the payment received allocable to the post-June 1986 investment in the contract is $520 ($13,000/$25,000 × $1,000).

Second, B determines the pre-July 1986 investment in the contract and the post-June 1986 investment in the contract allocable to the taxable year by dividing the pre-July 1986 and post-June 1986 investments in the contract by the applicable life expectancy multiple. The life expectancy multiple applicable to pre-July 1986 investment in the contract is B's life expectancy as of the original annuity starting date adjusted for annual payments and is determined under Table I of § 1.72-9 (15.1 (15.6 – 0.5)). The life expectancy multiple applicable to post-June 1986 investment in the contract is determined under Table V of § 1.72-9 (20.3 (20.8 – 0.5)). Thus, the pre-July 1986 investment in the contract allocable to each taxable year is $794.70 ($12,000 ÷ 15.1), and the post-June 1986 investment in the contract so allocable is $640.39 ($13,000 ÷ 20.3). Because the applicable portions of the total payment received in 1991 under the contract ($480 allocable to the pre-July 1986 investment in the contract and $520 allocable to the post-June 1986 investment in the contract) are treated as amounts received as an annuity and are excludable from gross income to the extent they do not exceed the portion of the corresponding investment in the contract allocable to 1991 ($794.70 pre-July 1986 investment in the contract and $640.39 post-June 1986 investment in the contract), the entire amount of each applicable portion of the total payment is excludable from gross income. B may elect, in the return filed for taxable year 1993, to redetermine amounts to be received as an annuity under the contract as of June 30, 1992. The extent to which the amounts received in 1993 or thereafter shall be considered amounts received as an annuity is determined as follows:

Pre-July 1986 investment in the contract allocable to taxable years 1991 and 1992 ($794.70 × 2)	$1,589.40
Less: Portion of total payments allocable to pre-July 1986 investment in the contract actually received as an annuity in taxable years 1991 and 1992	480.00
	1,109.40
Divided by: Life expectancy multiple applicable to pre-July 1986 investment in the contract for B, age 66 (14.4 – 0.5)	13.9
	79.81
Plus: Amount originally determined with respect to pre-July 1986 investment in the contract	794.70
Pre-July 1986 amount	874.51
Post-June 1986 investment in the contract allocable to taxable years 1991 and 1992 ($640.39 – 2)	$1,280.78
Less: Portion of total payments allocable to post-June 1986 investment in the contract actually received as an annuity in taxable years 1991 and 1992	520.00
	760.78
Divided by: Life expectancy multiple applicable to post-June 1986 investment in the contract for B, age 66 (19.2 – 0.5)	18.7
	40.68
Plus: Amount originally determined with respect to post-June 1986 investment in the contract	640.39
Post-June 1986 amount	681.07

(vi) The method of making an election to perform the separate computations illustrated in paragraph (d)(3)(v) of this section is described in § 1.72-6(d)(6).

(e) Exclusion ratio in the case of two or more annuity elements acquired for a single consideration. *(1)* (i) Where two or more annuity elements are provided under a contract described in paragraph (a)(2) of § 1.72-2, an exclusion ratio shall be determined for the contract as a whole and applied to all amounts received as an annuity under any of the annuity elements. To obtain this ratio, the investment in the contract determined in accordance with § 1.72-6 shall be divided by the aggregate of the expected returns found with respect to each of the annuity elements in accordance with § 1.72-5. For this purpose, it is immaterial that payments under one or more of the annuity elements involved have not commenced at the time when an amount is first received as an annuity under one or more of the other annuity elements.

(ii) The exclusion ratio found under subdivision (i) of this subparagraph does not apply to:

(a) An annuity element payable to a surviving annuitant under a joint and survivor annuity contract to which section 72(i) and paragraphs (b)(3) and (e)(3) of § 1.72-5 apply, or to

(b) A contract under which one or more of the constituent annuity elements provides for payments described in paragraph (b)(3) of § 1.72-2.

For rules with respect to a contract providing for annuity elements described in (b) of this subdivision, see subparagraph (2) of this paragraph.

(2) If one or more of the annuity elements under a contract described in paragraph (a)(2) of § 1.72-2 provides for payments to which paragraph (b)(3) of § 1.72-2 applies:

(i) With respect to the annuity elements to which paragraph (b)(3) of § 1.72-2 does not apply, an exclusion ratio shall be determined by dividing the portion of the investment in the entire contract which is properly allocable to all such elements (in the manner provided in paragraph (b)(3)(ii) of § 1.72-6) by the aggregate of the expected returns thereunder and such ratio shall be applied in the manner described in subdivision (i) of subparagraph (1); and

(ii) With respect to the annuity elements to which paragraph (b)(3) of § 1.72-2 does apply, the investment in the entire contract shall be reduced by the portion thereof found in subdivision (i) of this subparagraph and the resulting amount shall be used to determine the extent to which the aggregate of the payments received during the taxable year under all such elements is excludable from gross income. The amount so excludable shall be allocated to each recipient under such elements in the same ratio that the total of payments he receives each year bears to the total of the payments received by all such recipients during the year. The exclusion ratio with respect to the amounts so allocated shall be 100 percent. See paragraph (f)(2) of § 1.72-5 and paragraph (b)(3) of § 1.72-6.

(iii) In the case of a contract to which § 1.72-6(d) (relating to contracts in which amounts were invested both before July 1, 1986, and after June 30, 1986) applies, this paragraph (e) is applied in the manner prescribed in § 1.72-6(d) and, in particular, § 1.72-6(d)(5)(iv).

T.D. 6211, 11/14/56, amend T.D. 7043, 6/1/70, T.D. 7352, 4/9/75, T.D. 8115, 12/16/86.

PAR. 3. Section 1.72-4(a)(1)(i) is amended by deleting "72(o)" and inserting in lieu thereof "72(n)". As amended, § 1.72-4(a)(1)(i) reads as follows:

Proposed § 1.72-4 Exclusion ratio. [*For Preamble, see ¶ 150,135*]

• ***Caution:*** Proposed section 1.62-1 was finalized by TD 7399, 2/3/76. Proposed sections 1.72-4, 1.72-13, 1.101-2, 1.122-1, 1.402(a)-1, 1.402(e)-2, 1.402(e)-3, 1.403(a)-1, 1.403(a)-2, 1.405-3, 1.652(b)-1, 1.1304-2 and 11.402(e)(4)(B)-1 remain proposed.

(a) General rule. *(1)* (i) To determine the proportionate part of the total amount received each year as an annuity which is excludable from the gross income of a recipient in the taxable year of receipt (other than amounts received under (A) certain employee annuities described in section 72(d) and § 1.72-13, or (B) certain annuities described in section 72(n) and § 1.122-1), an exclusion ratio is to be determined for each contract. In general, this ratio is determined by dividing the investment in the contract as found under § 1.72-6 by the expected return under such contract as found under § 1.72-5. Where a single consideration is given for a particular contract which provides for two or more annuity elements, an exclusion ratio shall be determined for the contract as a whole by dividing the investment in such contract by the aggregate of the expected returns under all the annuity elements provided thereunder. However, where the provisions of paragraph (b)(3) of § 1.72-2 apply to payments received under such a contract, see paragraph (b)(3) of § 1.72-6.

* * * * *

§ 1.72-5 Expected return.

(a) Expected return for but one life. *(1)* If a contract to which section 72 applies provides that one annuitant is to receive a fixed monthly income for life, the expected return is determined by multiplying the total of the annuity payments to be received annually by the multiple shown in Table I or V (whichever is applicable) of § 1.72-9 under the age (as of the annuity starting date) and, if applicable, sex of the measuring life (usually the annuitant's). Thus, where a male purchases a contract before July 1, 1986, providing for an immediate annuity of $100 per month for his life and, as of the annuity starting date (in this case the date of purchase), the annuitant's age at his nearest birthday is 66, the expected return is computed as follows:

Monthly payment of $100 × 12 months equals annual payment of	$1,200
Multiple shown in Table 1, male, age 66	14.4
Expected return (1,200 × 14.4)	17,280

If, however, the taxpayer had purchased the contract after June 30, 1986, the expected return would be $23,040, determined by multiplying 19.2 (multiple shown in Table V, age 66) by $1,200.

(2) (i) If payments are to be made quarterly, semiannually, or annually, an adjustment of the applicable multiple shown in Table I or V (whichever is applicable) may be required. A further adjustment may be required where the interval between the annuity starting date and the date of the first payment is less than the interval between future payments. Neither adjustment shall be made, however, if the payments are to be made more frequently than quarterly. The amount of the adjustment, if any, is to be found in accordance with the following table:

If the number of whole months from the annuity starting date to the first payment date is—	0-1	2	3	4	5	6	7	8	9	10	11	12
And the payments under the contract are to be made:												
Annually	+0.5	+0.4	+0.3	+0.2	+0.1	0	0	−0.1	−0.2	−0.3	−0.4	−0.5
Semiannually	+.2	+.1	0	0	−.1	−.2						
Quarterly	+.1	0	−.1									

Thus, for a male, age 66, the multiple found in Table I, adjusted for quarterly payments the first of which is to be made one full month after the annuity starting date, is 14.5 (14.4 + 0.1); for semiannual payments the first of which is to be made six full months from the annuity starting date, the adjusted multiple is 14.2 (14.4 one full month from the annuity starting date, the adjusted multiple is 14.9 (14.4 + 0.5). If the annuitant in the example shown in subparagraph (1) of this paragraph were to receive an annual payment of $1,200 commencing 12 full months after his annuity starting date, the amount of the expected return would be $16,680 ($1,200 × 13.9 [14.4 − 0.5]). Similarly, for an annuitant, age 50, the multiple found in Table V, adjusted for quarterly payments the first of which is to be made one full month after the annuity starting date, is 33.2 (33.1 + 0.1); for semiannual payments the first of which is to be made six full months from the annuity starting date, the adjusted multiple is 32.9 (33.1 − 0.2); for annual payments the first of which is to be made one full month from the annuity starting date, the adjusted multiple is 33.6 (33.1 + 0.5).

(ii) Notwithstanding the table in subdivision (i) of this subparagraph, adjustments of multiples for early or other than monthly payments determined prior to February 19, 1956, under the table prescribed in paragraph 1(b)(4) of T.D. 6118 (19 FR 9897, C.B. 1955-1, 699), approved December 30, 1954, need not be redetermined.

(3) If the contract provides for fixed payments to be made to an annuitant until death or until the expiration of a specified limited period, whichever occurs earlier, the expected return of such temporary life annuity is determined by multiplying the total of the annuity payments to be received annually by the multiple shown in Table IV or VIII (whichever is applicable) of § 1.72-9 for the age (as of the annuity starting date) and, if applicable, sex of the annuitant and the nearest whole number of years in the specified period. For example, if a male annuitant, age 60 (at his nearest birthday), is to receive $60 per month for five years or until he dies, whichever is earlier, and there is no post-June 1986, investment in the contract, the expected return under such a contract is $3,456, computed as follows:

Monthly payments of $60 × 12 months equals annual payment of	$ 720
Multiple shown in Table IV for male, age 60, for term of 5 years	4.8
Expected return for 5 year temporary life annuity of $720 per year ($720 × 4.8)	$3,456

If the annuitant purchased the same contract after June 30, 1986, the expected return under the contract would be $3,528, computed as follows:

Monthly payments of $60 × 12 months equals annual payment of	$ 720.00
Multiple shown in Table VIII for annuitant, age 60, for term of 5 years	4.9
Expected return for 5-year temporary life annuity of $720 per year ($720 × 4.9)	$3,528.00

The adjustment provided by subparagraph (2) of this paragraph shall not be made with respect to the multiple found in Table IV or VIII (whichever is applicable).

(4) If the contract provides for payments to be made to an annuitant for the annuitant's lifetime, but the amount of the annual payments is to be decreased after the expiration of a specified limited period, the expected return is computed by considering the contract as a combination of a whole life annuity for the smaller amount plus a temporary life annuity for an amount equal to the difference between the larger and the smaller amount. For example, if a male annuitant, age 60, is to receive $150 per month for five years or until his earlier death, and is to receive $90 per month for the remainder of his lifetime after such five years, the expected return is computed as if the annuitant's contract consisted of a whole life annuity for $90 per month plus a five year temporary life annuity of $60 per month. In such circumstances, the expected return if there is no post-June 1986 investment in the contract is computed as follows:

Monthly payments of $90 × 12 months equals annual payment of	$ 1,080
Multiple shown in Table I for male, age 60	18.2
Expected return for whole life annuity of $1,080 per year	$19,656
Expected return for 5-year temporary life annuity of $720 per year (as found in subparagraph (3) of this paragraph (a))	$ 3,456
Total expected return	$23,112

If the annuitant purchased the same contract after June 30, 1986, the expected return would be $29,664, computed as follows:

Monthly payments of $90 × 12 months equals annual payment of	$ 1,080
Multiple shown in Table V for annuitant, age 60	24.2
Expected return for whole life annuity of $1,080 per year	$26,136
Plus: Expected return for 5-year temporary life annuity of $720 per year (as found in subparagraph (3) of this paragraph (a))	$ 3,528
Total expected return	$29,664

If payments are to be made quarterly, semiannually, or annually, an appropriate adjustment of the multiple found in Table I or V (whichever is applicable) for the whole life annuity should be made in accordance with subparagraph (2) of this paragraph.

(5) If the contract described in subparagraph (4) of this paragraph provided that the amount of the annual payments to the annuitant were to be increased (instead of decreased) after the expiration of a specified limited period, the expected return would be computed as if the annuitant's contract consisted of a whole life annuity for the larger amount minus a temporary life annuity for an amount equal to the difference between the larger and smaller amount. Thus, if the annuitant described in subparagraph (4) of this paragraph were to receive $90 per month for five years or until his earlier death, and to receive $150 per month for the remainder of his lifetime after such five years, the expected return would be computed by subtracting the expected return under a five year temporary life annuity of $60 per month from the expected return under a whole life annuity of $150 per month. In such circumstances, the expected return if there is no post-June 1986 investment in the contract is computed as follows:

Monthly payments of $150 × 12 months equals annual payment of	$ 1,800
Multiple shown in Table 1 (male, age 60)	18.2
Expected return for annuity for whole life of $1,800 per year	$32,760
Less expected return for 5-year temporary life annuity of $720 per year (as found in subparagraph (3))	$ 3,456
Net expected return	$29,304

If the annuitant purchased the same contract after June 30, 1986, the expected return would be $40,032, computed as follows:

Monthly payments of $150 × 12 months equals annual payments of	$ 1,800
Multiple shown in Table V (age 60)	24.2
Expected return for annuity for whole life of $1,800 per year	$43,560
Less expected return for 5-year temporary life annuity of $720 per year (as found in subparagraph (3) of this paragraph (a))	$ 3,528
Net expected return	$40,032

If payments are to be made quarterly, semiannually, or annually, an appropriate adjustment of the multiple found in Table I or V (whichever is applicable) for the whole life annuity should be made in accordance with subparagraph (2) of this paragraph.

(b) Expected return under joint and survivor and joint annuities. *(1)* In the case of a joint and survivor annuity contract involving two annuitants which provides the first annuitant with a fixed monthly income for life and, after the death of the first annuitant, provides an identical monthly income for life to a second annuitant, the expected return shall be determined by multiplying the total amount of the payments to be received annually by the multiple obtained from Table II or VI (whichever is applicable) of § 1.72-9 under the ages (as of the annuity starting date) and, if applicable, sexes of the living annuitants. For example, a husband purchases a joint and survivor annuity contract providing for payments of $100 per month for life and, after his death, for the same amount to his wife for the remainder of her life. As of the annuity starting date his age at his nearest birthday is 70 and that of his wife at her nearest birthday is 67. If there is no post-June 1986 investment in the contract, the expected return is computed as follows:

Monthly payments of $100 × 12 month equals annual payment of	$ 1,200
Multiple shown in Table II (male, age 70, female, age 67)	19.7
Expected return ($1,200 × 19.7)	$23,640

If the annuitants purchased the same contract after June 30, 1986, the expected return would be $26,400, computed as follows:

Monthly payments of $100 × 12 equals annual payment of	$ 1,200
Multiple shown in Table VI (ages 70, 67)	22.0
Expected return ($1,200 × 22.0)	$26,400

If payments are to be made quarterly, semiannually, or annually, an appropriate adjustment of the multiple found in Table II or VI (whichever is applicable) should be made in accordance with paragraph (a)(2) of this section.

(2) If a contract of the type described in subparagraph (1) of this paragraph provides that a different (rather than an identical) monthly income is payable to the second annuitant, the expected return is computed in the following manner. The applicable multiple in Table II or VI (whichever is applicable) is first found as in the example in subparagraph (1) of this paragraph. The multiple applicable to the first annuitant is then found in Table I or V (whichever is applicable) as though the contract were for a single life annuity. The multiple from Table I or V is then subtracted from the multiple obtained from Table II or VI and the resulting multiple is applied to the total payments to be received annually under the contract by the second annuitant. The result is the expected return with respect to the second annuitant. The portion of the expected return with respect to payments to be made during the first annuitant's life is then computed by applying the multiple found in Table I or V to the total annual payments to be received by such annuitant under the contract. The expected returns with respect to each of the annuitants separately are then aggregated to obtain the expected return under the entire contract.

Example (1). A husband purchases a joint and survivor annuity providing for payments of $100 per month for his life and, after his death, payments to his wife of $50 per month for her life. As of the annuity starting date his age at his nearest birthday is 70 and that of his wife at her nearest birthday is 67. There is no post-June 1986 investment in the

Multiple from Table II (male, age 70, female, age 67)	19.7
Multiple from Table I (male, age 70)	12.1
Difference (multiple applicable to second annuitant)	7.6
Portion of expected return, second annuitant ($600 × 7.6)	$ 4,560
Portion of expected return, first annuitant ($1,200 × 12.1)	$14,520
Expected return under the contract	$19,080

The expected return thus found, $19,080, is to be used in computing the amount to be excluded from gross income. Thus, if the investment in the contract in this example is $14,310, the exclusion ratio is $14,310 ÷ $19,080; or 75 percent. The amount excludable from each monthly payment made to the husband is 75 percent of $100, or $75, and the remaining $25 of each payment received by him shall be included in his gross income. After the husband's death, the amount excludable by the second annuitant (the surviving wife) would be 75 percent of each monthly payment of $50, or $37.50, and the remaining $12.50 of each payment shall be included in her gross income.

Example (2). If the same contract were purchased after June 30, 1986, the expected return would be $22,800, computed as follows:

Multiple from Table VI (ages 70, 67)	22.0
Multiple from Table V (age 70)	16.0
Difference (multiple applicable to second annuitant)	6.0
Portion of expected return, second annuitant ($600 × 6.0)	$ 3,600
Plus: Portion of expected return, first annuitant ($1,200 × 16.0)	$19,200
Expected return under the contract	$22,800

If the investment in the contract is $14,310, the exclusion ratio is $14,310 ÷ $22,800, or 62.8 percent. Thus, the husband would exclude $62.80 of each $100 payment received by him. After his death, his wife would exclude 62.8 percent, or $31.40, of each $50 monthly payment.

Example (3). If amounts were invested in the same contract both before July 1, 1986, and after June 30, 1986, and the election described in § 1.72-6(d)(6) were made, two exclusion ratios would be determined pursuant to § 1.72-6(d). Assume that the husband's total investment in the contract is $14,310 and that $7,310 is the pre-July 1986 investment in the contract. The pre-July 1986 exclusion ratio would be $7,310 ratio would be $7,000 ÷ $22,800, or 30.7 percent. The husband would exclude $69.00 ($38.30 + $30.70) of the $100 monthly payment received by him. The remaining $31.00 would be included in his gross income. After the husband's death, the amount excludable by his wife would be $34.50 (38.3 percent of $50 plus 30.7 percent of $50). The remaining $15.50 would be included in gross income.

The same method is used if the payments are to be increased after the death of the first annuitant. Thus, if the payments to be made until the husband's death were $50 per month and his widow were to receive $100 per month thereafter until her death, the 7.6 multiple in example (1) above would be applied to the $100 payments, yielding an expected return with respect to this portion of the annuity contract of $9,120 ($1,200 × 7.6). An expected return of $7,260 ($600 × 12.1) would be obtained with respect to the payments to be made to the husband, yielding a total expected return under the contract of $16,380 ($9,120 plus $7,260). If payments are to be made quarterly, semiannually, or annually, an appropriate adjustment of the multiples found in Tables I and II or Tables V and VI (whichever are applicable) should be made in accordance with paragraph (a)(2) of this section.

(3) In the case of a joint and survivor annuity contract in respect of which the first annuitant died in 1951, 1952, or 1953, and the basis of the surviving annuitant's interest in the contract was determinable under section 113(a)(5) of the Internal Revenue Code of 1939, such basis shall be considered the "aggregate of premiums or other consideration paid" by the surviving annuitant for the contract. (For rules governing this determination, see 26 CFR (1939) 39.22(b)(2)-2 and 39.113(a)(5)-1 (Regulations 118).) In determining such an annuitant's investment in the contract, such aggregate shall be reduced by any amounts received under the contract by the surviving annuitant before the annuity starting date, to the extent such amounts were excludable from his gross income at the time of receipt. The expected return of the surviving annuitant in such cases shall be determined in the manner prescribed in paragraph (a) of this section, as though the surviving annuitant alone were involved. For this purpose, the appropriate multiple for the survivor shall be obtained from Table I as of the annuity starting date determined in accordance with paragraph (b)(2)(i) of § 1.72-4.

(4) If a contract involving two annuitants provides for fixed monthly payments to be made as a joint life annuity until the death of the first annuitant to die (in other words, only as long as both remain alive), the expected return under such contract shall be determined by multiplying the total of the annuity payments to be received annually under the contract by the multiple obtained from Table IIA or VIA (whichever is applicable) of § 1.72-9 under the ages (as of the annuity starting date) and, if applicable, sexes of the annuitants. If, however, payments are to be made under the contract quarterly, semiannually, or annually, an appropriate adjustment of the multiple found in Table IIA or VIA shall be made in accordance with paragraph (a)(2) of this section.

(5) If a joint and survivor annuity contract involving two annuitants provides that a specified amount shall be paid during their joint lives and a different specified amount shall be paid to the survivor upon the death of whichever of the annuitants is the first to die, the following preliminary computation shall be made in all cases preparatory to determining the expected return under the contract:

(i) From Table II or VI (whichever is applicable), obtain the multiple under both of the annuitants' ages (as of the annuity starting date) and, if applicable, their appropriate sexes;

(ii) From Table IIA or VIA (whichever is applicable), obtain the multiple applicable to both annuitants' ages (as of the annuity starting date) and, if applicable, their appropriate sexes;

(iii) Apply the multiple found in subdivision (i) of this subparagraph to the total of the amounts to be received annually after the death of the first to die; and

(iv) Apply the multiple found in subdivision (ii) of this subparagraph to the difference between the total of the amounts to be received annually before and the total of the amounts to be received annually after the death of the first to die.

If the original annual payment is in excess of the annual payment to be made after the death of the first to die, the expected return is the sum of the amounts determined under subdivisions (iii) and (iv) of this subparagraph. This may be illustrated by the following examples:

Example (1). A husband purchases a joint and survivor annuity providing for payments of $100 a month for as long as both he and his wife live, and, after the death of the first to die, payments to the survivor of $75 a month for life. As of the annuity starting date, his age at his nearest birthday is 70 and that of his wife at her nearest birthday is 67. If there is no post-June 1986 investment in the contract, the expected return under the contract is computed as follows:

Multiple from Table II (male age 70, female age 67)	19.7
Multiple from Table IIA (male age 70, female age 67)	9.3
Portion of expected return ($900 × 19.7—sum per year after first death)	$17,730
Plus: Portion of expected return ($300 × 9.3—amount of change in sum at first death)	$ 2,790
Expected return under the contract	$20,520

The total expected return in this example, $20,520, is to be used in computing the amount to be excluded from gross income. Thus, if the investment in the contract is $17,887, the exclusion ratio is $17,887 monthly payment made while both are alive is 87.2 percent of $100, or $87.20, and the remaining $12.80 of each payment shall be included in gross income. After the death of the first to die, the amount excludable by the survivor shall be 87.2 percent of each monthly payment of $75, or $65.40, and the remaining $9.60 of each payment shall be included in gross income.

Example (2). Assume the same facts as in example (1), except that the contract is purchased after June 30, 1986.

The expected return under the contract is computed as follows:

Multiple from Table VI (ages 70, 67)	22.0
Multiple from Table VIA (ages 70, 67)	12.4
Portion of expected return ($900 × 22.0—sum per year after first death)	$19,800
Plus: Portion of expected return ($300 × 12.4—amount of change in sum at first death)	$ 3,720
Expected return under the contract	$23,520

Thus, if the investment in the contract is $17,887, the exclusion ratio is $17,887 ÷ $23,520, or 76.1 percent. The amount excludable from each monthly payment made while both are alive would be 76.1 percent of $100, or $76.10, and the remaining $23.90 of each payment would be included in gross income. After the death of the first to die, the amount excludable by the survivor would be 76.1 percent of each monthly payment of $75, or $57.08, and the remaining $17.92 of each payment would be included in gross income.

Example (3). Assume the same facts as in examples (1) and (2), except that the total investment in the contract is $17,887, and that the pre-July 1986 investment in the contract is $8,000. Assume also that one of the annuitants makes the election described in § 1.72-6(d)(6). Separate computations shall be performed pursuant to § 1.72-6(d) to determine the amount excludable from gross income. The pre-July 1986 exclusion ratio would be $8,000 ÷ $20,520, or 39 percent. The post-June 1986 exclusion ratio would be $9,887 ÷ $23,520, or 42 percent. The amount excludable from each monthly payment made while both are alive would be $81 ((.39 × 100) + (.42 income. After the death of the first to die, the amount excludable by the survivor would be $60.75 ((.39 × 75) + (.42 income.

If the original annual payment is less than the annual payment to be made after the death of the first to die, the expected return is the difference between the amounts determined under subdivisions (iii) and (iv) of this subparagraph. If, however, payments are to be made quarterly, semiannually, or annually under the contract, the multiples obtained from both Tables II and IIA or Tables VI and VIA (whichever are applicable) shall first be adjusted in a manner prescribed in paragraph (a)(2) of this section.

(6) If a contract provides for the payment of life annuities to two persons during their respective lives and, after the death of one (without regard to which one dies first), provides that the survivor shall receive for life both his own annuity payments and the payments made formerly to the deceased person, the expected return shall be determined in accordance with paragraph (e)(4) of this section.

(7) If paragraph (b)(3) of § 1.72-2 applies to payments provided under a contract and this paragraph applies to such payments, the principles of this paragraph shall be used in making the computations described in paragraph (d)(3) of § 1.72-4. This may be illustrated by the following examples, examples (1) through (3) of which assume that there is no post-June 1986 investment in the contract:

Example (1). Taxpayer A, a male age 63, pays $24,000 for a contract which provides that the proceeds (both income and return of capital) from eight units of an investment fund shall be paid monthly to him for his life and that after his death the proceeds from six such units shall be paid monthly to B, a female age 55, for her life. The portion of the investment in the contract allocable to each taxable year of A is $955.20 and that allocable to each taxable year of B is $716.40. This is determined in the following manner:

Multiple from Table II (male, age 63, and female, age 55)	28.1
Number of units to be paid, in effect, as a joint and survivor annuity	× 6
Number of total annual unit payments anticipatable with respect to the joint and survivor annuity element	168.6
Multiple from Table I (male, age 63)	16.2
Number of units to be paid, in effect, as a single life annuity	× 2
Number of total annual unit payments anticipatable with respect to A alone	32.4
Total number of unit payments anticipatable	201
Portion of investment in the contract allocable to unit payments ($24,000 ÷ 201) on an annual basis	$119.40
Number of units to A while he continues to live	× 8
Portion of the investment in the contract allocable to each taxable year of A	$955.20
Portion of investment in the contract allocable to unit payments ($24,000 ÷ 201) on an annual basis	$119.40
Number of units payable to B for her life after A's death	× 6
Portion of the investment in the contract allocable to each taxable year of B	$716.40

For the purpose of the above computation it is immaterial whether or not A lives to or beyond the life expectancy shown for him in Table I.

Example (2). Assume that Taxpayer A in example (1) receives payments for five years which are at least as large as the portion of the investment in the contract allocable to such years, but in the sixth year he receives a total of only $626.40 rather than the $955.20 allocable to such year. A is 69 and B is 61 at the beginning of the first monthly period for which an amount is payable in the seventh taxable year. A makes the election in that year provided under paragraph (d)(3) of § 1.72-4. The difference between the portion of the investment in the contract allocable to the sixth year and the amount actually received in that year is $328.80 ($955.20 less $626.40). In this case, 139.2 unit payments are anticipatable (on an annual basis), since the appropriate multiple from Table II of § 1.72-9, 23.2, multiplied by the number of units payable, in effect, as a joint and survivor annuity yields this result (6 for the two units which will cease to be paid at his death is 12.6, and the total number of unit payments anticipatable (on an annual basis) is, therefore, 164.4 (2 × 12.6 plus 139.2). Dividing the difference previously found ($328.80) by the total number of unit payments thus determined (164.4) indicates that A will have an additional allocation of the investment in the contract of $16 to the seventh and every succeeding full taxable year (8 units × $2), and B will have an additional allocation of the investment in the contract of $12 (6 units × $2) to each taxable year in which she receives 12 monthly payments subsequent to the death of A. The total allocable to each taxable year of A is, therefore, $971.20, and that allocable to each taxable year of B will be $728.40.

Example (3). If, in example (2), A had died at the end of the fifth year, in the sixth year B would have received a payment of $469.80 (that portion of the $626.40 that A would have received which is in the same ratio that 6 units bear to 8 units) and would thus have received $246.60 less than the portion of the investment in the contract originally determined to be allocable to each of her taxable years. In these circumstances, B would be entitled to elect to redetermine the portion of the investment in the contract allocable to the taxable year of election and all subsequent years. The new amount allocable thereto would be found by dividing the $246.60 difference by her life expectancy as of the first day of the first period for which she received an amount as an annuity in the seventh year of the annuity contract, and adding the result to her originally determined allocation of $716.40.

Example (4). On July 1, 1986, Taxpayer C, age 60, pays $28,000 for a contract which provides that the proceeds (both income and return of capital) from 10 units of an investment fund shall be paid monthly to C for C's life and that after C's death the proceeds from 4 such units shall be paid monthly to D, age 57, for D's life. The portion of the investment in the contract allocable to each taxable year of C is $1,037.00 and that allocable to each taxable year of D is $414.80. This is determined as follows:

Multiple from Table VI (ages 60, 57)	31.2
Number of units to be paid, in effect, as a joint and survivor annuity	× 4
Number of total annual unit payments anticipatable with respect to the joint and survivor annuity element	124.8
Multiple from Table V (age 60)	24.2
Number of units to be paid, in effect, as a single life annuity	× 6
Number of total annual unit payments anticipatable with respect to C alone	145.2
Total number of unit payments anticipatable	270
Portion of investment in the contracts allocable to unit payments ($28,000 / 270) on an annual basis	103.70
Number of units payable to C while C continues to live	× 10
Portion of the investment in the contract allocable to each taxable year of C	$1,037.00
Portion of investment in the contract allocable to unit payments ($28,000 / 270) on an annual basis	$103.70
Number of units payable to D for D's life after C's death	× 4
Portion of the investment in the contract allocable to each taxable year of D	$414.80

For purposes of the above computation it is immaterial whether or not C lives to or beyond the life expectancy shown in Table V.

Example (5). Assume the same facts as in example (4), except that C's total investment in the contract is $28,000, and C's pre-July 1986 investment in the contract is $16,000. If C makes the election described in § 1.72-6(d)(6), separate computations are required to determine the amount excludable from gross income with respect to the pre-July 1986 investment in the contract and the post-June 1986 investment in the contract. The annuitant shall apply the appropriate pre-July 1986 and post-June 1986 life expectancy multiples to the applicable portions of the units to be paid as a joint and survivor annuity, and as a single life annuity.

Pre-July 1986 Computation (all references to unit payments are to the pre-July 1986 applicable portion of such payments):

Multiple from Table II (male, age 60, female, age 57)	27.6
Number of units to be paid, in effect, as a joint and survivor annuity	× 4
Number of total annual unit payments anticipatable with respect to the joint and survivor annuity element	110.40
Multiple from Table I (male, age 60)	18.2
Number of units to be paid, in effect, as a single life annuity	× 6
Number of total annual unit payments anticipatable with respect to C alone	109.20
Total number of unit payments anticipatable	219.6
Portion of pre-July 1986 investment in the contract allocable to unit payments ($16,000 ÷ 219.60) on an annual basis	$72.86
Number of units payable to C while C continues to live	× 10
Portion of pre-July 1986 investment in the contract allocable to each taxable year of C	728.60
Portion of pre-July 1986 investment in the contract allocable to unit payments ($16,000 ÷ 219.60) on an annual basis	72.86
Number of units payable to D for D's life after C's death	× 4
Portion of pre-July 1986 investment in the contract allocable to each taxable year of D	$291.44

Post-June 1986 Computation (all references to unit payments are to the post-June 1986 applicable portion of such payments):

Multiple from Table VI (ages 60, 57)	31.2
Number of units to be paid, in effect, as a joint and survivor annuity	× 4
Number of total annual unit payments anticipatable with respect to the joint and survivor annuity element	124.80
Multiple from Table V (age 60)	24.2
Number of units to be paid, in effect, as a single life annuity	× 6
Number of total annual unit payments anticipatable with respect to C alone	145.20

Total number of unit payments anticipatable	270
Portion of post-June 1986 investment in the contract allocable to unit payments ($12,000 ÷ 270) on an annual basis	$44.44
Number of units payable to C while C continues to live	× 10
Portion of post-June 1986 investment in the contract allocable to each taxable year of C	$444.40
Portion of post-June 1986 investment in the contract allocable to unit payments ($12,000 ÷ 270) on an annual basis	44.44
Number of units payable to D for D's life after C's death	× 4
Portion of post-June 1986 investment in the contract allocable to each taxable year of D	$177.78
Total computation:	
Total portion of the investment in the contract allocable to each taxable year of C ($728.60 + $444.40)	$1,173.00
Total portion of the investment in the contract allocable to each taxable year of D ($291.44 + $177.78)	$469.22

Example (6). Assume that taxpayer C in example (4) receives payments for four years which are at least as large as the portion of the investment in the contract allocable to such years, but in the fifth year receives a total of only $600 rather than the $1,037 allocable to such year. C is 65 and D is 62 at the beginning of the first monthly period for which an amount is payable in the sixth taxable year. C makes the election in that year provided under paragraph (d)(3) of § 1.72-4. The difference between the portion of the investment in the contract allocable to the fifth year and the amount actually received in that year is $437 ($1,037 with respect to the joint and survivor annuity element, since the appropriate multiple from Table VI of § 1.72-9, 26.5, multiplied by the number of units payable, in effect, as a joint and survivor annuity yields this result (4 × 26.0). C's appropriate multiple from Table V of § 1.72-9 for the six units which will cease to be paid at C's death is 20.0, and the number of unit payments anticipatable with respect to C alone is 120 (6 × 20). The total number of unit payments anticipatable is, therefore, 226 (120 plus 106). Dividing the difference previously found ($437) by the total number of unit payments thus determined (226) indicates that C will have an additional allocation of the investment in the contract of $19.30 to the sixth and every succeeding full taxable year (10 units × $1.93), and D will have an additional allocation of the investment in the contract of $7.72 (4 units × $1.93) to each taxable year in which D receives 12 monthly payments subsequent to the death of C. The total allocable to each taxable year of C is, therefore, $1,056.30, and that allocable to each taxable year of D will be $422.52.

Example (7). If, in example (6), C had died at the end of the fourth year, in the fifth year D would have received a payment of $240 (that portion of the $600 that C would have received which is in the same ratio that 4 units bear to 10 units) and would thus have received $174.80 less than the portion of the investment in the contract allocable to each of D's taxable years. In these circumstances, D would be entitled to elect to redetermine the portion of the investment in the contract allocable to the taxable year of election and all subsequent years. The new amount allocable thereto would be found by dividing the $174.80 difference by D's life expectancy as of the first day of the first period for which D received an amount as an annuity in the sixth year of the annuity contract, and adding the result to D's originally determined allocation of $414.80.

(c) Expected return for term certain. In the case of a contract providing for specific periodic payments which are to be paid for a term certain such as a fixed number of months or years, without regard to life expectancy, the expected return is determined by multiplying the fixed number of years or months for which payments are to be made on or after the annuity starting date by the amount of the payment provided in the contract for each such period.

(d) Expected return with respect to amount certain. In the case of contracts involving no life or lives as a measurement of their duration, but under which a determinable total amount is to be paid in installments of lesser amounts paid at periodic intervals, the expected return shall be the total amount guaranteed. If an amount is to be paid periodically until a fund plus interest at a fixed rate is exhausted, but further payments may be made thereafter because of earnings at a higher interest rate, this paragraph shall apply to the total amount anticipatable as a result of the amount of the fund plus the fixed interest thereon. Any amount which may be paid as the result of earnings at a greater interest rate shall be disregarded in determining the expected return. If such an amount is later received, it shall be considered an amount not received as an annuity after the annuity starting date. See paragraph (b)(2) of § 1.72-11.

(e) Expected return where two or more annuity elements providing for fixed payments are acquired for a single consideration. *(1)* In the case of a contract described in paragraph (a)(2) of § 1.72-2, which provides for specified payments to be made under two or more annuity elements, the expected return shall be found for the contract as a whole by aggregating the expected returns found with respect to each annuity element. If individual life annuity elements are involved (including joint and survivor annuities where the primary annuitant died before January 1, 1954) the expected return for each of them shall be determined in the manner prescribed in paragraph (a) of this section. If joint and survivor annuity elements are involved, the expected return for such elements shall be determined under the appropriate subparagraph of paragraph (b) of this section. If terms certain or amounts certain are involved, the expected returns for such elements shall be determined under paragraph (c) or (d) of this section, respectively.

(2) The aggregate expected return found in accordance with the rules set forth in subparagraph (1) of this paragraph shall constitute the expected return for the contract as a whole. The investment in the contract shall be divided by the amount thus determined to obtain the exclusion ratio for the contract as a whole. This exclusion ratio shall be applied to all amounts received as a annuity under the contract by any recipient (in accordance with the provisions of § 1.72-4), except in the case of amounts received by a surviving annuitant under a joint and survivor annuity element to which the provisions of section 72(i) and paragraph (b)(3) of this section would apply if it were a separate contract. See subparagraph (3) of this paragraph.

(3) In the case of a contract providing two or more annuity elements, one of which is a joint and survivor annuity element of the type described in section 72(i) and paragraph (b)(3) of this section, the general exclusion ratio for the contract as a whole, for the purpose of computations with respect to all the other annuity elements shall be determined in

accordance with the principles of subparagraphs (1) and (2) of this paragraph. A special exclusion ratio shall thereafter be determined for surviving annuitant receiving payments under the annuity element described in section 72(i) and paragraph (b)(3) of this section by using the investment in the contract and the expected return determined in accordance with the provisions of paragraph (b)(3) of this section.

(4) In the case of a contract providing for payments to be made to two persons in the manner described in paragraph (b)(6) of this section, the expected return is to be computed as though there were two joint and survivor annuities under the same contract, in the following manner. First, the multiple appropriate to the ages (as of the annuity starting date) and, if applicable, sexes of the annuitants involved shall be found in Table II or VI (whichever is applicable) of § 1.72-9 and adjusted, if necessary, in the manner described in paragraph (a)(2) of this section. Second, the multiple so found shall be applied to the sum of the payments to be made each year to both annuitants. The result is the expected return for the contract as a whole.

(5) For rules relating to expected return where two or more annuity elements are acquired for a single consideration and one or more of such elements does not specify a fixed payment for each period, see paragraph (f) of this section.

(f) Expected return with respect to obligations providing for payments described in paragraph (b)(3) of § 1.72-2. *(1)* If a contract to which section 72 applies provides only for payments to be made in a manner described in paragraph (b)(3) of § 1.72-2, the expected return for such contract as a whole shall be an amount equal to the investment in the contract found in accordance with section 72(c)(1) and § 1.72-6, as adjusted for any refund feature in accordance with § 1.72-7.

(2) If a contract to which section 72 applies provides for annuity elements, one or more of which (but not all) provide for payments to be made in a manner described in paragraph (b)(3) of § 1.72-2:

(i) With respect to the portion of the contract providing for annuity elements to which paragraph (b)(3) of § 1.72-2 does not apply, the expected return shall be the aggregate of the expected returns found for each of such elements in accordance with the appropriate paragraph of this section; and

(ii) With respect to all annuity elements to which paragraph (b)(3) of § 1.72-2 does apply, the expected return for all such elements shall be an amount equal to the portion of the investment in the contract allocable to such elements in accordance with the provisions of paragraph (e)(2)(ii) of § 1.72-4 and paragraph (b)(3)(ii)(b) of § 1.72-6.

(g) Expected return with respect to contracts subject to § 1.72-6(d). In the case of a contract to which § 1.72-6(d) (relating to contracts in which amounts were invested both before July 1, 1986, and after June 30, 1986) applies, an expected return is computed using the multiples in Tables I through IV of § 1.72-9 with respect to the pre-July 1986 investment in the contract and a second expected return is computed using the multiples in Tables V through VIII of § 1.72-9 with respect to the post-June 1986 investment in the contract.

T.D. 6211, 11/14/56, amend T.D. 8115, 12/16/86.

---

§ 1.72-6 Investment in the contract.

Caution: The Treasury has not yet amended Reg § 1.72-6 to reflect changes made by P.L. 108-357.

(a) General rule. *(1)* For the purpose of computing the "investment in the contract", it is first necessary to determine the "aggregate amount of premiums or other consideration paid" for such contract. See section 72(c)(1). This determination is made as of the later of the annuity starting date of the contract or the date on which an amount is first received thereunder as an annuity. The amount so found is then reduced by the sum of the following amounts in order to find the investment in the contract:

(i) The total amount of any return of premiums or dividends received (including unrepaid loans or dividends applied against the principal or interest on such loans) on or before the date on which the foregoing determination is made, and

(ii) The total of any other amounts received with respect to the contract on or before such date which were excludable from the gross income of the recipient under the income tax law applicable at the time of receipt.

Amounts to which subdivision (ii) of this subparagraph applies shall include, for example, amounts considered to be return of premiums or other consideration paid under section 22(b)(2) of the Internal Revenue Code of 1939 and amounts considered to be an employer-provided death benefit under section 22(b)(1)(B) of such Code. For rules relating to the extent to which an employee or his beneficiary may include employer contributions in the aggregate amount of premiums or other consideration paid, see § 1.72-8. If the aggregate amount of premiums or other consideration paid for the contract includes amounts for which deductions were allowed under section 404 as contributions on behalf of a self-employed individual, such amounts shall not be included in the investment in the contract.

(2) For the purpose of subparagraph (1) of this paragraph, amounts received subsequent to the receipt of an amount as an annuity or subsequent to the annuity starting date, whichever is the later, shall be disregarded. See, however, § 1.72-11.

(3) The application of this paragraph may be illustrated by the following examples:

Example (1). In 1950, B purchased an annuity contract for $10,000 which was to provide him with an annuity of $1,000 per year for life. He received $1,000 in each of the years 1950, 1951, 1952, and 1953, prior to the annuity starting date (January 1, 1954). Under the Internal Revenue Code of 1939, $300 of each of these payments (3 percent of $10,000) was includible in his gross income, and the remaining $700 was excludable therefrom during each of the taxable years mentioned. In computing B's investment in the contract as of January 1, 1954, the total amount excludable from his gross income during the years 1950 through 1953 ($2,800) must be subtracted from the consideration paid ($10,000). Accordingly, B's investment in the contract as of January 1, 1954, is $7,200 ($10,000 less $2,800).

Example (2). In 1945, C contracted for an annuity to be paid to him beginning December 31, 1960. In 1945 and in each successive year until 1960, he paid a premium of $5,000. Assuming he receives no payments of any kind under the contract until the date on which he receives the first annual payment as an annuity (December 31, 1960), his investment in the contract as of the annuity starting date (December 31, 1959) will be $75,000 ($5,000 paid each year for the 15 years from 1945 to 1959, inclusive).

Example (3). Assume the same facts as in example (2), except that prior to the annuity starting date C has already received from the insurer dividends of $1,000 each in 1949, 1954, and 1959, such dividends not being includible in his gross income in any of those years. C's investment in the contract, as of the annuity starting date, will then be $72,000 ($75,000 – $3,000).

(b) Allocation of the investment in the contract where two or more annuity elements are acquired for a single consideration. *(1)* In the case of a contract described in § 1.72-2(a)(2) which provides for two or more annuity elements, the investments in the contract determined under paragraph (a) shall be allocated to each of the annuity elements in the ratio that the expected return under each annuity element bears to the aggregate of the expected returns under all the annuity elements. The exclusion ratio for the contract as a whole shall be determined by dividing the investment in the contract (after adjustment for the present value of any or all refund features) by the aggregate of the expected returns under all the annuity elements. This may be illustrated by the following examples:

Example (1). If a contract provides for annuity payments of $1,000 per year for life (with no refund feature) to both A and B, a male and female, respectively, each 70 years of age as of the annuity starting date, such contract is acquired for consideration of $19,575 (without regard to whether paid by A, B, or both), and there is no post-June 1986 investment in the contract, the investment in the contract shall be allocated by determining the exclusion ratio for the contract as a whole in the following manner:

Expectancy of A under Table 1 and § 1.72-5(a)(2), 11.8 (12.1 – 0.5), multiplied by $1,000	$11,600
Expectancy of B computed in a similar manner ($1,000 × 14.5 [15.0 – 0.5])	14,500
Total expected return	26,100

The exclusion ratio for both A and B is then $19,575 ÷ $26,100, or 75 percent. A and B shall each exclude from gross income three-fourths ($750) of each $1,000 annual payment received and shall include the remaining one-fourth ($250) of each $1,000 annual payment received in gross income.

Example (2). Assume the same facts as in example (1) except that of the total investment in the contract of $19,575, the pre-July 1986 investment in the contract is $10,000. If the election described in § 1.72-6(d)(6) is made with respect to the contract, the investment in the contract shall be allocated by determining an exclusion ratio for the contract as a whole based on separately computed exclusion ratios with respect to the pre-July 1986 investment in the contract and the post-June 1986 investment in the contract in the following manner:

Expectancy of A under Table I and § 1.72-5(a)(2), 11.6 (12.1 – 0.5), multiplied by $1,000	$11,600
Plus: Expectancy of B under Table I and § 1.72-5(a)(2), 14.5 (15.0 – 0.5), multiplied by $1,000	$14,500
Pre-July 1986 expected return	$26,100
Plus: Expectancy of A under Table V and § 1.72-5(a)(2), 15.5 (16.0 – 0.5), multiplied by $1,000	$15,500
Expectancy of B under Table V and § 1.72-5(a)(2), 15.5 (16.0 – 0.5), multiplied by $1,000	$15,500
Post-June 1986 expected return	$31,000
Pre-July 1986 exclusion ratio ($10,000 ÷ $26,100)	38.3
Post-June 1986 exclusion ratio ($9,575 ÷ 31,000)	30.9

A and B shall each exclude from gross income $692 (38.3 percent of $1,000 + 30.9 percent of $1,000) of each $1,000 payment and include the remaining $308 in gross income

(2) In the case of a contract providing for specified annual annuity payments to be made to two persons during their joint lives and the payment of the aggregate of the two individual payments to the survivor for his life, the investment in the contract shall be allocated in accordance with the provisions of subparagraph (1) of this paragraph. For this purpose, the investment in the contract (without regard to the fact that differing amounts may have been contributed by the two annuitants) shall be divided by the expected return determined in accordance with paragraph (e)(4) of § 1.72-5. The resulting exclusion ratio shall then be applied to any amounts received as an annuity by either annuitant.

(3) In the case of a contract providing two or more annuity elements, one or more of which provides for payments to be made in a manner described in paragraph (b)(3) of § 1.72-2, the investment in the contract shall be allocated to the various annuity elements in the following manner.

(i) If all the annuity elements provide for payments to be made in the manner described in paragraph (b)(3) of § 1.72-2, the investment in the contract shall be allocated on the basis of the amounts received by each recipient by apportioning the amount determined to be excludable under that section to each recipient in the same ratio as the total of the amounts received by him in the taxable year bears to the total of the amounts received by all recipients during the same period; and

(ii) If one or more, but not all, of the annuity elements provide for payments to be made in a manner described in paragraph (b)(3) of § 1.72-2:

(a) With respect to all annuity elements to which that section does not apply, the investment in the contract for all such elements shall be the portion of the investment in the contract as a whole (found in accordance with the provisions of this section) which is properly allocable to all such elements; and

(b) With respect to all annuity elements to which paragraph (b)(3) of § 1.72-2 does apply, the investment in the contract for all such elements shall be the investment in the contract as a whole (found in accordance with the provisions of this section) as reduced by the portion thereof determined under (a) of this subdivision.

For the purpose of determining, pursuant to (a) of this subdivision, the portion of the investment in the contract as a whole properly allocable to a particular annuity element, reference shall be made to the present value of such annuity element determined in accordance with paragraph (e)(1)(iii)(b) of § 1.101-2.

(iii) In the case of a contract to which paragraph (d) of this section applies, this paragraph (b) is applied in the manner prescribed in paragraph (d) and, in particular, paragraph (d)(5)(v) of this section.

(c) Special rules. *(1)* For the special rule for determining the investment in the contract for a surviving annuitant in cases where the prior annuitant of a joint and survivor annuity contract died in 1951, 1952, or 1953, see paragraph (b)(3) of § 1.72-5.

(2) For special rules relating to the determination of the investment in the contract where employer contributions are involved, see § 1.72-8. See also paragraph (b) of § 1.72-16 for a special rule relating to the determination of the premi-

ums or other consideration paid for a contract where an employee is taxable on the premiums paid for life insurance protection that is purchased by and considered to be a distribution from an exempt employees' trust.

(3) For the determination of an adjustment in investment in the contract in cases where a contract contains a refund feature, see § 1.72-7.

(4) In the case of "face-amount certificates" described in section 72(1), the amount of consideration paid for purposes of computing the investment in the contract shall include any amount added to the holder's basis by reason of section 1232(a)(3)(E) (relating to basis adjustment for amount of original issue discount ratably included in gross income as interest under section 1232(a)(3)).

(d) Pre-July 1986 and post-June 1986 investment in the contract. *(1)* This paragraph (d) applies to an annuity contract If—

(i) The investment in the contract includes a pre-July 1986 investment in the contract and a post-June 1966 investment in the contract (both as defined in § 1.72-6(d)(3));

(ii) The use of a multiple found in Tables I through VIII of § 1.72-9 is required to determine the expected return under the contract; and

(iii) The election described in paragraph (d)(6) of this section is made with respect to the contract.

(2) In the case of annuity contract to which this paragraph (d) applies—

(i) All computations required to determine the amount excludable from gross income shall be performed separately with respect to the pre-July 1986 investment in the contract and the post-June 1986 investment in the contract as if each such amount were the entire investment in the contract;

(ii) The multiples in Tables I through IV shall be used for computations involving the pre-July 1986 investment in the contract and the multiples in Tables V through VIII shall be used for computations involving the post-June 1986 investment in the contract; and

(iii) The amount excludable from gross income shall be the sum of the amounts determined under the separate computations required by paragraph (d)(2)(i) of this section.

(3) For purposes of the regulations under section 72, the pre-July 1986 investment in the contract and post-June 1986 investment in the contract are determined in accordance with the following rules:

(i) (A) Except as provided in § 1.72-9, if the annuity starting date of the contract occurs before July 1, 1986, the pre-July 1986 investment in the contract is the total investment in the contract as of the annuity starting date;

(B) Except as provided in § 1.72-9, if the annuity starting date of the contract occurs after June 30, 1986, and the contract does not provide for a disqualifying form of payment or settlement, the pre-July 1986 investment in the contract is the investment in the contract computed as of June 30, 1986, as if June 30, 1986, had been the later of the annuity starting date of the contract or the date on which an amount is first received thereunder as an annuity;

(C) If the annuity starting date of the contract occurs after June 30, 1986, and the contract provides, at the option of the annuitant or of any other person (including, in the case of an employee's annuity, an option exercisable only by, or with the consent of, the employer), for a disqualifying form of payment or settlement, the pre-July 1986 investment in the contract is zero (i.e., the total investment in the contract is post-June 1986 investment in the contract).

(ii) The post-June 1986 investment in the contract is the amount by which the total investment in the contract as of the annuity starting date exceeds the pre-July 1986 investment in the contract.

(iii) For purposes of paragraph (d)(3)(i) of this section, a disqualifying form of payment or settlement is any form of payment or settlement (whether or not selected) that permits the receipt of amounts under the contract in a form other than a life annuity. For example, each of the following options provides for a disqualifying form of payment or settlement:

(A) An option to receive a lump sum in full discharge of the obligation under the contract.

(B) An option to receive an amount under the contract after June 30, 1986, and before the annuity starting date.

(C) An option to receive an annuity for a period certain.

(D) An option to receive payments under a refund feature (within the meaning of paragraphs (b) and (c) of § 1.72-7) that is substantially equivalent to an annuity for a period certain.

(E) An option to receive a temporary life annuity (within the meaning of § 1.72-5(a)(3)) that is substantially equivalent to an annuity for a period certain.

An option to receive alternative forms of life annuity is not a disqualifying option for purposes of paragraph (d)(3)(i) of this section. Thus, if the sole options provided under a contract are a single life annuity and a joint and survivor life annuity, paragraph (d)(3)(i)(C) of this section does not apply to such contract.

(iv) For purposes of paragraph (d)(3)(iii) of this section, a refund feature is substantially equivalent to an annuity for a period certain if its value determined under Table VII of § 1.72-9 exceeds 50 percent. Similarly, a temporary life annuity is substantially equivalent to an annuity for a period certain if the multiple determined under Table VIII of § 1.72-9 exceeds 50 percent of the maximum duration of the annuity.

(4) In any separate computation under this paragraph (d) only the applicable portion of other amounts (such as the total expected return under the contract, or the total amount guaranteed under the contract as of the annuity starting date) shall be taken into account if the use of the entire amount in such computation is inconsistent with the use in the computation of only a portion of the investment in the contract. For example, such use is generally inconsistent if the computation requires a comparison of the investment in the contract and such other amount for the purpose of using the greater (or lesser) amount or the difference between the two. For purposes of the first sentence of this paragraph (d)(4), the applicable portion is the amount that bears the same ratio to the entire amount as the pre-July 1986, investment in the contract or the post-June 1986 investment in the contract, whichever is applicable, bears to the total investment in the contract as of the annuity starting date.

(5) Application to particular computations. (i) In the case of a contract to which this paragraph (d) applies, the exclusion ratio for purposes of § 1.72-4(a) is the sum of the exclusion ratios separately computed in accordance with this paragraph (d). The exclusion ratio with respect to the pre-July 1986 investment in the contract is determined by dividing the pre-July 1986 investment in the contract by the expected return as found under § 1.72-5 by applying the appropriate multiples of Tables I through IV of § 1.72-9. Similarly, the exclusion ratio with respect to the post-June 1986 investment in the contract is determined by dividing

the post-June 1986 investment in the contract by the expected return as found under § 1.72-5 by applying the appropriate multiples in Tables V through VIII of § 1.72-9.

(ii) The applicability of § 1.72-4(d)(2) to a contract to which this paragraph (d) applies shall be determined separately with respect to the post-June 1986 investment in the contract and the pre-July 1986 investment in the contract and in each such determination only the applicable portion of the total expected return under the contract shall be taken into account. If § 1.72-4(d)(2) applies with respect to either such investment in the contract, the separately computed exclusion ratio shall be considered to be the applicable portion of 100 percent.

(iii) If § 1.72-4(d)(3) applies to a contract to which this paragraph (d) applies—

(A) The applicable portions (as defined in paragraph (d)(4) of this section) of payments received under the contract for a taxable year shall be separately computed;

(B) The pre-July 1986 investment in the contract and the post-June 1986 investment in the contract shall be separately allocated to the taxable year; and

(C) The separate applicable portions of the payments received under the contract for the taxable year shall be considered to be amounts received as an annuity (for which the exclusion ratio is 100 percent) only to the extent they do not exceed the portions of the corresponding investments in the contract which are properly allocable to that year.

See the example in § 1.72-4(d)(3)(v).

(iv) If § 1.72-4(e) applies to a contract to which this paragraph (d) applies, the exclusion ratio shall be separately computed with respect to the pre-July 1986 investment in the contract and the post-June 1986 investment in the contract. For purposes of the separate computations under § 1.72-4(e)(2)(ii), only the applicable portion of payments received shall be taken into account and the exclusion ratio (100%) shall be applied to the separately computed portion allocated to each participant.

(v) If paragraph (b)(3) of this section applies to a contract to which this paragraph (d) applies, separate allocations are required with respect to the pre-July 1986 investment in the contract and the post-June 1986 investment in the contract. For purposes of the separate computations required to determine the portion of the investment in the contract properly allocable to a particular annuity element, only the applicable portion of the present value of the annuity element determined in accordance with § 1.101-2(e)(1)(iii)(b) is taken into account.

(vi) If § 1.72-7 applies to a contract to which this paragraph (d) applies, separate computations are required to determine the adjustment to the pre-July 1986 investment in the contract and the post-June 1986 investment in the contract. For purposes of such separate computations, only the applicable portions of the amounts described in § 1.72-7(b)(3)(ii), (c)(1)(ii)(B), (c)(2)(vii)(B), and (d)(1)(ii) are taken into account. Similarly, in the case of computations with respect to the guarantee of a specified amount under § 1.72-7(d)(1), only the applicable portion of such amount is taken into account.

(6) This paragraph (d) applies to a contract only if the first taxpayer to receive an amount as an annuity under the contract elects to perform separate computations with respect to the pre-July 1986 investment in the contract and the post-June 1986 investment in the contract as if each such amount were the entire investment in contract. If two or more annuitants receive an amount as an annuity under the contract at the same time (such as under a joint-and-last-survivorship annuity contract), and election by one of the annuitants is treated as an election by each of the annuitants. The election is made by attaching a statement to the first return filed by the taxpayer for the first taxable year in which an amount is received as an annuity under the contract. The statement must indicate that the taxpayer is electing to apply the provisions of paragraph (d) of § 1.72-6, and must also contain the name, address, and taxpayer identification number of each annuitant under the contract, and the amount of the pre-July 1986 investment in the contract.

(7) If the investment in the contract includes a post-June 1986 investment in the contract and the election described in paragraph (d)(6) of this section is not made—

(i) The amount excludable from gross income shall be determined without regard to the separate computations described in this paragraph (d); and

(ii) Only the multiples found in Tables V through VIII shall be used in determining the amount excludable from gross income.

T.D. 6211, 11/14/56, amend T.D. 6676, 9/16/63, T.D. 7311, 4/1/74, T.D. 8115, 12/16/86.

PAR. 2. In § 1.72-6, paragraph (e) is added to read as follows:

Proposed § 1.72-6 Investment in the contract. [*For Preamble, see ¶ 152,809*]

* * * * *

(e) Certain annuity contracts received in exchange for property. *(1) In general.* If an annuity contract is received in an exchange subject to § 1.1001-1(j), the aggregate amount of premiums or other consideration paid for the contract equals the amount realized attributable to the annuity contract, determined according to § 1.1001-1(j).

(2) Effective date. (i) In general. Except as provided in paragraph (e)(2)(ii), this paragraph (e) is applicable for annuity contracts received after October 18, 2006 in an exchange subject to § 1.1001-1(j).

(ii) This paragraph (e) is applicable for annuity contracts received after April 18, 2007 in an exchange subject to § 1.1001-1(j) if the following conditions are met—

(A) The issuer of the annuity contract is an individual;

(B) The obligations under the annuity contract are not secured, either directly or indirectly; and

(C) The property transferred in exchange for the annuity contract is not subsequently sold or otherwise disposed of by the transferee during the two-year period beginning on the date of the exchange. For purposes of this provision, a disposition includes without limitation a transfer to a trust (whether a grantor trust, a revocable trust, or any other trust) or to any other entity even if solely owned by the transferor.

§ 1.72-7 Adjustment in investment where a contract contains a refund feature.

(a) Definition of a contract containing a refund feature. A contract to which section 72 applies, contains a refund feature if:

(1) The total amount receivable as an annuity under such contract depends, in whole or in part, on the continuing life of one or more persons,

(2) The contract provides for payments to be made to a beneficiary or the estate of an annuitant on or after the death of the annuitant if a specified amount or a stated number of

payments has not been paid to the annuitant or annuitants prior to death, and

(3) Such payments are in the nature of a refund of the consideration paid. See paragraph (c)(1) of § 1.72-11.

(b) Adjustment of investment for the refund feature in the case of a single life annuity. Where a single life annuity contract to which section 72 applies contains a refund feature and the special rule of paragraph (d) of this section does not apply, the investment in the contract shall be adjusted in the following manner:

(1) Determine the number of years necessary for the guaranteed amount to be fully paid by dividing the maximum amount guaranteed as of the annuity starting date by the amount to be received annually under the contract to the extent such amount reduces the guaranteed amount. The number of years should be stated in terms of the nearest whole year, considering for this purpose a fraction of one-half or more as an additional whole year.

(2) Consult Table III or VII (whichever is applicable) of § 1.72-9 for the appropriate percentage under the whole number of years found in subparagraph (1) of this paragraph and the age (as of the annuity starting date) and, if applicable, sex of the annuitant.

(3) Multiply the percentage found in subparagraph (2) of this paragraph by whichever of the following is the smaller: (i) The investment in the contract found in accordance with § 1.72-6 or (ii) the total amount guaranteed as of the annuity starting date.

(4) Subtract the amount found in subparagraph (3) of this paragraph from the investment in the contract found in accordance with § 1.72-6.

The resulting amount is the investment in the contract adjusted for the present value of the refund feature without discount for interest and is to be used in determining the exclusion ratio to be applied to the payments received as an annuity. The percentage found in Tables III or VII shall not be adjusted in a manner described in paragraph (a)(2) of § 1.72-5. These principles may be illustrated by the following examples:

Example (1). On January 1, 1954, a husband, age 65, purchased for $21,053, an immediate installment refund annuity payable $100 per month for life. The contract provided that in the event the husband did not live long enough to recover the full purchase price, payments were to be made to his wife until the total payments under the contract equaled the purchase price. The investment in the contract adjusted for the purpose of determining the exclusion ratio is computed in the following manner:

Cost of the annuity contract (investment in the contract, unadjusted	$21,053
Amount to be received annually	$ 1,200
Number of years for which payment guaranteed ($21,053 divided by $1,200)	17.5
Rounded to nearest whole number of years	18
Percentage located in Table III for age 65 (age of the annuitant as of the annuity starting date) and 18 (the number of whole years) (percent)	30
Subtract value of the refund feature to the nearest dollar (30 percent of $21,053)	$ 6,316
Investment in the contract adjusted for the present value of the refund feature without discount for interest	$14,737

Example (2). Assume the same facts as in example (1), except that the total investment in the contract was made after June 30, 1986. The investment in the contract adjusted for the purpose of determining the exclusion ratio is computed as follows:

Cost of the annuity contract (investment in the contract, unadjusted	$21,053
Amount to be received annually	$ 1,200
Number of years for which payment guaranteed ($21,053 ÷ $1,200)	17.5
Rounded to nearest whole number of years	18
Percentage in Table VII for age 65 and 18 years (percent)	15
Subtract value of the refund feature to the nearest dollar (15 percent of $21,053)	$ 3,158
Investment in the contract adjusted for the present value of the refund feature without discount for interest	$17,895

Example (3). Assume the same facts as in example (1), except that the pre-July 1986 investment in the contract is $10,000 and the post-June 1986 investment in the contract is $11,053. If the annuitant makes the election described in § 1.72-6(d)(6), separate computations must be performed pursuant to § 1.72-6(d) to determine the adjusted investment in the contract. The pre-July 1986 investment in the contract and the post-June 1986 investment in the contract adjusted for the purpose of determining the exclusion ratios are, respectively, $7,000 and $9,395, determined as follows:

Pre-July 1986 investment in the contract (unadjusted)	$10,000
Pre-July 1986 portion of the amount to be received annually ($10,000/$21,053 × $1,200)	$570.00
Number of years for which payment guaranteed ($10,000 ÷ $570)	17.50
Rounded to nearest whole number of years	18
Percentage in Table III for age 65 and 18 years (percent)	30
Subtract value of refund feature to nearest dollar (30 percent of $10,000)	$ 3,000
Pre-July 1986 investment in the contract adjusted for the present value of the refund feature without discount for interest	$ 7,000
Post-June 1986 investment in the contract (unadjusted)	$11,053
Post-June 1986 portion of the amount to be received annually ($11,053 ÷ $21,053 × $1,200)	$ 630
Number of years for which payment guaranteed ($11,053 / $630)	17.54
Rounded to nearest whole number of years	18
Percentage in Table VII for age 65 and 18 years (percent)	15
Subtract value of the refund feature to the nearest dollar (15 percent of $11,053)	$ 1,658
Post-June 1986 investment in the contract adjusted for the present value of the refund feature without discount for interest	$ 9,395

If, in the above examples, the guaranteed amount had exceeded the investment in the contract (or applicable portion thereof), the percentage found in Table III or VII (whichever is applicable) should have been applied to the lesser of these amounts since any excess of the guaranteed amount over the investment in the contract (as found under § 1.72-6) would not have constituted a refund of premiums or other consideration paid. In such a case, however, a different multiple might have been obtained from Table III or VII (whichever is applicable) since the number of years for which payments were guaranteed would have been greater.

(c) Adjustment of investment for the refund feature in the case of a joint and survivor annuity. *(1)* Except as provided in paragraph (c)(2) of this section, if a joint and survivor annuity contract described in paragraph (b)(1), (2) or (6) of § 1.72-5 contains a refund feature and the special rule of paragraph (d) of this section does not apply, the investment in the contract shall be adjusted in the following manner:

(i) Find the percentage determined under the following formula:

$$V = \frac{\sum_{t=0}^{N-1} \frac{d_{x+t}}{l_x} \left[(N - \tfrac{1}{2} - t) - P \left(\frac{T_{y+t+1} - T_{y+t+M+1}}{l_y} \right) \right]}{N}$$

In which:

v =The percentage, rounded to the nearest whole percent,
x =The age at the nearest birthday of the primary annuitant,
y =The age at the nearest birthday of the survivor annuitant,
N =The guaranteed amount divided by the annual annuity payable to the primary annuitant, rounded to the nearest integer,
P =The annual annuity continued to the survivor annuitant divided by the annual annuity payable to the primary annuitant,

$M = \frac{N - 1/2 - t}{P}$

l_x =the number of survivors at age x,
d =$l_x - l_x{+}1$, and

$$T_x = \sum_{s=0}^{\infty} \tfrac{1}{2} (l_{x+s} + l_{x+s+1})$$

(ii) Multiply the percentage found in paragraph (c)(1)(i) of this section by the lesser of (A) the investment in the contract found in accordance with § 1.72-6, or (B) the total amount guaranteed as of the annuity starting date.

(iii) Subtract the amount found in paragraph (c)(1)(ii) of this section from the investment in the contract found in accordance with § 1.72-6.

In the case of a contract providing for payments to be made to two persons in the manner described in paragraph (b)(6) of § 1.72-5, this paragraph (c)(1) is applied as though the older person were the primary annuitant and the younger person were the survivor annuitant. For purposes of this paragraph (c)(1), the number of survivors at age$_x$(l_x) is determined under the following table:

x	lx
5	1000000.
6	999729.
7	999493.
8	999284.
9	999069.
10	998849.
11	998620.
12	998382.
13	998135.
14	997876.
15	997606.
16	997322.
17	997025.
18	996714.
19	996387.
20	996044.
21	995684.
22	995304.
23	994905.
24	994484.
25	994041.
26	993573.
27	993080.
28	992563.
29	992024.
30	991461.
31	990876.
32	990269.
33	989638.
34	988984.
35	988303.
36	987593.
37	986846.
38	986055.
39	985210.
40	984298.
41	983310.
42	982230.
43	981046.
44	979742.
45	978302.
46	976709.
47	974945.
48	972992.
49	970832.
50	968447.
51	966000.
52	963313.
53	960375.
54	957175.
55	953705.
56	949954.
57	945912.
58	941568.
59	936908.
60	931903.
61	926451.
62	920540.
63	914090.
64	907011.
65	899221.
66	890428.
67	880797.
68	870298.
69	858904.
70	846565.
71	832316.
72	816861.

73	800078.
74	781837.
75	762012.
76	740743.
77	717689.
78	692780.
79	665977.
80	637260.
81	607339.
82	575531.
83	541919.
84	506647.
85	469931.
86	432459.
87	394138.
88	355393.
89	316712.
90	278663.
91	242020.
92	207150.
93	174602.
94	144828.
95	118151.
96	94871.7
97	74863.6
98	58042.2
99	44176.1
100	32956.4
101	24044.8
102	17104.1
103	11815.5
104	7886.75
105	5054.94
106	3086.95
107	1778.82
108	955.465
109	470.955
110	208.668
111	80.7889
112	26.2340
113	6.69620
114	1.19385
115	.111460

(2) If the multiples in Tables I through IV of § 1.72-9 are used to determine any portion of the expected return under a contract described in paragraph (c)(1) of this section, only the post-June 1986 investment in the contract (if any) shall be adjusted in the manner described in paragraph (c)(1) of this section, and the pre-July 1986 investment in the contract shall, in the case of a contract described in paragraph (b)(1) or (6) of § 1.72-5, be adjusted in the following manner:

(i) Determine the number of years necessary for the guaranteed amount to be fully paid by dividing the maximum amount guaranteed as of the annuity starting date by the amount to be received annually under the contract. The number of years should be stated in terms of the nearest whole year, considering for this purpose a fraction of one-half or more as an additional whole year.

(ii) Consult Table III of § 1.72-9 for the appropriate percentages under the whole number of years found in subdivision (i) of this subparagraph and the age (as of the annuity starting date) and sex of each annuitant. If the annuitants are not of the same sex, substitute for the female annuitant a male annuitant 5 years younger, or for the male annuitant a female annuitant 5 years older, so that Table III will be entered in both cases with the ages of annuitants of the same sex.

(iii) Find the sum of the two percentages found in accordance with subdivision (ii) of this subparagraph.

(iv) To the age of the elder of the two annuitants (as determined under subdivision (ii) of this subparagraph), add the number of years (indicated in the table below) opposite the number of years by which such annuitants' ages differ:

Number of years difference in age (2 male annuitants or 2 female annuitants)	Addition to older age in years
0 to 1, inclusive	9
2 to 3, inclusive	8
4 to 5, inclusive	7
6 to 8, inclusive	6
9 to 11, inclusive	5
12 to 15, inclusive	4
16 to 20, inclusive	3
21 to 27, inclusive	2
28 to 42, inclusive	1
Over 42	0

(v) Consult Table III for the appropriate percentage under the whole number of years found in subdivision (i) of this subparagraph and the age and sex of the elder annuitant as adjusted under subdivision (iv) of this subparagraph.

(vi) Subtract the percentage obtained in subdivision (v) of this subparagraph from the sum of the percentages found under subdivision (iii) of this subparagraph. If the result is less than one, subdivisions (vii) and (viii) of this subparagraph shall be disregarded and no adjustment made to the investment in the contract.

(vii) Multiply the percentage found in subdivision (vi) of this subparagraph by whichever of the following is the smaller: (A) the investment in the contract found in accordance with § 1.72-6 or (B) the total amount guaranteed as of the annuity starting date.

(viii) Subtract the amount found in subdivision (vii) of this subparagraph from the investment in the contract found in accordance with § 1.72-6.

(3) The principles of this paragraph (c) may be illustrated by the following examples:

Example (1). Prior to July 1, 1986, Taxpayer A, a 70-year-old male, purchases a joint and last survivor annuity for $33,050. The contract provides for payments of $100 a month to be paid first to himself for life and then to B, his 40-year-old daughter, if she survives him. The contract further provides that in the event both die before ten years' payments have been made, payments will be continued to C, a beneficiary, or to C's estate, until ten years' payments have been made. If there is no post-June 1986 investment in the contract, the investment in the contract adjusted for the purpose of determining the exclusion ratio is computed in the following manner:

Cost of the annuity contract (investment in the contract unadjusted)	$33,050
Guaranteed amount ($1,200 × 10)	$12,000
Percentage in Table III for male, age 70 (or female, age 75) for duration of the guarantee (10)	21
Percentage in Table III for female, age 40 (or male, age 35) for duration of the guarantee (10)	2

Sum of percentage obtained	23
Difference in years of age between two males, aged 70 and 35 (or 2 females, aged 75 and 40)	35
Addition, in years, to older age	1
Percentage in Table III for male one year older than A	22
Difference between percentages obtained (23 percent less 22 percent)	1
Value of the refund feature to the nearest dollar (1 percent of $12,000)	$ 120
Investment in the contract adjusted for present value of the refund feature	$32,930

Example (2). The facts are the same as in example (1), except that the total investment in the contract was made after June 30, 1986, A is 73 years of age, and B is A's 70 year old spouse. The percentage determined under the formula in paragraph (c)(1)(i) of this section is two percent. Thus, the amount determined under paragraph (c)(1)(ii) of this section is $240 (2 percent of $12,000), and the investment in the contract adjusted for the present value of the refund feature is $32,810 ($33,050— $240).

(4) If an annuity described in paragraph (b) of § 1.72-5 contains a refund feature and the manner of determining the adjustment to the investment in the contract (or to any part of such investment) is not prescribed or requires use of the formula in paragraph (c)(1)(i) of this section, the Commissioner will determine the amount of the adjustment upon request. The request must contain the date of birth of each annuitant, the guaranteed amount, the annual annuity payable to each annuitant, and the annuity starting date. Send the request to the Commissioner of Internal Revenue, Attention: OP:E:EP:GA, Washington, D.C. 20224.

(d) Adjustment of investment in the contract where paragraph (b)(3) of § 1.72-2 applies to payments. *(1)* If paragraph (b)(3) of § 1.72-2 applies to payments to be made under a contract and this section also applies because of the provision for a refund feature, an adjustment shall be made to the investment in the contract in accordance with this paragraph before making the computations required by paragraph (d)(3) of § 1.72-4 and paragraph (d)(7) of § 1.72-5. In the case of the guarantee of a specified amount, the adjustment shall be made by applying the appropriate multiple from Table III or VII (whichever is applicable), as otherwise determined under this section, to the investment in the contract or the guaranteed amount, whichever is the lesser. The guarantee period shall be found by dividing the amount guaranteed by the amount determined by placing the payments received during the first taxable year (to guaranteed amount) on an annual basis. Thus, if monthly payments are first received by a taxpayer on a calendar year basis in August, his total payments (to the extent that they reduce the guaranteed amount) for the taxable year would be divided by 5 and multiplied by 12. The guaranteed amount would then be divided by the result of this computation to obtain the guarantee period. If the contract merely guarantees that proceeds from a unit or units of a fund shall be paid for a fixed number of years or the life (or lives) of an annuitant (or annuitants), whichever is the longer, the fixed number of years is the guarantee period. The appropriate percentage in Table III or VII shall be applied to whichever of the following is the smaller: (i) the investment in the contract; or (ii) the product of the payments received in the first taxable year, placed on an annual basis, multiplied by the number of years for which payment of the proceeds of a unit or units is guaranteed.

(2) The principles of this paragraph may be illustrated by the following examples:

Example (1). Taxpayer A, a 50-year-old male purchases for $25,000 a contract which provides for variable monthly payments to be paid to him for his life. The contract also provides that if he should die before receiving payments for fifteen years, payments shall continue according to the original formula to his estate or beneficiary until payments have been made for that period. Beginning with the month of September, A receives payments which total $450 for the first taxable year of receipt. This amount, placed on an annual basis, is $1,350 ($450 divided by 4, or $112.50; $112.50 multiplied by 12, or $1,350). If there is no post-June 1986 investment in the contract, the guaranteed amount is considered to be $20,250 ($1,350 × 15), and the multiple from Table III (found in the same manner as in paragraph (b) of this section), 9 percent, applied to $20,250 (since this amount is less than the investment in the contract), results in a refund adjustment of $1,822.50. The latter amount, subtracted from the investment in the contract of $25,000, results in an adjusted investment in the contract of $23,177.50. If A dies before receiving payments for 15 years and the remaining payments are made to B, his beneficiary, B shall exclude the entire amount of such payments from his gross income until the amounts so received by B, together with the amount received by A and excludable from A's gross income, equal or exceed $25,000. Any excess and any payments thereafter received by B shall be fully includible in gross income.

Example (2). Assume the same facts as in example (1), except that the total investment in the contract was made after June 30, 1986. The applicable multiple found in Table VII is 3 percent. When this is applied to the guaranteed amount of $20,250, it results in a refund adjustment of $607.50. The adjusted investment in the contract in $24,392.50 ($25,000 – $607.50).

(e) Adjustment of the investment in the contract where more than one annuity element is provided for a single consideration. In the case of contract to which paragraph (b) of § 1.72-6 applies for the purpose of allocating the investment in the contract to two or more annuity elements which are provided for a single consideration, if one or more of such elements involves a refund feature, the portion of the investment in the contract properly allocable to each such element shall be adjusted for the refund feature before aggregating all the investments in order to obtain the exclusion ratio which is to apply to the contract as a whole.

Example (1). If taxpayer A, an insured 70 years of age, upon maturity of an endowment policy which cost him a net amount of $86,000, elected a dual settlement consisting of (1) monthly payments for his life aggregating $4,146 per year with 10 years' payments certain, and (2) monthly payments for his 60-year-old brother, B, aggregating $2,820 per year with 20 years' payments certain, the exclusion ratio to be used by both A and B if there is no post-June 1986 investment in the contract would be determined in the following manner:

A's expected return (A's payments per year of $4,146 multiplied by his life expectancy from Table 1 of 12.1)	$ 50,166.60
B's expected return (B's payments per year of $2,820 multiplied by his life expectancy from Table 1 of 18.2)	$ 51,324.00
Sum of expected returns to be used in determining exclusion ratio	$101,490.60

Percentage of total expected return attributable to A's expectancy of the ($50,166.60 – $101,490.60)	49.4
Percentage of total expected return attributable to B's expectancy of the ($51,324 – $101,490.60)	50.6
Portion of investment in the contract allocable to A's annuity (49.4 percent of $86,000)	$ 42,484.00
Portion of investment in the contract allocable to B's annuity (50.6 percent of $86,000)	$ 43,516.00
Value of the refund feature with respect to A's annuity (percentage from Table III for male, age 70, and duration 10, or 21 percent, multiplied by lesser of guaranteed amount and allocable portion of investment in the contract $41,460)	$ 8,707.00
A's allocable portion of the investment in the contract adjusted for refund feature ($42,484 less $8,707.00)	$ 33,777.00
Value of the refund feature with respect to B's annuity (percentage from Table III for male, age 60, and duration 20, or 25 percent, multiplied by lesser of guaranteed amount and allocable portion of investment in the contract, $43,516)	$ 10,879.00
B's allocable portion of the investment in the contract adjusted for refund feature ($43,516 less $10,879.00)	$ 32,637.00
Sum of A's and B's allocable portions of the investment in the contract after adjustment for the refund feature	$ 66,414.00
Exclusion ratio for the contract as a whole (total adjusted investment in the contract, $66,414, divided by the total expected return from above, $101,490.60) (percent)	65.4

Example (2). Assume the same facts as in example (1) except that the total investment in the contract was made after June 30, 1986. The exclusion ratio to be used by both A and B would be 56.9 percent, determined as follows:

A's expected return (A's payments per year of $4,146 multiplied by his life expectancy from Table V of 16.0)	$ 66,336.00
B's expected return (B's payments per year of $2,820 multiplied by his life expectancy from Table V of 24.2)	$ 68,244.00
Sum of expected returns to be used in determining exclusion ratio	$134,580.00
Percentage of total expected return attributable to A's expectancy of life ($66,336.00 ÷ $134,580.00)	49.3
Percentage of total expected return attributable to B's expectancy of life ($68,244.00 ÷ $134,580.00)	50.7
Portion of investment in the contract allocable to A's annuity (49.3 percent of $86,000)	$ 42,398.00
Portion of investment in the contract allocable to B's annuity (50.7 percent of $86,000)	$ 43,602.00
Value of the refund feature with respect to A's annuity (percentage from Table VII for age 70 and duration 10, or 11 percent, multiplied by lesser of the guaranteed amount and allocable portion of investment in the contract, $41,460)	$ 4,560.60
A's allocable portion of the investment in the contract adjusted for refund feature ($42,398 less $4,560.60)	$ 37,837.40
Value of the refund feature with respect to B's annuity (percentage from Table VII for age 60 and duration 20, or 11 percent, multiplied by lesser of guaranteed amount and allocable portion of investment in the contract, $43,602)	$ 4,796.22
B's allocable portion of the investment in the contract adjusted for refund feature ($43,602 less $4,796.22)	$ 38,805.78
Sum of A's and B's allocable portions of the investment in the contract after adjustment for the refund feature	$ 76,643.18
Exclusion ratio for the contract as a whole (total adjusted investment in the contract, $76,643.18, divided by the total expected return from above, $134,580.00) (percent)	56.9

(f) Adjustment of investment in the contract with respect to contracts subject to § 1.72-6(d). In the case of a contract to which § 1.72-6(d) (relating to contracts in which amounts were invested both before July 1, 1986, and after June 30, 1986) applies, this section is applied in the manner prescribed in § 1.72-6(d) and, in particular, § 1.72-6(d)(5)(vi).

T.D. 6211, 11/14/56, amend T.D. 8115, 12/16/86.

§ 1.72-8 Effect of certain employer contributions with respect to premiums or other consideration paid or contributed by an employee.

Caution: The Treasury has not yet amended Reg § 1.72-8 to reflect changes made by P.L. 104-188, P.L. 97-34.

(a) Contributions in the nature of compensation. *(1) Amounts includible in gross income of employee under subtitle A of the Code or prior income tax laws.* Section 72(f) provides that for the purposes of section 72(c), (d), and (e), amounts contributed by an employer for the benefit of an employee or his beneficiaries shall constitute consideration paid or contributed by the employee to the extent that such amounts were includible in the gross income of the employee under subtitle A of the Code or prior income tax laws. Amounts to which this paragraph applies include, for example, contributions made by an employer to or under a trust or plan which fails to qualify under the provisions of section 401(a), provided that the employee's rights to such contributions are nonforfeitable at the time the contributions are made. See sections 402(b) and 403(c) and the regulations thereunder. This subparagraph also applies to premiums paid by an employer (other than premiums paid on behalf of an owner-employee) for life insurance protection for an employee if such premiums are includible in the gross income of the employee when paid. See § 1.72-16. However, such premiums shall only be considered as premiums and other consideration paid by the employee with respect to any benefits attributable to the contract providing the life insurance protection. See § 1.72-16.

(2) Amounts not includible in gross income of employee at time contributed if paid directly to employee at that time. Except as provided in subparagraph (3) of this paragraph, section 72(f) provides that for the purposes of section 72(c), (d), and (e), amounts contributed by an employer for the benefit of an employee or his beneficiaries shall constitute consideration paid or contributed by the employee to the extent that such amounts would not have been includible in the

gross income of the employee at the time contributed had they been paid directly to the employee at that time. Amounts to which this subparagraph applies include, for example, contributions made by an employer after December 31, 1950, and before January 1, 1963, if made on account of foreign services rendered by an employee during a period in which the employee qualified as a bona fide resident of a foreign country under section 911(a) of the Internal Revenue Code of 1954, or under section 116(a) section 116(a) of the Internal Revenue Code of 1939. In such a case, it would be immaterial whether such contributions were made under a qualified plan or otherwise. See subparagraph (4) of this paragraph for rules governing the determination of the amount of employer foreign service contributions to which this subparagraph applies. On the other hand, if contributions are made by an employer to a qualified plan at a time when compensation paid directly to the employee concerned with respect to the same services rendered would have been includible in the gross income of the employee, such as in the case of an employee of a State government where contributions are made in 1955 with respect to services rendered by the employee prior to the year 1939, this subparagraph does not apply to such contributions.

(3) Limitation. (i) In general. Except as provided in subdivision (ii) of this subparagraph, the provisions of subparagraph (2) of this paragraph shall not apply to amounts which were contributed by the employer after December 31, 1962, and which would not have been includible in the gross income of the employee by reason of the application of section 911, if such amounts had been paid directly to the employee at the time of contribution. Employer contributions attributable to foreign services performed by the employee after December 31, 1962, do not constitute, for purposes of section 72(c), (d), and (e), consideration paid or contributed by the employee.

(ii) Exception. The provisions of subdivision (i) of this subparagraph shall not apply to amounts which were contributed by the employer to provide pension or annuity credits (determined in accordance with the provisions of subparagraph (4) of this paragraph) to the extent such credits are—

(a) Attributable to foreign services performed before January 1, 1963, with respect to which the employee qualified for the benefits of section 911(a) (or corresponding provisions of prior revenue laws), and

(b) Provided pursuant to pension or annuity plan provisions in existence on March 12, 1962, and on that date applicable to such services.

Amounts described in this subdivision constitute, for purposes of section 72(c), (d), and (e), consideration paid or contributed by the employee even though such amounts are contributed by the employer after December 31, 1962.

(4) Determination of employer foreign service contributions which constitute consideration paid or contributed by employee. For purposes of subparagraphs (2) and (3)(ii) of this paragraph, employer foreign service contributions which constitute, for purposes of section 72(c), (d), and (e), consideration paid or contributed by the employee shall be determined as follows:

(i) Treatment of identifiable contributions. If, under the terms of the pension or annuity plan under which employer contributions were made, such contributions may be identified as—

(a) Attributable to foreign services performed before January 1, 1963, with respect to which the employee qualified for the benefits of section 911(a) (or corresponding provisions of prior revenue laws), and

(b) Made under pension or annuity plan provisions in existence on March 12, 1962, which were applicable to the services referred to in **(a)** of this subdivision on that date,

the amount of employer contributions so identified shall be considered paid or contributed by the employee.

(ii) Alternative rule for unidentifiable contributions. If employer contributions may not be identified in the manner described in subdivision (i) of this subparagraph, the amount of employer contributions attributable to foreign services performed before January 1, 1963, and considered paid or contributed by the employee shall be determined on the basis of an estimated allocation which is reasonable and consistent with the circumstances and the provisions of the pension or annuity plan under which such contributions are made. For example, if an employee's benefits under a pension or annuity plan, which is unchanged after March 12, 1962, are determined with respect to his basic compensation during his entire period of credited service, the amount of employer contributions considered paid or contributed by the employee shall be an amount which bears the same ratio to total employer contributions for such employee under the pension or annuity plan as his basic compensation attributable to foreign services performed before January 1, 1963, with respect to which he qualified for the benefits of section 911(a) (or corresponding provisions of prior revenue laws) bears to his total basic compensation. On the other hand, if an employee's benefits under a pension or annuity plan, which is unchanged after March 12, 1962, are determined with respect to his basic compensation during his final five years of credited service, the amount of employer contributions considered paid or contributed by the employee shall be an amount which bears the same ratio to total employer contributions for such employee as his number of years of credited service before January 1, 1963, with respect to which he qualified for the benefits of section 911(a) (or corresponding provisions of prior revenue laws) bears to his total number of years of credited service.

(5) Amounts not includible in gross income of employee under subtitle A of the Code or prior income tax laws. Amounts contributed by an employer which were not includible in the gross income of the employee under subtitle A of the Code or prior income tax laws, but which would have been includible therein had they been paid directly to the employee, do not constitute consideration paid or contributed by the employee for the purposes of section 72. For example, contributions made by an employer under a qualified employees' trust or plan, which contributions would have been includible in the gross income of the employee had such contributions been paid to him directly as compensation, do not constitute consideration paid or contributed by the employee. Accordingly, the aggregate amount of premiums or other consideration paid or contributed by an employee, insofar as compensatory employer contributions are concerned, consists solely of the (i) sum of all amounts actually contributed by the employee, plus (ii) contributions in the nature of compensation which are deemed to be paid or contributed by the employee under this paragraph.

(b) Contributions in the nature of death benefits. In the case of an employee's beneficiary, the aggregate amount of premiums or other consideration paid or deemed to be paid or contributed by the employee shall also include:

(1) Amounts (other than amounts paid as an annuity) to the extent such amounts are excludable from the benefici-

ary's gross income as a death benefit under section 101(b), and

(2) Any amount or amounts of death benefits which are treated as additional consideration contributed by the employee under section 101(b)(2)(D) and the regulations thereunder, or which were excludable from the beneficiary's gross income as a death benefit under section 22(b)(1)(B) of the Internal Revenue Code of 1939 and the regulations thereunder.

Accordingly, in the case of an employee's beneficiary, any such amount shall be added to any amount or amounts deemed paid or contributed by the employee under paragraph (a)(1) of this section and to any amounts actually contributed by the employee for the purpose of finding the aggregate amount of premiums or other consideration paid or contributed by the employee.

(c) Amounts "made available" to an employee or his beneficiary. Any amount which, although not actually paid, is made available to and includible in the gross income of an employee or his beneficiary under the rules of sections 402 and 403 and the regulations thereunder, shall be considered an amount contributed by the employee and shall be aggregated with amounts, if any, to which paragraphs (a) and (b) of this section apply for the purpose of determining the aggregate amount of premiums or other consideration paid by the employee.

(d) Amounts includible in gross income of employee when his rights under annuity contract change to nonforfeitable rights. Any amount which, by reason of section 403(d) and after the application of paragraph (b) of § 1.403(b)-1, is required to be included in an employee's gross income for the year when his rights under an annuity contract change from forfeitable to nonforfeitable rights shall be considered an amount contributed by the employee and shall be aggregated with amounts, if any, to which paragraphs (a), (b), and (c) of this section apply for the purpose of determining the aggregate amount of premiums or other consideration paid or contributed by the employee for such annuity contract. In other words, if, under section 403(d), an employee of an organization exempt from tax under section 501(a) or 521(a) is required to include an amount in gross income by reason of his rights under an annuity contract changing from forfeitable to nonforfeitable rights, such amount, to the extent it is not excludable from gross income under paragraph (b) of § 1.403(b)-1, shall be considered an amount contributed by such employee for the annuity contract.

T.D. 6211, 11/14/56, amend T.D. 6665, 7/15/63, T.D. 6783, 12/23/64.

---

§ 1.72-9 Tables.

Caution: The Treasury has not yet amended Reg § 1.72-9 to reflect changes made by P.L. 107-16.

The following tables are to be used in connection with computations under section 72 and the regulations thereunder. Tables, I, II, IIA, III, and IV are to be used if the investment in the contract does not include a post-June 1986 investment in the contract (as defined in § 1.72-6(d)(3)). Tables V, VI, VIA, VII, and VIII are to be used if the investment in the contract includes a post-June 1986 investment in the contract (as defined in § 1.72-6(d)(3)).

In the case of a contract under which amounts are received as an annuity after June 30, 1986, a taxpayer receiving such amounts may elect to treat the entire investment in the contract as post-June 1986 investment in the contract and thus apply Tables V through VIII. A taxpayer may make the election for any taxable year in which such amounts are received by attaching to the taxpayer's return for such taxable year a statement that the taxpayer is electing under § 1.72-9 to treat the entire investment in the contract as post-June 1986 investment in the contract. The statement must contain the taxpayer's name, address, and taxpayer identification number. The election is irrevocable and applies with respect to all amounts that the taxpayer receives as an annuity under the contract in the taxable year for which the election is made or in any subsequent taxable year. (Note that for purposes of the examples in §§ 1.72-4 through 1.72-11 the election described in this section is disregarded (i.e., it assumed that the taxpayer does not make an election under this section).) See also § 1.72-6(d)(3) for rules treating the entire investment in a contract as post-June 1986 investment in a contract if the annuity starting date of the contract is after June 30, 1986, and the contract provides for a disqualifying form of payment or settlement, such as an option to receive a lump sum in full discharge of the obligation under the contract. In addition, see § 1.72-6(d) for special rules concerning the tables to be used and the separate computations required if the investment in the contract includes both a pre-July 1986 investments in the contract and a post-June 1986 investment in the contract and the election described in § 1.72-6(d)(6) is made with respect to the contract. If (a) the terms of the contract involve a life or lives, and are such that the above tables cannot be correctly applied, and (b) the amounts received under the contract are at least partly "amounts received as an annuity" under a contract to which section 72 applies, the taxpayer may submit with his return an actuarial computation based upon the applicable annuity table (described below) with ages set back one year, showing the appropriate factors applied in his case, subject to the approval of the Commissioner upon examination of such return. The applicable annuity table is the 1937 Standard Annuity Table (if the investment in the contract does not include a post-June 1986 investment in the contract) or the gender-neutral version of the 1983 Basic Table (if the investment in the contract includes a post-June 1986 investment in the contract). In the case of a contract to which § 1.72-6(d) (relating to contracts in which amounts were invested both before July 1, 1986, and after June 30, 1986) applies, the actuarial computation shall be based on both tables in accordance with the principles of § 1.72-6(d). Computations involving factors to compensate for the effects of contingencies other than mortality, such as marriage or remarriage, re-employment, recovery from disability, or the like, will not be approved.

Annuity Valuation Tables

Tables I-IV apply to contracts that don't include a post-June '86 investment in the contract

(For use of these tables, see Chapter J)

Table I—Ordinary Life Annuities—One Life—Expected Return Multiples

Ages Male	Ages Female	Multiples	Ages Male	Ages Female	Multiples	Ages Male	Ages Female	Multiples
6	11	65.0	42	47	32.1	78	83	8.3
7	12	64.1	43	48	31.2	79	84	7.8
8	13	63.2	44	49	30.4	80	85	7.5
9	14	62.3	45	50	29.6	81	86	7.1
10	15	61.4	46	51	28.7	82	87	6.7
11	16	60.4	47	52	27.9	83	88	6.3
12	17	59.5	48	53	27.1	84	89	6.0
13	18	58.6	49	54	26.3	85	90	5.7
14	19	57.7	50	55	25.5	86	91	5.4
15	20	56.7	51	56	24.7	87	92	5.1
16	21	55.8	52	57	24.0	88	93	4.8
17	22	54.9	53	58	23.2	89	94	4.5
18	23	53.9	54	59	22.4	90	95	4.2
19	24	53.0	55	60	21.7	91	96	4.0
20	25	52.1	56	61	21.0	92	97	3.7
21	26	51.1	57	62	20.3	93	98	3.5
22	27	50.2	58	63	19.6	94	99	3.3
23	28	49.3	59	64	18.9	95	100	3.1
24	29	48.3	60	65	18.2	96	101	2.9
25	30	47.4	61	66	17.5	97	102	2.7
26	31	46.5	62	67	16.9	98	103	2.5
27	32	45.6	63	68	16.2	99	104	2.3
28	33	44.6	64	69	15.6	100	105	2.1
29	34	43.7	65	70	15.0	101	106	1.9
30	35	42.8	66	71	14.4	102	107	1.7
31	36	41.9	67	72	13.8	103	108	1.5
32	37	41.0	68	73	13.2	104	109	1.3
33	38	40.0	69	74	12.6	105	110	1.2
34	39	39.1	70	75	12.1	106	111	1.0
35	40	38.2	71	76	11.6	107	112	.8
36	41	37.3	72	77	11.0	108	113	.7
37	42	36.5	73	78	10.5	109	114	.6
38	43	35.6	74	79	10.1	110	115	.5
39	44	34.7	75	80	9.6	111	116	0
40	45	33.8	76	81	9.1			
41	46	33.0	77	82	8.7			

Table II—Ordinary Joint Life and Last Survivor Annuities—Two Lives—Expected Return Multiples

Male	Female	Ages: Male 6 Female 11	7 12	8 13	9 14	10 15	11 16	12 17	13 18	14 19	15 20	16 21	17 22	18 23	19 24	20 25
6	11	73.5	73.0	72.6	72.2	71.8	71.4	71.0	70.7	70.4	70.0	69.7	69.5	69.2	68.9	68.7
7	12	73.0	72.6	72.1	71.7	71.3	70.9	70.5	70.1	69.8	69.4	69.1	68.8	68.5	68.3	68.0
8	13	72.6	72.1	71.6	71.2	70.8	70.4	70.0	69.6	69.2	68.9	68.5	68.2	67.9	67.6	67.3
9	14	72.2	71.7	71.2	70.7	70.3	69.9	69.4	69.0	68.7	68.3	67.9	67.6	67.3	67.0	66.7
10	15	71.8	71.3	70.8	70.3	69.8	69.4	68.9	68.5	68.1	67.7	67.4	67.0	66.7	66.4	66.1
11	16	71.4	70.9	70.4	69.9	69.4	68.9	68.5	68.0	67.6	67.2	66.8	66.5	66.1	65.8	65.4
12	17	71.0	70.5	70.0	69.4	68.9	68.5	68.0	67.5	67.1	66.7	66.3	65.9	65.5	65.2	64.8
13	18	70.7	70.1	69.6	69.0	68.5	68.0	67.5	67.1	66.6	66.2	65.8	65.4	65.0	64.6	64.2
14	19	70.4	69.8	69.2	68.7	68.1	67.6	67.1	66.6	66.1	65.7	65.3	64.8	64.4	64.0	63.7
15	20	70.0	69.4	68.9	68.3	67.7	67.2	66.7	66.2	65.7	65.2	64.8	64.3	63.9	63.5	63.1
16	21	69.7	69.1	68.5	67.9	67.4	66.8	66.3	65.8	65.3	64.8	64.3	63.8	63.4	63.0	62.6
17	22	69.5	68.8	68.2	67.6	67.0	66.5	65.9	65.4	64.8	64.3	63.8	63.4	62.9	62.5	62.0
18	23	69.2	68.5	67.9	67.3	66.7	66.1	65.5	65.0	64.4	63.9	63.4	62.9	62.4	62.0	61.5
19	24	68.9	68.3	67.6	67.0	66.4	65.8	65.2	64.6	64.0	63.5	63.0	62.5	62.0	61.5	61.0
20	25	68.7	68.0	67.3	66.7	66.1	65.4	64.8	64.2	63.7	63.1	62.6	62.0	61.5	61.0	60.6

Table II—Ordinary Joint Life and Last Survivor Annuities—Two Lives—Expected Return Multiples—Continued

		Ages													
Male	Female	Male 21 Female 26	22 27	23 28	24 29	25 30	26 31	27 32	28 33	29 34	30 35	31 36	32 37	33 38	34 39
6	11	68.4	68.2	68.0	67.8	67.6	67.5	67.3	67.1	67.0	66.8	66.7	66.6	66.5	66.4
7	12	67.8	67.5	67.3	67.1	66.9	66.7	66.5	66.4	66.2	66.1	65.9	65.8	65.7	65.6
8	13	67.1	66.8	66.6	66.4	66.2	66.0	65.8	65.6	65.4	65.3	65.1	65.0	64.9	64.7
9	14	66.4	66.2	65.9	65.7	65.4	65.2	65.0	64.8	64.7	64.5	64.3	64.2	64.1	63.9
10	15	65.8	65.5	65.2	65.0	64.7	64.5	64.3	64.1	63.9	63.7	63.6	63.4	63.3	63.1
11	16	65.1	64.8	64.6	64.3	64.1	63.8	63.6	63.4	63.2	63.0	62.8	62.6	62.5	62.3
12	17	64.5	64.2	63.9	63.6	63.4	63.1	62.9	62.7	62.4	62.2	62.0	61.9	61.7	61.5
13	18	63.9	63.6	63.3	63.0	62.7	62.4	62.2	61.9	61.7	61.5	61.3	61.1	60.9	60.8
14	19	63.3	63.0	62.7	62.3	62.0	61.8	61.5	61.2	61.0	60.8	60.6	60.4	60.2	60.0
15	20	62.7	62.4	62.0	61.7	61.4	61.1	60.8	60.6	60.3	60.1	59.8	59.6	59.4	59.2
16	21	62.2	61.8	61.4	61.1	60.8	60.5	60.2	59.9	59.6	59.4	59.1	58.9	58.7	58.5
17	22	61.6	61.2	60.9	60.5	60.2	59.8	59.5	59.2	58.9	58.7	58.4	58.2	57.9	57.7
18	23	61.1	60.7	60.3	59.9	59.6	59.2	58.9	58.6	58.3	58.0	57.7	57.5	57.2	57.0
19	24	60.6	60.2	59.7	59.4	59.0	58.6	58.3	57.9	57.6	57.3	57.0	56.8	56.5	56.3
20	25	60.1	59.6	59.2	58.8	58.4	58.0	57.7	57.3	57.0	56.7	56.4	56.1	55.8	55.6
21	26	59.6	59.1	58.7	58.3	57.9	57.5	57.1	56.7	56.4	56.0	55.7	55.4	55.1	54.9
22	27	59.1	58.7	58.2	57.7	57.3	56.9	56.5	56.1	55.8	55.4	55.1	54.8	54.5	54.2
23	28	58.7	58.2	57.7	57.2	56.8	56.4	55.9	55.5	55.2	54.8	54.4	54.1	53.8	53.5
24	29	58.3	57.7	57.2	56.8	56.3	55.8	55.4	55.0	54.6	54.2	53.8	53.5	53.2	52.8
25	30	57.9	57.3	56.8	56.3	55.8	55.3	54.9	54.4	54.0	53.6	53.2	52.9	52.5	52.2
26	31	57.5	56.9	56.4	55.8	55.3	54.8	54.4	53.9	53.5	53.1	52.7	52.3	51.9	51.6
27	32	57.1	56.5	55.9	55.4	54.9	54.4	53.9	53.4	53.0	52.5	52.1	51.7	51.3	50.9
28	33	56.7	56.1	55.5	55.0	54.4	53.9	53.4	52.9	52.4	52.0	51.6	51.1	50.7	50.3
29	34	56.4	55.8	55.2	54.6	54.0	53.5	53.0	52.4	52.0	51.5	51.0	50.6	50.2	49.3
30	35	56.0	55.4	54.8	54.2	53.6	53.1	52.5	52.0	51.5	51.0	50.5	50.1	49.6	49.2
31	36	55.7	55.1	54.4	53.8	53.2	52.7	52.1	51.6	51.0	50.5	50.0	49.5	49.1	48.7
32	37	55.4	54.8	54.1	53.5	52.9	52.3	51.7	51.1	50.6	50.1	49.5	49.1	48.6	48.1
33	38	55.1	54.5	53.8	53.2	52.5	51.9	51.3	50.7	50.2	49.6	49.1	48.6	48.1	47.6
34	39	54.9	54.2	53.5	52.8	52.2	51.6	50.9	50.3	49.8	49.2	48.7	48.1	47.6	47.1

		Ages														
Male	Female	Male 35 Female 40	36 41	37 42	38 43	39 44	40 45	41 46	42 47	43 48	44 49	45 50	46 51	47 52	48 53	49 54
6	11	66.3	66.2	66.1	66.0	65.9	65.9	65.8	65.7	65.7	65.6	65.6	65.5	65.5	65.5	65.4
7	12	65.4	65.3	65.3	65.2	65.1	65.0	64.9	64.9	64.8	64.8	64.7	64.7	64.6	64.6	64.5
8	13	64.6	64.5	64.4	64.3	64.2	64.2	64.1	64.0	64.0	63.9	63.8	63.8	63.7	63.7	63.7
9	14	63.8	63.7	63.6	63.5	63.4	63.3	63.2	63.2	63.1	63.0	63.0	62.9	62.9	62.8	62.8
10	15	63.0	62.9	62.8	62.7	62.6	62.5	62.4	62.3	62.2	62.2	62.1	62.0	62.0	61.9	61.9
11	16	62.2	62.1	61.9	61.8	61.7	61.6	61.5	61.4	61.4	61.3	61.2	61.2	61.1	61.0	61.0
12	17	61.4	61.3	61.1	61.0	60.9	60.8	60.7	60.6	60.5	60.4	60.4	60.3	60.2	60.2	60.1
13	18	60.6	60.5	60.3	60.2	60.1	60.0	59.9	59.8	59.7	59.6	59.5	59.4	59.4	59.3	59.2
14	19	59.8	59.7	59.5	59.4	59.3	59.1	59.0	58.9	58.8	58.7	58.6	58.6	58.5	58.4	58.4
15	20	59.0	58.9	58.7	58.6	58.4	58.3	58.2	58.1	58.0	57.9	57.8	57.7	57.6	57.6	57.5
16	21	58.3	58.1	57.9	57.8	57.6	57.5	57.4	57.2	57.1	57.0	56.9	56.8	56.8	56.7	56.6
17	22	57.5	57.3	57.2	57.0	56.8	56.7	56.6	56.4	56.3	56.2	56.1	56.0	55.9	55.8	55.7
18	23	56.8	56.6	56.4	56.2	56.0	55.9	55.7	55.6	55.5	55.4	55.2	55.1	55.1	55.0	54.9
19	24	56.0	55.8	55.6	55.4	55.3	55.1	54.9	54.8	54.7	54.5	54.4	54.3	54.2	54.1	54.0
20	25	55.3	55.1	54.9	54.7	54.5	54.3	54.1	54.0	53.8	53.7	53.6	53.5	53.4	53.3	53.2
21	26	54.6	54.4	54.1	53.9	53.7	53.5	53.4	53.2	53.0	52.9	52.8	52.6	52.5	52.4	52.3
22	27	53.9	53.6	53.4	53.2	53.0	52.8	52.6	52.4	52.2	52.1	51.9	51.8	51.7	51.6	51.5
23	28	53.2	52.9	52.7	52.5	52.2	52.0	51.8	51.6	51.5	51.3	51.1	51.0	50.9	50.7	50.6
24	29	52.5	52.3	52.0	51.7	51.5	51.3	51.1	50.9	50.7	50.5	50.3	50.2	50.0	49.9	49.8
25	30	51.9	51.6	51.3	51.0	50.8	50.5	50.3	50.1	49.9	49.7	49.6	49.4	49.2	49.1	49.0
26	31	51.2	50.9	50.6	50.3	50.1	49.8	49.6	49.4	49.2	49.0	48.8	48.6	48.4	48.3	48.1
27	32	50.6	50.3	50.0	49.7	49.4	49.1	48.9	48.6	48.4	48.2	48.0	47.8	47.6	47.5	47.3
28	33	50.0	49.6	49.3	49.0	48.7	48.4	48.2	47.9	47.7	47.5	47.2	47.1	46.9	46.7	46.5
29	34	49.4	49.0	48.7	48.3	48.0	47.7	47.5	47.2	47.0	46.7	46.5	46.3	46.1	45.9	45.7
30	35	48.8	48.4	48.1	47.7	47.4	47.1	46.8	46.5	46.2	46.0	45.8	45.5	45.3	45.2	45.0
31	36	48.2	47.8	47.5	47.1	46.8	46.4	46.1	45.8	45.6	45.3	45.0	44.8	44.6	44.4	44.2
32	37	47.7	47.3	46.9	46.5	46.1	45.8	45.5	45.2	44.9	44.6	44.3	44.1	43.9	43.7	43.4
33	38	47.2	46.7	46.3	45.9	45.5	45.2	44.8	44.5	44.2	43.9	43.7	43.4	43.2	42.9	42.7
34	39	46.7	46.2	45.8	45.4	45.0	44.6	44.2	43.9	43.6	43.3	43.0	42.7	42.5	42.2	42.0

Table II—Ordinary Joint Life and Last Survivor Annuities—Two Lives—Expected Return Multiples—Continued

Male	Female	Ages: Male 50 Female 55	51 56	52 57	53 58	54 59	55 60	56 61	57 62	58 63	59 64	60 65	61 66	62 67	63 68
6	11	65.4	65.4	65.3	65.3	65.3	65.3	65.3	65.2	65.2	65.2	65.2	65.2	65.2	65.2
7	12	64.5	64.5	64.4	64.4	64.4	64.4	64.3	64.3	64.3	64.3	64.3	64.3	64.3	64.2
8	13	63.6	63.6	63.5	63.5	63.5	63.5	63.4	63.4	63.4	63.4	63.4	63.4	63.3	63.3
9	14	62.7	62.7	62.7	62.6	62.6	62.6	62.5	62.5	62.5	62.5	62.5	62.4	62.4	62.4
10	15	61.8	61.8	61.8	61.7	61.7	61.7	61.6	61.6	61.6	61.6	61.6	61.5	61.5	61.5
11	16	61.0	60.9	60.9	60.8	60.8	60.8	60.7	60.7	60.7	60.7	60.6	60.6	60.6	60.6
12	17	60.1	60.0	60.0	59.9	59.9	59.9	59.8	59.8	59.8	59.8	59.7	59.7	59.7	59.7
13	18	59.2	59.1	59.1	59.0	59.0	59.0	58.9	58.9	58.9	58.9	58.8	58.8	58.8	58.8
14	19	58.3	58.2	58.2	58.2	58.1	58.1	58.0	58.0	58.0	57.9	57.9	57.9	57.9	57.9
15	20	57.4	57.4	57.3	57.3	57.2	57.2	57.1	57.1	57.1	57.0	57.0	57.0	57.0	56.9
16	21	56.5	56.5	56.4	56.4	56.3	56.3	56.2	56.2	56.2	56.1	56.1	56.1	56.1	56.0
17	22	55.7	55.6	55.5	55.5	55.4	55.4	55.3	55.3	55.3	55.2	55.2	55.2	55.1	55.1
18	23	54.8	54.7	54.7	54.6	54.6	54.5	54.5	54.4	54.4	54.3	54.3	54.3	54.2	54.2
19	24	53.9	53.9	53.8	53.7	53.7	53.6	53.6	53.5	53.5	53.4	53.4	53.4	53.3	53.3
20	25	53.1	53.0	52.9	52.8	52.8	52.7	52.7	52.6	52.6	52.5	52.5	52.4	52.4	52.4
21	26	52.2	52.1	52.0	52.0	51.9	51.8	51.8	51.7	51.7	51.6	51.6	51.5	51.5	51.5
22	27	51.4	51.3	51.2	51.1	51.0	51.0	50.9	50.8	50.8	50.7	50.7	50.6	50.6	50.6
23	28	50.5	50.4	50.3	50.2	50.2	50.1	50.0	50.0	49.9	49.8	49.8	49.7	49.7	49.7
24	29	49.7	49.6	49.5	49.4	49.3	49.2	49.1	49.1	49.0	49.0	48.9	48.9	48.8	48.8
25	30	48.8	48.7	48.6	48.5	48.4	48.3	48.3	48.2	48.1	48.1	48.0	48.0	47.9	47.9
26	31	48.0	47.9	47.8	47.7	47.6	47.5	47.4	47.3	47.3	47.2	47.1	47.1	47.0	47.0
27	32	47.2	47.1	46.9	46.8	46.7	46.6	46.5	46.5	46.4	46.3	46.2	46.2	46.1	46.1
28	33	46.4	46.3	46.1	46.0	45.9	45.8	45.7	45.6	45.5	45.4	45.4	45.3	45.2	45.2
29	34	45.6	45.4	45.3	45.2	45.1	44.9	44.8	44.7	44.7	44.6	44.5	44.4	44.4	44.3
30	35	44.8	44.6	44.5	44.4	44.2	44.1	44.0	43.9	43.8	43.7	43.6	43.6	43.5	43.4
31	36	44.0	43.9	43.7	43.6	43.4	43.3	43.2	43.1	43.0	42.9	42.8	42.7	42.6	42.0
32	37	43.3	43.1	42.9	42.8	42.6	42.5	42.4	42.2	42.1	42.0	41.9	41.9	41.8	41.7
33	38	42.5	42.3	42.1	42.0	41.8	41.7	41.5	41.4	41.3	41.2	41.1	41.0	40.9	40.8
34	39	41.8	41.6	41.4	41.2	41.0	40.9	40.7	40.6	40.5	40.4	40.3	40.2	40.1	40.0

Male	Female	Ages: Male 64 Female 69	65 70	66 71	67 72	68 73	69 74	70 75	71 76	72 77	73 78	74 79	75 80	76 81	77 82	78 83
6	11	65.1	65.1	65.1	65.1	65.1	65.1	65.1	65.1	65.1	65.1	65.1	65.1	65.1	65.1	65.1
7	12	64.2	64.2	64.2	64.2	64.2	64.2	64.2	64.2	64.2	64.2	64.2	64.2	64.2	64.1	64.1
8	13	63.3	63.3	63.3	63.3	63.3	63.3	63.3	63.3	63.3	63.2	63.2	63.2	63.2	63.2	63.2
9	14	62.4	62.4	62.4	62.4	62.4	62.4	62.3	62.3	62.3	62.3	62.3	62.3	62.3	62.3	62.3
10	15	61.5	61.5	61.5	61.5	61.4	61.4	61.4	61.4	61.4	61.4	61.4	61.4	61.4	61.4	61.4
11	16	60.6	60.6	60.6	60.5	60.5	60.5	60.5	60.5	60.5	60.5	60.5	60.5	60.5	60.5	60.5
12	17	59.7	59.6	59.6	59.6	59.6	59.6	59.6	59.6	59.6	59.6	59.6	59.6	59.6	59.5	59.5
13	18	58.8	58.7	58.7	58.7	58.7	58.7	58.7	58.7	58.7	58.7	58.6	58.6	58.6	58.6	58.6
14	19	57.8	57.8	57.8	57.8	57.8	57.8	57.8	57.7	57.7	57.7	57.7	57.7	57.7	57.7	57.7
15	20	56.9	56.9	56.9	56.9	56.9	56.8	56.8	56.8	56.8	56.8	56.8	56.8	56.8	56.8	56.8
16	21	56.0	56.0	56.0	56.0	55.9	55.9	55.9	55.9	55.9	55.9	55.9	55.9	55.9	55.9	55.8
17	22	55.1	55.1	55.1	55.0	55.0	55.0	55.0	55.0	55.0	55.0	55.0	54.9	54.9	54.9	54.9
18	23	54.2	54.2	54.1	54.1	54.1	54.1	54.1	54.1	54.0	54.0	54.0	54.0	54.0	54.0	54.0
19	24	53.3	53.2	53.2	53.2	53.2	53.2	53.2	53.1	53.1	53.1	53.1	53.1	53.1	53.1	53.1
20	25	52.4	52.3	52.3	52.3	52.3	52.2	52.2	52.2	52.2	52.2	52.2	52.2	52.2	52.1	52.1
21	26	51.4	51.4	51.4	51.4	51.3	51.3	51.3	51.3	51.3	51.3	51.3	51.2	51.2	51.2	51.2
22	27	50.5	50.5	50.5	50.5	50.4	50.4	50.4	50.4	50.4	50.3	50.3	50.3	50.3	50.3	50.3
23	28	49.6	49.6	49.6	49.5	49.5	49.5	49.5	49.5	49.4	49.4	49.4	49.4	49.4	49.4	49.4
24	29	48.7	48.7	48.7	48.6	48.6	48.6	48.6	48.5	48.5	48.5	48.5	48.5	48.5	48.4	48.4
25	30	47.8	47.8	47.8	47.7	47.7	47.7	47.6	47.6	47.6	47.6	47.6	47.5	47.5	47.5	47.5
26	31	46.9	46.9	46.8	46.8	46.8	46.8	46.7	46.7	46.7	46.7	46.6	46.6	46.6	46.6	46.6
27	32	46.0	46.0	45.9	45.9	45.9	45.8	45.8	45.8	45.8	45.7	45.7	45.7	45.7	45.7	45.7
28	33	45.1	45.1	45.1	45.0	45.0	44.9	44.9	44.9	44.9	44.8	44.8	44.8	44.8	44.8	44.8
29	34	44.3	44.2	44.2	44.1	44.1	44.0	44.0	44.0	44.0	43.9	43.9	43.9	43.9	43.9	43.8
30	35	43.4	43.3	43.3	43.2	43.2	43.1	43.1	43.1	43.1	43.0	43.0	43.0	43.0	42.9	42.9
31	36	42.5	42.4	42.4	42.3	42.3	42.3	42.2	42.2	42.2	42.1	42.1	42.1	42.1	42.0	42.0
32	37	41.6	41.6	41.5	41.5	41.4	41.4	41.3	41.3	41.3	41.2	41.2	41.2	41.2	41.1	41.1
33	38	40.8	40.7	40.7	40.6	40.5	40.5	40.5	40.4	40.4	40.3	40.3	40.3	40.3	40.2	40.2
34	39	39.9	39.9	39.8	39.7	39.7	39.6	39.6	39.5	39.5	39.5	39.4	39.4	39.4	39.3	39.3

Table II—Ordinary Joint Life and Last Survivor Annuities—Two Lives—Expected Return Multiples—Continued

Male	Female	Ages: Male 79 / Female 64	80 / 85	81 / 86	82 / 87	83 / 88	84 / 89	85 / 90	86 / 91	87 / 92	66 / 93	89 / 94	90 / 95	91 / 96	92 / 97
6	11	65.1	65.1	65.1	65.1	65.1	65.1	65.1	65.1	65.1	65.0	65.0	65.0	65.0	65.0
7	12	64.1	64.1	64.1	64.1	64.1	64.1	64.1	64.1	64.1	64.1	64.1	64.1	64.1	64.1
8	13	63.2	63.2	63.2	63.2	63.2	63.2	63.2	63.2	63.2	63.2	63.2	63.2	63.2	63.2
9	14	62.3	62.3	62.3	62.3	62.3	62.3	62.3	62.3	62.3	62.3	62.3	62.3	62.3	62.3
10	15	61.4	61.4	61.4	61.4	61.4	61.4	61.4	61.4	61.4	61.4	61.4	61.4	61.4	61.4
11	16	60.5	60.5	60.5	60.5	60.5	60.5	60.4	60.4	60.4	60.4	60.4	60.4	60.4	60.4
12	17	59.5	59.5	59.5	59.5	59.5	59.5	59.5	59.5	59.5	59.5	59.5	59.5	59.5	59.5
13	18	58.6	58.6	58.6	58.6	58.6	58.6	58.6	58.6	58.6	58.6	58.6	58.6	58.6	58.6
14	19	57.7	57.7	57.7	57.7	57.7	57.7	57.7	57.7	57.7	57.7	57.7	57.7	57.7	57.7
15	20	56.8	56.8	56.8	56.8	56.8	56.8	56.7	56.7	56.7	56.7	56.7	56.7	56.7	56.7
16	21	55.8	55.8	55.8	55.8	55.8	55.8	55.8	55.8	55.8	55.8	55.8	55.8	55.8	55.8
17	22	54.9	54.9	54.9	54.9	54.9	54.9	54.9	54.9	54.9	54.9	54.9	54.9	54.9	54.9
18	23	54.0	54.0	54.0	54.0	54.0	54.0	54.0	54.0	54.0	54.0	54.0	54.0	54.0	53.9
19	24	53.1	53.1	53.1	53.0	53.0	53.0	53.0	53.0	53.0	53.0	53.0	53.0	53.0	53.0
20	25	52.1	52.1	52.1	52.1	52.1	52.1	52.1	52.1	52.1	52.1	52.1	52.1	52.1	52.1
21	26	51.2	51.2	51.2	51.2	51.2	51.2	51.2	51.2	51.2	51.2	51.2	51.2	51.2	51.2
22	27	50.3	50.3	50.3	50.3	50.3	50.2	50.2	50.2	50.2	50.2	50.2	50.2	50.2	50.2
23	28	49.4	49.3	49.3	49.3	49.3	49.3	49.3	49.3	49.3	49.3	49.3	49.3	49.3	49.3
24	29	48.4	48.4	48.4	48.4	48.4	48.4	48.4	48.4	48.4	48.4	48.4	48.4	48.4	48.4
25	30	47.5	47.5	47.5	47.5	47.5	47.5	47.5	47.5	47.4	47.4	47.4	47.4	47.4	47.4
26	31	46.6	46.6	46.6	46.6	46.5	46.5	46.5	46.5	46.5	46.5	46.5	46.5	46.5	46.5
27	32	45.7	45.6	45.6	45.6	45.6	45.6	45.6	45.6	45.6	45.6	45.6	45.6	45.6	45.6
28	33	44.7	44.7	44.7	44.7	44.7	44.7	44.7	44.7	44.7	44.7	44.7	44.7	44.7	44.7
29	34	43.8	43.8	43.8	43.8	43.8	43.8	43.8	43.8	43.8	43.7	43.7	43.7	43.7	43.7
30	35	42.9	42.9	42.9	42.9	42.9	42.9	42.8	42.8	42.8	42.8	42.8	42.8	42.8	42.8
31	36	42.0	42.0	42.0	42.0	42.0	41.9	41.9	41.9	41.9	41.9	41.9	41.9	41.9	41.9
32	37	41.1	41.1	41.1	41.1	41.0	41.0	41.0	41.0	41.0	41.0	41.0	41.0	41.0	41.0
33	38	40.2	40.2	40.2	40.2	40.1	40.1	40.1	40.1	40.1	40.1	40.1	40.1	40.1	40.1
34	39	39.3	39.3	39.3	39.3	39.2	39.2	39.2	39.2	39.2	39.2	39.2	39.2	39.2	39.2

Male	Female	Ages: Male 93 / Female 98	94 / 99	95 / 100	96 / 101	97 / 102	98 / 103	99 / 104	100 / 105	101 / 106	102 / 107	103 / 108	104 / 109	105 / 110	106 / 111	107 / 112	108 / 113
6	11	65.0	65.0	65.0	65.0	65.0	65.0	65.0	65.0	65.0	65.0	65.0	65.0	65.0	65.0	65.0	65.0
7	12	64.1	64.1	64.1	64.1	64.1	64.1	64.1	64.1	64.1	64.1	64.1	64.1	64.1	64.1	64.1	64.1
8	13	63.2	63.2	63.2	63.2	63.2	63.2	63.2	63.2	63.2	63.2	63.2	63.2	63.2	63.2	63.2	63.2
9	14	62.3	62.3	62.3	62.3	62.3	62.3	62.3	62.3	62.3	62.3	62.3	62.3	62.3	62.3	62.3	62.3
10	15	61.4	61.4	61.4	61.4	61.4	61.4	61.4	61.4	61.4	61.4	61.4	61.4	61.4	61.4	61.4	61.4
11	16	60.4	60.4	60.4	60.4	60.4	60.4	60.4	60.4	60.4	60.4	60.4	60.4	60.4	60.4	60.4	60.4
12	17	59.5	59.5	59.5	59.5	59.5	59.5	59.5	59.5	59.5	59.5	59.5	59.5	59.5	59.5	59.5	59.5
13	18	58.6	58.6	58.6	58.6	58.6	58.6	58.6	58.6	58.6	58.6	58.6	58.6	58.6	58.6	58.6	58.6
14	19	57.7	57.7	57.7	57.7	57.7	57.7	57.7	57.7	57.7	57.7	57.7	57.7	57.7	57.7	57.7	57.7
15	20	56.7	56.7	56.7	56.7	56.7	56.7	56.7	56.7	56.7	56.7	56.7	56.7	56.7	56.7	56.7	56.7
16	21	55.8	55.8	55.8	55.8	55.8	55.8	55.8	55.8	55.8	55.8	55.8	55.8	55.8	55.8	55.8	55.8
17	22	54.9	54.9	54.9	54.9	54.9	54.9	54.9	54.9	54.9	54.9	54.9	54.9	54.9	54.9	54.9	54.9
18	23	53.9	53.9	53.9	53.9	53.9	53.9	53.9	53.9	53.9	53.9	53.9	53.9	53.9	53.9	53.9	53.9
19	24	53.0	53.0	53.0	53.0	53.0	53.0	53.0	53.0	53.0	53.0	53.0	53.0	53.0	53.0	53.0	53.0
20	25	52.1	52.1	52.1	52.1	52.1	52.1	52.1	52.1	52.1	52.1	52.1	52.1	52.1	52.1	52.1	52.1
21	26	51.2	51.2	51.2	51.2	51.2	51.2	51.1	51.1	51.1	51.1	51.1	51.1	51.1	51.1	51.1	51.1
22	27	50.2	50.2	50.2	50.2	50.2	50.2	50.2	50.2	50.2	50.2	50.2	50.2	50.2	50.2	50.2	50.2
23	28	49.3	49.3	49.3	49.3	49.3	49.3	49.3	49.3	49.3	49.3	49.3	49.3	49.3	49.3	49.3	49.3
24	29	48.4	48.4	48.4	48.4	48.4	48.4	48.4	48.4	48.4	48.4	48.4	48.4	48.4	48.4	48.3	48.3
25	30	47.4	47.4	47.4	47.4	47.4	47.4	47.4	47.4	47.4	47.4	47.4	47.4	47.4	47.4	47.4	47.4
26	31	46.5	46.5	46.5	46.5	46.5	46.5	46.5	46.5	46.5	46.5	46.5	46.5	46.5	46.5	46.5	46.5
27	32	45.6	45.6	45.6	45.6	45.6	45.6	45.6	45.6	45.6	45.6	45.6	45.6	45.6	45.6	45.6	45.6
28	33	44.7	44.6	44.6	44.6	44.6	44.6	44.6	44.6	44.6	44.6	44.6	44.6	44.6	44.6	44.6	44.6
29	34	43.7	43.7	43.7	43.7	43.7	43.7	43.7	43.7	43.7	43.7	43.7	43.7	43.7	43.7	43.7	43.7
30	35	42.8	42.8	42.8	42.8	42.8	42.8	42.8	42.8	42.8	42.8	42.8	42.8	42.8	42.8	42.8	42.8
31	36	41.9	41.9	41.9	41.9	41.9	41.9	41.9	41.9	41.9	41.9	41.9	41.9	41.9	41.9	41.9	41.9
32	37	41.0	41.0	41.0	41.0	41.0	41.0	41.0	41.0	41.0	41.0	41.0	41.0	41.0	41.0	41.0	41.0
33	38	40.1	40.1	40.1	40.1	40.1	40.1	40.1	40.1	40.1	40.1	40.1	40.1	40.1	40.1	40.1	40.0
34	39	39.2	39.2	39.2	39.2	39.2	39.2	39.2	39.2	39.2	39.2	39.2	39.1	39.1	39.1	39.1	39.1

Table II—Ordinary Joint Life and Last Survivor Annuities—Two Lives—Expected Return Multiples—Continued

Male	Female	Ages: Male 35 / Female 40	36 / 41	37 / 42	38 / 43	39 / 44	40 / 45	41 / 46	42 / 47	43 / 48	44 / 49	45 / 50	46 / 51	47 / 52
35	40	46.2	45.7	45.3	44.8	44.4	44.0	43.6	43.3	43.0	42.6	42.3	42.0	41.8
36	41	45.7	45.2	44.8	44.3	43.9	43.5	43.1	42.7	42.3	42.0	41.7	41.4	41.1
37	42	45.3	44.8	44.3	43.8	43.4	42.9	42.5	42.1	41.8	41.4	41.1	40.7	40.4
38	43	44.8	44.3	43.8	43.3	42.9	42.4	42.0	41.6	41.2	40.8	40.5	40.1	39.8
39	44	44.4	43.9	43.4	42.9	42.4	41.9	41.5	41.0	40.6	40.2	39.9	39.5	39.2
40	45	44.0	43.5	42.9	42.4	41.9	41.4	41.0	40.5	40.1	39.7	39.3	38.9	38.6
41	46	43.6	43.1	42.5	42.0	41.5	41.0	40.5	40.0	39.6	39.2	38.8	38.4	38.0
42	47	43.3	42.7	42.1	41.6	41.0	40.5	40.0	39.6	39.1	38.7	38.2	37.8	37.5
43	48	43.0	42.3	41.8	41.2	40.6	40.1	39.6	39.1	38.6	38.2	37.7	37.3	36.9
44	49	42.6	42.0	41.4	40.8	40.2	39.7	39.2	38.7	38.2	37.7	37.2	36.8	36.4
45	50	42.3	41.7	41.1	40.5	39.9	39.3	38.8	38.2	37.7	37.2	36.8	36.3	35.9
46	51	42.0	41.4	40.7	40.1	39.5	38.9	38.4	37.8	37.3	36.8	36.3	35.9	35.4
47	52	41.8	41.1	40.4	39.8	39.2	38.6	38.0	37.5	36.9	36.4	35.9	35.4	35.0

Male	Female	Ages: Male 48 / Female 53	49 / 54	50 / 55	51 / 56	52 / 57	53 / 58	54 / 59	55 / 60	56 / 61	57 / 62	58 / 63	59 / 64	60 / 65
35	40	41.5	41.3	41.0	40.8	40.6	40.4	40.3	40.1	40.0	39.8	39.7	39.6	39.5
36	41	40.8	40.6	40.3	40.1	39.9	39.7	39.5	39.3	39.2	39.0	38.9	38.8	38.6
37	42	40.2	39.9	39.6	39.4	39.2	39.0	38.8	38.6	38.4	38.3	38.1	38.0	37.9
38	43	39.5	39.2	39.0	38.7	38.5	38.3	38.1	37.9	37.7	37.5	37.3	37.2	37.1
39	44	38.9	38.6	38.3	38.0	37.8	37.6	37.3	37.1	36.9	36.8	36.6	36.4	36.3
40	45	38.3	38.0	37.7	37.4	37.1	36.9	36.6	36.4	36.2	36.0	35.9	35.7	35.5
41	46	37.7	37.3	37.0	36.7	36.5	36.2	36.0	35.7	35.5	35.3	35.1	35.0	34.8
42	47	37.1	36.8	36.4	36.1	35.8	35.6	35.3	35.1	34.8	34.6	34.4	34.2	34.1
43	48	36.5	36.2	35.8	35.5	35.2	34.9	34.7	34.4	34.2	33.9	33.7	33.5	33.3
44	49	36.0	35.6	35.3	34.9	34.6	34.3	34.0	33.8	33.5	33.3	33.0	32.8	32.6
45	50	35.5	35.1	34.7	34.4	34.0	33.7	33.4	33.1	32.9	32.6	32.4	32.2	31.9
46	51	35.0	34.6	34.2	33.8	33.5	33.1	32.8	32.5	32.2	32.0	31.7	31.5	31.3
47	52	34.5	34.1	33.7	33.3	32.9	32.6	32.2	31.9	31.6	31.4	31.1	30.9	30.6
48	53	34.0	33.6	33.2	32.8	32.4	32.0	31.7	31.4	31.1	30.8	30.5	30.2	30.0
49	54	33.6	33.1	32.7	32.3	31.9	31.5	31.2	30.8	30.5	30.2	29.9	29.6	29.4
50	55	33.2	32.7	32.3	31.8	31.4	31.0	30.6	30.3	29.9	29.6	29.3	29.0	28.8
51	56	32.8	32.3	31.8	31.4	30.9	30.5	30.1	29.8	29.4	29.1	28.8	28.5	28.2
52	57	32.4	31.9	31.4	30.9	30.5	30.1	29.7	29.3	28.9	28.6	28.2	27.9	27.6
53	58	32.0	31.5	31.0	30.5	30.1	29.6	29.2	28.8	28.4	28.1	27.7	27.4	27.1
54	59	31.7	31.2	30.6	30.1	29.7	29.2	28.8	28.3	27.9	27.6	27.2	26.9	26.5
55	60	31.4	30.8	30.3	29.8	29.3	28.8	28.3	27.9	27.5	27.1	26.7	26.4	26.0
56	61	31.1	30.5	29.9	29.4	28.9	28.4	27.9	27.5	27.1	26.7	26.3	25.9	25.5
57	62	30.8	30.2	29.6	29.1	28.6	28.1	27.6	27.1	26.7	26.2	25.8	25.4	25.1
58	63	30.5	29.9	29.3	28.8	28.2	27.7	27.2	26.7	26.3	25.8	25.4	25.0	24.6
59	64	30.2	29.6	29.0	28.5	27.9	27.4	26.9	26.4	25.9	25.4	25.0	24.6	24.2
60	65	30.0	29.4	28.8	28.2	27.6	27.1	26.5	26.0	25.5	25.1	24.6	24.2	23.8

Table II—Ordinary Joint Life and Last Survivor Annuities—Two Lives—Expected Return Multiples—Continued

Male	Female	Ages: Male 61 / Female 66	62 / 67	63 / 68	64 / 69	65 / 70	66 / 71	67 / 72	68 / 73	69 / 74	70 / 75	71 / 76	72 / 77	73 / 78
35	40	39.4	39.3	39.2	39.1	39.0	38.9	38.9	38.8	38.8	38.7	38.7	38.6	38.6
36	41	38.5	38.4	38.3	38.2	38.2	38.1	38.0	38.0	37.9	37.9	37.8	37.8	37.7
37	42	37.7	37.6	37.5	37.4	37.3	37.3	37.2	37.1	37.1	37.0	36.9	36.9	36.9
38	43	36.9	36.8	36.7	36.6	36.5	36.4	36.4	36.3	36.2	36.2	36.1	36.0	36.0
39	44	36.2	36.0	35.9	35.8	35.7	35.6	35.5	35.5	35.4	35.3	35.3	35.2	35.2
40	45	35.4	35.3	35.1	35.0	34.9	34.8	34.7	34.6	34.6	34.5	34.4	34.4	34.3
41	46	34.6	34.5	34.4	34.2	34.1	34.0	33.9	33.8	33.8	33.7	33.6	33.5	33.5
42	47	33.9	33.7	33.6	33.5	33.4	33.2	33.1	33.0	33.0	32.9	32.8	32.7	32.7
43	48	33.2	33.0	32.9	32.7	32.6	32.5	32.4	32.3	32.2	32.1	32.0	31.9	31.9
44	49	32.5	32.3	32.1	32.0	31.8	31.7	31.6	31.5	31.4	31.3	31.2	31.1	31.1
45	50	31.8	31.6	31.4	31.3	31.1	31.0	30.8	30.7	30.6	30.5	30.4	30.4	30.3
46	51	31.1	30.9	30.7	30.5	30.4	30.2	30.1	30.0	29.9	29.8	29.7	29.6	29.5
47	52	30.4	30.2	30.0	29.8	29.7	29.5	29.4	29.3	29.1	29.0	28.9	28.8	28.7

Male	Female													
48	53	29.8	29.5	29.3	29.2	29.0	28.8	28.7	28.5	28.4	28.3	28.2	28.1	28.0
49	54	29.1	28.9	28.7	28.5	28.3	28.1	28.0	27.8	27.7	27.6	27.5	27.4	27.3
50	55	28.5	28.3	28.1	27.8	27.6	27.5	27.3	27.1	27.0	26.9	26.7	26.6	26.5
51	56	27.9	27.7	27.4	27.2	27.0	26.8	26.6	26.5	26.3	26.2	26.0	25.9	25.8
52	57	27.3	27.1	26.8	26.6	26.4	26.2	26.0	25.8	25.7	25.5	25.4	25.2	25.1
53	58	26.8	26.5	26.2	26.0	25.8	25.6	25.4	25.2	25.0	24.8	24.7	24.6	24.4
54	59	26.2	25.9	25.7	25.4	25.2	25.0	24.7	24.6	24.4	24.2	24.0	23.9	23.8
55	60	25.7	25.4	25.1	24.9	24.6	24.4	24.1	23.9	23.8	23.6	23.4	23.3	23.1
56	61	25.2	24.9	24.6	24.3	24.1	23.8	23.8	23.4	23.2	23.0	22.8	22.6	22.5
57	62	24.7	24.4	24.1	23.8	23.5	23.3	23.0	22.8	22.6	22.4	22.2	22.0	21.9
58	63	24.3	23.9	23.6	23.3	23.0	22.7	22.5	22.2	22.0	21.8	21.6	21.4	21.3
59	64	23.8	23.5	23.1	22.8	22.5	22.2	21.9	21.7	21.5	21.2	21.0	20.9	20.7
60	65	23.4	23.0	22.7	22.3	22.0	21.7	21.4	21.2	20.9	20.7	20.5	20.3	20.1
61	66	23.0	22.6	22.2	21.9	21.6	21.3	21.0	20.7	20.4	20.2	20.0	19.8	19.6
62	67	22.6	22.2	21.8	21.5	21.1	20.8	20.5	20.2	19.9	19.7	19.5	19.2	19.0
63	68	22.2	21.8	21.4	21.1	20.7	20.4	20.1	19.8	19.5	19.2	19.0	18.7	18.5
64	69	21.9	21.5	21.1	20.7	20.3	20.0	19.6	19.3	19.0	18.7	18.5	18.2	18.0
65	70	21.6	21.1	20.7	20.3	19.9	19.6	19.2	18.9	18.6	18.3	18.0	17.8	17.5
66	71	21.3	20.8	20.4	20.0	19.6	19.2	18.8	18.5	18.2	17.9	17.6	17.3	17.1
67	72	21.0	20.5	20.1	19.6	19.2	18.8	18.5	18.1	17.8	17.5	17.2	16.9	16.7
68	73	20.7	20.2	19.8	19.3	18.9	18.5	18.1	17.8	17.4	17.1	16.8	16.5	16.2
69	74	20.4	19.9	19.5	19.0	18.6	18.2	17.8	17.4	17.1	16.7	16.4	16.1	15.8
70	75	20.2	19.7	19.2	18.7	18.3	17.9	17.5	17.1	16.7	16.4	16.1	15.8	15.5
71	76	20.0	19.5	19.0	18.5	18.0	17.6	17.2	16.8	16.4	16.1	15.7	15.4	15.1
72	77	19.8	19.2	18.7	18.2	17.8	17.3	16.9	16.5	16.1	15.8	15.4	15.1	14.8
73	78	19.6	19.0	18.5	18.0	17.5	17.1	16.7	16.2	15.8	15.5	15.1	14.8	14.4

Table II—Ordinary Joint Life and Last Survivor Annuities—Two Lives—Expected Return Multiples—Continued

		Ages											
Male	Female	Male 74 Female 79	75 80	76 81	77 82	78 83	79 84	80 85	81 86	82 87	83 88	84 89	85 90
35	40	38.6	38.5	38.5	38.5	38.4	38.4	38.4	38.4	38.4	38.4	38.3	38.3
36	41	37.7	37.8	37.6	37.6	37.6	37.5	37.5	37.5	37.5	37.5	37.5	37.4
37	42	36.8	36.8	36.7	36.7	36.7	36.7	36.6	36.6	36.6	36.6	36.6	36.6
38	43	36.0	35.9	35.9	35.9	35.8	35.8	35.8	35.8	35.7	35.7	35.7	35.7
39	44	35.1	35.1	35.0	35.0	35.0	34.9	34.9	34.9	34.9	34.8	34.8	34.8
40	45	34.3	34.2	34.2	34.1	34.1	34.1	34.1	34.0	34.0	34.0	34.0	34.0
41	46	33.4	33.4	33.3	33.3	33.3	33.2	33.2	33.2	33.2	33.1	33.1	33.1
42	47	32.6	32.6	32.5	32.5	32.4	32.4	32.4	32.3	32.3	32.3	32.3	32.3
43	48	31.8	31.8	31.7	31.7	31.6	31.6	31.5	31.5	31.5	31.5	31.4	31.4
44	49	31.0	30.9	30.9	30.8	30.8	30.8	30.7	30.7	30.7	30.6	30.6	30.6
45	50	30.2	30.1	30.1	30.0	30.0	29.9	29.9	29.9	29.8	29.8	29.8	29.8
46	51	29.4	29.4	29.3	29.2	29.2	29.2	29.1	29.1	29.0	29.0	29.0	28.9
47	52	28.7	28.6	28.5	28.5	28.4	28.4	28.3	28.3	28.2	28.2	28.2	28.1
48	53	27.9	27.8	27.8	27.7	27.6	27.6	27.5	27.5	27.5	27.4	27.4	27.4
49	54	27.2	27.1	27.0	26.9	26.9	26.8	26.8	26.7	26.7	26.6	26.6	26.6
50	55	26.4	26.3	26.3	26.2	26.1	26.1	26.0	26.0	25.9	25.9	25.8	25.8
51	56	25.7	25.6	25.5	25.5	25.4	25.3	25.3	25.2	25.2	25.1	25.1	25.0
52	57	25.0	24.9	24.8	24.7	24.7	24.6	24.5	24.5	24.4	24.4	24.3	24.3
53	58	24.3	24.2	24.1	24.0	23.9	23.9	23.8	23.7	23.7	23.6	23.6	23.5
54	59	23.6	23.5	23.4	23.3	23.2	23.2	23.1	23.0	23.0	22.9	22.9	22.8
55	60	23.0	22.9	22.8	22.7	22.6	22.5	22.4	22.3	22.3	22.2	22.2	22.1
56	61	22.3	22.2	22.1	22.0	21.9	21.8	21.7	21.6	21.6	21.5	21.5	21.4
57	62	21.7	21.6	21.5	21.3	21.2	21.1	21.1	21.0	20.9	20.8	20.8	20.7
58	63	21.1	21.0	20.8	20.7	20.6	20.5	20.4	20.3	20.2	20.2	20.1	20.0
59	64	20.5	20.4	20.2	20.1	20.0	19.9	19.8	19.7	19.6	19.5	19.4	19.4
60	65	19.9	19.8	19.6	19.5	19.4	19.3	19.1	19.0	19.0	18.9	18.8	18.7
61	66	19.4	19.2	19.1	18.9	18.8	18.7	18.5	18.4	18.3	18.3	18.2	18.1
62	67	18.8	18.7	18.5	18.3	18.2	18.1	18.0	17.8	17.7	17.7	17.6	17.5
63	68	18.3	18.1	18.0	17.8	17.6	17.5	17.4	17.3	17.2	17.1	17.0	16.9
64	69	17.8	17.6	17.4	17.3	17.1	17.0	16.8	16.7	16.6	16.5	16.4	16.3

Male	Female												
65	70	17.3	17.1	16.9	16.7	16.6	16.4	16.3	16.2	16.0	15.9	15.8	15.8
66	71	16.9	16.6	16.4	16.3	16.1	15.9	15.8	15.6	15.5	15.4	15.3	15.2
67	72	16.4	16.2	16.0	15.8	15.6	15.4	15.3	15.1	15.0	14.9	14.8	14.7
68	73	16.0	15.7	15.5	15.3	15.1	15.0	14.8	14.6	14.5	14.4	14.3	14.2
69	74	15.6	15.3	15.1	14.9	14.7	14.5	14.3	14.2	14.0	13.9	13.8	13.7
70	75	15.2	14.9	14.7	14.5	14.3	14.1	13.9	13.7	13.6	13.4	13.3	13.2
71	76	14.8	14.5	14.3	14.1	13.8	13.6	13.5	13.3	13.1	13.0	12.8	12.7
72	77	14.5	14.2	13.9	13.7	13.5	13.2	13.0	12.9	12.7	12.5	12.4	12.3
73	78	14.1	13.8	13.6	13.3	13.1	12.9	12.7	12.5	12.3	12.1	12.0	11.8
74	79	13.8	13.5	13.2	13.0	12.7	12.5	12.3	12.1	11.9	11.7	11.6	11.4
75	80	13.5	13.2	12.9	12.6	12.4	12.2	11.9	11.7	11.5	11.4	11.2	11.0
76	81	13.2	12.9	12.6	12.3	12.1	11.8	11.6	11.4	11.2	11.0	10.8	10.7
77	82	13.0	12.6	12.3	12.1	11.8	11.5	11.3	11.1	10.8	10.7	10.5	10.3
78	83	12.7	12.4	12.1	11.8	11.5	11.2	11.0	10.7	10.5	10.3	10.1	10.0
79	84	12.5	12.2	11.8	11.5	11.2	11.0	10.7	10.5	10.2	10.0	9.8	9.6
80	85	12.3	11.9	11.6	11.3	11.0	10.7	10.4	10.2	10.0	9.7	9.5	9.3
81	86	12.1	11.7	11.4	11.1	10.7	10.5	10.2	9.9	9.7	9.5	9.3	9.1
82	87	11.9	11.5	11.2	10.8	10.5	10.2	10.0	9.7	9.4	9.2	9.0	8.8
83	88	11.7	11.4	11.0	10.7	10.3	10.0	9.7	9.5	9.2	9.0	8.7	8.5
84	89	11.6	11.2	10.8	10.5	10.1	9.8	9.5	9.3	9.0	8.7	8.5	8.3
85	90	11.4	11.0	10.7	10.3	10.0	9.6	9.3	9.1	8.8	8.5	8.3	8.1

Table II—Ordinary Joint Life and Last Survivor Annuities—Two Live—Expected Return Multiples—Continued

Male	Female	Ages											
		Male 86 Female 91	87 92	88 93	89 94	90 95	91 96	92 97	93 98	94 99	95 100	96 101	97 102
35	40	38.3	38.3	38.3	38.3	38.3	38.3	38.3	38.3	38.3	38.3	38.3	38.3
36	41	37.4	37.4	37.4	37.4	37.4	37.4	37.4	37.4	37.4	37.4	37.4	37.4
37	42	36.5	36.5	36.5	36.5	36.5	36.5	36.5	36.5	36.5	36.5	36.5	36.5
38	43	35.7	35.7	35.6	35.6	35.6	35.6	35.6	35.6	35.6	35.6	35.6	35.6
39	44	34.8	34.8	34.8	34.8	34.8	34.8	34.7	34.7	24.7	34.7	34.7	34.7
40	45	33.9	33.9	33.9	33.9	33.9	33.9	33.9	33.9	33.9	33.9	33.9	33.9
41	46	33.1	33.1	33.1	33.0	33.0	33.0	33.0	33.0	33.0	33.0	33.0	33.0
42	47	32.2	32.2	32.2	32.2	32.2	32.2	32.2	32.2	32.2	32.1	32.1	32.1
43	48	31.4	31.4	31.4	31.3	31.3	31.3	31.3	31.3	31.3	31.3	31.3	31.3
44	49	30.6	30.5	30.5	30.5	30.5	30.5	30.5	30.5	30.5	30.5	30.5	30.4
45	50	29.7	29.7	29.7	29.7	29.7	29.7	29.7	29.6	29.6	29.6	29.6	29.6
46	51	28.9	28.9	28.9	28.9	28.9	28.8	28.8	28.8	28.8	28.8	28.8	28.8
47	52	28.1	28.1	28.1	28.1	28.0	28.0	28.0	28.0	28.0	28.0	28.0	28.0
48	53	27.3	27.3	27.3	27.3	27.2	27.2	27.2	27.2	27.2	27.2	27.2	27.2
49	54	26.5	26.5	26.5	26.5	26.5	26.4	26.4	26.4	26.4	26.4	26.4	26.4
50	55	25.8	25.7	25.7	25.7	25.7	25.7	25.6	25.6	25.6	25.6	25.6	25.6
51	56	25.0	25.0	24.9	24.9	24.9	24.9	24.9	24.9	24.8	24.8	24.8	24.8
52	57	24.3	24.2	24.2	24.2	24.1	24.1	24.1	24.1	24.1	24.1	24.1	24.0
53	58	23.5	23.5	23.4	23.4	23.4	23.4	23.4	23.3	23.3	23.3	23.3	23.3
54	59	22.8	22.7	22.7	22.7	22.7	22.6	22.6	22.6	22.6	22.6	22.6	22.5
55	60	22.1	22.0	22.0	22.0	21.9	21.9	21.9	21.9	21.8	21.8	21.8	21.8
56	61	21.4	21.3	21.3	21.3	21.2	21.2	21.2	21.1	21.1	21.1	21.1	21.1
57	62	20.7	20.6	20.6	20.6	20.5	20.5	20.5	20.4	20.4	20.4	20.4	20.4
58	63	20.0	19.9	19.9	19.9	19.8	19.8	19.8	19.8	19.7	19.7	19.7	19.7
59	64	19.3	19.3	19.2	19.2	19.2	19.1	19.1	19.1	19.0	19.0	19.0	19.0

Male	Female	Ages										
		Male 98 Female 103	99 104	100 105	101 106	102 107	103 108	104 109	105 110	106 111	107 112	108 113
35	40	38.3	38.3	38.3	38.3	38.3	38.3	38.2	38.2	38.2	38.2	38.2
36	41	37.4	37.4	37.4	37.4	37.4	37.4	37.4	37.4	37.4	37.4	37.3
37	42	36.5	36.5	36.5	36.5	36.5	36.5	36.5	36.5	36.5	36.5	36.5
38	43	35.6	35.6	35.6	35.6	35.6	35.6	35.6	35.6	35.6	35.6	35.6
39	44	34.7	34.7	34.7	34.7	34.7	34.7	34.7	34.7	34.7	34.7	34.7
40	45	33.9	33.8	33.8	33.8	33.8	33.8	33.8	33.8	33.8	33.8	33.8
41	46	33.0	33.0	33.0	33.0	33.0	33.0	33.0	33.0	33.0	33.0	33.0
42	47	32.1	32.1	32.1	32.1	32.1	32.1	32.1	32.1	32.1	32.1	32.1
43	48	31.3	31.3	31.3	31.3	31.3	31.3	31.3	31.3	31.3	31.3	31.3

Male	Female											
44	49	30.4	30.4	30.4	30.4	30.4	30.4	30.4	30.4	30.4	30.4	30.4
45	50	29.6	29.6	29.6	29.6	29.6	29.6	29.6	29.6	29.6	29.6	29.6
46	51	28.8	28.8	28.8	28.8	28.8	28.8	28.8	28.8	28.8	28.8	28.7
47	52	28.0	28.0	28.0	28.0	28.0	28.0	28.0	27.9	27.9	27.9	27.9
48	53	27.2	27.2	27.2	27.2	27.2	27.1	27.1	27.1	27.1	27.1	27.1
49	54	26.4	26.4	26.4	26.4	26.4	26.3	26.3	26.3	26.3	26.3	26.3
50	55	25.6	25.6	25.6	25.6	25.6	25.6	25.6	25.6	25.5	25.5	25.5
51	56	24.8	24.8	24.8	24.8	24.8	24.8	24.8	24.8	24.8	24.8	24.7
52	57	24.0	24.0	24.0	24.0	24.0	24.0	24.0	24.0	24.0	24.0	24.0
53	58	23.3	23.3	23.3	23.3	23.3	23.3	23.2	23.2	23.2	23.2	23.2
54	59	22.5	22.5	22.5	22.5	22.5	22.5	22.5	22.5	22.5	22.5	22.5
55	60	21.8	21.8	21.8	21.8	21.8	21.8	21.8	21.8	21.8	21.7	21.7
56	61	21.1	21.1	21.1	21.1	21.1	21.0	21.0	21.0	21.0	21.0	21.0
57	62	20.4	20.4	20.4	20.3	20.3	20.3	20.3	20.3	20.3	20.3	20.3
58	63	19.7	19.7	19.7	19.6	19.6	19.6	19.6	19.6	19.6	19.6	19.6
59	64	19.0	19.0	19.0	19.0	19.0	18.9	18.9	18.9	18.9	18.9	18.9

Table II—Ordinary Joint Life and Last Survivor Annuities—Two Lives—Expected Return Multiples—Continued

		Ages											
Male	Female	Male 86 Female 91	87 92	88 93	89 94	90 95	91 96	92 97	93 96	94 99	95 100	96 101	97 102
60..........	65..........	18.7	18.6	18.6	18.5	18.5	18.5	18.4	18.4	18.4	18.4	18.3	18.3
61..........	66..........	18.1	18.0	17.9	17.9	17.9	17.8	17.8	17.8	17.7	17.7	17.7	17.7
62..........	67..........	17.4	17.4	17.3	17.3	17.2	17.2	17.1	17.1	17.1	17.1	17.0	17.0
63..........	68..........	16.8	16.8	16.7	16.7	16.6	16.6	16.5	16.5	16.5	16.4	16.4	16.4
64..........	69..........	16.2	16.2	16.1	16.1	16.0	16.0	15.9	15.9	15.9	15.8	15.8	15.8
65..........	70..........	15.7	15.6	15.5	15.5	15.4	15.4	15.3	15.3	15.3	15.2	15.2	15.2
66..........	71..........	15.1	15.0	15.0	14.9	14.8	14.8	14.7	14.7	14.7	14.6	14.6	14.6
67..........	72..........	14.6	14.5	14.4	14.4	14.3	14.2	14.2	14.1	14.1	14.1	14.1	14.0
68..........	73..........	14.1	14.0	13.9	13.8	13.8	13.7	13.6	13.6	13.6	13.5	13.5	13.5
69..........	74..........	13.6	13.5	13.4	13.3	13.2	13.2	13.1	13.1	13.0	13.0	13.0	12.9
70..........	75..........	13.1	13.0	12.9	12.8	12.7	12.7	12.6	12.5	12.5	12.5	12.4	12.4
71..........	76..........	12.6	12.5	12.4	12.3	12.2	12.2	12.1	12.1	12.0	12.0	11.9	11.9
72..........	77..........	12.1	12.0	11.9	11.8	11.8	11.7	11.6	11.6	11.5	11.5	11.4	11.4
73..........	78..........	11.7	11.6	11.5	11.4	11.3	11.2	11.2	11.1	11.0	11.0	11.0	10.9
74..........	79..........	11.3	11.2	11.1	11.0	10.9	10.8	10.7	10.7	10.6	10.6	10.5	10.5
75..........	80..........	10.9	10.8	10.7	10.5	10.5	10.4	10.3	10.2	10.2	10.1	10.1	10.0
76..........	81..........	10.5	10.4	10.3	10.2	10.1	10.0	9.9	9.8	9.7	9.7	9.7	9.6
77..........	82..........	10.2	10.0	9.9	9.8	9.7	9.6	9.5	9.4	9.3	9.3	9.2	9.2
78..........	83..........	9.8	9.7	9.5	9.4	9.3	9.2	9.1	9.0	9.0	8.9	8.9	8.8
79..........	84..........	9.5	9.3	9.2	9.2	8.9	8.8	8.8	8.7	8.6	8.5	8.5	8.4
80..........	85..........	9.2	9.0	8.9	8.7	8.6	8.5	8.4	8.3	8.3	8.2	8.1	8.1
81..........	86..........	8.9	8.7	8.6	8.4	8.3	8.2	8.1	8.0	7.9	7.9	7.8	7.7
82..........	87..........	8.6	8.4	8.3	8.1	8.0	7.9	7.8	7.7	7.6	7.5	7.5	7.4
83..........	88..........	8.3	8.2	8.0	7.9	7.7	7.6	7.5	7.4	7.3	7.2	7.2	7.1
84..........	89..........	8.1	7.9	7.8	7.6	7.5	7.3	7.2	7.1	7.0	7.0	6.9	6.8

		Ages										
Male	Female	Male 98 Female 103	99 104	100 105	101 106	102 107	103 108	104 109	105 110	106 111	107 112	108 113
60...........	65...........	18.3	18.3	18.3	18.3	18.3	18.3	18.3	18.2	18.2	18.2	18.2
61...........	66...........	17.7	17.7	17.6	17.6	17.6	17.6	17.6	17.6	17.6	17.6	17.5
62...........	67...........	17.0	17.0	17.0	17.0	17.0	17.0	16.9	16.9	16.9	16.9	16.9
63...........	68...........	16.4	16.4	16.4	16.3	16.3	16.3	16.3	16.3	16.3	16.3	16.2
64...........	69...........	15.8	15.8	15.7	15.7	15.7	15.7	15.7	15.7	15.7	15.7	15.6
65...........	70...........	15.2	15.2	15.1	15.1	15.1	15.1	15.1	15.1	15.1	15.0	15.0
66...........	71...........	14.6	14.6	14.5	14.5	14.5	14.5	14.5	14.5	14.5	14.4	14.4
67...........	72...........	14.0	14.0	14.0	14.0	13.9	13.9	13.9	13.9	13.9	13.9	13.8
68...........	73...........	13.5	13.4	13.4	13.4	13.4	13.4	13.3	13.3	13.3	13.3	13.2
69...........	74...........	12.9	12.9	12.9	12.8	12.8	12.8	12.8	12.8	12.8	12.7	12.7
70...........	75...........	12.4	12.4	12.3	12.3	12.3	12.3	12.3	12.2	12.2	12.2	12.1
71...........	76...........	11.9	11.9	11.8	11.8	11.8	11.8	11.7	11.7	11.7	11.7	11.6
72...........	77...........	11.4	11.4	11.3	11.3	11.3	11.3	11.2	11.2	11.2	11.2	11.1
73...........	78...........	10.9	10.9	10.9	10.8	10.8	10.8	10.7	10.7	10.7	10.7	10.6
74...........	79...........	10.5	10.4	10.4	10.4	10.3	10.3	10.3	10.3	10.2	10.2	10.1
75...........	80...........	10.0	10.0	9.9	9.9	9.9	9.8	9.8	9.8	9.8	9.7	...
76...........	81...........	9.6	9.5	9.5	9.5	9.4	9.4	9.4	9.4	9.3	9.3	...

Male	Female											
77	82	9.2	9.1	9.1	9.1	9.0	9.0	9.0	8.9	8.9	8.9	...
78	83	8.8	8.7	8.7	8.7	8.6	8.6	8.5	8.5	8.5	8.4	...
79	84	8.4	8.4	8.3	8.3	8.2	8.2	8.2	8.1	8.1	8.0	...
80	85	8.0	8.0	7.9	7.9	7.9	7.8	7.8	7.7	7.7	7.6	...
81	86	7.7	7.6	7.6	7.6	7.5	7.5	7.4	7.4	7.3	7.3	...
82	87	7.4	7.3	7.3	7.2	7.2	7.1	7.1	7.0	7.0	6.9	...
83	88	7.1	7.0	6.9	6.9	6.8	6.8	6.7	6.7	6.7	6.6	...
84	89	6.8	6.7	6.6	6.6	6.5	6.5	6.4	6.4	6.3	...	...

Table II—Ordinary Joint Life and Last Survivor Annuities—Two Lives—Expected Return Multiples—Continued

Male	Female	Ages										
		Male 86 Female 91	87 92	88 93	89 94	90 95	91 96	92 97	93 98	94 99	95 100	96 101
85	90	7.9	7.7	7.5	7.4	7.2	7.1	7.0	6.9	6.8	6.7	6.6
86	91	7.7	7.5	7.3	7.1	7.0	6.8	6.7	6.6	6.5	6.4	6.4
87	92	7.5	7.3	7.1	6.9	6.8	6.6	6.5	6.4	6.3	6.2	6.1
88	93	7.3	7.1	6.9	6.7	6.6	6.4	6.3	6.2	6.1	6.0	5.9
89	94	7.1	6.9	6.7	6.5	6.4	6.2	6.1	6.0	5.9	5.8	5.7
90	95	7.0	6.8	6.6	6.4	6.2	6.1	5.9	5.8	5.7	5.6	5.5
91	96	6.8	6.6	6.4	6.2	6.1	5.9	5.8	5.7	5.5	5.4	5.3
92	97	6.7	6.5	6.3	6.1	5.9	5.8	5.6	5.5	5.4	5.3	5.2
93	98	6.6	6.4	6.2	6.0	5.8	5.7	5.5	5.4	5.2	5.1	5.0
94	99	6.5	6.3	6.1	5.9	5.7	5.5	5.4	5.2	5.1	5.0	4.9
95	100	6.4	6.2	6.0	5.8	5.6	5.4	5.3	5.1	5.0	4.9	4.7
96	101	6.4	6.1	5.9	5.7	5.5	5.3	5.2	5.0	4.9	4.7	4.6
97	102	6.3	6.1	5.8	5.6	5.4	5.2	5.1	4.9	4.8	4.6	4.5
98	103	6.2	6.0	5.8	5.5	5.3	5.1	5.0	4.8	4.7	4.5	4.4
99	104	6.2	5.9	5.7	5.5	5.2	5.1	4.9	4.7	4.6	4.4	4.3

Male	Female	Ages										
		Male 97 Female 102	98 103	99 104	100 105	101 106	102 107	103 108	104 109	105 110	106 111
85	90	6.6	6.5	6.4	6.4	6.3	6.2	6.2	6.1	6.1	6.0
86	91	6.3	6.2	6.2	6.1	6.0	6.0	5.9	5.9	5.8	5.7
87	92	6.1	6.0	5.9	5.8	5.8	5.7	5.6	5.6	5.5	5.4
88	93	5.8	5.8	5.7	5.6	5.5	5.5	5.4	5.3	5.3	5.1
89	94	5.6	5.5	5.5	5.4	5.3	5.2	5.2	5.1	5.0	...
90	95	5.4	5.3	5.2	5.2	5.1	5.0	4.9	4.9	4.8	...
91	96	5.2	5.1	5.1	5.0	4.9	4.8	4.7	4.6	4.5	...
92	97	5.1	5.0	4.9	4.8	4.7	4.6	4.5	4.4	...	...
93	98	4.9	4.8	4.7	4.6	4.5	4.4	4.3	4.2	...	...
94	99	4.8	4.7	4.6	4.5	4.4	4.3	4.1	...	...	...
95	100	4.6	4.5	4.4	4.3	4.2	4.1	4.0	...	...	...
96	101	4.5	4.4	4.3	4.2	4.1	3.9	...	...	...	...
97	102	4.4	4.3	4.1	4.0	3.9	3.7	...	...	...	...
98	103	4.3	4.1	4.0	3.9	3.7	...	...	...	...	...
99	104	4.1	4.0	3.9	3.7	...	...	...	...	...	...

Table IIA—Annuities for Joint Life Only—Two Lives—Expected Return Multiples

Male	Female	Ages														
		Male 6 Female 11	7 12	8 13	9 14	10 15	11 16	12 17	13 18	14 19	15 20	16 21	17 22	18 23	19 24	20 25
6	11	56.6	56.1	55.7	55.1	54.6	54.1	53.5	52.9	52.3	51.7	51.1	50.5	49.8	49.1	48.4
7	12	56.1	55.7	55.2	54.7	54.2	53.7	53.1	52.6	52.0	51.4	50.8	50.2	49.5	48.9	48.2
8	13	55.7	55.2	54.8	54.3	53.8	53.3	52.8	52.2	51.6	51.1	50.5	49.9	49.2	48.6	47.9
9	14	55.1	54.7	54.3	53.8	53.3	52.9	52.3	51.8	51.3	50.7	50.1	49.5	48.9	48.3	47.7
10	15	54.6	54.2	53.8	53.3	52.9	52.4	51.9	51.4	50.9	50.3	49.8	49.2	48.6	48.0	47.4
11	16	54.1	53.7	53.3	52.9	52.4	52.0	51.5	51.0	50.5	50.0	49.4	48.8	48.3	47.7	47.1
12	17	53.5	53.1	52.8	52.3	51.9	51.5	51.0	50.6	50.1	49.6	49.0	48.5	47.9	47.3	46.7
13	18	52.9	52.6	52.2	51.8	51.4	51.0	50.6	50.1	49.6	49.1	48.6	48.1	47.5	47.0	46.4
14	19	52.3	52.0	51.6	51.3	50.9	50.5	50.1	49.6	49.2	48.7	48.2	47.7	47.2	46.6	46.1
15	20	51.7	51.4	51.1	50.7	50.3	50.0	49.6	49.1	48.7	48.2	47.8	47.3	46.8	46.2	45.7
16	21	51.1	50.8	50.5	50.1	49.8	49.4	49.0	48.6	48.2	47.8	47.3	46.8	46.3	45.8	45.3
17	22	50.5	50.2	49.9	49.5	49.2	48.8	48.5	48.1	47.7	47.3	46.8	46.4	45.9	45.4	44.9
18	23	49.8	49.5	49.2	48.9	48.6	48.3	47.9	47.5	47.2	46.8	46.3	45.9	45.4	45.0	44.5
19	24	49.1	48.9	48.6	48.3	48.0	47.7	47.3	47.0	46.6	46.2	45.8	45.4	45.0	44.5	44.0
20	25	48.4	48.2	47.9	47.7	47.4	47.1	46.7	46.4	46.1	45.7	45.3	44.9	44.5	44.0	43.6

Table IIA—Annuities for Joint Life Only—Two Lives—Expected Return Multiples—Continued

		Ages													
Male	Female	Male 21 Female 26	22 27	23 28	24 29	25 30	26 31	27 32	28 33	29 34	30 35	31 36	32 37	33 38	34 39
6	11	47.7	47.0	46.3	45.6	44.8	44.1	43.3	42.5	41.8	41.0	40.2	39.4	38.6	37.8
7	12	47.5	46.8	46.1	45.4	44.6	43.9	43.2	42.4	41.6	40.9	40.1	39.3	38.5	37.7
8	13	47.3	46.6	45.9	45.2	44.5	43.7	43.0	42.2	41.5	40.7	39.9	39.2	38.4	37.6
9	14	47.0	46.3	45.6	45.0	44.2	43.5	42.8	42.1	41.3	40.6	39.8	39.0	38.3	37.5
10	15	46.7	46.1	45.4	44.7	44.0	43.3	42.6	41.9	41.1	40.4	39.7	38.9	38.1	37.4
11	16	46.4	45.8	45.1	44.5	43.8	43.1	42.4	41.7	41.0	40.2	39.5	38.8	38.0	37.2
12	17	46.1	45.5	44.9	44.2	43.6	42.9	42.2	41.5	40.8	40.1	39.3	38.6	37.9	37.1
13	18	45.8	45.2	44.6	43.9	43.3	42.6	42.0	41.3	40.6	39.9	39.2	38.4	37.7	37.0
14	19	45.5	44.9	44.3	43.7	43.0	42.4	41.7	41.0	40.4	39.7	39.0	38.3	37.5	36.8
15	20	45.1	44.6	44.0	43.4	42.7	42.1	41.5	40.8	40.1	39.5	38.8	38.1	37.4	36.6
16	21	44.8	44.2	43.6	43.0	42.4	41.8	41.2	40.5	39.9	39.2	38.6	37.9	37.2	36.5
17	22	44.4	43.8	43.3	42.7	42.1	41.5	40.9	40.3	39.6	39.0	38.3	37.7	37.0	36.3
18	23	44.0	43.5	42.9	42.4	41.8	41.2	40.6	40.0	39.4	38.7	38.1	37.4	36.8	36.1
19	24	43.6	43.1	42.5	42.0	41.4	40.9	40.3	39.7	39.1	38.5	37.8	37.2	36.5	35.9
20	25	43.1	42.6	42.1	41.6	41.1	40.5	40.0	39.4	38.8	38.2	37.6	36.9	36.3	35.7
21	26	42.7	42.2	41.7	41.2	40.7	40.2	39.6	39.1	38.5	37.9	37.3	36.7	36.1	35.4
22	27	42.2	41.8	41.3	40.8	40.3	39.8	39.3	38.7	38.2	37.6	37.0	36.4	35.8	35.2
23	28	41.7	41.3	40.8	40.4	39.9	39.4	38.9	38.4	37.8	37.3	36.7	36.1	35.5	34.9
24	29	41.2	40.8	40.4	39.9	39.5	39.0	38.5	38.0	37.5	36.9	36.4	35.8	35.2	34.6
25	30	40.7	40.3	39.9	39.5	39.0	38.6	38.1	37.6	37.1	36.6	36.0	35.5	34.9	34.4
26	31	40.2	39.8	39.4	39.0	38.6	38.1	37.7	37.2	36.7	36.2	35.7	35.2	34.6	34.1
27	32	39.6	39.3	38.9	38.5	38.1	37.7	37.2	36.8	36.3	35.8	35.3	34.8	34.3	33.7
28	33	39.1	38.7	38.4	38.0	37.6	37.2	36.8	36.3	35.9	35.4	34.9	34.5	33.9	33.4
29	34	38.5	38.2	37.8	37.5	37.1	36.7	36.3	35.9	35.5	35.0	34.6	34.1	33.6	33.1
30	35	37.9	37.6	37.3	36.9	36.6	36.2	35.8	35.4	35.0	34.6	34.1	33.7	33.2	32.7
31	36	37.3	37.0	36.7	36.4	36.0	35.7	35.3	34.9	34.6	34.1	33.7	33.3	32.8	32.3
32	37	36.7	36.4	36.1	35.8	35.5	35.2	34.8	34.5	34.1	33.7	33.3	32.9	32.4	32.0
33	38	36.1	35.8	35.5	35.2	34.9	34.6	34.3	33.9	33.6	33.2	32.8	32.4	32.0	31.6
34	39	35.4	35.2	34.9	34.6	34.4	34.1	33.7	33.4	33.1	32.7	32.3	32.0	31.6	31.1

		Ages														
Male	Female	Male 35 Female 40	36 41	37 42	38 43	39 44	40 45	41 46	42 47	43 48	44 49	45 50	46 51	47 52	48 53	49 54
6	11	37.0	36.2	35.4	34.6	33.8	33.0	32.2	31.4	30.6	29.8	29.0	28.2	27.5	26.7	25.9
7	12	36.9	36.1	35.3	34.5	33.7	32.9	32.1	31.3	30.5	29.8	29.0	28.2	27.4	26.7	25.9
8	13	36.8	36.0	35.2	34.4	33.7	32.9	32.1	31.3	30.5	29.7	28.9	28.2	27.4	26.6	25.9
9	14	36.7	35.9	35.1	34.4	33.6	32.8	32.0	31.2	30.4	29.7	28.9	28.1	27.3	26.6	25.8
10	15	36.6	35.8	35.1	34.3	33.5	32.7	31.9	31.2	30.4	29.6	28.8	28.1	27.3	26.5	25.8
11	16	36.5	35.7	34.9	34.2	33.4	32.6	31.9	31.1	30.3	29.5	28.8	28.0	27.3	26.5	25.7
12	17	36.4	35.6	34.8	34.1	33.3	32.5	31.8	31.0	30.2	29.5	28.7	28.0	27.2	26.4	25.7
13	18	36.2	35.5	34.7	34.0	33.2	32.4	31.7	30.9	30.2	29.4	28.7	27.9	27.1	26.4	25.7
14	19	36.1	35.3	34.6	33.8	33.1	32.3	31.6	30.8	30.1	29.3	28.6	27.8	27.1	26.3	25.6
15	20	35.9	35.2	34.5	33.7	33.0	32.2	31.5	30.7	30.0	29.3	28.5	27.8	27.0	26.3	25.6
16	21	35.8	35.0	34.3	33.6	32.9	32.1	31.4	30.6	29.9	29.2	28.4	27.7	27.0	26.2	25.5
17	22	35.6	34.9	34.2	33.4	32.7	32.0	31.3	30.5	29.8	29.1	28.3	27.6	26.9	26.2	25.4
18	23	35.4	34.7	34.0	33.3	32.6	31.9	31.2	30.4	29.7	29.0	28.3	27.5	26.8	26.1	25.4
19	24	35.2	34.5	33.8	33.1	32.4	31.7	31.0	30.3	29.6	28.9	28.2	27.4	26.7	26.0	25.3
20	25	35.0	34.3	33.7	33.0	32.3	31.6	30.9	30.2	29.5	28.8	28.1	27.3	26.6	25.9	25.2
21	26	34.8	34.1	33.5	32.8	32.1	31.4	30.7	30.0	29.3	28.6	27.9	27.2	26.5	25.8	25.1
22	27	34.5	33.9	33.3	32.6	31.9	31.3	30.6	29.9	29.2	28.5	27.8	27.1	26.4	25.7	25.1
23	28	34.3	33.7	33.0	32.4	31.7	31.1	30.4	29.7	29.1	28.4	27.7	27.0	26.3	25.6	25.0
24	29	34.0	33.4	32.8	32.2	31.5	30.9	30.2	29.6	28.9	28.2	27.6	26.9	26.2	25.5	24.9
25	30	33.8	33.2	32.6	32.0	31.3	30.7	30.1	29.4	28.8	28.1	27.4	26.8	26.1	25.4	24.8
26	31	33.5	32.9	32.3	31.7	31.1	30.5	29.9	29.2	28.6	27.9	27.3	26.6	26.0	25.3	24.6
27	32	33.2	32.6	32.1	31.5	30.9	30.3	29.6	29.0	28.4	27.8	27.1	26.5	25.8	25.2	24.5
28	33	32.9	32.3	31.8	31.2	30.6	30.0	29.4	28.8	28.2	27.6	27.0	26.3	25.7	25.0	24.4
29	34	32.6	32.0	31.5	30.9	30.4	29.8	29.2	28.6	28.0	27.4	26.8	26.2	25.5	24.9	24.3
30	35	32.2	31.7	31.2	30.6	30.1	29.5	29.0	28.4	27.8	27.2	26.6	26.0	25.4	24.7	24.1
31	36	31.9	31.4	30.9	30.3	29.8	29.3	28.7	28.1	27.6	27.0	26.4	25.8	25.2	24.6	24.0
32	37	31.5	31.0	30.5	30.0	29.5	29.0	28.4	27.9	27.3	26.8	26.2	25.6	25.0	24.4	23.8
33	38	31.1	30.7	30.2	29.7	29.2	28.7	28.2	27.6	27.1	26.5	26.0	25.4	24.8	24.2	23.6
34	39	30.7	30.3	29.8	29.3	28.9	28.4	27.9	27.3	26.8	26.3	25.7	25.2	24.6	24.0	23.5

Table IIA—Annuities for Joint Life Only—Two Lives—Expected Return Multiples—Continued

Male	Female	Ages: Male 50 / Female 55	51 / 56	52 / 57	53 / 58	54 / 59	55 / 60	56 / 61	57 / 62	58 / 63	59 / 64	60 / 65	61 / 66	62 / 67	63 / 68
6	11	25.2	24.4	23.7	22.9	22.2	21.5	20.8	20.1	19.4	18.7	18.0	17.4	16.7	16.1
7	12	25.1	24.4	23.6	22.9	22.2	21.5	20.8	20.1	19.4	18.7	18.0	17.4	16.7	16.1
8	13	25.1	24.4	23.6	22.9	22.2	21.4	20.7	20.0	19.4	18.7	18.0	17.4	16.7	16.1
9	14	25.1	24.3	23.6	22.9	22.1	21.4	20.7	20.0	19.3	18.7	18.0	17.3	16.7	16.1
10	15	25.0	24.3	23.6	22.8	22.1	21.4	20.7	20.0	19.3	18.6	18.0	17.3	16.7	16.1
11	16	25.0	24.3	23.5	22.8	22.1	21.4	20.7	20.0	19.3	18.6	18.0	17.3	16.7	16.1
12	17	25.0	24.2	23.5	22.8	22.1	21.4	20.7	20.0	19.3	18.6	18.0	17.3	16.7	16.0
13	18	24.9	24.2	23.5	22.7	22.0	21.3	20.6	19.9	19.3	18.6	17.9	17.3	16.7	16.0
14	19	24.9	24.1	23.4	22.7	22.0	21.3	20.6	19.9	19.2	18.6	17.9	17.3	16.6	16.0
15	20	24.8	24.1	23.4	22.7	22.0	21.3	20.6	19.9	19.2	18.5	17.9	17.3	16.6	16.0
16	21	24.8	24.0	23.3	22.6	21.9	21.2	20.5	19.9	19.2	18.5	17.9	17.3	16.6	16.0
17	22	24.7	24.0	23.3	22.6	21.9	21.2	20.5	19.8	19.2	18.5	17.8	17.2	16.6	16.0
18	23	24.7	23.9	23.2	22.5	21.8	21.1	20.5	19.8	19.1	18.5	17.8	17.2	16.6	15.9
19	24	24.6	23.9	23.2	22.5	21.8	21.1	20.4	19.8	19.1	18.4	17.8	17.2	16.5	15.9
20	25	24.5	23.8	23.1	22.4	21.7	21.1	20.4	19.7	19.1	18.4	17.8	17.1	16.5	15.9
21	26	24.4	23.7	23.1	22.4	21.7	21.0	20.3	19.7	19.0	18.4	17.7	17.1	16.5	15.9
22	27	24.4	23.7	23.0	22.3	21.6	21.0	20.3	19.6	19.0	18.3	17.7	17.1	16.5	15.9
23	28	24.3	23.6	22.9	22.2	21.6	20.9	20.2	19.6	18.9	18.3	17.7	17.0	16.4	15.8
24	29	24.2	23.5	22.8	22.2	21.5	20.8	20.2	19.5	18.9	18.3	17.6	17.0	16.4	15.8
25	30	24.1	23.4	22.8	22.1	21.4	20.8	20.1	19.5	18.8	18.2	17.6	17.0	16.4	15.8
26	31	24.0	23.3	22.7	22.0	21.4	20.7	20.1	19.4	18.8	18.2	17.5	16.9	16.3	15.7
27	32	23.9	23.2	22.6	21.9	21.3	20.6	20.0	19.4	18.7	18.1	17.5	16.9	16.3	15.7
28	33	23.8	23.1	22.5	21.8	21.2	20.6	19.9	19.3	18.7	18.1	17.4	16.8	16.2	15.6
29	34	23.6	23.0	22.4	21.7	21.1	20.5	19.8	19.2	18.6	18.0	17.4	16.8	16.2	15.6
30	35	23.5	22.9	22.3	21.6	21.0	20.4	19.8	19.1	18.5	17.9	17.3	16.7	16.1	15.6
31	36	23.4	22.7	22.1	21.5	20.9	20.3	19.7	19.1	18.5	17.9	17.3	16.7	16.1	15.5
32	37	23.2	22.6	22.0	21.4	20.8	20.2	19.6	19.0	18.4	17.8	17.2	16.6	16.0	15.5
33	38	23.1	22.5	21.9	21.3	20.7	20.1	19.5	18.9	18.3	17.7	17.1	16.5	16.0	15.4
34	39	22.9	22.3	21.7	21.1	20.5	20.0	19.4	18.8	18.2	17.6	17.0	16.5	15.9	15.3

Male	Female	Ages: Male 64 / Female 69	65 / 70	66 / 71	67 / 72	68 / 73	69 / 74	70 / 75	71 / 76	72 / 77	73 / 78	74 / 79	75 / 80	76 / 81	77 / 82	78 / 83
6	11	15.5	14.9	14.3	13.7	13.1	12.6	12.0	11.5	11.0	10.5	10.0	9.6	9.1	8.7	8.2
7	12	15.5	14.9	14.3	13.7	13.1	12.6	12.0	11.5	11.0	10.5	10.0	9.6	9.1	8.7	8.2
8	13	15.5	14.9	14.3	13.7	13.1	12.6	12.0	11.5	11.0	10.5	10.0	9.6	9.1	8.7	8.2
9	14	15.5	14.9	14.3	13.7	13.1	12.6	12.0	11.5	11.0	10.5	10.0	9.5	9.1	8.7	8.2
10	15	15.4	14.8	14.3	13.7	13.1	12.6	12.0	11.5	11.0	10.5	10.0	9.5	9.1	8.7	8.2
11	16	15.4	14.8	14.2	13.7	13.1	12.6	12.0	11.5	11.0	10.5	10.0	9.5	9.1	8.7	8.2
12	17	15.4	14.8	14.2	13.7	13.1	12.5	12.0	11.5	11.0	10.5	10.0	9.5	9.1	8.6	8.2
13	18	15.4	14.8	14.2	13.6	13.1	12.5	12.0	11.5	11.0	10.5	10.0	9.5	9.1	8.6	8.2
14	19	15.4	14.8	14.2	13.6	13.1	12.5	12.0	11.5	11.0	10.5	10.0	9.5	9.1	8.6	8.2
15	20	15.4	14.8	14.2	13.6	13.1	12.5	12.0	11.5	11.0	10.5	10.0	9.5	9.1	8.6	8.2
16	21	15.4	14.8	14.2	13.6	13.1	12.5	12.0	11.5	11.0	10.5	10.0	9.5	9.1	8.6	8.2
17	22	15.4	14.8	14.2	13.6	13.0	12.5	12.0	11.5	10.9	10.5	10.0	9.5	9.1	8.6	8.2
18	23	15.3	14.7	14.2	13.6	13.0	12.5	12.0	11.4	10.9	10.4	10.0	9.5	9.1	8.6	8.2
19	24	15.3	14.7	14.1	13.6	13.0	12.5	12.0	11.4	10.9	10.4	10.0	9.5	9.1	8.6	8.2
20	25	15.3	14.7	14.1	13.6	13.0	12.5	11.9	11.4	10.9	10.4	10.0	9.5	9.0	8.6	8.2
21	26	15.3	14.7	14.1	13.5	13.0	12.5	11.9	11.4	10.9	10.4	9.9	9.5	9.0	8.6	8.2
22	27	15.3	14.7	14.1	13.5	13.0	12.4	11.9	11.4	10.9	10.4	9.9	9.5	9.0	8.6	8.2
23	28	15.2	14.6	14.1	13.5	13.0	12.4	11.9	11.4	10.9	10.4	9.9	9.5	9.0	8.6	8.2
24	29	15.2	14.6	14.0	13.5	12.9	12.4	11.9	11.4	10.9	10.4	9.9	9.5	9.0	8.6	8.2
25	30	15.2	14.6	14.0	13.5	12.9	12.4	11.9	11.4	10.9	10.4	9.9	9.5	9.0	8.6	8.2
26	31	15.1	14.6	14.0	13.4	12.9	12.4	11.9	11.3	10.8	10.4	9.9	9.4	9.0	8.6	8.2
27	32	15.1	14.5	14.0	13.4	12.9	12.4	11.8	11.3	10.8	10.4	9.9	9.4	9.0	8.6	8.2
28	33	15.1	14.5	13.9	13.4	12.9	12.3	11.8	11.3	10.8	10.3	9.9	9.4	9.0	8.6	8.2
29	34	15.0	14.5	13.9	13.4	12.8	12.3	11.8	11.3	10.8	10.3	9.9	9.4	9.0	8.6	8.1
30	35	15.0	14.4	13.9	13.3	12.8	12.3	11.8	11.3	10.8	10.3	9.8	9.4	9.0	8.5	8.1
31	36	14.9	14.4	13.8	13.3	12.8	12.2	11.7	11.2	10.8	10.3	9.8	9.4	8.9	8.5	8.1
32	37	14.9	14.3	13.8	13.3	12.7	12.2	11.7	11.2	10.7	10.3	9.8	9.4	8.9	8.5	8.1
33	38	14.8	14.3	13.8	13.2	12.7	12.2	11.7	11.2	10.7	10.2	9.8	9.3	8.9	8.5	8.1
34	39	14.8	14.2	13.7	13.2	12.7	12.2	11.7	11.2	10.7	10.2	9.8	9.3	8.9	8.5	8.1

Table IIA—Annuities for Joint Life Only—Two Lives—Expected Return Multiples—Continued

Male	Female	Male 79 Female 84	80 85	81 86	82 87	83 88	84 89	85 90	86 91	87 92	88 93	89 94	90 95	91 96	92 97	93 98
		Ages														
6	11	7.8	7.4	7.1	6.7	6.3	6.0	5.7	5.4	5.1	4.8	4.5	4.2	4.0	3.7	3.5
7	12	7.8	7.4	7.1	6.7	6.3	6.0	5.7	5.4	5.1	4.8	4.5	4.2	4.0	3.7	3.5
8	13	7.8	7.4	7.0	6.7	6.3	6.0	5.7	5.4	5.1	4.8	4.5	4.2	4.0	3.7	3.5
9	14	7.8	7.4	7.0	6.7	6.3	6.0	5.7	5.4	5.1	4.8	4.5	4.2	4.0	3.7	3.5
10	15	7.8	7.4	7.0	6.7	6.3	6.0	5.7	5.4	5.1	4.8	4.5	4.2	4.0	3.7	3.5
11	16	7.8	7.4	7.0	6.7	6.3	6.0	5.7	5.4	5.1	4.8	4.5	4.2	4.0	3.7	3.5
12	17	7.8	7.4	7.0	6.7	6.3	6.0	5.7	5.4	5.1	4.8	4.5	4.2	4.0	3.7	3.5
13	18	7.8	7.4	7.0	6.7	6.3	6.0	5.7	5.3	5.1	4.8	4.5	4.2	4.0	3.7	3.5
14	19	7.8	7.4	7.0	6.7	6.3	6.0	5.7	5.3	5.0	4.8	4.5	4.2	4.0	3.7	3.5
15	20	7.8	7.4	7.0	6.7	6.3	6.0	5.7	5.3	5.0	4.8	4.5	4.2	4.0	3.7	3.5
16	21	7.8	7.4	7.0	6.7	6.3	6.0	5.7	5.3	5.0	4.8	4.5	4.2	4.0	3.7	3.5
17	22	7.8	7.4	7.0	6.7	6.3	6.0	5.7	5.3	5.0	4.8	4.5	4.2	4.0	3.7	3.5
18	23	7.8	7.4	7.0	6.7	6.3	6.0	5.7	5.3	5.0	4.8	4.5	4.2	4.0	3.7	3.5
19	24	7.8	7.4	7.0	6.7	6.3	6.0	5.7	5.3	5.0	4.8	4.5	4.2	4.0	3.7	3.5
20	25	7.8	7.4	7.0	6.7	6.3	6.0	5.6	5.3	5.0	4.8	4.5	4.2	4.0	3.7	3.5
21	26	7.8	7.4	7.0	6.7	6.3	6.0	5.6	5.3	5.0	4.8	4.5	4.2	4.0	3.7	3.5
22	27	7.8	7.4	7.0	6.7	6.3	6.0	5.6	5.3	5.0	4.8	4.5	4.2	4.0	3.7	3.5
23	28	7.8	7.4	7.0	6.6	6.3	6.0	5.6	5.3	5.0	4.8	4.5	4.2	4.0	3.7	3.5
24	29	7.8	7.4	7.0	6.6	6.3	6.0	5.6	5.3	5.0	4.7	4.5	4.2	4.0	3.7	3.5
25	30	7.8	7.4	7.0	6.6	6.3	6.0	5.6	5.3	5.0	4.7	4.5	4.2	4.0	3.7	3.5
26	31	7.8	7.4	7.0	6.6	6.3	6.0	5.6	5.3	5.0	4.7	4.5	4.2	4.0	3.7	3.5
27	32	7.7	7.4	7.0	6.6	6.3	5.9	5.6	5.3	5.0	4.7	4.5	4.2	4.0	3.7	3.5
28	33	7.7	7.4	7.0	6.6	6.3	5.9	5.6	5.3	5.0	4.7	4.5	4.2	4.0	3.7	3.5
29	34	7.7	7.3	7.0	6.6	6.3	5.9	5.6	5.3	5.0	4.7	4.5	4.2	4.0	3.7	3.5
30	35	7.7	7.3	7.0	6.6	6.3	5.9	5.6	5.3	5.0	4.7	4.5	4.2	4.0	3.7	3.5
31	36	7.7	7.3	7.0	6.6	6.3	5.9	5.6	5.3	5.0	4.7	4.5	4.2	4.0	3.7	3.5
32	37	7.7	7.3	7.0	6.6	6.3	5.9	5.6	5.3	5.0	4.7	4.5	4.2	4.0	3.7	3.5
33	38	7.7	7.3	6.9	6.6	6.2	5.9	5.6	5.3	5.0	4.7	4.5	4.2	3.9	3.7	3.5
34	39	7.7	7.3	6.9	6.6	6.2	5.9	5.6	5.3	5.0	4.7	4.4	4.2	3.9	3.7	3.5

Male	Female	Male 94 Female 99	95 100	96 101	97 102	98 103	99 104	100 105	101 106	102 107	103 108	104 109	105 110	106 111	107 112	108 113
		Ages														
6	11	3.3	3.1	2.9	2.7	2.5	2.3	2.1	1.9	1.7	1.5	1.3	1.2	1.0	0.8	0.7
7	12	3.3	3.1	2.9	2.7	2.5	2.3	2.1	1.9	1.7	1.5	1.3	1.2	1.0	0.8	0.7
8	13	3.3	3.1	2.9	2.7	2.5	2.3	2.1	1.9	1.7	1.5	1.3	1.2	1.0	0.8	0.7
9	14	3.3	3.1	2.9	2.7	2.5	2.3	2.1	1.9	1.7	1.5	1.3	1.2	1.0	0.8	0.7
10	15	3.3	3.1	2.9	2.7	2.5	2.3	2.1	1.9	1.7	1.5	1.3	1.2	1.0	0.8	0.7
11	16	3.3	3.1	2.9	2.7	2.5	2.3	2.1	1.9	1.7	1.5	1.3	1.2	1.0	0.8	0.7
12	17	3.3	3.1	2.9	2.7	2.5	2.3	2.1	1.9	1.7	1.5	1.3	1.2	1.0	0.8	0.7
13	18	3.3	3.1	2.9	2.7	2.5	2.3	2.1	1.9	1.7	1.5	1.3	1.2	1.0	0.8	0.7
14	19	3.3	3.1	2.9	2.7	2.5	2.3	2.1	1.9	1.7	1.5	1.3	1.2	1.0	0.8	0.7
15	20	3.3	3.1	2.9	2.7	2.5	2.3	2.1	1.9	1.7	1.5	1.3	1.2	1.0	0.8	0.7
16	21	3.3	3.1	2.9	2.7	2.5	2.3	2.1	1.9	1.7	1.5	1.3	1.2	1.0	0.8	0.7
17	22	3.3	3.1	2.9	2.7	2.5	2.3	2.1	1.9	1.7	1.5	1.3	1.2	1.0	0.8	0.7
18	23	3.3	3.1	2.9	2.7	2.5	2.3	2.1	1.9	1.7	1.5	1.3	1.2	1.0	0.8	0.7
19	24	3.3	3.1	2.9	2.7	2.5	2.3	2.1	1.9	1.7	1.5	1.3	1.2	1.0	0.8	0.7
20	25	3.3	3.1	2.9	2.7	2.5	2.3	2.1	1.9	1.7	1.5	1.3	1.2	1.0	0.8	0.7
21	26	3.3	3.1	2.9	2.7	2.5	2.3	2.1	1.9	1.7	1.5	1.3	1.2	1.0	0.8	0.7
22	27	3.3	3.1	2.9	2.7	2.5	2.3	2.1	1.9	1.7	1.5	1.3	1.2	1.0	0.8	0.7
23	28	3.3	3.1	2.9	2.7	2.5	2.3	2.1	1.9	1.7	1.5	1.3	1.2	1.0	0.8	0.7
24	29	3.3	3.1	2.9	2.7	2.5	2.3	2.1	1.9	1.7	1.5	1.3	1.2	1.0	0.8	0.7
25	30	3.3	3.1	2.9	2.7	2.5	2.3	2.1	1.9	1.7	1.5	1.3	1.2	1.0	0.8	0.7
26	31	3.3	3.1	2.9	2.7	2.5	2.3	2.1	1.9	1.7	1.5	1.3	1.2	1.0	0.8	0.7
27	32	3.3	3.1	2.9	2.7	2.5	2.3	2.1	1.9	1.7	1.5	1.3	1.2	1.0	0.8	0.7
28	33	3.3	3.1	2.9	2.7	2.5	2.3	2.1	1.9	1.7	1.5	1.3	1.2	1.0	0.8	0.7
29	34	3.3	3.1	2.9	2.7	2.5	2.3	2.1	1.9	1.7	1.5	1.3	1.2	1.0	0.8	0.7
30	35	3.3	3.1	2.9	2.7	2.5	2.3	2.1	1.9	1.7	1.5	1.3	1.2	1.0	0.8	0.7
31	36	3.3	3.1	2.9	2.7	2.5	2.3	2.1	1.9	1.7	1.5	1.3	1.2	1.0	0.8	0.7
32	37	3.3	3.1	2.9	2.7	2.5	2.3	2.1	1.9	1.7	1.5	1.3	1.2	1.0	0.8	0.7
33	38	3.3	3.1	2.9	2.7	2.5	2.3	2.1	1.9	1.7	1.5	1.3	1.2	1.0	0.8	0.7
34	39	3.3	3.1	2.9	2.7	2.5	2.3	2.1	1.9	1.7	1.5	1.3	1.2	1.0	0.8	0.7

Table IIA—Annuities for Joint Life Only—Two Lives—Expected Return Multiples—Continued

Male	Female	Ages: Male 35 / Female 40	36 / 41	37 / 42	38 / 43	39 / 44	40 / 45	41 / 46	42 / 47	43 / 48	44 / 49	45 / 50	46 / 51	47 / 52
35	40	30.3	29.9	29.4	29.0	28.5	28.0	27.5	27.0	26.5	26.0	25.5	24.9	24.4
36	41	29.9	29.5	29.0	28.6	28.2	27.7	27.2	26.7	26.2	25.7	25.2	24.7	24.2
37	42	29.4	29.0	28.6	28.2	27.8	27.3	26.9	26.4	25.9	25.5	25.0	24.4	24.2
38	43	29.0	28.6	28.2	27.8	27.4	27.0	26.5	26.1	25.6	25.2	24.7	24.2	23.9
39	44	28.5	28.2	27.8	27.4	27.0	26.6	26.2	25.8	25.3	24.8	24.4	23.9	23.7
40	45	28.0	27.7	27.3	27.0	26.6	26.2	25.8	25.4	25.0	24.5	24.1	23.6	23.4
41	46	27.5	27.2	26.9	26.5	26.2	25.8	25.4	25.0	24.6	24.2	23.8	23.3	23.1
42	47	27.0	26.7	26.4	26.1	25.8	25.4	25.0	24.6	24.2	23.8	23.4	23.0	22.6
43	48	26.5	26.2	25.9	25.6	25.3	25.0	24.6	24.2	23.9	23.5	23.1	22.7	22.2
44	49	26.0	25.7	25.5	25.2	24.8	24.5	24.2	23.8	23.5	23.1	22.7	22.3	21.9
45	50	25.5	25.2	25.0	24.7	24.4	24.1	23.8	23.4	23.1	22.7	22.4	22.0	21.6
46	51	24.9	24.7	24.4	24.2	23.9	23.6	23.3	23.0	22.7	22.3	22.0	21.6	21.2
47	52	24.4	24.2	23.9	23.7	23.4	23.1	22.9	22.6	22.2	21.9	21.6	21.2	20.9

Male	Female	Ages: Male 48 / Female 53	49 / 54	50 / 55	51 / 56	52 / 57	53 / 58	54 / 59	55 / 60	56 / 61	57 / 62	58 / 63	59 / 64	60 / 65
35	40	23.8	23.3	22.7	22.1	21.6	21.0	20.4	19.8	19.3	18.7	18.1	17.5	17.0
36	41	23.6	23.1	22.5	22.0	21.4	20.8	20.3	19.7	19.1	18.6	18.0	17.4	16.9
37	42	23.4	22.9	22.3	21.8	21.2	20.7	20.1	19.6	19.0	18.4	17.9	17.3	16.8
38	43	23.2	22.6	22.1	21.6	21.1	20.5	20.0	19.4	18.9	18.3	17.8	17.2	16.7
39	44	22.9	22.4	21.9	21.4	20.9	20.3	19.8	19.3	18.7	18.2	17.7	17.1	16.6
40	45	22.7	22.2	21.7	21.2	20.7	20.1	19.6	19.1	18.6	18.0	17.5	17.0	16.5
41	46	22.4	21.9	21.4	20.9	20.4	19.9	19.4	18.9	18.4	17.9	17.4	16.9	16.3
42	47	22.1	21.6	21.2	20.7	20.2	19.7	19.2	18.7	18.2	17.7	17.2	16.7	16.2
43	48	21.8	21.4	20.9	20.5	20.0	19.5	19.0	18.6	18.1	17.6	17.1	16.6	16.1
44	49	21.5	21.1	20.6	20.2	19.8	19.3	18.8	18.4	17.9	17.4	16.9	16.4	15.9
45	50	21.2	20.8	20.4	19.9	19.5	19.1	18.6	18.1	17.7	17.2	16.7	16.3	15.8
46	51	20.9	20.5	20.1	19.7	19.2	18.8	18.4	17.9	17.5	17.0	16.6	16.1	15.6
47	52	20.5	20.1	19.8	19.4	19.0	18.5	18.1	17.7	17.3	16.8	16.4	15.9	15.5
48	53	20.2	19.8	19.4	19.1	18.7	18.3	17.9	17.5	17.0	16.6	16.2	15.7	15.3
49	54	19.8	19.5	19.1	18.8	18.4	18.0	17.6	17.2	16.8	16.4	16.0	15.5	15.1
50	55	19.4	19.1	18.8	18.4	18.1	17.7	17.3	16.9	16.6	16.2	15.8	15.3	14.9
51	56	19.1	18.8	18.4	18.1	17.8	17.4	17.0	16.7	16.3	15.9	15.5	15.1	14.7
52	57	18.7	18.4	18.1	17.8	17.4	17.1	16.8	16.4	16.0	15.7	15.3	14.9	14.5
53	58	18.3	18.0	17.7	17.4	17.1	16.8	16.4	16.1	15.8	15.4	15.1	14.7	14.3
54	59	17.9	17.6	17.3	17.0	16.8	16.4	16.1	15.8	15.5	15.1	14.8	14.4	14.1
55	60	17.5	17.2	16.9	16.7	16.4	16.1	15.8	15.5	15.2	14.9	14.5	14.2	13.9
56	61	17.0	16.8	16.6	16.3	16.0	15.8	15.5	15.2	14.9	14.6	14.3	13.9	13.6
57	62	16.6	16.4	16.2	15.9	15.7	15.4	15.1	14.9	14.6	14.3	14.0	13.7	13.4
58	63	16.2	16.0	15.8	15.5	15.3	15.1	14.8	14.5	14.3	14.0	13.7	13.4	13.1
59	64	15.7	15.5	15.3	15.1	14.9	14.7	14.4	14.2	13.9	13.7	13.4	13.1	12.8
60	65	15.3	15.1	14.9	14.7	14.5	14.3	14.1	13.9	13.6	13.4	13.1	12.8	12.6

Table IIA—Annuities for Joint Life Only—Two Lives—Expected Return Multiples—Continued

Male	Female	Ages: Male 61 / Female 66	62 / 67	63 / 68	64 / 69	65 / 70	66 / 71	67 / 72	68 / 73	69 / 74	70 / 74	71 / 76	72 / 77	73 / 78
35	40	16.4	15.8	15.3	14.7	14.2	13.7	13.1	12.6	12.1	11.6	11.1	10.7	10.2
36	41	16.3	15.8	15.2	14.7	14.1	13.6	13.1	12.6	12.1	11.6	11.1	10.6	10.2
37	42	16.2	15.7	15.1	14.6	14.1	13.6	13.0	12.5	12.0	11.5	11.1	10.6	10.1
38	43	16.1	15.6	15.1	14.5	14.0	13.5	13.0	12.5	12.0	11.5	11.0	10.6	10.1
39	44	16.0	15.5	15.0	14.5	13.9	13.4	12.9	12.4	11.9	11.5	11.0	10.5	10.1
40	45	15.9	15.4	14.9	14.4	13.9	13.4	12.9	12.4	11.9	11.4	11.0	10.5	10.0
41	46	15.8	15.3	14.8	14.3	13.8	13.3	12.8	12.3	11.8	11.4	10.9	10.5	10.0

Male	Female													
42	47	15.7	15.2	14.7	14.2	13.7	13.2	12.7	12.3	11.8	11.3	10.9	10.4	10.0
43	48	15.6	15.1	14.6	14.1	13.6	13.1	12.7	12.2	11.7	11.3	10.8	10.4	9.9
44	49	15.5	15.0	14.5	14.0	13.5	13.1	12.6	12.1	11.7	11.2	10.8	10.3	9.9
45	50	15.3	14.8	14.4	13.9	13.4	13.0	12.5	12.0	11.6	11.1	10.7	10.3	9.8
46	51	15.2	14.7	14.2	13.8	13.3	12.9	12.4	12.0	11.5	11.1	10.6	10.2	9.8
47	52	15.0	14.6	14.1	13.7	13.2	12.8	12.3	11.9	11.4	11.0	10.6	10.1	9.7
48	53	14.9	14.4	14.0	13.5	13.1	12.6	12.2	11.8	11.3	10.9	10.5	10.1	9.7
49	54	14.7	14.3	13.8	13.4	13.0	12.5	12.1	11.7	11.3	10.8	10.4	10.0	9.6
50	55	14.5	14.1	13.7	13.3	12.8	12.4	12.0	11.6	11.2	10.7	10.3	9.9	9.5
51	56	14.3	13.9	13.5	13.1	12.7	12.3	11.9	11.5	11.1	10.7	10.3	9.9	9.5
52	57	14.1	13.7	13.3	12.9	12.5	12.1	11.7	11.3	10.9	10.6	10.2	9.8	9.4
53	58	13.9	13.6	13.2	12.8	12.4	12.0	11.6	11.2	10.8	10.5	10.1	9.7	9.3
54	59	13.7	13.4	13.0	12.6	12.2	11.9	11.5	11.1	10.7	10.3	10.0	9.6	9.2
55	60	13.5	13.2	12.8	12.4	12.1	11.7	11.3	11.0	10.6	10.2	9.9	9.5	9.1
56	61	13.3	12.9	12.6	12.2	11.9	11.5	11.2	10.8	10.5	10.1	9.8	9.4	9.0
57	62	13.0	12.7	12.4	12.1	11.7	11.4	11.0	10.7	10.3	10.0	9.6	9.3	8.9
58	63	12.8	12.5	12.2	11.8	11.5	11.2	10.9	10.5	10.2	9.8	9.5	9.2	8.8
59	64	12.6	12.3	11.9	11.6	11.3	11.0	10.7	10.4	10.0	9.7	9.4	9.1	8.7
60	65	12.3	12.0	11.7	11.4	11.1	10.8	10.5	10.2	9.9	9.6	9.3	8.9	8.6
61	66	12.0	11.8	11.5	11.2	10.9	10.6	10.3	10.0	9.7	9.4	9.1	8.8	8.5
62	67	11.8	11.5	11.2	11.0	10.7	10.4	10.1	9.8	9.6	9.3	9.0	8.7	8.4
63	68	11.5	11.2	11.0	10.7	10.5	10.2	9.9	9.7	9.4	9.1	8.8	8.5	8.2
64	69	11.2	11.0	10.7	10.5	10.2	10.0	9.7	9.5	9.2	8.9	8.7	8.4	8.1
65	70	10.9	10.7	10.5	10.2	10.0	9.8	9.5	9.3	9.0	8.8	8.5	8.2	8.0
66	71	10.6	10.4	10.2	10.0	9.8	9.5	9.3	9.1	8.8	8.6	8.3	8.1	7.8
67	72	10.3	10.1	9.9	9.7	9.5	9.3	9.1	8.9	8.6	8.4	8.1	7.9	7.7
68	73	10.0	9.8	9.7	9.5	9.3	9.1	8.9	8.6	8.4	8.2	8.0	7.7	7.5
69	74	9.7	9.6	9.4	9.2	9.0	8.8	8.6	8.4	8.2	8.0	7.8	7.6	7.3
70	75	9.4	9.3	9.1	8.9	8.8	8.6	8.4	8.2	8.0	7.8	7.6	7.4	7.2
71	76	9.1	9.0	8.8	8.7	8.5	8.3	8.1	8.0	7.8	7.6	7.4	7.2	7.0
72	77	8.8	8.7	8.5	8.4	8.2	8.1	7.9	7.7	7.6	7.4	7.2	7.0	6.8
73	78	8.5	8.4	8.2	8.1	8.0	7.8	7.7	7.5	7.3	7.2	7.0	6.8	6.7

Table IIA—Annuities for Joint Life Only—Two Lives—Expected Return Multiples—Continued

		Ages												
Male	Female	Male 74 Female 79	75 80	76 81	77 82	78 83	79 84	80 85	81 86	82 87	83 88	84 89	85 90	86 91
35	40	9.7	9.3	8.9	8.5	8.1	7.7	7.3	6.9	6.6	6.2	5.9	5.6	5.3
36	41	9.7	9.3	8.9	8.4	8.0	7.7	7.3	6.9	6.6	6.2	5.9	5.6	5.3
37	42	9.7	9.3	8.8	8.4	8.0	7.6	7.3	6.9	6.5	6.2	5.9	5.6	5.3
38	43	9.7	9.2	8.8	8.4	8.0	7.6	7.2	6.9	6.5	6.2	5.9	5.6	5.3
39	44	9.6	9.2	8.8	8.4	8.0	7.6	7.2	6.9	6.5	6.2	5.9	5.6	5.3
40	45	9.6	9.2	8.8	8.4	8.0	7.6	7.2	6.9	6.5	6.2	5.9	5.5	5.2
41	46	9.6	9.2	8.7	8.3	7.9	7.6	7.2	6.8	6.5	6.2	5.8	5.5	5.2
42	47	9.5	9.1	8.7	8.3	7.9	7.5	7.2	6.8	6.5	6.2	5.8	5.5	5.2
43	48	9.5	9.1	8.7	8.3	7.9	7.5	7.2	6.8	6.5	6.1	5.8	5.5	5.2
44	49	9.5	9.0	8.6	8.2	7.9	7.5	7.1	6.8	6.4	6.1	5.8	5.5	5.2
45	50	9.4	9.0	8.6	8.2	7.8	7.5	7.1	6.8	6.4	6.1	5.8	5.5	5.2
46	51	9.4	9.0	8.6	8.2	7.8	7.4	7.1	6.7	6.4	6.1	5.8	5.5	5.2
47	52	9.3	8.9	8.5	8.1	7.8	7.4	7.1	6.7	6.4	6.1	5.8	5.5	5.2
48	53	9.3	8.9	8.5	8.1	7.7	7.4	7.0	6.7	6.4	6.0	5.7	5.4	5.1
49	54	9.2	8.8	8.4	8.1	7.7	7.3	7.0	6.7	6.3	6.0	5.7	5.4	5.1
50	55	9.1	8.8	8.4	8.0	7.7	7.3	7.0	6.6	6.3	6.0	5.7	5.4	5.1
51	56	9.1	8.7	8.3	8.0	7.6	7.3	6.9	6.6	6.3	6.0	5.7	5.4	5.1
52	57	9.0	8.6	8.3	7.9	7.6	7.2	6.9	6.6	6.2	5.9	5.6	5.4	5.1
53	58	8.9	8.6	8.2	7.9	7.5	7.2	6.9	6.5	6.2	5.9	5.6	5.3	5.1
54	59	8.9	8.5	8.2	7.8	7.5	7.1	6.8	6.5	6.2	5.9	5.6	5.3	5.0
55	60	8.8	8.4	8.1	7.7	7.4	7.1	6.8	6.4	6.1	5.8	5.6	5.3	5.0
56	61	8.7	8.4	8.0	7.7	7.3	7.0	6.7	6.4	6.1	5.8	5.5	5.3	5.0
57	62	8.6	8.3	7.9	7.6	7.3	7.0	6.7	6.4	6.1	5.8	5.5	5.2	5.0
58	63	8.5	8.2	7.9	7.5	7.2	6.9	6.6	6.3	6.0	5.7	5.5	5.2	4.9

59	64	8.4	8.1	7.8	7.5	7.1	6.8	6.5	6.3	6.0	5.7	5.4	5.2	4.9
60	65	8.3	8.0	7.7	7.4	7.1	6.8	6.5	6.2	5.9	5.6	5.4	5.1	4.9
61	66	8.2	7.9	7.6	7.3	7.0	6.7	6.4	6.1	5.9	5.6	5.3	5.1	4.8
62	67	8.1	7.8	7.5	7.2	6.9	6.6	6.4	6.1	5.8	5.5	5.3	5.0	4.8
63	68	8.0	7.7	7.4	7.1	6.8	6.6	6.3	6.0	5.7	5.5	5.2	5.0	4.7
64	69	7.8	7.6	7.3	7.0	6.7	6.5	6.2	5.9	5.7	5.4	5.2	4.9	4.7
65	70	7.7	7.4	7.2	6.9	6.6	6.4	6.1	5.9	5.6	5.4	5.1	4.9	4.7
66	71	7.6	7.3	7.1	6.8	6.5	6.3	6.0	5.8	5.5	5.3	5.1	4.8	4.6
67	72	7.4	7.2	6.9	6.7	6.4	6.2	6.0	5.7	5.5	5.2	5.0	4.8	4.6
68	73	7.3	7.0	6.8	6.6	6.3	6.1	5.9	5.6	5.4	5.2	4.9	4.7	4.5
69	74	7.1	6.9	6.7	6.4	6.2	6.0	5.8	5.5	5.3	5.1	4.9	4.7	4.5
70	75	7.0	6.8	6.5	6.3	6.1	5.9	5.7	5.4	5.2	5.0	4.8	4.6	4.4
71	76	6.8	6.6	6.4	6.2	6.0	5.8	5.6	5.3	5.1	4.9	4.7	4.5	4.3
72	77	6.6	6.4	6.3	6.1	5.9	5.7	5.5	5.3	5.0	4.9	4.7	4.5	4.3
73	78	6.5	6.3	6.1	5.9	5.7	5.5	5.3	5.1	5.0	4.8	4.6	4.4	4.2
74	79	6.3	6.1	6.0	5.8	5.6	5.4	5.2	5.0	4.9	4.7	4.5	4.3	4.1
75	80	6.1	6.0	5.8	5.6	5.5	5.3	5.1	4.9	4.8	4.6	4.4	4.2	4.1
76	81	6.0	5.8	5.6	5.5	5.3	5.2	5.0	4.8	4.7	4.5	4.3	4.1	4.0
77	82	5.8	5.6	5.5	5.3	5.2	5.0	4.9	4.7	4.5	4.4	4.2	4.1	3.9
78	83	5.6	5.5	5.3	5.2	5.0	4.9	4.7	4.6	4.4	4.3	4.1	4.0	3.8
79	84	5.4	5.3	5.2	5.0	4.9	4.7	4.6	4.5	4.3	4.2	4.0	3.9	3.7
80	85	5.2	5.1	5.0	4.9	4.7	4.6	4.5	4.3	4.2	4.1	3.9	3.8	3.6
81	86	5.0	4.9	4.8	4.7	4.6	4.5	4.3	4.2	4.1	3.9	3.8	3.7	3.6
82	87	4.9	4.8	4.7	4.5	4.4	4.3	4.2	4.1	4.0	3.8	3.7	3.6	3.5
83	88	4.7	4.6	4.5	4.4	4.3	4.2	4.1	3.9	3.8	3.7	3.6	3.5	3.4
84	89	4.5	4.4	4.3	4.2	4.1	4.0	3.9	3.8	3.7	3.6	3.5	3.4	3.3
85	90	4.3	4.2	4.1	4.1	4.0	3.9	3.8	3.7	3.6	3.5	3.4	3.3	3.2
86	91	4.1	4.1	4.0	3.9	3.8	3.7	3.6	3.6	3.5	3.4	3.3	3.2	3.1

Table IIA—Annuities for Joint Life Only—Two Lives—Expected Return Multiples—Continued

		Ages										
Male	Female	Male 87 Female 92	88 93	89 94	90 95	91 96	92 97	93 98	94 99	95 100	96 101	97 102
35	40	5.0	4.7	4.4	4.2	3.9	3.7	3.5	3.3	3.1	2.9	2.7
36	41	5.0	4.7	4.4	4.2	3.9	3.7	3.5	3.3	3.1	2.9	2.7
37	42	5.0	4.7	4.4	4.2	3.9	3.7	3.5	3.3	3.1	2.9	2.7
38	43	5.0	4.7	4.4	4.2	3.9	3.7	3.5	3.3	3.1	2.8	2.6
39	44	5.0	4.7	4.4	4.2	3.9	3.7	3.5	3.3	3.0	2.8	2.6
40	45	5.0	4.7	4.4	4.2	3.9	3.7	3.5	3.3	3.0	2.8	2.6
41	46	5.0	4.7	4.4	4.2	3.9	3.7	3.5	3.2	3.0	2.8	2.6
42	47	4.9	4.7	4.4	4.2	3.9	3.7	3.5	3.2	3.0	2.8	2.6
43	48	4.9	4.7	4.4	4.1	3.9	3.7	3.5	3.2	3.0	2.8	2.6
44	49	4.9	4.7	4.4	4.1	3.9	3.7	3.4	3.2	3.0	2.8	2.6
45	50	4.9	4.6	4.4	4.1	3.9	3.7	3.4	3.2	3.0	2.8	2.6
46	51	4.9	4.6	4.4	4.1	3.9	3.7	3.4	3.2	3.0	2.8	2.6
47	52	4.9	4.6	4.4	4.1	3.9	3.7	3.4	3.2	3.0	2.8	2.6
48	53	4.9	4.6	4.4	4.1	3.9	3.6	3.4	3.2	3.0	2.8	2.6
49	54	4.9	4.6	4.3	4.1	3.9	3.6	3.4	3.2	3.0	2.8	2.6
50	55	4.8	4.6	4.3	4.1	3.9	3.6	3.4	3.2	3.0	2.8	2.6
51	56	4.8	4.6	4.3	4.1	3.8	3.6	3.4	3.2	3.0	2.8	2.6
52	57	4.8	4.5	4.3	4.1	3.8	3.6	3.4	3.2	3.0	2.8	2.6
53	58	4.8	4.5	4.3	4.0	3.8	3.6	3.4	3.2	3.0	2.8	2.6
54	59	4.8	4.5	4.3	4.0	3.8	3.6	3.4	3.2	3.0	2.8	2.6
55	60	4.7	4.5	4.3	4.0	3.8	3.6	3.4	3.2	3.0	2.8	2.6
56	61	4.7	4.5	4.2	4.0	3.8	3.6	3.3	3.1	2.9	2.8	2.6
57	62	4.7	4.5	4.2	4.0	3.8	3.5	3.3	3.1	2.9	2.7	2.6
58	63	4.7	4.4	4.2	4.0	3.7	3.5	3.3	3.1	2.9	2.7	2.5
59	64	4.6	4.4	4.2	3.9	3.7	3.5	3.3	3.1	2.9	2.7	2.5

Male	Female	Ages: Male 98 / Female 103	99 / 104	100 / 105	101 / 106	102 / 107	103 / 108	104 / 109	105 / 110	106 / 111	107 / 112	108 / 113
35	40	2.5	2.3	2.1	1.9	1.7	1.5	1.3	1.2	1.0	0.8	0.7
36	41	2.5	2.3	2.1	1.9	1.7	1.5	1.3	1.2	1.0	0.8	0.7
37	42	2.5	2.3	2.1	1.9	1.7	1.5	1.3	1.1	1.0	0.8	0.7
38	43	2.5	2.3	2.1	1.9	1.7	1.5	1.3	1.1	1.0	0.8	0.7
39	44	2.4	2.3	2.1	1.9	1.7	1.5	1.3	1.1	1.0	0.8	0.7
40	45	2.4	2.2	2.1	1.9	1.7	1.5	1.3	1.1	1.0	0.8	0.7
41	46	2.4	2.2	2.1	1.9	1.7	1.5	1.3	1.1	1.0	0.8	0.7
42	47	2.4	2.2	2.0	1.9	1.7	1.5	1.3	1.1	1.0	0.8	0.7
43	48	2.4	2.2	2.0	1.9	1.7	1.5	1.3	1.1	1.0	0.8	0.7
44	49	2.4	2.2	2.0	1.9	1.7	1.5	1.3	1.1	1.0	0.8	0.7
45	50	2.4	2.2	2.0	1.8	1.7	1.5	1.3	1.1	1.0	0.8	0.7
46	51	2.4	2.2	2.0	1.8	1.7	1.5	1.3	1.1	1.0	0.8	0.7
47	52	2.4	2.2	2.0	1.8	1.7	1.5	1.3	1.1	1.0	0.8	0.7
48	53	2.4	2.2	2.0	1.8	1.7	1.5	1.3	1.1	1.0	0.8	0.7
49	54	2.4	2.2	2.0	1.8	1.7	1.5	1.3	1.1	1.0	0.8	0.7
50	55	2.4	2.2	2.0	1.8	1.6	1.5	1.3	1.1	1.0	0.8	0.7
51	56	2.4	2.2	2.0	1.8	1.6	1.5	1.3	1.1	1.0	0.8	0.7
52	57	2.4	2.2	2.0	1.8	1.6	1.5	1.3	1.1	1.0	0.8	0.7
53	58	2.4	2.2	2.0	1.8	1.6	1.5	1.3	1.1	1.0	0.8	0.7
54	59	2.4	2.2	2.0	1.8	1.6	1.5	1.3	1.1	1.0	0.8	0.7
55	60	2.4	2.2	2.0	1.8	1.6	1.4	1.3	1.1	1.0	0.8	0.7
56	61	2.4	2.2	2.0	1.8	1.6	1.4	1.3	1.1	1.0	0.8	0.7
57	62	2.4	2.2	2.0	1.8	1.6	1.4	1.3	1.1	0.9	0.8	0.7
58	63	2.4	2.2	2.0	1.8	1.6	1.4	1.3	1.1	0.9	0.8	0.7
59	64	2.3	2.2	2.0	1.8	1.6	1.4	1.3	1.1	0.9	0.8	0.7

Table IIA—Annuities for Joint Life Only—Two Lives—Expected Return Multiples—Continued

Male	Female	Ages: Male 87 / Female 92	88 / 93	89 / 94	90 / 95	91 / 96	92 / 97	93 / 98	94 / 99	95 / 100	96 / 101	97 / 102
60	65	4.6	4.4	4.1	3.9	3.7	3.5	3.3	3.1	2.9	2.7	2.5
61	66	4.6	4.3	4.1	3.9	3.7	3.5	3.3	3.1	2.9	2.7	2.5
62	67	4.5	4.3	4.1	3.9	3.7	3.5	3.3	3.1	2.9	2.7	2.5
63	68	4.5	4.3	4.1	3.8	3.6	3.4	3.2	3.0	2.9	2.7	2.5
64	69	4.5	4.2	4.0	3.8	3.6	3.4	3.2	3.0	2.8	2.7	2.5
65	70	4.4	4.2	4.0	3.8	3.6	3.4	3.2	3.0	2.8	2.6	2.5
66	71	4.4	4.2	4.0	3.8	3.6	3.4	3.2	3.0	2.8	2.6	2.4
67	72	4.3	4.1	3.9	3.7	3.5	3.3	3.1	3.0	2.8	2.6	2.4
68	73	4.3	4.1	3.9	3.7	3.5	3.3	3.1	2.9	2.8	2.6	2.4
69	74	4.2	4.0	3.8	3.6	3.5	3.3	3.1	2.9	2.7	2.6	2.4
70	75	4.2	4.0	3.8	3.6	3.4	3.2	3.1	2.9	2.7	2.5	2.4
71	76	4.1	3.9	3.8	3.6	3.4	3.2	3.0	2.9	2.7	2.5	2.3
72	77	4.1	3.9	3.7	3.5	3.3	3.2	3.0	2.8	2.7	2.5	2.3
73	78	4.0	3.8	3.7	3.5	3.3	3.1	3.0	2.8	2.6	2.5	2.3
74	79	3.9	3.8	3.6	3.4	3.3	3.1	2.9	2.8	2.6	2.4	2.3
75	80	3.9	3.7	3.5	3.4	3.2	3.0	2.9	2.7	2.6	2.4	2.2
76	81	3.8	3.6	3.5	3.3	3.2	3.0	2.8	2.7	2.5	2.4	2.2
77	82	3.7	3.6	3.4	3.3	3.1	3.0	2.8	2.6	2.5	2.3	2.2
78	83	3.7	3.5	3.4	3.2	3.1	2.9	2.7	2.6	2.4	2.3	2.1
79	84	3.6	3.4	3.3	3.1	3.0	2.8	2.7	2.5	2.4	2.2	2.1
80	85	3.5	3.4	3.2	3.1	2.9	2.8	2.6	2.5	2.3	2.2	2.0
81	86	3.4	3.3	3.1	3.0	2.9	2.7	2.6	2.4	2.3	2.1	2.0
82	87	3.3	3.2	3.1	2.9	2.8	2.7	2.5	2.4	2.2	2.1	2.0
83	88	3.2	3.1	3.0	2.9	2.7	2.6	2.5	2.3	2.2	2.0	1.9
84	89	3.1	3.0	2.9	2.8	2.7	2.5	2.4	2.3	2.1	2.0	1.9

Male	Female	Ages: Male 98 / Female 103	99 / 104	100 / 105	101 / 106	102 / 107	103 / 108	104 / 109	105 / 110	106 / 111	107 / 112	108 / 113
60	65	2.3	2.1	2.0	1.8	1.6	1.4	1.3	1.1	0.9	0.8	0.7
61	66	2.3	2.1	2.0	1.8	1.6	1.4	1.2	1.1	0.9	0.8	0.7
62	67	2.3	2.1	1.9	1.8	1.6	1.4	1.2	1.1	0.9	0.8	0.7
63	68	2.3	2.1	1.9	1.7	1.6	1.4	1.2	1.1	0.9	0.8	0.7
64	69	2.3	2.1	1.9	1.7	1.6	1.4	1.2	1.1	0.9	0.8	0.7
65	70	2.3	2.1	1.9	1.7	1.6	1.4	1.2	1.1	0.9	0.8	0.7
66	71	2.3	2.1	1.9	1.7	1.5	1.4	1.2	1.1	0.9	0.8	0.7
67	72	2.2	2.1	1.9	1.7	1.5	1.4	1.2	1.0	0.9	0.7	0.7
68	73	2.2	2.0	1.9	1.7	1.5	1.4	1.2	1.0	0.9	0.7	0.7
69	74	2.2	2.0	1.8	1.7	1.5	1.3	1.2	1.0	0.9	0.7	0.6
70	75	2.2	2.0	1.8	1.7	1.5	1.3	1.2	1.0	0.9	0.7	0.6
71	76	2.2	2.0	1.8	1.6	1.5	1.3	1.2	1.0	0.9	0.7	0.6
72	77	2.1	2.0	1.8	1.6	1.5	1.3	1.1	1.0	0.8	0.7	0.6
73	78	2.1	1.9	1.8	1.6	1.4	1.3	1.1	1.0	0.8	0.7	0.6
74	79	2.1	1.9	1.7	1.6	1.4	1.3	1.1	1.0	0.8	0.7	0.6
75	80	2.1	1.9	1.7	1.6	1.4	1.3	1.1	1.0	0.8	0.7	...
76	81	2.0	1.9	1.7	1.5	1.4	1.2	1.1	0.9	0.8	0.7	...
77	82	2.0	1.8	1.7	1.5	1.4	1.2	1.1	0.9	0.8	0.7	...
78	83	2.0	1.8	1.6	1.5	1.3	1.2	1.0	0.9	0.8	0.7	...
79	84	1.9	1.8	1.6	1.5	1.3	1.2	1.0	0.9	0.8	0.7	...
80	85	1.9	1.7	1.6	1.4	1.3	1.1	1.0	0.9	0.7	0.7	...
81	86	1.8	1.7	1.5	1.4	1.3	1.1	1.0	0.8	0.7	0.6	...
82	87	1.8	1.7	1.5	1.4	1.2	1.1	1.0	0.8	0.7	0.6	...
83	88	1.8	1.6	1.5	1.3	1.2	1.1	0.9	0.8	0.7	0.6	...
84	89	1.7	1.6	1.4	1.3	1.2	1.0	0.9	0.8	0.7	..	...

Table IIA—Annuities for Joint Life Only—Two Lives—Expected Return Multiples—Continued

Male	Female	Ages: Male 87 / Female 92	88 / 93	89 / 94	90 / 95	91 / 96	92 / 97	93 / 98	94 / 99	95 / 100	96 / 101
85	90	3.1	2.9	2.8	2.7	2.6	2.5	2.3	2.2	2.1	1.9
86	91	3.0	2.8	2.7	2.6	2.5	2.4	2.3	2.1	2.0	1.9
87	92	2.9	2.8	2.6	2.5	2.4	2.3	2.2	2.1	1.9	1.8
88	93	2.8	2.7	2.6	2.4	2.3	2.2	2.1	2.0	1.9	1.7
89	94	2.6	2.6	2.5	2.4	2.2	2.1	2.0	1.9	1.8	1.7
90	95	2.5	2.4	2.4	2.3	2.2	2.0	1.9	1.8	1.7	1.6
91	96	2.4	2.3	2.2	2.2	2.1	2.0	1.9	1.7	1.6	1.5
92	97	2.3	2.2	2.1	2.0	2.0	1.9	1.8	1.7	1.6	1.5
93	98	2.2	2.1	2.0	1.9	1.9	1.8	1.7	1.6	1.5	1.4
94	99	2.1	2.0	1.9	1.8	1.7	1.7	1.6	1.5	1.4	1.3
95	100	1.9	1.9	1.8	1.7	1.6	1.6	1.5	1.4	1.3	1.2
96	101	1.8	1.7	1.7	1.6	1.5	1.5	1.4	1.3	1.2	1.1
97	102	1.7	1.6	1.6	1.5	1.4	1.4	1.3	1.2	1.1	1.1
98	103	1.6	1.5	1.4	1.4	1.3	1.3	1.2	1.1	1.0	1.0
99	104	1.4	1.4	1.3	1.3	1.2	1.1	1.1	1.0	1.0	0.9

Male	Female	Ages: Male 97 / Female 102	98 / 103	99 / 104	100 / 105	101 / 106	102 / 107	103 / 108	104 / 109	105 / 110	106 / 111
85............	90............	1.8	1.7	1.5	1.4	1.3	1.1	1.0	0.9	0.8	0.7
86............	91............	1.7	1.6	1.5	1.3	1.2	1.1	1.0	0.8	0.7	0.7
87............	92............	1.7	1.6	1.4	1.3	1.2	1.1	0.9	0.8	0.7	0.6
88............	93............	1.6	1.5	1.4	1.3	1.1	1.0	0.9	0.8	0.7	0.6
89............	94............	1.6	1.4	1.3	1.2	1.1	1.0	0.9	0.7	0.7	...
90............	95............	1.5	1.4	1.3	1.2	1.0	0.9	0.8	0.7	0.6	...
91............	96............	1.4	1.3	1.2	1.1	1.0	0.9	0.8	0.7	0.6	...
92............	97............	1.4	1.3	1.1	1.0	0.9	0.8	0.7	0.7	..	...
93............	98............	1.3	1.2	1.1	1.0	0.9	0.8	0.7	0.6	..	...
94............	99............	1.2	1.1	1.0	0.9	0.8	0.7	0.7	..	..	...
95............	100............	1.1	1.0	1.0	0.9	0.8	0.7	0.6	..	..	...
96............	101............	1.1	1.0	0.9	0.8	0.7	0.7	..	..	..	...
97............	102............	1.0	0.9	0.8	0.7	0.7	0.6	..	..	..	...
98............	103............	0.9	0.8	0.7	0.7	0.6	..	..	..	..	...

99	104	0.8	0.7	0.7	0.6	..	..	..	..	..	..

Table III—Percent Value of Refund Feature

Ages		Duration of guaranteed amount—[Years]												
Male	Female	1	2	3	4	5	6	7	8	9	10	11	12	13
6	11	..	..	..	..	..	..	..	..	1	1	1	1	1
7	12	..	..	..	..	..	..	..	..	1	1	1	1	1
8	13	..	..	..	..	..	..	..	1	1	1	1	1	1
9	14	..	..	..	..	..	..	..	1	1	1	1	1	1
10	15	..	..	..	..	..	..	..	1	1	1	1	1	1
11	16	..	..	..	..	..	..	..	1	1	1	1	1	1
12	17	..	..	..	..	..	..	..	1	1	1	1	1	1
13	18	..	..	..	..	..	..	..	1	1	1	1	1	1
14	19	..	..	..	..	..	..	..	1	1	1	1	1	1
15	20	..	..	..	..	..	..	..	1	1	1	1	1	1
16	21	..	..	..	..	..	..	..	1	1	1	1	1	1
17	22	..	..	..	..	..	..	..	1	1	1	1	1	1
18	23	..	..	..	..	..	..	..	1	1	1	1	1	1
19	24	..	..	..	..	..	..	..	1	1	1	1	1	1
20	25	..	..	..	..	..	..	..	1	1	1	1	1	1
21	26	..	..	..	..	..	..	..	1	1	1	1	1	1
22	27	..	..	..	..	..	..	1	1	1	1	1	1	1
23	28	..	..	..	..	..	..	1	1	1	1	1	1	1
24	29	..	..	..	..	..	..	1	1	1	1	1	1	1
25	30	..	..	..	..	..	..	1	1	1	1	1	1	1
26	31	..	..	..	..	..	1	1	1	1	1	1	1	1
27	32	..	..	..	..	..	1	1	1	1	1	1	1	1
28	33	..	..	..	..	..	1	1	1	1	1	1	1	1
29	34	..	..	..	..	..	1	1	1	1	1	1	1	2
30	35	..	..	..	..	1	1	1	1	1	1	1	2	2
31	36	..	..	..	..	1	1	1	1	1	1	1	2	2
32	37	..	..	..	..	1	1	1	1	1	1	2	2	2
33	38	..	..	..	..	1	1	1	1	1	1	2	2	2
34	39	..	..	..	1	1	1	1	1	1	2	2	2	2
35	40	..	..	..	1	1	1	1	1	2	2	2	2	2
36	41	..	..	..	1	1	1	1	1	2	2	2	2	3
37	42	..	..	1	1	1	1	1	2	2	2	2	3	3
38	43	..	..	1	1	1	1	1	2	2	2	2	3	3
39	44	..	..	1	1	1	1	2	2	2	2	3	3	3
40	45	..	..	1	1	1	1	2	2	2	3	3	3	4
41	46	..	..	1	1	1	1	2	2	2	3	3	3	4
42	47	..	..	1	1	1	2	2	2	3	3	3	4	4
43	48	..	1	1	1	1	2	2	2	3	3	4	4	4
44	49	..	1	1	1	1	2	2	3	3	3	4	4	5
45	50	..	1	1	1	2	2	2	3	3	4	4	5	5
46	51	..	1	1	1	2	2	3	3	3	4	4	5	5
47	52	..	1	1	1	2	2	3	3	4	4	5	5	6
48	53	..	1	1	2	2	2	3	3	4	5	5	6	6
49	54	..	1	1	2	2	3	3	4	4	5	5	6	7
50	55	..	1	1	2	2	3	3	4	5	5	6	7	7
51	56	..	1	1	2	3	3	4	4	5	6	6	7	8
52	57	1	1	2	2	3	3	4	5	5	6	7	8	8
53	58	1	1	2	2	3	4	4	5	6	7	7	8	9
54	59	1	1	2	2	3	4	5	5	6	7	8	9	10
55	60	1	1	2	3	3	4	5	6	7	8	8	9	10
56	61	1	1	2	3	4	4	5	6	7	8	9	10	11
57	62	1	1	2	3	4	5	6	7	8	9	10	11	12
58	63	1	2	2	3	4	5	6	7	8	9	10	12	13
59	64	1	2	3	4	5	6	7	8	9	10	11	12	14
60	65	1	2	3	4	5	6	7	8	10	11	12	13	15
61	66	1	2	3	4	5	6	8	9	10	12	13	14	16
62	67	1	2	3	4	6	7	8	10	11	12	14	15	17
63	68	1	2	4	5	6	7	9	10	12	13	15	16	18
64	69	1	3	4	5	7	8	9	11	13	14	16	17	19
65	70	1	3	4	6	7	9	10	12	13	15	17	19	20
66	71	1	3	4	6	8	9	11	13	14	16	18	20	22
67	72	2	3	5	6	8	10	12	14	15	17	19	21	23
68	73	2	3	5	7	9	11	13	14	16	18	21	23	25
69	74	2	4	6	7	9	11	13	16	18	20	22	24	26
70	75	2	4	6	8	10	12	14	17	19	21	23	26	28
71	76	2	4	6	9	11	13	15	18	20	22	25	27	29
72	77	2	5	7	9	12	14	16	19	21	24	26	29	31
73	78	2	5	7	10	12	15	18	20	23	25	28	30	33
74	79	3	5	8	11	13	16	19	22	24	27	30	32	35
75	80	3	6	8	11	14	17	20	23	26	29	31	34	37
76	81	3	6	9	12	15	18	21	24	27	30	33	36	39
77	82	3	7	10	13	16	20	23	26	29	32	35	38	41
78	83	4	7	11	14	17	21	24	28	31	34	37	40	43
79	84	4	8	11	15	19	22	26	29	33	36	39	42	45

Table III—Percent Value of Refund Feature (continued)

Ages		Duration of guaranteed amount—[Years]												
Male	Female	1	2	3	4	5	6	7	8	9	10	11	12	13
80	85	4	8	12	16	20	24	27	31	34	38	41	44	47
81	86	4	9	13	17	21	25	29	33	36	40	43	46	49
82	87	5	9	14	18	23	27	31	35	38	42	45	48	51
83	88	5	10	15	19	24	28	33	37	40	44	47	50	53
84	89	5	11	16	21	26	30	34	38	42	46	49	52	55
85	90	6	11	17	22	27	32	36	41	44	48	51	55	57

Ages		Duration of guaranteed amount—[Years]												
Male	Female	14	15	16	17	18	19	20	21	22	23	24	25	26
6	11	1	1	1	1	1	1	1	1	1	1	2	2	2
7	12	1	1	1	1	1	1	1	1	1	1	2	2	2
8	13	1	1	1	1	1	1	1	1	1	1	2	2	2
9	14	1	1	1	1	1	1	1	1	1	1	2	2	2
10	15	1	1	1	1	1	1	1	1	1	2	2	2	2
11	16	1	1	1	1	1	1	1	1	1	2	2	2	2
12	17	1	1	1	1	1	1	1	1	1	2	2	2	2
13	18	1	1	1	1	1	1	1	1	2	2	2	2	2
14	19	1	1	1	1	1	1	1	1	2	2	2	2	2
15	20	1	1	1	1	1	1	1	1	2	2	2	2	2
16	21	1	1	1	1	1	1	1	2	2	2	2	2	2
17	22	1	1	1	1	1	1	1	2	2	2	2	2	2
18	23	1	1	1	1	1	1	2	2	2	2	2	2	2
19	24	1	1	1	1	1	2	2	2	2	2	2	2	2
20	25	1	1	1	1	1	2	2	2	2	2	2	2	3
21	26	1	1	1	1	2	2	2	2	2	2	2	3	3
22	27	1	1	1	1	2	2	2	2	2	2	3	3	3
23	28	1	1	1	2	2	2	2	2	2	2	3	3	3
24	29	1	1	2	2	2	2	2	2	2	3	3	3	3
25	30	1	1	2	2	2	2	2	2	3	3	3	3	3
26	31	1	2	2	2	2	2	2	3	3	3	3	3	4
27	32	2	2	2	2	2	2	3	3	3	3	3	4	4
28	33	2	2	2	2	2	3	3	3	3	3	4	4	4
29	34	2	2	2	2	2	3	3	3	3	4	4	4	5
30	35	2	2	2	2	3	3	3	3	4	4	4	5	5
31	36	2	2	2	3	3	3	3	4	4	4	5	5	5
32	37	2	2	3	3	3	3	4	4	4	5	5	5	6
33	38	2	3	3	3	3	4	4	4	5	5	5	6	6
34	39	3	3	3	3	4	4	4	5	5	5	6	6	7
35	40	3	3	3	4	4	4	5	5	5	6	6	7	7
36	41	3	3	4	4	4	5	5	5	6	6	7	7	8
37	42	3	3	4	4	4	5	5	6	6	7	7	8	8
38	43	3	4	4	4	5	5	6	6	7	7	8	8	9
39	44	4	4	4	5	5	6	6	7	7	8	8	9	9
40	45	4	4	5	5	6	6	7	7	8	8	9	9	10
41	46	4	5	5	6	6	7	7	8	8	9	9	10	11
42	47	5	5	5	6	6	7	8	8	9	9	10	11	12
43	48	5	5	6	6	7	8	8	9	9	10	11	12	12
44	49	5	6	6	7	7	8	9	9	10	11	12	12	13
45	50	6	6	7	7	8	9	9	10	11	12	12	13	14

Table III—Percent Value of Refund Feature (continued)

Ages		Duration of guaranteed amount—[Years]												
Male	Female	14	15	16	17	18	19	20	21	22	23	24	25	26
46	51	6	7	7	8	9	9	10	11	12	12	13	14	15
47	52	7	7	8	9	9	10	11	12	12	13	14	15	16
48	53	7	8	8	9	10	11	12	12	13	14	15	16	17
49	54	8	8	9	10	11	11	12	13	14	15	16	17	18
50	55	8	9	10	11	11	12	13	14	15	16	17	18	20
51	56	9	10	10	11	12	13	14	15	16	17	18	20	21
52	57	9	10	11	12	13	14	15	16	17	18	20	21	22
53	58	10	11	12	13	14	15	16	17	19	20	21	22	24
54	59	11	12	13	14	15	16	17	18	20	21	22	24	25
55	60	11	13	14	15	16	17	18	20	21	22	24	25	26
56	61	12	13	15	16	17	18	20	21	22	24	25	27	28
57	62	13	14	16	17	18	20	21	22	24	25	27	28	30
58	63	14	15	17	18	19	21	22	24	25	27	28	30	31
59	64	15	16	18	19	21	22	24	25	27	28	30	31	33
60	65	16	18	19	20	22	24	25	27	28	30	32	33	35
61	66	17	19	20	22	23	25	27	28	30	32	33	35	37
62	67	18	20	22	23	25	27	28	30	32	33	35	37	38
63	68	20	21	23	25	26	28	30	32	33	35	37	39	40
64	69	21	23	24	26	28	30	32	33	35	37	39	41	42
65	70	22	24	26	28	30	32	33	35	37	39	41	42	44

Male	Female													
66	71	24	26	28	29	31	33	35	37	39	41	43	44	46
67	72	25	27	29	31	33	35	37	39	41	43	45	46	48
68	73	27	29	31	33	35	37	39	41	43	45	47	48	50
69	74	28	30	33	35	37	39	41	43	45	47	48	50	52
70	75	30	32	34	37	39	41	43	45	47	49	50	52	54
71	76	32	34	36	39	41	43	45	47	49	51	52	54	56
72	77	34	36	38	41	43	45	47	49	51	53	54	56	58
73	78	35	38	40	43	45	47	49	51	53	55	56	58	59
74	79	37	40	42	45	47	49	51	53	55	57	58	60	61
75	80	39	42	44	47	49	51	53	55	57	58	60	62	63
76	81	41	44	46	49	51	53	55	57	59	60	62	63	65
77	82	43	46	48	51	53	55	57	59	61	62	64	65	66
78	83	45	48	50	53	55	57	59	61	62	64	65	67	68
79	84	48	50	53	55	57	59	61	63	64	66	67	68	70
80	85	50	52	55	57	59	61	63	64	66	67	69	70	71
81	86	52	54	57	59	61	63	65	66	68	69	70	72	73
82	87	54	56	59	61	63	65	66	68	69	71	72	73	74
83	88	56	58	61	63	65	66	68	70	71	72	73	74	75
84	89	58	60	63	65	67	68	70	71	73	74	75	76	77
85	90	60	62	65	67	68	70	71	73	74	75	76	77	..

Ages		Duration of guaranteed amount — [Years]								
Male	Female	27	28	29	30	31	32	33	34	35
6	11	2	2	2	2	2	2	2	2	2
7	12	2	2	2	2	2	2	2	2	3
8	13	2	2	2	2	2	2	2	2	3
9	14	2	2	2	2	2	2	2	3	3
10	15	2	2	2	2	2	2	3	3	3
11	16	2	2	2	2	2	2	3	3	3
12	17	2	2	2	2	2	3	3	3	3
13	18	2	2	2	2	2	3	3	3	3
14	19	2	2	2	2	3	3	3	3	3
15	20	2	2	2	3	3	3	3	3	3
16	21	2	2	3	3	3	3	3	3	4
17	22	2	2	3	3	3	3	3	4	4
18	23	2	3	3	3	3	3	4	4	4
19	24	3	3	3	3	3	4	4	4	4
20	25	3	3	3	3	4	4	4	4	5

Table III—Percent Value of Refund Feature (continued)

Ages		Duration of guaranteed amount — [Years]								
Male	Female	27	28	29	30	31	32	33	34	35
21	26	3	3	3	4	4	4	4	5	5
22	27	3	3	4	4	4	4	5	5	5
23	28	3	3	4	4	4	5	5	5	5
24	29	3	4	4	4	5	5	5	5	6
25	30	4	4	4	5	5	5	6	6	6
26	31	4	4	5	5	5	6	6	6	7
27	32	4	5	5	5	6	6	6	7	7
28	33	5	5	5	6	6	6	7	7	8
29	34	5	5	6	6	6	7	7	8	8
30	35	5	6	6	6	7	7	8	8	9
31	36	6	6	6	7	7	8	8	9	9
32	37	6	7	7	7	8	8	9	10	10
33	38	7	7	7	8	8	9	10	10	11
34	39	7	8	8	9	9	10	10	11	12
35	40	8	8	9	9	10	10	11	12	12
36	41	8	9	9	10	10	11	12	13	13
37	42	9	9	10	11	11	12	13	13	14
38	43	9	10	11	11	12	13	13	14	15
39	44	10	11	11	12	13	14	14	15	16
40	45	11	11	12	13	14	15	15	16	17
41	46	11	12	13	14	15	16	16	17	18
42	47	12	13	14	15	16	17	18	18	19
43	48	13	14	15	16	17	18	19	20	21
44	49	14	15	16	17	18	19	20	21	22
45	50	15	16	17	18	19	20	21	22	23
46	51	16	17	18	19	20	21	22	24	25
47	52	17	18	19	20	21	23	24	25	26
48	53	18	19	20	22	23	24	25	26	28
49	54	19	21	22	23	24	25	27	28	29
50	55	21	22	23	24	26	27	28	29	31
51	56	22	23	25	26	27	28	30	31	32
52	57	23	25	26	27	29	30	31	33	34
53	58	25	26	28	29	30	32	33	34	36
54	59	26	28	29	31	32	33	35	36	38
55	60	28	29	31	32	34	35	36	38	39
56	61	29	31	32	34	35	37	38	40	41
57	62	31	33	34	36	37	39	40	41	43
58	63	33	34	36	37	39	40	42	43	45
59	64	35	36	38	39	41	42	44	45	47
60	65	36	38	40	41	43	44	46	47	48

Male	Female									
61	66	38	40	41	43	44	46	47	49	50
62	67	40	42	43	45	46	48	49	51	52
63	68	42	44	45	47	48	50	51	52	54
64	69	44	46	47	49	50	52	53	54	55
65	70	46	47	49	50	52	53	55	56	57
66	71	48	49	51	52	54	55	56	58	59
67	72	50	51	53	54	56	57	58	59	61
68	73	52	53	55	56	57	59	60	61	62
69	74	53	55	56	58	59	60	62	63	64
70	75	55	57	58	60	61	62	62	64	65
71	76	57	59	60	61	63	64	65	66	67
72	77	59	60	62	63	64	65	66	67	68
73	78	61	62	64	65	66	67	68	69	70
74	79	63	64	65	66	67	68	69	70	71
75	80	64	66	67	68	69	70	71	72	72
76	81	66	67	68	69	70	71	72	73	..
77	82	68	69	70	71	72	73	74	..	..
78	83	69	70	71	72	73	74	..	..	..
79	84	71	72	73	74	75	..	..	..	..
80	85	72	73	74	75	..	..	..	..	..
81	86	74	75	75	..	..	..	..	..	..
82	87	75	76	..	..	..	..	..	..	..
83	88	76	..	..	..	..	..	..	..	..
84	89	..	..	..	..	..	..	..	..	..
85	90	..	..	..	..	..	..	..	..	..

Table III—Percent Value of Refund Feature (continued)

Ages		Duration of guaranteed amount—[Years]													
Male	Female	1	2	3	4	5	6	7	8	9	10	11	12	13	14
86	91	6	12	18	24	29	34	38	43	47	50	54	57	59	62
87	92	7	13	19	25	31	36	40	45	49	52	56	59	61	64
88	93	7	14	21	27	32	38	42	47	51	55	58	61	63	66
89	94	8	15	22	28	34	40	45	49	53	57	60	63	65	68
90	95	8	16	23	30	36	42	47	51	55	59	62	65	67	70
91	96	9	17	25	32	38	44	49	53	57	61	64	67	69	71
92	97	9	18	26	34	40	46	51	55	59	63	66	69	71	73
93	98	10	20	28	36	42	48	53	58	62	65	68	70	73	75
94	99	11	21	30	37	44	50	55	60	64	67	70	72	74	76
95	100	12	22	31	39	46	52	58	62	66	69	72	74	76	78
96	101	12	24	33	42	49	55	60	64	68	71	73	76	78	79
97	102	13	25	35	44	51	57	62	66	70	73	75	77	79	..
98	103	14	27	37	46	54	60	65	69	72	75	77	79	..	..
99	104	15	29	40	49	56	62	67	71	74	77	79	..	..	..
100	105	17	31	43	52	59	65	70	74	76	79	..	..	..	..
101	106	18	33	46	55	63	68	73	76	79	..	..	..	..	..
102	107	20	36	49	59	66	71	75	78	..	..	..	..	..	..
103	108	22	40	53	62	69	74	78	..	..	..	..	..	..	..
104	109	24	43	57	66	73	77	..	..	..	..	..	..	..	..
105	110	27	48	61	70	76	..	..	..	..	..	..	..	..	..
106	111		53	66	74	..	..	..	..	..	..	..	..	..	..
107	112	35	53	71	..	..	..	..	..	..	..	..	..	..	..
108	113	40	64	..	..	..	..	..	..	..	..	..	..	..	..

Ages		Duration of guaranteed amount—[Years]										
Male	Female	15	16	17	18	19	20	21	22	23	24	25
86	91	64	66	68	70	72	73	74	75	76	77	..
87	92	66	68	70	72	73	74	76	77	78	..	..
88	93	68	70	72	73	75	76	77	78	..	..	..
89	94	70	72	73	75	76	77	78	..	..	..	..
90	95	72	73	75	76	77	79	..	..	..	..	..
91	96	73	75	76	78	79	..	..	..	..	..	..
92	97	75	76	78	79	..	..	..	..	..	..	..
93	98	76	78	79	..	..	..	..	..	..	..	..
94	99	78	79	..	..	..	..	..	..	..	..	..
95	100	79	..	..	..	..	..	..	..	..	..	..

Table IV—Temporary Life Annuities[1]—One Life—Expected Return Multiples

Ages		Temporary period—maximum duration of annuity—[Years]									
Male	Female	1	2	3	4	5	6	7	8	9	10
0 to 8	0 to 13	1.0	2.0	3.0	4.0	5.0	6.0	7.0	8.0	8.9	9.9
9	14	1.0	2.0	3.0	4.0	5.0	6.0	7.0	8.0	8.9	9.9
10	15	1.0	2.0	3.0	4.0	5.0	6.0	7.0	8.0	8.9	9.9
11	16	1.0	2.0	3.0	4.0	5.0	6.0	7.0	8.0	8.9	9.9
12	17	1.0	2.0	3.0	4.0	5.0	6.0	7.0	8.0	8.9	9.9
13	18	1.0	2.0	3.0	4.0	5.0	6.0	7.0	8.0	8.9	9.9
14	19	1.0	2.0	3.0	4.0	5.0	6.0	7.0	8.0	8.9	9.9
15	20	1.0	2.0	3.0	4.0	5.0	6.0	7.0	8.0	8.9	9.9
16	21	1.0	2.0	3.0	4.0	5.0	6.0	7.0	8.0	8.9	9.9
17	22	1.0	2.0	3.0	4.0	5.0	6.0	7.0	8.0	8.9	9.9
18	23	1.0	2.0	3.0	4.0	5.0	6.0	7.0	8.0	8.9	9.9
19	24	1.0	2.0	3.0	4.0	5.0	6.0	7.0	8.0	8.9	9.9
20	25	1.0	2.0	3.0	4.0	5.0	6.0	7.0	8.0	8.9	9.9
21	26	1.0	2.0	3.0	4.0	5.0	6.0	7.0	8.0	8.9	9.9
22	27	1.0	2.0	3.0	4.0	5.0	6.0	7.0	8.0	8.9	9.9
23	28	1.0	2.0	3.0	4.0	5.0	6.0	7.0	8.0	8.9	9.9
24	29	1.0	2.0	3.0	4.0	5.0	6.0	7.0	7.9	8.9	9.9
25	30	1.0	2.0	3.0	4.0	5.0	6.0	7.0	7.9	8.9	9.9
26	31	1.0	2.0	3.0	4.0	5.0	6.0	7.0	7.9	8.9	9.9
27	32	1.0	2.0	3.0	4.0	5.0	6.0	7.0	7.9	8.9	9.9
28	33	1.0	2.0	3.0	4.0	5.0	6.0	7.0	7.9	8.9	9.9
29	34	1.0	2.0	3.0	4.0	5.0	6.0	6.9	7.9	8.9	9.9
30	35	1.0	2.0	3.0	4.0	5.0	6.0	6.9	7.9	8.9	9.9
31	36	1.0	2.0	3.0	4.0	5.0	6.0	6.9	7.9	8.9	9.9
32	37	1.0	2.0	3.0	4.0	5.0	6.0	6.9	7.9	8.9	9.9
33	38	1.0	2.0	3.0	4.0	5.0	6.0	6.9	7.9	8.9	9.9
34	39	1.0	2.0	3.0	4.0	5.0	5.9	6.9	7.9	8.9	9.8
35	40	1.0	2.0	3.0	4.0	5.0	5.9	6.9	7.9	8.9	9.8
36	41	1.0	2.0	3.0	4.0	5.0	5.9	6.9	7.9	8.9	9.8
37	42	1.0	2.0	3.0	4.0	5.0	5.9	6.9	7.9	8.8	9.8
38	43	1.0	2.0	3.0	4.0	5.0	5.9	6.9	7.9	8.8	9.8
39	44	1.0	2.0	3.0	4.0	4.9	5.9	6.9	7.9	8.8	9.8
40	45	1.0	2.0	3.0	4.0	4.9	5.9	6.9	7.8	8.8	9.7
41	46	1.0	2.0	3.0	4.0	4.9	5.9	6.9	7.8	8.8	9.7
42	47	1.0	2.0	3.0	4.0	4.9	5.9	6.9	7.8	8.8	9.7
43	48	1.0	2.0	3.0	4.0	4.9	5.9	6.9	7.8	8.8	9.7
44	49	1.0	2.0	3.0	4.0	4.9	5.9	6.8	7.8	8.7	9.7
45	50	1.0	2.0	3.0	3.9	4.9	5.9	6.8	7.8	8.7	9.6
46	51	1.0	2.0	3.0	3.9	4.9	5.9	6.8	7.8	8.7	9.6
47	52	1.0	2.0	3.0	3.9	4.9	5.9	6.8	7.7	8.7	9.6
48	53	1.0	2.0	3.0	3.9	4.9	5.9	6.8	7.7	8.6	9.5
49	54	1.0	2.0	3.0	3.9	4.9	5.8	6.8	7.7	8.6	9.5
50	55	1.0	2.0	3.0	3.9	4.9	5.8	6.8	7.7	8.6	9.5
51	56	1.0	2.0	3.0	3.9	4.9	5.8	6.7	7.7	8.6	9.4
52	57	1.0	2.0	3.0	3.9	4.9	5.8	6.7	7.6	8.5	9.4
53	58	1.0	2.0	2.9	3.9	4.9	5.8	6.7	7.6	8.5	9.3
54	59	1.0	2.0	2.9	3.9	4.8	5.8	6.7	7.6	8.4	9.3
55	60	1.0	2.0	2.9	3.9	4.8	5.8	6.7	7.5	8.4	9.2
56	61	1.0	2.0	2.9	3.9	4.8	5.7	6.6	7.5	8.4	9.2
57	62	1.0	2.0	2.9	3.9	4.8	5.7	6.6	7.5	8.3	9.1
58	63	1.0	2.0	2.9	3.9	4.8	5.7	6.6	7.4	8.3	9.1
59	64	1.0	2.0	2.9	3.9	4.8	5.7	6.5	7.4	8.2	9.0
60	65	1.0	2.0	2.9	3.8	4.8	5.6	6.5	7.3	8.1	8.9
61	66	1.0	2.0	2.9	3.8	4.7	5.6	6.5	7.3	8.1	8.8
62	67	1.0	2.0	2.9	3.8	4.7	5.6	6.4	7.2	8.0	8.8
63	68	1.0	2.0	2.9	3.8	4.7	5.6	6.4	7.2	7.9	8.7
64	69	1.0	1.9	2.9	3.8	4.7	5.5	6.3	7.1	7.9	8.6
65	70	1.0	1.9	2.9	3.8	4.6	5.5	6.3	7.1	7.8	8.5
66	71	1.0	1.9	2.9	3.8	4.6	5.4	6.2	7.0	7.7	8.4
67	72	1.0	1.9	2.9	3.7	4.6	5.4	6.2	6.9	7.6	8.3
68	73	1.0	1.9	2.8	3.7	4.6	5.4	6.1	6.8	7.5	8.2
69	74	1.0	1.9	2.8	3.7	4.5	5.3	6.1	6.8	7.4	8.0
70	75	1.0	1.9	2.8	3.7	4.5	5.3	6.0	6.7	7.3	7.9

[1] The multiples in this table are not applicable to annuities for a term certain; for such cases see paragraph (c) of § 1.72-5.

Table IV—Temporary Life Annuities[1]—One Life—Expected Return Multiples (continued)

Ages		Temporary period—maximum duration of annuity—[Years]									
Male	Female	1	2	3	4	5	6	7	8	9	10
71	76	1.0	1.9	2.8	3.7	4.5	5.2	5.9	6.6	7.2	7.8
72	77	1.0	1.9	2.8	3.6	4.4	5.2	5.8	6.5	7.1	7.6
73	78	1.0	1.9	2.8	3.6	4.4	5.1	5.8	6.4	7.0	7.5
74	79	1.0	1.9	2.8	3.6	4.3	5.0	5.7	6.3	6.8	7.3
75	80	1.0	1.9	2.7	3.5	4.3	5.0	5.6	6.2	6.7	7.1
76	81	1.0	1.9	2.7	3.5	4.2	4.9	5.5	6.1	6.5	7.0
77	82	1.0	1.9	2.7	3.5	4.2	4.8	5.4	5.9	6.4	6.8
78	83	1.0	1.9	2.7	3.4	4.1	4.7	5.3	5.8	6.2	6.6
79	84	1.0	1.8	2.7	3.4	4.1	4.7	5.2	5.7	6.1	6.4
80	85	1.0	1.8	2.6	3.4	4.0	4.6	5.1	5.5	5.9	6.2
81	86	1.0	1.8	2.6	3.3	3.9	4.5	5.0	5.4	5.7	6.0
82	87	1.0	1.8	2.6	3.3	3.9	4.4	4.8	5.2	5.6	5.8
83	88	.9	1.8	2.6	3.2	3.8	4.3	4.7	5.1	5.4	5.6
84	89	.9	1.8	2.5	3.2	3.7	4.2	4.6	4.9	5.2	5.4
85	90	.9	1.8	2.5	3.1	3.6	4.1	4.5	4.8	5.0	5.2
86	91	.9	1.8	2.5	3.1	3.6	4.0	4.3	4.6	4.8	5.0

[1] The multiples in this table are not applicable to annuities for a term certain; for such cases see paragraph (c) of § 1.72-5.

Ages		Temporary period—maximum duration of annuity—[Years]									
Male	Female	11	12	13	14	15	16	17	18	19	20
0 to 8	0 to 13	10.9	11.9	12.9	13.9	14.9	15.8	16.8	17.8	18.8	19.7
9	14	10.9	11.9	12.9	13.9	14.9	15.8	16.8	17.8	18.8	19.7
10	15	10.9	11.9	12.9	13.9	14.9	15.8	16.8	17.8	18.8	19.7
11	16	10.9	11.9	12.9	13.9	14.9	15.8	16.8	17.8	18.8	19.7
12	17	10.9	11.9	12.9	13.9	14.9	15.8	16.8	17.8	18.8	19.7
13	18	10.9	11.9	12.9	13.9	14.9	15.8	16.8	17.8	18.8	19.7
14	19	10.9	11.9	12.9	13.9	14.9	15.8	16.8	17.8	18.8	19.7
15	20	10.9	11.9	12.9	13.9	14.9	15.8	16.8	17.8	18.7	19.7
16	21	10.9	11.9	12.9	13.9	14.8	15.8	16.8	17.8	18.7	19.7
17	22	10.9	11.9	12.9	13.9	14.8	15.8	16.8	17.8	18.7	19.7
18	23	10.9	11.9	12.9	13.9	14.8	15.8	16.8	17.8	18.7	19.7
19	24	10.9	11.9	12.9	13.9	14.8	15.8	16.8	17.7	18.7	19.7
20	25	10.9	11.9	12.9	13.9	14.8	15.8	16.8	17.7	18.7	19.7
21	26	10.9	11.9	12.9	13.8	14.8	15.8	16.8	17.7	18.7	19.6
22	27	10.9	11.9	12.9	13.8	14.8	15.8	16.7	17.7	18.7	19.6
23	28	10.9	11.9	12.9	13.8	14.8	15.8	16.7	17.7	18.7	19.6
24	29	10.9	11.9	12.9	13.8	14.8	15.8	16.7	17.7	18.6	19.6
25	30	10.9	11.9	12.8	13.8	14.8	15.7	16.7	17.7	18.6	19.6
26	31	10.9	11.9	12.8	13.8	14.8	15.7	16.7	17.6	18.6	19.5
27	32	10.9	11.9	12.8	13.8	14.8	15.7	16.7	17.6	18.6	19.5
28	33	10.9	11.8	12.8	13.8	14.7	15.7	16.6	17.6	18.5	19.5
29	34	10.9	11.8	12.8	13.8	14.7	15.7	16.6	17.6	18.5	19.4
30	35	10.9	11.8	12.8	13.7	14.7	15.6	16.6	17.5	18.4	19.4
31	36	10.8	11.8	12.8	13.7	14.7	15.6	16.5	17.5	18.4	19.3
32	37	10.8	11.8	12.7	13.7	14.6	15.6	16.5	17.4	18.4	19.3
33	38	10.8	11.8	12.7	13.7	14.6	15.6	16.5	17.4	18.3	19.2
34	39	10.8	11.8	12.7	13.6	14.6	15.5	16.4	17.4	18.3	19.2
35	40	10.8	11.7	12.7	13.6	14.6	15.5	16.4	17.3	18.2	19.1
36	41	10.8	11.7	12.7	13.6	14.5	15.4	16.3	17.2	18.1	19.0
37	42	10.8	11.7	12.6	13.6	14.5	15.4	16.3	17.2	18.1	18.9
38	43	10.7	11.7	12.6	13.5	14.4	15.3	16.2	17.1	18.0	18.9
39	44	10.7	11.6	12.6	13.5	14.4	15.3	16.2	17.1	17.9	18.8
40	45	10.7	11.6	12.5	13.5	14.4	15.2	16.1	17.0	17.8	18.7
41	46	10.7	11.6	12.5	13.4	14.3	15.2	16.1	16.9	17.8	18.6
42	47	10.6	11.6	12.5	13.4	14.3	15.1	16.0	16.8	17.7	18.5
43	48	10.6	11.5	12.4	13.3	14.2	15.1	15.9	16.7	17.6	18.4
44	49	10.6	11.5	12.4	13.3	14.1	15.0	15.8	16.7	17.5	18.3
45	50	10.5	11.4	12.3	13.2	14.1	14.9	15.7	16.6	17.4	18.1

Table IV—Temporary Life Annuities[1]—One Life—Expected Return Multiples (continued)

Ages		Temporary period—maximum duration of annuity—[Years]									
Male	Female	11	12	13	14	15	16	17	18	19	20
46	51	10.5	11.4	12.3	13.2	14.0	14.8	15.7	16.5	17.2	18.0
47	52	10.5	11.4	12.2	13.1	13.9	14.7	15.6	16.3	17.1	17.8
48	53	10.4	11.3	12.2	13.0	13.8	14.7	15.4	16.2	17.0	17.7
49	54	10.4	11.3	12.1	12.9	13.8	14.6	15.3	16.1	16.8	17.5
50	55	10.3	11.2	12.0	12.9	13.7	14.5	15.2	16.0	16.7	17.4
51	56	10.3	11.1	12.0	12.8	13.6	14.3	15.1	15.8	16.5	17.2
52	57	10.2	11.1	11.9	12.7	13.5	14.2	14.9	15.6	16.3	17.0
53	58	10.2	11.0	11.8	12.6	13.4	14.1	14.8	15.5	16.1	16.8
54	59	10.1	10.9	11.7	12.5	13.2	14.0	14.6	15.3	15.9	16.5
55	60	10.1	10.9	11.6	12.4	13.1	13.8	14.5	15.1	15.7	16.3
56	61	10.0	10.8	11.5	12.3	13.0	13.7	14.3	14.9	15.5	16.1
57	62	9.9	10.7	11.4	12.2	12.8	13.5	14.1	14.7	15.3	15.8
58	63	9.8	10.6	11.3	12.0	12.7	13.3	13.9	14.5	15.0	15.5
59	64	9.8	10.5	11.2	11.9	12.5	13.2	13.7	14.3	14.8	15.3
60	65	9.7	10.4	11.1	11.7	12.4	13.0	13.5	14.0	14.5	15.0
61	66	9.6	10.3	11.0	11.6	12.2	12.8	13.3	13.8	14.2	14.7
62	67	9.5	10.2	10.8	11.4	12.0	12.5	13.1	13.5	14.0	14.3
63	68	9.4	10.0	10.7	11.3	11.8	12.3	12.8	13.2	13.7	14.0
64	69	9.3	9.9	10.5	11.1	11.6	12.1	12.5	13.0	13.3	13.7
65	70	9.1	9.8	10.3	10.9	11.4	11.9	12.3	12.7	13.0	13.3
66	71	9.0	9.6	10.2	10.7	11.2	11.6	12.0	12.4	12.7	13.0
67	72	8.9	9.5	10.0	10.5	10.9	11.3	11.7	12.0	12.3	12.6
68	73	8.7	9.3	9.8	10.3	10.7	11.1	11.4	11.7	12.0	12.2
69	74	8.6	9.1	9.6	10.0	10.4	10.8	11.1	11.4	11.6	11.8
70	75	8.4	8.9	9.4	9.8	10.2	10.5	10.8	11.0	11.2	11.4
71	76	8.3	8.7	9.2	9.6	9.9	10.2	10.4	10.7	10.9	11.0
72	77	8.1	8.6	8.9	9.3	9.6	9.9	10.1	10.3	10.5	10.6
73	78	7.9	8.3	8.7	9.0	9.3	9.6	9.8	9.9	10.1	10.2
74	79	7.7	8.1	8.5	8.8	9.0	9.2	9.4	9.6	9.7	9.8
75	80	7.6	7.9	8.2	8.5	8.7	8.9	9.1	9.2	9.3	9.4
76	81	7.4	7.7	8.0	8.2	8.4	8.6	8.7	8.8	8.9	9.0
77	82	7.1	7.5	7.7	7.9	8.1	8.3	8.4	8.5	8.5	8.6
78	83	6.9	7.2	7.4	7.6	7.8	7.9	8.0	8.1	8.2	8.2
79	84	6.7	7.0	7.2	7.3	7.5	7.6	7.7	7.7	7.8	7.8
80	85	6.5	6.7	6.9	7.1	7.2	7.3	7.3	7.4	7.4	7.4
81	86	6.3	6.5	6.6	6.8	6.9	6.9	7.0	7.0	7.1	..
82	87	6.0	6.2	6.4	6.5	6.5	6.6	6.7	6.7	...	..
83	88	5.8	6.0	6.1	6.2	6.2	6.3	6.3	..	...	..
84	89	5.6	5.7	5.8	5.9	5.9	6.0	...	..	...	..
85	90	5.3	5.5	5.5	5.6	5.6	..	...	..	...	..
86	91	5.1	5.2	5.3	5.3	...	..	...	..	...	..

[1] The multiples in this table are not applicable to annuities for a term certain; for such cases see paragraph (c) of § 1.72-5.

Ages		Temporary period—maximum duration of annuity—[Years]									
Male	Female	21	22	23	24	25	26	27	28	29	30
0 to 8	0 to 13	20.7	21.7	22.7	23.6	24.6	25.6	26.5	27.5	28.4	29.4
9	14	20.7	21.7	22.7	23.6	24.6	25.5	26.5	27.5	28.4	29.4
10	15	20.7	21.7	22.7	23.6	24.6	25.5	26.5	27.5	28.4	29.4
11	16	20.7	21.7	22.6	23.6	24.6	25.5	26.5	27.4	28.4	29.3
12	17	20.7	21.7	22.6	23.6	24.6	25.5	26.5	27.4	28.4	29.3
13	18	20.7	21.7	22.6	23.6	24.6	25.5	26.5	27.4	28.4	29.3
14	19	20.7	21.7	22.6	23.6	24.5	25.5	26.4	27.4	28.3	29.3
15	20	20.7	21.6	22.6	23.6	24.5	25.5	26.4	27.4	28.3	29.2
16	21	20.7	21.6	22.6	23.6	24.5	25.5	26.4	27.3	28.3	29.2
17	22	20.7	21.6	22.6	23.5	24.5	25.4	26.4	27.3	28.2	29.2
18	23	20.7	21.6	22.6	23.5	24.5	25.4	26.3	27.3	28.2	29.1
19	24	20.6	21.6	22.5	23.5	24.4	25.4	26.3	27.2	28.1	29.1
20	25	20.6	21.6	22.5	23.5	24.4	25.3	26.3	27.2	28.1	29.0

Table IV—Temporary Life Annuities[1]—One Life—Expected Return Multiples (continued)

Ages		Temporary period—maximum duration of annuity—[Years]									
Male	Female	21	22	23	24	25	26	27	28	29	30
21	26	20.6	21.5	22.5	23.4	24.4	25.3	26.2	27.1	28.0	28.9
22	27	20.6	21.5	22.5	23.4	24.3	25.3	26.2	27.1	28.0	28.9
23	28	20.6	21.5	22.4	23.4	24.3	25.2	26.1	27.0	27.9	28.8
24	29	20.5	21.5	22.4	23.3	24.2	25.2	26.1	27.0	27.8	28.7
25	30	20.5	21.4	22.4	23.3	24.2	25.1	26.0	26.9	27.8	28.6
26	31	20.5	21.4	22.3	23.2	24.1	25.0	25.9	26.8	27.7	28.5
27	32	20.4	21.3	22.3	23.2	24.1	25.0	25.8	26.7	27.6	28.4
28	33	20.4	21.3	22.2	23.1	24.0	24.9	25.8	26.6	27.5	28.3
29	34	20.3	21.2	22.1	23.0	23.9	24.8	25.7	26.5	27.4	28.2
30	35	20.3	21.2	22.1	23.0	23.8	24.7	25.6	26.4	27.2	28.1
31	36	20.2	21.1	22.0	22.9	23.8	24.6	25.5	26.3	27.1	27.9
32	37	20.2	21.1	21.9	22.8	23.7	24.5	25.4	26.2	27.0	27.8
33	38	20.1	21.0	21.9	22.7	23.6	24.4	25.2	26.0	26.8	27.6
34	39	20.0	20.9	21.8	22.6	23.5	24.3	25.1	25.9	26.7	27.4
35	40	20.0	20.8	21.7	22.5	23.3	24.2	25.0	25.7	26.5	27.2
36	41	19.9	20.7	21.6	22.4	23.2	24.0	24.8	25.6	26.3	27.0
37	42	19.8	20.6	21.5	22.3	23.1	23.9	24.6	25.4	26.1	26.8
38	43	19.7	20.5	21.4	22.2	23.0	23.7	24.5	25.2	25.9	26.6
39	44	19.6	20.4	21.2	22.0	22.8	23.6	24.3	25.0	25.7	26.4
40	45	19.5	20.3	21.1	21.9	22.6	23.4	24.1	24.8	25.5	26.1
41	46	19.4	20.2	21.0	21.7	22.5	23.2	23.9	24.6	25.2	25.9
42	47	19.3	20.1	20.8	21.6	22.3	23.0	23.7	24.3	25.0	25.6
43	48	19.2	19.9	20.7	21.4	22.1	22.8	23.4	24.1	24.7	25.3
44	49	19.0	19.8	20.5	21.2	21.9	22.6	23.2	23.8	24.4	25.0
45	50	18.9	19.6	20.3	21.0	21.7	22.3	22.9	23.5	24.1	24.6
46	51	18.7	19.4	20.1	20.8	21.5	22.1	22.7	23.2	23.8	24.3
47	52	18.6	19.3	19.9	20.6	21.2	21.8	22.4	22.9	23.4	23.9
48	53	18.4	19.1	19.7	20.4	21.0	21.5	22.1	22.6	23.1	23.5
49	54	18.2	18.9	19.5	20.1	20.7	21.2	21.7	22.2	22.7	23.1
50	55	18.0	18.7	19.3	19.8	20.4	20.9	21.4	21.9	22.3	22.7
51	56	17.8	18.4	19.0	19.6	20.1	20.6	21.1	21.5	21.9	22.3
52	57	17.6	18.2	18.7	19.3	19.8	20.2	20.7	21.1	21.5	21.8
53	58	17.4	17.9	18.5	19.0	19.4	19.9	20.3	20.7	21.0	21.3
54	59	17.1	17.7	18.2	18.7	19.1	19.5	19.9	20.2	20.6	20.8
55	60	16.9	17.4	17.9	18.3	18.7	19.1	19.5	19.8	20.1	20.3
56	61	16.6	17.1	17.5	18.0	18.4	18.7	19.0	19.3	19.6	19.8
57	62	16.3	16.8	17.2	17.6	18.0	18.3	18.6	18.9	19.1	19.3
58	63	16.0	16.5	16.9	17.2	17.6	17.9	18.1	18.4	18.6	18.8
59	64	15.7	16.1	16.5	16.8	17.1	17.4	17.7	17.9	18.1	18.2
60	65	15.4	15.8	16.1	16.4	16.7	17.0	17.2	17.4	17.5	17.7
61	66	15.1	15.4	15.7	16.0	16.3	16.5	16.7	16.9	17.0	17.1
62	67	14.7	15.0	15.3	15.6	15.8	16.0	16.2	16.3	16.4	16.5
63	68	14.4	14.6	14.9	15.1	15.3	15.5	15.7	15.8	15.9	16.0
64	69	14.0	14.3	14.5	14.7	14.9	15.0	15.2	15.3	15.3	15.4
65	70	13.6	13.8	14.1	14.2	14.4	14.5	14.6	14.7	14.8	14.9
66	71	13.2	13.4	13.6	13.8	13.9	14.0	14.1	14.2	14.2	14.3
67	72	12.8	13.0	13.2	13.3	13.4	13.5	13.6	13.7	13.7	13.7
68	73	12.4	12.6	12.7	12.8	12.9	13.0	13.1	13.1	13.2	13.2
69	74	12.0	12.1	12.3	12.4	12.4	12.5	12.6	12.6	12.6	12.6
70	75	11.6	11.7	11.8	11.9	12.0	12.0	12.0	12.1	12.1	12.1
71	76	11.2	11.3	11.3	11.4	11.5	11.5	11.5	11.6	11.6	...
72	77	10.7	10.8	10.9	10.9	11.0	11.0	11.0	11.0	...	...
73	78	10.3	10.4	10.4	10.5	10.5	10.5	10.5	...	...	...
74	79	9.9	9.9	10.0	10.0	10.1	10.1	...	...	...	...
75	80	9.5	9.5	9.6	9.6	9.6	...	...	...	...	...
76	81	9.1	9.1	9.1	9.1	...	...	...	...	...	...
77	82	8.6	8.7	8.7	...	...	...	...	...	...	...
78	83	8.2	8.3	...	...	...	...	...	...	...	...
79	84	7.8	...	...	...	...	...	...	...	...	...

[1] The multiples in this table are not applicable to annuities for a term certain; for such cases see paragraph (c) of § 1.72-5.

Table V—Ordinary Life Annuities One Life— Expected Return Multiples

Age	Multiple	Age	Multiple	Age	Multiple
5	76.6	43	39.6	80	9.5
6	75.6	44	38.7	81	8.9
7	74.7	45	37.7	82	8.4
8	73.7	46	36.8	83	7.9
9	72.7	47	35.9	84	7.4
10	71.7	48	34.9	85	6.9
11	70.7	49	34.0	86	6.5
12	69.7	50	33.1	87	6.1
13	68.8	51	32.2	88	5.7
14	67.8	52	31.3	89	5.3
15	66.8	53	30.4	90	5.0
16	65.8	54	29.5	91	4.7
17	64.6	55	28.6	92	4.4
18	63.9	56	27.7	93	4.1
19	62.9	57	26.8	94	3.9
20	61.9	58	25.9	95	3.7
21	60.9	59	25.0	96	3.4
22	59.9	60	24.2	97	3.2
23	59.0	61	23.3	98	3.0
24	58.0	62	22.5	99	2.8
25	57.0	63	21.6	100	2.7
26	56.0	64	20.8	101	2.5
27	55.1	65	20.0	102	2.3
28	54.1	66	19.2	103	2.1
29	53.1	67	18.4	104	1.9
30	52.2	68	17.6	105	1.8
31	51.2	69	16.8	106	1.6
32	50.2	70	16.0	107	1.4
33	49.3	71	15.3	108	1.3
34	48.3	72	14.6	109	1.1
35	47.3	73	13.9	110	1.0
36	46.4	74	13.2	111	.9
37	45.4	75	12.5	112	.8
38	44.4	76	11.9	113	.7
39	43.5	77	11.2	114	.6
40	42.5	78	10.6	115	.5
41	41.5	79	10.0		
42	40.6				

Table VI—Ordinary Joint Life and Last Survivor Annuities; Two Lives—Expected Return Multiples

Ages	5	6	7	8	9	10	11	12	13	14
5	83.8	83.3	82.8	82.4	82.0	81.6	81.2	80.9	80.6	80.3
6	83.3	82.8	82.3	81.8	81.4	81.0	80.6	80.3	79.9	79.6
7	82.8	82.3	81.8	81.3	80.9	80.4	80.0	79.6	79.3	78.9
8	82.4	81.8	81.3	80.8	80.3	79.9	79.4	79.0	78.6	78.3
9	82.0	81.4	80.9	80.3	79.8	79.3	78.9	78.4	78.0	77.6
10	81.6	81.0	80.4	79.9	79.3	78.8	78.3	77.9	77.4	77.0
11	81.2	80.6	80.0	79.4	78.9	78.3	77.8	77.3	76.9	76.4
12	80.9	80.3	79.6	79.0	78.4	77.9	77.3	76.8	76.3	75.9
13	80.6	79.9	79.3	78.6	78.0	77.4	76.9	76.3	75.8	75.3
14	80.3	79.6	78.9	78.3	77.6	77.0	76.4	75.9	75.3	74.8
15	80.0	79.3	78.6	77.9	77.3	76.6	76.0	75.4	74.9	74.3
16	79.8	79.0	78.3	77.6	76.9	76.3	75.6	75.0	74.4	73.9
17	79.5	78.8	78.0	77.3	76.6	75.9	75.3	74.6	74.0	73.4
18	79.3	78.5	77.8	77.0	76.3	75.6	74.9	74.3	73.6	73.0
19	79.1	78.3	77.5	76.8	76.0	75.3	74.6	73.9	73.3	72.6
20	78.9	78.1	77.3	76.5	75.8	75.0	74.3	73.6	72.9	72.3
21	78.7	77.9	77.1	76.3	75.5	74.8	74.0	73.3	72.6	71.9
22	78.6	77.7	76.9	76.1	75.3	74.5	73.8	73.0	72.3	71.6
23	78.4	77.6	76.7	75.9	75.1	74.3	73.5	72.8	72.0	71.3
24	78.3	77.4	76.6	75.7	74.9	74.1	73.3	72.6	71.8	71.1
25	78.2	77.8	76.4	75.6	74.8	73.9	73.1	72.3	71.6	70.8

Table VI—Ordinary Joint Life and Last Survivor Annuities; Two Lives—Expected Return Multiples (continued)

Ages	5	6	7	8	9	10	11	12	13	14
26	78.0	77.2	76.3	75.4	74.6	73.8	72.9	72.1	71.3	70.6
27	77.9	77.1	76.2	75.3	74.4	73.6	72.8	71.9	71.1	70.3
28	77.8	76.9	76.1	75.2	74.3	73.4	72.6	71.8	70.9	70.1
29	77.7	76.8	76.0	75.1	74.2	73.3	72.5	71.6	70.8	70.0
30	77.7	76.8	75.9	75.0	74.1	73.2	72.3	71.5	70.6	69.8
31	77.6	76.7	75.8	74.9	74.0	73.1	72.2	71.3	70.5	69.6
32	77.5	76.6	75.7	74.8	73.9	73.0	72.1	71.2	70.3	69.5
33	77.5	76.5	75.6	74.7	73.8	72.9	72.0	71.1	70.2	69.3
34	77.4	76.5	75.5	74.6	73.7	72.8	71.9	71.0	70.1	69.2
35	77.3	76.4	75.5	74.5	73.6	72.7	71.8	70.9	70.0	69.1
36	77.3	76.3	75.4	74.5	73.5	72.6	71.7	70.8	69.9	69.0
37	77.2	76.3	75.4	74.4	73.5	72.6	71.6	70.7	69.8	68.9
38	77.2	76.2	75.3	74.4	73.4	72.5	71.6	70.6	69.7	68.8
39	77.2	76.2	75.3	74.3	73.4	72.4	71.5	70.6	69.6	68.7
40	77.1	76.2	75.2	74.3	73.3	72.4	71.4	70.5	69.6	68.6
41	77.1	76.1	75.2	74.2	73.3	72.3	71.4	70.4	69.5	68.6
42	77.0	76.1	75.1	74.2	73.2	72.3	71.3	70.4	69.4	68.5
43	77.0	76.1	75.1	74.1	73.2	72.2	71.3	70.3	69.4	68.5
44	77.0	76.0	75.1	74.1	73.1	72.2	71.2	70.3	69.3	68.4
45	77.0	76.0	75.0	74.1	73.1	72.2	71.2	70.2	69.3	68.4
46	76.9	76.0	75.0	74.0	73.1	72.1	71.2	70.2	69.3	68.3
47	76.9	75.9	75.0	74.0	73.1	72.1	71.1	70.2	69.2	68.3
48	76.9	75.9	75.0	74.0	73.0	72.1	71.1	70.1	69.2	68.2
49	76.9	75.9	74.9	74.0	73.0	72.0	71.1	70.1	69.1	68.2
50	76.9	75.9	74.9	73.9	73.0	72.0	71.0	70.1	69.1	68.2
51	76.8	75.9	74.9	73.9	73.0	72.0	71.0	70.1	69.1	68.1
52	76.8	75.9	74.9	73.9	72.9	72.0	71.0	70.0	69.1	68.1
53	76.8	75.8	74.9	73.9	72.9	71.9	71.0	70.0	69.0	68.1
54	76.8	75.8	74.8	73.9	72.9	71.9	71.0	70.0	69.0	68.1
55	76.8	75.8	74.8	73.9	72.9	71.9	70.9	70.0	69.0	68.0
56	76.8	75.8	74.8	73.8	72.9	71.9	70.9	69.9	69.0	68.0
57	76.8	75.8	74.8	73.8	72.9	71.9	70.9	69.9	69.0	68.0
58	76.8	75.8	74.8	73.8	72.8	71.9	70.9	69.9	68.9	68.0
59	76.7	75.8	74.8	73.8	72.8	71.9	70.9	69.9	68.9	68.0
60	76.7	75.8	74.8	73.8	72.8	71.8	70.9	69.9	68.9	67.9
61	76.7	75.7	74.8	73.8	72.8	71.8	70.9	69.9	68.9	67.9
62	76.7	75.7	74.8	73.8	72.8	71.8	70.8	69.9	68.9	67.9
63	76.7	75.7	74.8	73.8	72.8	71.8	70.8	69.9	68.9	67.9
64	76.7	75.7	74.7	73.8	72.8	71.8	70.8	69.8	68.9	67.9
65	76.7	75.7	74.7	73.8	72.8	71.8	70.8	69.8	68.9	67.9
66	76.7	75.7	74.7	73.7	72.8	71.8	70.8	69.8	68.9	67.9
67	76.7	75.7	74.7	73.7	72.8	71.8	70.8	69.8	68.8	67.9
68	76.7	75.7	74.7	73.7	72.8	71.8	70.8	69.8	68.8	67.9
69	76.7	75.7	74.7	73.7	72.7	71.8	70.8	69.8	68.8	67.8
70	76.7	75.7	74.7	73.7	72.7	71.8	70.8	69.8	68.8	67.8
71	76.7	75.7	74.7	73.7	72.7	71.8	70.8	69.8	68.8	67.8
72	76.7	75.7	74.7	73.7	72.7	71.8	70.8	69.8	68.8	67.8
73	76.7	75.7	74.7	73.7	72.7	71.7	70.8	69.8	68.8	67.8
74	76.7	75.7	74.7	73.7	72.7	71.7	70.8	69.8	68.8	67.8
75	76.7	75.7	74.7	73.7	72.7	71.7	70.8	69.8	68.8	67.8
76	76.6	75.7	74.7	73.7	72.7	71.7	70.8	69.8	68.8	67.8
77	76.6	75.7	74.7	73.7	72.7	71.7	70.8	69.8	68.8	67.8
78	76.6	75.7	74.7	73.7	72.7	71.7	70.7	69.8	68.8	67.8
79	76.6	75.7	74.7	73.7	72.7	71.7	70.7	69.8	68.8	67.8
80	76.6	75.7	74.7	73.7	72.7	71.7	70.7	69.8	68.8	67.8
81	76.6	75.7	74.7	73.7	72.7	71.7	70.7	69.8	68.8	67.8
82	76.6	75.7	74.7	73.7	72.7	71.7	70.7	69.8	68.8	67.8
83	76.6	75.7	74.7	73.7	72.7	71.7	70.7	69.8	68.8	67.8
84	76.6	75.7	74.7	73.7	72.7	71.7	70.7	69.8	68.8	67.8
85	76.6	75.7	74.7	73.7	72.7	71.7	70.7	69.8	68.8	67.8
86	76.6	75.7	74.7	73.7	72.7	71.7	70.7	69.8	68.8	67.8
87	76.6	75.7	74.7	73.7	72.7	71.7	70.7	69.8	68.8	67.8

Table VI—Ordinary Joint Life and Last Survivor Annuities; Two Lives—Expected Return Multiples (continued)

Ages	5	6	7	8	9	10	11	12	13	14
88	76.6	75.7	74.7	73.7	72.7	71.7	70.7	69.8	68.8	67.8
89	76.6	75.7	74.7	73.7	72.7	71.7	70.7	69.7	68.8	67.8
90	76.6	75.6	74.7	73.7	72.7	71.7	70.7	69.7	68.8	67.8
91	76.6	75.6	74.7	73.7	72.7	71.7	70.7	69.7	68.8	67.8
92	76.6	75.6	74.7	73.7	72.7	71.7	70.7	69.7	68.8	67.8
93	76.6	75.6	74.7	73.7	72.7	71.7	70.7	69.7	68.8	67.8
94	76.6	75.6	74.7	73.7	72.7	71.7	70.7	69.7	68.8	67.8
95	76.6	75.6	74.7	73.7	72.7	71.7	70.7	69.7	68.8	67.8
96	76.6	75.6	74.7	73.7	72.7	71.7	70.7	69.7	68.8	67.8
97	76.6	75.6	74.7	73.7	72.7	71.7	70.7	69.7	68.8	67.8
98	76.6	75.6	74.7	73.7	72.7	71.7	70.7	69.7	68.8	67.8
99	76.6	75.6	74.7	73.7	72.7	71.7	70.7	69.7	68.8	67.8
100	76.6	75.6	74.7	73.7	72.7	71.7	70.7	69.7	68.8	67.8
101	76.6	75.6	74.7	73.7	72.7	71.7	70.7	69.7	68.8	67.8
102	76.6	75.6	74.7	73.7	72.7	71.7	70.7	69.7	68.8	67.8
103	76.6	75.6	74.7	73.7	72.7	71.7	70.7	69.7	68.8	67.8
104	76.6	75.6	74.7	73.7	72.7	71.7	70.7	69.7	68.8	67.8
105	76.6	75.6	74.7	73.7	72.7	71.7	70.7	69.7	68.8	67.8
106	76.6	75.6	74.7	73.7	72.7	71.7	70.7	69.7	68.8	67.8
107	76.6	75.6	74.7	73.7	72.7	71.7	70.7	69.7	68.8	67.8
108	76.6	75.6	74.7	73.7	72.7	71.7	70.7	69.7	68.8	67.8
109	76.6	75.6	74.7	73.7	72.7	71.7	70.7	69.7	68.8	67.8
110	76.6	75.6	74.7	73.7	72.7	71.7	70.7	69.7	68.8	67.8
111	76.6	75.6	74.7	73.7	72.7	71.7	70.7	69.7	68.8	67.8
112	76.6	75.6	74.7	73.7	72.7	71.7	70.7	69.7	68.8	67.8
113	76.6	75.6	74.7	73.7	72.7	71.7	70.7	69.7	68.8	67.8
114	76.6	75.6	74.7	73.7	72.7	71.7	70.7	69.7	68.8	67.8
115	76.6	75.6	74.7	73.7	72.7	71.7	70.7	69.7	68.8	67.8

Table VI.—Ordinary Joint Life and Last Survivor Annuities; Two Lives—Expected Return Multiples

Ages	15	16	17	18	19	20	21	22	23	24
15	73.8	73.3	72.9	72.4	72.0	71.6	71.3	70.9	70.6	70.3
16	73.3	72.8	72.3	71.9	71.4	71.0	70.7	70.3	70.0	69.6
17	72.9	72.3	71.8	71.3	70.9	70.5	70.0	69.7	69.3	69.0
18	72.4	71.9	71.3	70.8	70.4	69.0	69.5	69.9	68.7	68.3
19	72.0	71.4	70.9	70.4	69.8	69.4	68.9	68.5	68.1	67.7
20	71.6	71.0	70.5	69.9	69.4	68.8	68.4	67.9	67.5	67.1
21	71.3	70.7	70.0	69.5	68.9	68.4	67.9	67.4	66.9	66.5
22	70.9	70.3	69.7	69.0	68.5	67.9	67.4	66.9	66.4	65.9
23	70.6	70.0	69.3	68.7	68.1	67.5	66.9	66.4	65.9	65.4
24	70.3	69.6	69.0	68.3	67.7	67.1	66.5	65.9	65.4	64.9
25	70.1	69.3	68.6	68.0	67.3	66.7	66.1	65.5	64.9	64.4
26	69.8	69.1	68.3	67.6	67.0	66.3	65.7	65.1	64.5	63.9
27	69.6	68.8	68.1	67.3	66.7	66.0	65.3	64.7	64.1	63.5
28	69.3	68.6	67.8	67.1	66.4	65.7	65.0	64.3	63.7	63.1
29	69.1	68.4	67.6	66.8	66.1	65.4	64.7	64.0	63.3	62.7
30	69.0	68.2	67.4	66.6	65.8	65.1	64.4	63.7	63.0	62.3
31	68.8	68.0	67.2	66.4	65.6	64.8	64.1	63.4	62.7	62.0
32	68.6	67.8	67.0	66.2	65.4	64.6	63.8	63.1	62.4	61.7
33	68.5	67.6	66.8	66.0	65.2	64.4	63.6	62.8	62.1	61.4
34	68.3	67.5	66.6	65.8	65.0	64.2	63.4	62.6	61.9	61.1
35	68.2	67.4	66.5	65.6	64.8	64.0	63.2	62.4	61.6	60.9
36	68.1	67.2	66.4	65.5	64.7	63.8	63.0	62.2	61.4	60.6
37	68.0	67.1	66.2	65.4	64.5	63.7	62.8	62.0	61.2	60.4
38	67.9	67.0	66.1	65.2	64.4	63.5	62.7	61.8	61.0	60.2
39	67.8	66.9	66.0	65.1	64.2	63.4	62.5	61.7	60.8	60.0
40	67.7	66.8	65.9	65.0	64.1	63.3	62.4	61.5	60.7	59.9
41	67.7	66.7	65.8	64.9	64.0	63.1	62.3	61.4	60.5	59.7
42	67.6	66.7	65.7	64.8	63.9	63.0	62.2	61.3	60.4	59.6
43	67.5	66.6	65.7	64.8	63.8	62.9	62.1	61.2	60.3	59.4
44	67.5	66.5	65.6	64.7	63.8	62.9	62.0	61.1	60.2	59.3

Table VI.—Ordinary Joint Life and Last Survivor Annuities; Two Lives—Expected Return Multiples (continued)

Ages	15	16	17	18	19	20	21	22	23	24
45	67.4	66.5	65.5	64.6	63.7	62.8	61.9	61.0	60.1	59.2
46	67.4	66.4	65.4	64.6	63.6	62.7	61.8	60.9	60.0	59.1
47	67.3	66.4	65.4	64.5	63.6	62.6	61.7	60.8	59.9	59.0
48	67.3	66.3	65.4	64.4	63.5	62.6	61.6	60.7	59.8	58.9
49	67.2	66.3	65.3	64.4	63.5	62.5	61.6	60.7	59.7	58.8
50	67.2	66.2	65.3	64.3	63.4	62.5	61.5	60.6	59.7	58.8
51	67.2	66.2	65.3	64.3	63.4	62.4	61.5	60.5	59.6	58.7
52	67.1	66.2	65.2	64.3	63.3	62.4	61.4	60.5	59.6	58.6
53	67.1	66.2	65.2	64.2	63.3	62.3	61.4	60.4	59.5	58.6
54	67.1	66.1	65.2	64.2	63.2	62.3	61.3	60.4	59.5	58.5
55	67.1	66.1	65.1	64.2	63.2	62.3	61.3	60.4	59.4	58.5
56	67.0	66.1	65.1	64.1	63.2	62.2	61.3	60.3	59.4	58.4
57	67.0	66.1	65.1	64.1	63.2	62.2	61.2	60.3	59.3	58.4
58	67.0	66.0	65.1	64.1	63.1	62.2	61.2	60.3	59.3	58.4
59	67.0	66.0	65.0	64.1	63.1	62.1	61.2	60.2	59.3	58.3
60	67.0	66.0	65.0	64.1	63.1	62.1	61.2	60.2	59.2	58.3
61	67.0	66.0	65.0	64.0	63.1	62.1	61.1	60.2	59.2	58.3
62	66.9	66.0	65.0	64.0	63.1	62.1	61.1	60.2	59.2	58.2
63	66.9	66.0	65.0	64.0	63.0	62.1	61.1	60.1	59.2	58.2
64	66.9	65.9	65.0	64.0	63.0	62.1	61.1	60.1	59.2	58.2
65	66.9	65.9	65.0	64.0	63.0	62.0	61.1	60.1	59.1	58.2
66	66.9	65.9	64.9	64.0	63.0	62.0	61.1	60.1	59.1	58.2
67	66.9	65.9	64.9	64.0	63.0	62.0	61.1	60.1	59.1	58.1
68	66.9	65.9	64.9	64.0	63.0	62.0	61.0	60.1	59.1	58.1
69	66.9	65.9	64.9	63.9	63.0	62.0	61.0	60.0	59.1	58.1
70	66.9	65.9	64.9	63.9	63.0	62.0	61.0	60.0	59.1	58.1
71	66.9	65.9	64.9	63.9	62.9	62.0	61.0	60.0	59.1	58.1
72	66.9	65.9	64.9	63.9	62.9	62.0	61.0	60.0	59.0	58.1
73	66.8	65.9	64.9	63.9	62.9	62.0	61.0	60.0	59.0	58.1
74	66.8	65.9	64.9	63.9	62.9	62.0	61.0	60.0	59.0	58.1
75	66.8	65.9	64.9	63.9	62.9	61.9	61.0	60.0	59.0	58.1
76	66.8	65.9	64.9	63.9	62.9	61.9	61.0	60.0	59.0	58.0
76	66.8	65.9	64.9	63.9	62.9	61.9	61.0	60.0	59.0	58.0
77	66.8	65.9	64.9	63.9	63.9	62.9	61.0	60.0	59.0	58.0
78	66.8	65.8	64.9	63.9	62.9	61.9	61.0	60.0	59.0	58.0
79	66.8	65.8	64.9	63.9	62.9	61.9	61.0	60.0	59.0	58.0
80	66.8	65.9	64.9	63.9	62.9	61.9	60.9	60.0	59.0	58.0
81	66.8	65.8	64.9	63.9	62.9	61.9	60.9	60.0	59.0	58.0
82	66.8	65.8	64.9	63.9	62.9	61.9	60.9	60.0	59.0	58.0
83	66.8	65.8	64.9	63.9	62.9	61.9	60.9	60.0	59.0	58.0
84	66.8	65.8	64.8	63.9	62.9	61.9	60.9	60.0	59.0	58.0
85	66.8	65.8	64.8	63.9	62.9	61.9	60.9	60.0	59.0	58.0
86	66.8	65.8	64.8	63.9	62.9	61.9	60.9	60.0	59.0	58.0
87	66.8	65.8	64.8	63.9	62.9	61.9	60.9	60.0	59.0	58.0
88	66.8	65.8	64.8	63.9	62.9	61.9	60.9	60.0	59.0	58.0
89	66.8	65.8	64.8	63.9	62.9	61.9	60.9	60.0	59.0	58.0
90	66.8	65.8	64.8	63.9	62.9	61.9	60.9	60.0	59.0	58.0
91	66.8	65.8	64.8	63.9	62.9	61.9	60.9	60.0	59.0	58.0
92	66.8	65.8	64.8	63.9	62.9	61.9	60.9	59.9	59.0	58.0
93	66.8	65.8	64.8	63.9	62.9	61.9	60.9	59.9	59.0	58.0
94	66.8	65.8	64.8	63.9	62.9	61.9	60.9	59.9	59.0	58.0
95	66.8	65.8	64.8	63.9	62.9	61.9	60.9	59.9	59.0	58.0
96	66.8	65.8	64.8	63.9	62.9	61.9	60.9	59.9	59.0	58.0
97	66.8	65.8	64.8	63.9	62.9	61.9	60.9	59.9	59.0	58.0
98	66.8	65.8	64.8	63.9	62.9	61.9	60.9	59.9	59.0	58.0
99	66.8	65.8	64.8	63.9	62.9	61.9	60.9	59.9	59.0	58.0
100	66.8	65.8	64.8	63.9	62.9	61.9	60.9	59.9	59.0	58.0
101	66.8	65.8	64.8	63.9	62.9	61.9	60.9	59.9	59.0	58.0
102	66.8	65.8	64.8	63.9	62.9	61.9	60.9	59.9	59.0	58.0
103	66.8	65.8	64.8	63.9	62.9	61.9	60.9	59.9	59.0	58.0
104	66.8	65.8	64.8	63.9	62.9	61.9	60.9	59.9	59.0	58.0
105	66.8	65.8	64.8	63.9	62.9	61.9	60.9	59.9	59.0	58.0

Table VI.—Ordinary Joint Life and Last Survivor Annuities; Two Lives—Expected Return Multiples (continued)

Ages	15	16	17	18	19	20	21	22	23	24
106	66.8	65.8	64.8	63.9	62.9	61.9	60.9	59.9	59.0	58.0
107	66.8	65.8	64.8	63.9	62.9	61.9	60.9	59.9	59.0	58.0
108	66.8	65.8	64.8	63.9	62.9	61.9	60.9	59.9	59.0	58.0
109	66.8	65.8	64.8	63.9	62.9	61.9	60.9	59.9	59.0	58.0
110	66.8	65.8	64.8	63.9	62.9	61.9	60.9	59.9	59.0	58.0
111	66.8	65.8	64.8	63.9	62.9	61.9	60.9	59.9	59.0	58.0
112	66.8	65.8	64.8	63.9	62.9	61.9	60.9	59.9	59.0	58.0
113	66.8	65.8	64.8	63.9	62.9	61.9	60.9	59.9	59.0	58.0
114	66.8	65.8	64.8	63.9	62.9	61.9	60.9	59.9	59.0	58.0
115	66.8	65.8	64.8	63.9	62.9	61.9	60.9	59.9	59.0	58.0

Table VI—Ordinary Joint Life and Last Survivor Annuities; Two Lives—Expected Return Multiples

Ages	25	26	27	28	29	30	31	32	33	34
25	63.9	63.4	62.9	62.5	62.1	61.7	61.3	61.0	60.7	60.4
26	63.4	62.9	62.4	61.9	61.5	61.1	60.7	60.4	60.0	59.7
27	62.9	62.4	61.9	61.4	60.9	60.5	60.1	59.7	59.4	59.0
28	62.5	61.9	61.4	60.9	60.4	60.0	59.5	59.1	58.7	58.4
29	62.1	61.5	60.9	60.4	59.9	59.4	59.0	58.5	58.1	57.7
30	61.7	61.1	60.5	60.0	59.4	58.9	58.4	58.0	57.5	57.1
31	61.3	60.7	60.1	59.5	59.0	58.4	57.9	57.4	57.0	56.5
32	61.0	60.4	59.7	59.1	58.5	58.0	57.4	56.9	56.4	56.0
33	60.7	60.0	59.4	58.7	58.1	57.5	57.0	56.4	55.9	55.5
34	60.4	59.7	59.0	58.4	57.7	57.1	56.5	56.0	55.5	54.9
35	60.1	59.4	58.7	58.0	57.4	56.7	56.1	55.6	55.0	54.5
36	59.9	59.1	58.4	57.7	57.0	56.4	55.8	55.1	54.6	54.0
37	59.6	58.9	58.1	57.4	56.7	56.0	55.4	54.8	54.2	53.6
38	59.4	58.6	57.9	57.9	56.4	55.7	55.1	54.4	53.8	53.2
39	59.2	58.4	57.7	56.9	56.2	55.4	54.7	54.1	53.4	52.8
40	59.0	58.2	57.4	56.7	55.9	55.2	54.5	53.8	53.1	52.4
41	58.9	58.0	57.2	56.4	55.7	54.9	54.2	53.5	52.8	52.1
42	58.7	57.9	57.1	56.2	55.5	54.7	53.9	53.2	52.5	51.8
43	58.6	57.7	56.9	56.1	55.3	54.5	53.7	52.9	52.2	51.5
44	58.4	57.6	56.7	55.9	55.1	54.3	53.5	52.7	52.0	51.2
45	58.3	57.4	56.6	55.7	54.9	54.1	53.3	52.5	51.7	51.0
46	58.2	57.3	56.5	55.6	54.8	53.9	53.1	52.3	51.5	50.7
47	58.1	57.2	56.3	55.5	54.6	53.8	52.9	52.1	51.3	50.5
48	58.0	57.1	56.2	55.3	54.5	53.6	52.8	51.9	51.1	50.3
49	57.9	57.0	56.1	55.2	54.4	53.5	52.6	51.8	51.0	50.1
50	57.8	56.9	56.0	55.1	54.2	53.4	52.5	51.7	50.8	50.0
51	57.8	56.9	55.9	55.0	54.1	53.3	52.4	51.5	50.7	49.8
52	57.7	56.8	55.9	55.0	54.1	53.2	52.3	51.4	50.5	49.7
53	57.6	56.7	55.8	54.9	54.0	53.1	52.2	51.3	50.4	49.6
54	57.6	56.7	55.7	54.8	53.9	53.0	52.1	51.2	50.3	49.4
55	57.5	56.6	55.7	54.7	53.8	52.9	52.0	51.1	40.2	49.3
56	57.5	56.5	55.6	54.7	53.8	52.8	51.9	51.0	50.1	49.2
57	57.4	56.5	55.6	54.6	53.7	52.8	51.9	50.9	50.0	49.1
58	57.4	56.5	55.5	54.6	53.6	52.7	51.8	50.9	50.0	49.1
59	57.4	56.4	55.5	54.5	53.6	52.7	51.7	50.8	49.9	49.0
60	57.3	56.4	55.4	54.5	53.6	52.6	51.7	50.8	49.8	48.9
61	57.3	56.4	55.4	54.5	53.5	52.6	51.6	50.7	49.8	48.9
62	57.3	56.3	55.4	54.4	53.5	52.5	51.6	50.7	49.7	48.8
63	57.3	56.3	55.3	54.4	53.4	52.5	51.6	50.6	49.7	48.7
64	57.2	56.3	55.3	54.4	53.4	52.5	51.5	50.6	49.6	48.7
65	57.2	56.3	55.3	54.3	53.4	52.4	51.5	50.5	49.6	48.7
66	57.2	56.2	55.3	54.3	53.4	52.4	51.5	50.5	49.6	48.6
67	57.2	56.2	55.3	54.3	53.3	52.4	51.4	50.5	49.5	48.6
68	57.2	56.2	55.2	54.3	53.3	52.4	51.4	50.4	49.5	48.6
69	57.1	56.2	55.2	54.3	53.3	52.3	51.4	50.4	49.5	48.5
70	57.1	56.2	55.2	54.2	53.3	52.3	51.4	50.4	49.4	48.5
71	57.1	56.2	55.2	54.2	53.3	52.3	51.3	50.4	49.4	48.5
72	57.1	56.1	55.2	54.2	53.2	52.3	51.3	50.4	49.4	48.5

Table VI—Ordinary Joint Life and Last Survivor Annuities; Two Lives—Expected Return Multiples (continued)

Ages	25	26	27	28	29	30	31	32	33	34
73	57.1	56.1	55.2	54.2	53.2	52.3	51.3	50.3	49.4	48.4
74	57.1	56.1	55.2	54.2	53.2	52.3	51.3	50.3	49.4	48.4
75	57.1	56.1	55.1	54.2	53.2	52.2	51.3	50.3	49.4	48.4
76	57.1	56.1	55.1	54.2	53.2	52.2	51.3	50.3	49.3	48.4
77	57.1	56.1	55.1	54.2	53.2	52.2	51.3	50.3	49.3	48.4
78	57.1	56.1	55.1	54.2	53.2	52.2	51.3	50.3	49.3	48.4
79	57.1	56.1	55.1	54.1	53.2	52.2	51.2	50.3	49.3	48.4
80	57.1	56.1	55.1	54.1	53.2	52.2	51.2	50.3	49.3	48.3
81	57.0	56.1	55.1	54.1	53.2	52.2	51.2	50.3	49.3	48.3
82	57.0	56.1	55.1	54.1	53.2	52.2	51.2	50.3	49.3	48.3
83	57.0	56.1	55.1	54.1	53.2	52.2	51.2	50.3	49.3	48.3
84	57.0	56.1	55.1	54.1	53.2	52.2	51.2	50.3	49.3	48.3
85	57.0	56.1	55.1	54.1	53.2	52.2	51.2	50.2	49.3	48.3
86	57.0	56.1	55.1	54.1	53.1	52.2	51.2	50.2	49.3	48.3
87	57.0	56.1	55.1	54.1	53.1	52.2	51.2	50.2	49.3	48.3
88	57.0	56.1	55.1	54.1	53.1	52.2	51.2	50.2	49.3	48.3
89	57.0	56.1	55.1	54.1	53.1	52.2	51.2	50.2	49.3	48.3
90	57.0	56.1	55.1	54.1	53.1	52.2	51.2	50.2	49.3	48.3
91	57.0	56.1	55.1	54.1	53.1	52.2	51.2	50.2	49.3	48.3
92	57.0	56.1	55.1	54.1	53.1	52.2	51.2	50.2	49.3	48.3
93	57.0	56.1	55.1	54.1	53.1	52.2	51.2	50.2	49.3	48.3
94	57.0	56.0	55.1	54.1	53.1	52.2	51.2	50.2	49.3	48.3
95	57.0	56.0	55.1	54.1	53.1	52.2	51.2	50.2	49.3	48.3
96	57.0	56.0	55.1	54.1	53.1	52.2	51.2	50.2	49.3	48.3
97	57.0	56.0	55.1	54.1	53.1	52.2	51.2	50.2	49.3	48.3
98	57.0	56.0	55.1	54.1	53.1	52.2	51.2	50.2	49.3	48.3
99	57.0	56.0	55.1	54.1	53.1	52.2	51.2	50.2	49.3	48.3
100	57.0	56.0	55.1	54.1	53.1	52.2	51.2	50.2	49.3	48.3
101	57.0	56.0	55.1	54.1	53.1	52.2	51.2	50.2	49.3	48.3
102	57.0	56.0	55.1	54.1	53.1	52.2	51.2	50.2	49.3	48.3
103	57.0	56.0	55.1	54.1	53.1	52.2	51.2	50.2	49.3	48.3
104	57.0	56.0	55.1	54.1	53.1	52.2	51.2	50.2	49.3	48.3
105	57.0	56.0	55.1	54.1	53.1	52.2	51.2	50.2	49.3	48.3
106	57.0	56.0	55.1	54.1	53.1	52.2	51.2	50.2	49.3	48.3
107	57.0	56.0	55.1	54.1	53.1	52.2	51.2	50.2	49.3	48.3
108	57.0	56.0	55.1	54.1	53.1	52.2	51.2	50.2	49.3	48.3
109	57.0	56.0	55.1	54.1	53.1	52.2	51.2	50.2	49.3	48.3
110	57.0	56.0	55.1	54.1	53.1	52.2	51.2	50.2	49.3	48.3
111	57.0	56.0	55.1	54.1	53.1	52.2	51.2	50.2	49.3	48.3
112	57.0	56.0	55.1	54.1	53.1	52.2	51.2	50.2	49.3	48.3
113	57.0	56.0	55.1	54.1	53.1	52.2	51.2	50.2	49.3	48.3
114	57.0	56.0	55.1	54.1	53.1	52.2	51.2	50.2	49.3	48.3
115	57.0	56.0	55.1	54.1	53.1	52.2	51.2	50.2	49.3	48.3

Table VI.—Ordinary Joint Life and Last Survivor Annuities; Two Lives—Expected Return Multiples

Ages	35	36	37	38	39	40	41	42	43	44
35	54.0	53.5	53.0	52.6	52.2	51.8	51.4	51.1	50.8	50.5
36	53.5	53.0	52.5	52.0	51.6	51.2	50.8	50.4	50.1	49.8
37	53.0	52.5	52.0	51.5	51.0	50.6	50.2	49.8	49.5	49.1
38	52.6	52.0	51.5	51.0	50.5	50.0	49.6	49.2	48.8	48.5
39	52.2	51.6	51.0	50.5	50.0	49.5	49.1	48.6	48.2	47.8
40	51.8	51.2	50.6	50.0	49.5	49.0	48.5	48.1	47.6	47.2
41	51.4	50.8	50.2	49.6	49.1	48.5	48.0	47.5	47.1	46.7
42	51.1	50.4	49.8	49.2	48.6	48.1	47.5	47.0	46.6	46.1
43	50.8	50.1	49.5	48.8	48.2	47.6	47.1	46.6	46.0	45.6
44	50.5	49.8	49.1	48.5	47.8	47.2	46.7	46.1	45.6	45.1
45	50.2	49.5	48.8	48.1	47.5	46.9	46.3	45.7	45.1	44.6
46	50.0	49.2	48.5	47.8	47.2	46.5	45.9	45.3	44.7	44.1
47	49.7	49.0	48.3	47.5	46.8	46.2	45.5	44.9	44.3	43.7
48	49.5	48.8	48.0	47.3	46.6	45.9	45.2	44.5	43.9	43.3
49	49.3	48.5	47.8	47.0	46.3	45.6	44.9	44.2	43.6	42.9

Table VI.—Ordinary Joint Life and Last Survivor Annuities; Two Lives—Expected Return Multiples (continued)

Ages	35	36	37	38	39	40	41	42	43	44
50	49.2	48.4	47.6	46.8	46.0	45.3	44.6	43.9	43.2	42.6
51	49.0	48.2	47.4	46.6	45.8	45.1	44.3	43.6	42.9	44.2
52	48.8	48.0	47.2	46.4	45.6	44.8	44.1	43.3	42.6	41.9
53	48.7	47.9	47.0	46.2	45.4	44.6	43.9	43.1	42.4	41.7
54	48.6	47.7	46.9	46.0	45.2	44.4	43.6	42.9	42.1	41.4
55	48.5	47.6	46.7	45.9	45.1	44.2	43.4	42.7	41.9	41.2
56	48.3	47.5	46.6	45.8	44.9	44.1	43.3	42.5	41.7	40.9
57	48.3	47.4	46.5	45.6	44.8	43.9	43.1	42.3	41.5	40.7
58	48.2	47.3	46.4	45.5	44.7	43.8	43.0	42.1	41.3	40.5
59	48.1	47.2	46.3	45.4	44.5	43.7	42.8	42.0	41.2	40.4
60	48.0	47.1	46.2	45.3	44.4	43.6	42.7	41.9	41.0	40.2
61	47.9	47.0	46.1	45.2	44.3	43.5	42.6	41.7	40.9	40.0
62	47.9	47.0	46.0	45.1	44.2	43.4	42.5	41.6	40.8	39.9
63	47.8	46.9	46.0	45.1	44.2	43.3	42.4	41.5	40.6	39.8
64	47.8	46.8	45.9	45.0	44.1	43.2	42.3	41.4	40.5	39.7
65	47.7	46.8	45.9	44.9	44.0	43.1	42.2	41.3	40.4	39.6
66	47.7	46.7	45.8	44.9	44.0	43.1	42.2	41.3	40.4	39.5
67	47.6	46.7	45.8	44.8	43.9	43.0	42.1	41.2	40.3	39.4
68	47.6	46.7	45.7	44.8	43.9	42.9	42.0	41.1	40.2	39.3
69	47.6	46.6	45.7	44.8	43.8	42.9	42.0	41.1	40.2	39.3
70	47.5	46.6	45.7	44.7	43.8	42.9	41.9	41.0	40.1	39.2
71	47.5	46.6	45.6	44.7	43.8	42.8	41.9	41.0	40.1	39.1
72	47.5	46.6	45.6	44.7	43.7	42.8	41.9	40.9	40.0	39.1
73	47.5	46.5	45.6	44.6	43.7	42.8	41.8	40.9	40.0	39.0
74	47.5	46.5	45.6	44.6	43.7	42.7	41.8	40.9	39.9	39.0
75	47.4	46.5	45.5	44.6	43.6	42.7	41.8	40.8	39.9	39.0
76	47.4	46.5	45.5	44.6	43.6	42.7	41.7	40.8	39.9	38.9
77	47.4	46.5	45.5	44.6	43.6	42.7	41.7	40.8	39.8	38.9
78	47.4	46.4	45.5	44.5	43.6	42.6	41.7	40.7	39.8	38.9
79	47.4	46.4	45.5	44.5	43.6	42.6	41.7	40.7	39.8	38.9
80	47.4	46.4	45.5	44.5	43.6	42.6	41.7	40.7	39.8	38.8
81	47.4	46.4	45.5	44.5	43.5	42.6	41.6	40.7	39.8	38.8
82	47.4	46.4	45.4	44.5	43.5	42.6	41.6	40.7	39.7	38.8
83	47.4	46.4	45.4	44.5	43.5	42.6	41.6	40.7	39.7	38.8
84	47.4	46.4	45.4	44.5	43.5	42.6	41.6	40.7	39.7	38.8
85	47.4	46.4	45.4	44.5	43.5	42.6	41.6	40.7	39.7	38.8
86	47.3	46.4	45.4	44.5	43.5	42.5	41.6	40.6	39.7	38.8
87	47.3	46.4	45.4	44.5	43.5	42.5	41.6	40.6	39.7	38.7
88	47.3	46.4	45.4	44.5	43.5	42.5	41.6	40.6	39.7	38.7
89	47.3	46.4	45.4	44.4	43.5	42.5	41.6	40.6	39.7	38.7
90	47.3	46.4	45.4	44.4	43.5	42.5	41.6	40.6	39.7	38.7
91	47.3	46.4	45.4	44.4	43.5	42.5	41.6	40.6	39.7	39.7
92	47.3	46.4	45.4	44.4	44.4	43.5	42.5	41.6	40.6	38.7
93	47.3	46.4	45.4	43.5	42.5	41.6	40.6	39.7	39.7	38.7
94	47.3	46.4	45.4	44.4	43.5	42.5	41.6	40.6	39.7	38.7
95	47.3	46.4	45.4	44.4	43.5	42.5	41.6	40.6	39.7	38.7
96	47.3	46.4	45.4	44.4	43.5	42.5	41.6	40.6	39.7	38.7
97	47.3	46.4	45.4	44.4	43.5	42.5	41.6	40.6	39.6	38.7
98	47.3	46.4	45.4	44.4	43.5	42.5	41.6	40.6	39.6	38.7
99	47.3	46.4	45.4	44.4	43.5	42.5	41.5	40.6	39.6	38.7
100	47.3	46.4	45.4	44.4	43.5	42.5	41.5	40.6	39.6	38.7
101	47.3	46.4	45.4	44.4	43.5	42.5	41.5	40.6	39.6	38.7
102	47.3	46.4	45.4	44.4	43.5	42.5	41.5	40.6	39.6	38.7
103	47.3	46.4	45.4	44.4	43.5	42.5	41.5	40.6	39.6	38.7
104	47.3	46.4	45.4	44.4	43.5	42.5	41.5	40.6	39.6	38.7
105	47.3	46.4	45.4	44.4	43.5	42.5	41.5	40.6	39.6	38.7
106	47.3	46.4	45.4	44.4	43.5	42.5	41.5	40.6	39.6	38.7
107	47.3	46.4	45.4	44.4	43.5	42.5	41.5	40.6	39.6	38.7
108	47.3	46.4	45.4	44.4	43.5	42.5	41.5	40.6	39.6	38.7
109	47.3	46.4	45.4	44.4	43.5	42.5	41.5	40.6	39.6	38.7
110	47.3	46.4	45.4	44.4	43.5	42.5	41.5	40.6	39.6	38.7
111	47.3	46.4	45.4	44.4	43.5	42.5	41.5	40.6	39.6	38.7

Table VI.—Ordinary Joint Life and Last Survivor Annuities; Two Lives—Expected Return Multiples (continued)

Ages	35	36	37	38	39	40	41	42	43	44
112....	47.3	46.4	45.4	44.4	43.5	42.5	41.5	40.6	39.6	38.7
113....	47.3	46.4	45.4	44.4	43.5	42.5	41.5	40.6	39.6	38.7
114....	47.3	48.4	45.4	44.4	43.5	42.5	41.5	40.6	39.6	38.7
115....	47.3	46.4	45.4	44.4	43.5	42.5	41.5	40.6	39.6	38.7

Table VI—Ordinary Joint Life and Last Survivor Annuities; Two Lives— Expected Return Multiples

Ages	45	46	47	48	49	50	51	52	53	54
45.....	44.1	43.6	43.2	42.7	42.3	42.0	41.6	41.3	41.0	40.7
46.....	43.6	43.1	42.6	42.2	41.8	41.4	41.0	40.6	40.3	40.0
47.....	43.2	42.6	42.1	41.7	41.2	40.8	40.4	40.0	39.7	39.3
48.....	42.7	42.2	41.7	41.2	40.7	40.2	39.8	39.4	39.0	38.7
49.....	42.3	41.8	41.2	40.7	40.2	39.7	39.3	38.8	38.4	38.1
50.....	42.0	41.4	40.8	40.2	39.7	39.2	38.7	38.3	37.9	37.5
51.....	41.6	41.0	40.4	39.8	39.3	38.7	38.2	37.8	37.3	36.9
52.....	41.3	40.6	40.0	39.4	38.8	38.3	37.8	37.3	36.8	36.4
53.....	41.0	40.3	39.7	39.0	38.4	37.9	37.3	36.8	36.3	35.8
54.....	40.7	40.0	39.3	38.7	38.1	37.5	36.9	36.4	35.8	35.3
55.....	40.4	39.7	39.0	38.4	37.7	37.1	36.5	35.9	35.4	34.9
56.....	40.2	39.5	38.7	38.1	37.4	36.8	36.1	35.6	35.0	34.4
57.....	40.0	39.2	38.5	37.8	37.1	36.4	35.8	35.2	34.6	34.0
58.....	39.7	39.0	38.2	37.5	36.8	36.1	35.5	34.8	34.2	33.6
59.....	39.6	38.8	38.0	37.3	36.6	35.9	35.2	34.5	33.9	33.3
60.....	39.4	38.6	37.8	37.1	36.3	35.6	34.9	34.2	33.6	32.9
61.....	39.2	38.4	37.6	36.9	36.1	35.4	34.6	33.9	33.3	32.6
62.....	39.1	38.3	37.5	36.7	35.9	35.1	34.4	33.7	33.0	32.3
63.....	38.9	38.1	37.3	36.5	35.7	34.9	34.2	33.5	32.7	32.0
64.....	38.8	38.0	37.2	36.3	35.5	34.8	34.0	33.2	32.5	31.8
65.....	38.7	37.9	37.0	36.2	35.4	34.6	33.8	33.0	32.3	31.6
66.....	38.6	37.8	36.9	36.1	35.2	34.4	33.6	32.9	32.1	31.4
67.....	38.5	37.7	36.8	36.0	35.1	34.3	33.5	32.7	31.9	31.2
68.....	38.4	37.6	36.7	35.8	35.0	34.2	33.4	32.5	31.8	31.0
69.....	38.4	37.5	36.6	35.7	34.9	34.1	33.2	32.4	31.6	30.8
70.....	38.3	37.4	36.5	35.7	34.8	34.0	33.1	32.3	31.5	30.7
71.....	38.2	37.3	36.5	35.6	34.7	33.9	33.0	32.2	31.4	30.5
72.....	38.2	37.3	36.4	35.5	34.6	33.8	32.9	32.1	31.2	30.4
73.....	38.1	37.2	36.3	35.4	34.6	33.7	32.8	32.0	31.1	30.3
74.....	38.1	37.2	36.3	35.4	34.5	33.6	32.8	31.9	31.1	30.2
75.....	38.1	37.1	36.2	35.3	34.5	33.6	32.7	31.8	31.0	30.1
76.....	38.0	37.1	36.2	35.3	34.4	33.5	32.6	31.8	30.9	30.1
77.....	38.0	37.1	36.2	35.3	34.4	33.5	32.6	31.7	30.8	30.0
78.....	38.0	37.0	36.1	35.2	34.3	33.4	32.5	31.7	30.8	29.9
79.....	37.9	37.0	36.1	35.2	34.3	33.4	32.5	31.6	30.7	29.9
80.....	37.9	37.0	36.1	35.2	34.2	33.4	32.5	31.6	30.7	29.8
81.....	37.9	37.0	36.0	35.1	34.2	33.3	32.4	31.5	30.7	29.8
82.....	37.9	36.9	36.0	35.1	34.2	33.3	32.4	31.5	30.6	29.7
83.....	37.9	36.9	36.0	35.1	34.2	33.3	32.4	31.5	30.6	29.7
84.....	37.8	36.9	36.9	35.0	34.2	33.2	32.3	31.4	30.6	29.7
85.....	37.8	36.9	36.0	35.1	34.1	33.2	32.3	31.4	30.5	29.6
86.....	38.8	36.9	36.0	35.0	34.1	33.2	32.3	31.4	30.5	29.6
87.....	37.8	36.9	35.9	35.0	34.1	33.2	32.3	31.4	30.5	29.6
88.....	37.8	36.9	35.9	35.0	34.1	33.2	32.3	31.4	30.5	29.6
89.....	37.8	36.9	35.9	35.0	34.1	33.2	32.3	31.3	30.5	29.6
90.....	37.8	36.9	35.9	35.0	34.1	33.2	32.3	31.3	30.5	29.6
91.....	37.8	36.8	35.9	35.0	34.1	33.2	32.2	31.3	30.4	29.5
92.....	37.8	36.8	35.9	35.0	34.1	33.2	32.2	31.3	30.4	29.5
93.....	37.8	36.8	35.9	35.0	34.1	33.1	32.2	31.3	30.4	29.5
94.....	37.8	36.8	35.9	35.0	34.1	33.1	32.2	31.3	30.4	29.5
95.....	37.8	36.8	35.9	35.0	34.0	33.1	32.2	31.3	30.4	29.5
96.....	37.8	36.8	35.9	35.0	34.0	33.1	32.2	31.3	30.4	29.5
97.....	37.8	36.8	35.9	35.0	34.0	33.1	32.2	31.3	30.4	29.5
98.....	37.8	36.8	35.9	35.0	34.0	33.1	32.2	31.3	30.4	29.5

Table VI—Ordinary Joint Life and Last Survivor Annuities; Two Lives— Expected Return Multiples (continued)

Ages	45	46	47	48	49	50	51	52	53	54
99	37.8	36.8	35.9	35.0	34.0	33.1	32.2	31.3	30.4	29.5
101	37.8	36.8	35.9	35.0	34.0	33.1	32.2	31.3	30.4	29.5
102	37.8	36.8	35.9	35.0	34.0	33.1	32.2	31.3	30.4	29.5
103	37.7	36.8	35.9	34.9	34.0	33.1	32.2	31.3	30.4	29.5
104	37.7	36.8	35.9	34.9	34.0	33.1	32.2	31.3	30.4	29.5
105	37.7	36.8	35.9	34.9	34.0	33.1	32.2	31.3	30.4	29.5
106	37.7	36.8	35.9	34.9	34.0	33.1	32.2	31.3	30.4	29.5
107	37.7	36.8	35.9	34.9	34.0	33.1	32.2	31.3	30.4	29.5
108	37.7	36.8	35.9	34.9	34.0	33.1	32.2	31.3	30.4	29.5
109	37.7	36.8	35.9	34.9	34.0	33.1	32.2	31.3	30.4	29.5
110	37.7	36.8	35.9	34.9	34.0	33.1	32.2	31.3	30.4	29.5
111	37.7	36.8	35.9	34.9	34.0	33.1	32.2	31.3	30.4	29.5
112	37.7	36.8	35.9	34.9	34.0	33.1	32.2	31.3	30.4	29.5
113	37.7	36.8	35.9	34.9	34.0	33.1	32.2	31.3	30.4	29.5
114	37.7	36.8	35.9	34.9	34.0	33.1	32.2	31.3	30.4	29.5
115	37.7	36.8	35.9	34.9	34.0	33.1	32.2	31.3	30.4	29.5

Table VI—Ordinary Joint Life and Last Survivor Annuities; Two Lives—Expected Return Multiples

Ages	55	56	57	58	59	60	61	62	63	64
55	34.4	33.9	33.5	33.1	32.7	32.3	32.0	31.7	31.4	31.1
56	33.9	33.4	33.0	32.5	32.1	31.7	31.4	31.0	30.7	30.4
57	33.5	33.0	32.5	32.0	31.6	31.2	30.8	30.4	30.1	29.8
58	33.1	32.5	32.0	31.5	31.1	30.6	30.2	29.9	29.5	29.2
59	32.7	32.1	31.6	31.1	30.6	30.1	29.7	29.3	28.9	28.6
60	32.3	31.7	31.2	30.6	30.1	29.7	29.2	28.8	28.4	28.0
61	32.0	31.4	30.8	30.2	29.7	29.2	28.7	28.3	27.8	27.4
62	31.7	31.0	30.4	29.9	29.3	28.8	28.3	27.8	27.3	26.9
63	31.4	30.7	30.1	29.5	28.9	28.4	27.8	27.3	26.9	26.4
64	31.1	30.4	29.8	29.2	28.6	28.0	27.4	26.9	26.4	25.9
65	30.9	30.2	29.5	28.9	28.2	27.6	27.1	26.5	26.0	25.5
66	30.6	29.9	29.2	28.6	27.9	27.3	26.7	26.1	25.6	25.1
67	30.4	29.7	29.0	28.3	27.6	27.0	26.4	25.8	25.2	24.7
68	30.2	29.5	28.8	28.1	27.4	26.7	26.1	25.5	24.9	24.3
69	30.1	29.3	28.6	27.8	27.1	26.5	25.8	25.2	24.6	24.0
70	29.9	29.1	28.4	27.6	26.9	26.2	25.6	24.9	24.3	23.7
71	29.7	29.0	28.2	27.5	26.7	26.0	25.3	24.7	24.0	23.4
72	29.6	28.8	28.1	27.3	26.5	25.8	25.1	24.4	23.8	23.1
73	29.5	28.7	27.9	27.1	26.4	25.6	24.9	24.2	23.5	22.9
74	29.4	28.6	27.8	27.0	26.2	25.5	24.7	24.0	23.3	22.7
75	29.3	28.5	27.7	26.9	26.1	25.3	24.6	23.8	23.1	22.4
76	29.2	28.4	27.6	26.8	26.0	25.2	24.4	23.7	23.0	22.3
77	29.1	28.3	27.5	26.7	25.9	25.1	24.3	23.6	22.8	22.1
78	29.1	28.2	27.4	26.6	25.8	25.0	24.2	23.4	22.7	21.9
79	29.0	28.2	27.3	26.5	25.7	24.9	24.1	23.3	22.6	21.8
80	29.0	28.1	27.3	26.4	25.6	24.8	24.0	23.2	22.4	21.7
81	28.9	28.1	27.2	26.4	25.5	24.7	23.9	23.1	22.3	21.6
82	28.9	28.0	27.2	26.3	25.5	24.6	23.8	23.0	22.3	21.5
83	28.8	28.0	27.1	26.3	25.4	24.6	23.8	23.0	22.2	21.4
84	28.8	27.9	27.1	26.2	25.4	24.5	23.7	22.9	22.1	21.3
85	28.8	27.9	27.0	26.2	25.3	24.5	23.7	22.8	22.0	21.3
86	28.7	27.9	27.0	26.1	25.3	24.5	23.6	22.8	22.0	21.2
87	28.7	27.8	27.0	26.1	25.3	24.4	23.6	22.8	21.9	21.1
88	28.7	27.8	27.0	26.1	25.2	24.4	23.5	22.7	21.9	21.1
89	28.7	27.8	26.9	26.1	25.2	24.4	23.5	22.7	21.9	21.1
90	28.7	27.8	26.9	26.1	25.2	24.3	23.5	22.7	21.8	21.0
91	28.7	27.8	26.9	26.0	25.2	24.3	23.5	22.6	21.8	21.0
92	28.6	27.8	26.9	26.0	25.2	24.3	23.5	22.6	21.8	21.0
93	28.6	27.8	26.9	26.0	25.1	24.3	23.4	22.6	21.8	20.9
94	28.6	27.7	26.9	26.0	25.1	24.3	23.4	22.6	21.7	20.9
95	28.6	27.7	26.9	26.0	25.1	24.3	23.4	22.6	21.7	20.9
96	28.6	27.7	26.9	26.0	25.1	24.2	23.4	22.6	21.7	20.9

Table VI—Ordinary Joint Life and Last Survivor Annuities; Two Lives—Expected Return Multiples (continued)

Ages	55	56	57	58	59	60	61	62	63	64
97	28.6	27.7	26.8	26.0	25.1	24.2	23.4	22.5	21.7	20.9
98	28.6	27.7	26.8	26.0	25.1	24.2	23.4	22.5	21.7	20.9
99	28.6	27.7	26.8	26.0	25.1	24.2	23.4	22.5	21.7	20.9
100	28.6	27.7	26.8	26.0	25.1	24.2	23.4	22.5	21.7	20.8
101	28.6	27.7	26.8	25.9	25.1	24.2	23.4	22.5	21.7	20.8
102	28.6	27.7	26.8	25.9	25.1	24.2	23.3	22.5	21.7	20.8
103	28.6	27.7	26.8	25.9	25.1	24.2	23.3	22.5	21.7	20.8
104	28.6	27.7	26.8	25.9	25.1	24.2	23.3	22.5	21.6	20.8
105	28.6	27.7	26.8	25.9	25.1	24.2	23.3	22.5	21.6	20.8
106	28.6	27.7	26.8	25.9	25.1	24.2	23.3	22.5	21.6	20.8
107	28.6	27.7	26.8	25.9	25.1	24.2	23.3	22.5	21.6	20.8
108	28.6	27.7	26.8	25.9	25.1	24.2	23.3	22.5	21.6	20.8
109	28.6	27.7	26.8	25.9	25.1	24.2	23.3	22.5	21.6	20.8
110	28.6	27.7	26.8	25.9	25.1	24.2	23.3	22.5	21.6	20.8
111	28.6	27.7	26.8	25.9	25.0	24.2	23.3	22.5	21.6	20.8
112	28.6	27.7	26.8	25.9	25.0	24.2	23.3	22.5	21.6	20.8
113	28.6	27.7	26.8	25.9	25.0	24.2	23.3	22.5	21.6	20.8
114	28.6	27.7	26.8	25.9	25.0	24.2	23.3	22.5	21.6	20.8
115	28.6	27.7	26.8	25.9	25.0	24.2	23.3	22.5	21.6	20.8

Table VI—Ordinary Joint Life and Last Survivor Annuities; Two Lives—Expected Return Multiples

Ages	65	66	67	68	69	70	71	72	73	74
65	25.0	24.6	24.2	23.8	23.4	23.1	22.8	22.5	22.2	22.0
66	24.6	24.1	23.7	23.3	22.9	22.5	22.2	21.9	21.6	21.4
67	24.2	23.7	23.2	22.8	22.4	22.0	21.7	21.3	21.0	20.8
68	23.8	23.3	22.8	22.3	21.9	21.5	21.2	20.8	20.5	20.2
69	23.4	22.9	22.4	21.9	21.5	21.1	20.7	20.3	20.0	19.6
70	23.1	22.5	22.0	21.5	21.1	20.6	20.2	19.8	19.4	19.1
71	22.8	22.2	21.7	21.2	20.7	20.2	19.8	19.4	19.0	18.6
72	22.5	21.9	21.3	20.8	20.3	19.8	19.4	18.9	18.5	18.2
73	22.2	21.6	21.0	20.5	20.0	19.4	19.0	18.5	18.1	17.7
74	22.0	21.4	20.8	20.2	19.6	19.1	18.6	18.2	17.7	17.3
75	21.8	21.1	20.5	19.9	19.3	18.8	18.3	17.8	17.3	16.9
76	21.6	20.9	20.3	19.7	19.1	18.5	18.0	17.5	17.0	16.5
77	21.4	20.7	20.1	19.4	18.8	18.3	17.7	17.2	16.7	16.2
78	21.2	20.5	19.9	19.2	18.6	18.0	17.5	16.9	16.4	15.9
79	21.1	20.4	19.7	19.0	18.4	17.8	17.2	16.7	16.1	15.6
80	21.0	20.2	19.5	18.9	18.2	17.6	17.0	16.4	15.9	15.4
81	20.8	20.1	19.4	18.7	18.1	17.4	16.8	16.2	15.7	15.1
82	20.7	20.0	19.3	18.6	17.9	17.3	16.6	16.0	15.5	14.9
83	20.6	19.9	19.2	18.5	17.8	17.1	16.5	15.9	15.3	14.7
84	20.5	19.8	19.1	18.4	17.7	17.0	16.3	15.7	15.1	14.5
85	20.5	19.7	19.0	18.3	17.6	16.9	16.2	15.6	15.0	14.4
86	20.4	19.6	18.9	18.2	17.5	16.8	16.1	15.5	14.8	14.2
87	20.4	19.6	18.8	18.1	17.4	16.7	16.0	15.4	14.7	14.1
88	20.3	19.5	18.8	18.0	17.3	16.6	15.9	15.3	14.6	14.0
89	20.3	19.5	18.7	18.0	17.2	16.5	15.8	15.2	14.5	13.9
90	20.2	19.4	18.7	17.9	17.2	16.5	15.8	15.1	14.5	13.8
91	20.2	19.4	18.6	17.9	17.1	16.4	15.7	15.0	14.4	13.7
92	20.2	19.4	18.6	17.8	17.1	16.4	15.7	15.0	14.3	13.7
93	20.1	19.3	18.6	17.8	17.1	16.3	15.6	14.9	14.3	13.6
94	20.1	19.3	18.5	17.8	17.0	16.3	15.6	14.9	14.2	13.6
95	20.1	19.3	18.5	17.8	17.0	16.3	15.6	14.9	14.2	13.5
96	20.1	19.3	18.5	17.7	17.0	16.2	15.5	14.8	14.2	13.5
97	20.1	19.3	18.5	17.7	17.0	16.2	15.5	14.8	14.1	13.5
98	20.1	19.3	18.5	17.7	16.9	16.2	15.5	14.8	14.1	13.4
99	20.0	19.2	18.5	17.7	16.9	16.2	15.5	14.7	14.1	13.4
100	20.0	19.2	18.4	17.7	16.9	16.2	15.4	14.7	14.0	13.4
101	20.0	19.2	18.4	17.7	16.9	16.1	15.4	14.7	14.0	13.3
102	20.0	19.2	18.4	17.6	16.9	16.1	15.4	14.7	14.0	13.3
103	20.0	19.2	18.4	17.6	16.9	16.1	15.4	14.7	14.0	13.3

Table VI—Ordinary Joint Life and Last Survivor Annuities; Two Lives—Expected Return Multiples (continued)

Ages	65	66	67	68	69	70	71	72	73	74
104	20.0	19.2	18.4	17.6	16.9	16.1	15.4	14.7	14.0	13.3
105	20.0	19.2	18.4	17.6	16.8	16.1	15.4	14.6	13.9	13.3
106	20.0	19.2	18.4	17.6	16.8	16.1	15.3	14.6	13.9	13.3
107	20.0	19.2	18.4	17.6	16.8	16.1	15.3	14.6	13.9	13.2
108	20.0	19.2	18.4	17.6	16.8	16.1	15.3	14.6	13.9	13.2
109	20.0	19.2	18.4	17.6	16.8	16.1	15.3	14.6	13.9	13.2
110	20.0	19.2	18.4	17.6	16.8	16.1	15.3	14.6	13.9	13.2
111	20.0	19.2	18.4	17.6	16.8	16.0	15.3	14.6	13.9	13.2
112	20.0	19.2	18.4	17.6	16.8	16.0	15.3	14.6	13.9	13.2
113	20.0	19.2	18.4	17.6	16.8	16.0	15.3	14.6	13.9	13.2
114	20.0	19.2	18.4	17.6	16.8	16.0	15.3	14.6	13.9	13.2
115	20.0	19.2	18.4	17.6	16.8	16.0	15.3	14.6	13.9	13.2

Table VI—Ordinary Joint Life and Last Survivor Annuities; Two Lives—Expected Return Multiples

Ages	75	76	77	78	79	80	81	82	83	84
75	16.5	16.1	15.8	15.4	15.1	14.9	14.6	14.4	14.2	14.0
76	16.1	15.7	15.4	15.0	14.7	14.4	14.1	13.9	13.7	13.5
77	15.8	15.4	15.0	14.6	14.3	14.0	13.7	13.4	13.2	13.0
78	15.4	15.0	14.6	14.2	13.9	13.5	13.2	13.0	12.7	12.5
79	15.1	14.7	14.3	13.9	13.5	13.2	12.8	12.5	12.3	12.0
80	14.9	14.4	14.0	13.5	13.2	12.8	12.5	12.2	11.9	11.6
81	14.6	14.1	13.7	13.2	12.8	12.5	12.1	11.8	11.5	11.2
82	14.4	13.9	13.4	13.0	12.5	12.2	11.8	11.5	11.1	10.9
83	14.2	13.7	13.2	12.7	12.3	11.9	11.5	11.1	10.8	10.5
84	14.0	13.5	13.0	12.5	12.0	11.6	11.2	10.9	10.5	10.2
85	13.8	13.3	12.8	12.3	11.8	11.4	11.0	10.6	10.2	9.9
86	13.7	13.1	12.6	12.1	11.6	11.2	10.8	10.4	10.0	9.7
87	13.5	13.0	12.4	11.9	11.4	11.0	10.6	10.1	9.8	9.4
88	13.4	12.8	12.3	11.8	11.3	10.8	10.4	10.0	9.6	9.2
89	13.3	12.7	12.2	11.6	11.1	10.7	10.2	9.8	9.4	9.0
90	13.2	12.6	12.1	11.5	11.0	10.5	10.1	9.6	9.2	8.8
91	13.1	12.5	12.0	11.4	10.9	10.4	9.9	9.5	9.1	8.7
92	13.1	12.5	11.9	11.3	10.8	10.3	9.8	9.4	8.9	8.5
93	13.0	12.4	11.8	11.3	10.7	10.2	9.7	9.3	8.8	8.4
94	12.9	12.3	11.7	11.2	10.6	10.1	9.6	9.2	8.7	8.3
95	12.9	12.3	11.7	11.1	10.6	10.1	9.6	9.1	8.6	8.2
96	12.9	12.2	11.6	11.1	10.5	10.0	9.5	9.0	8.5	8.1
97	12.8	12.2	11.6	11.0	10.5	9.9	9.4	8.9	8.5	8.0
98	12.8	12.2	11.5	11.0	10.4	9.9	9.4	8.9	8.4	8.0
99	12.7	12.1	11.5	10.9	10.4	9.8	9.3	8.8	8.3	7.9
100	12.7	12.1	11.5	10.9	10.3	9.8	9.2	8.7	8.3	7.8
101	12.7	12.1	11.4	10.8	10.3	9.7	9.2	8.7	8.2	7.8
102	12.7	12.0	11.4	10.8	10.2	9.7	9.2	8.7	8.2	7.7
103	12.6	12.0	11.4	10.8	10.2	9.7	9.1	8.6	8.1	7.7
104	12.6	12.0	11.4	10.8	10.2	9.6	9.1	8.6	8.1	7.6
105	12.6	12.0	11.3	10.7	10.2	9.6	9.1	8.5	8.0	7.6
106	12.6	11.9	11.3	10.7	10.1	9.6	9.0	8.5	8.0	7.5
107	12.6	11.9	11.3	10.7	10.1	9.6	9.0	8.5	8.0	7.5
108	12.6	11.9	11.3	10.7	10.1	9.5	9.0	8.5	8.0	7.5
109	12.6	11.9	11.3	10.7	10.1	9.5	9.0	8.4	7.9	7.5
110	12.6	11.9	11.3	10.7	10.1	9.5	9.0	8.4	7.9	7.4
111	12.5	11.9	11.3	10.7	10.1	9.5	8.9	8.4	7.9	7.4
112	12.5	11.9	11.3	10.6	10.1	9.5	8.9	8.4	7.9	7.4
113	12.5	11.9	11.2	10.6	10.0	9.5	8.9	8.4	7.9	7.4
114	12.5	11.9	11.2	10.6	10.0	9.5	8.9	8.4	7.9	7.4
115	12.5	11.9	11.2	10.6	10.0	9.5	8.9	8.4	7.9	7.4

Table VI—Ordinary Joint Life and Last Survivor Annuities; Two Lives—Expected Return Multiples

Ages	85	86	87	88	89	90	91	92	93	94
85	9.6	9.3	9.1	8.9	8.7	8.5	8.3	8.2	8.0	7.9
86	9.3	9.1	8.8	8.6	8.3	8.2	8.0	7.8	7.7	7.6
87	9.1	8.8	8.5	8.3	8.1	7.9	7.7	7.5	7.4	7.2
88	8.9	8.6	8.3	8.0	7.8	7.6	7.4	7.2	7.1	6.9
89	8.7	8.3	8.1	7.8	7.5	7.3	7.1	6.9	6.8	6.6
90	8.5	8.2	7.9	7.6	7.3	7.1	6.9	6.7	6.5	6.4
91	8.3	8.0	7.7	7.4	7.1	6.9	6.7	6.5	6.3	6.2
92	8.2	7.8	7.5	7.2	6.9	6.7	6.5	6.3	6.1	5.9
93	8.0	7.7	7.4	7.1	6.8	6.5	6.3	6.1	5.9	5.8
94	7.9	7.6	7.2	6.9	6.6	6.4	6.2	5.9	5.8	5.6
95	7.8	7.5	7.1	6.8	6.5	6.3	6.0	5.8	5.6	5.4
96	7.7	7.3	7.0	6.7	6.4	6.1	5.9	5.7	5.5	5.3
97	7.6	7.3	6.9	6.6	6.3	6.0	5.8	5.5	5.3	5.1
98	7.6	7.2	6.8	6.5	6.2	5.9	5.6	5.4	5.2	5.0
99	7.5	7.1	6.7	6.4	6.1	5.8	5.5	5.3	5.1	4.9
100	7.4	7.0	6.6	6.3	6.0	5.7	5.4	5.2	5.0	4.8
101	7.3	6.9	6.6	6.2	5.9	5.6	5.3	5.1	4.9	4.7
102	7.3	6.9	6.5	6.2	5.8	5.5	5.3	5.0	4.8	4.6
103	7.2	6.8	6.4	6.1	5.8	5.5	5.2	4.9	4.7	4.5
104	7.2	6.8	6.4	6.0	5.7	5.4	5.1	4.8	4.6	4.4
105	7.1	6.7	6.3	6.0	5.6	5.3	5.0	4.8	4.5	4.3
106	7.1	6.7	6.3	5.9	5.6	5.3	5.0	4.7	4.5	4.2
107	7.1	6.6	6.2	5.9	5.5	5.2	4.9	4.6	4.4	4.2
108	7.0	6.6	6.2	5.8	5.5	5.2	4.9	4.6	4.3	4.1
109	7.0	6.6	6.2	5.8	5.5	5.1	4.8	4.5	4.3	4.1
110	7.0	6.6	6.2	5.8	5.4	5.1	4.8	4.5	4.3	4.0
111	7.0	6.5	6.1	5.7	5.4	5.1	4.8	4.5	4.2	4.0
112	7.0	6.5	6.1	5.7	5.4	5.0	4.7	4.4	4.2	3.9
113	6.9	6.5	6.1	5.7	5.4	5.0	4.7	4.4	4.2	3.9
114	6.9	6.5	6.1	5.7	5.3	5.0	4.7	4.4	4.1	3.9
115	6.9	6.5	6.1	5.7	5.3	5.0	4.7	4.4	4.1	3.9

Table VI—Ordinary Joint Life and Last Survivor Annuities; Two Lives—Expected Return Multiples

Ages	95	96	97	98	99	100	101	102	103	104
95	5.3	5.1	5.0	4.8	4.7	4.6	4.5	4.4	4.3	4.2
96	5.1	5.0	4.8	4.7	4.5	4.4	4.3	4.2	4.1	4.0
97	5.0	4.8	4.7	4.5	4.4	4.3	4.1	4.0	3.9	3.8
98	4.8	4.7	4.5	4.4	4.2	4.1	4.0	3.9	3.8	3.7
99	4.7	4.5	4.4	4.2	4.1	4.0	3.8	3.7	3.6	3.5
100	4.6	4.4	4.3	4.1	4.0	3.8	3.7	3.6	3.5	3.3
101	4.5	4.3	4.1	4.0	3.8	3.7	3.6	3.4	3.3	3.2
102	4.4	4.2	4.0	3.9	3.7	3.6	3.4	3.3	3.2	3.1
103	4.3	4.1	3.9	3.8	3.6	3.5	3.3	3.2	3.0	2.9
104	4.2	4.0	3.8	3.7	3.5	3.3	3.2	3.1	2.9	2.8
105	4.1	3.9	3.7	3.6	3.4	3.2	3.1	2.9	2.8	2.7
106	4.0	3.8	3.6	3.5	3.3	3.1	3.0	2.8	2.7	2.5
107	4.0	3.8	3.6	3.4	3.2	3.1	2.9	2.7	2.6	2.4
108	3.9	3.7	3.5	3.3	3.1	3.0	2.8	2.7	2.5	2.3
109	3.8	3.6	3.4	3.3	3.1	2.9	2.7	2.6	2.4	2.3
110	3.8	3.6	3.4	3.2	3.0	2.8	2.7	2.5	2.3	2.2
111	3.8	3.5	3.3	3.2	3.0	2.8	2.6	2.4	2.3	2.1
112	3.7	3.5	3.3	3.1	2.9	2.8	2.6	2.4	2.2	2.1
113	3.7	3.5	3.3	3.1	2.9	2.7	2.5	2.4	2.2	2.0
114	3.7	3.5	3.3	3.1	2.9	2.7	2.5	2.3	2.1	2.0
115	3.7	3.4	3.2	3.0	2.8	2.7	2.5	2.3	2.1	1.9

Table VI—Ordinary Joint Life and Last Survivor Annuities; Two Lives—Expected Return Multiples

Ages	105	106	107	108	109	110	111	112	113	114	115
105	2.5	2.4	2.3	2.2	2.1	2.0	2.0	1.9	1.8	1.8	1.8
106	2.4	2.3	2.2	2.1	2.0	1.9	1.8	1.7	1.7	1.6	1.6
107	2.3	2.2	2.1	1.9	1.8	1.7	1.7	1.6	1.5	1.5	1.4
108	2.2	2.1	1.9	1.8	1.7	1.6	1.5	1.5	1.4	1.3	1.3
109	2.1	2.0	1.8	1.7	1.6	1.5	1.4	1.3	1.3	1.2	1.1
110	2.0	1.9	1.7	1.6	1.5	1.4	1.3	1.2	1.1	1.1	1.0
111	2.0	1.8	1.7	1.5	1.4	1.3	1.2	1.1	1.0	.9	.9
112	1.9	1.7	1.6	1.5	1.3	1.2	1.1	1.0	.9	.8	.8
113	1.8	1.7	1.5	1.4	1.3	1.1	1.0	.9	.8	.7	.7
114	1.8	1.6	1.5	1.3	1.2	1.1	.9	.8	.7	.6	.6
115	1.8	1.6	1.4	1.3	1.1	1.0	.9	.8	.7	.6	.5

Table VIA—Annuities for Joint Life Only; Two Lives—Expected Return Multiples

Ages	5	6	7	8	9	10	11	12	13	14
5	69.5	69.0	68.4	67.9	67.3	66.7	66.1	65.5	64.8	64.1
6	69.0	68.5	68.0	67.5	66.9	66.4	65.8	65.1	64.5	63.8
7	68.4	68.0	67.5	67.0	66.5	66.0	65.4	64.8	64.2	63.5
8	67.9	67.5	67.0	66.6	66.1	65.5	65.0	64.4	63.8	63.2
9	67.3	66.9	66.5	66.1	65.6	65.1	64.6	64.0	63.4	62.8
10	66.7	66.4	66.0	65.5	65.1	64.6	64.1	63.6	63.0	62.5
11	66.1	65.8	65.4	65.0	64.6	64.1	63.6	63.1	62.6	62.1
12	65.5	65.1	64.8	64.4	64.0	63.6	63.1	62.7	62.2	61.7
13	64.8	64.5	64.2	63.8	63.4	63.0	62.6	62.2	61.7	61.2
14	64.1	63.8	63.5	63.2	62.8	62.5	62.1	61.7	61.2	60.7
15	63.4	63.1	62.9	62.6	62.2	61.9	61.5	61.1	60.7	60.2
16	62.7	62.4	62.2	61.9	61.6	61.3	60.9	60.5	60.1	59.7
17	61.9	61.7	61.5	61.2	60.9	60.6	60.3	59.9	59.6	59.2
18	61.2	61.0	60.7	60.5	60.2	60.0	59.7	59.3	59.0	58.6
19	60.4	60.2	60.0	59.8	59.5	59.3	59.0	58.7	58.4	58.0
20	59.6	59.4	59.2	59.0	58.8	58.6	58.3	58.0	57.7	57.4
21	58.8	58.7	58.5	58.3	58.1	57.8	57.6	57.3	57.1	56.8
22	58.0	57.8	57.7	57.5	57.3	57.1	56.9	56.6	56.4	56.1
23	57.2	57.0	56.9	56.7	56.5	56.4	56.1	55.9	55.7	55.4
24	56.3	56.2	56.1	55.9	55.8	55.6	55.4	55.2	55.0	54.7
25	55.5	55.4	55.2	55.1	55.0	54.8	54.6	54.4	54.2	54.0
26	54.6	54.5	54.4	54.3	54.1	54.0	53.8	53.7	53.5	53.3
27	53.8	53.7	53.6	53.4	53.3	53.2	53.0	52.9	52.7	52.5
28	52.9	52.8	52.7	52.6	52.5	52.4	52.2	52.1	51.9	51.7
29	52.0	51.9	51.8	51.7	51.6	51.5	51.4	51.3	51.1	51.0
30	51.1	51.0	51.0	50.9	50.8	50.7	50.6	50.4	50.3	50.2
31	50.2	50.2	50.1	50.0	49.9	49.8	49.7	49.6	49.5	49.3
32	49.3	49.3	49.2	49.1	49.0	49.0	48.9	48.8	48.6	48.5
33	48.4	48.4	48.3	48.2	48.2	48.1	48.0	47.9	47.8	47.7
34	47.5	47.5	47.4	47.4	47.3	47.2	47.1	47.0	47.0	46.8
35	46.6	46.6	46.5	46.5	46.4	46.3	46.3	46.2	46.1	46.0
36	45.7	45.7	45.6	45.6	45.5	45.4	45.4	45.3	45.2	45.1
37	44.8	44.7	44.7	44.6	44.6	44.5	44.5	44.4	44.3	44.3
38	43.9	43.8	43.8	43.7	43.7	43.6	43.6	43.5	43.5	43.4
39	42.9	42.9	42.9	42.8	42.8	42.7	42.7	42.6	42.6	42.5
40	42.0	42.0	42.0	41.9	41.9	41.8	41.8	41.7	41.7	41.6
41	41.1	41.1	41.0	41.0	41.0	40.9	40.9	40.8	40.8	40.7
42	40.2	40.1	40.1	40.1	40.1	40.0	40.0	39.9	39.9	39.8
43	39.2	39.2	39.2	39.2	39.1	39.1	39.1	39.0	39.0	39.0
44	38.3	38.3	38.3	38.3	38.2	38.2	38.2	38.1	38.1	38.1
45	37.4	37.4	37.4	37.3	37.3	37.3	37.3	37.2	37.2	37.2
46	36.5	36.5	36.5	36.4	36.4	36.4	36.4	36.3	36.3	36.3
47	35.6	35.6	35.5	35.5	35.5	35.5	35.5	35.4	35.4	35.4
48	34.7	34.7	34.6	34.6	34.6	34.6	34.6	34.5	34.5	34.5
49	33.8	33.8	33.7	33.7	33.7	33.7	33.7	33.7	33.6	33.6
50	32.9	32.9	32.8	32.8	32.8	32.8	32.8	32.8	32.7	32.7
51	32.0	32.0	31.9	31.9	31.9	31.9	31.9	31.9	31.9	31.8
52	31.1	31.1	31.1	31.0	31.0	31.0	31.0	31.0	31.0	30.9
53	30.2	30.2	30.2	30.2	30.1	30.1	30.1	30.1	30.1	30.1

Table VIA—Annuities for Joint Life Only; Two Lives—Expected Return Multiples (continued)

Ages	5	6	7	8	9	10	11	12	13	14
54	29.3	29.3	29.3	29.3	29.3	29.2	29.2	29.2	29.2	29.2
55	28.4	28.4	28.4	28.4	28.4	28.4	28.4	28.3	28.3	28.3
56	27.5	27.5	27.5	27.5	27.5	27.5	27.5	27.5	27.5	27.5
57	26.7	26.7	26.7	26.6	26.6	26.6	26.6	26.6	26.6	26.6
58	25.8	25.8	25.8	25.8	25.8	25.8	25.8	25.7	25.7	25.7
59	24.9	24.9	24.9	24.9	24.9	24.9	24.9	24.9	24.9	24.9
60	24.1	24.1	24.1	24.1	24.1	24.0	24.0	24.0	24.0	24.0
61	23.2	23.2	23.2	23.2	23.2	23.2	23.2	23.2	23.2	23.2
62	22.4	22.4	22.4	22.4	22.4	22.4	22.3	22.3	22.3	22.3
63	21.5	21.5	21.5	21.5	21.5	21.5	21.5	21.5	21.5	21.5
64	20.7	20.7	20.7	20.7	20.7	20.7	20.7	20.7	20.7	20.7
65	19.9	19.9	19.9	19.9	19.9	19.9	19.9	19.9	19.9	19.9
66	19.1	19.1	19.1	19.1	19.1	19.1	19.1	19.1	19.1	19.1
67	18.3	18.3	18.3	18.3	18.3	18.3	18.3	18.3	18.3	18.3
68	17.5	17.5	17.5	17.5	17.5	17.5	17.5	17.5	17.5	17.5
69	16.8	16.8	16.8	16.7	16.7	16.7	16.7	16.7	16.7	16.7
70	16.0	16.0	16.0	16.0	16.0	16.0	16.0	16.0	16.0	16.0
71	15.3	15.3	15.3	15.3	15.3	15.3	15.3	15.3	15.3	15.2
72	14.6	14.6	14.5	14.5	14.5	14.5	14.5	14.5	14.5	14.5
73	13.9	13.9	13.8	13.8	13.8	13.8	13.8	13.8	13.8	13.8
74	13.2	13.2	13.2	13.2	13.2	13.2	13.2	13.2	13.2	13.2
75	12.5	12.5	12.5	12.5	12.5	12.5	12.5	12.5	12.5	12.5
76	11.9	11.9	11.8	11.8	11.8	11.8	11.8	11.8	11.8	11.8
77	11.2	11.2	11.2	11.2	11.2	11.2	11.2	11.2	11.2	11.2
78	10.6	10.6	10.6	10.6	10.6	10.6	10.6	10.6	10.6	10.6
79	10.0	10.0	10.0	10.0	10.0	10.0	10.0	10.0	10.0	10.0
80	9.5	9.5	9.5	9.5	9.5	9.5	9.5	9.5	9.4	9.4
81	8.9	8.9	8.9	8.9	8.9	8.9	8.9	8.9	8.9	8.9
82	8.4	8.4	8.4	8.4	8.4	8.4	8.4	8.4	8.4	8.4
83	7.9	7.9	7.9	7.9	7.9	7.9	7.9	7.9	7.9	7.9
84	7.4	7.4	7.4	7.4	7.4	7.4	7.4	7.4	7.4	7.4
85	6.9	6.9	6.9	6.9	6.9	6.9	6.9	6.9	6.9	6.9
86	6.5	6.5	6.5	6.5	6.5	6.5	6.5	6.5	6.5	6.5
87	6.1	6.1	6.1	6.1	6.1	6.1	6.1	6.1	6.1	6.1
88	5.7	5.7	5.7	5.7	5.7	5.7	5.7	5.7	5.7	5.7
89	5.3	5.3	5.3	5.3	5.3	5.3	5.3	5.3	5.3	5.3
90	5.0	5.0	5.0	5.0	5.0	5.0	5.0	5.0	5.0	5.0
91	4.7	4.7	4.7	4.7	4.7	4.7	4.7	4.7	4.7	4.7
92	4.4	4.4	4.4	4.4	4.4	4.4	4.4	4.4	4.4	4.4
93	4.1	4.1	4.1	4.1	4.1	4.1	4.1	4.1	4.1	4.1
94	3.9	3.9	3.9	3.9	3.9	3.9	3.9	3.9	3.9	3.9
95	3.7	3.7	3.7	3.7	3.7	3.7	3.6	3.6	3.6	3.6
96	3.4	3.4	3.4	3.4	3.4	3.4	3.4	3.4	3.4	3.4
97	3.2	3.2	3.2	3.2	3.2	3.2	3.2	3.2	3.2	3.2
98	3.0	3.0	3.0	3.0	3.0	3.0	3.0	3.0	3.0	3.0
99	2.8	2.8	2.8	2.8	2.8	2.8	2.8	2.8	2.8	2.8
100	2.7	2.7	2.7	2.7	2.7	2.7	2.7	2.7	2.7	2.7
101	2.5	2.5	2.5	2.5	2.5	2.5	2.5	2.5	2.5	2.5
102	2.3	2.3	2.3	2.3	2.3	2.3	2.3	2.3	2.3	2.3
103	2.1	2.1	2.1	2.1	2.1	2.1	2.1	2.1	2.1	2.1
104	1.9	1.9	1.9	1.9	1.9	1.9	1.9	1.9	1.9	1.9
105	1.8	1.8	1.8	1.8	1.8	1.8	1.8	1.8	1.8	1.8
106	1.6	1.6	1.6	1.6	1.6	1.6	1.6	1.6	1.6	1.6
107	1.4	1.4	1.4	1.4	1.4	1.4	1.4	1.4	1.4	1.4
108	1.3	1.3	1.3	1.3	1.3	1.3	1.3	1.3	1.3	1.3
109	1.1	1.1	1.1	1.1	1.1	1.1	1.1	1.1	1.1	1.1
110	1.0	1.0	1.0	1.0	1.0	1.0	1.0	1.0	1.0	1.0
111	.9	.9	.9	.9	.9	.9	.9	.9	.9	.9
112	.8	.8	.8	.8	.8	.8	.8	.8	.8	.8
113	.7	.7	.7	.7	.7	.7	.7	.7	.7	.7
114	.6	.6	.6	.6	.6	.6	.6	.6	.6	.6
115	.5	.5	.5	.5	.5	.5	.5	.5	.5	.5

Table VIA—Annuities for Joint Life Only; Two Lives—Expected Return Multiples

Ages	15	16	17	18	19	20	21	22	23	24
15	59.8	59.3	58.8	58.2	57.6	57.0	56.4	55.8	55.1	54.5
16	59.3	58.8	58.3	57.8	57.2	56.7	56.1	55.5	54.8	54.2
17	58.8	58.3	57.8	57.3	56.8	56.3	55.7	55.1	54.5	53.9
18	58.2	57.8	57.3	56.9	56.4	55.9	55.3	54.7	54.2	53.5
19	57.6	57.2	56.8	56.4	55.9	55.4	54.9	54.4	53.8	53.2
20	57.0	56.7	56.3	55.9	55.4	54.9	54.5	53.9	53.4	52.8
21	56.4	56.1	55.7	55.3	54.9	54.5	54.0	53.5	53.0	52.4
22	55.8	55.5	55.1	54.7	54.4	53.9	53.5	53.0	52.5	52.0
23	55.1	54.8	54.5	54.2	53.8	53.4	53.0	52.5	52.1	51.6
24	54.5	54.2	53.9	53.5	53.2	52.8	52.4	52.0	51.6	51.1
25	53.8	53.5	53.2	52.9	52.6	52.2	51.9	51.5	51.1	50.6
26	53.0	52.8	52.5	52.3	52.0	51.6	51.3	50.9	50.5	50.1
27	52.3	52.1	51.8	51.6	51.3	51.0	50.7	50.3	50.0	49.6
28	51.5	51.3	51.1	50.9	50.6	50.3	50.0	49.7	49.4	49.0
29	50.8	50.6	50.4	50.2	49.9	49.7	49.4	49.1	48.8	48.4
30	50.0	49.8	49.6	49.4	49.2	49.0	48.7	48.4	48.1	47.8
31	49.2	49.0	48.9	48.7	48.5	48.3	48.0	47.8	47.5	47.2
32	48.4	48.2	48.1	47.9	47.7	47.5	47.3	47.1	46.8	46.5
33	47.6	47.4	47.3	47.1	47.0	46.8	46.6	46.3	46.1	45.9
34	46.7	46.6	46.5	46.3	46.2	46.0	45.8	45.6	45.4	45.2
35	45.9	45.8	45.7	45.5	45.4	45.2	45.1	44.9	44.7	44.4
36	45.0	44.9	44.8	44.7	44.6	44.4	44.3	44.1	43.9	43.7
37	44.2	44.1	44.0	43.9	43.8	43.6	43.5	43.3	43.2	43.0
38	43.3	43.2	43.1	43.0	42.9	42.8	42.7	42.5	42.4	42.2
39	42.4	42.4	42.3	42.2	42.1	42.0	41.9	41.7	41.6	41.4
40	41.6	41.5	41.4	41.3	41.2	41.1	41.0	40.9	40.8	40.6
41	40.7	40.6	40.5	40.5	40.4	40.3	40.2	40.1	40.0	39.8
42	39.8	39.7	39.7	39.6	39.5	39.4	39.4	39.3	39.1	39.0
43	38.9	38.9	38.8	38.7	38.7	38.6	38.5	38.4	38.3	38.2
44	38.0	38.0	37.9	37.9	37.8	37.7	37.7	37.6	37.5	37.4
45	37.1	37.1	37.0	37.0	36.9	36.9	36.8	36.7	36.6	36.5
46	36.2	36.2	36.2	36.1	36.1	36.0	35.9	35.9	35.8	35.7
47	35.3	35.3	35.3	35.2	35.2	35.1	35.1	35.0	34.9	34.9
48	34.5	34.4	34.4	34.4	34.3	34.3	34.2	34.2	34.1	34.0
49	33.6	33.5	33.5	33.5	33.4	33.4	33.4	33.3	33.2	33.2
50	32.7	32.7	32.6	32.6	32.6	32.5	32.5	32.4	32.4	32.3
51	31.8	31.8	31.8	31.7	31.7	31.7	31.6	31.6	31.5	31.5
52	30.9	30.9	30.9	30.9	30.8	30.8	30.8	30.7	30.7	30.6
53	30.0	30.0	30.0	30.0	30.0	29.9	29.9	29.9	29.8	29.8
54	29.2	29.2	29.1	29.1	29.1	29.1	29.0	29.0	29.0	28.9
55	28.3	28.3	28.3	28.3	28.2	28.2	28.2	28.2	28.1	28.1
56	27.4	27.4	27.4	27.4	27.4	27.3	27.3	27.3	27.3	27.2
57	26.6	26.6	26.5	26.5	26.5	26.5	26.5	26.5	26.4	26.4
58	25.7	25.7	25.7	25.7	25.7	25.6	25.6	25.6	25.6	25.6
59	24.9	24.8	24.8	24.8	24.8	24.8	24.8	24.8	24.7	24.7
60	24.0	24.0	24.0	24.0	24.0	23.9	23.9	23.9	23.9	23.9
61	23.2	23.2	23.1	23.1	23.1	23.1	23.1	23.1	23.1	23.0
62	22.3	22.3	22.3	22.3	22.3	22.3	22.3	22.2	22.2	22.2
63	21.5	21.5	21.5	21.5	21.5	21.4	21.4	21.4	21.4	21.4
64	20.7	20.7	20.7	20.6	20.6	20.6	20.6	20.6	20.6	20.6
65	19.9	19.8	19.8	19.8	19.8	19.8	19.8	19.8	19.8	19.8
66	19.1	19.0	19.0	19.0	19.0	19.0	19.0	19.0	19.0	19.0
67	18.3	18.3	18.3	18.3	18.2	18.2	18.2	18.2	18.2	18.2
68	17.5	17.5	17.5	17.5	17.5	17.5	17.5	17.5	17.4	17.4
69	16.7	16.7	16.7	16.7	16.7	16.7	16.7	16.7	16.7	16.7
70	16.0	16.0	16.0	16.0	16.0	16.0	15.9	15.9	15.9	15.9
71	15.2	15.2	15.2	15.2	15.2	15.2	15.2	15.2	15.2	15.2
72	14.5	14.5	14.5	14.5	14.5	14.5	14.5	14.5	14.5	14.5
73	13.8	13.8	13.8	13.8	13.8	13.8	13.8	13.8	13.8	13.8
74	13.2	13.1	13.1	13.1	13.1	13.1	13.1	13.1	13.1	13.1
75	12.5	12.5	12.5	12.5	12.5	12.5	12.5	12.5	12.5	12.5
76	11.8	11.8	11.8	11.8	11.8	11.8	11.8	11.8	11.8	11.8
77	11.2	11.2	11.2	11.2	11.2	11.2	11.2	11.2	11.2	11.2
78	10.6	10.6	10.6	10.6	10.6	10.6	10.6	10.6	10.6	10.6

Table VIA—Annuities for Joint Life Only; Two Lives—Expected Return Multiples (continued)

Ages	15	16	17	18	19	20	21	22	23	24
79	10.0	10.0	10.0	10.0	10.0	10.0	10.0	10.0	10.0	10.0
80	9.4	9.4	9.4	9.4	9.4	9.4	9.4	9.4	9.4	9.4
81	8.9	8.9	8.9	8.9	8.9	8.9	8.9	8.9	8.9	8.9
82	8.4	8.4	8.4	8.4	8.4	8.4	8.4	8.4	8.4	8.4
83	7.9	7.9	7.9	7.9	7.9	7.9	7.9	7.9	7.8	7.8
84	7.4	7.4	7.4	7.4	7.4	7.4	7.4	7.4	7.4	7.4
85	6.9	6.9	6.9	6.9	6.9	6.9	6.9	6.9	6.9	6.9
86	6.5	6.5	6.5	6.5	6.5	6.5	6.5	6.5	6.5	6.5
87	6.1	6.1	6.1	6.1	6.1	6.1	6.1	6.1	6.1	6.1
88	5.7	5.7	5.7	5.7	5.7	5.7	5.7	5.7	5.7	5.7
89	5.3	5.3	5.3	5.3	5.3	5.3	5.3	5.3	5.3	5.3
90	5.0	5.0	5.0	5.0	5.0	5.0	5.0	5.0	5.0	5.0
91	4.7	4.7	4.7	4.7	4.7	4.7	4.7	4.7	4.7	4.7
92	4.4	4.4	4.4	4.4	4.4	4.4	4.4	4.4	4.4	4.4
93	4.1	4.1	4.1	4.1	4.1	4.1	4.1	4.1	4.1	4.1
94	3.9	3.9	3.9	3.9	3.9	3.9	3.9	3.9	3.9	3.9
95	3.6	3.6	3.6	3.6	3.6	3.6	3.6	3.6	3.6	3.6
96	3.4	3.4	3.4	3.4	3.4	3.4	3.4	3.4	3.4	3.4
97	3.2	3.2	3.2	3.2	3.2	3.2	3.2	3.2	3.2	3.2
98	3.0	3.0	3.0	3.0	3.0	3.0	3.0	3.0	3.0	3.0
99	2.8	2.8	2.8	2.8	2.8	2.8	2.8	2.8	2.8	2.8
100	2.7	2.7	2.7	2.7	2.7	2.7	2.7	2.7	2.7	2.7
101	2.5	2.5	2.5	2.5	2.5	2.5	2.5	2.5	2.5	2.5
102	2.3	2.3	2.3	2.3	2.3	2.3	2.3	2.3	2.3	2.3
103	2.1	2.1	2.1	2.1	2.1	2.1	2.1	2.1	2.1	2.1
104	1.9	1.9	1.9	1.9	1.9	1.9	1.9	1.9	1.9	1.9
105	1.8	1.8	1.8	1.8	1.8	1.8	1.8	1.8	1.8	1.8
106	1.6	1.6	1.6	1.6	1.6	1.6	1.6	1.6	1.6	1.6
107	1.4	1.4	1.4	1.4	1.4	1.4	1.4	1.4	1.4	1.4
108	1.3	1.3	1.3	1.3	1.3	1.3	1.3	1.3	1.3	1.3
109	1.1	1.1	1.1	1.1	1.1	1.1	1.1	1.1	1.1	1.1
110	1.0	1.0	1.0	1.0	1.0	1.0	1.0	1.0	1.0	1.0
111	.9	.9	.9	.9	.9	.9	.9	.9	.9	.9
112	.8	.8	.8	.8	.8	.8	.8	.8	.8	.8
113	.7	.7	.7	.7	.7	.7	.7	.7	.7	.7
114	.6	.6	.6	.6	.6	.6	.6	.6	.6	.6
115	.5	.5	.5	.5	.5	.5	.5	.5	.5	.5

Table VIA—Annuities for Joint Life Only; Two Lives—Expected Return Multiples

Ages	25	26	27	28	29	30	31	32	33	34
25	50.2	49.7	49.2	48.6	48.1	47.5	46.9	46.2	45.6	44.9
26	49.7	49.2	48.7	48.2	47.7	47.1	46.5	45.9	45.3	44.6
27	49.2	48.7	48.3	47.8	47.3	46.7	46.2	45.6	45.0	44.3
28	48.6	48.2	47.8	47.3	46.8	46.3	45.8	45.2	44.6	44.0
29	48.1	47.7	47.3	46.8	46.4	45.9	45.4	44.8	44.3	43.7
30	47.5	47.1	46.7	48.3	45.9	45.4	44.9	44.4	43.9	43.3
31	46.9	46.5	46.2	45.8	45.4	44.9	44.5	44.0	43.5	42.9
32	46.2	45.9	45.6	45.2	44.8	44.4	44.0	43.5	43.0	42.5
33	45.6	45.3	45.0	44.6	44.3	43.9	43.5	43.0	42.6	42.1
34	44.9	44.6	44.3	44.0	43.7	43.3	42.9	42.5	42.1	41.6
35	44.2	44.0	43.7	43.4	43.1	42.7	42.4	42.0	41.6	41.1
36	43.5	43.3	43.0	42.7	42.4	42.1	41.8	41.4	41.0	40.6
37	42.8	42.5	42.3	42.1	41.8	41.5	41.2	40.8	40.5	40.1
38	42.0	41.8	41.6	41.4	41.1	40.8	40.6	40.2	39.9	39.5
39	41.3	41.1	40.9	40.7	40.4	40.2	39.9	39.6	39.3	39.0
40	40.5	40.3	40.1	39.9	39.7	39.5	39.2	39.0	38.7	38.4
41	39.7	39.5	39.4	39.2	39.0	38.8	38.5	38.3	38.0	37.7
42	38.9	38.8	38.6	38.4	38.3	38.1	37.8	37.6	37.4	37.1
43	38.1	38.0	37.8	37.7	37.5	37.3	37.1	36.9	36.7	36.4
44	37.3	37.2	37.0	36.9	36.7	36.6	36.4	36.2	36.0	35.8
45	36.5	36.3	36.2	36.1	36.0	35.8	35.6	35.5	35.3	35.1

46	35.6	35.5	35.4	35.3	35.2	35.0	34.9	34.7	34.5	34.4
47	34.8	34.7	34.6	34.5	34.4	34.3	34.1	34.0	33.8	33.6
48	34.0	33.9	33.8	33.7	33.6	33.5	33.4	33.2	33.1	32.9
49	33.1	33.0	33.0	32.9	32.8	32.7	32.6	32.4	32.3	32.2
50	32.3	32.2	32.1	32.1	32.0	31.9	31.8	31.7	31.5	31.4
51	31.4	31.4	31.3	31.2	31.2	31.1	31.0	30.9	30.8	30.6
52	30.6	30.5	30.5	30.4	30.3	30.3	30.2	30.1	30.0	29.9
53	29.7	29.7	29.6	29.6	29.5	29.5	29.4	29.3	29.2	29.1
54	28.9	28.9	28.8	28.8	28.7	28.6	28.6	28.5	28.4	28.3
55	28.1	28.0	28.0	27.9	27.9	27.8	27.8	27.7	27.6	27.5
56	27.2	27.2	27.1	27.1	27.0	27.0	26.9	26.9	26.8	26.7
57	26.4	26.3	26.3	26.3	26.2	26.2	26.1	26.1	26.0	25.9
58	25.5	25.5	25.5	25.4	25.4	25.4	25.3	25.3	25.2	25.1
59	24.7	24.7	24.6	24.6	24.6	24.5	24.5	24.5	24.4	24.3
60	23.9	23.8	23.8	23.8	23.8	23.7	23.7	23.6	23.6	23.5
61	23.0	23.0	23.0	23.0	22.9	22.9	22.9	22.8	22.8	22.7
62	22.2	22.2	22.2	22.1	22.1	22.1	22.1	22.0	22.0	21.9
63	21.4	21.4	21.3	21.3	21.3	21.3	21.3	21.2	21.2	21.2
64	20.6	20.6	20.5	20.5	20.5	20.5	20.5	20.4	20.4	20.4
65	19.8	19.8	19.7	19.7	19.7	19.7	19.7	19.6	19.6	19.6
66	19.0	19.0	19.0	18.9	18.9	18.9	18.9	18.9	18.8	18.8
67	18.2	18.2	18.2	18.2	18.2	18.1	18.1	18.1	18.1	18.1
68	17.4	17.4	17.4	17.4	17.4	17.4	17.4	17.3	17.3	17.3
69	16.7	16.7	16.7	16.6	16.6	16.6	16.6	16.6	16.6	16.6
70	15.9	15.9	15.9	15.9	15.9	15.9	15.9	15.9	15.8	15.8
71	15.2	15.2	15.2	15.2	15.2	15.2	15.2	15.1	15.1	15.1
72	14.5	14.5	14.5	14.5	14.5	14.5	14.5	14.4	14.4	14.4
73	13.8	13.8	13.8	13.8	13.8	13.8	13.8	13.8	13.7	13.7
74	13.1	13.1	13.1	13.1	13.1	13.1	13.1	13.1	13.1	13.1
75	12.5	12.5	12.5	12.4	12.4	12.4	12.4	12.4	12.4	12.4
76	11.8	11.8	11.8	11.8	11.8	11.8	11.8	11.8	11.8	11.8
77	11.2	11.2	11.2	11.2	11.2	11.2	11.2	11.2	11.2	11.1
78	10.6	10.6	10.6	10.6	10.6	10.6	10.6	10.6	10.6	10.5
79	10.0	10.0	10.0	10.0	10.0	10.0	10.0	10.0	10.0	10.0
80	9.4	9.4	9.4	9.4	9.4	9.4	9.4	9.4	9.4	9.4
81	8.9	8.9	8.9	8.9	8.9	8.9	8.9	8.9	8.9	8.9
82	8.4	8.4	8.3	8.3	8.3	8.3	8.3	8.3	8.3	8.3
83	7.8	7.8	7.8	7.8	7.8	7.8	7.8	7.8	7.8	7.8
84	7.4	7.4	7.4	7.4	7.4	7.4	7.4	7.4	7.4	7.4
85	6.9	6.9	6.9	6.9	6.9	6.9	6.9	6.9	6.9	6.9
86	6.5	6.5	6.5	6.5	6.5	6.5	6.5	6.5	6.5	6.5
87	6.1	6.1	6.1	6.1	6.1	6.1	6.1	6.1	6.1	6.1
88	5.7	5.7	5.7	5.7	5.7	5.7	5.7	5.7	5.7	5.7
89	5.3	5.3	5.3	5.3	5.3	5.3	5.3	5.3	5.3	5.3
90	5.0	5.0	5.0	5.0	5.0	5.0	5.0	5.0	5.0	5.0
91	4.7	4.7	4.7	4.7	4.7	4.7	4.7	4.7	4.7	4.7
92	4.4	4.4	4.4	4.4	4.4	4.4	4.4	4.4	4.4	4.4
93	4.1	4.1	4.1	4.1	4.1	4.1	4.1	4.1	4.1	4.1
94	3.9	3.9	3.9	3.9	3.9	3.9	3.9	3.9	3.9	3.9
95	3.6	3.6	3.6	3.6	3.6	3.6	3.6	3.6	3.6	3.6
96	3.4	3.4	3.4	3.4	3.4	3.4	3.4	3.4	3.4	3.4
97	3.2	3.2	3.2	3.2	3.2	3.2	3.2	3.2	3.2	3.2
98	3.0	3.0	3.0	3.0	3.0	3.0	3.0	3.0	3.0	3.0
99	2.8	2.8	2.8	2.8	2.8	2.8	2.8	2.8	2.8	2.8
100	2.7	2.7	2.7	2.7	2.7	2.7	2.7	2.7	2.7	2.7
101	2.5	2.5	2.5	2.5	2.5	2.5	2.5	2.5	2.5	2.5
102	2.3	2.3	2.3	2.3	2.3	2.3	2.3	2.3	2.3	2.3
103	2.1	2.1	2.1	2.1	2.1	2.1	2.1	2.1	2.1	2.1
104	1.9	1.9	1.9	1.9	1.9	1.9	1.9	1.9	1.9	1.9
105	1.8	1.8	1.8	1.8	1.8	1.8	1.8	1.8	1.8	1.8
106	1.6	1.6	1.6	1.6	1.6	1.6	1.6	1.6	1.6	1.6
107	1.4	1.4	1.4	1.4	1.4	1.4	1.4	1.4	1.4	1.4
108	1.3	1.3	1.3	1.3	1.3	1.3	1.3	1.3	1.3	1.3
109	1.1	1.1	1.1	1.1	1.1	1.1	1.1	1.1	1.1	1.1
110	1.0	1.0	1.0	1.0	1.0	1.0	1.0	1.0	1.0	1.0
111	.9	.9	.9	.9	.9	.9	.9	.9	.9	.9
112	.8	.8	.8	.8	.8	.8	.8	.8	.8	.8

113	.7	.7	.7	.7	.7	.7	.7	.7	.7	.7
114	.6	.6	.6	.6	.6	.6	.6	.6	.6	.6
115	.5	.5	.5	.5	.5	.5	.5	.5	.5	.5

Table VIA—Annuities for Joint Life Only; Two Lives—Expected Return Multiples

Ages	35	36	37	38	39	40	41	42	43	44
35	40.7	40.2	39.7	39.2	38.6	38.0	37.4	36.8	36.2	35.5
36	40.2	39.7	39.3	38.7	38.2	37.7	37.1	36.5	35.9	35.2
37	39.7	39.3	38.8	38.3	37.8	37.3	36.7	36.2	35.6	34.9
38	39.2	38.7	38.3	37.9	37.4	36.9	36.3	35.8	35.2	34.6
39	38.6	38.2	37.8	37.4	36.9	36.4	35.9	35.4	34.9	34.3
40	38.0	37.7	37.3	36.9	36.4	36.0	35.5	35.0	34.5	34.0
41	37.4	37.1	36.7	36.3	35.9	35.5	35.1	34.6	34.1	33.6
42	36.8	36.5	36.2	35.8	35.4	35.0	34.6	34.1	33.7	33.2
43	36.2	35.9	35.6	35.2	34.9	34.5	34.1	33.7	33.2	32.8
44	35.5	35.2	34.9	34.6	34.3	34.0	33.6	33.2	32.8	32.3
45	34.8	34.6	34.3	34.0	33.7	33.4	33.0	32.7	32.3	31.8
46	34.1	33.9	33.7	33.4	33.1	32.8	32.5	32.1	31.8	31.4
47	33.4	33.2	33.0	32.8	32.5	32.2	31.9	31.6	31.2	30.8
48	32.7	32.5	32.3	32.1	31.8	31.6	31.3	31.0	30.7	30.3
49	32.0	31.8	31.6	31.4	31.2	30.9	30.7	30.4	30.1	29.8
50	31.3	31.1	30.9	30.7	30.5	30.3	30.0	29.8	29.5	29.2
51	30.5	30.4	30.2	30.0	29.8	29.6	29.4	29.2	28.9	28.6
52	29.7	29.6	29.5	29.3	29.1	28.9	28.7	28.5	28.3	28.0
53	29.0	28.9	28.7	28.6	28.4	28.2	28.1	27.9	27.6	27.4
54	28.2	28.1	28.0	27.8	27.7	27.5	27.4	27.2	27.0	26.8
55	27.4	27.3	27.2	27.1	27.0	26.8	26.7	26.5	26.3	26.1
56	26.7	26.6	26.5	26.3	26.2	26.1	26.0	25.8	25.6	25.4
57	25.9	25.8	25.7	25.6	25.5	25.4	25.2	25.1	24.9	24.8
58	25.1	25.0	24.9	24.8	24.7	24.6	24.5	24.4	24.2	24.1
59	24.3	24.2	24.1	24.1	24.0	23.9	23.8	23.6	23.5	23.4
60	23.5	23.4	23.4	23.3	23.2	23.1	23.0	22.9	22.8	22.7
61	22.7	22.6	22.6	22.5	22.4	22.4	22.3	22.2	22.1	22.0
62	21.9	21.9	21.8	21.7	21.7	21.6	21.5	21.4	21.3	21.2
63	21.1	21.1	21.0	21.0	20.9	20.8	20.8	20.7	20.6	20.5
64	20.3	20.3	20.2	20.2	20.1	20.1	20.0	20.0	19.9	19.8
65	19.6	19.5	19.5	19.4	19.4	19.3	19.3	19.2	19.1	19.1
66	18.8	18.8	18.7	18.7	18.6	18.6	18.5	18.5	18.4	18.4
67	18.0	18.0	18.0	17.9	17.9	17.9	17.8	17.8	17.7	17.6
68	17.3	17.3	17.2	17.2	17.2	17.1	17.1	17.0	17.0	16.9
69	16.5	16.5	16.5	16.5	16.4	16.4	16.4	16.3	16.3	16.2
70	15.8	15.8	15.8	15.7	15.7	15.7	15.6	15.6	15.6	15.5
71	15.1	15.1	15.1	15.0	15.0	15.0	15.0	14.9	14.9	14.9
72	14.4	14.4	14.4	14.3	14.3	14.3	14.3	14.2	14.2	14.2
73	13.7	13.7	13.7	13.7	13.7	13.6	13.6	13.6	13.6	13.5
74	13.1	13.0	13.0	13.0	13.0	13.0	13.0	12.9	12.9	12.9
75	12.4	12.4	12.4	12.4	12.3	12.3	12.3	12.3	12.3	12.2
76	11.8	11.8	11.7	11.7	11.7	11.7	11.7	11.7	11.6	11.6
77	11.1	11.1	11.1	11.1	11.1	11.1	11.1	11.1	11.0	11.0
78	10.5	10.5	10.5	10.5	10.5	10.5	10.5	10.5	10.5	10.4
79	10.0	10.0	9.9	9.9	9.9	9.9	9.9	9.9	9.9	9.9
80	9.4	9.4	9.4	9.4	9.4	9.4	9.4	9.3	9.3	9.3
81	8.9	8.8	8.8	8.8	8.8	8.8	8.8	8.8	8.8	8.8
82	8.3	8.3	8.3	8.3	8.3	8.3	8.3	8.3	8.3	8.3
83	7.8	7.8	7.8	7.8	7.8	7.8	7.8	7.8	7.8	7.8
84	7.3	7.3	7.3	7.3	7.3	7.3	7.3	7.3	7.3	7.3
85	6.9	6.9	6.9	6.9	6.9	6.9	6.9	6.9	6.9	6.9
86	6.5	6.5	6.5	6.5	6.4	6.4	6.4	6.4	6.4	6.4
87	6.1	6.0	6.0	6.0	6.0	6.0	6.0	6.0	6.0	6.0
88	5.7	5.7	5.7	5.7	5.7	5.7	5.7	5.6	5.6	5.6
89	5.3	5.3	5.3	5.3	5.3	5.3	5.3	5.3	5.3	5.3
90	5.0	5.0	5.0	5.0	5.0	5.0	5.0	5.0	5.0	5.0
91	4.7	4.7	4.7	4.7	4.7	4.7	4.7	4.7	4.6	4.6
92	4.4	4.4	4.4	4.4	4.4	4.4	4.4	4.4	4.4	4.4
93	4.1	4.1	4.1	4.1	4.1	4.1	4.1	4.1	4.1	4.1
94	3.9	3.9	3.9	3.9	3.9	3.9	3.9	3.9	3.9	3.9

Table VIA—Annuities for Joint Life Only; Two Lives—Expected Return Multiples (continued)

95	3.6	3.6	3.6	3.6	3.6	3.6	3.6	3.6	3.6	3.6
96	3.4	3.4	3.4	3.4	3.4	3.4	3.4	3.4	3.4	3.4
97	3.2	3.2	3.2	3.2	3.2	3.2	3.2	3.2	3.2	3.2
98	3.0	3.0	3.0	3.0	3.0	3.0	3.0	3.0	3.0	3.0
99	2.8	2.8	2.8	2.8	2.8	2.8	2.8	2.8	2.8	2.8
100	2.7	2.7	2.7	2.7	2.7	2.7	2.7	2.7	2.6	2.6
101	2.5	2.5	2.5	2.5	2.5	2.5	2.5	2.5	2.5	2.5
102	2.3	2.3	2.3	2.3	2.3	2.3	2.3	2.3	2.3	2.3
103	2.1	2.1	2.1	2.1	2.1	2.1	2.1	2.1	2.1	2.1
104	1.9	1.9	1.9	1.9	1.9	1.9	1.9	1.9	1.9	1.9
105	1.8	1.8	1.8	1.8	1.8	1.8	1.8	1.8	1.8	1.8
106	1.6	1.6	1.6	1.6	1.6	1.6	1.6	1.6	1.6	1.6
107	1.4	1.4	1.4	1.4	1.4	1.4	1.4	1.4	1.4	1.4
108	1.3	1.3	1.3	1.3	1.3	1.3	1.3	1.3	1.3	1.3
109	1.1	1.1	1.1	1.1	1.1	1.1	1.1	1.1	1.1	1.1
110	1.0	1.0	1.0	1.0	1.0	1.0	1.0	1.0	1.0	1.0
111	.9	.9	.9	.9	.9	.9	.9	.9	.9	.9
112	.8	.8	.8	.8	.8	.8	.8	.8	.8	.8
113	.7	.7	.7	.7	.7	.7	.7	.7	.7	.7
114	.6	.6	.6	.6	.6	.6	.6	.6	.6	.6
115	.5	.5	.5	.5	.5	.5	.5	.5	.5	.5

Table VIA—Annuities for Joint Life Only; Two Lives—Expected Return Multiples

Ages	45	46	47	48	49	50	51	52	53	54
45	31.4	30.9	30.5	30.0	29.4	28.9	28.3	27.7	27.1	26.5
46	30.9	30.5	30.0	29.6	29.1	28.5	28.0	27.4	26.9	26.3
47	30.5	30.0	29.6	29.2	28.7	28.2	27.7	27.1	26.6	26.0
48	30.0	29.6	29.2	28.7	28.3	27.8	27.3	26.8	26.3	25.7
49	29.4	29.1	28.7	28.3	27.9	27.4	26.9	26.5	25.9	25.4
50	28.9	28.5	28.2	27.4	27.4	27.0	26.5	26.1	25.6	25.1
51	28.3	28.0	27.7	27.3	26.9	26.5	26.1	25.7	25.2	24.7
52	27.7	27.4	27.1	26.8	26.5	26.1	25.7	25.3	24.8	24.4
53	27.1	26.9	26.6	26.3	25.9	25.6	25.2	24.8	24.4	24.0
54	26.5	26.3	26.0	25.7	25.4	25.1	24.7	24.4	24.0	23.6
55	25.9	25.7	25.4	25.1	24.9	24.6	24.2	23.9	23.5	23.2
56	25.2	25.0	24.8	24.6	24.3	24.0	23.7	23.4	23.1	22.7
57	24.6	24.4	24.2	24.0	23.7	23.5	23.2	22.9	22.6	22.2
58	23.9	23.7	23.5	23.3	23.1	22.9	22.6	22.4	22.1	21.7
59	23.2	23.1	22.9	22.7	22.5	22.3	22.1	21.8	21.5	21.2
60	22.5	22.4	22.2	22.1	21.9	21.7	21.5	21.2	21.0	20.7
61	21.8	21.7	21.6	21.4	21.2	21.1	20.9	20.6	20.4	20.2
62	21.1	21.0	20.9	20.7	20.6	20.4	20.2	20.0	19.8	19.6
63	20.4	20.3	20.2	20.1	19.9	19.8	19.6	19.4	19.2	19.0
64	19.7	19.6	19.5	19.4	19.3	19.1	19.0	18.8	18.6	18.5
65	19.0	18.9	18.8	18.7	18.6	18.5	18.3	18.2	18.0	17.9
66	18.3	18.2	18.1	18.0	17.9	17.8	17.7	17.6	17.4	17.3
67	17.6	17.5	17.4	17.3	17.3	17.2	17.1	16.9	16.8	16.7
68	16.9	16.8	16.7	16.7	16.6	16.5	16.4	16.3	16.2	16.1
69	16.2	16.1	16.1	16.0	15.9	15.8	15.8	15.7	15.6	15.4
70	15.5	15.4	15.4	15.3	15.3	15.2	15.1	15.0	14.9	14.8
71	14.8	14.8	14.7	14.7	14.6	14.5	14.5	14.4	14.3	14.2
72	14.1	14.1	14.1	14.0	14.0	13.9	13.8	13.8	13.7	13.6
73	13.5	13.5	13.4	13.4	13.3	13.3	13.2	13.2	13.1	13.0
74	12.8	12.8	12.8	12.7	12.7	12.7	12.6	12.6	12.5	12.4
75	12.2	12.2	12.2	12.1	12.1	12.1	12.0	12.0	11.9	11.9
76	11.6	11.6	11.6	11.5	11.5	11.5	11.4	11.4	11.3	11.3
77	11.0	11.0	11.0	10.9	10.9	10.9	10.8	10.8	10.8	10.7
78	10.4	10.4	10.4	10.4	10.3	10.3	10.3	10.2	10.2	10.2
79	9.9	9.8	9.8	9.8	9.8	9.8	9.7	9.7	9.7	9.6
80	9.3	9.3	9.3	9.3	9.2	9.2	9.2	9.2	9.1	9.1
81	8.8	8.8	8.7	8.7	8.7	8.7	8.7	8.7	8.6	8.6
82	8.3	8.2	8.2	8.2	8.2	8.2	8.2	8.2	8.1	8.1
83	7.8	7.8	7.7	7.7	7.7	7.7	7.7	7.7	7.7	7.6

Table VIA—Annuities for Joint Life Only; Two Lives—Expected Return Multiples (continued)

Ages	45	46	47	48	49	50	51	52	53	54
84	7.3	7.3	7.3	7.3	7.3	7.2	7.2	7.2	7.2	7.2
85	6.8	6.8	8.8	6.8	6.8	6.8	6.8	6.8	6.8	6.7
86	6.4	6.4	6.4	6.4	6.4	6.4	6.4	6.4	6.3	6.3
87	6.0	6.0	6.0	6.0	6.0	6.0	6.0	6.0	6.0	5.9
88	5.6	5.6	5.6	5.6	5.6	5.6	5.6	5.6	5.6	5.6
89	5.3	5.3	5.3	5.3	5.3	5.3	5.2	5.2	5.2	5.2
90	5.0	4.9	4.9	4.9	4.9	4.9	4.9	4.9	4.9	4.9
91	4.6	4.6	4.6	4.6	4.6	4.6	4.6	4.6	4.6	4.6
92	4.4	4.4	4.4	4.3	4.3	4.3	4.3	4.3	4.3	4.3
93	4.1	4.1	4.1	4.1	4.1	4.1	4.1	4.1	4.1	4.1
94	3.9	3.9	3.8	3.8	3.8	3.8	3.8	3.8	3.8	3.8
95	3.6	3.6	3.6	3.6	3.6	3.6	3.6	3.6	3.6	3.6
96	3.4	3.4	3.4	3.4	3.4	3.4	3.4	3.4	3.4	3.4
97	3.2	3.2	3.2	3.2	3.2	3.2	3.2	3.2	3.2	3.2
98	3.0	3.0	3.0	3.0	3.0	3.0	3.0	3.0	3.0	3.0
99	2.8	2.8	2.8	2.8	2.8	2.8	2.8	2.8	2.8	2.8
100	2.6	2.6	2.6	2.6	2.6	2.6	2.6	2.6	2.6	2.6
101	2.5	2.5	2.5	2.5	2.5	2.5	2.5	2.5	2.5	2.5
102	2.3	2.3	2.3	2.3	2.3	2.3	2.3	2.3	2.3	2.3
103	2.1	2.1	2.1	2.1	2.1	2.1	2.1	2.1	2.1	2.1
104	1.9	1.9	1.9	1.9	1.9	1.9	1.9	1.9	1.9	1.9
105	1.8	1.8	1.8	1.8	1.8	1.8	1.8	1.8	1.8	1.8
106	1.6	1.6	1.6	1.6	1.6	1.6	1.6	1.6	1.6	1.6
107	1.4	1.4	1.4	1.4	1.4	1.4	1.4	1.4	1.4	1.4
108	1.3	1.3	1.3	1.3	1.3	1.3	1.3	1.3	1.3	1.3
109	1.1	1.1	1.1	1.1	1.1	1.1	1.1	1.1	1.1	1.1
110	1.0	1.0	1.0	1.0	1.0	1.0	1.0	1.0	1.0	1.0
111	.9	.9	.9	.9	.9	.9	.9	.9	.9	.9
112	.8	.8	.8	.8	.8	.8	.8	.8	.8	.8
113	.7	.7	.7	.7	.7	.7	.7	.7	.7	.7
114	.6	.6	.6	.6	.6	.6	.6	.6	.6	.6
115	.5	.5	.5	.5	.5	.5	.5	.5	.5	.5

Table VIA—Annuities for Joint Life Only; Two Lives—Expected Return Multiples

Ages	55	56	57	58	59	60	61	62	63	64
55	22.7	22.3	21.9	21.4	20.9	20.4	19.9	19.4	18.8	18.3
56	22.3	21.9	21.5	21.1	20.6	20.1	19.6	19.1	18.6	18.0
57	21.9	21.5	21.1	20.7	20.3	19.8	19.3	18.8	18.3	17.8
58	21.4	21.1	20.7	20.3	19.9	19.5	19.0	18.5	18.0	17.5
59	20.9	20.6	20.3	19.9	19.5	19.1	18.7	18.2	17.7	17.3
60	20.4	20.1	19.8	19.5	19.1	18.7	18.3	17.9	17.4	17.0
61	29.9	19.6	19.3	19.0	18.7	18.3	17.9	17.5	17.1	16.7
62	19.4	19.1	18.8	18.5	18.2	17.9	17.5	17.1	16.8	16.3
63	18.8	18.6	18.3	18.0	17.7	17.4	17.1	16.8	16.4	16.0
64	18.3	18.0	17.8	17.5	17.3	17.0	16.7	16.3	16.0	15.6
65	17.7	17.5	17.3	17.0	16.8	16.5	16.2	15.9	15.6	15.3
66	17.1	16.9	16.7	16.5	16.3	16.0	15.8	15.5	15.2	14.9
67	16.5	16.3	16.2	16.0	15.8	15.5	15.3	15.0	14.7	14.5
66	15.9	15.8	15.6	15.4	15.2	15.0	14.8	14.6	14.3	14.0
69	15.3	15.2	15.0	14.9	14.7	14.5	14.3	14.1	13.9	13.6
70	14.7	14.6	14.5	14.3	14.2	14.0	13.8	13.6	13.4	13.2
71	14.1	14.0	13.9	13.8	13.6	13.5	13.3	13.1	12.9	12.7
72	13.5	13.4	13.3	13.2	13.1	12.9	12.8	12.6	12.4	12.3
73	13.0	12.9	12.8	12.7	12.5	12.4	12.3	12.1	12.0	11.8
74	12.4	12.3	12.2	12.1	12.0	11.9	11.8	11.6	11.5	11.3
75	11.8	11.7	11.7	11.6	11.5	11.4	11.3	11.1	11.0	10.9
76	11.2	11.2	11.1	11.0	10.9	10.9	10.8	10.6	10.5	10.4
77	10.7	10.6	10.6	10.5	10.4	10.3	10.3	10.2	10.0	9.9
78	10.1	10.1	10.0	10.0	9.9	9.8	9.8	9.7	9.6	9.5
79	9.6	9.6	9.5	9.5	9.4	9.3	9.3	9.2	9.1	9.0
80	9.1	9.0	9.0	9.0	8.9	8.9	8.8	8.7	8.7	8.6

Table VIA—Annuities for Joint Life Only; Two Lives—Expected Return Multiples (continued)

Ages	55	56	57	58	59	60	61	62	63	64
81	8.6	8.5	8.5	8.5	8.4	8.4	8.3	8.3	8.2	8.1
82	8.1	8.1	8.0	8.0	8.0	7.9	7.9	7.8	7.8	7.7
83	7.6	7.6	7.6	7.5	7.5	7.5	7.4	7.4	7.3	7.3
84	7.2	7.1	7.1	7.1	7.1	7.0	7.0	7.0	6.9	6.9
85	6.7	6.7	6.7	6.7	6.6	6.6	6.6	6.5	6.5	6.5
86	6.3	6.3	6.3	6.3	6.2	6.2	6.2	6.2	6.1	6.1
87	5.9	5.9	5.9	5.9	5.9	5.8	5.8	5.8	5.8	5.7
88	5.6	5.5	5.5	5.5	5.5	5.5	5.5	5.4	5.4	5.4
89	5.2	5.2	5.2	5.2	5.2	5.1	5.1	5.1	5.1	5.1
90	4.9	4.9	4.9	4.9	4.9	4.8	4.8	4.8	4.8	4.8
91	4.6	4.6	4.6	4.6	4.6	4.5	4.5	4.5	4.5	4.5
92	4.3	4.3	4.3	4.3	4.3	4.3	4.3	4.2	4.2	4.2
93	4.1	4.1	4.0	4.0	4.0	4.0	4.0	4.0	4.0	4.0
94	3.8	3.8	3.8	3.8	3.8	3.8	3.8	3.8	3.8	3.7
95	3.6	3.6	3.6	3.6	3.6	3.6	3.6	3.6	3.5	3.5
96	3.4	3.4	3.4	3.4	3.4	3.4	3.4	3.3	3.3	3.3
97	3.2	3.2	3.2	3.2	3.2	3.2	3.2	3.2	3.1	3.1
98	3.0	3.0	3.0	3.0	3.0	3.0	3.0	3.0	3.0	3.0
99	2.8	2.8	2.8	2.8	2.8	2.8	2.8	2.8	2.8	2.8
100	2.6	2.6	2.6	2.6	2.6	2.6	2.6	2.6	2.6	2.6
101	2.5	2.4	2.4	2.4	2.4	2.4	2.4	2.4	2.4	2.4
102	2.3	2.3	2.3	2.3	2.3	2.3	2.3	2.3	2.3	2.2
103	2.1	2.1	2.1	2.1	2.1	2.1	2.1	2.1	2.1	2.1
104	1.9	1.9	1.9	1.9	1.9	1.9	1.9	1.9	1.9	1.9
105	1.8	1.8	1.8	1.8	1.8	1.8	1.7	1.7	1.7	1.7
106	1.6	1.6	1.6	1.6	1.6	1.6	1.6	1.6	1.6	1.6
107	1.4	1.4	1.4	1.4	1.4	1.4	1.4	1.4	1.4	1.4
108	1.3	1.3	1.3	1.3	1.3	1.3	1.3	1.3	1.3	1.3
109	1.1	1.1	1.1	1.1	1.1	1.1	1.1	1.1	1.1	1.1
110	1.0	1.0	1.0	1.0	1.0	1.0	1.0	1.0	1.0	1.0
111	.9	.9	.9	.9	.9	.9	.9	.9	.9	.9
112	.8	.8	.8	.8	.8	.8	.8	.8	.8	.8
113	.7	.7	.7	.7	.7	.7	.7	.7	.7	.7
114	.6	.6	.6	.6	.6	.6	.6	.6	.6	.6
115	.5	.5	.5	.5	.5	.5	.5	.5	.5	.5

Table VIA—Annuities for Joint Life Only; Two Lives—Expected Return Multiples

Ages	65	66	67	68	69	70	71	72	73	74
65	14.9	14.5	14.1	13.7	13.3	12.9	12.5	12.0	11.6	11.2
66	14.5	14.2	13.8	13.4	13.1	12.6	12.2	11.8	11.4	11.0
67	14.1	13.8	13.5	13.1	12.8	12.4	12.0	11.6	11.2	10.8
68	13.7	13.4	13.1	12.8	12.5	12.1	11.7	11.4	11.0	10.6
69	13.3	13.1	12.8	12.5	12.1	11.8	11.4	11.1	10.7	10.4
70	12.9	12.6	12.4	12.1	11.8	11.5	11.2	10.8	10.5	10.1
71	12.5	12.2	12.0	11.7	11.4	11.2	10.9	10.5	10.2	9.9
72	12.0	11.8	11.6	11.4	11.1	10.8	10.5	10.2	9.9	9.6
73	11.6	11.4	11.2	11.0	10.7	10.5	10.2	9.9	9.7	9.4
74	11.2	11.0	10.8	10.6	10.4	10.1	9.9	9.6	9.4	9.1
75	10.7	10.5	10.4	10.2	10.0	9.8	9.5	9.3	9.1	8.8
76	10.3	10.1	9.9	9.8	9.6	9.4	9.2	9.0	8.8	8.5
77	9.8	9.7	9.5	9.4	9.2	9.0	8.8	8.6	8.4	8.2
78	9.4	9.2	9.1	9.0	8.8	8.7	8.5	8.3	8.1	7.9
79	8.9	8.8	8.7	8.6	8.4	8.3	8.1	8.0	7.8	7.6
80	8.5	8.4	8.3	8.2	8.0	7.9	7.8	7.6	7.5	7.3
81	8.0	8.0	7.9	7.9	7.7	7.5	7.4	7.3	7.1	7.0
82	7.6	7.5	7.5	7.4	7.3	7.2	7.1	6.9	6.8	6.7
83	7.2	7.1	7.1	7.0	6.9	6.8	6.7	6.6	6.5	6.4
84	6.8	6.7	6.7	6.6	6.5	6.4	6.4	6.3	6.2	6.0
85	6.4	6.4	6.3	6.2	6.2	6.1	6.0	5.9	5.8	5.7
86	6.0	6.0	5.9	5.9	5.8	5.8	5.7	5.6	5.5	5.4
87	5.7	5.6	5.6	5.6	5.5	5.4	5.4	5.3	5.2	5.2

Table VIA—Annuities for Joint Life Only; Two Lives—Expected Return Multiples (continued)

Ages	65	66	67	68	69	70	71	72	73	74
88	5.3	5.3	5.3	5.2	5.2	5.1	5.1	5.0	5.0	4.9
89	5.0	5.0	5.0	4.9	4.9	4.8	4.8	4.7	4.7	4.6
90	4.7	4.7	4.7	4.6	4.6	4.6	4.5	4.5	4.4	4.4
91	4.5	4.4	4.4	4.4	4.3	4.3	4.3	4.2	4.2	4.1
92	4.2	4.2	4.1	4.1	4.1	4.1	4.0	4.0	3.9	3.9
93	3.9	3.9	3.9	3.9	3.9	3.8	3.8	3.8	3.7	3.7
94	3.7	3.7	3.7	3.7	3.6	3.6	3.6	3.6	3.5	3.5
95	3.5	3.5	3.5	3.5	3.4	3.4	3.4	3.4	3.3	3.3
96	3.3	3.3	3.3	3.3	3.3	3.2	3.2	3.2	3.2	3.1
97	3.1	3.1	3.1	3.1	3.1	3.1	3.0	3.0	3.0	3.0
98	2.9	2.9	2.9	2.9	2.9	2.9	2.9	2.9	2.8	2.8
99	2.8	2.8	2.8	2.7	2.7	2.7	2.7	2.7	2.7	2.6
100	2.6	2.6	2.6	2.6	2.6	2.5	2.5	2.5	2.5	2.5
101	2.4	2.4	2.4	2.4	2.4	2.4	2.4	2.4	2.3	2.3
102	2.2	2.2	2.2	2.2	2.2	2.2	2.2	2.2	2.2	2.2
103	2.1	2.1	2.1	2.1	2.1	2.0	2.0	2.0	2.0	2.0
104	1.9	1.9	1.9	1.9	1.9	1.9	1.9	1.9	.19	1.9
105	1.7	1.7	1.7	1.7	1.7	1.7	1.7	1.7	1.7	1.7
106	1.6	1.6	.16	1.6	1.6	1.6	1.6	1.6	1.5	1.5
107	1.4	1.4	1.4	1.4	1.4	1.4	1.4	1.4	1.4	1.4
108	1.3	1.3	1.3	1.3	1.3	1.3	1.3	1.3	1.3	1.3
109	1.1	1.1	1.1	1.1	1.1	1.1	1.1	1.1	1.1	1.1
110	1.0	1.0	1.0	1.0	1.0	1.0	1.0	1.0	1.0	1.0
111	.9	.9	.9	.9	.9	.9	.9	.9	.9	.9
112	.8	.8	.8	.8	.8	.8	.8	.8	.8	.8
113	.7	.7	.7	.7	.7	.6	.6	.6	.6	.6
114	.6	.6	.6	.6	.6	.6	.5	.5	.5	.5
115	.5	.5	.5	.5	.5	.5	.5	.5	.5	.5

Table VIA—Annuities for Joint Life Only; Two Lives—Expected Return Multiples

Ages	75	76	77	78	79	80	81	82	83	84
75	8.6	8.3	8.0	7.7	7.4	7.1	6.8	6.5	6.2	5.9
76	8.3	8.0	7.8	7.5	7.2	6.9	6.7	6.4	6.1	5.8
77	8.0	7.8	7.5	7.3	7.0	6.8	6.5	6.2	5.9	5.7
78	7.7	7.5	7.3	7.0	6.8	6.6	6.3	6.0	5.8	5.5
79	7.4	7.2	7.0	6.8	6.6	6.3	6.1	5.9	5.6	5.4
80	7.1	6.9	6.8	6.6	6.3	6.1	5.9	5.7	5.5	5.2
81	6.8	6.7	6.5	6.3	6.1	5.9	5.7	5.5	5.3	5.1
82	6.5	6.4	6.2	6.0	5.9	5.7	5.5	5.3	5.1	4.9
83	6.2	6.1	5.9	5.8	5.6	5.5	5.3	5.1	4.9	4.7
84	5.9	5.8	5.7	5.5	5.4	5.2	5.1	4.9	4.7	4.6
85	5.6	5.5	5.4	5.3	5.2	5.0	4.9	4.7	4.6	4.4
86	5.4	5.3	5.1	5.0	4.9	4.8	4.7	4.5	4.4	4.2
87	5.1	5.0	4.9	4.8	4.7	4.6	4.4	4.3	4.2	4.1
88	4.8	4.7	4.6	4.5	4.4	4.3	4.2	4.1	4.0	3.9
89	4.5	4.5	4.4	4.3	4.2	4.1	4.0	3.9	3.8	3.7
90	4.3	4.2	4.2	4.1	4.0	3.9	3.8	3.8	3.7	3.5
91	4.1	4.0	4.0	3.9	3.8	3.7	3.7	3.6	3.5	3.4
92	3.9	3.8	3.7	3.7	3.6	3.6	3.5	3.4	3.3	3.2
93	3.7	3.6	3.6	3.5	3.4	3.4	3.3	3.2	3.2	3.1
94	3.5	3.4	3.4	3.3	3.3	3.2	3.2	3.1	3.0	3.0
95	3.3	3.2	3.2	3.2	3.1	3.1	3.0	3.0	2.9	2.8
96	3.1	3.1	3.0	3.0	3.0	2.9	2.9	2.8	2.8	2.7
97	2.9	2.9	2.9	2.9	2.8	2.8	2.7	2.7	2.6	2.6
98	2.8	2.8	2.7	2.7	2.7	2.6	2.6	2.6	2.5	2.5
99	2.6	2.6	2.6	2.6	2.5	2.5	2.5	2.4	2.4	2.3
100	2.5	2.5	2.4	2.4	2.4	2.4	2.3	2.3	2.3	2.2
101	2.3	2.3	2.3	2.3	2.2	2.2	2.2	2.2	2.1	2.1
102	2.2	2.1	2.1	2.1	2.1	2.1	2.0	2.0	2.0	2.0
103	2.0	2.0	2.0	2.0	1.9	1.9	1.9	1.9	1.9	1.8
104	1.8	1.8	1.8	1.8	1.8	1.8	1.8	1.7	1.7	1.7

Table VIA—Annuities for Joint Life Only; Two Lives—Expected Return Multiples (continued)

Ages	75	76	77	78	79	80	81	82	83	84
105	1.7	1.7	1.7	1.7	1.6	1.6	1.6	1.6	1.6	1.6
106	1.5	1.5	1.5	1.5	1.5	1.5	1.5	1.5	1.5	1.4
107	1.4	1.4	1.4	1.4	1.4	1.4	1.3	1.3	1.3	1.3
108	1.3	1.2	1.2	1.2	1.2	1.2	1.2	1.2	1.2	1.2
109	1.1	1.1	1.1	1.1	1.1	1.1	1.1	1.1	1.1	1.1
110	1.0	1.0	1.0	1.0	1.0	1.0	1.0	1.0	1.0	1.0
111	.9	.9	.9	.9	.9	.9	.9	.9	.8	.8
112	.8	.8	.8	.7	.7	.7	.7	.7	.7	.7
113	.6	.6	.6	.6	.6	.6	.6	.6	.6	.6
114	.5	.5	.5	.5	.5	.5	.5	.5	.5	.5
115	.5	.5	.5	.5	.5	.5	.5	.5	.5	.5

Table VIA—Annuities for Joint Life Only; Two Lives—Expected Return Multiples

Ages	85	86	87	88	89	90	91	92	93	94
85	4.2	4.1	3.9	3.8	3.6	3.4	3.3	3.2	3.0	2.9
86	4.1	3.9	3.8	3.6	3.5	3.3	3.2	3.1	2.9	2.8
87	3.9	3.8	3.6	3.5	3.4	3.2	3.1	3.0	2.8	2.7
88	3.8	3.6	3.5	3.4	3.2	3.1	3.0	2.9	2.8	2.6
89	3.6	3.5	3.4	3.2	3.1	3.0	2.9	2.8	2.7	2.6
90	3.4	3.3	3.2	3.1	3.0	2.9	2.8	2.7	2.6	2.5
91	3.3	3.2	3.1	3.0	2.9	2.8	2.7	2.6	2.5	2.4
92	3.2	3.1	3.0	2.9	2.8	2.7	2.6	2.5	2.4	2.3
93	3.0	2.9	2.8	2.8	2.7	2.6	2.5	2.4	2.3	2.3
94	2.9	2.8	2.7	2.6	2.6	2.5	2.4	2.3	2.3	2.2
95	2.8	2.7	2.6	2.5	2.5	2.4	2.3	2.2	2.2	2.1
96	2.6	2.6	2.5	2.4	2.4	2.3	2.2	2.2	2.1	2.0
97	2.5	2.5	2.4	2.3	2.3	2.2	2.2	2.1	2.0	2.0
98	2.4	2.4	2.3	2.2	2.2	2.1	2.1	2.0	2.0	1.9
99	2.3	2.2	2.2	2.1	2.1	2.0	2.0	1.9	1.9	1.8
100	2.2	2.1	2.1	2.0	2.0	1.9	1.9	1.9	1.8	1.8
101	2.1	2.0	2.0	1.9	1.9	1.9	1.8	1.8	1.7	1.7
102	1.9	1.9	1.9	1.8	1.8	1.8	1.7	1.7	1.6	1.6
103	1.8	1.8	1.8	1.7	1.7	1.7	1.6	1.6	1.5	1.5
104	1.7	1.7	1.6	1.6	1.6	1.5	1.5	1.5	1.5	1.4
105	1.6	1.5	1.5	1.5	1.5	1.4	1.4	1.4	1.4	1.3
106	1.4	1.4	1.4	1.4	1.4	1.3	1.3	1.3	1.3	1.2
107	1.3	1.3	1.3	1.3	1.2	1.2	1.2	1.2	1.2	1.2
108	1.2	1.2	1.2	1.1	1.1	1.1	1.1	1.1	1.1	1.1
109	1.1	1.1	1.0	1.0	1.0	1.0	1.0	1.0	1.0	1.0
110	.9	.9	.9	.9	.9	.9	.9	.9	.9	.9
111	.8	.8	.8	.8	.8	.8	.8	.8	.8	.8
112	.7	.7	.7	.7	.7	.7	.7	.7	.7	.7
113	.6	.6	.6	.6	.6	.6	.6	.6	.6	.6
114	.5	.5	.5	.5	.5	.5	.5	.5	.5	.5
115	.5	.5	.5	.5	.5	.5	.5	.5	.5	.5

Table VIA—Annuities for Joint Life Only; Two Lives—Expected Return Multiples

Ages	95	96	97	98	99	100	101	102	103	104
95	2.0	2.0	1.9	1.8	1.8	1.7	1.6	1.6	1.5	1.4
96	2.0	1.9	1.9	1.8	1.7	1.7	1.6	1.5	1.5	1.4
97	1.9	1.9	1.8	1.7	1.7	1.6	1.6	1.5	1.4	1.3
98	1.8	1.8	1.7	1.7	1.6	1.6	1.5	1.5	1.4	1.3
99	1.8	1.7	1.7	1.6	1.6	1.5	1.5	1.4	1.4	1.3
100	1.7	1.7	1.6	1.6	1.5	1.5	1.4	1.4	1.3	1.3
101	1.6	1.6	1.6	1.5	1.5	1.4	1.4	1.3	1.3	1.2
102	1.6	1.5	1.5	1.5	1.4	1.4	1.3	1.3	1.2	1.2
103	1.5	1.5	1.4	1.4	1.4	1.3	1.3	1.2	1.2	1.1
104	1.4	1.4	1.3	1.3	1.3	1.3	1.2	1.2	1.1	1.1
105	1.3	1.3	1.3	1.2	1.2	1.2	1.2	1.1	1.1	1.0
106	1.2	1.2	1.2	1.2	1.1	1.1	1.1	1.1	1.0	1.0

Table VIA—Annuities for Joint Life Only; Two Lives—Expected Return Multiples (continued)

Ages	95	96	97	98	99	100	101	102	103	104
107	1.1	1.1	1.1	1.1	1.1	1.0	1.0	1.0	1.0	.9
108	1.0	1.0	1.0	1.0	1.0	1.0	1.0	.9	.9	.9
109	1.0	.9	.9	.9	.9	.9	.9	.9	.8	.8
110	.9	.9	.8	.8	.8	.8	.8	.8	.8	.8
111	.8	.8	.8	.8	.8	.7	.7	.7	.7	.7
112	.7	.7	.7	.7	.7	.7	.7	.7	.6	.6
113	.6	.6	.6	.6	.6	.6	.6	.6	.6	.6
114	.5	.5	.5	.5	.5	.5	.5	.5	.5	.5
115	.5	.5	.5	.5	.5	.5	.5	.5	.5	.5

Table VIA—Annuities for Joint Life Only; Two Lives—Expected Return Multiples

Ages	105	106	107	108	109	110	111	112	113	114	115
105	1.0	1.0	.9	.9	.8	.7	.7	.6	.6	.5	.5
106	1.0	.9	.9	.8	.8	.7	.7	.6	.6	.5	.5
107	.9	.9	.8	.8	.7	.7	.7	.6	.6	.5	.5
108	.9	.8	.8	.8	.7	.7	.6	.6	.5	.5	.5
109	.8	.8	.7	.7	.7	.7	.6	.6	.5	.5	.5
110	.7	.7	.7	.7	.7	.6	.6	.6	.5	.5	.5
111	.7	.7	.7	.6	.6	.6	.6	.5	.5	.5	.5
112	.6	.6	.6	.6	.6	.6	.5	.5	.5	.5	.5
113	.6	.6	.6	.5	.5	.5	.5	.5	.5	.5	.5
114	.5	.5	.5	.5	.5	.5	.5	.5	.5	.5	.5
115	.5	.5	.5	.5	.5	.5	.5	.5	.5	.5	.5

Table VII—Percent Value of Refund Feature; Duration of Guaranteed Amount

	Years—									
Age	1	2	3	4	5	6	7	8	9	10
5	0	0	0	0	0	0	0	0	0	0
6	0	0	0	0	0	0	0	0	0	0
7	0	0	0	0	0	0	0	0	0	0
8	0	0	0	0	0	0	0	0	0	0
9	0	0	0	0	0	0	0	0	0	0
10	0	0	0	0	0	0	0	0	0	0
11	0	0	0	0	0	0	0	0	0	0
12	0	0	0	0	0	0	0	0	0	0
13	0	0	0	0	0	0	0	0	0	0
14	0	0	0	0	0	0	0	0	0	0
15	0	0	0	0	0	0	0	0	0	0
16	0	0	0	0	0	0	0	0	0	0
17	0	0	0	0	0	0	0	0	0	0
18	0	0	0	0	0	0	0	0	0	0
19	0	0	0	0	0	0	0	0	0	0
20	0	0	0	0	0	0	0	0	0	0
21	0	0	0	0	0	0	0	0	0	0
22	0	0	0	0	0	0	0	0	0	0
23	0	0	0	0	0	0	0	0	0	0
24	0	0	0	0	0	0	0	0	0	0
25	0	0	0	0	0	0	0	0	0	0
26	0	0	0	0	0	0	0	0	0	0
27	0	0	0	0	0	0	0	0	0	0
28	0	0	0	0	0	0	0	0	0	0
29	0	0	0	0	0	0	0	0	0	0
30	0	0	0	0	0	0	0	0	0	0
31	0	0	0	0	0	0	0	0	0	0
32	0	0	0	0	0	0	0	0	0	0
33	0	0	0	0	0	0	0	0	0	0
34	0	0	0	0	0	0	0	0	0	0
35	0	0	0	0	0	0	0	0	0	0
36	0	0	0	0	0	0	0	0	0	0

Table VII—Percent Value of Refund Feature; Duration of Guaranteed Amount (continued)

	Years—									
Age	1	2	3	4	5	6	7	8	9	10
37	0	0	0	0	0	0	0	0	0	1
38	0	0	0	0	0	0	0	0	0	1
39	0	0	0	0	0	0	0	0	1	1
40	0	0	0	0	0	0	0	1	1	1
41	0	0	0	0	0	0	0	1	1	1
42	0	0	0	0	0	0	1	1	1	1
43	0	0	0	0	0	0	1	1	1	1
44	0	0	0	0	0	1	1	1	1	1
45	0	0	0	0	0	1	1	1	1	1
46	0	0	0	0	1	1	1	1	1	1
47	0	0	0	0	1	1	1	1	1	1
48	0	0	0	0	1	1	1	1	1	1
49	0	0	0	1	1	1	1	1	1	2
50	0	0	0	1	1	1	1	1	1	2
51	0	0	0	1	1	1	1	1	2	2
52	0	0	0	1	1	1	1	1	2	2
53	0	0	1	1	1	1	1	2	2	2
54	0	0	1	1	1	1	1	2	2	2
55	0	0	1	1	1	1	2	2	2	2
56	0	0	1	1	1	1	2	2	2	3
57	0	0	1	1	1	2	2	2	3	3
58	0	1	1	1	1	2	2	2	3	3
59	0	1	1	1	1	2	2	3	3	4
60	0	1	1	1	2	2	2	3	3	4
61	0	1	1	1	2	2	3	3	4	4
62	0	1	1	2	2	2	3	4	4	5
63	0	1	1	2	2	3	3	4	5	5
64	0	1	1	2	2	3	4	4	5	6
65	0	1	2	2	3	3	4	5	6	6
66	1	1	2	2	3	4	5	5	6	7
67	1	1	2	3	3	4	5	6	7	8
68	1	1	2	3	4	5	6	7	8	9
69	1	1	2	3	4	5	6	7	8	10
70	1	2	3	4	5	6	7	8	9	11
71	1	2	3	4	5	6	8	9	10	12
72	1	2	3	4	6	7	8	10	11	13
73	1	2	4	5	6	8	9	11	13	14
74	1	3	4	5	7	9	10	12	14	16
75	1	3	4	6	8	9	11	13	15	17
76	2	3	5	7	9	10	12	15	17	19
77	2	4	5	7	9	12	14	16	18	21
78	2	4	6	8	10	13	15	18	20	23
79	2	4	7	9	11	14	17	19	22	25
80	2	5	7	10	13	15	18	21	24	27
81	3	5	8	11	14	17	20	23	26	29
82	3	6	9	12	15	19	22	25	28	32
83	3	7	10	13	17	20	24	27	31	34
84	4	7	11	15	19	22	26	30	33	37
85	4	8	12	16	20	24	28	32	36	40
86	4	9	13	18	22	27	31	35	39	42
87	5	10	15	20	24	29	33	37	41	45
88	5	11	16	21	26	31	36	40	44	48
89	6	12	18	23	28	33	38	43	47	50
90	7	13	19	25	31	36	41	45	49	53
91	7	14	21	27	33	38	43	48	52	55
92	8	15	22	29	35	40	45	50	54	58
93	9	17	24	31	37	43	48	52	56	60
94	9	18	26	33	39	45	50	54	58	62
95	10	19	27	35	41	47	52	57	60	64
96	11	20	29	36	43	49	54	59	62	66
97	11	21	30	38	45	51	56	61	64	68

Table VII—Percent Value of Refund Feature; Duration of Guaranteed Amount (continued)

Age	Years— 1	2	3	4	5	6	7	8	9	10
98	12	23	32	40	47	53	58	63	66	69
99	13	24	34	42	49	55	60	65	68	71
100	14	26	36	44	52	58	63	67	70	73
101	14	27	38	47	54	60	65	69	72	75
102	15	29	40	49	56	62	67	71	74	77
103	17	31	42	52	59	65	69	73	76	78
104	18	33	45	55	62	67	72	75	78	80
105	19	36	48	58	65	70	74	77	80	82
106	21	38	51	61	68	73	77	79	82	84
107	23	42	55	64	71	75	79	81	84	85
108	25	45	58	67	73	78	81	83	85	87
109	28	49	62	71	76	80	83	85	87	88
110	31	52	66	74	79	82	85	87	88	89
111	34	57	70	77	82	85	87	88	90	91
112	37	61	73	80	84	87	88	90	91	92
113	41	66	77	83	86	88	90	91	92	93
114	45	70	80	85	88	90	92	93	93	94
115	50	75	83	88	90	92	93	94	94	95

Table VII—Percent Value of Refund Feature; Duration of Guaranteed Amount

Age	Years— 11	12	13	14	15	16	17	18	19	20
5	0	0	0	0	0	0	0	0	0	0
6	0	0	0	0	0	0	0	0	0	0
7	0	0	0	0	0	0	0	0	0	0
8	0	0	0	0	0	0	0	0	0	0
9	0	0	0	0	0	0	0	0	0	0
10	0	0	0	0	0	0	0	0	0	0
11	0	0	0	0	0	0	0	0	0	0
12	0	0	0	0	0	0	0	0	0	0
13	0	0	0	0	0	0	0	0	0	0
14	0	0	0	0	0	0	0	0	0	0
15	0	0	0	0	0	0	0	0	0	0
16	0	0	0	0	0	0	0	0	0	0
17	0	0	0	0	0	0	0	0	0	0
18	0	0	0	0	0	0	0	0	0	0
19	0	0	0	0	0	0	0	0	0	0
20	0	0	0	0	0	0	0	0	0	1
21	0	0	0	0	0	0	0	0	0	1
22	0	0	0	0	0	0	0	0	1	1
23	0	0	0	0	0	0	0	1	1	1
24	0	0	0	0	0	0	0	1	1	1
25	0	0	0	0	0	0	1	1	1	1
26	0	0	0	0	0	0	1	1	1	1
27	0	0	0	0	0	1	1	1	1	1
28	0	0	0	0	1	1	1	1	1	1
29	0	0	0	0	1	1	1	1	1	1
30	0	0	0	1	1	1	1	1	1	1
31	0	0	0	1	1	1	1	1	1	1
32	0	0	1	1	1	1	1	1	1	1
33	0	0	1	1	1	1	1	1	1	1
34	0	1	1	1	1	1	1	1	1	1
35	0	1	1	1	1	1	1	1	1	1
36	1	1	1	1	1	1	1	1	1	1
37	1	1	1	1	1	1	1	1	1	1
38	1	1	1	1	1	1	1	1	1	2
39	1	1	1	1	1	1	1	1	2	2
40	1	1	1	1	1	1	1	2	2	2
41	1	1	1	1	1	1	2	2	2	2

Table VII—Percent Value of Refund Feature; Duration of Guaranteed Amount (continued)

	Years—									
Age	11	12	13	14	15	16	17	18	19	20
42	1	1	1	1	1	2	2	2	2	2
43	1	1	1	1	2	2	2	2	2	3
44	1	1	1	2	2	2	2	2	3	3
45	1	1	2	2	2	2	2	3	3	3
46	1	2	2	2	2	2	3	3	3	3
47	1	2	2	2	2	2	3	3	3	4
48	2	2	2	2	2	3	3	3	4	4
49	2	2	2	2	3	3	3	4	4	4
50	2	2	2	3	3	3	3	4	4	5
51	2	2	3	3	3	3	4	4	4	5
52	2	2	3	3	3	4	4	5	5	5
53	2	3	3	3	4	4	5	5	5	6
54	3	3	3	4	4	4	5	5	6	7
55	3	3	4	4	4	5	5	6	7	7
56	3	3	4	4	5	5	6	7	7	8
57	3	4	4	5	5	6	6	7	8	9
58	4	4	5	5	6	6	7	8	9	9
59	4	5	5	6	6	7	8	9	9	10
60	4	5	6	6	7	8	9	10	10	11
61	5	6	6	7	8	9	10	10	11	13
62	5	6	7	8	9	10	11	12	13	14
63	6	7	8	9	10	11	12	13	14	15
64	7	8	8	9	10	12	13	14	15	17
65	7	8	9	10	12	13	14	15	17	18
66	8	9	10	12	13	14	15	17	18	20
67	9	10	11	13	14	15	17	18	20	22
68	10	11	13	14	15	17	19	20	22	24
69	11	12	14	15	17	19	20	22	24	26
70	12	14	15	17	19	20	22	24	26	28
71	13	15	17	18	20	22	24	26	28	30
72	15	17	18	20	22	24	26	28	30	32
73	16	18	20	22	24	26	28	31	33	35
74	18	20	22	24	26	28	31	33	35	37
75	19	22	24	26	28	31	33	35	38	40
76	21	24	26	28	31	33	36	38	40	43
77	23	26	28	31	33	36	38	41	43	45
78	25	28	31	33	36	38	41	43	46	48
79	28	30	33	36	38	41	44	46	48	51
80	30	33	36	38	41	44	46	49	51	53
81	32	35	38	41	44	47	49	51	54	56
82	35	38	41	44	47	49	52	54	56	58
83	38	41	44	47	49	52	54	57	59	61
84	40	44	47	49	52	55	57	59	61	63
85	43	46	49	52	55	57	59	62	63	65
86	46	49	52	55	57	60	62	64	66	67
87	48	52	55	57	60	62	64	66	68	69
88	51	54	57	60	62	64	66	68	70	71
89	54	57	60	62	65	67	68	70	72	73
90	56	59	62	64	67	69	70	72	74	75
91	59	62	64	67	69	71	72	74	75	76
92	61	64	66	69	71	72	74	75	77	78
93	63	66	68	70	72	74	75	77	78	79
94	65	68	70	72	74	75	77	78	79	80
95	67	69	72	74	75	77	78	79	81	82
96	69	71	73	75	77	78	80	81	82	83
97	70	73	75	77	78	80	81	82	83	84
98	72	74	76	78	79	81	82	83	84	85
99	74	76	78	79	81	82	83	84	85	86
100	75	78	79	81	82	83	84	85	86	86
101	77	79	81	82	83	84	85	86	87	87
102	79	81	82	83	84	85	86	87	88	88

Table VII—Percent Value of Refund Feature; Duration of Guaranteed Amount (continued)

Age	Years— 11	12	13	14	15	16	17	18	19	20
103	80	82	83	85	86	87	87	88	89	89
104	82	84	85	86	87	88	88	89	90	90
105	84	85	86	87	88	89	89	90	90	91
106	85	86	87	88	89	90	90	91	91	92
107	87	88	89	89	90	91	91	92	92	93
108	88	89	90	90	91	92	92	93	93	93
109	89	90	91	92	92	93	93	93	94	94
110	90	91	92	92	93	93	94	94	94	95
111	92	92	93	93	94	94	95	95	95	95
112	93	93	94	94	95	95	95	96	96	96
113	94	94	95	95	95	96	96	96	96	97
114	95	95	95	96	96	96	97	97	97	97
115	95	96	96	96	97	97	97	97	97	98

Table VII—Percent Value of Refund Feature; Duration of Guaranteed Amount

Age	Years— 21	22	23	24	25	26	27	28	29	30
5	0	0	0	0	0	0	0	0	0	0
6	0	0	0	0	0	0	0	0	0	0
7	0	0	0	0	0	0	0	0	0	0
8	0	0	0	0	0	0	0	0	0	1
9	0	0	0	0	0	0	0	0	1	1
10	0	0	0	0	0	0	0	1	1	1
11	0	0	0	0	0	0	1	1	1	1
12	0	0	0	0	0	0	1	1	1	1
13	0	0	0	0	0	1	1	1	1	1
14	0	0	0	0	1	1	1	1	1	1
15	0	0	0	1	1	1	1	1	1	1
16	0	0	1	1	1	1	1	1	1	1
17	0	0	1	1	1	1	1	1	1	1
18	0	1	1	1	1	1	1	1	1	1
19	1	1	1	1	1	1	1	1	1	1
20	1	1	1	1	1	1	1	1	1	1
21	1	1	1	1	1	1	1	1	1	1
22	1	1	1	1	1	1	1	1	1	1
23	1	1	1	1	1	1	1	1	1	1
24	1	1	1	1	1	1	1	1	1	1
25	1	1	1	1	1	1	1	1	1	1
26	1	1	1	1	1	1	1	1	1	1
27	1	1	1	1	1	1	1	1	1	2
28	1	1	1	1	1	1	1	1	2	2
29	1	1	1	1	1	1	1	2	2	2
30	1	1	1	1	1	1	2	2	2	2
31	1	1	1	1	1	2	2	2	2	2
32	1	1	1	1	2	2	2	2	2	2
33	1	1	1	2	2	2	2	2	2	2
34	1	1	2	2	2	2	2	2	2	3
35	1	2	2	2	2	2	2	2	3	3
36	2	2	2	2	2	2	2	3	3	3
37	2	2	2	2	2	2	3	3	3	3
38	2	2	2	2	2	3	3	3	3	4
39	2	2	2	2	3	3	3	3	4	4
40	2	2	3	3	3	3	3	4	4	4
41	2	3	3	3	3	3	4	4	4	5
42	3	3	3	3	3	4	4	4	5	5
43	3	3	3	4	4	4	4	5	5	6
44	3	3	4	4	4	4	5	5	6	6
45	3	4	4	4	5	5	5	6	6	7
46	4	4	4	5	5	5	6	6	7	7

Table VII—Percent Value of Refund Feature; Duration of Guaranteed Amount (continued)

Age	Years— 21	22	23	24	25	26	27	28	29	30
47	4	4	5	5	5	6	6	7	7	8
48	4	5	5	5	6	6	7	7	8	9
49	5	5	5	6	6	7	8	8	9	10
50	5	5	6	6	7	8	8	9	10	10
51	5	6	6	7	8	8	9	10	11	11
52	6	7	7	8	8	9	10	11	11	12
53	7	7	8	8	9	10	11	12	13	14
54	7	8	8	9	10	11	12	13	14	15
55	8	9	9	10	11	12	13	14	15	16
56	9	9	10	11	12	13	14	15	16	18
57	9	10	11	12	13	14	15	17	18	19
58	10	11	12	13	14	16	17	18	19	21
59	11	12	13	15	16	17	18	20	21	22
60	12	14	15	16	17	19	20	21	23	24
61	14	15	16	17	19	20	22	23	25	26
62	15	16	18	19	20	22	23	25	27	28
63	16	18	19	21	22	24	25	27	29	30
64	18	19	21	23	24	26	28	29	31	33
65	20	21	23	25	26	28	30	31	33	35
66	21	23	25	27	28	30	32	34	35	37
67	23	25	27	29	31	32	34	36	38	40
68	25	27	29	31	33	35	37	38	40	42
69	28	29	31	33	35	37	39	41	43	44
70	30	32	34	36	38	40	42	43	45	47
71	32	34	36	38	40	42	44	46	47	49
72	35	37	39	41	43	45	46	48	50	51
73	37	39	41	43	45	47	49	51	52	54
74	40	42	44	46	48	50	51	53	54	56
75	42	44	46	48	50	52	54	55	57	58
76	45	47	49	51	53	54	56	58	59	60
77	47	50	51	53	55	57	58	60	61	62
78	50	52	54	56	57	59	61	62	63	64
79	53	55	56	58	60	61	63	64	65	66
80	55	57	59	60	62	63	65	66	67	68
81	58	59	61	63	64	66	67	68	69	70
82	60	62	63	65	66	68	69	70	71	72
83	62	64	66	67	68	70	71	72	73	74
84	65	66	68	69	70	71	72	73	74	75
85	67	68	70	71	72	73	74	75	76	77
86	69	70	72	73	74	75	76	77	77	78
87	71	72	73	75	76	76	77	78	79	80
88	73	74	75	76	77	78	79	80	80	81
89	74	76	77	78	79	79	80	81	81	82
90	76	77	78	79	80	81	81	82	83	83
91	78	79	79	80	81	82	83	83	84	84
92	79	80	81	82	82	83	84	84	85	85
93	80	81	82	83	83	84	85	85	86	86
94	81	82	63	84	84	85	85	86	86	87
95	82	83	84	85	85	86	86	87	87	88
96	83	84	85	86	86	87	87	88	88	88
97	84	85	86	86	87	87	88	88	89	89
98	85	86	87	87	88	88	89	89	89	90
99	86	87	87	88	88	89	89	90	90	90
100	87	88	88	89	89	90	90	90	91	91
101	88	89	89	90	90	90	91	91	91	92
102	89	89	90	90	91	91	91	92	92	92
103	90	90	91	91	91	92	92	92	93	93
104	91	91	91	92	92	92	93	93	93	93
105	91	92	92	92	93	93	93	94	94	94
106	92	93	93	93	93	94	94	94	94	95
107	93	93	94	94	94	94	95	95	95	95

Table VII—Percent Value of Refund Feature; Duration of Guaranteed Amount (continued)

Age	Years—									
	21	22	23	24	25	26	27	28	29	30
108	94	94	94	94	95	95	95	95	95	96
109	94	95	95	95	95	95	96	96	96	96
110	95	95	95	96	96	96	96	96	96	96
111	96	96	96	96	96	96	97	97	97	97
112	96	96	96	97	97	97	97	97	97	97
113	97	97	97	97	97	97	97	98	98	98
114	97	97	97	98	98	98	98	98	98	98
115	98	98	98	98	98	98	98	98	98	98

Table VII—Percent Value of Refund Feature; Duration of Guaranteed Amount

Age	Years—									
	31	32	33	34	35	36	37	38	39	40
5	0	1	1	1	1	1	1	1	1	1
6	0	1	1	1	1	1	1	1	1	1
7	1	1	1	1	1	1	1	1	1	1
8	1	1	1	1	1	1	1	1	1	1
9	1	1	1	1	1	1	1	1	1	1
10	1	1	1	1	1	1	1	1	1	1
11	1	1	1	1	1	1	1	1	1	1
12	1	1	1	1	1	1	1	1	1	1
13	1	1	1	1	1	1	1	1	1	1
14	1	1	1	1	1	1	1	1	1	1
15	1	1	1	1	1	1	1	1	1	1
16	1	1	1	1	1	1	1	1	1	1
17	1	1	1	1	1	1	1	1	1	1
18	1	1	1	1	1	1	1	1	1	2
19	1	1	1	1	1	1	1	1	2	2
20	1	1	1	1	1	1	1	2	2	2
21	1	1	1	1	1	1	2	2	2	2
22	1	1	1	1	1	2	2	2	2	2
23	1	1	1	2	2	2	2	2	2	2
24	1	1	2	2	2	2	2	2	2	2
25	1	2	2	2	2	2	2	2	2	3
26	2	2	2	2	2	2	2	2	3	3
27	2	2	2	2	2	2	2	3	3	3
28	2	2	2	2	2	2	3	3	3	3
29	2	2	2	2	2	3	3	3	3	4
30	2	2	2	3	3	3	3	3	4	4
31	2	2	3	3	3	3	3	4	4	4
32	2	3	3	3	3	3	4	4	4	5
33	3	3	3	3	3	4	4	4	5	5
34	3	3	3	3	4	4	4	5	5	5
35	3	3	3	4	4	4	5	5	5	6
36	3	4	4	4	4	5	5	5	6	6
37	4	4	4	4	5	5	6	6	6	7
38	4	4	5	5	5	6	6	7	7	8
39	4	5	5	5	6	6	7	7	8	8
40	5	5	5	6	6	7	7	8	8	9
41	5	5	6	6	7	7	8	9	9	10
42	6	6	6	7	7	8	9	9	10	11
43	6	7	7	8	8	9	9	10	11	12
44	7	7	8	8	9	10	10	11	12	13
45	7	8	8	9	10	10	11	12	13	14
46	8	9	9	10	11	11	12	13	14	15
47	9	9	10	11	12	12	13	14	15	16
48	9	10	11	12	13	14	15	16	17	18
49	10	11	12	13	14	15	16	17	18	19
50	11	12	13	14	15	16	17	18	20	21
51	12	13	14	15	16	17	19	20	21	22

Table VII—Percent Value of Refund Feature; Duration of Guaranteed Amount (continued)

Age	Years— 31	32	33	34	35	36	37	38	39	40
52.....	13	14	15	17	18	19	20	21	23	24
53.....	15	16	17	18	19	20	22	23	24	26
54.....	16	17	18	19	21	22	23	25	26	28
55.....	17	18	20	21	22	24	25	27	28	30
56.....	19	20	21	23	24	26	27	29	30	32
57.....	20	22	23	25	26	28	29	31	32	34
58.....	22	24	25	27	28	30	31	33	34	36
59.....	24	25	27	28	30	32	33	35	36	38
60.....	26	27	29	31	32	34	35	37	38	40
61.....	28	29	31	33	34	36	37	39	40	42
62.....	30	32	33	35	36	38	40	41	42	44
63.....	32	34	35	37	39	40	42	43	45	46
64.....	34	36	38	39	41	42	44	45	47	48
65.....	37	38	40	42	43	45	46	47	49	50
66.....	39	41	42	44	45	47	48	50	51	52
67.....	41	43	45	46	48	49	50	52	53	54
68.....	44	45	47	48	50	51	52	54	55	56
69.....	46	48	49	51	52	53	54	56	57	58
70.....	48	50	51	53	54	55	57	58	59	60
71.....	51	52	54	55	56	57	59	60	61	62
72.....	53	54	56	57	58	59	60	62	62	63
73.....	55	57	58	59	60	61	62	63	64	65
74.....	57	59	60	61	62	63	64	65	66	67
75.....	59	61	62	63	64	65	66	67	68	69
76.....	62	63	64	65	66	67	68	69	69	70
77.....	64	65	66	67	68	69	70	70	71	72
78.....	66	67	68	69	70	70	71	72	73	73
79.....	67	68	69	70	71	72	73	73	74	75
80.....	69	70	71	72	73	74	74	75	76	76
81.....	71	72	73	74	74	75	76	76	77	78
82.....	73	74	74	75	76	77	77	78	78	79
83.....	74	75	76	77	77	78	79	79	80	80
84.....	76	77	77	78	79	79	80	80	81	81
85.....	78	78	79	79	80	81	81	82	82	83
86.....	79	80	80	81	81	82	82	83	83	84
87.....	80	81	81	82	83	83	83	84	84	85
88.....	82	82	83	83	84	84	85	85	85	86
89.....	83	83	84	84	85	85	85	86	86	87
90.....	84	84	85	85	86	86	86	87	87	87
91.....	85	85	86	86	87	87	87	88	88	88
92.....	86	86	87	87	87	88	88	88	89	89
93.....	87	87	87	88	88	88	89	89	89	90
94.....	87	88	88	88	89	89	89	90	90	90
95.....	88	88	89	89	89	90	90	90	91	91
96.....	89	89	89	90	90	90	91	91	91	91
97.....	89	90	90	90	91	91	91	91	92	92
98.....	90	90	91	91	91	91	92	92	92	92
99.....	91	91	91	92	92	92	92	92	93	93
100....	91	92	92	92	92	92	93	93	93	93
101....	92	92	92	93	93	93	93	93	94	94
102....	92	93	93	93	93	94	94	94	94	94
103....	93	93	93	94	94	94	94	94	94	95
104....	94	94	94	94	94	95	95	95	95	95
105....	94	94	95	95	95	95	95	95	95	95
106....	95	95	95	95	95	95	96	96	96	96
107....	95	95	96	96	96	96	96	96	96	96
108....	96	96	96	96	96	96	96	96	97	97
109....	96	96	96	97	97	97	97	97	97	97
110....	97	97	97	97	97	97	97	97	97	97
111....	97	97	97	97	97	97	98	98	98	98
112....	97	97	98	98	98	98	98	98	98	98

Table VII—Percent Value of Refund Feature; Duration of Guaranteed Amount (continued)

Age	Years— 31	32	33	34	35	36	37	38	39	40
113....	98	98	98	98	98	98	98	98	98	98
114....	98	98	98	98	98	98	98	98	98	99
115....	98	98	98	99	99	99	99	99	99	99

Table VIII—Temporary Life Annuities;[1] One Life—Expected Return Multiples (continued)

[See footnote at end of tables]

Temporary Period—Maximum Duration of Annuity

[1] The multiples in this table are not applicable to annuities for a term certain; for such cases see paragraph (c) of § 1.72-5.

Age	Years— 1	2	3	4	5	6	7	8	9	10
5......	1.0	2.0	3.0	4.0	5.0	6.0	7.0	8.0	9.0	10.0
6......	1.0	2.0	3.0	4.0	5.0	6.0	7.0	8.0	9.0	10.0
7......	1.0	2.0	3.0	4.0	5.0	6.0	7.0	8.0	9.0	10.0
8......	1.0	2.0	3.0	4.0	5.0	6.0	7.0	8.0	9.0	10.0
9......	1.0	2.0	3.0	4.0	5.0	6.0	7.0	8.0	9.0	10.0
10.....	1.0	2.0	3.0	4.0	5.0	6.0	7.0	8.0	9.0	10.0
11.....	1.0	2.0	3.0	4.0	5.0	6.0	7.0	8.0	9.0	10.0
12.....	1.0	2.0	3.0	4.0	5.0	6.0	7.0	8.0	9.0	10.0
13.....	1.0	2.0	3.0	4.0	5.0	6.0	7.0	8.0	9.0	10.0
14.....	1.0	2.0	3.0	4.0	5.0	6.0	7.0	8.0	9.0	10.0
15.....	1.0	2.0	3.0	4.0	5.0	6.0	7.0	8.0	9.0	10.0
16.....	1.0	2.0	3.0	4.0	5.0	6.0	7.0	8.0	9.0	10.0
17.....	1.0	2.0	3.0	4.0	5.0	6.0	7.0	8.0	9.0	10.0
18.....	1.0	2.0	3.0	4.0	5.0	6.0	7.0	8.0	9.0	10.0
19.....	1.0	2.0	3.0	4.0	5.0	6.0	7.0	8.0	9.0	10.0
20.....	1.0	2.0	3.0	4.0	5.0	6.0	7.0	8.0	9.0	10.0
21.....	1.0	2.0	3.0	4.0	5.0	6.0	7.0	8.0	9.0	10.0
22.....	1.0	2.0	3.0	4.0	5.0	6.0	7.0	8.0	9.0	10.0
23.....	1.0	2.0	3.0	4.0	5.0	6.0	7.0	8.0	9.0	10.0
24.....	1.0	2.0	3.0	4.0	5.0	6.0	7.0	8.0	9.0	10.0
25.....	1.0	2.0	3.0	4.0	5.0	6.0	7.0	8.0	9.0	10.0
26.....	1.0	2.0	3.0	4.0	5.0	6.0	7.0	8.0	9.0	10.0
27.....	1.0	2.0	3.0	4.0	5.0	6.0	7.0	8.0	9.0	10.0
28.....	1.0	2.0	3.0	4.0	5.0	6.0	7.0	8.0	9.0	10.0
29.....	1.0	2.0	3.0	4.0	5.0	6.0	7.0	8.0	9.0	10.0
30.....	1.0	2.0	3.0	4.0	5.0	6.0	7.0	8.0	9.0	10.0
31.....	1.0	2.0	3.0	4.0	5.0	6.0	7.0	8.0	9.0	10.0
32.....	1.0	2.0	3.0	4.0	5.0	6.0	7.0	8.0	9.0	10.0
33.....	1.0	2.0	3.0	4.0	5.0	6.0	7.0	8.0	9.0	10.0
34.....	1.0	2.0	3.0	4.0	5.0	6.0	7.0	8.0	9.0	10.0
35.....	1.0	2.0	3.0	4.0	5.0	6.0	7.0	8.0	9.0	10.0
36.....	1.0	2.0	3.0	4.0	5.0	6.0	7.0	8.0	9.0	10.0
37.....	1.0	2.0	3.0	4.0	5.0	6.0	7.0	8.0	9.0	9.9
38.....	1.0	2.0	3.0	4.0	5.0	6.0	7.0	8.0	9.0	9.9
39.....	1.0	2.0	3.0	4.0	5.0	6.0	7.0	8.0	9.0	9.9
40.....	1.0	2.0	3.0	4.0	5.0	6.0	7.0	8.0	8.9	9.9
41.....	1.0	2.0	3.0	4.0	5.0	6.0	7.0	8.0	8.9	9.9
42.....	1.0	2.0	3.0	4.0	5.0	6.0	7.0	8.0	8.9	9.9
43.....	1.0	2.0	3.0	4.0	5.0	6.0	7.0	7.9	8.9	9.9
44.....	1.0	2.0	3.0	4.0	5.0	6.0	7.0	7.9	8.9	9.9
45.....	1.0	2.0	3.0	4.0	5.0	6.0	7.0	7.9	8.9	9.9
46.....	1.0	2.0	3.0	4.0	5.0	6.0	6.9	7.9	8.9	9.9
47.....	1.0	2.0	3.0	4.0	5.0	6.0	6.9	7.9	8.9	9.9
48.....	1.0	2.0	3.0	4.0	5.0	6.0	6.9	7.9	8.9	9.9
49.....	1.0	2.0	3.0	4.0	5.0	6.0	6.9	7.9	8.9	9.9
50.....	1.0	2.0	3.0	4.0	5.0	5.9	6.9	7.9	8.9	9.8
51.....	1.0	2.0	3.0	4.0	5.0	5.9	6.9	7.9	8.9	9.8
52.....	1.0	2.0	3.0	4.0	5.0	5.9	6.9	7.9	8.8	9.8

53	1.0	2.0	3.0	4.0	5.0	5.9	6.9	7.9	8.8	9.8
54	1.0	2.0	3.0	4.0	4.9	5.9	6.9	7.9	8.8	9.8
55	1.0	2.0	3.0	4.0	4.9	5.9	6.9	7.8	8.8	9.7
56	1.0	2.0	3.0	4.0	4.9	5.9	6.9	7.8	8.8	9.7
57	1.0	2.0	3.0	4.0	4.9	5.9	6.9	7.8	8.8	9.7
58	1.0	2.0	3.0	4.0	4.9	5.9	6.9	7.8	8.7	9.7
59	1.0	2.0	3.0	4.0	4.9	5.9	6.8	7.8	8.7	9.6
60	1.0	2.0	3.0	3.9	4.9	5.9	6.8	7.8	8.7	9.6
61	1.0	2.0	3.0	3.9	4.9	5.9	6.8	7.7	8.7	9.6
62	1.0	2.0	3.0	3.9	4.9	5.8	6.8	7.7	8.6	9.5
63	1.0	2.0	3.0	3.9	4.9	5.8	6.8	7.7	8.6	9.5
64	1.0	2.0	3.0	3.9	4.9	5.8	6.7	7.6	8.5	9.4
65	1.0	2.0	3.0	3.9	4.9	5.8	6.7	7.6	8.5	9.3
66	1.0	2.0	2.9	3.9	4.8	5.8	6.7	7.6	8.4	9.3
67	1.0	2.0	2.9	3.9	4.8	5.7	6.6	7.5	8.4	9.2
68	1.0	2.0	2.9	3.9	4.8	5.7	6.6	7.5	8.3	9.1
69	1.0	2.0	2.9	3.9	4.8	5.7	6.6	7.4	8.2	9.0
70	1.0	2.0	2.9	3.9	4.8	5.6	6.5	7.3	8.1	8.9
71	1.0	2.0	2.9	3.8	4.7	5.6	6.5	7.3	8.1	8.8
72	1.0	2.0	2.9	3.8	4.7	5.6	6.4	7.2	8.0	8.7
73	1.0	2.0	2.9	3.8	4.7	5.5	6.3	7.1	7.9	8.6
74	1.0	1.9	2.9	3.8	4.6	5.5	6.3	7.0	7.7	8.4
75	1.0	1.9	2.9	3.8	4.6	5.4	6.2	6.9	7.6	8.3
76	1.0	1.9	2.8	3.7	4.6	5.4	6.1	6.8	7.5	8.1
77	1.0	1.9	2.8	3.7	4.5	5.3	6.0	6.7	7.3	7.9
78	1.0	1.9	2.8	3.7	4.5	5.2	5.9	6.6	7.2	7.7
79	1.0	1.9	2.8	3.6	4.4	5.1	5.8	6.4	7.0	7.5
80	1.0	1.9	2.8	3.6	4.4	5.1	5.7	6.3	6.8	7.3
81	1.0	1.9	2.8	3.6	4.3	5.0	5.6	6.1	6.6	7.0

[See footnote at end of tables]

Temporary Period—Maximum Duration of Annuity

Age	Years—									
	1	2	3	4	5	6	7	8	9	10
82	1.0	1.9	2.7	3.5	4.2	4.9	5.4	6.0	6.4	6.8
83	1.0	1.9	2.7	3.5	4.1	4.8	5.3	5.8	6.2	6.5
84	1.0	1.8	2.7	3.4	4.1	4.6	5.2	5.6	6.0	6.3
85	1.0	1.8	2.6	3.3	4.0	4.5	5.0	5.4	5.7	6.0
86	1.0	1.8	2.6	3.3	3.9	4.4	4.8	5.2	5.5	5.7
87	.9	1.8	2.5	3.2	3.8	4.3	4.7	5.0	5.3	5.5
88	.9	1.8	2.5	3.1	3.7	4.1	4.5	4.8	5.0	5.2
89	.9	1.8	2.5	3.1	3.6	4.0	4.3	4.6	4.8	4.9
90	.9	1.7	2.4	3.0	3.4	3.8	4.1	4.4	4.5	4.7
91	.9	1.7	2.4	2.9	3.3	3.7	4.0	4.2	4.3	4.4
92	.9	1.7	2.3	2.8	3.2	3.5	3.8	4.0	4.1	4.2
93	.9	1.7	2.3	2.7	3.1	3.4	3.6	3.8	3.9	4.0
94	.9	1.6	2.2	2.7	3.0	3.3	3.5	3.6	3.7	3.8
95	.9	1.6	2.2	2.6	2.9	3.1	3.3	3.4	3.5	3.6
96	.9	1.6	2.1	2.5	2.8	3.0	3.2	3.3	3.3	3.4
97	.9	1.6	2.1	2.4	2.7	2.9	3.0	3.1	3.2	3.2
98	.9	1.5	2.0	2.4	2.6	2.8	2.9	3.0	3.0	3.0
99	.9	1.5	2.0	2.3	2.5	2.6	2.7	2.8	2.8	2.8
100	.9	1.5	1.9	2.2	2.4	2.5	2.6	2.6	2.6	2.7
101	.8	1.4	1.8	2.1	2.3	2.4	2.4	2.5	2.5	2.5
102	.8	1.4	1.8	2.0	2.1	2.2	2.3	2.3	2.3	2.3
103	.8	1.4	1.7	1.9	2.0	2.1	2.1	2.1	2.1	2.1
104	.8	1.3	1.6	1.8	1.9	1.9	1.9	1.9	1.9	1.9
105	.8	1.3	1.5	1.7	1.7	1.8	1.8	1.8	1.8	1.8
106	.8	1.2	1.4	1.5	1.6	1.6	1.6	1.6	1.6	1.6
107	.7	1.1	1.3	1.4	1.4	1.4	1.4	1.4	1.4	1.4
108	.7	1.1	1.2	1.3	1.3	1.3	1.3	1.3	1.3	1.3
109	.7	1.0	1.1	1.1	1.1	1.1	1.1	1.1	1.1	1.1
110	.7	.9	1.0	1.0	1.0	1.0	1.0	1.0	1.0	1.0
111	.6	.8	.9	.9	.9	.9	.9	.9	.9	.9
112	.6	.7	.8	.8	.8	.8	.8	.8	.8	.8
113	.6	.6	.7	.7	.7	.7	.7	.7	.7	.7

114	.5	.6	.6	.6	.6	.6	.6	.6	.6	.6
115	.5	.5	.5	.5	.5	.5	.5	.5	.5	.5

Table VIII—Temporary Life Annuities;[1] One Life—Expected Return Multiples

[See footnote at end of table]

Period—Maximum Duration of Annuity

Age	Years— 11	12	13	14	15	16	17	18	19	20
5	11.0	12.0	13.0	14.0	15.0	16.0	17.0	18.0	19.0	19.9
6	11.0	12.0	13.0	14.0	15.0	16.0	17.0	18.0	19.0	19.9
7	11.0	12.0	13.0	14.0	15.0	16.0	17.0	18.0	19.0	19.9
8	11.0	12.0	13.0	14.0	15.0	16.0	17.0	18.0	18.9	19.9
9	11.0	12.0	13.0	14.0	15.0	16.0	17.0	18.0	18.9	19.9
10	11.0	12.0	13.0	14.0	15.0	16.0	17.0	18.0	18.9	19.9
11	11.0	12.0	13.0	14.0	15.0	16.0	17.0	17.9	18.9	19.9
12	11.0	12.0	13.0	14.0	15.0	16.0	17.0	17.9	18.9	19.9
13	11.0	12.0	13.0	14.0	15.0	16.0	17.0	17.9	18.9	19.9
14	11.0	12.0	13.0	14.0	15.0	16.0	16.9	17.9	18.9	19.9
15	11.0	12.0	13.0	14.0	15.0	16.0	16.9	17.9	18.9	19.9
16	11.0	12.0	13.0	14.0	15.0	16.0	16.9	17.9	18.9	19.9
17	11.0	12.0	13.0	14.0	15.0	15.9	16.9	17.9	18.9	19.9
18	11.0	12.0	13.0	14.0	15.0	15.9	16.9	17.9	18.9	19.9
19	11.0	12.0	13.0	14.0	15.0	15.9	16.9	17.9	18.9	19.9
20	11.0	12.0	13.0	14.0	14.9	15.9	16.9	17.9	18.9	19.9
21	11.0	12.0	13.0	14.0	14.9	15.9	16.9	17.9	18.9	19.9
22	11.0	12.0	13.0	14.0	14.9	15.9	16.9	17.9	18.9	19.9
23	11.0	12.0	13.0	13.9	14.9	15.9	16.9	17.9	18.9	19.9
24	11.0	12.0	13.0	13.9	14.9	15.9	16.9	17.9	18.9	19.9
25	11.0	12.0	13.0	13.9	14.9	15.9	16.9	17.9	18.9	19.9
26	11.0	12.0	12.9	13.9	14.9	15.9	16.9	17.9	18.9	19.9
27	11.0	12.0	12.9	13.9	14.9	15.9	16.9	17.9	18.9	19.9
28	11.0	12.0	12.9	13.9	14.9	15.9	16.9	17.9	18.9	19.8
29	11.0	12.0	12.9	13.9	14.9	15.9	16.9	17.9	18.9	19.8
30	11.0	11.9	12.9	13.9	14.9	15.9	16.9	17.9	18.8	19.8
31	11.0	11.9	12.9	13.9	14.9	15.9	16.9	17.9	18.8	19.8
32	11.0	11.9	12.9	13.9	14.9	15.9	16.9	17.8	18.8	19.8
33	11.0	11.9	12.9	13.9	14.9	15.9	16.9	17.8	18.8	19.8
34	10.9	11.9	12.9	13.9	14.9	15.9	16.8	17.8	18.8	19.8
35	10.9	11.9	12.9	13.9	14.9	15.9	16.8	17.8	18.8	19.7
36	10.9	11.9	12.9	13.9	14.9	15.8	16.8	17.8	18.8	19.7
37	10.9	11.9	12.9	13.9	14.9	15.8	16.8	17.8	18.7	19.7
38	10.9	11.9	12.9	13.9	14.8	15.8	16.8	17.8	18.7	19.7
39	10.9	11.9	12.9	13.9	14.8	15.8	16.8	17.7	18.7	19.6
40	10.9	11.9	12.9	13.8	14.8	15.8	16.7	17.7	18.7	19.6
41	10.9	11.9	12.9	13.8	14.8	15.8	16.7	17.7	18.6	19.6
42	10.9	11.9	12.8	13.8	14.8	15.7	16.7	17.6	18.6	19.5
43	10.9	11.9	12.8	13.8	14.8	15.7	16.7	17.6	18.6	19.5
44	10.9	11.8	12.8	13.8	14.7	15.7	16.6	17.6	18.5	19.4
45	10.9	11.8	12.8	13.8	14.7	15.7	16.6	17.5	18.5	19.4

[See footnote at end of table]

Temporary Period—Maximum Duration of Annuity

Age	Years— 11	12	13	14	15	16	17	18	19	20
46	10.9	11.8	12.8	13.7	14.7	15.6	16.6	17.5	18.4	19.3
47	10.8	11.8	12.8	13.7	14.7	15.6	16.5	17.5	18.4	19.3
48	10.8	11.8	12.7	13.7	14.6	15.6	16.5	17.4	18.3	19.2
49	10.8	11.8	12.7	13.7	14.6	15.5	16.4	17.4	18.3	19.2
50	10.8	11.7	12.7	13.6	14.6	15.5	16.4	17.3	18.2	19.1
51	10.8	11.7	12.7	13.6	14.5	15.4	16.3	17.2	18.1	19.0
52	10.8	11.7	12.6	13.6	14.5	15.4	16.3	17.2	18.0	18.9
53	10.7	11.7	12.6	13.5	14.4	15.3	16.2	17.1	18.0	18.8
54	10.7	11.6	12.6	13.5	14.4	15.3	16.2	17.0	17.9	18.7
55	10.7	11.6	12.5	13.4	14.3	15.2	16.1	16.9	17.8	18.6
56	10.7	11.6	12.5	13.4	14.3	15.1	16.0	16.8	17.6	18.4

Table VIII—Temporary Life Annuities;[1] One Life—Expected Return Multiples (continued)

57.....	10.6	11.5	12.4	13.3	14.2	15.1	15.9	16.7	17.5	18.3
58.....	10.6	11.5	12.4	13.3	14.1	15.0	15.8	16.6	17.4	18.1
59.....	10.6	11.4	12.3	13.2	14.0	14.9	15.7	16.4	17.2	17.9
60.....	10.5	11.4	12.3	13.1	13.9	14.7	15.5	16.3	17.0	17.7
61.....	10.5	11.3	12.2	13.0	13.8	14.6	15.4	16.1	16.8	17.5
62.....	10.4	11.3	12.1	12.9	13.7	14.5	15.2	15.9	16.6	17.2
63.....	10.3	11.2	12.0	12.8	13.6	14.3	15.0	15.7	16.3	17.0
64.....	10.3	11.1	11.9	12.7	13.4	14.1	14.8	15.5	16.1	16.7
65.....	10.2	11.0	11.8	12.5	13.2	13.9	14.6	15.2	15.8	16.3
66.....	10.1	10.9	11.6	12.4	13.1	13.7	14.4	14.9	15.5	16.0
67.....	10.0	10.8	11.5	12.2	12.9	13.5	14.1	14.7	15.2	15.6
68.....	9.9	10.6	11.4	12.0	12.7	13.3	13.8	14.3	14.8	15.3
69.....	9.8	10.5	11.2	11.8	12.4	13.0	13.5	14.0	14.4	14.8
70.....	9.6	10.3	11.0	11.6	12.2	12.7	13.2	13.7	14.0	14.4
71.....	9.5	10.2	10.8	11.4	11.9	12.4	12.9	13.3	13.6	13.9
72.....	9.4	10.0	10.6	11.2	11.7	12.1	12.5	12.9	13.2	13.5
73.....	9.2	9.8	10.4	10.9	11.4	11.8	12.1	12.5	12.7	13.0
74.....	9.0	9.6	10.1	10.6	11.0	11.4	11.7	12.0	12.3	12.5
75.....	8.8	9.4	9.9	10.3	10.7	11.0	11.3	11.6	11.8	12.0
76.....	8.6	9.1	9.6	10.0	10.3	10.6	10.9	11.1	11.3	11.4
77.....	8.4	8.9	9.3	9.7	10.0	10.2	10.5	10.6	10.8	10.9
78.....	8.2	8.6	9.0	9.3	9.6	9.8	10.0	10.2	10.3	10.4
79.....	7.9	8.3	8.7	9.0	9.2	9.4	9.5	9.7	9.8	9.8
80.....	7.7	8.0	8.3	8.6	8.8	9.0	9.1	9.2	9.3	9.3
81.....	7.4	7.7	8.0	8.2	8.4	8.5	8.6	8.7	8.8	8.8
82.....	7.1	7.4	7.6	7.8	8.0	8.1	8.2	8.2	8.3	8.3
83.....	6.8	7.1	7.3	7.4	7.5	7.6	7.7	7.8	7.8	7.8
84.....	6.5	6.7	6.9	7.0	7.1	7.2	7.3	7.3	7.3	7.4
85.....	6.2	6.4	6.6	6.7	6.7	6.8	6.8	6.9	6.9	6.9
86.....	5.9	6.1	6.2	6.3	6.4	6.4	6.4	6.5	6.5	6.5
87.....	5.6	5.8	5.9	5.9	6.0	6.0	6.0	6.1	6.1	6.1
88.....	5.3	5.4	5.5	5.6	5.6	5.6	5.7	5.7	5.7	5.7
89.....	5.1	5.1	5.2	5.3	5.3	5.3	5.3	5.3	5.3	5.3
90.....	4.8	4.9	4.9	4.9	5.0	5.0	5.0	5.0	5.0	5.0
91.....	4.5	4.6	4.6	4.6	4.7	4.7	4.7	4.7	4.7	4.7
92.....	4.3	4.3	4.3	4.4	4.4	4.4	4.4	4.4	4.4	4.4
93.....	4.0	4.1	4.1	4.1	4.1	4.1	4.1	4.1	4.1	4.1
94.....	3.8	3.8	3.9	3.9	3.9	3.9	3.9	3.9	3.9	3.9
95.....	3.6	3.6	3.6	3.6	3.7	3.7	3.7	3.7	3.7	3.7
96.....	3.4	3.4	3.4	3.4	3.4	3.4	3.4	3.4	3.4	3.4
97.....	3.2	3.2	3.2	3.2	3.2	3.2	3.2	3.2	3.2	3.2
98.....	3.0	3.0	3.0	3.0	3.0	3.0	3.0	3.0	3.0	3.0
99.....	2.8	2.8	2.8	2.8	2.8	2.8	2.8	2.8	2.8	2.8
100....	2.7	2.7	2.7	2.7	2.7	2.7	2.7	2.7	2.7	2.7
101....	2.5	2.5	2.5	2.5	2.5	2.5	2.5	2.5	2.5	2.5
102....	2.3	2.3	2.3	2.3	2.3	2.3	2.3	2.3	2.3	2.3
103....	2.1	2.1	2.1	2.1	2.1	2.1	2.1	2.1	2.1	2.1
104....	1.9	1.9	1.9	1.9	1.9	1.9	1.9	1.9	1.9	1.9
105....	1.8	1.8	1.8	1.8	1.8	1.8	1.8	1.8	1.8	1.8
106....	1.6	1.6	1.6	1.6	1.6	1.6	1.6	1.6	1.6	1.6
107....	1.4	1.4	1.4	1.4	1.4	1.4	1.4	1.4	1.4	1.4
108....	1.3	1.3	1.3	1.3	1.3	1.3	1.3	1.3	1.3	1.3
109....	1.1	1.1	1.1	1.1	1.1	1.1	1.1	1.1	1.1	1.1
110....	1.0	1.0	1.0	1.0	1.0	1.0	1.0	1.0	1.0	1.0
111....	.9	.9	.9	.9	.9	.9	.9	.9	.9	.9
112....	.8	.8	.8	.8	.8	.8	.8	.8	.8	.8
113....	.7	.7	.7	.7	.7	.7	.7	.7	.7	.7
114....	.6	.6	.6	.6	.6	.6	.6	.6	.6	.6
115....	.5	.5	.5	.5	.5	.5	.5	.5	.5	.5

Table VIII—Temporary Life Annuities;[1] One Life—Expected Return Multiples

[See footnote at end of table]

Temporary Period—Maximum Duration of Annuity

Years—

Table VIII—Temporary Life Annuities;[1] One Life—Expected Return Multiples (continued)

Age	21	22	23	24	25	26	27	28	29	30
5	20.9	21.9	22.9	23.9	24.9	25.9	26.9	27.9	28.9	29.9
6	20.9	21.9	22.9	23.9	24.9	25.9	26.9	27.9	28.9	29.9
7	20.9	21.9	22.9	23.9	24.9	25.9	26.9	27.9	28.9	29.9
8	20.9	21.9	22.9	23.9	24.9	25.9	26.9	27.9	28.9	29.8
9	20.9	21.9	22.9	23.9	24.9	25.9	26.9	27.9	28.9	29.8

[See footnote at end of table]

Temporary Period—Maximum Duration of Annuity

	Years—									
Age	21	22	23	24	25	26	27	28	29	30
10	20.9	21.9	22.9	23.9	24.9	25.9	26.9	27.9	28.8	29.8
11	20.9	21.9	22.9	23.9	24.9	25.9	26.9	27.9	28.8	29.8
12	20.9	21.9	22.9	23.9	24.9	25.9	26.9	27.8	28.8	29.8
13	20.9	21.9	22.9	23.9	24.9	25.9	26.9	27.8	28.8	29.8
14	20.9	21.9	22.9	23.9	24.9	25.9	26.8	27.8	28.8	29.8
15	20.9	21.9	22.9	23.9	24.9	25.9	26.8	27.8	28.8	29.8
16	20.9	21.9	22.9	23.9	24.9	25.8	26.8	27.8	28.8	29.8
17	20.9	21.9	22.9	23.9	24.9	25.8	26.8	27.8	28.8	29.8
18	20.9	21.9	22.9	23.9	24.8	25.8	26.8	27.8	28.8	29.7
19	20.9	21.9	22.9	23.9	24.8	25.8	26.8	27.8	28.8	29.7
20	20.9	21.9	22.9	23.8	24.8	25.8	26.8	27.8	28.7	29.7
21	20.9	21.9	22.9	23.8	24.8	25.8	26.8	27.8	28.7	29.7
22	20.9	21.9	22.8	23.8	24.8	25.8	26.8	27.7	28.7	29.7
23	20.9	21.9	22.8	23.8	24.8	25.8	26.7	27.7	28.7	29.7
24	20.9	21.8	22.8	23.8	24.8	25.8	26.7	27.7	28.7	29.6
25	20.9	21.8	22.8	23.8	24.8	25.7	26.7	27.7	28.6	29.6
26	20.8	21.8	22.8	23.8	24.8	25.7	26.7	27.7	28.6	29.6
27	20.8	21.8	22.8	23.8	24.7	25.7	26.7	27.6	28.6	29.5
28	20.8	21.8	22.8	23.7	24.7	25.7	26.6	27.6	28.6	29.5
29	20.8	21.8	22.8	23.7	24.7	25.7	26.6	27.6	28.5	29.5
30	20.8	21.8	22.7	23.7	24.7	25.6	26.6	27.5	28.5	29.4
31	20.8	21.8	22.7	23.7	24.6	25.6	26.6	27.5	28.4	29.4
32	20.8	21.7	22.7	23.7	24.6	25.6	26.5	27.5	28.4	29.3
33	20.8	21.7	22.7	23.6	24.6	25.5	26.5	27.4	28.4	29.3
34	20.7	21.7	22.7	23.6	24.6	25.5	26.4	27.4	28.3	29.2
35	20.7	21.7	22.6	23.6	24.5	25.5	26.4	27.3	28.2	29.2
36	20.7	21.6	22.6	23.5	24.5	25.4	26.3	27.3	28.2	29.1
37	20.7	21.6	22.6	23.5	24.4	25.4	26.3	27.2	28.1	29.0
38	20.6	21.6	22.5	23.4	24.4	25.3	26.2	27.1	28.0	28.9
39	20.6	21.5	22.5	23.4	24.3	25.2	26.1	27.0	27.9	28.8
40	20.6	21.5	22.4	23.3	24.3	25.2	26.1	27.0	27.8	28.7
41	20.5	21.4	22.4	23.3	24.2	25.1	26.0	26.9	27.7	28.6
42	20.5	21.4	22.3	23.2	24.1	25.0	25.9	26.8	27.6	28.5
43	20.4	21.3	22.2	23.2	24.0	24.9	25.8	26.6	27.5	28.3
44	20.4	21.3	22.2	23.1	24.0	24.8	25.7	26.5	27.3	28.2
45	20.3	21.2	22.1	23.0	23.9	24.7	25.6	26.4	27.2	28.0
46	20.2	21.1	22.0	22.9	23.8	24.6	25.4	26.2	27.0	27.8
47	20.2	21.1	21.9	22.8	23.6	24.5	25.3	26.1	26.8	27.6
48	20.1	21.0	21.8	22.7	23.5	24.3	25.1	25.9	26.6	27.4
49	20.0	20.9	21.7	22.6	23.4	24.2	25.0	25.7	26.4	27.1
50	19.9	20.8	21.6	22.4	23.2	24.0	24.8	25.5	26.2	26.9
51	19.8	20.7	21.5	22.3	23.1	23.8	24.6	25.3	25.9	26.6
52	19.7	20.6	21.4	22.1	22.9	23.6	24.3	25.0	25.7	26.3
53	19.6	20.4	21.2	22.0	22.7	23.4	24.1	24.7	25.3	25.9
54	19.5	20.3	21.0	21.8	22.5	23.2	23.8	24.4	25.0	25.6
55	19.3	20.1	20.8	21.6	22.2	22.9	23.5	24.1	24.6	25.2
56	19.2	19.9	20.6	21.3	22.0	22.6	23.2	23.7	24.3	24.7
57	19.0	19.7	20.4	21.1	21.7	22.3	22.8	23.4	23.8	24.3
58	18.8	19.5	20.2	20.8	21.4	21.9	22.5	22.9	23.4	23.8
59	18.6	19.3	19.9	20.5	21.1	21.6	22.0	22.5	22.9	23.2
60	18.4	19.0	19.6	20.2	20.7	21.2	21.6	22.0	22.4	22.7
61	18.1	18.7	19.3	19.8	20.3	20.7	21.1	21.5	21.8	22.1

Table VIII—Temporary Life Annuities;[1] One Life—Expected Return Multiples (continued)

Age										
62	17.8	18.4	18.9	19.4	19.9	20.3	20.6	21.0	21.2	21.5
63	17.5	18.1	18.5	19.0	19.4	19.8	20.1	20.4	20.6	20.8
64	17.2	17.7	18.1	18.6	18.9	19.3	19.5	19.8	20.0	20.2
65	16.8	17.3	17.7	18.1	18.4	18.7	18.9	19.2	19.3	19.5
66	16.5	16.9	17.3	17.6	17.9	18.1	18.3	18.5	18.7	18.8
67	16.1	16.4	16.8	17.1	17.3	17.5	17.7	17.9	18.0	18.1
68	15.6	16.0	16.3	16.5	16.7	16.9	17.1	17.2	17.3	17.4
69	15.2	15.5	15.7	16.0	16.1	16.3	16.4	16.5	16.6	16.7
70	14.7	15.0	15.2	15.4	15.5	15.7	15.8	15.8	15.9	15.9
71	14.2	14.4	14.6	14.8	14.9	15.0	15.1	15.2	15.2	15.2
72	13.7	13.9	14.1	14.2	14.3	14.4	14.4	14.5	14.5	14.5
73	13.2	13.3	13.5	13.6	13.7	13.7	13.8	13.8	13.8	13.9
74	12.6	12.8	12.9	13.0	13.0	13.1	13.1	13.1	13.2	13.2
75	12.1	12.2	12.3	12.4	12.4	12.5	12.5	12.5	12.5	12.5
76	11.5	11.6	11.7	11.8	11.8	11.8	11.8	11.9	11.9	11.9
77	11.0	11.1	11.1	11.2	11.2	11.2	11.2	11.2	11.2	11.2
78	10.4	10.5	10.5	10.6	10.6	10.6	10.6	10.6	10.6	10.6
79	9.9	9.9	10.0	10.0	10.0	10.0	10.0	10.0	10.0	10.0
80	9.4	9.4	9.4	9.4	9.5	9.5	9.5	9.5	9.5	9.5
81	8.8	8.9	8.9	8.9	8.9	8.9	8.9	8.9	8.9	8.9
82	8.3	8.4	8.4	8.4	8.4	8.4	8.4	8.4	8.4	8.4
83	7.8	7.9	7.9	7.9	7.9	7.9	7.9	7.9	7.9	7.9
84	7.4	7.4	7.4	7.4	7.4	7.4	7.4	7.4	7.4	7.4
85	6.9	6.9	6.9	6.9	6.9	6.9	6.9	6.9	6.9	6.9
86	6.5	6.5	6.5	6.5	6.5	6.5	6.5	6.5	6.5	6.5
87	6.1	6.1	6.1	6.1	6.1	6.1	6.1	6.1	6.1	6.1
88	5.7	5.7	5.7	5.7	5.7	5.7	5.7	5.7	5.7	5.7
89	5.3	5.3	5.3	5.3	5.3	5.3	5.3	5.3	5.3	5.3
90	5.0	5.0	5.0	5.0	5.0	5.0	5.0	5.0	5.0	5.0
91	4.7	4.7	4.7	4.7	4.7	4.7	4.7	4.7	4.7	4.7
92	4.4	4.4	4.4	4.4	4.4	4.4	4.4	4.4	4.4	4.4
93	4.1	4.1	4.1	4.1	4.1	4.1	4.1	4.1	4.1	4.1
94	3.9	3.9	3.9	3.9	3.9	3.9	3.9	3.9	3.9	3.9
95	3.7	3.7	3.7	3.7	3.7	3.7	3.7	3.7	3.7	3.7
96	3.4	3.4	3.4	3.4	3.4	3.4	3.4	3.4	3.4	3.4

[See footnote at end of table]

Temporary Period—Maximum Duration of Annuity

Age	Years— 21	22	23	24	25	26	27	28	29	30
97	3.2	3.2	3.2	3.2	3.2	3.2	3.2	3.2	3.2	3.2
98	3.0	3.0	3.0	3.0	3.0	3.0	3.0	3.0	3.0	3.0
99	2.8	2.8	2.8	2.8	2.8	2.8	2.8	2.8	2.8	2.8
100	2.7	2.7	2.7	2.7	2.7	2.7	2.7	2.7	2.7	2.7
101	2.5	2.5	2.5	2.5	2.5	2.5	2.5	2.5	2.5	2.5
102	2.3	2.3	2.3	2.3	2.3	2.3	2.3	2.3	2.3	2.3
103	2.1	2.1	2.1	2.1	2.1	2.1	2.1	2.1	2.1	2.1
104	1.9	1.9	1.9	1.9	1.9	1.9	1.9	1.9	1.9	1.9
105	1.8	1.8	1.8	1.8	1.8	1.8	1.8	1.8	1.8	1.8
106	1.6	1.6	1.6	1.6	1.6	1.6	1.6	1.6	1.6	1.6
107	1.4	1.4	1.4	1.4	1.4	1.4	1.4	1.4	1.4	1.4
108	1.3	1.3	1.3	1.3	1.3	1.3	1.3	1.3	1.3	1.3
109	1.1	1.1	1.1	1.1	1.1	1.1	1.1	1.1	1.1	1.1
110	1.0	1.0	1.0	1.0	1.0	1.0	1.0	1.0	1.0	1.0
111	.9	.9	.9	.9	.9	.9	.9	.9	.9	.9
112	.8	.8	.8	.8	.8	.8	.8	.8	.8	.8
113	.7	.7	.7	.7	.7	.7	.7	.7	.7	.7
114	.6	.6	.6	.6	.6	.6	.6	.6	.6	.6
115	.5	.5	.5	.5	.5	.5	.5	.5	.5	.5

Table VIII—Temporary Life Annuities;[1] One Life—Expected Return Multiples

[See footnote at end of table]

Temporary Period—Maximum Duration of Annuity

Table VIII—Temporary Life Annuities;[1] One Life—Expected Return Multiples (continued)

Age	Years— 31	32	33	34	35	36	37	38	39	40
5	30.8	31.8	32.8	33.8	34.8	35.8	36.8	37.7	38.7	39.7
6	30.8	31.8	32.8	33.8	34.8	35.8	36.8	37.7	38.7	39.7
7	30.8	31.8	32.8	33.8	34.8	35.8	36.7	37.7	38.7	39.7
8	30.8	31.8	32.8	33.8	34.8	35.7	36.7	37.7	38.7	39.7
9	30.8	31.8	32.8	33.8	34.8	35.7	36.7	37.7	38.7	39.6
10	30.8	31.8	32.8	33.8	34.7	35.7	36.7	37.7	38.6	39.6
11	30.8	31.8	32.8	33.8	34.7	35.7	36.7	37.7	38.6	39.6
12	30.8	31.8	32.8	33.7	34.7	35.7	36.7	37.6	38.6	39.6
13	30.8	31.8	32.7	33.7	34.7	35.7	36.6	37.6	38.6	39.5
14	30.8	31.8	32.7	33.7	34.7	35.7	36.6	37.6	38.6	39.5
15	30.8	31.7	32.7	33.7	34.7	35.6	36.6	37.6	38.5	39.5
16	30.8	31.7	32.7	33.7	34.6	35.6	36.6	37.5	38.5	39.4
17	30.7	31.7	32.7	33.7	34.6	35.6	36.5	37.5	38.5	39.4
18	30.7	31.7	32.7	33.6	34.6	35.6	36.5	37.5	38.4	39.4
19	30.7	31.7	32.6	33.6	34.6	35.5	36.5	37.4	38.4	39.3
20	30.7	31.7	32.6	33.6	34.5	35.5	36.4	37.4	38.3	39.3
21	30.7	31.6	32.6	33.6	34.5	35.5	36.4	37.4	38.3	39.2
22	30.6	31.6	32.6	33.5	34.5	35.4	36.4	37.3	38.2	39.2
23	30.6	31.6	32.5	33.5	34.4	35.4	36.3	37.3	38.2	39.1
24	30.6	31.5	32.5	33.5	34.4	35.3	36.3	37.2	38.1	39.0
25	30.6	31.5	32.5	33.4	34.3	35.3	36.2	37.1	38.1	39.0
26	30.5	31.5	32.4	33.4	34.3	35.2	36.2	37.1	38.0	38.9
27	30.5	31.4	32.4	33.3	34.2	35.2	36.1	37.0	37.9	38.8
28	30.5	31.4	32.3	33.3	34.2	35.1	36.0	36.9	37.8	38.7
29	30.4	31.4	32.3	33.2	34.1	35.0	35.9	36.8	37.7	38.6
30	30.4	31.3	32.2	33.1	34.1	35.0	35.8	36.7	37.6	38.5
31	30.3	31.2	32.2	33.1	34.0	34.9	35.8	36.6	37.5	38.3
32	30.3	31.2	32.1	33.0	33.9	34.8	35.6	36.5	37.4	38.2
33	30.2	31.1	32.0	32.9	33.8	34.7	35.5	36.4	37.2	38.0
34	30.1	31.0	31.9	32.8	33.7	34.6	35.4	36.2	37.1	37.9
35	30.1	31.0	31.8	32.7	33.6	34.4	35.3	36.1	36.9	37.7
36	30.0	30.9	31.7	32.6	33.5	34.3	35.1	35.9	36.7	37.4
37	29.9	30.8	31.6	32.5	33.3	34.1	34.9	35.7	36.5	37.2
38	29.8	30.7	31.5	32.3	33.2	34.0	34.7	35.5	36.2	37.0
39	29.7	30.5	31.4	32.2	33.0	33.8	34.5	35.3	36.0	36.7
40	29.6	30.4	31.2	32.0	32.8	33.6	34.3	35.0	35.7	36.4
41	29.4	30.2	31.0	31.8	32.6	33.3	34.1	34.7	35.4	36.0
42	29.3	30.1	30.9	31.6	32.4	33.1	33.8	34.4	35.1	35.7
43	29.1	29.9	30.7	31.4	32.1	32.8	33.5	34.1	34.7	35.3
44	28.9	29.7	30.5	31.2	31.9	32.5	33.2	33.8	34.3	34.9
45	28.8	29.5	30.2	30.9	31.6	32.2	32.8	33.4	33.9	34.4
46	28.5	29.3	30.0	30.6	31.3	31.9	32.4	33.0	33.5	33.9
47	28.3	29.0	29.7	30.3	30.9	31.5	32.0	32.5	33.0	33.4
48	28.1	28.7	29.4	30.0	30.6	31.1	31.6	32.1	32.5	32.9
49	27.8	28.4	29.0	29.6	30.2	30.7	31.1	31.5	31.9	32.3
50	27.5	28.1	28.7	29.2	29.7	30.2	30.6	31.0	31.4	31.7
51	27.2	27.8	28.3	28.8	29.3	29.7	30.1	30.4	30.7	31.0
52	26.8	27.4	27.9	28.4	28.8	29.2	29.5	29.8	30.1	30.3
53	26.5	27.0	27.4	27.9	28.3	28.6	28.9	29.2	29.4	29.6
54	26.1	26.5	27.0	27.4	27.7	28.0	28.3	28.5	28.7	28.9
55	25.6	26.1	26.5	26.8	27.1	27.4	27.6	27.8	28.0	28.1
56	25.2	25.6	25.9	26.2	26.5	26.7	26.9	27.1	27.2	27.3
57	24.7	25.0	25.3	25.6	25.8	26.0	26.2	26.3	26.5	26.5
58	24.1	24.4	24.7	25.0	25.2	25.3	25.5	25.6	25.7	25.7
59	23.6	23.8	24.1	24.3	24.4	24.6	24.7	24.8	24.9	24.9
60	23.0	23.2	23.4	23.6	23.7	23.8	23.9	24.0	24.0	24.1

[See footnote at end of table]

Temporary Period—Maximum Duration of Annuity

Age	Years— 31	32	33	34	35	36	37	38	39	40

Table VIII—Temporary Life Annuities;[1] One Life—Expected Return Multiples (continued)

61	22.3	22.5	22.7	22.9	23.0	23.1	23.1	23.2	23.2	23.3
62	21.7	21.9	22.0	22.1	22.2	22.3	22.3	22.4	22.4	22.4
63	21.0	21.1	21.3	21.4	21.4	21.5	21.5	21.6	21.6	21.6
64	20.3	20.4	20.5	20.6	20.6	20.7	20.7	20.7	20.8	20.8
65	19.6	19.7	19.8	19.8	19.9	19.9	19.9	19.9	19.9	20.0
66	18.9	19.0	19.0	19.1	19.1	19.1	19.1	19.1	19.1	19.1
67	18.2	18.2	18.3	18.3	18.3	18.3	18.3	18.3	18.4	18.4
68	17.4	17.5	17.5	17.5	17.5	17.6	17.6	17.6	17.6	17.6
69	16.7	16.7	16.8	16.8	16.8	16.8	16.8	16.8	16.8	16.8
70	16.0	16.0	16.0	16.0	16.0	16.0	16.0	16.0	16.0	16.0
71	15.3	15.3	15.3	15.3	15.3	15.3	15.3	15.3	15.3	15.3
72	14.6	14.6	14.6	14.6	14.6	14.6	14.6	14.6	14.6	14.6
73	13.9	13.9	13.9	13.9	13.9	13.9	13.9	13.9	13.9	13.9
74	13.2	13.2	13.2	13.2	13.2	13.2	13.2	13.2	13.2	13.2
75	12.5	12.5	12.5	12.5	12.5	12.5	12.5	12.5	12.5	12.5
76	11.9	11.9	11.9	11.9	11.9	11.9	11.9	11.9	11.9	11.9
77	11.2	11.2	11.2	11.2	11.2	11.2	11.2	11.2	11.2	11.2
78	10.6	10.6	10.6	10.6	10.6	10.6	10.6	10.6	10.6	10.6
79	10.0	10.0	10.0	10.0	10.0	10.0	10.0	10.0	10.0	10.0
80	9.5	9.5	9.5	9.5	9.5	9.5	9.5	9.5	9.5	9.5
81	8.9	8.9	8.9	8.9	8.9	8.9	8.9	8.9	8.9	8.9
82	8.4	8.4	8.4	8.4	8.4	8.4	8.4	8.4	8.4	8.4
83	7.9	7.9	7.9	7.9	7.9	7.9	7.9	7.9	7.9	7.9
84	7.4	7.4	7.4	7.4	7.4	7.4	7.4	7.4	7.4	7.4
85	6.9	6.9	6.9	6.9	6.9	6.9	6.9	6.9	6.9	6.9
86	6.5	6.5	6.5	6.5	6.5	6.5	6.5	6.5	6.5	6.5
87	6.1	6.1	6.1	6.1	6.1	6.1	6.1	6.1	6.1	6.1
88	5.7	5.7	5.7	5.7	5.7	5.7	5.7	5.7	5.7	5.7
89	5.3	5.3	5.3	5.3	5.3	5.3	5.3	5.3	5.3	5.3
90	5.0	5.0	5.0	5.0	5.0	5.0	5.0	5.0	5.0	5.0
91	4.7	4.7	4.7	4.7	4.7	4.7	4.7	4.7	4.7	4.7
92	4.4	4.4	4.4	4.4	4.4	4.4	4.4	4.4	4.4	4.4
93	4.1	4.1	4.1	4.1	4.1	4.1	4.1	4.1	4.1	4.1
94	3.9	3.9	3.9	3.9	3.9	3.9	3.9	3.9	3.9	3.9
95	3.7	3.7	3.7	3.7	3.7	3.7	3.7	3.7	3.7	3.7
96	3.4	3.4	3.4	3.4	3.4	3.4	3.4	3.4	3.4	3.4
97	3.2	3.2	3.2	3.2	3.2	3.2	3.2	3.2	3.2	3.2
98	3.0	3.0	3.0	3.0	3.0	3.0	3.0	3.0	3.0	3.0
99	2.8	2.8	2.8	2.8	2.8	2.8	2.8	2.8	2.8	2.8
100	2.7	2.7	2.7	2.7	2.7	2.7	2.7	2.7	2.7	2.7
101	2.5	2.5	2.5	2.5	2.5	2.5	2.5	2.5	2.5	2.5
102	2.3	2.3	2.3	2.3	2.3	2.3	2.3	2.3	2.3	2.3
103	2.1	2.1	2.1	2.1	2.1	2.1	2.1	2.1	2.1	2.1
104	1.9	1.9	1.9	1.9	1.9	1.9	1.9	1.9	1.9	1.9
105	1.8	1.8	1.8	1.8	1.8	1.8	1.8	1.8	1.8	1.8
106	1.6	1.6	1.6	1.6	1.6	1.6	1.6	1.6	1.6	1.6
107	1.4	1.4	1.4	1.4	1.4	1.4	1.4	1.4	1.4	1.4
108	1.3	1.3	1.3	1.3	1.3	1.3	1.3	1.3	1.3	1.3
109	1.1	1.1	1.1	1.1	1.1	1.1	1.1	1.1	1.1	1.1
110	1.0	1.0	1.0	1.0	1.0	1.0	1.0	1.0	1.0	1.0
111	.9	.9	.9	.9	.9	.9	.9	.9	.9	.9
112	.8	.8	.8	.8	.8	.8	.8	.8	.8	.8
113	.7	.7	.7	.7	.7	.7	.7	.7	.7	.7
114	.6	.6	.6	.6	.6	.6	.6	.6	.6	.6
115	.5	.5	.5	.5	.5	.5	.5	.5	.5	.5

T.D. 6211, 11/14/56, amend T.D. 6233, 5/14/57, T.D. 8115, 12/16/86.

§ 1.72-10 Effect of transfer of contracts on investment in the contract.

(a) If a contract to which section 72 applies, or any interest therein, is transferred for a valuable consideration, by assignment or otherwise, only the actual value of the consideration given for such transfer and the amount of premiums or other consideration subsequently paid by the transferee shall be included in the transferee's aggregate of premiums or other consideration paid. In accordance with the provisions of section 72(g)(3) and paragraph (b) of § 1.72-4, an annuity starting date shall be determined for the transferee without regard to the annuity starting date, if any, of the transferor. In determining the transferee's investment in the contract, the aggregate amount of premiums or other consideration paid shall be reduced by all amounts received by the transferee before the receipt of an amount as an annuity or before the annuity starting date, whichever is the later, to the extent that such amounts were excludable from his gross income under the applicable income tax law at the time of receipt. For the treatment of amounts received by the transferee subsequent to both the annuity starting date and the date of receipt of a payment as an annuity, but not received as annuity payments, see § 1.72-11. For a limitation on adjustments to the basis of annuity contracts sold, see section 1021.

(b) In the case of a transfer of such a contract without valuable consideration, the annuity starting date and the expected return under the contract shall be determined as though no such transfer had taken place. See paragraph (b) of § 1.72-4.

The transferee shall include the aggregate of premiums or other consideration paid or deemed to have been paid by his transferor in the aggregate of premiums or other consideration as though paid by him. In determining the transferee's investment in the contract, the transferee's aggregate amount of premiums or other consideration paid (as so found) shall be reduced by all amounts either received or deemed to have been received by himself or his transferor before the annuity starting date, or before the date on which an amount is first received as an annuity, whichever is the later, to the extent that such amounts were excludable from the gross income of the actual recipient under the applicable income tax law at the time of receipt. For treatment of amounts received subsequent to both the above dates by such transferee, but not received as annuity payments, see § 1.72-11.

T.D. 6211, 11/14/56.

---

§ 1.72-11 Amounts not received as annuity payments.

Caution: The Treasury has not yet amended Reg § 1.72-11 to reflect changes made by P.L. 99-514, P.L. 98-369, P.L. 97-248.

(a) Introductory. *(1)* This section applies to amounts received under a contract to which section 72 applies if either:

(i) Paragraph (b) of § 1.72-2 is inapplicable to such amounts.

(ii) Paragraph (b) of § 1.72-2 is applicable but the annuity payments received differ either in amount, duration, or both, from those originally provided under the contract, or

(iii) Paragraph (b) of § 1.72 is applicable, but such annuity payments are received by a beneficiary after the death of an annuitant (or annuitants) in full discharge of the obligation under the contract and solely because of a guarantee.

The payments referred to in subdivision (i) of this subparagraph include all amounts other than "amounts received as an annuity" as that term is defined in paragraph (b)(2) and (3) of § 1.72-2. If such amounts are received as dividends or payments in the nature of dividends, or as a return of premiums, see paragraph (b) of this section. If such amounts are paid in full discharge of the obligation under the contract and are in the nature of a refund of the consideration, see paragraph (c) of this section. If such amounts are paid upon the surrender, redemption, or maturity of the contract, see paragraph (d) of this section. The payments referred to in subdivision (ii) of this subparagraph include all annuity payments which are paid as the result of a modification or an exchange of the annuity obligations originally provided under a contract for different annuity obligations (whether or not such modification or exchange is accompanied by the payment of an amount to which subdivision (i) of this subparagraph applies). If the duration of the new annuity obligations differs from the duration of the old annuity obligations, paragraph (e) of this section applies to the new annuity obligations and paragraph (d) of this section applies to any lump sum payment received. If, however, the duration of the new annuity obligations is the same as the duration of the old obligations, paragraph (f) of this section applies to the new obligations and to any lump sum received in connection therewith. The annuity payments referred to in subdivision (iii) of this subparagraph are annuity payments which are made to a beneficiary after the death of annuitant (or annuitants) in full discharge of the obligations under a contract because of a provision in the contract requiring the payment of a guaranteed amount or minimum number of payments for a fixed period; see paragraph (c) of this section.

(2) The principles of this section apply, to the extent appropriate thereto, to amounts paid which are taxable under section 72 (except, for taxable years beginning before January 1, 1964, section 72(e)(3)) in accordance with sections 402 and 403 and the regulations thereunder. However, if contributions used to purchase the contract include amounts for which a deduction was allowed under section 404 as contributions on behalf of an owner-employee, the rules of this section are modified by the rules of paragraph (b) of § 1.72-17. Further, in applying the provisions of this section, the aggregate premiums or other consideration paid shall not include contributions on behalf of self-employed individuals to the extent that deductions were allowed under section 404 for such contributions. Nor, shall the aggregate of premiums or other consideration paid include amounts used to purchase life, accident, health, or other insurance protection for an owner-employee. See paragraph (b)(4) of § 1.72-16 and paragraph (c) of § 1.72-17. The principles of this section also apply to payments made in the manner described in paragraph (b)(3)(i) of § 1.72-2.

(b) Amounts received in the nature of dividends or similar distributions. *(1)* If dividends (or payments in the nature of dividends or a return of premiums or other consideration) are received under a contract to which section 72 applies and such payments are received before the annuity starting date or before the date on which an amount is first received as an annuity, whichever is the later, such payments are includible in the gross income of the recipient only to the extent that they, taken together with all previous payments received under the contract which were excludable from the gross income of the recipient under the applicable income tax law, exceed the aggregate of premiums or other consideration paid or deemed to have been paid by the recipient. Such payments shall also be subtracted from the consideration paid (or deemed paid) both for the purpose of determining an exclusion ration to be applied to subsequent amounts paid as an annuity and for the purpose of determining the applicability of section 72(d) and § 1.72-13, relating to employee contributions recoverable in three years.

(2) If dividends or payments in the nature of dividends are paid under a contract to which section 72 applies and such payments are received on or after the annuity starting date or the date on which an amount is first received as an annuity, whichever is later, such payments shall be fully includible in the gross income of the recipient. The receipt of such payments shall not affect the aggregate of premiums or other consideration paid nor the amounts contributed or deemed to have been contributed by an employee as otherwise calcu-

lated for purposes of section 72. Since the investment in the contract and the expected return are not affected by a payment which is fully includible in the gross income of the recipient under this rule, the exclusion ratio will not be affected by such payment and will continue to be applied to amounts received as annuity payments in the future as though such payment had not been made. This subparagraph shall apply to amounts received under a contract described in paragraph (b)(3)(i) of § 1.72-2 to the extent that the amounts received exceed the portion of the investment in the contract allocable to each taxable year in accordance with paragraph (d)(3) of § 1.72-4. Hence, such excess is fully includible in the gross income of the recipient.

(c) Amounts received in the nature of a refund of the consideration under a contract and in full discharge of the obligation thereof. *(1)* Any amount received under a contract to which section 72 applies, if it is at least in part a refund of the consideration paid, including amounts payable to a beneficiary after the death of an annuitant by reason of a provision in the contract for a life annuity with minimum period of payments certain or with a minimum amount which must be paid in any event, shall be considered an amount received in the nature of a refund of the consideration paid for such contract. If such an amount is in full discharge of an obligation to pay a fixed amount (whether in a lump sum or otherwise) or to pay amounts for a fixed number of years (including amounts described in paragraph (b)(3)(i) of § 1.72-2), it shall be included in the gross income of the recipient only to the extent that it, when added to amounts previously received under the contract which were excludable from gross income under the law applicable at the time of receipt, exceeds the aggregate of premiums or other consideration paid. See section 73(e)(2)(A). This paragraph shall not apply if the total of the amounts to be paid in discharge of the obligation can in any event exceed the total of the annuity payments which would otherwise fully discharge the obligation. For rules to be applied in such a case, see paragraph (e) of this section.

(2) The principles of subparagraph (1) of this paragraph may be illustrated by the following examples:

Example (1). A, a male employee, retired on December 31, 1954, at the age of 60. A life annuity of $75 per month was payable to him beginning January 31, 1955. The annuity contract guaranteed that if A did not live for at least ten years after his retirement his beneficiary, B, would receive the monthly payments for any balance of such ten-year period which remained at the date of A's death. Under section 72, A was deemed to have paid $3,600 toward the cost of the annuity. A lived for five years after his retirement receiving a total of $4,500 in annuity payments. After A's death, B began receiving the monthly payments of $75 beginning with the January 31, 1960 payment. B will exclude such payments from his gross income throughout 1960, 1961, and 1962, and will exclude only $18 of the first payment in 1963 from his gross income for that year. Thereafter, B will include the entire amount of all such payments in his gross income for the taxable year of receipt. This result is determined as follows:

A's investment in the contract (unadjusted)	$3,600
Multiple from Table III of § 1.72-9 for male, age 60, where duration of guaranteed amount is 10 years (percent)	11
Subtract value of the refund feature to the nearest dollar (11 percent of $3,600)	396
Investment in the contract adjusted for the present value of the refund feature without discount for interest	3,204
Aggregate of premiums or other consideration paid	3,600
A's exclusion ratio ($3,204 ÷ $16,380 [$900 × 18.2]) (percent)	19.6
Subtract amount excludable during five years A received payments (19.6 percent of $4,500 [$999 × 5])	882
Remainder of aggregate of premiums or other consideration paid excludable from gross income of B under section 72(e)	2,718

As a result of the above computation, the number of payment to B which will exhaust the remainder of consideration paid which is excludable from gross income of the recipient is 36⁶⁄₂₅ ($2,718 ÷ $75) and B will exclude the payments from his gross income for three years, then exclude only $18 of the first payment for the fourth year from his gross income, and thereafter include the entire amount of all payments he receives in his gross income.

Example (2). The facts are the same as in example (1), except that B, the beneficiary, elects to receive $50 per month for his life in lieu of the payments guaranteed under the original contractual obligation. Since such amounts will be received as an annuity and may, because of the length of time B may live, exceed the amount guaranteed, they are not amounts to which this paragraph applies. See paragraph (e) of this section.

Example (3). The facts are the same as in example (1), except that B, the beneficiary, elects to receive the remaining guaranteed amount in installments which are larger or smaller than the $75 per months provided until, under the terms of the contract, the guaranteed amount is exhausted. The rule of subparagraph (1) of this paragraph and the computation illustrated in example (1) apply to such installments since the total of such installments will not exceed the original amount guaranteed to be paid at A's death in any event.

Example (4). C pays $12,000 for a contract providing that he is to be paid an annuity of $1,000 per year for 15 years. His exclusion ratio is therefore 80 percent ($12,000 ÷ $15,000). He directs that the annuity is to be paid to D, his beneficiary, if he should die before the full 15-year period has expired. C dies after 5 years and D is paid $1,000 in 1960. D will include $200 ($1,000 − $800 [80 percent of $1,000]) in his gross income for the taxable year in which he receives the $1,000 since section 72(e) and this section do not apply to the annuity payments made in accordance with the provisions and during the term of the contract, D will continue with the same exclusion ratio used by C (80 percent).

Example (5). In 1954, E paid $50,000 into a fund and was promised an annual income for life the amount of which would depend in part upon the earnings realized from the investment of the fund in accordance with an agreed formula. The contract also specified that if E should die before ten years had elapsed, his beneficiary, F, would be paid the amounts determined annually under the formula until ten payments had been received by E and F together. E died in 1960, having received five payments totaling $30,900. Assuming that $22,000 of this amount was properly excludable from E's gross income prior to his death. F will exclude from his gross income the payments he receives until the taxable year in which his total receipts from the fund exceed $28,000 ($50,000 − $22,000). F will include any excess over the $28,000 in his gross income for that taxable year. Thereafter, F will include in his gross income the entire amount of any payments made to him from the fund.

Example (6). Assume the facts are the same as in example (1), except that the total investment in the contract is made after June 30, 1986, that A is to receive payments under the life annuity contract beginning on January 31, 1987, and that B will begin to receive the monthly payments on January 31, 1992. B will exclude the $75 monthly payments from gross income throughout 1992, 1993, and 1994. B will exclude only the first two monthly payments and $21 of the third monthly payment in 1995. This is determined as follows:

A's investment in the contract (unadjusted)	$3,600
Multiple from Table VII, age 60, 10 years (percent)	4
Subtract value of the refund feature (4 percent of $3,600	$144
Investment in the contract adjusted for the present value of the refund feature without discount for interest	$3,456
Aggregate of premiums or other consideration paid	$3,600.00
A's exclusion ratio ($3,456 ÷ $21,780 [$900 × 24.2]) (percent)	15.9
Subtract amount excludable during five years A received payments (15.9 percent of $4,500 [$900 × 5])	$715.50
Remainder of aggregate of premiums or other consideration paid excludable from gross income of B under section 72(e)	$2,884.50

As a result of the above computation, the number of payments to B which will exhaust the remainder of consideration paid which is excludable from gross income of the recipient is 38 23/50 ($2,884.50 ÷ 75) and B will exclude the payments from gross income for three years, then exclude only the first two monthly payments and $34.50 of the third. Thereafter B shall include the entire amount of all payments received in gross income.

(3) For the purpose of applying the rule contained in subparagraph (1) of this paragraph, it is immaterial whether the recipient of the amount received in full discharge of the obligation is the same person as the recipient of amounts previously received under the contract which were excludable from gross income, except in the case of a contract transferred for a valuable consideration, with respect to which see paragraph (a) of § 1.72-10. For the limit on the tax, for taxable years beginning before January 1, 1964, attributable to the receipt of a lump sum to which this paragraph applies, see paragraph (g) of this section.

(d) Amounts received upon the surrender, redemption, or maturity of a contract. *(1)* Any amount received upon the surrender, redemption, or maturity of a contract to which section 72 applies, which is not received as an annuity under the regulations of paragraph (b) of § 1.72-2, shall be included in the gross income of the recipient to the extent that it, when added to amounts previously received under the contract and which were excludable from the gross income of the recipient under the law applicable at the time of receipt, exceeds the aggregate of premiums or other consideration paid. See section 72(e)(2)(B). If amounts are to be received as an annuity, whether in lieu of or in addition to amounts described in the preceding sentence, such amounts shall be included in the gross income of the recipient in accordance with the provisions of paragraph (e) or (f) of this section, whichever is applicable. The rule stated in the first sentence of this paragraph shall not apply to payments received as an annuity or otherwise after the date of the first receipt of an amount as an annuity subsequent to the maturity, redemption, or surrender of the original contract. If amounts are so received and are other than amounts received as an annuity, they are includible in the gross income of the recipient. See section 72(e)(1)(A) and paragraph (b)(2) of this section.

(2) For the purpose of applying the rule contained in subparagraph (1) of this paragraph, it is immaterial whether the recipient of the amount received upon the surrender, redemption, or maturity of the contract is the same as the recipient of amounts previously received under the contract which were excludable from gross income, except in the case of a contract transferred for a valuable consideration, with respect to which see paragraph (a) of § 1.72-10. For the limit on the amount of tax, for taxable years beginning before January 1, 1964, attributable to the receipt of certain lump sums to which this paragraph applies, see paragraph (g) of this section.

(e) Periodic payments received for a different term. If, after the date on which an amount is first received as an annuity under a contract to which section 72 applies, the terms of the contract are modified or the annuity obligations are exchanged so that periodic payments are to be received for a different term than originally provided under the contract (whether or not accompanied by the receipt of a lump sum to which paragraph (d) of this section applies), the rules of this paragraph shall apply to such payments. Hence, the provisions of section 72(e) and paragraphs (b), (c), (d), and (f) of this section are inapplicable for the purpose of determining the includibility of such payments in gross income and the general principles of section 72 with respect to the use of an exclusion ratio shall be applied to such payments as if they were provided under a new contract received in exchange for the contract providing the original annuity payments. If such payments are received as the result of the surrender, redemption, or discharge of a contract to which section 72 applies, they shall be considered to be received as an annuity under a contract exchanged for the contract whose redemption, surrender, or discharge was involved. For the purpose of determining the extent to which the payments so received are to be included in the gross income of the recipient, an exclusion ratio shall be determined for such contract as of the later of January 1, 1954, or the first day of the first period for which an amount is received as an annuity thereunder, whichever is the later. See paragraph (b) of § 1.72-4. In determining the investment in the contract for this purpose, any lump sum amount received at the time of the exchange shall not be considered an amount to which paragraph (a)(2) of § 1.72-6 applies. However, such lump sum shall be subtracted from the aggregate of premiums or other consideration paid to the extent it is excludable as an amount not received as an annuity under this section as if it were an amount received before the annuity starting date of the contract obtained in exchange.

(f) Periodic payments received for the same term after a lump sum withdrawal. *(1)* If, after the date of the first receipt of a payment as an annuity, the annuitant receives a lump sum and is thereafter to receive annuity payments in a reduced amount under the contract for the same term, life, or lives as originally specified in the contract, a portion of the contract shall be considered to have been surrendered or redeemed in consideration of the payment of such lump sum and the exclusion ratio originally determined for the contract shall continue to apply to the amounts received as an annuity without regard to the fact that such amounts are less than the original amounts which were to be paid periodically. The lump sum shall be includible in the gross income of the recipient in accordance with the provisions of subparagraph (2) of this paragraph. However, except in the case of amounts to which sections 402 and 403 apply, the tax, for taxable years beginning before January 1, 1964, attributable to the inclusion of all or part of the lump sum in gross income shall not exceed the amount determined under section 72(e)(3) and paragraph (g) of this section. For taxable years beginning after December 31, 1963, such amounts may be taken into account in computations under sections 1301 through 1305 (relating to income averaging).

(2) There shall be excluded from gross income that portion of the lump sum which bears the same ratio to the aggregate premiums or other consideration paid for the contract, as reduced by all amounts previously received under the contract and excludable from the gross income of the recipient under the applicable income tax law, as:

(i) In the case of payments to be made in the manner described in paragraph (b)(2) of § 1.71-2, the amount of the reduction in the annuity payments to be made thereafter bears to the annuity payments originally provided under the contract, or

(ii) In the case of a contract providing for payments to be made in the manner described in paragraph (b)(3)(i) of § 1.72-2, the amount of the reduction in the number of units per period to be paid thereafter bears to the number of units per period payable under the contract immediately before the lump sum withdrawal.

(3) This paragraph may be illustrated by the following examples:

Example (1). Taxpayer A pays $20,000 for an annuity contract providing for payments to him of $100 per month for his life. At the annuity starting date he has a life expectancy of 20 years. His expected return is therefore $24,000 and the exclusion ratio is five-sixths. He continues to receive the original annuity payments for 5 years, receiving a total of $6,000, and properly excludes a total of $5,000 from his gross income in his income tax returns for those years. At the beginning of the next year, A agrees with the insurer to take a reduced annuity of $75 per month and a lump sum payment of $4,000 in cash. Of the lump sum he receives, he will include $250 and exclude $3,750 from his gross income for his taxable year of receipt, determined as follows:

Aggregate of premiums or other consideration paid	$20,000
Less amounts received as an annuity to the extent they were excludable from A's income	$5,000
Remainder of the consideration	$15,000
Ratio of the reduction in the amount of the annuity payments to the original annuity payments	25/$100 or ¼
Lump sum received	$4,000
Less one-fourth of the remainder of the consideration (¼ of $15,000)	$3,750
Portion of the lump sum includible in gross income	$250

For taxable years beginning before January 1, 1964, the limit on tax of section 72(e)(3), as in effect before such date, applies to the portion of the lump sum includible in gross income. For taxable years beginning after December 31, 1963, such portion may be taken into account in computations under sections 1301 through 1305 (relating to income averaging). If, in this example, the annuity were a pension payable to A as a retired employee, but the facts were otherwise the same (assuming that, for instance, the $20,000 aggregate of premiums or other consideration paid were A's contributions as determined under section 72(f) and § 1.72-8) the result would be the same except that the tax attributable to the inclusion of the $250 in A's gross income, for taxable years beginning before January 1, 1964, would not be limited by section 72(e)(3), as in effect before such date. If such a lump sum is received in a taxable year beginning after December 31, 1963, the portion of such sum includible in gross income may be taken into account in computations under sections 1301 through 1305 (relating to income averaging).

Example (2). Taxpayer B pays $30,000 for a contract providing for monthly payments to be made to him for 15 years with respect to the principal and earnings of 10 units of an investment fund. B receives $12,000 during the first 5 years of participation and of this amount he has properly excluded a total of $10,000 from his gross income in his income returns for the taxable years, since $2,000 of $2,400 he received in each such year represented his investment divided by the term of the annuity ($30,000 ÷ 15). At the beginning of the 6th year, B agrees to take $11,000 in a lump sum and thereafter to accept the payments arising with respect to five units for the remaining 10 years of payments in full discharge of the original obligations of the contract. B shall include $1,000 in his gross income for the 6th year as the result of the lump sum he receives and allocates $1,000 of his original investment in the contract to each of the remaining 10 years with respect to the payments which will continue, determined as follows:

Aggregate of premiums or other consideration paid	$30,000
Total amount received and excludable from gross income	$10,000
Remainder of the consideration	$20,000
Ratio of units discontinued to the total units originally provided	5/10 or ½
Lump sum received at the time of reduction in the number of units to be paid	$11,000
Less one-half of the remainder of the consideration (½ of $20,000)	$10,000
Portion of the lump sum received and includible in gross income	$1,000
Remainder of the consideration less the portion of such remainder attributable to the excludable portion of the lump sum ($20,000 − $10,000)	$10,000
Remainder of the consideration properly allocable to each taxable year for the remaining 10 years ($10,000 ÷ 10)	$1,000

For the taxable years beginning before January 1, 1964, the limit on tax of section 72(e)(3), as in effect before such date, applies to the portion of the lump sum received and includible in gross income. For taxable years beginning after December 31, 1963, such portion may be taken into account in computations under sections 1301 through 1305 (relating to income averaging).

(g) Limit on tax attributable to the receipt of a lump sum. *(1)* For taxable years beginning before January 1,

1964, if the entire amount of the proceeds received upon the redemption, maturity, surrender, or discharge of a contract to which section 72 applies is received in a lump sum and paragraph (c), (d), or (f) of this section is applicable in determining the portion of such amount which is includible in gross income, the tax attributable to such portion shall not exceed the tax which would have been attributable thereto had such portion been received ratably in the taxable year in which received and the 2 preceding taxable years. The amount of tax attributable to the includible portion of the lump sum received shall be the lesser of:

(i) The difference between the amount of tax for the taxable year of receipt computed by including such portion in gross income and the amount of tax for such taxable year computed by excluding such portion from gross income; or

(ii) The difference between the total amount of tax for the taxable year of receipt and the 2 preceding taxable years computed by including one-third of such portion in gross income for each of the 3 taxable years, and the total amount of the tax for the taxable year of receipt and the 2 preceding taxable years computed by entirely excluding such portion from the gross income of all 3 taxable years.

For the definition of "taxable year", see section 441(b). This subparagraph shall not apply, for taxable years beginning before January 1, 1964, to payments excepted from the application of section 72(e)(3), as in effect before such date, under the provisions of section 402 or 403. See paragraph (a) of § 1.72-2 and paragraph (d) of § 1.72-14.

(2) For taxable years beginning after December 31, 1963, any amount includible in gross income to which this section relates may be taken into account in computations under sections 1301 through 1305 (relating to income averaging).

(h) Amounts deemed to be paid or received by a transferee. Amounts deemed to have been paid or received by a transferee for the purposes of § 1.72-10 shall also be deemed to have been so paid or received by such transferee for the purposes of this section. Thus, if a donee is deemed to have paid the premiums or other consideration actually paid by his transferor for the purposes of section 72(g) and paragraph (b) of § 1.72-10, such consideration shall be deemed premiums or other consideration paid by the donee for the purposes of this section.

T.D. 6211, 11/14/56, amend T.D. 6676, 9/16/63, T.D. 6885, 6/1/66, T.D. 8115, 12/16/86.

§ 1.72-12 Effect of taking an annuity in lieu of a lump sum upon the maturity of a contract.

If a contract to which section 72 applies provides for the payment of a lump sum in full discharge of the obligation thereunder and the obligee entitled thereto, prior to receiving any portion of such lump sum and within 60 days after the date on which such lump sum first becomes payable, exercises an option or irrevocably agrees with the obligor to take, in lieu thereof, payments which will constitute "amounts received as an annuity", as that term is defined in paragraph (b) of § 1.72-2, no part of such lump sum shall be deemed to have been received by the obligee at the time he was first entitled thereto merely because he would have been entitled to such amount had he not exercised the option or made such an agreement with the obligor.

T.D. 6211, 11/14/56.

§ 1.72-13 Special rule for employee contributions recoverable in three years.

Caution: The Treasury has not yet amended Reg § 1.72-13 to reflect changes made by P.L. 99-514, P.L. 97-34.

(a) Amounts received as an annuity. *(1)* Section 72(d) provides a special rule for the treatment of amounts received as an annuity by an employee (or by the beneficiary or beneficiaries of an employee) under a contract to which section 72 applies. This special rule is applicable only in the event that:

(i) At least part of the consideration paid for the contract is contributed by the employer, and

(ii) The aggregate amount receivable as an annuity under such contract by the employee (or by his beneficiary or beneficiaries if the employee died before any amount was received as an annuity under the contract) within the 3-year period beginning on the date (whether or not before January 1, 1954) on which an amount is first received as an annuity equals or exceeds the total consideration contributed (or deemed contributed under section 72(f) and § 1.72-8) by the employee as of such date as reduced by all amounts previously received and excludable from the gross income of the recipient under the applicable income tax law.

In such an event, section 72(d) provides that all amounts received as an annuity under the contract during a taxable year to which the Code applies shall be excluded from gross income until the total of the amounts excluded under that section plus all amounts excluded under prior income tax laws equals or exceeds the consideration contributed (or deemed contributed) by the employee. The excess, if any, and all amounts received by any recipient thereafter (whether or not received as an annuity), shall be fully included in gross income. See paragraph (b) of this section.

(2) If the aggregate amount receivable as an annuity under the contract within three years from the date on which an amount is first received as an annuity thereunder will not equal or exceed the consideration contributed (or deemed contributed) by the employee in accordance with the provisions of § 1.72-8, computed as of such date, the special rule of section 72(d) shall not apply to amounts received as an annuity under the contract and the general rules of section 72 shall apply thereto.

(3) The aggregate of the amounts receivable as an annuity within the prescribed 3-year period shall be the total of all annuity payments anticipatable by an employee (or a beneficiary or beneficiaries of an employee, if the employee died before any amount was received as an annuity) under the contract as a whole as defined in paragraph (a) of § 1.72-2. See paragraph (a)(3) of § 1.72-2 for rules for determining what constitutes "the contract" in the case of distributions from an employees' trust or plan.

(4) If subparagraphs (1) and (3) of this paragraph apply to amounts received as an annuity under a contract, the rule prescribed in subparagraph (1) of this paragraph shall apply to all amounts so received thereunder regardless of the fact that they may be payable (i) to more than one beneficiary, (ii) for the same or different intervals, (iii) in different sums, or (iv) for a different period certain life, or lives.

(5) For purposes of section 72(d), contributions which are made with respect to a self-employed individual and which are allowed as a deduction under section 404(a) are not considered contributions by the employee, but such contributions are considered contributions by the employer. A contribution which is deemed paid in a prior taxable year under

the provisions of section 404(a)(6) shall be considered made with respect to a self-employed individual if the individual on whose behalf the contribution is made was self-employed for the taxable year in which the contribution is deemed paid, whether or not such individual is self-employed at the time the contribution is actually paid. Contributions with respect to a self-employed individual who is an owner-employee used to purchase life, accident, health, or other insurance protection for such owner-employee shall not be treated as consideration for the contract contributed by the employee in computing the employee contributions for purposes of section 72(d).

(b) Amounts not received as an annuity. If the rule of paragraph (a) of this section applies to a contract and, after the date on which an annuity payment is first received, amounts are received other than as an annuity under such contract in a taxable year to which the Code applies, they shall be included in the gross income of the recipient in accordance with the provisions of § 1.72-11. Thus, if such amounts are received as a dividend or a similar distribution after the date on which an amount is first received as an annuity under the contract, they shall be included in the gross income of the recipient (in accordance with section 72(e)(1)(A) and paragraph (b)(2) of § 1.72-11. All other amounts not received as an annuity shall be included in the gross income of the recipient in accordance with the provisions of section 72(e)(1)(B) and paragraph (c), (d), or (f), whichever is applicable, of § 1.72-11. See section 72(e)(2).

(c) Amounts received after the exhaustion of employee contributions. *(1)* Amounts received under a contract to which the rule of paragraph (a) of this section applies (whether or not such amounts are received as an annuity) shall be included in the gross income of the recipient if such amounts are received after the date on which the aggregate of all amounts excluded from gross income by the recipients under section 72(d) and prior income tax laws equalled or exceeded the consideration contributed (or deemed contributed) by the employee.

(2) If the rule of paragraph (a) of this section applies to amounts received by an employee (or his beneficiary or beneficiaries) under a joint and survivor annuity contract, payments made to a prior annuitant may entirely exhaust the amounts excludable from gross income. In such case, amounts paid to the surviving annuitant (or annuitants) shall be included in gross income by such recipients.

(d) Application of section 72(d) to a contract, trust, or plan providing for payments in a manner described in paragraph (b)(3)(i) of § 1.72-2. For the purpose of applying section 72(d) and this section, any amount received in the nature of a periodic payment under a contract, trust, or plan which provides for the payment of amounts in a manner described in paragraph (b)(3)(i) of § 1.72-2 shall be considered an amount received as an annuity notwithstanding the provisions of any other section of the regulations under section 72. The special exclusion rule of section 72(d) and paragraph (a) of this section shall apply to all amounts so received if the first amount received, when multiplied by the number of periodic payments to be made within the three years beginning on the date of its receipt, results in an amount in excess of the aggregate premiums or other consideration contributed (or deemed contributed) by the employee as of that date. If more than one series of periodic payments is to be paid under the same contract, trust, or plan, all payments anticipatable, whether because fixed in amount or determinable in the manner described in the preceding sentence, shall be aggravated for the purpose of determining the applicability of section 72(d) to the contract, trust, or plan as a whole.

(e) Inapplicability of section 72(d) and this section. Section 72(d) and this section do not apply to:

(1) Amounts received as proceeds of a life insurance contract to which section 101(a) applies, nor to

(2) Amounts paid to a surviving annuitant under a joint and survivor annuity contract to which paragraph (b)(3) of § 1.72-5 applies, nor to

(3) Amounts paid to an annuitant under chapter 73 of title 10 of the United States Code with respect to which section 72(o) and § 1.122-1 apply.

See also paragraph (d) of § 1.72-14.

T.D. 6211, 11/14/56, amend T.D. 6497, 10/19/60, T.D. 6676, 9/16/63, T.D. 7043, 6/1/70.

PAR. 4. Section 1.72-13(e)(3) is amended by deleting "72(o)" and inserting in lieu thereof "72(n)". As amended § 1.72-13(e)(3) reads as follows:

Proposed § 1.72-13 Special rule for employee contributions recoverable in three years. [*For Preamble, see ¶ 150,135*]

• ***Caution:*** Proposed section 1.62-1 was finalized by TD 7399, 2/3/76. Proposed sections 1.72-4, 1.72-13, 1.101-2, 1.122-1, 1.402(a)-1, 1.402(e)-2, 1.402(e)-3, 1.403(a)-1, 1.403(a)-2, 1.405-3, 1.652(b)-1, 1.1304-2 and 11.402(e)(4)(B)-1 remain proposed.

* * * * *

(e) Inapplicability of section 72(d) and this section. Section 72(d) and this section do not apply to: * * *

(3) Amounts paid to an annuitant under chapter 73 of title 10 of the United States Code with respect to which section 72(n) and § 1.122-1 apply.

§ 1.72-14 Exceptions from application of principles of section 72.

Caution: The Treasury has not yet amended Reg § 1.72-14 to reflect changes made by P.L. 98-369, P.L. 87-792.

(a) Payments of interest. If any amount is received under an agreement to pay interest on a sum or sums held by the obligor, such amount shall not be excludable from the gross income of the recipient under the provisions of section 72 to the extent that it is an actual interest payment. See section 72(j). An amount shall be considered to be held under an agreement to pay interest thereon if the amount payable after the term of the annuity (whether for a term certain or for a life or lives) is substantially equal to or larger than the aggregate amount of premiums or other consideration paid therefor. For this purpose, however, the aggregate amount of premiums or other consideration paid shall include all contributions made by an employer and not merely those to which section 72(f) applies.

(b) Alimony payments. To the extent that payments made to a wife are includible in her gross income by reason of either or both sections 71 and 682, they shall not be excluded from the wife's gross income under the principles of section 72 although made under a contract to which that section applies. However, section 72 shall apply in the case of amounts received under such a contract if a husband and wife are entitled to make and do make a single return jointly.

(c) Certain "face-amount certificates." The principles of section 72 do not apply to "face-amount certificates" described in section 72(1) which were issued before January 1, 1955.

(d) Employer plans. The provisions of §§ 1.72-1 to 1.72-13, inclusive, shall be disregarded to the extent that they are inconsistent with the treatment of amounts received provided in section 402 (relating to the taxability of a beneficiary of an employees' trust), section 403 (relating to the taxation of employee annuities), or the regulations under either of such sections.

T.D. 6211, 11/14/56.

---

§ 1.72-15 Applicability of section 72 to accident or health plans.

Caution: The Treasury has not yet amended Reg § 1.72-15 to reflect changes made by P.L. 94-455.

(a) Applicability of section. This section provides the rules for determining the taxation of amounts received from an employer-established plan which provides for distributions that are taxable under section 72 (or for distributions that are taxable under section 402(a)(2) or (e), or section 403(a)(2), in the case of lump sum distributions) and which also provides for distributions that may be excludable from gross income under section 104 or 105 as accident or health benefits. For example, this section will apply to a pension plan described in section 401 and exempt under section 501 which provides for the payment of pensions at retirement and the payment of an earlier pension in the event of permanent disability. This section will also apply to a profit-sharing plan described in section 401 and exempt under section 501 which provides for periodic distribution of the amount standing to the account of a participant during any period that the participant is absent from work due to a personal injury or sickness and for the distribution of any balance standing to the account of the participant upon his separation from service. For purposes of this section, the term "contributions of the employee" includes contributions by the employer which were includible in the employee's gross income. For special rules for taxable years ending before January 27, 1975, relating to certain accident or health benefits which were treated as distributions to which section 72 applied, see paragraph (i) of this section.

(b) General rule. Section 72 does not apply to any amount received as an accident or health benefit, and the tax treatment of any such amount shall be determined under sections 104 and 105. See paragraphs (c) and (d) of this section, paragraph (d) of § 1.104-1, and §§ 1.105-1 through 1.105-5. Section 72 (or, in the case of certain total distributions, section 402(a)(2) or section 403(a)(2)) does not apply to any amount which is received under a plan to which this section applies and which is not an accident or health benefit. See paragraph (e) of this section.

(c) Accident or health benefits attributable to employee contributions. *(1)* If a plan to which this section applies provides that any portion of the accident or health benefits is attributable to the contributions of the employee to such plan, then such portion of such benefits is excludable from gross income under section 104(a)(3) and paragraph (d) of § 1.104-1. Neither section 72 nor section 105 applies to any accident or health benefits (whether paid before or after retirement) attributable to contributions of the employee. Since such portion is excludable under section 104(a)(3), such portion is not subject to the dollar limitation of section 105(d) and if such portion is payable after the retirement of the employee, it is excludable without regard to the provisions of § 1.105-4 and section 72.

(2) In determining the taxation of any amounts received as accident or health benefits from a plan to which this section applies, the first step is to determine the portion, if any, of the contributions of the employee which is used to provide the accident or health benefits and the portion of the accident or health benefits attributable to such portion of the employee's contributions. If such a plan expressly provides that the accident or health benefits are provided in whole or in part by employee contributions and the portion of employee contributions to be used for such purpose, the contributions so used will be treated as used to provide accident or health benefits. However, if the plan does not expressly provide that the accident or health benefits are to be provided with employee contributions and the portion of employee contributions to be used for such purpose, it will be presumed that none of the employee contributions is used to provide such benefits. Thus, in the case of a contributory pension plan, it will be presumed that the disability pension is provided by employer contributions, unless the plan expressly provides otherwise, or in the case of a contributory profit-sharing plan providing that a portion of the amount standing to the account of each participant will be used to purchase accident or health insurance, it will be presumed that such insurance is purchased with employer contributions, unless the plan expressly provides otherwise. Similarly, unless the plan expressly provides otherwise, it will be presumed that if a contributory profit-sharing plan provides for periodic distributions from the account of a participant during any absence from work because of a personal injury or sickness, all such distributions which do not exceed the contributions of the employer plus earnings thereon are provided by employer contributions.

(3) Any employee contributions that are treated under subparagraph (2) of this paragraph as used to provide accident or health benefits shall not be included for any purpose under section 72 as employee contributions or as aggregate premiums or other consideration paid. Thus, in the case of a pension plan, or in the case of a profit-sharing plan providing that a portion of the amount standing to the account of each participant will be used to purchase accident or health insurance, any employee whose contributions are so used must make the adjustment provided by this subparagraph irrespective of whether such employee receives any accident or health benefits under such plan. However, in the case of a profit-sharing plan providing for periodic distributions from the account of a participant during any absence from work because of a personal injury or sickness, an adjustment under this subparagraph is required only when an employee receives distributions in excess of the employer contributions and earnings thereon or receives distributions consisting in whole or in part of his own contributions.

(4) If any of the employee contributions are treated under subparagraph (2) of this paragraph as used to provide any of the accident or health benefits, the portion of the benefits attributable to employee contributions shall be determined in accordance with § 1.105-1. Any accident or health benefits that are excludable under section 104(a)(3) shall not be included in the expected return for purposes of section 72.

(d) Accident or health benefits attributable to employer contributions. Any amounts received as accident or health benefits and not attributable to contributions of the employee are includible in gross income except to the extent that such amounts are excludable from gross income under section 105(b), (c), or (d) and the regulations thereunder. Thus, such amounts may be excludable under section 105(d) as payments under a wage continuation plan. However, if such payments, when added to other such payments attributable to employer contributions, exceed the limitations of section 105(d), then the excess is includible in gross income under section 105(a). Such excess is not excludable under section 72. See, however, paragraph (1) of this section, for special rules for taxable years ending before January 27, 1975, relating to certain accident or health benefits which were treated as distributions to which section 72 applied.

(e) Other benefits under the plan. The taxability of amounts that are received under a plan to which this section applies and that are not accident or health benefits is determined under section 72 (or, in the case of certain total distributions, under section 402(a)(2) or section 403(a)(2)) without regard to any exclusion or inclusion of accident or health benefits under sections 104 and 105. For example, the investment in the contract or aggregate premiums paid is determined without regard to the exclusion of any amount under section 104 or 105, and the annuity starting date is determined without regard to the receipt of any accident or health benefits. However, if any employee contributions are used to provide any accident or health benefits, the investment in the contract or aggregate premiums paid must be adjusted as provided in paragraph (c)(3) of this section.

(f) Examples. The principles of this section may be illustrated by the following examples:

Example (1). A, an employee, is a participant in a contributory pension plan described in section 401(a) and exempt under section 501(a). Such plan provides for the payment of a pension to each participant when he retires at age 65 or when he retires earlier if the retirement is due to permanent and total disability. In 1964, A, who was age 52, became totally and permanently disabled because of an injury, was hospitalized, and commenced to receive a pension of $74 a week under this plan. The weekly amounts received by A do not exceed 75 percent of his "regular weekly rate of wages" under section 105(d). A had contributed $11,500 to the plan. The plan does not expressly provide that any portion of the disability pension is purchased with employee contributions. Accordingly, it is presumed that no portion of the disability pension is purchased with A's contributions. The disability pension which A receives qualifies as payments under a wage continuation plan for purposes of section 105(d) and § 1.105-4, and if such payments are the only accident or health benefits which are attributable to the contributions of his employer, such payments are entirely excludable under section 105(d) until A reaches age 65, his mandatory retirement age under the plan. The payments which A receives after he becomes 65 are taxable under section 72. The payments which A receives do constitute an annuity as defined in paragraph (b) of § 1.72-2, but since the amounts which he will receive during the first three years after attaining age 65 exceed his contributions, he shall exclude under § 1.72-13 the entire amount of all payments that he receives as an annuity after attaining age 65 until such amounts equal his contributions to the plan, or $11,500. Thereafter, the payments that he receives under the plan are includible in gross income.

Example (2). B, an employee, is a participant in a contributory profit-sharing plan described in section 401(a) and exempt under section 501(a). Such plan provides that, in the event a participant is absent from work because of a personal injury or sickness, he will be paid $125 a week out of his account in such plan. Such weekly amount does, not exceed 75 percent of B's "regular weekly rate of wages" under section 105(d). Any amount standing to the account of a participant at the time of his separation from service will be paid to him at such time. During 1964, B incurred a personal injury, was hospitalized, and as a result was absent from work for nine weeks. He received nine weekly payments of $125, or a total of $1,125, on account of such absence from work. At the time B was injured, he had contributed $5,000 to the plan. The plan did not expressly provide that a participant's contributions are to be used to provide for the distributions during disability. Accordingly, it is presumed that B's contributions were not used to provide the accident or health benefits under the plan. Since these weekly payments are paid because of B's absence from work due to the injury, and since such payments are considered as attributable to contributions of his employer, such payments are required under section 105(a) to be included in B's gross income except to the extent that they are excludable under section 105(d). If B receives no other payments under a wage continuation plan attributable to contributions of his employer, during the first 30 days in the period of absence $75 of each weekly payment is excludable from gross income under section 105(d), but $50 of each weekly payment is includible in gross income under section 105(a). Amounts attributable to the period of absence in excess of 30 days are excludable from gross income under section 105(d) to the extent of $100 a week and includible in gross income under section 105(a) to the extent of $25 a week. The excludable portion of payments does not reduce B's investment in the contract or the amount of premiums considered to have been paid by B for purposes of any subsequent computations under section 72.

Example (3). The facts are the same as in example (2) except that B was absent from work for 130 weeks. At the time B was injured, his employer had contributed $10,000 to the plan on his account, and $6,000 of earnings of the plan had been allocated to his account. Thus, at the time he was injured, B's account included $21,000, and $14,000 of such amount consists of employer contributions of $10,000 plus earnings of $4,000 thereon. The first 112 weekly payments (totaling $14,000) which B receives are treated in the manner set forth in example (2). However, since the remaining payments exceed the employer contributions plus earnings thereon, such remaining payments are considered to be distributions of B's contributions plus earnings thereon. Since the total of such payments, or $2,250, is less than B's contributions to the plan, $5,000, the entire amount of such payments is excludable from B's gross income, but a corresponding adjustment with respect to the return of B's contributions shall be made to his consideration in determining the taxation of any lump sum paid to B upon separation from service.

(g) Payments to or on behalf of a self-employed individual. A self-employed individual is not considered an employee for purposes of section 105, relating to amounts received by employees under accident and health plans, nor for purposes of excluding under section 104(a)(3) amounts received by him under an accident and health plan as referred to in section 105(e). See section 105(g) and paragraph (a) of § 1.105-1. Therefore, the other paragraphs of this section are not applicable to amounts received by or on behalf of a self-employed individual. Except where accident or health benefits are provided through an insurance contract or an arrangement having the effect of insurance, all amounts received by or on behalf of a self-employed individual from a plan described in section 401(a) and exempt under section 501(a) or a plan described in section 403(a) shall be taxed as otherwise provided in section 72, 402, or 403. If the accident or health benefits are paid under an insurance contract or under an arrangement having the effect of insurance, section 104(a)(3) shall apply. Section 72 shall not apply to any amounts received under such circumstances. For the treatment of the amounts paid for such accident or health benefits, see section 404(e)(3) and paragraph (f) of § 1.404(e)-1.

(h) Medical benefits for retired employees, etc. Employer contributions to provide medical benefits described in section 401(h) under a qualified pension or annuity plan are not includible in the gross income of the employee on whose behalf such contributions were made. Similarly, if the trustee of a trust forming a part of a qualified pension plan applies employer contributions which have been contributed to provide medical benefits described in section 401(h) or earnings thereon, to purchase insurance contracts which provide such benefits, the amount so applied is not includible in the gross income of the employee on whose behalf such insurance was purchased. The payment of medical benefits described in section 401(h) as defined in paragraph (a) of § 1.401-14 under a plan established by an employer shall be treated in the same manner as the payment of any other accident or health benefits under an employer-established plan. See paragraphs (b), (c), and (d) of this section.

(i) Special rules. *(1) Special rule for taxable years ending before January 27, 1975.* A taxpayer who has reached retirement age, as defined in § 1.79-2(b)(3) (hereinafter referred to as "initial retirement age"), before January 27, 1975, and who has received payments under a plan described in paragraph (a) of this section, which are wage continuation benefits to which section 105(d) and this section apply, or which are treated as such by reason of the employee having so agreed under § 1.105-6, shall be entitled to an exclusion, in taxable years ending before January 27, 1975, with respect to payments received after initial retirement age but before mandatory retirement age, as defined in § 1.105-4(a)(3)(i)(B), which is the greater of:

(i) the amount actually excluded on an original return under section 72(b) or (d) with respect to payments received after initial retirement age, to the extent such amount does not exceed an amount properly excludable under section 72(b) or (d) if this paragraph and paragraph (b) of this section did not apply; or

(ii) the amount that would have been properly excludable under section 105(d) during the same period.

(2) Investment in the annuity contract. A taxpayer described in paragraph (i)(1) of this section, shall redetermine his investment in, consideration for, or basis of his annuity contract (hereinafter referred to in this paragraph as the "investment in the contract") in accordance with the applicable rules of section 72 and the regulations thereunder, and the rules of this paragraph. In making such redetermination the taxpayer's investment in his contract shall be decreased, by the excess (if any) of the amount which the taxpayer is entitled to exclude under paragraph (i)(1) of this section over the amount which could have been excluded under section 105(d) (subject to the limitations contained in such provision). Such investment in the contract shall be decreased only by the excess of the amount excluded under section 72 in taxable years ending before January 27, 1975, over the amount which could have been excluded under section 105(d) during the same period. For example, the investment in the contract shall not be decreased in the case of an individual who was retired from work on account of injury or sickness for a full taxable year, if the amount excluded under section 72 was less than $5,200, since the entire amount could have been excluded under section 105(d). On the other hand, if the amount excluded under section 72 was equal to or greater than $5,200 for a full taxable year, for example, $6,000 for the full taxable year, then $5,200 shall be treated as excluded under section 105(d) and the investment in the contract shall be reduced by $800 ($6,000 – $5,200).

(3) Surviving annuitants and beneficiaries. (i) The rights of a surviving annuitant or beneficiary, with respect to the application of the rules of section 72, shall be based on the employee's investment in his annuity contract, as adjusted in accordance with the provisions of this paragraph. Thus, where an employee dies after having recomputed his investment as provided in paragraph (i)(2) of this section, and his contract provided a survivorship element, the survivor would assume the employee's recomputed investment for purposes of determining excludability of amounts under section 72.

(ii) Where a beneficiary failed to increase the amount treated as an employee's contribution toward his annuity contract to reflect the employee death benefit under section 101(b) and § 1.72-8(b), because the employee had treated his initial retirement age as his annuity starting date, such beneficiary may apply section 101(b) as if the appropriate addition to basis had been made in the year of the employee's death, but only if the employee had not reached his mandatory retirement age (as defined in section 105-4(a)(3)(i)(B)). For purposes of this paragraph, the amount treated as the section 101(b) death benefit would be valued as of the date of the employee's death.

(4) Records. (i) For purposes of section 72(b) and (d), and this section, the taxpayer shall maintain such records as are necessary to substantiate the amount treated as his investment in his annuity contract.

(ii) The Commissioner may prescribe a form and instructions with respect to the taxpayer's past and current treatment of amounts received under section 72 or 105, and the taxpayer's computation, or recomputation, of his investment in his annuity contract. Such form may be required to be filed with the taxpayer's returns for years in which amounts are excluded under section 72 or 105.

(5) Cross references. (i) See section 72(b)(4) and § 1.72-4(b) with respect to annuity starting dates.

(ii) See §§ 1.72-8(b) and 1.101-2(a)(2) with respect to treating certain amounts received by an estate or beneficiary as employee death benefits.

(iii) See § 1.105-4(a)(3)(i)(B) for the definition of "mandatory retirement age."

(iv) See § 1.105-6 with respect to the application of section 105(d) to certain amounts received as retirement annuities before January 27, 1975, where the employee would otherwise have been eligible for benefits to which section 105(d) applies.

(6) Examples. The provisions of this paragraph may be illustrated by the following examples. In such examples assume that the plan does not expressly provide that any portion of the disability pension is purchased with employee contributions. Accordingly, it is presumed that no portion of the disability pension is purchased with employee contributions. Also, assume that in each case the taxpayer retired only after he had been absent from work for at least 30 days on account of personal injuries or sickness:

Example (1). A, a calendar year taxpayer, retired because of disability on January 1, 1968, his 58th birthday, receiving $80 per week ($4,160 per year) under a plan which qualifies as a wage continuation plan under section 105(d) and § 1.105-4. Under the plan, A's initial retirement age is age 60 (January 1, 1970), and his mandatory retirement age is 65 (January 1, 1975). A's consideration for the contract was $10,000. For payments received in 1968 and 1969 A excluded the entire amount under section 105(d). Payments received with respect to periods after A's initial retirement age (January 1, 1970) were excluded under section 72(d) until his entire $10,000 consideration for his contract had been excluded. Thus, A applied section 72(d) to exclude $4,160 each year for taxable years 1970 and 1971, and $1,680 ($10,000 – ($4,160 + $4,160)) for 1972. In late 1974 A realized that he was entitled to treat the full amount received under his annuity as excludable under section 105(d) rather than section 72 for the taxable years 1970 through 1974. Consequently, A filed amended returns for 1972 and 1973 excluding an additional $2,480 ($4,160 – $1,680) and $4,160, respectively, claiming refunds based upon such additional exclusions. Moreover, A's annuity starting date is January 1, 1975 (A's mandatory retirement age), and he excludes under section 72(d) for 1975, 1976, and 1977, $4,160, $4,160 and $1,680 ($10,000 – ($4,160 + $4,160)), respectively.

Example (2). B, a calendar year taxpayer retired because of disability, July 1, 1970, on his 58th birthday, receiving $1,000 per month under a plan which qualifies as a wage continuation plan for purposes of section 105(d) and § 1.105-4. Under the plan, B's initial retirement age is age 60 (July 1, 1972), and his mandatory retirement age is 65 (July 1, 1977). B's consideration for the contract was $25,000. For payments received in 1970 and 1971 B excluded under section 105(d) $2,600 and $5,200, respectively, of the $6,000 (6 × $1,000) and $12,000 (12 × $1,000) received under the plan. For the period January 1, 1972, through June 30, 1972, B excluded an additional $2,600 under section 105(d). For the period July 1, 1972 through December 31, 1972, B excluded under section 72(d)(1) the entire $6,000 in payments received under the plan. Similarly, under section 72(d)(1), B excluded the entire $12,000 in payments received under the plan in 1973, and in 1974 B excluded the remaining $7,000 of his annuity basis. In 1975, B realized that he will be entitled to take full advantage of the exclusion under section 105(d) for periods through June 30, 1977, when he would reach age 65. B need not file amended returns for 1972, 1973, and 1974, even though the amounts he excluded under section 72(d) (exceeded the amount he was entitled to exclude under section 105(d)). He must, however, recompute the amount that will be treated as his investment in his annuity contract. Thus, on July 1, 1977, B's annuity starting date, his investment in his annuity contract would be $13,000, recomputed as follows:

B's original investment	$25,000
Less amounts excluded under section 72 to the extent they exceed amounts that would have been excludable during the same period under section 105(d):	
1972 ($6,000 – 2,600)	3,400
1973 ($12,000 – 5,200)	6,800
1974 ($7,000 – 5,200)	1,800
Total	$12,000
B's recomputed investment in his annuity contract	13,000

Example (3). Assume the same facts as in example (2) except that B's investment in his annuity contract is $37,000, and he excluded under section 72(b) 16.9 percent, or $2,028, of the $12,000 received per year. Thus, for the period July 1, 1972 through December 31, 1972, B excluded under section 72(b) $1,014 (16.9 percent of $6,000), and $2,028 in both 1973 and 1974. B files amended returns for 1972, 1973 and 1974 claiming the exclusion under section 105(d). Thus, B restored to income $1,014 for 1972, and $2,028 for both 1973 and 1974, claiming $2,600 ($5,200 – $2,600) exclusion under section 105(d) for 1972 and a $5,200 exclusion in both 1973 and 1974. Thus, for 1972 B is entitled to an additional exclusion of $1,586 ($2,600 – $1,014), and, for both 1973 and 1974, an additional exclusion of $3,172 ($5,200 – $2,028). On July 1, 1977, B's investment in the contract is $37,000.

Example (4). C, a calendar year taxpayer, retired because of disability on January 1, 1965, his 58th birthday, receiving payments of $500 per month under a plan which qualifies as a wage continuation plan for purposes of section 105(d) and § 1.105-4. C had contributed $18,000 toward the cost of his annuity contract. Under the plan, C's initial retirement age is age 60 (January 1, 1967) and C's mandatory retirement age is age 70 (January 1, 1977). For taxable years 1965 and 1966 C excluded from gross income under section 105(d) $5,200 of the $6,200 (12 × $500) he received from his employer as wage continuation benefits. On January 1, 1967, C began excluding all of the benefits C received in accordance with the rules of section 72(d). Thus, for 1967, 1968 and 1969, C excluded 100 percent of the annuity payments. For his taxable years 1970 through 1973, C included in his gross income all annuity payments. In 1974, C realized that he will be entitled to use the exclusion under section 105(d) through December 31, 1976 (until he reaches age 70). In 1974, C filed a timely claim for refund for his taxable years 1971, 1972 and 1973 (refunds for taxable year 1970 and prior years were barred by the statute of limitations), and continues to claim the exclusion under section 105(d) for 1974, 1975 and 1976. For 1977, C treats January 1, 1977, as the annuity starting date, and treats $15,600 as the investment in the contract. The $15,600 represents the $18,000 original investment in the contract reduced by the excess of $2,400, of the amount excluded under section 72 for 1967, 1968 and 1969 ($18,000) over the amount excludable under section 105(d) ($5,200 × 3) for such years.

Example (5). (i) D, a calendar year taxpayer, retired because of disability on June 30, 1965, receiving $100 per month under a plan which qualifies as a wage contribution plan for purposes of section 105(d) and § 1.105-4. Under the plan, the initial retirement age of D, whose birthday is January 1, is age 60 (January 1, 1967), and D's mandatory retirement age is age 70 (January 1, 1977). D had contributed $6,000 toward the cost of the annuity contract under such plan. For 1965 and 1966, D excluded under section 105(d) the entire amount received under the plan ($600 and $1,200 respectively). For 1967 through 1973, D excluded $330 per year under section 72(b), or 27.5 percent of the $1,200 payment received under the plan per year.

(ii) In 1974, D realized that he will be entitled to use the exclusion provided in section 105(d) up until January 1, 1977, when he reaches his mandatory retirement age, and that he improperly applied section 72 to payments received in the years 1967 through 1973. In 1974, D filed a timely claim for refund with respect to the section 105(d) wage continuation benefits, for 1971, 1972 and 1973 (refunds for taxable year 1970 and prior years were barred by the statute of limitations), and continues to claim the section 105(d) exclusion for 1974, 1975 and 1976. D is entitled to an additional exclusion of $870 ($1,200 − $330) for each of the years 1971, 1972 and 1973.

(iii) Upon reaching mandatory retirement age on January 1, 1977, D treats such date as the annuity starting date, and treats $6,000 as the investment in the contract. The investment in the contract is not reduced, because the amount excluded under section 72(b) for 1967 through 1970 ($330 per year) does not exceed the amount excludable under section 105(d) ($1,200 per year), and the $330 per year excluded for 1971, 1972, and 1973 were restored to the investment in the contract. Therefore, assuming that D would be entitled to exclude 41.3 percent of the payments under the plan if the annuity starting date is January 1, 1977, D would be entitled to exclude $495.60 (41.3 percent of $1,200) per annum.

Example (6). Assume the facts stated in example (5) except that D's investment in his annuity contract is $100,000 and he received payments equaling $10,000 per year. Assume also, that D had excluded under section 72(b) 54.9 percent of the payments received under the plan through 1974. Consequently, he excluded $5,490 (54.9 percent of $10,000) from his gross income for the years 1967 through 1974. D need not file amended returns for 1971, 1972, 1973, and 1974, even though the amount he excluded under section 72(b) exceeded the amounts he was entitled to exclude under section 105(d). He must, however, recompute the amount that will be treated as his investment in his annuity contract. Thus, on January 1, 1977, D's annuity starting date, his investment in his annuity contract would be $97,680. This figure represents the original investment ($100,000) reduced by the amount excluded under section 72(b) for the years 1967-1974 (8 × $5,490 = $43,920) over the amount properly excludable during those years under section 105(d) ($5,200 × 8 = $41,600).

Example (7). Assume the same facts as in example (6) except that D's mandatory retirement age is 63 (January 1, 1970). D would redetermine his exclusion ratio for purposes of section 72(b) as of January 1, 1970, since D's mandatory retirement age is D's annuity starting date. D would treat $99,130 as his investment in his annuity contract as of such date for purposes of section 72(b). Assuming refunds for 1970 and prior taxable years were barred by the statute of limitations, the $99,130 represents the original investment of $100,000 reduced by the excess of the amount excluded under section 72(b) for 1967, 1968, and 1969 ($5,490 × 3 = $16,470) over the amount otherwise excludable during those years under section 105(d) ($5,200 × 3 = $15,600). Therefore, assuming that D would be entitled to exclude 61.2 of the payments received under the plan if the annuity starting date is January 1, 1970, D would be entitled to exclude $6,120 (61.2 percent of the $10,000 received under the plans) per annum for 1971 and subsequent years. However, D is not entitled to exclude the additional $630 ($6,120 − $5,490) for 1970, because credit or refund for 1970 and prior years is barred by the statute of limitations.

T.D. 6485, 7/29/60, amend T.D. 6676, 9/16/63, T.D. 6722, 4/13/64, T.D. 6770, 11/16/64, T.D. 7352, 4/9/75.

PAR. 2. Section 1.72-15 is amended by:

1. Revising paragraphs (d), (h), and (i).
2. Removing and reserving paragraph (f).

The revisions read as follows:

Proposed § 1.72-15 Applicability of section 72 to accident or health plans. [*For Preamble, see ¶ 152,901*]

* * * * *

(d) Accident or health benefits attributable to employer contributions. Any amounts received as accident or health benefits and not attributable to contributions of the employee are includible in gross income except to the extent that such amounts are excludable from gross income under section 105(b) or (c) and the regulations thereunder. See § 1.402(a)-1(e) for rules relating to the use of a qualified plan under section 401(a) to pay premiums for accident or health insurance.

* * * * *

(h) Medical benefits for retired employees, etc. See § 1.402(a)-1(e)(2) for rules relating to the payment of medical benefits described in section 401(h) under a qualified pension or annuity plan.

(i) Special rules. *(1) In general.* For purposes of section 72(b) and (d), and this section, the taxpayer shall maintain such records as are necessary to substantiate the amount treated as an investment in the taxpayer's annuity contract.

(2) Delegation to Commissioner. The Commissioner may prescribe a form and instructions with respect to the taxpayer's past and current treatment of amounts received under section 72 or 105, and the taxpayer's computation, or recomputation, of the taxpayer's investment in his or her annuity contract. This form may be required to be filed with the taxpayer's returns for years in which such amounts are excluded under section 72 or 105.

§ 1.72-16 Life insurance contracts purchased under qualified employee plans.

Caution: The Treasury has not yet amended Reg § 1.72-16 to reflect changes made by P.L. 104-188.

(a) Applicability of section. This section provides rules for the tax treatment of premiums paid under qualified pension, annuity, or profit-sharing plans for the purchase of life insurance contracts and rules for the tax treatment of the proceeds of such a life insurance contract and of annuity contracts purchased under such plans. For purposes of this section, the term "life insurance contract" means a retirement income, an endowment, or other contract providing life insurance protection. The rules of this section apply to plans covering only common-law employees as well as to plans covering self-employed individuals.

(b) Treatment of cost of life insurance protection. *(1)* The rules of this paragraph are applicable to any life insurance contract—

(i) Purchased as a part of a plan described in section 403(a), or

(ii) Purchased by a trust described in section 401(a) which is exempt from tax under section 501(a) if the proceeds of such contract are payable directly or indirectly to a participant in such trust or to a beneficiary of such participant. The proceeds of a contract described in subdivision (ii) of this subparagraph will be considered payable indirectly to a participant or beneficiary of such participant where they are payable to the trustee but under the terms of the plan the trustee is required to pay over all of such proceeds to the beneficiary.

(2) If under a plan or trust described in subparagraph (1) of this paragraph, amounts which were allowed as a deduction under section 404, or earnings of the trust, are applied

toward the purchase of a life insurance contract described in subparagraph (1) of this paragraph, the cost of the life insurance protection under such contract shall be included in the gross income of the participant for the taxable year or years in which such contributions or earnings are so applied.

(3) If the amount payable upon death at any time during the year exceeds the cash value of the insurance policy at the end of the year, the entire amount of such excess is considered current life insurance protection. The cost of such insurance will be considered to be a reasonable net premium cost, as determined by the Commissioner, for such amount of insurance for the appropriate period.

(4) The amount includible in the gross income of the employee under this paragraph shall be considered as premiums or other consideration paid or contributed by the employee only with respect to any benefits attributable to the contract (within the meaning of paragraph (a)(3) of § 1.72-2) providing the life insurance protection. However, if under the rules of this paragraph an owner-employee is required to include any amounts in his gross income, such amounts shall not in any case be treated as part of his investment in the contract.

(5) The determination of the cost of life insurance protection may be illustrated by the following example:

Example. An annual premium policy purchased by a qualified trust for a common-law employee provides an annuity of $100 per month upon retirement at age 65, with a minimum death benefit of $10,000. The insurance payable if death occurred in the first year would be $10,000. The cash value at the end of the first year is 0. The net insurance is therefore $10,000 minus 0, or $10,000. Assuming that the Commissioner has determined that a reasonable net premium cost for the employee's age is $5.85 per $1,000, the premium for $10,000 of life insurance is therefore $58.50, and this is the amount to be reported as income by the employee for his taxable year in which the premium is paid. The balance of the premium is the amount contributed for the annuity, which is not taxable to the employee under a plan meeting the requirements of section 401(a), except as provided under section 402(a). Assuming that the cash value at the end of the second year is $500, the net insurance would then be $9,500 for the second year. With a net 1-year term rate of $6.30 for the employee's age in the second year, the amount to be reported as income to the employee would be $59.85.

(6) This paragraph shall not apply if the trust has a right under any circumstances to retain any part of the proceeds of the life insurance contract. But see paragraph (c)(4) of this section relating to the taxability of the distribution of such proceeds to a beneficiary.

(c) Treatment of proceeds of life insurance and annuity contracts. *(1)* If under a qualified pension, annuity, or profit-sharing plan, there is purchased either—

(i) A life insurance contract described in paragraph (b)(1) of this section, and the employee either paid the cost of the insurance or was taxable on the cost of the insurance under paragraph (b) of this section, or

(ii) An annuity contract,

the amounts payable under any such contract by reason of the death of the employee are taxable under the rules of subparagraph (2) of this paragraph, except in the case of a joint and survivor annuity.

(2) (i) In the case of an annuity contract, the death benefit is the accumulation of the premiums (plus earnings thereon) which is intended to fund pension or other deferred benefits under a pension, annuity, or profit-sharing plan. Such death benefits are not in the nature of life insurance and are not excludable from gross income under section 101(a).

(ii) In the case of a life insurance contract under which there is a reserve accumulation which is intended to fund pension or other deferred benefits under a pension, annuity, or profit-sharing plan, such reserve accumulation constitutes the source of the cash value of the contract and approximates the amount of such cash value. The portion of the proceeds paid upon the death of the insured employee which is equal to the cash value immediately before death is not excludable from gross income under section 101(a). The remaining portion, if any, of the proceeds paid to the beneficiary by reason of the death of the insured employee—that is, the amount in excess of the cash value—constitutes current insurance protection and is excludable under section 101(a).

(iii) The death benefit under an annuity contract, or the portion of the death proceeds under a life insurance contract which is equal to the cash value of the contract immediately before death, constitutes a distribution under the plan consisting in whole or in part of deferred compensation and is taxable to the beneficiary in accordance with section 72(m)(3) and the provisions of this paragraph, except to the extent that the limited exclusion from income provided in section 101(b) is applicable.

(iv) In the case of a life insurance contract under which the benefits are paid at a date or dates later than the death of the employee, section 101(d) is applicable only to the portion of the benefits which is attributable to the amount excludable under section 101(a). The portion of such benefits which is attributable to the cash value of the contract immediately before death is taxable under section 72, and in such case, any amount excludable under section 101(b) is treated as additional consideration paid by the employee in accordance with section 101(b)(2)(D).

(3) The application of the rules under subparagraph (2) of this paragraph with respect to the taxability of proceeds of a life insurance contract paid by reason of the death of an insured common-law employee who has paid no contributions under the plan is illustrated by the following examples:

Example (1).

Total face amount of the contract payable in a lump sum at time of death	$25,000
Cash value of the contract immediately before death	11,000
Excess over cash value, excludable under section 101(a)	$14,000
Cash value subject to limited exclusion under section 101(b)	11,000
Excludable under section 101(b) (assuming that there is no other death benefit paid by or on behalf of any employer with respect to the employee)	5,000
Balance taxable in accordance with section 402(a)(2) or 403(a)(2) (assuming a total distribution in one taxable year of the distributee)	6,000
Portion of premiums taxed to employee under the provisions of paragraph (b) of this section and considered as contributions of the employee	940
Balance taxable as long-term capital gain	$ 5,060

Example (2). The facts are the same as in example (1), except that the contract provides that the beneficiary may elect within 60 days after the death of the employee either to take the $25,000 or to receive 10 annual installments of $3,000 each, and the beneficiary elects to receive the 10 installments. In addition, the employee's rights to the cash value immediately before his death were forfeitable at least to the extent of $5,000. Section 101(d) is applicable to the amount excludable under section 101(a), that is, $14,000. The portion of each annual installment of $3,000 which is attributable to this $14,000 is determined by allocating each installment in accordance with the ratio which this $14,000 bears to the total amount which was payable at death ($25,000). Accordingly, the portion of each annual installment which is subject to section 101(d) is $1,680 (14/25 of $3,000), of which $1,400 (1/10 of $14,000) is excludable under section 101(a), and the remaining $280 is includible in the gross income of the beneficiary. However, if the beneficiary is a surviving spouse as defined in section 101(d)(3), the exclusion provided by section 101(d)(1)(B) is applicable to such $280. The remaining portion of each annual $3,000 installment, $1,320, is attributable to the cash value of the contract and is treated under section 72, as follows:

Amount actually contributed by the employee.....	$ 0
Amount considered contributed by employee by reason of section 101(b)	$ 5,000
Portion of premiums taxed to employee under the provisions of paragraph (b) of this section and considered as contributions of the employee	$ 940
Investment in the contract	$ 5,940
Expected return, 10 × $1,320	$13,200
Exclusion ratio, $5,940 ÷ $13,200	0.45
Annual exclusion, 0.45 × $1,320	$ 594

Accordingly, $594 of the $1,320 portion of each annual installment is excludable each year under section 72, and the remaining $726 is includible. Thus, if the beneficiary is not a surviving spouse, a total of $1,006 ($280 plus $726) of each annual $3,000 installment is includible in income each year. If the beneficiary is a surviving spouse, and can exclude all of the $280 under section 101(d)(1)(B), the amount includible in gross income each year is $726 of each annual $3,000 installment.

(4) If an employee neither paid the total cost of the life insurance protection provided under a life insurance contract, nor was taxable under paragraph (b) of this section with respect thereto, no part of the proceeds of such a contract which are paid to the beneficiaries of the employee as a death benefit is excludable under section 101(a). The entire distribution is taxable to the beneficiaries under section 402(a) or 403(a) except to the extent that a limited exclusion may be allowable under section 101(b).

T.D. 6676, 9/16/63.

§ 1.72-17 Special rules applicable to owner-employees.

Caution: The Treasury has not yet amended Reg § 1.72-17 to reflect changes made by P.L. 98-369, P.L. 97-248, P.L. 97-34, P.L. 93-406.

(a) In general. Under section 401(c) and section 403(a), certain self-employed individuals may participate in qualified pension, annuity, and profit-sharing plans, and the amounts received by such individuals from such plans are taxable under section 72. Section 72(m) and this section contain special rules for the taxation of amounts received from qualified pension, profit-sharing, or annuity plans covering an owner-employee. For purposes of section 72 and the regulations thereunder, the term "employee" shall include the self-employed individual who is treated as an employee by section 401(c)(1) (see paragraph (b) of § 1.401-10), and the term "owner-employee" has the meaning assigned to it in section 401(c)(3) (see paragraph (d) of § 1.401-10). See also paragraph (a)(2) of § 1.401-10 for the rule for determining when a plan covers an owner-employee. For purposes of this section, a self-employed individual may not treat as consideration for the contract contributed by the employee any contributions under the plan for which deductions were allowed under section 404 and which, consequently, are considered employer contributions.

(b) Certain amounts received before annuity starting date. *(1)* The rules of this paragraph are applicable to amounts received from a qualified pension, profit-sharing, or annuity plan by an employee (or his beneficiary) who is or was an owner-employee with respect to such plan when such amounts—

(i) Are received before the annuity starting date; and

(ii) Are not received as an annuity.

For the definition of annuity starting date, see paragraph (b) of § 1.72-4 and subparagraph (4) of this paragraph. As to what constitutes amounts not received as an annuity, see paragraphs (c) and (d) of § 1.72.11.

(2) Amounts to which this paragraph applies shall be included in the recipient's gross income for the taxable year in which received. However, the sum of the amounts so included under this subparagraph in all taxable years shall not exceed the aggregate deductions allowed under section 404 for premiums or other consideration paid under the plan on behalf of the employee while he was an owner-employee, including any such deductions taken in the taxable year of receipt.

(3) Any amounts to which this paragraph applies and which are not includible in gross income under the rules of subparagraph (2) of this paragraph shall be subject to the provisions of section 72(e) and § 1.72-11. However, for taxable years beginning before January 1, 1964, section 72(e)(3), as in effect before such date, shall not apply to such amounts. For taxable years beginning after December 31, 1963, such amounts (other than amounts subject to a penalty under section 72(m)(5) and paragraph (e) of this section) may be taken into account in computations under sections 1301 through 1305 (relating to income averaging).

(4) Under section 401(d)(4), a qualified pension, profit-sharing, or annuity plan may not provide for distributions to an owner-employee before he reaches age 59½ years, except in the case of his earlier disability. Therefore, in the case of a distribution from a qualified plan to an individual for whom contributions have been made to the plan as an owner-employee, the annuity starting date cannot be prior to the time such individual attains the age 59½ years unless he is entitled to benefits before reaching such age because of his disability. For taxable years beginning after December 31, 1966, see section 72(m)(7) and paragraph (f) of this section for the meaning of disabled. For taxable years beginning before January 1, 1967, see section 213(g)(3) for the meaning of disabled.

(5) The rules of this paragraph are not applicable to amounts credited to an individual in his capacity as a policyholder of an annuity, endowment, or life insurance contract which are in the nature of a dividend or refund of premium, and which are applied in accordance with paragraph (a)(4) of § 1.404(a)-8 towards the purchase of benefits under the policy.

(6) The rules of this paragraph may be illustrated by the following example:

Example. B, a self-employed individual, received $8,000 as a distribution under a qualified pension plan before the annuity starting date. At the time of such distribution, $10,000 had been contributed (the whole amount being allowed as a deduction) under the plan on behalf of such individual while he was a common-law employee and $5,000 had been contributed under the plan on his behalf while he was an owner-employee, of which $2,500 was allowed as a deduction. In addition, B had contributed $1,000 on his own behalf as an employee under the plan. Of the $8,000, $2,500 (the amount allowed as a deduction with respect to contributions on behalf of the individual while he was an owner-employee) is includible in gross income under subparagraph (2) of this paragraph. With respect to the remaining $5,500, B has a basis of $3,500, consisting of the $2,500 contributed on his behalf while he was an owner-employee which was not allowed as a deduction and the $1,000 which B contributed as an employee. The difference between the $5,500 and B's basis of $3,500, or $2,000, is includible in gross income under section 72(e).

(c) Amounts paid for life, accident, health, or other insurance. Amounts used to purchase life, accident, health, or other insurance protection for an owner-employee shall not be taken into account in computing the following:

(1) The aggregate amount of premiums or other consideration paid for the contract for purposes of determining the investment in the contract under section 72(c)(1)(A) and § 1.72-6;

(2) The consideration for the contract contributed by the employee for purposes of section 72(d)(1) and § 1.72-13, which provide the method of taxing employees annuities where the employee's contributions will be recoverable within 3 years; and

(3) The aggregate premiums or other consideration paid for purposes of section 72(e)(1)(B) and § 1.72-11, which provide the rules for taxing amounts not received as annuities prior to the annuity starting date.

The cost of such insurance protection will be considered to be a reasonable net premium cost, as determined by the Commissioner, for the appropriate period.

(d) Amounts constructively received. *(1)* If during any taxable year an owner-employee assigns or pledges (or agrees to assign or pledge) any portion of his interest in a trust described in section 401(a) which is exempt from tax under section 501(a), or any portion of the value of a contract purchased as part of a plan described in section 403(a), such portion shall be treated as having been received by such owner-employee as a distribution from the trust or as an amount received under the contract during such taxable year.

(2) If during any taxable year an owner-employee receives, either directly or indirectly, any amount from any insurance company as a loan under a contract purchased by a trust described in section 401(a) which is exempt from tax under section 501(a) or purchased as part of a plan described in section 403(a), and issued by such insurance company, such amount shall be treated as an amount received under the contract during such taxable year. An owner-employee will be considered to have received an amount under a contract if a premium, which is otherwise in default, is paid by the insurance company in the form of a loan against the cash surrender value of the contract. Further, an owner-employee will be considered to have received an amount to which this subparagraph applies if an amount is received from the issuer of a face-amount certificate as a loan under such a certificate purchased as part of a qualified trust or plan.

(e) Penalties applicable to certain amounts received by owner-employees. *(1)* (i) The rules of this paragraph are applicable to amounts, to the extent includible in gross income, received from a trust described in section 401(a) or under a plan described in section 403(a) by or on behalf of an individual who is or has been an owner-employee with respect to such plan or trust—

(a) Which are received before the owner-employee reaches the age of 59½ years and which are attributable to contributions paid on behalf of such owner-employee (whether or not paid by him) while he was an owner-employee (see subdivision (ii) of this subparagraph),

(b) Which are in excess of the benefits provided for such owner-employee under the plan formula (see subdivision (iii) of this subparagraph), or

(c) Which are received by reason of a distribution of the owner-employee's entire interest under the provisions of section 401(e)(2)(E), relating to excess contributions on behalf of an owner-employee which are willfully made.

(ii) The amounts referred to in subdivision (i)(a) of this subparagraph do not include—

(a) Amounts received by reason of the owner-employee becoming disabled, or

(b) Amounts received by the owner-employee in his capacity as a policyholder of an annuity, endowment, or life insurance contract which are in the nature of a dividend or similar distribution. Amounts attributable to contributions paid on behalf of an owner-employee and which are paid to a person other than the owner-employee before the owner-employee dies or reaches the age 59½ shall be considered received by the owner-employee for purposes of this paragraph. For taxable years beginning after December 31, 1966, see section 72(m)(7) and paragraph (f) of this section for the meaning of disabled. For taxable years beginning before January 1, 1967, see section 213(g)(3) for the meaning of disabled. For taxable years beginning after December 31, 1968, if an amount is not included in the amounts referred to in subdivision (1)(a) of this subparagraph solely by reason of the owner-employee becoming disabled and if a penalty would otherwise be applicable with respect to all or a portion of such amount, then for the taxable year in which such amount is received, there must be submitted with the owner-employee's income tax return a doctor's statement as to the impairment, and a statement by the owner-employee with respect to the effect of such impairment upon his substantial gainful activity and the date such impairment occurred. For taxable years which are subsequent to the first taxable year beginning after December 31, 1968, with respect to which the statements referred to in the preceding sentence are submitted, the owner-employee may, in lieu of such statements, submit a statement declaring the continued existence (without substantial diminution) of the impairment and its continued effect upon his substantial gainful activity.

(iii) This paragraph applies to amounts described in subdivision (i)(b) of this subparagraph (relating to excess benefits) even though a portion of such amounts may be attributable to contributions made on behalf of an individual while he was not an owner-employee and even though the amounts are received by his successor. However, these amounts do not include the portion of a distribution to which section 402(a)(2) or 403(a)(2) (relating to certain total distributions in one taxable year) applies.

(iv) (a) For purposes of subdivision (i)(a) of this subparagraph, the portion of any distribution or payment attributable to contributions on behalf of an employee-participant while he was an owner-employee includes the contributions made on his behalf while he was an owner-employee and the increments in value attributable to such contributions.

(b) The increments in value of an individual's account may be allocated to contributions on his behalf while he was an owner-employee either by maintaining a separate account, or an accounting, which reflects the actual increment attributable to such contributions, or by the method described in (c) of this subdivision.

(c) Where an individual is covered under the same plan both as an owner-employee and as a nonowner-employee, the portion of the increment in value of his interest attributable to contributions made on his behalf while he was an owner-employee may be determined by multiplying the total increment in value in his account by a fraction. The numerator of the fraction is the total contributions made on behalf of the individual as an owner-employee, weighted for the number of years that each contribution was in the plan. The denominator is the total contributions made on behalf of the individual, whether or not an owner-employee, weighted for the number of years each contribution was in the plan. The contributions are weighted for the number of years in the plan by multiplying each contribution by the number of years it was in the plan. For purposes of this computation, any forfeiture allocated to the account of the individual is treated as a contribution to the account made at the time so allocated.

(d) The method described in (c) of this subdivision may be illustrated by the following example:

Example. B was a member of the XYZ Partnership and a participant in the partnership's profit-sharing plan which was created in 1963. Until the end of 1967, B's interest in the partnership was less than 10 percent. On January 1, 1968, B obtained an interest in excess of 10 percent in the partnership and continued to participate in the profit-sharing plan until 1972. During 1972, prior to the time he attained the age of 59½ years and during a time when he was not disabled, B withdrew his entire interest in the profit-sharing plan. At that time his interest was $15,000, $9,600 contributions and $5,400 increment attributable to the contributions. The portion of the increment attributable to contributions while B was an owner-employee is $667.80, determined as follows:

	A Contribution	B Number of years contri-bution was in trust—	C Contribution weighted for years in trust (A × B)
1972	$1,000	0	0
1971	800	1	800
1970	1,200	2	2,400
1969	600	3	1,800
1968	200	4	800
1967	400	5	2,000
1966	2,000	6	12,000
1965	1,000	7	7,000
1964	1,500	8	12,000
1963	900	9	8,100
	$9,600		46,900

Total weighted contributions as owner-employee (1968-1972)—$5,800.

Total weighted contributions—$46,900.

$$5{,}400 \times \frac{\$5{,}800}{46{,}900} = \$667.80$$

(2) (i) If the aggregate of the amounts to which this paragraph applies received by any person in his taxable year equals or exceeds $2,500, the tax with respect to such amount shall be the greater of—

(a) The increase in tax attributable to the inclusion of the amounts so received in his gross income for the taxable year in which received, or

(b) 110 percent of the aggregate increase in taxes, for such taxable year and the four immediately preceding taxable years, which would have resulted if such amounts had been included in such person's gross income ratably over such taxable years. However, if deductions were allowed under section 404 for contributions to the plan on behalf of the individual as an owner-employee for less than four prior taxable years (whether or not consecutive), the number of immediately preceding taxable years taken into account shall be the number of prior taxable years in which such deductions were allowed.

(ii) If the aggregate of the amounts to which this paragraph applies received by any person in his taxable year is less than $2,500, the tax with respect to such amounts shall be 110 percent of the increase in tax which results from including such amounts in the person's gross income for the taxable year in which received.

(3) (i) For purposes of making the ratable inclusion computations of subparagraph (2)(i) of this paragraph, the taxable income of the recipient for each taxable year involved (notwithstanding section 63, relating to definition of taxable income) shall be treated as being not less than the amount required to be treated as includible in the taxable year pursuant to the ratable inclusion.

(ii) For purposes of subparagraph (2)(i)(a) and (ii) of this paragraph, the recipient's taxable income (notwithstanding section 63, relating to definition of taxable income) shall be treated as being not less than the aggregate of the amounts to which this paragraph applies reduced by the deductions allowed the recipient for such taxable year under section 151 (relating to deductions for personal exemptions).

(iii) In any case in which the application of subdivision (i) or (ii) of this subparagraph results in an increase in taxable income for any taxable year, the resulting increase in taxes imposed by section 1 or 3 for such taxable year shall be reduced by the credit against tax provided by section 31 (tax withheld on wages) and section 39 (certain uses of gasoline and lubricating oil), but shall not be reduced by any other credits against tax.

(4) The application of the rules of subparagraphs (2)(i) and (3) of this paragraph may be illustrated by the following example:

Example. B, a sole proprietor and a calendar-year basis taxpayer, established a qualified pension trust to which he made annual contributions for 10 years of 10 percent of his earned income. B withdrew his entire interest in the trust during 1973 when he was 55 years old and not disabled and for which, without regard to the distribution, he had a net operating loss and for which he is allowed under section 151 a deduction for one personal exemption. The portion of the distribution includible in B's gross income is $25,750. In addition, B had a net operating loss for 1972. The other 3 taxable years involved in the computation under subparagraph (2)(i) of this paragraph were years of substantial income. For purposes of determining B's increase in tax attributable to the receipt of the $25,750 (before the application of the provisions of subparagraph (2)(i)(b) of this paragraph), B's taxable income for the year he received the $25,750 is treated, under subparagraph (3)(ii) of this paragraph, as being $25,000 ($25,750 minus $750, the amount of the deduction allowed for each personal exemption under section 151 for 1973). For purposes of determining whether 110 percent of the aggregate increase in taxes which would have resulted if 20 percent of the amount of the withdrawal had been included in B's gross income for the year of receipt and for each of the 4 preceding taxable years is greater (and thus is the amount of his increase in tax attributable to the receipt of the $25,750), B's taxable income for the taxable year of receipt, and for the immediately preceding taxable year, is treated, under subparagraph (3)(i) of this paragraph, as being $5,150 ($25,750 divided by 5).

(f) Meaning of disabled. *(1)* For taxable years beginning after December 31, 1966, section 72(m)(7) provides that an individual shall be considered to be disabled if he is unable to engage in any substantial gainful activity by reason of any medically determinable physical or mental impairment which can be expected to result in death or to be of long-continued and indefinite duration. In determining whether an individual's impairment makes him unable to engage in any substantial gainful activity, primary consideration shall be given to the nature and severity of his impairment. Consideration shall also be given to other factors such as the individual's education, training, and work experience. The substantial gainful activity to which section 72(m)(7) refers in the activity, or a comparable activity, in which the individual customarily engaged prior to the arising of the disability (or prior to retirement if the individual was retired at the time the disability arose).

(2) Whether or not the impairment in a particular case constitutes a disability is to be determined with reference to all the facts in the case. The following are examples of impairments which would ordinarily be considered as preventing substantial gainful activity:

(i) Loss of use of two limbs;

(ii) Certain progressive diseases which have resulted in the physical loss or atrophy of a limb, such as diabetes, multiple sclerosis, or Buerger's disease;

(iii) Diseases of the heart, lungs, or blood vessels which have resulted in major loss of heart or lung reserve as evidenced by X-ray, electrocardiogram, or other objective findings, so that despite medical treatment breathlessness, pain, or fatigue is produced on slight exertion, such as walking several blocks, using public transportation, or doing small chores;

(iv) Cancer which is inoperable and progressive;

(v) Damage to the brain or brain abnormality which has resulted in severe loss of judgment, intellect, orientation, or memory;

(vi) Mental diseases (e.g. psychosis or severe psychoneurosis) requiring continued institutionalization or constant supervision of the individual;

(vii) Loss or diminution of vision to the extent that the affected individual has a central visual acuity of no better than 20/200 in the better eye after best correction, or has a limitation in the fields of vision such that the widest diameter of the visual fields subtends an angle no greater than 20 degrees;

(viii) Permanent and total loss of speech;

(ix) Total deafness uncorrectible by a hearing aid.

The existence of one or more of the impairments described in this subparagraph (or of an impairment of greater severity) will not, however, in and of itself always permit a finding that an individual is disabled as defined in section 72(m)(7). Any impairment, whether of lesser or greater severity, must be evaluated in terms of whether it does in fact prevent the individual from engaging in his customary or any comparable substantial gainful activity.

(3) In order to meet the requirements of section 72(m)(7), an impairment must be expected either to continue for a long and indefinite period or to result in death. Ordinarily, a terminal illness because of disease or injury would result in disability. Indefinite is used in the sense that it cannot reasonably be anticipated that the impairment will, in the foreseeable future, be so diminished as no longer to prevent substantial gainful activity. For example, an individual who suffers a bone fracture which prevents him from working for an extended period of time will not be considered disabled, if his recovery can be expected in the foreseeable future; if the fracture persistently fails to knit, the individual would ordinarily be considered disabled.

(4) An impairment which is remediable does not constitute a disability within the meaning of section 72(m)(7). An individual will not be deemed disabled if, with reasonable effort and safety to himself, the impairment can be diminished to the extent that the individual will not be prevented by the impairment from engaging in his customary or any comparable substantial gainful activity.

(g) Years to which this section applies. This section applies to taxable years ending before September 3, 1974. For taxable years ending after September 2, 1974, see § 1.72-17A.

T.D. 6676, 9/16/63, amend T.D. 6885, 6/1/66, T.D. 6985, 12/26/68, T.D. 7114, 5/17/71, T.D. 7636, 8/9/79.

§ 1.72-17A Special rules applicable to employee annuities and distributions under deferred compensation plans to self-employed individuals and owner-employees.

Caution: The Treasury has not yet amended Reg § 1.72-17A to reflect changes made by P.L. 99-514, P.L. 98-369, P.L. 97-248, P.L. 97-34.

(a) In general. Section 72(m) and this section contain special rules for the taxation of amounts received from qualified pension, profit-sharing, or annuity plans covering an owner-employee. This section applies to such amounts for taxable years of the recipient ending after September 2, 1974, unless another date is specified. For purposes of this section, the term "employee" shall include the self-employed individual who is treated as an employee by section 401(c)(1), and the term "owner-employee" has the meaning assigned to it in section 401(c)(3). Paragraph (b) of this section provides rules dealing with the computation of consideration paid by self-employed individuals and paragraph (c) of this section provides rules dealing with such computation when insurance is purchased for owner-employees. Paragraph (d) of this section provides rules for constructive receipt and, for purposes of these rules, treats as an owner-employee an individual for whose benefit an individual retirement account or annuity described in section 408(a) or (b) is maintained after December 31, 1974. Paragraph (e) of this section provides rules for penalties provided by section 72(m)(5) with respect to certain distributions received by owner-employees or their successors. Paragraph (f) of this section provides rules for determining whether a person is disabled within the meaning of section 72(m)(7). See § 1.72-16, relating to life insurance contracts purchased under qualified employee plans, for rules under section 72(m)(3).

(b) Computation of consideration paid by self-employed individuals. Under section 72(m)(2), consideration paid or contributed for the contract by any self-employed individual shall for purposes of section 72 be deemed not to include any contributions paid or contributed under a plan described in paragraph (a), or any other plan of deferred compensation described in section 404(a) (whether or not qualified), if the contributions are—

(1) Paid under such plan with respect to a time during which the employee was an employee only by reason of sections 401(c)(1) and 404(a)(8), and

(2) Deductible under section 404 by the employer, including an employer within the meaning of sections 401(c)(4) and 404(a)(8), of such self-employed individual at the time of such payment, or subsequent to such time of payment.

For purposes of this paragraph the term "consideration paid or contributed for the contract" has the same meaning as under subparagraphs (1), (2), and (3) of paragraph (c) of this section.

(c) Amounts paid for life, accident, health, or other insurance. Under section 72(m)(2), amounts used to purchase life, accident, health, or other insurance protection for an owner-employee shall not be taken into account in computing the following:

(1) The aggregate amount of premiums or other consideration paid for the contract for purposes of determining the investment in the contract under section 72(c)(1)(A) and § 1.72-6;

(2) The consideration for the contract contributed by the employee for purposes of section 72(d)(1) and § 1.72-13, which provide the method of taxing employee's annuities where the employee's contributions will be recoverable within 3 years; and

(3) The aggregate premiums or other consideration paid for purposes of section 72(e)(1)(B) and § 1.72-11, which provide the rules for taxing amounts not received as annuities prior to the annuity starting date.

The cost of such insurance protection will be considered to be a reasonable net premium cost, as determined by the Commissioner, for the appropriate period.

(d) Amounts constructively received. *(1)* The references in this paragraph (d) to section 72(m)(4) are to that section as in effect on August 13, 1982. Section 236(b)(1) of the Tax Equity and Fiscal Responsibility Act of 1982 (96 Stat. 324) repealed section 72(m)(4), generally effective for assignments, pledges and loans made after August 13, 1982, and added section 72(p). See section 72(p) and § 1.72(p)-1 for rules governing the income tax treatment of certain assignments, pledges and loans from qualified employer plans made after August 13, 1982.

(2) Under section 72(m)(4)(A), if during any taxable year an owner-employee assigns or pledges (or agrees to assign or pledge) any portion of his interest in a trust described in section 401(a) which is exempt from tax under section 501(a), or any portion of the value of a contract purchased as part of a plan described in section 403(a), such portion shall be treated as having been received by such owner-employee as a distribution from the trust or as an amount received under the contract during such taxable year.

(3) (i) Under paragraphs (4)(A) and (6) of section 72(m), if after December 31, 1974, during any taxable year an individual for whose benefit an individual retirement account or annuity described in section 408(a) or (b) is maintained assigns or pledges (or agrees to assign or pledge) any portion of his interest in such account or annuity, such portion shall be treated as having been received by such individual as a distribution from such account or trust during such taxable year. See subsections (d) and (f) of section 408 and the regulations thereunder for the tax treatment of an amount treated as a distribution under this subparagraph.

(ii) Notwithstanding subdivision (i) of this subparagraph, if an individual retirement account or annuity, or portion thereof, is subject to the additional tax imposed by section 408(f), that amount shall be deemed not to be a distribution under section 72(m)(4)(A) and subdivision (i) of this subparagraph.

(4) Under section 72(m)(4)(B), if during any taxable year an owner-employee receives, either directly or indirectly, any amount from any insurance company as a loan under a contract purchased by a trust described in section 401(a) which is exempt from tax under section 501(a) or purchased as part of a plan described in section 403(a), and issued by such insurance company, such amount shall be treated as an amount received under the contract during such taxable year. An owner-employee will be considered to have received an amount under a contract if a premium, which is otherwise in default, is paid by the insurance company in the form of a loan against the cash surrender value of the contract. Further, an owner-employee will be considered to have received an amount to which this subparagraph applies if an amount is received from the issuer of a face-amount certificate as a loan under such a certificate purchased as part of a qualified trust or plan.

(e) Penalties applicable to certain amounts received with respect to owner-employees under section 72(m)(5). *(1)* (i) For taxable years of the recipient beginning after December 31, 1975, if any person receives an amount to which subparagraph (2) of this paragraph applies, his tax under chapter 1 for the taxable year in which such amount is received shall be increased by an amount equal to 10 percent of the portion of the amount so received which is includible in his gross income for such taxable year.

(ii) For taxable years of the recipient beginning before January 1, 1976, see subparagraph (3) of this paragraph.

(2) (i) This subparagraph is applicable to amounts, to the extent includible in gross income, received from a qualified trust described in section 401(a) or under a plan described in section 403(a) by or on behalf of an individual who is or has been an owner-employee with respect to such trust or plan—

(A) Which are received before the owner-employee reaches the age of 59½ years, and which are attributable to contributions paid on behalf of such owner-employee by his employer (that is employer contributions within the meaning of section 401(c)(5)(A) and the increments in value attributable to such employer contributions) and the increments in value attributable to contributions made by him as an owner-employee while he was an owner-employee (that is, the increments attributable to owner-employee contributions within the meaning of section 401(c)(5)(B), but not such contributions; see subdivision (ii) of this subparagraph).

(B) Which are in excess of the benefits provided for such owner-employee under the plan formula (see subdivision (iii) of this subparagraph), or

(C) Which are subject to the transitional rules with respect to willful excess contributions made on behalf of an owner-employee in his employer's taxable years which begin before January 1, 1976 (see subdivision (v) of this subparagraph).

(ii) The amounts referred to in subdivision (i)(A) of this subparagraph do not include—

(A) Amounts received by reason of the owner-employee becoming disabled (see paragraph (f) of this section).

(B) Amounts received by the owner-employee in his capacity as a policyholder of an annuity, endowment, or life insurance contract which are in the nature of a dividend or similar distribution, or

(C) Amounts attributable to contributions (and increments in value thereon) made for years for which the recipient was not an owner-employee.

If an amount is not included in the amounts referred to in subdivision (i)(A) of this subparagraph solely by reason of the owner-employee's becoming disabled and if a penalty would otherwise be applicable with respect to all or a portion of such amount, then for the owner-employee's taxable year in which such amount is received, there must be submitted with his income tax return a doctor's statement as to the impairment, and a statement by the owner-employee with respect to the effect of such impairment upon his substantial gainful activity and the date such impairment occurred. For taxable years which are subsequent to the first taxable year with respect to which the statements referred to in the preceding sentence are submitted, the owner-employee may, in lieu of such statements, submit a statement declaring the continued existence (without substantial diminution) of the impairment and its continued effect upon his substantial gainful activity.

(iii) This subparagraph applies to amounts described in subdivision (i)(B) of this subparagraph (relating to benefits in excess of the plan formula) even though a portion of such amounts may be attributable to contributions made on behalf of an individual while he was not an owner-employee and even if he is deceased and the amounts are received by his successor.

(iv) (A) The rules described in subdivisions (i)(A) and (iii) of this subparagraph, relating to the treatment under section 72(m)(5)(A)(i) of certain premature distributions, may be illustrated by the following example:

Example. (1) A was a member of the X partnership, consisting of partners A through I, and a participant in the partnership's qualified profit-sharing plan which was established on January 1, 1972. A's taxable years, the X partnership's taxable years, the plan years, and other relevant years are all calendar years at all relevant times. For the three calendar years, 1972 through 1974, A was an owner-employee in the X partnership. On January 1, 1975, new partners J and K became partners in the X partnership, and as of that date, each of partners A through K held a 1/11 interest in the capital and profits of the X partnership. on that date, A became a partner who was not an owner-employee. A continued in this status for the 2 calendar years 1975 and 1976. On January 1, 1977, when A was 50 years old and not disabled, he liquidated his interest in the X partnership and became an employee of an unrelated employer. On that date, A received a distribution representing his entire interest in the X partnership's plan of $54,000 cash in violation of the plan provision required by section 401(d)(4)(B). As of that date, the distribution was attributable to the following sources and times, computed by the plan in a manner consistent with the subparagraph:

Calendar years	X contributions on behalf of A deductible under sec. 404 A	A's contributions made as an employee B	Increments in value attributable to column A yearly contributions C	Increments in value attributable to column B yearly contributions D
1977	0	0	0	0
1976	$ 7,500	$ 2,500	$900	$300
1975	7,500	2,500	4,000	1,300
1974	7,500	2,500	1,800	700
1973	2,500	2,500	1,200	1,200
1972	2,500	2,500	1,300	1,300
Total	27,500	12,500	9,200	4,800

(2) The amount of the $54,000 distribution to which subdivision (i)(A) of this subparagraph applies is $20,000, computed as follows:

X contributions on behalf of A made in years A was an owner-employee:	
1974	$7,500
1973	2,500
1972	2,500
Total	12,500
Increments in value attributable to such contributions:	
1974	1,800
1973	1,200
1972	1,300
Total	4,300
Increments in value attributable to contributions made by A as an employee for years in which he was an owner-employee:	
1974	700
1973	1,200
1972	1,300
Total	3,200
Grand total	20,000

In this example, the $20,000 amount computed above would be includible in A's gross income for 1977 and would be subject to the 10 percent tax described in subparagraph (1)(i) of this paragraph.

(3) Subdivision (i)(A) of this subparagraph does not apply to the contributions made by X on behalf of A for 1976 and 1975 ($7,500 each year, totaling $15,000) nor to the increments in value attributable to those contributions ($900 for 1976 and $4,000 for 1975, totaling $4,900), because A was not an owner-employee with respect to these two years, 1976 and 1975, on account of which these employer contributions were made. For the same reason, subdivision (i)(A) of this subparagraph does not apply to the increments in value attributable to A's contributions for 1976 and 1975 ($300 and $1,300, respectively, totaling $1,600).

See section 4972(c) for the amount of employee contributions which is permitted to be contributed by an owner-employee (as an employee) without subjecting an owner-employee to the tax on excess contributions.

(4) Subdivision (i)(A) of this subparagraph does not apply to the contributions made by A, as an employee during the years when he was an owner-employee ($2,500 during each of the years 1972, 1973, and 1974, totaling $7,500), because the distribution was received in a taxable year of A ending after September 2, 1974; see subparagraph (3) of this paragraph. Furthermore, because the distribution of the amount of A's contributions ($12,500) constitutes consideration for the contract paid by A for purposes of section 72, the $7,500 amount described in the preceding sentence is not includible in his gross income, and that amount is not subject to the rules of this subparagraph; see subdivision (i) of this subparagraph, and paragraphs (b) and (c) of this section.

(B) The increments in value of an individual's account may be allocated to contributions on his behalf, by his employer or by such individual as an owner-employee, while he was an owner-employee either by maintaining a separate account, or an accounting, which reflects the actual increment attributable to such contributions, or by the method described in (C) of this subdivision.

(C) Where an individual is covered under the same plan both as an owner-employee and as a non-owner-employee, the portion of the increment in value of his interest attributable to contributions made on his behalf while he was an owner-employee may be determined by multiplying the total increment in value in his account by a fraction. The numerator of the fraction is the total contributions made on behalf of the individual as an owner-employee, weighted for the number of years that each contribution was in the plan. The denominator is the total contributions made on behalf of the individual, whether or not as an owner-employee, weighted for the number of years each contribution was in the plan. The contributions are weighted for the number of years in the plan by multiplying each contribution by the number of years it was in the plan. For purposes of this computation, any forfeiture allocated to the account of the individual is treated as a contribution to the account made at the time so allocated. For purposes of this computation, where the individual has received a prior distribution from such account, an appropriate adjustment must be made to reflect such prior distribution.

(D) The method described in (C) of this subdivision may be illustrated by the following example:

Example. B was a member of the XYZ Partnership and a participant in the partnership's profit-sharing plan which was created in 1973. Until the end of 1977, B's interest in the partnership was less than 10 percent. On January 1, 1978, B obtained an interest in excess of 10 percent in the partnership and continued to participate in the profit-sharing plan until 1982. During 1982, prior to the time he attained the age of 59½ years and during a time when he was not disabled, B, who had not received any prior plan distributions, withdrew his entire interest in the profit-sharing plan. At the time his interest was $15,000, $9,600 contributions and $5,400 increment attributable to the contributions. The portion of the increment attributable to contributions while B was an owner-employee is $667.80, determined as follows:

	Contribution A	Number of years contribution was in trust B	Contribution weighted for years in trust (A × B) C
1982	$1,000	0	0
1981	800	1	800
1980	1,200	2	2,400
1979	600	3	1,800
1978	200	4	800
1977	400	5	2,000
1976	2,000	6	12,000
1975	1,000	7	7,000
1974	1,500	8	12,000
1973	900	9	8,100
Total.....	9,600	....	46,900

Total weighted contributions as owner-employee (1978—1982) = $5,800.

Total weighted contributions = $46,900.

$$\$5{,}400 \times \frac{\$5{,}800}{\$46{,}900} = \$667.80$$

(E) (1) The rules set forth in subdivision (iv)(E)(2) of this subparagraph shall be used to determine the amounts to which subdivision (i)(A) of this subparagraph applies in the case of a distribution of less than the entire balance of the employee's account from a plan in which he has been covered at different times as owner-employee or as an employee other than an owner-employee.

(2) Distributions or payments from a plan for any employee taxable year shall be deemed to be attributable to contributions to the plan, and increments thereon, in the following order—

(i) Excess contributions, within the meaning of section 4972(b), designated as such by the trustee;

(ii) Employee contributions;

(iii) Employer contributions, other than those described in (i), and the increments in value attributable to the employee's own contributions and his employer's contributions on the basis of the taxable years of his employer in succeeding order of time whether or not the employee was an owner-employee for any such year.

For purposes of (iii) of this subdivision, the time of contributions made on the basis of any employer taxable year shall take into account the rule specified in section 404(a)(6), relating to time when contributions deemed made.

(v) The amounts referred to in subdivision (i)(C) of this subparagraph are amounts which are received by reason of a distribution of the owner-employee's entire interest under the provisions of section 401(e)(2)(E), as in effect on September 1, 1974, relating to excess contributions on behalf of an owner-employee which are willfully made. Notwithstanding the preceding sentence, an owner-employee's entire interest in all plans with respect to which he is an owner-employee (within the meaning of subsections (d)(8)(C) and (e)(2)(E)(ii) of section 401, as in effect on September 1, 1974) does not include any distribution or payment attributable to his employer's contributions or his own contributions made with respect to his employer's taxable years beginning after December 31, 1975. However, his entire interest in all plans does include all of the distribution or payment attributable to his employer's contributions and his own contributions made with respect to all of his employer's taxable years beginning before January 1, 1976, if any portion thereof is attributable in whole or in part to such a willful excess contribution and such entire interest is received because of a willful excess contribution pursuant to section 401(e)(2)(E)(ii). A distribution or payment is described in the preceding sentence even though it is received in an owner-employee's taxable year beginning after December 31, 1975. For purposes of computing the increments in value attributable to employer taxable years which begin before January 1, 1976, and such increments attributable to such years beginning after December 31, 1975, the rules specified in subdivision (iv)(B), (C), (D), and (E) of this subparagraph shall be applied to the extent applicable. See § 1.401(e)-4(c) for transitional rules with respect to contributions described in this subdivision.

(3) (i) For taxable years of the recipient beginning before January 1, 1976, the tax with respect to amounts to which subparagraph (2) of this paragraph applies shall be computed under subparagraphs (B), (C), (D), and (E) of section 72(m)(5) as such subparagraphs were in effect prior to the amendments made by subsections (g)(1) and (2)(A) of section 2001 of the Employee Retirement Income Security Act of 1974 (88 Stat. 957) except as provided in subdivisions (ii) and (iii) of this subparagraph (see paragraph (e) of § 1.72-17). For purposes of the preceding sentence, amounts to which subparagraph (2) of this paragraph applies in the case of an amount described in section 72(m)(5)(A)(i) shall be determined under subdivisions (i)(a) and (ii) of § 1.72-17(e)(1), except as provided in subdivision (ii) of this subparagraph. For purposes of the first sentence of this subdivision, amounts to which subparagraph (2) of this paragraph applies in the case of an amount described in section 72(m)(5)(A)(ii) shall be determined under subdivisions (i)(b) and (iii) of § 1.72-17(e)(1), except as provided in subdivision (iii) of this subparagraph.

(ii) For purposes of applying section 72(m)(5)(A)(i), after the amendment made by section 2001(h)(3) of such Act, and subdivisions (i)(a) and (ii) of § 1.72-17(e)(1), to a distribution or payment received in recipient taxable years ending after September 2, 1974, and beginning before January 1, 1976, with respect to contributions made on behalf of an owner-employee which were made by him as an owner-employee (that is, employee contributions within the meaning of section 401(c)(5)(B)) the portion of any distribution or payment attributable to such contributions shall not include such contributions but shall include the increments in value attributable to such contributions.

(iii) For purposes of applying section 72(m)(5)(D) and subdivisions (i)(b) and (iii) of § 1.72-17(e)(1) to recipient taxable years beginning after December 31, 1973, and beginning before January 1, 1976, in the case of distributions or payments made after December 31, 1973, the amounts to which section 402(a)(2) or 403(a)(2) applies after the amendments made by section 2005(b)(1) and (2) of such Act (88 Stat. 990 and 991) (which are amounts to which subdivision (i)(b) of § 1.72-17(e)(1) does not apply) shall be deemed to be the amount which is treated as a gain from the sale or exchange of a capital asset held for more than 6 months under either of such sections.

(f) Meaning of disabled. *(1)* Section 72(m)(7) provides that an individual shall be considered to be disabled if he is unable to engage in any substantial gainful activity by reason of any medically determinable physical or mental impairment which can be expected to result in death or to be of long-continued and indefinite duration. In determining whether an individual's impairment makes him unable to engage in any substantial gainful activity, primary consideration shall be given to the nature and severity of his impairment. Consideration shall also be given to other factors such as the individual's education, training, and work experience. The substantial gainful activity to which section 72(m)(7) refers is the activity, or a comparable activity, in which the individual customarily engaged prior to the arising of the disability or prior to retirement if the individual was retired at the time the disability arose.

(2) Whether or not the impairment in a particular case constitutes a disability is to be determined with reference to all the facts in the case. The following are examples of impairments which would ordinarily be considered as preventing substantial gainful activity:

(i) Loss of use of two limbs;

(ii) Certain progressive diseases which have resulted in the physical loss or atrophy of a limb, such as diabetes, multiple sclerosis, or Buerger's disease;

(iii) Diseases of the heart, lungs, or blood vessels which have resulted in major loss of heart or lung reserve as evidenced by X-ray, electrocardiogram, or other objective findings, so that despite medical treatment breathlessness, pain, or fatigue is produced on slight exertion, such as walking several blocks, using public transportation, or doing small chores;

(iv) Cancer which is inoperable and progressive;

(v) Damage to the brain or brain abnormality which has resulted in severe loss of judgment, intellect, orientation, or memory;

(vi) Mental diseases (e.g. psychosis or severe psychoneurosis) requiring continued institutionalization or constant supervision of the individual;

(vii) Loss or diminution of vision to the extent that the affected individual has a central visual acuity of no better than 20/200 in the better eye after best correction, or has a limitation in the fields of vision such that the widest diameter of the visual fields subtends an angle no greater than 20 degrees;

(viii) Permanent and total loss of speech;

(ix) Total deafness uncorrectible by a hearing aid.

The existence of one or more of the impairments described in this subparagraph (or of an impairment of greater severity) will not, however, in and of itself always permit a finding that an individual is disabled as defined in section 72(m)(7). Any impairment, whether of lesser or greater severity, must be evaluated in terms of whether it does in fact prevent the individual from engaging in his customary or any comparable substantial gainful activity.

(3) In order to meet the requirements of section 72(m)(7), an impairment must be expected either to continue for a long and indefinite period or to result in death. Ordinarily, a terminal illness because of disease or injury would result in disability. The term "indefinite" is used in the sense that it cannot reasonably be anticipated that the impairment will, in the foreseeable future, be so diminished as no longer to prevent substantial gainful activity. For example, an individual who suffers a bone fracture which prevents him from work-

ing for an extended period of time will not be considered disabled, if his recovery can be expected in the foreseeable future; if the fracture persistently fails to knit, the individual would ordinarily be considered disabled.

(4) An impairment which is remediable does not constitute a disability within the meaning of section 72(m)(7). An individual will not be deemed disabled if, with reasonable effort and safety to himself, the impairment can be diminished to the extent that the individual will not be prevented by the impairment from engaging in his customary or any comparable substantial gainful activity.

T.D. 7636, 8/9/79, amend T.D. 8894, 7/28/2000.

§ 1.72-18 Treatment of certain total distributions with respect to self-employed individuals.

(a) In general. The Self-Employed Individuals Tax Retirement Act of 1962 permits self-employed individuals to be treated as employees for purposes of participation in pension, profit-sharing, and annuity plans described in sections 401(a) and 403(a). In general, amounts received by a distributee or payee which are attributable to contributions made on behalf of a participant while he was self-employed are taxed in the same manner as amounts which are attributable to contributions made on behalf of a common-law employee. However, such amounts which are paid in one taxable year presenting the total distributions payable to a distributee or payee with respect to an employee are not eligible for the capital gains treatment of section 402(a)(2) or 403(a)(2). This section sets forth the treatment of such distributions, except where such a distribution is subject to the penalties of section 72(m)(5) and paragraph (e) of § 1.72-17.

(b) Distributions to which this section applies. *(1)* (i) Except as provided in subparagraphs (2) and (3) of this paragraph, this section applies to amounts distributed to a distributee in one taxable year of the distributee in the case of an employee's trust described in section 401(a) which is exempt under section 501(a), or to amounts paid to a payee in one taxable year of the payee in the case of an annuity plan described in section 403(a), which constitute the total distributions payable, or the total amounts payable, to the distributee or payee with respect to an employee.

(ii) For the total distributions or amounts payable to a distributee or payee to be considered paid within one taxable year of the distributee or payee for purposes of this section, all amounts to the credit of the employee-participant through the end of such taxable year which are payable to the distributee or payee must be distributed or paid within such taxable year. Thus, the provisions of this section are not applicable to a distribution or payment to a distributee or payee if the trust or plan retains any amounts after the close of such taxable year which are payable to the same distributee or payee even though the amounts retained may be attributable to contributions on behalf of the employee-participant while he was a common-law employee in the business with respect to which the plan was established.

(iii) For purposes of this section, the total amounts payable to a distributee or the amounts to the credit of the employee do not include United States Retirement Plan Bonds held by a trust to the credit of the employee. Thus, a distribution to a distributee by a qualified trust may constitute a distribution to which this section applies even though the trust retains retirement plan bonds registered in the name of the employee on whose behalf the distribution is made which are to be distributed to the same distributee. Moreover, the proceeds of a retirement bond received as part of a distribution which constitutes the total distributions payable to the distributee are not entitled to the special tax treatment of this section. See section 405(d) and paragraph (a)(1) of § 1.405-3.

(iv) If the amounts payable to a distributee from a qualified trust with respect to an employee-participant includes an annuity contract, such contract must be distributed along with all other amounts payable to the distributee in order to have a distribution to which this section applies. However, the proceeds of an annuity contract received in a total distribution will not be entitled to the tax treatment of this section unless the contract is surrendered in the taxable year of the distributee in which the total distribution was received.

(v) In the case of a qualified annuity plan, the term "total amounts" means all annuities payable to a payee. If more than one annuity contract is received under the plan by a distributee, this section shall not apply to an amount received on surrender of any such contracts unless all contracts under the plan payable to the payee are surrendered within one taxable year of the payee.

(vi) (a) The provisions of this section are applicable where the total amounts payable to a distributee or payee are paid within one taxable year of the distributee or payee whether or not a portion of the employee-participant's interest which is payable to another distributee or payee is paid within the same taxable year. However, a distributee or payee who, in prior taxable years received amounts (except amounts described in (b) of this subdivision) after the employee-participant ceases to be eligible for additional contributions to be made on his behalf, does not receive a distribution or payment to which this section applies, even though the total amount remaining to be paid to such distributee or payee with respect to such employee is paid within one taxable year. On the other hand, a distribution to a distributee or payee prior to the time that the employee-participant ceases to be eligible for additional contributions on his behalf does not preclude the application of this section to a later distribution to the same distributee or payee.

(b) The receipt of an amount which constitutes—

(1) A payment in the nature of a dividend or similar distribution to an individual in his capacity as a policyholder of an annuity, endowment, or life insurance contract, or

(2) A return of excess contributions which were not willfully made,

does not prevent the application of this section to a total distribution even though the amount is received after the employee-participant ceases to be eligible for additional contributions and in a taxable year other than the taxable year in which the total amount is received.

(vii) For purposes of this section, the total amounts payable to a distributee or payee, or the amounts to the credit of the employee, do not include any amounts which have been placed in a separate account for the funding of medical benefits described in section 401(h) as defined in paragraph (a) of § 1.401-14. Thus, a distribution by a qualified trust or annuity plan may constitute a distribution to which this section applies even though amounts attributable to the funding of section 401(h) medical benefits as defined in paragraph (a) of § 1.401-14 are not so distributed.

(2) This section shall apply—

(i) Only if the distribution or payment is made—

(a) On account of the employee's death at any time,

(b) After the employee has attained the age 59½ years, or

(c) After the employee has become disabled; and

(ii) Only to so much of the distribution or payment as is attributable to contributions made on behalf of an employee while he was a self-employed individual in the business with respect to which the plan was established. Any distribution or payment, or any portion thereof, which is not so attributable shall be subject to the rules of taxation which apply to any distribution or payment that is attributable to contributions on behalf of common-law employees.

For taxable years beginning after December 31, 1966, see section 72(m)(7) and paragraph (f) of § 1.72-17 for the meaning of disabled. For taxable years beginning before January 1, 1967, see section 213(g)(3) for the meaning of disabled. For taxable years beginning after December 31, 1968, if this section is applicable by reason of the distribution or payment being made after the employee has become disabled, then for the taxable year in which the amounts to which this section applies are distributed or paid, there shall be submitted with the recipient's income tax return a doctor's statement as to the nature and effect of the employee's impairment.

(3) This section shall not apply to—

(i) Distributions or payments to which the penalty provisions of section 72(m)(5) and paragraph (e) of § 1.72-17 apply,

(ii) Distributions or payments from a trust or plan made to or on behalf of an individual prior to the time such individual ceases to be eligible for additional contributions (except the contribution attributable to the last year of service) to be made to the trust or plan on his behalf as a self-employed individual, and

(iii) Distributions or payments made to the employee from a plan or trust unless contributions which were allowed as a deduction under section 404 have been made on behalf of such employee as a self-employed individual under such trust or plan for 5 or more taxable years (whether or not consecutive) prior to the taxable year in which such distributions or payments are made. Distributions or payments to which this section does not apply by reason of this subdivision are taxed as otherwise provided in section 72. However, for taxable years beginning before January 1, 1964, section 72(e)(3), as in effect before such date, is not applicable. For taxable years beginning after December 31, 1963, such distributions or payments may be taken into account in computations under sections 1301 through 1305 (relating to income averaging).

(4) The portion of any distribution or payment attributable to contributions on behalf of an employee-participant while he was self-employed includes the contributions made on his behalf while he was self-employed and the increments in value attributable to such contributions. Where the amounts to the credit of an employee-participant include amounts attributable to contributions on his behalf while he was a self-employed individual and amounts attributable to contributions on his behalf while he was a common-law employee, the increment in value attributable to the employee-participant's interest shall be allocated to the contributions on his behalf while he was self-employed either by maintaining a separate account, or an accounting, which reflects the actual increment attributable to such contributions, or by the method described in paragraph (e)(1)(iv)(c) of § 1.72-17. However, if the latter method is used, the numerator of the fraction is the total contributions made on behalf of the individual as a self-employed individual, weighted for the number of years that each contribution was in the plan.

(c) Amounts includible in gross income. *(1)* Where a total distribution or payment to which this section applies is made to one distributee or payee and includes the total amount remaining to the credit of the employee-participant on whose behalf the distribution or payment was made, the distributee or payee shall include in gross income an amount equal to the portion of the distribution or payment which exceeds the employee-participant's investment in the contract. For purposes of this paragraph, the investment in the contract shall be reduced by any amounts previously received from the plan or trust by or on behalf of the employee-participant which were excludable from gross income as a return of the investment in the contract.

(2) In the case of a distribution to which this section applies and which is made to more than one distributee or payee, each element of the amounts to the credit of an employee-participant shall be allocated among the several distributees or payees on the basis of the ratio of the value of the distributee's or payee's distribution or payment to the total amount to the credit of the employee-participant. The elements to be so allocated include the investment in the contract, the increments in value, and the portion of the amounts to the credit of the employee-participant which is attributable to the contributions on behalf of the employee-participant while he was a self-employed individual.

(d) Computation of tax. *(1)* The tax attributable to the amounts to which this section applies for the taxable year in which such amounts are received is the greater of—

(i) 5 times the increase in tax which would result from the inclusion in gross income of the recipient of 20 percent of so much of the amount so received as is includible in gross income, or

(ii) 5 times the increase which would result if the taxable income of the recipient for such taxable year equaled 20 percent of the excess of the aggregate of the amounts so received and includible in gross income over the amount of the deductions allowed the recipient for such taxable year under section 151 (relating to deduction for personal exemptions).

In any case in which the application of subdivision (ii) of this subparagraph results in an increase in taxable income for any taxable year, the resulting increase in taxes imposed by section 1 or 3 for such taxable year shall be reduced by the credit against tax provided by section 31 (tax withheld on wages), but shall not be reduced by any other credits against tax.

(2) The application of the rules of this paragraph may be illustrated by the following example:

Example. B, a sole proprietor and a calendar-year basis taxpayer, established a qualified pension trust to which he made annual contributions for 10 years of 10 percent of his earned income. B withdrew his entire interest in the trust during 1973, for which year, without regard to the distribution, he had a net operating loss and is allowed under section 151 a deduction for one personal exemption. At the time of the withdrawal, B was 64 years old. The amount of the distribution that is includible in his gross income is $25,750. Because of B's net operating loss, the tax attributable to the distribution is determined under the rule of subparagraph (1)(ii) of this paragraph. For purposes of determining the tax attributable to the $25,750, B's taxable income for 1973 is treated, under subparagraph (1)(ii) of this paragraph, as being 20 percent of $25,000 ($25,750 minus $750, the amount of the deduction allowed for each personal exemption under section 151 for 1973). Thus, under subparagraph

(1) of this paragraph, the tax attributable to the $25,750 would be 5 times the increase which would result if the taxable income of B for the taxable year he received such amount equaled $5,000. B has had no amounts withheld from wages and thus is not entitled to reduce the increase in taxes by the credit against tax provided in section 31 and may not reduce the increase in taxes by any other credits against tax.

T.D. 6676, 9/16/63, amend T.D. 6722, 4/13/64, T.D. 6885, 6/1/66, T.D. 6985, 12/26/68, T.D. 7114, 5/17/71.

§ 1.72(e)-1T Treatment of distributions where substantially all contributions are employee contributions (temporary).

Q-1. How did the Tax Reform Act (TRA) of 1984 change the law with regard to the treatment of non-annuity distributions (i.e., amounts distributed prior to the annuity starting date and not received as annuities) from a qualified plan that is treated as a single contract under section 72 and under which substantially all of the contributions are employee contributions?

A-1. (a) Prior to the amendment of section 72(e) by the TRA of 1984, nonannuity distributions from such a qualified plan generally were allocable, first, to nondeductible employee contributions and thus were not includible in gross income. After distributions equaled the balance of nondeductible employee contributions, further non-annuity distributions generally were includible in gross income.

(b) Pursuant to section 72(e)(7), as added by the TRA of 1984, non-annuity distributions from such a qualified plan that are allocable to investment in the plan after August 13, 1982 (as determined in accordance with section 72(e)(5)(B)), generally will be treated, first, as allocable to income and, second, as allocable to nondeductible employee contributions. Distributions allocable to income are includible in gross income. Distributions allocable to nondeductible employee contributions are not includible in gross income.

Q-2. To which qualified plans and contracts does section 72(e)(7) apply?

A-2. Section 72(e)(7) applies to any plan or contract under which substantially all of the contributions are employee contributions if—

(a) Such plan is described in section 401(a) and the related trust or trusts are exempt from tax under section 501(a); or

(b) Such contract is—

(1) Purchased by a trust described in (a) above,

(2) Purchased as part of a plan described in section 403(a), or

(3) Described in section 403(b).

Q-3. What is the definition of a qualified plan or contract under which substantially all of the contributions are employee contributions?

A-3. (a) A qualified plan or contract under which substantially all of the contributions are employee contributions is a plan or contract with respect to which 85 percent or more of the total contributions during the "representative period" are employee contributions. The "representative period" means the five-plan-year period preceding the plan year during which a distribution occurs. However, if less than 85 percent of the total contributions for all plan years during which the plan or contract is in existence prior to the plan year of distribution are employee contributions, then the plan or contract is not one with respect to which substantially all of the contributions are employee contributions.

(b) For purposes of the 85 percent test, contributions made to a predecessor plan or contract are aggregated with contributions to the plan or contract to which the 85 percent test is being applied (the successor plan or contract). For purposes of the preceding sentence, a predecessor plan or contract is a plan or contract the terms of which are substantially the same as the successor plan or contract.

Q-4. What is the definition of employee contributions for purposes of section 72(e)(7)?

A-4. For purposes of section 72(e)(7), employee contributions are those amounts contributed by the employee and those amounts considered contributed by the employee under section 72(f). For example, amounts contributed to a section 401(k) qualified cash or deferred arrangement, pursuant to an employee's election to defer such amounts, are employer contributions to the extent that such amounts are not currently includible in gross income. In addition, deductible employee contributions under section 72(o) are disregarded in their entirety (i.e., treated as neither employee contributions nor employer contributions) in determining whether substantially all the contributions are employee contributions.

Q-5. How is the 85 percent test of section 72(e)(7) applied to a qualified plan or contract?

A-5. (a) Except as provided in paragraphs (b), (c), and (d), the 85 percent test is applied separately with respect to each contract under section 72.

(b) If a single qualified plan described in section 401(a) or section 403(a) comprises more than one contract under section 72, regardless of whether such plan includes multiple trusts or combinations of profit-sharing and pension features, these contracts are aggregated for purposes of applying the 85 percent test. Thus, if substantially all of the contributions under a qualified plan comprising two contracts under section 72 are employee contributions, section 72(e)(5)(D) shall not apply to non-annuity distributions under either of the contracts.

(c) With respect to the plans maintained by the Federal Government or by instrumentalities of the Federal Government, the 85 percent test shall be applied by aggregating all such plans. This aggregation rule applies only to those plans that are actively administered by the Federal Government or an instrumentality thereof. Thus, if a plan of the Federal Government is administered by a commercial financial institution, it would not be aggregated with other plans of the Federal Government and its instrumentalities for purposes of applying the 85 percent test.

(d) In the case of a contract described in section 403(b), the 85 percent test is applied separately to each such contract.

Q-6. Is a loan from a qualified plan or contract described in section 72(e)(7) treated as a distribution under section 72(e)(4)(A)?

A-6. Yes. Pursuant to section 72(e)(4)(A), if an employee receives, either directly or indirectly, any amount as a loan from a qualified plan or contract described in section 72(e)(7), such amount shall be treated as a distribution from the plan or contract of an amount not received as an annuity. Similarly, if an employee assigns or pledges, or agrees to assign or pledge, any portion of the value of any qualified plan or contract, such portion shall be treated as a distribution from the plan or contract of an amount not received as an annuity.

Q-7. Does the five percent penalty for premature distributions from annuity contracts, as described in section 72(q), apply to distributions from a qualified plan or contract described in section 72(e)(7)?

A-7. No.

Q-8. When is section 72(e)(7) effective?

A-8. Section 72(e)(7) is effective for amounts received or loans made on or after October 17, 1984. For purposes of this effective date provision, loan amounts outstanding on October 16, 1984, which are renegotiated, extended, renewed, or revised after that date generally are treated as loans made on the date of the renegotiation, etc.

T.D. 8073, 1/29/86.

---

§ 1.72(p)-1 Loans treated as distributions.

Caution: The Treasury has not yet amended Reg § 1.72(p)-1 to reflect changes made by P.L. 107-16.

The questions and answers in this section provide guidance under section 72(p) pertaining to loans from qualified employer plans (including government plans and tax-sheltered annuities and employer plans that were formerly qualified). The examples included in the questions and answers in this section are based on the assumption that a bona fide loan is made to a participant from a qualified defined contribution plan pursuant to an enforceable agreement (in accordance with paragraph (b) of Q&A-3 of this section), with adequate security and with an interest rate and repayment terms that are commercially reasonable. (The particular interest rate used, which is solely for illustration, is 8.75 percent compounded annually.) In addition, unless the contrary is specified, it is assumed in the examples that the amount of the loan does not exceed 50 percent of the participant's nonforfeitable account balance, the participant has no other outstanding loan (and had no prior loan) from the plan or any other plan maintained by the participant's employer or any other person required to be aggregated with the employer under section 414(b), (c) or (m), and the loan is not excluded from section 72(p) as a loan made in the ordinary course of an investment program as described in Q&A-18 of this section. The regulations and examples in this section do not provide guidance on whether a loan from a plan would result in a prohibited transaction under section 4975 of the Internal Revenue Code or on whether a loan from a plan covered by Title I of the Employee Retirement Income Security Act of 1974 (88 Stat. 829) (ERISA) would be consistent with the fiduciary standards of ERISA or would result in a prohibited transaction under section 406 of ERISA. The questions and answers are as follows:

Q-1. In general, what does section 72(p) provide with respect to loans from a qualified employer plan?

A-1. (a) Loans. Under section 72(p), an amount received by a participant or beneficiary as a loan from a qualified employer plan is treated as having been received as a distribution from the plan (a deemed distribution), unless the loan satisfies the requirements of Q&A-3 of this section. For purposes of section 72(p) and this section, a loan made from a contract that has been purchased under a qualified employer plan (including a contract that has been distributed to the participant or beneficiary) is considered a loan made under a qualified employer plan.

(b) Pledges and assignments. Under section 72(p), if a participant or beneficiary assigns or pledges (or agrees to assign or pledge) any portion of his or her interest in a qualified employer plan as security for a loan, the portion of the individual's interest assigned or pledged (or subject to an agreement to assign or pledge) is treated as a loan from the plan to the individual, with the result that such portion is subject to the deemed distribution rule described in paragraph (a) of this Q&A-1. For purposes of section 72(p) and this section, any assignment or pledge of (or agreement to assign or to pledge) any portion of a participant's or beneficiary's interest in a contract that has been purchased under a qualified employer plan (including a contract that has been distributed to the participant or beneficiary) is considered an assignment or pledge of (or agreement to assign or pledge) an interest in a qualified employer plan. However, if all or a portion of a participant's or beneficiary's interest in a qualified employer plan is pledged or assigned as security for a loan from the plan to the participant or the beneficiary, only the amount of the loan received by the participant or the beneficiary, not the amount pledged or assigned, is treated as a loan.

Q-2. What is a qualified employer plan for purposes of section 72(p)?

A-2. For purposes of section 72(p) and this section, a qualified employer plan means—

(a) A plan described in section 401(a) which includes a trust exempt from tax under section 501(a);

(b) An annuity plan described in section 403(a);

(c) A plan under which amounts are contributed by an individual's employer for an annuity contract described in section 403(b);

(d) Any plan, whether or not qualified, established and maintained for its employees by the United States, by a State or political subdivision thereof, or by an agency or instrumentality of the United States, a State or a political subdivision of a State; or

(e) Any plan which was (or was determined to be) described in paragraph (a), (b), (c), or (d) of this Q&A-2.

Q-3. What requirements must be satisfied in order for a loan to a participant or beneficiary from a qualified employer plan not to be a deemed distribution?

A-3. (a) In general. A loan to a participant or beneficiary from a qualified employer plan will not be a deemed distribution to the participant or beneficiary if the loan satisfies the repayment term requirement of section 72(p)(2)(B), the level amortization requirement of section 72(p)(2)(C), and the enforceable agreement requirement of paragraph (b) of this Q&A-3, but only to the extent the loan satisfies the amount limitations of section 72(p)(2)(A).

(b) Enforceable agreement requirement. A loan does not satisfy the requirements of this paragraph unless the loan is evidenced by a legally enforceable agreement (which may include more than one document) and the terms of the agreement demonstrate compliance with the requirements of section 72(p)(2) and this section. Thus, the agreement must specify the amount and date of the loan and the repayment schedule. The agreement does not have to be signed if the agreement is enforceable under applicable law without being signed. The agreement must be set forth either—

(1) In a written paper document; or

(2) In a document that is delivered through an electronic medium under an electronic system that satisfies the requirements of § 1.401(a)-21 of this chapter.

Q-4. If a loan from a qualified employer plan to a participant or beneficiary fails to satisfy the requirements of Q&A-3 of this section, when does a deemed distribution occur?

A-4. (a) Deemed distribution. For purposes of section 72, a deemed distribution occurs at the first time that the requirements of Q&A-3 of this section are not satisfied, in form or in operation. This may occur at the time the loan is made or at a later date. If the terms of the loan do not require repayments that satisfy the repayment term requirement of section 72(p)(2)(B) or the level amortization requirement of section 72(p)(2)(C), or the loan is not evidenced by an enforceable agreement satisfying the requirements of paragraph (b) of Q&A-3 of this section, the entire amount of the loan is a deemed distribution under section 72(p) at the time the loan is made. If the loan satisfies the requirements of Q&A-3 of this section except that the amount loaned exceeds the limitations of section 72(p)(2)(A), the amount of the loan in excess of the applicable limitation is a deemed distribution under section 72(p) at the time the loan is made. If the loan initially satisfies the requirements of section 72(p)(2)(A), (B) and (C) and the enforceable agreement requirement of paragraph (b) of Q&A-3 of this section, but payments are not made in accordance with the terms applicable to the loan, a deemed distribution occurs as a result of the failure to make such payments. See Q&A-10 of this section regarding when such a deemed distribution occurs and the amount thereof and Q&A-11 of this section regarding the tax treatment of a deemed distribution.

(b) Examples. The following examples illustrate the rules in paragraph (a) of this Q&A-4 and are based upon the assumptions described in the introductory text of this section:

Example 1. (i) A participant has a nonforfeitable account balance of $200,000 and receives $70,000 as a loan repayable in level quarterly installments over five years.

(ii) Under section 72(p), the participant has a deemed distribution of $20,000 (the excess of $70,000 over $50,000) at the time of the loan, because the loan exceeds the $50,000 limit in section 72(p)(2)(A)(i). The remaining $50,000 is not a deemed distribution.

Example 2. (i) A participant with a nonforfeitable account balance of $30,000 borrows $20,000 as a loan repayable in level monthly installments over five years.

(ii) Because the amount of the loan is $5,000 more than 50% of the participant's nonforfeitable account balance, the participant has a deemed distribution of $5,000 at the time of the loan. The remaining $15,000 is not a deemed distribution. (Note also that, if the loan is secured solely by the participant's account balance, the loan may be a prohibited transaction under section 4975 because the loan may not satisfy 29 CFR 2550.408b-1(f)(2).)

Example 3. (i) The nonforfeitable account balance of a participant is $100,000 and a $50,000 loan is made to the participant repayable in level quarterly installments over seven years. The loan is not eligible for the section 72(p)(2)(B)(ii) exception for loans used to acquire certain dwelling units.

(ii) Because the repayment period exceeds the maximum five-year period in section 72(p)(2)(B)(i), the participant has a deemed distribution of $50,000 at the time the loan is made.

Example 4. (i) On August 1, 2002, a participant has a nonforfeitable account balance of $45,000 and borrows $20,000 from a plan to be repaid over five years in level monthly installments due at the end of each month. After making monthly payments through July 2003, the participant fails to make any of the payments due thereafter.

(ii) As a result of the failure to satisfy the requirement that the loan be repaid in level monthly installments, the participant has a deemed distribution. See paragraph (c) of Q&A-10 of this section regarding when such a deemed distribution occurs and the amount thereof.

Q-5. What is a principal residence for purposes of the exception in section 72(p)(2)(B)(ii) from the requirement that a loan be repaid in five years?

A-5. A-5: Section 72(p)(2)(B)(ii) provides that the requirement in section 72(p)(2)(B)(i) that a plan loan be repaid within five years does not apply to a loan used to acquire a dwelling unit which will within a reasonable time be used as the principal residence of the participant (a principal residence plan loan). For this purpose, a principal residence has the same meaning as a principal residence under section 121.

Q-6. In order to satisfy the requirements for a principal residence plan loan, is a loan required to be secured by the dwelling unit that will within a reasonable time be used as the principal residence of the participant?

A-6. A loan is not required to be secured by the dwelling unit that will within a reasonable time be used as the participant's principal residence in order to satisfy the requirements for a principal residence plan loan.

Q-7. What tracing rules apply in determining whether a loan qualifies as a principal residence plan loan?

A-7. The tracing rules established under section 163(h)(3)(B) apply in determining whether a loan is treated as for the acquisition of a principal residence in order to qualify as a principal residence plan loan.

Q-8. Can a refinancing qualify as a principal residence plan loan?

A-8. (a) Refinancings. In general, no, a refinancing cannot qualify as a principal residence plan loan. However, a loan from a qualified employer plan used to repay a loan from a third party will qualify as a principal residence plan loan if the plan loan qualifies as a principal residence plan loan without regard to the loan from the third party.

(b) Example. The following example illustrates the rules in paragraph (a) of this Q&A-8 and is based upon the assumptions described in the introductory text of this section:

Example. (i) On July 1, 2003, a participant requests a $50,000 plan loan to be repaid in level monthly installments over 15 years. On August 1, 2003, the participant acquires a principal residence and pays a portion of the purchase price with a $50,000 bank loan. On September 1, 2003, the plan loans $50,000 to the participant, which the participant uses to pay the bank loan.

(ii) Because the plan loan satisfies the requirements to qualify as a principal residence plan loan (taking into account the tracing rules of section 163(h)(3)(B)), the plan loan qualifies for the exception in section 72(p)(2)(B)(ii).

Q-9. Does the level amortization requirement of section 72(p)(2)(C) apply when a participant is on a leave of absence without pay?

A-9. (a) Leave of absence. The level amortization requirement of section 72(p)(2)(C) does not apply for a period, not longer than one year (or such longer period as may apply under section 414(u) and paragraph (b) of this Q&A-9), that a participant is on a bona fide leave of absence, either without pay from the employer or at a rate of pay (after applicable employment tax withholdings) that is less than the amount of the installment payments required under the terms of the loan. However, the loan (including interest that accrues during the leave of absence) must be repaid by the latest permissible term of the loan and the amount of the installments due after the leave ends must not be less than the amount required under the terms of the original loan.

(b) Military service. In accordance with section 414(u)(4), if a plan suspends the obligation to repay a loan made to an employee from the plan for any part of a period during which the employee is performing service in the uniformed services (as defined in 38 U.S.C. chapter 43), whether or not qualified military service, such suspension shall not be taken into account for purposes of section 72(p) or this section. Thus, if a plan suspends loan repayments for any part of a period during which the employee is performing military service described in the preceding sentence, such suspension shall not cause the loan to be deemed distributed even if the suspension exceeds one year and even if the term of the loan is extended. However, the loan will not satisfy the repayment term requirement of section 72(p)(2)(B) and the level amortization requirement of section 72(p)(2)(C) unless loan repayments resume upon the completion of such period of military service and the loan is repaid thereafter by amortization in substantially level installments over a period that ends not later than the latest permissible term of the loan.

(c) Latest permissible term of a loan. For purposes of this Q&A-9, the latest permissible term of a loan is the latest date permitted under section 72(p)(2)(B) (i.e., five years from the date of the loan, assuming that the replacement loan does not qualify for the exception at section 72(p)(2)(B)(ii) for principal residence plan loans) plus any additional period of suspension permitted under paragraph (b) of this Q&A-9.

(d) Examples. The following examples illustrate the rules of this Q&A-9 and are based upon the assumptions described in the introductory text of this section:

Example 1. (i) On July 1, 2003, a participant with a nonforfeitable account balance of $80,000 borrows $40,000 to be repaid in level monthly installments of $825 each over 5 years. The loan is not a principal residence plan loan. The participant makes 9 monthly payments and commences an unpaid leave of absence that lasts for 12 months. The participant was not performing military service during this period. Thereafter, the participant resumes active employment and resumes making repayments on the loan until the loan is repaid. The amount of each monthly installment is increased to $1,130 in order to repay the loan by June 30, 2008.

(ii) Because the loan satisfies the requirements of section 72(p)(2), the participant does not have a deemed distribution. Alternatively, section 72(p)(2) would be satisfied if the participant continued the monthly installments of $825 after resuming active employment and on June 30, 2008 repaid the full balance remaining due.

Example 2. (i) The facts are the same as in Example 1, except the participant was on leave of absence performing service in the uniformed services (as defined in chapter 43 of title 38, United States Code) for two years and the rate of interest charged during this period of military service is reduced to 6 percent compounded annually under 50 App. section 526 (relating to the Soldiers' and Sailors' Civil Relief Act Amendments of 1942). After the military service ends on April 2, 2006, the participant resumes active employment on April 19, 2006, continues the monthly installments of $825 thereafter, and on June 30, 2010, repays the full balance remaining due ($6,487).

(ii) Because the loan satisfies the requirements of section 72(p)(2) and paragraph (b) of this Q&A-9, the participant does not have a deemed distribution. Alternatively, section 72(p)(2) would also be satisfied if the amount of each monthly installment after April 19, 2006, is increased to $930 in order to repay the loan by June 30, 2010 (without any balance remaining due then).

Q-10. If a participant fails to make the installment payments required under the terms of a loan that satisfied the requirements of Q&A-3 of this section when made, when does a deemed distribution occur and what is the amount of the deemed distribution?

A-10. (a) Timing of deemed distribution. Failure to make any installment payment when due in accordance with the terms of the loan violates section 72(p)(2)(C) and, accordingly, results in a deemed distribution at the time of such failure. However, the plan administrator may allow a cure period and section 72(p)(2)(C) will not be considered to have been violated if the installment payment is made not later than the end of the cure period, which period cannot continue beyond the last day of the calendar quarter following the calendar quarter in which the required installment payment was due.

(b) Amount of deemed distribution. If a loan satisfies Q&A-3 of this section when made, but there is a failure to pay the installment payments required under the terms of the loan (taking into account any cure period allowed under paragraph (a) of this Q&A-10), then the amount of the deemed distribution equals the entire outstanding balance of the loan (including accrued interest) at the time of such failure.

(c) Example. The following example illustrates the rules in paragraphs (a) and (b) of this Q&A-10 and is based upon the assumptions described in the introductory text of this section:

Example. (i) On August 1, 2002, a participant has a nonforfeitable account balance of $45,000 and borrows $20,000 from a plan to be repaid over 5 years in level monthly installments due at the end of each month. After making all monthly payments due through July 31, 2003, the participant fails to make the payment due on August 31, 2003 or any other monthly payments due thereafter. The plan administrator allows a three-month cure period.

(ii) As a result of the failure to satisfy the requirement that the loan be repaid in level installments pursuant to section 72(p)(2)(C), the participant has a deemed distribution on November 30, 2003, which is the last day of the three-month cure period for the August 31, 2003 installment. The amount of the deemed distribution is $17,157, which is the outstanding balance on the loan at November 30, 2003. Alternatively, if the plan administrator had allowed a cure period through the end of the next calendar quarter, there would be a deemed distribution on December 31, 2003 equal to $17,282, which is the outstanding balance of the loan at December 31, 2003.

Q-11. Does section 72 apply to a deemed distribution as if it were an actual distribution?

A-11. (a) Tax basis. If the employee's account includes after-tax contributions or other investment in the contract under section 72(e), section 72 applies to a deemed distribution as if it were an actual distribution, with the result that all or a portion of the deemed distribution may not be taxable.

(b) Section 72(t) and (m). Section 72(t) (which imposes a 10 percent tax on certain early distributions) and section 72(m)(5) (which imposes a separate 10 percent tax on certain amounts received by a 5-percent owner) apply to a deemed distribution under section 72(p) in the same manner as if the deemed distribution were an actual distribution.

Q-12. Is a deemed distribution under section 72(p) treated as an actual distribution for purposes of the qualification requirements of section 401, the distribution provisions of section 402, the distribution restrictions of section 401(k)(2)(B) or 403(b)(11), or the vesting requirements of § 1.411(a)-7(d)(5) (which affects the application of a graded vesting schedule in cases involving a prior distribution)?

A-12. No; thus, for example, if a participant in a money purchase plan who is an active employee has a deemed distribution under section 72(p), the plan will not be considered to have made an in-service distribution to the participant in violation of the qualification requirements applicable to money purchase plans. Similarly, the deemed distribution is not eligible to be rolled over to an eligible retirement plan and is not considered an impermissible distribution of an amount attributable to elective contributions in a section 401(k) plan. See also § 1.402(c)-2, Q&A-4(d) and § 1.401(k)-1(d)(5)(ii).

Q-13. How does a reduction (offset) of an account balance in order to repay a plan loan differ from a deemed distribution?

A-13. (a) Difference between deemed distribution and plan loan offset amount. (1) Loans to a participant from a qualified employer plan can give rise to two types of taxable distributions—

(i) A deemed distribution pursuant to section 72(p); and

(ii) A distribution of an offset amount.

(2) As described in Q&A-4 of this section, a deemed distribution occurs when the requirements of Q&A-3 of this section are not satisfied, either when the loan is made or at a later time. A deemed distribution is treated as a distribution to the participant or beneficiary only for certain tax purposes and is not a distribution of the accrued benefit. A distribution of a plan loan offset amount (as defined in § 1.402(c)-2, Q&A-9(b)) occurs when, under the terms governing a plan loan, the accrued benefit of the participant or beneficiary is reduced (offset) in order to repay the loan (including the enforcement of the plan's security interest in the accrued benefit). A distribution of a plan loan offset amount could occur in a variety of circumstances, such as where the terms governing the plan loan require that, in the event of the participant's request for a distribution, a loan be repaid immediately or treated as in default.

(b) Plan loan offset. In the event of a plan loan offset, the amount of the account balance that is offset against the loan is an actual distribution for purposes of the Internal Revenue Code, not a deemed distribution under section 72(p). Accordingly, a plan may be prohibited from making such an offset under the provisions of section 401(a), 401(k)(2)(B) or 403(b)(11) prohibiting or limiting distributions to an active employee. See § 1.402(c)-2, Q&A-9(c), Example 6. See also Q&A-19 of this section for rules regarding the treatment of a loan after a deemed distribution.

Q-14. How is the amount includible in income as a result of a deemed distribution under section 72(p) required to be reported?

A-14. The amount includible in income as a result of a deemed distribution under section 72(p) is required to be reported on Form 1099-R (or any other form prescribed by the Commissioner).

Q-15. What withholding rules apply to plan loans?

A-15. To the extent that a loan, when made, is a deemed distribution or an account balance is reduced (offset) to repay a loan, the amount includible in income is subject to withholding. If a deemed distribution of a loan or a loan repayment by benefit offset results in income at a date after the date the loan is made, withholding is required only if a transfer of cash or property (excluding employer securities) is made to the participant or beneficiary from the plan at the same time. See §§ 35.3405-1, f-4, and 31.3405(c)-1, Q&A-9 and Q&A-11, of this chapter for further guidance on withholding rules.

Q-16. If a loan fails to satisfy the requirements of Q&A-3 of this section and is a prohibited transaction under section 4975, is the deemed distribution of the loan under section 72(p) a correction of the prohibited transaction?

A-16. No, a deemed distribution is not a correction of a prohibited transaction under section 4975. See §§ 141.4975-13 and 53.4941(e)-1(c)(1) of this chapter for guidance concerning correction of a prohibited transaction.

Q-17. What are the income tax consequences if an amount is transferred from a qualified employer plan to a participant or beneficiary as a loan, but there is an express or tacit understanding that the loan will not be repaid?

A-17. If there is an express or tacit understanding that the loan will not be repaid or, for any reason, the transaction does not create a debtor-creditor relationship or is otherwise not a bona fide loan, then the amount transferred is treated as an actual distribution from the plan for purposes of the Internal Revenue Code, and is not treated as a loan or as a deemed distribution under section 72(p).

Q-18. If a qualified employer plan maintains a program to invest in residential mortgages, are loans made pursuant to the investment program subject to section 72(p)?

A-18. (a) Residential mortgage loans made by a plan in the ordinary course of an investment program are not subject to section 72(p) if the property acquired with the loans is the primary security for such loans and the amount loaned does not exceed the fair market value of the property. An investment program exists only if the plan has established, in advance of a specific investment under the program, that a certain percentage or amount of plan assets will be invested in residential mortgages available to persons purchasing the property who satisfy commercially customary financial criteria. A loan will not be considered as made under an investment program if—

(1) Any of the loans made under the program matures upon a participant's termination from employment;

(2) Any of the loans made under the program is an earmarked asset of a participant's or beneficiary's individual account in the plan; or

(3) The loans made under the program are made available only to participants or beneficiaries in the plan.

(b) Paragraph (a)(3) of this Q&A-18 shall not apply to a plan which, on December 20, 1995, and at all times thereafter, has had in effect a loan program under which, but for paragraph (a)(3) of this Q&A-18, the loans comply with the conditions of paragraph (a) of this Q&A-18 to constitute residential mortgage loans in the ordinary course of an investment program.

(c) No loan that benefits an officer, director, or owner of the employer maintaining the plan, or their beneficiaries, will be treated as made under an investment program.

(d) This section does not provide guidance on whether a residential mortgage loan made under a plan's investment program would result in a prohibited transaction under section 4975, or on whether such a loan made by a plan covered by Title I of ERISA would be consistent with the fiduciary standards of ERISA or would result in a prohibited transaction under section 406 of ERISA. See 29 CFR 2550.408b-1.

Q-19. If there is a deemed distribution under section 72(p), is the interest that accrues thereafter on the amount of the deemed distribution an indirect loan for income tax purposes and what effect does the deemed distribution have on subsequent loans?

A-19. (a) General rule. Except as provided in paragraph (b) of this Q&A-19, a deemed distribution of a loan is treated as a distribution for purposes of section 72. Therefore, a loan that is deemed to be distributed under section 72(p) ceases to be an outstanding loan for purposes of section 72, and the interest that accrues thereafter under the plan on the amount deemed distributed is disregarded for purposes of applying section 72 to the participant or the beneficiary. Even though interest continues to accrue on the outstanding loan (and is taken into account for purposes of determining the tax treatment of any subsequent loan in accordance with paragraph (b) of this Q&A-19), this additional interest is not treated as an additional loan (and thus, does not result in an additional deemed distribution) for purposes of section 72(p). However, a loan that is deemed distributed under section 72(p) is not considered distributed for all purposes of the Internal Revenue Code. See Q&A-11 through Q&A-16 of this section.

(b) Effect on subsequent loans. (1) Application of section 72(p)(2)(A). A loan that is deemed distributed under section 72(p) (including interest accruing thereafter) and that has not been repaid (such as by a plan loan offset) is considered outstanding for purposes of applying section 72(p)(2)(A) to determine the maximum amount of any subsequent loan to the participant or beneficiary.

(2) Additional security for subsequent loans. If a loan is deemed distributed to a participant or beneficiary under section 72(p) and has not been repaid (such as by a plan loan offset), then no payment made thereafter to the participant or beneficiary is treated as a loan for purposes of section 72(p)(2) unless the loan otherwise satisfies section 72(p)(2) and this section and either of the following conditions is satisfied:

(i) There is an arrangement among the plan, the participant or beneficiary, and the employer, enforceable under applicable law, under which repayments will be made by payroll withholding. For this purpose, an arrangement will not fail to be enforceable merely because a party has the right to revoke the arrangement prospectively.

(ii) The plan receives adequate security from the participant or beneficiary that is in addition to the participant's or beneficiary's accrued benefit under the plan.

(3) Condition no longer satisfied. If, following a deemed distribution that has not been repaid, a payment is made to a participant or beneficiary that satisfies the conditions in paragraph (b)(2) of this Q&A-19 for treatment as a plan loan and, subsequently, before repayment of the second loan, the conditions in paragraph (b)(2) of this Q&A-19 are no longer satisfied with respect to the second loan (for example, if the loan recipient revokes consent to payroll withholding), the amount then outstanding on the second loan is treated as a deemed distribution under section 72(p).

Q-20. May a participant refinance an outstanding loan or have more than one loan outstanding from a plan?

A-20. (a) Refinancings and multiple loans. (1) General rule. A participant who has an outstanding loan that satisfies section 72(p)(2) and this section may refinance that loan or borrow additional amounts if, under the facts and circumstances, the loans collectively satisfy the amount limitations of section 72(p)(2)(A) and the prior loan and the additional loan each satisfy the requirements of section 72(p)(2)(B) and (C) and this section. For this purpose, a refinancing includes any situation in which one loan replaces another loan.

(2) Loans that repay a prior loan and have a later repayment date. For purposes of section 72(p)(2) and this section (including the amount limitations of section 72(p)(2)(A)), if a loan that satisfies section 72(p)(2) is replaced by a loan (a replacement loan) and the term of the replacement loan ends after the latest permissible term of the loan it replaces (the replaced loan), then the replacement loan and the replacement loan are both treated as outstanding on the date of the transaction. For purposes of the preceding sentence, the latest permissible term of the replaced loan is the latest date permitted under section 72(p)(2)(C) (i.e., five years from the original date of the replaced loan, assuming that the replaced loan does not qualify for the exception at section 72(p)(2)(B)(ii) for principal residence plan loans and that no additional period of suspension applied to the replaced loan under Q&A-9(b) of this section). Thus, for example, if the term of the replacement loan ends after the latest permissible term of the replaced loan and the sum of the amount of the replacement loan plus the outstanding balance of all other loans on the date of the transaction, including the replaced loan, fails to satisfy the amount limitations of section 72(p)(2)(A), then the replacement loan results in a deemed distribution. This paragraph (a)(2) does not apply to a replacement loan if the terms of the replacement loan would satisfy section 72(p)(2) and this section determined as if the replacement loan consisted of two separate loans, the replaced loan (amortized in substantially level payments over a period ending not later than the last day of the latest permissible term of the replaced loan) and, to the extent the amount of the replacement loan exceeds the amount of the replaced loan, a new loan that is also amortized in substantially level payments over a period ending not later than the last day of the latest permissible term of the replaced loan.

(b) Examples. The following examples illustrate the rules of this Q&A-20 and are based on the assumptions described in the introductory text of this section:

Example 1. (i) A participant with a vested account balance that exceeds $100,000 borrows $40,000 from a plan on January 1, 2005, to be repaid in 20 quarterly installments of $2,491 each. Thus, the term of the loan ends on December 31, 2009. On January 1, 2006, when the outstanding balance on the loan is $33,322, the loan is refinanced and is replaced by a new $40,000 loan from the plan to be repaid in 20 quarterly installments. Under the terms of the refinanced loan, the loan is to be repaid in level quarterly installments (of $2,491 each) over the next 20 quarters. Thus, the term of the new loan ends on December 31, 2010.

(ii) Under section 72(p)(2)(A), the amount of the new loan, when added to the outstanding balance of all other loans from the plan, must not exceed $50,000 reduced by the excess of the highest outstanding balance of loans from the plan during the 1-year period ending on December 31, 2005, over the outstanding balance of loans from the plan on January 1, 2006, with such outstanding balance to be determined immediately prior to the new $40,000 loan. Because the term of the new loan ends later than the term of the loan it replaces, under paragraph (a)(2) of this Q&A-20, both the new loan and the loan it replaces must be taken into account for purposes of applying section 72(p)(2), including the amount limitations in section 72(p)(2)(A). The amount of the new loan is $40,000, the outstanding balance on January 1, 2006, of the loan it replaces is $33,322, and the highest outstanding balance of loans from the plan during 2005 was $40,000. Accordingly, under section 72(p)(2)(A), the sum of the new loan and the outstanding balance on January 1, 2006, of the loan it replaces must not exceed $50,000 reduced by $6,678 (the excess of the $40,000 maximum outstanding loan balance during 2005 over the $33,322 outstanding balance on January 1, 2006, determined immediately prior to the new loan) and, thus, must not exceed $43,322. The sum of the new loan ($40,000) and the outstanding balance on January 1, 2006, of the loan it replaces ($33,322) is $73,322. Since $73,322 exceeds the $43,322 limit under section 72(p)(2)(A) by $30,000, there is a deemed distribution of $30,000 on January 1, 2006.

(iii) However, no deemed distribution would occur if, under the terms of the refinanced loan, the amount of the first 16 installments on the refinanced loan were equal to $2,907, which is the sum of the $2,491 originally scheduled quarterly installment payment amount under the first loan, plus $416 (which is the amount required to repay, in level quarterly installments over 5 years beginning on January 1, 2006, the excess of the refinanced loan over the January 1, 2006, balance of the first loan ($40,000 minus $33,322 equals $6,678)), and the amount of the 4 remaining installments was equal to $416. The refinancing would not be subject to paragraph (a)(2) of this Q&A-20 because the terms of the new loan would satisfy section 72(p)(2) and this section (including the substantially level amortization requirements of section 72(p)(2)(B) and (C)) determined as if the new loan consisted of 2 loans, one of which is in the amount of the first loan ($33,322) and is amortized in substantially level payments over a period ending December 31, 2009 (the last day of the term of the first loan) and the other of which is in the additional amount ($6,678) borrowed under the new loan. Similarly, the transaction also would not result in a deemed distribution (and would not be subject to paragraph (a)(2) of this Q&A-20) if the terms of the refinanced loan provided for repayments to be made in level quarterly installments (of $2,990 each) over the next 16 quarters.

Example 2. (i) The facts are the same as in Example 1(i), except that the applicable interest rate used by the plan when the loan is refinanced is significantly lower due to a reduction in market rates of interest and, under the terms of the refinanced loan, the amount of the first 16 installments on the refinanced loan is equal to $2,848 and the amount of the next 4 installments on the refinanced loan is equal to $406. The $2,848 amount is the sum of $2,442 to repay the first loan by December 31, 2009 (the term of the first loan), plus $406 (which is the amount to repay, in level quarterly installments over 5 years beginning on January 1, 2006, the $6,678 excess of the refinanced loan over the January 1, 2006, balance of the first loan).

(ii) The transaction does not result in a deemed distribution (and is not subject to paragraph (a)(2) of this Q&A-20) because the terms of the new loan would satisfy section 72(p)(2) and this section (including the substantially level amortization requirements of section 72(p)(2)(B) and (C)) determined as if the new loan consisted of 2 loans, one of which is in the amount of the first loan ($33,322) and is amortized in substantially level payments over a period ending December 31, 2009 (the last day of the term of the first loan), and the other of which is in the additional amount ($6,678) borrowed under the new loan. The transaction would also not result in a deemed distribution (and not be subject to paragraph (a)(2) of this Q&A-20) if the terms of the new loan provided for repayments to be made in level quarterly installments (of $2,931 each) over the next 16 quarters.

Q-21. Is a participant's tax basis under the plan increased if the participant repays the loan after a deemed distribution?

A-21. (a) Repayments after deemed distribution. Yes, if the participant or beneficiary repays the loan after a deemed distribution of the loan under section 72(p), then, for purposes of section 72(e), the participant's or beneficiary's investment in the contract (tax basis) under the plan increases by the amount of the cash repayments that the participant or beneficiary makes on the loan after the deemed distribution. However, loan repayments are not treated as after-tax contributions for other purposes, including sections 401(m) and 415(c)(2)(B).

(b) Example. The following example illustrates the rules in paragraph (a) of this Q&A-21 and is based on the assumptions described in the introductory text of this section:

Example. (i) A participant receives a $20,000 loan on January 1, 2003, to be repaid in 20 quarterly installments of $1,245 each. On December 31, 2003, the outstanding loan balance ($19,179) is deemed distributed as a result of a failure to make quarterly installment payments that were due on September 30, 2003 and December 31, 2003. On June 30, 2004, the participant repays $5,147 (which is the sum of the three installment payments that were due on September 30, 2003, December 31, 2003, and March 31, 2004, with interest thereon to June 30, 2004, plus the installment payment due on June 30, 2004). Thereafter, the participant resumes making the installment payments of $1,245 from September 30, 2004 through December 31, 2007. The loan repayments made after December 31, 2003 through December 31, 2007 total $22,577.

(ii) Because the participant repaid $22,577 after the deemed distribution that occurred on December 31, 2003, the participant has investment in the contract (tax basis) equal to $22,577 (14 payments of $1,245 each plus a single payment of $5,147) as of December 31, 2007.

Q-22. When is the effective date of section 72(p) and the regulations in this section?

A-22. (a) Statutory effective date. Section 72(p) generally applies to assignments, pledges, and loans made after August 13, 1982.

(b) Regulatory effective date. This section applies to assignments, pledges, and loans made on or after January 1, 2002.

(c) Loans made before the regulatory effective date—(1) General rule. A plan is permitted to apply Q&A-19 and Q&A-21 of this section to a loan made before the regulatory effective date in paragraph (b) of this Q&A-22 (and after the statutory effective date in paragraph (a) of this Q&A-22) if there has not been any deemed distribution of the loan before the transition date or if the conditions of paragraph (c)(2) of this Q&A-22 are satisfied with respect to the loan.

(2) Consistency transition rule for certain loans deemed distributed before the regulatory effective date. (i) The rules in this paragraph (c)(2) of this Q&A-22 apply to a loan made before the regulatory effective date in paragraph (b) of this Q&A-22 (and after the statutory effective date in paragraph (a) of this Q&A-22) if there has been any deemed distribution of the loan before the transition date.

(ii) The plan is permitted to apply Q&A-19 and Q&A-21 of this section to the loan beginning on any January 1, but only if the plan reported, in Box 1 of Form 1099-R, for a taxable year no later than the latest taxable year that would be permitted under this section (if this section had been in effect for all loans made after the statutory effective date in paragraph (a) of this Q&A-22), a gross distribution of an amount at least equal to the initial default amount. For purposes of this section, the initial default amount is the amount that would be reported as a gross distribution under Q&A-4 and Q&A-10 of this section and the transition date is the January 1 on which a plan begins applying Q&A-19 and Q&A-21 of this section to a loan.

(iii) If a plan applies Q&A-19 and Q&A-21 of this section to such a loan, then the plan, in its reporting and withholding on or after the transition date, must not attribute investment in the contract (tax basis) to the participant or beneficiary based upon the initial default amount.

(iv) This paragraph (c)(2)(iv) of this Q&A-22 applies if—

(A) The plan attributed investment in the contract (tax basis) to the participant or beneficiary based on the deemed distribution of the loan;

(B) The plan subsequently made an actual distribution to the participant or beneficiary before the transition date; and

(C) Immediately before the transition date, the initial default amount (or, if less, the amount of the investment in the contract so attributed) exceeds the participant's or beneficiary's investment in the contract (tax basis). If this paragraph (c)(2)(iv) of this Q&A-22 applies, the plan must treat the excess (the loan transition amount) as a loan amount that remains outstanding and must include the excess in the participant's or beneficiary's income at the time of the first actual distribution made on or after the transition date.

(3) Examples. The rules in paragraph (c)(2) of this Q&A-22 are illustrated by the following examples, which are based on the assumptions described in the introductory text of this section (and, except as specifically provided in the examples, also assume that no distributions are made to the participant and that the participant has no investment in the contract with respect to the plan). Example 1, Example 2, and Example 4 of this paragraph (c)(3) of this Q&A-22 illustrate the application of the rules in paragraph (c)(2) of this Q&A-22 to a plan that, before the transition date, did not treat interest accruing after the initial deemed distribution as resulting in additional deemed distributions under section 72(p). Example 3 of this paragraph (c)(3) of this Q&A-22 illustrates the application of the rules in paragraph (c)(2) of this Q&A-22 to a plan that, before the transition date, treated interest accruing after the initial deemed distribution as resulting in additional deemed distributions under section 72(p). The examples are as follows:

Example 1. (i) In 1998, when a participant's account balance under a plan is $50,000, the participant receives a loan from the plan. The participant makes the required repayments until 1999 when there is a deemed distribution of $20,000 as a result of a failure to repay the loan. For 1999, as a result of the deemed distribution, the plan reports, in Box 1 of Form 1099-R, a gross distribution of $20,000 (which is the initial default amount in accordance with paragraph (c)(2)(ii) of this Q&A-22) and, in Box 2 of Form 1099-R, a taxable amount of $20,000. The plan then records an increase in the participant's tax basis for the same amount ($20,000). Thereafter, the plan disregards, for purposes of section 72, the interest that accrues on the loan after the 1999 deemed distribution. Thus, as of December 31, 2001, the total taxable amount reported by the plan as a result of the deemed distribution is $20,000 and the plan's records show that the participant's tax basis is the same amount ($20,000). As of January 1, 2002, the plan decides to apply Q&A-19 of this section to the loan. Accordingly, it reduces the participant's tax basis by the initial default amount of $20,000, so that the participant's remaining tax basis in the plan is zero. Thereafter, the amount of the outstanding loan is not treated as part of the account balance for purposes of section 72. The participant attains age 59½ in the year 2003 and receives a distribution of the full account balance under the plan consisting of $60,000 in cash and the loan receivable. At that time, the plan's records reflect an offset of the loan amount against the loan receivable in the participant's account and a distribution of $60,000 in cash.

(ii) For the year 2003, the plan must report a gross distribution of $60,000 in Box 1 of Form 1099-R and a taxable amount of $60,000 in Box 2 of Form 1099-R.

Example 2. (i) The facts are the same as in Example 1, except that in 1999, immediately prior to the deemed distribution, the participant's account balance under the plan totals $50,000 and the participant's tax basis is $10,000. For 1999, the plan reports, in Box 1 of Form 1099-R, a gross distribution of $20,000 (which is the initial default amount in accordance with paragraph (c)(2)(ii) of this Q&A-22) and reports, in Box 2 of Form 1099-R, a taxable amount of $16,000 (the $20,000 deemed distribution minus $4,000 of tax basis ($10,000 times ($20,000/$50,000)) allocated to the deemed distribution). The plan then records an increase in tax basis equal to the $20,000 deemed distribution, so that the participant's remaining tax basis as of December 31, 1999, totals $26,000 ($10,000 minus $4,000 plus $20,000). Thereafter, the plan disregards, for purposes of section 72, the interest that accrues on the loan after the 1999 deemed distribution. Thus, as of December 31, 2001, the total taxable amount reported by the plan as a result of the deemed distribution is $16,000 and the plan's records show that the participant's tax basis is $26,000. As of January 1, 2002, the plan decides to apply Q&A-19 of this section to the loan. Accordingly, it reduces the participant's tax basis by the initial default amount of $20,000, so that the participant's remaining tax basis in the plan is $6,000. Thereafter, the amount of the outstanding loan is not treated as part of the account balance for purposes of section 72. The participant attains age 59½ in the year 2003 and receives a distribution of the full account balance under the plan consisting of $60,000 in cash and the loan receivable. At that time, the plan's records reflect an offset of the loan amount against the loan receivable in the participant's account and a distribution of $60,000 in cash.

(ii) For the year 2003, the plan must report a gross distribution of $60,000 in Box 1 of Form 1099-R and a taxable amount of $54,000 in Box 2 of Form 1099-R.

Example 3. (i) In 1993, when a participant's account balance in a plan is $100,000, the participant receives a loan of $50,000 from the plan. The participant makes the required loan repayments until 1995 when there is a deemed distribution of $28,919 as a result of a failure to repay the loan. For 1995, as a result of the deemed distribution, the plan reports, in Box 1 of Form 1099-R, a gross distribution of $28,919 (which is the initial default amount in accordance with paragraph (c)(2)(ii) of this Q&A-22) and, in Box 2 of Form 1099-R, a taxable amount of $28,919. For 1995, the plan also records an increase in the participant's tax basis for the same amount ($28,919). Each year thereafter through 2001, the plan reports a gross distribution equal to the interest accruing that year on the loan balance, reports a taxable amount equal to the interest accruing that year on the loan balance reduced by the participant's tax basis allocated to the gross distribution, and records a net increase in the participant's tax basis equal to that taxable amount. As of December 31, 2001, the taxable amount reported by the plan as a result of the loan totals $44,329 and the plan's records for purposes of section 72 show that the participant's tax basis totals the same amount ($44,329). As of January 1, 2002, the plan decides to apply Q&A-19 of this section. Accordingly, it reduces the participant's tax basis by the initial default amount of $28,919, so that the participant's remaining tax basis in the plan is $15,410 ($44,329 minus $28,919). Thereafter, the amount of the outstanding loan is not treated as part of the account balance for purposes of section 72. The participant attains age 59½ in the year 2003 and receives a distribution of the full account balance under the plan consisting of $180,000 in cash and the loan receivable equal to the $28,919 outstanding loan amount in 1995 plus interest accrued thereafter to the payment date in 2003. At that time, the plan's records reflect an offset of the loan amount against the loan receivable in the participant's account and a distribution of $180,000 in cash.

(ii) For the year 2003, the plan must report a gross distribution of $180,000 in Box 1 of Form 1099-R and a taxable amount of $164,590 in Box 2 of Form 1099-R ($180,000 minus the remaining tax basis of $15,410).

Example 4. (i) The facts are the same as in Example 1, except that in 2000, after the deemed distribution, the participant receives a $10,000 hardship distribution. At the time of the hardship distribution, the participant's account balance under the plan totals $50,000. For 2000, the plan reports, in Box 1 of Form 1099-R, a gross distribution of $10,000 and, in Box 2 of Form 1099-R, a taxable amount of $6,000 (the $10,000 actual distribution minus $4,000 of tax basis ($10,000 times ($20,000/$50,000)) allocated to this actual distribution). The plan then records a decrease in tax basis equal to $4,000, so that the participant's remaining tax basis as of December 31, 2000, totals $16,000 ($20,000 minus $4,000). After 1999, the plan disregards, for purposes of section 72, the interest that accrues on the loan after the 1999 deemed distribution. Thus, as of December 31, 2001, the total taxable amount reported by the plan as a result of the deemed distribution plus the 2000 actual distribution is $26,000 and the plan's records show that the participant's tax basis is $16,000. As of January 1, 2002, the plan decides to apply Q&A-19 of this section to the loan. Accordingly, it reduces the participant's tax basis by the initial default amount of $20,000, so that the participant's remaining tax basis in the plan is reduced from $16,000 to zero. However, because the $20,000 initial default amount exceeds $16,000, the plan records a loan transition amount of $4,000 ($20,000 minus $16,000). Thereafter, the amount of the outstanding loan, other than the $4,000 loan transition amount, is not treated as part of the account balance for purposes of section 72. The participant attains age 59½ in the year 2003 and receives a distribution of the full account balance under the plan consisting of $60,000 in cash and the loan receivable. At that time, the plan's records reflect an offset of the loan amount against the loan receivable in the participant's account and a distribution of $60,000 in cash.

(ii) In accordance with paragraph (c)(2)(iv) of this Q&A-22, the plan must report in Box 1 of Form 1099-R a gross distribution of $64,000 and in Box 2 of Form 1099-R a taxable amount for the participant for the year 2003 equal to $64,000 (the sum of the $60,000 paid in the year 2003 plus $4,000 as the loan transition amount).

(d) Effective date for Q&A-19(b)(2) and Q&A-20. Q&A-19(b)(2) and Q&A-20 of this section apply to assignments, pledges, and loans made on or after January 1, 2004.

T.D. 8894, 7/28/2000, amend T.D. 9021, 12/2/2002, T.D. 9169, 12/28/2004, T.D. 9294, 10/19/2006.

§ 1.73-1 Services of child.

(a) Compensation for personal services of a child shall, regardless of the provisions of State law relating to who is entitled to the earnings of the child, and regardless of whether the income is in fact received by the child, be deemed to be the gross income of the child and not the gross income of the parent of the child. Such compensation, therefore, shall be included in the gross income of the child and shall be reflected in the return rendered by or for such child. The income of a minor child is not required to be included in the gross income of the parent for income tax purposes. For requirements for making the return by such child, or for such child by his guardian, or other person charged with the care of his person or property, see section 6012.

(b) In the determination of taxable income or adjusted gross income, as the case may be, all expenditures made by the parent or the child attributable to amounts which are includible in the gross income of the child and not of the parent solely by reason of section 73 are deemed to have been paid or incurred by the child. In such determination, the child is entitled to take deductions not only for expenditures made on his behalf by his parent which would be commonly considered as business expenses, but also for other expenditures such as charitable contributions made by the parent in the name of the child and out of the child's earnings.

(c) For purposes of section 73, the term "parent" includes any individual who is entitled to the services of the child by reason of having parental rights and duties in respect of the child. See section 6201(c) and the regulations in Part 301 of this chapter (Regulations on Procedure and Administration) for assessment of tax against the parent in certain cases.

T.D. 6137, 7/12/55.

§ 1.74-1 Prizes and awards.

Caution: The Treasury has not yet amended Reg § 1.74-1 to reflect changes made by P.L. 99-514.

(a) Inclusion in gross income. *(1)* Section 74(a) requires the inclusion in gross income of all amounts received as prizes and awards, unless such prizes or awards qualify as an exclusion from gross income under subsection (b), or unless such prize or award is a scholarship or fellowship grant excluded from gross income by section 117. Prizes and awards which are includible in gross income include (but are not limited to) amounts received from radio and television giveaway shows, door prizes, and awards in contests of all types, as well as any prizes and awards from an employer to an employee in recognition of some achievement in connection with his employment.

(2) If the prize or award is not made in money but is made in goods or services, the fair market value of the goods or services is the amount to be included in income.

(b) Exclusion from gross income. Section 74(b) provides an exclusion from gross income of any amount received as a prize or award, if (1) such prize or award was made primarily in recognition of past achievements of the recipient in religious, charitable, scientific, educational, artistic, literary, or civic fields; (2) the recipient was selected without any action on his part to enter the contest or proceedings; and (3) the recipient is not required to render substantial future services as a condition to receiving the prize or award. Thus, such awards as the Nobel prize and the Pulitzer prize would qualify for the exclusion. Section 74(b) does not exclude prizes or awards from an employer to an employee in recognition of some achievement in connection with his employment.

(c) Scholarships and fellowship grants. See section 117 and the regulations thereunder for provisions relating to scholarships and fellowship grants.

T.D. 6137, 7/6/55.

PAR. 2. Section 1.74-1 is amended as follows:

(a) Paragraph (a)(1) is amended by—

(1) Removing the phrase "subsection (b)" and adding the phrase "subsections (b) and (c)" in its place, and

(2) Removing the word "any" in the last sentence and adding the word "most" in its place.

(b) Paragraph (b) is amended by—

(1) Removing the word "and" from the first sentence, and

(2) Removing "award." at the end of the first sentence and adding the language set forth below in its place.

(c) Paragraph (c) is removed and new paragraphs (c), (d), (e), (f), and (g) are added directly following paragraph (b) to read as set forth below.

Proposed § 1.74-1 Prizes and awards. [*For Preamble, see ¶ 151,137*]

* * * * *

(b) Exclusion from gross income. * * * award; and (4) the payor transfers the prize or award (and the prize or award is, in fact, transferred) to one or more governmental units or organizations described in paragraph (1) or (2) of section 170(c) pursuant to a designation by the recipient. Accordingly, awards such as the Nobel prize and the Pulitzer prize will qualify for the exclusion if the award is transferred by the payor to one or more qualifying organizations pursuant to a qualified designation by the recipient.

(c) Designation by recipient. *(1) In general.* To qualify for the exclusion under this section, the recipient must make a qualifying designation, in writing, within 45 days of the date the prize or award is granted (see paragraph (e)(3) of this section for a definition of "granted"). A qualifying designation is required to indicate only that a designation is being made. The document does not need to state on its face that the organization(s) are entities described in paragraph (1) and/or (2) of section 170(c) to result in a qualified designation. Furthermore, it is not necessary that the document do more than identify a class of entities from which the payor may select a recipient. However, designation of a specific nonqualified donee organization or designation of a class of recipients that may include nonqualified donee organizations is not a qualified designation. The following example illustrates the application of this section:

A distinguished ophthalmologist, S, is awarded the Nobel prize for medicine. S may designate that the prize money be given to a particular university that is described in section 170(c)(1), or to any university that is described in that section. However, S cannot designate that the award be given to a donee that is not described in section 170(c)(1), such as a foreign medical school. Selection of such a donee or inclusion of such a donee on a list of possible donees on S's designation would disqualify the designation.

(2) Prizes and awards granted before 60 days after date of publication of final regulations. In the case of prizes and awards granted before 60 days after the date of publication of final regulations, a qualifying designation may be made at any time prior to 105 days after date of publication of final regulations.

(d) Transferred by payor. An exclusion will not be available under this section unless the designated items or amounts are transferred by the payor to one or more qualified donee organizations. The provisions of this paragraph shall not be satisfied unless the items or amounts are transferred by the payor to one or more qualifying donee organizations no later than the due date of the return (without regard to extensions) for the taxable year in which the items or amounts would otherwise be includible in the recipient's gross income. A transfer may be accomplished by any method that results in the receipt of the items or amounts by one or more qualified donee organizations from the payor and does not involve a disqualifying use of the items or amounts. Delivery of items or amounts by a person associated with a payor (e.g., a contractual agent, licensee, or other representative of the payor) will satisfy the requirements of this section so long as the items or amounts are received by, or on behalf of, one or more qualified donee organizations. Possession of a prize or award by any person before a designation is made will not result in the disallowance of an exclusion unless a disqualifying use of the items or amounts is made before the items or amounts are returned to the payor for transfer to one or more qualified donee organizations (see paragraph (e)(2) of this section for a definition of "disqualifying use"). Accordingly, transfer of an item or amount to a nonqualified donee organization will not result in an ineffective transfer under this section if the item or amount is timely returned to the payor by the nonqualified donee organization before a disqualifying use of the item or amount is made and the item or amount is then transferred to a qualifying organization.

(e) Definitions. *(1)* For purposes of this section, "qualified donee organizations" means entities defined in section 170(c)(1) or (2) of the Code.

(2) For purposes of this section, the term "disqualifying use" means, in the case of cash or other intangibles, spending, depositing, investing or otherwise using the prize or award so as to ensure to the benefit of the recipient or any person other than the grantor or an entity described in section 170(c)(1) or (2). In the case of tangible items, the term "disqualifying use" means physical possession of the item for more than a brief period of time by any person other than the grantor or an entity described in section 170(c)(1) or (2). Thus, physical possession by the recipient or a person associated with the recipient may constitute a disqualifying use if the item is kept for more than a brief period of time. For example, receipt of an unexpected tangible award at a ceremony that otherwise comports with the requirements of this section will not constitute a disqualifying use unless the recipient fails to return the item to the payor as soon as practicable after receipt.

(3) For purposes of this section, an item will be considered "granted" when it is subject to the recipient's dominion and control to such an extent that it otherwise would be includible in the recipient's gross income.

(f) Charitable deduction not allowable. Neither the payor nor the recipient will be allowed a charitable deduction for the value of any prize or award that is excluded under this section.

(g) Qualified scholarships. See section 117 and the regulations thereunder for provisions relating to qualified scholarships.

Proposed § 1.74-2 Special exclusion for certain employee achievement awards. [*For Preamble, see ¶ 151,137*]

(a) General rule. *(1)* Section 74(c) provides an exclusion from gross income for the value of an employee achievement award (as defined in section 274(j)) received by an employee if the cost to the employer of the award does not exceed the amount allowable as a deduction to the employer for the cost of the award. Thus, where the cost to the employer of an employee achievement award is fully deductible after considering the limitation under section 274(j), the value representing the employer's cost of the award is excludable from the employee's gross income.

(2) Where the cost of an award to the employer is so disproportionate to the fair market value of the award that there is a significant likelihood that the award was given as disguised compensation, no portion of the award will qualify as an employee achievement award excludable under the provisions of this section (see also § 1.274-8(c)(1) and (4)).

(b) Excess deduction award. Where the cost to the employer of an employee achievement award exceeds the amount allowable as a deduction to the employer, the recipient must include in gross income an amount which is the greater of (1) the excess of such cost over the amount that is allowable as a deduction (but not to exceed the fair market value of the award) or (2) the excess of the fair market value of the award over the amount allowable as a deduction to the employer.

(c) Examples. The operation of this section may be illustrated by the following examples:

Example (1). An employer makes a qualifying length of service award to an employee in the form of a television set. Assume that the deduction limitation under section 274(j)(2) applicable to the award is $400. Assume also that the cost of the television set to the employer was $350, and that the fair market value of the television set is $475. The amount excludable is $475 (the full fair market value of the television set). This is true even though the fair market value exceeds both the cost of the television set to the employer and the $400 deduction allowable to the employer for non-qualified plan awards under section 274(j)(2)(A).

Example (2). Assume the same facts as in example (1) except that the fair market value of the television set is $900. Under these circumstances, the fair market value of the television set is so disproportionate to the cost of the item to the employer that the item will be considered payment of disguised compensation. As a result, no portion of the award will qualify as an employee achievement award. Since no portion of the award is excludable by the employee, the employer must report the full fair market value of the award as compensation on the employee's Form W-2.

Example (3). An employer makes a qualifying safety achievement award to an employee in the form of a pearl necklace. Assume that the deduction limitation under section 274(j) is $400. Assume also that the cost of the necklace to the employer is $425 and that the fair market value of the necklace is $475. The amount includible by the employee in gross income is the greater of (a) $25 (the difference between the cost of the item ($425) and the employer's deductible amount of $400) or (b) $75 (the amount by which the fair market value of the award ($475) exceeds the employer's deductible amount of $400). Accordingly, $75 is the amount includible in the employee's gross income. The remaining portion of the fair market value of the award (i.e., the $400 amount allowable as a deduction to the employer) is not included in the gross income of the employee. If the cost of the pearl necklace to the employer was $500 instead of $425, then $100 would be includible in the employee's gross income because the excess of the cost of the award over $400 (i.e., $100) is greater than the excess of the fair market value of the award over $400 (i.e., $75). The employer must report the $75, which is includible in the employee's gross income, as compensation on the employee's Form W-2.

Example (4). An employer invites its employees to attend a party it is sponsoring to benefit a charity. In order to encourage the employees to attend the party and to make contributions to the charity, the employer promises to match the employees' contributions and also provides expensive prizes to be awarded to contributing employees selected at random. Each employee receiving a prize must include the full fair market value of the prize in gross income because the prizes are not qualifying achievement awards under section 274(j) or de minimis fringe benefits under section 132(e). Since the prizes are not excludable, the employer must report the full fair market value of the prize as compensation on the employee's Form W-2.

(d) Special rules. *(1)* The exclusion provided by this section shall not be available for any award made by a sole proprietorship to the sole proprietor.

(2) In the case of an employer exempt from taxation under Subtitle A of the Code, any reference in this section to the amount allowable as a deduction to the employer shall be treated as a reference to the amount which would be allowable as a deduction to the employer if the employer were not exempt from taxation under Subtitle A of the Code.

(e) Exclusion for certain de minimis fringe benefits. Nothing contained in this section shall preclude the exclusion of the value of an employee award that is otherwise qualified for exclusion under section 132(e).

§ 1.75-1 Treatment of bond premiums in case of dealers in tax-exempt securities.

(a) In general. *(1)* Section 75 requires certain adjustments to be made by dealers in securities with respect to premiums paid on municipal bonds which are held for sale to customers in the ordinary course of the trade or business. The adjustments depend upon the method of accounting used by the taxpayer in computing the gross income from the trade or business. See paragraphs (b) and (c) of this section.

(2) The term "municipal bond" under section 75 means any obligation issued by a government or political subdivision thereof if the interest on the obligation is excludable from gross income under section 103. However, such term does not include an obligation—

(i) If the earliest maturity or call date of the obligation is more than 5 years from the date of acquisition by the taxpayer or the obligation is sold or otherwise disposed of by the taxpayer within 30 days after the date of acquisition by him, and

(ii) If, in case of an obligation acquired after December 31, 1957, the amount realized upon its sale (or, in the case of any other disposition, its fair market value at the time of disposition) is higher than its adjusted basis.

For purposes of this subparagraph, the amount realized on the sale of the obligation, or the fair market value of the obligation, shall not include any amount attributable to interest, and the adjusted basis shall be computed without regard to any adjustment for amortization of bond premium required under section 75 and section 1016(a)(6). For purposes of determining whether the obligation is sold or otherwise disposed of by the taxpayer within 30 days after the date of its acquisition by him, it is immaterial whether or not such 30-day period is entirely within one taxable year.

(3) The term "cost of securities sold" means the amount ascertained by subtracting the inventory value of the closing inventory of a taxable year from the sum of the inventory value of the opening inventory for such year and the cost of securities and other property purchased during such year which would properly be included in the inventory of the taxpayer if on hand at the close of the taxable year.

(b) Inventories not valued at cost. *(1)* In the case of a dealer in securities who computes gross income from his trade or business by the use of inventories and values such inventories on any basis other than cost, the adjustment required by section 75 is, except as provided in subparagraph (2) of this paragraph, the reduction of "cost of securities sold" by the amount equal to the amortizable bond premium which would be disallowed as a deduction under section 171(a) (2) with respect to the municipal bond if the dealer were an ordinary investor holding such bond. Such amortizable bond premium is computed under section 171(b) by reference to the cost or other original basis of the bond on the date of acquisition (determined without regard to section 1013, relating to inventory value on a subsequent date).

(2) With respect to an obligation acquired after December 31, 1957, which has as its earliest maturity or call date a date more than five years from the date on which it was acquired by the taxpayer, the following rules shall apply:

(i) If the taxpayer holds the obligation at the end of the taxable year, he is not required by section 75 to reduce the "cost of securities sold" for such year with respect to the obligation.

(ii) If the taxpayer sells or otherwise disposes of the obligation during the taxable year, he shall reduce the "cost of securities sold" for the taxable year of the sale or disposition unless he sold the obligation for more than its adjusted basis or otherwise disposed of it when its fair market value was more than its adjusted basis. For purposes of determining whether or not the taxpayer sold the obligation for more than its adjusted basis, or otherwise disposed of it when its fair market value was more than its adjusted basis, the amount realized on the sale of the obligation, or the fair market value of the obligation, shall not include any amount attributable to interest, and the adjusted basis shall be computed without regard to any adjustment for amortization of bond premium required under sections 75 and 1016(a)(6). The amount of the reduction referred to in the first sentence of this subdivision is the total amount by which the adjusted basis of the obligation would be required to be reduced under section 1016(a)(5) were the obligation subject to the amortizable bond premium provisions of section 171; that is, the amount of the amortizable bond premium attributable to the period during which the obligation was held which would be disallowed as a deduction under section 171(a)(2) if the taxpayer were an ordinary investor.

(3) This paragraph may be illustrated by the following examples:

Example (1). X, a dealer in securities who values his inventories on a basis other than cost, makes his income tax returns on the calendar year basis. On July 1, 1954, he bought, for $1,060 each, three municipal bonds (A, B, and C) having a face obligation of $1,000, and maturing on July 1, 1959. Bond A is sold on December 31, 1954, bond B is sold on December 31, 1955, and bond C is sold on June 30, 1956. For each bond the amortizable bond premium to maturity is $60, the period from date of acquisition to maturity is 60 months, and the amortizable bond premium per month is $1. The adjustment for each of the years 1954, 1955, and 1956 is as follows:

Bond	Date acquired	Date sold	Adjustment to "cost of securities sold" for— 1954	1955	1956
A	July 1, 1954	Dec. 31, 1954	$6		
B	July 1, 1954	Dec. 31, 1955	6	$12	
C	July 1, 1954	June 30, 1956	6	12	$6
Total			$18	$24	$6

Example (2). Y is a dealer in securities who values his inventories on a basis other than cost. He makes his income tax returns on the calendar year basis. On January 1, 1958, Y bought five bonds (D, E, F, G, and H) issued by various municipalities. Each bond has a face obligation of $1,000 and was purchased for $1,060. The interest on each is excludable from gross income under section 103. Bonds D, E, and F mature on December 31, 1962, and bonds G and H mature on December 31, 1967. The amortizable bond premium per month is $1 with respect to bonds D, E, and F, and is $.50 with respect to bonds G and H. The following table indicates the reduction in "cost of securities sold" which Y should make for the years shown, assuming that he sells the bonds on the dates and for the prices set forth:

Bond	Date sold	Sale price	Adjustment to "cost of securities sold" for— 1958	1959	1960
D	Feb. 1, 1959	$1,090	$12	$1	
E	Jan. 30, 1958	1,100	None		
F	Jan. 30, 1958	1,000	1		
G	Dec. 31, 1960	1,065	None	None	None
H	Dec. 31, 1960	1,050	None	None	$18
			13	1	18

An adjustment to "cost of securities sold" must be made with respect to bond D (even though it was ultimately sold at a gain) because the bond neither had an earliest maturity or call date of more than 5 years from the date on which Y acquired it, nor was it disposed of within 30 days after such date. An adjustment must be made for the years 1958 and 1959 since section 75(a)(1) requires that an adjustment be made with respect to such a bond at the close of each taxable year in which it is held. On the other hand, since bonds E, F, G, and H either were disposed of within 30 days after the date of such acquisition or had an earliest maturity or call date more than 5 years from the date of acquisition, and were acquired after December 31, 1957, it is necessary to determine whether Y disposed of them at a loss so as to require an adjustment under section 75. No adjustment is necessary with respect to bonds E and G because they were sold at a gain. An adjustment to "cost of securities sold" is required with respect to bonds F and H because they were sold at a loss. As in the case of bond D, an adjustment with respect to bond F is made in 1958 in accordance with section 75(a)(1); however, the adjustment with respect to bond H is made entirely in 1960, the taxable year in which Y sold that bond in accordance with the last sentence of section 75(a). If Y had acquired bonds before January 1, 1958, it would be unnecessary to determine whether they were disposed of at a loss since that factor is significant only with respect to bonds acquired on or after that date.

(c) Inventories not used or inventories valued at cost. *(1)* In the case of a dealer in securities who computes gross income from his trade or business without the use of inventories or by use of inventories valued at cost, the adjustment required by section 75 is a reduction of the adjusted basis of each municipal bond sold or otherwise disposed of during the taxable year. The amount of such reduction is the total amount by which the adjusted basis of the bond would be required to be reduced under section 1016(a)(5) were the bond subject to the amortizable bond premium provisions of section 171; that is, the amount of the amortizable bond premium attributable to the period during which the bond was held which would be disallowed as a deduction under section 171(a)(2) if the taxpayer were an ordinary investor.

(2) Subparagraph (1) of this paragraph may be illustrated by the following example:

Example. Z, a dealer in securities who values his inventories on the basis of cost, makes his income tax returns on the calendar year basis. On January 1, 1954, he buys, for $1,060 each, three municipal bonds (I, J, and K) having a face obligation of $1,000, and maturing on January 1, 1959. Bond I is sold on December 31, 1954, bond J is sold on June 30, 1955, and bond K is sold on December 31, 1956. For each bond, the amortizable bond premium to maturity is $60, the period from the date of acquisition to maturity is 60 months, and the amortizable bond premium per month is $1.

Bond	Date acquired	Date sold	Adjustment for— 1954	1955	1956
I	Jan. 1, 1954	Dec. 31, 1954	$12		
J	Jan. 1, 1954	June 30, 1955	None	$18	
K	Jan. 1, 1954	Dec. 31, 1956	None	None	$36

(d) Bonds acquired before July 1, 1950. Under section 203(c) of the Revenue Act of 1950, adjustment is required for a municipal bond acquired before July 1, 1950, only with respect to taxable years beginning on or after that date. Accordingly, if the municipal bond was acquired before July 1, 1950, then for purposes of section 75 the amortizable bond premium under section 171 must be computed after adjusting the bond premium to the extent proper to reflect unamortized bond premium for so much of the holding period (as determined under section 1223) as precedes the taxable year of the dealer beginning on or after July 1, 1950. Thus, in example (1) of paragraph (b) and in the example in paragraph (c) of this section, the first taxable year beginning on or after July 1, 1950, is, for each dealer, the taxable year beginning January 1, 1951. If each dealer had purchased for $1,060 on April 1, 1950, a municipal bond having a face obligation of $1,000 and maturing April 1, 1955, and had sold such bond on February 28, 1955, the adjustment under section 75 would be computed as follows:

	Dealer X	Dealer Z
Bond premium	$60	$60
Adjustment for holding period prior to Jan. 1, 1951	9	9
Amortizable bond premium to maturity, as adjusted	51	51
Amortizable bond premium per month	1	1
Total adjustments under sec. 22(o) 1939 Code, for years 1951—53	36	None
Adjustment under sec. 75 for 1954	12	None
Adjustment under sec. 75 for 1955	2	50

T.D. 6137, 7/6/55, amend T.D. 6647, 4/10/63.

§ 1.77-1 Election to consider Commodity Credit Corporation loans as income.

A taxpayer who receives a loan from the Commodity Credit Corporation may, at his election, include the amount of such loan in his gross income for the taxable year in which the loan is received. If a taxpayer makes such an election (or has made such an election under section 123 of the Internal Revenue Code of 1939 or under section 223(d) of the Revenue Act of 1939 (53 Stat 897)), then for subsequent taxable years he shall include in his gross income all amounts received during those years as loans from the Commodity Credit Corporation, unless he secures the permission of the Commissioner to change to a different method of accounting. Application for permission to change such method of accounting and the basis upon which the return is made shall be filed with the Commission of Internal Revenue, Washington 25, D.C., within 90 days after the beginning of the taxable year to be covered by the return.

T.D. 6137, 7/6/55.

§ 1.77-2 Effect of election to consider commodity credit loans as income.

(a) If a taxpayer elects or has elected under section 77, section 123 of the Internal Revenue Code of 1939, or section 223(d) of the Revenue Act of 1939 (53 Stat 897), as amended, to include in his gross income the amount of a loan from the Commodity Credit Corporation for the taxable year in which it is received, then—

(1) No part of the amount realized by the Commodity Credit Corporation upon the sale or other disposition of the commodity pledged for such loan shall be recognized as income to the taxpayer, unless the taxpayer receives an amount in addition to that advanced to him as the loan, in which event such additional amount shall be included in the gross income of the taxpayer for the taxable year in which it is received, and

(2) No deductible loss to the taxpayer shall be recognized on account of any deficiency realized by the Commodity Credit Corporation on such loan if the taxpayer was relieved from liability for such deficiency.

(b) The application of paragraph (a) of this section may be illustrated by the following example:

Example. A, a taxpayer who elected for his taxable year 1952 to include in gross income amounts received as loans from the Commodity Credit Corporation, received as loans $500 in 1952, $700 in 1953, and $900 in 1954. In 1956 all the pledged commodity was sold by the Commodity Credit Corporation for an amount $100 and $200 less than the loans with respect to the commodity pledged in 1952 and 1953, respectively, and for an amount $150 greater than the loan with respect to the commodity pledged in 1954. A, in making his return for 1956, shall include in gross income the sum of $150 if it is received during that year, but will not be allowed a deduction for the deficiencies of $100 and $200 unless he is required to satisfy such deficiencies and does satisfy them during that year.

T.D. 6137, 7/6/55.

§ 1.78-1 Dividends received from certain foreign corporations by certain domestic corporations choosing the foreign tax credit.

(a) Taxes deemed paid by certain domestic corporations treated as a section 78 dividend. Any reduction under section 907(a) of the foreign income taxes deemed to be paid with respect to foreign oil and gas extraction income does not affect the amount treated as a section 78 dividend. If a domestic corporation chooses to have the benefits of the foreign tax credit under section 901 for any taxable year, an amount which is equal to the foreign income taxes deemed to be paid by such corporation for such year under section 902(a) in accordance with §§ 1.902-1 and 1.902-2 or under section 960(a)(1) in accordance with § 1.960-7, shall, to the extent provided by this section, be treated as a dividend (hereinafter referred to as a section 78 dividend) received by such domestic corporation from the foreign corporation described in section 902(a) in accordance with §§ 1.902-1 and 1.902-2 or section 960(a)(1) in accordance with § 1.960-7, as the case may be. A section 78 dividend shall be treated as a dividend for all purposes of the Code, except that it shall not be treated as a dividend under section 245, relating to dividends received from certain foreign corporations, or increase the earnings and profits of the domestic corporation. For purposes of determining the source of a section 78 dividend in computing the limitation on the foreign tax credit under section 904, see § 1.902-1(h)(1) and the regulations under section 960. For special rules relating to the determination of the foreign tax credit under section 902 with respect to certain minimum distributions received from controlled foreign corporations and the effect of such rules upon the gross-up under section 78, see paragraph (c) of § 1.963-4. For rules respecting the reduction of foreign income taxes under section 6038(b) in applying section 902(a) in accordance with §§ 1.902-1 and 1.902-2 and section 960(a)(1) in accordance with § 1.960-7 where there has been a failure to furnish certain information and for an illustration of the effect of such reduction upon the amount of a section 78 dividend, see paragraph (1) of § 1.6038-2.

(b) Certain taxes not treated as a section 78 dividend. Foreign income taxes deemed paid by a domestic corporation under section 902(a) in accordance with §§ 1.902-1 and 1.902-2 or section 960(a)(1) in accordance with § 1.960-7 shall not, to the extent provided by paragraph (b) of § 1.960-3, be treated as a section 78 dividend where such taxes are imposed on certain distributions from the earnings and profits of a controlled foreign corporation attributable to an amount which is, or has been, included in gross income of the domestic corporation under section 951.

(c) United Kingdom income tax included in gross income under treaty. Any amount of United Kingdom income tax appropriate to a dividend paid by a corporation which is a resident of the United Kingdom shall not be treated as a section 78 dividend by a domestic corporation to the extent that such tax is included in the gross income of such domestic corporation in accordance with Article XIII(1) of the income tax convention between the United States and the United Kingdom, as amended by Article II of the supplementary protocol between such Governments signed on August 19, 1957 (9 UST 1331). See § 507.117 of this chapter, relating to credit against United States tax liability for income tax paid or deemed to have been paid to the United Kingdom.

(d) Taxable year in which section 78 dividend is received. A section 78 dividend shall be considered received in the taxable year of a domestic corporation in which—

(1) The corporation receives the dividend by reason of which there are deemed paid under section 902(a) in accordance with §§ 1.902-1 and 1.902-2 the foreign income taxes which give rise to such section 78 dividend, or

(2) The corporation includes in gross income under section 951(a) the amounts by reason of which there are deemed paid under section 960(a)(1) in accordance with § 1.960-7 the foreign income taxes which give rise to such section 78 dividend,

notwithstanding that such foreign income taxes may be carried back or carried over to another taxable year under section 904(d) and are deemed to be paid or accrued in such other taxable year.

(e) Effective dates for the application of section 78. *(1) In general.* This section shall apply to amounts of foreign income taxes deemed paid under section 902(a) in accordance with §§ 1.902-1 and 1.902-2 and section 960(a)(1) in accordance with 1.960-7 by reason of a distribution received by a domestic corporation—

(i) After December 31, 1964, or

(ii) Before January 1, 1965, in a taxable year of such domestic corporation beginning after December 31, 1962, but only to the extent that such distribution is made out of the accumulated profits of a foreign corporation for a taxable year of such foreign corporation beginning after December 31, 1962.

For special rules relating to determination of accumulated profits for such purposes, see the regulations under section 902.

(2) Amounts under section 951 treated as distributions. For purposes of this paragraph, any amount attributable to the earnings and profits for the taxable year of a first-tier corporation (as defined in paragraph (b)(1) of § 1.960-P) which is included in the gross income of a domestic corporation under section 951(a) shall be treated as a distribution received by such domestic corporation on the last day in such taxable year on which such first-tier corporation is a controlled foreign corporation.

(f) Illustrations. The application of this section may be illustrated by the examples provided in § 1.902-1, § 1.904-5, § 1.960-4, and § 1.963-4.

T.D. 6805, 3/8/65, amend T.D. 7120, 6/3/71, T.D. 7481, 4/15/77, T.D. 7490, 6/10/77, T.D. 7649, 10/17/79, T.D. 7961, 6/20/84.

§ 1.79-0 Group-term life insurance—definitions of certain terms.

The following definitions apply for purposes of section 79, this section, and §§ 1.79-1, 1.79-2, and 1.79-3.

Carried directly or indirectly. A policy of life insurance is "carried directly or indirectly" by an employer if—

(a) The employer pays any part of the cost of the life insurance directly or through another person; or

(b) The employer or two or more employers arrange for payment of the cost of the life insurance by their employees and charge at least one employee less than the cost of his or her insurance, as determined under Table I of § 1.79-3(d)(2), and at least one other employee more than the cost of his or her insurance, determined in the same way.

Employee. An "employee" is—

(a) A person who performs services if his or her relationship to the person for whom services are performed is the legal relationship of employer and employee described in § 31.3401(c)-1; or

(b) A full-time insurance salesperson described in section 7701(a)(20); or

(c) A person who formerly performed services as an employee.

A person who formerly performed services as an employee and currently performs services for the same employer as an independent contractor is considered an employee only with respect to insurance provided because of the person's former services as an employee.

Group of employees. A "group of employees" is all employees of an employer, or less than all employees if membership in the group is determined solely on the basis of age, marital status, or factors related to employment. Examples of factors related to employment are membership in a union some or all of whose members are employed by the employer, duties performed, compensation received, and length of service. Ordinarily the purchase of something other than group-term life insurance is not a factor related to employment. For example, if an employer provides credit life insurance to all employees who purchase automobiles, these employees are not a "group of employees" because membership is not determined solely on the basis of age, marital status, or factors related to employment. On the other hand, participation in an employer's pension, profit-sharing or accident and health plan is considered a factor related to employment even if employees are required to contribute to the cost of the plan. Ownership of stock in the employer corporation is not a factor related to employment. However, participation in an employer's stock bonus plan may be a factor related to employment and a "group of employees" may include employees who own stock in the employer corporation.

Permanent benefit. A "permanent benefit" is an economic value extending beyond one policy year (for example, a paid-up or cash surrender value) that is provided under a life insurance policy. However, the following features are not permanent benefits:

(a) A right to convert (or continue) life insurance after group life insurance coverage terminates:

(b) Any other feature that provides no economic benefit (other than current insurance protection) to the employee; or

(c) A feature under which term life insurance is provided at a level premium for a period of five years or less.

Policy. The term "policy" includes two or more obligations of an insurer (or its affiliates) that are sold in conjunction. Obligations that are offered or available to members of a group of employees are sold in conjunction if they are offered or available because of the employment relationship. The actuarial sufficiency of the premium charged for each obligation is not taken into account in determining whether the obligations are sold in conjunction. In addition, obligations may be sold in conjunction even if the obligations are contained in separate documents, each document is filed with and approved by the applicable state insurance commission, or each obligation is independent of any other obligation. Thus, a group of individual contracts under which life insurance is provided to a group of employees may be a policy. Similarly, two benefits provided to a group of employees, one term life insurance and the other a permanent benefit, may be a policy, even if one of the benefits is provided only to employees who decline the other benefit. However, an employer may elect to treat two or more obligations each of which provides no permanent benefits as separate policies if the premiums are properly allocated among such policies. An employer also may elect to treat an obligation which provides permanent benefits as a separate policy if—

(a) The insurer sells the obligation directly to the employee who pays the full cost thereof;

(b) The participation of the employer with respect to sales of the obligation to employees is limited to selection of the insurer and the type of coverage and to sales assistance activities such as providing employee lists to the insurer, permitting the insurer to use the employer's premises for solicitation, and collecting premiums through payroll deduction;

(c) The insurer sells the obligation on the same terms and in substantial amounts to individuals who do not purchase (and whose employers do not purchase) any other obligation from the insurer; and

(d) No employer-provided benefit is conditioned on purchase of the obligation.

T.D. 7623, 5/14/79, amend T.D. 7917, 10/6/83.

---

§ 1.79-1 Group-term life insurance—general rules.

(a) What is group-term life insurance? Life insurance is not group-term life insurance for purposes of section 79 unless it meets the following conditions:

(1) It provides a general death benefit that is excludable from gross income under section 101(a).

(2) It is provided to a group of employees.

(3) It is provided under a policy carried directly or indirectly by the employer.

(4) The amount of insurance provided to each employee is computed under a formula that precludes individual selection. This formula must be based on factors such as age, years of service, compensation, or position. This condition may be satisfied even if the amount of insurance provided is determined under a limited number of alternative schedules that are based on the amount each employee elects to contribute. However, the amount of insurance provided under each schedule must be computed under a formula that precludes individual selection.

(b) May group-term life insurance be combined with other benefits? No part of the life insurance provided under a policy that provides a permanent benefit is group-term life insurance unless—

(1) The policy or the employer designates in writing the part of the death benefit provided to each employee that is group-term life insurance; and

(2) The part of the death benefit that is provided to an employee and designated as the group-term life insurance benefit for any policy year is not less than the difference between the total death benefit provided under the policy and the employee's deemed death benefit (DDB) at the end of the policy year determined under paragraph (d)(3) of this section.

(c) May a group include fewer than 10 employees? *(1)* As a general rule, life insurance provided to a group of employees cannot qualify as group-term life insurance for purposes of section 79 unless, at some time during the calendar year, it is provided to at least 10 full-time employees who are members of the group of employees. For purposes of this rule, all life insurance provided under policies carried directly or indirectly by the employer is taken into account in determining the number of employees to whom life insurance is provided.

(2) The general rule of paragraph (c)(1) of this section does not apply if the following conditions are met:

(i) The insurance is provided to all full-time employees of the employer or, if evidence of insurability affects eligibility, to all full-time who provide evidence of insurability satisfactory to the insurer.

(ii) The amount of insurance provided is computed either as a uniform percentage of compensation or on the basis of coverage brackets established by the insurer. However, the amount computed under either method may be reduced in the case of employees who do not provide evidence of insurability satisfactory to the insurer. In general, no bracket may exceed 2½ times the next lower bracket and the lowest bracket must be at least 10 percent of the highest bracket. However, the insurer may establish a separate schedule of coverage brackets for employees who are over age 65, but no bracket in the over-65 schedule may exceed 2½ times the next lower bracket and the lowest bracket in the over-65 schedule must be at least 10 percent of the highest bracket in the basic schedule.

(iii) Evidence of insurability affecting employee's eligibility for insurance or the amount of insurance provided to that employee is limited to a medical questionnaire completed by the employee that does not require a physical examination.

(3) The general rule of paragraph (c)(1) of this section does not apply if the following conditions are met:

(i) The insurance if provided under a common plan to the employees of two or more unrelated employers.

(ii) The insurance is restricted to, but mandatory for, all employees of the employer who belong to or are represented by an organization (such as a union) that carries on substantial activities in addition to obtaining insurance.

(iii) Evidence of insurability does not affect an employee's eligibility for insurance or the amount of insurance provided to that employee.

(4) For purposes of paragraph (c)(2) and (3) of this section, employees are not taken into account if they are denied insurance for the following reasons:

(i) They are not eligible for insurance under the terms of the policy because they have not been employed for a waiting period, specified in the policy, which does not exceed six months.

(ii) They are part-time employees. Employees whose customary employment is for not more than 20 hours in any week, or 5 months in any calendar year, are presumed to be part-time employees.

(iii) They have reached the age of 65.

(5) For purposes of paragraph (c)(1) and (2) of this section, insurance is considered to be provided to an employee who elects not to receive insurance unless, in order to receive the insurance, the employee is required to contribute to the cost of benefits other than term life insurance. Thus, if an employee could receive term life insurance by contributing to its cost, the employee is taken into account in determining whether the insurance is provided to 10 or more employees even if such employee elects not to receive the insurance. However, an employee who must contribute to the cost of permanent benefits to obtain term life insurance is not taken into account in determining whether the term life insurance is provided to 10 or more employees unless the term life insurance is actually provided to such employee.

(d) How much must an employee receiving permanent benefits include in income? *(1) In general.* If an insurance policy that meets the requirements of this section provides permanent benefits to an employee, the cost of the permanent benefits reduced by the amount paid for permanent benefits by the employee is included in the employee's income. The cost of the permanent benefits is determined under the formula in paragraph (d)(2) of this section.

(2) Formula for determining cost of the permanent benefits. In each policy year the cost of the permanent benefits for any particular employee must be no less than:

$X (DDB_2—DDB_1)$

where

DDB_2 is the employee's deemed death benefit at the end of the policy year;

DDB_1 is the employee's deemed death benefit at the end of the preceding policy year; and

X is the net single premium for insurance (the premium for one dollar of paid-up whole-life insurance) at the employee's attained age at the beginning of the policy year.

(3) Formula for determining deemed death benefit. The deemed death benefit (DDB) at the end of any policy year for any particular employee is equal to—

R/Y

Where—

R is the net level premium reserve at the end of that policy year for all benefits provided to the employee by the policy or, if greater, the fair market value of the policy at the end of that policy year; and

Y is the net single premium for insurance (the premium for one dollar of paid-up, whole life insurance) at the employee's age at the end of that policy year.

(4) Mortality tables and interest rates used. For purposes of paragraph (d)(2) and (3) of this section, the net level premium reserve *(R)* and the net single premium *(X* or *Y)* shall be based on the 1958 CSO Mortality Table and 4 percent interest.

(5) Dividends. If an insurance policy that meets the requirements of this section provides permanent benefits, part or all of the dividends under the policy may be includible in the employee's income. If the employee pays nothing for the permanent benefits, all dividends under the policy that are actually or constructively received by the employee are includible in the employee's income. In all other cases, the amount of dividends included in the employee's income is equal to

(D + C)—(PI + DI + AP)

where

D is the total amount of dividends actually or constructively received under the policy by the employee in the current and all preceding taxable years of the employee;

C is the total cost of the permanent benefits for the current and all preceding taxable years of the employee determined under the formulas in paragraph (d)(2) and (6) of this section:

PI is the total amount of premium included in the employee's income under paragraph (d)(1) of this section for the current and all preceding taxable years of the employee;

DI is the total amount of dividends included in the employee's income under this paragraph (d)(5) in all preceding taxable years of the employee; and

AP is the total amount paid for permanent benefits by the employee in the current and all preceding taxable years of the employee.

(6) Different policy and taxable years. (i) If a policy year begins in one employee taxable year, the cost of the permanent benefits, determined under the formula in paragraph (d)(2) of this section, is allocated between the employee taxable years.

(ii) The cost of permanent benefits for a policy year is allocated first to the employee taxable year in which the policy year begins. The cost of permanent benefits allocated to that policy year is equal to:

F × *C*

where

F is the fraction of the premium for that policy year that is paid on or before the last day of the employee taxable year; and

C is the cost of permanent benefits for the policy year determined under the formula in paragraph (d)(2) of this section.

(iii) Any part of the cost of permanent benefits that is not allocated to the employee taxable year in which the policy year begins is allocated to the subsequent employee taxable year.

(iv) The cost of permanent benefits for an employee taxable year is the sum of the costs of permanent benefits allocated to that year under paragraph (d)(6)(ii) and (iii) of this section.

(7) Example. The provisions of this paragraph may be illustrated by the following example:

Example. An employer provides insurance to employee A under a policy that meets the requirements of this section. Under the policy, A, who is 47 years old, received $70,000 of group-term life insurance and elects to receive a permanent benefit under the policy. A pays $2 for each $1,000 of group-term life insurance through payroll deductions and the employer pays the remainder of the premium for the group-term life insurance. The employer also pays one half of the premium specified in the policy for the permanent benefit. A pays the other half of the premium for the permanent benefit through payroll deductions. The policy specifies that the annual premium paid for the permanent benefit is $300. However, the amount of premium allocated to the permanent benefit by the formula in paragraph (d)(2) of this section is $350. A is a calendar year taxpayer; the policy year begins January 1. In year 2000, $200 is includible in A's income because of insurance provided by the employer. This amount is computed as follows:

(1) Cost of permanent benefits	$350
(2) Amounts considered paid by A for permanent benefits (½ × $300)	150
(3) line (1) minus line (2)	200
(4) Cost of $70,000 of group-term life insurance under Table I of § 1.79-3	126
(5) Cost of $50,000 of group-term life insurance under Table 1 of § 1.79-3	90
(6) Cost of group-term life insurance in excess of $50,000 (line (4) minus line (5))	36
(7) Amount considered paid by A for group-term life insurance (70 × $2)	140
(8) Line (6) minus line (7) (but not less than 0)	0
(9) Amount includible in income (line (3) plus line (8))	200

(e) What is the effect of state law limits?. Section 79 does not apply to life insurance in excess of limits under applicable state law on the amount of life insurance that can be provided to an employee under a single contract of group-term life insurance.

(f) Cross references. *(1)* See section 79(b) and § 1.79-2 for rules relating to group-life insurance provided to certain retired individuals.

(2) See section 61(a) and the regulations thereunder for rules relating to life insurance not meeting the requirements of section 79, this section or § 1.79-2, such as insurance provided on the life of a non-employee (for example, an employee's spouse), insurance not provided as compensation for personal services performed as an employee, insurance not provided under a policy carried directly or indirectly by the employer, or permanent benefits.

(3) See sections 106 and § 1.106-1 for rules relating to certain insurance that does not provide general death benefits, such as travel insurance or accident and health insurance (including amounts payable under a double indemnity clause or rider).

(g) [Reserved.]

(h) Effective date. Section 1.79-0 applies to insurance provided in employee taxable years beginning on or after January 1, 1977 (except as provided in 26 CFR 1.79-1(g) (revised as of April 1, 1983) with respect to insurance provided in employee taxable years beginning in 1977). Sections 1.79-1 through 1.79-3 apply to insurance provided in employee taxable years beginning after December 31, 1982. See 26 CFR 1.79-1 through 1.79-3 (revised as of April 1, 1983) for rules applicable to insurance provided in employee taxable years beginning before January 1, 1983.

T.D. 6888, 7/6/66, amend T.D. 6999, 1/17/69, T.D. 7132, 7/13/71, T.D. 7236, 12/27/72,1/26/73, T.D. 7623, 5/14/79, T.D. 7917, 10/6/83, T.D. 7924, 12/1/83, T.D. 8821, 5/28/99, T.D. 9223, 8/26/2005.

§ 1.79-2 Exceptions to the rule of inclusion.

Caution: The Treasury has not yet amended Reg § 1.79-2 to reflect changes made by P.L. 98-369.

(a) In general. *(1)* Section 79(b) provides exceptions for the cost of group-term life insurance provided under certain policies otherwise described in section 79(a). The policy or policies of group-term life insurance which are described in section 79(a) but which qualify for one of the exceptions set forth in section 79(b) are described in paragraphs (b) through (d) of this section. Paragraph (b) of this section discusses the exception provided in section 79(b)(1); paragraph (c) of this section discusses the exception provided in section 79(b)(2); and paragraph (d) of this section discusses the exception provided in section 79(b)(3).

(2) (i) If a policy of group-term life insurance qualifies for an exception provided by section 79(b), then the amount equal to the cost of such insurance is excluded from the application of the provisions of section 79(a).

(ii) If a policy, or portion of a policy of group-term life insurance qualifies for an exception provided by section 79(b), the amount (if any) paid by the employee toward the purchase of such insurance is not to be taken into account as an amount referred to in section 79(a)(2). In the case of a policy or policies of group-term life insurance which qualify for an exception provided by section 79(b)(1) or (3), the amount paid by the employee which is not to be taken into account as an amount referred to in section 79(a)(2) is the amount paid by the employee for the particular policy or policies of group-term life insurance which qualify for an exception provided under such section. If the exception provided in section 79(b)(2) is applicable only to a portion of the group-term life insurance on the employee's life, the amount considered to be paid by the employee toward the purchase of such portion is the amount equal to the excess of the cost of such portion of the insurance over the amount otherwise includible in the employee's gross income with respect to the group-term life insurance on his life carried directly or indirectly by such employer.

(iii) The rules of this subparagraph may be illustrated by the following example:

Example. A is an employee of X Corporation and is also an employee of Y Corporation, a subsidiary of X Corporation. A is provided, under a separate plan arranged by each of his employers, group-term life insurance on his life. During his taxable year, under the group-term life insurance plan of X Corporation, A is provided $60,000 of group-term life insurance on his life, and A pays $360.00 toward the purchase of such insurance. Under the group-term life insurance plan of Y Corporation, A is provided $65,000 of group-term life insurance on his life, but does not pay any part of the cost of such insurance. At the beginning of his taxable year, A terminates his employment with the X Corporation after he has reached the retirement age with respect to such employer, and the policy carried by the X Corporation qualifies for the exception provided by section 79(b)(1). For that taxable year, the cost of the group-term life insurance on A's life which is provided under the plan of X Corporation is not taken into account in determining the amount includible in A's gross income under section 79(a), and A may not take into account as an amount described in section 79(a)(2) the $360.00 he pays toward the purchase of such insurance.

(b) Retired and disabled employees. *(1) In general.* Section 79(b)(1) provides an exception for the cost of group-term life insurance on the life of an individual which is provided under a policy or policies otherwise described in section 79(a) if the individual has terminated his employment (as defined in subparagraph (2) of this paragraph) with such employer and either has reached the retirement age with respect to such employer (as defined in subparagraph (3) of this paragraph), or has become disabled (as defined in subparagraph (4)(i) of this paragraph). If an individual who has terminated his employment attains retirement age or has become disabled during his taxable year, or if an employee who has attained retirement age or has become disabled terminates his employment during the taxable year, the exception provided by section 79(b)(1) applies only to the portion of the cost of group-term life insurance which is provided subsequent to the happening of the last event which qualifies the policy of insurance on the employee's life for the exception provided in such section.

(2) Termination of employment. For purposes of section 79(b)(1), an individual has terminated his employment with an employer providing such individual group-term life insurance when such individual no longer renders services to that employer as an employee of such employer.

(3) Retirement age. For purposes of section 79(b)(1) and this section, the meaning of the term "retirement age" is determined in accordance with the following rules—

(i) (a) If the employee is covered under a written pension or annuity plan of the employer providing such individual group-term life insurance on his life (whether or not such plan is qualified under section 401(a) or 403(a)), then his retirement age shall be considered to be the earlier of—

(1) The earliest age indicated by such plan at which an active employee has the right (or an inactive individual would have the right had he continued in employment) to retire without disability and without the consent of his employer and receive immediate retirement benefits computed at either the full rate or a rate proportionate to completed service as set forth in the normal retirement formula of the plan, i.e., without actuarial or similar reduction because of retirement before some later specified age, or

(2) The age at which it has been the practice of the employer to terminate, due to age, the services of the class of employees to which he last belonged.

(b) For purposes of (a) of this subdivision, if an employee is covered under more than one pension or annuity plan of the employer, his retirement age shall be determined with regard to that plan which covers that class of employees of the employer to which the employee last belonged. If the class of employees to which the employee last belonged is covered under more than one pension or annuity plan, then the employee's retirement age shall be determined with regard to that plan which covers the greatest number of the employer's employees.

(ii) In the absence of a written employee's pension or annuity plan described in subdivision (i) of this subparagraph, retirement age is the age, if any, at which it has been the practice of the employer to terminate, due to age, the services of the class of employees to which the particular employee last belonged, provided such age is reasonable in view of all the pertinent facts and circumstances.

(iii) If neither subdivision (i) or (ii) of this subparagraph applies, the retirement age is considered to be age 65.

(4) Disabled. (i) For taxable years beginning after December 31, 1966, an individual is considered disabled for purposes of section 79(b)(1) and subparagraph (1) of this paragraph if he is disabled within the meaning of section 72(m)(7) and paragraph (f) of § 1.72-17. For taxable years beginning before January 1, 1967, an individual is considered disabled for purposes of section 79(b)(1) and subparagraph (1) of this paragraph if he is disabled within the meaning of section 213(g)(3), relating to the meaning of disabled, but the determination of the individual's status shall be made without regard to the provisions of section 213(g)(4), relating to the determination of status.

(ii) (a) In any taxable year in which an individual seeks to apply the exception set forth in section 79(b)(1) by reason of his being disabled within the meaning of subdivision (i) of this subparagraph, and in which the aggregate amount of insurance on the individual's life subject to the rule of inclusion set forth in section 79(a) but determined without regard to the amount of any insurance subject to any exception set forth in section 79(b), is greater than $50,000 of such insurance, the substantiation required by (b) or (c) of this subdivision must be submitted with the individual's tax return.

(b) For the first taxable year for which the individual seeks to apply the exception set forth in section 79(b)(1) by reason of his being disabled within the meaning of subdivision (i) of this subparagraph, there must be submitted with his income tax return a doctor's statement as to his impairment. There must also be submitted with the return a statement by the individual with respect to the effect of the impairment upon his substantial gainful activity, and the date such impairment occurred. For subsequent taxable years, the taxpayer may, in lieu of such statements, submit a statement declaring the continued existence (without substantial diminution) of the impairment and its continued effect upon his substantial gainful activity.

(c) In lieu of the substantiation required to be submitted by (b) of this subdivision for the taxable year, the individual may submit a signed statement issued to him by the insurer to the effect that the individual is disabled within the meaning of subdivision (i) of this paragraph. Such statement must set forth the basis for the insurer's determination that the individual was so disabled, and for the first taxable year in which the individual is so disabled, the date such disability occurred.

(c) Employer or charity a beneficiary. *(1) General rule.* Section 79(b)(2) provides an exception with respect to the amounts referred to in section 79(a) for the cost of any portion of the group-term life insurance on the life of an employee provided during part or all of the taxable year of the employee under which the employer is directly or indirectly the beneficiary, or under which a person described in section 170(c) (relating to definition of charitable contributions) is the sole beneficiary, for the entire period during such taxable year for which the employee receives such insurance.

(2) Employer is a beneficiary. For purposes of section 79(b)(2) and subparagraph (1) of this paragraph, the determination of whether the employer is directly or indirectly the beneficiary under a policy or policies of group-term life insurance depends upon the facts and circumstances of the particular case. Such determination is not made solely with regard to whether the employer possesses all the incidents of ownership in the policy. Thus, for example, if the employer is the nominal beneficiary under a policy of group-term life insurance on the life of his employee but there is an arrangement whereby the employer is required to pay over all (or a portion) of the proceeds of such policy to the employee's estate or his beneficiary, the employer is not considered a beneficiary under such policy (or such portion of the policy).

(3) Charity a beneficiary. (i) For purposes of section 79(b)(2) and subparagraph (1) of this paragraph, a person described in section 170(c) is a beneficiary under a policy providing group-term life insurance if such person is designated the beneficiary under the policy by any assignment or designation of beneficiary under the policy which, under the law of the jurisdiction which is applicable to the policy, has the effect of making such person the beneficiary under such policy (whether or not such designation is revocable during the taxable year). Such a designation may be made by the employee with respect to any portion of the group-term life insurance on his life. However, no deduction is allowed under section 170, relating to charitable, etc., contributions and gifts, with respect to any such assignment or designation.

(ii) A person described in section 170(c) must be designated the sole beneficiary under the policy or portion of the policy. Such requirement is satisfied if the person described in section 170(c) is the beneficiary under such policy or portion of the policy, and there is no contingent or similar beneficiary under such policy or such portion other than a person described in section 170(c). A general "preference beneficiary clause" in a policy governing payment where there is no designated beneficiary in existence at the death of the employee will not of itself be considered to create a contingent or similar beneficiary. A person described in section 170(c) may be designated the beneficiary under a portion of the policy if such person is designated the sole beneficiary under a beneficiary designation which is expressed, for example, as a fraction of the amount of insurance on the insured's life.

(iii) If a person described in section 170(c) is designated under the policy (or portion thereof) and such person remains the beneficiary for the period beginning May 1, 1964, and ending with the close of the first taxable year of the employee ending after April 30, 1964, such person shall be treated as the beneficiary under the policy (or the portion thereof) for the period beginning January 1, 1964, and ending April 30, 1964.

(d) Insurance contracts purchased under qualified employee plans. *(1)* Section 79(b)(3) provides an exception with respect to the cost of any group-term life insurance which is provided under a life insurance contract purchased as a part of a plan described in section 403(a), or purchased by a trust described in section 401(a) which is exempt from tax under section 501(a) if the proceeds of such contract are payable directly or indirectly to a participant in such trust or to a beneficiary of such participant. The provisions of section 72(m)(3) and § 1.72-16 apply to the cost of such group-term life insurance, and, therefore, no part of such cost is excluded from the gross income of the employee by reason of the provisions of section 79.

(2) Whether the life insurance protection on an employee's life is provided under a qualified employee plan referred to in subparagraph (1) of this paragraph depends upon the provisions of such plan. In determining whether a pension, profit-sharing, stock bonus, or annuity plan satisfies the requirements for qualification set forth in sections 401(a) or 403(a), only group-term life insurance which is provided under such plan is taken into account.

T.D. 6888, 7/6/66, amend T.D. 6919, 5/17/67, T.D. 6985, 12/26/68, T.D. 7623, 5/14/79.

§ 1.79-3 Determination of amount equal to cost of group-term life insurance.

Caution: The Treasury has not yet amended Reg § 1.79-3 to reflect changes made by P.L. 100-647.

(a) In general. This section prescribes the rules for determining the amount equal to the cost of group-term life insurance on an employee's life which is to be included in his gross income pursuant to the rule of inclusion set forth in section 79(a). Such amount is determined by—

(1) Computing the cost of the portion of the group-term life insurance on the employee's life to be taken into account (determined in accordance with the rules set forth in paragraph (b) of this section) for each "period of coverage" (as defined in paragraph (c) of this section) and aggregating the costs so determined, then

(2) Reducing the amount determined under subparagraph (1) of this paragraph by the amount determined in accordance with the rules set forth in paragraph (e) of this section, relating to the amount paid by the employee toward the purchase of group-term life insurance.

(b) Determination of the portion of the group-term life insurance on the employee's life to be taken into account. *(1)* For each "period of coverage" (as defined in paragraph (c) of this section), the portion of the group-term life insurance to be taken into account in computing the amount includible in an employee's gross income for purposes of paragraph (a)(1) of this section is the sum of the proceeds payable upon the death of the employee under each policy, or portion of a policy, of group-term life insurance on such employee's life to which the rule of inclusion set forth in section 79(a) applies, less $50,000 of such insurance. Thus, the amount of any proceeds payable under a policy, or portion of a policy, which qualifies for one of the exceptions to the rule of inclusion provided by section 79(b) is not taken into account. For the regulations relating to such exceptions to the rule of inclusion, see § 1.79-2.

(2) For purposes of making the computation required by subparagraph (1) of this paragraph in any case in which the amount payable under the policy, or portion thereof, varies during the period of coverage, the amount payable under such policy during such period is considered to be the average of the amount payable under such policy at the beginning and the end of such period.

(3) (i) For purposes of making the computation required by subparagraph (1) of this paragraph in any case in which the amount payable under the policy is not payable as a specific amount upon the death of the employee in full discharge of the liability of the insurer, and such form of payment is not one of alternative methods of payment, the amount payable under such policy is the present value of the agreement by the insurer under the policy to make the payments to the beneficiary or beneficiaries entitled to such amounts upon the employee's death. For each period of coverage, such present value is to be determined as if the first and last day of such period is the date of death of the employee.

(ii) The present value of the agreement by the insurer under the policy to make payments shall be determined by the use of the mortality tables and interest rate employed by the insurer with respect to such a policy in calculating the amount held by the insurer (as defined in section 101(d)(2)), unless the Commissioner otherwise determines that a particular mortality table and interest rate, representative of the mortality table and interest rate used by commercial insurance companies with respect to such policies, shall be used to determine the present value of the policy for purposes of this subdivision.

(iii) For purposes of making the computation required by subdivision (i) of this subparagraph in any case in which it is necessary to determine the age of an employee's beneficiary and such beneficiary remains the same (under the policy, or the portion of the policy with respect to which the determination of the present value of the agreement of the insurer to pay benefits is being made) for the entire period during the employee's taxable year for which such policy is in effect, the age of such beneficiary is such beneficiary's age at his nearest birthday on June 30th of the calendar year.

(iv) If the policy of group-term life insurance on the employee's life is such that the present value of the agreement by the insurer under the policy to pay benefits cannot be determined by the rules prescribed in this subparagraph, the taxpayer may submit with his return a computation of such present value, consistent with the actuarial and other assumptions set forth in this subparagraph, showing the appropriate factors applied in his case. Each computation shall be subject to the approval of the Commissioner upon examination of such return.

(c) Period of coverage. For purposes of this section, the phrase "period of coverage" means any one calendar month period, or part thereof, during the employee's taxable year during which the employee is provided group-term life insurance on his life to which the rule of inclusion set forth in section 79(a) applies. The phrase "part thereof" as used in the preceding sentence means any continuous period which is less than the one calendar month period referred to in the preceding sentence for which premiums are charged by the insurer.

(d) The cost of the portion of the group-term life insurance on an employee's life. *(1)* This paragraph sets forth the rules for determining the cost, for each period of coverage, of the portion of the group-term life insurance on the employee's life to be taken into account in computing the amount includible in the employee's gross income for purposes of paragraph (a)(1) of this section. The portion of the group-term life insurance on the employee's life to be taken into account is determined in accordance with the provisions of paragraph (b) of this section. Table I, which is set forth in subparagraph (2) of this paragraph, determines the cost for each $1,000 of such portion of the group-term life insurance on the employee's life for each one-month period. The cost of the portion of the group-term life insurance on the employee's life for each period of coverage of one month is obtained by multiplying the number of thousand dollars of such insurance computed to the nearest tenth which is provided during such period by the appropriate amount set forth in Table I. In any case in which group-term life insurance is provided for a period of coverage of less than one month, the amount set forth in Table I is prorated over such period of coverage.

(2) For the cost of group-term life insurance provided after June 30, 1999, the following table sets forth the cost of $1,000 of group-term life insurance provided for one month, computed on the basis of 5-year age brackets. See 26 CFR § 1.79-3(d)(2) in effect prior to July 1, 1999, and contained in the 26 CFR part 1 edition revised as of April 1, 1999, for a table setting forth the cost of group-term life insurance provided before July 1, 1999. For purposes of Table I, the age of the employee is the employee's attained age on the last day of the employee's taxable year.

Table I.—Uniform Premiums for $1,000 of Group-Term Life Insurance Protection

5-year age bracket	Cost per $1,000 of protection for one month
Under 25	$0.05
25 to 29	.06
30 to 34	.08
35 to 39	.09
40 to 44	.10
45 to 49	.15
50 to 54	.23
55 to 59	.43
60 to 64	.66
65 to 69	1.27
70 and above	2.06

(3) The net premium cost of group-term life insurance as provided in Table I of subparagraph (2) of this paragraph applies only to the cost of group-term life insurance subject to the rule of inclusion set forth in section 79(a). Therefore, such net premium cost is not applicable to the determination of the cost of group-term life insurance provided under a policy which is not subject to such rule of inclusion.

(e) Effective date. *(1) General effective date for table.* Except as provided in paragraph (e)(2) of this section, the table in paragraph (d)(2) of this section is applicable July 1, 1999. Until January 1, 2000, an employer may calculate imputed income for all its employees under age 30 using the 5-year age bracket for ages 25 to 29.

(2) Effective date for table for purposes of § 1.79-0. For a policy of life insurance issued under a plan in existence on June 30, 1999, which would not be treated as carried directly or indirectly by an employer under § 1.79-0 (taking into account the Table I in effect on that date), until January 1, 2003, an employer may use either the table in paragraph (d)(2) of this section or the table in effect prior to July 1, 1999 (as described in paragraph (d)(2) of this section) for determining if the policy is carried directly or indirectly by the employer.

(f) Amount paid by the employee toward the purchase of group-term life insurance. *(1)* Except as otherwise provided in subparagraph (2) of this paragraph, if an employee pays any amount toward the purchase of group-term life insurance provided for a taxable year which is subject to the rule of inclusion set forth in section 79(a), the sum of all such amounts is the amount referred to in section 79(a)(2) and paragraph (a)(2) of this section. The rule of the preceding sentence applies even though the payments made by the employee are made with respect to a period of coverage during which no portion of the group-term life insurance on his life is taken into account under paragraph (b)(1) of this section.

(2) In determining the amount paid by the employee for purposes of section 79(a)(2) and paragraph (a)(2) of this section, there is not taken into account any amounts paid by the employee for group-term life insurance provided (or to be provided) for a different taxable year (other than amounts applicable to regular pay periods extending into the next taxable year). Thus, for example, if part of an employee's payment during a taxable year represents a prepayment for insurance to be provided after his retirement, such part does not reduce the amount includible in his gross income for the current taxable year. Furthermore, in determining such amount, there is not taken into account any amount paid by an employee toward the purchase of group-term life insurance which qualifies for one of the exceptions described in section 79(b). The amount paid by an employee toward the purchase of group-term life insurance which qualifies for one of the exceptions described in section 79(b) is determined under the rules of paragraph (a)(2) of § 1.79-2.

(3) If payments are made by the employer and his employees to provide group-term life insurance which is subject to the rule of inclusion set forth in section 79(a) as well as to provide other benefits for the employees, and if the amount paid by the employee toward the purchase of such insurance cannot be determined by the provisions of the policy or plan under which such benefits are provided, then the determination of the portion of the cost of group-term life insurance (computed in accordance with the provisions of this section) which is attributable to the contributions of the employee shall be made in accordance with the provisions of this subparagraph. The amount paid by the employee toward the purchase of all the group-term life insurance on his life for his taxable year (or for the portion of his taxable year if such portion is the basis of the computation) under such group policy shall be an amount determined first by ascertaining the total amount paid by all employees who are covered for multiple benefits which is allocable toward the purchase of group-term life insurance on their lives for the year, and then by ascertaining the pro rata portion of such total amount attributable to the individual employee. The total amount paid by all employees who are covered for multiple benefits which is allocable toward the purchase of group-term life insurance on their lives with respect to such year shall be an amount which bears the same ratio to the total

amount paid by all employees for multiple benefits with respect to such year as the aggregate premiums paid to the insurer for group-term life insurance on such employees' lives with respect to such year bears to the aggregate premiums paid to the insurer for such multiple benefits with respect to such year. The pro rata portion of such total amount attributable to the individual employee for the cost of group-term life insurance on his life shall be an amount which bears the same ratio to the total amount paid by all employees which is allocable toward the purchase of group-term insurance on their lives with respect to such year as the amount of group-term life insurance on the life of the employee at a specified time during the year, as determined by the employer, bears to the total amount of group-term life insurance on the lives of all employees insured for such multiple benefits at such time.

(g) Effect of provision of other benefits. *(1) In general.* This paragraph discusses the effect of the provision of certain benefits other than group-term life insurance on the life of the employee if the provision of such benefits is contingent upon the underwriting of group-term life insurance on the employee's life to which the rule of inclusion set forth in section 79(a).

(2) Dependent coverage. An amount equal to the cost of group-term life insurance on the life of the spouse or other family member of the employee which is provided under a policy of group-term life insurance carried directly or indirectly by his employer is not subject to the provisions of section 79 since it is not on the life of the employee. See paragraph (d)(2)(ii)(b) of § 1.61-2 for rules regarding the tax treatment of such insurance.

(3) Disability provisions. Payments made for disability benefits provided under a group-term life insurance contract are considered to constitute payments made for accident and health insurance. Thus, employer contributions to provide such benefits are excluded from gross income by reason of the provisions of section 106.

(4) Cost of other benefits. If a benefit described in this paragraph is provided under a policy under which both the employer and his employees contribute, then, except as otherwise provided in this subparagraph, the employer and the employees will be treated as contributing toward the payment of such benefit at the same rate as they contribute toward the cost of group-term life insurance on the employees' lives. A separate allocation of employer and employee contributions for such benefits is permissible only if—

(i) Such separate allocation is set forth in the group policy and is applicable to all the employees covered under such policy;

(ii) Such separate allocation is followed in transactions between the insurer and the group-policyholder; and

(iii) The allocation set forth in the policy satisfies the requirements of the law of the jurisdiction which is applicable to the contract regarding any minimum or maximum contribution rate by the employer or the employees.

T.D. 6888, 7/5/66, amend T.D. 7623, 5/14/79, T.D. 7924, 12/1/83, T.D. 8273, 11/17/89, T.D. 8424, 7/29/92, T.D. 8821, 5/28/99.

§ 1.79-4T Questions and answers relating to the nondiscrimination requirements for group-term life insurance (temporary).

Caution: The Treasury has not yet amended Reg § 1.79-4T to reflect changes made by P.L. 101-508.

Q-1. When does section 79, as amended by the Tax Reform Act of 1984, become effective?

A-1. (a) Generally, section 79, as amended, applies to taxable years (of the employee receiving insurance coverage) beginning after December 31, 1983. There are, however, several exceptions to this effective date where there is coverage under a group-term life insurance plan of the employer that was in existence on January 1, 1984, or a comparable successor to such a plan maintained by the employer or a successor employer.

(b) First, the new rules of section 79(b) and (e), that require the inclusion in income of a retired employee of amounts attributable to the cost of group-term life insurance in excess of $50,000 and that include former employees within the definition of the term "employee," will not apply to any employee who retired from employment on or before January 1, 1984.

(c) Second, in the case of an individual who retires after January 1, 1984, and before January 1, 1987, the new rules of section 79(b) and (e) do not apply if (1) the individual attained age 55 on or before January 1, 1984, and (2) the plan was maintained by the same employer who employed the individual during 1983, or by a successor employer.

(d) Third, in the case of an individual who retires after December 31, 1986, the new rules of section 79(b) and (e) do not apply if (1) the individual attained age 55 on or before January 1, 1984, (2) the plan was maintained by the same employer who employed the individual during 1983, or by a successor employer, and (3) the plan is not, after December 31, 1986, a discriminatory group-term life insurance plan (not taking into account any group-term life insurance coverage provided to employees who retired before January 1, 1987).

(e) For purposes of determining whether a plan is, after December 31, 1986, a discriminatory group-term life insurance plan, there shall be ignored any insurance coverage provided pursuant to a state law requirement that an insurer continue to provide insurance coverage for a period of time not in excess of two months following the termination of a policy.

Q-2. What is meant by a "group-term life insurance plan of the employer that was in existence on January 1, 1984"?

A-2. A group-term life insurance plan of the employer was in existence on January 1, 1984, only if the group policy or policies providing group-term life insurance benefits under the plan were executed on or before January 1, 1984, and were not terminated prior to such date. The applicability of section 79, as amended, to an employee will not be affected by the transfer of the employee between employers treated as a single employer under section 79(d)(7) if the employee continues, after the transfer, to be provided with group-term life insurance benefits under a plan that is comparable (determined under the principles set forth in Q&A 3) to the plan provided by the former employer.

Q-3. When is a plan of group-term life insurance a "comparable successor" to another such plan?

A-3. A plan of group-term life insurance will be a comparable successor to another plan of group-term life insurance (the first plan) only if the plan does not differ from the first plan in any significant aspect with respect to individuals who are potentially eligible for benefits provided under the grandfather provisions in Q&A 1. These individuals consist of those persons who are covered under a plan of group-term life insurance of the employer that was in existence on January 1, 1984, or a comparable successor to such a plan maintained by the employer or a successor employer, and who either retired on or before January 1, 1984, or who both attained age 55 on or before January 1, 1984, and were employed by the employer maintaining the plan (or a predecessor of that employer) during the year 1983. Accordingly, if significant additional or reduced benefits are provided only to individuals who are not described in the preceding sentence, the plan will be considered a comparable successor plan. A plan will not fail to be a comparable successor plan merely because the employer purchases a policy or policies identical to the employer's first plan from a different insurance company. If the new plan provides significant additional or reduced benefits (either as to the type or amount available) to employees, or provides benefits to a category of employees that was formerly excluded from participating in the plan, the plan is generally not a comparable successor to the first plan. However, a plan will not be considered as providing significant additional or reduced benefits merely because a participant's coverage is based on a percentage of compensation and the participant's compensation for the taxable year has been increased or decreased. Furthermore, a plan will not be considered a non-comparable successor plan merely because it is amended, either to decrease benefits provided to key employees or to increase benefits provided to non-key employees, solely in order to comply with the nondiscrimination requirements of section 79(d). Finally, a plan will not be considered a non-comparable successor plan merely because a policy that is part of a discriminatory plan is terminated in order to end discriminatory coverage.

Q-4. For purposes of determining the effective date of section 79, as amended by the Tax Reform Act of 1984, what is a "successor employer"?

A-4. A successor employer is an employer who employs a group of individuals formerly employed by another employer as a result of a business merger, acquisition or division.

Q-5. Under what circumstances will separate policies of group-term life insurance of an employer be considered to be a single plan in determining whether the employer's plan of group-term life insurance is discriminatory?

A-5. All policies providing group-term life insurance to a common key employee or key employees (as defined in this Q&A) carried directly or indirectly by an employer (or by a group of employers described in section 79(d)(7)) will be considered as a single plan for purposes of determining whether an employer's group-term life insurance plan is discriminatory. For example, if a key employee receives $50,000 of group-term life insurance coverage under one policy and the same key employee receives an additional $250,000 of coverage under a separate group-term life insurance policy, the two policies will be treated as a single plan in determining whether the group-term life insurance provided by the employer is discriminatory. If it is discriminatory, the key employees covered by either policy will not receive the benefit of section 79(a)(1) or section 79(c) for either policy. The result is the same even if each policy, considered alone, would be nondiscriminatory. A policy that provides group-term life insurance to a key employee and a policy under which the same key employee is eligible to receive group-term life insurance upon separation from service will be considered to provide group-term life insurance to a common key employee. In addition, an employer may treat two or more policies that do not provide group-term life insurance to a common key employee as constituting a single plan for purposes of satisfying the nondiscrimination provisions of section 79(d). For example, if the employer provides group-term life insurance coverage for non-key employees under one policy and provides group-term life insurance coverage for key employees under a second policy, the two policies may be considered together in determining whether the requirements of section 79(d) are satisfied with regard to the second policy. For purposes of this section, the term "key employee" has the meaning given to such term by paragraph (1) of section 416(i), except that subparagraph (A)(iv) of such paragraph shall be applied by not taking into account employees described in section 79(d)(3)(B) who are not participants in the plan. For purposes of this section, all references to "plan year" or "plan years" in section 416(g)(4)(C) and section 416(i) shall be deleted and replaced with "taxable year of the employer" or "taxable years of the employer," respectively.

Q-6. In the case of a discriminatory group-term life insurance plan, what amounts should be included in the gross income of a key employee?

A-6. (a) In the case of a discriminatory group-term life insurance plan, each key employee must include in gross income for the taxable year the cost of his or her insurance benefit for that year provided by the employer under the plan.

(b) The cost of group-term life insurance coverage provided by an employer for a key employee during the employee's taxable year is determined by apportioning the net premium (group premium less policy dividends, premium refunds or experience rating credits) allocable to the group-term life insurance coverage during the key employee's taxable year, less the actual cost allocated to other key employees pursuant to the method described in the subparagraph (d) of this answer, if applicable, among the covered employees. In the event that the employer has other forms and types of coverage with the same insurer, the employer must make a reasonable allocation of the total premiums paid to the insurer. For example, where an employer has both health insurance coverage and a plan of group-term life insurance with the same insurer, and there is no volume discount, the net premium for the plan of group-term life insurance must include the excess, if any, of the payments the employer makes for the health insurance coverage over the payments the employer would make for such coverage if the plan of group-term life insurance for which this calculation is being made did not exist.

(c) In general, the portion of the net premium for group-term life insurance that should be apportioned to a key employee, other than a key employee to whom the method in subparagraph (d) of this answer is applicable, is determined by: (1) Calculating a "tabular" premium for the entire group (with the exception of all key employees to whom the method in subparagraph (d) of this answer is applicable), in the manner described below, (2) determining the ratio of the total actual net premium (less the actual cost allocated to key employees pursuant to the method in the subparagraph (d) of this answer) to the total tabular premium and (3) multiplying the tabular premium for the key employee at his or her attained age by such ratio. Thus, if the total actual net premium is 125 percent of the total tabular premium for all covered employees and the tabular premium at the key employee's attained age is $2.00 per thousand per month, the cost for such employee would be $2.50 per thousand per month ($2.00 times 125 percent). For these purposes the table used to calculate tabular premiums will be determined as follows:

(i) If the group policy contains a reasonable table (based on recognized mortality assumptions) of premium rates on an attained age basis (which table may use age brackets not exceeding five years) with reference to which the group premium is determined, such table will be used;

(ii) If such table is not available, the 1960 Basic Group Table published by the Society of Actuaries will be used.

(d) In cases where the mortality charge for group-term life insurance coverage provided to a key employee is calculated separately by the insurer (for example, where the charge for the coverage provided to a key employee is based on a medical examination) and the amount of such mortality charge plus a proportionate share of the loading charge for the coverage provided to the group is higher than the amount that would be allocable to such employee under the allocation method in subparagraph (c) the cost of group-term life insurance coverage for that employee shall be that higher amount.

Q-7. Must all active and former employees be considered in applying the coverage tests in section 79(d)(3) to determine whether or not a plan of group-term life insurance is discriminatory with respect to coverage?

A-7. No. Generally, a plan of group-term life insurance which covers both active and former employees will not satisfy the nondiscrimination requirements of section 79(d) unless the coverage tests in section 79(d)(3) are satisfied with respect to both the active and the former employees of the employer, except to the extent they are excluded from tests for discrimination by application of the grandfather provisions set forth in Q&A 1. However, for purposes of determining whether a plan is discriminatory with respect to coverage, the coverage tests must be applied separately to active and former employees. In addition, if the plan limits participation by former employees to employees who retired from employment with the employer, then only retired employees must be considered in applying the coverage tests to former employees. Also, in applying the coverage tests in section 79(d)(3), the employer may make reasonable mortality assumptions regarding former employees who are not covered under the plan but must be considered in applying the coverage tests. Furthermore, only those former employees who terminated employment on or after the earliest date of termination from employment for any former employee covered by the plan must be considered. Finally, for purposes of determining whether a plan of group-term life insurance of the employer (or a successor employer) that was in existence on January 1, 1984 (or a comparable successor to such a plan) is discriminatory, after December 31, 1986, with respect to group-term life insurance coverage for former employees, coverage provided to employees who retired on or before December 31, 1986, shall not be taken into account.

Q-8. Will a group-term life insurance plan be considered discriminatory if active employees receive greater benefits as a percentage of compensation than former employees, or vice versa?

A-8. No. For purposes of determining whether a plan is discriminatory with respect to the type and amount of benefits available, insurance coverage for former employees must be tested separately from insurance coverage for active employees. For example, a group-term life insurance plan that provides group-term life insurance benefits equal to 200 percent of compensation for all active employees and 100 percent of final compensation (based on the average annual compensation for the final five years) for all former employees would satisfy the nondiscrimination requirements of section 79(d). However, a group-term life insurance plan that provides group-term life insurance benefits equal to 200 percent of compensation for all active employees and 100 percent of final compensation (based on the average annual compensation for the final five years) only for key employees who are no longer employed by the employer (or a successor employer) would not satisfy the nondiscrimination requirement of section 79(d)(2)(A).

Q-9. Under what circumstances will the amount of benefits available under a plan of group-term life insurance be considered not to discriminate in favor of participants who are key employees?

A-9. A plan of group-term life insurance will be considered not to discriminate in favor of participants who are key employees, as to the amount of benefits available, if the plan provides a fixed amount of insurance which is the same for all covered employees. In other circumstances, the determination of whether a plan is nondiscriminatory will be based on all of the facts and circumstances. Such plans will be considered not to discriminate in favor of participants who are key employees, as to the amount of benefits available, if the plan contains no group of employees described in the following sentence that, if tested separately, would fail to satisfy the requirements of section 79(d)(2)(A). The group subject to separate testing under the preceding sentence consists of a key employee and all other participants (including other key employees) who receive, under the plan, an amount of insurance (as a multiple of compensation (either total compensation or the basic or regular rate of compensation)) that is equal to or greater than the amount of insurance received by such key employee. As described in Q&As 7&8, active and former employees are tested separately under section 79(d)(2)(A).

Example. Assume that a plan of group-term life insurance has 500 participants, 10 of whom are key employees. Under the plan, 400 of the non-key employees receive an amount of insurance equal to 100 percent of compensation, while all of the key employees and 90 of the non-key employees receive an amount of insurance equal to 200 percent of compensation. The plan will be considered not to discriminate in favor of the participants who are key employees because, tested separately, the group of participants receiving an amount of insurance equal to or greater than 200 percent of compensation would satisfy the requirements of section 79(d)(2)(A) (by reason of section 79(d)(3)(A)(ii)). If one of the key employees received an amount of insurance equal to 300 percent of compensation, the plan would be considered to discriminate in favor of participants who are key employees, because, tested separately, the group consisting of the single key employee receiving an amount of insurance equal to or greater than 300 percent of compensation would fail to satisfy the requirements of section 79(d)(2)(A).

In determining the groups of employees that are tested separately for this purpose, allowance shall be made for reasonable differences in amount of insurance (as a multiple of compensation) due to rounding, the use of compensation brackets or other similar factors. Thus, if a plan bases group-term life insurance coverage on "compensation brackets," it is not intended that any participants will be treated as receiving an amount of insurance (as a multiple of compensation) that is greater (or less) than that of any other participant merely because the first participant's compensation is at the lower (or higher) end of a compensation bracket while the second participant's compensation is at the higher (or lower) end of a compensation bracket. However, any compensation brackets utilized by a plan will be examined to determine if the brackets, or compensation groupings, result in discrimination in favor of key employees. In addition, a plan does not meet the requirements for nondiscrimination as to the type and amount of benefits available under the plan unless all types of benefits (including permanent benefits) and all terms and conditions with respect to such benefits which are available to any participant who is a key employee are also available on a nondiscriminatory basis to non-key employee participants.

Q-10. How is additional coverage purchased by employees under a plan of group-term life insurance treated for purposes of determining whether a plan of group-term life insurance is discriminatory?

A-10. (a) The extent to which employees purchase additional coverage under a plan of group-term life insurance is not taken into account for purposes of determining whether a plan of group-term life insurance is discriminatory. For example, a plan providing insurance to all employees of 1 times annual compensation, which gives all employees the option to purchase additional insurance of 1 times annual compensation at their own expense, would not be considered discriminatory as to the type and amount of benefits available, even if the group (or groups) of participants who purchase additional insurance, if tested separately, would not satisfy the requirements of section 79(d)(2)(A). Solely for this purpose, the choice of an amount of group-term life insurance as a benefit under a cafeteria plan will be treated as the purchase of group-term life insurance by an employee. If additional insurance coverage is available to any key employee that is not available, on a nondiscriminatory basis, to non-key employees, the plan will be considered discriminatory, even if the full cost of such additional insurance coverage is paid by the employee(s) electing such benefits.

(b) If the employer bears a part of the expense of any additional coverage that is purchased by an employee under a plan of group-term life insurance, the additional insurance shall be treated, in part, as an amount of insurance provided by the employer under the plan and, in part, as an amount of insurance purchased by the employee. Except to the extent provided in subparagraph (a) above, the portion of insurance treated as an amount of insurance purchased by the employee is not taken into account for purposes of determining whether the plan is discriminatory. Whether such insurance (together with any other insurance provided by the employer under the plan) will cause the plan to be considered to discriminate in favor of participants who are key employees is determined under the rules of Q&A 9.

Q-11. What effect do the provisions of section 79(d)(1) have if a plan of group-term life insurance is discriminatory for only part of a year?

A-11. If a plan of group-term life insurance is discriminatory at any time during the key employee's taxable year, then it is a discriminatory group-term life insurance plan for that taxable year and the provisions of section 79(d)(1) will be applicable with respect to all group-term life insurance costs allocable to that employee for that year.

Q-12. Are the section 79(d) provisions independent from the requirements contained in Treas. Reg. § 1.79-1?

A-12. Yes. Treas. Reg. § 1.79-1(c)(1) provides that life insurance provided to a group of employees cannot qualify as group-term life insurance if it is provided to less than ten full-time employees unless certain requirements are satisfied. The satisfaction of these requirements does not guarantee that the plan will be nondiscriminatory, and vice versa. Treas. Reg. § 1.79-1(a)(4) provides that life insurance is not group-term life insurance unless the amount of insurance provided to each employee is computed under a formula that precludes individual selection. The mere fact that a life insurance policy is nondiscriminatory is not determinative as to whether the policy precludes individual selection, and vice versa.

T.D. 8073, 1/29/86.

---

§ 1.82-1 Payments for or reimbursements of expenses of moving from one residence to another residence attributable to employment or self-employment.

Caution: The Treasury has not yet amended Reg § 1.82-1 to reflect changes made by P.L. 103-66.

(a) Reimbursements in gross income. *(1) In general.* Any amount received or accrued, directly or indirectly, by an individual as a payment for or reimbursement of expenses of moving from one residence to another residence attributable to employment or self-employment is includible in gross income under section 82 as compensation for services in the taxable year received or accrued. For rules relating to the year a deduction may be allowed for expenses of moving from one residence to another residence, see section 217 and the regulations thereunder.

(2) Amounts received or accrued as reimbursement or payment. For purposes of this section, amounts are considered as being received or accrued by an individual as reimbursement or payment whether received in the form of money, property, or services. A cash basis taxpayer will include amounts in gross income under section 82 when they are received or treated as received by him. Thus, for example, if an employer moves an employee's household goods and personal effects from the employee's old residence to his new residence using the employer's facilities, the employee is considered as having received a payment in the amount of the fair market value of the services furnished at the time the services are furnished by the employer. If the employer pays a mover for moving the employee's household goods and personal effects, the employee is considered as having received the payment at the time the employer pays the mover, rather than at the time the mover moves the employee's household goods and personal effects. Where an employee receives a loan or advance from an employer to enable him to pay his moving expenses, the employee will not be deemed to have received a reimbursement of moving expenses until such time as he accounts to his employer if he is not required to repay such loan or advance and if he makes such accounting within a reasonable time. Such loan or advance will be deemed to be a reimbursement of moving expenses at the time of such accounting to the extent used by the employee for such moving expenses.

(3) Direct or indirect payments or reimbursements. For purposes of this section amounts are considered as being received or accrued whether received directly (paid or provided to an individual by an employer, a client, a customer, or similar person) or indirectly (paid to a third party on behalf of an individual by an employer, a client, a customer, or similar person). Thus, if an employer pays a mover for the expenses of moving an employee's household goods and personal effects from one residence to another residence, the employee has indirectly received a payment which is includible in his gross income under section 82.

(4) Expenses of moving from one residence to another residence. An expense of moving from one residence to another residence is any expenditure, cost, loss, or similar item paid or incurred in connection with a move from one residence to another residence. Moving expenses include (but are not limited to) any expenditure, cost, loss, or similar item directly or indirectly resulting from the acquisition, sale, or exchange of property, the transportation of goods or

property, or travel (by the taxpayer or any other person) in connection with a change in residence. Such expenses include items described in section 217(b) (relating to the definition of moving expenses), irrespective of the dollar limitations contained in section 217(b)(3) and the conditions contained in section 217(c), as well as items not described in section 217(b), such as a loss sustained on the sale or exchange of personal property, storage charges, taxes, or expenses of refitting rugs or draperies.

(5) Attributable to employment or self-employment. Any amount received or accrued from an employer, a client, a customer, or similar person in connection with the performance of services for such employer, client, customer, or similar person, is attributable to employment or self-employment. Thus, for example, if an employer reimburses an employee for a loss incurred on the sale of the employee's house, reimbursement is attributable to the performance of services if made because of the employer-employee relationship. Similarly, if an employer in order to prevent an employee's sustaining a loss on a sale of a house acquires the property from the employee at a price in excess of fair market value, the employee is considered to have received a payment attributable to employment to the extent that such payment exceeds the fair market value of the property.

(b) Effective date. *(1) In general.* Except as provided in subparagraph (2) of this paragraph, paragraph (a) of this section is applicable only to amounts received or accrued in taxable years beginning after December 31, 1969.

(2) Election with respect to payments or reimbursements for expenses paid or incurred before January 1, 1971. Paragraph (a) of this section does not apply with respect to moving expenses paid or incurred before January 1, 1971, in connection with the commencement of work by an employee at a new principal place of work where such employee had been notified by his employer on or before December 19, 1969, of such move and the employee makes an election under paragraph (h) of § 1.217-2.

T.D. 7197, 7/10/72, amend T.D. 7578, 12/19/78.

§ 1.83-1 Property transferred in connection with the performance of services.

Caution: The Treasury has not yet amended Reg § 1.83-1 to reflect changes made by P.L. 108-357, P.L. 104-188, P.L. 98-369.

(a) Inclusion in gross income. *(1) General rule.* Section 83 provides rules for the taxation of property transferred to an employee or independent contractor (or beneficiary thereof) in connection with the performance of services by such employee or independent contractor. In general, such property is not taxable under section 83(a) until it has been transferred (as defined in § 1.83-3(a)) to such person and become substantially vested (as defined in § 1.83-3(b)) in such person. In that case, the excess of—

(i) The fair market value of such property (determined without regard to any lapse restriction, as defined in § 1.83-3(i)) at the time that the property becomes substantially vested, over

(ii) The amount (if any) paid for such property,

shall be included as compensation in the gross income of such employee or independent contractor for the taxable year in which the property becomes substantially vested. Until such property becomes substantially vested the transferor shall be regarded as the owner of such property, and any income from such property received by the employee or independent contractor (or beneficiary thereof) or the right to the use of such property by the employee or independent contractor constitutes additional compensation and shall be included in the gross income of such employee or independent contractor for the taxable year in which such income is received or such use is made available. This paragraph applies to a transfer of property in connection with the performance of services even though the transferor is not the person for whom such services are performed.

(2) Life insurance. The cost of life insurance protection under a life insurance contract, retirement income contract, endowment contract, or other contract providing life insurance protection is taxable generally under section 61 and the regulations thereunder during the period such contract remains substantially nonvested (as defined in § 1.83-3(b)). For the taxation of life insurance protection under a split-dollar life insurance arrangement (as defined in § 1.61-22(b)(1) or (2)), see § 1.61-22.

(3) Cross references. For rules concerning the treatment of employers and other transferors of property in connection with the performance of services, see section 83(h) and § 1.83-6. For rules concerning the taxation of beneficiaries of an employees' trust that is not exempt under section 501(a), see section 402(b) and the regulations thereunder.

(b) Subsequent sale, forfeiture, or other disposition of nonvested property. *(1)* If substantially nonvested property (that has been transferred in connection with the performance of services) is subsequently sold or otherwise disposed of to a third party in an arm's length transaction while still substantially nonvested, the person who performed such services shall realize compensation in an amount equal to the excess of—

(i) The amount realized on such sale or other disposition, over

(ii) The amount (if any) paid for such property.

Such amount of compensation is includible in his gross income in accordance with his method of accounting. Two preceding sentences also apply when the person disposing of the property has received it in a non-arm's length transaction described in paragraph (c) of this section. In addition, section 83(a) and paragraph (a) of this section shall thereafter cease to apply with respect to such property.

(2) If substantially nonvested property that has been transferred in connection with the performance of services to the person performing such services is forfeited while still substantially nonvested and held by such person, the difference between the amount paid (if any) and the amount received upon forfeiture (if any) shall be treated as an ordinary gain or loss. This paragraph (b)(2) does not apply to property to which § 1.83-2(a) applies.

(3) This paragraph (b) shall not apply to, and no gain shall be recognized on, any sale, forfeiture, or other disposition described in this paragraph to the extent that any property received in exchange therefor is substantially nonvested. Instead, section 83 and this section shall apply with respect to such property received (as if it were substituted for the property disposed of).

(c) Dispositions of nonvested property not at arm's length. If substantially nonvested property (that has been transferred in connection with the performance of services) is disposed of in a transaction which is not at arm's length and the property remains substantially nonvested, the person who performed such services realizes compensation equal in amount to the sum of any money and the fair market value of any substantially vested property received in such disposition. Such amount of compensation is includible in his gross income in accordance with his method of accounting. However, such amount of compensation shall not exceed the fair market value of the property disposed of at the time of disposition (determined without regard to any lapse restriction), reduced by the amount paid for such property. In addition, section 83 and these regulations shall continue to apply with respect to such property, except that any amount previously includible in gross income under this paragraph (c) shall thereafter be treated as an amount paid for such property. For example, if in 1971 an employee pays $50 for a share of stock which has a fair market value of $100 and is substantially nonvested at that time and later in 1971 (at a time when the property still has a fair market value of $100 and is still substantially nonvested) the employee disposes of, in a transaction not at arm's length, the share of stock to his wife for $10, the employee realizes compensation of $10 in 1971. If in 1972, when the share of stock has a fair market value of $120, it becomes substantially vested, the employee realizes additional compensation in 1972 in the amount of $60 (the $120 fair market value of the stock less both the $50 price paid for the stock and the $10 taxed as compensation in 1971). For purposes of this paragraph, if substantially nonvested property has been transferred to a person other than the person who performed the services, and the transferee dies holding the property while the property is still substantially nonvested and while the person who performed the services is alive, the transfer which results by reason of the death of such transferee is a transfer not at arm's length.

(d) Certain transfers upon death. If substantially nonvested property has been transferred in connection with the performance of services and the person who performed such services dies while the property is still substantially nonvested, any income realized on or after such death with respect to such property under this section is income in respect of a decedent to which the rules of section 691 apply. In such a case the income in respect of such property shall be taxable under section 691 (except to the extent not includible under section 101(b)) to the estate or beneficiary of the person who performed the services, in accordance with section 83 and the regulations thereunder. However, if an item of income is realized upon such death before July 21, 1978, because the property became substantially vested upon death, the person responsible for filing decedent's income tax return for decedent's last taxable year may elect to treat such item as includible in gross income for decedent's last taxable year by including such item in gross income on the return or amended return filed for decedent's last taxable year.

(e) Forfeiture after substantial vesting. If a person is taxable under section 83(a) when the property transferred becomes substantially vested and thereafter the person's beneficial interest in such property is nevertheless forfeited pursuant to a lapse restriction, any loss incurred by such person (but not by a beneficiary of such person) upon such forfeiture shall be an ordinary loss to the extent the basis in such property has been increased as a result of the recognition of income by such person under section 83(a) with respect to such property.

(f) Examples. The provisions of this section may be illustrated by the following examples:

Example (1). On November 1, 1978, X corporation sells to E, an employee, 100 shares of X corporation stock at $10 per share. At the time of such sale the fair market value of the X corporation stock is $100 per share. Under the terms of the sale each share of stock is subject to a substantial risk of forfeiture which will not lapse until November 1, 1988. Evidence of this restriction is stamped on the face of E's stock certificates, which are therefore nontransferable (within the meaning of § 1.83-3(d)). Since in 1978 E's stock is substantially nonvested, E does not include any of such amount in his gross income as compensation in 1978. On November 1, 1988, the fair market value of the X corporation stock is $250 per share. Since the X corporation stock becomes substantially vested in 1988, E must include $24,000 (100 shares of X corporation stock × $250 fair market value per share less $10 price paid by E for each share) as compensation for 1988. Dividends paid by X to E on E's stock after it was transferred to E on November 1, 1973, are taxable to E as additional compensation during the period E's stock is substantially nonvested and are deductible as such by X.

Example (2). Assume the facts are the same as in example (1), except that on November 1, 1985, each share of stock of X corporation in E's hands could as a matter of law be transferred to a bona fide purchaser who would not be required to forfeit the stock if the risk of forfeiture materialized. In the event, however, that the risk materializes, E would be liable in damages to X. On November 1, 1985, the fair market value of the X corporation stock is $230 per share. Since E's stock is transferable within the meaning of § 1.83-3(d) in 1985, the stock is substantially vested and E must include $22,000 (100 shares of X corporation stock × $230 fair market value per share less $10 price paid by E for each share) as compensation for 1985.

Example (3). Assume the facts are the same as in example (1) except that, in 1984 E sells his 100 shares of X corporation stock in an arm's length sale to I, an investment company, for $120 per share. At the time of this sale each share of X corporation's stock has a fair market value of $200. Under paragraph (b) of this section, E must include $11,000 (100 shares of X corporation stock × $120 amount realized per share less $10 price paid by E per share) as compensation for 1984 notwithstanding that the stock remains nontransferable and is still subject to a substantial risk of forfeiture at the time of such sale. Under § 1.83-4(b)(2), I's basis in the X corporation stock is $120 per share.

T.D. 7554, 7/21/78, amend T.D. 9092, 9/11/2003.

§ 1.83-2 Election to include in gross income in year of transfer.

Caution: The Treasury has not yet amended Reg § 1.83-2 to reflect changes made by P.L. 99-514, P.L. 98-369.

(a) In general. If property is transferred (within the meaning of § 1.83-3(a)) in connection with the performance of services, the person performing such services may elect to include in gross income under section 83(b) the excess (if any) of the fair market value of the property at the time of transfer (determined without regard to any lapse restriction, as defined in § 1.83-3(i)) over the amount (if any) paid for such property, as compensation for services. The fact that the transferee has paid full value for the property transferred, realizing no bargain element in the transaction, does not preclude the use of the election as provided for in this section. If this election is made, the substantial vesting rules of section 83(a) and the regulations thereunder do not apply with respect to such property, and except as otherwise provided in section 83(d)(2) and the regulations thereunder (relating to the cancellation of a nonlapse restriction), any subsequent appreciation in the value of the property is not taxable as compensation to the person who performed the services.

Thus, property with respect to which this election is made shall be includible in gross income as of the time of transfer, even though such property is substantially nonvested (as defined in § 1.83-3(b)) at the time of transfer, and no compensation will be includible in gross income when such property becomes substantially vested (as defined in § 1.83-3(b)). In computing the gain or loss from the subsequent sale or exchange of such property, its basis shall be the amount paid for the property increased by the amount included in gross income under section 83(b). If property for which a section 83(b) election is in effect is forfeited while substantially nonvested, such forfeiture shall be treated as a sale or exchange upon which there is realized a loss equal to the excess (if any) of—

(1) The amount paid (if any) for such property, over,

(2) The amount realized (if any) upon such forfeiture.

If such property is a capital asset in the hands of the taxpayer, such loss shall be a capital loss. A sale or other disposition of the property that is in substance a forfeiture, or is made in contemplation of a forfeiture, shall be treated as a forfeiture under the two immediately preceding sentences.

(b) Time for making election. Except as provided in the following sentence, the election referred to in paragraph (a) of this section shall be filed not later than 30 days after the date the property was transferred (or, if later, January 29, 1970) and may be filed prior to the date of transfer. Any statement filed before February 15, 1970, which was amended not later than February 16, 1970, in order to make it conform to the requirements of paragraph (e) of this section, shall be deemed a proper election under section 83(b).

(c) Manner of making election. The election referred to in paragraph (a) of this section is made by filing one copy of a written statement with the internal revenue office with whom the person who performed the services files his return. In addition, one copy of such statement shall be submitted with this income tax return for the taxable year in which such property was transferred.

(d) Additional copies. The person who performed the services shall also submit a copy of the statement referred to in paragraph (c) of this section to the person for whom the services are performed. In addition, if the person who performs the services and the transferee of such property are not the same person, the person who performs the services shall submit a copy of such statement to the transferee of the property.

(e) Content of statement. The statement shall be signed by the person making the election and shall indicate that it is being made under section 83(b) of the Code, and shall contain the following information:

(1) The name, address and taxpayer identification number of the taxpayer;

(2) A description of each property with respect to which the election is being made;

(3) The date or dates on which the property is transferred and the taxable year (for example, "calendar year 1970" or "fiscal year ending May 31, 1970") for which such election was made;

(4) The nature of the restriction or restrictions to which the property is subject;

(5) The fair market value at the time of transfer (determined without regard to any lapse restriction, as defined in § 1.83-3(i)) of each property with respect to which the election is being made;

(6) The amount (if any) paid for such property; and

(7) With respect to elections made after July 21, 1978, a statement to the effect that copies have been furnished to other persons as provided in paragraph (d) of this section.

(f) Revocability of election. An election under section 83(b) may not be revoked except with the consent of the Commissioner. Consent will be granted only in the case where the transferee is under a mistake of fact as to the underlying transaction and must be requested within 60 days of the date on which the mistake of fact first became known to the person who made the election. In any event, a mistake as to the value, or decline in the value, of the property with respect to which an election under section 83(b) has been made or a failure to perform an act contemplated at the time of transfer of such property does not constitute a mistake of fact.

T.D. 7554, 7/21/78.

§ 1.83-3 Meaning and use of certain terms.

(a) Transfer. *(1) In general.* For purposes of section 83 and the regulations thereunder, a transfer of property occurs when a person acquires a beneficial ownership interest in such property (disregarding any lapse restriction, as defined in § 1.83-3(i)). For special rules applying to the transfer of a life insurance contract (or an undivided interest therein) that is part of a split-dollar life insurance arrangement (as defined in § 1.61-22(b)(1) or (2)), see § 1.61-22(g).

(2) Option. The grant of an option to purchase certain property does not constitute a transfer of such property. However, see § 1.83-7 for the extent to which the grant of the option itself is subject to section 83. In addition, if the amount paid for the transfer of property is an indebtedness secured by the transferred property, on which there is no personal liability to pay all or a substantial part of such indebtedness, such transaction may be in substance the same as the grant of an option. The determination of the substance of the transaction shall be based upon all the facts and circumstances. The factors to be taken into account include the type of property involved, the extent to which the risk that the property will decline in value has been transferred, and the likelihood that the purchase price will, in fact, be paid. See also § 1.83-4(c) for the treatment of forgiveness of indebtedness that has constituted an amount paid.

(3) Requirement that property be returned. Similarly, no transfer may have occurred where property is transferred under conditions that require its return upon the happening of an event that is certain to occur, such as the termination of employment. In such a case, whether there is, in fact, a transfer depends upon all the facts and circumstances. Factors which indicate that no transfer has occurred are described in paragraph (a)(4), (5), and (6) of this section.

(4) Similarity to option. An indication that no transfer has occurred is the extent to which the conditions relating to a transfer are similar to an option.

(5) Relationship to fair market value. An indication that no transfer has occurred is the extent to which the consideration to be paid the transferee upon surrendering the property does not approach the fair market value of the property at the time of surrender. For purposes of paragraph (a)(5) and (6) of this section, fair market value includes fair market value determined under the rules of § 1.83-5(a)(1), relating to the valuation of property subject to nonlapse restrictions. Therefore, the existence of a nonlapse restriction referred to in § 1.83-5(a)(1) is not a factor indicating no transfer has occurred.

(6) Risk of loss. An indication that no transfer has occurred is the extent to which the transferee does not incur the risk of a beneficial owner that the value of the property at the time of transfer will decline substantially. Therefore, for purposes of this (6), risk of decline in property value is not limited to the risk that any amount paid for the property may be lost.

(7) Examples. The provisions of this paragraph may be illustrated by the following examples:

Example (1). On January 3, 1971, X corporation sells for $500 to S, a salesman of X, 10 shares of stock in X corporation with a fair market value of $1,000. The stock is nontransferable and subject to return to the corporation (for $500) if S's sales do not reach a certain level by December 31, 1971. Disregarding the restriction concerning S's sales (since the restrictions is a lapse restriction), S's interest in the stock is that of a beneficial owner and therefore a transfer occurs on January 3, 1971.

Example (2). On November 17, 1972, W sells to E 100 shares of stock in W corporation with a fair market value of $10,000 in exchange for a $10,000 note without personal liability. The note requires E to make yearly payments of $2,000 commencing in 1973. E collects the dividends, votes the stock and pays the interest on the note. However, he makes no payments toward the face amount of the note. Because E has no personal liability on the note, and since E is making no payments towards the face amount of the note, the likelihood of E paying the full purchase price is in substantial doubt. As a result E has not incurred the risks of a beneficial owner that the value of the stock will decline. Therefore, no transfer of the stock has occurred on November 17, 1972, but an option to purchase the stock has been granted to E.

Example (3). On January 3, 1971, X corporation purports to transfer to E, an employee, 100 shares of stock in X corporation. The X stock is subject to the sole restriction that E must sell such stock to X on termination of employment for any reason for an amount which is equal to the excess (if any) of the book value of the X stock at termination of employment over book value on January 3, 1971. The stock is not transferable by E and the restrictions on transfer are stamped on the certificate. Under these facts and circumstances, there is no transfer of the X stock within the meaning of section 83.

Example (4). Assume the same facts as in example (3) except that E paid $3,000 for the stock and that the restriction required E upon termination of employment to sell the stock to M for the total amount of dividends that have been declared on the stock since September 2, 1971, or $3,000 whichever is higher. Again, under the facts and circumstances, no transfer of the X stock has occurred.

Example (5). On July 4, 1971, X corporation purports to transfer to G, an employee, 100 shares of X stock. The stock is subject to the sole restriction that upon termination of employment G must sell the stock to X for the greater of its fair market value at such time or $100, the amount G paid for the stock. On July 4, 1971 the X stock has a fair market value of $100. Therefore, G does not incur the risk of a beneficial owner that the value of the stock at the time of transfer ($100) will decline substantially. Under these facts and circumstances, no transfer has occurred.

(b) Substantially vested and substantially nonvested property. For purposes of section 83 and the regulations thereunder, property is substantially nonvested when it is subject to a substantial risk of forfeiture, within the meaning of paragraph (c) of this section, and is nontransferable, within the meaning of paragraph (d) of this section. Property is substantially vested for such purposes when it is either transferable or not subject to a substantial risk of forfeiture.

(c) Substantial risk of forfeiture. *(1) In general.* For purposes of section 83 and the regulations thereunder, whether a risk of forfeiture is substantial or not depends upon the facts and circumstances. A substantial risk of forfeiture exists where rights in property that are transferred are conditioned, directly or indirectly, upon the future performance (or refraining from performance) of substantial services by any person, or the occurrence of a condition related to a purpose of the transfer, and the possibility of forfeiture is substantial if such condition is not satisfied.

Property is not transferred subject to a substantial risk of forfeiture to the extent that the employer is required to pay the fair market value of a portion of such property to the employee upon the return of such property. The risk that the value of property will decline during a certain period of time does not constitute a substantial risk of forfeiture. A nonlapse restriction, standing by itself, will not result in a substantial risk of forfeiture.

(2) Illustrations of substantial risks of forfeiture. The regularity of the performance of services and the time spent in performing such services tend to indicate whether services required by a condition are substantial. The fact that the person performing services has the right to decline to perform such services without forfeiture may tend to establish that services are insubstantial. Where stock is transferred to an underwriter prior to a public offering and the full enjoyment of such stock is expressly or impliedly conditioned upon the successful completion of the underwriting, the stock is subject to a substantial risk of forfeiture. Where an employee receives property from an employer subject to a requirement that it be returned if the total earnings of the employer do not increase, such property is subject to a substantial risk of forfeiture. On the other hand, requirements that the property be returned to the employer if the employee is discharged for cause or for committing a crime will not be considered to result in a substantial risk of forfeiture. An enforceable requirement that the property be returned to the employer if the employee accepts a job with a competing firm will not ordinarily be considered to result in a substantial risk of forfeiture unless the particular facts and circumstances indicate to the contrary. Factors which may be taken into account in determining whether a covenant not to compete constitutes a substantial risk of forfeiture are the age of the employee, the availability of alternative employment opportunities, the likelihood of the employee's obtaining such other employment, the degree of skill possessed by the employee, the employee's health, and the practice (if any) of the employer to enforce such covenants. Similarly, rights in property transferred to a retiring employee subject to the sole requirement that it be returned unless he renders consulting services upon the request of his former employer will not be considered subject to a substantial risk of forfeiture unless he is in fact expected to perform substantial services.

(3) Enforcement of forfeiture condition. In determining whether the possibility of forfeiture is substantial in the case of rights in property transferred to an employee of a corporation who owns a significant amount of the total combined voting power or value of all classes of stock of the employer corporation or of its parent corporation, there will be taken into account (i) the employee's relationship to other stockholders and the extent of their control, potential control and possible loss of control of the corporation, (ii) the position

of the employee in the corporation and the extent to which he is subordinate to other employees, (iii) the employee's relationship to the officers and directors of the corporation, (iv) the person or persons who must approve the employee's discharge, and (v) past actions of the employer in enforcing the provisions of the restrictions. For example, if an employee would be considered as having received rights in property subject to a substantial risk of forfeiture, but for the fact that the employee owns 20 percent of the single class of stock in the transferor corporation, and if the remaining 80 percent of the class of stock is owned by an unrelated individual (or members of such an individual's family) so that the possibility of the corporation enforcing a restriction on such rights is substantial, then such rights are subject to a substantial risk of forfeiture. On the other hand, if 4 percent of the voting power of all the stock of a corporation is owned by the president of such corporation and the remaining stock is so diversely held by the public that the president, in effect, controls the corporation, then the possibility of the corporation enforcing a restriction on rights in property transferred to the president is not substantial, and such rights are not subject to a substantial risk of forfeiture.

(4) Examples. The rules contained in paragraph (c)(1) of this section may be illustrated by the following examples. In each example it is assumed that, if the conditions on transfer are not satisfied, the forfeiture provision will be enforced.

Example (1). On November 1, 1971, corporation X transfers in connection with the performance of services to E, an employee, 100 shares of corporation X stock for $90 per share. Under the terms of the transfer, E will be subject to a binding commitment to resell the stock to corporation X at $90 per share if he leaves the employment of corporation X for any reason prior to the expiration of a 2-year period from the date of such transfer. Since E must perform substantial services for corporation X and will not be paid more than $90 for the stock, regardless of its value, if he fails to perform such services during such 2-year period, E's rights in the stock are subject to a substantial risk of forfeiture during such period.

Example (2). On November 10, 1971, corporation X transfers in connection with the performance of services to a trust for the benefit of employees, $100x. Under the terms of the trust any child of an employee who is an enrolled full-time student at an accredited educational institution as a candidate for a degree will receive an annual grant of cash for each academic year the student completes as a student in good standing, up to a maximum of four years. E, an employee, has a child who is enrolled as a full-time student at an accredited college as a candidate for a degree. Therefore, E has a beneficial interest in the assets of the trust equalling the value of four cash grants. Since E's child must complete one year of college in order to receive a cash grant, E's interest in the trust assets are subject to a substantial risk of forfeiture to the extent E's child has not become entitled to any grants.

Example (3). On November 25, 1971, corporation X gives to E, an employee, in connection with his performance of services to corporation X, a bonus of 100 shares of corporation X stock. Under the terms of the bonus arrangement E is obligated to return the corporation X stock to corporation X if he terminates his employment for any reason. However, for each year occurring after November 25, 1971, during which E remains employed with corporation X, E ceases to be obligated to return 10 shares of the corporation X stock. Since in each year occurring after November 25, 1971, for which E remains employed he is not required to return 10 shares of corporation X's stock, E's rights in 10 shares each year for 10 years cease to be subject to a substantial risk of forfeiture for each year he remains so employed.

Example (4). (a) Assume the same facts as in example (3) except that for each year occurring after November 25, 1971, for which E remains employed with corporation X, X agrees to pay, in redemption of the bonus shares given to E if he terminates employment for any reason, 10 percent of the fair market value of each share of stock on the date of such termination of employment. Since corporation X will pay E 10 percent of the value of his bonus stock for each of the 10 years after November 25, 1971, in which he remains employed by X, and the risk of a decline in value is not a substantial risk of forfeiture, E's interest in 10 percent of such bonus stock becomes substantially vested in each of those years.

(b) The following chart illustrates the fair market value of the bonus stock and the fair market value of the portion of bonus stock that becomes substantially vested on November 25, for the following years:

Year	Fair market value of	
	All Stock	Portion of stock that becomes vested
1972	$200	$20
1973	300	30
1974	150	15
1975	150	15
1976	100	10

If E terminates his employment on July 1, 1977, when the fair market value of the bonus stock is $100, E must return the bonus stock to X, and X must pay, in redemption of the bonus stock, $50 (50 percent of the value of the bonus stock on the date of termination of employment). E has recognized income under section 83(a) and § 1.83-3(a) with respect to 50 percent of the bonus stock, and E's basis in that portion of the stock equals the amount of income recognized, $90. Under § 1.83-1(e), the $40 loss E incurred upon forfeiture ($90 basis less $50 redemption payment) is an ordinary loss.

Example (5). On January 7, 1971, corporation X, a computer service company, transfers to E, 100 shares of corporation X stock for $50. E is a highly compensated salesman who sold X's products in a three-state area since 1960. At the time of transfer each share of X stock has a fair market value of $100. The stock is transferred to E in connection with his termination of employment with X. Each share of X stock is subject to the sole condition that E can keep such share only if he does not engage in competition with X for a 5-year period in the three-state area where E had previously sold X's products. E, who is 45 years old, has no intention of retiring from the work force. In order to earn a salary comparable to his current compensation, while preventing the risk of forfeiture from arising, E will have to expend a substantial amount of time and effort in another industry or market to establish the necessary business contacts. Thus, under these facts and circumstances E's rights in the stock are subject to a substantial risk of forfeiture.

(d) Transferability of property. For purposes of section 83 and the regulations thereunder, the rights of a person in property are transferable if such person can transfer any interest in the property to any person other than the transferor of the property, but only if the rights in such property of such transferee are not subject to a substantial risk of forfeiture. Accordingly, property is transferable if the person performing the services or receiving the property can sell, assign, or pledge (as collateral for a loan, or as security for the performance of an obligation, or for any other purpose) his interest in the property to any person other than the transferor of such property and if the transferee is not required to give up the property or its value in the event the substantial risk of forfeiture materializes. On the other hand, property is not considered to be transferable merely because the person performing the services or receiving the property may designate a beneficiary to receive the property in the event of his death.

(e) Property. For purposes of section 83 and the regulations thereunder, the term "property" includes real and personal property other than either money or an unfunded and unsecured promise to pay money or property in the future. The term also includes a beneficial interest in assets (including money) which are transferred or set aside from the claims of creditors of the transferor, for example, in a trust or escrow account. See, however, § 1.83-8(a) with respect to employee trusts and annuity plans subject to section 402(b) and section 403(c). In the case of a transfer of a life insurance contract, retirement income contract, endowment contract, or other contract providing life insurance protection, or any undivided interest therein, the policy cash value and all other rights under such contract (including any supplemental agreements thereto and whether or not guaranteed), other than current life insurance protection, are treated as property for purposes of this section. However, in the case of the transfer of a life insurance contract, retirement income contract, endowment contract, or other contract providing life insurance protection, which was part of a split-dollar arrangement (as defined in § 1.61-22(b)) entered into (as defined in § 1.61-22(j)) on or before September 17, 2003, and which is not materially modified (as defined in § 1.61-22(j)(2)) after September 17, 2003, only the cash surrender value of the contract is considered to be property. Where rights in a contract providing life insurance protection are substantially nonvested, see § 1.83-1(a)(2) for rules relating to taxation of the cost of life insurance protection.

(f) Property transferred in connection with the performance of services. Property transferred to an employee or an independent contractor (or beneficiary thereof) in recognition of the performance of, or he refraining from performance of, services is considered transferred in connection with the performance of services within the meaning of section 83. The existence of other persons entitled to buy stock on the same terms and conditions as an employee, whether pursuant to a public or private offering may, however, indicate that in such circumstances a transfer to the employee is not in recognition of the performance of, or the refraining from performance of, services. The transfer of property is subject to section 83 whether such transfer is in respect of past, present, or future services.

(g) Amount paid. For purposes of section 83 and the regulations thereunder, the term "amount paid" refers to the value of any money or property paid for the transfer of property to which section 83 applies, and does not refer to any amount paid for the right to use such property or to receive the income therefrom. Such value does not include any stated or unstated interest payments. For rules regarding the calculation of the amount of unstated interest payments, see § 1.483-1(c). When section 83 applies to the transfer of property pursuant to the exercise of an option, the term "amount paid" refers to any amount paid for the grant of the option plus any amount paid as the exercise price of the option. For rules regarding the forgiveness of indebtedness treated as an amount paid, see § 1.83-4(c).

(h) Nonlapse restriction. For purposes of section 83 and the regulations thereunder, a restriction which by its terms will never lapse (also referred to as a "nonlapse restriction") is permanent limitation on the transferability of property—

(i) Which will require the transferee of the property to sell, or offer to sell, such property at a price determined under a formula, and

(ii) Which will continue to apply to and be enforced against the transferee or any subsequent holder (other than the transferor).

A limitation subjecting the property to a permanent right of first refusal in a particular person at a price determined under a formula is a permanent nonlapse restriction. Limitations imposed by registration requirements of State or Federal security laws or similar laws imposed with respect to sales or other dispositions of stock or securities are not nonlapse restrictions. An obligation to resell or to offer to sell property transferred in connection with the performance of services to a specific person or persons at its fair market value at the time of such sale is not a nonlapse restriction. See § 1.83-5(c) for examples of nonlapse restrictions.

(i) Lapse restriction. For purposes of section 83 and the regulations thereunder, the term "lapse restriction" means a restriction other than a nonlapse restriction as defined in paragraph (h) of this section, and includes (but is not limited to) a restriction that carries a substantial risk of forfeiture.

(j) Sales which may give rise to suit under section 16(b) of the Securities Exchange Act of 1934. *(1) In general.* For purposes of section 83 and the regulations thereunder if the sale of property at a profit within six months after the purchase of the property could subject a person to suit under section 16(b) of the Securities Exchange Act of 1934, the person's rights in the property are treated as subject to a substantial risk of forfeiture and as not transferable until the earlier of (i) the expiration of such six-month period, or (ii) the first day on which the sale of such property at a profit will not subject the person to suit under section 16(b) of the Securities Exchange Act of 1934. However, whether an option is "transferable by the optionee" for purposes of § 1.83-7(b)(2)(i) is determined without regard to section 83(c)(3) and this paragraph (j).

(2) Examples. The provisions of this paragraph may be illustrated by the following examples:

Example (1). On January 1, 1983, X corporation sells to P, a beneficial owner of 12% of X corporation stock, in connection with P's performance of services, 100 shares of X corporation stock at $10 per share. At the time of the sale the fair market value of the X corporation stock is $100 per share. P, as a beneficial owner of more 10% of X corporation stock, officer of X, is liable to suit under section 16(b) of the Securities Exchange Act of 1934 for recovery of any profit from any sale and purchase or purchase and sale of X corporation stock within a six-month period, but no other restrictions apply to the stock. Because the section 16(b) restriction is applicable to P, "P's rights in the 100 shares of stock purchased on January 1, 1983, are treated as subject to a substantial risk of forfeiture and as not transferable through June 29, 1983. P chooses not to make an election under section 83(b) and therefore does not include any amount with respect to the stock purchase in gross income as compensation on the date of purchase. On June 30, 1983, the fair market value of X corporation stock is $250 per share." P must include $24,000 (100 shares of X corporation stock by P for each share)) in gross income as compensation on June 30, 1983. If, in this example, restrictions other than section 16(b) applied to the stock, such other restrictions (but not section 16(b)) would be taken into account in determining whether the stock is subject to a substantial risk of forfeiture and is nontransferable for periods after June 29, 1983.

Example (2). Assume the same facts as in example (1) except that P is not an insider on or after May 1, 1983, and the section 16(b) restriction does not apply beginning on that date. On May 1, 1983, P must include in gross income as compensation the difference between the fair market value of the stock on that date and the amount paid for the stock.

Example (3). Assume the same facts as in example (1) except that on June 1, 1983, X corporation sells to P an additional 100 shares of X corporation stock at $20 per share. At the time of the sale the fair market value of the X corporation stock is $150 per share. On June 30, 1983, P must include $24,000 in gross income as compensation with respect to the January 1, 1983 purchase. On November 30, 1983, the fair market value of X corporation stock is $200 per share. Accordingly, on that date P must include $18,000 (100 shares of X corporation stock × $180 ($200 fair market value per share less $20 price paid by P for each share)) in gross income as compensation with respect to the June 1, 1983 purchase.

(3) Effective date. This paragraph applies property transferred after December 31, 1981.

(k) Special rule for certain accounting rules. *(1)* For purposes of section 83 and the regulations thereunder, property is subject to substantial risk of forfeiture and is not transferable so long as the property is subject to a restriction on transfer to comply with the "Pooling-of-Interests Accounting" rules set forth in Accounting Series Release Numbered 130 ((10/5/72) 37 FR 20937; 17 CFR 211.130) and Accounting Series Release Numbered 135 ((1/18/73) 38 FR 1734; 17 CFR 211.135).

(2) Effective date. This paragraph applies to property transferred after December 31, 1981.

T.D. 7554, 7/21/78, amend T.D. 8042, 8/5/85, T.D. 9092, 9/11/2003, T.D. 9223, 8/26/2005.

PAR. 2. Section 1.83-3 is amended as follows:

1. Paragraph (e) is amended by adding two new sentences after the first sentence.

2. Paragraph (l) is added.

The revision and addition read as follows:

Proposed § 1.83-3 Meaning and use of certain terms.
[*For Preamble, see ¶ 152,663*]

* * * * *

(e) Property. * * * Accordingly, property includes a partnership interest. The previous sentence is effective for transfers on or after the date final regulations are published in the Federal Register. * * *

* * * * *

(l) Special rules for the transfer of a partnership interest. *(1)* Subject to such additional conditions, rules, and procedures that the Commissioner may prescribe in regulations, revenue rulings, notices, or other guidance published in the Internal Revenue Bulletin (see § 601.601(d)(2)(ii)(b) of this chapter), a partnership and all of its partners may elect a safe harbor under which the fair market value of a partnership interest that is transferred in connection with the performance of services is treated as being equal to the liquidation value of that interest for transfers on or after the date final regulations are published in the Federal Register if the following conditions are satisfied:

(i) The partnership must prepare a document, executed by a partner who has responsibility for Federal income tax reporting by the partnership, stating that the partnership is electing, on behalf of the partnership and each of its partners, to have the safe harbor apply irrevocably as of the stated effective date with respect to all partnership interests transferred in connection with the performance of services while the safe harbor election remains in effect and attach the document to the tax return for the partnership for the taxable year that includes the effective date of the election.

(ii) Except as provided in paragraph (l)(1)(iii) of this section, the partnership agreement must contain provisions that are legally binding on all of the partners stating that—

(A) The partnership is authorized and directed to elect the safe harbor; and

(B) The partnership and each of its partners (including any person to whom a partnership interest is transferred in connection with the performance of services) agrees to comply with all requirements of the safe harbor with respect to all partnership interests transferred in connection with the performance of services while the election remains effective.

(iii) If the partnership agreement does not contain the provisions described in paragraph (l)(1)(ii) of this section, or the provisions are not legally binding on all of the partners of the partnership, then each partner in a partnership that transfers a partnership interest in connection with the performance of services must execute a document containing provisions that are legally binding on that partner stating that—

(A) The partnership is authorized and directed to elect the safe harbor; and

(B) The partner agrees to comply with all requirements of the safe harbor with respect to all partnership interests transferred in connection with the performance of services while the election remains effective.

(2) The specified effective date of the safe harbor election may not be prior to the date that the safe harbor election is executed. The partnership must retain such records as may be necessary to indicate that an effective election has been made and remains in effect, including a copy of the partnership's election statement under this paragraph (l), and, if applicable, the original of each document submitted to the partnership by a partner under this paragraph (l). If the partnership is unable to produce a record of a particular document, the election will be treated as not made, generally resulting in termination of the election. The safe harbor election also may be terminated by the partnership preparing a document, executed by a partner who has responsibility for Federal income tax reporting by the partnership, which states that the partnership, on behalf of the partnership and each of its partners, is revoking the safe harbor election on the stated effective date, and attaching the document to the tax return for the partnership for the taxable year that includes the effective date of the revocation.

§ 1.83-4 Special rules.

Caution: The Treasury has not yet amended Reg § 1.83-4 to reflect changes made by P.L. 108-357.

(a) Holding period. Under section 83(f), the holding period of transferred property to which section 83(a) applies shall begin just after such property is substantially vested. However, if the person who has performed the services in connection with which property is transferred has made an election under section 83(b), the holding period of such property shall begin just after the date such property is transferred. If property to which section 83 and the regulations thereunder apply is transferred at arm's length, the holding period of such property in the hands of the transferee shall be determined in accordance with the rules provided in section 1223.

(b) Basis. *(1)* Except as provided in paragraph (b)(2) of this section, if property to which section 83 and the regulations thereunder apply is acquired by any person (including a person who acquires such property in a subsequent transfer which is not at arm's length), while such property is still substantially nonvested, such person's basis for the property shall reflect any amount paid for such property and any amount includible in the gross income of the person who performed the services (including any amount so includible as a result of a disposition by the person who acquired such property.) Such basis shall also reflect any adjustments to basis provided under sections 1015 and 1016.

(2) If property to which § 1.83-1 applies is transferred at arm's length, the basis of the property in the hands of the transferee shall be determined under section 1012 and the regulations thereunder.

(c) Forgiveness of indebtedness treated as an amount paid. If an indebtedness that has been treated as an amount paid under § 1.83-1(a)(1)(ii) is subsequently cancelled, forgiven or satisfied for an amount less than the amount of such indebtedness, the amount that is not, in fact, paid shall be includible in the gross income of the service provider in the taxable year in which such cancellation, forgiveness or satisfaction occurs.

T.D. 7554, 7/21/78.

§ 1.83-5 Restrictions that will never lapse.

(a) Valuation. For purposes of section 83 and the regulations thereunder, in the case of property subject to a nonlapse restriction (as defined in § 1.83-3(h)), the price determined under the formula price will be considered to be the fair market value of the property unless established to the contrary by the Commissioner, and the burden of proof shall be on the commissioner with respect to such value. If stock in a corporation is subject to a nonlapse restriction which requires the transferee to sell such stock only at a formula price based on book value, a reasonable multiple of earnings or a reasonable combination thereof, the price so determined will ordinarily be regarded as determinative of the fair market value of such property for purposes of section 83. However, in certain circumstances the formula price will not be considered to be the fair market value of property subject to such a formula price restriction, even though the formula price restriction is a substantial factor in determining such value. For example, where the formula price is the current book value of stock, the book value of the stock at some time in the future may be a more accurate measure of the value of the stock than the current book value of the stock for purposes of determining the fair market value of the stock at the time the stock becomes substantially vested.

(b) Cancellation. *(1) In general.* Under section 83(d)(2), if a nonlapse restriction imposed on property that is subject to section 83 is cancelled, then, unless the taxpayer establishes—

(i) That such cancellation was not compensatory, and

(ii) That the person who would be allowed a deduction, if any, if the cancellation were treated as compensatory, will treat the transaction as not compensatory, as provided in paragraph (c)(2) of this section,

the excess of the fair market value of such property (computed without regard to such restriction) at the time of cancellation, over the sum of—

(iii) The fair market value of such property (computed by taking the restriction into account) immediately before the cancellation, and

(iv) The amount, if any, paid for the cancellation,

shall be treated as compensation for the taxable year in which such cancellation occurs. Whether there has been a noncompensatory cancellation of a nonlapse restriction under section 83(d)(2) depends upon the particular facts and circumstances. Ordinarily the fact that the employee or independent contractor is required to perform additional services or that the salary or payment of such a person is adjusted to take the cancellation into account indicates that such cancellation has a compensatory purpose. On the other hand, the fact that the original purpose of a restriction no longer exists may indicate that the purpose of such cancellation is noncompensatory. Thus, for example, if a so-called "buy-sell" restriction was imposed on a corporation's stock to limit ownership of such stock and is being cancelled in connection with a public offering of the stock, such cancellation will generally be regarded as noncompensatory. However, the mere fact that the employer is willing to forego a deduction under section 83(h) is insufficient evidence to establish a noncompensatory cancellation of a nonlapse restriction. The refusal by a corporation or shareholder to repurchase stock of the corporation which is subject to a permanent right of first refusal will generally be treated as a cancellation of a nonlapse restriction. The preceding sentence shall not apply where there is no nonlapse restriction, for example, where the price to be paid for the stock subject to the right of first refusal is the fair market value of the stock. Section 83(d)(2) and this (1) do not apply where immediately after the cancellation of a nonlapse restriction the property is still substantially nonvested and no section 83(b) election has been made with respect to such property. In such a case the rules of section 83(a) and § 1.83-1 shall apply to such property.

(2) Evidence of noncompensatory cancellation. In addition to the information necessary to establish the factors described in paragraph (b)(1) of this section, the taxpayer shall request the employer to furnish the taxpayer with a written statement indicating that the employer will not treat the cancellation of the nonlapse restriction as a compensatory event, and that no deduction will be taken with respect to such cancellation. The taxpayer shall file such written statement with his income tax return for the taxable year in which or with which such cancellation occurs.

(c) Examples. The provisions of this section may be illustrated by the following examples:

Example (1). On November 1, 1971, X corporation whose shares are closely held and not regularly traded, transfers to E, an employee, 100 shares of X corporation stock subject to the condition that, if he desires to dispose of such stock during the period of his employment, he must resell the stock to his employer at its then existing book value. In addition, E or E's estate is obligated to offer to sell the stock at his retirement or death to his employer at its then existing book value. Under these facts and circumstances, the restriction to which the shares of X corporation stock are subject is a nonlapse restriction. Consequently, the fair market value of the X stock is includible in E's gross income as compensation for taxable year 1971. However, in determining the fair market value of the X stock, the book value formula price will ordinarily be regarded as being determinative of such value.

Example (2). Assume the facts are the same as in example (1), except that the X stock is subject to the condition that if E desires to dispose of the stock during the period of his employment he must resell the stock to his employer at a multiple of earnings per share that is in this case a reasonable approximation of value at the time of transfer to E. In addition, E or E's estate is obligated to offer to sell the stock at his retirement or death to his employer at the same multiple of earnings. Under these facts and circumstances, the restriction to which the X corporation stock is subject is a nonlapse restriction. Consequently, the fair market value of the X stock is includible in E's gross income for taxable year 1971. However, in determining the fair market value of the X stock, the multiple-of-earnings formula price will ordinarily be regarded as determinative of such value.

Example (3). On January 4, 1971, X corporation transfers to E, an employee, 100 shares of stock in X corporation. Each such share of stock is subject to an agreement between X and E whereby E agrees that such shares are to be held solely for investment purposes and not for resale (a so-called investment letter restriction). E's rights in such stock are substantially vested upon transfer, causing the fair market value of each share of X corporation stock to be includible in E's gross income as compensation for taxable year 1971. Since such an investment letter restriction does not constitute a nonlapse restriction, in determining the fair market value of each share, the investment letter restriction is disregarded.

Example (4). On September 1, 1971, X corporation transfers to B, an independent contractor, 500 shares of common stock in X corporation in exchange for B's agreement to provide services in the construction of an office building on property owned by X corporation. X corporation has 100 shares of preferred stock outstanding and an additional 500 shares of common stock outstanding. The preferred stock has a liquidation value of $1,000 *x*, which is equal to the value of all assets owned by X. Therefore, the book value of the common stock in X corporation is $0. Under the terms of the transfer, if B wishes to dispose of the stock, B must offer to sell the stock to X for 150 percent of the then existing book value of B's common stock. The stock is also subject to a substantial risk of forfeiture until B performs the agreed-upon services. B makes a timely election under section 83(b) to include the value of the stock in gross income in 1971. Under these facts and circumstances, the restriction to which the shares of X corporation common stock are subject is a nonlapse restriction. In determining the fair market value of the X common stock at the time of transfer, the book value formula price would ordinarily be regarded as determinative of such value. However, the fair market value of X common stock at the time of transfer, subject to the book value restriction, is greater than $0 since B was willing to agree to provide valuable personal services in exchange for the stock. In determining the fair market value of the stock, the expected book value after construction of the office building would be given great weight. The likelihood of completion of construction would be a factor in determining the expected book value after completion of construction.

T.D. 7554, 7/21/78.

---

§ 1.83-6 Deduction by employer.

(a) Allowance of deduction. *(1) General rule.* In the case of a transfer of property in connection with the performance of services, or a compensatory cancellation of a nonlapse restriction described in section 83(d) and § 1.83-5, a deduction is allowable under section 162 or 212 to the person for whom the services were performed. The amount of the deduction is equal to the amount included as compensation in the gross income of the service provider under section 83(a), (b), or (d)(2), but only to the extent the amount meets the requirements of section 162 or 212 and the regulations thereunder. The deduction is allowed only for the taxable year of that person in which or with which ends the taxable year of the service provider in which the amount is included as compensation. For purposes of this paragraph, any amount excluded from gross income under section 79 or section 101(b) or subchapter N is considered to have been included in gross income.

(2) Special rule. For purposes of paragraph (a)(1) of this section, the service provider is deemed to have included the amount as compensation in gross income if the person for whom the services were performed satisfies in a timely manner all requirements of section 6041 or section 6041A, and the regulations thereunder, with respect to that amount of compensation. For purposes of the preceding sentence, whether a person for whom services were performed satisfies all requirements of section 6041 or section 6041A, and the regulations thereunder, is determined without regard to § 1.6041-3(c) (exception for payments to corporations). In the case of a disqualifying disposition of stock described in section 421(b), an employer that otherwise satisfies all requirements of section 6041 and the regulations thereunder will be considered to have done so timely for purposes of this paragraph (a)(2) if Form W-2 or Form W-2c, as appropriate, is furnished to the employee or former employee, and is filed with the federal government, on or before the date on which the employer files the tax return claiming the deduction relating to the disqualifying disposition.

(3) Exceptions. Where property is substantially vested upon transfer, the deduction shall be allowed to such person in accordance with his method of accounting (in conformity with sections 446 and 461). In the case of a transfer to an employee benefit plan described in § 1.162-10(a) or a transfer to an employees' trust or annuity plan described in section 404(a)(5) and the regulations thereunder, section 83(h) and this section do not apply.

(4) Capital expenditure, etc. No deduction is allowed under section 83(h) to the extent that the transfer of property constitutes a capital expenditure, an item of deferred expense, or an amount properly includible in the value of inventory items. In the case of a capital expenditure, for example, the basis of the property to which such capital expenditure relates shall be increased at the same time and to the same extent as any amount includible in the employee's gross income in respect of such transfer. Thus, for example, no deduction is allowed to a corporation in respect of a transfer of its stock to a promoter upon its organization, notwithstanding that such promoter must include the value of such stock in his gross income in accordance with the rules under section 83.

(5) Transfer of life insurance contract (or an undivided interest therein). (i) General rule. In the case of a transfer of a life insurance contract (or an undivided interest therein) described in § 1.61-22(c)(3) in connection with the performance of services, a deduction is allowable under paragraph (a)(1) of this section to the person for whom the services

were performed. The amount of the deduction, if allowable, is equal to the sum of the amount included as compensation in the gross income of the service provider under § 1.61-22(g)(1) and the amount determined under § 1.61-22(g)(1)(ii).

(ii) Effective date. (A) General rule. Paragraph (a)(5)(i) of this section applies to any split-dollar life insurance arrangement (as defined in § 1.61-22(b)(1) or (2)) entered into after September 17, 2003. For purposes of this paragraph (a)(5), an arrangement is entered into as determined under § 1.61-22(j)(1)(ii).

(B) Modified arrangements treated as new arrangements. If an arrangement entered into on or before September 17, 2003 is materially modified (within the meaning of § 1.61-22(j)(2)) after September 17, 2003, the arrangement is treated as a new arrangement entered into on the date of the modification.

(6) Effective date. Paragraphs (a)(1) and (2) of this section apply to deductions for taxable years beginning on or after January 1, 1995. However, taxpayers may also apply paragraphs (a)(1) and (2) of this section when claiming deductions for taxable years beginning before that date if the claims are not barred by the statute of limitations. Paragraphs (a)(3) and (4) of this section are effective as set forth in § 1.83-8(b).

(b) Recognition of gain or loss. Except as provided in section 1032, at the time of a transfer of property in connection with the performance of services the transferor recognizes gain to the extent that the transferor receives an amount that exceeds the transferor's basis in the property. In addition, at the time a deduction is allowed under section 83(h) and paragraph (a) of this section, gain or loss is recognized to the extent of the difference between (i) the sum of the amount paid plus the amount allowed as a deduction under section 83(h), and (ii) the sum of the taxpayer's basis in the property plus any amount recognized pursuant to the previous sentence.

(c) Forfeitures. If, under section 83(h) and paragraph (a) of this section, a deduction, an increase in basis, or a reduction of gross income was allowable (disregarding the reasonableness of the amount of compensation) in respect of a transfer of property and such property is subsequently forfeited, the amount of such deduction, increase in basis or reduction of gross income shall be includible in the gross income of the person to whom it was allowable for the taxable year of forfeiture. The basis of such property in the hands of the person to whom it is forfeited shall include any such amount includible in the gross income of such person, as well as any amount such person pays upon forfeiture.

(d) Special rules for transfers by shareholders. *(1) Transfers.* If a shareholder of a corporation transfers property to an employee of such corporation or to an independent contractor (or to a beneficiary thereof), in consideration of services performed for the corporation, the transaction shall be considered to be a contribution of such property to the capital of such corporation by the shareholder, and immediately thereafter a transfer of such property by the corporation to the employee or independent contractor under paragraphs (a) and (b) of this section. For purposes of this (1), such a transfer will be considered to be in consideration for services performed for the corporation if either the property transferred is substantially nonvested at the time of transfer or an amount is includible in the gross income of the employee or independent contractor at the time of transfer under § 1.83-1(a)(1) or § 1.83-2(a). In the case of such a transfer, any money or other property paid to the shareholder for such stock shall be considered to be paid to the corporation and transferred immediately thereafter by the corporation to the shareholder as a distribution to which section 302 applies. For special rules that may apply to a corporation's transfer of its own stock to any person in consideration of services performed for another corporation or partnership, see § 1.1032-3. The preceding sentence applies to transfers of stock and amounts paid for such stock occuring on or after May 16, 2000.

(2) Forfeiture. If, following a transaction described in paragraph (d)(1) of this section, the transferred property is forfeited to the shareholder, paragraph (c) of this section shall apply both with respect to the shareholder and with respect to the corporation. In addition, the corporation shall in the taxable year of forfeiture be allowed a loss (or realize a gain) to offset any gain (or loss) realized under paragraph (b) of this section. For example, if a shareholder transfers property to an employee of the corporation as compensation, and as a result the shareholder's basis of $200 *x* in such property is allocated to his stock in such corporation and such corporation recognizes a short-term capital gain of $800 *x*, and is allowed a deduction of $1,000 *x* on such transfer, upon a subsequent forfeiture of the property to the shareholder, the shareholder shall take $200 *x* into gross income, and the corporation shall take $1,000 *x* into gross income and be allowed a short-term capital loss of $800 *x*.

(e) Options. [Reserved.]

(f) Reporting requirements. [Reserved.]

T.D. 7554, 7/21/78, amend T.D. 8599, 7/18/95, T.D. 8883, 5/11/2000, T.D. 9092, 9/11/2003.

PAR. 3. Section 1.83-6 is amended by revising the first sentence of paragraph (b) to read as follows:

Proposed § 1.83-6 Deduction by employer. [*For Preamble, see ¶ 152,663*]

* * * * *

(b) Recognition of gain or loss. Except as provided in section 721 and section 1032, at the time of a transfer of property in connection with the performance of services the transferor recognizes gain to the extent that the transferor receives an amount that exceeds the transferor's basis in the property. * * *

* * * * *

§ 1.83-7 Taxation of nonqualified stock options.

(a) In general. If there is granted to an employee or independent contractor (or beneficiary thereof) in connection with the performance of services, an option to which section 421 (relating generally to certain qualified and other options) does not apply, section 83(a) shall apply to such grant if the option has a readily ascertainable fair market value (determined in accordance with paragraph (b) of this section) at the time the option is granted. The person who performed such services realizes compensation upon such grant at the time and in the amount determined under section 83(a). If section 83(a) does not apply to the grant of such an option because the option does not have a readily ascertainable fair market value at the time of grant, sections 83(a) and 83(b) shall apply at the time the option is exercised or otherwise disposed of, even though the fair market value of such option may have become readily ascertainable before such time. If the option is exercised, sections 83(a) and 83(b) apply to the transfer of property pursuant to such exercise, and the employee or independent contractor realizes compensation upon such transfer at the time and in the amount determined under section 83(a) or 83(b). If the option is sold or otherwise disposed of in an arm's length transaction, sections 83(a) and 83(b) apply to the transfer of money or other property received in the same manner as sections 83(a) and 83(b) would have applied to the transfer of property pursuant to an exercise of the option. The preceding sentence does not apply to a sale or other disposition of the option to a person related to the service provider that occurs on or after July 2, 2003. For this purpose, a person is related to the service provider if—

(1) The person and the service provider bear a relationship to each other that is specified in section 267(b) or 707(b)(1), subject to the modifications that the language "20 percent" is used instead of "50 percent" each place it appears in sections 267(b) and 707(b)(1), and section 267(c)(4) is applied as if the family of an individual includes the spouse of any member of the family; or

(2) The person and the service provider are engaged in trades or businesses under common control (within the meaning of section 52(a) and (b)); provided that a person is not related to the service provider if the person is the service recipient with respect to the option or the grantor of the option.

(b) Readily ascertainable defined. *(1) Actively traded on an established market.* Options have a value at the time they are granted, but that value is ordinarily not readily ascertainable unless the option is actively traded on an established market. If an option is actively traded on an established market, the fair market value of such option is readily ascertainable for purposes of this section by applying the rules of valuation set forth in § 20.2031-2.

(2) Not actively traded on an established market. When an option is not actively traded on an established market, it does not have a readily ascertainable fair market value unless its fair market value can otherwise be measured with reasonable accuracy. For purposes of this section, if an option is not actively traded on an established market, the option does not have a readily ascertainable fair market value when granted unless the taxpayer can show that all of the following conditions exist:

(i) The option is transferable by the optionee;

(ii) The option is exercisable immediately in full by the optionee;

(iii) The option or the property subject to the option is not subject to any restriction or condition (other than a lien or other condition to secure the payment of the purchase price) which has a significant effect upon the fair market value on the option; and

(iv) The fair market value of the option privilege is readily ascertainable in accordance with paragraph (b)(3) of this section.

(3) Option privilege. The option privilege in the case of an option to buy is the opportunity to benefit during the option's exercise period from any increase in the value of property subject to the option during such period, without risking any capital. Similarly, the option privilege in the case of an option to sell is the opportunity to benefit during the exercise period from a decrease in the value of property subject to the option. For example, if at some time during the exercise period of an option to buy, the fair market value of the property subject to the option is greater than the option's exercise price, a profit may be realized by exercising the option and immediately selling the property so acquired for its higher fair market value. Irrespective of whether any such gain may be realized immediately at the time an option is granted, the fair market value of an option to buy includes the value of the right to benefit from any future increase in the value of the property subject to the option (relative to the option exercise price), without risking any capital. Therefore, the fair market value of an option is not merely the difference that may exist at a particular time between the option's exercise price and the value of the property subject to the option, but also includes the value of the option privilege for the remainder of the exercise period. Accordingly, for purposes of this section, in determining whether the fair market value of an option is readily ascertainable, it is necessary to consider whether the value of the entire option privilege can be measured with reasonable accuracy. In determining whether the value of the option privilege is readily ascertainable, and in determining the amount of such value when such value is readily ascertainable, it is necessary to consider—

(i) Whether the value of the property subject to the option can be ascertained;

(ii) The probability of any ascertainable value of such property increasing or decreasing; and

(iii) The length of the period during which the option can be exercised.

(c) Reporting requirements. [Reserved.]

(d) This section applies on and after July 2, 2003. For transactions prior to that date, see § 1.83-7 as published in 26 CFR part 1 (revised as of April 1, 2003).

T.D. 7554, 7/21/78, amend T.D. 9067, 7/1/2003, T.D. 9148, 8/9/2004.

---

§ 1.83-8 Applicability of section and transitional rules.

Caution: The Treasury has not yet amended Reg § 1.83-8 to reflect changes made by P.L. 98-369.

(a) Scope of section 83. Section 83 is not applicable to—

(1) A transaction concerning an option to which section 421 applies;

(2) A transfer to or from a trust described in section 401(a) for the benefit of employees or their beneficiaries, or a transfer under an annuity plan that meets the requirements of section 404(a)(2) for the benefit of employees or their beneficiaries;

(3) The transfer of an option without a readily ascertainable fair market value (as defined in § 1.83-7(b)(1)); or

(4) The transfer of property pursuant to the exercise of an option with a readily ascertainable fair market value at the date of grant. Section 83 applies to a transfer to or from a trust or under an annuity plan for the benefit of employee, independent contractors, or their beneficiaries (except as provided in paragraph (a)(2) of this section), but to the extent a transfer is subject to section 402(b) or 403(c), section 83 applies to such a transfer only as provided for in section 402(b) or 403(c).

(b) Transitional rules. *(1) In general.* Except as otherwise provided in this paragraph, section 83 and the regulations thereunder shall apply to property transferred after June 30, 1969.

(2) Binding written contracts. Section 83 and the regulations thereunder shall not apply to property transferred pursuant to a binding written contract entered into before April 22, 1969. For purposes of this paragraph, a binding written contract means only a written contract under which the em-

ployee or independent contractor has an enforceable right to compel the transfer of property or to obtain damages upon the breach of such contract. A contract which provides that a person's right to such property is contingent upon the happening of an event (including the passage of time) may satisfy the requirements of this paragraph. However, if the event itself, or the determination of whether the event has occurred, rests with the board of directors or any other individual or group acting on behalf of the employer (other than an arbitrator), the contract will not be treated as giving the person an enforceable right for purposes of this paragraph.

The fact that the board of directors has the power (either expressly or impliedly) to terminate employment of an officer pursuant to a contract that contemplates the completion of services over a fixed or ascertainable period does not negate the existence of a binding written contract. Nor will the binding nature of the contract be negated by a provision in such contract which allows the employee or independent contractor to terminate the contract for any year and receive cash instead of property if such election would cause a substantial penalty, such as a forfeiture of part or all of the property received in connection with the performance of services in an earlier year.

(3) Options granted before April 22, 1969. Section 83 shall not apply to property received upon the exercise of an option granted before April 22, 1969.

(4) Certain written plans. Section 83 shall not apply to property transferred (whether or not by the exercise of an option) before May 1, 1970, pursuant to a written plan adopted and approved before July 1, 1969. A plan is to be considered as having been adopted and approved before July 1, 1969, only if prior to such date the transferor of the property undertook an ascertainable course of conduct which under applicable State law does not require further approval by the board of directors or the stockholders of any corporation. For example, if a corporation transfers property to an employee in connection with the performance of services pursuant to a plan adopted and approved before July 1, 1969, by the board of directors of such corporation, it is not necessary that the stockholders have adopted or approved such plan if State law does not require such approval. However, such approval is necessary if required by the articles of incorporation or the bylaws or if, by its terms, such plan will not become effective without such approval.

(5) Certain options granted pursuant to a binding written contract. Section 83 shall not apply to property transferred before January 1, 1973, upon the exercise of an option granted pursuant to a binding written contract (as defined in paragraph (b)(2) of this section) entered into before April 22, 1969, between a corporation and the transferor of such property requiring the transferor to grant options to employees of such corporation (or a subsidiary of such corporation) to purchase a determinable number of shares of stock of such corporation, but only if the transferee was an employee of such corporation (or a subsidiary of such corporation) on or before April 22, 1969.

(6) Certain tax free exchanges. Section 83 shall not apply to property transferred in exchange for (or pursuant to the exercise of a conversion privilege contained in) property transferred before July 1, 1969, or in exchange for property to which section 83 does not apply (by reason of paragraphs (1), (2), (3), or (4) of section 83(i)), if section 354, 355, 356, or 1036 (or so much of section 1031 as relates to section 1036) applies, or if gain or loss is not otherwise required to be recognized upon the exercise of such conversion privilege, and if the property received in such exchange is subject to restrictions and conditions substantially similar to those to which the property given in such exchange was subject.

T.D. 7554, 7/21/78.

§ 1.84-1 Transfer of appreciated property to political organizations.

(a) Transfer defined. A transfer after May 7, 1974, of property to a political organization (as defined in section 527(e)(1), and including a newsletter fund to the extent provided under section 527(g)) is treated as a sale of the property to the political organization if the fair market value of the property exceeds its adjusted basis. The transferor is treated as having realized an amount equal to the fair market value of the property on the date of the transfer. For purposes of this section, a transfer is any assignment, conveyance, or delivery of property other than a bona fide sale for an adequate and full consideration in money or money's worth, whether the transfer is in trust or otherwise, whether the transfer is direct or indirect and whether the property is real or personal, tangible or intangible. Thus, for example, a sale at less than fair market value (other than an ordinary trade discount), or a receipt of property by a political organization under an agency agreement entitling the organization to sell the property and retain all or a portion of the proceeds of the sale, is a transfer within the meaning, of this section. The term "transfer" also includes an illegal contribution of property.

(b) Amount realized. A transferor to whom this section applies realizes an amount equal to the fair market value of the property on the date of the transfer. For purposes of this section, the definition of fair market value set forth in § 1.170A-1(c)(2) and (3) is incorporated by reference.

(c) Amount recognized. A transferor to whom this section applies is treated as having sold the property to the political organization on the date of the transfer. Therefore, the rules of chapter 1 of subtitle A (relating to income tax) apply to the gain realized under this section as if this gain were an amount realized upon the sale of the property. These rules include those of section 55 an section 56 (relating to minimum tax for tax preference), section 306 (relating to disposition of certain stock), section 1201 (relating to the alternative tax on certain capital gains), section 1245 (relating to gain from dispositions of certain depreciable property), and section 1250 (relating to gain from dispositions of certain depreciable realty).

(d) Holding period. The holding period of property transferred to a political organization to which this section applies begins on the day after the date of acquisition of the property by the political organization.

T.D. 7671, 2/5/80.

§ 1.85-1 Unemployment compensation.

(a) Introduction. Section 85 prescribes rules relating to the inclusion in gross income of unemployment compensation (as defined in paragraph (b)(1) of this section) paid in taxable years beginning after December 31, 1978 pursuant to governmental programs. In general, these rules provide that unemployment compensation paid pursuant to governmental programs is includible in the gross income of a taxpayer if the taxpayer's modified adjusted gross income (as defined in paragraph (b)(2) of this section) exceeds a statutory base amount (as defined in paragraph (b)(3) of this section). If there is such an excess, however, the amount included in gross income is limited under paragraph (c)(1) of this section to the lesser of one-half of such excess or the amount of the unemployment compensation. If such taxpayer's modified adjusted gross income does not exceed the applicable statutory base amount, none of the unemployment compensation is included in the taxpayer's gross income.

(b) Definitions. *(1) Unemployment compensation.* (i) General rule. Except as provided in paragraph (b)(1)(iii) of this section, the term "unemployment compensation" means any amount received under a law of the United States, or of a State, which is in the nature of unemployment compensation. Thus, section 85 applies only to unemployment compensation paid pursuant to governmental programs and does not apply to amounts paid pursuant to private nongovernmental unemployment compensation plans (which are includible in income without regard to section 85). Generally, unemployment compensation programs are those designed to protect taxpayers against the loss of income caused by involuntary layoff. Ordinarily, unemployment compensation is paid in cash and on a periodic basis. The amount of the payments is usually computed in accordance with formula based on the taxpayer's length of prior employment and wages. Such payments, however, may be made in a lump sum or other than in cash or on some other basis.

(ii) Disability and worker's compensation payments. Amounts in the nature of the unemployment compensation also include cash disability payments made pursuant to a governmental program as a substitute for case unemployment payments to an unemployed taxpayer who is ineligible for such payments solely because of the disability. Usually these disability payments are paid in the same weekly amount and for the same period as the unemployment compensation benefits to which the unemployed taxpayer otherwise would have been entitled. Amounts received under workmen's compensation acts as compensation for personal injuries or sickness are not amounts in the nature of unemployment compensation. See section 104(a)(1) relating to the exclusion from gross income of such amounts.

(iii) Employee contributions to a governmental plan. If a governmental unemployment compensation program is funded in part by an employee's contribution which is not deductible by the employee, an amount paid to such employee under the program is not to be considered unemployment compensation until an amount equal to the total nondeductible contributions paid by the employee to such program has been paid to such employee.

(iv) Examples of governmental unemployment compensation programs. Governmental unemployment compensation programs include (but are not limited to) programs established under:

(A) A State law approved by the Secretary of Labor pursuant to section 3304 of the Internal Revenue Code of 1954.

(B) Chapter 85 of Title 5, United States Code, relating to unemployment compensation for Federal employees generally and for ex-servicemen.

(C) Trade Act of 1974, sections 231 and 232 (19 U.S.C. 2291 and 2292).

(D) Disaster Relief Act of 1974, section 407 (42 U.S.C. 5177).

(E) The Airline Deregulation Act of 1978 (49 U.S.C 1552(b)).

(F) The Railroad Unemployment Insurance Act, section 2 (45 U.S.C. 352).

(2) Modified adjusted gross income. The term "modified adjusted gross income" means the sum of the following amounts:

(i) Adjusted gross income (as defined in section 62);

(ii) All disability payments of the type that are eligible for exclusion from gross income under section 105(d); and

(iii) All amounts of unemployment compensation (as defined in paragraph (b)(1) of this section).

(3) Base amount. The term "base amount" means—

(i) $25,000 in the case of a joint return under section 6013.

(ii) Zero in the case of a taxpayer who—

(A) Is married (within the meaning of section 143) at the close of the taxable year,

(B) Does not file a joint return for such taxable year, and

(C) Does not live apart (as defined in paragraph (B)(4) of this section) from his or her spouse at all times during the taxable year.

(iii) $20,000 in the case of all other taxpayers.

(4) Living apart. A taxpayer does not "live apart" from his or her spouse at all times during a taxable year if for any period during the taxable year the taxpayer is a member of the same household as such taxpayer's spouse. A taxpayer is a member of a household for any period, including temporary absences due to special circumstances, during which the household is the taxpayer's place of abode. A temporary absence due to special circumstances includes a nonpermanent absence caused by illness, education, business, vacation, or military service.

(c) Limitations. *(1) General rule.* If for a taxable year, a taxpayer's modified adjusted gross income does not exceed the applicable statutory base amount, no amount of unemployment compensation is included in gross income for the taxable year. If there is such an excess, the taxpayer includes in gross income for the taxable year the lesser of the following:

(i) One-half of the excess of the taxpayer's modified adjusted gross income over such taxpayer's base amount, or

(ii) The amount of unemployment compensation.

(2) Exception for fraudulently received unemployment compensation. If a taxpayer fraudulently receives unemployment compensation under any governmental unemployment compensation program, then the entire amount of such fraudulently received unemployment compensation must be included in the taxpayer's gross income for the taxable year in which the benefits were received. Thus, the limitation in section 85 and in paragraph (c)(1) of this section, does not apply to such amounts.

(3) Examples. The application of this paragraph may be illustrated by the following examples:

Example (1). H and W are married taxpayers who for calendar year 1979 file a joint income tax return. During 1979 H receives $4,500 of disability income that is eligible for an exclusion under section 105(d). W works for part of 1979 and receives $20,000 as compensation and also receives $5,000 of unemployment compensation in 1979. Assume that H and W's adjusted gross income is $20,000. The modified adjusted gross income of H and W is $29,500 ($4,500 + $20,000 + $5,000). Since their modified adjusted gross income ($29,500) is greater than their base amount ($25,000), some of the unemployment compensation received by W must be included in their gross income on their 1979 joint income tax return. Under paragraph (c)(1) of this section, of the $5,000 which is unemployment compensation, the lesser of $2,250 (($29,500 – $25,000) ÷ 2) or $5,000 must be included in their gross income. Thus, $2,250 of the $5,000 received by W in 1979 is included in the gross income of H and W on their joint income tax return for 1979.

Example (2). Assume the same facts in example (1) except H received $5,000 of disability income that is eligible for an exclusion under section 105(d) and W receives $28,000 as compensation, and $4,000 which is unemployment compensation. Assume that H and W's adjusted gross income is $28,000. The modified adjusted gross income of H and W is $37,000 ($4,000 + $28,000 + $5,000). Since their modified adjusted gross income ($37,000) is greater than their base amount ($25,000), all of the unemployment compensation received by W must be included in their gross income on their 1979 joint income tax return. Under paragraph (c)(1) of this section, of the $4,000 which is unemployment compensation, the lesser of $6,000 (($37,000 – $25,000) ÷ 2) or $4,000 must be included in their gross income. Thus, all of the $4,000 unemployment compensation received by W is included in the gross income of H and W on their joint income tax return for 1979.

(d) Cross reference. See section 6050B, relating to the requirement that every person who makes payments of unemployment compensation aggregating $10 or more to any individual during any calendar year file an information return with the Internal Revenue Service.

T.D. 7705, 7/8/80.

§ 1.88-1 Nuclear decommissioning costs.

(a) In general. Section 88 provides that the amount of nuclear decommissioning costs directly or indirectly charged to the customers of a taxpayer that is engaged in the furnishing or sale of electric energy generated by a nuclear power plant must be included in the gross income of such taxpayer in the same manner as amounts charged for electric energy. For this purpose, decommissioning costs directly or indirectly charged to the customers of a taxpayer include all decommissioning costs that consumers are liable to pay by reason of electric energy furnished by the taxpayer during the taxable year, whether payable to the taxpayer, a trust, State government, or other entity, and even though the taxpayer may not control the investment or current expenditure of the amount and the amount may not be paid to the taxpayer at the time decommissioning costs are incurred. However, decommissioning costs payable to a taxpayer holding a qualified leasehold interest (as described in paragraph (b)(2)(ii) of § 1.468A-1) are included in the gross income of such taxpayer, and not in the gross income of the lessor.

(b) Examples. The following examples illustrate the application of the principles of paragraph (a) of this section:

Example (1). X corporation, an accrual method taxpayer engaged in the sale of electric energy generated by a nuclear power plant owned by X, is authorized by the public utility commission of State A to collect nuclear decommissioning costs from ratepayers residing in State A. With respect to the sale of electric energy, X includes in income amounts that have been billed to customers as well as estimated unbilled amounts that relate to energy provided by X after the previous billing but before the end of the taxable year ("accrued unbilled amounts"). The decommissioning costs are included in the monthly bills provided by X to its ratepayers and the entire amount billed is remitted directly to X. Under paragraph (a) of this section, the decommissioning costs must be included in the gross income of X in the same manner as amounts charged for electric energy (i.e., by including in income decommissioning costs that relate to amounts billed as well as decommissioning costs that relate to accrued unbilled amounts). The same rule would apply if the decommissioning costs charged to ratepayers were separately billed and the amounts billed were remitted to State A to be held in trust for the purpose of decommissioning the nuclear power plant owned by X. In that case, X must include in gross income decommissioning costs that relate to amounts billed as well as decommissioning costs that relate to accrued unbilled amounts.

Example (2). Assume the same facts as in Example (1), except that X and M, a municipality located in State A, have entered into a life-of-unit contract pursuant to which (i) M is entitled to 20 percent of the electric energy generated by the nuclear power plant owned by X, and (ii) M is obligated to pay 20 percent of the plant operating costs, including decommissioning costs, incurred by X. Under paragraph (a) of this section, the decommissioning costs that relate to electric energy consumed or distributed by M during any taxable year must be included in the gross income of X for such taxable year. The result contained in this example would be the same if M was a State or an agency or instrumentality of a State or a political subdivision thereof.

(c) Cross reference. For special rules relating to the deduction for amounts paid to a nuclear decommissioning fund, see § 1.468A-1 through § 1.468A-5, 1.468A-7, 1.468A-8.

(d) Effective date. *(1)* Section 88 and this section apply to nuclear decommissioning costs directly or indirectly charged to the customers of a taxpayer on or after July 18, 1984, and with respect to taxable years ending on or after such date.

(2) If the amount of nuclear decommissioning costs directly or indirectly charged to the customers of a taxpayer before July 18, 1984, was includible in gross income in a different manner than amounts charged for electric energy, such amount must be included in gross income for the taxable year in which includible in gross income under the method of accounting of the taxpayer that was in effect when such amount was charged to customers.

T.D. 8184, 2/29/88.

Proposed § 1.89(a)-1 Miscellaneous questions and answers relating to nondiscrimination rules for certain employee benefit plans. [*For Preamble, see ¶ 151,141*]

• ***Caution:*** This Notice of Proposed Rulemaking was partially withdrawn by Notice of Proposed Rulemaking 72-150, 08/06/2007. Reg. §§ 1.89(a)(1) and 1.89(k)-1 remain proposed.

• ***Caution:*** Q&A-6(c) and (d) of proposed regulation § 1.125-2 were withdrawn by notice of proposed rulemaking 62-216, 11/7/97, 62 Fed. Reg. 60196.

• *Caution:* Q&A-6(f) of proposed regulation § 1.125-2 was withdrawn on 11/7/97, 62 Fed. Reg. 60196.

Caution: The Treasury has not yet amended Reg § 1.89(a)-1 to reflect changes made by P.L. 101-140.

The following is a list of the questions addressed in this section:

Q–1: What are the section 89 nondiscrimination rules?

Q–2: What transitional and special rules are available to health plans under section 89?

Q–3: Under what circumstances may employees be disregarded for purposes of section 89 when the employees receive health coverage from other employers or when employees do not have a family or have a family whose members receive health coverage from another employer?

Q–4: What is a health plan under the section 89 nondiscrimination rules and to what extent are health plans comparable or aggregated for purposes of such rules?

Q–5: What is the testing methodology for applying the nondiscrimination rules under section 89?

Q–6: What is the period for testing whether the nondiscrimination rules of section 89 are satisfied?

Q–7: For purposes of applying section 89 to an employer's health plan, what rules apply for determining the employer-provided benefits and calculating the excess benefits?

Q–8: How are salary reduction contributions treated for purposes of the section 89 nondiscrimination tests?

Q–9: How is an excess benefit under the section 89 nondiscrimination rules to be determined with respect to health plans?

Q–10: What are the effective dates of the section 89 nondiscrimination and qualification rules?

Q-1. What are the section 89 nondiscrimination rules?

A-1. **(a) Nondiscrimination rules.** *(1) In general.* Section 89(a) provides that, notwithstanding any other provision of the tax law specifically excluding items from gross income (e.g., sections 79 and 106), the gross income of a highly compensated employee (as defined in section 414(q)) includes an amount equal to the employee's employer-provided benefit that is found to be discriminatory under the rules provided in this section. See paragraph (f)(3) of this Q&A-1 for the definition of "employer-provided benefit" for these nondiscrimination rules. The nondiscrimination requirements of section 89(a), however, do not affect the exclusion from gross income of death benefits under section 101(a) and accident and health benefits under sections 104 and 105.

(2) Timing of inclusion and deduction. The excess benefit for a testing year generally is treated as received on the last day of the testing year. Thus, the excess benefit for a testing year generally is included in a highly compensated employee's gross income for the employee's taxable year with or within which the testing year ends. Similarly, the excess benefit for a testing year generally is treated as paid by the employer on the last day of the testing year. Thus, the excess benefit for a testing year is deductible by the employer only for the taxable year of the employer with or within which the testing year ends. Also, for purposes of determining the deductibility of both employer-provided benefits that are not excess benefits and employer-provided benefits that are excess benefits, excess benefits are deemed to be attributable to the employer-provided benefits provided latest during the testing year. For purposes of determining the treatment of excess benefits under section 404, excess benefits are treated as paid under a plan or arrangement that defers the receipt of compensation or benefits to the extent that, under the rule of this paragraph (a)(2), the excess benefits are received after the end of the employer's taxable year in which the services creating the right to such compensation or benefits are performed. For these purposes, excess benefits are deemed to be attributable to employees' services performed latest in such testing year. Excess benefits are treated as paid under such a plan or arrangement even if they are received not more than a brief period (e.g., 2½ months) after the end of the employer's taxable year (see § 1.404(b)-1T) and even if the employer elects the rule of section 89(a)(2)(B) with respect to excess benefits. An employer's election of the rule of section 89(a)(2)(B) for a testing year must be made in writing by January 31 of the first calendar year following the calendar year in which the testing year ends. Such election, when made, must apply for all plans of the same type.

(b) Discriminatory employee benefit plan. *(1) In general.* A statutory employee benefit plan is a discriminatory employee benefit plan for a testing year unless, for such year, the plan satisfies the requirements of paragraphs (c) and (d) of this Q&A-1. Alternatively, in lieu of the requirements of paragraph (d) of this Q& A-1, an employer may elect to apply the requirements of paragraph (e) of this Q&A-1 to a statutory employee benefit plan. However, for testing years beginning in 1989, a statutory employee benefit plan is not treated as a discriminatory employee benefit plan for purposes of section 4976 if the excess benefits with respect to such plan are properly reported in accordance with section 89(1).

(2) Disability coverage. Generally, a plan (or portion thereof) that provides disability coverage is not subject to the requirements of paragraphs (c), (d) or (e) of this Q&A-1 for a testing year and, thus, may not be taken into account in determining whether any other accident or health plan satisfies the requirements of such paragraphs. For example, short-term sick pay, short-term and long-term disability plans, worker's compensation plans (as defined in paragraph (f)(1)((v) of this Q&A-1), plans described in section 104(a)(4) and (5) and similar wage continuation plans are not subject to the requirements of paragraphs (c), (d) or (e) of this Q&A-1, even if there are significant employer-provided benefits with respect to such plans. This paragraph (b)(2) does not apply with respect to disability coverage the benefits of which are excludable from gross income under section 105(b) or (c).

(3) No employer-provided benefit. If there is no employer-provided benefit (other than by reason of coverage under such plan being considered excess benefit) for a testing year, with respect to a plan that is otherwise subject to the nondiscrimination rules of section 89, such plan is not subject to the requirements of paragraphs (c), (d) or (e) of this Q&A-1 for such testing year. See Q&A-7 of this section to determine a plan's employer-provided benefit. An employer cannot take into account a plan (or portion thereof) providing no employer-provided benefit in determining whether other plans meet the requirements of paragraphs (c), (d) or (e) of this Q&A-1.

(4) Employers with only highly compensated employees. A statutory employee benefit plan is not subject to the re-

quirements of paragraphs (c), (d) or (e) of this Q&A-1 for a testing year if such plan is maintained by an employer that, for such year, only has employees who are highly compensated employees.

(c) Nondiscriminatory provisions requirement. *(1) In general.* A plan satisfies the requirement of this paragraph (c) and section 89(d)(1)(C) only if the plan does not contain any provision that (by its terms, operation, or otherwise) discriminates in favor of highly compensated employees. In making this determination, an employer must take into account all plans of the same type. For purposes of this requirement, an employer's election with respect to testing (e.g., designation of a testing day) is subject to the nondiscriminatory provisions requirement even though it is not required to be in the single written document required under section 89(k)(1)(A).

(2) Waiting periods under core health plans. If an employer has two or more core health plans with different waiting periods, the core health plans do not satisfy the nondiscriminatory provisions test of this paragraph (c) unless each plan satisfies the 50 percent eligibility test of paragraph (d)(3) of this Q&A-1 either on an individual basis or by inclusion in a group of comparable plans, under paragraph (b) of Q&A-4 of this section, that includes only one or more additional core health plans that have the same or shorter waiting periods. If a plan fails to satisfy this paragraph (c) by reason of this paragraph (c)(2), the excess benefit attributable to this failure is the employer-provided benefit under the plan that relates to the period of coverage that prevents the plan from being included in a group of comparable plans under the preceding sentence.

(3) Examples. The provisions of this paragraph (c) are illustrated in the following examples:

Example (1). Assume that an employer has 25 employees, 5 of whom are highly compensated employees. Two of the 20 nonhighly compensated employees have families. The employer provides employee-only health coverage with an employer-provided benefit of $2,000 to all employees, and provides the highly compensated employees with an additional plan providing employee-only coverage with an employer-provided benefit of $2,200. In addition, the employer provides family-only health coverage (with an employer-provided benefit of $2,000) to all of the nonhighly compensated employees, but makes such family-only coverage available to the highly compensated employees only if they pay the total cost of such coverage on an after-tax employee contribution basis. Thus, the highly compensated employees receive no employer-provided benefit with respect to such family-only coverage. The employer decides to treat all of its employees as having a family (see Q&A-3 of this section). The family-only coverage that is treated as received by employees without families may be used under the comparability rule of paragraph (c)(2) of Q&A-4 of this section to support the additional $2,200 employee-only coverage provided to highly compensated employees. Although after the application of the comparability rule, the $2,200 employee-only coverage for the highly compensated passes the 80 percent coverage test set forth in paragraph (e) of this Q&A-1, the nondiscriminatory provisions test is violated. This is because the coverage of 18 of the 20 nonhighly compensated employees is not meaningful because they are not in fact receiving benefits under the family-only coverage.

Example (2). A school district selects July 1 as its testing day. On that day, the school district has no part-time employees and only administrative personnel, regular faculty and maintenance personnel on its payroll. The designation of July 1 as the testing day does not constitute the designation of a testing day that is fairly representative of the employee pool and business operation of the school district and, therefore, such designation violates the nondiscriminatory provisions test.

Example (3). An employer that operates a department store selects July 1 as its testing day. Traditionally, the number of the employees employed by the employer on July 1 does not reasonably reflect the number of the employer's employees employed during most of its fiscal year. This designation violates the nondiscriminatory provisions test.

Example (4). Assume that an employer maintains numerous health plans (both core and noncore plans) for its 5,000 employees. All but one core health plan, Plan X, provides for a 3-month waiting period for new employees. Plan X provides coverage after 1 month of employment for certain executive personnel. This 1-month waiting period provision violates the nondiscriminatory provisions test of this paragraph (c) unless Plan X satisfies the 50 percent eligibility test of paragraph (d)(3) of this Q&A-1 either on an individual basis or by inclusion with another core health plan or plans with the same or shorter waiting periods in a group of comparable plans under paragraph (b) of Q&A-4 of this section. If the 1-month waiting period provision fails the nondiscriminatory provisions test of this paragraph (c), then the employer-provided benefit under Plan X that relates to coverage for the period between the first and third months of employment is treated as an excess benefit of each highly compensated employee eligible for coverage under Plan X after 1 month of employment.

(d) Eligibility and benefit requirements. *(1) In general.* A plan satisfies the requirements of this paragraph (d) only if the tests of paragraphs (d)(2), (d)(3), and (d)(4) of this Q&A-1 are satisfied.

(2) 90 percent/50 percent eligibility test. (i) In general. A plan satisfies this test only if at least 90 percent of all nonhighly compensated employees have available under all plans of the same type an employer-provided benefit that is at least 50 percent of the largest employer-provided benefit available under all such plans to any highly compensated employee. To the extent that an employee is eligible to be covered under two or more plans of different types (see paragraph (f)(2)(i) of this Q&A-1), but not fully under all such plans, the employee cannot be treated as eligible for the full employer-provided benefit of each plan for purposes of the 90 percent/50 percent test. Instead, the employer must use a reasonable, uniform, and nondiscriminatory allocation method to allocate to such employee only a reasonable portion of each plan's full employer-provided benefit. Whether a plan is available to an employee is determined under all of the facts and circumstances. For example, an HMO at a location distant from the location of the employer might not, under the facts and circumstances, be reasonably available to employees at the location of the employer. See Q&A-8 of this section for the treatment of salary reduction contributions under this test. Also, see Q&A-2 of this section for a transition rule for the 1989 testing year.

(ii) Example. The provisions of this paragraph (d)(2) are illustrated in the following example:

Example. An employer has 12 employees, 10 of whom are nonhighly compensated employees. The employer maintains two health plans. Plan A has an employer-provided benefit of $1,000. It is available to 9 of the 10 nonhighly compensated employees and both of the highly compensated employees. Plan B, a dental plan, has an employer-provided benefit of $500. It is available only to the two highly compensated employees. The health plans meet the requirements of this paragraph (d)(2). This is the result since 90 percent of the nonhighly compensated employees (9 of 10) have available to them an employer-provided benefit of $1,000, which is more than 50 percent of $1,500, the largest employer-provided benefit available to any highly compensated employee. Note that the dental plan in this example fails the 50 percent eligibility test set forth in paragraph (d)(3) of this Q& A-1.

(3) 50 percent eligibility test. (i) In general. A plan satisfies this test only if the plan satisfies the requirement of either paragraph (d)(3)(ii) or paragraph (d)(3)(iii) of this Q&A-1. An employee is eligible to participate in a plan only if, under all of the facts and circumstances, the employee is reasonably eligible to participate in such plan. See Q&A-4 of this section with respect to rules relating to the comparability and aggregation of health plans.

(ii) 50 percent eligibility. A plan satisfies the requirement of this paragraph (d)(3)(ii) only if at least 50 percent of the employees eligible to participate in the plan are nonhighly compensated employees.

(iii) Nondiscriminatory ratio. A plan satisfies the requirements of this paragraph (d)(3)(iii) only if the highly compensated eligibility percentage does not exceed the nonhighly compensated eligibility percentage. The highly compensated eligibility percentage is the percentage determined by dividing the number of highly compensated employees eligible to participate in the plan by the total number of highly compensated employees. The nonhighly compensated eligibility percentage is the percentage determined by the same method substituting nonhighly compensated employees for highly compensated employees.

(iv) Example. The provisions of this paragraph (d)(3) are illustrated in the following example:

Example. An employer maintains a plan providing for medical diagnostic examinations to a group of management personnel. Of this group, 10 percent are nonhighly compensated employees. Unless the plan can be treated as part of a group of comparable plans that passes the 50 percent eligibility test (see paragraph (b) of Q&A-4 of this section), the plan fails the tests described in this paragraph (d)(3).

(4) 75 percent benefits test. (i) In general. A plan satisfies the test of this paragraph (d)(4) only if the average employer-provided benefit actually received under all plans of the same type by nonhighly compensated employees is at least 75 percent of the average employer-provided benefit actually received under all plans of the same type by highly compensated employees. See paragraph (f)(2)(ii) of this Q&A-1 for a rule under which, in certain circumstances, plans that are not of the same type may be treated as plans of the same type for purposes of this paragraph (d)(4). Also, see Q&A-2 of this section for transition rules for the 1989 and 1990 testing years.

(ii) Example. The provisions of this paragraph (d)(4) are illustrated in the following example:

Example. An employer has 5 highly compensated employees and 15 nonhighly compensated employees. The employer maintains only one health plan with an employer-provided benefit of $1,500. All of the highly compensated employees and 10 of the nonhighly compensated employees participate in the plan. The employer's health plan does not meet the requirements of this paragraph (d)(4) since the average employer-provided benefit of the nonhighly compensated employees is only $1,000 ((10 × $1,500)/15), and this amount is less than 75 percent of the average employer-provided benefit of the highly compensated employees, which is $1,500 ((5 × $1,500)/5). In order to meet the requirements of this paragraph (d)(4), the average employer-provided benefit of the nonhighly compensated employees must be at least $1,125 (75 percent of $1,500) or the average employer-provided benefit of the highly compensated employees must be no more than $1,333.33 ($1000 is 75 percent of $1333.33).

(e) 80 percent coverage test. A plan that is a health plan or a group-term life insurance plan satisfies the requirements of this paragraph (e) only if at least 80 percent of the nonhighly compensated employees are covered under such plan and the plan meets the requirements of paragraph (c) of this Q&A-1 (the nondiscriminatory provisions test). Plans of the same type may pass the 80 percent test separately or together (e.g., by reason of health plans being comparable). See Q&A-4 of this section with respect to rules relating to comparability and aggregation. If any of an employer's plans of the same type are tested under this paragraph (e), all plans of the same type must be tested under the requirements of this paragraph (e). The employer must elect in writing to use this 80 percent test.

(f) Definitions. *(1) Statutory employee benefit plan.* (i) In general. The term "statutory employee benefit plan" means an accident or health plan (within the meaning of sections 106 and 105) or a group-term life insurance plan (within the meaning of section 79). Also, under section 89(i)(2), an employer may treat certain other plans as statutory employee benefit plans.

(ii) Health plan. In general, the term "health plan" means an accident or health plan under section 105 or 106, except to the extent the plan is a disability plan (see paragraph (b)(2) of this Q&A-1). In addition, a plan that provides payments for accidental death and dismemberment, or business travel accident insurance, is an accident or health plan because coverage under such plan is eligible for the exclusion under section 106. Furthermore, plan that provides for medical diagnostic procedures or physical examination is an accident or health plan because the plan is eligible for the exclusion under section 106.

(iii) Church plans. The term "statutory employee benefit plan" does not include a plan maintained by a church (as defined in section 3121(w)(3)(A)), including a qualified church-controlled organization within the meaning of section 3121(w)(3)(B)), if the plan is maintained exclusively for clergy and church employees, and their spouses and dependents.

(iv) Plans maintained by governments. A plan does not fail to be a statutory employee benefit plan merely because it is maintained by a state or local government or political subdivision or instrumentality thereof, by the District of Columbia, or by the federal government or a political subdivision or instrumentality thereof.

(v) Worker's compensation. The term "statutory employee benefit plan" does not include a worker's compensation plan that pays amounts from a sickness and disability fund maintained for employees under the laws of the United States, a state or the District of Columbia (i.e., a fund maintained pursuant to a worker's compensation act or statute in the nature of a worker's compensation act, the benefits from which are excludable under section 104(a)(1)). Thus such a plan is not subject to the nondiscrimination requirements of section 89. An employer may not take into account a worker's compensation plan (or portion thereof) in determining whether other plans meet the requirements of paragraphs (c), (d) or (e) of this Q&A-1. However, accident or health plans maintained by a government (as defined in paragraph (f)(1)(iv) of this Q&A-1) that provide benefits that are excludable from the income of the employee solely by reason of section 105(b) or (c) are not worker's compensation plans within the meaning of the first sentence of this paragraph (f)(1)(v) and thus are subject to the nondiscrimination requirements of section 89.

(2) Plans of the same type. (i) In general. Two or more plans are treated as plans of the same type if all of such plans are included in only one of the following categories: accident or health plans (sections 106 and 105); group-term life insurance (section 79); qualified group legal services plans (section 120); educational assistance programs (section 127); or dependent care assistance programs (section 129).

(ii) Election. For purposes of applying the requirements of paragraph (d)(4) of this Q&A-1 (the 75 percent benefits test) to plans of the same type other than health plans for a testing year, an employer may elect in writing to treat all plans of the types specified in the election as plans of the same type. Although this section is not available for purposes of determining whether the health plans of the employer satisfy the 75 percent benefits test, if such plans satisfy the 75 percent benefits test they may be taken into account in determining whether plans of the same type (e.g. group-term life insurance plans), other than health plans, satisfy such test. For any testing year, if an employer elects to take health plans into account in determining whether two or more plans of another type or types satisfy the 75 percent benefits test, all of the employer's health plans must be taken into account with all other plans of the type or types subject to the election. Thus, for example, if an employer elects to take its health plans into account in testing its group-term life insurance plans and dependent care assistance programs for purposes of the 75 percent benefits test, all such plans must be tested on an aggregated basis under the 75 percent benefits test.

(3) Employer-provided benefit. In the case of any health or group-term life insurance plan, the employer-provided benefit for purposes of this section is the value of the coverage under the plan that is attributable to employer contributions. For example, in the case of a health plan, the employer-provided benefit is the employer-provided portion of the value of the entitlement to receive payment on account of personal injury or sickness including medical care or reimbursements of specified medical expenses or other medical benefits, subject to various conditions and limits, rather than the value of the reimbursements, products, services and other benefits received pursuant to the health coverage. See Q&A-7 of this section for guidance relating to the value of health coverage. See section 89(g)(3)(C) for rules with respect to the value of coverage under a group-term life insurance plan. In the case of any other statutory employee benefit plan, an employee's employer-provided benefit under section 89 is the employer-provided portion of the value of the reimbursements, products, services and other benefits provided under the plan (rather than the value of the coverage or the entitlement to such benefits).

(4) Highly compensated employee. The term "highly compensated employee" is defined as that term is defined in section 414(q). For purposes of determining who is a highly compensated employee under section 89, the testing year is the determination year.

(5) Nonhighly compensated employee. The term "nonhighly compensated employee" is defined as each employee other than a highly compensated employee.

(6) Employee. (i) In general. The term "employee" generally means an individual who performs service for the employer maintaining the plan and who is either a common law employee of the employer, a self-employed individual treated as an employee under section 401(c)(1), or an individual who is treated as an employee with respect to the employer for purposes of the provision (e.g., section 106) that provides for the exclusion of the benefit being tested under section 89.

(ii) Leased employees. (A) In general. The term "employee" includes a leased employee who is treated as an employee of the employer-recipient pursuant to the provisions of section 414(n)(1)(A) or section 414(o)(2) and the regulations thereunder. In general, section 414(n) applies with respect to employee benefit plans covered by section 89 in the same manner as it applies with respect to qualified plans covered by section 401(a). Thus, the rule of section 414(n)(1)(B) permitting a recipient to take into account certain benefits provided by a leasing organization is available with respect to benefits subject to section 89. The safe harbor exception of section 414(n)(5), however, is not available with respect to section 89. In addition, the rule of § 1.414(n)-1(b)(10) regarding services performed on a "substantially full-time basis" is to be applied by appropriately adjusting the hour of service requirements to reflect the 6-month period of service requirement. Nevertheless, a leased employee may be disregarded by an employer-recipient when testing its health plans if the employer-recipient treats the health coverage received by the leased employee from the leasing organization as health coverage received from another employer and, on such basis, applies the rules of Q&A-3 of this section with respect to such leased employee. Notwithstanding the immediately preceding sentence, no leased employee described in this paragraph (f)(6)(ii) may be disregarded as having coverage from another employer unless the value of employer-provided core health benefits actually received by the leased employee from the leasing organization under its plan is at least 50 percent as valuable as the highest employer-provided core health benefit available to any highly compensated employee of the employer-recipient.

(B) Authority to issue additional requirements. The differing natures of employee benefit plans covered by section 89 and qualified plans covered by section 401(a) may require different rules in certain circumstances. The Commissioner may provide such rules, to the extent appropriate, through revenue rulings, notices, and other guidance of general applicability.

(iii) Excluded employees. In general, the term "employee" does not include employees who are excluded employees under section 89(h) and thus who are excluded from consideration in applying the nondiscrimination rules of section 89 with respect to other employees. For example, employees who are included in a unit of employees covered by a collective bargaining agreement are excluded employees only if there is evidence that the type of benefits provided under the plan being tested under section 89 was the subject of good faith bargaining and no employee in such collective bargaining unit of employees is eligible to receive or does receive any benefit under the plan or any plan of the same type.

(7) Core health benefits. Except as provided otherwise in this section, the terms "core health benefits," "core health coverage," and "core health plan" generally refer to coverage providing comprehensive major medical and hospitalization benefits and similar types of health benefits. Dental

care, vision care, accidental death and dismemberment, and disability coverage are examples of health benefits that generally are not core health plans. Also, any health coverage provided through a flexible spending arrangement (as defined in Q&A-7 of § 1.125-2) is not a core health benefit.

(g) Written election. In general, unless specifically provided otherwise, an election required to be in writing under this section must be in writing by January 31 of the first calendar year following the calendar year in which excess benefits for the testing year (without regard to whether there are such excess benefits for such year) would be treated as received under paragraph (a)(2) of this Q& A-1. However, if an employer makes an election under section 89(a)(2)(B) to delay the inclusion of excess benefits in income for one year, then any other written elections must be in writing by January 31 of the first calendar year following the calendar year in which excess benefits for the testing year (without regard to whether there are such excess benefits for such year) are treated as received under paragraph (a)(2) of this Q&A-1. See Q&A-1(a)(2) for the time for making the section 89(a)(2)(B) election. The elections must be written in a manner that will allow a reconstruction of the employer's method of testing.

Q-2. What transitional and special rules are available to health plans under section 89?

A-2. **(a) Transition rule for 75 percent benefits test.** *(1) In general.* With respect to the 1989 and 1990 testing years, an employer's health plans are deemed to satisfy paragraph (d)(4) of Q&A-1 of this section (the 75 percent benefits test) with respect to active employees for a testing year if the requirements of paragraphs (a)(2), (a)(3), and (a)(4) of this Q&A-2 are satisfied with respect to such testing year.

(2) Testing years ending in 1989 and 1990. The requirement of this paragraph (a)(2) is satisfied only if the testing year ends in either the 1989 calendar year or the 1990 calendar year. For purposes of this paragraph (a), a testing year that ends in 1989 is a 1989 testing year and a testing year that ends in 1990 is a 1990 testing year.

(3) Employer election. The requirement of this paragraph (a)(3) is satisfied only if the employer elects in writing the application of the transition rule in this paragraph (a) with respect to a testing year.

(4) Includible coverage for applicable group of employees. (i) In general. The requirement of this paragraph (a)(4) is satisfied for a testing year only if the employer-provided benefits (including the portion attributable to salary reduction contributions) under all health plans of the employer received by the applicable group of employees for the testing year are treated as excess benefits for such testing year. If an employer makes an election under paragraph (a) of this Q&A-2, then in determining whether the requirements of paragraphs (d)(2) and (d)(3) of Q& A-1 of this section (the 90 percent/50 percent eligibility test and the 50 percent eligibility test, respectively) are met, the employer may treat benefits that are includible in gross income by reason of this paragraph (a)(4) as attributable to after-tax employee contributions.

(ii) Applicable group of employees. (A) 1989 testing year. For a 1989 testing year, the applicable group of employees includes all active employees of the employer for such year who had more than a 5 percent ownership interest in the employer (determined in accordance with section 416(i)) at any time between January 1, 1988, and the end of the testing year, and the applicable number of the highly compensated active employees of the employer who receive the most compensation for the 1989 testing year. The applicable number for the preceding sentence is the number of employees representing 20 percent of the highly compensated active employees of the employer for the testing year, but in no event greater than 1,000 highly compensated employees and in no event less than 10 employees (or the total number of highly compensated employees of the employer if less than 10).

(B) 1990 testing year. For a 1990 testing year, the applicable group of employees includes all highly compensated active employees of the employer for such year who had more than a 5 percent ownership interest in the employer (determined in accordance with section 416(i)) at any time between January 1, 1989, and the end of the testing year, and the applicable number of highly compensated active employees of the employer (or all highly compensated active employees if the employer has fewer than the applicable number of such employees) who receive the most compensation for the 1990 testing year. The applicable number for the preceding sentence is the number of employees representing 40 percent of the highly compensated active employees of the employer for the testing year, but in no event greater than 2,000 highly compensated employees and in no event less than 50 employees (or the total number of highly compensated employees of the employer if less than 50).

(C) Compensation. For purposes of identifying those highly compensated employees who receive the greatest amount of compensation, "compensation" means "compensation" as defined in section 414(q)(7). In the case of two or more employees with the same amount of compensation, the employer may decide which of such employees is to be treated as receiving more compensation.

(b) Transition rule for 90 percent/50 percent eligibility test. If an employer's health plans are deemed to satisfy paragraph (d)(4) of Q&A-1 of this section (the 75 percent benefits test) by reason of paragraph (a) of this Q&A-2 for a testing year ending in 1989, then, for such testing year, such employer may elect in writing to apply the 90 percent/50 percent eligibility test of paragraph (d)(2) of Q&A-1 of this section with respect to active employees for such testing year by substituting "80 percent" for "90 percent" and by substituting "66 percent" for "50 percent" (i.e., the test may be treated as an 80 percent/66 percent eligibility test). The rule of this paragraph (b) is not applicable for purposes of determining excess benefits under section 89(b).

(c) Special rule for certain large employers. *(1) In general.* An employer's health plans are deemed to satisfy the requirements of paragraph (d) of Q&A-1 of this section (the eligibility and benefit requirements) with respect to active employees for a testing year if all of the requirements of paragraphs (c)(2) through (c)(7) of this Q&A-2 are satisfied for such testing year. In applying the requirements of paragraphs (c)(2) through (c)(7) of this Q&A-2, only nonexcludable employees are taken into account and, for such purpose, the excluded employee rules of section 89(h)(1)(A), (B), (C), and (D) are to be applied without regard to the last sentence of section 89(h)(1) and without regard to sections 89(h)(2) and 89(h)(3). Thus, for example, differences in eligibility waiting periods do not result in the loss of an employee's status as an excludable employee to the extent that the period with respect to such employee does not exceed the maximum period allowed under section 89(h) (e.g., 6 months for core health coverage). The nondiscriminatory provisions test of paragraph (c) of Q& A-1 of this section does not apply to waiting periods under core health plans as discussed in paragraph (c)(2) of Q& A-1 of this section with respect to plans tested under this paragraph (c). The rules of this paragraph (c) are not applicable for purposes of determining excess benefits under section 89(b).

(2) Employer election. The requirement of this paragraph (c)(2) is satisfied with respect to a testing year only if the employer elects in writing the application of the rule of this paragraph (c) with respect to such testing year. If any of an employer's health plans are tested under this paragraph (c), all of such employer's health plans must be tested under this paragraph (c).

(3) Minimum number of employees. The requirement of this paragraph (c)(3) is satisfied for a testing year only if the employer employs at least 5,000 active employees on at least 1 day in each quarter of such testing year.

(4) Minimum percentage of nonhighly compensated employees. The requirement of this paragraph (c)(4) is satisfied only if at least 90 percent of the employer's active employees are nonhighly compensated employees:

(5) Maximum percentage of highly compensated employees. The requirement of this paragraph (c)(5) is satisfied only if fewer than 3/4 percent (0.75 percent) of the employer's active employees have annual compensation (within the meaning of section 414(q)(7)) in excess of 200 percent of the dollar amount in effect under section 414(q)(1)(C) for the testing year.

(6) Health plan eligibility. (i) In general. The requirement of this paragraph (c)(6) is satisfied only if both of the tests in paragraphs (c)(6)(ii) and (c)(6)(iii) are satisfied. For purposes of this paragraph (c)(6), the rules of paragraph (b) of Q&A-3 of this section are available. However, for purposes of this paragraph (c)(6), the comparability rules of paragraph (c) of Q&A-4 of this section are not available.

(ii) 80 percent eligibility test. This test is satisfied only if at least 80 percent of the employees eligible to participate in each health plan of the employer are nonhighly compensated employees. For purposes of this paragraph (c)(6)(ii) the comparability rules of paragraph (b) of Q&A-4(b) of this section and the family eligibility test rules of Q& A-3(b) of this section are available.

(iii) 80 percent/80 percent eligibility test. This test is satisfied only if at least 80 percent of the nonhighly compensated employees of the employer have available to them under all health plans an employer-provided benefit that is at least 80 percent as valuable as the largest employer-provided benefit available under all such health plans to any highly compensated employee. The rules relating to the application of the 90 percent/50 percent eligibility test apply in making this determination.

(7) Benefits test. The requirement of this paragraph (c)(7) is satisfied only if at least 66 percent of the nonhighly compensated employees of the employer actually receive core health coverage with an employer-provided benefit that is at least 66 percent as valuable as the largest employer-provided benefit available under all health plans (including both core and noncore health coverage) to any highly compensated employee. In determining the largest employer-provided benefit available to a highly compensated employee, the rules applicable to the 75 percent benefits test apply, except that for this purpose salary reduction contributions are treated as employer contributions. For purposes of this paragraph (c)(7), the coverage rules of Q&A-3(c) of this section are available.

Q-3. Under what circumstances may employees be disregarded for purposes of section 89 when the employees receive health coverage from other employers or when employees do not have a family or have a family whose members receive health coverage from another employer?

A-3. **(a) In general.** For purposes of determining whether health plans providing coverage to the spouse and dependents (if any) of an employee (i.e., family-only coverage) satisfy the requirements of paragraph (d)(2) (the 90 percent/50 percent eligibility test) and paragraph (d)(3) (the 50 percent eligibility test) of Q& A-1 of this section, an employer may elect in writing to apply the rules of paragraph (b) of this Q&A-3. Also, for purposes of determining whether health plans satisfy the requirements of paragraph (d)(4) (the 75 percent benefits test) or paragraph (e) (the 80 percent coverage test) of Q&A-1 of this section, the employer may elect in writing to apply the rules of paragraph (c) of this Q& A-3.

(b) Eligibility tests. An employee who is eligible to receive family-only coverage under a health plan or would be eligible under the same terms and conditions as other eligible employees if the employee had a spouse and dependents may be treated as eligible to receive such family-only coverage without regard to whether the employee has a spouse and dependents. This is the case without regard to whether there is a requirement of an employee contribution or other employee election under the plan so long as any such election is uniformly available. If the employer applies the rule of this paragraph (b) with regard to any employee or any health plan, the employer must apply the rule uniformly with regard to all employees and health plans except to the extent such application would cause a plan to fail the nondiscriminatory provisions test of paragraph (c) of Q&A-1 of this section.

(c) 75 percent benefits test and 80 percent coverage test. *(1) Separate testing.* Except as otherwise provided in this paragraph (c), an employer may elect in writing to apply the requirements of paragraph (d)(4) or (e) of Q&A-1 of this section for a testing year by testing its health plan or plans that provide employee-only coverage separately from the health plan or plans that provide family-only coverage. If the employer tests family-only coverage separately from employee-only coverage, all family-only coverage must be tested together under this paragraph (c). Therefore, an employer may not separately test coverage provided to a spouse from coverage provided to a dependent. Separate testing may be elected under this paragraph (c)(1) without regard to the fact that family-only coverage is not available as a separate option to employees (i.e., the employee-only and family-only coverages are available or provided only as a package to the employee). No amendment to a written plan document is required to test separately under this paragraph (c)(1).

(2) Presumption of family status. In applying the requirements of paragraph (d)(4) or (e) of Q&A-1 of this section for a testing year to a health plan that provides family-only coverage, an employee does not fail to be treated as receiving family-only coverage merely because the employee does not have a spouse or dependents. This is the case without regard to whether the employer has elected separate testing in accordance with paragraph (c)(1) of this Q& A-3. Thus, for example, if an employer automatically provides an employee with family-only coverage (i.e., such coverage is provided on a nonelective, noncontributory basis) or automatically provides an employee with family-only coverage if the employee purchases employee-only coverage and the employee does purchase such employee-only coverage, the employee may be treated as having received the family-only coverage even though the employee does not have a spouse or dependents. However, see paragraph (c) of Q& A-1 of this section

with respect to the application of the nondiscriminatory provisions test to certain plans that provide family-only coverage.

(3) Other core health coverage. (i) Employer does not elect separate testing. If an employer does not elect to test plans providing employee-only coverage separately from plans that provide family-only coverage (as permitted under paragraph (c)(1) of this Q&A-3), an employee who has a family (as determined under this paragraph (c)) may be disregarded for purposes of applying the requirements of paragraphs (d)(4) and (e) of Q&A-1 of this section if either of the following two requirements are met. First, such employee and family members (if any) all receive core health coverage from another employer or from the spouse's or a dependent's employer. Second, if the employer does not provide a health plan that includes employer-provided family-only coverage, then the employee must receive core health coverage from another employer or from the spouse's or a dependent's employer.

(ii) Employer elects separate testing. If an employer elects to test employee-only coverage separately from family-only coverage (as permitted under paragraph (c)(1) of this Q&A-3), an employee may be disregarded for purposes of applying the requirements of paragraphs (d)(4) and (e) of Q&A-1 of this section with respect to the family-only coverage if such employee does not have a family (as determined under this paragraph (c)) or if such employee has a family and the family members all receive core health coverage from another employer or from the spouse's or a dependent's employer. Similarly, for purposes of applying the requirements of paragraphs (d)(4) and (e) of Q&A-1 of this section with respect to the employee-only coverage, an employee may be disregarded if the employee receives core health coverage from another employer or from a spouse's or a dependent's employer. In testing only the health plan or plans that provide employee-only coverage, employees are taken into account without regard to whether they have families.

(4) Sworn statements. (i) In general. An employer may not elect the rules of paragraph (c)(3) of this Q&A-3 unless the employer obtains and maintains adequate sworn statements that satisfy the requirements of paragraph (c)(4)(ii) of this Q&A-3. In the absence of an adequate sworn statement with respect to an employee or the application of paragraph (c)(4)(iii) of this Q&A-3, certain presumptions, set forth in section 89(g)(2)(C), are to be applied with respect to those facts that would otherwise have been provided on the sworn statement.

(ii) Adequate sworn statement. An adequate sworn statement must contain sufficient information to indicate whether the employee has a spouse or any dependents and, if so, the number of dependents and the current receipt by the employee and any spouse or dependents of core health coverage under a plan of another employer or the employer of the spouse or dependent. An employer cannot rely on sworn statements for testing years beginning after 1989 unless such statements are made under penalty of perjury and contain a designation of the employer-provided health coverage currently received by the employee under the employer's health plan or plans. In lieu of including information about the employer-provided health coverage being received by an employee under the employer's health plans, an employer may use any other reasonable method to enable it to determine, for each testing year, the extent to which an employee who is receiving core health coverage under a plan of another employer is also receiving employer-provided health coverage from the employer. A sworn statement is not required to be notarized or on a form approved in advance by the Commissioner. The rule of this paragraph (c)(4)(ii) is illustrated by the following example:

Example. As part of its open season on the selection of health plan coverage, an employer requests that an employee complete a form providing information about the employee's family status, number of dependents and whether the employee or the employee's spouse or dependents receive core health coverage through another employer or the employer of the spouse or a dependent. If the employee does receive other core health coverage, the form also requests the name of the other employer and, if applicable, the insurance company administering the program or providing the other coverage. At the bottom of the form, just above the signature block and date, is the following phrase: "Under penalties of perjury, I declare that the information I have furnished above, to the best of my knowledge and belief, is true, correct, and complete." This form satisfies the sworn statement requirement of section 89(g)(2)(B) and this Q&A-3 provided that the employer also is able to determine for each testing year, by other reasonable means, the extent to which employees who receive other core health coverage also receive health coverage from the employer.

(iii) Exception. If an employee is eligible to receive employee-only coverage under a core health plan of the employer with a substantial employer-provided benefit at no cost to the employee and such employee does not elect to receive any employee-only coverage under a core health plan of the employer, the employer may treat such employee as having completed an adequate sworn statement that the employee has core health coverage from another employer. Similarly, if an employee is eligible to receive family-only coverage under a core health plan of the employer with a substantial employer-provided benefit and at no cost, and such employee does not elect to receive any family-only coverage under a core health plan of the employer, the employer may treat such employee as having completed an adequate sworn statement that the employee has no family or has a family all the members of which receive other core health coverage. Even if a sworn statement is deemed to have been completed under this paragraph (c)(4)(iii), the employer must establish by other reasonable methods the extent to which employees described in this paragraph (c)(4)(iii) receive health coverage from such employer. For purposes of this paragraph (c)(4)(iii), the plan has a cost to the employee if the employee is required to make any after-tax or salary reduction contributions or to waive any other benefit (taxable or otherwise) in order to obtain the health coverage.

(iv) Frequency of sworn statements. An employer that elects to use sworn statements as permitted under this paragraph (c)(4) must obtain such statements on no less frequent a basis than once each 3-consecutive years. If the employer does not obtain sworn statements from substantially all of its employees or from a statistically valid random sample of all of its employees determined under statistical standards consistent with those in paragraph (d) of Q&A-5 of this section, the employer must obtain such sworn statements on an annual basis.

(5) Certain highly compensated employees. A highly compensated employee cannot be disregarded under paragraph (c)(3) of this Q&A-3 if such employee receives an employer-provided benefit under all health plans of the employer that is greater than 133-1/3 percent of the average employer-provided benefit under all such health plans received by nonhighly compensated employees (after applying the rule of paragraph (c)(6) of this Q&A-3). The rule of this

paragraph (c)(5) is applied separately with respect to employee-only coverage and family-only coverage if the employer elects under paragraph (c)(1) of this Q&A-3 to test such coverages separately.

(6) Certain nonhighly compensated employees. A nonhighly compensated employee may not be disregarded under paragraph (c)(3) of this Q&A-3 because of other core health coverage unless, at the time such other coverage ceases, such employee is eligible to elect coverage under any core health plan of the employer for which the employee was eligible (through election or otherwise) during the immediately preceding period in which the employee could have elected coverage (e.g. an open season). The election period for purposes of the rule in this paragraph (c)(6) must be no shorter than 30 days). This paragraph (c)(6) applies without regard to the reason for the cessation of the employee's other core health coverage and without regard to whether the employer's health plans otherwise permit employees to commence coverage at other than an open season. Similarly, a nonhighly compensated employee may not be disregarded as having no family or having a family with other coverage under paragraph (c)(3) of this Q&A-3 unless such employee is eligible to elect (on the same conditions set forth in the preceding two sentences) family-only coverage, upon a change in family status in which the employee acquires a family or upon a loss of such other coverage for a member of the family. This paragraph (c)(6) does not require that an employee be eligible to participate under a plan for which the employee would not previously have been eligible. In addition, any otherwise applicable eligibility conditions that would have barred participation during the immediately preceding open season, such as insurability, may continue to be applied with respect to eligibility resulting under this paragraph (c)(6) but only if such conditions exist at the time the other core health coverage ceases and such conditions are applied on a uniform, consistent and nondiscriminatory basis. However, in no event may an employer impose conditions on eligibility that were not previously applicable to such employee during the immediately preceding open season. Conditions that were previously applicable may be applied with regard to the facts in existence either at the time of previous eligibility or at the time the other core coverage ceases, as long as such application is on a uniform, consistent and nondiscriminatory basis. This paragraph (c)(6) is applicable only for plan years beginning after December 31, 1990.

(7) Eligibility requirement. An employer may not disregard employees under paragraph (c)(3) of this Q&A-3 for purposes of applying paragraph (e) of Q&A-1 of this section (the 80 percent coverage test) unless paragraph (e) of Q&A-1 of this section would be satisfied without use of the rules contained in such paragraph on the basis of eligibility to participate instead of coverage received.

Q-4. What is a health plan under the section 89 nondiscrimination rules and to what extent are health plans comparable or aggregated for purposes of such rules?

A-4. **(a) In general.** Except as otherwise provided in this section, a health plan is a uniform entitlement provided to employees with respect to payments on account of personal injury or sickness, including specified medical claims, expenses, products or services. Any difference in entitlement creates separate health plans. In addition, any difference in cost to different groups of employees, including the fact that salary reduction contributions are required for coverage that is identical to coverage that is otherwise employer-provided, creates separate plans. Each option as to coverage is treated as a separate health plan for purposes of section 89. However, paragraphs (b) through (f) of this Q&A-4 provide testing rules under which comparable health plans may be treated as a single health plan, rules when two or more health plans must be aggregated and treated as a single plan, and rules when separate health plans may be restructured. These rules apply solely for purposes of testing and calculating discriminatory excess with respect to an employer's health plans under the section 89 nondiscrimination rules, and do not require that the single written document required by Q&A-3 of § 1.89(k)-1 relating to any of such plans be modified to conform to the testing status of such plans under these rules.

(b) Comparable health plans for 50 percent eligibility test. For purposes of applying paragraph (d)(3) of Q&A-1 of this section (the 50 percent eligibility test), two or more health plans included in a group of comparable plans may be treated as a single health plan. A group of plans is comparable if the smallest employer-provided benefit available to any employee in any plan in the group is at least 95 percent of the largest employer-provided benefit available to any employee in any plan in the group. See paragraph (d) of this Q& A-4 for mandatory aggregation rules that may be applicable before the application of this paragraph (b).

(c) Comparable health plans for 80 percent coverage test. *(1) In general.* Except as otherwise provided in this paragraph (c), for purposes of applying paragraph (e) of Q&A-1 of this section (the 80 percent coverage test), two or more health plans included in a group of comparable plans, may be treated as a single health plan. A group of plans is comparable if the smallest employer-provided benefit available to any employee in any plan in the group is at least 90 percent of the largest employer-provided benefit available to any employee in any plan in the group. See paragraph (e) of this Q&A-4 for mandatory aggregation rules that may be applicable before the application of this paragraph (c).

(2) Alternative general comparability rule. At the employer's written election, a group of plans is comparable for purposes of applying paragraph (e) of Q&A-1 (the 80 percent coverage test) if the smallest employer-provided benefit available to any employee in any plan in the group is at least 80 percent of the largest employer-provided benefit available to any employee in any plan in the group. This alternative general comparability rule is available only if the employer applies the requirements of paragraph (e) of Q&A-1 by substituting "90 percent" for "80 percent." Thus, this alternative general comparability rule applies only if at least 90 percent of the nonhighly compensated employees are covered under the health plan or group of comparable plans being tested.

(3) Restriction on general comparability. If a plan fails to satisfy paragraph (d)(3) of Q&A-1 of this section (the 50 percent eligibility test) (the failed plan), the failed plan may not be included with any other plan in a group of comparable plans under paragraphs (c)(1) or (c)(2) of this Q&A-4 unless the following two requirements are met. First, the employer-provided benefit of the group of comparable plans must be within at least 95 percent of the employer-provided benefit of the failed plan. Second, the failed plan and the group of comparable plans, considered together, must be comparable under paragraph (c)(1) or (c)(2) of this Q&A-4. The following example illustrates the rules of this paragraph (c)(3):

Example. Assume that an employer with 25 employees, 5 of whom are highly compensated employees, provides all nonhighly compensated employees with a health plan with an employer-provided benefit of $3,000. In addition, the employer provides a health plan with an employer-provided benefit of $3,750 only to its highly compensated employees. The employer tests its health plans under the 80 percent coverage test of paragraph (e) of Q&A-1 of this section. Because the additional $3,750 health plan is available only to highly compensated employees and thus fails the 50 percent eligibility test, such plan may not be aggregated with the $3,000 plan unless the employer-provided benefit under the $3,750 plan is reduced to $3,158 ($3,000 is 95 percent of $3,158) or the employer-provided benefit under the other plan is increased to $3,562 (95 percent of $3,750).

(4) Deemed comparability rule. (i) Health plan outside comparability range. A health plan (or a group of health plans treated as a single health plan) that is not otherwise included with another health plan in a group of comparable plans (determined under paragraph (c)(1) through (3) of this Q&A-4) may be included in such group if the employer-provided benefit under the former health plan (or group of health plans) is greater than the employer-provided benefit under the latter health plan (or group of plans); the former health plan's nonhighly compensated coverage percentage is at least 80 percent of the highly compensated coverage percentage; and, after the inclusion of the former plan in a group with the latter plan, the nonhighly compensated coverage percentage remains at least 80 percent of the highly compensated coverage percentage for such group. No plan can be included under this rule if a plan with an employer-provided benefit smaller than the employer-provided benefit of the plan to be included has previously been included in the group of comparable plans under this rule. If the employer elects the alternative general comparability rule of paragraph (c)(2) of this Q& A-4, "90 percent" must be substituted for "80 percent" in the preceding sentence. If the deemed comparability rule of this paragraph (c)(4) is applied by treating a resulting group of comparable plans as a single health plan, the employer-provided benefit for such single health plan, except as provided in paragraph (c)(5)(i) of this section, is the largest employer-provided benefit of any plan included in the group.

(ii) Coverage percentages. For purposes of this paragraph (c)(4), a health plan's (or health plan group's) nonhighly compensated coverage percentage is the percentage determined by dividing the number of nonhighly compensated employees covered by the plan (or the group) by the total number of nonhighly compensated employees of the employer. A health plan's (or group's) highly compensated coverage percentage is the percentage determined in the same manner by reference only to highly compensated employees.

(iii) Examples. The following examples illustrate the application of the rules of this paragraph (c)(4):

Example (1). Assume that an employer maintains four health plans that constitute a group of comparable plans under the general comparability rule of paragraph (c)(1) of this Q&A-4. The employer also maintains another health plan that has too large an employer-provided benefit to permit it to be included in the group of comparable plans under the general comparability rule. Under this paragraph (c)(4), if the nonhighly compensated coverage percentage with respect to such plan is at least 80 percent of the highly compensated coverage percentage for such plan and if after inclusion of the plan with the group of four comparable plans, the resulting group of plans has a nonhighly compensated coverage percentage that is at least 80 percent of the highly compensated coverage percentage, then the plan may be included in the group of comparable health plans to form a new group of comparable plans.

Example (2). Assume the same facts as in Example 1, except that the other health plan has too small an employer-provided benefit to permit it to be included in a group of comparable plans under the general comparability rule of paragraph (c)(1) of this Q&A-4. If the nonhighly compensated coverage percentage for the group of comparable plans is at least 80 percent of the highly compensated coverage percentage for such group, and if, after inclusion of the other plan with the group of comparable plans, the resulting group of plans has a nonhighly compensated coverage percentage that is at least 80 percent of the highly compensated coverage percentage, then the group of comparable plans may be included with the other plan to form a new group of comparable plans.

(5) Employee cost comparability. (i) In general. Health plans may be treated as a group of comparable plans if such plans are available to all of the employees who are covered under any of such plans on the same terms and conditions and the difference in the annual employee costs between the plan in the group with the largest employee cost and the plan in the group with the smallest employee cost is not greater than $100 (adjusted for testing years beginning after 1989 in accordance with section 89(g)(1)(E)(v)). Two or more plans generally are not available on the same terms if the employee cost for one plan is in the form of after-tax employee contributions and the employee cost for another plan is in the form of salary reduction contributions. A health plan is available to an employee only if, under all of the facts and circumstances, the plan is reasonably available to such employee. The employer-provided benefit for a group of comparable plans determined under this paragraph (c)(5)(i) is deemed to be the largest employer-provided core health benefit of any plan included in the group under this paragraph (c)(5)(i). If both salary reduction contributions and after-tax employee contributions are required under each of the plans, the plans may be treated as comparable if the maximum total amount of such annual contributions under each plan does not differ from the maximum total amount of such contributions under any of the other plans by more than $100. The rules of this paragraph (c)(5)(i) are illustrated by the following examples:

Example (1). Assume that an employer maintains two health plans, Plan X and Plan Y. Plan X is provided to employees at no employee cost. Plan Y is available to employees under a cafeteria plan for $100 a year, to be paid through salary reduction contributions. These plans may not be treated as part of a group of comparable plans under an analysis that compares the after-tax employee contributions required for Plan X ($0) with the after-tax employee contributions required for Plan Y ($0) because Plan Y is not actually available for only $0 in after-tax employee contributions, but rather is available for $100 in salary reduction contributions. However, these plans may be treated as part of a group of comparable plans under an analysis that compares the salary reduction contributions of Plan X ($0) with the salary reduction contributions of Plan Y ($100) because the salary reduction contributions under each plan do not differ by more than $100 and neither plan has any required after-tax contributions.

Example (2). Assume that an employer maintains two health plans, Plan V and Plan W. Plan V is provided to employees for an after-tax employee contribution of $20 a year and a salary reduction contribution of $20 a year. Plan W is provided to employees for an after-tax employee contribution of $100 a year and a salary reduction contribution of $100 a year. These two plans may not be treated as part of a group of comparable plans under this paragraph (c)(5)(i) because the annual maximum total amount of after-tax and salary reduction contributions under Plan V ($40) differs from the maximum total amount of after-tax and salary reduction contributions for Plan W ($200) by more than $100.

(ii) Coordination rule. A health plan that is not included in a group of comparable plans under paragraph (c)(5)(i) of this Q&A-4 may be included with such group of comparable plans under the comparability rules of paragraphs (c)(1) through (c)(4) of this Q&A-4 if such plan and the group are otherwise comparable under such rules. The employer-provided benefit under the group of plans is to be determined under the rule of paragraph (c)(5)(i) of this Q&A-4.

(iii) Special employee cost rule. A health plan that is not otherwise included in a group of comparable plans may be included in a group with respect to an employee if the employer-provided benefit under the plan to be included is less than the employer-provided benefit of the plan within the group of comparable plans with the largest employer-provided benefit and, in the case of a nonhighly compensated employee, the employee is eligible on the same terms and conditions as other employees to participate in the plan in such group with the largest employer-provided benefit and the annual employee cost for the employee under the plan to be included is equal to or greater than the greatest employee cost for the employee under any plan in the group of comparable plans minus $100. Thus, the rule of this paragraph (c)(5)(iii) applies if a nonhighly compensated employee may choose a more expensive plan with a lesser employer-provided benefit than any plan in the group so long as the conditions of this paragraph (c)(5)(iii) are satisfied. A health plan is available to an employee only if, under all of the facts and circumstances, the plan is reasonably available to such employee. This paragraph (c)(5)(iii) may be applied with respect to a health plan and a group of comparable plans or with respect to two groups of comparable plans otherwise determined under paragraph (c)(1) through (c)(3) or (c)(5) of this Q&A-4. In such case, the employer-provided benefit of the group of comparable plans is the largest employer-provided benefit of any plan (whether or not that plan is a core health plan) in such group and the lowest employee cost permitted within the group of comparable plans is equal to the employee cost for the plan in such group with the largest employee cost minus $100. The rules of this paragraph (c)(5)(iii) are illustrated by the following examples:

Example (1). Assume that an employer permits all of its employees to elect coverage under one of two health plans: Plan A (with an employer-provided benefit of $3,000 and an employee contribution of $300) and Plan B (with an employer-provided benefit of $2,200 and an employee contribution of $500). These two plans may form a group of comparable plans under this paragraph (c)(5)(iii) because Plan B's employer-provided benefit is less than Plan A's employer-provided benefit and Plan B's required employee contribution of $500 is greater than $200 (i.e., Plan A's required employee contribution minus $100).

Example (2). Assume that an employer permits all of its employees to elect coverage under any one of four health plans: Plan A (with an employer-provided benefit of $2,000 and an employee contribution of $125); Plan B (with an employer-provided benefit of $2,500 and an employee contribution of $225); Plan C (with an employer-provided benefit of $3,000 and an employee contribution of $200); and Plan D (with an employer-provided benefit of $2,500 and an employee contribution of $300). Plans A, B, and C may be included in a group of comparable plans under the rules of paragraph (c)(5)(i). Plan D may be included in such group under the rules of paragraph (c)(5)(iii) with respect to all employees because Plan D's employer-provided benefit of $2,500 is less than Plan C's employer-provided benefit of $3,000 and Plan D's required employee contribution of $300 is greater than $125 (i.e., Plan B's required employee contribution of $225 minus $100).

Example (3). Assume that an employer permits all of its employees to elect coverage under one of three health plans: Plan A (with an employer-provided benefit of $3,000 and an employee contribution of $500); Plan B (with an employer-provided benefit of $2,700 and an employee contribution of $350); and Plan C (with an employer-provided benefit of $2,500 and an employee contribution of $450). Plans A and B are included in a group of comparable plans determined under paragraph (c)(1) of this Q&A-4 (i.e., 90 percent of $3,000 is $2,700). Plan C may be included in such group under the rules of this paragraph (c)(5)(iii) because Plan C's employer-provided benefit of $2,500 is less than Plan A's employer-provided benefit of $3,000 and Plan C's required employee contribution of $450 is greater than $400 (i.e., Plan A's required employee contribution of $500 minus $100).

(iv) Employee cost. For purposes of this paragraph (c)(5), the term "employee cost" refers to both the employee's after-tax employee contributions and salary reduction contributions that are required in order for the employee to receive coverage under the health plan. The de minimis employee cost comparability rule of this paragraph (c)(5) may be applied on the basis of either after-tax employee contributions or salary reduction contributions under a cafeteria plan, but not both. Thus, for example, health Plan X that is available for $50 in after-tax employee contributions and health Plan Y that is available for $100 in salary reduction contributions under a cafeteria plan may not be treated as comparable plans under this paragraph (c)(5).

(d) Mandatory aggregation of plans for the 50 percent eligibility test. *(1) In general.* For purposes of applying paragraph (d)(3) of Q&A-1 of this section (the 50 percent eligibility test), if an employee may receive coverage under two or more health plans the rules of this paragraph (d) must be applied with respect to such plans. In addition, such plans may not be included in a group of comparable plans under paragraph (b) of this Q&A-4 with regard to such employee until the rules of this paragraph (d) have been applied with respect to such plans. Such health plans must be aggregated into an additional, single health plan that provides all of the coverage provided under any of the separate plans. The additional plan is treated as having an employer-provided benefit equal to the sum of the employer-provided benefits of each of the included plans (with an appropriate adjustment to eliminate the multiple inclusion of overlapping coverage). A nonhighly compensated employee is treated as eligible for both the additional plan and the separate plans. A highly compensated employee is treated as eligible only for the additional plan and is no longer treated as eligible for the separate plans.

(2) Special rule for salary reduction contributions. Any employer-provided benefit that is a non-core health benefit and is attributable to salary reduction contributions available to any nonhighly compensated employee that, after application of paragraph (d)(1) of this Q&A-4, exceeds the greater of $2,000 (adjusted for testing years beginning after 1989 in accordance with 89(g)(1)(E)(v)) or the employee's actual

salary reduction contribution is not considered available to such employee. This paragraph (d)(2) is effective for plan years beginning after December 31, 1989.

(3) Examples. The provisions of this paragraph (d) are illustrated in the following examples:

Example (1). Assume that, under an employer's health program, an employee is permitted to elect coverage under one plan from among two health indemnity plans provided through insurance companies and two HMO plans. The indemnity and HMO plans are four alternative health coverages and thus an employer is not required to apply this paragraph (d).

Example (2). Assume the same facts as *Example 1.* In addition to electing one of the indemnity or HMO plans, an employee may also elect coverage under any one or more of the following plans: a dental plan, a vision plan and various levels of health coverage (up to and including $1000) under a health flexible spending arrangement (FSA). Under this paragraph (d), each of the indemnity and HMO plans must be aggregated with the 3 elective plans, before testing any of the plans under the 50 percent eligibility test.

Example (3). Employee X is a nonhighly compensated employee and may receive coverage under either Plan A or Plan B, each of which has an employer-provided benefit of $500, or under both Plans A and B. Under this paragraph (d), for Employee X, Plan A and Plan B must be aggregated to form an additional Plan AB for purposes of the 50 percent eligibility test. In addition, Plan AB is treated as having an employer-provided benefit equal to $1,000 (assuming no overlapping coverage). Thus, there are three health plans that each must pass the 50 percent eligibility test: Plan A ($500), Plan B ($500), and Plan AB ($1,000). Employee X is treated as eligible for all three plans.

Example (4). An employer maintains two health plans: Plan A ($500) and Plan B ($500). The following table illustrates all of the eligible employees for these two plans. In addition, HCE denotes a highly compensated employee and NCE denotes a nonhighly compensated employee.

Employee	Plan A	Plan B
HCE 1	500	500
HCE 2	500	Not Elig.
HCE 3	Not Elig.	500
HCE 4	500	500
NCE 1	500	500
NCE 2	Not Elig.	500
NCE 3	500	Not Elig.
NCE 4	500	Not Elig.
NCE 5	Not Elig.	500

The following table reflects the plans after the application of this paragraph (d):

Employee	Plan A	Plan B	Plan AB
HCE 1	Not Elig.	Not Elig.	1000
HCE 2	500	Not Elig.	Not Elig.
HCE 3	Not Elig.	500	Not Elig.
HCE 4	Not Elig.	Not Elig.	1000
NCE 1	500	500	1000
NCE 2	Not Elig.	500	Not Elig.
NCE 3	500	Not Elig.	Not Elig.
NCE 4	500	Not Elig.	Not Elig.
NCE 5	Not Elig.	500	Not Elig.

After application of this paragraph (d), there are three plans that must satisfy the 50 percent eligibility test. Plan A and Plan B satisfy the 50 percent eligibility test, both as separate plans and as plans included in a group of comparable plans under paragraph (b) of this Q&A-4. However, Plan AB fails the 50 percent eligibility test. See Q&A-9 for rules relating to the determination of the excess benefit with respect to a plan that fails to satisfy the 50 percent eligibility test.

Example (5). An employer maintains two health plans: Plan A ($1,000) and Plan B ($500). The following table illustrates all of the eligible employees for these two plans.

Employee	Plan A	Plan B
HCE 1	$1,000	$500
HCE 2	$1,000	$500
NCE 1-100	$1,000	Not Elig.

The following table reflects the plans after the application of this paragraph (d):

Employee	Plan A	Plan B	Plan AB
HCE 1	Not Elig.	Not Elig.	$1,500
HCE 2	Not Elig.	Not Elig.	$1,500
NCE 1-100	$1,000	Not Elig.	Not Elig.

After application of this paragraph (d), there are three plans that must pass the 50 percent eligibility test. Plan A passes the 50 percent eligibility test. Plan B is no longer available to any employee and is not required to be tested under the 50 percent eligibility test. However, Plan AB fails the 50 percent eligibility test. Under Q&A-9, an excess benefit must be imputed to HCEs 1 and 2 so that Plan AB may be included in a group of comparable plans under paragraph (b) of this Q&A-4.

(e) Mandatory aggregation of plans for the 80 percent coverage test. *(1) In general.* For purposes of applying paragraph (e) of Q& A-1 of this section (the 80 percent coverage test), if an employee receives coverage under two or more health plans the rules of this paragraph (e) must be applied with respect to such plans. In addition, such plans may not be included in a group of comparable plans under paragraph (c) of this Q&A-4 with regard to such employee until the rules of this paragraph (e) have been applied with respect to such plans. Such health plans must be aggregated into an additional, single health plan that provides all of the coverage that is provided under any of the separate plans. The additional plan is treated as having an employer-provided benefit equal to the sum of the employer-provided benefits of each of the included plans (with an appropriate adjustment to eliminate the multiple inclusion of overlapping coverage). A nonhighly compensated employee is treated as covered under both the additional plan, and the separate plans. A highly compensated employee is treated as covered under the additional plan and not covered under the separate plans.

(2) Exception. This paragraph (e) does not apply with respect to two or more health plans if at least 90 percent of the nonhighly compensated employees eligible for coverage under each plan are eligible for coverage under all of such plans on the same terms and conditions as other employees, and each plan (prior to application of the comparability rules of paragraph (c) of this Q&A-4) satisfies the 80 percent coverage test.

(3) Examples. The provisions of this paragraph (e) are illustrated by the following examples:

Example (1). Assume that an employer maintains two health plans, Plan A and Plan B. Each has an employer-provided benefit of $500. Also, each plan covers 45 percent of the employer's nonhighly compensated employees who are not covered by the other plan. Employee X, a highly compensated employee, and Employee Y, a nonhighly compensated employee, are covered by both Plan A and Plan B. Plan A and Plan B must be aggregated to form an additional single health plan because the exception of paragraph (e)(2) of this Q&A-4 does not apply. Thus, there are three health plans: Plan A ($500), Plan B ($500), and Plan AB ($1,000). The plans fail the 80 percent coverage test because Plan AB may not be included with Plan A and Plan B under any of the comparability rules of paragraph (c) of this Q&A-4. Thus, the employer-provided benefit under Plan AB must be reduced to $526 with respect to Employee X for all plans to pass the 80 percent coverage test.

Example (2). Assume that an employer maintains two health plans, Plan A and Plan B. Each has an employer-provided benefit of $500. Each plan is available on the same terms to all employees of the employer and covers over 80 percent of the employer's nonhighly compensated employees. Because these plans qualify for the exception of paragraph (e)(2) of this Q&A-4, the employer is not required to aggregate the plans under this paragraph (e). Plan A and Plan B each satisfy the 80 percent coverage test.

Example (3). An employer maintains two health plans. Plan A has an employer-provided benefit of $1,000 and Plan B has an employer-provided benefit of $500. The following table illustrates all of the eligible employees for these two plans. HCE denotes a highly compensated employee and NCE denotes a nonhighly compensated employee.

Employee	Plan A	Plan B
HCE 1	$1,000	$500
HCE 2	$1,000	Not Elig.
NCE 1	$1,000	$500
NCE 2-100	$1,000	Not Elig.

The following table reflects the plans after the application of this paragraph (e):

Employee	Plan A	Plan B	Plan AB
HCE 1	Not Elig.	Not Elig.	$1,500
HCE 2	$1,000	Not Elig.	Not Elig.
NCE 1	$1,000	$500	$1,500
NCE 2-100	$1,000	Not Elig.	Not Elig.

After application of this paragraph (e), there are three plans that must be comparable in order for the plans to pass the 80 percent coverage test. The plans fail the 80 percent coverage test even though Plans A and B may be included in a group of comparable plans under paragraph (c)(3) because Plan AB may not be included in a group of comparable plans with Plan A and Plan B under any of the rules of paragraph (c) of this Q&A-4 for inclusion in a group of comparable plans with Plans A and B. It does, however, pass the 50 percent eligibility test, and therefore Plan AB's employer-provided benefit may be reduced to $1,111 ($1000 is 90 percent of $1,111) and the health plans will be considered comparable.

(f) Permissive plan restructuring. For purposes of applying paragraphs (d)(3) and (e) of Q&A-1 of this section (the 50 percent eligibility test and the 80 percent coverage test, respectively) an employer may, in certain circumstances, restructure two or more health plans into two or more restructured health plans on the basis of the value of coverages under such plans. To the extent mandatory aggregation is applicable and if the employer decides to apply the comparability rules of this Q&A-4, such mandatory aggregation and comparability rules must be applied only prior to the application of the permissive restructuring rule of this paragraph (f). Pursuant to this rule, two or more health plans may be restructured into one health plan of common value and two or more plans of distinct values. In all cases, to the extent the values of any plans being restructured are equivalent, the values may be restructured into only one plan. In no case may the plan (or plans) with the lowest value be restructured into two or more plans with a lower value. Thus, for example, if an employer has three plans (after the application of the mandatory aggregation and the comparability rules of this Q&A-4), Plan A with an employer-provided benefit of $7,000, Plan B with an employer-provided benefit of $6,000 and Plan C with an employer-provided benefit of $4,000 the employer may restructure the three plans only in the following manner: a plan providing employer-provided benefits of $4000, $2000 and $1000 respectively.

(g) Authority to issue additional requirements. The Commissioner, in revenue rulings, notices and other publications of general applicability, may make any modification to, or issue such additional requirements for the application of, the rules contained in this Q&A-4 as may be necessary to ensure proper compliance with the intent of such rules and section 89(g)(1).

Q-5. What is the testing methodology for applying the nondiscrimination rules under section 89?

A-5. **(a) In general.** Except as otherwise provided in this Q&A-5, the determination of whether a statutory employee benefit plan is a discriminatory employee benefit plan for a testing year is made on the basis of all of the applicable facts with respect to the employees of the employer as of the testing day included within such testing year. Such facts generally are to be treated as in existence for the entire testing year.

(b) Adjustments to facts on the testing day. *(1) Changes in plan terms.* If the employer-provided benefit (actually provided or made available) of an employee who is taken into account on the testing day changes during the testing year (either before or after the testing day) in connection with any change in plan terms, the amount taken into account as such employee's employer-provided benefit for such testing year must be adjusted to reflect the employer-provided benefit for the portions of the testing year both before and after such change.

(2) Election changes by highly compensated employees. (i) In general. If the employer-provided benefit (actually provided or made available) of a highly compensated employee for a testing year who is taken into account on the testing day changes during the testing year (either before or after the testing day) solely on account of an election of the employee, the amount taken into account as such employee's employer-provided benefit for such testing year must be adjusted to reflect the employer-provided benefit for the portions of the testing year both before and after such change.

(ii) Special rule for the first quarter of each testing year. An employer must make the adjustments otherwise required under this paragraph (b)(2) for election changes during the first quarter of a testing year only for those election changes by employees who were highly compensated employees for the immediately preceding testing year and employees who, for the current testing year, either are among the 100 highly compensated employees who receive the most compensation for the current testing year or are 5 percent owners of the employer (as determined under section 416(i)).

(3) Distinction between changes in plan terms and election changes. A change in an employee's employer-provided benefit is treated as an election change only if such change is exclusively attributable to an election change by the employee that is not in connection with or otherwise related to any change in the terms of the plan or other plans of the same type available to the employee. Changes in an employee's employer-provided benefit are treated as attributable to changes in plan terms even if the changes are pursuant to an election of the employee that occurs in conjunction with any change in the terms of the plan (or of another plan of the same type available to such employee). Thus, for example, if during an open season or election period an employee elects to change health plan coverage and there is any change to any one or more of the health plans available to such employee during the open season, such employee's change in employer-provided benefit is treated as in connection with a change in plan terms even if the employee is not covered, either before or after the open season, by a health plan that changed. An increase or decrease in the after-tax employee contributions or employer contributions, including salary reduction contributions, is treated as a change in plan terms.

(4) Taking required adjustments into account. (i) In general. Adjustments taken into account under this paragraph (b) are to be taken into account as of the effective date of the change in the employer-provided benefit.

(ii) Adjustment period rule. (A) In general. If the requirements of paragraph (b)(4)(ii)(B) and (C) of this Q&A-5 are satisfied, an employer may on a uniform and consistent basis treat employer-provided benefit changes as having become effective as of the first day of the applicable adjustment period or periods.

(B) Adjustment period. The requirement of this paragraph (b)(4)(ii)(B) is satisfied only if the employer uses at least 24 adjustment periods for its testing year. Adjustment periods must be regular, uniform periods throughout the testing year. For example, an employer may use each 2-week pay period as an adjustment period.

(C) Applicable adjustment periods. The requirement of this paragraph (b)(4)(ii)(C) is satisfied only if, in the case of a nonhighly compensated employee, the lowest employer-provided benefit of such employee on any day during an adjustment period is taken into account for at least either the current adjustment period (i.e., the period during which the change in employer-provided benefit occurred) or the adjustment period immediately following the effective date of the benefit change. In the case of a highly compensated employee, the highest employer-provided benefit of such employee on any day during an adjustment period must be taken into account for at least either the current adjustment period or the adjustment period immediately following the effective date of the benefit change.

(5) Transition rule for 1989. (i) In general. For any testing year that begins prior to July 1, 1989, the employer may apply the nondiscrimination rules of section 89 (including the rules of Q&A-2 of this section) with respect to its health plans for such testing year in accordance with the rules in paragraph (b)(5)(ii) through (iv) of this Q&A-5.

(ii) Partial testing year. The facts with respect to all employees of the employer as of the testing day for the testing year are to be treated as in existence for the entire partial testing year. The partial testing year begins on the earliest of July 1, 1989; the testing day for such testing year; or the first day of the calendar month beginning three months before the end of the testing year. The last day of the partial testing year is the last day of such testing year.

(iii) Adjustments. The employer-provided benefit (received or made available) of an employee determined as of the testing day is to be adjusted for the partial testing year as required under this paragraph (b) for elections and plan design changes occurring during the partial testing year as if the partial testing year were the entire testing year.

(iv) Annualization of employer-provided benefit. The employer-provided benefit (received or made available) of an employee for the partial testing year (determined after the application of the other rules in this paragraph (b)(5)) is multiplied by the applicable fraction for the testing year and such product is deemed to be the employer-provided benefit (received or made available) of the employee for the testing year for purposes of applying the section 89 nondiscrimination tests to such testing year. The numerator of the applicable fraction for a testing year is the total number of calendar months in the testing year and the denominator of such fraction is the number of calendar months in the partial testing year.

(v) Transition rule inapplicable with respect to certain plans. (A) Changes in plan terms. The rule of this paragraph (b)(5) is not available with respect to a health plan that provides an employer-provided benefit for the partial testing year that is less, by more than a de minimis amount, than such plan's employer-provided benefit for the portion of the testing year that precedes the partial testing year. Thus, for example, the rule of this paragraph (b)(5) is not available if an employer amends its health plan to provide that employee contributions for coverage during the partial testing year are to be in the form of after-tax employee contributions rather than salary reduction contributions. See paragraph (c) of Q&A-1 of this section (the nondiscriminatory provisions test).

(B) New plans. The rule of this paragraph (b)(5) is not available with respect to a health plan that is first established, or coverage under a health plan that is first provided, on or after January 1, 1989, and that terminates or ceases to be provided before the end of the partial testing year. Also, such plan or coverage may fail to satisfy the requirement of section 89(k)(1)(E) (that a plan be established with the intention of being maintained for an indefinite period of time).

(C) Certain discriminatory plans. The rule of this paragraph (b)(5) is not applicable with regard to a plan unless, for the testing year, at least 25 percent of those employees eligible to participate in the plan are nonhighly compensated employees or such plan satisfies the alternative 50 percent eligibility test of paragraph (d)(3)(iii) of Q&A-1 of this section. The rules of Q&A-4 of this section are not available in determining whether a plan meets this 25 percent requirement.

(vi) Example. The rules of this paragraph (b)(5) are illustrated in the following example:

Example. Assume that an employer maintains several health plans, one of which has a plan year beginning on January 1, 1989. The employer elects to use a calendar year testing year for purposes of testing its health plans under section 89. Under this paragraph (b)(5), if the employer elects a testing day of July 1, 1989 (or any day after such date and before January 1, 1990), the employer may apply the testing day and benefit adjustment rules of section 89 to the period between July 1, 1989 and January 1, 1990 as if such period were the entire testing year. Thus, for example, only those benefit changes that occur during the partial testing year need to be taken into account under the rules of this paragraph (b). Then, employees' employer-provided benefits (received or made available) for the partial testing year are converted into employer-provided benefits for the full testing year by multiplying each of such benefits by two (i.e., 12/6, which is the applicable fraction, the numerator of which is the total number of calendar months in the testing year and the denominator of which is the number of calendar months in the partial testing year). The section 89 nondiscrimination tests are then applied with respect to such annualized employer-provided benefits.

(c) Testing day. The testing day is the single day within the testing year that is elected in writing as the testing day for purposes of applying the nondiscrimination tests of section 89 with respect to the testing year. The testing day is not required to be designated in the single written document required under section 89(k)(1)(A) (See Q&A-3 of § 1.89(k)-1). If a testing day is not elected in writing, the testing day is the last day of the testing year. All plans of the same type, and plans that are not of the same type but are treated as of the same type for nondiscrimination testing under section 89, must have the same testing day. The testing day for any testing year beginning after December 31, 1990, is the same testing day used for the immediately preceding testing year unless a change in such testing day is made with the consent of the Commissioner or is in accordance with such rules as the Commissioner may provide with respect to changes in testing days. The election of a testing day is subject to the requirements of the nondiscriminatory provisions test of paragraph (c) of Q&A-1 of this section. Thus, an employer's testing day must reasonably reflect the employee pool of the employer and the business of the employer throughout the year.

(d) Sampling. For purposes of determining whether a statutory employee benefit plan is a discriminatory employee benefit plan, an employer may elect in writing to apply the rules of paragraphs (d) and (e) of Q&A-1 of this section (the general eligibility and benefits tests and the alternative 80 percent coverage test, respectively), paragraph (c) of Q&A-2 of this section (the special rule for certain large employers), and paragraph (c)(4) of Q&A-3 of this section (relating to sworn statements) on the basis of a statistically valid random sample of the employer's employees. A sample is statistically valid for purposes of this paragraph (d) only if the statistical method and sample size result in at least a 95 percent probability that the results of the sample with respect to the applicable requirements have a margin of error not greater than 3 percent. Also, the statistical validity of the sample and statistical method and analysis must be confirmed in a written opinion of a qualified and independent third party.

Q-6. What is the period for testing whether the nondiscrimination rules of section 89 are satisfied?

A-6. **(a) Testing year.** *(1) In general.* An employer must apply the nondiscrimination tests of section 89 to its health plans and other statutory employee benefit plans on the basis of a testing year that begins on the first day of a calendar month and ends on the last day of a calendar month, regardless of the beginning of the plan year or years of such plans. Unless the employer elects otherwise in accordance with paragraph (a)(2) of this Q&A-6, the testing year for all statutory employee benefit plans is the calendar year.

(2) Election of different testing year. An employer may elect a uniform 12-month testing year other than the calendar year for purposes of applying the section 89 nondiscrimination tests to all plans of the same type. Thus, for example, an employer may elect to apply the section 89 nondiscrimination tests to all of its health plans on the basis of an April 1 to March 31 testing year. In addition, if the 75 percent benefits test is applied on an aggregate basis to plans of different types (e.g., health plans, group-term life insurance plans, and dependent care assistance programs) as though such plans were plans of the same type, the same testing year must be used with respect to all such plans.

(3) Election. An employer must make the election of a testing year described in paragraph (a)(2) of this Q&A-6 in writing prior to the commencement of the testing year to which the election relates. See paragraph (b)(3) of this Q&A-6 for a transition rule for 1989.

(b) First testing year in 1989. *(1) In general.* Notwithstanding paragraph (a) of this Q&A-6, for the first testing year applicable with respect to plans of the same type, the employer may elect to apply the section 89 nondiscrimination tests with respect to all plans of the same type on the basis of any 12-month period beginning on the first day of any calendar month beginning on or after January 1, 1989, but no later than the first day that any plan of such type first becomes subject to the section 89 nondiscrimination tests. The rule of this paragraph (b) is applicable even though not all of the plans of the same type are subject to the section 89 nondiscrimination tests for the entire first testing year. See paragraph (c) of this Q&A-6 for special rules applicable to the section 89 nondiscrimination tests in such cases. The rule of this paragraph (b)(1) is illustrated in the following example:

Example. Assume that an employer maintains three health plans, Plan A, Plan B and Plan C. Plan A's plan year begins on March 1, Plan B's plan year begins on July 1, and Plan C's plan year begins on September 1. The section 89 nondiscrimination rules apply to plan years that begin after December 31, 1988. For these plans, the employer may elect as its first testing year under section 89 any 12-month period beginning on or after January 1, 1989, and on or before March 1, 1989. This is the case even though not all of the health coverage provided during any of these possible first testing years is subject to the section 89 nondiscrimination tests.

(2) Short testing year. An employer may elect to apply the section 89 nondiscrimination tests to its first testing year commencing in 1989 with respect to all plans of the same type on the basis of a first testing year that is shorter than 12 months in duration. However, if an employer applies the section 89 nondiscrimination tests on the basis of such a short first testing year, the second testing year for such employer for such plans must be 12 months in duration. In addition, in no case may any employer-provided benefit subject to the section 89 nondiscrimination tests either be excluded from consideration in a testing year or considered in more than one testing year. The rule of this paragraph (b)(2) is illustrated in the following example:

Example. Assume that an employer's first testing year in 1989 for its health plans commences on March 1, 1989. The employer may elect to use a first testing year of March 1, 1989, to December 31, 1989, for all of its health plans. In such case, the employer's second testing year must commence on January 1, 1990, and must be 12 months in duration.

(3) Election. (i) First day. An employer must elect the first day of the first testing year beginning in 1989 with respect to plans of the same type in writing prior to the earlier of the first day of the second testing year for such plans or Jan-

uary 1, 1990. If an employer fails to make an election by such required date with respect to plans of the same type, the first day of the first testing year beginning in 1989 for all plans of such type is January 1, 1989.

(ii) Last day. If an employer uses a short testing year for the first testing year beginning in 1989 with respect to plans of the same type, the employer must elect the last day of such year in writing prior to such last day. Thus, for example, if an employer decides to begin the first testing year for its health plans on March 1, 1989, and, after such date, decides to use a calendar year testing year beginning in 1990, the employer must, before December 31, 1989, elect December 31, 1989, as the last day of the first testing year.

(c) Testing where not all plans are subject to section 89. *(1) In general.* If, during a testing year with respect to plans of the same type, there is any employer-provided benefit that is not subject to the section 89 nondiscrimination rules for the entire testing year, the rules of this paragraph (c) apply for purposes of testing and excess benefit calculations.

(2) Testing. All employer-provided benefits available or provided during the first testing year applicable with respect to plans of the same type are taken into account in applying the nondiscrimination tests of section 89. This is the case even if such employer-provided benefits are provided under a plan that is not yet subject to section 89. The rule of this paragraph (c)(2) is illustrated in the following example:

Example. Assume that an employer maintains three health plans. Plan A's plan year begins on March 1, Plan B's plan year begins on July 1, and Plan C's plan year begins on September 1. The section 89 nondiscrimination rules apply to plan years that begin after December 31, 1988. Assume further that the employer elects as its first testing year under section 89 the 12-month period beginning on March 1, 1989. For purposes of applying the nondiscrimination tests of section 89, all health coverage provided during this 12-month period, including coverage under Plans B and C from March 1, 1989, until July 1, 1989, and September 1, 1989, respectively, is taken into account.

(3) Excess benefit calculation. (i) In general. If, during a testing year with respect to plans of the same type, an employer-provided benefit under one plan is not yet subject to the section 89 nondiscrimination rules and another plan subject to section 89 fails to satisfy the nondiscrimination rules, the rules of this paragraph (c)(3) apply for purposes of calculating the amount of excess benefit (if any) that is attributable to employer-provided benefits subject to section 89 for such testing year. Plans that are not of the same type but are being tested under the 75 percent benefits test as if they were of the same type are to be treated as plans of the same type for purposes of this paragraph (c)(3).

(ii) Total excess benefit. The excess benefit for the testing year with respect to plans of the same type is calculated with regard to an employee under the generally applicable rules of section 89 as if all employer-provided benefits provided under such plans during such year were subject to section 89. See Q&A-9 of this section for rules governing the determination of excess benefits.

(iii) Excess benefit subject to section 89. (A) Determination with respect to the 90 percent/50 percent eligibility and 75 percent benefits tests. For purposes of determining excess benefit resulting from the failure of the employer to meet the requirements of paragraph (d)(2) or (d)(4) of Q&A-1 of this section, the portion of an excess benefit that is attributable to employer-provided benefits subject to section 89 for the testing year with respect to the plan or plans being tested is determined by multiplying the excess benefit determined under paragraph (c)(3)(ii) of this Q&A-6 by a fraction. The numerator of the fraction is the total employer-provided benefit for the highly compensated employee under the plan or plans being tested that are subject to section 89, and the denominator is the total employer-provided benefit for the highly compensated employee under the plan or plans being tested for the first testing year, whether or not they are subject to section 89. The rule of this paragraph (c)(3)(iii)(A) is illustrated by the following example:

Example. Assume that an employer maintains two health plans, Plan A and Plan B. The plan years for these plans and the effective dates for these plans for purposes of section 89 are January 1, 1989, and July 1, 1989, respectively. Plan A provides health coverage with an annual employer-provided benefit of $1,000, and Plan B provides health coverage with an annual, employer-provided benefit of $2,000. In each case, the employer-provided benefit for the 1989 year is the same as the benefit for the prior year. With regard to its health plans, the employer uses a 12-month testing year beginning on January 1, 1989. Thus, in applying the section 89 nondiscrimination tests, all health coverage under Plan B for this testing year must be taken into account. Assume that, for the 1989 testing year, the employer determines that a highly compensated employee who was in Plan A and Plan B for the entire testing year has an excess benefit of $500 for the testing period. The applicable fraction for this employee is $2,000/$3,000. The $2,000 numerator represents the annual employer-provided benefit of Plan A ($1,000) because it was subject to section 89 for the entire testing year plus ½ of the annual employer-provided benefit of Plan B ($2,000) because it was only subject to section 89 for ½ of the testing year. The denominator is the annual employer-provided benefit of Plans A and B. Thus, the employee is treated as having received an excess benefit in the amount of $333.33 (i.e., 66-⅔ percent of $500).

(B) Determination with respect to 50 percent eligibility and 80 percent coverage tests. If an excess benefit with regard to a highly compensated employee is attributable to a plan failing to meet the requirements of the 50 percent eligibility test or the 80 percent coverage test, then this paragraph (c)(3)(iii)(B) applies. The portion of an employee's excess benefit that is attributable to employer-provided benefits for the testing year with respect to the plan or plans being tested is determined by multiplying the excess benefit determined under paragraph (c)(3)(ii) of this Q&A-6 by a fraction. The numerator of the fraction is the number of months in the testing year that the plan or plans failing the applicable requirement is subject to section 89, and the denominator is the number of months that constitute such testing year. In the case of plans that have become subject to section 89 at different times during the testing year, which plans are aggregated under the mandatory aggregation requirements of paragraphs (d) and (e) of Q&A-4 of this section, the excess benefit is determined by calculating a weighted average for each of the originally separate plans in the aggregated plan and adding together such weighted averages. The weighted average for each plan is determined by multiplying the excess benefit by a fraction. The numerator of the fraction is the product of the total amount of the employer-provided benefit for the plan year (without regard to whether such coverage was subject to section 89 for the entire testing year) multiplied by the number of months that such plan has been subject to section 89. The denominator is the product of the total amount of the employer-provided benefit for all the plans in the aggregated plan (without regard to whether such coverage was subject to section 89 for the entire testing year) multiplied by the number of months in the testing year.

(d) Changes in testing year. *(1) In general.* Subject to paragraph (d)(2) of this Q&A-6, an employer may elect to change its testing year with respect to plans of the same type if such election is made in writing prior to the beginning of such new testing year. In no case may any such change result in any employer-provided benefit subject to the section 89 nondiscrimination tests not being included in any testing year or being included in more than one testing year. See also paragraph (b)(2) of this Q&A-6 (precluding changes in an employer's second testing year with respect to plans of the same type if the employer has elected a short first testing year for 1989).

(2) Commissioner approval. An employer's election to change its testing year with respect to plans of the same type subject to section 89 may be made without the prior approval of the Commissioner, provided that the first day of the new testing year is on or before January 1, 1991, such change otherwise meets the requirements of paragraph (d)(1) of this Q& A-6, and such change has no discriminatory effect. For all subsequent changes in testing years, the employer must obtain the prior approval of the Commissioner or must meet such requirements as the Commissioner may otherwise prescribe.

(3) Example. The provisions of this paragraph (d) are illustrated as follows:

Example. An employer is using the calendar year as its testing year for its health plans. On October 3, 1990, the employer designates the 12-month period beginning each December 1 as its new testing year, effective December 1, 1990. This is a permissible change in testing year. The result of this designation is that the employer's testing year beginning on January 1, 1990, is a short year ending on November 30, 1990.

Q-7. For purposes of applying section 89(a) to an employer's health plan, what rules apply for determining the employer-provided benefit and calculating the excess benefits?

A-7. **(a) In general.** For purposes of nondiscrimination testing under section 89, the employer-provided benefit under a health plan is the value of the health coverage under the plan that is attributable to employer contributions, determined in accordance with the rules in this Q&A-7. See paragraph (h) of this Q&A-7 for rules governing the determination of the excess benefit (if any) under section 89.

(b) Reasonable valuation methods. *(1) In general.* Prior to the effective date of procedures prescribed by the Secretary in accordance with section 89(g)(3)(B), employers may use any reasonable valuation method for valuing health coverage under each plan for purposes of applying the nondiscrimination tests of section 89. The employer must be able to demonstrate that its method for valuing such health coverage is actuarially reasonable. All features of a health plan must be taken into account under a reasonable method. However, unless the employer is using a reasonable cost method to value health coverage (in accordance with paragraph (c) of this Q&A-7), a reasonable valuation method may disregard those features that have a de minimis effect on the total value of the coverage under the plan and are not disproportionately available to highly compensated employees. The features that are disregarded cannot, in the aggregate, result in a more than de minimis effect on the total value of the plan. If a feature is disregarded as de minimis with respect to one health plan, it must be disregarded with respect to all health plans. An entitlement to a periodic medical diagnostic or physical examination, whether or not required as a condition of employment, is not considered to have a de minimis effect on the total value of the health coverage under the plan and thus the entitlement must be taken into account in valuing coverage even if the plan is available to nonhighly compensated employees on the same or a more favorable basis than it is to highly compensated employees and even for employees who do not actually undergo the covered examinations.

(2) Presumption where value is substantially unrelated to cost. If the employer is not using a cost method permitted under section 4980B to value health coverage (in accordance with paragraph (c) of this Q&A-7), a valuation method is presumed to be unreasonable if the relative values of the plans determined under such method do not reasonably reflect the relative values that would be determined for the plans using a cost method permitted under section 4980B. However, the fact that the relative values of the plans determined by the employer reasonably reflect the relative values of such plans under a cost method permitted under section 4980B does not mean that the valuation method is necessarily reasonable. The provisions of this paragraph (b)(2) are illustrated in the following example:

Example. Assume that an employer maintains three health plans for its employees and does not use a cost method permitted under section 4980B for purposes of determining the employer-provided benefits with respect to these plans. The applicable premiums under the cost method used under section 4980B(f)(4) for these plans are as follows: Plan A, $2,500; Plan B, $2,000; and Plan C, $2,100. Thus, Plan B's value under the cost method is 80 percent of Plan A's value, and Plan C's value is 84 percent of Plan A's value. Under the employer's valuation method, the values of the plans are as follows: Plan A, $1,600; Plan B, $2,400; and Plan C, $400. Thus, under the employer's valuation method, Plan B's value is 150 percent of the value of Plan A, and Plan C's value is 25 percent of Plan A's value. These relative values do not reasonably reflect the relative values under the section 4980B cost method. Thus, the presumption of this paragraph (b)(2) applies, and unless the employer can demonstrate otherwise, its valuation method is not considered reasonable.

(3) De minimis effect. A feature does not have a de minimis effect on the total value of coverage unless it is demonstrably difficult to value such feature and, if it were valued, the feature would be insignificant in value.

(4) Disproportionate ratio. A de minimis feature of a health plan is not considered to be disproportionately available to highly compensated employees if that feature, treated as a separate plan, meets the requirements of paragraph (d)(3) of Q&A-1 of this section (the 50 percent eligibility test). For purposes of this paragraph (b)(4), the availability of the feature is determined based on all health plans of the employer.

(c) Reasonable cost-method. *(1) In general.* An employer is deemed to be using a reasonable valuation method that satisfies the requirements of paragraph (b) of this Q&A-7 if the employer is using a reasonable cost method as described in this paragraph (c) to value its health coverage. The employer must be able to demonstrate that its method for determining the cost of health coverage is actuarially reasonable. The method that the employer uses to determine the applicable premium for purposes of the continuation coverage requirements for group health plans in accordance with section 4980B(f)(4) is deemed to be a reasonable cost method. If a health plan is not subject to the requirements of section 4980B, the employer may calculate cost on the basis of a method permitted to be used for determining an applicable premium under section 4980B(f)(4) as if such plan were subject to that section. A cost method does not fail to be a reasonable valuation method for purposes of section 89 merely because the calculation of cost takes into account the average annual cost under section 4980B(f)(4) of substantially similar coverage for the immediately preceding two years or the immediately preceding year if two years' data are not available or if data for the two years would not be reasonable to use under the facts and circumstances of the case.

(2) Certain permitted adjustments.(i) In general. An employer may elect in writing to make certain adjustments to the cost of health coverage in determining the value of such coverage under a reasonable cost method. These adjustments are intended to eliminate cost differences that are unrelated to the relative value of health coverage. These adjustments may be made only to the extent they have not already been taken into account (if permitted) under the method of determining the applicable premium under section 4980B. If an employer makes an adjustment of the type described in this paragraph (c)(2) with respect to one health plan, the employer must make that same type of adjustment for all health plans. Thus, if an employer maintains two plans providing identical coverage at two geographic locations and elects to make the geographic adjustment permitted in paragraph (c)(2)(ii) with respect to such plans, the employer must make a geographic adjustment to all plans at all locations since the values of these plans are compared to one another under the various tests contained in section 89.

(ii) Geographic adjustment. Costs may be adjusted to eliminate differences in cost solely attributable to the employer's operation in significantly separate geographic locations.

(iii) Demographic adjustment. Costs may be adjusted to eliminate differences in cost solely attributable to the different demographic characteristics (other than family status) of the participants in the plans.

(iv) Utilization adjustment. Costs may be adjusted to eliminate differences in costs solely attributable to differences in the utilization of coverage features common to two or more separate health plans. This adjustment must be made by allocating the total cost for a common feature among all the plans with such feature on the basis of the number of employees covered by such feature under each of the plans. The adjustment under this paragraph (c)(iv) is to be made only after all other adjustments that are permitted in this paragraph (c).

(d) Certain cost containment features. A valuation method is not unreasonable if it fails to make adjustments for bona fide cost containment features, such as second opinion requirements or requirements for physician approval prior to referral for specialized medical care. In addition, a valuation method generally is not reasonable if it makes adjustments based on the method of health benefit delivery (e.g., traditional indemnity plans, health maintenance organizations and preferred provider organizations).

(e) Consistency rule. With the exception of certain multiemployer plans (see section 89(g)(3)(E)), an employer must use the same valuation method (including any permitted adjustment under this Q&A-7) to value all of the health plans that are tested together under section 89.

(f) Health coverage under flexible spending arrangements. In the case of a health plan provided under a flexible spending arrangement (FSA) (as defined in Q&A-7 of § 1.125-2), the value of the coverage for a year generally is equal to the total cost (i.e., required premium or payment) of the coverage for the year, whether or not such cost is paid through employer contributions, including salary reduction contributions, or after-tax employee contributions. If an employer is separately testing employee-only health coverage and family-only health coverage (in accordance with paragraph (c) of Q&A-3 of this section) and health coverage under an FSA is applicable to employees and their family members, the employer may elect to treat 40 percent of the value of the coverage under the health FSA as family-only coverage and 60 percent of such value as employee-only coverage. This election must apply with respect to all employees who have a spouse or dependent. The rule of this paragraph (f) is illustrated in the following example:

Example. Assume that an employer maintains a cafeteria plan under which an employee may elect to reduce his or her salary by any amount of compensation for a year, to a maximum of $2,000, for reimbursements for health expenses. Assume further that the maximum reimbursement for any particular employee under the arrangement for a year is equal to the amount the employee has elected to reduce his or her salary for the year. This arrangement is a health flexible spending arrangement (FSA). Each different amount by which an employee may elect to reduce his or her salary for a year is a separate health plan under the FSA. The salary reduction contributions are employee premium payments for the level of health coverage elected for the year. For purposes of the 90 percent/50 percent eligibility test (if salary reduction contributions are treated as employer contributions under the rules of Q&A-8 of this section), the health plan under the FSA with the largest employer-provided benefit is the plan with a $2,000 maximum reimbursement. Because all employees may elect any level of coverage under the health FSA, all of the health plans included in the health FSA satisfy the 50 percent eligibility test. For purposes of the 75 percent benefits test, if an employee elects to receive health coverage under the FSA providing for the reimbursement of up to $1,200 of health expenses for a year, the value of such coverage received for the year is $1,200. This is the case without regard to whether the employee actually pays the total required premium for the coverage, as long as the employee receives the coverage. Finally, for purposes of the 80 percent coverage test, each different level of coverage under the health FSA is a separate health plan with a value equal to the cost of such level of coverage.

(g) Health coverage attributable to employer contributions. *(1) In general.* The portion of the value of the health coverage of a plan that is attributable to employer contributions is determined by multiplying the value of the health coverage of the plan (determined under paragraphs (b) through (f) of this Q&A-7) by a fraction. The numerator of the fraction is the employer-paid cost of the health plan, and the denominator of the fraction is the sum of the employer-paid cost and the employee-paid cost of the health plan. For this purpose, the cost of a health plan is its actual cost determined under the same method the employer uses to determine the applicable premium (for the same coverage) for health continuation coverage purposes under section 4980B(f)(4) without regard to any of the adjustments permitted in paragraph (c) of this Q&A-7 (other than the adjustment for utilization differences). If a health plan is not subject to the requirements of section 4980B, the employer may calculate cost on the basis of a method permitted to be used for determining an applicable premium under section 4980B(f)(4) as if such plan were subject to that section. For purposes of this Q&A-7, health coverage of a self-employed individual is deemed attributable to employer contributions to the extent that a deduction under section 162(m) is allowable with respect to the coverage. Also, the determination of the extent to which health coverage is attributable to employer or employee contributions is to be made without regard to whether an employee is permitted a deduction with respect to employee contributions under section 213.

(2) Exception. If, for a particular health plan, the employer-paid portion of the cost (treating salary reduction contributions as employer contributions) is less than or equal to 2 percent of the sum of the employer-paid cost and the employee-paid cost of such health plan, the employer may treat such health plan as providing no employer-provided benefit.

(3) Salary reduction contributions. See Q&A-8 of this section for the treatment of salary reduction contributions under a cafeteria plan as either employer or employee contributions.

(h) Calculation of excess benefit. The amount of a highly compensated employee's excess benefit under section 89(b) with respect to a health plan is the cost of the excess benefit based on its actual cost determined under the same method the employer uses to determine the applicable premium for the same coverage for health continuation coverage purposes under section 4980B(f)(4) without regard to any of the adjustments permitted in paragraph (c) of this Q&A-7 (other than the adjustment for utilization differences). This rule applies with respect to both highly compensated and nonhighly compensated employees. Thus, an employer must use the method it uses to determine the applicable premium for all coverage provided in making the determination of excess benefits. See Q&A-9 of this section for further guidance with respect to the determination of excess benefits.

Q-8. How are salary reduction contributions treated for purposes of the section 89 nondiscrimination tests?

A-8. **(a) Treatment of salary reduction contributions.** *(1) In general.* Except as otherwise provided (see, e.g., paragraphs (b) and (c) of this Q&A-8), salary reduction contributions are treated as employer contributions. Thus, for purposes of paragraph (d)(3) (the 50 percent eligibility test), paragraph (d)(4) (the 75 percent benefits test), and paragraph (e) (the 80 percent coverage test) of Q&A-1 of this section, the portion of the value of health coverage that is attributable to salary reduction contributions is treated as attributable to employer contributions and thus as an employer-provided benefit. See paragraph (d)(2) of Q&A-4 of this section for a special rule for the treatment of certain salary reduction contributions for purposes of the mandatory aggregation rule for the 50 percent eligibility test.

(2) Definition of salary reduction contributions. The term "salary reduction contributions" means all employer contributions that are excludable from the gross income of an employee by reason of section 125. Thus, all elective contributions under a cafeteria plan described in section 125 that are excludable from employees' gross incomes are salary reduction contributions, even if such amounts are available in cash or other taxable benefits only if the employee satisfies a specified condition under the plan (e.g., the completion of a statement that the employee has other health plan coverage). This is the case regardless of the manner in which such contributions are described under a plan. For example, amounts that are described as employer or company credits under a cafeteria plan are salary reduction contributions to the extent that such amounts are available to employees in cash or other taxable benefits under the plan, even if, for example, the plan defines salary reduction contributions as only those contributions that are directly and explicitly deducted from employees' regular salaries.

(b) 90 percent/50 percent eligibility test. *(1) In general.* Except as provided in paragraphs (b)(2) and (c) of this Q&A-8, for purposes of paragraph (d)(2) of Q& A-1 of this section (the 90 percent/50 percent eligibility test), salary reduction contributions are treated as employee contributions (rather than employer contributions) in computing the employer-provided benefit available to any employee.

(2) Election to treat as employer contributions. (i) In general. An employer may elect in writing to treat all salary reduction contributions as employer contributions for purposes of paragraph (d)(2) of Q&A-1 of this section (the 90 percent/50 percent eligibility test). An employer may not elect to treat some, but not all, salary reduction contributions as employer contributions. An employer election under this paragraph (b)(2) applies with respect to all salary reduction contributions with regard to plans of the same type whether or not the plans are part of the same cafeteria plan.

(ii) Requirements to qualify for election. (A) In general. In order to make an election under this paragraph (b)(2), an employer must meet the requirements of paragraphs (b)(2)(ii)(B) through (b)(2)(ii)(D) of this Q&A-8.

(B) Plan must be available on same terms. This requirement is satisfied only if all of the benefits available under each cafeteria plan are available on the same terms and conditions to all employees eligible to participate under such plans.

(C) Nonhighly compensated employees may not comprise a disproportionate portion of those eligible to participate. This requirement is satisfied only if the nonhighly compensated eligibility percentage for each cafeteria plan does not exceed the highly compensated eligibility percentage for each such plan. The nonhighly compensated eligibility percentage is the percentage determined by dividing the number of nonhighly compensated employees eligible to participate in the cafeteria plan by the total number of nonhighly compensated employees, and the highly compensated eligibility percentage is the percentage determined in the same manner by reference only to highly compensated employees.

(D) No highly compensated employee with benefits outside cafeteria plan. This requirement is satisfied only if no highly compensated employee eligible to participate in a cafeteria plan is eligible to participate in any other statutory employee benefit plan that is of the same type as a plan available under the cafeteria plan unless such other statutory employee benefit plan (whether inside or outside of a cafeteria plan) is available on the same terms and conditions to all nonhighly compensated employees that are eligible to participate in the cafeteria plan.

(c) Mandatory treatment of salary reduction contributions. *(1) In general.* Notwithstanding paragraphs (b)(1) and (b)(2) of this Q&A-8, if certain conditions set forth in paragraph (c)(2) or (c)(3) of this Q&A-8 are satisfied, an employer is required to treat some or all salary reduction contributions available to highly compensated employees as employer contributions, some or all salary reduction contributions available to nonhighly compensated employees as employee contributions, or both. Paragraph (c)(2) and (c)(3) of this Q&A-8 are applied separately. This mandatory treatment applies only for purposes of applying the 90 percent/50 percent eligibility test of paragraph (d)(2) of Q&A-1 of this section (including the 80 percent/66 percent and 80 percent/80 percent eligibility test alternatives set forth in paragraphs (b) and (c)(6)(iii) of Q&A-2 of this section).

(2) Highly compensated employees. (i) In general. In computing the largest employer-provided benefit available to a highly compensated employee (and for purposes of the excess benefit calculation under paragraph (e) of Q&A-9 of this section), core health coverage attributable to salary reduction contributions is treated as attributable to employer contributions (rather than employee contributions) to the extent that the portion of the core health coverage attributable to salary reduction contributions exceeds 100 percent of the portion of the core health coverage attributable to employer contributions (excluding salary reduction contributions). The rule of this paragraph (c)(2) applies only if the employer has not made the election described in paragraph (b)(2) of this Q& A-8.

(ii) Examples. The rule of this paragraph (c)(2) is illustrated by the following examples:

Example (1). Assume that a highly compensated employee may elect coverage under one of two health plans: Plan A has an employer-provided benefit of $4,000, which is attributable to non-salary reduction, employer contributions; and Plan B (a core health plan) has a total employer-provided benefit of $5,200 (i.e., $3,200 attributable to non-salary reduction, employer contributions and $2,000 attributable to salary reduction contributions). This paragraph (c)(2) does not require that any of the salary reduction contributions for Plan B be treated as employer contributions for purposes of determining the plan with the largest employer-provided benefit available to this highly compensated employee. Thus, for purposes of the 90 percent/50 percent eligibility test and assuming that the employer has not made the election under paragraph (b)(2) of this Q&A-8, Plan A is the plan with the largest employer-provided benefit available to this employee.

Example (2). Assume the same facts as Example 1, except that Plan B's total employer-provided benefit of $5,200 is comprised of $2,500 attributable to non-salary reduction, employer contributions and $2,700 attributable to salary reduction contributions. This paragraph (c)(2) requires that $200 of the salary reduction contributions for Plan B (i.e., the excess of the salary reduction contributions over the non-salary reduction, employer contributions) be treated as employer contributions for purposes of determining the plan with the largest employer-provided benefit available to this highly compensated employee. Thus, for purposes of the 90 percent/50 percent eligibility test, Plan B is treated as having an employer-provided benefit of $2,700. However, Plan A still is the plan with the largest employer-provided benefit available to this highly compensated employee.

Example (3). Assume the same facts as in Example 1, except that Plan B has a total employer-provided benefit of $8,000 (i.e., $3,500 attributable to non-salary reduction, employer contributions and $4,500 attributable to salary reduction contributions). This paragraph (c)(2) requires that $1,000 of the salary reduction contributions for Plan B (i.e., the excess of the salary reduction contributions over the non-salary reduction, employer contributions) be treated as employer contributions for purposes of determining the plan with the largest employer-provided benefit available to this highly compensated employee. Thus, for purposes of the 90 percent/50 percent eligibility test, Plan B is treated as having an employer-provided benefit of $4,500 and, accordingly, is the plan with the largest employer-provided benefit available to this highly compensated employee.

Example (4). Assume the same facts as in Example 3, except that the highly compensated employee also may elect health coverage under a flexible spending arrangement (FSA) providing for health expense reimbursements up to and including $5,000. Because health FSAs are not core health plans, this FSA is disregarded in applying this paragraph (c)(2). Thus, the manner in which such health FSA, the employer-provided benefit of which is wholly attributable to salary reduction contributions, is taken into account for purposes of the 90 percent/50 percent eligibility test depends upon whether salary reduction contributions are generally disregarded or are generally taken into account as employer contributions for purposes of such test.

Example (5). Assume the same facts as Example 3, except that the highly compensated employee also has available Plan C, a dental plan not funded through salary reduction and with an employer-provided benefit of $500. Since the dental plan is not a core health plan, it is not considered in determining whether salary reduction contributions are treated as employer contributions under this paragraph (c)(2). However, the employer-provided benefit of the dental plan is added to the total employer-provided benefit available to the highly compensated employee in determining the largest employer-provided benefit available to any highly compensated employee.

(3) Nonhighly compensated employees. In computing the employer-provided benefit available to a nonhighly compensated employee, core health coverage attributable to salary reduction contributions is treated as attributable to employee contributions (rather than employer contributions) to the extent that the portion of the core health coverage attributable to salary reduction contributions exceeds 100 percent of the portion of the core health coverage attributable to employer contributions (excluding salary reduction contributions). The rule of this paragraph (c)(3) applies only if the employer has made the election described in paragraph (b)(2) of this Q&A-8.

(4) Transition rule. This paragraph (c) does not apply with respect to testing years beginning before January 1, 1990.

(d) Certain part-time employees. See section 89(g)(3)(D)(i) for the treatment of salary reduction contributions for employees described in section 89(j)(5).

Q-9. How is an excess benefit under the section 89 nondiscrimination rules to be determined with respect to health plans?

A-9. **(a) In general.** A highly compensated employee's excess benefit under a discriminatory employee benefit plan that is a health plan for a testing year generally is determined in accordance with the rules for applying the requirements of section 89 for the testing year and with the modifications set forth in this Q&A-9. Because the method for determining excess benefits thus differs from the method for applying the nondiscrimination tests of section 89, a statutory employee benefit plan that is a discriminatory employee benefit plan under the nondiscrimination tests may, in some circumstances, not have any excess benefit under this Q&A-9. Similarly, a statutory employee benefit plan is treated as not having an excess benefit under this Q&A-9 if such plan satisfies the applicable nondiscrimination tests of section 89 and thus is not a discriminatory employee benefit plan. See paragraph (b) of Q&A-1 of this section. This is the case even if such plan would be determined to have an excess benefit under the rules of this Q&A-9 if such rules were applicable to such plan. See paragraph (h) of Q&A-7 of this section for the requirement that, for purposes of determining the amount of excess benefit, the value of the benefit of all employees must be determined under the same method the employer uses for determining the applicable premium for health continuation coverage purposes under section 4980B(f)(4) and the nondiscrimination tests reapplied on such basis. In addition, see paragraph (c) of Q&A-6 for rules relating to the determination of excess benefits for testing years beginning in 1989 if some, but not all, of the employer-provided benefits for such years are subject to the section 89 nondiscrimination rules.

(b) Determination made under failed requirements. *(1) In general.* A highly compensated employee's excess benefit under a discriminatory employee benefit plan is determined under the failed requirements of paragraphs (c), (d) and (e) of Q&A-1 of this section. Thus, for example, if each health plan satisfies the 50 percent eligibility test, but the health plans collectively fail to satisfy the 75 percent benefits test, excess benefits are to be determined only under the 75 percent benefits test. However, an employer may elect in writing to use the 80 percent coverage test to determine excess benefits without regard to whether it used that test in determining compliance with section 89. Similarly, the employer may elect in writing to use the tests described in paragraphs (c) and (d) of Q&A-1 of this section to determine excess benefits even if it initially used the 80 percent coverage test to determine whether its plans are discriminatory.

(2) Failure of more than one requirement. Where an employer's health plans of the same type fail to meet more than one requirement of Q&A-1 of this section, the excess benefit calculations for the failed requirements are to be made in the following order: the 50 percent eligibility test; the 90 percent/50 percent eligibility test; and the 75 percent benefits test. If a highly compensated employee is determined to have an excess benefit under the 50 percent eligibility test, then for purposes of determining such employee's excess benefit (if any) under the 90 percent/50 percent eligibility test, such employee's employer-provided benefit for purposes of the 90 percent/50 percent eligibility test excess benefit calculation is first reduced by the amount of such employee's excess benefit determined under the 50 percent eligibility test excess benefit calculation. If a portion of the employer-provided benefit of the plan that failed the 50 percent eligibility test is attributable to salary reduction contributions, then the same portion of an employee's excess benefit with respect to such plan is treated as attributable to salary reduction contributions. For purposes of determining excess benefits under the 75 percent benefit test, a highly compensated employee's employer-provided benefit under the plan or plans that failed the 50 percent eligibility test or the 90 percent/50 percent eligibility test (or both) is first reduced by the amount of such employee's excess benefit with respect to such test or tests.

(c) Highly compensated employees and the employer-provided benefit taken into account for purposes of determining excess benefit. *(1) In general.* For purposes of making the excess benefit calculations under this Q&A-9, all highly compensated employees who receive employer-provided benefits for a testing year under a plan or plans that fail the applicable nondiscrimination test are eligible to be treated as receiving excess benefits. This is the case even though such highly compensated employees were not taken into account for any reason on the testing day for such testing year. In addition, only employer-provided benefits that highly compensated employees actually receive for a testing year under a plan or plans that fail the applicable nondiscrimination test may be treated as excess benefits. Thus, for example, a highly compensated employee does not have an excess benefit with respect to a plan that fails the 50 percent eligibility test merely because such employee is eligible to receive, but does not actually receive, employer-provided benefits (e.g., health plan coverage) under such plan. Similarly, employer-provided benefits that highly compensated employees do not actually receive but were treated as having received under the rules providing for the annualization and adjustment of the employer-provided benefits for the testing day are not treated as excess benefits.

(2) Special rule. In the case of the first testing year beginning in 1989 of an employer that is using the transition rule included in paragraph (b)(5) of Q&A-5 of this section, the excess benefits (if any) for such testing year may be determined by reference to those employer-provided benefits that highly compensated employees actually receive for the partial testing year, annualized for the entire testing year as provided in paragraph (b)(5)(iv) of Q&A-5 of this section. If an employer elects to determine excess benefits in accordance with the preceding sentence, the employer must provide those highly compensated employees having excess benefits an opportunity to demonstrate that they actually received less employer-provided benefits during the portion of the testing year preceding the partial testing year than the deemed employer-provided benefits under paragraph (b)(5) of Q&A-5 of this section. If an employee makes such a demonstration, the employer must recalculate such employee's excess benefit based on the employer-provided benefits actually received for the entire testing year and make any amendments to required reports relating to such employee (e.g., Form W-2). This special rule is not available with respect to a plan for which paragraph (b)(5) of Q&A-5 of this section is inapplicable.

(d) 50 percent eligibility test. A highly compensated employee's excess benefit under a health plan that fails to satisfy the 50 percent eligibility test of paragraph (d)(3) of Q&A-1 of this section is equal to that portion of the employer-provided benefit actually received by such employee under the plan that is in excess of the maximum employer-provided benefit that such plan may have and be included in a group of comparable plans under paragraph (b) of Q&A-4 of this section that satisfies the 50 percent eligibility test. The rule of this paragraph (d) is illustrated as follows:

Example. An employer maintains two health plans, Plan A and Plan B. Plan A has an employer-provided benefit of $3,000 and is automatically provided to all employees of the employer other than those eligible for Plan B. Plan B has an employer-provided benefit of $4,000 and is available to all employees who earn more than $100,000. Plan B fails to satisfy the 50 percent eligibility test. As a result, each highly compensated employee who actually receives coverage under Plan B is treated as receiving an excess benefit with respect to such plan. The employer-provided benefit under Plan B must be reduced by $842 to $3,158 ($3,000 is 95 percent of $3,158), in order for Plan B to be included in a group of comparable plans with Plan A under paragraph (b) of Q&A-4 of this section. Thus, for a highly compensated employee who received a full $4,000 employer-provided benefit under Plan B, the amount of the excess benefit with respect to Plan B is $842.

(e) 90 percent/50 percent eligibility test. A highly compensated employee's excess benefit under plans of the same type that fail to satisfy the 90 percent/50 percent eligibility test of paragraph (d)(2) of Q&A-1 of this section is equal to that portion of the employer-provided benefit actually received by such employee under such plans that is in excess of 200 percent of the largest amount of employer-provided benefit available to at least 90 percent of the employer's nonhighly compensated employees. For this purpose, benefits attributable to salary reduction contributions by nonhighly compensated employees are not treated as employer-provided benefits, even if the employer has made the election provided under paragraph (b)(2) of Q&A-8 of this section. In addition, benefits with respect to highly compensated employees that are attributable to salary reduction contributions are not treated as employer-provided benefits except to the extent that such contributions are treated as employer contributions with regard to such employees under paragraph (c)(2) of Q&A-8 of this section. The rule of this paragraph (e) is illustrated as follows:

Example. Assume that an employer maintains numerous health plans for its employees. For a testing year, the largest employer-provided benefit available to any highly compensated employee, determined under the 90 percent/50 percent eligibility test, is $12,000. Because only 75 percent of the employer's nonhighly compensated employees have available to them an employer-provided benefit of at least $6,000, the employer's health plans fail to satisfy the 90 percent/50 percent eligibility test. As a result, the highly compensated employees who receive coverage under one or more health plans are treated as receiving an excess benefit. If, for this testing year, 90 percent of the employer's nonhighly compensated employees have available to them an employer-provided health benefit of at least $4,500, a highly compensated employee is treated as receiving an excess benefit to the extent such employee actually receives (rather than is eligible to receive) an employer-provided benefit under all health plans in excess of $9,000 (i.e., 200 percent of $4,500). If the largest amount of employer-provided benefit that is available to 90 percent of the employer's nonhighly compensated employees were $3,000 (instead of $4,500), a highly compensated employee's excess benefit would be the amount of such employee's employer-provided benefit that is in excess of $6,000. If no amount of employer-provided benefit is available to 90 percent or more of the nonhighly compensated employees, then all highly compensated employees have excess benefits equal to their total employer-provided benefits received for the testing year.

(f) 75 percent benefits test. *(1) In general.* A highly compensated employee's excess benefit under plans of the same type that fail to satisfy the 75 percent benefits test of paragraph (d)(4) of Q&A-1 of this section is determined under the rules of this paragraph (f). If plans of different types are tested together under paragraph (f)(2)(ii) of Q&A-1 of this section, then such plans are treated as plans of the same type for purposes of this paragraph (f).

(2) Reapply test. The 75 percent benefits test is to be reapplied for the testing year with respect to those plans of the same type by taking into account, in accordance with paragraph (c) of this Q&A-9, all highly compensated employees of the employer and the employer-provided benefits that such employees actually received for the testing year. If upon such reapplication of the 75 percent benefits test, such test is satisfied, there are no excess benefits under section 89(b) with respect to such test.

(3) Amount of excess benefit. Excess benefits under the 75 percent benefits test are determined by reducing the employer-provided benefit of the highly compensated employee or employees with the highest amount of employer-provided benefit for the testing year, under the 75 percent benefits test as reapplied in accordance with this paragraph (f), until either such employee's employer-provided benefit is equal to the next highest amount of employer-provided benefit for any highly compensated employee or if no next highest such employee exists, until the employee no longer has any employer-provided benefit. This method of reduction is then applied with respect to additional highly compensated employees (beginning with highly compensated employees with the highest remaining amounts of employer-provided benefits) until the 75 percent benefits test is satisfied in accordance with this paragraph (f). A highly compensated employee's excess benefit is equal to the total amount of such employee's employer-provided benefit that is reduced under this paragraph (f).

(g) 80 percent coverage test. *(1) In general.* A highly compensated employee's excess benefit under a plan that fails to satisfy the 80 percent coverage test of paragraph (e) of Q&A-1 of this section is equal to that portion of the employer-provided benefit received by such employee under the plan that is in excess of the maximum employer-provided benefit that such plan may have and be included in a group of comparable plans under paragraphs (c)(1) through (c)(4) of Q&A-4 of this section that satisfies the 80 percent coverage test.

(2) Examples. The rule of this paragraph (g) is illustrated in the following examples:

Example (1). An employer maintains numerous health plans. All but one of such employer's health plans are included in a group of comparable plans determined in accordance with paragraph (c)(5) of Q&A-4 of this section (employee cost comparability). Because over 80 percent of the employer's nonhighly compensated employees are covered by a plan included in the group of comparable plans, each of the plans in such group satisfies the 80 percent coverage test. The deemed employer-provided benefit for the group of comparable plans is $3,780. Plan F, which has an employer-provided benefit of $5,000, is not included in the group of comparable plans and thus such plan fails the 80 percent coverage test. If Plan F's employer-provided benefit were reduced by $800 to $4,200 ($3,780 is 90 percent of $4,200), it could be included in the group of comparable plans under the rules of paragraph (c)(1) of Q&A-4 of this section. Similarly, if Plan F's employer-provided benefit were reduced by $1,221 to $3,779, it could be included in the group of comparable plans under the rules of paragraph (c)(4) of Q&A-4 of this section. As a result, each highly compensated employee who receives coverage under Plan F is treated as receiving an excess benefit of $800 (the lesser of $800 and $1,221) with respect to such plan.

Example (2). Assume the same facts as Example 1 except that the plan that is not included in the group of comparable plans fails the 50 percent eligibility test of paragraph (b) of Q&A-4 of this section. Under paragraph (c)(3) of Q&A-4 of this section, the eligibility test must be satisfied before the plan may be included in a group of comparable plans in determining whether the 80 percent coverage test is satisfied. Thus, the excess benefit for Plan F must include the amount necessary to permit such plan to satisfy the 50 percent eligibility test. In this example, this would occur if Plan F's employer-provided benefit were reduced by $1,021 to $3,979 ($3,780 is 95 percent of $3,979).

Q-10. What are the effective dates of the section 89 nondiscrimination and qualification rules?

A-10. **(a) Effective date.** *(1) In general.* Except as otherwise provided in this Q&A-10, the nondiscrimination rules of sections 89(a)-(j) and 89(l)-(m) and the qualification rules of section 89(k) apply for plan years beginning after December 31, 1988.

(2) Collectively bargained plans. (i) In general. In the case of a collectively bargained plan that is adopted pursuant to one or more collective bargaining agreements ratified prior to March 1, 1986, section 89 does not apply to such plan with respect to employees included in a unit of employees covered by any of such collective bargaining agreements in years beginning before the earlier of January 1, 1991, or the date on which the last collective bargaining agreement relating to the plan expires (determined without regard to extensions after February 28, 1986).

(ii) Definition of collectively bargained plan. A collectively bargained plan is a plan covering only eligible individuals who are included in a unit of employees covered by an agreement that is a collective bargaining agreement entered into between employee representatives and one or more employers (as determined under section 7701(a)(46)). A plan that is maintained pursuant to two or more collective bargaining agreements is treated as two or more collectively bargained plans to the extent that the employer-provided benefits provided pursuant to the agreements are not uniform. Thus, for example, if a multiemployer plan is maintained pursuant to three collective bargaining agreements, two of which provide for an identical benefit structure and one of which provides for a different benefit structure, the plan is treated as two separate, collectively bargained plans for purposes of this paragraph (a)(2).

(iii) Plans benefiting non-collectively bargained employees. If a plan provides employer-provided benefits to employees who are included in a unit of employees covered by a collective bargaining agreement and to employees who are not included in any such unit of employees (i.e., non-collectively bargained employees), the non-collectively bargained employees are treated as covered by a plan that is not a collectively bargained plan for purposes of this paragraph (a)(2). Thus, the delayed effective date of paragraph (a)(2)(i) of this Q&A-10 is available only with respect to the portion of the plan that provides employer-provided benefits to the collectively bargained employees.

(iv) Treatment of collectively bargained employees as excludable employees. Unless the employer elects otherwise, employees who receive employer-provided benefits under a collectively bargained plan to which section 89 does not yet apply by reason of this paragraph (a)(2) are to be treated as excludable employees (i.e., as though they were described in section 89(h)) for purposes of applying the nondiscrimination tests of section 89 to plans that are subject to section 89. However, an employer may elect in writing not to treat such collectively bargained employees as excludable employees for purposes of applying section 89 to plans that are subject to section 89. Such an election must be made with respect to all collectively bargained employees, regardless of bargaining unit, and once made applies to all subsequent testing years. Such an election does not accelerate the otherwise applicable effective date with respect to the application of the qualification rules of section 89(k) to such collectively bargained plan or plans. However, if the employer makes an election under this paragraph (a)(2)(iv), then the nondiscrimination rules of section 89 are effective with respect to such plan or plans and thus a highly compensated employee within the group of otherwise excludable employees (i.e., nonexcludable by reason of such election), may have an excess benefit under section 89(b).

(v) Examples. The provisions of this paragraph (a)(2) are illustrated by the following examples:

Example (1). A collective bargaining agreement ratified in January 1986 is scheduled to expire on December 31, 1992. Such agreement provides for contributions by an employer to a multiemployer plan providing health coverage. Assuming that no employee who is included in the collective bargaining unit receives health coverage from the employer other than coverage under the multiemployer plan, the collective bargaining employees and their health coverage may be disregarded by the employer in applying the section 89 nondiscrimination tests for any period before January 1, 1991.

Example (2). Employer X maintains two health plans, Plan A (covering non-collectively bargained employees) and Plan B (covering collectively bargained employees). Plan B is a multiemployer plan that has an effective date for purposes of section 89 of January 1, 1991. Plan A is an insurance plan with a policy that expires on June 30, 1989. The collectively bargained employees receiving benefits under Plan B may be treated as excludable employees until January of 1991 and their health coverage may be disregarded by Employer X in applying the nondiscrimination tests of section 89 until that date. However, before that date, Employer X may elect to take such collectively bargained employees (and their employer-provided benefits) into account for purposes of testing Plan A for periods prior to January of 1991.

(b) Definition of plan year. *(1) In general.* Except as provided in paragraph (b)(2) or (b)(3) of this Q&A-10, for purposes of determining the applicable effective date of section 89 with respect to a plan, the plan year is the year that is designated as the plan year in the written plan. For plans other than health and group-term life insurance plans, if there is no such designation, the plan year is the calendar year. For purposes of this rule, the designation of a plan year solely for purposes of filing the Form 5500 is to be disregarded.

(2) Certain health and group-term life insurance plans. (i) Insured plans. If a health or group-term life insurance plan's plan year is not clearly ascertainable from a written plan document adopted and in existence on January 1, 1989, and the plan is provided under an arrangement through an insurance company, the policy year is the applicable plan year for effective date purposes. If there is no policy year, the employer may elect in writing either the limit/deductible year, the calendar year, or the employer's fiscal year as the applicable plan year for effective date purposes. If the employer does not make such an election, the applicable plan year is the calendar year. An arrangement is not provided through an insurance company for purposes of this paragraph (b) if the insurance company provides merely administrative services under the arrangement.

(ii) Self-insured plans. If a health or group-term life insurance plan's plan year is not clearly ascertainable from a written plan document adopted and in existence on January 1, 1989, and the coverage under such plan is not provided under an arrangement through an insurance company, the employer may elect in writing either the limit/deductible year, the calendar year, or the employer's fiscal year as the applicable plan year for effective date purposes. If the employer does not make such an election, the applicable plan year is the calendar year.

(iii) Limit/deductible year. The limit/deductible year is the year with respect to which the plan's benefit and deductible limits are applied, except that if different years are used for benefit limit purposes and for deductible limit purposes, it means the limit or deductible year that commences earlier in the calendar year.

(3) Special rule to prevent delay of the section 89 effective date. (i) In general. Notwithstanding paragraphs (b)(1) and (b)(2) of this Q&A-10, in the case of a health or group-term life insurance plan with respect to which the first day of the first plan year beginning after December 31, 1988 (determined under paragraphs (b)(1) and (b)(2)), is later during the calendar year than the first day of the first plan year (also determined under such paragraphs) beginning in 1988, the first plan year beginning after December 31, 1988, is deemed to begin on the day that is 12 months after the first day of the plan's first plan year beginning in 1988. Thus, section 89 becomes effective with respect to such plan on the first anniversary date of the plan's first plan year beginning in 1988. In addition, for purposes of this Q&A-10, a plan's last plan year beginning in 1988 is not treated as longer than 12 months in duration. Thus, for example, an agreement between an employer and insurance company to extend for longer than 12 months the last plan year of a health plan beginning in 1988 is not recognized for purposes of determining the applicable section 89 effective date with respect to such plan. Such plan is treated as commencing a new plan year on the day that is 12 months after the first day of the last plan year commencing in 1988.

(ii) Exceptions. (A) In general. Except as provided in paragraph (b)(3)(iii) of this Q&A-10, paragraph (b)(3)(i) of this Q&A-10 does not apply to the extent that any of the tests described in this paragraph (b)(3)(ii)(B) through (D) are satisfied.

(B) Three-month rule. A plan is a health plan and the first day of the plan's first plan year beginning after December 31, 1988, is not more than 3 months later during the calendar year than the first day of the plan's first plan year beginning in 1988 and the selection of the new plan year was for bona fide business reasons unrelated to section 89 (e.g., by reason of a merger or acquisition).

(C) New carrier rule. A plan is a health plan and the health coverage for the plan's first plan year beginning after December 31, 1988, is provided through an insurance arrangement with an insurance company unrelated to any insurance company that provided health coverage under the plan for the first day of the plan's first plan year beginning in 1988 and such change in insurance carriers and the selection of the new plan year were for bona fide business reasons unrelated to section 89.

(D) Uniform plan year. The first day of the plan's first plan year beginning after December 31, 1988, is the same day during the calendar year on which commenced in 1988 the plan year or years of the plan or plans of the same type that provided, in the aggregate, at least 25 percent of the total employer-provided benefits provided under all plans of the same type during 1988 and the selection of the new plan year was for bona fide business reasons unrelated to section 89. This rule may be applied in the case of a merger or acquisition by treating such transaction as having occurred on December 31, 1987.

(iii) Retroactive plan year changes. This paragraph (b)(3) is to be applied by disregarding any change in a plan year that is made after the commencement of such plan year.

(iv) Additional rules. The Commissioner may, through revenue rulings, notices, and other guidance of general applicability, provide such additional exceptions to paragraph (b)(3)(i) of this Q&A-10 as are appropriate if such exceptions do not have the effect of permitting employers to delay significantly the effective date of section 89 with respect to their plans without any significant, independent business reason.

(4) New plans. For purposes of this Q&A-10, a plan is not treated as a new plan commencing in calendar year 1989, unless such plan provides coverage and benefits that are substantially different from the coverage and benefits previously provided by a plan in calendar year 1988.

(5) Certain dispositions or acquisitions. If a person becomes or ceases to be a member of a group described in section 414(b), (c), (m) or (o) on or before December 31, 1988, the transitional rule of section 89(j)(8) is not applicable with respect to any plan of such person or of any member of such group unless the requirements of section 89 were met immediately before such change in the group. This determination is to be made as though section 89 (and this section) were effective with respect to all such plans of such person. Alternatively, for testing years beginning in 1989, the nondiscrimination rules of section 89 may be applied separately to the separate portions of the group under section 414(b), (c), (m) and (o) involved in the change of the group as if such portions did not become part of the same group until December 31, 1989.

Proposed § 1.89(k)-1 Qualification requirements for certain employee welfare benefit plans. [*For Preamble, see ¶ 151,141*]

• ***Caution:*** This Notice of Proposed Rulemaking was partially withdrawn by Notice of Proposed Rulemaking 72-150, 08/06/2007. Reg. §§ 1.89(a)(1) and 1.89(k)-1 remain proposed.

• ***Caution:*** Q&A-6(c) and (d) of proposed regulation § 1.125-2 were withdrawn by notice of proposed rulemaking 62-216, 11/7/97, 62 Fed. Reg. 60196.

• ***Caution:*** Q&A-6(f) of proposed regulation § 1.125-2 was withdrawn on 11/7/97, 62 Fed. Reg. 60196.

Caution: The Treasury has not yet amended Reg § 1.89(k)-1 to reflect changes made by P.L. 101-140.

The following is a list of the questions addressed in this section.

Q–1: What is required under section 89(k)?

Q–2: What plans must meet the requirements of section 89(k)?

Q–3: What is required under the writing requirement of section 89(k)(1)(A)?

Q–4: When is a plan legally enforceable within the meaning of section 89(k)(1)(B)?

Q–5: What constitutes reasonable notification of employees under section 89(k)(1)(C)?

Q–6: How does an employer meet the exclusive benefit requirement of section 89(k)(1)(D)?

Q–7: How is it determined whether a plan is established with the intent of being maintained for an indefinite period of time?

Q–8: What are the sanctions for failure to meet the qualification requirements of section 89(k)?

Q-1. What is required under section 89(k)?

A-1. **(a) In general.** Section 89(k) imposes the following requirements on employers maintaining certain employee benefit plans as described in Q&A-2 of this section: the plan must be in writing; employees within the class of employees designated in the plan as eligible for participation must have a legally enforceable right to participate and, if covered under such plan, to receive benefits; employees who are eligible to participate must be provided reasonable notice of the benefits available under such plan; the plan must be maintained for the exclusive benefit of employees; and the plan must be established with the intent that it will be maintained for an indefinite period of time.

(b) Definitions. *(1) Benefit.* For purposes of section 89(k), the term "benefit" or "benefits" means those payments, reimbursements, products and services provided under the plan to a participant on account of such participant's claim, need or event that is covered under the plan. For example, the fair market value of the use of an on-site child care facility by a participant is the benefit under a dependent care assistance program described in section 129. Similarly, reimbursement of a participant's expense incurred for a covered surgical procedure is a benefit under a health plan. Another example of a benefit under a plan is the payment of a death benefit under a group-term life insurance plan to which section 79 applies.

(2) Employer-provided benefit. With respect to section 89(k), the term "employer-provided benefit" means that portion of the benefits received by an individual that is attributable to employer contributions, including salary reduction contributions under a cafeteria plan. See paragraph (f)(3) of Q&A-1 of § 1.89(a)-1 for a definition of "employer-provided benefit" for purposes of the nondiscrimination rules under section 89.

(3) ERISA. The term "ERISA" refers to the Employee Retirement Income Security Act of 1974, as amended.

(4) Salary reduction contributions. The term "salary reduction contributions" means elective contributions under a cafeteria plan described in section 125 that would be taxable to an employee, but for section 125, by reason of such employee's right to receive such amounts as cash or other taxable benefits. See paragraph (a)(2) of Q&A-8 of § 1.89(a)-1 for further guidance regarding the term "salary reduction contributions."

Q-2. What plans must meet the requirements of section 89(k)?

A-2. **(a) In general.** *(1) Types of plans subject to section 89(k).* In general, the following plans are subject to section 89(k): an accident or health plan (sections 106 and 105); a plan of an employer providing group-term life insurance (section 79); a dependent care assistance program (section 129(d)); a qualified tuition reduction program (section 117(d)); a cafeteria plan (section 125(c)); a fringe benefit program providing no-additional-cost services, qualified employee discounts, or employer-operated eating facilities, the benefits from which are excludable from the gross income of the beneficiary under section 132; and a plan of which an organization covered by section 505 is a part. Section 89(k) applies to these plans without regard to whether they are statutory employee benefit plans subject to the nondiscrimination rules of section 89 and without regard to whether they are subject to Title I of ERISA. Also, section 89(k) applies to plans described in this paragraph (a)(1) even though they are maintained by employers that are state or local governments or by the federal government. Finally, except as provided in paragraph (f) of this Q&A-2, section 89(k) also applies to plans described in this paragraph (a)(1) even though they are maintained by organizations exempt from taxation under section 501(a).

(2) Plans maintained by an employer. For purposes of section 89(k), a plan "maintained by an employer" is any plan of, or subsidized by, an employer who employs participants in the plan. A plan is maintained by an employer even if the cost of such plan is borne by the employees through after-tax employee contributions, as long as the value of the coverage under the plan for any employee is greater than such employee's after-tax contributions. See section 79 and the regulations thereunder for rules relating to when a group-term life insurance plan is subject to section 79 and, therefore, to section 89(k). For purposes of this paragraph (a)(2), the term "employee" includes the spouse and dependents of an employee. See also Q&A-6 of this section with regard to individuals who may participate in a plan. In addition, plans of the type described in paragraph (a)(1) of this Q&A-2 that are maintained by one or more "employee organizations," as that term is defined in section 3(4) of ERISA, or that are maintained pursuant to one or more collective bargaining agreements, are maintained by one or more employers and must meet the requirements of section 89(k).

(b) Special rules with respect to accident or health plans. *(1) In general.* For purposes of section 89(k), an accident or health plan providing coverage that is excludable under section 106 must meet the requirements of section 89(k) if benefits under the plan are to be excludable under section 105(b) or (c) or, in the case of a death benefit under a plan described in paragraph (b)(2) of this Q&A-2, under section 101. If employer-provided benefits under an accident or health plan are not excludable under section 105(b) or (c) or section 101 (other than by reason of section 89), the plan is not required to comply with section 89(k). Thus, for example, employer-provided health plans (including plans that provide medical diagnostic examinations) must satisfy section 89(k) in order for the benefits thereunder to be excludable under section 105(b) or (c). An accident or health plan the entire cost of which is borne by the employees on an after-tax contributory basis (as determined under Q&A-7 of § 1.89(a)-1) is not required to meet the requirements of section 89(k). Thus, if employees' required after-tax contributions for health coverage are equal to or exceed the applicable premium for such coverage within the meaning of section 4980B(f)(4), then the health plan does not have an employer-provided benefit (determined under Q&A-7 of § 1.89(a)-1) and thus is not subject to section 89(k).

(2) Accidental death and dismemberment. In order for the employer-provided benefit under an accidental death and dismemberment plan to be excludable under section 101 or 105, the plan must meet the requirements of section 89(k). For purposes of section 89, an accidental death and dismemberment plan is a plan that provides insurance type coverage attributable to employer contributions that are excludable under section 106 and that provides only benefits excludable

from income under either section 105(c) or section 101 (where the benefits are payable on account of, and conditioned principally upon, the accidental death of the employee). If a plan provides for a general death benefit (described in § 1.79-1(a)(1)), it is not an accidental death and dismemberment plan.

(3) Disability and other sick pay plans. Sick pay plans and disability plans are subject to the requirements of section 89(k) only if employer-provided benefits under such plans are excludable from gross income upon receipt by the individual under section 105(b) or (c).

(4) Worker's compensation. A worker's compensation plan that pays amounts from a sickness and disability fund maintained for employees under the laws of the United States, a state or the District of Columbia (i.e., a fund maintained pursuant to a worker's compensation act or a statute in the nature of a worker's compensation act, the benefits from which are excludable under section 104(a)(1)) is not subject to the requirements of section 89(k). However, accident or health plans maintained by the United States, a state or the District of Columbia that provide benefits that are excludable from the income of an employee solely by reason of section 105(b) or (c) are not worker's compensation funds within the meaning of the preceding sentence and thus are subject to the requirements of section 89(k).

(5) Section 401(h) accounts. A section 4019h) account contained in a pension or annuity plan is subject to the requirements of section 89(k) with regard to benefits provided through such account.

(c) Special rules relating to dependent care assistance programs, group legal services plans and educational assistance programs. A dependent care assistance program (within the meaning of section 129(d)) must comply with section 89(k) without regard to whether the employer elects to treat such program as a statutory employee benefit plan as allowed under section 89(i)(2). Similarly, qualified group legal services plans (within the meaning of section 120(b)) and educational assistance programs (within the meaning of section 127(b)) must satisfy section 89(k) requirements, provided the applicable statutory provisions are in effect.

(d) Plans to which section 505 applies. A plan of which an organization covered by section 505 is a part must satisfy the requirements of section 89(k). Such plans include plans providing benefits through organizations described in section 501(c)(9) or 501(c)(17). If section 120 is in effect, plans providing benefits through organizations described in section 501(c)(20) must satisfy the requirements of section 89(k). The requirements of section 89(k) must be met by a plan even if the related organization qualifies as an organization that is part of a plan maintained pursuant to a collective bargaining agreement as described in section 505(a)(2).

(e) Multiemployer plans. If a plan is otherwise subject to section 89(k) and is a multiemployer plan within the meaning of section 3(37) of ERISA, that plan is maintained by all contributing employers and is subject to the requirements of section 89(k).

(f) Church plans. Employee benefit plans of a type described in paragraph (a)(1) of this Q&A-2 that are maintained by organizations described in section 3121(w) (i.e., churches or church-controlled organizations) exclusively for their employees and clergy (including the spouse or dependents of employees or clergy) are not subject to the requirements of section 89(k).

(g) Treatment of statutory employee benefit plans providing excess benefits. A statutory employee benefit plan that provides any amount of employer-provided benefits is subject to the requirements of section 89(k) even though the plan fails to satisfy the nondiscrimination requirements of section 89(a). Thus, for example, an employer-provided health plan that covers medical diagnostic examinations is subject to section 89(k) even if such health plan fails to satisfy the 50 percent eligibility test of section 89 and the entire value of the employer-provided coverage with respect to such plan is treated as an excess benefit under section 89(b).

(h) Dispositions and acquisitions. The rule of section 89(j)(8) does not apply with respect to the requirements of section 89(k). Thus, a plan that is subject to section 89(k) must continue to satisfy such requirements during the transition period (defined under section 89(j)(8)) without regard to the fact that the employer maintaining the plan has been involved in a merger, consolidation, or similar transaction.

(i) Effective date. Generally, see Q&A-10 of § 1.89(a)-1 for the effective date of the qualification requirements of section 89(k). However, the general effective date is subject to the transition rules set forth in this section.

(j) Coordination with ERISA provisions. The reporting, notification and written plan document requirements contained in this section are in addition to, and not in lieu of, any requirements otherwise imposed on employer-provided benefit plans by Title I of ERISA or any other provision of law. The rules contained herein apply for purposes of section 89(k) and no inference should be drawn therefrom regarding the requirements otherwise imposed by Title I of ERISA or any other law.

Q-3. What is required under the writing requirement of section 89(k)(1)(A)?

A-3. **(a) In general.** Section 89(k)(1)(A) requires a plan to be in writing. Generally, this means that all material terms of the plan must be contained, by direct inclusion, by incorporation by reference, or by a combination of these methods, in a single written document.

(b) Requirement of a single written document. *(1) In general.* The writing requirement of section 89(k) must be met with respect to a plan by a single written document. One such document may satisfy the writing requirement for more than one plan.

(2) Incorporation by reference. Written documents relating to the plan are treated as part of the single written document if they are specifically incorporated by reference in the single written document. Section 89(k)(1)(A) is satisfied with respect to a plan if the single written document with regard to such plan either contains all of the plan's material terms or, to the extent a material term is not contained in the single written document, incorporates by reference the document containing such term. Examples of documents which may be so incorporated in the single written document are: contracts with insurance providers; contracts with any other provider of benefits under the plan; contracts with plan administrators of, or consultants to, the plan; documents creating a trust or other funding instrument related to the plan; resolutions of the employer's governing body relating to the creation, operation, maintenance or termination of the plan; collective bargaining agreements; pronouncements made by the employer, an agent of the employer, a plan administrator or other person relating to or concerning a material term in the plan; and all plan-related documents required to be provided to any employee or filed with any regulatory agency or instrumentality of any federal, state, or local governmental body by statute, rule, or regulation, including but not limited to the documentation required to be provided to employ-

ees by the notice requirement of section 89(k)(1)(C) (see Q&A-5 of this section). There is no limitation on the number of single written documents that may incorporate a document by specific reference.

(c) Contents of single written document. *(1) In general.* Certain minimum information must be included in the single written document in order for the plan to satisfy the writing requirement of section 89(k)(1)(A). All material terms of the plan must be included in the single written document. If a material term of an insured plan is not defined in the single written document of the plan or in a document incorporated therein by reference, and such term is stated in the insurance contract, the term has the meaning given it by the insurance company's usual practice. See paragraph (c)(4) of this Q&A-3 for the definition of a material term of a plan. Further, the provisions required to be included in the single written document by paragraphs (c)(2) and (c)(3) of this Q&A-3 are deemed to be material terms.

(2) Recitation of certain qualification requirements. The single written document must contain a recitation of the qualification requirements contained in section 89(k)(1)(B) and (D). Thus, the single written document must state that the employer intends that the plan terms, including those relating to coverage and benefits, are legally enforceable and that the plan is maintained for the exclusive benefit of employees.

(3) Additional requirements under specific exclusion provision. The single written document must include any information or term required by any other applicable provision of the Code or accompanying regulation.

(4) Definition of a material term of a plan. The phrase "material term of a plan" generally means a term relating to an employee's rights to be covered by, participate in, or benefit under a plan. The following are examples of material terms of a plan: the eligibility rules governing plan participation; terms relating to the periods during which coverage or benefits are provided; descriptions of available benefits; the procedures governing participants' elections under the plan, including the period during which an election may be made, the extent to which elections are irrevocable, and the periods with respect to which elections are effective; the manner in which employer contributions may be made under the plan, such as by salary reduction agreements between a participant and the employer and by nonelective employer contributions, as well as any maximum limitation on employer contributions on behalf of any participant; terms relating to the timing or amount of salary reduction or employee contributions to the plan; terms relating to deductibles, co-payments or similar requirements, including any dollar limit on any benefit; conditions precedent or subsequent with regard to a participant's qualification or continued qualification for any coverage or benefit, including any limitations or restrictions relating to benefits, such as a pre-existing condition limitation; provisions relating to the procedure under which claims are to be made and evaluated for reimbursement; provisions relating to health continuation coverage under section 4980B; and the procedures or circumstances under which the plan may be terminated, including a statement, if applicable, that the plan may be terminated at will by the employer.

(d) Timing. *(1) In general.* Except as set forth in paragraph (d)(2) or (d)(3) of this Q&A-3, the material terms of the plan, as well as any amendment, extension, or modification of any of such material terms of the plan, must be in writing prior to the first day for which coverage is provided under an insured or insurance-type plan, or benefits are available under any other type of plan, or prior to the effective date of any amendment, extension or modification of such material terms, as the case may be.

(2) Certain plan modifications. (i) Clarifications of material terms. Where a plan modification constitutes merely a clarification to a material term (i.e., if the change merely clarifies an existing term in the plan and will have a de minimis impact on the individuals eligible or covered under the plan), the plan document need not reflect such modification until 120 days after the effective date of the modification or, if there is no separate effective date, until 120 days after the adoption of such amendment. A clarifying change generally includes a change in the plan language (either by addition or amendment) that reflects the previous intention of the employer with respect to a term of the plan. Whether the change is a clarifying change is to be determined not only by reference to the existing plan provisions and the notices provided to the employees, but also with regard to all of the facts and circumstances including, but not limited to, whether and the extent to which the amended language is consistent with the previous operation of the plan.

(ii) Extension of time where notice provided. If the employer provides reasonable notice satisfying the requirements of section 89(k)(1)(C) relating to the material terms of a plan to those entitled to notice under Q&A-5 of this section prior to the effective date of the plan or prior to the effective date of any addition or amendment to any material term of the plan (including any amendment to the terms contained in documents that are incorporated in the single written document by reference), then the time by which the single written document must meet the requirements of paragraph (d)(1) of this Q&A-3 to reflect such notice (or the related additions or amendments) is extended until 120 days after the effective date of the new plan or modification. However, this rule is available only if the notice contains a statement that the terms of the notice are legally enforceable.

(iii) Certain retroactive modifications. (A) In general. A modification to a material term of a plan does not fail to satisfy section 89(k)(1)(A) or this section merely because such modification applies retroactively to periods prior to the date of adoption of such modification if all of the conditions set forth in paragraph (d)(2)(iii)(B) through (F) are satisfied.

(B) Expansion of coverage or benefits. The modification must constitute an expansion of coverage or benefits under the plan (i.e., results in the plan having a larger value).

(C) Notification. Employees under the plan (including all employees covered under the plan for any portion of the period to which the retroactive coverage applies, regardless of whether they are currently covered) must be reasonably notified (within the meaning of Q&A-5 of this section determined without regard to the last sentence of paragraph (g)(2) of Q&A-5) of the modification within 60 days after its adoption.

(D) Plan amendment. The single written document must be amended to reflect the modification no later than 120 days after the adoption of the modification.

(E) Duration. The modification must continue in effect with respect to all eligible individuals with respect to the plan from the effective date of the modification until 12 months after the date of adoption.

(F) Nondiscrimination. The modification must not discriminate in favor of highly compensated employees.

(iv) Nonmaterial terms. Modification to any term contained in the single written document that is not a material term must be incorporated in the document no later than 120 days after the effective date of the modification or, if there is no separate effective date, no later than 120 days after the adoption of such amendment. Thus, to the extent that the single written document includes nonmaterial terms of the plan, such writing must accurately reflect such nonmaterial terms and any modifications thereto must be incorporated in the single written document within the time set forth in the preceding sentence.

(v) Examples. The requirements of this paragraph (d) are illustrated by the following examples:

Example (1). A plan is amended to change the level of employee contributions required to participate. This constitutes an amendment to a material term of the plan. If the employer properly notifies the employees prior to the amendment being effective, the single written document need not be amended to reflect such change until 120 days after the effective date of such change as long as the notice contains a statement that its terms are legally enforceable.

Example (2). An administration agreement incorporated by reference in the plan document is amended to change the timing of fees paid to the plan administrator. Unless the circumstances indicate that this is a material term, no amendment to the plan document is required until 120 days after the effective date of the new fee agreement. In such case, the single written document must be amended to reflect by specific reference (by an addendum or otherwise) the date of execution of the new fee agreement.

(3) Exception for certain on-site medical and eating facilities. Certain on-site medical and eating facilities are exempt from the requirements of section 89(k)(1)(A). An on-site medical facility is described in this paragraph (d)(3) if it is located and operates exclusively on a work-site of the employer and there is no physician care provided at the site at any time. A wellness program sponsored by the employer may be considered an on-site medical facility. A medical facility is not described in this paragraph (d)(3) unless access to the facility is available on the same terms to each member of a group of employees that is defined under a reasonable classification set up by the employer that does not discriminate in favor of highly compensated employees. An eating facility is described in this paragraph (d)(3) if it is described in and meets the requirements of section 132(e)(2).

(4) Transition rule. A plan is not required to meet the writing requirement of section 89(k)(1)(A) with respect to the first plan year beginning in 1989. For the subsequent plan year, a plan is not required to meet the writing requirement of section 89(k)(1)(A) before the later of the first day of such plan year, and the day following the end of the 12-month period beginning on the first day of the first plan year in 1989 that the plan is subject to section 89. For purposes of this transition rule, the extension of time due to a notice that is described in paragraph (d)(2)(ii) of this Q&A-3 is not available.

Q-4. When is a plan legally enforceable within the meaning of section 89(k)(1)(B)?

A-4. **(a) In general.** A plan is considered legally enforceable only if the conditions required for an employee to participate, receive coverage and obtain a benefit are definitely determinable under the terms of the plan and an employee satisfying such conditions is able to compel such participation, coverage and benefit.

(b) Employer discretion. *(1) Impermissible discretion.* (i) In general. A plan generally is not considered legally enforceable if a decision as to whether to grant or deny participation, coverage or a benefit is discretionary with the employer either pursuant to the terms of the plan or through the operation of the plan. Thus, except as provided in paragraph (b)(2) of this Q&A-4, a plan that permits the employer, either directly or indirectly, through the exercise of discretion, to grant or deny an employee the right to participate, receive coverage or obtain a benefit under the plan for which the employee is otherwise eligible or ineligible (but for the employer's exercise of discretion) violates the requirement of section 89(k)(1)(B). An employer is deemed to have exercised discretion in a manner inconsistent with section 89(k)(1)(B) if the employer imposes conditions or limitations on eligibility for coverage that are not contained in the single written document comprising the plan and have not been included in the notice described in paragraph (d)(2)(ii) of Q&A-3 of this section. Likewise, except as provided in paragraph (c) of this Q&A-4, a plan violates section 89(k)(1)(B) if the employer waives an otherwise applicable condition, restriction or other term contained in the plan if the single written document does not contain objective, clearly ascertainable criteria and procedures under which such condition, restriction or term may be waived. Finally, a plan violates section 89(k)(1)(B) if participation, coverage or benefits under the plan are subject to objective conditions that are within the control of the employer.

(ii) Employer. For purposes of this Q&A-4, the term "employer" includes the plan administrator, fiduciary, trustee, actuary, independent third party, and other persons. Thus, if a plan grants any person the discretion to deny or limit the availability of a plan benefit for which the employee may otherwise be eligible under the plan (but for the exercise of such discretion), and such exercise is not provided for under the terms of the plan through objective criteria or otherwise permissible under this Q& A-4, then the plan violates section 89(k)(1)(B).

(2) Permissible discretion. (i) In general. A plan may permit discretion with respect to the administration of the plan, including the application of objective criteria specifically set forth in the plan. In addition, a plan does not fail to meet the requirements of this Q&A-4 merely because discretion is exercised in accordance with a qualified medical opinion of a physician. Also, if plan coverage or benefits are limited to those employees who satisfy certain objective conditions that are clearly set forth in the single written document and are not generally subject to the employer's discretion, an employer may exercise discretion to the extent reasonably necessary to determine whether the objective conditions have been met.

(ii) Administrative discretion. Administrative discretion means a determination by the employer with respect to participation in, or coverage or benefits under, a plan or with respect to the general operation of a plan to the extent the exercise of such discretion is based exclusively on clearly defined and ascertainable criteria contained in the single written document. The following provisions that permit limited administrative discretion are examples of provisions that do not violate section 89(k)(1)(B), provided that the provisions are described in the single written document prior to the date a claim is incurred by a participant who is affected by the administrative discretion and, when the provisions are made effective, they apply only to claims that have not yet been incurred: a provision allowing for the commencement of benefits under the plan as soon as administratively feasible after a stated date or event; a provision granting the employer authority to determine whether an employee has satisfied the age and service requirements of the plan or is an excludable employee under section 89(h); and a provision stating that the benefits under the plan are limited to an amount equal to the reasonable and customary charge for such services.

(iii) Medical discretion. (A) In general. A health plan does not fail to be legally enforceable merely because coverage or benefits under the plan are conditioned on a qualified medical opinion of a physician. For example, the following plan provisions do not violate the requirements of this Q&A-4: the requirement of a qualified medical opinion of a physician that treatment or benefits are medically necessary or appropriate prior to the provisions of such treatment or benefits under a health plan; the requirement of a second opinion or other cost-containment feature of a health plan that is conditioned on a qualified medical opinion of a physician; and the inclusion under the plan of a managed care program. This is the case even if the qualified opinion is provided by a physician who is an employee of the employer.

(B) Managed care programs. A managed care program is a program that permits the provision of alternative medical care not otherwise available under a health plan for medical conditions that are covered under the plan. A managed care program must operate pursuant to conditions and procedures clearly ascertainable under the plan. That is, the availability of the program as well as a description of the types of cases that may qualify under the program must be contained in the single written document. Also, the provision of alternative medical care must be based on the consent of the employee and a qualified medical opinion of a physician. Such program may also be conditioned upon the consent of the employer.

(iv) Certain benefit limitations. A health plan does not include impermissible discretion merely because the plan limits certain benefits, such as reimbursements, for specified medical claims to those benefits that constitute the "prevailing" or "reasonable and customary" charge for the claim if such charge is determined in accordance with a reasonable, uniform, consistent and nondiscriminatory method. In addition, a health plan does not include impermissible discretion merely because such plan reimburses medical claims in excess of a "prevailing" or "reasonable and customary" charge if such reimbursements are authorized in accordance with reasonable, uniform, consistent, and nondiscriminatory claims review and reimbursement procedures set forth in the single written document.

(c) Certain retroactive modifications in the plan. A modification to a plan's material terms does not fail to satisfy section 89(k)(1)(B) merely because such modification applies retroactively to periods prior to the date of adoption of such modification if all of the conditions set forth in paragraph (d)(2)(iii) of Q&A-3 of this section are satisfied with respect to such modification.

(d) Examples. The requirements of this Q&A-4 are illustrated as follows:

Example (1). A plan does not fail to meet the requirements of section 89(k)(1)(B) because the employer grants benefits to an employee with a pre-existing medical condition in contravention of a specific plan term excluding coverage for any pre-existing conditions if the single written document is amended to reflect such expanded coverage, it is provided in a nondiscriminatory manner, and the expanded coverage continues in effect for a period of at least 12 continuous months from such amendment.

Example (2). A plan includes a managed care program which provides that upon the recommendation of the attending physician and the consent of both the insurer and the participant, the plan will reimburse alternative care (e.g., home health care expenses) instead of continued hospitalization. This program does not cause the plan to fail to meet the requirements of section 89(k)(1)(B).

Example (3). An employer maintains a health plan for former employees who retire from the employer on or after age 55 with at least 10 years of service if the employer consents to such employee's separation from service. Conditioning participation in this health plan on the employer's consent to the employee's separation constitutes impermissible discretion and violates section 89(k)(1)(B).

(e) Transition rule. A plan that is otherwise subject to the rules contained in section 89(k) is not required to comply with section 89(k)(1)(B) prior to the first day of the plan year following the first plan year beginning in 1989.

Q-5. What constitutes reasonable notification of employees under section 89(k)(1)(C)?

A-5. **(a) In general.** The employer or, if the plan is a multiemployer plan (within the meaning of section 3(37) of ERISA), the plan administrator must provide reasonable notice of the terms of a plan in order to satisfy section 89(k)(1)(C). Such reasonable notice must be provided to all eligible individuals (other than those individuals deriving their eligibility solely through another individual, such as dependents who derive their eligibility in a health plan through an employee). An eligible individual is an individual who participates under the plan or is described in the plan as eligible to participate. An otherwise eligible individual is an eligible individual even if participation under the plan is conditioned upon an election not yet made by such individual or the passage of a waiting period required by the plan. For purposes of this paragraph (a), an eligible individual also includes an individual who is a qualified beneficiary (as defined in section 4980B(g)(1)) under a health plan by reason of an occurrence of a qualifying event described in section 4980B(f)(3)(A), (C) or (E). Thus, such a qualified beneficiary must receive notice separate from the employee through whom such beneficiary derived eligibility in the health plan. See paragraph (g) of this Q&A-5 for rules regarding the timing of notice.

(b) Content of reasonable notice. The notice must contain a fair and complete summary of the material terms of the plan that are reasonably likely to be of significance to an eligible individual. These terms include at least the following: a general description of who is eligible to participate in the plan; a general description of the coverage or coverages offered (including the general types of benefits provided under the plan, basic limitations on such benefits, and required deductibles and co-payments); the timing and method of any election to participate; the cost to the employee relating to the plan, whether by way of salary reduction or employee contributions; the method by which a copy of the plan may be obtained; and the name and means of contacting a person from whom to request further information about the plan.

(c) Alternative form of compliance. For any plan other than an accident or health plan, in lieu of a notice meeting the requirements of paragraph (b) of this Q&A-5, the employer (or plan administrator, if the plan is a multiemployer plan) may furnish each eligible individual with a copy of the single written document and all related documents that have been incorporated by reference. This alternative cannot be used unless the single written document complies in all material respects with the requirements of 29 CFR § 2520.102-2 (style and format of summary plan description).

(d) Specific rule as to dependent care assistance programs. If a plan is a dependent care assistance program described in section 129, any notice to employees that is required for any plan year commencing on or after January 1, 1990, shall include a general description of the dependent care credit (under section 21), the relationship between the credit and participation in the dependent care assistance program, and the general circumstances under which the credit may be more advantageous to a taxpayer than the exclusion. If any other provision of law requires that a notice be provided to individuals eligible to participate in a dependent care assistance program, the requirements of this Q&A-5 are deemed satisfied to the extent such notice meets the requirements of this Q&A-5.

(e) Maintenance of single written document. The notice must contain a statement that the employer (or the plan administrator, if the plan is a multiemployer plan) shall make the single written document (including all related documents incorporated therein by reference) available for inspection upon reasonable notice. At a minimum, the following individuals shall be entitled to inspect and copy the single written document: any eligible individual; any other employee of the employer maintaining the plan; and any employee organization that represents employees of such employer. The document must be made available at no cost to the requesting individual at a reasonable time and place and, if a copy of the document is requested, a copy is to be provided at a cost no greater than that prescribed in § 601.702(f)(5)(iv)(B) of this Title.

(f) Method of notification. Notification to eligible individuals must be provided by the employer (or the plan administrator, if the plan is a multiemployer plan). For purposes of this paragraph (f), notice that otherwise meets the requirements of this Q&A-5 and is provided by an insurance company, health maintenance organization or other health care entity is considered to be provided by the employer. Notice must be provided to all eligible individuals (other than those individuals deriving their eligibility solely through another individual, such as dependents who derive their eligibility in a health plan through an employee). Except as otherwise stated in the final sentence of this paragraph (f), notice must be made in a manner consistent in all material respects with 29 CFR § 2520.104b-1(b)(1). If the employer elects to notify eligible individuals through the use of the alternative described in paragraph (c) of this Q&A-5, the notice must be provided to each such eligible individual either by hand or by mail with first class postage prepaid to the last known address of the eligible individual.

(g) Timing of notice. *(1) In general.* The notice required under section 89(k) must be provided prior to the first day on which coverage is provided under an insured or insurance-type plan or benefits are available under any other type of plan and prior to the effective date of any material amendment, extension or modification of such coverage or benefits, and no later than a reasonable time prior to the availability of any election with respect to participation under such plan. For purposes of this paragraph (g), the first date on which coverage is provided or benefits are available is the earliest date on which a claim may be incurred and be covered under coverage provided under a written document in existence on the date the claim is incurred.

(2) Plan modifications. If there is a modification to a material term of a plan (including any change in plan design that results in a modification of a material term), eligible individuals must be provided with notice of such modification no later than 60 days after the effective date of the modification. In addition, a notice of a retroactive modification will be treated as satisfying this paragraph (g)(2) if all of the conditions set forth in paragraph (d)(2)(iii) of Q&A-3 of this section are satisfied with respect to such modification.

(3) New employees. If an employee's participation in a plan is nonelective and begins within the employee's first 60 days of employment, the notice to such employee required under section 89(k)(1)(C) is not required prior to 60 days after the first day such employee is employed.

(4) Transition rule. With respect to a plan year beginning on or after January 1, 1989, a plan is not required to comply with this Q&A-5 prior to the later of July 1, 1989, or the first day of such plan year. The transition rule of this paragraph (g)(4) is solely for purposes of compliance with section 89(k)(1)(C). Use of the transition rule of this paragraph (g)(4) does not accelerate the first date by which the plan must meet the writing requirement of section 89(k)(1)(A).

(h) Examples. The requirements of this Q&A-5 are illustrated in the following examples:

Example (1). An employer has its open season relating to health plan selection from September 1 to October 1. Because the employer operates at several locations, employees are provided notice at different times. However, the employer ensures that all of its eligible individuals are notified during the period of time beginning 90 days before and ending on the first of September. The employer has notified eligible individuals on a timely basis.

Example (2). An election with respect to a plan is available on a continuous basis throughout the plan year. The employer provides the required notice to all eligible individuals 30 days prior to the beginning of the plan year. The employer has notified eligible individuals on a timely basis.

Example (3). A plan is amended effective June 1 to increase the maximum amount payable for a benefit provided under the plan. The amendment is adopted on May 1 and notice is provided to eligible individuals on that date. The amendment relates to a material term of the plan, and the employer has notified the eligible individuals on a timely basis.

Example (4). An employee begins employment on October 10. Under the terms of the employer's health plan, the employee becomes a participant in the plan as of the beginning of the next calendar month. If notice is provided to the employee no later than December 9, the employer has provided timely notice regardless of the fact that the employee becomes a participant on November 1.

Example (5). The facts are the same as in Example 4 except that the plan is elective. The notice is timely only if the employee is given notice prior to November 1.

Q-6. How does an employer meet the exclusive benefit requirement of section 89(k)(1)(D)?

A-6. **(a) In general.** A plan must be maintained for the exclusive benefit of those employees who participate in the plan. A plan may fail the requirement of this Q&A-6 by reason of its terms or operation. Whether this rule is satisfied is based on all of the facts and circumstances.

(b) Requirements as to the individuals who may participate in a plan. *(1) In general.* The exclusive benefit provisions are satisfied only if all of the participants in the plan or plans are common law employees of the employer or employers maintaining the plan. In the case of a voluntary employees' beneficiary association described in section 501(c)(9) (VEBA) that is part of a plan which must satisfy the requirements of section 89(k)(1)(D), those individuals who may participate in the plan include those who may be members of the VEBA under § 1.501(c)(9)-2(a).

(2) Deemed common law employees. An individual who is not a common law employee of an employer maintaining the plan and who receives coverage or benefits under such plan is deemed to be an employee for purposes of paragraph (b)(1) if the exclusion from gross income that is granted under the relevant provision of the Code (e.g., sections 79, 105, 106, 129 and 132) is available to such individual on the same basis that it is available to a common law employee. In addition, a qualified beneficiary, as defined in section 4980B(g)(1), is treated as a common law employee for purposes of paragraph (b)(1) of this Q&A-6 with respect to a health plan under which the qualified beneficiary receives continuation coverage.

(3) Certain nonemployees. (i) In general. An individual who is not a common law employee of the employer maintaining the plan, but who performs significant services for the employer in a capacity other than as an employee, and receives coverage or benefits under such plan may be disregarded in applying paragraph (b)(1) of this Q&A-6 if such individual pays for such coverage entirely on an after-tax basis. Thus, a nonemployee participant may be disregarded in applying paragraph (b)(1) of this Q&A-6 with respect to a health plan if the participant performs significant services for the employer and purchases the full coverage under the plan with after-tax contributions.

(ii) Self-employed individuals. A self-employed individual who is treated as an employee under section 401(c)(1) is treated as a common law employee of the employer for purposes of applying paragraph (b)(1) of this Q&A-6.

(4) Examples. The requirements of this paragraph (b) are illustrated by the following examples:

Example (1). Under section 132(f)(3), certain use of air transportation by a parent of an employee is treated as use by the employee for purposes of determining the excludability of the value of air transportation. The parent of the employee is deemed to be a common law employee for purposes of applying section 89(k) (1)(D) to a plan providing such air transportation because the air transportation provided to the parent is excludable from gross income under section 132.

Example (2). A health plan provides coverage with respect to the spouse and dependents of a common law employee-participant. Because the value of such coverage is excludable under section 106 and the benefits are excludable under section 105(b), the spouse and dependent children are deemed to be common law employees and the plan does not violate the exclusive benefit requirement of section 89(k) by reason of such coverage.

Example (3). An employer allows an independent contractor to purchase health care continuation coverage under section 4980B. The plan does not fail to meet the requirements of section 89(k) by reason of the participation of the independent contractor.

Example (4). A full-time life insurance salesman within the meaning of section 7701(a)(20) participates in an accident or health plan of an insurance company. Since this individual is treated as an employee for purposes of sections 105 and 106, the inclusion of such an individual in the plan does not violate the exclusive benefit requirement of section 89(k).

Example (5). A former employee of Employer X participates in Employer X's accident or health plan. Because this individual is treated as an employee of Employer X for purposes of sections 105 and 106, the former employee's inclusion in the plan does not violate the exclusive benefit requirement of section 89(k).

Example (6). An individual who is a leased employee with respect to the recipient under section 414(n) of the individual's services is treated as an employee of the recipient for purposes of sections 105 and 106, and thus, the inclusion of such leased employee in an accident or health plan of the recipient does not violate the exclusive benefit requirement of section 89(k).

Example (7). An individual who provides significant services to another person for a year but who is not a leased employee under section 414(n) of such person and is not otherwise an employee of such person is not treated as that person's employee for purposes of sections 105 and 106. However, the inclusion of such individual in an accident or health plan maintained by the employer does not violate the exclusive benefit requirement of section 89(k) if such individual's participation in such plan is fully paid for by such individual with after-tax contributions.

(c) Multiemployer plans. A multiple employer plan or a multiemployer plan maintained by two or more employers does not fail to satisfy the requirements of section 89(k)(1)(D) merely because employees of contributing employers participate in such plan or because the plan includes employees of an employee organization or of the plan.

(d) Rules under other sections of the Code relating to the individuals who may participate in a plan. Nothing in this Q&A-6 modifies any other section of the Code or the regulations specifically relating to who may participate in a plan. To the extent this Q&A-6 is more restrictive than another section of the Code or regulations, this Q&A-6 applies only for purposes of section 89. Notwithstanding the preceding sentence, the rules relating to who may participate in plans provided through organizations to which section 505 applies (i.e., organizations described in sections 501(c)(9) and 501(c)(17)) continue to be applicable to such organizations. Similarly, in addition to the rules contained in this Q&A-6, the rule contained in section 125(c)(1)(A) remains applicable in determining who may participate in a cafeteria plan.

(e) Example. The provisions of this Q&A-6 are illustrated in the following example:

Example. A self-insured health plan is funded through a voluntary employees' beneficiary association (within the meaning of section 501(c)(9)) which accepts employee contributions. Under the plan, the experience gain for a year is used to fund a part of the cost of the program for the following year by reducing the employee cost of participation (i.e., employee premiums) for all participants. The provision does not violate the exclusive benefit rule of section 89(k).

(f) Transition rule. A plan that is subject to the rules contained in section 89(k) is not required to comply with section 89(k)(1)(D) prior to the first day of the plan year following the first plan year beginning in 1989.

Q-7. How is it determined whether a plan is established with the intent of being maintained for an indefinite period of time?

A-7. **(a) In general.** Whether a plan is established with the intent that it will be maintained for an indefinite period of time as required by section 89(k)(1)(E) is to be determined on the basis of all of the facts and circumstances. For purposes of section 89(k)(1)(E), a plan generally is treated as established with the intent that it will be maintained for an indefinite period of time if it is established and maintained for at least a consecutive 12-month period.

(b) Plan modifications and terminations. *(1) In general.* Generally, a plan does not fail the requirement of section 89(k)(1)(E) merely because the employer reserves the right to modify or terminate the plan or because the plan is not renewed pursuant to a specific plan provision or is terminated. However, in certain circumstances, significant modifications in the coverage or benefits under the plan or a termination of coverage or benefits raises a presumption that the plan was not established with the intent that it continue for an indefinite period of time. A plan is not considered to be modified or terminated merely because of a change in the insurance carrier or health care provider if the coverage and benefits under the plan are not substantially changed.

(2) Coverage in effect for at least 12 consecutive months. The requirement of section 89(k)(1)(E) is not violated by reason of a material modification or termination of a plan, if such material modification or termination is effective on a prospective basis and the affected coverage (or substantially similar coverage) has been in effect for at least a consecutive 12-month period. This paragraph (b)(2) applies even if the plan contains a term specifying the intent of the employer to terminate the plan upon the expiration of a 12-month period.

(3) Coverage in effect for less than 12 consecutive months. For plan years beginning after December 31, 1989, special scrutiny will be given with respect to material modifications and terminations of a plan that occur before the terminated or modified coverage or benefits have been in effect for at least 12 consecutive months. Such a termination or modification will not violate the requirement of section 89(k)(1)(E) if the employer can demonstrate that there is a substantial, independent business reason for such termination or modification and that the termination or modification does not discriminate in favor of one or more highly compensated employees.

(4) Certain modifications. A retroactive modification to a plan does not cause the plan to fail to satisfy section 89(k)(1)(E) if all of the conditions set forth in paragraph (d)(2)(iii) of Q&A-3 of this section are satisfied with respect to such modification.

(c) Examples. The requirements of this Q&A-7 are illustrated in the following examples:

Example (1). An employer merges with another company. Pursuant to the merger and in order to consolidate operations, the surviving employer terminates the health coverage in mid-year for the merged company's employees and adds these employees to the plan maintained by the surviving company. The merger constitutes a valid business purpose for the termination of the health plan of the merged company and, thus, neither plan has failed the requirements of section 89(k)(1)(E).

Example (2). A dental plan is modified on July 1 to include coverage for certain orthodontic benefits. The plan year of the dental plan is the calendar year. The requirements of section 89(k)(1)(E) are not violated if the orthodontic benefits are eliminated from the plan on or after July 1 of the following year because the coverage would have been in effect for at least 12 consecutive months.

Example (3). An employer announces that employees who retire from the employer on or after age 55 with at least 10 years of service will receive employer-provided health coverage for 1 year after separation if such employees retire during a specified 2-month period. This plan does not fail to satisfy section 89(k)(1)(E) merely because the retirement window is only 2 months long, because such window is a coverage eligibility condition rather than a limitation on the period of coverage under the plan.

Example (4). A health plan with a broad range of coverage provided to all nonhighly compensated employees of an employer is in existence for only one day in a year. The employer designates this day as the testing day for its health plans. Under the facts of the case, a reasonable inference may be made that the intention of the employer in granting the coverage under the health plan in existence only on the testing day is to enhance the likelihood that the employer's other health plan will satisfy the nondiscrimination requirements of section 89. This plan fails the requirement of section 89(k)(1)(E). These circumstances may also result in a finding by the Commissioner that the plan or plans fail the nondiscriminatory provisions test of section 89(d)(1)(C).

Example (5). The requirement of section 89(k)(1)(E) may be violated if a plan is established under circumstances in which it is likely to benefit only one individual. For example, assume that a plan is adopted after an illness is diagnosed with respect to an individual and that the coverage provided relates to this illness. If the plan is terminated after the payment of these expenses, the plan may fail the permanency requirement. If this individual is a highly compensated employee these circumstances may also result in a finding by the Commissioner that the plan fails the nondiscriminatory provisions test of section 89(d)(1)(C).

(d) Exception for fringe benefits constituting no-additional-cost services and qualified employee discounts. The requirements of section 89(k)(1)(E) and this Q&A-7 do not apply to any plan providing no-additional-cost services as described in section 132(b) or to any plan providing qualified employee discounts as described in section 132(c).

Q-8. What are the sanctions for failure to meet the qualification requirements of section 89(k)?

A-8. **(a) In general.**

(1) Employer provided benefits. If a plan subject to section 89(k) fails to satisfy any of the requirements of that section, the employer-provided benefits under the plan generally are not eligible for any exclusion from gross income under Part III, Subchapter B, Chapter 1, Subtitle A, of the Code. For purposes of this Q&A-8, such benefits are termed "nonexcludable benefits". Thus, for example, employer-provided benefits provided under a health plan that fails to satisfy the requirements of section 89(k) are not excludable under section 105. See, however, the limit on the amount of the nonexcludable benefits under paragraph (c)(4) of this Q&A-8. In addition, see section 6652(k) with respect to certain sanctions that may be imposed on the employer with respect to the employer's responsibilities under section 89.

(2) Employee-provided benefits. Employee-provided benefits are not subject to section 89(k) and continue to be subject to any applicable exclusion including, for example, the exclusion provided in section 104(a)(3) with respect to accident and health plans.

(3) Determination of includible benefit. The includible benefit is determined by calculating the total amount of the benefits provided under the plan and then subtracting the amount of the employee-provided benefit. Determination of the amount of the employee-provided benefit must be made under the provisions of paragraph (d) of this Q&A-8 regarding the allocation of benefits.

(4) Section 89(b) excess benefits. Except as provided under paragraph (e) of this Q&A-8, benefits received under a plan that fails to satisfy section 89(k) include those bene-

fits received under coverage that constitutes an excess benefit under section 89(b). That is, for example, sections 101 and 105(b) and (c) are not applicable to benefits received under a discriminatory accident or health plan that also fails to satisfy section 89(k). In addition, a plan's failure to satisfy section 89(k) does not, in and of itself, affect the extent to which the coverage provided with respect to such plan (as opposed to the benefits under the plan) is eligible for an exclusion from gross income. Thus, for example, coverage under a health plan does not fail to be excludable under section 106 merely because the plan fails to satisfy section 89(k).

(b) De minimis failures to comply with section 89(k)(1)(A) and (C). *(1) In general.* If a plan fails to satisfy the writing or notice requirements of section 89(k) and such failure constitutes a de minimis failure (as defined in paragraph (b)(2) of this Q&A-8), then the plan will be deemed to have complied with the requirements of section 89(k) with respect to the failed requirement, provided that such failure is corrected within 90 days after the employer has notice of such failure.

(2) Definition of de minimis failure to comply. (i) In general. A failure constitutes a de minimis failure to comply only if the failure meets all of the requirements of paragraph (b)(2)(ii) of this Q&A-8. Whether a failure to comply is described in paragraph (b)(2)(ii) of this Q& A-8 is determined under all of the facts and circumstances.

(ii) Requirements for qualifying as a de minimis failure. (A) Good faith effort. The employer must have acted in good faith and must have made a reasonable effort to comply with the applicable requirement.

(B) No discriminatory effect. The failure must not have had the effect of causing the plan to discriminate in favor of one or more highly compensated employees.

(C) No retroactive reduction of coverage. Correction of the failure cannot require that coverage be reduced under the single written document (as that plan existed at the time of the failure). That is, a failure is not a de minimis failure if its correction requires that the coverage described in the single written document be reduced with retroactive effect to conform to the previous operation of the plan.

(iii) Examples. The requirements of paragraph (b)(2)(ii) of this Q&A-8 are illustrated by the following examples:

Example (1). An employer provides notice to its employees regarding a health plan. Despite the employer's good faith and reasonable efforts to provide timely notice, the notice is 1 week late. The notice complies with all other requirements of section 89(k). Provided that no facts or circumstances suggest otherwise, this is a de minimis failure to comply. The correction occurred when the notice was provided.

Example (2). Despite the employer's good faith and reasonable efforts, an employer fails to give notice to its employees with respect to nonelective coverage under a dental plan that has been added to the employer's health program. The employer has no knowledge (constructive or otherwise) of such failure. Only one employee incurs a covered expense under the dental program and the employee submits a claim to the employer notwithstanding the fact that the employee is not sure whether the claim is covered. If within 90 days of receiving notice of the failure the employer follows the single written document, reimburses the expense, and gives notice relating to such coverage (including the effective date of the dental plan), then the employer has corrected the failure to comply with the notice requirements.

(3) Correction. The terms "correct" and "correction" mean, with respect to a de minimis failure to comply, that the employer performs all the necessary acts in order to comply with section 89(k) and places the affected employees in a financial position not worse than that in which they would have been if the employer had been in full compliance with section 89(k). If a subsequent notice is given to correct a de minimis failure, such notice must reflect the original effective date relating to the coverage, benefit or other material term that is the subject of the notice and must indicate that the employer will honor (and the employer must in fact honor) claims incurred after such effective date (including those prior to the date of such correcting notice). This paragraph (b)(3) is illustrated in the following example:

Example. Despite the good faith and reasonable efforts of the employer, a benefit is denied by a plan administrator in contravention of the written terms of the plan. If at a later date payment is made under the plan and the employer otherwise places the participant in a financial position no worse than if the employer had complied (e.g., by paying the benefit, interest if applicable and any fees incurred in compelling payment), then the failure is a de minimis failure and there has been correction. If the employee cannot be put in the same financial position as if the employer had complied, the failure cannot be corrected and the employer has failed to meet the requirements of section 89(k).

(c) Determination of the amount of nonexcludable benefit. *(1) In general.* The amount of a nonexcludable benefit with respect to an employee under a plan that fails to satisfy section 89(k) (including any insurance-type plan) is the value of the benefits (rather than the coverage) either received by the employee under the plan during the plan year or received thereafter but incurred under coverage in effect during the plan year. Thus, the calculation of the amount of the nonexcludable benefit under section 89(k) is based on the plan year of the failed plan and not, as is the case with the determination of excess benefit under section 89(b), on the testing year of the employer. To the extent that the single written document does not reflect a plan year, the determination of the plan year shall be based on paragraph (b) of Q&A-10 of § 1.89(a)-1. Nonexcludable benefits under section 89(k) are treated as received by an employee at the time such benefits are actually received or, but for the employee's election to defer the receipt of such benefits, first become available for receipt. In no case, however, will the amount of a nonexcludable benefit with respect to an employee exceed the limit for such employee determined under paragraph (c)(4) of this Q&A-8.

(2) Definition of plan. (i) In general. The nonexcludable benefits with respect to a plan that fails to satisfy section 89(k) include all benefits received under such plan. Unless the special definition of plan set forth in paragraph (c)(2)(ii) of this Q&A-8 applies, the nonexcludable benefits are those benefits described in the single written document that relates to the failure under section 89(k).

(ii) Severable coverage. To the extent that the failure of a plan to satisfy section 89(k) is directly and exclusively related to a specific portion or aspect of coverage provided in a plan, such portion or aspect of the coverage may be treated as a separate plan for purposes of determining the nonexcludable benefits under a plan that fails to satisfy section 89(k). In such a case, the coverage remaining under the single written document after the severance of the coverage providing nonexcludable benefits does not fail to satisfy the requirements of section 89(k) solely by reason of the failure related to the severed coverage. This paragraph (c)(2)(ii) does not permit the severance of coverage of one individual from similar coverage provided to other individuals under the single written document.

(3) Examples. The requirements of paragraph (c)(1) and (2) of this Q& A-8 are illustrated by the following examples:

Example (1). An employer maintains a single health plan. During the plan year, the employer allows a claim for a preexisting condition in direct contravention of a provision in the plan. If the plan is not modified in accordance with paragraph (d)(2)(iii) of Q&A-3 of this section and if no correction occurs, coverage for that benefit is deemed to constitute a separate plan and the benefit thereunder is nonexcludable. However, unless a pattern or practice indicates that this provision was intended to be a part of the employer's health plan (e.g., by continuous operation in a similar manner), benefits properly paid with respect to the plan are not taxable by reason of the above described failure.

Example (2). An employer fails to notify certain eligible individuals who are not highly compensated employees concerning their eligibility to elect to have coverage under a health plan. Certain of the individuals fail to receive coverage under the plan and incur medical expenses that are not reimbursed due to the fact that the insurance company refuses to retroactively cover these individuals. The plan relating to the notice fails to comply with section 89(k) and all benefits described in the single written document that relates to the failure are nonexcludable to the recipients.

Example (3). A health program contained in a single written document is terminated. The plan provided core coverage and dental care. The portion of the program containing dental coverage recently became effective and the termination with respect to such coverage fails to meet the permanence requirement of section 89(k)(1)(E). The failed coverage under the dental program can reasonably be severed from the balance of the program. Thus, the dental coverage is treated as a separate plan and the benefits that were provided under such plan are nonexcludable. Other benefits provided under the single written document which relates to the failed plan however, are not affected by such failure.

Example (4). A benefit is mistakenly granted to a participant in that the benefit amount exceeds the dollar limitation described in the single written document. Unless the plan is modified in accordance with paragraph (d)(2)(iii) of Q&A-3 of this section, the operation of the plan in a manner inconsistent with the single written document violates the writing requirement of section 89(k). The amount of the benefit in excess of the dollar limitation may be treated as severable coverage and thus be nonexcludable without adverse impact upon the balance of the program.

Example (5). An employer maintains a core health plan. A participant incurs an expense that is determined by the plan administrator to be incurred for a benefit not covered by the plan. The benefit is denied by the plan administrator in contravention of the terms of the plan. Coverage for such benefit is actually available under the terms of the insurance contract that describes medical benefits and coverage. However, if the employer is not able to correct the failure on a timely basis, all benefits described in the single written document that relates to the failure are nonexcludable because the coverage involved is not reasonably severable from the general core coverage under the plan.

Example (6). A notice sent to participants fails to satisfy section 89(k). The notice contains a modification of a material term relating to cosmetic surgical procedures coverage. If the failure is not corrected, benefits received under the coverage of the type described in the notice are nonexcludable.

Example (7). A notice is sent to employee participants failing to disclose a material term of the plan. The material term does not relate to a particular coverage or benefit, but rather applies to all benefits under the plan. All benefits provided under the single written document related to the notice are nonexcludable unless such failure is corrected on a timely basis.

(4) Limit on nonexcludable amount. Notwithstanding any other provision of this Q&A-8, the amount of the employer-provided portion (see paragraph (d)(2) of this Q&A-8) of the nonexcludable benefits received by an employee (and the employee's spouse and dependents) during a taxable year of the employee under one or more accident and health plans that fail to satisfy section 89(k) (but do not fail to be accident or health plans under section 105 and 106) shall not exceed the sum of the following 4 amounts: 10 percent of the employee's compensation (before inclusion of the employer-provided benefit) from the employer maintaining the plan for the employee's taxable year, up to and including the dollar amount in effect for such year under section 414(q)(1)(C); 25 percent of the employee's compensation in excess of such dollar amount up to and including 200 percent of such dollar amount; 75 percent of the employee's compensation in excess of 200 percent of such dollar amount up to and including 300 percent of such dollar amount; and 100 percent of the employee's compensation in excess of 300 percent of such dollar amount. The limitation under this paragraph (c)(4) is applied after the determination of the employer-provided portion of the nonexcludable benefits described in paragraph (d)(2) of this Q&A-8, but before the coordination of nonexcludable benefits with excess benefits as described in paragraph (e) of this Q&A-8. Compensation of an employee as used in this paragraph (c)(4) is compensation as determined under section 414(q)(7) and with respect to the taxable year of the employee in which the nonexcludable benefit is received. Thus, for example, if an employee with compensation from the employer of $25,000 for a calendar year also receives $20,000 in employer-provided benefits under a health plan that fails to satisfy section 89(k), the maximum amount of nonexcludable benefit for such employee for such year is $2,500 (i.e., 10 percent of $25,000). The remaining $17,500 in benefits under the plan that failed to satisfy section 89(k) may be excludable from gross income under section 105. Finally, this paragraph (c)(4) does not apply if, in addition to failing one or more of the requirements of section 89(k), a plan also fails to be an accident or health plan under sections 106 and 105.

(d) Allocation between employer and employee contributions. *(1) In general.* Section 89(k) generally eliminates the otherwise available exclusions only with regard to benefits attributable to the employer-provided portion of the benefits received. Thus, for example, if a portion of the coverage provided under a plan is attributable to after-tax employee contributions, an allocation of the benefits under such plan must be made on the basis of the relative cost to the employer and the employee for the plan. Allocation is permitted, however, only to the extent that a nonexcludable benefit is directly related to the portion of the coverage under the plan that is attributable to employee contributions.

(2) Accident or health plans. If coverage provided under an accident or health plan is partially attributable to after-tax employee contributions, an allocation of the benefits under such plan is made in accordance with a method set forth in paragraphs (c), (d) or (e) of § 1.105-1 and the method per-

mitted to determine the applicable premium for a group health plan under section 4980B(f)(4) to determine the cost of a health plan. For purposes of this paragraph, coverage that is taxable by reason of being considered an excess benefit (as defined in section 89(b)) is not considered to be attributable to employee contributions to the plan. See paragraph (e) of this Q&A-8 for rules regarding coordination of sanctions.

(3) Group-term life insurance plans. The portion of coverage under a plan to which section 79 applies that is attributable to employee contributions must be computed in the manner set forth in § 1.79-3(e). In addition, the rule of paragraph (d)(1) of this Q&A-8 does not apply to certain benefits received under a group-term life insurance program subject to section 79. Thus, while the table value of coverage over $50,000 is taxable without regard to section 89, such coverage is not attributable to employee contributions for purposes of the rule in this paragraph (d). Similarly, coverage that is taxable by reason of being considered excess benefit (as defined in section 89(b)) is not considered to be attributable to employee contributions to the plan. See paragraph (e) of this Q&A-8 for rules regarding coordination of sanctions.

(4) Example. The following example illustrates the rule contained in this paragraph (d):

Example. Employer A maintains a plan under which it pays two-thirds of the annual premium cost on individual policies of accident and health insurance for its employees. The remainder of each employee's premium is paid through after-tax payroll deduction from the wages of the employee. The annual cost of coverage determined by the method permitted to determine the applicable premium (as defined in section 4980B(f)(4) for plans to which that section applies) for Employee X is $240, of which $160 is paid by the employer. Thus, two-thirds (160/240) of all amounts received by Employee X under such insurance policy are attributable to the contributions of the employer and are nonexcludable if the plan fails to meet the requirements of section 89(k).

(e) Coordination rules. *(1) Relationship between statutory employee benefit plans that fail to meet the section 89(k) requirements and nondiscrimination tests.* The employer-provided benefit (as defined in § 1.89(a)-1 for purposes of the section 89 nondiscrimination tests) with respect to a statutory employee benefit plan must be taken into account for purposes of nondiscrimination testing under section 89 even though the plan has failed the requirements of section 89(k). That is, unless the coverage under a statutory employee benefit plan is purchased by the employee with after-tax employee contributions (or is treated as having been purchased with after-tax employee contributions), the coverage is subject to section 89 nondiscrimination testing. For the purposes of this paragraph (e), coverage that is taxable by reason of being an excess benefit under section 89(b) is not treated as purchased with after-tax employee contributions. Thus, employer-provided benefits (as defined in paragraph (b) of Q&A-1 of this section) that are attributable to such excess benefits are nonexcludable benefits if the plan also fails section 89(k). Also, a group-term life insurance plan subject to section 79 must be considered for purposes of section 89 without regard to the fact that the cost of coverage is currently taxable to the extent provided in section 79 (those amounts in excess of $50,000) or by reason of being considered excess benefit under section 89(b).

(2) Coordination of sanctions where there is a failure of section 89(k) related to discriminatory coverage. (i) In general. If an individual has a nonexcludable benefit by reason of section 89(k), the treatment of that benefit and the related excess benefit under section 89(b) are coordinated by limiting the taxable amount of any employee to the greater of either the nonexcludable benefit or the excess benefit.

(ii) Nonexcludable benefit must be related to discriminatory coverage. Coordination of sanctions with respect to a nonexcludable benefit under section 89(k) and a discriminatory excess benefit under section 89(b) is available only when the nonexcludable benefit under section 89(k) is related to the excess benefit that is taxable by reason of its being contained in a discriminatory employee benefit plan under section 89(c). For this purpose, a plan means any specific option under the health program. The determination of relatedness is made on the basis of all of the facts and circumstances. Generally, if an employee is treated as having received an excess benefit under section 89(b) and the excess benefit relates to a failure to meet the requirements of paragraph (d)(2) (the 90 percent/50 percent eligibility test) or (d)(4) (the 75 percent benefits test) of Q&A-1 of § 1.89(a)-1, there is a presumption that such excess benefit does not relate to a plan (or portion thereof) that fails section 89(k). Thus, for example, an employee who receives employer-provided coverage with a value of $2,500 under an indemnity plan and employer-provided coverage with a value of $750 under a dental plan and who is treated as receiving an excess benefit of $1,000 under section 89(b) because these health plans fail to meet the requirements of the 75 percent benefits test or the 90 percent/50 percent eligibility test, and a nonexcludable benefit of $600 because the dental plan fails section 89(k), the entire $1,000 excess benefit is treated as attributable to the indemnity plan and the total includible amount would be $1,600 ($1,000 plus $600). If the employee received an excess benefit of $3,000 under section 89(b), then $500 of such excess benefit would be allocated to the dental plan and the total includible amount would be $3,100. If the dental plan failed the 50 percent eligibility test, then $750 of the excess benefit or the higher of the excess benefit if less than $750 of the excess benefit related to the dental plan under Q&A-9 of § 1.89(a)-1) or the $600 nonexcludable benefit would be includible in the employee's gross income.

(iii) Coordination where nonexcludable benefit received in taxable year other than the taxable year in which testing year ends. If a nonexcludable benefit under section 89(k) is received in a taxable year of the employee other than that taxable year in which ends the testing year for which there is a related excess benefit under section 89(b) (including any additional time permitted by reason of an election under section 89(a)(2)(B)) and if the benefits otherwise qualify for the coordination described in this paragraph (e), the rules of this paragraph (e)(2)(iii) apply. If the testing year ends in a later taxable year of the employee than the taxable year in which the nonexcludable benefit is received, the amount of the excess benefit that is included in gross income for the later taxable year is reduced (but not below zero) by the amount of nonexcludable benefit included in gross income for the earlier taxable year. Similarly, where the nonexcludable benefit is received in a later taxable year of the employee than the taxable year in which the testing year ends, the amount of the nonexcludable benefit included in gross income for the later year is reduced (but not below zero) by the amount of the excess benefit included for the earlier taxable year to which the nonexcludable benefit relates.

(iv) Examples. The provisions of this paragraph (e)(2) are illustrated by the following examples:

Example (1). Assume that an employer's testing year under section 89(a) is the calendar year. Plan A has a plan year beginning on July 1 and has an employer-provided benefit, based on its annual applicable premium, of $2,000. Employee X receives a reimbursement under Plan A on July 10 in the amount of $500. Assume that Plan A fails section 89(k). Assume further that Employee X has received $1,000 in excess benefit for the testing year, all of which relates to the total value of coverage under Plan A. For this calendar year, Employee X must include in gross income $1,000.

Example (2). Assume the same facts as in Example 1, except that the $500 reimbursement is $1,500. Employee X must include in income $1,500.

Example (3). Assume that an employer's testing year begins on July 1. Plan A has an applicable premium of $2,000 and its plan year is the 1991 calendar year. Employee X receives a reimbursement of $500 under Plan A on July 10, 1991. Assume that Plan A fails section 89(k). The employer determines that Employee X has $2,000 in excess benefit in the testing year that begins July 1, 1991, related to Plan A. For 1991, Employee X must include $500 in gross income. However, for 1992, Employee X may use that $500 as an offset against the amount of excess benefit related to the coverage under which the benefit was granted. Thus, Employee X is only required to include $1,500 in gross income for 1992 ($2,000 – $500).

Example (4). Assume the same facts as Example 3, except that Employee X received the reimbursement on June 10, 1991. Unless other facts indicate otherwise, no offset is available since the reimbursement did not relate to excess benefit calculated with regard to the 1991 testing year.

(f) Authority to limit nonexcludable benefits. The Commissioner, in revenue rulings, notices and other publications of general applicability, may limit the nonexcludable benefit that would otherwise be determined under section 89(k) and this proposed regulation to the extent the facts and circumstances indicate that the elimination of the otherwise available exclusions from gross income would be inconsistent with the purposes underlying the requirements of section 89(k). Among the facts and circumstances to be taken into account are the relationship between the plan's failure under section 89(k) and the employee's receipt of benefits under such plan, the extent to which the plan's failure was attributable to a reckless or intentional disregard of the requirements of section 89(k), and whether the imposition of the full sanction under section 89(k) would impose a hardship on the employee that is not justified by the nature and degree of the plan's failure.

PAR. 5. Section 1.101 is amended.

Proposed § 1.101 Statutory provisions; certain death benefits. [*For Preamble, see ¶ 150,135*]

• ***Caution:*** Proposed section 1.62-1 was finalized by TD 7399, 2/3/76. Proposed sections 1.72-4, 1.72-13, 1.101-2, 1.122-1, 1.402(a)-1, 1.402(e)-2, 1.402(e)-3, 1.403(a)-1, 1.403(a)-2, 1.405-3, 1.652(b)-1, 1.1304-2 and 11.402(e)(4)(B)-1 remain proposed.

[Code Sec. 101]

§ 1.101-1 Exclusion from gross income of proceeds of life insurance contracts payable by reason of death.

Caution: The Treasury has not yet amended Reg § 1.101-1 to reflect changes made by P.L. 105-34, P.L. 104-191, P.L. 97-248.

(a) *(1) In general.* Section 101(a)(1) states the general rule that the proceeds of life insurance policies, if paid by reason of the death of the insured, are excluded from the gross income of the recipient. Death benefit payments having the characteristics of life insurance proceeds payable by reason of death under contracts, such as workmen's compensation insurance contracts, endowment contracts, or accident and health insurance contracts, are covered by this provision. For provisions relating to death benefits paid by or on behalf of employers, see section 101(b) and § 1.101-2. The exclusion from gross income allowed by section 101(a) applies whether payment is made to the estate of the insured or to any beneficiary (individual, corporation, or partnership) and whether it is made directly or in trust. The extent to which this exclusion applies in cases where life insurance policies have been transferred for a valuable consideration is stated in section 101(a)(2) and in paragraph (b) of this section. In cases where the proceeds of a life insurance policy, payable by reason of the death of the insured, are paid other than in a single sum at the time of such death, the amounts to be excluded from gross income may be affected by the provisions of section 101(c) (relating to amounts held under agreements to pay interest) or section 101(d) (relating to amounts payable at a date later than death). See §§ 1.101-3 and 1.101-4. However, neither section 101(c) nor section 101(d) applies to a single sum payment which does not exceed the amount payable at the time of death even though such amount is actually paid at a date later than death.

(2) Cross references. For rules governing the taxability of insurance proceeds constituting benefits payable on the death of an employee—

(i) Under pension, profit-sharing, or stock bonus plans described in section 401(a) and exempt from tax under section 501(a), or under annuity plans described in section 403(a), see section 72(m)(3) and paragraph (c) of § 1.72-16;

(ii) Under annuity contracts to which § 1.403(b)-3 applies, see § 1.403(b)-7.

For the definition of a life insurance company, see section 801; or

(iii) Under eligible State deferred compensation plans described in section 457(b), see paragraph (c) of § 1.457-1.

(b) Transfers of life insurance policies. *(1)* In the case of a transfer, by assignment or otherwise, of a life insurance policy or any interest therein for a valuable consideration, the amount of the proceeds attributable to such policy or interest which is excludable from the transferee's gross income is generally limited to the sum of (i) the actual value of the consideration for such transfer, and (ii) the premiums and other amounts subsequently paid by the transferee (see section 101(a)(2) and example (1) of subparagraph (5) of this paragraph). However, this limitation on the amount excludable from the transferee's gross income does not apply (except in certain special cases involving a series of transfers), where the basis of the policy or interest transferred, for the purpose of determining gain or loss with respect to the transferee, is determinable, in whole or in part, by reference to the basis of such policy or interest in the hands of the transferor (see section 101(a)(2)(A) and examples (2) and (4) of subparagraph (5) of this paragraph). Neither does the limitation apply where the policy or interest therein is transferred to the insured, to a partner of the insured, to a partnership in which the insured is a partner, or to a corporation in which the insured is a shareholder or officer (see section 101(a)(2)(B)). For rules relating to gratuitous transfers, see subparagraph (2) of this paragraph. For special rules with respect to certain cases where a series of transfers is involved, see subparagraph (3) of this paragraph.

(2) In the case of a gratuitous transfer, by assignment or otherwise, of a life insurance policy or any interest therein, as a general rule the amount of the proceeds attributable to such policy or interest which is excludable from the transferee's gross income under section 101(a) is limited to the sum of (i) the amount which would have been excludable by the transferor (in accordance with this section) if no such transfer had taken place, and (ii) any premiums and other amounts subsequently paid by the transferee. See example (6) of subparagraph (5) of this paragraph. However, where the gratuitous transfer in question is made by or to the insured, a partner of the insured, a partnership in which the insured is a partner, or a corporation in which the insured is a shareholder or officer, the entire amount of the proceeds attributable to the policy or interest transferred shall be excludable from the transferee's gross income (see section 101(a)(2)(B) and example (7) of subparagraph (5) of this paragraph).

(3) In the case of a series of transfers, if the last transfer of a life insurance policy or an interest therein is for a valuable consideration—

(i) The general rule is that the final transferee shall exclude from gross income, with respect to the proceeds of such policy or interest therein, only the sum of—

(a) The actual value of the consideration paid by him, and

(b) The premiums and other amounts subsequently paid by him;

(ii) If the final transfer is to the insured, to a partner of the insured, to a partnership in which the insured is a partner, or to a corporation in which the insured is a shareholder or officer, the final transferee shall exclude the entire amount of the proceeds from gross income;

(iii) Except where subdivision (ii) of this subparagraph applies, if the basis of the policy or interest transferred, for the purpose of determining gain or loss with respect to the final transferee, is determinable, in whole or in part, by reference to the basis of such policy or interest therein in the hands of the transferor, the amount of the proceeds which is excludable by the final transferee is limited to the sum of—

(a) The amount which would have been excludable by his transferor if no such transfer had taken place, and

(b) Any premiums and other amounts subsequently paid by the final transferee himself.

(4) For the purposes of section 101(a)(2) and subparagraphs (1) and (3) of this paragraph, a "transfer for a valuable consideration" is any absolute transfer for value of a right to receive all or a part of the proceeds of a life insurance policy. Thus, the creation, for value, of an enforceable contractual right to receive all or a part of the proceeds of a policy may constitute a transfer for a valuable consideration of the policy or an interest therein. On the other hand, the pledging or assignment of a policy as collateral security is not a transfer for a valuable consideration of such policy or an interest therein, and section 101 is inapplicable to any amounts received by the pledgee or assignee.

(5) The application of this paragraph may be illustrated by the following examples:

Example (1). A pays premiums of $500 for an insurance policy in the face amount of $1,000 upon the life of B, and subsequently transfers the policy to C for $600. C receives the proceeds of $1,000 upon the death of B. The amount which C can exclude from his gross income is limited to $600 plus any premiums paid by C subsequent to the transfer.

Example (2). The X Corporation purchases for a single premium of $500 an insurance policy in the face amount of $1,000 upon the life of A, one of its employees, naming the X Corporation as beneficiary. The X Corporation transfers the policy to the Y Corporation in a tax-free reorganization (the policy having a basis for determining gain or loss in the hands of the Y Corporation determined by reference to its basis in the hands of the X Corporation). The Y Corporation receives the proceeds of $1,000 upon the death of A. The entire $1,000 is to be excluded from the gross income of the Y Corporation.

Example (3). The facts are the same as in example (2) except that, prior to the death of A, the Y Corporation transfers the policy to the Z Corporation for $600. The Z Corporation receives the proceeds of $1,000 upon the death of A. The amount which the Z Corporation can exclude from its gross income is limited to $600 plus any premiums paid by the Z Corporation subsequent to the transfer of the policy to it.

Example (4). The facts are the same as in example (3) except that, prior to the death of A, the Z Corporation transfers the policy to the M Corporation in a tax-free reorganization (the policy having a basis for determining gain or loss in the hands of the M Corporation determined by reference to its basis in the hands of the Z Corporation). The M Corporation receives the proceeds of $1,000 upon the death of A. The amount which the M Corporation can exclude from its gross income is limited to $600 plus any premiums paid by the Z Corporation and the M Corporation subsequent to the transfer of the policy to the Z Corporation.

Example (5). The facts are the same as in example (3) except that, prior to the death of A, the Z Corporation transfers the policy to the N Corporation, in which A is a shareholder. The N Corporation receives the proceeds of $1,000 upon the death of A. The entire $1,000 is to be excluded from the gross income of the N Corporation.

Example (6). A pays premiums of $500 for an insurance policy in the face amount of $1,000 upon his own life, and subsequently transfers the policy to his wife B for $600. B later transfers the policy without consideration to C, who is the son of A and B. C receives the proceeds of $1,000 upon the death of A. The amount which C can exclude from his gross income is limited to $600 plus any premiums paid by B and C subsequent to the transfer of the policy to B.

Example (7). The facts are the same as in example (6) except that, prior to the death of A, C transfers the policy without consideration to A, the insured. A's estate receives the proceeds of $1,000 upon the death of A. The entire $1,000 is to be excluded from the gross income of A's estate.

T.D. 6280, 12/16/57, amend T.D. 6783, 12/23/64, T.D. 7836, 9/23/82, T.D. 9340, 7/23/2007.

§ 1.101-2 Employees' death benefits.

Caution: The Treasury has not yet amended Reg § 1.101-2 to reflect changes made by P.L. 104-188, P.L. 98-369.

(a) In general. *(1)* Section 101(b) states the general rule that amounts up to $5,000 which are paid to the beneficiaries or the estate of an employee, or former employee, by or on behalf of an employer and by reason of the death of the employee shall be excluded from the gross income of the recipient. This exclusion from gross income applies whether payment is made to the estate of the employee or to any beneficiary (individual, corporation, or partnership), whether it is made directly or in trust, and whether or not it is made pursuant to a contractual obligation of the employer. The exclusion applies whether payment is made in a single sum or otherwise, subject to the provisions of section 101(c), relating to amounts held under an agreement to pay interest thereon (see § 1.101-3). The exclusion from gross income also applies to any amount not actually paid which is otherwise taxable to a beneficiary of an employee because it was made available as a distribution from an employee's trust.

(2) The exclusion does not apply to amounts constituting income payable to the employee during his life as compensation for his services, such as bonuses or payments for unused leave or uncollected salary, nor to certain other amounts with respect to which the deceased employee possessed, immediately before his death, a nonforfeitable right to receive the amounts while living (see section 101(b)(2)(B) and paragraph (d) of this section). Further, the exclusion does not apply to amounts received as an annuity under a joint and survivor annuity obligation where the employee was the primary annuitant and the annuity starting date occurred before the death of the employee (see section 101(b)(2)(C) and paragraph (e)(1)(ii) of this section). In the case of amounts received by a beneficiary as an annuity (but not as a survivor under a joint and survivor annuity with respect to which the employee was the primary annuitant), the exclusion is applied indirectly by means of the provisions of section 72 and the regulations thereunder (see section 101(b)(2)(D) and paragraph (e)(1)(iii) and (iv) of this section). Thus, for example, the exclusion applies to amounts which are received by a survivor of an employee retired on disability under the provisions of the Civil Service retirement law (5 U.S.C. 8301 or any former corresponding provisions of law) or the Retired Serviceman's Family Protection Plan or Survivor Benefit Plan (10 U.S.C. 1431 *et seq.*), provided such employee dies before attaining mandatory retirement age (as defined in § 1.105-4(a)(3)(i)(B)).

(3) The total amount excludable with respect to any employee may not exceed $5,000, regardless of the number of employers or the number of beneficiaries. For allocation of the exclusion among beneficiaries, see paragraph (c) of this section. For rules governing the taxability of benefits payable on the death of an employee under pension, profit-sharing, or stock bonus plans described in section 401(a) and exempt under section 501(a), under annuity plans described in section 403(a), or under annuity contracts to which paragraph (a) or (b) of § 1.403(b)-1 applies, see sections 72(m)(3), 402(a), and 403 and the regulations thereunder.

(b) Payments under certain employee benefit plans. *(1) In general.* Where a payment is made by reason of the death of an employee by an employer-provided welfare fund or a trust, including a stock bonus, pension, or profit-sharing trust described in section 401(a), or by an insurance company (if such payment does not constitute "life insurance" within the purview of section 101(a)), the payment shall be considered to have been made by or on behalf of the employer to the extent that it exceeds amounts contributed by, or deemed contributed by, the deceased employee.

(2) Cross references. For provisions governing the taxability of distributions payable on the death of an employee participant—

(i) Under a trust described in section 401(a) and exempt from tax under section 501(a), see paragraph (c) of § 1.72-16 and paragraph (a)(5) of § 1.402(a)-1;

(ii) Under an annuity plan described in section 403(a), see paragraph (c) of § 1.72-16 and paragraph (c) of § 1.403(a)-1;

(iii) Under annuity contracts to which paragraph (a) or (b) of § 1.403(b)-1 applies, see paragraph (c)(2) and (3) of § 1.403(b)-1;

(iv) Under eligible State deferred compensation plans described in section 457(b), see paragraph (c) of § 1.457-1.

(c) Allocation of the exclusion. *(1)* Where the aggregate payments by or on behalf of an employer or employers as death benefits to the beneficiaries or the estate of a deceased employee exceed $5,000, the $5,000 exclusion shall be apportioned among them in the same proportion as the amount received by or the present value of the amount payable to each bears to the total death benefits paid or payable by or on behalf of the employer or employers.

(2) The application of the rule in subparagraph (1) of this paragraph may be illustrated by the following example:

Example. The M Corporation, the employer of A, a deceased employee who died November 30, 1954, makes payments in 1955 to the beneficiaries of A as follows: $5,000 to W, A's widow, $2,000 to B, the son of A, and $3,000 to C, the daughter of A. No other amounts are paid by any other employer of A to his estate or beneficiaries. By application of the apportionment rule stated above, W, the widow, will exclude $2,500 ($5,000/$10,000, or one-half, of $5,000); B, the son, will exclude $1,000 ($2,000/$10,000, or one-fifth, of $5,000); and C, the daughter, will exclude $1,500 ($3,000/$10,000, or three-tenths, of $5,000).

(d) Nonforfeitable rights. *(1)* Except as provided in subparagraphs (3) and (4) of this paragraph, the exclusion provided by section 101(b) does not apply to amounts with respect to which the deceased employee possessed, immediately before his death, a nonforfeitable right to receive the amounts while living. Section 101(b)(2)(B). For the purpose of section 101(b) and this paragraph, an employee shall be considered to have had a nonforfeitable right with respect to—

(i) Any amount to which he would have been entitled—

(a) If he had made an appropriate election or demand, or

(b) Upon termination of his employment (see examples (5) and (6) of subparagraph (2) of this paragraph); or

(ii) The present value (immediately before his death) of—

(a) Amounts payable as an annuity (as defined in paragraph (b) of § 1.72-2, whether immediate or deferred) by or on behalf of the employer (see example (1) of subparagraph (2) of this paragraph), or

(b) Amounts which would have been so payable if the employee had terminated his employment and continued to live; or

(iii) Any amount to the extent it is paid in lieu of amounts described in either subdivision (i) or (ii) of this subparagraph. See examples (2), (3), and (4) of subparagraph (2) of this paragraph.

For purposes of subdivision (iii) of this subparagraph, any amount paid in discharge of an obligation which arose solely because of the existence of a particular fact or circumstance subsequent to the employee's death shall not be considered an amount paid in lieu of amounts described in subdivision (i) or (ii) of this subparagraph. Subdivision (iii) of this subparagraph shall apply, however, to the extent indicated therein, to amounts payable without regard to any such contingency (to the extent that such amounts are equal to or less than those described in subdivision (i) and (ii) of this subparagraph which are not paid). See paragraph (e)(I)(iii)(b) of this section for rules with respect to finding the present value of an annuity immediately before the employee's death.

(2) The application of paragraph (d)(1) of this section may be illustrated by the following examples, in which it is assumed that the plans are not "qualified plans" and that no employer is an organization referred to in section 170(b)(1)(A)(ii) or (vi) or a religious organization (other than a trust) which is exempt from tax under section 501(a):

Example (1). A, who was a participant under the X Company pension plan, retired on December 31, 1953. He had made no contributions to the plan. Upon his retirement, he became entitled to monthly payments of $100 payable for life, or 120 months certain. A died on October 31, 1954, having received 10 monthly payments of $100 each. After his death, the monthly payments became payable to his estate for the remaining 110 months certain. No exclusion from gross income is allowed to A's estate (or any beneficiary who receives the right to such payments from the estate), since the employee's right to the monthly payments was nonforfeitable at the date of his death. It will be noted that in this example it is unnecessary to consider the present value of the annuity to A just before his death since the payments to be made include only those certain to be made in any event under the plan whether or not A continued to live.

Example (2). C, a participant under the Y Company pension plan, died on December 15, 1954, while actively in the employment of the company, survived by a widow and minor children. Because of his years of service, he would have been entitled to an annuity for life, his own contributions to the plan and interest thereon being guaranteed, if he had retired or terminated his employment at a time immediately before his death. The plan further provides that—(a) if, but only if, an employee is survived by a widow and minor children, his widow is to receive an annuity for her life without regard to whether or not the employee had begun his annuity; (b) any payments made with respect to his widow's annuity are to reduce the guaranteed amount to an equal extent; and (c) if the employee is not so survived, the guaranteed amount is payable to his beneficiary or estate, but no amount is payable to anyone with respect to what would have been the widow's annuity. In view of these provisions, that portion of the present value of the annuity payable to C's widow which exceeds the guaranteed amount shall be considered paid neither as an amount, nor in lieu of an amount, which C had a nonforfeitable right to receive while living. The reason for this result is that the payment of such excess is contingent upon C's being survived by a widow and minor children, a circumstances existing subsequent to his death. Conversely, to the extent that the present value of the annuity payable to C's widow does not exceed the guaranteed amount, annuity payments attributable to such present value shall be considered paid in lieu of an amount which C had a nonforfeitable right to receive while living.

Example (3). D, a participant under the Y Company pension plan, died on January 1, 1955, while actively in the employment of the company. The Y Company plan provides that where an employee dies in service, the present value of the accumulated credits which he could have obtained at that time if he had instead separated from the service shall be paid in a single sum to his surviving spouse or to his estate if no widow survives him. The present value of D's accumulated credits, at the time of his death, was $10,000. However, the plan also provides that a surviving spouse may elect to take, in lieu of a single sum, an annuity the present value of which exceeds such sum by $2,500. D's widow elects to receive an annuity (the present value of which is $12,500). Therefore, $2,500 is an amount to which the exclusion of section 101(b) and this section shall apply.

Example (4). A, an employee of the X Company, continues to work after reaching the normal retirement age of 60 years, although he could have retired at that age and obtained an annuity of $3,000 per year for his life. A is not entitled to any part of the annuity while he is employed and receiving compensation. A dies at the age of 67 while still in active employment. Since he had passed normal retirement age, his additional years of service did not entitle him to a larger annuity at age 67 than that which he could have obtained at age 60. However, the plan of the X Company provides that in the event of an employee's death prior to separation from the service, his widow is to be paid an annuity for her life in the same amount per year as that which the employee could have obtained if he had instead retired; but if no widow survives him, the present value of the annuity which the employee could have obtained at a time just before his death is to be paid to a named beneficiary or the estate of the employee. Assuming that the present value of the annuity to A's widow, whose age is 61, is $36,000 and the present value of the annuity which would have been payable to A at age 67 if he had then retired is $23,500, the present value of the widow's annuity, to the extent of $23,500, is an amount which is payable in lieu of amounts which the employee had a nonforfeitable right to receive while living because it does not exceed the value of his nonforfeitable rights and is not otherwise paid. On the other hand, the $12,500 excess of the value of the widow's annuity ($36,000) over the value of the employee's annuity ($23,500) is an amount to which section 101(b) applies since the employee had no right to any part of it. If no other death benefits are payable, a $5,000 exclusion is available (see section 101(b)(2)(D) and paragraph (e) of this section.

Example (5). The trustee of the X Corporation noncontributory profit-sharing plan is required under the provisions of the plan to pay to the beneficiary of B, an employee of the X Corporation who died on July 1, 1955, the benefit due on account of the death of B. The provisions of the profit-sharing plan give each participating employee in case of termination of employment a 10-percent vested interest in the amount accumulated in his account for each year of participation in the plan. In case of death, the entire credit in the participant's account is to be paid to his beneficiary. At the time of B's death, he had been a participant for three years and the accumulation in his account was $8,000. After his death this amount is paid to his beneficiary. At the time of B's death, the amount distributable to him on account of termination of employment would have been $2,400 (30 percent of $8,000). The difference of $5,600 ($8,000 minus $2,400), payable to the beneficiary of B, is an amount payable solely by reason of B's death. Accordingly, $5,000 of the $5,600 may be excluded from the gross income of the beneficiary receiving such payment (assuming no other death benefits are involved). However, if it is assumed that the facts are the same as above, except that at the time of his death B has been a participant for 6 years, the amount distributable to him on account of termination of employment would have been $4,800 (60 percent of $8,000). The difference of $3,200 ($8,000 minus $4,800), payable to B's beneficiary, is an amount payable solely by reason of B's death. Accordingly, only $3,200 may be excluded from the gross income of the beneficiary receiving such payment (assuming no other death benefits are involved).

Example (6). The X Corporation instituted a trust, forming part of a pension plan, for its employees, the cost thereof being borne entirely by the corporation. The plan provides, in part, that after 10 or more years of service and attaining the age of 55, an employee can elect to retire and receive benefits before the normal retirement date contingent upon the employer's approval. If he retires without the employer's consent, or voluntarily leaves the company, no benefits are or will be payable. The plan further provides that if the employee is involuntarily separated or dies before retirement, he or his beneficiary, respectively, will receive a percentage of the reserve provided for the employee in the trust fund on the following basis: 10 to 15 years of service, 25 percent; 15 to 20 years of service, 50 percent; 20 to 25 years of service, 75 percent; 25 or more years of service, 100 percent. A, an employee of the X Corporation for 17 years, died at the age of 56 while in the employ of the corporation. At the time of his death, $15,000 was the reserve provided for him in the trust. His beneficiary receives $7,500, an amount equal to 50 percent of the reserve provided for A's retirement; accordingly, $5,000 of the $7,500 may be excluded from the gross income of the beneficiary receiving such payment (assuming no other death benefits are involved) since A, prior to his death, had only a forfeitable right to receive $7,500.

(3) (i) Notwithstanding the rule stated in subparagraph (1) of this paragraph and illustrated in subparagraph (2) of this paragraph, the exclusion from gross income provided by section 101(b) applies to the receipt of certain amounts, paid under "qualified" plans, with respect to which the deceased employee possessed, immediately before his death, a nonforfeitable right to receive the amounts while living (see section 101(b)(2)(B)(i) and (ii)). The payments to which this exclusion applies are—

(a) "Total distributions payable" by a stock bonus, pension, or profit-sharing trust described in section 401(a) which is exempt from tax under section 501(a), and

(b) "Total amounts" paid under an annuity contract under a plan described in section 403(a), provided such distributions or amounts are paid in full within one taxable year of the distributee (see example (3) of subdivision (ii) of this subparagraph). For the purposes of applying section 101(b), "total distributions payable" means the balance to the credit of an employee which becomes payable to a distributee on account of the employee's death, either before or after separation from the service (see section 402(a)(3)(C), the regulations thereunder, and examples (2) and (4) of subdivision (ii) of this subparagraph); and "total amounts" means the balance to the credit of an employee which becomes payable to the payee by reason of the employee's death, either before or after separation from the service (see section 403(a)(2)(B), the regulations thereunder, and example (1) of subdivision (ii) of this subparagraph). See subparagraph (4) of this paragraph relating to the exclusion of amounts which are received under annuity contracts purchased by certain exempt organizations and with respect to which the deceased employee possessed, immediately before his death, a nonforfeitable right to receive the amounts while living.

(ii) The application of the provisions of subdivision (i) of this subparagraph may be illustrated by the following examples:

Example (1). The widow of an employee elects, under a noncontributory "qualified" plan, to receive in a lump sum the present value of the annuity which C, the deceased employee, could have obtained at a time just before his death if he had retired at that time. Such present value is $6,000. Of this amount, $5,000 is excludable from the widow's gross income despite the fact that C had a nonforfeitable right to the amount in lieu of which the payment is made, since such payment is an amount to which subdivision (i) of this subparagraph applies (assuming no other death benefits are involved).

Example (2). The trustee of the X Corporation noncontributory, "qualified", profit-sharing plan is required under the provisions of the plan to pay to the beneficiary of B, an employee of the X Corporation who died on July 1, 1955, the benefit due on account of the death of B. The provisions of the profit-sharing plan give each participating employee, in case of termination of employment, a 10 percent vested interest in the amount accumulated in his account for each year of participation in the plan, but, in case of death, the entire credit to the participant's account is to be paid to his beneficiary. At the time of B's death, he had been a participant for five years. The accumulation in his account was $8,000, and the amount which would have been distributable to him in the event of termination of employment was $4,000 (50 percent of $8,000). After his death, $8,000 is paid to his beneficiary in a lump sum. (It may be noted that these are the same facts as in example (5) of subparagraph (2) of this paragraph except that the employee has been a participant for five years instead of three and the plan is a "qualified" plan.) It is immaterial that the employee had a nonforfeitable right to $4,000, because the payment of the $8,000 to the beneficiary is the payment of the "total distributions payable" within one taxable year of the distributee to which subdivision (i) of this subparagraph applies. Assuming no other death benefits are involved, the beneficiary may exclude $5,000 of the $8,000 payment from gross income.

Example (3). The facts are the same as in example (2) except that the beneficiary is entitled to receive only the $4,000 to which the employee had a nonforfeitable right and elects, 30 days after B's death, to receive it over a period of ten years. Since the "total distributions payable" are not paid within one taxable year of the distributee, no exclusion from gross income is allowable with respect to the $4,000.

Example (4). The X Corporation instituted a trust, forming part of a "qualified" profit-sharing plan for its employees, the cost thereof being borne entirely by the corporation. The plan provides, in part, that if, after 10 or more years of service, an employee leaves the employ of the corporation, either voluntarily or involuntarily, before retirement, a percentage of the reserve provided for the employee in the trust fund will be paid to the employee as follows: 10 to 15 years of service, 25 percent; 15 to 20 years of service, 50 percent; 20 to 25 years of service, 75 percent; 25 or more years of service, 100 percent. The plan further provides that if an employee dies before reaching retirement age, his beneficiary will receive a percentage of the reserve provided for the employee in the trust fund, on the same basis as shown in the preceding sentence. A, an employee of the X Corporation for 17 years, died before attaining retirement age while in the employ of the corporation. At the time of his death, $15,000 was the reserve provided for him in the trust fund. His beneficiary receives $7,500 in a lump sum, an amount equal to 50 percent of the reserve provided for A's retirement. The beneficiary may exclude from gross income (assuming no other death benefits are involved) $5,000 of the $7,500, since the latter amount constitutes "total distributions payable" paid within one taxable year of the distributee, to which subdivision (i) of this subparagraph applies.

(4) (i) Notwithstanding the rule stated in subparagraph (1) of this paragraph and illustrated in subparagraph (2) of this paragraph, the exclusion from gross income under section 101(b) also applies (but only to the extent provided in the next sentence) to amounts with respect to which the deceased employee possessed, immediately before his death, a nonforfeitable right to receive the amounts while living—

(a) If such amounts are paid under an annuity contract purchased by an employer which is an organization referred to in section 170(b)(1)(A)(ii) or (vi) or which is a religious organization (other than a trust) and which is exempt from tax under section 501(a).

(b) If such amounts are paid as part of a "total payment" with respect to the deceased employee; and

(c) If such "total payment" is paid in full within one taxable year of the payee beginning after December 31, 1957. However, the amount that is excludable under section 101(b) by reason of this subparagraph shall not exceed an amount which bears the same ratio to the amount which would be includible in the payee's gross income if it were not for the second sentence of section 101(b)(2)(B) and this subparagraph, as the amount contributed by the employer for the annuity contract that was excludable from the deceased employee's gross income under paragraph (b) of § 1.403(b)-1 bears to the total amount contributed by the employer for the annuity contract. See section 101(b)(2)(B)(iii). For purposes of this subparagraph, a "total payment" means a payment of the balance to the credit of an employee with respect to all "section 403(b) annuities" purchased by the employer which becomes payable to the payee by reason of the employee's death, either before or after separation from the service. An annuity contract will be regarded as a "section 403(b) annuity" if any amount contributed (or considered as contributed under paragraph (b)(2) of § 1.403(b)-1) by the employer for such contract was excludable from the employee's gross income under paragraph (b) of § 1.403(b)-1. Under this definition, therefore, an annuity contract may be regarded as a "section 403(b) annuity" even though some of the employer's contributions for the contract were not excludable from the employee's gross income under paragraph (b) of § 1.403(b)-1 because, for example, the employer was not an exempt organization when such contributions were paid. For purposes of computing the ratio described in this subdivision in such a case, the total amount contributed by the employer for the contract includes the amounts contributed by the employer when it was not an exempt organization.

(ii) This subparagraph does not relate to any amounts with respect to which the deceased employee did not possess, immediately before his death, a nonforfeitable right to receive the amounts while living. Such amounts are excludable under the provisions of section 101(b) without regard to section 101(b)(2)(B) and this subparagraph. Thus, if a "total payment" received by a beneficiary of a deceased employee under an annuity contract purchased by an organization described in subdivision (i)(a) of this subparagraph consists both of amounts with respect to which the deceased employee possessed, immediately before his death, a nonforfeitable right to receive the amounts while living and of amounts with respect to which the deceased employee did not possess such a nonforfeitable right, only those amounts with respect to which the deceased employee possessed such a nonforfeitable right are amounts to which this subparagraph applies. Therefore, for purposes of computing the ratio described in subdivision (i) of this subparagraph in such a case, there shall be taken into account only the employer contributions attributable to those amounts with respect to which the deceased employee possessed, immediately before his death, a nonforfeitable right to receive the amounts while living. See example (3) of subdivision (v) of this subparagraph. In no event, however, may the total amount excludable under section 101(b) with respect to any employee exceed $5,000 (see paragraph (a)(3) of this section).

(iii) (a) In any case when the deceased employee's interest in the employer's contributions for an annuity contract was forfeitable at the time the contributions were made but, at a subsequent date prior to his death, such interest changed to a nonforfeitable interest, then, for purposes of computing the ratio described in subdivision (i) of this subparagraph, the cash surrender value of the contract on the date of the change (except to the extent attributable to employee contributions) shall be considered as the amount contributed by the employer for the contract. In such a case, if only part of the deceased employee's interest in the annuity changed from a forfeitable to a nonforfeitable interest, then only the corresponding part of the cash surrender value of the contract on the date of the change shall be considered as the amount contributed by the employer for the contract. Similarly, if part of the deceased employee's interest in the annuity contract changed from a forfeitable to a nonforfeitable interest on a particular date and another part of his interest so changed on a subsequent date, it is necessary, in order to compute the amount contributed by the employer for the contract, to first determine (under the rules in the preceding sentence) the amount that is considered as the amount contributed by the employer with respect to each change, and then to add these amounts together. For purposes of computing the ratio described in subdivision (i) of this subparagraph in all of the above cases, the amount contributed by the employer that was excludable from the employee's gross income under paragraph (b) of § 1.403(b)-1 is that amount which, under paragraph (b)(2) of such section, was considered as employer contributions and which, under such paragraph (b) of § 1.403(b)-1, was excludable from the deceased employee's gross income for the taxable year in which the change occurred.

(b) This subdivision (iii) may be illustrated by the following examples:

Example (1). X Organization contributed $4,000 toward the purchase of an annuity contract for A, an employee who died in 1970. At the time they were made, A's interest in such contributions was forfeitable. A made no contributions toward the purchase of the annuity contract. On January 1, 1960, A's entire interest in the annuity contract changed to a nonforfeitable interest. At the time of such change, the cash surrender value of the contract was $5,000. For purposes of the ratio described in subdivision (i) of this subparagraph, the total amount contributed by X Organization for the annuity contract is $5,000. If any part of such $5,000 was excludable under paragraph (b) of § 1.403(b)-1 from A's gross income for his taxable year in which the change occurred, the amount so excludable shall be considered as the amount contributed for the contract by the employer that was excludable from the employee's gross income under paragraph (b) of § 1.403(b)-1.

Example (2). Assume the same facts as in example (1) except that only one-half of A's interest in the annuity contract changed to a nonforfeitable interest on January 1, 1960, and that no other part of his interest so changed during his lifetime. For purposes of the ratio described in subdivision (i) of this subparagraph, the total amount contributed by X Organization for the annuity contract is $2,500 (½ of the cash surrender value of the annuity contract on the date of the change). To the extent such $2,500 was, under paragraph (b) of § 1.403(b)-1, excludable from A's gross income for the taxable year of the change, it is considered as the amount contributed by the employer that was excludable under paragraph (b) of § 1.403(b)-1.

Example (3). Assume the same facts as in example (1) except that one-half of A's interest in the annuity contract changed to a nonforfeitable interest on January 1, 1960, and the other half of his interest changed to a nonforfeitable interest on January 1, 1965. On January 1, 1965, the cash surrender value of the annuity contract was $6,000. For purposes of the ratio described in subdivision (i) of this subparagraph, the total amount contributed by X organization for the annuity contract is $5,500 (i.e., ½ × $5,000 plus ½ × $6,000). The amount contributed by the employer that was excludable from A's gross income under paragraph (b) of § 1.403(b)-1 is an amount equal to the sum of the amount that was, under such paragraph, excludable from A's gross income for the taxable year during which the first change occurred and the amount that was, under such paragraph, excludable from A's gross income for the taxable year in which the second change occurred.

(iv) For purposes of this subparagraph, an annuity contract will be considered to have been purchased by an employer which is an organization referred to in section 170(b)(1)(A)(ii) or (vi) or which is a religious organization (other than a trust) and which is exempt from tax under section 501(a), if any of the contributions paid toward the purchase price of such contract by the employer were paid at a time when the employer was such an organization. Thus an annuity contract may be regarded as purchased by such an organization even though part of the organization's contributions for such annuity contract were paid at a time when the organization was not such an exempt organization.

(v) The application of this subparagraph may be illustrated by the following examples:

Example (1). The widow of A, a deceased employee, elects, under an annuity contract purchased for A by X Organization, to receive in a lump sum the present value of such annuity contract as of the date of A's death. Such present value is $6,000 and is received by the widow in a taxable year beginning after December 31, 1957. X Organization contributed $3,000 toward the purchase of the annuity contract and A contributed $2,000 toward such purchase. A's interest in X Organization's contributions was nonforfeitable at the time such contributions were made. Thus, just before his death, A's entire interest in the annuity contract was a nonforfeitable interest and, if he had retired at that time, he could have received the present value of $6,000. The whole amount of the $3,000 contributed by X Organization for the annuity contract was excludable from A's gross income under paragraph (b) of § 1.403(b)-1. This annuity contract was the only annuity contract purchased by X Organization for A and was not purchased as part of a qualified plan. However, all the contributions paid by X Organization were paid at a time when X Organization was an organization referred to in section 170(b)(1)(A)(ii) and exempt from tax under section 501(a). The amount that A's widow may exclude from gross income (assuming no other death benefits) is computed in the following manner:

(a) Amount includible in gross income without regard to second sentence of section 101(b)(2)(B) ($6,000 minus $2,000 contributed for contract by A)	$4,000
(b) Total employer contributions for the contract	$3,000
(c) Amount of employer contributions for the contract that was excludable under paragraph (b) of § 1.403(b)-1	$3,000
(d) Percent of total employer contributions for the contract that were excludable under paragraph (b) of § 1.403(b)-1 ((c)÷(b))	100%
(e) Amount to which section 101(b) exclusion applies ((d) × (a))	$4,000

Example (2). The facts are the same as in example (1) except that only $2,000 of X Organization's contributions for the annuity contract was excludable from A's gross income under paragraph (b) of § 1.403(b)-1 and that the remaining $1,000 was includible in A's gross income for the taxable years during which such amounts were contributed by X Organization. The amount that A's widow may exclude from gross income (assuming no other death benefits) is computed in the following manner:

(a) Amount includible in gross income without regard to second sentence of section 101(b)(2)(B) ($6,000 minus $2,000 contributed for contract by A and $1,000 of X Organization's contributions includible in A's gross income)	$3,000
(b) Total employer contributions for the contract	$3,000
(c) Amount of employer contributions for the contract that was excludable under paragraph (b) of § 1.403(b)-1	$2,000
(d) Percent of total employer contributions for the contract that were excludable under paragraph (b) of § 1.403(b)-1 ((c)÷(b))	67%
(e) Amount to which section 101(b) exclusion applies ((d) × (a))	$2,000

Example (3). The widow of B, a deceased employee, elects, under an annuity contract purchased for B by Y Organization, to receive in a lump sum the present value of such annuity contract as of the date of B's death. Such present value is $6,000 and is received by the widow in a taxable year beginning after December 31, 1957. Y Organization contributed $4,000 toward the purchase of the contract; whereas B made no contributions toward the purchase of the contract. This annuity contract was the only annuity contract purchased by Y Organization for B and was not purchased as part of a "qualified" plan. However, all the contributions paid by Y Organization were paid at a time when it was an organization referred to in section 170(b)(1)(A)(ii) and exempt from tax under section 501(a). B's interest in Y Organization's contributions was, at the time they were paid, forfeitable. However, prior to his death, one-half of B's interest in the annuity contract changed from a forfeitable to a nonforfeitable interest. Therefore, just before his death, B could have obtained $3,000 under the annuity contract if he had retired at that time. On the date of the change, the cash surrender value of the annuity contract was $5,000. As a result of the change, $1,500 was, under paragraph (b) of § 1.403(b)-1, excludable from B's gross income, and $600 was includible in his gross income for the taxable year in which the change occurred. Part of the value of the annuity contract on the date of the change was attributable to contributions made by Y Organization prior to January 1, 1958, and, consequently, was neither excludable from B's gross income under paragraph (b) of § 1.403(b)-1 nor includible in B's gross income (see paragraph (b) of § 1.403(d)-1). The amount that B's widow may exclude from gross income (assuming no other death benefits) is computed in the following manner:

(a) Amount of "total payment" with respect to which A had a forfeitable right at time of death (½ × $6,000)	$3,000
(b) Amount includible in gross income without regard to second sentence of section 101(b)(2)(B) (½ × $6,000 less $600 includible in B's gross income for year when his rights changed to nonforfeitable rights)	$2,400
(c) Total employer contributions for the contract (½ of cash surrender value of contract on date B's rights changed to nonforfeitable rights)	$2,500
(d) Amount of employer contributions for the contract that was excludable under paragraph (b) of § 1.403(b)-1	$1,500
(e) Percent of total employer contributions for the contract that were excludable under paragraph (b) of § 1.403(b)-1 ((d) ÷ (c))	60%
(f) Amount to which section 101(b) exclusion applies by reason of the second sentence of section 101(b)(2)(B) ((e) × (b))	$1,440
(g) Total amount to which section 101(b) exclusion applies ((a) + (f))	$4,440

(e) Annuity payments. *(1)* Where death benefits are paid in the form of annuity payments, the following rules shall govern for purposes of the exclusion provided in section 101(b):

(i) The exclusion from gross income provided by section 101(b) does not apply to amounts, paid as an annuity, with respect to which the employee possessed, immediately before his death, a nonforfeitable right to receive the amounts while living, or to amounts paid as an annuity in lieu thereof. See paragraph (d) of this section.

(ii) Under section 101(b)(2)(C), no exclusion is allowable for amounts received by a surviving annuitant under a joint and survivor's annuity contract if the annuity starting date (as defined in section 72(c)(4) and paragraph (b) of § 1.72-4) occurs before the death of the employee. If the annuity starting date occurs after the death of the employee, the joint and survivor's annuity contract shall be treated as an annuity to which section 101(b)(2)(D) applies. See subdivision (iii) of this subparagraph.

(iii) (a) Subject to the other limitations stated in section 101(b) and in this section (see section 101(b)(2)(D)), the amount to which the exclusion of section 101(b) shall apply, with respect to "amounts received as an annuity" (as defined in paragraph (b) of § 1.72-2) shall be the amount by which the present value of the annuity to be paid to the beneficiary, computed as of the date of the employee's death, exceeds the value (if any) of whichever of the following is the larger:

(1) Amounts contributed by the employee (determined in accordance with the provisions of section 72 and the regulations thereunder), or

(2) Amounts with respect to which the employee possessed, immediately before his death, a nonforfeitable right to receive the amounts while living, or amounts paid in lieu thereof (see paragraph (d) of this section).

(b) The present value of an annuity (immediately before the death of the employee), to the employee, or (immediately after the death of the employee), to his estate or beneficiary, shall be determined as follows:

(1) In the case of an annuity paid by an insurance company or by an organization (other than an insurance company) regularly engaged in issuing annuity contracts with an insurance company as the coinsurer or reinsurer of the obligations under the contract, by use of the discount interest rates and mortality tables used by the insurance company involved to determine the installment benefits; and

(2) In the case of an annuity issued after November 23, 1984, to which paragraph (e)(1)(iii)(b)(1) of this section is not applicable, by use of the appropriate tables in section 20.2031-7 of this chapter (Estate Tax Regulations).

(iv) Any amount subject to section 101(b)(2)(D) which is excludable under section 101(b) (see subdivision (iii) of this subparagraph) shall, for purposes of section 72, be treated as additional consideration paid by the employee. See paragraph (b) of § 1.72-8.

(v) Where more than one beneficiary, or more than one death benefit, is involved, the exclusion provided by section 101(b) shall be apportioned to the various beneficiaries and benefits in accordance with the proportion that the present value of each benefit bears to the total present value of all the benefits.

(2) The application of the principles of this paragraph may be illustrated by the following examples:

Example (1). (i) A died on January 1, 1969. Under the plan of the X Corporation, W, who is the widow of employee A, and who is 55 years old at the time of A's death, is entitled to an immediate annuity of $2,000 per year during her life and C, the minor child of A, is entitled to receive $1,000 per year for 15 years. A made no contributions under the plan and died while still employed by the X Corporation. At the time of A's death, the amount in his account is $18,000. Under the terms of the plan, this amount would have been distributable to him on account of voluntary termination of employment, but would not have been payable after his death except in the form of the annuities just described. This amount, accordingly, constitutes a nonforfeitable interest in lieu of which the annuities are paid. The exclusion does not apply, except to the extent that the present value of the annuities exceeds $18,000, whether or not the plan is "qualified", since the total of the amount in A's account will not be paid within one taxable year of the distributees. See subparagraph (1)(i) of this paragraph.

(ii) The computation of the exclusion applicable to the interests of W and C (assuming that the payments will not be made by an insurance company or some other organization regularly engaged in issuing annuity contracts) is, by application of the tables in § 20.2031-7 of this chapter (Estate Tax Regulations), as follows: The present value of W's interest is $26,243.60, determined by multiplying the annual payment of $2,000 by 13.1218 (the factor in Table I for a person aged 55); the present value of C's interest is $11,517.40, determined by multiplying the yearly payment of $1,000 by 11.5174 (the factor in Table II for payments for a term certain of 15 years). The present value of both annuities is $37,761 and (assuming no other death benefits are involved), the total amount excludable is $5,000, because the total present value of the annuities exceeds the employee's nonforfeitable interest by more than $5,000 ($37,761 minus $18,000 equal $19,761). The exclusion allocable to W's interest is $26,243.60/$37,761 times $5,000, or $3,474.96; the exclusion allocable to C's interest is $11,517.40/$37,761 times $5,000, or $1,525.04. That portion of the death benefit exclusion as so determined for each beneficiary is to be treated as consideration paid by the employee for purposes of section 72.

Example (2). The facts are the same as in example (1), except that the nonforfeitable interest of A, at the time of his death, amounted to $33,761. Since the present value of both annuities ($37,761) exceeds the value of such nonforfeitable interest by only $4,000, the latter amount is the total amount excludable from the gross income of the beneficiaries. This $4,000 exclusion is to be divided in the same proportions as those indicated in example (1). Thus, the exclusion allocable to W's interest is $26,243.60/$37,761 times $4,000, or $2,779.97; and the exclusion allocable to the interest of C is $11,517.40/$37,761 times $4,000, or $1,220.03. That portion of the death benefit exclusion as so determined for each beneficiary is to be treated as consideration paid by the employee for purposes of section 72.

(f) Distributions on behalf of a self-employed individual. *(1)* Under sections 401(c)(1) and 403(a)(3), certain self-employed individuals may be covered by a pension or profit-sharing plan described in section 401(a) and exempt under section 501(a) or under an annuity plan described in section 403(a). However, a payment pursuant to the provisions of any such plan by reason of the death of an individual who participated in such a plan as a self-employed individual immediately before his retirement or death to the beneficiary or estate of such individual does not qualify for the exclusion provided by section 101(b).

(2) The application of this paragraph may be illustrated by the following examples:

Example (1). From 1950 to 1965, A was an employee of B, a sole proprietor. In 1963, B established a qualified pension plan covering A and all other persons who had been employed by B for more than 3 years. In 1965, A acquired from B a 40-percent interest in the capital and profits of the business. A continued to participate in the pension plan as a self-employed individual. In 1970, A died and his widow, in compliance with one of the provisions of the pension plan, elected to receive all of the benefits accrued to A prior to his death in a lump-sum distribution. As A participated in the plan as a self-employed individual immediately prior to his death, A's widow may not exclude any portion of such distribution from her gross income under section 101(b).

Example (2). A, an attorney, is employed by the X Company in their legal department. He is covered by the pension plan that X has established for its employees. Under the terms of A's contract of employment with X, A is permitted to carry on the private practice of law in his off-duty hours. A establishes his own pension plan with respect to his earnings from his private practice. On A's death, his widow elected to receive a lump-sum distribution with respect to any benefits accrued to A under both X's pension plan and A's own pension plan. To the extent that such payment otherwise complies with the requirements of section 101(b), up to $5,000 of the amount paid by X may be excluded from her gross income. No part of the distribution from A's own pension plan may be excluded from her gross income under section 101(b) because A participated in the plan as a self-employed individual immediately before his death.

T.D. 6280, 12/16/57, amend T.D. 6722, 4/13/64, T.D. 6783, 12/23/64, T.D. 7043, 6/1/70, T.D. 7352, 4/9/75, T.D. 7428, 8/13/76, T.D. 7836, 9/23/82, T.D. 7955, 5/10/84, T.D. 8540, 6/9/94.

PAR. 6. Paragraph (d) of § 1.101-2 is amended by revising subparagraph (3)(i) and example (2) [sic -(4)] of subparagraph (3)(ii) to read as follows:

Proposed § 1.101-2 Employees' death benefits. [*For Preamble, see ¶ 150,135*]

• ***Caution:*** Proposed section 1.62-1 was finalized by TD 7399, 2/3/76. Proposed sections 1.72-4, 1.72-13, 1.101-2, 1.122-1, 1.402(a)-1, 1.402(e)-2, 1.402(e)-3, 1.403(a)-1, 1.403(a)-2, 1.405-3, 1.652(b)-1, 1.1304-2 and 11.402(e)(4)(B)-1 remain proposed.

* * * * *

(d) Nonforfeitable rights. * * *

(3) (i) Notwithstanding the rule stated in paragraph (d)(1) of this section and illustrated in paragraph (d)(2) of this section, the exclusion from gross income provided by section 101(b) applies to a lump sum distribution (as defined in section 402(e)(4)(A) and the regulations thereunder) with respect to which the deceased employee possessed, immediately before his death, a nonforfeitable right to receive the amounts while living (see section 101(b)(2)(B)(i) and (ii)). See paragraph (d)(4) of this section relating to the exclusion of amounts which are received under annuity contracts purchased by certain exempt organizations and with respect to which the deceased employee possessed, immediately before his death, a nonforfeitable right to receive the amounts while living.

(ii) The application of the provisions of paragraph (d)(3)(i) of this section may be illustrated by the following examples:

* * * * *

Example (2). The trustee of the X Corporation noncontributory, "qualified," profit-sharing plan is required under the provisions of the plan to pay to the beneficiary of B, an employee of the X Corporation who died on July 1, 1974, the benefit due on account of the death of B. The provisions of the profit-sharing plan give each participating employee, in case of termination of employment, a 10 percent vested interest in the amount accumulated in his account for each of the first 10 years of participation in the plan, but, in case of death, the entire balance to the credit of the participant's account is to be paid to his beneficiary. At the time of B's death, he had been a participant for five years. The accumulation in his account was $8,000, and the amount which would have been distributable to him in the event of termination of employment was $4,000 (50 percent of $8,000). After his death, $8,000 is paid to his beneficiary in a lump sum. (It may be noted that these are the same facts as in example (5) of subparagraph (2) of this paragraph except that the employee has been a participant for five years instead of three and the plan is a "qualified" plan.) It is immaterial that the employee had a nonforfeitable right to $4,000, because the payment of the $8,000 to the beneficiary is the payment of a lump sum distribution to which subdivision (i) of this subparagraph applies. Assuming no other death benefits are involved, the beneficiary may exclude $5,000 of the $8,000 payment from gross income.

Example (3). The facts are the same as in example (2) except that the beneficiary is entitled to receive only the

$4,000 to which the employee had a nonforfeitable right and elects, 30 days after B's death, to receive it over a period of ten years. Because the distribution is not a lump sum distribution and because B's interest is nonforfeitable, no exclusion from gross income is allowable with respect to the $4,000.

Example (4). The X Corporation instituted a trust, forming part of a "qualified" profit-sharing plan for its employees, the cost thereof being borne entirely by the corporation. The plan provides, in part, that if an employee leaves the employ of the corporation, either voluntarily or involuntarily, before retirement, 10 percent of the account balance provided for the employee in the trust fund will be paid to the employee for each of the first 10 years of service. The plan further provides that if an employee dies before reaching retirement age, his beneficiary will receive a percentage of the account balance provided for the employee in the trust fund, on the same basis as shown in the preceding sentence. A, an employee of the X Corporation for 5 years, died before attaining retirement age while in the employ of the corporation. At the time of his death, $15,000 was the account balance provided for him in the trust fund. His beneficiary receives $7,500 in a lump sum, an amount equal to 50 percent of the account balance provided for A's retirement. The beneficiary may exclude from gross income (assuming no other death benefits are involved) $5,000 of the $7,500, since the latter amount constitutes a lump sum distribution to which subdivision (i) of this subparagraph applies.

§ 1.101-3 Interest payments.

Caution: The Treasury has not yet amended Reg § 1.101-3 to reflect changes made by P.L. 104-188.

(a) Applicability of section 101(c). Section 101(c) provides that if any amount excluded from gross income by section 101(a) (relating to life insurance proceeds) or section 101(b) (relating to employees' death benefits) is held under an agreement to pay interest thereon, the interest payments shall be included in gross income. This provision applies to payments made (either by an insurer or by or on behalf of an employer) of interest earned on any amount so excluded from gross income which is held without substantial diminution of the principal amount during the period when such interest payments are being made or credited to the beneficiaries or estate of the insured or the employee. For example, if a monthly payment is $100, of which $99 represents interests and $1 represents diminution of the principal amount, the principal amount shall be considered held under an agreement to pay interest thereon and the interest payment shall be included in the gross income of the recipient. Section 101(c) applies whether the election to have an amount held under an agreement to pay interest thereon is made by the insured or employee or by his beneficiaries or estate, and whether or not an interest rate is explicitly stated in the agreement. Section 101(d), relating to the payment of life insurance proceeds at a date later than death, shall not apply to any amount to which section 101(c) applies. See section 101(d)(4). However, both section 101(c) and section 101(d) may apply to payments received under a single life insurance contract. For provisions relating to the application of this rule to payments received under a permanent life insurance policy with a family income rider attached, see paragraph (h) of § 1.101-4.

(b) Determination of "present value". For the purpose of determining whether section 101(c) or section 101(d) applies, the present value (at the time of the insured's death) of any amount which is to be paid at a date later than death shall be determined by the use of the interest rate and mortality tables used by the insurer in determining the size of the payments to be made.

T.D. 6280, 12/16/57, amend T.D. 6577, 10/27/61.

§ 1.101-4 Payment of life insurance proceeds at a date later than death.

Caution: The Treasury has not yet amended Reg § 1.101-4 to reflect changes made by P.L. 99-514, P.L. 98-369.

(a) In general. *(1)* (i) Section 101(d) states the provisions governing the exclusion from gross income of amounts (other than those to which section 101(c) applies) received under a life insurance contract and paid by reason of the death of the insured which are paid to a beneficiary on a date or dates later than the death of the insured. However, if the amounts payable as proceeds of life insurance to which section 101(a)(1) applies cannot in any event exceed the amount payable at the time of the insured's death, such amounts are fully excludable from the gross income of the recipient (or recipients) without regard to the actual time of payment and no further determination need be made under this section. Section 101(d)(1)(A) provides an exclusion from gross income of any amount determined by a proration, under applicable regulations, of "an amount held by an insurer with respect to any beneficiary". The quoted phrase is defined in section 101(d)(2). For the regulations governing the method of computation of this proration, see paragraphs (c) through (f) of this section. The prorated amounts are to be excluded from the gross income of the beneficiary regardless of the taxable year in which they are actually received (see example (2) of subparagraph (2) of this paragraph).

(ii) Section 101(d)(1)(B) provides an additional exclusion where life insurance proceeds are paid to the surviving spouse of an insured. For purposes of this exclusion, the term "surviving spouse" means the spouse of the insured as of the date of death, including a spouse legally separated, but not under a decree of absolute divorce (section 101(d)(3)). To the extent that the total payments, under one or more agreements, made in excess of the amounts determined by proration under section 101(d)(1)(A) do not exceed $1,000 in the taxable year of receipt, they shall be excluded from the gross income of the surviving spouse (whether or not payment of any part of such amounts is guaranteed by the insurer). Amounts excludable under section 101(d)(1)(B) are not "prorated" amounts.

(2) The principles of this paragraph may be illustrated by the following examples:

Example (1). A surviving spouse elects to receive all of the life insurance proceeds with respect to one insured, amounting to $150,000, in ten annual installments of $16,500 each, based on a certain guaranteed interest rate. The prorated amount is $15,000 ($150,000 ÷ 10). As the second payment, the insurer pays $17,850, which exceeds the guaranteed payment by $1,350 as the result of earnings of the insurer in excess of those required to pay the guaranteed installments. The surviving spouse shall include $1,850 in gross income and exclude $16,000— determined in the following manner:

Fixed payment (including guaranteed interest)	$16,500
Excess interest	1,350
Total payment	17,850
Prorated amount	15,000
Excess over prorated amount................	2,850
Annual excess over prorated amount excludable under section 101 (d) (1) (B)	1,000
Amount includible in gross income	1,850

Example (2). Assume the same facts as in example (1), except that the third and fourth annual installments, totalling $33,000 (2 × $16,500), are received in a single subsequent taxable year of the surviving spouse. The prorated amount of $15,000 of each annual installment, totalling $30,000, shall be excluded even though the spouse receives more than one annual installment in the single subsequent taxable year. However, the surviving spouse is entitled to only one exclusion of $1,000 under section 101(d)(1)(B) for each taxable year of receipt. The surviving spouse shall include $2,000 in her gross income for the taxable year with respect to the above installment payments ($33,000 less the sum of $30,000 plus $1,000).

Example (3). Assume the same facts as in example (1), except that the surviving spouse dies before receiving all ten annual installments and the remaining installments are paid to her estate or beneficiary. In such a case, $15,000 of each installment would continue to be excludable from the gross income of the recipient, but any amounts received in excess thereof would be fully includible.

(b) Amount held by an insurer. *(1)* For the purpose of the proration referred to in section 101(d)(1), an "amount held by an insurer with respect to any beneficiary" means an amount equal to the present value to such beneficiary (as of the date of death of the insured) of an agreement by the insurer under a life insurance policy (whether as an option or otherwise) to pay such beneficiary an amount or amounts at a date or dates later than the death of the insured (section 101(d)(2)). The present value of such agreement is to be computed as if the agreement under the life insurance policy had been entered into on the date of death of the insured, except that such value shall be determined by the use of the mortality table and interest rate used by the insurer in calculating payments to be made to the beneficiary under such agreement. Where an insurance policy provides an option for the payment of a specific amount upon the death of the insured in full discharge of the contract, such lump sum is the amount held by the insurer with respect to all beneficiaries (or their beneficiaries) under the contract. See, however, paragraph (e) of this section.

(2) In the case of two or more beneficiaries, the "amount held by the insurer" with respect to each beneficiary depends on the relationship of the different benefits payable to such beneficiaries. Where the amounts payable to two or more beneficiaries are independent of each other, the "amount held by the insurer with respect to each beneficiary" shall be determined and prorated over the periods involved independently. Thus, if a certain amount per month is to be paid to A for his life, and, concurrently, another amount per month is to be paid to B for his life, the "amount held by the insurer" shall be determined and prorated for both A and B independently, but the aggregate shall not exceed the total present value of such payments to both. On the other hand, if the obligation to pay B was contingent on his surviving A, the "amount held by the insurer" shall be considered an amount held with respect to both beneficiaries simultaneously. Furthermore, it is immaterial whether B is a named beneficiary or merely the ultimate recipient of payments for a term of years. For the special rules governing the computation of the proration of the "amount held by an insurer" in determining amounts excludable under the provisions of section 101 (d), see paragraphs (c) to (f), inclusive, of this section.

(3) Notwithstanding any other provision of this section, if the policy was transferred for a valuable consideration, the total "amount held by an insurer" cannot exceed the sum of the consideration paid plus any premiums or other consideration paid subsequent to the transfer if the provisions of section 101 (a) (2) and paragraph (b) of § 1.101-1 limit the excludability of the proceeds to such total.

(c) Treatment of payments for life to a sole beneficiary. If the contract provides for the payment of a specified lump sum, but, pursuant to an agreement between the beneficiary and the insurer, payments are to be made during the life of the beneficiary in lieu of such lump sum, the lump sum shall be divided by the life expectancy of the beneficiary determined in accordance with the mortality table used by the insurer in determining the benefits to be paid. However, if payments are to be made to the estate or beneficiary of the primary beneficiary in the event that the primary beneficiary dies before receiving a certain number of payments or a specified total amount, such lump sum shall be reduced by the present value (at the time of the insured's death) of amounts which may be paid by reason of the guarantee, in accordance with the provisions of paragraph (e) of this section, before making this calculation. To the extent that payments received in each taxable year do not exceed the amount found from the above calculation, they are "prorated amounts" of the "amount held by an insurer" and are excludable from the gross income of the beneficiary without regard to whether he lives beyond the life expectancy used in making the calculation. If the contract in question does not provide for the payment of a specific lump sum upon the death of the insured as one of the alternative methods of payment, the present value (at the time of the death of the insured) of the payments to be made the beneficiary, determined in accordance with the interest rate and mortality table used by the insurer in determining the benefits to be paid, shall be used in the above calculation in lieu of a lump sum.

(d) Treatment of payments to two or more beneficiaries. *(1) Unrelated payments.* If payments are to be made to two or more beneficiaries, but the payments to be made to each are to be made without regard to whether or not payments are made or continue to be made to the other beneficiaries, the present value (at the time of the insured's death) of such payments to each beneficiary shall be determined independently for each such beneficiary. The present value so determined shall then be divided by the term for which the payments are to be made. If the payments are to be made for the life of the beneficiary, the divisor shall be the life expectancy of the beneficiary. To the extent that payments received by a beneficiary do not exceed the amount found from the above calculation, they are "prorated amounts" of the "amount held by an insurer" with respect to such beneficiary and are excludable from the gross income of the beneficiary without regard to whether he lives beyond any life expectancy used in making the calculation. For the purpose of the calculation described above, both the "present value" of the payments to be made periodically and the "life expectancy" of the beneficiary shall be determined in accordance with the interest rate and mortality table used by the insurer in determining the benefits to be paid. If payments are to be made to the estate or beneficiary of a primary beneficiary in the event that such beneficiary dies before receiving a certain number of payments or a specified total amount, the "present value" of payments to such beneficiary shall not include the present value (at the time of the insured's death) of amounts which may be paid by reason of such a guarantee. See paragraph (e) of this section.

(2) Related payments. If payments to be made to two or more beneficiaries are in the nature of a joint and survivor annuity (as described in paragraph (b) of § 1.72-5), the present value (at the time of the insured's death) of the payments to be made to all such beneficiaries shall be divided by the life expectancy of such beneficiaries as a group. To the extent that the payments received by a beneficiary do not exceed the amount found from the above calculation, they are "prorated amounts" of the "amount held by an insurer" with respect to such beneficiary and are excludable from the gross income of the beneficiary without regard to whether all the beneficiaries involved live beyond the life expectancy used in making the calculation. For the purpose of the calculation described above, both the "present value" of the payments to be made periodically and the "life expectancy" of all the beneficiaries as a group shall be determined in accordance with the interest rate and mortality table used by the insurer in determining the benefits to be paid. If the contract provides that certain payments are to be made in the event that all the beneficiaries of the group die before a specified number of payments or a specified total amount is received by them, the present value of payments to be made to the group shall not include the present value (at the time of the insured's death) of amounts which may be paid by reason of such a guarantee. See paragraph (e) of this section.

(3) Payments to secondary beneficiaries. Payments made by reason of the death of a beneficiary (or beneficiaries) under a contract providing that such payments shall be made in the event that the beneficiary (or beneficiaries) die before receiving a specified number of payments or a specified total amount shall be excluded from the gross income of the recipient to the extent that such payments are made solely by reason of such guarantee.

(e) Treatment of present value of guaranteed payments. In the case of payments which are to be made for a life or lives under a contract providing that further amounts shall be paid upon the death of the primary beneficiary (or beneficiaries) in the event that such beneficiary (or beneficiaries) die before receiving a specified number of payments or a specified total amount, the present value (at the time of the insured's death) of all payments to be made under the contract shall not include, for purposes of prorating the amount held by the insurer, the present value of the payments which may be made to the estate or beneficiary of the primary beneficiary. In such a case, any lump sum amount used to measure the value of the amount held by an insurer with respect to the primary beneficiary must be reduced by the value at the time of the insured's death of any amounts which may be paid by reason of the guarantee provided for a secondary beneficiary or the estate of the primary beneficiary before prorating such lump sum over the life or lives of the primary beneficiaries. Such present value (of the guaranteed payment) shall be determined by the use of the interest rate and mortality tables used by the insurer in determining the benefits to be paid.

(f) Treatment of payments not paid periodically. Payments made to beneficiaries other than periodically shall be included in the gross income of the recipients, but only to the extent that they exceed amounts payable at the time of the death of the insured to each such beneficiary or, where no such amounts are specified, the present value of such payments at that time.

(g) Examples. The principles of this section may be illustrated by the following examples:

Example (1). A life insurance policy provides for the payment of $20,000 in a lump sum to the beneficiary at the death of the insured. Upon the death of the insured, the beneficiary elects an option to leave the proceeds with the company for five years and then receive payment of $24,000, having no claim of right to any part of such sum before the entire five years have passed. Upon the payment of the larger sum, $24,000, the beneficiary shall include $4,000 in gross income and exclude $20,000 therefrom. If it is assumed that the same insurer has determined the benefits to be paid, the same result would obtain if no lump sum amount were provided for at the death of the insured and the beneficiary were to be paid $24,000 five years later. In neither of these cases would the surviving spouse be able to exclude any additional amount from gross income since both cases involve an amount held by an insurer under an agreement to pay interest thereon to which section 101(c) applies, rather than an amount to be paid periodically after the death of the insured to which section 101 (d) applies.

Example (2). A life insurance policy provides that $1,200 per year shall be paid the sole beneficiary (other than a surviving spouse) until a fund of $20,000 and interest which accrues on the remaining balance is exhausted. A guaranteed rate of interest is specified, but excess interest may be credited according to the earnings of the insurer. Assuming that the fund will be exhausted in 20 years if only the guaranteed interest is actually credited, the beneficiary shall exclude $1,000 of each installment received ($20,000 divided by 20) and any installments received, whether by the beneficiary or his estate or beneficiary, in excess of 20 shall be fully included in the gross income of the recipient. If, instead, the excess interest were to be paid each year, any portion of each installment representing an excess over $1,000 would be fully includible in the recipient's gross income. Thus, if an installment of $1,350 were received, $350 of it would be included in gross income.

Example (3). Assume that the sole life insurance policy of a decedent provides only for the payment of $5,000 per year for the life of his surviving spouse, beginning with the insured's death. If the present value of the proceeds, determined by reference to the interest rate and the mortality table used by the insurance company, is $60,000, and such beneficiary's life expectancy is 20 years, $3,000 of each $5,000 payment ($60,000 divided by 20) is excludable as the prorated portion of the "amount held by an insurer". For each taxable year in which a payment is made, an additional $1,000 is excludable from the gross income of the surviving spouse. Hence, if she receives only one $5,000 payment in her taxable year, only $1,000 is includible in her gross income in that year with respect to such payment ($5,000 less the total amount excludable, $4,000). Assuming that the policy also provides for payments of $2,000 per year for 10 years to the daughter of the insured, the present value of the payments to the daughter is to be computed separately for the purpose of determining the excludable portion of each payment to her. Assuming that such present value is $15,000, $1,500 of each payment of $2,000 received by the daughter is excludable from her gross income ($15,000 divided by 10). The remaining $500 shall be included in the gross income of the daughter.

Example (4). Beneficiaries A and B, neither of whom is the surviving spouse of the insured, are each to receive annual payments of $1,800 for each of their respective lives upon the death of the insured. The contract does not provide for payments to be made in any other manner. Assuming that the present value of the payments to be made to A, whose life expectancy according to the insurer's mortality table is 30 years, is $36,000, A shall exclude $1,200 of each payment received ($36,000 divided by 30). Assuming that the present value of the payments to be made to B, whose life expectancy according to the insurer's mortality table is 20 years, is $27,000, B shall exclude $1,350 of each payment received ($27,000 divided by 20).

Example (5). A life insurance policy provides for the payment of $76,500 in a lump sum to the beneficiary, A, at the death of the insured. Upon the insured's death, however, A selects an option for the payment of $2,000 per year for her life and for the same amount to be paid after her death to B, her daughter, for her life. Assuming that since A is 51 years of age and her daughter is 28 years of age, the insurer determined the amount of the payments by reference to a mortality table under which the life expectancy for the lives of both A and B, joint and survivor, is 51 years, $1,500 of each $2,000 payment to either A or B ($76,500 divided by 51, or $1,500) shall be excluded from the gross income of the recipient. However, if A is the surviving spouse of the insured and no other contracts of insurance whose proceeds are to be paid to her at a date later than death are involved, A shall exclude the entire payment of $2,000 in any taxable year in which she receives but one such payment because of the additional exclusion under section 101 (d)(1)(B).

Example (6). Beneficiaries A and B, neither of whom is the surviving spouse of the insured, are each to receive annual payments of $1,800 for each of their respective lives upon the death of the insured, but after the death of either, the survivor is to receive the payments formerly made to the deceased beneficiary until the survivor dies. Assuming that the life expectancy, joint and survivor, of A and B in accordance with the mortality table used by the insurer is 32 years and assuming that the total present value of the benefits to both (determined in accordance with the interest rate used by the insurer), is $80,000, A and B shall each exclude $1,250 of each installment of $1,800 ($80,000 divided by the life expectancy, 32, multiplied by the fraction of the annual payment payable to each, one-half) until the death of either. Thereafter, the survivor shall exclude $2,500 of each installment of $3,600 ($80,000 divided by 32).

Example (7). A life insurance policy provides for the payment of $75,000 in a lump sum to the beneficiary, A, at the death of the insured. A, upon the insured's death, however, selects an option for the payment of $4,000 per year for life, with a guarantee that any part of the $75,000 lump sum not paid to A before his death shall be paid to B (or his estate), A's beneficiary. Assuming that, under the criteria used by the insurer in determining the benefits to be paid, the present value of the guaranteed amount to B is $13,500 and that A's life expectancy is 25 years, the lump sum shall be reduced by the present value of the guarantee to B ($75,000 less $13,500, or $61,500) and divided by A's life expectancy ($61,500 divided by 25, or $2,460). Hence, $2,460 of each $4,000 payment is excludable from A's gross income. If A is the surviving spouse of the insured and no other contracts of insurance whose proceeds are to be paid to her at a date later than death are involved, A shall exclude $3,460 of each $4,000 payment from gross income in any taxable year in which but one such payment is received. Under these facts, if any amount is paid to B by reason of the fact that A dies before receiving a total of $75,000, the residue of the lump sum paid to B shall be excluded from B's gross income since it is wholly in lieu of the present value of such guarantee plus the present value of the payments to be made to the first beneficiary, and is therefore entirely an "amount held by an insurer" paid at a date later than death (see paragraph (d)(3) of this section).

Example (8). Assume that an insurance policy does not provide for the payment of a lump sum, but provides for the payment of $1,200 per year for a beneficiary's life upon the death of the insured, and also provides that if ten payments are not made to the beneficiary before death a secondary beneficiary (whether named by the insured or by the first beneficiary) shall receive the remainder of the ten payments in similar installments. If, according to the criteria used by the insurance company in determining the benefits, the present value of the payments to the first beneficiary is $12,000 and the life expectancy of such beneficiary is 15 years, $800 of each payment received by the first beneficiary is excludable from gross income. Assuming that the same figures obtain even though the payments are to be made at the rate of $100 per month, the yearly exclusion remains the same unless more or less than twelve months' installments are received by the beneficiary in a particular taxable year. In such a case two-thirds of the total received in the particular taxable year with respect to such beneficiary shall be excluded from gross income. Under either of the above alternatives, any amount received by the second beneficiary by reason of the guarantee of ten payments is fully excludable from the beneficiary's gross income since it is wholly in lieu of the present value of such guarantee plus the present value of the payments to be made to the first beneficiary and is therefore entirely an "amount held by an insurer" paid at a date later than death (see paragraph (d)(3) of this section).

(h) Applicability of both section 101(c) and 101(d) to payments under a single life insurance contract. *(1) In general.* Section 101(d) shall not apply to interest payments on any amount held by an insurer under an agreement to pay interest thereon (see sections 101(c) and 101(d)(4) and § 1.101-3). On the other hand, both section 101(c) and section 101(d) may be applicable to payments received under a single life insurance contract, if such payments consist both of interest on an amount held by an insurer under an agreement to pay interest thereon and of amounts held by the insurer and paid on a date or dates later than the death of the insured. One instance when both section 101(c) and section 101(d) may be applicable to payments received under a single life insurance contract is in the case of a permanent life insurance policy with a family income rider attached. A typical family income rider is one which provides additional term insurance coverage for a specified number of years from the register date of the basic policy. Under the policy with such a rider, if the insured dies at any time during the term period, the beneficiary is entitled to receive (i) monthly payments of a specified amount commencing as of the date of death and continuing for the balance of the term period, and (ii) a lump sum payment of the proceeds under the basic policy to be paid at the end of the term period. If the insured dies after the expiration of the term period, the beneficiary receives only the proceeds under the basic policy. If the insured dies before the expiration of the term period, part of each monthly payment received by the beneficiary during the term period consists of interest on the proceeds of the basic policy (such proceeds being retained by the insurer until the end of the term period). The remaining part consists of an installment (principal plus interest) of the proceeds of the terms insurance purchased under the family income rider. The amount of term insurance which is provided under the family income rider is, therefore, that amount which, at the date of the insured's death, will provide proceeds sufficient to fund such remaining part of each monthly payment. Since the proceeds under the basic policy are held by the insurer until the end of the term period, that portion of each monthly payment which consists of interest on such proceeds is interest on an amount held by an insurer under an agreement to pay interest thereon and is includible in gross income under section 101(c). On the other hand, since the remaining portion of each monthly payment consists of an installment payment (principal plus interest) of the proceeds of the term insurance, it is a payment of an amount held by the insurer and paid on a date later than the death of the insured to which section 101(d) and this section applies (including the $1,000 exclusion allowed the surviving spouse under section 101(d)(1)(B)). The proceeds of the basic policy, when received in a lump sum at the end of the term period, are excludable from gross income under section 101(a).

(2) Example of tax treatment of amounts received under a family income rider. The following example illustrates the application of the principles contained in subparagraph (1) of this paragraph to payments received under a permanent life insurance policy with a family income rider attached:

Example. The sole life insurance policy of the insured provides for the payment of $100,000 to the beneficiary (the insured's spouse) on his death. In addition, there is attached to the policy a family income rider which provides that, if the insured dies before the 20th anniversary of the basic policy, the beneficiary shall receive (i) monthly payments of $1,000 commencing on the date of the insured's death and ending with the payment prior to the 20th anniversary of the basic policy, and (ii) a single payment of $100,000 payable on the 20th anniversary of the basic policy. On the date of the insured's death, the beneficiary (surviving spouse of the insured) is entitled to 36 monthly payments of $1,000 and to the single payment of $100,000 on the 20th anniversary of the basic policy. The value of the proceeds of the term insurance at the date of the insured's death is $28,409.00 (the present value of the portion of the monthly payments to which section 101(d) applies computed on the basis that the interest rate used by the insurer in determining the benefits to be paid under the contract is 2¼ percent). The amount of each monthly payment of $1,000 which is includible in the beneficiary's gross income is determined in the following manner:

(a) Total amount of monthly payment	$1,000.00
(b) Amount includible in gross income under section 101(c) as interest on the $100,000 proceeds under the basic policy held by the insurer until 20th anniversary of the basic policy (computed on the basis that the interest rate used by the insurer in determining the benefits to be paid under the contract is 2¼ percent)	185.00
(c) Amount to which section 101(d) applies *((a) minus (b))*	815.00
(d) Amount excludable from gross income under section 101(d) ($28,409 ÷ 36)	789.14
(e) Amount includible in gross income under section 101(d) without taking into account the $1,000 exclusion allowed the beneficiary as the surviving spouse *((c) minus (d))*	25.86

The beneficiary, as the surviving spouse of the insured, is entitled to exclude the amounts otherwise includible in gross income under section 101(d) (item *(e)*) to the extent such amounts do not exceed $1,000 in the taxable year of receipt. This exclusion is not applicable, however, with respect to the amount of each payment which is includible in gross income under section 101(c) (item *(b)*). In this example, therefore, the beneficiary must include $185 of each monthly payment in gross income (amount includible under section 101(c)), but may exclude the $25.86 which is otherwise includible under section 101(d). The payment of $100,000 which is payable to the beneficiary on the 20th anniversary of the basic policy will be entirely excludable from gross income under section 101(a).

(3) Limitation on amount considered to be an "amount held by an insurer". See paragraph (b)(3) of this section for a limitation on the amount which shall be considered an "amount held by an insurer" in the case of proceeds of life insurance which are paid subsequent to the transfer of the policy for a valuable consideration.

(4) Effective date. The provisions of this paragraph are applicable only with respect to amounts received during taxable years beginning after October 28, 1961, irrespective of the date of the death of the insured.

T.D. 6280, 12/16/57, amend T.D. 6577, 10/27/61.

§ 1.101-5 Alimony, etc., payments.

Caution: The Treasury has not yet amended Reg § 1.101-5 to reflect changes made by P.L. 98-369.

Proceeds of life insurance policies paid by reason of the death of the insured to his separated wife, or payment excludable as death benefits under section 101(b) paid to a deceased employee's separated wife, if paid to discharge legal obligations imposed by a decree of divorce or separate maintenance, by a written separation agreement executed after August 16, 1954, or by a decree of support entered after March 1, 1954, shall be included in the gross income of the separated wife if section 71 or 682 is applicable to the payments made. For definition of "wife", see section 7701(a)(17) and the regulations thereunder.

T.D. 6280, 12/16/57.

§ 1.101-6 Effective date.

Caution: The Treasury has not yet amended Reg § 1.101-6 to reflect changes made by P.L. 104-188, P.L. 97-248, P.L. 94-455.

(a) Except as otherwise provided in paragraph (h)(4) of § 1.101-4, the provisions of section 101 of the Internal Revenue Code of 1954 and §§ 1.101-1, 1.101-2, 1.101-3, 1.101-4, and 1.101-5 are applicable only with respect to amounts received by reason of the death of an insured or an employee occurring after August 16, 1954. In the case of such amounts, these sections are applicable even though the receipt of such amounts occurred in a taxable year beginning before January 1, 1954, to which the Internal Revenue Code of 1939 applies.

(b) Section 22(b)(1) of the Internal Revenue Code of 1939 and the regulations pertaining thereto shall apply to amounts received by reason of the death of an insured or an employee occurring before August 17, 1954, regardless of the date of receipt.

T.D. 6280, 12/16/57, amend T.D. 6577, 10/27/61.

§ 1.101-7 Mortality table used to determine exclusion for deferred payments of life insurance proceeds.

(a) Mortality table. Notwithstanding any provision of § 1.101-4 that otherwise would permit the use of a mortality table not described in this section, the mortality table set forth in § 1.72-7(c)(1) must be used to determine—

(1) The amount held by an insurer with respect to a beneficiary for purposes of section 101(d)(2) and § 1.101-4; and

(2) The period or periods with respect to which payments are to be made for purposes of section 101(d)(1) and § 1.101-4.

(b) Examples. The principles of this section may be illustrated by the following examples:

Example (1). A life insurance policy provides only for the payment of $5,000 per year for the life of the beneficiary. A, beginning with the insured's death. If A is 59 years of age at the time of the insured's death, the period with respect to which the payments are to be made is 25 years. This period is determined by using the mortality table set forth in § 1.72-7(c)(1), and is shown in Table V of § 1.72-9 (which contains life expectancy tables determined using this mortality table). If the present value of the proceeds, determined by reference to the interest rate used by the insurance company and the mortality table set forth in § 1.72-7(c)(1), is $75,000, $3,000 of each $5,000 payment ($75,000 divided by 25) is excluded from the gross income of A.

Example (2). A life insurance policy provides for the payment of $82,500 in a lump sum to the beneficiary, A, at the death of the insured. Upon the insured's death, however, A selects an option for the payment of $2,000 per year for life and for the same amount to be paid after A's death to B for B's life. If A is 51 years of age and B is 28 years of age at the death of the insured, the period with respect to which the payments are to be made is 55 years. This period is determined by using the mortality table set forth in § 1.72-7(c)(1), and is shown in Table VI of § 1.72-9 (which contains life expectancy tables determined using this mortality table). Accordingly $1,500 of each $2,000 payment ($82,500 divided by 55) is excluded from the gross income of the recipient.

(c) Effective date. This section applies to amounts received with respect to deaths occurring after October 22, 1986, in taxable years ending after October 22, 1986.

T.D. 8161, 9/18/87, amend T.D. 8272, 11/17/89.

Proposed § 1.101-8 Amounts paid with respect to terminally ill individuals. [*For Preamble, see ¶ 151,453*]

Caution: The Treasury has not yet amended Reg § 1.101-8 to reflect changes made by P.L. 104-188.

For purposes of section 101(a), a qualified accelerated death benefit (as defined in § 1.7702-2(d)), received on or after [date on which final regulations are published in the FEDERAL REGISTER]), is treated as an amount paid by reason of the death of the insured.

§ 1.102-1 Gifts and inheritances.

Caution: The Treasury has not yet amended Reg § 1.102-1 to reflect changes made by P.L. 99-514.

(a) General rule. Property received as a gift, or received under a will or under statutes of descent and distribution, is not includible in gross income, although the income from such property is includible in gross income. An amount of principal paid under a marriage settlement is a gift. However, see section 71 and the regulations thereunder for rules relating to alimony or allowances paid upon divorce or separation. Section 102 does not apply to prizes and awards (see section 74 and § 1.74-1) nor to scholarships and fellowship grants (see section 117 and the regulations thereunder).

(b) Income from gifts and inheritances. The income from any property received as a gift, or under a will or statute of descent and distribution shall not be excluded from gross income under paragraph (a) of this section.

(c) Gifts and inheritances of income. If the gift, bequest, devise, or inheritance is of income from property, it shall not be excluded from gross income under paragraph (a) of this section. Section 102 provides a special rule for the treatment of certain gifts, bequests, devises, or inheritances which by their terms are to be paid, credited, or distributed at intervals. Except as provided in section 663(a)(1) and paragraph (d) of this section, to the extent any such gift, bequest, devise, or inheritance is paid, credited, or to be distributed out of income from property, it shall be considered a gift, bequest, devise, or inheritance of income from property. Section 102 provides the same treatment for amounts of income from property which is paid, credited, or to be distributed under a gift or bequest whether the gift or bequest is in terms of a right to payments at intervals (regardless of income) or is in terms of a right to income. To the extent the amounts in either case are paid, credited, or to be distributed at intervals out of income, they are not to be excluded under section 102 from the taxpayer's gross income.

(d) Effect of subchapter J. Any amount required to be included in the gross income of a beneficiary under sections 652, 662, or 668 shall be treated for purposes of this section as a gift, bequest, devise, or inheritance of income from property. On the other hand, any amount excluded from the gross income of a beneficiary under section 663(a)(1) shall be treated for purposes of this section as property acquired by gift, bequest, devise, or inheritance.

(e) Income taxed to grantor or assignor. Section 102 is not intended to tax a donee upon the same income which is taxed to the grantor of a trust or assignor of income under section 61 or sections 671 through 677, inclusive.

T.D. 6220, 12/28/56.

PAR. 4. Section 1.102-1 is amended as follows:

(a) The last sentence of paragraph (a) is removed.

(b) A new paragraph (f) is added immediately following paragraph (e) to read as follows.

Proposed § 1.102-1 Gifts and inheritances. [*For Preamble, see ¶ 151,137*]

* * * * *

(f) Exclusions. *(1) In general.* Section 102 does not apply to prizes and awards (including employee achievement awards) (see section 74); certain de minimis fringe benefits (see section 132); any amount transferred by or for an employer to, or for the benefit of, an employee (see section 102(c)); or to qualified scholarships (see section 117).

(2) Employer/Employee transfers. For purposes of section 102(c), extraordinary transfers to the natural objects of an employer's bounty will not be considered transfers to, or for the benefit of, an employee if the employee can show that the transfer was not made in recognition of the employee's employment. Accordingly, section 102(c) shall not apply to amounts transferred between related parties (e.g., father and son) if the purpose of the transfer can be substantially attrib-

uted to the familial relationship of the parties and not to the circumstances of their employment.

§ 1.103-1 Interest upon obligations of a State, territory, etc.

Caution: The Treasury has not yet amended Reg § 1.103-1 to reflect changes made by P.L. 99-514, P.L. 94-455.

(a) Interest upon obligations of a State, territory, a possession of the United States, the District of Columbia, or any political subdivision thereof (hereinafter collectively or individually referred to as "State or local governmental unit") is not includable in gross income, except as provided under section 103(c) and (d) and the regulations thereunder.

(b) Obligations issued by or on behalf of any State or local governmental unit by constituted authorities empowered to issue such obligations are the obligations of such a unit. However, section 103(a)(1) and this section do not apply to industrial development bonds except as otherwise provided in section 103(c). See section 103(c) and §§ 1.103-7 through 1.103-12 for the rules concerning interest paid on industrial development bonds. See section 103(d) for rules concerning interest paid on arbitrage bonds. Certificates issued by a political subdivision for public improvements (such as sewers, sidewalks, streets, etc.) which are evidence of special assessments against specific property, which assessments become a lien against such property and which the political subdivision is required to enforce, are, for purposes of this section, obligations of the political subdivision even though the obligations are to be satisfied out of special funds and not out of general funds or taxes. The term "political subdivision", for purposes of this section denotes any division of any State or local governmental unit which is a municipal corporation or which has been delegated the right to exercise part of the sovereign power of the unit. As thus defined, a political subdivision of any State or local governmental unit may or may not, for purposes of this section, include special assessment districts so created, such as road, water, sewer, gas, light, reclamation, drainage, irrigation, levee, school, harbor, port improvement, and similar districts and divisions of any such unit.

T.D. 6220, 12/28/56, amend T.D. 7199, 7/31/72.

---

§ 5c.103-1 Leases and capital expenditures.

• *Caution:* Reg. § 5c.103-1, following, was issued under Code section 103 before the related provisions of that Code section were deleted by P.L. 99-514 (10/22/86). Provisions similar to, but not necessarily identical to, the provisions deleted from Code section 103 now appear in Code section 144.

For purposes of section 103(b)(6)(D) and § 1.103-10(b)(2)(iv)(b), the determination of whether property is leased and whether property is of a type that is ordinarily subject to a lease shall be made without regard to the characterization of the transaction as a lease under section 168(f)(8).

T.D. 7791, 10/20/81.

---

§ 5f.103-1 Obligations issued after December 31, 1982, required to be in registered form.

• *Caution:* Reg. § 5f.103-1, following, was issued under Code section 103 before the related provisions of that Code section were deleted by P.L. 99-514 (10/22/86). Provisions similar to, but not necessarily identical to, the provisions deleted from Code section 103 now appear in Code section 149.

Caution: The Treasury has not yet amended Reg § 5f.103-1 to reflect changes made by P.L. 101-239, P.L. 100-647.

(a) Registration; general rule. Interest on a registration-required obligation (as defined in paragraph (b) of this section) shall not be exempt from tax notwithstanding section 103(a) or any other provision of law, exclusive of any treaty obligation of the United States, unless the obligation is issued in registered form (as defined in paragraph (c) of this section).

(b) Registration-required obligation. For purposes of this section, the term "registration-required obligation" means any obligation except any one of the following:

(1) An obligation not of a type offered to the public. The determination as to whether an obligation is not of a type offered to the public shall be based on whether similar obligations are in fact publicly offered or traded.

(2) An obligation that has a maturity at the date of issue of not more than 1 year.

(3) An obligation issued before January 1, 1983. An obligation first issued before January 1, 1983, shall not be considered to have been issued on or after that date merely as a result of the existence of a right on the part of the holder of such obligation to convert the obligation from registered form into bearer form, or as a result of the exercise of such a right.

(4) An obligation described in § 5f.163-1(c) (relating to certain obligations issued to foreign persons).

(c) Registered form. *(1) General rule.* An obligation issued after January 20, 1987, pursuant to a binding contract entered into after January 20, 1987, is in registered form if—

(i) The obligation is registered as to both principal and any stated interest with the issuer (or its agent) and transfer of the obligation may be effected only by surrender of the old instrument and either the reissuance by the issuer of the old instrument to the new holder or the issuance by the issuer of a new instrument to the new holder,

(ii) The right to the principal of, and stated interest on, the obligation may be transferred only through a book entry system maintained by the issuer (or its agent) (as described in paragraph (c)(2) of this section), or

(iii) The obligation is registered as to both principal and any stated interest with the issuer (or its agent) and may be transferred through both of the methods described in subdivisions (i) and (ii).

(2) Special rule for registration of a book entry obligation. An obligation shall be considered transferable through a book entry system if the ownership of an interest in the obligation is required to be reflected in a book entry, whether or not physical securities are issued. A book entry is a record

of ownership that identifies the owner of an interest in the obligation.

(d) Effective date. The provisions of this section shall apply to obligations issued after December 31, 1982, unless issued on an exercise of a warrant for the conversion of a convertible obligation if such warrant or obligation was offered or sold outside the United States without registration under the Securities Act of 1933 and was issued before August 10, 1982.

(e) Special rules. The following special rules apply to obligations issued after January 20, 1987, pursuant to a binding contract entered into after January 20, 1987.

(1) An obligation that is not in registered form under paragraph (c) of this section is considered to be in bearer form.

(2) An obligation is not considered to be in registered form as of a particular time if it can be transferred at that time or at any time until its maturity by any means not described in paragraph (c) of this section.

(3) An obligation that as of a particular time is not considered to be in registered form by virtue of subparagraph (2) of this paragraph (e) and that, during a period beginning with a later time and ending with the maturity of the obligation, can be transferred only by a means described in paragraph (c) of this section, is considered to be in registered form at all times during such period.

(f) Examples. The application of this section may be illustrated by the following examples:

Example (1). Municipality X publicly offers its general debt obligations to United States persons. The obligations have a maturity at issue exceeding 1 year. The obligations are registration-required obligations under § 5f.103-1(b). When individual A buys an obligation, X issues an obligation in A's name evidencing A's ownership of the principal and interest under the obligation. A can transfer the obligation only by surrendering the obligation to X and by X issuing a new instrument to the new holder. The obligation is issued in registered form.

Example (2). Municipality Y issues a single obligation on January 4, 1983 to Bank M provided that (i) Bank M will not at any time transfer any interest in the obligation to any person unless the transfer is recorded on Municipality Y's records (except by means of a transfer permitted in (ii) of this example and (ii) interests in the obligation that are sold by Bank M (and any persons who acquire interests from M) will be reflected in book entries. C, an individual, buys an interest in Y's obligation from Bank M. Bank M receives the interest or principal payments with respect to C's interest in the obligation as agent for C. Bank M records interests in the Municipality Y obligation as agent of Municipality Y. Any transfer of C's interest must be reflected in a book entry in accordance with Bank M's agreement with Municipality Y. Since C's interest can only be transferred through a book entry system maintained by the issuer (or its agent), the obligation is considered issued in registered form. Interest received by C is excludable from gross income under section 103(a).

Example (3). Municipality Z wishes to sell its debt obligations having a maturity in excess of 1 year. The obligations are sold to Banks N, O, and P, all of which are located in Municipality Z. By their terms the obligations are freely transferable, although each of the banks has stated that it acquired the obligations for purposes of investment and not for resale. Obligations similar to the obligations sold by Municipality Z are traded in the market for municipal securities. The obligations issued by Municipality Z are of a type offered to the public and are therefore registration-required under § 5f.103-1(b).

Example (4). Corporation A issues an obligation that is registered with the corporation as to both principal and any stated interest. Transfer may be effected by the surrender of the old instrument and either the reissuance by the issuer of the old instrument to the new holder or the issuance by the issuer of a new instrument to the new holder. The obligation can be converted into a form in which the right to the principal of, or state interest on, the obligation may be effected by physical transfer of the obligation. Under § 5f.103-1(c) and (e), the obligation is not considered to be in registered form and is considered to be in bearer form.

Example (5). Corporation B issues its obligations in a public offering in bearer definitive form. Beginning at X months after the issuance of the obligations, a purchaser (either the original purchaser or a purchaser in the secondary market) may deliver the definitive bond in bearer form to the issuer in exchange for a registration receipt evidencing a book entry record of the ownership of the obligation. The issuer maintains the book entry system. The purchaser identified in the book entry as the owner of record has the right to receive a definitive bearer obligation at any time. Under § 5f.103-1(c) and (e), the obligation is not considered to be issued in registered form and is considered to be issued in bearer form. All purchasers of the obligation are considered to hold an obligation in bearer form.

Example (6). Corporation C issues obligations in bearer form. A foreign person purchases a definitive bearer obligation and then sells it to a United States person. At the time of the sale, the United States person delivers the bearer obligation to Corporation C and receives an obligation that is identical except that the obligation is registered as to both principal and any stated interest with the issuer or its agent and may be transferred at all times until its maturity only through a means described in § 5f.103-1(c). Under § 5f.103-1(e), the obligation is considered to be in registered form from the time it is delivered to Corporation C until its maturity.

(g) Cross-references. See section 103A(j)(1) for the registration requirement of certain mortgage subsidy bonds issued after December 31, 1981, and § 6a.103A-1(a)(5) for the definition of registered form for such obligations issued after December 31, 1981, and on or before December 31, 1982. See also section 103(h) (requiring registration of certain energy bonds issued on or after October 18, 1979).

T.D. 7852, 11/9/82, amend T.D. 8111, 12/16/86.

§ 1.103-2 Dividends from shares and stock of Federal agencies or instrumentalities.

(a) Issued before March 28, 1942. *(1)* Section 26 of the Federal Farm Loan Act of July 17, 1916 (12 U. S. C. 931), provides that Federal land banks and Federal land bank associations, including the capital and reserve or surplus therein and the income derived therefrom, shall be exempt from taxation, except taxes upon real estate. Section 7 of the Federal Reserve Act of December 23, 1913 (12 U. S. C. 531), provides that Federal reserve banks, including the capital stock and surplus therein and the income derived therefrom, shall be exempt from taxation, except taxes upon real estate. Section 13 of the Federal Home Loan Bank Act (12 U. S. C. 1433) provides that the Federal Home Loan Bank including its franchise, its capital, reserves, and surplus, its advances, and its income shall be exempt from all taxation, except taxes upon real estate. Section 5 (h) of the Home

Owners' Loan Act of 1933 (12 U. S. C. 1464 (h)) provides that shares of Federal savings and loan associations shall, both as to their value and the income therefrom, be exempt from all taxation (except surtaxes, estate, inheritance, and gift taxes) imposed by the United States. Under the above-mentioned provisions, income consisting of dividends on stock of Federal land banks, Federal land bank associations, Federal home loan banks, and Federal reserve banks is not, in the case of stock issued before March 28, 1942, includible in gross income. Income consisting of dividends on share accounts of Federal savings and loan associations is includible in gross income but, in the case of shares issued before March 28, 1942, is not subject to the normal tax on income. For taxability of such income in the case of such stock or shares issued on or after March 28, 1942, see section 6 of the Public Debt Act of 1942 (31 U. S. C. 742a) and paragraph (b) of this section. For the time at which a stock or share is issued within the meaning of this section, see paragraph (b) of this section.

(2) Regardless of the exemption from income tax of dividends paid on the stock of Federal reserve banks, dividends paid by member banks are treated like dividends of ordinary corporations.

(3) Dividends on the stock of the central bank for cooperatives, the production credit corporations, production credit associations, and banks for cooperatives, organized under the provisions of the Farm Credit Act of 1933 (12 U.S.C. 1138), constitute income to the recipients, subject to both the normal tax and surtax constitute income to the recipients, subject to both the normal tax and surtax (see section 63 of the Farm Credit Act of 1933 (12 U.S.C. 1138c)).

(b) Issued on or after March 28, 1942. *(1)* By virtue of the provisions of section 6 of the Public Debt Act of 1942 (31 U.S.C. 742a), the tax exemption provisions set forth in paragraph (a) of this section with respect to income consisting of dividends on stock of the Federal land banks, Federal land bank associations, and Federal reserve banks, or on share accounts of Federal savings and loan associations, are not applicable in the case of dividends on such stock or shares issued on or after March 28, 1942.

(2) For the purposes of this section, a stock or share is deemed to be issued at the time and to the extent that payment therefor is made to the agency or instrumentality. The date of issuance of the certificate or other evidence of ownership of such stock or share is not determinative if payment is made at an earlier or later date. Where old stock is retired in exchange for new stock of a different character or preference, the new stock shall be deemed to have been issued at the time of the exchange rather than when the old stock was paid for. These rules may be illustrated by the following examples:

Example (1). A, the owner of an investment share account, consisting of 10 shares, in a Federal savings and loan association, has a single certificate issued before March 28, 1942, evidencing such ownership. In order that A may dispose of half of such shares, the association at his request issues, after March 27, 1942, two 5-share certificates in substitution for the 10-share certificate. The shares evidenced by the two new certificates are deemed to have been issued before March 28, 1942, the shares having been paid for before such date.

Example (2). The X Bank, a member of a Federal reserve bank, owns 50 shares of Federal reserve bank stock, evidenced by a single stock certificate issued before March 28, 1942. On December 31, 1942, the X Bank reduces the amount of its capital stock, as a result of which it is required to reduce the amount of its Federal reserve bank stock to 40 shares. It surrenders the 50-share certificate to the Federal reserve bank and receives a new 40-share certificate. The 40 shares evidenced by such certificate are deemed to have been issued before March 28, 1942. On December 31, 1943, the X Bank increases the amount of its capital stock, as a result of which it is required to purchase 10 additional shares of the Federal reserve bank stock. The Federal reserve bank issues a 10-share certificate evidencing ownership of the new shares. Of the 50 shares then owned by the X Bank, 40 were issued prior to March 28, 1942, and 10 were issued after March 27, 1942.

Example (3). A, the owner of a savings share account in the amount of $100 in a Federal savings and loan association, has a passbook containing a certificate issued prior to March 28, 1942, evidencing such ownership. Subsequent to March 27, 1942, A deposits $10,000 in the account. With respect to the $10,000 deposit, the share is deemed to have been issued after March 27, 1942.

T.D. 6220, 12/28/56.

§ 5c.103-2 Leases and industrial development bonds.

• ***Caution:*** Reg. § 5c.103-2, following, was issued under Code section 103 before the related provisions of that Code section were deleted by P.L. 99-514 (10/22/86). Provisions similar to, but not necessarily identical to, the provisions deleted from Code section 103 now appear in Code section 142.

Caution: The Treasury has not yet amended Reg § 5c.103-2 to reflect changes made by P.L. 100-647, P.L. 99-514.

For purposes of section 103(b)(2), the determination of whether an obligation constitutes an industrial development bond shall be made without regard to the characterization of the transaction as a lease under section 168(f)(8).

T.D. 7800, 12/28/81.

§ 5f.103-2 Public approval of industrial development bonds.

• ***Caution:*** Reg. § 5f.103-2, following, was issued under Code section 103 before the related provisions of that Code section were deleted by P.L. 99-514 (10/22/86). Provisions similar to, but not necessarily identical to, the provisions deleted from Code section 103 now appear in Code section 147.

Caution: The Treasury has not yet amended Reg § 5f.103-2 to reflect changes made by P.L. 100-647, P.L. 99-514.

(a) General rule. An industrial development bond (within the meaning of § 1.103-7(b)(1) issued after December 31, 1982, shall be treated as an obligation not described in section 103(a) unless it is issued as part of an issue which satisfies the public approval requirement of section 103(k) and paragraph (c) of this section or is described in the exceptions set forth in paragraph (b) of this section.

(b) Exceptions. *(1) No extension of maturity.* Paragraph (a) of this section does not apply to a refunding obligation if—

(i) It refunds an obligation which was approved under section 103(k) and this section (or which is treated as approved pursuant to paragraph (f) of this section), and

(ii) It has a maturity date which is not later than the maturity date of the obligation to be refunded.

(2) Refunding of pre-July 1, 1982, obligation. Paragraph (a) of this section does not apply to an obligation issued solely to refund an obligation which—

(i) Was issued before July 1, 1982, and

(ii) Has a term which does not exceed 3 years.

The term of an obligation is determined without regard to whether it is a refunding obligation. With respect to the refunding of an issue also containing obligations with terms which exceed 3 years, paragraph (b)(2) applies only if the refunding issue proceeds are used solely to refund obligations with terms not exceeding 3 years and to pay reasonable incidental costs of the refunding (e.g., legal and accounting fees, printing costs, and rating fees) attributable thereto. Paragraph (b)(2) applies only to issues issued after December 31, 1982, the proceeds of which are used to refund issues issued prior to July 1, 1982. Thus, subsequent refundings of such refunding issues must satisfy the public approval requirement of section 103(k) and paragraph (c) of this section.

(c) Public approval requirement. *(1) In general.* An issue is publicly approved if prior to the date of issue the governmental unit(s) described in subparagraphs (2) and (3) this paragraph (c) approve the issue, in the manner described in paragraph (d) of this section. See paragraph (f) for rules pertaining to determining the scope of an approval and paragraph (g)(1) for the definition of "governmental unit".

(2) Issuer approval. The governmental unit (i) which will issue the obligations or (ii) on behalf of which the issue is to be issued must approve the issue ("issuer approval"). If the issuer is not a governmental unit, the governmental unit on behalf of which the issuer acts shall be determined in a manner consistent with determinations under § 1.103-1, and such unit must approve the issue. However, in the case of an issuer which issues obligations on behalf of more than one governmental unit (e.g., an authority which acts for two counties), any one of such units may give the issuer approval required by this paragraph (c)(2).

(3) Host approval. Each governmental unit the geographic jurisdiction (as defined in paragraph (g)(4)) of which contains the site of a facility to be financed by the issue must approve the issue ("host approval"). However, if the entire site of a facility to be financed by the issue is within the geographic jurisdiction of more than one governmental unit within a State (counting the State as a governmental unit within such State), then any one of such units may provide host approval for the issue with respect to that facility. For purposes of this paragraph (c)(3), if property to be financed by the issue is located within two or more governmental units but not entirely within either of such units, each portion of the property which is located entirely within the smallest respective governmental units may be treated as a separate facility. The issuer approval (as described in paragraph (c)(2)) may be treated as a host approval if the governmental unit giving the issuer approval is also a governmental unit described in this paragraph (c)(3). See paragraph (e)(2) with respect to host approval by a governmental unit with no applicable elected representative.

(d) Method of public approval. For purposes of this section, an issue is approved by a governmental unit only if—

(1) An applicable elected representative (as defined in paragraph (e)) of such unit approves the issue following a public hearing (as defined in paragraph (g)(2)) held in a location which, under the facts and circumstances, is convenient for residents of the unit, and for which there was reasonable public notice (as defined in paragraph (g)(3)), or

(2) A referendum of the voters of the unit (as defined in paragraph (g)(5)) approves the issue.

An approval may satisfy the requirements of this section without regard to the authority under State or local law for the acts constituting such approval. The location of hearing will be presumed convenient for residents of the unit if it is located in the approving governmental unit's capital or seat of government. If more than one governmental unit is required to provide a public hearing, such hearings may be combined as long as the combined hearing is a joint undertaking that provides all of the residents of the participating governmental units (i.e., those relying on such hearing as an element of public approval) a reasonable opportunity to be heard. The location of any combined hearing is presumed to provide a reasonable opportunity to be heard provided it is no farther than 100 miles from the seat of government of each participating governmental unit beyond whose geographic jurisdiction the hearing is conducted.

(e) Applicable elected representative. *(1) In general.* The applicable elected representative of a governmental unit means—

(i) Its elected legislative body,

(ii) Its chief elected executive officer,

(iii) In the case of a State, the chief elected legal officer of the State's executive branch of government, or

(iv) Any official elected by the voters of the unit and designated for purposes of this section by the unit's chief elected executive officer or by State or local law to approve issues for the unit.

For purposes of subdivisions (ii), (iii), and (iv) of this paragraph (e)(1), an official shall be considered elected by the voters of the unit only if he is popularly elected at-large by the voters of the governmental unit. If an official popularly elected at-large by the voters of a governmental unit is appointed or selected pursuant to State or local law to be the chief executive officer of the unit, such official is deemed to be an elected chief executive officer for purposes of this section but for no longer than his tenure as an official elected at-large. In the case of a bicameral legislature which is popularly elected, both chambers together constitute an applicable elected representative, but neither chamber does independently, unless so designated under paragraph (e)(1)(iv). If multiple elected legislative bodies of a governmental unit have independent legislative authority, however, the body with the more specific authority relating to the issue is the only legislative body described in paragraph (e)(1)(i) of this section. See paragraph (h), Example (7) of this section.

(2) Governmental unit with no applicable elected representative. (i) The applicable elected representatives of a governmental unit with no representative (but for this paragraph (e)(2) and section 103(k)(2)(E)(ii)) are deemed to be those of the next higher governmental unit (with an applicable elected representative) from which the governmental unit derives its authority. For purposes of this subparagraph (2), a governmental unit derives its authority from another unit which—

(A) Enacts a specific law (e.g., a provision in a State constitution, charter or statute) by or under which the governmental unit is created,

(B) Otherwise empowers or approves the creation of the governmental unit, or

(C) Appoints members to the governing body of the governmental unit.

In the case of a governmental unit with no applicable elected representative (but for this paragraph (e)(2)), any unit described in subdivision (A), (B), or (C) or this paragraph (e)(2)(i) may be treated as the next higher unit, without regard to the relative status of all of such units under State law.

(ii) In the case of a host approval (as required under paragraph (c)(3) of this section), a unit may be treated as the next higher unit, only if—

(A) The facility is located within its geographic jurisdiction, and

(B) Eligible individuals, if any, residing at the site of the facility are entitled to vote for the applicable elected representative of that unit (as determined under this paragraph (e)).

(3) On behalf of issuers. In the case of an issuer which is not a governmental unit but which issues bonds on behalf of a governmental unit, the applicable elected representative is any applicable elected representative of the unit on behalf of which the bonds are issued. If the unit on behalf of which the bonds are issued has no applicable elected representative (but for paragraph (e)(2) of this section), the applicable elected representative of the governmental unit is determined in the manner described in paragraph (e)(2).

(f) Scope of approval. *(1) In general.* Public approval is required by section 103(k) and this section for issues of industrial development bonds, except as otherwise provided in paragraph (a) and (b) of this section. An issue is treated as approved if the governmental units (described in paragraph (c) of this section in relation to the issue) have approved either—

(i) The issue (by approving each facility to be financed), not more than one year before the date of issue, or

(ii) A plan of financing for each facility financed by the issue pursuant to which the issue in question is timely issued (as required in paragraph (f)(3) of this section).

In either case, the scope of the approval is determined by the information, as specified in paragraph (f)(2), contained in the notice of hearing (when required) and the approval.

(2) Information required. A facility is within the scope of an approval if the notice of hearing (when required) and the approval contain—

(i) A general, functional description of the type and use of the facility to be financed (e.g., "a 10,000 square foot machine shop and hardware manufacturing plant", "400-room airport hotel building", "dock facility for supertankers", "convention center auditorium and sports arena with 25,000 seating capacity", "air and water pollution control facilities for oil refinery"),

(ii) The maximum aggregate face amount of obligations to be issued with respect to the facility,

(iii) The initial owner, operator, or manager of the facility,

(iv) The prospective location of the facility by its street address or, if none, by a general description designed to inform readers of its specific location.

An approval is valid for purposes of this section with respect to any issue used to provide publicly approved facilities, notwithstanding insubstantial deviations with respect to the maximum aggregate face amount of the bonds issued under the approval for the facility, the name of its initial owner, manager, or operator, or the type or location of the facility from that described in the approval. An approval or notice of public hearing will not be considered to be adequate if any of the items in subdivisions (i) through (iv) of this subparagraph (2), with respect to the facility to be financed, are unknown on the date of the approval or the date of the public notice.

(3) Timely issuance pursuant to a plan of financing. An issue is timely issued pursuant to a plan of financing for a facility if—

(i) The issue is issued no later than 3 years after the first issue pursuant to the plan, and

(ii) The first such issue in whole or in part issued pursuant to the plan was issued no later than 1 year after the date of approval.

(4) Facility— definition. For purposes of this paragraph (f), the term "facility" includes a tract or adjoining tracts of land, the improvements thereon and any personal property used in connection with such real property. Separate tracts of land (including improvements and connected personal property) may be treated as one facility only if they are used in an integrated operation.

(g) Definitions. For purposes of this section. *(1) Governmental unit.* Governmental unit has the same meaning as in § 1.103-1. Thus, a governmental unit is a State, territory, a possession of the United States, the District of Columbia, or any political subdivision thereof. The term "political subdivision" denotes any division of any State or local governmental unit which is a municipal corporation or which has been delegated the right to exercise part of the sovereign power of the unit.

(2) Public hearing. Public hearing means a forum providing a reasonable opportunity for interested individuals to express their views, both orally and in writing, on the proposed issue of bonds and the location and nature of a proposed facility to be financed. In general, a governmental unit may select its own procedure for the hearing, provided that interested individuals have a reasonable opportunity to express their views. Thus, it may impose reasonable requirements on persons who wish to participate in the hearing, such as a requirement that persons desiring to speak at the hearing so request in writing at least 24 hours before the hearing or that they limit their oral remarks to 10 minutes. For purposes of this public hearing requirement, it is not necessary, for example, that the applicable elected representative who will approve the bonds be present at the hearing, that a report on the hearing be submitted to that official, or that State administrative procedural requirements for public hearings in general be observed. However, compliance with such State procedural requirements (except those at variance with a specific requirement set forth in this section) will generally assure that the hearing satisfies the requirements of this section. The hearing may be conducted by any individual appointed or employed to perform such function by the governmental unit or its agencies, or by the issuer (if on behalf of issuer). Thus, for example, for bonds to be issued by an authority that acts on behalf of a county, the hearing may be conducted by the authority, the county, or an appointee or employee of either.

(3) Reasonable public notice. Reasonable public notice means published notice which is reasonably designed to inform residents of the affected governmental units, including residents of the issuing unit and the governmental unit where a facility is to be located, of the proposed issue. The notice must state the time and place for the hearing and contain the information contained in paragraph (f)(2) of this section. Notice is presumed reasonable if published no fewer than 14 days before the hearing. Except in the locality of the facility, publication is presumed to be reasonably designed to inform residents of the approving governmental unit if given in the same manner and same locations as required of the approving governmental unit for any other purposes for which applicable State or local law specifies a notice of public hearing requirement (including laws relating to notice of public meetings of the governmental unit). Notice is presumed reasonably designed to inform affected residents in the locality of the facility only if published in one or more newspapers of general circulation available to residents of that locality or if announced by radio or television broadcast to those residents.

(4) Geographic jurisdiction. Geographic jurisdiction is the are encompassed by the boundaries prescribed by State or local law for a governmental unit or, if there are no such boundaries, the area in which a unit may exercise such sovereign powers that make that unit a governmental unit for purposes of § 1.103-1 and this section.

(5) Voter referendum. A voter referendum is a vote by the voters of the affected governmental unit conducted in the manner and at such a time as voter referenda on matters relating to governmental spending or bond issuances by the governmental unit under applicable State and local law.

(h) Examples. The provisions of this section may be illustrated by the following examples:

Example (1). State X proposes to issue an industrial development bond, the proceeds of which are to finance a facility located entirely within the geographic jurisdiction of City Y (which is located in State X). Under the provisions of paragraph (c), only State X must approve the issue because State X is the issuer and the facility is to be located entirely within the State's geographic jurisdiction. Its applicable elected representative must approve the issue after the public notice and public hearing requirements are satisfied.

Example (2). (i) Industrial Development Authority X proposes to issue an industrial development bond, the proceeds of which are to finance a facility located entirely within the geographic jurisdiction of City Y (which is located in State Z). Authority X acts on behalf of State Z. Under the provisions of paragraph (c), only State Z must approve the issue because State Z is the governmental unit on behalf of which Authority X, the issuer, is acting and the facility is to be located entirely within its geographic jurisdiction.

(ii) State Z has a governor, an elected bicameral legislature and an appointed attorney general who is the chief legal officer of State Z. Under the laws of State Z, the attorney general must approve any issue of industrial development bonds. The approval by the attorney general is not a sufficient approval under this section, since the attorney general is not an applicable elected representative within the meaning of this section. Under the provisions of paragraphs (d) and (e), either the governor, both chambers of the legislature or any popularly elected official of the State who is designated for this purpose by the governor or by State law must approve the issue after the public notice and public hearing requirements are satisfied.

Example (3). (i) County Y, a county in State X, proposes to issue an industrial development bond, the proceeds of which are to finance a facility located entirely within its jurisdiction. Under the provisions of paragraph (c), only County Y must approve the issue because County Y is the issuer and the facility is to be located entirely within the geographic jurisdiction of County Y.

(ii) County Y has no elected officials or legislature. County Y derives its authority from State X which is the next higher governmental unit with an applicable elected representative. The laws of State X designate the attorney general, who is an official of State X elected at-large, as the official who must approve any issue of industrial development bonds for the State. Under this section, State X's attorney general is an applicable elected representative who may approve the issue after the public notice and public hearing requirements are satisfied.

Example (4). (i) City X, a city located in County Y and State Z, proposes to issue an industrial development bond, the proceeds of which are to finance a facility located entirely within the geographic jurisdiction of City X. Under the provisions of paragraph (c), only City X must approve the issue because it is the issuer and the facility is to be located entirely within the geographic jurisdiction of City X.

(ii) Mayor A, the chief elected executive officer of City X, has designated, for purposes of this section, Deputy Mayor B, an official of City X elected at-large, to approve industrial development bond issues for the city. Under the provisions of paragraph (e), Deputy Mayor B may approve the issue, since he is an applicable elected representative, after the public notice and public hearing requirements are satisfied.

Example (5). (i) County M proposes to issue an industrial development bond to finance a project located partly within the geographic jurisdiction of County M and partly within the geographic jurisdiction of County N. Both counties are located in State X. The part of the project in County N is also located partly within the geographic jurisdiction of City O and partly within the geographic jurisdiction of City P. Under the provisions of paragraph (c)(2), County M must give issuer approval. Additionally, under the provisions of paragraph (c)(3), either State X, County N, or both Cities O and P, must give host approval.

(ii) Counties M and N will approve the issue, but neither has any officials who are elected at-large by the voters of the respective governmental units. Both governmental units derive their authority from State X which is the next higher governmental unit with an applicable elected representative. Under the provisions of paragraph (e), an applicable elected representative of State X must approve the issue for Counties M and N after the public notice and public hearing requirements are satisfied.

Example (6). (i) County M proposes to issue an industrial development bond to finance two facilities. One facility is located entirely within the geographic jurisdiction of County M and the second facility is located partly within the geographic jurisdiction of County M and partly within the geographic jurisdiction of County N. The second facility is also located within the geographic jurisdictions of Cities O and P, which cities are located within the geographic jurisdiction of County N. Under the provisions of paragraph (c)(2), County M must give issuer approval. Additionally, under the provisions of paragraph (c)(3), either State X, County N, or both Cities O and P, must give host approval.

(ii) Counties M and N will approve the issue. Each has a chief elected executive officer. Under the provisions of paragraphs (d) and (e), the chief elected executive officer of each county may approve the issue, after the public notice and public hearing requirements are satisfied.

Example (7). (i) State X proposes to issue an industrial development bond to finance a facility located partly within the geographic jurisdiction of State X and partly within the geographic jurisdiction of State Y. That portion of the facility located in State Y is located entirely within the geographic jurisdiction of City Z. State X must give issuer approval. Additionally, either State Y or City Z must give host approval as that part of the facility to be located outside State X will be entirely within the geographic jurisdiction of each unit.

(ii) Under the provisions of paragraphs (d) and (e), the governor of State X may approve the issue, after the public notice and public hearing requirements are satisfied. City Z (assuming that it give host approval for the bond) has a city council and a school board, both of which are elected legislative bodies with independent jurisdiction. The authority of the school board is limited under State law to matters directly concerning the provision of public education. Under paragraph (e), the school board is not an applicable elected representative of City Z but the city council is an applicable elected representative of City Z. The city council may approve the issue after the public hearing and public notice requirements are satisfied.

Example (8). (i) Public Housing Authority M, a governmental unit, proposes to issue an industrial development bond to finance several housing projects with known sites located entirely within its geographic jurisdiction. M's geographic jurisdiction is coextensive with the combined geographic jurisdictions of Counties N and O. The projects are separately owned and managed. They are not adjacent to each other. The projects also are located in County N. Under the provisions of paragraph (c), M must give issuer approval.

(ii) M, which has no elected officials or legislature, was created by both Counties N and O pursuant to a special statute of State Q permitting such a joint undertaking. Both Counties N and O have an applicable elected representative. Under the provisions of paragraph (e)(2), either County N, County O, or State Q is deemed to be the next higher governmental unit with an applicable elected representative, and an applicable elected representative from any of these units may give the issuer approval for Authority M. Therefore, either the applicable representative of County N, County O, or State Q can give the issuer approval for Authority M.

(iii) For purposes of the host approval, the issuer approval by M will satisfy the host approval requirement only if the applicable elected representative of County N or State Q gives issuer approval for M. Under the provisions of paragraph (e)(2), the host approval requirement is satisfied only if qualified persons residing at the site of the facility are entitled to vote for the applicable elected representative who gave the approval (i.e., the representative of State Q or County N). However, if the applicable elected representative of O gave issuer approval for Authority M, a separate host approval would be required because the residents of the sites where the projects are located (i.e., County N) could not note for the applicable elected representative of County O.

(iv) Public Housing Authority M conducts a public hearing concerning prospective housing projects following notice thereof published in a newspaper of general circulation in County N. Additionally, M provides notice to the residents of O (which are also within M's jurisdiction) in the manner required for notice of public hearing for other purposes under State Q law. Following the public hearing, the chief elected executive officer of County N approves for Authority M prospective issues for the project. M issues two $7 million issues, one for each project. One issue is issued six months after the date of approval; the second issue is issued thirteen months thereafter. On these facts, only the first issue satisfied the public approval requirement of this section.

T.D. 7892, 5/6/83.

§ 1.103-3 Interest upon notes secured by mortgages executed to Federal agencies or instrumentalities.

Section 26 of the Federal Farm Loan Act (12 U.S.C. 931), and section 210 of such act, as added by section 2 of the act of March 4, 1923 (12 U.S.C 1111), provide that first mortgages executed to Federal land banks, joint-stock land banks, or Federal intermediate credit banks, and the income derived therefrom, shall be exempt from taxation. Accordingly, income consisting of interest on promissory notes held by such banks and secured by such first mortgages is not subject to the income tax.

T.D. 6220, 12/28/56.

§ 5c.103-3 Leases and arbitrage.

• ***Caution:*** Reg. § 5c.103-3, following, was issued under Code section 103 before the related provisions of that Code section were deleted by P.L. 99-514 (10/22/86). Provisions similar to, but not necessarily identical to, the provisions deleted from Code section 103 now appear in Code section 148.

Caution: The Treasury has not yet amended Reg § 5c.103-3 to reflect changes made by P.L. 100-647, P.L. 99-514.

In the case of a sale and leaseback transaction qualifying under section 168(f)(8), where the lessee's rental payments are substantially equal in timing and amount to the principal and interest payments on the lessor's note, the arbitrage provisions of section 103(c) and §§ 1.103-13, 1.103-14, and 1.103-15 shall apply to any obligations of the lessee (or party related to the lessee) without regard to the section 168(f)(8) lease transaction.

T.D. 7800, 12/28/81.

§ 5f.103-3 Information reporting requirements for certain bonds.

• ***Caution:*** Reg. § 5f.103-3, following, was issued under Code section 103 before the related provisions of that Code section were deleted by P.L. 99-514 (10/22/86). Provisions similar to, but not necessarily identical to, the provisions deleted from Code section 103 now appear in Code section 149.

Caution: The Treasury has not yet amended Reg § 5f.103-3 to reflect changes made by P.L. 101-239, P.L. 100-647.

(a) General rule. Under section 103(l), any private purpose bond issued after December 31, 1982 (including any obligation issued thereafter to refund private purpose bonds issued before December 31, 1982) shall be treated as an obligation not described in section 103(a) unless the information reporting requirement (as described in paragraph (c) of this section) is substantially satisfied with respect to the issue of which the bond is a part. For rules concerning bonds issued after December 31, 1986, see § 1.149(e)-1.

(b) Private purpose bonds. For purposes of this section, the term "private purpose bond" means—

(1) Any industrial development bond (as defined in section 103(b)(2) and § 1.103-7(b)(1)), or

(2) Any obligation which is issued as part of an issue all or a major portion of the proceeds of which are to be used directly or indirectly—

(i) To finance loans to individuals for educational or related expenses (hereinafter referred to as a "student loan bond"), or

(ii) By an organization described in section 501(c)(3) which is exempt from taxation by reason of section 501(a) (hereinafter referred to as "private exempt entity bond").

The meaning of the terms "major portion" and "directly or indirectly" shall be the same as under § 1.103-7. Student loan bonds include, but are not limited to, qualified scholarship funding bonds (as defined in section 103(e)).

(c) Information required. An obligation satisfies the requirements of section 103(l) and this section only if it is issued as part of an issue with respect to which the issuer, based on information and reasonable expectations determined as of the date of issue, submits on Form 8038 the information required therein, including—

(1) The name, address, and employer identification number of the issuer,

(2) The date of issue (as defined in paragraph (g)(1)),

(3) The face amount of the issue,

(4) The total purchase price of the issue,

(5) The amount allocated to a reasonably required reserve or replacement fund,

(6) The amount of lendable proceeds (as defined in paragraph (g)(4) of this section),

(7) The stated interest rate of each maturity (as defined in paragraph (g)(2) of this section) or, if the interest rate is variable, a description of the method under which the interest rate is computed,

(8) The term (as defined in paragraph (g)(3)) of each maturity,

(9) A general description of the property to be financed by the issue (including property financed by an obligation that will be refunded with the issue proceeds) which includes—

(i) The type of bond issued, that is, a student loan bond, a private exempt entity bond, or an industrial development bond and in the case of an industrial development bond described in section 103(b)(4), the subparagraph of section 103(b)(4) that describes the property, e.g., for a football stadium, that the property is described in section 103(b)(4)(B),

(ii) The recovery classes (as defined in section 168(c)(2)), if applicable, of the various items of financed property and the approximate amount of lendable proceeds attributable thereto,

(iii) The approximate amount of lendable proceeds attributable to land or other property not described in subdivision (ii),

(iv) In the case of obligations described in section 103(b)(6) or private exempt entity bonds, the four-digit Standard Industrial Classification Code of the facilities financed.

(10) If section 103(k) (relating to public approval requirement for industrial development bonds) applies to such issue, the name(s) of the approving governmental unit(s) and of the applicable elected representative(s) (as defined in section 103(k)(2)(E) and § 5f.103-2(e)) or a description of the voter referendum that approved the issue for such unit(s).

(11) The name, address, and employer identification number of—

(i) Each initial principal user (as defined in paragraph (g)(5) of this section) of any facilities provided with the proceeds of the issue,

(ii) The common parent, if any, of any affiliated group of corporations (as defined in section 1504(a) but determined without regard to the exceptions of section 1504(b)) of which such initial principal user is a member, and

(iii) Any person (not included under paragraph (c)(11)(i)) that is treated as a principal user under section 103(b)(6)(L), but only if the issue is treated as a separate issue under section 103(b)(6)(K).

The information to be supplied must be determined based on information and reasonable expectations as of the date of issue. Therefore, such statement need not be amended to report information learned subsequent to the date of issue. However, if the statement is filed after the date of issue it may reflect such information and the reasonable expectations of the issuer as of that date.

(d) Additional information. An issuer may supply the following information—

(1) The average maturity of the issue (as defined in section 103(b)(14)), and

(2) The average reasonably expected economic life (as defined in section 103(b)(14)) of the facility which is financed with the issue..

(e) Time for filing. The statement required by section 103(l) and this section shall be filed not later than the 15th day of the 2nd calendar month after the close of the calendar quarter in which the obligation is issued. It may be filed at any time before such date but must be complete based on facts and reasonable expectations as of the date of issue. The Secretary may grant an extension of time for filing the statement required under section 103(l) and this section if there is reasonable cause for the failure to file such statement in a timely fashion.

(f) Place for filing. Form 8038 is to be mailed to the Internal Revenue Service Center, Philadelphia, Pennsylvania 19255.

(g) Definitions. For purposes of this section—

(1) The term "date of issue" means the date on which the issuer physically exchanges the first of the obligations which are part of the issue for the underwriter's (or other purchaser's) funds. In the event that amounts are periodically advanced with respect to an issue, the date of issue is when the first of such obligations under the issue is created and the funds are advanced.

(2) The term "maturity" means those obligations of the issue having both the same maturity date and the same stated interest rate.

(3) The term "term of an issue" means the duration of the period beginning on the date of issue and ending on the latest maturity date of any obligation of the issue without regard to optional redemption dates.

(4) The term "lendable proceeds" means the amount of the original proceeds, net of amounts allocated to a reasonably required reserve or replacement fund. See generally § 1.103-13(b) and § 1.103-14(d) for further definitions.

(5) The term "initial principal user" means each person who as of the date of issue is obligated to use the facility to such an extent that under section 103(b)(6) such person would be treated as a principal user. With respect to organizations described in section 501(c)(3), however, such determination is made without regard to whether such organization is treated as an exempt organization under section 103(b)(3) and § 1.103-7(b)(2).

T.D. 7892, 5/6/83, amend T.D. 8129, 3/10/87, T.D. 8425, 8/11/92.

§ 1.103-4 Interest upon United States obligations.

(a) Issued before March 1, 1941. *(1)* Interest upon obligations of the United States issued on or before September 1, 1917, is exempt from tax. In the case of obligations issued by the United States after September 1, 1917, and in the case of obligations of a corporation organized under act of Congress, if such corporation is an instrumentality of the United States, the interest is exempt from tax only if and to the extent provided in the acts authorizing the issue thereof, as amended and supplemented.

(2) Interest on Treasury bonds issued before March 1, 1941, is exempt from Federal income taxes except surtaxes imposed upon the income or profits of individuals, associations, or corporations. However, interest on an aggregate of not exceeding $5,000 principal amount of such bonds is also exempt from surtaxes. Interest in excess of the interest on an aggregate of not exceeding $5,000 principal amount of such bonds is subject to surtax and must be included in gross income.

(3) Interest credited to postal savings accounts upon moneys deposited before March 1, 1941, in postal savings banks is wholly exempt from income tax.

(b) Issued on or after March 1, 1941. *(1)* Under the provisions of sections 4 and 5 of the Public Debt Act of 1941 (31 U.S.C. 742a), interest upon obligations issued on or after March 1, 1941, by the United States, or any agency or instrumentality thereof, shall not have any exemption, as such, from Federal income tax except in respect of any such obligations which the Federal Maritime Board and Maritime Administration (formerly United States Maritime Commission) or the Federal Housing Administration has, before March 1, 1941, contracted to issue at a future date. The interest on such obligations so contracted to be issued shall bear such tax-exemption privileges as were at the time of such contract provided in the law authorizing their issuance. For the purposes hereof, under section 4(a) of the Public Debt Act of 1941, a Territory and a possession of the United States (or any political subdivisions thereof), and the District of Columbia, and any agency or instrumentality of any one or more of the foregoing, shall not be considered as an agency or instrumentality of the United States.

(2) In the case of obligations issued as the result of a refunding operation, as, for example, where a corporation exchanges bonds for previously issued bonds, the refunding obligations are deemed, for the purposes of this section, to have been issued at the time of the exchange rather than at the time the original bonds were issued.

T.D. 6220, 12/28/56.

§ 1.103-5 Treasury bond exemption in the case of trusts or partnerships.

(a) When the income of a trust is taxable to beneficiaries, as in the case of a trust the income of which is to be distributed to the beneficiaries currently, each beneficiary is entitled to exemption as if he owned directly a proportionate part of the Treasury bonds held in trust. When, on the other hand, income is taxable to the trustee, as in the case of a trust the income of which is accumulated for the benefit of unborn or unascertained persons, the trust, as the owner of the bonds held in trust, is entitled to the exemption on account of such ownership. In general, see sections 652(b) and 662(b) and the regulations thereunder.

(b) As the income of a partnership is taxable to the individual partners, each partner is entitled to exemption as if he owned directly a proportionate part of the bonds held by the partnership. For rules relating to partially tax-exempt interest see section 702(a)(7) and the regulations thereunder.

T.D. 6220, 12/28/56.

§ 1.103-6 Interest upon United States obligations in the case of nonresident aliens and foreign corporations, not engaged in business in the United States.

By virtue of section 4 of the Victory Liberty Loan Act of March 3, 1919 (31 U.S.C. 750), amending section 3 of the Fourth Liberty Bond Act of July 9, 1918 (31 U.S.C. 750), the interest received on and after March 3, 1919, on bonds, notes, and certificates of indebtedness of the United States while beneficially owned by a nonresident alien individual, or a foreign corporation, partnership, or association, if such individual, corporation, partnership, or association is not engaged in business in the United States, is exempt from income taxes. Such exemption applies only to such bonds, notes, or certificates as have been issued before March 1, 1941. Interest derived by a nonresident alien individual, or by a foreign corporation, partnership, or association on such bonds, notes, or certificates issued on or after March 1, 1941, is subject to tax as in the case of taxpayers generally as provided in paragraph (b) of § 1.103-4.

T.D. 6220, 12/28/56.

§ 1.103-7 Industrial development bonds.

Caution: The Treasury has not yet amended Reg § 1.103-7 to reflect changes made by P.L. 100-647.

(a) In general. Under section 103(c)(1) and this section, an industrial development bond issued after April 30, 1968, shall be treated as an obligation not described in section 103(a)(1) and § 1.103-1. Accordingly, interest paid on such a bond is includible in gross income unless the bond was issued by a State, or local governmental unit to finance certain exempt facilities (see section 103(c)(4) and § 1.103-8), to finance an industrial park (see section 103(c)(5) and § 1.103-9), or as part of an exempt small issue (see section 103(c)(6) and § 1.103-10). For applicable rules when an industrial development bond is held by a substantial user (or a person related to a substantial user) of such an exempt facility, or an industrial park, or a facility financed with the proceeds of such an exempt small issue, see section 103(c)(7) and

§ 1.103-11. See also § 1.103-12 for the transitional provisions concerning the interest paid on certain industrial development bonds issued before January 1, 1969, and certain other industrial development bonds. Even if section 103(c) does not prevent a bond from being treated as an obligation described in section 103(a)(1) and § 1.103-1, such bond shall nevertheless be treated as an obligation which is not described in section 103(a)(1) and § 1.103-1 if under section 103(d) it is an arbitrage bond. For purposes of section 103(c), the term "issue" includes a single obligation such as a single note issued in connection with a bank loan as well as a series of notes or bonds.

(b) Industrial development bonds. *(1) Definition.* For purposes of this section, the term "industrial development bond" means any obligation—

(i) Which is issued as part of an issue all or a major portion of the proceeds of which are to be used directly or indirectly in any trade or business carried on by any person who is not an exempt person (as defined in subparagraph (2) of this paragraph), and

(ii) The payment of the principal or interest on which, under the terms of such obligation or any underlying arrangement (as described in subparagraph (4) of this paragraph), is in whole or in major part (i.e., major portion)—

(a) Secured by any interest in property used or to be used in a trade or business,

(b) Secured by any interest in payments in respect of property used or to be used in a trade or business, or

(c) To be derived from payments in respect of property, or borrowed money, used or to be used in a trade or business.

See subparagraphs (3) and (4) of this paragraph for the trade or business test and the security interest test respectively. See § 1.103-8(a)(6) to determine the amount of proceeds of an issue for which the amount payable during each annual period over the term of the issue is less than the amount of interest accruing thereon in such period, e.g., in the case of an issue sold by the issuer for less than its face amount.

(2) Exempt person. The term "exempt person" means a governmental unit as defined in this subparagraph, or an organization which is described in section 501(c)(3) and this subparagraph and is exempt from taxation under section 501(a). For purposes of this subparagraph, the term "governmental unit" means a State or local governmental unit (as defined in § 1.103-1). For purposes of this subparagraph, the term "governmental unit" also includes the United States of America (or an agency or instrumentality of the United States of America), but only in the case of obligations (i) issued on or before August 3, 1972, or (ii) issued after August 3, 1972, with respect to which a bond resolution or any other official action was taken and in reliance on such action either (a) construction of such facility to be financed with such obligations commenced or (b) a binding contract was entered into, or an irrevocable bid was submitted, prior to August 3, 1972, or (iii) issued after August 3, 1972, with respect to a program approved by Congress prior to such date but only if (a) a portion of such program has been financed by obligations issued prior to such date, to which section 103(a) applied pursuant to a ruling issued by the Commissioner or his delegate prior to such date and (b) construction of one or more facilities comprising a part of such program commenced prior to such date. For purposes of this subparagraph, a tax-exempt organization is an exempt person only with respect to a trade or business it carries on which is not an unrelated trade or business. Whether a particular trade or business carried on by a tax-exempt organization is an unrelated trade or business is determined by applying the rules of section 513(a) (relating to general rule for unrelated trade or business) and the regulations thereunder to the tax-exempt organization without regard to whether the organization is an organization subject to the tax imposed by section 511 (relating to imposition of tax on unrelated business income of charitable, etc., organizations).

(3) Trade or business test. (i) The trade or business test relates to the use of the proceeds of a bond issue. The test is met if all or a major portion of the proceeds of a bond issue is used in a trade or business carried on by a nonexempt person. For example, if all or a major portion of the proceeds of a bond issue is to be loaned to one or more private business users, or is to be used to acquire, construct, or reconstruct facilities to be leased or sold to such private business users, and such proceeds or facilities are to be used in trades or businesses carried on by them, such proceeds are to be used in a trade or business carried on by persons who are not exempt persons, and the debt obligations comprising the bond issue satisfy the trade or business test. If, however, less than a major portion of the proceeds of an issue is to be loaned to nonexempt persons or is to be used to acquire or construct facilities which will be used in a trade or business carried on by a nonexempt person, the debt obligations will not be industrial development bonds. Also, when publicly-owned facilities which are intended for general public use, such as toll roads or bridges, are constructed with the proceeds of a bond issue and used by nonexempt persons in their trades or businesses on the same basis as other members of the public, such use does not constitute a use in the trade or business of a nonexempt person for purposes of the trade or business test.

(ii) In determining whether a debt obligation meets the trade or business test, the indirect, as well as the direct, use of the proceeds is to be taken into account. For example, the debt obligations comprising a bond issue do not fail to satisfy the trade or business test merely because the State or local governmental unit uses the proceeds to engage in a series of financing transactions for property to be used by private business users in trades or businesses carried on by them. Similarly, if such proceeds are to be used to construct facilities to be leased or sold to any nonexempt person for use in a trade or business it carries on, such proceeds are to be used in a trade or business carried on by a nonexempt person and the debt obligations comprising such issue satisfy the trade or business test. If such proceeds are to be used to construct facilities to be leased or sold to an exempt person who will, in turn, lease or sell the facilities to a nonexempt person for use in a trade or business, such proceeds are to be used in a trade or business carried on by a nonexempt person and the debt obligations comprising such issue satisfy the trade or business test. In addition, proceeds will be treated as being used in the trade or business of a nonexempt person in situations involving other arrangements, whether in a single transaction or in a series of transactions, whereby a nonexempt person uses property acquired with the proceeds of a bond issue in its trade or business.

(iii) The use of more than 25 percent of the proceeds of an issue of obligations in the trades or businesses of nonexempt persons will constitute the use of a major portion of such proceeds in such manner. In the case of the direct or indirect use of the proceeds of an issue of obligations or the direct or indirect use of a facility constructed, reconstructed, or acquired with such proceeds, the use by all nonexempt persons in their trades or businesses must be aggregated to determine whether the trade or business test is satisfied. If more than 25 percent of the proceeds of a bond issue is used in the trades or businesses of nonexempt persons, the trade or business test is satisfied. For special rules with respect to the acquisition of the output of facilities, see subparagraph (5) of this paragraph.

(4) Security interest test. The security interest test relates to the nature of the security for, and the source of, the payment of either the principal or interest on a bond issue. The nature of the security for, and the source of, the payment may be determined from the terms of the bond indenture or on the basis of an underlying arrangement. An underlying arrangement to provide security for, or the source of, the payment of the principal or interest on an obligation may result from separate agreements between the parties or may be determined on the basis of all the facts and circumstances surrounding the issuance of the bonds. The property which is the security for, or the source of, the payment of either the principal or interest on a debt obligation need not be property acquired with bond proceeds. The security interest test is satisfied, if, for example, a debt obligation is secured by unimproved land or investment securities used, directly or indirectly, in any trade or business carried on by any private business user. A pledge of the full faith and credit of a State or local governmental unit will not prevent a debt obligation from otherwise satisfying the security interest test. For example, if the payment of either the principal or interest on a bond issue is secured by both a pledge of the full faith and credit of a State or local governmental unit and any interest in property used or to be used in a trade or business, the bond issue satisfies the security interest test. For rules with respect to the acquisition of the output of facilities see subparagraph (5) of this paragraph.

(5) Trade or business test and security interest test with respect to certain output contracts. (i) The use by one or more nonexempt persons of a major portion of the subparagraph (5) output of facilities such as electric energy, gas, or water facilities constructed, reconstructed, or acquired with the proceeds of an issue satisfies the trade or business test and the security interest test if such use has the effect of transferring to nonexempt persons the benefits of ownership of such facilities, and the burdens of paying the debt service on governmental obligations used directly or indirectly to finance such facilities, so as to constitute the indirect use by them of a major portion of such proceeds. Such benefits and burdens are transferred and a major portion of the proceeds of an issue is used indirectly by the users of the subparagraph (5) output of such a facility which is owned and operated by an exempt person where—

(a) (1) One nonexempt person agrees pursuant to a contract to take, or to take or pay for, a major portion (more than 25 percent) of the subparagraph (5) output (within the meaning of subdivision (ii) of this subparagraph) of such a facility (whether or not conditional upon the production of such output) or

(2) two or more nonexempt persons, each of which pays annually a guaranteed minimum payment exceeding 3 percent of the average annual debt service with respect to the obligations in question, agree, pursuant to contracts, to take, or to take or pay for, a major portion (more than 25 percent) of the subparagraph (5) output of such a facility (whether or not conditioned upon the production of such output), and

(b) Payment made or to be made with respect to such contract or contracts by such nonexempt person or persons exceeds a major part (more than 25 percent) of the total debt service with respect to such issue of obligations.

(ii) For purposes of this subparagraph—

(a) Where a contract described in subdivision (i) of this subparagraph may be extended by the issuer of obligations described therein, the term of the contract shall be considered to include the period for which such contract may be so extended.

(b) The subparagraph (5) output of a facility shall be determined by multiplying the number of units produced or to be produced by the facility in 1 year by the number of years in the contract term of the issue of obligations issued to provide such facility. The number of units produced or to be produced by a facility in 1 year shall be determined by reference to its nameplate capacity (or where there is no nameplate capacity, its maximum capacity) without any reduction for reserves or other unutilized capacity. The contract term of an issue begins on the date the output of a facility is first taken, pursuant to a take or a take or pay contract, by a nonexempt person and ends on the latest maturity date of any obligation of the issue (determined without regard to any optional redemption dates). If, however, on or before the date of issue of a prior issue of governmental obligations issued to provide a facility, the issuer makes a commitment in the bond indenture or related document to refinance such prior issue with one or more subsequent issues of governmental obligations, then the contract term of the issue shall be determined with regard to the latest redemption date of any obligation of the last such refinancing issue with respect to such facility (determined without regard to any optional redemption dates). Where it appears that the term of an issue (or the terms of two or more issues) is extended for purposes of extending the contract term of an issue and thereby increasing the subparagraph (5) output of the facility provided by such issue, the subparagraph (5) output of such facility shall be determined by the Commissioner without regard to the provisions of this subdivision *(b)*.

(c) The total debt service with respect to an issue of obligations shall be the total dollar amount (excluding any penalties) payable with respect to such issue over its entire term. The entire term of an issue begins on its date of issue and ends on the latest maturity date of any obligation of the issue (determined without regard to any optional redemption dates). If, however, on or before the date of issue of a prior issue of governmental obligations the issuer makes a commitment in the bond indenture or related document to refinance such prior issue with one or more subsequent issues of governmental obligations, the entire term of the issue shall be determined with regard to the latest redemption date of any obligation of the last such refinancing issue (determined without regard to any optional redemption dates).

(d) Two or more nonexempt persons who are related persons (within the meaning of section 103(c)(6)(C)) shall be treated as one nonexempt person.

(c) Examples. The application of the rules contained in section 103(c)(2) and (3) and paragraph (b) of this section are illustrated by the following examples:

Example (1). State A and corporation X enter into an arrangement under which A is to provide a factory which X will lease for 20 years. The arrangement provides (1) that A will issue $10 million of bonds, (2) that the proceeds of the bond issue will be used to purchase land and to construct and equip a factory in accordance with X's specifications, (3) that X will rent the facility (land, factory, and equipment) for 20 years at an annual rental equal to the amount necessary to amortize the principal and pay the interest on the outstanding bonds, and (4) that such payments by X and the facility itself will be the security for the bonds. The bonds are industrial development bonds since they are part of an issue of obligations (1) all of the proceeds of which are to be used (by purchasing land and constructing and equipping the factory) in a trade or business by a nonexempt person, and (2) the payment of the principal and interest on which is secured by the facility and payments to be made with respect thereto.

Example (2). The facts are the same as in example (1) except that (1) X will purchase the facility, and (2) annual payments equal to the amount necessary to amortize the principal and pay the interest on the outstanding bonds will be made by X. The bonds are industrial development bonds for the reasons set forth in example (1).

Example (3). State B and corporation X enter into an arrangement under which B is to loan $10 million to X. The arrangement provides (1) that B will issue $10 million of bonds, (2) that the proceeds of the bond issue will be loaned to X to provide additional working capital and to finance the acquisition of certain new machinery, (3) that X will repay the loan in annual installments equal to the amount necessary to amortize the principal and pay the interest on the outstanding bonds, and (4) that the payments on the loan and the machinery will be the security for only the payment of the principal on the bonds. The bonds are industrial development bonds since they are part of an issue of obligations (1) all of the proceeds of which are to be used in a trade or business by a nonexempt person, and (2) the payment of the principal on which is secured by payments to be made in respect of property to be used in a trade or business. The result would be the same if only the payment of the interest on the bonds were secured by payments on the loan and machinery.

Example (4). The facts are the same as in example (1), (2), or (3) except that the annual payments required to be made by corporation X exceed the amount necessary to amortize the principal and pay the interest on the outstanding bonds. The bonds are industrial development bonds for the reasons set forth in such examples. The fact that corporation X is required to pay an amount in excess of the amount necessary to pay the principal and interest on the bonds does not affect their status as industrial development bonds. Similarly, if the annual payments required to be made by corporation X were sufficient to pay only a major portion of either the principal or the interest on the outstanding bonds, the bonds would be industrial development bonds for the reasons set forth in such examples.

Example (5). The facts are the same as in example (1), (2), (3), or (4) except that the issuer is a political subdivision which has taxing power and the bonds are general obligation bonds. Since both the trade or business and the security interest tests are met, the bonds are industrial development bonds notwithstanding the fact that they constitute an unconditional obligation of the issuer payable from its general revenues.

Example (6). (a) State C issues its general obligation bonds to purchase land and construct a hotel for use by the general public (i.e., tourists, visitors, travelers on business, etc.). The bond indenture provides (1) that C will own and operate the project for the period required to redeem the bonds, and (2) that the project itself and the revenues derived therefrom are the security for the bonds. The bonds are not industrial development bonds since (1) the proceeds are to be used by an exempt person in a trade or business carried on by such person, and (2) a major portion of such proceeds is not to be used, directly or indirectly, in a trade or business carried on by a nonexempt person. Use of the hotel by hotel guests who are travelling in connection with trades or businesses of nonexempt persons is not an indirect use of the hotel by such nonexempt persons for purposes of section 103(c).

(b) The facts are the same as in paragraph (a) of this example except that corporation Y enters into a long-term agreement with C that Y will rent more than one-fourth of the rooms on an annual basis for a period approximately equal to one half of the term of the bonds. The bonds are industrial development bonds because (1) a major portion of the proceeds used to construct the hotel is to be used in the trade or business of corporation Y (a nonexempt person) and (2) a major portion of the principal and interest on such issue will be derived from payments in respect of the property used in the trade or business of Y.

Example (7). (a) State D and corporation Y enter into an agreement under which Y will lease for 20 years three floors of a 12-story office building to be constructed by D on land which it will acquire. D will occupy the grade floor and the remaining eight floors of the building. The portion of the costs of acquiring the land and constructing the building which are allocated to the space to be leased by Y is not in excess of 25 percent of the total costs of acquiring the land and constructing the building. Such costs, whether attributable to the acquisition of land or the construction of the building, were allocated to leased space in the same proportion that the reasonable rental value of such leased space bears to the reasonable rental value of the entire building. From the facts and circumstances presented, it is determined that such allocation was reasonable. The arrangement between D and Y provides that D will issue $10 million of bonds, that the proceeds of the bond issue will be used to purchase land and construct an office building, that Y will lease the designated floor space for 20 years at its reasonable rental value, and that such rental payments and the building itself shall be security for the bonds. The bonds are not industrial development bonds since a major portion of the proceeds is not to be used, directly or indirectly, in the trade or business of a nonexempt person.

(b) The facts are the same as in paragraph (a) of this example except that corporation Y will lease four floors, and the costs allocated to these floors are in excess of 25 percent of D's investment in the land and building. The bonds are industrial development bonds because (1) a major portion of the building is to be used in the trade or business of a nonexempt person, and (2) a major portion of the principal and interest on such issue is secured by the rental payments on the building.

Example (8). The facts are the same as in paragraph (b) of example (7) except that, instead of leasing any space to corporation Y, State D will lease the four floors to numerous unrelated private business users to be used in their trades or businesses. No lease will have a term exceeding 2 years. A major portion of the principal and interest will be paid from the revenues that D will derive from such leases. The fact that the activities of D, an exempt person, may amount to a trade or business of leasing property is not material, and the bonds are industrial development bonds for the reasons set forth in paragraph (b) of example (7). The result would be the same in the case of long-term leases.

Example (9). State E issues its obligations to finance the construction of dormitories for educational institution Z which is an organization described in section 501(c)(3) and exempt from tax under section 501(a). The dormitories are to be owned and operated by Z and their operation does not constitute an unrelated trade or business. The bonds are not industrial development bonds since the proceeds are to be used by an exempt person in a trade or business carried on by such person which is not an unrelated trade or business, as determined by applying section 513(a) to Z.

Example (10). State F issues its obligations to finance the construction of a toll road and the cost of erecting related facilities such as gasoline service stations and restaurants. Such related facilities represent less than 25 percent of the total cost of the project and are to be leased or sold to nonexempt persons. The toll road is to be owned and operated by F. The revenues from the toll road and from the rental of related facilities are the security for the bonds. The bonds are not industrial development bonds since a major portion of the proceeds is not to be used, directly or indirectly, in the trades or businesses of nonexempt persons. The fact that vehicles owned by nonexempt persons engaged in their trades or businesses may use the road in common with, or as a part of, the general public is not material.

Example (11). City G issues its obligations to finance the construction of a municipal auditorium which it will own and operate. The use of the auditorium will be open to anyone who wishes to use it for a short period of time on a rate-scale basis. The rights of such a user are only those of a transient occupant rather than the full legal possessory interests of a lessee. It is anticipated that the auditorium will be used by schools, church groups, and fraternities, and numerous commercial organizations. The revenues from the rentals of the auditorium and the auditorium building itself will be the security for the bonds. The bonds are not industrial development bonds because such use is not a use in the trade or business of a nonexempt person.

Example (12). The facts are the same as in example (11) except that one nonexempt person will have a 20-year rental agreement providing for exclusive use of the entire auditorium for more than 3 months of each year at a rental comparable to that charged short-term users. The bonds are industrial development bonds since such use is a use in the trade or business of a nonexempt person and, therefore, a major portion of the proceeds of the issue will be used in the trade or business of a nonexempt person and a major portion of the principal or interest on such issue will be secured by a facility used in such trade or business and by payments with respect to such facility.

Example (13). In order to construct an electric generating facility of a size sufficient to take advantage of the economies of scale: (1) City H will issue $50 million of its 25-year bonds and Z (a privately owned electric utility) will use $100 million of its funds for construction of a facility they will jointly own as tenants in common. (2) Each of the participants will share in the ownership, output, and operating expenses of the facility in proportion to its contribution to the cost of the facility, that is, one-third by H and two-thirds by Z. (3) H's bonds will be secured by H's ownership in the facility and by revenues to be derived from the sale of H's share of the annual output of the facilities. (4) Because H will need only 50 percent of its share of the annual output of the facility, it agrees to sell to Z 25 percent of its share of such annual output for a period of 20 years pursuant to a contract under which Z agrees to take or pay for such power in all events. The facility will begin operation, and Z will begin to receive power, 4 years after the City H obligations are issued. The contract term of the issue will, therefore, be 21 years. (5) H also agrees to sell the remaining 25 percent of its share of the annual output to numerous other private utilities under a prevailing rate schedule including demand charges. (6) No contracts will be executed obligating any person other than Z to purchase any specified amount of the power for any specified period of time and no one such person (other than Z) will pay a demand charge or other minimum payment under conditions which, under paragraph (b)(5) of this section, result in a transfer of the benefits of ownership and the burdens of paying the debt service on obligations used directly or indirectly to provide such facilities. The bonds are not industrial development bonds because H's one-third interest in the facility (financed with bond proceeds) shall be treated as a separate property interest and, although 25 percent of H's interest in the annual output of the facility will be used directly or indirectly in the trade or business of Z, a nonexempt person, under the rule of paragraph (b)(5) of this section, such portion constitutes less than a major portion of the subparagraph (5) output of the facility. If more than 25 percent of the subparagraph (5) output of the facility were to be sold to Z pursuant to the take or pay contract, the bonds would be industrial development bonds since they would be secured by H's ownership in the facility and revenues therefrom, and under the rules of paragraph (b)(5) of this section a major portion of the proceeds of the bond issue would be used in the trade or business of Z, a nonexempt person.

Example (14). J, a political subdivision of a State, will issue several series of bonds from time to time and will use the proceeds to rehabilitate urban areas. More than 25 percent of the proceeds of each issue will be used for the rehabilitation and construction of buildings which will be leased or sold to nonexempt persons for use in their trades or businesses. There is no limitation either on the number of issues or the aggregate amount of bonds which may be outstanding. No group of bondholders has any legal claim prior to any other bondholders or creditors with respect to specific revenues of J, and there is no arrangement whereby revenues from a particular project are paid into a trust or constructive trust, or sinking fund, or are otherwise segregated or restricted for the benefit of any group of bondholders. There is, however, an unconditional obligation by J to pay the principal and interest on each issue of bonds. Further, it is apparent that J requires the revenues from the lease or sale of buildings to nonexempt persons in order to pay in full the principal and interest on the bonds in question. The bonds are industrial development bonds because a major portion of the proceeds will be used in the trades or businesses of nonexempt persons and, pursuant to an underlying arrangement, payment of the principal and interest is, in major part, to be derived from payments in respect of property or borrowed money used in the trades or businesses of nonexempt persons.

Example (15). Power Authority K, a political subdivision created by the legislature in State X to own and operate certain power generating facilities, sells all of the power from its existing facilities to four private utility systems under contracts executed in 1970, whereby such four systems are required to take or pay for specified portions of the total power output until the year 2000. Currently, existing facilities supply all of the present needs of the four utility systems but their future power requirements are expected to increase substantially. K issues 20-year general obligation bonds to construct a large nuclear generating facility. A fifth private utility system contracts with K to take or pay for 30 percent of the subparagraph (5) output of the new facility. The balance of the power output of the new facility will be available for sale as required, but initially it is not anticipated there will be any need for such power. The revenues from the contract with the fifth private utility system will be sufficient to pay less than 25 percent of the principal or interest on the bonds. The balance, which will exceed 25 percent of the principal or interest on such bonds, will be paid from revenues from the contracts with the four systems from sale of power produced by the old facilities. The bonds will be industrial development bonds because a major portion of the proceeds will be used in the trade or business of a nonexempt person, and payment of the principal and interest, pursuant to an underlying arrangement, will be derived in major part from payments in respect of property used in the trades or businesses of nonexempt persons.

(d) Certain refunding issues. *(1) General rule.* In the case of an issue of obligations issued to refund the outstanding face amount of an issue of obligations, the proceeds of the refunding issue will be considered to be used for the purpose for which the proceeds of the issue to be refunded were used. The rules of this subparagraph shall apply regardless of the date of issuance of the issue to be refunded and shall apply to refunding issues to be issued to refund prior refunding issues.

(2) Obligations issued prior to effective date. In the case of an issue of obligations issued to refund the outstanding face amount of an issue of obligations issued on or before April 30, 1968 (or before January 1, 1969, if the transitional rules of § 1.103-12 are applicable) which would have been industrial development bonds within the meaning of section 103(c)(2) had they been issued after such date, the refunding issue shall not be considered to be an issue of industrial development bonds if it does not make funds available for any purpose other than the debt service on the obligations. For rules as to arbitrage bonds, see section 103(d).

(3) Examples. The provisions of this paragraph may be illustrated by the following examples:

Example (1). In 1969, State A issued $20 million of 20-year revenue bonds the proceeds of which were used to construct a sports facility which qualifies as an exempt facility described in section 103(c)(4)(B) and paragraph (c) of § 1.103-8. The sports facility will be owned and operated by X, a nonexempt person, for the use of the general public. In 1975, A issues $15 million of revenue bonds in order to refund the outstanding face amount of the 1969 issue. Since the proceeds of the 1969 issue were used for an exempt facility, the proceeds of the 1975 refunding issue will be considered to be used for the same purposes and section 103(c)(1) shall not apply to the 1975 refunding issue. The result would have been the same if the original issue had been issued in 1965. For rules as to a refunding obligation held by substantial users of facilities constructed with the proceeds of the issue refunded, see section 103(c)(7) and § 1.103-11.

Example (2). In 1967, prior to the effective date of section 103(c), city B issued $10 million of revenue bonds the proceeds of which were used to construct a manufacturing facility for corporation Y, a nonexempt person. Lease payments by Y were security for the bonds. In 1975, B issued $7 million of revenue bonds in order to retire the outstanding face amount of the 1967 issue. The interest rate of the 1975 issue is one and one-half percentage points lower than the interest rate on the 1967 issue. Both issues sold at par. All of the terms of the 1975 issue are the same as the terms of the 1967 issue with the exception of the interest rate. The 1975 refunding issue will not be considered to be an issue of industrial development bonds since the refunding issue will not make funds available for any purpose other than the debt service on the outstanding obligations.

Example (3). The facts are the same as in example (2) except that the interest rate on the refunding issue is the same as the interest rate on the issue to be refunded. Assume further that city B issued the 1975 refunding issue in order to extend the terms of the obligations issued in 1967 as the result of its inability to pay such obligations due to insufficient revenues. The results will be the same as in example (2) for the reasons stated therein.

T.D. 7199, 7/31/72, amend T.D. 7869, 1/12/83.

§ 1.103-8 Interest on bonds to finance certain exempt facilities.

• ***Caution:*** Reg. § 1.103-8, following, was issued under Code section 103 before the related provisions of that Code section were deleted by P.L. 99-514 (10/22/86). Provisions similar to, but not necessarily identical to, the provisions deleted from Code section 103 now appear in Code section 142.

Caution: The Treasury has not yet amended Reg § 1.103-8 to reflect changes made by P.L. 110-289, P.L. 107-16.

(a) In general. *(1) General rule.* (i) Under section 103(b)(4), interest paid on an issue of obligations issued by a State, or local governmental unit (as defined in § 1.103-1) is not includable in gross income if substantially all of the proceeds of such issue is to be used to provide one or more of the exempt facilities listed in subparagraphs (A) through (J) of section 103(b)(4) and in this section. However, interest on an obligation of such issue is includable in gross income if the obligation is held by a substantial user or a related person (as described in section 103(b)(8) and § 1.103-11). If substantially all of the proceeds of a bond issue is to be used to provide such exempt facilities, the debt obligations are treated as obligations described in section 103(a)(1) and § 1.103-1 even though such obligations are industrial development bonds as defined in section 103(b)(2) and § 1.103-7. Substantially all of the proceeds of an issue of governmental obligations are used to provide an exempt facility if 90 percent or more of such proceeds are so used. For purposes of this "substantially all" test, two rules apply. First, proceeds are reduced by amounts properly allocable on a pro rata basis between providing the exempt facility and other uses of the proceeds. Second, amounts used to provide an exempt facility include amounts paid or incurred which are chargeable to the facility's capital account or would be so chargeable either with a proper election by a taxpayer (for example, under section 266) or but for a proper election by a taxpayer to deduct such amounts. In the event the amount payable with respect to an issue during each annual period over its term is less than the amount of interest accruing thereon in such such period, *e.g.*, in the case of an issue sold by the issuer for less than its face amount, see paragraph (a)(6) of this section to determine the amount of proceeds of the issue.

(ii) The provisions of subdivision (i) of this subparagraph shall also apply to an issue of obligations substantially all of the proceeds of which is to be used to provide exempt facilities described in this section and for either or both of the following purposes: *(a)* To acquire or develop land as the site for an industrial park described in section 103(b)(5) and § 1.103-9, *(b)* to provide facilities to be used by an exempt person.

(iii) Section 103(b)(4) only becomes applicable where the bond issue meets both the trade or business and the security interest tests so that obligations are industrial development bonds within the meaning of section 103(b)(2). For rules as to exempt facilities including property functionally related and subordinate to such facilities, see subparagraph (3) of this paragraph. For rules with respect to the ultimate use of proceeds of obligations, see paragraph (4) of this subparagraph. For rules which limit the application of the provisions of this section see subparagraph (5) of this paragraph. For the interrelationship of the rules provided in this section and the exemption for certain small issues provided in section 103(b)(6), see § 1.103-10.

(2) Public use requirement. To qualify under section 103(b)(4) and this section as an exempt facility, a facility must serve or be available on a regular basis for general public use, or be a part of a facility so used, as contrasted with similar types of facilities which are constructed for the exclusive use of a limited number of nonexempt persons in their trades or businesses. For example, a private dock or wharf owned by or leased to, and serving only a single manufacturing plant would not qualify as a facility for general public use, but a hangar or repair facility at a municipal airport, or a dock or a wharf, would qualify even if it is owned by, or leased or permanently assigned to, a nonexempt person provided that such nonexempt person directly serves the general public, such as a common passenger carrier or freight carrier. Similarly, an airport owned or operated by a nonexempt person for general public use is a facility for public use, as is a dock or wharf which is a part of a public port. However, a landing strip which, by reason of a formal or informal agreement or by reason of geographic location, will not be available for general public use does not satisfy the public use requirement. Sewage or solid waste disposal facilities and air or water pollution control facilities, described in sections 103(b)(4)(E) and (F) and paragraphs (f) and (g) of this section, will be treated in all events as serving a general public use although they may be part of a nonpublic facility such as a manufacturing facility used in the trade or business of a nonexempt user.

(3) Functionally related and subordinate. An exempt facility includes any land, building, or other property functionally related and subordinate to such facility. Property is not functionally related and subordinate to a facility if it is not of a character and size commensurate with the character and size of such facility. Since substantially all of the proceeds of a bond issue must be used for the exempt facility (or for any combination of exempt facilities, industrial parks, and facilities to be used by exempt persons), including property functionally related and subordinate thereto, an insubstantial amount of the proceeds of a bond issue may be used for facilities which are neither exempt facilities (or a combination of exempt facilities, industrial parks and facilities to be used by exempt persons) nor functionally related and subordinate to exempt facilities. Thus, for example, where substantially all of the proceeds of an urban redevelopment bond issue are to be used by a State urban redevelopment agency for residential real property for family units within the meaning of section 103(b)(4)(A) and paragraph (b) of this section, an insubstantial amount may be used for an industrial or commercial project or for any other purpose that is not functionally related and subordinate to the residential real property for family units.

(4) Ultimate use of proceeds. The question whether substantially all of the proceeds of an issue of obligations are to be used to provide one or more of the exempt facilities listed in subparagraphs (A) through (J) of section 103(b)(4) and in this section is to be resolved by reference to the ultimate use of such proceeds. For example, such proceeds will be treated as used to provide residential rental property whether the State or local governmental unit (i) constructs such property and leases or sells it to any person who is not an exempt person for use in such person's trade or business of leasing such property; (ii) lends the proceeds to any such person for such purpose; or (iii) lends the proceeds to banks or other financial institutions in order to increase the supply of funds for mortgage lending under conditions requiring such banks or other financial institutions to use such proceeds only for further lending for residential rental property.

(5) Limitation. (i) A facility qualifies under this section only to the extent that there is a valid reimbursement allocation under § 1.150-2 with respect to expenditures that are incurred before the issue date of the bonds to provide the facility and that are to be paid with the proceeds of the issue. In addition, if the original use of the facility begins before the issue date of the bonds, the facility does not qualify under this section if any person that was a substantial user of the facility at any time during the 5-year period before the issue date or any related person to that user receives (directly or indirectly) 5 percent or more of the proceeds of the issue for the user's interest in the facility and is a substantial user of the facility at any time during the 5-year period after the issue date, unless—

(A) An official intent for the facility is adopted under § 1.150-2 within 60 days after the date on which acquisition, construction, or reconstruction of that facility commenced; and

(B) For an acquisition, no person that is a substantial user or related person after the acquisition date was also a substantial user more than 60 days before the date on which the official intent was adopted.

(ii) A facility, the original use of which commences (or the acquisition of which occurs) on or after the issue date of bonds to provide that facility, qualifies under this section only to the extent that an official intent for the facility is adopted under § 1.150-2 by the issuer of the bonds within 60 days after the commencement of the construction, reconstruction, or acquisition of that facility. Temporary construction or other financing of a facility prior to the issuance of the bonds to provide that facility will not cause that facility to be one that does not qualify under this paragraph (a)(5)(ii).

(iii) For purposes of paragraph (a)(5)(i) of this section, substantial user has the meaning used in section 147(a)(1), related person has the meaning used in section 144(a)(3), and a user that is a governmental unit within the meaning of § 1.103-1 is disregarded.

(iv) Except to the extent provided in §§ 1.142-4(d), 1.148-11A(i), and 1.150-2(j), this paragraph (a)(5) applies to bonds issued after June 30, 1993, and sold before July 8, 1997. See § 1.142-4(d) for rules relating to bonds sold on or after July 8, 1997.

(6) Deep discount obligations. (i) Except as otherwise provided in paragraph (a)(7) of this section, the proceeds of any issue of obligations sold by the issuer after June 4, 1982, shall include any imputed proceeds of the issue. The imputed proceeds of an issue equal the sum of the amounts of imputed proceeds for each annual period (hereinafter, bond year) over the term of the issue.

(ii) The amount of imputed proceeds for a bond year equals—

(a) The sum of the amounts of interest that will accrue with respect to each obligation that is part of the issue in such year, reduced (but not below zero) by

(b) The sum of the amounts of principal and interest that become payable with respect to the issue in that bond year.

(iii) Interest will be deemed to accrue with respect to an obligation on an amount that, as of the commencement of that year, is equal to the sum of—

(a) The purchase price (as defined in § 1.103-13(d)(2)) allocable to the obligation and

(b) The aggregate of the amounts of interest accruing in each prior bond year with respect to the obligation, reduced by all amounts that became payable with respect to the obligation in prior bond years. Any amount that becomes payable during the 30 day period following any bond year will be deemed to have become payable in such bond year. Thus, to the extent interest on an obligation accruing during a bond year does not become payable within 30 days from the end of such year, it is treated as reinvested under the same terms as the obligation. For purposes of this subparagraph (6), the rate at which such interest accrues is equal to the yield of the obligation. Yield is computed in the same manner as set forth in § 1.103-13(c)(1)(ii) for computing yield on governmental obligations (assuming annual compounding of interest). Such computations shall be made without regard to optional call dates.

(7) Deep discount obligations; special rules. (i) There are no imputed proceeds with respect to an obligation if—

(a) The obligation does not have a stated interest rate (determinable at the date of issue) that increases over the term of the obligation, and

(b) The purchase price of the obligation is at least 95 percent of its face amount.

At the option of the issuer, any obligation described in the preceding sentence may be disregarded in computing the imputed proceeds of the issue. Payments with respect to such obligations are also disregarded in determining the amount payable with respect to the issue in that bond year. If each obligation which is part of an issue is described in the subdivision (i), there are no imputed proceeds with respect to the issue.

(ii) If the actual rate at which interest is to accrue over the term of an obligation is indeterminable at the date of issue then, in computing the yield of the obligation for purposes of this paragraph, such rate shall be determined as if the conditions as of the date of issue will not change over the term of the obligation. Thus, for example, if interest on an obligation is to be paid semiannually at a rate equal to 80 percent of the yield on six month Treasury bills at the most recent public sale immediately prior to the corresponding interest payment date and the yield on six month Treasury bills sold immediately preceding the issue date is 10 percent, then the six month Treasury bill rate is deemed to be a constant 10 percent for purposes of determining the amount of imputed proceeds of the issue. Therefore, all interest payments on the obligation would be deemed to be made at a rate of 8 percent.

(8) Examples. The principles of this paragraph may be illustrated by the following examples:

Example (1). State A issues its bonds and plans to use substantially all of the proceeds from such bond issue to purchase land and build a facility which will be used for one of the purposes described in section 103(b)(4) and this section. The arrangement provides that (1) A will issue bonds with a face amount of $21 million and with all accrued interest payable annually, the proceeds of which (after deducting bond election costs, costs of publishing notices, attorneys' fees, printing costs, trustees' fees for fiscal agents, and similar expenses) will be $20 million; (2) $18 million of the proceeds of the bond issue will be used to purchase land and to construct such facility; (3) $2 million of the proceeds will be used for an unrelated facility which will be used by X, a nonexempt person, in a separate trade or business and for a purpose not described in section 103(b)(4) or (5); (4) X will rent both facilities for 20 years at an annual rental equal to the amount necessary to amortize the principal and pay the interest annually on the outstanding bonds; and (5) such payments by X and the facilities will be the security for the bonds. On these facts, substantially all of the proceeds will be used in connection with an exempt facility described in section 103(b)(4) and this section. Accordingly, section 103(b)(1) does not apply to the bonds unless such bonds are thereafter held by a person who is a substantial user of the facilities or a related person within the meaning of section 103(b)(13) and § 1.103-11.

Example (2). On July 1, 1982, State B sells an issue of its obligations to an underwriter in anticipation of a public offering. The initial offering price is $18,627,639.69 of which $17,000,000 is to be used to construct a pollution control facility described in section 103(b)(4)(F). X Corporation, a nonexempt person, is to use the facility and, in exchange, is obligated to pay an amount equal to the face amount of the issue when it becomes due. The obligations are issued on August 1, 1982. The face amount of the issue is $30,000,000. The issue is a term issue with all obligations maturing on August 1, 1987. The issue bears no stated rate of interest; there are no interest coupons on the obligations. The bonds are industrial development bonds with a yield (based upon annual compounding) of ten percent. Based on these facts, the amount of imputed proceeds with respect to the issue is determined as follows:

Date	Purchase price plus accumulated interest	Interest	Imputed proceeds
Aug. 1, 1983	$18,627,639.69	$1,862,763.97	$1,862,763.97
Aug. 1, 1984	20,490,403.66	2,049,040.37	2,049,040.37
Aug. 1, 1985	22,539,444.03	2,253,944.40	2,253,944.40
Aug. 1, 1986	24,793,388.43	2,479,338.84	2,479,338.84
Aug. 1, 1987	27,272,727.27	2,727,272.73	0
Total imputed proceeds			8,645,087.58

Therefore, proceeds of the issue equal $27,272,727.27 less issuance costs. Substantially all of the bond proceeds are not used to provide an exempt facility, and section 103(b)(1) applies to the issue.

Example (3). The facts are the same as example (2) except that the issue has a face amount and purchase price of $18,500,000. The issue also provides for one payment in addition to the redemption payment, in the amount of $10,267,668 payable on or after August 1, 1986, one year before maturity. Section 103(b)(1) applies to the issue.

Example (4). On July 1, 1982, City E sells an issue of industrial development bonds to provide for a convention facility, as described in section 103(b)(4)(C). Assume that the bonds are issued on that date as well. The issue has a face amount of $15,240,000 and a purchase price of $11,929,382.53. The estimated cost of the facility is $11,000,000. The bonds are "zero coupon" bonds, *i.e.,* there are no interest coupons. Each series is initially offered for less than 95 percent of its face amount. The issue matures serially over a five year period, with each series being allocated a part of the purchase price of the issue. The following chart indicates the purchase price and yield for each series and debt service for the issue:

Date	1983 series at 8 percent	1984 series at 8.5 percent	1985 series at 8.75 percent	1986 series at 9.25 percent	1987 series at 9.75 percent	Interest accruing on issue*	Amount due	Imputed proceeds
July 1, 1983	2,939,814.82	2,697,020.54	2,468,629.60	2,228,732.51	1,595,185.06			
	235,185.18	229,246.75	216,005.09	206,157.76	155,530.54	1,042,125.32	3,175,000	0
July 1, 1984		2,926,267.29	2,684,634.69	2,434,890.27	1,750,715.60			
		248,732.71	234,905.54	225,227.35	170,694.77	879,560.37	3,175,000	0
July 1, 1985			2,919,540.23	2,660,117.62	1,921,410.37			
			255,459.77	246,060.88	187,337.51	688,858.16	3,175,000	0
July 1, 1986				2,906,178.50	2,108,747.88			
				268,821.50	205,602.92	474,424.42	3,175,000	0
July 1, 1987					2,314,350.80			
					225,649.20	225,649.20	2,540,000	0
Total							15,240,000	

* This column (Interest accruing on the issue) contains the sums of the interest that accrues on each series in each bond year. The amount of interest accruing on the issue is computed by adding the amount of interest accruing on each series outstanding for that bond year (the bottom number in the line for each bond year). The amount of interest annually accruing on each series also is added to the purchase price of the series to determine the amount of interest accruing in subsequent years, inasmuch as there are no payments with respect to the outstanding series prior to maturity. Thus, the "principal" amount, of the top of the two numbers given in such line for each bond year, is the purchase price allocable to that series plus the amount of interest that accrued on that series in prior years.

There are no imputed proceeds because the amount payable on the issue in each bond year exceeds the total amount of interest accruing on the issue during such bond year. Section 103(b)(1) does not apply to the bonds unless such bonds are held by a person who is a substantial user of the facility or a related person within the meaning of section 103(b)(13) and § 1.103-11.

Example (5). On July 1, 1982, City C issues industrial development bonds in the face amount of $30 million to construct a sports facility described in section 103(b)(4)(B) to be leased to D, a nonexempt person, with payments on the bonds secured by the lease. C receives $30 million in exchange for the bonds which will be used to provide the facility. The bonds mature on July 1, 2002. Each bond provides for an annual interest payment equal to ten percent of the face amount of the bond, with the last payment thereon (on July 1, 2202) including a return of the principal amount of the bond. The proceeds of the issue are $30 million. Section 103(b)(1) does not apply to the bonds unless such bonds are held by a person who is a substantial user of the facility or a related person within the meaning of section 103(b)(13) and § 1.103-11.

Example (6). The facts are the same as example (5) except that each bond provides for an annual interest payment equal to nine percent of its face amount and is sold with the option to tender the bond to D for purchase at par 5 years after the sale date of July 1, 1982 (*i.e.,* the bonds are sold with a "put" option). Such bonds also provide a put option annually thereafter. There are no imputed proceeds (without regard to § 1.103-8(a)(7)), and the result is the same as example (5).

Example (7). On July 1, 1982, City F sells an issue of industrial development bonds in the face amount of $20 million to acquire a parking facility as described in section 103(b)(4)(D). The estimated cost of the facility is $17,800,000. The issue is issued on the same date and will mature serially over the following ten years. Each bond that is part of the issue bears annual interest coupons, each of which is in an amount equal to ten percent of the face amount of the bond. Each maturity has a face amount of $2,000,000. The issue is initially offered to the public for $19,700,000, allocable to each maturity as follows:

Maturity	Purchase price
July 1, 1983	$1,990,000
July 1, 1984	$1,980,000
July 1, 1985	$1,980,000
July 1, 1986	$1,970,000
July 1, 1987	$1,970,000
July 1, 1988	$1,970,000
July 1, 1989	$1,960,000
July 1, 1990	$1,960,000
July 1, 1991	$1,960,000
July 1, 1992	$1,960,000

Based on the foregoing issue proceeds equal $19,700,000 less issuance costs. There are no imputed proceeds with respect to this issue inasmuch as each bond pays interest at a constant rate in each bond year and the purchase price of each bond is at least 95 percent of its face amount. Substantially all of the proceeds are to be used to provide the exempt facility. Accordingly, section 103(b)(1) does not apply to the bonds unless such bonds are thereafter held by a person who is a substantial user of the facility or a related person within the meaning of section 103(b)(13) and § 1.103-11.

(b) Residential rental property. *(1) General rule for obligations issued after April 24, 1979.* Section 103(b)(1) shall not apply to any obligations which is issued after April 24, 1979, and is part of an issue substantially all of the proceeds of which are to be used to provide a residential rental project in which 20 percent or more of the units are to be occupied by individuals or families of low or moderate income (as defined in paragraph (b)(8)(v) of this section). In the case of a targeted area project, the minimum percentage of units which are to be occupied by individuals of low or moderate income is 15 percent. See generally § 1.103-7 for rules relating to refunding issues.

(2) Registration requirement. Any obligation (including any refunding obligation) issued after December 31, 1981, to provide a residential rental project must be issued as part of an issue, each obligation of which is in registered form (as defined in paragraph (b)(8)(ii) of this section).

(3) Transitional rule. For purposes of this section, obligations issued after April 24, 1979, may be treated as issued before April 25, 1979, if the transitional requirements of section 1104 of the Mortgage Subsidy Bond Tax Act of 1980 (94 Stat. 2670) are satisfied.

(4) Residential rental project. (i) In general. A residential rental project is a building or structure, together with any functionally related and subordinate facilities, containing one or more similarly constructed units—

(a) Which are used on other than a transient basis, and

(b) Which satisfy the requirements of paragraph (b)(5)(i) of this section and are available to members of the general public in accordance with the requirement of paragraph (a)(2) of this section.

Substantially all of each project must contain such units and functionally related and subordinate facilities. Hotels, motels, dormitories, fraternity and sorority houses, rooming houses, hospitals, nursing homes, sanitariums, rest homes, and trailer parks and courts for use on a transient basis are not residential rental projects.

(ii) Multiple buildings. (a) Proximate buildings or structures (hereinafter "buildings") which have similarly constructed units are treated as part of the same project if they are owned for Federal tax purposes by the same person and if the buildings are financed pursuant to a common plan.

(b) Buildings are proximate if they are located on a single tract of land. The term "tract" means any parcel or parcels of land which are contiguous except for the interposition of a road, street, stream or similar property. Otherwise, parcels are contiguous if their boundaries meet at one or more points.

(c) A common plan of financing exists if, for example, all such buildings are provided by the same issue or several issues subject to a common indenture.

(iii) Functionally related and subordinate facilities. Under paragraph (a)(3) of this section, facilities that are functionally related and subordinate to residential rental projects include facilities for use by the tenants, for example, swimming pools, other recreational facilities, parking areas, and other facilities which are reasonably required for the project, for example, heating and cooling equipment, trash disposal equipment or units for resident managers or maintenance personnel.

(iv) Owner-occupied residences. For purposes of section 103(b)(4)(A) and this paragraph (b), the term "residential rental project" does not include any building or structure which contains fewer than five units, one unit of which is occupied by an owner of the units.

(5) Requirement must be continuously satisfied. (i) Rental requirement. Once available for occupancy, each unit (as defined in paragraph (b)(8)(i) of this section) in a residential rental project must be rented or available for rental on a continuous basis during the longer of—

(a) the remaining term of the obligation, or

(b) the qualified project period (as defined in paragraph (b)(7) of this section).

(ii) Low or moderate income occupancy requirement. Individuals or families of low or moderate income must occupy that percentage of completed units in such project applicable to the project under paragraph (b)(1) of this section continuously during the qualified project period. For this purpose, a unit occupied by an individual or family who at the commencement of the occupancy is of low or moderate income is treated as occupied by such an individual or family during their tenancy in such unit, even though they subsequently cease to be of low or moderate income. Moreover, such unit is treated as occupied by an individual or family of low or moderate income until reoccupied, other than for a temporary period, at which time the character of the unit shall be redetermined. In no event shall such temporary period exceed 31 days.

(6) Effect of post-issuance noncompliance. (i) In general. Unless corrected within a reasonable period, noncompliance with the requirements of this paragraph (b) shall cause the project to be treated as other than a project described in section 103(b)(4)(A) and this paragraph (b) as of the date of issue. After an issue to provide such project ceases to qualify, subsequent conformity with the requirements will not alter the taxable status of such issue.

(ii) Correction of noncompliance. If the issuer corrects any noncompliance arising from events occurring after the issuance of the obligation within a reasonable period, such noncompliance *(e.g.,* an unauthorized sublease) shall not cause the project to be a project not described in this paragraph (b). A reasonable period is at least 60 days after such error is first discovered or would have been discovered by the exercise of reasonable diligence.

(iii) Involuntary loss. (a) The requirements of paragraph (b) shall cease to apply to a project in the event of involuntary noncompliance caused by fire, seizure, requisition, foreclosure, transfer of title by deed in lieu of foreclosure, change in a Federal law or an action of a Federal agency after the date of issue which prevents an issuer from enforcing the requirements of this paragraph, or condemnation or similar event but only if, within a reasonable period, either the obligation used to provide such project is retired or amounts received as a consequence of such event are used to provide a project which meets the requirement of section 103(b)(4)(A) and this paragraph (b).

(b) The provisions of paragraph (b)(6)(iii) *(a)* of this section shall cease to apply to a project subject to foreclosure, transfer of title by deed in lieu of foreclosure or similar event if, at anytime during that part of the qualified project period subsequent to such event, the obligor on the acquired purpose obligation (as defined in § 1.103-13(b)(4)(iv) *(a)*) or a related person (as defined in § 1.103-10(e)) obtains an ownership interest in such project for tax purposes.

(7) Qualified project period. The term "qualified project period" means—

(i) For obligations issued after April 24, 1979, and prior to September 4, 1982, a period of 20 years commencing on the later of the date that the project becomes available for occupancy or the date of issue of the obligations. The requirement of paragraph (b)(5)(ii) of this section shall be deemed met if the owner of the project contracts with a Federal or state agency to maintain at least 20 percent (or 15 percent in the case of targeted areas) of the units for low or moderate income individuals or families (as defined in paragraph (b)(8)(v) of this section) for 20 years in consideration for rent subsidies for such individuals or families for such period.

(ii) For obligations issued after September 3, 1982, a period beginning on the later of the first day on which at least 10 percent of the units in the project are first occupied or the date of issue of an obligation described in section 103(b)(4)(A) and this paragraph and ending on the later of the date—

(a) Which is 10 years after the date on which at least 50 percent of the units in the project are first occupied,

(b) Which is a qualified number of days after the date on which any of the units in the project is first occupied, or

(c) On which any assistance provided with respect to the project under section 8 of the United States Housing Act of 1937 terminates.

For purposes of this paragraph (b)(7)(ii), the term "qualified number of days" means 50 percent of the total number of days comprising the term of the obligation with the longest maturity in the issue used to provide the project. In the case of a refunding of such an issue, the longest maturity is equal to the sum of the period the prior issue was outstanding and the longest term of any refunding obligations.

(8) Other definitions. For purposes of this paragraph—

(i) Unit. The term "unit" means any accommodation containing separate and complete facilities for living, sleeping, eating, cooking, and sanitation. Such accommodations may be served by centrally located equipment, such as air conditioning or heating. Thus, for example, an apartment containing a living area, a sleeping area, bathing and sanitation facilities, and cooking facilities equipped with a cooking range, refrigerator, and sink, all of which are separate and distinct from other apartments, would constitute a unit.

(ii) In registered form. The term "in registered form" has the same meaning as in section 6049. With respect to obligations issued after December 31, 1982, such term shall have the same meaning as prescribed in section 103(j) (including the regulations thereunder).

(iii) Targeted area project. The term "targeted area project" means a project located in a qualified census tract (as defined in § 6a.103A-2(b)(4)) or an area of chronic economic distress (as defined in § 6a.103A-2(b)(5)).

(iv) Building or structure. The term "building or structure" generally means a discrete edifice or other man-made construction consisting of an independent foundation, outer walls, and roof. A single unit which is not an entire building but is merely a part of a building is not a building or structure within the meaning of this section. As such, while single townhouses are not buildings if their foundation, outer walls, and roof are not independent, detached houses and rowhouses are buildings.

(v) Low or moderate income. Individuals and families of low or moderate income shall be determined in a manner consistent with determinations of lower income families under section 8 of the United States Housing Act of 1937, as amended, except that the percentage of median gross income which qualifies as low or moderate income shall be 80 percent. Therefore, occupants of a unit are considered individuals or families of low or moderate income only if their adjusted income (computed in the manner prescribed with § 1.167(k)-3(b)(3)) does not exceed 80 percent of the median gross income for the area. Notwithstanding the foregoing, the occupants of a unit shall not be considered to be of low or moderate income if all the occupants are students (as defined in section 151(e)(4)), no one of whom is entitled to file a joint return under section 6013. The method of determining low or moderate income in effect on the date of issue will be determinative for such issue, even if such method is subsequently changed. In the event programs under § 8(f) of the Housing Act of 1937, as amended, are terminated prior to the date of issue, the applicable method shall be that in effect immediately prior to the date of such termination.

(9) Examples. The following examples illustrate the application of this paragraph (b).

Example (1). In August 1982, City X issues $10 million of registered bonds with a term of 20 years to be used to finance the construction of an apartment building to be available to members of the general public. X loans the proceeds of the bonds to Corporation M, the tax owner of the project. The loan is secured by a promissory note from M and a mortgage on the project. The mortgage requires annual payments sufficient to amortize the principal and interest on the bonds. Corporation M maintains 20 percent of the units in the project for low or moderate income individuals and meets all of the requirements of this section until 2002, at which time M converts the project to offices. The bonds are industrial development bonds, but because the proceeds are used for construction of residential rental property, which is an exempt facility under section 103(b)(4)(A) and paragraph (b) of this section, section 103(b)(1) does not apply.

Example (2). The facts are the same as in example (1), except that the building is constructed adjacent to a factory, and the factory employees are to be given preference in selecting tenants. The bonds are industrial development bonds and the facility is not an exempt facility under section 103(b)(4)(A) and paragraph (b) of this section because it is not a facility constructed for use by the general public.

Example (3). The facts are the same as in example (1), except that the proceeds of the obligation are provided to N, a cooperative housing corporation, to finance the construction of a cooperative housing project. N sells stock in such cooperative to shareholders, some of whom occupy the units in the cooperative and some of whom rent the units to other persons. Such project is not a residential rental project within the meaning of section 103(b)(4)(A) and § 1.103-8(b) because less than all of the units in the building are used for rental. Further, the bonds are mortgage subsidy bonds under section 103A because more than a significant portion of the proceeds are used to provide financing for residences, some of which are owner-occupied and some of which are used in the trade or business of rental.

Example (4). On February 1, 1984, County Z issues registered obligations with a term of 3 years and loans the proceeds to Corporation V to construct a garden apartment project for tenants who are 65 years or older. The mortgage on the project secures the loan. At the end of 3 years, V obtains permanent financing for the project from a commercial lender. The project is not a targeted area project. V has not contracted with any Federal or state agency to provide rental assistance under section 8 of the United States Housing Act of 1937. As a condition for providing financing for construction, Z requires that the deed to the project contain a covenant that requires the project be used for elderly tenants and restricts occupancy of 20 percent of the units in the project to individuals or families of low or moderate income. Further, the deed provides that "Such covenant shall run with and bind the land, from the date that ten percent of the units in the project are first occupied until ten years after the date that at least half the units are first occupied. The right to enforce these restrictions is vested in County Z." In 1990, however, less than 20 percent of the units are occupied by families or individuals of low or moderate incomes, and three months after learning of this condition County Z had not commenced enforcement of the covenant. Although on the date of issue the proceeds of the obligation were used to provide a residential rental project, the obligation will not be treated as providing a residential rental project within the meaning of section 103(b)(4)(A) as of February 1, 1984, because the project did not meet the requirements of this paragraph for at least 10 years after at least 50 percent of the units are first occupied.

Example (5). On January 15, 1983, State X issues registered obligations with a term of 15 years, the proceeds of which are loaned to Corporation P to construct an apartment building. The project will be a "targeted area project", within the meaning of § 1.103-8(b)(8)(iii). Corporation P intends to rent all the units to individuals for their residences, maintaining 15 percent of the units in the project for individuals having low or moderate incomes, for 15 years. In 1988, however, Corporation P converts 80 percent of the units to condominiums. Corporation P repays the loan to State X which, in turn, redeems the obligations. The obligations are not used to provide a residential rental project within the meaning of section 103(b)(4)(A), and all the interest paid or to be paid on such obligations will be includable in gross income.

Example (6). On January 15, 1984, State Z issues registered obligations with a term of 15 years the proceeds of which will be used to acquire and renovate a residential apartment building. Z sells the project to Corporation U and receives a 30-year mortgage. On June 1, 1985, the first occupants of the project commence their tenancies. At least 50 percent of the units in the project are occupied on July 1, 1985. On January 15, 1988, Z issues 35-year refunding bonds the proceeds of which are used to retire the obligations issued in 1984. The prior issue will be discharged by March 15, 1988. In order to meet the requirement of § 1.103-8(b)(5)(ii), at least 20 percent of such units must be occupied by individuals of low or moderate income until January 1, 2005.

Example (7). The facts are the same as in example (6) except that in 1987, the apartment building is substantially destroyed by fire. The building was insured at its fair market value. U does not intend to reconstruct the building but uses a portion of the insurance proceeds to repay the unpaid balance of the mortgage. Z uses this amount to redeem the outstanding bonds at the first available call date. Since the project was substantially destroyed by fire and the outstanding bonds are retired at the first available call date, the requirements of section 103(b)(4)(A) and this paragraph (b) are satisfied with respect to the obligations.

Example (8). The facts are the same as in example (6) except that in 1987 U defaults on the mortgage, and Z obtains title to the project without instituting foreclosure proceedings. Z sells the project to S and uses the proceeds to retire the outstanding bonds. Since S did not obtain the project with obligations described in section 103(b)(4), S is not required to meet the requirements of section 103(b)(4)(A) and this paragraph. Further, the 1984 obligations are obligations described in section 103(b)(4)(A).

Example (9). In September 1983, State W issues $10 million of registered bonds with a term of 3 years, the proceeds of which are to be loaned to Corporation V to finance the construction of an apartment building in a rural community. At the end of 3 years, V obtains permanent financing from Federal Agency T. Agency T will not allow the deed to contain any restrictive covenant relating to the use of the project. Under Federal law, however, T requires that V maintain all of the units in the project for rental to low-income farm workers for the term of the mortgage, which is 20 years. Further, the mortgage between T and V provides that if T determines that low-income housing is no longer required in the community in which the project is constructed then the repayment of the mortgage may be accelerated. T determines as of the date of issue that low-income housing will be needed in the community for at least 20 years. In 1987, the project fails to meet the requirements of § 1.103-8(b)(5)(ii), relating to occupancy by individuals or families of low or moderate income. Further, T does not require V to correct the failure. Based on the foregoing, the bonds issued by W will be treated as described in section 103(b)(4)(A).

Example (10). The facts are the same as in example (9) except that in 1987, the Federal law is amended to provide that Agency T may not enforce its low-income occupancy requirement. The result is the same.

Example (11). The facts are the same as in example (9) except that in 1987 Agency T determines that due to a change in circumstances in the community in which the project is located low-income rental housing is no longer required. As such, T requires V to repay the mortgage. Since the obligations have been repaid, W has no legal right to enforce the requirements of paragraph (b) with respect to the project. Subsequent nonconformity of the project with the requirements of § 1.103-8(b) under these circumstances will not cause the obligations issued by W to be industrial development bonds within the meaning of section 103(b)(1).

(10) Obligations issued before April 25, 1979. (i) General rules. Section 103(b)(1) shall not apply to obligations issued before April 25, 1979, which are part of an issue substantially all of the proceeds of which are to be used to provide residential real property for family units. In order to qualify under this paragraph (b) as an exempt facility, the facility must satisfy the public use requirement of paragraph (a)(2) of this section by being available for use by members of the general public.

(ii) Family units defined. For purposes of this paragraph (b) the term "family unit" means a building or any portion thereof which contains complete living facilities which are to be used on other than a transient basis by one or more persons, and facilities functionally related and subordinate thereto. Thus, an apartment which is to be used on other than a transient basis as a residence by a single person or by a family and which contains complete facilities for living, sleeping, eating, cooking, and sanitation, constitutes a family unit. Such a unit may be served by centrally located machinery and equipment as in a typical apartment building. To qualify as a family unit, the living facilities must be a separate, self-contained building or constitute one unit in a building substantially all of which consists of similar units, together with functionally related and subordinate facilities and areas. Hotels, motels, dormitories, fraternity and sorority houses, rooming houses, hospitals, sanitariums, rest homes, and trailer parks and courts for use on a transient basis do not constitute residential real property for family units.

(iii) Functionally related and subordinate facilities. Under paragraph (a)(3) of this section, facilities which are functionally related and subordinate to residential real property actually used for family units include, for example, facilities for use by the occupants such as a swimming pool, a parking area, and recreational facilities.

(c) Sports facilities. *(1) General rule.* Section 103(b)(4)(B) provides that section 103(b)(1) shall not apply to obligations by a State or local governmental unit which are part of an issue substantially all of the proceeds of which are to be used to provide sports facilities. In order to qualify as an exempt facility under section 103(b)(4)(B) and this paragraph, the facility must satisfy the public use requirement of paragraph (a)(2) of this section by being available for use by members of the general public either as participants or as spectators.

(2) Sports facility defined. (i) For purposes of section 103(b)(4)(B) and this paragraph, the term "sports facilities" includes both outdoor and indoor facilities. The facility may be designed either as a spectator or as a participation facility. For example, the term includes both indoor and outdoor stadiums for baseball, football, ice hockey, or other sports events, as well as facilities for the participation of the general public in sports activities, such as golf courses, ski slopes, swimming pools, tennis courts, and gymnasiums. The term does not include, however, facilities such as a golf course, swimming pool, or tennis court, which are constructed for use by members of a private club or as integral or subordinate parts of a hotel or motel, or the use of which will be restricted to a special class or group or to guests of a particular hotel or motel, since they are not facilities for the use of the general public as required by paragraph (a)(2) of this section.

(ii) Under paragraph (a)(3) of this section, facilities which are functionally related and subordinate to a sports facility, such as a parking lot, clubhouse, ski slope warming house, bath house, or ski tow, are considered to be part of a sports facility. A ski lodge which consists primarily of overnight accommodations is not functionally related and subordinate to a sports facility.

(d) Convention or trade show facilities. *(1) General rule.* Section 103(b)(4)(C) provides that section 103(b)(1) shall not apply to obligations issued by a State or local governmental unit which are a part of an issue substantially all of the proceeds of which are to be used to provide convention or trade show facilities. In order to qualify under section 103(b)(4)(C) and this paragraph as an exempt facility, the facility must satisfy the public use requirement of paragraph (a)(2) of this section by being available for an appropriate charge or rental, on a rate scale basis, for use by members of the general public. The public use requirement is not satisfied if the use of a convention or trade show facility is limited by long-term leases to a single user or group of users.

(2) Convention or trade show facilities defined. For purposes of section 103(b)(4)(C) and this paragraph, the term "convention or trade show facilities" means special-purpose buildings or structures, such as meeting halls and display areas, which are generally used to house a convention or trade show, including, under paragraph (a)(3) of this section, facilities functionally related and subordinate to such facilities such as parking lots or railroad sidings. A hotel or motel which is available to the general public, whether or not it is intended primarily to house persons attending or participating in a convention or trade show, is neither a convention or trade show facility nor functionally related and subordinate thereto.

(e) Certain transportation facilities. *(1) General rule.* Section 103(b)(4)(D) provides that section 103(b)(1) shall not apply to obligations issued by a State or local governmental unit which are part of an issue substantially all of the proceeds of which are to be used to provide (i) airports, docks, wharves, mass commuting facilities, or public parking facilities, or (ii) storage or training facilities directly related to any such facility. In order to qualify under section 103(b)(4)(D) and this paragraph as an exempt facility, the facility must satisfy the public use requirement of paragraph (a)(2) of this section by being available for use by members of the general public or for use by common carriers or charter carriers which serve members of the general public. A dock or wharf which is part of a public port (or a public port to be constructed in accordance with a plan which has been finally adopted on the date the obligations in question are issued) satisfies the public use test. A parking lot will be available for use by the general public unless more than an insubstantial portion thereof will be used exclusively by or for the benefit of a nonexempt person by reason of a formal or informal agreement or by reason of the remote geographic location of the facility.

(2) Definitions. For purposes of section 103(b)(4)(D) and this paragraph—

(i) With respect to bonds sold at or before 5:00 p.m. EST on December 29, 1978, an airport includes service accommodations for the public such as terminals, retail stores in such terminals, runways, hangars, loading facilities, repair shops, parking areas, and facilities which, under paragraph (a)(3) of this section, are functionally related and subordinate to the airport, such as facilities for the preparation of in-flight meals, restaurants, and accommodations for temporary or overnight use by passengers, and other facilities functionally related to the needs or convenience of passengers, shipping companies, and airlines. The term "airport" does not include a landing strip which, by reason of a formal or informal agreement, or by reason of geographic location, will not be available for general public use.

(ii) With respect to bonds sold after 5:00 p.m. EST on December 29, 1978—

(a) An airport includes facilities which are directly related and essential to—

(1) Servicing aircraft or enabling aircraft to take off and land, or

(2) Transferring passengers or cargo to or from aircraft.

A facility does not satisfy either of the foregoing requirements if the facility need not be located at, or in close proximity to, the take-off and landing area in order to perform its function. Examples of facilities which satisfy those requirements are terminals, runways, hangars, loading facilities, repair shops, and land-based navigation aids such as radar installation.

(b) Under paragraph (a)(3) of this section, an airport includes facilities other than those described in paragraph (e)(2)(ii)(a) only if they are functionally related and subordinate to an airport (as defined in paragraph (e)(2)(ii)(a)). A facility (or part thereof) is not functionally related and subordinate to an airport if the facility (or part thereof)—

(1) Is not of a character and size commensurate with the character and size of the airport at or adjacent to which the facility is located, or

(2) Is not located at or adjacent to that airport.

A facility may satisfy the character and size requirement although it provides minimal benefits to other airports. For example, a facility for the preparation of in-flight meals which has capacity sufficient to prepare all in-flight meals for aircraft departing the airport where the facility is located qualifies although some meals may be consumed in transit between other airports. Other examples of facilities functionally related and subordinate to an airport are restaurants and retail stores located in terminals, ground transportation parking areas, and accommodations for temporary or overnight use by passengers. Unimproved land (including agricultural land) that is adjacent to an airport and that is impaired by a significant level of airport noise is functionally related and subordinate to the airport if after its acquisition that land will not be converted to a use that is incompatible with the level of airport noise. Adjacent land with existing improvements also may be functionally related and subordinate to an airport by reason of impairment by a significant level of airport noise but only if the use of such land before its acquisition is incompatible with the airport noise level, its use after acquisition is to be compatible, and the post-acquisition use will be essentially different from the pre-acquisition use. Notwithstanding the foregoing, an interest in such improved land acquired solely to mitigate damages attributable to airport noise is treated as functionally related and subordinate to the airport. Thus, for example, amounts allocated to imposing a servitude on improved land adjacent to an airport restricting its future use to uses compatible with airport noise are treated as amounts allocated to property functionally related and subordinate to an airport. For the purpose of determining whether land is impaired by a significant level of airport noise, any generally accepted noise estimating methodology may be used. For example, a Noise Exposure Forecast (NEF), a method for composite noise rating recommended by the Federal Aviation Administration to measure the impact of airport noise, may be used for this purpose. Compatibility may be determined by reference to regulations or general guidelines published by the Federal Aviation Administration under section 102 of the Aviation Safety and Noise Abatement Act of 1979 (49 U.S.C. 2102), or sections 11(3)(C) and 18(a)(4) of the Airport and Airway Development Act of 1970, as amended (49 U.S.C. 1711(3)(C) and 1718(a)(4)), concerning uses of land impaired by a significant level of airport noise, or, where available, by reference to the airport compatibility plan specifically addressing what constitutes a compatible use of that land.

(c) As an illustration of the rules of this paragraph (e)(2)(ii), an office building (or office space within a building) or a computer facility, either of which serves a systemwide or regional function of an airline, is not considered part of an airport since that facility is not described in either paragraph (e)(2)(ii)(a) or (b). However, a maintenance or overhaul facility which services aircraft is considered part of an airport under paragraph (e)(2)(ii)(a) since that facility is directly related and essential to servicing aircraft and must be located where aircraft take off and land in order to perform its function.

(d) A hotel located at or adjacent to an airport satisfies the requirements of paragraph (e)(2)(ii)(b), that is, it is of a character and size commensurate with the character and size of the airport at or adjacent to which it is located, if the number of quest rooms in the hotel is reasonable for the size of the airport, taking into account the current and projected passenger usage of the terminal facility. If the hotel contains meeting rooms, the number and size of these rooms must be in reasonable proportion to the number of guest rooms in the hotel. Limited recreational facilities will not prevent the hotel from being of a character and size commensurate with the character and size of the airport.

(iii) A dock or wharf includes property which, under paragraph (a)(3) of this section, is functionally related and subordinate to a dock or wharf such as the structure alongside which a vessel docks, the equipment needed to receive and to discharge cargo and passengers from the vessel, such as cranes and conveyors, related storage, handling, office, and passenger areas, and similar facilities.

(iv) A mass commuting facility includes real property together with improvements and personal property used therein, such as machinery, equipment, and furniture, serving the general public commuting on a day-to-day basis by bus, subway, rail, ferry, or other conveyance which moves over prescribed routes. Such property also includes terminals and facilities which, under paragraph (a)(3) of this section, are functionally related and subordinate to the mass commuting facility, such as parking garages, car barns, and repair shops. Use of mass commuting facilities by noncommuters in common with commuters is immaterial. Thus, a terminal leased to a common carrier bus line which serves both commuters and long distance travelers would qualify as an exempt facility.

(3) Related storage and training facility. Section 103(b)(4)(D) includes only those storage and training facilities which are both (i) directly related to a facility to which subparagraph (1)(i) or (ii) of this paragraph applies and (ii) physically located on or adjacent to such a facility. For example, a storage facility would include a grain elevator, silo, warehouse, or oil and gas storage tank used in connection with a dock or wharf located on or adjacent to such dock or wharf. Similarly, a training facility would include a building located at or adjacent to an airport for the training of flight personnel or a paved area immediately adjoining a bus garage used to train bus drivers.

(4) Examples. The principles of this paragraph may be illustrated by the following examples:

Example (1). B Airport Authority, a political subdivision of State A, owns and operates B Airport. B Airport Authority adds several runways. In view of the expanded area impaired by significant levels of airport noise, the Authority proposes to issue bonds the proceeds of which are to be used to acquire a hospital located adjacent to the airport. The noise level on the acquired property is 40 NEF. By reference to a noise exposure map setting forth noncompatible land uses and by reference to guidelines published by the Federal Aviation Administration, it is established that continued use of the land for a hospital is not compatible with the noise level. Prior to issuing the bonds, B contracts to lease the property to Corporation C to be used for warehouse space. Within 18 months of the bonds' issuance C will remodel the hospital (previously owned by D, who is unrelated to C) with its own funds and rent the facility as a warehouse. Use as a warehouse is determined to be compatible with the level of airport noise impairing the land. The improved land and prospective revenues from the facility's rental are security for the proposed issuance. Based on the foregoing, the acquired land satisfies the public use test. Furthermore, it is functionally related and subordinate to the airport because the improvements are to be used in an essentially different matter than prior to the land's acquisition. The bonds are industrial development bonds. However, section 103(b)(1) does not apply unless the provisions of section 103(b)(8) and § 1.103-11 apply.

Example (2). The facts are the same as in Example (1) except that a substantial portion of the proceeds of the bond issue is allocated to the acquisition of a limited interest in an additional tract of land (also impaired by airport noise measured at 40 NEF) on which an office building stands. The limited interest holds B harmless for damages caused by airport noise and restricts uses of the tract after the building is retired to those compatible with noise levels caused by the airport. Based on the foregoing, such interest satisfies the public use test. Furthermore, the interest is functionally related and subordinate to the airport because it is solely to mitigate damage attributable to airport noise, in part by restricting future land uses. The bonds are industrial development bonds. However, section 103(b)(1) does not apply unless the provisions of section 103(b)(8) or § 1.103-11 apply.

Example (3). On June 1, 1982, M Airport Authority, a political subdivision of State O, issues obligations, the proceeds of which are loaned to X Corporation, a nonexempt person. X uses the proceeds to construct a hotel adjacent to the main terminal building at M Airport. X will be unconditionally liable for repayment of the proposed obligations. The hotel will be used to provide temporary and overnight accommodations for airline passengers using M Airport. The number of rooms in the hotel is reasonable for an airport of M's size, taking into account the current and projected passenger usage of the terminal facility. In addition to guest rooms, the hotel will contain a restaurant, small retail stores (such as a gift shop and newsstand), and limited recreation facilities (such as a swimming pool). The hotel will also contain several multipurpose rooms suitable for use as meeting rooms. The number and size of these rooms will be in reasonable proportion to the number and size of the guest rooms in the hotel. Use of the guest rooms, restaurant and stores, recreational facilities, and meeting rooms by air passengers arriving at or departing from M Airport will be incidental to the use of the hotel by air passengers for temporary and overnight accommodations. The hotel is of a character and size commensurate with the character and size of M Airport. Consequently, applying the provisions of § 1.103-8(e)(2), the hotel is functionally related and subordinate to M Airport. The obligations are industrial development bonds. Section 103(b)(1) does not apply to the obligations, however, unless the provisions of section 103(b)(10) and § 1.103-11 apply.

Example (4). On June 1, 1982, N Airport Authority, a political subdivision of State P, issues obligations the proceeds of which are loaned to Y Corporation, a nonexempt person. Y uses the proceeds to construct a hotel adjacent to the main terminal building at N Airport. Y Corporation will be unconditionally liable for repayment of the proposed obligations. The hotel will contain extensive recreational facilities, including a large roof-top swimming pool, tennis courts, and a health club. In addition, facilities for conferences consisting of a ballroom-sized meeting room capable of being partitioned by movable panels and several smaller meeting rooms will be constructed. The number of rooms in the hotel will substantially exceed the number which is reasonable based on the current and projected passenger usage of the terminal facility. Because of the presence of extensive recreational and conference facilities, as well as the presence of on excessive number of rooms at the hotel, the hotel fails to be of a character and size commensurate with the character and size commensurate with the character and size of N Airport. The result would be the same if the hotel did not have extensive recreational facilities. Consequently, the hotel is not functionally related and subordinate to N Airport under § 1.103-8(e)(2). The obligations are industrial development bonds and interest thereon is not excluded from gross income by reason of subsection (a)(1) or (b)(4) of section 103.

(f) Certain public utility facilities. *(1) General rule.* (i) Section 103(b)(4)(E) provides that section 103(b)(1) shall not apply to obligations issued by a State or local governmental unit which are part of an issue substantially all of the proceeds of which are to be used to provide sewage disposal facilities, solid waste disposal facilities, or facilities for the local furnishing of electric energy or gas. In order to qualify under section 103(b)(4)(E) as an exempt facility, the facility must satisfy the public use requirement of paragraph (a)(2) of this section. A public utility facility described in this subparagraph (with the exception of sewage and solid waste disposal facilities which will be treated in all events as serving the general public) will satisfy the public use requirement only if such facility, or the output thereof, is available for use by members of the general public.

(ii) A facility for the local furnishing of electric energy or gas is, for purposes of applying the public use test in paragraph (a)(2) of this section, available for use by members of the general public if (a) the owner or operator of the facility is obligated, by a legislative enactment, local ordinance, regulation, or the equivalent thereof, to furnish electric energy or gas to all persons who desire such services and who are within the service area of the owner or operator of such facility, and (b) it is reasonably expected that such facility will serve or be available to a large segment of the general public in such service area. For rules with respect to facilities for the furnishing of water, see paragraph (h) of this section.

(2) Definitions. For purposes of section 103(b)(4)(E) and this paragraph—

(i) The term "sewage disposal facilities" means any property used for the collection, storage, treatment, utilization, processing, or final disposal of sewage.

(ii) (a) The term "solid waste disposal facilities" means any property or portion thereof used for the collection, storage, treatment, utilization, processing, or final disposal of solid waste. Only expenditures for that portion of property which is a solid waste disposal facility qualify as expenditures for solid waste disposal facilities. The fact that a facility which otherwise qualifies as a solid waste disposal facility operates at a profit will not, of itself, disqualify the facility as an exempt facility. However, whether a collection or storage facility qualifies as a solid waste disposal facility depends upon all of the facts and circumstances. Thus, land and facilities for the collection of materials to form a slag heap which is not preliminary to the recycling or other final disposal of such materials within a reasonable period of time will not qualify. The term does not include facilities for collection, storage, or disposal of liquid or gaseous waste except where such facilities are facilities which, under paragraph (a)(3) of this section, are functionally related and subordinate to a solid waste disposal facility.

(b) The term "solid waste" shall have the same meaning as in section 203(4) of the Solid Waste Disposal Act (42 U.S.C. 3252(4)), except that for purposes of this paragraph, material will not qualify as solid waste unless, on the date of issue of the obligations issued to provide the facility to dispose of such waste material, it is property which is useless, unused, unwanted, or discarded solid material, which has no market or other value at the place where it is located. Thus, where any person is willing to purchase such property, at any price, such material is not waste. Where any person is willing to remove such property at his own expense but is not willing to purchase such property at any price, such material is waste. Section 203(4) of the Solid Waste Disposal Act provides that:

(4) The term "solid waste" means garbage, refuge, and other discarded solid materials, including solid-waste materials resulting from industrial, commercial, and agricultural operations, and from community activities, but does not include solids or dissolved material in domestic sewage or other significant pollutants in water resources, such as silt, dissolved or suspended solids in industrial waste water effluents, dissolved materials in irrigation return flows or other common water pollutants.

(c) A facility which disposes of solid waste by reconstituting, converting, or otherwise recycling it into material which is not waste shall also qualify as a solid waste disposal facility if solid waste (within the meaning of *(b)* of this subdivision (ii)) constitutes at least 65 percent, by weight or volume, of the total materials introduced into the recycling process. Such a recycling facility shall not fail to qualify as a solid waste disposal facility solely because it operates at a profit.

(d) For rules relating to property which has both a solid waste disposal function and a function other than the disposal of solid waste, see § 17.1 of this chapter.

(iii) The term "facilities for the local furnishing of electric energy or gas" means property which—

(a) Is either property of a character subject to the allowance for depreciation provided in section 167 or land,

(b) Is used to produce, collect, generate, transmit, store, distribute, or convey electric energy or gas.

(c) Is used in the trade or business of furnishing electric energy or gas, and

(d) Is a part of a system providing service to the general populace of one or more communities or municipalities, but in no event more than 2 contiguous counties (or a political equivalent) whether or not such counties are located in one State.

For purposes of this subdivision, a city which is not within, or does not consist of, one or more counties (or a political equivalent) shall be treated as a county (or a political equivalent). A facility for the generation of electric energy otherwise qualifying under this subdivision will not be disqualified because it is connected to a system for interconnection with other public utility systems for the emergency transfer of electric energy.

The facilities need not be located in the area served by them. Also, the term "facilities for the local furnishing of electric energy or gas" does not include coal, oil, gas, nuclear cores, or other materials performing a similar function.

(g) Air or water pollution control facilities. *(1) General rule.* Section 103(b)(4)(F) provides that section 103(b)(1) shall not apply to obligations issued by a State or local governmental unit which are part of an issue substantially all of the proceeds of which are to be used to provide air or water pollution control facilities. Such facilities are in all events treated as serving the general public and, thus, satisfy the public use requirement of paragraph (a)(2) of this section.

(2) Definitions. (i) For purposes of section 103(b)(4)(F) and this paragraph, property is a pollution control facility to the extent that the test of either subdivision (iii) or (iv) of this subparagraph is satisfied, but only if—

(a) It is property which is described in subdivision (ii) of this subparagraph and is either of a character subject to the allowance for depreciation provided in section 167 or land, and

(b) Either (1) a Federal, State, or local agency exercising jurisdiction has certified that the facility, as designed, is in furtherance of the purpose of abating or controlling atmospheric pollutants or contaminants, or water pollution, as the case may be, or (2) the facility is designed to meet or exceed applicable Federal, State, and local requirements for the control of atmospheric pollutants or contaminants, or water pollution, as the case may be, in effect at the time the obligations, the proceeds of which are to be used to provide such facilities, are issued.

(ii) Property is described in this subdivision if it is property to be used, in whole or in part, to abate or control water or atmospheric pollution or contamination by removing, altering, disposing, or storing pollutants, contaminants, wastes, or heat. In the case of property to be used to control water pollution, such property includes the necessary intercepting sewers, pumping, power, and other equipment, and their appurtenances. For rules relating to facilities which remove pollutants from fuel or certain other items, see subdivision (vi) of this subparagraph.

(iii) In the case of an expenditure for property which is designed for no significant purpose other than the control of pollution, the total expenditure for such property satisfies the test of this subdivision. Thus, where property which is to serve no function other than the control of pollution is to be added to an existing manufacturing or production facility, the total expenditure for such property satisfies the test of this subdivision, Also, if an expenditure for property would not be made but for the purpose of controlling pollution, and if the expenditure has no significant purpose other than the purpose of pollution control, the total expenditure for such property satisfies the test of this subdivision even though such property serves one or more functions in addition to its function as a pollution control facility.

(iv) In the case of property to be placed in service for the purpose of controlling pollution and for a significant purpose other than controlling pollution, only the incremental cost of such facility satisfies the test of this subdivision. The "incremental cost" of property is the excess of its total cost over that portion of its cost expended for a purpose other than the control of pollution.

(v) An expenditure has a significant purpose other than the control of pollution if it results in an increase in production or capacity, or in a material extension of the useful life of a manufacturing or production facility or a part thereof.

(vi) [Reserved]

(h) Water facilities. *(1) General rule.* Section 103(b)(4)(G) provides that section 103(b)(1) shall not apply to obligations issued by a State or local governmental unit which are part of an issue substantially all of the proceeds of which are to be used to provide facilities for the furnishing of water which are available, on reasonable demand, to members of the general public. A water facility will satisfy the public use test of paragraph (a)(2) of this section if it will provide water, on reasonable demand, to any member of the general public within the service area of the water system of which such facility is a part.

(2) Definition. For purposes of section 103(b)(4)(G) and this paragraph, the "water facilities" include artesian wells,

reservoirs, dams, related equipment and pipelines, and other facilities used to furnish water for domestic, industrial, irrigation, or other purposes.

(3) Effective date. The provisions of this paragraph apply in the case of facilities provided by obligations issued after January 1, 1969. In the case of facilities provided by obligations issued on or before such date to which section 103(b) is applicable, the provisions of paragraph (f) of this section shall apply. For such purposes, wherever the term "local furnishing of electric energy or gas appears in paragraph (f) of this section, such term shall be deemed to read "local furnishing of electric energy, gas, or water."

(i) Examples. The application of section 103(b)(4) and this section are illustrated by the following examples:

Example (1). City B plans to issue $10 million of bonds to be used to construct a sports stadium. The revenues from the facility and the facility itself will be the security for the bonds. A professional football team rents the facility on a long-term lease for part of the year and a professional baseball team rents the sports facility for the remainder of the year. Tickets are sold by the teams to the general public. The bonds are industrial development bonds, but since the proceeds are used for a spectator facility for general public use, which is an exempt facility under section 103(b)(4)(B) and paragraph (c) of this section, section 103(b)(1) does not apply unless the provisions of section 103(b)(8) and § 1.103-11 apply.

Example (2). City C plans to issue $10 million of bonds to be used to construct a convention hall which it will own. City C plans to lease the convention hall for 25 years to corporation Y, a nonexempt person, which will operate and maintain it. The terms of the lease obligate Y to make the convention hall generally available for civic, business, and recreational shows, meetings, performances, and similar activities serving or benefiting the community. Lease payments from Y and the facility will be security for the bonds. The bonds are industrial development bonds, but since the proceeds are to be used for a facility for general public use, which is an exempt facility under section 103(b)(4)(C) and paragraph (d) of this section, section 103(b)(1) does not apply unless the provisions of section 103(b)(8) and § 1.103-11 apply.

Example (3). City D issues $100 million of its bonds and uses the proceeds to finance the construction of an airport for the use of the general public. D will own and operate the airport. A major portion of the rentable space in the terminal building is leased on a long-term basis to common carrier and non-scheduled airlines. The bonds will be secured by the airport landing and runway charges and by payments with respect to such long-term leases from such commercial airlines. Such commercial airline payments are expected to constitute more than 50 percent of the total revenues from the airport. The bonds are industrial development bonds, but since the proceeds are to be used for an airport for use by the general public and by carriers serving the general public, which is an exempt facility under section 103(b)(4)(D) and paragraph (e) of this section, section 103(b)(1) does not apply unless the provisions of section 103(b)(13) and § 1.103-11 apply. The result would be the same if D hired an airport management firm to operate the airport.

Example (4). City E issues $6 million of its bonds and uses the proceeds to finance construction of a landing strip for airplanes to be located adjacent to the factories of corporations Y and Z. The landing strip will be used in the trades or businesses of Y and Z and by any number of the general public wishing to use it. However, due to its location, general public use will be negligible. The lease payments by Y and Z for the use of the facility are the security for the bonds. The bonds are industrial development bonds and the facility is not an exempt facility under section 103(b)(4)(D) and paragraph (c) of this section because it is not a facility constructed for general public use.

Example (5). State F and corporation Z enter into an arrangement which provides that F will issue $10 million of its bonds and use the proceeds to construct a facility for Z the only purpose of which is to control air and water pollution at Z's plant. The principal and interest on the bonds will be secured by the charges which F will impose on Z. The bonds are industrial development bonds, but since the proceeds are to be used for air and water pollution facilities designed to abate pollution by private persons, such facilities are for the benefit of the general public and are exempt facilities under section 103(b)(4)(F) and paragraph (g) of this section. Accordingly, section 103(b)(1) does not apply unless the provisions of section 103(b)(13) and § 1.103-11 apply.

Example (6). City G issues $20 million of its bonds and will use $6 million to finance residential rental property which qualifies as an exempt facility under section 103(b)(4)(A) and paragraph (b) of this section, $9 million to finance construction of a stadium which qualifies as an exempt facility under section 103(b)(4)(B) and paragraph (c) of this section, and $5 million for convention facilities which qualify as exempt facilities under section 103(b)(4)(C) and paragraph (d) of this section. The facilities will be used in the trades or businesses of nonexempt persons and rental payments with respect to such facilities and the facilities themselves will be the security for the bonds. The bonds are industrial development bonds, but since all the proceeds are to be used for facilities which are exempt facilities under section 103(b)(4), section 103(b)(1) does not apply unless the provisions of section 133(b)(13) and § 1.103-11 apply. The result would be the same, if; instead of using $9 million to finance construction of a stadium, the $9 million were used to finance construction of a capital building. [Reg. § 1.103-8].

T.D. 7199, 7/31/72, amend T.D. 7362, 6/17/75, T.D. 7511, 9/30/77, T.D. 7737, 11/14/80, T.D. 7840, 10/12/82, T.D. 7848, 11/10/82, T.D. 7869, 1/12/83, T.D. 8476, 6/14/93, T.D. 8538, 5/5/94, T.D. 8718, 5/8/97.

PAR. 2. Section 1.103-8 is amended by revising paragraph (b)(1), (b)(3) and paragraph (b)(4)(i) and (ii), by adding a new paragraph (b)(4)(v), by revising paragraph (b)(5), paragraph (b)(7)(ii), and paragraph (b)(8)(v), by revising Example (3) of paragraph (b)(9), and by adding new Example (12) and Example (13) to follow Example (11) of paragraph (b)(9). These revised and added provisions read as follows:

Proposed § 1.103-8 Interest on bonds to finance certain exempt facilities. [*For Preamble, see ¶ 151,037*]

* * * * *

• ***Caution:*** Proposed reg. § 1.103-8, following, was issued under Code section 103 before the related provisions of that Code section were deleted by P.L. 99-514 (10/22/86). Provisions similar to, but not necessarily identical to, the provisions deleted from Code section 103 now appear in Code section 142.

(b) Residential rental property. *(1) General rule for obligations issued after April 24, 1979.* Section 103(b)(1) shall not apply to any obligation which is issued after April 24, 1979, and is part of an issue substantially all of the proceeds of which are to be used to provide a residential rental project in which 20 percent or more of the units in the project that are to be provided with the proceeds of the issue (other than those units to be provided with an insubstantial amount of the proceeds of the issue as permitted under paragraph (a)(3) of this section) are to be occupied by individuals or familes of low or moderate income (as defined in paragraph (b)(8)(v) of this section). See paragraph (b)(4)(v) with respect to mixed-use projects. In the case of a targeted area project, the minimum percentage is 15 percent. See generally § 1.103-7 for rules relating to refunding issues.

* * * * *

(3) Transitional rule. For purposes of this section, obligations issued after April 24, 1979, may be treated as issued before April 25, 1979, if the transitional requirements of section 1104 of the Mortgage Subsidy Bond Tax Act of 1980 (94 Stat. 2670), as amended by section 614 of the Tax Reform Act of 1984 (98 Stat. 914), are satisfied.

(4) Residential rental project. (i) In general. A residential rental project is a building or structure, together with any facilities functionally related and subordinate thereto, containing one or more similarly constructed units that—

(a) Are not used on a transient basis, and

(b) Satisfy the requirements of paragraph (b)(5)(i) of this section and are available to members of the general public in accordance with the requirements of paragraph (a)(2) of this section.

Although a residential rental project may include other property, such as commercial office space, special rules apply to such mixed-use projects (see paragraph (b)(4)(v)). Hotels, motels, dormitories, fraternity and sorority houses, rooming houses, hospitals, nursing homes, sanitariums, and rest homes are not residential rental projects (but, with respect to obligations issued prior to January 1, 1986, only if such facilities are for use on a transient basis). In addition, trailer parks and courts for use on a transient basis are not residential rental projects.

(ii) Multiple buildings and partial use of buildings (a) Proximate buildings or structures that have similarly constructed units are treated as part of the same project if they are owned for Federal tax purposes by the same person and they are financed pursuant to a common plan.

(b) Buildings or structures are proximate if they are located on a single tract of land. The term "tract" means any parcel or parcels of land that either are contiguous or are contiguous except for the interposition of a road, street, stream or similar property. Parcels are contiguous in their boundaries meet at one or more points.

(c) Similarly constructed units located in a single building and financed pursuant to a common plan of financing are treated as part of the same project.

(d) A common plan of financing exists if, for example, all such buildings or similarly constructed units are provided by the same issue or several issues subject to a common indenture.

* * * * *

(v) Mixed-use projects. (a) For purposes of this paragraph (b), a mixed-use project is a building or structure, together with any facilities functionally related and subordinate thereto, containing—

(1) One or more similarly constructed units rented or available for rental that, in the aggregate, meet the low or moderate income occupancy requirement of paragraph (b)(5)(ii), and

(2) Other property the use of which is unrelated to such units, e.g., commercial office space, owner-occupied residences, and units that, in the aggregate, do not meet the low or moderate income occupancy requirement of paragraph (b)(5)(ii) ("nonqualifying property").

(b) For purposes of determining whether, in the case of a mixed-use project, substantially all of the proceeds of the issue are to be used to provide a residential rental project, only the proceeds to be used to provide the units described in paragraph (b)(4)(v)(a)(1) and the other portions of the project allocable to such units are treated as being used to provide a residential rental project. Other portions of the project allocable to such units include—

(1) The allocable portion of property benefitting both such units and the nonqualifying property (e.g., common elements), and

(2) All property benefitting only such units (e.g., reactional facilities used only by occupants of the units described in paragraph (b)(4)(v)(a)(1)).

(c) In determining whether, in the case of a mixed-use project, substantially all of the proceeds of an issue are to be used to provide a residential rental project, the cost of property that will benefit, directly or indirectly, both the units described in paragraph (b)(4)(v)(a)(1) and the nonqualifying property must be allocated between such units and the nonqualifying property. For example, in the case of a mixed-use project part of which is to be used for commercial purposes, the cost of the building's foundation must be allocated between the commercial portion of the building and the units described in paragraph (b)(4)(v)(a)(1). The allocation of the cost of such common elements may be made according to any reasonable method that properly reflects the proportionate benefit to be derived, directly or indirectly, by the units described in paragraph (b)(4)(v)(a)(1) and the nonqualifying property. Allocating the cost of such common elements based on the ratio of the total floor space in the building or structure that is to be used for nonqualifying property to all other floor space in the building or structure is, generally, a reasonable method; however, in the case of any common elements with respect to which an allocation according to this method does not reasonably reflect the relative benefits to be derived, directly or indirectly, by the units described in paragraph (b)(4)(v)(a)(1) and the nonqualifying property, the allocation may not be made according to this method. For example, this method would not be a reasonable method for making the allocation in the case of a residential rental project one-half of the floor space of which is used for shopping space where three-fourths of the parking lot for the building will be used to serve the shopping space and the balance of the parking lot will be used to serve tenants of the units described in paragraph (b)(4)(v)(a)(1); the cost of constructing the parking lot must be allocated based on the proportion of the parking lot to be used, directly or indirectly, by the tenants of the units described in paragraph (b)(4)(v)(a)(1) and by the owners and tenants of the nonqualifying portion of the project.

(5) Requirements must be continuously satisfied. (i) Rental requirement. Once available for occupancy, each unit (as defined in paragraph (b)(8)(i) of this section) in a resi-

dential rental project that was provided with the proceeds of an issue described in section 103(b)(4)(A) (other than those units provided with an insubstantial amount of the proceeds of the issue as permitted under paragraph (a)(3) of this section) must be rented or available for rental on a continuous basis for the longer of—

(a) The remaining term of the obligation, or

(b) The qualified project period (as defined in paragraph (b)(7) of this section).

(ii) Low or moderate income occupancy requirement. Individuals or families of low or moderate income must occupy that percentage of completed units in the project that were provided with the proceeds of an issue described in section 103(b)(4)(A) (other than those units provided with an insubstantial amount of the proceeds of the issue as permitted under paragraph (a)(3) of this section) applicable to the project under paragraph (b)(1) of this section continuously during the qualified project period. For this purpose, a unit occupied by an individual or family who at the commencement of the occupancy is of low or moderate income is treated as occupied by an individual or family of low or moderate income even though the individual or family ceases to be of low or moderate income during the period of their occupancy. Moreover, such unit is treated as occupied by an individual or family of low or moderate income until reoccupied, other than for a temporary period not in excess of 31 days, at which time a redetermination of whether the unit is occupied by an individual or family of low or moderate income shall be made.

*   *   *   *   *

(7) Qualified project period. * * *

(ii) For obligations issued after September 3, 1982, a period beginning on the later of the first day on which at least 10 percent of the units in the project that are provided with the proceeds of the issue are first occupied or the date of issue of an obligation described in section 103(b)(4)(A) and this paragraph and ending on the later of the date—

(a) Which is 10 years after the date on which at least 50 percent of the units in the project that are provided with the proceeds of the issue are first occupied,

(b) Which is a qualified number of days after the date on which any of the units in the project that are provided with the proceeds of the issue are first occupied, or

(c) On which any assistance provided with respect to the project under section 8 of the United States Housing Act of 1937 terminates.

For purposes of this paragraph (b)(7)(ii), the term "qualified number of days" means 50 percent of the total number of days comprising the term of the obligation with the longest maturity in the issue used to provide the project. In the case of a refunding of such an issue, the longest maturity is equal to the sum of the period the prior issue was outstanding and the longest term of any refunding obligations.

(8) Other definitions. * * *

(v) Low or moderate income. Individuals and families of low or moderate income shall be determined in a manner consistent with determinations of lower income families under section 8 of the United States Housing Act of 1937, as amended, except that the percentage of median gross income that qualifies as low or moderate income shall be 80 percent of the median gross income for the area with adjustments for smaller and larger families. Therefore, occupants of a unit are considered individuals or families of low or moderate income only if their adjusted income (computed in the manner prescribed in § 1.167(k)-3(b)(3)) does not exceed 80 percent of the median gross income for the area with adjustments for smaller and larger families. With respect to obligations issued prior to January 1, 1986, a determination of low or moderate income shall be made in accordance with the requirements of this paragraph (b)(8)(v) except that median gross income for the area need not be adjusted for family size. Notwithstanding the foregoing, the occupants of a unit shall not be considered to be of low or moderate income if all the occupants are students (as defined in section 151(e)(4)), no one of whom is entitled to file a joint return under section 6013. The method of determining low or moderate income in effect on the date of issue will be determinative for such issue even if such method is subsequently changed. In the event programs under section 8(f) of the Housing Act of 1937, as amended, are terminated prior to the date of issue, the applicable method shall be that in effect immediately prior to the date of such termination.

(9) Examples. * * *

Example (3). The facts are the same as in example (1), except that the proceeds of the obligation are provided to N, a cooperative housing corporation. N uses the proceeds to finance the construction of a portion of a cooperative housing project. The balance of the project is financed with the proceeds of a note that is not described in section 103(a). Shares in the cooperative carrying the rights to occupy the units in the portion of the project financed with the proceeds of the obligation issued by City X will be sold to shareholders who will rent the units to other persons. The balance of the shares in the cooperative, carrying the rights to occupy more than half of the space in the project, will be sold to individuals who will occupy the units themselves. The project is a residential rental project within the meaning of section 103(b)(4)(A) and this paragraph (b).

*   *   *   *   *

Example (12). In July 1985, County X issues a $10 million issue of industrial development bonds to be used to finance the construction of a building to be owned by Corporation W. Corporation W will construct a 10 story building. The first 2 floors of the building will be made available for commercial use. The remaining 8 floors will consist of similarly constructed units that will be made available as residences on a rental basis to members of the general public. Corporation W uses substantially all of the proceeds of the issue to finance the 8 floors of the building to be made available as rental units, the portions of the building benefitting, directly or indirectly, only the rental units, and the portions of the building benefitting, directly or indirectly, both the rental units and the commercial space that are properly allocable to the rental units. The remainder of the building is financed other than with the proceeds of an obligation described in section 103(a). Corporation W will make 20 percent of the rental units available to low or moderate income individuals, and all of the other requirements of this section are met. The obligations are used to provide a residential rental project within the meaning of section 103(b)(4)(A) and this section, and the obligations are described in section 103(a).

Example (13). The facts are the same as in example (12), except that Corporation W uses the proceeds of the issue to finance the entire building including the 2 floors to be available for commercial use. The cost of the 2 floors available for commercial use, including those portions of the building that benefit both the commercial space and the rental units that are properly allocable to the commercial space, is $2 million. Under paragraph (b)(4)(v) of this section, the building is a residential rental project. However, substantially all of the proceeds of the issue are not used to provide a residential rental project since, in making this determination, proceeds used to provide nonqualifying property are treated as not used to provide a residential rental project. Therefore, the obligations are not described in section 103(b)(4)(A) and this paragraph (b).

* * * * *

Section 1.103-8 (relating to exemption for interest on bonds to finance certain exempt facilities) is amended by revising paragraph (h) thereof. The revised provisions read as folows:

Proposed § 1.103-8 Interest on bonds to finance certain exempt facilities. [*For Preamble, see ¶ 150,971*]

* * * * *

• ***Caution:*** Proposed reg. § 1.103-8, following, was issued under Code section 103 before the related provisions of that Code section were deleted by P.L. 99-514 (10/22/86). Provisions similar to, but not necessarily identical to, the provisions deleted from Code section 103 now appear in Code section 142.

(h) Water facilities. *(1) General rule for obligations issued after November 6, 1978.* Section 103(b)(4)(G) provides that section 103(b)(1) shall not apply to any obligation issued after November 6, 1978, by (or on behalf of) a State or local governmental unit which is issued as part of an issue substantially all of the proceeds of which are to be used to provide facilities for the furnishing of water for any purpose if certain requirements are met. In order to qualify under section 103(b)(4)(G) and this paragraph as an exempt facility, the facility must satisfy the requirements established by subparagraph (3) of this paragraph.

(2) Facilities for the furnishing of water defined. For purposes of section 103(b)(4)(G) and this paragraph, the term "facilities for the furnishing of water" means those components of a system for the distribution of water to customers that are necessary for the collection, treatment, and distribution of water to a service area, and other functionally related and subordinate components as defined in § 1.103-8(a)(3). For a component to come within this definition, it must be part of a system which, when viewed as a whole, is for the distribution of water to customers. A system or component does not come within this definition if it is a production facility that merely uses water in the production process (e.g., a cooling pond, or equipment using water internally within a manufacturing plant). For exemple, an extension of a pipeline to carry water to a single industrial user from a qualified system is a qualified component because the system as a whole quantifies, but the internal water facilities of a private plant would not be a quantified component. In general a series of dams will not constitute a single system but each will constitute a separate system. Components of a dam or reservoir used to generate electric energy, such as generators and turbines, will not qualify as facilities for the furnishing of water (of course they may qualify as components for the local furnishing of electric energy under section 103(b)(4)(E) or as components used in hydroelectric generating facilities qualifying under section 103(b)(4)(H)). However, a reservoir or dam does not necessarily fail to qualify as facilities for the furnishing of water solely because one use of the water is to produce electricity if at least 90 percent of the water is available for other purposes, such as irrigation and domestic consumption, in addition to producing electricity.

(3) Additional requirements. (i) The facility must make its water available to members of the general public. For this purpose, the general public includes electric utility, industrial, agricultural, and commercial users. In order to make its water available to the general public, a facility must make available to residential users within its service area, municipal water districts within its service area, or any combination thereof, at least 25 percent of its capacity (which must be a considerable quantity in absolute terms). Except with respect to residential users and municipal water districts, a water facility is not required to make available water to all segments of the general public in order to qualify under this subdivision (i). For example, if an industrial user agrees to "take or pay for" the entrie capacity of a reservoir (but is guaranteed only 25 to 75 percent of the capacity), the facility will comply with this subdivision (i), provided the remainder of the water will be made available to residential users or municipal water districts within the service area. However, a facility is not considered to make water available to the general public merely because it is available for swimming, water skiing, and other recreational activities. A water facility is not required to make its water available to the general public immediately after its construction in order to qualify under this subdivision (i); it is sufficient that the facility is available to serve the general public. For example, if a pipeline is built to serve a sparsely inhabited region which lacks water, the pipeline meets the requirements of this subdivision (i) if it will serve the general public that the new source of water reasonably may be expected to cause to move into the region.

(ii) The facility must be operated either by—

(A) A governmental unit, within the meaning of § 1.103-7(b)(2), or the United States government or an agency or instrumentality thereof, or

(B) A regulated public water utility whose rates for the furnishing or sale of the water are required to be established or approved by a State or political subdivision thereof, by an agency or instrumentality of the United States, or by a public service or public utility commission or other similar body of any State or political subdivision thereof.

A governmental unit or a regulated public water utility is considered to operate a facility only if it has responsibility and control over the repairs and maintenance of the facility. For example, if an industrial user leases the facility on a long-term basis, and it either controls the maintenance and repair of the facility, or bears these costs, then the facility fails to meet the requirement that it be operated by a governmental unit or a regulated public water utility.

* * * * *

These amendments are proposed to be issued under the authority contained in section 7805 of the Internal Revenue Code of 1954 (68A Stat. 917, 26 U.S.C. 7805).

Section 1.103-8 is amended by adding two new sentences at the end of paragraph (a)(1)(i) and by revising paragraph (g). The new and revised provisions read as follows:

Proposed § 1.103-8 Interest on bonds to finance certain exempt facilities. [*For Preamble, see ¶ 150,243*]

• *Caution:* Proposed reg. § 1.103-8, following, was issued under Code section 103 before the related provisions of that Code section were deleted by P.L. 99-514 (10/22/86). Provisions similar to, but not necessarily identical to, the provisions deleted from Code section 103 now appear in Code section 142.

(a) In general. *(1) General rule.* (i) [made final by T.D. 7511, 9/30/77]

* * * * *

(g) Air or water pollution control facilities. *(1) General rule.* Section 103(c)(4)(F) provides that section 103(c)(1) shall not apply to obligations issued by a State of local governmental unit which are part of an issue substantially all of the proceeds of which are to be used to provide air or water pollution control facilities. Such facilities are in all events treated as serving the general public and thus satisfy the public use requirement of paragraph (a)(2) of this section. Proceeds are used to provide air or water pollution control facilities if they are used to provide property which satisfies the requirements of paragraph (g)(2) and (3) of this section. Where property has a function other than to abate or control water or atmospheric pollution or contamination (hereinafter referred to as "control of pollution"), only the incremental cost of such property is taken into account as an expenditure to provide an air or water pollution control facility. Rules to determine whether property has any function other than the control of pollution are provided in paragraph (g)(2) and (3) of this section. Rules to determine the incremental cost of such property are provided in paragraph (g)(3) of this section.

(2) Definitions. (i) Property is a pollution control facility if it is property described in paragraph (g)(2)(ii) of this section and if either (A) a Federal, State, or local agency exercising jurisdiction has certified that the facility, as designed, is in furtherance of the purpose of abating or controlling atmospheric pollutants or contaminants, or water pollution, as the case may be, or (B) the facility is designed to meet or exceed applicable Federal, State, and local requirements for the control of atmospheric contaminants, or water pollution, as the case may be, in effect at the time the obligations, the proceeds of which are to be used to provide such facilities, are issued.

(ii) Property is described in this subdivision if it (A) is either of a character subject to the allowance for depreciation provided in section 167 or land, and (B) is used in whole or in part to abate or control water or atmospheric pollution or contamination by removing, altering, disposing, or storing pollutants, contaminants, waste or heat (hereinafter individually and collectively referred to as a pollutant). Property is not described in the preceding sentence unless it is a unit which is discrete and which performs in whole or in part one or more of the functions referred to in such sentence and which cannot be further reduced in size without losing one of such characteristics. The term "pollutant" does not include any material or heat unless such material or heat is in a state or form such that its discharge or release would result in water or atmospheric pollution or contamination. Property is not described in this subdivision to the extent that such property avoids the creation of pollutants. Property which is used solely for the processing or manufacturing of material or heat after such material or heat is no longer a pollutant is not property described in this subdivision. Property is not a pollution control facility to the extent that such property treats or processes a material in such a manner as to prevent the discharge or release of pollutants when such material is subsequently used. Property to be used in the control of water pollution includes the necessary intercepting sewers, pumping, power, and other equipment, and their appurtenances. Such property is necessary if it removes, alters, disposes of, or stores a pollutant or is functionally related and subordinate to property used to control water pollution. In the case of property which removes pollutants from fuel, see paragraph (g)(2)(iv) of this section. For inclusion, as property described in this subdivision, of property functionally related and subordinate to an exempt pollution control facility, see paragraph (a)(3) of this section.

(iii) Property is not used for the control of pollution to the extent that it—

(A) Is designed to prevent the release of pollutants in a major accident,

(B) Prevents the release of materials or heat which would endanger the employees of the trade or business in which such property is used (as determined for example by Federal, State, or local employee occupational health or safety standards),

(C) Is used to control materials or heat that traditionally have been controlled because their release would constitute a nuisance,

(D) Controls the release of hazardous materials or heat that would cause an immediate risk of substantial damage or injury to property or persons, or

(E) Controls materials or heat in essentially the same manner as the user of such property has previously controlled such material or heat as a customary practice for reasons other than compliance with pollution control requirements. If such user previously has not generated such material or heat at the location where such material or heat is controlled, such customary practice shall be determined by reference to the use of similar property by similarly situated users.

For example, property is used in the manner described in paragraph (g)(2)(C) of this section and is not used to control pollution if such property is used to control from an uncontrolled level of 200 units to a level of 100 units the release of materials that traditionally has been controlled to that level because such release would constitute a nuisance. However, if pollution control requirements limit the level of emissions to 60 units, the use of the property to reduce and control the level of emissions from 100 units to 60 units is a use for pollution control. If the method of allocation described in paragraph (g)(3)(iii) of this section is used to allocate the cost of the functions of property used to control materials from a level of 200 units to a level of 60 units, factor Y in the ratio must include the present value of gross capital costs necessary to acquire a facility that limits the release of emissions to a level of 100 units and the present value of estimated expenses necessary to operate or maintain such facility.

(iv) A facility that removes elements or compounds from fuel which would be released as pollutants when such fuels are burned is not a pollution control facility whether or not such facility is used in connection with a plant or property where such fuels are burned. Such a nonqualifying facility includes all property used to remove such elements or compounds from fuel. Related facilities for the handling and treatment of wastes and other pollutants resulting from that removal process (including the elements and compounds removed) will qualify as pollution control facilities if such facilities meet the requirements of this paragraph.

(3) Allocation. (i) If property described in paragraph (g)(2) of this section is used to control pollution and also has a function other than the control of pollution, only the incremental cost of such property is taken into account as an expenditure to provide air or water pollution control facilities. The incremental cost of such property is the portion of the cost of the property which is allocable to the control of pollution (as determined under paragraph (g)(3)(ii) or (iii) of this section). Examples of functions of property other than the control of pollution are an economic benefit to the user resulting from use of the property and a function described in paragraph (g)(2)(iii) of this section. The term "economic benefit" means gross income or cost savings resulting from any increase in production or capacity, production efficiencies, the production of a byproduct, the extension of the useful life of other property which is not described in paragraph (g)(2) of this section, and any other identifiable cost savings, such as savings resulting from the use, reuse, or recycling of items recovered. For purposes of the preceding sentence, where that part of property which controls pollution makes unnecessary the use of any property which otherwise would be necessary but for the use of the property which controls pollution, the term "cost savings" includes capital expenditures and operating and maintenance expenses which need not be incurred as a result of the use of the pollution control property. In the case of property which (A) controls pollution, (B) results in an economic benefit, and (C) has a nonproductive function other than the control of pollution such as employee safety, which is solely related to the facility, the allocation of the cost of the property between the pollution control function and the economic benefit includes any allocation of cost to such other nonproductive function, and no other allocation of cost to such nonproductive function is necessary.

(ii) The portion of the cost of property allocable to the control of pollution is determined by an allocation of the cost of such property between the property's pollution control function and any other functions that clearly reflects a separation of costs for each function of the property. The method of allocation described in paragraph (g)(3)(iii) of this section is presumed to clearly reflect such a separation of the costs of such functions. Notwithstanding the preceding sentence, an allocation of costs on the basis of accounting principles may overcome such presumption if such allocation is of adequate detail and specificity to clearly reflect a separation of costs for each function of the property.

(iii) In the case of property which results in an economic benefit, the portion of the cost of such property allocable to the control of pollution is the cost of the property reduced by the amount, if any, determined by applying to such cost the following ratio:

$$\frac{Y}{C + E}$$

where *Y* is the present value of all estimated economic benefits, net of any selling expenses, to be realized over the useful life of such property to the person in whose trade or business such property is used; *C* is the present value of payments (other than interest), present and future, necessary to acquire ownership of the property, less its estimated salvage value, adjusted for the burden of Federal income taxes; and *E* is the present value of all estimated expenses to be paid or incurred in operating and maintaining the property, including utilities, labor, property taxes (or payments in lieu of such taxes), State and local income taxes, insurance, and interest expense. In this ratio, if the sum of $C + E$ is less than *Y*, such sum shall be treated as being equal to *Y*. Where $C + E$ is used in determining *Y*, because an alternative facility need not be built, $C + E$ shall not be less than zero. Present value shall be computed by use of a discount rate of 12½ percent. The sum of $C + E$, expressed as present values, is an amount equal to the gross return to capital invested by the owner of the property which is sufficient to permit payment of Federal income tax, recover the investment, receive a net rate of return on invested capital of 12½ percent, and to recover other estimated costs of operating and maintaining the property. The two terms in the denominator are defined as follows:

$$E = PV(E_t)$$

$$C = \frac{PV(O_t) - PV(a_t) - mPV(d_t)}{1 - m}$$

where

PV( ) = present value of the terms enclosed within parenthesis (i.e., the sum of the discounted values of the indicated quantities),

E_t = estimated expenses each year, when

$t = 1, 2, 3, \ldots$ n, n being the last year of the period used in the computation,

O_t = outlays each year necessary to acquire ownership of the property,

a = investment credit,

m = tax rate, and

d_t = depreciation deduction allowable each year.

This formula is to be applied to the manner set forth in example (1) of paragraph (g)(5) of this section. In the definition of *C* above, the outlays, $O \pm T$, are the repayments of principal of a privately financed loan which would be sufficient to enable the user to acquire the property; the associated interest payments for such a loan are included in the term "estimated expenses", *E*. Therefore, no other computation is made for depreciation or any rental or purchase payments on such property, since such items are already taken into account. All estimated expenses other than interest shall be computed with reference to the useful life of the property to the person in whose trade or business such property is used. The outlays necessary to acquire ownership of the property and the interest expense shall be determined on the basis of (A) acquisition of the property by a loan equal to the cost of the property discharged by equal annual amortization payments, (B) the market rate of interest (as of any date during the 90 day period preceding the date of issue) for capital construction for the owner or operator of such property, or, if such rate is not known, the prime rate on any such date, and (C) an assumed maturity equal to the lesser of the useful life of the property used in determining *Y* or the term of the governmental obligations. In determining *m* the surtax exemption shall be disregarded; in determining $d \pm T$, depreciation shall be computed by use of the straight line method based on the same useful life of the property as is used in computing *Y*.

(4) Effective date. The provisions of this paragraph apply to obligations issued after August 20, 1975, except that, at the option of the issuer, the provisions of this paragraph prescribed by T.D. 7199, as corrected August 11, 1972 (37 FR 16177), shall apply to obligations issued before November 19, 1975, or to obligations issued with respect to facilities the construction, reconstruction, or acquisition (including, in the case of an acquisition, a binding contract to acquire such facility) of which commences before November 19, 1975.

(5) Examples. The principles of this paragraph may be illustrated by the following examples:

Example (1). (a) Company A, engaged in processing ore, is required under applicable law to limit emissions causing air pollution from its plant and plans to install equipment costing $9 million that will remove the pollutants generated in the processing of the ore and convert the pollutants into ore concentrate that can be used in A's business or can be sold. The equipment is discrete property used to abate or control air pollution by removing, altering, storing, or disposing of a pollutant. The equipment also functions in part to protect the safety of employees operating the equipment. The equipment will be acquired and placed in service in 1977. Company A intends to finance the equipment with 20-year industrial development bonds. The equipment has a useful life of 20 years to A. Company A allocates the $9 million cost of the property between its pollution control function and its productive function by the method described in paragraph (g)(3)(iii) of this section.

(b) On the basis of the current market price for ore concentrate, the annual economic benefit from the recovered ore is estimated to be $588,750. The total economic benefit over the equipment's useful life is $11,775,000, which has a present value on the date of issue, at a 12½ percent discount rate, of $4,263,346.79. The operating and maintenance expense of the equipment over its useful life is estimated on the basis of current costs to be $10,875,000, which accrues ratably over the 20-year period and which has a present value on the date of issue, at a 12½ percent discount rate, of $3,937,485.89. To apply the formula in paragraph (g)(3)(iii) of this section, it is also necessary to know the present value of the annual interest expense which would be incurred, and the present value of company A's annual investment in the facility, determined as if the $9 million facility were financed on the basis of a loan amortized by equal annual payments. Interest expense is computed by use of an interest rate of 10 percent to the user on a 20-year obligation of $9 million discharged by equal annual payments.

The equal annual payments, computed by use of the formula

$$A = P\frac{i}{1-(1+i)^n}$$ are $1,057,136.62 when

A = amount of annual repayment of principal and interest payable at the end of any year,

P = $9 million, the total amount borrowed,

i = .10 (i.e., a 10 percent rate of interest), and

n = 20, the term of the loan, in years.

The following 3 step calculation is used to determine the present value of all annual payments of principal and the present value of all annual payments of interest:

(1) Compute the present value of annual payments by use of the formula

$$PV(A_t) = A\frac{1-(1+r)^n}{\text{percent discount rate)};}$$ when r = .125 (i.e., a 12½

(2) Compute the present value of principal repayments by use of the formula

$$PV(a_1) = \frac{a_1}{1+r}\left[\frac{1-\left(\frac{1+i}{1+r}\right)^n}{1-\frac{1+i}{1+r}}\right]$$

when

a ±1 = the first year's principal repayment and *a ±1 = A − iP*

(3) Compute the present value of interest payments by use of the formula

PV (I ±T) = PV (A ±T) − PV (a ±T)

$$PV(I_t) = PV(A_t) - PV(a_t)$$

when PV (I ±T) = present value of annual interest payments over the term of the loan. By use of the 3 step calculation, the total of the present values of all annual payments of principal is determined to be $2,275,499.19 and the total of the present values of all annual payments of interest is determined to be $5,379,600.65. The equipment will not have any salvage value at the end of its useful life.

(c) Using the method of allocation described in paragraph (g)(3)(iii) of this section, including a 12½ percent discount rate, the portion of the cost of the equipment allocable to pollution control is determined as follows:

Y = $4,263,346.79, the present value of the gross economic benefit realized over the equipment's useful life.

E = $9,317,086.54, the present value of the operating expense ($3,937,485.89) plus the present value of the interest expense ($5,379,600.65).

$$C = \$156{,}474.74 \text{ or } \frac{PV(O_t) - a - mPV(d_t)}{1 - m}$$

where the present value of the outlays of principal (*O ±T*) is $2,275,499.19, the investment credit *(a)* is $630,000, the rate of tax *(m)* is 48 percent, and the present value of the depreciation deductions (*d ±T*) is $3,258,609.01. Thus, *C* is computed as follows:

$$\frac{\$2{,}275{,}499.19 - \$630{,}000 - .48\ (\$3{,}258{,}609.01)}{1 - .48}$$

The portion of the cost of the equipment allocable to the pollution control function is:

$$\$9{,}000{,}000 - \$9{,}000{,}000\left(\frac{\$4{,}263{,}346.79}{\$156{,}474.74 + \$9{,}317{,}086.54}\right) \text{ or}$$

$$\$9{,}000{,}000 - \$4{,}050{,}232.01 = \$4{,}949{,}767.99$$

Thus, $4,949,767.99 of the cost of the equipment is allocable to pollution control.

Example (2). Company B operates a recovery boiler to recover valuable chemicals that can be used in its manufacturing process. In the course of operating the recovery boiler gases containing particulate material are generated which, when emitted into the environment, are in violation of new local air pollution control standards. To comply with local air pollution control standards, B plans to replace the existing recovery boiler with a new recovery boiler that is based on the latest manufacturing technology. As a result of more efficient combustion, fewer gases are generated and less particulate material is discharged. Company B also plans to acquire a new electrostatic precipitator to be used in conjunction with the new recovery boiler. The new recovery boiler when operated with the electrostatic precipitator does not violate the local air pollution control standards. The electrostatic precipitator is property described in paragraph (g)(2)(i) and (ii) of this section used to remove, alter, store, or dispose of pollutants. To the extent that the cost of the electrostatic precipitator is not allocable to the recovery of any chemicals, the cost of the electrostatic precipitator qualifies as an expenditures to provide a pollution control facility. The new recovery boiler avoids the creation of pollutants by generating fewer gases and discharging less particulate material. Therefore neither the new recovery boiler nor any part of it is property described in paragraph (g)(2)(i) and (ii) of this section used to remove, alter, store, or dispose of pollutants. The recovery boiler is not an exempt facility under section 103(c)(4)(F).

Example (3). C, an oil company, intends to construct a refinery in State X. A "sour" gas stream containing hydrocarbons and hydrogen sulphide will result from the refining process. Pollution control laws in State X limit the amount of sulphur dioxide that C can release into the environment. To comply with the State law, C must install amine absorbers, DEA strippers, and Claus-Beavon sulphur units (or functionally equivalent facilities) at the refinery. The amine absorbers will separate the "sour" gas into an amine solution containing hydrogen sulphide and a gas containing hydrocarbons. The hydrocarbon gas will be burned as fuel in the refinery. DEA strippers will remove the hydrogen sulphide from the amine solution. The hydrogen-sulphide will be converted into sulphur by the Claus-Beavon sulphur recovery units and sold. Because the amine absorbers pretreat a fuel by removing hydrogen sulphide from the "sour" gas, the amine absorbers are not exempt facilities under section 103(c)(4) (F). To the extent that the cost of the DEA strippers and the Claus-Beavon facilities is not allocable to the function of sulphur production, the cost of such facilities qualifies as an expenditure to provide pollution control facilities.

Example (4). D proposes to use water from an adjacent river to cool new machinery at its plant. Heat realized in the course of operating the new machinery will be transferred to the water. Because the heated water would destroy marine life and thus constitute a risk to the general environment, local pollution control requirements do not permit D to release heated water into the river. To comply with the local pollution control requirements D plans to install a closed-loop facility consisting of pipes, cooling towers, and related equipment which will enable D to cool the water and reuse it in manufacturing. The closed-loop facility is discrete property used to abate or control water pollution. The cost of the closed-loop facility is allocable to the control of pollution to the extent that such cost is not allocable to any cost savings resulting from the reuse or recycling of water or any cost savings resulting because an alternate facility need not be constructed which would, without any pollution control restrictions, be an adequate facility to cycle water to and from the manufacturing plant. Accordingly, if an allocation of costs is made under paragraph (g)(3)(iii) of this section to determine the portion of the cost of the closed-loop facility allocable to pollution control, factor Y in the ratio must include the present value of gross capital costs necessary to acquire the alternate facility plus the present value of estimated expenses necessary to operate or maintain the alternate facility. These capital costs and estimated expenses are determined in the same manner as C and E in the ratio. The portion of the cost of the closed-loop facility allocable to pollution control is determined by reducing the cost of the facility by an amount determined by applying to such cost the ratio

$$\frac{C^1 + E^1}{C + E}$$

where C^1 and E^1 are the present values of the capital costs necessary to acquire the alternative facility and the estimated expenses to operate and maintain such facility and C and E are the present values of the costs and expenses of the closed-loop facility. Thus, assume that the cooling tower costs $10,000,000 and that the cost of the pipes, pumps and other equipment interconnecting with the machinery is $2,000,000. Assume further that the present value of such costs plus the present value of the operating and maintenance expenses for such property is $20,000,000. Also assume that the present value of the gross capital costs of the alternate facility necessary to bring water to the machinery and return it to the river is $5,000,000 and that the present value of the operating and maintenance expenses for such alternate facility is $7,000,000. The portion of the cost of the closed-loop facility allocable to pollution control under paragraph (g)(3)(iii) of this section is $12,000,000—

$$\left(\$12{,}000{,}000 \times \frac{12{,}000}{20{,}000}\right)$$

or $4,800,000.

Example (5). E, a utility, plans to construct an electric generating plant powered by nuclear fuel. The plant will be located adjacent to city Y. The plant will have several types of facilities to prevent the release of radioactive materials into the air or water. The containment facility, the emergency core cooling system, and the emergency service water system will be designed to function in the event of a major accident, such as a loss of coolant. Under paragraph (g)(2)(iii) of this section, property designed to prevent a release of radioactive materials which would occur only in the event of a major accident is not property used for pollution control. Thus, expenditures for the containment facility, the emergency core cooling system, and the emergency service water system are not expenditures for a pollution control facility under section 103(c)(4)(F). The plant will also contain radwaste systems that will treat gas and liquid waste streams and solid waste materials containing radioactive materials which arise in the ordinary course of the plant operations. The radwaste systems are designed to prevent injury to the employees of the plant and the residents of city Y which would result if the material were released. Consequently, under paragraph (g)(2)(iii)(B) and (D) of this section, property used in the radwaste systems is not used for pollution control, and expenditures for such property are not expenditures for a pollution control facility under section 103(c)(4)(F). Water used in the generating plant will be pumped through a cooling facility the sole function of which is to cool the heated water prior to the discharge of the water into an adjacent river. The cooling facility is discrete property used to abate or control water pollution by altering the heated water into a nonpollutant. The cost of the cooling facility is an expenditure for a pollution control facility to the extent that such cost is not allocable to any cost savings resulting because an alternate facility need not be constructed which, without regard to any pollution control requirements, would be an adequate facility to cycle water to and from the manufacturing plant.

Example (6). F intends to construct a facility that generates electricity by use of a turbine which by design requires a water cooled condensor to operate at peak efficiency. The only source of water available to F is an underground spring from which F can pump limited amounts of water. In order to cool the condensor with the available water, F installs a closed-loop facility which will enable F to cool and reuse the water. The closed-loop facility is property which is used in electric generating plants as a customary practice and for reasons other than compliance with pollution control requirements to dispose of heat in water which is reused when an adequate water source is not available at the plant location. Accordingly, under the last sentence of paragraph (g)(2)(ii)(B) of this section, the closed-loop facility is not used to control pollution and is not a pollution control facility.

Example (7). G, a manufacturing company, uses a mineral in its manufacturing process which generates pollutants in violation of local pollution control requirements. To comply with local pollution control requirements, G plans to construct equipment that will wash the mineral with water so that the mineral will not generate pollutants when used in the manufacturing process. The fact that the equipment treats or processes the mineral in such a manner as to prevent the discharge or release of pollutants when the mineral is subsequently used does not qualify the equipment as a pollution control facility. Accordingly, none of the cost of the equipment qualifies as an expenditure to provide a pollution control facility. However, any additional equipment that treats water used to wash the mineral may qualify under paragraph (g)(2) of this section as property used to control pollution.

Example (8). Company H operates a manufacturing facility and is required by State pollution laws to lower the amount of waste which it emits into the environment. To satisfy this requirement H installs a series of three machines. The first machine converts the waste into a chemical which is not a pollutant. The second machine grinds the chemical into a powder and the third machine packages the powdered chemical for sale. The first machine is discrete property used to abate or control pollution. Since the chemical which leaves the first machine is not a pollutant, and the second and third machines are used solely for the processing of the chemical, none of the cost of the second and third machines qualifies as an expenditure to provide air or water pollution control facilities. The first machine is the smallest unit of property which functions to control pollution. Since the first machine functions both to control pollution and to produce an economic benefit (a chemical which when processed and packaged can be sold) only the incremental cost of the machine is taken into account as an expenditure to provide air or water pollution control facilities. If an allocation of costs is made under paragraph (g)(3)(iii) of this section to determine the portion of the cost of the first machine allocable to pollution control, factor Y in the ratio must include the present value of the unprocessed chemical resulting from the operation of the first machine.

Example (9). Company J, a mining company, intends to construct a tailings basin and an overflow treatment facility. Waste in the form of a slurry of water and tailings from the production of iron ore pellets will be pumped to the tailings basin where the tailings will settle and the water will be recycled and reused. The overflow treatment facility treats any slurry which overflows from the basin. The overflow treatment facility removes the tailings from the slurry prior to discharge of the residue into an adjacent river. Local pollution control laws prohibit the discharge of tailings into public watercourses. The basin is property which controls material in essentially the same manner as similarly situated users previously have controlled such material as a customary practice for reasons other than compliance with pollution control requirements. Accordingly, the tailings basin is not an exempt facility under section 103(c)(4)(F). The overflow treatment facility is discrete property used to abate or control water pollution, and the cost of the overflow treatment facility qualifies as an expenditure to provide pollution control facilities.

* * * * *

§ 17.1 Industrial development bonds used to provide solid waste disposal facilities; temporary rules.

• ***Caution:*** Reg. § 17.1, following, was issued under Code section 103 before the related provisions of that Code section were deleted by P.L. 99-514 (10/22/86). Provisions similar to, but not necessarily identical to, the provisions deleted from Code section 103 now appear in Code section 142.

Caution: The Treasury has not yet amended Reg § 17.1 to reflect changes made by P.L. 100-647, P.L. 99-514.

(a) In general. Section 103(c)(4)(E) provides that section 103(c)(1) shall not apply to obligations issued by a State or local governmental unit which are part of an issue substantially all the proceeds of which are used to provide solid waste disposal facilities. Section 1.103-8(f) of this chapter provides general rules with respect to such facilities and defines such facilities. In the case of property which has both a solid waste disposal function and a function other than the disposal of solid waste, only the portion of the cost of the property allocable to the function of solid waste disposal (as determined under paragraph (b) of this section) is taken into account as an expenditure to provide solid waste disposal facilities. A facility which otherwise qualifies as a solid waste disposal facility will not be treated as having a function other than solid waste disposal merely because material or heat which has utility or value is recovered or results from the disposal process. Where materials or heat are recovered, the waste disposal function includes the processing of such materials or heat which occurs in order to put them into the form in which the materials or heat are in fact sold or used, but does not include further processing which converts the materials or heat into other products.

(b) Allocation. The portion of the cost of property allocable to solid waste disposal is determined by allocating the cost of such property between the property's solid waste disposal function and any other functions by any method which, with reference to all the facts and circumstances with respect to such property, reasonably reflects a separation of costs for each function of the property.

(c) Example. The principles of this paragraph may be illustrated by the following example:

Example. Company A intends to construct a new facility to process solid waste which City X will deliver to the facility. City X will pay a disposal fee for each ton of solid waste that City X dumps at the facility. The waste will be processed by A in a manner which separates metals, glass, and similar materials. As separated, some of such items are commercially saleable; but A does not intend to sell the metals and glass until the metals are further separated, sorted, sized, and cleaned and the glass is pulverized. The metals and pulverized glass will then be sold to commercial users. The waste disposal function includes such processing of the metals and glass, but no further processing is included.

The remaining waste will be burned in an incinerator. Gases generated by the incinerator will be cleaned by use of an electrostatic precipitator. To reduce the size and cost of the electrostatic precipitator, the incinerator exhaust gases will be cooled and reduced in volume by means of a heat exchange process using boilers. The precipitator is functionally related and subordinate to disposal of the waste residue and is therefore property used in solid waste disposal. The heat can be used by A to produce steam. Company B operates an adjacent electric generating facility and B can use steam to power its turbine-generator. B needs steam with certain physical characteristics and as a result A's boilers, heat exchanger and related equipment are somewhat more costly than might be required to produce steam for some other uses. The disposal function includes the equipment actually used to put the heat into the form in which it is sold.

Company A intends to construct pipes to carry the steam from A's boiler to B's facility. When converted to such steam the heat is in the form in which sold, and therefore the disposal function does not include subsequent transporting of the steam by pipes. Similarly, if A installed generating equipment and used the steam to generate electricity, the disposal function would not include the generating equipment, since such equipment transforms the commercially saleable steam into another form of energy.

T.D. 7362, 6/17/75.

§ 1.103-9 Interest on bonds to finance industrial parks.

Caution: The Treasury has not yet amended Reg § 1.103-9 to reflect changes made by P.L. 100-647, P.L. 99-514.

(a) General rule. *(1)* Under section 103(c)(5), interest paid on an issue of obligations issued by a State or local governmental unit (as defined in § 1.103-1) is not includable in gross income if substantially all of the proceeds of such issue is to be used to finance the acquisition or development of land as the site for an industrial park (referred to in this section as "industrial park bonds"). However, interest on an obligation of such an issue is includable in gross income if the obligation is held by a substantial user or a related person (as described in section 103(c)(7) and § 1.103-11). If substantially all of the proceeds of a bond issue is to be so used to finance an industrial park, the debt obligations are treated as obligations described in section 103(a)(1) and § 1.103-1 even though such obligations are industrial development bonds within the meaning of section 103(c)(2) and § 1.103-7. Whether substantially all of the proceeds of an issue of governmental obligations are used to finance an industrial park is determined consistently with the rules for exempt facilities in § 1.103-8(a)(1)(i).

(2) The provisions of subparagraph (1) of this paragraph shall also apply to an issue of obligations substantially all of the proceeds of which is to be used to acquire or develop land as the site for an industrial park described in section 103(c)(5) and this section and for either or both of the following purposes: (i) To finance exempt facilities described in section 103(c)(4) and § 1.103-8, (ii) to finance facilities to be used by an exempt person.

(3) Section 103(c)(5) only becomes applicable where the bond issue meets both the trade or business and the security interest tests so that the obligations are industrial development bonds within the meaning of section 103(c)(2). For the interrelationship of the rules provided in this section and the exemption for certain small issues provided in section 103(c)(6), see § 1.103-10.

(b) Definition of an industrial park. For purposes of section 103(c)(5) and this section, the term "industrial park" means a tract of land, other than a tract of land intended for use by a single enterprise, suitable primarily for use as building sites by a group of enterprises engaged in industrial, distribution, or wholesale businesses if either—

(1) The control and administration of the tract is vested in an exempt person (within the meaning of paragraph (b)(2) of § 1.103-7), or

(2) The uses of the tract are normally (i) regulated by protective minimum restrictions, ordinarily including the size of individual sites, parking and loading regulations, and building setback lines, and (ii) designed to be compatible, under a comprehensive plan, with the community in which the industrial park is located and with the uses of the surrounding land.

(c) Development of land defined. For purposes of section 103(c)(5) and this section, the term "development of land" includes the provision of certain improvements to an industrial park site if such improvements are incidental to the use of the land as an industrial park. Such incidental improvements include the building or installation of incidental water, sewer, sewage and waste disposal, drainage, or similar facilities (whether surface, subsurface, or both). Such incidental improvements include the provision of incidental transportation facilities, such as hard-surface roads (including curbs and gutters) and railroad spurs and sidings; power distribution facilities, such as gas and electric lines; and communication facilities. The provision of structures or buildings of any kind is not included within the meaning of the term "development of land," except for those structures or buildings which are necessary in connection with the incidental improvements encompassed by the term, such as, for example, a water pumphouse and storage tank needed in connection with the incidental provision of water facilities in an industrial park.

(d) Examples. The application of the rules contained in section 103(c)(5) and this section are illustrated by the following examples:

Example (1). City A and corporations X, Y, and Z (unrelated companies) enter into an arrangement under which A is to acquire a tract of land suitable for use as an industrial park. The arrangement provides that: (1) A will issue $10 million of bonds to be used for the acquisition and development of a suitable tract of land; (2) the tract will be controlled and administered by A, pursuant to a comprehensive zoning plan, for the use of a group of enterprises; (3) A will install necessary water, sewer, and drainage facilities on the tract; (4) A will sell substantial portions of the developed tract to X for use as a factory site and to Y for use as a warehouse site; (5) A will lease a sizeable portion of the tract to Z for 20 years as a distribution center site; and (6) the developed tract and the proceeds from the sale or lease of parts of the tract will be the security for the bonds. The bonds are industrial development bonds. Since, however, the proceeds of the issue are to be used for the acquisition and development of a tract of land as the site for an industrial park under section 103(c)(5), section 103(c)(1) does not apply unless the provisions of section 103(c)(7) and § 1.103-11 apply.

Example (2). The facts are the same as in example (1) except that $1 million of the proceeds of the $10 million issue are to be used for the construction of a factory by corporation W or X. The bonds are industrial development bonds. Under these circumstances, substantially all of the proceeds are treated as used or to be used for the acquisition and development of a tract of land as the site for an industrial park described in section 103(c)(5). Accordingly, section

103(c)(1) does not apply unless the provisions of section 103(c)(7) and § 1.103-11 apply.

T.D. 7511, 9/30/77.

§ 1.103-10 Exemption for certain small issues of industrial development bonds.

• ***Caution:*** Reg. § 1.103-10, following, was issued under Code section 103 before the related provisions of that Code section were deleted by P.L. 99-514 (10/22/86). Provisions similar to, but not necessarily identical to, the provisions deleted from Code section 103 now appear in Code section 144.

Caution: The Treasury has not yet amended Reg § 1.103-10 to reflect changes made by P.L. 107-16, P.L. 104-188, P.L. 100-647, P.L. 99-514.

(a) In general. Section 103(b)(6) applies to certain industrial development bond issues (referred to in this section as "exempt small issues") and bonds issued to refund certain issues (referred to in this section as "exempt small refunding issues"). If an issue is an exempt small issue or an exempt small refunding issue, then under the requirements of section 103(b)(6) and this section the interest paid on the debt obligations is not includable in gross income, and the obligations are treated as obligations described in section 103(a)(1) and § 1.103-1, even though such obligations are industrial development bonds as defined in section 103(b)(2) and § 1.103-7. However, interest on an obligation of such an issue is includable in gross income if the obligation is held by a substantial user of the financed facilities or a related person (as described in section 103(b)(7) and § 1.103-11). Section 103(b)(6) only becomes applicable where the bond issue meets both the trade or business and the security interest tests so that the obligations are industrial development bonds within the meaning of section 103(b)(2). For bonds issued before January 1, 1979, in taxable years ending before such date, and for capital expenditures made before January 1, 1979, with respect to such bonds, paragraphs (b), (c), and (d) of this section shall be applied by substituting $5 million for $10 million.

(b) Small issue exemption. *(1) $1 million or less.* Section 103(b)(6)(A) provides that section 103(b)(1) shall not apply to any debt obligation issued by a State or local governmental unit as part of an issue where—

(i) The aggregate authorized face amount of such issue (determined by aggregating the outstanding face amount of any prior exempt small issues described in paragraph (d) of this section and the face amount of the issue of obligations in question) is $1 million or less; and

(ii) Substantially all of the proceeds of such issue is to be used for the acquisition, construction, reconstruction, or improvement of land or property of a character subject to the allowance for depreciation under section 167. Proceeds which are loaned to a borrower for use as working capital or to finance inventory are not used in the manner described in the preceding sentence. Whether substantially all of the proceeds of an issue of governmental obligations are used in such manner is determined consistently with the rules for exempt facilities in § 1.103-8(a)(1)(i). Any obligation which is an industrial development bond within the meaning of section 103(b)(2) and which satisfies the $1 million small issue exemption requirements is an exempt small issue. See paragraph (b)(1) of this section for the treatment of refunding issues of $1 million or less.

(2) $10 million or less. (i) Under section 103(b)(6)(D), the issuing State or local governmental unit may elect to have an aggregate authorized face amount of $10 million or less, in lieu of the $1 million exemption otherwise provided for in section 103(b)(6)(A), with respect to issues of obligations that are industrial development bonds (within the meaning of section 103(b)(2)) issued after October 24, 1968. If the election is made in a timely manner, the bonds will be treated as obligations of a State or local governmental unit described in section 103(a)(1) and § 1.103-1 if the sum of—

(a) The aggregate face amount of the issue including the aggregate outstanding face amount of any prior $1 million or $10 million exempt small issues taken into account under section 103(b)(6)(B) and paragraph (d) of this section, and

(b) The aggregate amount of "section 103(b)(6)(D) capital expenditures" (within the meaning of paragraph (b)(2)(ii) of this section), is $10 million or less. In the case of an issue of obligations that qualified for exemption under section 103(b)(6)(A) and this paragraph, if a section (b)(6)(D) capital expenditure made after the date of issue has the effect of making taxable the interest on the issue, under section 103(b)(6)(G) the loss of tax exemption for the interest shall begin only with the date on which the expenditure that caused the issue to cease to qualify under the $10 million limit was paid or incurred. See paragraph (b)(2)(vi) of this section for the time and manner in which the issuer may elect the $10 million exemption. See section 103(b)(6)(H) and paragraph (c)(2) of this section for the treatment of certain refinancing issues of $10 million of less.

(ii) The term "section 103(b)(6)(D) capital expenditure" is defined in this subdivision. Special rules for applying such definition in the case of certain expenditures paid or incurred by a State or local governmental unit are prescribed in subdivision (iii) of this subparagraph. Except as excluded by subdivision (iv) or (v) of this subparagraph, an expenditure (regardless of how paid, whether in cash, notes, or stock in a taxable or nontaxable transaction) is a section 103(b)(6)(D) capital expenditure if—

(a) The capital expenditure was financed other than out of the proceeds of issues to the extent such issues are taken into account under paragraph (b)(2)(i)(a) of this section.

(b) The capital expenditures were paid or incurred during the 6-year period which begins 3 years before the date of issuance of the issue in question and ends 3 years after such date,

(c) The principal user of the facility in connection with which the property resulting from the capital expenditures is used and the principal user of the facility financed by the proceeds of the issue in question is the same person or are two or more related persons (as defined in section 103(b)(6)(C) and paragraph (e) of this section),

(d) Both facilities referred to in *(c)* of this subdivision were (during the period described in (b) of this subdivision or a part thereof) located in the same incorporated municipality or in the same county outside of the incorporated municipalities in such county), and

(e) The capital expenditures were properly chargeable to the capital account of any person or State or local governmental unit (whether or not such person is the principal user of the facility or a related person) determined, for this purpose, without regard to any rule of the Code which permits expenditures properly chargeable to capital account to be treated as current expenses. With respect to obligations issued on or after August 8, 1972, determinations under the preceding sentence shall be made by including any expenditure which may, under any rule or election under the Code, be treated as a capital expenditure (whether or not such expenditure is so treated). With respect to obligations issued on or after August 8, 1972, for purposes of this subparagraph, capital expenditures made with respect to a contiguous or integrated facility which is located on both sides of a border between two or more political jurisdictions are made with respect to a facility located in all such jurisdictions and, therefore, shall be treated as if they were made in each such political jurisdiction.

(iii) Amounts properly chargeable to capital account under subdivision (ii)(e) of this subparagraph include capital expenditures made by a State or local governmental unit with respect to an exempt facility or an industrial park, within the 6-year period described in subdivision (ii)(b) of this subparagraph, out of the proceeds of bond issues to which section 103(b)(1) did not apply by reason of section 103(b)(4) or (5) (relating to certain exempt activities and industrial parks). Thus, for example, the cost to the lessor of a leased plantsite financed out of the proceeds of an issue for an exempt air pollution control facility under section 103(b)(4)(F) and paragraph (g) of § 1.103-8 would constitute a section 103(b)(6)(D) capital expenditure. However, in the case of an industrial park, only the land costs allocated on an area basis to the plantsite and the actual cost of any improvements made on the plantsite, or to be used principally in connection with the actual plantsite occupied by a principal user or a related person, shall be taken into account as capital expenditures. Where the actual amount of capital expenditures made with respect to a facility by a person (including a State or local governmental unit) other than the user of such facility (or a related person) cannot be ascertained, the fair market value of the property with respect to which the capital expenditures were made, at the time of such capital expenditures, shall be deemed to be the amount of such capital expenditures. In the case of a transaction which is not in form a purchase but which is treated as a purchase for Federal income tax purposes, the purchase price for Federal income tax purposes shall constitute a capital expenditure.

(iv) A section 103(b)(6)(D) capital expenditure shall not include any "excluded expenditure" described in (a) through (e) of this subdivision (iv).

(a) A capital expenditure is an excluded expenditure if either it is made by a public utility company which is not the principal user of the facility financed by the proceeds of the issue in question (or a related person) with respect to property of such company, or it is made by a State or local governmental unit with respect to property of such unit, and if in either case it meets all of the following three conditions: Such property of such company or unit (as the case may be) must be used to provide gas, water, sewage disposal services, electric energy, or telephone service. Such property must be installed in, or connected to, the facility but must not consist of property which is such an integral part of the facility that the cost of such property is ordinarily included as part of the acquisition, construction, or reconstruction cost of such facility. Such property must be of a type normally paid for by the user (or a related person) in the form of periodic fees based upon time or use.

(b) A capital expenditure is an excluded expenditure if it is made by a person other than the user, a related person, or a State or local governmental unit and if it is made with respect to tangible personal property (within the meaning of paragraph (c) of § 1.48-1), or intangible personal property, leased to the user (or a related person) of a facility. However, the preceding sentence shall apply only if such personal property is leased by the manufacturer of such tangible or intangible personal property, or by a person in the trade or business of leasing property the same as, or similar to, such personal property, and only if, pursuant to general business practice, property of such type is ordinarily the subject of a lease.

(c) A capital expenditure is an excluded expenditure if it is made to replace property damaged or destroyed by fire, storm, or other casualty, to the extent that these expenditures do not exceed in dollar amount the fair market value (determined immediately before the casualty) of the property replaced.

(d) A capital expenditure is an excluded expenditure if it is required by a change made after the date of issue in a Federal or State law, or a local ordinance which has general application, or if it is required by a change made after such date in rules and regulations of general application issued under such law or ordinance.

(e) A capital expenditure is an excluded expenditure if it is required by or arises out of circumstances which could not reasonably be foreseen on the date of issue or which arise out of a mistake of law or fact. However, the aggregate dollar amount taken into account under this subdivision (e) with respect to any issue may not exceed $1 million. With respect to expenditures incurred prior to December 11, 1971, the dollar amount specified in the preceding sentence shall be $250,000.

(v) (a) If the assets of a corporation are acquired by another corporation in a transaction to which section 381(a) (relating to carryovers in certain corporate acquisitions) applies, the exchange of consideration by the acquiring corporation for such assets is not a section 103(b)(6)(D) capital expenditure by such acquiring corporation.

(b) However, if an exchange referred to in (a) of this subdivision occurs during the 6-year period beginning 3 years before the date of issuance of an issue of obligations and ending 3 years after such date, the transferor and transferee shall be treated as having been related persons for the portion of such 6-year period preceding the date of the exchange for purposes of determining whether section 103(b)(6)(D) capital expenditures have been made. For purposes of this subdivision (b), the date of an exchange to which section 381 applies shall be the date of distribution or transfer within the meaning of paragraph (b) of § 1.381(b)-1.

(c) If section 351(a) applies to a transfer of property to a corporation solely in exchange for its stock or securities, the issuance of such stock or securities in such exchange is not a section 103(b)(6)(D) capital expenditure by such corporation.

(d) However, if such a transfer referred to in (c) of this subdivision occurs during the 6-year period beginning 3 years before the date of issuance of an issue of obligations and ending 3 years after such date, and if, with respect to the property transferred, expenditures made within such period would have been section 103(b)(6)(D) capital expenditures if the transferor and transferee had been related persons for such period, then such expenditures shall be considered to be section 103(b)(6)(D) capital expenditures made by the transferee. In addition, if a transferor and transferee are related persons immediately following such transfer, such transferor and transferee shall also be treated as having been related persons for the portion of such 6-year period preceding the date of such transfer.

(e) For purposes of this subdivision (v), the term "issue of obligations" means an issue being tested for purposes of qualifying or continuing to qualify under an election pursuant to section 103(b)(6)(D) as to which an amount which would be a section 103(b)(6)(D) capital expenditure solely be reason of (b) or (d) of this subdivision must be taken into account.

(f) If with respect to an issue of obligations an expenditure would not have been a section 103(b)(6)(D) capital expenditure but for the application of (b) or (d) of this subdivision, and if such section 103(b)(6)(D) capital expenditure has the effect of making taxable the interest on an issue of obligations which qualified for exemption under section 103(b)(6)(A) and this paragraph, the loss of tax exemption for such interest shall begin not earlier than the date of such exchange or transfer referred to in this subdivision (v).

(vi) The issuer may make the election provided by section 103(b)(6)(D) and this paragraph (b)(2) (assuming that the bonds otherwise qualify under section 103(b)(6) by noting the election affirmatively at or before the time of issuance of the issue in question on its books or records with respect to the issue. The term "books or records" includes the bond resolution or other similar legislation for the issue in question as well as the bond transcript or other compilation of bond and bond-related documents. If the issuer fails to make an election at the time and in the manner prescribed in this paragraph (b)(2), the issue will not be treated as described in section 103(b)(6)(D), and interest thereon will be includible in gross income.

(c) Refunding or refinancing issue exemption. *(1) $1 million or less refunding issue.* Section 103(b)(6)(A) also provides that section 103(b)(1) shall not apply to any debt obligation issued by a State or local governmental unit as part of an issue the aggregate authorized face amount of which is $1 million or less, if substantially all of the proceeds of such issue are to be used—

(i) To redeem part or all of a prior issue substantially all of the proceeds of which were used to acquire, construct, reconstruct, or improve land or property of a character subject to the allowance for depreciation, or

(ii) To redeem part or all of a prior exempt small refunding issue.

(2) $10 million or less refinancing issue. Section 103(b)(6)(H) provides that section 103(b)(1) shall not apply to any debt obligation issued by a governmental unit as part of an issue which is $10 million or less if the condition of section 103(b)(6)(H) is met and if substantially all of the proceeds are to be used—

(i) To redeem part or all of one or more prior exempt small issues, or

(ii) To redeem part or all of one or more prior exempt small refunding issues.

The condition of section 103(b)(6)(H) is that an election by the issuer of the $10 million exemption in lieu of the $1 million limit for a refunding issue may be made only if each prior issue being redeemed is an issue which qualified either for the $1 million exemption or, by reason of an election under section 103(b)(6)(D), for the $10 million exemption. In addition, in applying the capital expenditures test under section 103(b)(6)(D)(ii) and paragraph (b)(2)(i)(b) of this section to refinancing issues, section 103(b)(6)(D) capital expenditures are taken into account only for purposes of determining whether prior issues which were made under the section 103(b)(6)(D) election qualified under section 103(b)(6)(A) and would have continued to qualify under that section but for the redemption.

(d) Certain prior issues taken into account. *(1) In general.* Section 103(b)(6)(B) provides, in effect, that if (i) a prior issue specified in subparagraph (2) of this paragraph is an exempt small issue (including for this purpose an exempt small refunding issue) under section 103(b)(6)(A) and this section, and (ii) such prior issue is outstanding at the time of issuance of a subsequent issue, then in determining the aggregate face amount of such subsequent issue (for purposes of determining whether such issue is a $1 million of $10 million exempt small issue under section 103(b)(6)(A) and this section) there shall be taken into account the outstanding face amount of such prior exempt small issue. For purposes of this paragraph, the outstanding face amount of a prior exempt small issue does not include the face amount of any obligation which is to be redeemed from the proceeds of such subsequent issue.

(2) Prior issues specified. The face amount of an outstanding prior exempt small issue is taken into account under subparagraph (1) of this paragraph if—

(i) The proceeds of both the prior exempt small issue and of the subsequent issue (whether or not the State or local governmental unit issuing such obligation is the same unit for each such issue) are or will be used primarily with respect to facilities located or to be located in the same incorporated municipality or located or to be located in the same county outside of an incorporated municipality in such county (and, for purposes of this subdivision, on or after August 8, 1972, a contiguous or integrated facility which is located on both sides of a border between two or more political jurisdictions shall be treated as if it is entirely within each such political jurisdiction), and

(ii) The principal user of the financial facilities referred to in subdivision (i) of this subparagraph is or will be the same person or two or more related persons (as defined in section 103(b)(6)(C) and paragraph (e) of this section).

(3) Rules of application. The rules of this paragraph shall apply—

(i) Only in the case of outstanding prior exempt small issues which are industrial development bonds to which section 103(b)(1) would have applied but for the provisions of section 103(b)(6). Thus, for example, the provisions of this paragraph do not apply in respect of a prior issue of obligations issued on or before April 30, 1968. In addition, the provisions of this paragraph do not apply in respect of a prior issue for an exempt facility under section 103(b)(4) and § 1.103-8, or for an industrial park under section 103(b)(5) and § 1.103-9, whether or not the issue might also have qualified as an exempt small issue under section 103(b)(6)(A) and this section.

(ii) To all prior exempt small issues which meet the requirements of this paragraph. Thus, for example, in determining the aggregate face amount of an issue under section 103(b)(6)(A), the outstanding face amount of prior $1 million or $10 million exempt small issues which meet the requirements of this paragraph shall be taken into account in determining the aggregate face amount of a subsequent issue being tested for the $1 million small issue exemption. Similarly, in determining the aggregate face amount of an issue under section 103(b)(6)(A) and (D), the outstanding face amount of prior $1 million or $10 million exempt small issues which meet the requirements of this paragraph shall be taken into account in determining the aggregate face amount of a subsequent issue being tested for the $10 million small issue exemption.

(e) Related persons. For purposes of section 103(b) and §§ 1.103-7 through 1.103-11, the term "related person" means a person who is related to another person if, on the date of issue of obligations—

(1) The relationship between such persons would result in a disallowance of losses under section 267 (relating to disallowance of losses, etc., between related taxpayers) and section 707(b) (relating to losses disallowed, etc., between partners and controlled partnerships) and the regulations thereunder, or

(2) Such persons are members of the same controlled group of corporations, as defined in section 1563(a), relating to definition of controlled group of corporations (except that "more than 50 percent" shall be substituted for "at least 80 percent" each place it appears in section 1563(a)) and the regulations thereunder.

(f) Disqualification of certain small issues. *(1)* Section 103(b)(6) shall not apply to any obligation issued after April 24, 1979, which is part of an issue, a significant portion of the proceeds of which are to be used directly or indirectly to provide residential real property for family units. For purposes of the preceding sentence, the term "residential real property for family units" means residential rental projects (within the meaning of § 1.103-8(b)) and owner-occupied residences (within the meaning of section 103A).

(2) For purposes of paragraph (f)(1), a significant portion of the proceeds of an issue are used to provide residential real property for family units if 5 percent or more of the proceeds are so used.

(g) Examples. The application of the rules contained in section 103(b)(6) and this section are illustrated by the following examples:

Example (1). County A and corporation X enter into an arrangement under which the county will provide a factory which X will lease for 25 years. The arrangement provides (1) that A will issue $1 million of bonds on March 1, 1970, (2) that the proceeds of the bond issue will be used to acquire land in County A (but not in an incorporated municipality) and to construct and equip a factory on such land in accordance with X's specifications, (3) that X will rent the facility for 25 years at an annual rental equal to the amount necessary to amortize the principal and pay the interest on the outstanding bonds, and (4) that such payments by X and the facility itself shall be the security for the bonds. Although the bonds issued are industrial development bonds, the bonds are an exempt small issue under section 103(b)(6)(A) and this section since the aggregate authorized face amount of the bond issue is $1 million or less and all of the proceeds of the bond issue are to be used to acquire and improve land and acquire and construct depreciable property. The result would be the same if the arrangement provided that X would purchase the facility from A.

Example (2). The facts are the same as in example (1) except that, instead of acquiring land and constructing a new factory, the arrangement provides that A will acquire a vacant existing factory building and rebuild and equip the building in accordance with X's specifications. The bonds are an exempt small issue for the same reasons as in example (1).

Example (3). The facts are the same as in example (1) or *(2)* except that the financed facilities are additions to facilities which were financed by an issue of bonds to which section 103(b)(1) does not apply because such bonds were issued prior to May 1, 1968, or were subject to the transitional provisions of § 1.103-12. The bonds are an exempt small issue since neither of the prior bond issues are taken into account under section 103(b)(6)(B) and this section in determining the status of industrial development bonds which are issued after April 30, 1968, and which are not subject to the transitional provisions of § 1.103-12.

Example (4). The facts are the same as in example (1) except that, subsequently, corporation X proposes to County A that A build a $400,000 warehouse located in Town M (an unincorporated town located in County A) for X under terms similar to the factory arrangement described in example (1). On the proposed issue date of the subsequent bond issue, $600,000 of the first exempt small issue will be outstanding. If A issues $400,000 of bonds for such purposes, the bonds will be an exempt small issue under section 103(b)(6) and this section since, under the rules of section 103(b)(6)(B) and paragraph (d) of this section, if the aggregate authorized face amount of the new issue and the outstanding prior exempt small issue will be $1 million or less, the new issue will be an exempt small issue. If, however, the aggregate authorized face amount of the prior issue outstanding on the date of the subsequent issue were in excess of $600,000, the subsequent issue would not qualify as an exempt small issue because (1) the combined aggregate face amount of the outstanding prior issue and the new issue would be in excess of $1 million, (2) the facilities financed by both issues are to be located in unincorporated areas in the same county, (3) the same taxpayer will be the principal user of both facilities, and (4) but for the rules of section 103(b)(6)(B) and paragraph (d) of this section the prior issue would be an exempt small issue.

Example (5). The facts are the same as in example (1) except that subsequently corporation X proposes to City P and City R (incorporated municipalities located in County A) that P and R each issue bonds and each build $1 million facilities to be located in Cities P and R for the use of X under terms similar to the arrangement in example (1). Each of the $1 million issues will be an exempt small issue because each proposed facility is located within a different incorporated municipality and the proceeds of the prior outstanding exempt small issue were used to construct facilities outside of an incorporated area.

Example (6). The facts are the same as in example (1) except that $95,000 of the $1 million will be used by the corporation as working capital. The bonds are an exempt small issue for the same reason as in example (1) since substantially all of the proceeds will be used for the acquisition of land and the construction of depreciable property.

Example (7). The facts are the same as in example (1) except that on November 1, 1969, County A issued $10 million of industrial development bonds, all of the proceeds of which were issued for the acquisition of land as the site for an industrial park within the meaning of section 103(b)(5) and § 1.103-9. The proceeds of the $1 million of bonds issued in 1970 will be used to construct a factory for corporation X to be located in the industrial park. The bonds issued in 1970 are industrial development bonds within the meaning of section 103(b)(2) and § 1.103-7. Since, however, the prior 1969 issue is not an issue to which section 103(b)(6)(A) applied (see paragraph (d)(3)(i) of this section), the bonds issued in 1970 are an exempt small issue for the reasons stated in example (1).

Example (8). County B enters into three separate arrangements with three unrelated corporations whereby the county will provide separate storage facilities for each corporation.

The arrangement provides (1) that the county will issue bonds and loan to each corporation $250,000 of the proceeds which will be used to acquire land in the county and to construct the facilities, (2) that the rental payments by the corporations will be equal to the amount necessary to amortize the principal and pay the interest on any outstanding bonds issued by the county, and (3) that the payments by the corporations and the facilities themselves shall be the security for the industrial development bonds. For convenience, the county issues one series of bonds in the face amount of $750,000 rather than three separate series of bonds of $250,000 each. The issue is an exempt small issue under section 103(b)(6)(A) and paragraph (b)(1) of this section since the aggregate authorized face amount of the bond issue is $1 million or less, and all of the proceeds of the bond issue are to be used to acquire and improve land and acquire and construct depreciable property.

Example (9). City C and corporation Y enter into an arrangement under which C will provide a factory which Y will lease for 25 years. The arrangement provides (1) that C will issue $4 million of bonds on March 1, 1969, after making the election under section 103(b)(6)(D) and paragraph (b)(2) of this section, (2) that the proceeds of the bond issue will be used to acquire land in the city and to construct and equip a factory on such land in accordance with Y's specifications, (3) that Y will rent the facilities for 25 years at an annual rental equal to the amount necessary to amortize the principal and pay the interest on the outstanding bonds, (4) that such payments by Y and the facility itself shall be the security for the bonds, and (5) that, if corporation Y pays or incurs capital expenditures in excess of $1 million within 3 years from the date of issue which disqualify the bonds as an exempt small issue under section 103(b)(6)(D), it will either furnish funds to C to redeem such bonds at par or at a premium, or increase the rental payments to C in an amount sufficient to pay a premium interest rate. Although the bonds issued are industrial development bonds, they are an exempt small issue under section 103(b)(6)(A) by reason of the election under section 103(b)(6)(D) and paragraph (b)(2) of this section, since the aggregate authorized face amount of the bond issue is $5 million or less and all of the proceeds of the bond issue are to be used to acquire and improve land and acquire and construct depreciable property. The provisions for redemption of the bonds or an increase in rental if the bonds are disqualified as an exempt small issue under section 103(b)(6)(A) will not disqualify an otherwise valid election under section 103(b)(6)(D) and paragraph (b)(2) of this section.

Example (10). The facts are the same as in example (9) except that corporation Y subsequently proposed to the city that it build a $1 million warehouse next to the plant for the use of Y under terms similar to the factory arrangement. Assume further that the factory building was completed by March 1, 1970, and that on January 15, 1972, the proposed issue date of the subsequent bond issue, $2 million of the first exempt small issue will be outstanding. In determining the aggregate authorized face amount of the new issue, the original face amount of a prior outstanding issue must be reduced by that portion which is to be redeemed before it is added to the face amount of the new issue. Therefore, if the city issues $3 million of bonds to redeem the remaining $2 million of bonds and to construct the warehouse the bonds will be an exempt small issue under section 103(b)(6)(A) if an election is made under section 103(b)(6)(D) and paragraph (b)(2) of this section since (1) the face amount of the new issue ($3 million), plus (2) the face amount of the prior outstanding exempt small issue minus the amount of such issue to be refunded ($2 million minus $2 million), plus (3) capital expenditures during the preceding 3 years financed other than out of the proceeds of outstanding issues to which section 103(b)(6)(A) and paragraph (b) of this section applied ($2 million), do not exceed $5 million. If, however, the amount of the January 15, 1972, issue were $3½ million, the issue would not qualify as an exempt small issue under section 103(b)(6)(A) and paragraph (b)(2) of this section.

Example (11). The facts are the same as in example (9), except that on June 15, 1971, Y purchases from an unrelated motor carrier business a warehouse terminal in the same city at a cost of $250,000 and tractor-trailers and other automotive equipment based at the terminal at a cost of $1 million. This subsequent expenditure by Y has the effect of making the interest on the city C bonds includable in the gross income of the holders of such bonds as of June 15, 1971, because the face amount of the March 1, 1969, issue ($4 million) plus the subsequent capital expenditures within 3 years of the date of issue $1,250,000) exceed $5 million. (See section 103(b)(6)(D) and paragraph (b)(2)(i) of this section.)

Example (12). The facts are the same as in example (9), except that in March, 1970, Y will move $3 million of additional used machinery and equipment into the factory from its factory in another city. The expenditures for such machinery, and equipment were incurred by Y more than 3 years prior to the date of issue of the bonds. The transfer of such used equipment into city C does not constitute a section 103(b)(6)(D) capital expenditure within the meaning of paragraph (b)(2)(ii) of this section since the expenditures with respect to such property were incurred more than 3 years prior to the date of issue of the bonds. Had the capital expenditures with respect to such property been incurred during the 6-year period beginning 3 years before the date of issue of the bonds and in the 3 years after such date, they would constitute section 103(b)(6)(D) capital expenditures.

Example (13). The facts are the same as in example (9), except that in March 1970, corporation Y enters into an arrangement with respect to machinery and equipment to be used in the facility. The arrangement is labeled by the parties as a lease but is treated as a sale for Federal income tax purposes. The amount treated as the purchase price of the machinery and equipment is a section 103(b)(6)(D) capital expenditure.

Example (14). On February 1, 1970, city D issues $5 million of its bonds to finance construction of an addition to the manufacturing plant of corporation Z. The bonds will be secured by the facility and lease payments to be made by Z which will be sufficient to pay the principal and interest on such bonds. Assume that the bonds qualify as an exempt small issue under section 103(b)(6)(A) pursuant to an election under section 103(b)(6)(D) and paragraph (b)(2) of this section. On February 1, 1971, D plans to issue $1 million of its bonds to construct a pollution control facility to be leased to Z for use at its manufacturing plant. The rental payments from the lease will be sufficient to pay the principal and interest on the bonds. The bonds will be secured by such facility and the lease payments. Capital expenditures for the pollution control facility will be paid or incurred beginning before February 1, 1973. Although the pollution control facility is an exempt facility under section 103(b)(4)(F) and paragraph (g) of § 1.103-8, amounts used for the pollution control facility shall be considered to be a section 103(b)(6)(D) capital expenditure and the interest on the February 1, 1970, issue will become taxable as of the date such capital expenditure began to be paid or incurred. See section 103(b)(6)(G) and paragraph (b)(2)(i) of this section.

Example (15). On February 1, 1970, City E issues $500,000 of its bonds to acquire and develop an industrial park within the meaning of section 103(b)(5) and paragraph (b) of § 1.103-9. The park consists of 100 acres and is divided into one 50 acre plantsite and 4 smaller sites. The aggregate acquisition cost of the undeveloped land is $150,000 or an average per acre cost of $1,500. Roads, sidewalks, sewers, utilities, sewage, and waste disposal facilities serving the entire industrial park cost $300,000. On September 1, 1970, E. leases to corporation Y for 30 years the 50 acre plantsite (with an allocated cost of $75,000) and a railroad spur track from the railroad right of way to Y's plantsite for Y's exclusive use. The spur track was constructed using $50,000 of the proceeds of the industrial park bond issue. E also proposes to issue on September 1, 1970, $4,875,000 of its bonds to construct and equip a building on the leased plantsite to be leased to Y at an additional rental sufficient to pay the principal and interest on this issue of bonds. The September 1, 1970, issue will be an exempt small issue under section 103(b)(6)(A) pursuant to an election under section 103(b)(6)(D) and paragraph (b)(2) of this section since the sum of the amount of the second issue ($4,875,000) and the capital expenditures allocated to the plantsite ($75,000 for 50 acres of land plus $50,000 for the railroad spur tract, totaling $125,000) does not exceed $5 million. The sum of $300,000 which was spent in development of the industrial park provided facilities which will serve or benefit the users generally and hence under paragraph (b)(2)(iii) of this section is not considered to have provided facilities as to which Y will be the principal user.

Example (16). On June 1, 1970, corporation Z simultaneously enters into separate arrangements with City F and City G under which each city will issue a $5 million exempt small issue of bonds the proceeds of which will be used by Z to construct separate facilities in each city. By June 1, 1971, the facilities have been completed in the respective cities. On January 1, 1972, Cities F and G, through a valid legal proceeding, merge into a new City FG. Since in this case F and G were separate cities on June 1, 1970 (the date of the bond issues), the factories are not considered to be located in the same incorporated municipality. Accordingly, each $5 million issue by City F and G will continue to qualify as an exempt small issue.

Example (17). On June 1, 1973, City H issues an exempt small issue of $4.75 million to finance a facility of corporation S to be located in City H. On October 1, 1974, S and corporation T, previously unrelated to S, consummated a statutory merger which qualifies as a reorganization described in section 368(a)(1)(A) and thus as a transaction described in section 381(a). In the transaction, T transferred to S assets with a fair market value of $1.5 million in exchange for stock of S, $300,000 of securities of S, and $100,000 cash. On March 23, 1971, T made $400,000 of capital expenditures for an addition to its factory located in City H. For purposes of testing the H issue of June 1, 1973, such expenditures would have been section 103(b)(6)(D) capital expenditures if T and S had been related persons. Under the provisions of paragraph (b)(2)(v) *(a)* of this section, the exchange of $1.5 million of stock, securities, and cash by S does not constitute a section 103(b)(6)(D) capital expenditure. Since, however, S and T are treated as related persons starting 3 years prior to the date of issue of the obligations, the $400,000 of expenditures by T constitute section 103(b)(6)(D) capital expenditures. Thus, the interest on the June 1, 1973, issue of obligations would become taxable (since the $5 million limit would be exceeded) on the date of the merger.

Example (18). In 1965 City I issues $10 million of industrial development bonds to construct and equip a factory for corporation Z. In 1975 the remaining principal amount of the bonds outstanding is $4.1 million. If I issues $4.5 million of bonds to redeem the balance of the prior issue, and for other purposes, such issue cannot qualify as an exempt small issue under section 103(b)(6)(D) and paragraph (b)(2) of this section even though at the time of issue the interest on the 1965 bonds was tax-exempt since the prior issue must be one which qualified under section 103(b)(6)(A) and this section. Further, the 1975 issue will be an issue of industrial development bonds notwithstanding the provisions of paragraph (d)(2) of § 1.103-7 which provides that certain bonds issued to refund an issue of obligations issued on or before April 30, 1968 (or January 1, 1969, in certain cases) will not be so treated. Paragraph (d)(2) of § 1.103-7 is not applicable because the 1975 issue makes funds available for a purpose other than the debt service obligation on the 1965 bonds.

Example (19). In 1969 City J issues $4 million of industrial development bonds which qualify as an exempt small issue under section 103(b)(6)(A) pursuant to an election under section 103(b)(6)(D) and paragraph (b)(2) of this section. In 1971, by reason of a $2 million addition to the factory built with the proceeds of the issue, the 1969 exempt small issue loses its tax-exempt status. In 1972, the city issues a $5 million issue to redeem the prior 1969 issue. The redemption issue will not qualify as an exempt small issue since the prior 1969 issue did not continue to qualify under section 103(b)(6)(A) and this section.

T.D. 7199, 7/31/72, amend T.D. 7511, 9/30/77, T.D. 7840, 10/12/82, T.D. 8086, 5/1/86.

PAR. 2. Section 1.103-10 is amended by adding a new sentence after the second sentence of paragraph (b)(2)(i); by deleting "(e)" and adding "(f)" in lieu thereof in the first sentence of paragraph (b)(2)(iv) introductory text and by adding a new subdivision (f) at the end of subdivision (iv) thereof; by adding two new sentences after the first sentence of paragraph (d)(1); by revising paragraph (d)(2)(ii); by adding two new flush sentences at the end of paragraph (d)(2); by revising the introductory text of paragraph (g); and by adding a new paragraph (h). The revised and added provisions read as follows:

Proposed § 1.103-10 Exemption for certain small issues of industrial development bonds. [*For Preamble, see ¶ 151,059*]

* * * * *

• ***Caution:*** Proposed reg. § 1.103-10, following, was issued under Code section 103 before the related provisions of that Code section were deleted by P.L. 99-514 (10/22/86). Provisions similar to, but not necessarily identical to, the provisions deleted from Code section 103 now appear in Code section 144.

(b) Small issue exemption. * * *

(2) $10 million or less. (i) * * * All capital expenditures described in paragraph (b)(2)(ii) with respect to each principal user and each related person must be aggregated with the issue of obligations in question for purposes of determining whether the $10 million limitation of section 103(b)(6)(D) is exceeded. * * *

(iv) * * *

(f) A capital expenditure with respect to a facility other than the bond-financed facility ("other facility") is an excluded expenditure if the principal user of the other facility does not become a principal user of the facility financed by the proceeds of the issue in question (" bond-financed facility") until after the last day of the test period described in paragraph (i)(3)(ii) of this section. In addition, a capital expenditure with respect to an "other facility" becomes an excluded expenditure on and after the date the principal user of the other facility ceases to use the bond-financed facility; if, however, the issue financing the bond-financed facility lost its tax-exempt status on or before that date, this sentence will not apply to restore its tax-exempt status. * * *

* * * * *

(d) Certain prior issues taken into account. *(1) In general.* * * * Thus, the outstanding face amount of all prior issues specified in paragraph (d)(2) with respect to each principal user and each related person and taken into account under this paragraph (d)(1) must be aggregated with the issue of obligations in question for purposes of determining whether the $1 million limitation of section 103(b)(6)(A) or the $10 million limitation of section 103(b)(6)(D) has been exceeded with respect to the issue in question. The outstanding face amount of the prior exempt small issue is the principal amount outstanding at the time of issuance of the subsequent exempt small issue. * * *

(2) Prior issues specified. * * *

(ii) The principal user of the facilities described in paragraph (d)(2)(i) of this section is the same person or two or more related persons (as defined in section 103(b)(6)(C) and in paragraph (e) of this section) at any time on or after the date of issue of the subsequent issue but before the expiration of the test period described in paragraph (i)(3)(ii) of this section with respect to the subsequent issue.

The loss of tax exemption with respect to the interest on the subsequent issue shall be effective on the date of issue of the subsequent issue. For purposes of this paragraph (d), when a person ceases to use a facility financed by either the prior issue or the subsequent issue, the prior issue will no longer be taken into account under paragraph (d)(1) with respect to the subsequent issue; if, however, the subsequent issue loses its tax-exempt status on or before the date the person ceases to use either of the facilities described in this subparagraph, this paragraph will not apply to restore the tax-exempt status of the subsequent issue. * * *

* * * * *

(g) Examples. The application of the rules contained in section 103(b)(6) and in paragraphs (a) through (f) of this section are illustrated by the following examples: * * *

* * * * *

(h) Rules relating to principal users. *(1) Definition of principal user.* For purposes of section 103(b)(6) and § 1.103-10, the term "principal user" means a person who is a principal owner, a principal lessee, a principal output purchaser, or an "other" principal user. The term "principal user" also includes a person who is related to another person who is a principal user under section 103(b)(6)(C) and paragraph (e) of this section, unless the other person ceased to use the facility before the two persons become related. For purposes of this paragraph (h)—

(i) Principal owner. A principal owner is a person who at any time holds more than a 10-percent ownership interest (by value) in the facility or, if no person holds more than a 10-percent ownership interest, then the person (or persons in the case of multiple equal owners) who holds the largest ownership interest in the facility. A person is treated as holding an ownership interest if such person is an owner for Federal income tax purposes generally. Thus, for example, where a facility constructed on land subject to a ground lease has an economic useful life less than the noncancellable portion of the term of the ground lease, the ground lessor shall not, merely by reason of that reversionary interest, be treated as the principal user of the facility before the ground lease expires.

(ii) Principal lessee. A principal lessee is a person who at any time leases more than 10 percent of the facility (disregarding portions used by the lessee under a short-term lease). The portion of a facility leased to a lessee is generally determined by reference to its fair rental value. A short-term lease is one which has a term of one year or less, taking into account all options to renew and reasonably anticipated renewals.

(iii) Principal output purchaser. A principal output purchaser is any person who purchases output of an electric or thermal energy, gas, water, or other similar facility, unless the total output purchased by such person during each one-year period beginning with the date the facility is placed in service is 10 percent or less of the facility's output during each such period.

(iv) Other principal user. An "other" principal user is a person who enjoys a use of the facility (other than a short-term use) in a degree comparable to the enjoyment of a principal owner or a principal lessee, taking into account all the relevant facts and circumstances, such as the person's participation in control over use of the facility or its remote or proximate geographic location. For example, a party to a contract who would be treated as a lessee using more than 10 percent of a facility on a long-term basis but for the special rules of section 7701(e)(3) and (5) (relating to service contracts for certain energy and water facilities and low-income housing) is an "other" principal user. A short-term use means use that is comparable to use under a short-term lease.

(2) Operating rules. (i) In determining whether a person is a principal user of a facility, it is irrelevant where in a chain of use such person's use occurs. For example, where a sublessee subleases more than 10 percent of a facility from a lessee, both the lessee and the sublessee are principal lessees.

(ii) In determining whether a person owns or uses more than 10 percent of a facility or whether he uses it for more than one year, the person is treated as owning or using the facility to the extent that any person related to such person under section 103(b)(6)(C) and paragraph (e) of this section owns or uses the facility. For purposes of the preceding sentence, the term "use" includes use pursuant to an output purchase arrangement.

(iii) Co-owners or co-lessees who are collectively treated as a partnership subject to subchapter K under section 761(a) are not treated as principal users merely by reason of their ownership of partnership interests; such ownership is, however, taken into account in determining whether persons are related under section 103(b)(6)(C) and paragraph (e) of this section.

(iv) For purposes of this section, a principal user of a facility is treated as ceasing to use the facility when he ceases to own, lease, purchase the output of, or otherwise use the facility, as the case may be. A person who is a principal user of a facility because he is related to another person who is a principal user is treated as ceasing to use the facility when the other person ceases to use the facility or when the two persons cease to be related. A principal user who ceases to use a facility continues to be a principal user. See, however, paragraph (b)(2)(iv) *(f)* of this section (relating to excluded expenditures), paragraph (d)(2) (relating to prior issues), and paragraph (h)(1) (defining principal user), which may apply when a principal user ceases to use a facility.

(3) Special rule for exempt persons. If an exempt person, as defined in section 103(b)(3) and § 1.103-7(b)(2), is a principal user of a facility financed with an issue of obligations described in section 103(b)(6), the following amounts must be aggregated with the issue in determining whether the $1 million limit of section 103(b)(6)(A) or the $10 million limit of section 103(b)(6)(D) has been exceeded:

(i) The outstanding face amount of any prior exempt small issue of industrial development bonds described in paragraph (d) of this section that financed a facility of which the exempt person is a principal user,

(ii) For purposes of the $10 million limitation, capital expenditures described in paragraph (b)(2)(ii) of this section paid or incurred with respect to other facilities used by the exempt person in an unrelated trade or business (within the meaning of section 513 and § 1.513-1) and of which the exempt person is a principal user, and

(iii) Any section 103(b)(6)(D) capital expenditures paid or incurred with respect to the facility financed by the issue in question.

(4) Examples. The application of the rule of section 103(b)(6) and this paragraph (h) is illustrated by the following examples:

Example (1). On September 1, 1986, City L, after making the section 103(b)(6)(D) election, issues $8 million of obligations to finance the costs of acquiring a newly constructed warehouse within City L, owned by Corporation Z, a non-exempt person, which thus is a principal user of the warehouse. Beginning on September 1, 1986, the entire warehouse is leased to Corporation Y, an unrelated non-exempt person, for a 2-year term; thus, Y is also a principal user of the warehouse. On June 30, 1986, Y ceases to lease the warehouse. On October 1, 1988, Y incurs $20 million of capital expenditures in connection with its purchase of an office building in City L. Although Y continues to be a principal user of the warehouse under paragraph (h)(2)(iv) of this section, Y's capital expenditures after the date it ceases to use the warehouse are excluded expenditures under paragraph (b)(2)(iv) *(f)* of this section. Accordingly, the $20 million Y incurred with respect to the office building is not taken into account for purposes of determining whether the $10 million limitation of section 103(b)(6)(D) has been exceeded.

Example (2). The facts are the same as in Example (1), except that on October 1, 1985, City L issued an exempt small issue to finance acquisition of a newly constructed office building in the amount of $5 million, of which $4 million is outstanding on September 1, 1986. On December 1, 1988, Corporation Z leases 15 percent (by fair rental value) of the office building financed by the 1985 issue for a 2-year term. Thus, beginning on December 1, 1988, Z is a principal user of the office building. On December 1, 1988, Z still owns the warehouse financed by the 1986 issue. Because Z became a principal user of the office building before the end of the 3-year test period described in paragraph (i)(3)(ii) of this section with respect to the 1986 issue, the $4 million outstanding amount of the 1985 issue must be aggregated with the $8 million 1986 issue for purposes of determining whether the 1986 issue has exceeded the $10 million limitation of section 103(b)(6)(D). Because the sum of the two issues ($4 million of the prior 1985 issue outstanding on September 1, 1986, and the $8 million subsequent issue issued on September 1, 1986) exceeds $10 million, the interest on the 1986 issue ceases to be tax-exempt on September 1, 1986. Had Z's lease begun after September 1, 1989, the two issues would not have to be aggregated.

Example (3). On June 1, 1985, City O issues $15 million of its obligations to finance an expansion of a hospital owned by H, an organization described in section 501(c)(3) exempt from taxation under section 501(a). None of the proceeds of the issue will be used by H in an unrelated trade or business or in the trade or business of non-exempt persons. On November 1, 1986, City O, after making the section 103(b)(6)(D) election, issues $5 million of its obligations to construct a medical office building which will be owned by H for Federal income tax purposes and which will be entirely leased (for terms in excess of one year) to physicians, none of whom will lease over 10 percent of the building by value. On July 1, 1987, H incurs a $500,000 capital expenditure for permanent improvements to the medical office building. In addition, on August 1, 1987, W, a non-exempt person related to H, incurs a $1 million capital expenditure with respect to a facility that W owns within City O and uses in its trade or business. For purposes of determining whether the $10 million limitation of section 103(b)(6)(D) has been exceeded with respect to the November 1, 1986, issue for the medical office building, H must take into account the $5 million issue, the $500,000 of capital expenditures made with respect to the medical office building, and W's $1 million capital expenditure.

Because the sum of these amounts is less than $10 million, interest on the issue does not cease to be tax-exempt. H is not required to take into account the June 1, 1985, issue financing the hospital expansion because that issue is not an exempt small issue as defined in section 103(b)(6) (see paragraph (h)(3)(i) of this section) and because the cost of the facility financed by the June 1, 1985, issue is neither a section 103(b)(6)(D) capital expenditure with respect to the medical office building owned by H (see paragraph (h)(3)(iii) of this section) nor a section 103(b)(6)(D) capital expenditure for a separate facility used by H in an unrelated trade or business (see paragraph (h)(3)(ii) of this section).

* * * * *

PAR. 2. Section 1.103-10 is amended by adding a new paragraph (i) immediately following paragraph (h) therein. The new paragraph reads as follows:

Proposed § 1.103-10 Exemption for certain small issues of industrial development bonds. [*For Preamble, see ¶ 151,057*]

* * * * *

• ***Caution:*** Proposed reg. § 1.103-10, following, was issued under Code section 103 before the related provisions of that Code section were deleted by P.L. 99-514 (10/22/86). Provisions similar to, but not necessarily identical to, the provisions deleted from Code section 103 now appear in Code section 144.

(i) $40 million limitation for beneficiaries of small issues of industrial development bonds. *(1) General rule.* Section 103(b)(6) and § 1.103-10(a) do not apply to an issue of obligations ("issue in question") if—

(i) The portion of the aggregate authorized face amount of the issue in question allocated to any test-period beneficiary, as defined in paragraph (i)(3) of this section, of the issue, plus

(ii) The portion of the outstanding principal amount of prior bonds, as defined in paragraph (i)(2) of this section, allocated—

(a) To the test-period beneficiary described in paragraph (i)(1)(i) of this section, or

(b) To a person who at any time during the test period of the issue in question is related to such beneficiary,

exceeds $40 million. If interest on the issue in question would, but for this paragraph and section 103(b)(15), be exempt from Federal income taxation solely because of section 103(b)(6), the issue is treated as an issue of obligations not described in section 103(a) on and after the date of issuance. For purposes of this paragraph (i), the aggregate authorized face amount of the issue in question and the outstanding principal amount of a prior bond shall be determined without regard to section 103(b)(6) (B) or (D) (requiring certain amounts of prior issues or capital expenditures to be taken into account in determining the aggregate face amount of the issue in question or of the prior bond).

(2) Prior bonds. For purposes of this paragraph (i), "prior bonds" means prior or simultaneous issues of industrial development bonds described in paragraph (4), (5), or (6) of section 103(b) the interest on which is exempt from tax pursuant to section 103(a), including such bonds issued before January 1, 1984. For purposes of paragraph (i)(1)(ii) of this section, "outstanding principal amount of prior bonds" means the principal amount that is outstanding at the time of issuance of the issue in question, not including the amount to be redeemed from the proceeds of the issue in question. Thus, the outstanding principal amount of prior bonds does not include the portion of the original face amount that has been discharged, nor does it include any amount to be issued in the future.

(3) Test-period beneficiary. (i) In general. For purposes of this paragraph (i), a "test-period beneficiary" of the issue in question or of an issue of prior bonds means any person who at any time during the test period for the issue is a principal user, as defined in paragraph (h)(1) of this section, of a facility financed by the proceeds of the issue, including a person who is related to a principal user. For purposes of the preceding sentence, a person shall be treated as related to a principal user only if that person is related to such user within the meaning of section 103(b)(6)(C) and paragraph (e) of this section at any time during the test period, and such user has not ceased to use the facility before the persons became related. See paragraph (h)(2)(iv) of this section for circumstances in which a person will be treated as ceasing to use a facility. A test-period beneficiary does not cease to be a test-period beneficiary if he ceases to use the facility; the portion of the issue allocated to the test-period beneficiary continues to be so allocated until the issue is no longer outstanding.

(ii) Test period. The "test period" for an issue means the 3-year period beginning on the later of the date the facility financed by the proceeds of the issue is placed in service or the date of issue of such issue. A facility shall be considered as being placed in service at the time the facility is placed in a condition or state of readiness and availability for a specifically assigned function. If separate facilities are financed by an issue and the facilities are placed in service at different times, there shall be separate test periods for the portions of the issue financing each separate facility. If a single facility (consisting of separately depreciable items of property) is placed in service in stages, then the entire facility will be deemed placed in service when its last portion is placed in service.

(4) Allocation of issue. (i) In general. The portion of the amount of an issue allocated to a test-period beneficiary is the highest percent of the facility financed by proceeds of the issue that the beneficiary owned or used on a regular basis during the test period. For example, a person that owns the entire facility shall be allocated 100 percent of the issue; a person that leases 90 percent of a facility for two years of the test period and leases 35 percent for the third year shall be allocated 90 percent of the issue.

(ii) Portion allocable to lessee and output purchaser. The portion of a facility used by a lessee is generally determined by reference to its fair rental value. The portion of a facility used by a principal output purchaser, as defined in paragraph (h)(1)(iii) of this section, is the highest portion of the facility's total output purchased by such purchaser during any of the three years of the test period.

(iii) Portion allocable to related person. The portion of an issue allocable to a person who is a test-period beneficiary because he is related to a principal user is the same portion allocated to such principal user.

(iv) Double allocation. The total amount of an issue allocated to test-period beneficiaries may exceed 100 percent of its outstanding face amount, such as when one test-period beneficiary is an owner and another person leases the facility for over a year. However, if a beneficiary is the owner of all or a portion of a facility that is leased to or otherwise used by such beneficiary or by a related person, then the portion of the issue the proceeds of which were used to finance the facility is allocated only once to the beneficiary. For example, if Corporation X owns an undivided 50 percent of a facility while related Corporation Y is the lessee of 60 percent of the facility, the portion of the issue financing the facility allocable to X is 80 percent (50 percent plus 30 percent), because one-half of the 60-percent portion used by Y (30 percent) is considered attributable to the portion owned by X.

(v) Allocation of remainder of issue to owners. If the portion of an issue allocated to all test-period beneficiaries of the bond-financed facility (other than related persons) is less than 100 percent, the remainder shall be allocated to test-period beneficiaries who are owners of the facility in proportion to the amount of the issue otherwise allocable to such persons by reason of their ownership interests during the test period.

(vi) Bond redeemed before person becomes principal user. If all or some of the outstanding principal amount of the issue in question or of prior bonds is redeemed other than from the proceeds of a refunding issue described in section 103(a) either before or as soon as reasonably practicable after a person becomes a test-period beneficiary with respect to the issue in question, but in no event later than 180 days after the date such person becomes a test-period beneficiary, then the amount of the issue so redeemed will not be allocated to such person (or to a related person) in determining whether the issue in question exceeds the $40 million limitation. With respect to obligations that are issued after August 22, 1986 paragraph (i)(4)(vi) shall not apply if the terms of the issue provide for a delay in redemption a principal purpose of which is to benefit from the 180-day period referred to therein. In the case of a person who becomes a test-period beneficiary before February 21, 1986, bonds redeemed before August 22, 1986 shall be considered redeemed as soon as reasonably practicable for purposes of the first sentence of this paragraph (i)(4)(vi) and the 180-day limitation referred to therein shall not apply.

(5) Treatment of certain successors as test-period beneficiaries. If a corporation, partnership, or other entity which is a test-period beneficiary with respect to one or more issues transfers substantially all of its properties to another person (or to two or more related persons within the meaning of section 103(b)(6)(C)), or if a corporation acquires the assets of a test-period beneficiary in a transaction described in section 381(a), the transferee shall be treated as a test-period beneficiary with respect to such issues and shall be allocated the portion of such issues that were allocated to the transferor prior to the transfer. The preceding sentence shall not apply to the extent that it would result in double allocation of an issue, such as in the case of a transfer to a related person. This paragraph (i)(5) shall apply regardless of whether gain is required to be recognized by the transferor for Federal income tax purposes and regardless of whether the transferor remains in existence after the transfer. If the transferor remains in existence after the transfer, this paragraph (i)(5) shall not relieve the transferor of its allocation of any issue. This paragraph (i)(5) shall apply only for purposes of determining the tax exemption of issues of which the transferee becomes the test-period beneficiary after the transfer described herein.

(6) Examples. The application of section 103(b)(15) and this paragraph (i) may be illustrated by the following examples:

Example (1). On September 1, 1986, City M issues a $9 million obligation to finance acquisition of a newly constructed shopping center that is placed in service on September 1, 1986, and is owned and managed by Corporation X. Half of the shopping center (determined by fair rental value) is leased for a term exceeding 1 year to Corporation Y. X owns 60 percent of the shares of Y. The other half of the shopping center (also determined by fair rental value) is leased in equal shares for a term exceeding 1 year to A and B, two unrelated corporations. As of September 1, 1986, $30 million of prior issues of obligations are outstanding and are allocable to X as a test-period beneficiary under the rules of § 1.103-10(i)(4). As of that date there is no prior issue of obligations outstanding and allocable to Y, A, or B as test-period beneficiaries. Because X owns 100 percent of the shopping center, 100 percent of the 1986 issue ($9 million) is allocated to X. Therefore, for purposes of determining whether the 1986 issue exceeds the $40 million limitation of section 103(b)(15), the $30 million of outstanding prior issues must be added to the $9 million 1986 issue. Because Y leases 50 percent of the shopping center, 50 percent of the 1986 issue ($4.5 million) is allocated to Y. Although Y is related to X under section 103(b)(15)(E), the $4.5 million of the 1986 issue that is allocated to Y is not added to the $39 million allocated to X under paragraph (i)(4)(iv) of this section since such amount has already been allocated to X as owner of the shopping center. Because A and B each leases 25 percent of the shopping center, each is allocated 25 percent ($2.25 million) of the 1986 issue.

Example (2). The facts are the same as in *Example (1)* except that A owns a 60-percent interest in an airport hotel described in § 1.103-8(e)(2)(ii) *(d)* and, because of such ownership interest, is allocated $15 million of prior outstanding obligations described in section 103(b)(4)(D). In addition, County N issues $25 million of obligations described in section 103(b)(4)(E) on October 1, 1986, to finance construction of a solid-waste disposal facility that will be owned by C, A's wholly-owned subsidary corporation. In this case, with respect to the September 1, 1986 issue, A is allocated the $15 million prior issue that is outstanding with respect to A's share of the airport hotel bond and the $2.25 million that is A's allocable share of the September 1, 1986, issue for a total of $17.25 million. Because the solid waste disposal facility bonds had not yet been issued when the September 1, 1986, obligation was issued, no portion of the $25 million of obligations to finance C's solid-waste disposal facility will be treated as part of A's allocable obligations with respect to the September 1, 1986, issue even though A and C are related persons. In addition, even though A and C are related persons and even though on the date of issue of the solid-waste disposal bonds C will be allocated more than $40 million of outstanding obligations for purposes of section 103(b)(15) (including A's $17.25 million of outstanding prior obligations), the $40 million limitation of section 103(b)(15) does not render the interest on the October 1, 1986, bonds taxable since the October 1, 1986 issue, qualifies for tax exemption under section 103(b)(4), and the $40 million limitation of section 103(b)(15) does not apply to render taxable bonds issued under section 103(b)(4).

Example (3). On October 1, 1986, City K issues an $8 million issue of obligations exempt under section 103(b)(6) to finance acquisition of a newly-constructed manufacturing plant owned by Corporation L. On October 1, 1986, Corporation M has $35 million of prior outstanding obligations allocable to it under section 103(b)(15). On October 1, 1986, L has no prior outstanding obligations allocable to itself. On April 1, 1988, M acquires 100 percent of the stock of L, which still owns the plant financed by the 1986 issue. Since M and L became related to each other during the 3-year test period of the 1986 issue and L had not ceased to use the facility, the $8 million issue is allocated to M under section 103(b)(15). This allocation causes the 1986 issue to exceed the $40 million limitation of section 103(b)(15) and the interest upon the issue to become taxable on and after October 1, 1986. However, if at least $3 million of the 1986 issue or of other issues allocated to M are redeemed as soon as reasonably practicable, and no later than 180 days after M's acquisition of L's stock then the 1986 issue would not exceed the $40 million limitation.

Example (4). The facts are the same as in *Example (3),* except the October 1, 1986, bonds were issued on January 1, 1985, the plant acquired with the proceeds of the issue was placed in service on January 1, 1985, and M had $39 million of prior outstanding obligations allocable to it on January 1, 1985. Because M and L became related to each other after the test period for the January 1, 1985, issue ended, M is not a test-period beneficiary, and the January 1, 1985, issue does not exceed the $40 million limitation of section 103(b)(15). However, if either M or L subsequently becomes a test-period beneficiary of an issue of obligations, then the outstanding principal amount of the January 1, 1985, issue and of the other issues allocable to M would be taken into account in applying the $40 million limitation to that issue.

§ 1.103-11 Bonds held by substantial users.

• ***Caution:*** Reg. § 1.103-11, following, was issued under Code section 103 before the related provisions of that Code section were deleted by P.L. 99-514 (10/22/86). Provisions similar to, but not necessarily identical to, the provisions deleted from Code section 103 now appear in Code section 147.

Caution: The Treasury has not yet amended Reg § 1.103-11 to reflect changes made by P.L. 100-647, P.L. 99-514.

(a) In general. Section 103(c) (4), (5), or (6) (relating respectively to interest on bonds to finance certain exempt facilities, interest on bonds to finance industrial parks, and the exemption for certain small issues of industrial development bonds) does not apply, as provided in section 103(c)(7), with respect to any obligation for any period during which such obligation is held either by a person who is a substantial user of the facilities with respect to which the proceeds of such obligation were used or by a related person (within the meaning of section 103(e)(6)(C) and paragraph (e) of § 1.103-10). Therefore, in such a case, interest paid on such an obligation is includable in the gross income of a substantial user (or related person) for any period during which such obligation is held by such user (or related person).

(b) Substantial user. In general, a substantial user of a facility includes any nonexempt person who regularly uses a part of such facility in his trade or business. However, unless a facility, or a part thereof, is constructed, reconstructed, or acquired specifically for a nonexempt person or persons, such a nonexempt person shall be considered to be a substantial user of a facility only if (1) the gross revenue derived by such user with respect to such facility is more than 5 percent of the total revenue derived by all users of such facility or (2) the amount of area of the facility occupied by such user is more than 5 percent of the entire usable area of the facility. Under certain facts and circumstances, where a nonexempt person has a contractual or preemptive right to the exclusive use of property or a portion of property, such person may be a substantial user of such property. A substantial user may also be a lessee or sublessee of all or any portion of the facility. A licensee or similar person may also be a substantial user where his use is regular and is not merely a casual, infrequent, or sporadic use of the facility. Absent special circumstances, individuals who are physically present on or in the facility as employees of a substantial user shall not be deemed to be substantial users.

(c) Examples. The application of section 103(c)(7) and this section are illustrated by the following examples:

Example (1). Pursuant to an arrangement with corporation X, County A issues $4 million of its bonds (an exempt small issue under section 103(c)(6)(A) pursuant to an election under section 103(c)(6)(D) and paragraph (b)(2) of § 1.103-10) and will use the proceeds to finance construction of a manufacturing facility which is to be leased to X for an annual rental of $500,000. X subleases space to a restaurant operator at an annual rental of $25,000 for the operation of a canteen and lunch counter for the convenience of X's employees. The canteen is required to be open at least 5 days each week (except holidays) from 8:30 a.m. to 5 p.m., and the lunch counter must be in operation during the noon hour. The canteen regularly sells cigarettes, candy, and soft drinks, and uses advertising displays and dispensers with product names. The space physically occupied and the amount of revenue derived by the restaurant operator are more than 5 percent of the respective amounts with respect to the entire facility. Both X and the restaurant operator are substantial users. However, absent special circumstances none of X's employees, the employees of the restaurant operator, or the customers or salesmen who regularly visit the premises to do business either with X or the restaurant operator are substantial users. Similarly, the manufacturers, distributors, and dealers of products sold in the canteen ordinarily are not substantial users.

Example (2). The facts are the same as in example (1) except that X rents food and beverage vending machines from a local dealer. The machines are regularly serviced by the local dealer under a contract with X. Title to and ownership of the machines are retained by the dealer. The local dealer is not deemed to be a substantial user if the revenue derived by such dealer from, and the space occupied by, such machines do not exceed 5 percent of the respective amounts with respect to the entire facility.

Example (3). City B proposes to issue $2 million of bonds which qualify as an exempt small issue under section 103(c)(6)(A) pursuant to an election under section 103(c)(6)(D) and paragraph (b)(2) of § 1.103-10 in order to construct a medical building for certain physicians and dentists. The facility will contain 30 offices to be leased on equal terms and for the same rental rates to each physician or dentist for use in his trade or business. Each physician or dentist will be a substantial user of the facility since the facility is being constructed specifically for such physicians and dentists. The result would be the same in the case of an office building for general commercial use.

Example (4). City C proposes to expand the airport it owns and operates with the proceeds of its bonds which qualify as bonds issued for an exempt facility under section 103(c)(4)(D) and paragraph (e) of § 1.103-8 and which are secured by a pledge of airport revenues. The airport is serviced by several commercial airlines which have long-term agreements with C for the use of runways, terminal space, and hangar and storage facilities. Each of the airlines either occupies more than 5 percent of the usable space of, or derives more than 5 percent of the revenue derived with respect to, the airport. C also leases counter and vehicle servicing and parking areas to car rental companies, space for restaurants, kiosks for the sale of newspapers and magazines, and space for the operations of a charter plane company. The latter operates its own planes, offers flying lessons and services, and stores private planes for local businesses and individuals. An airport limousine company has an exclusive franchise for passenger pickup at the terminal. Other taxi, transfer, freight, and express companies regularly deliver passengers and freight to the terminal but do not have space regularly assigned to them, nor do they have operating agreements with C. Various business concerns have advertising product displays in the terminal building. In addition to regular telephone service, coin-operated telephones, provided by the telephone company, are located throughout the terminal, at locations specified by C. None of the above exceed the 5-percent limitations of paragraph (b) of this section and the bond proceeds will not be specifically used for any of them. Only the commercial airlines, which violate the 5-percent limitations, are substantial users of the airport.

Example (5). City D issues $25 million of its revenue bonds and will use $10 million of the proceeds to finance construction of a sports facility which qualifies as an exempt facility under section 103(c)(4)(B) and paragraph (c) of § 1.103-8, $8 million to acquire and develop land as the site for an industrial park within the meaning of section 103(c)(5) and § 1.103-9, and $7 million to finance the construction of an office building to be used exclusively by the city, an exempt person. The revenues from the sports facility and the industrial park and all the facilities themselves will be the security for the bonds. The sports facility and the industrial park sites will be used in the trades or businesses of nonexempt persons. The bonds are industrial development bonds, but under the provisions of paragraph (a)(1) of § 1.103-8 and paragraph (a) of § 1.103-9, the interest on the $25 million issue will not be includable in gross income. However, the interest on bonds held shall be includable in the gross income of a substantial user of either the sports facility or the industrial park if such substantial user holds any of the obligations of the $25 million issue. The 5-percent limitations of paragraph (b) of this section are applied separately with respect to each facility.

Example (6). Authority E issues $4 million of bonds which qualify as an exempt small issue under section 103(c)(6)(A) pursuant to an election under section 103(c)(6)(D) and paragraph (b)(2) of § 1.103-10 in order to construct a bank building on the grounds of an airport. In addition, E issues $40 million to expand the airport. The bank will not derive revenue in excess of 5 percent of the revenue derived with respect to the airport nor will it occupy more than 5 percent of the usable area of such airport. The bank will be a substantial user of the bank building constructed with the proceeds of the $4 million issue since the facility was constructed specifically for the bank. However, the bank will not be a substantial user with respect to the airport because it does not exceed the 5-percent limitations of paragraph (b) of this section. Had E issued one issue of $44 million in order to expand the airport and construct a bank building, the bank would be a substantial user of the entire facility since the $44 million issue was being used to construct a facility a portion of which was specifically for the bank.

T.D. 7199, 7/31/72.

---

§ 1.103-16 Obligations of certain volunteer fire departments.

• ***Caution:*** Reg. § 1.103-16, following, was issued under Code section 103 before the related provisions of that Code section were deleted by P.L. 99-514 (10/22/86). Provisions similar to, but not necessarily identical to, the provisions deleted from Code section 103 now appear in Code section 150.

Caution: The Treasury has not yet amended Reg § 1.103-16 to reflect changes made by P.L. 100-647, P.L. 99-514.

(a) General rule. An obligation of a volunteer fire department issued after December 31, 1980, shall be treated as an obligation of a political subdivision of a State for purposes of section 103(a)(1) if—

(1) The volunteer fire department is a qualified volunteer fire department within the meaning of paragraph (b) of this section, and

(2) Substantially all of the proceeds of the issue of which the obligation is a part are to be used for the acquisition, construction, reconstruction, or improvement of a fire house or fire truck used or to be used by the qualified volunteer fire department.

An obligation of a volunteer fire department shall not be treated as an obligation of a political subdivision of a State for purposes of section 103(a)(1) unless both conditions set forth in this paragraph (a) are satisfied. Thus, for example, if an obligation is issued by an ambulance and rescue squad that is a qualified volunteer fire department as required by paragraph (a)(1) of this section, but substantially all of the proceeds of the issue of which the obligation is a part are to be used for the furnishing of emergency medical services, rather than for the purposes specified in paragraph (a)(2) of this section, the obligation shall not be treated as an obligation of a political subdivision of a State for purposes of section 103(a)(1).

(b) Definition of qualified volunteer fire department. For purposes of this section, the term "qualified volunteer fire department" means an organization—

(1) That is organized and operated to provide firefighting services or emergency medical services in an area within the jurisdiction of a political subdivision, and

(2) That is required to furnish firefighting services by written agreement with the political subdivision, and

(3) That serves persons in an area within the jurisdiction of the political subdivision that is not provided with any other firefighting services. The requirement of paragraph (b)(2) of this section that a qualified volunteer fire department be required to furnish firefighting services by written agreement with the political subdivision may be satisfied by an ordinance or statute of the political subdivision that establishes, regulates, or funds the volunteer fire department. A volunteer fire department does not fail to satisfy the requirement of paragraph (b)(3) of this section by furnishing or receiving firefighting services on an emergency basis, or by cooperative agreement with other fire departments, to or from areas outside of the area that the volunteer fire department is organized and operated to serve. The fact that tax revenues of a political subdivision served by a volunteer fire department contribute toward the support of the volunteer fire department in the form of salary, purchase of equipment, or other defrayment of expenses will not prevent the volunteer fire department from being a "qualified volunteer fire department" within the meaning of this paragraph (b). Moreover, an obligation of a volunteer fire department receiving such support may qualify as an obligation of a political subdivision within the meaning of section 103(a)(1) independently of section 103(i) and this section if the requirements of section 103(a)(1) are satisfied. See § 1.103-1(b) for rules relating to qualification under section 103(a)(1).

(c) "Substantially all" test. Substantially all of the proceeds of an issue are used for the purposes specified in paragraph (a)(2) of this section if 90 percent or more of the proceeds are so used. Thus, for example, if more than 10 percent of the proceeds of an obligation issued by a qualified volunteer fire department are used for the purchase of an ambulance or for rescue equipment not to be used in providing fire fighting services, interest on the obligation is not exempt from tax under section 103(i) and this section. In computing this percentage—

(1) Costs are allocated between providing a firehouse or firetruck and other uses of the proceeds on a pro rata basis; and

(2) The rules set forth in § 1.103-8(a)(1)(i), relating to amounts allocable to exempt and nonexempt uses and amounts chargeable to capital account, apply.

(d) Refunding issues. An obligation which is part of an issue issued by a qualified volunteer fire department after December 31, 1980, part or all of the proceeds of which issue are used directly or indirectly to pay principal, interest, call premium, or reasonable incidental costs of refunding a prior issue qualifies as an obligation of a political subdivision under section 103(i) and this section only if—

(1) The prior issue was issued by a qualified volunteer fire department;

(2) Substantially all of the proceeds of the prior issue were used for the purposes described in paragraph (a)(2) of this section;

(3) The prior issue was issued after December 31, 1980; and

(4) The refunding issue is issued not more than 180 days before the date on which the last obligation of the prior issue is discharged (within the meaning of § 1.103-13)(b)(11)).

(e) Examples. The provisions of this section may be illustrated by the following examples:

Example (1). The County M Volunteer Fire and Rescue Association provides firefighting, ambulance, and emergency medical services in County M. The board of county commissioners of County M contracts with the County M Volunteer Fire and Rescue Association for these services, and County M is not served by any other firefighting association. On August 1, 1981, the Association issues an obligation for funds to purchase a new fire truck, a new ambulance, and rescue equipment not to be used for fighting fires. Funds to be used for the purchase of the ambulance and rescue equipment constitute more than 10 percent of the proceeds of the obligation. Thus, substantially all of the proceeds of the obligations are not used for one of the purposes described in paragraph (a)(2) of this section. Although the County M Volunteer Fire and Rescue Association is a qualified volunteer fire department under paragraph (b) of this section because it provides firefighting and emergency medical services in an area within County M which is not provided with any other firefighting services and is required to provide these services by written agreement with County M, the August 1, 1981, obligation of County M Volunteer Fire and Rescue Association will not be treated as an obligation of a political subdivision of a State under section 103(i) and paragraph (a) of this section because substantially all of the proceeds of the obligation are not to be used for a purpose described in section 103(i)(l)(B) and paragraph (a)(2) of this section. Accordingly, interest on the August 1, 1981, obligation of County M Volunteer Fire and Rescue Association is not exempt from gross income under section 103(a)(1).

Example (2). County N Volunteer Fire Department provides firefighting services in County N by contract with the county, which is not served by any other firefighting association. On June 15, 1982, County N Volunteer Fire Department issues its obligation for funds to construct an addition to its firehouse to house a rescue squad, the rescue squad's vehicle, and rescue equipment not to be used in firefighting. Although the County N Volunteer Fire Department is a qualified volunteer fire department under paragraph (b) of this section, interest on its June 15, 1982, obligation will not be exempt from tax under section 103(i) and this section because the proceeds of this obligation will not be used for the purposes described in paragraph (a) of this section.

Example (3). The County O Volunteer Fire and Rescue Association provides firefighting, ambulance, and emergency medical services in County O. The board of county commissioners of County O contracts with the County O Volunteer Fire and Rescue Association for these services, and County O is not served by any other firefighting association. On September 1, 1983, the Association issues its obligations for funds to construct a new building to house its firefighting, ambulance, and rescue functions. Although the ambulance and rescue equipment will occupy space in the projected facility, the cost allocable on a pro rata basis to providing housing for the ambulance and rescue equipment represents less than 10 percent of the proceeds of the obligations. Thus, substantially all of the proceeds of the obligations are used for one of the purposes described in paragraph (a)(2) of this section. The County O Volunteer Fire and Rescue Association is a qualified volunteer fire department under paragraph (b) of this section because it provides firefighting and emergency medical services in an area within County O which is not provided with any other firefighting services and is required to provide these services by written agreement with County O. The obligations of County O Volunteer Fire and Rescue Association will be treated as obligations of a political subdivision of a State under section 103(i) and paragraph (a) of this section because the obligations are those of a qualified volunteer fire department and because substantially all of the proceeds of the obligations are to be used for a purpose described in section 103(i)(1)(B) and paragraph (a)(2) of this section. Accordingly, interest on the September 1, 1983, issue of obligations of County O Volunteer Fire and Rescue Association is exempt from gross income under section 103(a)(1).

T.D. 7901, 7/19/83.

---

§ 1.103(n)-1T Limitation on aggregate amount of private activity bonds (temporary).

Caution: The Treasury has not yet amended Reg § 1.103(n)-1T to reflect changes made by P.L. 100-647, P.L. 99-514.

Q-1. What does section 103(n) provide?

A-1. Interest on an issue of private activity bonds will not be tax exempt unless the aggregate amount of bonds issued pursuant to that issue, when added to (i) the aggregate amount of private activity bonds previously issued by the issuing authority during the calendar year and (ii) the portion of that year's private activity bond limit that the issuing authority has elected to carry forward to a future year, does not exceed the issuing authority's private activity bond limit for that calendar year. See A-4 of § 1.103(n)-4T with respect to private activity bonds issued under a carryforward election.

Q-2. What is the effective date of section 103(n)?

A-2. In general, section 103(n) applies to private activity bonds issued after December 31, 1983. Section 103(n) does not apply to any issue of obligations, however, if there was an inducement resolution (or other comparable preliminary approval) for the project before June 19, 1984, and the issue for such project is issued before January 1, 1985. An issue of obligations will be considered to be issued for the project pursuant to the inducement resolution in existence before June 19, 1984, to the extent that the nature, character, and purpose of the facility has not changed in any material way, and to the extent that the capacity of the facility has not increased materially; in addition, the issue of obligations must be for the same or a related initial owner, manager, or operator. See § 1.103-10(e) for the definition of related persons. See A-16 of § 1.103(n)-3T with respect to certain projects preliminarily approved before October 19, 1983. The transitional rules provided by section 631(c) of the Tax Reform Act of 1984 do not apply to section 103(n). See § 1.103-13(b)(6) for the rules relating to the date of issue of obligations.

Q-3. If an issue of private activity bonds causes the issuer's private activity bond limit to be exceeded, what is the effect on that issue?

A-3. If an issue of private activity bonds causes the issuing authority's private activity bond limit to be exceeded, no portion of that issue will be treated as obligations described in section 103(a), and interest paid on the issue will be subject to Federal income taxation.

Q-4. If an issue of private activity bonds causes the issuer's private activity bond limit to be exceeded, what is the effect on previous issues of private activity bonds that met the requirements of section 103(n) when issued?

A-4. Private activity bonds issued as part of an issue that met the private activity bond limit when issued continue to meet the requirements of section 103(n) even though a subsequent issue causes the aggregate amount of private activity bonds issued by an issuing authority to exceed the authority's private activity bond limit for the calendar year.

Example. The following example illustrates the provisions of A-3 and A-4 of this § 1.103(n)-1T:

Example. The State ceiling for State Z for 1986 is $200 million. City M, within the State, and State Z itself are authorized to issue private activity bonds. Under the allocation formula provided by the Governor of State Z, City M has a private activity bond limit of $50 million; the balance of the State ceiling is allocated to State Z. On June 1, 1986, City M issues a $75 activity bonds. On September 1, 1986, State Z issues a $150 million issue of private activity bonds. Based on these facts, the obligations of City M do not meet the requirements of section 103(n) since the aggregate amount of private activity bonds issued by City M in 1986 exceeded its private activity bond limit for such year; thus, such obligations are not described in section 103(a). That the State Z issue caused the aggregate amount of private activity bonds issued in the State during 1986 to exceed the State ceiling does not cause such obligations to fail to meet the requirements of section 103(n).

Q-5. What is the aggregate amount of private activity bonds issued as part of an issue?

A-5. The aggregate amount of private activity bonds issued as part of an issue is the face amount of the issue.

T.D. 7981, 10/2/84.

§ 1.103(n)-2T Private activity bond defined (temporary).

Caution: The Treasury has not yet amended Reg § 1.103(n)-2T to reflect changes made by P.L. 100-647, P.L. 99-514.

Q-1. What is the definition of the term "private activity bond"?

A-1. In general, for purposes of §§ 1.103(n)-1T through 1.103(n)-6T, the term "private activity bond" means any industrial development bond or student loan bond the interest on which is exempt from tax under section 103(a) (without application of section 103(n)). See § 1.103-7(b) for the definition of the term "industrial development bond." See A-17 of this § 1.103(n)-2T for the definition of the term "student loan bond." There are five exceptions to the general definition of the term "private activity bond"; the exceptions include the exception for the Texas Veterans Bond Program, the residential rental property exception, the exception for certain facilities described in section 103(b)(4)(C) or (D), and the refunding obligation exception. These exceptions are described in A-2 through A-16 of this § 1.103(n)-2T. In addition, the term "private activity bond" does not include any issue of obligations if there was an inducement resolution (or other comparable preliminary approval) for the project before June 19, 1984, and the issue for that project is issued before January 1, 1985. See A-2 of § 1.103(n)-1T.

Q-2. To which obligations does the exception for the Texas Veterans Bond Program apply?

A-2. The term "private activity bond" does not include general obligation bonds issued under the Texas Veterans Bond Program if the proceeds of the issue, other than an amount that is not a major portion of the proceeds, are used to make loans of up to $20,000 for the purchase of land for purposes authorized by such program as in effect on June 19, 1984. The use of the proceeds may be established by the affidavit of the veteran receiving the loan. For purposes of this exception to the definition of the term "private activity bond," the use of more than 25 percent of the proceeds of an issue of obligations will constitute the use of a major portion of such proceeds.

Q-3. To which obligations does the residential rental property exception apply?

A-3. The term "private activity bond" does not include any obligation issued to private projects for residential rental property (including property functionally related and subordinate to any such facility), as described in section 103(b)(4)(A) and § 1.103-8(b). In addition, the term "private activity bond" does not include any housing program obligation under section 11(b) of the United States Housing Act of 1937.

Q-4. To which obligations does the exception for certain facilities described in section 103(b)(4)(C) or (D) apply?

A-4. Section 103(n)(7)(C) provides that the term "private activity bond" does not include any obligation issued as part of an issue to provide convention or trade show facilities, as described in section 103(b)(4)(C) and § 1.103-8(d) (including property functionally related and subordinate to any such facilities), if the property so described is owned by, or on behalf of, a governmental unit. In addition, the term "private activity bond" does not include any obligation issued as part of an issue to provide airports, docks, wharfs, mass commuting facilities, or storage or training facilities directly related to any of the foregoing facilities, as described in section 103(b)(4)(D) and § 1.103-8(e) (including property functionally related and subordinate to any such facilities), if the property so described is owned by, or on behalf of, a governmental unit. See § 1.103-8(a)(3), in general, for the definition of the term "functionally related and subordinate." For purposes of this exception to the definition of the term "private activity bond," the term "mass commuting facilities" includes "qualified mass commuting vehicles," as defined in section 103(b)(9), that are associated with a mass commuting facility described in § 1.103-8(e)(2)(iv). Obligations issued as part of an issue to provide parking facilities, as described in section 103(b)(4)(D), are not excepted from the definition of the term "private activity bond;" however, parking facilities may be functionally related and subordinate to another facility described in section 103(b)(4)(C) or (D).

Q-5. When is property described in section 103(b)(4)(C) or (D) owned by, or on behalf of, a governmental unit?

A-5. In general, property described in section 103(b)(4)(C) or (D) will be considered to be owned by a governmental unit if a governmental unit is the owner of the property for Federal income tax purposes generally. See A-5 of § 1.103(n)-3T for the definition of the term "governmental unit". In general, property described in section 103(b)(4) (C) or (D) will be considered to be owned on behalf of a governmental unit if a constituted authority empowered to issue obligations on behalf of a governmental unit is the owner of the property for Federal income tax purposes generally. Whether the property is owned by, or on behalf of, a governmental unit will be determined on the basis of the facts and circumstances of each particular case. The fact that the governmental unit's or constituted authority's obligation to pay principal and interest on an obligation is limited to revenues from fees collected from users of the property provided with the proceeds of such obligation will not, in itself, cause such property to be treated as not owned by, or on behalf of, the governmental unit. In order to qualify for the exception described in section 103(n)(7)(C), the property must be owned by, or on behalf of, the governmental unit throughout the term of the issue. See A-10 of this § 1.103(n)-2T with respect to the consequences of a transfer of ownership.

Q-6. Will property described in section 103(b)(4)(C) or (D) that is leased to a non-governmental entity be treated as owned by, or on behalf of, a governmental unit if the lessee is the owner of the property for Federal income tax purposes generally solely by reason of the length of the lease?

A-6. If property, or any portion thereof, is leased to a non-governmental entity and if, for Federal income tax purposes generally, the lessee is the owner of the property solely by reason of the length of the lease, then, for purposes of §§ 1.103(n)-1T through 1.103(n)-6T (but not for other Federal income tax purposes, such as whether payments under the lease constitute deductible rental payments), the governmental unit will be treated as the owner of the property if the lessee elects not to claim depreciation or an investment credit with respect to such property. See A-7 of this § 1.103(n)-2T for the rules describing the method of making this election. For purposes of §§ 1.103(n)-1T through 1.103(n)-6T, the term "non-governmental entity" means a person other than a governmental unit or a constituted authority empowered to issue obligations on behalf of a governmental unit. The fact that a non-governmental entity lessee elects not to claim depreciation or an investment credit with respect to property does not, however, ensure that the property will be treated as owned by, or on behalf of a governmental unit for purposes of §§ 1.103(n)-1T through 1.103(n)-6T. Thus, for example, if the lessee is the owner of the property for Federal income tax purposes generally other than solely because of the length of the lease, the obligations issued as part of the issue are private activity bonds notwithstanding that the lessee elected not to claim depreciation or an investment credit with respect to the property.

Similarly, even if a governmental unit is the owner of property for Federal income tax purposes generally, the property will not be treated as owned by, or on behalf of, a governmental unit for purposes of §§ 1.103(n)-1T through 1.103(n)-6T if the lease under which such property is leased to a non-governmental entity provides for significant front end loading of rental accruals or payments. See A-12 of this § 1.103(n)-2T with respect to significant front end loading of rental accruals or payments.

Q-7. What must a lessee do in order to elect not to take depreciation or an investment credit with respect to property described in section 103(b)(4)(C) or (D)?

A-7. The lessee must make the election at the time the lease is executed. The election must include a description of the property with respect to which the election is being made; the name, address, and TIN of the issuing authority; the name, address, and TIN of the lessee; and the date and face amount of the issue the proceeds of which are to be used to provide the property. The election must be signed by the lessee, if a natural person, or by a duly authorized official of the lessee. The issuing authority must be provided with a copy of the election. The issuing authority and the lessee must retain copies of the election in their respective records for the entire term of the lease. In addition, the lease, and any publicly recorded document recorded in lieu of such lease, must state that neither the lessee nor any successor in interest under the lease may claim depreciation or an investment credit with respect to such property. This election may be made with respect to property whether or not such property otherwise would be eligible for depreciation or an investment tax credit. See section 7701(a)(41) for the definition of the term "TIN."

Q-8. Is the election not to claim depreciation or an investment credit revocable?

A-8. No, the election is irrevocable. In addition, the election is binding on all successors in interest under the lease regardless of whether the obligations remain outstanding. If a successor in interest claims depreciation or an investment credit with respect to property for which such an election has been made, such property will be considered transferred to a non-governmental entity. See A-10 of this § 1.103(n)-2T with respect to the consequences of such a transfer.

Q-9. Where obligations are issued to provide all or any portion of a facility described in section 103(b)(4)(C) or (D), must all of the property described in section 103(b)(4)(C) or (D) that is part of such facility be owned by, or on behalf of, a governmental unit in order for such obligations to qualify for the exception to the definition of the term "private activity bond" provided in section 103(n)(7)(C)?

A-9. Generally, yes. If obligations are issued to provide all or any portion of a facility described in section 103(b)(4)(C) or (D), the obligations comprising such issue will not qualify for the exception to the definition of the term "private activity bond" provided in section 103(n)(7)(C) unless all of the property described in section 103(b)(4)(C) or (D) that is part of (or functionally related and subordinate to) the facility being financed is owned by, or on behalf of, a governmental unit throughout the term of the issue. For this purpose, the facility being financed will be construed to include the entire airport, dock, etc., under consideration and not merely the part of the facility being provided with the proceeds of the issue. For example, the term facility, when used in reference to an airport, will be considered to include all property that is part of, or included in, that airport under § 1.103-8(e)(2)(ii)(a), including all property functionally related and subordinate thereto under § 1.103-8(a)(3) and (e)(2)(ii)(b). Thus, if the proceeds of an issue are used to provide a hangar at an airport described in section 103(b)(4)(D), that airport is considered as being financed with such issue, and if any portion of that airport, including property functionally related and subordinate thereto, is treated as owned by a non-governmental entity, that issue does not qualify for the exception of the definition of the term "private activity bond" provided in section 103(n)(7)(C).

There are three exceptions to this rule, however. First, if any property otherwise would be considered part of the facility financed and such property was not provided with proceeds of any obligation described in section 103(a), such property will not be considered part of the facility being financed.

Second, if any property otherwise would be considered part of the facility being financed and such property was part of such facility on or before October 5, 1984, such property will not be considered part of the facility being financed. For this purpose, property will be considered part of the facility on or before October 5, 1984, if any person was under a binding contract to acquire or construct such property to be a part of such facility on October 5, 1984.

Third, property will not be considered part of the facility being financed if such property (i) is land, a building, a structural component of a building, or other structure (other than tangible personal property (other than an air conditioning or heating unit)) and such property is not physically supported by, does not physically support, and is not physically connected to any property provided with the proceeds of obligations that qualify for the exception to the definition of the term "private activity bond" provided in section 103(n)(7)(C), or (ii) is tangible personal property (other than an air conditioning or heating unit). For this purpose, contiguous parcels of land will not be considered to support, to be supported by, or to be physically connected to each other, and insignificant physical connections (such as a connection by a sidewalk) will be disregarded. For purposes of this A-9, the term "tangible personal property" shall have the meaning given to it under section 48(a)(1)(A) and § 1.48-1(c).

*Examples.*The following examples illustrate the provisions of A-9 of this § 1.103(n)-2T:

Example (1). On January 1, 1986, Governmental Unit M issues industrial development bonds to provide an airport, as described in section 103(b)(4)(D), which will consist of land, runways, a terminal and a functionally related and subordinate hotel. The hotel will be leased to N, a non-governmental entity. The lease does not call for significant front end loading of rental accruals or payments. For Federal income tax purposes generally, M will own the entire airport except that N will be the owner of the hotel solely by reason of the length of the lease. N properly elects not to claim depreciation of an investment credit with respect to the hotel. The industrial development bonds are not private activity bonds.

Example (2). The facts are the same as in Example (1) except that N does not make the election and claims depreciation with respect to the hotel. The entire issue of industrial development bonds is treated as an issue of private activity bonds.

Example (3). The facts are the same as in Example (2) except that the hotel is provided other than with the proceeds of an obligation described in section 103(a). The issue for the remainder of the airport qualifies for the exception to the definition of the term "private activity bond" provided in section 103(n)(7)(C).

Example (4). The facts are the same as in Example (2) except that the hotel, including the hotel parking lot, the hotel grounds, and the parcel of land on which they rest, are provided with a separate issue of industrial development bonds. There are no significant connections between the hotel and the airport. The issue for the hotel is an issue of private activity bonds. The issue for the remainder of the airport qualifies for the exception to the definition of the term "private activity bonds" provided in section 103(n)(7)(C).

Example (5). The facts are the same as Example (4) except that the hotel is constructed upon land provided with the proceeds of the issue used to provide the remainder of the airport. Both issues are treated as issues of private activity bonds.

Example (6). On June 30, 1983, construction began on the City NN airport, which consists of land, runways, a terminal, and hangars. Corporation XX (a non-governmental entity) owns for Federal income tax purposes generally several of the hangars, which it financed with obligations described in section 103(a) issued on June 30, 1983. On March 1, 1985, at a time when XX still owns the hangars, City NN issues an issue of obligations described in section 103(b)(4)(D) to enlarge the terminal at the City NN airport. City NN will own the addition to the terminal for Federal income tax purposes generally. The obligations comprising the March 1, 1985, issue will not be private activity bonds.

Q-10. What are the consequences if a governmental unit ceases to be treated as owning property described in section 103(b)(4)(C) or (D) where the property was provided by obligations that were not private activity bonds on the date of issue due to the exception provided in section 103(n)(7)(C)?

A-10. The obligations outstanding on the date such ownership ceases are private activity bonds and are treated as if they are the last private activity bonds issued by the issuer in the calendar year in which the transfer of ownership occurs. Thus, if the aggregate amount of bonds issued pursuant to such issue, when added to the aggregate amount of the other private activity bonds actually issued or treated as issued under this A-10 by the issuer during such year and the amount of any carryforward elections made during the year, exceeds the issuer's private activity bond limit for such year, the obligations are not described in section 103(a) as of the date on which transfer of ownership occurs; if such obligations do not comply with the requirements of section 103(n), the obligations will be treated as not described in section 103(a) as of the date such ownership ceases. However, if on the date of issue the issuer intended to transfer ownership of such property to a non-governmental entity during the term of the issue, then the obligations are treated as the last private activity bonds actually issued or treated as issued under this A-10 by the issuer during the year in which such obligations were actually issued; if such obligations do not comply with the requirements of section 103(n), the obligations will be treated as not described in section 103(a) as of the date of issue. The exception to the definition of the term "private activity bond" for facilities described in section 103(b)(4)(C) and (D) only applies if the property is owned by, or on behalf of, a governmental unit while all or any part of the issue or any refunding issue remains outstanding.

If all or a portion of the property is sold to a non-governmental entity for its fair market value and all of the proceeds from the sale (except for a de minimis amount less than $5,000) are used within six months to redeem outstanding obligations, the obligations will not be treated as private entity bonds.

Q-11. What are the consequences if private activity bonds are issued to provide additions to a facility that was provided with obligations that were not private activity bonds when issued by virtue of the exception provided in section 103(n)(7)(C) and such additions are not treated as owned by a governmental unit?

A-11. In order to qualify for the exception to the definition of the term "private activity bond" for obligations described in section 103(b)(4)(C) or (D), all of the property described in section 103(b)(4) (C) or (D) that is part of the facility provided with the proceeds generally must be owned by, or on behalf of, a governmental unit. See A-9 of this § 1.103 (n)-2T. However, if the proceeds of an issue of private activity bonds are used to make additions to a facility (other than additions that are not considered to be part of the facility under A-9 of this § 1.103(n)-2T) that was provided with another issue of industrial development bonds that were not private activity bonds when issued by virtue of the exception provided in section 103(n)(7)(C), then the prior issue will not cease to qualify for that exception. Nevertheless, for purposes of determining the aggregate amount of private activity bonds issued during the year that the issue to provide the addition to the previously financed facility is issued, the portion of the prior issue outstanding on the date of issue of the issue to provide the addition will be treated as part of the issue to provide the addition.

Example. The following example illustrates the provisions of A-11 of this § 1.103(n)-2T:

Example. On March 1, 1986, City P issues a $100 million issue of industrial development bonds to provide an airport, as described in section 103(b)(4)(D). City P uses substantially all of the proceeds to acquire land and to construct runways and a terminal on that land. No other property is constructed on the land. City P is the owner of the land and the terminal for Federal income tax purposes generally. Thus, the obligations comprising the March 1, 1986, issue are not private activity bonds when issued. On September 1, 1988, City P leases a portion of the land adjacent to the terminal to Corporation V (a non-governmental entity) under a true lease for Federal income tax purposes. City P's private activity bond limit for 1988 is $100 million, and as of September 30, 1988, City P has not issued any private activity bond during 1988. On September 30, 1988, City P issues a $20 million issue of industrial development bonds, the proceeds of which are to be used to construct a hotel that is functionally related and subordinate to the airport. The hotel is to be constructed on the land that P leased to Corporation V. The hotel will be owned by Corporation V for Federal income tax purposes generally. On September 30, 1988, the outstanding face amount of the March 1, 1986, issue is $100 million. Although the obligations comprising the March 1, 1986, issue will not become private activity bonds as a result of the subsequent issue, on September 30, 1988, City P is treated as issuing a $120 million issue of private activity bonds. Since that amount exceeds City P's private activity bond limit, the $20 million issue of private activity bonds issued on September 30, 1988, does not meet the requirements of section 103(n). In addition, any subsequent issuance of private activity bonds by City P during 1988 will fail to meet the requirements of section 103(n). The March 1, 1986, issue continues to be described in section 103(a).

Q-12. Section 103(n)(7)(C)(iv) provides that the exception for certain facilities described in section 103(b)(4)(C) or (D) shall not apply in any case where the facility is leased under a lease that has "significant front end loading of rental accruals or payments" mean?

A-12. Where a lease requires rental payments that are significantly higher in the early years of the lease than in later years, the lease calls for significant front end loading of rental accruals or payments. A lease that provides for flat rental payments during the entire lease term does not violate the prohibition against significant front end loading of rent. In addition, a lease may provide for adjustments in rent for inflation or deflation, provided that such adjustments are to be made on the basis of a generally recognized price index. In addition, a lease may provide that rental payments are to be determined, in whole or part, based on a percentage of income, production, etc., provided that the percentage rate is kept constant (or increases) over the term of the lease and that the threshold, if any, above which the percentage applies is kept constant (or decreases) over the term of the lease. Thus, for example, a lease that requires rental payments throughout the term of the lease of $100,000 per year plus 5 percent of the gross income from the facility in excess of $500,000 does not violate the prohibition against significant front end loading of rent.

*Examples.*The following examples illustrate the provisions of A-4 through A-12 of this § 1.103(n)-2T:

Example (1). On February 1, 1985, County Z issues obligations with a term of 30 years. Substantially all of the proceeds of the obligations are to be used to provide a trade show facility as described in section 103(b)(4)(C). Z leases the entire facility to Corporation S. For Federal income tax purposes generally, S is treated as the owner of the facility solely by reason of the length of the lease. The lease provides that the lessee will elect not to claim depreciation or an investment credit with respect to the facility and that S will provide Z with a copy of the election. S makes the election, retains it in its records, and provides County Z with a copy. The lease provides that neither the lessee nor any successor in interest will claim a deduction for depreciation or an investment credit with respect to such facility. The obligations are not private activity bonds on the date of issue, provided that the lease does not call for significant front end loading of rental accruals or payments.

Example (2). The facts are the same as in Example (1) except that on February 1, 1986, S assigns the lease to Corporation T. For its taxable year ending March 31, 1986, Corporation T claims depreciation with respect to the trade show facility. The obligations outstanding on the date Corporation T claims depreciation on its Federal income tax return are treated as the last private activity bonds actually issued or treated as issued by County Z during 1986, and such obligations must comply with the requirements of section 103(n). In addition, Corporation T is not entitled to claim depreciation or an investment credit with respect to the trade show facility during the balance of the term of the lease and will be subject to the applicable penalties for so claiming depreciation.

Example (3). The facts are the same as in Example (1) except that the obligations are redeemed on January 31, 1998; on January 31, 1999, S assigns the lease to Corporation X; and on its Federal income tax return for calendar year 1999, Corporation X claims depreciation with respect to the facility. The obligations are not private activity bonds provided that the lease does not call for significant front end loading of rental accruals or payments. However, X is not entitled to claim depreciation or an investment credit with respect to the trade show facility during the balance of the term of the lease and will be subject to the applicable penalties for so claiming those items.

Q-13. To which obligations does the refunding obligation exception apply?

A-13. The term "private activity bond" does not include any refunding obligation to the extent specified in this A-13. The term "refunding obligation" means an obligation that is part of an issue of obligations the proceeds of which are used to pay any principal or interest on any other issue of obligations described in section 103(a) (referred to as the prior issue). The term "refunding obligation" does not include any obligations issued more than 180 days before the prior issue is discharged ("advance refundings"). The exception for refunding obligations only applies to the extent that the aggregate amount of the refunding issue does not exceed the outstanding face amount of the prior issue, or portion thereof, being refunded. Thus, for example, in the case of an obligation part of the proceeds of which are to be used to refund a prior issue of private activity bonds and part of the proceeds of which are to be used to provide a pollution control facility under section 103(b)(4)(F), those proceeds to be used to refund all or any part of the principal amount of the prior issue are not the proceeds of a private activity bond; the balance of the proceeds are the proceeds of a private activity bond. The refunding obligation exception does not apply to obligations to the extent that amounts are used to pay the costs of issuing refunding obligations. If an issue of obligations consists of both obligations that qualify for the refunding obligation exception and private activity bonds that do not meet the requirements of section 103(n), the entire issue is treated as consisting of obligations not described in section 103(a).

Q-14. Does the refunding obligation exception apply to obligations issued to refund a prior issue of student loan bonds?

A-14. In the case of any student loan bond, the refunding obligation exception applies only if, in addition to the requirements stated in A-13 of this § 1.103(n)-2T, the maturity date of the funding obligation is not later than the later of (i) the maturity date of the obligation to be refunded, or (ii) the date 17 years after the date on which the refunded obligation was issued (or, in the case of a series of refundings, the date on which the original obligation was issued).

Q-15. What is the "maturity date" of an obligation?

A-15. For purposes of section 103(n), the "maturity date" of an obligation is the date on which interest ceases to accrue and the obligation may either be paid or redeemed without penalty. The date is determined without regard to optional redemption dates (including those at the option of holders). If the issuer is required by the obligations or the indenture to redeem portions of obligations or to make payments of principal with respect to obligations in specified amounts and at specified times, such mandatory redemptions or payments shall be treated as separate obligations.

Q-16. Where private activity bonds are refunded with other obligations described in section 103(a), does the refunding obligation exception apply to the extent that the aggregate amount of the refunding obligations exceeds the outstanding principal amount of the prior issue due to the use of a portion of the proceeds of the refunding issue to fund a reasonably required reserve or replacement fund?

A-16. Whether the prior issue was issued prior to January 1, 1984, or thereafter, the refunding obligation exception to the definition of the term "private activity bond" only applies to the extent that the aggregate amount of the refunding obligation does not exceed the outstanding principal amount of the prior issue. Thus, the additional obligations issued to provide for a reasonably required reserve or replacement fund are private activity bonds.

Q-17. What is a "student loan bond"?

A-17. The term "student loan bond" means an obligation that is issued as part of an issue all or a major portion of the proceeds of which are to be used directly or indirectly to finance loans to individuals for educational expenses. For purposes of this A-17, the use of more than 25 percent of the proceeds of an issue of obligations to finance loans to individuals for educational expenses will constitute the use of a major portion of such proceeds in such manner.

T.D. 7981, 10/2/84.

---

§ 1.103(n)-3T Private activity bond limit (temporary).

Caution: The Treasury has not yet amended Reg § 1.103(n)-3T to reflect changes made by P.L. 107-16, P.L. 100-647, P.L. 99-514.

Q-1. What is the "State ceiling"?

A-1. In general, the State ceiling applicable to each State and the District of Columbia for any calendar year prior to 1987 shall be the greater of $200 million or an amount equal to $150 multiplied by the State's (or the District of Columbia's) population. In the case of any territory or possession of the United States, the State ceiling for any calendar year prior to 1987 shall be an amount equal to $150 multiplied by the population of such territory or possession. In the case of calendar years after 1986, the two preceding sentences shall be applied by substituting "$100" for "$150." In the case of any State that had an excess bond amount for 1983, the State ceiling for calendar year 1984 shall be the sum of the State ceiling determined under the general rule plus 50 percent of the excess bond amount for 1983. The excess bond amount for 1983 is the excess (if any) of (i) the aggregate amount of private activity bonds issued by issuing authorities in such State during the first 9 months of calendar year 1983 multiplied by 4/3, over (ii) the State ceiling determined under the general rule for 1984. For purposes of determining the State ceiling amount applicable to any any State for calendar year 1984, an issuer may rely upon the State ceiling amount published by the Treasury Department for such calender year. However, an issuer may compute a different excess bond amount for 1983 where the issuer or the State in which the issuer is located has made a more accurate determination of the amount of private activity bonds issued by issuing authorities in the issuer's State during 1983. See A-7 of this § 1.103(n)-3T for rules regarding a State containing constitutional home rule cities.

Q-2. What is the private activity bond limit for a State agency?

A-2. Under section 103(n)(2) the private activity bond limit for any agency of the State authorized to issue private activity bonds for any calendar year shall be 50 percent of the State ceiling for such year unless the State provides for a different allocation. For this purpose, the State is considered an agency. See, however, A-17 of this § 1.103(n)-3T with respect to the penalty for failure to comply with the requirements of section 631(a)(3) of the Tax Reform Act of 1984.

Q-3. How is private activity bond limit determined where a State has more than one agency?

A-3. If any State has more than one agency (including the State) authorized to issue private activity bonds, all such agencies shall be treated as a single agency for purposes of determining the aggregate private activity bond limit available for all such agencies. Each of the State agencies is treated as having jurisdiction over the entire State. Therefore, under A-8 of this § 1.103(n)-3T the aggregate private activity bond limit for all the State agencies is allocated to the State since it possesses the broadest sovereign powers of any of the State agencies. Each other State agency's private activity bond limit is zero until it is assigned part of the private activity bond limit of another governmental unit pursuant to these regulations.

Q-4. What is a State agency?

A-4. A State agency is an agency authorized by a State to issue private activity bonds on behalf of the State. In addition, a special purpose governmental unit that derives its sovereign powers from the State and may exercise its sovereign powers throughout the State is a State agency. See A-5 of this § 1.103(n)-3T for the definition of the term "special purpose governmental unit." The term "State agency" does not include issuing authorities empowered by a State at the request of another governmental unit within the State to issue private activity bonds to provide facilities within the jurisdiction of such other governmental unit. For example, if County O requests the legislature of State P to create an issuing authority empowered to issue obligations to provide pollution control facilities in County O, the authority is not a State agency.

*Examples.*The following examples illustrate the provisions of A-3 and A-4 of this § 1.103(n)-3T:

Example (1). For 1987 State Q has a State ceiling of $200 million. Neither the Governor nor the legislature of State Q has provided a formula for allocating the State ceiling different from that provided by section 103(n)(2) and (3). State Q has authorized the following State agencies to issue private activity bonds on its behalf: Authority M, Authority N, and Authority O. The aggregate private activity bond limit available for State agencies of State Q is $100 million. As of January 1, 1987, none of this aggregate private activity bond limit has been assigned to any of Authorities M, N, or O. On January 1, 1987, Authority M issues $25 million of private activity bonds. During 1987, the duly authorized official designated by State Q to allocate the aggregate private activity bond limit among the three authorities does not allocate any of the State's private activity bond limit to Authority M. The January 1, 1987, issue does not meet the requirements of section 103(n) since Authority M has no private activity bond limit for 1987.

Example (2). Under the laws of State U, only the State legislature can create constituted authorities empowered to issue private activity bonds on behalf of governmental units within State U. Authority R was created by the State U legislature at the request of County X. Authority R was created by the State U legislature at the request of County X. Authority R is a constituted authority empowered to issue private activity bonds on behalf of County X to provide facilities located in County X. Authority S was created by the legislature to issue private activity bonds to provide pollution control facilities throughout the State. Authority S is a State agency as defined in A-4 of this § 1.103(n)-3T. Authority R it is not a State agency.

Q-5. What is a governmental unit?

A-5. The term "governmental unit" has the meaning given such term by § 1.103-1. For purposes of §§ 1.103(n)-1T through 1.103(n)-6T, a governmental unit is either a general purpose governmental unit or a special purpose governmental unit. The term "general purpose governmental unit" means a State, territory, possession of the United States, the District of Columbia, or any general purpose political subdivision thereof. The term "general purpose political subdivision" denotes any division of government that possesses the right to exercise police powers, the power to tax, and the power of eminent domain and that is governed, at least in part, by popularly elected officials. (*e.g.,*county, city, town, township, parish, village). The term "special purpose governmental unit" means any governmental unit as defined in § 1.103-1 other than a general purpose governmental unit. For example, a sewer authority with the power of eminent domain but without police powers is a special purpose governmental unit. A constituted authority empowered to issue private activity bonds on behalf of a governmental unit is not a governmental unit.

Q-6. What is the private activity bond limit for a general purpose governmental unit other than a State, the District of Columbia, a territory, or a possession?

A-6. The private activity bond limit for any such general purpose governmental unit for any calendar year is an amount equal to the general purpose governmental unit's proportionate share of 50 percent of the State ceiling amount for such calendar year. See A-10 of this § 1.103(n)-3T with respect to the rules for providing a different allocation. The proportionate share of a general purpose governmental unit is an amount that bears the same ratio to 50 percent of the State ceiling for such year as the population of the jurisdiction of such general purpose governmental unit bears to the population of the entire State, District of Columbia, territory, or possession in which its jurisdiction falls. See however, A-17 of this § 1.103(n)-3T with respect to the penalty for failure to comply with the requirements of section 631(a)(3) of the Tax Reform Act of 1984. See A-9 of this § 1.103(n)-3T with respect to the private activity bond limit of issuing authorities other than general purpose governmental units.

Q-7. What is the private activity bond limit for a general purpose governmental unit in a State with one or more constitutional homes rule cities?

A-7. The private activity bond limit for a constitutional home rule city for any calendar year is an amount equal to the constitutional home rule city's proportionate share of 100 percent of the State ceiling amount for the calendar year. The proportionate share of a constitutional home rule city is an amount that bears the same ratio to the State ceiling for such year as the population of the jurisdiction of such constitutional home rule city bears to the population of the entire State. The private activity bond limit for issuers other than constitutional home rule cities is computed in the manner described in A-2 through A-6 of this § 1.103(n)-3T, except that in computing the private activity bond limit for issuers other than such constitutional home rule cities, the State ceiling amount for any calendar year shall be reduced by the aggregate private activity bond limit for all constitutional home rule cities in the State. The term "constitutional home rule city" means, with respect to any calendar year, any political subdivision of a State that, under a State constitution that was adopted in 1970 and effective on July 1, 1971, had home rule powers on the first day of the calendar year. See, however, A-17 of this § 1.103(n)-3T with respect to the penalty for failure to comply with the requirements of section 631(a)(3) of the Tax Reform Act of 1984.

Q-8. How is the private activity bond limit of an issuing authority determined under section 103(n)(3) when there are overlapping jurisdictions?

A-8. If an area is within the jurisdiction of two or more governmental units, that area will be treated as only within the jurisdiction of the governmental unit having jurisdiction over the smallest geographical area. However, the governmental unit with jurisdiction over the smallest geographical area may enter into a written agreement to allocate all or a designated portion of such overlapping area to the governmental unit having jurisdiction over the next smallest geographical area. Where two or more issuing authorities, whether governmental units or constituted authorities, have authority to issue private activity bonds and both issuing authorities have jurisdiction over the identical geographical area, that area will be treated as only within the jurisdiction of the one having the broadest sovereign powers. However, the issuing authority having the broadest sovereign powers may enter into a written agreement to allocate all or a designated portion of such area to the one with the narrower sovereign powers. All written agreements entered into pursuant to this A-8 must be retained by the assignee in its records for the term of all private activity bonds it issues in each calendar year to which such agreement applies. See A-9 of this § 1.103(n)-3T with respect to the private activity bond limit of issuing authorities other than general purpose governmental units.

Q-9. What is the private activity bond limit of an issuing authority (other than a State agency) that is not a general purpose governmental unit?

A-9. A constituted authority empowered to issue private activity bonds on behalf of a governmental unit is treated as having jurisdiction over the same geographical area as the governmental unit on behalf of which it is empowered to issue private activity bonds. Since a governmental unit has broader sovereign powers than a constituted authority empowered to issue private activity bonds on its behalf, a constituted authority has a private activity bond limit under section 103(n)(2) and (3) of zero. Similarly, a special purpose governmental unit is treated for purposes of section 103(n) as having jurisdiction over the same geographical area as that of the general purpose governmental unit or units from which the special purpose governmental unit derives its sovereign powers. Since a general purpose governmental unit has broader sovereign powers than a special purpose governmental unit, a special purpose governmental unit has a private activity bond limit under section 103(n)(2) and (3) of zero. An issuer of qualified scholarship funding bonds, as defined in section 103(e), is treated for purposes of section 103(n) as issuing on behalf of the State or political subdivision or subdivisions that requested its organization or its exercise of power to issue bonds. See A-13 and A-14 of this § 103(n)-3T with respect to assignments of private activity bond limit. For purposes of §§ 1.103(n)-1T through 1.103(n)-6T, a special purpose governmental unit shall be considered to derive its authority from the smallest general purpose governmental unit that—

(i) Enacts a specific law (e.g., a provision of a State constitution, charter, or statute) by or under which the special purpose governmental unit is created, or

(ii) Otherwise empowers, approves, or requests the creation of the special purpose governmental unit, or

(iii) Appoints members to the governing body of the special purpose governmental unit, and within which general purpose governmental unit falls the entire area in which such special purpose governmental unit may exercise its sovereign powers. If no one general purpose governmental unit meets such criteria (e.g., a regional special purpose governmental unit that exercises its sovereign powers within three counties pursuant to a separate ordinance adopted by each such county), such special purpose governmental unit shall be considered to derive its sovereign powers from each of the general purpose governmental units comprising the combination of smallest general purpose governmental units within which falls the entire area in which such special purpose governmental unit may exercise its sovereign powers and each of which meets (i), (ii), or (iii) above.

Q-10. Does the issue comply with the requirements of section 103(n) under the following circumstances? Based on the most recent estimate of the resident population of State Y published by the Bureau of the Census before the beginning of 1988, the State ceiling for State Y is $200 million. Based on the same estimate, the population of City Q is one-fourth of the population of State Y. No part of the geographical area within the jurisdiction of City Q is within the jurisdiction of any other governmental unit with jurisdiction over a smaller geographical area. There are no constitutional home rule cities in State Y. Neither the Governor nor the legislature of State Y has provided a different formula for allocating the State ceiling than that provided by section 103(n)(2) and (3); thus, City Q's private activity bond limit for 1988 is $25 million (.25 × .50 × $200 million). As of March 1, 1988, City Q has issued $15 million of private activity bonds during calendar year 1988, none of which were issued pursuant to a carryforward election made in a prior year. On March 1, 1988, City Q will issue $5 million of private activity bonds to provide a pollution control facility as described in section 103(b)(4)(F). C, a duly authorized official of City Q responsible for issuing the bonds, provides a statement that will be included in the bond indenture or a related document providing that—

(i) Under section 103(n)(2) and (3) of the Internal Revenue Code, City Q has a private activity bond limit of $25 million for calendar year 1988 (.25 × .50 × $200 million), none of which has been assigned to it by another governmental unit,

(ii) State Y has not provided a different method of allocating the State ceiling.

(iii) City Q has not assigned any portion of its private activity bond limit to a constituted authority empowered to issue private activity bonds on its behalf, or to any other governmental unit,

(iv) City Q has not elected to carry forward any of its private activity bond limit for 1988 to another calendar year, nor has City Q in any prior year made a carryforward election for the pollution control facility.

(v) The aggregate amount of private activity bonds issued by City Q during 1988 is $15 million, and

(vi) The issuance of $5 million of private activity bonds on March 1, 1988, will not violate the requirements of section 103(n) and the regulations thereunder.

In addition, C provides the certification described in section 103(n)(12)(A).

A-10. Based on these facts, the issue meets the requirements of section 103(n) and §§ 1.103(n)-1T through 1.103(n)-6T. See § 1.103-13(b)(8) for the definition of the terms "bond indenture" and "related documents."

Q-11. May a State provide a different formula for allocating the state ceiling?

A-11. A State, by law enacted at any time, may provide a different formula for allocating the State ceiling among the governmental units in the State (other than constitutional home rule cities) having authority to issue private activity bonds, subject to the limitation provided in A-12 of this § 1.103(n)-3T. The governor of a State may proclaim a different formula for allocating the State ceiling among the governmental units in such State having authority to issue private activity bonds. The authority of the governor to proclaim a different formula shall not apply after the earlier of (i) the first day of the first calendar year beginning after the legislature of the State has met in regular session for more than 60 days after July 18, 1984, and (ii) the effective date of any State legislation dealing with the allocation of the State ceiling. If, on or before either date, the governor of any State exercises the authority to provide a different allocation, such allocation shall be effective until the date specified in (ii) of the immediately preceding sentence. Unless otherwise provided in a State constitutional amendment or by a law changing the home rule provisions adopted in the manner provided by the State constitution, the allocation of that portion of the State ceiling that is allocated to any constitutional home rule city may not be changed by the governor or State legislature unless such city agrees to such different allocation.

Q-12. Where a State provides an allocation formula different from that provided in section 103(n)(2) and (3), which allocation formula applies to obligations issued prior to the adoption of the different allocation formula?

A-12. Where a State provides a different allocation formula, the determination as to whether a particular bond issue meets the requirements of section 103(n) will be based upon the allocation formula in effect at the time such bonds were issued. The amount that may be reallocated pursuant to the later allocation formula is limited to the State ceiling for such year reduced by the amount of private activity bonds issued under the prior allocation formula in effect for such year.

Q-13. May an issuing authority assign a portion of its private activity bond limit to another issuing authority if the governor or legislature has not provided for an allocation formula different from that provided in section 103(n)(2) and (3)?

A-13. Except as provided in this A-13 or in A-8, A-14, or A-15 of this § 1.103(n)-3T, no issuing authority may assign, directly or indirectly, all or any portion of its private activity bond limit to any other issuing authority, and no such attempted assignment will be effective. However, a general purpose governmental unit may assign a portion of its private activity bond limit to (i) a constituted authority empowered to issue private activity bonds on behalf of the assigning governmental unit, and (ii) a special purpose governmental unit deriving sovereign powers from the governmental unit making the assignment. In addition, a State may assign a portion of its private activity bond limit to a constituted authority empowered to issue private activity bonds on behalf of any governmental unit within such State and to any governmental unit within such State. Finally, an issuing authority that is assigned all or a portion of the private activity bond limit of a governmental unit pursuant to the immediately preceding two sentences may assign such amount or any part thereof to the governmental unit from which it received the assignment. None of these permissible types of assignments shall be effective, however, unless made in writing by a duly authorized official of the governmental unit making the assignment and a record of the assignment is maintained by the assignee for the term of all private activity bonds it issues in each calendar year to which such assignment applies. None of these permissible types of assignments shall be effective if made retroactively; provided, however, that retroactive assignments may be made during 1984. In addition, except as provided in A-15 of this § 1.103(n)-3T, a purported assignment by a governmental unit of a portion of its private activity bond limit to an issuing authority will be ineffective to the extent that private activity bonds issued by such authority provide facilities not located within the jurisdiction of the governmental unit making the assignment, unless the sole beneficiary of the facility is the governmental unit attempting to make the assignment. Similarly, except as provided in A-15 of this § 1.103(n)-3T, a governmental unit may not allocate a portion of its private activity bond limit to an issue of obligations to provide a facility not located within the jurisdiction of that governmental unit unless the sole beneficiary of the facility is the governmental unit attempting to allocate its private activity bond limit to the issue. If an issuing authority issues an issue of obligations a portion of the proceeds of which are to be used to provide a facility not within its jurisdiction other than one described in the immediately preceding sentence, that issue will not meet the requirements of section 103(n) unless an issuing authority within the jurisdiction of which the facility is to be located specifically allocates a portion of its private activity bond limit to such issue equal to the amount of proceeds to be used to provide such facility.

Q-14. May an issuing authority assign a portion of its private activity bond limit to another issuing authority if the governor or legislature has provided for an allocation formula different from that provided in section 103(n)(2) and (3)?

A-14. Yes, under certain conditions. In providing a different formula for allocating the State ceiling, a State may permit an issuing authority to assign all or a portion of its private activity bond limit to other issuing authorities within the State, provided that such assignment is made in writing and a record of that assignment is maintained by the assignee in its records for the term of all private activity bonds it issues in each calendar year to which such assignment applies and a record of that assignment is maintained during such period by the public official responsible for making allocations of the State ceiling to issuing authorities within the State. The preceding sentence will only apply where the different formula expressly permits such assignments. Notwithstanding this A-14, no assignments may be made to regional authorities without compliance with the provisions of A-15 of this § 1.103(n)-3T.

Q-15. ; May a general purpose governmental unit assign a portion of its private activity bond limit to a regional authority empowered to issue private activity bonds on behalf of two or more general purpose governmental units?

A-15. Yes, under certain conditions. In order for an issue of private activity bonds issued by such a regional authority to meet the requirements of section 103(n), each of the governmental units on behalf of which the regional authority issues private activity bonds must assign to the regional authority a portion of its private activity bond limit based on the ratio of its population to the aggregate population of all such governmental units. The governmental unit within the jurisdiction of which the facility to be provided by the private activity bonds will be located, however, may elect to treat the regional authority as if it were a constituted authority empowered to issue such obligations solely on behalf of that governmental unit and, therefore, may assign a portion of its limit to the authority solely to provide the facility within its jurisdiction. Similarly, if a facility will solely benefit one governmental unit, that governmental unit may make the election described in the preceding sentence. In addition, any of the governmental units on behalf of which the regional authority issues private activity bonds, other than the governmental unit within the jurisdiction of which the facility will be located, may elect to be treated as if it had not empowered the authority to issue that issue of private activity bonds on its behalf. In providing a different formula for allocating the State ceiling, a State may permit a governmental unit to assign all or a portion of its private activity bond limit to a constituted authority empowered to issue private activity bonds on behalf of two or more governmental units, all of which are located within the State. The preceding sentence will only apply where the different formula expressly so provides. The principles of this A-15 shall not apply to any regional authority created with a principal purpose of avoiding the restrictions provided in A-13 or A-14 of this § 1.103(n)-3T. The principles of this A-15 shall also apply to a special purpose governmental unit providing facilities located within the jurisdiction of two or more general purpose governmental units from which it derives sovereign powers.

*Examples.*The following examples illustrate the provisions of A-8 through A-15 of this section:

Example (1). Authority ZZ is empowered by City Y to issue obligations on its behalf to provide financing for pollution control facilities located within the jurisdiction of City Y and the geographical area within 10 miles of the limits of City Y. Authority ZZ has no sovereign powers. Although the authority of Authority ZZ to issue obligations enables it to provide facilities located outside of the jurisdiction of City Y, Authority ZZ is treated as having jurisdiction over the same geographical area as City Y. Since City Y has broader sovereign powers than Authority ZZ, under section 103(n)(3) Authority ZZ has a private activity bond limit of zero. On March 31, 1985, Authority ZZ issues $5 million of private activity bonds. City Y has not assigned any portion of its private activity bond limit to Authority ZZ. Thus, the March 31, 1985, issue of private activity bonds is treated as an issue of obligations not described in section 103(a), and the interest on such obligations is subject to Federal income taxation.

Example (2). In 1972, State S, State T, and State V empowered Authority Z to issue industrial development bonds on behalf of the three States and to provide port facilities in a harbor serving residents of all three States. S, T, and V have populations of 1,000,000, 2,000,000, and 7,000,000, respectively. Authority Z will issue $100 million of private activity bonds on September 1, 1985, to finance construction of a dock to be located in State S. The obligations will not meet the requirements of section 103(n) unless S, T, and V assign a portion of their private activity bond limits to Authority Z pursuant to one of three methods. First, S, T, and V may assign $10 million, $20 million, and $70 million, respectively, of their private activity bond limits to Authority Z for this issue. Second, S, T, and V may assign $100 million, $0, and $0, respectively, of their private activity bond limits to Authority Z for this issue. Third, either T or V (but not S) may allocate $0 of its private activity bond limit to Authority Z for purposes of this issue, and the remaining two States may allocate the $100 million based upon their respective populations. For instance, if T were to allocate $0 for purposes of this issue, S and V must allocate $12.5 million and $87.5 million, respectively, of their private activity bond limits to Authority Z.

Q-16. Must an issuing authority allocate any of its private activity bond limit to certain preliminarily approved projects?

A-16. Yes. Section 631(a)(3) of the Tax Reform Act of 1984 provides that, with respect to certain projects preliminarily approved by an issuing authority before October 19, 1983, the issuing authority shall allocate its share of the private activity bond limit for the calendar year during which the obligations are to be issued first to those projects. For purposes of this A-16 and A-17 and A-18 of this § 1.103(n)-3T, a general purpose governmental unit will be treated as having preliminarily approved a project if the project was preliminarily approved by it, by a constituted authority empowered to issue private activity bonds on its behalf, or by a special purpose governmental unit treated as having jurisdiction over the same geographical area as the general purpose governmental unit. Thus, if a project was approved by a constituted authority, the governmental unit on behalf of which such issue is to be issued must assign a portion of its private activity bond limit to the authority pursuant to section 631(a)(3) of the Act. If a project was preliminarily approved by a constituted authority empowered to issue private activity bonds on behalf or more than one general purpose governmental unit or a special purpose governmental unit that derives its sovereign powers from more than one general purpose governmental unit, the project will be considered approved by each of such general purpose governmental units in proportion to their relative populations. The projects that receive priority under section 631(a)(3) of the Act and this A-16 are those with respect to which—

(i) There was an inducement resolution (or other comparable preliminary approval) for a project before October 19, 1983, by an issuing authority,

(ii) A substantial user of the project notified such issuing authority—

(A) By August 17, 1984, that it intended to claim its rights under section 631(a)(3) of the Tax Reform Act of 1984, and

(B) By December 31, 1984, as to the calendar year in which it expects the obligations to provide the project to be issued, and

(iii) Construction of such project began before October 19, 1983, or a substantial user was under a binding obligation on that date to incur significant expenditures with respect to the project.

For purposes of the preceding sentence, the term "significant expenditures" means expenditures that equal or exceed the lesser of $15 million or 20 percent of the estimated cost of the facilities. An issuing authority may require, as part of the submission required by (ii)(B) of this A-16, that a substantial user specify the aggregate amount of private activity bonds necessary for the project. Section 631(a)(3) does not apply to a project to the extent that the aggregate amount of obligations required for such project exceeds the amount, if any, provided for in the inducement resolution or resolutions in existence with respect to such project before October 19, 1983, or in the statement that may be required by the issuing authority as part of the submission required by (ii)(B) of this A-16. Similarly, section 631(a)(3) does not apply to a project to the extent of any material change in its nature, character, purpose, or capacity. Section 631(a)(3) does not apply to a project if the owner, operator, or manager of such project is not the same (or a related person) as the owner, operator, or manager named in the latest inducement resolution with respect to such project in existence before October 19, 1983. Section 631(a)(3) of the Act does not apply to any project if the obligations to provide the project are not issued in the year specified in the submission required by (ii)(B) of this A-16. In addition, section 631(a)(3) of the Act does not apply to any project to the extent that the amount of obligations to be issued for such project exceeds the share of the State ceiling to which the issuing authority that authorized the project is entitled as determined under section 103(n)(2) and (3) without regard to any alternative formula for allocating the State ceiling. The requirements of section 631(a)(3) will not apply where a State statute specifically so provides.

Q-17. What is the penalty for failure to comply with the requirements of section 631(a)(3) of the Act?

A-17. If any issuing authority fails to comply with the requirements of section 631(a)(3) of the Act, its private activity bond limit for the calendar year following the year in which the failure occurs shall be reduced by the amount of private activity bonds with respect to which the failure occurs. This penalty applies whether the issuing authority's private activity bond limit is determined under the formula provided under section 103(n)(2) and (3) or a different formula provided under section 103(n)(6). The penalty is imposed on the issuing authority that failed to comply with the requirements of section 631(a)(3) or, if in the year in which the penalty is imposed the issuing authority does not have a sufficient private activity bond limit to absorb the entire penalty, on the general purpose governmental unit treated as having jurisdiction over the same geographical area as the issuing authority. For purposes of this A-17, the general purpose governmental unit's private activity bond limit includes the private activity bond limit of each issuing authority treated as having preliminarily approved the project under A-16 of this § 1.103(n)-3T. Thus, for example, if a governmental unit failed to comply with the requirements of section 631(a)(3) of the Act with respect to a $5 million issue to be issued in 1985, and that governmental unit is assigned $15 million of the State ceiling for 1986 pursuant to a formula provided under section 103(n)(6), that governmental unit has a private activity bond limit of $10 million for 1986. Similarly, where a project that was preliminarily approved by an issuing authority that is not a governmental unit qualifies for $10 million of priority under section 631(a)(3) of the Act is not allocated a total of $10 million by the governmental unit on behalf of which the issuing authority is empowered to issue private activity bonds, the issuing authority's private activity bond limit, if any, for the year following this failure is reduced by $10 million; if the issuing authority's private activity bond limit for the year following the failure is less than $10 million, the private activity bond limit of the governmental unit on behalf of which the private activity bonds would have been issued had the failure not occurred (including if necessary, on a proportionate basis, the private activity bond limit purported to have been assigned to each of the other constituted authorities empowered to issue private activity bonds on behalf of the governmental unit and each special purpose governmental unit deriving all or part of its sovereign powers from the governmental unit) is reduced by the difference between $10 million and the reduction made in the issuing authority's private activity bond limit with respect to such failure.

Q-18. Will a penalty be assessed for failure to allocate private activity bond limit to all projects that meet the requirements section 631(a)(3) if the amount of obligations required by all such projects preliminarily approved by (or treated as having been preliminarily approved by) an issuing authority exceeds the private activity bond limit of such issuing authority?

A-18. No penalty will be assessed if priority is given to those eligible projects for which substantial expenditures were incurred before October 19, 1983. An issuer may define the term "substantial expenditures" in any reasonable manner based on the relevant facts and circumstances and its private activity bond limit.

*Examples.*The following examples illustrate the provisions of A-16 through A-18:

Example (1). On October 1, 1983, County S approved an inducement resolution for the issuance of up to $30 million of industrial development bonds to provide a pollution control facility described in section 103(b)(4)(F) for Corporation R. On October 5, 1983, R contracted with Corporation Q to begin construction of the pollution control facility immediately, and construction began on October 10, 1983. Not later than August 17, 1984, Corporation R notified County S that it intended to seek priority under section 631(a)(3) of the Tax Reform Act of 1984. In addition, prior to December 31, 1984, Corporation R notified County S that it expected the County to issue $25 million of industrial development bonds for its project during calendar year 1985. Under section 103(n)(3), County S has a private activity bond limit of $50 million for calendar year 1985, and neither the Governor nor the legislature of the State has provided a different allocation formula under section 103(n)(6). There are no other projects approved by County S that have rights under section 631(a)(3). On March 1, 1985, County S issues $25 million of industrial development bonds for the pollution control facility for Corporation R. If County S allocates less than $25 million of its private activity bond limit to that project, its private activity bond limit for 1986 will be reduced by the difference between $25 million and the amount County S actually allocates to the project.

Example (2). The facts are the same as in Example (1) except that during 1984 Corporation R fails to notify County S of the year in which it expects the obligations to be issued. Upon such failure the pollution control facility no longer qualifies for priority under section 631(a)(3), and County S will not be penalized if it does not not allocate any of its private activity bond limit for 1985, or any future year, to that project.

Example (3). The facts are the same as in Example (1) except that under section 103(n)(3) County S has a private activity bond limit of $10 million for 1985. County S will not be penalized if it allocates $10 million of its private activity bond limit to the project.

Example (4). The facts are the same as in Example (3) except that on December 31, 1984, the Governor of the State provides a different allocation from that provided under section 103(n)(2) and (3). (The State has not enacted a statute specifically providing that section 631(a)(3) does not apply.) The different allocation provides that the entire State ceiling is allocated to the State and that the State will allocate the State ceiling to issuing authorities for specific projects on a first-come, first-served basis. Corporation R qualifies for the special rights granted by section 631(a)(3) of the Tax Reform Act to the extent of County S's private activity bond limit as determined under section 103(n)(3), *i.e.*,$10 million. If the State fails to assign to County S $10 million of the State ceiling or if County S, after receiving such assignment, fails to allocate $10 million of private activity bond limit to the project, County S's private activity bond limit (if any) for 1986 will be reduced by the difference between $10 million and the amount of private activity bond limit allocated to the project.

Example (5). The facts are the same as in Example (1) except that Corporation R notifies County S that it only requires $15 million for the pollution control facility, County S only issues $15 million of private activity bonds for the pollution control facility, and County S only allocates $15 million of its private activity bond limit to such obligations. County S will not be penalized for not allocating more than $15 million of its private activity bond limit to Corporation R even though the original inducement resolution provided for up to $25 million.

T.D. 7981, 10/2/84.

§ 1.103(n)-4T Elective carryforward of unused private activity bond limit (temporary).

Caution: The Treasury has not yet amended Reg § 1.103(n)-4T to reflect changes made by P.L. 107-16, P.L. 100-647, P.L. 99-514.

Q-1. May an issuing authority carry forward any of its unused private activity bond limit for a calendar year?

A-1. In any calendar year after 1983 in which an issuing authority's private activity bond limit exceeds the aggregate amount of private activity bonds issued during such calendar year by such issuing authority, such issuing authority may elect to treat all, or any portion, of such excess as a carryforward for any one or more projects described in A-5 of this § 1.103(n)-4T (carryforward projects).

Q-2. How is the election to carry forward an issuing authority's unused private activity bond limit made?

A-2. (i) An issuing authority may make the election by means of a statement, signed by an authorized public official responsible for making allocations of such issuing authority's private activity bond limit, that the issuing authority elects to carry forward its unused private activity bond limit. The statement shall be filed with the Internal Revenue Service Center, Philadelphia, Pennsylvania 19255. Except with respect to elections to carry forward any unused private activity bond limit for calendar year 1984, the election must be filed prior to the end of the calendar year with respect to which the issuing authority has the unused private activity bond limit; elections with respect to unused private activity bond limit for calendar year 1984 must be filed prior to February 26, 1985. The statement is to be titled "Carryforward election under section 103(n)."

(ii) The statement required by (i) of this A-2 shall contain the following information:

(A) The name, address, and TIN of the issuing authority,

(B) The issuing authority's private activity bond limit for the calendar year,

(C) The aggregate amount of private activity bonds issued by the issuing authority during the calendar year for which the election is being made,

(D) The unused private activity bond limit of the issuing authority, and

(E) For each carryforward project—

(1) A description of the project, including its address (by its street address or, if none, by a general description designed to indicate its specific location) and the general type of facility (e.g., an airport described in section 103(b)(4)(D)),

(2) The name, address, and TIN of the initial owner, operator, or manager, and

(3) The amount to be carried forward for the project.

(iii) For purposes of (ii)(E) of this A-2, in the case of a carryforward project for which the initial owner, operator, or manager is to be selected pursuant to a competitive bidding process, the election may include up to 3 prospective addresses for the project and the name, address, and TIN of more than one prospective initial owner, operator, or manager, if prior to the end of the calendar year for which the election is made—

(A) In the case of elections for calendar years other than 1984, the issuing authority has taken preliminary official action approving the undertaking of the carryforward project,

(B) All persons included as prospective owners, operators, or managers have met all applicable conditions (if any) to submit proposals to provide the project, and

(C) The issuing authority has expended (or has entered into binding contracts to expend) in connection with the planning and construction of the carryforward project the lesser of $500,000 or 2½ percent of the carryforward amount.

(iv) For purposes of (ii) of this A-2, in the case of a carryforward election for the purpose of issuing student loan bonds, the statement need not include the address of a facility or the name, address, and TIN of an initial owner, operator, or manager of a project but shall state that the carryforward election is for the purpose of issuing student loan bonds.

Q-3. Is a carryforward election revocable?

A-3. Any carryforward election, and any specification contained therein, shall be irrevocable after the last day of the calendar year in which the election is made. Thus, for example, obligations issued to finance a carryforward project with a different initial owner, operator, or manager from the owner, operator, or manager specified in the carryforward election shall not be issued pursuant to such carryforward election. An insubstantial deviation from a specification contained in a carryforward election shall not prevent obligations from being issued pursuant to such carryforward election. In addition, where a carryforward election is made with respect to more than one carryforward project, a substantial deviation with respect to one carryforward project shall not prevent obligations from being issued pursuant to such carryforward election with respect to the other carryforward projects.

Q-4. How is a carryforward used?

A-4. Any private activity bonds issued during the three calendar years (six calendar years in the case of a project described in section 103(b)(4)(F)) following the calendar year in which the carryforward election was first made with respect to a carryforward project shall not be taken into account in determining whether the issue meets the requirements of section 103(n). If, however, the amount of private activity bonds issued for the carryforward project exceeds the amount of the carryforward elected with respect to the project, then the portion of the issue that exceeds the carryforward shall be taken into account in determining whether the issue meets with the requirements of section 103(n); if that portion of the issue does not meet the requirements of section 103(n) then the entire issue is treated as consisting of obligations not described in section 103(a). Carryforwards elected with respect to any project shall be used in the order of the calendar years in which they arose. Thus, for example, if an issuing authority makes carryforward elections in 1986 and 1988 for a carryforward project and issues private activity bonds for that project in 1989 and 1990, the obligations issued in 1989 will be applied to the 1986 carryforward election to the extent thereof.

Q-5. For what projects may a carryforward election be made?

A-5. A carryforward election may be made for any project described in section 103(b)(4) or (5), and for the purpose of issuing student loan bonds. Thus, for example, an issuing authority may elect to carry forward its unused private activity bond limit in order to provide a sports facility described in section 103(b)(4)(B). In addition, a governmental unit may elect to carry forward its unused private activity bond limit in order to issue qualified scholarship funding bonds. An issuing authority may not, however, elect to carry forward its unused private activity bond limit in order to issue an exempt small issue of industrial development bonds under section 103(b)(6).

T.D. 7981, 10/2/84, amend T.D. 8001, 12/26/84.

§ 1.103(n)-5T Certification of no consideration for allocation (temporary).

Caution: The Treasury has not yet amended Reg § 1.103(n)-5T to reflect changes made by P.L. 100-647, P.L. 99-514.

Q-1. Who must certify that there was no consideration for an allocation?

A-1. Section 103(n)(12)(A) provides that, with respect to any private activity bond allocated any portion of the State ceiling, the private activity bond will not be described under section 103(a) unless the public official, if any, responsible for such allocation ("responsible public official") certifies under penalties of perjury that to the best of his knowledge the allocation of the State ceiling to that private activity bond was not made in consideration of any bribe, gift, gratuity, or direct or indirect contribution to any political campaign. With respect to any issue of private activity bonds, the responsible public official is the official or officer of the issuing authority that in fact is responsible for choosing which individual projects will be allocated a portion of the State ceiling. If a body of several individuals is responsible for such choices, any one member of such body qualifies as the responsible public official.

Q-2. What is the penalty for willfully making an allocation in consideration of any bribe, gift, gratuity, or direct or indirect contribution to any political campaign?

A-2. Section 103(n)(12)(B) provides that any person willfully making an allocation of any portion of the State ceiling in consideration of any bribe, gift, gratuity, or direct or indirect contribution to any political campaign will be subject to criminal penalty as though the allocation were a willful attempt to evade tax imposed by the Internal Revenue Code.

T.D. 7981, 10/2/84.

§ 1.103(n)-6T Determinations of population (temporary).

Caution: The Treasury has not yet amended Reg § 1.103(n)-6T to reflect changes made by P.L. 100-647, P.L. 99-514.

Q-1. What is the proper method for determining population?

A-1. All determinations of population must be made with respect to any calendar year on the basis of the most recent census estimate (whether final or provisional) of the resident population of the State or other governmental unit published by the Bureau of the Census in the "Current Population Reports" series before the beginning of the calendar year.

However, determinations of the population of a general purpose governmental unit (other than a State, territory, or possession) within a State, territory, or possession may not be based on estimates that do not contain estimates for all of the general purpose governmental units within such State, territory, or possession. Thus, a county may not determine its population on the basis of a census estimate that does not provide an estimate of the population of the other general purpose governmental units within the State (*e.g.*, cities, towns). If no census estimate is available for all such general purpose governmental units, the most recent decennial census of population may be relied on.

Example. The following example illustrates the provisions of A-1 of this § 1.103(n)-6T:

Example. County Q is located within State R. There are no constitutional home rule cities in State R. State R has not adopted a formula for allocating the State ceiling different from the formula provided in section 103(n)(2) and (3). The geographical area within the jurisdiction of County Q is not within the jurisdiction of any other governmental unit having jurisdiction over a smaller geographical area. As of December 31, 1984, the Bureau of the Census has published the following estimates of resident population: "Current Population Reports; Series P-25: Population Estimates and Projections, Estimates of the Population of States: July 1, 1981–1983" and "Current Population Reports; Series P-26: Local Population Estimates: Population of State R, Counties, Incorporated Places, and Minor Civil Divisions: July 1, 1981–1982." The most recent population estimate for State R available prior to 1985 provides population estimates as of July 1, 1983. The most recent population estimates for County Q available prior to 1985 is the estimate for July 1, 1982. Assuming that the State ceiling for State R for 1985 is in excess of $200 million (*i.e.,* $150 multiplied by the estimated population of State R as of July 1, 1983, exceeds $200 million), County Q may determine its private activity bond limit by using the following formula:

$P = \$150 \times .5 \times W \times Y/Z$, where,

P = County Q's private activity bond limit,

W = the July 1, 1983, population estimate for State R,

Y = the July 1, 1982, population estimate for County Q, and

Z = the July 1, 1982, population estimate for State R.

If the State ceiling for State R is not in excess of $200 million, County Q may determine its private activity bond limit by using the following formula:

$P = \$200{,}000{,}000 \times .5 \times Y/Z$, where

P, Y, and Z have the same meaning as above.

T.D. 7981, 10/2/84.

§ 1.103(n)-7T Election to allocate State ceiling to certain facilities for local furnishing of electricity (temporary).

Caution: The Treasury has not yet amended Reg § 1.103(n)-7T to reflect changes made by P.L. 100-647, P.L. 99-514.

(a) Election. *(1) In general.* The issuing authorities of the State of New York ("New York") may elect to use in 1984 up to one-half of the amount that would have been New York's State ceiling (as defined in section 103(n)(4) and A-1 of § 1.103(n)-3T) for calendar years 1985, 1986, and 1987 for the purpose of issuing obligations to provide facilities for the local furnishing of electric energy described in section 644(a) of the Tax Reform Act of 1984 (the "Act"). For purposes of this paragraph, New York's State ceiling for calendar years 1985, 1986, and 1987 is considered equal to the State ceiling for 1984 (without taking into account any increase in the State ceiling for 1984 as a result of an election under section 644(b) and this section).

(2) Procedure. The election shall be made by filing the statement described in this paragraph (a)(2) with the Internal Revenue Service Center, Philadelphia, Pennsylvania, on or before December 31, 1984. The statement shall be titled "Allocation election under section 644 of the Tax Reform

Act of 1984," shall be signed by the Governor of New York or his authorized representative, and shall contain the following information:

(i) The name, address, and TIN of the issuing authority (or authorities) that is expected to issue the obligations for the facilities described in section 644(a) of the Act pursuant to the election described in section 644(b) of the Act and this section, and

(ii) The amount of the State ceiling for each of calendar years 1985, 1986, and 1987 with respect to which the election is made.

(b) Effect of election. *(1) In 1984.* The amount of the State ceiling for calendar years 1985, 1986, and 1987 with respect to which the election is made will be considered part of New York's State ceiling for calendar year 1984. For purposes of section 644(b) of the Act, such amount will be considered used in 1984 only to the extent that obligations are issued in 1984 to provide facilities for the local furnishing of electric energy described in section 644(a) of the Act, or to the extent that a proper election is made on or before December 31, 1984 (and is not revoked or amended between the time it is made and the end of 1984) pursuant to section 103(n)(10) and § 1.103(n)-4T to carry forward all or part of such amount to provide such facilities during the carryforward period applicable to calendar year 1984 State ceiling.

(2) In 1985, 1986, and 1987. An election under section 644(b) of the Act and this section to use in calendar year 1984 an amount of New York's State ceiling for a subsequent calendar year reduces the State ceiling for such subsequent calendar year by the amount with respect to which the election is made, whether or not such amount is considered used in 1984 pursuant to this paragraph (b). Thus, no obligations may be issued pursuant to the election described in section 644(b) of the Act and this section to provide a facility other than the facilities for the furnishing of electric energy described in section 644(a) of the Act.

(3) Other effects. An election or the failure to make an election under section 644(b) of the Act and this section shall not affect any otherwise applicable rule that permits an issuing authority, for any calendar year, to—

(i) Allocate a portion of its private activity bond limit,

(ii) Issue obligations within its private activity bond limit, or

(iii) Elect under section 103(n)(10) and § 1.103(n)-4T to carry forward any portion of its private activity bond limit, in order to issue obligations to provide a facility described in section 644(a) of the Act.

(c) Revocation of election. An election made under section 644(b) of the Act and this section may not be revoked or amended. An insubstantial deviation from a specification contained in an election under section 644(b) of the Act and this section shall not prevent obligations from being issued pursuant to such election.

T.D. 8001, 12/26/84.

§ 6a.103A-1 Interest on mortgage subsidy bonds.

• ***Caution:*** Reg. § 6a.103A-1, following, was issued under Code section 103A before the related provisions of that Code section were deleted by P.L. 99-514 (10/22/86). Provisions similar to, but not necessarily identical to, the provisions deleted from Code section 103A now appear in Code section 143.

Caution: The Treasury has not yet amended Reg § 6a.103A-1 to reflect changes made by P.L. 100-647, P.L. 99-514.

(a) In general. *(1) Mortgage subsidy bond.* A mortgage subsidy bond shall be treated as an obligation not described in section 103(a)(1) or (a)(2). Thus, the interest on a mortgage subsidy bond is includable in gross income and subject to Federal income taxation.

(2) Exceptions. Any qualified mortgage bond and any qualified veterans' mortgage bond shall not be treated as a mortgage subsidy bond. See § 6a.103A-2 with respect to requirements of qualified mortgage bonds and § 6a.103A-3 with respect to requirements of qualified veterans' mortgage bonds.

(3) Additional requirement. In addition to the requirements of § 6a.103A-2, § 6a.103A-3, and this section, qualified mortgage bonds and qualified veterans' mortgage bonds shall be subject to the requirements of section 103(c) and the regulations thereunder.

(4) Advance refunding. On or after December 5, 1980, no tax-exempt obligation may be issued for the advance refunding of a mortgage subsidy bond (determined without regard to section 103A(b)(2) or § 6a.103A-1(a)(2)). An obligation issued for the refunding of a mortgage subsidy bond will be considered to be an advance refunding obligation if it is issued more than 180 days before the prior issue is discharged.

(5) Registration. Any obligation that is part of a qualified mortgage bond issue or qualified veterans' mortgage bond issue and which is issued after December 31, 1981, must be in registered form. The term "in registered form" has the same meaning as in § 1.6049-2(d). Thus, in general, an obligation is issued in registered form if it is registered as to both principal and interest and if its transfer must be effected by the surrender of the old instrument to the issuer and by either the reissuance of the old instrument to a new holder or the issuance of a new instrument to a new holder.

(b) Definitions. For purposes of § 6a.103A-2, § 6a.103A-3, and this section the following definitions apply:

(1) Mortgage subsidy bond. (i) The term "mortgage subsidy bond" means any obligation which is issued as part of an issue a significant portion of the proceeds of which is to be used directly or indirectly to provide mortgages on owner-occupied residences.

(ii) For purposes of subdivision (i), a significant portion of the proceeds of an issue is used to provide mortgages if 5 percent or more of the proceeds are so used.

(2) Mortgage. The term "mortgage" includes deeds of trust, conditional sales contracts, pledges, agreements to hold title in escrow, and any other form of owner financing.

(3) Bond. The term "bond" means any obligation. The term "obligation" means any evidence of indebtedness.

(4) State. (i) The term "State" includes a possession of the United States and the District of Columbia.

(ii) For purposes of subdivision (i), obligations issued by or on behalf of any State or local governmental unit by constituted authorities empowered to issue such obligations are the obligations of such governmental unit. See § 1.103-1(b).

(5) Proceeds. The term "proceeds" includes original proceeds and investment proceeds. The terms "original proceeds" and "investment proceeds" shall have the same meaning as in § 1.103-13(b)(2). Unless otherwise provided in § 6a.103A-2 or this section, however, amounts earned from the investment of proceeds which are derived from qualified mortgage bonds in nonmortgage investments may not be commingled for the purposes of accounting for expenditures with other non-bond amounts, and such proceeds are investment proceeds even though not treated as investment proceeds for purposes of section 103(c). Repayments of principal on mortgages shall be treated as proceeds of an issue. Amounts (such as State appropriations or surplus funds) which are provided by the issuer or a private lender in conjunction with a qualified mortgage bond or a qualified veterans' mortgage bond shall not be treated as proceeds of a mortgage subsidy bond under this section. However, fees which are paid by a participating financial institution pursuant to an agreement with the issuer whereby such institution receives the right to originate or service mortgages and which are retained by an issuer are treated as original proceeds of the issue. Amounts provided by the issuer or a private lender may be treated as proceeds of an issue for purposes of section 103(c).

(6) Single-family and owner-occupied residences. Except for purposes of § 6a.103A-2(g) and (h)(2)(ii), the terms "single-family" and "owner-occupied," when used with respect to residences, include two-, three-, and four-family residences—

(i) One unit of which is occupied by the owner of the units, and

(ii) Which were first occupied as a residence at least 5 years before the mortgage is executed.

T.D. 7780, 6/29/81, amend T.D. 7794, 11/5/81.

§ 1.103A-2 Qualified mortgage bond.

• ***Caution:*** Reg. § 1.103A-2, following, was issued under Code section 103A before the related provisions of that Code section were deleted by P.L. 99-514 (10/22/86). Provisions similar to, but not necessarily identical to, the provisions deleted from Code section 103A now appear in Code section 143.

Caution: The Treasury has not yet amended Reg § 1.103A-2 to reflect changes made by P.L. 101-239, P.L. 100-647.

(a) –(j) [Reserved]

(k) Information reporting requirement. *(1) In general.* An issue meets the requirements of this paragraph only if the issuer in good faith attempted to meet the information reporting requirements of this paragraph. Except as otherwise provided in paragraph (k)(5)(iv) of this section, the requirements of this paragraph apply to qualified veterans' mortgage bonds issued after July 18, 1984, and to qualified mortgage bonds issued after December 31, 1984. With respect to bonds issued after December 31, 1986, see the regulations under section 149(e).

(2) Information required. (i) The issuer must, based on information and reasonable expectations determined as of the date of issue, submit on Form 8038 the information required therein; the issuer need not however, include the information required by Form 8038 that is relevant only to obligations described in section 103(l)(1) and the regulations thereunder. The information that must be submitted includes—

(A) The name, address, and employer identification number of the issuer,

(B) The date of issue,

(C) The face amount of each obligation which is part of the issue,

(D) The total purchase price of the issue,

(E) The amount allocated to a reasonably required reserve or replacement fund,

(F) The amount of lendable proceeds,

(G) The stated interest rate of each maturity,

(H) The term of each maturity,

(I) In the case of an issue of qualified mortgage bonds, whether the issuer has elected under § 6a.103A-2(i)(4)(v) to pay arbitrage to the United States,

(J) In the case of an issue of qualified mortgage bonds, the issuer's market limitation as of the date of issue (as defined in § 6a.103A-2(g)), the amount of qualified mortgage bonds that the issuer has elected not to issue under section 25(c)(2) and the regulations thereunder, and the aggregate amount of qualified mortgage bonds issued to date by the issuer during the calendar year, and

(K) In the case of an issue of qualified veterans' mortgage bonds, the issuer's State veterans limit (as defined in section 103A(o)(3)(B) and the regulations thereunder) and the aggregate amount of qualified veterans' mortgage bonds issued to date by the issuer during the calendar year and prior to the date of issue of the issue for which the Form 8038 is being submitted.

(ii) With respect to issues issued after December 31, 1984, the issuer must submit a report containing information on the borrowers of the original proceeds of such issues. The report must be filed for each reporting period in which the original proceeds of any of such issues are used to provide mortgages. The issuer is not responsible for false information provided by a borrower if the issuer did not know or have reason to know that the information was false. The report must be filed on the form prescribed by the Internal Revenue Service. If no form is prescribed, or if the form prescribed is not readily available, the issuer may use its own form provided that such form is in the format set forth in paragraph (k)(3) of this section and contains the information required by this paragraph (k)(2)(ii). The report must be titled "Qualified Mortgage Bond Information Report" or "Qualified Veterans' Mortgage Bond Information Report", and must include the name, address, and TIN of the issuer, the reporting period for which the information is provided, and the following tables containing information concerning the borrowers of the original proceeds of the issues subject to the requirements of this paragraph (k)(2)(ii) with respect to mortgages provided during the reporting period for which the report is filed:

(A) A table titled "Number of Mortgage Loans by Income and Acquisition Cost" showing the number of mortgage loans (other than those issued in connection with qualified home improvement and rehabilitation loans) made during the reporting period according to the annualized gross income of the borrowers (categorized in the following intervals of income: $0-$9,999; $10,000-$19,999; $20,000-$29,999; $30,000-$39,999; $40,000-$49,999; $50,000-$74,999; and $75,000 or more) and according to the acquisition cost of each residence being financed (categorized in the following intervals of acquisition cost: $0-$19,999; $20,000-$39,999; $40,000-$59,999; $60,000-$79,999; $80,000-$99,999; $100,000-$119,999; $120,000-$149,999; $150,000-$199,999; and $200,000 or more). For each interval of income and acquisition cost the table must also be categorized according to the number of borrowers that—

(1) Did not have a present ownership interest in a principal residence at any time during the 3-year period ending on the date the mortgage is executed (i.e., satisfied the 3-year requirement) and purchased residences in targeted areas,

(2) Satisfied the 3-year requirement and purchased residences not located in targeted areas,

(3) Did have a present ownership interest in a principal residence at any time during the 3-year period ending on the date the mortgage is executed (i.e., did not satisfy the 3-year requirement) and purchased residences in targeted areas, and

(4) Did not satisfy the 3-year requirement and purchased residences not located in targeted areas. With respect to issues of qualified veterans' mortgage bonds, for each interval of income and acquisition cost the table need only be categorized according to the number of borrowers that satisfied the 3-year requirement and the number of borrowers that failed to satisfy the 3-year requirement.

(B) A table titled "Volume of Mortgage Loans by Income and Acquisition Cost" showing the total principal amount of the mortgage loans (other than qualified home improvement and rehabilitation loans) provided during the reporting period according to annualized gross income (categorized in the same intervals of income as the preceding table) and according to the acquisition cost of the residences acquired (categorized in the same acquisition cost intervals as the preceding table). For each interval of income and acquisition cost the table must also be categorized according to the total principal amount of the mortgage loans of borrowers that—

(1) Satisfied the 3-year requirement and purchased residences in targeted areas,

(2) Satisfied the 3-year requirement and purchased residences not located in targeted areas,

(3) Did not satisfy the 3-year requirement and purchased residences in targeted areas, and

(4) Did not satisfy the 3-year requirement and purchased residences not located in targeted areas. With respect to issues of qualified veterans' mortgage bonds, for each interval of income and acquisition cost the table need only be categorized according to the total principal amount of the mortgage loans of borrowers that satisfied the 3-year requirement and the total principal amount of the mortgage loans of borrowers that did not satisfy the 3-year requirement.

(C) For issues other than qualified veterans' mortgage bonds, a table titled "Mortgage Subsidy Bonds for Qualified Home Improvement and Rehabilitation Loans" showing the number of borrowers obtaining qualified home improvement loans and qualified rehabilitation loans and the total of the principal amounts of such loans; the information contained in the table must also be categorized according to whether the residences with respect to which the loans were provided are located in targeted areas.

(3) Format. (i) With respect to the report required by paragraph (k)(2)(ii) of this section, if no form is prescribed by the Internal Revenue Service, or if the prescribed form is not readily available, the issuer must submit the report in the format specified in this paragraph (k)(3).

(ii) With respect to issues of qualified mortgage bonds, the format of the report specified in this paragraph (k)(3) is the following:

Qualified Mortgage Bond Information Report

Name of issuer:
Address of issuer:
TIN of issuer:
Reporting period:

Number of Mortgage Loans by Income and Acquisition Cost

3-year requirement: Annualized gross monthly income of borrowers	Satisfied		Not Satisfied		
	Nontargeted area	Targeted area	Nontargeted area	Targeted area	Totals
$0 to $9,999					
$10,000 to $19,999					
$20,000 to $29,999					
$30,000 to $39,999					
$40,000 to $49,999					
$50,000 to $74,999					
$75,000 or more					
Total					

3-year requirement: Annualized gross monthly income of borrowers	Satisfied		Not Satisfied		
	Nontargeted area	Targeted area	Nontargeted area	Targeted area	Totals
Acquisition Cost					
$0 to $19,999					
$20,000 to $39,999					
$40,000 to $59,999					
$60,000 to $79,999					
$80,000 to $99,999					
$100,000 to $119,999					
$120,000 to $149,999					
$150,000 to $199,999					
$200,000 or more					
Total					

Volume of Mortgage Loans by Income and Acquisition Cost

3-year requirement: Annualized gross monthly income of borrowers	Satisfied		Not Satisfied		
	Nontargeted area	Targeted area	Nontargeted area	Targeted area	Totals
$0 to $9,999					
$10,000 to 19,999					
$20,000 to 29,999					
$30,000 to $39,999					
$40,000 to $49,999					
$50,000 to $74,999					
$75,000 or more					
Total					

3-year requirement: Annualized gross monthly income of borrowers	Satisfied		Not Satisfied		
	Nontargeted area	Targeted area	Nontargeted area	Targeted area	Totals
Acquisition Cost					
$0 to $19,999					
$20,000 to $39,999					
$40,000 to $59,999					
$60,000 to $79,999					
$80,000 to $99,999					
$100,000 to $119,999					
$120,000 to $149,999					
$150,000 to $199,999					
$200,000 or more					
Total					

Mortgage Subsidy Bonds for Qualified Home Improvement and Rehabilitation Loans

	Nontargeted area	Targeted area	Totals
Number of qualified home improvement loans			
Volume of qualified home improvement loans			
Number of qualified rehabilitation loans ...			
Volume of qualified rehabilitation loans ...			

Qualified Veterans' Mortgage Bond Information Report

Name of issuer:
Address of issuer:
TIN of issuer:
Reporting period:

Number of Mortgage Loans by Income and Acquisition Cost

3-year requirement: annualized gross monthly income of borrowers	Satisfied	Not satisfied	Totals
$0 to $99,999			
$10,000 to $19,000			
$20,000 to $29,999			
$30,000 to $39,999			
$40,000 to $49,999			
$50,000 to $74,999			
$75,000 or more			
Total			

3-year requirement: annualized gross monthly income of borrowers	Satisfied	Not satisfied	Totals
Acquisition Cost			
$0 to $19,999			
$20,000 to $39,999			
$40,000 to $59,999			
$60,000 to $79,999			
$80,000 to $99,999			
$100,000 to $119,999			
$120,000 to $149,999			
$150,000 to $199,999			
$200,000 or more			
Total			

Volume of Mortgage Loans by Income and Acquisition Cost

3-year requirement: annualized gross monthly income of borrowers	Satisfied	Not satisfied	Totals
$0 to $9,999			
$10,000 to $19,999			
$20,000 to $29,999			
$30,000 to $39,999			
$40,000 to $49,999			
$50,000 to $74,999			
$75,000 or more			
Total			
Acquisition Cost			
$0 to $19,999			
$20,000 to $39,999			
$40,000 to $59,999			
$60,000 to $79,999			

$80,000 to $99,999	
$100,000 to $119,999	
$120,000 to $149,999	
$150,000 to $199,999	
$200,000 or more	
Total	

(4) Definitions and special rules. (i) For purposes of this paragraph the term "annualized gross income" means the borrower's gross monthly income multiplied by 12. Gross monthly income is the sum of monthly gross pay, any additional income from investments, pensions, Veterans Administration (VA) compensation, part-time employment, bonuses, dividends, interest, current overtime pay, net rental income, etc., and other income (such as alimony and child support, if the borrower has chosen to disclose such income). Information with respect to gross monthly income may be obtained from available loan documents, e.g., the sum of lines 23D and 23E on the Application for VA or FmHA Home Loan Guaranty or for HUD/FHA Insured Mortgage (VA Form 26-1802a, HUD 92900, Jan. 1982), or the total line from the Gross Monthly Income section of FHLMC Residential Loan Application form (FHLMC 65 Rev. 8/78). With respect to obligations issued prior to October 1, 1985, issuers may submit data based on annualized gross income or, instead, based on the adjusted income (as defined in § 1.167(k)-3(b)(3)) of the mortgagor's family for the previous calendar year. If data is submitted based on adjusted income, the issuer must note this fact in the report.

(ii) For purposes of this paragraph, the term "reporting period" means the following periods:

(A) The period beginning January 1, 1985, and ending on September 30, 1985,

(B) The period beginning on October 1, 1985, and ending on June 30, 1986, and

(C) After June 30, 1986, each 1-year period beginning July 1 and ending June 30.

(iii) See the regulations under section 103(l) for the definitions of the terms "date of issue", "maturity", and "term of issue".

(iv) For purposes of this paragraph, verification of information concerning a borrower's gross monthly income with other available information concerning the borrower's income (e.g., Federal income tax returns) is not required. In determining whether a borrower acquiring a residence in a targeted area satisfies the 3-year requirement, the issuer may rely on a statement signed by the borrower.

(5) Time for filing. (i) The report required by paragraph (k)(2)(i) of this section shall be filed not later than the 15th day of the second calendar month after the close of the calendar quarter in which the obligation is issued. The statement may be filed at any time before such date but must be complete based on facts and reasonable expectations as of the date of issue. The statement need not be amended to report information learned subsequent to the date of issue or to reflect changed circumstances with respect to the issuer.

(ii) The report required by paragraph (k)(2)(ii) of this section (relating to use of proceeds) shall be filed not later than the 15th day of the second calendar month after the close of the reporting period, except that the report for the reporting period ending September 30, 1985, is due not later than February 15, 1986. The report may be filed at any time before such date but must be complete based on facts and reasonable expectations as of the date the report is filed. The report need not be amended to reflect information learned subsequent to the date the report is filed or to reflect changed circumstances with respect to any borrower.

(iii) The Commissioner may grant an extension of time for the filing of a report required by paragraph (k)(2)(i) or (ii) of this section if there is reasonable cause for the failure to file such report in a timely fashion.

(iv) An issue of qualified veterans' mortgage bonds issued after July 18, 1984, and prior to January 1, 1985, will be treated as satisfying the information reporting requirement of this paragraph if a Form 8038 with respect to the issue is properly filed not later than February 15, 1985; the report described in paragraph (k)(2)(ii) of this section need not be filed with respect to such issues.

(6) Place for filing. The reports required by paragraph (k)(2)(i) and (ii) of this section are to be filed at the Internal Revenue Service Center, Philadelphia, Pennsylvania 19255.

(l) Policy statement. *(1) In general.* (i) For obligations issued after December 31, 1984, an issue meets the requirements of this paragraph only if the applicable elected representative of the governmental unit which is the issuer (or on behalf of which the issuing authority is empowered to issue qualified mortgage bonds) has published (after a public hearing following reasonable public notice) the report described in paragraph (l)(3) of this section by the last day of the year preceding the year in which such issue is issued and a copy of such report has been submitted to the Commissioner on or before such last day. The Commissioner may grant an extension of time for publishing and filing the report if there is reasonable cause for the failure to publish or file such report in a timely fashion. The requirements of this paragraph will be treated as met if the issuer in good faith attempted to meet the policy statement requirements of this paragraph.

(ii) With respect to reports required by paragraph (l)(1)(i) of this section to be published and submitted to the Commissioner not later than December 31, 1984, the Commissioner has determined that there is reasonable cause for the failure to publish or file such reports in a timely fashion; such a report will be considered published and filed in a timely fashion if, not later than March 11, 1985, the report is published (after a public hearing following reasonable public notice) and a copy is submitted to the Commissioner. In addition, any report submitted not later than December 31, 1984, with respect to which an issuer in good faith attempted to satisfy the requirements of section 103A(j)(5) shall be treated as substantially satisfying the requirement of this paragraph. For example, with respect to a report submitted not later than December 31, 1984, an issuer shall not be treated as failing to satisfy the requirements of section 103A(j)(5) based on the fact that (A) the notice of public hearing failed to state the manner in which affected residents may obtain copies of the proposed report prior to the hearing, or (B) the proposed report was not available prior to or at the public hearing. With respect to reports required to be published and submitted to the Commissioner not later than December 31, 1986, the Commissioner has determined that there is a reasonable cause for the failure to publish and file such reports in a timely fashion; such reports will be considered published and filed in a timely fashion if, not later than December 31, 1987, the report is published (after having a public hearing following reasonable public notice) and a copy is submitted to the Commissioner.

(2) Definitions and special rules. (i) In the case of an issuer that issues qualified mortgage bonds on behalf of one or more governmental units, a single report may be filed provided that such report is signed (A) by the applicable elected

representative of each governmental unit on whose behalf obligations have been issued during any preceding calendar year or (B) by the Governor of the State in which the issuer is located.

(ii) See notice 103(k)(2)(E) and the regulations thereunder for the definition of the term "applicable elected representative".

(iii) In the case of qualified mortgage bonds issued by, or on behalf of, a governmental unit that did not reasonably expect during the preceding calendar year to issue (or have issued on its behalf by any other issuer) qualified mortgage bonds during the current calendar year, the requirements of this paragraph will be treated as met if the applicable governmental unit which is the issuer (or on behalf of which the issuing authority is empowered to issue qualified mortgage bonds) has published (after a public hearing following reasonable public notice) the report described in paragraph (l)(3) of this section prior to the issuance of any qualified mortgage bonds and a copy of such report has been submitted to the Commissioner prior to such issuance.

(iv) For purposes of this paragraph a report will be considered to be "published" when the applicable elected representative of the governmental unit has made copies of the report available for distribution to the public. Reasonable public notice of the manner in which copies of the report may be obtained must be provided; such notice may be included as part of the public notice required by paragraph (l)(4) of this section.

(3) Report. (i) A report is described in this paragraph (l)(3) if it contains the issuer's name, TIN, and the title "Policy Report Under Section 103A" stated on the cover page of the report and if it includes—

(A) A statement of the policies of the issuer with respect to housing, development, and low-income housing assistance which such issuer is to follow in issuing qualified mortgage bonds and mortgage credit certificates, and

(B) An assessment of the compliance of such issuer during the 1-year period preceding the date of the report with—

(1) The statement of policy on qualified mortgage bonds and mortgage credit certificates that was set forth in the previous report, if any, of the issuer, and

(2) The intent of Congress that State and local governments are expected to use their authority to issue qualified mortgage bonds and mortgage credit certificates to the greatest extent feasible (taking into account prevailing interest rates and conditions in the housing market) to assist lower income families to afford home ownership before assisting higher income families.

(ii) For example, a report described in this paragraph (l)(3) may (but is not required to) contain—

(A) A specific statement of the policies with respect to housing, development, and low-income housing assistance which the issuer is to follow in issuing qualified mortgage bonds and mortgage credit certificates, including, for example, a statement as to—

(1) With respect to housing policies, (i) whether the proceeds will be used to provide financing for the acquisition of residences, to provide qualified home improvement loans, or to provide qualified rehabilitation loans; (ii) whether all or a portion of the proceeds will be targeted to new, existing, or any other particular class or type of housing; (iii) how the existence of a need or absence of a need for such targeting has been determined; (iv) the method by which the proceeds will be targeted; (v) any other pertinent information relating to the issuer's housing policies; and (vi) how the housing policies relate to the issuer's development and low-income housing assistance policies;

(2) With respect to development policies, (i) whether all or a portion of the proceeds will be targeted to specific areas (including targeted areas as described in § 6a.103A-2(b)(3)); (ii) a description of the areas to which the proceeds will be targeted; (iii) the reasons for selecting such areas; (iv) whether proceeds targeted to each area are to be used to finance redevelopment of existing housing or new construction; (v) any other pertinent information relating to the issuer's development policies; and (vi) how the development policies relate to the issuer's low-income housing assistance policies; and

(3) With respect to low-income housing assistance policies, (i) whether all or a portion of the proceeds will be targeted to low-income (i.e., 80 percent of median income), moderate-income (i.e., 100 percent of median income), or any other class of borrowers; (ii) the method by which the proceeds will be targeted to such borrowers; and (iii) any other pertinent information relating to the issuer's low-income housing assistance policies;

(B) An assessment of the compliance of the governmental unit or issuing authority during the twelve-month period ending with the date of the report with the statement of housing, development, and low-income housing assistance policies with respect to qualified mortgage bonds and mortgage credit certificates that were set forth in the report, if any, published in the preceding year with respect to such governmental unit, including, for example, a statement as to whether the governmental unit or issuing authority successfully implemented its policies and, if not, an analysis of the reasons for such failure; and

(C) An assessment of the compliance of the governmental unit or issuing authority during the twelve-month period ending with the date of the report with the intent of Congress that State and local governments are expected to use their authority to issue qualified mortgage bonds and mortgage credit certificates to the greatest extent feasible (taking into account prevailing interest rates and conditions in the housing market) to assist lower income families to afford home ownership before assisting higher income families, including, for example, a description of (1) the method used by the governmental unit or issuing authority to distribute proceeds, (2) whether and how that method enabled the governmental unit or issuing authority to assist lower income families before higher income families, and (3) any income levels that have been defined and used by the governmental unit or issuing authority in connection with distribution of the proceeds (no specific definition of lower income and higher income is imposed on governmental units or issuing authorities).

(iii) For purposes of the assessments of compliance required by paragraph (l)(3)(i)(B) of this section to be included in the report, the "date of the report" means June 30. For purposes of the report required to be filed prior to January 1, 1986, an issuer need not perform these assessments of compliance with respect to any period prior to January 1, 1985.

(iv) An issuer that fails to establish policies with respect to the criteria provided in paragraph (l)(3)(i) of this section will not be treated as failing to satisfy the requirements of this paragraph. Thus, for example, an issuer may state in its report that none of the proceeds of the issue will be targeted to specific areas. Similarly, an issuer that fails to successfully implement its policies will not be treated as failing to satisfy the requirements of this paragraph.

(4) Public hearing. The public hearing required by paragraph (l)(1) of this section means a forum providing a reasonable opportunity for interested individuals to express their views, both orally and in writing, on the report that the applicable representative proposes to publish to satisfy the requirements of this paragraph (l). A public hearing held prior to January 1, 1985, will not fail to satisfy the requirements of this paragraph (l)(4) merely because the proposed policy statement was not available prior to the public hearing. In general, a governmental unit may select its own procedure for the hearing, provided that interested individuals have a reasonable opportunity to express their views. Thus, it may impose reasonable requirements on persons who wish to participate in the hearing, such as a requirement that persons desiring to speak at the hearing so request in writing at least 24 hours before the hearing or that they limit their oral remarks to 10 minutes. For purposes of this public hearing requirement, it is not necessary that the applicable elected representative who will publish the report be present at the hearing, that a report on the hearing be submitted to that official, or that State administrative procedural requirements for public hearings in general be observed. However, compliance with such State procedural requirements (except those at variance with a specific requirement set forth in this paragraph) will generally assure that the hearing satisfies the requirements of this paragraph. The hearing may be conducted by any individual appointed or employed to perform such function by the governmental unit, its agencies, or by the issuer. Thus, for example, for a report to be issued by an issuing authority that acts on behalf of a county, the hearing may be conducted by the issuing authority, the county, or an appointee or employee of either.

(5) Reasonable public notice. (i) The reasonable public notice required by paragraph (l)(1) of this section means published notice which is reasonably designed to inform residents of the geographical area within the jurisdiction of the governmental unit that will publish the report. The notice must state the time and place for the hearing and contain the information required by paragraph (l)(5)(ii) of this section. Notice is presumed reasonable if published no fewer than 14 days before the hearing. Notice is presumed reasonably designed to inform affected residents only if published in one or more newspapers of general circulation available to residents of that locality or if announced by radio or television broadcast to those residents.

(ii) The notice of hearing described in this paragraph (l)(5) must state—

(A) The time and place for the hearing,

(B) Any applicable limitations regarding participation in the hearing,

(C) With respect to any notice of hearing published after December 31, 1984, the manner in which affected residents may obtain copies of the proposed report prior to the hearing, and

(D) With respect to any notice of hearing published after December 31, 1984, that the hearing will involve the issuer's policies with respect to housing, development, and low-income housing assistance which the issuer is to follow in issuing qualified mortgage bonds and mortgage credit certificates.

(6) Procedure for public hearings of multiple jurisdiction issuers. In the case of an issuer that issues qualified mortgage bonds on behalf of two or more governmental units ("multiple jurisdiction issuer"), each governmental unit on whose behalf the issuer reasonably expects to issue qualified mortgage bonds during the succeeding calendar year must hole a public hearing following reasonable public notice prior to the publication of the report required by this paragraph. A multiple jurisdiction issuer may hold a combined hearing as long as the combined hearing is a joint undertaking that provides all residents of the participating governmental units (i.e., each governmental unit on whose behalf qualified mortgage bonds were issued by the authority and each governmental unit on whose behalf the authority reasonably expects to issue qualified mortgage bonds during the succeeding calendar year) a reasonable opportunity to be heard. The location of any combined hearing is presumed to provide a reasonable opportunity for all affected residents to be heard if it is no farther than 100 miles from the seat of government of each participating governmental unit beyond whose geographic jurisdiction the hearing is conducted.

(7) Place for filing. The report is to be filed with the Internal Revenue Service Center, Philadelphia, Pennsylvania 19255.

(m) State certification requirements. *(1) In general.* An issue meets the requirements of this paragraph only if the issuer in good faith attempted to meet the State certification requirements of this paragraph. The requirements of this paragraph apply to obligations issued after December 31, 1984; see section 149(e) and the regulations thereunder with respect to obligations issued after December 31, 1986.

(2) Certification. (i) An issue satisfied the requirements of section 103A(j)(4) and this paragraph (m)(2) only if the State official designated by law (or, if there is no State official, the Governor) certifies on or before the later of the date of issue or October 3, 1985, following a request for such certification by the issuer, that, as of the date the certification is executed, the issue meets the requirements of section 103A(g) and the regulations thereunder (relating to volume limitation). In the case of any constitutional home rule city, the certification shall be made by the chief executive officer of the city. To the extent consistent with State and local law, the Governor (or the chief executive officer of any constitutional home rule city) may delegate the responsibility to execute the certification required by this paragraph.

(ii) The certifying official need not perform an independent investigation in order to determine whether the issue meets the requirements of section 103A(g). In determining the aggregate amount of qualified mortgage bonds previously issued by an issuer during a calendar year, the certifying official may rely on copies of the reports submitted, to date, by the issuer pursuant to section 103A(j)(3) for other issues of qualified mortgage bonds issued during that year and copies of any elections previously made pursuant to section 25(c)(2) not to issue qualified mortgage bonds, together with an affidavit executed by an officer of the issuer responsible for issuing the bonds stating that the issuer has not, to date during the calendar year, issued any other qualified mortgage bonds, the amount, if any, of the issuer's market limitation that it has, to date during the calendar year, surrendered to other issuing authorities, and that it has not, to date during the calendar year, made any other elections not to issue qualified mortgage bonds. If, based on such information, the certifying official determines that, as of the date the certification is executed, the issue will not exceed the issuer's market limitation for the year, the official may certify that the issue meets the requirements of section 103A(g).

(3) Special rule. If 15 days elapse after the issuer files a proper request for the certification described in paragraph

(m)(2) of this section and the issuer has not received from the State official designated by law (or, if there is no State official, the Governor) certification that the issue meets the requirements of section 103A(g) and § 6a.103A-2(g) or, in the alternative, a statement that the issue does not meet such requirements, the issuer may, instead, submit an affidavit executed by an officer of the issuer responsible for issuing the bonds stating that—

(i) The issue meets the requirements of section 103(A)(g) and § 6a.103A-2(g),

(ii) At least 15 days before the execution of the affidavit the issuer filed a proper request for the certification described in paragraph (m)(2) of this section, and

(iii) The State official designated by law (or, if there is no State official, the Governor) has not provided the certification described in paragraph (m)(2) of this section. In the case of obligations issued prior to October 4, 1985 the preceding sentence shall be applied by substituting "30 days" for "15 days". For purposes of this paragraph, a request for certification is proper if the request includes the reports and affidavits described in paragraph (m)(2)(ii) of this section.

(4) Filing. The certification (or affidavit) required by this paragraph shall be filed with the Internal Revenue Service Center, Philadelphia, PA 19255. The certification (or affidavit) shall be submitted with the Form 8038 required to be filed by section 103A(j)(3) and paragraph (k) of this § 1.103A-2. The Commissioner may grant an extension of time for filing the certification (or affidavit) if there is a reasonable cause for the failure to file such statement in a timely fashion.

(5) Effect of certification. The fact that an issuer obtains the certification (or affidavit) described in this paragraph does not ensure that the requirements of paragraph (g) of § 6a.103A-2 are met. Obligations that do not meet the requirements of paragraph (g) of § 6a.103A-2 are not described in section 103(a).

T.D. 8049, 8/29/85, amend T.D. 8129, 3/10/87.

§ 6a.103A-2 Qualified mortgage bond.

• ***Caution:*** Reg. § 6a.103A-2, following, was issued under Code section 103A before the related provisions of that Code section were deleted by P.L. 99-514 (10/22/86). Provisions similar to, but not necessarily identical to, the provisions deleted from Code section 103A now appear in Code section 143.

Caution: The Treasury has not yet amended Reg § 6a.103A-2 to reflect changes made by P.L. 105-34, P.L. 101-508, P.L. 100-647, P.L. 99-514.

(a) In general. *(1) Qualified mortgage bond.* A qualified mortgage bond shall not be treated as a mortgage subsidy bond, and the interest on a qualified mortgage bond will be exempt from Federal income taxation.

(2) Termination date. No obligation issued after December 31, 1987, shall be treated as part of a qualified mortgage bond issue.

(b) Definitions and special rules. For purposes of this section and § 6a.103A-1, the following definitions apply:

(1) Qualified mortgage bond. The term "qualified mortgage bond" means one or more obligations issued by a State or any political subdivision thereof (hereinafter referred to as "governmental unit") as part of an issue—

(i) All of the original proceeds of which, net of the costs of issuing the obligations and proceeds invested in a reasonably required reserve fund (such net amount hereinafter in this section referred to as "lendable proceeds"), are to be used to finance owner-occupied residences, and

(ii) Which meets each of the requirements of § 6a.103A-1 and this section.

A qualified mortgage bond does not include any bond that is an industrial development bond under section 103(b).

(2) Constitutional home rule city. The term "constitutional home rule city" means, with respect to any calendar year, any political subdivision of a State which, under a State constitution which was adopted in 1970 and effective on July 1, 1971, had home rule powers on the 1st day of the calendar year.

(3) Targeted area residence. The term "targeted area residence" means a residence in an area which is either—

(i) A qualified census tract, or

(ii) An area of chronic economic distress.

(4) Qualified census tract. (i) The term "qualified census tract" means a census tract in which 70 percent or more of the families have an income which is 80 percent or less of the State-wide median family income.

(ii) The determination under subdivision (i) shall be made on the basis of the most recent decennial census for which data are available. With respect to any particular bond issue, such determination may be based upon the decennial census data available 3 months prior to the date of issuance and shall not be affected by official changes to such data during or after such 3-month period.

(iii) The term "census tract" means a census tract as defined by the Secretary of Commerce.

(5) Areas of chronic economic distress. (i) The term "area of chronic economic distress" means an area designated by a State as meeting the standards established by that State for purposes of this subparagraph and approved by the Secretary and by the Secretary of Housing and Urban Development in accordance with the criteria set forth in (iii) of this subparagraph. A State may withdraw such designation at any time, with reasonable cause. Such withdrawal shall be effective upon notification by the State to the Assistant Secretary for Housing/Federal Housing Commissioner of the Department of Housing and Urban Development. Such withdrawal shall not affect the tax-exempt status of any outstanding issue of obligations.

(ii) For purposes of making a designation under this subparagraph, withdrawing a designation, or making any other submission, "State" means the governor of a State, or a State official commissioned by the governor or by State statute for such purposes.

(iii) The following criteria will be used in evaluating a proposed designation of an area of chronic economic distress:

(A) The condition of the housing stock, including the age of the housing and the number of abandoned and substandard residential units. Data pertinent to this criterion include the number and percentage of housing units that were constructed prior to 1940, the average age of the housing stock, the number and percentage of abandoned housing units, and the number and percentage of substandard residential units.

(B) The need of area residents for owner financing under a qualified mortgage bond issue as indicated by low per capital income, a high percentage of families in poverty, a high number of welfare recipients, and high unemployment rates. Data pertinent to this criterion include the per capita income of the population in the area, the number and percentage of families eligible to receive food stamps from a program pursuant to 7 U.S.C. 2011, the number and percentage of families eligible to receive payments under the Aid to Families with Dependent Children program, and the unemployment rate.

(C) The potential for use of owner financing under a qualified mortgage bond issue to improve housing conditions in the area. Data pertinent to this criterion include the number and percentage of owner-occupied homes that are substandard, the number and percentage of families that are low- or moderate-income renters, and the number and percentage of substandard units in the area that will be improved through the use of owner financing provided by the proceeds of a qualified mortgage bond issue.

(D) The existence of a housing assistance plan which provides a displacement program and a public improvements and services program (similar to the Housing Assistance Plan (HAP) required by the Department of Housing and Urban Development under the Community Development Block Grant program (42 U.S.C. section 5301 *et seq.)).*

This determination shall be based upon the most recent data available. The certification described in subdivision (iv)(C) shall satisfy the criteria set forth in subdivisions (C) and (D). A certification described in (iv)(D) shall satisfy the criteria set forth in subdivisions (A) and (B): *Provided,* That the majority of the households in the proposed area have incomes less than 80 percent of the median income for the standard metropolitan statistical area (SMSA) in which the proposed area is located or, if the proposed area is not within a SMSA, less than 80 percent of the median income for the State.

(iv) A proposal by the State that an area be approved as an area of chronic economic distress shall contain the following information:

(A) A description of the proposed area by its geographical limits.

(B) Maps of the State and of areas within the State that are qualified census tracts and existing or proposed areas of chronic economic distress.

(C) Where applicable, a certification of the local Area Manager of the Department of Housing and Urban Development in which the proposed area is located that the proposed area is a Neighborhood Strategy Area (NSA) under 24 CFR 570.301(c) promulgated pursuant to the Community Development Block Grant program or an area comparable to a NSA which has been reviewed and approved by the Area Manager as meeting the standards for an NSA.

(D) Where applicable, a certification from the HUD Area Manager with jurisdiction over the proposed area that the proposed area is within a geographic area which has been declared eligible for grants under the Urban Development Action Grant Program, Pursuant to 24 CFR 570.452, by the Secretary of Housing and Urban Development.

(E) Statistical and descriptive information pertinent to the criteria enumerated in subdivision (iii) of this subparagraph, and a succinct statement of how the information furnished satisfies those criteria. Such statistical information shall be based upon the most recent data available.

(F) If the State so desires, a written request for a conference prior to any adverse decision on the proposed designation.

(G) A certification by the Governor or designated official that the proposed designation conforms to these regulations.

(v) The proposed designation and the information furnished with it as required by subdivision (iv) of this subparagraph shall be submitted in triplicate to the Assistant Secretary for Housing/Federal Housing Commissioner of the Department of Housing and Urban Development (Attention: Office of State Agency and Bond Financed Programs, Rm. 6138, 451 7th Street, SW., Washington, D.C. 20410).

(vi) Only those areas of chronic economic distress that have been previously designated by the State and approved in accordance with this subparagraph at least 3 months prior to the date of issuance need to be taken into account for any particular bond issue. Residences located in areas designated as areas of chronic economic distress approved in accordance with this subparagraph within such 3-month period or after the date of issue, however, may be treated as targeted area residences. However, for purposes of paragraph (h)(2), relating to the specified portion of proceeds to be placed in targeted areas, and paragraph (i)(3)(ii)(A), relating to the 1½ year temporary period, only areas approved as areas of chronic economic distress in accordance with his subparagraph at the time of issue may be taken into consideration.

(6) Standard metropolitan statistical area. A standard metropolitan statistical area ("SMSA") is an area in and around a city of 50,000 inhabitants or more (or equivalent area) and defined by the Secretary of Commerce as an SMSA.

(7) Statistical area. The term "statistical area" means—

(i) An SMSA,

(ii) Any county (or portion thereof) which is not within an SMSA, or

(iii) If there is insufficient recent statistical information with respect to a county (or portion thereof) described in subdivision (ii) of this subparagraph, such other area as may be designated by the Commissioner, upon proper application, as a substitute for such county (or portion thereof).

For purposes of subdivisions (ii) and (iii) of this subparagraph, in Alaska, the entire State, and in Louisiana, a parish, shall be treated in a manner similar to a county.

(8) Acquisition cost. (i) The term "acquisition cost" means the cost of acquiring a residence from the seller as a completed residential unit. Acquisition cost includes the following:

(A) All amounts paid, either in cash or in kind, by the purchaser (or a related party or for the benefit of the purchaser) to the seller (or a related party or for the benefit of the seller) as consideration for the residence.

(B) If a residence is incomplete, the reasonable cost of completing the residence whether or not the cost of completing construction is to be financed with bond proceeds. For example, where a mortgagor purchases a building which is so incomplete that occupancy of the building is not permitted under local law, the acquisition cost includes the cost of completing the building so that occupancy of the building is permitted.

(C) Where a residence is purchased subject to a ground rent, the capitalized value of the ground rent. Such value shall be calculated using a discount rate equal to the yield on the issue (as defined in § 6a.103A-2(i)(2)(vi)).

(ii) The term "acquisition cost" does not include the following:

(A) The usual and reasonable settlement or financing costs. Settlement costs include titling and transfer costs, title insurance, survey fees, or other similar costs. Financing costs include credit reference fees, legal fees, appraisal expenses, "points" which are paid by the buyer (but not the seller, even though borne by the mortgagor through a higher purchase price) or other costs of financing the residence. However, such amounts will be excluded in determining acquisition cost only to the extent that the amounts do not exceed the usual and reasonable costs which would be paid by the buyer where financing is not provided through a qualified mortgage bond issue. For example, if the purchaser agrees to pay to the seller more than a pro rata share of property taxes, such excess shall be treated as part of the acquisition cost of a residence.

(B) The value of services performed by the mortgagor or members of the mortgagor's family in completing the residence. For purposes of the preceding sentence, the family of an individual shall include only the individual's brothers and sisters (whether by the whole or half blood), spouse, ancestors, and lineal descendants. For example, where the mortgagor builds a home alone or with the help of family members, the acquisition cost includes the cost of materials provided and work performed by subcontractors (whether or not related to the mortgagor) but does not include the imputed cost of any labor actually performed by the mortgagor or a member of the mortgagor's family in constructing the residence. Similarly, where the mortgagor purchases an incomplete residence the acquisition cost includes the cost of material and labor paid by the mortgagor to complete the residence but does not include the imputed value of the mortgagor's labor or the labor of the mortgagor's family in completing the residence.

(C) The cost of land which has been owned by the mortgagor for at least 2 years prior to the date on which construction of the residence begins.

(iii) The following examples illustrate the provisions of subparagraph (8):

Example (1). A contracts with B, a builder of single-family residences, for the purchase of a residence. Under the terms of the contract, B will deliver a residential unit to A that contains an uncompleted recreation room and an unfinished third floor and which lacks a garage. Normally, a completed recreation room, a finished third floor and a garage are provided as part of the residence built by B. The contract price for the residence is $58,000. At the same time, A contracts with C, an affiliate of B, to complete the recreation room and third floor and to construct the garage for a contract price of $10,000. C will perform this work after A receives title to the unit from B. Under § 6a.103A-2(b)(8)(i)(A), the acquisition cost of A's completed residential unit is $68,000, which represents the contract price of the residence plus the cost of completion of the recreation room and third floor and construction of the garage.

Example (2). E owns a single-family residence which E has listed for sale. D contracts to purchase E's residence, and the contract provides for a selling price of $30,000. D also agrees to pay an unsecured debt in the amount of $5,000, which E owes to X, a local bank. D further agrees to purchase from E the refrigerator, stove, washer, and dryer located in E's residence for $500. Such amount is equal to the fair market value of such personalty. D also agrees to purchase the light fixtures, curtain rods, and wall-to-wall carpeting for a fair market value price of $700. Under § 6a.103A-2(b)(8)(i)(A), the acquisition cost of D's completed residential unit is $35,700. Such amount includes the $5,000 unsecured debt paid off by D. The $500 paid for the refrigerator, stove, washer, and dryer are not included because such items are not included within the definition of a residence under § 6a.103A-2(d)(4). Such definition does include, however, the light fixtures, curtain rods, and wall-to-wall carpeting purchased by D.

Example (3). F contracts with G to purchase G's home for $40,000. After purchasing the residence, F pays a party unrelated to G $3,000 for painting, minor repairs, and refinishing the floors. Under § 6a.103A-2(b)(8)(i)(A), the acquisition cost of the residence is $40,000. Such fix-up expenses are not treated as part of the acquisition costs. If G had incurred such fix-up expenses, however, F may not reduce his acquisition cost of the residence by such amounts.

(9) Qualified home improvement loan. (i) The term "qualified home improvement loan" means the financing (whether or not secured by a mortgage), in an amount which does not exceed $15,000 with respect to any residence, of alterations, repairs, and improvements on, or in connection with, an existing single-family, owner-occupied residence by the owner thereof, but only if such items substantially protect or improve the basic livability or energy efficiency of the residence.

(ii) Alterations, repairs, or improvements that satisfy the requirement of subdivision (i) of this subparagraph include the renovation of plumbing or electric systems, the installation of improved heating or air conditioning systems, the addition of living space, or the renovation of a kitchen area. Items that will not be considered to substantially protect or improve the basic livability of the residence include swimming pools, tennis courts, saunas, or other recreational or entertainment facilities.

(iii) If—

(A) Two or more qualified home improvement loans are provided for the same residence, whether or not by the same lender, and

(B) Any person who had a present ownership interest in such residence at the time the previous qualified home improvement loan or loans were made has a present ownership interest in the residence at the time the subsequent qualified home improvement loan is made,

then the allowable amount of the subsequent qualified home improvement loan shall be reduced by the amount, at origination, of any previous qualified home improvement loan, so that the sum of such loans does not exceed $15,000.

(iv) The following example illustrates the provisions of subparagraph (9):

Example. A and B jointly own a residence located in Town M. They obtain a qualified home improvement loan for $10,000 from Town M. A acquires B's interest in the residence. A applies to State X for a qualified home improvement loan. The maximum amount of a qualified home improvement loan which may be made by State X is $5,000, the amount that when added to the $10,000 previous loan from Town M does not exceed $15,000.

(10) Qualified rehabilitation loans. (i) The term "qualified rehabilitation loan" means any owner financing provided in connection with—

(A) A qualified rehabilitation, or

(B) The acquisition of a residence with respect to which there has been a qualified rehabilitation,

but only if the mortgagor to whom such financing is provided is the first resident of the residence after completion of the rehabilitation. Where there are two or more mortgagors of a rehabilitation loan, the first residency requirement is met if any of the mortgagors meets the first residency requirement.

(ii) The term "qualified rehabilitation" means any rehabilitation of a residence if—

(A) There is a period of at least 20 years between the date on which the building was first used and the date on which physical work on such rehabilitation begins,

(B) 75 percent or more of the existing external walls of such building are retained in place as external walls in the rehabilitation process, and

(C) The expenditures for such rehabilitation are 25 percent or more of the mortgagor's adjusted basis in the residence (including the land on which the residence is located).

(iii) For purposes of (A) and (B), the rules applicable to the investment tax credit for qualified rehabilitated buildings under section 48(g)(1)(A)(iii) and (B) shall apply. However, unlike section 48(g)(1)(B), once a building meets the 20-year test, more than one rehabilitation of that building within a 20-year period may qualify as a qualified rehabilitation.

(iv) The adjusted basis to the mortgagor is the mortgagor's adjusted basis for purposes of determining gain or loss on the sale or exchange of a capital asset (as defined in section 1221). The mortgagor's adjusted basis shall be determined as of the date of completion of the rehabilitation, or, if later, the date the mortgagor acquires the residence, *i.e.*, the date on which the mortgagor includes in basis any amounts expended for rehabilitation that are expended for capital assets.

(v) The amounts expended by the mortgagor for rehabilitation include all amounts expended for rehabilitation regardless of whether the amounts expended were financed from the proceeds of the loan or from other sources, and regardless of whether the expenditure is a capital expenditure, so long as the expenditure is made during the rehabilitation of the residence and is reasonably related to the rehabilitation of the residence. The value of services performed by the mortgagor or members of the mortgagor's family (as used in § 6a.103A-2(b)(8)(ii)(B)) in rehabilitating the residence will not be included in determining the rehabilitation expenditures for purposes of the 25-percent test.

(vi) Where a mortgagor purchases a residence that has been substantially rehabilitated, the 25-percent test is determined by comparing the total expenditures made by the seller for the rehabilitation of the residence with the acquisition cost of the residence to the mortgagor. The total expenditures made by the seller for rehabilitation do not include the cost of acquiring the building or land but do include all amounts directly expended by the seller in rehabilitating the building (excluding overhead and other indirect charges).

(c) Good faith compliance efforts. *(1) Mortgage eligibility requirements.* An issue of qualified mortgage bonds which fails to meet one or more of the requirements of paragraphs (d), (e), (f), and (j) of this section shall be treated as meeting such requirements if each of the following provisions is met.

(i) The issuer in good faith attempted to meet all such requirements before the mortgages were executed. Good faith requires that the trust indenture, participation agreements with loan originators, and other relevant instruments contain restrictions that permit the financing of mortgages only in accordance with such requirements. In addition, the issuer must establish reasonable procedures to ensure compliance with such requirements. Such procedures include reasonable investigations by the issuer or its agent to determine that the mortgages satisfy such requirements.

(ii) Ninety-five percent or more of the lendable proceeds (as defined in § 6a.103A-2(b)(1)) that were devoted to owner financing were devoted to residences with respect to which, at the time the mortgages were executed or assumed, all such requirements were met. In determining whether the proceeds are devoted to owner financing which meets such requirements, the issuer may rely on an affidavit of the mortgagor that the property is located within the issuer's jurisdiction and an affidavit of the mortgagor and the seller that the requirements of § 6a.103A-2(f) are met. The issuer may also rely on his own or his agent's examination of copies of income tax returns which were filed with the Internal Revenue Service and which are provided by the mortgagor or obtained by the issuer or loan originator in accordance with the procedures set forth in § 301.6103(c)-1 which indicate that, during the preceding 3 years, the mortgagor did not claim deductions for taxes or interest on indebtedness with respect to real property constituting his principal residence, in addition to an affidavit of the mortgagor that the requirements of § 6a.103A-2(e) are met. The mortgagor may also provide the issuer or his agent with an affidavit that the mortgagor was not required to file such return in accordance with section 6012 during one or all of the preceding 3 years. Where a particular mortgage fails to meet more than one of these requirements, the amount of the mortgage will be taken into account only once in determining whether the 95-percent requirement is met. However, all of the defects in the mortgage must be corrected pursuant to paragraph (c)(1)(iii) of this section.

(iii) Any failure to meet such requirements is corrected within a reasonable period after such failure is discovered. For example, where a mortgage fails to meet one or more of such requirements those failures can be corrected by calling the nonqualifying mortgage or by replacing the nonqualifying mortgage with a qualifying mortgage.

Example (1). State X issues obligations to be used to provide mortgages for owner-occupied residences. X contracts with bank M to originate and service the mortgages. The trust indenture and participation agreement require that the mortgages meet the mortgage eligibility requirements referred to in paragraph (c)(1). In addition, pursuant to procedures established by X, M obtains a signed affidavit from each applicant that the applicant intends to occupy the property as his or her principal residence within 60 days after the final closing and thereafter to maintain the property as his or her principal residence. Further, M obtains from each applicant copies certified by the Internal Revenue Service of the applicant's Federal tax returns for the preceding 3 years and examines each statement to determine whether the applicant has claimed a deduction for taxes on real property which was the applicant's principal residence pursuant to section 164(a)(1) or a deduction pursuant to section 163 for interest paid on a mortgage secured by real property which was the applicant's principal residence. Also in accordance with X's procedures, M obtains from each applicant a signed affidavit as to facts that are sufficient for M to determine whether the residence is located within X's jurisdiction and affidavits from the seller and the buyer that the purchase price and the new mortgage requirements have been met, and neither M nor X knows or has reason to believe that such affidavits are false. The mortgage instrument provides that the mortgage may not be assumed by another person unless X determines that the principal residence, 3-year, and purchase price requirements are met at the time of the assumption. These facts are sufficient evidence of the good faith of the issuer and meet the requirements of paragraph (c)(1)(i). Further, if 95 percent of the lendable proceeds are devoted to owner financing which according to these procedures meet the requirements of paragraphs (d), (e), (f), and (i), then the issue meets the requirements of paragraph (c)(1)(ii).

Example (2). State Y issues obligations to be used to provide mortgages for owner-occupied residences. Y contracts with bank N to originate and service the mortgages. The trust indenture and participation agreement require that the mortgagor certify compliance with the requirements referred to in paragraph (c)(1). By itself, this certification is not sufficient evidence of the good faith of the issuer to meet the requirements referred to in paragraph (c)(1).

Example (3). The facts are the same as in Example 1, except that M discovers through a verification procedure required by X that, at the time of closing, A fraudulently executed the residency affidavit. Instead of occupying the property as a principal residence, A leased the property to B for one year. A did not use the property as his residence during the lease term. Thus, at the time that A's mortgage was executed the residence failed to meet the requirements of paragraph (d) of this section.

More than 95 percent of the lendable proceeds of the issue were devoted to residences which met all the requirements referred to in paragraph (c)(1) at the time the mortgages were executed. Furthermore, pursuant to a provision in the mortgage instrument M called the loan. Any failures with respect to other mortgages are corrected by M. Based on these facts, the issue meets the requirements of subparagraph (c)(1).

Example (4). The facts are the same as in Example (1), except that the issuer requires copies of the applicant's signed tax returns that were filed with the Internal Revenue Service for the preceding 3 years but does not require that such returns be certified. If 95 percent of the lendable proceeds are devoted to owner financing which according to these procedures meet the requirements of paragraphs (d), (e), (f), and (i), then the issue meets the requirements of paragraph (c)(1)(ii).

(2) Nonmortgage eligibility requirements. An issue of qualified mortgage bonds which fails to meet one or more of the requirements of paragraphs (g), (h), and (i) of this section and § 6a.103A-1(a)(5) shall be treated as meeting such requirements if each of the following provisions is met.

(i) The issuer in good faith attempted to meet all such requirements. This good faith requirement will be met if all reasonable steps are taken by the issuer to ensure that the issue complies with these requirements.

(ii) Any failure to meet such requirements is due to inadvertent error, *e.g.*, mathematical error, after taking reasonable steps to comply with such requirements.

(iii) The following examples illustrate the application of this subparagraph (2):

Example (1). City X issues obligations to finance owner-occupied residences. However, despite taking all reasonable steps to determine accurately the size of the market share limitation, as provided in paragraph (g)(3), the limit is exceeded because the amount of the mortgages originated in the area during the past 3 years is incorrectly computed as a result of mathematical error. Such facts are sufficient evidence of the good faith of the issuer to meet the requirements of paragraph (c)(2).

Example (2). City Y issues $25 million of bonds to finance single-family, owner-occupied homes. Attorney A gives an opinion that the bonds satisfy the arbitrage requirements of § 6a.103A-2(i) and § 6a.103A-1(a)(3). In fact, however, the legal conclusion reached by A is erroneous, and the bonds do not meet the requirements of § 6a.103A-2(i). The issue does not meet the requirements of subparagraph (c)(2) because the erroneous opinion does not constitute inadvertent error.

(d) Residence requirements. *(1) In general.* An issue meets the requirements of this paragraph only if all of the residences for which owner financing is provided under the issue meet the requirements of this paragraph. A residence meets the requirements of this paragraph only if—

(i) It is a single-family residence (as defined in § 6a.103A-1(b)(6)) which, at the time the mortgage is executed or assumed, can reasonably be expected by the issuer to become the principal residence of the mortgagor within a reasonable time after the financing is provided; and

(ii) It is located within the jurisdiction of the authority issuing the obligation.

(2) Affidavit. The requirements of subparagraph (1)(i) of this paragraph may normally be met if the mortgagor executes an affidavit of his intent to use the residence as his principal residence within a reasonable time (*e.g.*, 60 days) after the financing is provided.

(3) Principal residence. Whether a residence is used as a principal residence depends upon all the facts and circumstances of each case, including the good faith of the mortgagor. A residence which is primarily intended to be used in a trade or business shall not satisfy the requirements of this paragraph. For purposes of the preceding sentence, any use of a residence which does not qualify for a deduction allowable for certain expenses incurred in connection with the business use of a home under section 280A shall not be considered as a use in a trade or business. Except for certain owner-occupied residences described in paragraph (b)(6) of § 6a.103A-1, a residence more than 15 percent of the total area of which is reasonably expected to be used primarily in a trade or business does not satisfy the requirements of this subparagraph. Further, a residence used as an investment property or a recreational home does not satisfy the requirements of this subparagraph.

(4) Residence. (i) The term "residence" includes stock held by a tenant-stockholder in a cooperative housing corporation (as those terms are defined in section 216(b)(1) and (2)). It does not include property such as an appliance, a piece of furniture, a radio, *etc.*, which, under applicable local law, is not a fixture. The term also includes factory-made housing which is permanently fixed to real property. The determination of whether factory-made housing is permanently fixed to real property shall be made on the basis of the facts and circumstances of each particular case.

(ii) Land. Land appurtenant to a residence shall be considered as part of the residence only if such land reasonably maintains the basic livability of the residence and does not provide, other than incidentally, a source of income to the mortgagor.

(5) Examples. The following examples illustrate the application of this paragraph (d):

Example (1). A contracts to purchase a new residence from B. Since B is unable to move from the residence until 1 month after the scheduled closing date, A agrees to lease the residence to B for 1 month at a rent equal to the fair rental value. A applies for a mortgage to be provided from the proceeds of a qualified mortgage bond. In light of all the facts and circumstances in the case, the fact that A temporarily leases the residence to B does not prevent the residence from being considered as property that can reasonably be expected to be used as A's principal residence within a reasonable period of time after financing is provided.

Example (2). C contracts to purchase a new residence located on 2 acres of land in city X. City X has a zoning regulation which prevents the subdividing of any lot in that part of the city for use as a private residence into parcels of less than 2 acres. In light of all the facts and circumstances in the case, the fact that the residence is located on 2 acres of land appurtenant to the residence does not prevent the entire property from being considered as property to be used by C as a residence.

Example (3). D contracts to purchase a new residence located on 40 acres of land that D intends to farm. Any financing provided for the purchase of that portion of the property intended to be farmed will not be considered as financing provided for an owner-occupied residence.

(e) 3-year requirement. *(1) In general.* An issue meets the requirements of this paragraph only if each of the mortgagors to whom owner financing is provided under the issue meets the requirements of this paragraph. A mortgagor meets the requirements of this paragraph only if the mortgagor had no present ownership interest in a principal residence at any time during the 3-year period prior to the date on which the mortgage is executed. For purposes of the preceding sentence, the mortgagor's interest in the residence with respect to which the financing is being provided shall not be taken into account.

(2) Exceptions. Subparagraph (1) shall not apply with respect to—

(i) Any financing provided with respect to a targeted area residence (as defined in § 6a.103A-2(b)(3)),

(ii) Any qualified home improvement loan (as defined in § 6a.103A-2(b)(10)), and

(iii) Any qualified rehabilitation loan (as defined in § 6a.103A-2(b)(10)), and

(3) Multiple mortgagors. In the event that there is more than one mortgagor with respect to a particular residence, each of such mortgagors must meet the 3-year requirement. A person who is liable under a note secured by the mortgage but who does not have a present ownership interest in a residence subject to the mortgage need not meet the 3-year requirement. For example, where a parent of a home purchaser cosigns the note for a child but the parent takes no interest in the residence, it is not necessary that the parent meet the 3-year requirement since the parent is not a mortgagor of the residence.

(4) Included interests. Examples of interests which constitute present ownership interests are the following:

(i) A fee simple interest;

(ii) A joint tenancy, a tenancy in common, or tenancy by the entirety;

(iii) The interest of a tenant-shareholder in a cooperative;

(iv) A life estate;

(v) A land contract (*i.e.*, a contract pursuant to which possession and the benefits and burdens of ownership are transferred although legal title is not transferred until some later time); and

(vi) An interest held in trust for the mortgagor (whether or not created by the mortgagor) that would constitute a present ownership interest if held directly by the mortgagor.

(5) Excluded interests. Examples of interests which do not constitute present ownership interests are the following:

(i) A remainder interest;

(ii) A lease with or without an option to purchase;

(iii) A mere expectancy to inherit an interest in a principal residence;

(iv) The interest that a purchaser of a residence acquires on the execution of a purchase contract; and

(v) An interest in other than a principal residence during the previous 3 years.

(f) Purchase price requirements. *(1) In general.* An issue meets the requirements of this paragraph only if the acquisition cost (as defined in § 6a.103A-2(b)(8)) of each residence, other than a targeted area residence, for which owner financing is provided does not exceed 90 percent of the average area purchase price applicable to such residence. In the case of a targeted area residence (as defined in § 6a.103A-2(b)(3)), the acquisition cost may not exceed 110 percent of the average area purchase price applicable to such residence.

(2) Exception. Paragraph (1) shall not apply with respect to any qualified home improvement loan (as defined in § 6a.103A-2(b)(9)).

(3) Average area purchase price. The term "average area purchase price" means, with respect to any residence, the average purchase price of all single-family residences in the statistical area (as defined in § 6a.103A-2(b)(7)) in which the residence being financed is located for the most recent 12-month period for which sufficient statistical information is available. The determination whether a particular residence meets the purchase price requirement shall be made as of the date on which the commitment to provide the financing is made or, if earlier, the date of purchase of the residence.

(4) Special rules. (i) In the case of a qualified rehabilitation loan, the requirements of this paragraph are met if the mortgagor's adjusted basis in the property as of the completion of the rehabilitation (including the cost of the rehabilitation) meets the requirements of paragraph (f)(1). For this purpose, a rehabilitated residence is to be treated as a residence which has been previously occupied.

(ii) The determination of average area purchase price shall be made separately with respect to—

(A) Residences which have not been previously occupied;

(B) Residences which have been previously occupied; and

(C) One-family, two-family, three-family, and four-family residences.

(5) Safe harbor limitation. (i) For purposes of meeting the requirements of this paragraph, an issuer may rely upon average area purchase price limitations published by the Treasury Department for the statistical area in which a residence is located. These safe harbor limitations will be effective for the period stated at the time of publication. An issuer may use a limitation different from such safe harbor limitation for any statistical area (as defined in § 6a.103A-2(b)(7)) for which the issuer has more accurate and comprehensive data.

(ii) The following example illustrates the application of subparagraph (5)(i):

Example. The average area purchase price safe harbor limitation for new single-family residences published by the Treasury Department for the second half of 1981 for the jurisdiction of governmental unit X is $41,500. However, on July 1, 1981, X determines that its average area purchase price for new single-family residences is actually $43,000. Such determination is based on a comprehensive survey of residential housing sales in the jurisdiction over the previous calendar year. The data accumulated are based on records maintained by the county clerk's office in X's jurisdiction, which enables X to compute average area purchase prices separately for new and used residences and for one-, two-, three-, and four-family residences. X cannot reasonably update such data more often than once a year. X may use average area purchase prices computed from these data for mortgages made from July 1, 1981, through June 30, 1982, rather than the safe harbor published by the Treasury Department.

(g) Limitation on aggregate amount of qualified mortgage bonds issued during any calendar year. *(1) In general.* An issue meets the requirements of this section only if the aggregate amount of bonds issued pursuant thereto, when added to the sum of (i) the aggregate amount of qualified mortgage bonds previously issued by the issuing authority during the calendar year and (ii) the amount of qualified mortgage bonds which the issuing authority previously elected not to issue under section 25(c)(2)(A)(ii) and the regulations thereunder during the calendar year, does not exceed the applicable limit ("market limitation") for such authority for such calendar year.

(2) State housing finance agency. Except as provided in paragraph (g)(4) of this section, the market limitation for any State housing finance agency for any calendar year shall be 50 percent of the State ceiling for such year. For purposes of the preceding sentence, if any State has more than one housing finance agency all such agencies shall be treated as a single agency.

(3) Other issuers. Except as provided in paragraph (g)(4), the market limitation for any issuing authority (other than a State housing finance agency) for any calendar year is an amount equal to that authority's proportionate share of 50 percent of the State ceiling amount for such calendar year. The proportionate share is an amount which bears the same ratio to 50 percent of the State ceiling for such year as—

(i) The average annual aggregate principal amount of mortgages executed during the immediately preceding 3 calendar years for single-family, owner-occupied residences located within the jurisdiction of such issuing authority, bears to

(ii) An average determined in the same way for the entire State.

(4) Constitutional home rule city. (i) In determining the market limitation for any constitutional home rule city (as defined in paragraph (b)(2) of this section), subparagraph (3) shall be applied by substituting "100 percent" for "50 percent."

(ii) In a State with one or more constitutional home rule cities, in computing the market limitation for issuers other than constitutional home rule cities, the State ceiling amount for any calendar year shall be reduced by the aggregate market limitation for such year for all constitutional home rule cities in the State.

(5) Overlapping jurisdictions. (i) For purposes of subparagraph (3) of this paragraph, if an area is within the jurisdiction of two or more governmental units, such area shall be treated as only within the jurisdiction of the unit having jurisdiction over the smallest geographical area. However, the governmental unit with jurisdiction over the smallest geographical area may enter into a written agreement to allocate all or a designated portion of such overlapping area to the governmental unit having jurisdiction over the next smallest geographical area.

(ii) Where two governmental units have authority to issue mortgage subsidy bonds and both governmental units have jurisdiction over the identical geographical area, the aggregate principal amount of mortgages on residences located within that area shall be allocated to the governmental unit having broader sovereign powers.

(6) State ceiling. (i) Except as provided in paragraph (g)(6)(v), the State ceiling applicable to any State for any calendar year shall be the greater of—

(A) 9 percent of the average annual aggregate principal amount of mortgages executed during the immediately preceding 3 calendar years for single-family, owner-occupied residences located within the jurisdiction of such State, or

(B) $200,000,000.

Only single-family owner-occupied residences (without regard to the definition of such term under § 6a.103A-1(b)(6)) may be used in determining the market limitation regardless of whether or not residences with up to four family units are to be financed by the program. First and second mortgages or mortgages used to refinance an existing mortgage shall be used in making such determination. Liens, special assessments, and similar encumbrances may not be taken into consideration.

(ii) For mortgages on residences with more than one family unit, the full amount of the mortgage shall be applied toward the market limitation and not merely that portion allocable to the owner-occupied unit.

(iii) For purposes of determining the State ceiling amount applicable to any State for any calendar year an issuer may rely upon the State ceiling amount published by the Treasury Department for such calendar year. An issuer may rely on a different State ceiling amount than such safe-harbor limitation where the issuer has made a more accurate and comprehensive determination of such amount.

(iv) The following example illustrates the application of subparagraphs (3) and (6) of this paragraph (g):

Example. Pursuant to the allocation rule provided in subparagraph (3), City Y determines that its maximum market limitation in 1981 is $15,000,000. This determination is based on records maintained by the county clerk's office from which data for the preceding 3 years have been accumulated by City Y as to the number of sales of single-family homes in City Y's jurisdiction, the purchase price in each such sales transaction, the number of such sales that were financed by mortgages and the volume of second mortgages and refinancing on previously purchased owner-occupied single-family residences. This information, combined with estimates made by City Y of the average mortgage-loan-to-purchase-price ratio and the ratio of sales of single-family, owner-occupied residences to all sales of single-family residences from a representative sample of sales transactions, enables Y to estimate the preceding 3 years' annual aggregate mortgage volume by using the following formula:

$$v = \tfrac{1}{3} \sum_{l=t-3}^{t-1} (u_l - w_l - x_l - y_l - z_l) + a_l$$

where:

v = the preceding 3 years' average annual aggregate volume of mortgages on single-family, owner-occupied residences in City Y.

v_l +24 number of sales of single-family residences,

w_l +24 average purchase price of all sales,

x_l +24 percent of all sales transactions that were financed with mortgages,

y_l +24 estimated average mortgage-loan-to-purchase-price ratio,

z_l +24 estimated percent of sales that were owner-occupied residences,

a_l +24 total volume of second mortgages and refinancing on previously purchased owner-occupied, single-family residences,

i = the annual period of calculation, and

t = the current year.

City Y determines its applicable limit for 1981 based on the following formula:

L = 0.5 (v/s) r, where

L = market limitation for City Y for the current year,

s = the preceding 3 years' average annual aggregate volume of mortgages on single-family, owner-occupied residences in State X, and

r = ceiling for State X *(i.e.,* r = the greater of .09s or $200,000,000).

City Y may use the Treasury estimate of s which will be published with the mortgage volume safe harbor limitation. City Y may rely on its determination of its market limitation for obligations issued during 1981.

(v) Reduction in State ceiling. If for any calendar year an issuer of mortgage credit certificates, as defined in section 25 and the regulations thereunder, fails to meet the requirements of section 25(d)(2) and the regulations thereunder, relating to the limit on the aggregate amount of mortgage credit certificates that may be issued, the applicable State ceiling under paragraph (g)(6)(i) of this section for the State in which the program operates will be reduced by 1.25 times the correction amount (as defined in section 25(f)(2) and the regulations thereunder) with respect to that failure for the calendar year following the calendar year in which the Commissioner determines the correction amount with respect to that failure.

(7) Excess obligations. Where an issue of obligations when added to the aggregate amount of bonds issued by the same issuing authority in the same calendar year exceeds the market limitation determined in accordance with this paragraph (g), no portion of the issue will be treated as a qualified mortgage bond issue, and interest on such obligations shall be subject to Federal income taxation. However, previously issued qualified mortgage bond issues which met the market limitation at the time of their issuance will not cease to be qualified mortgage bond issues even though a subsequent issue causes the aggregate amount of obligations to exceed such limitation for a calendar year.

(8) Transitional rule obligations. In applying this paragraph (g) to any calendar year, there shall not be taken into account any bond which, by reason of section 1104 of the Mortgage Subsidy Bond Tax Act of 1980 (94 Stat. 2670) (relating to transitional rules), receives the same tax treatment as bonds issued on or before April 24, 1979.

(9) Procedure for providing a different allocation. (i) A State may, by law enacted after December 5, 1980, provide a different formula for allocating the State ceiling amount among the governmental units in such State (other than constitutional home rule jurisdictions) having authority to issue qualified mortgage bonds.

(ii) The governor of any State may proclaim a different formula than provided in subparagraphs (g)(2) and (g)(3) for allocating the State ceiling amount among the governmental units in such State having authority to issue qualified mortgage bonds. The authority of the governor to proclaim a different formula shall not apply after the earlier of—

(A) The 1st day of the 1st calendar year beginning after the 1st calendar year after 1980 during which the legislature of the State met in regular session, or

(B) The effective date of any State legislation dealing with such ceiling enacted after December 5, 1980.

If, on or before either date, the governor of any State exercises the authority to provide a different allocation, such allocation shall be effective until the date specified in (B).

(iii) Unless otherwise provided in a State constitutional amendment or by law changing the home rule provisions adopted in the manner provided by the State constitution, the allocation of that portion of the State ceiling which is allocated to any constitutional home rule city may not be changed by the governor or State legislature unless such city agrees to such different allocation.

(iv) Where a State elects to make a different allocation in accordance with subdivision (i) or (ii) of this subparagraph, the determination as to whether a particular bond issue meets the requirements of paragraph (g) of this section will be based upon the allocation in effect at the time such bonds were issued. Moreover, the authority to provide for a different allocation may not be used directly or indirectly to increase the State ceiling amount.

(v) An issuing authority located in a State with one or more constitutional home rule cities may use an alternative method to those provided in subparagraphs (2), (3), and (4) for determining such issuing authority's market limitation if, prior to issuing any obligations for the calendar year, it demonstrates to the satisfaction of the Commissioner that—

(A) The use of the methods provided in subparagraph (2), (3), or (4) would impose an unreasonable hardship on the issuing authority, and

(B) Such alternative method is reasonable.

(h) Portion of loans required to be placed in targeted areas. *(1) In general.* An issue meets the requirements of this paragraph only if—

(i) The portion of the lendable proceeds (as defined in § 6a.103A-2(b)(1)) of the issue specified in subparagraph (2) is made available for owner financing of targeted area residences (as defined in § 6a.103A-2(b)(3)) for at least 1 year after the date on which owner financing is first made available with respect to targeted area residences, and

(ii) The issuer attempts with reasonable diligence to place such proceeds in qualified mortgages.

Proceeds are considered first made available with respect to targeted area residences on the date on which any financing of mortgages with the lendable proceeds of an issue first becomes available. Reasonable diligence requires that the issuer and the loan originators use reasonable efforts in trying to place mortgages in targeted areas, such as by advertising that mortgage funds are available for targeted areas. Reasonable diligence is not shown by merely providing in the governing instruments that the required amount be set aside for targeted areas.

(2) Specified portion. The specified portion of lendable proceeds of an issue required to be made available in targeted areas is the lesser of—

(i) 20 percent of the lendable proceeds, or

(ii) 40 percent of the average annual aggregate principal amount of mortgages executed during the immediately preceding 3 calendar years for single-family, owner-occupied residences in targeted areas within the jurisdiction of the issuing authority.

(3) Safe harbor. For purposes of computing the required portion of proceeds specified in subparagraph (2)(ii) of this paragraph, where such provision is applicable, an issuer may rely upon the amount produced by the following formula:

$P = .2(X/Y \times Z)$, where

P = Required portion to be made available in targeted areas,

X = Average annual aggregate principal amount of mortgages executed during the immediately preceding 3 calendar years for single-family, owner-occupied residences within the State in which the issuing jurisdiction is located,

Y = The total population within the State, based on the most recent decennial census for which data are available, and

Z = The total population in the targeted areas located within the issuer's jurisdiction, based on the most recent decennial census for which data are available.

The issuing jurisdiction may use the Treasury Department estimate of X which will be published with the mortgage volume safe harbor limitation.

(4) Minimum amount. (i) The specified portion required to be made available in targeted areas is a minimum amount. More than the minimum amount may be (but need not be) made available in targeted areas.

(ii) With respect to any proceeds not required to be made available in targeted areas, the requirements of this paragraph do not abrogate the requirement of the arbitrage rules that due diligence be used in placing lendable proceeds into mortgages.

(i) Arbitrage and investment gain. *(1) In general.* An issue meets the requirements of this paragraph only if such issue meets the requirements of subparagraphs (2), (3), and (4) of this paragraph. For purposes of these requirements, all determinations of yield, effective interest rates, and amounts required to be paid or credited to mortgagors under paragraph (i)(4)(i) of this section shall be made on an actuarial basis taking into account the present value of money. The requirements of section 103A(i) and this paragraph are applicable in addition to the requirements of section 103(c) and §§ 1.103-13, 1.103-14, and 1.103-15.

(2) Effective rate of mortgage interest not to exceed bond yield by more than 1 percentage point. (i) Maximum yield. An issue of qualified mortgage bonds shall be treated as meeting the requirements of this subparagraph only if the excess of—

(A) The effective rate of interest on the mortgages financed by the issue, over

(B) The yield on the issue,

is not greater over the term of the issue than 1 percentage point.

(ii) Effective rate of interest. (A) In determining the effective rate of interest on any mortgage for purposes of this subparagraph, there shall be taken into account all fees, charges, and other amounts borne by the mortgagor which are attributable to the mortgage or to the bond issue. Such amounts include points, commitment fees, origination fees, servicing fees, and prepayment penalties paid by the mortgagor.

(B) Items that shall be treated as borne by the mortgagor and shall be taken into account in calculating the effective rate of interest also include—

(1) All points, commitment fees, origination fees, or similar charges borne by the seller of the property;

(2) The excess of any amounts received from any person other than the mortgagor by any person in connection with the acquisition of the mortgagor's interest in the property over the usual and reasonable costs incurred by a person acquiring like property where owner financing is not provided through the use of qualified mortgage bonds.

(C) The following items shall not be treated as borne by the mortgagor and shall not be taken into account in calculating the effective rate of interest:

(1) Any expected rebate of arbitrage profit (as required by § 6a.103A-2(i)(4)).

(2) Any application fee, survey fee, credit report fee, insurance fee or similar settlement or financing cost to the extent such amount does not exceed amounts charged in such area in cases where owner financing is not provided through the use of qualified mortgage bonds. For example, amounts paid for FHA, VA, or similar private mortgage insurance on an individual's mortgage need not be taken into account so long as such amounts do not exceed the amounts charged in the area with respect to a similar mortgage that is not financial with qualified mortgage bonds. Premiums charged for pool mortgage insurance will be considered amounts in excess of the usual and reasonable amounts charged for insurance in cases where owner financing is not provided through the use of qualified mortgage bonds.

(D) (1) Where amounts other than those derived from the proceeds of a mortgage subsidy bond are used to finance single-family residences such amounts will not be treated as the proceeds of a qualified mortgage bond issue and will not be subject to the limitations set forth in subparagraphs (2), (3), and (4) of this paragraph (i). Such amounts may, however, be treated as proceeds for purposes of the requirements of section 103(c) and the regulations thereunder. Thus, the portion of the mortgage pool financed by the proceeds of a qualified mortgage bond issue will be subject to the limitations of subparagraphs (2), (3), and (4) of this paragraph (i), while the portion not provided with bond proceeds will not be subject to such limitations. The interest rate, points, origination fees, servicing fees, and other amounts charged with respect to that portion of a mortgage loan financed with non-bond amounts may not exceed the reasonable and customary amount which would be charged where financing is not provided through a qualified mortgage bond issue. Where the charge does exceed such reasonable and customary amount, any excess will be taken into account in computing the effective interest rate on the portion of the loan provided with the proceeds of the qualified mortgage bond issue. Furthermore, where such fees and other charges are less than the reasonable and customary charges, the issuer may not allocate that portion of the charges on the loan amounts made with bond proceeds which is equal to such differential to loan amounts made with non-bond proceeds.

(2) If any mortgage is allocated to two or more sources of funds, the receipt of amounts which are described in paragraph (i)(2)(ii)(A) and (B) of this section, repayments of principal, or payments of interest on such mortgage must be allocated to each source of funds.

(E) The effective rate of interest on any mortgage shall be determined in a manner consistent with actuarial methods and shall take into account the discounted value of all amounts from the time received to an amount equal to the "purchase price" of the mortgage. Such discount rate is the effective rate of interest on the mortgages. The "purchase price" of a mortgage means the net amount loaned to the mortgagor. For example, if a mortgage loan is in the amount of $30,000 and the mortgagor is charged one point ($300) as an origination fee which amount is deducted from loan proceeds available to the mortgagor, the purchase price is $29,700. If interest on an issue is paid semiannually, all regular monthly mortgage payments and prepayments of principal may be treated as being received at the end of each semiannual debt service period.

(1) If interest on an issue is paid semiannually, all regular monthly mortgage payments may be treated as being received at the end of each semiannual debt service period.

(2) Prepayments of principal shall be treated as being received on the last day of the month in which the issuer reasonably expects to receive such prepayments.

(F) The rate shall be determined on a composite basis for all mortgages financed by the issue.

(iii) Example. The following example illustrate the provisions of subparagraph (2)(ii) of this paragraph:

Example. Purchaser A contracts with seller B, who is represented by real estate agent C, for the purchase of B's residence for $65,000. A applies to County X for a mortgage provided by the proceeds of a qualified mortgage bond. County X requires that agent C provide it with a principal residence affidavit as well as verify the purchase price of the residence and the location of the purchasers previous residences. Due to the increased administrative burden imposed on agent C by County X, C charges B a real estate commission of 8 percent ($5,200), rather than 6 percent ($3,900). The normal real estate commission is 6 percent. Since the 8 percent commission charged by C and paid by B is in excess of the usual and reasonable real estate commission where owner financing is not provided through the use of qualified mortgage bonds, 2 percent ($1,300) shall be treated as borne by A and taken into account in calculating the effective rate of interest on the mortgage.

(iv) Prepayment assumption In determining the affective rate of interest on mortgages, it shall be assumed that the mortgage prepayment rate for mortgages made out of both original proceeds and mortgages that the issuer expects with reasonable certainty to be made out of prepayments of principal will be equal to 100 percent of the rate set forth in the most recent mortgage maturity experience table for mortgages having the same term insured under section 203 of the National Housing Act and published by the Federal Housing Administration in "Survivorship and Decrement Tables for HUD/FHA Home MORTGAGE Insurance Program" for the region, or, if available, the State in which the residence is located. For purposes of applying these tables, either the original balance method or the declining balance method of calculating mortgage loan prepayments may be used. For proceeds used to finance qualified home improvement loans or shorter term qualified rehabilitation loans for which there are no comparable FHA mortgage maturity experience tables, the assumption used by the issuer as to the rate of prepayment shall be based upon the reasonable expectations of the issuer, as reflected, where applicable, by the issuer's prior experience with such loans.

(v) Net losses. The projected net losses on the mortgage pool (after foreclosure and payment of insurance proceeds), based on the most recent default experience for the area in which the residences are located, shall be taken into consideration in calculating the effective rate of interest on the mortgages. However, where mortgages provided under an issue are insured with FHA, VA, or private mortgage insurance, in conjunction with pool mortgage insurance, the expected net losses will be presumed to be zero. In the event that the actual losses on the mortgage pool exceed the projected net losses which were taken into consideration in calculating the effective rate of interest on the mortgages, investment proceeds earned from nonmortgage assets may be used to recover the excess losses and need not be paid or credited to the mortgagors under § 6a.103A-2(i)(4).

(vi) Yield on the issue. (A) The yield on an issue of qualified mortgage bonds shall be calculated on the basis of—

(1) The issue price, and

(2) An expected maturity for the bonds which is consistent with the prepayment assumption required under subparagraph (2)(iv) of this paragraph.

The expected maturity will be considered consistent with such prepayment assumption if all prepayments are assumed to be used to call bonds proportionately (i.e., a "strip" call). The preceding sentence shall not apply to prepayments of mortgages provided from original proceeds to the extent such prepayments are used to provide mortgages.

(B) For purposes of (1) of this subdivision (vi), the term "issue price" shall have the same meaning as in section 1232(b)(2). Thus, in general, such term means the initial offering price to the public, not including bond houses and brokers, or similar persons or organizations acting in the capacity of underwriters or wholesalers, at which price a substantial amount of such obligations were sold or, if privately placed, the price paid by the first buyer of such obligations or the acquisition cost of the first buyer.

(3) Nonmortgage investments. (i) Maximum investment. Except as provided in subdivision (ii) of this subparagraph, an issue meets the requirements of this subparagraph only if—

(A) At no time during any bond year does the aggregate amount invested in nonmortgage investments, *e.g.*, reasonably required reserve funds, with a yield materially higher than the yield on the issue exceed 150 percent of the debt service on the issue for the current bond year, and

(B) Such aggregate amount invested in nonmortgage assets with a yield materially higher than the yield on the issue is promptly and appropriately reduced as mortgages are repaid.

The amount subject to the maximum investment rule in subdivision (i)(A) of this subparagraph includes the original bond proceeds, investment proceeds and repayments of principal on the mortgages. For purposes of subdivision (B), the amount described in subdivision (A) shall be considered promptly and appropriately reduced if beginning in the first bond year after the expiration of the temporary period for original proceeds described in subdivision (ii)(A) of this subparagraph, such amount is reduced within 30 days of the beginning of each bond year by an amount equal to the difference between the average scheduled monthly mortgage receipts for the bond year (excluding any receipts that were scheduled with respect to mortgages that were discharged in the preceding bond year) and the average scheduled monthly mortgage receipts for the preceding bond year.

(ii) Temporary periods. Subparagraph (3)(i) of this paragraph shall not apply to—

(A) Proceeds (including prepayments of principal designated to be used to acquire additional mortgages) of the issue invested for an initial temporary period not to exceed 1 year (1½ years for proceeds required to be set aside for placing mortgages in targeted areas) until such proceeds are needed for mortgages, and

(B) Repayments of principal and interest on mortgages that are contributed to a bona fide debt service fund (as defined in § 1.103-13(b)(12)) and invested for a 13-month temporary period as provided in § 1.103-14(b)(10).

(iii) Debt service defined. For purposes of subparagraph (3)(i)(A) of this paragraph, the debt service on the issue for any bond year is the scheduled amount of interest and amortization of principal payable for such year with respect to such issue. There shall not be taken into account amounts scheduled with respect to any bond which has been retired before the beginning of the bond year.

(iv) Nonmortgage investments. A nonmortgage investment is any investment other than an investment in a qualified mortgage. For example, a mortgage-secured certificate or obligation is a nonmortgage investment. Investment earnings from participation fees (described in § 6a.103A-1(b)(5)) are treated as investment proceeds on nonmortgage investments unless such fees are used to pay debt service or to finance owner occupied residences.

(v) Bonds issued after June 30, 1993. Section 1.148-2(f)(2)(iv) applies to bonds issued after June 30, 1993, in lieu of this paragraph (i)(3).

(4) Arbitrage and investment gains to be used to reduce costs of owner financing. (i) Rebate requirement. An issue shall be treated as meeting the requirements of this subparagraph only if an amount equal to the sum of

(A) The excess of—

(1) The net amount earned on all nonmortgage investments pursuant to subparagraph (3)(i) and (ii) of this paragraph (other than investments attributable to an excess described in this subdivision (A)) over

(2) The amount which would have been earned if the investments were invested at a rate equal to the yield on the issue, plus

(B) Any income attributable to the excess described in subdivision (A).

shall be paid or credited to the mortgagors as rapidly as practicable. Such amount may be disproportionately distributed to the mortgagors if the larger portion of such amount is distributed to lower income mortgagors. The determination of the excess described in subdivision (A) shall take into account any reinvestment of nonmortgage investment receipts and any gain or loss realized on the disposition of nonmortgage investments. In addition, where nonmortgage investments are retained by the issuer after retirement of an issue, any unrealized gains or losses as of the date of retirement of such issue must be taken into account, in calculating the amount to be rebated to the mortgagors. The amount described in subdivision (A) *(2)* is the amount that would have been earned if the investments in nonmortgage obligations were invested at a rate equal to the yield on the issue calculated in the same manner as provided in § 6a.103A-2(i)(2)(vi) and by using the same compounding method. For purposes of subdivision (B), any income attributable to the excess described in subdivision (A) shall be taken into account whether or not such income exceeds the yield on the bonds.

(ii) Computation period. Whether earnings are amounts described in subdivision (i)(A) or (B) of this subparagraph shall be determined by making computations on an annual basis. For example, if at the end of the first year the earnings on nonmortgage investments exceed the amount that could have been earned if such investments were invested at the bond yield, the amount of earnings equal to such difference constitutes an excess described in subdivision (i)(A) of this subparagraph. In the following year, investment proceeds earned on such excess must be taken into account, whether or not such earnings exceed the yield on the bonds, and may not be treated as "negative arbitrage" .

(iii) Paid or credited. For purposes of subdivision (i) of this subparagraph, amounts are paid or credited to mortgagors as rapidly as practicable if such amounts are paid or credited to such mortgagors at the time the mortgagor discharges the mortgage, for example, through prepayment of the entire principal amount or through making the last regular payment on the mortgage. The amount paid or credited to the mortgagors must have a present value at least equal to the present value of the amount described in subdivision (i) of this subparagraph, using the yield on the bonds as the discount rate. In the case of prepayments, the cumulative amount required to be rebated under subparagraph (4)(i) of this paragraph may be determined as of a date before the actual prepayment but not more than 1 year earlier than the date of prepayment. Except as provided in subparagraph (2)(v) or subparagraph (4)(iv) of this paragraph, such amount may not be subject to the claim of any party, *e.g.*, a bondholder, and may not be paid over to any party other than the mortgagor or the United States.

(iv) Reduction where issuer does not use full 1 percentage point. (A) The amount required to be paid or credited to mortgagors under subparagraph (4)(i) of this paragraph shall be reduced by the amount which (if it were treated as an interest payment made by mortgagors) would result in the excess referred to in subparagraph (2)(i) of this paragraph being equal to 1 percentage point. Such amount shall be fixed and determined as of the yield determination date. This fixed dollar amount may be received by the issuer at any time but may not be adjusted for the time of payment. Such fixed dollar amount shall be equal to the difference between the purchase price of mortgages financed by the proceeds of the issue and the present value of expected payments of principal and interest on such mortgages, using a discount rate equal to the bond yield plus 1 percentage point.

(B) The following example illustrates the provisions of subparagraph (4)(iv)(A) of this paragraph:

Example. In 1981, County X issues obligations to provide mortgages for owner-occupied residences. The yield paid on the obligations is 10 percent and the effective rate of interest on the mortgages provided by the proceeds of such obligations is 9.75 percent. X maintains a reasonably required reserve fund which is invested at 15 percent and intends to recover that additional amount computed in the manner described in subparagraph (4)(iv) which could have been earned from investment of the proceeds in mortgages with an effective interest rate of 11 percent from the arbitrage earned from the reserve fund nonmortgage assets. X plans to recover such amount from the arbitrage over a period of 3 years; thus, X will not recover such amount until 1984. X may not adjust the amount to be received to account for the time when such amount will be received.

(v) Election to pay United States. Subparagraph (4)(i) of this paragraph shall be satisfied with respect to any issue if the issuer elects in writing before issuing the obligations to pay over to the United States—

(A) Not less frequently than once each 5 years after the date of issue, an amount equal to 90 percent of the aggregate amount described in subdivision (i) earned during such period (and not theretofore paid to the United States), and

(B) Not later than 30 days after the redemption of the last obligation, 100 percent of such aggregate amount not theretofore paid to the United States.

(j) New mortgages. *(1) In general.* An issue meets the requirements of this paragraph only if no part of the proceeds of such issue is to be used to acquire or replace an existing mortgage. All of the lendable proceeds must be used to provide mortgage loans to persons who did not have a mortgage (whether or not paid off) on the residence securing the mortgage note at any time prior to the execution of the mortgage.

(2) Exceptions. For purposes of this paragraph, the replacement of—

(i) Construction period loans,

(ii) Bridge loans or similar temporary initial financing, and

(iii) In the case of a qualified rehabilitation, an existing mortgage, shall not be treated as the acquisition or replacement of an existing mortgage. Generally, temporary initial financing is any financing which has a term of 24 months or less.

(3) Assumptions. An issue meets the requirement of this paragraph only if a mortgage with respect to which owner financing has been provided under such issue may be assumed only if the requirements of paragraphs (d), (e), and (f) of this section are met with respect to such assumption. The determination of whether these requirements are met is based upon the facts as they exist at the time of the assumption as if the loan were being made for the first time. For example, the purchase price requirement is to be determined by reference to the average area purchase price at the time of the assumption and not when the mortgage was originally placed. If the bond documents and relevant mortgage instruments provide that a mortgage may be assumed only if the issuer has determined that the conditions stated in this subparagraph are satisfied, the good faith and 95-percent requirements of paragraph (c)(1)(i) and (ii) of this section will be considered satisfied with respect to the requirements of this subparagraph at the time the mortgages were executed. However, any failure to meet the requirements of this subparagraph at the time a mortgage is assumed is subject to the remedy requirement in paragraph (c)(1)(iii) of this section.

(4) Examples. The following examples illustrate the application of this paragraph (j):

Example (1). In June 1981 mortgagor A obtained a mortgage from a private lending institution in order to construct a house on land which A purchased without a mortgage in May 1981. In January 1982 A applies to obtain permanent financing on the residence from a program sponsored by State housing finance agency Y. Such program is funded with the proceeds of qualified mortgage bonds. If A meets the other requirements of this section, A qualifies for such permanent financing since the replacing of construction financing is not treated as the acquisition or replacement of an existing mortgage.

Example (2). In June 1981 mortgagor B purchased a new residence in a targeted area but was unable to sell his former residence. Therefore, B obtained temporary financing for his new residence until his former residence was sold. In October 1981 B applies to County Z to obtain financing from a program funded with proceeds of qualified mortgage bonds. Such financing is needed by B to replace the temporary financing for his new residence. If B meets the other requirements of this section, the mortgage qualifies for such permanent financing since the permanent financing replaces temporary initial financing.

Example (3). In 1979 mortgagor C purchased a residence but was unable to obtain financing from a program sponsored by County W because such program prohibited loans from the program which were in excess of 80 percent of the fair market value of the property. Therefore, in 1979 C obtained financing from a private lending institution with the intention of refinancing when he accumulated sufficient equity in the property. In 1981 C has accumulated sufficient equity in the property so as to comply with the requirements of the program. C applies to County W to refinance under the program, which is funded with the proceeds of qualified mortgage bonds. Even if C met the other requirements of this section, the mortgage would fail to meet the requirement of paragraph (j) since such a mortgage would replace an existing mortgage.

Example (4). In 1969 mortgagor D purchased a residence and obtained financing from a private lending institution. In 1981 D applies to County U for a loan for the rehabilitation of the property and for the refinancing of the existing mortgage. The program is funded with qualified mortgage bonds. If D meets the other requirements of this section the mortgage qualifies for such permanent financing since the replacement of the mortgage is not treated as the replacement or acquisition of an existing mortgage.

Example (5). In 1950 mortgagor E purchased a residence, obtaining a mortgage from a private lending institution to finance the purchase price. In 1980 E completed repaying the mortgage. In 1981 E applies for a loan from a program sponsored by State housing finance agency X and funded with the proceeds of qualified mortgage bonds. The mortgage does not meet the requirements of paragraph (j) since E had a previous mortgage on his residence, even though such mortgage was previously released.

(k) Information reporting requirement. See § 1.103A-2(k) for rules relating to section 103A(j)(3).

(l) Policy statement. See § 1.103A-2(l) for rules relating to section 103A(j)(5).

(m) State certification. See § 1.103A-2(m) for rules relating to section 103A(j)(4).

T.D. 7780, 6/29/81, amend T.D. 7794, 11/5/81, T.D. 7817, 5/19/82, T.D. 7819, 6/4/82, T.D. 7821, 6/24/82, T.D. 7995, 12/7/84, T.D. 8023, 5/3/85, T.D. 8049, 8/29/85, T.D. 8476, 6/14/93.

PAR. 41. Paragraph (i)(2)(vi)(B) of § 6a.103A-2 is amended by removing the phrase "section 1232(b)(2)" and adding in its place the phrase "section 1273(b)".

Proposed § 6a.103A-2 [Amended] [*For Preamble, see ¶ 151,065*]

• ***Caution:*** Prop reg § 1.482-2 was finalized by T.D. 8204, 5/20/88. Prop regs §§ 1.163-7, 1.446-2, 1.483-1 through -5, 1.1001-1, 1.1012-1, 1.1271 through -3, 1.1272-1, 1.1273-1, 1.1273-2, 1.1274-1 throught -7, 1.1274A-1, 1.1275-1 through -3, and 1.1275-5 were withdrawn by the Treasury on 12/22/92, 57 Fed. Reg. 67050. Prop reg § 1.1275-4 was superseded by the Treasury on 12/16/94, Fed. Reg. 59, 64884, which was finalized by T.D. 8674, 6/11/96.

Caution: The Treasury has not yet amended Reg § 6a.103A-2 to reflect changes made by P.L. 100-647.

§ 6a.103A-3 Qualified veterans' mortgage bonds.

• *Caution:* Reg. § 6a.103A-3, following, was issued under Code section 103A before the related provisions of that Code section were deleted by P.L. 99-514 (10/22/86). Provisions similar to, but not necessarily identical to, the provisions deleted from Code section 103A now appear in Code section 143.

Caution: The Treasury has not yet amended Reg § 6a.103A-3 to reflect changes made by P.L. 100-647, P.L. 99-514.

(a) In general. A qualified veterans' mortgage bond shall not be treated as a mortgage subsidy bond, and the interest shall be exempt from Federal income taxation.

(b) Qualified veterans' mortgage bond. *(1)* With respect to obligations issued prior to July 19, 1984, the term "qualified veterans' mortgage bond" means any issue of obligations—

(i) Which meets the requirements of § 6a.103A-1, § 6a.103A-2(j)(1) and (2), and this section;

(ii) Substantially all of the proceeds of which are to be used to provide financing for single-family, owner-occupied residences (which meet the requirements of § 6a.103A-1(b)(6) and § 6a.103A-2(d)) for veterans; and

(iii) Payment of the principal and interest on which is secured by a pledge of the full faith and credit of the issuing State.

A qualified veterans' mortgage bond does not include any bond that is an industrial development bond under section 103(b).

(2) With respect to obligations issued after July 18, 1984, the term "qualified veterans' mortgage bond" means any issue of obligations—

(i) Which meets the requirements of § 6.103A-1, § 6a.103A-2(d) (relating to residence requirements), (j)(1) and (2) (relating to new mortgage requirement), and (k) (relating to information reporting requirement), and this section;

(ii) Substantially all of the proceeds of which are to be used to provide financing for qualified veterans; and

(iii) Payment of the principal and interest on which is secured by a pledge of the full faith and credit of the issuing State.

A qualified veterans' mortgage bond does not include any bond that is an industrial development bond under section 103(b).

(c) Qualified veteran. *(1)* An issue meets the requirements of this paragraph only if each of the mortgagors to whom owner financing is provided is a qualified veteran.

(2) With respect to obligations issued prior to July 19, 1984, the term "qualified veteran" means any veteran.

(3) With respect to obligations issued after July 18, 1984, the term "qualified veteran" means any veteran who—

(i) Served on active duty at some time before January 1, 1977, and

(ii) Applied for financing before the later of—

(A) The date 30 years after the date on which such veteran left active service, or

(B) January 1, 1985.

(4) The term "veteran" shall have the same meaning as in 38 U.S.C. 101(2), that is, a person who served in the active military, naval, or air service, and who was discharged or released therefrom under conditions other than dishonorable.

(d) Husband and wife. For purposes of this section, if a residence is to be owned by a husband and wife as joint tenants, as tenants by the entirety, or as community property, and if one spouse is a veteran, then both spouses shall be treated as satisfying the requirements of paragraph (c) of this section.

(e) Substantially all. For purposes of this section, the term "substantially all" shall have the same meaning as in § 1.103-8.

(f) Qualified home improvement loan. The term "qualified home improvement loan" means the financing (whether or not secured by a mortgage) of alterations, repairs, and improvements on, or in connection with, an existing single-family, owner-occupied residence by a veteran who is the owner thereof. The alterations, repairs, and improvements, however, must substantially protect or improve the basic livability or energy efficiency of the property, such as the renovation of plumbing or electric systems, the installation of improved heating or air conditioning systems, the addition of living space, or the renovation of a kitchen area. Items that will not be considered to substantially protect or improve the basic livability of the property include swimming pools, tennis courts, saunas, or other recreational or entertainment facilities.

(g) Volume limitation. *(1) In general.* In the case of obligations issued after June 22, 1984, an issue meets the requirements of this paragraph only if the aggregate amount of obligations issued pursuant thereto, when added to the aggregate amount of qualified veterans' mortgage bonds previously issued by the State during the calendar year, does not exceed the State veterans limit for such calendar year. In determining the aggregate amount of qualified veterans' mortgage bonds issued in calendar year 1984, obligations issued prior to June 23, 1984, shall not be taken into account.

(2) State veterans limit. (i) The State veterans limit for any State is the amount equal to—

(A) The aggregate amount of qualified veterans' mortgage bonds issued by the State during the period beginning on January 1, 1979, and ending on June 22, 1984 (not including the amount of any qualified veterans' mortgage bonds actually issued during the calendar year, or the applicable portion of 1984, in such period for which the amount of such bonds was the lowest), divided by

(B) The number (not to exceed 5) of calendar years after 1978 and before 1985 during which the State issued qualified veterans' mortgage bonds.

In determining the number of calendar years after 1978 and before 1985 during which the State issued qualified veterans' mortgage bonds, any qualified veterans' mortgage bonds issued after June 22, 1984, shall not be taken into account. A State that did not issue qualified veterans' mortgage bonds during the period beginning on January 1, 1979, and ending on June 22, 1984, may not issue qualified veterans' mortgage bonds after June 22, 1984.

(ii) In the case of any obligation which has a term of 1 year or less and which was issued to provide financing for property taxes, the amount taken into account under this paragraph with respect to such obligation shall be 1/15 of its principal amount.

(3) Examples. The following examples illustrate the provisions of this paragraph:

Example (1). State R issued the following issues of qualified veterans' mortgage bonds: a $200 million issue on March 31, 1979, a $150 million issue on May 1, 1980, a $75 million issue on September 1, 1981, a $200 million issue on June 5, 1982, a $125 million issue on March 1, 1983, a $60 million issue on April 1, 1984, and a $100 million issue on September 1, 1984. R issued no other issues of qualified veterans' mortgage bonds during the period beginning January 1, 1979, and ending on December 31, 1984. The aggregate amount of qualified veterans' mortgage bonds issued during the period January 1, 1984, through June 22, 1984 ($60 million), is not taken into account in determining R's State veterans limit because that is the lowest aggregate amount of qualified veterans' mortgage bonds issued during the calendar year or the applicable portion of 1984, in the period beginning on January 1, 1979, and ending on June 22, 1984. Thus, R's State veterans limit is $150 million ($750 million (which is the sum of $200 million, $150 million, $75 million, $200 million, and $125 million) divided by 5). The September 1, 1984, issue is not included in determining the State veterans limit because that issue was issued after June 22, 1984. The September 1, 1984, issue of qualified veterans' mortgage bonds meets the requirements of § 6a.103A-3(g) since the aggregate amount of qualified veterans' mortgage bonds issued in calendar year 1984 (not including obligations issued prior to June 23, 1984), does not exceed the State veterans limit.

Example (2). State S issued a $100 million issue of qualified veterans' mortgage bonds on March 31, 1984. S issued no other issues of qualified veterans' mortgage bonds during the period beginning on January 1, 1979, and ending on June 22, 1984. The aggregate amount of qualified veterans' mortgage bonds issued in the calendar year, or the applicable portion of 1984, in the period January 1, 1979, through June 22, 1984, for which the amount of bonds was the lowest is zero. Thus, the State veterans limit for S is $100 million (($100 million minus $0) divided by 1).

(h) Good faith compliance efforts. *(1) Mortgage eligibility requirements.* An issue of qualified veterans' mortgage bonds issued after July 18, 1984, which fails to meet the requirements of section 103A(o)(1), § 6a.103A-2(d) relating to residence requirements), and § 6a.103A-2(j)(1) and (2) (relating to new mortgage requirements) shall be treated as meeting such requirements if each of the following provisions is complied with:

(i) The issuer in good faith attempted to meet all such requirements before the mortgages were executed. Good faith requires that the trust indenture, participation agreements with loan originators, and other relevant instruments contain restrictions that permit the financing of residences only in accordance with such requirements. in addition, the issuer must establish reasonable procedures to ensure compliance with such requirements. Such procedures include reasonable investigations by the issuer to satisfy such requirements.

(ii) Ninety-five percent or more of the lendable proceeds (as defined in § 6a.103A-2(b)(1)) that were devoted to owner-financing were devoted to residences with respect to which, at the time the mortgages were executed, all such requirements were met. In determining whether a person is a qualified veteran the issuer may rely on copies of the mortgagor's certificate of discharge indicating that the mortgagor served on active duty at some time before January 1, 1977, and stating the date on which the mortgagor left active service provided that neither the issuer nor its agent knows or has reason to believe that such affidavit is false. Where a particular mortgage fails to meet more than one of these requirements, the amount of the mortgage will be taken into account only once in determining whether the 95-percent requirement is met. However, all of the defects in the mortgage must be corrected pursuant to subdivision (iii).

(iii) Any failure to meet such requirements is corrected within a reasonable period after such failure is discovered. For example, failures can be corrected by calling the nonqualifying mortgage or by replacing the nonqualifying mortgage with a qualifying mortgage.

(2) Nonmortgage eligibility requirements. An issue of qualified veterans' mortgage bonds issued after July 18, 1984, which fails to meet the requirements of paragraph (g) of this section shall be treated as meeting such requirements if each of the requirements of § 6a.103A-2(c)(2)(i) and (ii) is met.

T.D. 7780, 6/29/81, amend T.D. 7995, 12/7/84.

---

§ 1.104-1 Compensation for injuries or sickness.

Caution: The Treasury has not yet amended Reg § 1.104-1 to reflect changes made by P.L. 107-134, P.L. 104-188, P.L. 101-239, P.L. 97-473, P.L. 94-455.

(a) In general. Section 104(a) provides an exclusion from gross income with respect to certain amounts described in paragraphs (b), (c), (d) and (e) of this section, which are received for personal injuries or sickness, except to the extent that such amounts are attributable to (but not in excess of) deductions allowed under section 213 (relating to medical, etc., expenses) for any prior taxable year. See section 213 and the regulations thereunder.

(b) Amounts received under workmen's compensation acts. Section 104(a)(1) excludes from gross income amounts which are received by an employee under a workmen's compensation act (such as the Longshoremen's and Harbor Workers' Compensation Act, 33 U.S.C., c. 18), or under a statute in the nature of a workmen's compensation act which provides compensation to employees for personal injuries or sickness incurred in the course of employment. Section 104(a)(1) also applies to compensation which is paid under a workmen's compensation act to the survivor or survivors of a deceased employee. However, section 104(a)(1) does not apply to a retirement pension or annuity to the extent that it is determined by reference to the employee's age or length of service, or the employee's prior contributions, even though the employee's retirement is occasioned by an occupational injury or sickness. Section 104(a)(1) also does not apply to amounts which are received as compensation for a nonoccupational injury or sickness nor to amounts received as compensation for an occupational injury or sickness to the extent that they are in excess of the amount provided in the applicable workmen's compensation act or acts. See, however, §§ 1.105-1 through 1.105-5 for rules relating to exclusion of such amounts from gross income.

(c) Damages received on account of personal injuries or sickness. Section 104(a)(2) excludes from gross income the amount of any damages received (whether by suit or agreement) on account of personal injuries or sickness. The term "damages received (whether by suit or agreement)" means an amount received (other than workmen's compensation) through prosecution of a legal suit or action based upon tort or tort type rights, or through a settlement agreement entered into in lieu of such prosecution.

(d) Accident or health insurance. Section 104(a)(3) excludes from gross income amounts received through accident or health insurance for personal injuries or sickness (other than amounts received by an employee, to the extent that such amounts (1) are attributable to contributions of the employer which were not includible in the gross income of the employee, or (2) are paid by the employer). Similar treatment is also accorded to amounts received under accident or health plans and amounts received from sickness or disability funds. See section 105(e) and § 1.105-5. If, therefore, an individual purchases a policy of accident or health insurance out of his own funds, amounts received thereunder for personal injuries or sickness are excludable from his gross income under section 104(a)(3). See, however, section 213 and the regulations thereunder as to the inclusion in gross income of amounts attributable to deductions allowed under section 213 for any prior taxable year. Section 104(a)(3) also applies to amounts received by an employee for personal injuries or sickness from a fund which is maintained exclusively by employee contributions. Conversely, if an employer is either the sole contributor to such a fund, or is the sole purchaser of a policy of accident or health insurance for his employees (on either a group or individual basis), the exclusion provided under section 104(a)(3) does not apply to any amounts received by his employees through such fund or insurance. If the employer and his employees contribute to a fund or purchase insurance which pays accident or health benefits to employees, section 104(a)(3) does not apply to amounts received thereunder by employees to the extent that such amounts are attributable to the employer's contributions. See § 1.105-1 for rules relating to the determination of the amount attributable to employer contributions. Although amounts paid by or on behalf of an employer to an employee for personal injuries or sickness are not excludable from the employee's gross income under section 104(a)(3), they may be excludable therefrom under section 105. See §§ 1.105-1 through 1.105-5, inclusive. For treatment of accident or health benefits paid to or on behalf of a self-employed individual by a trust described in section 401(a) which is exempt under section 501(a) or under a plan described in section 403(a), see paragraph (g) of § 1.72-15.

(e) Amounts received as pensions, etc., for certain personal injuries or sickness. *(1)* Section 104(a)(4) excludes from gross income amounts which are received as a pension, annuity, or similar allowance for personal injuries or sickness resulting from active service in the armed forces of any country, or in the Coast and Geodetic Survey, or the Public Health Service. For purposes of this section, that part of the retired pay of a member of an armed force, computed under formula No. 1 or 2 of 10 U.S.C. 1401, or under 10 U.S.C. 1402(d), on the basis of years of service, which exceeds the retired pay that he would receive if it were computed on the basis of percentage of disability is not considered as a pension, annuity, or similar allowance for personal injury or sickness, resulting from active service in the armed forces of any country, or in the Coast and Geodetic Survey, or the Public Health Service (see 10 U.S.C. 1403 (formerly 37 U.S.C. 272(h), section 402(h) of the Career Compensation Act of 1949)). See paragraph (a)(3)(i) *(a)* of § 1.105-4 for the treatment of retired pay in excess of the part computed on the basis of percentage of disability as amounts received through a wage continuation plan. For the rules relating to certain reduced uniformed services retirement pay, see paragraph (c)(2) of § 1.22-1. For rules relating to a waiver by a member or former member of the uniformed services of a portion of disability retired pay in favor of a pension or compensation receivable under the laws administered by the Veterans Administration (38 U.S.C. 3105), see § 1.122-1(e)(3). For rules relating to a reduction of the disability retired pay of a member or former member of the uniformed services under the Dual Compensation Act of 1964 (5 U.S.C. 5531) by reason of Federal employment, see § 1.122-1(c)(4).

(2) Section 104(a)(4) excludes from gross income amounts which are received by a participant in the Foreign Service Retirement and Disability System in a taxable year of such participant ending after September 8, 1960, as a disability annuity payable under the provisions of section 831 of the Foreign Service Act of 1946, as amended (22 U.S.C. 1081; 60 Stat. 1021). However, if any amount is received by a survivor of a disabled or incapacitated participant, such amount is not excluded from gross income by reason of the provisions of section 104(a)(4).

(3) Section 104(a)(4) excludes from gross income amounts which are received by a participant in the Retired Serviceman's Family Protection Plan as a disability annuity payable under the provisions of 10 U.S.C. 1431. However, if any amount is received by a survivor of a disabled or incapacitated participant, such amount is not excluded from gross income by reason of the provisions of section 104(a)(4).

T.D. 6169, 4/13/56, amend T.D. 6722, 4/13/64, T.D. 7043, 6/1/70.

§ 1.105-1 Amounts attributable to employer contributions.

(a) In general. Under section 105(a), amounts received by an employee through accident or health insurance for personal injuries or sickness must be included in his gross income to the extent that such amounts (1) are attributable to contributions of the employer which were not includible in the gross income of the employee, or (2) are paid by the employer, unless such amounts are excluded therefrom under section 105(b), (c), or (d). For purposes of this section, the term "amounts received by an employee through an accident or health plan" refers to any amounts received through accident or health insurance, and also to any amounts which, under section 105(e), are treated as being so received. See § 1.105-5. In determining the extent to which amounts received for personal injuries or sickness by an employee through an accident or health plan are subject to the provisions of section 105(a), rather than section 104(a)(3), the provisions of paragraphs (b), (c), (d), and (e) of this section shall apply. A self-employed individual is not an employee for purposes of section 105 and §§ 1.105-1 through 1.105-5. See paragraph (g) of § 1.72-15. Thus, such an individual will not be treated as an employee with respect to benefits described in section 105 received from a plan in which he participates as an employee within the meaning of section 401(c)(1) at the time he, his spouse, or any of his dependents becomes entitled to receive such benefits.

(b) Noncontributory plans. All amounts received by employees through an accident or health plan which is financed solely by their employer, either by payment of premiums on an accident or health insurance policy (whether on a group or individual basis), by contributions to a fund which pays accident or health benefits, or by direct payment of the benefits under the plan, are subject to the provisions of section 105(a), except to the extent that they are excludable under section 105(b), (c), or (d). This rule may be illustrated by the following examples:

Example (1). Employer A maintains a plan for his employees which provides that he will continue to pay regular wages to employees who are absent from work due to sickness or personal injuries. Employees make no contributions to the plan and all benefits are paid by the employer. Amounts received by employees under the plan are subject to section 105(a), and must be included in gross income unless excluded therefrom under section 105(b), (c), or (d).

Example (2). Pursuant to a State nonoccupational disability benefits law, employer B maintains an accident and health plan for his employees. Although under the State law B is authorized to withhold from his employees' wages a specified amount for employee contributions to the State fund, in actual practice B does not so withhold and makes all contributions out of his own funds. All amounts received by B's employees from the State fund are subject to section 105(a), and must be included in gross income unless excluded therefrom under section 105(b), (c), or (d).

(c) Contributory plans. *(1)* In the case of amounts received by an employee through an accident or health plan which is financed partially by his employer and partially by contributions of the employee, section 105(a) applies to the extent that such amounts are attributable to contributions of the employer which were not includible in the employee's gross income. The portion of such amounts which is attributable to such contributions of the employer shall be determined in accordance with paragraph (d) of this section in the case of an insured plan, or paragraph (e) of this section in the case of a noninsured plan. As used in this section, the phrase "contributions of the employer" means employer contributions which were not includible in the gross income of the employee. See section 106 for the exclusion from an employee's gross income of employer contributions to accident or health plans.

(2) A separate determination of the portion of the amounts received under the accident or health plan which is attributable to the contributions of the employer shall be made with respect to each class of employees in any case where the plan provides that some classes of covered employees contribute but others do not, or that the employer will make different contributions for different classes of employees, or that different classes of employees will make different contributions, and where in any such case both the contributions of the employer on account of each such class of employees and the contributions of such class of employees can be ascertained. For example, if employees contribute during the first year of employment but not thereafter, there will have to be a separate determination for first year employees, provided that the amount of the contributions of the employer on account of first-year employees and the contributions of such first-year employees can be ascertained for the required periods to apply the rules of paragraph (d) or (e) of this section. If in such a case the contributions of the employer to the plan on account of first-year employees are not distinguishable from his other contributions to the plan, then the determination shall be made for all employees under the plan, and such determination shall be used by all employees under the plan.

(3) Except as provided in paragraph (c)(2) of § 1.72-15, if the plan provides accident or health benefits as well as other benefits for the employees, and if the respective contributions made by the employer and the employees to provide the accident or health benefits cannot be ascertained, the determination of the portion of the accident or health benefits received under such plan which is attributable to the contributions of the employer shall be made in accordance with the rules of paragraph (d) or (e) of this section on the basis of the contributions of the employer and of the employees to the entire plan.

(4) A determination of the portion attributable to the contributions of the employer, once made in accordance with the rules of this section, shall as to such portion be used for all purposes. For example, if an employee receives amounts under a wage continuation plan during the month of January and terminates his services during February, the portion of such amounts which is attributable to the contributions of the employer may be determined in order to provide the employee with such information at the time he is provided his Form W-2. The determination made for such purpose will also be used by the employee to report his income for his taxable year in which such amounts are received, without regard to the experience under the plan for the rest of the year.

(d) Insured plans. *(1) Individual policies.* If an amount is received from an insurance company by an employee under an individual policy of accident or health insurance purchased by contributions of the employer and the employee, the portion of the amount received which is attributable to the employer's contributions shall be an amount which bears the same ratio to the amount received as the portion of the premiums paid by the employer for the current policy year bears to the total premiums paid by the employer and the employee for that year. This rule may be illustrated by the following example:

Example. Employer A maintains a plan whereby he pays two-thirds of the annual premium cost on individual policies of accident and health insurance for his employees. The remainder of each employee's premium is paid by a payroll deduction from the wages of the employee. The annual premium for employee X is $24, of which $16 is paid by the employer. Thus, $\frac{16}{24}$ or two-thirds of all amounts received by X under such insurance policy are attributable to the contributions of the employer and are subject to section 105(a), and the remaining one-third of such amounts is excludable from X's gross income under section 104(a)(3).

(2) Group policies. If the accident or health coverage is provided under or is a part of a group insurance policy purchased by contributions of the employer and of the employees, and the net premiums for such coverage for a period of at least three policy years are known at the beginning of the calendar year, the portion of any amount received by an employee which is attributable to the contributions of the employer for such coverage shall be an amount which bears the same ratio to the amount received, as the portion of the net premiums contributed by the employer for the last three policy years which are known at the beginning of the calendar year, bears to the total of the net premiums contributed by the employer and all employees for such policy years. If the net premiums for such coverage for a period of at least three policy years are not known at the beginning of the calendar year but are known for at least one policy year, such determination shall be made by using the net premiums for such coverage which are known at the beginning of the calendar

year. If the net premiums for such coverage are not known at the beginning of the calendar year for even one policy year, such determination shall be made by using either (i) a reasonable estimate of the net premiums for the first policy year, or (ii) if the net premiums for a policy year are ascertained during the calendar year, by using such net premiums. These rules may be illustrated by the following example:

Example. An employer maintains a plan under which a portion of the cost of a group policy of accident and health insurance for his employees is paid through payroll deductions from wages of the employees. The remainder of the cost is borne by the employer. The policy year begins on November 1 and ends on October 31. The net premium for the policy year ended October 31, 1954, is not known on January 1, 1955, because certain retroactive premium adjustments, such as dividends and credits, are not determinable until after January 1. Therefore, for purposes of this computation the last three policy years are the policy years ended October 31, 1951, 1952, and 1953. The net premium for the policy year ended October 31, 1953, was $8,000, of which the employer contributed $3,000; the net premium for the policy year ended October 31, 1952, was $9,000, of which the employer contributed $3,500; and the net premium for the policy year ended October 31, 1951, was $7,000, of which the employer contributed $1,500. The portion of any amount received under the policy by an employee at any time during 1955 which is attributable to the contributions of the employer is to be determined by using the ratio of $8,000 ($3,000 plus $3,500 plus $1,500) to $24,000 ($8,000 plus $9,000 plus $7,000. Thus

$$\frac{\$8{,}000}{\$24{,}000}$$

or

one-third, of the amounts received by an employee at any time during 1955 is attributable to contributions of the employer.

(e) Noninsured plans. If the accident or health benefits are a part of a noninsured plan to which the employer and the employees contribute, and such plan has been in effect for at least three years before the beginning of the calendar year, the portion of the amount received which is attributable to the employer's contributions shall be an amount which bears the same ratio to the amount received as the contributions of the employer for the period of three calendar years next preceding the year of receipt bear to the total contributions of the employer and all the employees for such period. If, at the beginning of the calendar year of receipt, such plan has not been in effect for three years but has been in effect for at least one year, such determination shall be based upon the contributions made during the 1-year or 2-year period during which the plan has been in effect. If such plan has not been in effect for one full year at the beginning of the calendar year of receipt, such determination may be based upon the portion of the year of receipt preceding the time when the determination is made, or such determination may be made periodically (such as monthly or quarterly) and used throughout the succeeding period. For example, if an employee terminates his services on April 15, 1955, and 1955 is the first year the plan has been in effect, such determination may be based upon the contributions of the employer and the employees during the period beginning with January 1 and ending with April 15, or during the month of March, or during the quarter consisting of January, February, and March.

T.D. 6169, 4/13/56, amend T.D. 6485, 7/29/60, T.D. 6722, 4/13/64.

§ 7.105-1 Questions and answers relating to exclusions of certain disability income payments.

Caution: The Treasury has not yet amended Reg § 7.105-1 to reflect changes made by P.L. 98-21.

The following questions and answers relate to the exclusion of certain disability income payments under section 105(d) of the Internal Revenue Code of 1954, as amended by section 505(a) and (c) of the Tax Reform Act of 1976 (90 Stat. 1566):

Q-1. What effect on the sick pay exclusion does the new law have?

A-1. The "sick pay" provisions of prior law (which allowed a limited exclusion from gross income of sick pay received before mandatory retirement age by active employees temporarily absent from work because of sickness or injury, as well as by disability retirees) have been replaced by provisions of the new law (which provide for a limited exclusion of disability payments but restrict its application to individuals retired on disability who meet certain requirements as to permanent and total disability, age, etc.) (Q-4). As a result of the more restrictive provisions of the new law, many taxpayers who qualified for the exclusion in previous taxable years will not be eligible to claim the disability payments exclusion beginning with the effective date of the new law.

Q-2. What is the effective date of the new law relating to disability exclusion?

A-2. The disability income exclusion and related annuity provisions of the Tax Reform Act of 1976 are effective for taxable years beginning on or after January 1, 1977. In addition, the Tax Reduction and Simplification Act of 1977 allows certain taxpayers to begin excluding pension or annuity costs in taxable years beginning in 1976. In the case of a retiree who uses the cash receipts and disbursements method of accounting, the new law applies to payments received on or after the effective date even if the payment is for a period before the effective date. Thus, a payment for December 1976 that is received in January 1977 by a calendar-year, cash-basis taxpayer is controlled by the new law.

Q-3. What are disability payments?

A-3. In general, disability payments are amounts constituting wages or payments in lieu of wages made under provisions of a plan providing for the payment of such amounts to an employee for a period during which the employee is absent from work on account of permanent and total disability. Amounts paid to such an employee after mandatory retirement age is attained are not wages or payments in lieu of wages for purposes of the disability income exclusion.

Q-4. Who is eligible to exclude disability payments?

A-4. A taxpayer who receives disability payments in lieu of wages under a plan providing for the payment of such amounts may qualify for the exclusion provided all of the following requirements are met:

(1) The taxpayer has not reached age 65 (see Q-9) before the end of the taxable year;

(2) The taxpayer has not reached mandatory retirement age (see Q-8) before the beginning of the taxable year;

(3) The taxpayer retired on disability (see Q-10) (or if retired prior to January 1, 1977 and did not retire on disability, would have been eligible to retire on disability at the time of such retirement);

(4) The taxpayer was permanently and totally disabled (see Q-11) when the taxpayer retired (or if the taxpayer retired before January 1, 1977, was permanently and totally disabled on January 1, 1976 or January 1, 1977); and

(5) The taxpayer has not made an irrevocable election not to claim the disability income exclusion (see Q-17 through Q-19).

Q-5. What limitations are placed on the amounts excludable?

A-5. The amount of disability income that is excludable:

(a) Cannot exceed the amount of the disability income payments received for any pay period;

(b) Cannot exceed a maximum weekly rate of $100 per taxpayer. Thus, the maximum disability income exclusion allowable on a joint return (see Q-7) in the usual case where one spouse receives disability payments, generally, would be $5,200, and if both spouses received disability payments the maximum exclusion, generally, would be $10,400 ($5,200 for each spouse);

(c) Cannot exceed, in the case of a disability income payment for a period of less than a week, a prorated portion of the amount otherwise excludable for that week (see Q-6); and

(d) Cannot exceed, for the entire taxable year, the total amount otherwise excludable for such taxable year reduced, dollar for dollar, by the amount by which the taxpayer's adjusted gross income (determined without regard to the disability income exclusion) exceeds $15,000. Where a disability income exclusion is claimed by either or both spouses on a joint return, the taxpayer's adjusted gross income means the total adjusted gross income of both spouses combined (determined without regard to the disability income exclusion) (see also Q-7).

Q-6. On what occasion is a taxpayer likely to receive part-week disability payments? How do you prorate such payments?

A-6. Such part-week payments may be received when one of the following events occurs after the first day of the taxpayer's normal workweek: (a) the disability retirement commences; (b) the taxpayer reaches mandatory retirement age in a taxable year prior to the taxable year in which such taxpayer attains age 65; or (c) the taxpayer dies. To prorate a part-week disability income payment for purposes of the exclusion, the taxpayer must:

(1) Determine the "daily exclusion," which is the lesser of—

(a) The taxpayer's daily rate of disability pay, or

(b) $100 divided by the number of days in the taxpayers normal workweek.

(2) Multiply the daily exclusion by the number of days for which the part-week payment was made.

Thus, for a taxpayer whose normal workweek was Monday through Friday and whose retirement on permanent and total disability began on Wednesday, the first disability income payment would include a payment for a part-week consisting of three days. Assuming that the daily exclusion determined in (1), above, is $20, the taxpayer's exclusion for the first week would be $60 ($20 × 3).

Q-7. What filing restrictions apply to a married taxpayer who claims a disability income exclusion?

A-7. A taxpayer married at the close of the taxable year who lived with his or her spouse at any time during such taxable year must file a joint return in order to claim the disability income exclusion. However, a taxpayer married at the close of the taxable year who lived apart from his or her spouse for the entire taxable year may claim the exclusion on either a joint or separate return.

Q-8. What is "mandatory retirement age"?

A-8. Generally, mandatory retirement age is the age at which the taxpayer would have been required to retire under the employer's retirement program, had the taxpayer not become disabled.

Q-9. Does a taxpayer reach age 65 on the day before his or her 65th birthday for purposes of the disability income exclusion, as is the case for purposes of the exemption for age and the credit for the elderly?

A-9. No. For purposes of the disability income exclusion, a taxpayer reaches age 65 on the day of his or her 65th birthday anniversary. Thus, a taxpayer whose 65th birthday occurs on January 1, 1978, is not considered to reach age 65 during 1977, for purposes of the disability income exclusion.

Q-10. What does "retired on disability" mean?

A-10. Generally, it means that an employee has ceased active employment in all respects because of a disability and has retired under a disability provision of a plan for employees. However, an employee who has actually ceased active employment in all respects because of a disability may be treated as "retired on disability" even though the employee has not yet gone through formal "retirement" procedures, as for example, where an employer carries the disabled employee in a non-retired status under the disability provisions of the plan solely for the purpose of continuing such employee's eligibility for certain employer-provided fringe benefits. In addition, such an employee may be treated as "retired on disability" even though the initial period immediately following his or her ceasing of employment on account of a disability must first be used against accumulated "sick leave" or "annual leave" prior to the employee being formally placed in disability retirement status.

Q-11. What is permanent and total disability?

A-11. It is the inability to engage in any substantial gainful activity by reason of any medically determinable physical or mental impairment that:

(a) Can be expected to result in death;

(b) Has lasted for a continuous period of not less than 12 month; or

(c) Can be expected to last for a continuous period of not less than 12 months. The substantial gainful activity referred to is not limited to the activity, or a comparable activity, in which the individual customarily engaged prior to such individual's retirement on disability. See § 7.105-2 for additional information relating to substantial gainful activity.

Q-12. If a taxpayer retired on disability but it is not clear until the following taxable year that the disability as of the date of such retirement was permanent and total (so that the employee did not exclude any amount as disability income in the earlier taxable year), may the taxpayer file an amended return to claim the disability income exclusion for the taxable year in which such taxpayer retired on disability which was permanent and total?

A-12. Yes.

Q-13. What proof must a taxpayer furnish to establish the existence of permanent and total disability?

A-13. If retired on disability before January 1, 1977: A certificate from a qualified physician attesting that—

(a) The taxpayer was permanently and totally disabled on January 1, 1976 or January 1, 1977; or

(b) The records of the Veterans Administration show that the taxpayer was permanently and totally disabled as defined in 38 CFR 3.340 or 3.342 on January 1, 1976 or January 1, 1977.

If retired on disability during 1977 or thereafter: A certificate from a qualified physician attesting that—

(a) The taxpayer was permanently and totally disabled on the date he or she retired; or (b) The records of the Veterans Administration show that the taxpayer was permanently and totally disabled as defined in 38 CFR 3.340 or 3.342 on the date he or she retired.

In either case, the taxpayer must attach the certificate or a copy of the certificate to his or her income tax return. The certificate shall give the physician's name and address. No certificate from any employer is required with regard to the determination of permanent and total disability.

Q-14. For what period does a taxpayer eligible (see Q-4) for the disability income exclusion (without regard to the $15,000 income phaseout explained in Q-5) continue to be eligible for such exclusion?

A-14. Unless the taxpayer earlier makes the irrevocable election not to claim the disability income exclusion described in Q-17 through Q-19, such taxpayer continues to be eligible until the earlier of:

(a) The beginning of the taxable year in which the taxpayer reaches age 65; and

(b) The day on which the taxpayer reaches mandatory retirement age.

Q-15. May a taxpayer while eligible (see Q-4) for the disability income exclusion under the new law, exclude any applicable pension or annuity costs?

A-15. No. This is true even though while eligible for the disability income exclusion, such taxpayer is unable to exclude any amount of the disability income payments because of the $15,000 income phaseout (see Q-5).

Q-16. When will a taxpayer who is eligible (see Q-4) to exclude disability income payments (without regard to the $15,000 phaseout explained in Q-5) under the new law be able to exclude any applicable pension or annuity costs?

A-16. In general, such a taxpayer will begin to exclude any of his or her pension or annuity costs under applicable rules of the Code beginning on the first day of the taxable year in which he or she attains age 65 or, if mandatory retirement age is attained in an earlier taxable year, beginning on the day the taxpayer attains mandatory retirement age.

Q-17. May a taxpayer who is eligible (see Q-4) to exclude disability income payments (without regard to the $15,000 phaseout explained in Q-5) under the new law begin to exclude applicable pension or annuity costs in an earlier taxable year?

A-17. Yes, but such a taxpayer must make the election described in Q-18 and Q-19 in which case the taxpayer would no longer be eligible for the disability income exclusion.

Q-18. What is an election not to claim the disability income exclusion?

A-18. It is an irrevocable election for the taxable year for which the election is made, and each taxable year thereafter. If such an election is made the taxpayer will begin to recover tax-free, out of the payments, his or her annuity costs as provided under the applicable provision of the Code.

Q-19. How does a taxpayer who is eligible to exclude disability income payments (without regard to the $15,000 phaseout explained in Q-5) under the new law make this election?

A-19. The election is made by means of a statement attached to the taxpayer's income tax return (or amended return) for the taxable year in which the taxpayer wishes to have the applicable annuity rule apply. The statement shall set forth the taxpayer's qualifications to make the election (i.e., that the taxpayer is eligible (see Q-4) to exclude disability income payments (without regard to the $15,000 income phaseout explained in Q-5)) and that such taxpayer irrevocably elects not to claim the benefit of excluding disability income payments under section 105(d), as amended, for such taxable year and each taxable year thereafter. The election cannot be made for any taxable year beginning before January 1, 1976.

Q-20. Did the changes made by the Tax Reduction and Simplification Act provide any relief to taxpayers eligible for the sick pay exclusion in taxable years beginning in 1976?

A-20. Yes. As originally enacted, the more restrictive provisions of the disability income exclusion applied to taxable years beginning in 1976. The Tax Reduction and Simplification Act postponed the effective date of these provisions for 1 year. Thus, taxpayers may claim the sick pay exclusion in taxable years beginning in 1976.

T.D. 7450, 12/22/76, amend T.D. 7544, 5/3/78.

§ 1.105-2 Amounts expended for medical care.

Section 105(b) provides an exclusion from gross income with respect to the amounts referred to in section 105(a) (see § 1.105-1) which are paid, directly or indirectly, to the taxpayer to reimburse him for expenses incurred for the medical care (as defined in section 213(e)) of the taxpayer, his spouse, and his dependents (as defined in section 152). However, the exclusion does not apply to amounts which are attributable to (and not in excess of) deductions allowed under section 213 (relating to medical, etc., expenses) for any prior taxable year. See section 213 and the regulations thereunder. Section 105(b) applies only to amounts which are paid specifically to reimburse the taxpayer for expenses incurred by him for the prescribed medical care. Thus, section 105(b) does not apply to amounts which the taxpayer would be entitled to receive irrespective of whether or not he incurs expenses for medical care. For example, if under a wage continuation plan the taxpayer is entitled to regular wages during a period of absence from work due to sickness or injury, amounts received under such plan are not excludable from his gross income under section 105(b) even though the taxpayer may have incurred medical expenses during the period of illness. Such amounts may, however, be excludable from his gross income under section 105(d). See § 1.105-4. If the amounts are paid to the taxpayer solely to reimburse him for expenses which he incurred for the prescribed medical care, section 105(b) is applicable even though such amounts are paid without proof of the amount of the actual expenses incurred by the taxpayer, but section 105(b) is not applicable to the extent that such amounts exceed the amount of the actual expenses for such medical care. If the taxpayer incurs an obligation for medical care, payment to the obligee in discharge of such obligation shall constitute indirect payment to the taxpayer as reimbursement for medical care. Similarly, payment to or on behalf of the taxpayer's spouse or dependents shall constitute indirect payment to the taxpayer.

T.D. 6169, 4/13/56.

§ 7.105-2 Substantial gainful activity.

Caution: The Treasury has not yet amended Reg § 7.105-2 to reflect changes made by P.L. 98-21.

(a) Purpose. This section defines substantial gainful activity for purposes of section 105(d) and § 7.105-1, prescribes rules for determining whether a taxpayer has the ability to engage in substantial gainful activity, and provides examples of the application of the definition and rules in specific factual situations.

(b) Definition. Substantial gainful activity is the performance of significant duties over a reasonable period of time in work for remuneration or profit (or in work of a type generally performed for remuneration or profit).

(c) General rules. *(1)* Full-time work under competitive circumstances generally indicates ability to engage in substantial gainful activity.

(2) Work performed in self-care or the taxpayer's own household tasks, and nonremunerative work performed in connection with hobbies, institutional therapy or training, school attendance, clubs, social programs, and similar activities is not substantial gainful activity. However, the nature of the work performed may be evidence of ability to engage in substantial gainful activity.

(3) The fact that a taxpayer is unemployed for any length of time is not, of itself, conclusive evidence of inability to engage in substantial gainful activity.

(4) Regular performance of duties by a taxpayer in a full-time, competitive work situation at a rate of pay at or above the minimum wage will conclusively establish the taxpayer's ability to engage in substantial gainful activity. For purposes of paragraphs (c)(4) and (c)(5) of this section, the minimum wage is the minimum wage prescribed by section 6(a)(1) of the Fair Labor Standards Act of 1938, as amended, 29 U.S.C. 206(a)(1).

(5) Regular performance of duties by a taxpayer in a part-time, competitive work situation at a rate of pay at or above the minimum wage will conclusively establish the taxpayer's ability to engage in substantial gainful activity, if the duties are performed at the employer's convenience.

(6) In situations other than those described in paragraphs (c)(4) and (c)(5) of this section, other factors, such as the nature of the duties performed, may establish a taxpayer's ability to engage in substantial gainful activity.

(d) Examples. The following examples illustrate the application of the definition in paragraph (b) of this section and the rules in paragraph (c) of this section in specific factual situations. In examples 1 through 5, the facts establish that the taxpayers are able to engage in substantial gainful activity and, therefore, are not entitled to claim the disability income exclusion of section 105(d). In examples 6 through 9, the facts do not, of themselves, establish the taxpayers' ability or inability to engage in substantial gainful activity. In these situations, all the facts and circumstances must be examined to determine whether the taxpayers are able to engage in substantial gainful activity.

Example (1). Before retirement on disability, taxpayer worked for a hotel as night desk clerk. After retirement, the taxpayer is hired by another hotel as night desk clerk at a rate of pay exceeding the minimum wage. Since the taxpayer regularly performs duties in a full-time competitive work situation at a rate of pay at or above the minimum wage, he or she is able to engage in substantial gainful activity.

Example (2). A taxpayer who retired on disability from employment as a sales clerk is employed as a full-time babysitter at a rate of pay equal to the minimum wage. Since the taxpayer regularly performs duties in a full-time, competitive work situation at a rate of pay at or above the minimum wage, he or she is able to engage in substantial gainful activity.

Example (3). A taxpayer retired on disability from employment as a teacher because of terminal cancer. The taxpayer's physician recommended continuing employment for therapeutic reasons and taxpayer accepted employment as a part-time teacher at a rate of pay in excess of the minimum wage. The part-time teaching work is done at the employer's convenience. Even though the taxpayer's illness is terminal, the employment was recommended for therapeutic reasons, and the work is part-time, the fact that the work is done at the employer's convenience demonstrates that the taxpayer is able to engage in substantial gainful activity.

Example (4). A taxpayer who retired on disability, is employed full-time in a competitive work situation that is less demanding than his or her former position. The rate of pay exceeds the minimum wage but is about half of the taxpayers's rate of pay in the former position. It is immaterial that the new work activity is less demanding or less gainful than the work in which the taxpayer was engaged before his or her retirement on disability. Since the taxpayer regularly performs duties in a full-time, competitive work situation at a rate of pay at or above the minimum wage, he or she is able to engage in substantial gainful activity.

Example (5). A taxpayer who retired on disability from employment as a bookkeeper drives trucks for a charitable organization at the taxpayer's convenience. The taxpayer receives no compensation, but duties of this nature generally are performed for remuneration or profit. Some weeks the taxpayer works 10 hours, some weeks 40 hours, and over the year the taxpayer works an average of 20 hours per week. Even though the taxpayer receives no compensation, works part-time, and at his or her convenience, the nature of the duties performed and the average number of hours worked per week conclusively establish the taxpayer's ability to engage in substantial gainful activity.

Example (6). A taxpayer who retired on disability was instructed by a doctor that uninterrupted bedrest was vital to the treatment of his or or her disability. However, because of financial need, the taxpayer secured new employment in a sedentary job. After attempting the new employment for approximately two months, the taxpayer was physically unable to continue the employment. The fact that the taxpayer attempted to work and did, in fact, work for two months, does not, of itself, conclusively establish the taxpayer's ability to engage in substantial gainful activity.

Example (7). A taxpayer who retired on disability accepted employment with a former employer on a trial basis. The purpose of the employment was to determine whether the taxpayer was employable. The trial period continued for an extended period of time and the taxpayer was paid at a rate equal to the minimum wage. However, because of the taxpayer's disability only light duties of a nonproductive make-work nature were assigned. Unless the activity is both substantial and gainful, the taxpayer is not engaged in substantial gainful activity. The activity was gainful because the taxpayer was paid at a rate at or above the minimum wage. However, the activity was not substantial because the duties were of a nonproductive, make-work nature. Accordingly, these facts do not, of themselves, establish the taxpayer's ability to engage in substantial gainful activity.

Example (8). A taxpayer who retired on disability from employment as a bookkeeper lives with a relative who manages several motel units. The taxpayer assisted the relative for one or two hours a day by performing duties such as washing dishes, answering phones, registering guests, and bookkeeping. The taxpayer can select the times during the day when he or she feels most fit to perform the tasks undertaken. Work of this nature, performed off and on during the day at the taxpayer's convenience, is not activity of a "substantial and gainful" nature even if the individual is paid for the work. The performance of these duties does not, of itself, show that the taxpayer is able to engage in substantial gainful activity.

Example (9). A taxpayer who retired on disability because of a physical or mental impairment accepts sheltered employment in a protected environment under an institutional program. Sheltered employment is offered in sheltered workshops, hospitals and similar institutions, homebound programs, and Veterans Administration domiciliaries. Typically, earnings are lower in sheltered employment than in commercial employment. Consequently, impaired workers normally do not seek sheltered employment if other employment is available. The acceptance of sheltered employment by an impaired taxpayer does not necessarily establish his or her ability to engage in substantial gainful activity.

T.D. 7544, 5/3/78.

§ 1.105-3 Payments unrelated to absence from work.

Section 105(c) provides an exclusion from gross income with respect to the amounts referred to in section 105(a) to the extent that such amounts (a) constitute payments for the permanent loss or permanent loss of use of a member or function of the body, or the permanent disfigurement, of the taxpayer, his spouse, or a dependent (as defined in section 152), and (b) are computed with reference to the nature of the injury without regard to the period the employee is absent from work. Loss of use or disfigurement shall be considered permanent when it may reasonably be expected to continue for the life of the individual. For purposes of section 105(c), loss or loss of use of a member or function of the body includes the loss or loss of use of an appendage of the body, the loss of an eye, the loss of substantially all of the vision of an eye, and the loss of substantially all of the hearing in one or both ears. The term "disfigurement" shall be given a reasonable interpretation in the light of all the particular facts and circumstances. Section 105(c) does not apply if the amount of the benefits is determined by reference to the period the employee is absent from work. For example, if an employee is absent from work as a result of the loss of an arm, and under the accident and health plan established by his employer, he is to receive $125 a week so long as he is absent from work for a period not in excess of 52 weeks, section 105(c) is not applicable to such payments. See, however, section 105(d) and § 1.105-4. However, for purposes of section 105(c), it is immaterial whether an amount is paid in a lump sum or in installments. Section 105(c) does not apply to amounts which are treated as workmen's compensation under paragraph (b) of § 1.104-1, or to amounts paid by reason of the death of the employee (see section 101).

T.D. 6169, 4/13/56.

§ 1.105-4 Wage continuation plans.

Caution: The Treasury has not yet amended Reg § 1.105-4 to reflect changes made by P.L. 98-21.

(a) In general. *(1)* Subject to the limitations provided in this section, section 105(d) provides an exclusion from gross income with respect to amounts referred to in section 105(a) which are paid to an employee through a wage continuation plan and which constitute wages or payments in lieu of wages for a period during which the employee is absent from work on account of personal injuries or sickness.

(2) (i) Section 105(d) is applicable only if the wages or payments in lieu of wages are paid pursuant to a wage continuation plan. (See § 1.105-6 for special rules for employees retired before January 27, 1975). The term "wage continuation plan" means an accident or health plan, as defined in § 1.105-5, under which wages, or payments in lieu of wages, are paid to an employee for a period during which he is absent from work on account of a personal injury or sickness. Such term includes plans under which payments are continued as long as the employee is absent from work on account of personal injury or sickness. It includes plans under which there is a limitation on the period for which benefits will be paid, such as 13 or 26 weeks, and also plans under which benefits are continued until the employee is either able to return to work or reaches mandatory retirement age. Such term also includes a plan under which wages or payments in lieu of wages are paid to an employee who is absent from work on account of personal injury or sickness, even though the plan also provides that wages or payments in lieu of wages may be paid to an employee who is absent from work for reasons other than a personal injury or sickness.

(ii) Section 105(d) is applicable if, and only if, the employee is absent from work and such absence is due to a personal injury or sickness. Thus, if an employer has a plan for continuing the wages of employees when they are absent from work, regardless of the cause of the absence from work, section 105(d) is applicable to any payments made under this plan to an employee whose absence from work is in fact due to a personal injury or sickness. On the other hand, although the terms of a plan provide that benefits are to be continued only as long as the employee is absent from work on account of a personal injury or sickness, section 105(d) does not apply to payments made to an employee for a period of absence from work where such absence is not in fact due to a personal injury or sickness.

(3) (i) (A) Section 105(d) applies only to amounts attributable to periods during which the employee would be at work were it not for a personal injury or sickness. Thus, an employee is not absent from work if he is not expected to work because, for example, he has reached mandatory retirement age. If a plan provides that an employee, who is absent from work on account of a personal injury or sickness, will receive a disability pension or annuity as long as he is disabled, section 105(d) is applicable to any payments that he receives under this plan before reaching mandatory retirement age, as defined in paragraph (a)(3)(i)(B) of this section. Thus, section 105(d) would not apply to the payments that an employee receives after reaching mandatory retirement age. The disability retired pay received by a member on the retired list pursuant to section 402 of the Career Compensation Act of 1949 (63 Stat. 802) or chapter 61 of title 10, United States Code (10 U.S.C. 1201 *et seq.*) which is in excess of the amounts excludable under section 104(a)(4) and paragraph (e) of § 1.104-1 shall be excluded from gross income subject to the limitations of section 105(d) and this section, if such pay is received before the member reaches

mandatory retirement age. See § 1.72-15 for additional rules relating to the tax treatment of disability pensions. For the rules relating to certain reduced uniformed services retirement pay, see paragraph (c)(2) of § 1.122-1. For rules relating to a waiver by a member or former member of the uniformed services of a portion of disability retired pay in favor of a pension of compensation receivable under the laws administered by the Veterans Administration (38 U.S.C. 3105), see § 1.122-1(c)(3).

(B) The term "mandatory retirement age" as used in paragraph (a)(3)(i)(A) of this section means the age set by an employer for the mandatory retirement of employees in the class to which the taxpayer last belonged, unless such age has been set at an age higher than that at which it has been the practice of the employer to terminate, due to age, the services of such employees, or for purposes of tax avoidance. Where no age is set for mandatory retirement, such term means age 65, or, if higher, the age at which it has been the practice of the employer to terminate, due to age, the service of the class of employees to which the taxpayer last belonged.

(ii) Similarly, an employee who incurs a personal injury or sickness during his paid vacation is not allowed to exclude under section 105(d) any of the vacation pay which he receives, since he is not absent from work on account of the personal injury or sickness. Likewise, a teacher who becomes sick during the summer or other vacation period when he is not expected to teach, is not entitled to any exclusion under section 105(d) for the summer or vacation period. However, if an employee who would otherwise be at work during a particular period is absent from work and his absence is in fact due to a personal injury or sickness, a payment which he receives for such period under a wage continuation plan is subject to section 105(d).

(4) A period of absence from work shall commence the moment the employee first becomes absent from work and shall end the moment the employee first returns to work. However, the exclusion provided under section 105(d) is applicable only to payments attributable to a period of absence from work which is due to a personal injury or sickness, and to payments attributable to a period when the employee would have been at work but for such personal injury or sickness.

(5) For the purpose of section 105(d), whether an employee is absent from work depends upon all the circumstances. For example, an employee, who is a farm hand and who lives upon the premises of his employer, is absent from work when he is unable to work even though he remains on the premises of his employer. A member of the Armed Forces, who on a particular day has no assigned duties but to stand ready for duty, is absent from work if he is unable to answer any duty call that may be made upon him. An employee is not absent from work when he performs any services for his employer at his usual place or places of employment, whether or not the services are the usual services performed by the employee. Furthermore, the employee is not absent from work when he performs substantial services for his employer, even though they are performed at a place other than his usual place of employment. Thus, if an employee returns to his usual place or places of employment and performs any services for his employer, he has returned to work, but if he merely holds occasional short conferences concerning his work with other employees or clients while hospitalized or at home recuperating, such conferences do not constitute a return to work.

(b) Determination of amount attributable to period of absence. The amount which is paid to an employee as wages or payments in lieu of wages for a period of absence from work due to a personal injury or sickness shall be determined by reference to the plan under which the amount is paid, and to the contract, statute, or regulation which provides the terms of the employment. However, unless the plan, contract, statute, or regulation provides otherwise, it will be presumed that no wages or plan benefits are attributable to days (or portions of days) which are not normal working days for the particular employee. Also, section 105(d) does not apply to amounts earned prior to or subsequent to the period of absence from work, even though received during such period. These rules may be illustrated by the following examples:

Example (1). Employee A, who receives regular wages of $70 per week, normally works five days (Monday through Friday) during each week. A is absent from work on a Friday and the succeeding Monday (two working days) on account of a personal injury, but receives his regular wages with respect to such period of absence under his employer's accident and health plan. Unless the plan of A's employer, or the contract, statute, or regulation under which A is employed, provides otherwise, it will be presumed that A is not paid with respect to nonworking days (Saturday and Sunday). Therefore, the amount received by A with respect to his period of absence from work due to injury is $28, which is two days regular wages. If the plan, or the employment contract, statute, or regulation had provided that wages were paid on a 7-day per week basis and that A must be available for call to work on Saturday and Sunday, A's daily wage would have been $10, and the amount attributable to the period of absence would have been $40 ($10 per day for four days).

Example (2). Employee B is a salesman who is paid on a commission basis. The employer purchases for B an accident and health insurance policy which provides that B shall receive $50 per week during any period (after a 7-day waiting period) that he is unable to work due to personal injuries or sickness. B incurs a personal injury and is incapacitated for two weeks. He receives $50 under the insurance policy with respect to the second week of absence. In addition, during the 2-week period of absence he receives a check for $40 from his employer as his commission on a sale which he made before becoming incapacitated. Section 105(d) applies to the $50 received through the insurance policy, but does not apply to the $40 commission which B earned prior to the period of absence from work.

(c) Limitation in the case of absence from work due to sickness for periods commencing prior to January 1, 1964. *(1)* In the case of a period of absence from work on account of sickness commencing prior to January 1, 1964, the exclusion provided by section 105(d) does not apply to amounts attributable to the first seven calendar days of each such period, unless the employee is hospitalized on account of sickness for at least one day during the period of absence from work. This 7-day rule applies to each period of absence from work because of sickness, regardless of the frequency of such absences or the closeness in time to any prior period of absence from work because of sickness. For example, employee A becomes absent from work because of sickness on Friday, October 4, 1963, and returns to work on the morning of Monday, October 14, 1963. He suffers a relapse and again becomes absent from work on the afternoon of Monday, October 14, 1963. A's return to work on the morning of Monday, October 14, 1963, terminates the first period of absence from work because of sickness, and a new period of absence from work because of sickness begins on the afternoon of Monday, October 14, 1963. The 7-day limitation does not apply if the absence from work is due to personal injury. These rules may be illustrated by the following examples:

Example (1). Employee C normally works five days (Monday through Friday) during each week. On Saturday, October 5, 1963 (a nonworking day), C becomes sick and as a result, he does not return to work until Thursday, October 17, 1963. The period of absence from work due to sickness commences on Monday, October 7, 1963, and terminates when C returns to work on Thursday, October 17, 1963. If C is not hospitalized during such period of absence from work, section 105(d) does not apply to amounts which C receives under his employer's wage continuation plan attributable to the 7-day period commencing Monday, October 7, 1963, and ending Sunday, October 13, 1963, inclusive.

Example (2). Employee D incurs a personal injury which causes him to be absent from work two days. His regular wages are continued during this period in accordance with the wage continuation plan of his employer. Since D's absence from work was due to a personal injury, rather than a sickness, the 7-day waiting period does not apply, and, subject to the other requirements of section 150(d), D is entitled to an exclusion with respect to the amounts received under the employer's plan attributable to the 2-day period of absence.

(2) For the purpose of starting the 7-day waiting period, if the period of absence due to sickness commences after the start of a working day, the amount received with respect to the portion of such day that the employee is absent from work shall be considered the amount attributable to the first calendar day of the period of absence from work due to sickness. This rule may be illustrated by the following example:

Example. Employee E normally works from 9 a.m. until 5:30 p.m. on five days (Monday through Friday) during each week. From noon on Friday, September 6, 1963, until noon on Monday, September 16, 1963, E is absent from work on account of sickness but is not hospitalized at any time during this period. Section 105(d) does not apply to amounts received by E under his employer's wage continuation plan which are attributable to the calendar period beginning September 6, 1963, and ending September 12, 1963, inclusive. However, if the other requirements of section 105(d) are met, E may exclude from gross income amounts attributable to the period beginning September 13, 1963, and ending at noon on September 16, 1963, inclusive.

(3) If the absence from work is due to sickness, the amount attributable to the first seven calendar days of such absence includes all amounts paid for such seven calendar days, regardless of the number of work days included in such seven calendar days. For example, if on one of such seven calendar days an employee would have worked two 8-hour shifts, the amount he is paid for the two shifts is considered to be an amount attributable to only one calendar day.

(4) An employee is considered to be hospitalized for one day only if he is admitted to and confined in a hospital as a bed patient for at least one hospital day. Entry into a hospital as an in-and-out patient does not constitute hospitalization for purposes of section 105(d). The same applies to mere entry into the out-patient ward or the emergency ward of a hospital.

(d) Exclusion not applicable to the extent that amounts exceed a weekly rate of $100 for periods of absence commencing prior to January 1, 1964. *(1) In general.* Amounts received under a wage continuation plan, attributable to periods of absence commencing before January 1, 1964, which are not excludable from gross income as being attributable to contributions of the employee (see § 1.105-1) must be included in gross income under section 105(d) to the extent that the weekly rate of such amounts exceeds $100. Thus, an employee, who receives $50 under his employer's wage continuation plan on account of his being absent from work for two days due to a personal injury, cannot exclude the entire $50 under section 105(d) if the weekly rate of such benefits exceeds $100. If an employee receives payments under a wage continuation plan for less than a full pay period, the excludability of such payments shall be determined under subparagraph (2) of this paragraph. In all other cases, the weekly rate and excludability of such payments under a wage continuation plan shall be determined under subparagraph (3) of this paragraph. If, with respect to any pay period or portion thereof, the employee receives amounts under two or more wage continuation plans (whether such plans are maintained by or for the same employer or by different employers), the weekly rate and excludability of amounts received under each plan shall be determined under subparagraph (3) of this paragraph and the weekly rate for purposes of section 105(d) shall be the sum of all such weekly rates. This rule may be illustrated by the following examples.

Example (1). An employee whose weekly salary is $120 is covered by two wage continuation plans maintained by his employer. Plan A is a contributory insured plan to which the employee contributes 60 percent of the premiums and which provides a weekly payment of $30. Plan B is a salary continuation plan completely financed by the employer. Since 60 percent of the cost of plan A is contributed by the employee, 60 percent of the weekly payment of $30 ($18) is excluded from gross income under section 104(a)(3). The remainder of each weekly payment ($12) is the weekly rate of plan A. Since the employer pays the entire cost of plan B, the weekly rate of this plan is the total amount paid per week. In the case of an employee whose weekly wages of $120 are continued under plan B, the weekly rate for the employee for purposes of section 105(d) is $132 ($120 from plan B, plus $12 from plan A).

Example (2). Assume in Example (1) that plan A provides a waiting period of four calendar days while plan B is effective immediately. For the first four days of absence the weekly rate for purposes of section 105(d) is $120, and for periods after the first four days the weekly rate for purposes of section 105(d) is $132.

(2) Daily exclusion. If an employee receives payments under a wage continuation plan for less than a full pay period, the extent to which such benefits are excludable under section 105(d) shall be determined by computing the daily rate of the benefits which can be excluded under section 105(d). Such daily rate is determined by dividing the weekly rate at which wage continuation payments are excludable ($100) by the number of work days in a normal work week. This rule may be illustrated by the following example:

Example. Employee E is covered by a wage continuation plan maintained by his employer providing that E's regular salary of $220 semi-monthly will be continued in case he is absent from work on account of a personal injury or sickness. E is absent from work on account of a personal injury for three days and under the plan he received $66 as wage continuation payments. The extent to which the $66 is excludable under section 105(d) shall be determined by dividing $100 by 5, the number of work days in a normal work week for E, resulting in a daily exclusion of $20 and a total exclusion of $60.

(3) Determination of weekly rate at which amounts are paid under a wage continuation plan. (i) For purposes of this subparagraph the pay period of a particular wage continuation plan shall be determined by reference to such plan. If, in the usual operation of the plan, benefits are paid for the same periods as regular wages, then the pay period of such benefits shall be the period for which a payment of wages is ordinarily made to the employee by the employer. If plan benefits are ordinarily paid for different periods than regular wages then the pay period of such benefits shall be the period for which payment of such benefits is ordinarily made.

(ii) The weekly rate shall be determined in accordance with the following rules:

(a) Weekly pay period. If benefits are paid on the basis of a weekly pay period, the weekly rate at which such benefits are paid shall be the weekly amount of such benefits.

(b) Biweekly pay period. If benefits are paid on the basis of a biweekly pay period, the weekly rate at which such benefits are paid shall be one-half of the biweekly rate.

(c) Semimonthly pay period. If benefits are paid on the basis of a semimonthly pay period, the weekly rate at which such benefits are paid shall be the semimonthly rate multiplied by 24 and divided by 52.

(d) Monthly pay period. If benefits are paid on the basis of a monthly pay period, the weekly rate at which such benefits are paid shall be the monthly rate multiplied by 12 and divided by 52.

(e) Other pay periods. If benefits are paid on the basis of a period other than a period described in (a) through (d), of this subdivision the weekly rate at which such benefits are paid shall be determined by ascertaining the annual rate at which such benefits are paid and dividing such annual rate by 52.

(f) Examples. The operation of the rules of this subdivision may be illustrated by the following examples:

Example (1). A's employer maintains a noncontributory plan which provides for the continuation of regular salary during periods of absence from work due to personal injury or sickness. A, an office employee, receives regular salary of $520 per month, and he is paid on the basis of a monthly pay period. Since benefits under the salary continuation plan are paid for the same periods as regular salary, the pay period of the plan is monthly. For purposes of section 105(d), the weekly rate at which benefits are paid to A under the plan is $120, determined as follows:

$520 (monthly rate) × 12	$6,240	(annual rate)
$\frac{\$6,240}{52}$	$120	(weekly rate)

Example (2). B, a factory employee of the same employer, is paid regular wages on the basis of a 10-day pay period. B's regular wages are $200 per pay period. If B is absent from work for 15 days, the weekly rate of the amount he receives under his employer's plan will be determined as follows:

$\frac{365 \times \$200}{10}$	$7,300	(annual rate)
$\frac{\$7,300}{52}$	$140.38	(weekly rate)

(iii) If the weekly rate for purposes of section 105(d) (as determined in subdivision (ii) of this subparagraph) does not exceed $100, the amount received which is not attributable to the 7-day waiting period described in paragraph (c) of this section is fully excludable from gross income. If the weekly rate for purposes of section 105(d) (as determined in subdivision (ii) of this subparagraph) exceeds $100, the amount received which is not attributable to the 7-day waiting period provided in paragraph (c) of this section is only partially excludable. The excludable portion of such amount shall bear the same ratio to such amount as $100 bears to the weekly rate for purposes of section 105(d). This rule may be illustrated by the following example:

Example. The weekly rate of benefits in the case of employee A in example (1) of subdivision (ii) of this subparagraph was $120. If A does not receive amounts under any other plan, this is the weekly rate for purposes of section 105(d). Assume that A is absent from work on account of a personal injury for one full month and receives full pay of $520 for such period of absence. Since there is no waiting period requirement, the exclusion is $433.33 computed as follows:

$$\frac{\$100}{\$120} \times \$520 \text{ or } \$433.33.$$

(e) Limitation in the case of absence from work on account of personal injury or sickness for periods commencing after December 31, 1963. *(1)* In the case of periods of absence from work on account of sickness or personal injury commencing after December 31, 1963, the exclusion provided by section 105(d) does not apply to amounts attributable to the first 30 calendar days of each such period, if such amounts are at a rate which exceeds 75 percent of the employee's "regular weekly rate of wages", as determined under subparagraph (5) of this paragraph. If the amounts are at a rate of 75 percent or less of the employee's "regular weekly rate of wages", the exclusion provided by section 105(d) does not apply to amounts attributable to the first 7 calendar days of each such period, unless the employee is hospitalized on account of personal injury or sickness for at least one day during the period of absence from work. The 7- or 30-day waiting period (whichever is applicable) applies to each period of absence from work because of personal injury or sickness, regardless of the frequency of such absences or the closeness in time to any prior period of absence from work because of personal injury or sickness. The waiting period is to be counted by beginning with the first work day for which the employee was absent. These rules may be illustrated by the following examples:

Example (1). Employee A is absent from work because of sickness on Tuesday, January 7, 1964, and returns to work on the morning of Thursday, February 13, 1964. He suffers a relapse and again becomes absent from work on the afternoon of Thursday, February 13, 1964. A's return to work on the morning of Thursday, February 13, 1964, terminates the first period of absence from work because of sickness, and a new period of absence from work because of sickness begins on the afternoon of Thursday, February 13, 1964.

Example (2). Employee B normally works five days (Monday through Friday) during each week. On Saturday, January 11, 1964 (a nonworking day), B becomes sick or injured and as a result he does not return to work until Monday, February 17, 1964. The period of absence from work commences on Monday, January 13, 1964, and terminates when B returns to work on Monday, February 17, 1964. Assuming B receives amounts under his employer's wage continuation plan at a rate exceeding 75 percent of his "regular weekly rate of wages" (as determined under subparagraph (5) of this paragraph), the exclusion provided by section 105(d) does not apply to amounts B receives under his employer's wage continuation plan which are attributable to the 30-day period commencing Monday, January 13, 1964, and ending Tuesday, February 11, 1964, inclusive. If B receives amounts under his employer's wage continuation plan at a rate which is 75 percent or less of his "regular weekly rate of wages" and he is not hospitalized during the period of absence from work, the exclusion provided by section 105(d) does not apply to amounts B receives which are attributable to the 7-day period commencing Monday, January 13, 1964, and ending Sunday, January 19, 1964, inclusive.

Example (3). Employee C is sick or incurs a personal injury which causes him to be absent from work for two weeks. He receives amounts under his employer's wage continuation plan at a rate which is 75 percent or less of his "regular weekly rate of wages" (as determined under subparagraph (5) of this paragraph) and is hospitalized from the eighth through the eleventh day of his absence. Since C was hospitalized on account of personal injury or sickness for at least one day during the period of absence, the 7-day waiting period does not apply, and, subject to the other requirements of section 105(d), C is entitled to an exclusion with respect to the amounts received under his employer's plan attributable to the two-week period of absence. If C were receiving amounts under his employer's wage continuation plan at a rate exceeding 75 percent of his "regular weekly rate of wages", he would not be entitled to an exclusion under section 105(d).

(2) For the purpose of starting the 7- or 30-day waiting period, whichever is applicable, if the period of absence commences after the start of a working day, the amount received with respect to the portion of such day that the employee is absent from work shall be considered an amount attributable to the first calendar day of the period of absence from work. This rule may be illustrated by the following example:

Example. Employee D normally works from 9 a.m. until 5:30 p.m. on five days (Monday through Friday) during each week. From noon on Wednesday, January 8, 1964, until noon on Monday, February 17, 1964, D is absent from work on account of personal injury or sickness but is not hospitalized at any time during this period. D receives amounts under his employer's wage continuation plan at a rate not exceeding 75 percent of his "regular weekly rate of wages" (as determined under subparagraph (5) of this paragraph). Section 105(d) does not apply to amounts received by D under his employer's wage continuation plan which are attributable to the calendar period beginning January 8, 1964, and continuing through January 14, 1964, inclusive. However, if the other requirements of section 105(d) are met, D may exclude from gross income amounts attributable to the remainder of the period of absence, ending at noon on Monday, February 17, 1964.

(3) If the exclusion is subject to a 7- or 30-calendar-day waiting period, any amount attributable to such 7- or 30-calendar-day waiting period includes all amounts paid therefor, regardless of the number of work days included in such 7 or 30 calendar days. For example, if on one of the days included in the waiting period, an employee would have worked two 8-hour shifts, the amount he is paid for the two shifts is considered to be attributable to only one calendar day.

(4) An employee is considered to be hospitalized for one day only if he is admitted to and confined in a hospital as a bed patient for at least one hospital day. Entry into a hospital as an in-and-out-patient does not constitute hospitalization for purposes of section 105(d). The same applies to mere entry into the out-patient ward or the emergency ward of a hospital.

(5) (i) In general, the "regular weekly rate of wages", for purposes of section 105(d), shall be the average weekly wages paid for the last four weekly periods falling within a full pay period or full pay periods immediately preceding the commencement of the period of absence. If the employee was absent from work for three or more normal working days during any such pay period, and the amount of wages paid for such pay period was less than the amount of wages paid for the immediately preceding pay period during which the employee was not absent from work for three or more normal working days, then the amount of wages paid for the weekly period or weekly periods falling wholly or partly within the pay period during which each such absence occurred shall not be used in the determination of "regular weekly rate of wages". In such a case, there shall be substituted the amount of wages paid for the last weekly period or weekly periods falling within the pay period or pay periods immediately preceding the pay period or pay periods in which such absence or absences occurred during which the employee was not absent from work for three or more normal working days.

(a) In order to compute wages paid for the last four weekly periods falling within a full pay period or full pay periods immediately preceding the commencement of the period of absence, or any substituted weekly periods therefor, it will be necessary to convert the wages paid for any pay period other than a weekly pay period into a weekly rate or weekly rates of payment of such wages in accordance with the rules stated in subdivision (iv) of this subparagraph. Such weekly rate or weekly rates of wage payments are then used in determining the wages for the last four weekly periods falling within a full pay period or full pay periods immediately preceding the commencement of the period of absence, or any substituted weekly periods therefor.

(b) If the employee does not have four weekly periods falling within a full pay period or full pay periods preceding his absence during which he was not absent from work for three or more normal working days, then the greatest number of available weekly periods shall be used, consistent with the rules set forth in this subdivision (i), in determining the "regular weekly rate of wages."

(c) If the employee has been employed for a full pay period or more preceding his absence, and has worked for the number of days in a normal work week, but was absent from work for three or more normal working days during each of the pay periods preceding his absence, then the "regular weekly rate of wages" shall be determined by multiplying the employee's actual wages paid for the total number of normal working days in the pay period immediately preceding the employee's absence by the number of days that the employee is expected to work in a normal work week, and by dividing the product by the number of normal work days in such pay period for which wages were paid.

(d) If the employee has not been employed for a full pay period preceding his absence, and has worked for the number of days in a normal work week, the "regular weekly rate of wages" shall be determined by multiplying the employee's actual wages paid for the total number of normal working days preceding the employee's absence by the number of days that the employee is expected to work in a normal work week, and by dividing the product by the number of normal work days for which wages were paid.

(e) If the employee has not worked the number of days in a normal work week, then there is no "regular weekly rate of wages," and the employee will not be permitted an exclusion under section 105(d) for amounts attributable to the first 30 calendar days in the period of absence.

(f) Wages paid by a former employer shall not be used in the determination of "regular weekly rate of wages" as described in this subparagraph.

(ii) In the case of a wage continuation plan of an employer under which the benefits are computed as a specified percentage of average wages, the formula for computing the employee's average wages included in the plan may be used (in lieu of the formula provided in subdivision (i) of this subparagraph) for determining the "regular weekly rate of wages" for purposes of section 105(d), if under the plan—

(a) The definition of wages does not include any items which are not considered "wages" as defined in subdivision (iii) of this subparagraph.

(b) The period for computing average wages is not less than twenty-eight successive calendar days, does not end earlier than five months preceding the date on which the period of absence commences, and is one in which the employee was at work at least 35 percent of the normal working time, and

(c) The period and formula for computing average wages are applied uniformly with respect to all employees eligible to receive benefits under the plan. A plan will not fail to meet the conditions of this subdivision merely because different portions of the employee's wages are averaged over different periods for purposes of computing his average wages, so long as each such period meets the requirements in (b) and (c) of this subdivision.

(iii) For the purpose of determining "regular weekly rate of wages" under subdivision (i) or (ii) of this subparagraph, whichever is applicable, an employee's wages shall comprise basic salary, fees, commissions, tips, gratuities, overtime, and any other type of taxable compensation which is normally paid for services. However, wages shall not include any type of compensation which is not normally paid, such as bonuses and incentive payments. An employee's compensation, for the purpose of determining his "regular weekly rate of wages", will not include any compensation which is not currently includible in gross income. For example, an employee's wages for the purpose of this subdivision shall not include deferred compensation paid by the employer which is not includible in gross income until received by the employee, such as employer contributions to a qualified annuity under section 403(a), or employer contributions to an accident or health plan excluded under section 106.

(iv) The following rules shall be used to convert wages for pay periods other than weekly pay periods into weekly rates of wage payments to be used in determining "regular weekly rate of wages" as described in subdivision (i) of this subparagraph.

(a) If wages are paid biweekly, the weekly rate of wage payments shall be one-half of the biweekly wages paid.

(b) If the employee is paid semimonthly, the weekly rate of wage payments shall be the semimonthly wages paid multiplied by 24 and divided by 52.

(c) If wages are paid monthly, the weekly rate of wage payments shall be the monthly wages paid multiplied by 12 and divided by 52.

(d) If wages are paid on the basis of a pay period other than a period described in (a) through (c) of this subdivision, the weekly rate of wage payments shall be determined by ascertaining the annual rate of wage payments and dividing by 52.

(e) For the purpose of this subparagraph, if separate portions of an employee's wages are paid on the basis of different pay periods, the weekly rate or weekly rates of wage payments of each portion of wages paid with respect to each pay period shall first be determined under the rules set forth in (a) through (d) of this subdivision and the average weekly rate of each portion of wages, determined in accordance with the rules set forth in subdivision (i) of this subparagraph, shall be aggregated to determine the employee's "regular weekly rate of wages" for purposes of section 105(d).

(v) The provisions of subdivisions (i), (iii) and (iv) of this subparagraph may be illustrated by the following examples:

Example (1). Employee A is a salesman who is paid a basic salary of $60 per week and, in addition, is paid commissions on a weekly basis. A became ill and did not report for work beginning Monday, February 17, 1964. For the four-week period preceding the commencement of the period of absence, A was paid the following:

Week of—	Basic salary	Commissions	Total weekly wages
Jan. 20, 1964	$60	$10	$ 70
Jan. 27, 1964	60	50	110
Feb. 3, 1964	60	30	90
Feb. 10, 1964	60	40	100
Total 4-week wages			370

A's wages, under the rules set forth in subdivision (iii) of this subparagraph, consist of basic salary plus commissions. Since the amount of A's average weekly wages paid for the last four weekly periods falling within the four pay periods immediately preceding the commencement of his period of absence from work is $92.50 ($370 ÷ 4), such amount is considered as the "regular weekly rate of wages" (as computed under subdivision (i) of this subparagraph) for purposes of section 105(d).

Example (2). Assume, in example (1), that A normally works five days during each week (Monday through Friday) and that he was also absent from work for any reason from Monday, February 3, 1964, through Wednesday, February 5, 1964. Since A was absent from work for three normal working days during the pay period of February 3, 1964, and was paid a lesser amount of wages for such pay period than in the immediately preceding pay period during which he was not absent from work (week of January 27), the weekly pay period beginning January 27, 1964 is substituted for the weekly pay period beginning February 3, 1964 in the determination of "regular weekly rate of wages" (as computed under subdivision (i) of this subparagraph) for purposes of section 105(d). The "regular weekly rate of wages" is calculated to be $97.50, as follows:

Week of:	Total wages
February 10	$100
January 27 (substitute for week of Feb. 3)	110
January 27	110
January 20	70
	390 ÷ 4 = $97.50

Example (3). Employee B is a salesman who is paid a basic salary of $75 and, in addition, is paid commissions for semimonthly periods ending on the 15th day and the last day of each month. He was absent from work on account of a personal injury beginning Monday, February 17, 1964. He was paid the following amounts:

Pay period	Salary	Commissions	Total wages
Feb. 1-15, 1964	$75	$60	$135
Jan. 16-31, 1964	75	50	125

The four weekly periods falling within full pay periods preceding the commencement of the period of absence are the weeks beginning February 9, February 2, January 26, and January 19. B's wages are converted to weekly rates of wage payments per pay period in accordance with the rule set forth in subdivision (iv) **(b)** of this subparagraph as follows:

$135 × 24 = $3240.00 (annual rate)

$$\frac{\$3240.00}{52} = \$62.31 \text{ (weekly rate)}$$

From January 16-31, inclusive:

$125 × 24 = $3000.00 (annual rate)

$$\frac{\$3000.00}{52} = \$57.69 \text{ (weekly rate)}$$

The weekly rates are then used in determining the wages for four weekly periods falling within the pay periods immediately preceding the commencement of B's absence. B's "regular weekly rate of wages" (as computed under subdivision (i) of this subparagraph) is calculated to be $60.17, as follows:

February 9-15, inclusive	$62.31
February 2-8, inclusive	62.31
January 26-February 1, inclusive (6/7 × $57.69 + 1/7 × $62.31)	58.35
January 19-25, inclusive	57.69
	240.66 ÷ 4 = $60.17

Example (4). Employee C is paid semimonthly on the 5th and 20th of each month and he began working for his present employer at the beginning of the semi-monthly pay period commencing Tuesday, January 21, 1964. C received total wages of $200 for the pay period of January 21, 1964 through February 5, 1964, inclusive. He was not absent during that pay period. C became sick and was absent from work beginning February 7, 1964. Since employee C does not have four weekly periods falling within a full pay period or full pay periods preceding his absence, the average wages for the last two weekly periods falling within such full pay period will be C's "regular weekly rate of wages" (as computed under subdivision (i) of this subparagraph) for purposes of section 105(d), determined to be $92.31, as follows:

$200 × 24 = $4800 (annual rate)

$$\frac{\$4800}{52} = \$92.31 \text{ (weekly rate)}$$

Example (5). Employee D, an office worker, is paid weekly and is expected to work five days during each week. He has been employed by his present employer for three weeks, but has been absent from work for three normal work days in each of the weeks preceding his illness. He became ill and was absent from work on Monday, February 17, 1964. During the weekly pay period immediately preceding his absence (week of February 10) D was paid $48 salary. He was paid for two working days during such weekly pay period. D's "regular weekly rate of wages" (as computed under subdivision (i) of this subparagraph), is calculated to be $120.00, determined as follows:

$$\frac{\$48 \text{ (total wages)} \times 5 \text{ (normal work days in week)}}{2 \text{ (number of workdays for which wages were paid)}} = \$120.000$$

Example (6). Employee E is an hourly worker who is paid a salary of $1.25 per hour. E is paid basic salary on a biweekly basis for the periods beginning every other Thursday and ending every other Wednesday. E is also paid monthly for his overtime work and is compensated for such work at one and one-half times the hourly rate. E worked 16 hours of overtime for his employer during the month of January. E was injured and could not report for work on Friday, February 21, 1964. E returned to work on Monday, March 16, 1964. E was paid as follows for the pay periods indicated:

Pay period	Hours		Salary per hour		Total
	Regular	Overtime	Regular	Overtime	Salary
Month of January, 1964		16		$1.875	$ 30
Jan. 23-Feb. 5, 1964 inclusive	80		$1.25		100
Feb. 6-19, 1964, inclusive	80		1.25		100

Under the rule set forth in subdivision (iv)(e) of this subparagraph, the weekly rates of payment of salary and overtime must be determined separately. Since basic salary is paid biweekly, the weekly rate of payment is determined to be one-half of $100.00, or $50.00. The full pay period immediately preceding the commencement of E's absence for overtime compensation ended on January 31, 1964. E's overtime earnings are converted to a weekly rate for such period, as follows:

\$30.00 (overtime pay) × 12 = \$360.00 (annual rate)

$$\frac{\$360.00}{52} = \$6.93 \text{ (weekly rate)}$$

The average wages for the last four weekly periods falling within pay periods immediately preceding the commencement of E's absence with respect to basic salary (weeks of February 13, 6, January 30, and 23) is \$50.00. The average wages for the last four weekly periods falling within the pay period immediately preceding the commencement of E's absence with respect to overtime compensation (weeks of January 25, 18, 11, and 4) is \$6.93. Accordingly, E's "regular weekly rate of wages" (as computed under subdivision (i) of this subparagraph) for the purpose of section 105(d) is \$56.93.

(6) (i) Amounts paid under a wage continuation plan must be converted to a weekly rate in order to determine the percentage of benefits paid in relation to the employee's "regular weekly rate of wages", since such percentage is used in determining the waiting period, if any, after which an exclusion is allowable under section 105(d). In order to calculate the weekly rate at which benefits are being paid, reference is made to the particular wage continuation plan. If, in the usual operation of the plan, benefits are paid for the same periods as regular wages, then the pay period of such benefits shall be the period for which a payment of wages is ordinarily made to the employee by the employer. If plan benefits are ordinarily paid for different periods than regular wages, then the pay period of such benefits shall be the period for which payment of such benefits is ordinarily made.

(ii) The weekly rate at which the benefits are paid under a wage continuation plan shall be determined in accordance with the following rules:

(a) If benefits are paid on the basis of a weekly pay period, the weekly rate at which such benefits are paid shall be the weekly amount of such benefits.

(b) If benefits are paid on the basis of a biweekly pay period, the weekly rate at which such benefits are paid shall be one-half of the bi-weekly rate.

(c) If benefits are paid on the basis of a semimonthly pay period, the weekly rate at which such benefits are paid shall be the semimonthly rate multiplied by 24 and divided by 52.

(d) If benefits are paid on the basis of a monthly pay period, the weekly rate at which such benefits are paid shall be the monthly rate multiplied by 12 and divided by 52.

(e) If benefits are paid on the basis of a period other than a period described in (a) through (d) of this subdivision the weekly rate at which such benefits are paid shall be determined by ascertaining the annual rate at which such benefits are paid and dividing such annual rate by 52.

(iii) The principles of subdivisions (i) and (ii) of this subparagraph may be illustrated by the following example:

Example. A's employer maintains a noncontributory plan which provides for a monthly benefit of \$400 during periods of absence from work due to personal injury or sickness. A, a salesman, receives regular salary of \$520 per calendar month plus commissions, depending upon the amount of sales made by A during the month. During the month of January 1964, A was paid commissions of \$180. A received a total benefit of \$200 for an absence of two weeks because of illness occurring in February 1964. He was not hospitalized. Since benefits under the salary continuation plan are paid for the same period as regular wages, the pay period of the plan is monthly. A's "regular weekly rate of wages", determined in accordance with the rules set forth in subparagraph (5)(i) of this paragraph is

$$\$161.54 \quad \frac{(\$700 \times 12)}{52}$$

For purposes of determining the percentage of benefits paid in relation to A's "regular weekly rate of wages", the weekly rate of the benefits are calculated to be \$92.31, as follows:

\$400 (monthly rate) × 12 = \$4,800 (annual rate)

$$\frac{\$4,800}{52} \times \$92.31 \text{ (weekly rate)}$$

Since \$92.31 does not exceed 75 percent of A's "regular weekly rate of wages", A is entitled to an exclusion under section 105(d) for the second week of absence, subject to the other limitations provided in this section.

(iv) For the purpose of determining whether or not the rate of benefits paid under a wage continuation plan for a period of absence exceeds 75 percent of the employee's "regular weekly rate of wages" (as determined under subparagraph (5) of this paragraph), it is necessary to ascertain the average percentage of benefits paid in relation to the employee's "regular weekly rate of wages" for the first 30 calendar days in the period of absence. Such percentage is derived from a fraction, the numerator of which is the sum of benefits paid (attributable to employer contributions) for the period of absence occurring within the first 30 calendar days, and the denominator of which is the collective sum of the employee's "regular weekly rate of wages" during such period. This rule may be illustrated by the following examples:

Example (1). Employee A is paid a semimonthly basic salary of \$150 plus commissions. He normally works five days during each week (Monday through Friday). During the month of January 1964, A received wages of \$150 plus commissions of \$66.67 for each of the semimonthly pay periods. A became ill on Monday, February 3, 1964, and as a result was absent from work until Monday, February 17, 1964, but was not hospitalized. Under the noncontributory wage continuation plan of A's employer, A received no benefits for the first three working days' absence (Monday through Wednesday) and was paid benefits at the rate of \$100 a week thereafter. A's "regular weekly rate of wages," determined under the rules set forth in subparagraph (5) of this paragraph, is \$100. A is considered to have received average benefits at a rate of 70 percent of his "regular weekly rate of wages", computed as follows:

(1) Week of absence	(2) Benefits paid weekly rate	(3) Regular weekly rate of wages
1—Feb. 3	\$ 40	\$100
2—Feb. 10	100	100
Totals	140	200

Average percentage of benefits paid—140/200 = 70%. Accordingly, A may exclude amounts attributable to the second week of absence, subject to the other limitations of section 105(d).

Example (2). Assume, in example (1), that A did not return to work until Thursday, February 20, 1964. A is considered to have received average benefits at the rate of 76.92 percent of his "regular weekly rate of wages", computed as follows:

(1) Week of absence	(2) Benefits paid weekly rate	(3) Regular weekly rate of wages
1—Feb. 3	$ 40	$100
2—Feb. 10	100	100
2⅗—Feb. 17	60[1]	60[1]
Totals	200	260

[1] Three-fifths of 100.

Average percentage of benefits paid—$^{200}/_{260}$ = 76.92%. Accordingly, A would not be permitted any exclusion under section 105(d).

(v) If with respect to any pay period or portion thereof the employee receives amounts under two or more wage continuation plans (whether such plans are maintained by or for the same employers or by different employers), the weekly rate for purposes of section 105(d) shall be the sum of the weekly rates received under all plans. This rule may be illustrated by the following example:

Example. An employee who is absent because of personal injuries or sickness receives $100 biweekly under wage continuation plan A maintained by his employer. He contributes one-half of the premiums for maintenance of the plan. Under wage continuation plan B maintained by his employer the employee receives $400 monthly. Plan B is noncontributory. The weekly rate at which benefits are paid for the purpose of section 105(d) is computed as follows:

Plan A— $\frac{\$100}{2}$ = $ 50.00 (weekly rate)

25.00 (less amount attributable to employee contributions (½))

25.00 (weekly rate of Plan A)

Plan B— $\frac{\$400 \times 12}{52}$ = 92.31 (weekly rate of Plan B)

$117.31 (combined weekly rate at which benefits are paid)

The $25 attributable to contributions made by the employee under Plan A would be subject to section 104(a)(3).

(f) Amount of exclusion for periods of absence commencing after December 31, 1963. *(1) In general.* Amounts received under a wage continuation plan attributable to periods of absence commencing after December 31, 1963, and which are not excludable from gross income as being attributable to contributions of the employee (see § 1.105-1) are excludable from gross income of the employee to the extent that such amounts do not exceed—

(i) A weekly rate of $75, during the first 30 calendar days in the period of absence; and

(ii) A weekly rate of $100, after the first 30 calendar days in the period of absence.

For example, an employee who normally works five days during each week is absent from work for two days, is hospitalized during his absence, and receives $75 under his employer's wage continuation plan, which amount is at a rate of 75 percent of his "regular weekly rate of wages". The employee cannot exclude the entire $75 under section 105(d), if the weekly rate of such benefits exceeds $75.

(2) Daily exclusion. An employee receiving payments under a wage continuation plan must, in order to determine the amount of the exclusion under section 105(d), compute the daily rate of the benefits. Such daily rate is determined, for amounts attributable to the first 30 calendar days in the period of absence, by dividing the weekly rate at which benefits are paid (as determined under paragraph (e)(6)(ii) of this section), or the maximum weekly rate at which wage continuation payments are excludable ($75), whichever is lower, by the number of work days in a normal work week. In the case of amounts attributable to days in a period of absence after the first 30 calendar days, the daily rate for such period is determined by dividing the weekly rate at which benefits are paid (as determined under paragraph (e)(6)(ii) of this section), or the maximum weekly rate at which wage continuation payments are excludable ($100), whichever is lower, by the number of work days in a normal work week. The daily rate or daily rates of exclusion are then multiplied by the number of normal work days in the period of absence for which an exclusion is allowable in order to determine the total allowable exclusion. These rules may be illustrated by the following examples:

Example (1). Employee A is a salesman receiving salary and commissions on a weekly basis. His employer maintains a noncontributory wage continuation plan which provides for the continuation of A's basic salary of $80 per week during periods of absence. A was absent from work on account of sickness from Monday, February 3, 1964, through Sunday, March 15, 1964, but was not hospitalized. His normal work week is from Monday through Friday. The weekly amount of benefits paid to A ($80) does not exceed 75 percent of his "regular weekly rate of wages" as defined in paragraph (e)(5) of this section. Under section 105 (d), the daily rate of exclusion for amounts attributable to the first 30 calendar days in the period of absence, excluding the first 7 days thereof (Monday, February 10, 1964, through Tuesday, March 3, 1964, inclusive) is limited to $15 ($75, maximum weekly rate of exclusion divided by 5 (number of normal work days in week)). The daily rate of exclusion for amounts attributable to the period of absence in excess of 30 calendar days (Wednesday, March 4, 1964, through Sunday, March 15, 1964, inclusive) is limited to $16 ($80, weekly rate of benefits divided by 5). Thus, the total exclusion permitted to employee A by section 105(d) is $383.00 ($15 × 17 work days ($255) + $16 × 8 work days ($128)).

Example (2). Assume the facts in example (1) except that A is paid benefits at the rate of $500 a month during periods of absence. The weekly rate of the benefits computed under the rules stated in paragraph (e)(6)(ii) of this section is $115.38, which amount does not exceed 75 percent of his "regular weekly rate of wages" as defined in paragraph (e)(5) of this section. Under section 105(d), the daily rate of exclusion for amounts attributable to the first 30 calendar days in the period of absence, excluding the first 7 days thereof (Monday, February 10, 1964, through Tuesday, March 3, 1964, inclusive) is limited to $15 ($75, maximum weekly rate of exclusion divided by 5). The daily rate of exclusion for amounts attributable to the period of absence in excess of 30 calendar days (Wednesday, March 4, 1964, through Sunday, March 15, 1964, inclusive) is limited to $20 ($100, maximum weekly rate of exclusion divided by 5). Thus, the total exclusion permitted to employee A by section 105(d) is $415.00 ($15 × 17 work days ($255) + $20 × 8 work days ($160)).

Example (3). Employee B, an office worker works five days during each week (Monday through Friday) and receives a salary of $85 per week. His employer maintains a noncontributory wage continuation plan which provides for no benefits during the first three days of absence, the continuation of full salary for one week thereafter and benefits at the rate of $65 per week thereafter. B was absent from work on account of sickness from Monday, March 16, 1964, through Tuesday, March 31, 1964, and was hospitalized from Wednesday, March 18, through Tuesday, March 24. B received total benefits of $137 for the period of absence, which does not exceed 75 percent of his "regular weekly rate of wages" as determined under paragraph (e)(5) of this section. B is permitted an exclusion under section 105(d) of $127 calculated as follows:

Period of absence	Weekly rate of benefits	Maximum weekly rate of exclusion	Daily rate of exclusion	Days of absence in period	Maximum exclusion
Mar. 16-18	0	$75	0	3	0
Mar. 19-25	$85	75	$15	5	$ 75
Mar. 26-31	65	75	13	4	52
Total exclusion					$127

(g) Definitions. The term "personal injury" as used in this section, means an externally caused sudden hurt or damage to the body brought about by an identifiable event. The term "sickness" as used in this section, means mental illnesses and all bodily infirmities and disorders other than "personal injuries". Diseases, whether resulting from the occupation or otherwise, are not considered personal injuries, but they are treated as a sickness.

T.D. 6169, 4/13/56, amend T.D. 6177, 5/29/56, T.D. 6485, 7/29/60, T.D. 6770, 11/16/64, T.D. 6888, 7/5/66, amend T.D. 7043, 6/1/70, T.D. 7352, 4/9/75.

PAR. 3. Section 1.105-4 is removed.

Proposed § 1.105-4 [*For Preamble, see ¶ 152,901*]

§ 1.105-4 [Removed]

§ 1.105-5 Accident and health plans.

Caution: The Treasury has not yet amended Reg § 1.105-5 to reflect changes made by P.L. 94-455.

(a) In general. Sections 104(a)(3) and 105(b), (c), and (d) exclude from gross income certain amounts received through accident or health insurance. Section 105(e) provides that for purposes of sections 104 and 105 amounts received through an accident or health plan for employees, and amounts received from a sickness and disability fund for employees maintained under the law of a State, a Territory, or the District of Columbia, shall be treated as amounts received through accident or health insurance. In general, an accident or health plan is an arrangement for the payment of amounts to employees in the event of personal injuries or sickness. A plan may cover one or more employees, and there may be different plans for different employees or classes of employees. An accident or health plan may be either insured or noninsured, and it is not necessary that the plan be in writing or that the employee's rights to benefits under the plan be enforceable. However, if the employee's rights are not enforceable, an amount will be deemed to be received under a plan only if, on the date the employee became sick or injured, the employee was covered by a plan (or a program, policy, or custom having the effect of a plan) providing for the payment of amounts to the employee in the event of personal injuries or sickness, and notice or knowledge of such plan was reasonably available to the employee. It is immaterial who makes payment of the benefits provided by the plan. For example, payment may be made by the employer, a welfare fund, a State sickness or disability benefits fund, an association of employers or employees, or by an insurance company.

(b) Self-employed individuals. Under section 105(g), a self-employed individual is not treated as an employee for purposes of section 105. Therefore, for example, benefits paid under an accident or health plan as referred to in section 105(e) to or on behalf of an individual who is self-employed in the business with respect to which the plan is established will not be treated as received through accident and health insurance for purposes of sections 104(a)(3) and 105.

T.D. 6169, 4/13/56, amend T.D. 6722, 4/13/64.

§ 1.105-6 Special rules for employees retired before January 27, 1975.

Caution: The Treasury has not yet amended Reg § 1.105-6 to reflect changes made by P.L. 98-21.

(a) Application of section 105(d) to amounts received as retirement annuities. An employee who retired from work before January 27, 1975, receiving payments under his employer-established plan (to which § 1.72-15(a) applies) which payments were not treated as amounts received under a wage continuation plan for purposes of section 105(d), may, as of the date the employee retired, treat such plan as such a wage continuation plan to the extent such payments are received prior to mandatory retirement age (as described in § 1.105-4(a)(3)(i)(B)), if—

(1) His employer had in operation at the time of his retirement a program providing accident and health benefits under a wage continuation plan to which section 105(d) would apply;

(2) The employer certifies, under procedures approved in advance under paragraph (c) of this section, that the employee would have been eligible for wage continuation benefits, under the terms and conditions of his employer's plan, because of personal injuries or sickness;

(3) At the time of the employee's retirement there was no substantive difference between the benefits being actually received and the benefits he would have received had he retired under his employer's wage continuation plan; and

(4) The employee agrees to the adjustments and conditions required by the Commissioner with respect to amounts

excluded under section 72 (b) or (d) in taxable years ending before January 27, 1975.

(b) Filing requirements. *(1)* the Certification required in paragraph (a)(2) and the agreement required in paragraph (a)(4) of this section shall be filed on or before April 15, 1977, with the return, or timely amended return or claim, made for the taxable year in which the employee reached retirement age as described in § 1.79-2(b)(3), or, for the first taxable year for which the taxpayer files an income tax return claiming an exclusion under section 105(d), as provided in paragraph (a) of this section.

(2) The Commissioner may prescribe a form and instructions with respect to the agreement provided for in paragraph (a)(4) of this section.

(c) Employer certification. *(1) Advance approval of procedures.* Any reasonable and consistently applied procedures, approved in advance by the Internal Revenue Service, which require the employee to provide the employer or the insurer with medical documentation sufficient to show that an illness or disability existed as of the date of the employee's retirement, which would have entitled him to retire on account of personal injuries or sickness alone, are sufficient for purposes of this paragraph.

(2) Place of submission. Request for advance approval of procedures for certification shall be submitted to the district director.

(d) Cross reference. For special rules pertaining to taxpayers retired on disability before January 27, 1975, see § 1.72-15(i).

T.D. 7352, 4/9/75.

PAR. 4. Section 1.105-6 is removed.

Proposed § 1.105-6 [*For Preamble, see ¶ 152,901*]

§ 1.105-6 [Removed]

§ 1.105-11 Self-insured medical reimbursement plan.

Caution: The Treasury has not yet amended Reg § 1.105-11 to reflect changes made by P.L. 97-34.

(a) In general. Under section 105(a), amounts received by an employee through a self-insured medical reimbursement plan which are attributable to contributions of the employer, or are paid by the employer, are included in the employee's gross income unless such amounts are excludable under section 105(b). For amounts reimbursed to a highly compensated individual to be fully excludable from such individual's gross income under section 105(b), the plan must satisfy the requirements of section 105(h) and this section. Section 105(h) is not satisfied if the plan discriminates in favor of highly compensated individuals as to eligibility to participate or benefits. All or a portion of the reimbursements or payments on behalf of such individuals under a discriminatory plan are not excludable from gross income under section 105(b). However, benefits paid to participants who are not highly compensated individuals may be excluded from gross income if the requirements of section 105(b) are satisfied, even if the plan is discriminatory.

(b) Self-insured medical reimbursement plan. *(1) General rule.* (i) Definition. A self-insured medical reimbursement plan is a separate written plan for the benefit of employees which provides for reimbursement of employee medical expenses referred to in section 105(b). A plan or arrangement is self-insured unless reimbursement is provided under an individual or group policy of accident or health insurance issued by a licensed insurance company or under an arrangement in the nature of a prepaid health care plan that is regulated under federal or state law in a manner similar to the regulation of insurance companies. Thus, for example, a plan of a health maintenance organization, established under the Health Maintenance Organization Act of 1973, would qualify as a prepaid health care plan. In addition, this section applies to a self-insured medical reimbursement plan, determined in accordance with the rules of this section, maintained by an employee organization described in section 501(c)(9).

(ii) Shifting of risk. A plan underwritten by a policy of insurance or a prepaid health care plan that does not involve the shifting of risk to an unrelated third party is considered self-insured for purposes of this section. Accordingly, a cost-plus policy or a policy which in effect merely provides administrative or bookkeeping services is considered self-insured for purposes of this section. However, a plan is not considered self-insured merely because one factor the insurer uses in determining the premium is the employer's prior claims experience.

(iii) Captive insurance company. A plan underwritten by a policy of insurance issued by a captive insurance company is not considered self-insured for purposes of this section if for the plan year the premiums paid by companies unrelated to the captive insurance company equal or exceed 50 percent of the total premiums received and the policy of insurance is similar to policies sold to such unrelated companies.

(2) Other rules. The rules of this section apply to a self-insured portion of an employer's medical plan or arrangement even if the plan is in part underwritten by insurance. For example, if an employer's medical plan reimburses employees for benefits not covered under the insured portion of an overall plan, or for deductible amounts under the insured portions, such reimbursement is subject to the rules of this section. However, a plan which reimburses employees for premiums paid under an insured plan is not subject to this section. In addition, medical expense reimbursements not described in the plan are not paid pursuant to a plan for the benefit of employees, and therefore are not excludable from gross income under section 105(b). Such reimbursements will not affect the determination of whether or not a plan is discriminatory.

(c) Prohibited discrimination. *(1) In general.* A self-insured medical reimbursement plan does not satisfy the requirements of section 105(h) and this paragraph for a plan year unless the plan satisfies subparagraphs (2) and (3) of this paragraph. However, a plan does not fail to satisfy the requirements of this paragraph merely because benefits under the plan are offset by benefits paid under a self-insured or insured plan of the employer or another employer, or by benefits paid under Medicare or other Federal or State law or similar Foreign law. A self-insured plan may take into account the benefits provided under another plan only to the extent that the type of benefit subject to reimbursement is the same under both plans. For example, an amount reimbursed to an employee for a hospital expense under a medical plan maintained by the employer of the employee's spouse may be offset against the self-insured benefit where the self-insured plan covering the employee provides the same type of hospital expense benefit.

(2) Eligibility to participate. (i) Percentage test. A plan satisfies the requirements of this subparagraph if it benefits—

(A) Seventy percent or more of all employees, or

(B) Eighty percent or more of all the employees who are eligible to benefit under the plan if 70 percent or more of all employees are eligible to benefit under the plan.

(ii) Classification test. A plan satisfies the requirements of this subparagraph if it benefits such employees as qualify under a classification of employees set up by the employer which is found by the Internal Revenue Service not to be discriminatory in favor of highly compensated individuals. In general, this determination will be made based upon the facts and circumstances of each case, applying the same standards as are applied under section 410(b)(1)(B) (relating to qualified pension, profit-sharing and stock bonus plans), without regard to the special rules in section 401(a)(5) concerning eligibility to participate.

(iii) Exclusion of certain employees. Under section 105(h)(3), for purposes of subparagraph (2) of this section, there may be excluded from consideration:

(A) Employees who have not completed 3 years of service prior to the beginning of the plan year. For purposes of this section years of service may be determined by any method that is reasonable and consistent. A determination made in the same manner as (and not requiring service in excess of how) a year of service is determined under section 410(a)(3) shall be deemed to be reasonable. For purposes of the 3-year rule, all of an employee's years of service with the employer prior to a separation from service are not taken into account. For purposes of the 3-year rule, an employee's years of service prior to age 25, as a part-time or seasonal employee, as a member of a collective bargaining unit, or as a nonresident alien, as each is described in this subdivision, are not excluded by reason of being so described from counting towards satisfaction of the rule. In addition, if the employer is a predecessor employer (determined in a manner consistent with section 414(a)), service for such predecessor is treated as service for the employer.

(B) Employees who have not attained age 25 prior to the beginning of the plan year.

(C) Part-time employees whose customary weekly employment is less than 35 hours, if other employees in similar work with the same employer (or, if no employees of the employer are in similar work, in similar work in the same industry and location) have substantially more hours, and seasonal employees whose customary annual employment is less than 9 months, if other employees in similar work with the same employer (or, if no employees of the employer are in similar work, in similar work in the same industry and location) have substantially more months. Notwithstanding the preceding sentence, any employee whose customary weekly employment is less than 25 hours or any employee whose customary annual employment is less than 7 months may be considered as a part-time or seasonal employee.

(D) Employees who are included in a unit of employees covered by an agreement between employee representatives and one or more employers which the Commissioner finds to be a collective bargaining agreement, if accident and health benefits were the subject of good faith bargaining between such employee representatives and such employer or employers. For purposes of determining whether such bargaining occurred, it is not material that such employees are not covered by another medical plan or that the plan was not considered in such bargaining.

(E) Employees who are nonresident aliens and who receive no earned income (within the meaning of section 911(b) and the regulations thereunder) from the employer which constitutes income from sources within the United States (within the meaning of section 861(a)(3) and the regulations thereunder).

(3) Nondiscriminatory benefits. (i) In general. In general, benefits subject to reimbursement under a plan must not discriminate in favor of highly compensated individuals. Plan benefits will not satisfy the requirements of this subparagraph unless all the benefits provided for participants who are highly compensated individuals are provided for all other participants. In addition, all the benefits available for the dependents of employees who are highly compensated individuals must also be available on the same basis for the dependents of all other employees who are participants. A plan that provides optional benefits to participants will be treated as providing a single benefit with respect to the benefits covered by the option provided that (A) all eligible participants may elect any of the benefits covered by the option and (B) there are either no required employee contributions or the required employee contributions are the same amount. This test is applied to the benefits subject to reimbursement under the plan rather than the actual benefit payments or claims under the plan. The presence or absence of such discrimination will be determined by considering the type of benefit subject to reimbursement provided highly compensated individuals, as well as the amount of the benefit subject to reimbursement. A plan may establish a maximum limit for the amount of reimbursement which may be paid a participant for any single benefit, or combination of benefits. However, any maximum limit attributable to employer contributions must be uniform for all participants and for all dependents of employees who are participants and may not be modified by reason of a participant's age or years of service. In addition, if a plan covers employees who are highly compensated individuals, and the type or the amount of benefits subject to reimbursement under the plan are in proportion to employee compensation, the plan discriminates as to benefits.

(ii) Discriminatory operation. Not only must a plan not discriminate on its face in providing benefits in favor of highly compensated individuals, the plan also must not discriminate in favor of such employees in actual operation. The determination of whether plan benefits discriminate in operation in favor of highly compensated individuals is made on the basis of the facts and circumstances of each case. A plan is not considered discriminatory merely because highly compensated individuals participating in the plan utilize a broad range of plan benefits to a greater extent than do other employees participating in the plan. In addition, if a plan (or a particular benefit provided by a plan) is terminated, the termination would cause the plan benefits to be discriminatory if the duration of the plan (or benefit) has the effect of discriminating in favor of highly compensated individuals. Accordingly, the prohibited discrimination may occur where the duration of a particular benefit coincides with the period during which a highly compensated individual utilizes the benefit.

(iii) Retired employees. To the extent that an employer provides benefits under a self-insured medical reimbursement plan to a retired employee that would otherwise be excludible from gross income under section 105(b), determined without regard to section 105(h), such benefits shall not be considered a discriminatory benefit under this paragraph (c). The preceding sentence shall not apply to a retired employee who was a highly compensated individual unless the type, and the dollar limitations, of benefits provided retired employees who were highly compensated individuals are the same for all other retired participants. If this subdivision applies to a retired participant, that individual is not considered an employee for purposes of determining the highest paid 25 percent of all employees under paragraph (d) of this section solely by reason of receiving such plan benefits.

(4) Multiple plans, etc. (i) General rule. An employer may designate two or more plans as constituting a single plan that is intended to satisfy the requirements of section 105(h)(2) and paragraph (c) of this section, in which case all plans so designated shall be considered as a single plan in determining whether the requirements of such section are satisfied by each of the separate plans. A determination that the combination of plans so designated does not satisfy such requirements does not preclude a determination that one or more of such plans, considered separately, satisfies such requirements. A single plan document may be utilized by an employer for two or more separate plans provided that the employer designates the plans that are to be considered separately and the applicable provisions of each separate plan.

(ii) Other rules. If the designated combined plan discriminates as to eligibility to participate or benefits, the amount of excess reimbursement will be determined under the rules of section 105(h)(7) and paragraph (e) of this section by taking into account all reimbursements made under the combined plan.

(iii) H.M.O. participants. For purposes of section 105(h)(2)(A) and paragraph (c)(2) of this section, a self-insured plan will be deemed to benefit an employee who has enrolled in a health maintenance organization (HMO) that is offered on an optional basis by the employer in lieu of coverage under the self-insured plan if, with respect to that employee, the employer's contributions to the HMO plan equal or exceed those that would be made to the self-insured plan, and if the HMO plan is designated in accordance with subdivision (i) with the self-insured plan as a single plan. For purposes of section 105(h) and this section, except as provided in the preceding sentence, employees covered by, and benefits under, the HMO plan are not treated as part of the self-insured plan.

(d) Highly compensated individuals defined. For purposes of section 105(h) and this section, the term "highly compensated individual" means an individual who is—

(1) One of the 5 highest paid officers,

(2) A shareholder who owns (with the application of section 318) more than 10 percent in value of the stock of the employer, or

(3) Among the highest paid 25 percent of all employees (including the 5 highest paid officers, but not including employees excludable under paragraph (c)(2)(iii) of this section who are not participants in any self-insured medical reimbursement plan of the employer, whether or not designated as a single plan under paragraph (c)(4) of this section, or in a health maintenance organization plan).

The status of an employee as an officer or stockholder is determined with respect to a particular benefit on the basis of the employee's officer status or stock ownership at the time during the plan year at which the benefit is provided. In calculating the highest paid 25 percent of all employees, the number of employees included will be rounded to the next highest number. For example, if there are 5 employees, the top two are in the highest paid 25 percent. The level of an employee's compensation is determined on the basis of the employee's compensation for the plan year. For purposes of the preceding sentence, fiscal year plans may determine employee compensation on the basis of the calendar year ending within the plan year.

(e) Excess reimbursement of highly compensated individual. *(1) In general.* For purposes of section 105(h) and this section, a reimbursement paid to a highly compensated individual is an excess reimbursement if it is paid pursuant to a plan that fails to satisfy the requirements of paragraph (c)(2) or (c)(3) for the plan year. The amount reimbursed to a highly compensated individual which constitutes an excess reimbursement is not excludable from such individual's gross income under section 105(b).

(2) Discriminatory benefit. In the case of a benefit available to highly compensated individuals but not to all other participants (or which otherwise discriminates in favor of highly compensated individuals as opposed to other participants), the amount of excess reimbursement equals the total amount reimbursed to the highly compensated individual with respect to the benefit.

(3) Discriminatory coverage. In the case of benefits (other than discriminatory benefits described in subparagraph (2)) paid to a highly compensated individual under a plan which fails to satisfy the requirements of paragraph (c)(2) relating to nondiscrimination in eligibility to participate, the amount of excess reimbursement is determined by multiplying the total amount reimbursed to the individual by a fraction. The numerator of the fraction is the total amount reimbursed during that plan year to all highly compensated individuals. The denominator of the fraction is the total amount reimbursed during that plan year to all participants. In computing the fraction and the total amount reimbursed to the individual, discriminatory benefits described in subparagraph (2) are not taken into account. Accordingly, any amount which is included in income by reason of the benefit's not being available to all other participants will not be taken into account.

(4) Examples. The provisions of this paragraph are illustrated by the following examples:

Example (1). Corporation M maintains a self-insured medical reimbursement plan which covers all employees. The plan provides the following maximum limits on the amount of benefits subject to reimbursement: $5,000 for officers and $1,000 for all other participants. During a plan year Employee A, one of the 5 highest paid officers, received reimbursements in the amount of $4,000. Because the amount of benefits provided for highly compensated individuals is not provided for all other participants, the plan benefits are discriminatory. Accordingly, Employee A received an excess reimbursement of $3,000 ($4,000 – $1,000) which constitutes a benefit available to highly compensated individuals, but not to all other participants.

Example (2). Corporation N maintains a self-insured medical reimbursement plan which covers all employees. The plan provides a broad range of medical benefits subject to reimbursement for all participants. However, only the 5 highest paid officers are entitled to dental benefits. During the plan year Employee B, one of the 5 highest paid officers, received dental payments under the plan in the amount of $300. Because dental benefits are provided for highly compensated individuals, and not for all other participants, the plan discriminates as to benefits. Accordingly, Employee B received an excess reimbursement in the amount of $300.

Example (3). Corporation O maintains a self-insured medical reimbursement plan which discriminates as to eligibility by covering only the highest paid 40% of all employees. Benefits subject to reimbursement under the plan are the same for all participants. During a plan year Employee C, a highly compensated individual, received benefits in the amount of $1,000. The amount of excess reimbursement paid Employee C during the plan year will be calculated by multiplying the $1,000 by a fraction determined under subparagraph (3).

Example (4). Corporation P maintains a self-insured medical reimbursement plan for its employees. Benefits subject to reimbursement under the plan are the same for all plan participants. However, the plan fails the eligibility tests of section 105(h)(3)(A) and thereby discriminates as to eligibility. During the 1980 plan year Employee D, a highly compensated individual, was hospitalized for surgery and incurred medical expenses of $4,500 which were reimbursed to D under the plan. During that plan year the Corporation P medical plan paid $50,000 in benefits under the plan, $30,000 of which constituted benefits paid to highly compensated individuals. The amount of excess reimbursement not excludable by D under section 105(b) is $2,700

$$\left(\$4{,}500 \times \frac{\$30{,}000}{\$50{,}000}\right)$$

Example (5). Corporation Q maintains a self-insured medical reimbursement plan for its employees. The plan provides a broad range of medical benefits subject to reimbursement for participants. However, only the five highest paid officers are entitled to dental benefits. In addition, the plan fails the eligibility test of section 105(h)(3)(A) and thereby discriminates as to eligibility. During the calendar 1981 plan year, Employee E, a highly compensated individual, received dental benefits under the plan in the amount of $300, and no other employee received dental benefits. In addition, Employee E was hospitalized for surgery and incurred medical expenses reimbursement for which was available to all participants, of $4,500 which were reimbursed to E under the plan. Because dental benefits are only provided for highly compensated individuals, Employee E received an excess reimbursement under paragraph (e)(2) above in the amount of $300. For the 1981 plan year, the Corporation Q medical plan paid $50,300 in total benefits under the plan, $30,300 of which constituted benefits paid to highly compensated individuals. In computing the fraction under paragraph (e)(3), discriminatory benefits described in paragraph (e)(2) are not taken into account. Therefore, the amount of excess reimbursement not excludable to Employee E with respect to the $4,500 of medical expenses incurred is $2,700

$$\left(\$4{,}500 \times \frac{\$30{,}000}{\$50{,}000}\right)$$

and the total amount of excess reimbursements includable in E's income for 1981 is $3,000.

Example (6). (i) Corporation R maintains a calendar year self-insured medical reimbursement plan which covers all employees. The type of benefits subject to reimbursement under the plan include all medical care expenses as defined in section 213(e). The amount of reimbursement available to any employee for any calendar year is limited to 5 percent of the compensation paid to each employee during the calendar year. The amount of compensation and reimbursement paid to Employees A– F for the calendar year is as follows:

Employee	Compensation	Reimbursable amount paid
A	$100,000	$5,000
B	25,000	1,250
C	15,000	750
D	10,000	500
E	10,000	500
F	8,000	400
		8,400

(ii) Because the amount of benefits subject to reimbursement under the plan is in proportion to employee compensation the plan discriminates as to benefits. In addition, Employees A and B are highly compensated individuals. The amount of excess reimbursement paid Employees A and B during the plan year will be determined under paragraph (e)(2). Because benefits in excess of $400 (Employee F's maximum benefit) are provided for highly compensated individuals and not for all other participants, Employees A and B received respectively, an excess reimbursement of $4,600 and $850.

(f) Certain controlled groups. For purposes of applying the provisions of section 105(h) and this section, all employees who are treated as employed by a single employer under section 414(b) and (c), and the regulations thereunder (relating to special rules for qualified pension, profit-sharing and stock bonus plans), shall be treated as employed by a single employer.

(g) Exception for medical diagnostic procedures. *(1) In general.* For purposes of applying section 105(h) and this section, reimbursements paid under a plan for medical diagnostic procedures for an employee, but not a dependent, are not considered to be a part of a plan described in this section. The medical diagnostic procedures include routine medical examinations, blood tests, and X-rays. Such procedures do not include expenses incurred for the treatment, cure or testing of a known illness or disability, or treatment or testing for a physical injury, complaint or specific symptom of a bodily malfunction. For example, a routine dental examination with X-rays is a medical diagnostic procedure, but X-rays and treatment for a specific complaint are not. In addition, such procedures do not include any activity undertaken for exercise, fitness, nutrition, recreation, or the general improvement of health. The diagnostic procedures must be performed at a facility which provides no services (directly or indirectly) other than medical, and ancillary, services. For purposes of the preceding sentence, physical proximity between a medical facilities and nonmedical facility will not for that reason alone cause the medical facility not to qualify. For example, an employee's annual physical examination conducted at the employee's personal physician's office is not considered a part of the medical reimbursement plan and therefore is not subject to the nondiscrimination requirements. Accordingly, the amount reimbursed may be excludable from the employee's income if the requirements of section 105(b) are satisfied.

(2) Transportation, etc. expenses. Transportation expenses primarily for an allowable diagnostic procedure are included within the exception described in this paragraph, but only to the extent they are ordinary and necessary. Transportation undertaken merely for the general improvement of health, or in connection with a vacation, is not within the scope of this exception, nor are any incidental expenses for food or lodging; therefore, amounts reimbursed for such expenses may be excess reimbursements under paragraph (e).

(h) Time of inclusion. Excess reimbursements (determined under paragraph (e)) paid to a highly compensated individual for a plan year will be considered as received in the taxable year of the individual in which (or with which) the plan year ends. The particular plan year to which reimbursements relate shall be determined under the plan provisions. In the absence of plan provisions reimbursements shall be attributed to the plan year in which payment is made. For example, under a calendar year plan an excess reimbursement paid to A in 1981 on account of an expense incurred and subject to reimbursement for the 1980 plan year under the terms of the plan will be considered as received in 1980 by A.

(i) Self-insured contributory plan. A medical plan subject to this section may provide for employer and employee contributions. See § 1.105-1(c). The tax treatment of reimbursements attributable to employee contributions is determined under section 104(a)(3). The tax treatment of reimbursements attributable to employer contributions is determined under section 105. The amount of reimbursements which are attributable to contributions of the employer shall be determined in accordance with § 1.105-1(e).

(j) Effective date. Section 105(h) and this section are effective for taxable years beginning after December 31, 1979 and for amounts reimbursed after December 31, 1979. In determining plan discrimination and the taxability of excess reimbursements made for a plan year beginning in 1979 and ending in 1980, a plan's eligibility and benefit requirements as well as actual reimbursements made in the plan year during 1979, will not be taken into account. In addition, this section does not apply to claims which are filed in 1979 and paid in 1980.

(k) Special rules. *(1) Relation to cafeteria plans.* If a self-insured medical reimbursement plan is included in a cafeteria plan as described in section 125, the rules of this section will determine the status of a benefit as a taxable or nontaxable benefit, and the rules of section 125 will determine whether an employee is taxed as though he elected all available taxable benefits (including taxable benefits under a discriminatory medical reimbursement plan). This rule is illustrated by the following example:

Example. Corporation M maintains a cafeteria plan described in section 125. Under the plan an officer of the corporation may elect to receive medical benefits provided by a self-insured medical reimbursement plan which is subject to the rules of this section. However, the self-insured medical reimbursement plan fails the nondiscrimination rules under paragraph (c) of this section. Accordingly, the amount of excess reimbursement is taxable to the officer participating in the medical reimbursement plan pursuant to section 105(h) and this section. Therefore, the self-insured medical reimbursement plan will be considered a taxable benefit under section 125 and the regulations thereunder.

(2) Benefit subject to reimbursement. For purposes of this section, a benefit subject to reimbursement is a benefit described in the plan under which a claim for reimbursement or for a payment directly to the health service provider may be filed by a plan participant. It does not refer to actual claims or benefit reimbursements paid under a plan.

T.D. 7754, 1/13/81.

PARAGRAPH 1. Paragraph (f) of § 1.105-11 is amended by striking out "section 414(b) and (c)" and inserting in lieu thereof "section 414(b), (c), or (m)."

Proposed § 1.105-11 [Amended] [*For Preamble, see ¶ 150,825*]

§ 1.106-1 Contributions by employer to accident and health plans.

The gross income of an employee does not include contributions which his employer makes to an accident or health plan for compensation (through insurance or otherwise) to the employee for personal injuries or sickness incurred by him, his spouse, or his dependents, as defined in section 152. The employer may contribute to an accident or health plan either by paying the premium (or a portion of the premium) on a policy of accident or health insurance covering one or more of his employees, or by contributing to a separate trust or fund (including a fund referred to in section 105(e)) which provides accident or health benefits directly or through insurance to one or more of his employees. However, if such insurance policy, trust, or fund provides other benefits in addition to accident or health benefits, section 106 applies only to the portion of the employer's contribution which is allocable to accident or health benefits. See paragraph (d) of § 1.104-1 and §§ 1.105-1 through 1.105-5, inclusive, for regulations relating to exclusion from an employee's gross income of amounts received through accident or health insurance and through accident or health plans.

T.D. 6169, 4/13/56.

PAR. 2.

Section 1.106-1 is amended by redesignating the existing text as paragraph (a), revising the first sentence of paragraph (a), and adding a new paragraph (b) to read as follows:

Proposed § 1.106-1 Contributions by employer to accident and health plans. [*For Preamble, see ¶ 151,085*]

(a) Except as set forth in paragraph (b) of this section, the gross income of an employee does not include contributions which his employer makes to an accident or health plan for compensation (through insurance or otherwise) to the employee for personal injuries or sickness incurred by him, his spouse, or his dependents, as defined in section 152. * * *

(b) In situations involving group health plans that do not comply with section 162(k), the exclusion described in paragraph (a) of this section is not available to highly compensated employees (as defined in section 414(q)). See § 1.162-26 (regarding continuation coverage requirements of group health plans).

PAR. 5. Section 1.106-1 is amended by revising the first sentence and adding a new sentence at the end of the paragraph to read as follows:

Proposed § 1.106-1 Contributions by employer to accident and health plans. [*For Preamble, see ¶ 152,901*]

The gross income of an employee does not include the contributions which the employer makes to an accident or health plan for compensation (through insurance or otherwise) to the employee for personal injuries or sickness incurred by the employee, the employee's spouse, or the employee's dependents (as defined in section 152 determined without regard to section 152(b)(1), (b)(2), or (d)(1)(B)). * * * For the treatment of the payment of premiums for accident or health insurance from a qualified trust under section 401(a), see §§ 1.72-15 and 1.402(a)-1(e).

§ 1.107-1 Rental value of parsonages.

(a) In the case of a minister of the gospel, gross income does not include (1) the rental value of a home, including utilities, furnished to him as a part of his compensation, or (2) the rental allowance paid to him as part of his compensation to the extent such allowance is used by him to rent or otherwise provide a home. In order to qualify for the exclusion, the home or rental allowance must be provided as remuneration for services which are ordinarily the duties of a minister of the gospel. In general, the rules provided in § 1.1402(c)-5 will be applicable to such determination. Examples of specific services the performance of which will be considered duties of a minister for purposes of section 107 include the performance of sacerdotal functions, the conduct of religious worship, the administration and maintenance of religious organizations and their integral agencies, and the performance of teaching and administrative duties at theological seminaries. Also, the service performed by a qualified minister as an employee of the United States (other than as a chaplain in the Armed Forces, whose service is considered to be that of a commissioned officer in his capacity as such, and not as a minister in the exercise of his ministry), or a State, Territory, or possession of the United States, or a political subdivision of any of the foregoing, or the District of Columbia, is in the exercise of his ministry provided the service performed includes such services as are ordinarily the duties of a minister.

(b) For purposes of section 107, the term "home" means a dwelling place (including furnishings) and the appurtenances thereto, such as a garage. The term "rental allowance" means an amount paid to a minister to rent or otherwise provide a home if such amount is designated as rental allowance pursuant to official action taken prior to January 1, 1958, by the employing church or other qualified organization, or if such amount is designated as rental allowance pursuant to official action taken in advance of such payment by the employing church or other qualified organization when paid after December 31, 1957. The designation of an amount as rental allowance may be evidenced in an employment contract, in minutes of or in a resolution by a church or other qualified organization or in its budget, or in any other appropriate instrument evidencing such official action. The designation referred to in this paragraph is a sufficient designation if it permits a payment or a part thereof to be identified as a payment of rental allowance as distinguished from salary or other remuneration.

(c) A rental allowance must be included in the minister's gross income in the taxable year in which it is received, to the extent that such allowance is not used by him during such taxable year to rent or otherwise provide a home. Circumstances under which a rental allowance will be deemed to have been used to rent or provide a home will include cases in which the allowance is expended (1) for rent of a home, (2) for purchase of a home, and (3) for expenses directly related to providing a home. Expenses for food and servants are not considered for this purpose to be directly related to providing a home. Where the minister rents, purchases, or owns a farm or other business property in addition to a home, the portion of the rental allowance expended in connection with the farm or business property shall not be excluded from his gross income.

T.D. 6239, 6/14/57, amend T.D. 6691, 12/2/63.

§ 1.108-1 Stock-for-debt exception not to apply in de minimis cases.

[Reserve]

T.D. 8532, 3/17/94, amend T.D. 9304, 12/21/2006.

§ 1.108-2 Acquisition of indebtedness by a person related to the debtor.

(a) General rules. The acquisition of outstanding indebtedness by a person related to the debtor from a person who is not related to the debtor results in the realization by the debtor of income from discharge of indebtedness (to the extent required by section 61(a)(12) and section 108) in an amount determined under paragraph (f) of this section. Income realized pursuant to the preceding sentence is excludible from gross income to the extent provided in section 108(a). The rules of this paragraph apply if indebtedness is acquired directly by a person related to the debtor in a direct acquisition (as defined in paragraph (b) of this section) or if a holder of indebtedness becomes related to the debtor in an indirect acquisition (as defined in paragraph (c) of this section).

(b) Direct acquisition. An acquisition of outstanding indebtedness is a direct acquisition under this section if a person related to the debtor (or a person who becomes related to the debtor on the date the indebtedness is acquired) acquires the indebtedness from a person who is not related to the debtor. Notwithstanding the foregoing, the Commissioner may provide by Revenue Procedure or other published guidance that certain acquisitions of indebtedness described in the preceding sentence are not direct acquisitions for purposes of this section.

(c) Indirect acquisition. *(1) In general.* An indirect acquisition is a transaction in which a holder of outstanding indebtedness becomes related to the debtor, if the holder acquired the indebtedness in anticipation of becoming related to the debtor.

(2) Proof of anticipation of relationship. In determining whether indebtedness was acquired by a holder in anticipation of becoming related to the debtor, all relevant facts and circumstances will be considered. Such facts and circumstances include, but are not limited to, the intent of the parties at the time of the acquisition, the nature of any contacts between the parties (or their respective affiliates) before the acquisition, the period of time for which the holder held the indebtedness, and the significance of the indebtedness in proportion to the total assets of the holder group (as defined in paragraph (c)(5) of this section). For example, if a holder acquired the indebtedness in the ordinary course of its portfolio investment activities and the holder's acquisition of the indebtedness preceded any discussions concerning the acquisition of the holder by the debtor (or by a person related to the debtor) or the acquisition of the debtor by the holder (or by a person related to the holder), as the case may be, these facts, taken together, would ordinarily establish that the holder did not acquire the indebtedness in anticipation of becoming related to the debtor. The absence of discussions between the debtor and the holder (or their respective affiliates), however, does not by itself establish that the holder did not acquire the indebtedness in anticipation of becoming related to the debtor (if, for example, the facts and circumstances show that the holder was considering a potential acquisition of or by the debtor, or the relationship is created within a relatively short period of time of the acquisition, or the indebtedness constitutes a disproportionate portion of the holder group's assets).

(3) Indebtedness acquired within 6 months of becoming related. Notwithstanding any other provision of this paragraph (c), a holder of indebtedness is treated as having acquired the indebtedness in anticipation of becoming related to the debtor if the holder acquired the indebtedness less than 6 months before the date the holder becomes related to the debtor.

(4) Disclosure of potential indirect acquisition. (i) In general. If a holder of outstanding indebtedness becomes related to the debtor under the circumstances described in paragraph (c)(4)(ii) or (iii) of this section, the debtor is required to attach the statement described in paragraph (c)(4)(iv) of this section to its tax return (or to a qualified amended return within the meaning of § 1.6664-2(c)(3)) for the taxable year in which the debtor becomes related to the holder, unless the debtor reports its income on the basis that the holder ac-

quired the indebtedness in anticipation of becoming related to the debtor. Disclosure under this paragraph (c)(4) is in addition to, and is not in substitution for, any disclosure required to be made under section 6662, 6664 or 6694.

(ii) Indebtedness represents more than 25 percent of holder group's assets. (A) In general. Disclosure under this paragraph (c)(4) is required if, on the date the holder becomes related to the debtor, indebtedness of the debtor represents more than 25 percent of the fair market value of the total gross assets of the holder group (as defined in paragraph (c)(5) of this section).

(B) Determination of total gross assets. In determining the total gross assets of the holder group, total gross assets do not include any cash, cash item, marketable stock or security, short-term indebtedness, option, futures contract, notional principal contract, or similar item (other than indebtedness of the debtor), nor do total gross assets include any asset in which the holder has substantially reduced its risk of loss. In addition, total gross assets do not include any ownership interest in or indebtedness of a member of the holder group.

(iii) Indebtedness acquired within 6 to 24 months of becoming related. Disclosure under this paragraph (c)(4) is required if the holder acquired the indebtedness 6 months or more before the date the holder becomes related to the debtor, but less than 24 months before that date.

(iv) Contents of statement. A statement under this paragraph (c)(4) must include the following—

(A) A caption identifying the statement as disclosure under § 1.108-2(c);

(B) An identification of the indebtedness with respect to which disclosure is made;

(C) The amount of such indebtedness and the amount of income from discharge of indebtedness if section 108(e)(4) were to apply;

(D) Whether paragraph (c)(4)(ii) or (iii) of this section applies to the transaction; and

(E) A statement describing the facts and circumstances supporting the debtor's position that the holder did not acquire the indebtedness in anticipation of becoming related to the debtor.

(v) Failure to disclose. In addition to any other penalties that may apply, if a debtor fails to provide a statement required by this paragraph (c)(4), the holder is presumed to have acquired the indebtedness in anticipation of becoming related to the debtor unless the facts and circumstances clearly establish that the holder did not acquire the indebtedness in anticipation of becoming related to the debtor.

(5) Holder group. For purposes of this paragraph (c), the holder group consists of the holder of the indebtedness and all persons who are both—

(i) Related to the holder before the holder becomes related to the debtor; and

(ii) Related to the debtor after the holder becomes related to the debtor.

(6) Holding period. (i) Suspensions. The running of the holding periods set forth in paragraphs (c)(3) and (c)(4)(iii) of this section is suspended during any period in which the holder or any person related to the holder is protected (directly or indirectly) against risk of loss by an option, a short sale, or any other device or transaction.

(ii) Tacking. For purposes of paragraphs (c)(3) and (c)(4)(iii) of this section, the period for which a holder held the debtor's indebtedness includes—

(A) The period for which the indebtedness was held by a corporation to whose attributes the holder succeeded pursuant to section 381; and

(B) The period (ending on the date on which the holder becomes related to the debtor) for which the indebtedness was held continuously by members of the holder group (as defined in paragraph (c)(5) of this section).

(d) Definitions. *(1) Acquisition date.* For purposes of this section, the acquisition date is the date on which a direct acquisition of indebtedness or an indirect acquisition of indebtedness occurs.

(2) Relationship. For purposes of this section, persons are considered related if they are related within the meaning of sections 267(b) or 707(b)(1). However—

(i) Sections 267(b) and 707(b)(1) are applied as if section 267(c)(4) provided that the family of an individual consists of the individual's spouse, the individual's children, grandchildren, and parents, and any spouse of the individual's children or grandchildren; and

(ii) Two entities that are treated as a single employer under subsection (b) or (c) of section 414 are treated as having a relationship to each other that is described in section 267(b).

(e) Exceptions. *(1) Indebtedness retired within one year.* This section does not apply to a direct or indirect acquisition of indebtedness with a stated maturity date on or before the date that is one year after the acquisition date, if the indebtedness is, in fact, retired on or before its stated maturity date.

(2) Acquisitions by securities dealers. (i) This section does not apply to a direct acquisition or an indirect acquisition of indebtedness by a dealer that acquires and disposes of such indebtedness in the ordinary course of its business of dealing in securities if—

(A) The dealer accounts for the indebtedness as a security held primarily for sale to customers in the ordinary course of business;

(B) The dealer disposes of the indebtedness (or it matures while held by the dealer) within a period consistent with the holding of the indebtedness for sale to customers in the ordinary course of business, taking into account the terms of the indebtedness and the conditions and practices prevailing in the markets for similar indebtedness during the period in which it is held; and

(C) The dealer does not sell or otherwise transfer the indebtedness to a person related to the debtor (other than in a sale to a dealer that in turn meets the requirements of this paragraph (e)(2)).

(ii) A dealer will continue to satisfy the conditions of this paragraph (e)(2) with respect to indebtedness that is exchanged for successor indebtedness in a transaction in which unrelated holders also exchange indebtedness of the same issue, provided that the conditions of this paragraph (e)(2) are met with respect to the successor indebtedness.

(iii) For purposes of this paragraph (e)(2), if the period consistent with the holding of indebtedness for sale to customers in the ordinary course of business is 30 days or less, the dealer is considered to dispose of indebtedness within that period if the aggregate principal amount of indebtedness of that issue sold by the dealer to customers in the ordinary course of business (or that mature and are paid while held by the dealer) in the calendar month following the month in which the indebtedness is acquired equals or exceeds the aggregate principal amount of indebtedness of that issue held in the dealer's inventory at the close of the month in which the indebtedness is acquired. If the period consistent with the holding of indebtedness for sale to customers in the ordinary course of business is greater than 30 days, the dealer is considered to dispose of the indebtedness within that period if the aggregate principal amount of indebtedness of that issue sold by the dealer to customers in the ordinary course of business (or that mature and are paid while held by the dealer) within that period equals or exceeds the aggregate principal amount of indebtedness of that issue held in inventory at the close of the day on which the indebtedness was acquired.

(f) Amount of discharge of indebtedness income realized. *(1) Holder acquired the indebtedness by purchase on or less than six months before the acquisition date.* Except as otherwise provided in this paragraph (f), the amount of discharge of indebtedness income realized under paragraph (a) of this section is measured by reference to the adjusted basis of the related holder (or of the holder that becomes related to the debtor) in the indebtedness on the acquisition date if the holder acquired the indebtedness by purchase on or less than six months before the acquisition date. For purposes of this paragraph (f), indebtedness is acquired "by purchase" if the indebtedness in the hands of the holder is not substituted basis property within the meaning of section 7701(a)(42). However, indebtedness is also considered acquired by purchase within six months before the acquisition date if the holder acquired the indebtedness as transferred basis property (within the meaning of section 7701(a)(43)) from a person who acquired the indebtedness by purchase on or less than six months before the acquisition date.

(2) Holder did not acquire the indebtedness by purchase on or less than six months before the acquisition date. Except as otherwise provided in this paragraph (f), the amount of discharge of indebtedness income realized under paragraph (a) of this section is measured by reference to the fair market value of the indebtedness on the acquisition date if the holder (or the transferor to the holder in a transferred basis transaction) did not acquire the indebtedness by purchase on or less than six months before the acquisition date.

(3) Acquisitions of indebtedness in nonrecognition transactions. [Reserved]

(4) Avoidance transactions. The amount of discharge of indebtedness income realized by the debtor under paragraph (a) of this section is measured by reference to the fair market value of the indebtedness on the acquisition date if the indebtedness is acquired in a direct or an indirect acquisition in which a principal purpose for the acquisition is the avoidance of federal income tax.

(g) Correlative adjustments. *(1) Deemed issuance.* For income tax purposes, if a debtor realizes income from discharge of its indebtedness in a direct or an indirect acquisition under this section (whether or not the income is excludible under section 108(a)), the debtor's indebtedness is treated as new indebtedness issued by the debtor to the related holder on the acquisition date (the deemed issuance). The new indebtedness is deemed issued with an issue price equal to the amount used under paragraph (f) of this section to compute the amount realized by the debtor under paragraph (a) of this section (i.e., either the holder's adjusted basis or the fair market value of the indebtedness, as the case may be). Under section 1273(a)(1), the excess of the stated redemption price at maturity (as defined in section 1273(a)(2)) of the indebtedness over its issue price is original issue discount (OID) which, to the extent provided in sections 163 and 1272, is deductible by the debtor and includible in the gross income of the related holder. Notwithstanding the foregoing, the Commissioner may provide by Revenue Procedure or other published guidance that the indebtedness is not treated as newly issued indebtedness for purposes of designated provisions of the income tax laws.

(2) Treatment of related holder. The related holder does not recognize any gain or loss on the deemed issuance described in paragraph (g)(1) of this section. The related holder's adjusted basis in the indebtedness remains the same as it was immediately before the deemed issuance. The deemed issuance is treated as a purchase of the indebtedness by the related holder for purposes of section 1272(a)(7) (pertaining to reduction of original issue discount where a subsequent holder pays acquisition premium) and section 1276 (pertaining to acquisitions of debt at a market discount).

(3) Loss deferral on disposition of indebtedness acquired in certain exchanges. (i) Any loss otherwise allowable to a related holder on the disposition at any time of indebtedness acquired in a direct or indirect acquisition (whether or not any discharge of indebtedness income was realized under paragraph (a) of this section) is deferred until the date the debtor retires the indebtedness if—

(A) The related holder acquired the debtor's indebtedness in exchange for its own indebtedness; and

(B) The issue price of the related holder's indebtedness was not determined by reference to its fair market value (e.g., the issue price was determined under section 1273(b)(4) or 1274(a) or any other provision of applicable law).

(ii) Any comparable tax benefit that would otherwise be available to the holder, debtor, or any person related to either, in any other transaction that directly or indirectly results in the disposition of the indebtedness is also deferred until the date the debtor retires the indebtedness.

(4) Examples. The following examples illustrate the application of this paragraph (g). In each example, all taxpayers are calendar-year taxpayers, no taxpayer is insolvent or under the jurisdiction of a court in a title 11 case and no indebtedness is qualified farm indebtedness described in section 108(g).

Example (1). (i) P, a domestic corporation, owns 70 percent of the single class of stock of S, a domestic corporation. S has outstanding indebtedness that has an issue price of $10,000,000 and provides for monthly interest payments of $80,000 payable at the end of each month and a payment at maturity of $10,000,000. The indebtedness has a stated maturity date of December 31, 1994. On January 1, 1992, P purchases S's indebtedness from I, an individual not related to S within the meaning of paragraph (d)(2) of this section, for cash in the amount of $9,000,000. S repays the indebtedness in full at maturity.

(ii) Under section 61(a)(12), section 108(e)(4), and paragraphs (a) and (f) of this section, S realizes $1,000,000 of income from discharge of indebtedness on January 1, 1992.

(iii) Under paragraph (g)(1) of this section, the indebtedness is treated as issued to P on January 1, 1992, with an issue price of $9,000,000. Under section 1273(a), the $1,000,000 excess of the stated redemption price at maturity of the indebtedness ($10,000,000) over its issue price ($9,000,000) is original issue discount, which is includible in gross income by P and deductible by S over the remaining term of the indebtedness under sections 163(e) and 1272(a).

(iv) Accordingly, S deducts and P includes in income original issue discount, in addition to stated interest, as follows: in 1992, $289,144.88; in 1993, $331,286.06; and in 1994, $379,569.06.

Example (2). The facts are the same as in Example 1, except that on January 1, 1993, P sells S's indebtedness to J, who is not related to S within the meaning of paragraph (d)(2) of this section, for $9,400,000 in cash. J holds S's indebtedness to maturity. On January 1, 1993, P's adjusted basis in S's indebtedness is $9,289,144.88. Accordingly, P realizes gain in the amount of $110,855.12 upon the disposition. S and J continue to deduct and include the original issue discount on the indebtedness in accordance with Example 1. The amount of original issue discount includible by J is reduced by the $110,855.12 acquisition premium as provided in section 1272(a)(7).

Example (3). The facts are the same as in Example 1, except that on February 1, 1992 (one month after P purchased S's indebtedness), S retires the indebtedness for an amount of cash equal to the fair market value of the indebtedness. Assume that the fair market value of the indebtedness is $9,022,621.41, which in this case equals the issue price of the indebtedness determined under paragraph (g)(1) of this section ($9,000,000) plus the accrued original issue discount through February 1 ($22,621.41). Section 1.61-12(c)(3) provides that if indebtedness is repurchased for a price that is exceeded by the issue price of the indebtedness plus the amount of discount already deducted, the excess is income from discharge of indebtedness. Therefore, S does not realize income from discharge of indebtedness. The result would be the same if P had contributed the indebtedness to the capital of S. Under section 108(e)(6), S would be treated as having satisfied the indebtedness with an amount of money equal to P's adjusted basis and, under section 1272(d)(2), P's adjusted basis is equal to $9,022,621.41.

Example (4). (i) P, a domestic corporation, owns 70 percent of the single class of stock of S, a domestic corporation. On January 1, 1986, P issued indebtedness that has an issue price of $5,000,000 and provides for no stated interest payments and a payment at maturity of $10,000,000. The indebtedness has a stated maturity date of December 31, 1995. On January 1, 1992, S purchases P's indebtedness from K, a partnership not related to P within the meaning of paragraph (d)(2) of this section, for cash in the amount of $6,000,000. The sum of the debt's issue price and previously deducted original issue discount is $7,578,582.83. P repays the indebtedness in full at maturity.

(ii) Under section 61(a)(12), section 108(e)(4), and paragraphs (a) and (f) of this section, P realizes $1,578,582.83 in income from discharge of indebtedness ($7,578,582.83 minus $6,000,000) on January 1, 1992.

(iii) Under paragraph (g)(1) of this section, the indebtedness is treated as issued to S on January 1, 1992, with an issue price of $6,000,000. Under section 1273(a), the $4,000,000 excess of the stated redemption price at maturity of the indebtedness ($10,000,000) over its issue price ($6,000,000) is original issue discount, which is includible in gross income by S and deductible by P over the remaining term of the indebtedness under sections 163(e) and 1272(a).

(iv) Accordingly, P deducts and S includes in income original issue discount as follows: in 1992, $817,316.20; in 1993, $928,650.49; in 1994, $1,055,150.67; and in 1995, $1,198,882.64.

(h) Effective date. This section applies to any transaction described in paragraph (a) and in either paragraph (b) or (c) of this section with an acquisition date on or after March 21, 1991. Although this section does not apply to direct or indirect acquisitions occurring before March 21, 1991, section 108(e)(4) is effective for any transaction after December 31, 1980, subject to the rules of section 7 of the Bankruptcy Tax Act of 1980 (Pub. L. 96-589, 94 Stat. 3389, 3411). Taxpayers may use any reasonable method of determining the amount of discharge of indebtedness income realized and the treatment of correlative adjustments under section 108(e)(4) for acquisitions of indebtedness before March 21, 1991, if such method is applied consistently by both the debtor and related holder.

T.D. 8460, 12/28/92.

§ 1.108-3 Intercompany losses and deductions.

(a) General rule. This section applies to certain losses and deductions from the sale, exchange, or other transfer of property between corporations that are members of a consolidated group or a controlled group (an intercompany transaction). See section 267(f) (controlled groups) and § 1.1502-13 (consolidated groups) for applicable definitions. For purposes of determining the attributes to which section 108(b) applies, a loss or deduction not yet taken into account under section 267(f) or § 1.1502-13 (an intercompany loss or deduction) is treated as basis described in section 108(b) that the transferor retains in property. To the extent a loss not yet taken into account is reduced under this section, it cannot subsequently be taken into account under section 267(f) or § 1.1502-13. For example, if S and B are corporations filing a consolidated return, and S sells land with a $100 basis to B for $90 and the $10 loss is deferred under section 267(f) and § 1.1502-13, the deferred loss is treated for purposes of section 108(b) as $10 of basis that S has in land (even though S has no remaining interest in the land sold to B) and is subject to reduction under section 108(b)(2)(E). Similar principles apply, with appropriate adjustments, if S and B are members of a controlled group and S's loss is deferred only under section 267(f).

(b) Effective date. This section applies with respect to discharges of indebtedness occurring on or after September 11, 1995.

T.D. 8597, 7/12/95.

§ 1.108-4 Election to reduce basis of depreciable property under section 108(b)(5) of the Internal Revenue Code.

(a) Description. An election under section 108(b)(5) is available whenever a taxpayer excludes discharge of indebtedness income (COD income) from gross income under sections 108(a)(1)(A), (B), or (C) (concerning title 11 cases, insolvency, and qualified farm indebtedness, respectively). See sections 108(d)(2) and (3) for the definitions of title 11 case and insolvent. See section 108(g)(2) for the definition of qualified farm indebtedness.

(b) Time and manner. To make an election under section 108(b)(5), a taxpayer must enter the appropriate information on Form 982, Reduction of Tax Attributes Due to Discharge of Indebtedness (and Section 1082 Basis Adjustment), and attach the form to the timely filed (including extensions) Federal income tax return for the taxable year in which the taxpayer has COD income that is excluded from gross income under section 108(a). An election under this section may be revoked only with the consent of the Commissioner.

(c) Effective date. This section applies to elections concerning discharges of indebtedness occurring on or after October 22, 1998.

T.D. 8787, 10/21/98.

§ 1.108-5 Time and manner for making election under the Omnibus Budget Reconciliation Act of 1993.

(a) Description. Section 108(c)(3)(C), as added by section 13150 of the Omnibus Budget Reconciliation Act of 1993 (Public Law 103-66, 107 Stat. 446), allows certain noncorporate taxpayers to elect to treat certain indebtedness described in section 108(c)(3) that is discharged after December 31, 1992, as qualified real property business indebtedness. This discharged indebtedness is excluded from gross income to the extent allowed by section 108.

(b) Time and manner for making election. The election described in this section must be made on the timely-filed (including extensions) Federal income tax return for the taxable year in which the taxpayer has discharge of indebtedness income that is excludible from gross income under section 108(a). The election is to be made on a completed Form 982, in accordance with that Form and its instructions.

(c) Revocability of election. The election described in this section is revocable with the consent of the Commissioner.

(d) Effective date. The rules set forth in this section are effective December 27, 1993.

T.D. 8688, 12/11/96, amend T.D. 8787, 10/21/98.

§ 1.108-6 Limitations on the exclusion of income from the discharge of qualified real property business indebtedness.

(a) Indebtedness in excess of value. With respect to any qualified real property business indebtedness that is discharged, the amount excluded from gross income under section 108(a)(1)(D) (concerning discharges of qualified real property business indebtedness) shall not exceed the excess, if any, of the outstanding principal amount of that indebtedness immediately before the discharge over the net fair market value of the qualifying real property, as defined in § 1.1017-1(c)(1), immediately before the discharge. For purposes of this section, net fair market value means the fair market value of the qualifying real property (notwithstanding section 7701(g)), reduced by the outstanding principal amount of any qualified real property business indebtedness (other than the discharged indebtedness) that is secured by such property immediately before and after the discharge. Also, for purposes of section 108(c)(2)(A) and this section, outstanding principal amount means the principal amount of indebtedness together with all additional amounts owed that, immediately before the discharge, are equivalent to principal, in that interest on such amounts would accrue and compound in the future, except that outstanding principal amount shall not include amounts that are subject to section 108(e)(2) and shall be adjusted to account for unamortized premium and discount consistent with section 108(e)(3).

(b) Overall limitation. The amount excluded from gross income under section 108(a)(1)(D) shall not exceed the aggregate adjusted bases of all depreciable real property held by the taxpayer immediately before the discharge (other than depreciable real property acquired in contemplation of the discharge) reduced by the sum of any—

(1) Depreciation claimed for the taxable year the taxpayer excluded discharge of indebtedness from gross income under section 108(a)(1)(D); and

(2) Reductions to the adjusted bases of depreciable real property required under section 108(b) or section 108(g) for the same taxable year.

(c) Effective date. This section applies to discharges of qualified real property business indebtedness occurring on or after October 22, 1998.

T.D. 8787, 10/21/98.

§ 1.108-7 Reduction of attributes.

(a) In general. *(1)* If a taxpayer excludes discharge of indebtedness income (COD income) from gross income under section 108(a)(1)(A), (B), or (C), then the amount excluded shall be applied to reduce the following tax attributes of the taxpayer in the following order:

(i) Net operating losses.

(ii) General business credits.

(iii) Minimum tax credits.

(iv) Capital loss carryovers.

(v) Basis of property.

(vi) Passive activity loss and credit carryovers.

(vii) Foreign tax credit carryovers.

(2) The taxpayer may elect under section 108(b)(5), however, to apply any portion of the excluded COD income to reduce first the basis of depreciable property to the extent the excluded COD income is not so applied, the taxpayer must then reduce any remaining tax attributes in the order specified in section 108(b)(2). If the excluded COD income exceeds the sum of the taxpayer's tax attributes, the excess is permanently excluded from the taxpayer's gross income. For rules relating to basis reductions required by sections 108(b)(2)(E) and 108(b)(5), see sections 1017 and 1.1017-1. For rules relating to the time and manner for making an election under section 108(b)(5), see § 1.108-4.

(b) Carryovers and carrybacks. The tax attributes subject to reduction under section 108(b)(2) and paragraph (a)(1) of this section that are carryovers to the taxable year of the discharge, or that may be carried back to taxable years preceding the year of the discharge, are taken into account by the taxpayer for the taxable year of the discharge or the preceding years, as the case may be, before such attributes are reduced pursuant to section 108(b)(2) and paragraph (a)(1) of this section.

(c) Transactions to which section 381 applies. If a taxpayer realizes COD income that is excluded from gross income under section 108(a) either during or after a taxable year in which the taxpayer is the distributor or transferor of assets in a transaction described in section 381(a), any tax attributes to which the acquiring corporation succeeds, including the basis of property acquired by the acquiring corporation in the transaction, must reflect the reductions required by section 108(b). For this purpose, all attributes listed in section 108(b)(2) immediately prior to the transaction described in section 381(a), but after the determination of tax for the year of the distribution or transfer of assets, including basis of property, will be available for reduction under section 108(b)(2). However, the basis of stock or securities of the acquiring corporation, if any, received by the taxpayer in exchange for the transferred assets shall not be available for reduction under section 108(b)(2).

(d) Examples. The following examples illustrate the application of this section:

Example (1). (i) Facts. In Year 4, X, a corporation in a title 11 case, is entitled under section 108(a)(1)(A) to exclude from gross income $100,000 of COD income. For Year 4, X has gross income in the amount of $50,000. In each of Years 1 and 2, X had no taxable income or loss. In Year 3, X had a net operating loss of $100,000, the use of which when carried over to Year 4 is not subject to any restrictions other than those of section 172.

(ii) Analysis. Pursuant to paragraph (b) of this section, X takes into account the net operating loss carryover from Year 3 in computing its taxable income for Year 4 before any portion of the COD income excluded under section 108(a)(1)(A) is applied to reduce tax attributes. Thus, the amount of the net operating loss carryover that is reduced under section 108(b)(2) and paragraph (a) of this section is $50,000.

Example (2). (i) Facts. The facts are the same as in Example 1, except that in Year 4 X sustains a net operating loss in the amount of $100,000. In addition, in each of Years 2 and 3, X reported taxable income in the amount of $25,000.

(ii) Analysis. Pursuant to paragraph (b) of this section and section 172, the net operating loss sustained in Year 4 is carried back to Years 2 and 3 before any portion of the COD income excluded under section 108(a)(1)(A) is applied to reduce tax attributes. Thus, the amount of the net operating loss that is reduced under section 108(b)(2) and paragraph (a) of this section is $50,000.

Example (3). (i) Facts. In Year 2, X, a corporation in a title 11 case, has outstanding debts of $200,000 and a depreciable asset that has an adjusted basis of $75,000 and a fair market value of $100,000. X has no other assets or liabilities. X has a net operating loss of $80,000 that is carried over to Year 2 but has no general business credit, minimum tax credit, or capital loss carryovers. Under a plan of reorganization, X transfers its asset to Corporation Y in exchange for Y stock with a value of $100,000. X distributes the Y stock to its creditors in exchange for release of their claims against X. X's shareholders receive nothing in the transaction. The transaction qualifies as a reorganization under section 368(a)(1)(G) that satisfies the requirements of section 354(b)(1)(A) and (B). For Year 2, X has gross income of $10,000 (without regard to any income from the discharge of indebtedness) and is allowed a depreciation deduction of $10,000 in respect of the asset. In addition, it generates no general business credits.

(ii) Analysis. On the distribution of Y stock to X's creditors, under section 108(a)(1)(A), X is entitled to exclude from gross income the debt discharge amount of $100,000. (Under section 108(e)(8), X is treated as satisfying $100,000 of the debt owed the creditors for $100,000, the fair market value of the Y stock transferred to those creditors.) In Year 2, X has no taxable income or loss because its gross income is exactly offset by the depreciation deduction. As a result of the depreciation deduction, X's basis in the asset is reduced by $10,000 to $65,000. Pursuant to paragraph (c) of this section, the amount of X's net operating loss to which Y succeeds pursuant to section 381 and the basis of X's property transferred to Y must take into account the reductions required by section 108(b). Pursuant to paragraph (a) of this section, X's net operating loss carryover in the amount of $80,000 is reduced by $80,000 of the COD income excluded under section 108(a)(1). In addition, X's basis in the asset is reduced by $20,000, the extent to which the COD income excluded under section 108(a)(1) did not reduce the net operating loss. Accordingly, as a result of the reorganization, there is no net operating loss to which Y succeeds under section 381. Pursuant to section 361, X recognizes no gain or loss on the transfer of its property to Y. Pursuant to section 362(b), Y's basis in the asset acquired from X is $45,000.

Example (4). (i) Facts. The facts are the same as in Example 3, except that X elects under section 108(b)(5) to reduce first the basis of its depreciable asset.

(ii) Analysis. As in Example 3, on the distribution of Y stock to X's creditors, under section 108(a)(1)(A), X is entitled to exclude from gross income the debt discharge amount of $100,000. In addition, in Year 2, X has no taxable income or loss because its gross income is exactly offset by the depreciation deduction. As a result of the depreciation deduction, X's basis in the asset is reduced by $10,000 to $65,000. Pursuant to paragraph (c) of this section, the amount of X's net operating loss to which Y succeeds pursuant to section 381 and the basis of X's property transferred to Y must take into account the reductions required by section 108(b). As a result of the election under section 108(b)(5), X's basis in the asset is reduced by $65,000 to $0. In addition, X's net operating loss is reduced by $35,000, the extent to which the amount excluded from income under section 108(a)(1)(A) does not reduce X's asset basis. Accordingly, as a result of the reorganization, Y succeeds to X's net operating loss in the amount of $45,000 under section 381. Pursuant to section 361, X recognizes no gain or loss on the transfer of its property to Y. Pursuant to section 362(b), Y's basis in the asset acquired from X is $0.

(e) Effective date. This section applies to discharges of indebtedness occurring on or after May 10, 2004.

T.D. 9080, 7/17/2003, amend T.D. 9127, 5/10/2004.

PAR. 2. Section 1.108-7 is added to read as follows:

Proposed § 1.108-7 Reduction of attributes. [*For Preamble, see ¶ 152,431*]

[The text of the proposed § 1.108-7 is the same as the text for § 1.108-7T published elsewhere in this issue of the Federal Register]. [*See T.D. 9080, 7/18/2003, 68 Fed. Reg. 138.*]

PAR. 2. Section 1.108-7 is amended by:

1. Redesignating paragraphs (d) and (e) as paragraphs (e) and (f), respectively.

2. Adding new paragraph (d).

3. Adding paragraph (e) Example 5 and Example 6 to newly-redesignated paragraph (e).

4. Revising newly-redesignated paragraph (f).

The additions and revision read as follows:

Proposed § 1.108-7 Reduction of attributes. [*For Preamble, see ¶ 152,431*]

[The text of the proposed § 1.108-7 is the same as the text for § 1.108-7T published elsewhere in this issue of the Federal Register]. [*See T.D. 9080, 7/18/2003, 68 Fed. Reg. 138.*]

Proposed § 1.108-8 Indebtedness satisfied by partnership interest. [*For Preamble, see ¶ 153,069*]

(a) In general. For purposes of determining income of a debtor from discharge of indebtedness (COD income), if a debtor partnership transfers a capital or profits interest in the partnership to a creditor in satisfaction of its recourse or nonrecourse indebtedness (a debt-for-equity exchange), the partnership is treated as having satisfied the indebtedness with an amount of money equal to the fair market value of the partnership interest.

(b) Determination of fair market value. *(1) In general.* For purposes of paragraph (a) of this section, the fair market value of a partnership interest transferred by a debtor partnership to a creditor in satisfaction of the debtor partnership's indebtedness (debt-for-equity interest) is the liquidation value of the debt-for-equity interest, where liquidation value equals the amount of cash that the creditor would receive with respect to the debt-for-equity interest if, immediately after the transfer, the partnership sold all of its assets (including goodwill, going concern value, and any other intangibles associated with the partnership's operations) for cash equal to the fair market value of those assets and then liquidated, if--

(i) The debtor partnership determines and maintains the capital accounts of its partners in accordance with the capital accounting rules of § 1.704-1(b)(2)(iv);

(ii) The creditor, debtor partnership, and its partners treat the fair market value of the indebtedness as being equal to the liquidation value of the debt-for-equity interest for purposes of determining the tax consequences of the debt-for-equity exchange;

(iii) The debt-for-equity exchange is an arm's-length transaction; and

(iv) Subsequent to the debt-for-equity exchange, neither the partnership redeems nor any person related to the partnership purchases the debt-for-equity interest as part of a plan at the time of the debt-for-equity exchange which has as a principal purpose the avoidance of COD income by the partnership.

(2) Exception. If the requirements in paragraph (b)(1) of this section are not satisfied, all the facts and circumstances will be considered in determining the fair market value of a debt-for-equity interest for purposes of paragraph (a) of this section.

(c) Example. The following example illustrates the provisions of this section:

Example. (i) AB partnership has $1,000 of outstanding indebtedness owed to C. In an arm's-length transaction, C agrees to cancel the $1,000 indebtedness in exchange (debt-for-equity exchange) for an interest (debt-for-equity interest) in AB. AB's partnership agreement provides that its partners' capital accounts will be determined and maintained in accordance with the capital accounting rules in § 1.704-1(b)(2)(iv). The fair market value of the $1,000 indebtedness is $700 at the time of the debt-for-equity exchange. Under § 1.704-1(b)(2)(iv)(b), C's capital account is increased by $700 as a result of the debt-for-equity exchange. This amount equals the liquidation value of C's debt-for-equity interest, which is the amount of cash that C would receive with respect to that interest if AB partnership sold all of its assets for cash equal to the fair market value of those assets and then liquidated. C, AB partnership, and its partners treat the fair market value of the indebtedness as being equal to the liquidation value of C's debt-for-equity interest ($700) for purposes of determining the tax consequences of the debt-for-equity exchange. Subsequent to the debt-for-equity exchange, neither AB partnership redeems nor any person related to AB partnership purchases C's debt-for-equity interest as part of a plan at the time of the debt-for-equity exchange which has as a principal purpose the avoidance of COD income by AB partnership.

(ii) Because the requirements in paragraph (b)(1) of this section are satisfied, the fair market value of C's debt-for-equity interest in AB partnership for purposes of determining AB partnership's COD income is the liquidation value of C's debt-for-equity interest, or $700. Accordingly, AB partnership is treated as satisfying the $1,000 indebtedness with $700 under section 108(e)(8).

(d) Effective/applicability date. This section applies to debt-for-equity exchanges occurring on or after the date that these regulations are published as final regulations in the Federal Register.

§ 1.109-1 Exclusion from gross income of lessor of real property of value of improvements erected by lessee.

(a) Income derived by a lessor of real property upon the termination, through forfeiture or otherwise, of the lease of such property and attributable to buildings erected or other improvements made by the lessee upon the leased property is excluded from gross income. However, where the facts disclose that such buildings or improvements represent in whole or in part a liquidation in kind of lease rentals, the exclusion from gross income shall not apply to the extent that such buildings or improvements represent such liquidation. The exclusion applies only with respect to the income realized by the lessor upon the termination of the lease and has no application to income, if any, in the form of rent, which may be derived by a lessor during the period of the lease and attributable to buildings erected or other improvements made by the lessee. It has no application to income which may be realized by the lessor upon the termination of the lease but not attributable to the value of such buildings or improvements. Neither does it apply to income derived by the lessor subsequent to the termination of the lease incident to the ownership of such buildings or improvements.

(b) The provisions of this section may be illustrated by the following example:

Example. The A Corporation leased in 1945 for a period of 50 years unimproved real property to the B Corporation under a lease providing that the B Corporation erect on the leased premises an office building costing $500,000, in addition to paying the A Corporation a lease rental of $10,000 per annum beginning on the date of completion of the improvements, the sum of $100,000 being placed in escrow for the payment of the rental. The building was completed on January 1, 1950. The lease provided that all improvements made by the lessee on the leased property would become the absolute property of the A Corporation on the termination of the lease by forfeiture or otherwise and that the lessor would become entitled on such termination to the remainder of the sum, if any, remaining in the escrow fund. The B Corporation forfeited its lease on January 1, 1955, when the improvements had a value of $100,000. Under the provisions of section 109, the $100,000 is excluded from gross income. The amount of $50,000 representing the remainder in the escrow fund is forfeited to the A Corporation and is included in the gross income of that taxpayer. As to the basis of the property in the hands of the A Corporation, see § 1.1019-1.

T.D. 6220, 12/28/56.

§ 1.110-1 Qualified lessee construction allowances.

(a) Overview. Amounts provided to a lessee by a lessor for property to be constructed and used by the lessee pursuant to a lease are not includible in the lessee's gross income if the amount is a qualified lessee construction allowance under paragraph (b) of this section.

(b) Qualified lessee construction allowance. *(1) In general.* A qualified lessee construction allowance means any amount received in cash (or treated as a rent reduction) by a lessee from a lessor—

(i) Under a short-term lease of retail space;

(ii) For the purpose of constructing or improving qualified long-term real property for use in the lessee's trade or business at that retail space; and

(iii) To the extent the amount is expended by the lessee in the taxable year received on the construction or improvement of qualified long-term real property for use in the lessee's trade or business at that retail space.

(2) Definitions. (i) Qualified long-term real property is nonresidential real property under section 168(e)(2)(B) that is part of, or otherwise present at, the retail space referred to in paragraph (b)(1)(i) of this section and which reverts to the lessor at the termination of the lease. Thus, qualified long-term real property does not include property qualifying as section 1245 property under section 1245(a)(3).

(ii) Short-term lease is a lease (or other agreement for occupancy or use) of retail space for 15 years or less (as determined pursuant to section 168(i)(3)).

(iii) Retail space is nonresidential real property under section 168(e)(2)(B) that is leased, occupied, or otherwise used by the lessee in its trade or business of selling tangible personal property or services to the general public. The term retail space includes not only the space where the retail sales are made, but also space where activities supporting the retail activity are performed (such as an administrative office, a storage area, and employee lounge). Examples of services typically sold to the general public include services provided by hair stylists, tailors, shoe repairmen, doctors, lawyers, accountants, insurance agents, stock brokers, securities dealers (including dealers who sell securities out of inventory), financial advisors and bankers. For purposes of this paragraph (b)(2)(iii), a taxpayer is selling to the general public if the products or services for sale are made available to the general public, even if the product or service is targeted to certain customers or clients.

(3) Purpose requirement. An amount will meet the requirement in paragraph (b)(1)(ii) of this section only to the extent that the lease agreement for the retail space expressly provides that the construction allowance is for the purpose of constructing or improving qualified long-term real property for use in the lessee's trade or business at the retail space. An ancillary agreement between the lessor and the lessee providing for a construction allowance, executed contemporaneously with the lease or during the term of the lease, is considered a provision of the lease agreement for purposes of the preceding sentence, provided the agreement is executed before payment of the construction allowance.

(4) Expenditure requirement. (i) In general. Expenditures referred to in paragraph (b)(1)(iii) of this section may be treated as being made first from the lessee's construction allowance. Tracing of the construction allowance to the actual lessee expenditures for the construction or improvement of qualified long-term real property is not required. However, the lessee should maintain accurate records of the amount of the qualified lessee construction allowance received and the expenditures made for qualified long-term real property.

(ii) Time when expenditures deemed made. For purposes of paragraph (b)(1)(iii) of this section, an amount is deemed to have been expended by a lessee in the taxable year in which the construction allowance was received by the lessee if—

(A) The amount is expended by the lessee within 8½ months after the close of the taxable year in which the amount was received; or

(B) The amount is a reimbursement from the lessor for amounts expended by the lessee in a prior year and for which the lessee has not claimed any depreciation deductions.

(5) Consistent treatment by lessor. Qualified long-term real property constructed or improved with any amount excluded from a lessee's gross income by reason of paragraph (a) of this section must be treated as nonresidential real property owned by the lessor (for purposes of depreciation under 168(e)(2)(B) and determining gain or loss under section 168(i)(8)(B)). For purposes of the preceding sentence, the lessor must treat the construction allowance as fully expended in the manner required by paragraph (b)(1)(iii) of this section unless the lessor is notified by the lessee in writing to the contrary. General tax principles apply for purposes of determining when the lessor may begin depreciation of its nonresidential real property. The lessee's exclusion from gross income under paragraph (a) of this section, however, is not dependent upon the lessor's treatment of the property as nonresidential real property.

(c) Information required to be furnished. *(1) In general.* The lessor and the lessee described in paragraph (b) of this section who are paying and receiving a qualified lessee construction allowance, respectively, must furnish the information described in paragraph (c)(3) of this section in the time and manner prescribed in paragraph (c)(2) of this section.

(2) Time and manner for furnishing information. The requirement to furnish information under paragraph (c)(1) of this section is met by attaching a statement with the information described in paragraph (c)(3) of this section to the lessor's or the lessee's, as applicable, timely filed (including extensions) Federal income tax return for the taxable year in which the construction allowance was paid by the lessor or received by the lessee (either in cash or treated as a rent reduction), as applicable. A lessor or a lessee may report the required information for several qualified lessee construction allowances on a combined statement. However, a lessor's or a lessee's failure to provide information with respect to each lease will be treated as a separate failure to provide information for purposes of paragraph (c)(4) of this section.

(3) Information required. (i) Lessor. The statement provided by the lessor must contain the lessor's name (and, in the case of a consolidated group, the parent's name), employer identification number, taxable year and the following information for each lease:

(A) The lessee's name (in the case of a consolidated group, the parent's name).

(B) The address of the lessee.

(C) The employer identification number of the lessee.

(D) The location of the retail space (including mall or strip center name, if applicable, and store name).

(E) The amount of the construction allowance.

(F) The amount of the construction allowance treated by the lessor as nonresidential real property owned by the lessor.

(ii) Lessee. The statement provided by the lessee must contain the lessee's name (and, in the case of a consolidated group, the parent's name), employer identification number, taxable year and the following information for each lease:

(A) The lessor's name (in the case of a consolidated group, the parent's name).

(B) The address of the lessor.

(C) The employer identification number of the lessor.

(D) The location of the retail space (including mall or strip center name, if applicable, and store name).

(E) The amount of the construction allowance.

(F) The amount of the construction allowance that is a qualified lessee construction allowance under paragraph (b) of this section.

(4) Failure to furnish information. A lessor or a lessee that fails to furnish the information required in this paragraph (c) may be subject to a penalty under section 6721.

(d) Effective date. This section is applicable to leases entered into on or after October 5, 2000.

T.D. 8901, 9/1/2000.

---

§ 1.111-1 Recovery of certain items previously deducted or credited.

Caution: The Treasury has not yet amended Reg § 1.111-1 to reflect changes made by P.L. 99-514, P.L. 98-369.

(a) General. Section 111 provides that income attributable to the recovery during any taxable year of bad debts, prior taxes, and delinquency amounts shall be excluded from gross income to the extent of the "recovery exclusion" with respect to such items. The rule of exclusion so prescribed by statute applies equally with respect to all other losses, expenditures and accruals made the basis of deductions from gross income for prior taxable years, including war losses referred to in section 127 of the Internal Revenue Code of 1939, but not including deductions with respect to depreciation, depletion, amortization, or amortizable bond premiums. The term "recovery exclusion" as used in this section means an amount equal to the portion of the bad debts, prior taxes, and delinquency amounts (the items specifically referred to in section 111), and of all other items subject to the rule of exclusion which, when deducted or credited for a prior taxable year, did not result in a reduction of any tax of the taxpayer under subtitle A (other than the accumulated earnings tax imposed by section 531 or the personal holding company tax imposed by section 541) of the Internal Revenue Code of 1954 or corresponding provisions of prior income tax laws (other than the World War II excess profits tax imposed under subchapter E, chapter 2 of the Internal Revenue Code of 1939).

(1) Section 111 items. The term "section 111 items" as used in this section means bad debts, prior taxes, delinquency amounts, and all other items subject to the rule of exclusion, for which a deduction or credit was allowed for a prior taxable year. If a bad debt was previously charged against a reserve by a taxpayer on the reserve method of treating bad debts, it was not deducted, and it is therefore not considered a section 111 item. Bad debts, prior taxes, and delinquency amounts are defined in section 111(b)(1), (2), and (3), respectively. An example of a delinquency amount is interest on delinquent taxes. An example of the other items not expressly referred to in section 111 but nevertheless subject to the rule of exclusion is a loss sustained upon the sale of stock and later recovered, in whole or in part, through an action against the party from whom such stock had been purchased.

(2) Definition of "recovery". Recoveries result from the receipt of amounts in respect of the previously deducted or credited section 111 items, such as from the collection or sale of a bad debt, refund or credit of taxes paid, or cancellation of taxes accrued. Care should be taken in the case of bad debts which were treated as only partially worthless in prior years to distinguish between the item described in section 111, that is, the part of such debt which was deducted, and the part not previously deducted, which is not a section 111 item and is considered the first part collected. The collection of the part not deducted is not considered a "recovery". Furthermore, the term "recovery" does not include the gain resulting from the receipt of an amount on account of a section 111 item which, together with previous such receipts, exceeds the deduction or credit previously allowed for such item. For instance, a $100 corporate bond purchased for $40 and later deducted as worthless is subsequently collected to the extent of $50. The $10 gain (excess of $50 collection over $40 cost) is not a recovery of a section 111 item. Such gain is in no case excluded from gross income under section 111, regardless of whether the $40 recovery is or is not excluded.

(3) Treatment of debt deducted in more than one year by reason of partial worthlessness. In the case of a bad debt deducted in part for two or more prior years, each such deduction of a part of the debt is considered a separate section 111 item. A recovery with respect to such debt is considered first a recovery of those items (or portions thereof), resulting from such debt, for which there are recovery exclusions. If there are recovery exclusions for two or more items resulting from the same bad debt, such items are considered recovered in the order of the taxable years for which they were deducted, beginning with the latest. The recovery exclusion for any such item is determined by considering the recovery exclusion with respect to the prior year for which such item was deducted as being first used to offset all other applicable recoveries in the year in which the bad debt is recovered.

(4) Special provisions as to worthless bonds, etc., which are treated as capital losses. Certain bad debts arising from the worthlessness of securities and certain nonbusiness bad debts are treated as losses from the sale or exchange of capital assets. See sections 165(g) and 166(d). The amounts of the deductions allowed for any year under section 1211 on account of such losses for such year are considered to be section 111 items. Any part of such losses which, under section 1211, is a deduction for a subsequent year through the capital loss carryover (any later receipt of an amount with respect to such deducted loss is a recovery) is considered a section 111 item for the year in which such loss was sustained.

(b) Computation of recovery exclusion. *(1) Amount of recovery exclusion allowable for year of recovery.* For the year of any recovery, the section 111 items which were deducted or credited for one prior year are considered as a group and the recovery thereon is considered separately from recoveries of any items which were deducted or credited for other years. This recovery is excluded from gross income to the extent of the recovery exclusion with respect to this group of items as (i) determined for the original year for which such items were deducted or credited (see subparagraph (2) of this paragraph) and (ii) reduced by the excludable recoveries in intervening years on account of all section 111 items for such original year. A taxpayer claiming a recovery exclusion shall submit, at the time the exclusion is claimed, the computation of the recovery exclusion claimed for the original year for which the items were deducted or credited, and computations showing the amount recovered in intervening years on account of the section 111 items deducted or credited for the original year.

(2) Determination of recovery exclusion for original year for which items were deducted or credited. (i) The recovery exclusion for the taxable year for which section 111 items were deducted or credited (that is, the "original taxable year") is the portion of the aggregate amount of such deductions and credits which could be disallowed without causing an increase in any tax of the taxpayer imposed under subtitle A (other than the accumulated earnings tax imposed by section 531 or the personal holding company tax imposed by section 541) of the Internal Revenue Code of 1954 or corresponding provisions of prior income tax laws (other than the World War II excess profits tax imposed under subchapter E, chapter 2 of the Internal Revenue Code of 1939). For the purpose of such recovery exclusion, consideration must be given to the effect of net operating loss carryovers and carrybacks or capital loss carryovers.

(ii) This rule shall be applied by determining the recovery exclusion as the aggregate amount of the section 111 items for the original year for which such items were deducted or credited reduced by whichever of the following amounts is the greater:

(a) The difference between (1) the taxable income for such original year and (2) the taxable income computed without regard to the section 111 items for such original year.

(b) In the case of a taxpayer subject to any income tax in lieu of normal tax or surtax or both (except the alternative tax on capital gains imposed by section 1201, which is disregarded), the difference between (1) the income subject to such tax for such original year and (2) the income subject to such tax computed without regard to the section 111 items for such original year.

(Neither the amount determined under (1) nor the amount under (2) of (a) or (b) of this subdivision shall in any case be considered less than zero.) For this determination of the recovery exclusion, the aggregate of the section 111 items must be further decreased by the portion thereof which caused a reduction in tax in preceding or succeeding taxable years through any net operating loss carryovers or carrybacks or capital loss carryovers affected by such items. This decrease is the aggregate of the largest amount determined for each of such preceding and succeeding years under (a) and (b) of this subdivision, the computation of each carryover or carryback to the preceding or succeeding year being made under (1) of (a) and (b) of this subdivision with regard to the section 111 items for the original year and such computation being made under (2) of (a) and (b) of this subdivision without regard to such items. For the purpose of the preceding sentence, the computations under both (1) and (2) of (a) and (b) of this subdivision shall be made without regard to any section 111 items for such preceding or succeeding year and the carryovers and carrybacks to such year shall be determined without regard to any section 111 items for years subsequent to the original year.

(iii) The determination of the recovery exclusion for original taxable years subject to the provisions of the Internal Revenue Code of 1939 shall be made under 26 CFR (1939) 39.22(b)(12)-1(b)(2) (Regulations 118).

(3) Example. The provisions of this paragraph may be illustrated by the following example:

Example. A single individual with no dependents has for his 1954 taxable year the following income and deductions:

	With deduction of section 111 items	Without deduction of section 111 items
Gross income	$25,000	$25,000
Less deductions:		
Depreciation	20,000	20,000
Business bad debts and taxes	6,300	
Personal exemption	600	600
	26,900	20,600
Taxable income or (loss)	(1,900)	4,400
Adjustment under section 172 (d) (3)	600	
Net operating loss	(1,300)	

The full amount of the net operating loss of $1,300 is carried back and allowed as a deduction for 1952. The aggregate of the section 111 items for 1954 is $6,300 (bad debts and taxes). The recovery exclusion on account of section 111 items for 1954 is $600, determined by reducing the $6,300 aggregate of the section 111 items by $5,700, i.e., the sum of (1) the difference between the amount of the taxable income for 1954 computed without regard to the section 111 items ($4,400) and the amount of the taxable income for 1954) (not less than zero) computed by taking such items into account, and (2) the amount of the net operating loss ($1,300) which caused the reduction in tax for 1952 by reason of the carryback provisions. If in 1956 the taxpayer recovers $400 of the bad debts, all of the recovery is excluded from the income by reason of the recovery exclusion of $600 determined for the original year 1954. If in 1957 the taxpayer recovers an additional $300 of the bad debts, only $200 is excluded from gross income. That is, the recovery exclusion of $600 determined for the original year 1954 is reduced by the $400 recovered in 1956, leaving a balance of $200 which is used in 1957. The balance of the amount recovered in 1957, $100 ($300 less $200), is included in gross income for 1957.

(c) Provisions as to taxes imposed by section 531 (relating to the accumulated earnings tax) and section 541 (relating to the tax on personal holding companies). A recovery exclusion allowed for purposes of subtitle A (other than section 531 or section 541) of the Internal Revenue Code of 1954 shall also be allowed for the purpose of determining the accumulated earnings tax under section 531 or the personal holding company tax under section 541 regardless of whether or not the section 111 items on which such recovery exclusion is based resulted in a reduction of the tax under section 531 or section 541 of the Internal Revenue Code of 1954 (or corresponding provisions of prior income tax laws) for the prior taxable year. Furthermore, if there is recovery of a section 111 item which was not allowable as a deduction or credit for the prior taxable year for purposes of subtitle A (not including section 531 or section 541) or corresponding provisions of prior income tax laws (other than subchapter E, chapter 2 of the Internal Revenue Code of 1939, relating to World War II excess profits tax), but was allowable for such prior taxable year in determining the tax under section 531 or section 541 (or corresponding provisions of prior income tax laws) then for the purpose of determining the tax under section 531 or section 541 a recovery exclusion shall be allowable with respect to such recovery if the section 111 item did not result in a reduction of the tax under section 531 or section 541 (or corresponding provisions of prior income tax laws).

T.D. 6220, 12/28/56.

---

§ 1.112-1 Combat zone compensation of members of the armed forces.

Caution: The Treasury has not yet amended Reg § 1.112-1 to reflect changes made by P.L. 104-117.

(a) Combat zone compensation exclusion. *(1) Amount excluded.* In addition to the exemptions and credits otherwise applicable, section 112 excludes from gross income the following compensation of members of the Armed Forces:

(i) Enlisted personnel. Compensation received for active service as a member below the grade of commissioned officer in the Armed Forces of the United States for any month during any part of which the member served in a combat zone or was hospitalized at any place as a result of wounds, disease, or injury incurred while serving in the combat zone.

(ii) Commissioned officers. Compensation not exceeding the monthly dollar limit received for active service as a commissioned officer in the Armed Forces of the United States for any month during any part of which the officer served in a combat zone or was hospitalized at any place as a result of wounds, disease, or injury incurred while serving in the combat zone. The monthly dollar limit is the monthly amount excludable from the officer's income under section 112(b) as amended. Beginning in 1966, the monthly dollar limit for periods of active service after 1965 became $500. As of September 10, 1993, the monthly dollar limit continues to be $500.

(2) Time limits on exclusion during hospitalization. Compensation received for service for any month of hospitalization that begins more than 2 years after the date specified by the President in an Executive Order as the date of the termination of combatant activities in the combat zone cannot be excluded under section 112. Furthermore, compensation received while hospitalized after January 1978 for wounds, disease, or injury incurred in the Vietnam combat zone designated by Executive Order 11216 cannot be excluded under section 112.

(3) Special terms. A commissioned warrant officer is not a commissioned officer under section 112(b) and is entitled to the exclusion allowed to enlisted personnel under section 112(a). Compensation, for the purpose of section 112, does not include pensions and retirement pay. Armed Forces of the United States is defined (and members of the Armed Forces are described) in section 7701(a)(15).

(4) Military compensation only. Only compensation paid by the Armed Forces of the United States to members of the Armed Forces can be excluded under section 112, except for compensation paid by an agency or instrumentality of the United States or by an international organization to a member of the Armed Forces whose military active duty status continues during the member's assignment to the agency or instrumentality or organization on official detail. Compensation paid by other employers (whether private enterprises or governmental entities) to members of the Armed Forces cannot be excluded under section 112 even if the payment is made to supplement the member's military compensation or is labeled by the employer as compensation for active service in the Armed Forces of the United States. Compensation paid to civilian employees of the federal government, including civilian employees of the Armed Forces, cannot be excluded under section 112, except as provided in section 112(d)(2) (which extends the exclusion to compensation of civilian employees of the federal government in missing status due to the Vietnam conflict).

(b) Service in combat zone. *(1) Active service.* The exclusion under section 112 applies only if active service is performed in a combat zone. A member of the Armed Forces is in active service if the member is actually serving in the Armed Forces of the United States. Periods during which a member of the Armed Forces is absent from duty on account of sickness, wounds, leave, internment by the enemy, or other lawful cause are periods of active service. A member of the Armed Forces in active service in a combat zone who becomes a prisoner of war or missing in action in the combat zone is deemed, for the purpose of section 112, to continue in active service in the combat zone for the period for which the member is treated as a prisoner of war or as missing in action for military pay purposes.

(2) Combat zone status. Except as provided in paragraphs (e) and (f) of this section, service is performed in a combat zone only if it is performed in an area which the President of the United States has designated by Executive Order, for the purpose of section 112, as an area in which Armed Forces of the United States are or have been engaged in combat, and only if it is performed on or after the date designated by the President by Executive Order as the date of the commencing of combatant activities in that zone and on or before the date designated by the President by Executive Order as the date of the termination of combatant activities in that zone.

(3) Partial month service. If a member of the Armed Forces serves in a combat zone for any part of a month, the member is entitled to the exclusion for that month to the same extent as if the member has served in that zone for the entire month. If a member of the Armed Forces is hospitalized for a part of a month as a result of wounds, disease, or injury incurred while serving in that zone, the member is entitled to the exclusion for the entire month.

(4) Payment time and place. The time and place of payment are irrelevant in considering whether compensation is excludable under section 112; rather, the time and place of the entitlement to compensation determine whether the compensation is excludable under section 112. Thus, compensation can be excluded under section 112 whether or not it is received outside a combat zone, or while the recipient is hospitalized, or in a year different from that in which the service was rendered for which the compensation is paid, provided that the member's entitlement to the compensation fully accrued in a month during which the member served in the combat zone or was hospitalized as a result of wounds, disease, or injury incurred while serving in the combat zone. For this purpose, entitlement to compensation fully accrues upon the completion of all actions required of the member to receive the compensation. Compensation received by a member of the Armed Forces for services rendered while in active service can be excluded under section 112 even though payment is received subsequent to discharge or release from active service. Compensation credited to a deceased member's account for a period subsequent to the established date

of the member's death and received by the member's estate can be excluded from the gross income of the estate under section 112 to the same extent that it would have been excluded from the gross income of the member had the member lived and received the compensation.

(5) Examples of combat zone compensation. The rules of this section are illustrated by the following examples:

Example (1). On January 5, outside of a combat zone, an enlisted member received basic pay for active duty services performed from the preceding December 1 through December 31. On December 4 (and no other date), the member performed services within a combat zone. The member may exclude from income the entire payment received on January 5, although the member served in the combat zone only one day during December, received the payment outside of the combat zone, and received the payment in a year other than the year in which the combat zone services were performed.

Example (2). From March through December, an enlisted member became entitled to 25 days of annual leave while serving in a combat zone. The member used all 25 days of leave in the following year. The member may exclude from income the compensation received for those 25 days, even if the member performs no services in the combat zone in the year the compensation is received.

Example (3). From March through December, a commissioned officer became entitled to 25 days of annual leave while serving in a combat zone. During that period the officer also received basic pay of $1,000 per month from which the officer excluded from income $500 per month (exhausting the monthly dollar limit under section 112 for that period). The officer used all 25 days of leave in the following year. The officer may not exclude from income any compensation received in the following year related to those 25 days of leave, since the officer had already excluded from income the maximum amount of combat zone compensation for the period in which the leave was earned.

Example (4). In November, while serving in a combat zone, an enlisted member competing for a cash award submitted an employee suggestion. After November, the member neither served in a combat zone nor was hospitalized for wounds incurred in the combat zone. In June of the following year, the member's suggestion was selected as the winner of the competition and the award was paid. The award can be excluded from income as combat zone compensation although granted and received outside of the combat zone, since the member completed the necessary action to win the award (submission of the suggestion) in a month during which the member served in the combat zone.

Example (5). In July, while serving in a combat zone, an enlisted member voluntarily reenlisted. After July, the member neither served in a combat zone nor was hospitalized for wounds incurred in the combat zone. In February of the following year, the member received a bonus as a result of the July reenlistment. The reenlistment bonus can be excluded from income as combat zone compensation although received outside of the combat zone, since the member completed the necessary action for entitlement to the reenlistment bonus in a month during which the member served in the combat zone.

Example (6). In July, while serving outside a combat zone, an enlisted member voluntarily reenlisted. In February of the following year, the member, while performing services in a combat zone, received a bonus as a result of the July reenlistment. The reenlistment bonus cannot be excluded from income as combat zone compensation although received while serving in the combat zone, since the member completed the necessary action for entitlement to the reenlistment bonus in a month during which the member had neither served in the combat zone nor was hospitalized for wounds incurred while serving in a combat zone.

(c) Hospitalization. *(1) Presumption of combat zone injury.* If an individual is hospitalized for wound, disease, or injury while serving in a combat zone, the wound, disease, or injury will be presumed to have been incurred while serving in a combat zone, unless the contrary clearly appears. In certain cases, however, a wound, disease, or injury may have been incurred while serving in a combat zone even though the individual was not hospitalized for it while so serving. In exceptional cases, a wound, disease, or injury will not have been incurred while serving in a combat zone even though the individual was hospitalized for it while so serving.

(2) Length of hospitalization. An individual is hospitalized only until the date the individual is discharged from the hospital.

(3) Examples of combat zone injury. The rules of this paragraph (c) are illustrated by the following examples:

Example (1). An individual is hospitalized for a disease in the combat zone where the individual has been serving for three weeks. The incubation period of the disease is two to four weeks. The disease is incurred while serving in the combat zone.

Example (2). The facts are the same as in Example 1 except that the incubation period of the disease is one year. The disease is not incurred while serving in the combat zone.

Example (3). A member of the Air Force, stationed outside the combat zone, is shot while participating in aerial combat over the combat zone, but is not hospitalized until returning to the home base. The injury is incurred while serving in a combat zone.

Example (4). An individual is hospitalized for a disease three weeks after having departed from a combat zone. The incubation period of the disease is two to four weeks. The disease is incurred while serving in a combat zone.

(d) Married members. The exclusion under section 112 applies without regard to the marital status of the recipient of the compensation. If both spouses meet the requirements of the statute, then each spouse is entitled to the benefit of an exclusion. In the case of a husband and wife domiciled in a State recognized for Federal income tax purposes as a community property State, any exclusion from gross income under section 112 operates before apportionment of the gross income of the spouses under community property law. For example, a husband and wife are domiciled in a community property State and the member spouse is entitled, as a commissioned officer, to the benefit of the exclusion under section 112(b) of $500 for each month. The member receives $7,899 as compensation for active service for 3 months in a combat zone. Of that amount, $1,500 is excluded from gross income under section 112(b) and $6,399 is taken into account in determining the gross income of both spouses.

(e) Service in area outside combat zone. *(1) Combat zone treatment.* For purposes of section 112, a member of the Armed Forces who performs military service in an area outside the area designated by Executive Order as a combat zone is deemed to serve in that combat zone while the member's service is in direct support of military operations in that zone and qualifies the member for the special pay for duty subject to hostile fire or imminent danger authorized under section 310 of title 37 of the United States Code, as amended (37 U.S.C. 310) (hostile fire/imminent danger pay).

(2) Examples of combat zone treatment. The examples in this paragraph (e)(2) are based on the following circumstances: Certain areas, airspace, and adjacent waters are designated as a combat zone for purposes of section 112 as of May 1. Some members of the Armed Forces are stationed in the combat zone; others are stationed in two foreign countries outside the combat zone, named Nearby Country and Destination Country.

Example (1). B is a member of an Armed Forces ground unit stationed in the combat zone. On May 31, B's unit crosses into Nearby Country. B performs military service in Nearby Country in direct support of the military operations in the combat zone from June 1 through June 8 that qualifies B for hostile fire/imminent danger pay. B does not return to the combat zone during June. B is deemed to serve in the combat zone from June 1 through June 8. Accordingly, B is entitled to the exclusion under section 112 for June. Of course, B is also entitled to the exclusion for any month (May, in this example) in which B actually served in the combat zone.

Example (2). B is a member of an Armed Forces ground unit stationed in the combat zone. On May 31, B's unit crosses into Nearby Country. On June 1, B is wounded while performing military service in Nearby Country in direct support of the military operations in the combat zone that qualifies B for hostile fire/imminent danger pay. On June 2, B is transferred for treatment to a hospital in the United States. B is hospitalized from June through October for those wounds. B is deemed to have incurred the wounds while serving in the combat zone on June 1. Accordingly, B is entitled to the exclusion under section 112 for June through October. Of course, B is also entitled to the exclusion for any month (May, in this example) in which B actually served in the combat zone.

Example (3). B is stationed in Nearby Country for the entire month of June as a member of a ground crew servicing combat aircraft operating in the combat zone. B's service in Nearby Country during June does not qualify B for hostile fire/imminent danger pay. Accordingly, B is not deemed to serve in the combat zone during June and is not entitled to the exclusion under section 112 for that month.

Example (4). B is assigned to an air unit stationed in Nearby Country for the entire month of June. In June, members of air units of the Armed Forces stationed in Nearby Country fly combat and supply missions into and over Destination Country in direct support of military operations in the combat zone. B flies combat missions over Destination Country from Nearby Country from June 1 through June 8. B's service qualifies B for hostile fire/imminent danger pay. Accordingly, B is deemed to serve in the combat zone during June and is entitled to the exclusion under section 112. The result would be the same if B were to fly supply missions into Destination Country from Nearby Country in direct support of operations in the combat zone qualifying B for hostile fire/imminent danger pay.

Example (5). Assigned to an air unit stationed in Nearby Country, B was killed in June when B's plane crashed on returning to the airbase in Nearby Country. B was performing military service in direct support of the military operations in the combat zone at the time of B's death. B's service also qualified B for hostile fire/imminent danger pay. B is deemed to have died while serving in the combat zone or to have died as a result of wounds, disease, or injury incurred while serving in the combat zone for purposes of section 692(a) and section 692(b) (providing relief from certain income taxes for members of the Armed Forces dying in a combat zone or as a result of wounds, disease, or injury incurred while serving in a combat zone) and section 2201 (providing relief from certain estate taxes for members of the Armed Forces dying in a combat zone or by reason of combat-zone-incurred wounds). The result would be the same if B's mission had been a supply mission instead of a combat mission.

Example (6). In June, B was killed as a result of an off-duty automobile accident while leaving the airbase in Nearby Country shortly after returning from a mission over Destination Country. At the time of B's death, B was not performing military duty qualifying B for hostile fire/imminent danger pay. B is not deemed to have died while serving in the combat zone or to have died as the result of wounds, disease, or injury incurred while serving in the combat zone. Accordingly, B does not qualify for the benefits of section 692(a), section 692(b), or section 2201.

Example (7). B performs military service in Nearby Country from June 1 through June 8 in direct support of the military operations in the combat zone. Nearby Country is designated as an area in which members of the Armed Forces qualify for hostile fire/imminent danger pay due to imminent danger, even though members in Nearby Country are not subject to hostile fire. B is deemed to serve in the combat zone from June 1 through June 8. Accordingly, B is entitled to the exclusion under section 112 for June.

(f) Nonqualifying presence in combat zone. *(1) Inapplicability of exclusion.* The following members of the Armed Forces are not deemed to serve in a combat zone within the meaning of section 112(a)(1) or section 112(b)(1) or to be hospitalized as a result of wounds, disease, or injury incurred while serving in a combat zone within the meaning of section 112(a)(2) or section 112(b)(2)—

(i) Members present in a combat zone while on leave from a duty station located outside a combat zone;

(ii) Members who pass over or through a combat zone during the course of a trip between two points both of which lie outside a combat zone; or

(iii) Members present in a combat zone solely for their own personal convenience.

(2) Exceptions for temporary duty or special pay. Paragraph (f)(1) of this section does not apply to members of the Armed Forces who—

(i) Are assigned on official temporary duty to a combat zone (including official temporary duty to the airspace of a combat zone); or

(ii) Qualify for hostile fire/imminent danger pay.

(3) Examples of nonqualifying presence and its exceptions. The examples in this paragraph (f)(3) are based on the following circumstances: Certain areas, airspace, and adjacent waters are designated as a combat zone for purposes of section 112 as of May 1. Some members of the Armed Forces are stationed in the combat zone; others are stationed in two foreign countries outside the combat zone, named Nearby Country and Destination Country.

Example (1). B is a member of the Armed Forces assigned to a unit stationed in Nearby Country. On June 1, B voluntarily visits a city within the combat zone while on leave. B is not deemed to serve in a combat zone since B is present in a combat zone while on leave from a duty station located outside a combat zone.

Example (2). B is a member of the Armed Forces assigned to a unit stationed in Nearby Country. During June, B takes authorized leave and elects to spend the leave period by visiting a city in the combat zone. While on leave in the combat zone, B is subject to hostile fire qualifying B for hostile fire/imminent danger pay. Although B is present in the combat zone while on leave from a duty station outside the combat zone, B qualifies for the exclusion under section 112 because B qualifies for hostile fire/imminent danger pay while in the combat zone.

Example (3). B is a member of the Armed Forces assigned to a ground unit stationed in the combat zone. During June, B takes authorized leave and elects to spend the leave period in the combat zone. B is not on leave from a duty station located outside a combat zone, nor is B present in a combat zone solely for B's own personal convenience. Accordingly, B's combat zone tax benefits continue while B is on leave in the combat zone.

Example (4). B is assigned as a navigator to an air unit stationed in Nearby Country. On June 4, during the course of a flight between B's home base in Nearby Country and another base in Destination Country, the aircraft on which B serves as a navigator flies over the combat zone. B is not on official temporary duty to the airspace of the combat zone and does not qualify for hostile fire/imminent danger pay as a result of the flight. Accordingly, B is not deemed to serve in a combat zone since B passes over the combat zone during the course of a trip between two points both of which lie outside the combat zone without either being on official temporary duty to the combat zone or qualifying for hostile fire/imminent danger pay.

Example (5). B is a member of the Armed Forces assigned to a unit stationed in Nearby Country. B enters the combat zone on a 3-day pass. B is not on official temporary duty and does not qualify for hostile fire/imminent danger pay while present in the combat zone. Accordingly, B is not deemed to serve in a combat zone since B is present in the combat zone solely for B's own personal convenience.

Example (6). B, stationed in Nearby Country, is a military courier assigned on official temporary duty to deliver military pouches in the combat zone and in Destination Country. On June 1, B arrives in the combat zone from Nearby Country, and on June 2, B departs for Destination Country. Although B passes through the combat zone during the course of a trip between two points outside the combat zone, B is nevertheless deemed to serve in a combat zone while in the combat zone because B is assigned to the combat zone on official temporary duty.

Example (7). B is a member of an Armed Forces ground unit stationed in Nearby Country. On June 1, B took authorized leave and elected to spend the leave period by visiting a city in the combat zone. On June 2, while on leave in the combat zone, B was wounded by hostile fire qualifying B for hostile fire/imminent danger pay. On June 3, B was transferred for treatment to a hospital in the United States. B is hospitalized from June through October for those wounds. Although B was present in the combat zone while on leave from a duty station outside the combat zone, B is deemed to have incurred the wounds while serving in the combat zone on June 2, because B qualified for hostile fire/imminent danger pay while in the combat zone. Accordingly, B is entitled to the exclusion under section 112 for June through October.

Example (8). The facts are the same as in Example 7 except that B dies on September 1 as a result of the wounds incurred in the combat zone. B is deemed to have died as a result of wounds, disease, or injury incurred while serving in the combat zone for purposes of section 692(a) and section 692(b) (providing relief from certain income taxes for members of the Armed Forces dying in a combat zone or as a result of wounds, disease, or injury incurred while serving in a combat zone) and section 2201 (providing relief from certain estate taxes for members of the Armed Forces dying in a combat zone or by reason of combat-zone-incurred wounds).

T.D. 6220, 12/28/56, amend T.D. 6906, 12/28/66, T.D. 7066, 11/10/70, T.D. 8489, 9/9/93.

§ 1.113-1 Mustering-out payments for members of the Armed Forces.

Caution: The Treasury has not yet amended Reg § 1.113-1 to reflect changes made by P.L. 101-508.

For the purposes of the exclusion from gross income under section 113 of mustering-out payments with respect to service in the Armed Forces, mustering-out payments are payments made to any recipients pursuant to the provisions of 38 U.S.C. 2105 (formerly section 5 of the Mustering-out Payment Act of 1944 and section 505 of the Veterans' Readjustment Assistance Act of 1952).

T.D. 6220, 12/28/56.

Proposed § 1.117-0 Outline of regulations pertaining to scholarships and fellowship grants. [*For Preamble, see ¶ 151,121*]

• ***Caution:*** Prop reg 1.6041-3 was withdrawn by the notice of proposed rulemaking issued on 4/22/96, 61 Fed. Reg. 17614. Prop. regs. 1.117-0 through -6 remain proposed.

(a) Section 1.117-1. Exclusion of amounts received as a scholarship or fellowship grant in taxable years beginning before 1987, but only in the case of scholarships and fellowships granted before August 17, 1986.

(b) Section 1.117-2. Limitations applicable to taxable years beginning before 1987, but only in the case of scholarships and fellowships granted before August 17, 1986.

(c) Section 1.117-3. Definitions applicable to taxable years beginning before 1987, but only in the case of scholarships and fellowships granted before August 17, 1986.

(d) Section 1.117-4. Items not considered as scholarships or fellowship grants in taxable years beginning before 1987, but only in the case of scholarships and fellowships granted before August 17, 1986.

(e) Section 1.117-5. Federal grants requiring future service as a federal employee pertaining to taxable years beginning before 1987, but only in the case of scholarships and fellowships granted before August 17, 1986.

(f) Section 1.117-6. Qualified scholarships.

§ 1.117-1 Exclusion of amounts received as a scholarship or fellowship grant.

Caution: The Treasury has not yet amended Reg § 1.117-1 to reflect changes made by P.L. 99-514.

(a) In general. Any amount received by an individual as a scholarship at an educational institution or as a fellowship grant, including the value of contributed services and accommodations, shall be excluded from the gross income of the recipient, subject to the limitations set forth in section 117(b) and § 1.117-2. The exclusion from gross income of an amount which is a scholarship or fellowship grant is controlled solely by section 117. Accordingly, to the extent that a scholarship or a fellowship grant exceeds the limitations of section 117(b) and § 1.117-2, it is includible in the gross income of the recipient notwithstanding the provisions of section 102 relating to exclusion from gross income of gifts, or section 74(b) relating to exclusion from gross income of certain prizes and awards. For definitions, see § 1.117-3.

(b) Exclusion of amounts received to cover expenses. *(1)* Subject to the limitations provided in subparagraph (2) of this paragraph, any amount received by an individual to cover expenses for travel (including meals and lodging while traveling and an allowance for travel of the individual's family), research, clerical help, or equipment is excludable from gross income provided that such expenses are incident to a scholarship or fellowship grant which is excludable from gross income under section 117(a)(1). If, however, only a portion of a scholarship or fellowship grant is excludable from gross income under section 117(a)(1) because of the part-time employment limitation contained in section 117(b)(1) or because of the expiration of the 36-month period described in section 117(b)(2)(B), only the amount received to cover expenses incident to such excludable portion is excludable from gross income. The requirement that these expenses be incident to the scholarship or the fellowship grant means that the expenses of travel, research, clerical help, or equipment must be incurred by the individual in order to effectuate the purpose for which the scholarship or the fellowship grant was awarded.

(2) (i) In the case of a scholarship or fellowship grant which is awarded after July 28, 1956, the exclusion provided under subparagraph (1) of this paragraph is not applicable unless the amount received by the individual is specifically designated to cover expenses for travel, research, clerical help, or equipment.

(ii) In the case of a scholarship or fellowship grant awarded before July 29, 1956, the exclusion provided under subparagraph (1) of this paragraph is not applicable unless the recipient establishes, by competent evidence, that the amount was received to cover expenses for travel, research, clerical help, or equipment, but such amount need not be specifically designated. The fact that the recipient actually incurred expenses for travel, research, clerical help, or equipment is not sufficient to establish that the amount was received to cover such expenses.

(iii) The exclusion provided under subparagraph (1) of this paragraph is applicable only to the extent that the amount received for travel, research, clerical help, or equipment is actually expended for such expenses by the recipient during the term of the scholarship or fellowship grant and within a reasonable time before and after such term.

(3) The portion of any amount received to cover the expenses described in subparagraph (1) of this paragraph which is not actually expended for such expenses within the exclusion period described in subparagraph (2) of this paragraph shall, if not returned to the grantor within this period, be included in the gross income of the recipient for the taxable year in which such exclusion period expires.

T.D. 6186, 6/29/56, amend T.D. 6456, 3/22/60.

PAR. 3. Section 1.117-1 is amended by revising the heading to read as set forth below, inserting "and before August 17, 1986," after "July 28, 1956," in the first sentence of paragraph (b)(2)(i), and adding a new paragraph (c) to read as follows:

Proposed § 1.117-1 Exclusion of amounts received as a scholarship or fellowship grant in taxable years beginning before 1987, but only in the case of scholarships and fellowships granted before August 17, 1986. [*For Preamble, see ¶ 151,121*]

* * * * *

• ***Caution:*** Prop reg 1.6041-3 was withdrawn by the notice of proposed rulemaking issued on 4/22/96, 61 Fed. Reg. 17614. Prop. regs. 1.117-0 through -6 remain proposed.

(c) Special rule; termination date; cross reference. For purposes of this section, all references to section 117 within this section are to section 117 as in effect prior to its amendment by the Tax Reform Act of 1986, unless otherwise indicated. This section does not apply to amounts granted after August 16, 1986, except to the extent that amounts granted after August 16, 1986, and before January 1, 1987, and received prior to January 1, 1987, are attributable to expenditures incurred before January 1, 1987. See § 1.117-6(f) for rules relating to when a scholarship or fellowship is granted for purposes of section 117 as amended by the 1986 Act.

§ 1.117-2 Limitations.

Caution: The Treasury has not yet amended Reg § 1.117-2 to reflect changes made by P.L. 99-514.

(a) Individuals who are candidates for degrees. *(1) In general.* Under the limitations provided by section 117(b)(1) in the case of an individual who is a candidate for a degree at an educational institution, the exclusion from gross income shall not apply (except as otherwise provided in subparagraph (2) of this paragraph) to that portion of any amount received as payment for teaching, research, or other services in the nature of part-time employment required as a condition to receiving the scholarship or fellowship grant. Payments for such part-time employment shall be included in the gross income of the recipient in an amount determined by reference to the rate of compensation ordinarily paid for similar services performed by an individual who is not the recipient of a scholarship or a fellowship grant. A typical example of employment under this subparagraph is the case of an individual who is required, as a condition to receiving the scholarship or the fellowship grant, to perform part-time teaching services. A requirement that the individual shall furnish periodic reports to the grantor of the scholarship or the fellowship grant for the purpose of keeping the grantor informed as to the general progress of the individual shall not be deemed to constitute the performance of services in the nature of part-time employment.

(2) Exception. If teaching, research, or other services are required of all candidates (whether or not recipients of scholarships or fellowship grants) for a particular degree as a condition to receiving the degree, such teaching, research, or other services on the part of the recipient of a scholarship or fellowship grant who is a candidate for such degree shall not be regarded as part-time employment within the meaning of this paragraph. Thus, if all candidates for a particular educa-

tion degree are required, as part of their regular course of study or curriculum, to perform part-time practice teaching services, such services are not to be regarded as part-time employment within the meaning of this paragraph.

(b) Individuals who are not candidates for degrees. *(1) Conditions for exclusion.* In the case of an individual who is not a candidate for a degree at an educational institution, the exclusion from gross income of an amount received as a scholarship or a fellowship grant shall apply (to the extent provided in subparagraph (2) of this paragraph) only if the grantor of the scholarship or fellowship grant is—

(i) An organization described in section 501(c)(3) which is exempt from tax under section 501(a),

(ii) The United States or an instrumentality or agency thereof, or a State, a territory, or a possession of the United States, or any political subdivision thereof, or the District of Columbia, or

(iii) For taxable years beginning after December 31, 1961, a foreign government, an international organization, or a binational or multinational educational and cultural foundation or commission created or continued pursuant to section 103 of the Mutual Educational and Cultural Exchange Act of 1961 (22 U.S.C. 2453).

(2) Extent of exclusion. (i) In the case of an individual who is not a candidate for a degree, the amount received as a scholarship or a fellowship grant which is excludable from gross income under section 117(a)(1) shall not exceed an amount equal to $300 times the number of months for which the recipient received amounts under the scholarship or fellowship grant during the taxable year. In determining the number of months during the period for which the recipient received amounts under a scholarship or fellowship grant, computation shall be made on the basis of whole calendar months. A whole calendar month means a period of time terminating with the day of the succeeding month numerically corresponding to the day of the month of its beginning, less one, except that if there be no corresponding day of the succeeding month the period terminates with the last day of the succeeding month. For purposes of this computation a fractional part of a calendar month consisting of a period of time including 15 days or more shall be considered to be a whole calendar month and a fractional part of a calendar month consisting of a period of time including 14 days or less shall be disregarded. For example, if an individual receives a fellowship grant on September 13 which is to expire on June 12 of the following year, the grant shall be considered to have extended for a period of 9 months. If in the preceding example the grant expired on June 27, instead of June 12, the grant shall be considered to have extended for a period of 10 months.

(ii) No exclusion shall be allowed under section 117(a)(1) to an individual who is not a candidate for a degree after the recipient has, as an individual who is not a candidate for a degree, been entitled to an exclusion under that section for a period of 36 months. This limitation applies if the individual has received any amount which was either excluded or excludable from his gross income under section 117(a)(1) for any prior 36 months, whether or not consecutive. For example, if the individual received a fellowship grant of $7,200 for 3 years (which he elected to receive in 36 monthly installments of $200), his exclusion period would be exhausted even though he did not in any of the 36 months make use of the maximum exclusion. Accordingly, such individual would be entitled to no further exclusion from gross income with respect to any additional grants which he may receive as an individual who is not a candidate for a degree.

(iii) If an individual who is not a candidate for a degree receives amounts from more than one scholarship or fellowship grant during the taxable year, the total amounts received in the taxable year shall be aggregated for the purpose of computing the amount which may be excludable from gross income for such taxable year. If amounts are received from more than one scholarship or fellowship grant during the same month or months within the taxable year, such month or months shall be counted only once for the purpose of determining the number of months for which the individual received such amounts under the scholarships or fellowship grants during the taxable year. For example, if an individual receives a fellowship grant from one source for the months of January to June of the taxable year and also receives a fellowship grant from another source for the months of March through December of the same taxable year, he shall be considered to have received amounts for 12 months of the taxable year. See example (4) in subparagraph (3) of this paragraph for further illustration.

(3) Examples. The application of this paragraph may be further illustrated by the following examples, it being assumed that in each example the grantor is a grantor who is described in section 117(b)(2)(A) and subparagraph (1) of this paragraph:

Example (1). B, an individual who files his return on the calendar year basis, is awarded a post-doctorate fellowship grant in March 1955. The grant is to commence on September 1, 1955, and is to end on May 31, 1956, so that it will extend over a period of 9 months. The amount of the fellowship grant is $4,500 and B receives this amount in monthly installments of $500 on the first day of each month commencing September 1, 1955. During the taxable year 1955, B receives a total of $2,000 with respect to the 4-month period September through December, inclusive. He may exclude $1,200 from gross income in the taxable year 1955 ($300 × 4) and must include the remaining $800 in gross income for that year. For the year 1956, he will exclude $1,500 ($300 × 5) from gross income with respect to the $2,500 which he receives in that year and must include in gross income $1,000.

Example (2). Assume the same facts as in example (1) except that B receives the full amount of the grant ($4,500) on September 1, 1955. Since the amount received in the taxable year 1955 is for the full term of the fellowship grant (9 months), B may exclude $2,700 ($300 × 9) from gross income for the taxable year 1955. The remaining $1,800 must be included in gross income for that year.

Example (3). C, an individual who files his return on the calendar year basis, is awarded a post-doctorate fellowship grant in March 1955. The amount of the grant is $4,500 for a period commencing on September 1, 1955, and ending 24 months thereafter. C receives a full amount of the grant on September 1, 1955. C may exclude from gross income for the taxable year 1955, the full amount of the grant ($4,500) since this amount does not exceed an amount equal to $300 times the number of months (24) for which he received the amount of the grant during that taxable year.

Example (4). (i) F, an individual who files his return on the calendar year basis, is awarded a post-doctorate fellowship grant (Grant A) for two years commencing June 1, 1955, in the amount of $4,800. He elects to receive his grant in monthly installments of $200 commencing June 1, 1955. On March 1, 1956, F is awarded another post-doctorate fellowship grant (Grant B) for two years commencing September 1, 1956, in the amount of $7,200. He elects to receive this grant in monthly installments of $300 commencing September 1, 1956.

(ii) For the calendar year 1955, F receives $1,400 from Grant A which he is entitled to exclude from gross income since it does not exceed an amount equal to $300 times the number of months (7) for which he received amounts under the grant in the taxable year.

(iii) For the calendar year 1956, F receives $3,600 as the aggregate of amounts received under fellowship grants ($2,400 from Grant A and $1,200 from Grant B). F will be entitled to exclude the entire amount of $3,600 from gross income for the calendar year 1956 since such amount does not exceed an amount equal to $300 times the number of months (12) for which he received amounts under the grants in the taxable year.

(iv) For the calendar year 1957, F receives $4,600 as the aggregate of amounts received under fellowship grants ($1,000 from Grant A and $3,600 from Grant B). F will be entitled to exclude $3,600 ($300 × 12) from gross income for the calendar year 1957 and he will have to include $1,000 in gross income.

(v) For the calendar year 1958, F receives $2,400 from Grant B. F is entitled to exclude $1,500 ($300 × 5) from gross income for the calendar year 1958 and he will have to include $900 in gross income. While F receives amounts under fellowship Grant B for 8 months during the calendar year 1958, he is limited to an amount equal to $300 times 5 (months) because of the fact that he has already been entitled to exclude (and has in fact excluded) amounts received as a fellowship grant for a period of 31 months. Accordingly, he can only exclude amounts received under the fellowship grant for 5 months during the calendar year 1958, because of the 36-month limitation period. The fact that he was entitled to exclude only $1,400 ($200 a month for 7 months) instead of the maximum amount of $2,100 ($300 × 7) in 1955, is immaterial and the limitation period of 36 months is applicable.

(vi) The following chart illustrates the computation of the number of months for which F received amounts under the fellowship grants during the respective taxable years and the computation of the total amounts received under the fellowship grants during each taxable year:

Period for which received and source	Number of months	Amounts received
1955		
June 1 to December 31	7	
Grant A		$ 1,400
Grant B		none
Aggregate	7	$ 1,400
1956		
January 1 to August 31	8	
Grant A		$ 1,600
Grant B		none
September 1 to December 31	4	
Grant A		800
Grant B		1,200
Aggregate	12	$ 3,600
1957		
January 1 to May 31	5	
Grant A		$ 1,000
Grant B		1,500
June 1 to December 31	7	
Grant A		none
Grant B		2,100
Aggregate	12	$ 4,600
1958		
January 1 to August 31	8	
Grant A		none
Grant B		$ 2,400
Aggregate	8	$ 2,400

T.D. 6186, 6/29/56, amend T.D. 6782, 12/23/64.

PAR. 4. Section 1.117-2 is amended by revising the heading to read as set forth below, inserting "and before August 17, 1986," after "December 31, 1961," in the first sentence of paragraph (b)(1)(iii), and adding a new paragraph (c) to read as follows:

Proposed § 1.117-2 Limitations applicable to taxable years beginning before 1987, but only in the case of scholarships and fellowships granted before August 17, 1986. [*For Preamble, see ¶ 151,121*]

* * * * *

• ***Caution:*** Prop reg 1.6041-3 was withdrawn by the notice of proposed rulemaking issued on 4/22/96, 61 Fed. Reg. 17614. Prop. regs. 1.117-0 through -6 remain proposed.

(c) Special rule; termination date; cross reference. For purposes of this section, all references to section 117 within this section are to section 117 as in effect prior to its amendment by the Tax Reform Act of 1986, unless otherwise indicated. This section does not apply to amounts granted after August 16, 1986, except to the extent that amounts granted after August 16, 1986, and before January 1, 1987, and received prior to January 1, 1987, are attributable to expenditures incurred before January 1, 1987. See § 1.117-6(f) for rules relating to when a scholarship or fellowship is granted for purposes of section 117 as amended by the 1986 Act.

§ 1.117-3 Definitions.

Caution: The Treasury has not yet amended Reg § 1.117-3 to reflect changes made by P.L. 99-514.

(a) Scholarship. A scholarship generally means an amount paid or allowed to, or for the benefit of, a student, whether an undergraduate or a graduate, to aid such individual in pursuing his studies. The term includes the value of contributed services and accommodations (see paragraph (d) of this section) and the amount of tuition, matriculation, and other fees which are furnished or remitted to a student to aid him in pursuing his studies. The term also includes any amount received in the nature of a family allowance as a part of a scholarship. However, the term does not include any amount provided by an individual to aid a relative, friend, or other individual in pursuing his studies where the grantor is motivated by family or philanthropic considerations. If an educational institution maintains or participates in a plan whereby the tuition of a child of a faculty member of such institution is remitted by any other participating educational institution attended by such child, the amount of the tuition so remitted shall be considered to be an amount received as a scholarship.

(b) Educational institution. For definition of "educational organization" paragraphs (a) and (b) of section 117 adopt the definition of that term which is prescribed in section 151(e)(4). Accordingly, for purposes of section 117 the term "educational organization" means only an educational organization which normally maintains a regular faculty and curriculum and normally has a regularly organized body of students in attendance at the place where its educational activities are carried on. See section 151(e)(4) and regulations thereunder.

(c) Fellowship grant. A fellowship grant generally means an amount paid or allowed to, or for the benefit of, an individual to aid him in the pursuit of study or research. The term includes the value of contributed services and accommodations (see paragraph (d) of this section) and the amount of tuition, matriculation, and other fees which are furnished or remitted to an individual to aid him in the pursuit of study or research. The term also includes any amount received in the nature of a family allowance as a part of a fellowship grant. However, the term does not include any amount provided by an individual to aid a relative, friend, or other individual in the pursuit of study or research where the grantor is motivated by family or philanthropic considerations.

(d) Contributed services and accommodations. The term "contributed services and accommodations" means such services and accommodations as room, board, laundry service, and similar services or accommodations which are received by an individual as a part of a scholarship or fellowship grant.

(e) Candidate for a degree. The term "candidate for a degree" means an individual, whether an undergraduate or a graduate, who is pursuing studies or conducting research to meet the requirements for an academic or professional degree conferred by colleges or universities. It is not essential that such study or research be pursued or conducted at an educational institution which confers such degrees if the purpose thereof is to meet the requirements for a degree of a college or university which does confer such degrees. A student who receives a scholarship for study at a secondary school or other educational institution is considered to be a "candidate for a degree."

T.D. 6186, 6/29/56, amend T.D. 8032, 7/1/85.

PAR. 5. Section 1.117-3 is amended by revising the heading to read as set forth below, inserting "of the Internal Revenue Code of 1954" after "151(e)(4)" in the first sentence of paragraph (b), inserting "of the Internal Revenue Code of 1954" after "151(e)(4)" in the last sentence of paragraph (b), and adding a new paragraph (f) to read as follows:

Proposed § 1.117-3 Definitions applicable to taxable years beginning before 1987, but only in the case of scholarships and fellowships granted before August 17, 1986. [*For Preamble, see ¶ 151,121*]

* * * * *

• ***Caution:*** Prop reg 1.6041-3 was withdrawn by the notice of proposed rulemaking issued on 4/22/96, 61 Fed. Reg. 17614. Prop. regs. 1.117-0 through -6 remain proposed.

(f) Special rule; termination date; cross reference. For purposes of this section, all references to section 117 within this section are to section 117 as in effect prior to its amendment by the Tax Reform Act of 1986, unless otherwise indicated. This section does not apply to amounts granted after August 16, 1986, except to the extent that amounts granted after August 16, 1986, and before January 1, 1987, and received prior to January 1, 1987, are attributable to expenditures incurred before January 1, 1987. See § 1.117-6(f) for rules relating to when a scholarship or fellowship is granted for purposes of section 117 as amended by the 1986 Act.

§ 1.117-4 Items not considered as scholarships or fellowship grants.

Caution: The Treasury has not yet amended Reg § 1.117-4 to reflect changes made by P.L. 107-16, P.L. 99-514.

The following payments or allowances shall not be considered to be amounts received as a scholarship or a fellowship grant for the purpose of section 117:

(a) Educational and training allowances to veterans. Educational and training allowances to a veteran pursuant to section 400 of the Servicemen's Readjustment Act of 1944 (58 Stat 287) or pursuant to 38 USC 1631 (formerly section 231 of the Veterans' Readjustment Assistance Act of 1952).

(b) Allowances to members of the Armed Forces of the United States. Tuition and subsistence allowances to members of the Armed Forces of the United States who are students at an educational institution operated by the United States or approved by the United States for their education and training, such as the United States Naval Academy and the United States Military Academy.

(c) Amounts paid as compensation for services or primarily for the benefit of the grantor. *(1)* Except as provided in paragraph (a) of § 1.117-2 and § 1.117-5, any amount paid or allowed to, or on behalf of, an individual to enable him to pursue studies or research, if such amount represents either compensation for past, present, or future employment services or represents payment for services which are subject to the direction or supervision of the grantor.

(2) Any amount paid or allowed to, or on behalf of, an individual to enable him to pursue studies or research primarily for the benefit of the grantor.

However, amounts paid or allowed to, or on behalf of, an individual to enable him to pursue studies or research are considered to be amounts received as a scholarship or fellowship grant for the purpose of section 117 if the primary purpose of the studies or research is to further the education and training of the recipient in his individual capacity and the amount provided by the grantor for such purpose does not represent compensation or payment for the services described in subparagraph (1) of this paragraph. Neither the fact that the recipient is required to furnish reports of his progress to the grantor, nor the fact that the results of his studies or research may be of some incidental benefit to the grantor shall, of itself, be considered to destroy the essential character of such amount as a scholarship or fellowship grant.

T.D. 6186, 6/29/56, amend T.D. 8032, 7/1/85.

PAR. 6. Section 1.117-4 is amended as follows:

1. The heading is revised as set forth below.

2. The first sentence is revised by inserting "(a) Applicability." before "The".

3. Paragraphs (a), (b), and (c) are redesignated as paragraphs (1), (2), and (3).

4. Paragraphs (1) and (2) of paragraph (3) as redesignated are redesignated as paragraphs (i) and (ii).

5. The second sentence of paragraph (3)(ii) as redesignated is amended by removing "subparagraph (1)" and adding in its place "subparagraph (i)".

6. A new paragraph (b) is added to read as set forth below.

Proposed § 1.117-4 Items not considered as scholarships or fellowship grants in taxable years beginning before 1987, but only in the case of scholarships and fellowships granted before August 17, 1986. [*For Preamble, see ¶ 151,121*]

* * * * *

• ***Caution:*** Prop reg 1.6041-3 was withdrawn by the notice of proposed rulemaking issued on 4/22/96, 61 Fed. Reg. 17614. Prop. regs. 1.117-0 through -6 remain proposed.

(b) Special rule; termination date; cross reference. For purposes of this section, all references to section 117 within this section are to section 117 as in effect prior to its amendment by the Tax Reform Act of 1986, unless otherwise indicated. This section does not apply to amounts granted after August 16, 1986, except to the extent that amounts granted after August 16, 1986, and before January 1, 1987, and received prior to January 1, 1987, are attributable to expenditures incurred before January 1, 1987. See § 1.117-6(f) for rules relating to when a scholarship or fellowship is granted for purposes of section 117 as amended by the 1986 Act.

§ 1.117-5 Federal grants requiring future service as a federal employee.

Caution: The Treasury has not yet amended Reg § 1.117-5 to reflect changes made by P.L. 99-514.

(a) In general. Under section 117(c), amounts received by an individual under a federal program as a scholarship or grant for qualified tuition and expenses at an institution of higher education are excluded from the gross income of the recipient even though the recipient is required to perform future service as a federal employee. See paragraph (c) of this section for the definitions of the terms "qualified tuition and expenses" and "institution of higher education."

(b) Exception for uniformed services scholarship programs. The requirements of this section do not apply to amounts received before 1985 by a member of a uniformed service who entered training before 1981 under the Armed Forces Health Professions Scholarship Program, National Public Health Service Corps Scholarship Training Program, or other substantially similar federal programs requiring the recipient to work for a uniformed federal service after completion of studies. These awards are governed by section 4 of Pub. L. 93-483 as amended by Pub. L. 95-171, Pub. L. 95-600 and Pub. L. 96-167. See section 101(3) of title 37, United States Code for the definition of the term "uniformed service."

(c) Definitions. *(1) Qualified tuition and related expenses.* For purposes of section 117(c) and this section, qualified tuition and related expenses are those amounts which under the terms of the federal program are required to be used and in fact are used for payment of:

(i) Tuition and fees that are required for the recipient's enrollment or attendance at an institution of higher education; and

(ii) Those amounts used for payment of fees, books, supplies and equipment required for courses of instruction at such an institution.

Incidental expenses are not considered related expenses and thus are not excludable from gross income under section 117(c). Incidental expenses include room and board at an institution of higher education, expenses for travel (including expenses for meals and lodging incurred during travel and allowances for travel of the recipient's family), research, clerical help, equipment and other expenses which are not required for enrollment at the institution or in a course of instruction at such institution.

(2) Institution of higher education. To qualify as an institution of higher education under this section, the institution must be a public or other nonprofit institution in any state which—

(i) Admits as regular students only individuals who have a certificate of graduation from a high school or the recognized equivalent of such a certificate;

(ii) Is legally authorized within the state to provide a program of education beyond high school; and

(iii) Provides an education program for which it awards a bachelor's or higher degree or which is acceptable for full credit towards such a degree, or which trains and prepares students for gainful employment in a recognized health profession. For purposes of this section, recognized health professions are those health professions which are supervised or monitored by appropriate state or federal agencies or governing professional associations and which require members to be currently licensed or certified in order to practice.

(3) Service as a federal employee. (i) In general. Except as otherwise provided in paragraph (c)(3)(ii) of this section, service as a federal employee refers to employment of the recipient by the federal government to work directly for the federal government. Thus, federal grants or scholarships which do not require the recipient to work directly for the federal government are not governed by the rules of this section.

(ii) Service in a health manpower shortage area. For purposes of this section an obligation under a grant for the recipient to serve in a health related field in a health manpower shortage area as designated by the Secretary of Health and Human Services according to the criteria of the Public Health Services Act (42 U.S.C. 254(e)) and the regulations promulgated thereunder (42 CFR 5.1-5.4) will be considered an obligation to serve as a federal employee.

(d) Records required for exclusion from gross income. To exclude amounts received under federal programs requiring future services as a federal employee, the recipient must maintain records that establish that the amounts received under such programs were used for qualified tuition and related expenses as defined in paragraph (c)(1) of this section. Qualifying uses may be established by providing to the Service, upon request, copies of relevant bills, receipts, cancelled checks or other convenient documentation or records which clearly reflect the use of the money received under the grant. The recipient must also submit, upon request, documentation establishing receipt of the grant and setting out the terms and requirements of the particular grant.

(e) Applicability of rules of §§ 117(a) and 117(b). Except where a different rule has been expressly provided in this section, amounts received under federal grants requiring future service as a federal employee, and which meet the requirements for exclusion from gross income under this section, are subject to the rules, limitations and definitions specified in sections 117(a) and (b) of the Code and §§ 1.117-1 through 1.117-4.

(f) Effective date. Except as provided in paragraph (b) of this section, this section will apply to amounts received after December 31, 1980 under federal programs which meet the requirements of this section.

T.D. 8032, 7/1/85.

PAR. 7. Section 1.117-5 is amended by revising the heading to read as set forth below, adding a second sentence to paragraph (f), and adding a new paragraph (g) to read as follows:

Proposed § 1.117-5 Federal grants requiring future service as a federal employee pertaining to taxable years beginning before 1987, but only in the case of scholarships and fellowships granted before August 17, 1986. [*For Preamble, see ¶ 151,121*]

* * * * *

• ***Caution:*** Prop reg 1.6041-3 was withdrawn by the notice of proposed rulemaking issued on 4/22/96, 61 Fed. Reg. 17614. Prop. regs. 1.117-0 through -6 remain proposed.

(f) Effective date. * * * This section does not apply to amounts granted after August 16, 1986, except to the extent that amounts granted after August 16, 1986, and before January 1, 1987, and received prior to January 1, 1987, are attributable to expenditures incurred before January 1, 1987.

(g) Special rule; cross reference. For purposes of this section, all references to section 117 within this section are to section 117 as in effect prior to its amendment by the Tax Reform Act of 1986, unless otherwise indicated. See § 1.117-6(f) for rules relating to when a scholarship or fellowship is granted for purposes of section 117 as amended by the 1986 Act.

Proposed § 1.117-6 Qualified scholarships. [*For Preamble, see ¶ 151,121*]

Caution: The Treasury has not yet amended Reg § 1.117-6 to reflect changes made by P.L. 100-647.

• ***Caution:*** Prop reg 1.6041-3 was withdrawn by the notice of proposed rulemaking issued on 4/22/96, 61 Fed. Reg. 17614. Prop. regs. 1.117-0 through -6 remain proposed.

(a) Outline of provisions. This outline lists the paragraphs contained in § 1.117-6.

(a) Outline of provisions.

(b) Exclusion of qualified scholarships.

(c) Definitions.

(1) Qualified scholarship.

(2) Qualified tuition and related expenses.

(3) Scholarship or fellowship grant.

(i) In general.

(ii) Items not considered as scholarships or fellowship grants.

(4) Candidate for a degree.

(5) Educational organization.

(6) Examples.

(d) Inclusion of qualified scholarships and qualified tuition reductions representing payment for services.

(1) In general.

(2) Payment for services.

(3) Determination of amount of scholarship or fellowship grant representing payment for services.

(4) Characterization of scholarship or fellowship grants representing payment for services for purposes of the reporting and withholding requirements.

(5) Examples.

(e) Recordkeeping requirements.

(f) Effective date.

(1) In general.

(2) When a scholarship or fellowship is granted.

(3) Scholarships or fellowships granted before August 17, 1986.

(i) In general.

(ii) Amounts received in subsequent academic periods that were not initially described as fixed cash amounts or readily determinable amounts.

(iii) Examples.

(4) Expenditures incurred before January 1, 1987.

(g) Reporting and withholding requirements.

(h) Characterization of scholarship or fellowship grants exceeding amounts permitted to be excluded from gross income for purposes of the standard deduction and filing requirements for dependents.

(b) Exclusion of qualified scholarships. *(1)* Gross income does not include any amount received as a qualified scholarship by an individual who is a candidate for a degree at an educational organization described in section 170(b)(1)(A)(ii), subject to the rules set forth in paragraph (d) of this section. Generally, any amount of a scholarship or fellowship grant that is not excludable under section 117 is includable in the gross income of the recipient for the taxable year in which such amount is received, notwithstanding the provisions of section 102 (relating to exclusion from gross incomes of gifts). However, see section 127 and the regulations thereunder for rules permitting an exclusion from gross income for certain educational assistance payments. See also section 162 and the regulations thereunder for the deductibility as a trade or business expense of the educational expenses of an individual who is not a candidate for a degree.

(2) If the amount of a scholarship or fellowship grant eligible to be excluded as a qualified scholarship under this paragraph cannot be determined when the grant is received because expenditures for qualified tuition and related expenses have not yet been incurred, then that portion of any amount received as a scholarship or fellowship grant that is not used for qualified tuition and related expenses within the academic period to which the scholarship or fellowship grant applies must be included in the gross income of the recipient for the taxable year in which such academic period ends.

(c) Definitions. *(1) Qualified scholarship.* For purposes of this section, a *qualified scholarship* is any amount received by an individual as a scholarship or fellowship grant (as defined in paragraph (c)(3) of this section), to the extent the individual establishes that, in accordance with the conditions of the grant, such amount was used for qualified tuition and related expenses (as defined in paragraph (c)(2) of this section). To be considered a qualified scholarship, the terms of the scholarship or fellowship grant need not expressly require that the amounts received be used for tuition and related expenses. However, to the extent that the terms of the grant specify that any portion of the grant cannot be used for tuition and related expenses or designate any portion of the grant for purposes other than tuition and related expenses (such as for room and board, or for a meal allowance), such amounts are not amounts received as a qualified scholarship. See paragraph (e) of this section for rules relating to recordkeeping requirements for establishing amounts used for qualified tuition and related expenses.

(2) Qualified tuition and related expenses. For purposes of this section, *qualified tuition and related expenses* are—

(i) Tuition and fees required for the enrollment or attendance of a student at an educational organization described in section 170(b)(1)(A)(ii); and

(ii) Fees, books, supplies, and equipment required for courses of instruction at such an educational organization.

In order to be treated as related expenses under this section, the fees, books, supplies, and equipment must be required of all students in the particular course of instruction. Incidental expenses are not considered related expenses. Incidental expenses include expenses incurred for room and board, travel, research, clerical help, and equipment and other expenses that are not required for either enrollment or attendance at an educational organization, or in a course of instruction at such educational organization. See paragraph (c)(6), Example (1) of this section.

(3) Scholarship or fellowship grant. (i) In general. Generally, a *scholarship or fellowship grant* is a cash amount paid or allowed to, or for the benefit of, an individual to aid such individual in the pursuit of study or research. A scholarship or fellowship grant also may be in the form of a reduction in the amount owed by the recipient to an educational organization for tuition, room and board, or any other fee. A scholarship or fellowship grant may be funded by a governmental agency, college or university, charitable organization, business, or other source. To be considered a scholarship or fellowship grant for purposes of this section, any amount received need not be formally designated as a scholarship. For example, an "allowance" is treated as a scholarship if it meets the definition set forth in this paragraph. However, a scholarship or fellowship grant does not include any amount provided by an individual to aid a relative, friend, or other individual in the pursuit of study or research if the grantor is motivated by family or philanthropic considerations.

(ii) Items not considered as scholarships or fellowship grants. The following payments or allowances are not considered to be amounts received as a scholarship or fellowship grant for purposes of section 117:

(A) Educational and training allowances to a veteran pursuant to section 400 of the Servicemen's Readjustment Act of 1944 (58 Stat. 287) or pursuant to 38 U.S.C. 1631 (formerly section 231 of the Veteran's Readjustment Assistance Act of 1953).

(B) Tuition and subsistence allowances to members of the Armed Forces of the United States who are students at an educational institution operated by the United States or approved by the United States for their education and training, such as the United States Naval Academy and the United States Military Academy.

(4) Candidate for a degree. For purposes of this section, a candidate for a degree is—

(i) A primary or secondary school student;

(ii) An undergraduate or graduate student at a college or university who is pursuing studies or conducting research to meet the requirement for an academic or professional degree; or

(iii) A full-time or part-time student at an educational organization described in section 170(b)(1)(A)(ii) that—

(A) Provides an educational program that is acceptable for full credit towards a bachelor's or higher degree, or offers a program of training to prepare students for gainful employment in a recognized occupation, and

(B) Is authorized under Federal or State law to provide such a program and is accredited by a nationally recognized accreditation agency.

The student may pursue studies or conduct research at an educational organization other than the one conferring the degree provided that such study or research meets the requirements of the educational organization granting the degree. See paragraph (c)(6), Examples (2) and (3) of this section.

(5) Educational organization. For purposes of this section, an *educational organization* is an organization described under section 170(b)(1)(A)(ii) and the regulations thereunder. An educational organization is described in section 170(b)(1)(A)(ii) if it has as its primary function the presentation of formal instruction, and it normally maintains a regular faculty and curriculum and normally has a regularly enrolled body of pupils or students in attendance at the place where its educational activities are regularly carried on. See paragraph (c)(6), Example (4) of this section.

(6) Examples. The provisions of this paragraph may be illustrated by the following examples:

Example (1). On September 1, 1987, A receives a scholarship from University U for academic year 1987-1988. A is enrolled in a writing course at U. Suggested supplies for the writing course in which A is enrolled include a word processor, but students in the course are not required to obtain a word processor. Any amount used for suggested supplies is not an amount used for qualified tuition and related expenses for purposes of this section. Thus, A may not include the cost of a word processor in determining the amount received by A as a qualified scholarship.

Example (2). B is a scholarship student during academic year 1987-1988 at Technical School V located in State W. B is enrolled in a program to train individuals to become data processors. V is authorized by State W to provide this program and is accredited by an appropriate accreditation agency. B is a candidate for a degree for purposes of this section. Thus, B may exclude from gross income any amount received as a qualified scholarship, subject to the rules set forth in paragraph (d) of this section.

Example (3). C holds a Ph.D in chemistry. On January 31, 1988, Foundation X awards C a fellowship. During 1988 C pursues chemistry research at Research Foundation Y, supported by the fellowship grant from X. C is not an employee of either foundation. C is not a candidate for a degree for purposes of this section. Thus, the fellowship grant from X must be included in C's gross income.

Example (4). On July 1, 1987, D receives a $500 scholarship to take a correspondence course from School Z. D receives and returns all lessons to Z through the mail. No students are in attendance at Z's place of business. D is not attending an educational organization described in section 170(b)(1)(A)(ii) for purposes of this section. Thus, the $500 scholarship must be included in D's gross income.

(d) Inclusion of qualified scholarships and qualified tuition reductions representing payment for services. *(1) In general.* The exclusion from gross income under this section does not apply to that portion of any amount received as a qualified scholarship or qualified tuition reduction (as defined under section 117(d)) that represents payment for teaching, research, or other services by the student required as a condition to receiving the qualified scholarship or qualified tuition reduction, regardless of whether all candidates for the degree are required to perform such services. The provisions of this paragraph (d) apply not only to cash amounts received in return for such services, but also to amounts by which the tuition or related expenses of the person who performs services are reduced, whether or not pursuant to a tuition reduction plan described in section 117(d).

(2) Payment for services. For purposes of this section, a scholarship or fellowship grant represents payment for services when the grantor requires the recipient to perform services in return for the granting of the scholarship or fellowship. A requirement that the recipient pursue studies, research, or other activities primarily for the benefit of the grantor is treated as a requirement to perform services. A requirement that a recipient furnish periodic reports to the grantor for the purpose of keeping the grantor informed as to the general progress of the individual, however, does not constitute the performance of services. A scholarship or fellowship grant conditioned upon either past, present, or future teaching, research, or other services by the recipient represents payment for services under this section. See paragraph (d)(5), Examples (1), (2), (3) and (4) of this section.

(3) Determination of amount of scholarship or fellowship grant representing payment for services. If only a portion of a scholarship or fellowship grant represents payment for services, the grantor must determine the amount of the scholarship or fellowship grant (including any reduction in tuition or related expenses) to be allocated to payment for services. Factors to be taken into account in making this allocation include, but are not limited to, compensation paid by—

(i) The grantor for similar services performed by students with qualifications comparable to those of the scholarship recipient, but who do not receive scholarship or fellowship grants;

(ii) The grantor for similar services performed by full-time or part-time employees of the grantor who are not students; and

(iii) Educational organizations, other than the grantor of the scholarship or fellowship, for similar services performed either by students or other employees.

If the recipient includes in gross income the amount allocated by the grantor to payment for services and such amount represents reasonable compensation for those services, then any additional amount of a scholarship or fellowship grant received from the same grantor that meets the requirements of paragraph (b) of this section is excludable from gross income. See paragraph (d)(5), Examples (5) and (6) of this section.

(4) Characterization of scholarship or fellowship grants representing payment for services for purposes of the reporting and withholding requirements. Any amount of a scholarship or fellowship grant that represents payment for services (as defined in paragraph (d)(2) of this section) is considered wages for purposes of sections 3401 and 3402 (relating to withholding for income taxes), section 6041 (relating to returns of information), and section 6051 (relating to reporting wages of employees). The application of sections 3101 and 3111 (relating to the Federal Insurance Contributions Act (FICA)), or section 3301 (relating to the Federal Unemployment Tax Act (FUTA)) depends upon the nature of the employment and the status of the organization. See sections 3121(b), 3306(c), and the regulations thereunder.

(5) Examples. The provisions of this paragraph may be illustrated by the following examples:

Example (1). On November 15, 1987, A receives a $5,000 qualified scholarship (as defined paragraph (c)(1) of this section) for academic year 1988-1989 under a federal program requiring A's future service as a federal employee. The $5,000 scholarship represents payment for services for purposes of this section. Thus, the $5,000 must be included in A's gross income as wages.

Example (2). B receives a $10,000 scholarship from V Corporation on June 4, 1987, for academic year 1987-1988. As a condition to receiving the scholarship, B agrees to work for V after graduation. B has no previous relationship with V. The $10,000 scholarship represents payment for future services for purposes of this section. Thus, the $10,000 scholarship must be included in B's gross income as wages.

Example (3). On March 15, 1987, C is awarded a fellowship for academic year 1987-1988 to pursue a research project the nature of which is determined by the grantor, University W. C must submit a paper to W that describes the research results. The paper does not fulfill any course requirements. Under the terms of the grant, W may publish C's results, or otherwise use the results of C's research. C is treated as performing services for W. Thus, C's fellowship from W represents payment for services and must be included in C's gross income as wages.

Example (4). On September 27, 1987, D receives a qualified scholarship (as defined in paragraph (c)(1) of this section) from University X for academic year 1987-1988. As a condition to receiving the scholarship, D performs services as a teaching assistant for X. Such services are required of all candidates for a degree at X. The amount of D's scholarship from X is equal to the compensation paid by X to teaching assistants who are part-time employees and not students at X. D's scholarship from X represents payment for services. Thus, the entire amount of D's scholarship from X must be included in D's gross income as wages.

Example (5). On June 11, 1987, E receives a $6,000 scholarship for academic year 1987-1988 from University Y. As a condition to receiving the scholarship, E performs services as a researcher for Y. Other researchers who are not scholarship recipients receive $2,000 for similar services for the year. Therefore, Y allocates $2,000 of the scholarship amount to compensation for services performed by E. Thus, the portion of the scholarship that represents payment for services, $2,000, must be included in E's gross income as wages. However, if E establishes expenditures of $4,000 for qualified tuition and related expenses (as defined in paragraph (c)(2) of this section), then $4,000 of E's scholarship is excludable from E's gross income as a qualified scholarship.

Example (6). During 1987 F is employed as a research assistant to a faculty member at University Z. F receives a salary from Z that represents reasonable compensation for the position of research assistant. In addition to salary, F receives from Z a qualified tuition reduction (as defined in section 117(d)) to be used to enroll in an undergraduate course at Z. F includes the salary in gross income. Thus, the qualified tuition reduction does not represent payment for services and therefore, is not includable in F's gross income.

(e) Recordkeeping requirements. In order to be eligible to exclude from gross income any amount received as a qualified scholarship (as defined in paragraph (c)(1) of this section), the recipient must maintain records that establish amounts used for qualified tuition and related expenses (as defined in paragraph (c)(2) of this section) as well as the total amount of qualified tuition and related expenses. Such amounts may be established by providing to the Service, upon request, copies of relevant bills, receipts, canceled checks, or other documentation or records that clearly reflect the use of the money. The recipient must also submit, upon request, documentation that established receipt of the grant, notification date of the grant, and the conditions and requirements of the particular grant. Subject to the rules set forth in paragraph (d) of this section, qualified scholarship amounts are excludable without the need to trace particular grant dollars to particular expenditures for qualified tuition and related expenses.

(f) Effective date. *(1) In general.* The rules of this section generally apply to taxable years beginning on or after January 1, 1987. However, section 117, as in effect prior to its amendment by the Tax Reform Act of 1986 (1986 Act), continues to apply to scholarships and fellowships granted before August 17, 1986, whenever received. In addition, section 117, as in effect prior to its amendment by the 1986 Act, applies in the case of scholarships and fellowships granted after August 16, 1986, and before January 1, 1987, to the extent of any amount received prior to January 1, 1987, that is attributable to expenditures incurred before January 1, 1987.

(2) When a scholarship or fellowship is granted. For purposes of this section, a scholarship or fellowship is granted when the grantor either notifies the recipient of the award or notifies an organization or institution acting on behalf of a specified recipient of the award to be provided to such recipient. If the notification is sent by mail, notification occurs as of the date the notice is postmarked. If evidence of a postmark does not exist, the date on the award letter is treated as the notification data.

(3) Scholarships or fellowships granted before August 17, 1986. (i) In general. For purposes of this section, a scholarship or fellowship is considered granted before August 17, 1986, to the extent that, in a notice of award made before that date, the grantor made a firm commitment to provide the recipient with a fixed cash amount or a readily determinable amount. A notice of award is treated as containing a firm commitment even if the scholarship or fellowship grant is subject to a condition that the recipient remain in good standing or maintain a specific grade point average. In addition, a requirement that the recipient file a financial statement on an annual basis to show continuing financial need is not treated as a requirement to reapply to the grantor. If a scholarship or fellowship, initially awarded before August 17, 1986, is granted for a period exceeding one academic period (for example, a semester), amounts received in subsequent academic periods are treated as granted before August 17, 1986, only if—

(A) The amount awarded for the first academic period is described in the original notice of award as a fixed cash amount or readily determinable amount;

(B) The original notice of award contains a firm commitment by the grantor to provide the scholarship or fellowship grant for more than one academic period; and

(C) The recipient is not required to reapply to the grantor in order to receive the scholarship or fellowship grant in future academic periods.

Scholarship or fellowship amounts treated as granted before August 17, 1986, must be applied against qualified tuition and related expenses before any amount of a scholarship or fellowship treated as granted after August 16, 1986, may be eligible for exclusion as a qualified scholarship.

(ii) Amounts received in subsequent academic periods that were not initially described as fixed cash amounts or readily determinable amounts. If the notice of award of a scholarship or fellowship grant satisfies the requirements of paragraph (f)(3)(i) of this section but does not describe the amount to be received in subsequent academic periods as either a fixed cash amount or readily determinable amount, then the amount received in each subsequent academic period that is treated as granted before August 17, 1986, may not exceed the amount granted for the initial academic period. To the extent that any amount received in a subsequent academic period, under the same notice of award, exceeds the amount received in the initial academic period, the excess amount is treated as a scholarship or fellowship granted after August 16, 1986.

(iii) Examples. The provisions of this paragraph may be illustrated by the following examples:

Example (1). On January 7, 1985, A receives a notice of award under a federal program of a $500 scholarship for the academic period Spring 1985. A receives the $500 in February 1988. For purposes of this section the $500 scholarship is granted before August 17, 1986, and thus is subject to section 117 prior to its amendment by the 1986 Act.

Example (2). On May 7, 1986, B received a notice of award of a scholarship in the amount of $4,000 annually for four years. The total amount of this scholarship is a fixed cash amount. Thus, $16,000, the total amount of the scholarship for all four years, is subject to section 117 prior to its amendment by the 1986 Act.

Example (3). On May 7, 1986, C is notified of the award of the Y scholarship that will pay for C's tuition, room, and board for four years. The total amount of the Y scholarship is readily determinable. Thus, the total amount of the Y scholarship for all four years is subject to section 117 prior to its amendment by the 1986 Act.

Example (4). On May 7, 1986, D is notified that she is the recipient of a scholarship to attend university Z. The scholarship is not conditioned upon the performance of services by D. The notice provides that Z will award scholarship funds for four years and specifies that D will receive $5,000 during the first year. D is not required to reapply in order to receive scholarship funds during years 2 through 4. However, the notice does not specify the scholarship funds to be received in years 2 through 4. The $5,000 received in year 1 is treated as granted before August 17, 1986, because this amount is a fixed cash amount described in the notice of award. In addition, because Z has made a specific commitment to provide scholarship funds during years 2 through 4 without requiring D to reapply for the scholarship, an amount from Z not exceeding $5,000 per year is treated as granted before August 17, 1986, during years 2 through 4. Thus, if D receives $4,000 from Z in year 2, the entire $4,000 is treated as granted before August 17, 1986. If, in year 3, D receives $6,000 from Z, only $5,000 of the amount received is treated as granted before August 17, 1986. The additional $1,000 received in year 3 is treated as granted after August 16, 1986. Whether this additional $1,000 is excludable from D's gross income depends upon the amount of qualified tuition and related expenses (as defined in paragraph (c)(2) of this section) incurred by D in year 3. Thus, if D's qualified tuition and related expenses for year 3 are $6,000, the entire $6,000 is excludable from D's gross income.

Example (5). Assume the same facts as in Example (4) except that D's qualified tuition and related expenses in year 3 are $5,500. D excludes the $5,000 that is treated as granted before August 17, 1986. However, this $5,000 must be applied against the total qualified tuition and related expenses of $5,500 owed by D for year 3 before any amount received from a scholarship or fellowship granted after August 16, 1986, may be excluded. The additional $1,000 received by D that is treated as granted after August 16, 1986, is excludable to the extent of $500, the amount by which qualified tuition and related expenses exceed the amount that is treated as granted before August 17, 1986. The remaining $500 scholarship amount must be included in D's gross income.

Example (6). Assume the same facts as in Example (4) except that D's qualified tuition and related expenses for year 3 are $5,000. The amount of D's qualified tuition and related expenses for year 3 is equal to the scholarship amount from Z treated as granted before August 17, 1986. Thus, no part of the $1,000 treated as granted after August 16, 1986, is excludable from D's gross income.

(4) Expenditures incurred before January 1, 1987. In the case of scholarships and fellowships granted after August 16, 1986, and before January 1, 1987, amounts received prior to January 1, 1987, that are attributable to expenditures incurred prior to January 1, 1987, are subject to section 117 as in effect prior to its amendment by the 1986 Act. For purposes of this section, an expenditure is incurred when it becomes properly due and payable by the recipient. However, expenditures relating to an academic period beginning after December 31, 1986, paid by the recipient before January 1, 1987, prior to the time when the recipient is billed for such expenditures, are not treated as expenditures incurred before January 1, 1987. Thus, if in December 1986 an educational organization billed a scholarship recipient for expenses relating to the academic period beginning in January 1987, and the recipient used scholarship amounts received prior to January 1, 1987, to pay the expenses on January 5, 1987, the scholarship amounts used to pay such expenses are considered attributable to expenditures incurred prior to January 1, 1987. If, however, on December 31, 1986, a scholarship recipient used scholarship amount to pay expenses relating to the academic period beginning in January 1987, before the recipient was billed for such expenses, the amounts used are not treated as attributable to expenditures incurred before January 1, 1987.

(g) Reporting and withholding requirements. For return of information requirements, see section 6041, 6051, and the regulations thereunder. For withholding from scholarships or fellowship grants representing payment for services, see sections 3401, 3402, and the regulations thereunder. For withholding from scholarships or fellowship grants of nonresident aliens, see section 1441 and the regulations thereunder. For the application of FICA, see sections 3101 and 3111. For the application of FUTA, see section 3301.

(h) Characterization of scholarship or fellowship grants exceeding amounts permitted to be excluded from gross income for purposes of the standard deduction and filing requirements for dependents. For purposes of section 63(c)(5) (relating to the standard deduction for dependents) and section 6012(a)(1)(C)(i) (relating to dependents required to make returns of income), any amount of a scholarship or fellowship grant in excess of the amount permitted to be excluded from gross income under paragraph (b) of this section is considered earned income. For example, on June 11, 1987, A, a student who has no other earned or unearned income for the year and can be claimed as a dependent on another taxpayer's return of tax, receives a $1,000 scholarship for room and board. The $1,000 must be included in A's gross income because it is not a qualified scholarship under paragraph (b) of this section. However, for purposes of sections 63(c)(5) and 6012(a)(1)(C)(i), the $1,000 is earned income. Accordingly, A is not required to file a return of tax for 1987 because A's gross income ($1,000) does not exceed A's standard deduction ($1,000) and A has no unearned income.

§ 1.118-1 Contributions to the capital of a corporation.

> ***Caution:*** The Treasury has not yet amended Reg § 1.118-1 to reflect changes made by P.L. 99-514, P.L. 98-369, P.L. 95-600, P.L. 94-455.

In the case of a corporation, section 118 provides an exclusion from gross income with respect to any contribution of money or property to the capital of the taxpayer. Thus, if a corporation requires additional funds for conducting its business and obtains such funds through voluntary pro rata payments by its shareholders, the amounts so received being credited to its surplus account or to a special account, such amounts do not constitute income, although there is no increase in the outstanding shares of stock of the corporation. In such a case the payments are in the nature of assessments upon, and represent an additional price paid for, the shares of stock held by the individual shareholders, and will be treated as an addition to and as a part of the operating capital of the company. Section 118 also applies to contributions to capital made by persons other than shareholders. For example, the exclusion applies to the value of land or other property contributed to a corporation by a governmental unit or by a civic group for the purpose of inducing the corporation to locate its business in a particular community, or for the purpose of enabling the corporation to expand its operating facilities. However, the exclusion does not apply to any money or property transferred to the corporation in consideration for goods or services rendered, or to subsidies paid for the purpose of inducing the taxpayer to limit production. See section 362 for the basis of property acquired by a corporation through a contribution to its capital by its stockholders or by nonstockholders.

T.D. 6220, 12/28/56.

§ 1.118-2 Contribution in aid of construction.

(a) Special rule for water and sewerage disposal utilities. *(1) In general.* For purposes of section 118, the term contribution to the capital of the taxpayer includes any amount of money or other property received from any person (whether or not a shareholder) by a regulated public utility that provides water or sewerage disposal services if—

(i) The amount is a contribution in aid of construction under paragraph (b) of this section;

(ii) In the case of a contribution of property other than water or sewerage disposal facilities, the amount satisfies the expenditure rule under paragraph (c) of this section; and

(iii) The amount (or any property acquired or constructed with the amount) is not included in the taxpayer's rate base for ratemaking purposes.

(2) Definitions. (i) Regulated public utility has the meaning given such term by section 7701(a)(33), except that such term does not include any utility which is not required to provide water or sewerage disposal services to members of the general public in its service area.

(ii) Water or sewerage disposal facility is defined as tangible property described in section 1231(b) that is used predominately (80% or more) in the trade or business of furnishing water or sewerage disposal services.

(b) Contribution in aid of construction. *(1) In general.* For purposes of section 118(c) and this section, the term contribution in aid of construction means any amount of money or other property contributed to a regulated public utility that provides water or sewerage disposal services to the extent that the purpose of the contribution is to provide for the expansion, improvement, or replacement of the utility's water or sewerage disposal facilities.

(2) Advances. A contribution in aid of construction may include an amount of money or other property contributed to a regulated public utility for a water or sewerage disposal facility subject to a contingent obligation to repay the amount, in whole or in part, to the contributor (commonly referred to as an advance). For example, an amount received by a utility from a developer to construct a water facility pursuant to an agreement under which the utility will pay the developer a percentage of the receipts from the facility over a fixed period may constitute a contribution in aid of construction. Whether an advance is a contribution or a loan is determined under general principles of federal tax law based on all the facts and circumstances. For the treatment of any amount of a contribution in aid of construction that is repaid by the utility to the contributor, see paragraphs (c)(2)(ii) and (d)(2) of this section.

(3) Customer connection fee. (i) In general. Except as provided in paragraph (b)(3)(ii) of this section, a customer connection fee is not a contribution in aid of construction under this paragraph (b) and generally is includible in income. The term customer connection fee includes any amount of money or other property transferred to the utility representing the cost of installing a connection or service line (including the cost of meters and piping) from the utility's main water or sewer lines to the line owned by the customer or potential customer. A customer connection fee also includes any amount paid as a service charge for starting or stopping service.

(ii) Exceptions. (A) Multiple customers. Money or other property contributed for a connection or service line from the utility's main line to the customer's or the potential customer's line is not a customer connection fee if the connection or service line serves, or is designed to serve, more than one customer. For example, a contribution for a split service line that is designed to serve two customers is not a customer connection fee. On the other hand, if a water or sewerage disposal utility treats an apartment or office building as one utility customer, then the cost of installing a connection or service line from the utility's main water or sewer lines serving that single customer is a customer connection fee.

(B) Fire protection services. Money or other property contributed for public and private fire protection services is not a customer connection fee.

(4) Reimbursement for a facility previously placed in service. (i) In general. If a water or sewerage disposal facility is placed in service by the utility before an amount is contributed to the utility, the contribution is not a contribution in aid of construction under this paragraph (b) with respect to the cost of the facility unless, no later than 8½ months after the close of the taxable year in which the facility was placed in service, there is an agreement, binding under local law, that the utility is to receive the amount as reimbursement for the cost of acquiring or constructing the facility. An order or tariff, binding under local law, that is issued or approved by the applicable public utility commission requiring current or prospective utility customers to reimburse the utility for the cost of acquiring or constructing the facility, is a binding agreement for purposes of the preceding sentence. If an agreement exists, the basis of the facility must be reduced by the amount of the expected contributions. Appropriate adjustments must be made if actual contributions differ from expected contributions.

(ii) Example. The application of paragraph (b)(4)(i) of this section is illustrated by the following example:

Example. M, a calendar year regulated public utility that provides water services, spent $1,000,000 for the construction of a water facility that can serve 200 customers. M placed the facility in service in 2000. In June 2001, the public utility commission that regulates M approves a tariff requiring new customers to reimburse M for the cost of constructing the facility by paying a service availability charge of $5,000 per lot. Pursuant to the tariff, M expects to receive reimbursements for the cost of the facility of $100,000 per year for the years 2001 through 2010. The reimbursements are contributions in aid of construction under paragraph (b) of this section because no later than 8½ months after the close of the taxable year in which the facility was placed in service there was a tariff, binding under local law, approved by the public utility commission requiring new customers to reimburse the utility for the cost of constructing the facility. The basis of the $1,000,000 facility is zero because the expected contributions equal the cost of the facility.

(5) Classification by ratemaking authority. The fact that the applicable ratemaking authority classifies any money or other property received by a utility as a contribution in aid of construction is not conclusive as to its treatment under this paragraph (b).

(c) Expenditure rule. *(1) In general.* An amount satisfies the expenditure rule of section 118(c)(2) if the amount is expended for the acquisition or construction of property described in section 118(c)(2)(A), the amount is paid or incurred before the end of the second taxable year after the taxable year in which the amount was received as required by section 118(c)(2)(B), and accurate records are kept of contributions and expenditures as provided in section 118(c)(2)(C).

(2) Excess amount. (i) Includible in the utility's income. An amount received by a utility as a contribution in aid of construction that is not expended for the acquisition or construction of water or sewerage disposal facilities as required by paragraph (c)(1) of this section (the excess amount) is not a contribution to the capital of the taxpayer under paragraph (a) of this section. Except as provided in paragraph (c)(2)(ii) of this section, such excess amount is includible in the utility's income in the taxable year in which the amount was received.

(ii) Repayment of excess amount. If the excess amount described in paragraph (c)(2)(i) of this section is repaid, in whole or in part, either—

(A) Before the end of the time period described in paragraph (c)(1) of this section, the repayment amount is not includible in the utility's income; or

(B) After the end of the time period described in paragraph (c)(1) of this section, the repayment amount may be deducted by the utility in the taxable year in which it is paid or incurred to the extent such amount was included in income.

(3) Example. The application of this paragraph (c) is illustrated by the following example:

Example. M, a calendar year regulated public utility that provides water services, received a $1,000,000 contribution in aid of construction in 2000 for the purpose of constructing a water facility. To the extent that the $1,000,000 exceeded the actual cost of the facility, the contribution was subject to being returned. In 2001, M built the facility at a cost of $700,000 and returned $200,000 to the contributor. As of the end of 2002, M had not returned the remaining $100,000. Assuming accurate records are kept, the requirement under section 118(c)(2) is satisfied for $700,000 of the contribution. Because $200,000 of the contribution was returned within the time period during which qualifying expenditures could be made, this amount is not includible in M's income. However, the remaining $100,000 is includible in M's income for its 2000 taxable year (the taxable year in which the amount was received) because the amount was neither spent nor repaid during the prescribed time period. To the extent M repays the remaining $100,000 after year 2002, M would be entitled to a deduction in the year such repayment is paid or incurred.

(d) Adjusted basis. *(1) Exclusion from basis.* Except for a repayment described in paragraph (d)(2) of this section, to the extent that a water or sewerage disposal facility is acquired or constructed with an amount received as a contribution to the capital of the taxpayer under paragraph (a) of this section, the basis of the facility is reduced by the amount of the contribution. To the extent the water or sewerage disposal facility is acquired as a contribution to the capital of the taxpayer under paragraph (a) of this section, the basis of the contributed facility is zero.

(2) Repayment of contribution. If a contribution to the capital of the taxpayer under paragraph (a) of this section is repaid to the contributor, either in whole or in part, then the repayment amount is a capital expenditure in the taxable year in which it is paid or incurred, resulting in an increase in the property's adjusted basis in such year. Capital expenditures allocated to depreciable property under paragraph (d)(3) of this section may be depreciated over the remaining recovery period for that property.

(3) Allocation of contributions. An amount treated as a capital expenditure under this paragraph (d) is to be allocated proportionately to the adjusted basis of each property acquired or constructed with the contribution based on the relative cost of such property.

(4) Example. The application of this paragraph (d) is illustrated by the following example:

Example. A, a calendar year regulated public utility that provides water services, received a $1,000,000 contribution in aid of construction in 2000 as an advance from B, a developer, for the purpose of constructing a water facility. To the extent that the $1,000,000 exceeds the actual cost of the facility, the contribution is subject to being returned. Under the terms of the advance, A agrees to pay to B a percentage of the receipts from the facility over a fixed period, but limited to the cost of the facility. In 2001, A builds the facility at a cost of $700,000 and returns $300,000 to B. In 2002, A pays $20,000 to B out of the receipts from the facility. Assuming accurate records are kept, the $700,000 advance is a contribution to the capital of A under paragraph (a) of this section and is excludable from A's income. The basis of the $700,000 facility constructed with this contribution to capital is zero. The $300,000 excess amount is not a contribution to the capital of A under paragraph (a) of this section because it does not meet the expenditure rule described in paragraph (c)(1) of this section. However, this excess amount is not includible in A's income pursuant to paragraph (c)(2)(ii) of this section since the amount is repaid to B within the required time period. The repayment of the $300,000 excess amount to B in 2001 is not treated as a capital expenditure by A. The $20,000 payment to B in 2002 is treated as a capital expenditure by A in 2002 resulting in an increase in the adjusted basis of the water facility from zero to $20,000.

(e) Statute of limitations. *(1) Extension of statute of limitations.* Under section 118(d)(1), the statutory period for assessment of any deficiency attributable to a contribution to capital under paragraph (a) of this section does not expire before the expiration of 3 years after the date the taxpayer notifies the Secretary in the time and manner prescribed in paragraph (e)(2) of this section.

(2) Time and manner of notification. Notification is made by attaching a statement to the taxpayer's federal income tax return for the taxable year in which any of the reportable items in paragraphs (e)(2)(i) through (iii) of this section occur. The statement must contain the taxpayer's name, address, employer identification number, taxable year, and the following information with respect to contributions of property other than water or sewerage disposal facilities that are subject to the expenditure rule described in paragraph (c) of this section—

(i) The amount of contributions in aid of construction expended during the taxable year for property described in section 118(c)(2)(A) (qualified property) as required under paragraph (c)(1) of this section, identified by taxable year in which the contributions were received;

(ii) The amount of contributions in aid of construction that the taxpayer does not intend to expend for qualified property as required under paragraph (c)(1) of this section, identified by taxable year in which the contributions were received; and

(iii) The amount of contributions in aid of construction that the taxpayer failed to expend for qualified property as required under paragraph (c)(1) of this section, identified by taxable year in which the contributions were received.

(f) Effective date. This section is applicable for any money or other property received by a regulated public utility that provides water or sewerage disposal services on or after January 11, 2001.

T.D. 8936, 1/10/2001.

§ 1.119-1 Meals and lodging furnished for the convenience of the employer.

Caution: The Treasury has not yet amended Reg § 1.119-1 to reflect changes made by P.L. 100-647, P.L. 99-514.

(a) Meals. *(1) In general.* The value of meals furnished to an employee by his employer shall be excluded from the employee's gross income if two tests are met: (i) The meals are furnished on the business premises of the employer, and (ii) the meals are furnished for the convenience of the employer. The question of whether meals are furnished for the convenience of the employer is one of fact to be determined by analysis of all the facts and circumstances in each case. If the tests described in subdivisions (i) and (ii) of this subparagraph are met, the exclusion shall apply irrespective of whether under an employment contract or a statute fixing the terms of employment such meals are furnished as compensation.

(2) Meals furnished without a charge. (i) Meals furnished by an employer without charge to the employee will be regarded as furnished for the convenience of the employer if such meals are furnished for a substantial noncompensatory business reason of the employer. If an employer furnishes meals as a means of providing additional compensation to his employee (and not for a substantial noncompensatory business reason of the employer), the meals so furnished will not be regarded as furnished for the convenience of the employer. Conversely, if the employer furnishes meals to his employee for a substantial noncompensatory business reason, the meals so furnished will be regarded as furnished for the convenience of the employer, even though such meals are also furnished for a compensatory reason. In determining the reason of an employer for furnishing meals, the mere declaration that meals are furnished for a noncompensatory business reason is not sufficient to prove that meals are furnished for the convenience of the employer, but such determination will be based upon an examination of all the surrounding facts and circumstances. In subdivision (ii) of this subparagraph, there are set forth some of the substantial noncompensatory business reasons which occur frequently and which justify the conclusion that meals furnished for such a reason are furnished for the convenience of the employer. In subdivision (iii) of this subparagraph, there are set forth some of the business reasons which are considered to be compensatory and which, in the absence of a substantial noncompensatory business reason, justify the conclusion that meals furnished for such a reason are not furnished for the convenience of the employer. Generally, meals furnished before or after the working hours of the employee will not be regarded as furnished for the convenience of the employer, but see subdivision (ii)(d) and (f) of this subparagraph for some exceptions to this general rule. Meals furnished on nonworking days do not qualify for the exclusion under section 119. If the employee is required to occupy living quarters on the business premises of his employer as a condition of his employment (as defined in paragraph (b) of this section), the exclusion applies to the value of any meal furnished without charge to the employee on such premises.

(ii) (a) Meals will be regarded as furnished for a substantial noncompensatory business reason of the employer when the meals are furnished to the employee during his working hours to have the employee available for emergency call during his meal period. In order to demonstrate that meals are furnished to the employee to have the employee available for emergency call during the meal period, it must be shown that emergencies have actually occurred, or can reasonably be expected to occur, in the employer's business which have resulted, or will result, in the employer calling on the employee to perform his job during his meal period.

(b) Meals will be regarded as furnished for a substantial noncompensatory business reason of the employer when the meals are furnished to the employee during his working hours because the employer's business is such that the employee must be restricted to a short meal period, such as 30 or 45 minutes, and because the employee could not be expected to eat elsewhere in such a short meal period. For example, meals may qualify under this subdivision when the employer is engaged in a business in which the peak work load occurs during the normal lunch hours. However, meals cannot qualify under this subdivision (b) when the reason for restricting the time of the meal period is so that the employee can be let off earlier in the day.

(c) Meals will be regarded as furnished for a substantial noncompensatory business reason of the employer when the meals are furnished to the employee during his working hours because the employee could not otherwise secure proper meals within a reasonable meal period. For example, meals may qualify under this subdivision (c) when there are insufficient eating facilities in the vicinity of the employer's premises.

(d) A meal furnished to a restaurant employee or other food service employee for each meal period in which the employee works will be regarded as furnished for a substantial noncompensatory business reason of the employer, irrespective of whether the meal is furnished during, immediately before, or immediately after the working hours of the employee.

(e) If the employer furnishes meals to employees at a place of business and the reason for furnishing the meals to each of substantially all of the employees who are furnished the meals is a substantial noncompensatory business reason of the employer, the meals furnished to each other employee will also be regarded as furnished for a substantial noncompensatory business reason of the employer.

(f) If an employer would have furnished a meal to an employee during his working hours for a substantial noncompensatory business reason, a meal furnished to such an employee immediately after his working hours because his duties prevented him from obtaining a meal during his working hours will be regarded as furnished for a substantial noncompensatory business reason.

(iii) Meals will be regarded as furnished for a compensatory business reason of the employer when the meals are furnished to the employee to promote the morale or goodwill of the employee, or to attract prospective employees.

(3) Meals furnished with a charge. (i) If an employer provides meals which an employee may or may not purchase, the meals will not be regarded as furnished for the convenience of the employer. Thus, meals for which a charge is made by the employer will not be regarded as furnished for the convenience of the employer if the employee has a choice of accepting the meals and paying for them or of not paying for them and providing his meals in another manner.

(ii) If an employer furnishes an employee meals for which the employee is charged an unvarying amount (for example, by subtraction from his stated compensation) irrespective of whether he accepts the meals, the amount of such flat charge made by the employer for such meals is not, as such, part of the compensation includible in the gross income of the employee; whether the value of the meals so furnished is excludable under section 119 is determined by applying the rules of subparagraph (2) of this paragraph. If meals furnished for an unvarying amount are not furnished for the convenience of the employer in accordance with the rules of subparagraph (2) of this paragraph, the employee shall include in gross income the value of the meals regardless of whether the value exceeds or is less than the amount charged for such meals. In the absence of evidence to the contrary, the value of the meals may be deemed to be equal to the amount charged for them.

(b) Lodging. The value of lodging furnished to an employee by the employer shall be excluded from the employee's gross income if three tests are met:

(1) The lodging is furnished on the business premises of the employer,

(2) The lodging is furnished for the convenience of the employer, and

(3) The employee is required to accept such lodging as a condition of his employment.

The requirement of subparagraph (3) of this paragraph that the employee is required to accept such lodging as a condition of his employment means that he be required to accept the lodging in order to enable him properly to perform the duties of his employment. Lodging will be regarded as furnished to enable the employee properly to perform the duties of his employment when, for example, the lodging is furnished because the employee is required to be available for duty at all times or because the employee could not perform the services required of him unless he is furnished such lodging. If the tests described in subparagraphs (1), (2), and (3) of this paragraph are met, the exclusion shall apply irrespective of whether a charge is made, or whether, under an employment contract or statute fixing the terms of employment, such lodging is furnished as compensation. If the employer furnishes the employee lodging for which the employee is charged an unvarying amount irrespective of whether he accepts the lodging, the amount of the charge made by the employer for such lodging is not, as such, part of the compensation includible in the gross income of the employee; whether the value of the lodging is excludable from gross income under section 119 is determined by applying the other rules of this paragraph. If the tests described in subparagraph (1), (2), and (3) of this paragraph are not met, the employee shall include in gross income the value of the lodging regardless of whether it exceeds or is less than the amount charged. In the absence of evidence to the contrary, the value of the lodging may be deemed to be equal to the amount charged.

(c) Business premises of the employer. *(1) In general.* For purposes of this section, the term "business premises of the employer" generally means the place of employment of the employee. For example, meals and lodging furnished in the employer's home to a domestic servant would constitute meals and lodging furnished on the business premises of the employer. Similarly, meals furnished to cowhands while herding their employer's cattle on leased land would be regarded as furnished on the business premises of the employer.

(2) Certain camps. For taxable years beginning after December 31, 1981, in the case of an individual who is furnished lodging by or on behalf of his employer in a camp (as defined in paragraph (d) of this section) in a foreign country (as defined in § 1.911-2(h)), the camp shall be considered to be part of the business premises of the employer.

(d) Camp defined. *(1) In general.* For the purposes of paragraph (c)(2) of this section, a camp is lodging that is all of the following:

(i) Provided by or on behalf of the employer for the convenience of the employer because the place at which the employee renders services is in a remote area where satisfactory housing is not available to the employee on the open market within a reasonable commuting distance of that place;

(ii) Located, as near as practicable, in the vicinity of the place at which the employee renders services; and

(iii) Furnished in a common area or enclave which is not available to the general public for lodging or accommodations and which normally accommodates ten or more employees.

(2) Satisfactory housing. For purposes of paragraph (d)(1)(i) of this section, facts and circumstances that may be relevant in determining whether housing available to the employee is satisfactory include, but are not limited to, the size and condition of living space and the availability and quality of utilities such as water, sewers or other waste disposal facilities, electricity, or heat. The general environment in which housing is located (e.g. climate, prevalence of insects, etc.) does not of itself make housing unsatisfactory. The general environment is relevant, however, if housing is inadequate to protect the occupants from environmental conditions. The individual employee's income level is not relevant in determining whether housing is satisfactory; it may, however, be relevant in determining whether satisfactory housing is available to the employee (see paragraph (d)(3)(i)(B) of this section).

(3) Availability of satisfactory housing. (i) Facts and circumstances. For purposes, facts and circumstances to be considered in determining whether satisfactory housing is available to the employee on the open market include but are not limited to:

(A) The number of housing units available on the open market in relation to the number of housing units required for the employer's employees;

(B) The cost of housing available on the open market;

(C) The quality of housing available on the open market; and

(D) The presence of warfare or civil insurrection within the area where housing would be available which would subject U.S. citizens to unusual risk of personal harm or property loss.

(ii) Presumptions. Satisfactory housing will generally be considered to be unavailable to the employee on the open market if either of the following conditions is satisfied:

(A) The foreign government requires the employer to provide housing for its employees other than housing available on the open market; or

(B) An unrelated person awarding work to the employer requires that the employer's employees occupy housing specified by such unrelated person.

The condition of either paragraph (d)(3)(ii)(A) or (B) of this section is not satisfied if the requirement described therein and imposed either by a foreign government or unrelated person applies primarily to U.S. employers and not to a significant number of third country employers or applies primarily to employers of U.S. employees and not to a significant number of employers of third country employees.

(4) Reasonable commuting distance. For purposes of paragraph (d)(1)(i) of this section, in determining whether a commuting distance is reasonable, the accessibility of the place at which the employee renders services due to geographic factors, the quality of the roads, the customarily available transportation, and the usual travel time (at the time of day such travel would be required) to the place at which the employee renders services shall be taken into account.

(5) Common area or enclave. A cluster of housing units does not satisfy paragraph (d)(1)(iii) of this section if it is adjacent to or surrounded by substantially similar housing available to the general public. Two or more common areas or enclaves that house employees who work on the same project (for example, a highway project) are considered to be one common area or enclave in determining whether they normally accommodate ten or more employees.

(e) Rules. The exclusion provided by section 119 applies only to meals and lodging furnished in kind by or on behalf of an employer to his employee. If the employee has an option to receive additional compensation in lieu of meal or lodging in kind, the value of such meals and lodging is not excludable from gross income under section 119. However, the mere fact that an employee, at his option, may decline to accept meals tendered in kind will not of itself require inclusion of the value thereof in gross income. Cash allowances for meals or lodging received by an employee are includible in gross income to the extent that such allowances constitute compensation.

(f) Examples. The provisions of section 119 may be illustrated by the following examples:

Example (1). A waitress who works from 7 a.m. to 4 p.m. is furnished without charge two meals a work day. The employer encourages the waitress to have her breakfast on his business premises before starting work, but does not require her to have breakfast there. She is required, however, to have her lunch on such premises. Since the waitress is a food service employee and works during the normal breakfast and lunch periods, the waitress is permitted to exclude from her gross income both the value of the breakfast and the value of the lunch.

Example (2). The waitress in example (1) is allowed to have meals on the employer's premises without charge on her days off. The waitress is not permitted to exclude the value of such meals from her gross income.

Example (3). A bank teller who works from 9 a.m. to 5 p.m. is furnished his lunch without charge in a cafeteria which the bank maintains on its premises. The bank furnishes the teller such meals in order to limit his lunch period to 30 minutes since the bank's peak work load occurs during the normal lunch period. If the teller had to obtain his lunch elsewhere, it would take him considerably longer than 30 minutes for lunch, and the bank strictly enforces the 30-minute time limit. The bank teller may exclude from his gross income the value of such meals obtained in the bank cafeteria.

Example (4). Assume the same facts as in example (3), except that the bank charges the bank teller an unvarying rate per meal regardless of whether he eats in the cafeteria. The bank teller is not required to include in gross income such flat amount charged as part of his compensation, and he is entitled to exclude from his gross income the value of the meals he receives for such flat charge.

Example (5). A Civil Service employee of a State is employed at an institution and is required by his employer to be available for duty at all times. The employer furnishes the employee with meals and lodging at the institution without charge. Under the applicable State statute, his meals and lodging are regarded as part of the employee's compensation. The employee would nevertheless be entitled to exclude the value of such meals and lodging from his gross income.

Example (6). An employee of an institution is given the choice of residing at the institution free of charge, or of residing elsewhere and receiving a cash allowance in addition to his regular salary. If he elects to reside at the institution, the value to the employee of the lodging furnished by the employer will be includible in the employee's gross income because his residence at the institution is not required in order for him to perform properly the duties of his employment.

Example (7). A construction worker is employed at a construction project at a remote job site in Alaska. Due to the inaccessibility of facilities for the employees who are working at the job site to obtain food and lodging and the prevailing weather conditions, the employer is required to furnish meals and lodging to the employee at the camp site in order to carry on the construction project. The employee is required to pay $40 a week for the meals and lodging. The weekly charge of $40 is not, as such, part of the compensation includible in the gross income of the employee, and under paragraphs (a) and (b) of this section the value of the meals and lodging is excludable from his gross income.

Example (8). A manufacturing company provides a cafeteria on its premises at which its employees can purchase their lunch. There is no other eating facility located near the company's premises, but the employee can furnish his own meal by bringing his lunch. The amount of compensation which any employee is required to include in gross income is not reduced by the amount charged for the meals, and the meals are not considered to be furnished for the convenience of the employer.

Example (9). A hospital maintains a cafeteria on its premises where all of its 230 employees may obtain a meal during their working hours. No charge is made for these meals. The hospital furnishes such meals in order to have each of 210 of the employees available for any emergencies that may occur, and it is shown that each such employee is at times called upon to perform services during his meal period. Although the hospital does not require such employees to remain on the premises during meal periods, they rarely leave the hospital during their meal period. Since the hospital furnishes meals to each of substantially all of its employees in order to have each of them available for emergency call during his meal period, all of the hospital employees who obtain their meals in the hospital cafeteria may exclude from their gross income the value of such meals.

T.D. 6220, 12/28/56, amend T.D. 6745, 7/8/64, T.D. 8006, 1/17/85.

§ 1.120-1 Statutory subsistence allowance received by police. [Repealed provision]

(a) Section 120 excludes from the gross income of an individual employed as a police official by a State, Territory, or possession of the United States, by any of their political subdivisions, or by the District of Columbia, any amount received as a statutory subsistence allowance to the extent that such allowance does not exceed $5 per day. For purposes of this section, the term "statutory subsistence allowance" means an amount which is designated as a subsistence allowance under the laws of a State, a Territory, or a possession of the United States, any political subdivision of any of the foregoing, or the District of Columbia and which is paid to an individual who is employed as a police official of such governmental unit. A subsistence allowance paid to a police official by any of the foregoing governmental units which is not so provided by statute may not be excluded from gross income under the provisions of section 120. The term "police official" includes an employee of any of the foregoing governmental units who has police duties, such as a sheriff, a detective, a policeman, or a State police trooper, however designated.

(b) The exclusion provided by section 120 is to be computed on a daily basis, that is, for each day for which the statutory allowance is paid. If the statute providing the allowance does not specify the daily amount of such allowance, the allowance shall be converted to a daily basis for the purpose of applying the limitation provided herein. For example, if a State statute provides for a weekly subsistence allowance, the daily amount is to be determined by dividing the weekly amount by the number of days for which the allowance is paid. Thus, if a State trooper receives a weekly statutory subsistence allowance of $40 for 5 days of the week, the daily amount would be $8, that is, $40 divided by 5. However, for purposes of this section, only $5 per day may be excluded, or $25 on a weekly basis.

(c) Expenses in respect of which the allowance under section 120 is paid may not be deducted under any provision of the income tax laws except to the extent that (1) such expenses exceed the amount of the exclusion, and (2) the excess is otherwise allowable as a deduction. For example, if a State statute provides a subsistence allowance of $3 per day and the taxpayer, a State trooper, incurs expenditures of $4.50 for meals while away from home overnight on official police duties only $3 would be excludable under this section. Expenses relating to such exclusion ($3) may not be deducted under any provision of the income tax laws. However, the remaining $1.50 may be an allowable deduction under section 162 as traveling expenses while away from home in the performance of official duties. See § 1.162-2.

(d) In the case of taxable years ending after September 30, 1958, section 120 and this section do not apply to amounts received as a statutory subsistence allowance for any day after September 30, 1958.

T.D. 6220, 12/28/56, amend T.D. 6318, 9/26/58.

PARAGRAPH 1. Section 1.120-1, relating to statutory subsistence allowances received by police, is deleted.

Proposed § 1.120-1 [Deleted] [*For Preamble, see ¶ 150,581*]

Proposed § 1.120-1 Amounts received under a qualified group legal services plan. [*For Preamble, see ¶ 150,581*]

Caution: The Treasury has not yet amended Reg § 1.120-2 to reflect changes made by P.L. 102-227, P.L. 101-508, P.L. 101-239, P.L. 100-647, P.L. 99-514.

(a) Exclusion from gross income. The gross income of an employee, or the employee's spouse or dependent, does not include—

(1) Amounts contributed by an employer on behalf of the employee, spouse or dependent under a qualifed group legal services plan described in § 1.120-2,

(2) The value of legal services provided the employee, spouse or dependent under the plan, or

(3) Amounts paid to the employee, spouse or dependent under the plan as reimbursement for the cost of personal legal services provided to the employee, spouse or dependent.

(b) Definitions. For rules relating to the meaning of the terms "employee," "employer," "spouse," and "dependent" see paragraph (d)(3) and (4) and paragraph (i) of § 1.120-2.

(c) Effective date. This section is effective with respect to employer contributions made on behalf of, and legal services provided to, an employee, spouse or dependent on or after the first day of the period of plan qualification (as determined under § 1.120-3(d)) and in taxable years of the employee, spouse or dependent beginning after December 31, 1976, and ending before January 1, 1982.

Proposed § 1.120-2 Qualified group legal services plan. [*For Preamble, see ¶ 150,581*]

(a) In general. In general, a qualified group legal services plan is a plan established and maintained by an employer under which the employer provides employees, or their spouses or dependents, personal legal services by preparing, or providing in advance for, all or part of the legal fees for the services. To be a qualified plan, the plan must satisfy the requirements described in paragraphs (b) through (h) of this section and be recognized as a qualified plan by the Internal Revenue Service. Section 1.120-3 provides rules under which a plan must apply to the Internal Revenue Service for recognition as a qualified plan.

(b) Separate written plan. The plan must be a separate written plan of the employer. For purposes of this section—

(1) Plan. The term "plan" implies a permanent as distinguished from a temporary program. Thus, although the employer may reserve the right to change or terminate the plan, and to discontinue contributions thereunder, the abandonment of the plan for any reason other than a business necessity soon after it has taken effect will be evidence that the plan from its inception was not a *bona fide* plan for the benefit of employees generally (see paragraph (d) of this section). Such evidence will be given special weight if, for example, a plan is abandoned soon after extensive benefits are provided to persons with respect to whom discrimination in plan benefits is prohibited (see paragraph (e) of this section).

(2) Separate plan. The requirement that the plan be a separate plan means that the plan may not provide benefits which are not personal legal services within the meaning of paragraph (c) of this section. For example, the requirement for a separate plan is not satisfied if personal legal services are provided under an employee benefit plan that also provides pension, disability, life insurance, medical or other such non-legal benefits. The requirement for a separate plan does not, however, preclude a single plan from being adopted by more than one employer.

(c) Personal legal services. *(1) In general.* In general, benefits under the plan must consist of, or be provided with respect to, only personal legal services that are specified in the plan. The plan must specifically prohibit a diversion or use of any funds of the plan for purposes other than the providing of personal legal services for the participants. In general, a personal legal service is a legal service (within the meaning of subparagraph (3) of this paragraph) provided to a participant employee, spouse or dependent which is not directly connected with or pertaining to—

(i) A trade or business of the employee, spouse or dependent,

(ii) The management, conservation or preservation of property held by the employee, spouse or dependent for the production of income, or

(iii) The production or collection of income by the employee, spouse or dependent.

(2) Certain personal legal services. Notwithstanding subparagraph (1)(ii) and (iii) of this paragraph, the following (if legal services within the meaning of subparagraph (3)) are considered personal legal services—

(i) A legal service provided to a participant with respect to securing, increasing or collecting alimony under a decree of divorce (or payments in lieu of alimony) or the division or redivision of community property under the community property laws of a State,

(ii) A legal service provided to a participant as heir or legatee of a decedent, or as beneficiary under a testamentary trust, in protecting or asserting rights to property of a decedent, or

(iii) A legal service provided to a participant with respect to the participant's claim for damages, other than compensatory damages, for personal injury.

(3) Legal services. (i) Services of a lawyer. In general, a legal service is a service performed by a lawyer if the performing of the service constitutes the practice of law.

(ii) Services of a person not a lawyer. A legal service may include a service performed by a person who is not a lawyer, if the service is performed under the direction or control of a lawyer, in connection with a legal service (within the meaning of subdivision (i)) performed by the lawyer, and the fee for the service is included in the legal fee of the lawyer. Examples of services to which this subdivision (ii) may apply are the services of an accountant, a researcher, a paralegal, a law clerk, an investigator or a searcher of title to real property.

(iii) Court fees. Amounts payable to a court in connection with the presentation, litigation or appeal from a matter before a court is considered the cost of a legal service. For example, benefits under the plan may be provided with respect to a court filing fee, a fee for service of summons or other process, the cost of a transcript of trial or the posting of bail bond.

(iv) Other fees or charges. An amount payable to a competent governmental authority (for example, the United States, a State or any subdivision thereof) is considered the cost of a legal service, if the amount is payable with respect to the filing or registration of a legal document (for example, a deed or will). However, any amount payable directly or indirectly to a governmental authority is not the cost of a legal service, if the amount is in the nature of a tax. For example, although a plan may provide for payment of an amount payable to a county for the filing or registration of a deed to real property, a plan may not provide for payment of an amount in the nature of a tax on the transfer of title to real property.

(4) Limited initial consultation. A plan is not other than a qualified plan merely because in connection with providing personal legal services, the plan provides a specified "limited initial consultation" benefit without restricting the benefit to personal legal services. An "initial consultation" is a consultation, the purpose of which is to determine whether a plan participant is in need of a personal legal service and, if so, whether the required personal legal service may be provided under the plan. An initial consultation must not include document preparation or review, or representation of the participant. An initial consultation benefit is "limited", if under the plan it is limited either in time (e.g., no more than 4 hours of initial consultation during any year) or number (e.g., no more than 4 initial consultations during any year).

(d) Exclusive benefit. *(1) In general.* The plan must benefit only employees of the employer, including individuals who are employees within the meaning of paragraph (i)(1) of this section, or the spouses or dependents of employees.

(2) Plans to which more than one employer contributes. In the case of a plan to which more than one employer contributes, in determining whether the plan is for the exclusive benefit of an employer's employees, or their spouses or dependents, the employees of any employer who maintains the plan are considered the employees of each employer who maintains the plan.

(3) Spouses of employees. In general, for purposes of determining whether a plan is for the exclusive benefit of an employer's employees, or their spouses or dependents, the determination of whether an individual is a spouse of an employee is made at the time the legal services are provided to the individual. The term "spouse" includes a surviving spouse of a deceased employee. Although, in general, the term "spouse" does not include a person legally separated from an employee under a decree of divorce or separate maintenance, a legal service provided to an employee's former spouse after the issuing of a decree of divorce, annulment or separate maintenance from the employee is considered a service provided to the spouse of an employee, if the service relates to the divorce, annulment or separation. For purposes of this section and § 1.120-1, the term "spouse" includes an individual to whom benefits may be provided under this subparagraph.

(4) Dependents of employees. For purposes of determining whether a plan is for the exclusive benefit of an employer's employees, or their spouses or dependents, benefits provided to the following individuals are considered benefits provided to a dependent of an employee:

(i) An individual who is a dependent of an employee within the meaning of section 152 for the taxable year of the employee within which the legal services are provided to the individual;

(ii) An individual who is described in paragraph (h)(2) of this section (relating to certain surviving dependents) at the time the legal services are provided to the individual; or

(iii) An individual who is a dependent of an employee within the meaning of section 152 for the taxable year of the employee ending on the date of the employee's death, under age 21 on the date of the employee's death, and under age 21 at the time the legal services are provided to the individual.

For purposes of this section and § 1.120-1, the term "dependent" means an individual to whom benefits may be provided under this subparagraph.

(5) Estates of employees. A plan is for the exclusive benefit of the employer's employees, or their spouses or dependents, notwithstanding that the plan provides benefits to the personal representative of a deceased employee, or spouse or dependent, with respect to the estate of the deceased.

(e) Prohibited discrimination. *(1) In general.* The plan must benefit the employer's employees generally. Among those benefited may be employees who are officers, shareholders, self-employed or highly compensated. A plan is not for the benefit of employees generally, however, if the plan discriminates in favor of employees described in the preceding sentence, or their spouses or dependents, in eligibility requirements (see subparagraph (2) of this paragraph) or in contributions or benefits (see subparagraph (3) of this paragraph).

(2) Eligibility to participate. A plan need not provide benefits for all employees (or their spouses or dependent). A plan must, however, benefit those employees (or their spouses or dependents) who qualify under a classification of employees set up by the employer which is found by the Internal Revenue Service not to discriminate in favor of employees who are officers, shareholders, self-employed or highly compensated, or their spouses or dependents. In general, this determination shall be made by applying the same standards as are applied under section 410(b)(1)(B) (relating to qualified pension, profit-sharing and stock bonus plans), without regard to section 401(a)(5). For purposes of making this determination, there shall be excluded from consideration employees not covered by the plan who are included in a unit of employees covered by an agreement which the Secretary of Labor finds to be a collective bargaining agreement between employee representatives and one or more employers, if the Internal Revenue Service finds that group legal services plan benefits were the subject of good faith bargaining between the employee representatives and the employer or employers. For purposes of determining whether such bargaining occurred, it is not material that the employees are not covered by another plan or that the employer's present plan was not considered in the bargaining.

(3) Contributions and benefits. (i) In general. Employer contributions under the plan or benefits provided under the plan must not discriminate in favor of employees who are officers, shareholders, self-employed or highly compensated, or their spouses or dependents, as against other employees, or their spouses or dependents, covered by the plan. This does not mean that contributions or benefits may not vary. Variations in contributions or benefits may be provided so long as the plan, viewed as a whole for the benefit of employees in general, with all its attendant circumstances, does not discriminate in favor of those with respect to whom discrimination is prohibited. Thus, contributions or benefits which vary by reason of a formula which takes into account years of service with the employer, or other factors, are not prohibited unless those factors discriminate in favor of employees who are officers, shareholders, self-employed or highly compensated, or their spouses or dependents. Under this subparagraph (3), if a plan covers employees who are highly compensated, and benefits under the plan uniformly increase as compensation increases, the plan is not a qualified plan.

(ii) Relative utilization of plan benefits. Not only must a plan not discriminate on its face in employer contributions or plan benefits in favor of employees who are officers, shareholders, self-employed or highly compensated, or their spouses or dependents, the plan also must not discriminate in favor of such employees, or their spouses or dependents, in actual operation. Accordingly, the extent to which such employees, or their spouses or dependents, as a group, utilize plan benefits must be compared to the extent to which all other employees, or their spouses or dependents, as a group, utilize plan benefits. A plan is not other than a qualified plan for a plan year merely because, relative to their number, those employees, or their spouses or dependents, with respect to whom discrimination is prohibited utilize plan benefits to a greater extent than do other employees, or their spouses or dependents. However, a persistent pattern of greater relative utilization of plan benefits by the group of employees who are officers, shareholders, self-employed or highly compensated, or their spouses or dependents, may be evidence that the plan discriminates in favor of such employees and is not for the benefit of employees generally. Such evidence will be considered, together with all other pertinent facts and circumstances, to determine whether the plan improperly discriminates in actual operation.

(f) Contribution limitation. *(1) In general.* Under section 120(c)(3), a plan is a qualified plan for a plan year only if no more than 25% of the amount contributed by the employer under the plan for the plan year is contributed on behalf of the limitation class described in subparagraph (2). A plan satisfies the requirements of section 120(c)(3) for a plan year (as determined under the plan) if either—

(i) The plan satisfies the requirements of subparagraph (3), or

(ii) The percentage determined under subparagraph (4) is 25% or less, and the plan is not other than a qualified plan by reason of subparagraph (5).

(2) Limitation class. The limitation class consists of—

(i) Shareholders. Individuals who, on any day of the plan year, own more than 5% of the total number of shares of outstanding stock of the employer, or

(ii) Owners. In the case of an employer's trade or business which is not incorporated, individuals who on any day of the plan year, own more than 5% of the capital or profits interest in the employer, and

(iii) Spouses and dependents. Individuals who are spouses or dependents of shareholders or owners described in subdivision (i) or (ii).

For purposes of determining stock ownership, the attribution rules described in paragraph (i)(4) of this section apply. The regulations prescribed under section 414(c) are applicable in determining an individual's interest in the capital or profits of an unincorporated trade or business.

(3) Disregarding allocation rules. (i) Plans providing legal services directly. If a plan is one under which legal services are provided directly to a participant, the plan will satisfy the requirements of section 120(c)(3), without regard to the allocation rules described in subparagraphs (4) and (5) of this paragraph, if the plan satisfies the following requirement. The plan must provide and be operated so that no legal service may be provided to a member of the limitation class if to provide the service would cause the fair market value of legal services provided to date during the plan year to members of the limitation class to exceed 25% of the fair market value of the legal services provided under the plan to date during the plan year.

(ii) Plans providing reimbursement for the cost of legal services. If a plan is one under which a participant is reimbursed for the cost of legal services, the plan will satisfy the requirements of section 120(c)(3), without regard to the allocation rules described in subparagraphs (4) and (5) of this paragraph, if the plan satisfies the following requirement. The plan must provide and be operated so that no amount may be paid to a member of the limitation class if the payment would cause amounts paid to date during the plan year to members of the limitation class to exceed 25% of the amounts paid under the plan to date during the plan year.

(iii) Limitation class; special rule. For purposes of this subparagraph (3) an individual is a member of the limitation class only if the individual is a member (within the meaning of subparagraph (2)) on or before the date on which the determination described in subdivision (ii) or (iii) is required to be made.

(iv) Example. The provisions of subdivision (iii) of this subparagraph may be illustrated by the following example:

Example. (A) Plan X is a qualified group legal services plan under which plan participants are reimbursed for the cost of personal legal services specified in the plan. The plan includes a provision satisfying the requirements of subdivision (ii) of this subparagraph. The plan year is the calendar year.

(B) A, an individual, is a participant in Plan X. On March 18, 1981, A is paid an amount under the plan. On June 21, 1981, A purchases shares of stock of the employer maintaining the plan. As a result of the purchase A owns more than 5% of the total number of shares of outstanding stock of the employer. Accordingly, under subparagraph (2) of this paragraph, A is a member of the limitation class for the plan year 1981. On August 14, 1981, A sells the shares of stock purchased on June 21, 1981, and no longer owns more than 5% of the total number of shares of outstanding stock of the employer. On October 9, 1981, A is paid an additional amount under the plan.

(C) For purposes of the determination required by subdivision (ii) of this subparagraph, if the determination is made for a date after March 17, 1981, and before June 21, 1981, the amount paid to A on March 18, 1981, is not considered an amount paid to a member of the limitation class. If the determination is made for a date after June 20, 1981, the amount paid to A on March 18, 1981, is considered an amount paid to a member of the limitation class. With respect to a determination made for a date after October 8, 1981, the amount paid to A on October 9, 1981, is considered an amount paid to a member of the limitation class.

(4) Contribution allocation. (i) Equal benefits. In general, if under a plan the same benefits are made available to each participant, the percentage of the amount contributed by the employer for a plan year that is considered contributed on behalf of the limitation class is equal to the number of participants who are members of the limitation class at any time during the plan year, divided by the number of individuals who are participants in the plan at any time during the plan year.

(ii) Unequal benefits. In general, if under the plan different benefits are made available to different participants or different classes of participants, the percentage of the amount contributed by the employer for a plan year that is considered contributed on behalf of the limitation class is equal to the fair market value (as of the first day of the plan year) of those benefits available under the plan to participants who are members of the limitation class at any time during the plan year, divided by the fair market value (as of the first day of the plan year) of those benefits available under the plan to all individuals who are participants in the plan at any time during the plan year.

(iii) Individual premiums. Notwithstanding subdivision (i) or (ii) of this subparagraph, if benefits are provided under the plan in exchange for the employer's prepayment or payment of a premium, and the amount of the prepayment or premium is determined by taking into account the circumstances of individual participants or classes of participants, the percentage of the amount contributed by the employer for a plan year that is considered contributed on behalf of the limitation class is equal to the sum of the prepayments or premiums paid for the plan year on behalf of participants who are members of the limitation class at any time during the plan year, divided by the sum of the prepayments or premiums paid for the plan year. A prepayment or premium is paid for the plan year if it is paid with respect to legal services provided or made available during the plan year. This subdivision (iii) will apply if, for example, equal benefits are provided each participant under the plan in exchange for the employer's payment of a premium with respect to each participant employee, and the amount of the premium varies, taking into account the employee's income level, the number and ages of the employee's dependents or other such factors.

(5) Relative utilization of plan benefits. (i) Application. The extent to which members of the limitation class, as a class, utilize plan benefits shall be taken into account in determining the percentage of amounts contributed by the employer that is considered contributed on behalf of the limitation class. The rules described in this subparagraph (5) are in addition to those described in subparagraph (4) of this paragraph, and a plan may be other than a qualified plan by reason of the application of this subparagraph (5), notwithstanding that the percentage determined under subparagraph (4) is 25% or less.

(ii) Computation. Under this subparagraph (5), if during any three successive plan years, benefits paid to or with respect to the limitation class (as determined for each plan year) exceed 25% of all benefits paid under the plan during the three years, the plan is not a qualified plan for the next succeeding plan year.

(iii) Reapplication for recognition as a qualified plan. A plan that is not a qualified plan for a plan year by reason of this subparagraph (5), may reapply under § 1.120-3 for recognition as a qualified plan for any plan year following the first plan year for which it is not a qualified plan. A plan so reapplying will be recognized as a qualified plan for any plan year for which recognition is sought only if the plan is a qualified plan under this subparagraph (5) for the first plan year for which such recognition is sought and otherwise satisfies the requirements of section 120 and this section.

(g) Employer contributions. *(1) In general.* Employer contributions under the plan may be made only—

(i) To insurance companies, or to organizations or persons that provide personal legal services, or indemnification against the cost of personal legal services, in exchange for a prepayment or payment of a premium,

(ii) To organizations or trusts described in section 501(c)(20),

(iii) To organizations described in section 501(c) that are permitted by that section to receive payments from an employer for support of a qualified group legal services plan, except that the organization shall pay or credit the contribution to an organization or trust described in section 501(c)(20),

(iv) As prepayment to providers of legal services under the plan, or

(v) A combination of the above.

(2) Prepayment required. For purposes of subparagraph (1)(i) and (iv), employer contributions are considered prepayments or premiums only if a contribution made with respect to benefits reasonably anticipated to be provided under the plan during any month is made on or before the tenth day of the month.

(h) Employee contributions. *(1) In general.* A plan is not a qualified plan if it permits participants to contribute under the plan other than as described in subparagraphs (2) and (3) of this paragraph.

(2) Certain separated employees and surviving spouses and dependents. A plan will not be other than a qualified plan merely because the plan allows—

(i) A separated former employee,

(ii) A surviving spouse of a deceased employee, or

(iii) An individual who is a dependent of an employee within the meaning of section 152 for the taxable year of the employee ending on the date of the death of the employee,

to elect to continue as a participant under the plan on a self-contributory basis for a period not to exceed one year after the separation or death.

(3) Certain employee contributions in lieu of employer contributions. This subparagraph (3) applies with respect to a plan that—

(i) Is maintained pursuant to an agreement that the Secretary of Labor finds to be a collective bargaining agreement between employee representatives and one or more employers, and

(ii) Provides that an employer is required to contribute (or contribute in full) on behalf of a participant employee only if the employee completes a minimum number of hours of service with the employer within a stated period ending on or before the date the contribution is otherwise required to be made by the employer.

Such a plan is not other than a qualified plan merely because it permits a participant employee to contribute under the plan an amount not required to be contributed by the employer because the employee fails to complete the minumum number of hours. However, no amount may be contributed by an employee under this subparagraph (3) unless employer contributions on behalf of participant employees are required to be made monthly or more often, and at least one employer contribution is made on behalf of the employee under the plan before the contribution by the employee is made under the plan. In addition, a plan shall not be a qualified plan for a plan year by reason of this subparagraph (3), if amounts contributed by employees under this subparagraph (3) during the plan year exceed 5% of the total amount contributed under the plan during the plan year.

(i) Definitions. For purposes of this section, § 1.120-1 and § 1.120-3—

(1) Employee. The term "employee" includes—

(i) A retired, disabled or laid-off employee,

(ii) A present employee who is on leave, as, for example, in the Armed Forces of the United States,

(iii) An individual who is self-employed within the meaning of section 401(c)(1), or

(iv) A separated former employee who is covered by the plan by reason of paragraph (h)(2)(i) of this section (relating to employee contributions).

(2) Employer. An individual who owns the entire interest in an unincorporated trade or business is treated as his or her own employer. A partnership is treated as the employer of each partner who is an employee within the meaning of section 401(c)(1).

(3) Officer. An officer is an individual who is an officer within the meaning of regulations prescribed under section 414(c).

(4) Shareholder. The term "shareholder" includes an individual who is a shareholder as determined by the attribution rules under section 1563(d) and (e), without regard to section 1563(e)(3)(C).

(5) Highly compensated. The term "highly compensated" has the same meaning as it does for purposes of section 410(b)(1)(B).

§ 1.120-3 Notice of application for recognition of status of qualified group legal services plan.

(a) In general. In order for a plan to be a qualified group legal services plan for purposes of the exclusion from gross income provided by section 120(a), the plan must give notice to the Internal Revenue Service that it is applying for recognition of its status as a qualified plan. Paragraph (b) of this section describes how the notice is to be filed for the plan. Paragraph (c) of this section describes the action that the Internal Revenue Service will take in response to the notice submitted for the plan. Paragraph (d) of this section describes the period of plan qualification.

(b) Filing of notice. *(1) In general.* A notice of application for recognition of the status of a qualified group legal services plan must be filed with the key district director of internal revenue as described in § 601.201(n). The notice must be filed on Form 1024, Application for Recognition of Exemption Under Section 501(a) or for Determination Under Section 120, with the accompanying Schedule L, and must contain the information required by the form and any accompanying instructions. The form may be filed by either the employer adopting the plan or the person administering the plan. No Form 1024 and Schedule L may be filed for a plan before an employer adopts the plan, or proposes to adopt the plan contingent only upon the recognition of the plan as a qualified plan.

(2) Plans to which more than one employer contributes. In general, for purposes of section 120 the adoption of a plan by an employer constitutes the adoption of a separate plan to which that employer alone contributes, notwithstanding that, in form, the employer purports to adopt a plan with respect to which the employer is one of two or more contributing employers. Accordingly, a separate Schedule L must be filed pursuant to the instructions accompanying Form 1024 for each employer adopting a plan.

(3) Certain collectively bargained plans. Notwithstanding subparagraph (2) of this paragraph, if a plan to which more than one employer contributes is a plan to which this subparagraph (3) applies, the plan is treated as a single plan for purposes of section 120. Accordingly, only one Form 1024 and Schedule L is required to be filed for the plan, regardless of the number of employers originally adopting the plan. In addition, once a Form 1024 and Schedule L is filed, no additional filing is required with respect to an employer who thereafter adopts the plan. In general, this subparagraph (3) applies to any plan that is maintained pursuant to a collective bargaining agreement between employee representatives and more than one employer who is required by the plan instrument or other agreement to contribute to the plan with respect to employees (or their spouses or dependents) participating in the plan. This subparagraph does not apply, however, if all employers required to contribute to the plan are corporations which are members of a controlled group of corporations within the meaning of section 1563(a), determined without regard to section 1563(e)(3)(C). If all employers required to contribute to the plan are corporations which are members of such a controlled group, the filing requirements described in subparagraph (2) of this paragraph

apply, notwithstanding that the plan is maintained pursuant to a collective bargaining agreement.

(c) Internal Revenue Service action on notice of application for recognition. The Internal Revenue Service will issue to the person submitting Form 1024 and Schedule L a ruling or determination letter stating that the plan is or is not a qualified group legal services plan. For general procedural rules, see § 601.201(a) through (n), as that section relates to rulings and determination letters.

(d) Period of plan qualification. *(1) In general.* In the case of a favorable determination, the plan will be considered a qualified group legal services plan. If a Form 1024 and Schedule L required to be filed by or on behalf of an employer is filed before—

(i) The end of the first plan year (as determined under the plan),

(ii) The end of the plan year within which the employer adopts the plan, or

(iii) July 29, 1980, the period of plan qualification with respect to the employer will begin on the date the plan is adopted by the employer (or, if later, January 1, 1977). If the form and schedule are not filed before the latest of the dates described in subdivisions (i), (ii) and (iii), the period of plan qualification with respect to the employer will begin on the date of filing. In any case in which either the Form 1024 or Schedule L filed by or on behalf of an employer is incomplete, the date of filing is the date on which the incomplete form or schedule is filed, if the necessary additional information is provided at the request of the Commissioner within the additional time period allowed by the Commissioner. If the additional information is not provided within the additional time period, allowed, the date of filing is the date on which the additional information is filed. If no separate Form 1024 and Schedule L are required to be filed by or on behalf of an employer (see paragraph (b)(3) of this section), the period of plan qualification with respect to the employer will begin on the date the plan is adopted by the employer (or, if later, January 1, 1977). In any case in which a plan is materially modified to conform to the requirements of section 120, either before or after a Form 1024 and Schedule L are filed, the period of plan qualification will not include any period before the effective date of the modification.

(2) Plans in existence on June 4, 1976. (i) Notwithstanding paragraph (d)(1) of this section, a written group legal services plan providing for employer contributions which was in existence on June 4, 1976, will be considered a qualified group legal services plan for the period January 1, 1977, through April 2, 1977. However, if the plan is maintained pursuant to one or more agreements which were in effect on October 4, 1976, and which the Secretary of Labor finds to be collective bargaining agreements, the period of deemed qualification will extend beyond April 2, 1977, and end on the date on which the last of the collective bargaining agreements relating to the plan terminates. Extensions of a bargaining agreement which are agreed to after October 4, 1976, are to be disregarded. The period of deemed qualification for a plan maintained pursuant to a collective bargaining agreement will not, however, extend beyond December 31, 1981.

(ii) A written group legal services plan will be considered to have been in existence on June 4, 1976, if on or before that date the plan was reduced to writing and adopted by one or more employers. No amounts need have been contributed under the plan as of June 4, 1976.

(iii) Notwithstanding that a plan is a qualified plan for the period of deemed qualification described in this paragraph (d)(2), the rules of paragraphs (c) and (d)(1) of this section still apply with respect to a Form 1024 and Schedule L filed for the plan. For example, if a Form 1024 and Schedule L filed by or on behalf of a employer are filed before the latest of the 3 dates described in paragraph (d)(1) of this section, in the case of a favorable determination the plan will be a qualified plan from the date the plan is adopted by the employer (or, if later, January 1, 1977), and any period of deemed qualification and the period of qualification based upon the favorable determination will overlap. However, in the case of a plan to which this paragraph (d)(2) applies, if a Form 1024 and Schedule L required to be filed by or on behalf of an employer is not filed before the latest of the 3 dates described in paragraph (d)(1) of this section, the following rules shall apply. In general, if Form 1024 and Schedule L are filed before the end of the plan year following the plan year with or within which the plan's period of deemed qualification expires, in the event of a favorable determination the plan will be a qualified plan with respect to the employer beginning on the earlier of the day following the date on which the period of deemed qualification expires or the date on which the Form 1024 and Schedule L are filed. The period of plan qualification with respect to an employer cannot, however, include any period before the employer adopts the plan. If the Form 1024 and Schedule L are not filed before the end of the plan year following the plan year with or within which the plan's period of deemed qualification expires, in the case of a favorable determination the plan will be a qualified plan with respect to an employer from the later of the date of filing or adoption of the plan by the employer. The rules described in paragraph (d)(1) of this section relating to incomplete filings and plan modifications apply with respect to a filing described in this paragraph (d)(2).

(e) Effective date. This section is effective for notices of application for recognition of the status of a qualified group legal services plan filed after May 29, 1980.

T.D. 7696, 4/28/80.

§ 1.121-1 Exclusion of gain from sale or exchange of a principal residence.

(a) In general. Section 121 provides that, under certain circumstances, gross income does not include gain realized on the sale or exchange of property that was owned and used by a taxpayer as the taxpayer's principal residence. Subject to the other provisions of section 121, a taxpayer may exclude gain only if, during the 5-year period ending on the date of the sale or exchange, the taxpayer owned and used the property as the taxpayer's principal residence for periods aggregating 2 years or more.

(b) Residence. *(1) In general.* Whether property is used by the taxpayer as the taxpayer's residence depends upon all the facts and circumstances. A property used by the taxpayer as the taxpayer's residence may include a houseboat, a house trailer, or the house or apartment that the taxpayer is entitled to occupy as a tenant-stockholder in a cooperative housing corporation (as those terms are defined in section 216(b)(1) and (2)). Property used by the taxpayer as the taxpayer's residence does not include personal property that is not a fixture under local law.

(2) Principal residence. In the case of a taxpayer using more than one property as a residence, whether property is used by the taxpayer as the taxpayer's principal residence

depends upon all the facts and circumstances. If a taxpayer alternates between 2 properties, using each as a residence for successive periods of time, the property that the taxpayer uses a majority of the time during the year ordinarily will be considered the taxpayer's principal residence. In addition to the taxpayer's use of the property, relevant factors in determining a taxpayer's principal residence, include, but are not limited to—

(i) The taxpayer's place of employment;

(ii) The principal place of abode of the taxpayer's family members;

(iii) The address listed on the taxpayer's federal and state tax returns, driver's license, automobile registration, and voter registration card;

(iv) The taxpayer's mailing address for bills and correspondence;

(v) The location of the taxpayer's banks; and

(vi) The location of religious organizations and recreational clubs with which the taxpayer is affiliated.

(3) Vacant land. (i) In general. The sale or exchange of vacant land is not a sale or exchange of the taxpayer's principal residence unless—

(A) The vacant land is adjacent to land containing the dwelling unit of the taxpayer's principal residence;

(B) The taxpayer owned and used the vacant land as part of the taxpayer's principal residence;

(C) The taxpayer sells or exchanges the dwelling unit in a sale or exchange that meets the requirements of section 121 within 2 years before or 2 years after the date of the sale or exchange of the vacant land; and

(D) The requirements of section 121 have otherwise been met with respect to the vacant land.

(ii) Limitations. (A) Maximum limitation amount. For purposes of section 121(b)(1) and (2) (relating to the maximum limitation amount of the section 121 exclusion), the sale or exchange of the dwelling unit and the vacant land are treated as one sale or exchange. Therefore, only one maximum limitation amount of $250,000 ($500,000 for certain joint returns) applies to the combined sales or exchanges of vacant land and the dwelling unit. In applying the maximum limitation amount to sales or exchanges that occur in different taxable years, gain from the sale or exchange of the dwelling unit, up to the maximum limitation amount under section 121(b)(1) or (2), is excluded first and each spouse is treated as excluding one-half of the gain from a sale or exchange to which section 121(b)(2)(A) and § 1.121-2(a)(3)(i) (relating to the limitation for certain joint returns) apply.

(B) Sale or exchange of more than one principal residence in 2-year period. If a dwelling unit and vacant land are sold or exchanged in separate transactions that qualify for the section 121 exclusion under this paragraph (b)(3), each of the transactions is disregarded in applying section 121(b)(3) (restricting the application of section 121 to only 1 sale or exchange every 2 years) to the other transactions but is taken into account as a sale or exchange of a principal residence on the date of the transaction in applying section 121(b)(3) to that transaction and the sale or exchange of any other principal residence.

(C) Sale or exchange of vacant land before dwelling unit. If the sale or exchange of the dwelling unit occurs in a later taxable year than the sale or exchange of the vacant land and after the date prescribed by law (including extensions) for the filing of the return for the taxable year of the sale or exchange of the vacant land, any gain from the sale or exchange of the vacant land must be treated as taxable on the taxpayer's return for the taxable year of the sale or exchange of the vacant land. If the taxpayer has reported gain from the sale or exchange of the vacant land as taxable, after satisfying the requirements of this paragraph (b)(3) the taxpayer may claim the section 121 exclusion with regard to the sale or exchange of the vacant land (for any period for which the period of limitation under section 6511 has not expired) by filing an amended return.

(4) Examples. The provisions of this paragraph (b) are illustrated by the following examples:

Example (1). Taxpayer A owns 2 residences, one in New York and one in Florida. From 1999 through 2004, he lives in the New York residence for 7 months and the Florida residence for 5 months of each year. In the absence of facts and circumstances indicating otherwise, the New York residence is A's principal residence. A would be eligible for the section 121 exclusion of gain from the sale or exchange of the New York residence, but not the Florida residence.

Example (2). Taxpayer B owns 2 residences, one in Virginia and one in Maine. During 1999 and 2000, she lives in the Virginia residence. During 2001 and 2002, she lives in the Maine residence. During 2003, she lives in the Virginia residence. B's principal residence during 1999, 2000, and 2003 is the Virginia residence. B's principal residence during 2001 and 2002 is the Maine residence. B would be eligible for the 121 exclusion of gain from the sale or exchange of either residence (but not both) during 2003.

Example (3). In 1991 Taxpayer C buys property consisting of a house and 10 acres that she uses as her principal residence. In May 2005 C sells 8 acres of the land and realizes a gain of $110,000. C does not sell the dwelling unit before the due date for filing C's 2005 return, therefore C is not eligible to exclude the $110,000 of gain. In March 2007 C sells the house and remaining 2 acres realizing a gain of $180,000 from the sale of the house. C may exclude the $180,000 of gain. Because the sale of the 8 acres occurred within 2 years from the date of the sale of the dwelling unit, the sale of the 8 acres is treated as a sale of the taxpayer's principal residence under paragraph (b)(3) of this section. C may file an amended return for 2005 to claim an exclusion for $70,000 ($250,000 - $180,000 gain previously excluded) of the $110,000 gain from the sale of the 8 acres.

Example (4). In 1998 Taxpayer D buys a house and 1 acre that he uses as his principal residence. In 1999 D buys 29 acres adjacent to his house and uses the vacant land as part of his principal residence. In 2003 D sells the house and 1 acre and the 29 acres in 2 separate transactions. D sells the house and 1 acre at a loss of $25,000. D realizes $270,000 of gain from the sale of the 29 acres. D may exclude the $245,000 gain from the 2 sales.

(c) Ownership and use requirements. *(1) In general.* The requirements of ownership and use for periods aggregating 2 years or more may be satisfied by establishing ownership and use for 24 full months or for 730 days (365 x 2). The requirements of ownership and use may be satisfied during nonconcurrent periods if both the ownership and use tests are met during the 5-year period ending on the date of the sale or exchange.

(2) Use. (i) In establishing whether a taxpayer has satisfied the 2-year use requirement, occupancy of the residence is required. However, short temporary absences, such as for vacation or other seasonal absence (although accompanied with rental of the residence), are counted as periods of use.

(ii) Determination of use during periods of out-of-residence care. If a taxpayer has become physically or mentally incapable of self-care and the taxpayer sells or exchanges property that the taxpayer owned and used as the taxpayer's principal residence for periods aggregating at least 1 year during the 5-year period preceding the sale or exchange, the taxpayer is treated as using the property as the taxpayer's principal residence for any period of time during the 5-year period in which the taxpayer owns the property and resides in any facility (including a nursing home) licensed by a State or political subdivision to care for an individual in the taxpayer's condition.

(3) Ownership. (i) Trusts. If a residence is owned by a trust, for the period that a taxpayer is treated under sections 671 through 679 (relating to the treatment of grantors and others as substantial owners) as the owner of the trust or the portion of the trust that includes the residence, the taxpayer will be treated as owning the residence for purposes of satisfying the 2-year ownership requirement of section 121, and the sale or exchange by the trust will be treated as if made by the taxpayer.

(ii) Certain single owner entities. If a residence is owned by an eligible entity (within the meaning of § 301.7701-3(a) of this chapter) that has a single owner and is disregarded for federal tax purposes as an entity separate from its owner under § 301.7701-3 of this chapter, the owner will be treated as owning the residence for purposes of satisfying the 2-year ownership requirement of section 121, and the sale or exchange by the entity will be treated as if made by the owner.

(4) Examples. The provisions of this paragraph (c) are illustrated by the following examples. The examples assume that § 1.121-3 (relating to the reduced maximum exclusion) does not apply to the sale of the property. The examples are as follows:

Example (1). Taxpayer A has owned and used his house as his principal residence since 1986. On January 31, 1998, A moves to another state. A rents his house to tenants from that date until April 18, 2000, when he sells it. A is eligible for the section 121 exclusion because he has owned and used the house as his principal residence for at least 2 of the 5 years preceding the sale.

Example (2). Taxpayer B owns and uses a house as her principal residence from 1986 to the end of 1997. On January 4, 1998, B moves to another state and ceases to use the house. B's son moves into the house in March 1999 and uses the residence until it is sold on July 1, 2001. B may not exclude gain from the sale under section 121 because she did not use the property as her principal residence for at least 2 years out of the 5 years preceding the sale.

Example (3). Taxpayer C lives in a townhouse that he rents from 1993 through 1996. On January 18, 1997, he purchases the townhouse. On February 1, 1998, C moves into his daughter's home. On May 25, 2000, while still living in his daughter's home, C sells his townhouse. The section 121 exclusion will apply to gain from the sale because C owned the townhouse for at least 2 years out of the 5 years preceding the sale (from January 19, 1997 until May 25, 2000) and he used the townhouse as his principal residence for at least 2 years during the 5-year period preceding the sale (from May 25, 1995 until February 1, 1998).

Example (4). Taxpayer D, a college professor, purchases and moves into a house on May 1, 1997. He uses the house as his principal residence continuously until September 1, 1998, when he goes abroad for a 1-year sabbatical leave. On October 1, 1999, 1 month after returning from the leave, D sells the house. Because his leave is not considered to be a short temporary absence under paragraph (c)(2) of this section, the period of the sabbatical leave may not be included in determining whether D used the house for periods aggregating 2 years during the 5-year period ending on the date of the sale. Consequently, D is not entitled to exclude gain under section 121 because he did not use the residence for the requisite period.

Example (5). Taxpayer E purchases a house on February 1, 1998, that he uses as his principal residence. During 1998 and 1999, E leaves his residence for a 2-month summer vacation. E sells the house on March 1, 2000. Although, in the 5-year period preceding the date of sale, the total time E used his residence is less than 2 years (21 months), the section 121 exclusion will apply to gain from the sale of the residence because, under paragraph (c)(2) of this section, the 2-month vacations are short temporary absences and are counted as periods of use in determining whether E used the residence for the requisite period.

(d) Depreciation taken after May 6, 1997. *(1) In general.* The section 121 exclusion does not apply to so much of the gain from the sale or exchange of property as does not exceed the portion of the depreciation adjustments (as defined in section 1250(b)(3)) attributable to the property for periods after May 6, 1997. Depreciation adjustments allocable to any portion of the property to which the section 121 exclusion does not apply under paragraph (e) of this section are not taken into account for this purpose.

(2) Example. The provisions of this paragraph (d) are illustrated by the following example:

Example. On July 1, 1999, Taxpayer A moves into a house that he owns and had rented to tenants since July 1, 1997. A took depreciation deductions totaling $14,000 for the period that he rented the property. After using the residence as his principal residence for 2 full years, A sells the property on August 1, 2001. A's gain realized from the sale is $40,000. A has no other section 1231 or capital gains or losses for 2001. Only $26,000 ($40,000 gain realized - $14,000 depreciation deductions) may be excluded under section 121. Under section 121(d)(6) and paragraph (d)(1) of this section, A must recognize $14,000 of the gain as unrecaptured section 1250 gain within the meaning of section 1(h).

(e) Property used in part as a principal residence. *(1) Allocation required.* Section 121 will not apply to the gain allocable to any portion (separate from the dwelling unit) of property sold or exchanged with respect to which a taxpayer does not satisfy the use requirement. Thus, if a portion of the property was used for residential purposes and a portion of the property (separate from the dwelling unit) was used for non-residential purposes, only the gain allocable to the residential portion is excludable under section 121. No allocation is required if both the residential and non-residential portions of the property are within the same dwelling unit. However, section 121 does not apply to the gain allocable to the residential portion of the property to the extent provided by paragraph (d) of this section.

(2) Dwelling unit. For purposes of this paragraph (e), the term dwelling unit has the same meaning as in section 280A(f)(1), but does not include appurtenant structures or other property.

(3) Method of allocation. For purposes of determining the amount of gain allocable to the residential and non-residential portions of the property, the taxpayer must allocate the basis and the amount realized between the residential and the

non-residential portions of the property using the same method of allocation that the taxpayer used to determine depreciation adjustments (as defined in section 1250(b)(3)), if applicable.

(4) Examples. The provisions of this paragraph (e) are illustrated by the following examples:

Example (1). Non-residential use of property not within the dwelling unit.

(i) Taxpayer A owns a property that consists of a house, a stable and 35 acres. A uses the stable and 28 acres for non-residential purposes for more than 3 years during the 5-year period preceding the sale. A uses the entire house and the remaining 7 acres as his principal residence for at least 2 years during the 5-year period preceding the sale. For periods after May 6, 1997, A claims depreciation deductions of $9,000 for the non-residential use of the stable. A sells the entire property in 2004, realizing a gain of $24,000. A has no other section 1231 or capital gains or losses for 2004.

(ii) Because the stable and the 28 acres used in the business are separate from the dwelling unit, the allocation rules under this paragraph (e) apply and A must allocate the basis and amount realized between the portion of the property that he used as his principal residence and the portion of the property that he used for non-residential purposes. A determines that $14,000 of the gain is allocable to the non-residential-use portion of the property and that $10,000 of the gain is allocable to the portion of the property used as his residence. A must recognize the $14,000 of gain allocable to the non-residential-use portion of the property ($9,000 of which is unrecaptured section 1250 gain within the meaning of section 1(h), and $5,000 of which is adjusted net capital gain). A may exclude $10,000 of the gain from the sale of the property.

Example (2). Non-residential use of property not within the dwelling unit and rental of the entire property.

(i) In 1998 Taxpayer B buys a property that includes a house, a barn, and 2 acres. B uses the house and 2 acres as her principal residence and the barn for an antiques business. In 2002, B moves out of the house and rents it to tenants. B sells the property in 2004, realizing a gain of $21,000. Between 1998 and 2004 B claims depreciation deductions of $4,800 attributable to the antiques business. Between 2002 and 2004 B claims depreciation deductions of $3,000 attributable to the house. B has no other section 1231 or capital gains or losses for 2004.

(ii) Because the portion of the property used in the antiques business is separate from the dwelling unit, the allocation rules under this paragraph (e) apply. B must allocate basis and amount realized between the portion of the property that she used as her principal residence and the portion of the property that she used for non-residential purposes. B determines that $4,000 of the gain is allocable to the non-residential portion of the property and that $17,000 of the gain is allocable to the portion of the property that she used as her principal residence.

(iii) B must recognize the $4,000 of gain allocable to the non-residential portion of the property (all of which is unrecaptured section 1250 gain within the meaning of section 1(h)). In addition, the section 121 exclusion does not apply to the gain allocable to the residential portion of the property to the extent of the depreciation adjustments attributable to the residential portion of the property for periods after May 6, 1997 ($3,000). Therefore, B may exclude $14,000 of the gain from the sale of the property.

Example (3). Non-residential use of a separate dwelling unit.

(i) In 2002 Taxpayer C buys a 3-story townhouse and converts the basement level, which has a separate entrance, into a separate apartment by installing a kitchen and bathroom and removing the interior stairway that leads from the basement to the upper floors. After the conversion, the property constitutes 2 dwelling units within the meaning of paragraph (e)(2) of this section. C uses the first and second floors of the townhouse as his principal residence and rents the basement level to tenants from 2003 to 2007. C claims depreciation deductions of $2,000 for that period with respect to the basement apartment. C sells the entire property in 2007, realizing gain of $18,000. C has no other section 1231 or capital gains or losses for 2007.

(ii) Because the basement apartment and the upper floors of the townhouse are separate dwelling units, C must allocate the gain between the portion of the property that he used as his principal residence and the portion of the property that he used for non-residential purposes under paragraph (e) of this section. After allocating the basis and the amount realized between the residential and non-residential portions of the property, C determines that $6,000 of the gain is allocable to the non-residential portion of the property and that $12,000 of the gain is allocable to the portion of the property used as his residence. C must recognize the $6,000 of gain allocable to the non-residential portion of the property ($2,000 of which is unrecaptured section 1250 gain within the meaning of section 1(h), and $4,000 of which is adjusted net capital gain). C may exclude $12,000 of the gain from the sale of the property.

Example (4). Separate dwelling unit converted to residential use. The facts are the same as in Example 3 except that in 2007 C incorporates the basement of the townhouse into his principal residence by eliminating the kitchen and building a new interior stairway to the upper floors. C uses all 3 floors of the townhouse as his principal residence for 2 full years and sells the townhouse in 2010, realizing a gain of $20,000. Under section 121(d)(6) and paragraph (d) of this section, C must recognize $2,000 of the gain as unrecaptured section 1250 gain within the meaning of section 1(h). Because C used the entire 3 floors of the townhouse as his principal residence for 2 of the 5 years preceding the sale of the property, C may exclude the remaining $18,000 of the gain from the sale of the house.

Example (5). Non-residential use within the dwelling unit, property depreciated. Taxpayer D, an attorney, buys a house in 2003. The house constitutes a single dwelling unit but D uses a portion of the house as a law office. D claims depreciation deductions of $2,000 during the period that she owns the house. D sells the house in 2006, realizing a gain of $13,000. D has no other section 1231 or capital gains or losses for 2006. Under section 121(d)(6) and paragraph (d) of this section, D must recognize $2,000 of the gain as unrecaptured section 1250 gain within the meaning of section 1(h). D may exclude the remaining $11,000 of the gain from the sale of her house because, under paragraph (e)(1) of this section, she is not required to allocate gain to the business use within the dwelling unit.

Example (6). Non-residential use within the dwelling unit, property not depreciated. The facts are the same as in Example 5, except that D is not entitled to claim any depreciation deductions with respect to her business use of the house. D may exclude $13,000 of the gain from the sale of her house because, under paragraph (e)(1) of this section, she is not required to allocate gain to the business use within the dwelling unit.

(f) Effective date. This section is applicable for sales and exchanges on or after December 24, 2002. For rules on electing to apply the provisions of this section retroactively, see § 1.121-4(j).

T.D. 6856, 10/19/65, amend T.D. 7614, 4/26/79, T.D. 9030, 12/23/2002.

§ 1.121-2 Limitations.

Caution: The Treasury has not yet amended Reg § 1.121-2 to reflect changes made by P.L. 110-142.

(a) Dollar limitations. *(1) In general.* A taxpayer may exclude from gross income up to $250,000 of gain from the sale or exchange of the taxpayer's principal residence. A taxpayer is eligible for only one maximum exclusion per principal residence.

(2) Joint owners. If taxpayers jointly own a principal residence but file separate returns, each taxpayer may exclude from gross income up to $250,000 of gain that is attributable to each taxpayer's interest in the property, if the requirements of section 121 have otherwise been met.

(3) Special rules for joint returns. (i) In general. A husband and wife who make a joint return for the year of the sale or exchange of a principal residence may exclude up to $500,000 of gain if—

(A) Either spouse meets the 2-year ownership requirements of § 1.121-1(a) and (c);

(B) Both spouses meet the 2-year use requirements of § 1.121-1(a) and (c); and

(C) Neither spouse excluded gain from a prior sale or exchange of property under section 121 within the last 2 years (as determined under paragraph (b) of this section).

(ii) Other joint returns. For taxpayers filing jointly, if either spouse fails to meet the requirements of paragraph (a)(3)(i) of this section, the maximum limitation amount to be claimed by the couple is the sum of each spouse's limitation amount determined on a separate basis as if they had not been married. For this purpose, each spouse is treated as owning the property during the period that either spouse owned the property.

(4) Examples. The provisions of this paragraph (a) are illustrated by the following examples. The examples assume that § 1.121-3 (relating to the reduced maximum exclusion) does not apply to the sale of the property. The examples are as follows:

Example (1). Unmarried Taxpayers A and B own a house as joint owners, each owning a 50 percent interest in the house. They sell the house after owning and using it as their principal residence for 2 full years. The gain realized from the sale is $256,000. A and B are each eligible to exclude $128,000 of gain because the amount of realized gain allocable to each of them from the sale does not exceed each taxpayer's available limitation amount of $250,000.

Example (2). The facts are the same as in Example 1, except that A and B are married taxpayers who file a joint return for the taxable year of the sale. A and B are eligible to exclude the entire amount of realized gain ($256,000) from gross income because the gain realized from the sale does not exceed the limitation amount of $500,000 available to A and B as taxpayers filing a joint return.

Example (3). During 1999, married Taxpayers H and W each sell a residence that each had separately owned and used as a principal residence before their marriage. Each spouse meets the ownership and use tests for his or her respective residence. Neither spouse meets the use requirement for the other spouse's residence. H and W file a joint return for the year of the sales. The gain realized from the sale of H's residence is $200,000. The gain realized from the sale of W's residence is $300,000. Because the ownership and use requirements are met for each residence by each respective spouse, H and W are each eligible to exclude up to $250,000 of gain from the sale of their individual residences. However, W may not use H's unused exclusion to exclude gain in excess of her limitation amount. Therefore, H and W must recognize $50,000 of the gain realized on the sale of W's residence.

Example (4). Married Taxpayers H and W sell their residence and file a joint return for the year of the sale. W, but not H, satisfies the requirements of section 121. They are eligible to exclude up to $250,000 of the gain from the sale of the residence because that is the sum of each spouse's dollar limitation amount determined on a separate basis as if they had not been married ($0 for H, $250,000 for W).

Example (5). Married Taxpayers H and W have owned and used their principal residence since 1998. On February 16, 2001, H dies. On September 24, 2001, W sells the residence and realizes a gain of $350,000. Pursuant to section 6013(a)(3), W and H's executor make a joint return for 2001. All $350,000 of the gain from the sale of the residence may be excluded.

Example (6). Assume the same facts as Example 5, except that W does not sell the residence until January 31, 2002. Because W's filing status for the taxable year of the sale is single, the special rules for joint returns under paragraph (a)(3) of this section do not apply and W may exclude only $250,000 of the gain.

(b) Application of section 121 to only 1 sale or exchange every 2 years. *(1) In general.* Except as otherwise provided in § 1.121-3 (relating to the reduced maximum exclusion), a taxpayer may not exclude from gross income gain from the sale or exchange of a principal residence if, during the 2-year period ending on the date of the sale or exchange, the taxpayer sold or exchanged other property for which gain was excluded under section 121. For purposes of this paragraph (b)(1), any sale or exchange before May 7, 1997, is disregarded.

(2) Example. The following example illustrates the rules of this paragraph (b). The example assumes that § 1.121-3 (relating to the reduced maximum exclusion) does not apply to the sale of the property. The example is as follows:

Example. Taxpayer A owns a townhouse that he uses as his principal residence for 2 full years, 1998 and 1999. A buys a house in 2000 that he owns and uses as his principal residence. A sells the townhouse in 2002 and excludes gain realized on its sale under section 121. A sells the house in 2003. Although A meets the 2-year ownership and use requirements of section 121, A is not eligible to exclude gain from the sale of the house because A excluded gain within the last 2 years under section 121 from the sale of the townhouse.

(c) Effective date. This section is applicable for sales and exchanges on or after December 24, 2002. For rules on electing to apply the provisions of this section retroactively, see § 1.121-4(j).

T.D. 6856, 10/19/65, amend T.D. 7614, 4/26/79, T.D. 9030, 12/23/2002.

§ 1.121-3 Reduced maximum exclusion for taxpayers failing to meet certain requirements.

(a) In general. In lieu of the limitation under section 121(b) and § 1.121-2, a reduced maximum exclusion limitation may be available for a taxpayer who sells or exchanges property used as the taxpayer's principal residence but fails to satisfy the ownership and use requirements described in § 1.121-1(a) and (c) or the 2-year limitation described in § 1.121-2(b).

(b) Primary reason for sale or exchange. In order for a taxpayer to claim a reduced maximum exclusion under section 121(c), the sale or exchange must be by reason of a change in place of employment, health, or unforeseen circumstances. If a safe harbor described in this section applies, a sale or exchange is deemed to be by reason of a change in place of employment, health, or unforeseen circumstances. If a safe harbor described in this section does not apply, a sale or exchange is by reason of a change in place of employment, health, or unforeseen circumstances only if the primary reason for the sale or exchange is a change in place of employment (within the meaning of paragraph (c) of this section), health (within the meaning of paragraph (d) of this section), or unforeseen circumstances (within the meaning of paragraph (e) of this section). Whether the requirements of this section are satisfied depends upon all the facts and circumstances. Factors that may be relevant in determining the taxpayer's primary reason for the sale or exchange include (but are not limited to) the extent to which—

(1) The sale or exchange and the circumstances giving rise to the sale or exchange are proximate in time;

(2) The suitability of the property as the taxpayer's principal residence materially changes;

(3) The taxpayer's financial ability to maintain the property is materially impaired;

(4) The taxpayer uses the property as the taxpayer's residence during the period of the taxpayer's ownership of the property;

(5) The circumstances giving rise to the sale or exchange are not reasonably foreseeable when the taxpayer begins using the property as the taxpayer's principal residence; and

(6) The circumstances giving rise to the sale or exchange occur during the period of the taxpayer's ownership and use of the property as the taxpayer's principal residence.

(c) Sale or exchange by reason of a change in place of employment. *(1) In general.* A sale or exchange is by reason of a change in place of employment if, in the case of a qualified individual described in paragraph (f) of this section, the primary reason for the sale or exchange is a change in the location of the individual's employment.

(2) Distance safe harbor. A sale or exchange is deemed to be by reason of a change in place of employment (within the meaning of paragraph (c)(1) of this section) if—

(i) The change in place of employment occurs during the period of the taxpayer's ownership and use of the property as the taxpayer's principal residence; and

(ii) The qualified individual's new place of employment is at least 50 miles farther from the residence sold or exchanged than was the former place of employment, or, if there was no former place of employment, the distance between the qualified individual's new place of employment and the residence sold or exchanged is at least 50 miles.

(3) Employment. For purposes of this paragraph (c), employment includes the commencement of employment with a new employer, the continuation of employment with the same employer, and the commencement or continuation of self-employment.

(4) Examples. The following examples illustrate the rules of this paragraph (c):

Example (1). A is unemployed and owns a townhouse that she has owned and used as her principal residence since 2003. In 2004 A obtains a job that is 54 miles from her townhouse, and she sells the townhouse. Because the distance between A's new place of employment and the townhouse is at least 50 miles, the sale is within the safe harbor of paragraph (c)(2) of this section and A is entitled to claim a reduced maximum exclusion under section 121(c)(2).

Example (2). B is an officer in the United States Air Force stationed in Florida. B purchases a house in Florida in 2002. In May 2003 B moves out of his house to take a 3-year assignment in Germany. B sells his house in January 2004. Because B's new place of employment in Germany is at least 50 miles farther from the residence sold than is B's former place of employment in Florida, the sale is within the safe harbor of paragraph (c)(2) of this section and B is entitled to claim a reduced maximum exclusion under section 121(c)(2).

Example (3). C is employed by Employer R at R's Philadelphia office. C purchases a house in February 2002 that is 35 miles from R's Philadelphia office. In May 2003 C begins a temporary assignment at R's Wilmington office that is 72 miles from C's house, and moves out of the house. In June 2005 C is assigned to work in R's London office. C sells her house in August 2005 as a result of the assignment to London. The sale of the house is not within the safe harbor of paragraph (c)(2) of this section by reason of the change in place of employment from Philadelphia to Wilmington because the Wilmington office is not 50 miles farther from C's house than is the Philadelphia office. Furthermore, the sale is not within the safe harbor by reason of the change in place of employment to London because C is not using the house as her principal residence when she moves to London. However, C is entitled to claim a reduced maximum exclusion under section 121(c)(2) because, under the facts and circumstances, the primary reason for the sale is the change in C's place of employment.

Example (4). In July 2003 D, who works as an emergency medicine physician, buys a condominium that is 5 miles from her place of employment and uses it as her principal residence. In February 2004, D obtains a job that is located 51 miles from D's condominium. D may be called in to work unscheduled hours and, when called, must be able to arrive at work quickly. Because of the demands of the new job, D sells her condominium and buys a townhouse that is 4 miles from her new place of employment. Because D's new place of employment is only 46 miles farther from the condominium than is D's former place of employment, the sale is not within the safe harbor of paragraph (c)(2) of this section. However, D is entitled to claim a reduced maximum exclusion under section 121(c)(2) because, under the facts and circumstances, the primary reason for the sale is the change in D's place of employment.

(d) Sale or exchange by reason of health. *(1) In general.* A sale or exchange is by reason of health if the primary reason for the sale or exchange is to obtain, provide, or facilitate the diagnosis, cure, mitigation, or treatment of disease, illness, or injury of a qualified individual described in paragraph (f) of this section, or to obtain or provide medical or personal care for a qualified individual suffering from a disease, illness, or injury. A sale or exchange that is merely beneficial to the general health or well-being of an individual is not a sale or exchange by reason of health.

(2) Physician's recommendation safe harbor. A sale or exchange is deemed to be by reason of health if a physician (as defined in section 213(d)(4)) recommends a change of residence for reasons of health (as defined in paragraph (d)(1) of this section).

(3) Examples. The following examples illustrate the rules of this paragraph (d):

Example (1). In 2003 A buys a house that she uses as her principal residence. A is injured in an accident and is unable to care for herself. A sells her house in 2004 and moves in with her daughter so that the daughter can provide the care that A requires as a result of her injury. Because, under the facts and circumstances, the primary reason for the sale of A's house is A's health, A is entitled to claim a reduced maximum exclusion under section 121(c)(2).

Example (2). H's father has a chronic disease. In 2003 H and W purchase a house that they use as their principal residence. In 2004 H and W sell their house in order to move into the house of H's father so that they can provide the care he requires as a result of his disease. Because, under the facts and circumstances, the primary reason for the sale of their house is the health of H's father, H and W are entitled to claim a reduced maximum exclusion under section 121(c)(2).

Example (3). H and W purchase a house in 2003 that they use as their principal residence. Their son suffers from a chronic illness that requires regular medical care. Later that year their son begins a new treatment that is available at a hospital 100 miles away from their residence. In 2004 H and W sell their house so that they can be closer to the hospital to facilitate their son's treatment. Because, under the facts and circumstances, the primary reason for the sale is to facilitate the treatment of their son's chronic illness, H and W are entitled to claim a reduced maximum exclusion under section 121(c)(2).

Example (4). B, who has chronic asthma, purchases a house in Minnesota in 2003 that he uses as his principal residence. B's doctor tells B that moving to a warm, dry climate would mitigate B's asthma symptoms. In 2004 B sells his house and moves to Arizona to relieve his asthma symptoms. The sale is within the safe harbor of paragraph (d)(2) of this section and B is entitled to claim a reduced maximum exclusion under section 121(c)(2).

Example (5). In 2003 H and W purchase a house in Michigan that they use as their principal residence. H's doctor tells H that he should get more outdoor exercise, but H is not suffering from any disease that can be treated or mitigated by outdoor exercise. In 2004 H and W sell their house and move to Florida so that H can increase his general level of exercise by playing golf year-round. Because the sale of the house is merely beneficial to H's general health, the sale of the house is not by reason of H's health. H and W are not entitled to claim a reduced maximum exclusion under section 121(c)(2).

(e) Sale or exchange by reason of unforeseen circumstances. *(1) In general.* A sale or exchange is by reason of unforeseen circumstances if the primary reason for the sale or exchange is the occurrence of an event that the taxpayer could not reasonably have anticipated before purchasing and occupying the residence. A sale or exchange by reason of unforeseen circumstances (other than a sale or exchange deemed to be by reason of unforeseen circumstances under paragraph (e)(2) or (3) of this section) does not qualify for the reduced maximum exclusion if the primary reason for the sale or exchange is a preference for a different residence or an improvement in financial circumstances.

(2) Specific event safe harbors. A sale or exchange is deemed to be by reason of unforeseen circumstances (within the meaning of paragraph (e)(1) of this section) if any of the events specified in paragraphs (e)(2)(i) through (iii) of this section occur during the period of the taxpayer's ownership and use of the residence as the taxpayer's principal residence:

(i) The involuntary conversion of the residence.

(ii) Natural or man-made disasters or acts of war or terrorism resulting in a casualty to the residence (without regard to deductibility under section 165(h)).

(iii) In the case of a qualified individual described in paragraph (f) of this section—

(A) Death;

(B) The cessation of employment as a result of which the qualified individual is eligible for unemployment compensation (as defined in section 85(b));

(C) A change in employment or self-employment status that results in the taxpayer's inability to pay housing costs and reasonable basic living expenses for the taxpayer's household (including amounts for food, clothing, medical expenses, taxes, transportation, court-ordered payments, and expenses reasonably necessary to the production of income, but not for the maintenance of an affluent or luxurious standard of living);

(D) Divorce or legal separation under a decree of divorce or separate maintenance; or

(E) Multiple births resulting from the same pregnancy.

(3) Designation of additional events as unforeseen circumstances. The Commissioner may designate other events or situations as unforeseen circumstances in published guidance of general applicability and may issue rulings addressed to specific taxpayers identifying other events or situations as unforeseen circumstances with regard to those taxpayers (see § 601.601(d)(2) of this chapter).

(4) Examples. The following examples illustrate the rules of this paragraph (e):

Example (1). In 2003 A buys a house in California. After A begins to use the house as her principal residence, an earthquake causes damage to A's house. A sells the house in 2004. The sale is within the safe harbor of paragraph (e)(2)(ii) of this section and A is entitled to claim a reduced maximum exclusion under section 121(c)(2).

Example (2). H works as a teacher and W works as a pilot. In 2003 H and W buy a house that they use as their principal residence. Later that year W is furloughed from her job for six months. H and W are unable to pay their mortgage and reasonable basic living expenses for their household during the period W is furloughed. H and W sell their house in 2004. The sale is within the safe harbor of paragraph (e)(2)(iii)(C) of this section and H and W are entitled to claim a reduced maximum exclusion under section 121(c)(2).

Example (3). In 2003 H and W buy a two-bedroom condominium that they use as their principal residence. In 2004

W gives birth to twins and H and W sell their condominium and buy a four-bedroom house. The sale is within the safe harbor of paragraph (e)(2)(iii)(E) of this section, and H and W are entitled to claim a reduced maximum exclusion under section 121(c)(2).

Example (4). In 2003 B buys a condominium in a high-rise building and uses it as his principal residence. B's monthly condominium fee is $X. Three months after B moves into the condominium, the condominium association replaces the building's roof and heating system. Six months later, B's monthly condominium fee doubles in order to pay for the repairs. B sells the condominium in 2004 because he is unable to afford the new condominium fee along with a monthly mortgage payment. The safe harbors of paragraph (e)(2) of this section do not apply. However, under the facts and circumstances, the primary reason for the sale, the doubling of the condominium fee, is an unforeseen circumstance because B could not reasonably have anticipated that the condominium fee would double at the time he purchased and occupied the property. Consequently, the sale of the condominium is by reason of unforeseen circumstances and B is entitled to claim a reduced maximum exclusion under section 121(c)(2).

Example (5). In 2003 C buys a house that he uses as his principal residence. The property is located on a heavily traveled road. C sells the property in 2004 because C is disturbed by the traffic. The safe harbors of paragraph (e)(2) of this section do not apply. Under the facts and circumstances, the primary reason for the sale, the traffic, is not an unforeseen circumstance because C could reasonably have anticipated the traffic at the time he purchased and occupied the house. Consequently, the sale of the house is not by reason of unforeseen circumstances and C is not entitled to claim a reduced maximum exclusion under section 121(c)(2).

Example (6). In 2003 D and her fiancé E buy a house and live in it as their principal residence. In 2004 D and E cancel their wedding plans and E moves out of the house. Because D cannot afford to make the monthly mortgage payments alone, D and E sell the house in 2004. The safe harbors of paragraph (e)(2) of this section do not apply. However, under the facts and circumstances, the primary reason for the sale, the broken engagement, is an unforeseen circumstance because D and E could not reasonably have anticipated the broken engagement at the time they purchased and occupied the house. Consequently, the sale is by reason of unforeseen circumstances and D and E are each entitled to claim a reduced maximum exclusion under section 121(c)(2).

Example (7). In 2003 F buys a small condominium that she uses as her principal residence. In 2005 F receives a promotion and a large increase in her salary. F sells the condominium in 2004 and purchases a house because she can now afford the house. The safe harbors of paragraph (e)(2) of this section do not apply. Under the facts and circumstances, the primary reason for the sale of the house, F's salary increase, is an improvement in F's financial circumstances. Under paragraph (e)(1) of this section, an improvement in financial circumstances, even if the result of unforeseen circumstances, does not qualify for the reduced maximum exclusion by reason of unforeseen circumstances under section 121(c)(2).

Example (8). In April 2003 G buys a house that he uses as his principal residence. G sells his house in October 2004 because the house has greatly appreciated in value, mortgage rates have substantially decreased, and G can afford a bigger house. The safe harbors of paragraph (e)(2) of this section do not apply. Under the facts and circumstances, the primary reasons for the sale of the house, the changes in G's house value and in the mortgage rates, are an improvement in G's financial circumstances. Under paragraph (e)(1) of this section, an improvement in financial circumstances, even if the result of unforeseen circumstances, does not qualify for the reduced maximum exclusion by reason of unforeseen circumstances under section 121(c)(2).

Example (9). H works as a police officer for City X. In 2003 H buys a condominium that he uses as his principal residence. In 2004 H is assigned to City X's K-9 unit and is required to care for the police service dog at his home. Because H's condominium association does not permit H to have a dog in his condominium, in 2004 he sells the condominium and buys a house. The safe harbors of paragraph (e)(2) of this section do not apply. However, under the facts and circumstances, the primary reason for the sale, H's assignment to the K-9 unit, is an unforeseen circumstance because H could not reasonably have anticipated his assignment to the K-9 unit at the time he purchased and occupied the condominium. Consequently, the sale of the condominium is by reason of unforeseen circumstances and H is entitled to claim a reduced maximum exclusion under section 121(c)(2).

Example (10). In 2003, J buys a small house that she uses as her principal residence. After J wins the lottery, she sells the small house in 2004 and buys a bigger, more expensive house. The safe harbors of paragraph (e)(2) of this section do not apply. Under the facts and circumstances, the primary reason for the sale of the house, winning the lottery, is an improvement in J's financial circumstances. Under paragraph (e)(1) of this section, an improvement in financial circumstances, even if the result of unforeseen circumstances, does not qualify for the reduced maximum exclusion under section 121(c)(2).

(f) Qualified individual. For purposes of this section, qualified individual means—

(1) The taxpayer;

(2) The taxpayer's spouse;

(3) A co-owner of the residence;

(4) A person whose principal place of abode is in the same household as the taxpayer; or

(5) For purposes of paragraph (d) of this section, a person bearing a relationship specified in sections 152(a)(1) through 152(a)(8) (without regard to qualification as a dependent) to a qualified individual described in paragraphs (f)(1) through (4) of this section, or a descendant of the taxpayer's grandparent.

(g) Computation of reduced maximum exclusion. *(1)* The reduced maximum exclusion is computed by multiplying the maximum dollar limitation of $250,000 ($500,000 for certain joint filers) by a fraction. The numerator of the fraction is the shortest of the period of time that the taxpayer owned the property during the 5-year period ending on the date of the sale or exchange; the period of time that the taxpayer used the property as the taxpayer's principal residence during the 5-year period ending on the date of the sale or exchange; or the period of time between the date of a prior sale or exchange of property for which the taxpayer excluded gain under section 121 and the date of the current sale or exchange. The numerator of the fraction may be expressed in days or months. The denominator of the fraction is 730 days or 24 months (depending on the measure of time used in the numerator).

(2) Examples. The following examples illustrate the rules of this paragraph (g):

Example (1). Taxpayer A purchases a house that she uses as her principal residence. Twelve months after the purchase, A sells the house due to a change in place of her employment. A has not excluded gain under section 121 on a prior sale or exchange of property within the last 2 years. A is eligible to exclude up to $125,000 of the gain from the sale of her house (12/24 x $250,000).

Example (2). (i) Taxpayer H owns a house that he has used as his principal residence since 1996. On January 15, 1999, H and W marry and W begins to use H's house as her principal residence. On January 15, 2000, H sells the house due to a change in W's place of employment. Neither H nor W has excluded gain under section 121 on a prior sale or exchange of property within the last 2 years.

(ii) Because H and W have not each used the house as their principal residence for at least 2 years during the 5-year period preceding its sale, the maximum dollar limitation amount that may be claimed by H and W will not be $500,000, but the sum of each spouse's limitation amount determined on a separate basis as if they had not been married. (See § 1.121-2(a)(3)(ii).)

(iii) H is eligible to exclude up to $250,000 of gain because he meets the requirements of section 121. W is not eligible to exclude the maximum dollar limitation amount. Instead, because the sale of the house is due to a change in place of employment, W is eligible to claim a reduced maximum exclusion of up to $125,000 of the gain (365/730 x $250,000). Therefore, H and W are eligible to exclude up to $375,000 of gain ($250,000 + $125,000) from the sale of the house.

(h) Effective dates. Paragraphs (a) and (g) of this section are applicable for sales and exchanges on or after December 24, 2002. Paragraphs (b) through (f) of this section are applicable for sales and exchanges on or after August 13, 2004.

T.D. 6856, 10/19/65, amend T.D. 7614, 4/26/79, T.D. 9030, 12/23/2002, T.D. 9152, 8/13/2004.

---

§ 1.121-4 Special rules.

(a) Property of deceased spouse. *(1) In general.* For purposes of satisfying the ownership and use requirements of section 121, a taxpayer is treated as owning and using property as the taxpayer's principal residence during any period that the taxpayer's deceased spouse owned and used the property as a principal residence before death if—

(i) The taxpayer's spouse is deceased on the date of the sale or exchange of the property; and

(ii) The taxpayer has not remarried at the time of the sale or exchange of the property.

(2) Example. The provisions of this paragraph (a) are illustrated by the following example. The example assumes that § 1.121-3 (relating to the reduced maximum exclusion) does not apply to the sale of the property. The example is as follows:

Example. Taxpayer H has owned and used a house as his principal residence since 1987. H and W marry on July 1, 1999 and from that date they use H's house as their principal residence. H dies on August 15, 2000, and W inherits the property. W sells the property on September 1, 2000, at which time she has not remarried. Although W has owned and used the house for less than 2 years, W will be considered to have satisfied the ownership and use requirements of section 121 because W's period of ownership and use includes the period that H owned and used the property before death.

(b) Property owned by spouse or former spouse. *(1) Property transferred to individual from spouse or former spouse.* If a taxpayer obtains property from a spouse or former spouse in a transaction described in section 1041(a), the period that the taxpayer owns the property will include the period that the spouse or former spouse owned the property.

(2) Property used by spouse or former spouse. A taxpayer is treated as using property as the taxpayer's principal residence for any period that the taxpayer has an ownership interest in the property and the taxpayer's spouse or former spouse is granted use of the property under a divorce or separation instrument (as defined in section 71(b)(2)), provided that the spouse or former spouse uses the property as his or her principal residence.

(c) Tenant-stockholder in cooperative housing corporation. A taxpayer who holds stock as a tenant-stockholder in a cooperative housing corporation (as those terms are defined in section 216(b)(1) and (2)) may be eligible to exclude gain under section 121 on the sale or exchange of the stock. In determining whether the taxpayer meets the requirements of section 121, the ownership requirements are applied to the holding of the stock and the use requirements are applied to the house or apartment that the taxpayer is entitled to occupy by reason of the taxpayer's stock ownership.

(d) Involuntary conversions. *(1) In general.* For purposes of section 121, the destruction, theft, seizure, requisition, or condemnation of property is treated as a sale of the property.

(2) Application of section 1033. In applying section 1033 (relating to involuntary conversions), the amount realized from the sale or exchange of property used as the taxpayer's principal residence is treated as being the amount determined without regard to section 121, reduced by the amount of gain excluded from the taxpayer's gross income under section 121.

(3) Property acquired after involuntary conversion. If the basis of the property acquired as a result of an involuntary conversion is determined (in whole or in part) under section 1033(b) (relating to the basis of property acquired through an involuntary conversion), then for purposes of satisfying the requirements of section 121, the taxpayer will be treated as owning and using the acquired property as the taxpayer's principal residence during any period of time that the taxpayer owned and used the converted property as the taxpayer's principal residence.

(4) Example. The provisions of this paragraph (d) are illustrated by the following example:

Example. (i) On February 18, 1999, fire destroys Taxpayer A's house which has an adjusted basis of $80,000. A had owned and used this property as her principal residence for 20 years prior to its destruction. A's insurance company pays A $400,000 for the house. A realizes a gain of $320,000 ($400,000 - $80,000). On August 27, 1999, A purchases a new house at a cost of $100,000.

(ii) Because the destruction of the house is treated as a sale for purposes of section 121, A will exclude $250,000 of the realized gain from A's gross income. For purposes of section 1033, the amount realized is then treated as being $150,000 ($400,000 - $250,000) and the gain realized is $70,000 ($150,000 amount realized - $80,000 basis). A elects under section 1033 to recognize only $50,000 of the gain ($150,000 amount realized - $100,000 cost of new house). The remaining $20,000 of gain is deferred and A's basis in the new house is $80,000 ($100,000 cost - $20,000 gain not recognized).

(iii) A will be treated as owning and using the new house as A's principal residence during the 20-year period that A owned and used the destroyed house.

(e) Sales or exchanges of partial interests. *(1) Partial interests other than remainder interests.* (i) In general. Except as provided in paragraph (e)(2) of this section (relating to sales or exchanges of remainder interests), a taxpayer may apply the section 121 exclusion to gain from the sale or exchange of an interest in the taxpayer's principal residence that is less than the taxpayer's entire interest if the interest sold or exchanged includes an interest in the dwelling unit. For rules relating to the sale or exchange of vacant land, see § 1.121-1(b)(3).

(ii) Limitations. (A) Maximum limitation amount. For purposes of section 121(b)(1) and (2) (relating to the maximum limitation amount of the section 121 exclusion), sales or exchanges of partial interests in the same principal residence are treated as one sale or exchange. Therefore, only one maximum limitation amount of $250,000 ($500,000 for certain joint returns) applies to the combined sales or exchanges of the partial interests. In applying the maximum limitation amount to sales or exchanges that occur in different taxable years, a taxpayer may exclude gain from the first sale or exchange of a partial interest up to the taxpayer's full maximum limitation amount and may exclude gain from the sale or exchange of any other partial interest in the same principal residence to the extent of any remaining maximum limitation amount, and each spouse is treated as excluding one-half of the gain from a sale or exchange to which section 121(b)(2)(A) and § 1.121-2(a)(3)(i)(relating to the limitation for certain joint returns) apply.

(B) Sale or exchange of more than one principal residence in 2-year period. For purposes of applying section 121(b)(3) (restricting the application of section 121 to only 1 sale or exchange every 2 years), each sale or exchange of a partial interest is disregarded with respect to other sales or exchanges of partial interests in the same principal residence, but is taken into account as of the date of the sale or exchange in applying section 121(b)(3) to that sale or exchange and the sale or exchange of any other principal residence.

(2) Sales or exchanges of remainder interests. (i) In general. A taxpayer may elect to apply the section 121 exclusion to gain from the sale or exchange of a remainder interest in the taxpayer's principal residence.

(ii) Limitations. (A) Sale or exchange of any other interest. If a taxpayer elects to exclude gain from the sale or exchange of a remainder interest in the taxpayer's principal residence, the section 121 exclusion will not apply to a sale or exchange of any other interest in the residence that is sold or exchanged separately.

(B) Sales or exchanges to related parties. This paragraph (e)(2) will not apply to a sale or exchange to any person that bears a relationship to the taxpayer that is described in section 267(b) or 707(b).

(iii) Election. The taxpayer makes the election under this paragraph (e)(2) by filing a return for the taxable year of the sale or exchange that does not include the gain from the sale or exchange of the remainder interest in the taxpayer's gross income. A taxpayer may make or revoke the election at any time before the expiration of a 3-year period beginning on the last date prescribed by law (determined without regard to extensions) for the filing of the return for the taxable year in which the sale or exchange occurred.

(3) Example. The provisions of this paragraph (e) are illustrated by the following example:

Example. In 1991 Taxpayer A buys a house that A uses as his principal residence. In 2004 A's friend B moves into A's house and A sells B a 50% interest in the house realizing a gain of $136,000. A may exclude the $136,000 of gain. In 2005 A sells his remaining 50% interest in the home to B realizing a gain of $138,000. A may exclude $114,000 ($250,000 - $136,000 gain previously excluded) of the $138,000 gain from the sale of the remaining interest.

(f) No exclusion for expatriates. The section 121 exclusion will not apply to any sale or exchange by an individual if the provisions of section 877(a) (relating to the treatment of expatriates) applies to the individual.

(g) Election to have section not apply. A taxpayer may elect to have the section 121 exclusion not apply to a sale or exchange of property. The taxpayer makes the election by filing a return for the taxable year of the sale or exchange that includes the gain from the sale or exchange of the taxpayer's principal residence in the taxpayer's gross income. A taxpayer may make an election under this paragraph (g) to have section 121 not apply (or revoke an election to have section 121 not apply) at any time before the expiration of a 3-year period beginning on the last date prescribed by law (determined without regard to extensions) for the filing of the return for the taxable year in which the sale or exchange occurred.

(h) Residences acquired in rollovers under section 1034. If a taxpayer acquires property in a transaction that qualifies under section 1034 (section 1034 property) for the nonrecognition of gain realized on the sale or exchange of another property and later sells or exchanges such property, in determining the period of the taxpayer's ownership and use of the property under section 121 the taxpayer may include the periods that the taxpayer owned and used the section 1034 property as the taxpayer's principal residence (and each prior residence taken into account under section 1223(7) in determining the holding period of the section 1034 property).

(i) [Reserved].

(j) Election to apply regulations retroactively. Taxpayers who would otherwise qualify under § § 1.121-1 through 1.121-4 to exclude gain from a sale or exchange of a principal residence before December 24, 2002 but on or after May 7, 1997, may elect to apply § § 1.121-1 through 1.121-4 for any years for which the period of limitation under section 6511 has not expired. The taxpayer makes the election under this paragraph (j) by filing a return for the taxable year of the sale or exchange that does not include the gain from the sale or exchange of the taxpayer's principal residence in the taxpayer's gross income. Taxpayers who have filed a return for the taxable year of the sale or exchange may elect to apply the provisions of these regulations for any years for which the period of limitation under section 6511 has not expired by filing an amended return.

(k) Audit protection. The Internal Revenue Service will not challenge a taxpayer's position that a sale or exchange of a principal residence occurring before December 24, 2002 but on or after May 7, 1997, qualifies for the section 121 exclusion if the taxpayer has made a reasonable, good faith effort to comply with the requirements of section 121. Compliance with the provisions of the regulations project under section 121 (REG-105235-99 (2000-2 C.B. 447)) generally will be considered a reasonable, good faith effort to comply with the requirements of section 121.

(l) Effective date. This section is applicable for sales and exchanges on or after December 24, 2002. For rules on electing to apply the provisions retroactively, see paragraph (j) of this section.

T.D. 6856, 10/19/65, amend T.D. 7614, 4/26/79, T.D. 7927, 12/15/83, T.D. 9030, 12/23/2002.

§ 1.121-5 Suspension of 5-year period for certain members of the uniformed services and Foreign Service.

(a) In general. Under section 121(d)(9), a taxpayer who is serving (or whose spouse is serving) on qualified official extended duty as a member of the uniformed services or Foreign Service of the United States may elect to suspend the running of the 5-year period of ownership and use during such service but for not more than 10 years. The election does not suspend the running of the 5-year period for any period during which the running of the 5-year period with respect to any other property of the taxpayer is suspended by an election under section 121(d)(9).

(b) Manner of making election. The taxpayer makes the election under section 121(d)(9) and this section by filing a return for the taxable year of the sale or exchange of the taxpayer's principal residence that does not include the gain in the taxpayer's gross income.

(c) Application of election to closed years. A taxpayer who would otherwise qualify under §§ 1.121-1 through 1.121-4 to exclude gain from a sale or exchange of a principal residence on or after May 7, 1997, may elect to apply section 121(d)(9) and this section for any years for which a claim for refund is barred by operation of any law or rule of law by filing an amended return before November 11, 2004.

(d) Example. The provisions of this section are illustrated by the following example:

Example. B purchases a house in Virginia in 2003 that he uses as his principal residence for 3 years. For 8 years, from 2006 through 2014, B serves on qualified official extended duty as a member of the Foreign Service of the United States in Brazil. In 2015 B sells the house. B did not use the house as his principal residence for 2 of the 5 years preceding the sale. Under section 121(d)(9)and this section, however, B may elect to suspend the running of the 5-year period of ownership and use during his 8-year period of service with the Foreign Service in Brazil. If B makes the election, the 8-year period is not counted in determining whether B used the house for 2 of the 5 years preceding the sale. Therefore, B may exclude the gain from the sale of the house under section 121.

(e) Effective date. This section is applicable for sales and exchanges on or after May 7, 1997.

T.D. 9152, 8/13/2004.

PAR. 7. Section 1.122 is amended.

Proposed § 1.122 Statutory provisions; certain reduced uniformed services retirement pay. [*For Preamble, see ¶ 150,135*]

• ***Caution:*** Proposed section 1.62-1 was finalized by TD 7399, 2/3/76. Proposed sections 1.72-4, 1.72-13, 1.101-2, 1.122-1, 1.402(a)-1, 1.402(e)-2, 1.402(e)-3, 1.403(a)-1, 1.403(a)-2, 1.405-3, 1.652(b)-1, 1.1304-2 and 11.402(e)(4)(B)-1 remain proposed.

[Code Sec. 122]

§ 1.122-1 Applicable rules relating to certain reduced uniformed services retirement pay.

Caution: The Treasury has not yet amended Reg § 1.122-1 to reflect changes made by P.L. 104-188.

(a) Rule applicable prior to January 1, 1966. In the case of a member or former member of the uniformed services of the United States (as defined in 37 U.S.C. 101(3)) who has made an election under subchapter I of chapter 73 of title 10 of the United States Code (also referred to in this section as the Retired Serviceman's Family Protection plan (10 U.S.C. 1431)) to receive a reduced amount of retired or retainer pay, gross income shall include the amount of any reduction made in his retired or retainer pay before January 1, 1966, by reason of such election, unless such reduction, or portion thereof, is otherwise excluded from gross income under part III of subchapter B of chapter 1 of the Internal Revenue Code of 1954 or any other provision of law.

(b) Rule applicable after December 31, 1965. *(1)* In a case of a member or former member of the uniformed services of the United States (as defined in 37 U.S.C. 101(3)), gross income shall not include the amount of any reduction made in his or her retired or retainer pay after December 31, 1965, by reason of—

(i) An election made under the Retired Serviceman's Family Protection Plan (10 U.S.C. 1431), or

(ii) The provisions of subchapter II of chapter 73 of title 10 of the United States Code (also referred to in this section as the Survivor Benefit Plan (10 U.S.C. 1447)).

(2) (i) In a case where a member or former member of the uniformed services has, pursuant to the election described in paragraph (a) of this section, received before January 1, 1966, a reduced amount of retired or retainer pay, he shall, after December 31, 1965, exclude from gross income under section 122(b) and this subdivision all amounts received as uniformed services retired or retainer pay until there has been so excluded an amount of retired or retainer pay equal to the "consideration for the contract" (as described in subdivision (iii) of this subparagraph).

(ii) Upon the death of a member or former member of the uniformed services, where the "consideration for the contract" (as described in subdivision (iii) of this subparagraph) has not been excluded in whole or in part from gross income under section 122(b) and subdivision (i) of this subparagraph, the survivor of such member who is receiving an annuity under chapter 73 of title 10 of the United States Code shall, after December 31, 1965, exclude from gross income under section 72(o) and this subdivision such annuity payments received after December 31, 1965, until there has been so excluded annuity payments equalling the portion of the "consideration for the contract" not previously excluded under subdivision (i) of this subparagraph.

(iii) The term "consideration for the contract" as used in this subparagraph means—

(a) The total amount of the reductions, if any, before January 1, 1966, in retired or retainer pay by reason of an election under subchapter I of chapter 73 of title 10 of the United States Code, plus

(b) The total amount, if any, deposited by the serviceman at any time pursuant to the provisions of section 1438 or 1452(d) of title 10 of the United States Code, plus

(c) The total amount, if any, excludable from income under section 101(b)(2)(D) and paragraph (a)(2) of § 1.101-2 with respect to a survivor annuity provided by such retired or retainer pay, minus

(d) The total amount, if any, excluded from income before January 1, 1966, pursuant to the provisions of section 72(b) and (d) with respect to a survivor annuity provided by such retired or retainer pay.

(iv) In determining whether there has been a recovery of the "consideration for the contract" under subdivision (i) of this subparagraph, the exclusion of retired pay from income after December 31, 1965, under sections 104(a)(4) and 105(d) shall not be considered as recovery of all or part of the "consideration for the contract."

(c) Special rules. In any of the following situations, the computation of the excludable portion of disability retired pay received by the member or former member of the uniformed services shall be governed by the following rules:

(1) An exclusion under section 122(a) and paragraph (b)(1) of this section is applicable only in the taxable year in which a reduction in retired pay is made under the Retired Serviceman's Family Protection Plan (10 U.S.C. 1431) or the Survivor Benefit Plan (10 U.S.C. 1447).

(2) Where the member or former member of the uniformed services is entitled to exclude the whole or a portion of his retired pay under the provisions of section 104(a)(4) or section 105(d) and under section 122(a) and paragraph (b)(1) of this section, the exclusion under section 122(a) and paragraph (b)(1) of this section shall be applied prior to the exclusions under sections 104(a)(4) and 105(d).

(3) Where the member or former member of the uniformed services waives a portion of his disability retired pay, or such retired pay reduced under the Retired Serviceman's Family Protection Plan (10 U.S.C. 1431) or the Survivor Benefit Plan (10 U.S.C. 1447), in favor of a non-taxable pension or compensation receivable under laws administered by the Veterans Administration (38 U.S.C. 3105), the waived amount of such disability retired pay, or reduced amount thereof, shall first be subtracted from any amounts which are excludable under the provisions of sections 104(a)(4) or 105(d) so as to reduce the amounts otherwise excludable under those sections.

(4) Where the member or former member of the uniformed services receives (before any forfeiture) disability retired pay (whether or not reduced under the Retired Serviceman's Family Protection Plan or Survivor Benefit Plan) which is partially excludable under section 104(a)(4), and also forfeits a portion of such disability retired pay under the Dual Compensation Act of 1964 (5 U.S.C. 5531 or any former corresponding provision of law), the amount of the forfeiture under such Act shall be applied against disability retired pay (before any forfeiture) in the same proportion that the excludable portion of such pay under section 104(a)(4) bears to the total amount of such pay after subtraction of any reduction under the Retired Serviceman's Family Protection Plan (10 U.S.C. 1431)) or the Survivor Benefit Plan (10 U.S.C. 1447).

(5) The exclusion provided by section 122(b) and paragraph (b)(2)(i) of this section shall be available with respect to repayments made upon removal from the temporary disability retired list even though such repayments were previously excluded from gross income under section 104(a)(4) or 105(d).

However, the exclusion permitted by the prior sentence will apply only to the extent the repaid amount has not been previously excluded under section 122(b) and paragraph (b)(2)(i) of this section.

(d) Examples with respect to the Retired Serviceman's Family Protection Plan. The rules discussed in this section relating to the Retired Serviceman's Family Protection Plan (10 U.S.C. 1431) may be illustrated by the following examples:

Example (1). A, a member of the uniformed services, retires on January 1, 1963, and receives nondisability retired pay computed to be 60 percent of his active duty pay of $10,000 per year, or $6,000 per year, based upon 24 years of service. He elects, under the Retired Serviceman's Family Protection Plan (10 U.S.C. 1431), to provide his survivor with an annuity equal to one-fourth of his reduced retired pay. His retired pay of $6,000 is reduced by $600, to $5,400, in order to provide a survivor annuity of $1,350 per year or $112.50 per month. For 1963, 1964, and 1965, A must include in gross income the unreduced amount of retired pay, or $6,000. For 1966 and subsequent years, he may exclude under section 122(a) and paragraph (b)(1) of this section the $600 total annual reductions to provide the survivor annuity, and may, for 1966, further exclude from gross income under section 122(b) and paragraph (b)(2)(i) of this section the $1,800 "consideration for the contract," i.e., the total reductions which were made in 1963, 1964, and 1965, to provide the survivor annuity. Accordingly, A will include $3,600 of retired pay in gross income for 1966 ($6,000 minus the sum of $600 and $1,800).

Example (2). Assume the facts in Example (1) except that A retires on disability resulting from active service and his disability is rated at 40 percent. The entire amount of disability retirement pay, prior to and including 1966, is excludable from gross income under sections 104(a)(4) and 105(d), and in 1966, section 122(a). Assume further that A attains retirement age on December 31, 1966, dies on January 1, 1967, and his widow then begins receiving a survivor annuity under the Retired Serviceman's Family Protection Plan (10 U.S.C. 1431). A's widow may exclude from gross income in 1967 and 1968 under section 72(o) and paragraph (b)(2)(ii) of this section, the $1,800 of "consideration for the contract," i.e., the reductions in 1963, 1964, and 1965 to provide the survivor annuity. Thus, A's widow will exclude all of the survivor annuity she receives in 1967 ($1,350) and $450 of the $1,350 annuity received in 1968. In addition, if A had not attained retirement age at the time of his death, his widow would, under section 101 and paragraph (a)(2) of § 1.101-2, exclude up to $5,000 subject to the limitations of paragraph (b)(2)(ii) of this section.

Example (3). Assume, in the previous example, that A dies on January 1, 1965, and his widow then begins receiving a survivor annuity. Assume further that A's widow is entitled to exclude under section 72(b) $1,000 of the $1,350 she received in 1965. Under section 72(o) and paragraph (b)(2)(ii) of this section, A's widow for 1966 will exclude the $200 remaining consideration for the contract ($1,200 – $1,000) and will include $1,150 of the survivor annuity in gross income.

Example (4). B, a member of the uniformed services, retires on January 1, 1966, after 32 years of active military service, and receives disability retirement pay under section 1401 of title 10, limited to 75 percent of his active duty pay of $15,000 per year, or $11,250. His disability rating is 30 percent. B has not reached retirement age (as defined in § 1.79-2(b)(3)). He elects under the Retired Serviceman's Family Protection Plan (10 U.S.C. 1431) to provide his survivor with an annuity equal to one-half of his reduced retired pay and, for that purpose, his retired pay of $11,250 is reduced by $1,250 to provide an annuity of $5,000 per year. B also elects to waive retired pay in the amount of $1,000 in order to receive disability compensation in like amount under laws administered by the Veterans Administration. In addition, B is required to forfeit $4,088 of his retired pay under the Dual Compensation Act of 1964, 5 U.S.C. 5532, $11,250 – $1,000 = $10,250 less one-half of excess thereof over $2,074) and by reason of his Federal employment is not entitled to an exclusion of his retired pay under section 105(d). B's taxable retired pay for 1966 is $3,002, computed as follows:

Gross retired pay		$11,250
Less: Section 122(a) exclusion		(1,250)
Reduced retired pay		10,000
Less: Retired pay waived to receive V.A. compensation		(1,000)
Adjusted retired pay—		9,000
Less:		
(i) Excludable retired pay computed under section 104(a)(4) as limited by 10 U.S.C. 1403	$4,500	
(ii) Less: Retired pay, not to exceed (i), waived to receive V.A. compensation	(1,000)	
(iii) Net disability exclusion		(3,500)
Taxable retired pay before adjustment for Dual Compensation forfeiture		5,500
Less:		
Adjustment for Dual Compensation forfeiture of $4,088		
$\frac{5500}{9000} \times \$4,088 = \$2,498$ (rounded)		(2,498)
Net taxable retired pay		3,002

Example (5). C, a member of the uniformed services retires on January 1, 1966, and receives disability retirement pay of $11,250 per year, which is reduced by $1,250 to provide a survivor annuity, and $1,000 of which is waived in order to receive disability compensation in like amount under laws administered by the Veterans Administration. C has not reached retirement age for purposes of section 105(d) and is not employed by the Federal Government. C's taxable disability retirement pay for 1966 is $300 computed as follows:

Adjusted retired pay		$9,000
Less:		
(i) Excludable retired pay under section 104(a)(4) as limited by 10 U.S.C. 1403	$4,500	
(ii) Excludable retired pay under section 105(d)	5,200	
(iii) Total	9,700	
(iv) Less: Retired pay, not to exceed (iii), waived to receive V.A. compensation	(1,000)	
(v) Net disability and "sick pay" exclusion		(8,700)
Net taxable retired pay		300

Example (6). D, a member of the uniformed services, retires for physical disability resulting from active service on January 1, 1966, after 35 years of service and with a disability rated at 20 percent. His active duty pay is $4,000 per year and he attained retirement age prior to retirement. He had an election in effect under the Retired Serviceman's Family Protection Plan to provide his survivor with an annuity and his retired pay is reduced therefor by $500 per year. He waives $1,300 of his retired pay in order to receive compensation from the Veterans Administration in like amount. His taxable retired pay for 1966 is $1,200 computed as follows:

Gross retired pay (75% × $4,000)		$3,000
Less: Section 122(a) exclusion		(500)
Reduced retired pay		2,500
Less: V.A. waiver		(1,300)
Adjusted retired pay		1,200
Less:		
(i) Section 104(a)(4) exclusion	$800	
(ii) Less: Retired pay, not to exceed (i), waived to receive V.A. compensation	(800)	
(iii) Net disability exclusion	0	
Net taxable retired pay		1,200

(e) Principles applicable to the Survivor Benefit Plan. The principles illustrated by the examples set forth in paragraph (d) of this section apply to an annuity under the Survivor Benefit Plan (10 U.S.C. 1447).

T.D. 7043, 6/1/70, amend T.D. 7562, 8/30/78.

PAR. 8. Section 1.122-1 is amended by deleting "72(o)" each place it appears and inserting in lieu thereof "72(n)". As amended, § 1.122-1(b)(2)(ii) and examples (2) and (3) of § 1.122-(d) read as follows:

Proposed § 1.122-1 Applicable rules relating to certain reduced uniformed services retirement pay. [*For Preamble, see ¶ 150,135*]

• ***Caution:*** Proposed section 1.62-1 was finalized by TD 7399, 2/3/76. Proposed sections 1.72-4, 1.72-13, 1.101-2, 1.122-1, 1.402(a)-1, 1.402(e)-2, 1.402(e)-3, 1.403(a)-1, 1.403(a)-2, 1.405-3, 1.652(b)-1, 1.1304-2 and 11.402(e)(4)(B)-1 remain proposed.

* * * * *

(b) Rule applicable after December 31, 1965. * * *

(2) * * *

(ii) Upon the death of a member or former member of the uniformed services, where the "consideration for the contract" (as described in paragraph (b)(2)(iii) of this section has not been excluded in whole or in part from gross income under section 122(b) and (b)(2)(i) of this section, the survivor of such member who is receiving an annuity under chapter 73 of title 10 of the United States Code shall, after December 31, 1965, exclude from gross income under section 72(n) and this section such annuity payments received after December 31, 1965, until there has been so excluded annuity payments equalling the portion of the "consideration for the contract" not previously excluded under paragraph (b)(2)(i) of this section.

* * * * *

(d) Examples. The rules discussed in paragraph (a) of this section may be illustrated by the following examples:

* * * * *

Example (2). Assume the facts in Example (1) except that A retires on disability resulting from active service and his disability is rated at 40 percent. The entire amount of disability retirement pay, prior to and including 1966, is excludable from gross income under sections 104(a)(4) and 105(d), and in 1966, section 122(a). Assume further that A attains retirement age on December 31, 1966, dies on January 1, 1967, and his widow then begins receiving a survivor annuity under the Retired Serviceman's Family Protection Plan (10 U.S.C. 1431). A's widow may exclude from gross income in 1967 and 1968 under section 72(n) and paragraph (b)(2)(ii) of this section, the $1,800 of "consideration for the contract" i.e., the reductions in 1963, 1964, and 1965 to provide the survivor annuity. Thus, A's widow will exclude all of the survivor annuity she receives in 1967 ($1,350) and $450 of the $1,350 annuity received in 1968. In addition, if A had not attained retirement age at the time of his death, his widow would, under section 101 and paragraph (a)(2) of § 1.101-2, exclude up to $5,000 subject to the limitations of paragraph (b)(2)(ii) of this section.

Example (3). Assume, in the previous example, that A dies on January 1, 1965, and his widow then begins receiving a survivor annuity. Assume further that A's widow is entitled to exclude under section 72(b) $1,000 of the $1,350 she received in 1965. Under section 72(n) and paragraph (b)(2)(ii) of this section, A's widow for 1966 will exclude the $200 remaining consideration for the contract ($1,200 – $1,000) and will include $1,150 of the survivor annuity in gross income.

* * * * *

§ 1.123-1 Exclusion of insurance proceeds for reimbursement of certain living expenses.

(a) In general. *(1)* Gross income does not include insurance proceeds received by an individual on or after January 1, 1969, pursuant to the terms of an insurance contract for indemnification of the temporary increase in living expenses resulting from the loss of use or occupancy of his principal residence, or a part thereof, due to damage or destruction by fire, storm, or other casualty. The term "other casualty" has the same meaning assigned to such term under section 165(c)(3). The exclusion also applies in the case of an individual who is denied access to his principal residence by governmental authorities because of the occurrence (or threat of occurrence) of such a casualty. The amount excludable under this section is subject to the limitation set forth in paragraph (b) of this section.

(2) This exclusion applies to amounts received as reimbursement or compensation for the reasonable and necessary increase in living expenses incurred by the insured and members of his household to maintain their customary standard of living during the loss period.

(3) This exclusion does not apply to an insurance recovery for the loss of rental income. Nor does the exclusion apply to any insurance recovery which compensates for the loss of, or damage to, real or personal property. See section 165(c)(3) relating to casualty losses; section 1231 relating to gain on an involuntary conversion of a capital asset held for more than 1 year (6 months for taxable years beginning before 1977; 9 months for taxable years beginning in 1977); and section 1033 relating to recognition of gain on an involuntary conversion. In the case of property used by an insured partially as a principal residence and partially for other purposes, the exclusion does not apply to the amount of insurance proceeds which compensates for the portion of increased expenses attributable to the nonresidential use of temporary replacement property during the loss period. In the case of denial of access to a principal residence by governmental authority, the exclusion provided by this section does not apply to an insurance recovery received by an individual as reimbursement for living expenses incurred by reason of a governmental condemnation or order not related to a casualty or the threat of a casualty.

(4) (i) Subject to the limitation set forth in paragraph (b), the amount excludable is the amount which is identified by the insurer as being paid exclusively for increased living expenses resulting from the loss of use or occupancy of the principal residence and pursuant to the terms of the insurance contract.

(ii) When a lump-sum insurance settlement includes, but does not specifically identify, compensation for property damage, loss of rental income, and increased living expenses, the amount of such settlement allocable to living expenses shall, in the case of uncontested claims, be that portion of the settlement which bears the same ratio to the total recovery as the amount of claimed increased living expense bears to the total amount of claimed losses and expenses, to the extent not in excess of the coverage limitations specified in the contract for such losses and expenses.

(iii) In the case of a lump-sum settlement involving contested claims, the insured shall establish the amount reasonably allocable to increased living expenses, consistent with the terms of the contract and other facts of the particular case.

(iv) In no event may the amount of a lump-sum settlement which is allocable to increased living expenses exceed the coverage limitation specified in the contract for increased living expenses. Where, however, a coverage limitation is applicable to the total amount payable for increased living expenses and, for example, loss of rental income, the amount of an unitemized settlement which is allocable to increased living expenses may not exceed the portion of the applicable coverage limitation which bears the same ratio to such limitation as the amount of increased living expenses bears to the sum of the amount of such increased living expenses and the amount, if any, of lost rental income.

(5) The portion of any insurance recovery for increased living expenses which exceeds the limitation set forth in paragraph (b) shall be included in gross income under section 61 of the Code.

(b) Limitation. *(1) Amount excludable.* The amount excludable under this section is limited to amounts received which are not in excess of the amount by which (i) total actual living expenses incurred by the insured and members of his household which result from the loss of use or occupancy of their residence exceed (ii) the total normal living expenses which would have been incurred during the loss period but are not incurred as a result of the loss of use or occupancy of the principal residence. Generally, the excludable amount represents such excess expenses actually incurred by reason of a casualty, or threat thereof, for renting suitable housing and for extraordinary expenses for transportation, food, utilities, and miscellaneous services during the period of repair or replacement of the damaged principal residence or denial of access by governmental authority.

(2) Actual living expenses. For purposes of this section, actual living expenses are the reasonable and necessary expenses incurred as a result of the loss of use or occupancy of the principal residence to maintain the insured and members of his household in accordance with their customary standard of living. Actual living expenses must be of such a nature as to qualify as a reimbursable expense under the terms of the applicable insurance contract without regard to monetary limitations upon coverage. Generally, actual living expenses include the cost during the loss period of temporary housing, utilities furnished at the place of temporary housing, meals obtained at restaurants which customarily would have been prepared in the residence, transportation, and other miscellaneous services. To the extent that the loss of use or occupancy of the principal residence results merely in an increase in the amount expended for items of living expenses normally incurred, such as food and transportation, only the increase in such costs shall be considered as actual living expenses in computing the limitation.

(3) Normal living expenses not incurred. Normal living expenses consist of the same categories of expenses comprising actual living expenses which would have been incurred but are not incurred as a result of the casualty or threat thereof. If the loss of use of the residence results in a decrease in the amount normally expended for a living expense item during the loss period, the item of normal living expense is considered not to have been incurred to the extent of the decrease for purposes of computing the limitation.

(4) Examples. The application of this paragraph (b) may be illustrated by the following examples:

Example (1). On March 1, 1970, A's principal residence, a dwelling owned by A no part of which was rented to others or used for nonresidential purposes, was extensively damaged by fire. The damaged residence was under repair during the entire month of March making it necessary for A and his spouse to obtain temporary lodging and to take their meals at a restaurant. A and his spouse incur expenses of $200 for lodging at a motel, $180 for meals which customarily would have been prepared in his residence, and $25 for commercial laundry service which customarily would have been done by A's wife. A makes (directly or through mortgage insurance), or remains liable for, the required March payment of $190 on the mortgage note on his residence. The mortgage payment results from a contractual obligation having no causal relationship to the occurrence of the casualty and is not considered as an actual living expense resulting from the loss of use of the residence. A's customary commuting expense of $40 for bus fares to and from work is decreased by $20 for the month because of the motel's closer proximity to his place of employment. Other transportation expenses remain stable. Since there has been a decrease in the amount of A's customary bus fares, normal transportation expenses are considered not to have been incurred to the extent of the decrease. Finally, A does not incur customary expenses of $150 for food obtained for home preparation, $75 for utilities expenses, and $10 for laundry cleansers. The limitation upon the excludable amount of an insurance recovery for excess living expenses is $150, computed as follows:

LIVING EXPENSES

	Actual resulting from casualty	Normal not incurred	Increase (decrease)
Housing	$200.00		$200.00
Utilities		$ 75.00	(75.00)
Meals	180.00	150.00	30.00
Transportation		20.00	(20.00)
Laundry	25.00	10.00	15.00
Total	405.00	255.00	150.00

Example (2). Assume the same facts as in example (1) except that the damaged residence is not owned by A but is rented to him for $100 per month and that the risk of loss is upon the lessor. Since A would not have incurred the normal rental of $100 for March, the excludable amount is limited to $50 ($150 as in previous example less $100 normal rent not incurred).

(c) Principal residence. Whether or not property is used by the insured taxpayer and members of his household as their principal residence depends upon all the facts and circumstances in each case. For purposes of this section, a principal residence may be a dwelling or an apartment leased to the insured as well as a dwelling or apartment owned by the insured.

T.D. 7118, 6/1/71, amend T.D. 7728, 10/31/80.

Proposed § 1.125-0 Table of contents. [*For Preamble, see ¶ 152,897*]

This section lists captions contained in §§ 1.125-1, 1.125-2, 1.125-5, 1.125-6 and § 1.125-7.

§ 1.125-1 Cafeteria plans; general rules.

(a) Definitions.

(b) General rules.

(c) Written plan requirements.

(d) Plan year requirements.

(e) Grace period.

(f) Run-out period.

(g) Employee for purpose of Section 125.

(h) After-tax employee contributions.

(i) Prohibited taxable benefits.

(j) Coordination with other rules.

(k) Group-term life insurance.

(l) COBRA premiums.

(m) Payment or reimbursement of employees' individual accident and health insurance premiums.

(n) Section 105 rules for accident and health plan offered through a cafeteria plan.

(o) Prohibition against deferred compensation.

(p) Benefits relating to more than one year.

(q) Nonqualified benefits.

(r) Employer contributions to a cafeteria plan.

(s) Effective/applicability date.

§ 1.125-2 Cafeteria plans; elections.

(a) Rules relating to making elections and revoking elections.

(b) Automatic elections.

(c) Election rules for salary reduction contributions to HSAs.

(d) Optional election for new employees.

(e) Effective/applicability date.

§ 1.125-5 Flexible spending arrangements.

(a) Definition of flexible spending arrangement.

(b) Flex-credits allowed.

(a) Use-or-lose rule.

(d) Uniform coverage rules applicable to health FSAs.

(e) Required period of coverage for a health FSA, dependent care FSA and adoption assistance FSA.

(f) Coverage on a month-by-month or expense-by-expense basis prohibited.

(g) FSA administrative practices.

(h) Qualified benefits permitted to be offered through a FSA.

(i) Section 129 rules for dependent care assistance program offered through a cafeteria plan.

(j) Section 137 rules for adoption assistance program offered through a cafeteria plan.

(k) FSAs and the rules governing the tax-favored treatment of employer-provided health benefits.

(l) Section 105(h) requirements.

(m) HSA-compatible FSAs-limited-purpose health FSAs and post-deductible health FSAs.

(n) Qualified HSA distributions.

(o) FSA experience gains or forfeitures.

(p) Effective/applicability date.

§ 1.125-6 Substantiation of expenses for all cafeteria plans.

(a) Cafeteria plan payments and reimbursements.

(b) Rules for claims substantiation for cafeteria plans.

(c) Debit cards—overview.

(d) Mandatory rules for all debit cards usable to pay or reimburse medical expenses.

(e) Substantiation of expenses incurred at medical care providers and certain other stores with Drug Stores and Pharmacies merchant category code.

(f) Inventory information approval system.

(g) Debit cards used to pay or reimburse dependent care assistance.

(h) Effective/applicability date.

§ 1.125-7 Cafeteria plan nondiscrimination rules.

(a) Definitions.

(b) Nondiscrimination as to eligibility.

(c) Nondiscrimination as to contributions and benefits.

(d) Key employees.

(e) Section 125(g)(2) safe harbor for cafeteria plans providing health benefits.

(f) Safe harbor test for premium-only-plans.

(g) Permissive disaggregation for nondiscrimination testing.

(h) Optional aggregation of plans for nondiscrimination testing.

(i) Employees of certain controlled groups.

(j) Time to perform nondiscrimination testing.

(k) Discrimination in actual operation prohibited.

(l) Anti-abuse rule.

(m) Tax treatment of benefits in a cafeteria plan.

(n) Employer contributions to employees' Health Savings Accounts.

(o) Effective/applicability date.

PAR. 2. In § 1.125-1, as proposed May 7, 1984 (49 FR 19321) and as amended March 23, 2000 (65 FR 15587), Q&A-8 is amended by removing the last four sentences of A-8 and adding a sentence in their place to read as follows:

Proposed § 1.125-1 Questions and answers relating to cafeteria plan. [*For Preamble, see ¶ 152,127*]

* * * * *

Q-8. What requirements apply to participants' elections under a cafeteria plan?

A-8. * * * However, a cafeteria plan may permit a participant to revoke a benefit election after the period of coverage has commenced and make a new election with respect to the remainder of the period of coverage if both the revocation and the new election are permitted under § 1.125-4.

* * * * *

Proposed § 1.125-1 Cafeteria plans; general rules. [*For Preamble, see ¶ 152,897*]

(a) Definitions. The definitions set forth in this paragraph (a) apply for purposes of section 125 and the regulations.

(1) The term cafeteria plan means a separate written plan that complies with the requirements of section 125 and the regulations, that is maintained by an employer for the benefit of its employees and that is operated in compliance with the requirements of section 125 and the regulations. All participants in a cafeteria plan must be employees. A cafeteria plan must offer at least one permitted taxable benefit (as defined in paragraph (a)(2) of this section) and at least one qualified benefit (as defined in paragraph (a)(3) of this section). A cafeteria plan must not provide for deferral of compensation (except as specifically permitted in paragraph (o) of this section).

(2) The term permitted taxable benefit means cash and certain other taxable benefits treated as cash for purposes of section 125. For purposes of section 125, cash means cash compensation (including salary reduction), payments for annual leave, sick leave, or other paid time off and severance pay. A distribution from a trust described in section 401(a) is not cash for purposes of section 125. Other taxable benefits treated as cash for purposes of section 125 are:

(i) Property;

(ii) Benefits attributable to employer contributions that are currently taxable to the employee upon receipt by the employee; and

(iii) Benefits purchased with after-tax employee contributions, as described in paragraph (h) of this section.

(3) Qualified benefit. Except as otherwise provided in section 125(f) and paragraph (q) of this section, the term qualified benefit means any benefit attributable to employer contributions to the extent that such benefit is not currently taxable to the employee by reason of an express provision of the Internal Revenue Code (Code) and which does not defer compensation (except as provided in paragraph (o) of this section). The following benefits are qualified benefits that may be offered under a cafeteria plan and are excludible from employees' gross income when provided in accordance with the applicable provisions of the Code—

(A) Group-term life insurance on the life of an employee in an amount that is less than or equal to the $50,000 excludible from gross income under section 79(a), but not combined with any permanent benefit within the meaning of § 1.79-0;

(B) An accident and health plan excludible from gross income under section 105 or 106, including self-insured medical reimbursement plans (such as health FSAs described in § 1.125-5);

(C) Premiums for COBRA continuation coverage (if excludible under section 106) under the accident and health plan of the employer sponsoring the cafeteria plan or premiums for COBRA continuation coverage of an employee of the employer sponsoring the cafeteria plan under an accident and health plan sponsored by a different employer;

(D) An accidental death and dismemberment insurance policy (section 106);

(E) Long-term or short-term disability coverage (section 106);

(F) Dependent care assistance program (section 129);

(G) Adoption assistance (section 137);

(H) A qualified cash or deferred arrangement that is part of a profit-sharing plan or stock bonus plan, as described in paragraph (o)(3) of this section (section 401(k));

(I) Certain plans maintained by educational organizations (section 125(d)(2)(C) and paragraph (o)(3)(iii) of this section); and

(J) Contributions to Health Savings Accounts (HSAs) (sections 223 and 125(d)(2)(D)).

(4) Dependent. The term dependent generally means a dependent as defined in section 152. However, the definition of dependent is modified to conform with the underlying Code section for the qualified benefit. For example, for purposes of a benefit under section 105, the term dependent means a dependent as defined in section 152, determined without regard to section 152(b)(1), (b)(2) or (d)(1)(B).

(5) Premium-only-plan. A premium-only-plan is a cafeteria plan that offers as its sole benefit an election between cash (for example, salary) and payment of the employee share of the employer-provided accident and health insurance premium (excludible from the employee's gross income under section 106).

(b) General rules. *(1) Cafeteria plans.* Section 125 is the exclusive means by which an employer can offer employees an election between taxable and nontaxable benefits without the election itself resulting in inclusion in gross income by the employees. Section 125 provides that cash (including certain taxable benefits) offered to an employee through a nondiscriminatory cafeteria plan is not includible in the employee's gross income merely because the employee has the opportunity to choose among cash and qualified benefits (within the meaning of section 125(e)) through the cafeteria plan. Section 125(a), (d)(1). However, if a plan offering an employee an election between taxable benefits (including cash) and nontaxable qualified benefits does not meet the section 125 requirements, the election between taxable and nontaxable benefits results in gross income to the employee, regardless of what benefit is elected and when the election is made. An employee who has an election among nontaxable benefits and taxable benefits (including cash) that is not through a cafeteria plan that satisfies section 125 must include in gross income the value of the taxable benefit with the greatest value that the employee could have elected to receive, even if the employee elects to receive only the nontaxable benefits offered. The amount of the taxable benefit is includible in the employee's income in the year in which the employee would have actually received the taxable benefit if the employee had elected such benefit. This is the result even if the employee's election between the nontaxable benefits and taxable benefits is made prior to the year in which the employee would actually have received the taxable benefits. See paragraph (q) in § 1.125-1 for nonqualified benefits.

(2) Nondiscrimination rules for qualified benefits. Accident and health plan coverage, group-term life insurance coverage, and benefits under a dependent care assistance program or adoption assistance program do not fail to be qualified benefits under a cafeteria plan merely because they are includible in gross income because of applicable nondiscrimination requirements (for example, sections 79(d), 105(h),129(d), 137(c)(2)). See also §§ 1.105-11(k) and 1.125-7.

(3) Examples. The following examples illustrate the rules of paragraph (b)(1) of this section.

Example (1). Distributions from qualified pension plan used for health insurance premiums. (i) Employer A maintains a qualified section 401(a) retirement plan for employees. Employer A also provides accident and health insurance (as described in section 106) for employees and former employees, their spouses and dependents. The health insurance premiums are partially paid through a cafeteria plan. None of Employer A's employees are public safety officers. Employer A's health plan allows former employees to elect to have distributions from the qualified retirement plan applied to pay for the health insurance premiums through the cafeteria plan.

(ii) Amounts distributed from the qualified retirement plan which the former employees elect to have applied to pay health insurance premiums through the cafeteria plan are includible in their gross income. The same result occurs if distributions from the qualified retirement plan are applied directly to reimburse section 213(d) medical care expenses incurred by a former employee or his or her spouse or dependents. These distributions are includible in their income, and are not cash for purposes of section 125. The plan is not a cafeteria plan with respect to former employees.

Example (2). Severance pay used to pay COBRA premiums. Employer B maintains a cafeteria plan, which offers employees an election between cash and employer-provided accident and health insurance (excludible from employees' gross income under section 106). Employer B pays terminating employees severance pay. The cafeteria plan also allows a terminating employee to elect between receiving severance pay and using the severance pay to pay the COBRA premiums for the accident and health insurance. These provisions in the cafeteria plan are consistent with the requirements in section 125.

(4) Election by participants. (i) In general. A cafeteria plan must offer participants the opportunity to elect between at least one permitted taxable benefit and at least one qualified benefit. For example, if employees are given the opportunity to elect only among two or more nontaxable benefits, the plan is not a cafeteria plan. Similarly, a plan that only offers the election among salary, permitted taxable benefits, paid time off or other taxable benefits is not a cafeteria plan. See section 125(a), (d). See § 1.125-2 for rules on elections.

(ii) Premium-only-plan. A cafeteria plan may be a premium-only-plan.

(iii) Examples. The following examples illustrate the rules of paragraph (b)(4)(i) of this section.

Example (1). No election. Employer C covers all its employees under its accident and health plan (excludible from employees' gross income under section 106). Coverage is mandatory (that is, employees have no election between cash and the Employer C's accident and health plan). This plan is not a cafeteria plan, because the plan offers employees no election between taxable and nontaxable benefits. The accident and health coverage is excludible from employees' gross income.

Example (2). Election between cash and at least one qualified benefit. Employer D offers its employees a plan with an election between cash and an employer-provided accident and health plan (excludible from employees' gross income under section 106). If the plan also satisfies all the other requirements of section 125, the plan is a cafeteria plan because it offers an election between at least one taxable benefit and at least one nontaxable qualified benefit.

Example (3). Election between employer flex-credits and qualified benefits. Employer E offers its employees an election between an employer flex-credit (as defined in paragraph (b) in § 1.125-5) and qualified benefits. If an employee does not elect to apply the entire employer flex-credit to qualified benefits, the employee will receive no cash or other taxable benefit for the unused employer flex-credit. The plan is not a cafeteria plan because it does not offer an election between at least one taxable benefit and at least one nontaxable qualified benefit.

Example (4). No election between cash and qualified benefits for certain employees. (i) Employer F maintains a calendar year plan offering employer-provided accident and health insurance coverage which includes employee-only and family coverage options.

(ii) The plan provides for an automatic enrollment process when a new employee is hired, or during the annual election period under the plan: only employees who certify that they have other health coverage are permitted to elect to receive cash. Employees who cannot certify are covered by the accident and health insurance on a mandatory basis. Employer F does not otherwise request or collect information from employees regarding other health coverage as part of the enrollment process. If the employee has a spouse or child, the employee can elect between cash and family coverage.

(iii) When an employee is hired, the employee receives a notice explaining the plan's automatic enrollment process. The notice includes the salary reduction amounts for employee-only coverage and family coverage, procedures for certifying whether the employee has other health coverage, elections for family coverage, information on the time by which a certification or election must be made, and the period for which a certification or election will be effective. The notice is also given to each current employee before the beginning of each plan year, (except that the notice for a current employee includes a description of the employee's existing coverage, if any).

(iv) For a new employee, an election to receive cash or to have family coverage is effective if made when the employee is hired. For a current employee, an election is effective if made prior to the start of each calendar year or under any other circumstances permitted under § 1.125-4. An election for any prior year carries over to the next succeeding plan year unless changed. Certification that the employee has other health coverage must be made annually.

(v) Contributions used to purchase employer-provided accident and health coverage under section 125 are not includible in an employee's gross income if the employee can elect cash. Section 125 does not apply to the employee-only coverage of an employee who cannot certify that he or she has other health coverage and, therefore, does not have the ability to elect cash in lieu of health coverage.

(5) No deferred compensation. Except as provided in paragraph (o) of this section, in order for a plan to be a cafeteria plan, the qualified benefits and the permitted taxable benefits offered through the cafeteria plan must not defer compensation. For example, a cafeteria plan may not provide for retirement health benefits for current employees beyond the current plan year or group-term life insurance with a permanent benefit, as defined under § 1.79-0.

(c) Written plan requirements. *(1) General rule.* A cafeteria plan must contain in writing the information described in this paragraph (c), and depending on the qualified benefits offered in the plan, may also be required to contain additional information described in paragraphs (c)(2) and (c)(3) of this section. The cafeteria plan must be adopted and effective on or before the first day of the cafeteria plan year to which it relates. The terms of the plan must apply uniformly to all participants. The cafeteria plan document may be comprised of multiple documents. The written cafeteria plan must contain all of the following information—

(i) A specific description of each of the benefits available through the plan, including the periods during which the benefits are provided (the periods of coverage);

(ii) The plan's rules governing participation, and specifically requiring that all participants in the plan be employees;

(iii) The procedures governing employees' elections under the plan, including the period when elections may be made, the periods with respect to which elections are effective, and providing that elections are irrevocable, except to the extent that the optional change in status rules in § 1.125-4 are included in the cafeteria plan;

(iv) The manner in which employer contributions may be made under the plan, (for example, through an employee's salary reduction election or by nonelective employer contributions (that is, flex-credits, as defined in paragraph (b) in § 1.125-5) or both);

(v) The maximum amount of employer contributions available to any employee through the plan, by stating:

(A) The maximum amount of elective contributions (i.e., salary reduction) available to any employee through the plan, expressed as a maximum dollar amount or a maximum percentage of compensation or the method for determining the maximum dollar amount; and

(B) For contributions to section 401(k) plans, the maximum amount of elective contributions available to any employee through the plan, expressed as a maximum dollar amount or maximum percentage of compensation that may be contributed as elective contributions through the plan by employees.

(vi) The plan year of the cafeteria plan;

(vii) If the plan offers paid time off, the required ordering rule for use of nonelective and elective paid time off in paragraph (o)(4) of this section;

(viii) If the plan includes flexible spending arrangements (as defined in § 1.125-5(a)), the plan's provisions complying with any additional requirements for those FSAs (for example, the uniform coverage rule and the use-or-lose rules in paragraphs (d) and (c) in § 1.125-5);

(ix) If the plan includes a grace period, the plan's provisions complying with paragraph (e) of this section; and

(x) If the plan includes distributions from a health FSA to employees' HSAs, the plan's provisions complying with paragraph (n) in § 1.125-5.

(2) Additional requirements under sections 105(h), 129, and 137. A written plan is required for self-insured medical reimbursement plans (§ 1.105-11(b)(1)(i)), dependent care assistance programs (section 129(d)(1)), and adoption assistance (section 137(c)). Any of these plans or programs offered through a cafeteria plan that satisfies the written plan requirement in this paragraph (c) for the benefits under these plans and programs also satisfies the written plan requirements in § 1.105-11(b)(1)(i), section 129(d)(1), and section 137(c) (whichever is applicable). Alternatively, a self-insured medical reimbursement plan, a dependent care assistance program, or an adoption assistance program is permitted to satisfy the requirements in § 1.105-11(b)(1)(i), section 129(d)(1), or section 137(c) (whichever is applicable) through a separate written plan, and not as part of the written cafeteria plan.

(3) Additional requirements under section 401(k). See § 1.401(k)-1(e)(7) for additional requirements that must be satisfied in the written plan if the plan offers deferrals into a section 401(k) plan.

(4) Cross-reference allowed. In describing the benefits available through the cafeteria plan, the written cafeteria plan need not be self-contained. For example, the written cafeteria plan may incorporate by reference benefits offered through other separate written plans, such as a section 401(k) plan, or coverage under a dependent care assistance program (section 129), without describing in full the benefits established through these other plans. But, for example, if the cafeteria plan offers different maximum levels of coverage for dependent care assistance programs, the descriptions in the separate written plan must specify the available maximums.

(5) Amendments to cafeteria plan. Any amendment to the cafeteria plan must be in writing. A cafeteria plan is permitted to be amended at any time during a plan year. However, the amendment is only permitted to be effective for periods after the later of the adoption date or effective date of the amendment. For an amendment adding a new benefit, the cafeteria plan must pay or reimburse only those expenses for new benefits incurred after the later of the amendment's adoption date or effective date.

(6) Failure to satisfy written plan requirements. If there is no written cafeteria plan, or if the written plan fails to satisfy any of the requirements in this paragraph (c) (including cross-referenced requirements), the plan is not a cafeteria plan and an employee's election between taxable and nontaxable benefits results in gross income to the employee.

(7) Operational failure. (i) In general. If the cafeteria plan fails to operate according to its written plan or otherwise fails to operate in compliance with section 125 and the regulations, the plan is not a cafeteria plan and employees' elections between taxable and nontaxable benefits result in gross income to the employees.

(ii) Failure to operate according to written cafeteria plan or section 125. Examples of failures resulting in section 125 not applying to a plan include the following—

(A) Paying or reimbursing expenses for qualified benefits incurred before the later of the adoption date or effective date of the cafeteria plan, before the beginning of a period of coverage or before the later of the date of adoption or effective date of a plan amendment adding a new benefit;

(B) Offering benefits other than permitted taxable benefits and qualified benefits;

(C) Operating to defer compensation (except as permitted in paragraph (o) of this section);

(D) Failing to comply with the uniform coverage rule in paragraph (d) in § 1.125-5;

(E) Failing to comply with the use-or-lose rule in paragraph (c) in § 1.125-5;

(F) Allowing employees to revoke elections or make new elections, except as provided in § 1.125-4 and paragraph (a) in § 1.125-2;

(G) Failing to comply with the substantiation requirements of § 1.125-6;

(H) Paying or reimbursing expenses in an FSA other than expenses expressly permitted in paragraph (h) in § 1.125-5;

(I) Allocating experience gains other than as expressly permitted in paragraph (o) in § 1.125-5;

(J) Failing to comply with the grace period rules in paragraph (e) of this section; or

(K) Failing to comply with the qualified HSA distribution rules in paragraph (n) in § 1.125-5.

(d) Plan year requirements. *(1) Twelve consecutive months.* The plan year must be specified in the cafeteria plan. The plan year of a cafeteria plan must be twelve consecutive months, unless a short plan year is allowed under this paragraph (d). A plan year is permitted to begin on any day of any calendar month and must end on the preceding day in the immediately following year (for example, a plan year that begins on October 15, 2007, must end on October 14, 2008). A calendar year plan year is a period of twelve consecutive months beginning on January 1 and ending on December 31 of the same calendar year. A plan year specified in the cafeteria plan is effective for the first plan year of a cafeteria plan and for all subsequent plan years, unless changed as provided in paragraph (d)(2) of this section.

(2) Changing plan year. The plan year is permitted to be changed only for a valid business purpose. A change in the plan year is not permitted if a principal purpose of the change in plan year is to circumvent the rules of section 125 or these regulations. If a change in plan year does not satisfy this subparagraph, the attempt to change the plan year is ineffective and the plan year of the cafeteria plan remains the same.

(3) Short plan year. A short plan year of less than twelve consecutive months is permitted for a valid business purpose.

(4) Examples. The following examples illustrate the rules in paragraph (d) of this section:

Example (1). Employer with calendar year. Employer G, with a calendar taxable year, first establishes a cafeteria plan effective July 1, 2009. The cafeteria plan specifies a calendar plan year. The first cafeteria plan year is the period beginning on July 1, 2009, and ending on December 31, 2009. Employer G has a business purpose for a short first cafeteria plan year.

Example (2). Employer changes insurance carrier. Employer H establishes a cafeteria plan effective January 1, 2009, with a calendar year plan year. The cafeteria plan offers an accident and health plan through Insurer X. In March 2010, Employer H contracts to provide accident and health insurance through another insurance company, Y. Y's accident and health insurance is offered on a July 1-June 30 benefit year. Effective July 1, 2010, Employer H amends the plan to change to a July 1-June 30 plan year. Employer H has a business purpose for changing the cafeteria plan year and for the short plan year ending June 30, 2010.

(5) Significance of plan year. The plan year generally is the coverage period for benefits provided through the cafeteria plan to which annual elections for these benefits apply. Benefits elected pursuant to the employee's election for a plan year generally may not be carried forward to subsequent plan years. However, see the grace period rule in paragraph (e) of this section.

(e) Grace period. *(1) In general.* A cafeteria plan may, at the employer's option, include a grace period of up to the fifteenth day of the third month immediately following the end of each plan year. If a cafeteria plan provides for a grace period, an employee who has unused benefits or contributions relating to a qualified benefit (for example, health flexible spending arrangement (health FSA) or dependent care assistance) from the immediately preceding plan year, and who incurs expenses for that same qualified benefit during the grace period, may be paid or reimbursed for those expenses from the unused benefits or contributions as if the expenses had been incurred in the immediately preceding plan year. A grace period is available for all qualified benefits described in paragraph (a)(3) of this section, except that the grace period does not apply to paid time off and elective contributions under a section 401(k) plan. The effect of the grace period is that the employee may have as long as 14 months and 15 days (that is, the 12 months in the current cafeteria plan year plus the grace period) to use the benefits or contributions for a plan year before those amounts are forfeited under the use-or-lose rule in paragraph (c) in § 1.125-5. If the grace period is added to a cafeteria plan through an amendment, all requirements in paragraph (c) of this section must be satisfied.

(2) Grace period optional features. A grace period provision may contain any or all of the following—

(i) The grace period may apply to some qualified benefits described in paragraph (a)(3) of this section, but not to others;

(ii) The grace period provision may limit the amount of unused benefits or contributions available during the grace period. The limit must be uniform and apply to all participants. However, the limit must not be based on a percentage of the amount of the unused benefits or contributions remaining at the end of the immediately prior plan year;

(iii) The last day of the grace period may be sooner than the fifteenth day of the third month immediately following the end of the plan year (that is, the grace period may be shorter than two and one half months);

(iv) The grace period provision is permitted to treat expenses for qualified benefits incurred during the grace period either as expenses incurred during the immediately preceding plan year or as expenses incurred during the current plan year (for example, the plan may first apply the unused contributions or benefits from the immediately preceding year to pay or reimburse grace period expenses and then, when the unused contributions and benefits from the prior year are exhausted, the grace period expenses may be paid from current year contributions and benefits.); and

(v) The grace period provision may permit the employer to defer the allocation of expenses described in paragraph (e)(2)(iv) of this section until after the end of the grace period.

(3) Grace period requirements. A grace period must satisfy the requirements in paragraph (c) of this section and all of the following requirements:

(i) The grace period provisions in the cafeteria plan (including optional provisions in paragraph (e)(2) of this section) must apply uniformly to all participants in the cafeteria plan, determined as of the last day of the plan year. Participants in the cafeteria plan through COBRA and participants who were participants as of the last day of the plan year but terminate during the grace period are participants for purposes of the grace period. See § 54.4980B-2, Q&A-8 of this chapter;

(ii) The grace period provision in the cafeteria plan must state that unused benefits or contributions relating to a particular qualified benefit may only be used to pay or reimburse expenses incurred with respect to the same qualified benefit. For example, unused amounts elected to pay or reimburse medical expenses in a health FSA may not be used to pay or reimburse dependent care expenses incurred during the grace period; and

(iii) The grace period provision in the cafeteria plan must state that to the extent any unused benefits or contributions from the immediately preceding plan year exceed the expenses for the qualified benefit incurred during the grace period, those remaining unused benefits or contributions may not be carried forward to any subsequent period (including any subsequent plan year), cannot be cashed-out and must be forfeited under the use-or-lose rule. See paragraph (c) in § 1.125-5

(4) Examples. The following examples illustrate the rules in this paragraph (e).

Example (1). Expenses incurred during grace period and immediately following plan year. (i) Employer I's calendar year cafeteria plan includes a grace period allowing all participants to apply unused benefits or contributions remaining at the end of the plan year to qualified benefits incurred during the grace period immediately following that plan year. The grace period for the plan year ending December 31, 2009, ends on March 15, 2010.

(ii) Employee X timely elected salary reduction of $1,000 for a health FSA for the plan year ending December 31, 2009. As of December 31, 2009, X has $200 remaining unused in his health FSA. X timely elected salary reduction for a health FSA of $1,500 for the plan year ending December 31, 2010.

(iii) During the grace period from January 1 through March 15, 2010, X incurs $300 of unreimbursed medical expenses (as defined in section 213(d)). The unused $200 from the plan year ending December 31, 2009, is applied to pay or reimburse $200 of X's $300 of medical expenses incurred during the grace period. Therefore, as of March 16, 2010, X has no unused benefits or contributions remaining for the plan year ending December 31, 2009.

(iv) The remaining $100 of medical expenses incurred between January 1 and March 15, 2010, is paid or reimbursed from X's health FSA for the plan year ending December 31, 2010. As of March 16, 2010, X has $1,400 remaining in the health FSA for the plan year ending December 31, 2010.

Example (2). Unused benefits exceed expenses incurred during grace period. Same facts as Example 1, except that X incurs $150 of section 213(d) medical expenses during the grace period (January 1 through March 15, 2010). As of March 16, 2010, X has $50 of unused benefits or contributions remaining for the plan year ending December 31, 2009. The unused $50 cannot be cashed-out, converted to any other taxable or nontaxable benefit, or used in any other plan year (including the plan year ending December 31, 2009). The unused $50 is subject to the use-or-lose rule in paragraph (c) in § 1.125-5 and is forfeited. As of March 16, 2010, X has the entire $1,500 elected in the health FSA for the plan year ending December 31, 2010.

Example (3). Terminated participants. (i) Employer J's cafeteria plan includes a grace period allowing all participants to apply unused benefits or contributions remaining at the end of the plan year to qualified benefits incurred during the grace period immediately following that plan year. For the plan year ending on December 31, 2009, the grace period ends March 15, 2010.

(ii) Employees A, B, C, and D each timely elected $1,200 salary reduction for a health FSA for the plan year ending December 31, 2009. Employees A and B terminated employment on September 15, 2009. Each has $500 of unused benefits or contributions in the health FSA.

(iii) Employee A elected COBRA for the health FSA. Employee A is a participant in the cafeteria plan as of December 31, 2009, the last day of the 2009 plan year. Employee A has $500 of unused benefits or contributions available during the grace period for the 2009 plan year (ending March 15, 2010).

(iv) Employee B did not elect COBRA for the health FSA. Employee B is not a participant in the cafeteria plan as of December 31, 2009. The grace period does not apply to Employee B.

(v) Employee C has $500 of unused benefits in his health FSA as of December 31, 2009, and terminated employment on January 15, 2010. Employee C is a participant in the cafeteria plan as of December 31, 2009 and has $500 of unused benefits or contributions available during the grace period ending March 15, 2010, even though he terminated employment on January 15, 2010.

(vi) Employee D continues to work for Employer H throughout 2009 and 2010, also has $500 of unused benefits or contributions in his health FSA as of December 31, 2009, but made no health FSA election for 2010. Employee D is a participant in the cafeteria plan as of December 31, 2009 and has $500 of unused benefits or contributions available during the grace period ending March 15, 2010, even though he is not a participant in a health FSA for the 2010 plan year.

(f) Run-out period. A cafeteria plan is permitted to contain a run-out period as designated by the employer. A run-out period is a period after the end of the plan year (or grace period) during which a participant can submit a claim for reimbursement for a qualified benefit incurred during the plan year (or grace period). Thus, a plan is also permitted to provide a deadline on or after the end of the plan year (or grace period) for submitting a claim for reimbursement for the plan year. Any run-out period must be provided on a uniform and consistent basis with respect to all participants.

(g) Employee for purposes of section 125. *(1) Current employees, former employees.* The term employee includes any current or former employee (including any laid-off employee or retired employee) of the employer. See paragraph (g)(3) of this section concerning limits on participation by former employees. Specifically, the term employee includes the following—

(i) Common law employee;

(ii) Leased employee described in section 414(n);

(iii) Full-time life insurance salesman (as defined in section 7701(a)(20)); and

(iv) A current employee or former employee described in paragraphs (g)(1)(i) through (iii) of this section.

(2) Self-employed individual not an employee. (i) In general. The term employee does not include a self-employed individual or a 2-percent shareholder of an S corporation, as defined in paragraph (g)(2)(ii) of this subsection. For example, a sole proprietor, a partner in a partnership, or a director solely serving on a corporation's board of directors (and not otherwise providing services to the corporation as an employee) is not an employee for purposes of section 125, and thus is not permitted to participate in a cafeteria plan. However, a sole proprietor may sponsor a cafeteria plan covering the sole proprietor's employees (but not the sole proprietor). Similarly, a partnership or S corporation may sponsor a cafeteria plan covering employees (but not a partner or 2-percent shareholder of an S corporation).

(ii) Two percent shareholder of an S corporation. A 2-percent shareholder of an S corporation has the meaning set forth in section 1372(b).

(iii) Certain dual status individuals. If an individual is an employee of an employer and also provides services to that employer as an independent contractor or director (for example, an individual is both a director and an employee of a C corp), the individual is eligible to participate in that employer's cafeteria plan solely in his or her capacity as an employee. This rule does not apply to partners or to 2-percent shareholders of an S corporation.

(iv) Examples. The following examples illustrate the rules in paragraphs (g)(2)(ii) and (g)(2)(iii) of this section:

Example (1). Two-percent shareholders of an S corporation. (i) Employer K, an S corporation, maintains a cafeteria plan for its employees (other than 2-percent shareholders of an S corporation). Employer K's taxable year and the plan year are the calendar year. On January 1, 2009, individual Z owns 5 percent of the outstanding stock in Employer K. Y, who owns no stock in Employer K, is married to Z. Y and Z are employees of Employer K. Z is a 2-percent shareholder in Employer K (as defined in section 1372(b)). Y is also a 2-percent shareholder in Employer K by operation of the attribution rules in section 318(a)(1)(A)(i).

(ii) On July 15, 2009, Z sells all his stock in Employer K to an unrelated third party, and ceases to be a 2-percent shareholder. Y and Z continue to work as employees of Employer K during the entire 2009 calendar year. Y and Z are ineligible to participate in Employer K's cafeteria plan for the 2009 plan year.

Example (2). Director and employee. T is an employee and also a director of Employer L, a C corp that sponsors a cafeteria plan. The cafeteria plan allows only employees of Employer L to participate in the cafeteria plan. T's annual compensation as an employee is $50,000; T is also paid $3,000 annually in director's fees. T makes a timely election to salary reduce $5,000 from his employee compensation for dependent care benefits. T makes no election with respect to his compensation as a director. T may participate in the cafeteria plan in his capacity as an employee of Employer L.

(3) Limits on participation by former employees. Although former employees are treated as employees, a cafeteria plan may not be established or maintained predominantly for the benefit of former employees of the employer. Such a plan is not a cafeteria plan.

(4) No participation by the spouse or dependent of an employee. (i) Benefits allowed to participant's spouse or dependents but not participation. The spouse or dependents of employees may not be participants in a cafeteria plan unless they are also employees. However, a cafeteria plan may provide benefits to spouses and dependents of participants. For example, although an employee's spouse may benefit from the employee's election of accident and health insurance coverage or of coverage through a dependent care assistance program, the spouse may not participate in a cafeteria plan (that is, the spouse may not be given the opportunity to elect or purchase benefits offered by the plan).

(ii) Certain elections after employee's death. An employee's spouse is not a participant in a cafeteria plan merely because the spouse has the right, upon the death of the employee, to elect among various settlement options or to elect among permissible distribution options with respect to the deceased employee's benefits through a section 401(k) plan, Health Savings Account, or certain group-term life insurance offered through the cafeteria plan. See § 54.4980B-2, Q&A 8 and § 54.4980B-4, Q&A-1 of this chapter on COBRA rights of a participant's spouse or dependents.

(5) Employees of certain controlled groups. All employees who are treated as employed by a single employer under section 414(b), (c), (m), or (o) are treated as employed by a single employer for purposes of section 125. Section 125(g)(4); section 414(t).

(h) After-tax employee contributions. *(1) Certain after-tax employee contributions treated as cash.* In addition to the cash benefits described in paragraph (a)(2) of this section, in general, a benefit is treated as cash for purposes of section 125 if the benefit does not defer compensation (except as provided in paragraph (o) of this section) and an employee who receives the benefit purchases such benefit with after-tax employee contributions or is treated, for all purposes under the Code (including, for example, reporting and withholding purposes), as receiving, at the time that the benefit is received, cash compensation equal to the full value of the benefit at that time and then purchasing the benefit with after-tax employee contributions. Thus, for example, long-term disability coverage is treated as cash for purposes of section 125 if the cafeteria plan provides that an employee may purchase the coverage through the cafeteria plan with after-tax employee contributions or provides that the employee receiving such coverage is treated as having received cash compensation equal to the value of the coverage and then as having purchased the coverage with after-tax employee contributions. Also, for example, a cafeteria plan may offer employees the opportunity to purchase, with after-tax employee contributions, group-term life insurance on the life of an employee (providing no permanent benefits), an accident and health plan, or a dependent care assistance program.

(2) Accident and health coverage purchased for someone other than the employee's spouse or dependents with after-tax employee contributions. If the requirements of section 106 are satisfied, employer-provided accident and health coverage for an employee and his or her spouse or dependents is excludible from the employee's gross income. The fair market value of coverage for any other individual, provided with respect to the employee, is includible in the employee's gross income. § 1.106-1; § 1.61-21(a)(4), and § 1.61-21(b)(1). A cafeteria plan is permitted to allow employees to elect accident and health coverage for an individual who is not the spouse or dependent of the employee as a taxable benefit.

(3) Example. The following example illustrates the rules of this paragraph (h):

Example. Accident and health plan coverage for individuals who are not a spouse or dependent of an employee. (i) Employee C participates in Employer M's cafeteria plan. Employee C timely elects salary reduction for employer-provided accident and health coverage for himself and for accident and health coverage for his former spouse. C's former spouse is not C's dependent. A former spouse is not a spouse as defined in section 152.

(ii) The fair market value of the coverage for the former spouse is $1,000. Employee C has $1,000 includible in gross income for the accident and health coverage of his former spouse, because the section 106 exclusion applies only to employer-provided accident and health coverage for the employee or the employee's spouse or dependents.

(iii) No payments or reimbursements received under the accident and health coverage result in gross income to Employee C or to the former spouse. The result is the same if the $1,000 for coverage of C's former spouse is paid from C's after-tax income outside the cafeteria plan.

(i) Prohibited taxable benefits. Any taxable benefit not described in paragraph (a)(2) of this section and not treated as cash for purposes of section 125 in paragraph (h) of this section is not permitted to be included in a cafeteria plan. A plan that offers taxable benefits other than the taxable benefits described in paragraph (a)(2) and (h) of this section is not a cafeteria plan.

(j) Coordination with other rules. *(1) In general.* If a benefit is excludible from an employee's gross income when provided separately, the benefit is excludible from gross income when provided through a cafeteria plan. Thus, a qualified benefit is excludible from gross income if both the rules under section 125 and the specific rules providing for the exclusion of the benefit from gross income are satisfied. For example, if the nondiscrimination rules for specific qualified benefits (for example, sections 79(d), 105(h), 129(d)(2), 137(c)(2)) are not satisfied, those qualified benefits are includible in gross income. Thus, if $50,000 in group-term life insurance is offered through a cafeteria plan, the nondiscrimination rules in section 79(d) must be satisfied in order to exclude the coverage from gross income.

(2) Section 125 nondiscrimination rules. Qualified benefits are includible in the gross income of highly compensated participants or key employees if the nondiscrimination rules of section 125 are not satisfied. See § 1.125-7.

(3) Taxable benefits. If a benefit that is includible in gross income when offered separately is offered through a cafeteria plan, the benefit continues to be includible in gross income.

(k) Group-term life insurance. *(1) In general.* In addition to offering up to $50,000 in group-term life insurance coverage excludible under section 79(a), a cafeteria plan may offer coverage in excess of that amount. The cost of coverage in excess of $50,000 in group-term life insurance coverage provided under a policy or policies carried directly or indirectly by one or more employers (taking into account all coverage provided both through a cafeteria plan and outside a cafeteria plan) is includible in an employee's gross income. Group-term life insurance combined with permanent benefits, within the meaning of § 1.79-0, is a prohibited benefit in a cafeteria plan.

(2) Determining cost of insurance includible in employee's gross income. (i) In general. If the aggregate group-term life insurance coverage on the life of the employee

(under policies carried directly or indirectly by the employer) exceeds $50,000, all or a portion of the insurance is provided through a cafeteria plan, and the group-term life insurance is provided through a plan that meets the nondiscrimination rules of section 79(d), the amount includible in an employee's gross income is determined under paragraphs (k)(2)(i)(A) through (C) of this section. For each employee—

(A) The entire amount of salary reduction and employer flex-credits through a cafeteria plan for group-term life insurance coverage on the life of the employee is excludible from the employee's gross income, regardless of the amount of employer-provided group-term life insurance on the employee's life (that is, whether or not the coverage provided to the employee both through the cafeteria plan and outside the cafeteria plan exceeds $50,000);

(B) The cost of the group-term life insurance in excess of $50,000 of coverage is includible in the employee's gross income. The amount includible in the employee's income is determined using the rules of § 1.79-3 and Table I (Uniform Premiums for $1,000 of Group-Term Life Insurance Protection). See subparagraph (C) of this paragraph (k)(2)(i) for determining the amount paid by the employee for purposes of reducing the Table I amount includible in income under § 1.79-3.

(C) In determining the amount paid by the employee toward the purchase of the group-term life insurance for purposes of § 1.79-3, only an employee's after-tax contributions are treated as an amount paid by the employee.

(ii) Examples. The rules in this paragraph (k) are illustrated by the following examples, in which the group-term life insurance coverage satisfies the nondiscrimination rules in section 79(d), provides no permanent benefits, is for a 12-month period, is the only group-term life insurance coverage provided under a policy carried directly or indirectly by the employer, and applies Table I (Uniform Premiums for $1,000 of Group-Term Life Insurance Protection) effective July 1, 1999:

Example (1). Excess group-term life insurance coverage provided through salary reduction in a cafeteria plan. (i) Employer N provides group-term life insurance coverage to its employees only through its cafeteria plan. Employer N's cafeteria plan allows employees to elect salary reduction for group-term life insurance. Employee B, age 42, elected salary reduction of $200 for $150,000 of group-term life insurance. None of the group-term life insurance is paid through after-tax employee contributions.

(ii) B's $200 of salary reduction for group-term life insurance is excludible from B's gross income under paragraph (k)(2)(i)(A).

(iii) B has a total of $150,000 of group-term life insurance. The group-term life insurance in excess of the dollar limitation of section 79 is $100,000 (150,000-50,000).

(iv) The Table I cost is $120 for $100,000 of group-term life insurance for an individual between ages 40 to 44. The Table I cost of $120 is reduced by zero (because B paid no portion of the group-term life insurance with after-tax employee contributions), under paragraphs (k)(2)(i)(A)-(B) of this section.

(v) The amount includible in B's gross income for the $100,000 of excess group-term life insurance is $120.

Example (2). Excess group-term life insurance coverage provided through salary reduction in a cafeteria plan where employee purchases a portion of group-term life insurance coverage with after-tax contributions. (i) Same facts as Example 1, except that B elected salary reduction of $100 and makes an after-tax contribution of $100 toward the purchase of group-term life insurance coverage.

(ii) B's $100 of salary reduction for group-term life insurance is excludible from B's gross income, under paragraph (k)(2)(i)(A) of this section.

(iii) B has a total of $150,000 of group-term life insurance. The group-term life insurance in excess of the dollar limitation of section 79 is $100,000 (150,000-50,000).

(iv) The Table I cost is $120 for $100,000 of group-term life insurance for an individual between ages 40 to 44, under (k)(2)(i)(B). The Table I cost of $120 is reduced by $100 (because B paid $100 for the group-term life insurance with after-tax employee contributions), under paragraphs (k)(2)(i)(B) and (k)(2)(i)(C) of this section.

(v) The amount includible in B's gross income for the $100,000 of excess group-term life insurance coverage is $20.

Example (3). Excess group-term life insurance coverage provided through salary reduction in a cafeteria plan and outside a cafeteria plan. (i) Same facts as Example 1 except that Employer N also provides (at no cost to employees) group-term life insurance coverage equal to each employee's annual salary. Employee B's annual salary is $150,000. B has $150,000 of group-term life insurance directly from Employer N, and also $150,000 coverage through Employer N's cafeteria plan.

(ii) B's $200 of salary reduction for group-term life insurance is excludible from B's gross income, under paragraph (k)(2)(i)(A) of this section.

(iii) B has a total of $300,000 of group-term life insurance. The group-term life insurance in excess of the dollar limitation of section 79 is $250,000 (300,000-50,000).

(iv) The Table I cost is $300 for $250,000 of group-term life insurance for an individual between ages 40 to 44. The Table I cost of $300 is reduced by zero (because B paid no portion of the group-term life insurance with after-tax employee contributions), under paragraphs (k)(2)(i)(B) and (k)(2)(i)(C) of this section.

(v) The amount includible in B's gross income for the $250,000 of excess group-term life insurance is $300.

Example (4). Excess group-term life insurance coverage provided through salary reduction in a cafeteria plan and outside a cafeteria plan. (i) Same facts as Example 3 except that Employee C's annual salary is $30,000. C has $30,000 of group-term life insurance coverage provided directly from Employer N, and elects an additional $30,000 of coverage for $40 through Employer N's cafeteria plan. C is 42 years old.

(ii) C's $40 of salary reduction for group-term life insurance is excludible from C's gross income, under paragraph (k)(2)(i)(A) of this section.

(iii) C has a total of $60,000 of group-term life insurance. The group-term life insurance in excess of the dollar limitation of section 79 is $10,000 (60,000-50,000).

(iv) The Table I cost is $12 for $10,000 of group-term life insurance for an individual between ages 40 to 44. The Table I cost of $12 is reduced by zero (because C paid no portion of the group-term life insurance with after-tax employee contributions), under paragraphs (k)(2)(i)(B) and (k)(2)(i)(C) of this section.

(v) The amount includible in C's gross income for the $10,000 of excess group-term life insurance coverage is $12.

(l) COBRA premiums. *(1) Paying COBRA premiums through a cafeteria plan.* Under § 1.125-4(c)(3)(iv), COBRA premiums for an employer-provided group health plan are qualified benefits if:

(i) The premiums are excludible from an employee's income under section 106; or

(ii) The premiums are for the accident and health plan of the employer sponsoring the cafeteria plan, even if the fair market value of the premiums is includible in an employee's gross income. See also paragraph (e)(2) in § 1.125-5 and § 54.4980B-2, Q&A-8 of this chapter for COBRA rules for health FSAs.

(2) Example. The following example illustrates the rules of this paragraph (l):

Example. COBRA premiums. (i) Employer O maintains a cafeteria plan for full-time employees, offering an election between cash and employer-provided accident and health insurance and other qualified benefits. Employees A, B, and C participate in the cafeteria plan. On July 1, 2009, Employee A has a qualifying event (as defined in § 54.4980B-4 of this chapter).

(ii) Employee A was a full-time employee and became a part-time employee and for that reason, is no longer covered by Employer O's accident and health plan. Under § 1.125-4(f)(3)(ii), Employee A changes her election to salary reduce to pay her COBRA premiums.

(iii) Employee B previously worked for another employer, quit and elected COBRA. Employee B begins work for Employer O on July 1, 2009, and becomes eligible to participate in Employer O's cafeteria plan on July 1, 2009, but will not be eligible to participate in Employer O's accident and health plan until October 1, 2009. Employee B elects to salary reduce to pay COBRA premiums for coverage under the accident and health plan sponsored by B's former employer.

(iv) Employee C and C's spouse are covered by Employer O's accident and health plan until July 1, 2009, when C's divorce from her spouse became final. C continues to be covered by the accident and health plan. On July 1, 2009, C requests to pay COBRA premiums for her former spouse (who is not C's dependent (as defined in section 152)) with after-tax employee contributions.

(v) Salary reduction elections for COBRA premiums for Employees A and B are qualified benefits for purposes of section 125 and are excludible from the gross income of Employees A and B. Employer O allows A and B to salary reduce for these COBRA premiums.

(vi) Employer O allows C to pay for COBRA premiums for C's former spouse, with after-tax employee contributions because although accident and health coverage for C's former spouse is permitted in a cafeteria plan, the premiums are includible in C's gross income.

(vii) The operation of Employer O's cafeteria plan satisfies the requirements of this paragraph (l).

(m) Payment or reimbursement of employees' individual accident and health insurance premiums. *(1) In general.* The payment or reimbursement of employees' substantiated individual health insurance premiums is excludible from employees' gross income under section 106 and is a qualified benefit for purposes of section 125.

(2) Example. The following example illustrates the rule of this paragraph (m):

Example. Payment or reimbursement of premiums.

(i) Employer P's cafeteria plan offers the following benefits for employees who are covered by an individual health insurance policy. The employee substantiates the expenses for the premiums for the policy (as required in paragraph (b)(2) in § 1.125-6) before any payments or reimbursements to the employee for premiums are made. The payments or reimbursements are made in the following ways:

(ii) The cafeteria plan reimburses each employee directly for the amount of the employee's substantiated health insurance premium;

(iii) The cafeteria plan issues the employee a check payable to the health insurance company for the amount of the employee's health insurance premium, which the employee is obligated to tender to the insurance company;

(iv) The cafeteria plan issues a check in the same manner as (iii), except that the check is payable jointly to the employee and the insurance company; or

(vi) Under these circumstances, the individual health insurance policies are accident and health plans as defined in § 1.106-1. This benefit is a qualified benefit under section 125.

(n) Section 105 rules for accident and health plan offered through a cafeteria plan. *(1) General rule.* In order for an accident and health plan to be a qualified benefit that is excludible from gross income if elected through a cafeteria plan, the cafeteria plan must satisfy section 125 and the accident and health plan must satisfy section 105(b) and (h).

(2) Section 105(b) requirements in general. Section 105(b) provides an exclusion from gross income for amounts paid to an employee from an employer-funded accident and health plan specifically to reimburse the employee for certain expenses for medical care (as defined in section 213(d)) incurred by the employee or the employee's spouse or dependents during the period for which the benefit is provided to the employee (that is, when the employee is covered by the accident and health plan).

(o) Prohibition against deferred compensation. *(1) In general.* Any plan that offers a benefit that defers compensation (except as provided in this paragraph (o)) is not a cafeteria plan. See section 125(d)(2)(A). A plan that permits employees to carry over unused elective contributions, after-tax contributions, or plan benefits from one plan year to another (except as provided in paragraphs (e), (o)(3) and (4) and (p) of this section) defers compensation. This is the case regardless of how the contributions or benefits are used by the employee in the subsequent plan year (for example, whether they are automatically or electively converted into another taxable or nontaxable benefit in the subsequent plan year or used to provide additional benefits of the same type). Similarly, a cafeteria plan also defers compensation if the plan permits employees to use contributions for one plan year to purchase a benefit that will be provided in a subsequent plan year (for example, life, health or disability if these benefits have a savings or investment feature, such as whole life insurance). See also Q&A-5 in § 1.125-3, prohibiting deferring compensation from one cafeteria plan year to a subsequent cafeteria plan year. See paragraph (e) of this section for grace period rules. A plan does not defer compensation merely because it allocates experience gains (or forfeitures) among participants in compliance with paragraph (o) in § 1.125-5.

(2) Effect if a plan includes a benefit that defers the receipt of compensation or a plan operates to defer compensation. If a plan violates paragraph (o)(1) of this section, the

availability of an election between taxable and nontaxable benefits under such a plan results in gross income to the employees.

(3) Cash or deferred arrangements that may be offered in a cafeteria plan. (i) In general. A cafeteria plan may offer the benefits set forth in this paragraph (o)(3), even though these benefits defer compensation.

(ii) Elective contributions to a section 401(k) plan. A cafeteria plan may permit a covered employee to elect to have the employer, on behalf of the employee, pay amounts as contributions to a trust that is part of a profit-sharing or stock bonus plan or rural cooperative plan (within the meaning of section 401(k)(7)), which includes a qualified cash or deferred arrangement (as defined in section 401(k)(2)). In addition, after-tax employee contributions under a qualified plan subject to section 401(m) are permitted through a cafeteria plan. The right to make such contributions does not cause a plan to fail to be a cafeteria plan merely because, under the qualified plan, employer matching contributions (as defined in section 401(m)(4)(A)) are made with respect to elective or after-tax employee contributions.

(iii) Additional permitted deferred compensation arrangements. A plan maintained by an educational organization described in section 170(b)(1)(A)(ii) to the extent of amounts which a covered employee may elect to have the employer pay as contributions for post-retirement group life insurance is permitted through a cafeteria plan, if—

(A) All contributions for such insurance must be made before retirement; and

(B) Such life insurance does not have a cash surrender value at any time.

(iv) Contributions to HSAs. Contributions to covered employees' HSAs as defined in section 223 (but not contributions to Archer MSAs).

(4) Paid time off. (i) In general. A cafeteria plan is permitted to include elective paid time off (that is, vacation days, sick days or personal days) as a permitted taxable benefit through the plan by permitting employees to receive more paid time off than the employer otherwise provides to the employees on a nonelective basis, but only if the inclusion of elective paid time off through the plan does not operate to permit the deferral of compensation. In addition, a plan that only offers the choice of cash or paid time off is not a cafeteria plan and is not subject to the rules of section 125. In order to avoid deferral of compensation, the cafeteria plan must preclude any employee from using the paid time off or receiving cash, in a subsequent plan year, for any portion of such paid time off remaining unused as of the end of the plan year. (See paragraph (o)(4)(iii) of this section for the deadline to cash out unused elective paid time off.) For example, a plan that offers employees the opportunity to purchase paid time off (or to receive cash or other benefits through the plan in lieu of paid time off) is not a cafeteria plan if employees who purchase the paid time off for a plan year are allowed to use any unused paid time off in a subsequent plan year. This is the case even though the plan does not permit the employee to convert, in any subsequent plan year, the unused paid time off into any other benefit.

(ii) Ordering of elective and nonelective paid time off. In determining whether a plan providing paid time off operates to permit the deferral of compensation, a cafeteria plan must provide that employees are deemed to use paid time off in the following order:

(A) Nonelective paid time off. Nonelective paid time off (that is, paid time off with respect to which the employee has no election) is used first;

(B) Elective paid time off. Elective paid time off is used after all nonelective paid time off is used.

(iii) Cashing out or forfeiture of unused elective paid time off, in general. The cafeteria plan must provide that all unused elective paid time off (determined as of the last day of the plan year) must either be paid in cash (within the time specified in this paragraph (o)(4)) or be forfeited. This provision must apply uniformly to all participants in the cafeteria plan.

(A) Cash out of unused elective paid time off. A plan does not operate to permit the deferral of compensation merely because the plan provides that an employee who has not used all elective paid time off for a plan year receives in cash the value of such unused paid time off. The employee must receive the cash on or before the last day of the cafeteria plan's plan year to which the elective contributions used to purchase the unused elective paid time off relate.

(B) Forfeiture of unused elective paid time off. If the cafeteria plan provides for forfeiture of unused elective paid time off, the forfeiture must be effective on the last day of the plan year to which the elective contributions relate.

(iv) No grace period for paid time off. The grace period described in paragraph (e) of this section does not apply to paid time off.

(v) Examples. The following examples illustrate the rules of this paragraph (o)(4):

Example (1). Plan cashes out unused elective paid time off on or before the last day of the plan year. (i) Employer Q provides employees with two weeks of paid time off for each calendar year. Employer Q's human resources policy (that is, outside the cafeteria plan), permits employees to carry over one nonelective week of paid time off to the next year. Employer Q maintains a calendar year cafeteria plan that permits the employee to purchase, with elective contributions, an additional week of paid time off.

(ii) For the 2009 plan year, Employee A (with a calendar tax year), timely elects to purchase one additional week of paid time off. During 2009, Employee A uses only two weeks of paid time off. Employee A is deemed to have used two weeks of nonelective paid time off and zero weeks of elective paid time off.

(iii) Pursuant to the cafeteria plan, the plan pays Employee A the value of the unused elective paid time off week in cash on December 31, 2009. Employer Q includes this amount on the 2009 Form W-2 for Employee A. This amount is included in Employee A's gross income in 2009. The cafeteria plan's terms and operations do not violate the prohibition against deferring compensation.

Example (2). Unused nonelective paid time off carried over to next plan year. (i) Same facts as Example 1, except that Employee A uses only one week of paid time off during the year. Pursuant to the cafeteria plan, Employee A is deemed to have used one nonelective week, and having retained one nonelective week and one elective week of paid time off. Employee A receives in cash the value of the unused elective paid time off on December 31, 2009. Employer Q includes this amount on the 2009 Form W-2 for Employee A. Employee A must report this amount as gross income in 2009.

(ii) Pursuant to Employer Q's human resources policy, Employee A is permitted to carry over the one nonelective week of paid time off to the next year. Nonelective paid time off is not part of the cafeteria plan (that is, neither Employer Q nor the cafeteria plan permit employees to exchange nonelective paid time off for other benefits).

(iii) The cafeteria plan's terms and operations do not violate the prohibition against deferring compensation.

Example (3). Forfeiture of unused elective paid time off. Same facts as Example 2, except that pursuant to the cafeteria plan, Employee A forfeits the remaining one week of elective paid time off. The cafeteria plan's terms and operations do not violate the prohibition against deferring compensation.

Example (4). Unused elective paid time off carried over to next plan year. Same facts as Example 1, except that Employee A uses only two weeks of paid time off during the 2009 plan year, and, under the terms of the cafeteria plan, Employee A is treated as having used the two nonelective weeks and as having retained the one elective week. The one remaining week (that is, the elective week) is carried over to the next plan year (or the value thereof used for any other purpose in the next plan year). The plan operates to permit deferring compensation and is not a cafeteria plan.

Example (5). Paid time off exchanged for accident and health insurance premiums. Employer R provides employees with four weeks of paid time off for a year. Employer R's calendar year cafeteria plan permits employees to exchange up to one week of paid time off to pay the employee's share of accident and health insurance premiums. For the 2009 plan year, Employee B (with a calendar tax year), timely elects to exchange one week of paid time off (valued at $769) to pay accident and health insurance premiums for 2009. The $769 is excludible from Employee B's gross income under section 106. The cafeteria plan's terms and operations do not violate the prohibition against deferring compensation.

(p) Benefits relating to more than one year. *(1) Benefits in an accident and health insurance policy relating to more than one year.* Consistent with section 125(d), an accident and health insurance policy may include certain benefits, as set forth in this paragraph (p)(1), without violating the prohibition against deferred compensation.

(i) Permitted benefits. The following features or benefits of insurance policies do not defer compensation—

(A) Credit toward the deductible for unreimbursed covered expenses incurred in prior periods;

(B) Reasonable lifetime maximum limit on benefits;

(C) Level premiums;

(D) Premium waiver during disability;

(E) Guaranteed policy renewability of coverage, without further evidence of insurability (but not guaranty of the amount of premium upon renewal);

(F) Coverage for a specified accidental injury;

(G) Coverage for a specified disease or illness, including payments at initial diagnosis of the specified disease or illness, and progressive payments of a set amount per month following the initial diagnosis (sometimes referred to as progressive diagnosis payments); and

(H) Payment of a fixed amount per day (or other period) of hospitalization.

(ii) Requirements of permitted benefits. All benefits described in paragraph (p)(1)(i) of this section must in addition satisfy all of the following requirements—

(A) No part of any benefit is used in one plan year to purchase a benefit in a subsequent plan year;

(B) The policies remain in force only so long as premiums are timely paid on a current basis, and, irrespective of the amount of premiums paid in prior plan years, if the current premiums are not paid, all coverage for new diseases or illnesses lapses. See paragraph (p)(1)(i)(D), allowing premium waiver during disability;

(C) There is no investment fund or cash value to rely upon for payment of premiums; and

(D) No part of any premium is held in a separate account for any participant or beneficiary, or otherwise segregated from the assets of the insurance company.

(2) Benefits under a long-term disability policy relating to more than one year. A long-term disability policy paying disability benefits over more than one year does not violate the prohibition against deferring compensation.

(3) Reasonable premium rebates or policy dividends. Reasonable premium rebates or policy dividends paid with respect to benefits provided through a cafeteria plan do not constitute impermissible deferred compensation if such rebates or dividends are paid before the close of the 12-month period immediately following the cafeteria plan year to which such rebates and dividends relate.

(4) Mandatory two-year election for vision or dental insurance. When a cafeteria plan offers vision or dental insurance that requires a mandatory two-year coverage period, but not longer (sometimes referred to as a "two-year lock-in"), the mandatory two-year coverage period does not result in deferred compensation in violation of section 125(d)(2), provided both of the following requirements are satisfied—

(i) The premiums for each plan year are paid no less frequently than annually; and

(ii) In no event does a cafeteria plan use salary reduction or flex-credits relating to the first year of a two-year election to apply to vision or dental insurance for the second year of the two-year election.

(5) Using salary reduction amounts from one plan year to pay accident and health insurance premiums for the first month of the immediately following plan year.

(i) In general. Salary reduction amounts from the last month of one plan year of a cafeteria plan may be applied to pay accident and health insurance premiums for insurance during the first month of the immediately following plan year, if done on a uniform and consistent basis with respect to all participants (based on the usual payroll interval for each group of participants).

(ii) Example. The following example illustrates the rules in this paragraph (p)(5):

Example. Salary reduction payments in December of calendar plan year to pay accident and health insurance premiums for January. Employer S maintains a calendar year cafeteria plan. The cafeteria plan offers employees a salary reduction election for accident and health insurance. The plan provides that employees' salary reduction amounts for the last pay period in December are applied to pay accident and health insurance premiums for the immediately following January. All employees are paid bi-weekly. For the plan year ending December 31, 2009, Employee C elects salary reduction of $3,250 for accident and health coverage. For the last pay period in December 2009, $125 (3,250/26) is applied to the accident and health insurance premium for January 2010. This plan provision does not violate the prohibition against deferring compensation.

(q) Nonqualified benefits. *(1) In general.* The following benefits are nonqualified benefits that are not permitted to be offered in a cafeteria plan—

(i) Scholarships described in section 117;

(ii) Employer-provided meals and lodging described in section 119;

(iii) Educational assistance described in section 127;

(iv) Fringe benefits described in section 132;

(v) Long-term care insurance, or any product which is advertised, marketed or offered as long-term care insurance;

(vi) Long-term care services (but see paragraph (q)(3) of this section);

(vii) Group-term life insurance on the life of any individual other than an employee (whether includible or excludible from the employee's gross income);

(viii) Health reimbursement arrangements (HRAs) that provide reimbursements up to a maximum dollar amount for a coverage period and that all or any unused amount at the end of a coverage period is carried forward to increase the maximum reimbursement amount in subsequent coverage periods;

(ix) Contributions to Archer MSAs (section 220); and

(x) Elective deferrals to a section 403(b) plan.

(2) Nonqualified benefits not permitted in a cafeteria plan. The benefits described in this paragraph (q) are not qualified benefits or taxable benefits or cash for purposes of section 125 and thus may not be offered in a cafeteria plan regardless of whether any such benefit is purchased with after-tax employee contributions or on any other basis. A plan that offers a nonqualified benefit is not a cafeteria plan. Employees' elections between taxable and nontaxable benefits through such plan result in gross income to the participants for any benefit elected. See section 125(f). See paragraph (q)(3) of this section for special rule on long-term care insurance purchased through an HSA.

(3) Long-term care insurance or services purchased through an HSA. Although long-term care insurance is not a qualified benefit and may not be offered in a cafeteria plan, a cafeteria plan is permitted to offer an HSA as a qualified benefit, and funds from the HSA may be used to pay eligible long-term care premiums on a qualified long-term care insurance contract or for qualified long-term care services.

(r) Employer contributions to a cafeteria plan. *(1) Salary reduction-in general.* The term employer contributions means amounts that are not currently available (after taking section 125 into account) to the employee but are specified in the cafeteria plan as amounts that an employee may use for the purpose of electing benefits through the plan. A plan may provide that employer contributions may be made, in whole or in part, pursuant to employees' elections to reduce their compensation or to forgo increases in compensation and to have such amounts contributed, as employer contributions, by the employer on their behalf. See also § 1.125-5 (flexible spending arrangements). Also, a cafeteria plan is permitted to require employees to elect to pay the employees' share of any qualified benefit through salary reduction and not with after-tax employee contributions. A cafeteria plan is also permitted to pay reasonable cafeteria plan administrative fees through salary reduction amounts, and these salary reduction amounts are excludible from an employee's gross income.

(2) Salary reduction as employer contribution. Salary reduction contributions are employer contributions. An employee's salary reduction election is an election to receive a contribution by the employer in lieu of salary or other compensation that is not currently available to the employee as of the effective date of the election and that does not subsequently become currently available to the employee.

(3) Employer flex-credits. A cafeteria plan may also provide that the employer contributions will or may be made on behalf of employees equal to (or up to) specified amounts (or specified percentages of compensation) and that such nonelective contributions are available to employees for the election of benefits through the plan.

(4) Elective contributions to a section 401(k) plan. See § 1.401(k)-1 for general rules relating to contributions to section 401(k) plans.

(s) Effective/applicability date. It is proposed that these regulations apply on and after plan years beginning on or after January 1, 2009, except that the rule in paragraph (k)(2)(i)(B) of this section is effective as of the date the proposed regulations are published in the Federal Register.

Proposed § 1.125-2 Cafeteria plans; elections. [*For Preamble, see ¶ 152,897*]

(a) Rules relating to making and revoking elections. *(1) Elections in general.* A plan is not a cafeteria plan unless the plan provides in writing that employees are permitted to make elections among the permitted taxable benefits and qualified benefits offered through the plan for the plan year (and grace period, if applicable). All elections must be irrevocable by the date described in paragraph (a)(2) of this section except as provided in paragraph (a)(4) of this section. An election is not irrevocable if, after the earlier of the dates specified in paragraph (a)(2) of this section, employees have the right to revoke their elections of qualified benefits and instead receive the taxable benefits for such period, without regard to whether the employees actually revoke their elections.

(2) Timing of elections. In order for employees to exclude qualified benefits from employees' gross income, benefit elections in a cafeteria plan must be made before the earlier of—

(i) The date when taxable benefits are currently available; or

(ii) The first day of the plan year (or other coverage period).

(3) Benefit currently available to an employee-in general. Cash or another taxable benefit is currently available to the employee if it has been paid to the employee or if the employee is able currently to receive the cash or other taxable benefit at the employee's discretion. However, cash or another taxable benefit is not currently available to an employee if there is a significant limitation or restriction on the employee's right to receive the benefit currently. Similarly, a benefit is not currently available as of a date if the employee may under no circumstances receive the benefit before a particular time in the future. The determination of whether a benefit is currently available to an employee does not depend on whether it has been constructively received by the employee for purposes of section 451.

(4) Exceptions to rule on making and revoking elections. If a cafeteria plan incorporates the change in status rules in § 1.125-4, to the extent provided in those rules, an employee who experiences a change in status (as defined in § 1.125-4) is permitted to revoke an existing election and to make a new election with respect to the remaining portion of the period of coverage, but only with respect to cash or other taxa-

ble benefits that are not yet currently available. See paragraph (c)(1) of this section for a special rule for changing elections prospectively for HSA contributions and paragraph (r)(4) in § 1.125-1 for section 401(k) elections. Also, only an employee of the employer sponsoring a cafeteria plan is allowed to make, revoke or change elections in the employer's cafeteria plan. The employee's spouse, dependent or any other individual other than the employee may not make, revoke or change elections under the plan.

(5) Elections not required on written paper documents. A cafeteria plan does not fail to meet the requirements of section 125 merely because it permits employees to use electronic media for such transactions. The safe harbor in § 1.401(a)-21 applies to electronic elections, revocations and changes in elections under section 125.

(6) Examples. The following examples illustrate the rules in this paragraph (a):

Example (1). Election not revocable during plan year. Employer A's cafeteria plan offers each employee the opportunity to elect, for a plan year, between $5,000 cash for the plan year and a dependent care assistance program of up to $5,000 of dependent care expenses incurred by the employee during the plan year. The cafeteria plan requires employees to elect between these benefits before the beginning of the plan year. After the year has commenced, employees are prohibited from revoking their elections. The cafeteria plan allows revocation of elections based on changes in status (as described in § 1.125-4). Employees who elected the dependent care assistance program do not include the $5,000 cash in gross income. The cafeteria plan satisfies the requirements in this paragraph (a).

Example (2). Election revocable during plan year. Same facts as Example 1 except that Employer A's cafeteria plan allows employees to revoke their elections for dependent care assistance at any time during the plan year and receive the unused amount of dependent care assistance as cash. The cafeteria plan fails to satisfy the requirements in this paragraph (a), and is not a cafeteria plan. All employees are treated as having received the $5,000 in cash even if they do not revoke their elections. The same result occurs even though the cash is not payable until the end of the plan year.

(b) Automatic elections. *(1) In general.* For new employees or current employees who fail to timely elect between permitted taxable benefits and qualified benefits, a cafeteria plan is permitted, but is not required, to provide default elections for one or more qualified benefits (for example, an election made for any prior year is deemed to be continued for every succeeding plan year, unless changed).

(2) Example. The following example illustrates the rules in this paragraph (b):

Example. Automatic elections for accident and health insurance. (i) Employer B maintains a calendar year cafeteria plan. The cafeteria plan offers accident and health insurance with an option for employee-only or family coverage. All employees are eligible to participate in the cafeteria plan immediately upon hire.

(ii) The cafeteria plan provides for an automatic enrollment process: Each new employee and each current employee is automatically enrolled in employee-only coverage under the accident and health insurance plan, and the employee's salary is reduced to pay the employee's share of the accident and health insurance premium, unless the employee affirmatively elects cash. Alternatively, if the employee has a spouse or child, the employee can elect family coverage.

(iii) When an employee is hired, the employee receives a notice explaining the automatic enrollment process and the employee's right to decline coverage and have no salary reduction. The notice includes the salary reduction amounts for employee-only coverage and family coverage, procedures for exercising the right to decline coverage, information on the time by which an election must be made, and the period for which an election is effective. The notice is also given to each current employee before the beginning of each subsequent plan year, except that the notice for a current employee includes a description of the employee's existing coverage, if any.

(iv) For a new employee, an election to receive cash or to have family coverage rather than employee-only coverage is effective if made when the employee is hired. For a current employee, an election is effective if made prior to the start of each calendar year or under any other circumstances permitted under § 1.125-4. An election made for any prior year is deemed to be continued for every succeeding plan year, unless changed.

(v) Contributions used to purchase accident and health insurance through a cafeteria plan are not includible in the gross income of the employee solely because the plan provides for automatic enrollment as a default election whereby the employee's salary is reduced each year to pay for a portion of the accident and health insurance through the plan (unless the employee affirmatively elects cash).

(c) Election rules for salary reduction contributions to HSAs. *(1) Prospective elections and changes in salary reduction elections allowed.* Contributions may be made to an HSA through a cafeteria plan. A cafeteria plan offering HSA contributions through salary reduction may permit employees to make prospective salary reduction elections or change or revoke salary reduction elections for HSA contributions (for example, to increase or decrease salary reduction elections for HSA contributions) at any time during the plan year, effective before salary becomes currently available. If a cafeteria plan offers HSA contributions as a qualified benefit, the plan must—

(i) Specifically describe the HSA contribution benefit;

(ii) Allow a participant to prospectively change his or her salary reduction election for HSA contributions on a monthly basis (or more frequently); and

(iii) Allow a participant who becomes ineligible to make HSA contributions to prospectively revoke his or her salary reduction election for HSA contributions.

(2) Example. The following example illustrates the rules in this paragraph (c):

Example. Prospective HSA salary reduction elections. (i) A cafeteria plan with a calendar plan year allows employees to make salary reduction elections for HSA contributions through the plan. The cafeteria plan permits employees to prospectively make, change or revoke salary contribution elections for HSA contributions, limited to one election, change or revocation per month.

(ii) Employee M participates in the cafeteria plan. Before salary becomes currently available to M, M makes the following elections. On January 2, 2009, M elects to contribute $100 for each pay period to an HSA, effective January 3, 2009. On March 15, 2009, M elects to reduce the HSA contribution to $35 per pay period, effective April 1, 2009. On May 1, 2009, M elects to discontinue all HSA contributions, effective May 15, 2009. The cafeteria plan implements all of Employee M's elections,

(iii) The cafeteria plan's operation is consistent with the section 125 election, change and revocation rules for HSA contributions.

(d) Optional election for new employees. A cafeteria plan may provide new employees 30 days after their hire date to make elections between cash and qualified benefits. The election is effective as of the employee's hire date. However, salary reduction amounts used to pay for such an election must be from compensation not yet currently available on the date of the election. The written cafeteria plan must provide that any employee who terminates employment and is rehired within 30 days after terminating employment (or who returns to employment following an unpaid leave of absence of less than 30 days) is not a new employee eligible for the election in this paragraph (d).

(e) Effective/applicability date. It is proposed that these regulations apply on and after plan years beginning on or after January 1, 2009.

PAR. 3. In § 1.125-2, as proposed March 7, 1989 (54 FR 9460) and as amended March 23, 2000 (65 FR 15587), A-6 is amended by removing A-6(b), A-6(c), and A-6(d), redesignating A-6(e) as paragraph A-6(b), removing the last 5 sentences of A-6(a) and adding a sentence in their place to read as follows:

Proposed § 1.125-2 Miscellaneous cafeteria plan questions and answers. [*For Preamble, see ¶ 152,127*]

* * * * *

Q-6. In what circumstance may participants revoke existing elections and make new elections under a cafeteria plan?

A-6. * * * (a) * * * However, to the extent permitted under § 1.125-4, the terms of a cafeteria plan may permit a participant to revoke an existing election and to make a new election with respect to the remaining portion of the period of coverage.

* * * * *

§ 1.125-3 Effect of the Family and Medical Leave Act on the operation of cafeteria plans.

The following questions and answers provide guidance on the effect of the Family and Medical Leave Act (FMLA), 29 U.S.C. 2601 et seq., on the operation of cafeteria plans:

Q-1. May an employee revoke coverage or cease payment of his or her share of group health plan premiums when taking unpaid FMLA, 29 U.S.C. 2601 et seq., leave?

A-1. Yes. An employer must either allow an employee on unpaid FMLA leave to revoke coverage, or continue coverage but allow the employee to discontinue payment of his or her share of the premium for group health plan coverage (including a health flexible spending arrangement (FSA)) under a cafeteria plan for the period of the FMLA leave. See 29 CFR 825.209(e). FMLA does not require that an employer allow an employee to revoke coverage if the employer pays the employee's share of premiums. As discussed in Q&A-3, if the employer continues coverage during an FMLA leave, the employer may recover the employee's share of the premiums when the employee returns to work. FMLA also provides the employee a right to be reinstated in the group health plan coverage (including a health FSA) provided under a cafeteria plan upon returning from FMLA leave if the employee's group health plan coverage terminated while on FMLA leave (either by revocation or due to nonpayment of premiums). Such an employee is entitled, to the extent required under FMLA, to be reinstated on the same terms as prior to taking FMLA leave (including family or dependent coverage), subject to any changes in benefit levels that may have taken place during the period of FMLA leave as provided in 29 CFR 825.215(d)(1). See 29 CFR 825.209(e) and 825.215(d). In addition, such an employee has the right to revoke or change elections under § 1.125-4 (e.g., because of changes in status or cost or coverage changes as provided under § 1.125-4) under the same terms and conditions as are available to employees participating in the cafeteria plan who are working and not on FMLA leave.

Q-2. Who is responsible for making premium payments under a cafeteria plan when an employee on FMLA leave continues group health plan coverage?

A-2. FMLA provides that an employee is entitled to continue group health plan coverage during FMLA leave whether or not that coverage is provided under a health FSA or other component of a cafeteria plan. See 29 CFR 825.209(b). FMLA permits an employer to require an employee who chooses to continue group health plan coverage while on FMLA leave to be responsible for the share of group health premiums that would be allocable to the employee if the employee were working, and, for this purpose, treats amounts paid pursuant to a pre-tax salary reduction agreement as amounts allocable to the employee. However, FMLA requires the employer to continue to contribute the share of the cost of the employee's coverage that the employer was paying before the employee commenced FMLA leave. See 29 CFR 825.100(b) and 825.210(a).

Q-3. What payment options are required or permitted to be offered under a cafeteria plan to an employee who continues group health plan coverage while on unpaid FMLA leave, and what is the tax treatment of these payments?

A-3. (a) In general. Subject to the limitations described in paragraph (b) of this Q&A-3, a cafeteria plan may offer one or more of the following payment options, or a combination of these options, to an employee who continues group health plan coverage (including a health FSA) while on unpaid FMLA leave; provided that the payment options for employees on FMLA leave are offered on terms at least as favorable as those offered to employees not on FMLA leave. These options are referred to in this section as pre-pay, pay-as-you-go, and catch-up. See also the FMLA notice requirements at 29 CFR 825.301(b)(1)(iv).

(1) Pre-pay. (i) Under the pre-pay option, a cafeteria plan may permit an employee to pay, prior to commencement of the FMLA leave period, the amounts due for the FMLA leave period. However, FMLA provides that the employer may not mandate that an employee pre-pay the amounts due for the leave period. See 29 CFR 825.210(c)(3) and (4).

(ii) Contributions under the pre-pay option may be made on a pre-tax salary reduction basis from any taxable compensation (including from unused sick days or vacation days). However, see Q&A-5 of this section regarding additional restrictions on pre-tax salary reduction contributions when an employee's FMLA leave spans two cafeteria plan years.

(iii) Contributions under the pre-pay option may also be made on an after-tax basis.

(2) Pay-as-you-go. (i) Under the pay-as-you-go option, employees may pay their share of the premium payments on the same schedule as payments would have been made if the employee were not on leave or under any other payment schedule permitted by the Labor Regulations at 29 CFR 825.210(c) (e.g., on the same schedule as payments are made under section 4980B (relating to coverage under the Consolidated Omnibus Budget Reconciliation Act (COBRA), 26

U.S.C. 4980B), under the employer's existing rules for payment by employees on leave without pay, or under any other system voluntarily agreed to between the employer and the employee that is not inconsistent with this section or with 29 CFR 825.210(c)).

(ii) Contributions under the pay-as-you-go option are generally made by the employee on an after-tax basis. However, contributions may be made on a pre-tax basis to the extent that the contributions are made from taxable compensation (e.g., from unused sick days or vacation days) that is due the employee during the leave period.

(iii) An employer is not required to continue the group health coverage of an employee who fails to make required premium payments while on FMLA leave, provided that the employer follows the notice procedures required under FMLA. See 29 CFR 825.212. However, if the employer chooses to continue the health coverage of an employee who fails to pay his or her share of the premium payments while on FMLA leave, FMLA permits the employer to recoup the premiums (to the extent of the employee's share). See 29 CFR 825.212(b). Such recoupment may be made as set forth in paragraphs (a)(3)(i) and (ii) of this Q&A-3. See also Q&A-6 of this section regarding coverage under a health FSA when an employee fails to make the required premium payments while on FMLA leave.

(3) Catch-up. (i) Under the catch-up option, the employer and the employee may agree in advance that the group coverage will continue during the period of unpaid FMLA leave, and that the employee will not pay premiums until the employee returns from the FMLA leave. Where an employee is electing to use the catch-up option, the employer and the employee must agree in advance of the coverage period that: the employee elects to continue health coverage while on unpaid FMLA leave; the employer assumes responsibility for advancing payment of the premiums on the employee's behalf during the FMLA leave; and these advance amounts are to be paid by the employee when the employee returns from FMLA leave.

(ii) When an employee fails to make required premium payments while on FMLA leave, an employer is permitted to utilize the catch-up option to recoup the employee's share of premium payments when the employee returns from FMLA leave. See, e.g., 29 CFR 825.212(b). If the employer chooses to continue group coverage under these circumstances, the prior agreement of the employee, as set forth in paragraph (a)(3)(i) of this Q&A-3, is not required.

(iii) Contributions under the catch-up option may be made on a pre-tax salary reduction basis from any available taxable compensation (including from unused sick days and vacation days) after the employee returns from FMLA leave. The cafeteria plan may provide for the catch-up option to apply on a pre-tax salary reduction basis if premiums have not been paid on any other basis (i.e., have not been paid under the pre-pay or pay-as-you-go options or on a catch-up after-tax basis).

(iv) Contributions under the catch-up option may also be made on an after-tax basis.

(b) Exceptions. Whatever payment options are offered to employees on non-FMLA leave must be offered to employees on FMLA leave. In accordance with 29 CFR 825.210(c), cafeteria plans may offer one or more of the payment options described in paragraph (a) of this Q&A-3, with the following exceptions:

(1) FMLA does not permit the pre-pay option to be the sole option offered to employees on FMLA leave. However, the cafeteria plan may include pre-payment as an option for employees on FMLA leave, even if such option is not offered to employees on non-FMLA leave-without-pay.

(2) FMLA allows the catch-up option to be the sole option offered to employees on FMLA leave if and only if the catch-up option is the sole option offered to employees on non-FMLA leave-without-pay.

(3) If the pay-as-you-go option is offered to employees on non-FMLA leave-without-pay, the option must also be offered to employees on FMLA leave. The employer may also offer employees on FMLA leave the pre-pay option and/or the catch-up option.

(c) Voluntary waiver of employee payments. In addition to the foregoing payment options, an employer may voluntarily waive, on a nondiscriminatory basis, the requirement that employees who elect to continue group health coverage while on FMLA leave pay the amounts the employees would otherwise be required to pay for the leave period.

(d) Example. The following example illustrates this Q&A-3:

Example. (i) Employer Y allows employees to pay premiums for group health coverage during an FMLA leave on an after-tax basis while the employee is on unpaid FMLA leave. Under the terms of Y's cafeteria plan, if an employee elects to continue health coverage during an unpaid FMLA leave and fails to pay one or more of the after-tax premium payments due for that coverage, the employee's salary after the employee returns from FMLA leave is reduced to cover unpaid premiums (i.e. the premiums that were to be paid by the employee on an after-tax basis during the FMLA leave, but were paid by the employer instead).

(ii) In this Example, Y's cafeteria plan satisfies the conditions in this Q&A-3. Y's cafeteria plan would also satisfy the conditions in this Q&A-3 if the plan provided for coverage to cease in the event the employee fails to make a premium payment when due during an unpaid FMLA leave.

Q-4. Do the special FMLA requirements concerning payment of premiums by an employee who continues group health plan coverage under a cafeteria plan apply if the employee is on paid FMLA leave?

A-4. No. The Labor Regulations provide that, if an employee's FMLA leave is paid leave as described at 29 CFR 825.207 and the employer mandates that the employee continue group health plan coverage while on FMLA leave, the employee's share of the premiums must be paid by the method normally used during any paid leave (e.g., by pre-tax salary reduction if the employee's share of premiums were paid by pre-tax salary reduction before the FMLA leave began). See 29 CFR 825.210(b).

Q-5. What restrictions apply to contributions when an employee's FMLA leave spans two cafeteria plan years?

A-5. (a) No amount will be included in an employee's gross income due to participation in a cafeteria plan during FMLA leave, provided that the plan complies with other generally applicable cafeteria plan requirements. Among other requirements, a plan may not operate in a manner that enables employees on FMLA leave to defer compensation from one cafeteria plan year to a subsequent cafeteria plan year. See section 125(d)(2).

(b) The following example illustrates this Q&A-5:

Example. (i) Employee A elects group health coverage under a calendar year cafeteria plan maintained by Employer X. Employee A's premium for health coverage is $100 per month throughout the 12-month period of coverage. Employee A takes FMLA leave for 12 weeks beginning on October 31 after making 10 months of premium payments totaling $1,000 (10 months x $100 = $1,000). Employee A elects to continue health coverage while on FMLA leave and utilizes the pre-pay option by applying his or her unused sick days in order to make the required premium payments due while he or she is on FMLA leave.

(ii) Because A cannot defer compensation from one plan year to a subsequent plan year, A may pre-pay the premiums due in November and December (i.e., $100 per month) on a pre-tax basis, but A cannot pre-pay the premium payment due in January on a pre-tax basis. If A participates in the cafeteria plan in the subsequent plan year, A must either prepay for January on an after-tax basis or use another option (e.g., pay-as-you-go, catch-up, reduction in unused sick days, etc.) to make the premium payment due in January.

Q-6. Are there special rules concerning employees taking FMLA leave who participate in health FSAs offered under a cafeteria plan?

A-6. (a) In general. (1) A group health plan that is a flexible spending arrangement (FSA) offered under a cafeteria plan must conform to the generally applicable rules in this section concerning employees who take FMLA leave. Thus, to the extent required by FMLA (see 29 CFR 825.209(b)), an employer must—

(i) Permit an employee taking FMLA leave to continue coverage under a health FSA while on FMLA leave; and

(ii) If an employee is on unpaid FMLA leave, either—

(A) Allow the employee to revoke coverage; or

(B) Continue coverage, but allow the employee to discontinue payment of his or her share of the premium for the health FSA under the cafeteria plan during the unpaid FMLA leave period.

(2) Under FMLA, the plan must permit the employee to be reinstated in health coverage upon return from FMLA leave on the same terms as if the employee had been working throughout the leave period, without a break in coverage. See 29 CFR 825.214(a) and 825.215(d)(1) and paragraph (b)(2) of this Q&A-6. In addition, under FMLA, a plan may require an employee to be reinstated in health coverage upon return from a period of unpaid FMLA leave, provided that employees who return from a period of unpaid leave not covered by the FMLA are also required to resume participation upon return from leave.

(b) Coverage. (1) Regardless of the payment option selected under Q&A-3 of this section, for so long as the employee continues health FSA coverage (or for so long as the employer continues the health FSA coverage of an employee who fails to make the required contributions as described in Q&A-3(a)(2)(iii) of this section), the full amount of the elected health FSA coverage, less any prior reimbursements, must be available to the employee at all times, including the FMLA leave period.

(2) (i) If an employee's coverage under the health FSA terminates while the employee is on FMLA leave, the employee is not entitled to receive reimbursements for claims incurred during the period when the coverage is terminated. If an employee subsequently elects or the employer requires the employee to be reinstated in the health FSA upon return from FMLA leave for the remainder of the plan year, the employee may not retroactively elect health FSA coverage for claims incurred during the period when the coverage was terminated. Upon reinstatement into a health FSA upon return from FMLA leave (either because the employee elects reinstatement or because the employer requires reinstatement), the employee has the right under FMLA: to resume coverage at the level in effect before the FMLA leave and make up the unpaid premium payments, or to resume coverage at a level that is reduced and resume premium payments at the level in effect before the FMLA leave. If an employee chooses to resume health FSA coverage at a level that is reduced, the coverage is prorated for the period during the FMLA leave for which no premiums were paid. In both cases, the coverage level is reduced by prior reimbursements.

(ii) FMLA requires that an employee on FMLA leave have the right to revoke or change elections (because of events described in § 1.125-4) under the same terms and conditions that apply to employees participating in the cafeteria plan who are not on FMLA leave. Thus, for example, if a group health plan offers an annual open enrollment period to active employees, then, under FMLA, an employee on FMLA leave when the open enrollment is offered must be offered the right to make election changes on the same basis as other employees. Similarly, if a group health plan decides to offer a new benefit package option and allows active employees to elect the new option, then, under FMLA, an employee on FMLA leave must be allowed to elect the new option on the same basis as other employees.

(3) The following examples illustrate the rules in this Q&A-6:

Example 1. (i) Employee B elects $1,200 worth of coverage under a calendar year health FSA provided under a cafeteria plan, with an annual premium of $1,200. Employee B is permitted to pay the $1,200 through pre-tax salary reduction amounts of $100 per month throughout the 12-month period of coverage. Employee B incurs no medical expenses prior to April 1. On April 1, B takes FMLA leave after making three months of contributions totaling $300 (3 months x $100 = $300). Employee B's coverage ceases during the FMLA leave. Consequently, B makes no premium payments for the months of April, May, and June, and B is not entitled to submit claims or receive reimbursements for expenses incurred during this period. Employee B returns from FMLA leave and elects to be reinstated in the health FSA on July 1.

(ii) Employee B must be given a choice of resuming coverage at the level in effect before the FMLA leave (i.e., $1,200) and making up the unpaid premium payments ($300), or resuming health FSA coverage at a level that is reduced on a prorata basis for the period during the FMLA leave for which no premiums were paid (i.e., reduced for 3 months or 1/4 of the plan year) less prior reimbursements (i.e., $0) with premium payments due in the same monthly amount payable before the leave (i.e., $100 per month). Consequently, if B chooses to resume coverage at the level in effect before the FMLA leave, B's coverage for the remainder of the plan year would equal $1,200 and B's monthly premiums would be increased to $150 per month for the remainder of the plan year, to make up the $300 in premiums missed ($100 per month plus $50 per month ($300 divided by the remaining 6 months)). If B chooses prorated coverage, B's coverage for the remainder of the plan year would equal $900, and B would resume making premium payments of $100 per month for the remainder of the plan year.

Example 2. (i) Assume the same facts as Example 1 except that B incurred medical expenses totaling $200 in February and obtained reimbursement of these expenses.

(ii) The results are the same as in Example 1, except that if B chooses to resume coverage at the level in effect before the FMLA leave, B's coverage for the remainder of the year would equal $1,000 ($1,200 reduced by $200) and the monthly payments for the remainder of the year would still equal $150. If instead B chooses prorated coverage, B's coverage for the remainder of the plan year would equal $700 ($1,200 prorated for 3 months, and then reduced by $200) and the monthly payments for the remainder of the year would still equal $100.

Example 3. (i) Assume the same facts as Example 1 except that, prior to taking FMLA leave, B elects to continue health FSA coverage during the FMLA leave. The plan permits B (and B elects) to use the catch-up payment option described in Q&A-3 of this section, and as further permitted under the plan, B chooses to repay the $300 in missed payments on a ratable basis over the remaining 6-month period of coverage (i.e., $50 per month).

(ii) Thus, B's monthly premium payments for the remainder of the plan year will be $150 ($100 + $50).

Q-7. Are employees entitled to non-health benefits while taking FMLA leave?

A-7. FMLA does not require an employer to maintain an employee's non-health benefits (e.g., life insurance) during FMLA leave. An employee's entitlement to benefits other than group health benefits under a cafeteria plan during a period of FMLA leave is to be determined by the employer's established policy for providing such benefits when the employee is on non-FMLA leave (paid or unpaid). See 29 CFR 825.209(h). Therefore, an employee who takes FMLA leave is entitled to revoke an election of non-health benefits under a cafeteria plan to the same extent as employees taking non-FMLA leave are permitted to revoke elections of non-health benefits under a cafeteria plan. For example, election changes are permitted due to changes of status or upon enrollment for a new plan year. See § 1.125-4. However, FMLA provides that, in certain cases, an employer may continue an employee's non-health benefits under the employer's cafeteria plan while the employee is on FMLA leave in order to ensure that the employer can meet its responsibility to provide equivalent benefits to the employee upon return from unpaid FMLA. If the employer continues an employee's non-health benefits during FMLA leave, the employer is entitled to recoup the costs incurred for paying the employee's share of the premiums during the FMLA leave period. See 29 CFR 825.213(b). Such recoupment may be on a pre-tax basis. A cafeteria plan must, as required by FMLA, permit an employee whose coverage terminated while on FMLA leave (either by revocation or nonpayment of premiums) to be reinstated in the cafeteria plan on return from FMLA leave. See 29 CFR 825.214(a) and 825.215(d).

Q-8. What is the applicability date of the regulations in this section?

A-8. This section is applicable for cafeteria plan years beginning on or after January 1, 2002.

T.D. 8966, 10/16/2001.

---

§ 1.125-4 Permitted election changes.

(a) Election changes. A cafeteria plan may permit an employee to revoke an election during a period of coverage and to make a new election only as provided in paragraphs (b) through (g) of this section. Section 125 does not require a cafeteria plan to permit any of these changes. See paragraph (h) of this section for special provisions relating to qualified cash or deferred arrangements, and paragraph (i) of this section for special definitions used in this section.

(b) Special enrollment rights. *(1) In general.* A cafeteria plan may permit an employee to revoke an election for coverage under a group health plan during a period of coverage and make a new election that corresponds with the special enrollment rights provided in section 9801(f).

(2) Examples. The following examples illustrate the application of this paragraph (b):

Example (1). (i) Employer M provides health coverage for its employees pursuant to a plan that is subject to section 9801(f). Under the plan, employees may elect either employee-only coverage or family coverage. M also maintains a calendar year cafeteria plan under which qualified benefits, including health coverage, are funded through salary reduction. M's employee, A, is married to B and they have a child, C. In accordance with M's cafeteria plan, Employee A elects employee-only health coverage before the beginning of the calendar year. During the year, A and B adopt a child, D. Within 30 days thereafter, A wants to revoke A's election for employee-only health coverage and obtain family health coverage for A's spouse, C, and D as of the date of D's adoption. Employee A satisfies the conditions for special enrollment of an employee with a new dependent under section 9801(f)(2), so that A may enroll in family coverage under M's accident or health plan in order to provide coverage effective as of the date of D's adoption.

(ii) M's cafeteria plan may permit A to change A's salary reduction election to family coverage for salary not yet currently available. The increased salary reduction is permitted to reflect the cost of family coverage from the date of adoption. (A's adoption of D is also a change in status, and the election of family coverage is consistent with that change in status. Thus, under paragraph (c) of this section, M's cafeteria plan could permit A to elect family coverage prospectively in order to cover B, C, and D for the remaining portion of the period of coverage.)

Example (2). (i) The employer plans and permissible coverage are the same as in Example 1. Before the beginning of the calendar year, Employee E elects employee-only health coverage under M's cafeteria plan. Employee E marries F during the plan year. F's employer, N, offers health coverage to N's employees, and, prior to the marriage, F had elected employee-only coverage. Employee E wants to revoke the election for employee-only coverage under M's cafeteria plan, and is considering electing family health coverage under M's plan or obtaining family health coverage under N's plan.

(ii) M's cafeteria plan may permit E to change E's salary reduction election to reflect the change to family coverage under M's accident or health plan because the marriage would result in special enrollment rights under section 9801(f), pursuant to which an election of family coverage under M's accident or health plan would be required to be effective no later than the first day of the first calendar month beginning after the completed request for enrollment is received by the plan. Since no retroactive coverage is required in the event of marriage under section 9801(f), E's salary reduction election may only be changed on a prospective basis. (E's marriage to F is also a change in status under paragraph (c) of this section, as illustrated in Example 1 of paragraph (c)(4) of this section.)

(c) Changes in status. *(1) Change in status rule.* A cafeteria plan may permit an employee to revoke an election during a period of coverage with respect to a qualified benefits plan (defined in paragraph (i)(8) of this section) to which this paragraph (c) applies and make a new election for the remaining portion of the period (referred to in this section as an election change) if, under the facts and circumstances—

(i) A change in status described in paragraph (c)(2) of this section occurs; and

(ii) The election change satisfies the consistency rule of paragraph (c)(3) of this section.

(iii) Application to other qualified benefits. [Reserved]

(2) Change in status events. The following events are changes in status for purposes of this paragraph (c):

(i) Legal marital status. Events that change an employee's legal marital status, including the following: marriage; death of spouse; divorce; legal separation; and annulment.

(ii) Number of dependents. Events that change an employee's number of dependents, including the following: birth; death; adoption; and placement for adoption.

(iii) Employment status. Any of the following events that change the employment status of the employee, the employee's spouse, or the employee's dependent: a termination or commencement of employment; a strike or lockout; a commencement of or return from an unpaid leave of absence; and a change in worksite. In addition, if the eligibility conditions of the cafeteria plan or other employee benefit plan of the employer of the employee, spouse, or dependent depend on the employment status of that individual and there is a change in that individual's employment status with the consequence that the individual becomes (or ceases to be) ligible under the plan, then that change constitutes a change in employment under this paragraph (c) (e.g., if a plan only applies to salaried employees and an employee switches from salaried to hourly-paid with the consequence that the employee ceases to be eligible for the plan, then that change constitutes a change in employment status under this paragraph (c)(2)(iii)).

(iv) Dependent satisfies or ceases to satisfy eligibility requirements. Events that cause an employee's dependent to satisfy or cease to satisfy eligibility requirements for coverage on account of attainment of age, student status, or any similar circumstance.

(v) Residence. A change in the place of residence of the employee, spouse, or dependent.

(vi) Adoption assistance. For purposes of adoption assistance provided through a cafeteria plan, the commencement or termination of an adoption proceeding.

(3) Consistency rule. (i) Application to accident or health coverage and group-term life insurance. An election change satisfies the requirements of this paragraph (c)(3) with respect to accident or health coverage or group-term life insurance only if the election change is on account of and corresponds with a change in status that affects eligibility for coverage under an employer's plan. A change in status that affects eligibility under an employer's plan includes a change in status that results in an increase or decrease in the number of an employee's family members or dependents who may benefit from coverage under the plan.

(ii) Application to other qualified benefits. An election change satisfies the requirements of this paragraph (c)(3) with respect to other qualified benefits if the election change is on account of and corresponds with a change in status that affects eligibility for coverage under an employer's plan. An election change also satisfies the requirements of this paragraph (c)(3) if the election change is on account of and corresponds with a change in status that effects expenses described in section 129 including employment-related expenses as defined in section 21(b)(2)) with respect to dependent care assistance, or expenses described in section 137 (including qualified adoption expenses as defined in section 137(d)) with respect to adoption assistance.

(iii) Application of consistency rule. If the change in status is the employee's divorce, annulment or legal separation from a spouse, the death of a spouse or dependent, or a dependent ceasing to satisfy the eligibility requirements for coverage, an employee's election under the cafeteria plan to cancel accident or health insurance coverage for any individual other than the spouse involved in the divorce, annulment or legal separation, the deceased spouse or dependent, or the dependent that ceased to satisfy the eligibility requirements for coverage, respectively, fails to correspond with that change in status. Thus, if a dependent dies or ceases to satisfy the eligibility requirements for coverage, the employee's election to cancel accident or health coverage for any other dependent, for the employee, or for the employee's spouse fails to correspond with that change in status. In addition, if an employee, spouse, or dependent gains eligibility for coverage under a family member plan (as defined in paragraph (i)(5) of this section) as a result of a change in marital status under paragraph (c)(2)(i) of this section or a change in employment status under paragraph (c)(2)(iii) of this section, an employee's election under the cafeteria plan to cease or decrease coverage for that individual under the cafeteria plan corresponds with that change in status only if coverage for that individual becomes applicable or is increased under the family member plan. With respect to group-term life insurance and disability coverage (as defined in paragraph (i)(4) of this section), an election under a cafeteria plan to increase coverage (or an election to decrease coverage) in response to a change in status described in paragraph (c)(2) of this section is deemed to correspond with that change in status as required by paragraph (c)(3)(i) of this section.

(iv) Exception for COBRA. If the employee, spouse, or dependent becomes eligible for continuation coverage under the group health plan of the employee's employer as provided in section 4980B or any similar state law, a cafeteria plan may permit the employee to elect to increase payments under the employer's cafeteria plan in order to pay for the continuation coverage.

(4) Examples. The following examples illustrate the application of this paragraph (c):

Example (1). (i) Employer M provides health coverage (including a health FSA) for its employees through its cafeteria plan. Before the beginning of the calendar year, Employee A elects employee-only health coverage under M's cafeteria plan and elects salary reduction contributions to fund coverage under the health FSA. Employee A marries B during the year. Employee B's employer, N, offers health coverage to N's employees (but not including any health FSA), and, prior to the marriage, B had elected employee-only coverage. Employee A wants to revoke the election for employee-only coverage, and is considering electing family health coverage under M's plan or obtaining family health coverage under N's plan.

(ii) Employee A's marriage to B is a change in status under paragraph (c)(2)(i) of this section, pursuant to which B has become eligible for coverage under M's health plan under paragraph (c)(3)(i) of this section. Two possible election changes by A correspond with the change in status: Employee A may elect family health coverage under M's plan to cover A and B; or A may cancel coverage under M's plan, if B elects family health coverage under N's plan to cover A and B. Thus, M's cafeteria plan may permit A to make either election change.

(iii) Employee A may also increase salary reduction contributions to fund coverage for B under the health FSA.

Example (2). (i) Employee C, a single parent, elects family health coverage under a calendar year cafeteria plan maintained by Employer O. Employee C and C's 21-year old child, D, are covered under O's health plan. During the year, D graduates from college. Under the terms of the health plan, dependents over the age of 19 must be full-time students to receive coverage. Employee C wants to revoke C's election for family health coverage and obtain employee-only coverage under O's cafeteria plan.

(ii) D's loss of eligibility for coverage under the terms of the health plan is a change in status under paragraph (c)(2)(iv) of this section. A revocation of C's election for family coverage and new election for employee-only coverage corresponds with the change in status. Thus, O's cafeteria plan may permit C to elect employee-only coverage.

Example (3). (i) Employee E is married to F and they have one child, G. Employee E is employed by Employer P, and P maintains a calendar year cafeteria plan that allows employees to elect no health coverage, employee-only coverage, employee-plus-one-dependent coverage, or family coverage. Under the plan, before the beginning of the calendar year, E elects family health coverage for E, F, and G. E and F divorce during the year and F loses eligibility for coverage under P's plan. G does not lose eligibility for health coverage under P's plan upon the divorce. E now wants to revoke E's election under the cafeteria plan and elect no coverage.

(ii) The divorce is a change in status under paragraph (c)(2)(i). A change in the cafeteria plan election to cancel health coverage for F is consistent with that change in status. However, an election change to cancel E's or G's health coverage does not satisfy the consistency rule under paragraph (c)(3)(iii) of this section regarding cancellation of coverage for an employee's other dependents in the event of divorce. Therefore, the cafeteria plan may not permit E to elect no coverage. However, an election to change to employee-plus-one-dependent health coverage would correspond with the change in status, and thus the cafeteria plan may permit E to elect employee-plus-one-dependent health coverage.

(iii) In addition, under paragraph (f)(4) of this section, if F makes an election change to cover G under F's employer's plan, then E may make a corresponding change to elect employee-only coverage under P's cafeteria plan.

Example (4). (i) Employer R maintains a calendar year cafeteria plan under which full-time employees may elect coverage under one of three benefit package options provided under an accident or health plan: an indemnity option or either of two HMO options for employees who work in the respective service areas of the two HMOs. Employee A, who works in the service area of HMO #1, elects the HMO #1 option. During the year, A is transferred to another work location which is outside the HMO #1 service area and inside the HMO #2 service area.

(ii) The transfer is a change in status under paragraph (c)(2)(iii) of this section (relating to a change in worksite), and, under the consistency rule in paragraph (c)(3) of this section, the cafeteria plan may permit A to make an election change to elect the indemnity option or HMO #2 or to cancel accident or health coverage.

(iii) The change in work location has no effect on A's eligibility under R's health FSA, so no change in A's health FSA is authorized under this paragraph (c).

Example (5). (i) Employer S maintains a calendar year cafeteria plan that allows employees to elect coverage under an accident or health plan providing indemnity coverage and coverage under a health FSA. Prior to the beginning of the calendar year, Employee B elects employee-only indemnity coverage, and elects salary reduction contributions of $600 during the year to fund coverage under the health FSA for up to $600 of reimbursements for the year. Employee B's spouse, C, has employee-only coverage under an accident or health plan maintained by C's employer. During the year, C terminates employment and loses coverage under that plan. B now wants to elect family coverage under S's accident or health plan and increase B's FSA election.

(ii) C's termination of employment is a change in status under paragraph (c)(2)(iii) of this section, and the election change satisfies the consistency rule of paragraph (c)(3) of this section. Therefore, the cafeteria plan may permit B to elect family coverage under S's accident or health plan and to increase B's FSA coverage.

Example (6). (i) Employer T provides group-term life insurance coverage as described under section 79. Under T's plan, an employee may elect life insurance coverage in an amount up to $50,000. T also maintains a calendar year cafeteria plan under which qualified benefits, including the group-term life insurance coverage, are funded through salary reduction. Employee D has a spouse and a child. Before the beginning of the year, D elects $10,000 of group-term life insurance coverage. During the year, D is divorced.

(ii) The divorce is a change in status under paragraph (c)(2)(i) of this section. Under paragraph (c)(3)(iii) of this section, either an increase or a decrease in coverage is consistent with this change in status. Thus, T's cafeteria plan may permit D to increase or to decrease D's group-term life insurance coverage.

Example (7). (i) Employee E is married to F and they have one child, G. Employee E's employer, U, maintains a cafeteria plan under which employees may elect no coverage, employee-only coverage, or family coverage under a group health plan maintained by U, and may make a separate vision coverage election under the plan. Before the beginning of the calendar year, E elects family health coverage and no vision coverage under U's cafeteria plan. Employee F's employer, V, maintains a cafeteria plan under which employees may elect no coverage, employee-only coverage, or family coverage under a group health plan maintained by V, and may make a separate vision coverage election under the plan. Before the beginning of the calendar year, F elects no health coverage and employee-only vision coverage under V's plan. During the year, F terminates employment with V and loses vision coverage under V's plan. Employee E now wants to elect family vision coverage under U's group health plan.

(ii) F's termination of employment is a change in status under paragraph (c)(2)(iii) of this section, and the election change satisfies the consistency rule of paragraph (c)(3) of this section. Therefore, U's cafeteria plan may permit E to elect family vision coverage (covering E and G as well as F) under U's group health plan.

Example (8). (i) Before the beginning of the year, Employee H elects to participate in a cafeteria plan maintained by H's employer, W. However, in order to change the election during the year so as to cancel coverage, and by prior understanding with W, H terminates employment and resumes employment one week later.

(ii) In this Example 8, under the facts and circumstances, a principal purpose of the termination of employment was to alter the election, and reinstatement of employment was understood at the time of termination. Accordingly, H does not have a change in status under paragraph (c)(2)(iii) of this section.

(iii) However, H's termination of employment would constitute a change in status, permitting a cancellation of coverage during the period of unemployment, if H's original cafeteria plan election for the period of coverage was reinstated upon resumption of employment (for example, if W's cafeteria plan contains a provision requiring an employee who resumes employment within 30 days, without any other intervening event that would permit a change in election, to return to the election in effect prior to termination of employment).

(iv) If, instead, H terminates employment and cancels coverage during a period of unemployment, and then returns to work more than 30 days following termination of employment, the cafeteria plan may permit H the option of returning to the election in effect prior to termination of employment or making a new election under the plan. Alternatively, the cafeteria plan may prohibit H from returning to the plan during that plan year.

Example (9). (i) Employee A has one child, B. Employee A's employer, X, maintains a calendar year cafeteria plan that allows employees to elect coverage under a dependent care FSA. Prior to the beginning of the calendar year, A elects salary reduction contributions of $4,000 during the year to fund coverage under the dependent care FSA for up to $4,000 of reimbursements for the year. During the year, B reaches the age of 13, and A wants to cancel coverage under the dependent care FSA.

(ii) When B turns 13, B ceases to satisfy the definition of qualifying individual under section 21(b)(1) of the Internal Revenue Code. Accordingly, B's attainment of age 13 is a change in status under paragraph (c)(2)(iv) of this section that affects A's employment-related expenses as defined in section 21(b)(2). Therefore, A may make a corresponding change under X's cafeteria plan to cancel coverage under the dependent care FSA.

Example (10). (i) Employer Y maintains a calendar year cafeteria plan under which full-time employees may elect coverage under either an indemnity option or an HMO. Employee C elects the employee-only indemnity option. During the year, C marries D. D has two children from a previous marriage, and has family group health coverage in a cafeteria plan sponsored by D's employer, Z. C wishes to change from employee-only indemnity coverage to HMO coverage for the family. D wishes to cease coverage in Z's group health plan and certifies to Z that D will have family coverage under C's plan (and Z has no reason to believe the certification is incorrect).

(ii) The marriage is a change in status under paragraph (c)(2)(i) of this section. Under the consistency rule in paragraph (c)(3) of this section, Y's cafeteria plan may permit C to change his or her salary reduction contributions to reflect the change from employee-only indemnity to HMO family coverage, and Z may permit D to revoke coverage under Z's cafeteria plan.

(d) Judgment, decree, or order. *(1) Conforming election change.* This paragraph (d) applies to a judgment, decree, or order order) resulting from a divorce, legal separation, annulment, or change in legal custody (including a qualified medical child support order as defined in section 609 of the Employee Retirement Income Security Act of 1974 (Public Law 93-406 (88 Stat. 829))) that requires accident or health coverage for an employee's child or for a foster child who is a dependent of the employee. A cafeteria plan will not fail to satisfy section 125 if it—

(i) Changes the employee's election to provide coverage for the child if the order requires coverage for the child under the employee's plan; or

(ii) Permits the employee to make an election change to cancel coverage for the child if:

(A) The order requires the spouse, former spouse, or other individual to provide coverage for the child; and

(B) That coverage is, in fact, provided.

(2) Example. The following example illustrates the application of this paragraph (d):

Example. (i) Employer M maintains a calendar year cafeteria plan that allows employees to elect no health coverage, employee-only coverage, employee-plus-one-dependent coverage, or family coverage. M's employee, A, is married to B and they have one child, C. Before the beginning of the year, A elects employee-only health coverage. Employee A divorces B during the year and, pursuant to A's divorce agreement with B, M's health plan receives a qualified medical child support order (as defined in section 609 of the Employee Retirement Income Security Act of 1974) during the plan year. The order requires M's health plan to cover C.

(ii) Under this paragraph (d), M's cafeteria plan may change A's election from employee-only health coverage to employee-plus-one-dependent coverage in order to cover C.

(e) Entitlement to Medicare or Medicaid. If an employee, spouse, or dependent who is enrolled in an accident or health plan of the employer becomes entitled to coverage (i.e., becomes enrolled) under Part A or Part B of Title XVIII of the Social Security Act (Medicare) (Public Law 89-97 (79 Stat. 291)) or Title XIX of the Social Security Act (Medicaid) (Public Law 89-97 (79 Stat. 343)), other than coverage consisting solely of benefits under section 1928 of the Social Security Act (the program for distribution of pediatric vaccines), a cafeteria plan may permit the employee to make a prospective election change to cancel or reduce coverage of that employee, spouse, or dependent under the accident or health plan. In addition, if an employee, spouse, or dependent who has been entitled to such coverage under Medicare or Medicaid loses eligibility for such coverage, the cafeteria plan may permit the employee to make a prospective election to commence or increase coverage of that employee, spouse, or dependent under the accident or health plan.

(f) Significant cost or coverage changes. *(1) In general.* Paragraphs (f)(2) through (5) of this section set forth rules for election changes as a result of changes in cost or coverage. This paragraph (f) does not apply to an election change with respect to a health FSA (or on account of a change in cost or coverage under a health FSA).

(2) Cost changes. (i) Automatic changes. If the cost of a qualified benefits plan increases (or decreases) during a period of coverage and, under the terms of the plan, employees are required to make a corresponding change in their payments, the cafeteria plan may, on a reasonable and consistent basis, automatically make a prospective increase (or decrease) in affected employees' elective contributions for the plan.

(ii) Significant cost changes. If the cost charged to an employee for a benefit package option (as defined in paragraph (i)(2) of this section) significantly increases or significantly decreases during a period of coverage, the cafeteria plan may permit the employee to make a corresponding change in election under the cafeteria plan. Changes that may be made include commencing participation in the cafeteria plan for the option with a decrease in cost, or, in the case of an increase in cost, revoking an election for that coverage and, in lieu thereof, either receiving on a prospective basis coverage under another benefit package option providing similar coverage or dropping coverage if no other benefit package option providing similar coverage is available. For example, if the cost of an indemnity option under an accident or health plan significantly increases during a period of coverage, employees who are covered by the indemnity option may make a corresponding prospective increase in their payments or may instead elect to revoke their election for the indemnity option and, in lieu thereof, elect coverage under another benefit package option including an HMO option (or drop coverage under the accident or health plan if no other benefit package option is offered).

(iii) Application of cost changes. For purposes of paragraphs (f)(2)(i) and (ii) of this section, a cost increase or decrease refers to an increase or decrease in the amount of the elective contributions under the cafeteria plan, whether that increase or decrease results from an action taken by the employee (such as switching between full-time and part-time status) or from an action taken by an employer (such as reducing the amount of employer contributions for a class of employees).

(iv) Application to dependent care. This paragraph (f)(2) applies in the case of a dependent care assistance plan only if the cost change is imposed by a dependent care provider who is not a relative of the employee. For this purpose, a relative is an individual who is related as described in section 152(a)(1) through (8), incorporating the rules of section 152(b)(1) and (2).

(3) Coverage changes. (i) Significant curtailment without loss of coverage. If an employee (or an employee's spouse or dependent) has a significant curtailment of coverage under a plan during a period of coverage that is not a loss of coverage as described in paragraph (f)(3)(ii) of this section (for example, there is a significant increase in the deductible, the copay, or the out-of-pocket cost sharing limit under an accident or health plan), the cafeteria plan may permit any employee who had been participating in the plan and receiving that coverage to revoke his or her election for that coverage and, in lieu thereof, to elect to receive on a prospective basis coverage under another benefit package option providing similar coverage. Coverage under a plan is significantly curtailed only if there is an overall reduction in coverage provided under the plan so as to constitute reduced coverage generally. Thus, in most cases, the loss of one particular physician in a network does not constitute a significant curtailment.

(ii) Significant curtailment with loss of coverage. If an employee (or the employee's spouse or dependent) has a significant curtailment that is a loss of coverage, the plan may permit that employee to revoke his or her election under the cafeteria plan and, in lieu thereof, to elect either to receive on a prospective basis coverage under another benefit package option providing similar coverage or to drop coverage if no similar benefit package option is available. For purposes of this paragraph (f)(3)(ii), a loss of coverage means a complete loss of coverage under the benefit package option or other coverage option (including the elimination of a benefits package option, an HMO ceasing to be available in the area where the individual resides, or the individual losing all coverage under the option by reason of an overall lifetime or annual limitation). In addition, the cafeteria plan may, in its discretion, treat the following as a loss of coverage—

(A) A substantial decrease in the medical care providers available under the option (such as a major hospital ceasing to be a member of a preferred provider network or a substantial decrease in the physicians participating in a preferred provider network or an HMO);

(B) A reduction in the benefits for a specific type of medical condition or treatment with respect to which the employee or the employee's spouse or dependent is currently in a course of treatment; or

(C) Any other similar fundamental loss of coverage.

(iii) Addition or improvement of a benefit package option. If a plan adds a new benefit package option or other coverage option, or if coverage under an existing benefit package option or other coverage option is significantly improved during a period of coverage, the cafeteria plan may permit eligible employees (whether or not they have previously made an election under the cafeteria plan or have previously elected the benefit package option) to revoke their election under the cafeteria plan and, in lieu thereof, to make an election on a prospective basis for coverage under the new or improved benefit package option.

(4) Change in coverage under another employer plan. A cafeteria plan may permit an employee to make a prospective election change that is on account of and corresponds with a change made under another employer plan (including a plan of the same employer or of another employer) if—

(i) The other cafeteria plan or qualified benefits plan permits participants to make an election change that would be permitted under paragraphs (b) through (g) of this section (disregarding this paragraph (f)(4)); or

(ii) The cafeteria plan permits participants to make an election for a period of coverage that is different from the period of coverage under the other cafeteria plan or qualified benefits plan.

(5) Loss of coverage under other group health coverage. A cafeteria plan may permit an employee to make an election on a prospective basis to add coverage under a cafeteria plan for the employee, spouse, or dependent if the employee, spouse, or dependent loses coverage under any group health coverage sponsored by a governmental or educational institution, including the following—

(i) A State's children's health insurance program (SCHIP) under Title XXI of the Social Security Act;

(ii) A medical care program of an Indian Tribal government (as defined in section 7701(a)(40)), the Indian Health Service, or a tribal organization;

(iii) A State health benefits risk pool; or

(iv) A Foreign government group health plan.

(6) Examples. The following examples illustrate the application of this paragraph (f):

Example (1). (i) A calendar year cafeteria plan is maintained pursuant to a collective bargaining agreement for the benefit of Employer M's employees. The cafeteria plan offers various benefits, including indemnity health insurance and a health FSA. As a result of mid-year negotiations, premiums for the indemnity health insurance are reduced in the middle of the year, insurance co-payments for office visits are reduced under the indemnity plan by an amount which constitutes a significant benefit improvement, and an HMO option is added.

(ii) Under these facts, the reduction in health insurance premiums is a reduction in cost. Accordingly, under paragraph (f)(2)(i) of this section, the cafeteria plan may automatically decrease the amount of salary reduction contributions of affected participants by an amount that corresponds to the premium change. However, the plan may not permit employees to change their health FSA elections to reflect the mid-year change in copayments under the indemnity plan.

(iii) Also, the decrease in co-payments is a significant benefit improvement and the addition of the HMO option is an addition of a benefit package option. Accordingly, under paragraph (f)(3)(ii) of this section, the cafeteria plan may permit eligible employees to make an election change to elect the indemnity plan or the new HMO option. However, the plan may not permit employees to change their health FSA elections to reflect differences in co-payments under the HMO option.

Example (2). (i) Employer N sponsors an accident or health plan under which employees may elect either employee-only coverage or family health coverage. The 12-month period of coverage under N's cafeteria plan begins January 1, 2001. N's employee, A, is married to B. Employee A elects employee-only coverage under N's plan. B's employer, O, offers health coverage to O's employees under its accident or health plan under which employees may elect either employee-only coverage or family coverage. O's plan has a 12-month period of coverage beginning September 1, 2001. B maintains individual coverage under O's plan at the time A elects coverage under N's plan, and wants to elect no coverage for the plan year beginning on September 1, 2001, which is the next period of coverage under O's accident or health plan. A certifies to N that B will elect no coverage under O's accident or health plan for the plan year beginning on September 1, 2001 and N has no reason to believe that A's certification is incorrect.

(ii) Under paragraph (f)(4)(ii) of this section, N's cafeteria plan may permit A to change A's election prospectively to family coverage under that plan effective September 1, 2001.

Example (3). (i) Employer P sponsors a calendar year cafeteria plan under which employees may elect either employee-only or family health coverage. Before the beginning of the year, P's employee, C, elects family coverage under P's cafeteria plan. C also elects coverage under the health FSA for up to $200 of reimbursements for the year to be funded by salary reduction contributions of $200 during the year. C is married to D, who is employed by Employer Q. Q does not maintain a cafeteria plan, but does maintain an accident or health plan providing its employees with employee-only coverage. During the calendar year, Q adds family coverage as an option under its health plan. D elects family coverage under Q's plan, and C wants to revoke C's election for health coverage and elect no health coverage under P's cafeteria plan for the remainder of the year.

(ii) Q's addition of family coverage as an option under its health plan constitutes a new coverage option described in paragraph (f)(3)(ii) of this section. Accordingly, pursuant to paragraph (f)(4)(i) of this section, P's cafeteria plan may permit C to revoke C's health coverage election if D actually elects family health coverage under Q's accident or health plan. Employer P's plan may not permit C to change C's health FSA election.

Example (4). (i) Employer R maintains a cafeteria plan under which employees may elect accident or health coverage under either an indemnity plan or an HMO. Before the beginning of the year, R's employee, E elects coverage under the HMO at a premium cost of $100 per month. During the year, E decides to switch to the indemnity plan, which charges a premium of $140 per month.

(ii) E's change from the HMO to indemnity plan is not a change in cost or coverage under this paragraph (f), and none of the other election change rules under paragraphs (b) through (e) of this section apply.

(iii) Although R's health plan may permit E to make the change from the HMO to the indemnity plan, R's cafeteria plan may not permit E to make an election change to reflect the increased premium. Accordingly, if E switches from the HMO to the indemnity plan, E may pay the $40 per month additional cost on an after-tax basis.

Example (5). (i) Employee A is married to Employee B and they have one child, C. Employee A's employer, M, maintains a calendar year cafeteria plan that allows employees to elect coverage under a dependent care FSA. Child C attends X's on site child care center at an annual cost of $3,000. Prior to the beginning of the year, A elects salary reduction contributions of $3,000 during the year to fund coverage under the dependent care FSA for up to $3,000 of reimbursements for the year. Employee A now wants to revoke A's election of coverage under the dependent care FSA, because A has found a new child care provider.

(ii) The availability of dependent care services from the new child care provider (whether the new provider is a household employee or family member of A or B or a person who is independent of A and B) is a significant change in coverage similar to a benefit package option becoming available. Because the FSA is a dependent care FSA rather than a health FSA, the coverage rules of this section apply and M's cafeteria plan may permit A to elect to revoke A's previous election of coverage under the dependent care FSA, and make a corresponding new election to reflect the cost of the new child care provider.

Example (6). (i) Employee D is married to Employee E and they have one child, F. Employee D's employer, N, maintains a calendar year cafeteria plan that allows employees to elect coverage under a dependent care FSA. Child F is cared for by Y, D's household employee, who provides child care services five days a week from 9 a.m. to 6 p.m. at an annual cost in excess of $5,000. Prior to the beginning of the year, D elects salary reduction contributions of $5,000 during the year to fund coverage under the dependent care FSA for up to $5,000 of reimbursements for the year. During the year, F begins school and, as a result, Y's regular hours of work are changed to five days a week from 3 p.m. to 6 p.m. Employee D now wants to revoke D's election under the dependent care FSA, and make a new election under the dependent care FSA to an annual cost of $4,000 to reflect a reduced cost of child care due to Y's reduced hours.

(ii) The change in the number of hours of work performed by Y is a change in coverage. Thus, N's cafeteria plan may permit D to reduce D's previous election under the dependent care FSA to $4,000.

Example (7). (i) Employee G is married to Employee H and they have one child, J. Employee G's employer, O, maintains a calendar year cafeteria plan that allows employees to elect coverage under a dependent care FSA. Child J is cared for by Z, G's household employee, who is not a relative of G and who provides child care services at an annual cost of $4,000. Prior to the beginning of the year, G elects salary reduction contributions of $4,000 during the year to fund coverage under the dependent care FSA for up to $4,000 of reimbursements for the year. During the year, G raises Z's salary. Employee G now wants to revoke G's election under the dependent care FSA, and make a new election under the dependent care FSA to an annual amount of $4,500 to reflect the raise.

(ii) The raise in Z's salary is a significant increase in cost under paragraph (f)(2)(ii) of this section, and an increase in election to reflect the raise corresponds with that change in status. Thus, O's cafeteria plan may permit G to elect to increase G's election under the dependent care FSA.

Example (8). (i) Employer P maintains a calendar year cafeteria plan that allows employees to elect employee-only, employee plus one dependent, or family coverage under an indemnity plan. During the middle of the year, Employer P gives its employees the option to select employee-only or family coverage from an HMO plan. P's employee, J, who had elected employee plus one dependent coverage under the indemnity plan, decides to switch to family coverage under the HMO plan.

(ii) Employer P's midyear addition of the HMO option is an addition of a benefit package option. Under paragraph (f) of this section, Employee J may change his or her salary reduction contributions to reflect the change from indemnity to HMO coverage, and also to reflect the change from employee plus one dependent to family coverage (however, an election of employee-only coverage under the new option would not correspond with the addition of a new option). Employer P may not permit J to change J's health FSA election.

(g) Special requirements relating to the Family and Medical Leave Act. An employee taking leave under the Family and Medical Leave Act (FMLA) (Public Law 103-3 (107 Stat. 6)) may revoke an existing election of accident or health plan coverage and make such other election for the remaining portion of the period of coverage as may be provided for under the FMLA. See § 1.125-3 for additional rules.

(h) Elective contributions under a qualified cash or deferred arrangement. The provisions of this section do not apply with respect to elective contributions under a qualified cash or deferred arrangement (within the meaning of section 401(k)) or employee contributions subject to section 401(m). Thus, a cafeteria plan may permit an employee to modify or revoke elections in accordance with section 401(k) and (m) and the regulations thereunder.

(i) Definitions. Unless otherwise provided, the definitions in paragraphs (i)(1) though (8) of this section apply for purposes of this section.

(1) Accident or health coverage. Accident or health coverage means coverage under an accident or health plan as defined in regulations under section 105.

(2) Benefit package option. A benefit package option means a qualified benefit under section 125(f) that is offered under a cafeteria plan, or an option for coverage under an underlying accident or health plan (such as an indemnity option, an HMO option, or a PPO option under an accident or health plan).

(3) Dependent. A dependent means a dependent as defined in section 152, except that, for purposes of accident or health coverage, any child to whom section 152(e) applies is treated as a dependent of both parents, and, for purposes of dependent care assistance provided through a cafeteria plan, a dependent means a qualifying individual (as defined in section 21(b)(1)) with respect to the employee.

(4) Disability coverage. Disability coverage means coverage under an accident or health plan that provides benefits due to personal injury or sickness, but does not reimburse expenses incurred for medical care (as defined in section 213(d)) of the employee or the employee's spouse and dependents. For purposes of this section, disability coverage includes payments described in section 105(c).

(5) Family member plan. A family member plan means a cafeteria plan or qualified benefit plan sponsored by the employer of the employee's spouse or the employee's dependent.

(6) FSA, health FSA. An FSA means a qualified benefits plan that is a flexible spending arrangement as defined in section 106(c)(2) . A health FSA means a health or accident plan that is an FSA.

(7) Placement for adoption. Placement for adoption means placement for adoption as defined in regulations under section 9801.

(8) Qualified benefits plan. A qualified benefits plan means an employee benefit plan governing the provision of one or more benefits that are qualified benefits under section 125(f). A plan does not fail to be a qualified benefits plan merely because it includes an FSA, assuming that the FSA meets the requirements of section 125 and the regulations thereunder.

(9) Similar coverage. Coverage for the same category of benefits for the same individuals (e.g., family to family or single to single). For example, two plans that provide coverage for major medical are considered to be similar coverage. For purposes of this definition, a health FSA is not similar coverage with respect to an accident or health plan that is not a health FSA. A plan may treat coverage by another employer, such as a spouse's or dependent's employer, as similar coverage.

(j) Effective date. *(1) General rule.* Except as provided in paragraph (j)(2) of this section, this section is applicable for cafeteria plan years beginning on or after January 1, 2001.

(2) Delayed effective date for certain provisions. The following provisions are applicable for cafeteria plan years beginning on or after January 1, 2002: paragraph (c) of this section to the extent applicable to qualified benefits other than an accident or health plan or a group-term life insurance plan; paragraph (d)(1)(ii)(B) of this section (relating to a spouse, former spouse, or other individual obtaining accident or health coverage for an employee's child in response to a judgment, decree, or order); paragraph (f) of this section (rules for election changes as a result of cost or coverage changes); and paragraph (i)(9) of this section (defining similar coverage).

T.D. 8878, 3/22/2000, amend T.D. 8921, 1/09/2001, T.D. 8966, 10/16/2001.

Proposed § 1.125-5 Flexible spending arrangements.
[*For Preamble, see ¶ 152,897*]

(a) Definition of flexible spending arrangement. *(1) In general.* An FSA generally is a benefit program that provides employees with coverage which reimburses specified, incurred expenses (subject to reimbursement maximums and any other reasonable conditions). An expense for qualified benefits must not be reimbursed from the FSA unless it is incurred during a period of coverage. See paragraph (e) of this section. After an expense for a qualified benefit has been incurred, the expense must first be substantiated before the expense is reimbursed. See paragraphs (a) through (f) in § 1.125-6.

(2) Maximum amount of reimbursement. The maximum amount of reimbursement that is reasonably available to an employee for a period of coverage must not be substantially in excess of the total salary reduction and employer flex-credit for such participant's coverage. A maximum amount of reimbursement is not substantially in excess of the total salary reduction and employer flex-credit if such maximum amount is less than 500 percent of the combined salary reduction and employer flex-credit. A single FSA may provide participants with different levels of coverage and maximum amounts of reimbursement. See paragraph (r) in § 1.125-1 and paragraphs (b) and (d) in this section for the definition of salary reduction, employer flex-credit, and uniform coverage rule.

(b) Flex-credits allowed. *(1) In general.* An FSA in a cafeteria plan must include an election between cash or taxable benefits (including salary reduction) and one or more qualified benefits, and may include, in addition, "employer flex-credits." For this purpose, flex-credits are non-elective employer contributions that the employer makes for every employee eligible to participate in the employer's cafeteria plan, to be used at the employee's election only for one or more qualified benefits (but not as cash or a taxable benefit). See § 1.125-1 for definitions of qualified benefits, cash and taxable benefits.

(2) Example. The following example illustrates the rules in this paragraph (b):

Example. Flex-credit. Contribution to health FSA for employees electing employer-provided accident and health plan. Employer A maintains a cafeteria plan offering employees an election between cash or taxable benefits and premiums for employer-provided accident and health insurance or coverage through an HMO. The plan also provides an employer contribution of $200 to the health FSA of every employee who elects accident and health insurance or HMO coverage. In addition, these employees may elect to reduce their salary to make additional contributions to their health FSAs. The benefits offered in this cafeteria plan are consistent with the requirements of section 125 and this paragraph (b).

(c) Use-or-lose rule. *(1) In general.* An FSA may not defer compensation. No contribution or benefit from an FSA may be carried over to any subsequent plan year or period of coverage. See paragraph (k)(3) in this section for specific exceptions. Unused benefits or contributions remaining at the end of the plan year (or at the end of a grace period, if applicable) are forfeited.

(2) Example. The following example illustrates the rules in this paragraph (c):

Example. Use-or-lose rule. (i) Employer B maintains a calendar year cafeteria plan, offering an election between cash and a health FSA. The cafeteria plan has no grace period.

(ii) Employee A plans to have eye surgery in 2009. For the 2009 plan year, Employee A timely elects salary reduction of $3,000 for a health FSA. During the 2009 plan year, Employee A learns that she cannot have eye surgery performed, but incurs other section 213(d) medical expenses totaling $1,200. As of December 31, 2009, she has $1,800 of unused benefits and contributions in the health FSA. Consistent with the rules in this paragraph (c), she forfeits $1,800.

(d) Uniform coverage rules applicable to health FSAs. *(1) Uniform coverage throughout coverage period—in general.* The maximum amount of reimbursement from a health FSA must be available at all times during the period of coverage (properly reduced as of any particular time for prior reimbursements for the same period of coverage). Thus, the maximum amount of reimbursement at any particular time during the period of coverage cannot relate to the amount that has been contributed to the FSA at any particular time prior to the end of the plan year. Similarly, the payment schedule for the required amount for coverage under a health FSA may not be based on the rate or amount of covered claims incurred during the coverage period. Employees' salary reduction payments must not be accelerated based on employees' incurred claims and reimbursements.

(2) Reimbursement available at all times. Reimbursement is deemed to be available at all times if it is paid at least monthly or when the total amount of the claims to be submitted is at least a specified, reasonable minimum amount (for example, $50).

(3) Terminated participants. When an employee ceases to be a participant, the cafeteria plan must pay the former participant any amount the former participant previously paid for coverage or benefits to the extent the previously paid amount relates to the period from the date the employee ceases to be a participant through the end of that plan year. See paragraph (e)(2) in this section for COBRA elections for health FSAs.

(4) Example. The following example illustrates the rules in this paragraph (d):

Example. Uniform coverage. (i) Employer C maintains a calendar year cafeteria plan, offering an election between cash and a health FSA. The cafeteria plan prohibits accelerating employees' salary reduction payments based on employees' incurred claims and reimbursements.

(ii) For the 2009 plan year, Employee N timely elects salary reduction of $3,000 for a health FSA. Employee N pays the $3,000 salary reduction amount through salary reduction of $250 per month throughout the coverage period. Employee N is eligible to receive the maximum amount of reimbursement of $3,000 at all times throughout the coverage period (reduced by prior reimbursements).

(iii) N incurs $2,500 of section 213(d) medical expenses in January, 2009. The full $2,500 is reimbursed although Employee N has made only one salary reduction payment of $250. N incurs $500 in medical expenses in February, 2009. The remaining $500 of the $3,000 is reimbursed. After Employee N submits a claim for reimbursement and substantiates the medical expenses, the cafeteria plan reimburses N for the $2,500 and $500 medical expenses. Employer C's cafeteria plan satisfies the uniform coverage rule.

(5) No uniform coverage rule for FSAs for dependent care assistance or adoption assistance. The uniform coverage rule applies only to health FSAs and does not apply to FSAs for dependent care assistance or adoption assistance. See paragraphs (i) and (j) of this section for the rules for FSAs for dependent care assistance and adoption assistance.

(e) Required period of coverage for a health FSA, dependent care FSA and adoption assistance FSA. *(1) Twelve-month period of coverage—in general.* An FSA's period of coverage must be 12 months. However, in the case of a short plan year, the period of coverage is the entire short plan year. See paragraph (d) in § 1.125-1 for rules on plan years and changing plan years.

(2) COBRA elections for health FSAs. For the application of the health care continuation rules of section 4980B of the Code to health FSAs, see Q&A-2 in § 54.4980B-2 of this chapter.

(3) Separate period of coverage permitted for each qualified benefit offered through FSA. Dependent care assistance, adoption assistance, and a health FSA are each permitted to have a separate period of coverage, which may be different from the plan year of the cafeteria plan.

(f) Coverage on a month-by-month or expense-by-expense basis prohibited. In order for reimbursements from an accident and health plan to qualify for the section 105(b) exclusion, an employer-funded accident and health plan offered through a cafeteria plan may not operate in a manner that enables employees to purchase the accident and health plan coverage only for periods when employees expect to incur medical care expenses. Thus, for example, if a cafeteria plan permits employees to receive accident and health plan coverage on a month-by-month or an expense-by-expense basis, reimbursements from the accident and health plan fail to qualify for the section 105(b) exclusion. If, however, the period of coverage under an accident and health plan offered through a cafeteria plan is twelve months and the cafeteria plan does not permit an employee to elect specific amounts of coverage, reimbursement, or salary reduction for less than twelve months, the cafeteria plan does not operate to enable participants to purchase coverage only for periods during which medical care will be incurred. See § 1.125-4 and paragraph (a) in § 1.125-2 regarding the revocation of elections during a period of coverage on account of changes in family status.

(g) FSA administrative practices. *(1) Limiting health FSA enrollment to employees who participate in the employer's accident and health plan.* At the employer's option, a cafeteria plan is permitted to provide that only those employees who participate in one or more specified employer-provided accident and health plans may participate in a health FSA. See § 1.125-7 for nondiscrimination rules.

(2) Interval for employees' salary reduction contributions. The cafeteria plan is permitted to specify any interval for employees' salary reduction contributions. The interval specified in the plan must be uniform for all participants.

(h) Qualified benefits permitted to be offered through an FSA. Dependent care assistance (section 129), adoption assistance (section 137) and a medical reimbursement arrangement (section 105(b)) are permitted to be offered through an FSA in a cafeteria plan.

(i) Section 129 rules for dependent care assistance program offered through a cafeteria plan. *(1) General rule.* In order for dependent care assistance to be a qualified benefit that is excludible from gross income if elected through a cafeteria plan, the cafeteria plan must satisfy section 125 and the dependent care assistance must satisfy section 129.

(2) Dependent care assistance in general. Section 129(a) provides an employee with an exclusion from gross income both for an employer-funded dependent care assistance program and for amounts paid or incurred by the employer for dependent care assistance provided to the employee, if the amounts are paid or incurred through a dependent care assistance program. See paragraph (a)(4) in § 1.125-6 on when dependent care expenses are incurred.

(3) Reimbursement exclusively for dependent care assistance. A dependent care assistance program may not provide reimbursements other than for dependent care expenses; in particular, if an employee has dependent care expenses less than the amount specified by salary reduction, the plan may not provide other taxable or nontaxable benefits for any portion of the specified amount not used for the reimbursement of dependent care expenses. Thus, if an employee has elected coverage under the dependent care assistance program and the period of coverage has commenced, the employee must not have the right to receive amounts from the program other than as reimbursements for dependent care expenses. This is the case regardless of whether coverage under the program is purchased with contributions made at the employer's discretion, at the employee's discretion, or pursuant to a collective bargaining agreement. Arrangements formally outside of the cafeteria plan providing for the adjustment of an employee's compensation or an employee's receipt of any other benefits on the basis of the assistance or reimbursements received by the employee are considered in determining whether a dependent care benefit is a dependent care assistance program under section 129.

(j) Section 137 rules for adoption assistance program offered through a cafeteria plan. *(1) General rule.* In order for adoption assistance to be a qualified benefit that is excludible from gross income if elected through a cafeteria plan, the cafeteria plan must satisfy section 125 and the adoption assistance must satisfy section 137.

(2) Adoption assistance in general. Section 137(a) provides an employee with an exclusion from gross income for amounts paid or expenses incurred by the employer for qualified adoption expenses in connection with an employee's adoption of a child, if the amounts are paid or incurred through an adoption assistance program. Certain limits on amount of expenses and employee's income apply.

(3) Reimbursement exclusively for adoption assistance. Rules and requirements similar to the rules and requirements in paragraph (i)(3) of this section for dependent care assistance apply to adoption assistance.

(k) FSAs and the rules governing the tax-favored treatment of employer-provided health benefits. *(1) Medical expenses.* Health plans that are flexible spending arrangements, as defined in paragraph (a)(1) of this section, must conform to the generally applicable rules under sections 105 and 106 in order for the coverage and reimbursements under such plans to qualify for tax-favored treatment under such sections. Thus, health FSAs must qualify as accident and health plans. See paragraph (n) in § 1.125-1. A health FSA is only permitted to reimburse medical expenses as defined in section 213(d). Thus, for example, a health FSA is not permitted to reimburse dependent care expenses.

(2) Limiting payment or reimbursement to certain section 213(d) medical expenses. A health FSA is permitted to limit payment or reimbursement to only certain section 213(d) medical expenses (except health insurance, long-term care services or insurance). See paragraph (q) in § 1.125-1. For example, a health FSA in a cafeteria plan is permitted to provide in the written plan that the plan reimburses all section 213(d) medical expenses allowed to be paid or reimbursed under a cafeteria plan except over-the-counter drugs.

(3) Application of prohibition against deferred compensation to medical expenses. (i) Certain advance payments for orthodontia permitted. A cafeteria plan is permitted, but is not required to, reimburse employees for orthodontia services before the services are provided but only to the extent that the employee has actually made the payments in advance of the orthodontia services in order to receive the services. These orthodontia services are deemed to be incurred when the employee makes the advance payment. Reimburs-

ing advance payments does not violate the prohibition against deferring compensation.

(ii) Example. The following example illustrates the rules in paragraph (k)(3):

Example. Advance payment to orthodontist. Employer D sponsors a calendar year cafeteria plan which offers a health FSA. Employee K elects to salary reduce $3,000 for a health FSA for the 2009 plan year. Employee K's dependent requires orthodontic treatment. K's accident and health insurance does not cover orthodontia. The orthodontist, following the normal practice, charges $3,000, all due in 2009, for treatment, to begin in 2009 and end in 2010. K pays the $3,000 in 2009. In 2009, Employer D's cafeteria plan may reimburse $3,000 to K, without violating the prohibition against deferring compensation in section 125(d)(2).

(iii) Reimbursements for durable medical equipment. A health FSA in a cafeteria plan that reimburses employees for equipment (described in section 213(d)) with a useful life extending beyond the period of coverage during which the expense is incurred does not provide deferred compensation. For example, a health FSA is permitted to reimburse the cost of a wheelchair for an employee.

(4) No reimbursement of premiums for accident and health insurance or long-term care insurance or services. A health FSA is not permitted to treat employees' premium payments for other health coverage as reimbursable expenses. Thus, for example, a health FSA is not permitted to reimburse employees for payments for other health plan coverage, including premiums for COBRA coverage, accidental death and dismemberment insurance, long-term disability or short-term disability insurance or for health coverage under a plan maintained by the employer of the employee or the employer of the employee's spouse or dependent. Also, a health FSA is not permitted to reimburse expenses for long-term care insurance premiums or for long-term care services for the employee or employee's spouse or dependent. See paragraph (q) in § 1.125-1 for nonqualified benefits

(l) Section 105(h) requirements. Section 105(h) applies to health FSAs. Section 105(h) provides that the exclusion provided by section 105(b) is not available with respect to certain amounts received by a highly compensated individual (as defined in section 105(h)(5)) from a discriminatory self-insured medical reimbursement plan, which includes health FSAs. See § 1.105-11. For purposes of section 105(h), coverage by a self-insured accident and health plan offered through a cafeteria plan is an optional benefit (even if only one level and type of coverage is offered) and, for purposes of the optional benefit rule in § 1.105-11(c)(3)(i), employer contributions are treated as employee contributions to the extent that taxable benefits are offered by the plan.

(m) HSA-compatible FSAs-limited-purpose health FSAs and post-deductible health FSAs. *(1) In general.* Limited-purpose health FSAs and post-deductible health FSAs which satisfy all the requirements of section 125 are permitted to be offered through a cafeteria plan.

(2) HSA-compatible FSAs. Section 223(a) allows a deduction for certain contributions to a "Health Savings Account" (HSA) (as defined in section 223(d)). An eligible individual (as defined in section 223(c)(1)) may contribute to an HSA. An eligible individual must be covered under a "high deductible health plan" (HDHP) and not, while covered under an HDHP, under any health plan which is not an HDHP. A general purpose health FSA is not an HDHP and an individual covered by a general purpose health FSA is not eligible to contribute to an HSA. However, an individual covered by an HDHP (and who otherwise satisfies section 223(c)(1)) does not fail to be an eligible individual merely because the individual is also covered by a limited-purpose health FSA or post-deductible health FSA (as defined in this paragraph (m)) or a combination of a limited-purpose health FSA and a post-deductible health FSA.

(3) Limited-purpose health FSA. A limited-purpose health FSA is a health FSA described in the cafeteria plan that only pays or reimburses permitted coverage benefits (as defined in section 223(c)(2)(C)), such as vision care, dental care or preventive care (as defined for purposes of section 223(c)(2)(C)). See paragraph (k) in this section.

(4) Post-deductible health FSA. (i) In general. A post-deductible health FSA is a health FSA described in the cafeteria plan that only pays or reimburses medical expenses (as defined in section 213(d)) for preventive care or medical expenses incurred after the minimum annual HDHP deductible under section 223(c)(2)(A)(i) is satisfied. See paragraph (k) in this section. No medical expenses incurred before the annual HDHP deductible is satisfied may be reimbursed by a post-deductible FSA, regardless of whether the HDHP covers the expense or whether the deductible is later satisfied. For example, even if chiropractic care is not covered under the HDHP, expenses for chiropractic care incurred before the HDHP deductible is satisfied are not reimbursable at any time by a post-deductible health FSA.

(ii) HDHP and health FSA deductibles. The deductible for a post-deductible health FSA need not be the same amount as the deductible for the HDHP, but in no event may the post-deductible health FSA or other coverage provide benefits before the minimum annual HDHP deductible under section 223(c)(2)(A)(i) is satisfied (other than benefits permitted under a limited-purpose health FSA). In addition, although the deductibles of the HDHP and the other coverage may be satisfied independently by separate expenses, no benefits may be paid before the minimum annual deductible under section 223(c)(2)(A)(i) has been satisfied. An individual covered by a post-deductible health FSA (if otherwise an eligible individual) is an eligible individual for the purpose of contributing to the HSA.

(5) Combination of limited-purpose health FSA and post-deductible health FSA. An FSA is a combination of a limited-purpose health FSA and post-deductible health FSA if each of the benefits and reimbursements provided under the FSA are permitted under either a limited-purpose health FSA or post-deductible health FSA. For example, before the HDHP deductible is satisfied, a combination limited-purpose and post-deductible health FSA may reimburse only preventive, vision or dental expenses. A combination limited-purpose and post-deductible health FSA may also reimburse any medical expense that may otherwise be paid by an FSA (that is, no insurance premiums or long-term care benefits) that is incurred after the HDHP deductible is satisfied.

(6) Substantiation. The substantiation rules in this section apply to limited-purpose health FSAs and to post-deductible health FSAs. In addition to providing third-party substantiation of medical expenses, a participant in a post-deductible health FSA must provide information from an independent third party that the HDHP deductible has been satisfied. A participant in a limited-purpose health FSA must provide information from an independent third-party that the medical expenses are for vision care, dental care or preventive care.

(7) Plan amendments. See paragraph (c) in § 1.125-1 on the required effective date for amendments adopting or

changing limited-purpose, post-deductible or combination limited-purpose and post-deductible health FSAs.

(n) Qualified HSA distributions. *(1) In general.* A health FSA in a cafeteria plan is permitted to offer employees the right to elect qualified HSA distributions described in section 106(e). No qualified HSA distribution may be made in a plan year unless the employer amends the health FSA written plan with respect to all employees, effective by the last day of the plan year, to allow a qualified HSA distribution satisfying all the requirements in this paragraph (n). See also section 106(e)(5)(B). In addition, a distribution with respect to an employee is not a qualified HSA distribution unless all of the following requirements are satisfied—

(i) No qualified HSA distribution has been previously made on behalf of the employee from this health FSA;

(ii) The employee elects to have the employer make a qualified HSA distribution from the health FSA to the HSA of the employee;

(iii) The distribution does not exceed the lesser of the balance of the health FSA on—

(A) September 21, 2006; or

(B) The date of the distribution;

(iv) For purposes of this paragraph (n)(1), balances as of any date are determined on a cash basis, without taking into account expenses incurred but not reimbursed as of a date, and applying the uniform coverage rule in paragraph (d) in this section;

(v) The distribution is made no later than December 31, 2011; and

(vi) The employer makes the distribution directly to the trustee of the employee's HSA.

(2) Taxation of qualified HSA distributions. A qualified HSA distribution from the health FSA covering the participant to his or her HSA is a rollover to the HSA (as defined in section 223(f)(5)) and thus is generally not includible in gross income. However, if the participant is not an eligible individual (as defined in section 223(c)(1)) at any time during a testing period following the qualified HSA distribution, the amount of the distribution is includible in the participant's gross income and he or she is also subject to an additional 10 percent tax (with certain exceptions). Section 106(e)(3).

(3) No effect on health FSA elections, coverage, use-or-lose rule. A qualified HSA distribution does not alter an employee's irrevocable election under paragraph (a) of § 1.125-2, or constitute a change in status under § 1.125-4(a). If a qualified HSA distribution is made to an employee's HSA, even if the balance in a health FSA is reduced to zero, the employee's health FSA coverage continues to the end of the plan year. Unused benefits and contributions remaining at the end of a plan year (or at the end of a grace period, if applicable) must be forfeited.

(o) FSA experience gains or forfeitures. *(1) Experience gains in general.* An FSA experience gain (sometimes referred to as forfeitures in the use-or-lose rule in paragraph (c) in this section) with respect to a plan year (plus any grace period following the end of a plan year described in paragraph (e) in § 1.125-1), equals the amount of the employer contributions, including salary reduction contributions, and after-tax employee contributions to the FSA minus the FSA's total claims reimbursements for the year. Experience gains (or forfeitures) may be—

(i) Retained by the employer maintaining the cafeteria plan; or

(ii) If not retained by the employer, may be used only in one or more of the following ways—

(A) To reduce required salary reduction amounts for the immediately following plan year, on a reasonable and uniform basis, as described in paragraph (o)(2) of this section;

(B) Returned to the employees on a reasonable and uniform basis, as described in paragraph (o)(2) of this section; or

(C) To defray expenses to administer the cafeteria plan.

(2) Allocating experience gains among employees on reasonable and uniform basis. If not retained by the employer or used to defray expenses of administering the plan, the experience gains must be allocated among employees on a reasonable and uniform basis. It is permissible to allocate these amounts based on the different coverage levels of employees under the FSA. Experience gains allocated in compliance with this paragraph (o) are not a deferral of the receipt of compensation. However, in no case may the experience gains be allocated among employees based (directly or indirectly) on their individual claims experience. Experience gains may not be used as contributions directly or indirectly to any deferred compensation benefit plan.

(3) Example. The following example illustrates the rules in this paragraph (o):

Example. Allocating experience gains. (i) Employer L maintains a cafeteria plan for its 1,200 employees, who may elect one of several different annual coverage levels under a health FSA in $100 increments from $500 to $2,000.

(ii) For the 2009 plan year, 1,000 employees elect levels of coverage under the health FSA. For the 2009 plan year, the health FSA has an experience gain of $5,000.

(iii) The $5,000 may be allocated to all participants for the plan year on a per capita basis weighted to reflect the participants' elected levels of coverage.

(iv) Alternatively, the $5,000 may be used to reduce the required salary reduction amount under the health FSA for all 2009 participants (for example, a $500 health FSA for the next year is priced at $480) or to reimburse claims incurred above the elective limit in 2010 as long as such reimbursements are made on a reasonable and uniform level.

(p) Effective/applicability date. It is proposed that these regulations apply on and after plan years beginning on or after January 1, 2009.

Proposed § 1.125-6 Substantiation of expenses for all cafeteria plans. [*For Preamble, see ¶ 152,897*]

(a) Cafeteria plan payments and reimbursements. *(1) In general.* A cafeteria plan may pay or reimburse only those substantiated expenses for qualified benefits incurred on or after the later of the effective date of the cafeteria plan and the date the employee is enrolled in the plan. This requirement applies to all qualified benefits offered through the cafeteria plan. See paragraph (b) of this section for substantiation rules.

(2) Expenses incurred. (i) Employees' medical expenses must be incurred during the period of coverage. In order for reimbursements to be excludible from gross income under section 105(b), the medical expenses reimbursed by an accident and health plan elected through a cafeteria plan must be incurred during the period when the participant is covered by the accident and health plan. A participant's period of coverage includes COBRA coverage. See § 54.4980B-2 of this chapter. Medical expenses incurred before the later of the effective date of the plan and the date the employee is enrolled

in the plan are not incurred during the period for which the employee is covered by the plan. However, the actual reimbursement of covered medical care expenses may be made after the applicable period of coverage.

(ii) When medical expenses are incurred. For purposes of this rule, medical expenses are incurred when the employee (or the employee's spouse or dependents) is provided with the medical care that gives rise to the medical expenses, and not when the employee is formally billed, charged for, or pays for the medical care.

(iii) Example. The following example illustrates the rules in this paragraph (a)(2):

Example. Medical expenses incurred after termination. (i) Employer E maintains a cafeteria plan with a calendar year plan year. The cafeteria plan provides that participation terminates when an individual ceases to be an employee of Employer E, unless the former employee elects to continue to participate in the health FSA under the COBRA rules in § 54.4980B-2 of this chapter. Employee G timely elects to salary reduce $1,200 to participate in a health FSA for the 2009 plan year. As of June 30, 2009, Employee G has contributed $600 toward the health FSA, but incurred no medical expenses. On June 30, 2009, Employee G terminates employment and does not continue participation under COBRA. On July 15, 2009, G incurs a section 213(d) medical expense of $500.

(ii) Under the rules in paragraph (a)(2) of this section, the cafeteria plan is prohibited from reimbursing any portion of the $500 medical expense because, at the time the medical expense is incurred, G is not a participant in the cafeteria plan.

(3) Section 105(b) requirements for reimbursement of medical expenses through a cafeteria plan. (i) In general. In order for medical care reimbursements paid to an employee through a cafeteria plan to be excludible under section 105(b), the reimbursements must be paid pursuant to an employer-funded accident and health plan, as defined in section 105(e) and §§ 1.105-2 and 1.105-5.

(ii) Reimbursement exclusively for section 213(d) medical expenses. A cafeteria plan benefit through which an employee receives reimbursements of medical expenses is excludable under section 105(b) only if reimbursements from the plan are made specifically to reimburse the employee for medical expenses (as defined in section 213(d)) incurred by the employee or the employee's spouse or dependents during the period of coverage. Amounts paid to an employee as reimbursement are not paid specifically to reimburse the employee for medical expenses if the plan provides that the employee is entitled, or operates in a manner that entitles the employee, to receive the amounts, in the form of cash (for example, routine payment of salary) or any other taxable or nontaxable benefit irrespective of whether the employee (or the employee's spouse or dependents) incurs medical expenses during the period of coverage. This rule applies even if the employee will not receive such amounts until the end or after the end of the period. A plan under which employees (or their spouses and dependents) will receive reimbursement for medical expenses up to a specified amount and, if they incur no medical expenses, will receive cash or any other benefit in lieu of the reimbursements is not a benefit qualifying for the exclusion under sections 106 and 105(b). See § 1.105-2. This is the case without regard to whether the benefit was purchased with contributions made at the employer's discretion, at the employee's discretion (for example, by salary reduction election), or pursuant to a collective bargaining agreement.

(iii) Other arrangements. Arrangements formally outside of the cafeteria plan that adjust an employee's compensation or an employee's receipt of any other benefits on the basis of the expenses incurred or reimbursements the employee receives are considered in determining whether the reimbursements are through a plan eligible for the exclusions under sections 106 and 105(b).

(4) Reimbursements of dependent care expenses. (i) Dependent care expenses must be incurred. In order to satisfy section 129, dependent care expenses may not be reimbursed before the expenses are incurred. For purposes of this rule, dependent care expenses are incurred when the care is provided and not when the employee is formally billed, charged for, or pays for the dependent care.

(ii) Dependent care provided during the period of coverage. In order for dependent care assistance to be provided through a dependent care assistance program eligible for the section 129 exclusion, the care must be provided to or on behalf of the employee during the period for which the employee is covered by the program. For example, if for a plan year, an employee elects a dependent care assistance program providing for reimbursement of dependent care expenses, only reimbursements for dependent care expenses incurred during that plan year are provided from a dependent care assistance program within the scope of section 129. Also, for purposes of this rule, expenses incurred before the later of the program's effective date and the date the employee is enrolled in the program are not incurred during the period when the employee is covered by the program. Similarly, if the dependent care assistance program furnishes the dependent care in-kind (for example, through an employer-maintained child care facility), only dependent care provided during the plan year of coverage is provided through a dependent care assistance program within the meaning of section 129. See also § 1.125-5 for FSA rules.

(iii) Period of coverage. In order for dependent care assistance through a cafeteria plan to be provided through a dependent care assistance program eligible for the section 129 exclusion, the plan may not operate in a manner that enables employees to purchase dependent care assistance only for periods during which the employees expect to receive dependent care assistance. If the period of coverage for a dependent care assistance program offered through a cafeteria plan is twelve months (or, in the case of a short plan year, at least equal to the short plan year) and the plan does not permit an employee to elect specific amounts of coverage, reimbursement, or salary reduction for less than twelve months, the plan is deemed not to operate to enable employees to purchase coverage only for periods when dependent care assistance will be received. See paragraph (a) in § 1.125-2 and § 1.125-4 regarding the revocation of elections during the period of coverage on account of changes in family status. See paragraph (e) in this section for required period of coverage for dependent care assistance.

(iv) Examples. The following examples illustrate the rules in paragraphs (a)(4)(i)-(iii) of this section:

Example (1). Initial non-refundable fee for child care. (i) Employer F maintains a calendar year cafeteria plan, offering employees an election between cash and qualified benefits, including dependent care assistance. Employee M has a one-year old dependent child. Employee M timely elected $5,000 of dependent care assistance for 2009. During the entire 2009 plan year, Employee M satisfies all the requirements in section 129 for dependent care assistance.

(ii) On February 1, 2009, Employee M pays an initial non-refundable fee of $500 to a licensed child care center (unrelated to Employer F or to Employee M), to reserve a space at the child care center for M's child. The child care center's monthly charges for child care are $1,200. When the child care center first begins to care for M's child, the $500 non-refundable fee is applied toward the first month's charges for child care.

(iii) On March 1, 2009, the child care center begins caring for Employee M's child, and continues to care for the child through December 31, 2009. On March 1, 2009, M pays the child care center $700 (the balance of the $1,200 in charges for child care to be provided in March 2009). On April 1, 2009, M pays the child care center $1,200 for the child care to be provided in April 2009.

(iv) Dependent care expenses are incurred when the services are provided. For dependent care services provided in March 2009, the $500 nonrefundable fee paid on February 1, 2009, and the $700 paid on March 1, 2009 may be reimbursed on or after the later of the date when substantiated or April 1, 2009. For dependent care services provided in April 2009, the $1,200 paid on April 1, 2009 may be reimbursed on or after the later of the date when substantiated or May 1, 2009.

Example (2). Non-refundable fee forfeited. Same facts as Example 1, except that the child care center never cared for M's child (who was instead cared for at Employer F's onsite child care facility). Because the child care center never provided child care services to Employee M's child, the $500 non-refundable fee is not reimbursable.

(v) Optional spend-down provision. At the employer's option, the written cafeteria plan may provide that dependent care expenses incurred after the date an employee ceases participation in the cafeteria plan (for example, after termination) and through the last day of that plan year (or grace period immediately after that plan year) may be reimbursed from unused benefits, if all of the requirements of section 129 are satisfied.

(vi) Example. The following example illustrates the rules in paragraph (a)(4)(v) of this section:

Example. Terminated employee's post-termination dependent care expenses. (i) For calendar year 2009, Employee X elects $5,000 salary reduction for dependent care assistance through Employer G's cafeteria plan. X works for Employer G from January 1 through June 30, 2009, when X terminates employment. As of June 30, 2009, X had paid $2,500 in salary reduction and had incurred and was reimbursed for $2,000 of dependent care expenses.

(ii) X does not work again until October 1, 2009, when X begins work for Employer H. X was employed by Employer H from October 1, 2009 through December 31, 2009. During this period, X also incurred $500 of dependent care expenses. During all the periods of employment in 2009, X satisfied all requirements in section 129 for excluding payments for dependent care assistance from gross income.

(iii) Employer G's cafeteria plan allows terminated employees to "spend down" unused salary reduction amounts for dependent care assistance, if all requirements of section 129 are satisfied. After X's claim for $500 of dependent care expenses is substantiated, Employer G's cafeteria plan reimburses X for $500 (the remaining balance) of dependent care expenses incurred during X's employment for Employer H between October 1, 2009 and December 31, 2009. Employer G's cafeteria plan and operation are consistent with section 125.

(b) Rules for claims substantiation for cafeteria plans.

(1) Substantiation required before reimbursing expenses for qualified benefits. This paragraph (b) sets forth the substantiation requirements that a cafeteria plan must satisfy before paying or reimbursing any expense for a qualified benefit.

(2) All claims must be substantiated. As a precondition of payment or reimbursement of expenses for qualified benefits, a cafeteria plan must require substantiation in accordance with this section. Substantiating only a percentage of claims, or substantiating only claims above a certain dollar amount, fails to comply with the substantiation requirements in § 1.125-1 and this section.

(3) Substantiation by independent third-party. (i) In general. All expenses must be substantiated by information from a third-party that is independent of the employee and the employee's spouse and dependents. The independent third-party must provide information describing the service or product, the date of the service or sale, and the amount. Self-substantiation or self-certification of an expense by an employee does not satisfy the substantiation requirements of this paragraph (b). The specific requirements in sections 105(b), 129, and 137 must also be satisfied as a condition of reimbursing expenses for qualified benefits. For example, a health FSA does not satisfy the requirements of section 105(b) if it reimburses employees for expenses where the employees only submit information describing medical expenses, the amount of the expenses and the date of the expenses but fail to provide a statement from an independent third-party (either automatically or subsequent to the transaction) verifying the expenses. Under § 1.105-2, all amounts paid under a plan that permits self-substantiation or self-certification are includible in gross income, including amounts reimbursed for medical expenses, whether or not substantiated. See paragraph (m) in § 1.125-5 for additional substantiation rules for limited-purpose and post-deductible health FSAs.

(ii) Rules for substantiation of health FSA claims using an explanation of benefits provided by an insurance company. (A) Written statement from an independent third-party. If the employer is provided with information from an independent third-party (such as an "explanation of benefits" (EOB) from an insurance company) indicating the date of the section 213(d) medical care and the employee's responsibility for payment for that medical care (that is, coinsurance payments and amounts below the plan's deductible), and the employee certifies that any expense paid through the health FSA has not been reimbursed and that the employee will not seek reimbursement from any other plan covering health benefits, the claim is fully substantiated without the need for submission of a receipt by the employee or further review.

(B) Example. The following example illustrates the rules in this paragraph (b)(3):

Example. Explanation of benefits. (i) During the plan year ending December 31, 2009, Employee Q is a participant in the health FSA sponsored by Employer J and is enrolled in Employer J's accident and health plan.

(ii) On March 1, 2009, Q visits a physician's office for medical care as defined in section 213(d). The charge for the physician's services is $150. Under the plan, Q is responsible for 20 percent of the charge for the physician's services (that is, $30). Q has sufficient FSA coverage for the $30 claim.

(iii) Employer J has coordinated with the accident and health plan so that Employer J or its agent automatically receives an EOB from the plan indicating that Q is responsible for payment of 20 percent of the $150 charged by the physician. Because Employer J has received a statement from an independent third-party that Q has incurred a medical expense, the date the expense was incurred, and the amount of the expense, the claim is substantiated without the need for J to submit additional information regarding the expense. Employer J's FSA reimburses Q the $30 medical expense without requiring Q to submit a receipt or a statement from the physician. The substantiation rules in paragraph (b) in this section are satisfied.

(4) Advance reimbursement of expenses for qualified benefits prohibited. Reimbursing expenses before the expense has been incurred or before the expense is substantiated fails to satisfy the substantiation requirements in § 1.105-2, § 1.125-1 and this section.

(5) Purported loan from employer to employee. In determining whether, under all the facts and circumstances, employees are being reimbursed for unsubstantiated claims, special scrutiny will be given to other arrangements such as employer-to-employee loans based on actual or projected employee claims.

(6) Debit cards. For purposes of this section, a debit card is a debit card, credit card, or stored value card. See also paragraphs (c) through (g) of this section for additional rules on payments or reimbursements made through debit cards.

(c) Debit cards-overview. *(1) Mandatory rules for all debit cards usable to pay or reimburse medical expenses.* Paragraph (d) of this section sets forth the mandatory procedures for debit cards to substantiate section 213(d) medical expenses. These rules apply to all debit cards used to pay or reimburse medical expenses. Paragraph (e) of this section sets forth additional substantiation rules that may be used for medical expenses incurred at medical care providers and certain stores with the Drug Stores and Pharmacies merchant category code. Paragraph (f) in this section sets forth the requirements for an inventory information approval system which must be used to substantiate medical expenses incurred at merchants or service providers that are not medical care providers or certain stores with the Drug Stores and Pharmacies merchant category code and that may be used for medical expenses incurred at all merchants.

(2) Debit cards used for dependent care assistance. Paragraph (g) of this section sets forth additional rules for debit cards usable for reimbursing dependent care expenses.

(3) Additional guidance. The Commissioner may prescribe additional guidance of general applicability, published in the Internal Revenue Bulletin (see § 601.601(d)(2)(ii)(b) of this chapter), to provide additional rules for debit cards.

(d) Mandatory rules for all debit cards usable to pay or reimburse medical expenses. A health FSA paying or reimbursing section 213(d) medical expenses through a debit card must satisfy all of the following requirements—

(1) Before any employee participating in a health FSA receives the debit card, the employee agrees in writing that he or she will only use the card to pay for medical expenses (as defined in section 213(d)) of the employee or his or her spouse or dependents, that he or she will not use the debit card for any medical expense that has already been reimbursed, that he or she will not seek reimbursement under any other health plan for any expense paid for with a debit card, and that he or she will acquire and retain sufficient documentation (including invoices and receipts) for any expense paid with the debit card.

(2) The debit card includes a statement providing that the agreements described in paragraph (d)(1) of this section are reaffirmed each time the employee uses the card.

(3) The amount available through the debit card equals the amount elected by the employee for the health FSA for the cafeteria plan year, and is reduced by amounts paid or reimbursed for section 213(d) medical expenses incurred during the plan year.

(4) The debit card is automatically cancelled when the employee ceases to participate in the health FSA.

(5) The employer limits use of the debit card to—

(i) Physicians, dentists, vision care offices, hospitals, other medical care providers (as identified by the merchant category code);

(ii) Stores with the merchant category code for Drugstores and Pharmacies if, on a location by location basis, 90 percent of the store's gross receipts during the prior taxable year consisted of items which qualify as expenses for medical care described in section 213(d); and

(iii) Stores that have implemented the inventory information approval system under paragraph (f).

(6) The employer substantiates claims based on payments to medical care providers and stores described in paragraphs (d)(5)(i) and (ii) of this section in accordance with either paragraph (e) or paragraph (f) of this section.

(7) The employer follows all of the following correction procedures for any improper payments using the debit card—

(i) Until the amount of the improper payment is recovered, the debit card must be de-activated and the employee must request payments or reimbursements of medical expenses from the health FSA through other methods (for example, by submitting receipts or invoices from a merchant or service provider showing the employee incurred a section 213(d) medical expense);

(ii) The employer demands that the employee repay the cafeteria plan an amount equal to the improper payment;

(iii) If, after the demand for repayment of improper payment (as described in paragraph (d)(7)(ii) of this section), the employee fails to repay the amount of the improper charge, the employer withholds the amount of the improper charge from the employee's pay or other compensation, to the full extent allowed by applicable law;

(iv) If any portion of the improper payment remains outstanding after attempts to recover the amount (as described in paragraph (d)(7)(ii) and (iii) of this section), the employer applies a claims substitution or offset to resolve improper payments, such as a reimbursement for a later substantiated expense claim is reduced by the amount of the improper payment. So, for example, if an employee has received an improper payment of $200 and subsequently submits a substantiated claim for $250 incurred during the same coverage period, a reimbursement for $50 is made; and

(v) If, after applying all the procedures described in paragraph (d)(7)(ii) through (iv) of this section, the employee remains indebted to the employer for improper payments, the employer, consistent with its business practice, treats the improper payment as it would any other business indebtedness.

(e) Substantiation of expenses incurred at medical care providers and certain other stores with Drug Stores and Pharmacies merchant category code.

(1) In general. A health FSA paying or reimbursing section 213(d) medical expenses through a debit card is permitted to comply with the substantiation provisions of this paragraph (e), instead of complying with the provisions of paragraph (f), for medical expenses incurred at providers described in paragraph (e)(2) of this section.

(2) Medical care providers and certain other stores with Drug Stores and Pharmacies merchant category code. Medical expenses may be substantiated using the methods described in paragraph (e)(3) of this section if incurred at physicians, pharmacies, dentists, vision care offices, hospitals, other medical care providers (as identified by the merchant category code) and at stores with the Drug Stores and Pharmacies merchant category code, if, on a store location-by-location basis, 90 percent of the store's gross receipts during the prior taxable year consisted of items which qualify as expenses for medical care described in section 213(d).

(3) Claims substantiation for copayment matches, certain recurring medical expenses and real-time substantiation. If all of the requirements in this paragraph (e)(3) are satisfied, copayment matches, certain recurring medical expenses and medical expenses substantiated in real-time are substantiated without the need for submission of receipts or further review.

(i) Matching copayments—multiples of five or fewer. If an employer's accident or health plan covering the employee (or the employee's spouse or dependents) has copayments in specific dollar amounts, and the dollar amount of the transaction at a medical care provider equals an exact multiple of not more than five times the dollar amount of the copayment for the specific service (for example, pharmacy benefit copayment, copayment for a physician's office visit) under the accident or health plan covering the specific employee-cardholder, then the charge is fully substantiated without the need for submission of a receipt or further review.

(A) Tiered copayments. If a health plan has multiple copayments for the same benefit, (for example, tiered copayments for a pharmacy benefit), exact matches of multiples or combinations of up to five copayments are similarly fully substantiated without the need for submission of a receipt or further review.

(B) Copayment match must be exact multiple. If the dollar amount of the transaction is not an exact multiple of the copayment (or an exact match of a multiple or combination of different copayments for a benefit in the case of multiple copayments), the transaction must be treated as conditional pending confirmation of the charge, even if the amount is less than five times the copayment.

(C) No match for multiple of six or more times copayment. If the dollar amount of the transaction at a medical care provider equals a multiple of six or more times the dollar amount of the copayment for the specific service, the transaction must be treated as conditional pending confirmation of the charge by the submission of additional third-party information. See paragraph (d) of this section. In the case of a plan with multiple copayments for the same benefit, if the dollar amount of the transaction exceeds five times the maximum copayment for the benefit, the transaction must also be treated as conditional pending confirmation of the charge by the submission of additional third-party information. In these cases, the employer must require that additional third-party information, such as merchant or service provider receipts, be submitted for review and substantiation, and the third-party information must satisfy the requirements in paragraph (b)(3) of this section.

(D) Independent verification of copayment required. The copayment schedule required under the accident or health plan must be independently verified by the employer. Statements or other representations by the employee are not sufficient. Self-substantiation or self-certification of an employee's copayment in connection with copayment matching procedures through debit cards or otherwise does not constitute substantiation. If a plan's copayment matching system relies on an employee to provide a copayment amount without verification of the amount, claims have not been substantiated, and all amounts paid from the plan are included in gross income, including amounts paid for medical care whether or not substantiated. See paragraph (b) in this section.

(4) Certain recurring medical expenses. Automatic payment or reimbursement satisfies the substantiation rules in this paragraph (e) for payment of recurring expenses that match expenses previously approved as to amount, medical care provider and time period (for example, for an employee who refills a prescription drug on a regular basis at the same provider and in the same amount). The payment is substantiated without the need for submission of a receipt or further review.

(5) Real-time substantiation. If a third party that is independent of the employee and the employee's spouse and dependents (for example, medical care provider, merchant, or pharmacy benefit manager) provides, at the time and point of sale, information to verify to the employer (including electronically by email, the internet, intranet or telephone) that the charge is for a section 213(d) medical expense, the expense is substantiated without the need for further review.

(6) Substantiation requirements for all other medical expenses paid or reimbursed through a health FSA debit card. All other charges to the debit card (other than substantiated copayments, recurring medical expenses or real-time substantiation, or charges substantiated through the inventory information approval system described in paragraph (f) of this section) must be treated as conditional, pending substantiation of the charge through additional independent third-party information describing the goods or services, the date of the service or sale and the amount of the transaction. All such debit card payments must be substantiated, regardless of the amount of the payment.

(f) Inventory information approval system. *(1) In general.* An inventory information approval system that complies with this paragraph (f) may be used to substantiate payments made using a debit card, including payments at merchants and service providers that are not described in paragraph (e)(2) of this section. Debit card transactions using this system are fully substantiated without the need for submission of a receipt by the employee or further review.

(2) Operation of inventory information approval system. An inventory information approval system must operate in the manner described in this paragraph (f)(2).

(i) When an employee uses the card, the payment card processor's or participating merchant's system collects information about the items purchased using the inventory control information (for example, stock keeping units (SKUs)). The system compares the inventory control information for the items purchased against a list of items, the purchase of which qualifies as expenses for medical care under section 213(d) (including nonprescription medications).

(ii) The section 213(d) medical expenses are totaled and the merchant's or payment card processor's system approves the use of the card only for the amount of the section 213(d) medical expenses eligible for coverage under the health FSA (taking into consideration the uniform coverage rule in paragraph (d) of § 1.125-5);

(iii) If the transaction is only partially approved, the employee is required to tender additional amounts, resulting in a split-tender transaction. For example, if, after matching inventory information, it is determined that all items purchased are section 213(d) medical expenses, the entire transaction is approved, subject to the coverage limitations of the health FSA;

(iv) If, after matching inventory information, it is determined that only some of the items purchased are section 213(d) medical expenses, the transaction is approved only as to the section 213(d) medical expenses. In this case, the merchant or service-provider must request additional payment from the employee for the items that do not satisfy the definition of medical care under section 213(d);

(v) The merchant or service-provider must also request additional payment from the employee if the employee does not have sufficient health FSA coverage to purchase the section 213(d) medical items;

(vi) Any attempt to use the card at non-participating merchants or service-providers must fail.

(3) Employer's responsibility for ensuring inventory information approval system's compliance with § 1.105-2, § 1.125-1, § 1.125-6 and recordkeeping requirements. An employer that uses the inventory information approval system must ensure that the inventory information approval system complies with the requirements in §§ 1.105-2, 1.125-1, and § 1.125-6 for substantiating, paying or reimbursing section 213(d) medical expenses and with the recordkeeping requirements in section 6001.

(g) Debit cards used to pay or reimburse dependent care assistance. *(1) In general.* An employer may use a debit card to provide benefits under its dependent care assistance program (including a dependent care assistance FSA). However, dependent care expenses may not be reimbursed before the expenses are incurred. See paragraph (a)(4) in this section. Thus, if a dependent care provider requires payment before the dependent care services are provided, the expenses cannot be reimbursed at the time of payment through use of a debit card or otherwise.

(2) Reimbursing dependent care assistance through a debit card. An employer offering a dependent care assistance FSA may adopt the following method to provide reimbursements for dependent care expenses through a debit card—

(i) At the beginning of the plan year or upon enrollment in the dependent care assistance program, the employee pays initial expenses to the dependent care provider and substantiates the initial expenses by submitting to the employer or plan administrator a statement from the dependent care provider substantiating the dates and amounts for the services provided.

(ii) After the employer or plan administrator receives the substantiation (but not before the date the services are provided as indicated by the statement provided by the dependent care provider), the plan makes available through the debit card an amount equal to the lesser of—

(A) The previously incurred and substantiated expense; or

(B) The employee's total salary reduction amount to date.

(iii) The card may be used to pay for subsequently incurred dependent care expenses.

(iv) The amount available through the card may be increased in the amount of any additional dependent care expenses only after the additional expenses have been incurred.

(3) Substantiating recurring dependent care expenses. Card transactions that collect information matching expenses previously substantiated and approved as to dependent care provider and time period may be treated as substantiated without further review if the transaction is for an amount equal to or less than the previously substantiated expenses. Similarly, dependent care expenses previously substantiated and approved through nonelectronic methods may also be treated as substantiated without further review. In both cases, if there is an increase in previously substantiated amounts or a change in the dependent care provider, the employee must submit a statement or receipt from the dependent care provider substantiating the claimed expenses before amounts relating to the increased amounts or new providers may be added to the card.

(4) Example. The following example illustrates the rules in this paragraph (g):

Example. Recurring dependent care expenses. (i) Employer K sponsors a dependent care assistance FSA through its cafeteria plan. Salary reduction amounts for participating employees are made on a weekly payroll basis, which are available for dependent care coverage on a weekly basis. As a result, the amount of available dependent care coverage equals the employee's salary reduction amount minus claims previously paid from the plan. Employer K has adopted a payment card program for its dependent care FSA.

(ii) For the plan year ending December 31, 2009, Employee F is a participant in the dependent care FSA and elected $5,000 of dependent care coverage. Employer K reduces F's salary by $96.15 on a weekly basis to pay for coverage under the dependent care FSA.

(iii) At the beginning of the 2009 plan year, F is issued a debit card with a balance of zero. F's childcare provider, ABC Daycare Center, requires a $250 advance payment at the beginning of the week for dependent care services that will be provided during the week. The dependent care services provided for F by ABC qualify for reimbursement under section 129. However, because as of the beginning of the plan year, no services have yet been provided, F cannot be reimbursed for any of the amounts until the end of the first week of the plan year (that is, the week ending January 5, 2009), after the services have been provided.

(iv) F submits a claim for reimbursement that includes a statement from ABC with a description of the services, the amount of the services, and the dates of the services. Employer K increases the balance of F's payment card to $96.15 after the services have been provided (i.e., the lesser of F's salary reduction to date or the incurred dependent care expenses). F uses the card to pay ABC $96.15 on the first day of the next week (January 8, 2009) and pays ABC the remaining balance due for that week ($153.85) by check.

(v) To the extent that this card transaction and each subsequent transaction is with ABC and is for an amount equal to or less than the previously substantiated amount, the charges are fully substantiated without the need for the submission by F of a statement from the provider or further review by the employer. However, the subsequent amount is not made available on the card until the end of the week when the services have been provided. Employer K's dependent care debit card satisfies the substantiation requirements of this paragraph (g).

(h) Effective/applicability date. It is proposed that these regulations apply on and after plan years beginning on or after January 1, 2009. However, the effective dates for the previously issued guidance on debit cards, which is incorporated in this section, remain applicable.

Proposed § 1.125-7 Cafeteria plan nondiscrimination rules. [*For Preamble, see ¶ 152,897*]

(a) Definitions. *(1) In general.* The definitions set forth in this paragraph (a) apply for purposes of section 125(b), (c), (e) and (g) and this section.

(2) Compensation. The term compensation means compensation as defined in section 415(c)(3).

(3) Highly compensated individual. (i) In general. The term highly compensated individual means an individual who is—

(A) An officer;

(B) A five percent shareholder (as defined in paragraph (a)(8) of this section); or

(C) Highly compensated.

(ii) Spouse or dependent. A spouse or a dependent of any highly compensated individual described in (a)(3)(i) of this section is a highly compensated individual. Section 125(e).

(4) Highly compensated participant. The term highly compensated participant means a highly compensated individual who is eligible to participate in the cafeteria plan.

(5) Nonhighly compensated individual. The term nonhighly compensated individual means an individual who is not a highly compensated individual.

(6) Nonhighly compensated participant. The term nonhighly compensated participant means a participant who is not a highly compensated participant.

(7) Officer. The term officer means any individual or participant who for the preceding plan year (or the current plan year in the case of the first year of employment) was an officer. Whether an individual is an officer is determined based on all the facts and circumstances, including the source of the individual's authority, the term for which he or she is elected or appointed, and the nature and extent of his or her duties. Generally, the term officer means an administrative executive who is in regular and continued service. The term officer implies continuity of service and excludes individuals performing services in connection with a special and single transaction. An individual who merely has the title of an officer but not the authority of an officer, is not an officer. Similarly, an individual without the title of an officer but who has the authority of an officer is an officer. Sole proprietorships, partnerships, associations, trusts and labor organizations also may have officers. See §§ 301.7701-1 through -3

(8) Five percent shareholder. A five percent shareholder is an individual who in either the preceding plan year or current plan year owns more than five percent of the voting power or value of all classes of stock of the employer, determined without attribution.

(9) Highly compensated. The term highly compensated means any individual or participant who for the preceding plan year (or the current plan year in the case of the first year of employment) had compensation from the employer in excess of the compensation amount specified in section 414(q)(1)(B), and, if elected by the employer, was also in the top-paid group of employees (determined by reference to section 414(q)(3)) for such preceding plan year (or for the current plan year in the case of the first year of employment).

(10) Key employee. A key employee is a participant who is a key employee within the meaning of section 416(i)(1) at any time during the preceding plan year. A key employee covered by a collective bargaining agreement is a key employee.

(11) Collectively bargained plan. A collectively bargained plan is a plan or the portion of a plan maintained under an agreement which is a collective bargaining agreement between employee representatives and one or more employers, if there is evidence that cafeteria plan benefits were the subject of good faith bargaining between such employee representatives and such employer or employers.

(12) Year of employment. For purposes of section 125(g)(3)(B)(i), a year of employment is determined by reference to the elapsed time method of crediting service. See § 1.410(a)-7.

(13) Premium-only-plan. A premium-only-plan is described in paragraph (a)(5) in § 1.125-1.

(14) Statutory nontaxable benefits. Statutory nontaxable benefits are qualified benefits that are excluded from gross income (for example, an employer-provided accident and health plan excludible under section 106 or a dependent care assistance program excludible under section 129). Statutory nontaxable benefits also include group-term life insurance on the life of an employee includible in the employee's gross income solely because the coverage exceeds the limit in section 79(a).

(15) Total benefits. Total benefits are qualified benefits and permitted taxable benefits.

(b) Nondiscrimination as to eligibility. *(1) In general.* A cafeteria plan must not discriminate in favor of highly compensated individuals as to eligibility to participate for that plan year. A cafeteria plan does not discriminate in favor of highly compensated individuals if the plan benefits a group of employees who qualify under a reasonable classification established by the employer, as defined in § 1.410(b)-4(b), and the group of employees included in the classification satisfies the safe harbor percentage test or the unsafe harbor percentage component of the facts and circumstances test in § 1.410(b)-4(c). (In applying the § 1.410(b)-4 test, substitute highly compensated individual for highly compensated employee and substitute nonhighly compensated individual for nonhighly compensated employee).

(2) Deadline for participation in cafeteria plan. Any employee who has completed three years of employment (and who satisfies any conditions for participation in the cafeteria plan that are not related to completion of a requisite length of employment) must be permitted to elect to participate in the cafeteria plan no later than the first day of the first plan year beginning after the date the employee completed three years of employment (unless the employee separates from service before the first day of that plan year).

(3) The safe harbor percentage test. (i) In general. For purposes of the safe harbor percentage test and the unsafe harbor percentage component of the facts and circumstances test, if the cafeteria plan provides that only employees who have completed three years of employment are permitted to participate in the plan, employees who have not completed three years of employment may be excluded from consideration. However, if the cafeteria plan provides that employees are allowed to participate before completing three years of employment, all employees with less than three years of employment must be included in applying the safe harbor per-

centage test and the unsafe harbor percentage component of the facts and circumstances test. See paragraph (g) of this section for a permissive disaggregation rule.

(ii) Employees excluded from consideration. In addition, for purposes of the safe harbor percentage test and the unsafe harbor percentage component of the facts and circumstances test, the following employees are excluded from consideration—

(A) Employees (except key employees) covered by a collectively bargained plan as defined in paragraph (a)(11) of this section;

(B) Employees who are nonresident aliens and receive no earned income (within the meaning of section 911(d)(2)) from the employer which constitutes income from sources within the United States (within the meaning of section 861(a)(3)); and

(C) Employees participating in the cafeteria plan under a COBRA continuation provision.

(iv [sic iii]) Examples. The following examples illustrate the rules in paragraph (b) of this section:

Example (1). Same qualified benefit for same salary reduction amount. Employer A has one employer-provided accident and health insurance plan. The cost to participants electing the accident and health plan is $10,000 per year for single coverage. All employees have the same opportunity to salary reduce $10,000 for accident and health plan. The cafeteria plan satisfies the eligibility test.

Example (2). Same qualified benefit for unequal salary reduction amounts. Same facts as Example 1 except the cafeteria plan offers nonhighly compensated employees the election to salary reduce $10,000 to pay premiums for single coverage. The cafeteria plan provides an $8,000 employer flex-credit to highly compensated employees to pay a portion of the premium, and provides an election to them to salary reduce $2,000 to pay the balance of the premium. The cafeteria plan fails the eligibility test.

Example (3). Accident and health plans of unequal value. Employer B's cafeteria plan offers two employer-provided accident and health insurance plans: Plan X, available only to highly compensated participants, is a low-deductible plan. Plan Y, available only to nonhighly compensated participants, is a high deductible plan (as defined in section 223(c)(2)). The annual premium for single coverage under Plan X is $15,000 per year, and $8,000 per year for Plan Y. Employer B's cafeteria plan provides that highly compensated participants may elect salary reduction of $15,000 for coverage under Plan X, and that nonhighly compensated participants may elect salary reduction of $8,000 for coverage under Plan Y. The cafeteria plan fails the eligibility test.

Example (4). Accident and health plans of unequal value for unequal salary reduction amounts. Same facts as Example 3, except that the amount of salary reduction for highly compensated participants to elect Plan X is $8,000. The cafeteria plan fails the eligibility test.

(c) Nondiscrimination as to contributions and benefits. *(1) In general.* A cafeteria plan must not discriminate in favor of highly compensated participants as to contributions and benefits for a plan year.

(2) Benefit availability and benefit election. A cafeteria plan does not discriminate with respect to contributions and benefits if either qualified benefits and total benefits, or employer contributions allocable to statutory nontaxable benefits and employer contributions allocable to total benefits, do not discriminate in favor of highly compensated participants. A cafeteria plan must satisfy this paragraph (c) with respect to both benefit availability and benefit utilization. Thus, a plan must give each similarly situated participant a uniform opportunity to elect qualified benefits, and the actual election of qualified benefits through the plan must not be disproportionate by highly compensated participants (while other participants elect permitted taxable benefits). Qualified benefits are disproportionately elected by highly compensated participants if the aggregate qualified benefits elected by highly compensated participants, measured as a percentage of the aggregate compensation of highly compensated participants, exceed the aggregate qualified benefits elected by nonhighly compensated participants measured as a percentage of the aggregate compensation of nonhighly compensated participants. A plan must also give each similarly situated participant a uniform election with respect to employer contributions, and the actual election with respect to employer contributions for qualified benefits through the plan must not be disproportionate by highly compensated participants (while other participants elect to receive employer contributions as permitted taxable benefits). Employer contributions are disproportionately utilized by highly compensated participants if the aggregate contributions utilized by highly compensated participants, measured as a percentage of the aggregate compensation of highly compensated participants, exceed the aggregate contributions utilized by nonhighly compensated participants measured as a percentage of the aggregate compensation of nonhighly compensated participants.

(3) Example. The following example illustrates the rules in paragraph (c) of this section:

Example. Contributions and benefits test. Employer C's cafeteria plan satisfies the eligibility test in paragraph (b) of this section. Highly compensated participants in the cafeteria plan elect aggregate qualified benefits equaling 5 percent of aggregate compensation; nonhighly compensated participants elect aggregate qualified benefits equaling 10 percent of aggregate compensation. Employer C's cafeteria plan passes the contribution and benefits test.

(d) Key employees. *(1) In general.* If for any plan year, the statutory nontaxable benefits provided to key employees exceed 25 percent of the aggregate of statutory nontaxable benefits provided for all employees through the cafeteria plan, each key employee includes in gross income an amount equaling the maximum taxable benefits that he or she could have elected for the plan year. However, see safe harbor for premium-only-plans in paragraph (f) of this section.

(2) Example. The following example illustrates the rules in paragraph (d) of this section:

Example. (i) Key employee concentration test. Employer D's cafeteria plan offers all employees an election between taxable benefits and qualified benefits. The cafeteria plan satisfies the eligibility test in paragraph (b) of this section. Employer D has two key employees and four nonhighly compensated employees. The key employees each elect $2,000 of qualified benefits. Each nonhighly compensated employee also elects $2,000 of qualified benefits. The qualified benefits are statutory nontaxable benefits.

(ii) Key employees receive $4,000 of statutory nontaxable benefits and nonhighly compensated employees receive $8,000 of statutory nontaxable benefits, for a total of $12,000. Key employees receive 33 percent of statutory nontaxable benefits (4,000/12,000). Because the cafeteria plan provides more than 25 percent of the aggregate of statutory nontaxable benefits to key employees, the plan fails the key employee concentration test.

(e) Safe harbor for cafeteria plans providing health benefits. *(1) In general.* A cafeteria plan that provides health benefits is not treated as discriminatory as to benefits and contributions if:

(i) Contributions under the plan on behalf of each participant include an amount which equals 100 percent of the cost of the health benefit coverage under the plan of the majority of the highly compensated participants similarly situated, or equals or exceeds 75 percent of the cost of the health benefit coverage of the participant (similarly situated) having the highest cost health benefit coverage under the plan, and

(ii) Contributions or benefits under the plan in excess of those described in paragraph (e)(1)(i) of this section bear a uniform relationship to compensation.

(2) Similarly situated. In determining which participants are similarly situated, reasonable differences in plan benefits may be taken into account (for example, variations in plan benefits offered to employees working in different geographical locations or to employees with family coverage versus employee-only coverage).

(3) Health benefits. Health benefits for purposes of this rule are limited to major medical coverage and exclude dental coverage and health FSAs.

(4) Example. The following example illustrates the rules in paragraph (e) of this section:

Example. (i) All 10 of Employer E's employees are eligible to elect between permitted taxable benefits and salary reduction of $8,000 per plan year for self-only coverage in the major medical health plan provided by Employer E. All 10 employees elect $8,000 salary reduction for the major medical plan.

(ii) The cafeteria plan satisfies the section 125(g)(2) safe harbor for cafeteria plans providing health benefits.

(f) Safe harbor test for premium-only-plans. *(1) In general.* A premium-only-plan (as defined in paragraph (a)(13) of this section) is deemed to satisfy the nondiscrimination rules in section 125(c) and this section for a plan year if, for that plan year, the plan satisfies the safe harbor percentage test for eligibility in paragraph (b)(3) of this section.

(2) Example. The following example illustrates the rules in paragraph (f) of this section:

Example. Premium-only-plan. (i) Employer F's cafeteria plan is a premium-only-plan (as defined in paragraph (a)(13) of this section). The written cafeteria plan offers one employer-provided accident and health plan and offers all employees the election to salary reduce same amount or same percentage of the premium for self-only or family coverage. All key employees and all highly compensated employees elect salary reduction for the accident and health plan, but only 20 percent of nonhighly compensated employees elect the accident and health plan.

(ii) The premium-only-plan satisfies the nondiscrimination rules in section 125(b) and (c) and this section.

(g) Permissive disaggregation for nondiscrimination testing. *(1) General rule.* If a cafeteria plan benefits employees who have not completed three years of employment, the cafeteria plan is permitted to test for nondiscrimination under this section as if the plan were two separate plans—

(i) One plan benefiting the employees who completed one day of employment but less than three years of employment; and

(ii) Another plan benefiting the employees who have completed three years of employment.

(2) Disaggregated plans tested separately for eligibility test and contributions and benefits test. If a cafeteria plan is disaggregated into two separate plans for purposes of nondiscrimination testing, the two separate plans must be tested separately for both the nondiscrimination as to eligibility test in paragraph (b) of this section and the nondiscrimination as to contributions and benefits test in paragraph (c) of this section.

(h) Optional aggregation of plans for nondiscrimination testing. An employer who sponsors more than one cafeteria plan is permitted to aggregate two or more of the cafeteria plans for purposes of nondiscrimination testing. If two or more cafeteria plans are aggregated into a combined plan for this purpose, the combined plan must satisfy the nondiscrimination as to eligibility test in paragraph (b) of this section and the nondiscrimination as to contributions and benefits test in paragraph (c) of this section, as though the combined plan were a single plan. Thus, for example, in order to satisfy the benefit availability and benefit election requirements in paragraph (c)(2) of this section, the combined plan must give each similarly situated participant a uniform opportunity to elect qualified benefits and the actual election of qualified benefits by highly compensated participants must not be disproportionate. However, if a principal purpose of the aggregation is to manipulate the nondiscrimination testing requirements or to otherwise discriminate in favor of highly compensated individuals or participants, the plans will not be permitted to be aggregated for nondiscrimination testing.

(i) Employees of certain controlled groups. All employees who are treated as employed by a single employer under section 414(b), (c), (m), or (o) are treated as employed by a single employer for purposes of section 125. Section 125(g)(4); section 414(t).

(j) Time to perform nondiscrimination testing. *(1) In general.* Nondiscrimination testing must be performed as of the last day of the plan year, taking into account all non-excludable employees (or former employees) who were employees on any day during the plan year.

(2) The following example illustrates the rules in paragraph (j) of this section:

Example. When to perform discrimination testing. (i) Employer H employs three employees and maintains a calendar year cafeteria plan. During the 2009 plan year, Employee J was an employee the entire calendar year, Employee K was an employee from May 1, through August 31, 2009, and Employee L worked from January 1, 2009 to April 15, 2009, when he retired.

(ii) Nondiscrimination testing for the 2009 plan year must be performed on December 31, 2009, taking into account employees J, K, and L's compensation in the preceding year.

(k) Discrimination in actual operation prohibited. In addition to not discriminating as to either benefit availability or benefit utilization, a cafeteria plan must not discriminate in favor of highly compensated participants in actual operation. For example, a plan may be discriminatory in actual operation if the duration of the plan (or of a particular nontaxable benefit offered through the plan) is for a period during which only highly compensated participants utilize the plan (or the benefit). See also the key employee concentration test in section 125(b)(2).

(l) Anti-abuse rule. *(1) Interpretation.* The provisions of this section must be interpreted in a reasonable manner consistent with the purpose of preventing discrimination in favor of highly compensated individuals, highly compensated participants and key employees.

(2) Change in plan testing procedures. A plan will not be treated as satisfying the requirements of this section if there are repeated changes to plan testing procedures or plan provisions that have the effect of manipulating the nondiscrimination testing requirements of this section, if a principal purpose of the changes was to achieve this result.

(m) Tax treatment of benefits in a cafeteria plan. *(1) Nondiscriminatory cafeteria plan.* A participant in a nondiscriminatory cafeteria plan (including a highly compensated participant or key employee) who elects qualified benefits is not treated as having received taxable benefits offered through the plan, and thus the qualified benefits elected by the employee are not includible in the employee's gross income merely because of the availability of taxable benefits. But see paragraph (j) in § 1.125-1 on nondiscrimination rules for sections 79(d), 105(h), 129(d), and 137(c)(2), and limitations on exclusion.

(2) Discriminatory cafeteria plan. A highly compensated participant or key employee participating in a discriminatory cafeteria plan must include in gross income (in the participant's taxable year within which ends the plan year with respect to which an election was or could have been made) the value of the taxable benefit with the greatest value that the employee could have elected to receive, even if the employee elects to receive only the nontaxable benefits offered.

(n) Employer contributions to employees' Health Savings Accounts. If an employer contributes to employees' Health Savings Accounts (HSAs) through a cafeteria plan (as defined in § 54.4980G-5 of this chapter) those contributions are subject to the nondiscrimination rules in section 125 and this section and are not subject to the comparability rules in section 4980G. See §§ 54.4980G-0 through 54.4980G-5 of this chapter.

(o) Effective/applicability date. It is proposed that these regulations apply on and after plan years beginning on or after January 1, 2009.

§ 16A.126-0 Effective dates.

These temporary regulations shall apply to any payments received under a contract signed by the taxpayer and the appropriate agency after September 30, 1979.

T.D. 7778, 5/18/81.

§ 16A.126-1 Certain cost sharing payments—in general.

(a) Introduction. In general, section 126 provides that recipients of payments made after September 30, 1979 under certain conservation, reclamation and restoration programs may exclude all or a portion of those payments from income if the payments do not substantially increase the annual income derived by the taxpayer from the affected property. For purposes of this section, the term "payment" as used in section 126 means payment of the economic benefit, if any, conferred upon the taxpayer upon receipt of the improvement. An increase in annual income is substantial if it exceeds the greater of 10 percent of the average annual income derived from the affected property prior to receipt of the improvement or an amount equal to $2.50 times the number of affected acres. The amount of gross income which a taxpayer realizes upon the receipt of a section 126 payment is the value of the section 126 improvement, reduced by the sum of the excludable portion and the taxpayer's share of the cost of the improvement (if any).

(b) Definitions. For purposes of this section, the term:

(1) "Cost of the improvement" means the sum of amounts paid by a government and the taxpayer, whether or not with borrowed funds, for the improvement.

(2) "Section 126 cost" means the cost of the improvement less the sum of

(i) Any government payments under a program which is not listed in section 126(a).

(ii) Any portion of a government payment under a program which is listed in section 126(a) which the Secretary of Agriculture has not certified is primarily for purposes of conservation,

(iii) Any government payment to the taxpayer which is in the nature of rent or compensation for services.

(3) "Value of the section 126 improvement" means the fair market value of the improvement multiplied by a fraction, the numerator of which is the section 126 cost and the denominator of which is the cost of the improvement.

(4) "Affected acreage" means the acres affected by the improvement.

(5) "Excludable portion" means the present fair market value of the right to receive annual income from the affected acreage of the greater of 10 percent of the prior average annual income from the affected acreage or $2.50 times the number of affected acres.

(6) "Prior average annual income" means the average of the gross receipts from the affected acreage for the last three taxable years preceding the taxable year in which installation of the improvement is commenced.

(7) "Section 126 improvement" means the portion of the improvement equal to the percentage which government payments made to the taxpayer, which the Secretary of Agriculture has certified were made primarily for the purpose of conservation, bear to the cost of the improvement.

(c) Income realized upon receipt of a section 126 improvement. *(1) Section 126 exclusion applied.* Unless a taxpayer elects not to have section 126 apply, the amount of gross income realized on receipt of the section 126 improvement is the value of the section 126 improvement less the sum of the taxpayer's share of the cost of the improvement and the excludable portion.

(2) Section 126 exclusion not applied. If a taxpayer elects under section 126(c) not to have section 126 apply in whole or in part, the amount realized on the receipt of the section 126 improvement is the value of the section 126 improvement less the sum of the taxpayer's share of the cost of the improvement and the excludable portion that applies, if any.

(d) Payments under watershed programs. *(1) Programs within section 126(a)(9).* Section 126(a)(9) covers certain programs affecting small watersheds.

These programs must be administered by the Secretary of Agriculture and be determined by the Commissioner to be substantially similar to the type of program described in section 126(a)(1) through (8). The Commissioner has determined that section 126 improvements made in connection with small watersheds are within the scope of section 126(a)(9) if they are made under one of the following programs:

(A) The Watershed Protection and Flood Prevention Act, Pub. L. 566, 68 Stat. 666, as amended (16 U.S.C. 1001, *et seq.*), as funded by the Act of November 9, 1979, Pub. L. 96-108, 93 Stat. 834.

(B) Flood Prevention Projects, Pub. L. 86-468, sec. 1, 74 Stat. 131, as amended (16 U.S.C. 1006a); Pub. L. 78-534, sec. 2, 58 Stat. 889 (33 U.S.C. 701a-1); Pub. L. 78-534, sec. 13, 58 Stat. 905;

(C) Emergency Watershed Protection, Pub. L. 81-516, sec. 216, 64 Stat. 184 (33 U.S.C. 701b-1), and

(D) Colorado River Basin Salinity Control Act, Pub. L. 93-320, 88 Stat. 266:

(1) Title 1. —Programs downstream from Imperial Dam, and

(2) Title 2. —Measures upstream from Imperial Dam.

(2) Other programs. The Commissioner may announce further determinations under section 126(a)(9) from time to time in the Internal Revenue Bulletin.

(3) Small watershed defined. A watershed is a "small watershed" under this paragraph and section 126(a)(9) if the watershed or subwatershed does not exceed 250,000 acres and does not include any single structure providing more than 12,500 acre-feet of floodwater detention capacity, nor more than 25,000 acre-feet of total capacity.

(e) Basis of property not increased by reason of excludable amounts. Notwithstanding any provision of section 1016 (relating to adjustments to basis) to the contrary, basis of any property does not include any amount which is excludable from gross income under section 126.

(f) Cross reference. For rules relating to the recapture as ordinary income of the gain from the disposition (within 20 years of the date of receipt) of property for which an exclusion is claimed for a section 126 improvement, see section 1255 and the regulations thereunder.

(g) Examples. The provisions of this section are illustrated by the following examples:

Example (1). In 1981, 100 acres of the taxpayer's land is reclaimed under a Rural Abandoned Mine Program contract with the Soil Conservation Service of the U.S. Department of Agriculture. The total cost of the improvement is $700,000. USDA pays $690,000, the taxpayer $10,000. The Secretary of Agriculture certifies that 95% of the $690,000 USDA payment was primarily for the purpose of conservation. Therefore, $34,500 ($690,000 × .05) is a nonsection 126 payment. $150,000 of USDA's payment is compensation for the taxpayer's service in the reclamation project and is includable in gross income as compensation for services. The taxpayer has $20,000 of allowable deductions in 1981, $15,500 of which are properly attributable to the USDA payment. Based on all the facts and circumstances, the value of the improvement is $21,000. The taxpayer elects not to have section 126 apply. The taxpayer computes the amount which is included in gross income as a result of receipt of the improvement as follows:

(1)

Cost of improvement	$ 700,000
Nonsection 126 payment	(34,500)
Compensation for services	(150,000)
Current deductions	(15,500)
Section 126 cost	500,000

(2)

Value of improvement	21,000
Multiplied by section 126 cost	× 500,000
Cost of improvement	700,000
Value of section 126 improvement	15,000

(3)

Value of 126 improvement	15,000
(Taxpayer's contribution)	10,000
Amount included in gross income	5,000

Example (2). The facts are the same as example (1) except that section 126 applies. Based on all the facts and circumstances, the present fair market value of the right to receive annual income from the property of 10 percent of the prior average annual income of the affected acreage prior to the receipt of the improvement is $1,380 and the present fair market value of the right to receive $250 ($2.50 × 100 acres) is $1,550. The excludable portion is, therefore, $1,550. The taxpayer computes the amount included in gross income as follows:

Value of section 126 improvement	$15,000
(Taxpayer's contribution)	(10,000)
(Excludable portion)	(1,550)
Amount included in income	3,450

Example (3). The facts are the same as example (2) except that the present value of 10 percent of the prior average annual income is $5,600. The taxpayer realizes no income as a result of receipt of the section 126 project.

(1)

(1)

Value of section 126 improvement	$15,000
(Taxpayer's contribution)	(10,000)
(Excludable portion)	(5,600)
Amount included in income	0

Example (4). In 1983, the taxpayer signs a contract under the water bank program under which he will maintain 20 acres of undisturbed wetlands as a wildfowl preserve. In return he will receive $90 an acre as rent from the government. Although the payment is made under a program listed in section 126(a) and the Secretary of Agriculture has certified that the entire amount of payment was made primarily for the purpose of conservation, there is no income eligible for section 126 exclusion because the full payment is rent. The rent is included in full in gross income.

Example (5). In 1980, the taxpayer reforests 200 acres of nonindustrial private forest land by planting tree seedlings. The taxpayer pays the full cost of the reforestation, $15,000. Under the cost-sharing provisions of the forestry incentives program, the taxpayer receives a reimbursement from USDA of $12,000. The Secretary of Agriculture certifies that 100% of the USDA payment is primarily for the purpose of conservation. Assume that the excludable portion is $3,500 and that based on all the facts and circumstances, the value of the improvement is $15,000. The amount which is includable in income is the value of the section 126 improvement, reduced by the excludable portion and the taxpayer's share of the cost of the improvement. Therefore the taxpayer includes $8,500 in gross income as a result of the USDA payment, computed as follows:

Value of the section 126 improvement	$15,000
(Excludable portion)	(3,500)
(Taxpayer's contribution)	(3,000)
Amount included in gross income	8,500

T.D. 7778, 5/18/81.

§ 16A.126-2 Section 126 elections.

(a) Election for section 126 not to apply in whole or in part. A taxpayer may elect under section 126(c) not to have section 126 apply to all or any part of an improvement described in section 126.

(b) Application of the section 126 exclusion. To the extent the section 126 exclusion applies, the taxpayer should so indicate on an attachment to the tax return (or amended return) for the taxable year in which the taxpayer received the last payment made by a government for the improvement. The attachment should state the dollar amount of the section 126 cost funded by a government payment, the value of the section 126 improvement, and the amount that the taxpayer is excluding under section 126.

T.D. 7778, 5/18/81.

§ 1.127-1 Amounts received under a qualified educational assistance program.

Caution: The Treasury has not yet amended Reg § 1.127-1 to reflect changes made by P.L. 107-16, P.L. 106-170, P.L. 104-188, P.L. 103-66, P.L. 101-508, P.L. 98-611.

(a) Exclusion from gross income. The gross income of an employee does not include—

(1) Amounts paid to, or on behalf of the employee under a qualified educational assistance program described in § 1.127-2, or

(2) The value of education provided to the employee under such a program.

(b) Disallowance of excluded amounts as credit or deduction. Any amount excluded from the gross income of an employee under paragraph (a) of this section shall not be allowed as a credit or deduction to such employee under any other provision of this part.

(c) Amounts received under a nonqualified program. Any amount received under an educational assistance program that is not a "qualified program" described in § 1.127-2 will not be excluded from gross income under paragraph (a) of this section. All or part of the amounts received under such a nonqualified program may, however, be excluded under section 117 or deducted under section 162 or section 212 (as the case may be), if the requirements of such section are satisfied.

(d) Definitions. For rules relating to the meaning of the terms "employee" and "employer", see paragraph (h) of § 1.127-2.

(e) Effective date. This section is effective for taxable years of the employee beginning after December 31, 1978, and before January 1, 1984.

T.D. 7898, 7/5/83.

§ 1.127-2 Qualified educational assistance program.

Caution: The Treasury has not yet amended Reg § 1.127-2 to reflect changes made by P.L. 104-188.

(a) In general. A qualified educational assistance program is a plan established and maintained by an employer under which the employer provides educational assistance to employees. To be a qualified program, the requirements described in paragraphs (b) through (g) of this section must be satisfied. It is not required that a program be funded or that the employer apply to the Internal Revenue Service for a determination that the plan is a qualified program. However, under § 601.201 (relating to rulings and determination letters), an employer may request that the Service determine whether a plan is a qualified program.

(b) Separate written plan. The program must be a separate written plan of the employer. This requirement means that the terms of the program must be set forth in a separate document or documents providing only educational assistance within the meaning of paragraph (c) of this section. The requirement for a separate plan does not, however, preclude an educational assistance program from being part of a more comprehensive employer plan that provides a choice of nontaxable benefits to employees.

(c) Educational assistance. *(1) In general.* The benefits provided under the program must consist solely of educational assistance. The term "educational assistance" means—

(i) The employer's payment of expenses incurred by or on behalf of an employee for education, or

(ii) The employer's provision of education to an employee.

(2) Alternative benefits. Benefits will not be considered to consist solely of educational assistance if the program, in form or in actual operation, provides employees with a choice between educational assistance and other remuneration includible in the employee's gross income.

(3) Certain benefits not considered educational assistance. The term "educational assistance" does not include the employer's payment for, or provision of—

(i) Tools or supplies (other than textbooks) that the employee may retain after completing a course of instruction,

(ii) Meals, lodging, or transportation, or

(iii) Education involving sports, games, or hobbies, unless such education involves the business of the employer or is required as part of a degree program. The phrase "sports, games, or hobbies" does not include education that instructs employees how to maintain and improve health so long as such education does not involve the use of athletic facilities or equipment and is not recreational in nature.

(4) Education defined. As used in section 127, § 1.127-1, and this section, the term "education" includes any form of instruction or training that improves or develops the capabilities of an individual. Education paid for or provided under a qualified program may be furnished directly by the employer, either alone or in conjunction with other employers, or through a third party such as an educational institution. Education is not limited to courses that are job related or part of a degree program.

(d) Exclusive benefit. The program may benefit only the employees of the employer, including, at the employer's option, individuals who are employees within the meaning of paragraph (h)(1) of this section. A program that provides benefits to spouses or dependents of employees is not a qualified program within the meaning of this section.

(e) Prohibited discrimination. *(1) Eligibility for benefits.* The program must benefit the employer's employees generally. Among those benefited may be employees who are officers, shareholders, self-employed or highly compensated. A program is not for the benefit of employees generally, however, if the program discriminates in favor of employees described in the preceding sentence (or in favor of their spouses and dependents who are themselves employees) in requirements relating to eligibility for benefits. Thus, although a program need not provide benefits for all employees, it must benefit those employees who qualify under a classification of employees that does not discriminate in favor of the employees with respect to whom discrimination is prohibited. The classification of employees to be considered benefited will consist of that group of employees who are actually eligible for educational assistance under the program, taking into account the eligibility requirements set forth in the written plan, the eligibility requirements reflected in the types of educational assistance available under the program, and any other conditions that may affect the availability of benefits under the program. Thus, for example, if an employer's plan provides that all employees are eligible for educational assistance, yet limits that assistance to courses of study leading to postgraduate degrees in fields relating to the employer's business, then only those employees able to pursue such a course of study are considered actually eligible for educational assistance under the program. Whether any classification of employees discriminates in favor of employees with respect to whom discrimination is prohibited will generally be determined by applying the same standards as are applied under section 410(b)(1)(B) (relating to qualified pension, profit-sharing and stock bonus plans), without regard to section 401(a)(5). For purposes of making this determination, there shall be excluded from consideration employees not covered by the program who are included in a unit of employees covered by an agreement which the Secretary of Labor finds to be a collective bargaining agreement between employee representatives and one or more employers, if the Internal Revenue Service finds that educational assistance benefits were the subject of good faith bargaining between the employee representatives and the employer or employers. For purposes of determining whether such bargaining occurred, it is not material that the employees are not covered by another educational assistance program or that the employer's present program was not considered in the bargaining.

(2) Factors not considered in determining the existence of prohibited discrimination. A program shall not be considered discriminatory under this paragraph (e) merely because—

(i) Different types of educational assistance available under the program are utilized to a greater degree by employees with respect to whom discrimination is prohibited than by other employees, or

(ii) With respect to a course of study for which benefits are otherwise available, successful completion of the course, attaining a particular course grade, or satisfying a reasonable condition subsequent (such as remaining employed for one year after completing the course) are required or considered in determining the availability of benefits.

(f) Benefit limitation. *(1) In general.* Under section 127(b)(3), a program is a qualified program for a program year only if no more than 5% of the amounts paid or incurred by the employer for educational assistance benefits during the year are provided to the limitation class described in subparagraph (2). For purposes of this paragraph (f), the program year must be specified in the written plan as either the calendar year or the taxable year of the employer.

(2) Limitation class. The limitation class consists of—

(i) Shareholders. Individuals who, on any day of the program year, own more than 5% of the total number of shares of outstanding stock of the employer, or

(ii) Owners. In the case of an employer's trade or business which is not incorporated, individuals who, on any day of the program year, own more than 5% of the capital or profits interest in the employer, and

(iii) Spouses or dependents. Individuals who are spouses or dependents of shareholders or owners described in subdivision (i) or (ii). For purposes of determining stock ownership, the attribution rules described in paragraph (h)(4) of this section apply. The regulations prescribed under section 414(c) are applicable in determining an individual's interest in the capital or profits of an unincorporated trade or business.

(g) Notification of employees. A program is not a qualified program unless employees eligible to participate in the program are given reasonable notice of the terms and availability of the program.

(h) Definitions. For purposes of this section and § 1.127-1—

(1) Employee. The term "employee" includes—

(i) A retired disabled or laid-off employee,

(ii) A present employee who is on leave, as for example, in the Armed Forces of the United States, or

(iii) An individual who is self-employed within the meaning of section 401(c)(1).

(2) Employer. An individual who owns the entire interest in an unincorporated trade or business shall be treated as his or her own employer. A partnership is treated as the employer of each partner who is an employee within the meaning of section 401(c)(1).

(3) Officer. An officer is an individual who is an officer within the meaning of regulations prescribed under section 414(c).

(4) Shareholder. The term "shareholder" includes an individual who is a shareholder as determined by the attribution rules under section 1563(d) and (e), without regard to section 1563(e)(3)(C).

(5) Highly compensated. The term "highly compensated" has the same meaning as it does for purposes of section 410(b)(1)(B).

(i) Substantiation. An employee receiving payments under a qualified educational assistance program must be prepared to provide substantiation to the employer such that it is reasonable to believe that payments or reimbursements made under the program constitute educational assistance within the meaning of paragraph (c) of this section.

T.D. 7898, 7/5/83.

§ 1.132-0 Outline of regulations under section 132.

The following is an outline of regulations in this section relating to exclusions from gross income for certain fringe benefits:

§ 1.132-0 Outline of regulations under section 132.

§ 1.132-1 Exclusion from gross income for certain fringe benefits.

(a) In general.

(b) Definition of employee.

(1) No-additional-cost services and qualified employee discounts.

(2) Working condition fringes.

(3) On-premises athletic facilities.

(4) De minimis fringes.

(5) Dependent child.

(c) Special rules for employers— effect of section 414.

(d) Customers not to include employees.

(e) Treatment of on-premises athletic facilities.

(1) In general.

(2) Premises of the employer.

(3) Application of rules to membership in an athletic facility.

(4) Operation by the employer.

(5) Nonapplicability of nondiscrimination rules.

(f) Nonapplicability of section 132 in certain cases.

(1) Tax treatment provided for in another section.

(2) Limited statutory exclusions.

(g) Effective date.

§ 1.132-2 No-additional-cost services.

(a) In general.

(1) Definition.

(2) Excess capacity services.

(3) Cash rebates.

(4) Applicability of nondiscrimination rules.

(5) No substantial additional cost.

(6) Payments for telephone service.

(b) Reciprocal agreements.

(c) Example.

§ 1.132-3 Qualified employee discounts.

(a) In general.

(1) Definition.

(2) Qualified property or services.

(3) No reciprocal agreement exception.

(4) Property of services provided without charge, at a reduced price, or by rebates.

(5) Property or services provided directly by the employer or indirectly through a third party.

(6) Applicability of nondiscrimination rules.

(b) Employee discount.

(1) Definition.

(2) Price to customers.

(3) Damaged, distressed, or returned goods.

(c) Gross profit percentage.

(1) In general.

(2) Line of business.

(3) Generally accepted accounting principles

(d) Treatment of leased sections of department stores.

(1) In general.

(2) Employees of the leased section.

(e) Excess discounts.

§ 1.132-4 Line of business limitation.

(a) In general.

(1) Applicability.

(2) Definition.

(3) Aggregation of two-digit classifications.

(b) Grandfather rule for certain retail stores.

(1) In general.

(2) Taxable year of affiliated group.

(3) Definition of "sales" .

(4) Retired and disabled employees.

(5) Increase of employee discount.

(c) Grandfather rule for telephone service provided to predivestiture retirees.

(d) Special rule for certain affiliates of commercial airlines.

(1) General rule.

(2) "Airline affiliated group" defined.

(3) "Qualified affiliate" defined.

(e) Grandfather rule for affiliated groups operating airlines.

(f) Special rule for qualified air transportation organizations.

(g) Relaxation of line of business requirement.

(h) Line of business requirement does not expand benefits eligible for exclusion.

§ 1.132-5 Working condition fringes.

(a) In general.

(1) Definition.

(2) Trade or business of the employee.

(b) Vehicle allocation rules.

(1) In general.

(2) Use of different employer-provided vehicles.

(3) Provision of a vehicle and chauffeur services.

(c) Applicability of substantiation requirements of sections 162 and 274(d).

(1) In general.

(2) Section 274(d) requirements.

(d) Safe harbor substantiation rules.

(1) In general.

(2) Period for use of safe harbor rules.

(e) Safe harbor substantiation rule for vehicles not used for personal purposes.

(f) Safe harbor substantiation rule for vehicles not available to employees for personal use other than commuting.

(g) Safe harbor substantiation rule for vehicles used in connection with the business of farming that are available to employees for personal use.

(1) In general.

(2) Vehicles available to more than one individual.

(3) Examples.

(h) Qualified nonpersonal use vehicles.

(1) In general.

(2) Shared usage of qualified nonpersonal use vehicles.

(i) [Reserved].

(j) Application of section 280F.

(k) Aircraft allocation rule.

(l) [Reserved].

(m) Employer-provided transportation for security concerns.

(1) In general.

(2) Demonstration of bona fide business-oriented security concerns.

(3) Application of security rules to spouses and dependents.

(4) Working condition safe harbor for travel on employer-provided aircraft.

(5) Bodyguard/chauffeur provided for a bona fide business-oriented security concern.

(6) Special valuation rule for government employees.
(7) Government employer and employee defined.
(8) Examples.
(n) Product testing.
(1) In general.
(2) Employer-imposed limits.
(3) Discriminating classifications.
(4) Factors that negate the existence of a product testing program.
(5) Failure to meet the requirements of this paragraph (n).
(6) Example.
(o) Qualified automobile demonstration use.
(1) In general.
(2) Full-time automobile salesman.
(3) Demonstration automobile.
(4) Substantial restrictions on personal use.
(5) Sales area.
(6) Applicability of substantiation requirements of sections 162 and 274(d).
(7) Special valuation rules.
(p) Parking.
(1) In general.
(2) Reimbursement of parking expenses.
(3) Parking on residential property
(4) Dates of applicability
(q) Nonapplicability of nondiscrimination rules.
(r) Volunteers.
(1) In general.
(2) Limit on application of this paragraph.
(3) Definitions.
(4) Example.
§ 1.132-6 De minimis fringes.
(a) In general.
(b) Frequency.
(1) Employee-measured frequency.
(2) Employer-measured frequency.
(c) Administrability.
(d) Special rules.
(1) Transit passes.
(2) Occasional meal money or local transportation fare.
(3) Use of special rules or examples to establish a general rule.
(4) Benefits exceeding value and frequency limits.
(e) Examples
(1) Benefits excludable from income.
(2) Benefits not excludable as de minimis fringes.
(f) Nonapplicability of nondiscrimination rules.
§ 1.132-7 Employer-operated eating facilities.
(a) In general.
(1) Conditions for exclusion.
(2) Employer-operated eating facility for employees.
(3) Operation by the employer.
(4) Example.
(b) Direct operating costs.
(1) In general.
(2) Multiple dining rooms or cafeterias.
(3) Payment to operator of facility.
(c) Valuation of non-excluded meals provided at an employer-operated eating facility for employees.
§ 1.132-8 Fringe benefit nondiscrimination rules.
(a) Application of nondiscrimination rules.
(1) General rule.
(2) Consequences of discrimination.
(3) Scope of the nondiscrimination rules provided in this section.
(b) Aggregation of employees.
(1) Section 132(a)(1) and (2).
(2) Section 132(e)(2).
(3) Classes of employees who may be excluded.
(c) Availability on substantially the same terms.
(1) General rule.
(2) Certain terms relating to priority.
(d) Testing for discrimination.
(1) Classification test.
(2) Classifications that are per se discriminatory
(3) Former employees.
(4) Restructuring of benefits.
(5) Employer-operated eating facilities for employees
(e) Cash bonuses or rebates.
(f) Highly compensated employee.
(1) Government and non-government employees.
(2) Former employees.
§ 1.132-9 Qualified transportation fringes.
(a) Table of contents.
(b) Questions and answers.

T.D. 8256, 7/6/89, amend T.D. 8457, 12/29/92, T.D. 8933, 1/10/2001.

---

§ 1.132-1 Exclusion from gross income for certain fringe benefits.

Caution: The Treasury has not yet amended Reg § 1.132-1 to reflect changes made by 103-66.

(a) In general. Gross income does not include any fringe benefit which qualifies as a—

(1) No-additional-cost service,

(2) Qualified employee discount,

(3) Working condition fringe, or

(4) De minimis fringe.

Special rules apply with respect to certain on-premises gyms and other athletic facilities (§ 1.132-1(e)), demonstration use of employer-provided automobiles by full-time automobile salesmen (§ 1.132-5(o)), parking provided to an employee on or near the business premises of the employer (§ 1.132-5(p)), and on-premises eating facilities (§ 1.132-7).

(b) Definition of employee. *(1) No-additional-cost services and qualified employee discounts.* For purposes of section 132(a)(1) (relating to no-additional-cost services) and section 132(a)(2) (relating to qualified employee discounts), the term "employee" (with respect to a line of business of an employer) means—

(i) Any individual who is currently employed by the employer in the line of business,

(ii) Any individual who was formerly employed by the employer in the line of business and who separated from service with the employer in the line of business by reason of retirement or disability, and

(iii) Any widow or widower of an individual who died while employed by the employer in the line of business or who separated from service with the employer in the line of business by reason of retirement or disability.

For purposes of this paragraph (b)(1), any partner who performs services for a partnership is considered employed by the partnership. In addition, any use by the spouse or dependent child (as defined in paragraph (b)(5) of this section) of the employee will be treated as use by the employee. For purposes of section 132(a)(1) (relating to no-additional-cost services), any use of air transportation by a parent of an employee (determined without regard to section 132(f)(1)(B) and paragraph (b)(1)(iii) of this section) will be treated as use by the employee.

(2) Working condition fringes. For purposes of section 132(a)(3) (relating to working condition fringes), the term "employee" means—

(i) Any individual who is currently employed by the employer,

(ii) Any partner who performs services for the partnership,

(iii) Any director of the employer, and

(iv) Any independent contractor who performs services for the employer.

Notwithstanding anything in this paragraph (b)(2) to the contrary, an independent contractor who performs services for the employer cannot exclude the value of parking or the use of consumer goods provided pursuant to a product testing program under § 1.132-5(n); in addition, any director of the employer cannot exclude the value of the use of consumer goods provided pursuant to a product testing program under § 1.132-5(n).

(3) On-premises athletic facilities. For purposes of section 132(h)(5) (relating to on-premises athletic facilities), the term "employee" means—

(i) Any individual who is currently employed by the employer,

(ii) Any individual who was formerly employed by the employer and who separated from service with the employer by reason of retirement or disability, and

(iii) Any widow or widower of an individual who died while employed by the employer or who separated from service with the employer by reason of retirement or disability.

For purposes of this paragraph (b)(3), any partner who performs services for a partnership is considered employed by the partnership. In addition, any use by the spouse or dependent child (as defined in paragraph (b)(5) of this section) of the employee will be treated as use by the employee.

(4) De minimis fringes. For purposes of section 132(a)(4) (relating to de minimis fringes), the term "employee" means any recipient of a fringe benefit.

(5) Dependent child. The term "dependent child" means any son, stepson, daughter, or stepdaughter of the employee who is a dependent of the employee, or both of whose parents are deceased and who has not attained age 25. Any child to whom section 152(e) applies will be treated as the dependent of both parents.

(c) Special rules for employers—Effect of section 414. All employees treated as employed by a single employer under section 414(b), (c), (m), or (o) will be treated as employed by a single employer for purposes of this section. Thus, employees of one corporation that is part of a controlled group of corporations may under certain circumstances be eligible to receive section 132 benefits from the other corporations that comprise the controlled group. However, the aggregation of employers described in this paragraph (c) does not change the other requirements for an exclusion, such as the line of business requirement. Thus, for example, if a controlled group of corporations consists of two corporations that operate in different lines of business, the corporations are not treated as operating in the same line of business even though the corporations are treated as one employer.

(d) Customers not to include employees. For purposes of section 132 and the regulations thereunder, the term "customer" means any customer who is not an employee. However, the preceding sentence does not apply to section 132(c)(2) (relating to the gross profit percentage for determining a qualified employee discount). Thus, an employer that provides employee discounts cannot exclude sales made to employees in determining the aggregate sales to customers.

(e) Treatment of on-premises athletic facilities. *(1) In general.* Gross income does not include the value of any on-premises athletic facility provided by an employer to its employees. For purposes of section 132(h)(5) and this paragraph (e), the term "on-premises athletic facility" means any gym or other athletic facility (such as a pool, tennis court, or golf course)—

(i) Which is located on the premises of the employer,

(ii) Which is operated by the employer, and

(iii) Substantially all of the use of which during the calendar year is by employees of the employer, their spouses, and their dependent children.

For purposes of paragraph (e)(1)(iii) of this section, the term "dependent children" has the same meaning as the plural of the term "dependent child" in paragraph (b)(5) of this section. The exclusion of this paragraph (e) does not apply to any athletic facility if access to the facility is made available to the general public through the sale of memberships, the rental of the facility, or a similar arrangement.

(2) Premises of the employer. The athletic facility need not be located on the employer's business premises. However, the athletic facility must be located on premises of the employer. The exclusion provided in this paragraph (e) applies whether the premises are owned or leased by the employer; in addition, the exclusion is available even if the employer is not a named lessee on the lease so long as the employer pays reasonable rent. The exclusion provided in this paragraph (e) does not apply to any athletic facility that is a facility for residential use. Thus, for example, a resort with accompanying athletic facilities (such as tennis courts, pool, and gym) would not qualify for the exclusion provided in this paragraph (e). An athletic facility is considered to be located on the employer's premises if the facility is located on the premises of a voluntary employees' beneficiary association funded by the employer.

(3) Application of rules to membership in an athletic facility. The exclusion provided in this paragraph (e) does not apply to any membership in an athletic facility (including health clubs or country clubs) unless the facility is owned (or leased) and operated by the employer and substantially all the use of the facility is by employees of the employer, their spouses, and their dependent children. Therefore, membership in a health club or country club not meeting the

rules provided in this paragraph (e) would not qualify for the exclusion.

(4) Operation by the employer. An employer is considered to operate the athletic facility if the employer operates the facility through its own employees, or if the employer contracts out to another to operate the athletic facility. For example, if an employer hires an independent contractor to operate the athletic facility for the employer's employees, the facility is considered to be operated by the employer. In addition, if an athletic facility is operated by more than one employer, it is considered to be operated by each employer. For purposes of paragraph (e)(1)(iii) of this section, substantially all of the use of a facility that is operated by more than one employer must be by employees of the various employers, their spouses, and their dependent children. Where the facility is operated by more than one employer, an employer that pays rent either directly to the owner of the premises or to a sublessor of the premises is eligible for the exclusion. If an athletic facility is operated by a voluntary employees' beneficiary association funded by an employer, the employer is considered to operate the facility.

(5) Nonapplicability of nondiscrimination rules. The nondiscrimination rules of section 132 and section 1.132-8 do not apply to on-premises athletic facilities.

(f) Nonapplicability of section 132 in certain cases. *(1) Tax treatment provided for in another section.* If the tax treatment of a particular fringe benefit is expressly provided for in another section of Chapter 1 of the Internal Revenue Code of 1986, section 132 and the applicable regulations (except for section 132(e) and the regulations thereunder) do not apply to such fringe benefit. For example, because section 129 provides an exclusion from gross income for amounts paid or incurred by an employer for dependent care assistance for an employee, the exclusions under section 132 and this section do not apply to the provision by an employer to an employee of dependent care assistance. Similarly, because section 117(d) applies to tuition reductions, the exclusions under section 132 do not apply to free or discounted tuition provided to an employee by an organization operated by the employer, whether the tuition is for study at or below the graduate level. Of course, if the amounts paid by the employer are for education relating to the employee's trade or business of being an employee of the employer so that, if the employee paid for the education, the amount paid could be deducted under section 162, the costs of the education may be eligible for exclusion as a working condition fringe.

(2) Limited statutory exclusions. If another section of Chapter 1 of the Internal Revenue Code of 1986 provides an exclusion from gross income based on the cost of the benefit provided to the employee and, such exclusion is a limited amount, section 132 and the regulations thereunder may apply to the extent the cost of the benefit exceeds the statutory exclusion.

(g) Effective date. Sections 1.132-0, 1.132-1, 1.132-2, 1.132-3, 1.132-4, 1.132-5, 1.132-6, 1.132-7 and 1.132-8 are effective as of January 1, 1989, except that sections 1.132-1(b)(1) with respect to the use of air transportation by a parent of an employee and 1.132-4(d) are effective as of January 1, 1985. Furthermore, in § 1.132-5, the eleventh sentence of paragraph (m)(1), Example 6 and 7 in paragraph (m)(8), and paragraphs (m)(2)(i), (m)(2)(v), (m)(3)(iv), (m)(6), (m)(7), and (r) are effective December 30, 1992; however, taxpayers may treat the rules as applicable to benefits provided on or after January 1, 1989. For the applicable rules relating to employer-provided transportation for security concerns prior to December 30, 1992, see § 1.132-5(m) (as contained in 26 CFR part 1 (§§ 1.61 to 1.169) revised April 1, 1992). See sections 1.132-IT, 1.132-2T, 1.132-3T, 1.132-4T, 1.132-5T, 1.132-6T, 1.132-7T and 1.132-8T for rules in effect for benefits received from January 1, 1985, to December 31, 1988.

T.D. 8256, 7/6/89, amend T.D. 8457, 12/29/92.

---

§ 1.132-1T Exclusion from gross income of certain fringe benefits — 1985 through 1988 (Temporary).

(a) In general. Gross income does not include any fringe benefit which qualifies as a—

(1) no-additional-cost service,

(2) qualified employee discount,

(3) working condition fringe, or

(4) de minimis fringe.

Special rules apply with respect to certain on-premises gyms and other athletic facilities (§ 1.132-1T(e)), demonstration use of employer-provided automobiles by full-time automobile salesmen (§ 1.132-5T(n)), parking provided to an employee on or near the business premises of the employer (§ 1.132-5T(o)), and on-premises eating facilities (§ 1.132-7T).

(b) Definition of employee. *(1) No-additional-cost services and qualified employee discounts.* For purposes of section 132(a)(1) (relating to no-additional-cost services) and section 132(a)(2) (relating to qualified employee discounts), the term "employee" (with respect to a line of business of an employer) means—

(i) any individual who is currently employed by the employer in the line of business,

(ii) any individual who was formerly employed by the employer in the line of business and who separated from service with the employer in the line of business by reason of retirement or disability, and

(iii) any widow or widower of an individual who died while employed by the employer in the line of business or who separated from service with the employer in the line of business by reason of retirement or disability.

For purposes of this paragraph (b)(1), any partner who performs services for a partnership is considered employed by the partnership. In addition, any use by the spouse or dependent child (as defined in this paragraph (b)) of the employee will be treated as use by the employee.

(2) Working condition fringes. For purposes of section 132(a)(3) (relating to working condition fringes), the term "employee" means—

(i) any individual who is currently employed by the employer,

(ii) any partner who performs services for the partnership,

(iii) any director of the employer, and

(iv) any independent contractor who performs services for the employer.

Notwithstanding anything in this paragraph (b)(2) to the contrary, any independent contractor who performs services for the employer cannot exclude the value of parking or the use of consumer goods provided pursuant to a product testing program under § 1.132-5T(n); in addition, any director of the employer cannot exclude the value of the use of consumer goods provided pursuant to a product testing program under § 1.132-5T(n).

(3) De minimis fringe. For purposes of section 132(a)(4) (relating to de minimis fringes), the term "employee" means any recipient of a fringe benefit.

(4) Dependent child. For purposes of this paragraph (b), the term "dependent child" means any son, stepson, daughter, or stepdaughter, of the employee who is a dependent of the employee, or both of whose parents are deceased. Any child to whom section 152(e) applies will be treated as the dependent of both parents.

(c) Special rules for employers—Effect of section 414. All employees treated as employed by a single employer under section 414(b), (c), or (m) will be treated as employed by a single employer for purposes of this section. Thus, employees of one corporation that is part of a controlled group of corporations may under certain circumstances be eligible to receive section 132 benefits from the other corporations that comprise the controlled group. However, the aggregation of employers described in this paragraph (c) does not change the other requirements for an exclusion, such as the line of business requirement. Thus, for example, if a controlled group of corporations consists of two corporations that operate in different lines of business, the corporations are not treated as operating in the same line of business even though the corporations are treated as one employer.

(d) Customers not to include employees. For purposes of section 132 and the regulations thereunder, the term "customer" means customers who are not employees. However, the preceding sentence does not apply to section 132(c)(2) (relating to the gross profit percentage for determining a qualified employee discount). Thus, an employer that provides employee discounts cannot exclude sales made to employees in determining the aggregate sales to customers.

(e) Treatment of on-premises athletic facilities. *(1) In general.* Gross income does not include the value of any on-premises athletic facility provided by the employer to its employees. For purposes of section 132 and this paragraph (e), the term "on-premises athletic facility" means any gym or other athletic facility (such as a pool, tennis court, or golf course)—

(i) which is located on the premises of the employer,

(ii) which is operated by the employer, and

(iii) where substantially all of the use of which is, during the calendar year, by employees of the employer, their spouses, and their dependent children.

For purposes of this paragraph (e)(1)(iii), the term "dependent children" has the same meaning as the plural of the term "dependent child" in paragraph (b)(4) of this section. The exclusion of this paragraph (e) does not apply to any athletic facility if access to the facility is made available to the general public through the sale of memberships, the rental of the facility, etc.

(2) Premises of the employer. The athletic facility need not be located on the employer's business premises. However, the athletic facility must be located on premises of the employer. The exclusion provided in this paragraph (e) applies whether the premises are owned or leased by the employer; in addition, the exclusion is available even if the employer is not a named lessee on the lease so long as the employer pays reasonable rent. The exclusion provided in this paragraph (e) does not apply to any athletic facility that is a facility for residential use. Thus, for example, a resort with accompanying athletic facilities (such as tennis courts, pool, and gym) would not qualify for the exclusion provided in this paragraph (e).

(3) Application of rules to membership in an athletic facility. The exclusion provided in this paragraph (e) does not apply to any membership in an athletic facility (including health clubs or country clubs) unless the facility is owned (or leased) and operated by the employer and substantially all the use of the facility is by employees of the employer, their spouses, and their dependent children. Therefore, membership in a health club or country club not meeting the rules provided in this paragraph (e) would not qualify for the exclusion.

(4) Operation by the employer. An employer is considered to operate the athletic facility if the employer itself operates the facility through its own employees, or if the employer contracts out to another to operate the athletic facility. For example, if an employer hires an independent contractor to operate the athletic facility for the employer's employees, the facility is considered to be operated by the employer. In addition, if an athletic facility is operated by more than one employer, it is considered to be operated by each employer. For purposes of paragraph (e)(1)(iii) of this section, substantially all the use of a facility operated by more than one employer must be by employees of all of the employers, their spouses, and their dependent children. Where the facility is operated by more than one employer, an employer that either pays rent directly to the owner of the premises or pays rent to a named lessor of the premises is eligible for the exclusion.

(5) Nonapplicability of nondiscrimination rules. The nondiscrimination rules of section 132 and § 1.132-8T do not apply to on-premises athletic facilities.

(f) Nonapplicability of section 132. If the tax treatment of a particular fringe benefit is expressly provided for in another section of Chapter 1, section 132 and the applicable regulations (except for section 132(e) and the regulations thereunder) do not apply to such fringe benefit. For example, since section 129 provides an exclusion from gross income for amounts paid or incurred by the employer for dependent care assistance for an employee, the exclusions under section 132 and this section do not apply to the provision by an employer to an employee of dependent care assistance.

T.D. 8063, 12/18/85, amend T.D. 8256, 7/6/89.

§ 1.132-2 No-additional-cost services.

(a) In general. *(1) definition.* Gross income does not include the value of a no-additional-cost service. A "no-additional-cost service" is any service provided by an employer to an employee for the employee's personal use if—

(i) The service is offered for sale by the employer to its customers in the ordinary course of the line of business of the employer in which the employee performs substantial services, and

(ii) The employer incurs no substantial additional cost in providing the service to the employee (including foregone revenue and excluding any amount paid by or on behalf of the employee for the service).

For rules relating to the line of business limitation, see section 1.132-4. For purposes of this section, a service will not be considered to be offered for sale by the employer to its customers if that service is primarily provided to employees and not to the employer's customers.

(2) Excess capacity services. Services that are eligible for treatment as no-additional-cost services include excess capacity services such as hotel accommodations; transportation by aircraft, train, bus, subway, or cruise line; and telephone

services. Services that are not eligible for treatment as no-additional-cost services are non-excess capacity services such as the facilitation by a stock brokerage firm of the purchase of stock. Employees who receive non-excess capacity services may, however, be eligible for a qualified employee discount of up to 20 percent of the value of the service provided. See section 1.132-3.

(3) Cash rebates. The exclusion for a no-additional-cost service applies whether the service is provided at no charge or at a reduced price. The exclusion also applies if the benefit is provided through a partial or total cash rebate of an amount paid for the service.

(4) Applicability of nondiscrimination rules. The exclusion for a no-additional-cost service applies to highly compensated employees only if the service is available on substantially the same terms to each member of a group of employees that is defined under a reasonable classification set up by the employer that does not discriminate in favor of highly compensated employees. See § 1.132-8.

(5) No substantial additional cost. (i) In general. The exclusion for a no-additional-cost service applies only if the employer does not incur substantial additional cost in providing the service to the employee. For purposes of the preceding sentence, the term "cost" includes revenue that is forgone because the service is provided to an employee rather than a nonemployee. (For purposes of determining whether any revenue is forgone, it is assumed that the employee would not have purchased the service unless it were available to the employee at the actual price charged to the employee.) Whether an employer incurs substantial additional cost must be determined without regard to any amount paid by the employee for the service. Thus, any reimbursement by the employee for the cost of providing the service does not affect the determination of whether the employer incurs substantial additional cost.

(ii) Labor intensive services. An employer must include the cost of labor incurred in providing services to employees when determining whether the employer has incurred substantial additional cost. An employer incurs substantial additional cost, whether non-labor costs are incurred, if a substantial amount of time is spent by the employer or its employees in providing the service to employees. This would be the result whether the time spent by the employer or its employees in providing the services would have been "idle," or if the services were provided outside normal business hours. An employer generally incurs no substantial additional cost, however, if the services provided to the employee are merely incidental to the primary service being provided by the employer. For example, the in-flight services of a flight attendant and the cost of in-flight meals provided to airline employees traveling on a space-available basis are merely incidental to the primary service being provided (i.e., air transportation). Similarly, maid service provided to hotel employees renting hotel rooms on a space-available basis is merely incidental to the primary service being provided (i.e., hotel accommodations).

(6) Payments for telephone service. Payment made by an entity subject to the modified final judgment (as defined in section 559(c)(5) of the Tax Reform Act of 1984) of all or part of the cost of local telephone service provided to an employee by a person other than an entity subject to the modified final judgment shall be treated as telephone service provided to the employee by the entity making the payment for purposes of this section. The preceding sentence also applies to a rebate of the amount paid by the employee for the service and a payment to the person providing the service. This paragraph (a)(6) applies only to services and employees described in section 1.132-4(c). For a special line of business rule relating to such services and employees, see section 1.132-4(c).

(b) Reciprocal agreements. For purposes of the exclusion from gross income for a no-additional-cost service, an exclusion is available to an employee of one employer for a no-additional-cost service provided by an unrelated employer only if all of the following requirements are satisfied—

(1) The service provided to such employee by the unrelated employer is the same type of service generally provided to nonemployee customers by both the line of business in which the employee works and the line of business in which the service is provided to such employee (so that the employee would be permitted to exclude from gross income the value of the service if such service were provided directly by the employee's employer);

(2) Both employers are parties to a written reciprocal agreement under which a group of employees of each employer, all of whom perform substantial services in the same line of business, may receive no-additional-cost services from the other employer; and

(3) Neither employer incurs any substantial additional cost (including forgone revenue) in providing such service to the employees of the other employer, or pursuant to such agreement. If one employer receives a substantial payment from the other employer with respect to the reciprocal agreement, the paying employer will be considered to have incurred a substantial additional cost pursuant to the agreement, and consequently services performed under the reciprocal agreement will not qualify for exclusion as no-additional-cost services.

(c) Example. The rules of this section are illustrated by the following example:

Example. Assume that a commercial airline permits its employees to take personal flights on the airline at no charge and receive reserved seating. Because the employer forgoes potential revenue by permitting the employees to reserve seats, employees receiving such free flights are not eligible for the no-additional-cost exclusion.

T.D. 8256, 7/6/89.

§ 1.132-2T No-additional-cost service—1985 through 1988 (Temporary).

(a) In general. *(1) Definition.* Gross income does not include the value of a no-additional-cost service. The term "no-additional-cost service" means any service provided by an employer to an employee for the employee's personal use if—

(i) the service is offered for sale to customers in the ordinary course of the line of business of the employer in which the employee performs substantial services, and

(ii) the employer incurs no substantial additional cost in providing the service to the employee (including forgone revenue and excluding any amount paid by or on behalf of the employee for the service).

For rules relating to the line of business limitation, see § 1.132-4T.

(2) Examples. Services that are eligible for treatment as no-additional-cost services are excess capacity services such as hotel accommodations; transportation by aircraft, train, bus, subway, or cruise line; and telephone services. Services that are not eligible for treatment as no-additional-cost ser-

vices are non-excess capacity services such as the facilitation by a stock brokerage firm of the purchase of stock. Employees who receive non-excess capacity services may, however, be eligible for a qualified employee discount of up to 20 percent of the value of the service provided. See § 1.132-3T.

(3) Cash rebates. The exclusion for a no-additional-cost service applies whether the service is provided at no charge or at a reduced price. The exclusion also applies if the benefit is provided through a partial or total cash rebate of an amount paid for the service.

(4) Applicability of nondiscrimination rules. The exclusion for a no-additional-cost service applies to officers, owners, and highly compensated employees only if the service is available on substantially the same terms to each member of a group of employees that is defined under a reasonable classification set up by the employer that does not discriminate in favor of officers, owners, or highly compensated employees. See § 1.132-8T.

(5) No substantial additional cost. (i) In general. The exclusion for a no-additional-cost service applies only if the employer does not incur substantial additional cost in providing the service to the employee. For purposes of the preceding sentence, the term "cost" includes revenue that is forgone because the service is provided to an employee rather than a nonemployee. (For purposes of determining whether any revenue is forgone, it is assumed that the employee would not have purchased the service unless it were available to the employee at the actual price charged to the employee.) Whether an employer incurs substantial additional cost must be determined without regard to any amount paid by the employee for the service. Thus, any reimbursement by the employee for the cost of providing the service does not affect the determination of whether the employer incurs substantial additional cost.

(ii) Labor intensive services. An employer must include the cost of labor incurred in providing services to employees when determining whether the employer has incurred substantial additional cost. An employer incurs substantial additional cost, whether or not non-labor costs are incurred, if a substantial amount of time is spent by the employer or its employees in providing the service to employees. This would be the result whether or not the time spent by the employer or its employees in providing the services would have been "idle", or if the services were provided outside normal business hours. An employer generally incurs no substantial additional cost, however, if the employee services provided are merely incidental to the primary service being provided by the employer. For example, the in-flight services of a flight attendant provided to airline employees traveling on a space-available basis are merely incidental to the primary service being provided (i.e., air transportation). In addition, the cost of in-flight meals provided to airline employees is not considered substantial in relation to the air transportation being provided.

(b) Reciprocal agreements. For purposes of the exclusion for a no-additional-cost service, any service provided by an employer to an employee of another employer shall be treated as provided by the employer of such employee if all of the following requirements are satisfied:

(1) The service is provided pursuant to a written reciprocal agreement between the employers under which a group of employees of each employer, all of whom perform substantial services in the same line of business, may receive no-additional-cost services from the other employer;

(2) The service provided pursuant to the agreement to the employees of both employers is the same type of service provided by the employers to customers both in the line of business in which the employees perform substantial services and the line of business in which the service is provided to customers; and

(3) Neither employer incurs substantial additional cost (including forgone revenue) in providing the service to the employees of the other employer or pursuant to the agreement. If one employer receives a substantial payment from the other employer with respect to the reciprocal agreement, the paying employer will be considered to have incurred a substantial additional cost pursuant to the agreement.

T.D. 8063, 12/18/85, amend T.D. 8256, 7/6/89.

§ 1.132-3 Qualified employee discounts.

(a) In general. *(1) Definition.* Gross income does not include the value of a qualified employee discount. A "qualified employee discount" is any employee discount with respect to qualified property or services provided by an employer to an employee for use by the employee to the extent the discount does not exceed—

(i) The gross profit percentage multiplied by the price at which the property is offered to customers in the ordinary course of the employer's line of business, for discounts on property, or

(ii) Twenty percent of the price at which the service is offered to customers, for discounts on services.

(2) Qualified property or services. (i) In general. The term "qualified property or services" means any property or services that are offered for sale to customers in the ordinary course of the line of business of the employer in which the employee performs substantial services. For rules relating to the line of business limitation, see section 1.132-4.

(ii) Exception for certain property. The term "qualified property" does not include real property and it does not include personal property (whether tangible or intangible) of a kind commonly held for investment. Thus, an employee may not exclude from gross income the amount of an employee discount provided on the purchase of securities, commodities, or currency, or of either residential or commercial real estate, whether or not the particular purchase is made for investment purposes.

(iii) Property and services not offered in ordinary course of business. The term "qualified property or services" does not include any property or services of a kind that is not offered for sale to customers in the ordinary course of the line of business of the employer. For example, employee discounts provided on property or services that are offered for sale primarily to employees and their families (such as merchandise sold at an employee store or through an employer-provided catalog service) may not be excluded from gross income. For rules relating to employer-operated eating facilities, see section 1.132-7, and for rules relating to employer-operated on-premises athletic facilities, see section 1.132-1(e).

(3) No reciprocal agreement exception. The exclusion for a qualified employee discount does not apply to property or services provided by another employer pursuant to a written reciprocal agreement that exists between employers to provide discounts on property and services to employees of the other employer.

(4) Property or services provided without charge, at a reduced price, or by rebates. The exclusion for a qualified em-

ployee discount applies whether the property or service is provided at no charge (in which case only part of the discount may be excludable as a qualified employee discount) or at a reduced price. The exclusion also applies if the benefit is provided through a partial or total cash rebate of an amount paid for the property or service.

(5) Property or services provided directly by the employer or indirectly through a third party. A qualified employee discount may be provided either directly by the employer or indirectly through a third party. For example, an employee of an appliance manufacturer may receive a qualified employee discount on the manufacturer's appliances purchased at a retail store that offers such appliances for sale to customers. The employee may exclude the amount of the qualified employee discount whether the employee is provided the appliance at no charge or purchases it at a reduced price, or whether the employee receives a partial or total cash rebate from either the employer-manufacturer or the retailer. If an employee receives additional rights associated with the property that are not provided by the employee's employer to customers in the ordinary course of the line of business in which the employee performs substantial services (such as the right to return or exchange the property or special warranty rights), the employee may only receive a qualified employee discount with respect to the property and not the additional rights. Receipt of such additional rights may occur, for example, when an employee of a manufacturer purchases property manufactured by the employee's employer at a retail outlet.

(6) Applicability of nondiscrimination rules. The exclusion for a qualified employee discount applies to highly compensated employees only if the discount is available on substantially the same terms to each member of a group of employees that is defined under a reasonable classification set up by the employer that does not discriminate in favor of highly compensated employees. See § 1.132-8.

(b) Employee discount. *(1) Definition.* The term "employee discount" means the excess of—

(i) The price at which the property or service is being offered by the employer for sale to customers, over

(ii) The price at which the property or service is provided by the employer to an employee for use by the employee. A transfer of property by an employee without consideration is treated as use by the employee for purposes of this section. Thus, for example, if an employee receives a discount on property offered for sale by his employer to customers and the employee makes a gift of the property to his parent, the property will be considered to be provided for use by the employee; thus, the discount will be eligible for exclusion as a qualified employee discount.

(2) Price to customers. (i) Determined at time of sale. In determining the amount of an employee discount, the price at which the property or service is being offered to customers at the time of the employee's purchase is controlling. For example, assume that an employer offers a product to customers for $20 during the first six months of a calendar year, but at the time the employee purchases the product at a discount, the price at which the product is being offered to customers is $25. In this case, the price from which the employee discount is measured is $25. Assume instead that, at the time the employee purchases the product at a discount, the price at which the product is being offered to customers is $15 and the price charged the employee is $12. The employee discount is measured from $15, the price at which the product is offered for sale to customers at the time of the employee purchase. Thus, the employee discount is $15 − $12, or $3.

(ii) Quantity discount not reflected. The price at which a property or service is being offered to customers cannot reflect any quantity discount unless the employee actually purchases the requisite quantity of the property or service.

(iii) Price to employer's customers controls. In determining the amount of an employee discount, the price at which a property or service is offered to customers of the employee's employer is controlling. Thus, the price at which the property is sold to the wholesale customers of a manufacturer will generally be lower than the price at which the same property is sold to the customers of a retailer. However, see paragraph (a)(5) of this section regarding the effect of a wholesaler providing to its employees additional rights not provided to customers of the wholesaler in the ordinary course of its business.

(iv) Discounts to discrete customer or consumer groups. Subject to paragraph (2)(ii) of this section, if an employer offers for sale property or services at one or more discounted prices to discrete customer or consumer groups, and sales at all such discounted prices comprise at least 35 percent of the employer's gross sales for a representative period, then in determining the amount of an employee discount, the price at which such property or service is being offered to customers for purposes of this section is a discounted price. The applicable discounted price is the current undiscounted price, reduced by the percentage discount at which the greatest percentage of the employer's discounted gross sales are made for such representative period. If sales at different percentage discounts equal the same percentage of the employer's gross sales, the price at which the property or service is being provided to customers may be reduced by the average of the discounts offered to each of the two groups. For purposes of this section, a representative period is the taxable year of the employer immediately preceding the taxable year in which the property or service is provided to the employee at a discount. If more than one employer would be aggregated under section 414(b), (c), (m), or (o), and not all of the employers have the same taxable year, the employers required to be aggregated must designate the 12-month period to be used in determining gross sales for a representative period. The 12-month period designated, however, must be used on a consistent basis.

(v) Examples. The rules provided in this paragraph (b)(2) are illustrated by the following examples:

Example (1). Assume that a wholesale employer offers property for sale to two discrete customer groups at differing prices. Assume further that during the prior taxable year of the employer, 70 percent of the employer's gross sales are made at a 15 percent discount and 30 percent at no discount. For purposes of this paragraph (b)(2), the current undiscounted price at which the property or service is being offered by the employer for sale to customers may be reduced by the 15 percent discount.

Example (2). Assume that a retail employer offers a 20 percent discount to members of the American Bar Association, a 15 percent discount to members of the American Medical Association, and a ten percent discount to employees of the Federal Government. Assume further that during the prior taxable year of the employer, sales to American Bar Association members equal 15 percent of the employer's gross sales, sales to American Medical Association members equal 20 percent of the employer's gross sales, and sales to Federal Government employees equal 25 percent of the employer's gross sales. For purposes of this paragraph (b)(2), the current undiscounted price at which the property or service is being offered by the employer for sale to customers may be reduced by the ten percent Federal Government discount.

(3) Damaged, distressed, or returned goods. If an employee pays at least fair market value for damaged, distressed, or returned property, such employee will not have income attributable to such purchase.

(c) Gross profit percentage. *(1) In general.* (i) General rule. An exclusion from gross income for an employee discount on qualified property is limited to the price at which the property is being offered to customers in the ordinary course of the employer's line of business, multiplied by the employer's gross profit percentage. The term "gross profit percentage" means the excess of the aggregate sales price of the property sold by the employer to customers (including employees) over the employer's aggregate cost of the property, then divided by the aggregate sales price.

(ii) Calculation of gross profit percentage. The gross profit percentage must be calculated separately for each line of business based on the aggregate sales price and aggregate cost of property in that line of business for a representative period.

For purposes of this section, a representative period is the taxable year of the employer immediately preceding the taxable year in which the discount is available. For example, if the aggregate amount of sales of property in an employer's line of business for the prior taxable year was $800,000, and the aggregate cost of the property for the year was $600,000, the gross profit percentage would be 25 percent ($800,000 minus $600,000, then divided by $800,000). If two or more employers are required to aggregate under section 414(b), (c), (m), or (o) (aggregated employer), and if all of the aggregated employers do not share the same taxable year, then the aggregated employers must designate the 12-month period to be used in determining the gross profit percentage. The 12-month period designated, however, must be used on a consistent basis. If an employee performs substantial services in more than one line of business, the gross profit percentage of the line of business in which the property is sold determines the amount of the excludable employee discount.

(iii) Special rule for employers in their first year of existence. An employer in its first year of existence may estimate the gross profit percentage of a line of business based on its mark- up from cost. Alternatively, an employer in its first year of existence may determine the gross profit percentage by reference to an appropriate industry average.

(iv) Redetermination of gross profit percentage. If substantial changes in an employer's business indicate at any time that it is inappropriate for the prior year's gross profit percentage to be used for the current year, the employer must, within a reasonable period, redetermine the gross profit percentage for the remaining portion of the current year as if such portion of the year were the first year of the employer's existence.

(2) Line of business. In general, an employer must determine the gross profit percentage on the basis of all property offered to customers (including employees) in each separate line of business. An employer may instead select a classification of property that is narrower than the applicable line of business. However, the classification must be reasonable. For example, if an employer computes gross profit percentage according to the department in which products are sold, such classification is reasonable. Similarly, it is reasonable to compute gross profit percentage on the basis of the type of merchandise sold (such as high mark-up and low mark-up classifications). It is not reasonable, however, for an employer to classify certain low mark-up products preferred by certain employees (such as highly compensated employees) with high mark-up products or to classify certain high mark-up products preferred by other employees with low mark-up products.

(3) Generally accepted accounting principles. In general, the aggregate sales price of property must be determined in accordance with generally accepted accounting principles. An employer must compute the aggregate cost of property in the same manner in which it is computed for the employer's Federal income tax liability; thus, for example, section 263A and the regulations thereunder apply in determining the cost of property.

(d) Treatment of leased sections of department stores. *(1) In general.* (i) General rule. For purposes of determining whether employees of a leased section of a department store may receive qualified employee discounts at the department store and whether employees of the department store may receive qualified employee discounts at the leased section of the department store, the leased section is treated as part of the line of business of the person operating the department store, end employees of the leased section are treated as employees of the person operating the department store as well as employees of their employer. The term "leased section of a department store" means a section of a department store where substantially all of the gross receipts of the leased section are from over-the-counter sales of property made under a lease, license, or similar arrangement where it appears to the general public that individuals making such sales are employed by the department store. A leased section of a department store which, in connection with the offering of beautician services, customarily makes sales of beauty aids in the ordinary course of business is deemed to derive substantially all of its gross receipts from over-the-counter sales of property.

(ii) Calculation of gross profit percentage. For purposes of paragraph (d) of this section, when calculating the gross profit percentage of property and services sold at a department store, sales of property and services sold at the department store, as well as sales of property and services sold at the leased section, are considered. The rule provided in the preceding sentence does not apply, however, if it is more reasonable to calculate the gross profit percentage for the department store and leased section separately, or if it would be inappropriate to combine them (such as where either the department store or the leased section but not both provides employee discounts).

(2) Employers of the leased section. (i) Definition. For purposes of this paragraph (d), "employees of the leased section" means all employees who perform substantial services at the leased section of the department store regardless of whether the employees engage in over-the-counter sales of property or services. The term "employee" has the same meaning as in section 132(f) and § 1.132-1(b)(1).

(ii) Discounts offered to either department store employees or employees of the leased section. If the requirements of this paragraph (d) are satisfied, employees of the leased section may receive qualified employee discounts at the department store whether or not employees of the department store are offered discounts at the leased section. Similarly, employees of the department store may receive a qualified employee discount at the leased section whether or not employees of the leased section are offered discounts at the department store.

(e) Excess discounts. Unless excludable under a provision of the Internal Revenue Code of 1986 other than section 132(a)(2), an employee discount provided on property is excludable to the extent of the gross profit percentage multiplied by the price at which the property is being offered for sale to customers. If an employee discount exceeds the gross profit percentage, the excess discount is includible in the employee's income. For example, if the discount on employer-purchased property is 30 percent and the employer's gross profit percentage for the period in the relevant line of business is 25 percent, then 5 percent of the price at which the property is being offered for sale to customers is includible in the employee's income. With respect to services, an employee discount of up to 20 percent may be excludable. If an employee discount exceeds 20 percent, the excess discount is includible in the employee's income. For example, assume that a commercial airline provides a pass to each of its employees permitting the employees to obtain a free round-trip coach ticket with a confirmed seat to any destination the airline services. Neither the exclusion of section 132(a)(1) (relating to no-additional-cost services) nor any other statutory exclusion applies to a flight taken primarily for personal purposes by an employee under this program. However, an employee discount of up to 20 percent may be excluded as a qualified employee discount. Thus, if the price charged to customers for the flight taken is $300 (under restrictions comparable to those actually placed on travel associated with the employee airline ticket), $60 is excludible from gross income as a qualified employee discount and $240 is includible in gross income.

T.D. 8256, 7/6/89.

§ 1.132-3T Qualified employee discount—1985 through 1988 (Temporary).

(a) In general. *(1) Definition.* Gross income does not include the value of a qualified employee discount. The term "qualified employee discount" means any employee discount with respect to qualified property or services provided by an employer to an employee for the employee's personal use to the extent the discount does not exceed—

(i) the gross profit percentage of the price at which the property is offered to customers, for discounts on property, or

(ii) 20 percent of the price at which the services are offered to customers, for discounts on services.

(2) Qualified property or services. (i) In general. The term "qualified property or services" means any property or services that are offered for sale to customers in the ordinary course of the line of business of the employer in which the employee performs substantial services. For rules relating to the line of business limitation, see § 1.132-4T.

(ii) Exception for certain property. The term "qualified property" does not include real property and it does not include personal property (whether tangible or intangible) of a kind commonly held for investment. Thus, an employee may not exclude from gross income the amount of an employee discount provided on the purchase of either residential or commercial real estate, securities, commodities, or currency, whether or not the particular purchase is made for investment purposes.

(iii) Property and services not offered in ordinary course of business. The term "qualified property or services" does not include any property or services of a kind that is not offered for sale to customers in the ordinary course of the line of business of the employer. For example, employee discounts provided on property or services that are offered for sale only to employees and their families (such as merchandise sold at an employee store or through an employer-provided catalog service) may not be excluded from gross income.

(3) No reciprocal agreement exception. The exclusion for a qualified employee discount does not apply to property or services provided by another employer pursuant to a written reciprocal agreement that exists between employers to provide discounts on property and services to employees of the other employer.

(4) Cash or third-party rebates. (i) Property or services provided without charge or at a reduced price. The exclusion for a qualified employee discount applies whether the property or service is provided at no charge (in which case only part of the discount may be excludable as a qualified employee discount) or at a reduced price. The exclusion also applies if the benefit is provided through a partial or total cash rebate of an amount paid for the property or service.

(ii) Property or services provided directly by the employer or indirectly through a third party. A qualified employee discount may be provided either directly by the employer or indirectly through a third party. For example, an employee of an appliance manufacturer may receive a qualified employee discount on the manufacturer's appliances purchased at a retail store that offers such appliances for sale to customers. The employee may exclude the amount of the qualified employee discount whether the employee is provided the appliance at no charge or purchases it at a reduced price, or whether the employee receives a partial or total cash rebate from either the employer-manufacturer or the retailer. If an employee receives additional rights associated with the property that are not provided by the employee's employer to customers in the ordinary course of the line of business in which the employee performs substantial services (such as the right to return or exchange the property or special warranty rights), the employee may only receive a qualified employee discount with respect to the property and not the additional rights. Receipt of such additional rights may occur, for example, when an employee of a manufacturer purchases property manufactured by the employee's employer at a retail outlet.

(5) Applicability of nondiscrimination rules. The exclusion for a qualified employee discount applies to officers, owners, and highly compensated employees only if the discount is available on substantially the same terms to each member of a group of employees that is defined under a reasonable classification set up by the employer that does not discriminate in favor of officers, owners, or highly compensated employees. See § 1.132-8T.

(b) Employee discount. *(1) Definition.* The term "employee discount" means the excess of —

(i) the price at which the property or service is being offered by the employer for sale to customers, over

(ii) the price at which the property or service is provided by the employer to an employee for use by the employee.

A transfer of property by an employee without consideration is considered use by the employee for purposes of this section. Thus, for example, if an employee receives a discount on property offered for sale by his employer to customers and the employee makes a gift of the property to his parent, the property will be considered to be provided for use by the employee, thus enabling the discount to be eligible for exclusion as a qualified employee discount.

(2) Price to customers. (i) Determined at time of sale. In determining the amount of an employee discount, the price at which the property or service is being offered to customers at the time of the employee's purchase is controlling. For example, assume that an employer offers a product to customers for $20 during the first six months of a calendar year, but at the time the employee purchases the product at a discount, the price at which the product is being offered to customers is $25. In this case, the price from which the employee discount is measured is $25.

(ii) Quantity discount not reflected. The price referred to in paragraph (b)(2)(i) of this section cannot reflect any quantity discount unless the employee actually purchases the requisite quantity of the property or service.

(iii) Customers of employee's employer controls. In determining the amount of an employee discount, the price at which the property or service is offered to customers of the employee's employer is controlling. Thus, the price at which property is sold to the wholesale customers of a manufacturer will generally be lower than the price at which the same property is sold to the customers of a retailer. However, see paragraph (a)(4)(ii) of this section regarding the effect of a wholesaler providing to its employees additional rights not provided to customers of the wholesaler in the ordinary course of its business.

(iv) Discounts to discrete customer or consumer groups. In determining the amount of an employee discount, if an employer offers for sale property or services at one or more discounted prices to discrete customer or consumer groups, and sales at all such discounted prices comprise at least 35 percent of the employer's gross sales for a representative period, then the price at which property or service is being offered to customers is a discounted price. The applicable discounted price is the current undiscounted price, reduced by the percentage discount at which the greatest percentage of the employer's gross sales are made for such representative period. If sales at different percentage discounts equal the same percentage of the employer's gross sales, the price at which the property or service is being provided to customers may be reduced by the average of the two group discounts. For purposes of this section, a representative period is the taxable year of the employer immediately preceding the taxable year in which the property or service is provided to the employee at a discount. If more than one employer would be aggregated under section 414 (b), (c), or (m), and all of the employers do not have the same taxable year, the employers required to be aggregated must designate the 12-month period to be used in determining gross sales for a representative period.

(v) Examples. The rules provided in this paragraph (b) (2) are illustrated by the following examples:

Example (1). Assume that a wholesale employer offers property for sale to two discrete customer groups at differing prices. Assume further that during the prior taxable year of the employer, 70 percent of the employer's gross sales are made at a 15-percent discount and 30 percent at no discount. The current undiscounted price at which the property or service is being offered by the employer for sale to customers may be reduced by the 15-percent discount.

Example (2). Assume that a retail employer offers a 20 percent discount to members of the American Bar Association, a 15 percent discount to members of the American Medical Association, and a ten percent discount to employees of the Federal Government. Assume further that during the prior taxable year of the employer, sales to American Bar Association members equal 15 percent of the employer's gross sales, sales to American Medical Association members equal 20 percent of the employer's gross sales, and sales to Federal Government employees equal 25 percent of the employer's gross sales. The current undiscounted price at which the property or service is being offered by the employer for sale to customers may be reduced by the ten percent Federal Government discount.

(3) Damaged, distressed, or returned goods. If an employee pays at least fair market value for damaged, distressed, or returned property, such employee will not have income attributable to such purchase.

(c) Gross profit percentage. *(1) In general.* (i) General rule. An exclusion from gross income for an employee discount on qualified property is limited to the price at which the property is being offered to customers in the ordinary course of the employer's line of business, multiplied by the employer's gross profit percentage. The term "gross profit percentage" means the excess of the aggregate sales price of the property sold by the employer to customers (including employees) over the employer's aggregate cost of the property, then divided by the aggregate sales price.

(ii) Calculation of gross profit percentage. The gross profit percentage must be calculated separately for each line of business based on the aggregate sales price and aggregate cost of property in that line of business for a representative period. For purposes of this section, a representative period is the taxable year of the employer immediately preceding the taxable year in which the discount is available. For example, if the aggregate sales of property in an employer's line of business for the prior taxable year were $800,000, and the aggregate cost of the property for the year were $600,000, the gross profit percentage would be 25 percent ($800,000 minus $600,000, then divided by $800,000). If more than one employer would be aggregated under section 414 (b), (c), or (m), and all of the employers do not have the same taxable year, the employers required to be aggregated must designate the 12-month period to be used in determining the gross profit percentage. If an employee performs substantial services in more than one line of business, the gross profit percentage of the line of business in which the property is sold determines the amount of the excludable employee discount.

(iii) Special rule for employers in their first year of existence. An employer in its first year of existence may estimate the gross profit percentage of a line of business based on its mark-up from cost. Alternatively, an employer in its first year of existence may determine the gross profit percentage by reference to an appropriate industry average.

(iv) Redetermination of gross profit percentage. If substantial changes in an employer's business indicate at any time that it is inappropriate for the prior years' gross profit percentage to be used for the current year, the employer must, within a reasonable period, redetermine the gross profit percentage for the remaining portion of the current year as if such portion of the year were the first year of the employer's existence.

(2) Line of business. In general, an employer must determine the gross profit percentage on the basis of all property offered to customers (including employees) in each separate line of business. An employer may instead select a classification of property that is narrower than the applicable line of business. However, such classification must be reasonable. For example, if an employer computes gross profit percentage according to the department in which products are sold, such classification is reasonable. Similarly, it is reasonable to compute gross profit percentage on the basis of the type

of merchandise sold (such as high mark-up and low mark-up classifications). It is not reasonable, however, for an employer to classify certain low mark-up products preferred by certain employees (such as officers, owners, and highly compensated employees) with high mark-up products or to classify certain high mark-up products preferred by other employees with low mark-up products.

(3) Generally accepted accounting principles. In general, the aggregate sales price of property must be determined in accordance with generally accepted accounting principles. An employer must compute the aggregate cost of property in the same manner in which it is computed for the employer's Federal income tax liability, pursuant to the inventory rules in section 471 and the regulations thereunder.

(d) Treatment of leased sections of department stores. *(1) In general.* (i) General rule. For purposes of determining whether employees of a leased section of a department store may receive qualified employee discounts at the department store and whether employees of the department store may receive qualified employee discounts at the leased section of the department store, the leased section is treated as part of the line of business of the person operating the department store, and employees of the leased section are treated as employees of the person operating the department store as well as employees of their employer. The term "leased section of a department store" means a section of a department store where substantially all of the gross receipts of the leased section are over-the-counter sales of property made under a lease, license, or similar arrangement where it appears to the general public that individuals making such sales are employed by the department store. An example of a leased section of a department store is a cosmetics firm that leases floor space from a department store.

(ii) Calculation of gross profit percentage. When calculating the gross profit percentage of property and services sold at the department store under paragraph (c) of this section, sales of property and services sold at the department store, as well as sales of property and services sold at the leased section, are considered. The rule provided in the preceding sentence does not apply, however, if it is reasonable to calculate the gross profit percentage for the department store and leased section separately, or if it would be inappropriate to combine them (such as where either the department store or the leased section, but not both, provides employee discounts).

(2) Employees of the leased section. (i) Definition. For purposes of this paragraph (d), "employees of the leased section" means all employees who perform substantial services at the leased section regardless of whether the employees engage in over-the-counter sales of property or services. The term "employee" has the same meaning as in section 132 (f).

(ii) Discounts offered to either department store employees or employees of the leased section. If the requirements of this paragraph (d) are satisfied, employees of the leased section may receive qualified employee discounts at the department store regardless of whether employees of the department store are offered discounts at the leased section. Similarly, regardless of whether employees of the leased section are offered discounts at the department store, employees of the department store may receive qualified employee discounts at the leased section.

(e) Excess discounts. Unless excludable under a statutory provision other than section 132 (a) (2), an employee discount provided on property is excludable to the extent of the gross profit percentage multiplied by the price at which the property is being offered for sale to customers. If an employee discount exceeds the gross profit percentage, the excess discount is includible in the employee's income. For example, if the discount on property is 30 percent and the employer's gross profit percentage for the period in the relevant line of business is 25 percent, then 5 percent of the price at which the property is being offered for sale to customers is includible in the employee's income. With respect to services, an employee discount of up to 20 percent may be excludable. If an employee discount exceeds 20 percent, the excess discount is includible in the employee's income.

T.D. 8063, 12/18/85, amend T.D. 8256, 7/6/89.

§ 1.132-4 Line of business limitation.

(a) In general. *(1) Applicability.* (i) General rule. A no-additional-cost service or a qualified employee discount provided to an employee is only available with respect to property or services that are offered for sale to customers in the ordinary course of the same line of business in which the employee receiving the property or service performs substantial services. Thus, an employee who does not perform substantial services in a particular line of business of the employer may not exclude from income under section 132(a)(1) or (a)(2) the value of services or employee discounts received on property or services in that line of business. For rules that relax the line of business requirement, see paragraphs (b) through (g) of this section.

(ii) Property and services sold to employees rather than customers. Because the property or services must be offered for sale to customers in the ordinary course of the same line of business in which the employee performs substantial services, the line of business limitation is not satisfied if the employer's products or services are sold primarily to employees of the employer, rather than to customers. Thus, for example, an employer in the banking line of business is not considered in the variety store line of business if the employer establishes an employee store that offers variety store items for sale to the employer's employees. See § 1.132-7 for rules relating to employer-operated eating facilities, and see § 1.132-1(e) for rules relating to employer-operated on-premises athletic facilities.

(iii) Performance of substantial services in more than one line of business. An employee who performs services in more than one of the employer's lines of business may only exclude no-additional-cost services and qualified employee discounts in the lines of business in which the employee performs substantial services.

(iv) Performance of services that directly benefit more than one line of business. (A) In general. An employee who performs substantial services that directly benefit more than one line of business of an employer is treated as performing substantial services in all such lines of business. For example, an employee who maintains accounting records for an employer's three lines of business may receive qualified employee discounts in all three lines of business. Similarly, if an employee of a minor line of business of an employer that is significantly interrelated with a major line of business of the employer performs substantial services that directly benefit both the major and the minor lines of business, the employee is treated as performing substantial services for both the major and the minor lines of business.

(B) Examples. The rules provided in this paragraph (a)(1)(iv) are illustrated by the following examples:

Example (1). Assume that employees of units of an employer provide repair or financing services, or sell by catalog, with respect to retail merchandise sold by the employer. Such employees may be considered to perform substantial services for the retail merchandise line of business under paragraph (a)(1)(iv)(A) of this section.

Example (2). Assume that an employer operates a hospital and a laundry service. Assume further that some of the gross receipts of the laundry service line of business are from laundry services sold to customers other than the hospital employer. Only the employees of the laundry service who perform substantial services which directly benefit the hospital line of business (through the provision of laundry services to the hospital) will be treated as performing substantial services for the hospital line of business. Other employees of the laundry service line of business will not be treated as employees of the hospital line of business.

Example (3). Assume the same facts as in example (2), except that the employer also operates a chain of dry cleaning stores. Employees who perform substantial services which directly benefit the dry cleaning stores but who do not perform substantial services that directly benefit the hospital line of business will not be treated as performing substantial services for the hospital line of business.

(2) Definition. (i) In general. An employer's line of business is determined by reference to the Enterprise Standard Industrial Classification Manual (ESIC Manual) prepared by the Statistical Policy Division of the U.S. Office of Management and Budget. An employer is considered to have more than one line of business if the employer offers for sale to customers property or services in more than one two-digit code classification referred to in the ESIC Manual.

(ii) Examples. Examples of two-digit classifications are general retail merchandise stores; hotels and other lodging places; auto repair, services, and garages; and food stores.

(3) Aggregation of two-digit classifications. If, pursuant to paragraph (a)(2) of this section, an employer has more than one line of business, such lines of business will be treated as a single line of business where and to the extent that one or more of the following aggregation rules apply:

(i) If it is uncommon in the industry of the employer for any of the separate lines of business of the employer to be operated without the others, the separate lines of business are treated as one line of business.

(ii) If it is common for a substantial number of employees (other than those employees who work at the headquarters or main office of the employer) to perform substantial services for more than one line of business of the employer, so that determination of which employees perform substantial services for which line or lines of business would be difficult, then the separate lines of business of the employer in which such employees perform substantial services are treated as one line of business. For example, assume that an employer operates a delicatessen with an attached service counter at which food is sold for consumption on the premises. Assume further that most but not all employees work both at the delicatessen and at the service counter. Under the aggregation rule of this paragraph (a)(3)(ii), the delicatessen and the service counter are treated as one line of business.

(iii) If the retail operations of an employer that are located on the same premises are in separate lines of business but would be considered to be within one line of business under paragraph (a)(2) of this section if the merchandise offered for sale in such lines of business were offered for sale at a department store, then the operations are treated as one line of business. For example, assume that on the same premises an employer sells both women's apparel and jewelry. Because, if sold together at a department store, the operations would be part of the same line of business, the operations are treated as one line of business.

(b) Grandfather rule for certain retail stores. *(1) In general.* The line of business limitation may be relaxed under the special grandfather rule of this paragraph (b). Under this special grandfather rule, if—

(i) On October 5, 1983, at least 85 percent of the employees of one member of an affiliated group (as defined in section 1504 without regard to subsections (b)(2) and (b)(4) thereof) ("first member") were entitled to receive employee discounts at retail department stores operated by another member of the affiliated group ("second member"), and

(ii) More than 50 percent of the previous year's sales of the affiliated group are attributable to the operation of retail department stores,

then, for purposes of the exclusion from gross income of a qualified employee discount, the first member is treated as engaged in the same line of business as the second member (the operator of the retail department stores). Therefore, employees of the first member of the affiliated group may exclude from income qualified employee discounts received at the retail department stores operated by the second member. However, employees of the second member of the affiliated group may not under this paragraph (b)(1) exclude any discounts received on property or services offered for sale to customers by the first member of the affiliated group.

(2) Taxable year of affiliated group. If not all of the members of an affiliated group have the same taxable year, the affiliated group must designate the 12-month period to be used in determining the "previous year's sales" (as referred to in the grandfather rule of this paragraph (b)). The 12-month period designated, however, must be used on a consistent basis.

(3) Definition of "sales". For purposes of this paragraph (b), the term "sales" means the gross receipts of an affiliated group, based upon the accounting methods used by its members.

(4) Retired and disabled employees. For purposes of this paragraph (b), an employee includes any individual who was, or whose spouse was, formerly employed by the first member of an affiliated group and who separated from service with the member by reason of retirement or disability if the second member of the group provided employee discounts to that individual on October 5, 1983.

(5) Increase of employee discount. If, after October 5, 1983, the employee discount described in this paragraph (b) is increased, the grandfather rule of this paragraph (b) does not apply to the amount of the increase. For example, if on January 1, 1989, the employee discount is increased from ten percent to 15 percent, the grandfather rule will not apply to the additional five percent discount.

(c) Grandfather rule for telephone service provided to pre-divestiture retirees. All entities subject to the modified final judgment (as defined in section 559(c)(5) of the Tax Reform Act of 1984) shall be treated as a single employer engaged in the same line of business for purposes of determining whether telephone service provided to certain employees is a no-additional-cost service. The preceding sentence applies only in the case of an employee who by reason of retirement or disability separated before January 1, 1984, from the service of an entity subject to the modified final judgment. This paragraph (c) only applies to services provided to such employees as of January 1, 1984. For a special no-additional-cost service rule relating to such employees and such services, see § 1.132-2(a)(6).

(d) Special rule for certain affiliates of commercial airlines. *(1) General rule.* If a qualified affiliate is a member of an airline affiliated group and employees of the qualified affiliate who are directly engaged in providing airline-related services are entitled to no-additional-cost service with respect to air transportation provided by such other member, then, for purposes of applying § 1.132-2 (relating to no-additional-cost services with respect to such air transportation), such qualified affiliate shall be treated as engaged in the same line of business as such other member.

(2) "Airline affiliated group" defined. An "airline affiliated group" is an affiliated group (as defined in section 1504(a)) one of whose members operates a commercial airline that provides air transportation to customers on a per-seat basis.

(3) "Qualified affiliate" defined. A "qualified affiliate" is any corporation that is predominantly engaged in providing airline-related services. The term "airline-related services" means any of the following services provided in connection with air transportation:

(i) Catering,

(ii) Baggage handling,

(iii) Ticketing and reservations,

(iv) Flight planning and weather analysis, and

(v) Restaurants and gift shops located at an airport.

(e) Grandfather rule for affiliated groups operating airlines. The line of business limitation may be relaxed under the special grandfather rule of this paragraph (e). Under this special grandfather rule, if, as of September 12, 1984—

(1) An individual—

(i) Was an employee (within the meaning of § 1.132-1(b)) of one member of an affiliated group (as defined in section 1504(a)) ("first corporation"), and

(ii) Was eligible for no-additional-cost services in the form of air transportation provided by another member of such affiliated group ("second corporation"),

(2) At least 50 percent of the individuals performing services for the first corporation were, or had been employees of, or had previously performed services for, the second corporation, and

(3) The primary business of the affiliated group was air transportation of passengers,

then, for purposes of applying sections 132(a)(1) and (2), with respect to no-additional-cost services and qualified employee discounts provided after December 31, 1984, for that individual by the second corporation, the first corporation is treated as engaged in the same air transportation line of business as the second corporation. For purposes of the preceding sentence, an employee of the second corporation who is performing services for the first corporation is also treated as an employee of the first corporation.

(f) Special rule for qualified air transportation organizations. A qualified air transportation organization is treated as engaged in the line of business of providing air transportation with respect to any individual who performs services for the organization if those services are performed primarily for persons engaged in providing air transportation, and are of a kind which (if performed on September 12, 1984) would qualify the individual for no-additional-cost services in the form of air transportation. The term "qualified air transportation organization" means any organization—

(1) If such organization (or a predecessor) was in existence on September 12, 1984,

(2) If such organization is—

(i) A tax-exempt organization under section 501(c)(6) whose membership is limited to entities engaged in the transportation by air of individuals or property for compensation or hire, or

(ii) Is a corporation all the stock of which is owned entirely by entities described in paragraph (f)(2)(i) of this section, and

(3) If such organization is operated in furtherance of the activities of its members or owners.

(g) Relaxation of line of business requirement. The line of business requirement may be relaxed under an elective grandfather rule provided in section 4977. For rules relating to the section 4977 election, see § 54.4977-1T.

(h) Line of business requirement does not expend benefits eligible for exclusion. The line of business requirement limits the benefits eligible for the no-additional-cost service and qualified employee discount exclusions to property or services provided by an employer to its customers in the ordinary course of the line of business of the employer in which the employee performs substantial services. The requirement is intended to ensure that employers do not offer, on a tax-free or reduced basis, property or services to employees that are not offered to the employer's customers, even if the property or services offered to the customers and the employees are within the same line of business (as defined in this section).

T.D. 8256, 7/6/89.

§ 1.132-4T Line of business limitation—1985 through 1988 (Temporary).

(a) In general. *(1) Applicability.* (i) General rule. A no-additional-cost service or qualified employee discount provided to an employee must be for property or services that are offered for sale to customers in the ordinary course of the same line of business in which the employee receiving the property or service performs substantial services. Thus, an employee who does not perform substantial services in a particular line of business of the employer may not exclude the value of services or employee discounts received on property or services in that line of business.

(ii) Property and services sold to employees rather than customers. Since the property or services must be offered for sale to customers in the ordinary course of the same line of business in which the employee performs substantial services, the line of business limitation is not satisfied if the employer's products or services are sold to employees of the employer, rather than to customers. Thus, for example, an employer in the banking line of business is not considered in the variety store line of business if the employer establishes an employee store that offers variety store items for sale to the employer's employees.

(iii) Performance of substantial services in more than one line of business. An employee who performs services in more than one of the employer's lines of business may only exclude no-additional-cost services and qualified employee discounts in the lines of business in which the employee performs substantial services.

(iv) Performance of services that directly benefit more than one line of business. (A) In general. An employee who performs substantial services that directly benefit more than one line of business of an employer is treated as performing substantial services in all such lines of business. For example, an employee who maintains accounting records for an employer's three lines of business may receive qualified employee discounts in all three lines of business.

(B) Significantly interrelated minor line of business. The employees of a minor line of business of an employer that is significantly interrelated with a major line of business of the employer who perform substantial services that directly benefit both the major and the minor lines of business are treated as employees of both the major and the minor lines of business. Employees of the minor line of business who do not perform substantial services which directly benefit the major line of business are not treated as employees of the major line of business. A minor line of business is significantly interrelated with a major line of business when, for example, the activity of the minor line of business is directly related to but is a minor part of the major line of business (such as laundry services provided at a hospital).

(C) Examples. The rules provided in this paragraph are illustrated in the following examples:

Example (1). Assume that employees of units of an employer provide repair or financing services, or sell by catalog, with respect to retail merchandise sold by the employer. Such employees may be considered as employees of the retail merchandise line of business under this paragraph (a)(1)(iv).

Example (2). Assume that an employer operates a hospital and a laundry service. Assume further that some of the gross receipts of the laundry service line of business are from laundry services sold to customers other than the hospital employer. Only the employees of the laundry service who perform substantial services which directly benefit the hospital line of business (through the provision of laundry services to the hospital) will be treated as employees of the hospital line of business. Other employees of the laundry service line of business will not be treated as employees of the hospital line of business.

Example (3). Assume the same facts as in example (2), except that the minor line of business also operates a chain of dry cleaning stores. Employees who perform substantial services which directly benefit the dry cleaning stores but who do not perform substantial services that directly benefit the hospital line of business will not be treated as employees of the hospital line of business.

(2) Definition. (i) In general. An employer's line of business is determined by reference to the Enterprise Standard Industrial Classification Manual (ESIC Manual) prepared by the Statistical Policy Division of the U.S. Office of Management and Budget. An employer is considered to have more than one line of business if the employer offers for sale to customers property or services in more than one two-digit code classification referred to in the ESIC Manual.

(ii) Examples. Examples of two-digit classifications are general retail merchandise stores; hotels and other lodging places; auto repair, services, and garages; and food stores.

(3) Aggregation of two-digit classifications. If, pursuant to paragraph (a) (2) of this section, an employer has more than one line of business, such lines of business will be treated as a single line of business where and to the extent that one or more of the following aggregation rules apply:

(i) If it is uncommon in the industry of the employer for any of the separate lines of business of the employer to be operated without the others, the separate lines of business are treated as one line of business.

(ii) If it is common for a substantial number of employees (other than those employees who work at the headquarters or main office of the employer) to perform substantial services for more than one line of business of the employer, so that determination of which employees perform substantial services for which line of business would be difficult, then the separate lines of business of the employer in which such employees perform substantial services are treated as one line of business. For example, assume that an employer operates a delicatessen with an attached service counter at which food is sold for consumption on the premises. Assume further that most but not all employees work both at the delicatessen and at the service counter. The delicatessen and the service counter are treated as one line of business.

(iii) If the retail operations of an employer that are located on the same premises are in separate lines of business but would be considered to be within one line of business under paragraph (a)(2) of this section if the merchandise offered for sale in such lines of business were offered for sale at a department store, then the operations are treated as one line of business. For example, assume that on the same premises an employer sells both women's apparel and jewelry. Since, if sold together at a department store, the operations would be part of the same line of business, the operations are treated as one line of business.

(b) Grandfather rule for certain retail stores. *(1) In general.* The line of business limitation may be relaxed under a special grandfather rule. If—

(i) on October 5, 1983, 85 percent of the employees of one member of an affiliated group (as defined in section 1504 without regard to subsections (b)(2) and (b)(4) thereof) were entitled to employee discounts at retail department stores operated by another member of the affiliated group, and

(ii) more than 50 percent of the current year's sales of the affiliated group are attributable to the operation of retail department stores,

then for purposes of the exclusion from gross income of a qualified employee discount, the first member is treated as engaged in the same line of business as the second member (the operator of the retail department stores). Therefore, employees of the first member of the affiliated group may exclude qualified employee discounts received at the retail department stores operated by the second member. However, employees of the second member of the affiliated group may not exclude any discounts received on property or services offered for sale to customers by the first member of the affiliated group.

(2) Taxable year of affiliated group. If all of the members do not have the same taxable year, the affiliated group must designate the 12-month period to be used in determining the "current year's sales" (as referred to in this paragraph (b)). The 12-month period designated, however, must be used consistently.

(3) Definition of "sales". For purposes of this paragraph (b), the term "sales" means the gross receipts of the affiliated group, based upon the accounting methods used by its members.

(4) Retired and disabled employees. For purposes of this paragraph (b), an employee includes any individual who was, or whose spouse was, formerly employed by the first

member of the affiliated group and who separated from service with the member by reason of retirement or disability if the second member of the group provided employee discounts to such individuals on October 5, 1983.

(5) Increase of employee discount. If, after October 5, 1983, the employee discount described in this paragraph (b) is increased, the grandfather rule of this paragraph (b) does not apply to the amount of the increase. For example, if on January 1, 1985, the employee discount is increased from ten percent to 15 percent, the grandfather rule will not apply to the additional five percent discount.

(c) Relaxation of line of business requirement. The line of business requirement may be relaxed under an elective grandfather rule provided in section 4977. For rules relating to the section 4977 election, see § 54.4977-1.

T.D. 8063, 12/18/85, amend T.D. 8256, 7/6/89.

§ 1.132-5 Working condition fringes.

Caution: The Treasury has not yet amended Reg § 1.132-5 to reflect changes made by 102-486.

(a) In general. *(1) Definition.* Gross income does not include the value of a working condition fringe. A "working condition fringe" is any property or service provided to an employee of an employer to the extent that, if the employee paid for the property or service, the amount paid would be allowable as a deduction under section 162 or 167.

(i) A service or property offered by an employer in connection with a flexible spending account is not excludable from gross income as a working condition fringe. For purposes of the preceding sentence, a flexible spending account is an agreement (whether or not written) entered into between an employer and an employee that makes available to the employee over a time period a certain level of unspecified non-cash benefits with a pre-determined cash value.

(ii) If, under section 274 or any other section, certain substantiation requirements must be met in order for a deduction under section 162 or 167 to be allowable, then those substantiation requirements apply when determining whether a property or service is excludable as a working condition fringe.

(iii) An amount that would be deductible by the employee under a section other than section 162 or 167, such as section 212, is not a working condition fringe.

(iv) A physical examination program provided by the employer is not excludable as a working condition fringe even if the value of such program might be deductible to the employee under section 213. The previous sentence applies without regard to whether the employer makes the program mandatory to some or all employees.

(v) A cash payment made by an employer to an employee will not qualify as a working condition fringe unless the employer requires the employee to—

(A) Use the payment for expenses in connection with a specific or pre-arranged activity or undertaking for which a deduction is allowable under section 162 or 167,

(B) Verify that the payment is actually used for such expenses, and

(C) Return to the employer any part of the payment not so used.

(vi) The limitation of section 67(a) (relating to the two-percent floor on miscellaneous itemized deductions) is not considered when determining the amount of a working condition fringe. For example, assume that an employer provides a $1,000 cash advance to Employee A and that the conditions of paragraph (a)(1)(v) of this section are not satisfied. Even to the extent A uses the allowance for expenses for which a deduction is allowable under section 162 or 167, because such cash payment is not a working condition fringe, section 67(a) applies. The $1,000 payment is includible in A's gross income and subject to income and employment tax withholding. If, however, the conditions of paragraph (a)(1)(v) of this section are satisfied with respect to the payment, then the amount of A's working condition fringe is determined without regard to section 67(a). The $1,000 payment is excludible from A's gross income and not subject to income and employment tax reporting and withholding.

(2) Trade or business of the employee. (i) General. If the hypothetical payment for a property or service would be allowable as a deduction with respect to a trade or business of an employee other than the employee's trade or business of being an employee of the employer, it cannot be taken into account for purposes of determining the amount, if any, of the working condition fringe.

(ii) Examples. The rule of paragraph (a)(2)(i) of this section may be illustrated by the following examples:

Example (1). Assume that, unrelated to company X's trade or business and unrelated to employee A's trade or business of being an employee of company X, A is a member of the board of directors of company Y. Assume further that company X provides A with air transportation to a company Y board of director's meeting. A may not exclude from gross income the value of the air transportation to the meeting as a working condition fringe. A may, however, deduct such amount under section 162 if the section 162 requirements are satisfied. The result would be the same whether the air transportation was provided in the form of a flight on a commercial airline or a seat on a company X airplane.

Example (2). Assume the same facts as in example (1) except that A serves on the board of directors of company Z and company Z regularly purchases a significant amount of goods and services from company X. Because of the relationship between Company Z and A's employer, A's membership on Company Z's board of directors is related to A's trade or business of being an employee of Company X. Thus, A may exclude from gross income the value of air transportation to board meetings as a working condition fringe.

Example (3). Assume the same facts as in example (1) except that A serves on the board of directors of a charitable organization. Assume further that the service by A on the charity's board is substantially related to company X's trade or business. In this case, A may exclude from gross income the value of air transportation to board meetings as a working condition fringe.

Example (4). Assume the same facts as in example (3) except that company X also provides A with the use of a company X conference room which A uses for monthly meetings relating to the charitable organization. Also assume that A uses company X's copy machine and word processor each month in connection with functions of the charitable organization. Because of the substantial business benefit that company X derives from A's service on the board of the charity, A may exclude as a working condition fringe the value of the use of company X property in connection with the charitable organization.

(b) Vehicle allocation rules. *(1) In general.* (i) General rule. In general, with respect to an employer-provided vehicle, the amount excludable as a working condition fringe is the amount that would be allowable as a deduction under section 162 or 167 if the employee paid for the availability of the vehicle. For example, assume that the value of the availability of an employer-provided vehicle for a full year is $2,000, without regard to any working condition fringe (i.e., assuming all personal use). Assume further that the employee drives the vehicle 6,000 miles for his employer's business and 2,000 miles for reasons other than the employer's business. In this situation, the value of the working condition fringe is $2,000 multiplied by a fraction, the numerator of which is the business-use mileage (6,000 miles) and the denominator of which is the total mileage (8,000 miles). Thus, the value of the working condition fringe is $1,500. The total amount includible in the employee's gross income on account of the availability of the vehicle is $500 ($2,000 − $1,500). For purposes of this section, the term "vehicle" has the meaning given the term in § 1.61-21(e)(2). Generally, when determining the amount of an employee's working condition fringe, miles accumulated on the vehicle by all employees of the employer during the period in which the vehicle is available to the employee are considered. For example, assume that during the year in which the vehicle is available to the employee in the above example, other employees accumulate 2,000 additional miles on the vehicle (while the employee is not in the automobile). In this case, the value of the working condition fringe is $2,000 multiplied by a fraction, the numerator of which is the business-use mileage by the employee (including all mileage (business and personal) accumulated by other employees) (8,000 miles) and the denominator of which is the total mileage (including all mileage accumulated by other employees) (10,000 miles). Thus, the value of the working condition fringe is $1,600; the total amount includible in the employee's gross income on account of the availability of the vehicle is $400 ($2,000 − $1,600). If, however, substantially all of the use of the automobile by other employees in the employer's business is limited to a certain period, such as the last three months of the year, the miles driven by the other employees during that period would not be considered when determining the employee's working condition fringe exclusion. Similarly, miles driven by other employees are not considered if the pattern of use of the employer-provided automobiles is designed to reduce Federal taxes. For example, assume that an employer provides employees A and B each with the availability of an employer-provided automobile and that A uses the automobile assigned to him 80 percent for the employer's business and that B uses the automobile assigned to him 30 percent for the employer's business. If A and B alternate the use of their assigned automobiles each week in such a way as to achieve a reduction in federal taxes, then the employer may count only miles placed on the automobile by the employee to whom the automobile is assigned when determining each employee's working condition fringe.

(ii) Use by an individual other than the employee. For purposes of this section, if the availability of a vehicle to an individual would be taxed to an employee, use of the vehicle by the individual is included in references to use by the employee.

(iii) Provision of an expensive vehicle for personal use. If an employer provides an employee with a vehicle that an employee may use in part for personal purposes, there is no working condition fringe exclusion with respect to the personal miles driven by the employee; if the employee paid for the availability of the vehicle, he would not be entitled to deduct under section 162 or 167 any part of the payment attributable to personal miles. The amount of the inclusion is not affected by the fact that the employee would have chosen the availability of a less expensive vehicle. Moreover, the result is the same even though the decision to provide an expensive rather than an inexpensive vehicle is made by the employer for bona fide noncompensatory business reasons.

(iv) Total value inclusion. In lieu of excluding the value of a working condition fringe with respect to an automobile, an employer using the automobile lease valuation rule of § 1.61-21(d) may include in an employee's gross income the entire Annual Lease Value of the automobile. Any deduction allowable to the employee under section 162 or 167 with respect to the automobile may be taken on the employee's income tax return. The total inclusion rule of this paragraph (b)(1)(iv) is not available if the employer is valuing the use or availability of a vehicle under general valuation principles or a special valuation rule other than the automobile lease valuation rule. See §§ 1.162-25 and 1.162-25T for rules relating to the employee's deduction.

(v) Shared usage. In calculating the working condition fringe benefit exclusion with respect to a vehicle provided for use by more than one employee, an employer shall compute the working condition fringe in a manner consistent with the allocation of the value of the vehicle under section 1.61-21(c)(2)(ii)(B).

(2) Use of different employer-provided vehicles. The working condition fringe exclusion must be applied on a vehicle-by-vehicle basis. For example, assume that automobile Y is available to employee D for 3 days in January and for 5 days in March, and automobile Z is available to D for a week in July. Assume further that the Daily Lease Value, as defined in § 1.61-21(d)(4)(ii), of each automobile is $50. For the eight days of availability of Y in January and March, D uses Y 90 percent for business (by mileage). During July, D uses Z 60 percent for business (by mileage). The value of the working condition fringe is determined separately for each automobile. Therefore, the working condition fringe for Y is $360 ($400 × .90) leaving an income inclusion of $40. The working condition fringe for Z is $210 ($350 × .60), leaving an income inclusion of $140. If the value of the availability of an automobile is determined under the Annual Lease Value rule for one period and Daily Lease Value rule for a second period (see § 1.61-21(d)), the working condition fringe exclusion must be calculated separately for the two periods.

(3) Provision of a vehicle and chauffeur services. (i) General rule. In general, with respect to the value of chauffeur services provided by an employer, the amount excludable as a working condition fringe is the amount that would be allowable as a deduction under section 162 or 167 if the employee paid for the chauffeur services. The working condition fringe with respect to a chauffeur is determined separately from the working condition fringe with respect to the vehicle. An employee may exclude from gross income the excess of the value of the chauffeur services over the value of the chauffeur services for personal purposes (such as commuting) as determined under § 1.61-21(b)(5). See § 1.61-21(b)(5) for additional rules and examples concerning the valuation of chauffeur services. See § 1.132-5(m)(5) for rules relating to an exclusion from gross income for the value of bodyguard/chauffeur services. When determining whether miles placed on the vehicle are for the employer's business, miles placed on the vehicle by a chauffeur between the chauffeur's residence and the place at which the chauffeur picks up (or drops off) the employee are with respect to

the employee (but not the chauffeur) considered to be miles placed on the vehicle for the employer's business and thus eligible for the working condition fringe exclusion. Thus, because miles placed on the vehicle by a chauffeur between the chauffeur's residence and the place at which the chauffeur picks up (or drops off) the employee are not considered business miles with respect to the chauffeur, the value of the availability of the vehicle for commuting is includible in the gross income of the chauffeur. For general and special rules concerning the valuation of the use of employer-provided vehicles, see paragraphs (b) through (f) of § 1.61-21.

(ii) Examples. The rules of paragraph (b)(3)(i) of this section are illustrated by the following examples:

Example (1). Assume that an employer makes available to an employee an automobile and a chauffeur. Assume further that the value of the chauffeur services determined in accordance with § 1.61-21 is $30,000 and that the chauffeur spends 30 percent of each workday driving the employee for personal purposes. There may be excluded from the employee's income 70 percent of $30,000, or $21,000, leaving an income inclusion with respect to the chauffeur services of $9,000.

Example (2). Assume that the value of the availability of an employer-provided vehicle for a year is $4,850 and that the value of employer-provided chauffeur services with respect to the vehicle for the year is $20,000. Assume further that 40 percent of the miles placed on the vehicle are for the employer's business and that 60 percent are for other purposes. In addition, assume that the chauffeur spends 25 percent of each workday driving the employee for personal purposes (i.e., 2 hours). The value of the chauffeur services includible in the employee's income is 25 percent of $20,000, or $5,000. The excess of $20,000 over $5,000 or $15,000 is excluded from the employee's income as a working condition fringe. The amount excludable as a working condition fringe with respect to the vehicle is 40 percent of $4,850, or $1,940 and the amount includible is $4,850 – $1,940, or $2,910.

(c) Applicability of substantiation requirements of sections 162 and 274(d). *(1) In general.* The value of property or services provided to an employee may not be excluded from the employee's gross income as a working condition fringe, by either the employer or the employee, unless the applicable substantiation requirements of either section 274(d) or section 162 (whichever is applicable) and the regulations thereunder are satisfied. The substantiation requirements of section 274(d) apply to an employee even if the requirements of section 274 do not apply to the employee's employer for deduction purposes (such as when the employer is a tax-exempt organization or a governmental unit).

(2) Section 274(d) requirements. The substantiation requirements of section 274(d) are satisfied by "adequate records or sufficient evidence corroborating the [employee's] own statement". Therefore, such records or evidence provided by the employee, and relied upon by the employer to the extent permitted by the regulations promulgated under section 274(d), will be sufficient to substantiate a working condition fringe exclusion.

(d) Safe harbor substantiation rules. *(1) In general.* § 1.274-6T provides that the substantiation requirements of section 274(d) and the regulations thereunder may be satisfied, in certain circumstances, by using one or more of the safe harbor rules prescribed in § 1.274-6T. If the employer uses one of the safe harbor rules prescribed in § 1.274-6T during a period with respect to a vehicle (as defined in § 1.61-21(e)(2)), that rule must be used by the employer to substantiate a working condition fringe exclusion with respect to that vehicle during the period. An employer that is exempt from Federal income tax may still use one of the safe harbor rules (if the requirements of that section are otherwise met during a period) to substantiate a working condition fringe exclusion with respect to a vehicle during the period. If the employer uses one of the methods prescribed in § 1.274-6T during a period with respect to an employer-provided vehicle, that method may be used by an employee to substantiate a working condition fringe exclusion with respect to the same vehicle during the period, as long as the employee includes in gross income the amount allocated to the employee pursuant to § 1.274-6T and this section. (See § 1.61-21(c)(2) for other rules concerning when an employee must include in income the amount determined by the employer.) If, however, the employer uses the safe harbor rule prescribed in § 1.274-6T(a)(2) or (3) and the employee without the employer's knowledge uses the vehicle for purposes other than de minimis personal use (in the case of the rule prescribed in § 1.274-6T(a)(2)), or for purposes other than de minimis personal use and commuting (in the case of the rule prescribed in § 1.274-6T(a)(3)), then the employee must include an additional amount in income for the unauthorized use of the vehicle.

(2) Period for use of safe harbor rules. The rules prescribed in this paragraph (d) assume that the safe harbor rules prescribed in § 1.274-6T are used for a one-year period. Accordingly, references to the value of the availability of a vehicle, amounts excluded as a working condition fringe, etc., are based on a one-year period. If the safe harbor rules prescribed in § 1.274-6T are used for a period of less than a year, the amounts referred to in the previous sentence must be adjusted accordingly. For purposes of this section, the term "personal use" has the same meaning as prescribed in § 1.274-6T(e)(5).

(e) Safe harbor substantiation rule for vehicles not used for personal purposes. For a vehicle described in § 1.274-6T(a)(2) (relating to certain vehicles not used for personal purposes), the working condition fringe exclusion is equal to the value of the availability of the vehicle if the employer uses the method prescribed in § 1.274-6T(a)(2).

(f) Safe harbor substantiation rule for vehicles not available to employees for personal use other than commuting. For a vehicle described in § 1.274-6T(a)(3) (relating to certain vehicles not used for personal purposes other than commuting), the working condition fringe exclusion is equal to the value of the availability of the vehicle for purposes other than commuting if the employer uses the method prescribed in § 1.274-6T(a)(3). This rule applies only if the special rule for valuing commuting use, as prescribed in § 1.61-21(f), is used and the amount determined under the special rule is either included in the employee's income or reimbursed by the employee.

(g) Safe harbor substantiation rule for vehicles used in connection with the business of farming that are available to employees for personal use. *(1) In general.* For a vehicle described in § 1.274-6T(b) (relating to certain vehicles used in connection with the business of farming), the working condition fringe exclusion is calculated by multiplying the value of the availability of the vehicle by 75 percent.

(2) Vehicles available to more than one individual. If the vehicle is available to more than one individual, the employer must allocate the gross income inclusion attributable to the vehicle (25 percent of the value of the availability of the vehicle) among the employees (and other individuals whose use would not be attributed to an employee) to whom

the vehicle was available. This allocation must be done in a reasonable manner to reflect the personal use of the vehicle by the individuals. An amount that would be allocated to a sole proprietor reduces the amounts that may be allocated to employees but is otherwise to be disregarded for purposes of this paragraph (g). For purposes of this paragraph (g), the value of the availability of a vehicle may be calculated as if the vehicle were available to only one employee continuously and without regard to any working condition fringe exclusion.

(3) Examples. The following examples illustrate a reasonable allocation of gross income with respect to an employer-provided vehicle between two employees:

Example (1). Assume that two farm employees share the use of a vehicle that for a calendar year is regularly used directly in connection with the business of farming and qualifies for use of the rule in § 1.274-6T(b). Employee A uses the vehicle in the morning directly in connection with the business of farming and employee B uses the vehicle in the afternoon directly in connection with the business of farming. Assume further that employee B takes the vehicle home in the evenings and on weekends. The employer should allocate all the income attributable to the availability of the vehicle to employee B.

Example (2). Assume that for a calendar year, farm employees C and D share the use of a vehicle that is regularly used directly in connection with the business of farming and qualifies for use of the rule in § 1.274-6T(b). Assume further that the employees alternate taking the vehicle home in the evening and alternate the availability of the vehicle for personal purposes on weekends. The employer should allocate the income attributable to the availability of the vehicle for personal use (25 percent of the value of the availability of the vehicle) equally between the two employees.

Example (3). Assume the same facts as in example (2) except that C is the sole proprietor of the farm. Based on these facts, C should allocate the same amount of income to D as was allocated to D in example (2). No other income attributable to the availability of the vehicle for personal use should be allocated.

(h) Qualified nonpersonal use vehicles. *(1) In general.* Except as provided in paragraph (h)(2) of this section, 100 percent of the value of the use of a qualified nonpersonal use vehicle (as described in § 1.274-5T(k)) is excluded from gross income as a working condition fringe, provided that, in the case of a vehicle described in paragraph (k)(3) through (8) of that section, the use of the vehicle conforms to the requirements of that paragraph.

(2) Shared usage of qualified nonpersonal use vehicles. In general, a working condition fringe under paragraph (h) of this section is available to the driver and all passengers of a qualified nonpersonal use vehicle. However, a working condition fringe under this paragraph (h) is available only with respect to the driver and not with respect to any passengers of a qualified nonpersonal use vehicle described in § 1.274-5T(k)(2)(ii)(L) or (P). In this case, the passengers must comply with provisions of this section (excluding this paragraph (h)) to determine the applicability of the working condition fringe exclusion. For example, if an employer provides a passenger bus with a capacity of 25 passengers to its employees for purposes of transporting employees to and/or from work, the driver of the bus may exclude from gross income as a working condition fringe 100 percent of the value of the use of the vehicle. The value of the commuting use of the employer-provided bus by the employee-passengers is includible in their gross incomes. See § 1.61-21(f) for a special rule to value the commuting-only use of employer-provided vehicles.

(i) [Reserved]

(j) Application of section 280F. In determining the amount, if any, of an employee's working condition fringe, section 280F and the regulations thereunder do not apply. For example, assume that an employee has available for a calendar year an employer-provided automobile with a fair market value of $28,000. Assume further that the special rule provided in § 1.61-21(d) is used yielding an Annual Lease Value, as defined in § 1.61-21(d), of $7,750, and that all of the employee's use of the automobile is for the employer's business. The employee would be entitled to exclude as a working condition fringe the entire Annual Lease Value, despite the fact that if the employee paid for the availability of the automobile, an income inclusion would be required under § 1.280F-6(d)(1). This paragraph (j) does not affect the applicability of section 280F to the employer with respect to such employer-provided automobile, nor does it affect the applicability of section 274 to either the employer or the employee. For rules concerning substantiation of an employee's working condition fringe, see paragraph (c) of this section.

(k) Aircraft allocation rule. In general, with respect to a flight on an employer-provided aircraft, the amount excludable as a working condition fringe is the amount that would be allowable as a deduction under section 162 or 167 if the employee paid for the flight on the aircraft. For example, if employee P and P's spouse fly on P's employer's airplane primarily for business reasons of P's employer so that P could deduct the expenses relating to the trip to the extent of P's payments, the value of the flights is excludable from gross income as a working condition fringe. However, if P's children accompany P on the trip primarily for personal reasons, the value of the flights by P's children are includible in P's gross income. See § 1.61-21(g) for special rules for valuing personal flights on employer-provided aircraft.

(l) [Reserved]

(m) Employer-provided transportation for security concerns. *(1) In general.* The amount of a working condition fringe exclusion with respect to employer-provided transportation is the amount that would be allowable as a deduction under section 162 or 167 if the employee paid for the transportation. Generally, if an employee pays for transportation taken for primarily personal purposes, the employee may not deduct any part of the amount paid. Thus, the employee may not generally exclude the value of employer-provided transportation as a working condition fringe if such transportation is primarily personal. If, however, for bona fide business-oriented security concerns, the employee purchases transportation that provides him or her with additional security, the employee may generally deduct the excess of the amount actually paid for the transportation over the amount the employee would have paid for the same mode of transportation absent the bona fide business-oriented security concerns. This is the case whether or not the employee would have taken the same mode of transportation absent the bona fide business-oriented security concerns. With respect to a vehicle, the phrase "the same mode of transportation" means use of the same vehicle without the additional security aspects, such as bulletproof glass. With respect to air transportation, the phrase "the same mode of transportation" means comparable air transportation. These same rules apply to the determination of an employee's working condition fringe exclusion. For example, if an employer provides an employee with a vehicle for commuting and, because of bona fide business-oriented security concerns, the vehicle is specially designed for security, then the employee may exclude from gross income the value of the special security design as a working condition fringe. The employee may not exclude the value of the commuting from income as a working condition fringe because commuting is a nondeductible personal expense. However, if an independent security study meeting the requirements of paragraph (m)(2)(v) of this section has been performed with respect to a government employee, the government employee may exclude the value of the personal use (other than commuting) of the employer-provided vehicle that the security study determines to be reasonable and necessary for local transportation. Similarly, if an employee travels on a personal trip in an employer-provided aircraft for bona fide business-oriented security concerns, the employee may exclude the excess, if any, of the vale of the flight over the amount the employee would have paid for the same mode of transportation, but for the bona fide business-oriented security concerns. Because personal travel is a nondeductible expense, the employee may not exclude the total value of the trip as a working condition fringe.

(2) Demonstration of bona fide business-oriented security concerns. (i) In general. For purposes of this paragraph (m), a bona fide business-oriented security concern exists only if the facts and circumstances establish a specific basis for concern regarding the safety of the employee. A generalized concern for an employee's safety is not a bona fide business-oriented security concern. Once a bona fide business-oriented security concern is determined to exist with respect to a particular employee, the employer must periodically evaluate the situation for purposes of determining whether the bona fide business-oriented security concern still exists. Example of factors indicating a specific basis for concern regarding the safety of an employee are—

(A) A threat of death or kidnapping of, or serious bodily harm to, the employee or a similarly situated employee because of either employee's status as an employee of the employer; or

(B) A recent history of violent terrorist activity (such as bombings) in the geographic area in which the transportation is provided, unless that activity is focused on a group of individuals which does not include the employee (or a similarly situated employee of an employer), or occurs to a significant degree only in a location within the geographic area where the employee does not travel.

(ii) Establishment of overall security program. Notwithstanding anything in paragraph (m)(2)(i) of this section to the contrary, no bona fide business-oriented security concern will be deemed to exist unless the employee's employer establishes to the satisfaction of the Commissioner that an overall security program has been provided with respect to the employee involved. An overall security program is deemed to exist if the requirements of paragraph (m)(2)(iv) of this section are satisfied (relating to an independent security study).

(iii) Overall security program. (A) Defined. An overall security program is one in which security is provided to protect the employee on a 24-hour basis. The employee must be protected while at the employee's residence, while commuting to and from the employee's workplace, and while at the employee's workplace. In addition, the employee must be protected while traveling both at home and away from home, whether for business or personal purposes. An overall security program must include the provision of a bodyguard/chauffeur who is trained in evasive driving techniques; an automobile specially equipped for security; guards, metal detectors, alarms, or similar methods of controlling access to the employee's workplace and residence; and, in appropriate cases, flights on the employer's aircraft for business and personal reasons.

(B) Application. There is no overall security program when, for example, security is provided at the employee's workplace but not at the employee's residence. In addition, the fact that an employer requires an employee to travel on the employer's aircraft, or in an employer-provided vehicle that contains special security features, does not alone constitute an overall security program. The preceding sentence applies regardless of the existence of a corporate or other resolution requiring the employee to travel in the employer's aircraft or vehicle for personal as well as business reasons.

(iv) Effect of an independent security study. An overall security program with respect to an employee is deemed to exist if the conditions of this paragraph (m)(2)(iv) are satisfied:

(A) A security study is performed with respect to the employer and the employee (or a similarly situated employee of the employer) by an independent security consultant;

(B) The security study is based on an objective assessment of all facts and circumstances;

(C) The recommendation of the security study is that an overall security program (as defined in paragraph (m)(2)(iii) of this section) is not necessary and the recommendation is reasonable under the circumstances; and

(D) The employer applies the specific security recommendations contained in the security study to the employee on a consistent basis.

The value of transportation-related security provided pursuant to a security study that meets the requirements of this paragraph (m)(2)(iv) may be excluded from income if the security study conclusions are reasonable and, but for the bona fide business-oriented security concerns, the employee would not have had such security. No exclusion from income applies to security provided by the employer that is not recommended in the security study. Security study conclusions may be reasonable even if, for example, it is recommended that security be limited to certain geographic areas, as in the case in which air travel security is provided only in certain foreign countries.

(v) Independent security study with respect to government employees. For purposes of establishing the existence of an overall security program under paragraph (m)(2)(ii) of this section with respect to a particular government employee, a security study conducted by the government employer (including an agency or instrumentality thereof) will be treated as a security study pursuant to paragraph (m)(2)(iv) of this section if, in lieu of the conditions of paragraphs (m)(2)(iv)(A) through (D) of this section, the following conditions are satisfied:

(A) The security study is conducted by a person expressly designated by the government employer as having the responsibility and independent authority to determine both the need for employer-provided security and the appropriate protective services in response to that determination;

(B) The security study is conducted in accordance with written internal procedures that require an independent and objective assessment of the facts and circumstances, such as the nature of the threat to the employee, the appropriate security response to that threat, an estimate of the length of time protective services will be necessary, and the extent to which employer-provided transportation may be necessary during the period of protection;

(C) With respect to employer-provided transportation, the security study evaluates the extent to which personal use, including commuting, by the employee and the employee's spouse and dependents may be necessary during the period of protection and makes a recommendation as to what would be considered reasonable personal use during that period; and

(D) The employer applies the specific security recommendations contained in the study to the employee on a consistent basis.

(3) Application of security rules to spouses and dependents. (i) In general. If a bona fide business-oriented security concern exists with respect to an employee (because, for example, threats are made on the life of an employee), the bona fide business-oriented security concern is deemed to exist with respect to the employee's spouse and dependents to the extent provided in this paragraph (m)(3).

(ii) Certain transportation. If a working condition fringe exclusion is available under this paragraph (m) for transportation in a vehicle or aircraft provided for a bona fide business-oriented security concern with respect to an employee, the requirements of this paragraph (m) are deemed to be satisfied with respect to transportation in the same vehicle or aircraft provided at the same time to the employee's spouse and dependent children.

(iii) Other. Except as provided in paragraph (m)(3)(ii) of this section, a bona fide business oriented security concern is deemed to exist for the spouse and dependent children of the employer only if the requirements of paragraph (m)(2)(iii) or (iv) of this section are applied independently to such spouse and dependent children.

(iv) Spouses and dependents of government employees. The security rules of this paragraph (m)(3) apply to the spouse and dependents of a government employee. However, the value of local vehicle transportation provided to the government employee's spouse and dependents for personal purposes, other than commuting, during the period that a bona fide business-oriented security concern exists with respect to the government employee will not be included in the government employee's gross income if the personal use is determined to be reasonable and necessary by the security study described in paragraph (m)(2)(v) of this section.

(4) Working condition safe harbor for travel on employer-provided aircraft. Under the safe harbor rule of this paragraph (m)(4), if, for a bona fide business-oriented security concern, the employer requires that an employee travel on an employer-provided aircraft for a personal trip, the employer and the employee may exclude from the employee's gross income, as a working condition fringe, the excess value of the aircraft trip over the safe harbor airfare without having to show what method of transportation the employee would have flown but for the bona fide business-oriented security concern. For purposes of the safe harbor rule of this paragraph (m)(4), the value of the safe harbor airfare is determined under the non-commercial flight valuation rule of § 1.61-21(g) (regardless of whether the employer or employee elects to use such valuation rule) by multiplying an aircraft multiple of 200-percent by the applicable cents-per-mile rates and the number of miles in the flight and then adding the applicable terminal charge. The value of the safe harbor airfare determined under this paragraph (m)(4) must be included in the employee's income (to the extent not reimbursed by the employee) regardless of whether the employee or the employer uses the special valuation rule of § 1.61-21(g). The excess of the value of the aircraft trip over this amount may be excluded from gross income as a working condition fringe. If, for a bona fide business-oriented security concern, the employer requires that an employee's spouse and dependents travel on an employer-provided aircraft for a personal trip, the special rule of this paragraph (m)(4) is available to exclude the excess value of the aircraft trips over the safe harbor airfares.

(5) Bodyguard/chauffeur provided for a bona fide business-oriented security concern. If an employer provides an employee with vehicle transportation and a bodyguard/chauffeur for a bona fide business-oriented security concern, and but for the bona fide business-oriented security concern the employee would not have had a bodyguard or a chauffeur, then the entire value of the services of the bodyguard/chauffeur is excludable from gross income as a working condition fringe. For purposes of this section, a bodyguard/chauffeur must be trained in evasive driving techniques. An individual who performs services as a driver for an employee is not a bodyguard/chauffeur if the individual is not trained in evasive driving techniques. Thus, no part of the value of the services of such an individual is excludable from gross income under this paragraph (m)(5). (See paragraph (b)(3) of this section for rules relating to the determination of the working condition fringe exclusion for chauffeur services.)

(6) Special valuation rule for government employees. If transportation is provided to a government employee for commuting during the period that a bona fide business-oriented security concern under § 1.132-5(m) exists, the commuting use may be valued by reference to the values set forth in § 1.61-21(e)(1)(i) or (f)(3) (vehicle cents-per-mile or commuting valuation of $1.50 per one-way commute, respectively) without regard to the additional requirements contained in § 1.61-21(e) or (f) and is deemed to have met the requirements of § 1.61-21(c).

(7) Government employer and employee defined. For purposes of this paragraph (m), "government employer" includes any Federal, state, or local government unit, and any agency or instrumentality thereof. A "government employee" is any individual who is employed by the government employer.

(8) Examples. The provisions of this paragraph (m) may be illustrated by the following examples:

Example (1). Assume that in response to several death threats on the life of A, the president of X a multinational company, X establishes an overall security program for A, including an alarm system at A's home and guards at A's workplace, the use of a vehicle that is specially equipped with alarms, bulletproof glass, and armor plating, and a bodyguard/chauffeur. Assume further that A is driven for both personal and business reasons in the vehicle. Also, assume that but for the bona fide business-oriented security concerns, no part of the overall security program would have been provided to A. With respect to the transportation provided for security reasons, A may exclude as a working condition fringe the value of the special security features of the vehicle and the value attributable to the bodyguard/chauffeur. Thus, if the value of the specially equipped vehicle is $40,000, and the value of the vehicle without the security features is $25,000, A may determine A's inclusion in income attributable to the vehicle as if the vehicle were worth $25,000. A must include in income the value of the availability of the vehicle for personal use.

Example (2). Assume that B is the chief executive officer of Y, a multinational corporation. Assume further that there have been kidnapping attempts and other terrorist activities in the foreign countries in which B performs services and that at least some of such activities have been directed against B or similarly situated employees. In response to these activities, Y provides B with an overall security program, including an alarm system at B's home and bodyguards at B's workplace, a bodyguard/chauffeur, and a vehicle specially designed for security during B's overseas travels. In addition, assume that Y requires B to travel in Y's airplane for business and personal trips taken to, from, and within these foreign countries. Also, assume that but for bona fide business-oriented security concerns, no part of the overall security program would have been provided to B. B may exclude as a working condition fringe the value of the special security features of the automobile and the value attributable to the bodyguards and the bodyguard/chauffeur. B may also exclude the excess, if any, of the value of the flights over the amount A would have paid for the same mode of transportation but for the security concerns. As an alternative to the preceding sentence, B may use the working condition safe harbor described in paragraph (m)(4) of this section and exclude as a working condition fringe the excess, if any, of the value of personal flights in the Y airplane over the safe harbor airfare determined under the method described in paragraph (m)(4) of this section. If this alternative is used, B must include in income the value of the availability of the vehicle for personal use and the value of the safe harbor.

Example (3). Assume the same facts as in example (2) except that Y also requires B to travel in Y's airplane within the United States, and provides B with a chauffeur-driven limousine for business and personal travel in the United States. Assume further that Y also requires B's spouse and dependents to travel in Y's airplane for personal flights in the United States. If no bona fide business-oriented security concern exists with respect to travel in the United States, B may not exclude from income any portion of the value of the availability of the chauffeur or limousine for personal use in the United States. Thus, B must include in income the value of the availability of the vehicle and chauffeur for personal use. In addition, B may not exclude any portion of the value attributable to personal flights by B or B's spouse and dependents on Y's airplane. Thus, B must include in income the value attributable to the personal use of Y's airplane. See section 1.61-21 for rules relating to the valuation of an employer-provided vehicle and chauffeur, and personal flights on employer-provided airplanes.

Example (4). Assume that company Z retains an independent security consultant to perform a security study with respect to its chief executive officer. Assume further that, based on an objective assessment of the facts and circumstances, the security consultant reasonably recommends that 24-hour protection is not necessary but that the employee be provided security at his workplace and for ground transportation, but not for air transportation. If company Z follows the recommendations on a consistent basis, an overall security program will be deemed to exist with respect to the workplace and ground transportation security only.

Example (5). Assume the same facts as in example (4) except that company Z only provides the employee security while commuting to and from work, but not for any other ground transportation. Because the recommendations of the independent security study are not applied on a consistent basis, an overall security program will not be deemed to exist. Thus, the value of commuting to and from work is not excludable from income. However, the value of a bodyguard with professional security training who does not provide chauffeur or other personal services to the employee or any member of the employee's family may be excludable as a working condition fringe if such expense would be otherwise allowable as a deduction by the employee under section 162 or 167.

Example (6). J is a United States District Judge. At the beginning of a 3-month criminal trial in J's court, a member of J's family receives death threats. M, the division (within government agency W) responsible for evaluating threats and providing protective services to the Federal judiciary, directs its threat analysis unit to conduct a security study with respect to J and J's family. The study is conducted pursuant to internal written procedures that require an independent and objective assessment of any threats to members of the federal judiciary and their families, a statement of the requisite security response, if any, to a particular threat (including the form of transportation to be furnished to the employee as part of the security program), and a description of the circumstances under which local transportation for the employee and the employee's spouse and dependents may be necessary for personal reasons during the time protective services are provided. M's study concludes that a bona fide business-oriented security concern exists with respect to J and J's family and determines that 24-hour protection of J and J's family is not necessary, but that protection is necessary during the course of the criminal trial whenever J or J's family is away from home. Consistent with that recommendation, J is transported every day in a government vehicle for both personal and business reasons and is accompanied by two bodyguard/chauffeurs who have been trained in evasive driving techniques. In addition, J's spouse is driven to and from work and J's children are driven to and from school and occasional school activities. Shortly after the trial is concluded, M's threat analysis unit determines that J and J's family no longer need special protection because the danger posed by the threat no longer exists and, accordingly, vehicle transportation is no longer provided. Because the security study conducted by M complies with the conditions of § 1.132-5(m)(2)(v), M has satisfied the requirement for an independent security study and an overall security program with respect to J is deemed to exist. Thus, with respect to the transportation provided for security concerns, J may exclude as a working condition fringe the value of any special security features of the government vehicle and the value attributable to the two bodyguard/chauffeurs. See Example (1) of this paragraph (m)(8). The value of vehicle transportation provided to J and J's family for personal reasons, other than commuting, may also be excluded during the period of protection, because its provision was consistent with the recommendation of the security study.

Example (7). Assume the same facts as in Example (6) and that J's one-way commute between home and work is 10 miles. Under paragraph (m)(6) of this section, the Federal government may value transportation provided to J for commuting purposes pursuant to the value set forth in either the vehicle cents-per-mile rule of § 1.61-21(e) or the commuting valuation rule of § 1.61-21(f). Because the commuting valuation rule yields the least amount of taxable income to J under the circumstances, W values the transportation provided to J for commuting at $1.50 per one-way commute, even though J is a control employee within the meaning of § 1.61-21(f)(6).

(n) Product testing. *(1) In general.* The fair market value of the use of consumer goods, which are manufactured for sale to nonemployees, for product testing and evaluation by an employee of the manufacturer outside the employer's workplace, is excludible from gross income as a working condition fringe if—

(i) Consumer testing and evaluation of the product is an ordinary and necessary business expense of the employer;

(ii) Business reasons necessitate that the testing and evaluation of the product be performed off the employer's business premises by employees (i.e., the testing and evaluation cannot be carried out adequately in the employer's office or in laboratory testing facilities);

(iii) The product is furnished to the employee for purposes of testing and evaluation;

(iv) The product is made available to the employee for no longer than necessary to test and evaluate its performance and (to the extent not exhausted) must be returned to the employer at completion of the testing and evaluation period;

(v) The employer imposes limits on the employee's use of the product that significantly reduce the value of any personal benefit to the employee; and

(vi) The employee must submit detailed reports to the employer on the testing and evaluation.

The length of the testing and evaluation period must be reasonable in relation to the product being tested.

(2) Employer-imposed limits. The requirement of paragraph (n)(1)(v) of this section is satisfied if—

(i) The employer places limits on the employee's ability to select among different models or varieties of the consumer product that is furnished for testing and evaluation purposes; and

(ii) The employer generally prohibits use of the product by persons other than the employee and, in appropriate cases, requires the employee, to purchase or lease at the employee's own expense the same type of product as that being tested (so that personal use by the employee's family will be limited). In addition, any charge by the employer for the personal use by an employee of a product being tested shall be taken into account in determining whether the requirement of paragraph (n)(1)(v) of this section is satisfied.

(3) Discriminating classifications. If an employer furnishes products under a testing and evaluation program only, or presumably, to certain classes of employees (such as highly compensated employees, as defined in § 1.132-8(g)), this fact may be relevant when determining whether the products are furnished for testing and evaluation purposes or for compensation purposes, unless the employer can show a business reason for the classification of employees to whom the products are furnished (e.g., that automobiles are furnished for testing and evaluation by an automobile manufacturer to its design engineers and supervisory mechanics).

(4) Factors that negate the existence of a product testing program. If an employer fails to tabulate and examine the results of the detailed reports submitted by employees within a reasonable period of time after expiration of the testing period, the program will not be considered a product testing program for purposes of the exclusion of this paragraph (n). Existence of one or more of the following factors may also establish that the program is not a bona fide product testing program for purposes of the exclusion of this paragraph (n):

(i) The program is in essence a leasing program under which employees lease the consumer goods from the employer for a fee;

(ii) The nature of the product and other considerations are insufficient to justify the testing program; or

(iii) The expense of the program outweighs the benefits to be gained from testing and evaluation.

(5) Failure to meet the requirements of this paragraph (n). The fair market value of the use of property for product testing and evaluation by an employee outside the employee's workplace, under a product testing program that does not meet all of the requirements of this paragraph (n), is not excludable from gross income as a working condition fringe under this paragraph (n).

(6) Example. The rules of this paragraph (n) may be illustrated by the following example:

Example. Assume that an employer that manufactures automobiles establishes a product testing program under which 50 of its 5,000 employees test and evaluate the automobiles for 30 days. Assume further that the 50 employees represent a fair cross-section of all of the employees of the employer, such employees submit detailed reports to the employer on the testing and evaluation, the employer tabulates and examines the test results within a reasonable time, and the use of the automobiles is restricted to the employees. If the employer imposes the limits described in paragraph (n)(2) of this section, the employees may exclude the value of the use of the automobile during the testing and evaluation period.

(o) Qualified automobile demonstration use. *(1) In general.* The value of qualified automobile demonstration use is excludable from gross income as a working condition fringe. "Qualified automobile demonstration use" is any use of a demonstration automobile by a full-time automobile salesman in the sales area in which the automobile dealer's sales office is located if—

(i) Such use is provided primarily to facilitate the salesman's performance of services for the employer; and

(ii) There are substantial restrictions on the personal use of the automobile by the salesman.

(2) Full-time automobile salesman. (i) Defined. The term "full-time automobile salesman" means any individual who—

(A) Is employed by an automobile dealer;

(B) Customarily spends at least half of a normal business day performing the functions of a floor salesperson or sales manager;

(C) Directly engages in substantial promotion and negotiation of sales to customers;

(D) Customarily works a number of hours considered full-time in the industry (but at a rate not less than 1,000 hours per year); and

(E) Derives at least 25 percent of his or her gross income from the automobile dealership directly as a result of the activities described in paragraphs (o)(2)(i)(B) and (C) of this section.

For purposes of paragraph (o)(2)(i)(E) of this section, income is not considered to be derived directly as a result of activities described in paragraphs (o)(2)(i)(B) and (C) of this section to the extent that the income is attributable to an individual's ownership interest in the dealership. An individual will not be considered to engage in direct sales activities if the individual's sales-related activities are substantially limited to review of sales price offers from customers. An individual, such as the general manager of an automobile dealership, who receives a sales commission on the sale of an automobile is not a full-time automobile salesman unless the requirements of this paragraph (o)(2)(i) are met. The exclusion provided in this paragraph (o) is available to an individual who meets the definition of this paragraph (o)(2)(i) whether the individual performs services in addition to those described in this paragraph (o)(2)(i). For example, an individual who is an owner of the automobile dealership but who otherwise meets the requirements of this paragraph (o)(2)(i) may exclude from gross income the value of qualified automobile demonstration use. However, the exclusion of this paragraph (o) is not available to owners of large automobile dealerships who do not customarily engage in significant sales activities.

(ii) Use by an individual other than a full-time automobile salesman. Personal use of a demonstration automobile by an individual other than a full-time automobile salesman is not treated as a working condition fringe. Therefore, any personal use, including commuting use, of a demonstration automobile by a part-time salesman, automobile mechanic, or other individual who is not a full-time automobile salesman is not "qualified automobile demonstration use" and thus not excludable from gross income. This is the case whether or not the personal use is within the sales area (as defined in paragraph (o)(5) of this section).

(3) Demonstration automobile. The exclusion provided in this paragraph (o) applies only to qualified use of a demonstration automobile. A demonstration automobile is an automobile that is—

(i) Currently in the inventory of the automobile dealership; and

(ii) Available for test drives by customers during the normal business hours of the employee.

(4) Substantial restrictions on personal use. Substantial restrictions on the personal use of a demonstration automobile exist when all of the following conditions are satisfied:

(i) Use by individuals other than the full-time automobile salesmen (e.g., the salesman's family) is prohibited;

(ii) Use for personal vacation trips is prohibited;

(iii) The storage of personal possessions in the automobile is prohibited; and

(iv) The total use by mileage of the automobile by the salesman outside the salesman's normal working hours is limited.

(5) Sales area. (i) In general. Qualified automobile demonstration use consists of use in the sales area in which the automobile dealer's sales office is located. The sales area is the geographic area surrounding the automobile dealer's sales office from which the office regularly derives customers.

(ii) Sales area safe harbor. With respect to a particular full-time salesman, the automobile dealer's sales area may be treated as the area within a radius of the larger of—

(A) 75 miles or

(B) The one-way commuting distance (in miles) of the particular salesman from the dealer's sales office.

(6) Applicability of substantiation requirements of sections 162 and 274(d). Notwithstanding anything in this section to the contrary, the value of the use of a demonstration automobile may not be excluded from gross income as a working condition fringe, by either the employer or the employee, unless, with respect to the restrictions of paragraph (o)(4) of this section, the substantiation requirements of section 274(d) and the regulations thereunder are satisfied. See section 1.132-5(c) for general and safe harbor rules relating to the applicability of the substantiation requirements of section 274(d).

(7) Special valuation rules. See § 1.61-21(d)(6)(ii) for special rules that may be used to value the availability of demonstration automobiles.

(p) Parking. *(1) In general.* The value of parking provided to an employee on or near the business premises of the employer is excludable from gross income as a working condition fringe under the special rule of this paragraph (p). If the rules of this paragraph (p) are satisfied, the value of parking is excludable from gross income whether the amount paid by the employee for parking would be deductible under section 162. The working condition fringe exclusion applies whether the employer owns or rents the parking facility or parking space.

(2) Reimbursement of parking expenses. A reimbursement to the employee of the ordinary and necessary expenses of renting a parking space on or near the business premises of the employer is excludable from gross income as a working condition fringe, if, but for the parking expense, the employee would not have been entitled to receive and retain such amount from the employer. If, however an employee is entitled to retain a general transportation allowance or a similar benefit whether or not the employee has parking expenses, no portion of that allowance is excludable from gross income under this paragraph (p) even if it is used for parking expenses.

(3) Parking on residential property. With respect to an employee, this paragraph (p) does not apply to any parking facility or space located on property owned or leased by the employee for residential purposes.

(4) Dates of applicability. This paragraph (p) applies to benefits provided before January 1, 1993. For benefits provided after December 31, 1992, see § 1.132-9.

(q) Nonapplicability of nondiscrimination rules. Except to the extent provided in paragraph (n)(3) of this section (relating to discriminating classifications of a product testing program), the nondiscrimination rules of section 132(h)(1) and § 1.132-8 do not apply in determining the amount, if any, of a working condition fringe.

(r) Volunteers. *(1) In general.* Solely for purposes of section 132(d) and paragraph (a)(1) of this section, a bona fide volunteer (including a director or officer) who performs services for an organization exempt from tax under section 501(a), or for a government employer (as defined in paragraph (m)(7) of this section), is deemed to have a profit motive under section 162.

(2) Limit on application of this paragraph. This paragraph (r) shall not be used to support treatment of the bona fide volunteer as having a profit motive for purposes of any provision of the Internal Revenue Code of 1986 (Code) other than section 132(d). Nothing in this paragraph (r) shall be interpreted as determining the employment status of a bona fide volunteer for purposes of any section of the Code other than section 132(d).

(3) Definitions. (i) Bona fide volunteer. For purposes of this paragraph (r), an individual is considered a "bona fide volunteer" if the individual does not have a profit motive for purposes of section 162. For example, an individual is considered a "bona fide volunteer" if the total value of the benefits provided with respect to the volunteer services is substantially less than the total value of the volunteer services the individual provides to an exempt organization or government employer.

(ii) Liability insurance coverage for a bona fide volunteer. For purposes of this paragraph (r), the receipt of liability insurance coverage by a volunteer, or an exempt organization or government employer's undertaking to indemnify the volunteer for liability, does not by itself confer a profit motive on the volunteer, provided the insurance coverage or indemnification relates to acts performed by the volunteer in the discharge of duties, or the performance of services, on behalf of the exempt organization or government employer.

(4) Example. The following example illustrates the provisions of paragraph (r) of this section.

Example. A is a manager and full-time employee of P, a tax-exempt organization described in section 501(c)(3). B is a member of P's board of directors. Other than $25 to defray expenses for attending board meetings, B receives no compensation for serving as a director and does not have a profit motive. Therefore, B is a bona fide volunteer by application of paragraph (r)(3)(i) of this section and is deemed to have a profit motive under paragraph (r)(1) of this section for purposes of section 132(d). In order to provide liability insurance coverage, P purchases a policy that covers actions arising from A's and B's activities performed as part of their duties to P. The value of the policy and payments made to or on behalf of A under the policy are excludable from A's gross income as a working condition fringe, because A has a profit motive under section 162 and would be able to deduct payments for liability insurance coverage had he paid for it himself. The receipt of liability insurance coverage by B does not confer a profit motive on B by application of paragraph (r)(3)(ii) of this section. Thus, the value of the policy and payments made to or on behalf of B under the policy are excludable from B's income as a working condition fringe. For the year in which the liability insurance coverage is provided to A and B, P may exclude the value of the benefit on the Form W-2 it issues to A or on any Form 1099 it might otherwise issue to B.

(s) Application of section 274(a)(3). *(1) In general.* If an employer's deduction under section 162(a) for dues paid or incurred for membership in any club organized for business, pleasure, recreation, or other social purpose is disallowed by section 274(a)(3), the amount, if any, of an employee's working condition fringe benefit relating to an employer-provided membership in the club is determined without regard to the application of section 274(a) to the employee. To be excludible as a working condition fringe benefit, however, the amount must otherwise qualify for deduction by the employee under section 162(a). If an employer treats the amount paid or incurred for membership in any club organized for business, pleasure, recreation, or other social purpose as compensation under section 274(e)(2), then the expense is deductible by the employer as compensation and no amount may be excluded from the employee's gross income as a working condition fringe benefit. See § 1.274-2(f)(2)(iii)(A).

(2) Treatment of tax-exempt employers. In the case of an employer exempt from taxation under subtitle A of the Internal Revenue Code, any reference in this paragraph (s) to a deduction disallowed by section 274(a)(3) shall be treated as a reference to the amount which would be disallowed as a deduction by section 274(a)(3) to the employer if the employer were not exempt from taxation under subtitle A of the Internal Revenue Code.

(3) Examples. The following examples illustrate this paragraph (s):

Example (1). Assume that Company X provides Employee B with a country club membership for which it paid $20,000. B substantiates, within the meaning of paragraph (c) of this section, that the club was used 40 percent for business purposes. The business use of the club (40 percent) may be considered a working condition fringe benefit, notwithstanding that the employer's deduction for the dues allocable to the business use is disallowed by section 274(a)(3), if X does not treat the club membership as compensation under section 274(e)(2). Thus, B may exclude from gross income $8,000 (40 percent of the club dues, which reflects B's business use). X must report $12,000 as wages subject to withholding and payment of employment taxes (60 percent of the value of the club dues, which reflects B's personal use). B must include $12,000 in gross income. X may deduct as compensation the amount it paid for the club dues which reflects B's personal use provided the amount satisfies the other requirements for a salary or compensation deduction under section 162.

Example (2). Assume the same facts as Example 1 except that Company X treats the $20,000 as compensation to B under section 274(e)(2). No portion of the $20,000 will be considered a working condition fringe benefit because the section 274(a)(3) disallowance will apply to B. Therefore, B must include $20,000 in gross income.

(t) Application of section 274(m)(3). *(1) In general.* If an employer's deduction under section 162(a) for amounts paid or incurred for the travel expenses of a spouse, dependent, or other individual accompanying an employee is disallowed by section 274(m)(3), the amount, if any, of the employee's working condition fringe benefit relating to the employer-provided travel is determined without regard to the application of section 274(m)(3). To be excludible as a working condition fringe benefit, however, the amount must otherwise qualify for deduction by the employee under section 162(a). The amount will qualify for deduction and for exclusion as a working condition fringe benefit if it can be adequately shown that the spouse's, dependent's, or other accompanying individual's presence on the employee's business trip has a bona fide business purpose and if the employee substantiates the travel within the meaning of paragraph (c) of this section. If the travel does not qualify as a working condition fringe benefit, the employee must include in gross income as a fringe benefit the value of the employer's payment of travel expenses with respect to a spouse, dependent, or other individual accompanying the employee on business travel. See §§ 1.61-21(a)(4) and 1.162-2(c). If an employer treats as compensation under section 274(e)(2) the amount paid or incurred for the travel expenses of a spouse, dependent, or other individual accompanying an employee, then the expense is deductible by the employer as compensation and no amount may be excluded from the employee's gross income as a working condition fringe benefit. See § 1.274-2(f)(2)(iii)(A).

(2) Treatment of tax-exempt employers. In the case of an employer exempt from taxation under subtitle A of the Internal Revenue Code, any reference in this paragraph (t) to a deduction disallowed by section 274(m)(3) shall be treated as a reference to the amount which would be disallowed as a deduction by section 274(m)(3) to the employer if the employer were not exempt from taxation under subtitle A of the Internal Revenue Code.

T.D. 8256, 7/6/89, amend T.D. 8451, 12/4/92 T.D. 8457, 12/29/92, T.D. 8666, 5/29/96, T.D. 8933, 1/10/2001.

PAR. 2. Section 1.132-5 paragraph (h) is revised to read as follows:

Proposed § 1.132-5 Working condition fringes. [*For Preamble, see ¶ 153,001*]

* * * * *

(h) Qualified nonpersonal use vehicles. *(1) In general.* Except as provided in paragraph (h)(2) of this section, 100 percent of the value of the use of a qualified nonpersonal use vehicle (as described in § 1.274-5(k)) is excluded from gross income as a working condition fringe, provided that, in the case of a vehicle described in § 1.274-5(k)(3) through (8), the use of the vehicle conforms to the requirements of that paragraph.

(2) Shared usage of qualified nonpersonal use vehicles. In general, a working condition fringe under this paragraph (h) is available to the driver and all passengers of a qualified nonpersonal use vehicle. However, a working condition fringe under this paragraph (h) is available only with respect to the driver and not with respect to any passengers of a qualified nonpersonal use vehicle described in § 1.274-5(k)(2)(ii)(L) or (P).

* * * * *

§ 1.132-5T Working condition fringe—1985 through 1988 (Temporary).

(a) In general. *(1) Definition.* Gross income does not include the value of a working condition fringe. The term "working condition fringe" means any property or service provided to an employee of an employer to the extent that, if the employee paid for the property or service, the amount paid would be allowable as a deduction under section 162 or 167. If, under section 274 or any other section, certain substantiation requirements must be met in order for a deduction under section 162 or 167 to be allowable, those substantiation requirements apply to the determination of a working condition fringe. An amount that would be deductible by the employee under, for example, section 212 is not a working condition fringe.

(2) Trade or business of the employee. If the hypothetical payment for the property or service would be allowable as a deduction with respect to a trade or business of the employee other than the employee's trade or business of being an employee of the employer, it cannot be taken into account for purposes of determining the amount, if any, of the working condition fringe. For example, assume that, unrelated to company X's trade or business and unrelated to company X's employee's trade or business of being an employee of company X, the employee is a member of the board of directors of company Y. Assume further that company X provides the employee with air transportation to a company Y board of director's meeting. The employee may not exclude the value of the air transportation to the meeting as a working condition fringe. The employee may, however, deduct such amount under section 162 if the section 162 requirements are satisfied. The result would be the same whether the air transportation was provided in the form of a flight on a commercial airline or a seat on a company X airplane.

(b) Vehicle allocation rules. *(1) In general.* (i) General rule. In general, with respect to an employer-provided vehicle, the amount excludable as a working condition fringe is the amount that would be allowable as a deduction under section 162 or 167 if the employee paid for the availability of the vehicle. For example, assume that the value of the availability of an employer-provided vehicle for a full year is $2,000, without regard to any working condition fringe (i.e., assuming all personal use). Assume further that the employee drives the vehicle 6,000 miles for his employer's business and 2,000 miles for reasons other than the employer's business. In this situation, the value of the working condition fringe is $2,000 multiplied by a fraction, the numerator of which is the business-use mileage (6,000 miles) and the denominator of which is the total mileage (8,000 miles). Thus, the value of the working condition fringe is $1,500. The total amount includible in the employee's gross income on account of the availability of the vehicle is $500. For purposes of this section, the term "vehicle" has the same meaning given the term in § 1.61-2T(e)(2). Generally, when determining the amount of an employee's working condition fringe, miles accumulated on the vehicle by all employees of the employer during the period in which the vehicle is available to the employee must be considered. For example, assume that an employee of the employer is provided the availability of an automobile for one year. Assume further that during the year, the automobile is regularly used in the employer's business by other employees. All miles accumulated on the automobile by all employees of the employer during the year must be considered. If, however, substantially all the use of the automobile by other employees in the employer's business is permitted during a certain period, such as the last three months of the year, the miles driven by the other employees during that period would not be considered when determining the employee's working condition fringe exclusion.

(ii) Use by an individual other than the employee. For purposes of this section, if the availability of a vehicle to an individual would be taxed to an employee, use of the vehicle by the individual is included in references to use by the employee.

(iii) Provision of an expensive vehicle for personal use. Assume an employer provides an employee with an expensive vehicle that an employee may use in part for personal purposes. Even though the decision to provide an expensive rather than an inexpensive vehicle is made by the employer for bona fide noncompensatory business reasons, there is no working condition fringe exclusion with respect to the personal miles driven by the employee. If the employee paid for the availability of the vehicle, he would not be entitled to deduct any part of the payment attributable to personal miles.

(2) Use of different employer-provided automobiles. The working condition fringe exclusion must be applied on an automobile by automobile basis. For example, assume that automobile Y is available to employee D for 3 days in January and for 5 days in March, and automobile Z is available to D for a week in July. Assume further that the Daily Lease Value, as defined in § 1.61-2T, of each automobile is $50. For the eight days of availability of Y in January and March, D uses Y 90 percent for business (by mileage). During July, D uses Z 60 percent for business (by mileage). The value of the working condition fringe is determined separately for each automobile. Therefore, the working condition fringe for Y is $360 ($400 × .90) leaving an income inclusion of $40. The working condition fringe for Z is $210 ($350 × .60) leaving an income inclusion of $140. If the value of the availability of an automobile is determined under the Annual Lease Value rule for one period and Daily Lease Value rule for a second period (see § 1.61-2T), the working condition fringe exclusion must be calculated separately for the two periods.

(c) Applicability of sections 162 and 274(d). *(1) In general.* The value of property or services provided to an employee may not be excluded from the employee's gross income as a working condition fringe, by either the employer or the employee, unless the applicable substantiation requirements of either section 274(d) or section 162 (whichever is applicable) and the regulations thereunder are satisfied. With respect to listed property, the substantiation requirements of section 274(d) and the regulations thereunder do not apply to the determination of an employee's working condition fringe exclusion prior to the date that those requirements apply to the first taxable year of the employer beginning after December 31, 1985. For example, if an employer's first taxable year beginning after December 31, 1985, begins on July 1, 1986, with respect to listed property, the substantiation requirements of section 274(d) apply as of that date. The substantiation requirements of section 274(d) apply to an employee even if the requirements of section 274 do not apply to the employee's employer for deduction purposes (such as when the employer is a tax-exempt organization or a governmental unit); in these cases, the requirements of section 274 (d) apply to the employee as of January 1, 1986.

(2) Section 274(d) requirements. The substantiation requirements of section 274(d) are satisfied by "adequate records or sufficient evidence corroborating the [employee's] own statement". Therefore, such records or evidence provided by the employee, and relied upon by the employer to the extent permitted by the regulations promulgated under section 274 (d), will be sufficient to substantiate a working condition fringe exclusion.

(d) Safe harbor rules. *(1) In general.* Section 1.274-6T provides that the substantiation requirements of section 274(d) and the regulations thereunder may be satisfied, in certain circumstances, by using one or more of the safe harbor rules prescribed in § 1.274-6T. If the employer uses one of the safe harbor rules prescribed in § 1.274-6T during a period with respect to a vehicle (as defined in § 1.61-2T), that rule must be used by the employer to substantiate a working condition fringe exclusion with respect to that vehicle during the period. An employer that is exempt from Federal income tax may still use one of the safe harbor rules (if the requirements of that section are otherwise met during a period) to substantiate a working condition fringe exclusion with respect to a vehicle during the period. If the employer uses one of the methods prescribed in § 1.274-6T during a period with respect to an employer-provided vehicle, that method may be used by an employee to substantiate a working condition fringe exclusion with respect to the same vehicle during the period, as long as the employee includes in gross income the amount allocated to the employee pursuant to § 1.274-6T and this section. (See § 1.61-2T(c)(2)(i) for other rules concerning when an employee must include in income the amount determined by the employer.) If, however, the employer uses the safe harbor rule prescribed in § 1.274-6T(a)(2) or (3) and the employee without the employer's knowledge uses the vehicle for purposes other than de minimis personal use (in the case of the rule prescribed in § 1.274-6T(a)(2)), or for purposes other than de minimis personal use and commuting (in the case of the rule prescribed in § 1.274-6T(a)(3)), then the employee must include additional income for the unauthorized use of the vehicle.

(2) Period for use of safe harbor rules. The rules prescribed in this paragraph (d) assume that the safe harbor rules prescribed in § 1.274-6T are used for a one-year period. Accordingly, references to the value of the availability of a vehicle, amounts excluded as a working condition fringe, etc., are based on a one-year period. If the safe harbor rules prescribed in § 1.274-6T are used for a period of less than a year, the amounts referenced in the previous sentence must be adjusted accordingly. For purposes of this section, the term "personal use" has the same meaning as prescribed in § 1.274-6T(e)(5).

(e) Vehicles not available to employees for personal use. For a vehicle described in § 1.274-6T(a)(2) (relating to certain vehicles not used for personal purposes), the working condition fringe exclusion is equal to the value of the availability of the vehicle if the employer uses the method prescribed in § 1.274-6T(a)(2).

(f) Vehicles not available to employees for personal use other than commuting. For a vehicle described in § 1.274-6T(a)(3) (relating to certain vehicles not used for personal purposes other than commuting), the working condition fringe exclusion is equal to the value of the availability of the vehicle for purposes other than commuting if the employer uses the method prescribed in § 1.274-6T (a) (3). This rule applies only if the special rule for valuing commuting use, as prescribed in § 1.61-2T, is used and the amount determined under the special rule is either included in the employee's income or reimbursed by the employee.

(g) Vehicles used in connection with the business of farming that are available to employees for personal use. *(1) In general.* For a vehicle described in § 1.274-6T(b) (relating to certain vehicles used in connection with the business of farming), the working condition fringe exclusion is calculated by multiplying the value of the availability of the vehicle by 75 percent.

(2) Vehicles available to more than one individual. If the vehicle is available to more than one individual, the employer must allocate the gross income attributable to the vehicle (25 percent of the value of the availability of the vehicle) among the employees (and other individuals whose use would not be attributed to an employee) to whom the vehicle was available. This allocation must be done in a reasonable manner to reflect the personal use of the vehicle by the individuals. An amount that would be allocated to a sole proprietor reduces the amounts that may be allocated to employees but are otherwise to be disregarded for purposes of this paragraph (g). For purposes of this paragraph (g), the value of the availability of a vehicle may be calculated as if the vehicle were available to only one employee continuously and without regard to any working condition fringe exclusion.

(3) Examples. The following examples illustrate a reasonable allocation of gross income with respect to an employer-provided vehicle between two employees:

Example (1). Assume that two farm employees share the use of a vehicle which for a calendar year is regularly used directly in connection with the business of farming and qualifies for use of the rule in § 1.274-6T(b). Employee A uses the vehicle in the morning directly in connection with the business of farming and employee B uses the vehicle in the afternoon directly in connection with the business of farming. Assume further that employee B takes the vehicle home in the evenings and on weekends. The employer should allocate all the income attributable to the availability of the vehicle to employee B.

Example (2). Assume that for a calendar year, farm employees C and D share the use of a vehicle that is regularly used directly in connection with the business of farming and qualifies for use of the rule in § 1.274-6T(b). Assume further that the employees alternate taking the vehicle home in the evening and alternate the availability of the vehicle for personal purposes on weekends. The employer should allocate the income attributable to the availability of the vehicle for personal use (25 percent of the value of the availability of the vehicle) equally between the two employees.

Example (3). Assume the same facts as in example (2) except that C is the sole proprietor of the farm. Based on these facts, C should allocate the same amount of income to D as was allocated to D in example (2). No other income attributable to the availability of the vehicle for personal use should be allocated.

(h) Qualified non-personal use vehicles. Effective January 1, 1985, 100 percent of the value of the use of a qualified nonpersonal use vehicle (as described in § 1.274-5T(k)) is excluded from gross income as a working condition fringe, provided that, in the case of a vehicle described in paragraph (k) (3) through (7) of that section, the use of the vehicles conforms to the requirements of that paragraph.

(i) [Reserved]

(j) Application of section 280F. In determining the amount, if any, of an employee's working condition fringe, section 280F and the regulations thereunder do not apply. For example, assume that an employee has available for a calendar year an employer-provided automobile with a fair market value of $28,000. Assume further that the special rule provided in § 1.61-2T is used and that the Annual Lease Value, as defined in § 1.61-2T, is $7,750, and that all of the employee's use of the automobile is in the employer's business. The employee would be entitled to exclude the entire Annual Lease Value as a working condition fringe, despite the fact that if the employee paid for the availability of the automobile, an income inclusion would be required under § 1.280F-5T(d)(1). This paragraph (j) does not affect the applicability of section 280F to the employer with respect to such employer-provided automobile, nor does it affect the applicability of section 274. For rules concerning substantiation of an employee's working condition fringe, see paragraph (c) of this section.

(k) Aircraft allocation rule. In general, with respect to a flight on an employer-provided aircraft, the amount excludable as a working condition fringe is the amount that would be allowable as a deduction under section 162 or 167 if the employee paid for the flight on the aircraft. For example, if employee P flies on P's employer's airplane primarily for business reasons of P's employer, the value of P's flight is excludable as a working condition fringe. However, if P's spouse and children accompany P on such airplane trip primarily for personal reasons, the value of the flights by P's spouse and children are includible in P's gross income. See § 1.61-2T(g) for special rules for valuing personal flights.

(l) [Reserved]

(m) Employer-provided transportation for security concerns. *(1) In general.* The amount of a working condition fringe exclusion with respect to employer-provided transportation is the amount that would be allowable as a deduction under section 162 or 167 if the employee paid for the transportation. Generally, if an employee pays for transportation taken for primarily personal purposes, the employee may not deduct any part of the amount paid. Thus, the employee may not generally exclude the value of employer-provided transportation as a working condition fringe if such transportation is primarily personal. If, however, for bona fide business-oriented security concerns, the employee purchases transportation that provides him or her with additional security, the employee may generally deduct the excess of the amount paid for the transportation over the lesser amount the employee would have paid for the same mode of transportation absent the bona fide business-oriented security concerns. With respect to a vehicle, the phrase "the same mode of transportation" means use of the same vehicle without the additional security aspects, such as bulletproof glass. With respect to air transportation, the phrase "the same mode of transportation" means comparable air transportation. These same rules apply to the determination of an employee's working condition fringe exclusion. For example, if an employer provides an employee with an automobile for commuting and, for bona fide business-oriented security concerns, the automobile is specially designed for security, then the employee may exclude the value of the special security design as a working condition fringe if the employee's automobile would not have had such security design but for the bona fide business-oriented security concerns. The employee may not exclude the value of the commuting from income as a working condition fringe because commuting is a nondeductible personal expense. Similarly, if an employee travels on a personal trip in an employer-provided aircraft for bona fide business-oriented security concerns, the employee may exclude the excess, if any, of the value of the flight over the amount the employee would have paid for comparable air transportation, but for the bona fide business-oriented security concerns. Because personal travel is a nondeductible expense, the employee may not exclude the total value of the trip as a working condition fringe.

(2) Demonstration of bona fide business-oriented security concerns. (i) In general. For purposes of this paragraph (m), the existence of a bona fide business-oriented security concern for the furnishing of a specific form of transportation to an employee is determined on the basis of all the facts and circumstances within the following guidelines:

(A) Services performed outside the United States. With respect to an employee performing services for an employer in a geographic area other than the United States, a factor indicating a bona fide business-oriented security concern is a recent history of violent terrorist activity in such geographic area (such as bombings or abductions for ransom), unless such activity is focused on a group of individuals which does not include the employee or a similarly situated employee or on a section of the geographic area which does not include the employee.

(B) Services performed in the United States. With respect to an employee performing services for an employer in the United States, a factor indicating a bona fide business-oriented security concern is threats on the life of the employee or on the life of a similarly situated employee because of the employee's status as an employee of the employer.

(ii) Establishment of overall security program. Notwithstanding anything in paragraph (m)(2)(i) of this section to the contrary, no bona fide business-oriented security concern will be deemed to exist unless the employee's employer establishes an overall security program with respect to the employee involved.

(iii) Overall security program. (A) Definition. An overall security program is one in which security is provided to protect the employee on a 24-hour basis. The employee must be protected while at the employee's residence, while commuting to and from the employee's workplace, and while at the employee's workplace. In addition, the employee must be protected while traveling, whether for business or personal purposes. An overall security program would include the provision of a bodyguard/driver who is trained in evasive driving techniques; an automobile specially equipped for security; guards, metal detectors, alarms, or similar methods of controlling access to the employee's workplace and residence; and, in appropriate cases, flights on the employer's aircraft for business and personal reasons.

(B) Application. There is no overall security program when, for example, security is provided at the employee's workplace but not at the employee's residence. In addition, the fact that an employer requires an employee to travel on the employer's aircraft, or in an employer-provided vehicle that contains special security features, does not alone constitute an overall security program. The preceding sentence applies regardless of the existence of a corporate or other resolution requiring the employee to travel in the employer's airplane or vehicle for personal as well as business reasons. Similarly, the existence of an independent security study particular to the employer and its employees, or to the employee involved, does not alone constitute an overall security program.

(iv) Effect of an independent security study. An overall security program with respect to an employee is deemed to exist even though security is not provided to an employee on a 24-hour basis if the conditions of this paragraph (m)(2)(iv) are satisfied:

(A) A security study is performed with respect to the employer and the employee (or a similarly situated employee) by an independent security consultant;

(B) The security study is based on an objective assessment of all the facts and circumstances;

(C) The recommendation of the security study is that an overall security program (as defined in paragraph (m)(2)(iii) of this section) is not necessary and such recommendation is reasonable under the circumstances; and

(D) The employer applies the specific security recommendations contained in the security study to the employee on a consistent basis.

The value of the security provided pursuant to a security study that meets the requirements of this paragraph (m)(2)(iv) may be excluded from income, if the security study conclusions are reasonable and, but for the bona fide business-oriented security concerns, the employee would not have had such security. No exclusion from income applies to security provided by the employer that is not recommended in the security study. Security study conclusions may be reasonable even if, for example, it is recommended that security be limited to certain geographic areas, as in the case where air travel security is provided only in certain foreign countries.

(v) Application of security rules to spouses and dependents. The availability of a working condition fringe exclusion based on the existence of a bona fide business-oriented security concern with respect to the spouse and dependents of an employee is determined separately for such spouse and dependents under the rules established in this paragraph (m).

(vi) Working condition safe harbor. Under the special rule of this paragraph (m)(2)(vi), if, for a bona fide business-oriented security concern, the employer requires that the employee travel on an employer-provided aircraft for a personal trip, the employer and the employee may exclude, as a working condition fringe, the excess value of the trip over comparable first-class airfare without having to show that but for the bona fide business-oriented security concerns, the employee would have flown first-class on a commercial aircraft. If the special valuation rule provided in § 1.61-2T is used, the excess over the amount determined by multiplying an aircraft multiple of 200-percent by the base aircraft valuation formula may be excluded as a working condition fringe.

(3) Examples. The provisions of this paragraph (m) may be illustrated by the following examples:

Example (1). Assume that in response to several death threats on the life of A, the president of a multinational company (company X), company X establishes an overall security program for A, including an alarm system at A's home and guards at A's workplace, the use of a vehicle that is specially equipped with alarms, bulletproof glass, and armor plating and a bodyguard/driver who is trained in evasive driving techniques. Assume further that A is driven for both personal and business reasons in the vehicle. Also, assume that but for the bona fide business-oriented security concerns, no part of the overall security program would have been provided to A. With respect to the transportation provided for security reasons, A may exclude as a working condition fringe the value of the special security features of the vehicle and the value attributable to the bodyguard/driver. Thus, if the value of the specially equipped vehicle is $40,000, and the value of the vehicle without the security features is $25,000, A may determine A's income attributable to the vehicle as if the vehicle were worth $25,000. A must include in income the value of the availability of the vehicle for personal use.

Example (2). Assume that B is the chief executive officer of a multinational corporation (company Y). Assume further that there have been kidnapping attempts and other terrorist activities in the foreign countries in which B performs services and that at least some of such activities have been directed against B or similarly situated employees. In response to these activities, company Y provides B with an overall security program, including an alarm system at B's home and bodyguards at B's workplace, a bodyguard/driver who is trained in evasive driving techniques, and a vehicle specially designed for security during B's overseas travels. In addition, assume that company Y requires B to travel in company Y's airplane for business and personal trips taken to, from, and within these foreign countries. Also, assume that but for bona fide business-oriented security concerns, no part of the overall security program would have been provided to B. B may exclude as a working condition fringe the value of the special security features of the automobile and the value attributable to the bodyguards and the bodyguard/driver. B may also exclude as a working condition fringe the excess, if any, of the value of personal flights in the company Y airplane over first-class airfare (as determined under the special valuation rule provided in § 1.61-2T if the safe harbor described in paragraph (m)(2)(vi) of this section is used). B must include in income the value of the availability of the vehicle for personal use and the lesser of the value of first-class airfare or the value of the flight determined under § 1.61-2T for each personal flight taken by B in company Y's airplane.

Example (3). Assume the same facts as in example (2) except that company Y also requires B to travel in company Y's airplane within the United States, and provides B with a chauffeur-driven limousine for business and personal travel in the United States. Assume further that company Y also requires B's spouse and dependents to travel in company Y's airplane for personal flights in the United States. If no bona fide business-oriented security concern exists with respect to travel in the United States, B may not exclude any portion of the value of the availability of the driver or limousine for personal use in the United States. Thus, B must include in income the value of the availability of the vehicle and driver for personal use. In addition, B may not exclude any portion of the value attributable to personal flights by B or B's spouse and dependents on company Y's airplane. Thus, B must include in income the value attributable to the personal use of company Y's airplane. See § 1.61-2T for rules relating to the valuation of personal flights on employer-provided airplanes.

Example (4). Assume that company Z retains an independent security consultant to perform a security study with respect to its chief executive officer. Assume further that, based on an objective assessment of the facts and circumstances, the security consultant reasonably recommends that the employee be provided security at his workplace and for ground transportation, but not for air transportation. If company Z follows the recommendations on a consistent basis, an overall security program will be deemed to exist with respect to the workplace and ground transportation security only.

Example (5). Assume the same facts as in example (4) except that company Z only provides the employee security while commuting to and from work, but not for any other ground transportation. Since the recommendations of the independent security study are not applied on a consistent basis, an overall security program will not be deemed to exist.

(n) Product testing. *(1) In general.* The fair market value of the use of consumer goods, which are manufactured for sale to nonemployees, for product testing and evaluation by an employee outside the employer's workplace is excludable as a working condition fringe if—

(i) Consumer testing and evaluation of the product is an ordinary and necessary business expense of the employer,

(ii) Business reasons necessitate that the testing and evaluation of the product be performed off the employer's business premises by employees (i.e., the testing and evaluation cannot be carried out adequately in the employer's office or in laboratory testing facilities),

(iii) The product is furnished to the employee for purposes of testing and evaluation,

(iv) The product is made available to the employee for no longer than necessary to test and evaluate its performance and must be returned to the employer at completion of the testing and evaluation period,

(v) The employer imposes limitations of the employee's use of the product which significantly reduce the value of any personal benefit to the employee, and

(vi) The employee must submit detailed reports to the employer on the testing and evaluation.

The length of the testing and evaluation period must be reasonable in relation to the product being tested.

(2) Employer-imposed limitations. The requirement of paragraph (n)(1)(v) of this section is satisfied if—

(i) The employer places limitations on the employee's ability to select among different models or varieties of the consumer product that is furnished for testing and evaluation purposes,

(ii) The employer's policy provides for the employee, in appropriate cases, to purchase or lease at his or her own expense the same type of product as that being tested (so that personal use by the employee's family will be limited), and

(iii) The employer generally prohibits use of the product by members of the employee's family.

(3) Discriminating classifications. If an employer furnishes products under a testing and evaluation program only to officers, owners, or highly compensated employees, this fact may be considered in a determination of whether the products are furnished for testing and evaluation purposes or for compensation purposes, unless the employer can show a business reason for the classification of employees to whom the products are furnished (e.g., that automobiles are furnished for testing and evaluation by an automobile manufacturer to its design engineers and supervisory mechanics).

(4) Factors that negate the existence of a product testing program. If an employer fails to tabulate and examine the results of the detailed reports within a reasonable period of time after expiration of the testing period, the program will not be considered a product testing program. Existence of one or more of the following factors may also establish that the program is not a bona fide product testing program:

(i) The program is in essence a leasing program under which employees lease the consumer goods from the employer for a fee;

(ii) The nature of the product and other considerations are insufficient to justify the testing program; or

(iii) The expense of the program outweighs the benefits to be gained from testing and evaluation.

(5) Failure to meet the requirements of this paragraph (n). The fair market value of the use of property for product testing and evaluation by an employee outside the employee's workplace, under a product testing program that does not meet all of the requirements of this paragraph (n), is not excludable as a working condition fringe.

(6) Example. Assume that an employer that manufactures automobiles establishes a product testing program under which 50 of its 5,000 employees test and evaluate the automobiles for 30 days. Assume further that the 50 employees represent a fair cross section of all of the employees of the employer, such employees submit detailed reports to the employer on the testing and evaluation, the employer tabulates and examines the test results within a reasonable time, and the use of the automobiles is restricted to the employees. If the rules of paragraph (n) (2) of this section are also met, the employees may exclude the value of the use of the automobile during the testing and evaluation period.

(o) Qualified automobile demonstration use. *(1) In general.* The value of qualified automobile demonstration use is excludable from gross income as a working condition fringe. The term "qualified automobile demonstration use" means any use of a demonstration automobile by a full-time automobile salesman in the sales area in which the automobile dealer's sales office is located if—

(i) Such use is provided primarily to facilitate the salesman's performance of services for the employer, and

(ii) There are substantial restrictions on the personal use of the automobile by the salesman.

(2) Full-time automobile salesman. (i) Definition. The term "full-time automobile salesman" means any individual who—

(A) Is employed by an automobile dealer,

(B) Customarily spends substantially all of a normal business day on the sales floor selling automobiles to customers of the automobile dealership,

(C) Customarily works a number of hours considered full-time in the industry (but at a rate not less than 1,000 hours per year), and

(D) Derives at least 85 percent of his or her gross income from the automobile dealership directly as a result of such automobile sales activities. An individual, such as the general manager of an automobile dealership, who receives a sales commission on the sale of an automobile is not a full-time automobile salesman unless the requirements of this paragraph (o)(2)(i) are met. The exclusion provided in this paragraph (o) is available to an individual who meets the definition of this paragraph (o)(2)(i) regardless of whether the individual performs services in addition to those described in this paragraph (o)(2)(i). For example, an individual who is an owner of the automobile dealership but who otherwise meets the requirements of this paragraph (o)(2)(i) may exclude from gross income the value of qualified automobile demonstration use.

(ii) Use by an individual other than a full-time automobile salesman. Personal use of a demonstration automobile by an individual other than a full-time automobile salesman is not treated as a working condition fringe. Therefore, any personal use, including commuting use, of a demonstration automobile by a part-time salesman, automobile mechanic, manager, or other individual is not "qualified automobile demonstration use" and thus not excludable from gross income.

(3) Demonstration automobile. The exclusion provided in this paragraph (o) applies only to qualified use of a demonstration automobile. A demonstration automobile is an automobile that is—

(i) Currently in the inventory of the automobile dealership, and

(ii) Available for test drives by customers during the normal business hours of the employee.

(4) Substantial restrictions on personal use. Substantial restrictions on the personal use of demonstration automobiles exist when all of the following conditions are satisfied:

(i) Use by individuals other than the full-time automobile salesmen (e.g., the salesman's family) is prohibited,

(ii) Use for personal vacation trips is prohibited,

(iii) The storage of personal possessions in the automobile is prohibited, and

(iv) The total use by mileage of the automobile by the salesman outside the salesman's normal working hours is limited.

(5) Sales area. (i) In general. Qualified automobile demonstration use must be use in the sales area in which the automobile dealer's sales office is located. The sales area is the geographic area surrounding the automobile dealer's sales office from which the office regularly derives customers.

(ii) Sales area safe harbor. With respect to a particular full-time salesman, the automobile dealer's sales area may be treated as the larger of the area within a 75 mile radius of the dealer's sales office, or the one-way commuting distance (in miles) of the particular salesman.

(p) Parking. *(1) In general.* The value of parking provided to an employee on or near the business premises of the employer is excludable from gross income as a working condition fringe. The working condition fringe exclusion applies whether the employer owns or rents the parking facility or parking space.

(2) Reimbursement of parking expenses. Any reimbursement to the employee of the ordinary and necessary expenses of renting a parking space on or near the business premises of the employer is excludable as a working condition fringe. The preceding sentence does not apply, however, to cash payments that are not actually used for renting a parking space. Thus, that part of a general transportation allowance that is not used for parking is not excludable as a working condition fringe under this paragraph (p).

(3) Parking on residential property. With respect to an employee, this paragraph (p) does not apply to any parking facility or space located on property owned or leased for residential purposes by the employee.

(q) Nonapplicability of nondiscrimination rules. Except to the extent provided in paragraph (n)(3) of this section, the nondiscrimination rules of section 132(h)(1) and § 1.132-8T do not apply in determining the amount, if any, of a working condition fringe.

T.D. 8063, 12/18/85, amend T.D. 8256, 7/16/89.

§ 1.132-6 De minimis fringes.

Caution: The Treasury has not yet amended Reg § 1.132-6 to reflect changes made by 102-486.

(a) In general. Gross income does not include the value of a de minimis fringe provided to an employee. The term "de minimis fringe" means any property or service the value of which is (after taking into account the frequency with which similar fringes are provided by the employer to the employer's employees) so small as to make accounting for it unreasonable or administratively impracticable.

(b) Frequency. *(1) Employee-measured frequency.* Generally, the frequency with which similar fringes are provided by the employer to the employer's employees is determined by reference to the frequency with which the employer provides the fringes to each individual employee. For example, if an employer provides a free meal in kind to one employee on a daily basis, but not to any other employee, the value of the meals is not de minimis with respect to that one employee even though with respect to the employer's entire workforce the meals are provided "infrequently."

(2) Employer-measured frequency. Notwithstanding the rule of paragraph (b)(1) of this section, except for purposes of applying the special rules of paragraph (d)(2) of this section, where it would be administratively difficult to determine frequency with respect to individual employees, the frequency with which similar fringes are provided by the employer to the employer's employees is determined by reference to the frequency with which the employer provides the fringes to the workforce as a whole. Therefore, under this rule, the frequency with which any individual employee receives such a fringe benefit is not relevant and in some circumstances, the de minimis fringe exclusion may apply with respect to a benefit even though a particular employee receives the benefit frequently. For example, if an employer exercises sufficient control and imposes significant restrictions on the personal use of a company copying machine so that at least 85 percent of the use of the machine is for business purposes, any personal use of the copying machine by particular employees is considered to be a de minimis fringe.

(c) Administrability. Unless excluded by a provision of chapter 1 of the Internal Revenue Code of 1986 other than section 132(a)(4), the value of any fringe benefit that would not be unreasonable or administratively impracticable to account for is includible in the employee's gross income. Thus, except as provided in paragraph (d)(2) of this section, the provision of any cash fringe benefit is never excludable under section 132(a) as a de minimis fringe benefit. Similarly except as otherwise provided in paragraph (d) of this section, a cash equivalent fringe benefit (such as a fringe benefit provided to an employee through the use of a gift certificate or charge or credit card) is generally not excludable under section 132(a) even if the same property or service acquired (if provided in kind) would be excludable as a de minimis fringe benefit. For example, the provision of cash to an employee for a theatre ticket that would itself be excludable as a de minimis fringe (see paragraph (e)(1) of this section) is not excludable as a de minimis fringe.

(d) Special rules. *(1) Transit passes.* A public transit pass provided at a discount to defray an employee's commuting costs may be excluded from the employee's gross income as a de minimis fringe if such discount does not exceed $21 in any month. The exclusion provided in this paragraph (d)(1) also applies to the provision of tokens or fare cards that enable an individual to travel on the public transit system if the value of such tokens and fare cards in any month does not exceed by more than $21 the amount the employee paid for the tokens and fare cards for such month. Similarly, the exclusion of this paragraph (d)(1) applies to the provision of a voucher or similar instruments that is exchangeable solely for tokens, fare cards, or other instruments that enable the employee to use the public transit system if the value of such vouchers and other instruments in any month does not exceed $21. The exclusion of this paragraph (d)(1) also applies to reimbursements made by an employer to an employee after December 31, 1988, to cover the cost of commuting on a public transit system, provided the employee does not receive more than $21 in such reimbursements for commuting costs in any given month. The reimbursement must be made under a bona fide reimbursement arrangement. A reimbursement arrangement will be treated as bona fide if the employer establishes appropriate procedures for verifying on a periodic basis that the employee's use of public transportation for commuting is consistent with the value of the benefit provided by the employer for that purpose. The amount of in-kind public transit commuting benefits and reimbursements provided during any month that are excludible under this paragraph (d)(1) is limited to $21. For months ending before July 1, 1991, the amount is $15 per month. The exclusion provided in this paragraph (d)(1) does not apply to the provision of any benefit to defray public transit expenses incurred for personal travel other than commuting.

(2) Occasional meal money or local transportation fare. (i) General rule. Meals, meal money or local transportation fare provided to an employee is excluded as a de minimis fringe benefit if the benefit provided is reasonable and is provided in a manner that satisfies the following three conditions:

(A) Occasional basis. The meals, meal money or local transportation fare is provided to the employee on an occasional basis. Whether meal money or local transportation fare is provided to an employee on an occasional basis will depend upon the frequency i.e. the availability of the benefit and regularity with which the benefit is provided by the employer to the employee. Thus, meals, meal money, or local transportation fare or a combination of such benefits provided to an employee on a regular or routine basis is not provided on an occasional basis.

(B) Overtime. The meals, meal money or local transportation fare is provided to an employee because overtime work necessitates an extension of the employee's normal work schedule. This condition does not fail to be satisfied merely because the circumstances giving rise to the need for overtime work are reasonably foreseeable.

(C) Meal money. In the case of a meal or meal money, the meal or meal money is provided to enable the employee to work overtime. Thus, for example, meals provided on the employer's premises that are consumed during the period that the employee works overtime or meal money provided for meals consumed during such period satisfy this condition.

In no event shall meal money or local transportation fare calculated on the basis of the number of hours worked (e.g., $1.00 per hour for each hour over eight hours) be considered a de minimis fringe benefit.

(ii) Applicability of other exclusions for certain means and for transportation provided for security concerns. The value of meals furnished to an employee, an employee's spouse, or any of the employee's dependents by or on behalf of the employee's employer for the convenience of the employer is excluded from the employee's gross income if the meals are furnished on the business premises of the employer (see section 119). (For purposes of the exclusion under section 119, the definitions of an employee under § 1.132-1(b) do not apply.) If, for a bona fide business-oriented security concern, an employer provides an employee vehicle transportation that is specially designed for security (for example, the vehicle is equipped with bulletproof glass and armor plating), and the conditions of § 1.132-5(m) are satisfied, the value of the special security design is excludable from gross income as a working condition fringe if the employee would not have had such special security design but for the bona fide business-oriented security concern.

(iii) Special rule for employer-provided transportation provided in certain circumstances. (A) Partial exclusion of value. If an employer provides transportation (such as taxi fare) to an employee for use in commuting to and/or from work because of unusual circumstances and because, based on the facts and circumstances, it is unsafe for the employee to use other available means of transportation, the excess of the value of each one-way trip over $1.50 per one-way commute is excluded from gross income. The rule of this paragraph (d)(2)(iii) is not available to a control employee as defined in § 1.61-21(f)(5) and (6).

(B) "Unusual circumstances". Unusual circumstances are determined with respect to the employee receiving the transportation and are based on all facts and circumstances. An example of unusual circumstances would be when an employee is asked to work outside of his normal work hours (such as being called to the workplace at 1:00 am when the employee normally works from 8:00 am to 4:00 pm). Another example of unusual circumstances is a temporary change in the employee's work schedule (such as working from 12 midnight to 8:00 am rather than from 8:00 am to 4:00 pm for a two-week period).

(C) "Unsafe conditions". Factors indicating whether it is unsafe for an employee to use other available means of transportation are the history of crime in the geographic area surrounding the employee's workplace or residence and the time of day during which the employee must commute.

(3) Use of special rules or examples to establish a general rule. The special rules provided in this paragraph (d) or examples provided in paragraph (e) of this section may not be used to establish any general rule permitting exclusion as a de minimis fringe. For example, the fact that $252 (i.e., $21 per month for 12 months) worth of public transit passes can be excluded from gross income as a de minimis fringe in 1992 does not mean that any fringe benefit with a value equal to or less than $252 may be excluded as a de minimis fringe. As another example, the fact that the commuting use of an employer-provided vehicle more than one day a month is an example of a benefit not excludable as a de minimis fringe (see paragraph (e)(2) of this section) does not mean that the commuting use of a vehicle up to 12 times per year is excludable from gross income as a de minimis fringe.

(4) Benefits exceeding value and frequency limits. If a benefit provided to an employee is not de minimis because either the value or frequency exceeds a limit provided in this paragraph (d), no amount of the benefit is considered to be a de minimis fringe. For example, if, in 1992, an employer provides a $50 monthly public transit pass, the entire $50 must be included in income, not just the excess value over $21.

(e) Examples. *(1) Benefits excludable from income.* Examples of de minimis fringe benefits are occasional typing of personal letters by a company secretary; occasional personal use of an employer's copying machine, provided that the employer exercises sufficient control and imposes significant restrictions on the personal use of the machine so that at least 85 percent of the use of the machine is for business purposes; occasional cocktail parties, group meals, or picnics for employees and their guests; traditional birthday or holiday gifts of property (not cash) with a low fair market value; occasional theater or sporting event tickets; coffee, doughnuts, and soft drinks; local telephone calls; and flowers, fruit, books, or similar property provided to employees under special circumstances (e.g., on account of illness, outstanding performance, or family crisis).

(2) Benefits not excludable as de minimis fringes. Examples of fringe benefits that are not excludable from gross income as de minimis fringes are: season tickets to sporting or theatrical events; the commuting use of an employer-provided automobile or other vehicle more than one day a month; membership in a private country club or athletic facility, regardless of the frequency with which the employee uses the facility; employer-provided group-term life insurance on the life of the spouse or child of an employee; and use of employer-owned or leased facilities (such as an apartment, hunting lodge, boat, etc.) for a weekend. Some amount of the value of certain of these fringe benefits may be excluded from income under other statutory provisions, such as the exclusion for working condition fringes. See § 1.132-5.

(f) Nonapplicability of nondiscrimination rules. Except to the extent provided in § 1.132-7, the nondiscrimination rules of section 132(h)(1) and § 1.132-8 do not apply in determining the amount, if any, of a de minimis fringe. Thus, a fringe benefit may be excludable as a de minimis fringe even if the benefit is provided exclusively to highly compensated employees of the employer.

T.D. 8256, 7/6/89, amend T.D. 8389, 11/5/92.

§ 1.132-6T De minimis fringe—1985 through 1988 (Temporary).

(a) In general. Gross income does not include the value of a de minimis fringe provided to an employee. The term "de minimis fringe" means any property or service the value of which is (after taking into account the frequency with which similar fringes are provided by the employer to the employer's employees) so small as to make accounting for it unreasonable or administratively impracticable.

(b) Frequency. Generally, the frequency with which similar fringes are provided by the employer to the employer's employees is determined by reference to the frequency with which the employer provides the fringe to each individual employee. For example, if an employer provides a free meal to one employee on a daily basis, but not to any other employee, the value of the meals is not de minimis with respect to that one employee even though with respect to the employer's entire workforce the meals are provided "infrequently." However, where it would be administratively difficult to determine frequency with respect to individual employees, the frequency with which similar fringes are provided by the employer to the employer's employees is determined by reference to the frequency with which the employer provides the fringes to the employees and not the frequency with which individual employees receive them. In these cases, if an employer occasionally provides a fringe benefit of de minimis value to the employer's employees, the de minimis fringe exclusion may apply even though a particular employee receives the benefit frequently. For example, if an employer exercises sufficient control and imposes significant restrictions on the personal use of a company copying machine so that at least 85 percent of the use of the machine is for business purposes, any personal use of the copying machine by particular employees is considered to be a de minimis fringe.

(c) Administrability. Unless excluded by a statutory provision other than section 132(a)(4), the value of any fringe benefit that would not be unreasonable or administratively impracticable to account for must be included in the employee's gross income. Thus, except as otherwise provided in this section, the provision of any cash fringe benefit (or any fringe benefit provided to an employee through the use of a charge or credit card) is not excludable as a de minimis fringe. For example, the provision of cash to an employee for personal entertainment is not excludable as a de minimis fringe.

(d) Special rules. *(1) Transit passes.* A transit pass provided to an employee at a discount not exceeding $15 per month may be excluded as a de minimis fringe. The exclusion provided in this paragraph (d) also applies to the provision of $15 in tokens or fare cards that enable an individual to travel on the transit system. The exclusion provided in this paragraph (d) does not apply to any provision of cash or other benefit to defray transit expenses incurred for personal travel.

(2) Occasional meal money or local transportation fare. Occasional meal money or local transportation fare provided to an employee because overtime work necessitates an extension of the employee's normal workday is excluded as a de minimis fringe.

(3) Use of special rules to establish a general rule. The special rules provided in this paragraph (d) may not be used to establish any general rule. For example, the fact that $180 ($15 per month for 12 months) worth of transit passes can be excluded in a year does not mean that any fringe benefit with a value equal to or less than $180 may be excluded as a de minimis fringe.

(4) Benefits exceeding value and frequency limitations. If the benefit provided to an employee is not de minimis because either the value or frequency exceeds a limit provided in this paragraph (d), no amount of the benefit is considered to be de minimis. For example, if an employer provides a $20 monthly transit pass, the entire $20 must be included in income, not just the excess value over $15.

(e) Nonapplicability of nondiscrimination rules. Except to the extent provided in § 1.132-7T, the nondiscrimination rules of section 132(h)(1) and § 1.132-8T do not apply. Thus, for example, a fringe benefit may be a de minimis fringe even if the benefit is provided exclusively to officers of the employer.

(f) Examples. *(1) Benefits excludable from income.* Examples of de minimis fringe benefits are occasional typing of personal letters by a company secretary; occasional personal use of an employer's copying machine, provided that the employer exercises sufficient control and imposes significant restrictions on the personal use of the machine so that at least 85 percent of the use of the machine is for business purposes; occasional cocktail parties or picnics for employees and their guests; traditional holiday gifts of property (not cash) with a low fair market value; occasional theatre or sporting event tickets; and coffee and doughnuts.

(2) Benefits not excludable as de minimis fringes. Examples of fringe benefits that are not excludable from income as de minimis fringes are: season tickets to sporting or theatrical events; the commuting use of an employer-provided automobile or other vehicle more than once a month; membership in a private country club or athletic facility, regardless of the frequency with which the employee uses the facility; and use of employer-owned or leased facilities (such as an apartment, hunting lodge, boat, etc.) for a weekend. Some amount of the value of these fringe benefits may be excluded under other statutory provisions, such as the exclusion for working condition fringes. See § 1.132-5T.

T.D. 8063, 12/18/85, amend T.D. 8256, 7/6/89.

§ 1.132-7 Employer-operated eating facilities.

(a) In general. *(1) Condition for exclusion.* (i) General rule. The value of meals provided to employees at an employer-operated eating facility for employees is excludable from gross income as a de minimis fringe only if on an annual basis, the revenue from the facility equals or exceeds the direct operating costs of the facility.

(ii) Additional condition for highly compensated employees. With respect to any highly compensated employee, an exclusion is available under this section only if the condition set out in paragraph (a)(l)(i) of this section is satisfied and access to the facility is available on substantially the same terms to each member of a group of employees that is defined under a reasonable classification set up by the employer that does not discriminate in favor of highly compensated employees. See § 1.132-8. For purposes of this paragraph (a)(1)(ii), each dining room or cafeteria in which meals are served is treated as a separate eating facility, whether each such dining room or cafeteria has its own kitchen or other food-preparation area.

(2) Employer-operated eating facility for employees. An employer-operated eating facility for employees is a facility that meets all of the following conditions—

(i) The facility is owned or leased by the employer,

(ii) The facility is operated by the employer,

(iii) The facility is located on or near the business premises of the employer, and

(iv) The meals furnished at the facility are provided during, or immediately before or after, the employee's workday.

For purposes of this section, the term "meals" means food, beverages, and related services provided at the facility. If an employer can reasonably determine the number of meals that are excludable from income by the recipient employees under section 119, the employer may, in determining whether the requirement of paragraph (a)(1)(i) of this section is satisfied, disregard all costs and revenues attributable to such meals provided to such employees. If an employer can reasonably determine the number of meals received by volunteers who receive food and beverages at a hospital, free or at a discount, the employer may, in determining whether the requirement of paragraph (a)(1)(i) of this section is satisfied, disregard all costs and revenues attributable to such meals provided to such volunteers. If an employer charges nonemployees a greater amount than employees, in determining whether the requirement of paragraph (a)(1)(i) of this section is satisfied, the employer must disregard all costs and revenues attributable to such meals provided to such nonemployees.

(3) Operation by the employer. If an employer contracts with another to operate an eating facility for its employees, the facility is considered to be operated by the employer for purposes of this section. If an eating facility is operated by more than one employer, it is considered to be operated by each employer.

(4) Example. The provisions of this paragraph (a)(2) may be illustrated by the following example:

Example (1). Assume that a not-for-profit hospital system maintains cafeterias for the use of its employees and volunteers. Only the employees are charged for food service at the cafeteria and the policy of the hospital is to charge the employees only for the costs of food, beverage and labor directly attributable to the meal. Most of the cafeterias within the system furnish more free meals to volunteers than they serve paid meals to employees. For purposes of this paragraph, as long as the employer can accurately determine the number of meals received free or at a discount by volunteers, the employer may disregard all the costs and revenues attributable to such meals provided to volunteers. Therefore, for purposes of this paragraph, the costs of the hospital system for furnishing meals to employees who pay for them are the costs to be compared to determine if the revenues from the facility equal or exceed direct operating costs of the facility's service to employees.

(b) Direct operating costs. *(1) In general.* For purposes of this section, the direct operating costs of an eating facility are—

(i) The cost of food and beverages, and

(ii) The cost of labor for personnel whose services relating to the facility are performed primarily on the premises of the eating facility.

Direct operating costs do not include the labor cost attributable to personnel whose services relating to the facility are not performed primarily on the premises of the eating facility. Thus, for example, the labor costs attributable to cooks, waiters and waitresses are included in direct operating costs, but the labor cost attributable to a manager of an eating facility whose services relating to the facility are not primarily performed on the premises of the eating facility is not included in direct operating costs. If an employee performs services relating to the facility both on and off the premises of the eating facility, only the portion of the total labor cost of the employee relating to the facility that bears the same proportion to such total labor cost as time spent on the premises bears to total time spent performing services relating to the facility is included in direct operating costs. For example, assume that 60 percent of the services of a cook in the above example are not related to the eating facility. Only 40 percent of the total labor cost of the cook is includible in direct operating costs. For purposes of this section, labor costs include all compensation required to be reported on a Form W-2 for income tax purposes and related employment taxes paid by the employer. In determining the direct operating costs of an eating facility, the employer may include as part of the facility, vending machines that are provided by the employer and located on the same premises as the other eating facilities operated by the employer.

(2) Multiple dining rooms or cafeterias. The direct operating costs test may be applied separately for each dining room or cafeteria. Alternatively, the direct operating costs test may be applied with respect to all the eating facilities operate by the employer.

(3) Payment to operator of facility. If an employer contracts with another to operate an eating facility for its employees, the direct operating costs of the facility consist both of direct operating costs, if any, incurred by the employer

and the amount paid to the operator of the facility to the extent that such amount is attributable to what would be direct operating costs if the employer operated the facility directly.

(c) Valuation of non-excluded meals provided at an employer-operated eating facility for employees. If the exclusion for meals provided at an employer-operated eating facility for employees is not available, the recipient of meals provided at such facility must include in income the amount by which the fair market value of the meals provided exceeds the sum of—

(1) the amount, if any, paid for the meals, and

(2) the amount, if any, specifically excluded by another section of chapter 1 of this subtitle.

For special valuation rules relating to such meals, see § 1.61-21(j)

T.D. 8256, 7/6/89.

§ 1.132-7T Treatment of employer-operated eating facilities—1985 through 1988 (Temporary).

(a) In general. *(1) General rule.* The value of meals provided to employees at an employer-operated eating facility for employees is excludable from gross income as a de minimis fringe only if—

(i) On an annual basis, the revenue from the facility equals or exceeds the direct operating costs of the facility, and

(ii) With respect to any officer, owner or highly compensated employee, access to the facility is available on substantially the same terms to each member of a group of employees that is defined under a reasonable classification set up by the employer that does not discriminate in favor of officers, owners, and highly compensated employees. See § 1.132-8T.

(2) Employer-operated eating facility for employees. An employer-operated eating facility for employees is a facility that meets all of the following conditions—

(i) The facility is owned or leased by the employer,

(ii) The facility is operated by the employer,

(iii) The facility is located on or near the business premises of the employer,

(iv) Substantially all of the use of the facility is by employees of the employer operating the facility, and

(v) The meals furnished at the facility are provided during, or immediately before or after, the employee's workday.

For purposes of this section, the term "meals" means food, beverages, and related services provided at the facility. If an employer can determine the number of employees who receive meals that are excludable from income under section 119, the employer may, in determining whether the requirement of paragraph (a)(1)(i) of this section is satisfied, disregard all costs and revenues attributable to such meals provided to such employees. For purposes of this section, each dining room or cafeteria in which meals are served is treated as a separate eating facility, regardless of whether each such dining room or cafeteria has its own kitchen or other food-preparation area.

(3) Operation by the employer. If an employer contracts with another to operate an eating facility for its employees, the facility is considered to be operated by the employer for purposes of this section. If an eating facility is operated by more than one employer, it is considered to be operated by each employer.

(b) Direct operating costs. The direct operating costs test must be applied separately for each dining room or cafeteria. For purposes of this section, the direct operating costs of an eating facility are (1) the cost of food and beverages and (2) the cost of labor for personnel whose services relating to the facility are performed primarily on the premises of the eating facility. Direct operating costs do not include the cost of labor for personnel whose services relating to the facility are not performed primarily on the premises of the eating facility. Thus, for example, the labor cost for cooks, waiters, and waitresses is included in direct operating costs, but the labor cost for a manager of an eating facility whose services relating to the facility are not primarily performed on the premises of the eating facility is not included in direct operating costs. If an employee performs services both on and off the premises of the eating facility, only the applicable percentage of the total labor cost of the employee that bears the same proportion as time spent on the premises bears to total time is included in direct operating costs. For example, assume that 60 percent of the services of the cooks in the above example are not related to the eating facility. Only 40 percent of the total labor cost of the cooks is includible in direct operating costs. For purposes of this section, labor costs include all compensation required to be reported on a Form W-2 for income tax purposes and related employment taxes paid by the employer.

(c) Valuation of non-excluded meals provided at an employer-operated eating facility for employees. If the exclusion for meals provided at an employer-operated eating facility for employees is not available, the recipient of meals provided at such facility must include in income the amount by which the fair market value of the meals provided exceeds the sum of (1) the amount, if any, paid for the meals, and (2) the amount, if any, specifically excluded by another section of the Code. For special valuation rules relating to such meals see § 1.61-2T(j).

T.D. 8063, 12/18/85, amend T.D. 8256, 7/6/89.

§ 1.132-8 Fringe benefit nondiscrimination rules.

Caution: The Treasury has not yet amended Reg § 1.132-8 to reflect changes made by P.L. 104-188.

(a) Application of nondiscrimination rules. *(1) General rule.* A highly compensated employee who receives a no-additional-cost service, a qualified employee discount or a meal provided at an employer-operated eating facility for employees shall not be permitted to exclude such benefit from his or her income unless the benefit is available on substantially the same terms to:

(i) All employees of the employer; or

(ii) A group of employees of the employer which is defined under a reasonable classification set up by the employer that does not discriminate in favor of highly compensated employees. See paragraph (f) of this section for the definition of a highly compensated employee.

(2) Consequences of discrimination. (i) In general. If an employer maintains more than one fringe benefit program, i.e., either different fringe benefits being provided to the same group of employees, or different classifications of employees or the same fringe benefit being provided to two or more classifications of employees, the nondiscrimination requirements of section 132 will generally be applied separately to each such program. Thus, a determination that one fringe benefit program discriminates in favor of highly compensated employees generally will not cause other fringe

benefit programs covering the same highly compensated employees to be treated as discriminatory. If the fringe benefits provided to a highly compensated individual do not satisfy the nondiscrimination rules provided in this section, such individual shall be unable to exclude from gross income any portion of the benefit. For example, if an employer offers a 20 percent discount (which otherwise satisfies the requirements for a qualified employee discount) to all non-highly compensated employees and a 35 percent discount to all highly compensated employees, the entire value of the 35 percent discount (not just the excess over 20 percent) is includible in the gross income and wages of the highly compensated employees who make purchases at a discount.

(ii) Exception. (A) Related fringe benefit programs. If one of a group of fringe benefit programs discriminates in favor of highly compensated employees, no related fringe benefit provided to such highly compensated employees under any other fringe benefit program may be excluded from the gross income of such highly compensated employees. For example, assume a department store provides a 20 percent merchandise discount to all employees under one fringe benefit program. Assume further that under a second fringe benefit program, the department store provides an additional 15 percent merchandise discount to a group of employees defined under a classification which discriminates in favor of highly compensated employees. Because the second fringe benefit program is discriminatory, the 15 percent merchandise discount provided to the highly compensated employees is not a qualified employee discount. In addition, because the 20 percent merchandise discount provided under the first fringe benefit program is related to the fringe benefit provided under the second fringe benefit program, the 20 percent merchandise discount provided the highly compensated employees is not a qualified employee discount. Thus, the entire 35 percent merchandise discount provided to the highly compensated employees is includible in such employees' gross incomes.

(B) Employer-operated eating facilities for employees. For purposes of paragraph (a)(2)(ii)(A) of this section, meals at different employer-operated eating facilities for employees are not related fringe benefits, so that a highly compensated employee may exclude from gross income the value of a meal at a nondiscriminatory facility even though any meals provided to him or her at a discriminatory facility cannot be excluded.

(3) Scope of the nondiscrimination rules provided in this section. The nondiscrimination rules provided in this section apply only to fringe benefits provided pursuant to section 132(a)(1), (a)(2), and (e)(2). These rules have no application to any other employee benefit that may be subject to nondiscrimination requirements under any other section of the Code.

(b) Aggregation of employees. *(1) Section 132(a)(1) and (2).* For purposes of determining whether the exclusions for no-additional-cost services and qualified employee discounts are available to highly compensated employees, the nondiscrimination rules of this section are applied by aggregating the employees of all related employers (as defined in § 1.132-1(c)), except that employees in different lines of business (as defined in § 1.132-4) are not to be aggregated. Thus, in general, for purposes of this section, the term "employees of the employer" refers to all employees of the employer and any other entity that is a member of a group described in sections 414(b), (c), (m), or, (o) and that performs services within the same line of business as the employer which provides the particular fringe benefit. Employees in different lines of business will be aggregated, however, if the line of business limitation has been relaxed pursuant to paragraphs (b) through (g) of § 1.132-4.

(2) Section 132(e)(2). For purposes of determining whether the exclusions for meals provided at employer-operated eating facilities are available to highly compensated, the nondiscrimination rules of this section are applied by aggregating the employees of all related employers (as defined in § 1.132-1(c)) who regularly work at or near the premises on which the eating facility is located, except that employees in different lines of business (as defined in § 1.132-4) are not to be aggregated. The nondiscrimination rules of this section are applied separately to each eating facility. Each dining room or cafeteria in which meals are served is treated as a separate eating facility, regardless of whether each such dining room or cafeteria has its own kitchen or other food-preparation area.

(3) Classes of employees who may be excluded. For purposes of applying the nondiscrimination rules of this section to a particular fringe benefit program, there may be excluded from consideration employees who may be excluded from consideration under section 89 (h), as enacted by the Tax Reform Act of 1986, Public Law 99-514, 100 Stat. 2085 (1986) and amended by the Technical and Miscellaneous Revenue Act of 1988, Public Law 100-647, 102 Stat. 3342 (1988).

(c) Availability on substantially the same terms. *(1) General rule.* The determination of whether a benefit is available on substantially the same terms shall be made upon the basis of the facts and circumstances of each situation. In general, however, if any one of the terms or conditions governing the availability of a particular benefit to one or more employees varies from any one of the terms or conditions governing the availability of a benefit made available to one or more other employees, such benefit shall not be considered to be available on substantially the same terms except to the extent otherwise provided in paragraph (2) below. For example, if a department store provides a 20 percent qualified employee discount to all of its employees on all merchandise, the substantially the [sic] same terms requirement will be satisfied. Similarly, if the discount provided to all employees is 30 percent on certain merchandise (such as apparel), and 20 percent on all other merchandise, the substantially the [sic] same terms requirement will be satisfied. However, if a department store provides a 20 percent qualified employee discount to all employees, but as to the employees in certain departments, the discount is available upon hire, and as to the remaining departments, the discount is only available when an employee has completed a specified term of services, the 20 percent discount is not available on substantially the same terms to all of the employees of the employer. Similarly, if a greater discount is given to employees with more seniority, full-time work status, or a particular job description, such benefit (i.e., the discount) would not be available to all employees eligible for the discount on substantially the same terms, except to the extent otherwise provided in paragraph (2) below. These examples also apply to no-additional-cost-services. Thus, if an employer charges non-highly compensated employees for a no-additional-cost service and does not charge highly compensated employees (or charges highly compensated employees a lesser amount), the substantially the same terms requirement will not be satisfied.

(2) Certain terms relating to priority. Certain fringe benefits made available to employees are available only in limited quantities that may be insufficient to meet employee de-

mand. This situation may occur either because of employer policy (such as where an employer determines that only a certain number of units of a specific product will be made available to employees each year) or because of the nature of the fringe benefit (such as where an employer provides a no-additional-cost transportation service that is limited to the number of seats available just before departure). Under these circumstances, an employer may find it necessary to establish some method of allocating the limited fringe benefits among the employees eligible to receive the fringe benefits. The employer may establish the priorities described below.

(i) Priority on a first come, first served, or similar basis. A benefit shall not fail to be treated as available to a group of employees on substantially the same terms merely because the employer allocates the benefit among such employees on a "first come, first served" or lottery basis, provided that the same notice of the terms of availability is given to all employees in the group and the terms under which the benefit is provided to employees within the group are otherwise the same with respect to all employees. For purposes of the preceding sentence, a program that gives priority to employees who are the first to submit written requests for the benefit will constitute priority on a "first come, first served" basis. Similarly, if the employer regularly engages in the practice of allocating benefits on a priority basis to employees demonstrating a critical need, such benefit shall not fail to be treated as available on substantially the same terms to all of the employees with respect to whom such priority status is available as long as the determination is based upon uniform and objective criteria which have been communicated to all employees in the group of eligible employees. An example of a critical need would be priority transportation given to an employee in the event of a medical emergency involving the employee (or a member of the employee's immediate family) or a recent death in the employee's immediate family. Frustrated vacation plans or forfeited deposits would not be treated as giving rise to particularly critical needs.

(ii) Priority on the basis of seniority. Solely for purposes of § 1.132-8, a benefit shall not fail to be treated as available to a group of employees of the employer on substantially the same terms merely because the employer allocates the benefit among such employees on a seniority basis provided that:

(A) the same notice of the terms of availability is given to all employees in the group; and

(B) the average value of the benefit provided for each nonhighly compensated employee is at least 75% of that provided for each highly compensated employee. For purposes of this test, the average value of the benefit provided for each nonhighly compensated (highly compensated) employee is determined by taking the sum of the fair market values of such benefit provided to all the nonhighly compensated (highly compensated) employees, determined in accordance with section 1.61-21, and then dividing that sum by the total number of nonhighly compensated (highly compensated) employees of the employer. For purposes of determining the average value of the benefit provided for each employee, all employees of the employer are counted, including those who are not eligible to receive the benefit from the employer.

(d) Testing for discrimination. *(1) Classification test.* In the event that a benefit described in section 132(a)(1), (a)(2) or (e)(2) is not available on substantially the same terms to all of the employees of the employer, no exclusion shall be available to a highly compensated employee for such benefit unless the program under which the benefit is provided satisfies the nondiscrimination standards set forth in this section. The nondiscrimination standard of this section will be satisfied only if the benefit is available on substantially the same terms to a group of employees of the employer which is defined under a reasonable classification established by the employer that does not discriminate in favor of highly compensated employees. The determination of whether a particular classification is discriminatory will generally depend upon the facts and circumstances involved, based upon principles similar to those applied for purposes of section 410(b)(2)(A)(i) or, for years commencing prior to January 1, 1988, section 410(b)(1)(B). Thus, in general, except as otherwise provided in this section, if a benefit is available on substantially the same terms to a group of employees which, when compared with all of the other employees of the employer, constitutes a nondiscriminatory classification under section 410(b)(2)(A)(i) (or, if applicable, section 410(b)(1)(B)), it shall be deemed to be nondiscriminatory.

(2) Classifications that are per se discriminatory. A classification that, on its face, makes fringe benefits available principally to highly compensated employees is per se discriminatory. In addition, a classification that is based on either an amount or rate of compensation is per se discriminatory if it favors those with the higher amount or rate of compensation. On the other hand, a classification that is based on factors such as seniority, full-time vs. part-time employment, or job description is not per se discriminatory but may be discriminatory as applied to the workforce of a particular employer.

(3) Former employees. When determining whether a classification is discriminatory, former employees shall be tested separately from other employees of the employer. Therefore, a classification is not discriminatory solely because the employer does not make fringe benefits available to any former employee. Whether a classification of former employees discriminates in favor of highly compensated employees will depend upon the particular facts and circumstances.

(4) Restructuring of benefits. For purposes of testing whether a particular group of employees would constitute a discriminatory classification for purposes of this section, an employer may restructure its fringe benefit program as described in this paragraph. If a fringe benefit is provided to more than one group of employees, and one or more such groups would constitute a discriminatory classification if considered by itself, then for purposes of this section, the employer may restructure its fringe benefit program so that all or some of the members of such group may be aggregated with another group, provided that each member of the restructured group will have available to him or her the same benefit upon the same terms and conditions. For example, assume that all highly compensated employees of an employer have fewer than five years of service and all nonhighly compensated employees have over five years of service. If the employer provided a five percent discount to employees with under five years of service and a ten percent discount to employees with over five years of service, the discount program available to the highly compensated employees would not satisfy the nondiscriminatory classification test; however, as a result of the rule described in this paragraph (d)(4), the employer could structure the program to consist of a five percent discount for all employees and a five percent additional discount for nonhighly compensated employees.

(5) Employer-operated eating facilities for employees. (i) General rule. If access to an employer-operated eating facility for employees is available to a classification of employees that discriminates in favor of highly compensated employees, then the classification will not be treated as

discriminating in favor of highly compensated employees unless the facility is used by one or more executive group employees more than a de minimis amount.

(ii) Executive group employee. For purposes of this paragraph (d)(5), an employee is an "executive group employee" if the definition of paragraph (f)(1) of this section is satisfied. For purposes of identifying such employees, the phrase "top one percent of the employees" is substituted for the phrase "top ten percent of the employees" in section 414(q)(4) (relating to the definition of "top-paid group").

(e) Cash bonuses or rebates. A cash bonus or rebate provided to an employee by an employer that is determined with reference to the value of employer-provided property or services purchased by the employee, is treated as an equivalent employee discount. For example, assume a department store provides a 20 percent merchandise discount to all employees under a fringe benefit program. In addition, assume that the department store provides cash bonuses to a group of employees defined under a classification which discriminates in favor of highly compensated employees. Assume further that such cash bonuses equal 15 percent of the value of merchandise purchased by each employee. This arrangement is substantively identical to the example described in paragraph (e)(2)(i) of this section concerning related fringe benefit programs. Thus, both the 20 percent merchandise discount and the 15 percent cash bonus provided to the highly compensated employees are includible in such employees' gross incomes.

(f) Highly compensated employee. *(1) Government and non-government employees.* A highly compensated employee of any employer is any employee who, during the year or the preceding year—

(i) Was a 5-percent owner,

(ii) Received compensation from the employer in excess of $75,000,

(iii) Received compensation from the employer in excess of $50,000 and was in the top-paid group of employees for such year, or

(iv) Was at any time an officer and received compensation greater than 150 percent of the amount in effect under section 415(c)(1)(A) for such year.

For purposes of determining whether an employee is a highly compensated employee, the rules of sections 414(q), (s), and (t) apply.

(2) Former employees. A former employee shall be treated as a highly compensated employee if—

(i) The employee was a highly compensated employee when the employee separated from service, or

(ii) The employee was a highly compensated employee at any time after attaining age 55.

T.D. 8256, 7/6/89.

---

§ 1.132-8T Nondiscrimination rules—1985 through 1988 (Temporary).

Caution: The Treasury has not yet amended Reg § 1.132-8T to reflect changes made by P.L. 101-239.

(a) Application of nondiscrimination rules. *(1) General rule.* To qualify under section 132 for the exclusions for no-additional-cost services, qualified employee discounts, or meals provided at employer-operated eating facilities for employees, the fringe benefit must be available on substantially the same terms to each member of a group of employees which is defined under a reasonable classification set up by the employer that does not discriminate in favor of officers, owners, or highly compensated employees (the "prohibited group employees").

(2) Consequences of discrimination. If the availability of or the provision of the fringe benefit does not satisfy the nondiscrimination rules provided in this section, the exclusion applies only to those employees (if any) who receive the benefit and who are not prohibited group employees. For example, if an employer offers a 20 percent discount (which otherwise satisfies the requirements for a qualified employee discount) to all nonprohibited group employees and a 35 percent discount to all prohibited group employees, the entire value of the 35 percent discount (not just the excess over 20 percent) is includible in the gross income and wages of the prohibited group employees who make purchases at a discount.

(3) Scope of the nondiscrimination rules provided in this section. The nondiscrimination rules provided in this section apply only to fringe benefits provided pursuant to section 132 (a) (1), (a) (2), and (e) (2). These rules have no application to any other employee benefit that may be subject to nondiscrimination requirements under any other section of the Code.

(b) Coverage requirement. *(1) Section 132(a)(1) and (2).* For purposes of the exclusions for no-additional-cost services and qualified employee discounts, the nondiscrimination rules of this section are applied by aggregating the employees of all related employers (as defined in § 1.132-1T(c)), but without aggregating employees in different lines of business (as defined in § 1.132-4T). Employees in different lines of business will be aggregated, however, if the line of business limitation has been relaxed pursuant to either § 1.132-4T(b) or (c). Except as provided in paragraph (e) of this section, the nondiscrimination rules of this section are generally applied separately to each fringe benefit program of an employer.

(2) Section 132(e)(2). For purposes of the exclusion for meals provided at employer-operated eating facilities for employees, the nondiscrimination rules of this section are applied by aggregating the employees of all related employers, without regard to different lines of business, who regularly work at or near the premises on which the eating facility is located. The nondiscrimination rules of this section are applied separately to each eating facility. Each dining room or cafeteria in which meals are served is treated as a separate eating facility, regardless of whether each such dining room or cafeteria has its own kitchen or other food-preparation area.

(3) Classes of employees who may be excluded. Except as otherwise provided in this section, for purposes of applying the nondiscrimination rules of this section to a particular fringe benefit program, there may be excluded from consideration the following classes of employees provided that, with respect to each class (other than the class described in paragraph (b)(3)(iii) of this section), all employees in the class are excluded from participating in the particular fringe benefit program—

(i) all part-time or seasonal employees who are (or who are reasonably expected to be) credited with less than 1,000 hours (or such lesser number required for the program) of service during a calendar year;

(ii) all employees who are included in a unit of employees covered by an agreement which the Secretary of Labor finds to be a collective bargaining agreement between employee representatives and one or more employers, if there is evidence that the particular fringe benefit program was the subject of good faith bargaining between such employee representatives and such employer or employers (and if, after March 31, 1984, the additional condition of section 7701(a)(46) is satisfied);

(iii) all employees who are nonresident aliens and who receive no earned income (within the meaning of section 911(d)(2)) from the employer which constitutes income from services within the United States (within the meaning of section 861(a)(3));

(iv) all employees who have not completed at least one year (or such lesser period required for the program) of service with the employer;

(v) all employees who have separated from the service of the employer in a year prior to the current year (regardless of the reason for the separation);

(vi) all employees who have separated from the service of the employer in a year prior to the current year except for retired and/or disabled employees (either with or without a time limit based on a set number of years since separation from the service of the employer); and

(vii) all employees of a leased section of a department store.

(c) Classification requirement. *(1) General rule.* The determination of whether a particular classification established by an employer discriminates in favor of the prohibited group will depend on the facts and circumstances involved, based on principles similar to those applied in the qualified plan area (see section 410(b)(1)(B) and the regulations thereunder). In general, except as otherwise provided in this section, a classification that would be determined to be nondiscriminatory pursuant to the application of the nondiscrimination standards that are applied in the qualified plan area shall be deemed to be nondiscriminatory for purposes of section 132.

(2) Classifications that are per se discriminatory. A classification that, on its face, makes fringe benefits available only to prohibited group employees is per se discriminatory, and no exclusion from gross income is available to any prohibited group employee under section 132. In addition, a classification that is based on either an amount or rate of compensation is per se discriminatory if it favors those with the higher amount or rate of compensation. On the other hand, a classification that is based on factors such as seniority, full-time vs. part-time employment, or job description is not per se discriminatory but may be discriminatory as applied to the workforce of a particular employer.

(3) Former employees. When determining whether a classification is discriminatory, former employees shall not be considered together with other employees of the employer. Therefore, a classification is not discriminatory if the employer does not make the fringe benefits available to any former employee. Whether a classification of former employees discriminates in favor of prohibited group employees will depend on the facts and circumstances. The rules of this section shall apply separately to the former employee classification.

(4) Employer-operated eating facilities for employees. (i) General rule. If access to an employer-operated eating facility for employees is available to a classification of employees that discriminates in favor of highly compensated employees, the classification will not be treated as discriminating in favor of the prohibited group employees unless the facility is used, more than a de minimis amount, by any executive group employee.

(ii) Executive group employees. For purposes of this paragraph (c)(4), the term "executive group employees" has the same meaning as the term "prohibited group employees" (as defined in paragraph (g) of this section), except that for purposes of identifying highly compensated employees—

(A) The exception provided in paragraph (g)(1)(i)(A) of this section does not apply, and

(B) The phrase "highest-paid one percent of all employees of an employer" is substituted for the phrase "highest-paid ten percent of all employees of an employer" in paragraph (g)(1)(ii)(A) of this section.

(d) Substantially-the-same-terms requirement. *(1) General rule.* Fringe benefits available to a particular classification of employees must be available to each employee in the classification on substantially the same terms. The determination of whether this requirement is met shall depend on the facts and circumstances involved. For example, if a department store provides a 20 percent qualified employee discount to its employees on all merchandise, the substantially-the-same-terms requirement will be satisfied. Similarly, if the discount provided to all employees is 30 percent on certain merchandise (such as apparel), and 20 percent on all other merchandise, the substantially-the-same-terms requirement will be satisfied. However, if the discount provided is 20 percent on all merchandise for hourly employees and 30 percent on all merchandise for salaried employees, the substantially-the-same-terms requirement will not be satisfied. In addition, if the percentage discount varies depending on either an employee's amount or rate of compensation, or volume of purchases, the substantially-the-same-terms requirement will not be satisfied. In order to determine whether such a discount program satisfies the nondiscrimination requirements of section 132, each group of employees that does receive fringe benefits on substantially the same terms must be treated as a separate classification. However, subject to the rules of paragraph (e)(2) of this section, an employer may divide a fringe benefit program into two programs for purposes of aggregating groups of employees. See Example (1) of paragraph (d)(3) of this section.

(2) Terms relating to priority. Certain fringe benefits made available to employees are available only in limited quantities that may be insufficient to meet employee demand. This may occur either because of employer policy (such as where an employer determines that only a certain number of units of a specific product will be made available to employees each year) or because of the nature of the fringe benefit (such as where an employer provides a no-additional-cost transportation service that is limited to the number of seats available just before departure). Under these circumstances, an employer may find it necessary to establish some method of allocating the limited fringe benefits among the employees eligible to receive the fringe benefits. An allocation among employees on a "first-come, first-served" basis will not violate the substantially-the-same-terms requirement provided that such an allocation is not discriminatory in practice. In addition, an allocation among employees on a lottery basis will not violate the substantially-the-same-terms requirement provided that such an allocation is nondiscriminatory in practice. For example, assume that an employer has a limited number of a particular benefit to offer to its employees. Assume further that the employees interested in receiving the benefit submit their names to the employer who then selects a number of names, at random, equal to the number of fringe benefits available. This lottery system would not

violate the substantially-the-same-terms requirement. An allocation among employees on other than a "first-come, first-served", lottery, or similar basis will violate the substantially-the-same-terms requirement. Therefore, an allocation based on seniority, full-time vs. part-time employment, or job description will violate the substantially-the-same-terms requirement. In order to determine whether such a fringe benefit program satisfies the nondiscrimination requirements of section 132, each group of employees that does receive fringe benefits on substantially the same terms must be treated as a separate classification. For purposes of this rule, the last two sentences of paragraph (d)(1) of this section apply.

(3) Examples. The following examples illustrate the provisions of this paragraph (d):

Example (1). Assume that with respect to a benefit available in limited quantities an employer provides priority to employees based on seniority. Assume further that all non-prohibited group employees have ten years of seniority and all prohibited group employees have nine years seniority. If each of these groups were tested separately, the benefits offered to prohibited group employees would be discriminatory under this section. In this case, the employer could divide the fringe benefit program provided to non-prohibited group employees into two parts: one relating to nine years of seniority and one relating to an additional year of seniority. As restructured in this manner, all employees receive the benefit relating to nine years seniority and only non-prohibited group employees receive the benefit relating to an additional year of seniority. Both groups (all employees and all non-prohibited group employees) are nondiscriminatory groups.

Example (2). Assume that prices charged to prohibited group employees at an employer-operated eating facility for employees are lower than prices charged to non-prohibited group employees. The substantially-the-same requirement is not satisfied.

(4) Disproportionate use of eating facility. If access to an employer-operated eating facility for employees is technically available on substantially-the-same-terms to (i) all employees who regularly work at or near the premises on which the eating facility is located (the employee group), or (ii) a nondiscriminatory classification of the employee group, but in practice a highly disproportionate number of the prohibited group employees in the employee group, compared to the non-prohibited group employees in the employee group, use the facility, the substantially-the-same-terms requirement will not be satisfied unless no member of the executive group eats there more than a de minimis amount.

(e) Aggregation of separate fringe benefit programs. *(1) General rule.* If an employer maintains more than one fringe benefit program, i.e., two or more classifications of employees providing either identical or different fringe benefits, the nondiscrimination requirements of section 132 will generally be applied separately to each such program. Thus, a determination that one fringe benefit program discriminates in favor of prohibited group employees generally will not cause other fringe benefit programs covering the same prohibited group employees to be treated as discriminatory.

(2) Exception. (i) Related fringe benefit programs. If one of a group of fringe benefit programs discriminates in favor of prohibited group employees, no related fringe benefit provided to such prohibited group employees under any other fringe benefit program may be excluded from the gross income of such prohibited group employees. For example, assume a department store provides a 20 percent merchandise discount to all employees under one fringe benefit program. Assume further that under a second fringe benefit program, the department store provides an additional 15 percent merchandise discount to a group of employees defined under a classification which discriminates in favor of the prohibited group. Because the second fringe benefit program is discriminatory, the 15 percent merchandise discount provided to the prohibited group employees is not a qualified employee discount. In addition, because the 20 percent merchandise discount provided under the first fringe benefit program is related to the fringe benefit provided under the second fringe benefit program, the 20 percent merchandise discount provided the prohibited group employees is not a qualified employee discount. Thus, the entire 35 percent merchandise discount provided to the prohibited group employees is includible in such employees' gross incomes.

(ii) Employer-operated eating facilities for employees. For purposes of paragraph (e)(2)(i) of this section, meals at different employer-operated eating facilities for employees are not related fringe benefits, so that a prohibited group employee may exclude the value of a meal at a nondiscriminatory facility even though any meals provided to him or her at the discriminatory facility cannot be excluded.

(f) Cash bonuses or rebates. A cash bonus or rebate provided to an employee by an employer that is determined pursuant to the value of employer-provided property or services purchased by the employee, is treated as an equivalent employee discount. For example, assume a department store provides a 20 percent merchandise discount to all employees under a fringe benefit program. In addition, assume that the department store provides cash bonuses to a group of employees defined under a classification which discriminates in favor of the prohibited group. Assume further that such cash bonuses equal 15 percent of the value of merchandise purchased by each employee. This arrangement is substantively identical to the example described in paragraph (e)(2) of this section. Thus, both the 20 percent merchandise discount and the 15 percent cash bonus provided to the prohibited group employees are includible in such employees' gross incomes.

(g) Prohibited group employees. *(1) Highly compensated.* (i) General rule. Except as otherwise provided in this paragraph (g)(1)(i), any employee of an employer who has (or is reasonably expected to have) compensation during a calendar year equal to or greater than the employer's base compensation amount is highly compensated. There are two exceptions to this rule:

(A) any employee who has (or is reasonably expected to have) compensation during a calendar year equal to or greater than $50,000 is highly compensated, regardless of whether such compensation is in excess of the base compensation amount, and

(B) any employee who is reasonably expected to have compensation during a calendar year equal to or less than $20,000 is not highly compensated, unless no employee of the employer is reasonably expected to have compensation equal to or greater than $35,000.

The determination of whether an employee is a highly compensated employee will be determined based on the entire employee workforce of all employers aggregated pursuant to the rules of section 414(b), (c), or (m) without regard to the regular workplace of the employees.

(ii) Base compensation amount. (A) General rule. The term "base compensation amount" is defined as that amount corresponding to the lowest annual compensation amount received by the highest-paid ten percent of all employees of an employer (the number of employees in the top ten percent will be increased to the next highest integer if necessary), determined on the basis of the preceding calendar year. For purposes of this paragraph (g)(1)(ii), the term "employer" includes all entities that would be aggregated pursuant to the rules of section 414(b), (c), or (m).

(B) Employees that are excluded. For purposes of determining the base compensation amount with respect to a fringe benefit program, employees described in paragraph (b)(3) of this section are excluded whether or not they are covered under the fringe benefit program, except that (1) employees described in paragraph (b)(3)(ii) of this section are taken into account with respect to the program even if they are excluded under paragraph (b)(3), and (2) employees described in paragraph (b)(3)(i) and (iv) of this section are taken into account with respect to the program unless they are excluded under paragraph (b)(3).

(C) Exception to preceding calendar year rule. In the case of an employer's first year of operation, or where an employer's business has changed significantly from the prior calendar year (e.g., due to an acquisition or merger), the employer must make a good faith attempt to either determine or adjust the base compensation amount for the current year based on reasonable estimates of current year compensation.

(iii) Compensation. The term "compensation" is defined as the amount reportable on a Form W-2 as income. Amounts that would be excluded from income but for section 132(h)(1) are not included in compensation for purposes of this paragraph (g)(1). Compensation includes amounts received from all entities which would be treated as a single employer under section 414(b), (c), or (m) and is not restricted to amounts received with respect to any one line of business.

(iv) Employee. Generally, for purposes of determining whether an employee is highly compensated under this paragraph (g)(1), the term "employee" does not include any individual who does not perform services for the employer as an employee during the calendar year. For example, if an employer has active employees, retired or disabled employees, and widows or widowers who are "employees" under section 132(f)(1)(B), the general rule (described in paragraph (g)(1)(i) of this section) applies only to the active employees.

(2) Owner. (i) General rule. For purposes of this section, the term "owner" means any employee who owns a one percent or greater interest in either the employer or in any entity that would be aggregated with the employer pursuant to the rules of section 414(b), (c), or (m). In addition, such an employee shall be treated as an owner of all entities that would be aggregated with the employer pursuant to the rules of section 414(b), (c), or (m).

(ii) Determining ownership. Ownership in a corporation shall be determined pursuant to the rules of section 318(a). For purposes of determining ownership in an entity other than a corporation, the rules of section 318(a) shall apply in a manner similar to the way in which they apply for purposes of determining ownership in a corporation. For noncorporate interests, capital or profits interest must be substituted for stock.

(3) Officer. (i) Non-government. For purposes of this section, an officer of a non-government employer is any employee who is appointed, confirmed, or elected by the Board or shareholders of the employer. An employee who is an officer of an employer shall be treated as an officer of all entities treated as a single employer pursuant to section 414(b), (c), or (m). The number of officers is not to exceed one-percent of the total number of employees of all entities treated as a single employer pursuant to section 414(b), (c), or (m) (increased to the next highest integer, if necessary). If the number of officers exceeds one-percent of all employees, then the limitation is to be applied to employees in descending order of compensation (as defined in paragraph (g)(1)(iii) of this section). Thus, if an employer with 1,000 employees has 11 board-appointed officers, the employee with the least compensation of those officers would not be an officer under this paragraph (g)(3)(i). In determining the total number of employees with respect to a fringe benefit program, employees described in paragraph (b)(3) of this section are excluded whether or not they are covered under the fringe benefit program, except that (A) employees described in paragraph (b)(3)(ii) of this section are taken into account with respect to the program even if they are excluded under paragraph (b)(3), and (B) employees described in paragraph (b)(3)(i) and (iv) of this section are taken into account with respect to the program unless they are excluded under paragraph (b)(3).

(ii) Government. For purposes of this section, an officer of a government employer is any—

(A) Elected official,

(B) Federal employee appointed by the President and confirmed by the Senate. However, in the case of any commissioned officer of the United States Armed Forces, an officer is any employee with the rank of brigadier general or rear admiral (lower half) or above, and

(C) State or local executive officer comparable to individuals described in paragraphs (g)(3)(ii)(A) and (B) of this section. For purposes of this paragraph (g)(3)(ii), the term "government" includes any Federal, state, or local governmental unit, and any agency or instrumentality thereof.

(4) Former employees. [Reserved]

T.D. 8063, 12/18/85, amend T.D. 8256, 7/6/89.

§ 1.132-9 Qualified transportation fringes.

(a) Table of contents. This section contains a list of the questions and answers in § 1.132-9.

(1) General rules.

Q-1. What is a qualified transportation fringe?

Q-2. What is transportation in a commuter highway vehicle?

Q-3. What are transit passes?

Q-4. What is qualified parking?

Q-5. May qualified transportation fringes be provided to individuals who are not employees?

Q-6. Must a qualified transportation fringe benefit plan be in writing?

(2) Dollar limitations.

Q-7. Is there a limit on the value of qualified transportation fringes that may be excluded from an employee's gross income?

Q-8. What amount is includible in an employee's wages for income and employment tax purposes if the value of the qualified transportation fringe exceeds the applicable statutory monthly limit?

Q-9. Are excludable qualified transportation fringes calculated on a monthly basis?

Q-10. May an employee receive qualified transportation fringes from more than one employer?

(3) Compensation reduction.

Q-11. May qualified transportation fringes be provided to employees pursuant to a compensation reduction agreement?

Q-12. What is a compensation reduction election for purposes of section 132(f)?

Q-13. Is there a limit to the amount of the compensation reduction?

Q-14. When must the employee have made a compensation reduction election and under what circumstances may the amount be paid in cash to the employee?

Q-15. May an employee whose qualified transportation fringe costs are less than the employee's compensation reduction carry over this excess amount to subsequent periods?

(4) Expense reimbursements.

Q-16. How does section 132(f) apply to expense reimbursements?

Q-17. May an employer provide nontaxable cash reimbursement under section 132(f) for periods longer than one month?

Q-18. What are the substantiation requirements if an employer distributes transit passes?

Q-19. May an employer choose to impose substantiation requirements in addition to those described in this regulation?

(5) Special rules for parking and vanpools.

Q-20. How is the value of parking determined?

Q-21. How do the qualified transportation fringe rules apply to van pools?

(6) Reporting and employment taxes.

Q-22. What are the reporting and employment tax requirements for qualified transportation fringes?

(7) Interaction with other fringe benefits.

Q-23. How does section 132(f) interact with other fringe benefit rules?

(8) Application to individuals who are not employees.

Q-24. May qualified transportation fringes be provided to individuals who are partners, 2-percent shareholders of S-corporations, or independent contractors?

(9) Effective date.

Q-25. What is the effective date of this section?

(b) Questions and answers.

Q-1. What is a qualified transportation fringe?

A-1. (a) The following benefits are qualified transportation fringe benefits:

(1) Transportation in a commuter highway vehicle.

(2) Transit passes.

(3) Qualified parking.

(b) An employer may simultaneously provide an employee with any one or more of these three benefits.

Q-2. What is transportation in a commuter highway vehicle?

A-2. Transportation in a commuter highway vehicle is transportation provided by an employer to an employee in connection with travel between the employee's residence and place of employment. A commuter highway vehicle is a highway vehicle with a seating capacity of at least 6 adults (excluding the driver) and with respect to which at least 80 percent of the vehicle's mileage for a year is reasonably expected to be—

(a) For transporting employees in connection with travel between their residences and their place of employment; and

(b) On trips during which the number of employees transported for commuting is at least one-half of the adult seating capacity of the vehicle (excluding the driver).

Q-3. What are transit passes?

A-3. A transit pass is any pass, token, farecard, voucher, or similar item (including an item exchangeable for fare media) that entitles a person to transportation—

(a) On mass transit facilities (whether or not publicly owned); or

(b) Provided by any person in the business of transporting persons for compensation or hire in a highway vehicle with a seating capacity of at least 6 adults (excluding the driver).

Q-4. What is qualified parking?

A-4. (a) Qualified parking is parking provided to an employee by an employer—

(1) On or near the employer's business premises; or

(2) At a location from which the employee commutes to work (including commuting by carpool, commuter highway vehicle, mass transit facilities, or transportation provided by any person in the business of transporting persons for compensation or hire).

(b) For purposes of section 132(f), parking on or near the employer's business premises includes parking on or near a work location at which the employee provides services for the employer. However, qualified parking does not include—

(1) The value of parking provided to an employee that is excludable from gross income under section 132(a)(3) (as a working condition fringe), or

(2) Reimbursement paid to an employee for parking costs that is excludable from gross income as an amount treated as paid under an accountable plan. See § 1.62-2.

(c) However, parking on or near property used by the employee for residential purposes is not qualified parking.

(d) Parking is provided by an employer if

(1) The parking is on property that the employer owns or leases;

(2) The employer pays for the parking; or

(3) The employer reimburses the employee for parking expenses (see Q/A-16 of this section for rules relating to cash reimbursements).

Q-5. May qualified transportation fringes be provided to individuals who are not employees?

A-5. An employer may provide qualified transportation fringes only to individuals who are currently employees of the employer at the time the qualified transportation fringe is provided. The term employee for purposes of qualified transportation fringes is defined in § 1.132-1(b)(2)(i). This term includes only common law employees and other statutory employees, such as officers of corporations. See Q/A-24 of this section for rules regarding partners, 2-percent shareholders, and independent contractors.

Q-6. Must a qualified transportation fringe benefit plan be in writing?

A-6. No. Section 132(f) does not require that a qualified transportation fringe benefit plan be in writing.

Q-7. Is there a limit on the value of qualified transportation fringes that may be excluded from an employee's gross income?

A-7. (a) Transportation in a commuter highway vehicle and transit passes. Before January 1, 2002, up to $65 per month is excludable from the gross income of an employee for transportation in a commuter highway vehicle and transit passes provided by an employer. On January 1, 2002, this amount is increased to $100 per month.

(b) Parking. Up to $175 per month is excludable from the gross income of an employee for qualified parking.

(c) Combination. An employer may provide qualified parking benefits in addition to transportation in a commuter highway vehicle and transit passes.

(d) Cost-of-living adjustments. The amounts in paragraphs (a) and (b) of this Q/A-7 are adjusted annually, beginning with 2000, to reflect cost-of-living. The adjusted figures are announced by the Service before the beginning of the year.

Q-8. What amount is includible in an employee's wages for income and employment tax purposes if the value of the qualified transportation fringe exceeds the applicable statutory monthly limit?

A-8. (a) Generally, an employee must include in gross income the amount by which the fair market value of the benefit exceeds the sum of the amount, if any, paid by the employee and any amount excluded from gross income under section 132(a)(5). Thus, assuming no other statutory exclusion applies, if an employer provides an employee with a qualified transportation fringe that exceeds the applicable statutory monthly limit and the employee does not make any payment, the value of the benefits provided in excess of the applicable statutory monthly limit is included in the employee's wages for income and employment tax purposes. See § 1.61-21(b)(1).

(b) The following examples illustrate the principles of this Q/A-8:

Example (1). (i) For each month in a year in which the statutory monthly transit pass limit is $100 (i.e., a year after 2001), Employer M provides a transit pass valued at $110 to Employee D, who does not pay any amount to Employer M for the transit pass.

(ii) In this Example 1, because the value of the monthly transit pass exceeds the statutory monthly limit by $10, $120 ($110--$100, times 12 months) must be included in D's wages for income and employment tax purposes for the year with respect to the transit passes.

Example (2). (i) For each month in a year in which the statutory monthly qualified parking limit is $175, Employer M provides qualified parking valued at $195 to Employee E, who does not pay any amount to M for the parking.

(ii) In this Example 2, because the fair market value of the qualified parking exceeds the statutory monthly limit by $20, $240 ($195--$175, times 12 months) must be included in Employee E's wages for income and employment tax purposes for the year with respect to the qualified parking.

Example (3). (i) For each month in a year in which the statutory monthly qualified parking limit is $175, Employer P provides qualified parking with a fair market value of $220 per month to its employees, but charges each employee $45 per month.

(ii) In this Example 3, because the sum of the amount paid by an employee ($45) plus the amount excludable for qualified parking ($175) is not less than the fair market value of the monthly benefit, no amount is includible in the employee's wages for income and employment tax purposes with respect to the qualified parking.

Q-9. Are excludable qualified transportation fringes calculated on a monthly basis?

A-9. (a) In general. Yes. The value of transportation in a commuter highway vehicle, transit passes, and qualified parking is calculated on a monthly basis to determine whether the value of the benefit has exceeded the applicable statutory monthly limit on qualified transportation fringes. Except in the case of a transit pass provided to an employee, the applicable statutory monthly limit applies to qualified transportation fringes used by the employee in a month. Monthly exclusion amounts are not combined to provide a qualified transportation fringe for any month exceeding the statutory limit. A month is a calendar month or a substantially equivalent period applied consistently.

(b) Transit passes. In the case of transit passes provided to an employee, the applicable statutory monthly limit applies to the transit passes provided by the employer to the employee in a month for that month or for any previous month in the calendar year. In addition, transit passes distributed in advance for more than one month, but not for more than twelve months, are qualified transportation fringes if the requirements in paragraph (c) of this Q/A-9 are met (relating to the income tax and employment tax treatment of advance transit passes). The applicable statutory monthly limit under section 132(f)(2) on the combined amount of transportation in a commuter highway vehicle and transit passes may be calculated by taking into account the monthly limits for all months for which the transit passes are distributed. In the case of a pass that is valid for more than one month, such as an annual pass, the value of the pass may be divided by the number of months for which it is valid for purposes of determining whether the value of the pass exceeds the statutory monthly limit.

(c) Rule if employee's employment terminates. (1) Income tax treatment. The value of transit passes provided in advance to an employee with respect to a month in which the individual is not an employee is included in the employee's wages for income tax purposes.

(2) Reporting and employment tax treatment. Transit passes distributed in advance to an employee are excludable from wages for employment tax purposes under sections 3121, 3306, and 3401 (FICA, FUTA, and income tax withholding) if the employer distributes transit passes to the employee in advance for not more than three months and, at the time the transit passes are distributed, there is not an established date that the employee's employment will terminate (for example, if the employee has given notice of retirement) which will occur before the beginning of the last month of the period for which the transit passes are provided. If the employer distributes transit passes to an employee in advance for not more than three months and at the time the transit passes are distributed there is an established date that the employee's employment will terminate, and the employee's employment does terminate before the beginning of the last month of the period for which the transit passes are provided, the value of transit passes provided for months beginning after the date of termination during which the employee is not employed by the employer is included in the employee's wages for employment tax purposes. If transit passes are distributed in advance for more than three months, the value of transit passes provided for the months during which the employee is not employed by the employer is includible in the employee's wages for employment tax purposes regardless of whether at the time the transit passes were distributed there was an established date of termination of the employee's employment.

(d) Examples. The following examples illustrate the principles of this Q/A-9:

Example (1). (i) Employee E incurs $150 for qualified parking used during the month of June of a year in which the statutory monthly parking limit is $175, for which E is reimbursed $150 by Employer R. Employee E incurs $180 in expenses for qualified parking used during the month of July of that year, for which E is reimbursed $180 by Employer R.

(ii) In this Example 1, because monthly exclusion amounts may not be combined to provide a benefit in any month greater than the applicable statutory limit, the amount by which the amount reimbursed for July exceeds the applicable statutory monthly limit ($180 minus $175 equals $5) is includible in Employee E's wages for income and employment tax purposes.

Example (2). (i) Employee F receives transit passes from Employer G with a value of $195 in March of a year (for which the statutory monthly transit pass limit is $65) for January, February, and March of that year. F was hired during January and has not received any transit passes from G.

(ii) In this Example 2, the value of the transit passes (three months times $65 equals $195) is excludable from F's wages for income and employment tax purposes.

Example (3). (i) Employer S has a qualified transportation fringe benefit plan under which its employees receive transit passes near the beginning of each calendar quarter for that calendar quarter. All employees of Employer S receive transit passes from Employer S with a value of $195 on March 31 for the second calendar quarter covering the months April, May, and June (of a year in which the statutory monthly transit pass limit is $65).

(ii) In this Example 3, because the value of the transit passes may be calculated by taking into account the monthly limits for all months for which the transit passes are distributed, the value of the transit passes (three months times $65 equals $195) is excludable from the employees' wages for income and employment tax purposes.

Example (4). (i) Same facts as in Example 3, except that Employee T, an employee of Employer S, terminates employment with S on May 31. There was not an established date of termination for Employee T at the time the transit passes were distributed.

(ii) In this Example 4, because at the time the transit passes were distributed there was not an established date of termination for Employee T, the value of the transit passes provided for June ($65) is excludable from T's wages for employment tax purposes. However, the value of the transit passes distributed to Employee T for June ($65) is not excludable from T's wages for income tax purposes.

(iii) If Employee T's May 31 termination date was established at the time the transit passes were provided, the value of the transit passes provided for June ($65) is included in T's wages for both income and employment tax purposes.

Example (5). (i) Employer F has a qualified transportation fringe benefit plan under which its employees receive transit passes semi-annually in advance of the months for which the transit passes are provided. All employees of Employer F, including Employee X, receive transit passes from F with a value of $390 on June 30 for the 6 months of July through December (of a year in which the statutory monthly transit pass limit is $65). Employee X's employment terminates and his last day of work is August 1. Employer F's other employees remain employed throughout the remainder of the year.

(ii) In this Example 5, the value of the transit passes provided to Employee X for the months September, October, November, and December ($65 times 4 months equals $260) of the year is included in X's wages for income and employment tax purposes. The value of the transit passes provided to Employer F's other employees is excludable from the employees' wages for income and employment tax purposes.

Example (6). (i) Each month during a year in which the statutory monthly transit pass limit is $65, Employer R distributes transit passes with a face amount of $70 to each of its employees. Transit passes with a face amount of $70 can be purchased from the transit system by any individual for $65.

(ii) In this Example 6, because the value of the transit passes distributed by Employer R does not exceed the applicable statutory monthly limit ($65), no portion of the value of the transit passes is included as wages for income and employment tax purposes.

Q-10. May an employee receive qualified transportation fringes from more than one employer?

A-10. (a) General rule. Yes. The statutory monthly limits described in Q/A-7 of this section apply to benefits provided by an employer to its employees. For this purpose, all employees treated as employed by a single employer under section 414(b), (c), (m), or (o) are treated as employed by a single employer. See section 414(t) and § 1.132-1(c). Thus, qualified transportation fringes paid by entities under common control under section 414(b), (c), (m), or (o) are combined for purposes of applying the applicable statutory monthly limit. In addition, an individual who is treated as a leased employee of the employer under section 414(n) is treated as an employee of that employer for purposes of section 132. See section 414(n)(3)(C).

(b) Examples. The following examples illustrate the principles of this Q/A-10:

Example (1). (i) During a year in which the statutory monthly qualified parking limit is $175, Employee E works for Employers M and N, who are unrelated and not treated as a single employer under section 414(b), (c), (m), or (o). Each month, M and N each provide qualified parking benefits to E with a value of $100.

(ii) In this Example 1, because M and N are unrelated employers, and the value of the monthly parking benefit provided by each is not more than the applicable statutory monthly limit, the parking benefits provided by each employer are excludable as qualified transportation fringes assuming that the other requirements of this section are satisfied.

Example (2). (i) Same facts as in Example 1, except that Employers M and N are treated as a single employer under section 414(b).

(ii) In this Example 2, because M and N are treated as a single employer, the value of the monthly parking benefit provided by M and N must be combined for purposes of determining whether the applicable statutory monthly limit has been exceeded. Thus, the amount by which the value of the parking benefit exceeds the monthly limit ($200 minus the monthly limit amount of $175 equals $25) for each month in the year is includible in E's wages for income and employment tax purposes.

Q-11. May qualified transportation fringes be provided to employees pursuant to a compensation reduction agreement?

A-11. Yes. An employer may offer employees a choice between cash compensation and any qualified transportation fringe. An employee who is offered this choice and who elects qualified transportation fringes is not required to include the cash compensation in income if—

(a) The election is pursuant to an arrangement described in Q/A-12 of this section;

(b) The amount of the reduction in cash compensation does not exceed the limitation in Q/A-13 of this section;

(c) The arrangement satisfies the timing and reimbursement rules in Q/A-14 and 16 of this section; and

(d) The related fringe benefit arrangement otherwise satisfies the requirements set forth elsewhere in this section.

Q-12. What is a compensation reduction election for purposes of section 132(f)?

A-12. (a) Election requirements generally. A compensation reduction arrangement is an arrangement under which the employer provides the employee with the right to elect whether the employee will receive either a fixed amount of cash compensation at a specified future date or a fixed amount of qualified transportation fringes to be provided for a specified future period (such as qualified parking to be used during a future calendar month). The employee's election must be in writing or another form, such as electronic, that includes, in a permanent and verifiable form, the information required to be in the election. The election must contain the date of the election, the amount of the compensation to be reduced, and the period for which the benefit will be provided. The election must relate to a fixed dollar amount or fixed percentage of compensation reduction. An election to reduce compensation for a period by a set amount for such period may be automatically renewed for subsequent periods.

(b) Automatic election permitted. An employer may provide under its qualified transportation fringe benefit plan that a compensation reduction election will be deemed to have been made if the employee does not elect to receive cash compensation in lieu of the qualified transportation fringe, provided that the employee receives adequate notice that a compensation reduction will be made and is given adequate opportunity to choose to receive the cash compensation instead of the qualified transportation fringe. See § 1.401(a)-21 of this chapter for rules permitting the use of electronic media to make participant elections with respect to employee benefit arrangements.

Q-13. Is there a limit to the amount of the compensation reduction?

A-13. Yes. Each month, the amount of the compensation reduction may not exceed the combined applicable statutory monthly limits for transportation in a commuter highway vehicle, transit passes, and qualified parking. For example, for a year in which the statutory monthly limit is $65 for transportation in a commuter highway vehicle and transit passes, and $175 for qualified parking, an employee could elect to reduce compensation for any month by no more than $240 ($65 plus $175) with respect to qualified transportation fringes. If an employee were to elect to reduce compensation by $250 for a month, the excess $10 ($250 minus $240) would be includible in the employee's wages for income and employment tax purposes.

Q-14. When must the employee have made a compensation reduction election and under what circumstances may the amount be paid in cash to the employee?

A-14. (a) The compensation reduction election must satisfy the requirements set forth under paragraphs (b), (c), and (d) of this Q/A-14.

(b) Timing of election. The compensation reduction election must be made before the employee is able currently to receive the cash or other taxable amount at the employee's discretion. The determination of whether the employee is able currently to receive the cash does not depend on whether it has been constructively received for purposes of section 451. The election must specify that the period (such as a calendar month) for which the qualified transportation fringe will be provided must not begin before the election is made. Thus, a compensation reduction election must relate to qualified transportation fringes to be provided after the election. For this purpose, the date a qualified transportation fringe is provided is—

(1) The date the employee receives a voucher or similar item; or

(2) In any other case, the date the employee uses the qualified transportation fringe.

(c) Revocability of elections. The employee may not revoke a compensation reduction election after the employee is able currently to receive the cash or other taxable amount at the employee's discretion. In addition, the election may not be revoked after the beginning of the period for which the qualified transportation fringe will be provided.

(d) Compensation reduction amounts not refundable. Unless an election is revoked in a manner consistent with paragraph (c) of this Q/A-14, an employee may not subsequently receive the compensation (in cash or any form other than by payment of a qualified transportation fringe under the employer's plan). Thus, an employer's qualified transportation fringe benefit plan may not provide that an employee who ceases to participate in the employer's qualified transportation fringe benefit plan (such as in the case of termination of employment) is entitled to receive a refund of the amount by which the employee's compensation reductions exceed the actual qualified transportation fringes provided to the employee by the employer.

(e) Examples. The following examples illustrate the principles of this Q/A-14:

Example (1). (i) Employer P maintains a qualified transportation fringe benefit arrangement during a year in which the statutory monthly limit is $100 for transportation in a commuter highway vehicle and transit passes (2002 or later) and $180 for qualified parking. Employees of P are paid cash compensation twice per month, with the payroll dates being the first and the fifteenth day of the month. Under P's arrangement, an employee is permitted to elect at any time before the first day of a month to reduce his or her compensation payable during that month in an amount up to the applicable statutory monthly limit ($100 if the employee elects coverage for transportation in a commuter highway vehicle or a mass transit pass, or $180 if the employee chooses qualified parking) in return for the right to receive qualified transportation fringes up to the amount of the election. If such an election is made, P will provide a mass transit pass for that month with a value not exceeding the compensation reduction amount elected by the employee or will reimburse the cost of other qualified transportation fringes used by the employee on or after the first day of that month up to the compensation reduction amount elected by the employee. Any compensation reduction amount elected by the employee for the month that is not used for qualified transportation fringes is not refunded to the employee at any future date.

(ii) In this Example 1, the arrangement satisfies the requirements of this Q/A-14 because the election is made before the employee is able currently to receive the cash and the election specifies the future period for which the qualified transportation fringes will be provided. The arrangement would also satisfy the requirements of this Q/A-14 and Q/A-13 of this section if employees are allowed to elect to reduce compensation up to $280 per month ($100 plus $180).

(iii) The arrangement would also satisfy the requirements of this Q/A-14 (and Q/A-13 of this section) if employees are allowed to make an election at any time before the first or the fifteenth day of the month to reduce their compensation payable on that payroll date by an amount not in excess of one-half of the applicable statutory monthly limit (depending on the type of qualified transportation fringe elected by the employee) and P provides a mass transit pass on or after the applicable payroll date for the compensation reduction amount elected by the employee for the payroll date or reimburses the cost of other qualified transportation fringes used by the employee on or after the payroll date up to the compensation reduction amount elected by the employee for that payroll date.

Example (2). (i) Employee Q elects to reduce his compensation payable on March 1 of a year (for which the statutory monthly mass transit limit is $65) by $195 in exchange for a mass transit voucher to be provided in March. The election is made on the preceding February 27. Employee Q was hired in January of the year. On March 10 of the year, the employer of Employee Q delivers to Employee Q a mass transit voucher worth $195 for the months of January, February, and March.

(ii) In this Example 2, $65 is included in Employee Q's wages for income and employment tax purposes because the compensation reduction election fails to satisfy the requirement in this Q/A-14 and Q/A-12 of this section that the period for which the qualified transportation fringe will be provided not begin before the election is made to the extent the election relates to $65 worth of transit passes for January of the year. The $65 for February is not taxable because the election was for a future period that includes at least one day in February.

(iii) However, no amount would be included in Employee Q's wages as a result of the election if $195 worth of mass transit passes were instead provided to Q for the months of February, March, and April (because the compensation reduction would relate solely to fringes to be provided for a period not beginning before the date of the election and the amount provided does not exceed the aggregate limit for the period, i.e., the sum of $65 for each of February, March, and April). See Q/A-9 of this section for rules governing transit passes distributed in advance for more than one month.

Example (3). (i) Employee R elects to reduce his compensation payable on March 1 of a year (for which the statutory monthly parking limit is $175) by $185 in exchange for reimbursement by Employer T of parking expenses incurred by Employee R for parking on or near Employer T's business premises during the period beginning after the date of the election through March. The election is made on the preceding February 27. Employee R incurs $10 in parking expenses on February 28 of the year, and $175 in parking expenses during the month of March. On April 5 of the year, Employer T reimburses Employee R $185 for the parking expenses incurred on February 28, and during March, of the year.

(ii) In this Example 3, no amount would be includible in Employee R's wages for income and employment tax purposes because the compensation reduction related solely to parking on or near Employer R's business premises used during a period not beginning before the date of the election and the amount reimbursed for parking used in any one month does not exceed the statutory monthly limitation.

Q-15. May an employee whose qualified transportation fringe costs are less than the employee's compensation reduction carry over this excess amount to subsequent periods?

A-15. (a) Yes. An employee may carry over unused compensation reduction amounts to subsequent periods under the plan of the employee's employer.

(b) The following example illustrates the principles of this Q/A-15:

Example. (i) By an election made before November 1 of a year for which the statutory monthly mass transit limit is $65, Employee E elects to reduce compensation in the amount of $65 for the month of November. E incurs $50 in employee-operated commuter highway vehicle expenses during November for which E is reimbursed $50 by Employer R, E's employer. By an election made before December, E elects to reduce compensation by $65 for the month of December. E incurs $65 in employee-operated commuter highway vehicle expenses during December for which E is reimbursed $65 by R. Before the following January, E elects to reduce compensation by $50 for the month of January. E incurs $65 in employee-operated commuter highway vehicle expenses during January for which E is reimbursed $65 by R because R allows E to carry over to the next year the $15 amount by which the compensation reductions for November and December exceeded the employee-operated commuter highway vehicle expenses incurred during those months.

(ii) In this Example, because Employee E is reimbursed in an amount not exceeding the applicable statutory monthly limit, and the reimbursement does not exceed the amount of employee-operated commuter highway vehicle expenses incurred during the month of January, the amount reimbursed ($65) is excludable from E's wages for income and employment tax purposes.

Q-16. How does section 132(f) apply to expense reimbursements?

A-16. (a) In general. The term qualified transportation fringe includes cash reimbursement by an employer to an employee for expenses incurred or paid by an employee for transportation in a commuter highway vehicle or qualified parking. The term qualified transportation fringe also includes cash reimbursement for transit passes made under a bona fide reimbursement arrangement, but, in accordance with section 132(f)(3), only if permitted under paragraph (b) of this Q/A-16. The reimbursement must be made under a bona fide reimbursement arrangement which meets the rules of paragraph (c) of this Q/A-16. A payment made before the date an expense has been incurred or paid is not a reimbursement. In addition, a bona fide reimbursement arrangement does not include an arrangement that is dependent solely upon an employee certifying in advance that the employee will incur expenses at some future date.

(b) Special rule for transit passes. (1) In general. The term qualified transportation fringe includes cash reimbursement for transit passes made under a bona fide reimbursement arrangement, but, in accordance with section 132(f)(3), only if no voucher or similar item that may be exchanged only for a transit pass is readily available for direct distribution by the employer to employees. If a voucher is readily available, the requirement that a voucher be distributed in-kind by the employer is satisfied if the voucher is distributed by the employer or by another person on behalf of the employer (for example, if a transit operator credits amounts to the employee's fare card as a result of payments made to the operator by the employer).

(2) Voucher or similar item. For purposes of the special rule in paragraph (b) of this Q/A-16, a transit system voucher is an instrument that may be purchased by employers from a voucher provider that is accepted by one or more mass transit operators (e.g., train, subway, and bus) in an area as fare media or in exchange for fare media. Thus, for example, a transit pass that may be purchased by employers directly from a voucher provider is a transit system voucher.

(3) Voucher provider. The term voucher provider means any person in the trade or business of selling transit system vouchers to employers, or any transit system or transit operator that sells vouchers to employers for the purpose of direct distribution to employees. Thus, a transit operator might or might not be a voucher provider. A voucher provider is not, for example, a third-party employee benefits administrator that administers a transit pass benefit program for an employer using vouchers that the employer could obtain directly.

(4) Readily available. For purposes of this paragraph (b), a voucher or similar item is readily available for direct distribution by the employer to employees if and only if an employer can obtain it from a voucher provider that—

(i) does not impose fare media charges that cause vouchers to not be readily available as described in paragraph (b)(5) of this section; and

(ii) does not impose other restrictions that cause vouchers to not be readily available as described in paragraph (b)(6) of this section.

(5) Fare media charges. For purposes of paragraph (b)(4) of this section, fare media charges relate only to fees paid by the employer to voucher providers for vouchers. The determination of whether obtaining a voucher would result in fare media charges that cause vouchers to not be readily available as described in this paragraph (b) is made with respect to each transit system voucher. If more than one transit system voucher is available for direct distribution to employees, the employer must consider the fees imposed for the lowest cost monthly voucher for purposes of determining whether the fees imposed by the voucher provider satisfy this paragraph. However, if transit system vouchers for multiple transit systems are required in an area to meet the transit needs of the individual employees in that area, the employer has the option of averaging the costs applied to each transit system voucher for purposes of determining whether the fare media charges for transit system vouchers satisfy this paragraph. Fare media charges are described in this paragraph (b)(5), and therefore cause vouchers to not be readily available, if and only if the average annual fare media charges that the employer reasonably expects to incur for transit system vouchers purchased from the voucher provider (disregarding reasonable and customary delivery charges imposed by the voucher provider, e.g., not in excess of $15) are more than 1 percent of the average annual value of the vouchers for a transit system.

(6) Other restrictions. For purposes of paragraph (b)(4) of this section, restrictions that cause vouchers to not be readily available are restrictions imposed by the voucher provider other than fare media charges that effectively prevent the employer from obtaining vouchers appropriate for distribution to employees. Examples of such restrictions include—

(i) Advance purchase requirements. Advance purchase requirements cause vouchers to not be readily available only if the voucher provider does not offer vouchers at regular intervals or fails to provide the voucher within a reasonable period after receiving payment for the voucher. For example, a requirement that vouchers may be purchased only once per year may effectively prevent an employer from obtaining vouchers for distribution to employees. An advance purchase requirement that vouchers be purchased not more frequently than monthly does not effectively prevent the employer from obtaining vouchers for distribution to employees.

(ii) Purchase quantity requirements. Purchase quantity requirements cause vouchers to not be readily available if the voucher provider does not offer vouchers in quantities that are reasonably appropriate to the number of the employer's employees who use mass transportation (for example, the voucher provider requires a $1,000 minimum purchase and the employer seeks to purchase only $200 of vouchers).

(iii) Limitations on denominations of vouchers that are available. If the voucher provider does not offer vouchers in denominations appropriate for distribution to the employer's employees, vouchers are not readily available. For example, vouchers provided in $5 increments up to the monthly limit are appropriate for distribution to employees, while vouchers available only in a denomination equal to the monthly limit are not appropriate for distribution to employees if the amount of the benefit provided to the employer's employees each month is normally less than the monthly limit.

(7) Example. The following example illustrates the principles of this paragraph (b):

Example. (i) Company C in City X sells mass transit vouchers to employers in the metropolitan area of X in various denominations appropriate for distribution to employees. Employers can purchase vouchers monthly in reasonably appropriate quantities. Several different bus, rail, van pool, and ferry operators service X, and a number of the operators accept the vouchers either as fare media or in exchange for fare media. To cover its operating expenses, C imposes on each voucher a 50 cents charge, plus a reasonable and customary $15 charge for delivery of each order of vouchers. Employer M disburses vouchers purchased from C to its employees who use operators that accept the vouchers and M reasonably expects that $55 is the average value of the voucher it will purchase from C for the next calendar year.

(ii) In this Example, vouchers for X are readily available for direct distribution by the employer to employees because the expected cost of the vouchers disbursed to M's employees for the next calendar year is not more than 1 percent of the value of the vouchers (50 cents divided by $55 equals 0.91 percent), the delivery charges are disregarded because they are reasonable and customary, and there are no other restrictions that cause the vouchers to not be readily available. Thus, any reimbursement of mass transportation costs in X would not be a qualified transportation fringe.

(c) Substantiation requirements. Employers that make cash reimbursements must establish a bona fide reimbursement arrangement to establish that their employees have, in fact, incurred expenses for transportation in a commuter highway vehicle, transit passes, or qualified parking. For purposes of section 132(f), whether cash reimbursements are made under a bona fide reimbursement arrangement may vary depending on the facts and circumstances, including the method or methods of payment utilized within the mass transit system. The employer must implement reasonable procedures to ensure that an amount equal to the reimbursement was incurred for transportation in a commuter highway vehicle, transit passes, or qualified parking. The expense must be substantiated within a reasonable period of time. An expense substantiated to the payor within 180 days after it has been paid will be treated as having been substantiated within a reasonable period of time. An employee certification at the time of reimbursement in either written or electronic form may be a reasonable reimbursement procedure depending on the facts and circumstances. Examples of reasonable reimbursement procedures are set forth in paragraph (d) of this Q/A-16.

(d) Illustrations of reasonable reimbursement procedures. The following are examples of reasonable reimbursement procedures for purposes of paragraph (c) of this Q/A-16. In each case, the reimbursement is made at or within a reasonable period after the end of the events described in paragraphs (d)(1) through (d)(3) of this section.

(1) An employee presents to the employer a parking expense receipt for parking on or near the employer's business premises, the employee certifies that the parking was used by the employee, and the employer has no reason to doubt the employee's certification.

(2) An employee either submits a used time-sensitive transit pass (such as a monthly pass) to the employer and certifies that he or she purchased it or presents an unused or used transit pass to the employer and certifies that he or she purchased it and the employee certifies that he or she has not previously been reimbursed for the transit pass. In both cases, the employer has no reason to doubt the employee's certification.

(3) If a receipt is not provided in the ordinary course of business (e.g., if the employee uses metered parking or if used transit passes cannot be returned to the user), the employee certifies to the employer the type and the amount of expenses incurred, and the employer has no reason to doubt the employee's certification.

Q-17. May an employer provide nontaxable cash reimbursement under section 132(f) for periods longer than one month?

A-17. (a) General rule. Yes. Qualified transportation fringes include reimbursement to employees for costs incurred for transportation in more than one month, provided the reimbursement for each month in the period is calculated separately and does not exceed the applicable statutory monthly limit for any month in the period. See Q/A-8 and 9 of this section if the limit for a month is exceeded.

(b) Example. The following example illustrates the principles of this Q/A-17:

Example. (i) Employee R pays $100 per month for qualified parking used during the period from April 1 through June 30 of a year in which the statutory monthly qualified parking limit is $175. After receiving adequate substantiation from Employee R, R's employer reimburses R $300 in cash on June 30 of that year.

(ii) In this Example, because the value of the reimbursed expenses for each month did not exceed the applicable statutory monthly limit, the $300 reimbursement is excludable from R's wages for income and employment tax purposes as a qualified transportation fringe.

Q-18. What are the substantiation requirements if an employer distributes transit passes?

A-18. There are no substantiation requirements if the employer distributes transit passes. Thus, an employer may distribute a transit pass for each month with a value not more than the statutory monthly limit without requiring any certification from the employee regarding the use of the transit pass.

Q-19. May an employer choose to impose substantiation requirements in addition to those described in this regulation?

A-19. Yes.

Q-20. How is the value of parking determined?

A-20. Section 1.61-21(b)(2) applies for purposes of determining the value of parking.

Q-21. How do the qualified transportation fringe rules apply to van pools?

A-21. (a) Van pools generally. Employer and employee-operated van pools, as well as private or public transit-operated van pools, may qualify as qualified transportation fringes. The value of van pool benefits which are qualified transportation fringes may be excluded up to the applicable statutory monthly limit for transportation in a commuter highway vehicle and transit passes, less the value of any transit passes provided by the employer for the month.

(b) Employer-operated van pools. The value of van pool transportation provided by or for an employer to its employees is excludable as a qualified transportation fringe, provided the van qualifies as a commuter highway vehicle as defined in section 132(f)(5)(B) and Q/A-2 of this section. A van pool is operated by or for the employer if the employer purchases or leases vans to enable employees to commute together or the employer contracts with and pays a third party to provide the vans and some or all of the costs of operating the vans, including maintenance, liability insurance and other operating expenses.

(c) Employee-operated van pools. Cash reimbursement by an employer to employees for expenses incurred for transportation in a van pool operated by employees independent of their employer are excludable as qualified transportation fringes, provided that the van qualifies as a commuter highway vehicle as defined in section 132(f)(5)(B) and Q/A-2 of this section. See Q/A-16 of this section for the rules governing cash reimbursements.

(d) Private or public transit-operated van pool transit passes. The qualified transportation fringe exclusion for transit passes is available for travel in van pools owned and operated either by public transit authorities or by any person in the business of transporting persons for compensation or hire. In accordance with paragraph (b) of Q/A-3 of this section, the van must seat at least 6 adults (excluding the driver). See Q/A-16(b) and (c) of this section for a special rule for cash reimbursement for transit passes and the substantiation requirements for cash reimbursement.

(e) Value of van pool transportation benefits. Section 1.61-21(b)(2) provides that the fair market value of a fringe benefit is based on all the facts and circumstances. Alternatively, transportation in an employer-provided commuter highway vehicle may be valued under the automobile lease valuation rule in § 1.61-21(d), the vehicle cents-per-mile rule in § 1.61-21(e), or the commuting valuation rule in § 1.61-21(f). If one of these special valuation rules is used, the employer must use the same valuation rule to value the use of the commuter highway vehicle by each employee who share the use. See § 1.61-21(c)(2)(i)(B).

(f) Qualified parking prime member. If an employee obtains a qualified parking space as a result of membership in a car or van pool, the applicable statutory monthly limit for qualified parking applies to the individual to whom the parking space is assigned. This individual is the prime member. In determining the tax consequences to the prime member, the statutory monthly limit amounts of each car pool member may not be combined. If the employer provides access to the space and the space is not assigned to a particular individual, then the employer must designate one of its employees as the prime member who will bear the tax consequences. The employer may not designate more than one prime member for a car or van pool during a month. The employer of the prime member is responsible for including the value of the qualified parking in excess of the statutory monthly limit in the prime member's wages for income and employment tax purposes.

Q-22. What are the reporting and employment tax requirements for qualified transportation fringes?

A-22. (a) Employment tax treatment generally. Qualified transportation fringes not exceeding the applicable statutory monthly limit described in Q/A-7 of this section are not wages for purposes of the Federal Insurance Contributions Act (FICA), the Federal Unemployment Tax Act (FUTA), and federal income tax withholding. Any amount by which an employee elects to reduce compensation as provided in Q/A-11 of this section is not subject to the FICA, the FUTA, and federal income tax withholding. Qualified transportation fringes exceeding the applicable statutory monthly limit described in Q/A-7 of this section are wages for purposes of the FICA, the FUTA, and federal income tax withholding and are reported on the employee's Form W-2, Wage and Tax Statement.

(b) Employment tax treatment of cash reimbursement exceeding monthly limits. Cash reimbursement to employees (for example, cash reimbursement for qualified parking) in excess of the applicable statutory monthly limit under section 132(f) is treated as paid for employment tax purposes when actually or constructively paid. See §§ 31.3121(a)-2(a), 31.3301-4, 31.3402(a)-1(b) of this chapter. Employers must report and deposit the amounts withheld in addition to reporting and depositing other employment taxes. See Q/A-16 of this section for rules governing cash reimbursements.

(c) Noncash fringe benefits exceeding monthly limits. If the value of noncash qualified transportation fringes exceeds the applicable statutory monthly limit, the employer may elect, for purposes of the FICA, the FUTA, and federal income tax withholding, to treat the noncash taxable fringe benefits as paid on a pay period, quarterly, semi-annual, annual, or other basis, provided that the benefits are treated as paid no less frequently than annually.

Q-23. How does section 132(f) interact with other fringe benefit rules?

A-23. For purposes of section 132, the terms working condition fringe and de minimis fringe do not include any qualified transportation fringe under section 132(f). If, however, an employer provides local transportation other than transit passes (without any direct or indirect compensation reduction election), the value of the benefit may be excludable, either totally or partially, under fringe benefit rules other than the qualified transportation fringe rules under section 132(f). See §§ 1.132-6(d)(2)(i) (occasional local transportation fare), 1.132-6(d)(2)(iii) (transportation provided under unusual circumstances), and 1.61-21(k) (valuation of local transportation provided to qualified employees). See also Q/A-4(b) of this section.

Q-24. May qualified transportation fringes be provided to individuals who are partners, 2-percent shareholders of S-corporations, or independent contractors?

A-24. (a) General rule. Section 132(f)(5)(E) states that self-employed individuals who are employees within the meaning of section 401(c)(1) are not employees for purposes of section 132(f). Therefore, individuals who are partners, sole proprietors, or other independent contractors are not employees for purposes of section 132(f). In addition, under section 1372(a), 2-percent shareholders of S corporations are treated as partners for fringe benefit purposes. Thus, an individual who is both a 2-percent shareholder of an S corporation and a common law employee of that S corporation is not considered an employee for purposes of section 132(f). However, while section 132(f) does not apply to individuals who are partners, 2-percent shareholders of S corporations, or independent contractors, other exclusions for working condition and de minimis fringes may be available as described in paragraphs (b) and (c) of this Q/A-24. See §§ 1.132-1(b)(2) and 1.132-1(b)(4).

(b) Transit passes. The working condition and de minimis fringe exclusions under section 132(a)(3) and (4) are available for transit passes provided to individuals who are partners, 2-percent shareholders, and independent contractors. For example, tokens or farecards provided by a partnership to an individual who is a partner that enable the partner to commute on a public transit system (not including privately-operated van pools) are excludable from the partner's gross income if the value of the tokens and farecards in any month does not exceed the dollar amount specified in § 1.132-6(d)(1). However, if the value of a pass provided in a month exceeds the dollar amount specified in § 1.132-6(d)(1), the full value of the benefit provided (not merely the amount in excess of the dollar amount specified in § 1.132-6(d)(1)) is includible in gross income.

(c) Parking. The working condition fringe rules under section 132(d) do not apply to commuter parking. See § 1.132-5(a)(1). However, the de minimis fringe rules under section 132(e) are available for parking provided to individuals who are partners, 2-percent shareholders, or independent contractors that qualifies under the de minimis rules. See § 1.132-6(a) and (b).

(d) Example. The following example illustrates the principles of this Q/A-24:

Example. (i) Individual G is a partner in partnership P. Individual G commutes to and from G's office every day and parks free of charge in P's lot.

(ii) In this Example, the value of the parking is not excluded under section 132(f), but may be excluded under section 132(e) if the parking is a de minimis fringe under § 1.132-6.

Q-25. What is the effective date of this section?

A-25. (a) Except as provided in paragraph (b) of this Q/A-25, this section is applicable for taxable years beginning after December 31, 2001. For this purpose, an employer may assume that the employee taxable year is the calendar year.

The last sentence of paragraph (b)(5) of Q/A-16 of this section (relating to whether transit system vouchers for transit passes are readily available) is effective for taxable years beginning after December 31, 2003. For this purpose, an employer may assume that the employee taxable year is the calendar year.

T.D. 8933, 1/10/2001, amend T.D. 9294, 10/19/2006.

§ 1.133-1T Questions and answers relating to interest on certain loans used to acquire employer securities (temporary).

Caution: The Treasury has not yet amended Reg § 1.133-1T to reflect changes made by P.L. 104-188, P.L. 101-508, P.L. 101-239, P.L. 99-514.

Q-1. What does section 133 provide?

A-1. In general, section 133 provides that certain commercial lenders may exclude from gross income fifty percent of the interest received with respect to securities acquisition loans. A securities acquisition loan is any loan to an employee stock ownership plan (ESOP) (as defined in section 4975(e)(7)) that qualifies as an exempt loan under §§ 54.4975-7 and -11 to the extent that the proceeds are used to acquire employer securities (within the meaning of section 409(l)) for the ESOP. A loan made to a corporation sponsoring an ESOP (or to a person related to such corporation under section 133(b)(2)) may also qualify as a securities acquisition loan to the extent and for the period that the proceeds are (a) loaned to the corporation's ESOP under a loan that qualifies as an exempt loan under §§ 54.4975-7 and -11 and that has substantially similar terms as the loan from the commercial lender to the sponsoring corporation, and (b) used to acquire employer securities for the ESOP. The terms of the loan between the commercial lender and the sponsoring corporation (or a related corporation) and the loan between such corporation and the ESOP shall be treated as substantially similar only if the timing and rate at which employer securities would be released from encumbrance if the loan from the commercial lender were the exempt loan under the applicable rule of § 54.4975-7(b)(8) are substantially similar to the timing and rate at which employer securities will actually be released from encumbrance in accordance with such rule. For this purpose, if the loan from the commercial lender to the sponsoring corporation states a variable rate of interest and the loan between the corporation and the ESOP states a fixed rate of interest, whether the terms of the loans are substantially similar shall be determined at the time the obligations are initially issued by taking into account the adjustment interval on the variable rate loan and the maturity of the fixed rate loan. For example, if the rate on the loan from the commercial lender to the sponsoring corporation adjusts each six months and the loan from the corporation to the ESOP has a ten year term, the initial interest rate on the variable rate loan could be compared to the rate on the fixed rate loan by comparing the yields on 6 month and ten year Treasury obligations. Similarly, if the rates on the two loans are based on different compounding assumptions, whether the terms of the loans are substantially similar shall be determined by taking into account the different compounding assumptions. A securities acquisition loan may be evidenced by any note, bond, debenture, or certificate. Also, section 133(b)(2) provides that certain loans between related persons are not securities acquisition loans. In addition, a loan from a commercial lender to an ESOP or sponsoring corporation to purchase employer securities will not be treated as a securities acquisition loan to the extent that such loan is used, either directly or indirectly, to purchase employer securities from any other qualified plan, including any other ESOP, maintained by the employer or any other corporation which is a member of the same controlled group (as defined in section 409(l)(4)).

Q-2. What lenders are eligible to receive the fifty percent interest exclusion?

A-2. Under section 133(a), a bank (within the meaning of section 581), an insurance company to which subchapter L applies, or a corporation (other than a subchapter S corporation) actively engaged in the business of lending money may exclude from gross income fifty percent of the interest received with respect to a securities acquisition loan (as defined in Q&A-1 of § 1.133-1T). For purposes of section 133(a)(3), a corporation is actively engaged in the business of lending money if it lends money to the public on a regular and continuing basis (other than in connection with the purchase by the public of goods and services from the lender or a related party). A corporation is not actively engaged in the business of lending money if a predominant share of the original value of the loans it makes to unrelated parties (other than in connection with the purchase by the public of goods and services from the lender or a related party) are securities acquisition loans.

Q-3. May loans which qualify for the fifty percent interest exclusion under section 133 be syndicated to other lending institutions?

A-3. Securities acquisition loans under section 133 may be syndicated to other lending institutions provided that such lending institutions are described in section 133(a)(1), (2) or (3) and the loan was originated by a qualified holder. Subsequent holders of the debt instrument may qualify for the partial interest exclusion of section 133 if such holders satisfy the requirements of section 133 and such loan does not fail to be a securities acquisition loan under section 133(b)(2).

Q-4. When is section 133 effective?

A-4. Section 133 applies to securities acquisition loans made after July 18, 1984, and used to acquire employer securities after July 18, 1984. The provision does not apply to loans made after July 18, 1984, to the extent that such loans are renegotiations, directly or indirectly, of loans outstanding on such date. A loan extended to an ESOP or sponsoring corporation after July 18, 1984, will be treated as a renegotiation of an outstanding loan if the loan proceeds are used to refinance acquisitions of employer securities made prior to July 19, 1984. For example, if an ESOP borrowed money prior to July 19, 1984, to purchase employer securities and after July 18, 1984, borrows other funds from the same or a different commercial lender to repay the first loan, the second loan will be treated as a renegotiation of an outstanding loan to the extent of the repaid amount. Similarly, if, after July 18, 1984, an ESOP sells employer securities, uses the proceeds to retire a pre-July 19, 1984, loan and obtains a second loan to acquire replacement employer securities, the second loan will be treated as a renegotiation of an outstanding loan.

T.D. 8073, 1/29/86.

---

§ 1.141-0 Table of contents.

This section lists the captioned paragraphs contained in §§ 1.141-1 through 1.141-16.

§ 1.141-1 Definitions and rules of general application.

(a) In general.

(b) Certain general definitions.

(c) Elections.

(d) Related parties.

§ 1.141-2 Private activity bond tests.

(a) Overview.

(b) Scope.

(c) General definition of private activity bond.

(d) Reasonable expectations and deliberate actions.

(1) In general.

(2) Reasonable expectations test.

(3) Deliberate action defined.

(4) Special rule for dispositions of personal property in the ordinary course of an established governmental program.

(5) Special rule for general obligation bond programs that finance a large number of separate purposes.

(e) When a deliberate action occurs.

(f) Certain remedial actions.

(g) Examples.

§ 1.141-3 Definition of private business use.

(a) General rule.

(1) In general.

(2) Indirect use.

(3) Aggregation of private business use.

(b) Types of private business use arrangements.

(1) In general.

(2) Ownership.

(3) Leases.

(4) Management contracts.

(5) Output contracts.

(6) Research agreements.

(7) Other actual or beneficial use.

(c) Exception for general public use.

(1) In general.

(2) Use on the same basis.

(3) Long-term arrangements not treated as general public use.

(4) Relation to other use.

(d) Other exceptions.

(1) Agents.

(2) Use incidental to financing arrangements.

(3) Exceptions for arrangements other than arrangements resulting in ownership of financed property by a nongovernmental person.

(4) Temporary use by developers.

(5) Incidental use.

(6) Qualified improvements.

(e) Special rule for tax assessment bonds.

(f) Examples.

(g) Measurement of private business use.

(1) In general.

(2) Measurement period.

(3) Determining average percentage of private business use.

(4) Determining the average amount of private business use for a 1-year period.

(5) Common areas.

(6) Allocation of neutral costs.

(7) Commencement of measurement of private business use.

(8) Examples.

§ 1.141-4 Private security or payment test.

(a) General rule.

(1) Private security or payment.

(2) Aggregation of private payments and security.

(3) Underlying arrangement.

(b) Measurement of private payments and security.

(1) Scope.

(2) Present value measurement.

(c) Private payments.

(1) In general.

(2) Payments taken into account.

(3) Allocation of payments.

(d) Private security.

(1) In general.

(2) Security taken into account.

(3) Pledge of unexpended proceeds.

(4) Secured by any interest in property or payments.

(5) Payments in respect of property.

(6) Allocation of security among issues.

(e) Generally applicable taxes.

(1) General rule.

(2) Definition of generally applicable taxes.

(3) Special charges.

(4) Manner of determination and collection.

(5) Payments in lieu of taxes.

(f) Certain waste remediation bonds.

(1) Scope.

(2) Persons that are not private users.

(3) Persons that are private users.

(g) Examples.

§ 1.141-5 Private loan financing test.

(a) In general.

(b) Measurement of test.

(c) Definition of private loan.

(1) In general.

(2) Application only to purpose investments.

(3) Grants.

(4) Hazardous waste remediation bonds.

(d) Tax assessment loan exception.

(1) General rule.

(2) Tax assessment loan defined.

(3) Mandatory tax or other assessment.

(4) Specific essential governmental function.

(5) Equal basis requirement.

(6) Coordination with private business tests.

(e) Examples.

§ 1.141-6 Allocation and accounting rules.

(a) Allocation of proceeds to expenditures.

(b) Allocation of proceeds to property. [Reserved]

(c) Special rules for mixed use facilities. [Reserved]

(d) Allocation of proceeds to common areas. [Reserved]

(e) Allocation of proceeds to bonds. [Reserved]

(f) Treatment of partnerships. [Reserved]

(g) Examples. [Reserved]

§ 1.141-7 Special rules for output facilities.

(a) Overview.

(b) Definitions.

(1) Available output.

(2) Measurement period.

(3) Sale at wholesale.

(4) Take contract and take or pay contract.

(5) Requirements contract.

(6) Nonqualified amount.

(c) Output contracts.

(1) General rule.

(2) Take contract or take or pay contract.

(3) Requirements contract.
(4) Output contract properly characterized as a lease.
(d) Measurement of private business use.
(e) Measurement of private security or payment.
(f) Exceptions for certain contracts.
(1) Small purchases of output.
(2) Swapping and pooling arrangements.
(3) Short-term output contracts.
(4) Certain conduit parties disregarded.
(g) Special rules for electric output facilities used to provide open access.
(1) Operation of transmission facilities by nongovernmental persons.
(2) Certain use by nongovernmental persons under output contracts.
(3) Ancillary services.
(4) Exceptions to deliberate action rules.
(5) Additional transactions as permitted by the Commissioner.
(h) Allocations of output facilities and systems.
(1) Facts and circumstances analysis.
(2) Illustrations.
(3) Transmission and distribution contracts.
(4) Allocation of payments.
(i) Examples.

§ 1.141-8 $15 million limitation for output facilities.

(a) In general.
(1) General rule.
(2) Reduction in $15 million output limitation for outstanding issues.
(3) Benefits and burdens test applicable.
(b) Definition of project.
(1) General rule.
(2) Separate ownership.
(3) Generating property.
(4) Transmission and distribution.
(5) Subsequent improvements.
(6) Replacement property.
(c) Examples.

§ 1.141-9 Unrelated or disproportionate use test.

(a) General rules.
(1) Description of test.
(2) Application of unrelated or disproportionate use test.
(b) Unrelated use.
(1) In general.
(2) Use for the same purpose as government use.
(c) Disproportionate use.
(1) Definition of disproportionate use.
(2) Aggregation of related uses.
(3) Allocation rule.
(d) Maximum use taken into account.
(e) Examples.

§ 1.141-10 Coordination with volume cap. [Reserved]

§ 1.141-11 Acquisition of nongovernmental output property. [Reserved]

§ 1.141-12 Remedial actions.

(a) Conditions to taking remedial action.
(1) Reasonable expectations test met.
(2) Maturity not unreasonably long.
(3) Fair market value consideration.
(4) Disposition proceeds treated as gross proceeds for arbitrage purposes.
(5) Proceeds expended on a governmental purpose.
(b) Effect of a remedial action.
(1) In general.
(2) Effect on bonds that have been advance refunded.
(c) Disposition proceeds.
(1) Definition.
(2) Allocating disposition proceeds to an issue.
(3) Allocating disposition proceeds to different sources of funding.
(d) Redemption or defeasance of nonqualified bonds.
(1) In general.
(2) Special rule for dispositions for cash.
(3) Notice of defeasance.
(4) Special limitation.
(5) Defeasance escrow defined.
(e) Alternative use of disposition proceeds.
(1) In general.
(2) Special rule for use by 501(c)(3) organizations.
(f) Alternative use of facility.
(g) Rules for deemed reissuance.
(h) Authority of Commissioner to provide for additional remedial actions.
(i) Effect of remedial action on continuing compliance.
(j) Nonqualified bonds.
(1) Amount of nonqualified bonds.
(2) Allocation of nonqualified bonds.
(k) Examples.

§ 1.141-13 Refunding issues.

(a) In general.
(b) Application of private business use test and private loan financing test.
(1) Allocation of proceeds.
(2) Determination of amount of private business use.
(c) Application of private security or payment test.
(1) Separate issue treatment.
(2) Combined issue treatment.
(3) Special rule for arrangements not entered into in contemplation of the refunding issue.
(d) Multipurpose issue allocations.
(1) In general.
(2) Exceptions.
(e) Application of reasonable expectations test to certain refunding bonds.
(f) Special rule for refundings of certain general obligation bonds.
(g) Examples.

§ 1.141-14 Anti-abuse rules.

(a) Authority of Commissioner to reflect substance of transactions.

(b) Examples.

§ 1.141-15 Effective dates.

(a) Scope.

(b) Effective dates.

(1) In general.

(2) Certain short-term arrangements.

(3) Certain prepayments.

(c) Refunding bonds.

(d) Permissive application of regulations.

(e) Permissive retroactive application of certain sections.

(f) Effective dates for certain regulations relating to output facilities.

(1) General rule.

(2) Transition rule for requirements contracts.

(g) Refunding bonds for output facilities.

(h) Permissive retroactive application.

(i) Permissive application of certain regulations relating to output facilities.

(j) Effective dates for certain regulations relating to refundings.

(k) Effective/applicability dates for certain regulations relating to generally applicable taxes and payments in lieu of tax.

§ 1.141-16 Effective dates for qualified private activity bond provisions.

(a) Scope.

(b) Effective dates.

(c) Permissive application.

(d) Certain remedial actions.

(1) General rule.

(2) Special rule for allocations of nonqualified bonds.

T.D. 8712, 1/10/97, amend T.D. 8757, 1/21/98, T.D. 8941, 1/17/2001, T.D. 9016, 9/19/2002, T.D. 9085, 8/1/2003, T.D. 9150, 8/12/2004, T.D. 9234, 12/16/2005, T.D. 9429, 10/20/2008.

PAR. 2. Section 1.141-0 is amended by adding an entry for § 1.141-1(e), revising entries for § 1.141-6, and adding an entry for § 1.141-15(k) and (l) as follows:

Proposed § 1.141-0 Table of Contents [*For Preamble, see ¶ 152,807*]

* * * * *

§ 1.141-1 Definitions and rules of general application

* * * * *

(e) Partnerships.

(1) In general.

(2) Governmental partnerships.

* * * * *

§ 1.141-6 Allocation and accounting rules

(a) Allocation of proceeds to expenditures, property, and uses in general.

(1) Allocations to expenditures.

(2) Allocations within property; general pro rata allocation method.

(3) Allocations of sources of funds to ultimate uses of financed property.

(4) Manner and time for electing to apply special allocation methods for mixed-use projects; final allocations generally.

(b) Special rules on reasonable proportionate allocation methods for mixed-use projects.

(1) In general.

(2) Definition of a mixed-use project.

(c) The discrete physical portion allocation method.

(1) In general.

(2) The measure of a discrete portion.

(3) Allocations to expenditures for discrete portions.

(4) Allocations of uses to discrete portions.

(5) Certain reallocations among discrete portions.

(d) The undivided portion allocation method.

(1) In general.

(2) The measure of an undivided portion.

(3) Allocations to expenditures for undivided portions.

(4) Allocations of uses to undivided portions.

(e) Certain general operating rules for mixed-use project allocations.

(1) In general.

(2) Governmental ownership requirement for undivided portion and discrete portion allocations.

(3) Sources of funds for mixed-use project allocations.

(4) Common areas.

(5) Allocations regarding multiple issues.

(f) Special rules for bond redemptions in anticipation of unqualified use.

(g) Special rules for applying the undivided portion allocation method to mixed-use output facilities.

(1) In general.

(2) Governmental ownership requirement for mixed-use output facilities.

(3) The measure of an undivided portion of a mixed-use output facility.

(h) Allocations of private payments.

(i) Allocations of proceeds to common costs of the issue.

(j) Allocations of proceeds to bonds.

(k) Examples.

§ 1.141-7 Special Rules for Output Facilities

* * * * *

§ 1.141-15 Effective dates

* * * * *

(k) Effective date for certain regulations related to allocation and accounting.

(l) Permissive retroactive application of certain regulations.

* * * * *

§ 1.141-1 Definitions and rules of general application.

(a) In general. For purposes of §§ 1.141-0 through 1.141-16, the following definitions and rules apply: the definitions in this section, the definitions in § 1.150-1, the definition of placed in service under § 1.150-2(c), the definition of grant under § 1.148-6(d)(4)(iii), the definition of reasonably required reserve or replacement fund in § 1.148-2(f), and the following definitions under § 1.148-1: bond year, commingled fund, fixed yield issue, higher yielding investments, investment, investment proceeds, issue price, issuer, nonpurpose investment, purpose investment, qualified guarantee, qualified hedge, reasonable expectations or reasonableness, rebate amount, replacement proceeds, sale proceeds, variable yield issue, and yield.

(b) Certain general definitions. *Common areas* means portions of a facility that are equally available to all users of a facility on the same basis for uses that are incidental to the primary use of the facility. For example, hallways and elevators generally are treated as common areas if they are used by the different lessees of a facility in connection with the primary use of that facility.

Consistently applied means applied uniformly to account for proceeds and other amounts.

Deliberate action is defined in § 1.141-2(d)(3).

Discrete portion means a portion of a facility that consists of any separate and discrete portion of a facility to which use is limited, other than common areas. A floor of a building and a portion of a building separated by walls, partitions, or other physical barriers are examples of a discrete portion.

Disposition is defined in § 1.141-12(c)(1).

Disposition proceeds is defined in § 1.141-12(c)(1).

Essential governmental function is defined in § 1.141-5(d)(4)(ii).

Financed means constructed, reconstructed, or acquired with proceeds of an issue.

Governmental bond has the same meaning as in § 1.150-1(b), except that, for purposes of § 1.141-13, governmental bond is defined in § 1.141-13(b)(2)(iv).

Governmental person means a state or local governmental unit as defined in § 1.103-1 or any instrumentality thereof. It does not include the United States or any agency or instrumentality thereof.

Hazardous waste remediation bonds is defined in § 1.141-4(f)(1).

Measurement period is defined in § 1.141-3(g)(2).

Nongovernmental person means a person other than a governmental person.

Output facility means electric and gas generation, transmission, distribution, and related facilities, and water collection, storage, and distribution facilities.

Private business tests means the private business use test and the private security or payment test of section 141(b).

Proceeds means the sale proceeds of an issue (other than those sale proceeds used to retire bonds of the issue that are not deposited in a reasonably required reserve or replacement fund). Proceeds also include any investment proceeds from investments that accrue during the project period (net of rebate amounts attributable to the project period). Disposition proceeds of an issue are treated as proceeds to the extent provided in § 1.141-12. The Commissioner may treat any replaced amounts as proceeds.

Project period means the period beginning on the issue date and ending on the date that the project is placed in service. In the case of a multipurpose issue, the issuer may elect to treat the project period for the entire issue as ending on either the expiration of the temporary period described in § 1.148-2(e)(2) or the end of the fifth bond year after the issue date.

Public utility property means public utility property as defined in section 168(i)(10).

Qualified bond means a qualified bond as defined in section 141(e).

Renewal option means a provision under which either party has a legally enforceable right to renew the contract. Thus, for example, a provision under which a contract is automatically renewed for 1-year periods absent cancellation by either party is not a renewal option (even if it is expected to be renewed).

Replaced amounts means replacement proceeds other than amounts that are treated as replacement proceeds solely because they are sinking funds or pledged funds.

Weighted average maturity is determined under section 147(b).

Weighted average reasonably expected economic life is determined under section 147(b). The reasonably expected economic life of property may be determined by reference to the class life of the property under section 168.

(c) Elections. Elections must be made in writing on or before the issue date and retained as part of the bond documents, and, once made, may not be revoked without the permission of the Commissioner.

(d) Related parties. Except as otherwise provided, all related parties are treated as one person and any reference to "person" includes any related party.

T.D. 6272, 11/25/57, amend T.D. 6792, 1/14/65, T.D. 7123, 6/8/71, T.D. 8712, 1/10/97, T.D. 9234, 12/16/2005.

PAR. 3. Section 1.141-1 is amended by adding additional definitions under paragraph (b) and by adding a new paragraph (e) as follows:

Proposed § 1.141-1 Definitions and rules of general application [*For Preamble, see ¶ 152,807*]

* * * * *

(b) Certain general definitions.

***** De minimis permitted private business use means the amount of private business use permitted for proceeds of tax-exempt bonds without causing such bonds to be classified as private activity bonds under section 141.

* * * * * Financed property means, except as otherwise provided, any project (as defined in § 1.141-6(b)(2)(ii)) to which proceeds of an issue of tax-exempt bonds are allocated under § 1.141-6.

***** Governmental use or government use means any use that is not private business use under § 1.141-3.

***** Private business use means use by a person other than a governmental person in a trade or business, as more particularly defined in § 1.141-3.

* * * * *

(e) Partnerships. *(1) In general.* Except as provided in paragraph (e)(2) of this section, a partnership (as defined under section 7701(a)(2)) is treated as a separate entity that is a nongovernmental person for purposes of section 141.

(2) Governmental partnerships. For purposes of section 141, in the case of a partnership (as defined in section 7701(a)(2)) in which each of the partners is a governmental person (as defined in § 1.141-1(b)), the partnership is disregarded as a separate entity and is treated as an aggregate of its partners.

§ 1.141-2 Private activity bond tests.

(a) Overview. Interest on a private activity bond is not excludable from gross income under section 103(a) unless the bond is a qualified bond. The purpose of the private activity bond tests of section 141 is to limit the volume of tax-exempt bonds that finance the activities of nongovernmental persons, without regard to whether a financing actually transfers benefits of tax-exempt financing to a nongovernmental person. The private activity bond tests serve to identify arrangements that have the potential to transfer the benefits of tax-exempt financing, as well as arrangements that actually transfer these benefits. The regulations under section 141 may not be applied in a manner that is inconsistent with these purposes.

(b) Scope. Sections 1.141-0 through 1.141-16 apply generally for purposes of the private activity bond limitations under section 141.

(c) General definition of private activity bond. Under section 141, bonds are private activity bonds if they meet either the private business use test and private security or payment test of section 141(b) or the private loan financing test of section 141(c). The private business use and private security or payment tests are described in §§ 1.141-3 and 1.141-4. The private loan financing test is described in § 1.141-5.

(d) Reasonable expectations and deliberate actions. *(1) In general.* An issue is an issue of private activity bonds if the issuer reasonably expects, as of the issue date, that the issue will meet either the private business tests or the private loan financing test. An issue is also an issue of private activity bonds if the issuer takes a deliberate action, subsequent to the issue date, that causes the conditions of either the private business tests or the private loan financing test to be met.

(2) Reasonable expectations test. (i) In general. In general, the reasonable expectations test must take into account reasonable expectations about events and actions over the entire stated term of an issue.

(ii) Special rule for issues with mandatory redemption provisions. An action that is reasonably expected, as of the issue date, to occur after the issue date and to cause either the private business tests or the private loan financing test to be met may be disregarded for purposes of those tests if—

(A) The issuer reasonably expects, as of the issue date, that the financed property will be used for a governmental purpose for a substantial period before the action;

(B) The issuer is required to redeem all nonqualifying bonds (regardless of the amount of disposition proceeds actually received) within 6 months of the date of the action;

(C) The issuer does not enter into any arrangement with a nongovernmental person, as of the issue date, with respect to that specific action; and

(D) The mandatory redemption of bonds meets all of the conditions for remedial action under § 1.141-12(a).

(3) Deliberate action defined. (i) In general. Except as otherwise provided in this paragraph (d)(3), a deliberate action is any action taken by the issuer that is within its control. An intent to violate the requirements of section 141 is not necessary for an action to be deliberate.

(ii) Safe harbor exceptions. An action is not treated as a deliberate action if—

(A) It would be treated as an involuntary or compulsory conversion under section 1033; or

(B) It is taken in response to a regulatory directive made by the federal government. See § 1.141-7(g)(4).

(4) Special rule for dispositions of personal property in the ordinary course of an established governmental program. (i) In general. Dispositions of personal property in the ordinary course of an established governmental program are not treated as deliberate actions if—

(A) The weighted average maturity of the bonds financing that personal property is not greater than 120 percent of the reasonably expected actual use of that property for governmental purposes;

(B) The issuer reasonably expects on the issue date that the fair market value of that property on the date of disposition will be not greater than 25 percent of its cost; and

(C) The property is no longer suitable for its governmental purposes on the date of disposition.

(ii) Reasonable expectations test. The reasonable expectation that a disposition described in paragraph (d)(4)(i) of this section may occur in the ordinary course while the bonds are outstanding will not cause the issue to meet the private activity bond tests if the issuer is required to deposit amounts received from the disposition in a commingled fund with substantial tax or other governmental revenues and the issuer reasonably expects to spend the amounts on governmental programs within 6 months from the date of commingling.

(iii) Separate issue treatment. An issuer may treat the bonds properly allocable to the personal property eligible for this exception as a separate issue under § 1.150-1(c)(3).

(5) Special rule for general obligation bond programs that finance a large number of separate purposes. The determination of whether bonds of an issue are private activity bonds may be based solely on the issuer's reasonable expectations as of the issue date if all of the requirements of paragraphs (d)(5)(i) through (vii) of this section are met.

(i) The issue is an issue of general obligation bonds of a general purpose governmental unit that finances at least 25 separate purposes (as defined in § 1.150-1(c)(3)) and does not predominantly finance fewer than 4 separate purposes.

(ii) The issuer has adopted a fund method of accounting for its general governmental purposes that makes tracing the bond proceeds to specific expenditures unreasonably burdensome.

(iii) The issuer reasonably expects on the issue date to allocate all of the net proceeds of the issue to capital expenditures within 6 months of the issue date and adopts reasonable procedures to verify that net proceeds are in fact so expended. A program to randomly spot check that 10 percent of the net proceeds were so expended generally is a reasonable verification procedure for this purpose.

(iv) The issuer reasonably expects on the issue date to expend all of the net proceeds of the issue before expending proceeds of a subsequent issue of similar general obligation bonds.

(v) The issuer reasonably expects on the issue date that it will not make any loans to nongovernmental persons with the proceeds of the issue.

(vi) The issuer reasonably expects on the issue date that the capital expenditures that it could make during the 6-month period beginning on the issue date with the net proceeds of the issue that would not meet the private business tests are not less than 125 percent of the capital expenditures to be financed with the net proceeds of the issue.

(vii) The issuer reasonably expects on the issue date that the weighted average maturity of the issue is not greater than

120 percent of the weighted average reasonably expected economic life of the capital expenditures financed with the issue. To determine reasonably expected economic life for this purpose an issuer may use reasonable estimates based on the type of expenditures made from a fund.

(e) When a deliberate action occurs. A deliberate action occurs on the date the issuer enters into a binding contract with a nongovernmental person for use of the financed property that is not subject to any material contingencies.

(f) Certain remedial actions. See § 1.141-12 for certain remedial actions that prevent a deliberate action with respect to property financed by an issue from causing that issue to meet the private business use test or the private loan financing test.

(g) Examples. The following examples illustrate the application of this section:

Example (1). Involuntary action. City B issues bonds to finance the purchase of land. On the issue date, B reasonably expects that it will be the sole user of the land for the entire term of the bonds. Subsequently, the federal government acquires the land in a condemnation action. B sets aside the condemnation proceeds to pay debt service on the bonds but does not redeem them on their first call date. The bonds are not private activity bonds because B has not taken a deliberate action after the issue date. See, however, § 1.141-14(b), Example 2.

Example (2). Reasonable expectations test—involuntary action. The facts are the same as in Example 1, except that, on the issue date, B reasonably expects that the federal government will acquire the land in a condemnation action during the term of the bonds. On the issue date, the present value of the amount that B reasonably expects to receive from the federal government is greater than 10 percent of the present value of the debt service on the bonds. The terms of the bonds do not require that the bonds be redeemed within 6 months of the acquisition by the federal government. The bonds are private activity bonds because the issuer expects as of the issue date that the private business tests will be met.

Example (3). Reasonable expectations test—mandatory redemption. City C issues bonds to rehabilitate an existing hospital that it currently owns. On the issue date of the bonds, C reasonably expects that the hospital will be used for a governmental purpose for a substantial period. On the issue date, C also plans to construct a new hospital, but the placed in service date of that new hospital is uncertain. C reasonably expects that, when the new hospital is placed in service, it will sell or lease the rehabilitated hospital to a private hospital corporation. The bond documents require that the bonds must be redeemed within 6 months of the sale or lease of the rehabilitated hospital (regardless of the amount actually received from the sale). The bonds meet the reasonable expectations requirement of the private activity bond tests if the mandatory redemption of bonds meets all of the conditions for a remedial action under § 1.141-12(a).

Example (4). Dispositions in the ordinary course of an established governmental program. City D issues bonds with a weighted average maturity of 6 years for the acquisition of police cars. D reasonably expects on the issue date that the police cars will be used solely by its police department, except that, in the ordinary course of its police operations, D sells its police cars to a taxicab corporation after 5 years of use because they are no longer suitable for police use. Further, D reasonably expects that the value of the police cars when they are no longer suitable for police use will be no more than 25 percent of cost. D subsequently sells 20 percent of the police cars after only 3 years of actual use. At that time, D deposits the proceeds from the sale of the police cars in a commingled fund with substantial tax revenues and reasonably expects to spend the proceeds on governmental programs within 6 months of the date of deposit. D does not trace the actual use of these commingled amounts. The sale of the police cars does not cause the private activity bond tests to be met because the requirements of paragraph (d)(4) of this section are met.

T.D. 8712, 1/10/97, amend T.D. 8757, 1/21/98, T.D. 9016, 9/19/2002.

§ 1.141-3 Definition of private business use.

(a) General rule. *(1) In general.* The private business use test relates to the use of the proceeds of an issue. The 10 percent private business use test of section 141(b)(1) is met if more than 10 percent of the proceeds of an issue is used in a trade or business of a nongovernmental person. For this purpose, the use of financed property is treated as the direct use of proceeds. Any activity carried on by a person other than a natural person is treated as a trade or business. Unless the context or a provision clearly requires otherwise, this section also applies to the private business use test under sections 141(b)(3) (unrelated or disproportionate use), 141(b)(4) ($15 million limitation for certain output facilities), and 141(b)(5) (the coordination with the volume cap where the nonqualified amount exceeds $15 million).

(2) Indirect use. In determining whether an issue meets the private business use test, it is necessary to look to both the indirect and direct uses of proceeds. For example, a facility is treated as being used for a private business use if it is leased to a nongovernmental person and subleased to a governmental person or if it is leased to a governmental person and then subleased to a nongovernmental person, provided that in each case the nongovernmental person's use is in a trade or business. Similarly, the issuer's use of the proceeds to engage in a series of financing transactions for property to be used by nongovernmental persons in their trades or businesses may cause the private business use test to be met. In addition, proceeds are treated as used in the trade or business of a nongovernmental person if a nongovernmental person, as a result of a single transaction or a series of related transactions, uses property acquired with the proceeds of an issue.

(3) Aggregation of private business use. The use of proceeds by all nongovernmental persons is aggregated to determine whether the private business use test is met.

(b) Types of private business use arrangements. *(1) In general.* Both actual and beneficial use by a nongovernmental person may be treated as private business use. In most cases, the private business use test is met only if a nongovernmental person has special legal entitlements to use the financed property under an arrangement with the issuer. In general, a nongovernmental person is treated as a private business user of proceeds and financed property as a result of ownership; actual or beneficial use of property pursuant to a lease, or a management or incentive payment contract; or certain other arrangements such as a take or pay or other output-type contract.

(2) Ownership. Except as provided in paragraph (d)(1) or (d)(2) of this section, ownership by a nongovernmental person of financed property is private business use of that property. For this purpose, ownership refers to ownership for federal income tax purposes.

(3) Leases. Except as provided in paragraph (d) of this section, the lease of financed property to a nongovernmental person is private business use of that property. For this purpose, any arrangement that is properly characterized as a lease for federal income tax purposes is treated as a lease. In determining whether a management contract is properly characterized as a lease, it is necessary to consider all of the facts and circumstances, including the following factors—

(i) The degree of control over the property that is exercised by a nongovernmental person; and

(ii) Whether a nongovernmental person bears risk of loss of the financed property.

(4) Management contracts. (i) Facts and circumstances test. Except as provided in paragraph (d) of this section, a management contract (within the meaning of paragraph (b)(4)(ii) of this section) with respect to financed property may result in private business use of that property, based on all of the facts and circumstances. A management contract with respect to financed property generally results in private business use of that property if the contract provides for compensation for services rendered with compensation based, in whole or in part, on a share of net profits from the operation of the facility.

(ii) Management contract defined. For purposes of this section, a management contract is a management, service, or incentive payment contract between a governmental person and a service provider under which the service provider provides services involving all, a portion of, or any function of, a facility. For example, a contract for the provision of management services for an entire hospital, a contract for management services for a specific department of a hospital, and an incentive payment contract for physician services to patients of a hospital are each treated as a management contract.

(iii) Arrangements generally not treated as management contracts. The arrangements described in paragraphs (b)(4)(iii)(A) through (D) of this section generally are not treated as management contracts that give rise to private business use.

(A) Contracts for services that are solely incidental to the primary governmental function or functions of a financed facility (for example, contracts for janitorial, office equipment repair, hospital billing, or similar services).

(B) The mere granting of admitting privileges by a hospital to a doctor, even if those privileges are conditioned on the provision of de minimis services, if those privileges are available to all qualified physicians in the area, consistent with the size and nature of its facilities.

(C) A contract to provide for the operation of a facility or system of facilities that consists predominantly of public utility property, if the only compensation is the reimbursement of actual and direct expenses of the service provider and reasonable administrative overhead expenses of the service provider.

(D) A contract to provide for services, if the only compensation is the reimbursement of the service provider for actual and direct expenses paid by the service provider to unrelated parties.

(iv) Management contracts that are properly treated as other types of private business use. A management contract with respect to financed property results in private business use of that property if the service provider is treated as the lessee or owner of financed property for federal income tax purposes, unless an exception under paragraph (d) of this section applies to the arrangement.

(5) Output contracts. See § 1.141-7 for special rules for contracts for the purchase of output of output facilities.

(6) Research agreements. (i) Facts and circumstances test. Except as provided in paragraph (d) of this section, an agreement by a nongovernmental person to sponsor research performed by a governmental person may result in private business use of the property used for the research, based on all of the facts and circumstances.

(ii) Research agreements that are properly treated as other types of private business use. A research agreement with respect to financed property results in private business use of that property if the sponsor is treated as the lessee or owner of financed property for federal income tax purposes, unless an exception under paragraph (d) of this section applies to the arrangement.

(7) Other actual or beneficial use. (i) In general. Any other arrangement that conveys special legal entitlements for beneficial use of bond proceeds or of financed property that are comparable to special legal entitlements described in paragraphs (b)(2), (3), (4), (5), or (6) of this section results in private business use. For example, an arrangement that conveys priority rights to the use or capacity of a facility generally results in private business use.

(ii) Special rule for facilities not used by the general public. In the case of financed property that is not available for use by the general public (within the meaning of paragraph (c) of this section), private business use may be established solely on the basis of a special economic benefit to one or more nongovernmental persons, even if those nongovernmental persons have no special legal entitlements to use of the property. In determining whether special economic benefit gives rise to private business use it is necessary to consider all of the facts and circumstances, including one or more of the following factors—

(A) Whether the financed property is functionally related or physically proximate to property used in the trade or business of a nongovernmental person;

(B) Whether only a small number of nongovernmental persons receive the special economic benefit; and

(C) Whether the cost of the financed property is treated as depreciable by any nongovernmental person.

(c) Exception for general public use. *(1) In general.* Use as a member of the general public (general public use) is not private business use. Use of financed property by nongovernmental persons in their trades or businesses is treated as general public use only if the property is intended to be available and in fact is reasonably available for use on the same basis by natural persons not engaged in a trade or business.

(2) Use on the same basis. In general, use under an arrangement that conveys priority rights or other preferential benefits is not use on the same basis as the general public. Arrangements providing for use that is available to the general public at no charge or on the basis of rates that are generally applicable and uniformly applied do not convey priority rights or other preferential benefits. For this purpose, rates may be treated as generally applicable and uniformly applied even if—

(i) Different rates apply to different classes of users, such as volume purchasers, if the differences in rates are customary and reasonable; or

(ii) A specially negotiated rate arrangement is entered into, but only if the user is prohibited by federal law from paying the generally applicable rates, and the rates established are as comparable as reasonably possible to the generally applicable rates.

(3) Long-term arrangements not treated as general public use. An arrangement is not treated as general public use if the term of the use under the arrangement, including all renewal options, is greater than 200 days. For this purpose, a right of first refusal to renew use under the arrangement is not treated as a renewal option if—

(i) The compensation for the use under the arrangement is redetermined at generally applicable, fair market value rates that are in effect at the time of renewal; and

(ii) The use of the financed property under the same or similar arrangements is predominantly by natural persons who are not engaged in a trade or business.

(4) Relation to other use. Use of financed property by the general public does not prevent the proceeds from being used for a private business use because of other use under this section.

(d) Other exceptions. *(1) Agents.* Use of proceeds by nongovernmental persons solely in their capacity as agents of a governmental person is not private business use. For example, use by a nongovernmental person that issues obligations on behalf of a governmental person is not private business use to the extent the nongovernmental person's use of proceeds is in its capacity as an agent of the governmental person.

(2) Use incidental to financing arrangements. Use by a nongovernmental person that is solely incidental to a financing arrangement is not private business use. A use is solely incidental to a financing arrangement only if the nongovernmental person has no substantial rights to use bond proceeds or financed property other than as an agent of the bondholders. For example, a nongovernmental person that acts solely as an owner of title in a sale and leaseback financing transaction with a city generally is not a private business user of the property leased to the city, provided that the nongovernmental person has assigned all of its rights to use the leased facility to the trustee for the bondholders upon default by the city. Similarly, bond trustees, servicers, and guarantors are generally not treated as private business users.

(3) Exceptions for arrangements other than arrangements resulting in ownership of financed property by a nongovernmental person. (i) Arrangements not available for use on the same basis by natural persons not engaged in a trade or business. Use by a nongovernmental person pursuant to an arrangement, other than an arrangement resulting in ownership of financed property by a nongovernmental person, is not private business use if—

(A) The term of the use under the arrangement, including all renewal options, is not longer than 100 days;

(B) The arrangement would be treated as general public use, except that it is not available for use on the same basis by natural persons not engaged in a trade or business because generally applicable and uniformly applied rates are not reasonably available to natural persons not engaged in a trade or business; and

(C) The property is not financed for a principal purpose of providing that property for use by that nongovernmental person.

(ii) Negotiated arm's-length arrangements. Use by a nongovernmental person pursuant to an arrangement, other than an arrangement resulting in ownership of financed property by a nongovernmental person, is not private business use if—

(A) The term of the use under the arrangement, including all renewal options, is not longer than 50 days;

(B) The arrangement is a negotiated arm's-length arrangement, and compensation under the arrangement is at fair market value; and

(C) The property is not financed for a principal purpose of providing that property for use by that nongovernmental person.

(4) Temporary use by developers. Use during an initial development period by a developer of an improvement that carries out an essential governmental function is not private business use if the issuer and the developer reasonably expect on the issue date to proceed with all reasonable speed to develop the improvement and property benefited by that improvement and to transfer the improvement to a governmental person, and if the improvement is in fact transferred to a governmental person promptly after the property benefited by the improvement is developed.

(5) Incidental use. (i) General rule. Incidental uses of a financed facility are disregarded, to the extent that those uses do not exceed 2.5 percent of the proceeds of the issue used to finance the facility. A use of a facility by a nongovernmental person is incidental if—

(A) Except for vending machines, pay telephones, kiosks, and similar uses, the use does not involve the transfer to the nongovernmental person of possession and control of space that is separated from other areas of the facility by walls, partitions, or other physical barriers, such as a night gate affixed to a structural component of a building (a nonpossessory use);

(B) The nonpossessory use is not functionally related to any other use of the facility by the same person (other than a different nonpossessory use); and

(C) All nonpossessory uses of the facility do not, in the aggregate, involve the use of more than 2.5 percent of the facility.

(ii) Illustrations. Incidental uses may include pay telephones, vending machines, advertising displays, and use for television cameras, but incidental uses may not include output purchases.

(6) Qualified improvements. Proceeds that provide a governmentally owned improvement to a governmentally owned building (including its structural components and land functionally related and subordinate to the building) are not used for a private business use if—

(i) The building was placed in service more than 1 year before the construction or acquisition of the improvement is begun;

(ii) The improvement is not an enlargement of the building or an improvement of interior space occupied exclusively for any private business use;

(iii) No portion of the improved building or any payments in respect of the improved building are taken into account under section 141(b)(2)(A) (the private security test); and

(iv) No more than 15 percent of the improved building is used for a private business use.

(e) Special rule for tax assessment bonds. In the case of a tax assessment bond that satisfies the requirements of § 1.141-5(d), the loan (or deemed loan) of the proceeds to the borrower paying the assessment is disregarded in determining whether the private business use test is met. However, the use of the loan proceeds is not disregarded in determining whether the private business use test is met.

(f) Examples. The following examples illustrate the application of paragraphs (a) through (e) of this section. In each example, assume that the arrangements described are the only arrangements with nongovernmental persons for use of the financed property.

Example (1). Nongovernmental ownership. State A issues 20-year bonds to purchase land and equip and construct a factory. A then enters into an arrangement with Corporation X to sell the factory to X on an installment basis while the bonds are outstanding. The issue meets the private business use test because a nongovernmental person owns the financed facility. See also § 1.141-2 (relating to the private activity bond tests), and § 1.141-5 (relating to the private loan financing test).

Example (2). Lease to a nongovernmental person. (i) The facts are the same as in Example 1, except that A enters into an arrangement with X to lease the factory to X for 3 years rather than to sell it to X. The lease payments will be made annually and will be based on the tax-exempt interest rate on the bonds. The issue meets the private business use test because a nongovernmental person leases the financed facility. See also § 1.141-14 (relating to anti-abuse rules).

The facts are the same as in Example 2(i), except that the annual payments made by X will equal fair rental value of the facility and exceed the amount necessary to pay debt service on the bonds for the 3 years of the lease. The issue meets the private business use test because a nongovernmental person leases the financed facility and the test does not require that the benefits of tax-exempt financing be passed through to the nongovernmental person.

Example (3). Management contract in substance a lease. City L issues 30-year bonds to finance the construction of a city hospital. L enters into a 15-year contract with M, a nongovernmental person that operates a health maintenance organization relating to the treatment of M's members at L's hospital. The contract provides for reasonable fixed compensation to M for services rendered with no compensation based, in whole or in part, on a share of net profits from the operation of the hospital. However, the contract also provides that 30 percent of the capacity of the hospital will be exclusively available to M's members and M will bear the risk of loss of that portion of the capacity of the hospital so that, under all of the facts and circumstances, the contract is properly characterized as a lease for federal income tax purposes. The issue meets the private business use test because a nongovernmental person leases the financed facility.

Example (4). Ownership of title in substance a leasehold interest. Nonprofit corporation R issues bonds on behalf of City P to finance the construction of a hospital. R will own legal title to the hospital. In addition, R will operate the hospital, but R is not treated as an agent of P in its capacity as operator of the hospital. P has certain rights to the hospital that establish that it is properly treated as the owner of the property for federal income tax purposes. P does not have rights, however, to directly control operation of the hospital while R owns legal title to it and operates it. The issue meets the private business use test because the arrangement provides a nongovernmental person an interest in the financed facility that is comparable to a leasehold interest. See paragraphs (a)(2) and (b)(7)(i) of this section.

Example (5). Rights to control use of property treated as private business use—parking lot. Corporation C and City D enter into a plan to finance the construction of a parking lot adjacent to C's factory. Pursuant to the plan, C conveys the site for the parking lot to D for a nominal amount, subject to a covenant running with the land that the property be used only for a parking lot. In addition, D agrees that C will have the right to approve rates charged by D for use of the parking lot. D issues bonds to finance construction of the parking lot on the site. The parking lot will be available for use by the general public on the basis of rates that are generally applicable and uniformly applied. The issue meets the private business use test because a nongovernmental person has special legal entitlements for beneficial use of the financed facility that are comparable to an ownership interest. See paragraph (b)(7)(i) of this section.

Example (6). Other actual or beneficial use—hydroelectric enhancements. J, a political subdivision, owns and operates a hydroelectric generation plant and related facilities. Pursuant to a take or pay contract, J sells 15 percent of the output of the plant to Corporation K, an investor-owned utility. K is treated as a private business user of the plant. Under the license issued to J for operation of the plant, J is required by federal regulations to construct and operate various facilities for the preservation of fish and for public recreation. J issues its obligations to finance the fish preservation and public recreation facilities. K has no special legal entitlements for beneficial use of the financed facilities. The fish preservation facilities are functionally related to the operation of the plant. The recreation facilities are available to natural persons on a short-term basis according to generally applicable and uniformly applied rates. Under paragraph (c) of this section, the recreation facilities are treated as used by the general public. Under paragraph (b)(7) of this section, K's use is not treated as private business use of the recreation facilities because K has no special legal entitlements for beneficial use of the recreation facilities. The fish preservation facilities are not of a type reasonably available for use on the same basis by natural persons not engaged in a trade or business. Under all of the facts and circumstances (including the functional relationship of the fish preservation facilities to property used in K's trade or business) under paragraph (b)(7)(ii) of this section, K derives a special economic benefit from the fish preservation facilities. Therefore, K's private business use may be established solely on the basis of that special economic benefit, and K's use of the fish preservation facilities is treated as private business use.

Example (7). Other actual or beneficial use—pollution control facilities. City B issues obligations to finance construction of a specialized pollution control facility on land that it owns adjacent to a factory owned by Corporation N. B will own and operate the pollution control facility, and N will have no special legal entitlements to use the facility. B, however, reasonably expects that N will be the only user of the facility. The facility will not be reasonably available for use on the same basis by natural persons not engaged in a trade or business. Under paragraph (b)(7)(ii) of this section, because under all of the facts and circumstances the facility is functionally related and is physically proximate to property used in N's trade or business, N derives a special economic benefit from the facility. Therefore, N's private business use may be established solely on the basis of that special economic benefit, and N's use is treated as private business use of the facility. See paragraph (b)(7)(ii) of this section.

Example (8). General public use—airport runway.

(i) City I issues bonds and uses all of the proceeds to finance construction of a runway at a new city-owned airport. The runway will be available for take-off and landing by any operator of an aircraft desiring to use the airport, including general aviation operators who are natural persons not engaged in a trade or business. It is reasonably expected that most of the actual use of the runway will be by private air carriers (both charter airlines and commercial airlines) in connection with their use of the airport terminals leased by those carriers. These leases for the use of terminal space provide no priority rights or other preferential benefits to the air carriers for use of the runway. Moreover, under the leases the lease payments are determined without taking into account the revenues generated by runway landing fees (that is, the lease payments are not determined on a "residual" basis). Although the lessee air carriers receive a special economic benefit from the use of the runway, this economic benefit is not sufficient to cause the air carriers to be private business users, because the runway is available for general public use. The issue does not meet the private business use test. See paragraphs (b)(7)(ii) and (c) of this section.

(ii) The facts are the same as in Example 8(i), except that the runway will be available for use only by private air carriers. The use by these private air carriers is not general public use, because the runway is not reasonably available for use on the same basis by natural persons not engaged in a trade or business. Depending on all of the facts and circumstances, including whether there are only a small number of lessee private air carriers, the issue may meet the private business use test solely because the private air carriers receive a special economic benefit from the runway. See paragraph (b)(7)(ii) of this section.

(iii) The facts are the same as in Example 8(i), except that the lease payments under the leases with the private air carriers are determined on a residual basis by taking into account the net revenues generated by runway landing fees. These leases cause the private business use test to be met with respect to the runway because they are arrangements that convey special legal entitlements to the financed facility to nongovernmental persons. See paragraph (b)(7)(i) of this section.

Example (9). General public use—airport parking garage. City S issues bonds and uses all of the proceeds to finance construction of a city-owned parking garage at the city-owned airport. S reasonably expects that more than 10 percent of the actual use of the parking garage will be by employees of private air carriers (both charter airlines and commercial airlines) in connection with their use of the airport terminals leased by those carriers. The air carriers' use of the parking garage, however, will be on the same basis as passengers and other members of the general public using the airport. The leases for the use of the terminal space provide no priority rights to the air carriers for use of the parking garage, and the lease payments are determined without taking into account the revenues generated by the parking garage. Although the lessee air carriers receive a special economic benefit from the use of the parking garage, this economic benefit is not sufficient to cause the air carriers to be private business users, because the parking garage is available for general public use. The issue does not meet the private business use test. See paragraphs (b)(7)(ii) and (c) of this section.

Example (10). Long-term arrangements not treated as general public use—insurance fund. Authority T deposits all of the proceeds of its bonds in its insurance fund and invests all of those proceeds in tax-exempt bonds. The insurance fund provides insurance to a large number of businesses and natural persons not engaged in a trade or business. Each participant receives insurance for a term of 1 year. The use by the participants, other than participants that are natural persons not engaged in a trade or business, is treated as private business use of the proceeds of the bonds because the participants have special legal entitlements to the use of bond proceeds, even though the contractual rights are not necessarily properly characterized as ownership, leasehold, or similar interests listed in paragraph (b) of this section. Use of the bond proceeds is not treated as general public use because the term of the insurance is greater than 200 days. See paragraphs (b)(7)(i) and (c)(3) of this section.

Example (11). General public use—port road. Highway Authority W uses all of the proceeds of its bonds to construct a 25-mile road to connect an industrial port owned by Corporation Y with existing roads owned and operated by W. Other than the port, the nearest residential or commercial development to the new road is 12 miles away. There is no reasonable expectation that development will occur in the area surrounding the new road. W and Y enter into no arrangement (either by contract or ordinance) that conveys special legal entitlements to Y for the use of the road. Use of the road will be available without restriction to all users, including natural persons who are not engaged in a trade or business. The issue does not meet the private business use test because the road is treated as used only by the general public.

Example (12). General public use of governmentally owned hotel. State Q issues bonds to purchase land and construct a hotel for use by the general public (that is, tourists, visitors, and business travelers). The bond documents provide that Q will own and operate the project for the term of the bonds. Q will not enter into a lease or license with any user for use of rooms for a period longer than 200 days (although users may actually use rooms for consecutive periods in excess of 200 days). Use of the hotel by hotel guests who are travelling in connection with trades or businesses of nongovernmental persons is not a private business use of the hotel by these persons because the hotel is intended to be available and in fact is reasonably available for use on the same basis by natural persons not engaged in a trade or business. See paragraph (c)(1) of this section.

Example (13). General public use with rights of first refusal. Authority V uses all of the proceeds of its bonds to construct a parking garage. At least 90 percent of the spaces in the garage will be available to the general public on a monthly first-come, first-served basis. V reasonably expects that the spaces will be predominantly leased to natural persons not engaged in a trade or business who have priority rights to renew their spaces at then current fair market value rates. More than 10 percent of the spaces will be leased to nongovernmental persons acting in a trade or business. These leases are not treated as arrangements with a term of use greater than 200 days. The rights to renew are not treated as renewal options because the compensation for the spaces is redetermined at generally applicable, fair market value rates that will be in effect at the time of renewal and the use of the spaces under similar arrangements is predominantly by natural persons who are not engaged in a trade or business. The issue does not meet the private business use test because at least 90 percent of the use of the parking garage is general public use. See paragraph (c)(3) of this section.

Example (14). General public use with a specially negotiated rate agreement with agency of United States. G, a sewage collection and treatment district, operates facilities that were financed with its bonds. F, an agency of the United States, has a base located within G. Approximately 20 percent of G's facilities are used to treat sewage produced by F under a specially negotiated rate agreement. Under the specially negotiated rate agreement, G uses its best efforts to charge F as closely as possible the same amount for its use of G's services as its other customers pay for the same amount of services, although those other customers pay for services based on standard district charges and tax levies. F is prohibited by federal law from paying for the services based on those standard district charges and tax levies. The use of G's facilities by F is on the same basis as the general public. See paragraph (c)(2)(ii) of this section.

Example (15). Arrangements not available for use by natural persons not engaged in a trade or business—federal use of prisons. Authority E uses all of the proceeds of its bonds to construct a prison. E contracts with federal agency F to house federal prisoners on a space-available, first-come, first-served basis, pursuant to which F will be charged approximately the same amount for each prisoner as other persons that enter into similar transfer agreements. It is reasonably expected that other persons will enter into similar agreements. The term of the use under the contract is not longer than 100 days, and F has no right to renew, although E reasonably expects to renew the contract indefinitely. The prison is not financed for a principal purpose of providing the prison for use by F. It is reasonably expected that during the term of the bonds, more than 10 percent of the prisoners at the prison will be federal prisoners. F's use of the facility is not general public use because this type of use (leasing space for prisoners) is not available for use on the same basis by natural persons not engaged in a trade or business. The issue does not meet the private business use test, however, because the leases satisfy the exception of paragraph (d)(3)(i) of this section.

Example (16). Negotiated arm's-length arrangements—auditorium reserved in advance.

(i) City Z issues obligations to finance the construction of a municipal auditorium that it will own and operate. The use of the auditorium will be open to anyone who wishes to use it for a short period of time on a rate-scale basis. Z reasonably expects that the auditorium will be used by schools, church groups, sororities, and numerous commercial organizations. Corporation H, a nongovernmental person, enters into an arm's-length arrangement with Z to use the auditorium for 1 week for each year for a 10-year period (a total of 70 days), pursuant to which H will be charged a specific price reflecting fair market value. On the date the contract is entered into, Z has not established generally applicable rates for future years. Even though the auditorium is not financed for a principal purpose of providing use of the auditorium to H, H is not treated as using the auditorium as a member of the general public because its use is not on the same basis as the general public. Because the term of H's use of the auditorium is longer than 50 days, the arrangement does not meet the exception under paragraph (d)(3)(ii) of this section.

(ii) The facts are the same as in Example 16(i), except that H will enter into an arm's-length arrangement with Z to use the auditorium for 1 week for each year for a 4-year period (a total of 28 days), pursuant to which H will be charged a specific price reflecting fair market value. H is not treated as a private business user of the auditorium because its contract satisfies the exception of paragraph (d)(3)(ii) of this section for negotiated arm's-length arrangements.

(g) Measurement of private business use. *(1) In general.* In general, the private business use of proceeds is allocated to property under § 1.141-6. The amount of private business use of that property is determined according to the average percentage of private business use of that property during the measurement period.

(2) Measurement period. (i) General rule. Except as provided in this paragraph (g)(2), the measurement period of property financed by an issue begins on the later of the issue date of that issue or the date the property is placed in service and ends on the earlier of the last date of the reasonably expected economic life of the property or the latest maturity date of any bond of the issue financing the property (determined without regard to any optional redemption dates). In general, the period of reasonably expected economic life of the property for this purpose is based on reasonable expectations as of the issue date.

(ii) Special rule for refundings of short-term obligations. For an issue of short-term obligations that the issuer reasonably expects to refund with a long-term financing (such as bond anticipation notes), the measurement period is based on the latest maturity date of any bond of the last refunding issue with respect to the financed property (determined without regard to any optional redemption dates).

(iii) Special rule for reasonably expected mandatory redemptions. If an issuer reasonably expects on the issue date that an action will occur during the term of the bonds to cause either the private business tests or the private loan financing test to be met and is required to redeem bonds to meet the reasonable expectations test of § 1.141-2(d)(2), the measurement period ends on the reasonably expected redemption date.

(iv) Special rule for ownership by a nongovernmental person. The amount of private business use resulting from ownership by a nongovernmental person is the greatest percentage of private business use in any 1-year period.

(v) Anti-abuse rule. If an issuer establishes the term of an issue for a period that is longer than is reasonably necessary for the governmental purposes of the issue for a principal purpose of increasing the permitted amount of private business use, the Commissioner may determine the amount of private business use according to the greatest percentage of private business use in any 1-year period.

(3) Determining average percentage of private business use. The average percentage of private business use is the average of the percentages of private business use during the 1-year periods within the measurement period. Appropriate adjustments must be made for beginning and ending periods of less than 1 year.

(4) Determining the average amount of private business use for a 1-year period. (i) In general. The percentage of private business use of property for any 1-year period is the average private business use during that year. This average is determined by comparing the amount of private business use during the year to the total amount of private business use and use that is not private business use (government use) during that year. Paragraphs (g)(4)(ii) through (v) of this section apply to determine the average amount of private business use for a 1-year period.

(ii) Uses at different times. For a facility in which actual government use and private business use occur at different times (for example, different days), the average amount of private business use generally is based on the amount of time that the facility is used for private business use as a percentage of the total time for all actual use. In determining the total amount of actual use, periods during which the facility is not in use are disregarded.

(iii) Simultaneous use. In general, for a facility in which government use and private business use occur simultaneously, the entire facility is treated as having private business use. For example, a governmentally owned facility that is leased or managed by a nongovernmental person in a manner that results in private business use is treated as entirely used for a private business use. If, however, there is also private business use and actual government use on the same basis, the average amount of private business use may be determined on a reasonable basis that properly reflects the proportionate benefit to be derived by the various users of the facility (for example, reasonably expected fair market value of use). For example, the average amount of private business use of a garage with unassigned spaces that is used for government use and private business use is generally based on the number of spaces used for private business use as a percentage of the total number of spaces.

(iv) Discrete portion. For purposes of this paragraph (g), measurement of the use of proceeds allocated to a discrete portion of a facility is determined by treating that discrete portion as a separate facility.

(v) Relationship to fair market value. For purposes of paragraphs (g)(4)(ii) through (iv) of this section, if private business use is reasonably expected as of the issue date to have a significantly greater fair market value than government use, the average amount of private business use must be determined according to the relative reasonably expected fair market values of use rather than another measure, such as average time of use. This determination of relative fair market value may be made as of the date the property is acquired or placed in service if making this determination as of the issue date is not reasonably possible (for example, if the financed property is not identified on the issue date). In general, the relative reasonably expected fair market value for a period must be determined by taking into account the amount of reasonably expected payments for private business use for the period in a manner that properly reflects the proportionate benefit to be derived from the private business use.

(5) Common areas. The amount of private business use of common areas within a facility is based on a reasonable method that properly reflects the proportionate benefit to be derived by the users of the facility. For example, in general, a method that is based on the average amount of private business use of the remainder of the entire facility reflects proportionate benefit.

(6) Allocation of neutral costs. Proceeds that are used to pay costs of issuance, invested in a reserve or replacement fund, or paid as fees for a qualified guarantee or a qualified hedge must be allocated ratably among the other purposes for which the proceeds are used.

(7) Commencement of measurement of private business use. Generally, private business use commences on the first date on which there is a right to actual use by the nongovernmental person. However, if an issuer enters into an arrangement for private business use a substantial period before the right to actual private business use commences and the arrangement transfers ownership or is an arrangement for other long-term use (such as a lease for a significant portion of the remaining economic life of financed property), private business use commences on the date the arrangement is entered into, even if the right to actual use commences after the measurement period. For this purpose, 10 percent of the measurement period is generally treated as a substantial period.

(8) Examples. The following examples illustrate the application of this paragraph (g):

Example (1). Research facility. University U, a state owned and operated university, owns and operates a research facility. U proposes to finance general improvements to the facility with the proceeds of an issue of bonds. U enters into sponsored research agreements with nongovernmental persons that result in private business use because the sponsors will own title to any patents resulting from the research. The governmental research conducted by U and the research U conducts for the sponsors take place simultaneously in all laboratories within the research facility. All laboratory equipment is available continuously for use by workers who perform both types of research. Because it is not possible to predict which research projects will be successful, it is not reasonably practicable to estimate the relative revenues expected to result from the governmental and nongovernmental research. U contributed 90 percent of the cost of the facility and the nongovernmental persons contributed 10 percent of the cost. Under this section, the nongovernmental persons are using the facility for a private business use on the same basis as the government use of the facility. The portions of the costs contributed by the various users of the facility provide a reasonable basis that properly reflects the proportionate benefit to be derived by the users of the facility. The nongovernmental persons are treated as using 10 percent of the proceeds of the issue.

Example (2). Stadium.

(i) City L issues bonds and uses all of the proceeds to construct a stadium. L enters into a long-term contract with a professional sports team T under which T will use the stadium 20 times during each year. These uses will occur on nights and weekends. L reasonably expects that the stadium will be used more than 180 other times each year, none of which will give rise to private business use. This expectation is based on a feasibility study and historical use of the old stadium that is being replaced by the new stadium. There is no significant difference in the value of T's uses when compared to the other uses of the stadium, taking into account the payments that T is reasonably expected to make for its use. Assuming no other private business use, the issue does not meet the private business use test because not more than 10 percent of the use of the facility is for a private business use.

(ii) The facts are the same as in Example 2(i), except that L reasonably expects that the stadium will be used not more than 60 other times each year, none of which will give rise to private business use. The issue meets the private business use test because 25 percent of the proceeds are used for a private business use.

Example (3). Airport terminal areas treated as common areas. City N issues bonds to finance the construction of an airport terminal. Eighty percent of the leasable space of the terminal will be leased to private air carriers. The remaining 20 percent of the leasable space will be used for the term of the bonds by N for its administrative purposes. The common areas of the terminal, including waiting areas, lobbies, and hallways are treated as 80 percent used by the air carriers for purposes of the private business use test.

T.D. 8712, 1/10/97, amend T.D. 8967, 11/19/2001.

§ 1.141-4 Private security or payment test.

(a) General rule. *(1) Private security or payment.* The private security or payment test relates to the nature of the security for, and the source of, the payment of debt service on an issue. The private payment portion of the test takes into account the payment of the debt service on the issue that is directly or indirectly to be derived from payments (whether or not to the issuer or any related party) in respect of property, or borrowed money, used or to be used for a private business use. The private security portion of the test takes into account the payment of the debt service on the issue that is directly or indirectly secured by any interest in property used or to be used for a private business use or payments in respect of property used or to be used for a private business use. For additional rules for output facilities, see § 1.141-7.

(2) Aggregation of private payments and security. For purposes of the private security or payment test, payments taken into account as private payments and payments or property taken into account as private security are aggregated. However, the same payments are not taken into account as both private security and private payments.

(3) Underlying arrangement. The security for, and payment of debt service on, an issue is determined from both the terms of the bond documents and on the basis of any underlying arrangement. An underlying arrangement may result from separate agreements between the parties or may be determined on the basis of all of the facts and circumstances surrounding the issuance of the bonds. For example, if the payment of debt service on an issue is secured by both a pledge of the full faith and credit of a state or local governmental unit and any interest in property used or to be used in a private business use, the issue meets the private security or payment test.

(b) Measurement of private payments and security. *(1) Scope.* This paragraph (b) contains rules that apply to both private security and private payments.

(2) Present value measurement. (i) Use of present value. In determining whether an issue meets the private security or payment test, the present value of the payments or property taken into account is compared to the present value of the debt service to be paid over the term of the issue.

(ii) Debt service. (A) Debt service paid from proceeds. Debt service does not include any amount paid or to be paid from sale proceeds or investment proceeds. For example, debt service does not include payments of capitalized interest funded with proceeds.

(B) Adjustments to debt service. Debt service is adjusted to take into account payments and receipts that adjust the yield on an issue for purposes of section 148(f). For example, debt service includes fees paid for qualified guarantees under section 1.148-4(f) and is adjusted to take into account payments and receipts on qualified hedges under § 1.148-4(h).

(iii) Computation of present value. (A) In general. Present values are determined by using the yield on the issue as the discount rate and by discounting all amounts to the issue date. See, however, § 1.141-13 for special rules for refunding bonds.

(B) Fixed yield issues. For a fixed yield issue, yield is determined on the issue date and is not adjusted to take into account subsequent events.

(C) Variable yield issues. The yield on a variable yield issue is determined over the term of the issue. To determine the reasonably expected yield as of any date, the issuer may assume that the future interest rate on a variable yield bond will be the then-current interest rate on the bonds determined under the formula prescribed in the bond documents. A deliberate action requires a recomputation of the yield on the variable yield issue to determine the present value of payments under that arrangement. In that case, the issuer must use the yield determined as of the date of the deliberate action for purposes of determining the present value of payments under the arrangement causing the deliberate action. See paragraph (g) of this section, Example 3.

(iv) Application to private security. For purposes of determining the present value of debt service that is secured by property, the property is valued at fair market value as of the first date on which the property secures bonds of the issue.

(c) Private payments. *(1) In general.* This paragraph (c) contains rules that apply to private payments.

(2) Payments taken into account. (i) Payments for use. (A) In general. Both direct and indirect payments made by any nongovernmental person that is treated as using proceeds of the issue are taken into account as private payments to the extent allocable to the proceeds used by that person. Payments are taken into account as private payments only to the extent that they are made for the period of time that proceeds are used for a private business use. Payments for a use of proceeds include payments (whether or not to the issuer) in respect of property financed (directly or indirectly) with those proceeds, even if not made by a private business user. Payments are not made in respect of financed property if those payments are directly allocable to other property being directly used by the person making the payment and those payments represent fair market value compensation for that other use. See paragraph (g) of this section, Example 4 and Example 5. See also paragraph (c)(3) of this section for rules relating to allocation of payments to the source or sources of funding of property.

(B) Payments not to exceed use. Payments with respect to proceeds that are used for a private business use are not taken into account to the extent that the present value of those payments exceeds the present value of debt service on those proceeds. Payments need not be directly derived from a private business user, however, to be taken into account. Thus, if 7 percent of the proceeds of an issue is used by a person over the measurement period, payments with respect to the property financed with those proceeds are taken into account as private payments only to the extent that the present value of those payments does not exceed the present value of 7 percent of the debt service on the issue.

(C) Payments for operating expenses. Payments by a person for a use of proceeds do not include the portion of any payment that is properly allocable to the payment of ordinary and necessary expenses (as defined under section 162) directly attributable to the operation and maintenance of the financed property used by that person. For this purpose, general overhead and administrative expenses are not directly attributable to those operations and maintenance. For example, if an issuer receives $5,000 rent during the year for use of space in a financed facility and during the year pays $500 for ordinary and necessary expenses properly allocable to the operation and maintenance of that space and $400 for general overhead and general administrative expenses properly allocable to that space, $500 of the $5,000 received would not be considered a payment for the use of the proceeds allocable to that space (regardless of the manner in which that $500 is actually used).

(ii) Refinanced debt service. Payments of debt service on an issue to be made from proceeds of a refunding issue are taken into account as private payments in the same proportion that the present value of the payments taken into account as private payments for the refunding issue bears to the present value of the debt service to be paid on the refunding issue. For example, if all the debt service on a note is paid with proceeds of a refunding issue, the note meets the private security or payment test if (and to the same extent that) the refunding issue meets the private security or payment test. This paragraph (c)(2)(ii) does not apply to payments that arise from deliberate actions that occur more than 3 years after the retirement of the prior issue that are not reasonably expected on the issue date of the refunding issue. For purposes of this paragraph (c)(2)(ii), whether an issue is a refunding issue is determined without regard to § 1.150-1(d)(2)(i) (relating to certain payments of interest).

(3) Allocation of payments. (i) In general. Private payments for the use of property are allocated to the source or different sources of funding of property. The allocation to the source or different sources of funding is based on all of the facts and circumstances, including whether an allocation is consistent with the purposes of section 141. In general, a private payment for the use of property is allocated to a source of funding based upon the nexus between the payment and both the financed property and the source of funding. For this purpose, different sources of funding may include different tax-exempt issues, taxable issues, and amounts that are not derived from a borrowing, such as revenues of an issuer (equity).

(ii) Payments for use of discrete property. Payments for the use of a discrete facility (or a discrete portion of a facility) are allocated to the source or different sources of funding of that discrete property.

(iii) Allocations among two or more sources of funding. In general, except as provided in paragraphs (c)(3)(iv) and (v) of this section, if a payment is made for the use of property financed with two or more sources of funding (for example, equity and a tax-exempt issue), that payment must be allocated to those sources of funding in a manner that reasonably corresponds to the relative amounts of those sources of funding that are expended on that property. If an issuer has not retained records of amounts expended on the property (for example, records of costs of a building that was built 30 years before the allocation), an issuer may use reasonable estimates of those expenditures. For this purpose, costs of issuance and other similar neutral costs are allocated ratably among expenditures in the same manner as in § 1.141-3(g)(6). A payment for the use of property may be allocated to two or more issues that finance property according to the relative amounts of debt service (both paid and accrued) on the issues during the annual period for which the payment is made, if that allocation reasonably reflects the economic substance of the arrangement. In general, allocations of payments according to relative debt service reasonably reflect the economic substance of the arrangement if the maturity of the bonds reasonably corresponds to the reasonably expected economic life of the property and debt service payments on the bonds are approximately level from year to year.

(iv) Payments made under an arrangement entered into in connection with issuance of bonds. A private payment for the use of property made under an arrangement that is entered into in connection with the issuance of the issue that finances that property generally is allocated to that issue. Whether an arrangement is entered into in connection with the issuance of an issue is determined on the basis of all of the facts and circumstances. An arrangement is ordinarily treated as entered into in connection with the issuance of an issue if—

(A) The issuer enters into the arrangement during the 3-year period beginning 18 months before the issue date; and

(B) The amount of payments reflects all or a portion of debt service on the issue.

(v) Allocations to equity. A private payment for the use of property may be allocated to equity before payments are allocated to an issue only if—

(A) Not later than 60 days after the date of the expenditure of those amounts, the issuer adopts an official intent (in a manner comparable to § 1.150-2(e)) indicating that the issuer reasonably expects to be repaid for the expenditure from a specific arrangement; and

(B) The private payment is made not later than 18 months after the later of the date the expenditure is made or the date the project is placed in service.

(d) Private security. *(1) In general.* This paragraph (d) contains rules that relate to private security.

(2) Security taken into account. The property that is the security for, or the source of, the payment of debt service on an issue need not be property financed with proceeds. For example, unimproved land or investment securities used, directly or indirectly, in a private business use that secures an issue provides private security. Private security (other than financed property and private payments) for an issue is taken into account under section 141(b), however, only to the extent it is provided, directly or indirectly, by a user of proceeds of the issue.

(3) Pledge of unexpended proceeds. Proceeds qualifying for an initial temporary period under § 1.148-2(e)(2) or (3) or deposited in a reasonably required reserve or replacement fund (as defined in § 1.148-2(f)(2)(i)) are not taken into account under this paragraph (d) before the date on which those amounts are either expended or loaned by the issuer to an unrelated party.

(4) Secured by any interest in property or payments. Property used or to be used for a private business use and payments in respect of that property are treated as private security if any interest in that property or payments secures the payment of debt service on the bonds. For this purpose, the phrase any interest in is to be interpreted broadly and includes, for example, any right, claim, title, or legal share in property or payments.

(5) Payments in respect of property. The payments taken into account as private security are payments in respect of property used or to be used for a private business use. Except as otherwise provided in this paragraph (d)(5) and paragraph (d)(6) of this section, the rules in paragraphs (c)(2)(i)(A) and (B) and (c)(2)(ii) of this section apply to determine the amount of payments treated as payments in respect of property used or to be used for a private business use. Thus, payments made by members of the general public for use of a facility used for a private business use (for example, a facility that is the subject of a management contract that results in private business use) are taken into account as private security to the extent that they are made for the period of time that property is used by a private business user.

(6) Allocation of security among issues. In general, property or payments from the disposition of that property that are taken into account as private security are allocated to each issue secured by the property or payments on a reasonable basis that takes into account bondholders' rights to the payments or property upon default.

(e) Generally applicable taxes. *(1) General rule.* For purposes of the private security or payment test, generally applicable taxes are not taken into account (that is, are not payments from a nongovernmental person and are not payments in respect of property used for a private business use).

(2) Definition of generally applicable taxes. A generally applicable tax is an enforced contribution exacted pursuant

to legislative authority in the exercise of the taxing power that is imposed and collected for the purpose of raising revenue to be used for governmental or public purposes. A generally applicable tax must have a uniform tax rate that is applied to all persons of the same classification in the appropriate jurisdiction and a generally applicable manner of determination and collection.

(3) Special charges. A special charge (as defined in this paragraph (e)(3)) is not a generally applicable tax. For this purpose, a special charge means a payment for a special privilege granted or regulatory function (for example, a license fee), a service rendered (for example, a sanitation services fee), a use of property (for example, rent), or a payment in the nature of a special assessment to finance capital improvements that is imposed on a limited class of persons based on benefits received from the capital improvements financed with the assessment. Thus, a special assessment to finance infrastructure improvements in a new industrial park (such as sidewalks, streets, streetlights, and utility infrastructure improvements) that is imposed on a limited class of persons composed of property owners within the industrial park who benefit from those improvements is a special charge. By contrast, an otherwise qualified generally applicable tax (such as a generally applicable ad valorem tax on all real property within a governmental taxing jurisdiction) or an eligible PILOT under paragraph (e)(5) of this section that is based on such a generally applicable tax is not treated as a special charge merely because the taxes or PILOTs received are used for governmental or public purposes in a manner which benefits particular property owners.

(4) Manner of determination and collection. (i) In general. A tax does not have a generally applicable manner of determination and collection to the extent that one or more taxpayers make any impermissible agreements relating to payment of those taxes. An impermissible agreement relating to the payment of a tax is taken into account whether or not it is reasonably expected to result in any payments that would not otherwise have been made. For example, if an issuer uses proceeds to make a grant to a taxpayer to improve property, agreements that impose reasonable conditions on the use of the grant do not cause a tax on that property to fail to be a generally applicable tax. If an agreement by a taxpayer causes the tax imposed on that taxpayer not to be treated as a generally applicable tax, the entire tax paid by that taxpayer is treated as a special charge, unless the agreement is limited to a specific portion of the tax.

(ii) Impermissible agreements. The following are examples of agreements that cause a tax to fail to have a generally applicable manner of determination and collection: an agreement to be personally liable on a tax that does not generally impose personal liability, to provide additional credit support such as a third party guarantee, or to pay unanticipated shortfalls; an agreement regarding the minimum market value of property subject to property tax; and an agreement not to challenge or seek deferral of the tax.

(iii) Permissible agreements. The following are examples of agreements that do not cause a tax to fail to have a generally applicable manner of determination and collection: an agreement to use a grant for specified purposes (whether or not that agreement is secured); a representation regarding the expected value of the property following the improvement; an agreement to insure the property and, if damaged, to restore the property; a right of a grantor to rescind the grant if property taxes are not paid; and an agreement to reduce or limit the amount of taxes collected to further a bona fide governmental purpose. For example, an agreement to abate taxes to encourage a property owner to rehabilitate property in a distressed area is a permissible agreement.

(5) Payments in lieu of taxes. A tax equivalency payment or other payment in lieu of a tax ("PILOT") is treated as a generally applicable tax if it meets the requirements of paragraphs (e)(5)(i) through (iv) of this section—

(i) Maximum amount limited by underlying generally applicable tax. The PILOT is not greater than the amount imposed by a statute for a generally applicable tax in each year.

(ii) Commensurate with a generally applicable tax. The PILOT is commensurate with the amount imposed by a statute for a generally applicable tax in each year under the commensurate standard set forth in this paragraph (e)(5)(ii). For this purpose, except as otherwise provided in this paragraph (e)(5)(ii), a PILOT is commensurate with a generally applicable tax only if it is equal to a fixed percentage of the generally applicable tax that would otherwise apply in each year or it reflects a fixed adjustment to the generally applicable tax that would otherwise apply in each year. A PILOT based on a property tax does not fail to be commensurate with the property tax as a result of changes in the level of the percentage of or adjustment to that property tax for a reasonable phase-in period ending when the subject property is placed in service (as defined in § 1.150-2(c)). A PILOT based on a property tax must take into account the current assessed value of the property for property tax purposes for each year in which the PILOT is paid and that assessed value must be determined in the same manner and with the same frequency as property subject to the property tax. A PILOT is not commensurate with a generally applicable tax, however, if the PILOT is set at a fixed dollar amount (for example, fixed debt service on a bond issue) that cannot vary with changes in the level of the generally applicable tax on which it is based.

(iii) Use of PILOTs for governmental or public purposes. The PILOT is to be used for governmental or public purposes for which the generally applicable tax on which it is based may be used.

(iv) No special charges. The PILOT is not a special charge under paragraph (e)(3) of this section.

(f) Certain waste remediation bonds. *(1) Scope.* This paragraph (f) applies to bonds issued to finance hazardous waste clean-up activities on privately owned land (hazardous waste remediation bonds).

(2) Persons that are not private users. Payments from nongovernmental persons who are not (other than coincidentally) either users of the site being remediated or persons potentially responsible for disposing of hazardous waste on that site are not taken into account as private security. This paragraph (f)(2) applies to payments that secure (directly or indirectly) the payment of principal of, or interest on, the bonds under the terms of the bonds. This paragraph (f)(2) applies only if the payments are made pursuant to either a generally applicable state or local taxing statute or a state or local statute that regulates or restrains activities on an industry-wide basis of persons who are engaged in generating or handling hazardous waste, or in refining, producing, or transporting petroleum, provided that those payments do not represent, in substance, payment for the use of proceeds. For this purpose, a state or local statute that imposes payments that have substantially the same character as those described in Chapter 38 of the Code are treated as generally applicable taxes.

(3) Persons that are private users. If payments from nongovernmental persons who are either users of the site being

remediated or persons potentially responsible for disposing of hazardous waste on that site do not secure (directly or indirectly) the payment of principal of, or interest on, the bonds under the terms of the bonds, the payments are not taken into account as private payments. This paragraph (f)(3) applies only if at the time the bonds are issued the payments from those nongovernmental persons are not material to the security for the bonds. For this purpose, payments are not material to the security for the bonds if—

(i) The payments are not required for the payment of debt service on the bonds;

(ii) The amount and timing of the payments are not structured or designed to reflect the payment of debt service on the bonds;

(iii) The receipt or the amount of the payment is uncertain (for example, as of the issue date, no final judgment has been entered into against the nongovernmental person);

(iv) The payments from those nongovernmental persons, when and if received, are used either to redeem bonds of the issuer or to pay for costs of any hazardous waste remediation project; and

(v) In the case when a judgment (but not a final judgment) has been entered by the issue date against a nongovernmental person, there are, as of the issue date, costs of hazardous waste remediation other than those financed with the bonds that may be financed with the payments.

(g) Examples. The following examples illustrate the application of this section:

Example (1). Aggregation of payments. State B issues bonds with proceeds of $10 million. B uses $9.7 million of the proceeds to construct a 10-story office building. B uses the remaining $300,000 of proceeds to make a loan to Corporation Y. In addition, Corporation X leases 1 floor of the building for the term of the bonds. Under all of the facts and circumstances, it is reasonable to allocate 10 percent of the proceeds to that 1 floor. As a percentage of the present value of the debt service on the bonds, the present value of Y's loan repayments is 3 percent and the present value of X's lease payments is 8 percent. The bonds meet the private security or payment test because the private payments taken into account are more than 10 percent of the present value of the debt service on the bonds.

Example (2). Indirect private payments. J, a political subdivision of a state, will issue several series of bonds from time to time and will use the proceeds to rehabilitate urban areas. Under all of the facts and circumstances, the private business use test will be met with respect to each issue that will be used for the rehabilitation and construction of buildings that will be leased or sold to nongovernmental persons for use in their trades or businesses. Nongovernmental persons will make payments for these sales and leases. There is no limitation either on the number of issues or the aggregate amount of bonds that may be outstanding. No group of bondholders has any legal claim prior to any other bondholders or creditors with respect to specific revenues of J, and there is no arrangement whereby revenues from a particular project are paid into a trust or constructive trust, or sinking fund, or are otherwise segregated or restricted for the benefit of any group of bondholders. There is, however, an unconditional obligation by J to pay the principal of, and the interest on, each issue. Although not directly pledged under the terms of the bond documents, the leases and sales are underlying arrangements. The payments relating to these leases and sales are taken into account as private payments to determine whether each issue of bonds meets the private security or payment test.

Example (3). Computation of payment in variable yield issues.

(i) City M issues general obligation bonds with proceeds of $10 million to finance a 5-story office building. The bonds bear interest at a variable rate that is recomputed monthly according to an index that reflects current market yields. The yield that the interest index would produce on the issue date is 6 percent. M leases 1 floor of the office building to Corporation T, a nongovernmental person, for the term of the bonds. Under all of the facts and circumstances, T is treated as using more than 10 percent of the proceeds. Using the 6 percent yield as the discount rate, M reasonably expects on the issue date that the present value of lease payments to be made by T will be 8 percent of the present value of the total debt service on the bonds. After the issue date of the bonds, interest rates decline significantly, so that the yield on the bonds over their entire term is 4 percent. Using this actual 4 percent yield as the discount rate, the present value of lease payments made by T is 12 percent of the present value of the actual total debt service on the bonds. The bonds are not private activity bonds because M reasonably expected on the issue date that the bonds would not meet the private security or payment test and because M did not take any subsequent deliberate action to meet the private security or payment test.

(ii) The facts are the same as Example 3(i), except that 5 years after the issue date M leases a second floor to Corporation S, a nongovernmental person, under a long-term lease. Because M has taken a deliberate action, the present value of the lease payments must be computed. On the date this lease is entered into, M reasonably expects that the yield on the bonds over their entire term will be 5.5 percent, based on actual interest rates to date and the then-current rate on the variable yield bonds. M uses this 5.5 percent yield as the discount rate. Using this 5.5 percent yield as the discount rate, as a percentage of the present value of the debt service on the bonds, the present value of the lease payments made by S is 3 percent. The bonds are private activity bonds because the present value of the aggregate private payments is greater than 10 percent of the present value of debt service.

Example (4). Payments not in respect of financed property. In order to further public safety, City Y issues tax assessment bonds the proceeds of which are used to move existing electric utility lines underground. Although the utility lines are owned by a nongovernmental utility company, that company is under no obligation to move the lines. The debt service on the bonds will be paid using assessments levied by City Y on the customers of the utility. Although the utility lines are privately owned and the utility customers make payments to the utility company for the use of those lines, the assessments are payments in respect of the cost of relocating the utility line. Thus, the assessment payments are not made in respect of property used for a private business use. Any direct or indirect payments to Y by the utility company for the undergrounding are, however, taken into account as private payments.

Example (5). Payments from users of proceeds that are not private business users taken into account. City P issues general obligation bonds to finance the renovation of a hospital that it owns. The hospital is operated for P by D, a nongovernmental person, under a management contract that results in private business use under § 1.141-3. P will use the revenues from the hospital (after the required payments to D and the payment of operation and maintenance expenses) to pay the debt service on the bonds. The bonds meet the private security or payment test because the revenues from the hospital are payments in respect of property used for a private business use.

Example (6). Limitation of amount of to amount of private business use not determined annually. City Q issues bonds with a term of 15 years and uses the proceeds to construct an office building. The debt service on the bonds is level throughout the 15-year term. Q enters into a 5-year lease with Corporation R under which R is treated as a user of 11 percent of the proceeds. R will make lease payments equal to 20 percent of the annual debt service on the bonds for each year of the lease. The present value of R's lease payments is equal to 12 percent of the present value of the debt service over the entire 15-year term of the bonds. If, however, the lease payments taken into account as private payments were limited to 11 percent of debt service paid in each year of the lease, the present value of these payments would be only 8 percent of the debt service on the bonds over the entire term of the bonds. The bonds meet the private security or payment test, because R's lease payments are taken into account as private payments in an amount not to exceed 11 percent of the debt service of the bonds.

Example (7). Allocation of payments to funds not derived from A borrowing. City Z purchases property for $1,250,000 using $1,000,000 of proceeds of its tax increment bonds and $250,000 of other revenues that are in its redevelopment fund. Within 60 days of the date of purchase, Z declared its intent to sell the property pursuant to a redevelopment plan and to use that amount to reimburse its redevelopment fund. The bonds are secured only by the incremental property taxes attributable to the increase in value of the property from the planned redevelopment of the property. Within 18 months after the issue date, Z sells the financed property to Developer M for $250,000, which Z uses to reimburse the redevelopment fund. The property that M uses is financed both with the proceeds of the bonds and Z's redevelopment fund. The payments by M are properly allocable to the costs of property financed with the amounts in Z's redevelopment fund. See paragraphs (c)(3)(i) and (v) of this section.

Example (8). Allocation of payments to different sources of funding— improvements. In 1997, City L issues bonds with proceeds of $8 million to finance the acquisition of a building. In 2002, L spends $2 million of its general revenues to improve the heating system and roof of the building. At that time, L enters into a 10-year lease with Corporation M for the building providing for annual payments of $1 million to L. The lease payments are at fair market value, and the lease payments do not otherwise have a significant nexus to either the issue or to the expenditure of general revenues. Eighty percent of each lease payment is allocated to the issue and is taken into account under the private payment test because each lease payment is properly allocated to the sources of funding in a manner that reasonably corresponds to the relative amounts of the sources of funding that are expended on the building.

Example (9). Security not provided by users of proceeds not taken into account. County W issues certificates of participation in a lease of a building that W owns and covenants to appropriate annual payments for the lease. A portion of each payment is specified as interest. More than 10 percent of the building is used for private business use. None of the proceeds of the obligations are used with respect to the building. W uses the proceeds of the obligations to make a grant to Corporation Y for the construction of a factory that Y will own. Y makes no payments to W, directly or indirectly, for its use of proceeds, and Y has no relationship to the users of the leased building. If W defaults under the lease, the trustee for the holders of the certificates of participation has a limited right of repossession under which the trustee may not foreclose but may lease the property to a new tenant at fair market value. The obligations are secured by an interest in property used for a private business use. However, because the property is not provided by a private business user and is not financed property, the obligations do not meet the private security or payment test.

Example (10). Allocation of payments among issues. University L, a political subdivision, issued three separate series of revenue bonds during 1989, 1991, and 1993 under the same bond resolution. L used the proceeds to construct facilities exclusively for its own use. Bonds issued under the resolution are equally and ratably secured and payable solely from the income derived by L from rates, fees, and charges imposed by L for the use of the facilities. The bonds issued in 1989, 1991, and 1993 are not private activity bonds. In 1997, L issues another series of bonds under the resolution to finance additional facilities. L leases 20 percent of the new facilities for the term of the 1997 bonds to nongovernmental persons who will use the facilities in their trades or businesses. The present value of the lease payments from the nongovernmental users will equal 15 percent of the present value of the debt service on the 1997 bonds. L will commingle all of the revenues from all its bond-financed facilities in its revenue fund. The present value of the portion of the lease payments from nongovernmental lessees of the new facilities allocable to the 1997 bonds under paragraph (d) of this section is less than 10 percent of the present value of the debt service on the 1997 bonds because the bond documents provide that the bonds are equally and ratably secured. Accordingly, the 1997 bonds do not meet the private security test. The 1997 bonds meet the private payment test, however, because the private lease payments for the new facility are properly allocated to those bonds (that is, because none of the proceeds of the prior issues were used for the new facilities). See paragraph (c) of this section.

Example (11). Generally applicable tax. (i) Authority N issues bonds to finance the construction of a stadium. Under a long-term lease, Corporation X, a professional sports team, will use more than 10 percent of the stadium. X will not, however, make any payments for this private business use. The security for the bonds will be a ticket tax imposed on each person purchasing a ticket for an event at the stadium. The portion of the ticket tax attributable to tickets purchased by persons attending X's events will, on a present value basis, exceed 10 percent of the present value of the debt service on N's bonds. The bonds meet the private security or payment test. The ticket tax is not a generally applicable tax and, to the extent that the tax receipts relate to X's events, the taxes are payments in respect of property used for a private business use.

(ii) The facts are the same as Example 11(i), except that the ticket tax is imposed by N on tickets purchased for events at a number of large entertainment facilities within the N's jurisdiction (for example, other stadiums, arenas, and concert halls), some of which were not financed with tax-exempt bonds. The ticket tax is a generally applicable tax and therefore the revenues from this tax are not payments in respect of property used for a private business use. The receipt of the ticket tax does not cause the bonds to meet the private security or payment test.

T.D. 8712, 1/10/97, amend T.D. 9429, 10/20/2008.

§ 1.141-5 Private loan financing test.

(a) In general. Bonds of an issue are private activity bonds if more than the lesser of 5 percent or $5 million of the proceeds of the issue is to be used (directly or indirectly) to make or finance loans to persons other than governmental persons. Section 1.141-2(d) applies in determining whether the private loan financing test is met. In determining whether the proceeds of an issue are used to make or finance loans, indirect, as well as direct, use of the proceeds is taken into account.

(b) Measurement of test. In determining whether the private loan financing test is met, the amount actually loaned to a nongovernmental person is not discounted to reflect the present value of the loan repayments.

(c) Definition of private loan. *(1) In general.* Any transaction that is generally characterized as a loan for federal income tax purposes is a loan for purposes of this section. In addition, a loan may arise from the direct lending of bond proceeds or may arise from transactions in which indirect benefits that are the economic equivalent of a loan are conveyed. Thus, the determination of whether a loan is made depends on the substance of a transaction rather than its form. For example, a lease or other contractual arrangement (for example, a management contract or an output contract) may in substance constitute a loan if the arrangement transfers tax ownership of the facility to a nongovernmental person. Similarly, an output contract or a management contract with respect to a financed facility generally is not treated as a loan of proceeds unless the agreement in substance shifts significant burdens and benefits of ownership to the nongovernmental purchaser or manager of the facility.

(2) Application only to purpose investments. (i) In general. A loan may be either a purpose investment or a nonpurpose investment. A loan that is a nonpurpose investment does not cause the private loan financing test to be met. For example, proceeds invested in loans, such as obligations of the United States, during a temporary period, as part of a reasonably required reserve or replacement fund, as part of a refunding escrow, or as part of a minor portion (as each of those terms are defined in § 1.148-1 or § 1.148-2) are generally not treated as loans under the private loan financing test.

(ii) Certain prepayments treated as loans. Except as otherwise provided, a prepayment for property or services, including a prepayment for property or services that is made after the date that the contract to buy the property or services is entered into, is treated as a loan for purposes of the private loan financing test if a principal purpose for prepaying is to provide a benefit of tax-exempt financing to the seller. A prepayment is not treated as a loan for purposes of the private loan financing test if—

(A) Prepayments on substantially the same terms are made by a substantial percentage of persons who are similarly situated to the issuer but who are not beneficiaries of tax-exempt financing;

(B) The prepayment is made within 90 days of the reasonably expected date of delivery to the issuer of all of the property or services for which the prepayment is made; or

(C) The prepayment meets the requirements of § 1.148-1(e)(2)(iii)(A) or (B) (relating to certain prepayments to acquire a supply of natural gas or electricity).

(iii) Customary prepayments. The determination of whether a prepayment satisfies paragraph (c)(2)(ii)(A) of this section is generally made based on all the facts and circumstances. In addition, a prepayment is deemed to satisfy paragraph (c)(2)(ii)(A) of this section if—

(A) The prepayment is made for—

(1) Maintenance, repair, or an extended warranty with respect to personal property (for example, automobiles or electronic equipment); or

(2) Updates or maintenance or support services with respect to computer software; and

(B) The same maintenance, repair, extended warranty, updates or maintenance or support services, as applicable, are regularly provided to nongovernmental persons on the same terms.

(iv) Additional prepayments as permitted by the Commissioner. The Commissioner may, by published guidance, set forth additional circumstances in which a prepayment is not treated as a loan for purposes of the private loan financing test.

(3) Grants. (i) In general. A grant of proceeds is not a loan. Whether a transaction may be treated as a grant or a loan depends on all of the facts and circumstances.

(ii) Tax increment financing. (A) In general. Generally, a grant using proceeds of an issue that is secured by generally applicable taxes attributable to the improvements to be made with the grant is not treated as a loan, unless the grantee makes any impermissible agreements relating to the payment that results in the taxes imposed on that taxpayer not to be treated as generally applicable taxes under § 1.141-4(e).

(B) Amount of loan. If a grant is treated as a loan under this paragraph (c)(3), the entire grant is treated as a loan unless the impermissible agreement is limited to a specific portion of the tax. For this purpose, an arrangement with each unrelated grantee is treated as a separate grant.

(4) Hazardous waste remediation bonds. In the case of an issue of hazardous waste remediation bonds, payments from nongovernmental persons that are either users of the site being remediated or persons potentially responsible for disposing of hazardous waste on that site do not establish that the transaction is a loan for purposes of this section. This paragraph (c)(4) applies only if those payments do not secure the payment of principal of, or interest on, the bonds (directly or indirectly), under the terms of the bonds and those payments are not taken into account under the private payment test pursuant to § 1.141-4(f)(3).

(d) Tax assessment loan exception. *(1) General rule.* For purposes of this section, a tax assessment loan that satisfies the requirements of this paragraph (d) is not a loan for purposes of the private loan financing test.

(2) Tax assessment loan defined. A tax assessment loan is a loan that arises when a governmental person permits or requires property owners to finance any governmental tax or assessment of general application for an essential governmental function that satisfies each of the requirements of paragraphs (d)(3) through (5) of this section.

(3) Mandatory tax or other assessment. The tax or assessment must be an enforced contribution that is imposed and collected for the purpose of raising revenue to be used for a specific purpose (that is, to defray the capital cost of an improvement). Taxes and assessments do not include fees for services. The tax or assessment must be imposed pursuant to a state law of general application that can be applied equally to natural persons not acting in a trade or business and per-

sons acting in a trade or business. For this purpose, taxes and assessments that are imposed subject to protest procedures are treated as enforced contributions.

(4) Specific essential governmental function. (i) In general. A mandatory tax or assessment that gives rise to a tax assessment loan must be imposed for one or more specific, essential governmental functions.

(ii) Essential governmental functions. For purposes of paragraph (d) of this section, improvements to utilities and systems that are owned by a governmental person and that are available for use by the general public (such as sidewalks, streets and street-lights; electric, telephone, and cable television systems; sewage treatment and disposal systems; and municipal water facilities) serve essential governmental functions. For other types of facilities, the extent to which the service provided by the facility is customarily performed (and financed with governmental bonds) by governments with general taxing powers is a primary factor in determining whether the facility serves an essential governmental function. For example, parks that are owned by a governmental person and that are available for use by the general public serve an essential governmental function. Except as otherwise provided in this paragraph (d)(4)(ii), commercial or industrial facilities and improvements to property owned by a nongovernmental person do not serve an essential governmental function. Permitting installment payments of property taxes or other taxes is not an essential governmental function.

(5) Equal basis requirement. (i) In general. Owners of both business and nonbusiness property benefiting from the financed improvements must be eligible, or required, to make deferred payments of the tax or assessment giving rise to a tax assessment loan on an equal basis (the equal basis requirement). A tax or assessment does not satisfy the equal basis requirement if the terms for payment of the tax or assessment are not the same for all taxed or assessed persons. For example, the equal basis requirement is not met if certain property owners are permitted to pay the tax or assessment over a period of years while others must pay the entire tax or assessment immediately or if only certain property owners are required to prepay the tax or assessment when the property is sold.

(ii) General rule for guarantees. A guarantee of debt service on bonds, or of taxes or assessments, by a person that is treated as a borrower of bond proceeds violates the equal basis requirement if it is reasonable to expect on the date the guarantee is entered into that payments will be made under the guarantee.

(6) Coordination with private business tests. See §§ 1.141-3 and 1.141-4 for rules for determining whether tax assessment loans cause the bonds financing those loans to be private activity bonds under the private business use and the private security or payment tests.

(e) Examples. The following examples illustrate the application of this section:

Example (1). Turnkey contract not treated as a loan. State agency Z and federal agency H will each contribute to rehabilitate a project owned by Z. H can only provide its funds through a contribution to Z to be used to acquire the rehabilitated project on a turnkey basis from an approved developer. Under H's turnkey program, the developer must own the project while it is rehabilitated. Z issues its notes to provide funds for construction. A portion of the notes will be retired using the H contribution, and the balance of the notes will be retired through the issuance by Z of long-term bonds. Z lends the proceeds of its notes to Developer B as construction financing and transfers title to B for a nominal amount. The conveyance is made on condition that B rehabilitate the property and reconvey it upon completion, with Z retaining the right to force reconveyance if these conditions are not satisfied. B must name Z as an additional insured on all insurance. Upon completion, B must transfer title to the project back to Z at a set price, which price reflects B's costs and profit, not fair market value. Further, this price is adjusted downward to reflect any cost-underruns. For purposes of section 141(c), this transaction does not involve a private loan.

Example (2). Essential government function requirement not met. City D creates a special taxing district consisting of property owned by nongovernmental persons that requires environmental clean-up. D imposes a special tax on each parcel within the district in an amount that is related to the expected environmental clean-up costs of that parcel. The payment of the tax over a 20-year period is treated as a loan by the property owners for purposes of the private loan financing test. The special district issues bonds, acting on behalf of D, that are payable from the special tax levied within the district, and uses the proceeds to pay for the costs of environmental clean-up on the property within the district. The bonds meet the private loan financing test because more than 5 percent of the proceeds of the issue are loaned to nongovernmental persons. The issue does not meet the tax assessment loan exception because the improvements to property owned by a nongovernmental person are not an essential governmental function under section 141(c)(2). The issue also meets the private business tests of section 141(b).

T.D. 8712, 1/10/97, amend T.D. 9085, 8/1/2003.

§ 1.141-6 Allocation and accounting rules.

(a) Allocation of proceeds to expenditures. For purposes of §§ 1.141-1 through 1.141-15, the provisions of § 1.148-6(d) apply for purposes of allocating proceeds to expenditures. Thus, allocations generally may be made using any reasonable, consistently applied accounting method, and allocations under section 141 and section 148 must be consistent with each other.

(b) Allocation of proceeds to property. [Reserved]

(c) Special rules for mixed use facilities. [Reserved]

(d) Allocation of proceeds to common areas. [Reserved]

(e) Allocation of proceeds to bonds. [Reserved]

(f) Treatment of partnerships. [Reserved]

(g) Examples. [Reserved]

T.D. 8712, 1/10/97.

PAR. 4. Section 1.141-6 is revised to read as follows:

Proposed § 1.141-6 Allocation and accounting rules [*For Preamble, see ¶ 152,807*]

(a) Allocations of proceeds to expenditures, property, and uses in general. *(1) Allocations to expenditures.* Except as otherwise provided in this section, for purposes of §§ 1.141-1 through 1.141-15, the provisions of § 1.148-6(d) apply for purposes of allocating proceeds and other sources of funds to expenditures (as contrasted with investments). Except as otherwise provided in this section, allocations of proceeds and other sources of funds to expenditures generally may be made using any reasonable, consistently applied accounting method. Allocations of proceeds to expenditures under section 141 and section 148 must be consistent with each other. For purposes of the consistency requirements in this paragraph (a), it is permissible to employ an allocation method under paragraph (a)(2), (c), or (d) of this section (for example, the general pro rata allocation method under paragraph (a)(2) of this section) to allocate sources of funds within a particular project for purposes of section 141 in conjunction with an accounting method allowed under § 1.148-6(d) (for example, the first-in, first out method) to determine the allocation of proceeds or other sources of funds to expenditures for that project.

(2) Allocations within property; the general pro rata allocation method. Except as otherwise provided in this section, proceeds and other sources of funds allocated to capital expenditures for a project (as defined in paragraph (b)(2)(ii) of this section) under section 148 and paragraph (a)(1) of this section are treated as allocated ratably throughout that project in proportion to the relative amounts of proceeds and other funds spent on that project (the general pro rata allocation method). For example, if a building is financed with proceeds and other funds and the issuer allocates the proceeds and other funds to the capital expenditures of the building using a gross proceeds spent first allocation method under section 148 and paragraph (a)(1) of this section, the proceeds and other sources of funds so allocated to the building are treated as being allocated ratably throughout the building under this paragraph (a)(2).

(3) Allocations of sources of funds to ultimate uses of financed property. Except as otherwise provided in this section, if financed property is financed with two or more sources of funding (including two or more tax-exempt governmental bond issues), those sources of funding must be allocated to multiple uses (that is, governmental use and private business use) of that financed property in proportion to the relative amounts of those sources of funding expended on that financed property.

(4) Manner and time for electing to apply special allocation methods for mixed-use projects; final allocations generally. If an issuer is making an election under paragraph (c) or (d) of this section to use one of the special allocation methods for mixed-use projects, the issuer must make this election in writing by noting in its records the method of allocation chosen and the preliminary amounts and sources of funds it expects to allocate to specific discrete or undivided portions within the mixed-use project. The time for making this election is on or before the start of the measurement period. An issuer must make final allocations of proceeds and other funds under this section by noting in its records the final amounts of such allocations. The time for making these final allocations is set forth in the timing rules under § 1.148-6(d)(1)(iii). Except as otherwise provided in this section, once the time for making final allocations under § 1.148-6(d)(1)(iii) has passed, allocations cannot be changed.

(5) References to proceeds. For purposes of this section, except where the context clearly requires otherwise (for example, in references to "proceeds" of taxable bonds) and regardless of whether expressly specified, references to proceeds generally are intended to refer to proceeds of tax-exempt governmental bonds.

(b) Special rules on reasonable proportionate allocation methods for mixed-use projects. *(1) In general.* Once proceeds and other sources of funds are allocated to a mixed-use project (as defined in paragraph (b)(2) of this section) under section 148 and paragraph(a)(1) of this section, there are three methods for allocating those proceeds and other sources of funds to capital expenditures (as defined in § 1.150-1(b)) within the mixed-use project. These methods are the general pro rata allocation method in paragraph (a)(2) of this section, the discrete physical portion allocation method, and the undivided portion allocation method. Allocations will be made under the general pro rata allocation method unless the issuer elects to use either the discrete portion method or the undivided portion method and meets the requirements for making such election under paragraph (a)(4) of this section and using such a method. The discrete portion and undivided portion allocation methods are elective and permit, to the extent provided, proceeds to be allocated to a portion of a mixed-use project based on a consistent application of a permitted reasonable allocation method that properly reflects the proportionate benefit to be derived by the various users of those portions of the mixed-use project. Paragraph (c) of this section sets forth the rules for the discrete physical portion allocation method and paragraph (d) of this section sets forth the rules for the undivided portion allocation method. Paragraph (e) of this section sets forth certain general operating rules for all mixed-use project allocations. Paragraph (g) of this section provides special rules for applying the undivided portion allocation method to output facilities.

(2) Definition of a mixed-use project. (i) In general. For purposes of this section, the term mixed-use project means a project (as defined in paragraph (b)(2)(ii) of this section) that, absent the application of the special elective allocation methods for mixed-use projects under paragraphs (c) and (d) of this section, is reasonably expected as of the issue date to have private business use in excess of de minimis permitted private business use.

(ii) Definition of project. (A) In general. For purposes of this section, the term project means one or more facilities or capital projects, including land, buildings, equipment, or other property, that meets each of the following requirements:

(1) The facilities or capital projects are functionally related or integrated and are located on the same site or on reasonably proximate adjacent sites;

(2) The facilities or capital projects are reasonably expected to be placed in service within the same 12-month period; and

(3) The proceeds and other sources of funds that are expended on the facilities or capital projects are expended pursuant to the same plan of financing.

(B) Subsequent improvements or replacements. Subsequent improvements and replacements of portions of a project that are within the size, function, and usable space of the original design of the project are treated as part of that same project even if placed in service beyond the 12-month period in paragraph (b)(2)(ii)(A)(2) of this section. Thus, for example, improvements and replacements of damaged walls or worn-out fixtures within an original building that do not expand the scope or function of usable space are part of the original project.

(c) Discrete physical portion allocation method. *(1) In general.* An issuer may elect the discrete physical portion allocation method when a mixed-use project can be separated into discrete portions (as defined in § 1.141-1(b)). With a proper election, an issuer may use the discrete physical portion allocation method to allocate proceeds and qualified equity to capital expenditures for a discrete portion within a mixed-use project and to allocate those sources of funds to uses. The issuer must use a reasonable, consistently applied allocation method that reflects the proportionate benefits to be derived by the various users of the discrete portions to determine the aggregate amount of proceeds and qualified equity allocable to a particular discrete portion in a mixed-use project.

(2) The measure of a discrete portion. An issuer is treated as using a reasonable allocation method that reflects the proportionate benefits if the issuer determines the amount of proceeds and qualified equity to be allocated to the discrete portions based on reasonable discrete portion benchmarks. These benchmarks generally include expected actual costs of the discrete portions, a percentage of total space of the mixed-use project to be used in the discrete portion, a percentage of the total fair market value of the mixed-use project that will be associated with the discrete portion, or another objective measure that is reasonable based on all the facts and circumstances. A discrete portion benchmark other than relative fair market value may not be used to make an allocation to a discrete portion that is reasonably expected to be used for private business use if an allocation to that same discrete portion using relative fair market value, determined as of the start of the measurement period, would result in a significantly greater percentage of the total capital expenditures of the project being allocated to such discrete portion.

(3) Allocations to expenditures for discrete portions. Except as otherwise provided in this section, an issuer may determine how each source of funds (for example, proceeds or qualified equity) spent on a mixed-use project is allocated among discrete portions of that project. For example, proceeds may be specially allocated to capital expenditures for costs of a discrete portion that is reasonably expected to be used for governmental use (or for de minimis permitted private business use), and qualified equity may be specially allocated to capital expenditures for costs of a discrete portion that is reasonably expected to be used for private business use.

(4) Allocations of uses to discrete portions. In applying the measurement rules under § 1.141-3(g) to measure ongoing use of a discrete portion of a mixed-use project, the measurement rules under § 1.141-3(g) generally apply to the same extent and in the same manner that they otherwise would. If an issuer properly elects to apply the discrete physical portion allocation method, the financed property is limited to the discrete portion to which any proceeds are allocated under paragraph (c)(3) of this section, and under § 1.141-3(g)(4)(iv), the only use of the mixed-use project that is taken into account is the use of the discrete portions to which proceeds are specially allocated.

(5) Certain reallocations among discrete portions. An issuer may reallocate in whole, but not in part, proceeds and qualified equity that it allocated to capital expenditures for one discrete portion of a mixed-use project under paragraph (c)(3) of this section to another discrete portion of the same mixed-use project if the proportionate benefits to be derived by the users of the two discrete portions are reasonably comparable both at the time of the original allocation and at the time of the reallocation. For purposes of this paragraph (c)(5), the proportionate benefits are reasonably comparable only if the measures of the discrete portion benchmarks are within five percent of each other. In determining whether the proportionate benefits of the discrete portions are reasonably comparable at the time of the reallocation, the same discrete portion benchmark used originally to determine the discrete portions and the fair market value of the discrete portions as of the time of the reallocation must be used. Reallocations under this paragraph (c)(5) may be made only once every five years.

(d) The undivided portion allocation method. *(1) In general.* An issuer may elect the undivided portion allocation method to make allocations with respect to a mixed-use project, provided that the undivided portions to which the allocations are made generally represent fixed percentages of the use of the entire mixed-use project (for example, a fixed percentage of unreserved parking spaces in a parking garage). The measures of the undivided portions may be based on physical or nonphysical characteristics of the project. In addition, the undivided portion allocation method may be applied separately to a discrete portion within a mixed-use project for which the issuer has elected to apply the discrete physical portion allocation method in which event the references in this paragraph (d) to mixed-use project generally shall be deemed to mean that discrete portion within which the undivided portion allocation method is applied separately. Upon a proper election, an issuer may, to the extent provided, use the undivided portion allocation method both to allocate proceeds or qualified equity to capital expenditures for the undivided portions and to allocate those sources of funds to uses of the mixed-use project. The issuer must use a reasonable consistently applied allocation method that properly reflects the proportionate benefit to be derived by the various users of the mixed-use project to determine the amount of proceeds or qualified equity allocable to a particular undivided portion of a mixed use project. See paragraph (g) of this section for special rules for output facilities. To apply the undivided portion allocation method, the following conditions must be met:

(A) The issuer must reasonably expect as of the start of the measurement period that private business use and governmental use of the mixed-use project will occur simultaneously and be on the same basis (within the meaning of § 1.141-3(g)(4)(iii)) or will occur at different times (within the meaning of § 1.141-3(g)(4)(ii)); and

(B) The issuer must reasonably expect as of the start of the measurement period that private business use allocated to the proceeds under paragraph (d)(4) of this section will not exceed de minimis permitted private business use.

(2) The measure of an undivided portion. An issuer is treated as using a reasonable allocation method that reflects the proportionate benefits if the issuer determines the amount of proceeds and qualified equity to be allocated to the undivided portions based on reasonable undivided portion benchmarks. Such benchmarks generally include a measure of how many units produced from the facility will be used by the various users, a percentage of the space in the mixed-use project to be used by the various users (for example, a percentage of the number of parking spaces or a percentage of square feet of usable leased office space), a percentage of the fair market value of the mixed-use project that will be used by the various users (for example, a dollar amount per parking space for a percentage of a total number of parking spaces or a dollar amount per square foot for a percentage of usable leased office space), a percentage of time that the project will be used by the various users (determined in a manner consistent with § 1.141-3(g)(4)(ii)), or another objective measure, which may include the present value of reasonably expected revenues associated with each user's use in circumstances in which no other measure is reasonably workable (for example, expected revenues from space in a research facility in which the qualified and nonqualified research is operationally fungible), that is reasonable based on all the facts and circumstances. An undivided

portion benchmark other than relative fair market value may not be used to make an allocation to an undivided portion that is reasonably expected to be used for private business use if an allocation to that same undivided portion using relative fair market values, determined as of the start of the measurement period, would result in a significantly greater percentage of the total capital expenditures of the project being allocated to such undivided portion. For example, if a private business and a governmental person use a financed facility each for 50 percent of the time, but the relative fair market value of the private business use is significantly greater than 50 percent because the private business uses the facility during prime hours, the relative fair market values of the undivided portions must be used as the undivided portion benchmark.

(3) Allocations to expenditures for undivided portions. Except as otherwise provided in this section, proceeds are specially allocated to capital expenditures for costs of an undivided portion that is reasonably expected to be used for governmental use (or for de minimis permitted private business use). Qualified equity is specially allocated to capital expenditures for costs of an undivided portion of a mixed-use project that is reasonably expected to be used for private business use.

(4) Allocations of uses to undivided portions. (i) General rule. If an issuer elects to apply the undivided portion allocation method, then for purposes of section 141, the financed property is the mixed-use project. In measuring ongoing use of a mixed-use project, the measurement rules under § 1.141-3(g) (or § 1.141-7 in the case of an undivided portion of a mixed-use project that is an output facility) apply to the same extent and in the same manner that they otherwise would to the mixed-use project. However, under the undivided portion allocation method, after measuring private business use of the mixed-use project, subject to the limits in paragraph (d)(4)(ii) of this section, private business use of the mixed-use project is specially allocated to the undivided portion of that project financed with qualified equity (as contrasted with the entire mixed-use project) for purposes of determining whether the issue meets the private business use test. Corresponding allocation rules apply to the undivided portion of a mixed-use project that is financed with proceeds and that is reasonably expected to be used for governmental use (or for de minimis permitted private business use). Thus, subject to the limitations in paragraph (d)(4)(ii) of this section, governmental use is specially allocated to the undivided portion that is financed with proceeds. Private business use of the mixed-use project that is properly allocated under this paragraph to an undivided portion financed with qualified equity is not private business use of proceeds. To determine whether the undivided portion to which proceeds are allocated is used for private business use, the measurement rules under § 1.141-3(g) (or § 1.141-7 for output facilities) apply, taking into account the special allocation rules for the undivided portion allocation method under this section.

(ii) Limit on amount targeted. In any year, the percentage of private business use of the mixed-use project, as determined under the measurement rules for any one-year period under § 1.141-3(g)(4), that is specially allocated to an undivided portion financed with qualified equity cannot exceed the percentage of capital expenditures of the mixed-use project used to determine that undivided portion and allocated to that undivided portion. The percentage of governmental use (and de minimis permitted private business use), as determined in the same manner, that is specially allocated to an undivided portion financed with proceeds cannot exceed the percentage of capital expenditures of the mixed-use project used to determine that undivided portion and allocated to that undivided portion. Similarly, for output facilities, the percentage of private business use of the mixed-use project, as determined under § 1.141-7, that may be targeted to an undivided portion cannot exceed the percentage of capital expenditures of the mixed-use project allocated to that undivided portion.

(iii) Consistency requirement. In applying the measurement rules under § 1.141-3(g) to a mixed-use project for which an issuer has employed the undivided portion allocation method, the issuer must use the same measurement method (for example, costs, quantity, or fair market value) that it used as its benchmark measure to make the allocations to the undivided portions of the mixed-use project under this section. For example, if the issuer made an allocation to an undivided portion using a time-based allocation, the issuer must measure private business use using a time-based allocation.

(e) Certain general operating rules for mixed-use project allocations. *(1) In general.* This paragraph (e) provides certain general operating rules for allocations regarding mixed-use projects under this section.

(2) Governmental ownership requirement for discrete physical portion and undivided portion allocation methods. Except in the case of an output facility, an issuer may make an election to apply the discrete physical portion or the undivided portion allocation method only if the mixed-use project is wholly-owned by governmental persons. An issuer may elect to apply the undivided portion method to a mixed-use project that is an output facility in which non-governmental persons own undivided ownership interests if those interests meet the requirements of paragraph (g)(2) of this section.

(3) Sources of funds for mixed-use project allocations. (i) In general. For purposes of applying the permitted allocation methods for mixed-use projects under paragraphs (c) and (d) of this section, the only sources of funds that may be allocated to the mixed-use project are proceeds and qualified equity (as defined in paragraph (e)(3)(ii) of this section).

(ii) Definition of qualified equity. Except as otherwise provided in special rules for anticipatory redemption bonds in paragraph (f) of this section, for purposes of this section, the term qualified equity means only proceeds of taxable bonds and funds that are not derived from proceeds of a borrowing that are spent on the same mixed-use project as the proceeds of the applicable tax-exempt governmental bonds. By contrast, for example, qualified equity does not include equity interests in real property or tangible personal property. Further, qualified equity does not include any funds spent on subsequent improvements and replacements (including any subsequent improvements or replacements described in paragraph (b)(2)(ii)(B) of this section).

(4) Common areas. Common areas may not be treated as separate discrete portions of mixed-use projects. Proceeds or qualified equity used to finance capital expenditures for common areas are allocated ratably to the discrete portions of the mixed-use project in the same manner that funds for other capital expenditures of the mixed-use project are allocated.

(5) Allocations regarding multiple issues. If proceeds of more than one issue are allocated under section 148 and paragraph (a)(1) of this section to capital expenditures of a mixed-use project, and the issuer elects to apply the discrete portion or undivided portion allocation method to such

mixed-use project, then proceeds of those issues are allocated ratably to capital expenditures for a discrete portion or undivided portion to which any proceeds are allocated in proportion to their relative shares of the total proceeds of such issues in the aggregate used for such mixed-use project.

(f) Special rules for bond redemptions in anticipation of unqualified use. *(1) In general.* Amounts other than proceeds of tax-exempt bonds that are used to retire a tax-exempt governmental bond (anticipatory redemption bond) are treated as qualified equity if the following requirements are met:

(i) Allocations to anticipatory redemption bonds are made in a manner similar to § 1.141-12(j)(2), and the anticipatory redemption bonds are retired within the time prescribed below in anticipation of a deliberate action that otherwise would cause the project to have private business use in excess of de minimis permitted private business use. An anticipatory redemption bond is redeemed in anticipation of the deliberate act when it is retired at least five years before its otherwise-scheduled maturity date or mandatory sinking fund redemption date and it is retired within a period that starts one year before the deliberate act occurs and ends 91 days before the deliberate act occurs;

(ii) The issuer must not reasonably expect at the start of the measurement period that the project would be a mixed-use project, and for the first five years of the measurement period, the project must not be used in a manner that would cause private business use of the project to exceed de minimis permitted private business use; and

(iii) The term of the issue of which the anticipatory redemption bond is a part must be no longer than is reasonably necessary for the governmental purpose of the issue (within the meaning of § 1.148-1(c)(4)).

(2) Allocation of qualified equity. Amounts that are treated as qualified equity under this paragraph (f) may be allocated to a discrete portion or undivided portion of a project in a manner provided in the discrete physical portion allocation method under paragraph (c) of this section or the undivided portion allocation method under paragraph (d) of this section if such allocation would have satisfied the applicable allocation method had that portion been identified for purposes of financing it in a new issue at the time of the retirement of anticipatory redemption bond. Allocations under this paragraph (f) cannot later be changed.

(3) Allocations of use. Use of a project to which this paragraph (f) applies is allocated in accordance with the discrete physical portion allocation method or undivided portion allocation method, as applied under the immediately preceding paragraph.

(4) Relationship to § 1.141-12. Anticipatory redemption bonds that are treated as qualified equity under this paragraph (f) have a comparable effect on continuing compliance as remedial actions under § 1.141-12 and need not be further remediated under § 1.141-12.

(g) Special rules for applying the undivided portion allocation method to mixed-use output facilities. *(1) In general.* This paragraph (g) sets forth certain special rules regarding how to apply the undivided portion allocation method to a mixed-use project that is an output facility.

(2) Governmental ownership requirement for mixed-use output facilities. An issuer may elect to apply the undivided portion method to a mixed-use project that is an output facility if it is wholly-owned by governmental persons or if it has multiple undivided ownership interests which are owned by governmental persons or private businesses, provided that all owners of the undivided ownership interests share the ownership, output, and operating expenses in proportion to their contributions to the costs of the output facility.

(3) The measure of an undivided portion of a mixed-use output facility. The measure of an undivided portion of a mixed-use project that is an output facility is based on a reasonable proportionate allocation method that properly reflects the proportionate benefit to be derived by the various users of the mixed-use project. For an output facility that has multiple undivided ownership interests that meet the requirements of paragraph (g)(2) of this section, those undivided ownership interests are treated as undivided portions. In addition, for purposes of determining the measure of proportionate benefit to be derived from users of an output facility (or of an undivided ownership interest in an output facility treated as an undivided portion) as a result of output contracts, the measure of an undivided portion is based on a benchmark equal to the proportionate share of available output (as defined in § 1.141-7(b)(1)) to be received by the user. For purposes of determining the measure of an undivided portion of an output facility based on the proportionate share of available output, the facts and circumstances test under § 1.141-7(h) governs allocations of output contracts to output facilities.

(h) Allocations of private payments. Private payments for financed property are allocated in accordance with § 1.141-4. Thus, private payments for a mixed-use project for which an election is made to apply the discrete physical portion allocation method are allocated under § 1.141-4(c)(3)(ii), and private payments for a mixed-use project for which an election is made to apply the undivided portion allocation method are allocated under 1.141-4(c)(3) without regard to the undivided portions. However, payments under output contracts that result in private business use are allocated to the undivided portion financed with qualified equity (notwithstanding § 1.141-4(c)(3)(v) (regarding certain allocations of private payments to equity)) in the same manner as the private business use from such contracts is allocated to that undivided portion under paragraph (d)(4) of this section.

(i) Allocations of proceeds to common costs of an issue. Proceeds of tax-exempt bonds allocated to expenditures for common costs (for example, issuance costs, qualified guarantee fees, or reasonably required reserve or replacement funds) are allocated in accordance with § 1.141-3(g)(6). Common costs allocable to a mixed-use project for which an election has been made to apply the undivided portion or discrete physical portion allocation method are allocated ratably to the discrete portions or undivided portion of the mixed-use project to which proceeds are allocated.

(j) Allocations of proceeds to bonds. In general, proceeds of tax-exempt bonds are allocated to bonds in accordance with the rules for allocations of proceeds to bonds for separate purposes of multipurpose issues in § 1.141-13(d). In the case of an issue that is not a multipurpose issue, proceeds are allocated to bonds ratably in a manner similar to the allocation of proceeds to projects under the general pro rata allocation method in paragraph (a)(2) of this section.

(k) Examples. The following examples illustrate the application of this section:

Example (1). Discrete portions of a mixed-use project. City A constructs a 10-story office building, having 100x square foot of office space, and costing $100x. Each floor has an equal amount of office space. Assume the building has no common areas. City A reasonably expects to use the first six floors for governmental use (and possibly for de minimis permitted private business use). City A will lease the top four floors to Corporation B for private business use. City A wants to divide the mixed-use project into two discrete portions and to allocate proceeds to the first six floors and qualified equity to the top four floors. City A treats the first six floors as one discrete portion (the Governmental Portion) and the top four floors as another discrete portion (the Private Business Portion). City A proposes to determine how much of the $100x can be allocated to each discrete portion using relative square feet of usable office space. The percentage of the $100x that would be allocated to the Private Business Portion using relative fair market values, determined at the start of the measurement period, would not be significantly greater than the amount that will be allocated using relative square footage. Relative square footage is an appropriate discrete portion benchmark because it is an objective measure that properly reflects the proportionate benefit to be derived by the various users. City A finances the costs of the Governmental Portion ($60x) with proceeds of tax-exempt governmental bonds (the Bonds) and the costs of the Private Business Portion ($40x) with qualified equity which consists of taxable bonds (the qualified equity). City A allocates Bond proceeds to capital expenditures for the costs of the Governmental Portion (that is, $60x for capital costs of six specific floors of the building). City A allocates the qualified equity to capital expenditures for the costs of the Private Business Portion (that is, $40x for capital costs of four specific floors of the building). The financed property to which proceeds of the Bonds are allocated is the Governmental Portion. For purposes of measuring ongoing use of the Bond proceeds, use of the Private Business Portion will be disregarded, but any private business use of the six specific floors which comprise the Governmental Portion will be taken into account during the measurement period. The proceeds of the Bonds are treated as used for the Governmental Portion and ongoing compliance depends on the amount of private business use of that Governmental Portion over the term of the applicable measurement period. Thus, if more than 10 percent of the specific physically discrete floors which comprise the Governmental Portion of the mixed-use project (that is, more than $6x of the proceeds or 6x square feet of the office space within the Governmental Portion) were used for private business use during the measurement period as a result of deliberate actions, then the Bonds would violate the private business use test.

Example (2). Reallocations among discrete portions. City A constructs a 10-story office building having 100x square feet of office space, and costing $100x. The top five floors are to be leased to a private business, Corporation B. Before the start of the measurement period, City A appropriately elected a discrete physical portion allocation method using a relative square footage measure and allocated $50x of proceeds to the first five floors (the Governmental Portion) and $50x in qualified equity to the top five floors (the Private Business Portion). After the time for finalizing allocations has passed, Corporation B defaults on its lease for the top five floors of the building and vacates the building. Corporation C, another private business, expresses interest in leasing office space, but Corporation C wants to lease the first five floors of the building rather than the top five floors previously leased by Corporation B. City A wants to reallocate the proceeds used for the Private Business Portion to the Governmental Portion. City A plans to use the Private Business Portion for governmental use. At the time of both the original allocation and this reallocation the measures of the Private Business Portion and Governmental Portion under the applicable discrete portion benchmarks are within five percent of each other. City A determines that the measures of the two discrete portions are reasonably comparable at the time of the reallocation by using the benchmarks of relative square footage and the then-current fair market values of the two discrete portions. This reallocation between discrete portions is permissible.

Example (3). Undivided portions of a mixed-use project. City A constructs a 10-story office building, having 100x square foot of office space, and costing $100x. City A has not identified specific space to be leased to any specific private business. Instead, City A reasonably expects to use 70 percent of the office space in the building for governmental use (or possibly for de minimis permitted private business use) (the Governmental Portion). City A reasonably expects that it will lease out a maximum of 30 percent of the office space to one or more private businesses in unspecified locations in the building (the Private Business Portion). City A wants to allocate this mixed-use project between two undivided portions and target the expected private business use to the undivided portion financed with qualified equity. City A determines how much of the $100x can be financed with tax-exempt governmental bonds based on relative square feet of usable office space. This undivided portion benchmark is an objective measure that properly reflects the proportionate benefit to be derived by the various users. City A finances 70 percent of the costs of the building ($70x) with proceeds (the Bonds) and 30 percent ($30x) of those costs with qualified equity which consists of taxable bonds (the Qualified Equity). Bond proceeds are allocated to capital expenditures for the costs of the Governmental Portion. Qualified Equity is allocated to capital expenditures for the costs of the Private Business Portion. For purposes of measuring ongoing use of the mixed-use project, private business use and governmental use of the entire 10-story office building is considered. As long as average private business use of the mixed-use project under the measurement rules does not exceed 30 percent in a particular year, that private business use is allocated to the Private Business Portion. Thus, none of that private business use is allocated to the Governmental Portion, and that private business use is disregarded for purposes of determining whether there is private business use of the proceeds allocated to the Governmental Portion. If average private business use of the mixed-use project increases to 45 percent in a subsequent year, a maximum of 30 percent of that private business use is properly allocable to the Private Business Portion and thereby disregarded in determining ongoing use of the Governmental Portion. Private business use in excess of the 30 percent properly allocable to the Private Business Portion (for example, 15 percent of private business use) would be allocated to the Governmental Portion. Conversely, if private business use of the mixed-use project in a subsequent year decreased to 20 percent, all 20 percent of the private use would be allocated to the Private Business Portion and thereby disregarded for purposes of measuring private use of the proceeds in that year. Because there would be governmental use in that year in excess of the 70 percent that is properly allocable to the Governmental use Portion, the governmental use in excess of 70 percent (for example, 10 percent of governmental use) would be allocated to the Private Business Portion.

Example (4). Revenue-based undivided portion of research facility. University A is a state university. University A owns and operates research facilities. In 2008, University A plans to build a new research facility (the 2008 Mixed-Use Research Project), which it expects will be used for both qualified research arrangements for governmental use (Governmental Research) and nonqualified research arrangements for private business use (Private Business Research). University A wants to allocate the 2008 mixed-use research facility between two undivided portions for Governmental Research and for Private Business Research and to target Private Business Research to the undivided portion financed with equity. University A proposes to make this allocation using a revenue-based undivided portion benchmark. All of University A's research activities will have the following operational characteristics:

(i) The research facilities are continuously available for both Governmental Research and Private Business Research;

(ii) Governmental Research and Private Business Research take place simultaneously in the same research facilities; and

(iii) The same research may relate to one or more research projects involving both Governmental Research and Private Business Research. University A also has a reasonable basis for determining the percentage of revenues that will be derived from Private Business Research and Governmental Research. During the past five years, of the total revenues, net of royalties and licenses, from University A's research facilities, the percentage of revenues from Governmental Research and the percentage of revenues from Private Business Research (on a present value basis) have not changed. University A reasonably expects that this split of revenues will continue with the 2008 Mixed-Use Research Project. Under all the facts and circumstances, including, among other things, the nature of the particular research arrangements (for example, the governmental or private business nature of particular research grantors or contractual terms that result in governmental use or private business use) and historic actual revenues and future expected revenues from research arrangements of a particular nature, net of royalties and licenses, the only objective measurable benchmark that can reasonably distinguish the Governmental Research portion from the Private Business Research portion is the expected percentage of revenues each will generate. Therefore, University A will be using a reasonable method for determining the undivided portions of the 2008 mixed-use research facility if it bases the portions on the revenues each is expected to generate.

Example (5). Output facility. Authority A is a governmental person that owns and operates an electric transmission facility. Prior to 2009, Authority A used its equity to pay capital expenditures of $1000x for the facility. In 2009, Authority A wants to make capital improvements to the facility in the amount of $100x. Authority A reasonably expects that, after completion of such capital improvements, 54 percent of the available output from the facility, as determined under § 1.141-7, will be sold under output contracts for governmental use and that 46 percent of such available output will be sold under output contracts for private business use. Authority A wants to allocate this 2009 project for capital improvements (the 2009 Mixed-Use Output Project) between two undivided portions based on proportionate measures of available output and to finance the maximum eligible undivided portion with tax-exempt governmental bonds (assuming use of the maximum 10 percent de minimis amount of private business use permitted for tax-exempt governmental bonds). Authority A treats a 60 percent undivided portion of the 2009 Mixed-Use Output Project as one undivided portion (the Governmental Portion), which it reasonably expects to use for output contracts involving 90 percent governmental use (representing 54 percent of the available output), plus 10 percent private business use (representing 6 percent of the available output). Authority A treats a 40 percent undivided portion of the 2009 Mixed-Use Output Project as another undivided portion (the Private Business Portion), which it reasonably expects to use for output contracts involving private business use. Authority A determines the measures of these two undivided portions based on relative shares of available output, as determined under § 1.141-7. This measure uses a reasonable proportionate allocation method which properly reflects the proportionate benefit to be derived by the various users. On January 1, 2009, Authority A issues bonds with proceeds of $60x (the Bonds) to finance the Governmental Portion of the 2009 Mixed-Use Output Project and uses $40 million of funds that are not derived from proceeds of a borrowing (the Qualified Equity) to finance the Private Business Portion of the 2009 Mixed-Use Output Project. Authority A allocates Bond proceeds to capital expenditures for the costs of the Governmental Portion and Qualified Equity to capital expenditures for the costs of the Private Business Portion. For purposes of measuring ongoing use of the Governmental Portion financed with the Bond proceeds, use of the Private Business Portion is disregarded, but any private business use of the Governmental Portion will be taken into account during the measurement period. So long as the actual amount of private business use of the Governmental Portion's share of available output does not exceed 6 percent, the Bonds will not be private activity bonds.

Example (6). Treatment of retirement of bonds. City B issues bonds to build a parking garage (the Garage), costing $100x, that it will own and operate. At the start of the measurement period, City B reasonably expects that the only use of the garage will be governmental use. The term of the issue is no longer than reasonably necessary for the governmental purpose of the issue. During the first six years of the measurement period, the garage is used as the issuer expected. In year seven of the measurement period, however, City B expects that in less than one year it will enter into a contract with Corporation C, a private business, which will cause 20 percent of the Garage to be used for private business use. More than 90 days before entering into a binding contract with Corporation C, City B uses $20x of funds other than proceeds of tax-exempt bonds to retire bonds and City B determines the bonds to be retired on a pro rata basis. The applicable bonds will be retired at least 5 years prior to their scheduled maturity dates. As of the date of the anticipatory redemption, the Garage qualifies as a mixed-use project, and City B applies paragraph (f) of this section and allocates the $20x that was used to redeem the bonds to an undivided portion to which the private business use will be allocated. If City B failed to meet the requirements of paragraph (f) of this section, amounts that City B used to redeem the bonds would not be qualified equity.

§ 1.141-7 Special rules for output facilities.

(a) Overview. This section provides special rules to determine whether arrangements for the purchase of output from an output facility cause an issue of bonds to meet the private business tests. For this purpose, unless otherwise stated, water facilities are treated as output facilities. Sections 1.141-3 and 1.141-4 generally apply to determine whether other types of arrangements for use of an output facility cause an issue to meet the private business tests.

(b) Definitions. For purposes of this section and § 1.141-8, the following definitions and rules apply:

(1) Available output. The available output of a facility financed by an issue is determined by multiplying the number of units produced or to be produced by the facility in one year by the number of years in the measurement period of that facility for that issue.

(i) Generating facilities. The number of units produced or to be produced by a generating facility in one year is determined by reference to its nameplate capacity or the equivalent (or where there is no nameplate capacity or the equivalent, its maximum capacity), which is not reduced for reserves, maintenance or other unutilized capacity.

(ii) Transmission and other output facilities. (A) In general. For transmission, distribution, cogeneration, and other output facilities, available output must be measured in a reasonable manner to reflect capacity.

(B) Electric transmission facilities. Measurement of the available output of all or a portion of electric transmission facilities may be determined in a manner consistent with the reporting rules and requirements for transmission networks promulgated by the Federal Energy Regulatory Commission (FERC). For example, for a transmission network, the use of aggregate load and load share ratios in a manner consistent with the requirements of the FERC may be reasonable. In addition, depending on the facts and circumstances, measurement of the available output of transmission facilities using thermal capacity or transfer capacity may be reasonable.

(iii) Special rule for facilities with significant unutilized capacity. If an issuer reasonably expects on the issue date that persons that are treated as private business users will purchase more than 30 percent of the actual output of the facility financed with the issue, the Commissioner may determine the number of units produced or to be produced by the facility in one year on a reasonable basis other than by reference to nameplate or other capacity, such as the average expected annual output of the facility. For example, the Commissioner may determine the available output of a financed peaking electric generating unit by reference to the reasonably expected annual output of that unit if the issuer reasonably expects, on the issue date of bonds that finance the unit, that an investor-owned utility will purchase more than 30 percent of the actual output of the facility during the measurement period under a take or pay contract, even if the amount of output purchased is less than 10 percent of the available output determined by reference to nameplate capacity. The reasonably expected annual output of the generating facility must be consistent with the capacity reported for prudent reliability purposes.

(iv) Special rule for facilities with a limited source of supply. If a limited source of supply constrains the output of an output facility, the number of units produced or to be produced by the facility must be determined by reasonably taking into account those constraints. For this purpose, a limited source of supply shall include a physical limitation (for example, flow of water), but not an economic limitation (for example, cost of coal or gas). For example, the available output of a hydroelectric unit must be determined by reference to the reasonably expected annual flow of water through the unit.

(2) Measurement period. The measurement period of an output facility financed by an issue is determined under § 1.141-3(g).

(3) Sale at wholesale. A sale at wholesale means a sale of output to any person for resale.

(4) Take contract and take or pay contract. A take contract is an output contract under which a purchaser agrees to pay for the output under the contract if the output facility is capable of providing the output. A take or pay contract is an output contract under which a purchaser agrees to pay for the output under the contract, whether or not the output facility is capable of providing the output.

(5) Requirements contract. A requirements contract is an output contract, other than a take contract or a take or pay contract, under which a nongovernmental person agrees to purchase all or part of its output requirements.

(6) Nonqualified amount. The nonqualified amount with respect to an issue is determined under section 141(b)(8).

(c) Output contracts. *(1) General rule.* The purchase pursuant to a contract by a nongovernmental person of available output of an output facility (output contract) financed with proceeds of an issue is taken into account under the private business tests if the purchase has the effect of transferring the benefits of owning the facility and the burdens of paying the debt service on bonds used (directly or indirectly) to finance the facility (the benefits and burdens test). See paragraph (c)(4) of this section for the treatment of an output contract that is properly characterized as a lease for Federal income tax purposes. See paragraphs (d) and (e) of this section for rules regarding measuring the use of, and payments of debt service for, an output facility for determining whether the private business tests are met. See also § 1.141-8 for rules for when an issue that finances an output facility (other than a water facility) meets the private business tests because the nonqualified amount of the issue exceeds $15 million.

(2) Take contract or take or pay contract. The benefits and burdens test is met if a nongovernmental person agrees pursuant to a take contract or a take or pay contract to purchase available output of a facility.

(3) Requirements contract. (i) In general. A requirements contract may satisfy the benefits and burdens test under paragraph (c)(3)(ii) or (iii) of this section. See § 1.141-15(f)(2) for special effective dates for the application of this paragraph (c)(3) to issues financing facilities subject to requirements contracts.

(ii) Requirements contract similar to take contract or take or pay contract. A requirements contract generally meets the benefits and burdens test to the extent that it contains contractual terms that obligate the purchaser to make payments that are not contingent on the output requirements of the purchaser or that obligate the purchaser to have output requirements. For example, a requirements contract with an industrial purchaser meets the benefits and burdens test if the purchaser enters into additional contractual obligations with the issuer or another governmental unit not to cease operations. A requirements contract does not meet the benefits and burdens test, however, by reason of a provision that requires the purchaser to pay reasonable and customary damages (including liquidated damages) in the event of a default, or a provision that permits the purchaser to pay a specified amount to terminate the contract while the purchaser has requirements, in each case if the amount of the payment is reasonably related to the purchaser's obligation to buy requirements that is discharged by the payment.

(iii) Wholesale requirements contract. (A) In general. A requirements contract that is a sale at wholesale (a wholesale requirements contract) may satisfy the benefits and burdens test, depending on all the facts and circumstances.

(B) Significant factors. Significant factors that tend to establish that a wholesale requirements contract meets the benefits and burdens test include, but are not limited to—

(1) The term of the contract is substantial relative to the term of the issue or issues that finance the facility; and

(2) The amount of output to be purchased under the contract represents a substantial portion of the available output of the facility.

(C) Safe harbors. A wholesale requirements contract does not meet the benefits and burdens test if—

(1) The term of the contract, including all renewal options, does not exceed the lesser of 5 years or 30 percent of the term of the issue; or

(2) The amount of output to be purchased under the contract (and any other requirements contract with the same purchaser or a related party with respect to the facility) does not exceed 5 percent of the available output of the facility.

(iv) Retail requirements contract. Except as otherwise provided in this paragraph (c)(3), a requirements contract that is not a sale at wholesale does not meet the benefits and burdens test.

(4) Output contract properly characterized as a lease. Notwithstanding any other provision of this section, an output contract that is properly characterized as a lease for Federal income tax purposes shall be tested under the rules contained in §§ 1.141-3 and 1.141-4 to determine whether it is taken into account under the private business tests.

(d) Measurement of private business use. If an output contract results in private business use under this section, the amount of private business use generally is the amount of output purchased under the contract.

(e) Measurement of private security or payment. The measurement of payments made or to be made by nongovernmental persons under output contracts as a percent of the debt service of an issue is determined under the rules provided in § 1.141-4.

(f) Exceptions for certain contracts. *(1) Small purchases of output.* An output contract for the use of a facility is not taken into account under the private business tests if the average annual payments to be made under the contract do not exceed 1 percent of the average annual debt service on all outstanding tax-exempt bonds issued to finance the facility, determined as of the effective date of the contract.

(2) Swapping and pooling arrangements. An agreement that provides for swapping or pooling of output by one or more governmental persons and one or more nongovernmental persons does not result in private business use of the output facility owned by the governmental person to the extent that—

(i) The swapped output is reasonably expected to be approximately equal in value (determined over periods of three years or less); and

(ii) The purpose of the agreement is to enable each of the parties to satisfy different peak load demands, to accommodate temporary outages, to diversify supply, or to enhance reliability in accordance with prudent reliability standards.

(3) Short-term output contracts. An output contract with a nongovernmental person is not taken into account under the private business tests if—

(i) The term of the contract, including all renewal options, is not longer than 3 years;

(ii) The contract either is a negotiated, arm's-length arrangement that provides for compensation at fair market value, or is based on generally applicable and uniformly applied rates; and

(iii) The output facility is not financed for a principal purpose of providing that facility for use by that nongovernmental person.

(4) Certain conduit parties disregarded. A nongovernmental person acting solely as a conduit for the exchange of output among governmentally owned and operated utilities is disregarded in determining whether the private business tests are met with respect to financed facilities owned by a governmental person.

(g) Special rules for electric output facilities used to provide open access. *(1) Operation of transmission facilities by nongovernmental persons.* (i) In general. The operation of an electric transmission facility by a nongovernmental person may result in private business use of the facility under § 1.141-3 and this section based on all the facts and circumstances. For example, a transmission facility is generally used for a private business use if a nongovernmental person enters into a contract to operate the facility and receives compensation based, in whole or in part, on a share of net profits from the operation of the facility.

(ii) Certain use by independent transmission operators. A contract for the operation of an electric transmission facility by an independent entity, such as a regional transmission organization or an independent system operator (independent transmission operator), does not constitute private business use of the facility if—

(A) The facility is owned by a governmental person;

(B) The operation of the facility by the independent transmission operator is approved by the FERC under one or more provisions of the Federal Power Act (16 U.S.C. 791a through 825r) (or by a state authority under comparable provisions of state law);

(C) No portion of the compensation of the independent transmission operator is based on a share of net profits from the operation of the facility; and

(D) The independent transmission operator does not bear risk of loss of the facility.

(2) Certain use by nongovernmental persons under output contracts. (i) Transmission facilities. The use of an electric transmission facility by a nongovernmental person pursuant to an output contract does not constitute private business use of the facility if—

(A) The facility is owned by a governmental person;

(B) The facility is operated by an independent transmission operator in a manner that satisfies paragraph (g)(1)(ii) of this section; and

(C) The facility is not financed for a principal purpose of providing that facility for use by that nongovernmental person.

(ii) Distribution facilities. The use of an electric distribution facility by a nongovernmental person pursuant to an output contract does not constitute private business use of the facility if—

(A) The facility is owned by a governmental person;

(B) The facility is available for use on a nondiscriminatory, open access basis by buyers and sellers of electricity in accordance with rates that are generally applicable and uniformly applied within the meaning of § 1.141-3(c)(2); and

(C) The facility is not financed for a principal purpose of providing that facility for use by that nongovernmental person (other than a retail end-user).

(3) Ancillary services. The use of an electric output facility to provide ancillary services required to be offered as part of an open access transmission tariff under rules promulgated by the FERC under the Federal Power Act (16 U.S.C. 791a through 825r) (or by a state regulatory authority under comparable provisions of state law) does not result in private business use.

(4) Exceptions to deliberate action rules. (i) Mandated wheeling. Entering into a contract for the use of electric transmission or distribution facilities is not treated as a deliberate action under § 1.141-2(d) if—

(A) The contract is entered into in response to (or in anticipation of) an order by the United States under sections 211 and 212 of the Federal Power Act (16 U.S.C. 824j and 824k) (or a state regulatory authority under comparable provisions of state law); and

(B) The terms of the contract are bona fide and arm's-length, and the consideration paid is consistent with the provisions of section 212(a) of the Federal Power Act.

(ii) Actions taken to implement non-discriminatory, open access. An action is not treated as a deliberate action under § 1.141-2(d) if it is taken to implement the offering of non-discriminatory, open access tariffs for the use of electric transmission or distribution facilities in a manner consistent with rules promulgated by the FERC under sections 205 and 206 of the Federal Power Act (16 U.S.C. 824d and 824e) (or comparable provisions of state law). This paragraph (g)(4)(ii) does not apply, however, to the sale, exchange, or other disposition (within the meaning of section 1001(a)) of transmission or distribution facilities to a nongovernmental person.

(iii) Application of reasonable expectations test to certain current refunding bonds. An action taken or to be taken with respect to electric transmission or distribution facilities refinanced by an issue is not taken into account under the reasonable expectations test of § 1.141-2(d) if—

(A) The action is described in paragraph (g)(4)(i) or (ii) of this section;

(B) The bonds of the issue are current refunding bonds that refund bonds originally issued before February 23, 1998; and

(C) The weighted average maturity of the refunding bonds is not greater than the remaining weighted average maturity of the prior bonds.

(5) Additional transactions as permitted by the Commissioner. The Commissioner may, by published guidance, set forth additional circumstances in which the use of electric output facilities in a restructured electric industry does not constitute private business use.

(h) Allocations of output facilities and systems. *(1) Facts and circumstances analysis.* Whether output sold under an output contract is allocated to a particular facility (for example, a generating unit), to the entire system of the seller of that output (net of any uses of that system output allocated to a particular facility), or to a portion of a facility is based on all the facts and circumstances. Significant factors to be considered in determining the allocation of an output contract to financed property are the following:

(i) The extent to which it is physically possible to deliver output to or from a particular facility or system.

(ii) The terms of a contract relating to the delivery of output (such as delivery limitations and options or obligations to deliver power from additional sources).

(iii) Whether a contract is entered into as part of a common plan of financing for a facility.

(iv) The method of pricing output under the contract, such as the use of market rates rather than rates designed to pay debt service of tax-exempt bonds used to finance a particular facility.

(2) Illustrations. The following illustrate the factors set forth in paragraph (h)(1) of this section:

(i) Physical possibility. Output from a generating unit that is fed directly into a low voltage distribution system of the owner of that unit and that cannot physically leave that distribution system generally must be allocated to those receiving electricity through that distribution system. Output may be allocated without regard to physical limitations, however, if exchange or similar agreements provide output to a purchaser where, but for the exchange agreements, it would not be possible for the seller to provide output to that purchaser.

(ii) Contract terms relating to performance. A contract to provide a specified amount of electricity from a system, but only when at least that amount of electricity is being generated by a particular unit, is allocated to that unit. For example, a contract to buy 20 MW of system power with a right to take up to 40 percent of the actual output of a specific 50 MW facility whenever total system output is insufficient to meet all of the seller's obligations generally is allocated to the specific facility rather than to the system.

(iii) Common plan of financing. A contract entered into as part of a common plan of financing for a facility generally is allocated to the facility if debt service for the issue of bonds is reasonably expected to be paid, directly or indirectly, from payments under the contract.

(iv) Pricing method. Pricing based on the capital and generating costs of a particular turbine tends to indicate that output under the contract is properly allocated to that turbine.

(3) Transmission and distribution contracts. Whether use under an output contract for transmission or distribution is allocated to a particular facility or to a transmission or distribution network is based on all the facts and circumstances, in a manner similar to paragraphs (h)(1) and (2) of this section. In general, the method used to determine payments under a contract is a more significant contract term for this purpose than nominal contract path. In general, if reasonable and consistently applied, the determination of use of transmission or distribution facilities under an output contract may be based on a method used by third parties, such as reliability councils.

(4) Allocation of payments. Payments for output provided by an output facility financed with two or more sources of funding are generally allocated under the rules in § 1.141-4(c).

(i) Examples. The following examples illustrate the application of this section:

Example (1). Joint ownership. Z, an investor-owned electric utility, and City H agree to construct an electric generating facility of a size sufficient to take advantage of the economies of scale. H will issue $50 million of its 24-year bonds, and Z will use $100 million of its funds for construction of a facility they will jointly own as tenants in common. Each of the participants will share in the ownership, output, and operating expenses of the facility in proportion to its contribution to the cost of the facility, that is, one-third by H and two-thirds by Z. H's bonds will be secured by H's ownership interest in the facility and by revenues to be derived from its share of the annual output of the facility. H will need only 50 percent of its share of the annual output of the facility during the first 20 years of operations. It agrees to sell 10 percent of its share of the annual output to Z for a period of 20 years pursuant to a contract under which Z agrees to take that power if available. The facility will begin operation, and Z will begin to receive power, 4 years after the H bonds are issued. The measurement period for the property financed by the issue is 20 years. H also will sell the remaining 40 percent of its share of the annual output to numerous other private utilities under contracts of three years or less that satisfy the exception under paragraph (f)(3) of this section. No other contracts will be executed obligating any person to purchase any specified amount of the power for any specified period of time. No person (other than Z) will make payments that will result in a transfer of the burdens of paying debt service on bonds used directly or indirectly to provide H's share of the facilities. The bonds are not private activity bonds, because H's one-third interest in the facility is not treated as used by the other owners of the facility. Although 10 percent of H's share of the annual output of the facility will be used in the trade or business of Z, a nongovernmental person, under this section, that portion constitutes not more than 10 percent of the available output of H's ownership interest in the facility.

Example (2). Wholesale requirements contract. (i) City J issues 20-year bonds to acquire an electric generating facility having a reasonably expected economic life substantially greater than 20 years and a nameplate capacity of 100 MW. The available output of the facility under paragraph (b)(1) of this section is approximately 17,520,000 MWh (100 MW x 24 hours x 365 days x 20 years). On the issue date, J enters into a contract with T, an investor-owned utility, to provide T with all of its power requirements for a period of 10 years, commencing on the issue date. J reasonably expects that T will actually purchase an average of 30 MW over the 10-year period. The contract is taken into account under the private business tests pursuant to paragraph (c)(3) of this section because the term of the contract is substantial relative to the term of the issue and the amount of output to be purchased is a substantial portion of the available output.

(ii) Under paragraph (d) of this section, the amount of reasonably expected private business use under this contract is approximately 15 percent (30 MW x 24 hours x 365 days x 10 years, or 2,628,000 MWh) of the available output. Accordingly, the issue meets the private business use test. J reasonably expects that the amount to be paid for an average of 30 MW of power (less the operation and maintenance costs directly attributable to generating that 30 MW of power), will be more than 10 percent of debt service on the issue on a present-value basis. Accordingly, the issue meets the private security or payment test because J reasonably expects that payment of more than 10 percent of the debt service will be indirectly derived from payments by T. The bonds are private activity bonds under paragraph (c) of this section. Further, if 15 percent of the sale proceeds of the issue is greater than $15 million and the issue meets the private security or payment test with respect to the $15 million output limitation, the bonds are also private activity bonds under section 141(b)(4). See § 1.141-8.

Example (3). Retail contracts. (i) State Agency M, a political subdivision, issues bonds in 2003 to finance the construction of a generating facility that will be used to furnish electricity to M's retail customers. In 2007, M enters into a 10-year contract with industrial corporation I. Under the contract, M agrees to supply I with all of its power requirements during the contract term, and I agrees to pay for that power at a negotiated price as it is delivered. The contract does not require I to pay for any power except to the extent I has requirements. In addition, the contract requires I to pay reasonable and customary liquidated damages in the event of a default by I, and permits I to terminate the contract while it has requirements by paying M a specified amount that is a reasonable and customary amount for terminating the contract. Any damages or termination payment by I will be reasonably related to I's obligation to buy requirements that is discharged by the payment. Under paragraph (c)(3) of this section, the contract does not meet the benefits and burdens test. Thus, it is not taken into account under the private business tests.

(ii) The facts are the same as in paragraph (i) of this Example 3, except that the contract requires I to make guaranteed minimum payments, regardless of I's requirements, in an amount such that the contract does not meet the exception for small purchases in paragraph (f)(1) of this section. Under paragraph (c)(3)(ii) of this section, the contract meets the benefits and burdens test because it obligates I to make payments that are not contingent on its output requirements. Thus, it is taken into account under the private business tests.

Example (4). Allocation of existing contracts to new facilities. Power Authority K, a political subdivision created by the legislature in State X to own and operate certain power generating facilities, sells all of the power from its existing facilities to four private utility systems under contracts executed in 1999, under which the four systems are required to take or pay for specified portions of the total power output until the year 2029. Existing facilities supply all of the present needs of the four utility systems, but their future power requirements are expected to increase substantially beyond the capacity of K's current generating system. K issues 20-year bonds in 2004 to construct a large generating facility. As part of the financing plan for the bonds, a fifth private utility system contracts with K to take or pay for 15 percent of the available output of the new facility. The balance of the output of the new facility will be available for sale as required, but initially it is not anticipated that there will be any need for that power. The revenues from the contract with the fifth private utility system will be sufficient to pay less than 10 percent of the debt service on the bonds (determined on a present value basis). The balance, which will exceed 10 percent of the debt service on the bonds, will be paid from revenues derived from the contracts with the four systems initially from sale of power produced by the old facilities. The output contracts with all the private utilities are allocated to K's entire generating system. See paragraphs (h)(1) and (2) of this section. Thus, the bonds meet the private business use test because more than 10 percent of the proceeds will be used in the trade or business of a nongovernmental person. In addition, the bonds meet the private security or payment test because payment of more than 10 percent of the debt service, pursuant to underlying arrangements, will be derived from payments in respect of property used for a private business use.

Example (5). Allocation to displaced resource. Municipal utility MU, a political subdivision, purchases all of the electricity required to meet the needs of its customers (1,000 MW) from B, an investor-owned utility that operates its own electric generating facilities, under a 50-year take or pay contract. MU does not anticipate that it will require additional electric resources, and any new resources would produce electricity at a higher cost to MU than its cost under its contract with B. Nevertheless, B encourages MU to construct a new generating plant sufficient to meet MU's requirements. MU issues obligations to construct facilities that will produce 1,000 MW of electricity. MU, B, and I, another investor-owned utility, enter into an agreement under which MU assigns to I its rights under MU's take or pay contract with B. Under this arrangement, I will pay MU, and MU will continue to pay B, for the 1,000 MW. I's payments to MU will at least equal the amounts required to pay debt service on MU's bonds. In addition, under paragraph (h)(1)(iii) of this section, the contract among MU, B, and I is entered into as part of a common plan of financing of the MU facilities. Under all the facts and circumstances, MU's assignment to I of its rights under the original take or pay contract is allocable to MU's new facilities under paragraph (h) of this section. Because I is a nongovernmental person, MU's bonds are private activity bonds.

Example (6). Operation of transmission facilities by regional transmission organization. (i) Public Power Agency D is a political subdivision that owns and operates electric generation, transmission and distribution facilities. In 2003, D transfers operating control of its transmission system to a regional transmission organization (RTO), a nongovernmental person, pursuant to an operating agreement that is approved by the FERC under sections 205 and 206 of the Federal Power Act. D retains ownership of its facilities. No portion of the RTO's compensation is based on a share of net profits from the operation of D's facilities, and the RTO does not bear any risk of loss of those facilities. Under paragraph (g)(1)(ii) of this section, the RTO's use of D's facilities does not constitute a private business use.

(ii) Company A is located in D's service territory. In 2004, Power Supplier E, a nongovernmental person, enters into a 10-year contract with A to supply A's electricity requirements. The electricity supplied by E to A will be transmitted over D's transmission and distribution facilities. D's distribution facilities are available for use on a nondiscriminatory, open access basis by buyers and sellers of electricity in accordance with rates that are generally applicable and uniformly applied within the meaning of § 1.141-3(c)(2). D's facilities are not financed for a principal purpose of providing the facilities for use by E. Under paragraph (g)(2) of this section, the contract between A and E does not result in private business use of D's facilities.

Example (7). Certain actions not treated as deliberate actions. The facts are the same as in Example 6 of this paragraph (i), except that the RTO's compensation is based on a share of net profits from operating D's facilities. In addition, D had issued bonds in 1994 to finance improvements to its transmission system. At the time D transfers operating control of its transmission system to the RTO, D chooses to apply the private activity bond regulations of §§ 1.141-1 through 1.141-15 to the 1994 bonds. The operation of D's facilities by the RTO results in private business use under § 1.141-3 and paragraph (g)(1)(i) of this section. Under the special exception in paragraph (g)(4)(ii) of this section, however, the transfer of control is not treated as a deliberate action. Accordingly, the transfer of control does not cause the 1994 bonds to meet the private activity bond tests.

Example (8). Current refunding. The facts are the same as in Example 7 of this paragraph (i), and in addition D issues bonds in 2004 to currently refund the 1994 bonds. The weighted average maturity of the 2004 bonds is not greater than the remaining weighted average maturity of the 1994 bonds. D chooses to apply the private activity bond regulations of §§ 1.141-1 through 1.141-15 to the refunding bonds. In general, reasonable expectations must be separately tested on the date that refunding bonds are issued under § 1.141-2(d). Under the special exception in paragraph (g)(4)(iii) of this section, however, the transfer of the financed facilities to the RTO need not be taken into account in applying the reasonable expectations test to the refunding bonds.

T.D. 9016, 9/19/2002.

---

§ 1.141-8 $15 million limitation for output facilities.

(a) In general. *(1) General rule.* Section 141(b)(4) provides a special private activity bond limitation (the $15 million output limitation) for issues 5 percent or more of the proceeds of which are to be used to finance output facilities (other than a facility for the furnishing of water). Under this rule, an issue consists of private activity bonds under the private business tests of section 141(b)(1) and (2) if the nonqualified amount with respect to output facilities financed by the proceeds of the issue exceeds $15 million. The $15 million output limitation applies in addition to the private business tests of section 141(b)(1) and (2). Under section 141(b)(4) and paragraph (a)(2) of this section, the $15 million output limitation is reduced in certain cases. Specifically, an issue meets the test in section 141(b)(4) if both of the following tests are met:

(i) More than $15 million of the proceeds of the issue to be used with respect to an output facility are to be used for a private business use. Investment proceeds are disregarded for this purpose if they are not allocated disproportionately to the private business use portion of the issue.

(ii) The payment of the principal of, or the interest on, more than $15 million of the sale proceeds of the portion of the issue used with respect to an output facility is (under the terms of the issue or any underlying arrangement) directly or indirectly—

(A) Secured by any interest in an output facility used or to be used for a private business use (or payments in respect of such an output facility); or

(B) To be derived from payments (whether or not to the issuer) in respect of an output facility used or to be used for a private business use.

(2) Reduction in $15 million output limitation for outstanding issues. (i) General rule. In determining whether an issue 5 percent or more of the proceeds of which are to be used with respect to an output facility consists of private activity bonds under the $15 million output limitation, the $15 million limitation on private business use and private security or payments is applied by taking into account the aggregate nonqualified amounts of any outstanding bonds of other issues 5 percent or more of the proceeds of which are or will be used with respect to that output facility or any other output facility that is part of the same project.

(ii) Bonds taken into account. For purposes of this paragraph (a)(2), in applying the $15 million output limitation to an issue (the later issue), a tax-exempt bond of another issue (the earlier issue) is taken into account if—

(A) That bond is outstanding on the issue date of the later issue;

(B) That bond will not be redeemed within 90 days of the issue date of the later issue in connection with the refunding of that bond by the later issue; and

(C) 5 percent or more of the sale proceeds of the earlier issue financed an output facility that is part of the same project as the output facility that is financed by 5 percent or more of the sale proceeds of the later issue.

(3) Benefits and burdens test applicable. (i) In general. In applying the $15 million output limitation, the benefits and burdens test of § 1.141-7 applies, except that "$15 million" is applied in place of "10 percent", or "5 percent" as appropriate.

(ii) Earlier issues for the project. If bonds of an earlier issue are outstanding and must be taken into account under paragraph (a)(2) of this section, the nonqualified amount for that earlier issue is multiplied by a fraction, the numerator of which is the adjusted issue price of the earlier issue as of the issue date of the later issue, and the denominator of which is the issue price of the earlier issue. Pre-issuance accrued interest as defined in § 1.148-1(b) is disregarded for this purpose.

(b) Definition of project. *(1) General rule.* For purposes of paragraph (a)(2) of this section, project has the meaning provided in this paragraph. Facilities that are functionally related and subordinate to a project are treated as part of that same project. Facilities having different purposes or serving different customer bases are not ordinarily part of the same project. For example, the following are generally not part of the same project—

(i) Generation, transmission and distribution facilities;

(ii) Separate facilities designed to serve wholesale customers and retail customers; and

(iii) A peaking unit and a baseload unit (regardless of the location of the units).

(2) Separate ownership. Except as otherwise provided in this paragraph (b)(2), facilities that are not owned by the same person are not part of the same project. If different governmental persons act in concert to finance a project, however (for example as participants in a joint powers authority), their interests are aggregated with respect to that project to determine whether the $15 million output limitation is met. In the case of undivided ownership interests in a single output facility, property that is not owned by different persons is treated as separate projects only if the separate interests are financed—

(i) With bonds of different issuers; and

(ii) Without a principal purpose of avoiding the limitation in this section.

(3) Generating property. (i) Property on same site. In the case of generation and related facilities, project means property located at the same site.

(ii) Special rule for generating units. Separate generating units are not part of the same project if one unit is reasonably expected, on the issue date of each issue that finances the units, to be placed in service more than 3 years before the other. Common facilities or property that will be functionally related to more than one generating unit must be allocated on a reasonable basis. If a generating unit already is constructed or is under construction (the first unit) and bonds are to be issued to finance an additional generating unit (the second unit), all costs for any common facilities paid or incurred before the earlier of the issue date of bonds to finance the second unit or the commencement of construction of the second unit are allocated to the first unit. At the time that bonds are issued to finance the second unit (or, if earlier, upon commencement of construction of that unit), any remaining costs of the common facilities may be allocated between the first and second units so that in the aggregate the allocation is reasonable.

(4) Transmission and distribution. In the case of transmission or distribution facilities, project means functionally related or contiguous property. Separate transmission or distribution facilities are not part of the same project if one facility is reasonably expected, on the issue date of each issue that finances the facilities, to be placed in service more than 2 years before the other.

(5) Subsequent improvements. (i) In general. An improvement to generation, transmission or distribution facilities that is not part of the original design of those facilities (the original project) is not part of the same project as the original project if the construction, reconstruction, or acquisition of that improvement commences more than 3 years after the original project was placed in service and the bonds issued to finance that improvement are issued more than 3 years after the original project was placed in service.

(ii) Special rule for transmission and distribution facilities. An improvement to transmission or distribution facilities that is not part of the original design of that property is not part of the same project as the original project if the issuer did not reasonably expect the need to make that improvement when it commenced construction of the original project and the construction, reconstruction, or acquisition of that improvement is mandated by the federal government or a state regulatory authority to accommodate requests for wheeling.

(6) Replacement property. For purposes of this section, property that replaces existing property of an output facility is treated as part of the same project as the replaced property unless—

(i) The need to replace the property was not reasonably expected on the issue date or the need to replace the property occurred more than 3 years before the issuer reasonably expected (determined on the issue date of the bonds financing the property) that it would need to replace the property; and

(ii) The bonds that finance (and refinance) the output facility have a weighted average maturity that is not greater than 120 percent of the reasonably expected economic life of the facility.

(c) Example. The application of the provisions of this section is illustrated by the following example:

Example. (i) Power Authority K, a political subdivision, intends to issue a single issue of tax-exempt bonds at par with a stated principal amount and sale proceeds of $500 million to finance the acquisition of an electric generating facility. No portion of the facility will be used for a private business use, except that L, an investor-owned utility, will purchase 10 percent of the output of the facility under a take contract and will pay 10 percent of the debt service on the bonds. The nonqualified amount with respect to the bonds is $50 million.

(ii) The maximum amount of tax-exempt bonds that may be issued for the acquisition of an interest in the facility in paragraph (i) of this Example is $465 million (that is, $450 million for the 90 percent of the facility that is governmentally owned and used plus a nonqualified amount of $15 million).

T.D. 9016, 9/19/2002.

§ 1.141-9 Unrelated or disproportionate use test.

(a) General rules. *(1) Description of test.* Under section 141(b)(3) (the unrelated or disproportionate use test), an issue meets the private business tests if the amount of private business use and private security or payments attributable to unrelated or disproportionate private business use exceeds 5 percent of the proceeds of the issue. For this purpose, the private business use test is applied by taking into account only use that is not related to any government use of proceeds of the issue (unrelated use) and use that is related but disproportionate to any government use of those proceeds (disproportionate use).

(2) Application of unrelated or disproportionate use test. (i) Order of application. The unrelated or disproportionate use test is applied by first determining whether a private

business use is related to a government use. Next, private business use that relates to a government use is examined to determine whether it is disproportionate to that government use.

(ii) Aggregation of unrelated and disproportionate use. All the unrelated use and disproportionate use financed with the proceeds of an issue are aggregated to determine compliance with the unrelated or disproportionate use test. The amount of permissible unrelated and disproportionate private business use is not reduced by the amount of private business use financed with the proceeds of an issue that is neither unrelated use nor disproportionate use.

(iii) Deliberate actions. A deliberate action that occurs after the issue date does not result in unrelated or disproportionate use if the issue meets the conditions of § 1.141-12(a).

(b) Unrelated use. *(1) In general.* Whether a private business use is related to a government use financed with the proceeds of an issue is determined on a case-by-case basis, emphasizing the operational relationship between the government use and the private business use. In general, a facility that is used for a related private business use must be located within, or adjacent to, the governmentally used facility.

(2) Use for the same purpose as government use. Use of a facility by a nongovernmental person for the same purpose as use by a governmental person is not treated as unrelated use if the government use is not insignificant. Similarly, a use of a facility in the same manner both for private business use that is related use and private business use that is unrelated use does not result in unrelated use if the related use is not insignificant. For example, a privately owned pharmacy in a governmentally owned hospital does not ordinarily result in unrelated use solely because the pharmacy also serves individuals not using the hospital. In addition, use of parking spaces in a garage by a nongovernmental person is not treated as unrelated use if more than an insignificant portion of the parking spaces are used for a government use (or a private business use that is related to a government use), even though the use by the nongovernmental person is not directly related to that other use.

(c) Disproportionate use. *(1) Definition of disproportionate use.* A private business use is disproportionate to a related government use only to the extent that the amount of proceeds used for that private business use exceeds the amount of proceeds used for the related government use. For example, a private use of $100 of proceeds that is related to a government use of $70 of proceeds results in $30 of disproportionate use.

(2) Aggregation of related uses. If two or more private business uses of the proceeds of an issue relate to a single government use of those proceeds, those private business uses are aggregated to apply the disproportionate use test.

(3) Allocation rule. If a private business use relates to more than a single use of the proceeds of the issue (for example, two or more government uses of the proceeds of the issue or a government use and a private use), the amount of any disproportionate use may be determined by—

(i) Reasonably allocating the proceeds used for the private business use among the related uses;

(ii) Aggregating government uses that are directly related to each other; or

(iii) Allocating the private business use to the government use to which it is primarily related.

(d) Maximum use taken into account. The determination of the amount of unrelated use or disproportionate use of a facility is based on the maximum amount of reasonably expected government use of a facility during the measurement period. Thus, no unrelated use or disproportionate use arises solely because a facility initially has excess capacity that is to be used by a nongovernmental person if the facility will be completely used by the issuer during the term of the issue for more than an insignificant period.

(e) Examples. The following examples illustrate the application of this section:

Example (1). School and remote cafeteria. County X issues bonds with proceeds of $20 million and uses $18.1 million of the proceeds for construction of a new school building and $1.9 million of the proceeds for construction of a privately operated cafeteria in its administrative office building, which is located at a remote site. The bonds are secured, in part, by the cafeteria. The $1.9 million of proceeds is unrelated to the government use (that is, school construction) financed with the bonds and exceeds 5 percent of $20 million. Thus, the issue meets the private business tests.

Example (2). Public safety building and courthouse. City Y issues bonds with proceeds of $50 million for construction of a new public safety building ($32 million) and for improvements to an existing courthouse ($15 million). Y uses $3 million of the bond proceeds for renovations to an existing privately operated cafeteria located in the courthouse. The bonds are secured, in part, by the cafeteria. Y's use of the $3 million for the privately operated cafeteria does not meet the unrelated or disproportionate use test because these expenditures are neither unrelated use nor disproportionate use.

Example (3). Unrelated garage. City Y issues bonds with proceeds of $50 million for construction of a new public safety building ($30.5 million) and for improvements to an existing courthouse ($15 million). Y uses $3 million of the bond proceeds for renovations to an existing privately operated cafeteria located in the courthouse. The bonds are secured, in part, by the cafeteria. Y also uses $1.5 million of the proceeds to construct a privately operated parking garage adjacent to a private office building. The private business use of the parking garage is unrelated to any government use of proceeds of the issue. Since the proceeds used for unrelated uses and disproportionate uses do not exceed 5 percent of the proceeds, the unrelated or disproportionate use test is not met.

Example (4). Disproportionate use of garage. County Z issues bonds with proceeds of $20 million for construction of a hospital with no private business use ($17 million); renovation of an office building with no private business use ($1 million); and construction of a garage that is entirely used for a private business use ($2 million). The use of the garage is related to the use of the office building but not to the use of the hospital. The private business use of the garage results in $1 million of disproportionate use because the proceeds used for the garage ($2 million) exceed the proceeds used for the related government use ($1 million). The bonds are not private activity bonds, however, because the disproportionate use does not exceed 5 percent of the proceeds of the issue.

Example (5). Bonds for multiple projects.

(i) County W issues bonds with proceeds of $80 million for the following purposes: (1) $72 million to construct a County-owned and operated waste incinerator; (2) $1 million for a County-owned and operated facility for the temporary storage of hazardous waste prior to final disposal; (3) $1 million to construct a privately owned recycling facility located at a remote site; and (4) $6 million to build a garage adjacent to the County-owned incinerator that will be leased to Company T to store and repair trucks that it owns and uses to haul County W refuse. Company T uses 75 percent of its trucks to haul materials to the incinerator and the remaining 25 percent of its trucks to haul materials to the temporary storage facility.

(ii) The $1 million of proceeds used for the recycling facility is used for an unrelated use. The garage is related use. In addition, 75 percent of the use of the $6 million of proceeds used for the garage is allocable to the government use of proceeds at the incinerator. The remaining 25 percent of the proceeds used for the garage ($1.5 million) relates to the government use of proceeds at the temporary storage facility. Thus, this portion of the proceeds used for the garage exceeds the proceeds used for the temporary storage facility by $0.5 million and this excess is disproportionate use (but not unrelated use). Thus, the aggregate amount of unrelated use and disproportionate use financed with the proceeds of the issue is $1.5 million. Alternatively, under paragraph (c)(3)(iii) of this section, the entire garage may be treated as related to the government use of the incinerator and, under that allocation, the garage is not disproportionate use. In either event, section 141(b)(3) limits the aggregate unrelated use and disproportionate use to $4 million. Therefore, the bonds are not private activity bonds under this section.

T.D. 8712, 1/10/97.

§ 1.141-10 Coordination with volume cap.

[Reserved]

T.D. 8712, 1/10/97.

§ 1.141-11 Acquisition of nongovernmental output property.

[Reserved]

T.D. 8712, 1/10/97.

§ 1.141-12 Remedial actions.

(a) Conditions to taking remedial action. An action that causes an issue to meet the private business tests or the private loan financing test is not treated as a deliberate action if the issuer takes a remedial action described in paragraph (d), (e), or (f) of this section with respect to the nonqualified bonds and if all of the requirements in paragraphs (a)(1) through (5) of this section are met.

(1) Reasonable expectations test met. The issuer reasonably expected on the issue date that the issue would meet neither the private business tests nor the private loan financing test for the entire term of the bonds. For this purpose, if the issuer reasonably expected on the issue date to take a deliberate action prior to the final maturity date of the issue that would cause either the private business tests or the private loan financing test to be met, the term of the bonds for this purpose may be determined by taking into account a redemption provision if the provisions of § 1.141-2(d)(2)(ii)(A) through (C) are met.

(2) Maturity not unreasonably long. The term of the issue must not be longer than is reasonably necessary for the governmental purposes of the issue (within the meaning of § 1.148-1(c)(4)). Thus, this requirement is met if the weighted average maturity of the bonds of the issue is not greater than 120 percent of the average reasonably expected economic life of the property financed with the proceeds of the issue as of the issue date.

(3) Fair market value consideration. Except as provided in paragraph (f) of this section, the terms of any arrangement that results in satisfaction of either the private business tests or the private loan financing test are bona fide and arm's-length, and the new user pays fair market value for the use of the financed property. Thus, for example, fair market value may be determined in a manner that takes into account restrictions on the use of the financed property that serve a bona fide governmental purpose.

(4) Disposition proceeds treated as gross proceeds for arbitrage purposes. The issuer must treat any disposition proceeds as gross proceeds for purposes of section 148. For purposes of eligibility for temporary periods under section 148(c) and exemptions from the requirement of section 148(f) the issuer may treat the date of receipt of the disposition proceeds as the issue date of the bonds and disregard the receipt of disposition proceeds for exemptions based on expenditure of proceeds under § 1.148-7 that were met before the receipt of the disposition proceeds.

(5) Proceeds expended on a governmental purpose. Except for a remedial action under paragraph (d) of this section, the proceeds of the issue that are affected by the deliberate action must have been expended on a governmental purpose before the date of the deliberate action.

(b) Effect of a remedial action. *(1) In general.* The effect of a remedial action is to cure use of proceeds that causes the private business use test or the private loan financing test to be met. A remedial action does not affect application of the private security or payment test.

(2) Effect on bonds that have been advance refunded. If proceeds of an issue were used to advance refund another bond, a remedial action taken with respect to the refunding bond proportionately reduces the amount of proceeds of the advance refunded bond that is taken into account under the private business use test or the private loan financing test.

(c) Disposition proceeds. *(1) Definition.* Disposition proceeds are any amounts (including property, such as an agreement to provide services) derived from the sale, exchange, or other disposition (disposition) of property (other than investments) financed with the proceeds of an issue.

(2) Allocating disposition proceeds to an issue. In general, if the requirements of paragraph (a) of this section are met, after the date of the disposition, the proceeds of the issue allocable to the transferred property are treated as financing the disposition proceeds rather than the transferred property. If a disposition is made pursuant to an installment sale, the proceeds of the issue continue to be allocated to the transferred property. If an issue does not meet the requirements for remedial action in paragraph (a) of this section or the issuer does not take an appropriate remedial action, the proceeds of the issue are allocable to either the transferred property or the disposition proceeds, whichever allocation produces the greater amount of private business use and private security or payments.

(3) Allocating disposition proceeds to different sources of funding. If property has been financed by different sources of funding, for purposes of this section, the disposition proceeds from that property are first allocated to the outstanding bonds that financed that property in proportion to the principal amounts of those outstanding bonds. In no event may disposition proceeds be allocated to bonds that are no longer outstanding or to a source of funding not derived from a borrowing (such as revenues of the issuer) if the disposition

proceeds are not greater than the total principal amounts of the outstanding bonds that are allocable to that property. For purposes of this paragraph (c)(3), principal amount has the same meaning as in § 1.148-9(b)(2) and outstanding bonds do not include advance refunded bonds.

(d) Redemption or defeasance of nonqualified bonds. *(1) In general.* The requirements of this paragraph (d) are met if all of the nonqualified bonds of the issue are redeemed. Proceeds of tax-exempt bonds must not be used for this purpose, unless the tax-exempt bonds are qualified bonds, taking into account the purchaser's use of the facility. If the bonds are not redeemed within 90 days of the date of the deliberate action, a defeasance escrow must be established for those bonds within 90 days of the deliberate action.

(2) Special rule for dispositions for cash. If the consideration for the disposition of financed property is exclusively cash, the requirements of this paragraph (d) are met if the disposition proceeds are used to redeem a pro rata portion of the nonqualified bonds at the earliest call date after the deliberate action. If the bonds are not redeemed within 90 days of the date of the deliberate action, the disposition proceeds must be used to establish a defeasance escrow for those bonds within 90 days of the deliberate action.

(3) Notice of defeasance. The issuer must provide written notice to the Commissioner of the establishment of the defeasance escrow within 90 days of the date the defeasance escrow is established.

(4) Special limitation. The establishment of a defeasance escrow does not satisfy the requirements of this paragraph (d) if the period between the issue date and the first call date of the bonds is more than 10½ years.

(5) Defeasance escrow defined. A defeasance escrow is an irrevocable escrow established to redeem bonds on their earliest call date in an amount that, together with investment earnings, is sufficient to pay all the principal of, and interest and call premium on, bonds from the date the escrow is established to the earliest call date. The escrow may not be invested in higher yielding investments or in any investment under which the obligor is a user of the proceeds of the bonds.

(e) Alternative use of disposition proceeds. *(1) In general.* The requirements of this paragraph (e) are met if—

(i) The deliberate action is a disposition for which the consideration is exclusively cash;

(ii) The issuer reasonably expects to expend the disposition proceeds within two years of the date of the deliberate action;

(iii) The disposition proceeds are treated as proceeds for purposes of section 141 and are used in a manner that does not cause the issue to meet either the private business tests or the private loan financing test, and the issuer does not take any action subsequent to the date of the deliberate action to cause either of these tests to be met; and

(iv) If the issuer does not use all of the disposition proceeds for an alternative use described in paragraph (e)(1)(iii) of this section, the issuer uses those remaining disposition proceeds for a remedial action that meets paragraph (d) of this section.

(2) Special rule for use by 501(c)(3) organizations. If the disposition proceeds are to be used by a 501(c)(3) organization, the nonqualified bonds must in addition be treated as reissued for purposes of sections 141, 145, 147, 149, and 150 and, under this treatment, satisfy all of the applicable requirements for qualified 501(c)(3) bonds. Thus, beginning on the date of the deliberate action, nonqualified bonds that satisfy these requirements must be treated as qualified 501(c)(3) bonds for all purposes, including sections 145(b) and 150(b).

(f) Alternative use of facility. The requirements of this paragraph (f) are met if—

(1) The facility with respect to which the deliberate action occurs is used in an alternative manner (for example, used for a qualifying purpose by a nongovernmental person or used by a 501(c)(3) organization rather than a governmental person);

(2) The nonqualified bonds are treated as reissued, as of the date of the deliberate action, for purposes of sections 55 through 59 and 141, 142, 144, 145, 146, 147, 149 and 150, and under this treatment, the nonqualified bonds satisfy all the applicable requirements for qualified bonds throughout the remaining term of the nonqualified bonds;

(3) The deliberate action does not involve a disposition to a purchaser that finances the acquisition with proceeds of another issue of tax-exempt bonds; and

(4) Any disposition proceeds other than those arising from an agreement to provide services (including disposition proceeds from an installment sale) resulting from the deliberate action are used to pay the debt service on the bonds on the next available payment date or, within 90 days of receipt, are deposited into an escrow that is restricted to the yield on the bonds to pay the debt service on the bonds on the next available payment date.

(g) Rules for deemed reissuance. For purposes of determining whether bonds that are treated as reissued under paragraphs (e) and (f) of this section are qualified bonds—

(1) The provisions of the Code and regulations thereunder in effect as of the date of the deliberate action apply; and

(2) For purposes of paragraph (f) of this section, section 147(d) (relating to the acquisition of existing property) does not apply.

(h) Authority of Commissioner to provide for additional remedial actions. The Commissioner may, by publication in the Federal Register or the Internal Revenue Bulletin, provide additional remedial actions, including making a remedial payment to the United States, under which a subsequent action will not be treated as a deliberate action for purposes of § 1.141-2.

(i) Effect of remedial action on continuing compliance. Solely for purposes of determining whether deliberate actions that are taken after a remedial action cause an issue to meet the private business tests or the private loan financing test—

(1) If a remedial action is taken under paragraph (d), (e), or (f) of this section, the private business use or private loans resulting from the deliberate action are not taken into account for purposes of determining whether the bonds are private activity bonds; and

(2) After a remedial action is taken, the amount of disposition proceeds is treated as equal to the proceeds of the issue that had been allocable to the transferred property immediately prior to the disposition. See paragraph (k) of this section, Example 5.

(j) Nonqualified bonds. *(1) Amount of nonqualified bonds.* The percentage of outstanding bonds that are nonqualified bonds equals the highest percentage of private business use in any 1-year period commencing with the deliberate action.

(2) Allocation of nonqualified bonds. Allocations to nonqualified bonds must be made on a pro rata basis, except that, for purposes of paragraph (d) of this section (relating to redemption or defeasance), an issuer may treat bonds with longer maturities (determined on a bond-by-bond basis) as the nonqualified bonds.

(k) Examples. The following examples illustrate the application of this section:

Example (1). Disposition proceeds less than outstanding bonds used to retire bonds. On June 1, 1997, City C issues 30-year bonds with an issue price of $10 million to finance the construction of a hospital building. The bonds have a weighted average maturity that does not exceed 120 percent of the reasonably expected economic life of the building. On the issue date, C reasonably expects that it will be the only user of the building for the entire term of the bonds. Six years after the issue date, C sells the building to Corporation P for $5 million. The sale price is the fair market value of the building, as verified by an independent appraiser. C uses all of the $5 million disposition proceeds to immediately retire a pro rata portion of the bonds. The sale does not cause the bonds to be private activity bonds because C has taken a remedial action described in paragraph (d) of this section so that P is not treated as a private business user of bond proceeds.

Example (2). Lease to nongovernmental person. The facts are the same as in Example 1, except that instead of selling the building, C, 6 years after the issue date, leases the building to P for 7 years and uses other funds to redeem all of the $10 million outstanding bonds within 90 days of the deliberate act. The bonds are not treated as private activity bonds because C has taken the remedial action described in paragraph (d) of this section.

Example (3). Sale for less than fair market value. The facts are the same as in Example 1, except that the fair market value of the building at the time of the sale to P is $6 million. Because the transfer was for less than fair market value, the bonds are ineligible for the remedial actions under this section. The bonds are private activity bonds because P is treated as a user of all of the proceeds and P makes a payment ($6 million) for this use that is greater than 10 percent of the debt service on the bonds, on a present value basis.

Example (4). Fair market value determined taking into account governmental restrictions. The facts are the same as in Example 1, except that the building was used by C only for hospital purposes and C determines to sell the building subject to a restriction that it be used only for hospital purposes. After conducting a public bidding procedure as required by state law, the best price that C is able to obtain for the building subject to this restriction is $4.5 million from P. C uses all of the $4.5 million disposition proceeds to immediately retire a pro rata portion of the bonds. The sale does not cause the bonds to be private activity bonds because C has taken a remedial action described in paragraph (d) of this section so that P is not treated as a private business user of bond proceeds.

Example (5). Alternative use of disposition proceeds. The facts are the same as in Example 1, except that C reasonably expects on the date of the deliberate action to use the $5 million disposition proceeds for another governmental purpose (construction of governmentally owned roads) within two years of receipt, rather than using the $5 million to redeem outstanding bonds. C treats these disposition proceeds as gross proceeds for purposes of section 148. The bonds are not private activity bonds because C has taken a remedial action described in paragraph (e) of this section. After the date of the deliberate action, the proceeds of all of the outstanding bonds are treated as used for the construction of the roads, even though only $5 million of disposition proceeds was actually used for the roads.

Example (6). Alternative use of financed property. The facts are the same as in Example 1, except that C determines to lease the hospital building to Q, an organization described in section 501(c)(3), for a term of 10 years rather than to sell the building to P. In order to induce Q to provide hospital services, C agrees to lease payments that are less than fair market value. Before entering into the lease, an applicable elected representative of C approves the lease after a noticed public hearing. As of the date of the deliberate action, the issue meets all the requirements for qualified 501(c)(3) bonds, treating the bonds as reissued on that date. For example, the issue meets the two percent restriction on use of proceeds of finance issuance costs of section 147(g) because the issue pays no costs of issuance from disposition proceeds in connection with the deemed reissuance. C and Q treat the bonds as qualified 501(c)(3) bonds for all purposes commencing with the date of the deliberate action. The bonds are treated as qualified 501(c)(3) bonds commencing with the date of the deliberate action.

Example (7). Deliberate action before proceeds are expended on a governmental purpose. County J issues bonds with proceeds of $10 million that can be used only to finance a correctional facility. On the issue date of the bonds, J reasonably expects that it will be the sole user of the bonds for the useful life of the facility. The bonds have a weighted average maturity that does not exceed 120 percent of the reasonably expected economic life of the facility. After the issue date of the bonds, but before the facility is placed in service, J enters into a contract with the federal government pursuant to which the federal government will make a fair market value, lump sum payment equal to 25 percent of the cost of the facility. In exchange for this payment, J provides the federal government with priority rights to use of 25 percent of the facility. J uses the payment received from the federal government to defease the nonqualified bonds. The agreement does not cause the bonds to be private activity bonds because J has taken a remedial action described in paragraph (d) of this section. See paragraph (a)(5) of this section.

Example (8). Compliance after remedial action. In 1997, City G issues bonds with proceeds of $10 million to finance a courthouse. The bonds have a weighted average maturity that does not exceed 120 percent of the reasonably expected economic life of the courthouse. G uses $1 million of the proceeds for a private business use and more than 10 percent of the debt service on the issue is secured by private security or payments. G later sells one-half of the courthouse property to a nongovernmental person for cash. G immediately redeems 60 percent of the outstanding bonds. This percentage of outstanding bonds is based on the highest private business use of the courthouse in any 1-year period commencing with the deliberate action. For purposes of subsequently applying section 141 to the issue, G may continue to use all of the proceeds of the outstanding bonds in the same manner (that is, for both the courthouse and the existing private business use) without causing the issue to meet the private business use test. The issue, however, continues to meet the private security or payment test. The result would be the same if D, instead of redeeming the bonds, established a defeasance escrow for those bonds, provided that the requirement of paragraph (d)(4) of this section was met.

T.D. 8712, 1/10/97.

PAR. 3. In § 1.141-12, paragraphs (j) and (k) Example 8 are revised to read as follows:

Proposed § 1.141-12 Remedial actions. [*For Preamble, see ¶ 152,439*]

• ***Caution:*** This Notice of Proposed Rulemaking was partially finalized by TD 9150, 08/12/2004. Reg. §§ 1.141-12 and 1.141-15 remain proposed.

* * * * *

(j) Nonqualified bonds. *(1) Amount of nonqualified bonds.* The nonqualified bonds are a portion of the outstanding bonds in an amount that, if the remaining bonds were issued on the date on which the deliberate action occurs, the remaining bonds would not satisfy the private business use test or private loan financing test, as applicable. For this purpose, the amount of private business use is the greatest percentage of private business use in any one-year period commencing with the deliberate action.

(2) Allocation of nonqualified bonds. Allocations of nonqualified bonds must be made on a pro rata basis, except that, for purposes of paragraph (d) of this section (relating to redemption or defeasance), an issuer may treat any bonds of an issue as the nonqualified bonds so long as—

(i) The remaining weighted average maturity of the issue, determined as of the date on which the nonqualified bonds are redeemed or defeased (determination date), and excluding from the determination the nonqualified bonds redeemed or defeased by the issuer in accordance with this section, is not greater than

(ii) The remaining weighted average maturity of the issue, determined as of the determination date, but without regard to the redemption or defeasance of any bonds (including the nonqualified bonds) occurring on the determination date.

(k) * * *

Example (8). Compliance after remedial action. In 2000, City G issues bonds with proceeds of $10 million to finance a courthouse. The bonds have a weighted average maturity that does not exceed 120 percent of the reasonably expected economic life of the courthouse. G uses $1 million of the proceeds for a private business use and more than 10 percent of the debt service on the issue is secured by private security or payments. In 2004, in a bona fide and arm's length arrangement, G enters into a management contract with a nongovernmental person that results in private business use of 40 percent of the courthouse per year during the remaining term of the bonds. G immediately redeems the nonqualified bonds, or 44.44 percent of the outstanding bonds. This is the portion of the outstanding bonds that, if the remaining bonds were issued on the date on which the deliberate action occurs, the remaining bonds would not satisfy the private business use test, if the amount of private business use is the greatest percentage of private business use in any one-year period commencing with the deliberate action (50 percent). This percentage is computed by dividing the percentage of the facility used for a government use (50 percent) by the minimum amount of government use required (90 percent), and subtracting the resulting percentage (55.56 percent) from 100 percent (44.44 percent). For purposes of subsequently applying section 141 to the issue, G may continue to use all of the proceeds of the outstanding bonds in the same manner (that is, for the courthouse and the private business use) without causing the issue to meet the private business use test. The issue, however, continues to meet the private security or payment test. The result would be the same if G, instead of redeeming the bonds, established a defeasance escrow for those bonds, provided that the requirement of paragraph (d)(4) of this section was met.

§ 1.141-13 Refunding issues.

(a) In general. Except as provided in this section, a refunding issue and a prior issue are tested separately under section 141. Thus, the determination of whether a refunding issue consists of private activity bonds generally does not depend on whether the prior issue consists of private activity bonds.

(b) Application of private business use test and private loan financing test. *(1) Allocation of proceeds.* In applying the private business use test and the private loan financing test to a refunding issue, the proceeds of the refunding issue are allocated to the same expenditures and purpose investments as the proceeds of the prior issue.

(2) Determination of amount of private business use. (i) In general. Except as provided in paragraph (b)(2)(ii) of this section, the amount of private business use of a refunding issue is determined under § 1.141-3(g), based on the measurement period for that issue (for example, without regard to any private business use that occurred prior to the issue date of the refunding issue).

(ii) Refundings of governmental bonds. In applying the private business use test to a refunding issue that refunds a prior issue of governmental bonds, the amount of private business use of the refunding issue is the amount of private business use—

(A) During the combined measurement period; or

(B) At the option of the issuer, during the period described in paragraph (b)(2)(i) of this section, but only if, without regard to the reasonable expectations test of § 1.141-2(d), the prior issue does not satisfy the private business use test, based on a measurement period that begins on the first day of the combined measurement period and ends on the issue date of the refunding issue.

(iii) Combined measurement period. (A) In general. Except as provided in paragraph (b)(2)(iii)(B) of this section, the combined measurement period is the period that begins on the first day of the measurement period (as defined in § 1.141-3(g)) for the prior issue (or, in the case of a series of refundings of governmental bonds, the first issue of governmental bonds in the series) and ends on the last day of the measurement period for the refunding issue.

(B) Transition rule for refundings of bonds originally issued before May 16, 1997. If the prior issue (or, in the case of a series of refundings of governmental bonds, the first issue of governmental bonds in the series) was issued before May 16, 1997, then the issuer, at its option, may treat the combined measurement period as beginning on the date (the transition date) that is the earlier of December 19, 2005 or the first date on which the prior issue (or an earlier issue in the case of a series of refundings of governmental bonds) became subject to the 1997 regulations (as defined in § 1.141-15(b)). If the issuer treats the combined measurement period as beginning on the transition date in accordance with this paragraph (b)(2)(iii)(B), then paragraph (c)(2) of this section shall be applied by treating the transition date as the issue date of the earliest issue, by treating the bonds as reissued on the transition date at an issue price equal to the value of the bonds (as determined under § 1.148-4(e)) on that date, and by disregarding any private security or private payments before the transition date.

(iv) Governmental bond. For purposes of this section, the term governmental bond means any bond that, when issued, purported to be a governmental bond, as defined in § 1.150-1(b), or a qualified 501(c)(3) bond, as defined in section 145(a).

(v) Special rule for refundings of qualified 501(c)(3) bonds with governmental bonds. For purposes of applying this paragraph (b)(2) to a refunding issue that refunds a qualified 501(c)(3) bond, any use of the property refinanced by the refunding issue before the issue date of the refunding issue by a 501(c)(3) organization with respect to its activities that do not constitute an unrelated trade or business under section 513(a) is treated as government use.

(c) Application of private security or payment test. *(1) Separate issue treatment.* If the amount of private business use of a refunding issue is determined based on the measurement period for that issue in accordance with paragraph (b)(2)(i) or (b)(2)(ii)(B) of this section, then the amount of private security and private payments allocable to the refunding issue is determined under § 1.141-4 by treating the refunding issue as a separate issue.

(2) Combined issue treatment. If the amount of private business use of a refunding issue is determined based on the combined measurement period for that issue in accordance with paragraph (b)(2)(ii)(A) of this section, then the amount of private security and private payments allocable to the refunding issue is determined under § 1.141-4 by treating the refunding issue and all earlier issues taken into account in determining the combined measurement period as a combined issue. For this purpose, the present value of the private security and private payments is compared to the present value of the debt service on the combined issue (other than debt service paid with proceeds of any refunding bond). Present values are computed as of the issue date of the earliest issue taken into account in determining the combined measurement period (the earliest issue). Except as provided in paragraph (c)(3) of this section, present values are determined by using the yield on the combined issue as the discount rate. The yield on the combined issue is determined by taking into account payments on the refunding issue and all earlier issues taken into account in determining the combined measurement period (other than payments made with proceeds of any refunding bond), and based on the issue price of the earliest issue. In the case of a refunding of only a portion of the original principal amount of a prior issue, the refunded portion of the prior issue is treated as a separate issue and any private security or private payments with respect to the prior issue are allocated ratably between the combined issue and the unrefunded portion of the prior issue in a consistent manner based on relative debt service. See paragraph (b)(2)(iii)(B) of this section for special rules relating to certain refundings of governmental bonds originally issued before May 16, 1997.

(3) Special rule for arrangements not entered into in contemplation of the refunding issue. In applying the private security or payment test to a refunding issue that refunds a prior issue of governmental bonds, the issuer may use the yield on the prior issue to determine the present value of private security and private payments under arrangements that were not entered into in contemplation of the refunding issue. For this purpose, any arrangement that was entered into more than 1 year before the issue date of the refunding issue is treated as not entered into in contemplation of the refunding issue.

(d) Multipurpose issue allocations. *(1) In general.* For purposes of section 141, unless the context clearly requires otherwise, § 1.148-9(h) applies to allocations of multipurpose issues (as defined in § 1.148-1(b)), including allocations involving the refunding purposes of the issue. An allocation under this paragraph (d) may be made at any time, but once made may not be changed. An allocation is not reasonable under this paragraph (d) if it achieves more favorable results under section 141 than could be achieved with actual separate issues. The issue to be allocated and each of the separate issues under the allocation must consist of one or more tax-exempt bonds. Allocations made under this paragraph (d) and § 1.148-9(h) must be consistent for purposes of section 141 and section 148.

(2) Exceptions. This paragraph (d) does not apply for purposes of sections 141(c)(1) and 141(d)(1).

(e) Application of reasonable expectations test to certain refunding bonds. An action that would otherwise cause a refunding issue to satisfy the private business tests or the private loan financing test is not taken into account under the reasonable expectations test of § 1.141-2(d) if—

(1) The action is not a deliberate action within the meaning of § 1.141-2(d)(3); and

(2) The weighted average maturity of the refunding bonds is not greater than the weighted average reasonably expected economic life of the property financed by the prior bonds.

(f) Special rule for refundings of certain general obligation bonds. Notwithstanding any other provision of this section, a refunding issue does not consist of private activity bonds if—

(1) The prior issue meets the requirements of § 1.141-2(d)(5) (relating to certain general obligation bond programs that finance a large number of separate purposes); or

(2) The refunded portion of the prior issue is part of a series of refundings of all or a portion of an issue that meets the requirements of § 1.141-2(d)(5).

(g) Examples. The following examples illustrate the application of this section:

Example (1). Measuring private business use. In 2002, Authority A issues tax-exempt bonds that mature in 2032 to acquire an office building. The measurement period for the 2002 bonds under § 1.141-3(g) is 30 years. At the time A acquires the building, it enters into a 10-year lease with a nongovernmental person under which the nongovernmental person will use 5 percent of the building in its trade or business during each year of the lease term. In 2007, A issues bonds to refund the 2002 bonds. The 2007 bonds mature on the same date as the 2002 bonds and have a measurement period of 25 years under § 1.141-3(g). Under paragraph (b)(2)(ii)(A) of this section, the amount of private business use of the proceeds of the 2007 bonds is 1.67 percent, which equals the amount of private business use during the combined measurement period (5 percent of ⅓ of the 30-year combined measurement period). In addition, the 2002 bonds do not satisfy the private business use test, based on a measurement period beginning on the first day of the measurement period for the 2002 bonds and ending on the issue date of the 2007 bonds, because only 5 percent of the proceeds of the 2002 bonds are used for a private business use during that period. Thus, under paragraph (b)(2)(ii)(B) of this section, A may treat the amount of private business use of the 2007 bonds as 1 percent (5 percent of ⅕ of the 25-year measurement period for the 2007 bonds). The 2007 bonds do not satisfy the private business use test.

Example (2). Combined issue yield computation. (i) On January 1, 2000, County B issues 20-year bonds to finance the acquisition of a municipal auditorium. The 2000 bonds have a yield of 7.7500 percent, compounded annually, and an issue price and par amount of $100 million. The debt service payments on the 2000 bonds are as follows:

Date	Debt service
1/1/01	$9,996,470
1/1/02	9,996,470
1/1/03	9,996,470
1/1/04	9,996,470
1/1/05	9,996,470
1/1/06	9,996,470
1/1/07	9,996,470
1/1/08	9,996,470
1/1/09	9,996,470
1/1/10	9,996,470
1/1/11	9,996,470
1/1/12	9,996,470
1/1/13	9,996,470
1/1/14	9,996,470
1/1/15	9,996,470
1/1/16	9,996,470
1/1/17	9,996,470
1/1/18	9,996,470
1/1/19	9,996,470
1/1/20	9,996,470
	199,929,400

(ii) On January 1, 2005, B issues 15-year bonds to refund all of the outstanding 2000 bonds maturing after January 1, 2005 (in the aggregate principal amount of $86,500,000). The 2005 bonds have a yield of 6.0000 percent, compounded annually, and an issue price and par amount of $89,500,000. The debt service payments on the 2005 bonds are as follows:

Date	Debt service
1/1/06	$9,215,167
1/1/07	9,215,167
1/1/08	9,215,167
1/1/09	9,215,167
1/1/10	9,215,167
1/1/11	9,215,167
1/1/12	9,215,167
1/1/13	9,215,167
1/1/14	9,215,167
1/1/15	9,215,167
1/1/16	9,215,167
1/1/17	9,215,167
1/1/18	9,215,167
1/1/19	9,215,167
1/1/20	9,215,167
	138,227,511

(iii) In accordance with § 1.141-15(h), B chooses to apply § 1.141-13 (together with the other provisions set forth in § 1.141-15(h)), to the 2005 bonds. For purposes of determining the amount of private security and private payments with respect to the 2005 bonds, the 2005 bonds and the refunded portion of the 2000 bonds are treated as a combined issue under paragraph (c)(2) of this section. The yield on the combined issue is determined in accordance with §§ 1.148-4, 1.141-4(b)(2)(iii) and 1.141-13(c)(2). Under this methodology, the yield on the combined issue is 7.1062 percent per year compounded annually, illustrated as follows:

Date	Previous debt service on refunded portion of prior issue	Refunding debt service	Total debt service	Present value on 1/1/00
1/1/00	....	....	....	($86,500,000.00)
1/1/01	6,689,793	....	6,689,793	6,245,945.33
1/1/02	6,689,793	....	6,689,793	5,831,545.62
1/1/03	6,689,793	....	6,689,793	5,444,640.09
1/1/04	6,689,793	....	6,689,793	5,083,404.58
1/1/05	6,689,793	....	6,689,793	4,746,135.95
1/1/06	....	9,215,167	9,215,167	6,104,023.84
1/1/07	....	9,215,167	9,215,167	5,699,040.20
1/1/08	....	9,215,167	9,215,167	5,320,926.00
1/1/09	....	9,215,167	9,215,167	4,967,898.55
1/1/10	....	9,215,167	9,215,167	4,638,293.40
1/1/11	....	9,215,167	9,215,167	4,330,556.57
1/1/12	....	9,215,167	9,215,167	4,043,237.15
1/1/13	....	9,215,167	9,215,167	3,774,980.51
1/1/14	....	9,215,167	9,215,167	3,524,521.90
1/1/15	....	9,215,167	9,215,167	3,290,680.46
1/1/16	....	9,215,167	9,215,167	3,072,353.70
1/1/17	....	9,215,167	9,215,167	2,868,512.26
1/1/18	....	9,215,167	9,215,167	2,678,195.09
1/1/19	....	9,215,167	9,215,167	2,500,504.89
1/1/20	....	9,215,167	9,215,167	2,334,603.90
	33,448,965	138,227,511	171,676,470.00	0.00

Example (3). Determination of private payments allocable to combined issue. The facts are the same as in Example 2. In addition, on January 1, 2001, B enters into a contract with a nongovernmental person for the use of the auditorium. The contract results in a private payment in the amount of $500,000 on each January 1 beginning on January 1, 2001, and ending on January 1, 2020. Under paragraph (c)(2) of this section, the amount of the private payments allocable to the combined issue is determined by treating the refunded portion of the 2000 bonds ($86,500,000 principal amount) as a separate issue, and by allocating the total private payments ratably between the combined issue and the unrefunded portion of the 2000 bonds ($13,500,000 principal amount) based on relative debt service, as follows:

Date	Private payments	Debt service on unrefunded portion of prior issue	Debt service on combined issue	Percentage of private payments allocable to combined issue	Amount of private payments allocable to combined issue
1/1/01	$500,000	$3,306,677	$6,689,793	66.92	$334,608
1/1/02	500,000	3,306,677	6,689,793	66.92	334,608
1/1/03	500,000	3,306,677	6,689,793	66.92	334,608
1/1/04	500,000	3,306,677	6,689,793	66.92	334,608
1/1/05	500,000	3,306,677	6,689,793	66.92	334,608
1/1/06	500,000	....	9,215,167	100.00	500,000
1/1/07	500,000	....	9,215,167	100.00	500,000
1/1/08	500,000	....	9,215,167	100.00	500,000
1/1/09	500,000	....	9,215,167	100.00	500,000
1/1/10	500,000	....	9,215,167	100.00	500,000
1/1/11	500,000	....	9,215,167	100.00	500,000
1/1/12	500,000	....	9,215,167	100.00	500,000
1/1/13	500,000	....	9,215,167	100.00	500,000
1/1/14	500,000	....	9,215,167	100.00	500,000
1/1/15	500,000	....	9,215,167	100.00	500,000
1/1/16	500,000	....	9,215,167	100.00	500,000
1/1/17	500,000	....	9,215,167	100.00	500,000
1/1/18	500,000	....	9,215,167	100.00	500,000
1/1/19	500,000	....	9,215,167	100.00	500,000
1/1/20	500,000	....	9,215,167	100.00	500,000
	$10,000,000	$16,533,385	$171,676,476	....	$9,173,039

Example (4). Refunding taxable bonds and qualified bonds. (i) In 1999, City C issues taxable bonds to finance the construction of a facility for the furnishing of water. The bonds are secured by revenues from the facility. The facility is managed pursuant to a management contract with a nongovernmental person that gives rise to private business use. In 2007, C terminates the management contract and takes over the operation of the facility. In 2009, C issues bonds to refund the 1999 bonds. On the issue date of the 2009 bonds, C reasonably expects that the facility will not be used for a private business use during the term of the 2009 bonds. In addition, during the term of the 2009 bonds, the facility is not used for a private business use. Under paragraph (b)(2)(i) of this section, the 2009 bonds do not satisfy the private business use test because the amount of private business use is based on the measurement period for those bonds and therefore does not take into account any private business use that occurred pursuant to the management contract.

(ii) The facts are the same as in paragraph (i) of this Example 4, except that the 1999 bonds are issued as exempt facility bonds under section 142(a)(4). The 2009 bonds do not satisfy the private business use test.

Example (5). Multipurpose issue. In 2001, State D issues bonds to finance the construction of two office buildings, Building 1 and Building 2. D expends an equal amount of the proceeds on each building. D enters into arrangements that result in 8 percent of Building 1 and 12 percent of Building 2 being used for a private business use during the measurement period under § 1.141-3(g). These arrangements result in a total of 10 percent of the proceeds of the 2001 bonds being used for a private business use. In 2006, D purports to allocate, under paragraph (d) of this section, an equal amount of the outstanding 2001 bonds to Building 1 and Building 2. D also enters into another private business use arrangement with respect to Building 1 that results in an additional 2 percent (and a total of 10 percent) of Building 1 being used for a private business use during the measurement period. An allocation is not reasonable under paragraph (d) of this section if it achieves more favorable results under section 141 than could be achieved with actual separate issues. D's allocation is unreasonable because, if permitted, it would result in more than 10 percent of the proceeds of the 2001 bonds being used for a private business use.

Example (6). Non-deliberate action. In 1998, City E issues bonds to finance the purchase of land and construction of a building (the prior bonds). On the issue date of the prior bonds, E reasonably expects that it will be the sole user of the financed property for the entire term of the bonds. In 2003, the federal government acquires the financed property in a condemnation action. In 2006, E issues bonds to refund the prior bonds (the refunding bonds). The weighted average maturity of the refunding bonds is not greater than the reasonably expected economic life of the financed property. In general, under § 1.141-2(d) and this section, reasonable expectations must be separately tested on the issue date of a refunding issue. Under paragraph (e) of this section, however, the condemnation action is not taken into account in applying the reasonable expectations test to the refunding bonds because the condemnation action is not a deliberate action within the meaning of § 1.141-2(d)(3) and the weighted average maturity of the refunding bonds is not greater than the weighted average reasonably expected economic life of the property financed by the prior bonds. Thus, the condemnation action does not cause the refunding bonds to be private activity bonds.

Example (7). Non-transitioned refunding of bonds subject to 1954 Code.

In 1985, County F issues bonds to finance a court house. The 1985 bonds are subject to the provisions of the Internal Revenue Code of 1954. In 2006, F issues bonds to refund all of the outstanding 1985 bonds. The weighted average maturity of the 2006 bonds is longer than the remaining weighted average maturity of the 1985 bonds. In addition, the 2006 bonds do not satisfy any transitional rule for refundings in the Tax Reform Act of 1986, 100 Stat. 2085 (1986). Section 141 and this section apply to determine whether the 2006 bonds are private activity bonds including whether, for purposes of § 1.141-13(b)(2)(ii)(B), the 1985 bonds satisfy the private business use test based on a measurement period that begins on the first day of the combined measurement period for the 2006 bonds and ends on the issue date of the 2006 bonds.

T.D. 8712, 1/10/97, amend T.D. 9234, 12/16/2005.

PAR. 5. Section 1.141-13 is amended by revising paragraph (d)(1) and paragraph (g) Example 5 to read as follows:

Proposed § 1.141-13 Refunding issues [*For Preamble, see ¶ 152,807*]

* * * * *

(d) Multipurpose issue allocations. *(1) In general.* For purposes of section 141, unless the context clearly requires otherwise, § 1.148-9(h) applies to allocations of multipurpose issues (as defined in § 1.148-1(b)), including allocations involving the refunding purposes of the issue. An allocation under this paragraph (d) may be made at any time, but once made may not be changed. An allocation is not reasonable under this paragraph (d) if it achieves more favorable results under section 141 than could be achieved with actual separate issues. Each of the separate issues under the allocation must consist of one or more tax-exempt bonds. Allocations made under this paragraph (d) and § 1.148-9(h) must be consistent for purposes of section 141 and section 148.

* * * * *

(g) Examples. * * *

Example (5). Multipurpose issue. (i) In 2006, State D issues bonds to finance the construction of two office buildings, Building 1 and Building 2. D expends an equal amount of the proceeds on each building. D enters into arrangements that result in private business use of 8 percent of Building 1 and 12 percent of Building 2 during the measurement period under § 1.141-3(g). In addition, D enters into arrangements that result in private payments in percentages equal to that private business use. These arrangements result in a total of 10 percent of the proceeds of the 2006 bonds being used for a private business use and for private payments. In 2007, D purports to make a multipurpose issue allocation under paragraph (d) of this section of the outstanding 2006 bonds, allocating the issue into two separate issues of equal amounts with one issue allocable to Building 1 and the second allocable to Building 2. An allocation is unreasonable under paragraph (d) of this section if it achieves more favorable results under section 141 than could be achieved with actual separate issues. D's allocation is unreasonable because, if permitted, it would allow more favorable results under section 141 for the 2006 bonds (for example, private business use and private payments which exceeds the aggregate 10 percent permitted de minimis amounts for the 2006 bonds allocable to Building 2) than could be achieved with actual separate issues. In addition, if D's purported allocation was intended to result in two separate issues of tax-exempt governmental bonds (versus tax-exempt private activity bonds), the allocation would violate paragraph (d) of this section in the first instance because the allocation to the separate issue for Building 2 would fail to qualify separately as an issue of tax-exempt governmental bonds as a result of its 12 percent of private business use and private payments, which exceed the 10 percent permitted de minimis amounts.

(ii) The facts are the same as in paragraph (i) of this Example 5, except that D enters into arrangements that result in 8 percent private business use for Building 1, and it expects no private business use of Building 2. In 2007, D allocates an equal amount of the outstanding 2006 bonds to Building 1 and Building 2. D selects particular bonds for each separate issue such that the allocation does not achieve a more favorable result than could have been achieved by issuing actual separate issues. D uses the same allocation for purposes of both section 141 and 148. D's allocation is reasonable.

(iii) The facts are the same as in paragraph (ii) of this Example 5, except that as part of the same issue, D issues bonds for a privately used airport. The airport bonds if issued as a separate issue would be qualified private activity bonds. The remaining bonds if issued separately from the airport bonds would be governmental bonds. Treated as one issue, however, the bonds are taxable private activity bonds. Therefore, D makes its allocation of the bonds under §§ 1.141-13(d) and 1.150-1(c)(3) into 3 separate issues on or before the issue date. Assuming all other applicable requirements are met, the bonds of the respective issues will be tax-exempt qualified private activity bonds or governmental bonds.

* * * * *

§ 1.141-14 Anti-abuse rules.

(a) Authority of Commissioner to reflect substance of transactions. If an issuer enters into a transaction or series of transactions with respect to one or more issues with a principal purpose of transferring to nongovernmental persons (other than as members of the general public) significant benefits of tax-exempt financing in a manner that is inconsistent with the purposes of section 141, the Commissioner may take any action to reflect the substance of the transaction or series of transactions, including—

(1) Treating separate issues as a single issue for purposes of the private activity bond tests;

(2) Reallocating proceeds to expenditures, property, use, or bonds;

(3) Reallocating payments to use or proceeds;

(4) Measuring private business use on a basis that reasonably reflects the economic benefit in a manner different than as provided in § 1.141-3(g); and

(5) Measuring private payments or security on a basis that reasonably reflects the economic substance in a manner different than as provided in § 1.141-4.

(b) Examples. The following examples illustrate the application of this section:

Example (1). Reallocating proceeds to indirect use. City C issues bonds with proceeds of $20 million for the stated purpose of financing improvements to roads that it owns. As a part of the same plan of financing, however, C also agrees to make a loan of $7 million to Corporation M from its general revenues that it otherwise would have used for the road improvements. The interest rate of the loan corresponds to the interest rate on a portion of the issue. A principal purpose of the financing arrangement is to transfer to M significant benefits of the tax-exempt financing. Although C actually allocates all of the proceeds of the bonds to the road improvements, the Commissioner may reallocate a portion of the proceeds of the bonds to the loan to M because a principal purpose of the financing arrangement is to transfer to M significant benefits of tax-exempt financing in a manner that is inconsistent with the purposes of section 141. The bonds are private activity bonds because the issue meets the private loan financing test. The bonds also meet the private business tests. See also §§ 1.141-3(a)(2), 1.141-4(a)(1), and 1.141-5(a), under which indirect use of proceeds and payments are taken into account.

Example (2). Taking into account use of amounts derived from proceeds that would be otherwise disregarded. County B issues bonds with proceeds of $10 million to finance the purchase of land. On the issue date, B reasonably expects that it will be the sole user of the land. Subsequently, the federal government acquires the land for $3 million in a condemnation action. B uses this amount to make a loan to Corporation M. In addition, the interest rate on the loan reflects the tax-exempt interest rate on the bonds and thus is substantially less than a current market rate. A principal purpose of the arrangement is to transfer to M significant benefits of the tax-exempt financing. Although the condemnation action is not a deliberate action, the Commissioner may treat the condemnation proceeds as proceeds of the issue because a principal purpose of the arrangement is to transfer to M significant benefits of tax-exempt financing in a manner inconsistent with the purposes of section 141. The bonds are private activity bonds.

Example (3). Measuring private business use on an alternative basis. City F issues bonds with a 30-year term to finance the acquisition of an industrial building having a remaining reasonably expected useful economic life of more than 30 years. On the issue date, F leases the building to Corporation G for 3 years. F reasonably expects that it will be the sole user of the building for the remaining term of the bonds. Because of the local market conditions, it is reasonably expected that the fair rental value of the industrial building will be significantly greater during the early years of the term of the bonds than in the later years. The annual rental payments are significantly less than fair market value, reflecting the interest rate on the bonds. The present value of these rental payments (net of operation and maintenance expenses) as of the issue date, however, is approximately 25 percent of the present value of debt service on the issue. Under § 1.141-3, the issue does not meet the private business tests, because only 10 percent of the proceeds are used in a trade or business by a nongovernmental person. A principal purpose of the issue is to transfer to G significant benefits of tax-exempt financing in a manner inconsistent with the purposes of section 141. The method of measuring private business use over the reasonably expected useful economic life of financed property is for the administrative convenience of issuers of state and local bonds. In cases where this method is used in a manner inconsistent with the purposes of section 141, the Commissioner may measure private business use on another basis that reasonably reflects economic benefit, such as in this case on an annual basis. If the Commissioner measures private business use on an annual basis, the bonds are private activity bonds because the private payment test is met and more than 10 percent of the proceeds are used in a trade or business by a nongovernmental person.

Example (4). Treating separate issues as a single issue. City D enters into a development agreement with Corporation T to induce T to locate its headquarters within D's city limits. Pursuant to the development agreement, in 1997 D will issue $20 million of its general obligation bonds (the 1997 bonds) to purchase land that it will grant to T. The development agreement also provides that, in 1998, D will issue $20 million of its tax increment bonds (the 1998 bonds), secured solely by the increase in property taxes in a special taxing district. Substantially all of the property within the special taxing district is owned by T or D. T will separately enter into an agreement to guarantee the payment of tax increment to D in an amount sufficient to retire the 1998 bonds. The proceeds of the 1998 bonds will be used to finance improvements owned and operated by D that will not give rise to private business use. Treated separately, the 1997 issue meets the private business use test, but not the private security or payment test; the 1998 issue meets the private security or payment test, but not the private business use test. A principal purpose of the financing plan including the two issues is to transfer significant benefits of tax-exempt financing to T for its headquarters. Thus, the 1997 issue and the 1998 issue may be treated by the Commissioner as a single issue for purposes of applying the private activity bond tests. Accordingly, the bonds of both the 1997 issue and the 1998 issue may be treated as private activity bonds.

Example (5). Reallocating proceeds. City E acquires an electric generating facility with a useful economic life of more than 40 years and enters into a 30-year take or pay contract to sell 30 percent of the available output to investor-owned utility M. E plans to use the remaining 70 percent of available output for its own governmental purposes. To finance the entire cost of the facility, E issues $30 million of its series A taxable bonds at taxable interest rates and $70 million series B bonds, which purport to be tax-exempt bonds, at tax-exempt interest rates. E allocates all of M's private business use to the proceeds of the series A bonds and all of its own government use to the proceeds of the series B bonds. The series A bonds have a weighted average maturity of 15 years, while the series B bonds have a weighted average maturity of 26 years. M's payments under the take or pay contract are expressly determined by reference to 30 percent of M's total costs (that is, the sum of the debt service required to be paid on both the series A and the series B bonds and all other operating costs). The allocation of all of M's private business use to the series A bonds does not reflect economic substance because the series of transactions transfers to M significant benefits of the tax-exempt interest rates paid on the series B bonds. A principal purpose of the financing arrangement is to transfer to M significant benefits of the tax-exempt financing. Accordingly, the Commissioner may allocate M's private business use on a pro rata basis to both the series B bonds as well as the series A bonds, in which case the series B bonds are private activity bonds.

Example (6). Allocations respected. The facts are the same as in Example 5, except that the debt service component of M's payments under the take or pay contract is based exclusively on the amounts necessary to pay the debt service on the taxable series A bonds. E's allocation of all of M's private business use to the series A bonds is respected because the series of transactions does not actually transfer benefits of tax-exempt interest rates to M. Accordingly, the series B bonds are not private activity bonds. The result would be the same if M's payments under the take or pay contract were based exclusively on fair market value pricing, rather than the tax-exempt interest rates on E's bonds. The result also would be the same if the series A bonds and the series B bonds had substantially equivalent weighted average maturities and E and M had entered into a customary contract providing for payments based on a ratable share of total debt service. E would not be treated by the Commissioner in any of these cases as entering into the contract with a principal purpose of transferring the benefits of tax-exempt financing to M in a manner inconsistent with the purposes of section 141.

T.D. 8712, 1/10/97.

§ 1.141-15 Effective dates.

* * * * *

(a) Scope. The effective dates of this section apply for purposes of §§ 1.141-1 through 1.141-6(a), 1.141-7 through 1.141-14, 1.145-1 through 1.145-2, 1.150-1(a)(3) and the definition of bond documents contained in § 1.150-1(b).

(b) Effective dates. *(1) In general.* Except as otherwise provided in this section, §§ 1.141-0 through 1.141-6(a), 1.141-9 through 1.141-12, 1.141-14, 1.145-1 through 1.145-2(c), and the definition of bond documents contained in § 1.150-1(b) (the 1997 regulations) apply to bonds issued on or after May 16, 1997, that are subject to section 1301 of the Tax Reform Act of 1986 (100 Stat. 2602).

(2) Certain short-term arrangements. The provisions of § 1.141-3 that refer to arrangements for 200 days, 100 days, or 50 days apply to any bond sold on or after November 20, 2001 and may be applied to any bond outstanding on November 20, 2001 to which § 1.141-3 applies.

(3) Certain prepayments. Except as provided in paragraph (c) of this section, paragraphs (c)(2)(ii), (c)(2)(iii) and (c)(2)(iv) of § 1.141-5 apply to bonds sold on or after October 3, 2003. Issuers may apply paragraphs (c)(2)(ii), (c)(2)(iii) and (c)(2)(iv) of § 1.141-5, in whole but not in part, to bonds sold before October 3, 2003 that are subject to § 1.141-5.

(c) Refunding bonds. Except as otherwise provided in this section, the 1997 regulations (defined in paragraph (b)(1) of this section) do not apply to any bonds issued on or after May 16, 1997, to refund a bond to which those regulations do not apply unless—

(1) The refunding bonds are subject to section 1301 of the Tax Reform Act of 1986 (100 Stat. 2602); and

(2) (i) The weighted average maturity of the refunding bonds is longer than—

(A) The weighted average maturity of the refunded bonds; or

(B) In the case of a short-term obligation that the issuer reasonably expects to refund with a long-term financing (such as a bond anticipation note), 120 percent of the weighted average reasonably expected economic life of the facilities financed; or

(ii) A principal purpose for the issuance of the refunding bonds is to make one or more new conduit loans.

(d) Permissive application of regulations. Except as provided in paragraph (e) of this section, the 1997 regulations (defined in paragraph (b)(1) of this section) may be applied in whole, but not in part, to actions taken before February 23, 1998, with respect to—

(1) Bonds that are outstanding on May 16, 1997, and subject to section 141; or

(2) Refunding bonds issued on or after May 16, 1997, that are subject to 141.

(e) Permissive application of certain sections. The following sections may each be applied to any bonds—

(1) Section 1.141-3(b)(4);

(2) Section 1.141-3(b)(6); and

(3) Section 1.141-12.

(f) Effective dates for certain regulations relating to output facilities. *(1) General rule.* Except as otherwise provided in this section, §§ 1.141-7 and 1.141-8 apply to bonds sold on or after November 22, 2002, that are subject to section 1301 of the Tax Reform Act of 1986 (100 Stat. 2602).

(2) Transition rule for requirements contracts. For bonds otherwise subject to §§ 1.141-7 and 1.141-8, § 1.141-7(c)(3) applies to output contracts entered into on or after September 19, 2002. An output contract is treated as entered into on or after that date if it is amended on or after that date, but only if the amendment results in a change in the parties to the contract or increases the amount of requirements covered by the contract by reason of an extension of the contract term or a change in the method for determining such requirements. For purposes of this paragraph (f)(2)—

(i) The extension of the term of a contract causes the contract to be treated as entered into on the first day of the additional term;

(ii) The exercise by a party of a legally enforceable right that was provided under a contract before September 19, 2002, on terms that were fixed and determinable before such date, is not treated as an amendment of the contract. For example, the exercise by a purchaser after September 19, 2002 of a renewal option that was provided under a contract before that date, on terms identical to the original contract, is not treated as an amendment of the contract; and

(iii) An amendment that increases the amount of requirements covered by the contract by reason of a change in the method for determining such requirements is treated as a separate contract that is entered into as of the effective date of the amendment, but only with respect to the increased output to be provided under the contract.

(g) Refunding bonds for output facilities. Except as otherwise provided in paragraph (h) or (i) of this section, §§ 1.141-7 and 1.141-8 do not apply to any bonds sold on or after November 22, 2002, to refund a bond to which §§ 1.141-7 and 1.141-8 do not apply unless—

(1) The refunding bonds are subject to section 1301 of the Tax Reform Act of 1986 (100 Stat. 2602); and

(2) (i) The weighted average maturity of the refunding bonds is longer than—

(A) The weighted average maturity of the refunded bonds; or

(B) In the case of a short-term obligation that the issuer reasonably expects to refund with a long-term financing (such as a bond anticipation note), 120 percent of the weighted average reasonably expected economic life of the facilities financed; or

(ii) A principal purpose for the issuance of the refunding bonds is to make one or more new conduit loans.

(h) Permissive retroactive application. Except as provided in paragraphs (d), (e) or (i) of this section, §§ 1.141-1 through 1.141-6(a), 1.141-7 through 1.141-14, 1.145-1 through 1.145-2, 1.149(d)-1(g), 1.150-1(a)(3), the definition of bond documents contained in § 1.150-1(b) and § 1.150-1(c)(3)(ii) may be applied by issuers in whole, but not in part, to—

(1) Outstanding bonds that are sold before February 17, 2006, and subject to section 141; or

(2) Refunding bonds that are sold on or after February 17, 2006, and subject to section 141.

(i) Permissive application of certain regulations relating to output facilities. Issuers may apply §§ 1.141-7(f)(3) and 1.141-7(g) to any bonds.

(j) Effective dates for certain regulations relating to refundings. Except as otherwise provided in this section, §§ 1.141-13, 1.145-2(d), 1.149(d)-1(g), 1.150-1(a)(3) and 1.150-1(c)(3)(ii) apply to bonds that are sold on or after February 17, 2006, and that are subject to the 1997 regulations (defined in paragraph (b)(1) of this section).

(k) Effective/applicability dates for certain regulations relating to generally applicable taxes and payments in lieu of tax. *(1) In general.* Except as otherwise provided in paragraphs (k)(2) and (k)(3) of this section, revised §§ 1.141-4(e)(2), 1.141-4(e)(3) and 1.141-4(e)(5) apply to bonds sold on or after October 24, 2008 that are otherwise subject to the 1997 Regulations (defined in paragraph (b)(1) of this section).

(2) Transitional rule for certain refundings. Paragraph (k)(1) does not apply to bonds that are issued to refund bonds if—

(i) Either—

(A) The refunded bonds (or the original bonds in a series of refundings) were sold before October 24, 2008, or

(B) The refunded bonds (or the original bonds in a series of refundings) satisfied the transitional rule for projects substantially in progress under paragraph (k)(3) of this section; and

(ii) The weighted average maturity of the refunding bonds does not exceed the remaining weighted average maturity of the refunded bonds.

(3) Transitional rule for certain projects substantially in progress. Paragraph (k)(1) of this section does not apply to bonds issued for projects for which all of the following requirements are met:

(i) A governmental person (as defined in § 1.141-1) took official action evidencing its preliminary approval of the project before October 19, 2006, and the plan of finance for the project in place at that time contemplated financing the project with tax-exempt bonds to be paid or secured by PILOTs.

(ii) Before October 19, 2006, significant expenditures were paid or incurred with respect to the project or a contract was entered into to pay or incur significant expenditures with respect to the project.

(iii) The bonds for the project (excluding refunding bonds) are issued on or before December 31, 2009.

T.D. 8712, 1/10/97, amend T.D. 8757, 1/21/98, T.D. 8941, 1/17/2001, T.D. 8967, 11/19/2001, T.D. 9016, 9/19/2002, T.D. 9085, 8/1/2003, T.D. 9234, 12/16/2005, T.D. 9429, 10/20/2008.

PAR. 6. Section 1.141-15 is amended by revising paragraph (a) and (i) and adding paragraphs (k) and (l) to read as follows:

Proposed § 1.141-15 Effective Dates [*For Preamble, see ¶ 152,807*]

(a) Scope. The effective dates of this section apply for purposes of §§ 1.141-1 through 1.141-14, 1.145-1 through 1.145-2, 1.150-1(a)(3) and the definition of bond documents contained in § 1.150-1(b).

* * * * *

(i) Permissive application of certain regulations relating to output facilities.

(1) Issuers may apply § 1.141-7(f)(3) and § 1.141-7(g) to any bonds used to finance output facilities.

(2) Issuers may apply § 1.141-6 to any bonds used to finance output facilities that are sold on or after the date that is 60 days after the date of publication of the Treasury decisions adopting these rules as final regulations in the Federal Register

* * * * *

(k) Effective date for certain regulations relating to allocation and accounting. Except as otherwise provided in this section, §§ 1.141-1(e), 1.141-6, 1.141-13(d), and 1.145-2(b)(4), (b)(5), and (c)(3) apply to bonds that are sold on or after the date that is 60 days after the date of publication of the Treasury decisions adopting these rules as final regulations in the Federal Register and that are subject to the 1997 Final Regulations.

(l) Permissive retroactive application of certain regulations. Issuers may apply § 1.141-13(d) to bonds to which § 1.141-13 applies.

PAR. 4. Section 1.141-15 is amended as follows:

1. Paragraph (b)(4) is added.

2. Paragraph (e) is revised.

The amendments read as follows:

Proposed § 1.141-15 Effective dates. [*For Preamble, see ¶ 152,439*]

• ***Caution:*** This Notice of Proposed Rulemaking was partially finalized by TD 9150, 08/12/2004. Reg. §§ 1.141-12 and 1.141-15 remain proposed.

* * * * *

(b) Effective dates. * * *

(4) Certain remedial actions. For bonds subject to § 1.141-12, the provisions of § § 1.141-12(j) and 1.141-12(k), Example 8, apply to deliberate actions that occur on or after the date of publication of final regulations in the Federal Register and may be applied by issuers to deliberate actions that occur on or after April 21, 2003 and before the date of publication of final regulations in the Federal Register.

* * * * *

(e) Permissive application of certain sections. *(1) In general.* Except as otherwise provided in paragraph (b)(4) of this section and this paragraph (e), the following sections may each be applied by issuers to any bonds—

(i) Section 1.141-3(b)(4);

(ii) Section 1.141-3(b)(6); and

(iii) Section 1.141-12.

(2) Transition rule for pre-effective date bonds. For purposes of paragraphs (e)(1) and (h) of this section, issuers may apply § 1.141-12 to bonds issued before May 16, 1997, without regard to paragraph (d)(4) thereof with respect to deliberate actions that occur on or after April 21, 2003.

* * * * *

§ 1.141-16 Effective dates for qualified private activity bond provisions.

(a) Scope. The effective dates of this section apply for purposes of §§ 1.142-0 through 1.142-2, 1.144-0 through 1.144-2, 1.147-0 through 1.147-2, and 1.150-4.

(b) Effective dates. Except as otherwise provided in this section, the regulations designated in paragraph (a) of this section apply to bonds issued on or after May 16, 1997, (the effective date).

(c) Permissive application. The regulations designated in paragraph (a) of this section may be applied by issuers in whole, but not in part, to bonds outstanding on the effective date. For this purpose, issuers may apply § 1.142-2 without regard to paragraph (c)(3) thereof to failures to properly use proceeds that occur on or after April 21, 2003.

(d) Certain remedial actions. *(1) General rule.* The provisions of § 1.142-2(e) apply to failures to properly use proceeds that occur on or after August 13, 2004 and may be applied by issuers to failures to properly use proceeds that occur on or after May 14, 2004, provided that the bonds are subject to § 1.142-2.

(2) Special rule for allocations of nonqualified bonds. For purposes of § 1.142-2(e)(2), in addition to the allocation methods permitted in § 1.142-2(e)(2), an issuer may treat bonds with the longest maturities (determined on a bond-by-bond basis) as the nonqualified bonds, but only with respect to failures to properly use proceeds that occur on or after May 14, 2004, with respect to bonds sold before August 13, 2004.

T.D. 8712, 1/10/97, amend T.D. 9150, 8/12/2004.

§ 1.142-0 Table of contents.

This section lists the captioned paragraphs contained in §§ 1.142-1 through 1.142-3.

§ 1.142-1 Exempt facility bonds.

(a) Overview.

(b) Scope.

(c) Effective dates.

§ 1.142-2 Remedial actions.

(a) General rule.

(b) Reasonable expectations requirement.

(c) Redemption or defeasance.

(1) In general.

(2) Notice of defeasance.

(3) Special limitation.

(4) Special rule for dispositions of personal property.

(5) Definitions.

(d) When a failure to properly use proceeds occurs.

(1) Proceeds not spent.

(2) Proceeds spent.

(e) Nonqualified bonds.

(1) Amount of nonqualified bonds.

(2) Allocation of nonqualified bonds.

§ 1.142-3 Refunding issues. [Reserved]

T.D. 8712, 1/10/97, T.D. 9150, 8/12/2004.

§ 1.142-1 Exempt facility bonds.

(a) Overview. Interest on a private activity bond is not excludable from gross income under section 103(a) unless the bond is a qualified bond. Under section 141(e)(1)(A), an exempt facility bond issued under section 142 may be a qualified bond. Under section 142(a), an exempt facility bond is any bond issued as a part of an issue using 95 percent or more of the proceeds for certain exempt facilities.

(b) Scope. Sections 1.142-0 through 1.142-3 apply for purposes of the rules for exempt facility bonds under section 142, except that, with respect to net proceeds that have been spent, § 1.142-2 does not apply to bonds issued under section 142(d) (relating to bonds issued to provide qualified residential rental projects) and section 142(f)(2) and (4) (relating to bonds issued to provide local furnishing of electric energy or gas).

(c) Effective dates. For effective dates of §§ 1.142-0 through 1.142-2, see § 1.141-16.

T.D. 6272, 11/25/57, amend T.D. 6455, 3/1/60, T.D. 6581, 12/5/61, T.D. 6792, 1/14/65, T.D. 7269, 4/12/73, T.D. 8712, 1/10/97.

§ 1.142-2 Remedial actions.

(a) General rule. If less than 95 percent of the net proceeds of an exempt facility bond are actually used to provide an exempt facility, and for no other purpose, the issue will be treated as meeting the use of proceeds requirement of section 142(a) if the issue meets the condition of paragraph (b) of this section and the issuer takes the remedial action described in paragraph (c) of this section.

(b) Reasonable expectations requirement. The issuer must have reasonably expected on the issue date that 95 percent of the net proceeds of the issue would be used to provide an exempt facility and for no other purpose for the entire term of the bonds (disregarding any redemption provisions). To meet this condition the amount of the issue must have been based on reasonable estimates about the cost of the facility.

(c) Redemption or defeasance. *(1) In general.* The requirements of this paragraph (c) are met if all of the nonqualified bonds of the issue are redeemed on the earliest call date after the date on which the failure to properly use the proceeds occurs under paragraph (d) of this section. Proceeds of tax-exempt bonds (other than those described in paragraph (d)(1) of this section) must not be used for this purpose. If the bonds are not redeemed within 90 days of the date on which the failure to properly use proceeds occurs, a defeasance escrow must be established for those bonds within 90 days of that date.

(2) Notice of defeasance. The issuer must provide written notice to the Commissioner of the establishment of the defeasance escrow within 90 days of the date the escrow is established.

(3) Special limitation. The establishment of a defeasance escrow does not satisfy the requirements of this paragraph (c) if the period between the issue date and the first call date is more than 10½ years.

(4) Special rule for dispositions of personal property. For dispositions of personal property exclusively for cash, the requirements of this paragraph (c) are met if the issuer expends the disposition proceeds within 6 months of the date of the disposition to acquire replacement property for the same qualifying purpose of the issue under section 142.

(5) Definitions. For purposes of paragraph (c)(4) of this section, disposition proceeds means disposition proceeds as defined in § 1.141-12(c).

(d) When a failure to properly use proceeds occurs. *(1) Proceeds not spent.* For net proceeds that are not spent, a failure to properly use proceeds occurs on the earlier of the date on which the issuer reasonably determines that the financed facility will not be completed or the date on which the financed facility is placed in service.

(2) Proceeds spent. For net proceeds that are spent, a failure to properly use proceeds occurs on the date on which an action is taken that causes the bonds not to be used for the qualifying purpose for which the bonds were issued.

(e) Nonqualified bonds. *(1) Amount of nonqualified bonds.* For purposes of this section, the nonqualified bonds are a portion of the outstanding bonds in an amount that, if the remaining bonds were issued on the date on which the failure to properly use the proceeds occurs, at least 95 percent of the net proceeds of the remaining bonds would be used to provide an exempt facility. If no proceeds have been spent to provide an exempt facility, all of the outstanding bonds are nonqualified bonds.

(2) Allocation of nonqualified bonds. Allocations of nonqualified bonds must be made on a pro rata basis, except that an issuer may treat any bonds of an issue as the nonqualified bonds so long as—

(i) The remaining weighted average maturity of the issue, determined as of the date on which the nonqualified bonds are redeemed or defeased (determination date), and excluding from the determination the nonqualified bonds redeemed or defeased by the issuer to meet the requirements of paragraph (c) of this section, is not greater than

(ii) The remaining weighted average maturity of the issue, determined as of the determination date, but without regard to the redemption or defeasance of any bonds (including the nonqualified bonds) occurring on the determination date.

T.D. 6272, 11/25/57, amend T.D. 8712, 1/10/97, T.D. 9150, 8/12/2004.

§ 1.142-3 Refunding issues.

[Reserved]

T.D. 8712, 1/10/97.

§ 1.142-4 Use of proceeds to provide a facility.

(a) In general. [Reserved].

(b) Reimbursement allocations. If an expenditure for a facility is paid before the issue date of the bonds to provide that facility, the facility is described in section 142(a) only if the expenditure meets the requirements of § 1.150-2 (relating to reimbursement allocations). For purposes of this paragraph (b), if the proceeds of an issue are used to pay principal of or interest on an obligation other than a State or local bond (for example, temporary construction financing of the conduit borrower), that issue is not a refunding issue, and, thus, § 1.150-2(g) does not apply.

(c) Limitation on use of facilities by substantial users. *(1) In general.* If the original use of a facility begins before the issue date of the bonds to provide the facility, the facility is not described in section 142(a) if any person that was a substantial user of the facility at any time during the 5-year period before the issue date or any related person to that user receives (directly or indirectly) 5 percent or more of the proceeds of the issue for the user's interest in the facility and is a substantial user of the facility at any time during the 5-year period after the issue date, unless—

(i) An official intent for the facility is adopted under § 1.150-2 within 60 days after the date on which acquisition, construction, or reconstruction of that facility commenced; and

(ii) For an acquisition, no person that is a substantial user or related person after the acquisition date was also a substantial user more than 60 days before the date on which the official intent was adopted.

(2) Definitions. For purposes of paragraph (c)(1) of this section, substantial user has the meaning used in section 147(a)(1), *related person* has the meaning used in section 144(a)(3), and a user that is a governmental unit within the meaning of § 1.103-1 is disregarded.

(d) Effective date. *(1) In general.* This section applies to bonds sold on or after July 8, 1997. See § 1.103-8(a)(5) for rules applicable to bonds sold before that date.

(2) Elective retroactive application. An issuer may apply this section to any bond sold before July 8, 1997.

T.D. 8718, 5/8/97.

---

§ 1.142(a)(5)-1 Exempt facility bonds: Sewage facilities.

(a) In general. Under section 103(a), a private activity bond is a tax-exempt bond only if it is a qualified bond. A qualified bond includes an exempt facility bond, defined as any bond issued as part of an issue 95 percent or more of the net proceeds of which are used to provide a facility specified in section 142. One type of facility specified in section 142(a) is a sewage facility. This section defines the term sewage facility for purposes of section 142(a).

(b) Definitions. *(1) Sewage facility defined.* A sewage facility is property—

(i) Except as provided in paragraphs (b)(2) and (d) of this section, used for the secondary treatment of wastewater; however, for property treating wastewater reasonably expected to have an average daily raw wasteload concentration of biochemical oxygen demand (BOD) that exceeds 350 milligrams per liter as oxygen (measured at the time the influent enters the facility) (the BOD limit), this paragraph (b)(1)(i) applies only to the extent the treatment is for wastewater having an average daily raw wasteload concentration of BOD that does not exceed the BOD limit;

(ii) Used for the preliminary and/or primary treatment of wastewater but only to the extent used in connection with secondary treatment (without regard to the BOD limit described in paragraph (b)(1)(i) of this section);

(iii) Used for the advanced or tertiary treatment of wastewater but only to the extent used in connection with and after secondary treatment;

(iv) Used for the collection, storage, use, processing, or final disposal of—

(A) Wastewater, which property is necessary for such preliminary, primary, secondary, advanced, or tertiary treatment; or

(B) Sewage sludge removed during such preliminary, primary, secondary, advanced, or tertiary treatment (without regard to the BOD limit described in paragraph (b)(1)(i) of this section);

(v) Used for the treatment, collection, storage, use, processing, or final disposal of septage (without regard to the BOD limit described in paragraph (b)(1)(i) of this section); and

(vi) Functionally related and subordinate to property described in this paragraph (b)(1), such as sewage disinfection property.

(2) Special rules and exceptions. (i) Exception to BOD limit. A facility treating wastewater with an average daily raw wasteload concentration of BOD exceeding the BOD limit will not fail to qualify as a sewage facility described in paragraph (b)(1) of this section to the extent that the failure to satisfy the BOD limit results from the implementation of a federal, state, or local water conservation program (for example, a program designed to promote water use efficiency that results in BOD concentrations beyond the BOD limit).

(ii) Anti-abuse rule for BOD limit. A facility does not satisfy the BOD limit if there is any intentional manipulation of the BOD level to circumvent the BOD limit (for example, increasing the volume of water in the wastewater before the influent enters the facility with the intention of reducing the BOD level).

(iii) Authority of commissioner. In appropriate cases upon application to the Commissioner, the Commissioner may determine that facilities employing technologically advanced or innovative treatment processes qualify as sewage facilities if it is demonstrated that these facilities perform functions that are consistent with the definition of sewage facilities described in paragraph (b)(1) of this section.

(3) Other applicable definitions. (i) Advanced or tertiary treatment means the treatment of wastewater after secondary treatment. Advanced or tertiary treatment ranges from biological treatment extensions to physical-chemical separation techniques such as denitrification, ammonia stripping, carbon adsorption, and chemical precipitation.

(ii) Nonconventional pollutants are any pollutants that are not listed in 40 CFR 401.15, 401.16, or app. A to part 423.

(iii) Preliminary treatment means treatment that removes large extraneous matter from incoming wastewater and renders the incoming wastewater more amenable to subsequent treatment and handling.

(iv) Pretreatment means a process that preconditions wastewater to neutralize or remove toxic, priority, or nonconventional pollutants that could adversely affect sewers or inhibit a preliminary, primary, secondary, advanced, or tertiary treatment operation.

(v) Primary treatment means treatment that removes material that floats or will settle, usually by screens or settling tanks.

(vi) Priority pollutants are those pollutants listed in app. A to 40 CFR part 423.

(vii) Secondary treatment means the stage in sewage treatment in which a bacterial process (or an equivalent process) consumes the organic parts of wastes, usually by trickling filters or an activated sludge process.

(viii) Sewage sludge is defined in 40 CFR 122.2 and includes septage.

(ix) Toxic pollutants are those pollutants listed in 40 CFR 401.15.

(c) Other property not included in the definition of a sewage facility. Property other than property described in paragraph (b)(1) of this section is not a sewage facility. Thus, for example, property is not a sewage facility, or functionally related and subordinate property, if the property is used for pretreatment of wastewater (whether or not this treatment is necessary to perform preliminary, primary, secondary, advanced, or tertiary treatment), or the related collection, storage, use, processing, or final disposal of the wastewater. In addition, property used to treat, process, or use wastewater subsequent to the time the wastewater can be discharged into navigable waters, as defined in 33 U.S.C. 1362, is not a sewage facility.

(d) Allocation of costs. In the case of property that has both a use described in paragraph (b)(1) of this section (a sewage treatment function) and a use other than sewage treatment, only the portion of the cost of the property allocable to the sewage treatment function is taken into account as an expenditure to provide sewage facilities. The portion of the cost of property allocable to the sewage treatment function is determined by allocating the cost of that property between the property's sewage treatment function and any other uses by any method which, based on all the facts and circumstances, reasonably reflects a separation of costs for each use of the property.

(e) Effective date. *(1) In general.* This section applies to issues of bonds issued after February 21, 1995.

(2) Refundings. In the case of a refunding bond issued to refund a bond to which this section does not apply, the issuer need not apply this section to that refunding bond. This paragraph (e)(2) applies only if the weighted average maturity of the refunding bonds, as described in section 147(b), is not greater than the remaining weighted average maturity of the refunded bonds.

T.D. 8576, 12/22/94.

Proposed § 1.142(a)(6)-1 Exempt facility bonds: solid waste disposal facilities. [*For Preamble, see ¶ 152,527*]

(a) In general. Section 103(a) provides that, generally, interest on a state or local bond is not included in gross income. However, this exclusion does not apply to any private activity bond that is not a qualified bond. Section 141(e) defines qualified bond to include an exempt facility bond that meets certain requirements. Section 142(a) defines exempt facility bond as any bond issued as part of an issue 95 percent or more of the net proceeds of which are to be used to provide a facility specified in section 142(a). One type of facility specified in section 142(a) is a solid waste disposal facility. This section defines the term solid waste disposal facility for purposes of section 142(a).

(b) Solid waste disposal facility. *(1) In general.* The term solid waste disposal facility means a facility to the extent that the facility is—

(i) Used to perform a solid waste disposal function (within the meaning of paragraph (b)(2) of this section);

(ii) Used to perform a preliminary function (within the meaning of paragraph (b)(3) of this section); or

(iii) Functionally related and subordinate (within the meaning of § 1.103-8(a)(3)) to a facility that is used to perform a solid waste disposal function or a preliminary function.

(2) Solid waste disposal function. A solid waste disposal function is the processing of solid waste (as defined in paragraph (c) of this section) in—

(i) A final disposal process (as defined in paragraph (d) of this section);

(ii) A conversion process (as defined in paragraph (e) of this section);

(iii) A recovery process (as defined in paragraph (f) of this section); or

(iv) A transformation process (as defined in paragraph (g) of this section).

(3) Preliminary function. A preliminary function is the collection, separation, sorting, storage, treatment, processing, disassembly, or handling of solid material that is preliminary and directly related to a solid waste disposal function. However, no portion of a collection, separation, sorting, storage, treatment, processing, disassembly, or handling activity is a preliminary function unless, for each year while the issue is outstanding, more than 50 percent, by weight or volume, of the total materials that result from the entire activity is solid waste.

(4) Mixed-function facilities. Paragraph (h) of this section provides rules for determining the portion of a facility that is a solid waste disposal facility for a facility that is used to perform—

(i) A solid waste disposal function or a preliminary function; and

(ii) Another function.

(c) Solid waste. *(1) In general.* For purposes of this section, the term solid waste means garbage, refuse, and other discarded solid materials (as defined in paragraph (c)(2) of this section), including solid'waste materials resulting from industrial, commercial, and agricultural operations, and from community activities, but does not include solids or dissolved material in domestic sewage or other significant pollutants in water resources, such as silt, dissolved or suspended solids in industrial waste water effluents, dissolved materials in irrigation return flows or other common water pollutants. Liquid or gaseous waste is not solid waste.

(2) Garbage, refuse and other discarded solid materials. (i) In general. For purposes of paragraph (c)(1) of this section, garbage, refuse and other discarded solid materials means material that is solid and that is introduced into a final disposal process, conversion process, recovery process, or transformation process unless the material is described in paragraph (c)(2)(ii), (iii), (iv), (v) or (vi) of this section.

(ii) Certain material introduced into a conversion process. Material is described in this paragraph (c)(2)(ii) if the material is introduced into a conversion process and the material is—

(A) A fossil fuel; or

(B) Any material that is grown, harvested, produced, mined, or otherwise created for the principal purpose of converting the material to heat, hot water, steam, or another useful form of energy. For example, organic material that is closed-loop biomass under section 45(c) is described in this paragraph (c)(2)(ii) if the material is introduced into a conversion process. Material is not treated as described in this paragraph (c)(2)(ii) just because an operation is performed on the material to make the material more conducive to being converted to heat, hot water, or steam. For example, if material that is not otherwise grown, harvested, produced, mined, or created for the principal purpose of converting the material to a useful form of energy is formed into pellets to make the material more conducive to being incinerated to produce steam, the creation of pellets does not cause the material to be produced or created for the principal purpose of converting the material to steam.

(iii) Certain material introduced into a recovery process. Material is described in this paragraph (c)(2)(iii) if the material is introduced into a recovery process, and the material is a precious metal.

(iv) Certain material introduced into a transformation process. [Reserved].

(v) Certain hazardous material. Material is described in this paragraph (c)(2)(v) if the material is hazardous material and it is disposed of at a facility that is subject to final permit requirements under subtitle C of title II of the Solid Waste Disposal Act (as in effect on October 22, 1986, the date of the enactment of the Tax Reform Act of 1986). See section 142(h)(1).

(vi) Radioactive material. Material is described in this paragraph (c)(2)(vi) if the material is radioactive.

(d) Final disposal process. The term final disposal process means—

(1) The placement of material in a landfill; or

(2) The incineration of material without any useful energy being captured.

(e) Conversion process. The term conversion process means a process in which material is incinerated and heat, hot water, or steam is created and captured as useful energy. The conversion process begins with the incineration of material and ends at the point at which the latest of heat, hot water, or steam is created. Thus, the conversion process ends before any transfer or distribution of heat, hot water or steam.

(f) Recovery process. *(1) In general.* The term recovery process means a process that starts with the melting or re-pulping of material to return the material to a form in which the material previously existed for use in the fabrication of an end product and ends immediately before the material is processed in the same or substantially the same way that virgin material is processed to fabricate the end product. For example, melting non-virgin metal to fabricate a metal product is not a recovery process if virgin metal is melted in the same or substantially the same process to fabricate the product.

(2) End products fabricated entirely from non-virgin material. If an end product is fabricated entirely from non-virgin material, the recovery process ends immediately before the non-virgin material is processed in the same or substantially the same way that virgin material is processed in a comparable fabrication process that uses only virgin material or a combination of virgin and non-virgin material. For example, if new paper is fabricated entirely from re-pulped, non-virgin material, the recovery process ends immediately before the non-virgin material is processed in the same or substantially the same manner that virgin material is processed in the fabrication of paper made only with virgin material, or with a mixture of virgin and non-virgin material.

(3) Refurbishing, repair, or similar activities. Refurbishing, repair, or similar activities are not recovery processes.

(g) Transformation process. [Reserved].

(h) Mixed-function facilities. *(1) In general.* Except to the extent provided in paragraph (h)(2) of this section, if a facility is used to perform both a solid waste disposal function or a preliminary function and another function, then the costs of the facility allocable to the solid waste disposal function or the preliminary function are determined using any reasonable method, based on all the facts and circumstances. See § 1.103-8(a)(1) for rules relating to which amounts are used to provide an exempt facility.

(2) Mixed inputs. (i) In general. Except as provided in paragraph (h)(2)(ii) of this section, for each final disposal process, conversion process, recovery process, or transformation process, the percentage of costs of the property used to perform such process that are allocable to a solid waste disposal function equals the lowest percentage of solid waste processed in that process in any year while the issue is outstanding. The percentage of solid waste processed in such process for any year is the percentage, by weight or volume, of the total materials processed in that process that constitute solid waste for that year.

(ii) Special rule for mixed-input processes if at least 80 percent of the materials processed are solid waste. For each final disposal process, conversion process, recovery process, or transformation process, all of the costs of the property used to perform such process are allocable to a solid waste disposal function if, for each year while the issue is outstanding, solid waste constitutes at least 80 percent, by weight or volume, of the total materials processed in the process.

(i) Examples. The following examples illustrate the application of this section:

Example (1). Final disposal process. Garbage trucks collect solid material at curbside from businesses and residences and dump the material in a landfill owned by Company A. The landfill is not subject to final permit requirements under subtitle C of title II of the Solid Waste Disposal Act (as in effect on the date of the enactment of the Tax Reform Act of 1986). The placement of material in the landfill is a final disposal process. The solid material placed in the landfill is solid waste under paragraph (c) of this section. Therefore, the landfill is a solid waste disposal facility.

Example (2). Recovery process. Company B re-pulps magazines and cleans the pulp. After cleaning, B mixes the pulp with virgin material and uses the mixed material to produce rolls of paper towels. Before the mixing, the re-pulped material is not processed in the same or substantially the same way that virgin material is processed to produce the paper towels. The process starting with the re-pulping of the magazines and ending immediately before the re-pulped material is mixed with the virgin material is a recovery process. The magazines introduced into the recovery process are solid waste. Therefore, the property that re-pulps the magazines and the property that cleans the re-pulped material are used to perform a solid waste disposal function.

Example (3). Preliminary function. Company C owns a paper mill. At the mill, logs from nearby timber operations are processed through a machine that removes bark. The stripped logs are used to manufacture paper. The stripped bark falls onto a conveyor belt that transports the bark to a storage bin used to briefly store the bark until C feeds the bark into a boiler. The conveyor belt and storage bin are used only for these purposes. The boiler is used only to create steam by burning the bark, and the steam is used to generate electricity. The creation of steam from the stripped bark is a conversion process that starts with the incineration of the stripped bark. The conversion process is a solid waste disposal function. The conveyor belt performs a collection activity that is preliminary and that is directly related to the solid waste disposal function. The storage bin performs a storage function that is preliminary and that is directly related to the solid waste disposal function. Thus, the conveyor belt and storage bin are solid waste disposal facilities. The removal of the bark does not have a sufficient nexus to the conversion process to be directly related to the conversion process; the process of removing the bark does not become directly related to the conversion process merely because it results in material that will be waste used in the conversion process.

Example (4). Mixed-input facility. Company D owns an incinerator financed by an issue and uses the incinerator exclusively to burn coal (a fossil fuel) and other solid material to create steam that is used to generate electricity. Each year while the issue is outstanding, 30 percent by volume and 40 percent by weight of the solid material that D processes in the conversion process is a fossil fuel. The remainder of the solid material processed is neither a fossil fuel nor material that was grown, harvested, produced, mined, or otherwise created for the principal purpose of converting the material to heat, hot water, steam, or another useful form of energy. Seventy percent of the costs of the property used to perform the conversion process are allocable to a solid waste disposal function.

Example (5). Mixed-function facility. Company E owns and operates a facility financed by an issue and uses the facility exclusively to sort damaged bottles from bottles that may be re-filled. The damaged bottles are directly introduced into a process that melts them for use in the fabrication of an end product. The melting process is a recovery process. Each year while the issue is outstanding, more than 50 percent, by weight or volume, of all of the bottles that pass out of the sorting process are damaged bottles that are processed in a recovery process. The sorting facility performs a preliminary function, but it also performs another function. The costs of the sorting facility allocable to the preliminary function are determined using any reasonable method, based on all the facts and circumstances.

(j) Effective date. *(1) In general.* Except as provided in paragraph (j)(2) of this section, this section applies to bonds that are— (i) Sold on or after the date that is 60 days after the date of publication of final regulations in the Federal Register; and

(ii) Subject to section 142.

(2) Certain refunding bonds. An issuer is not required to apply this section to bonds described in paragraph (j)(1) of this section that are issued to refund a bond to which this section does not apply if the weighted average maturity of the refunding bonds is not longer than the weighted average maturity of the refunded bonds.

§ 1.142(f)(4)-1 Manner of making election to terminate tax-exempt bond financing.

(a) Overview. Section 142(f)(4) permits a person engaged in the local furnishing of electric energy or gas (a local furnisher) that uses facilities financed with exempt facility bonds under section 142(a)(8) and that expands its service area in a manner inconsistent with the requirements of sections 142(a)(8) and (f) to make an election to ensure that those bonds will continue to be treated as exempt facility bonds. The election must meet the requirements of paragraphs (b) and (c) of this section.

(b) Time for making election. *(1) In general.* An election under section 142(f)(4)(B) must be filed with the Internal Revenue Service on or before 90 days after the date of the service area expansion that causes bonds to cease to meet the requirements of sections 142(a)(8) and (f).

(2) Date of service area expansion. For the purposes of this section, the date of the service area expansion is the first date on which the local furnisher is authorized to collect revenue for the provision of service in the expanded area.

(c) Manner of making election. An election under section 142(f)(4)(B) must be captioned "ELECTION TO TERMINATE TAX-EXEMPT BOND FINANCING", must be signed under penalties of perjury by a person who has authority to sign on behalf of the local furnisher, and must contain the following information—

(1) The name of the local furnisher;

(2) The tax identification number of the local furnisher;

(3) The complete address of the local furnisher;

(4) The date of the service area expansion;

(5) Identification of each bond issue subject to the election, including the complete name of each issue, the tax identification number of each issuer, the report number of the information return filed under section 149(e) for each issue, the issue date of each issue, the CUSIP number (if any) of the bond with the latest maturity of each issue, the issue price of each issue, the adjusted issue price of each issue as of the date of the election, the earliest date on which the bonds of each issue may be redeemed, and the principal amount of bonds of each issue to be redeemed on the earliest redemption date;

(6) A statement that the local furnisher making the election agrees to the conditions stated in section 142(f)(4)(B); and

(7) A statement that each issuer of the bonds subject to the election has received written notice of the election.

(d) Effect on section 150(b). Except as provided in paragraph (e) of this section, if a local furnisher files an election within the period specified in paragraph (b) of this section, section 150(b) does not apply to bonds identified in the election during and after that period.

(e) Effect of failure to meet agreements. If a local furnisher fails to meet any of the conditions stated in an election pursuant to paragraph (c)(6) of this section, the election is invalid.

(f) Corresponding provisions of the Internal Revenue Code of 1954. Section 103(b)(4)(E) of the Internal Revenue Code of 1954 set forth corresponding requirements for the exclusion from gross income of the interest on bonds issued for facilities for the local furnishing of electric energy or gas. For the purposes of this section any reference to sections 142(a)(8) and (f) of the Internal Revenue Code of 1986 includes a reference to the corresponding portion of section 103(b)(4)(E) of the Internal Revenue Code of 1954.

(g) Effective dates. This section applies to elections made on or after January 19, 2001.

T.D. 8941, 1/17/2001.

§ 1.143(g)-1 Requirements related to arbitrage.

(a) In general. Under section 143, for an issue to be an issue of qualified mortgage bonds or qualified veterans' mortgage bonds (together, mortgage revenue bonds), the requirements of section 143(g) must be satisfied. An issue satisfies the requirements of section 143(g) only if such issue meets the requirements of paragraph (b) of this section and, in the case of an issue 95 percent or more of the net proceeds of which are to be used to provide residences for veterans, such issue also meets the requirements of paragraph (c) of this section. The requirements of section 143(g) and this section are applicable in addition to the requirements of section 148 and §§ 1.148-0 through 1.148-11.

(b) Effective rate of mortgage interest not to exceed bond yield by more than 1.125 percentage points. *(1)*

Maximum yield. An issue shall be treated as meeting the requirements of this paragraph (b) only if the excess of the effective rate of interest on the mortgages financed by the issue, over the yield on the issue, is not greater over the term of the issue than 1.125 percentage points.

(2) Effective rate of interest. (i) In determining the effective rate of interest on any mortgage for purposes of this paragraph (b), there shall be taken into account all fees, charges, and other amounts borne by the mortgagor that are attributable to the mortgage or to the bond issue. Such amounts include points, commitment fees, origination fees, servicing fees, and prepayment penalties paid by the mortgagor.

(ii) Items that shall be treated as borne by the mortgagor and shall be taken into account in calculating the effective rate of interest also include—

(A) All points, commitment fees, origination fees, or similar charges borne by the seller of the property; and

(B) The excess of any amounts received from any person other than the mortgagor by any person in connection with the acquisition of the mortgagor's interest in the property over the usual and reasonable acquisition costs of a person acquiring like property when owner-financing is not provided through the use of mortgage revenue bonds.

(iii) The following items shall not be treated as borne by the mortgagor and shall not be taken into account in calculating the effective rate of interest—

(A) Any expected rebate of arbitrage profit under paragraph (c) of this section; and

(B) Any application fee, survey fee, credit report fee, insurance charge or similar settlement or financing cost to the extent such amount does not exceed amounts charged in the area in cases when owner-financing is not provided through the use of mortgage revenue bonds. For example, amounts paid for Federal Housing Administration, Veterans' Administration, or similar private mortgage insurance on an individual's mortgage, or amounts paid for pool mortgage insurance on a pool of mortgages, are not taken into account so long as such amounts do not exceed the amounts charged in the area with respect to a similar mortgage, or pool of mortgages, that is not financed with mortgage revenue bonds. For this purpose, amounts paid for pool mortgage insurance include amounts paid to an entity (for example, the Government National Mortgage Association, the Federal National Mortgage Association (FNMA), the Federal Home Loan Mortgage Corporation, or other mortgage insurer) to directly guarantee the pool of mortgages financed with the bonds, or to guarantee a pass-through security backed by the pool of mortgages financed with the bonds.

(C) The following example illustrates the provisions of this paragraph (b)(2)(iii):

Example. Housing Authority X issues bonds intended to be qualified mortgage bonds under section 143(a). At the time the bonds are issued, X enters into an agreement with a group of mortgage lending institutions (lenders) under which the lenders agree to originate and service mortgages that meet certain specified requirements. After originating a specified amount of mortgages, each lender issues a "pass-though security" (each, a PTS) backed by the mortgages and sells the PTS to X. Under the terms of the PTS, the lender pays X an amount equal to the regular monthly payments on the mortgages (less certain fees), whether or not received by the lender (plus any prepayments and liquidation proceeds in the event of a foreclosure or other disposition of any mortgages). FNMA guarantees the timely payment of principal and interest on each PTS. From the payments received from each mortgagor, the lender pays a fee to FNMA for its guarantee of the PTS. The amounts paid to FNMA do not exceed the amounts charged in the area with respect to a similar pool of mortgages that is not financed with mortgage revenue bonds. Under this paragraph (b)(2)(iii), the fees for the guarantee provided by FNMA are an insurance charge because the guarantee is pool mortgage insurance. Because the amounts charged for the guarantee do not exceed the amounts charged in the area with respect to a similar pool of mortgages that is not financed with mortgage revenue bonds, the amounts charged for the guarantee are not taken into account in computing the effective rate of interest on the mortgages financed with X's bonds.

(3) Additional rules. To the extent not inconsistent with the Tax Reform Act of 1986, Public Law 99-514 (the 1986 Act), or subsequent law, § 6a.103A-2(i)(2) (other than paragraphs (i)(2)(i) and (i)(2)(ii)(A) through (C)) of this chapter applies to provide additional rules relating to compliance with the requirement that the effective rate of mortgage interest not exceed the bond yield by more than 1.125 percentage points.

(c) Arbitrage and investment gains to be used to reduce costs of owner-financing. As provided in section 143(g)(3), certain earnings on nonpurpose investments must either be paid or credited to mortgagors, or paid to the United States, in certain circumstances. To the extent not inconsistent with the 1986 Act or subsequent law, § 6a.103A-2(i)(4) of this chapter applies to provide guidance relating to compliance with this requirement.

(d) Effective dates. *(1) In general.* Except as otherwise provided in this section, § 1.143(g)-1 applies to bonds sold on or after May 23, 2005, that are subject to section 143.

(2) Permissive retroactive application in whole. Except as provided in paragraph (d)(4) of this section, issuers may apply § 1.143(g)-1, in whole, but not in part, to bonds sold before May 23, 2005, that are subject to section 143.

(3) Bonds subject to the Internal Revenue Code of 1954. Except as provided in paragraph (d)(4) of this section and subject to the applicable effective dates for the corresponding statutory provisions, an issuer may apply § 1.143(g)-1, in whole, but not in part, to bonds that are subject to section 103A(i) of the Internal Revenue Code of 1954.

(4) Special rule for pre-July 1, 1993 bonds. To the extent that an issuer applies this section to bonds issued before July 1, 1993, § 6a.103A-2(i)(3) of this chapter also applies to the bonds.

T.D. 9204, 5/20/2005.

---

§ 1.144-0 Table of contents.

This section lists the captioned paragraphs contained in §§ 1.144-1 and 1.144-2.

§ 1.144-1 Qualified small issue bonds, qualified student loan bonds, and qualified redevelopment bonds.

(a) Overview.

(b) Scope.

(c) Effective dates.

§ 1.144-2 Remedial actions.

T.D. 8712, 1/10/97.

---

§ 1.144-1 Qualified small issue bonds, qualified student loan bonds, and qualified redevelopment bonds.

(a) Overview. Interest on a private activity bond is not excludable from gross income under section 103(a) unless the bond is a qualified bond. Under section 141(e)(1)(D), a qualified small issue bond issued under section 144(a) may be a qualified bond. Under section 144(a), any qualified small issue bond is any bond issued as a part of an issue 95 percent or more of the proceeds of which are to be used to provide certain manufacturing facilities or certain depreciable farm property and which meets other requirements. Under section 141(e)(1)(F) a qualified redevelopment bond issued under section 144(c) is a qualified bond. Under section 144(c), a qualified redevelopment bond is any bond issued as a part of an issue 95 percent or more of the net proceeds of which are to be used for one or more redevelopment purposes and which meets certain other requirements.

(b) Scope. Sections 1.144-0 through 1.144-2 apply for purposes of the rules for small issue bonds under section 144(a) and qualified redevelopment bonds under section 144(c), except that § 1.144-2 does not apply to the requirements for qualified small issue bonds under section 144(a)(4) (relating to the limitation on capital expenditures) or under section 144(a)(10) (relating to the aggregate limit of tax-exempt bonds per taxpayer).

(c) Effective dates. For effective dates of §§ 1.144-0 through 1.144-2, see § 1.141-16.

T.D. 8712, 1/10/97.

§ 1.144-2 Remedial actions.

The remedial action rules of § 1.142-2 apply to qualified small issue bonds issued under section 144(a) and to qualified redevelopment bonds issued under section 144(c), for this purpose treating those bonds as exempt facility bonds and the qualifying purposes for those bonds as exempt facilities.

T.D. 8712, 1/10/97.

§ 1.145-0 Table of contents.

This section lists the captioned paragraphs contained in §§ 1.145-1 and 1.145-2.

§ 1.145-1 Qualified 501(c)(3) bonds.

(a) Overview.

(b) Scope.

(c) Effective dates.

§ 1.145-2 Application of private activity bond regulations.

(a) In general.

(b) Modification of private business tests.

(c) Exceptions.

(1) Certain provisions relating to governmental programs.

(2) Costs of issuance.

(d) Issuance costs financed by prior issue.

T.D. 8712, 1/10/97, amend T.D. 9234, 12/16/20005

§ 1.145-1 Qualified 501(c)(3) bonds.

(a) Overview. Interest on a private activity bond is not excludable from gross income under section 103(a) unless the bond is a qualified bond. Under section 141(e)(1)(G), a qualified 501(c)(3) bond issued under section 145 is a qualified bond. Under section 145, a qualified 501(c)(3) bond is any bond issued as a part of an issue that satisfies the requirements of sections 145(a) through (d).

(b) Scope. Sections 1.145-0 through 1.145-2 apply for purposes of section 145(a).

(c) Effective dates. For effective dates of §§ 1.145-0 through 1.145-2, see § 1.141-15.

T.D. 8712, 1/10/97.

§ 1.145-2 Application of private activity bond regulations.

(a) In general. Except as provided in this section, §§ 1.141-0 through 1.141-15 apply to section 145(a). For example, under this section, § 1.141-1, and section 1.141-2, an issue ceases to be an issue of qualified 501(c)(3) bonds if the issuer or a conduit borrower 501(c)(3) organization takes a deliberate action, subsequent to the issue date, that causes the issue to fail to comply with the requirements of sections 141(e) and 145 (such as an action that results in revocation of exempt status of the 501(c)(3) organization).

(b) Modification of private business tests. In applying § 1.141-0 through 1.141-15 to section 145(a)—

(1) References to governmental persons include 501(c)(3) organizations with respect to their activities that do not constitute unrelated trades or businesses under section 513(a);

(2) References to "10 percent" and "proceeds" in the context of the private business use test and the private security or payment test mean "5 percent" and "net proceeds"; and

(3) References to the private business use test in §§ 1.141-2 and 1.141-12 include the ownership test of section 145(a)(1).

(c) Exceptions. *(1) Certain provisions relating to governmental programs.* The following provisions do not apply to section 145: § 1.141-2(d)(4) (relating to the special rule for dispositions of personal property in the ordinary course of an established governmental program) and § 1.141-2(d)(5) (relating to the special rule for general obligation bond programs that finance a large number of separate purposes).

(2) Costs of issuance. Section 1.141-3(g)(6) does not apply to section 145(a)(2) to the extent that it provides that costs of issuance are allocated ratably among the other purposes for which the proceeds are used. For purposes of section 145(a)(2), costs of issuance are treated as private business use.

(d) Issuance costs financed by prior issue. Solely for purposes of applying the private business use test to a refunding issue under § 1.141-13, the use of proceeds of the prior issue (or any earlier issue in a series of refundings) to pay issuance costs of the prior issue (or the earlier issue) is treated as a government use.

T.D. 8712, 1/10/97, amend T.D. 9234, 12/16/2005.

PAR. 7. Section 1.145-2 is amended by adding paragraphs (b)(4), (b)(5), and (c)(3) to read as follows:

Proposed § 1.145-2 Application of Private Activity Bond Regulations [*For Preamble, see ¶ 152,807*]

* * * * *

(b) * * *

(4) References to governmental bonds in § 1.141-6 mean qualified 501(c)(3) bonds.

(5) References to ownership by governmental persons in § 1.141-6 mean ownership by governmental persons or 501(c)(3) organizations.

(c) * * *

(3) Partnerships. Section 1.141-1(e)(2) does not apply for purposes of section 145(a)(1). For purposes of section 145(a)(2), in the case of a partnership (as defined in section 7701(a)(2)) in which each of the partners is a governmental person or a section 501(c)(3) organization, the partnership is disregarded as a separate entity and is treated as an aggregate of its partners.

§ 1.147-0 Table of contents.

This section lists the captioned paragraphs contained in §§ 1.147-1 and 1.147-2.

§ 1.147-1 Other requirements applicable to certain private activity bonds.

(a) Overview.

(b) Scope.

(c) Effective dates.

§ 1.147-2 Remedial actions.

T.D. 8712, 1/10/97.

§ 1.147-1 Other requirements applicable to certain private activity bonds.

(a) Overview. Interest on a private activity bond is not excludable from gross income under section 103(a) unless the bond is a qualified bond. Under section 147, certain requirements must be met for a private activity bond to qualify as a qualified bond.

(b) Scope. Sections 1.147-0 through 1.147-2 apply for purposes of the rules in section 147 for qualified private activity bonds that permit use of proceeds to acquire land for environmental purposes (section 147(c)(3)), permit use of proceeds for certain rehabilitations (section 147(d)(2) and (3)), prohibit use of proceeds to finance skyboxes, airplanes, gambling establishments and similar facilities (section 147(e)), and require public approval (section 147(f)), but not for the rules limiting use of proceeds to acquire land or existing property under sections 147(c)(1) and (2), and (d)(1).

(c) Effective dates. For effective dates of §§ 1.147-0 through 1.147-2, see § 1.141-16.

T.D. 8712, 1/10/97.

§ 1.147-2 Remedial actions.

The remedial action rules of § 1.142-2 apply to the rules in section 147 for qualified private activity bonds that permit use of proceeds to acquire land for environmental purposes (section 147(c)(3)), permit use of proceeds for certain rehabilitations (section 147(d)(2) and (3)), prohibit use of proceeds to finance skyboxes, airplanes, gambling establishments and similar facilities (section 147(e)), and require public approval (section 147(f)), for this purpose treating those private activity bonds subject to the rules under section 147 as exempt facility bonds and the qualifying purposes for those bonds as exempt facilities.

T.D. 8712, 1/10/97.

§ 1.147(b)-1 Bond maturity limitation-treatment of working capital.

Section 147(b) does not apply to proceeds of a private activity bond issue used to finance working capital expenditures.

T.D. 8476, 6/14/93.

Proposed § 1.147(f)-1 Public approval of private activity bonds. [*For Preamble, see ¶ 153,057*]

(a) In general. Interest on a private activity bond is excludable from gross income under section 103(a) only if the bond meets the requirements for a qualified bond under section 141(e) and other applicable requirements under section 103. In order to be a qualified bond under section 141(e), one of the requirements that must be met is the public approval requirement under section 147(f). This section provides guidance on the public approval requirement under section 147(f). In addition, to the extent not inconsistent with this section, the Tax Reform Act of 1986 (Pub. L. 99-514), or subsequent law, § 5f.103-2 of this chapter continues to apply for purposes of the public approval requirement under section 147(f).

(b) Scope, content, process, and timing for public approvals. *(1) In general.* This paragraph (b) provides guidance on the scope, content, process, and timing required for public approval of an issue of private activity bonds under section 147(f). In general, except as otherwise provided in this section, to meet the public approval requirement under section 147(f) for an issue (as defined in § 1.150-1) of private activity bonds, reasonable public notice (as defined in paragraph (c)(3) of this section) must be given in advance for a public hearing (as defined in paragraph (c)(2) of this section), a public hearing must be held, and the applicable governmental units under section 147(f)(2)(A) must provide public approval within the time set forth in paragraph (b)(8) of this section and in the manner set forth in section 147(f)(2)(B).

(2) General rule on information required for a reasonable public notice and public approval. Except as otherwise provided in this section, a facility (as defined in paragraph (c) of this section) to be financed with an issue is within the scope of a public approval under section 147(f) if the reasonable public notice of the public hearing and the public approval include the information set forth in paragraphs (b)(2)(i) through (iv) of this section.

(i) The facility. The information includes a general functional description of the type and use of the facility to be financed with the issue. For this purpose, a facility description generally is sufficient if it identifies the facility by reference to a particular category of exempt facility bond to be issued (for example, an exempt facility bond for an airport under section 142(a)(1) or an enterprise zone facility bond under section 1394(a)), or if not an exempt facility bond, by reference to another general category of private activity bond, together with accompanying information on the type and use of the facility to be financed with the issue (for example, a qualified small issue bond under section 144(b) for a manufacturing facility, a qualified 501(c)(3) bond under section 145 for a hospital facility and working capital expenditures, or a qualified mortgage bond for qualified mortgage loans for single-family housing residences under section 143).

(ii) The maximum stated principal amount of bonds. The information includes the maximum stated principal amount of the issue of private activity bonds to be issued to finance the facility.

(iii) The name of the initial owner or principal user of the facility. The information includes the name of the expected initial owner or principal user (as defined under section 144(a)) of the facility. The name provided may be either the name of the legal owner or principal user of the facility or, alternatively, the name of the true beneficial party of interest for such legal owner or user (for example, the name of a 501(c)(3) organization which is the sole member of a limited liability company owner).

(iv) The location of the facility. The information includes a general description of the prospective location of the facility by street address, reference to boundary streets or other geographic boundaries, or other description of the specific geographic location that is reasonably designed to inform readers of the location. For a facility involving multiple capital projects located on the same site, or on adjacent or reasonably proximate sites with similar uses, a consolidated description of the location of those capital projects may provide a sufficient description of the location of the facility. For example, a facility for a 501(c)(3) educational entity involving multiple buildings on the entity's main urban college campus may describe the location of the facility by reference to the outside street boundaries of that campus with a reference to any noncontiguous features of that campus.

(3) Special rule for mortgage revenue bonds. Mortgage revenue bonds under section 143 are treated as within the scope of a public approval under paragraph (b)(2) of this section if the reasonable public notice of the public hearing and the public approval state that the bonds are to be issued under section 143, the maximum stated principal amount of mortgage revenue bonds expected to be issued, and a general description of the geographic jurisdiction in which the residences to be financed with the proceeds of the mortgage revenue bonds are expected to be located, recognizing the issuer jurisdictional limitations on such financing under section 143(c)(1)(B) (for example, residences located throughout a state for an issuer with a statewide jurisdiction or residences within a particular local geographic jurisdiction, such as within a city or county, for a local issuer). In applying paragraph (b)(2) of this section to mortgage revenue bonds, no information is required on specific names of mortgage loan borrowers or specific locations of individual residences to be financed.

(4) Special rule for qualified student loan bonds. Qualified student loan bonds under section 144(b) are treated as within the scope of a public approval under paragraph (b)(2) of this section if the reasonable public notice of the public hearing and the public approval state that the bonds will be issued under section 144(b), the maximum stated principal amount of qualified student loan bonds expected to be issued for qualified student loans, and a general description of the type of student loan program that the loans are to be made under (for example, a Federally-guaranteed student loan program under the Higher Education Act of 1965 or a state supplemental student loan program). In applying paragraph (b)(2) of this section to qualified student loan bonds, and recognizing that these bonds do not finance facilities, no information is required with respect to names of specific student loan borrowers or locations of facilities.

(5) Special rule for certain qualified 501(c)(3) bonds. Qualified 501(c)(3) bonds under section 145 to be used to finance loans described in section 147(b)(4)(B) (without regard to any election under section 147(b)(4)(A)) are treated as within the scope of a public approval under paragraph (b)(2) of this section if both of the following requirements are met—

(i) Pre-issuance general public approval. Within the time period defined in paragraph (b)(8) of this section, public approval is obtained after reasonable public notice of a public hearing is provided and a public hearing is held. For this purpose, a facility is treated as described in a public notice of a public hearing and public approval if the notice and public approval provide that the bonds will be qualified 501(c)(3) bonds to be used to finance loans described in section 147(b)(4)(B), the maximum stated principal amount of bonds expected to be issued to finance loans to other 501(c)(3) organizations or governmental units as described in section 147(b)(4)(B), a general description of the type of facility to be financed with such loans (for example, loans for hospital facilities or college facilities), and a statement that an additional public approval that includes specific project information will be obtained before any such loans are originated; and

(ii) Post-issuance public approval for specific loans. Before a loan described in section 147(b)(4)(B) is originated, a supplemental public approval for the bonds to be used to finance that loan is obtained, and that supplemental public approval meets all the requirements of section 147(f) and this section applied by treating the bonds to be used to finance such loan as if they were reissued for purpose of section 147(f) (applied without regard to this paragraph (b)(5)).

(6) Deviations in public approval information. (i) In general. Except as otherwise provided in this paragraph (b)(6), a substantial deviation between the information required to be provided in a public notice of public hearing and public approval under paragraph (b)(2) of this section and actual information causes that issue to fail to meet the public approval requirement under section 147(f). Conversely, insubstantial deviations between information required to be provided in a notice of public hearing and public approval and actual information do not cause a failure to meet section 147(f). In general, for purposes of this paragraph (b)(6), the determination of whether a deviation is substantial is based on all the facts and circumstances. However, a change in the fundamental nature or type of a project is a substantial deviation.

(ii) Certain insubstantial deviations in public approval information. For purposes of this paragraph (b)(6), the following deviations are treated as insubstantial deviations:

(A) Use of proceeds. A deviation between the amount of proceeds of the issue that the notice of public hearing and public approval stated would be used for a facility and the amount of proceeds actually used for that facility is insubstantial if the amount of the difference does not exceed an amount equal to five percent (5%) of the net proceeds (as defined in section 150(a)(3)) of the issue.

(B) Initial owner or principal user. A deviation between the initial owner or principal user of the facility named in a notice of public hearing and public approval and the actual initial owner or principal user of the facility is treated as insubstantial if such parties are related parties (as defined in § 1.150-1) on the issue date of the issue.

(iii) Special rule to address certain substantial deviations in public approval information. A substantial deviation between the information required to be conveyed in the notice of public hearing and the public approval under paragraph (b)(2) and the actual information does not cause that issue to fail to meet the public approval requirement under section 147(f) if the following requirements are met:

(A) Original public approval and reasonable expectations. The issuer obtained a timely public approval (as set forth in paragraph (b)(8) of this section) for the issue in accordance with section 147(f) and, on the issue date of the issue, the issuer reasonably expected there would be no substantial deviations between the information required to be conveyed in the notice of public hearing and public approval and actual information.

(B) Unexpected events or unforeseen changes in circumstances. As a result of unexpected events or unforeseen changes in circumstances that arise after the issue date of the issue, the issuer determines that it cannot use some or all of the proceeds in the manner provided in the public approval either because such use is no longer feasible or viable, or because the cost of the facility was less than expected so the issuer did not need all of the proceeds specified in the public approval for the facility.

(C) Supplemental public approval. Before using the proceeds of the bonds that are affected by the substantial deviation for a different use, the issuer obtains a supplemental public approval for those bonds, and that supplemental public approval meets all the requirements of section 147(f) applied by treating those bonds as if they were reissued for purpose of section 147(f).

(7) Certain timing requirements. Except as otherwise provided in this section, a public approval of an issue under section 147(f) is timely only if the issuer obtains the public approval within one year before the issue date (as defined in section 1.150-1) of the issue. For a plan of financing described in section 147(f)(2)(C), public approval is timely for the plan of financing if the issuer obtains public approval for the plan of financing within one year before the issue date of the first issue issued under the plan of financing and the issuer issues all issues under the plan of financing within three years after the issue date of such first issue.

(c) Definitions. Unless otherwise stated, for purposes of this section, the following definitions apply:

(1) Facility. In general, for purposes of this section and section 5f.103-2, the term facility means one or more capital projects, including land, buildings, equipment, and other property to be financed with an issue that is located on the same site, or adjacent or proximate sites used for similar purposes, and that is subject to the public approval requirement under section 147(f). For an issue of mortgage revenue bonds under section 143 or qualified student loan bonds under section 144(b), the term facility means the mortgage loans or qualified student loans to be financed with the proceeds of the issue. For an issue of qualified 501(c)(3) bonds under section 145, the term facility means a facility, as defined in the first sentence of this paragraph (c)(1), and also includes working capital expenditures to be financed with proceeds of the issue.

(2) Public hearing. The term public hearing means a forum providing a reasonable opportunity for interested individuals to express their views, both orally and in writing, on the proposed issue of bonds and the location and nature of the proposed facility to be financed. In general, a governmental unit may select its own procedure for a public hearing, provided that interested individuals have a reasonable opportunity to express their views. Thus, a governmental unit may impose reasonable requirements on persons who wish to participate in the hearing, such as a requirement that persons desiring to speak at the hearing make a written request to speak at least 24 hours before the hearing or that they limit their oral remarks to a prescribed time. If a governmental unit provides reasonable public notice for a public hearing and receives no timely requests to participate in the hearing, then the governmental unit may cancel the hearing and, for purposes of this section, the public hearing requirement will be treated as met. For purposes of this public hearing requirement, it is unnecessary, for example, to have the applicable elected representative of the approving governmental unit present at the hearing, to submit a report on the hearing to that applicable elected representative, or to meet State administrative procedural requirements for public hearings. Except to the extent in conflict with a specific requirement of this paragraph (c)(2), compliance with State procedural requirements for public hearings generally satisfies the requirements of this paragraph (c)(2). A public hearing may be conducted by an individual appointed or employed to perform such function by the governmental unit or its agencies, or by the issuer. Thus, for example, for bonds to be issued by an authority that acts on behalf of a county, the hearing may be conducted by the authority, the county, or an appointee of either.

(3) Reasonable public notice. Reasonable public notice means notice that is reasonably designed to inform residents of the affected governmental units, including residents of the issuing governmental unit and the governmental unit where a facility is to be located, of the proposed issue. The notice must state the time and place for the public hearing and contain the information required under paragraph (b) of this section. Notice is presumed reasonable if given no fewer than seven (7) business days before the public hearing in one of the ways permitted by this paragraph (c)(2). Notice is treated as reasonably designed to inform affected residents of an approving governmental unit if it is given in one of the following ways:

(i) Newspaper publication. Public notice may be given by publication in one or more newspapers of general circulation available to the residents of the governmental unit.

(ii) Radio or television broadcast. Public notice may be given by radio or television broadcast to the residents of the governmental unit.

(iii) Governmental unit Web site posting. Public notice may be given by electronic posting on the approving governmental unit's Web site for its residents, provided that the governmental unit regularly uses that Web site to inform its residents about events affecting the residents (including notice of public meetings of the governmental unit) and the governmental unit offers a reasonable, publicly known alternative method for obtaining this information for residents without access to computers (such as phone recordings).

(iv) Alternative State law public notice procedures. Public notice may be given in a way that is permitted under a general State law for public notices for public hearings for the approving governmental unit.

(4) Writing. Unless specifically stated otherwise in this section, if permitted by the governmental unit, the term writing includes electronic communication.

(5) Mortgage revenue bonds. The term mortgage revenue bonds means qualified mortgage bonds under section 143(a) of the Code or qualified veterans' mortgage bonds under section 143(b) of the Code.

(d) Special rule on required governmental unit approvals for certain types of financings. In applying section 147(f)(2) and § 5f.103-2(c) of this chapter to mortgage revenue bonds under section 143, to qualified student loan bonds under section 144(b), and to the portion of an issue of qualified 501(c)(3) bonds under section 145 that finance working capital expenditures, the governmental unit by or on behalf of which those types of bonds are issued is treated as the only governmental unit required to provide a public approval and no separate public approval is required by a host governmental unit with respect to the location, if any, of a financed facility.

(e) Effective/applicability date. Except as otherwise provided in this section, § 1.147(f)-1 applies to bonds that are sold on or after the date of publication of final regulations in the Federal Register and that are subject to section 147(f).

§ 13.4 Arbitrage bonds; temporary rules.

• ***Caution:*** Reg. § 13.4, following, was issued under Code section 103 before the related provisions of that Code section were deleted by P.L. 99-514 (10/22/86). Provisions similar to, but not necessarily identical to, the provisions deleted from Code section 103 now appear in Code section 148.

(a) In general. *(1) Arbitrage bonds.* Section 103(d)(1) provides that any arbitrage bond (as such term is defined in section 103(d)(2)) shall be treated as an obligation not described in section 103(a)(1). Thus, the interest on an obligation which would have been excluded from gross income pursuant to the provisions of section 103(a)(1) will be included in gross income and subject to Federal income taxation if such obligation is an arbitrage bond. Under section 103(d)(2), an obligation is an arbitrage bond if it is issued by a governmental unit as part of an issue of obligations (for purposes of this section referred to as "governmental obligations") all of a major portion of the proceeds of which are (i) reasonably expected to be used directly or indirectly to acquire certain obligations or securities (for purposes of this section referred to as "acquired obligations") which may reasonably be expected, at the time of issuance of such governmental obligations, to produce a yield over the term of the issue of such governmental obligations which is materially higher (taking into account any discount or premium) than the yield on such issue, or (ii) reasonably expected to be used to replace funds which were used directly or indirectly to acquire such acquired obligations. For rules as to industrial development bonds, see section 103(c).

(2) Definitions. (i) For purposes of this section, the term "governmental unit" means a State, the District of Columbia, a Territory, or a possession of the United States, or any political subdivision of any of the foregoing.

(ii) For purposes of this section, the term "securities" has the same meaning as in section 165(g)(2)(A) and (B).

(3) Materially higher. For purposes of this section, the yield produced by acquired obligations is not "materially higher" than the yield produced by an issue of governmental obligations if it is reasonably expected, at the time of issue of such governmental obligations, that the adjusted yield (computed in accordance with subparagraphs (4) and (5) of this paragraph) to be produced by the acquired obligations will not exceed the adjusted yield (computed in accordance with subparagraphs (4) and (5) of this paragraph) to be produced by the issue of governmental obligations by more than one-eighth of 1 percentage point. In the case of an issue of governmental obligations issued on or before July 1, 1972, the percentage specified in the preceding sentence shall be one-half of 1 percentage point.

(4) Yield. (i) For purposes of this section, "yield" shall be computed using the "interest cost per annum" method in accordance with subdivision (ii) or (iii) of this subparagraph (as the case may be) or any other method satisfactory to the Commissioner which is consistent with generally accepted principles of computing yield. In the case of acquired obligations, the yield to be produced by such obligations shall be computed as if all acquired obligations comprised a single issue of obligations. Thus, for example, if the governmental unit acquires two blocks of Federal obligations, with different interest rates and maturity periods for each block, the yield on such acquired obligations shall be computed as if one issue of obligations with different interest rates and maturity periods had been acquired. The maturity period of each acquired obligation shall be the period that the governmental unit reasonably expects to hold such obligation.

(ii) If all the governmental or acquired obligations of an issue have a single interest rate (expressed in dollars per $1,000 for face amount of bonds), yield shall be computed using the following 4 steps:

(a) Step (1). Compute the total number of bond years for the issue by multiplying the number of bonds (treating each $1,000 of face value as one bond for purposes of this computation) of each maturity by the length of the maturity period (expressed in years and fractions thereof) and then adding together the amount determined for each maturity period.

(b) Step (2). Compute the total interest payable on the issue by multiplying the total number of bond years (as computed in step (1)) by the amount payable, expressed in dollars, as interest on each $1,000 of bonds for 1 year.

(c) Step (3). Compute the net interest in dollars for the issue by adding the amount, in dollars, of any discount to, or by subtracting the amount, in dollars, of any premium from, the total interest payable on the issue.

(d) Step (4). Compute yield by dividing the net interest by the product obtained by multiplying the total number of bond years for the issue by 10.

(iii) If governmental or acquired obligations of an issue have different interest rates (expressed in dollars per $1,000 of face amount of bonds), yield shall be computed using the following 4 steps:

(a) Step (1). Compute the total number of bond years for each group of bonds bearing the same interest rate (treating each $1,000 of face value as one bond for purposes of this computation) in the manner described in step 1 of subdivision (ii) of this subparagraph.

(b) Step (2). Compute the total interest payable on the issue by multiplying the total number of bond years for each group of bonds bearing the same interest rate (as computed in step (1)) by the amount payable, expressed in dollars, as interest on each $1,000 of bonds for 1 year, and then adding together the amounts determined for each group.

(c) Step (3). Compute net interest in the manner described in step (3) of subdivision (ii) of this subparagraph.

(d) Step (4). Compute the yield produced by the issue in the manner described in step (4) of subdivision (ii) of this subparagraph.

(iv) For purposes of this section, the same method of computing yield shall be used to compute the yield to be produced by an issue of governmental obligations and to compute the yield to be produced by acquired obligations acquired with the proceeds of such issue of governmental obligations.

(v) The following example illustrates the provisions of this subparagraph:

Example. Assume an issue of $200,000 ($1,000 per bond) with a stated interest (expressed in dollars per bond) of $50 on bonds maturing in 1, 2, or 3 years, a stated interest of $60 on bonds maturing in 4, 5, 6, or 7 years and a stated interest of $70 on bonds maturing in 8, 9, or 10 years. Assume also that a price of $101 has been bid for the issue. The yield on the issue is determined in accordance with the table below:

	Amount	Rate	Years to maturity	Bond years	Total bond years at interest rate	×	Interest rate	=	Interest cost
	$10,000	$50	1	10					
	5,000	50	2	10					
	25,000	50	3	75					
					95		$50		$ 4,750
	10,000	60	4	40					
	10,000	60	5	50					
	30,000	60	6	180					
	50,000	60	7	350					
					620		60		37,200
	20,000	70	8	160					
	25,000	70	9	225					
	15,000	70	10	150					
					535		70		37,450
Totals	200,000				1,250				79,400
Less premium									2,000
Net interest cost									$77,400
Divide by: Product of total bond years (1,250), multiplied by 10)									12,500
Yield (Percent)									6,192

(5) Adjusted yield. (i) For purposes of this section, "adjusted yield" shall be computed in accordance with subparagraph (4) of this paragraph, except that in the case of—

(a) Acquired obligations, an amount equal to the sum of the administrative costs reasonably expected to be incurred in purchasing, carrying, and selling or redeeming such obligations shall be treated as a premium on the purchase price of such acquired obligations.

(b) An issue of governmental obligations, an amount equal to the sum of the reasonably expected administrative costs of issuing, carrying, and repaying such issue of obligations shall be treated as a discount on the selling price of such issue of governmental obligation.

(ii) The provisions of subdivision (i) of this subparagraph may be illustrated by the following examples:

Example (1). State Z issues $15 million of obligations all of which will mature in 10 years. The obligations are sold at $1,000 each (par) to yield 6 percent interest. The adjusted yield produced by such issue of obligations will be determined as follows, assuming the following administrative expenses of issuing, carrying, and repaying such issue of obligations are reasonably expected:

Issuing costs:		
Printing	$12,500	
Financial advisors	25,000	
Counsel fees	12,500	
Total		$50,000
Carrying costs, paying agent and trustees fees		10,000
Repaying costs, paying agent		3,000
Total administrative costs		63,000

Bond years (15,000 × 10 years)	150,000
Interest cost per $1,000 bond per year	60
Total interest cost	9,000,000
Discount or premium	0
Plus adjustments	63,000
Net interest cost	9,063,000
Divide by product of bond years (150,000) multiplied by 10	1,500,000
Adjusted yield	6.042%

Example (2). State Z uses the net proceeds of the issue of obligations described in Example (1) to acquire $114,922,000 of students' notes at par of $1,000 each under a student loan program. The students' notes will all mature in 10 years, and all have a stated interest of 7½ percent. Expenses of the program include printing of forms ($5,000), financial advisors' fees ($11,000), counsel fees ($12,000), trustees' fees ($5,000), fees for the collecting agents and various banks which administer the loans ($100,000), advertising expenses ($10,000), credit reference checks ($20,000), and general office overhead ($5,000). Of the expenses listed in the preceding sentence, only those indicated on the following table constitute adjustments to yield in order to determine the adjusted yield to be produced by the students' notes:

Purchasing costs:		
Printing forms	$ 5,000	
Financial advisors	11,000	
Counsel fees	12,000	
Total		$28,000
Carrying costs, Trustees fees		5,000

Total administrative costs	33,000
Bond years (14,922 × 10 years)	149,220
Interest receivable per $1,000 note per year	75
Total interest receivable	11,191,500
Discount or premium	0
Minus adjustments	33,000
Net interest receivable	11,158,500
Divide by product of bond years (149,220) multiplied by 10	1,492,200
Adjusted yield	7.478%

(b) Rule with respect to certain governmental programs. *(1) General rule.* Subject to the limitations of subparagraph (3) of this paragraph, any obligations which are part of an issue of governmental obligations the proceeds of which are reasonably expected to be used to finance certain governmental programs (described in subparagraph (2) of this paragraph) are not arbitrage obligations.

(2) Governmental programs. A governmental program is described in this subparagraph if—

(i) The program involves the acquisition of acquired purpose obligations to carry out the purposes of such program (which obligations, for purposes of this paragraph, are referred to as "acquired program obligations");

(ii) At least 90 percent of all such acquired program obligations, by amount of cost outstanding, are evidences of loans to a substantial number of persons representing the general public, loans to exempt persons within the meaning of section 103(c)(3), or loans to provide housing and related facilities, or any combination of the foregoing;

(iii) At least 90 percent of all of the amounts received by the governmental unit with respect to acquired program obligations shall be used for one or more of the following purposes: To pay the principal or interest or otherwise to service the debt on governmental obligations relating to the governmental program; to reimburse the governmental unit, or to pay, for administrative costs of issuing such governmental obligations; to reimburse the governmental unit, or to pay, for administrative and other costs and anticipated future losses directly related to the program financed by such governmental obligations; to make additional loans for the same general purposes specified in such program; or to redeem and retire governmental obligations at the next earliest possible date of redemption; and

(iv) Requires that any person (or any related person, as defined in section 103(c)(6)(C)) from whom the governmental unit may, under the program, acquire acquired program obligations shall not, pursuant to an arrangement, formal or informal, purchase the governmental obligations in an amount related to the amount of the acquired program obligations to be acquired from such person by the governmental unit.

(3) Limitations. The provisions of subparagraph (1) of this paragraph shall apply only if it is reasonably expected that—

(i) A major portion of the proceeds of such issue of governmental obligations, including proceeds represented by repayments of principal and interest received by the governmental unit with respect to acquired program obligations, shall not be invested for more than a temporary period (within the meaning of section 103(d)(4)(A)), in acquired obligations (other than acquired program obligations) which produce a materially higher yield than the yield produced over the term of the issue by such governmental obligations, and

(ii) (a) The adjusted yield (computed in accordance with paragraph (a)(4) and (5) of this section) to be produced by acquired program obligations shall not exceed the adjusted yield (computed in accordance with paragraph (a)(4) and (5) of this section) to be produced by such issue of governmental obligations by more than 1½ percentage points, or

(b) Where the difference in the adjusted yields described in subdivision (ii)(a) of this subparagraph is expected to exceed 1½ percentage points, the amounts to be obtained as a result of the difference in such adjusted yields shall not exceed the amount necessary to pay expenses (including losses resulting from bad debts) reasonably expected to be incurred as a direct result of administering the program to be financed with the proceeds of such issue of governmental obligations, to the extent that such amounts are not payable with funds appropriated from other sources.

(4) Examples. The following examples illustrate governmental programs described in subparagraph (2) of this paragraph:

Example (1). State A issues obligations the proceeds of which are to be used to purchase certain home mortgage notes from commercial banks. The purpose of the governmental program is to encourage the construction of low income residential housing by creating a secondary market for mortgage notes and thereby increasing the availability of mortgage money for low income housing. The legislation provides that the adjusted yield produced by the mortgage notes to be acquired will not exceed the adjusted yield produced by such issue of obligations by more than 1½ percentage points. Amounts received as interest and principal payments on the mortgage notes are to be used for one or more of the following purposes: (1) To service the debt on the governmental obligations, (2) to retire such obligations at their earliest possible date of redemption, (3) to purchase additional mortgage notes. The governmental program is one which is described in subparagraph (2) of this paragraph and the governmental obligations are not arbitrage bonds.

Example (2). State B issues obligations the proceeds of which are to be used to make loans directly to students and to purchase from commercial banks promissory notes made by students as the result of loans made to them by such banks. The legislation authorizing the student loan program provides that the purpose of the program is to enable financially disadvantaged students to continue their studies. The legislation also provides that purchases will be made from banks only where such banks agree that an amount at least equal to the purchase price will be devoted to new or additional student loans. It is reasonably expected that the difference in adjusted yields between the issue of governmental obligations by State B and the students' notes will be 1¾ percentage points. It is also reasonably expected that the amount necessary to pay the expenses (other than expenses taken into account in computing adjusted yield) enumerated in subparagraph (3)(ii)(b) of this paragraph, directly incurred as a result of administering State B's student loan program, such as, for example, losses resulting from bad debts, insurance costs, bookkeeping expenses, advertising expenses, credit reference checks, appraisals, title searches, general office overhead, service fees for collecting agents and various banks which administer the loans, and salaries of employees not paid from other sources, will not require a difference in adjusted yields in excess of 1½ percentage points. The governmental program is one which is described in subparagraph (2) of this paragraph. Since, however, the difference in adjusted yields produced by the students' notes and the issue of State B obligations is reasonably expected to exceed 1½ percentage points, and since State B cannot show that 1¾ percentage points is necessary to cover such expenses, the provisions of subparagraph (1) of this paragraph shall not apply to the issue of State B obligations. If, however, State B reasonably expected that 1¾ percentage points would be necessary to cover such expenses, the provisions of subparagraph (1) of this paragraph would apply and the governmental obligations would not be arbitrage bonds.

Example (3). Authority C issues obligations the proceeds of which are to be used to purchase land to be sold to veterans. The governmental unit will receive purchase-money mortgage notes secured by mortgages on the land from the veterans in return for such land. The purpose of the program is to enable veterans to acquire land at reduced cost. The adjusted yield produced by the mortgage notes is not reasonably expected to exceed the adjusted yield produced by the issue of obligations issued by Authority C by more than 1½ percentage points. Amounts received as interest and principal payments on the mortgage notes are to be used for one or more of the following purposes: (1) To pay the administrative costs directly related to the program, (2) to service the debt on the governmental obligations, (3) to retire such governmental obligations at their earliest possible call date, (4) to purchase additional land to be sold to veterans. The governmental program is one which is described in subparagraph (2) of this paragraph and the governmental obligations are not arbitrage bonds.

(c) Effective date. The provisions of this section will apply with respect to obligations issued after October 9, 1969, and before final regulations are promulgated.

Because of the need for immediate guidance with respect to the provisions contained in this Treasury decision, it is found impracticable to issue it with notice and public procedure thereon under subsection (b) of section 553 of title 5 of the United States Code or subject to the effective date limitation of subsection (d) of that section.

T.D. 7072, 11/12/70, amend T.D. 7174, 5/26/72, T.D. 7273, 4/27/73.

---

§ 1.148-0 Scope and table of contents.

(a) Overview. Under section 103(a), interest on certain obligations issued by States and local governments is excludable from the gross income of the owners. Section 148 was enacted to minimize the arbitrage benefits from investing gross proceeds of tax-exempt bonds in higher yielding investments and to remove the arbitrage incentives to issue more bonds, to issue bonds earlier, or to leave bonds outstanding longer than is otherwise reasonably necessary to accomplish the governmental purposes for which the bonds were issued. To accomplish these purposes, section 148 restricts the direct and indirect investment of bond proceeds in higher yielding investments and requires that certain earnings on higher yielding investments be rebated to the United States. Violation of these provisions causes the bonds in the issue to become arbitrage bonds, the interest on which is not excludable from the gross income of the owners under section 103(a). The regulations in §§ 1.148-1 through 1.148-11 apply in a manner consistent with these purposes.

(b) Scope. Sections 1.148-1 through 1.148-11 apply generally for purposes of the arbitrage restrictions on State and local bonds under section 148.

(c) Table of contents. This paragraph (c) lists the table of contents for §§ 1.148-1, 1.148-2, 1.148-3, 1.148-4, 1.148-5, 1.148-6, 1.148-7, 1.148-8, 1.148-9. 1.148-10 and 1.148-11.

§ 1.148-1 Definitions and elections.

(a) In general.

(b) Certain definitions.

(c) Definition of replacement proceeds.

(1) In general.

(2) Sinking fund.

(3) Pledged fund.

(4) Other replacement proceeds.

(d) Elections.

(e) Investment-type property.

(1) In general.

(2) Prepayments.

(3) Certain hedges.

§ 1.148-2 General arbitrage yield restriction rules.

(a) In general.

(b) Reasonable expectations.

(1) In general.

(2) Certification of expectations.

(c) Intentional acts.

(d) Materially higher yielding investments.

(1) In general.

(2) Definitions of materially higher yield.

(3) Mortgage loans.

(e) Temporary periods.

(1) In general.

(2) General 3-year temporary period for capital projects and qualified mortgage loans.

(3) Temporary period for restricted working capital expenditures.

(4) Temporary period for pooled financings.

(5) Temporary period for replacement proceeds.

(6) Temporary period for investment proceeds.

(7) Other amounts.

(f) Reserve or replacement funds.

(1) General 10 percent limitation on funding with sale proceeds.

(2) Exception from yield restriction for reasonably required reserve or replacement funds.

(3) Certain parity reserve funds.

(g) Minor portion.

(h) Certain waivers permitted.

§ 1.148-3 General arbitrage rebate rules.

(a) In general.

(b) Definition of rebate amount.

(c) Computation of future value of a payment or receipt.

(d) Payments and receipts.

(1) Definition of payments.

(2) Definition of receipts.

(3) Special rules for commingled funds.

(e) Computation dates.

(1) In general.

(2) Final computation date.

(f) Amount of required rebate installment payment.
(1) Amount of interim rebate payments.
(2) Amount of final rebate payment.
(3) Future value of rebate payments.
(g) Time and manner of payment.
(h) Penalty in lieu of loss of tax exemption.
(1) In general.
(2) Interest on underpayments.
(3) Waivers of the penalty.
(4) Application to alternative penalty under § 1.148-7.
(i) Recovery of overpayment of rebate.
(1) In general.
(2) Limitations on recovery.
(j) Examples.
(k) Bona fide debt service fund exception.

§ 1.148-4 Yield on an issue of bonds.

(a) In general.
(b) Computing yield on a fixed yield issue.
(1) In general.
(2) Yield on certain fixed yield bonds subject to mandatory or contingent early redemption.
(3) Yield on certain fixed yield bonds subject to optional early redemption.
(4) Yield recomputed upon transfer of certain rights associated with the bond.
(5) Special aggregation rule treating certain bonds as a single fixed yield bond.
(6) Examples.
(c) Computing yield on a variable yield issue.
(1) In general.
(2) Payments on bonds included in yield for a computation period.
(3) Example.
(d) Conversion from variable yield issue to fixed yield issue.
(e) Value of bonds.
(1) Plain par bonds.
(2) Other bonds.
(f) Qualified guarantees.
(1) In general.
(2) Interest savings.
(3) Guarantee in substance.
(4) Reasonable charge.
(5) Guarantee of purpose investments.
(6) Allocation of qualified guarantee payments.
(7) Refund or reduction of guarantee payments.
(g) Yield on certain mortgage revenue and student loan bonds.
(h) Qualified hedging transactions.
(1) In general.
(2) Qualified hedge defined.
(3) Accounting for qualified hedges.
(4) Certain variable yield bonds treated as fixed yield bonds.
(5) Contracts entered into before issue date of hedged bond.
(6) Authority of the Commissioner.

§ 1.148-5 Yield and valuation of investments.

(a) In general.
(b) Yield on an investment.
(1) In general.
(2) Yield on a separate class of investments.
(3) Investments to be held beyond issue's maturity or beyond temporary period.
(4) Consistent redemption assumptions on purpose investments.
(5) Student loan special allowance payments included in yield.
(c) Yield reduction payments to the United States.
(1) In general.
(2) Manner of payment.
(3) Applicability of special yield reduction rule.
(d) Value of investments.
(1) In general.
(2) Mandatory valuation of yield restricted investments at present value.
(3) Mandatory valuation of certain investments at fair market value.
(4) Special transition rule for transferred proceeds.
(5) Definition of present value of an investment.
(6) Definition of fair market value.
(e) Administrative costs of investments.
(1) In general.
(2) Qualified administrative costs on nonpurpose investments.
(3) Qualified administrative costs on purpose investments.

§ 1.148-6 General allocation and accounting rules.

(a) In general.
(1) Reasonable accounting methods required.
(2) Bona fide deviations from accounting method.
(b) Allocation of gross proceeds to an issue.
(1) One-issue rule and general ordering rules.
(2) Universal cap on value of nonpurpose investments allocated to an issue.
(c) Fair market value limit on allocations to nonpurpose investments.
(d) Allocation of gross proceeds to expenditures.
(1) Expenditures in general.
(2) Treatment of gross proceeds invested in purpose investments.
(3) Expenditures for working capital purposes.
(4) Expenditures for grants.
(5) Expenditures for reimbursement purposes.
(6) Expenditures of certain commingled investment proceeds of governmental issues.
(7) Payments to related parties.
(e) Special rules for commingled funds.
(1) In general.
(2) Investments held by a commingled fund.
(3) Certain expenditures involving a commingled fund.
(4) Fiscal periods.

(5) Unrealized gains and losses on investments of a commingled fund.

(6) Allocations of commingled funds serving as common reserve funds or sinking funds.

§ 1.148-7 Spending exceptions to the rebate requirement.

(a) Scope of section.

(1) In general.

(2) Relationship of spending exceptions.

(3) Spending exceptions not mandatory.

(b) Rules applicable for all spending exceptions.

(1) Special transferred proceeds rules.

(2) Application of multipurpose issue rules.

(3) Expenditures for governmental purposes of the issue.

(4) De minimis rule.

(5) Special definition of reasonably required reserve or replacement fund.

(6) Pooled financing issue.

(c) 6-month exception.

(1) General rule.

(2) Additional period for certain bonds.

(3) Amounts not included in gross proceeds.

(4) Series of refundings.

(d) 18-month exception.

(1) General rule.

(2) Extension for reasonable retainage.

(3) Gross proceeds.

(4) Application to multipurpose issues.

(e) 2-year exception.

(1) General rule.

(2) Extension for reasonable retainage.

(3) Definitions.

(f) Construction issue.

(1) Definition.

(2) Use of actual facts.

(3) Ownership requirement.

(g) Construction expenditures.

(1) Definition.

(2) Certain acquisitions under turnkey contracts treated as construction expenditures.

(3) Constructed personal property.

(4) Specially developed computer software.

(5) Examples.

(h) Reasonable retainage definition.

(i) Available construction proceeds.

(1) Definition in general.

(2) Earnings on a reasonably required reserve or replacement fund.

(3) Reasonable expectations test for future earnings.

(4) Issuance costs.

(5) One and one-half percent penalty in lieu of arbitrage rebate.

(6) Payments on purpose investments and repayments of grants.

(7) Examples.

(j) Election to treat portion of issue used for construction as separate issue.

(1) In general.

(2) Example.

(k) One and one-half percent penalty in lieu of arbitrage rebate.

(1) In general.

(2) Application to reasonable retainage.

(3) Coordination with rebate requirement.

(l) Termination of 1 section percent penalty.

(1) Termination after initial temporary period.

(2) Termination before end of initial temporary period.

(3) Application to reasonable retainage.

(4) Example.

(m) Payment of penalties.

§ 1.148-8 Small issuer exception to rebate requirement.

(a) Scope.

(b) General taxing powers.

(c) Size limitation.

(1) In general.

(2) Aggregation rules.

(3) Certain refunding bonds not taken into account.

(d) Pooled financings.

(1) Treatment of pool issuer.

(2) Treatment of conduit borrowers.

(e) Refunding issues.

(1) In general.

(2) Multipurpose issues.

§ 1.148-9 Arbitrage rules for refunding issues.

(a) Scope of application.

(b) Transferred proceeds allocation rule.

(1) In general.

(2) Special definition of principal amount.

(3) Relation of transferred proceeds rule to universal cap rule.

(4) Limitation on multi-generational transfers.

(c) Special allocation rules for refunding issues.

(1) Allocations of investments.

(2) Allocations of mixed escrows to expenditures for principal, interest, and redemption prices on a prior issue.

(d) Temporary periods in refundings.

(1) In general.

(2) Types of temporary periods in refundings.

(e) Reasonably required reserve or replacement funds in refundings.

(f) Minor portions in refundings.

(g) Certain waivers permitted.

(h) Multipurpose issue allocations.

(1) Application of multipurpose issue allocation rules.

(2) Rules on allocations of multipurpose issues.

(3) Separate purposes of a multipurpose issue.

(4) Allocations of bonds of a multipurpose issue.

(5) Limitation on multi-generation allocations.

(i) Operating rules for separation of prior issues into refunded and unrefunded portions.

(1) In general.

(2) Allocations of proceeds and investments in a partial refunding.

(3) (3) References to prior issue.

§ 1.148-10 Anti-abuse rules and authority of commissioner.

(a) Abusive arbitrage device.

(1) In general.

(2) Abusive arbitrage device defined.

(3) Exploitation of tax-exempt interest rates.

(4) Overburdening the tax-exempt market.

(b) Consequences of overburdening the tax-exempt bond market.

(1) In general.

(2) Application.

(c) Anti-abuse rules on excess gross proceeds of advance refunding issues.

(1) In general.

(2) Definition of excess gross proceeds.

(3) Special treatment of transferred proceeds.

(4) Special rule for crossover refundings.

(5) Special rule for gross refundings.

(d) Examples.

(e) Authority of the Commissioner to clearly reflect the economic substance of a transaction.

(f) Authority of the Commissioner to require an earlier date for payment of rebate.

(g) Authority of the Commissioner to waive regulatory limitations.

§ 1.148-11 Effective dates.

(a) In general.

(b) Elective retroactive application in whole.

(1) In general.

(2) No elective retroactive application for 18-month spending exception.

(3) No elective retroactive application for hedges of fixed rate issues.

(4) No elective retroactive application for safe harbor for establishing fair market value for guaranteed investment contracts and investments purchased for a yield restricted defeasance escrow.

(c) Elective retroactive application of certain provisions.

(1) Retroactive application of overpayment recovery provisions.

(2) Certain allocations of multipurpose issues.

(3) Special limitation.

(d) Transition rule excepting certain state guarantee funds from the definition of replacement proceeds.

(1) Certain perpetual trust funds.

(2) Permanent University Fund.

(e) Transition rule regarding special allowance payments.

(f) Transition rule regarding applicability of yield reduction rule.

(g) Provisions applicable to certain bonds sold before effective date.

(h) Safe harbor for establishing fair market value for guaranteed investment contracts and investments purchased for a yield restricted defeasance escrow.

(i) Special rule for certain broker's commissions and similar fees.

(j) Certain prepayments.

T.D. 8418, 5/12/92, amend T.D. 8476, 6/14/92, T.D. 8538, 5/5/94, T.D. 8718, 5/8/97, T.D. 9085, 8/1/2003, T.D. 9097, 12/10/2003.

PAR. 2. Section 1.148-0(c) is amended as follows:

1. Add entry for new paragraph (d)(4) in the table of contents for § 1.148-3.

2. Revise entry for paragraph (d) in the table of contents for § 1.148-8.

3. Remove entries for paragraph (d)(1) and paragraph (d)(2) in the table of contents for § 1.148-8.

4. Add entries for new paragraphs (k), (k)(1), (k)(2), (k)(3) and (k)(4) in the table of contents for § 1.148-11.

The revised and added provisions read as follows:

Proposed § 1.148-0 Scope and Table of Contents. [*For Preamble, see ¶ 152,909*]

* * * * *

§ 1.148-3 General arbitrage rebate rules.

* * * * *

(d) * * *

(4) Cost-of living adjustment.

* * * * *

§ 1.148-8 Small issuer exception to rebate requirement.

* * * * *

(d) Pooled financings—treatment of conduit borrowers.

* * * * *

§ 1.148-11 Effective dates.

* * * * *

(k) Certain arbitrage guidance updates.

(1) In general.

(2) Permissive earlier application.

(3) Rebate overpayment recovery.

(4) Small issuer exception to rebate requirement for conduit borrowers of pooled financings.

* * * * *

§ 1.148-1 Definitions and elections.

Caution: The Treasury has not yet amended Reg § 1.148-1 to reflect changes made by P.L. 109-58.

(a) In general. The definitions in this section and the definitions under section 150 apply for purposes of section 148 and §§ 1.148-1 through 1.148-11.

(b) Certain definitions. The following definitions apply:

Accounting method means both the overall method used to account for gross proceeds of an issue (e.g., the cash method or a modified accrual method) and the method used to account for or allocate any particular item within that overall accounting method (e.g., accounting for investments, expenditures, allocations to and from different sources, and particular items of the foregoing).

Annuity contract means annuity contract as defined in section 72.

Available amount means available amount as defined in § 1.148-6(d)(3)(iii).

Bona fide debt service fund means a fund, which may include proceeds of an issue, that—

(1) Is used primarily to achieve a proper matching of revenues with principal and interest payments within each bond year; and

(2) Is depleted at least once each bond year, except for a reasonable carryover amount not to exceed the greater of:

the earnings on the fund for the immediately preceding bond year; or one-twelfth of the principal and interest payments on the issue for the immediately preceding bond year.

Bond year means, in reference to an issue, each 1-year period that ends on the day selected by the issuer. The first and last bond years may be short periods. If no day is selected by the issuer before the earlier of the final maturity date of the issue or the date that is 5 years after the issue date, bond years end on each anniversary of the issue date and on the final maturity date.

Capital project or capital projects means all capital expenditures, plus related working capital expenditures to which the de minimis rule under § 1.148-6(d)(3)(ii)(A) applies, that carry out the governmental purposes of an issue. For example, a capital project may include capital expenditures for one or more buildings, plus related start-up operating costs.

Commingled fund means any fund or account containing both gross proceeds of an issue and amounts in excess of $25,000 that are not gross proceeds of that issue if the amounts in the fund or account are invested and accounted for collectively, without regard to the source of funds deposited in the fund or account. An open-end regulated investment company under section 851, however, is not a commingled fund.

Computation date means each date on which the rebate amount for an issue is computed under § 1.148-3(e).

Computation period means the period between computation dates. The first computation period begins on the issue date and ends on the first computation date. Each succeeding computation period begins on the date immediately following the computation date and ends on the next computation date.

Consistently applied means applied uniformly within a fiscal period and between fiscal periods to account for gross proceeds of an issue and any amounts that are in a commingled fund.

De minimis amount means—

(1) In reference to original issue discount (as defined in section 1273(a)(1)) or premium on an obligation—

(i) An amount that does not exceed 2 percent multiplied by the stated redemption price at maturity; plus

(ii) Any original issue premium that is attributable exclusively to reasonable underwriters' compensation; and

(2) In reference to market discount (as defined in section 1278(a)(2)(A)) or premium on an obligation, an amount that does not exceed 2 percent multiplied by the stated redemption price at maturity.

Economic accrual method (also known as the constant interest method or actuarial method) means the method of computing yield that is based on the compounding of interest at the end of each compounding period.

Fair market value means fair market value as defined in § 1.148-5(d)(6).

Fixed rate investment means any investment whose yield is fixed and determinable on the issue date.

Fixed yield bond means any bond whose yield is fixed and determinable on the issue date using the assumptions and rules provided in § 1.148-4(b).

Fixed yield issue means any issue if each bond that is part of the issue is a fixed yield bond.

Gross proceeds means any proceeds and replacement proceeds of an issue.

Guaranteed investment contract includes any nonpurpose investment that has specifically negotiated withdrawal or reinvestment provisions and a specifically negotiated interest rate, and also includes any agreement to supply investments on two or more future dates (e.g., a forward supply contract).

Higher yielding investments means higher yielding investments as defined in section 148(b)(1).

Investment means any investment property as defined in sections 148(b)(2) and 148(b)(3), and any other tax-exempt bond.

Investment proceeds means any amounts actually or constructively received from investing proceeds of an issue.

Investment-type property is defined in paragraph (e) of this section.

Issue price means, except as otherwise provided, issue price as defined in sections 1273 and 1274. Generally, the issue price of bonds that are publicly offered is the first price at which a substantial amount of the bonds is sold to the public. Ten percent is a substantial amount. The public does not include bond houses, brokers, or similar persons or organizations acting in the capacity of underwriters or wholesalers. The issue price does not change if part of the issue is later sold at a different price. The issue price of bonds that are not substantially identical is determined separately. The issue price of bonds for which a bona fide public offering is made is determined as of the sale date based on reasonable expectations regarding the initial public offering price. If a bond is issued for property, the applicable Federal tax-exempt rate is used in lieu of the Federal rate in determining the issue price under section 1274. The issue price of bonds may not exceed their fair market value as of the sale date.

Issuer generally means the entity that actually issues the issue, and, unless the context or a provision clearly requires otherwise, each conduit borrower of the issue. For example, rules imposed on issuers to account for gross proceeds of an issue apply to a conduit borrower to account for any gross proceeds received under a purpose investment. Provisions regarding elections, filings, liability for the rebate amount, and certifications of reasonable expectations apply only to the actual issuer.

Multipurpose issue means an issue the proceeds of which are used for two or more separate purposes determined in accordance with § 1.148-9(h).

Net sale proceeds means sale proceeds, less the portion of those sale proceeds invested in a reasonably required reserve or replacement fund under section 148(d) and as part of a minor portion under section 148(e).

Nonpurpose investment means any investment property, as defined in section 148(b), that is not a purpose investment.

Payment means a payment as defined in § 1.148-3(d) for purposes of computing the rebate amount, and a payment as defined in § 1.148-5(b) for purposes of computing the yield on an investment.

Plain par bond means a qualified tender bond or a bond—

(1) Issued with not more than a de minimis amount of original issue discount or premium;

(2) Issued for a price that does not include accrued interest other than pre-issuance accrued interest;

(3) That bears interest from the issue date at a single, stated, fixed rate or that is a variable rate debt instrument under section 1275, in each case with interest unconditionally payable at least annually; and

(4) That has a lowest stated redemption price that is not less than its outstanding stated principal amount.

Plain par investment means an investment that is an obligation—

(1) Issued with not more than a de minimis amount of original issue discount or premium, or, if acquired on a date other than the issue date, acquired with not more than a de minimis amount of market discount or premium;

(2) Issued for a price that does not include accrued interest other than pre-issuance accrued interest;

(3) That bears interest from the issue date at a single, stated, fixed rate or that is a variable rate debt instrument under section 1275, in each case with interest unconditionally payable at least annually; and

(4) That has a lowest stated redemption price that is not less than its outstanding stated principal amount.

Pre-issuance accrued interest means amounts representing interest that accrued on an obligation for a period not greater than one year before its issue date but only if those amounts are paid within one year after the issue date.

Proceeds means any sale proceeds, investment proceeds, and transferred proceeds of an issue. Proceeds do not include, however, amounts actually or constructively received with respect to a purpose investment that are properly allocable to the immaterially higher yield under § 1.148-2(d) or section 143(g) or to qualified administrative costs recoverable under § 1.148-5(e).

Program investment means a purpose investment that is part of a governmental program in which—

(1) The program involves the origination or acquisition of purpose investments;

(2) At least 95 percent (90 percent for qualified student loans under section 144(b)(1)(A)) of the cost of the purpose investments acquired under the program represents one or more loans to a substantial number of persons representing the general public, States or political subdivisions, 501(c)(3) organizations, persons who provide housing and related facilities, or any combination of the foregoing;

(3) At least 95 percent of the receipts from the purpose investments are used to pay principal, interest, or redemption prices on issues that financed the program, to pay or reimburse administrative costs of those issues or of the program, to pay or reimburse anticipated future losses directly related to the program, to finance additional purpose investments for the same general purposes of the program, or to redeem and retire governmental obligations at the next earliest possible date of redemption;

(4) The program documents prohibit any obligor on a purpose investment financed by the program or any related party to that obligor from purchasing bonds of an issue that finance the program in an amount related to the amount of the purpose investment acquired from that obligor; and

(5) The issuer has not waived the right to treat the investment as a program investment.

Purpose investment means an investment that is acquired to carry out the governmental purpose of an issue.

Qualified administrative costs means qualified administrative costs as defined in § 1.148-5(e).

Qualified guarantee means a qualified guarantee as defined in § 1.148-4(f).

Qualified hedge means a qualified hedge as defined in § 1.148-4(h)(2).

Reasonable expectations or reasonableness. An issuer's expectations or actions are reasonable only if a prudent person in the same circumstances as the issuer would have those same expectations or take those same actions, based on all the objective facts and circumstances. Factors relevant to a determination of reasonableness include the issuer's history of conduct concerning stated expectations made in connection with the issuance of obligations, the level of inquiry by the issuer into factual matters, and the existence of covenants, enforceable by bondholders, that require implementation of specific expectations. For a conduit financing issue, factors relevant to a determination of reasonableness include the reasonable expectations of the conduit borrower, but only if, under the circumstances, it is reasonable and prudent for the issuer to rely on those expectations.

Rebate amount means 100 percent of the amount owed to the United States under section 148(f)(2), as further described in § 1.148-3.

Receipt means a receipt as defined in § 1.148-3(d) for purposes of computing the rebate amount, and a receipt as defined in § 1.148-5(b) for purposes of computing yield on an investment.

Refunding escrow means one or more funds established as part of a single transaction or a series of related transactions, containing proceeds of a refunding issue and any other amounts to provide for payment of principal or interest on one or more prior issues. For this purpose, funds are generally not so established solely because of—

(1) The deposit of proceeds of an issue and replacement proceeds of the prior issue in an escrow more than 6 months apart, or

(2) The deposit of proceeds of completely separate issues in an escrow.

Replacement proceeds is defined in paragraph (c) of this section.

Restricted working capital expenditures means working capital expenditures that are subject to the proceeds-spent-last rule in § 1.148-6(d)(3)(i) and are ineligible for any exception to that rule.

Sale proceeds means any amounts actually or constructively received from the sale of the issue, including amounts used to pay underwriters' discount or compensation and accrued interest other than pre-issuance accrued interest. Sale proceeds also include, but are not limited to, amounts derived from the sale of a right that is associated with a bond, and that is described in § 1.148-4(b)(4). See also § 1.148-4(h)(5) treating amounts received upon the termination of certain hedges as sale proceeds.

Stated redemption price means the redemption price of an obligation under the terms of that obligation, including any call premium.

Transferred proceeds means transferred proceeds as defined in § 1.148-9 (or the applicable corresponding provision of prior law).

Unconditionally payable means payable under terms in which—

(1) Late payment or nonpayment results in a significant penalty to the borrower or reasonable remedies to the lender, and

(2) It is reasonably certain on the issue date that the payment will actually be made.

Value means value determined under § 1.148-4(e) for a bond, and value determined under § 1.148-5(d) for an investment.

Variable yield bond means any bond that is not a fixed yield bond.

Variable yield issue means any issue that is not a fixed yield issue.

Yield means yield computed under § 1.148-4 for an issue, and yield computed under § 1.148-5 for an investment.

Yield restricted means required to be invested at a yield that is not materially higher than the yield on the issue under section 148(a) and § 1.148-2.

(c) Definition of replacement proceeds. *(1) In general.* Amounts are replacement proceeds of an issue if the amounts have a sufficiently direct nexus to the issue or to the governmental purpose of the issue to conclude that the amounts would have been used for that governmental purpose if the proceeds of the issue were not used or to be used for that governmental purpose. For this purpose, governmental purposes include the expected use of amounts for the payment of debt service on a particular date. The mere availability or preliminary earmarking of amounts for a governmental purpose, however, does not in itself establish a sufficient nexus to cause those amounts to be replacement proceeds. Replacement proceeds include, but are not limited to, sinking funds, pledged funds, and other replacement proceeds described in paragraph (c)(4) of this section, to the extent that those funds or amounts are held by or derived from a substantial beneficiary of the issue. A substantial beneficiary of an issue includes the issuer and any related party to the issuer, and, if the issuer is not a state, the state in which the issuer is located. A person is not a substantial beneficiary of an issue solely because it is a guarantor under a qualified guarantee.

(2) Sinking fund. Sinking fund includes a debt service fund, redemption fund, reserve fund, replacement fund, or any similar fund, to the extent reasonably expected to be used directly or indirectly to pay principal or interest on the issue.

(3) Pledged fund. (i) In general. A pledged fund is any amount that is directly or indirectly pledged to pay principal or interest on the issue. A pledge need not be cast in any particular form but, in substance, must provide reasonable assurance that the amount will be available to pay principal or interest on the issue, even if the issuer encounters financial difficulties. A pledge to a guarantor of an issue is an indirect pledge to secure payment of principal or interest on the issue. A pledge of more than 50 percent of the outstanding stock of a corporation that is a conduit borrower of the issue is not treated as a pledge for this purpose, unless the corporation is formed or availed of to avoid the creation of replacement proceeds.

(ii) Negative pledges. An amount is treated as pledged to pay principal or interest on an issue if it is held under an agreement to maintain the amount at a particular level for the direct or indirect benefit of the bondholders or a guarantor of the bonds. An amount is not treated as pledged under this paragraph (c)(3)(ii), however, if—

(A) The issuer or a substantial beneficiary may grant rights in the amount that are superior to the rights of the bondholders or the guarantor; or

(B) The amount does not exceed reasonable needs for which it is maintained, the required level is tested no more frequently than every 6 months, and the amount may be spent without any substantial restriction other than a requirement to replenish the amount by the next testing date.

(4) Other replacement proceeds. (i) Bonds outstanding longer than necessary. (A) In general. Replacement proceeds arise to the extent that the issuer reasonably expects as of the issue date that—

(1) The term of an issue will be longer than is reasonably necessary for the governmental purposes of the issue, and

(2) There will be available amounts during the period that the issue remains outstanding longer than necessary. Whether an issue is outstanding longer than necessary is determined under § 1.148-10. Replacement proceeds are created under this paragraph (c)(4)(i)(A) at the beginning of each fiscal year during which an issue remains outstanding longer than necessary in an amount equal to available amounts of the issuer as of that date.

(B) Safe harbor against creation of replacement proceeds. As a safe harbor, replacement proceeds do not arise under paragraph (c)(4)(i)(A) of this section—

(1) For the portion of an issue that is to be used to finance restricted working capital expenditures, if that portion is not outstanding longer than 2 years;

(2) For the portion of an issue (including a refunding issue) that is to be used to finance or refinance capital projects, if that portion has a weighted average maturity that does not exceed 120 percent of the average reasonably expected economic life of the financed capital projects, determined in the same manner as under section 147(b); or

(3) For the portion of an issue that is a refunding issue, if that portion has a weighted average maturity that does not exceed the remaining weighted average maturity of the prior issue, and the issue of which the prior issue is a part satisfies paragraph (c)(4)(i)(B)(1) or (2) of this section.

(ii) Bonds financing a working capital reserve. (A) In general. Except as otherwise provided in paragraph (c)(4)(ii)(B) of this section, replacement proceeds arise to the extent a working capital reserve is, directly or indirectly, financed with the proceeds of the issue (regardless of the expenditure of proceeds of the issue). Thus, for example, if an issuer that does not maintain a working capital reserve borrows to fund a working capital reserve, the issuer will have replacement proceeds. To determine the amount of a working capital reserve maintained, an issuer may use the average amount maintained as a working capital reserve during annual periods of at least 1 year, the last of which ends within 1 year before the issue date. For example, the amount of a working capital reserve may be computed using the average of the beginning or ending monthly balances of the amount maintained as a reserve (net of unexpended gross proceeds) during the 1 year period preceding the issue date.

(B) Exception to creation of replacement proceeds. Replacement proceeds do not arise under paragraph (c)(4)(ii)(A) of this section with respect to an issue—

(1) All of the net proceeds of which are spent within 6 months of the issue date under section 148(f)(4)(B)(iii)(I); or

(2) That is not subject to the rebate requirement under the exception provided by section 148(f)(4)(D).

(d) Elections. Except as otherwise provided, any required elections must be made in writing, and, once made, may not be revoked without the permission of the Commissioner.

(e) Investment-type property. *(1) In general.* Investment-type property includes any property, other than property described in section 148(b)(2)(A), (B), (C) or (E), that is held principally as a passive vehicle for the production of income. For this purpose, production of income includes any benefit based on the time value of money.

(2) Prepayments. (i) In general. (A) Generally. Except as otherwise provided in this paragraph (e)(2), a prepayment for property or services, including a prepayment for property or services that is made after the date that the contract to buy the property or services is entered into, also gives rise to investment-type property if a principal purpose for prepaying is to receive an investment return from the time the prepayment is made until the time payment otherwise would be made. A prepayment does not give rise to investment-type property if—

(1) Prepayments on substantially the same terms are made by a substantial percentage of persons who are similarly situated to the issuer but who are not beneficiaries of tax-exempt financing;

(2) The prepayment is made within 90 days of the reasonably expected date of delivery to the issuer of all of the property or services for which the prepayment is made; or

(3) The prepayment meets the requirements of paragraph (e)(2)(iii)(A) or (B) of this section.

(B) Example. The following example illustrates an application of this paragraph (e)(2)(i):

Example. Prepayment after contract is executed. In 1998, City A enters into a ten-year contract with Company Y. Under the contract, Company Y is to provide services to City A over the term of the contract and in return City A will pay Company Y for its services as they are provided. In 2004, City A issues bonds to finance a lump sum payment to Company Y in satisfaction of City A's obligation to pay for Company Y's services to be provided over the remaining term of the contract. The use of bond proceeds to make the lump sum payment constitutes a prepayment for services under paragraph (e)(2)(i) of this section, even though the payment is made after the date that the contract is executed.

(ii) Customary prepayments. The determination of whether a prepayment satisfies paragraph (e)(2)(i)(A)(1) of this section is generally made based on all the facts and circumstances. In addition, a prepayment is deemed to satisfy paragraph (e)(2)(i)(A)(1) of this section if—

(A) The prepayment is made for—

(1) Maintenance, repair, or an extended warranty with respect to personal property (for example, automobiles or electronic equipment); or

(2) Updates or maintenance or support services with respect to computer software; and

(B) The same maintenance, repair, extended warranty, updates or maintenance or support services, as applicable, are regularly provided to nongovernmental persons on the same terms.

(iii) Certain prepayments to acquire a supply of natural gas or electricity. (A) Natural gas prepayments. A prepayment meets the requirements of this paragraph (e)(2)(iii)(A) if—

(1) It is made by or for one or more utilities that are owned by a governmental person, as defined in § 1.141-1(b) (each of which is referred to in this paragraph (e)(2)(iii)(A) as the issuing municipal utility), to purchase a supply of natural gas; and

(2) At least 90 percent of the prepaid natural gas financed by the issue is used for a qualifying use. Natural gas is used for a qualifying use if it is to be—

(i) Furnished to retail gas customers of the issuing municipal utility who are located in the natural gas service area of the issuing municipal utility, provided, however, that gas used to produce electricity for sale shall not be included under this paragraph (e)(2)(iii)(A)(2)(i);

(ii) Used by the issuing municipal utility to produce electricity that will be furnished to retail electric customers of the issuing municipal utility who are located in the electricity service area of the issuing municipal utility;

(iii) Used by the issuing municipal utility to produce electricity that will be sold to a utility that is owned by a governmental person and furnished to retail electric customers of the purchaser who are located in the electricity service area of the purchaser;

(iv) Sold to a utility that is owned by a governmental person if the requirements of paragraph (e)(2)(iii)(A)(2)(i), (ii) or (iii) of this section are satisfied by the purchaser (treating the purchaser as the issuing municipal utility); or

(v) Used to fuel the pipeline transportation of the prepaid gas supply acquired in accordance with this paragraph (e)(2)(iii)(A).

(B) Electricity prepayments. A prepayment meets the requirements of this paragraph (e)(2)(iii)(B) if—

(1) It is made by or for one or more utilities that are owned by a governmental person (each of which is referred to in this paragraph (e)(2)(iii)(B) as the issuing municipal utility) to purchase a supply of electricity; and

(2) At least 90 percent of the prepaid electricity financed by the issue is used for a qualifying use. Electricity is used for a qualifying use if it is to be—

(i) Furnished to retail electric customers of the issuing municipal utility who are located in the electricity service area of the issuing municipal utility; or

(ii) Sold to a utility that is owned by a governmental person and furnished to retail electric customers of the purchaser who are located in the electricity service area of the purchaser.

(C) Service area. For purposes of this paragraph (e)(2)(iii), the service area of a utility owned by a governmental person consists of—

(1) Any area throughout which the utility provided, at all times during the 5-year period ending on the issue date—

(i) In the case of a natural gas utility, natural gas transmission or distribution service; and

(ii) In the case of an electric utility, electricity distribution service; and

(2) Any area recognized as the service area of the utility under state or Federal law.

(D) Retail customer. For purposes of this paragraph (e)(2)(iii), a retail customer is a customer that purchases natural gas or electricity, as applicable, other than for resale.

(E) Commodity swaps. A prepayment does not fail to meet the requirements of this paragraph (e)(2)(iii) by reason of any commodity swap contract that may be entered into between the issuer and an unrelated party (other than the gas or electricity supplier), or between the gas or electricity supplier and an unrelated party (other than the issuer), so long as each swap contract is an independent contract. A swap contract is an independent contract if the obligation of each party to perform under the swap contract is not dependent on performance by any person (other than the other party to the swap contract) under another contract (for example, a gas or electricity supply contract or another swap contract); provided, however, that a commodity swap contract will not fail to be an independent contract solely because the swap contract may terminate in the event of a failure of a gas or electricity supplier to deliver gas or electricity for which the swap contract is a hedge.

(F) Remedial action. Issuers may apply principles similar to the rules of § 1.141-12, including § 1.141-12(d) (relating to redemption or defeasance of nonqualified bonds) and § 1.141-12(e) (relating to alternative use of disposition proceeds), to cure a violation of paragraph (e)(2)(iii)(A)(2) or (e)(2)(iii)(B)(2) of this section. For this purpose, the amount of nonqualified bonds is determined in the same manner as for output contracts taken into account under the private business tests, including the principles of § 1.141-7(d), treating nonqualified sales of gas or electricity under this paragraph (e)(2)(iii) as satisfying the benefits and burdens test under § 1.141-7(c)(1).

(iv) Additional prepayments as permitted by the Commissioner. The Commissioner may, by published guidance, set forth additional circumstances in which a prepayment does not give rise to investment-type property.

(3) Certain hedges. Investment-type property also includes the investment element of a contract that is a hedge (within the meaning of § 1.148-4(h)(2)(i)(A)) and that contains a significant investment element because a payment by the issuer relates to a conditional or unconditional obligation by the hedge provider to make a payment on a later date. See § 1.148-4(h)(2)(ii) relating to hedges with a significant investment element.

T.D. 8418, 5/12/92, amend T.D. 8476, 6/14/93, T.D. 8538, 5/5/94, T.D. 8718, 5/8/97, T.D. 9085, 8/1/2003.

§ 1.148-1A Definitions and elections.

(a) [Reserved]. For guidance see § 1.148-1.

(b) Certain definitions. *Investment-type property.* See § 1.148-1(b). Investment-type property also includes a contract that would be a hedge (within the meaning of § 1.148-4(h)) except that it contains a significant investment element.

(c) through (c)(4)(i) [Reserved]. For guidance see § 1.148-1.

(4) (ii) Bonds financing a working capital reserve. (A) In general. Except as otherwise provided in § 1.148-1(c)(4)(ii)(B), replacement proceeds arise to the extent a working capital reserve is, directly or indirectly, financed with the proceeds of the issue (regardless of the expenditure of proceeds of the issue). Thus, for example, if an issuer that does not maintain a working capital reserve borrows to fund such a reserve, the issuer will have replacement proceeds. To determine the amount of a working capital reserve maintained, an issuer may use the average amount maintained as a working capital reserve during annual periods of at least one year, the last of which ends within a year before the issue date. For example, the amount of a working capital reserve may be computed using the average of the beginning or ending monthly balances of the amount maintained as a reserve (net of unexpended gross proceeds) during the one year period preceding the issue date.

T.D. 8538, 5/5/94, amend T.D. 8718, 5/8/97.

§ 1.148-2 General arbitrage yield restriction rules.

Caution: The Treasury has not yet amended Reg § 1.148-2 to reflect changes made by P.L. 105-34.

(a) In general. Under section 148(a), the direct or indirect investment of the gross proceeds of an issue in higher yielding investments causes the bonds of the issue to be arbitrage bonds. The investment of proceeds in higher yielding investments, however, during a temporary period described in paragraph (e) of this section, as part of a reasonably required reserve or replacement fund described in paragraph (f) of this section, or as part of a minor portion described in paragraph (g) of this section does not cause the bonds of the issue to be arbitrage bonds. Bonds are not arbitrage bonds under this section as a result of an inadvertent, insubstantial error.

(b) Reasonable expectations. *(1) In general.* Except as provided in paragraph (c) of this section, the determination of whether an issue consists of arbitrage bonds under section 148(a) is based on the issuer's reasonable expectations as of the issue date regarding the amount and use of the gross proceeds of the issue.

(2) Certification of expectations. (i) In general. An officer of the issuer responsible for issuing the bonds must, in good faith, certify the issuer's expectations as of the issue date. The certification must state the facts and estimates that form the basis for the issuer's expectations. The certification is evidence of the issuer's expectations, but does not establish any conclusions of law or any presumptions regarding either the issuer's actual expectations or their reasonableness.

(ii) Exceptions to certification requirement. An issuer is not required to make a certification for an issue under paragraph (b)(2)(i) of this section if—

(A) The issuer reasonably expects as of the issue date that there will be no unspent gross proceeds after the issue date, other than gross proceeds in a bona fide debt service fund (e.g., equipment lease financings in which the issuer purchases equipment in exchange for an installment payment note); or

(B) The issue price of the issue does not exceed $1,000,000.

(c) Intentional acts. The taking of any deliberate, intentional action by the issuer or person acting on its behalf after the issue date in order to earn arbitrage causes the bonds of the issue to be arbitrage bonds if that action, had it been expected on the issue date, would have caused the bonds to be arbitrage bonds. An intent to violate the requirements of section 148 is not necessary for an action to be intentional.

(d) Materially higher yielding investments. *(1) In general.* The yield on investments is materially higher than the yield on the issue to which the investments are allocated if the yield on the investments over the term of the issue exceeds the yield on the issue by an amount in excess of the applicable definition of materially higher set forth in paragraph (d)(2) of this section. If yield restricted investments in the same class are subject to different definitions of materially higher, the applicable definition of materially higher that produces the lowest permitted yield applies to all the investments in the class. The yield on the issue is determined under § 1.148-4. The yield on investments is determined under § 1.148-5.

(2) Definitions of materially higher yield. (i) General rule for purpose and nonpurpose investments. For investments

that are not otherwise described in this paragraph (d)(2), materially higher means one-eighth of 1 percentage point.

(ii) Refunding escrows and replacement proceeds. For investments in a refunding escrow or for investments allocable to replacement proceeds, materially higher means one-thousandth of 1 percentage point.

(iii) Program investments. For program investments that are not described in paragraph (d)(2)(iv) of this section, materially higher means 1 and one-half percentage points.

(iv) Student loans. For qualified student loans that are program investments, materially higher means 2 percentage points.

(v) Tax-exempt investments. For investments that are tax-exempt bonds and are not investment property under section 148(b)(3), no yield limitation applies.

(3) Mortgage loans. Qualified mortgage loans that satisfy the requirements of section 143(g) are treated as meeting the requirements of this paragraph (d).

(e) Temporary periods. *(1) In general.* During the temporary periods set forth in this paragraph (e), the proceeds and replacement proceeds of an issue may be invested in higher yielding investments without causing bonds in the issue to be arbitrage bonds. This paragraph (e) does not apply to refunding issues (see § 1.148-9).

(2) General 3-year temporary period for capital projects and qualified mortgage loans. (i) In general. The net sale proceeds and investment proceeds of an issue reasonably expected to be allocated to expenditures for capital projects qualify for a temporary period of 3 years beginning on the issue date (the 3-year temporary period). The 3-year temporary period also applies to the proceeds of qualified mortgage bonds and qualified veterans' mortgage bonds by substituting qualified mortgage loans in each place that capital projects appears in this paragraph (e)(2). The 3-year temporary period applies only if the issuer reasonably expects to satisfy the expenditure test, the time test, and the due diligence test. These rules apply separately to each conduit loan financed by an issue (other than qualified mortgage loans), with the expenditure and time tests measured from the issue date of the issue.

(A) Expenditure test. The expenditure test is met if at least 85 percent of the net sale proceeds of the issue are allocated to expenditures on the capital projects by the end of the 3-year temporary period.

(B) Time test. The time test is met if the issuer incurs within 6 months of the issue date a substantial binding obligation to a third party to expend at least 5 percent of the net sale proceeds of the issue on the capital projects. An obligation is not binding if it is subject to contingencies within the issuer's or a related party's control.

(C) Due diligence test. The due diligence test is met if completion of the capital projects and the allocation of the net sale proceeds of the issue to expenditures proceed with due diligence.

(ii) 5-year temporary period. In the case of proceeds expected to be allocated to a capital project involving a substantial amount of construction expenditures (as defined in § 1.148-7), a 5-year temporary period applies in lieu of the 3-year temporary period if the issuer satisfies the requirements of paragraph (e)(2)(i) of this section applied by substituting "5 years" in each place that "3 years" appears, and both the issuer and a licensed architect or engineer certify that the longer period is necessary to complete the capital project.

(3) Temporary period for restricted working capital expenditures. (i) General rule. The proceeds of an issue that are reasonably expected to be allocated to restricted working capital expenditures within 13 months after the issue date qualify for a temporary period of 13 months beginning on the issue date. Paragraph (e)(2) of this section contains additional temporary period rules for certain working capital expenditures that are treated as part of a capital project.

(ii) Longer temporary period for certain tax anticipation issues. If an issuer reasonably expects to use tax revenues arising from tax levies for a single fiscal year to redeem or retire an issue, and the issue matures by the earlier of 2 years after the issue date or 60 days after the last date for payment of those taxes without interest or penalty, the temporary period under paragraph (e)(3)(i) of this section is extended until the maturity date of the issue.

(4) Temporary period for pooled financings. (i) In general. Proceeds of a pooled financing issue reasonably expected to be used to finance purpose investments qualify for a temporary period of 6 months while held by the issuer before being loaned to a conduit borrower. Any otherwise available temporary period for proceeds held by a conduit borrower, however, is reduced by the period of time during which those proceeds were held by the issuer before being loaned. For example, if the proceeds of a pooled financing issue loaned to a conduit borrower would qualify for a 3-year temporary period, and the proceeds are held by the issuer for 5 months before being loaned to the conduit borrower, the proceeds qualify for only an additional 31-month temporary period after being loaned to the conduit borrower. Except as provided in paragraph (e)(4)(iv) of this section, this paragraph (e)(4) does not apply to any qualified mortgage bond or qualified veterans' mortgage bond under section 143.

(ii) Loan repayments. (A) Amount held by the issuer. The temporary period under this paragraph (e)(4) for proceeds from the sale or repayment of any loan that are reasonably expected to be used to make or finance new loans is 3 months.

(B) Amounts re-loaned to conduit borrowers. Any temporary period for proceeds held by a conduit borrower under a new loan from amounts described in paragraph (e)(4)(ii)(A) of this section is determined by treating the date the new loan is made as the issue date and by reducing the temporary period by the period the amounts were held by the issuer following the last repayment.

(iii) Construction issues. If all or a portion of a pooled financing issue qualifies as a construction issue under § 1.148-7(b)(6), paragraph (e)(4)(i) of this section is applied by substituting "2 years" for "6 months."

(iv) Amounts re-loaned for qualified mortgage loans. The temporary period under this paragraph (e)(4) for proceeds from the sale, prepayment, or repayment of any qualified mortgage loan that are reasonably expected to be used to make or finance new qualified mortgage loans is 3 years.

(5) Temporary period for replacement proceeds. (i) In general. Except as otherwise provided, replacement proceeds qualify for a temporary period of 30 days beginning on the date that the amounts are first treated as replacement proceeds.

(ii) Temporary period for bona fide debt service funds. Amounts in a bona fide debt service fund for an issue qualify for a temporary period of 13 months. If only a portion of a fund qualifies as a bona fide debt service fund, only that portion qualifies for this temporary period.

(6) Temporary period for investment proceeds. Except as otherwise provided in this paragraph (e), investment proceeds qualify for a temporary period of 1 year beginning on the date of receipt.

(7) Other amounts. Gross proceeds not otherwise eligible for a temporary period described in this paragraph (e) qualify for a temporary period of 30 days beginning on the date of receipt.

(f) Reserve or replacement funds. *(1) General 10 percent limitation on funding with sale proceeds.* An issue consists of arbitrage bonds if sale proceeds of the issue in excess of 10 percent of the stated principal amount of the issue are used to finance any reserve or replacement fund, without regard to whether those sale proceeds are invested in higher yielding investments. If an issue has more than a de minimis amount of original issue discount or premium, the issue price (net of pre-issuance accrued interest) is used to measure the 10-percent limitation in lieu of stated principal amount. This rule does not limit the use of amounts other than sale proceeds of an issue to fund a reserve or replacement fund.

(2) Exception from yield restriction for reasonably required reserve or replacement funds. (i) In general. The investment of amounts that are part of a reasonably required reserve or replacement fund in higher yielding investments will not cause an issue to consist of arbitrage bonds. A reasonably required reserve or replacement fund may consist of all or a portion of one or more funds, however labelled, derived from one or more sources. Amounts in a reserve or replacement fund in excess of the amount that is reasonably required are not part of a reasonably required reserve or replacement fund.

(ii) Size limitation. The amount of gross proceeds of an issue that qualifies as a reasonably required reserve or replacement fund may not exceed an amount equal to the least of 10 percent of the stated principal amount of the issue, the maximum annual principal and interest requirements on the issue, or 125 percent of the average annual principal and interest requirements on the issue. If an issue has more than a de minimis amount of original issue discount or premium, the issue price of the issue (net of pre-issuance accrued interest) is used to measure the 10 percent limitation in lieu of its stated principal amount. For a reserve or replacement fund that secures more than one issue (e.g. a parity reserve fund), the size limitation may be measured on an aggregate basis.

(iii) Valuation of investments. Investments in a reasonably required reserve or replacement fund may be valued in any reasonable, consistently applied manner that is permitted under § 1.148-5.

(iv) 150 percent debt service limitation on investment in nonpurpose investments for certain private activity bonds. Section 148(d)(3) contains additional limits on the amount of gross proceeds of an issue of private activity bonds, other than qualified 501(c)(3) bonds, that may be invested in higher yielding nonpurpose investments without causing the bonds to be arbitrage bonds. For purposes of these rules, initial temporary period means the temporary periods under paragraphs (e)(2), (e)(3), and (e)(4) of this section and under § 1.148-9(d)(2)(i), (ii), and (iii).

(3) Certain parity reserve funds. The limitation contained in paragraph (f)(1) of this section does not apply to an issue if the master legal document authorizing the issuance of the bonds (e.g., a master indenture) was adopted before August 16, 1986, and that document—

(i) Requires a reserve or replacement fund in excess of 10 percent of the sale proceeds, but not more than maximum annual principal and interest requirements;

(ii) Is not amended after August 31, 1986 (other than to permit the issuance of additional bonds as contemplated in the master legal document); and

(iii) Provides that bonds having a parity of security may not be issued by or on behalf of the issuer for the purposes provided under the document without satisfying the reserve fund requirements of the indenture.

(g) Minor portion. Under section 148(e), a bond of an issue is not an arbitrage bond solely because of the investment in higher yielding investments of gross proceeds of the issue in an amount not exceeding the lesser of—

(1) 5 percent of the sale proceeds of the issue; or

(2) $100,000.

(h) Certain waivers permitted. On or before the issue date, an issuer may elect to waive the right to invest in higher yielding investments during any temporary period under paragraph (e) of this section or as part of a reasonably required reserve or replacement fund under paragraph (f) of this section. At any time, an issuer may waive the right to invest in higher yielding investments as part of a minor portion under paragraph (g) of this section.

T.D. 8418, 5/12/92, amend T.D. 8476, 6/14/93, T.D. 8538, 5/5/94, T.D. 8718, 5/8/97.

§ 1.148-2A General arbitrage yield restriction rules.

(a) through (b)(2)(i) [Reserved]. For guidance see § 1.148-2.

(b) *(2)* (ii) Exceptions to certification requirement.

An issuer is not required to make a certification for an issue under § 1.148-2(b)(2)(i) if—

(A) The issuer reasonably expects as of the issue date that there will be no unspent gross proceeds after the issue date, other than gross proceeds in a bona fide debt service fund (e.g., *equipment lease* financings in which the issuer purchases equipment in exchange for an installment payment note); or

(B) The issue price of the issue does not exceed $1,000,000.

T.D. 8538, 5/5/94, amend T.D. 8718, 5/8/97.

§ 1.148-3 General arbitrage rebate rules.

(a) In general. Section 148(f) requires that certain earnings on nonpurpose investments allocable to the gross proceeds of an issue be paid to the United States to prevent the bonds in the issue from being arbitrage bonds. The arbitrage that must be rebated is based on the difference between the amount actually earned on nonpurpose investments and the amount that would have been earned if those investments had a yield equal to the yield on the issue.

(b) Definition of rebate amount. As of any date, the rebate amount for an issue is the excess of the future value, as of that date, of all receipts on nonpurpose investments over the future value, as of that date, of all payments on nonpurpose investments.

(c) Computation of future value of a payment or receipt. The future value of a payment or receipt at the end of any period is determined using the economic accrual method and equals the value of that payment or receipt when it is paid or received (or treated as paid or received), plus interest assumed to be earned and compounded over the period at a rate equal to the yield on the issue, using the same compounding interval and financial conventions used to compute that yield.

(d) Payments and receipts. *(1) Definition of payments.* For purposes of this section, payments are—

(i) Amounts actually or constructively paid to acquire a nonpurpose investment (or treated as paid to a commingled fund);

(ii) For a nonpurpose investment that is first allocated to an issue on a date after it is actually acquired (e.g., an investment that becomes allocable to transferred proceeds or to replacement proceeds) or that becomes subject to the rebate requirement on a date after it is actually acquired (e.g., an investment allocated to a reasonably required reserve or replacement fund for a construction issue at the end of the 2-year spending period), the value of that investment on that date;

(iii) For a nonpurpose investment that was allocated to an issue at the end of the preceding computation period, the value of that investment at the beginning of the computation period;

(iv) On the last day of each bond year during which there are amounts allocated to gross proceeds of an issue that are subject to the rebate requirement, and on the final maturity date, a computation credit of $1,000; and

(v) Yield reduction payments on nonpurpose investments made pursuant to § 1.148-5(c).

(2) Definition of receipts. For purposes of this section, receipts are—

(i) Amounts actually or constructively received from a nonpurpose investment (including amounts treated as received from a commingled fund), such as earnings and return of principal;

(ii) For a nonpurpose investment that ceases to be allocated to an issue before its disposition or redemption date (e.g., an investment that becomes allocable to transferred proceeds of another issue or that ceases to be allocable to the issue pursuant to the universal cap under § 1.148-6) or that ceases to be subject to the rebate requirement on a date earlier than its disposition or redemption date (e.g., an investment allocated to a fund initially subject to the rebate requirement but that subsequently qualifies as a bona fide debt service fund), the value of that nonpurpose investment on that date; and

(iii) For a nonpurpose investment that is held at the end of a computation period, the value of that investment at the end of that period.

(3) Special rules for commingled funds. Section 1.148-6(e) provides special rules to limit certain of the required determinations of payments and receipts for investments of a commingled fund.

(e) Computation dates. *(1) In general.* For a fixed yield issue, an issuer may treat any date as a computation date. For a variable yield issue, an issuer—

(i) May treat the last day of any bond year ending on or before the latest date on which the first rebate amount is required to be paid under paragraph (f) of this section (the first required payment date) as a computation date but may not change that treatment after the first payment date; and

(ii) After the first required payment date, must consistently treat either the end of each bond year or the end of each fifth bond year as computation dates and may not change these computation dates after the first required payment date.

(2) Final computation date. The date that an issue is discharged is the final computation date. For an issue retired within 3 years of the issue date, however, the final computation date need not occur before the end of 8 months after the issue date or during the period in which the issuer reasonably expects that any of the spending exceptions under § 1.148-7 will apply to the issue.

(f) Amount of required rebate installment payment. *(1) Amount of interim rebate payments.* The first rebate installment payment must be made for a computation date that is not later than 5 years after the issue date. Subsequent rebate installment payments must be made for a computation date that is not later than 5 years after the previous computation date for which an installment payment was made. A rebate installment payment must be in an amount that, when added to the future value, as of the computation date, of previous rebate payments made for the issue, equals at least 90 percent of the rebate amount as of that date.

(2) Amount of final rebate payment. For the final computation date, a final rebate payment must be paid in an amount that, when added to the future value of previous rebate payments made for the issue, equals 100 percent of the rebate amount as of that date.

(3) Future value of rebate payments. The future value of a rebate payment is determined under paragraph (c) of this section. This value is computed by taking into account recoveries of overpayments.

(g) Time and manner of payment. Each rebate payment must be paid no later than 60 days after the computation date to which the payment relates. Any rebate payment paid within this 60-day period may be treated as paid on the computation date to which it relates. A rebate payment is paid when it is filed with the Internal Revenue Service at the place or places designated by the Commissioner. A payment must be accompanied by the form provided by the Commissioner for this purpose.

(h) Penalty in lieu of loss of tax exemption. *(1) In general.* The failure to pay the correct rebate amount when required will cause the bonds of the issue to be arbitrage bonds, unless the Commissioner determines that the failure was not caused by willful neglect and the issuer promptly pays a penalty to the United States. If no bond of the issue is a private activity bond (other than a qualified 501(c)(3) bond), the penalty equals 50 percent of the rebate amount not paid when required to be paid, plus interest on that amount. Otherwise, the penalty equals 100 percent of the rebate amount not paid when required to be paid, plus interest on that amount.

(2) Interest on underpayments. Interest accrues at the underpayment rate under section 6621, beginning on the date the correct rebate amount is due and ending on the date 10 days before it is paid.

(3) Waivers of the penalty. The penalty is automatically waived if the rebate amount that the issuer failed to pay plus interest is paid within 180 days after discovery of the failure, unless, the Commissioner determines that the failure was due to willful neglect, or the issue is under examination by the Commissioner at any time during the period beginning on the date the failure first occurred and ending on the date 90 days after the receipt of the rebate amount. Generally, extensions of this 180-day period and waivers of the penalty in other cases will be granted by the Commissioner only in unusual circumstances. For purposes of this paragraph (h)(3),

willful neglect does not include a failure that is attributable solely to the permissible retroactive selection of a short first bond year if the rebate amount that the issuer failed to pay is paid within 60 days of the selection of that bond year.

(4) Application to alternative penalty under § 1.148-7. Paragraphs (h)(1), (2), and (3) of this section apply to failures to pay penalty payments under § 1.148-7 (alternative penalty amounts) by substituting alternative penalty amounts for rebate amount and the last day of each spending period for computation date.

(i) Recovery of overpayment of rebate. *(1) In general.* An issuer may recover an overpayment for an issue of tax-exempt bonds by establishing to the satisfaction of the Commissioner that the overpayment occurred. An overpayment is the excess of the amount paid to the United States for an issue under section 148 over the sum of the rebate amount for the issue as of the most recent computation date and all amounts that are otherwise required to be paid under section 148 as of the date the recovery is requested.

(2) Limitations on recovery. (i) An overpayment may be recovered only to the extent that a recovery on the date that it is first requested would not result in an additional rebate amount if that date were treated as a computation date.

(ii) Except for overpayments of penalty in lieu of rebate under section 148(f)(4)(C)(vii) and § 1.148-7(k), an overpayment of less than $5,000 may not be recovered before the final computation date.

(j) Examples. The provisions of this section may be illustrated by the following examples.

Example (1). Calculation and payment of rebate for a fixed yield issue.

(i) Facts. On January 1, 1994, City A issues a fixed yield issue and invests all the sale proceeds of the issue ($49 million). There are no other gross proceeds. The issue has a yield of 7.0000 percent per year compounded semiannually (computed on a 30 day month/360 day year basis). City A receives amounts from the investment and immediately expends them for the governmental purpose of the issue as follows:

Date	Amount
2/1/94	$ 3,000,000
5/1/94	5,000,000
1/1/95	5,000,000
9/1/95	20,000,000
3/1/96	22,000,000

(ii) First computation date.

(A) City A chooses January 1, 1999, as its first computation date. This date is the latest date that may be used to compute the first required rebate installment payment. The rebate amount as of this date is computed by determining the future value of the receipts and the payments for the investment. The compounding interval is each 6-month (or shorter) period and the 30 day month/360 day year basis is used because these conventions were used to compute yield on the issue. The future value of these amounts, plus the computation credit, as of January 1, 1999, is:

Date	Receipts (Payments)	FV (7.0000 percent)
1/1/94	($ 49,000,000)	($ 69,119,339)
2/1/94	3,000,000	4,207,602
5/1/94	5,000,000	6,893,079
1/1/95	5,000,000	6,584,045
1/1/95	(1,000)	(1,317)
9/1/95	20,000,000	25,155,464
1/1/96	(1,000)	(1,229)
3/1/96	22,000,000	26,735,275
1/1/97	(1,000)	(1,148)
Rebate amount (1/01/99)		$ 452,432

(B) City A pays 90 percent of the rebate amount ($407,189) to the United States within 60 days of January 1, 1999.

(iii) Second computation date.

(A) On the next required computation date, January 1, 2004, the future value of the payments and receipts is:

Date	Receipts (Payments)	FV (7.0000 percent)
1/1/99	$ 452,432	$ 638,200
Rebate amount (1/01/04)		$ 638,200

(B) As of this computation date, the future value of the payment treated as made on January 1, 1999, is $574,380, which equals at least 90 percent of the rebate amount as of this computation date ($638,200 x 0.9), and thus no additional rebate payment is due as of this date.

(iv) Final computation date.

(A) On January 1, 2009, City A redeems all the bonds, and thus this date is the final computation date. The future value of the receipts and payments as of this date is:

Date	Receipts (Payments)	FV (7.0000 percent)
1/1/04	$ 638,200	$ 900,244
1/1/09	(1,000)	(1,000)
Rebate amount (1/01/09)		$ 899,244

(B) As of this computation date, the future value of the payment made on January 1, 1999, is $810,220 and thus an additional rebate payment of $89,024 is due. This payment reflects the future value of the 10 percent unpaid portion, and thus would not be owed had the issuer paid the full rebate amount as of any prior computation date.

Example (2). Calculation and payment of rebate for a variable yield issue.

(i) Facts. On July 1, 1994, City B issues a variable yield issue and invests all of the sale proceeds of the issue ($30 million). There are no other gross proceeds. As of July 1, 1999, there are nonpurpose investments allocated to the issue. Prior to July 1, 1999, City B receives amounts from nonpurpose investments and immediately expends them for the governmental purpose of the issue as follows:

Date	Amount
8/1/1994	$ 5,000,000
7/1/1995	8,000,000
12/1/1995	17,000,000
7/1/1999	650,000

(ii) First computation date.

(A) City B treats the last day of the fifth bond year (July 1, 1999) as a computation date. The yield on the variable yield issue during the first computation period (the period beginning on the issue date and ending on the first computation date) is 6.0000 percent per year compounded semiannually. The value of the nonpurpose investments allocated to the issue as of July 1, 1999, is $3 million. The rebate amount as of July 1, 1999, is computed by determining the future value of the receipts and the payments for the nonpurpose investments. The compounding interval is each 6-month (or shorter) period and the 30 day month/360 day year basis is used because these conventions were used to compute yield on the issue. The future value of these amounts and of the computation date credits as of July 1, 1999, is:

Date	Receipts (Payments)	FV (6.0000 percent)
7/1/1994	($ 30,000,000)	($ 40,317,491)
8/1/1994	5,000,000	6,686,560
7/1/1995	(1,000)	(1,267)
7/1/1995	8,000,000	10,134,161
12/1/1995	17,000,000	21,011,112
7/1/1996	(1,000)	(1,194)
7/1/1997	(1,000)	(1,126)
7/1/1998	(1,000)	(1,061)
7/1/1999	3,000,000	3,000,000
7/1/1999	650,000	650,000
7/1/1999	(1,000)	(1,000)
Rebate amount (7/01/1999)		$ 1,158,694

(B) City B pays 90 percent of the rebate amount ($1,042,824.60) to the United States within 60 days of July 1, 1999.

(iii) Next computation date.

(A) On July 1, 2004, City B redeems all of the bonds. Thus, the next computation date is July 1, 2004. On July 30, 1999, City B chose to compute rebate for periods following the first computation period by treating the end of each fifth bond year as a computation date. The yield during the second computation period is 5.0000 percent per year compounded semiannually. The computation of the rebate amount as of this date reflects the value of the nonpurpose investments allocated to the issue at the end of the prior computation period. On July 1, 2004, City B sells those nonpurpose investments for $3,925,000 and expends that amount for the governmental purpose of the issue.

(B) As of July 1, 2004, the future value of the rebate amount computed as of July 1, 1999, and of all other payments and receipts is:

Date	Receipts (Payments)	FV (5.0000 percent)
7/1/1999	$1,158,694	$1,483,226
7/1/1999	(3,000,000)	(3,840,254)
7/1/2000	(1,000)	(1,218)
7/1/2001	(1,000)	(1,160)
7/1/2002	(1,000)	(1,104)
7/1/2003	(1,000)	(1,051)
7/1/2004	(2,000)	(2,000)
7/1/2004	3,925,000	3,925,000
		$1,561,439

(C) As of this computation date, the future value of the payment made on July 1, 1999, is $1,334,904 and thus an additional rebate payment of $226,535 is due.

(D) If the yield during the second computation period were, instead, 7.0000 percent, the rebate amount computed as of July 1, 1999, would be $1,320,891. The future value of the payment made on July 1, 1999, would be $1,471,007, and, therefore, City B would have overpaid the rebate amount by $150,116.

(k) Bona fide debt service fund exception. Under section 148(f)(4)(A), the rebate requirement does not apply to amounts in certain bona fide debt service funds. An issue with an average annual debt service that is not in excess of $2,500,000 may be treated as satisfying the $100,000 limitation in section 148(f)(4)(A)(ii).

T.D. 8418, 5/12/92, amend T.D. 8476, 6/14/93, T.D. 8538, 5/5/94, T.D. 8718, 5/8/97.

PAR. 3. Section 1.148-3 is amended by revising paragraph (d)(1)(iv) and adding a new paragraph (d)(4) as follows:

Proposed § 1.148-3 General arbitrage rebate rules. [*For Preamble, see ¶ 152,909*]

* * * * *

(d) * * *

(1) * * *

(iv) On the last day of each bond year during which there are amounts allocated to gross proceeds of an issue that are subject to the rebate requirement, and on the final maturity date, a computation credit of $1,400 for any bond year ending in 2007 and, for bond years ending after 2007, a computation credit in the amount determined under paragraph (d)(4) of this section; and

* * * * *

(4) Cost-of-living adjustment. For any calendar year after 2007, the $1,400 computation credit set forth in paragraph (d)(1)(iv) shall be increased by an amount equal to such dollar amount multiplied by the cost-of-living adjustment determined under section 1(f)(3) for such year as modified by this paragraph (d)(4). In applying section 1(f)(3) to determine this cost-of-living adjustment, the reference to "calendar year 1992" in section 1(f)(3)(B) shall be changed to "calendar year 2006." If any such increase determined under this paragraph (d)(4) is not a multiple of $10, such increase shall be rounded to the nearest multiple thereof.

* * * * *

PAR. 4. Section 1.148-3(j) is amended by revising Example 2(iii)(D) to read as follows:

Proposed § 1.148-3 General arbitrage rebate rules. [*For Preamble, see ¶ 152,909*]

* * * * *

(j) * * *

Example (2). * * *

(iii) * * *

(D) If the yield during the second computation period were, instead, 7.0000 percent, the rebate amount computed as of July 1, 2004, would be $1,320,891. The future value of the payment made on July 1, 1999, would be $1,471,007. Although the future value of the payment made on July 1, 1999 ($1,471,007), exceeds the rebate amount computed as of July 1, 2004 ($1,320,891), § 1.148-3(i) limits the amount recoverable as a defined overpayment of rebate under section 148 to the excess of the total "amount paid" over the sum of the amount determined under the future value method to be the "rebate amount" as of the most recent computation date and all other amounts that are otherwise required to be paid under section 148 as of the date the recovery is requested. Because the total amount that the issuer paid on July 1, 1999 ($1,042,824.60), does not exceed the rebate amount as of July 1, 2004 ($1,320,891), the issuer would not be entitled to recover any overpayment of rebate in this case.

* * * * *

§ 1.148-3A General arbitrage rebate rules.

(a) through (h)(2) [Reserved]. For guidance see § 1.148-3.

(h) *(3) Waivers of the penalty.* For purposes of § 1.148-3(h)(3), willful neglect does not include a failure that is attributable solely to the permissible retroactive selection of a short first bond year if the rebate amount that the issuer failed to pay is paid within 60 days of the selection of that bond year.

T.D. 8538, 5/5/94, amend T.D. 8718, 5/8/97.

§ 1.148-4 Yield on an issue of bonds.

(a) In general. The yield on an issue of bonds is used to apply investment yield restrictions under section 148(a) and to compute rebate liability under section 148(f). Yield is computed under the economic accrual method using any consistently applied compounding interval of not more than one year. A short first compounding interval and a short last compounding interval may be used. Yield is expressed as an annual percentage rate that is calculated to at least four decimal places (e.g., 5.2525 percent). Other reasonable, standard financial conventions, such as the 30 days per month/360 days per year convention, may be used in computing yield but must be consistently applied. The yield on an issue that would be a purpose investment (absent section 148(b)(3)(A)) is equal to the yield on the conduit financing issue that financed that purpose investment. The Commissioner may permit issuers of qualified mortgage bonds or qualified student loan bonds to use a single yield for two or more issues.

(b) Computing yield on a fixed yield issue. *(1) In general.* (i) Yield on an issue. The yield on a fixed yield issue is the discount rate that, when used in computing the present value as of the issue date of all unconditionally payable payments of principal, interest, and fees for qualified guarantees on the issue and amounts reasonably expected to be paid as fees for qualified guarantees on the issue, produces an amount equal to the present value, using the same discount rate, of the aggregate issue price of bonds of the issue as of the issue date. Further, payments include certain amounts properly allocable to a qualified hedge. Yield on a fixed yield issue is computed as of the issue date and is not affected by subsequent unexpected events, except to the extent provided in paragraphs (b)(4) and (h)(3) of this section.

(ii) Yield on a bond. Yield on a fixed yield bond is computed in the same manner as yield on a fixed yield issue.

(2) Yield on certain fixed yield bonds subject to mandatory or contingent early redemption. (i) In general. The yield on a fixed yield issue that includes a bond subject to mandatory early redemption or expected contingent redemption is computed by treating that bond as redeemed on its reasonably expected early redemption date for an amount equal to its value on that date. Reasonable expectations are determined on the issue date. A bond is subject to mandatory early redemption if it is unconditionally payable in full before its final maturity date. A bond is subject to a contingent redemption if it must be, or is reasonably expected to be, redeemed prior to final maturity upon the occurrence of a contingency. A contingent redemption is taken into account only if the contingency is reasonably expected to occur, in which case the date of occurrence of the contingency must be reasonably estimated. For example, if bonds are reasonably expected to be redeemed early using excess revenues from general or special property taxes or benefit assessments or similar amounts, the reasonably expected redemption schedule is used to determine yield. For purposes of this paragraph (b)(2)(i), excess proceeds calls for issues for which the requirements of § 1.148-2(e)(2) or (3) are satisfied, calamity calls, and refundings do not cause a bond to be subject to early redemption. The value of a bond is determined under paragraph (e) of this section.

(ii) Substantially identical bonds subject to mandatory early redemption. If substantially identical bonds of an issue are subject to specified mandatory redemptions prior to final maturity (e.g., a mandatory sinking fund redemption requirement), yield on that issue is computed by treating those bonds as redeemed in accordance with the redemption schedule for an amount equal to their value. Generally, bonds are substantially identical if the stated interest rate, maturity, and payment dates are the same. In computing the yield on an issue containing bonds described in this paragraph (b)(2)(ii), each of those bonds must be treated as redeemed at its present value, unless the stated redemption price at maturity of the bond does not exceed the issue price of the bond by more than one-fourth of one percent multiplied by the product of the stated redemption price at maturity and the number of years to the weighted average maturity date of the substantially identical bonds, in which case each of those bonds must be treated as redeemed at its outstanding stated principal amount, plus accrued, unpaid interest. Weighted average maturity is determined by taking into account the mandatory redemption schedule.

(3) Yield on certain fixed yield bonds subject to optional early redemption. (i) In general. If a fixed yield bond is subject to optional early redemption and is described in paragraph (b)(3)(ii) of this section, the yield on the issue containing the bond is computed by treating the bond as redeemed at its stated redemption price on the optional redemption date that would produce the lowest yield on the issue.

(ii) Fixed yield bonds subject to special yield calculation rule. A fixed yield bond is described in this paragraph (b)(3)(ii) only if it—

(A) Is subject to optional redemption within five years of the issue date, but only if the yield on the issue computed by assuming all bonds in the issue subject to redemption within 5 years of the issue date are redeemed at maturity is more than one-eighth of one percentage point higher than the yield on that issue computed by assuming all bonds subject to optional redemption within 5 years of the issue date are redeemed at the earliest date for their redemption;

(B) Is issued at an issue price that exceeds the stated redemption price at maturity by more than one-fourth of one percent multiplied by the product of the stated redemption price at maturity and the number of complete years to the first optional redemption date for the bond; or

(C) Bears interest at increasing interest rates (i.e., a stepped coupon bond).

(4) Yield recomputed upon transfer of certain rights associated with the bond. For purposes of § 1.148-3, as of the date of any transfer, waiver, modification, or similar transaction (collectively, a transfer) of any right that is part of the terms of a bond or is otherwise associated with a bond (e.g., a redemption right), in a transaction that is separate and apart from the original sale of the bond, the issue is treated as if it were retired and a new issue issued on the date of the transfer (reissued). The redemption price of the retired issue and the issue price of the new issue equal the aggregate values of all the bonds of the issue on the date of the transfer. In computing yield on the new issue, any amounts received

by the issuer as consideration for the transfer are taken into account.

(5) Special aggregation rule treating certain bonds as a single fixed yield bond. Two variable yield bonds of an issue are treated in the aggregate as a single fixed yield bond if—

(i) Aggregate treatment would result in the single bond being a fixed yield bond; and

(ii) The terms of the bonds do not contain any features that could distort the aggregate fixed yield from what the yield would be if a single fixed yield bond were issued. For example, if an issue contains a bond bearing interest at a floating rate and a related bond bearing interest at a rate equal to a fixed rate minus that floating rate, those two bonds are treated as a single fixed yield bond only if neither bond may be redeemed unless the other bond is also redeemed at the same time.

(6) Examples. The provisions of this paragraph (b) may be illustrated by the following examples.

Example (1). No early call.

(i) Facts. On January 1, 1994, City A issues an issue consisting of four identical fixed yield bonds. The stated final maturity date of each bond is January 1, 2004, and no bond is subject to redemption before this date. Interest is payable on January 1 of each year at a rate of 6.0000 percent per year on the outstanding principal amount. The total stated principal amount of the bonds is $20 million. The issue price of the bonds $20,060,000.

(ii) Computation. The yield on the issue is computed by treating the bonds as retired at the stated maturity under the general rule of § 1.148-4(b)(1). The bonds are treated as redeemed for their stated redemption prices. The yield on the issue is 5.8731 percent per year compounded semiannually, computed as follows:

Date	Payments	PV (5.8731 percent)
1/1/1995	$ 1,200,000	$ 1,132,510
1/1/1996	1,200,000	1,068,816
1/1/1997	1,200,000	1,008,704
1/1/1998	1,200,000	951,973
1/1/1999	1,200,000	898,433
1/1/2000	1,200,000	847,903
1/1/2001	1,200,000	800,216
1/1/2002	1,200,000	755,210
1/1/2003	1,200,000	712,736
1/1/2004	21,200,000	11,883,498
		$20,060,000

Example (2). Mandatory calls.

(i) Facts. The facts are the same as in Example 1. In this case, however, the bonds are subject to mandatory sinking fund redemption on January 1 of each year, beginning January 1, 2001. On each sinking fund redemption date, one of the bonds is chosen by lottery and is required to be redeemed at par plus accrued interest.

(ii) Computation. Because the bonds are subject to specified redemptions, yield on the issue is computed by treating the bonds as redeemed in accordance with the redemption schedule under § 1.148-4(b)(2)(ii). Because the bonds are not sold at a discount, the bonds are treated as retired at their stated redemption prices. The yield on the issue is 5.8678 percent per year compounded semiannually, computed as follows:

Date	Payments	PV (5.8678 percent)
1/1/1995	$ 1,200,000	$ 1,132,569
1/1/1996	1,200,000	1,068,926
1/1/1997	1,200,000	1,008,860
1/1/1998	1,200,000	952,169
1/1/1999	1,200,000	898,664
1/1/2000	1,200,000	848,166
1/1/2001	6,200,000	4,135,942
1/1/2002	5,900,000	3,714,650
1/1/2003	5,600,000	3,327,647
1/1/2004	5,300,000	2,972,407
		$20,060,000

Example (3). Optional early call.

(i) Facts. On January 1, 1994, City C issues an issue consisting of three bonds. Each bond has a stated principal amount of $10 million dollars and is issued for par. Bond X bears interest at 5 percent per year and matures on January 1, 1999. Bond Y bears interest at 6 percent per year and matures on January 1, 2002. Bond Z bears interest at 7 percent per year and matures on January 1, 2004. Bonds Y and Z are callable by the issuer at par plus accrued interest after December 31, 1998.

(ii) Computation.

(A) The yield on the issue computed as if each bond is outstanding to its maturity is 6.0834 percent per year compounded semiannually, computed as follows:

Date	Payments	PV (6.0834 percent)
1/1/1995	$ 1,800,000	$ 1,695,299
1/1/1996	1,800,000	1,596,689
1/1/1997	1,800,000	1,503,814
1/1/1998	1,800,000	1,416,342
1/1/1999	11,800,000	8,744,830
1/1/2000	1,300,000	907,374
1/1/2001	1,300,000	854,595
1/1/2002	11,300,000	6,996,316
1/1/2003	700,000	408,190
1/1/2004	10,700,000	5,876,551
		$30,000,000

(B) The yield on the issue computed as if all bonds are called at the earliest date for redemption is 5.9126 percent per year compounded semiannually, computed as follows:

Date	Payments	PV (5.9126 percent)
1/1/1995	$ 1,800,000	$ 1,698,113
1/1/1996	1,800,000	1,601,994
1/1/1997	1,800,000	1,511,315
1/1/1998	1,800,000	1,425,769
1/1/1999	31,800,000	23,762,809
		$30,000,000

(C) Because the yield on the issue computed by assuming all bonds in the issue subject to redemption within 5 years of the issue date are redeemed at maturity is more than one-eighth of one percentage point higher than the yield on the issue computed by assuming all bonds subject to optional redemption within 5 years of the issue date are redeemed at the earliest date for their redemption, each bond is treated as redeemed on the date that would produce the lowest yield for the issue. The lowest yield on the issue would result from a redemption of all the bonds on January 1, 1999.

Thus, the yield on the issue is 5.9126 percent per year compounded semiannually.

(c) Computing yield on a variable yield issue. *(1) In general.* The yield on a variable yield issue is computed separately for each computation period. The yield for each computation period is the discount rate that, when used in computing the present value as of the first day of the computation period of all the payments of principal and interest and fees for qualified guarantees that are attributable to the computation period, produces an amount equal to the present value, using the same discount rate, of the aggregate issue price (or deemed issue price, as determined in paragraph (c)(2)(iv) of this section) of the bonds of the issue as of the first day of the computation period. The yield on a variable yield bond is computed in the same manner as the yield on a variable yield issue. Except as provided in paragraph (c)(2) of this section, yield on any fixed yield bond in a variable yield issue is computed in the same manner as the yield on a fixed yield issue as provided in paragraph (b) of this section.

(2) Payments on bonds included in yield for a computation period. (i) Payments in general: The payments on a bond that are attributable to a computation period include any amounts actually paid during the period for principal on the bond. Payments also include any amounts paid during the current period both for interest accruing on the bond during the current period and for interest accruing during the prior period that was included in the deemed issue price of the bond as accrued unpaid interest at the start of the current period under this paragraph (c)(2). Further, payments include any amounts properly allocable to fees for a qualified guarantee of the bond for the period and to any amounts properly allocable to a qualified hedge for the period.

(ii) Payments at actual redemption. If a bond is actually redeemed during a computation period, an amount equal to the greater of its value on the redemption date or the actual redemption price is a payment on the actual redemption date.

(iii) Payments for bonds outstanding at end of computation period. If a bond is outstanding at the end of a computation period, a payment equal to the bond's value is taken into account on the last day of that period.

(iv) Issue price for bonds outstanding at beginning of next computation period. A bond outstanding at the end of a computation period is treated as if it were immediately reissued on the next day for a deemed issue price equal to the value from the day before as determined under paragraph (c)(2)(iii) of this section.

(3) Example. The provisions of this paragraph (c) may be illustrated by the following example.

Example. On January 1, 1994, City A issues an issue of identical plain par bonds in an aggregate principal amount of $1,000,000. The bonds pay interest at a variable rate on each June 1 throughout the term of the issue. The entire principal amount of the bonds plus accrued, unpaid interest is payable on the final maturity date of January 1, 2000. No bond year is selected. On June 1, 1994, 1995, 1996, 1997, and 1998, interest in the amounts of $30,000, $55,000, $57,000, $56,000, and $45,000 is paid on the bonds. From June 1, 1998, to January 1, 1999, $30,000 of interest accrues on the bonds. From January 1, 1999, to June 1, 1999, another $35,000 of interest accrues. On June 1, 1999, the issuer actually pays $65,000 of interest. On January 1, 2000, $1,000,000 of principal and $38,000 of accrued interest are paid. The payments for the computation period starting on the issue date and ending on January 1, 1999, include all annual interest payments paid from the issue date to June 1, 1998. Because the issue is outstanding on January 1, 1999, it is treated as redeemed on that date for amount equal to its value ($1,000,000 plus accrued, unpaid interest of $30,000 under paragraph (e)(1) of this section). Thus, $1,030,000 is treated as paid on January 1, 1999. The issue is then treated as reissued on January 1, 1999, for $1,030,000. The payments for the next computation period starting on January 1, 1999, and ending on January 1, 2000, include the interest actually paid on the bonds during that period ($65,000 on June 1, 1999, plus $38,000 paid on January 1, 2000). Because the issue was actually redeemed on January 1, 2000, an amount equal to its stated redemption price is also treated as paid on January 1, 2000.

(d) Conversion from variable yield issue to fixed yield issue. For purposes of determining yield under this section, as of the first day on which a variable yield issue would qualify as a fixed yield issue if it were newly issued on that date (A conversion date), that issue is treated as if it were reissued as a fixed yield issue on the conversion date. The redemption price of the variable yield issue and the issue price of the fixed yield issue equal the aggregate values of all the bonds on the conversion date. Thus, for example, for plain par bonds (e.g., tender bonds), the deemed issue price would be the outstanding principal amount, plus accrued unpaid interest. If the conversion date occurs on a date other than a computation date, the issuer may continue to treat the issue as a variable yield issue until the next computation date, at which time it must be treated as converted to a fixed yield issue.

(e) Value of bonds. *(1) Plain par bonds.* Except as otherwise provided, the value of a plain par bond is its outstanding stated principal amount, plus accrued unpaid interest. The value of a plain par bond that is actually redeemed or treated as redeemed is its stated redemption price on the redemption date, plus accrued, unpaid interest.

(2) Other bonds. The value of a bond other than a plain par bond on a date is its present value on that date. The present value of a bond is computed under the economic accrual method taking into account all the unconditionally payable payments of principal, interest, and fees for a qualified guarantee to be paid on or after that date and using the yield on the bond as the discount rate, except that for purposes of § 1.148-6(b)(2) (relating to the universal cap), these values may be determined by consistently using the yield on the issue of which the bonds are a part. To determine yield on fixed yield bonds, see paragraph (b)(1) of this section. The rules contained in paragraphs (b)(2) and (b)(3) of this section apply for this purpose. In the case of bonds described in paragraph (b)(2)(ii) of this section, the present value of those bonds on any date is computed using the yield to the final maturity date of those bonds as the discount rate. In determining the present value of a variable yield bond under this paragraph (e)(2), the initial interest rate on the bond established by the interest index or other interest rate setting mechanism is used to determine the interest payments on that bond.

(f) Qualified guarantees. *(1) In general.* Fees properly allocable to payments for a qualified guarantee for an issue (as determined under paragraph (f)(6) of this section) are treated as additional interest on that issue under section 148. A guarantee is a qualified guarantee if it satisfies each of the requirements of paragraphs (f)(2) through (f)(4) of this section.

(2) Interest savings. As of the date the guarantee is obtained, the issuer must reasonably expect that the present

value of the fees for the guarantee will be less than the present value of the expected interest savings on the issue as a result of the guarantee. For this purpose, present value is computed using the yield on the issue, determined with regard to guarantee payments, as the discount rate.

(3) Guarantee in substance. The arrangement must create a guarantee in substance. The arrangement must impose a secondary liability that unconditionally shifts substantially all of the credit risk for all or part of the payments, such as payments for principal and interest, redemption prices, or tender prices, on the guaranteed bonds. Reasonable procedural or administrative requirements of the guarantee do not cause the guarantee to be conditional. In the case of a guarantee against failure to remarket a qualified tender bond, commercially reasonable limitations based on credit risk, such as limitations on payment in the event of default by the primary obligor or the bankruptcy of a long-term credit guarantor, do not cause the guarantee to be conditional. The guarantee may be in any form. The guarantor may not be a co-obligor. Thus, the guarantor must not expect to make any payments other than under a direct-pay letter of credit or similar arrangement for which the guarantor will be reimbursed immediately. The guarantor and any related parties together must not use more than 10 percent of the proceeds of the portion of the issue allocable to the guaranteed bonds.

(4) Reasonable charge. (i) In general. Fees for a guarantee must not exceed a reasonable, arm's-length charge for the transfer of credit risk. In complying with this requirement, the issuer may not rely on the representations of the guarantor.

(ii) Fees for services other than transfer of credit risk must be separately stated. A fee for a guarantee must not include any payment for any direct or indirect services other than the transfer of credit risk, unless the compensation for those other services is separately stated, reasonable, and excluded from the guarantee fee. Fees for the transfer of credit risk include fees for the guarantor's overhead and other costs relating to the transfer of credit risk. For example, a fee includes payment for services other than transfer of credit risk if—

(A) It includes payment for the cost of underwriting or remarketing bonds or for the cost of insurance for casualty to bond-financed property;

(B) It is refundable upon redemption of the guaranteed bond before the final maturity date and the amount of the refund would exceed the portion of the fee that had not been earned; or

(C) The requirements of § 1.148-2(e)(2) (relating to temporary periods for capital projects) are not satisfied, and the guarantor is not reasonably assured that the bonds will be repaid if the project to be financed is not completed.

(5) Guarantee of purpose investments. Except for guarantees of qualified mortgage loans and qualified student loans, a guarantee of payments on a purpose investment is a qualified guarantee of the issue if all payments on the purpose investment reasonably coincide with payments on the related bonds and the payments on the purpose investment are unconditionally payable no more than 6 months before the corresponding interest payment and 12 months before the corresponding principal payments on the bonds. This paragraph (f)(5) only applies if, in addition to satisfying the other requirements of this paragraph (f), the guarantee is, in substance, a guarantee of the bonds allocable to that purpose investment and to no other bonds except for bonds that are equally and ratably secured by purpose investments of the same conduit borrower.

(6) Allocation of qualified guarantee payments. (i) In general. Payments for a qualified guarantee must be allocated to bonds and to computation periods in a manner that properly reflects the proportionate credit risk for which the guarantor is compensated. Proportionate credit risk for bonds that are not substantially identical may be determined using any reasonable, consistently applied method. For example, this risk may be based on the ratio of the total principal and interest paid and to be paid on a guaranteed bond to the total principal and interest paid and to be paid on all bonds of the guaranteed issue. An allocation method generally is not reasonable, for example, if a substantial portion of the fee is allocated to the construction portion of the issue and a correspondingly insubstantial portion is allocated to the later years covered by the guarantee. Reasonable letter of credit set up fees may be allocated ratably during the initial term of the letter of credit. Upon an early redemption of a variable yield bond, fees otherwise allocable to the period after the redemption are allocated to remaining outstanding bonds of the issue or, if none remain outstanding, to the period before the redemption.

(ii) Safe harbor for allocation of qualified guarantee fees for variable yield issues. An allocation of non-level payments for a qualified guarantee for variable yield bonds is treated as meeting the requirements of paragraph (f)(6)(i) of this section if, for each bond year for which the guarantee is in effect, an equal amount (or for any short bond year, a proportionate amount of the equal amount) is treated as paid as of the beginning of that bond year. The present value of the annual amounts must equal the fee for the guarantee allocated to that bond, with present value computed as of the first day the guarantee is in effect by using as the discount rate the yield on the variable yield bonds covered by the guarantee, determined without regard to any fee allocated under this paragraph (f)(6)(ii).

(7) Refund or reduction of guarantee payments. If as a result of an investment of proceeds of a refunding issue in a refunding escrow, there will be a reduction in, or refund of, payments for a guarantee (savings), the savings must be treated as a reduction in the payments on the refunding issue.

(g) Yield on certain mortgage revenue and student loan bonds. For purposes of section 148 and this section, section 143(g)(2)(C)(ii) applies to the computation of yield on an issue of qualified mortgage bonds or qualified veterans' mortgage bonds. For purposes of applying section 148 and section 143(g) with respect to purpose investments allocable to a variable yield issue of qualified mortgage bonds, qualified veterans' mortgage bonds, or qualified student loan bonds that is reasonably expected as of the issue date to convert to a fixed yield issue, the yield may be computed over the term of the issue, and, if the yield is so computed, paragraph (d) of this section does not apply to the issue. As of any date, the yield over the term of the issue is based on—

(1) With respect to any bond of the issue that has not converted to a fixed and determinable yield on or before that date, the actual amounts paid or received to that date and the amounts that are reasonably expected (as of that date) to be paid or received with respect to that bond over the remaining term of the issue (taking into account prepayment assumptions under section 143(g)(2)(B)(iv), if applicable); and

(2) With respect to any bond of the issue that has converted to a fixed and determinable yield on or before that date, the actual amounts paid or received before that bond converted, if any, and the amount that was reasonably expected (on the date that bond converted) to be paid or re-

ceived with respect to that bond over the remaining term of the issue (taking into account prepayment assumptions under section 143(g)(2)(B)(iv), if applicable).

(h) Qualified hedging transactions. *(1) In general.* Payments made or received by an issuer under a qualified hedge (as defined in paragraph (h)(2) of this section) relating to bonds of an issue are taken into account (as provided in paragraph (h)(3) of this section) to determine the yield on the issue. Except as provided in paragraphs (h)(4) and (h)(5)(ii)(E) of this section, the bonds to which a qualified hedge relates are treated as variable yield bonds from the issue date of the bonds. This paragraph (h) applies solely for purposes of sections 143(g), 148, and 149(d).

(2) Qualified hedge defined. Except as provided in paragraph (h)(5) of this section, the term *qualified hedge* means a contract that satisfies each of the following requirements:

(i) Hedge. (A) In general. The contract is entered into primarily to modify the issuer's risk of interest rate changes with respect to a bond (a hedge). For example, the contract may be an interest rate swap, an interest rate cap, a futures contract, a forward contract, or an option.

(B) Special rule for fixed rate issues. If the contract modifies the issuer's risk of interest rate changes with respect to a bond that is part of an issue that, absent the contract, would be a fixed rate issue, the contract must be entered into—

(1) No later than 15 days after the issue date (or the deemed issue date under paragraph (d) of this section) of the issue; or

(2) No later than the expiration of a qualified hedge with respect to bonds of that issue that satisfies paragraph (h)(2)(i)(B)(1) of this section; or

(3) No later than the expiration of a qualified hedge with respect to bonds of that issue that satisfies either paragraph (h)(2)(i)(B)(2) of this section or this paragraph (h)(2)(i)(B)(3).

(C) Contracts with certain acquisition payments. If a hedge provider makes a single payment to the issuer (e.g., a payment for an off-market swap) in connection with the acquisition of a contract, the issuer may treat a portion of that contract as a hedge provided—

(1) The hedge provider's payment to the issuer and the issuer's payments under the contract in excess of those that it would make if the contract bore rates equal to the on-market rates for the contract (determined as of the date the parties enter into the contract) are separately identified in a certification of the hedge provider; and

(2) The payments described in paragraph (h)(2)(i)(C)(1) of this section are not treated as payments on the hedge.

(ii) No significant investment element. (A) In general. The contract does not contain a significant investment element. Except as provided in paragraph (h)(2)(ii)(B) of this section, a contract contains a significant investment element if a significant portion of any payment by one party relates to a conditional or unconditional obligation by the other party to make a payment on a different date. Examples of contracts that contain a significant investment element are a debt instrument held by the issuer; an interest rate swap requiring any payments other than periodic payments, within the meaning of § 1.446-3 (periodic payments) (e.g., a payment for an off-market swap or prepayment of part or all of one leg of a swap); and an interest rate cap requiring the issuer's premium for the cap to be paid in a single, up-front payment.

(B) Special level payment rule for interest rate caps. An interest rate cap does not contain a significant investment element if—

(1) All payments to the issuer by the hedge provider are periodic payments;

(2) The issuer makes payments for the cap at the same time as periodic payments by the hedge provider must be made if the specified index (within the meaning of § 1.446-3) of the cap is above the strike price of the cap; and

(3) Each payment by the issuer bears the same ratio to the notional principal amount (within the meaning of § 1.446-3) that is used to compute the hedge provider's payment, if any, on that date.

(iii) Parties. The contract is entered into between the issuer or the political subdivision on behalf of which the issuer issues the bonds (collectively referred to in this paragraph (h) as the issuer) and a provider that is not a related party (the hedge provider).

(iv) Hedged bonds.The contract covers, in whole or in part, all of one or more groups of substantially identical bonds in the issue (i.e., all of the bonds having the same interest rate, maturity, and terms). Thus, for example, a qualified hedge may include a hedge of all or a pro rata portion of each interest payment on the variable rate bonds in an issue for the first 5 years following their issuance. For purposes of this paragraph (h), unless the context clearly requires otherwise, hedged bonds means the specific bonds or portions thereof covered by a hedge.

(v) Interest based contract.The contract is primarily interest based. A contract is not primarily interest based unless—

(A) The hedged bond, without regard to the contract, is either a fixed rate bond, a variable rate debt instrument within the meaning of § 1.1275-5 provided the rate is not based on an objective rate other than a qualified inverse floating rate or a qualified inflation rate, a tax-exempt obligation described in § 1.1275-4(d)(2), or an inflation-indexed debt instrument within the meaning of § 1.1275-7; and

(B) As a result of treating all payments on (and receipts from) the contract as additional payments on (and receipts from) the hedged bond, the resulting bond would be substantially similar to either a fixed rate bond, a variable rate debt instrument within the meaning of § 1.1275-5 provided the rate is not based on an objective rate other than a qualified inverse floating rate or a qualified inflation rate, a tax-exempt obligation described in § 1.1275-4(d)(2), or an inflation-indexed debt instrument within the meaning of § 1.1275-7. For this purpose, differences that would not prevent the resulting bond from being substantially similar to another type of bond include a difference between the index used to compute payments on the hedged bond and the index used to compute payments on the hedge where one index is substantially the same, but not identical to, the other; the difference resulting from the payment of a fixed premium for a cap (e.g., payments for a cap that are made in other than level installments); and the difference resulting from the allocation of a termination payment where the termination was not expected as of the date the contract was entered into.

(vi) Payments closely correspond. The payments received by the issuer from the hedge provider under the contract correspond closely in time to either the specific payments being hedged on the hedged bonds or specific payments required to be made pursuant to the bond documents, regardless of the hedge, to a sinking fund, debt service fund, or similar fund maintained for the issue of which the hedged bond is a part.

(vii) Source of payments. Payments to the hedge provider are reasonably expected to be made from the same source of funds that, absent the hedge, would be reasonably expected to be used to pay principal and interest on the hedged bonds.

(viii) Identification. The contract must be identified by the actual issuer on its books and records maintained for the hedged bonds not later than 3 days after the date on which the issuer and the hedge provider enter into the contract. The identification must specify the hedge provider, the terms of the contract, and the hedged bonds. The identification must contain sufficient detail to establish that the requirements of this paragraph (h)(2) and, if applicable, paragraph (h)(4) of this section are satisfied. In addition, the existence of the hedge must be noted on the first form relating to the issue of which the hedged bonds are a part that is filed with the Internal Revenue Service on or after the date on which the contract is identified pursuant to this paragraph (h)(2)(viii).

(3) Accounting for qualified hedges. (i) In general. Except as otherwise provided in paragraph (h)(4) of this section, payments made or received by the issuer under a qualified hedge are treated as payments made or received, as appropriate, on the hedged bonds that are taken into account in determining the yield on those bonds. These payments are reasonably allocated to the hedged bonds in the period to which the payments relate, as determined under paragraph (h)(3)(iii) of this section. Payments made or received by the issuer include payments deemed made or received when a contract is terminated or deemed terminated under this paragraph (h)(3). Payments reasonably allocable to the modification of risk of interest rate changes and to the hedge provider's overhead under this paragraph (h) are included as payments made or received under a qualified hedge.

(ii) Exclusions from hedge. If any payment for services or other items under the contract is not expressly treated by paragraph (h)(3)(i) of this section as a payment under the qualified hedge, the payment is not a payment with respect to a qualified hedge.

(iii) Timing and allocation of payments. Except as provided in paragraphs (h)(3)(iv) and (h)(5) of this section, payments made or received by the issuer under a qualified hedge are taken into account in the same period in which those amounts would be treated as income or deductions under § 1.446-4 (without regard to § 1.446-4(a)(2)(iv)) and are adjusted as necessary to reflect the end of a computation period and the start of a new computation period.

(iv) Termination payments. (A) Termination defined. A termination of a qualified hedge includes any sale or other disposition of the hedge by the issuer or the acquisition by the issuer of an offsetting hedge. A deemed termination occurs when the hedged bonds are redeemed or when a hedge ceases to be a qualified hedge of the hedged bonds. In the case of an assignment by a hedge provider of its remaining rights and obligations under the hedge to a third party or a modification of the hedging contract, the assignment or modification is treated as a termination with respect to the issuer only if it results in a deemed exchange of the hedge and a realization event under section 1001 to the issuer.

(B) General rule. A payment made or received by an issuer to terminate a qualified hedge, including loss or gain realized or deemed realized, is treated as a payment made or received on the hedged bonds, as appropriate. The payment is reasonably allocated to the remaining periods originally covered by the terminated hedge in a manner that reflects the economic substance of the hedge.

(C) Special rule for terminations when bonds are redeemed. Except as otherwise provided in this paragraph (h)(3)(iv)(C) and in paragraph (h)(3)(iv)(D) of this section, when a qualified hedge is deemed terminated because the hedged bonds are redeemed, the fair market value of the qualified hedge on the redemption date is treated as a termination payment made or received on that date. When hedged bonds are redeemed, any payment received by the issuer on termination of a hedge, including a termination payment or a deemed termination payment, reduces, but not below zero, the interest payments made by the issuer on the hedged bonds in the computation period ending on the termination date. The remainder of the payment, if any, is reasonably allocated over the bond years in the immediately preceding computation period or periods to the extent necessary to eliminate the excess.

(D) Special rules for refundings. To the extent that the hedged bonds are redeemed using the proceeds of a refunding issue, the termination payment is accounted for under paragraph (h)(3)(iv)(B) of this section by treating it as a payment on the refunding issue, rather than the hedged bonds. In addition, to the extent that the refunding issue is redeemed during the period to which the termination payment has been allocated to that issue, paragraph (h)(3)(iv)(C) of this section applies to the termination payment by treating it as a payment on the redeemed refunding issue.

(E) Safe harbor for allocation of certain termination payments. A payment to terminate a qualified hedge does not result in that hedge failing to satisfy the applicable provisions of paragraph (h)(3)(iv)(B) of this section if the payment is allocated in accordance with this paragraph (h)(3)(iv)(E). For an issue that is a variable yield issue after termination of a qualified hedge, an amount must be allocated to each date on which the hedge provider's payment, if any, would have been made had the hedge not been terminated. The amounts allocated to each date must bear the same ratio to the notional principal amount (within the meaning of § 1.446-3) that would have been used to compute the hedge provider's payment, if any, on that date, and the sum of the present values of those amounts must equal the present value of the termination payment. Present value is computed as of the day the qualified hedge is terminated, using the yield on the hedged bonds, determined without regard to the termination payment. The yield used for this purpose is computed for the period beginning on the first date the qualified hedge is in effect and ending on the date the qualified hedge is terminated. On the other hand, for an issue that is a fixed yield issue after termination of a qualified hedge, the termination payment is taken into account as a single payment on the date it is paid.

(4) Certain variable yield bonds treated as fixed yield bonds. (i) In general. Except as otherwise provided in this paragraph (h)(4), if the issuer of variable yield bonds enters into a qualified hedge, the hedged bonds are treated as fixed yield bonds paying a fixed interest rate if:

(A) Maturity. The term of the hedge is equal to the entire period during which the hedged bonds bear interest at variable interest rates, and the issuer does not reasonably expect that the hedge will be terminated before the end of that period.

(B) Payments closely correspond. Payments to be received under the hedge correspond closely in time to the hedged portion of payments on the hedged bonds. Hedge payments received within 15 days of the related payments on the hedged bonds generally so correspond.

(C) Aggregate payments fixed. Taking into account all payments made and received under the hedge and all payments on the hedged bonds (i.e., after netting all payments), the issuer's aggregate payments are fixed and determinable as of a date not later than 15 days after the issue date of the hedged bonds. Payments on bonds are treated as fixed for purposes of this paragraph (h)(4)(i)(C) if payments on the bonds are based, in whole or in part, on one interest rate, payments on the hedge are based, in whole or in part, on a second interest rate that is substantially the same as, but not identical to, the first interest rate and payments on the bonds would be fixed if the two rates were identical. Rates are treated as substantially the same if they are reasonably expected to be substantially the same throughout the term of the hedge. For example, an objective 30-day tax-exempt variable rate index or other objective index may be substantially the same as an issuer's individual 30-day interest rate.

(ii) Accounting. Except as otherwise provided in this paragraph (h)(4)(ii), in determining yield on the hedged bonds, all the issuer's payments on the hedged bonds and all payments made and received on a hedge described in paragraph (h)(4)(i) of this section are taken into account. If payments on the bonds and payments on the hedge are based, in whole or in part, on variable interest rates that are substantially the same within the meaning of paragraph (h)(4)(i)(C) of this section (but not identical), yield on the issue is determined by treating the variable interest rates as identical. For example, if variable rate bonds bearing interest at a weekly rate equal to the rate necessary to remarket the bonds at par are hedged with an interest rate swap under which the issuer receives payments based on a short-term floating rate index that is substantially the same as, but not identical to, the weekly rate on the bonds, the interest payments on the bonds are treated as equal to the payments received by the issuer under the swap for purposes of computing the yield on the bonds.

(iii) Effect of termination. (A) In general. Except as otherwise provided in this paragraph (h)(4)(iii) and paragraph (h)(5) of this section, the issue of which the hedged bonds are a part is treated as if it were reissued as of the termination date of the qualified hedge covered by paragraph (h)(4)(i) of this section in determining yield on the hedged bonds for purposes of § 1.148-3. The redemption price of the retired issue and the issue price of the new issue equal the aggregate values of all the bonds of the issue on the termination date. In computing the yield on the new issue for this purpose, any termination payment is accounted for under paragraph (h)(3)(iv) of this section, applied by treating the termination payment as made or received on the new issue under this paragraph (h)(4)(iii).

(B) Effect of early termination. Except as otherwise provided in this paragraph (h)(4)(iii), the general rules of paragraph (h)(4)(i) of this section do not apply in determining the yield on the hedged bonds for purposes of § 1.148-3 if the hedge is terminated or deemed terminated within 5 years after the issue date of the issue of which the hedged bonds are a part. Thus, the hedged bonds are treated as variable yield bonds for purposes of § 1.148-3 from the issue date.

(C) Certain terminations disregarded. This paragraph (h)(4)(iii) does not apply to a termination if, based on the facts and circumstances (e.g., taking into account both the termination and any qualified hedge that immediately replaces the terminated hedge), there is no change in the yield.

(5) Contracts entered into before issue date of hedged bond. (i) In general. A contract does not fail to be a hedge under paragraph (h)(2)(i) of this section solely because it is entered into before the issue date of the hedged bond. However, that contract must be one to which either paragraph (h)(5)(ii) or (h)(5)(iii) of this section applies.

(ii) Contracts expected to be closed substantially contemporaneously with the issue date of hedged bond. (A) Application. This paragraph (h)(5)(ii) applies to a contract if, on the date the contract is identified, the issuer reasonably expects to terminate or otherwise close (terminate) the contract substantially contemporaneously with the issue date of the hedged bond.

(B) Contract terminated. If a contract to which this paragraph (h)(5)(ii) applies is terminated substantially contemporaneously with the issue date of the hedged bond, the amount paid or received, or deemed to be paid or received, by the issuer in connection with the issuance of the hedged bond to terminate the contract is treated as an adjustment to the issue price of the hedged bond and as an adjustment to the sale proceeds of the hedged bond for purposes of section 148. Amounts paid or received, or deemed to be paid or received, before the issue date of the hedged bond are treated as paid or received on the issue date in an amount equal to the future value of the payment or receipt on that date. For this purpose, future value is computed using yield on the hedged bond without taking into account amounts paid or received (or deemed paid or received) on the contract.

(C) Contract not terminated. If a contract to which this paragraph (h)(5)(ii) applies is not terminated substantially contemporaneously with the issue date of the hedged bond, the contract is deemed terminated for its fair market value as of the issue date of the hedged bond. Once a contract has been deemed terminated pursuant to this paragraph (h)(5)(ii)(C), payments on and receipts from the contract are no longer taken into account under this paragraph (h) for purposes of determining yield on the hedged bond.

(D) Relation to other requirements of a qualified hedge. Payments made in connection with the issuance of a bond to terminate a contract to which this paragraph (h)(5)(ii) applies do not prevent the contract from satisfying the requirements of paragraph (h)(2)(vi) of this section.

(E) Fixed yield treatment. A bond that is hedged with a contract to which this paragraph (h)(5)(ii) applies does not fail to be a fixed yield bond if, taking into account payments on the contract and the payments to be made on the bond, the bond satisfies the definition of fixed yield bond. See also paragraph (h)(4) of this section.

(iii) Contracts expected not to be closed substantially contemporaneously with the issue date of hedged bond. (A) Application. This paragraph (h)(5)(iii) applies to a contract if, on the date the contract is identified, the issuer does not reasonably expect to terminate the contract substantially contemporaneously with the issue date of the hedge bond.

(B) Contract terminated. If a contract to which this paragraph (h)(5)(iii) applies is terminated in connection with the issuance of the hedged bond, the amount paid or received, or deemed to be paid or received, by the issuer to terminate the contract is treated as an adjustment to the issue price of the hedged bond and as an adjustment to the sale proceeds of the hedged bond for purposes of section 148.

(C) Contract not terminated. If a contract to which this paragraph (h)(5)(iii) applies is not terminated substantially contemporaneously with the issue date of the hedged bond, no payments with respect to the hedge made by the issuer before the issue date of the hedged bond are taken into account under this section.

(iv) Identification. The identification required under paragraph (h)(2)(viii) of this section must specify the reasonably expected governmental purpose, issue price, maturity, and issue date of the hedged bond, the manner in which interest is reasonably expected to be computed, and whether paragraph (h)(5)(ii) or (h)(5)(iii) of this section applies to the contract. If an issuer identifies a contract under this paragraph (h)(5)(iv) that would be a qualified hedge with respect to the anticipated bond, but does not issue the anticipated bond on the identified issue date, the contract is taken into account as a qualified hedge of any bond of the issuer that is issued for the identified governmental purpose within a reasonable interval around the identified issue date of the anticipated bond.

(6) Authority of the Commissioner. The Commissioner, by publication of a revenue ruling or revenue procedure (see § 601.601(d)(2) of this chapter), may specify contracts that, although they do not meet the requirements of paragraph (h)(2) of this section, are qualified hedges or, although they do not meet the requirements of paragraph (h)(4) of this section, cause the hedged bonds to be treated as fixed yield bonds.

T.D. 8418, 5/12/92, amend T.D. 8476, 6/14/93, T.D. 8538, 5/5/94, T.D. 8718, 5/8/97, T.D. 8838, 9/3/99.

PAR. 5. Section 1.148-4(a) is revised to read as follows:

Proposed § 1.148-4 Yield on an issue of bonds. [*For Preamble, see ¶ 152,909*]

(a) In general. The yield on an issue of bonds is used to apply investment yield restrictions under section 148(a) and to compute rebate liability under section 148(f). Yield is computed under the economic accrual method using any consistently applied compounding interval of not more than one year. A short first compounding interval and a short last compounding interval may be used. Yield is expressed as an annual percentage rate that is calculated to at least four decimal places (for example, 5.2525 percent). Other reasonable, standard financial conventions, such as the 30 days per month/360 days per year convention, may be used in computing yield but must be consistently applied. The yield on an issue that would be a purpose investment (absent section 148(b)(3)(A)) is equal to the yield on the conduit financing issue that financed that purpose investment.

* * * * *

PAR. 6. Section 1.148-4 is amended by:

1. Revising paragraph (b)(3)(i), and adding a new sentence at the end of paragraph (h)(2)(ii)(A).

2. Revising the heading and introductory text of paragraph (h)(2)(v).

3. Amending paragraph (h)(2)(v)(B) by revising the last sentence.

4. Adding paragraphs (h)(2)(v)(B)(1), (2) and (3).

5. Adding a new sentence at the end of paragraph (h)(2)(vi).

6. Revising the heading and first sentence of paragraph (h)(2)(viii).

7. Amending paragraph (h)(3)(iv)(B) by adding a new sentence immediately after the first sentence.

8. Adding a new sentence at the end of paragraph (h)(4)(i)(C).

The revised and added provisions read as follows:

Proposed § 1.148-4 Yield on an issue of bonds. [*For Preamble, see ¶ 152,909*]

* * * * *

(b) * * *

(3) Yield on certain fixed yield bonds subject to optional early redemption. (i) In general. If a fixed yield bond is subject to optional early redemption and is described in paragraph (b)(3)(ii) of this section, the yield on the issue containing the bond is computed by treating the bond as redeemed at its stated redemption price on the optional redemption date that would produce the lowest yield on that bond.

* * * * *

(h) * * *

(2) * * *

(ii) * * *

(A) * * * For purposes of applying the definition of periodic payment under § 1.446-3 to determine whether a hedge has a significant investment element under this paragraph (h)(2)(ii)(A), the definition of "specified index" under § 1.446-3 (upon which periodic payments are required to be based) is deemed also to include payments an issuer receives under a hedge that are computed to be equal to the issuer's cost of funds, such as the issuer's actual market-based tax-exempt variable interest rate on its bonds.

* * * * *

(v) Interest-based contract and size and scope of hedge. The contract is primarily interest-based (for example, a hedge based on a debt index rather than an equity index). In addition, the size and scope of the hedge under the contract is limited to that which is reasonably necessary to hedge the issuer's risk with respect to interest rate changes on the hedged bonds. For example, a contract is limited to hedging an issuer's risk with respect to interest rate changes on the hedged bonds if the hedge is based on the issuer's principal amount of bonds and reasonably expected interest requirements rather than based on a greater notional amount or an interest rate level greater than the expected interest requirements. A contract is not primarily interest based unless—

* * * * *

(B) * * * For this purpose, differences that would not prevent the resulting bond from being substantially similar to another type of bond or to result in overhedging include:

(1) A difference between the interest rate used to compute payments on the hedged bond and the interest rate used to compute payments on the hedge where one interest rate is substantially the same as, but not identical to, the other. For this purpose, if an interest rate swap under which the issuer pays the hedge provider a fixed interest payment and receives from the hedge provider a floating interest rate that is based on a taxable interest rate or a taxable market interest rate index, the floating rate on the hedge and the variable rate on the hedged bonds will be treated as being substantially the same only if:

(i) The difference between the interest rate on the issuer's hedged bonds and the floating interest rate on the hedge does not exceed one quarter of one percent (.25 percent, or 25 basis points) on the date that the issuer enters into the hedge; and

(ii) For a three-year period that ends on the date the issuer enters into the hedge, the average difference between the issuer's actual tax-exempt interest rate on comparable variable-rate bonds (or, if no such comparable bonds exist, rates from a reasonable tax-exempt interest rate index, such as the SIFMA Municipal Swap Index, for that same period) and interest rates determined in the same manner as the floating interest rate on the hedge and as of the same dates as the issuer's comparable variable-rate bonds (or the tax-exempt market index, if applicable) does not exceed one-quarter of one percent (.25 percent, or 25 basis points). For example, if the floating rate on the hedge is 67 percent of LIBOR, then 67 percent of LIBOR, determined as of the same dates as the issuer's actual interest rates (or tax-exempt market index, if applicable) is compared to those actual interest rates (or the tax-exempt market index, if applicable) for the three-year period ending on the date the hedge is entered into and the differences are averaged to determine whether the average difference exceeds one-quarter of one percent. For this purpose, a reasonable sample may be used if the sample for the issuer's actual rates (or tax-exempt market index rates, if applicable) and the sample of floating rates used for the hedge are determined as of the same dates.

(2) A difference resulting from the payment of a fixed premium for a cap (for example, payments for a cap that are made in other than level installments).

(3) A difference resulting from the allocation of a termination payment if the termination was unexpected as of the date that the parties entered into the hedge contract.

(vi) * * * For this purpose, such payments will be treated as corresponding closely in time under this paragraph (h)(2)(vi) if they are made within 60 calendar days of each other.

* * * * *

(viii) Reasonably contemporaneous identification. The contract must be identified by the actual issuer on its books and records maintained for the hedged bonds not later than 15 calendar days after the date on which the issuer and the hedge provider enter into the hedge contract. * * *

(3) * * *

(iv) * * *

(B) * * * The amount of the termination payment in a termination or deemed termination is equal to the fair market value of the qualified hedge on the date of the termination. * * *

* * * * *

(4) * * *

(i) * * *

(C) * * * Except for an anticipatory hedge that is terminated or otherwise closed substantially contemporaneously with the hedged bond in accordance with paragraph (h)(5)(ii) or (h)(5)(iii) of this section, a hedge based on a taxable interest rate or taxable interest index (for example, the London Interbank Offered Rate or LIBOR) does not meet the requirements of this paragraph (C).

* * * * *

§ 1.148-4A Yield on an issue of bonds.

(a) through (b)(4) [Reserved]. For guidance see § 1.148-4.

(b) *(5) Special aggregation rule treating certain bonds as a single fixed yield bond.* Two variable yield bonds of an issue are treated in the aggregate as a single fixed yield bond if—

(i) Aggregate treatment would result in the single bond being a fixed yield bond; and

(ii) The terms of the bonds do not contain any features that could distort the aggregate fixed yield from what the yield would be if a single fixed yield bond were issued. For example, if an issue contains a bond bearing interest at a floating rate and a related bond bearing interest at a rate equal to a fixed rate minus that floating rate, those two bonds are treated as a single fixed yield bond only if neither bond may be redeemed unless the other bond is also redeemed at the same time.

(c) through (f) [Reserved]. For guidance see § 1.148-4.

(g) Yield on certain mortgage revenue and student loan bonds. For purposes of section 148 and § 1.148-4, section 143(g)(2)(C)(ii) applies to the computation of yield on an issue of qualified mortgage bonds or qualified veterans' mortgage bonds. For purposes of applying sections 148 and 143(g) to a variable yield issue of qualified mortgage bonds, qualified veterans' mortgage bonds, or qualified student loan bonds, the yield on that issue is computed over the term of the issue, and § 1.148-4(d) does not apply to the issue. As of any date before the final maturity date, the yield over the term of the issue is based on the actual amounts paid or received to that date and the amounts that are reasonably expected (as of that date) to be paid or received over the remaining term of the issue.

(h) Qualified hedging transactions. *(1) In general.* Payments made or received by an issuer under a qualified hedge (as defined in § 1.148-4(h)(2)) relating to bonds of an issue are taken into account (as provided in paragraph (h)(3) of this section) to determine the yield on the issue. Except as provided in paragraphs (h)(4) and (h)(5)(ii)(C) of this section, the bonds to which a qualified hedge relates are treated as variable yield bonds. These hedging rules apply solely for purposes of sections 143(g), 148, and 149(d).

(2) (i) through (vi) [Reserved]. For guidance see § 1.148-4(h)(2).

(vii) Timing and duration. For a contract to be a qualified hedge under § 1.148-4(h)(2), payments must not begin to accrue under the contract on a date earlier than the issue date of the hedged bonds and must not accrue longer than the hedged interest payments on the hedged bonds.

(viii) [Reserved]. For guidance see § 1.148-4(h).

(ix) Identification. For a contract to be a qualified hedge under § 1.148-4(h)(2), the contract must be identified by the actual issuer on its books and records maintained for the hedge bonds not later than three days after the date on which the parties enter into the contract. The identification must specify the hedge provider, the terms of the contract, and the hedged bonds. The identification must contain sufficient detail to establish that the requirements of § 1.148-4(h)(2), and if applicable, paragraph (h)(4) of this section are satisfied. The existence of the hedge must be noted on all forms filed with the Internal Revenue Service for the issue on or after the date on which the hedge is entered into.

(3) Accounting for qualified hedges (i) In general. Except as otherwise provided in paragraph (h)(4) of this section, payments made or received by the issuer under a qualified hedge are treated as payments made or received, as appropriate, on the hedged bonds that are taken into account in determining the yield on those bonds. These payments are reasonably allocated to the hedged bonds in the period to which the payments relate, as determined under paragraph (h)(3)(iii) of this section. Payments made or received by the issuer include payments deemed made or received when a contract is terminated or deemed terminated under this paragraph (h)(3). Payments reasonably allocable to the reduction

of risk of interest rate changes and to the hedge provider's overhead under this paragraph (h) are included as payments made or received under a qualified hedge.

(ii) Exclusions from hedge. Payments for services or other items under the contract that are not expressly treated as payments under the qualified hedge under paragraph (h)(3)(i) of this section are not payments with respect to a qualified hedge.

(iii) Timing and allocation of payments. The period to which a payment made by the issuer relates is determined under general Federal income tax principles, including, without limitation, § 1.446-3, and adjusted as necessary to reflect the end of a computation period and the start of a new computation period. Except as provided in paragraphs (h)(3)(iv) and (h)(5)(ii) of this section, a payment received by the issuer is taken into account in the period that the interest payment that the payment hedges is required to be made.

(iv) Termination payments. (A) Termination defined. A termination of a qualified hedge includes any sale or other disposition of the hedge by the issuer, or the acquisition by the issuer of an offsetting hedge. A deemed termination occurs when the hedged bonds are redeemed and when a hedge ceases to be a qualified hedge of the hedged bonds. In the case of an assignment by a hedge provider of its remaining rights and obligations on the hedge to a third party or a modification of the hedging contract, the assignment or modification is treated as a termination with respect to the issuer only if it results in a deemed exchange of the hedge and a realization event under section 1001.

(B) General rule. A payment made or received by an issuer to terminate a qualified hedge, including loss or gain realized or deemed realized, is treated as a payment made or received on the hedged bonds, as appropriate. The payment is reasonably allocated to the remaining periods originally covered by the terminated hedge in a manner that reflects the economic substance of the hedge.

(C) Special rule for terminations when bonds are redeemed. Except as otherwise provided in this paragraph (h)(3)(iv)(C) and in paragraph (h)(3)(iv)(D) of this section, when a qualified hedge is deemed terminated because the hedged bonds are redeemed, the fair market value of the contract on the redemption date is treated as a termination payment made or received on that date. When hedged bonds are redeemed, any payment received by the issuer on termination of a hedge, including a termination payment or a deemed termination payment, reduces, but not below zero, the interest payments made by the issuer on the hedged bonds in the computation period ending on the termination date. The remainder of the payment, if any, is reasonably allocated over the bond years in the immediately preceding computation period or periods to the extent necessary to eliminate the excess.

(D) Special rules for refundings. To the extent that the hedged bonds are redeemed using the proceeds of a refunding issue, the termination payment is accounted for under paragraph (h)(3)(iv)(B) of this section by treating it as a payment on the refunding issue, rather than the hedged bonds. In addition, to the extent that the refunding issue, rather than the hedged bonds, has been redeemed, paragraph (h)(3)(iv)(C) of this section applies to the termination payment by treating it as a payment on the redeemed refunding issue.

(E) Safe harbor for certain non-level payments. A non-level payment to terminate a hedge does not result in that hedge failing to satisfy the applicable provisions of paragraph (h)(3)(iv)(B) of this section if the payment is allocated to each bond year for which the hedge would have been in effect in accordance with this paragraph (h)(3)(iv)(E). For a variable yield issue, an equal amount (or for any short bond year, a proportionate amount of the equal amount) must be allocated to each bond year such that the sum of the present values of the annual amounts equals the present value of the non-level payment. Present value is computed as of the day the hedge is terminated, using the yield on the hedged bonds, determined without regard to the non-level payment. The yield used for this purpose is computed for the period beginning on the first date the hedge is in effect and ending on the date the hedge is terminated. On the other hand, for a fixed yield issue, the non-level payment is taken into account as a single payment on the date it is paid.

(4) Certain variable yield bonds treated as fixed yield bonds. (i) In general. Except as otherwise provided in this paragraph (h)(4), if the issuer of variable yield bonds enters into a qualified hedge, the hedged bonds are treated as fixed yield bonds paying a fixed interest rate if:

(A) Start date. The date on which payments begin to accrue on the hedge is not later than 15 days after the issue date of the hedged bonds.

(B) Maturity. The term of the hedge is equal to the entire period during which the hedged bonds bear interest at variable interest rates.

(C) Payments closely correspond. Payments to be received under the hedge correspond closely in time to the hedged portion of the payments on the hedged bonds. Hedge payments received within 15 days of the related payments on the hedged bonds generally so correspond.

(D) Aggregate payments fixed. Taking into account all payments made and received under the hedge and all payments on the hedged bonds (i.e., after netting all payments), the issuer's aggregate payments are fixed and determinable as of a date not later than 15 days after the issue date of the hedged bonds. Payments on bonds are treated as fixed for purposes of this paragraph (h)(4)(i)(D) if payments on the bonds are based, in whole or in part, on one interest rate, payments on the hedge are based, in whole or in part, on a second interest rate that is substantially the same as, but not identical to, the first interest rate and payments on the bonds would be fixed if the two rates were identical. Rates are treated as substantially the same if they are reasonably expected to be substantially the same throughout the term of the hedge. For example, an objective 30-day tax-exempt variable rate index or other objective index (e.g., J.J. Kenny Index, PSA Municipal swap index, a percentage of LIBOR) may be substantially the same as an issuer's individual 30-day interest rate.

(ii) Accounting. Except as otherwise provided in this paragraph (h)(4)(ii), in determining yield on the hedged bonds, all the issuer's actual interest payments on the hedged bonds and all payments made and received on a hedge described in paragraph (h)(4)(i) of this section are taken into account. If payments on the bonds and payments on the hedge are based, in whole or in part, on variable interest rates that are substantially the same within the meaning of paragraph (h)(4)(i)(D) of this section (but not identical), yield on the issue is determined by treating the variable interest rates as identical. For example, if variable rate bonds bearing interest at a weekly rate equal to the rate necessary to remarket the bonds at par are hedged with an interest rate swap under which the issuer receives payments based on a short-term floating rate index that is substantially the same as, but not identical to, the weekly rate on the bonds, the interest payments on the bonds are treated as equal to the payments received by the issuer under the swap for purposes of computing the yield on the bonds.

(iii) Effect of termination. (A) In general. Except as otherwise provided in this paragraph (h)(4)(iii) and paragraph (h)(5) of this section, the issue of which the hedged bonds are a part is treated as if it were reissued as of the termination date of the qualified hedge covered by paragraph (h)(4)(i) of this section in determining yield on the hedged bonds for purposes of § 1.148-3. The redemption price of the retired issue and the issue price of the new issue equal the aggregate values of all the bonds of the issue on the termination date. In computing the yield on the new issue for this purpose, any termination payment is accounted for under paragraph (h)(3)(iv) of this section, applied by treating the termination payment as made or received on the new issue under this paragraph (h)(4)(iii).

(B) Effect of early termination. Except as otherwise provided in this paragraph (h)(4)(iii), the general rules of paragraph (h)(4)(i) of this section do not apply in determining the yield on the hedged bonds for purposes of § 1.148-3 if the hedge is terminated or deemed terminated within 5 years after the issue date of the issue of which the hedged bonds are a part. Thus, the hedged bonds are treated as variable yield bonds for purposes of § 1.148-3 from the issue date.

(C) Certain terminations disregarded. This paragraph (h)(4)(iii) does not apply to a termination if, based on the facts and circumstances (e.g., taking into account both the termination and any qualified hedge that immediately replaces the terminated hedge), there is no change in the yield. In addition, this paragraph (h)(4)(iii) does not apply to a termination caused by the bankruptcy or insolvency of the hedge provider if the Commissioner determines that the termination occurred without any action by the issuer (other than to protect its rights under the hedge).

(5) Special rules for certain hedges. (i) Certain acquisition payments. A payment to the issuer by the hedge provider (e.g., an up-front payment for an off-market swap) in connection with the acquisition of a hedge that, but for that payment, would be a qualified hedge, does not cause the hedge to fail to be a qualified hedge provided the payment to the issuer and the issuer's payments under the hedge in excess of those that it would make if the hedge bore rates equal to the on-market rates for the hedge are separately identified in a certification of the hedge provider and not taken into account in determining the yield on the issue of which the hedged bonds are a part. The on-market rates are determined as of the date the parties enter into the contract.

(ii) Anticipatory hedges. (A) In general. A contract does not fail to be a hedge under § 1.148-4(h)(2)(i)(A) solely because it is entered into with respect to an anticipated issuance of tax-exempt bonds. The identification required under § 1.148-4T(h)(2)(ix) must specify the reasonably expected governmental purpose, principal amount, and issue date of the hedged bonds, and the manner in which interest is reasonably expected to be computed.

(B) Special rules. Payments made in connection with the issuance of a bond to terminate or otherwise close (*terminate*) an anticipatory hedge of that bond do not prevent the hedge from satisfying the requirements of § 1.148-4(h)(2)(vi) and paragraph (h)(2)(vii) of this section. Amounts received or deemed to be received by the issuer in connection with the issuance of the hedged bonds to terminate an anticipatory hedge are treated as proceeds of the hedged bonds.

(C) Fixed yield treatment. A bond that is hedged with an anticipatory hedge is a fixed yield bond if, taking into account payments on the hedge that are made or fixed on or before the issue date of the bond and the payments to be made on the bond, the bond satisfies the definition of fixed yield bond. See also paragraph (h)(4) of this section.

(6) Authority of the Commissioner. (i) In general. A contract is not a qualified hedge if the Commissioner determines, based on all the facts and circumstances, that treating the contract as a qualified hedge would provide a material potential for arbitrage, or a principal purpose for entering into the contract is that arbitrage potential. For example, a contract that requires a substantial nonperiodic payment may constitute, in whole or part, an embedded loan, investment-type property, or other investment.

(ii) Other qualified hedges. The Commissioner, by publication of a revenue ruling or revenue procedure, may specify contracts that do not otherwise meet the requirements of § 1.148-4(h)(2) as qualified hedges and contracts that do not otherwise meet the requirements of paragraph (h)(4) of this section as causing the hedged bonds to be treated as fixed yield bonds.

(iii) Recomputation of yield. If an issuer enters into a hedge that is not properly identified, fails to properly associate an anticipatory hedge with the hedged bonds, or otherwise fails to meet the requirements of this section, the Commissioner may recompute the yield on the issue taking the hedge into account if the failure to take the hedge into account distorts that yield or otherwise fails to clearly reflect the economic substance of the transaction.

T.D. 8538, 5/5/94, amend T.D. 8718, 5/8/97.

§ 1.148-5 Yield and valuation of investments.

(a) In general. This section provides rules for computing the yield and value of investments allocated to an issue for various purposes under section 148.

(b) Yield on an investment. *(1) In general.* Except as otherwise provided, the yield on an investment allocated to an issue is computed under the economic accrual method, using the same compounding interval and financial conventions used to compute the yield on the issue. The yield on an investment allocated to an issue is the discount rate that, when used in computing the present value as of the date the investment is first allocated to the issue of all unconditionally payable receipts from the investment, produces an amount equal to the present value of all unconditionally payable payments for the investment. For this purpose, payments means amounts to be actually or constructively paid to acquire the investment, and receipts means amounts to be actually or constructively received from the investment, such as earnings and return of principal. The yield on a variable rate investment is determined in a manner comparable to the determination of the yield on a variable rate issue. For an issue of qualified mortgage bonds, qualified veterans' mortgage bonds, or qualified student loan bonds on which interest is paid semiannually, all regular monthly loan payments to be received during a semiannual debt service period may be treated as received at the end of that period. In addition, for any conduit financing issue, payments made by the conduit borrower are not treated as paid until the conduit borrower ceases to receive the benefit of earnings on those amounts.

(2) Yield on a separate class of investments. (i) In general. For purposes of the yield restriction rules of section 148(a)

and § 1.148-2, yield is computed separately for each class of investments. For this purpose, in determining the yield on a separate class of investments, the yield on each individual investment within the class is blended with the yield on other individual investments within the class, whether or not held concurrently, by treating those investments as a single investment. The yields on investments that are not within the same class are not blended.

(ii) Separate classes of investments. Each of the following is a separate class of investments—

(A) Each category of yield restricted purpose investment and program investment that is subject to a different definition of materially higher under § 1.148-2(d)(2);

(B) Yield-restricted nonpurpose investments; and

(C) All other nonpurpose investments;

(iii) Permissive application of single investment rules to certain yield restricted investments for all purposes of section 148. For all purposes of section 148, if an issuer reasonably expects as of the issue date to establish and maintain a sinking fund solely to reduce the yield on the investments in a refunding escrow, then the issuer may treat all of the yield restricted nonpurpose investments in the refunding escrow and that sinking fund as a single investment having a single yield, determined under this paragraph (b)(2). Thus, an issuer may not treat the nonpurpose investments in a reasonably required reserve fund and a refunding escrow as a single investment having a single yield under this paragraph (b)(2)(iii).

(iv) Mandatory application of single investment rules for refunding escrows for all purposes of section 148. For all purposes of section 148, in computing the yield on yield restricted investments allocable to proceeds (i.e., sale proceeds, investment proceeds, and transferred proceeds) of a refunding issue that are held in one or more refunding escrows, the individual investments are treated as a single investment having a single yield, whether or not held concurrently. For example, this single investment includes both the individual investments allocable to sale and investment proceeds of a refunding issue that are held in one refunding escrow for a prior issue and the investments allocable to transferred proceeds of that refunding issue that are held in another refunding escrow.

(3) Investments to be held beyond issue's maturity or beyond temporary period. In computing the yield on investments allocable to an issue that are to be held beyond the reasonably expected redemption date of the issue, those investments are treated as sold for an amount equal to their value on that date. In computing the yield on investments that are held beyond an applicable temporary period under § 1.148-2, for purposes of § 1.148-2 those investments may be treated as purchased for an amount equal to their fair market value as of the end of the temporary period.

(4) Consistent redemption assumptions on purpose investments. The yield on purpose investments allocable to an issue is computed using the same redemption assumptions used to compute the yield on the issue. Yield on purpose investments allocable to an issue of qualified mortgage bonds and qualified veterans' mortgage bonds must be determined in a manner that is consistent with, and using the assumptions required by, section 143(g)(2)(B).

(5) Student loan special allowance payments included in yield. Except as provided in § 1.148-11(e), the yield on qualified student loans is computed by including as receipts any special allowance payments made by the Secretary of Education pursuant to section 438 of the Higher Education Act of 1965.

(c) Yield reduction payments to the United States. *(1) In general.* In determining the yield on an investment to which this paragraph (c) applies, any amount paid to the United States in accordance with this paragraph (c), including a rebate amount, is treated as a payment for that investment that reduces the yield on that investment.

(2) Manner of payment. (i) In general. Except as otherwise provided in paragraph (c)(2)(ii) of this section, an amount is paid under this paragraph (c) if it is paid to the United States at the same time and in the same manner as rebate amounts are required to be paid or at such other time or in such manner as the Commissioner may prescribe. For example, yield reduction payments must be made on or before the date of required rebate installment payments as described in §§ 1.148-3(f), (g), and (h). The provisions of § 1.148-3(i) apply to payments made under this paragraph (c).

(ii) Special rule for purpose investments. For purpose investments allocable to an issue—

(A) No amounts are required to be paid to satisfy this paragraph (c) until the earlier of the end of the tenth bond year after the issue date of the issue or 60 days after the date on which the issue is no longer outstanding; and

(B) For payments made prior to the date on which the issue is retired, the issuer need not pay more than 75 percent of the amount otherwise required to be paid as of the date to which the payment relates.

(3) Applicability of special yield reduction rule. (i) Covered investments. This paragraph (c) applies to—

(A) Nonpurpose investments allocable to proceeds of an issue that qualified for one of the temporary periods available for capital projects, restricted working capital expenditures, pooled financings, or investment proceeds under § 1.148-2(e)(2), (e)(3), (e)(4), or (e)(6), respectively;

(B) Investments allocable to a variable yield issue during any computation period in which at least 5 percent of the value of the issue is represented by variable yield bonds, unless the issue is an issue of hedge bonds (as defined in section 149(g)(3)(A));

(C) Nonpurpose investments allocable to transferred proceeds of—

(1) A current refunding issue to the extent necessary to reduce the yield on those investments to satisfy yield restrictions under section 148(a); or

(2) An advance refunding issue to the extent that investment of the refunding escrows allocable to the proceeds, other than transferred proceeds, of the refunding issue in zero-yielding nonpurpose investments is insufficient to satisfy yield restrictions under section 148(a);

(D) Purpose investments allocable to qualified student loans under a program described in section 144(b)(1)(A);

(E) Nonpurpose investments allocable to gross proceeds of an issue in a reasonably required reserve or replacement fund or in a fund that, except for its failure to satisfy the size limitation in § 1.148-2(f)(2)(ii), would qualify as a reasonably required reserve or replacement fund, but only to the extent that—

(1) The value of the nonpurpose investments in the fund is not greater than 15 percent of the stated principal amount of the issue, as computed under § 1.148-2(f)(2)(ii), or

(2) The amounts in the fund (other than investment earnings) are not reasonably expected to be used to pay debt service on the issue other than in connection with reductions in the amount required to be in that fund (e.g., a reserve fund for a revolving fund loan program);

(F) Nonpurpose investments allocated to replacement proceeds of a refunded issue as a result of the application of the universal cap to amounts in a refunding escrow (see § 1.148-11(c)(1)(ii)); and

(G) Investments described in § 1.148-11(f).

(ii) Exception to yield reduction payments rule for advance refunding issues. Paragraph (c)(1) of this section does not apply to investments allocable to gross proceeds of an advance refunding issue, other than —

(A) Transferred proceeds to which paragraph (c)(3)(i)(C) of this section applies;

(B) Replacement proceeds to which paragraph (c)(3)(i)(F) of this section applies; and

(C) Transferred proceeds to which paragraph (c)(3)(i)(E) of this section applies, but only to the extent necessary to satisfy yield restriction under section 148(a) on those proceeds treating all investments allocable to those proceeds as a separate class.

(d) Value of investments. *(1) In general.* Except as otherwise provided, the value of an investment (including a payment or receipt on the investment) on a date must be determined using one of the following valuation methods consistently for all purposes of section 148 to that investment on that date:

(i) Plain par investment—outstanding principal amount. A plain par investment may be valued at its outstanding stated principal amount, plus any accrued unpaid interest on that date.

(ii) Fixed rate investment—present value. A fixed rate investment may be valued at its present value on that date.

(iii) Any investment—fair market value. An investment may be valued at its fair market value on that date.

(2) Mandatory valuation of yield restricted investments at present value. Any yield restricted investment must be valued at present value. For example, a purpose investment or an investment allocable to gross proceeds in a refunding escrow after the expiration of the initial temporary period must be valued at present value. See, however, paragraph (b)(3) of this section.

(3) Mandatory valuation of certain investments at fair market value. (i) In general. Except as provided in paragraphs (d)(2), (d)(3)(ii), and (d)(4) of this section, an investment must be valued at fair market value on the date that it is first allocated to an issue or first ceases to be allocated to an issue as a consequence of a deemed acquisition or deemed disposition. For example, if an issuer deposits existing investments into a sinking fund for an issue, those investments must be valued at fair market value as of the date first deposited into the fund.

(ii) Exception to fair market value requirement for transferred proceeds allocations, universal cap allocations, and commingled funds. Paragraph (d)(3)(i) of this section does not apply if the investment is allocated from one issue to another issue as a result of the transferred proceeds allocation rule under § 1.148-9(b) or the universal cap rule under § 1.148-6(b)(2), provided that both issues consist exclusively of tax-exempt bonds. In addition, paragraph (d)(3)(i) of this section does not apply to investments in a commingled fund (other than a bona fide debt service fund) unless it is an investment being initially deposited in or withdrawn from a commingled fund described in § 1.148-6(e)(5)(iii).

(4) Special transition rule for transferred proceeds. The value of a nonpurpose investment that is allocated to transferred proceeds of a refunding issue on a transfer date may not exceed the value of that investment on the transfer date used for purposes of applying the arbitrage restrictions to the refunded issue.

(5) Definition of present value of an investment. Except as otherwise provided, present value of an investment is computed under the economic accrual method, using the same compounding interval and financial conventions used to compute the yield on the issue. The present value of an investment on a date is equal to the present value of all unconditionally payable receipts to be received from and payments to be paid for the investment after that date, using the yield on the investment as the discount rate.

(6) Definition of fair market value. (i) In general. The fair market value of an investment is the price at which a willing buyer would purchase the investment from a willing seller in a bona fide, arm's-length transaction. Fair market value generally is determined on the date on which a contract to purchase or sell the nonpurpose investment becomes binding (i.e., the trade date rather than the settlement date). Except as otherwise provided in this paragraph (d)(6), an investment that is not of a type traded on an established securities market, within the meaning of section 1273, is rebuttably presumed to be acquired or disposed of for a price that is not equal to its fair market value. The fair market value of a United States Treasury obligation that is purchased directly from the United States Treasury is its purchase price.

(ii) Safe harbor for establishing fair market value for certificates of deposit. This paragraph (d)(6)(ii) applies to a certificate of deposit that has a fixed interest rate, a fixed payment schedule, and a substantial penalty for early withdrawal. The purchase price of such a certificate of deposit is treated as its fair market value on the purchase date if the yield on the certificate of deposit is not less than—

(A) The yield on reasonably comparable direct obligations of the United States; and

(B) The highest yield that is published or posted by the provider to be currently available from the provider on reasonably comparable certificates of deposit offered to the public.

(iii) Safe harbor for establishing fair market value for guaranteed investment contracts and investments purchased for a yield restricted defeasance escrow. The purchase price of a guaranteed investment contract and the purchase price of an investment purchased for a yield restricted defeasance escrow will be treated as the fair market value of the investment on the purchase date if all of the following requirements are satisfied:

(A) The issuer makes a bona fide solicitation for the purchase of the investment. A bona fide solicitation is a solicitation that satisfies all of the following requirements:

(1) The bid specifications are in writing and are timely forwarded to potential providers.

(2) The bid specifications include all material terms of the bid. A term is material if it may directly or indirectly affect the yield or the cost of the investment.

(3) The bid specifications include a statement notifying potential providers that submission of a bid is a representation that the potential provider did not consult with any other potential provider about its bid, that the bid was determined

without regard to any other formal or informal agreement that the potential provider has with the issuer or any other person (whether or not in connection with the bond issue), and that the bid is not being submitted solely as a courtesy to the issuer or any other person for purposes of satisfying the requirements of paragraph (d)(6)(iii)(B)(1) or (2) of this section.

(4) The terms of the bid specifications are commercially reasonable. A term is commercially reasonable if there is a legitimate business purpose for the term other than to increase the purchase price or reduce the yield of the investment. For example, for solicitations of investments for a yield restricted defeasance escrow, the hold firm period must be no longer than the issuer reasonably requires.

(5) For purchases of guaranteed investment contracts only, the terms of the solicitation take into account the issuer's reasonably expected deposit and drawdown schedule for the amounts to be invested.

(6) All potential providers have an equal opportunity to bid. For example, no potential provider is given the opportunity to review other bids (i.e., a last look) before providing a bid.

(7) At least three reasonably competitive providers are solicited for bids. A reasonably competitive provider is a provider that has an established industry reputation as a competitive provider of the type of investments being purchased.

(B) The bids received by the issuer meet all of the following requirements:

(1) The issuer receives at least three bids from providers that the issuer solicited under a bona fide solicitation meeting the requirements of paragraph (d)(6)(iii)(A) of this section and that do not have a material financial interest in the issue. A lead underwriter in a negotiated underwriting transaction is deemed to have a material financial interest in the issue until 15 days after the issue date of the issue. In addition, any entity acting as a financial advisor with respect to the purchase of the investment at the time the bid specifications are forwarded to potential providers has a material financial interest in the issue. A provider that is a related party to a provider that has a material financial interest in the issue is deemed to have a material financial interest in the issue.

(2) At least one of the three bids described in paragraph (d)(6)(iii)(B)(1) of this section is from a reasonably competitive provider, within the meaning of paragraph (d)(6)(iii)(A)(7) of this section.

(3) If the issuer uses an agent to conduct the bidding process, the agent did not bid to provide the investment.

(C) The winning bid meets the following requirements:

(1) Guaranteed investment contracts. If the investment is a guaranteed investment contract, the winning bid is the highest yielding bona fide bid (determined net of any broker's fees).

(2) Other investments. If the investment is not a guaranteed investment contract, the following requirements are met:

(i) The winning bid is the lowest cost bona fide bid (including any broker's fees). The lowest cost bid is either the lowest cost bid for the portfolio or, if the issuer compares the bids on an investment-by-investment basis, the aggregate cost of a portfolio comprised of the lowest cost bid for each investment. Any payment received by the issuer from a provider at the time a guaranteed investment contract is purchased (e.g., an escrow float contract) for a yield restricted defeasance escrow under a bidding procedure meeting the requirements of this paragraph (d)(6)(iii) is taken into account in determining the lowest cost bid.

(ii) The lowest cost bona fide bid (including any broker's fees) is not greater than the cost of the most efficient portfolio comprised exclusively of State and Local Government Series Securities from the United States Department of the Treasury, Bureau of Public Debt. The cost of the most efficient portfolio of State and Local Government Series Securities is to be determined at the time that bids are required to be submitted pursuant to the terms of the bid specifications.

(iii) If State and Local Government Series Securities from the United States Department of the Treasury, Bureau of Public Debt are not available for purchase on the day that bids are required to be submitted pursuant to terms of the bid specifications because sales of those securities have been suspended, the cost comparison of paragraph (d)(6)(iii)(C)(2)(ii) of this section is not required.

(D) The provider of the investments or the obligor on the guaranteed investment contract certifies the administrative costs that it pays (or expects to pay, if any) to third parties in connection with supplying the investment.

(E) The issuer retains the following records with the bond documents until three years after the last outstanding bond is redeemed:

(1) For purchases of guaranteed investment contracts, a copy of the contract, and for purchases of investments other than guaranteed investment contracts, the purchase agreement or confirmation.

(2) The receipt or other record of the amount actually paid by the issuer for the investments, including a record of any administrative costs paid by the issuer, and the certification under paragraph (d)(6)(iii)(D) of this section.

(3) For each bid that is submitted, the name of the person and entity submitting the bid, the time and date of the bid, and the bid results.

(4) The bid solicitation form and, if the terms of the purchase agreement or the guaranteed investment contract deviated from the bid solicitation form or a submitted bid is modified, a brief statement explaining the deviation and stating the purpose for the deviation. For example, if the issuer purchases a portfolio of investments for a yield restricted defeasance escrow and, in order to satisfy the yield restriction requirements of section 148, an investment in the winning bid is replaced with an investment with a lower yield, the issuer must retain a record of the substitution and how the price of the substitute investment was determined. If the issuer replaces an investment in the winning bid portfolio with another investment, the purchase price of the new investment is not covered by the safe harbor unless the investment is bid under a bidding procedure meeting the requirements of this paragraph (d)(6)(iii).

(5) For purchases of investments other than guaranteed investment contracts, the cost of the most efficient portfolio of State and Local Government Series Securities, determined at the time that the bids were required to be submitted pursuant to the terms of the bid specifications.

(e) Administrative costs of investments. *(1) In general.* Except as otherwise provided in this paragraph (e), an allocation of gross proceeds of an issue to a payment or a receipt on an investment is not adjusted to take into account any costs or expenses paid, directly or indirectly, to purchase, carry, sell, or retire the investment (administrative costs). Thus, these administrative costs generally do not increase the payments for, or reduce the receipts from, investments.

(2) Qualified administrative costs on nonpurpose investments. (i) In general. In determining payments and receipts on nonpurpose investments, qualified administrative costs are taken into account. Thus, qualified administrative costs increase the payments for, or decrease the receipts from, the investments. Qualified administrative costs are reasonable, direct administrative costs, other than carrying costs, such as separately stated brokerage or selling commissions, but not legal and accounting fees, recordkeeping, custody, and similar costs. General overhead costs and similar indirect costs of the issuer such as employee salaries and office expenses and costs associated with computing the rebate amount under section 148(f) are not qualified administrative costs. In general, administrative costs are not reasonable unless they are comparable to administrative costs that would be charged for the same investment or a reasonably comparable investment if acquired with a source of funds other than gross proceeds of tax-exempt bonds.

(ii) Special rule for administrative costs of nonpurpose investments in certain regulated investment companies and commingled funds. Qualified administrative costs include all reasonable administrative costs, without regard to the limitation on indirect costs under paragraph (e)(2)(i) of this section, incurred by:

(A) Regulated investment companies. A publicly offered regulated investment company (as defined in section 67(c)(2)(B)); and

(B) External commingled funds. A widely held commingled fund in which no investor in the fund owns more than 10 percent of the beneficial interest in the fund. For purposes of this paragraph (e)(2)(ii)(B), a fund is treated as widely held only if, during the immediately preceding fixed, semiannual period chosen by the fund (e.g., semiannual periods ending June 30 and December 31), the fund had a daily average of more than 15 investors that were not related parties, and the daily average amount each investor had invested in the fund was not less than the lesser of $500,000 and 1 percent of the daily average of the total amount invested in the fund. For purposes of this paragraph (e)(2)(ii)(B), an investor will be treated as owning not more than 10 percent of the beneficial interest in the fund if, on the date of each deposit by the investor into the fund, the total amount the investor and any related parties have on deposit in the fund is not more than 10 percent of the total amount that all investors have on deposit in the fund. For purposes of the preceding sentence, the total amount that all investors have on deposit in the fund is equal to the sum of all deposits made by the investor and any related parties on the date of those deposits and the closing balance in the fund on the day before those deposits. If any investor in the fund owns more than 10 percent of the beneficial interest in the fund, the fund does not qualify under this paragraph (e)(2)(ii)(B) until that investor makes sufficient withdrawals from the fund to reduce its beneficial interest in the fund to 10 percent or less.

(iii) Special rule for guaranteed investment contracts and investments purchased for a yield restricted defeasance escrow. (A) In general. An amount paid for a broker's commission or similar fee with respect to a guaranteed investment contract or investments purchased for a yield restricted defeasance escrow is a qualified administrative cost if the fee is reasonable within the meaning of paragraph (e)(2)(i) of this section.

(B) Safe harbor. (1) In general. A broker's commission or similar fee with respect to the acquisition of a guaranteed investment contract or investments purchased for a yield restricted defeasance escrow is reasonable within the meaning of paragraph (e)(2)(i) of this section to the extent that—

(i) The amount of the fee that the issuer treats as a qualified administrative cost does not exceed the lesser of:

(A) $30,000 and

(B) 0.2% of the computational base or, if more, $3,000; and

(ii) For any issue, the issuer does not treat as qualified administrative costs more than $85,000 in brokers' commissions or similar fees with respect to all guaranteed investment contracts and investments for yield restricted defeasance escrows purchased with gross proceeds of the issue.

(2) Computational base. For purposes of paragraph (e)(2)(iii)(B)(1) of this section, computational base shall mean—

(i) For a guaranteed investment contract, the amount of gross proceeds the issuer reasonably expects, as of the date the contract is acquired, to be deposited in the guaranteed investment contract over the term of the contract, and

(ii) For investments (other than guaranteed investment contracts) to be deposited in a yield restricted defeasance escrow, the amount of gross proceeds initially invested in those investments.

(3) Cost-of-living adjustment. In the case of a calendar year after 2004, each of the dollar amounts in paragraph (e)(2)(iii)(B)(1) of this section shall be increased by an amount equal to—

(i) Such dollar amount; multiplied by

(ii) The cost-of-living adjustment determined under section 1(f)(3) for such calendar year by using the language "calendar year 2003" instead of "calendar year 1992" in section 1(f)(3)(B).

(4) Rounding. If any increase determined under paragraph (e)(2)(iii)(B)(3) of this section is not a multiple of $1,000, such increase shall be rounded to the nearest multiple thereof.

(5) Applicable year for cost-of-living adjustment. The cost-of-living adjustments under paragraph (e)(2)(iii)(B)(3) of this section shall apply to the safe harbor amounts under paragraph (e)(2)(iii)(B)(1) of this section based on the year the guaranteed investment contract or the investments for the yield restricted defeasance escrow, as applicable, are acquired.

(6) Cost-of-living adjustment to determine remaining amount of per-issue safe harbor. (i) In general. This paragraph (e)(2)(iii)(B)(6) applies to determine the portion of the safe harbor amount under paragraph (e)(2)(iii)(B)(1)(ii) of this section, as modified by paragraph (e)(2)(iii)(B)(3) of this section (the per-issue safe harbor), that is available (the remaining amount) for any year (the determination year) if the per-issue safe harbor was partially used in one or more prior years.

(ii) Remaining amount of per-issue safe harbor. The remaining amount of the per-issue safe harbor for any determination year is equal to the per-issue safe harbor for that year, reduced by the portion of the per-issue safe harbor used in one or more prior years.

(iii) Portion of per-issue safe harbor used in prior years. The portion of the per-issue safe harbor used in any prior year (the prior year) is equal to the total amount of broker's commissions or similar fees paid in connection with guaranteed investment contracts or investments for a yield restricted defeasance escrow acquired in the prior year that the issuer treated as qualified administrative costs for the issue, multiplied by a fraction the numerator of which is the per-issue safe harbor for the determination year and the denominator of which is the per-issue safe harbor for the prior year. See paragraph (e)(2)(iii)(C) Example 2 of this section.

(C) Examples. The following examples illustrate the application of the safe harbor in paragraph (e)(2)(iii)(B) of this section:

Example (1). Multipurpose issue. In 2003, the issuer of a multipurpose issue uses brokers to acquire the following investments with gross proceeds of the issue: a guaranteed investment contract for amounts to be deposited in a construction fund (construction GIC), Treasury securities to be deposited in a yield restricted defeasance escrow (Treasury investments) and a guaranteed investment contract that will be used to earn a return on what otherwise would be idle cash balances from maturing investments in the yield restricted defeasance escrow (the float GIC). The issuer deposits $22,000,000 into the construction GIC and reasonably expects that no further deposits will be made over its term. The issuer uses $8,040,000 of the proceeds to purchase the Treasury investments. The issuer reasonably expects that it will make aggregate deposits of $600,000 to the float GIC over its term. The brokers' fees are $30,000 for the construction GIC, $16,080 for the Treasury investments and $3,000 for the float GIC. The issuer has not previously treated any brokers' commissions or similar fees as qualified administrative costs. The issuer may claim all $49,080 in brokers' fees for these investments as qualified administrative costs because the fees do not exceed the safe harbors in paragraph (e)(2)(iii)(B) of this section. Specifically, each of the brokers' fees equals the lesser of $30,000 and 0.2% of the computational base (or, if more, $3,000) (i.e., lesser of $30,000 and 0.2% x $22,000,000 for the construction GIC; lesser of $30,000 and 0.2% x $8,040,000 for the Treasury investments; and lesser of $30,000 and $3,000 for the float GIC). In addition, the total amount of brokers' fees claimed by the issuer as qualified administrative costs ($49,080) does not exceed the per-issue safe harbor of $85,000.

Example (2). Cost-of-living adjustment. In 2003, an issuer issues bonds and uses gross proceeds of the issue to acquire two guaranteed investment contracts. The issuer pays a total of $50,000 in brokers' fees for the two guaranteed investment contracts and treats these fees as qualified administrative costs. In a year subsequent to 2003 (Year Y), the issuer uses gross proceeds of the issue to acquire two additional guaranteed investment contracts, paying a total of $20,000 in broker's fees for the two guaranteed investment contracts, and treats those fees as qualified administrative costs. For Year Y, applying the cost-of-living adjustment under paragraph (e)(2)(iii)(B)(3) of this section, the safe harbor dollar limits under paragraph (e)(2)(iii)(B)(1) of this section are $3,000, $32,000 and $90,000. The remaining amount of the per-issue safe harbor for Year Y is $37,059 ($90,000-[$50,000 x $90,000/$85,000]). The broker's fees in Year Y do not exceed the per-issue safe harbor under paragraph (e)(2)(iii)(B)(1)(ii) (as modified by paragraph (e)(2)(iii)(B)(3)) of this section because the broker's fees do not exceed the remaining amount of the per-issue safe harbor determined under paragraph (e)(2)(iii)(B)(6) of this section for Year Y. In a year subsequent to Year Y (Year Z), the issuer uses gross proceeds of the issue to acquire an additional guaranteed investment contract, pays a broker's fee of $15,000 for the guaranteed investment contract, and treats the broker's fee as a qualified administrative cost. For Year Z, applying the cost-of-living adjustment under paragraph (e)(2)(iii)(B)(3) of this section, the safe harbor dollar limits under paragraph (e)(2)(iii)(B)(1) of this section are $3,000, $33,000 and $93,000. The remaining amount of the per-issue safe harbor for Year Z is $17,627 ($93,000—[($50,000 x $93,000/$85,000) + ($20,000 x $93,000/$90,000)]). The broker's fee incurred in Year Z does not exceed the per-issue safe harbor under paragraph (e)(2)(iii)(B)(1)(ii) (as modified by paragraph (e)(2)(iii)(B)(3)) of this section because the broker's fee does not exceed the remaining amount of the per-issue safe harbor determined under paragraph (e)(2)(iii)(B)(6) of this section for Year Z. See paragraph (e)(2)(iii)(B)(6) of this section.

(3) Qualified administrative costs on purpose investments. (i) In general. In determining payments and receipts on purpose investments, qualified administrative costs described in this paragraph (e)(3) paid by the conduit borrower are taken into account. Thus, these costs increase the payments for, or decrease the receipts from, the purpose investments. This rule applies even if those payments merely reimburse the issuer. Although the actual payments by the conduit borrower may be made at any time, for this purpose, a pro rata portion of each payment made by a conduit borrower is treated as a reimbursement of reasonable administrative costs, if the present value of those payments does not exceed the present value of the reasonable administrative costs paid by the issuer, using the yield on the issue as the discount rate.

(ii) Definition of qualified administrative costs of purpose investments. (A) In general. Except as otherwise provided in this paragraph (e)(3)(ii), qualified administrative costs of a purpose investment means—

(1) Costs or expenses paid, directly or indirectly, to purchase, carry, sell, or retire the investment; and

(2) Costs of issuing, carrying, or repaying the issue, and any underwriters' discount.

(B) Limitation on program investments. For a program investment, qualified administrative costs include only those costs described in paragraph (e)(3)(ii)(A)(2) of this section.

T.D. 8418, 5/12/92, amend T.D. 8476, 6/14/93, T.D. 8538, 5/5/94, T.D. 8718, 5/8/97, T.D. 8801, 12/29/98, T.D. 9097, 12/10/2003.

PAR. 7. Section 1.148-5(c) is amended by:

1. Removing existing paragraph (c)(3)(ii).

2. Adding introductory language to paragraph (c)(3).

3. Removing the heading in paragraph (c)(3)(i) and redesignating the existing text in paragraph (c)(3)(i)(A) as the text in paragraph (c)(3)(i).

4. Redesignate existing paragraphs (c)(3)(i)(B), (c)(3)(i)(C), (c)(3)(i)(D), (c)(3)(i)(E), (c)(3)(i)(F), and (c)(3)(i)(G) as paragraphs (c)(3)(ii), (c)(3)(iii), (c)(3)(iv), (c)(3)(v), (c)(3)(vi), and (c)(3)(vii), respectively.

5. Redesignate existing paragraphs (c)(3)(i)(C)(1) and (c)(3)(i)(C)(2) as paragraphs (c)(3)(iii)(A) and (c)(3)(iii)(B), respectively, in newly redesignated paragraph (c)(3)(iii).

6. Redesignate existing paragraphs (c)(3)(i)(E)(1) and (c)(3)(i)(E)(2) as paragraphs (c)(3)(v)(A) and (c)(3)(v)(B), respectively, in newly redesignated paragraph (c)(3)(v).

7. Amend newly redesignated paragraph (c)(3)(i), (c)(3)(ii), (c)(3)(iii), (c)(3)(iv), (c)(3)(v), (c)(3)(vi) and (c)(3)(vii) by adding headings to each paragraph.

8. Revise newly redesignated paragraph (c)(3)(v).

9. Revise newly redesignated paragraph (c)(3)(vi).

10. Amend newly redesignated paragraph (c)(3)(vii) by removing the period at the end of the paragraph and replacing it with a semicolon.

11. Amending paragraph (c)(3) by adding new paragraphs (c)(3)(viii) and (c)(3)(ix).

The revised and added provisions read as follows:

Proposed § 1.148-5 Yield and valuation of investments.
[*For Preamble, see ¶ 152,909*]

* * * * *

(c) * * *

(3) Applicability of special yield reduction rule. Except as otherwise expressly provided in paragraphs (c)(3)(i) through (ix) of this section, paragraph (c) applies only to investments listed in paragraphs (c)(3)(i) through (c)(3)(ix) of this section that are allocated to proceeds of an issue other than gross proceeds of an advance refunding issue.

(i) Nonpurpose investments allocated to proceeds of an issue that qualified for certain temporary periods. * * *

(ii) Investments allocable to certain variable yield issues. * * *

(iii) Nonpurpose investments allocable to certain transferred proceeds. * * *

(A) * * *

(B) * * *

(iv) Purpose investments allocable to certain qualified student loans. * * *

(v) Nonpurpose investments allocable to gross proceeds in certain reserve funds. Nonpurpose investments allocable to gross proceeds of an issue in a reasonably required reserve or replacement fund or a fund that, except for its failure to satisfy the size limitation in § 1.148-2(f)(2)(ii), would qualify as a reasonably required reserve or replacement fund, but only to the extent the requirements in paragraphs (c)(3)(v)(A) or (B) of this section are met. This paragraph (c)(3)(v) includes nonpurpose investments described in this paragraph that are allocable to transferred proceeds of an advance refunding issue, but only to the extent necessary to satisfy yield restriction under section 148(a) on those proceeds treating all investments allocable to those proceeds as a separate class.

(A) * * *

(B) * * *

(vi) Nonpurpose investments allocable to certain replacement proceeds of refunded issues. Nonpurpose investments allocated to replacement proceeds of a refunded issue, including a refunded issue that is an advance refunding issue, as a result of the application of the universal cap to amounts in a refunding escrow;

(vii) Investments allocable to replacement proceeds under a certain transition rule. * * *

(viii) Nonpurpose investments allocable to proceeds when SLGS are unavailable. Nonpurpose investments allocable to proceeds of an issue, including an advance refunding issue, that an issuer purchases on a date when the issuer is unable to purchase State and Local Government Series Securities (SLGS) because the U.S. Department of Treasury, Bureau of Public Debt, has suspended sales of those securities; and

(ix) Nonpurpose investments allocable to proceeds of certain variable-yield advance refunding issues. Nonpurpose investments allocable to proceeds of a variable-yield advance refunding issue (the hedged bond issue) deposited in a yield restricted defeasance escrow if—

(A) The issuer has entered into a qualified hedge under § 1.148-4(h)(2) with respect to all of the variable-yield bonds of the issue allocable to the yield restricted defeasance escrow and that hedge is in the form of a variable-to-fixed interest rate swap under which the issuer pays the hedge provider a fixed interest rate and receives from the hedge provider a floating interest rate;

(B) Such qualified hedge covers a period beginning on the issue date of the hedged bond issue and ending on or after the date on which the final payment is to be made from the yield restricted defeasance escrow; and

(C) The issuer restricts the yield on the yield restricted defeasance escrow to a yield that is not greater than the yield on the hedged bond issue, determined by taking into account the issuer's fixed payments to be made under the hedge and by assuming that the issuer's variable yield payments to be paid on the hedged bonds are equal to the floating payments to be received by the issuer under the qualified hedge and are paid on the same dates (that is, such yield reduction payments can only be made to address basis risk differences between the variable yield payments on the hedged bonds and the floating payments received on the hedge).

* * * * *

PAR. 8. Section 1.148-5(d)(6) is amended by revising paragraphs (d)(6)(iii)(A)(1) and (d)(6)(iii)(A)(6) to read as follows:

Proposed § 1.148-5 Yield and valuation of investments.
[*For Preamble, see ¶ 152,909*]

* * * * *

(d) * * *

(6) * * *

(iii) * * *

(A) * * *

(1) The bid specifications are in writing and are timely forwarded, or are made available on an internet website or other similar electronic media that is regularly used to post bid specifications, to potential bidders. For purposes of this paragraph (d)(6)(iii)(A), a writing includes a hard copy, a fax, or an electronic e-mail copy.

* * * * *

(6) All potential providers have an equal opportunity to bid. If the bidding process affords any opportunity for a potential provider to review other bids before providing a bid, then providers have an equal opportunity to bid only if all potential providers have an equal opportunity to review other bids. Thus, no potential provider may be given an opportunity to review other bids that is not equally given to all potential providers (that is, no exclusive "last look").

* * * * *

PAR. 9. Section 1.148-5(e)(2) is amended by revising the second sentence of paragraph (e)(2)(ii)(B) to read as follows:

Proposed § 1.148-5 Yield and valuation of investments.
[*For Preamble, see ¶ 152,909*]

* * * * *

(e) * * *

(2) * * *

(ii) * * *

(B) External commingled funds. * * * For purposes of this paragraph (e)(2)(ii)(B), a fund is treated as widely held only if, during the immediately preceding fixed, semiannual period chosen by the fund (for example, semiannual periods ending June 30 and December 31), the fund had a daily average of more than 15 investors that were not related parties, and at least 16 of the unrelated investors each maintained a daily average amount invested in the fund that was not less than the lesser of $500,000 and one percent (1%) of the daily average of the total amount invested in the fund (with it being understood that additional smaller investors will not disqualify the fund). * * *

* * * * *

§ 1.148-5A Yield and valuation of investments.

(a) through (b)(2)(ii) [Reserved]. For guidance see § 1.148-5.

(b) *(2)* (iii) Permissive application of single investment rules to certain yield restricted investments for all purposes of section 148. For all purposes of section 148, an issuer may treat all of the yield restricted nonpurpose investments in a refunding escrow and a sinking fund that is reasonably expected as of the issue date to be maintained to reduce the yield on the investments in the refunding escrow as a single investment having a single yield, determined under § 1.148(b)(2).

(iv) through (c)(1) [Reserved]. For guidance see § 1.148-5.

(c) *(2) Manner of payment.* (i) In general. Except as otherwise provided in § 1.148-5(c)(2)(ii), an amount is paid under § 1.148-5(c) if it is paid to the United States at the same time and in the same manner as rebate amounts are required to be paid or at such other time or in such manner as the Commissioner may prescribe. For example, yield reduction payments must be made on or before the date of required rebate installment payments as described in § 1.148-3(f). The date a payment is required to be paid is determined without regard to § 1.148-3(h). An amount that is paid untimely is not taken into account under this paragraph (c) unless the Commissioner determines that the failure to pay timely is not due to willful neglect. The provisions of § 1.148-3(i) apply to payments made under § 1.148-5(c).

(ii) through (c)(3)(i) [Reserved]. For guidance see § 1.148-5.

(ii) Exception to yield reduction payments rule for advance refunding issues. Section 1.148-5(c)(1) does not apply to investments allocable to gross proceeds of an advance refunding issue, other than—

(A) Transferred proceeds to which § 1.148-5(c)(3)(i)(C) applies;

(B) Replacement proceeds to which § 1.148-5(c)(3)(i)(F) applies; and

(C) Transferred proceeds to which § 1.148-5(c)(3)(i)(E) applies, but only to the extent necessary to satisfy yield restriction under section 148(a) on those proceeds treating all investments allocable to those proceeds as a separate class.

(d) *(1) through (d)(3)(i) [Reserved].* For guidance see § 1.148-5.

(ii) Exception to fair market value requirement for transferred proceeds allocations, universal cap allocations, and commingled funds. Section 1.148-5(d)(3)(i) does not apply if the investment is allocated from one issue to another issue as a result of the transferred proceeds allocation rule under § 1.148-9(b) or the universal cap rule under § 1.148-6(b)(2), provided that both issues consist exclusively of tax-exempt bonds. In addition, § 1.148-5(d)(3)(i) does not apply to investments in a commingled fund (other than a bona fide debt service fund) unless it is an investment being initially deposited in or withdrawn from a commingled fund described in § 1.148-6(e)(5)(iii).

(e) *(1) through (e)(2)(ii)(A) [Reserved].* For guidance see § 1.148-5.

(ii) (B) External commingled funds. For any semiannual period, a commingled fund satisfies the 10 percent requirement of § 1.148-5(e)(2)(ii)(B) if —

(1) Based on average amounts on deposit, this requirement was satisfied for the prior semiannual period; and

(2) The fund does not accept deposits that would cause it to fail to meet this requirement.

(iii) Special rule for guaranteed investment contracts. For a guaranteed investment contract, a broker's commission or similar fee paid on behalf of either an issuer or the provider is treated as an administrative cost and, except in the case of an issue that satisfies section 148(f)(4)(D)(i), is not a qualified administrative cost to the extent that the present value of the commission, as of the date the contract is allocated to the issue, exceeds the present value of annual payments equal to .05 percent of the weighted average amount reasonably expected to be invested each year of the term of the contract. For this purpose, present value is computed using the taxable discount rate used by the parties to compute the commission or, if not readily ascertainable, a reasonable taxable discount rate.

T.D. 8538, 5/5/94, amend T.D. 8718, 5/8/97.

§ 1.148-6 General allocation and accounting rules.

(a) In general. *(1) Reasonable accounting methods required.* An issuer may use any reasonable, consistently applied accounting method to account for gross proceeds, investments, and expenditures of an issue.

(2) Bona fide deviations from accounting method. An accounting method does not fail to be reasonable and consistently applied solely because a different accounting method is used for a bona fide governmental purpose to consistently account for a particular item. Bona fide governmental purposes may include special state law restrictions imposed on specific funds or actions to avoid grant forfeitures.

(3) Absence of allocation and accounting methods. If an issuer fails to maintain books and records sufficient to establish the accounting method for an issue and the allocation of the proceeds of that issue, the rules of this section are applied using the specific tracing method. This paragraph (a)(3) applies to bonds issued on or after May 16, 1997.

(b) Allocation of gross proceeds to an issue. *(1) One-issue rule and general ordering rules.* Except as otherwise provided, amounts are allocable to only one issue at a time as gross proceeds, and if amounts simultaneously are proceeds of one issue and replacement proceeds of another issue, those amounts are allocable to the issue of which they are proceeds. Amounts cease to be allocated to an issue as proceeds only when those amounts are allocated to an expenditure for a governmental purpose, are allocated to transferred proceeds of another issue, or cease to be allocated to that issue at retirement of the issue or under the universal cap of paragraph (b)(2) of this section. Amounts cease to be allocated to an issue as replacement proceeds only when those amounts are allocated to an expenditure for a governmental purpose, are no longer used in a manner that causes those amounts to be replacement proceeds of that issue, or cease to be allocated to that issue because of the retirement of the issue or the application of the universal cap under paragraph (b)(2) of this section. Amounts that cease to be allocated to an issue as gross proceeds are eligible for allocation to another issue. Under § 1.148-10(a), however, the rules in this paragraph (b)(1) do not apply in certain cases involving abusive arbitrage devices.

(2) Universal cap on value of nonpurpose investments allocated to an issue. (i) Application. The rules in this paragraph (b)(2) provide an overall limitation on the amount of gross proceeds allocable to an issue. Although the universal cap generally may be applied at any time in the manner described in this paragraph (b)(2), it need not be applied on any otherwise required date of application if its application on that date would not result in a reduction or reallocation of gross proceeds of an issue. For this purpose, if an issuer reasonably expects as of the issue date that the universal cap will not reduce the amount of gross proceeds allocable to the issue during the term of the issue, the universal cap need not be applied on any date on which an issue actually has all of the following characteristics—

(A) No replacement proceeds are allocable to the issue, other than replacement proceeds in a bona fide debt service fund or a reasonably required reserve or replacement fund;

(B) The net sale proceeds of the issue—

(1) Qualified for one of the temporary periods available for capital projects, restricted working capital expenditures, or pooled financings under § 1.148-2(e)(2), (e)(3), or (e)(4), and those net sales proceeds were in fact allocated to expenditures prior to the expiration of the longest applicable temporary period; or

(2) were deposited in a refunding escrow and expended as originally expected;

(C) The issue does not refund a prior issue that, on any transfer date, has unspent proceeds allocable to it;

(D) None of the bonds are retired prior to the date on which those bonds are treated as retired in computing the yield on the issue; and

(E) No proceeds of the issue are invested in qualified student loans or qualified mortgage loans.

(ii) General rule. Except as otherwise provided below, amounts that would otherwise be gross proceeds allocable to an issue are allocated (and remain allocated) to the issue only to the extent that the value of the nonpurpose investments allocable to those gross proceeds does not exceed the value of all outstanding bonds of the issue. For this purpose, gross proceeds allocable to cash, tax-exempt bonds that would be nonpurpose investments (absent section 148(b)(3)(A)), qualified student loans, and qualified mortgage loans are treated as nonpurpose investments. The values of bonds and investments are determined under § 1.148-4(e) and § 1.148-5(d), respectively. The value of all outstanding bonds of the issue is referred to as the universal cap. Thus, for example, the universal cap for an issue of plain par bonds is equal to the outstanding stated principal amount of those bonds plus accrued interest.

(iii) Determination and application of the universal cap. Except as otherwise provided, beginning with the first bond year that commences after the second anniversary of the issue date, the amount of the universal cap and the value of the nonpurpose investments must be determined as of the first day of each bond year. For refunding and refunded issues, the cap and values must be determined as of each date that, but for this paragraph (b)(2), proceeds of the refunded issue would become transferred proceeds of the refunding issue, and need not otherwise be determined in the bond year in which that date occurs. All values are determined as of the close of business on each determination date, after giving effect to all payments on bonds and payments for and receipts on investments on that date.

(iv) General ordering rule for allocations of amounts in excess of the universal cap. (A) In general. If the value of all nonpurpose investments allocated to the gross proceeds of an issue exceeds the universal cap for that issue on a date as of which the cap is determined under paragraph (b)(2)(iii) of this section, nonpurpose investments allocable to gross proceeds necessary to eliminate that excess cease to be allocated to the issue, in the following order of priority—

(1) First, nonpurpose investments allocable to replacement proceeds;

(2) Second, nonpurpose investments allocable to transferred proceeds; and

(3) Third, nonpurpose investments allocable to sale proceeds and investment proceeds.

(B) Re-allocation of certain amounts. Except as provided in § 1.148-9(b)(3), amounts that cease to be allocated to an issue as a result of the application of the universal cap may only be allocated to another issue as replacement proceeds.

(C) Allocations of portions of investments. Portions of investments to which this paragraph (b)(2)(iv) applies are allocated under either the ratable method or the representative method in the same manner as allocations of portions of investments to transferred proceeds under § 1.148-9(c).

(v) Nonpurpose investments in a bona fide debt service fund not counted. For purposes of this paragraph (b)(2), nonpurpose investments allocated to gross proceeds in a bona fide debt service fund for an issue are not taken into account in determining the value of the nonpurpose investments, and those nonpurpose investments remain allocated to the issue.

(c) Fair market value limit on allocations to nonpurpose investments. Upon a purchase or sale of a nonpurpose investment, gross proceeds of an issue are not allocated to a payment for that nonpurpose investment in an amount greater than, or to a receipt from that nonpurpose investment in an amount less than, the fair market value of the nonpurpose investment as of the purchase or sale date. For purposes of this paragraph (c) only, the fair market value of a nonpurpose investment is adjusted to take into account qualified administrative costs allocable to the investment.

(d) Allocation of gross proceeds to expenditures. *(1) Expenditures in general.* (i) General rule. Reasonable accounting methods for allocating funds from different sources to expenditures for the same governmental purpose include any of the following methods if consistently applied: a specific tracing method; a gross proceeds spent first method; a first-in, first-out method; or a ratable allocation method.

(ii) General limitation. An allocation of gross proceeds of an issue to an expenditure must involve a current outlay of cash for a governmental purpose of the issue. A current outlay of cash means an outlay reasonably expected to occur not later than 5 banking days after the date as of which the allocation of gross proceeds to the expenditure is made.

(iii) Timing. An issuer must account for the allocation of proceeds to expenditures not later than 18 months after the later of the date the expenditure is paid or the date the project, if any, that is financed by the issue is placed in service.

This allocation must be made in any event by the date 60 days after the fifth anniversary of the issue date or the date 60 days after the retirement of the issue, if earlier. This paragraph (d)(1)(iii) applies to bonds issued on or after May 16, 1997.

(2) Treatment of gross proceeds invested in purpose investments. (i) In general. Gross proceeds of an issue invested in a purpose investment are allocated to an expenditure on the date on which the conduit borrower under the purpose investment allocates the gross proceeds to an expenditure in accordance with this paragraph (d).

(ii) Exception for qualified mortgage loans and qualified student loans. If gross proceeds of an issue are allocated to a purpose investment that is a qualified mortgage loan or a qualified student loan, those gross proceeds are allocated to an expenditure for the governmental purpose of the issue on the date on which the issuer allocates gross proceeds to that purpose investment.

(iii) Continuing allocation of gross proceeds to purpose investments. Regardless of whether gross proceeds of a conduit financing issue invested in a purpose investment have been allocated to an expenditure under paragraph (d)(2)(i) or (ii) of this section, with respect to the actual issuer those gross proceeds continue to be allocated to the purpose investment until the sale, discharge, or other disposition of the purpose investment.

(3) Expenditures for working capital purposes. (i) In general. Except as otherwise provided in this paragraph (d)(3) or paragraph (d)(4) of this section, proceeds of an issue may only be allocated to working capital expenditures as of any date to the extent that those working capital expenditures exceed available amounts (as defined in paragraph (d)(3)(iii) of this section) as of that date (i.e., a "proceeds-spent-last" method). For this purpose, proceeds include replacement proceeds described in § 1.148-1(c)(4).

(ii) Exceptions. (A) General de minimis exception. Paragraph (d)(3)(i) of this section does not apply to expenditures to pay—

(1) Any issuance costs of the issue or any qualified administrative costs within the meaning of § 1.148-5(e)(2)(i) or (ii), or § 1.148-5(e)(3)(ii)(A);

(2) Fees for qualified guarantees of the issue or payments for a qualified hedge for the issue;

(3) Interest on the issue for a period commencing on the issue date and ending on the date that is the later of three years from the issue date or one year after the date on which the project is placed in service;

(4) Amounts paid to the United States under §§ 1.148-3, 1.148-5(c), or 1.148-7 for the issue;

(5) Costs, other than those described in paragraphs (d)(3)(ii)(A)(1) through (4) of this section, that do not exceed 5 percent of the sale proceeds of an issue and that are directly related to capital expenditures financed by the issue (e.g., initial operating expenses for a new capital project);

(6) Principal or interest on an issue paid from unexpected excess sale or investment proceeds; and

(7) Principal or interest on an issue paid from investment earnings on a reserve or replacement fund that are deposited in a bona fide debt service fund.

(B) Exception for extraordinary items. Paragraph (d)(3)(i) of this section does not apply to expenditures for extraordinary, nonrecurring items that are not customarily payable from current revenues, such as casualty losses or extraordinary legal judgments in amounts in excess of reasonable insurance coverage. If, however, an issuer or a related party maintains a reserve for such items (e.g., a self-insurance fund) or has set aside other available amounts for such expenses, gross proceeds within that reserve must be allocated to expenditures only after all other available amounts in that reserve are expended.

(C) Exception for payment of principal and interest on prior issues. Paragraph (d)(3)(i) of this section does not apply to expenditures for payment of principal, interest, or redemption prices on a prior issue and, for a crossover refunding issue, interest on that issue.

(D) No exceptions if replacement proceeds created. The exceptions provided in this paragraph (d)(3)(ii) do not apply if the allocation merely substitutes gross proceeds for other amounts that would have been used to make those expenditures in a manner that gives rise to replacement proceeds. For example, if a purported reimbursement allocation of proceeds of a reimbursement bond does not result in an expenditure under § 1.150-2, those proceeds may not be allocated to pay interest on an issue that, absent this allocation, would have been paid from the issuer's current revenues.

(iii) Definition of available amount. (A) In general. For purposes of this paragraph (d)(3), available amount means any amount that is available to an issuer for working capital expenditure purposes of the type financed by an issue. Except as otherwise provided, available amount excludes proceeds of the issue but includes cash, investments, and other amounts held in accounts or otherwise by the issuer or a related party if those amounts may be used by the issuer for working capital expenditures of the type being financed by an issue without legislative or judicial action and without a legislative, judicial, or contractual requirement that those amounts be reimbursed.

(B) Reasonable working capital reserve treated as unavailable. A reasonable working capital reserve is treated as unavailable. Any working capital reserve is reasonable if it does not exceed 5 percent of the actual working capital expenditures of the issuer in the fiscal year before the year in which the determination of available amounts is made. For this purpose only, in determining the working capital expenditures of an issuer for a prior fiscal year, any expenditures (whether capital or working capital expenditures) that are paid out of current revenues may be treated as working capital expenditures.

(C) Qualified endowment funds treated as unavailable. For a 501(c)(3) organization, a qualified endowment fund is treated as unavailable. A fund is a qualified endowment fund if—

(1) The fund is derived from gifts or bequests, or the income thereon, that were neither made nor reasonably expected to be used to pay working capital expenditures;

(2) Pursuant to reasonable, established practices of the organization, the governing body of the 501(c)(3) organization designates and consistently operates the fund as a permanent endowment fund or quasi-endowment fund restricted as to use; and

(3) There is an independent verification that the fund is reasonably necessary as part of the organization's permanent capital.

(D) Application to statutory safe harbor for tax and revenue anticipation bonds. For purposes of section 148(f)(4)(B)(iii)(II),available amount has the same meaning as in paragraph (d)(3)(iii) of this section, except that the otherwise-permitted reasonable working capital reserve is treated as part of the available amount.

(4) Expenditures for grants. (i) In general. Gross proceeds of an issue that are used to make a grant are allocated to an expenditure on the date on which the grant is made.

(ii) Characterization of repayments of grants. If any amount of a grant financed by gross proceeds of an issue is repaid to the grantor, the repaid amount is treated as unspent proceeds of the issue as of the repayment date unless expended within 60 days of repayment.

(iii) Definition of grant. Grant means a transfer for a governmental purpose of money or property to a transferee that is not a related party to or an agent of the transferor. The transfer must not impose any obligation or condition to directly or indirectly repay any amount to the transferor. Obligations or conditions intended solely to assure expenditure of the transferred moneys in accordance with the governmental purpose of the transfer do not prevent a transfer from being a grant.

(5) Expenditures for reimbursement purposes. In allocating gross proceeds of issues of reimbursement bonds (as defined in § 1.150-2)) to certain expenditures, § 1.150-2 applies. In allocating gross proceeds to an expenditure to reimburse a previously paid working capital expenditure, paragraph (d)(3) of this section applies. Thus, if the expenditure is described in paragraph (d)(3)(ii) of this section or there are no available amounts on the date a working capital expenditure is made and there are no other available amounts on the date of the reimbursement of that expenditure, gross proceeds are allocated to the working capital expenditure as of the date of the reimbursement.

(6) Expenditures of certain commingled investment proceeds of governmental issues. This paragraph (d)(6) applies to any issue of governmental bonds, any issue of private activity bonds issued to finance a facility that is required by section 142 to be owned by a governmental unit, and any portion of an issue that is not treated as consisting of private activity bonds under section 141(b)(9). Investment proceeds of the issue (other than investment proceeds held in a refunding escrow) are treated as allocated to expenditures for a governmental purpose when the amounts are deposited in a commingled fund with substantial tax or other revenues from governmental operations of the issuer and the amounts are reasonably expected to be spent for governmental purposes within 6 months from the date of the commingling. In establishing these reasonable expectations, an issuer may use any reasonable accounting assumption and is not bound by the proceeds-spent-last assumption generally required for working capital expenditures under paragraph (d)(3) of this section.

(7) Payments to related parties. Any payment of gross proceeds of the issue to a related party of the payor is not an expenditure of those gross proceeds.

(e) Special rules for commingled funds. *(1) In general.* An accounting method for gross proceeds of an issue in a commingled fund, other than a bona fide debt service fund, is reasonable only if it satisfies the requirements of paragraphs (e)(2) through (6) of this section in addition to the other requirements of this section.

(2) Investments held by a commingled fund. (i) Required ratable allocations. Not less frequently than as of the close of each fiscal period, all payments and receipts (including deemed payments and receipts) on investments held by a commingled fund must be allocated (but not necessarily distributed) among the different investors in the fund. This allocation must be based on a consistently applied, reasonable ratable allocation method.

(ii) Safe harbors for ratable allocation methods. Reasonable ratable allocation methods include, without limitation, methods that allocate these items in proportion to either—

(A) The average daily balances of the amounts in the commingled fund from different investors during a fiscal period (as described in paragraph (e)(4) of this section); or

(B) The average of the beginning and ending balances of the amounts in the commingled fund from different investors for a fiscal period that does not exceed one month.

(iii) Definition of investor. For purposes of this paragraph (e), the term investor means each different source of funds invested in a commingled fund. For example, if a city invests gross proceeds of an issue and tax revenues in a commingled fund, it is treated as two different investors.

(3) Certain expenditures involving a commingled fund. If a ratable allocation method is used under paragraph (d) of this section to allocate expenditures from the commingled fund, the same ratable allocation method must be used to allocate payments and receipts on investments in the commingled fund under paragraph (e)(2) of this section.

(4) Fiscal periods. The fiscal year of a commingled fund is the calendar year unless the fund adopts another fiscal year. A commingled fund may use any consistent fiscal period that does not exceed three months (e.g., a daily, weekly, monthly, or quarterly fiscal period).

(5) Unrealized gains and losses on investments of a commingled fund. (i) Mark-to-market requirement for internal commingled funds with longer-term investment portfolios. Except as otherwise provided in this paragraph (e), in the case of a commingled fund in which the issuer and any related party own more than 25 percent of the beneficial interests in the fund (an internal commingled fund), the fund must treat all its investments as if sold at fair market value either on the last day of the fiscal year or the last day of each fiscal period. The net gains or losses from these deemed sales of investments must be allocated to all investors of the commingled fund during the period since the last allocation.

(ii) Exception for internal commingled funds with shorter-term investment portfolios. If the remaining weighted average maturity of all investments held by a commingled fund during a particular fiscal year does not exceed 18 months, and the investments held by the commingled fund during that fiscal year consist exclusively of obligations, the mark-to-market requirement of paragraph (e)(5)(i) of this section does not apply.

(iii) Exception for commingled reserve funds and sinking funds. The mark-to-market requirement of paragraph (e)(5)(i) of this section does not apply to a commingled fund that operates exclusively as a reserve fund, sinking fund, or replacement fund for two or more issues of the same issuer.

(6) Allocations of commingled funds serving as common reserve funds or sinking funds. (i) Permitted ratable allocation methods. If a commingled fund serves as a common reserve fund, replacement fund, or sinking fund for two or more issues (a commingled reserve), after making reasonable adjustments to account for proceeds allocated under paragraph (b)(1) or (b)(2) of this section, investments held by that commingled fund must be allocated ratably among the issues served by the commingled fund in accordance with one of the following methods—

(A) The relative values of the bonds of those issues under § 1.148-4(e);

(B) The relative amounts of the remaining maximum annual debt service requirements on the outstanding principal amounts of those issues; or

(C) The relative original stated principal amounts of the outstanding issues.

(ii) Frequency of allocations. An issuer must make any allocations required by this paragraph (e)(6) as of a date at least every 3 years and as of each date that an issue first becomes secured by the commingled reserve. If relative original principal amounts are used to allocate, allocations must also be made on the retirement of any issue secured by the commingled reserve.

T.D. 8418, 5/12/93, amend T.D. 8476, 6/14/93, T.D. 8538, 5/5/94, T.D. 8712, 1/10/97, T.D. 8718, 5/8/97.

§ 1.148-6A General allocation and accounting rules.

(a) through (d)(3)(iii)(B) [Reserved]. For guidance see § 1.148-6.

(d) *(3)* (iii) (C) Qualified endowment funds treated as unavailable. For a 501(c)(3) organization, a qualified endowment fund is treated as unavailable. A fund is a qualified endowment fund if —

(1) The fund is derived from gifts or bequests, or the income thereon, that were neither made nor reasonably expected to be used to pay working capital expenditures;

(2) Pursuant to reasonable, established practices of the organization, the governing body of the 501(c)(3) organization designates and consistently operates the fund as a permanent endowment fund or quasi-endowment fund restricted as to use; and

(3) There is an independent verification (e.g., from an independent certified public accountant) that the fund is reasonably necessary as part of the organization's permanent capital.

T.D. 8538, 5/5/94, amend T.D. 8718, 5/8/97.

§ 1.148-7 Spending exceptions to the rebate requirement.

Caution: The Treasury has not yet amended Reg § 1.148-7 to reflect changes made by P.L. 105-34.

(a) Scope of section. *(1) In general.* This section provides guidance on the spending exceptions to the arbitrage rebate requirement of section 148(f)(2). These exceptions are the 6-month exception in section 148(f)(4)(B) (the 6-month exception), the 18-month exception under paragraph (d) of this section (the 18-month exception), and the 2-year construction exception under section 148(f)(4)(C) (the 2-year exception) (collectively, the spending exceptions).

(2) Relationship of spending exceptions. Each of the spending exceptions is an independent exception to arbitrage rebate. For example, a construction issue may qualify for the 6-month exception or the 18-month exception even though the issuer makes one or more elections under the 2-year exception with respect to the issue.

(3) Spending exceptions not mandatory. Use of the spending exceptions is not mandatory. An issuer may apply the arbitrage rebate requirement to an issue that otherwise satisfies a spending exception. If an issuer elects to pay penalty in lieu of rebate under the 2-year exception, however, the issuer must apply those penalty provisions.

(b) Rules applicable for all spending exceptions. The provisions of this paragraph (b) apply for purposes of applying each of the spending exceptions.

(1) Special transferred proceeds rules. (i) Application to prior issues. For purposes of applying the spending exceptions to a prior issue only, proceeds of the prior issue that become transferred proceeds of the refunding issue continue to be treated as unspent proceeds of the prior issue. If the prior issue satisfies one of the spending exceptions, the proceeds of the prior issue that are excepted from rebate under that spending exception are not subject to rebate either as proceeds of the prior issue or as transferred proceeds of the refunding issue.

(ii) Application to refunding issues. (A) In general. The only spending exception applicable to refunding issues is the 6-month exception. For purposes of applying the 6-month exception to a refunding issue only, proceeds of the prior issue that become transferred proceeds of the refunding issue generally are not treated as proceeds of the refunding issue and need not be spent for the refunding issue to satisfy that spending exception. Even if the refunding issue qualifies for that spending exception, those transferred proceeds are subject to rebate as proceeds of the refunding issue unless an exception to rebate applied to those proceeds as proceeds of the prior issue.

(B) Exception. For purposes of applying the 6-month exception to refunding issues, those transferred proceeds of the refunding issue excluded from the gross proceeds of the prior issue under the special definition of gross proceeds in paragraph (c)(3) of this section, and those that transferred from a prior taxable issue, are generally treated as gross proceeds of the refunding issue. Thus, for the refunding issue to qualify for the 6-month exception, those proceeds must be spent within 6 months of the issue date of the refunding issue, unless those amounts continue to be used in a manner that does not cause those amounts to be gross proceeds under paragraph (c)(3) of this section.

(2) Application of multipurpose issue rules. Except as otherwise provided, if any portion of an issue is treated as a separate issue allocable to refunding purposes under § 1.148-9(h) (relating to multipurpose issues), for purposes of this section, that portion is treated as a separate issue.

(3) Expenditures for governmental purposes of the issue. For purposes of this section, expenditures for the governmental purpose of an issue include payments for interest, but not principal, on the issue, and for principal or interest on another issue of obligations. The preceding sentence does not apply for purposes of the 18-month and 2-year exceptions if those payments cause the issue to be a refunding issue.

(4) De minimis rule. Any failure to satisfy the final spending requirement of the 18-month exception or the 2-year exception is disregarded if the issuer exercises due diligence to complete the project financed and the amount of the failure does not exceed the lesser of 3 percent of the issue price of the issue or $250,000.

(5) Special definition of reasonably required reserve or replacement fund. For purposes of this section only, a reasonably required reserve or replacement fund also includes any fund to the extent described in § 1.148-5(c)(3)(i)(E) or (G).

(6) Pooled financing issue. (i) In general. Except as otherwise provided in this paragraph (b)(6), the spending exceptions apply to a pooled financing issue as a whole, rather than to each loan separately.

(ii) Election to apply spending exceptions separately to each loan. (A) In general. At the election (made on or before the issue date) of the issuer of a pooled financing issue, the spending exceptions are applied separately to each conduit loan, and the applicable spending requirements for a loan begin on the earlier of the date the loan is made, or the first day following the 1-year period beginning on the issue date of the pooled financing issue. If this election is made, the rebate requirement applies to, and none of the spending exceptions are available for, gross proceeds of the pooled financing bonds before the date on which the spending requirements for those proceeds begin.

(B) Application of spending exceptions. If the issuer makes the election under this paragraph (b)(6)(ii), the rebate requirement is satisfied for proceeds used to finance a particular conduit loan to the extent that the loan satisfies a spending exception or the small issuer exception under § 1.148-8, regardless of whether any other conduit loans allocable to the issue satisfy such an exception. A pooled financing issue is an issue of arbitrage bonds, however, unless the entire issue satisfies the requirements of section 148. An issuer may pay rebate for some conduit loans and 1 3/4 percent penalty for other conduit loans from the same pooled financing issue. The 1 1/2 percent penalty is computed separately for each conduit loan.

(C) Elections under 2-year exception. If the issuer makes the election under this paragraph (b)(6)(ii), the issuer may make all elections under the 2-year exception separately for each loan. Elections regarding a loan that otherwise must be made by the issuer on or before the issue date instead may be made on or before the date the loan is made (but not later than 1 year after the issue date).

(D) Example. The operation of this paragraph (b)(6) is illustrated by the following example:

Example. Pooled financing issue. On January 1, 1994, Authority J issues bonds. As of the issue date, J reasonably expects to use the proceeds of the issue to make loans to City K, County L, and City M. J does not reasonably expect to use more than 75 percent of the available construction proceeds of the issue for construction expenditures. On or before the issue date, J elects to apply the spending exceptions separately for each loan, with spending requirements beginning on the earlier of the date the loan is made or the first day following the 1-year period beginning on the issue date. On February 1, 1994, J loans a portion of the proceeds to K, and K reasonably expects that 45 percent of those amounts will be used for construction expenditures. On the date this loan is made, J elects under paragraph (j) of this section to treat 60 percent of the amount loaned to K as a separate construction issue, and also elects the 1 1/2 percent penalty under paragraph (k) of this section for the separate construction issue. On March 1, 1994, J loans a portion of the proceeds to L, and L reasonably expects that more than 75 percent of those amounts will be used for construction expenditures. On March 1, 1995, J loans the remainder of the proceeds to M, and none of those amounts will be used for construction expenditures. J must satisfy the rebate requirement for all gross proceeds before those amounts are loaned. For the loan to K, the spending periods begin on February 1, 1994, and the 1 1/2 percent penalty must be paid for any failure to meet a spending requirement for the portion of the loan to K that is treated as a separate construction issue. Rebate must be paid on the remaining portion of the loan to K, unless that portion qualifies for the 6-month exception. For the loan to L, the spending periods begin on March 1, 1994, and the rebate requirement must be satisfied unless the 6-month, 18-month, or the 2-year exception is satisfied with respect to those amounts. For the loan to M, the spending periods begin on January 2, 1995, and the rebate requirement must be satisfied for those amounts unless the 6-month or 18-month exception is satisfied.

(c) 6-month exception. *(1) General rule.* An issue is treated as meeting the rebate requirement if—

(i) The gross proceeds (as modified by paragraph (c)(3) of this section) of the issue are allocated to expenditures for the governmental purposes of the issue within the 6-month period beginning on the issue date (the 6-month spending period); and

(ii) The rebate requirement is met for amounts not required to be spent within the 6-month spending period (excluding earnings on a bona fide debt service fund).

(2) Additional period for certain bonds. The 6-month spending period is extended for an additional 6 months in certain circumstances specified under section 148(f)(4)(B)(ii).

(3) Amounts not included in gross proceeds. For purposes of paragraph (c)(1)(i) of this section only, gross proceeds has the meaning used in § 1.148-1, except it does not include amounts—

(i) In a bona fide debt service fund;

(ii) In a reasonably required reserve or replacement fund (see § 1.148-7(b)(5));

(iii) That, as of the issue date, are not reasonably expected to be gross proceeds but that become gross proceeds after the end of the 6-month spending period;

(iv) Representing sale or investment proceeds derived from payments under any purpose investment of the issue; and

(v) Representing repayments of grants (as defined in § 1.148-6(d)(4)) financed by the issue.

(4) Series of refundings. If a principal purpose of a series of refunding issues is to exploit the difference between taxable and tax-exempt interest rates by investing proceeds during the temporary periods provided in § 1.148-9(d), the 6-month spending period for all issues in the series begins on the issue date of the first issue in the series.

(d) 18-month exception. *(1) General rule.* An issue is treated as meeting the rebate requirement if all of the following requirements are satisfied—

(i) 18-Month expenditure schedule met. The gross proceeds (as defined in paragraph (d)(3) of this section) are allocated to expenditures for a governmental purpose of the issue in accordance with the following schedule (the 18-month expenditure schedule) measured from the issue date—

(A) At least 15 percent within 6 months (the first spending period);

(B) At least 60 percent within 12 months (the second spending period); and

(C) 100 percent within 18 months (the third spending period).

(ii) Rebate requirement met for amounts not required to be spent. The rebate requirement is met for all amounts not required to be spent in accordance with the 18-month expenditure schedule (other than earnings on a bona fide debt service fund).

(iii) Issue qualifies for initial temporary period. All of the gross proceeds (as defined in paragraph (d)(3)(i) of this section) of the issue qualify for the initial temporary period under § 1.148-2(e)(2).

(2) Extension for reasonable retainage. An issue does not fail to satisfy the spending requirement for the third spend-

ing period as a result of a reasonable retainage if the reasonable retainage is allocated to expenditures within 30 months of the issue date. Reasonable retainage has the meaning under paragraph (h) of this section, as modified to refer to net sale proceeds on the date 18 months after the issue date.

(3) Gross proceeds. (i) Definition of gross proceeds. For purposes of paragraph (d)(1) of this section only, gross proceeds means gross proceeds as defined in paragraph (c)(3) of this section, as modified to refer to "18 months" in paragraph (c)(3)(iii) of this section in lieu of '6 months."

(ii) Estimated earnings. For purposes of determining compliance with the first two spending periods under paragraph (d)(1)(i) of this section, the amount of investment proceeds included in gross proceeds of the issue is determined based on the issuer's reasonable expectations on the issue date.

(4) Application to multipurpose issues. This paragraph (d) does not apply to an issue any portion of which is treated as meeting the rebate requirement under paragraph (e) of this section (relating to the 2-year exception).

(e) 2-year exception. *(1) General rule.* A construction issue is treated as meeting the rebate requirement for available construction proceeds if those proceeds are allocated to expenditures for governmental purposes of the issue in accordance with the following schedule (the 2-year expenditure schedule), measured from the issue date—

(i) At least 10 percent within 6 months (the first spending period);

(ii) At least 45 percent within 1 year (the second spending period);

(iii) At least 75 percent within 18 months (the third spending period); and

(iv) 100 percent within 2 years (the fourth spending period).

(2) Extension for reasonable retainage. An issue does not fail to satisfy the spending requirement for the fourth spending period as a result of unspent amounts for reasonable retainage (as defined in paragraph (h) of this section) if those amounts are allocated to expenditures within 3 years of the issue date.

(3) Definitions. For purposes of the 2-year exception, the following definitions apply:

(i) Real property means land and improvements to land, such as buildings or other inherently permanent structures, including interests in real property. For example, real property includes wiring in a building, plumbing systems, central heating or air-conditioning systems, pipes or ducts, elevators, escalators installed in a building, paved parking areas, roads, wharves and docks, bridges, and sewage lines.

(ii) Tangible personal property means any tangible property other than real property, including interests in tangible personal property. For example, tangible personal property includes machinery that is not a structural component of a building, subway cars, fire trucks, automobiles, office equipment, testing equipment, and furnishings.

(iii) Substantially completed. Construction may be treated as substantially completed when the issuer abandons construction or when at least 90 percent of the total costs of the construction reasonably expected, as of that date, to be financed with the available construction proceeds have been allocated to expenditures.

(f) Construction issue. *(1) Definition.* Construction issue means any issue that is not a refunding issue if—

(i) The issuer reasonably expects, as of the issue date, that at least 75 percent of the available construction proceeds of the issue will be allocated to construction expenditures (as defined in paragraph (g) of this section) for property owned by a governmental unit or a 501(c)(3) organization; and

(ii) Any private activity bonds that are part of the issue are qualified 501(c)(3) bonds or private activity bonds issued to finance property to be owned by a governmental unit or a 501(c)(3) organization.

(2) Use of actual facts. For the provisions of paragraphs (e) through (m) of this section that apply based on the issuer's reasonable expectations, an issuer may elect on or before the issue date to apply all of those provisions based on actual facts, except that this election does not apply for purposes of determining whether an issue is a construction issue under paragraph (f)(1) of this section if the 1½ percent penalty election is made under paragraph (k) of this section.

(3) Ownership requirement. (i) In general. A governmental unit or 501(c)(3) organization is treated as the owner of property if it would be treated as the owner for Federal income tax purposes. For obligations issued on behalf of a State or local governmental unit, the entity that actually issues the bonds is treated as a governmental unit.

(ii) Safe harbor for leases and management contracts. Property leased by a governmental unit or a 501(c)(3) organization is treated as owned by the governmental unit or 501(c)(3) organization if the lessee complies with the requirements of section 142(b)(1)(B). For a bond described in section 142(a)(6), the requirements of section 142(b)(1)(B) apply as modified by section 146(h)(2).

(g) Construction expenditures. *(1) Definition.* Except as otherwise provided, construction expenditures means capital expenditures (as defined in § 1.150-1) that are allocable to the cost of real property or constructed personal property (as defined in paragraph (g)(3) of this section). Except as provided in paragraph (g)(2) of this section, construction expenditures do not include expenditures for acquisitions of interests in land or other existing real property.

(2) Certain acquisitions under turnkey contracts treated as construction expenditures. Expenditures are not for the acquisition of an interest in existing real property other than land if the contract between the seller and the issuer requires the seller to build or install the property (e.g., a turnkey contract), but only to the extent that the property has not been built or installed at the time the parties enter into the contract.

(3) Constructed personal property. Constructed personal property means tangible personal property (or, if acquired pursuant to a single acquisition contract, properties) or specially developed computer software if—

(i) A substantial portion of the property or properties is completed more than 6 months after the earlier of the date construction or rehabilitation commenced and the date the issuer entered into an acquisition contract;

(ii) Based on the reasonable expectations of the issuer, if any, or representations of the person constructing the property, with the exercise of due diligence, completion of construction or rehabilitation (and delivery to the issuer) could not have occurred within that 6-month period; and

(iii) If the issuer itself builds or rehabilitates the property, not more than 75 percent of the capitalizable cost is attributable to property acquired by the issuer (e.g., components, raw materials, and other supplies).

(4) Specially developed computer software. Specially developed computer software means any programs or routines used to cause a computer to perform a desired task or set of tasks, and the documentation required to describe and maintain those programs, provided that the software is specially developed and is functionally related and subordinate to real property or other constructed personal property.

(5) Examples. The operation of this paragraph (g) is illustrated by the following examples:

Example (1). Purchase of construction materials. City A issues bonds to finance a new office building. A uses proceeds of the bonds to purchase materials to be used in constructing the building, such as bricks, pipes, wires, lighting, carpeting, heating equipment, and similar materials. Expenditures by A for the construction materials are construction expenditures because those expenditures will be capitalizable to the cost of the building upon completion, even though they are not initially capitalizable to the cost of existing real property. This result would be the same if A hires a third-party to perform the construction, unless the office building is partially constructed at the time that A contracts to purchase the building.

Example (2). Turnkey contract. City B issues bonds to finance a new office building. B enters into a turnkey contract with developer D under which D agrees to provide B with a completed building on a specified completion date on land currently owned by D. Under the agreement, D holds title to the land and building and assumes any risk of loss until the completion date, at which time title to the land and the building will be transferred to B. No construction has been performed by the date that B and D enter into the agreement. All payments by B to D for construction of the building are construction expenditures because all the payments are properly capitalized to the cost of the building, but payments by B to D allocable to the acquisition of the land are not construction expenditures.

Example (3). Right-of-way. P, a public agency, issues bonds to finance the acquisition of a right-of-way and the construction of sewage lines through numerous parcels of land. The right-of-way is acquired primarily through P's exercise of its powers of eminent domain. As of the issue date, P reasonably expects that it will take approximately 2 years to acquire the entire right-of-way because of the time normally required for condemnation proceedings. No expenditures for the acquisition of the right-of-way are construction expenditures because they are costs incurred to acquire an interest in existing real property.

Example (4). Subway cars. City C issues bonds to finance new subway cars. C reasonably expects that it will take more than 6 months for the subway cars to be constructed to C's specifications. The subway cars are constructed personal property. Alternatively, if the builder of the subway cars informs C that it will only take 3 months to build the subway cars to C's specifications, no payments for the subway cars are construction expenditures.

Example (5). Fractional interest in property. U, a public agency, issues bonds to finance an undivided fractional interest in a newly constructed power-generating facility. U contributes its ratable share of the cost of building the new facility to the project manager for the facility. U's contributions are construction expenditures in the same proportion that the total expenditures for the facility qualify as construction expenditures.

Example (6). Park land. City D issues bonds to finance the purchase of unimproved land and the cost of subsequent improvements to the land, such as grading and landscaping, necessary to transform it into a park. The costs of the improvements are properly capitalizable to the cost of the land, and therefore, are construction expenditures, but expenditures for the acquisition of the land are not.

(h) Reasonable retainage definition. Reasonable retainage means an amount, not to exceed 5 percent of available construction proceeds as of the end of the fourth spending period, that is retained for reasonable business purposes relating to the property financed with the proceeds of the issue. For example, a reasonable retainage may include a retention to ensure or promote compliance with a construction contract in circumstances in which the retained amount is not yet payable, or in which the issuer reasonably determines that a dispute exists regarding completion or payment.

(i) Available construction proceeds. *(1) Definition in general.* Available construction proceeds has the meaning used in section 148(f)(4)(C)(vi). For purposes of this definition, earnings include earnings on any tax-exempt bond. Pre-issuance accrued interest and earnings thereon may be disregarded. Amounts that are not gross proceeds as a result of the application of the universal cap under § 1.148-6(b)(2) are not available construction proceeds.

(2) Earnings on a reasonably required reserve or replacement fund. Earnings on any reasonably required reserve or replacement fund are available construction proceeds only to the extent that those earnings accrue before the earlier of the date construction is substantially completed or the date that is 2 years after the issue date. An issuer may elect on or before the issue date to exclude from available construction proceeds the earnings on such a fund. If the election is made, the rebate requirement applies to the excluded amounts from the issue date.

(3) Reasonable expectations test for future earnings. For purposes of determining compliance with the spending requirements as of the end of each of the first three spending periods, available construction proceeds include the amount of future earnings that the issuer reasonably expected as of the issue date.

(4) Issuance costs. Available construction proceeds do not include gross proceeds used to pay issuance costs financed by an issue, but do include earnings on such proceeds. Thus, an expenditure of gross proceeds of an issue for issuance costs does not count toward meeting the spending requirements. The expenditure of earnings on gross proceeds used to pay issuance costs does count toward meeting those requirements. If the spending requirements are met and the proceeds used to pay issuance costs are expended by the end of the fourth spending period, those proceeds and the earnings thereon are treated as having satisfied the rebate requirement.

(5) One and one-half percent penalty in lieu of arbitrage rebate. For purposes of the spending requirements of paragraph (e) of this section, available construction proceeds as of the end of any spending period are reduced by the amount of penalty in lieu of arbitrage rebate (under paragraph (k) of this section) that the issuer has paid from available construction proceeds before the last day of the spending period.

(6) Payments on purpose investments and repayments of grants. Available construction proceeds do not include—

(i) Sale or investment proceeds derived from payments under any purpose investment of the issue; or

(ii) Repayments of grants (as defined in § 1.148-6(d)(4)) financed by the issue.

(7) Examples. The operation of this paragraph (i) is illustrated by the following examples:

Example (1). Treatment of investment earnings. City F issues bonds having an issue price of $10,000,000. F deposits all of the proceeds of the issue into a construction fund to be used for expenditures other than costs of issuance. F estimates on the issue date that, based on reasonably expected expenditures and rates of investment, earnings on the construction fund will be $800,000. As of the issue date and the end of each of the first three spending periods, the amount of available construction proceeds is $10,800,000. To qualify as a construction issue, F must reasonably expect on the issue date that at least $8,100,000 (75 percent of $10,800,000) will be used for construction expenditures. In order to meet the 10 percent spending requirement at the end of the first spending period, F must spend at least $1,080,000. As of the end of the fourth spending period, F has received $1,100,000 in earnings. In order to meet the spending requirement at the end of the fourth spending period, however, F must spend all of the $11,100,000 of actual available construction proceeds (except for reasonable retainage not exceeding $555,000).

Example (2). Treatment of investment earnings without a reserve fund. City G issues bonds having an issue price of $11,200,000. G does not elect to exclude earnings on the reserve fund from available construction proceeds. G uses $200,000 of proceeds to pay issuance costs and deposits $1,000,000 of proceeds into a reasonably required reserve fund. G deposits the remaining $10,000,000 of proceeds into a construction fund to be used for construction expenditures. On the issue date, G reasonably expects that, based on the reasonably expected date of substantial completion and rates of investment, total earnings on the construction fund will be $800,000, and total earnings on the reserve fund to the date of substantial completion will be $150,000. G reasonably expects that substantial completion will occur during the fourth spending period. As of the issue date, the amount of available construction proceeds is $10,950,000 ($10,000,000 originally deposited into the construction fund plus $800,000 expected earnings on the construction fund and $150,000 expected earnings on the reserve fund). To qualify as a construction issue, G must reasonably expect on the issue date that at least $8,212,500 will be used for construction expenditures.

Example (3). Election to exclude earnings on a reserve fund. The facts are the same as Example 2, except that G elects on the issue date to exclude earnings on the reserve fund from available construction proceeds. The amount of available construction proceeds as of the issue date is $10,800,000.

(j) Election to treat portion of issue used for construction as separate issue. *(1) In general.* For purposes of paragraph (e) of this section, if any proceeds of an issue are to be used for construction expenditures, the issuer may elect on or before the issue date to treat the portion of the issue that is not a refunding issue as two, and only two, separate issues, if—

(i) One of the separate issues is a construction issue as defined in paragraph (f) of this section;

(ii) The issuer reasonably expects, as of the issue date, that this construction issue will finance all of the construction expenditures to be financed by the issue; and

(iii) The issuer makes an election to apportion the issue under this paragraph (j)(1) in which it identifies the amount of the issue price of the issue allocable to the construction issue.

(2) Example. The operation of this paragraph (j) is illustrated by the following example.

Example. City D issues bonds having an issue price of $19,000,000. On the issue date, D reasonably expects to use $10,800,000 of bond proceeds (including investment earnings) for construction expenditures for the project being financed. D deposits $10,000,000 in a construction fund to be used for construction expenditures and $9,000,000 in an acquisition fund to be used for acquisition of equipment not qualifying as construction expenditures. D estimates on the issue date, based on reasonably expected expenditures and rates of investment, that total earnings on the construction fund will be $800,000 and total earnings on the acquisition fund will be $200,000. Because the total construction expenditures to be financed by the issue are expected to be $10,800,000, the maximum available construction proceeds for a construction issue is $14,400,000 ($10,800,000 divided by 0.75). To determine the maximum amount of the issue price allocable to a construction issue, the estimated investment earnings allocable to the construction issue are subtracted. The entire $800,000 of earnings on the construction fund are allocable to the construction issue. Only a portion of the $200,000 of earnings on the acquisition fund, however, are allocable to the construction issue. The total amount of the available construction proceeds that is expected to be used for acquisition is $3,600,000 ($14,400,000 − $10,800,000). The portion of earnings on the acquisition fund that is allocable to the construction issue is $78,261 ($200,000 × $3,600,000/$9,200,000). Accordingly, D may elect on or before the issue date to treat up to $13,521,739 of the issue price as a construction issue ($14,400,000 − $800,000 − $78,261). D's election must specify the amount of the issue price treated as a construction issue. The balance of the issue price is treated as a separate nonconstruction issue that is subject to the rebate requirement unless it meets another exception to arbitrage rebate. Because the financing of a construction issue is a separate governmental purpose under § 1.148-9(h), the election causes the issue to be a multipurpose issue under that section.

(k) One and one-half percent penalty in lieu of arbitrage rebate. *(1) In general.* Under section 148(f)(4)(C)(vii), an issuer of a construction issue may elect on or before the issue date to pay a penalty (the 1½ percent penalty) to the United States in lieu of the obligation to pay the rebate amount on available construction proceeds upon failure to satisfy the spending requirements of paragraph (e) of this section. The 1½ percent penalty is calculated separately for each spending period, including each semiannual period after the end of the fourth spending period, and is equal to 1.5 percent times the underexpended proceeds as of the end of the spending period. For each spending period, underexpended proceeds equal the amount of available construction proceeds required to be spent by the end of the spending period, less the amount actually allocated to expenditures for the governmental purposes of the issue by that date. The 1½ percent penalty must be paid to the United States no later than 90 days after the end of the spending period to which it relates. The 1½ percent penalty continues to apply at the end of each spending period and each semiannual period thereafter until the earliest of the following—

(i) The termination of the penalty under paragraph (l) of this section;

(ii) The expenditure of all of the available construction proceeds; or

(iii) The last stated final maturity date of bonds that are part of the issue and any bonds that refund those bonds.

(2) Application to reasonable retainage. If an issue meets the exception for reasonable retainage except that all retainage is not spent within 3 years of the issue date, the issuer must pay the 1½ percent penalty to the United States for any reasonable retainage that was not so spent as of the close of the 3-year period and each later spending period.

(3) Coordination with rebate requirement. The rebate requirement is treated as met with respect to available construction proceeds for a period if the 1½ percent penalty is paid in accordance with this section.

(l) Termination of 1½ percent penalty. *(1) Termination after initial temporary period.* The issuer may terminate the 1½percent penalty after the initial temporary period (a section 148(f)(4)(C)(viii) penalty termination) if—

(i) Not later than 90 days after the earlier of the end of the initial temporary period or the date construction is substantially completed, the issuer elects to terminate the 1½ percent penalty; provided that solely for this purpose, the initial temporary period may be extended by the issuer to a date ending 5 years after the issue date;

(ii) Within 90 days after the end of the initial temporary period, the issuer pays a penalty equal to 3 percent of the unexpended available construction proceeds determined as of the end of the initial temporary period, multiplied by the number of years (including fractions of years computed to 2 decimal places) in the initial temporary period;

(iii) For the period beginning as of the close of the initial temporary period, the unexpended available construction proceeds are not invested in higher yielding investments; and

(iv) On the earliest date on which the bonds may be called or otherwise redeemed, with or without a call premium, the unexpended available construction proceeds as of that date (not including any amount earned after the date on which notice of the redemption was required to be given) must be used to redeem the bonds. Amounts used to pay any call premium are treated as used to redeem bonds. This redemption requirement may be met by purchases of bonds by the issuer on the open market at prices not exceeding fair market value. A portion of the annual principal payment due on serial bonds of a construction issue may be paid from the unexpended amount, but only in an amount no greater than the amount that bears the same ratio to the annual principal due that the total unexpended amount bears to the issue price of the construction issue.

(2) Termination before end of initial temporary period. If the construction to be financed by the construction issue is substantially completed before the end of the initial temporary period, the issuer may elect to terminate the 1½ percent penalty before the end of the initial temporary period (a section 148(f)(4)(C)(ix) penalty termination) if—

(i) Before the close of the initial temporary period and not later than 90 days after the date the construction is substantially completed, the issuer elects to terminate the 1½ percent penalty;

(ii) The election identifies the amount of available construction proceeds that will not be spent for the governmental purposes of the issue; and

(iii) The issuer has met all of the conditions for a section 148(f)(4)(C)(viii) penalty termination, applied as if the initial temporary period ended as of the date the required election for a section 148(f)(4)(C)(ix) penalty termination is made. That penalty termination election satisfies the required election for a section 148(f)(4)(C)(viii) termination.

(3) Application to reasonable retainage. Solely for purposes of determining whether the conditions for terminating the 1½ percent penalty are met, reasonable retainage may be treated as spent for a governmental purpose of the construction issue. Reasonable retainage that is so treated continues to be subject to the 1½ percent penalty.

(4) Example. The operation of this paragraph (l) is illustrated by the following example.

Example. City I issues a construction issue having a 20-year maturity and qualifying for a 3-year initial temporary period. The bonds are first subject to optional redemption 10 years after the issue date at a premium of 3 percent. I elects, on or before the issue date, to pay the 1½ percent penalty in lieu of arbitrage rebate. At the end of the 3-year temporary period, the project is not substantially completed, and $1,500,000 of available construction proceeds of the issue are unspent. At that time, I reasonably expects to need $500,000 to complete the project. I may terminate the 1½ percent penalty in lieu of arbitrage rebate with respect to the excess $1,500,000 by electing to terminate within 90 days of the end of the initial temporary period; paying a penalty to the United States of $135,000 (3 percent of $1,500,000 multiplied by 3 years); restricting the yield on the investment of unspent available construction proceeds for 7 years until the first call date, although any portion of these proceeds may still be spent on the project prior to that call date; and using the available construction proceeds that, as of the first call date, have not been allocated to expenditures for the governmental purposes of the issue to redeem bonds on that call date. If I fails to make the termination election, I is required to pay the 1½ percent penalty on unspent available construction proceeds every 6 months until the latest maturity date of bonds of the issue (or any bonds of another issue that refund such bonds).

(m) Payment of penalties. Each penalty payment under this section must be paid in the manner provided in § 1.148-3(g). See § 1.148-3(h) for rules on failures to pay penalties under this section.

T.D. 8476, 6/14/93.

---

§ 1.148-8 Small issuer exception to rebate requirement.

Caution: The Treasury has not yet amended Reg § 1.148-8 to reflect changes made by P.L. 107-16, P.L. 105-34.

(a) Scope. Under section 148(f)(4)(D), bonds issued to finance governmental activities of certain small issuers are treated as meeting the arbitrage rebate requirement of section 148(f)(2) (the "small issuer exception"). This section provides guidance on the small issuer exception.

(b) General taxing powers. The small issuer exception generally applies only to bonds issued by governmental units with general taxing powers. A governmental unit has general taxing powers if it has the power to impose taxes (or to cause another entity to impose taxes) of general applicability which, when collected, may be used for the general purposes of the issuer. The taxing power may be limited to a specific type of tax, provided that the applicability of the tax is not limited to a small number of persons. The governmental unit's exercise of its taxing power may be subject to procedural limitations, such as voter approval requirements, but may not be contingent on approval by another governmental unit. See, also, section 148(f)(4)(D)(iv).

(c) Size limitation. *(1) In general.* An issue (other than a refunding issue) qualifies for the small issuer exception only if the issuer reasonably expects, as of the issue date, that the aggregate face amount of all tax-exempt bonds (other than private activity bonds) issued by it during that calendar year will not exceed $5,000,000; or the aggregate face amount of all tax-exempt bonds of the issuer (other than private activity bonds) actually issued during that calendar year does not exceed $5,000,000. For this purpose, if an issue has more than a de minimis amount of original issue discount or premium, aggregate face amount means the aggregate issue price of that issue (determined without regard to pre-issuance accrued interest).

(2) Aggregation rules. The following aggregation rules apply for purposes of applying the $5,000,000 size limitation under paragraph (c)(1) of this section.

(i) On-behalf-of issuers. An issuer and all entities (other than political subdivisions) that issue bonds on behalf of that issuer are treated as one issuer.

(ii) Subordinate entities. (A) In general. Except as otherwise provided in paragraph (d) of this section and section 148(f)(4)(D)(iv), all bonds issued by a subordinate entity are also treated as issued by each entity to which it is subordinate. An issuer is subordinate to another governmental entity if it is directly or indirectly controlled by the other entity within the meaning of § 1.150-1(e).

(B) Exception for allocations of size limitation. If an entity properly makes an allocation of a portion of its $5,000,000 size limitation to a subordinate entity (including an on behalf of issuer) under section 148(f)(4)(D)(iv), the portion of bonds issued by the subordinate entity under the allocation is treated as issued only by the allocating entity and not by any other entity to which the issuing entity is subordinate. These allocations are irrevocable and must bear a reasonable relationship to the benefits received by the allocating unit from issues issued by the subordinate entity. The benefits to be considered include the manner in which—

(1) Proceeds are to be distributed;

(2) The debt service is to be paid;

(3) The facility financed is to be owned;

(4) The use or output of the facility is to be shared; and

(5) Costs of operation and maintenance are to be shared.

(iii) Avoidance of size limitation. An entity formed or availed of to avoid the purposes of the $5,000,000 size limitation and all entities that would benefit from the avoidance are treated as one issuer. Situations in which an entity is formed or availed of to avoid the purposes of the $5,000,000 size limitation include those in which the issuer—

(A) Issues bonds which, but for the $5,000,000 size limitation, would have been issued by another entity; and

(B) Does not receive a substantial benefit from the project financed by the bonds.

(3) Certain refunding bonds not taken into account. In applying the $5,000,000 size limitation, there is not taken into account the portion of an issue that is a current refunding issue to the extent that the stated principal amount of the refunding bond does not exceed the portion of the outstanding stated principal amount of the refunded bond paid with proceeds of the refunding bond. For this purpose, principal amount means, in reference to a plain par bond, its stated principal amount plus accrued unpaid interest, and in reference to any other bond, its present value.

(d) Pooled financings. *(1) Treatment of pool issuer.* To the extent that an issuer of a pooled financing is not an ultimate borrower in the financing and the conduit borrowers are governmental units with general taxing powers and not subordinate to the issuer, the pooled financing is not counted towards the $5,000,000 size limitation of the issuer for purposes of applying the small issuer exception to its other issues. The issuer of the pooled financing issue is, however, subject to the rebate requirement for any unloaned gross proceeds.

(2) Treatment of conduit borrowers. A loan to a conduit borrower in a pooled financing qualifies for the small issuer exception, regardless of the size of either the pooled financing or of any loan to other conduit borrowers, only if—

(i) The bonds of the pooled financing are not private activity bonds;

(ii) None of the loans to conduit borrowers are private activity bonds; and

(iii) The loan to the conduit borrower meets all the requirements of the small issuer exception.

(e) Refunding issues. *(1) In general.* Sections 148(f)(4)(D)(v) and (vi) provide restrictions on application of the small issuer exception to refunding issues.

(2) Multipurpose issues. The multipurpose issue allocation rules of § 1.148-9(h) apply for purposes of determining whether refunding bonds meet the requirements of section 148(f)(4)(D)(v).

T.D. 8418, 5/12/92, amend T.D. 8476, 6/14/93.

PAR. 10. Section 1.148-8(d) is revised to read as follows:

Proposed § 1.148-8 Small Issuer Exception to Rebate Requirement. [*For Preamble, see ¶ 152,909*]

* * * * *

(d) Pooled financings—treatment of conduit borrowers. A loan to a conduit borrower in a pooled financing qualifies for the small issuer exception, regardless of the size of either the pooled financing or of any loan to other conduit borrowers, only if—

(1) The bonds of the pooled financing are not private activity bonds;

(2) None of the loans to conduit borrowers are private activity bonds; and

(3) The loan to the conduit borrower meets all the requirements of the small issue exception.

* * * * *

§ 1.148-9 Arbitrage rules for refunding issues.

(a) Scope of application. This section contains special arbitrage rules for refunding issues. These rules apply for all purposes of section 148 and govern allocations of proceeds, bonds, and investments to determine transferred proceeds, temporary periods, reasonably required reserve or replacement funds, minor portions, and separate issue treatment of certain multipurpose issues.

(b) Transferred proceeds allocation rule. *(1) In general.* When proceeds of the refunding issue discharge any of the outstanding principal amount of the prior issue, proceeds of the prior issue become transferred proceeds of the refunding issue and cease to be proceeds of the prior issue. The amount of proceeds of the prior issue that becomes transferred proceeds of the refunding issue is an amount equal to the proceeds of the prior issue on the date of that discharge multiplied by a fraction—

(i) The numerator of which is the principal amount of the prior issue discharged with proceeds of the refunding issue on the date of that discharge; and

(ii) The denominator of which is the total outstanding principal amount of the prior issue on the date immediately before the date of that discharge.

(2) Special definition of principal amount. For purposes of this section, principal amount means, in reference to a plain par bond, its stated principal amount, and in reference to any other bond, its present value.

(3) Relation of transferred proceeds rule to universal cap rule. (i) In general. Paragraphs (b)(1) and (c) of this section apply to allocate transferred proceeds and corresponding investments to a refunding issue on any date required by those paragraphs before the application of the universal cap rule of § 1.148-6(b)(2) to reallocate any of those amounts. To the extent nonpurpose investments allocable to proceeds of a refunding issue exceed the universal cap for the issue on the date that amounts become transferred proceeds of the refunding issue, those transferred proceeds and corresponding investments are reallocated back to the issue from which they transferred on that same date to the extent of the unused universal cap on that prior issue.

(ii) Example. The following example illustrates the application of this paragraph of (b)(3):

Example. On January 1, 1995, $100,000 of nonpurpose investments allocable to proceeds of issue A become transferred proceeds of issue B under § 1.148-9, but the unused portion of issue B's universal cap is $75,000 as of that date. On January 1, 1995, issue A has unused universal cap in excess of $25,000. Thus, $25,000 of nonpurpose investments representing the transferred proceeds are immediately reallocated back to issue A on January 1, 1995, and are proceeds of issue A. On the next transfer date under § 1.148-9, the $25,000 receives no priority in determining transferred proceeds as of that date but is treated the same as all other proceeds of issue A subject to transfer.

(4) Limitation on multi-generational transfers. This paragraph (b)(4) contains limitations on the manner in which proceeds of a first generation issue that is refunded by a refunding issue (a second generation issue) become transferred proceeds of a refunding issue (a third generation issue) that refunds the second generation issue. Proceeds of the first generation issue that become transferred proceeds of the third generation issue are treated as having a yield equal to the yield on the refunding escrow allocated to the second generation issue (i.e., as determined under § 1.148-5(b)(2)(iv)). The determination of the transferred proceeds of the third generation issue does not affect compliance with the requirements of section 148, including the determination of the amount of arbitrage rebate with respect to or the yield on the refunding escrow, of the second generation issue.

(c) Special allocation rules for refunding issues. *(1) Allocations of investments.* (i) In general. Except as otherwise provided in this paragraph (c), investments purchased with sale proceeds or investment proceeds of a refunding issue must be allocated to those proceeds, and investments not purchased with those proceeds may not be allocated to those proceeds (i.e., a specific tracing method).

(ii) Allocations to transferred proceeds. When proceeds of a prior issue become transferred proceeds of a refunding issue, investments (and the related payments and receipts) of proceeds of the prior issue that are held in a refunding escrow for another issue are allocated to the transferred proceeds under the ratable allocation method described in paragraph (c)(1)(iii) of this section. Investments of proceeds of the prior issue that are not held in a refunding escrow for another issue are allocated to the transferred proceeds by application of the allocation methods described in paragraph (c)(1)(iii) or (iv) of this section, consistently applied to all investments on a transfer date.

(iii) Ratable allocation method. Under the ratable allocation method, a ratable portion of each nonpurpose and purpose investment of proceeds of the prior issue is allocated to transferred proceeds of the refunding issue.

(iv) Representative allocation method. (A) In general. Under the representative allocation method, representative portions of the portfolio of nonpurpose investments and the portfolio of purpose investments of proceeds of the prior issue are allocated to transferred proceeds of the refunding issue. Unlike the ratable allocation method, this representative allocation method permits an allocation of particular whole investments. Whether a portion is representative is based on all the facts and circumstances, including, without limitation, whether the current yields, maturities, and current unrealized gains or losses on the particular allocated investments are reasonably comparable to those of the unallocated investments in the aggregate. In addition, if a portion of nonpurpose investments is otherwise representative, it is within the issuer's discretion to allocate the portion from whichever source of funds it deems appropriate, such as a reserve fund or a construction fund for a prior issue.

(B) Mark-to-market safe harbor for representative allocation method. In addition to other representative allocations, a specific allocation of a particular nonpurpose investment to transferred proceeds (e,g., of lower yielding investments) is treated as satisfying the representative allocation method if that investment is valued at fair market value on the transfer date in determining the payments and receipts on that date, but only if the portion of the nonpurpose investments that transfers is based on the relative fair market value of all nonpurpose investments.

(2) Allocations of mixed escrows to expenditures for principal, interest, and redemption prices on a prior issue. (i) In general. Except for amounts required or permitted to be accounted for under paragraph (c)(2)(ii) of this section, proceeds of a refunding issue and other amounts that are not proceeds of a refunding issue that are deposited in a refunding escrow (a mixed escrow) must be accounted for under this paragraph (c)(2)(i). Those proceeds and other amounts must be allocated to expenditures for principal, interest, or stated redemption prices on the prior issue so that the expenditures of those proceeds do not occur faster than ratably with expenditures of the other amounts in the mixed escrow. During the period that the prior issue has unspent proceeds, however, these allocations must be ratable (with reasonable adjustments for rounding) both between sources for expenditures (i.e., proceeds and other amounts) and between uses (i.e., principal, interest, and stated redemption prices on the prior issue).

(ii) Exceptions. (A) Mandatory allocation of certain nonproceeds to earliest expenditures. If amounts other than proceeds of the refunding issue are deposited in a mixed escrow, but before the issue date of the refunding issue those amounts had been held in a bona fide debt service fund or a fund to carry out the governmental purpose of the prior issue (e.g., a construction fund), those amounts must be allocated to the earliest maturing investments in the mixed escrow.

(B) Permissive allocation of non-proceeds to earliest expenditures. Excluding amounts covered by paragraph (c)(2)(ii)(A) of this section and subject to any required earlier expenditure of those amounts, any amounts in a mixed escrow that are not proceeds of a refunding issue may be allocated to the earliest maturing investments in the mixed escrow, provided that those investments mature and the proceeds thereof are expended before the date of any expenditure from the mixed escrow to pay any principal of the prior issue.

(d) Temporary periods in refundings. *(1) In general.* Proceeds of a refunding issue may be invested in higher yielding investments under section 148(c) only during the temporary periods described in paragraph (d)(2) of this section.

(2) Types of temporary periods in refundings. The available temporary periods for proceeds of a refunding issue are as follows:

(i) General temporary period for refunding issues. Except as otherwise provided in this paragraph (d)(2), the temporary period for proceeds (other than transferred proceeds) of a refunding issue is the period ending 30 days after the issue date of the refunding issue.

(ii) Temporary periods for current refunding issues. (A) In general. Except as otherwise provided in paragraph (d)(2)(ii)(B) of this section, the temporary period for proceeds (other than transferred proceeds) of a current refunding issue is 90 days.

(B) Temporary period for short-term current refunding issues. The temporary period for proceeds (other than transferred proceeds) of a current refunding issue that has an original term to maturity of 270 days or less may not exceed 30 days. The aggregate temporary periods for proceeds (other than transferred proceeds) of all current refunding issues described in the preceding sentence that are part of the same series of refundings is 90 days. An issue is part of a series of refundings if it finances or refinances the same expenditures for a particular governmental purpose as another issue.

(iii) Temporary periods for transferred proceeds. (A) In general. Except as otherwise provided in paragraph (d)(2)(iii)(B) of this section, each available temporary period for transferred proceeds of a refunding issue begins on the date those amounts become transferred proceeds of the refunding issue and ends on the date that, without regard to the discharge of the prior issue, the available temporary period for those proceeds would have ended had those proceeds remained proceeds of the prior issue.

(B) Termination of initial temporary period for prior issue in an advance refunding. The initial temporary period under § 1.148-2(e)(2) and (3) for the proceeds of a prior issue that is refunded by an advance refunding issue (including transferred proceeds) terminates on the issue date of the advance refunding issue.

(iv) Certain short-term gross proceeds. Except for proceeds of a refunding issue held in a refunding escrow, proceeds otherwise reasonably expected to be used to pay principal or interest on the prior issue, replacement proceeds not held in a bona fide debt service fund, and transferred proceeds, the temporary period for gross proceeds of a refunding issue is the 13-month period beginning on the date of receipt.

(e) Reasonably required reserve or replacement funds in refundings. In addition to the requirements of § 1.148-2(f), beginning on the issue date of a refunding issue, a reserve or replacement fund for a refunding issue or a prior issue is a reasonably required reserve or replacement fund under section 148(d) that may be invested in higher yielding investments only if the aggregate amount invested in higher yielding investments under this paragraph (e) for both the refunding issue and the prior issue does not exceed the size limitations under § 1.148-2(f)(2) and (f)(3), measured by reference to the refunding issue only (regardless of whether proceeds of the prior issue have become transferred proceeds of the refunding issue).

(f) Minor portions in refundings. Beginning on the issue date of the refunding issue, gross proceeds not in excess of a minor portion of the refunding issue qualify for investment in higher yielding investments under section 148(e), and gross proceeds not in excess of a minor portion of the prior issue qualify for investment in higher yielding investments under either section 148(e) or § 149(d)(3)(A)(v), whichever is applicable. Minor portion is defined in § 1.148-2(g).

(g) Certain waivers permitted. On or before the issue date, an issuer may waive the right to invest in higher yielding investments during any temporary period or as part of a reasonably required reserve or replacement fund. At any time, an issuer may waive the right to invest in higher yielding investments as part of a minor portion.

(h) Multipurpose issue allocations. *(1) Application of multipurpose issue allocation rules.* The portion of the bonds of a multipurpose issue reasonably allocated to any separate purpose under this paragraph (h) is treated as a separate issue for all purposes of section 148 except the following—

(i) Arbitrage yield. Except to the extent that the proceeds of an issue are allocable to two or more conduit loans that are tax-exempt bonds, determining the yield on a multipurpose issue and the yield on investments for purposes of the arbitrage yield restrictions of section 148 and the arbitrage rebate requirement of section 148(f);

(ii) Rebate amount. Except as provided in paragraph (h)(1)(i) of this section, determining the rebate amount for a multipurpose issue, including subsidiary matters with respect to that determination, such as the computation date credit under § 1.148-3(d)(1), the due date for payments, and the $100,000 bona fide debt service fund exception under section 148(f)(4)(A)(ii);

(iii) Minor portion. Determining the minor portion of an issue under section 148(e);

(iv) Reasonably required reserve or replacement fund. Determining the portion of an issue eligible for investment in higher yielding investments as part of a reasonably required reserve or replacement fund under section 148(d); and

(v) Effective date. Applying the provisions of § 1.148-11(b) (relating to elective retroactive application of §§ 1.148-1 through 1.148-10 to certain issues).

(2) Rules on allocations of multipurpose issues. (i) In general. This paragraph (h) applies to allocations of multipurpose issues, including allocations involving the refunding purposes of the issue. Except as otherwise provided in this paragraph (h), proceeds, investments, and bonds of a multipurpose issue may be allocated among the various separate purposes of the issue using any reasonable, consistently applied allocation method. An allocation is not reasonable if it achieves more favorable results under section 148 or 149(d) than could be achieved with actual separate issues. An allocation under this paragraph (h) may be made at any time, but once made may not be changed.

(ii) Allocations involving certain common costs. A ratable allocation of common costs (as described in paragraph (h)(3)(ii) of this section) among the separate purposes of the multipurpose issue is generally reasonable. If another allocation method more accurately reflects the extent to which any separate purpose of a multipurpose issue enjoys the economic benefit or bears the economic burden of certain common costs, that allocation method may be used.

(3) Separate purposes of a multipurpose issue. (i) In general. Separate purposes of a multipurpose issue include refunding a separate prior issue, financing a separate purpose investment, financing a construction issue (as defined in § 1.148-7(f)), and any clearly discrete governmental purpose reasonably expected to be financed by that issue. In general, all integrated or functionally related capital projects that qualify for the same initial temporary period under § 1.148-2(e)(2) are treated as having a single governmental purpose. The separate purposes of a refunding issue include the separate purposes of the prior issue, if any. Separate purposes may be treated as a single purpose if the proceeds used to finance those purposes are eligible for the same initial temporary period under section 148(c). For example, the use of proceeds of a multipurpose issue to finance separate qualified mortgage loans may be treated as a single purpose.

(ii) Financing common costs. Common costs of a multipurpose issue are not separate purposes. Common costs include issuance costs, accrued interest, capitalized interest on the issue, a reserve or replacement fund, qualified guarantee fees, and similar costs properly allocable to the separate purposes of the issue.

(iii) Example. The following example illustrates the application of this paragraph (h)(3).

Example. On January 1, 1994, Housing Authority of State A issues a $10 million issue (the 1994 issue) at an interest rate of 10 percent to finance qualified mortgage loans for owner-occupied residences under section 143. During 1994, A originates $5 million in qualified mortgage loans at an interest rate of 10 percent. In 1995, the market interest rates for housing loans falls to 8 percent and A is unable to originate further loans from the 1994 issue. On January 1, 1996, A issues a $5 million issue (the 1996 issue) at an interest rate of 8 percent to refund partially the 1994 issue. Under paragraph (h) of this section, A treats the portion of the 1994 issue used to originate $5 million in loans as a separate issue comprised of that group of purpose investments. A allocates those purpose investments representing those loans to that separate unrefunded portion of the issue. In addition, A treats the unoriginated portion of the 1994 issue as a separate issue and allocates the nonpurpose investments representing the unoriginated proceeds of the 1994 issue to the refunded portion of the issue. Thus, when proceeds of the 1996 issue are used to pay principal on the refunded portion of the 1994 issue that is treated as a separate issue under paragraph (h) of this section, only the portion of the 1994 issue representing unoriginated loan funds invested in nonpurpose investments transfer to become transferred proceeds of the 1996 issue.

(4) Allocations of bonds of a multipurpose issue. (i) Reasonable allocation of bonds to portions of issue. After reasonable adjustment of the issue price of a multipurpose issue to account for common costs, the portion of the bonds of a multipurpose issue allocated to a separate purpose must have an issue price that bears the same ratio to the aggregate issue price of the multipurpose issue as the portion of the sale proceeds of the multipurpose issue used for that separate purpose bears to the aggregate sale proceeds of the multipurpose issue. For a refunding issue used to refund two or more prior issues, the portion of the sales proceeds allocated to the refunding of a separate prior issue is based on the present value of the refunded debt service on that prior issue, using the yield on investments in the refunding escrow allocable to the entire refunding issue as the discount rate.

(ii) Safe harbor for pro rata allocation method for bonds. The use of the relative amount of sales proceeds used for each separate purpose to ratably allocate each bond or a ratable number of substantially identical whole bonds is a reasonable method for allocating bonds of a multipurpose issue.

(iii) Safe harbor for allocations of bonds used to finance separate purpose investments. An allocation of a portion of the bonds of a multipurpose issue to a particular purpose investment is generally reasonable if that purpose investment has principal and interest payments that reasonably coincide in time and amount to principal and interest payments on the bonds allocated to that purpose investment.

(iv) Rounding of bond allocations to next whole bond denomination permitted. An allocation that rounds each resulting fractional bond up or down to the next integral multiple of a permitted denomination of bonds of that issue not in excess of $100,000 does not prevent the allocation from satisfying this paragraph (h)(4).

(v) Restrictions on allocations of bonds to refunding purposes. For each portion of a multipurpose issue that is used to refund a separate prior issue, a method of allocating bonds of that issue is reasonable under this paragraph (h) only if, in addition to the requirements of paragraphs (h)(1) and (h)(2) of this section, the portion of the bonds allocated to the refunding of that prior issue—

(A) Results from a pro rata allocation under paragraph (h)(4)(ii) of this section;

(B) Reflects aggregate principal and interest payable in each bond year that is less than, equal to, or proportionate to, the aggregate principal and interest payable on the prior issue in each bond year;

(C) Results from an allocation of all the bonds of the entire multipurpose issue in proportion to the remaining weighted average economic life of the capital projects financed or refinanced by the issue, determined in the same manner as under section 147(b); or

(D) Results from another reasonable allocation method, but only to the extent that the application of the allocation methods provided in this paragraph (h)(4)(v) is not permitted under state law restrictions applicable to the bonds, reasonable terms of bonds issued before, or subject to a master indenture that became effective prior to, July 1, 1993, or other similar restrictions or circumstances. This paragraph (h)(4)(v)(D) shall be strictly construed and is available only if it does not result in a greater burden on the market for tax-exempt bonds than would occur using one of the other allocation methods provided in this paragraph (h)(4)(v). (See also § 1.148-11(c)(2).)

(vi) Exception for refundings of interim notes. Paragraph (h)(4)(v) of this section need not be applied to refunding bonds issued to provide permanent financing for one or more projects if the prior issue had a term of less than 3 years and was sold in anticipation of permanent financing, but only if the aggregate term of all prior issues sold in anticipation of permanent financing was less than 3 years.

(5) Limitation on multi-generation allocations. This paragraph (h) does not apply to allocations of a multipurpose refunded issue unless that refunded issue is refunded directly by an issue to which this paragraph (h) applies. For example, if a 1994 issue refunds a 1984 multipurpose issue, which in

turn refunded a 1980 multipurpose issue, this paragraph (h) applies to allocations of the 1984 issue for purposes of allocating the refunding purposes of the 1994 issue, but does not permit allocations of the 1980 issue.

(i) Operating rules for separation of prior issue into refunded and unrefunded portions. *(1) In general.* For purposes of paragraph (h)(3)(i) of this section, the separate purposes of a prior issue include the refunded and unrefunded portions of the prior issue. Thus, the refunded and unrefunded portions are treated as separate issues under paragraph (h)(1) of this section. Those separate issues must satisfy the requirements of paragraphs (h) and (i) of this section. The refunded portion of the bonds of a prior issue is based on a fraction the numerator of which is the principal amount of the prior issue to be paid with proceeds of the refunding issue and the denominator of which is the outstanding principal amount of the bonds of the prior issue, each determined as of the issue date of the refunding issue. (See also paragraph (b)(2) of this section.

(2) Allocations of proceeds and investments in a partial refunding. As of the issue date of a partial refunding issue under this paragraph (i), unspent proceeds of the prior issue are allocated ratably between the refunded and unrefunded portions of the prior issue and the investments allocable to those unspent proceeds are allocated in the manner required for the allocation of investments to transferred proceeds under paragraph (c)(1)(ii) of this section.

(3) References to prior issue. If the refunded and unrefunded portions of a prior issue are treated as separate issues under this paragraph (i), then, except to the extent that the context clearly requires otherwise (e.g., references to the aggregate prior issue in the mixed escrow rule in paragraph (c)(2) of this section), all references in this section to a prior issue refer only to the refunded portion of that prior issue.

T.D. 8418, 5/12/92, amend T.D. 8476, 6/14/93, T.D. 8538, 5/5/94, T.D. 8718, 5/8/97.

§ 1.148-9A Arbitrage rules for refunding issues.

(a) through (c)(2)(ii)(A) [Reserved]. For guidance see § 1.148-9.

(c) *(2)* (ii) (B) Permissive allocation of non-proceeds to earliest expenditures. Excluding amounts covered by § 1.148-9(c)(2)(ii)(A) and subject to any required earlier expenditure of those amounts, any amounts in a mixed escrow that are not proceeds of a refunding issue may be allocated to the earliest maturing investments in the mixed escrow, provided that those investments mature and the proceeds thereof are expended before the date of any expenditure from the mixed escrow to pay any principal of the prior issue.

(d) through (h)(4)(v) [Reserved]. For guidance see § 1.148-9.

(h) *(4)* (vi) Exception for refundings of interim notes. Section 1.148-9(h)(4)(v) need not be applied to refunding bonds issued to provide permanent financing for one or more projects if the prior issue had a term of less than 3 years and was sold in anticipation of permanent financing, but only if the aggregate term of all prior issues sold in anticipation of permanent financing was less than 3 years.

T.D. 8538, 5/5/94, amend T.D. 8718, 5/8/97.

§ 1.148-10 Anti-abuse rules and authority of commissioner.

(a) Abusive arbitrage device. *(1) In general.* Bonds of an issue are arbitrage bonds under section 148 if an abusive arbitrage device under paragraph (a)(2) of this section is used in connection with the issue. This paragraph (a) is to be applied and interpreted broadly to carry out the purposes of section 148, as further described in § 1.148-0. Except as otherwise provided in paragraph (c) of this section, any action that is expressly permitted by section 148 or §§ 1.148-1 through 1.148-11 is not an abusive arbitrage device (e.g., investment in higher yielding investments during a permitted temporary period under section 148(c)).

(2) Abusive arbitrage device defined. Any action is an abusive arbitrage device if the action has the effect of—

(i) Enabling the issuer to exploit the difference between tax-exempt and taxable interest rates to obtain a material financial advantage; and

(ii) Overburdening the tax-exempt bond market.

(3) Exploitation of tax-exempt interest rates. An action may exploit tax-exempt interest rates under paragraph (a)(2) of this section as a result of an investment of any portion of the gross proceeds of an issue over any period of time, notwithstanding that, in the aggregate, the gross proceeds of the issue are not invested in higher yielding investments over the term of the issue.

(4) Overburdening the tax-exempt market. An action overburdens the tax-exempt bond market under paragraph (a)(2)(ii) of this section if it results in issuing more bonds, issuing bonds earlier, or allowing bonds to remain outstanding longer than is otherwise reasonably necessary to accomplish the governmental purposes of the bonds, based on all the facts and circumstances. Whether an action is reasonably necessary to accomplish the governmental purposes of the bonds depends on whether the primary purpose of the transaction is a bona fide governmental purpose (e.g., an issue of refunding bonds to achieve a debt service restructuring that would be issued independent of any arbitrage benefit). An important factor bearing on this determination is whether the action would reasonably be taken to accomplish the governmental purpose of the issue if the interest on the issue were not excludable from gross income under section 103(a) (assuming that the hypothetical taxable interest rate would be the same as the actual tax-exempt interest rate). Factors evidencing an overissuance include the issuance of an issue the proceeds of which are reasonably expected to exceed by more than a minor portion the amount necessary to accomplish the governmental purposes of the issue, or an issue the proceeds of which are, in fact, substantially in excess of the amount of sale proceeds allocated to expenditures for the governmental purposes of the issue. One factor evidencing an early issuance is the issuance of bonds that do not qualify for a temporary period under § 1.148-2(e)(2), (e)(3), or (e)(4). One factor evidencing that bonds may remain outstanding longer than necessary is a term that exceeds the safe harbors against the creation of replacement proceeds under § 1.148-1(c)(4)(i)(B). These factors may be outweighed by other factors, however, such as bona fide cost underruns or long-term financial distress.

(b) Consequences of overburdening the tax-exempt bond market. *(1) In general.* An issue that overburdens the tax-exempt bond market (within the meaning of paragraph (a)(4) of this section) is subject to the following special limitations—

(i) Special yield restriction. Investments are subject to the definition of materially higher yield under § 1.148-2(d) that is equal to one-thousandth of 1 percent. In addition, each investment is treated as a separate class of investments under § 1.148-5(b)(2)(ii), the yield on which may not be blended with that of other investments.

(ii) Certain regulatory provisions inapplicable. The provisions of § 1.148-5(c) (relating to yield reduction payments) and § 1.148-5(e)(2) and (3) (relating to recovery of qualified administrative costs) do not apply.

(iii) Restrictive expenditure rule. Proceeds are not allocated to expenditures unless the proceeds-spent-last rule under § 1.148-6(d)(3)(i) is satisfied, applied by treating those proceeds as proceeds to be used for restricted working capital expenditures. For this purpose, available amount includes a reasonable working capital reserve as defined in § 1.148-6(d)(3)(iii)(B).

(2) Application. The provisions of this paragraph (b) only apply to the portion of an issue that, as a result of actions taken (or actions not taken) after the issue date, overburdens the market for tax-exempt bonds, except that for an issue that is reasonably expected as of the issue date to overburden the market, those provisions apply to all of the gross proceeds of the issue.

(c) Anti-abuse rules on excess gross proceeds of advance refunding issues. *(1) In general.* Except as otherwise provided in this paragraph (c), an abusive arbitrage device is used and bonds of an advance refunding issue are arbitrage bonds if the issue has excess gross proceeds.

(2) Definition of excess gross proceeds. Excess gross proceeds means all gross proceeds of an advance refunding issue that exceed an amount equal to 1 percent of sale proceeds of the issue, other than gross proceeds allocable to—

(i) Payment of principal, interest, or call premium on the prior issue;

(ii) Payment of pre-issuance accrued interest on the refunding issue, and interest on the refunding issue that accrues for a period up to the completion date of any capital project for which the prior issue was issued, plus one year;

(iii) A reasonably required reserve or replacement fund for the refunding issue or investment proceeds of such a fund;

(iv) Payment of costs of issuance of the refunding issue;

(v) Payment of administrative costs allocable to repaying the prior issue, carrying and repaying the refunding issue, or investments of the refunding issue;

(vi) Transferred proceeds that will be used or maintained for the governmental purpose of the prior issue;

(vii) Interest on purpose investments;

(viii) Replacement proceeds in a sinking fund for the refunding issue;

(ix) Qualified guarantee fees for the refunding issue or the prior issue; and

(x) Fees for a qualified hedge for the refunding issue.

(3) Special treatment of transferred proceeds. For purposes of this paragraph (c), all unspent proceeds of the prior issue as of the issue date of the refunding issue are treated as transferred proceeds of the advance refunding issue.

(4) Special rule for crossover refundings. An advance refunding issue is not an issue of arbitrage bonds under this paragraph (c) if all excess gross proceeds of the refunding issue are used to pay interest that accrues on the refunding issue before the prior issue is discharged, and no gross proceeds of any refunding issue are used to pay interest on the prior issue or to replace funds used directly or indirectly to pay such interest (other than transferred proceeds used to pay interest on the prior issue that accrues for a period up to the completion date of the project for which the prior issue was issued, plus one year, or proceeds used to pay principal that is attributable to accrued original issue discount).

(5) Special rule for gross refundings. This paragraph (c)(5) applies if an advance refunding issue (the *series B issue*) is used together with one or more other advance refunding issues (the *series A issues*) in a gross refunding of a prior issue, but only if the use of a gross refunding method is required under bond documents that were effective prior to November 6, 1992. These advance refunding issues are not arbitrage bonds under this paragraph (c) if—

(i) All excess gross proceeds of the series B issue and each series A issue are investment proceeds used to pay principal and interest on the series B issue;

(ii) At least 99 percent of all principal and interest on the series B issue is paid with proceeds of the series B and series A issues or with the earnings on other amounts in the refunding escrow for the prior issue;

(iii) The series B issue is discharged not later than the prior issue; and

(iv) As of any date, the amount of gross proceeds of the series B issue allocated to expenditures does not exceed the aggregate amount of expenditures before that date for principal and interest on the series B issue, and administrative costs of carrying and repaying the series B issue, or of investments of the series B issue.

(d) Examples. The provisions of this section are illustrated by the following examples:

Example (1). Mortgage sale. In 1982, City issued its revenue issue (the 1982 issue) and lent the proceeds to Developer to finance a low-income housing project under former section 103(b)(4)(A) of the 1954 Code. In 1994, Developer encounters financial difficulties and negotiates with City to refund the 1982 issue. City issues $10 million in principal amount of its 8 percent bonds (the 1994 issue). City lends the proceeds of the 1994 issue to Developer. To evidence Developer's obligation to repay that loan, Developer, as obligor, issues a note to City (the City note). Bank agrees to provide Developer with a direct-pay letter of credit pursuant to which Bank will make all payments to the trustee for the 1994 issue necessary to meet Developer's obligations under the City note. Developer pays Bank a fee for the issuance of the letter of credit and issues a note to Bank (the Bank note). The Bank note is secured by a mortgage on the housing project and is guaranteed by FHA. The Bank note and the 1994 issue have different prepayment terms. The City does not reasonably expect to treat prepayments of the Bank note as gross proceeds of the 1994 issue. At the same time or pursuant to a series of related transactions, Bank sells the Bank note to Investor for $9.5 million. Bank invests these monies together with its other funds. In substance, the transaction is a loan by City to Bank, under which Bank enters into a series of transactions that, in effect, result in Bank retaining $9.5 million in amounts treated as proceeds of the 1994 issue. Those amounts are invested in materially higher yielding investments that provide funds sufficient to equal or exceed the Bank's liability under the letter of credit. Alternatively, the letter of credit is investment property in a sinking fund for the 1994 issue provided by Developer, a substantial beneficiary of the financing. Because, in substance, Developer acquires the $10 million principal amount letter of credit for a fair market value purchase price of $9.5 million, the letter of credit is a materially higher yielding investment. Neither result would change if Developer's obligation under the Bank note is contingent on Bank performing its obligation under the letter of credit. Each characterization causes the bonds to be arbitrage bonds.

Example (2). Bonds outstanding longer than necessary for yield-blending device.

(i) Longer bond maturity to create sinking fund. In 1994, Authority issues an advance refunding issue (the refunding issue) to refund a 1982 prior issue (the prior issue). Under current market conditions, Authority will have to invest the refunding escrow at a yield significantly below the yield on the refunding issue. Authority issues its refunding issue with a longer weighted average maturity than otherwise necessary primarily for the purpose of creating a sinking fund for the refunding issue that will be invested in a guaranteed investment contract. The weighted average maturity of the refunding issue is less than 120 percent of the remaining average economic life of the facilities financed with the proceeds of the prior issue. The guaranteed investment contract has a yield that is higher than the yield on the refunding issue. The yield on the refunding escrow blended with the yield on the guaranteed investment contract does not exceed the yield on the issue. The refunding issue uses an abusive arbitrage device and the bonds of the issue are arbitrage bonds under section 148(a).

(ii) Refunding of noncallable bonds. The facts are the same as in paragraph (i) of this Example 2 except that instead of structuring the refunding issue to enable it to take advantage of sinking fund investments, Authority will also refund other long-term, non-callable bonds in the same refunding issue. There are no savings attributable to the refunding of the non-callable bonds (e.g., a low-to-high refunding). The Authority invests the portion of the proceeds of the refunding issue allocable to the refunding of the noncallable bonds in the refunding escrow at a yield that is higher than the yield on the refunding issue, based on the relatively long escrow period for this portion of the refunding. The Authority invests the other portion of the proceeds of the refunding issue in the refunding escrow at a yield lower than the yield on the refunding issue. The blended yield on all the investments in the refunding escrow for the prior issues does not exceed the yield on the refunding issue. The portion of the refunding issue used to refund the noncallable bonds, however, was not otherwise necessary and was issued primarily to exploit the difference between taxable and tax-exempt rates for that long portion of the refunding escrow to minimize the effect of lower yielding investments in the other portion of the escrow. The refunding issue uses an abusive arbitrage device and the bonds of the issue are arbitrage bonds.

(iii) Governmental purpose. In paragraphs (i) and (ii) of this Example 2, the existence of a governmental purpose for the described financing structures would not change the conclusions unless Authority clearly established that the primary purpose for the use of the particular structure was a bona fide governmental purpose. The fact that each financing structure had the effect of eliminating significant amounts of negative arbitrage is strong evidence of a primary purpose that is not a bona fide governmental purpose. Moreover, in paragraph (i) of this Example 2, the structure of the refunding issue coupled with the acquisition of the guaranteed investment contract to lock in the investment yield associated with the structure is strong evidence of a primary purpose that is not a bona fide governmental purpose.

Example (3). Window refunding.

(i) Authority issues its 1994 refunding issue to refund a portion of the principal and interest on its outstanding 1985 issue. The 1994 refunding issue is structured using zero-coupon bonds that pay no interest or principal for the 5-year period following the issue date. The proceeds of the 1994 refunding issue are deposited in a refunding escrow to be used to pay only the interest requirements of the refunded portion of the 1985 issue. Authority enters into a guaranteed investment contract with a financial institution, G, under which G agrees to provide a guaranteed yield on revenues invested by Authority during the 5-year period following the issue date. The guaranteed investment contract has a yield that is no higher than the yield on the refunding issue. The revenues to be invested under this guaranteed investment contract consist of the amounts that Authority otherwise would have used to pay principal and interest on the 1994 refunding issue. The guaranteed investment contract is structured to generate receipts at times and in amounts sufficient to pay the principal and redemption requirements of the refunded portion of the 1985 issue. A principal purpose of these transactions is to avoid transferred proceeds. Authority will continue to invest the unspent proceeds of the 1985 issue that are on deposit in a refunding escrow for its 1982 issue at a yield equal to the yield on the 1985 issue and will not otherwise treat those unspent proceeds as transferred proceeds of the 1994 refunding issue. The 1994 refunding issue is an issue of arbitrage bonds since those bonds involve a transaction or series of transactions that overburdens the market by leaving bonds outstanding longer than is necessary to obtain a material financial advantage based on arbitrage. Specifically, Authority has structured the 1994 refunding issue to make available for the refunding of the 1985 issue replacement proceeds rather than proceeds so that the unspent proceeds of the 1985 issue will not become transferred proceeds of the 1994 refunding issue.

(ii) The result would be the same in each of the following circumstances:

(A) The facts are the same as in paragraph (i) of this Example 3 except that Authority does not enter into the guaranteed investment contract but instead, as of the issue date of the 1994 refunding issue, reasonably expects that the released revenues will be available for investment until used to pay principal and interest on the 1985 issue.

(B) The facts are the same as in paragraph (i) of this Example 3 except that there are no unspent proceeds of the 1985 issue and Authority invests the released revenues at a yield materially higher than the yield on the 1994 issue.

(C) The facts are the same as in paragraph (i) of this Example 3 except that Authority uses the proceeds of the 1994 issue for capital projects instead of to refund a portion of the 1985 issue.

Example (4). Sale of conduit loan. On January 1, 1994, Authority issues a conduit financing issue (the 1994 Conduit financing issue) and uses the proceeds to purchase from City, an unrelated party, a tax-exempt bond of City (the City note). The proceeds of the 1994 conduit financing issue are to be used to advance refund a prior conduit financing issue that was issued in 1988 and used to make a loan to City. The 1994 conduit financing issue and the City note each have a yield of 8 percent on January 1, 1994. On June 30, 1996, interest rates have decreased and Authority sells the City note to D, a person unrelated to either City or Authority. Based on the sale price of the City note and treating June 30, 1996 as the issue date of the City note, the City note has a 6 percent yield. Authority deposits the proceeds of the sale of the City note into an escrow to redeem the bonds of the 1994 conduit financing issue on January 1, 2001. The escrow is invested in nonpurpose investments having a yield of 8 percent. For purposes of section 149(d), City and Authority are related parties and, therefore, the issue date of the City note is treated as being June 30, 1996. Thus, the City note is an advance refunding of Authority's 1994 conduit financing issue. Interest on the City note is not exempt from Federal income tax from the date it is sold to D under section 149(d), because, by investing the escrow investments at a yield of 8 percent instead of a yield not materially higher than 6 percent, the sale of the City note employs a device to obtain a material financial advantage, based on arbitrage, apart from the savings attributable to lower interest rates. In addition, the City note is not a tax-exempt bond because the note is the second advance refunding of the original bond under section 149(d)(3). The City note also employs an abusive arbitrage device and is an arbitrage bond under section 148.

Example (5). Re-refunding.

(i) On January 1, 1984, City issues a tax-exempt issue (the 1984 Issue) to finance the cost of constructing a prison. The 1984 issue has a 7 percent yield and a 30-year maturity. The 1984 issue is callable at any time on or after January 1, 1994. On January 1, 1990, City issues a refunding issue (the 1990 Issue) to advance refund the 1984 issue. The 1990 issue has an 8 percent yield and a 30-year maturity. The 1990 issue is callable at any time on or after January 1, 2000. The proceeds of the 1990 issue are invested at an 8 percent yield in a refunding escrow for the 1984 issue (the original 1984 escrow) in a manner sufficient to pay debt service on the 1984 issue until maturity (i.e., an escrow to maturity). On January 1, 1994, City issues a refunding issue (the 1994 issue). The 1994 issue has a 6 percent yield and a 30-year maturity. City does not invest the proceeds of the 1994 issue in a refunding escrow for the 1990 issue in a manner sufficient to pay a portion of the debt service until, and redeem a portion of that issue on, January 1, 2000. Instead, City invests those proceeds at a 6 percent yield in a new refunding escrow for a portion of the 1984 issue (the new 1984 escrow) in a manner sufficient to pay debt service on a portion of the 1984 issue until maturity. City also liquidates the investments allocable to the proceeds of the 1990 issue held in the original 1984 escrow and reinvests those proceeds in an escrow to pay a portion of the debt service on the 1990 issue itself until, and redeem a portion of that issue on, January 1, 2000 (the 1990 escrow). The 1994 bonds are arbitrage bonds an employ an abusive device under section 149(d)(4). Although, in form, the proceeds of the 1994 issue are used to pay principal on the 1984 issue, this accounting for the use of the proceeds of the 1994 issue is an unreasonable, inconsistent accounting method under § 1.148-6(a). Moreover, since the proceeds of the 1990 issue were set aside in an escrow to be used to retire the 1984 issue, the use of proceeds of the 1994 issue for that same purpose involves a replacement of funds invested in higher yielding investments under section 148(a)(2). Thus, using a reasonable, consistent accounting method and giving effect to the substance of the transaction, the proceeds of the 1994 issue are treated as used to refund the 1990 issue and are allocable to the 1990 escrow. The proceeds of the 1990 issue are treated as used to refund the 1984 issue and are allocable to the investments in the new 1984 escrow. The proceeds of the 1990 issue allocable to the nonpurpose investments in the new 1984 escrow become transferred proceeds of the 1994 issue as principal is paid on the 1990 issue from amounts on deposit in the 1990 escrow. As a result, the yield on nonpurpose investments allocable to the 1994 issue is materially higher than the yield on the 1994 issue, causing the bonds of the 1994 issue to be arbitrage bonds. In addition, the transaction employs a device under section 149(d)(4) to obtain a material financial advantage based on arbitrage, other than savings attributable to lower interest rates.

(ii) The following changes in the facts do not affect the conclusion that the 1994 issue consists of arbitrage bonds—

(1) The 1990 issue is a taxable issue;

(2) The original 1984 escrow is used to pay the 1994 issue (rather than the 1990 issue); or

(3) The 1994 issue is used to retire the 1984 issue within 90 days of January 1, 1994.

(e) Authority of the Commissioner to clearly reflect the economic substance of a transaction. If an issuer enters into a transaction for a principal purpose of obtaining a material financial advantage based on the difference between tax-exempt and taxable interest rates in a manner that is inconsistent with the purposes of section 148, the Commissioner may exercise the Commissioner's discretion to depart from the rules of § 1.148-1 through § 1.148-11 as necessary to clearly reflect the economic substance of the transaction. For this purpose, the Commissioner may recompute yield on an issue or on investments, reallocate payments and receipts on investments, recompute the rebate amount on an issue, treat a hedge as either a qualified hedge or not a qualified hedge, or otherwise adjust any item whatsoever bearing upon the investments and expenditures of gross proceeds of an issue. For example, if the amount paid for a hedge is specifically based on the amount of arbitrage earned or expected to be earned on the hedged bonds, a principal purpose of entering into the contract is to obtain a material financial advantage based on the difference between tax-exempt and taxable interest rates in a manner that is inconsistent with the purposes of section 148.

(f) Authority of the Commissioner to require an earlier date for payment of rebate. If the Commissioner determines that an issue is likely to fail to meet the requirements of § 1.148-3 and that a failure to serve a notice of demand for payment on the issuer will jeopardize the assessment or collection of tax on interest paid or to be paid on the issue, the date that the Commissioner serves notice on the issuer is treated as a required computation date for payment of rebate for that issue.

(g) Authority of the Commissioner to waive regulatory limitations. Notwithstanding any specific provision in §§ 1.148-1 through 1.148-11, the Commissioner may prescribe extensions of temporary periods, larger reasonably required reserve or replacement funds, or consequences of failures or remedial action under section 148 in lieu of or in addition to other consequences of those failures, or take other action, if the Commissioner finds that good faith or other similar circumstances so warrant, consistent with the purposes of section 148.

T.D. 8284, 1/25/90, amend T.D. 8418, 5/12/92, T.D. 8476, 6/14/93, T.D. 8538, 5/5/94, T.D. 8718, 5/8/97.

§ 1.148-10A Anti-abuse rules and authority of Commissioner.

(a) through (b)(1) [Reserved]. For guidance see § 1.148-10.

(b) *(2) Application.* The provisions of § 1.148-10(b) only apply to the portion of an issue that, as a result of actions taken (or actions not taken) after the issue date, overburdens the market for tax-exempt bonds, except that for an issue that is reasonably expected as of the issue date to overburden the market, those provisions apply to all of the gross proceeds of the issue.

(c) through (c)(2)(viii) [Reserved]. For guidance see § 1.148-10.

(2) (ix) For purposes of § 1.148-10(c)(2), excess gross proceeds do not include gross proceeds allocable to fees for a qualified hedge for the refunding issue.

T.D. 8538, 5/5/94, amend T.D. 8718, 5/8/97.

§ 1.148-11 Effective dates.

(a) In general. Except as otherwise provided in this section, §§ 1.148-1 through § 1.148-11 apply to bonds sold on or after July 8, 1997.

(b) Elective retroactive application in whole. *(1) In general.* Except as otherwise provided in this section, and subject to the applicable effective dates for the corresponding statutory provisions, an issuer may apply the provisions of §§ 1.148-1 through 1.148-11 in whole, but not in part, to any issue that is outstanding on July 8, 1997, and is subject to section 148(f) or to sections 103(c)(6) or 103A(i) of the Internal Revenue Code of 1954, in lieu of otherwise applicable regulations under those sections.

(2) No elective retroactive application for 18-month spending exception. The provisions of § 1.148-7(d) (relating to the 18-month spending exception) may not be applied to any issue issued on or before June 30, 1993.

(3) No elective retroactive application for hedges of fixed rate issues. The provisions of § 1.148-4(h0(2)(i)(B) (relating to hedges of fixed rate issues) may not be applied to any bond sold on or before July 8, 1997.

(4) No elective retroactive application for safe harbor for establishing fair market value for guaranteed investment contracts and investments purchased for a yield restricted defeasance escrow. The provisions of §§ 1.148-5(d)(6)(iii) (relating to the safe harbor for establishing fair market value of guaranteed investment contracts and yield restricted defeasance escrow investments) and 1.148-5(e)(2)(iv) (relating to a special rule for yield restricted defeasance escrow investments) may not be applied to any bond sold before December 30, 1998.

(c) Elective retroactive application of certain provisions and special rules. *(1) Retroactive application of overpayment recovery provisions.* An issuer may apply the provisions of § 1.148-3(i) to any issue that is subject to section 148(f) or to sections 103(c)(6) or 103A(i) of the Internal Revenue Code of 1954.

(2) Certain allocations of multipurpose issues. An allocation of bonds to a refunding purpose under § 1.148-9(h) may be adjusted as necessary to reflect allocations made between May 18, 1992, and August 15, 1993, if the allocations satisfied the corresponding prior provision of § 1.148-11(j)(4) under applicable prior regulations.

(3) Special limitation. The provisions of § 1.148-9 apply to issues issued before August 15, 1993, only if the issuer in good faith estimates the present value savings, if any, associated with the effect of the application of that section on refunding escrows, using any reasonable accounting method, and applies those savings, if any, to redeem outstanding tax-exempt bonds of the applicable issue at the earliest possible date on which those bonds may be redeemed or otherwise retired. These savings are not reduced to take into account any administrative costs associated with applying these provisions retroactively.

(d) Transition rule excepting certain state guarantee funds from the definition of replacement proceeds. *(1) Certain perpetual trust funds.* A guarantee by a fund created and controlled by a State and established pursuant to its constitution does not cause the amounts in the fund to be pledged funds treated as replacement proceeds if—

(i) Substantially all of the corpus of the fund consists of nonfinancial assets, revenues derived from these assets, gifts, and bequests;

(ii) The corpus of the guarantee fund may be invaded only to support specifically designated essential governmental functions (designated functions) carried on by political subdivisions with general taxing powers;

(iii) Substantially all of the available income of the fund is required to be applied annually to support designated functions;

(iv) The issue guaranteed consists of general obligations that are not private activity bonds substantially all of the proceeds of which are to be used for designated functions;

(v) The fund satisfied each of the requirements of paragraphs (d)(1)(i) through (d)(1)(iii) of this section on August 16, 1986; and

(vi) The guarantee is not attributable to a deposit to the fund made after May 14, 1989, unless—

(A) The deposit is attributable to the sale or other disposition of fund assets; or

(B) Prior to the deposit, the outstanding amount of the bonds guaranteed by the fund did not exceed 250 percent of the lower of the cost or fair market value of the fund.

(2) Permanent university fund. Replacement proceeds do not include amounts allocable to investments of the fund described in section 648 of Public Law 98-369.

(e) Transition rule regarding special allowance payments. Section 1.148-5(b)(5) applies to any bond issued after January 5, 1990, except a bond issued exclusively to refund a bond issued before January 6, 1990, if the amount of the refunding bond does not exceed 101 percent of the amount of the refunded bond, and the maturity date of the refunding bond is not later than the date that is 17 years after the date on which the refunded bond was issued (or, in the case of a series of refundings, the date on which the original bond was issued), but only if § 1.148-2(d)(2)(iv) is applied by substituting 1 and one-half percentage points for 2 percentage points.

(f) Transition rule regarding applicability of yield reduction rule. Section 1.148-5(c) applies to nonpurpose investments allocable to replacement proceeds of an issue that are held in a reserve or replacement fund to the extent that—

(1) Amounts must be paid into the fund under a constitutional provision, statute, or ordinance adopted before May 3, 1978;

(2) Under that provision, amounts paid into the fund (and investment earnings thereon) can be used only to pay debt service on the issues; and

(3) The size of the payments made into the fund is independent of the size of the outstanding issues or the debt service thereon.

(g) Provisions applicable to certain bonds sold before effective date. Except for bonds to which paragraph (b)(1) of this section applies—

(1) Section 1.148-11A provides rules applicable to bonds sold after June 6, 1994, and before July 8, 1997; and

(2) Sections 1.148-1 through 1.148-11 as in effect on July 1, 1993 (see 26 CFR part 1 as revised April 1, 1994), and § 1.148-11A(i) (relating to elective retroactive application of certain provisions) provide rules applicable to certain issues issued before June 7, 1994.

(h) Safe harbor for establishing fair market value for guaranteed investment contracts and investments purchased for a yield restricted defeasance escrow. The provisions of § 1.148-5(d)(6)(iii) are applicable to bonds sold on or after March 1, 1999. Issuers may apply these provisions to bonds sold on or after December 30, 1998, and before March 1, 1999.

(i) Special rule for certain broker's commissions and similar fees. Section 1.148-5(e)(2)(iii) applies to bonds sold on or after February 9, 2004. In the case of bonds sold before February 9, 2004, that are subject to § 1.148-5 (pre-effective date bonds), issuers may apply § 1.148-5(e)(2)(iii), in whole but not in part, with respect to transactions entered into on or after December 11, 2003. If an issuer applies § 1.148-5(e)(2)(iii) to pre-effective date bonds, the per-issue safe harbor in § 1.148-5(e)(2)(iii)(B)(1)(ii) is applied by taking into account all brokers' commissions or similar fees with respect to guaranteed investment contracts and investments for yield restricted defeasance escrows that the issuer treats as qualified administrative costs for the issue, including all such commissions or fees paid before February 9, 2004. For purposes of §§ 1.148-5(e)(2)(iii)(B)(3) and 1.148-5(e)(2)(iii)(B)(6) (relating to cost-of-living adjustments), transactions entered into before 2003 are treated as entered into in 2003.

(j) Certain prepayments. Section 1.148-1(e)(1) and (2) apply to bonds sold on or after October 3, 2003. Issuers may apply § 1.148-1(e)(1) and (2), in whole but not in part, to bonds sold before October 3, 2003 that are subject to § 1.148-1.

T.D. 8418, 5/12/92, amend T.D. 8476, 6/14/93, T.D. 8538, 5/5/94, T.D. 8718, 5/8/97, T.D. 9085, 8/1/2003, T.D. 9097, 12/10/2003.

PAR. 11. Section 1.148-11 is revised by adding new paragraph (k) as follows:

Proposed § 1.148-11 Effective Dates. [*For Preamble, see ¶ 152,909*]

* * * * *

(k) Certain arbitrage guidance updates.

(1) In general. Sections 1.148-3(d)(1)(iv); 1.148-3(d)(4); 1.148-4(a); 1.148-4(b)(3)(i); 1.148-4(h)(2)(ii)(A); 1.148-4(h)(2)(v); 1.148-4(h)(2)(vi); 1.148-4(h)(2)(viii); 1.148-4(h)(3)(iv)(B); 1.148-4(h)(4)(i)(C); 1.148-5(c)(3); 1.148-5(d)(6)(iii)(A) and 1.148-5(e)(2)(ii)(B), as in effect on the effective date of the final regulations (the revised provisions), apply to bonds sold on or after the date that is 90 days after publication of the final regulations in the Federal Register, for bonds subject to such applicable section of the regulations as in effect before the effective date of the final regulations.

(2) Permissive earlier application. To the extent provided in paragraphs (k)(2)(i) through (vi) of this section, issuers may apply the proposed regulations to bonds sold before the date that is 90 days after publication of the final regulations in the Federal Register.

(i) Section 1.148-3(d)(1)(iv) and § 1.148-3(d)(4) may be applied for bond years ending on or after the date of publication of the proposed regulations in the Federal Register for bonds to which 1.148-3(d)(1)(iv) applies.

(ii) Section 1.148-4(b)(3)(i) may be applied for bonds sold on or after the date of publication of the proposed regulations in the Federal Register for bonds to which that section applies.

(iii) Sections 1.148-4(h)(2)(ii)(A), 1.148-4(h)(2)(v), 1.148-4(h)(2)(vi), 1.148-4(h)(2)(viii), 1.148-4(h)(3)(iv)(B), and 1.148-4(h)(4)(i)(C) may be applied, in whole but not in part, for qualified hedges entered into on or after the date of publication of the proposed regulations in the Federal Register for bonds to which § 1.148-4(h) applies.

(iv) Section 1.148-5(c)(3) may be applied for investments purchased on or after the date of publication of the proposed regulations in the Federal Register for bonds to which that section applies.

(v) Section 1.148-5(d)(6)(iii)(A) may be applied to guaranteed investment contracts entered into on or after the date of publication of the proposed regulations in the Federal Register for bonds to which § 1.148-5(d)(6)(iii) applies.

(vi) Section 1.148-5(e)(2)(ii)(B) may be applied with respect to investors investing in the fund on or after the date of publication of the proposed regulations in the Federal Register for bonds to which that section applies.

(3) Rebate overpayment recovery. Section 1.148-3(j) applies to bonds subject to § 1.148-3(i).

(4) Small issuer exception to rebate requirement for conduit borrowers of pooled financings. Section 1.148-8(d) applies to bonds issued after May 17, 2006.

§ 1.148-11A Effective dates.

(a) through (c)(3) [Reserved]. For guidance see § 1.148-11.

(c) *(4) Retroactive application of overpayment recovery provisions.* An issuer may apply the provisions of § 1.148-3(i) to any issue that is subject to section 148(f) or to sections 103(c)(6) or 103A(i) of the Internal Revenue Code of 1954.

(d) through (h) [Reserved]. For guidance see § 1.148-11.

(i) Transition rules for certain amendments. *(1) In general.* Section 1.103-8(a)(5), §§ 1.148-1, 1.148-2, 1.148-3, 1.148-4, 1.148-5, 1.148-6, 1.148-7, 1.148-8, 1.148-9, 1.148-10, 1.148-11, 1.149(d)-1, and 1.150-1 as in effect on June 7, 1994 (see 26 CFR part 1 as revised April 1, 1997), and §§ 1.148-1A through 1.148-11A, 1.149(d)-1A, and 1.150-1A apply, in whole, but not in part—

(i) To bonds sold after June 6, 1994, and before July 8, 1997;

(ii) To bonds issued before July 1, 1993, that are outstanding on June 7, 1994, if the first time the issuer applies sections 1.148-1 through 1.148-11 as in effect on June 7, 1994 (see 26 CFR part 1 as revised April 1, 1997), to the bonds under § 1.148-11(b) or (c) is after June 6, 1994, and before July 8, 1997;

(iii) At the option of the issuer, to bonds to which §§ 1.148-1 through 1.148-11, as in effect on July 1, 1993 (see 26 CFR part 1 as revised April 1, 1994), apply, if the bonds are outstanding on June 7, 1994, and the issuer applies § 1.103- 8(a)(5), §§ 1.148-1, 1.148-2, 1.148-3, 1.148-4, 1.148-5, 1.148-6, 1.148-7, 1.148-8, 1.148-9, 1.148-10, 1.148-11, 1.149(d)-1, and 1.150-1 as in effect on June 7, 1994 (see

26 CFR part 1 as revised April 1, 1997), and §§ 1.148-1A through 1.148-11A, 1.149(d)-1A, and 1.150-1A to the bonds before July 8, 1997.

(2) Special rule. For purposes of paragraph (i)(1) of this section, any reference to a particular paragraph of §§ 1.148-1T, 1.148-2T, 1.148-3T, 1.148-4T, 1.148-5T, 1.148-6T, 1.148-9T, 1.148-10T, 1.148-11T, 1.149(d)-1T, or 1.150-1T shall be applied as a reference to the corresponding paragraph of §§ 1.148-1A, 1.148-2A, 1.148-3A, 1.148-4A, 1.148-5A, 1.148-6A, 1.148-9A, 1.148-10A, 1.148-11A, 1.149(d)-1A, or 1.150-1A, respectively.

(3) Identification of certain hedges. For any hedge entered into after June 18, 1993, and on or before June 6, 1994, that would be a qualified hedge within the meaning of § 1.148-4(h)(2), as in effect on June 7, 1994 (see 26 CFR part 1 as revised April 1, 1997), except that the hedge does not meet the requirements of § 1.148-4A(h)(2)(ix) because the issuer failed to identify the hedge not later than 3 days after which the issuer and the provider entered into the contract, the requirements of § 1.148-4A(h)(2)(ix) are treated as met if the contract is identified by the actual issuer on its books and records maintained for the hedged bonds not later than July 8, 1997.

T.D. 8538, 5/5/94, amend T.D. 8718, 5/8/97.

§ 1.149(b)-1 Federally guaranteed bonds.

(a) General rule. Under section 149(b) and this section, nothing in section 103(a) or in any other provision of law shall be construed to provide an exemption from Federal income tax for interest on any bond issued as part of an issue that is federally guaranteed.

(b) Exceptions. Pursuant to section 149(b)(3)(B), section 149(b)(1) and paragraph (a) of this section do not apply to—

(1) Investments in obligations issued pursuant to section 21B(d)(3) of the Federal Home Loan Bank Act, as amended by section 511 of the Financial Institutions Reform, Recovery, and Enforcement Act of 1989, or any successor provision; or

(2) Any investments that are held in a refunding escrow (as defined in § 1.148-1).

(c) Effective date. This section applies to investments made after June 30, 1993.

T.D. 8476, 6/14/93.

§ 1.149(d)-1 Limitations on advance refundings.

(a) General rule. Under section 149(d) and this section, nothing in section 103(a) or in any other provision of law shall be construed to provide an exemption from Federal income tax for interest on any bond issued as part of an issue described in paragraphs (2), (3), or (4) of section 149(d).

(b) Advance refunding issues that employ abusive devices. *(1) In general.* An advance refunding issue employs an abusive device and is described in section 149(d)(4) if the issue violates any of the anti-abuse rules under § 1.148-10.

(2) Failure to pay required rebate. An advance refunding issue is described in section 149(d)(4) if the issue fails to meet the requirements of § 1.148-3. This paragraph (b)(2) applies to any advance refunding issue issued after August 31, 1986.

(3) Mixed escrows invested in tax-exempt bonds. An advance refunding issue is described in section 149(d)(4) if—

(i) Any of the proceeds of the issue are invested in a refunding escrow in which a portion of the proceeds are invested in tax-exempt bonds and a portion of the proceeds are invested in nonpurpose investments;

(ii) The yield on the tax-exempt bonds in the refunding escrow exceeds the yield on the issue;

(iii) The yield on all the investments (including investment property and tax-exempt bonds) in the refunding escrow exceeds the yield on the issue; and

(iv) The weighted average maturity of the tax-exempt bonds in the refunding escrow is more than 25 percent greater or less than the weighted average maturity of the nonpurpose investments in the refunding escrow, and the weighted average maturity of nonpurpose investments in the refunding escrow is greater than 60 days.

(4) Tax-exempt conduit loans. For purposes of applying section 149(d) to a conduit financing issue that finances any conduit loan that is a tax-exempt bond, the actual issuer of a conduit financing issue and the conduit borrower of that conduit financing issue are treated as related parties. Thus, the issue date of the conduit loan does not occur prior to the date on which the actual issuer of the conduit financing issue sells, exchanges, or otherwise disposes of that conduit loan, and the use of the proceeds of the disposition to pay debt service on the conduit financing issue causes the conduit loan to be a refunding issue. See § 1.148-10(d), Example 4.

(c) Unrefunded debt service remains eligible for future advance refunding. For purposes of section 149(d)(3)(A)(i), any principal or interest on a prior issue that has not been paid or provided for by any advance refunding issue is treated as not having been advance refunded.

(d) Application of arbitrage regulations. *(1) Application of multipurpose issue rules.* For purposes of sections 149(d)(2) and (3)(A)(i), (ii), and (iii), the provisions of the multipurpose issue rule in § 1.148-9(h) apply, except that the limitation in § 1.148-9(h)(5) is disregarded.

(2) General mixed escrow rules. For purposes of section 149(d), the provisions of § 1.148-9(c) (relating to mixed escrows) apply, except that those provisions do not apply for purposes of section 149(d)(2) and (d)(3)(A)(i) and (ii) to amounts that were not gross proceeds of the prior issue before the issue date of the refunding issue.

(3) Temporary periods and minor portions. Section 1.148-9(d) and (f) contains rules applicable to temporary periods and minor portions for advance refunding issues.

(4) Definitions. Section 1.148-1 applies for purposes of section 149(d).

(e) Taxable refundings. *(1) In general.* Except as provided in paragraph (e)(2) of this section, for purposes of section 149(d)(3)(A)(i), an advance refunding issue the interest on which is not excludable from gross income under section 103(a) (i.e., a taxable advance refunding issue) is not taken into account. In addition, for this purpose, an advance refunding of a taxable issue is not taken into account unless the taxable issue is a conduit loan of a tax-exempt conduit financing issue.

(2) Use to avoid section 149(d)(3)(A)(i). A taxable issue is taken into account under section 149(d)(3)(A)(i) if it is issued to avoid the limitations of that section. For example, in the case of a refunding of a tax-exempt issue with a taxable advance refunding issue that is, in turn, currently refunded with a tax-exempt issue, the taxable advance refunding issue is taken into account under section 149(d)(3)(A)(i) if the two

tax-exempt issues are outstanding concurrently for more than 90 days.

(f) Redemption at first call date. *(1) General rule.* Under sections 149(d)(3)(A)(ii) and (iii) (the first call requirement), bonds refunded by an advance refunding must be redeemed on their first call date if the savings test under section 149(d)(3)(B)(i) (the savings test) is satisfied. The savings test is satisfied if the issuer may realize present value debt service savings (determined without regard to administrative expenses) in connection with the issue of which the refunding bond is a part.

(2) First call date. First call date means the earliest date on which a bond may redeemed (or, if issued before 1986, on the earliest date on which that bond may be redeemed at a redemption price not in excess of 103 percent of par). If, however, the savings test is not met with respect to the date described in the preceding sentence (i.e., there are no present value savings if the refunded bonds are retired on that date), the first call date is the first date thereafter on which the bonds can be redeemed and on which the savings test is met.

(3) Application of savings test to multipurpose issues. Except as otherwise provided in this paragraph (f)(3), the multipurpose issue rules in § 1.148-9(h) apply for purposes of the savings test. If any separate issue in a multipurpose issue increases the aggregate present value debt service savings on the entire multipurpose issue or reduces the present value debt service losses on that entire multipurpose issue, that separate issue satisfies the savings test.

(g) Limitation on advance refundings of private activity bonds. Under section 149(d)(2) and this section, interest on a bond is not excluded from gross income if any portion of the issue of which the bond is a part is issued to advance refund a private activity bond (other than a qualified 501(c)(3) bond). For this purpose, the term private activity bond—

(1) Includes a qualified bond described in section 141(e) (other than a qualified 501(c)(3) bond), regardless of whether the refunding issue consists of private activity bonds under § 1.141-13; and

(2) Does not include a taxable bond.

(h) Effective dates. *(1) In general.* Except as provided in this paragraph (h), this section applies to bonds issued after June 30, 1993, to which §§ 1.148-1 through 1.148-11 apply, including conduit loans that are treated as issued after June 30, 1993, under paragraph (b)(4) of this section. In addition, this section applies to any issue to which the election described in § 1.148-11(b)(1) is made.

(2) Special effective date for paragraph (b)(3). Paragraph (b)(3) of this section applies to any advance refunding issue issued after May 28, 1991.

(3) Special effective date for paragraph (f)(3). Paragraph (f)(3) of this section applies to bonds sold on or after July 8, 1997 and to any issue to which the election described in § 1.148-11(b)(1) is made. See § 1.148-11A(i) for rules relating to certain bonds sold before July 8, 1997.

(4) Special effective date for paragraph (g). See § 1.141-15 for the applicability date of paragraph (g) of this section.

T.D. 8418, 5/12/92, amend T.D. 8476, 6/14/93, T.D. 8538, 5/5/94, T.D. 8718, 5/8/97, T.D. 9234, 12/16/2005.

§ 1.149(d)-1A Limitations on advance refundings.

(a) through (f)(2) [Reserved]. For guidance see § 1.149(d)-1.

(f) *(3) Application of savings test to multipurpose issues.* Except as otherwise provided in this paragraph (f)(3), the multipurpose issue rules in § 1.148-9(h) apply for purposes of the savings test. If any separate issue in a multipurpose issue increases the aggregate present value debt service savings on the entire multipurpose issue or reduces the present value debt service losses on that entire multipurpose issue, that separate issue satisfies the savings test.

T.D. 8538, 5/5/94, amend T.D. 8718, 5/8/97.

§ 1.149(e)-1 Information reporting requirements for tax-exempt bonds.

(a) General rule. Interest on a bond is included in gross income unless certain information with respect to the issue of which the bond is a part is reported to the Internal Revenue Service in accordance with the requirements of this section. This section applies to any bond if the issue of which the bond is a part is issued after December 31, 1986 (including any bond issued to refund a bond issued on or before December 31, 1986).

(b) Requirements for private activity bonds. *(1) In general.* If the issue of which the bond is a part is an issue of private activity bonds, the issuer must comply with the following requirements—

(i) Not later than the 15th day of the second calendar month after the close of the calendar quarter in which the issue is issued, the issuer must file with the Internal Revenue Service a completed information reporting form prescribed for this purpose;

(ii) If any bond that is part of the issue is taken into account under section 146 (relating to volume cap on private activity bonds), the state certification requirement of paragraph (b)(2) of this section must be satisfied; and

(iii) If any bond that is part of the issue is a qualified mortgage bond or qualified veterans' mortgage bond (within the meaning of section 143(a) or (b) or section 103A(c)(1) or (3) as in effect on the day before enactment of the Tax Reform Act of 1986), the issuer must submit the annual report containing information on the borrowers of the original proceeds of the issue as required under § 1.103A-2(k)(2)(ii) and (k)(3) through (k)(6).

(2) State certification with respect to volume cap. (i) In general. If an issue is subject to the volume cap under section 146, a state official designated by state law (if there is no such official, then the governor or the governor's delegate) must certify that the issue meets the requirements of section 146, and a copy of this certification must be attached to the information reporting form filed with respect to the issue. In the case of any constitutional home rule city (as defined in section 146(d)(3)(C)), the preceding sentence is applied by substituting "city" for "state" and "chief executive officer" for "governor."

(ii) Certification. The certifying official need not perform an independent investigation in order to certify that the issue meets the requirements of section 146. For example, if the certifying official receives an affidavit that was executed by an officer of the issuer who is responsible for issuing the bonds and that sets forth, in brief and summary terms, the facts necessary to determine that the issue meets the requirements of section 146 and if the certifying official has compared the information in that affidavit to other readily available information with respect to that issuer (e.g., previous affidavits and certifications for other private activity bonds issued by that issuer), the certifying official may rely on the affidavit.

(c) Requirements for governmental bonds. *(1) Issue price of $100,000 or more.* If the issue of which the bond is a part has an issue price of $100,000 or more and is not an issue of private activity bonds, then, not later than the 15th day of the second calendar month after the close of the calendar quarter in which the issue is issued, the issuer must file with the Internal Revenue Service a completed information reporting form prescribed for this purpose.

(2) Issue price of less than $100,000. (i) In general. If the issue of which the bond is a part has an issue price of less than $100,000 and is not an issue of private activity bonds, the issuer must file with the Internal Revenue Service one of the following information reporting forms within the prescribed period—

(A) Separate return. Not later than the 15th day of the second calendar month after the close of the calendar quarter in which the issue is issued, a completed information reporting form prescribed for this purpose with respect to that issue; or

(B) Consolidated return. Not later than February 15 of the calendar year following the calendar year in which the issue is issued, a completed information form prescribed for this purpose with respect to all issues to which this paragraph (c)(2) applies that were issued by the issuer during the calendar year and for which information was not reported on a separate information return pursuant to paragraph (c)(2)(i)(A) of this section.

(ii) Bond issues issued before January 1, 1992. Paragraph (c)(2)(i)(A) of this section does not apply if the issue of which the bond is a part is issued before January 1, 1992.

(iii) Extended filing date for first and second calendar quarters of 1992. If the issue of which the bond is a part is issued during the first or second calendar quarter of 1992, the prescribed period for filing an information reporting form with respect to that issue pursuant to paragraph (c)(2)(i)(A) of this section is extended until November 16, 1992.

(d) Filing of forms and special rules. *(1) Completed form.* For purposes of this section—

(i) Good faith effort. An information reporting form is treated as completed if the issuer (or a person acting on behalf of the issuer) has made a good faith effort to complete the form (taking into account the instructions to the form).

(ii) Information. In general, information reporting forms filed pursuant to this section must be completed on the basis of available information and reasonable expectations as of the date the issue is issued. Forms that are filed on a consolidated basis pursuant to paragraph (c)(2)(i)(B) of this section, however, may be completed on the basis of information readily available to the issuer at the close of the calendar year to which the form relates, supplemented by estimates made in good faith.

(iii) Certain information not required. An issuer need not report to the Internal Revenue Service any information specified in the first sentence of section 149(e)(2) that is not required to be reported to the Internal Revenue Service pursuant to the information reporting forms prescribed under that section and the instructions to those forms.

(2) Manner of filing. (i) Place for filing. The information reporting form must be filed with the Internal Revenue Service at the address specified on the form or in the instructions to the form.

(ii) Extension of time. The Commissioner may grant an extension of time to file any form or attachment required under this section if the Commissioner determines that the failure to file in a timely manner was not due to willful neglect. The Commissioner may make this determination with respect to an issue or to a class of issues.

(e) Definitions. For purposes of this section only. *(1) Private activity bond.* The term "private activity bond" has the meaning given that term in section 141(a) of the Internal Revenue Code, except that the term does not include any bond described in section 1312(c) of the Tax Reform Act of 1986 to which of section 1312 or 1313 of the Tax Reform Act of 1986 applies.

(2) Issue. (i) In general. Except as otherwise provided in this paragraph (e)(2), bonds are treated as part of the same issue only if the bonds are issued—

(A) By the same issuer;

(B) On the same date; and

(C) Pursuant to a single transaction or to a series of related transactions.

(ii) Draw-down loans, commercial paper, etc (A) Bonds issued during the same calendar year may be treated as part of the same tissue if the bonds are issued—

(1) Pursuant to a loan agreement under which amounts are to be advanced periodically ("draw-down loan"); or

(2) With a term not exceeding 270 days.

(B) In addition, the bonds must be equally and ratably secured under a single indenture or loan agreement and issued pursuant to a common financing arrangement (e.g., pursuant to the same official statement that is periodically updated to reflect changing factual circumstances). In the case of bonds issued pursuant to a draw-down loan that meets the requirements of the preceding sentence, bonds issued during different calendar years may be treated as part of the same issue if all the amounts to be advanced pursuant to the draw-down loan are reasonably expected to be advanced within three years of the date of issue of the first bond.

(iii) Leases and installment sales. Bonds other than private activity bonds may be treated as part of the same issue if—

(A) The bonds are issued pursuant to a single agreement that is in the form of a lease or installment sales agreement; and

(B) All of the property covered by that agreement is reasonably expected to be delivered within three years of the date of issue of the first bond.

(iv) Qualified 501(c)(3) bonds. If an issuer elects under section 141(b)(9) to treat a portion of an issue as a qualified 501(c)(3) bond, that portion is treated as a separate issue.

(3) Date of issue. (i) Bond. The date of issue of a bond is the date determined under § 1.150-1.

(ii) Issue. The date of issue of an issue of bonds is the date of issue of the first bond that is part of the issue. See paragraphs (e)(2)(ii) and (iii) of this section for rules relating to draw-down loans, commercial paper, etc., and leases and installment sales.

(iii) Bonds to which prior law applied. Notwithstanding the provisions of this paragraph (e)(3), an issue for which an information report was required to be filed under section 103(l) or section 103A(j)(3) is treated as issued prior to January 1, 1987.

(4) Issue price. The term "issue price" has the same meaning given the term under § 1.148-1(b).

T.D. 8425, 8/11/92.

§ 1.149(g)-1 Hedge bonds.

(a) Certain definitions. Except as otherwise provided, the definitions set forth in § 1.148-1 apply for purposes of section 149(g) and this section. In addition, the following terms have the following meanings:

Reasonable expectations means reasonable expectations (as defined in § 1.148-1), as modified to take into account the provisions of section 149(f)(2)(B).

Spendable proceeds means net sale proceeds (as defined in § 1.148-1).

(b) Applicability of arbitrage allocation and accounting rules. Section 1.148-6 applies for purposes of section 149(g), except that an expenditure that results in the creation of replacement proceeds (other than amounts in a bona fide debt service fund or a reasonably required reserve or replacement fund) is not an expenditure for purposes of section 149(g).

(c) Refundings. *(1) Investment in tax-exempt bonds.* A bond issued to refund a bond that is a tax-exempt bond by virtue of the rule in section 149(g)(3)(B) is not a tax-exempt bond unless the gross proceeds of that refunding bond (other than proceeds in a refunding escrow for the refunded bond) satisfy the requirements of section 149(g)(3)(B).

(2) Anti-abuse rule. A refunding bond is treated as a hedge bond unless there is a significant governmental purpose for the issuance of that bond (e.g., an advance refunding bond issued to realize debt service savings or to relieve the issuer of significantly burdensome document provisions, but not to otherwise hedge against future increases in interest rates).

(d) Effective date. This section applies to bonds issued after June 30, 1993 to which §§ 1.148-1 through 1.148-11 apply. In addition, this section applies to any issue to which the election described in § 1.148-11(b)(1) is made.

T.D. 8476, 6/14/93.

§ 3.1 Scope of section 607 of the Act and the regulations in this part.

(a) In general. The regulations prescribed in this part provide rules for determining the income tax liability of any person a party to an agreement with the Secretary of Commerce establishing a capital construction fund (for purposes of this part referred to as the "fund") authorized by section 607 of the Merchant Marine Act, 1936, as amended (for purposes of this part referred to as the "Act"). With respect to such parties, section 607 of the Act in general provides for the nontaxability of certain deposits of money or other property into the fund out of earnings or gains realized from the operation of vessels covered in an agreement, gains realized from the sale or other disposition of agreement vessels or proceeds from insurance for indemnification for loss of agreement vessels, earnings from the investment or reinvestment of amounts held in a fund, and gains with respect to amounts or deposits in the fund. Transitional rules are also provided for the treatment of "old funds" existing on or before the effective date of the Merchant Marine Act of 1970 (see § 3.10).

(b) Cross references. For rules relating to eligibility for a fund, deposits, and withdrawals and other aspects, see the regulations prescribed by the Secretary of Commerce in titles 46 (Merchant Marine) and 50 (Fisheries) of the Code of Federal Regulations.

(c) Code. For purposes of this part, the term "Code" means the Internal Revenue Code of 1954, as amended.

T.D. 7398, 1/23/76.

§ 3.2 Ceiling on deposits.

(a) In general. *(1) Total ceiling.* Section 607(b) of the Act provides a ceiling on the amount which may be deposited by a party for a taxable year pursuant to an agreement. The amount which a party may deposit into a fund may not exceed the sum of the following subsections:

(i) The lower of (a) the taxable income (if any) of the party for such year (computed as provided in chapter 1 of the Code but without regard to the carryback of any net operating loss or net capital loss and without regard to section 607 of the Act) or (b) taxable income (if any) of such party for such year attributable under paragraph (b) of this section to the operation of agreement vessels (as defined in paragraph (f) of this section) in the foreign or domestic commerce of the United States or in the fisheries of the United States (see section 607(b)(1)(A) of the Act),

(ii) Amounts allowable as a deduction under section 167 of the Code for such year with respect to the agreement vessels (see section 607(b)(1)(B) of the Act),

(iii) The net proceeds (if not included in subdivision (i) of this paragraph) from (a) the sale or other disposition of any agreement vessels or (b) insurance or indemnity attributable to any agreement vessels (see section 607(b)(1)(C) of the Act and paragraph (c) of this section), and

(iv) Earnings and gains from the investment or reinvestment of amounts held in such fund (see section 607(b)(1)(D) of the Act and paragraph (d) and (g) of this section).

(2) Overdeposits. (i) If for any taxable year an amount is deposited into the fund under a subceiling computed under subparagraph (1) of this paragraph which is in excess of the amount of such subceiling for such year, then at the party's option such excess (or any portion thereof) may—

(a) Be treated as a deposit into the fund for that taxable year under another available subceiling, or

(b) Be treated as not having been deposited for the taxable year and thus, at the party's option, may be disposed of either by it being—

(1) Treated as a deposit into the fund under any subceiling available in the first subsequent taxable year in which a subceiling is available, in which case such amount shall be deemed to have been deposited on the first day of such subsequent taxable year, or

(2) Repaid to the party from the fund.

(ii) (a) When a correction is made for overdeposit, proper adjustment shall be made with respect to all items for all taxable years affected by the overdeposit, such as, for example, amounts in each account described in § 3.4, treatment of nonqualified withdrawals, the consequences of qualified withdrawals and the treatment of losses realized or treated as realized by the fund. Thus, for example, if the party chooses to have the fund repay to him the amount of an overdeposit, amounts in each account, basis of assets, and any affected item will be determined as though no deposit and repayment had been made. Accordingly, in such a case, if there are insufficient amounts in an account to cover a repayment of an overdeposit (as determined before correcting the overdeposit), and the party had applied the proceeds of a qualified withdrawal from such account towards the purchase of a qualified vessel (within the meaning of § 3.11(a)(2)), then such account and the basis of the vessel shall be adjusted as of the time such withdrawal was made and proceeds were applied, and repayment shall be made from such account as adjusted. If a party chooses to treat the amount of an overdeposit as a deposit under a subceiling for a subsequent year, similar adjustments to affected items shall be made. If the amount of a withdrawal would have exceeded the amount in the fund (determined after adjusting all affected amounts by reason of correcting the overdeposit), the withdrawal to the extent of such shall be treated as a repayment made at the time the withdrawal was made.

(b) If the accounts (as defined in § 3.4) that were increased by reason of excessive deposits contain sufficient amounts at the time the overdeposit is discovered to repay the party, the party may, at his option, demand repayment of such excessive deposits from such accounts in lieu of making the adjustments required by (a) of this subdivision (ii).

(iii) During the period beginning with the day after the date an overdeposit was actually made and ending with the date it was disposed of in accordance with subdivision (i)(b) of this subparagraph, there shall be included in the party's gross income for each taxable year the earnings attributed to any amount of overdeposit on hand during such a year. The earnings attributable to any amount of overdeposit on hand during a taxable year shall be an amount equal to the product of—

(a) The average daily earnings for each one dollar in the fund (as determined in subdivision (iv) of this subparagraph),

(b) The amount of overdeposit (as determined in subdivision (vi) of this subparagraph), and

(c) The number of days during the taxable year the overdeposit existed.

(iv) For purposes of subdivision (iii)(a) of this subparagraph, the average daily earnings for each dollar in the fund shall be determined by dividing the total earnings of the fund for the taxable year by the sum of the products of—

(a) Any amount on hand during the taxable year (determined under subdivision (v) of this subparagraph), and

(b) The number of days during the taxable year such amount was on hand in the fund.

(v) For purposes of this subparagraph—

(a) An amount on hand in the fund or an overdeposit shall not be treated as on hand on the day deposited but shall be treated as on hand on the day withdrawn, and

(b) The fair market value of such amounts on hand for purposes of this subparagraph shall be determined as provided in § 20.2031-2 of the Estate Tax Regulations of this chapter but without applying the blockage and other special rules contained in paragraph (e) thereof.

(vi) For purposes of subdivision (iii) *(b)* of this subparagraph, the amount of overdeposit on hand at any time is an amount equal to—

(a) The amount deposited into the fund under a subceiling computed under subparagraph (1) of this paragraph which is in excess of the amount of such subceiling, less

(b) The sum of—

(1) Amounts described in (a) of this subdivision (vi) treated as a deposit under another subceiling for the taxable year pursuant to subdivision (i) of this subparagraph,

(2) Amounts described in (a) of this subdivision (vi) disposed of (or treated as disposed of) in accordance with subdivision (i) or (ii) of this subparagraph prior to such time.

(vii) To the extent earnings attributed under subdivision (iii) of this subparagraph represent a deposit for any taxable year in excess of the subceiling described in subparagraph (1)(iv) of this paragraph for receipts from the investment or reinvestment of amounts held in the fund, such attributed earnings shall be subject to the rules of this subparagraph for overdeposits.

(3) Underdeposit caused by audit adjustment. [Reserved]

(4) Requirements for deficiency deposits. [Reserved]

(b) Taxable income attributable to the operation of an agreement vessel. *(1) In general.* For purposes of this section, taxable income attributable to the operation of an agreement vessel means the amount, if any, by which the gross income of a party for the taxable year from the operation of an agreement vessel (as defined in paragraph (f) of this section) exceeds the allowable deductions allocable to such operation (as determined under subparagraph (3) of this paragraph). The term "taxable income attributable to the operation of the agreement vessels" means the sum of the amounts described in the preceding sentence separately computed with respect to each agreement vessel (or share therein) or, at the party's option, computed in the aggregate.

(2) Gross income. (i) Gross income from the operation of agreement vessels means the sum of the revenues which are derived during the taxable year from the following:

(a) Revenues derived from the transportation of passengers, freight, or mail in such vessels, including amounts from contracts for the charter of such vessels to others, from operating differential subsidies, from collections in accordance with pooling agreements and from insurance or indemnity net proceeds relating to the loss of income attributable to such agreement vessels.

(b) Revenues derived from the operation of agreement vessels relating to commercial fishing activities, including the transportation of fish, support activities for fishing vessels, charters for commercial fishing, and insurance or indemnity net proceeds relating to the loss of income attributable to such agreement vessels.

(c) Revenues from the rental, lease, or use by others of terminal facilities, revenues from cargo handling operations and rug and lighter operations, and revenues from other services or operations which are incidental and directly related to the operation of an agreement vessel. Thus, for example, agency fees, commissions, and brokerage fees derived by the party at his place of business for effecting transactions for services incidental and directly related to shipping for the accounts of other persons are includible in gross income from the operation of agreement vessels where the transaction is of a kind customarily consummated by the party for his own account at such place of business.

(d) Dividends, interest, and gains derived from assets set aside and reasonably retained to meet regularly occurring obligations relating to the shipping or fishing business directly connected with the agreement vessel which obligations cannot at all times be met from the current revenues of the business because of layups or repairs, special surveys, fluctuations in the business, and reasonably foreseeable strikes (whether or not a strike actually occurs), and security amounts retained by reason of participation in conferences, pooling agreements, or similar agreements.

(ii) The items of gross income described in subdivision (i)(c) and (d) of this subparagraph shall be considered to be derived from the operations of a particular agreement vessel in the same proportion that the sum of items of gross income described in subdivision (i)(a) and (b) of this subparagraph which are derived from the operations of such agreement vessel bears to the party's total gross income for the taxable year from operations described in subdivision (i)(a) and (b) of this subparagraph.

(iii) In the case of a party who uses his own or leased agreement vessels to transport his own products, the gross income attributable to such vessel operations is an amount determined to be an arm's length charge for such transportation. The arm's length charge shall be determined by applying the principles of section 482 of the Code and the regulations thereunder as if the party transporting the product and the owner of the product were not the same person but were controlled taxpayers within the meaning of § 1.482-1(a)(4) of the Income Tax Regulations of this chapter. Gross income attributable to the operation of agreement vessels does not include amounts for which the party is allowed a deduction for percentage depletion under sections 611 and 613 of the Code.

(3) Deductions. From the gross income attributable to the operation of an agreement vessel or vessels as determined under subparagraph (2) of this paragraph, there shall be deducted, in accordance with the principles of § 1.861-8 of the Income Tax Regulations of this chapter, the expenses, losses, and other deductions definitely related and therefore allocated and apportioned thereto and a ratable part of any expenses, losses, or other deductions which are not definitely related to any gross income of the party. Thus, for example, if a party has gross income attributable to the operation of an agreement vessel and other gross income and has a particular deduction definitely related to both types of gross income, such deduction must be apportioned between the two types of gross income on a reasonable basis in determining the taxable income attributable to the operation of the agreement vessel.

(4) Net operating and capital loss deductions. The taxable income of a party attributable to the operation of agreement vessels shall be computed without regard to the carryback of any net operating loss deduction allowed by section 172 of the Code, the carryback of any net capital loss deduction allowed by section 165(f) of the Code, or any reduction in taxable income allowed by section 607 of the Act.

(5) Method of accounting. Taxable income must be computed under the method of accounting which the party uses for Federal income tax purposes. Such method may include a method of reporting whereby items of revenue and expense properly allocable to voyages in progress at the end of any accounting period are eliminated from the computation of taxable income for such accounting period and taken into account in the accounting period in which the voyage is completed.

(c) Net proceeds from transactions with respect to agreement vessels. [Reserved]

(d) Earnings and gains from the investment or reinvestment of amounts held in a fund. *(1) In general.* (i) Earnings and gains received or accrued by a party from the investment or reinvestment of assets in a fund is the total amount of any interest or dividends received or accrued, and gains realized, by the party with respect to assets deposited in, or purchased with amounts deposited in, such fund. Such earnings and gains are therefore required to be included in the gross income of the party unless such amount, or a portion thereof, is not taken into account under section 607(d)(1)(C) of the Act and § 3.3(b)(2)(ii) by reason of a deposit or deemed deposit into the fund. For rules relating to receipts from the sale or other disposition of nonmoney deposits into the fund, see paragraph (g) of this section.

(ii) Earnings received or accrued by a party from investment or reinvestment of assets in a fund include the ratable monthly portion of original issue discount included in gross income pursuant to section 1232(a)(3) of the Code. Such ratable monthly portion shall be deemed to be deposited into the ordinary income account of the fund, but an actual deposit representing such ratable monthly portion shall not be made. For basis of a bond or other evidence of indebtedness issued at a discount, see § 3.3(b)(2)(ii)(b).

(2) Gain realized. (i) The gain realized with respect to assets in the fund is the excess of the amount realized (as defined in section 1001(b) of the Code and the regulations thereunder) by the fund on the sale or other disposition of a fund asset over its adjusted basis (as defined in section 1011 of the Code) to the fund. For the adjusted basis of nonmoney deposits, see paragraph (g) of this section.

(ii) Property purchased by the fund (including property considered under paragraph (g)(1)(iii) of this section as purchased by the fund) which is withdrawn from the fund in a qualified withdrawal (as defined in § 3.5) is treated as a disposition to which subdivision (i) of this subparagraph applies. For purposes of determining the amount by which the balance within a particular account will be reduced in the manner provided in § 3.6(b) (relating to order of application of qualified withdrawals against accounts) and for purposes of determining the reduction in basis of a vessel, barge, or container (or share therein) pursuant to § 3.6(c), the value of the property is its fair market value on the day of the qualified withdrawal.

(3) Holding Period. Except as provided in paragraph (g) of this section, the holding period of fund assets shall be determined under section 1223 of the Code.

(e) Leased vessels. In the case of a party who is a lessee of an agreement vessel, the maximum amount which such lessee may deposit with respect to any agreement vessel by reason of section 607(b)(1)(B) of the Act and paragraph (a)(1)(ii) of this section (relating to depreciation allowable) for any period shall be reduced by the amount (if any) which, under an agreement entered into under section 607 of the Act, the owner is required or permitted to deposit for such period with respect to such vessel by reason of section 607(b)(1)(B) of the Act and paragraph (a)(1)(ii) of this section. The amount of depreciation depositable by the lessee under this paragraph is the amount of depreciation deductible by the lessor on its income tax return, reduced by the amount described in the preceding sentence or the amount set forth in the agreement, whichever is lower.

(f) Definition of agreement vessel. For purposes of this section, the term "agreement vessel" (as defined in § 3.11(a)(3) and 46 CFR 390.6) includes barges and containers which are the complement of an agreement vessel and which are provided for in the agreement, agreement vessels which have been contracted for or are in the process of construction, and any shares in an agreement vessel. Solely for purposes of this section, a party is considered to have a "share" in an agreement vessel if he has a right to use the vessel to generate income from its use whether or not the party would be considered as having a proprietary interest in the vessel for purposes of State or Federal law. Thus, a partner may enter into an agreement with respect to his share of the vessel owned by the partnership and he may make deposits of his distributive share of the sum of the four subceilings described in paragraph (a)(1) of this section. Notwithstanding the provisions of subchapter K of the Code (relating to the taxation of partners and partnerships), the Internal Revenue Service will recognize, solely for the purposes of applying this part, an agreement by an owner of a share in an agreement vessel even though the "share" arrangement is a partnership for purposes of the Code.

(g) Special rules for nonmoney deposits and withdrawals. *(1) In general.* (i) Deposits may be made in the form of money or property of the type permitted to be deposited under the agreement. (For rules relating to the types of property which may be deposited into the fund, see 46 CFR 390.7(d), and 50 CFR 259.) For purposes of this paragraph, the term "property" does not include money.

(ii) Whether or not the election provided for in subparagraph (2) of this paragraph is made—

(a) The amount of any property deposit, and the fund's basis for property deposited in the fund, is the fair market value of the property at the time deposited, and

(b) The fund's holding period for the property begins on the day after the deposit is made.

(iii) Unless such an election is made, deposits of property into a fund are considered to be a sale at fair market value of the property, a deposit of cash equal to such fair market value, and a purchase by the fund of such property for cash. Thus, in the absence of the election, the difference between the fair market value of such property deposited and its adjusted basis shall be taken into account as gain or loss for purposes of computing the party's income tax liability for the year of deposit.

(iv) For fund's basis and holding period of assets purchased by the fund, see paragraph (d)(2) and (3) of this section.

(2) Election not to treat deposits of property other than money as a sale or exchange at the time of deposit. A party may elect to treat a deposit of property as if no sale or other taxable event had occurred on the date of deposit. If such election is made, in the taxable year the fund disposes of the property, the party shall recognize as gain or loss the amount he would have recognized on the day the property was deposited into the fund had the election not been made. The party's holding period with respect to such property shall not include the period of time such property was held by the fund. The election shall be made by a statement to that effect, attached to the party's Federal income tax return for the taxable year to which the deposit relates, or, if such return is filed before such deposit is made, attached to the party's return for the taxable year during which the deposit is actually made.

(3) Effect of qualified withdrawal of property deposited pursuant to election. If property deposited into a fund, with respect to which an election under subparagraph (2) of this paragraph is made, is withdrawn from the fund in a qualified withdrawal (as defined in § 3.5) such withdrawal is treated as a disposition of such property resulting in recognition by the party of gain or loss (if any) as provided in subparagraph (2) of this paragraph with respect to nonfund property. In addition, such withdrawal is treated as a disposition of such property by the fund resulting in recognition of gain or loss by the party with respect to fund property to the extent the fair market value of the property on the date of withdrawal is greater or less (as the case may be) than the adjusted basis of the property to the fund on such date. For purposes of determining the amount by which the balance within a particular account will be reduced in the manner provided in § 3.6(b) (relating to order of application of qualified withdrawals against accounts) and for purposes of determining the reduction in basis of a vessel, barge, or container (or share therein) pursuant to § 3.6(c), the value of the property is its fair market value on the day of the qualified withdrawal. For rules relating to the effect of a qualified withdrawal of property purchased by the fund (including deposited property considered under subparagraph (1)(iii) of this paragraph as purchased by the fund), see paragraph (d)(2)(ii) of this section.

(4) Effect of nonqualified withdrawal of property deposited pursuant to election. If property deposited into a fund with respect to which an election under subparagraph (2) of this paragraph is made, is withdrawn from the fund in a nonqualified withdrawal (as defined in § 3.7(b)), no gain or loss is to be recognized by the party with respect to fund property or nonfund property but an amount equal to the adjusted basis of the property to the fund is to be treated as a nonqualified withdrawal. Thus, such amount is to be applied against the various accounts in the manner provided in § 3.7(c), such amount is to be taken into account in computing the party's taxable income as provided in § 3.7(d), and such amount is to be subject to interest to the extent provided for in § 3.7(e). In the case of withdrawals to which this subparagraph applies, the adjusted basis of the property in the hands of the party is the adjusted basis on the date of deposit, increased or decreased by the adjustments made to such property while held in the fund, and in determining the period for which the party has held the property there shall be included, in addition to the period the fund held the property, the period for which the party held the property before the date of deposit of the property into the fund. For rules relating to the basis and holding period of property purchased by the fund (including deposited property considered under subparagraph (1)(ii) of this paragraph as purchased by the fund) and withdrawn in a nonqualified withdrawal see § 3.7(f).

(5) Examples. The provisions of this paragraph are illustrated by the following examples:

Example (1). X Corporation, which uses the calendar year as its taxable year, maintains a fund described in § 3.1. X's taxable income (determined without regard to section 607 of the Act) is $100,000, of which $80,000 is taxable income attributable to the operation of agreement vessels (as determined under paragraph (b)(1) of this section). Under the agreement, X is required to deposit into the fund all earnings and gains received from the investment or reinvestment of amounts held in the fund, an amount equal to the net proceeds from transactions referred to in § 3.2(c), and an amount equal to 50 percent of its earnings attributable to the operation of agreement vessels provided that such 50 percent does not exceed X's taxable income from all sources for the year of deposit. The agreement permits X to make voluntary deposits of amounts equal to 100 percent of its earnings attributable to the operation of agreement vessels, subject to the limitation with respect to taxable income from all sources. The agreement also provides that deposits attributable to such earnings may be in the form of cash or other property. On March 15, 1973, X deposits, with respect to its 1972 earnings attributable to the operation of agreement vessels, stock with a fair market value at the time of deposit of $80,000 and an adjusted basis to X of $10,000. Such deposit represents agreement vessel income of $80,000. At the time of deposit, such stock had been held by X for a period exceeding 6 months. X does not elect under subparagraph (2) of this paragraph to defer recognition of the gain. Accordingly, under subparagraph (1)(iii) of this paragraph, the deposit is treated as a deposit of $80,000 and X realizes a long-term capital gain of $70,000 on March 15, 1973.

Example (2). The facts are the same as in example (1), except that X elects in accordance with subparagraph (2) of this paragraph not to treat the deposit as a sale or exchange. On July 1, 1974, the fund sells the stock for $85,000. The basis to the fund of the stock is $80,000 (see subparagraph (1)(ii)(a) of this paragraph). With respect to nonfund property, X recognizes $70,000 of long-term capital gain on the sale includible in its gross income for 1974. With respect to fund property, X realizes $5,000 of long-term capital gain (the difference between the amount received by the fund on the sale of the stock, $85,000, and the basis to the fund of the stock, $80,000), an amount equal to which is required to be deposited into the fund with respect to 1974, as a gain from the investment or reinvestment of amounts held in the fund. Since the fund held the stock for a period exceeding 6 months, the $5,000 is allocated to the fund's capital gain account under § 3.4(c).

Example (3). The facts are the same as in example (2), except that the fund sells the stock on July 1, 1974, for $75,000. As the basis to the fund of the stock is $80,000, with respect to fund property, X realizes a long-term capital loss on the sale (the difference between the amount received by the fund on the sale of the stock, $75,000, and the basis to the fund of the stock, $80,000), of $5,000, an amount equal to which is required to be charged against the fund's capital gain account under § 3.4(e). Under subparagraph (2) of this paragraph, X recognizes $70,000 of long-term capital gain with respect to nonfund property on the sale which is includible in its gross income for 1974.

Example (4). The facts are the same as in example (2), except that on July 1, 1974, X makes a qualified withdrawal (as defined in § 3.5(a)) of the stock and uses it to pay indebtedness pursuant to § 3.5(b). On the disposition by X considered to occur under subparagraph (3) of this paragraph on the qualified withdrawal, X recognizes $70,000 of long-term capital gain with respect to nonfund property, which is includible in its gross income for 1974, and a long-term capital gain of $5,000 with respect to fund property, an amount equal to which is allocated to the fund's capital gain account under § 3.4(c). The fund is treated as having a qualified withdrawal of an amount equal to the fair market value of the stock on the day of withdrawal, $85,000 (see subparagraph (3) of this paragraph). In addition, $85,000 is applied against the various accounts in the order provided in § 3.6(b). The basis of the vessel with respect to which the indebtedness was incurred is to be reduced as provided in § 3.6(c).

Example (5). The facts are the same as in example (2), except that X withdraws the stock from the fund in a nonqualified withdrawal (as defined in § 3.7(b)). Under subparagraph (4) of this paragraph, X recognizes no gain or loss with respect to fund or nonfund property on such withdrawal. An amount equal to the basis of the stock to the fund ($80,000) is applied against the various accounts in the order provided in § 3.7(c), and is taken into account in computing X's taxable income for 1974 as provided in § 3.7(d). In addition, X must pay interest on the withdrawal as provided in § 3.7(e). The basis to X of the stock is $10,000 notwithstanding the fact that the fair market value of such stock was $85,000 on the day of withdrawal (see subparagraph (4) of this paragraph).

T.D. 7398, 1/23/76.

PAR. 36. Paragraph (d) of § 3.2 is amended by removing the phrase "ratable monthly portion" every place it appears and adding in its place the word "amount", and by removing the phrase "section 1232(a)(3)" every place it appears and adding in its place the phrase "section 1272".

Proposed § 3.2 [Amended] [*For Preamble, see ¶ 151,065*]

• ***Caution:*** Prop reg § 1.482-2 was finalized by T.D. 8204, 5/20/88. Prop regs §§ 1.163-7, 1.446-2, 1.483-1 through -5, 1.1001-1, 1.1012-1, 1.1271 through -3, 1.1272-1, 1.1273-1, 1.1273-2, 1.1274-1 throught -7, 1.1274A-1, 1.1275-1 through -3, and 1.1275-5 were withdrawn by the Treasury on 12/22/92, 57 Fed. Reg. 67050. Prop reg § 1.1275-4 was superseded by the Treasury on 12/16/94, Fed. Reg. 59, 64884, which was finalized by T.D. 8674, 6/11/96.

PARAGRAPH 1. Section 3.2, as adopted by Treasury Decision 7398, is amended by revising paragraphs (a)(3) and (4), (c), and (g)(2). These revised provisions read as follows:

Proposed § 3.2 Ceiling on deposits. [*For Preamble, see ¶ 150,183*]

(a) In general. * * *

(3) Underdeposit caused by audit adjustment. (i) If, upon an audit of a party's Federal income tax return, the district director, or director of an Internal Revenue Service center, makes an adjustment which increases the amount of a subceiling (as defined in subparagraph (1) of this paragraph) in a taxable year over the amount of such subceiling as determined when such return was filed, and if the party complies with the requirements of subparagraph (4) of this paragraph, then the party may make a deficiency deposit which will reduce the party's taxable income or be excluded from gross income (as the case may be) for purposes of determining the tax on the party's taxable income for that taxable year.

(ii) Such deficiency deposit shall not exceed the excess (if any) between (a) subceiling allowable under section 607(b) of the Act and paragraph (a)(1) of this section, as determined on audit, or under the agreement of the party with the Secretary of Commerce, whichever is lower, and (b) the subceiling determined when the party's return was filed.

(iii) A deficiency deposit will be related to the fund's subceiling in the manner provided in subparagraphs (1) and (2) of this paragraph in the taxable year to which it relates. The reduction in the party's taxable income or the exclusion from gross income (as the case may be) occasioned by a deficiency deposit will not, however, be allowed for the purpose of determining interest, additional amounts, or assessable penalties, computed with respect to the tax on the party's taxable income prior to the allowance of such reduction or exclusion. For example, in the case of a calendar year taxpayer, if a deposit is made in 1972 of an amount equal to an amount of earnings from shipping operations in 1971, and in 1974 a deficiency deposit is made which represents the portion of taxable income from 1971 that resulted from adjustments made upon an audit by the Internal Revenue Service, then the amounts deposited in 1972 and 1974 would both reduce taxable income for 1971. In such a case, interest, additional amounts, or assessable penalties will be due in the manner and under the conditions specified in the Code, applied by treating payment of the tax as having been made on the date the tax is paid or the deficiency deposit is actually made in the fund, whichever is earlier. No interest shall be allowed on a credit or refund arising from the application of this subparagraph.

(iv) For purposes of determining the order of withdrawals under § 3.6(b) and § 3.7(c) and interest on nonqualified withdrawals under § 3.7(e), these deposits will be treated under § 3.3(b)(4)(i) as having been made on the date they were actually made.

(4) Requirements for deficiency deposits. (i) In order for the deficiency deposit under subparagraph (3) of this paragraph to be allowed—

(a) There must be a determination described in subdivision (ii) of this subparagraph of the party's income tax liability determined without regard to any deficiency deposit,

(b) The adjustment made by the district director, or director of an Internal Revenue Service center, referred to in subparagraph (3)(i) of this paragraph, must not have resulted from an underpayment described in section 6653(a) (relating to negligence or intentional disregard of rules and regulations) or section 6653(b) (relating to fraud) of the Code,

(c) The deficiency deposit must be made by the party on, or within 90 days after, the date of such determination and prior to the filing of a claim under subdivision (iii) of this subparagraph for deduction for deficiency deposits.[,]

(d) The claim under subdivision (iii) of this subparagraph must be filed within 120 days after such determination, and

(e) The adjustment to the party's tax liability occasioned by the reduction in the party's taxable income or the exclusion from the party's gross income (as the case may be) under subparagraph (3) of this paragraph must not be prohibited by section 6215 or 6512 of the Code (with respect to Tax Court decision), the statute of limitations, or any other law or rule of law.

(ii) A determination of the party's income tax liability shall, for purposes of this subparagraph, be established in the following manner:

(a) A closing agreement made under section 7121 of the Code. For purposes of subdivision (i)(c) of this subparagraph, the date such agreement is approved by the Commissioner shall be the date of determination.

(b) An agreement signed by the district director, director of the service center with which the party files its annual return, or by such other official to whom authority to sign the agreement is delegated, and by or on behalf of the party, which agreement sets forth the total amount of the party's income tax liability for the taxable year or years and has been sent to the party at his last known address by either registered or certified mail. For purposes of subdivision (i)(c) of this subparagraph, if such agreement is sent by registered mail, the date of registration is considered the date of determination; if sent by certified mail, the date of postmark on the sender's receipt for such mail is considered the date of determination. If the party makes a deficiency deposit before such registration or postmark date but on or after the date the district director, director of the service center or other official has signed the agreement, the date of signature district director or director of the service center or other official is considered the date of final determination,

(c) A decision of the United States Tax Court which has become final, as prescribed in section 7481 of the Code,

(d) A decision of a court of the United States (other than the United States Tax Court) which has become final. The date upon which a judgment of a court becomes final, which is the date of the determination in such cases, must be determined upon the basis of the facts in the particular case. For example, a judgment of a United States District Court becomes final upon the expiration of the time allowed for taking an appeal, if no such appeal is duly taken within such time; and a judgment of the United States Court of Claims becomes final upon the expiration of the time allowed for filing a petition for certiorari if no such petition is duly filed within such time.

(iii) A claim for deduction for a deficiency deposit shall be made in duplicate, shall be dated and signed by the party and shall contain or be verified by, a written declaration that it is made under the penalties of perjury. The claim shall also contain the following information:

(a) The name and address of the party;

(b) The amount of the deficiency determined with respect to the party's income tax and the taxable year or years involved; the amount of the unpaid deficiency or, if the deficiency has been paid in whole or in part, the date of payment and the amount thereof; a statement as to how the deficiency was established, if unpaid; or if paid in whole or in part, how it was established that any portion of the amount paid was a deficiency at the time when paid and, in either case whether it was by an agreement under subdivision (ii)(b) of this subparagraph, by a closing agreement under section 7121, or by a decision of the Tax Court or court judgment and the date thereof; if established by a final judgment in a suit against the United States for refund, the date of payment of the deficiency, the date the claim for refund was filed, and the date the suit was brought; if established by a Tax Court decision or court judgment, a copy thereof shall be attached, together with an explanation of how the decision became final; if established by an agreement under subdivision (ii)(b) of this subparagraph, a copy of such agreement shall be attached;

(c) The amount and date of the deposit with respect to which the claim for the deduction or exclusion for the deficiency deposit is filed and a copy of the deposit receipt for such deposit;

(d) The amount claimed as a deduction or exclusion for deficiency deposit; and

(e) Such other information as may be required by the Commissioner or his delegate.

* * * * *

(c) Net proceeds from transactions with respect to agreement vessels. *(1) Gross proceeds from disposition of agreements vessels.* (i) Except as provided in subparagraph (6) of this paragraph, with respect to installment sales, the gross proceeds from the sale or other disposition (including certain mortgages treated for purposes of this part as a disposition) of an agreement vessel is the total amount realized or to be realized by the party from the sale or other disposition of such vessel, including any property (whether or not a vessel) and evidences of indebtedness and contract rights received, whether or not they constitute an amount realized under section 1001(b) of the Code and the regulations thereunder, but only to the extent not included in taxable income under paragraph (b) of this section. Notwithstanding the preceding sentence, gross proceeds does not include any property to the extent received without recognition of gain under both the Act and the Code. For purposes of this paragraph, sale or other disposition does not include any transaction between persons related within the meaning of subparagraph (3)(ii) of this paragraph which has as its primary purpose the creation of an allowable subceiling under section 607(b)(1)(C) of the Act and paragraph (a)(1)(iii) of this section.

(ii) Gross proceeds does not include interest on obligations received by the party from the sale or other disposition of an agreement vessel, but does include amounts received as the result of the forfeiture of collateral for the payment of purchase-money obligations and amounts received from the mortgaging of a qualified vessel. (For rules requiring the deposit of net proceeds from the mortgaging of a qualified vessel into the capital account of the fund, see 46 CFR § 390.11(b) and 50 CFR § 259).

(2) Net proceeds. Net proceeds from the sale or other disposition of an agreement vessel is the greater of—

(i) The sum of—

(a) The gain recognized (before application of this part) upon a sale or other disposition and

(b) The gain recognized under section 607(g)(5) of the Act upon such sale or other disposition which is not taken into account under (a) of this subdivision, or

(ii) The excess of the gross proceeds (as defined in subparagraph (1) of this paragraph) over the sum of—

(a) Amounts necessarily paid or incurred in connection with the sale or other disposition and

(b) The amounts of any indebtedness assumed by the purchaser of such vessel, subject to which the purchaser acquires the vessel, or secured by such vessel which the party must satisfy out of the proceeds of the sale or other disposition.

(3) Deposits of net proceeds. (i) For purposes of this part, any net proceeds deposited for the year of sale or other disposition shall be treated as an amount realized that year. In the case of the sale or other disposition of properties which include at least one agreement vessel, or share therein, for a lump sum, the gross proceeds shall be allocated between agreement vessels and other property in proportion to the aggregate fair market values of each of the two types of property on the date of the sale or other disposition. For purposes of determining the amount of net proceeds permitted to be deposited pursuant to this paragraph as a result of such a sale or other disposition, the party may use the aggregate gross proceeds that were allocated to the agreement vessels or, if less than the entire aggregate net proceeds is deposited, may further allocate the gross proceeds among each vessel or share therein. In order not to take gain into account, as provided by section 607(d)(1)(B) of the Act, the party must deposit an amount equal to the entire net proceeds realized or to be realized with respect to the agreement vessel sold or otherwise disposed of. Such deposit must be in the form of money and securities and stock of a type specified in section 607(c) of the Act other than securities or stock issued by the party or a person related to the party (as described in subdivision (ii) of this subparagraph); however, if the purchaser or transferee is not related to the party (as described in subdivision (ii) of this subparagraph), the deposit may include any intangible property received on such sale or other disposition.

(ii) For purposes of the preceding sentence a person is a related person to another person [if]—

(a) The relationship between such persons would result in disallowance of losses under section 267 or 707(b) of the Code, or

(b) Such persons are members of the same controlled group of corporations (as defined in section 1563(a) of the Code, except that "more than 50 percent" shall be substituted for "at least 80 percent" each place it appears therein).

(4) Related purchaser. In the event the party and the purchaser are owned or controlled directly or indirectly by the same interests within the meaning of section 482 of the Code and the regulations thereunder, the amount realized or to be realized shall be the fair market value of the vessels sold or otherwise disposed of. In such case, the party shall furnish evidence sufficient, in the opinion of the Secretary of Commerce, to establish that the amount realized or to be realized is the fair market value.

(5) Net proceeds from insurance or indemnity. Where the net proceeds of insurance or indemnity are received in more than one payment, the deposit of such net proceeds shall relate to the taxable year of receipt. The net proceeds from insurance or indemnity attributable to an agreement vessel under a contract of insurance or indemnity as compensation for damages done to the vessel (other than amounts intended to compensate for loss of profits) is the greater of—

(i) The sum of—

(a) The gain recognized (before application of this part) under such a contract and

(b) The gain recognized under section 607(g)(5) of the Act upon such contract which is not taken into account under (a) of this subdivision,

(ii) The excess of the gross proceeds the party received under such contract over the sum of—

(a) The amounts necessarily paid or incurred purely for the collection of such compensation and

(b) The amount of any indebtedness secured by such vessel which the party was required to satisfy out of the amount of such insurance of indemnity received.

(6) Installment sale of agreement vessel. (i) If the party deposits in a fund net proceeds from the sale or other disposition of an agreement vessel, gain from the disposition of the vessel may be reported under the installment method if such method is otherwise available under section 453 of the Code. If an installment obligation is not deposited into the fund, the ceiling on deposits described in paragraph (a) of this section is not increased by the income which consists of interest on each installment payment.

(ii) If the party properly elects the installment method under section 453 of the Code with respect to the sale or other disposition of an agreement vessel, then—

(a) The evidences of indebtedness of the purchaser (within the meaning of section 453(b) of the Code) which are not deposited into the fund shall not be considered to be gross proceeds or net proceeds,

(b) For purposes of this subparagraph, for each taxable year the amount of net proceeds realized and required to be deposited shall be the amount determined under subdivision (iii) of this subparagraph or, if the "short-cut" method is permitted, under subdivision (v) of this subparagraph,

(c) If the net proceeds so determined for a year are not timely deposited, the provisions of subdivision (vi) of this paragraph shall apply, and

(d) The income (other than interest) on each installment payment shall be deemed to consist of any gain which is treated as ordinary income by reason of the application of section 1245(a)(1) of the Code until all such gain is reported, then any gain which is treated as ordinary income by reason of the application of section 607(g)(5) of the Act and § 3.6(e) until all such gain has been reported, and the remaining portion (if any) of such income shall be deemed to consist of gain to which neither section 1245(a)(1) nor section 607(g)(5) of the Act and § 3.6(e) applies.

(iii) With respect to the sale or other disposition of an agreement vessel, the amount of net proceeds for any taxable year which must be timely deposited is equal to the greater of (a) the gain which would be recognized in that taxable year if the deposit were not made or (b) an amount equal to (1) the installment payment (within the meaning of § 1.453-4(c) of the Income Tax Regulations of this chapter) received during the taxable year minus (2) the sum of the expenses necessarily paid or incurred (or so treated under subdivision (iv) of this subparagraph during such taxable year in connection with the installment sale and amounts of any indebtedness which the party must satisfy out of the proceeds of the sale in such taxable year. For purposes of this subdivision (iii), but not subdivision (iv) of this subparagraph, the amount in (b) of this subdivision shall not be less than zero.

(iv) If for any taxable year the amount in subdivision (iii)(a) of this subparagraph exceeds the amount in subdivision (iii) (b) of this subparagraph, then such excess is an unabsorbed portion of expenses and indebtedness, which shall be treated as an expense or indebtedness described in subdivision (iii)(b)(2) of this subparagraph in the subsequent taxable year. Thus, for example, if the amount in subdivision (iii)(b) of this subparagraph is less than zero, such excess is the sum of such amount and the amount in subdivision (iii)(a) of this subparagraph.

(v) The "short-cut" method of this subdivision is permitted if the purchaser takes the vessel subject to, or assumes, a liability which was a lien on the vessel, and the amount of such liability at the time of the sale was in excess of the party's adjusted basis in such vessel. In such a case, the amount of net proceeds for any taxable year which must be timely deposited is equal to the gain recognized for the taxable year under section 453 of the Code and the regulations thereunder.

(vi) With respect to any sale or other disposition of an agreement vessel, deposits of net proceeds realized (determined under subdivision (iii) or (v) of this subparagraph) shall be contingent deposits until there is deposited the entire net proceeds to be realized (determined without regard to this paragraph) from such sale or other disposition or from the earlier disposition or satisfaction of installment obligations received pursuant to such sale or other disposition. If for any taxable year such net proceeds are not timely deposited pursuant to subdivision (iii) or (v) of this subparagraph, all amounts previously deposited with respect to such sale or other disposition shall be withdrawn in a nonqualified withdrawal under § 3.7, and such withdrawal shall be considered to have taken place on the last day of the party's first taxable year during which the net proceeds (which were not deposited) were received. See 46 CFR § 390 and 50 CFR Part 259.

(vii) The provisions of this subparagraph are illustrated by the following examples:

Example (1). X Corporation, which uses the calendar year as its taxable year and maintains a fund described in § 3.1 contracts to sell an agreement vessel (with an adjusted basis of $20,000) used in its shipping business for $200,000 plus a sufficient amount of interest so that section 483 does not apply. Thus, the gain realized is $180,000. The terms of the sale are that the purchaser is to assume the outstanding amount ($90,000) of a purchase-money mortgage, followed by 10 equal semi-annual principal payments of $11,000 for the 5 consecutive taxable years after the year of sale. Under § 1.453-4(c) of the Income Tax Regulations of this chapter, the excess of the mortgage ($90,000) over X's adjusted basis ($20,000), or $70,000, is included as a payment received in the year of sale. Since under section 453(b)(2)(A) of the Code payments in the taxable year of sale may not exceed 30 percent of the selling price (30% of $200,000 = $60,000), X may not elect under section 453 of the Code to report the gain under the installment method and the provisions of this subparagraph do not apply to such sale.

Example (2). (a) Assume the same facts as in example (1) except that X sells the vessel in 1972 when it has an adjusted basis of $100,000 and the terms of payment of the selling price of $200,000 are the assumption for an outstanding amount of a purchase-money mortgage of $50,000, a cash downpayment of $50,000 in 1972 (the year of the sale), and principal payments of $20,000 per year for the next 5 years. Thus, since the outstanding amount of the purchase-money mortgage ($50,000) is not greater than the vessel's adjusted basis ($100,000), the "contract price" within the meaning of § 1.453-4(c) of the Income Tax Regulations of this chapter is $150,000 i.e., downpayment, $50,000, plus 5 payments of $20,000 each, $100,000. Assume further that X incurred $10,000 in selling expenses of the type described in subdivision (iii)(b)(2) of this subparagraph. Thus, X's gain on the sale is $90,000 (i.e., selling price, $200,000 minus adjusted basis, $100,000, minus selling expenses, $10,000) and the gross profit realized or to be realized when the property is paid for (within the meaning of § 1.453-1(b) of the Income Tax Regulations of this chapter) is also $90,000.

(b) X properly elects to report the sale under the installment method under section 453 of the Code since payments in the year of sale ($50,000) do not exceed 30 percent of the selling price of $200,000, or $60,000.

(c) Since X has elected under section 453 of the Code to report gain on the installment method, in order to defer the gain on the sale as provided by section 607(d)(1)(B) of the Act and § 3.3(b)(2)(i), subdivision (ii)(c) of this subparagraph requires that X must timely deposit into the fund the net proceeds for each taxable year in which received.

(d) For each taxable year, the net proceeds which must be timely deposited under subdivision (iii) of this subparagraph are determined as follows:

	1972	Next 5 yrs
(1) Installment payment	$50,000	$20,000
(2) Multiply by gross profit percentage: gross profit ($90,000) divided by contract price ($150,000) (percent)	60	60
(3) Gain recognized	$30,000	$12,000
(4) Selling expenses	$10,000	0
(5) Indebtedness which party must satisfy	0	0
(6) Sum of lines (4) and (5)	10,000	0
(7) Line (1) minus line (6)	40,000	$20,000
(8) Required deposit: greater of line (3) or (7)	40,000	20,000

In the above computation, there is no unabsorbed portion of expenses and indebtedness under subdivision (iv) of this subparagraph since for no taxable year does line (3) exceed line (7).

(e) For purposes of subdivision (vi) of this subparagraph, the entire net proceeds determined under subparagraph (2) of this paragraph which must be deposited before any deposits will no longer be contingent deposits is the excess of the gross proceeds to be realized of $200,000 (i.e., the sum of the mortgage assumed, $50,000, the downpayment, $50,000, and the 5 annual $20,000 payments, $100,000) over the sum of selling expenses ($10,000) and the amount of the mortgage assumed ($50,000), or $140,000.

(f) Of the $90,000 gain to be recognized upon sale of the vessel, assume that $60,000 would be recognized as ordinary income by reason of the application of section 1245(a)(1) of the Code (relating to depreciation recapture), $20,000 would be recognized as ordinary income under section 607(g)(5) of the Act and § 3.6(e)(1) (relating to ordinary income treatment of certain gains), and $10,000 would be recognized as gain from the sale or exchange of property to which section 1231 of the Code applies. Under § 1.1245-6(d) of the Income Tax Regulations of this chapter and § 3.6(e)(1), the $80,000 of ordinary income (i.e., $60,000 plus $20,000) is treated as recognized first. Thus, under section 607(e) of the Act and § 3.4, the deposit of the entire net proceeds of $140,000 will result in the following additions to the fund accounts in the years indicated in the table below:

[In thousands]

Year	Payment (1)	Net proceeds (2)	Gain (3)	Ordinary income account (4)	Capital income account (5)	Capital account (6)
1972	$ 50	$ 40	$30	$30	....	$10
1973	20	20	12	12	....	8
1974	20	20	12	12	....	8
1975	20	20	12	12	....	8
1976	20	20	12	12	....	8
1977	20	20	12	2	10	8
Total	150	140	90	80	10	50

Example (3). (a) Assume the same facts as in example (2) except that X's adjusted basis in the vessel at the time of sale is $30,000, the sale price is $150,000, and the terms of payment are the assumption of the outstanding amount of a purchase-money mortgage of $45,000, cash downpayment of $25,000, and principal payments of $40,000 per year for the next 2 years. Under § 1.453-4(c) of the Income Tax Regulations of this chapter, the excess ($15,000) of the outstanding amount of the purchase-money mortgage assumed ($45,000) over X's adjusted basis in the vessel ($30,000) is treated as a payment received in the year of sale and thus, the payments in the year of sale are the sum of such excess, $15,000, and the downpayment, $25,000, or $40,000. Accordingly, the "contract price" is $120,000, i.e., the payments in the year of sale, $40,000, plus two payments of $40,000 each. Selling expenses remain at $10,000 in the year of sale. Thus, X's gain on the sale is $110,000 (i.e., selling price, $150,000, minus adjusted basis, $30,000, minus selling expenses $10,000) and the gross profit realized or to be realized when the property is paid for (within the meaning of § 1.453-1(b) of the Income Tax Regulations of this chapter) is also $110,000.

(b) X properly elects to report the sale under the installment method under section 453 of the Code since payments in the year of sale ($40,000) do not exceed 30 percent of the selling price of $150,000, or $45,000.

(c) Since X has elected under section 453 of the Code to report gain on the installment method, in order to defer the gain on the sale as provided by section 607(d)(1)(B) of the Act and § 3.3(b)(2)(i), subdivision (ii)(b) of this subparagraph requires that X must timely deposit into the fund the net proceeds for each taxable year in which received.

(d) For each taxable year, the net proceeds which must be timely deposited under subdivision (iii) of this subparagraph are determined as follows:

	1972	1973	1974
(1) Installment payment	$40,000	$40,000	$40,000
(2) Multiply by gross profit percentage: gross profit ($110,000) divided contract price ($120,000) (percent)	91⅔	91⅔	91⅔
(3) Gain recognized	$36,667	$36,667	$36,667
(4) Selling expenses	$10,000	0	0
(5) Indebtedness which party must satisfy	0	0	0
(6) Unabsorbed portion of expenses and indebtedness under subdivision (iv) of subparagraph: line (10)(e) from preceding year	......	$ 6,667	$ 3,333
(7) Sum of lines (4), (5), and (6)	$10,000	6,667	3,333
(8) Excess of line (1) over line (7)	30,000	33,333	36,667
(9) Required deposit: greater of line (3) or line (8)	36,667	36,667	36,667
(10) Unabsorbed portion carried forward to subsequent year:			

(a) Line 3	36,667	36,667	36,667
(b) Line 1	40,000	40,000	40,000
(c) Line 7	10,000	6,667	3,333
(d) Line (b) minus line (c)	30,000	33,333	36,667
(e) If line (a) exceeds line (d), the excess	6,667	3,333[1]	......

[1] Difference due to rounding.

(e) Since the outstanding amount of the purchase-money mortgage ($45,000) exceeds X's adjusted basis in the vessel ($30,000), X is permitted to use the "short-cut" method under subdivision (v) of this subparagraph, requiring the deposit of X's gain from the sale in each year ($36,667, as determined under line (3) of (d) of this example), which gives the same result as the determination under subdivision (iii) of this subparagraph.

Example (4). (a) Assume the same facts as in example (1) except that X sells the vessel in 1972 when it has an adjusted basis of $106,000 and the terms of payment of the selling price of $150,000 are the assumption of an outstanding amount of a purchase-money mortgage of $90,000, no payment in the year of sale, and principal payments of $19,000, $21,000, and $20,000, respectively, for the next 3 years. Thus, since the outstanding amount of the purchase-money mortgage ($90,000) is not greater than the vessel's adjusted basis ($106,000), the "contract price" within the meaning of § 1.453-4(c) of the Income Tax Regulations of this chapter is $60,000, i.e., the sum of the 3 annual payments. Assume further that X incurred $20,000 in selling expenses of the type described in subdivision (iii)(b)(2) of this subparagraph. Thus, X's gain on the sale is $24,000 (i.e., selling price, $150,000, minus adjusted basis $106,000, minus selling expenses, $20,000) and the gross profit realized or to be realized when the property is paid for (within the meaning of § 1.453-1(b) of the Income Tax Regulations of this chapter) is also $24,000. (b) X properly elects to report the sale under the installment method under section 453 of the Code since payments in the year of sale ($0) do not exceed 30 percent of the selling price of $150,000, or $45,000. (c) Since X has elected under section 453 of the Code to report gain on the installment method, in order to defer the gain on the sale as provided by section 607(d)(1)(B) of the Act and § 3.3(b)(2)(i), subdivision (ii)(b) of this subparagraph requires that X must timely deposit into the fund the net proceeds for each taxable year in which received. (d) For each taxable year, the net proceeds which must be timely deposited under subdivision (iii) of this subparagraph are determined as follows:

	1972	1973	1974	1975
(1) Installment payment	0	$19,000	$21,000	$20,000
(2) Multiply by gross profit percentage: gross profit ($24,000) divided contract price ($60,000) (percent)	40	40	40	40
(3) Gain recognized	0	$ 7,600	$ 8,400	$ 8,000
(4) Selling expenses	$20,000	0	0	0
(5) Indebtedness which party must satisfy	0	0	0	0
(6) Unabsorbed portion of expenses and indebtedness under subdivision (iv) of subparagraph: line (10)(e) from preceding year	......	$20,000	$ 8,600	0
(7) Sum of lines (4), (5), and (6)	$20,000	20,000	8,600	0
(8) Excess of line (1) over line (7)	0	0	12,400	$20,000
(9) Required deposit: greater of line (3) or line (8)	0	7,600	12,400	20,000
(10) Unabsorbed portion carried forward to subsequent year:				
(a) Line 3	0	7,600	8,400	8,000
(b) Line 1	0	19,000	21,000	20,000
(c) Line 3	20,000	20,000	8,600	0
(d) Line (b) minus line (c)	(20,000)	(1,000)	12,400	20,000
(a) If line (e) exceeds line (d), the excess	20,000	8,600	......	......

(g) Special rules for nonmoney deposits and withdrawals. * * *

(2) Election not to treat deposits of property other than money as a sale or exchange at the time of deposit. A party may elect to treat a deposit of property as if no sale or other taxable event had occurred on the date of deposit. If such election is made, in the taxable year the fund disposes of the property, or the party disposes of the fund in a transaction which is treated as not constituting a nonqualified withdrawal by reason of the application of § 3.8(b)(2) or (c), then the party shall as gain or loss with respect to nonfund property the amount he would have recognized on the day the property was deposited into the fund had the election not been made. The party's holding period with respect to such property shall not include the period of time such property was held by the fund. If the party disposes of a fund which contains property subject to the election provided by this subparagraph in a transaction which is treated as not constituting a nonqualified withdrawal by reason of the application of § 3.8(b)(1) then for purposes of determining the basis of property received by the party in such transaction, the basis of property in the fund subject to such election is the party's, not the fund's, adjusted basis for such property. The election shall be made by a statement to that effect, attached

to the party's Federal income tax return for the taxable year to which the deposit relates, or, if such return is filed before such deposit is made, attached to the party's return for the taxable year during which the deposit is actually made. Such statement shall also contain, or shall be considered as containing, an agreement by the party to be bound by the rules of this paragraph.

* * * * *

§ 3.3 Nontaxability of deposits.

(a) In general. Section 607(d) of the Act sets forth the rules concerning the income tax effects of deposits made with respect to ceilings described in section 607(b) and § 3.2. The specific treatment of deposits with respect to each of the subceilings is set forth in paragraph (b) of this section.

(b) Treatment of deposits. *(1) Earnings of agreement vessels.* Section 607(d)(1)(A) of the Act provides that taxable income of the party (determined without regard to section 607 of the Act) shall be reduced by an amount equal to the amount deposited for the taxable year out of amounts referred to in section 607(b)(1)(A) of the Act and § 3.2(a)(1)(i). For computation of the foreign tax credit see paragraph (i) of this section.

(2) Net proceeds from agreement vessels and fund earnings. (i) (a) Section 607(d)(1)(B) provides that gain from a transaction referred to in section 607(b)(1)(C) of the Act and § 3.2(a)(1)(iii) (relating to ceilings on deposits of net proceeds from the sale or other disposition of agreement vessels) is not to be taken into account for purposes of the Code if an amount equal to the net proceeds from transactions referred to in such sections is deposited in the fund. Such gain is to be excluded from gross income of the party for the taxable year to which such deposit relates. Thus, the gain will not be taken into account in applying section 1231 of the Code for the year to which the deposit relates.

(b) [Reserved]

(ii) (a) Section 607(d)(1)(C) of the Act provides that the earnings (including gains and losses) from the investment and reinvestment of amounts held in the fund and referred to in section 607(b)(1)(D) of the Act and § 3.2(a)(1)(iv) shall not be taken into account for purposes of the Code if an amount equal to such earnings is deposited into the fund. Such earnings are to be excluded from the gross income of the party for the taxable year to which such deposit relates. *(b)* However, for purposes of the basis adjustment under section 1232(a)(3)(E) of the Code, the ratable monthly portion of original issue discount included in gross income shall be determined without regard to section 607(d)(1)(C) of the Act.

(iii) In determining the tax liability of a party to whom subparagraph (1) of this paragraph applies, taxable income, determined after application of subparagraph (1) of this paragraph, is in effect reduced by the portion of deposits which represent gain or earnings respectively referred to in subdivision (i) or (ii) of this subparagraph. The excess, if any, of such portion over taxable income determined after application of subparagraph (1) of this paragraph is taken into account in computing the net operating loss (under section 172 of the Code) for the taxable year to which such deposits relate.

(3) Time for making deposits. (i) This section applies with respect to an amount only if such amount is deposited in the fund pursuant to the agreement and not later than the time provided in subdivision (ii), (iii), or (iv) of this subparagraph for the making of such deposit or the date the Secretary of Commerce provides, whichever is earlier.

(ii) Except as provided in subdivision (iii) or (iv) of this subparagraph, a deposit may be made not later than the last day prescribed by law (including extensions thereof) for filing the party's Federal income tax return for the taxable year to which such deposit relates.

(iii) If the party is a subsidized operator under an operating-differential subsidy contract, and does not receive on or before the 59th day preceding such last day, payment of all or part of the accrued operating-differential subsidy payable for the taxable year, the party may deposit an amount equivalent to the unpaid accrued operating-differential subsidy on or before the 60th day after receipt of payment of the accrued operating-differential subsidy.

(iv) A deposit pursuant to § 3.2(a)(3)(i) (relating to underdeposits caused by audit adjustments) must be made on or before the date prescribed for such a deposit in § 3.2(a)(4).

(4) Date of deposits. (i) Except as otherwise provided in subdivisions (ii) and (iii) of this subparagraph (with respect to taxable years beginning after December 31, 1969, and prior to January 1, 1972), in § 3.2(a)(2)(i), or in § 3.10(b), deposits made in a fund within the time specified in subparagraph (3) of this paragraph are deemed to have been made on the date of actual deposit.

(ii) (a) For taxable years beginning after December 31, 1969, and prior to January 1, 1971, where an application for a fund is filed by a taxpayer prior to January 1, 1972, and an agreement is executed and entered into by the taxpayer prior to March 1, 1972,

(b) For taxable years beginning after December 31, 1970, and prior to January 1, 1972, where an application for a fund is filed by a taxpayer prior to January 1, 1973, and an agreement is executed and entered into by the taxpayer prior to March 1, 1973, and

(c) For taxable years beginning after December 31, 1971, and prior to January 1, 1975, where an agreement is executed and entered into by the taxpayer on or prior to the due date, with extensions, for the filing of his Federal income tax return for such taxable year, deposits in a fund which are made within 60 days after the date of execution of the agreement, or on or before the due date, with extensions thereof, for the filing of his Federal income tax return for such taxable year or years, whichever date shall be later, shall be deemed to have been made on the date of the actual deposit or as of the close of business of the last regular business day of each such taxable year or years to which such deposits relate, whichever day is earlier.

(iii) Notwithstanding subdivision (ii) of this subparagraph, for taxable years beginning after December 31, 1970, and ending prior to January 1, 1972, deposits made later than the last date permitted under subdivision (ii) but on or before January 9, 1973, in a fund pursuant to an agreement with the Secretary of Commerce, acting by and through the Administrator of the National Oceanic and Atmospheric Administration, shall be deemed to have been made on the date of the actual deposit or as of the close of business of the last regular business day of such taxable year, whichever is earlier.

(c) Determination of earnings and profits. [Reserved]

(d) Accumulated earnings tax. As provided in section 607(d)(1)(E) of the Act amounts, while held in the fund, are not to be taken into account in computing the "accumulated taxable income" of the party within the meaning of section

531 of the Code. Amounts while held in the fund are considered held for the purpose of acquiring, constructing, or reconstructing a qualified vessel or barges and containers which are part of the complement of a qualified vessel or the payment of the principal on indebtedness incurred in connection with any such acquisition, construction, or reconstruction. Thus, for example, if the reasonable needs of the business (within the meaning of section 537 of the Code) justify a greater amount of accumulation for providing replacement vessels than can be satisfied out of the fund, such greater amount accumulated outside of the fund shall be considered to be accumulated for the reasonable needs of the business. For a further example, although amounts in the fund are not taken into account in applying the tax imposed by section 531 of the Code, to the extent there are amounts in a fund to provide for replacing a vessel, amounts accumulated outside of the fund to replace the same vessel are not considered to be accumulated for the reasonable needs of the business.

(e) Nonapplicability of section 1231. If an amount equivalent to gain from a transaction referred to in section 607(b)(1)(C) of the Act and § 3.2(c)(1) and (5) is deposited into the fund and, therefore, such gain is not taken into account in computing gross income under the provisions of paragraph (b)(2) of this section, then such gain will not be taken into account for purposes of the computations under section 1231 of the Code.

(f) Deposits of capital gains. In respect of capital gains which are not included in the gross income of the party by virtue of a deposit to which section 607(d) of the Act and this section apply, the following provisions of the Code do not apply: the minimum tax for tax preferences imposed by section 56 of the Code; the alternative tax imposed by section 1201 of the Code on the excess of the party's net long-term capital gain over his net short-term capital loss; and, in the case of a taxpayer other than a corporation, the deduction provided by section 1202 of the Code of 50 percent of the amount of such excess. However, section 56 may apply upon a nonqualified withdrawal with respect to amounts treated under § 3.7(d)(2) as being made out of the capital gain account.

(g) Deposits of dividends. The deduction provided by section 243 of the Code (relating to the deductions for dividends from a domestic corporation received by a corporation shall not apply in respect of dividends (earned on assets held in the fund) which are deposited into a fund, and which, by virtue of such deposits and the provisions of section 607(d) of the Act and this section, are not included in the gross income of the party.

(h) Presumption of validity of deposit. All amounts deposited in the fund shall be presumed to have been deposited pursuant to an agreement unless, after an examination of the facts upon the request of the Commissioner of Internal Revenue or his delegate, the Secretary of Commerce determines otherwise. The Commissioner or his delegate will request such a determination where there is a substantial question as to whether a deposit is made in accordance with an agreement.

(i) Special rules for application of the foreign tax credit. *(1) In general.* For purposes of computing the limitation under section 904 of the Code on the amount of the credit provided by section 901 of the Code (relating to the foreign tax credit) the party's taxable income from any source without the United States and the party's entire taxable income are to be determined after application of section 607(d) of the Act. Thus, amounts deposited for the taxable year with respect to amounts referred to in section 607(b)(1)(A) of the Act and § 3.2(a)(1)(i) (relating to taxable income attributable to the operation of agreement vessels) shall be treated as a deduction in arriving at the party's taxable income from sources without the United States (subject to the apportionment rules in subparagraph (2) of this paragraph) and the party's entire taxable income for the taxable year. Amounts deposited with respect to gain described in section 607(d)(1)(B) of the Act and § 3.2(c) (relating to net proceeds from the sale or other disposition of an agreement vessel and net proceeds from insurance or indemnity) and amounts deposited with respect to earnings described in section 607(d)(1)(C) of the Act and paragraph (b)(2)(ii) (relating to earnings from the investment and reinvestment of amounts held in a fund) of this section are not taken into account for purposes of the Code and hence are not included in the party's taxable income from sources without the United States or in the party's entire taxable income for purposes of this paragraph.

(2) Apportionment of taxable income attributable to agreement vessels. For purposes of computing the overall limitation under section 904(a)(2) of the Code the amount of the deposit made with respect to taxable income attributable to agreement vessels pursuant to § 3.2(a)(1)(i) which is allocable to sources without the United States is the total amount of such deposit multiplied by a fraction the numerator of which is the gross income from sources without the United States from the operation of agreement vessels and the denominator of which is the total gross income from the operation of agreement vessels computed as provided in § 3.2(b)(2). For purposes of this paragraph gross income from sources without the United States attributable to the operation of agreement vessels is to be determined under sections 861 through 863 of the Code and under the taxpayer's usual method of accounting provided such method is reasonable and in keeping with sound accounting practice. Any computation under the per-country limitation of section 904(a)(1) shall be made in the manner consistent with the provisions of the preceding sentences of this subparagraph.

T.D. 7398, 1/23/76.

PAR. 37. Paragraph (b) of § 3.3 is amended by removing the phrase "section 1232(a)(3)(E)" every place it appears and adding in its place the phrase "section 1272(d)(2)", and by removing the phrase "ratable monthly portion" every place it appears and adding in its place the word "amount".

Proposed § 3.3 [Amended] [*For Preamble, see ¶ 151,065*]

• ***Caution:*** Prop reg § 1.482-2 was finalized by T.D. 8204, 5/20/88. Prop regs §§ 1.163-7, 1.446-2, 1.483-1 through -5, 1.1001-1, 1.1012-1, 1.1271 through -3, 1.1272-1, 1.1273-1, 1.1273-2, 1.1274-1 throught -7, 1.1274A-1, 1.1275-1 through -3, and 1.1275-5 were withdrawn by the Treasury on 12/22/92, 57 Fed. Reg. 67050. Prop reg § 1.1275-4 was superseded by the Treasury on 12/16/94, Fed. Reg. 59, 64884, which was finalized by T.D. 8674, 6/11/96.

PAR. 2. Section 3.3, as adopted by Treasury Decision 7398, is amended by revising paragraph (b)(2)(i)(b) and paragraph (c). These revised provisions read as follows:

Proposed § 3.3 Nontaxability of deposits. [*For Preamble, see ¶ 150,183*]

* * * * *

(b) Treatment of deposit. * * *

(2) Net proceeds from agreement vessels and fund earnings. (i) (a) * * *

(b) However, if (1) a party transfers a vessel, (2) the basis of the property the party receives is determined by reference to the basis of such vessel or such vessel's basis in the hands of the transferee is determined by reference to its basis in the hands of the party, (3) the party deposits the net proceeds of the transfer into the fund, and (4) by reason of applying 607(d)(1)(B) of the Act the party's gain is not taken into account, then for the purpose of determining the basis of such property received, of such vessel in the hands of the transferee, or both (as the case may be) such gain shall be treated as if it were recognized. The provisions of this subdivision (b) are illustrated in example (4) of § 3.6(e)(7)(ii).

* * * * *

(c) Determination of earnings and profits. Under section 607(d)(1)(D) of the Act, in general the earnings and profits of any corporation (within the meaning of section 316 of the Code) shall be determined without regard to this part. Thus, for example—

(1) Although certain amounts deposited into the fund reduce taxable income and certain other amounts deposited into the fund result in an exclusion from gross income, earnings and profits of the corporation are not reduced by the amount of such deposits.

(2) Earnings and profits are not increased when amounts withdrawn from the fund are included in income under § 3.7(d).

(3) For purposes of the third sentence of section 312(f)(1) of the Code (see § 1.312-7(c) of the Income Tax Regulations of this chapter), the reduction in basis provided by § 3.6(c) of a qualified vessel purchased with fund assets or, in certain circumstances, of a vessel other than a qualified vessel is not a proper adjustment for earnings and profits purposes and thus, the depreciation deduction with respect to, and the gain or loss on the sale of, such a vessel shall, for earnings and profits purposes, be determined as if such reduction had not been made.

(4) The earnings (including gains and losses) from the investment and reinvestment of amounts held in the fund is a proper adjustment for earnings and profits purposes.

(5) Interest determined under § 3.7 which is allowed as a deduction under section 163 of the Code is allowed as a deduction in computing earnings and profits.

(6) The gain or loss recognized by a party on the disposition by the fund of property subject to an election under § 3.2(g)(2) not to recognize gain or loss upon the deposit is a proper adjustment for earnings and profits purposes.

(7) Deposits of property considered to be a sale under § 3.2(g)(1)(iii) increase or decrease earnings and profits by the amount of gain or loss included in the party's income from the taxable year.

* * * * *

§ 3.4 Establishment of accounts.

(a) In general. Section 607(e)(1) of the Act requires that three bookkeeping or memorandum accounts are to be established and maintained within the fund: The capital account, the capital gain account, and the ordinary income account. Deposits of the amounts under the subceilings in section 607(b) of the Act and § 3.2 are allocated among the accounts under section 607(e) of the Act and this section.

(b) Capital account. The capital account shall consist of:

(1) Amounts referred to in section 607(b)(1)(B) of the Act and § 3.2(a)(1)(ii) (relating to deposits for depreciation),

(2) Amounts referred to in section 607(b)(1)(C) of the Act and § 3.2(a)(1)(iii) (relating to deposits of net proceeds from the sale or other disposition of agreement vessels) other than that portion thereof which represents gain not taken into account for purposes of computing gross income by reason of section 607(d)(1)(B) of the Act and § 3.3(b)(2) (relating to nontaxability of gain from the sale or other disposition of an agreement vessel),

(3) Amounts representing 85 percent of any dividend received by the fund with respect to which the party would, but for section 607(d)(1)(C) of the Act and § 3.3(b)(2)(ii) (relating to nontaxability of deposits of earnings from investment and reinvestment of amounts held in a fund), be allowed a deduction under section 243 of the Code, and

(4) Amounts received by the fund representing interest income which is exempt from taxation under section 103 of the Code.

(c) Capital gain account. The capital gain account shall consist of amounts which represent the excess of (1) deposits of long-term capital gains on property referred to in section 607(b)(1)(C) and (D) of the Act and § 3.2(a)(1)(iii) and (iv) (relating respectively to certain agreement vessels and fund assets), over (2) amounts representing losses from the sale or exchange of assets held in the fund for more than 6 months (for purposes of this section referred to as "long-term capital losses"). For purposes of this paragraph and paragraph (d)(2) of this section, an agreement vessel disposed of at a gain shall be treated as a capital asset to the extent that gain thereon is not treated as ordinary income, including gain which is ordinary income under section 607(g)(5) of the Act (relating to treatment of gain on disposition of a vessel with a reduced basis) and § 3.6(e) or under section 1245 of the Code (relating to gain from disposition of certain depreciable property). For provisions relating to the treatment of short-term capital gains on certain transactions involving agreement vessels or realized by the fund, see paragraph (d) of this section. For rules relating to the treatment of capital losses on assets held in the fund, see paragraph (e) of this section.

(d) Ordinary income account. The ordinary income account shall consist of:

(1) Amounts referred to in section 607(b)(1)(A) of the Act and § 3.2(a)(1)(i) (relating to taxable income attributable to the operation of an agreement vessel),

(2) Amounts representing (i) deposits of gains from the sale or exchange of capital assets held for 6 months or less (for purposes of this section referred to as "short-term capital gains") referred to in section 607(b)(1)(C) or (D) of the Act and § 3.2(a)(1)(iii) and (iv) (relating respectively to certain agreement vessels and fund assets), reduced by (ii) amounts representing losses from the sale or exchange of capital assets held in the fund for 6 months or less (for purposes of this section referred to as "short-term capital losses"). For rules relating to the treatment of certain agreement vessels as capital assets, see paragraph (c) of this section,

(3) Amounts representing interest (not including any tax-exempt interest referred to in section 607(e)(2)(D) of the Act and paragraph (b)(4) of this section) and other ordinary in-

come received on assets held in the fund (not including any dividend referred to in section 607(e)(2)(C) of the Act and subparagraph (5) of this paragraph),

(4) Amounts representing ordinary income from a transaction (involving certain net proceeds with respect to an agreement vessel) described in section 607(b)(1)(C) of the Act and § 3.2(a)(1)(iii), including gain which is ordinary income under section 607(g)(5) of the Act and § 3.6(e) (relating to treatment of gain on the disposition of a vessel with a reduced basis) or under section 1245 of the Code (relating to gain from disposition of certain depreciable property), and

(5) Fifteen percent of any dividend referred to in section 607(e)(2)(C) of the Act and paragraph (b)(3) of this section received on any assets held in the fund.

(e) Limitation on deduction for capital losses on assets held in a fund. Except on termination of a fund, long-term (and short-term) capital losses on assets held in the fund shall be allowed only as an offset to long-term (and short-term) capital gains on assets held in the fund, but only if such gains are deposited into the fund, and shall not be allowed as an offset to any capital gains on assets not held in the fund. The net long-term capital loss of the fund for the taxable year shall reduce the earliest long-term capital gains in the capital gain account at the beginning of the taxable year and the net short-term capital loss for the taxable year shall reduce the earliest short-term capital gains remaining in the ordinary income account at the beginning of the taxable year. Any such losses that are in excess of the capital gains in the respective accounts shall reduce capital gains deposited into the respective accounts in subsequent years (without regard to section 1212, relating to capital loss carrybacks and carryovers). On termination of a fund, any net long-term capital loss in the capital gain account and any net short-term capital loss remaining in the ordinary income account is to be taken into account for purposes of computing the party's taxable income for the year of termination as a long-term or short-term (as the case may be) capital loss recognized in the year the fund is terminated. With respect to the determination of the basis to a fund of assets held in such fund, see § 3.2(g).

T.D. 7398, 1/23/76, amend T.D. 7728, 10/31/80, T.D. 7831, 9/3/82.

§ 3.5 Qualified withdrawals.

(a) In general. *(1)* A qualified withdrawal is one made from the fund during the taxable year which is in accordance with section 607(f)(1) of the Act, the agreement, and with regulations prescribed by the Secretary of Commerce and which is for the acquisition, construction, or reconstruction of a qualified vessel (as defined in § 3.11(a)(2)) or barges and containers which are part of the complement of a qualified vessel (or shares in such vessels, barges, and containers), or for the payment of the principal of indebtedness incurred in connection with the acquisition, construction, or reconstruction of such qualified vessel (or a barge or container which is part of the complement of a qualified vessel).

(2) For purposes of this section the term "share" is used to reflect an interest in a vessel and means a proprietary interest in a vessel such as, for example, that which results from joint ownership. Accordingly, a share within the meaning of § 3.2(f) (relating to the definition of "agreement vessel" for the purpose of making deposits) will not necessarily be sufficient to be treated as a share within the meaning of this section.

(3) For purposes of this section, the term "acquisition" means any of the following:

(i) Any acquisition, but only to the extent the basis of the property acquired in the hands of the transferee is its cost. Thus, for example, if a party transfers a vessel and $1 million in an exchange for another vessel which qualifies for nonrecognition of gain or loss under section 1031(a) of the Code (relating to like-kind exchange), there is an acquisition to the extent of $1 million.

(ii) With respect to a lessee's interest in a vessel, expenditures which result in increasing the amounts with respect to which a deduction for depreciation (or amortization in lieu thereof) is allowable.

(iii) [Reserved]

(b) Payments on indebtedness. Payments on indebtedness may constitute qualified withdrawals only if the party shows to the satisfaction of the Secretary of Commerce a direct connection between incurring the indebtedness and the acquisition, construction, or reconstruction of a qualified vessel or its complement of barges and containers whether or not the indebtedness is secured by the vessel or its complement of barges and containers. The fact that an indebtedness is secured by an interest in a qualified vessel, barge, or container is insufficient by itself to demonstrate the necessary connection.

(c) Payments to related persons. Notwithstanding paragraph (a) of this section, payments from a fund to a person owned or controlled directly or indirectly by the same interests as the party within the meaning of section 482 of the Code and the regulations thereunder are not to be treated as qualified withdrawals unless the party demonstrates to the satisfaction of the Secretary of Commerce that no part of such payment constitutes a dividend, a return of capital, or a contribution to capital under the Code.

(d) Treatment of fund upon failure to fulfill obligations. Section 607(f)(2) of the Act provides that if the Secretary of Commerce determines that any substantial obligation under the agreement is not being fulfilled, he may, after notice and opportunity for hearing to the party, treat the entire fund, or any portion thereof, as having been withdrawn as a nonqualified withdrawal. In determining whether a party has breached a substantial obligation under the agreement, the Secretary will consider among other things, (1) the effect of the party's action or omission upon his ability to carry out the purposes of the fund and for which qualified withdrawals are permitted under section 607(f)(1) of the Act, and (2) whether the party has made material misrepresentations in connection with the agreement or has failed to disclose material information. For the income tax treatment of nonqualified withdrawals, see § 3.7.

T.D. 7398, 1/23/76.

PAR. 3. Section 3.5, as adopted by Treasury Decision 7398, is amended by revising paragraph (a)(3)(iii) to read as follows:

Proposed § 3.5 Qualified withdrawals. [*For Preamble, see ¶ 150,183*]

(a) In general. * * *

(3) * * *

(iii) The receipt of property (which is a qualified vessel or barges and containers which are part of the complement of a qualified vessel (or shares therein)) by a parent corporation in liquidation of an 80-percent-or-more controlled subsidiary corporation in which the parent's basis for the property is determined under section 334(b)(2) of the Code by reference to its basis for the subsidiary's stock, but only if (a) the subsidiary a plan of liquidation not more than 30 days after the date of the transaction described in section 334(b)(2)(B) of the Code (or, in the case of a series of transactions, the date of the first such transaction) and (b) the property is actually distributed within days of such transaction (or first transaction), provided, however, that the amount of the qualified withdrawal for such purpose shall be limited to the lower of the fair market value of such property on the date of such transaction (or of the first such transaction) reduced by the amount of any liability secured by such property and the allocable amount of any unsecured liability of the subsidiary or the parent's basis for the stock of the subsidiary allocable to such property. For purposes of the preceding sentence, an allocable amount of liability or basis of stock shall be determined by reference to the relative gross fair market values of the assets of the subsidiary.

* * * * *

§ 3.6 Tax treatment of qualified withdrawals.

(a) In general. Section 607(g) of the Act and this section provide rules for the income tax treatment of qualified withdrawals including the income tax treatment on the disposition of assets acquired with fund amounts.

(b) Order of application of qualified withdrawals against accounts. A qualified withdrawal from a fund shall be treated as being made: first, out of the capital account; second out of the capital gain account; and third, out of the ordinary income account. Such withdrawals will reduce the balance within a particular account on a first-in-first-out basis, the earliest qualified withdrawals reducing the items within an account in the order in which they were actually deposited or deemed deposited in accordance with this part. The date funds are actually withdrawn from the fund determines the time at which withdrawals are considered to be made.

(c) Reduction of basis. *(1)* If any portion of a qualified withdrawal for the acquisition, construction or reconstruction of a vessel, barge, or container (or share therein) is made out of the ordinary income account, the basis of such vessel, barge, or container (or share therein) shall be reduced by an amount equal to such portion.

(2) If any portion of a qualified withdrawal for the acquisition, construction, or reconstruction of a vessel, barge, or container (or share therein) is made out of the capital gain account, the basis of such vessel, barge, or container (or share therein) shall be reduced by an amount equal to—

(i) Five-eighths of such portion, in the case of a corporation (other than an electing small business corporation, as defined in section 1371 of the Code), or

(ii) One-half of such portion, in the case of any other person.

(3) If any portion of a qualified withdrawal to pay the principal of an indebtedness is made out of the ordinary income account or the capital gain account, then the basis of the vessel, barge, or container (or share therein) with respect to which such indebtedness was incurred is reduced in the manner provided by subparagraphs (1) and (2) of this paragraph. If the aggregate amount of such withdrawal from the ordinary income account and capital gain account would cause a basis reduction in excess of the party's basis in such vessel, barge, or container (or share therein), the excess is applied against the basis of other vessels, barges, or containers (or shares therein) owned by the party at the time of withdrawal in the following order: (i) Vessels, barges, or containers (or shares therein) which were the subject of qualified withdrawals in the order in which they were acquired, constructed, or reconstructed; (ii) agreement vessels (as defined in section 607(k)(3) of the Act and § 3.11(a)(3)) and barges and containers which are part of the complement of an agreement vessel (or shares therein) which were not the subject of qualified withdrawals, in the order in which such vessels, barges, or containers (or shares therein) were acquired by the party; and (iii) other vessels, barges, and containers (or shares therein), in the order in which they were acquired by the party. Any amount of a withdrawal remaining after the application of this subparagraph is to be treated as a nonqualified withdrawal. If the indebtedness was incurred to acquire two or more vessels, barges, or containers (or shares therein), then the basis reduction in such vessels, barges, or containers (or shares therein) is to be made pro rata in proportion to the adjusted basis of such vessels, barges, or containers (or shares therein) computed, however, without regard to this section and adjustments under section 1016(a)(2) and (3) of the Code for depreciation or amortization.

(d) Basis for depreciation. For purposes of determining the allowance for depreciation under section 167 of the Code in respect of any property which has been acquired, constructed, or reconstructed from qualified withdrawals, the adjusted basis for determining gain on such property is determined after applying paragraph (c) of this section. In the case of reductions in the basis of any property resulting from the application of paragraph (c)(3) of this section, the party may adopt a method of accounting whereby (1) payments shall reduce the basis of the property on the day such payments are actually made, or (2) payments made at any time during the first half of the party's taxable year shall reduce the basis of the property on the first day of the taxable year, and payments made at any time during the second half of the party's taxable year shall reduce the basis of the property on the first day of the succeeding taxable year. For requirements respecting the change of methods of accounting, see § 1.446-1(e)(3) of the Income Tax Regulations of this chapter.

(e) Ordinary income treatment of gain from disposition of property acquired with qualified withdrawals. [Reserved]

T.D. 7398, 1/23/76.

PAR. 4. Section 3.6, as adopted by Treasury Decision 7398, is amended by revising paragraph (e) to read as follows:

Proposed § 3.6 Tax treatment of qualified withdrawals.
[*For Preamble, see ¶ 150,183*]

* * * * *

(e) Ordinary income treatment of gain from disposition of property acquired with qualified withdrawals. *(1)* (i) Under section 607(g)(5) of the Act and this paragraph, if any property the basis of which was reduced under paragraph (c) of this section is disposed of, then except as otherwise provided in this paragraph any gain realized on such disposition (after application of section 1245 of the Code) to the extent provided in subparagraph (2) of this paragraph shall be recognized and treated as an amount referred to in section 607(h)(3)(A) of the Act and § 3.7 (relating to nonqualified withdrawals) which was withdrawn on the date of such disposition. Accordingly, notwithstanding any provision of the

Code, the amount of such gain shall be included in the gross income of the party as an item of ordinary income for the taxable year in which the disposition occurred. In the case of a partnership holding any such property, see subparagraph (8) of this paragraph. In the case of a sale of such property which is reported under the installment method, see subparagraph (9) of this paragraph.

(ii) Interest on gain referred to in subdivision (i) of this subparagraph shall not attach under section 607(h)(3)(C) of the Act and § 3.7(e) unless the disposition occurred within 1 year of final delivery from the shipyard or within 1 year of first loading of the vessel, and the Secretary of Commerce determines that such disposition was not for a purpose for which the funds is established. Interest shall not attach in the case of an involuntary conversion.

(iii) If an amount representing the net proceeds (as defined in § 3.2(c)(2)) from the disposition is deposited into the fund pursuant to § 3.2(c)(3), the agreement, and the regulations prescribed by the Secretary of Commerce, such gain referred to in subdivision (i) of this subparagraph is to be excluded from gross income (and interest shall not be payable on such amount) and is to be treated as gain to which section 607(d)(1)(B) of the Act and § 3.3(b)(2) apply. The portion of such deposit which represents amounts that if not deposited would be treated as ordinary income under section 1245(a)(1) of the Code or as gain attributable to the reduction in basis under paragraph (c) section is considered a deposit in accordance with section 607(b)(1)(C) of the Act (relating to net proceeds from the sale of an agreement vessel) and must be allocated to the ordinary income account of the fund in accordance with § 3.4(d)(4).

(2) (i) The amount of gain included in gross income of the party as an item of ordinary income by reason of section 607(g)(5) of the Act and subparagraph (1)(i) of this paragraph shall be determined pursuant to section 1245 of the Code (including the exceptions and limitations in subsection (b) (other than paragraph (5) thereof)), applied in the manner and only to the extent prescribed in subparagraphs (3) and (4) of this paragraph, except that for purposes of this determination the exceptions and limitations in section 1245(b)(3) and (4) of the Code shall not apply unless a closing agreement is properly entered into under section 7121 of the Code which meets the requirements of subdivisions (ii) and (iii) of this subparagraph.

(ii) For a closing agreement to meet the requirements of this subdivision, it must (a) provide that the provisions of this paragraph shall apply for purposes of determining the consequences of the exchange, (b) be signed by the Assistant Commissioner (Technical or his delegate and by the party disposing of the vessel and, in the case of a transaction to which subparagraph (5) of this paragraph applies, the transferee of such vessel, and (c) be consistent with the examples set out in subparagraph (7)(i) of this paragraph.

(iii) For a closing agreement to meet the requirements of this subdivision, the party must make application therefor on or before the later of the applicable following dates:

(a) [90 days after the date this document is published in the FEDERAL REGISTER as a final regulation], or

(b) The last day prescribed by law (including extensions thereof) for filing the party's Federal income tax return for the taxable year in which the exchange occurs, or the date on which such return is actually filed, whichever is earlier.

For purposes of this subdivision (iii), a party makes application for a closing agreement by mailing a signed proposed agreement which meets the requirements of subdivision (ii) of this subparagraph to the Commissioner of Internal Revenue, Attention: T:FP:T, Washington, D.C. 20224. If the execution of such agreement by the Service prior to any particular date is desired, the party should make such application prior to 90 days before such date.

(3) The amount of gain to which section 1245 of the Code actually applies shall be determined first and without regard to section 607(g)(5) of the Act and subparagraph (1)(i) of this paragraph. Then the amount of gain to which section 607(g)(5) and subparagraph (1) of this paragraph apply shall be determined pursuant to the rules of section 1245 of the Code, applied in the manner and to the extent described in subparagraph (2) of this paragraph.

(4) For the purposes of determining the amount of gain to which section 607(g)(5) of the Act and subparagraph (1)(i) of this paragraph apply, the following rules are prescribed:

(i) For such purposes, any reduction in basis under paragraph (c) of this section (whether in respect of the same or other property) allowed to the party or any other person shall be treated as an adjustment reflected in adjusted basis on account of deductions for depreciation within the meaning of section 1245(a)(2) of the Code (relating to definition of recomputed basis).

(ii) For such purposes, the rules of subparagraph (5) of this paragraph shall apply with respect to transfers to which section 1245(b)(3) of the Code applies (relating to certain transfers where the transferee's basis is determined with reference to the transferor's basis) and, in the case of a distribution from a partnership, the rules of subparagraph (8) of this paragraph shall also apply.

(iii) For such purposes, the rules of subparagraph (6) of this paragraph shall apply with respect to a disposition described in section 1031 of the Code (relating to like-kind exchanges) and rules consistent with the principles of such subparagraph shall apply to a conversion with respect to which section 1033(a)(1) of the Code applies (relating to involuntary conversion into similar property). However, for such purpose, section 1245(b)(4) of the Code shall not apply to a conversion with respect to which an election under section 1033(a)(3) of the Code has been made.

(iv) (a) For such purposes, if there is reflected in the adjusted basis of a vessel reductions in basis made (whether in respect of such vessel or another vessel) under section 607(g)(2), (3), or (4) of the Act (1) by reason of paragraph (c)(3)(i), (ii), or (iii) of this section and (2) not by such reason, then any such gain recognized shall be treated as reducing any such reductions in basis in the order in which they were made, the earliest first. For any taxable year in which reductions of a character described in both (1) and (2) of this subdivision (a) were made, those described in (1) of this subdivision (a) shall be deemed to have occurred first.

(b) Notwithstanding (a) of this subdivision (iv), a party may, at his option, treat all reductions of a character described in (a)(1) of this subdivision (iv) as having occurred first.

(5) If the basis of a vessel in the hands of a transferee is determined (without regard to section 607(g)(5) of the Act and this paragraph) by reference to its basis in the hands of the transferor by reason of the application of section 332, 351, 361, 371(a), 374(a), 721, or 731 of the Code, and if a closing agreement is properly entered into pursuant to subparagraph (2) of this paragraph, then—

(i) The amount of gain recognized under section 607(g)(5) of the Act and subparagraph (1)(i) of this paragraph shall not exceed the excess of the amount of gain recognized to the transferor on the transfer of such vessel (determined without regard to section 607(g)(5) of the Act and subparagraph (1)(i) of this paragraph) over the amount of such gain to which section 1245(a)(1) of the Code actually applies.

(ii) Immediately after the transfer the amount of the reduction in basis under paragraph (c) of this section treated as an adjustment reflected in the adjusted basis of the vessel in the hands of the transferee shall be an amount equal to—

(a) The amount of such reduction treated as an adjustment reflected in the adjusted basis of the vessel in the hands of the transferor immediately before the disposition, minus

(b) The amount of gain recognized under section 607(g)(5) of the Act and subparagraph (1)(i) of this paragraph (determined without regard to section 607(d)(1)(B) of the Act and § 3.3(b)(2)(i)(a)).

(iii) Immediately after the transfer, the character of the reduction in basis under paragraph (c) of this section treated as an adjustment reflected in the adjusted basis of the vessel in the hands of the transferee shall be the same as it was in the hands of the transferor, reduced by, under subparagraph (4)(iv) of this paragraph, the amount of gain described in subdivision (ii)(b) of this subparagraph.

(iv) Immediately after the transfer, the basis of the property received shall be determined in accordance with the Code, but without taking into account any gain which would have been recognized by the party under section 607(g)(5) of the Act had the closing agreement not been signed but which was not recognized by reason of subdivision (i) of this subparagraph.

(v) In the case of any distribution from a partnership, the provisions of this subparagraph shall apply in the manner, and only to the extent, prescribed in subparagraph (8)(iii) of this paragraph.

(6) If a vessel is exchanged for a vessel and gain (determined without regard to section 607(g)(5) of the Act and this paragraph) is not recognized in whole or in part under section 1031 of the Code (relating to like-kind exchanges), and if a closing agreement is properly entered into pursuant to subparagraph (2) of this paragraph, then—

(i) The amount of gain recognized under section 607(g)(5) of the Act and subparagraph (1)(i) of this paragraph shall not exceed the sum of—

(a) The excess of the amount of gain recognized on such disposition (determined without regard to section 607(g)(5) of the Act and subparagraph (1)(i) of this paragraph) over the amount of such gain to which section 1245(a)(1) of the Code actually applies, plus

(b) The fair market value of the vessel acquired which is not a qualified vessel, but (1) only if there was reflected in the adjusted basis of the vessel exchanged reductions in basis made (whether in respect of such vessel or another vessel) under section 607(g)(2), (3), or (4) of the Act other than reductions in basis applied to any vessel by reason of paragraph (c)(3)(i), (ii), or (iii) of this section, and (2) only to the extent of such reductions in basis, and (3) then of amounts not taken into account under (a) of this subdivision, plus

(c) The fair market value of property acquired which is not a vessel and which is not taken into account under (a) of this subdivision.

(ii) Immediately after the exchange the amount of the reduction in basis under paragraph (c) of this section treated as an adjustment reflected in the adjusted basis of the vessel acquired shall be an amount equal to—

(a) The amount of such reduction treated as an adjustment reflected in the adjusted basis of the vessel exchanged immediately before the disposition, minus

(b) The amount of gain recognized under section 607(g)(5) of the Act and subparagraph (1)(i) of this paragraph (determined without regard to section 607(d)(1)(B) of the Act and § 3.3(b)(2)(i)(a)).

(iii) Immediately after the transfer, the character of the reduction in basis under paragraph (c) of this section treated as an adjustment reflected in the adjusted basis of the vessel acquired shall be the same as it was in the vessel exchanged, reduced by, under subparagraph (4)(iv) of this paragraph, the amount of gain described in subdivision (ii)(b) of this subparagraph.

(iv) Immediately after the exchange, the basis of the property received shall be determined in accordance with section 1031(d) of the Code, without taking into account any gain which would have been recognized by the party under section 607(g)(5) of the Act had the closing agreement not been signed but which was not recognized by reason of subdivision (i) of this subparagraph.

(7) (i) Closing agreements that will satisfy the requirements of subparagraph (2)(ii) of this paragraph can be illustrated by the following sample closing agreements.

Example (1). Proposed exchange to which section 1031 of the Code (relating to like-kind exchanges) will apply.

CLOSING AGREEMENT AS TO FINAL DETERMINATION COVERING SPECIFIC MATTERS

This closing agreement, made in triplicate under and in pursuance of section 7121 of the Internal Revenue Code of 1954 by and between ________ and the Commissioner of Internal Revenue:

Whereas, taxpayer proposes to exchange a __ (type) ________ vessel named ________ U.S. Coast Guard Registry number ________ (hereinafter "first vessel"), to ________ for a __ (type) __ vessel named ________, U.S. Coast Guard

Registry number ________ (hereinafter "second vessel") [and other consideration],[1]

Whereas, the taxpayer and Commissioner desire to finally determine the effect of such proposed exchange under section 607 of the Merchant Marine Act, 1936, as amended (hereinafter "Act"), the Treasury Regulations thereunder (26 CFR Part 3), and the Internal Revenue Code of 1954 (hereinafter "Code"), and

Whereas, if the proposed exchange qualifies under the provisions of section 1031 of the Code, then

It has been determined for Federal income tax purposes that the provisions of Treasury Regulations 26 CFR § 3.6(e) as in force this date shall apply for purposes of determining—

1. The amount of gain to be taken into account by the taxpayer under section 607(g)(5) of the Act,

2. The amounts of adjusted basis, and adjustments reflected in the adjusted basis, of the second vessel in the hands of the taxpayer immediately after the exchange,

3. The treatment of such amounts of the adjustments reflected in the adjusted basis of the second vessel immediately after the exchange as attributable to reductions in basis of the second vessel in the hands of the taxpayer under section 607(g)(2), (3), and (4) of the Act by reason of qualified withdrawals by the taxpayer from a capital construction fund (whether or not it has such a fund), and

4. All other consequences of the proposed exchange.

Whereas, the determinations as set forth above are hereby agreed to by said taxpayer.

Now, this closing agreement witnesseth, that the said taxpayer and said Commissioner of Internal Revenue hereby mutually agree that the determinations as set forth above shall be final and conclusive, subject, however, to reopening in the event of fraud, malfeasance, or misrepresentation of material fact, and provided that any change or modification of applicable statutes will render this agreement ineffective to the extent that it is dependent upon such statutes.

In witness whereof, the above parties have subscribed their names to these presents, in triplicate.

Signed this ________ day of ________, 19__

____

(Taxpayer)

____

By ________________________________

____

(Title)

Commissioner of Internal Revenue

By ________________________________

Assistant Commissioner (Technical)

Date ________________________________

Example (2). Proposed transfer of vessel in an exchange to which subparagraph (5) of this paragraph will apply (relating to certain transfers where the transferee's basis is determined with reference to the transferor's basis).

CLOSING AGREEMENT AS TO FINAL DETERMINATION COVERING SPECIFIC MATTERS

This closing agreement, made in quadruplicate under and in pursuance of section 7121 of the Internal Revenue Code of 1954 by and between ________ (hereinafter "transferor"), ________ (hereinafter "transferee"), and the Commissioner of Internal Revenue:

Whereas, transferor proposes to transfer a __ (type) __ vessel named ________ U.S. Coast Guard Registry number ________ to transferee for *[stock] [stock and securities] [partnership interest]*[2] [of, in][2] transferee [and other consideration].[3]

Whereas, the transferor, transferee, and Commissioner desire to finally determine the effect, of such proposed exchange, under section 607 of the Merchant Marine Act, 1936, as amended (hereinafter "Act"), the Treasury Regulations thereunder (26 CFR Part 3), and the Internal Revenue Code of 1954 (hereinafter "Code"), and

Whereas, if the proposed exchange qualifies under the provisions of section ________ of the Code, then

It has been determined for Federal income tax purposes that the provisions of Treasury Regulations 26 CFR § 3.6(e) as in force this date shall apply for purposes of determining—

1. The amount of gain to be taken into account by the transferor under section 607(g)(5) of the Act.

2. The amounts of adjusted basis, and adjustments reflected in the adjusted basis, of the vessel in the hands of the transferee immediately after the exchange, including for purposes of applying section 607(g)(5) to a subsequent transaction involving such vessel by the transferee,

3. The treatment of such amounts, of the adjustments reflected in the adjusted basis of the vessel immediately after the exchange, as attributable to reductions in basis of the vessel in the hands of the transferee under section 607(g)(2), (3), and (4) of the Act by reason of qualified withdrawals by the transferee from a capital construction fund (whether or not it has such a fund),

4. The adjusted basis in the hands of the transferor of the stock, securities, or partnership interest in the transferee received in exchange for the vessel, and

5. All other consequences of the proposed exchange.

Whereas, the determinations as set forth above are hereby agreed to by said transferor and transferee.

Now, this closing agreement witnesseth, that the said transferor, said transferee, and said Commissioner of Internal Revenue hereby mutually agree that the determinations as set forth above shall be final and conclusive, subject, however, to reopening in the event of fraud, malfeasance, or misrepresentation of material fact, and provided that any change or modification of applicable statutes will render this agreement ineffective to the extent that it is dependent upon such statutes.

In witness whereof, the above parties have subscribed their names to these presents, in quadruplicate.

Signed this ________ day of ________, 19__

____

(Transferor)

By ________________________________

____

(Title)

____

(Transferee)

By ________________________________

____

(Title)

Commissioner of Internal Revenue

By ________________________________

____

Assistant Commissioner (Technical)

Date ________________________________

(ii) The provisions of subparagraphs (1) through (6) of this paragraph are illustrated by the following examples:

Example (1). X Corporation, which maintains a fund described in § 3.1, exchanges qualified vessel A for qualified vessel B in a transaction in which no gain or loss is recognized under section 1031 (relating to like-kind exchange) of the Code, determined without regard to the Act and section 1245 of the Code. Prior to the exchange, a closing agreement is properly entered into under section 7121 of the Code which meets the requirements of subparagraph (2) of this paragraph. Vessel A had been purchased for $2 million, of which $1.5 million was attributable to a qualified withdrawal from the ordinary income account of the fund. Depreciation of $100,000 had been allowed (the amount allowable) on vessel A and, before any depreciation is allowed or allowable on vessel B, X sells vessel B for cash of $2.1 million. Under section 1245(b)(4) of the Code (relating to dispositions of property without recognition of gain or loss by reason of section 1031 of the Code) no gain is recognized under section 1245(a)(1) of the Code upon the exchange not-

1 Do not identify other consideration. Delete if inapplicable.

2 Delete inapplicable terms or insert other appropriate term. Do NOT further identify consideration, such as number of shares or class of stock.

3 Insert proper term or delete if inapplicable, but do not further identify other consideration.

withstanding the depreciation of $100,000 allowed with respect to vessel A. Since the only property received in the exchange is a qualified vessel, and since the closing agreement was properly entered into, under subparagraph (6)(i) of this paragraph no gain is recognized under section 607(g)(5) of the Act and subparagraph (1)(4) of this subparagraph.

Under subparagraph (6)(iii) of this paragraph, X's basis in vessel B just before the sale is the same as that of vessel A, or $400,000, *i.e.*, cost of $2 million reduced by $1.5 million qualified withdrawal (see paragraph (c)(1) of this section) and by $100,000 allowed as depreciation. Immediately after the exchange, the amount of depreciation adjustments reflected in adjusted basis under § 1.1245-2(c)(4) of the Income Tax Regulations of this chapter (determined without regard to this section) is $100,000, and the amount of the reduction in basis under paragraph (c) of this section treated as an adjustment reflected in adjusted basis under subparagraph (6)(ii) of this paragraph is $1.5 million. Gain recognized on the sale is $1.7 million, i.e., amount realized, $2.1 million, minus adjusted basis, $400,000. The first $100,000 of gain on the sale is gain to which section 1245(a)(1) of the Code applies, and the next $1.5 million of gain on the sale is gain to which subparagraph (1)(i) of this paragraph applies. Thus, $1.6 million of gain is included as ordinary income in X's gross income for the taxable year of the sale. The remaining $100,000 of gain may be treated as gain from the sale or exchange of property described in section 1231 of the Code.

Example (2). Assume the same facts as in example (1), except that X deposits the net proceeds from the sale into the fund in the manner described in subparagraph (1)(iii) of this paragraph. Under § 3.3(b)(2), X recognizes no gain on the sale, and the net proceeds of $2.1 million on the sale (see § 3.2(c)(2)) are allocated to the following accounts in the following amounts: $100,000 to the ordinary income account as gain to which section 1245 of the Code applies (see § 3.4(d)(4)), $1.5 million to the ordinary income account in accordance with subparagraph (1)(iii) of this paragraph (see § 3.4(d)(4)), $100,000 to the capital gain account (see § 3.4(c)), assuming X had purchased vessel A more than 6 months before its sale of vessel B (see section 1223(1) of the Code), and $400,000 to the capital account (see § 3.4(b)(2)).

Example (3). Assume the same facts as in example (1), except that X received vessel B, with a fair market value of $1 million, and $1 million in cash in exchange for vessel A and did not sell vessel B. Since section 1031(b) of the Code limits the amount of gain recognized to $1 million, subparagraph (6)(i) of this paragraph limits application of subparagraph (1) of this paragraph, but only after application of section 1245 of the Code. Under section 1245(a)(1) of the Code, the first $100,000 of recognized gain is treated as ordinary income. Under subparagraph (6)(i) of this paragraph, the amount of gain recognized under subparagraph (1)(i) of this paragraph is limited to $900,000, i.e., the $1 million of gain recognized under section 1031(b) of the Code less the $100,000 of such gain to which section 1245 of the Code applies. Accordingly, the amount of the reduction in basis under paragraph (c) of this section treated as an adjustment reflected in adjusted basis under subparagraph (6)(ii) of this paragraph of vessel B is $600,000, i.e., the amount of adjustments reflected in the adjusted basis of vessel A immediately before the disposition ($1.5 million) less the amount of gain recognized under subparagraph (1)(i) of this paragraph ($900,000). The basis of vessel B is equal to $400,000, computed in accordance with section 1031(d) of the Code, i.e., the basis in vessel A of $400,000 less cash received of $1 million plus gain recognized of $1 million.

Example (4). Assume that in example 3 X deposits the net proceeds from the exchange into the fund in the manner described in subparagraph (1)(iii) of this paragraph. Assume further that there were no selling expenses connected with the exchange and, at the time of the exchange, vessel A was not security for any mortgage. Since by reason of the application of subparagraph (6)(i) of this paragraph vessel B was received without recognition of gain under section 607(g)(5) of the Act, and since under § 3.2(c)(1)(i) gross proceeds does not include any property to the extent received without recognition of gain under the Act and the Code, the gross proceeds is equal to the amount of cash received, i.e., $1 million. Since X had no expenses described in § 3.2(c)(2)(ii) to reduce gross proceeds, and since the sum of the gain recognized on the exchange (before application of this part), $1 million, plus the gain recognized under section 607(g)(5) of the Act and subparagraph (6)(i) of this paragraph not taken into account in computing the gain of $1 million, zero, is not greater than the net proceeds, the net proceeds is also $1 million. By reason of the deposit, X recognizes no gain on the exchange and the entire $1 million of net proceeds is allocated to the ordinary income account in accordance with subparagraph (1)(iii) of this paragraph, i.e., $100,000 as gain to which section 1245(a)(1) of the Code would have applied and $900,000 as gain to which subparagraph (1)(i) of this paragraph would have applied had there been no deposit (see § 3.4(d)(4)). The amount of adjustments reflected in the adjusted basis of vessel B is determined in the same manner as in example (3). Since under § 3.3(b)(2)(i) (b) the $1 million of gain not recognized by reason of the deposit into the fund is treated as recognized for purposes of determining vessel B's basis, vessel B's basis is $400,000 as determined in example (3).

Example (5). (i) Assume the same facts as in example (1), except that X did not sell vessel B and vessel B is not a qualified vessel. Assume further that the fair market value of vessel B is $2.2 million. As stated in example (1), the limitation provided by section 1245(b)(4) of the Code prevents recognition of any gain under section 1245 of the Code notwithstanding the $100,000 of depreciation allowed with respect to vessel A. the only property received in the exchange is vessel B, which is not a qualified vessel, and since no gain is recognized under section 1245 of the Code, under subparagraph (6)(i) of this paragraph the amount of gain recognized under section 607(g)(5) of the Act and subparagraph (1)(i) of this paragraph is limited to the amount in subparagraph (6)(i)(b) of this paragraph. Since the fair market value of vessel B, $2.2 million, exceeds the reduction in basis of vessel A by virtue of paragraph (c) of this section, $1.5 million, subparagraph (6)(i)(b) of this paragraph limits the amount of gain recognized under section 607(g)(5) of the Act and subparagraph (1)(i) of this paragraph to $1.5 million, which is included in X's gross income as an item of ordinary income in the taxable year of the exchange. Further, since under subparagraph (3) of this paragraph the determination of gain under section 1245(b)(4) of the Code is made without regard to section 607(g)(5) of the Act and this paragraph, no part of this gain of $1.5 million is considered gain to which section 1245 of the Code applies.

(ii) If the entire $1.5 million of adjustments reflected in the adjusted basis of vessel A under paragraph (c) of this section were amounts applied under paragraph (c)(3)(i), (ii), or (iii) of this section by reason of qualified withdrawals to pay the principal of indebtedness incurred with respect to vessels other than vessel A, then the amount in subparagraph (6)(i)(b) of this paragraph would be zero and, accordingly, by reason of the application of subparagraph (6)(i) of this paragraph no gain would be recognized under section 607(g)(5) of the Act.

(iii) The results would be the same as stated in subdivision (i) of this example if there had been no closing agreement whether or not vessel B is a qualified vessel.

(8) If a partnership holds any property the basis of which was reduced under paragraph (c) of this section, then—

(i) For purposes of subparagraph (1)(i) of this paragraph, the term "disposition" includes a distribution by the partnership.

(ii) If a partner sells or exchanges all or a part of his interest in the partnership or receives a distribution from the partnership, then for purposes of applying section 751(c) of the Code (relating to unrealized receivables of a partnership) the amount of such gain to which section 607(g)(5) of the Act and subparagraph (1)(i) of this paragraph would apply if the property were sold by a partnership at its fair market value shall be treated as gain to which section 1245(a) of the Code would have applied.

(iii) [Reserved]

(9) Gain from a disposition to which subparagraph (1) of this paragraph applies may be reported under the installment method if such method is otherwise available under section 453 of the Code. In such case, the income (other than interest) on each installment payment shall be deemed to consist of any gain which is treated as ordinary income by reason of the application of section 1245(a)(1) of the Code until all such gain is reported, then any gain to which this paragraph applies until all such gain has been reported, and the remaining portion (if any) of such income shall be deemed to consist of gain to which this paragraph does not apply.

§ 3.7 Tax treatment of nonqualified withdrawals.

(a) In general. Section 607(h) of the Act provides rules for the tax treatment of nonqualified withdrawals, including rules for adjustments to the various accounts of the fund, the inclusion of amounts in income, and the payment of interest with respect to such amounts.

(b) Nonqualified withdrawals defined. Except as provided in section 607 of the Act and § 3.8 (relating to certain corporate reorganizations, changes in partnerships, and transfers by reason of death) any withdrawal from a fund which is not a qualified withdrawal shall be treated as a nonqualified withdrawal which is subject to tax in accordance with section 607(h) of the Act and the provisions of this section. Examples of nonqualified withdrawals are amounts remaining in a fund upon termination of the fund, and withdrawals which are treated as nonqualified withdrawals under section 607(f)(2) of the Act and § 3.5(d) (relating to failure by a party to fulfill substantial obligation under agreement) or under the second sentence of section 607(g)(4) of the Act and § 3.6(c)(3) (relating to payments against indebtedness in excess of basis).

(c) Order of application of nonqualified withdrawals against deposits. A nonqualified withdrawal from a fund shall be treated as being made: First, out of the ordinary income account; second, out of the capital gain account; and third, out of the capital account. Such withdrawals will reduce the balance within a particular account on a first-in-first-out basis, the earliest nonqualified withdrawals reducing the items within an account in the order in which they were actually deposited or deemed deposited in accordance with this part. Nonqualified withdrawals for research, development, and design expenses incident to new and advanced ship design, machinery, and equipment, and any amount treated as a nonqualified withdrawal under the second sentence of section 607(g)(4) of the Act and § 3.6(c)(3), shall be applied against the deposits within a particular account on a last-in-first-out basis. The date funds are actually withdrawn from the fund determines the time at which withdrawals are considered to be made. For special rules concerning the withdrawal of contingent deposits of net proceeds from the installment sale of an agreement vessel, see § 3.2(c)(6).

(d) Inclusion in income. *(1)* Any portion of a nonqualified withdrawal which, under paragraph (c) of this section, is treated as being made out of the ordinary income account is to be included in gross income as an item of ordinary income for the taxable year in which the withdrawal is made.

(2) Any portion of a nonqualified withdrawal which, under paragraph (c) of this section, is treated as being made out of the capital gain account is to be included in income as an item of long-term capital gain recognized during the taxable year in which the withdrawal is made.

(3) For effect upon a party's taxable income of capital losses remaining in a fund upon the termination of a fund (which, under paragraph (b) of this section, is treated as a nonqualified withdrawal of amounts remaining in the fund) see § 3.4(e).

(e) Interest. *(1)* For the period on or before the last date prescribed by law, including extensions thereof, for filing the party's Federal income tax return for the taxable year during which a nonqualified withdrawal is made, no interest shall be payable under section 6601 of the Code in respect of the tax on any item which is included in gross income under paragraph (d) of this section, and no addition to such tax for such period shall be payable under section 6651 of the Code. In lieu of the interest and additions to tax under such sections, simple interest on the amount of the tax attributable to any item included in gross income under paragraph (d) of this section is to be paid at the rate of interest determined for the year of withdrawal under subparagraph (2) of this paragraph. Such interest is to be charged for the period from the last date prescribed for payment of tax for the taxable year for which such item was deposited in the fund to the last date for payment of tax for the taxable year in which the withdrawal is made. Both dates are to be determined without regard to any extensions of time for payment. Interest determined under this paragraph which is paid within the taxable year shall be allowed as a deduction for such year under section 163 of the Code. However, such interest is to be treated as part of the party's tax for the year of withdrawal for purposes of collection and in determining any interest or additions to tax for the year of withdrawal under section 6601 or 6651, respectively, of the Code.

(2) For purposes of section 607(h)(3)(C)(ii) of the Act, and for purposes of certain dispositions of vessels constructed, reconstructed, or acquired with qualified withdrawals described in § 3.6(e), the applicable rate of interest for any nonqualified withdrawal—

(i) Made in a taxable year beginning in 1970 and 1971 is 8 percent.

(ii) Made in a taxable year beginning after 1971, the rate for such year as determined and published jointly by the Secretary of the Treasury or his delegate and the Secretary of Commerce, such rate shall bear a relationship to 8 percent which the Secretaries determine to be comparable to the relationship which the money rates and investment yields for the calendar year immediately preceding the beginning of the taxable year bear to the money rates and investment yields for the calendar year 1970. The determination of the applicable rate for any such taxable year will be computed by multiplying 8 percent by the ratio which (a) the average yield on 5-year Treasury securities for the calendar year immediately preceding the beginning of such taxable year, bears to (b) the average yield on 5-year Treasury securities for the calendar year 1970. The applicable rate so determined shall be computed to the nearest one-hundredth of 1 percent. If such a determination and publication is made, the latest published percentage shall apply for any taxable year beginning in the calendar year with respect to which publication is made.

(3) No interest shall be payable in respect of taxes on amounts referred to in section 607(h)(2)(i) and (ii) of the Act (relating to withdrawals for research and development and payments against indebtedness in excess of basis) or in the case of any nonqualified withdrawal arising from the application of the recapture provision of section 606(5) of the Merchant Marine Act, 1936, as in effect on December 31, 1969.

(f) Basis and holding period in the case of property purchased by the fund or considered purchased by the fund. In the case of a nonqualified withdrawal of property other than money which was purchased by the fund (including deposited property considered under § 3.2(g)(1)(ii) as purchased by the fund), the adjusted basis of the property in the hands of the party is its adjusted basis to the fund on the day of the withdrawal. In determining the period for which the taxpayer has held the property withdrawn in a nonqualified withdrawal, there shall be included only the period beginning with the date on which the withdrawal occurred. For basis and holding period in the case of nonqualified withdrawals of property other than money deposited into the fund, see § 3.2(g)(4).

T.D. 7398, 1/23/76.

§ 3.8 Certain corporate reorganizations and changes in partnerships, and certain transfers on death. [Reserved]

T.D. 7398, 1/23/76.

PAR. 5.

Section 3.8, as adopted by Treasury Decision 7398, is revised to read as follows:

Proposed § 3.8 Certain corporate reorganizations and changes in partner (and certain transfers on death). *[For Preamble, see ¶ 150,183]*

(a) In general. Section 607(i) of the Act and this section provide rules for certain corporate reorganizations, changes in partnerships, and certain transfers on death. Except as provided in paragraphs (b) and (c) of this section, any transfer of a fund from one taxpayer to another is a nonqualified withdrawal of the entire fund whether or not the transfer is voluntary, involuntary, or by operation of law.

(b) Certain transfers to corporations and partnerships. *(1)* If (i) a party which is a corporation transfers property (including property held in a fund) in a transaction to which section 381 of the Code applies, or a party which is a partnership transfers property (including property held in a fund) to a partnership which is treated as a continuation of the transferor partnership under the provisions of subchapter K of the Code, and (ii) the transfer of the fund has been approved by the Secretary of Commerce, then such transfer will be treated as if it did not constitute a nonqualified withdrawal and, if the fund included property subject to an election under § 3.2(g)(2), the transferee shall, for purposes of this part, be treated as if it had made such election. For purposes of determining the basis of property received in a transaction described in this subparagraph which involves the transfer of a fund including property subject to an election under § 3.2(g)(2), see § 3.2(g)(2).

(2) If a party transfers property, including property held in a fund) to a corporation solely in an exchange for stock or securities in which no gain or loss is recognized by reason of section 351(a) of the Code, the transfer of the fund will be treated as if it did not constitute a nonqualified withdrawal, but only if on or before the last day prescribed by law (including extensions thereof) for filing the party's Federal income tax return for the taxable year in which the transfer occurs, or the date on which such return is actually filed, whichever is earlier (or, if later, on or before [90 days after the date this document is published in the FEDERAL REGISTER as a final regulation])—

(i) The transfer of the fund to, and maintenance of the fund by, the corporation has been approved by the Secretary of Commerce, and

(ii) A closing agreement under section 7121 of the Code which meets the requirements of paragraph (e) of this section has been applied for by the party and the corporation.

For purposes of this paragraph, a closing agreement has been applied for when a signed proposed agreement which meets the requirements of paragraph (e) of this section is mailed to the Commissioner of Internal Revenue, Attention: T:FP:T, Washington, D.C. 20224. If the execution of such agreement by the Service prior to any particular date is desired, such application should be made prior to 90 days before such date.

(3) If by reason of subparagraph (2) of this paragraph, a transfer of a fund does not constitute a nonqualified withdrawal, then—

(i) The consequences to the transferee shall be determined under paragraph (d) of this section,

(ii) If the fund includes property covered by an election under § 3.2(g)(2) (relating to an election not to treat deposits of property other than money as a sale or exchange at the time of deposit), then with respect to such property the party shall under § 3.2(g)(2) recognize on the date of such transfer the amount of gain or loss it would have recognized under § 3.2(g)(1)(iii) (had the election not been made) on the day the property was deposited in the fund.

(iii) For purposes of determining the party's basis for the stock or securities of the transferee received by the party in the exchange—

(a) The basis of the assets in the fund that were transferred shall be considered to be the fund's basis for the property (see § 3.2(g)(1)(ii) for manner of determining such basis with respect to contributed property), and

(b) With respect to property in the fund to which subdivision (ii) of this subparagraph applies, the party's basis (as determined under (a) of this subdivision) for stock or securities received in the exchange for such property shall not be increased by the amount of gain (or decreased by the amount of loss) under § 3.2(g)(2) referred to in such subdivision (ii), and

(iv) The party's basis of the stock or securities of the transferee received by him in the exchange shall be the party's basis of the properties transferred (determined by taking into account the provisions of subdivision (iii) of this subparagraph) reduced by the sum of—

(a) The amount in the ordinary income account (see § 3.4(d)), and

(b) Five-eights (in the case of a corporation (other than an electing small business corporation, as defined in section 1371 of the Code)) or one-half (in the case of any other person) of the amount in the capital gain account (see § 3.4(c)).

(c) Transfers on death. *(1)* If a party who is an individual dies, the transfer of a fund and property held therein to an executor or administrator of the decedent's estate, or to any other person by reason of his death, will be treated as if it did not constitute a nonqualified withdrawal, but only if on or before the last day prescribed by law (including extensions thereof) for filing the party's Federal income tax return for the taxable year in which the transfer occurs, or the date on which such return is actually filed, whichever is earlier (or, if later, on or before [90 days after the date this document is published in the FEDERAL REGISTER is a final regulation])—

(i) Such executor, administrator, or other person receives approval for his maintenance of the fund from the Secretary of Commerce, and

(ii) A closing agreement under section 7121 of the Code which meets the requirements of paragraph (e) of this section has been applied for by such executor, administrator, or other person. For purposes of this subparagraph, a closing agreement has been applied for when a signed proposed agreement which meets the requirements of paragraph (e) of this section is mailed to the Commissioner of Internal Revenue, Attention: T:FP:T, Washington, D.C. 20224. If the execution of such agreement by the Service prior to any particular date is desired, such application should be made prior to 90 days before such date.

(2) If (i) By reason of the application of subparagraph (1) of this paragraph, the transfer of a fund from the individual who died to the executor or administrator of the decedent's estate was treated as if it did not constitute a nonqualified withdrawal,

(ii) The fund passes from the decedent's estate to another person or persons, and

(iii) Such passing of the fund does not constitute in whole or in part a sale or exchange (see § 1.1014-4(a)(3) of the Income Tax Regulations of this chapter), then the passing of such fund from the decedent's estate to such other person will also be treated as if it did not constitute a nonqualified withdrawal, but only if the requirements of subparagraph (3) of this paragraph are satisfied.

(3) The requirements of this subparagraph are satisfied with respect to the passing of a fund from a decedent's estate to another person if on or before the last day prescribed by law (including extensions thereof) for filing the estate's Federal income tax return for the taxable year in which the passing occurs, or the date on which such return is actually filed whichever is earlier (or, if later, on or before [90 days after the date this document is published in the FEDERAL REGISTER as a final regulation])—

(i) The passing of the fund to, and maintenance of the fund by, such other person has been approved by the Secretary of Commerce, and

(ii) A closing agreement under section 7121 of the Code which meets the requirements of paragraph (e) of this section has been applied for by such other person and the executor or administrator of the decedent's estate.

For purposes of this subparagraph, a closing agreement has been applied for when a signed proposed agreement which meets the requirements of paragraph (e) of this section is mailed to the Commissioner of Internal Revenue, Attention: T:FP:T, Washington, D.C. 20224. If the execution of such agreement by the Service prior to any particular date is desired, such application should be made prior to 90 days before such date.

(4) If a fund is transferred from an individual by reason of his death to his estate or from his estate to another person and the fund includes property covered by an election under § 3.2(g)(2) (relating to an election not to treat deposits of property other than money as a sale or exchange at the time of deposit), then with respect to such property the individual or estate shall under § 3.2(g)(2) recognize on the date of death or transfer the amount of gain or loss it would have recognized under § 3.2(g)(1)(iii) (had the election not been made) on the date the property was paragraphs (b)(3)(ii) and (c)(4) of this section) shall carry over from the transferor to the transferee. If the transferee is a party to an existing fund, the assets of the funds and the respective accounts within the funds, shall be combined. Thus, for example, each item in the combined fund shall retain its character as an item which was deposited into the capital account, the capital gain account, or the ordinary income account, as the case may be, on the date on which they were deposited into each original fund.

(e) Closing agreement. *(1)* For a closing agreement to meet the requirements of paragraph (b)(2), (c)(1), or (c)(3) of this section, it must (a) provide that the provisions of this section shall apply for purposes of determining the consequences of the transfer of the fund, (b) be signed by the Assistant Commissioner (Technical) or his delegate, the person transferring the fund (other than a decedent and the person receiving the fund, and (c) be consistent with the examples set out in subparagraph (2) of this paragraph.

(2) The provisions of subparagraph (1) of this paragraph can be illustrated by the following sample closing agreements:

Example (1). Proposed transfer of fund in an exchange to which section 351(a) of the Code (relating to transfer to controlled corporation) will apply.

CLOSING AGREEMENT AS TO FINAL DETERMINATION COVERING SPECIFIC MATTERS

This closing agreement, made in quadruplicate under and in pursuance of section 7121 of the Internal Revenue Code of 1954 by and between __________ (hereinafter "transferor"), __________ (hereinafter "transferee"), and Commissioner of Internal Revenue.

Whereas, transferor proposes to transfer property (including property held in its capital construction fund as described in Treasury Regulations 26 CFR § 3.1(a), hereinafter "fund") to transferee for stock or securities, or both,[4] of transferee,

4 Do NOT further identify stock or securities.

Whereas the transfer of the fund to, and maintenance of the fund by, transferee was approved by the Secretary of Commerce on __________, 19__,

Whereas, the transferor, transferee, and Commissioner desire to finally determine the effect, of such proposed exchange, under section 607 of the Merchant Marine Act, 1936, as amended (hereinafter "Act"), the Treasury Regulations thereunder (26 CFR Part 3), and the Internal Revenue Code of 1954 (hereinafter "Code"), and

Whereas, if the proposed exchange qualifies under the provisions of section 351(a) of the Code, then

It has been determined for Federal income tax purposes that the provisions of Treasury Regulations 26 CFR § 3.8 as in force this date shall apply for purposes of determining—

1. If the fund includes property covered by an election under § 3.2(g)(2), the amount of gain to be taken into account by the transferor under 26 CFR §§ 3.2(g)(2) and 3.8(b)(3)(ii),

2. The transferor's basis of the stock or securities, or both, received in the exchange from the transferee,

3. The tax attributes of the fund and property in the fund in the hands of the transferee, and

4. All other consequences of the proposed exchange.

Whereas, the determinations as set forth above are hereby agreed to by said transferor and transferee.

Now, this closing agreement witnesseth, that the said taxpayer and said Commissioner of Internal Revenue hereby mutually agree that the determinations as set forth above shall be final and conclusive, subject, however, to reopening in the event of fraud, malfeasance, or misrepresentation of material fact, and provided that any change or modification of applicable statutes will render this agreement ineffective to the extent that it is dependent upon such statutes.

In witness whereof, the above parties have subscribed their names to these presents, in quadruplicate.

Signed this ________ day of ________, 19__

____
(Transferor)

By ________________________________
(Title)

____
(Transferee)

By ________________________________

____
(Title)

Commissioner of Internal Revenue

By ________________________________
Assistant Commissioner (Technical)

Date ________________________________

Example (2). Maintenance of fund by decedent's estate.

CLOSING AGREEMENT AS TO FINAL DETERMINATION COVERING SPECIFIC MATTERS

This closing agreement, made in triplicate under and in pursuance of section 7121 of the Internal Revenue Code of 1954 by and between ________ and the Commissioner of Internal Revenue:

Whereas property was held in a capital construction fund as described in Treasury Regulations 26 CFR § 3.1(a) (hereinafter "fund") maintained by ________ (hereinafter "decedent") who died on ________, 19__,

Whereas by reason of the death of the decedent the fund passed from decedent to the taxpayer as ________ (executor or administrator) ________ of decedent's estate,

Whereas the maintenance of the fund by the taxpayer was approved by the Secretary of Commerce on ________, 19__, and

Whereas, the taxpayer and Commissioner desire to finally determine the effect of the passing of the fund from decedent to taxpayer, under section 607 of the Merchant Marine Act, 1936, as amended (hereinafter "Act"), the Treasury Regulations thereunder (26 CFR Part 3), and the Internal Revenue Code of 1954 (hereinafter "Code"), then

It has been determined for Federal income tax purposes that the provisions of Treasury Regulations 26 CFR § 3.8 as in force this date shall apply for purposes of determining—

1. If the fund includes property covered by an election under § 3.2(g)(2), the amount of gain to be taken into account by the decedent under 26 CFR §§ 3.2(g)(2) and 3.8(c)(4),

2. The tax attributes of the fund and property in the fund in the hands of the taxpayer, and

3. All other consequences of the transaction.

Whereas, the determinations as set forth above are hereby agreed to by said taxpayer.

Now, this closing agreement witnesseth, that the said taxpayer and said Commissioner of Internal Revenue hereby mutually agree that the determinations as set forth above shall be final and conclusive, subject, however, to reopening in the event of fraud, malfeasance, or misrepresentation of material fact, and provided that any change or modification of applicable statutes will render this agreement ineffective to the extent that it is dependent upon such statutes.

In witness whereof, the above parties have subscribed their names to these presents, in triplicate.

Signed this ________ day of ________, 19__

____
(Taxpayer)

By ________________________________

____
(Title)

Commissioner of Internal Revenue

By ________________________________
Assistant Commissioner (Technical)

Date ________________________________

Example (3). Proposed transfer of fund from a decedent's estate to another person.

CLOSING AGREEMENT AS TO FINAL DETERMINATION COVERING SPECIFIC MATTERS

This closing agreement, made in quadruplicate under and in pursuant of section 7121 of the Internal Revenue Code of 1954 by and between ________ (hereinafter "transferor"), ________ (hereinafter "transferee") and the Commissioner of Internal Revenue:

Whereas, transferor proposes to transfer property held in its capital construction fund as described in Treasury Regulations 26 CFR § 3.1(a) (hereinafter "fund") to transferee,

Whereas the transfer of the fund to, and maintenance of the fund by, transferee was approved by the Secretary of Commerce on ________, 19__ transferor,

Whereas, the transferee, and Commissioner desire to finally determine the effect, of such proposed exchange, under section 607 of the Merchant Marine Act, 1936, as amended (hereinafter "Act"), the Treasury regulations thereunder (26 CFR Part 3), and the Internal Revenue Code of 1954 (hereinafter "Code"), and

Whereas, if the proposed transfer qualifies as meeting the conditions of subdivisions (i), (ii), and (iii) of Treasury Regulations 26 CFR § 3.8(c)(2), then

It has been determined for Federal income tax purposes that the provisions of Treasury Regulations 26 CFR § 3.8 as in force this date shall apply for purposes of determining—

1. If the fund includes property covered by an election under § 3.2(g)(2), the amount of gain to be taken into account by the transferor under 26 CFR §§ 3.2(g)(2) and 3.8(c)(4),

2. The tax attributes of the fund and property in the fund in the hands of the transferee, and

3. All other consequences of the proposed exchange.

Whereas, the determination as set forth above are hereby agreed to by said transferor and transferee.

Now, this closing agreement witnesseth, that the said taxpayer and said Commissioner of Internal Revenue hereby mutually agree that the determinations as set forth above shall be final and conclusive, subject, however, to reopening in the event of fraud, malfeasance, or misrepresentation of material fact, and provided that any change or modification of applicable statutes will render this agreement ineffective to the extent that it is dependent upon such statutes.

In witness whereof, the above parties have subscribed their names to these presents, in quadruplicate.

Signed this ______ day of ______, 19__

____

(Transferor)

By ______________________________

____

(Title)

____

(Transferee)

By ______________________________

____

(Title)

Commissioner of Internal Revenue

By ______________________________

Assistant Commissioner (Technical)

Date ______________________________

§ 3.9 Consolidated returns. [Reserved]

T.D. 7398, 1/23/76.

§ 3.10 Transitional rules for existing funds.

(a) In general. Section 607(j) of the Act provides that any person who was maintaining a fund or funds under section 607 of the Merchant Marine Act, 1936 prior to its amendment by the Merchant Marine Act of 1970 (for purposes of this part referred to as "old fund") may continue to maintain such old fund in the same manner as under prior law subject to the limitations contained in section 607(j) of the Act. Thus, a party may not simultaneously maintain such old fund and a new fund established under the Act.

(b) Extension of agreement to new fund. If a person enters into an agreement under the Act to establish a new fund, he may agree to the extension of such agreement to some or all of the amounts in the old fund and transfer the amounts in the old fund to which the agreement is to apply from the old fund to the new fund. If an agreement to establish a new fund is extended to amounts from an old fund, each item in the old fund to which such agreement applies shall be considered to be transferred to the appropriate account in the manner provided for in § 3.8(d) in the new fund in a nontaxable transaction which is in accordance with the provisions of the agreement under which such old fund was maintained. For purposes of determining the amount of interest under section 607(h)(3)(C) of the Act and § 3.7(e), the date of deposit of any item so transferred shall be deemed to be July 1, 1971, or the date of the deposit in the old fund, whichever is the later.

T.D. 7398, 1/23/76.

§ 3.11 Definitions.

(a) As used in the regulations in this part and as defined in section 607(k) of the Act—

(1) The term "eligible vessel" means any vessel—

(i) Constructed in the United States, and if reconstructed, reconstructed in the United States,

(ii) Documented under the laws of the United States, and

(iii) Operated in the foreign or domestic commerce of the United States or in the fisheries of the United States.

Any vessel which was constructed outside of the United States but documented under the laws of the United States on April 15, 1970, or constructed outside the United States for use in the U.S. foreign trade pursuant to a contract entered into before April 15, 1970, shall be treated as satisfying the requirements of subdivision (i) of this subparagraph and the requirements of subparagraph (2)(i) of this section.

(2) The term "qualified vessel" means any vessel—

(i) Constructed in the United States and, if reconstructed, reconstructed in the United States,

(ii) Documented under the laws of the United States, and

(iii) Which the person maintaining the fund agrees with the Secretary of Commerce will be operated in the U.S. foreign, Great Lakes, or noncontiguous domestic trade or in the fisheries of the United States.

(3) The term "agreement vessel" means any eligible vessel or qualified vessel which is subject to an agreement entered into under section 607 of the Act.

(4) The term "vessel" includes cargo handling equipment which the Secretary of Commerce determines is intended for use primarily on the vessel. The term "vessel" also includes an ocean-going towing vessel or an ocean-going barge or comparable towing vessel or barge operated in the Great Lakes.

(b) Insofar as the computation and collection of taxes are concerned, other terms used in the regulations in this part, except as otherwise provided in the Act or this part, have the same meaning as in the Code and the regulations thereunder.

T.D. 7398, 1/23/76.

§ 1.150-1 Definitions.

(a) Scope and effective date. *(1) In general.* Except as otherwise provided, the definitions in this section apply for all purposes of sections 103 and 141 through 150.

(2) Effective date. (i) In general. Except as otherwise provided in this paragraph (a)(2), this section applies to issues issued after June 30, 1993 to which §§ 1.148-1 through 1.148-11 apply. In addition, this section (other than paragraph (c)(3) of this section) applies to any issue to which the election described in § 1.148-11(b)(1) is made.

(ii) Special effective date for paragraphs (c)(1), (c)(4)(iii), and (c)(6). Paragraphs (c)(1), (c)(4)(iii), and (c)(6) of this section apply to bonds sold on or after July 8, 1997, and to any issue to which the election described in § 1.148-11(b)(1) is made. See § 1.148-11A(i) for rules relating to certain bonds sold before July 8, 1997.

(3) Exceptions to general effective date. See § 1.141-15 for the applicability date of the definition of bond documents contained in paragraph (b) of this section and the effective date of paragraph (c)(3)(ii) of this section.

(b) Certain general definitions. The following definitions apply:

Bond means any obligation of a State or political subdivision thereof under section 103(c)(1).

Bond documents means the bond indenture or resolution, transcript of proceedings, and any related documents.

Capital expenditure means any cost of a type that is properly chargeable to capital account (or would be so chargeable with a proper election or with the application of the definition of placed in service under § 1.150-2(c)) under general Federal income tax principles. For example, costs incurred to acquire, construct, or improve land, buildings, and equipment generally are capital expenditures. Whether an expenditure is a capital expenditure is determined at the time the expenditure is paid with respect to the property. Future changes in law do not affect whether an expenditure is a capital expenditure.

Conduit borrower means the obligor on a purpose investment (as defined in § 1.148-1). For example, if an issuer invests proceeds in a purpose investment in the form of a loan, lease, installment sale obligation, or similar obligation to another entity and the obligor uses the proceeds to carry out the governmental purpose of the issue, the obligor is a conduit borrower.

Conduit financing issue means an issue the proceeds of which are used or are reasonably expected to be used to finance at least one purpose investment representing at least one conduit loan to one conduit borrower.

Conduit loan means a purpose investment (as defined in § 1.148-1).

Governmental bond means any bond of an issue of tax-exempt bonds in which none of the bonds are private activity bonds.

Issuance costs means costs to the extent incurred in connection with, and allocable to, the issuance of an issue within the meaning of section 147(g). For example, issuance costs include the following costs but only to the extent incurred in connection with, and allocable to, the borrowing: underwriters' spread; counsel fees; financial advisory fees; rating agency fees; trustee fees; paying agent fees; bond registrar, certification, and authentication fees; accounting fees; printing costs for bonds and offering documents; public approval process costs; engineering and feasibility study costs; guarantee fees, other than for qualified guarantees (as defined in § 1.148-4(f)); and similar costs.

Issue date means, in reference to an issue, the first date on which the issuer receives the purchase price in exchange for delivery of the evidence of indebtedness representing any bond included in the issue. Issue date means, in reference to a bond, the date on which the issuer receives the purchase price in exchange for that bond. In no event is the issue date earlier than the first day on which interest begins to accrue on the bond or bonds for Federal income tax purposes.

Obligation means any valid evidence of indebtedness under general Federal income tax principles.

Pooled financing issue means an issue the proceeds of which are to be used to finance purpose investments representing conduit loans to two or more conduit borrowers, unless those conduit loans are to be used to finance a single capital project.

Private activity bond means a private activity bond (as defined in section 141).

Qualified mortgage loan means a mortgage loan with respect to an owner-occupied residence acquired with the proceeds of an obligation described in section 143(a)(1) or 143(b) (or applicable prior law).

Qualified student loan means a student loan acquired with the proceeds of an obligation described in section 144(b)(1).

Related party means, in reference to a governmental unit or a 501(c)(3) organization, any member of the same controlled group, and, in reference to any person that is not a governmental unit or 501(c)(3) organization, a related person (as defined in section 144(a)(3)).

Taxable bond means any obligation the interest on which is not excludable from gross income under section 103.

Tax-exempt bond means any bond the interest on which is excludable from gross income under section 103(a). For purposes of section 148, tax-exempt bond includes:

(1) An interest in a regulated investment company to the extent that at least 95 percent of the income to the holder of the interest is interest that is excludable from gross income under section 103(a); and

(2) A certificate of indebtedness issued by the United States Treasury pursuant to the Demand Deposit State and Local Government Series program described in 31 CFR part 344.

Working capital expenditure means any cost that is not a capital expenditure. Generally, current operating expenses are working capital expenditures.

(c) Definition of issue. *(1) In general.* Except as otherwise provided in this paragraph (c), the term issue means two or more bonds that meet all of the following requirements:

(i) Sold at substantially the same time. The bonds are sold at substantially the same time. Bonds are treated as sold at substantially the same time if they are sold less than 15 days apart.

(ii) Sold pursuant to the same plan of financing. The bonds are sold pursuant to the same plan of financing. Factors material to the plan of financing include the purposes for the bonds and the structure of the financing. For example, generally—

(A) Bonds to finance a single facility or related facilities are part of the same plan of financing;

(B) Short-term bonds to finance working capital expenditures and long-term bonds to finance capital projects are not part of the same plan of financing; and

(C) Certificates of participation in a lease and general obligation bonds secured by tax revenues are not part of the same plan of financing.

(iii) Payable from same source of funds. The bonds are reasonably expected to be paid from substantially the same source of funds, determined without regard to guarantees from parties unrelated to the obligor.

(2) Exception for taxable bonds. Taxable bonds and tax-exempt bonds are not part of the same issue under this paragraph (c). The issuance of tax-exempt bonds in a transaction (or series of related transactions) that includes taxable bonds, however, may constitute an abusive arbitrage device under § 1.148-10(a) or a device to avoid other limitations in sections 103 and 141 through 150 (for example, structures involving windows or unreasonable allocations of bonds).

(3) Exception for certain bonds financing separate purposes. (i) In general. Bonds may be treated as part of separate issues if the requirements of this paragraph (c)(3) are satisfied. Each of these separate issues must finance a separate purpose (e.g., refunding a separate prior issue, financing a separate purpose investment, financing integrated or func-

tionally related capital projects, and financing any clearly discrete governmental purpose). Each of these separate issues independently must be a tax-exempt bond (e.g., a governmental bond or a qualified mortgage bond). The aggregate proceeds, investments, and bonds in such a transaction must be allocated between each of the separate issues using a reasonable, consistently applied allocation method. If any separate issue consists of refunding bonds, the allocation rules in § 1.148-9(h) must be satisfied. An allocation is not reasonable if it achieves more favorable results under sections 103 and 141 to 150 than could be achieved with actual separate issues. All allocations under this paragraph (c)(3) must be made in writing on or before the issue date.

(ii) Exceptions. This paragraph (c)(3) does not apply for purposes of sections 141, 144(a), 148, 149(d) and 149(g).

(4) Special rules for certain financings. (i) Draw-down loans. Bonds issued pursuant to a draw-down loan are treated as part of a single issue. The issue date of that issue is the first date on which the aggregate draws under the loan exceed the lesser of $50,000 or 5 percent of the issue price.

(ii) Commercial paper. (A) In general. Short-term bonds having a maturity of 270 days or less (commercial paper) issued pursuant to the same commercial paper program may be treated as part of a single issue, the issue date of which is the first date the aggregate amount of commercial paper issued under the program exceeds the lesser of $50,000 or 5 percent of the aggregate issue price of the commercial paper in the program. A commercial paper program is a program to issue commercial paper to finance or refinance the same governmental purpose pursuant to a single master legal document. Commercial paper is not part of the same commercial paper program unless issued during an 18-month period, beginning on the deemed issue date. In addition, commercial paper issued after the end of this 18-month period may be treated as part of the program to the extent issued to refund commercial paper that is part of the program, but only to the extent that—

(1) There is no increase in the principal amount outstanding; and

(2) The program does not have a term in excess of—

(i) 30 years; or

(ii) The period reasonably necessary for the governmental purposes of the program.

(B) Safe harbor. The requirement of paragraph (c)(4)(ii)(A)(2) of this section is treated as satisfied if the weighted average maturity of the issue does not exceed 120 percent of the weighted average expected economic life of the property financed by the issue.

(iii) Certain general obligation bonds. Except as otherwise provided in paragraph (c)(2) of this section, bonds that are secured by a pledge of the issuer's full faith and credit (or a substantially similar pledge) and sold and issued on the same dates pursuant to a single offering document may be treated as part of the same issue if the issuer so elects on or before the issue date.

(5) Anti-abuse rule. In order to prevent the avoidance of sections 103 and 141 through 150 and the general purposes thereof, the Commissioner may treat bonds as part of the same issue or as part of separate issues to clearly reflect the economic substance of a transaction.

(6) Sale date. The sale date of a bond is the first day on which there is a binding contract in writing for the sale or exchange of the bond.

(d) Definition of refunding issue and related definitions. *(1) General definition of refunding issue.* Refunding issue means an issue of obligations the proceeds of which are used to pay principal, interest, or redemption price on another issue (a prior issue, as more particularly defined in paragraph (d)(5) of this section), including the issuance costs, accrued interest, capitalized interest on the refunding issue, a reserve or replacement fund, or similar costs, if any, properly allocable to that refunding issue.

(2) Exceptions and special rules. For purposes of paragraph (d)(1) of this section, the following exceptions and special rules apply—

(i) Payment of certain interest. An issue is not a refunding issue if the only principal and interest that is paid with proceeds of the issue (determined without regard to the multipurpose issue rules of § 1.148-9(h)) is interest on another issue that—

(A) Accrues on the other issue during a one-year period including the issue date of the issue that finances the interest;

(B) Is a capital expenditure; or

(C) Is a working capital expenditure to which the de minimis rule of § 1.148-6(d)(3)(ii)(A) applies.

(ii) Certain issues with different obligors. (A) In general. An issue is not a refunding issue to the extent that the obligor (as defined in paragraph (d)(2)(ii)(B) of this section) of one issue is neither the obligor of the other issue nor a related party with respect to the obligor of the other issue.

(B) Definition of obligor. The obligor of an issue means the actual issuer of the issue, except that the obligor of the portion of an issue properly allocable to an investment in a purpose investment means the conduit borrower under that purpose investment. The obligor of an issue used to finance qualified mortgage loans, qualified student loans, or similar program investments (as defined in § 1.148-1) does not include the ultimate recipient of the loan (e.g., the homeowner, the student).

(iii) Certain special rules for purpose investments. For purposes of this paragraph (d), the following special rules apply:

(A) Refunding of a conduit financing issue by a conduit loan refunding issue. Except as provided in paragraph (d)(2)(iii)(B) of this section, the use of the proceeds of an issue that is used to refund an obligation that is a purpose investment (a conduit refunding issue) by the actual issuer of the conduit financing issue determines whether the conduit refunding issue is a refunding of the conduit financing issue (in addition to a refunding of the obligation that is the purpose investment).

(B) Recycling of certain payments under purpose investments. A conduit refunding issue is not a refunding of a conduit financing issue to the extent that the actual issuer of the conduit financing issue reasonably expects as of the date of receipt of the proceeds of the conduit refunding issue to use those amounts within 6 months (or, if greater, during the applicable temporary period for those amounts under section 148(c) or under applicable prior law) to acquire a new purpose investment. Any new purpose investment is treated as made from the proceeds of the conduit financing issue.

(C) Application to tax-exempt loans. For purposes of this paragraph (d), obligations that would be purpose investments (absent section 148(b)(3)(A)) are treated as purpose investments.

(iv) Substance of transaction controls. In the absence of other applicable controlling rules under this paragraph (d), the determination of whether an issue is a refunding issue is based on the substance of the transaction in light of all the facts and circumstances.

(v) Certain integrated transactions in connection with asset acquisition not treated as refunding issues. If, within six months before or after a person assumes (including taking subject to) obligations of an unrelated party in connection with an asset acquisition (other than a transaction to which section 381(a) applies if the person assuming the obligation is the acquiring corporation within the meaning of section 381(a)), the assumed issue is refinanced, the refinancing issue is not treated as a refunding issue.

(3) Current refunding issue. Current refunding issue means:

(i) Except as provided in paragraph (d)(3)(ii) of this section, a refunding issue that is issued not more than 90 days before the last expenditure of any proceeds of the refunding issue for the payment of principal or interest on the prior issue; and

(ii) In the case of a refunding issue issued before 1986.

(A) A refunding issue that is issued not more than 180 days before the last expenditure of any proceeds of the refunding issue for the payment of principal or interest on the prior issue; or

(B) A refunding issue if the prior issue had a term of less than 3 years and was sold in anticipation of permanent financing, but only if the aggregate term of all prior issues sold in anticipation of permanent financing was less than 3 years.

(4) Advance refunding issue. Advance refunding issue means a refunding issue that is not a current refunding issue.

(5) Prior issue. Prior issue means an issue of obligations all or a portion of the principal, interest, or call premium on which is paid or provided for with proceeds of a refunding issue. A prior issue may be issued before, at the same time as, or after a refunding issue. If the refunded and unrefunded portions of a prior issue are treated as separate issues under § 1.148-9(i), for the purposes for which that section applies, except to the extent that the context clearly requires otherwise, references to a prior issue refer only to the refunded portion of that prior issue.

(e) Controlled group means a group of entities controlled directly or indirectly by the same entity or group of entities within the meaning of this paragraph (e). *(1) Direct control.* The determination of direct control is made on the basis of all the relevant facts and circumstances. One entity or group of entities (the controlling entity) generally controls another entity or group of entities (the controlled entity) for purposes of this paragraph if the controlling entity possesses either of the following rights or powers and the rights or powers are discretionary and non-ministerial—

(i) The right or power both to approve and to remove without cause a controlling portion of the governing body of the controlled entity; or

(ii) The right or power to require the use of funds or assets of the controlled entity for any purpose of the controlling entity.

(2) Indirect control. If a controlling entity controls a controlled entity under the test in paragraph (e)(1) of this section, then the controlling entity also controls all entities controlled, directly or indirectly, by the controlled entity or entities.

(3) Exception for general purpose governmental entities. An entity is not a controlled entity under this paragraph (e) if the entity possesses substantial taxing, eminent domain, and police powers. For example, a city possessing substantial amounts of each of these sovereign powers is not a controlled entity of the state.

T.D. 8394, 1/27/92, amend T.D. 8418, 5/12/92, T.D. 8476, 6/14/93, T.D. 8538, 5/5/94, T.D. 8712, 1/10/97, T.D. 8718, 5/8/97, T.D. 9234, 12/16/2005.

PAR. 2. Section 1.150-1 is amended as follows:

1. Paragraph (a)(2)(iii) is added.

2. Paragraphs (d)(2)(ii) and (d)(2)(v) are revised.

The added and revised provisions read as follows:

Proposed § 1.150-1 Definitions. [*For Preamble, see ¶ 152,255*]

(a) * * *

(2) * * *

(iii) Special effective date for paragraphs (d)(2)(ii) and (d)(2)(v). Paragraphs (d)(2)(ii) and (d)(2)(v) of this section apply to bonds sold on or after the date of publication of final regulations in the Federal Register, and may be applied by issuers in whole, but not in part, to any issue that is sold on or after April 10, 2002.

* * * * *

(d) * * *

(2) * * *

(ii) Certain issues with different obligors. (A) In general. An issue is not a refunding issue to the extent that the obligor (as defined in paragraph (d)(2)(ii)(B) of this section) of one issue is neither the obligor of the other issue nor a related party with respect to the obligor of the other issue. The determination of whether persons are related for this purpose is generally made immediately before the issuance of the refinancing issue. This paragraph (d)(2)(ii)(A) does not apply to any issue that is issued in connection with a transaction to which section 381(a) applies.

(B) Definition of obligor. The obligor of an issue means the actual issuer of the issue, except that the obligor of the portion of an issue properly allocable to an investment in a purpose investment means the conduit borrower under that purpose investment. The obligor of an issue used to finance qualified mortgage loans, qualified student loans, or similar program investments (as defined in § 1.148-1) does not include the ultimate recipient of the loan (e.g., the homeowner, the student).

(C) Certain integrated transactions. If, within six months before or after a person assumes (including taking subject to) obligations of an unrelated party in connection with an acquisition transaction (other than a transaction to which section 381(a) applies), the assumed issue is refinanced, the refinancing issue is not a refunding issue. An acquisition transaction is a transaction in which a person acquires from an unrelated party—

(1) Assets (other than an equity interest in an entity);

(2) Stock of a corporation with respect to which a valid election under section 338 is made; or

(3) Control of a governmental unit or a 501(c)(3) organization through the acquisition of stock, membership interests or otherwise.

(D) Special rule for affiliated persons. Paragraphs (d)(2)(ii)(A) and (C) of this section do not apply to any issue that is issued in connection with a transaction between affiliated persons (as defined in paragraph (d)(2)(ii)(E) of this section), unless—

(1) The refinanced issue is redeemed on the earliest date on which it may be redeemed (or otherwise within 90 days after the date of issuance of the refinancing issue); and

(2) The refinancing issue is treated for all purposes of sections 103 and 141 through 150 as financing the assets that were financed with the refinanced issue.

(E) Affiliated persons. For purposes of paragraph (d)(2)(ii)(D) of this section, persons are affiliated persons if—

(1) At any time during the six months prior to the transaction, more than 5 percent of the voting power of the governing body of either person is in the aggregate vested in the other person and its directors, officers, owners, and employees; or

(2) During the one-year period beginning six months prior to the transaction, the composition of the governing body of the acquiring person (or any person that controls the acquiring person) is modified or established to reflect (directly or indirectly) representation of the interests of the acquired person or the person from whom assets are acquired (or there is an agreement, understanding, or arrangement relating to such a modification or establishment during that one-year period).

(F) Reverse acquisitions. Notwithstanding any other provision of this paragraph (d)(2)(ii), a refinancing issue is a refunding issue if the obligor of the refinanced issue (or any person that is related to the obligor of the refinanced issue immediately before the transaction) has or obtains in the transaction the right to appoint the majority of the members of the governing body of the obligor of the refinancing issue (or any person that controls the obligor of the refinancing issue). See paragraph (d)(2)(v) Example 2 of this section.

* * * * *

(v) Examples. The provisions of this paragraph (d)(2) are illustrated by the following examples:

Example (1). Consolidation of 501(c)(3) hospital organizations.

(i) A and B are unrelated hospital organizations described in section 501(c)(3). A has assets with a fair market value of $175 million, and is the obligor of outstanding tax-exempt bonds in the amount of $75 million. B has assets with a fair market value of $145 million, and is the obligor of outstanding tax-exempt bonds in the amount of $50 million. In response to significant competitive pressures in the healthcare industry, and for other substantial business reasons, A and B agree to consolidate their operations. To accomplish the consolidation, A and B form a new 501(c)(3) hospital organization, C. A and B each appoint one-half of the members of the initial governing body of C. Subsequent to the initial appointments, C's governing body is self-perpetuating. On December 29, 2003, State Y issues bonds with sale proceeds of $129 million and lends the entire sale proceeds to C. The 2003 bonds are collectively secured by revenues of A, B and C. Simultaneously with the issuance of the 2003 bonds, C acquires the sole membership interest in each of A and B. C's ownership of these membership interests entitles C to exercise exclusive control over the assets and operations of A and B. C uses the $129 million of sale proceeds of the 2003 bonds to defease the $75 million of bonds on which A was the obligor, and the $50 million of bonds on which B was the obligor. All of the defeased bonds will be redeemed on the first date on which they may be redeemed. In addition, C treats the 2003 bonds as financing the same assets as the defeased bonds. The 2003 bonds do not constitute a refunding issue because the obligor of the 2003 bonds (C) is neither the obligor of the defeased bonds nor a related party with respect to the obligors of those bonds immediately before the issuance of the 2003 bonds. In addition, the requirements of paragraph (d)(2)(ii)(D) of this section have been satisfied.

(ii) The facts are the same as in paragraph (i) of this Example 1, except that C acquires the membership interests in A and B subject to the obligations of A and B on their respective bonds, and the 2003 bonds are sold within six months after the acquisition by C of the membership interests. The 2003 bonds do not constitute a refunding issue.

Example (2). Reverse acquisition. D and E are unrelated hospital organizations described in section 501(c)(3). D has assets with a fair market value of $225 million, and is the obligor of outstanding tax-exempt bonds in the amount of $100 million. E has assets with a fair market value of $100 million. D and E agree to consolidate their operations. On May 18, 2004, Authority Z issues bonds with sale proceeds of $103 million and lends the entire sale proceeds to E. Simultaneously with the issuance of the 2004 bonds, E acquires the sole membership interest in D. In addition, D obtains the right to appoint the majority of the members of the governing body of E. E uses the $103 million of sale proceeds of the 2004 bonds to defease the bonds of which D was the obligor. All of the defeased bonds will be redeemed on the first date on which they may be redeemed. In addition, E treats the 2004 bonds as financing the same assets as the defeased bonds. The 2004 bonds constitute a refunding issue because the obligor of the defeased bonds (D) obtains in the transaction the right to appoint the majority of the members of the governing body of the obligor of the 2004 bonds (E). See paragraph (d)(2)(ii)(F) of this section.

Example (3). Relinquishment of control. The facts are the same as in Example 2, except that D does not obtain the right, directly or indirectly, to appoint any member of the governing body of E. Rather, E obtains the right both to approve and to remove without cause each member of the governing body of D. In addition, prior to being acquired by E, D experiences financial difficulties as a result of mismanagement. Thus, as part of E's acquisition of D, all of the former members of D's governing body resign their positions and are replaced with persons appointed by E. The 2004 bonds do not constitute a refunding issue.

* * * * *

§ 1.150-1A Definitions.

(a) through (b) [Reserved]. For guidance see § 1.150-1.

(c) Definition of issue. *(1) In general.* Except as otherwise provided, the provisions of this paragraph (c) apply for all purposes of sections 103 and 141 through 150. Except as otherwise provided in this paragraph (c), two or more bonds are treated as part of the same issue if all of the following factors are present:

(i) Sold at substantially the same time. The bonds are sold at substantially the same time. Bonds are treated as sold at substantially the same time if they are sold less than 15 days apart. For this purpose only, a variable yield bond is treated as sold on its issue date.

(ii) Sold pursuant to the same plan of financing. The bonds are sold pursuant to the same plan of financing. Factors material to the plan of financing include the purposes for the bonds and the structure of the financing. For example, generally —

(A) Bonds to finance a single facility or related facilities are part of the same plan of financing;

(B) Short-term bonds to finance working capital expenditures and long-term bonds to finance capital projects are not part of the same plan of financing; and

(C) Certificates of participation in a lease and general obligation bonds secured by tax revenues are not part of the same plan of financing.

(iii) Payable from same source of funds. The bonds are reasonably expected to be paid from substantially the same source of funds, determined without regard to guarantees from parties unrelated to the obligor.

(2) through (4)(ii) [Reserved]. For guidance see §§ 1.150-1(c)(3) through (c)(4)(ii)

(iii) Certain general obligation bonds. Bonds are part of the same issue if secured by a pledge of the issuer's full faith and credit (or a substantially similar pledge) and sold and issued on the same dates pursuant to a single offering document.

(5) [Reserved]. For guidance see § 1.150-1(c)(5).

(6) Sale date. The sale date of a bond is the first day on which there is a binding contract in writing for the sale or exchange of the bond.

T.D. 8538, 5/5/94, amend T.D. 8718, 5/8/97.

---

§ 1.150-2 Proceeds of bonds used for reimbursement.

(a) Table of contents. This table of contents contains a listing of the headings contained in § 1.150-2.

(a) Table of contents.

(b) Scope.

(c) Definitions.

(d) General operating rules for reimbursement expenditures.

(1) Official intent.

(2) Reimbursement period.

(3) Nature of expenditure.

(e) Official intent rules.

(1) Form of official intent.

(2) Project description in official intent.

(3) Reasonableness of official intent.

(f) Exceptions to general operating rules.

(1) De minimis exception.

(2) Preliminary expenditures exception.

(g) Special rules on refundings.

(1) In general — once financed, not reimbursed.

(2) Certain proceeds of prior issue used for reimbursement treated as unspent.

(h) Anti-abuse rules.

(1) General rule.

(2) One-year step transaction rule.

(i) Authority of the Commissioner to prescribe rules.

(j) Effective date.

(1) In general.

(2) Transitional rules.

(b) Scope. This section applies to reimbursement bonds (as defined in paragraph (c) of this section) for all purposes of sections 103 and 141 to 150.

(c) Definitions. The following definitions apply:

Issuer means—

(1) For any private activity bond (excluding a qualified 501(c)(3) bond, qualified student loan bond, qualified mortgage bond, or qualified veterans' mortgage bond), the entity that actually issues the reimbursement bond; and

(2) For any bond not described in paragraph (1) of this definition, either the entity that actually issues the reimbursement bond or, to the extent that the reimbursement bond proceeds are to be loaned to a conduit borrower, that conduit borrower.

Official intent means an issuer's declaration of intent to reimburse an original expenditure with proceeds of an obligation.

Original expenditure means an expenditure for a governmental purpose that is originally paid from a source other than a reimbursement bond.

Placed in service means, with respect to a facility, the date on which, based on all the facts and circumstances—

(1) The facility has reached a degree of completion which would permit its operation at substantially its design level; and

(2) The facility is, in fact, in operation at such level.

Reimbursement allocation means an allocation in writing that evidences an issuer's use of proceeds of a reimbursement bond to reimburse an original expenditure. An allocation made within 30 days after the issue date of a reimbursement bond may be treated as made on the issue date.

Reimbursement bond means the portion of an issue allocated to reimburse an original expenditure that was paid before the issue date.

(d) General operating rules for reimbursement expenditures. Except as otherwise provided, a reimbursement allocation is treated as an expenditure of proceeds of a reimbursement bond for the governmental purpose of the original expenditure on the date of the reimbursement allocation only if:

(1) Official intent. Not later than 60 days after payment of the original expenditure, the issuer adopts an official intent for the original expenditure that satisfies paragraph (e) of this section.

(2) Reimbursement period. (i) In general. The reimbursement allocation is made not later than 18 months after the later of—

(A) The date the original expenditure is paid; or

(B) The date the project is placed in service or abandoned, but in no event more than 3 years after the original expenditure is paid.

(ii) Special rule for small issuers. In applying paragraph (d)(2)(i) of this section to an issue that satisfies section 148(f)(4)(D)(i)(I) through (IV), the "18 month" limitation is changed to "3 years" and the "3-year" maximum reimbursement period is disregarded.

(iii) Special rule for long-term construction projects. In applying paragraph (d)(2)(i) to a construction project for which both the issuer and a licensed architect or engineer certify that at least 5 years is necessary to complete construction of the project, the maximum reimbursement period is changed from "3 years" to "5 years."

(3) Nature of expenditure. The original expenditure is a capital expenditure, a cost of issuance for a bond, an expenditure described in § 1.148-6(d)(3)(ii)(B) (relating to certain extraordinary working capital items), a grant (as defined in § 1.148-6(d)(4)), a qualified student loan, a qualified mortgage loan, or a qualified veterans' mortgage loan.

(e) Official intent rules. An official intent satisfies this paragraph (e) if:

(1) Form of official intent. The official intent is made in any reasonable form, including issuer resolution, action by an appropriate representative of the issuer (e.g., a person authorized or designated to declare official intent on behalf of the issuer), or specific legislative authorization for the issuance of obligations for a particular project.

(2) Project description in official intent. (i) In general. The official intent generally describes the project for which the original expenditure is paid and states the maximum principal amount of obligations expected to be issued for the project. A project includes any property, project, or program (e.g., highway capital improvement program, hospital equipment acquisition, or school building renovation).

(ii) Fund accounting. A project description is sufficient if it identifies, by name and functional purpose, the fund or account from which the original expenditure is paid (e.g., parks and recreation fund — recreational facility capital improvement program).

(iii) Reasonable deviations in project description. Deviations between a project described in an official intent and the actual project financed with reimbursement bonds do not invalidate the official intent to the extent that the actual project is reasonably related in function to the described project. For example, hospital equipment is a reasonable deviation from hospital building improvements. In contrast, a city office building rehabilitation is not a reasonable deviation from highway improvements.

(3) Reasonableness of official intent. On the date of the declaration, the issuer must have a reasonable expectation (as defined in § 1.148-1(b)) that it will reimburse the original expenditure with proceeds of an obligation. Official intents declared as a matter of course or in amounts substantially in excess of the amounts expected to be necessary for the project (e.g., blanket declarations) are not reasonable. Similarly, a pattern of failure to reimburse actual original expenditures covered by official intents (other than in extraordinary circumstances) is evidence of unreasonableness. An official intent declared pursuant to a specific legislative authorization is rebuttably presumed to satisfy this paragraph (e)(3).

(f) Exceptions to general operating rules. *(1) De minimis exception.* Paragraphs (d)(1) and (d)(2) of this section do not apply to costs of issuance of any bond or to an amount not in excess of the lesser of $100,000 or 5 percent of the proceeds of the issue.

(2) Preliminary expenditures exception. Paragraphs (d)(1) and (d)(2) of this section do not apply to any preliminary expenditures, up to an amount not in excess of 20 percent of the aggregate issue price of the issue or issues that finance or are reasonably expected by the issuer to finance the project for which the preliminary expenditures were incurred. Preliminary expenditures include architectural, engineering, surveying, soil testing, reimbursement bond issuance, and similar costs that are incurred prior to commencement of acquisition, construction, or rehabilitation of a project, other than land acquisition, site preparation, and similar costs incident to commencement of construction.

(g) Special rules on refundings. *(1) In general.* Once financed, not reimbursed. Except as provided in paragraph (g)(2) of this section, paragraph (d) of this section does not apply to an allocation to pay principal or interest on an obligation or to reimburse an original expenditure paid by another obligation. Instead, such an allocation is analyzed under rules on refunding issues. See § 1.148-9.

(2) Certain proceeds of prior issue used for reimbursement treated as unspent. In the case of a refunding issue (or series of refunding issues), proceeds of a prior issue purportedly used to reimburse original expenditures are treated as unspent proceeds of the prior issue unless the purported reimbursement was a valid expenditure under applicable law on reimbursement expenditures on the issue date of the prior issue.

(h) Anti-abuse rules. *(1) General rule.* A reimbursement allocation is not an expenditure of proceeds of an issue under this section if the allocation employs an abusive arbitrage device under § 1.148-10 to avoid the arbitrage restrictions or to avoid the restrictions under sections 142 through 147.

(2) One-year step transaction rule. (i) Creation of replacement proceeds. A purported reimbursement allocation is invalid and thus is not an expenditure of proceeds of an issue if, within 1 year after the allocation, funds corresponding to the proceeds of a reimbursement bond for which a reimbursement allocation was made are used in a manner that results in the creation of replacement proceeds (as defined in § 1.148-1) of that issue or another issue. The preceding sentence does not apply to amounts deposited in a bona fide debt service fund (as defined in § 1.148-1).

(ii) Example. The provisions of paragraph (h)(2)(i) of this section are illustrated by the following example.

Example. On January 1, 1994, County A issues an issue of 7 percent tax-exempt bonds (the 1994 issue) and makes a purported reimbursement allocation to reimburse an original expenditure for specified capital improvements. A immediately deposits funds corresponding to the proceeds subject to the reimbursement allocation in an escrow fund to provide for payment of principal and interest on its outstanding 1991 issue of 9 percent tax-exempt bonds (the prior issue). The use of amounts corresponding to the proceeds of the reimbursement bonds to create a sinking fund for another issue within 1 year after the purported reimbursement allocation invalidates the reimbursement allocation. The proceeds retain their character as unspent proceeds of the 7 percent issue upon deposit in the escrow fund. Accordingly, the proceeds are subject to the 7 percent yield restriction of the 1994 issue instead of the 9 percent yield restriction of the prior issue.

(i) Authority of the commissioner to prescribe rules. The Commissioner may by revenue ruling or revenue procedure (see § 601.601(d)(2)(ii)(b) of this chapter) prescribe rules for the expenditure of proceeds of reimbursement bonds in circumstances that do not otherwise satisfy this section.

(j) Effective date. *(1) In general.* The provisions of this section apply to all allocations of proceeds of reimbursement bonds issued after June 30, 1993.

(2) Transitional rules. (i) Official intent. An official intent is treated as satisfying the official intent requirement of paragraph (d)(1) of this section if it—

(A) Satisfied the applicable provisions of § 1.103-8(a)(5) as in effect prior to July 1, 1993, (as contained in 26 CFR part 1 revised as of April 1, 1993) and was made prior to that date, or

(B) Satisfied the applicable provisions of § 1.103-18 as in effect between January 27, 1992, and June 30, 1993, (as contained in 26 CFR part 1 revised as of April 1, 1993) and was made during that period.

(ii) Certain expenditures of private activity bonds. For any expenditure that was originally paid prior to August 15, 1993, and that would have qualified for expenditure by reimbursement from the proceeds of a private activity bond under T.D. 7199, § 1.103-8(a)(5), 1972-2 C.B. 45 (See § 601.601(d)(2)(i)(b) of this chapter.), the requirements of that section may be applied in lieu of this section.

T.D. 8476, 6/14/93.

§ 1.150-4 Change in use of facilities financed with tax-exempt private activity bonds.

(a) Scope. This section applies for purposes of the rules for change of use of facilities financed with private activity bonds under sections 150(b)(3) (relating to qualified 501(c)(3) bonds), 150(b)(4) (relating to certain exempt facility bonds and small issue bonds), 150(b)(5) (relating to facilities required to be owned by governmental units or 501(c)(3) organizations), and 150(c).

(b) Effect of remedial actions. *(1) In general.* Except as provided in this section, the change of use provisions of sections 150(b)(3) through (5), and 150(c) apply even if the issuer takes a remedial action described in §§ 1.142-2, 1.144-2, or 1.145-2.

(2) Exceptions. (i) Redemption. If nonqualified bonds are redeemed within 90 days of a deliberate action under § 1.145-2(a) or within 90 days of the date on which a failure to properly use proceeds occurs under § 1.142-2 or § 1.144-2, sections 150(b)(3) through (5) do not apply during the period between that date and the date on which the nonqualified bonds are redeemed.

(ii) Alternative qualifying use of facility. If a bond-financed facility is used for an alternative qualifying use under §§ 1.145-2 and 1.141-12(f), sections 150(b)(3) and (5) do not apply because of the alternative use.

(iii) Alternative use of disposition proceeds. If disposition proceeds are used for a qualifying purpose under §§ 1.145-2 and 1.141-12(e), 1.142-2(c)(4), or 1.144-2, sections 150(b)(3) through (5) do not apply because of the deliberate action that gave rise to the disposition proceeds after the date on which all of the disposition proceeds have been expended on the qualifying purpose. If all of the disposition proceeds are so expended within 90 days of the date of the deliberate action, however, sections 150(b)(3) through (5) do not apply because of the deliberate action.

(c) Allocation rules. *(1) In general.* If a change in use of a portion of the property financed with an issue of qualified private activity bonds causes section 150(b)(3), (b)(4), or (b)(5) to apply to an issue, the bonds of the issue allocable to that portion under section 150(c)(3) are the same as the nonqualified bonds determined for purposes of §§ 1.142-1, 1.144-1, and 1.145-1, except that bonds allocable to all common areas are also allocated to that portion.

(2) Special rule when remedial action is taken. If an issuer takes a remedial action with respect to an issue of private activity bonds under §§ 1.142-2, 1.144-2, or 1.145-2, the bonds of the issue allocable to a portion of property are the same as the nonqualified bonds determined for purposes of those sections.

(d) Effective dates. For effective dates of this section, see § 1.141-16.

T.D. 8712, 1/10/97.

§ 1.150-5 Filing notices and elections.

(a) In general. Notices and elections under the following sections must be filed with the Internal Revenue Service, 1111 Constitution Avenue, NW, Attention: T:GE:TEB:O, Washington, DC 20224 or such other place designated by publication of a notice in the Internal Revenue Bulletin—

(1) Section 1.141-12(d)(3);

(2) Section 1.142(f)(4)-1; and

(3) Section 1.142-2(c)(2).

(b) Effective dates. This section applies to notices and elections filed on or after January 19, 2001.

T.D. 8941, 1/17/2001.

§ 1.151-1 Deductions for personal exemptions.

Caution: The Treasury has not yet amended Reg § 1.151-1 to reflect changes made by P.L. 104-188, P.L. 103-66, P.L. 101-508, P.L. 99-514.

(a) In general. *(1)* In computing taxable income, an individual is allowed a deduction for the exemptions specified in section 151. Such exemptions are: (i) The exemptions for an individual taxpayer and spouse (the so-called personal exemptions); (ii) the additional exemptions for a taxpayer attaining the age of 65 years and spouse attaining the age of 65 years (the so-called old-age exemptions); (iii) the additional exemptions for a blind taxpayer and a blind spouse; and (iv) the exemptions for dependents of the taxpayer.

(2) A nonresident alien individual who is a bona fide resident of Puerto Rico during the entire taxable year and subject to tax under section 1 or 1201(b) is allowed as deductions the exemptions specified in section 151, even though as to the United States such individual is a nonresident alien. See section 876 and the regulations thereunder, relating to alien residents of Puerto Rico.

(b) Exemptions for individual taxpayer and spouse (so-called personal exemptions). Section 151(b) allows an exemption for the taxpayer and an additional exemption for the spouse of the taxpayer if a joint return is not made by the taxpayer and his spouse, and if the spouse, for the calendar year in which the taxable year of the taxpayer begins, has no gross income and is not the dependent of another taxpayer. Thus, a husband is not entitled to an exemption for his wife on his separate return for the taxable year beginning in a calendar year during which she has any gross income (though insufficient to require her to file a return). Since, in the case of a joint return, there are two taxpayers (although under section 6013 there is only one income for the two taxpayers on such return, i.e., their aggregate income), two exemptions are allowed on such return, one for each taxpayer spouse. If in any case a joint return is made by the taxpayer and his spouse, no other person is allowed an exemption for such spouse even though such other person would have been entitled to claim an exemption for such spouse as a dependent if such joint return had not been made.

(c) Exemptions for taxpayer attaining the age of 65 and spouse attaining the age of 65 (so-called old-age exemption). *(1)* Section 151(c) provides an additional exemption for the taxpayer if he has attained the age of 65 before the close of his taxable year. An additional exemption is also allowed to the taxpayer for his spouse if a joint return is not made by the taxpayer and his spouse and if the spouse has attained the age of 65 before the close of the taxable year of the taxpayer and, for the calendar year in which the taxable year of the taxpayer begins, the spouse has no gross income and is not the dependent of another taxpayer. If a husband and wife make a joint return, an old-age exemption will be allowed as to each taxpayer spouse who has attained the age of 65 before the close of the taxable year for which the joint return is made. The exemptions under section 151(c) are in addition to the exemptions for the taxpayer and spouse under section 151(b).

(2) In determining the age of an individual for the purposes of the exemption for old age, the last day of the taxable year of the taxpayer is the controlling date. Thus, in the event of a separate return by a husband, no additional exemption for old age may be claimed for his spouse unless such spouse has attained the age of 65 on or before the close of the taxable year of the husband. In no event shall the additional exemption for old age be allowed with respect to a spouse who dies before attaining the age of 65 even though such spouse would have attained the age of 65 before the close of the taxable year of the taxpayer. For the purposes of the old-age exemption, an individual attains the age of 65 on the first moment of the day preceding his sixty-fifth birthday Accordingly, an individual whose sixty-fifth birthday falls on January 1 in a given year attains the age of 65 on the last day of the calendar year immediately preceding.

(d) Exemptions for the blind. *(1)* Section 151(d) provides an additional exemption for the taxpayer if he is blind at the close of his taxable year. An additional exemption is also allowed to the taxpayer for his spouse if the spouse is blind and, for the calendar year in which the taxable year of the taxpayer begins, has no gross income and is not the dependent of another taxpayer. The determination of whether the spouse is blind shall be made as of the close of the taxable year of the taxpayer, unless the spouse dies during such taxable year, in which case such determination shall be made as of the time of such death.

(2) The exemptions for the blind are in addition to the exemptions for the taxpayer and spouse under section 151(b) and are also in addition to the exemptions under section 151(c) for taxpayers and spouses attaining the age of 65 years. Thus, a single individual who has attained the age of 65 before the close of his taxable year and who is blind at the close of his taxable year is entitled, in addition to so-called personal exemption, to two further exemptions, one by reason of his age and the other by reason of his blindness. If a husband and wife make a joint return, an exemption for the blind will be allowed as to each taxpayer spouse who is blind at the close of the taxable year for which the joint return is made.

(3) A taxpayer claiming an exemption allowed by section 151(d) for a blind taxpayer and a blind spouse shall, if the individual for whom the exemption is claimed is not totally blind as of the last day of the taxable year of the taxpayer (or, in the case of a spouse who dies during such taxable year, as of the time of such death), attach to his return a certificate from a physician skilled in the diseases of the eye or a registered optometrist stating that as of the applicable status determination date in the opinion of such physician or optometrist (i) the central visual acuity of the individual for whom the exemption is claimed did not exceed 20/200 in the better eye with correcting lenses or (ii) such individual's visual acuity was accompanied by a limitation in the fields of vision such that the widest diameter of the visual field subtends an angle no greater than 20 degrees. If such individual is totally blind as of the status determination date there shall be attached to the return a statement by the person or persons making the return setting forth such fact.

(4) Notwithstanding subparagraph (3) of this paragraph, this subparagraph may be applied where the individual for whom an exemption under section 151(d) is claimed is not totally blind, and in the certified opinion of an examining physician skilled in the diseases of the eye there is no reasonable probability that the individual's visual acuity will ever improve beyond the minimum standards described in subparagraph (3) of this paragraph. In this event, if the examination occurs during a taxable year for which the exemption is claimed, and the examining physician certifies that, in his opinion, the condition is irreversible, and a copy of this certification is filed with the return for that taxable year, then a statement described in subparagraph (3) of this paragraph need not be attached to such individual's return for subsequent taxable years so long as the condition remains irreversible. The taxpayer shall retain a copy of the certified opinion in his records, and a statement referring to such opinion shall be attached to future returns claiming the section 151(d) exemption.

T.D. 6231, 4/25/57, amend T.D. 7114, 5/17/71, T.D. 7230, 12/21/72.

---

§ 1.151-2 Additional exemptions for dependents.

Caution: The Treasury has not yet amended Reg § 1.151-2 to reflect changes made by 108-311, P.L. 106-554, P.L. 104-188, P.L. 103-66, P.L. 101-508, P.L. 100-647, P.L. 99-514, P.L. 98-369, P.L. 97-34, P.L. 95-600.

(a) Section 151(e) allows to a taxpayer an exemption for each dependent (as defined in section 152) whose gross income (as defined in section 61) for the calendar year in which the taxable year of the taxpayer begins is less than the amount provided in section 151(e)(1)(A) applicable to the taxable year of the taxpayer, or who is a child of the taxpayer and who—

(1) Has not attained the age of 19 at the close of the calendar year in which the taxable year of the taxpayer begins, or

(2) Is a student, as defined in paragraph (b) of § 1.151-3.

No exemption shall be allowed under section 151(e) for any dependent who has made a joint return with his spouse under section 6013 for the taxable year beginning in the calendar year in which the taxable year of the taxpayer begins. The amount provided in section 151(e)(1)(A) is $750 in the case of a taxable year beginning after December 31, 1972; $700 in the case of a taxable year beginning after December 31, 1971, and before January 1, 1973; $650 in the case of a taxable year beginning after December 31, 1970, and before January 1, 1972; $625 in the case of a taxable year beginning after December 31, 1969, and before January 1, 1971; and $600 in the case of a taxable year beginning before January 1, 1970. For special rules in the case of a taxpayer whose taxable year is a fiscal year ending after December 31, 1969, and beginning before January 1, 1973, see section 21(d) and the regulations thereunder.

(b) The only exemption allowed for a dependent of the taxpayer is that provided by section 151(e). The exemptions provided by section 151(c) (old-age exemptions) and section 151(d) (exemptions for the blind) are allowed only for the taxpayer or his spouse. For example, where a taxpayer provides the entire support for his father who meets all the requirements of a dependent, he is entitled to only one exemption for his father (section 151(e)), even though his father is over the age of 65.

T.D. 6231, 4/25/57, amend T.D. 7114, 5/17/71.

§ 1.151-3 Definitions.

Caution: The Treasury has not yet amended Reg § 1.151-3 to reflect changes made by 108-311.

(a) Child. For purposes of section 151(e), 152, and the regulations thereunder, the term "child" means a son, stepson, daughter, stepdaughter, adopted son, adopted daughter, or for taxable years beginning after December 31, 1958, a child who is a member of an individual's household if the child was placed with the individual by an authorized placement agency for legal adoption pursuant to a formal application filed by the individual with the agency (see paragraph (c)(2) of § 1.152-2), or, for taxable years beginning after December 31, 1969, a foster child (if such foster child satisfies the requirements set forth in paragraph (b) of § 1.152-1 with respect to the taxpayer) of the taxpayer.

(b) Student. For purposes of section 151(e) and section 152(d), and the regulations thereunder, the term "student" means an individual who during each of 5 calendar months during the calendar year in which the taxable year of the taxpayer begins is a full-time student at an educational institution or is pursuing a full-time course of institutional on-farm training under the supervision of an accredited agent of an educational institution or of a State or political subdivision of a State. An example of "institutional on-farm training" is that authorized by 38 U.S.C. 1652 (formerly section 252 of the Veterans' Readjustment Assistance Act of 1952), as described in section 252 of such act. A full-time student is one who is enrolled for some part of 5 calendar months for the number of hours or courses which is considered to be full-time attendance. The 5 calendar months need not be consecutive. School attendance exclusively at night does not constitute full-time attendance. However, full-time attendance at an educational institution may include some attendance at night in connection with a full-time course of study.

(c) Educational institution. For purposes of sections 151(e) and 152, and the regulations thereunder, the term "educational institution" means a school maintaining a regular faculty and established curriculum, and having an organized body of students in attendance. It includes primary and secondary schools, colleges, universities, normal schools, technical schools, mechanical schools, and similar institutions, but does not include non-educational institutions, on-the-job training, correspondence schools, night schools, and so forth.

T.D. 6231, 4/25/57, amend T.D. 7051, 7/8/70.

§ 1.151-4 Amount of deduction for each exemption under section 151.

Caution: The Treasury has not yet amended Reg § 1.151-4 to reflect changes made by P.L. 107-16, P.L. 103-66, P.L. 101-508, P.L. 99-514, P.L. 97-34, P.L. 95-600.

The amount allowed as a deduction for each exemption under section 151 is (a) $750 in the case of a taxable year beginning after December 31, 1972; (b) $700 in the case of a taxable year beginning after December 31, 1971, and before January 1, 1973; (c) $650 in the case of a taxable year beginning after December 31, 1970, and before January 1, 1972; (d) $625 in the case of a taxable year beginning after December 31, 1969, and before January 1, 1971; and (e) $600 in the case of a taxable year beginning before January 1, 1970. For special rules in the case of a fiscal year ending after December 31, 1969, and beginning before January 1, 1973, see section 21(d) and the regulations thereunder.

T.D. 7114, 5/17/71.

Proposed § 1.9300-1 [*For Preamble, see ¶ 152,823*]

[The text of proposed § 1.9300-1 is the same as the text of § 1.9300-1T published elsewhere in this issue of the Federal Register.] [See T.D. 9301, 12/12/2006, 71 Fed. Reg. 238.]

§ 1.9300-1T Reduction in taxable income for housing Hurricane Katrina displaced individuals.

(a) In general. For a taxable year beginning in 2005 or 2006, a taxpayer who is a natural person may reduce taxable income by $500 for each Hurricane Katrina displaced individual (as defined in paragraph (e)(1) of this section) to whom the taxpayer provides housing free of charge in, or on the site of, the taxpayer's principal residence for a period of 60 consecutive days ending in the taxable year. A taxpayer may not claim the reduction in taxable income unless the taxpayer includes the taxpayer identification number of the Hurricane Katrina displaced individual on the taxpayer's income tax return.

(b) Provision of housing. *(1) Principal residence.* For purposes of this section, the term principal residence has the same meaning as in section 121 and the regulations thereunder. See § 1.121-1(b)(1) and (b)(2).

(2) Legal interest required. A taxpayer is treated as providing housing for purposes of this section only if the taxpayer is an owner or lessee (including a co-owner or co-lessee) of the residence.

(3) Compensation for providing housing. (i) In general. No reduction in taxable income is allowed under this section to a taxpayer who receives rent or any other amount from any source in connection with the provision of housing.

(ii) Amounts in connection with the provision of housing. For purposes of this section, amounts in connection with the provision of housing include (but are not limited to) amounts for rent and utilities. Amounts for telephone calls, food, clothing, and transportation are examples of amounts not in connection with the provision of housing.

(c) Limitations. *(1) Dollar limitation.* (i) In general. The reduction under paragraph (a) of this section may not exceed the maximum dollar limitation reduced by the amount of the reduction under this section for all prior taxable years. The maximum dollar limitation is—

(A) $2,000 in the case of an unmarried individual;

(B) $2,000 in the case of a husband and wife who file a joint income tax return; and

(C) $1,000 in the case of a married individual who files a separate income tax return.

(ii) Married individuals with separate principal residences. The limitations in paragraphs (c)(1)(i)(B) and (c)(1)(i)(C) of this section apply without regard to whether the married individuals occupy the same principal residence. A person is treated as married for purposes of this section if the individual is treated as married under section 7703.

(2) Spouse or dependent of the taxpayer. No reduction is allowed for a Hurricane Katrina displaced individual who is the spouse or dependent of the taxpayer.

(3) Individual taken into account only once. A taxpayer may not reduce taxable income under paragraph (a) of this section with respect to a Hurricane Katrina displaced individual who was taken into account by the taxpayer for any prior taxable year.

(4) Taxpayers occupying the same principal residence. A Hurricane Katrina displaced individual may be taken into account by only one taxpayer occupying the same principal residence for all taxable years.

(d) Substantiation. A taxpayer claiming a reduction under this section must prepare and maintain records sufficient to show entitlement to the reduction as provided in Form 8914 (Exemption Amount for Taxpayers Housing Individuals Displaced by Hurricane Katrina) or other forms, instructions, publications or guidance published by the IRS.

(e) Definitions. The following definitions apply for purposes of this section.

(1) Hurricane Katrina displaced individual. The term Hurricane Katrina displaced individual means any natural person if the following requirements are met—

(i) The person's principal place of abode on August 28, 2005, was in the Hurricane Katrina disaster area (as defined in paragraph (e)(2) of this section);

(ii) The person was displaced from that abode; and

(iii) If the abode was located outside the Hurricane Katrina core disaster area (as defined in paragraph (e)(3) of this section)—

(A) The abode was damaged by Hurricane Katrina; or

(B) The person was evacuated from that abode by reason of Hurricane Katrina.

(2) Hurricane Katrina disaster area. The term Hurricane Katrina disaster area means the states of Alabama, Florida, Louisiana, and Mississippi.

(3) Hurricane Katrina core disaster area. The term Hurricane Katrina core disaster area means the portion of the Hurricane Katrina disaster area designated by the President to warrant individual or individual and public assistance from the federal government under the Robert T. Stafford Disaster Relief and Emergency Assistance Act (42 U.S.C. 5170).

(f) Examples. The provisions of this section are illustrated by the following examples in which each Hurricane Katrina displaced individual, who is not a dependent or spouse of the taxpayer, is provided housing (within the meaning of paragraph (b) of this section) in, or on the site of, the taxpayer's principal residence for a period of at least 60 consecutive days ending in the applicable taxable year. The examples are as follows:

Example (1). Taxpayer A provides housing to N, a Hurricane Katrina displaced individual, from September 1, 2005, until March 10, 2006. Under paragraphs (a) and (c)(3) of this section, A may reduce taxable income by $500 on A's 2005 income tax return or A's 2006 income tax return, but not both, with respect to N.

Example (2). The facts are the same as in Example 1 except that A and B, A's unmarried roommate and co-lessee, provide housing to N. Under paragraphs (a) and (c)(4) of this section, either A or B, but not both, may reduce taxable income by $500 for 2005 with respect to N. If either A or B reduces taxable income for 2005 with respect to N, neither A nor B may reduce taxable income with respect to N for 2006.

Example (3). Unmarried roommates and co-lessees C and D provide housing to eight Hurricane Katrina displaced individuals during 2005. Under paragraphs (a) and (c)(1)(i)(A) of this section, C and D each may reduce taxable income by $2,000 on their 2005 income tax returns.

Example (4). (i) H and W are married to each other and provide housing to a Hurricane Katrina displaced individual, O, in 2005. H and W file their 2005 income tax return married filing jointly. Under paragraphs (a) and (c)(4) of this section, H and W may reduce taxable income by $500 on their 2005 income tax return with respect to O.

(ii) In 2006, H and W provide housing to O and to another Hurricane Katrina displaced individual, P. H and W file their 2006 income tax return married filing separately. Because H and W reduced their 2005 taxable income with respect to O, under paragraph (c)(3) of this section, neither H nor W may reduce taxable income on their 2006 income tax return with respect to O. Under paragraphs (a) and (c)(4) of this section, either H or W, but not both, may reduce taxable income by $500 on his or her 2006 income tax return with respect to P.

(g) Effective date. This section applies for taxable years beginning after December 31, 2004, and before January 1, 2007, and ending on or after December 11, 2006.

T.D. 9301, 12/11/2006.

§ 1.152-1 General definition of a dependent.

Caution: The Treasury has not yet amended Reg § 1.152-1 to reflect changes made by 108-311.

(a) *(1)* For purposes of the income taxes imposed on individuals by chapter 1 of the Code, the term "dependent" means any individual described in paragraphs (1) through (10) of section 152(a) over half of whose support, for the calendar year in which the taxable year of the taxpayer begins, was received from the taxpayer.

(2) (i) For purposes of determining whether or not an individual received, for a given calendar year, over half of his support from the taxpayer, there shall be taken into account the amount of support received from the taxpayer as compared to the entire amount of support which the individual received from all sources, including support which the individual himself supplied. The term "support" includes food, shelter, clothing, medical and dental care, education, and the like. Generally, the amount of an item of support will be the amount of expense incurred by the one furnishing such item. If the item of support furnished an individual is in the form of property or lodging, it will be necessary to measure the amount of such item of support in terms of its fair market value.

(ii) In computing the amount which is contributed for the support of an individual, there must be included any amount which is contributed by such individual for his own support, including income which is ordinarily excludable from gross income, such as benefits received under the Social Security Act (42 USC ch 7). For example, a father receives $800 social security benefits, $400 interest, and $1,000 from his son during 1955, all of which sums represent his sole support during that year. The fact that the social security benefits of $800 are not includible in the father's gross income does not prevent such amount from entering into the computation of the total amount contributed for the father's support. Consequently, since the son's contribution of $1,000 was less than one-half of the father's support ($2,200) he may not claim his father as a dependent.

(iii) (a) For purposes of determining the amount of support furnished for a child (or children) by a taxpayer for a given calendar year, an arrearage payment made in a year subsequent to a calendar year for which there is an unpaid liability shall not be treated as paid either during that calendar year or in the year of payment, but no amount shall be treated as an arrearage payment to the extent that there is an unpaid liability (determined without regard to such payment) with respect to the support of a child for the taxable year of payment; and

(b) Similarly, payments made prior to any calendar year (whether or not made in the form of a lump sum payment in settlement of the parent's liability for support) shall not be treated as made during such calendar year, but payments made during any calendar year from amounts set aside in trust by a parent in a prior year, shall be treated as made during the calendar year in which paid.

(b) Section 152(a)(9) applies to any individual (other than an individual who at any time during the taxable year was the spouse, determined without regard to section 153, of the taxpayer) who lives with the taxpayer and is a member of the taxpayer's household during the entire taxable year of the taxpayer. An individual is not a member of the taxpayer's household if at any time during the taxable year of the taxpayer the relationship between such individual and the taxpayer is in violation of local law. It is not necessary under section 152(a)(9) that the dependent be related to the taxpayer. For example, foster children may qualify as dependents. It is necessary, however, that the taxpayer both maintain and occupy the household. The taxpayer and dependent will be considered as occupying the household for such entire taxable year notwithstanding temporary absences from the household due to special circumstances. A nonpermanent failure to occupy the common abode by reason of illness, education, business, vacation, military service, or a custody agreement under which the dependent is absent for less than six months in the taxable year of the taxpayer, shall be considered temporary absence due to special circumstances. The fact that the dependent dies during the year shall not deprive the taxpayer of the deduction if the dependent lived in the household for the entire part of the year preceding his death. Likewise, the period during the taxable year preceding the birth of an individual shall not prevent such individual from qualifying as a dependent under section 152(a)(9). Moreover, a child who actually becomes a member of the taxpayer's household during the taxable year shall not be prevented from being considered a member of such household for the entire taxable year, if the child is required to remain in a hospital for a period following its birth, and if such child would otherwise have been a member of the taxpayer's household during such period.

(c) In the case of a child of the taxpayer who is under 19 or who is a student, the taxpayer may claim the dependency exemption for such child provided he has furnished more than one-half of the support of such child for the calendar year in which the taxable year of the taxpayer begins, even though the income of the child for such calendar year may be equal to or in excess of the amount determined pursuant to § 1.151-2 applicable to such calendar year. In such a case, there may be two exemptions claimed for the child: One on the parent's (or stepparent's) return, and one on the child's return. In determining whether the taxpayer does in fact furnish more than one-half of the support of an individual who is a child, as defined in paragraph (a) of § 1.151-3, of the taxpayer and who is a student, as defined in paragraph (b) of § 1.151-3, a special rule regarding scholarships applies. Amounts received as scholarships, as defined in paragraph (a) of § 1.117-3, for study at an educational institution shall not be considered in determining whether the taxpayer furnishes more than one-half the support of such individual. For example, A has a child who receives a $1,000 scholarship to the X college for one year. A contributes $500, which constitutes the balance of the child's support for that year. A may claim the child as a dependent, as the $1,000 scholarship is not counted in determining the support of the child. For purposes of this paragraph, amounts received for tuition payments and allowances by a veteran under the provisions of the Servicemen's Readjustment Act of 1944 (58 Stat 284) or the Veterans' Readjustment Assistance Act of 1952 (38 USC ch 38) are not amounts received as scholarships. See also § 1.117-4. For definition of the terms "child," "student," and "educational institution," as used in this paragraph, see § 1.151-3.

T.D. 6231, 4/25/57, amend T.D. 6304, 8/22/58, T.D. 6441, 1/4/60, T.D. 6663, 7/10/63, T.D. 7099, 3/19/71, T.D. 7114, 5/17/71.

§ 1.152-2 Rules relating to general definition of dependent.

Caution: The Treasury has not yet amended Reg § 1.152-2 to reflect changes made by 108-311, P.L. 94-455.

(a) *(1)* Except as provided in subparagraph (2) of this paragraph, to qualify as a dependent an individual must be a citizen or resident of the United States or be a resident of the Canal Zone, the Republic of Panama, Canada, or Mexico, or, for taxable years beginning after December 31, 1971, a national of the United States, at some time during the calendar year in which the taxable year of the taxpayer begins. A resident of the Republic of the Philippines who was born to or legally adopted by the taxpayer in the Philippine Islands before January 1, 1956, at a time when the taxpayer was a member of the Armed Forces of the United States, may also be claimed as a dependent if such resident otherwise qualifies as a dependent. For definition of "Armed Forces of the United States," see section 7701(a)(15).

(2) (i) For any taxable year beginning after December 31, 1957, a taxpayer who is a citizen, or, for any taxable year beginning after December 31, 1971, a national, of the United States is permitted, under section 152(b)(3)(B) to treat as a dependent his legally adopted child who lives with him, as a member of his household, for the entire taxable year and who, but for the citizenship, nationality, or residence requirements of section 152(b)(3) and subparagraph (1) of this paragraph, would qualify as a dependent of the taxpayer for such taxable year.

(ii) Under section 152(b)(3)(B) and this subparagraph, it is necessary that the taxpayer both maintain and occupy the household. The taxpayer and his legally adopted child will be considered as occupying the household for the entire taxable year of the taxpayer notwithstanding temporary absences from the household due to special circumstances. A nonpermanent failure to occupy the common abode by reason of illness, education, business, vacation, military service, or a custody agreement under which the legally adopted child is absent for less than six months in the taxable year of the taxpayer shall be considered temporary absence due to special circumstances. The fact that a legally adopted child dies during the year shall not deprive the taxpayer of the deduction if the child lived in the household for the entire part of the year preceding his death. The period during the taxable year preceding the birth of a child shall not prevent such child from qualifying as a dependent under this subparagraph. Moreover, a legally adopted child who actually becomes a member of the taxpayer's household during the taxable year shall not be prevented from being considered a member of such household for the entire taxable year, if the child is required to remain in a hospital for a period following its birth and if such child would otherwise have been a member of the taxpayer's household during such period.

(iii) For purposes of section 152(b)(3)(B) and this subparagraph, any child whose legal adoption by the taxpayer (a citizen or national of the United States) becomes final at any time before the end of the taxable year of the taxpayer shall not be disqualified as a dependent of such taxpayer by reason of his citizenship, nationality, or residence, provided the child lived with the taxpayer and was a member of the taxpayer's household for the entire taxable year in which the legal adoption became final. For example, A, a citizen of the United States who makes his income tax returns on the basis of the calendar year, is employed in Brazil by an agency of the United States Government. In October 1958 he takes into his household C, a resident of Brazil who is not a citizen of the United States, for the purpose of initiating adoption proceedings. C lives with A and is a member of his household for the remainder of 1958 and for the entire calendar year 1959. On July 1, 1959, the adoption proceedings were completed and C became the legally adopted child of A. If C otherwise qualifies as a dependent, he may be claimed as a dependent by A for 1959.

(b) A payment to a wife which is includible in her gross income under section 71 or section 682 shall not be considered a payment by her husband for the support of any dependent.

(c) *(1)* For purposes of determining the existence of any of the relationships specified in section 152(a) or (b)(1), a legally adopted child of an individual shall be treated as a child of such individual by blood.

(2) For any taxable year beginning after December 31, 1958, a child who is a member of an individual's household also shall be treated as a child of such individual by blood if the child was placed with the individual by an authorized placement agency for legal adoption pursuant to a formal application filed by the individual with the agency. For purposes of this subparagraph an authorized placement agency is any agency which is authorized by a State, the District of Columbia, a possession of the United States, a foreign country, or a political subdivision of any of the foregoing to place children for adoption. A taxpayer who claims as a dependent a child placed with him for adoption shall attach to his income tax return a statement setting forth the name of the child for whom the dependency deduction is claimed, the name and address of the authorized placement agency, and the date the formal application was filed with the agency.

(3) The application of this paragraph may be illustrated by the following example:

Example. On March 1, 1959, D, a resident of the United States, made formal application to an authorized child placement agency for the placement of E, a resident of the United States, with him for legal adoption. On June 1, 1959, E was placed with D for legal adoption. During the year 1959 E received over one-half of his support from D. D may claim E as a dependent for 1959. Since E was a resident of the United States, his qualification as a dependent is in no way based on the provisions of section 152(b)(3)(B). Therefore, it is immaterial that E was not a member of D's household during the entire taxable year.

(4) For purposes of determining the existence of any of the relationships specified in section 152(a) or (b)(1), a foster child of an individual (if such foster child satisfies the requirements set forth in paragraph (b) of § 1.152-1 with respect to such individual) shall, for taxable years beginning after December 31, 1969, be treated as a child of such individual by blood. For purposes of this subparagraph, a foster child is a child who is in the care of a person or persons (other than the parents or adopted parents of the child) who care for the child as their own child. Status as a foster child is not dependent upon or affected by the circumstances under which the child became a member of the household.

(d) In the case of a joint return it is not necessary that the prescribed relationship exist between the person claimed as a dependent and the spouse who furnishes the support; it is sufficient if the prescribed relationship exists with respect to either spouse. Thus, a husband and wife making a joint return may claim as a dependent a daughter of the wife's brother (wife's niece) even though the husband is one who furnishes the chief support. The relationship of affinity once existing will not terminate by divorce or the death of a spouse. For example, a widower may continue to claim his deceased wife's father (his father-in-law) as a dependent provided he meets the other requirements of section 151.

T.D. 6231, 4/25/57, amend T.D. 6441, 1/4/60, T.D. 6663, 7/10/63, T.D. 7051, 7/8/70, T.D. 7291, 12/3/73.

PAR. 2. Section 1.152-2 is amended by revising paragraph (c)(2) to read as follows:

Proposed § 1.152-2 Rules relating to general definition of dependent. [*For Preamble, see ¶ 152,101*]

* * * * *

(c) * * *

(2) For any taxable year beginning after December 31, 2000, a child who is a member of an individual's household will be treated as a child of that individual by blood if the child was placed with the individual by an authorized placement agency for legal adoption pursuant to a formal application filed by the individual with the agency. For purposes of this paragraph (c)(2), an authorized placement agency is any agency that is authorized by a State, the District of Columbia, a possession of the United States, a foreign country, or a political subdivision of any of the foregoing to place children for adoption. An authorized placement agency also includes biological parents and other persons authorized by state law to place children for legal adoption.

* * * * *

§ 1.152-3 Multiple support agreements.

Caution: The Treasury has not yet amended Reg § 1.152-3 to reflect changes made by 108-311.

(a) Section 152(c) provides that a taxpayer shall be treated as having contributed over half of the support of an individual for the calendar year (in cases where two or more taxpayers contributed to the support of such individual) if—

(1) No one person contributed over half of the individual's support,

(2) Each member of the group which collectively contributed more than half of the support of the individual would have been entitled to claim the individual as a dependent but for the fact that he did not contribute more than one-half of such support,

(3) The member of the group claiming the individual as a dependent contributed more than 10 percent of the individual's support, and

(4) Each other person in the group who contributed more than 10 percent of such support furnishes to the taxpayer claiming the dependent a written declaration that such other person will not claim the individual as a dependent for any taxable year beginning in such calendar year.

(b) Examples. Application of the rule contained in paragraph (a) of this section may be illustrated by the following examples:

Example (1). During the taxable year, brothers A, B, C, and D contributed the entire support of their mother in the following percentages: A, 30 percent; B, 20 percent; C, 29 percent; and D, 21 percent. Any one of the brothers, except for the fact that he did not contribute more than half of her support, would have been entitled to claim his mother as a dependent. Consequently, any one of the brothers could claim a deduction for the exemption of the mother if he obtained a written declaration (as provided in paragraph (a)(4) of this section) from each of the other brothers. Even though A and D together contributed more than one-half the support of the mother, A, if he wished to claim his mother as a dependent, would be required to obtain written declarations from B, C, and D, since each of those three contributed more than 10 percent of the support and, but for the failure to contribute more than half of the mother's support, would have been entitled to claim his mother as a dependent.

Example (2). During the taxable year, E, an individual who resides with his son, S, received his entire support for that year as follows:

Source	Percentage of total
Social Security	25
N, an unrelated neighbor	11
B, a brother	14
D, a daughter	10
S, a son	40
Total received by E	100

B, D, and S are persons each of whom, but for the fact that none contributed more than half of E's support, could claim E as a dependent for the taxable year. The three together contributed 64 percent of E's support, and, thus, each is a member of the group to be considered for the purpose of section 152(c). B and S are the only members of such group who can meet all the requirements of section 152(c), and either one could claim E as a dependent for his taxable year if he obtained a written declaration (as provided in paragraph (a)(4) of this section) signed by the other, and furnished the other information required by the return with respect to all the contributions to E. Inasmuch as D did not contribute more than 10 percent of E's support, she is not entitled to claim E as a dependent for the taxable year nor is she required to furnish a written declaration with respect to her contributions to E. N contributed over 10 percent of the support of E, but, since he is an unrelated neighbor, he does not qualify as a member of the group for the purpose of the multiple support agreement under section 152(c).

(c) *(1)* The member of a group of contributors who claims an individual as a dependent for a taxable year beginning before January 1, 2002, under the multiple support agreement provisions of section 152(c) must attach to the member's income tax return for the year of the deduction a written declaration from each of the other persons who contributed more than 10 percent of the support of such individual and who, but for the failure to contribute more than half of the support of the individual, would have been entitled to claim the individual as a dependent.

(2) The taxpayer claiming an individual as a dependent for a taxable year beginning after December 31, 2001, under the multiple support agreement provisions of section 152(c) must provide with the income tax return for the year of the deduction—

(i) A statement identifying each of the other persons who contributed more than 10 percent of the support of the individual and who, but for the failure to contribute more than half of the support of the individual, would have been entitled to claim the individual as a dependent; and

(ii) A statement indicating that the taxpayer obtained a written declaration from each of the persons described in section 152(c)(2) waiving the right to claim the individual as a dependent.

(3) The taxpayer claiming the individual as a dependent for a taxable year beginning after December 31, 2001, must retain the waiver declarations and should be prepared to furnish the waiver declarations and any other information necessary to substantiate the claim, which may include a statement showing the names of all contributors (whether or not members of the group described in section 152(c)(2)) and the amount contributed by each to the support of the claimed dependent.

T.D. 6231, 4/25/57, amend T.D. 6663, 7/10/63, T.D. 8989, 4/23/2002, T.D. 9040, 1/30/2003.

§ 1.152-4 Special rule for a child of divorced or separated parents or parents who live apart.

Caution: The Treasury has not yet amended Reg § 1.152-4 to reflect changes made by 108-311, P.L. 98-369.

(a) In general. A taxpayer may claim a dependency deduction for a child (as defined in section 152(f)(1)) only if the child is the qualifying child of the taxpayer under section 152(c) or the qualifying relative of the taxpayer under section 152(d). Section 152(c)(4)(B) provides that a child who is claimed as a qualifying child by parents who do not file a joint return together is treated as the qualifying child of the parent with whom the child resides for a longer period of time during the taxable year or, if the child resides with both parents for an equal period of time, of the parent with the higher adjusted gross income. However, a child is treated as the qualifying child or qualifying relative of the noncustodial parent if the custodial parent releases a claim to the exemption under section 152(e) and this section.

(b) Release of claim by custodial parent. *(1) In general.* Under section 152(e)(1), notwithstanding section 152(c)(1)(B), (c)(4), or (d)(1)(C), a child is treated as the qualifying child or qualifying relative of the noncustodial parent (as defined in paragraph (d) of this section) if the requirements of paragraphs (b)(2) and (b)(3) of this section are met.

(2) Support, custody, and parental status. (i) In general. The requirements of this paragraph (b)(2) are met if the parents of the child provide over one-half of the child's support for the calendar year, the child is in the custody of one or both parents for more than one-half of the calendar year, and the parents--

(A) Are divorced or legally separated under a decree of divorce or separate maintenance;

(B) Are separated under a written separation agreement; or

(C) Live apart at all times during the last 6 months of the calendar year whether or not they are or were married.

(ii) Multiple support agreement. The requirements of this paragraph (b)(2) are not met if over one-half of the support of the child is treated as having been received from a taxpayer under section 152(d)(3).

(3) Release of claim to child. The requirements of this paragraph (b)(3) are met for a calendar year if--

(i) The custodial parent signs a written declaration that the custodial parent will not claim the child as a dependent for any taxable year beginning in that calendar year and the noncustodial parent attaches the declaration to the noncustodial parent's return for the taxable year; or

(ii) A qualified pre-1985 instrument, as defined in section 152(e)(3)(B), applicable to the taxable year beginning in that calendar year, provides that the noncustodial parent is entitled to the dependency exemption for the child and the noncustodial parent provides at least $600 for the support of the child during the calendar year.

(c) Custody. A child is in the custody of one or both parents for more than one-half of the calendar year if one or both parents have the right under state law to physical custody of the child for more than one-half of the calendar year.

(d) Custodial parent. *(1) In general.* The custodial parent is the parent with whom the child resides for the greater number of nights during the calendar year, and the noncustodial parent is the parent who is not the custodial parent. A child is treated as residing with neither parent if the child is emancipated under state law. For purposes of this section, a child resides with a parent for a night if the child sleeps--

(i) At the residence of that parent (whether or not the parent is present); or

(ii) In the company of the parent, when the child does not sleep at a parent's residence (for example, the parent and child are on vacation together).

(2) Night straddling taxable years. A night that extends over two taxable years is allocated to the taxable year in which the night begins.

(3) Absences. (i) Except as provided in paragraph (d)(3)(ii) of this section, for purposes of this paragraph (d), a child who does not reside (within the meaning of paragraph (d)(1) of this section) with a parent for a night is treated as residing with the parent with whom the child would have resided for the night but for the absence.

(ii) A child who does not reside (within the meaning of paragraph (d)(1) of this section) with a parent for a night is treated as not residing with either parent for that night if it cannot be determined with which parent the child would have resided or if the child would not have resided with either parent for the night.

(4) Special rule for equal number of nights. If a child is in the custody of one or both parents for more than one-half of the calendar year and the child resides with each parent for an equal number of nights during the calendar year, the parent with the higher adjusted gross income for the calendar year is treated as the custodial parent.

(5) Exception for a parent who works at night. If, in a calendar year, due to a parent's nighttime work schedule, a child resides for a greater number of days but not nights with the parent who works at night, that parent is treated as the custodial parent. On a school day, the child is treated as residing at the primary residence registered with the school.

(e) Written declaration. *(1) Form of declaration.* (i) In general. The written declaration under paragraph (b)(3)(i) of this section must be an unconditional release of the custodial parent's claim to the child as a dependent for the year or years for which the declaration is effective. A declaration is not unconditional if the custodial parent's release of the right to claim the child as a dependent requires the satisfaction of any condition, including the noncustodial parent's meeting of an obligation such as the payment of support. A written declaration must name the noncustodial parent to whom the exemption is released. A written declaration must specify the year or years for which it is effective. A written declaration that specifies all future years is treated as specifying the first taxable year after the taxable year of execution and all subsequent taxable years.

(ii) Form designated by IRS. A written declaration may be made on Form 8332, Release/Revocation of Release of Claim to Exemption for Child by Custodial Parent, or successor form designated by the IRS. A written declaration not on the form designated by the IRS must conform to the substance of that form and must be a document executed for the sole purpose of serving as a written declaration under this section. A court order or decree or a separation agreement may not serve as a written declaration.

(2) Attachment to return. A noncustodial parent must attach a copy of the written declaration to the parent's return for each taxable year in which the child is claimed as a dependent.

(3) Revocation of written declaration. (i) In general. A parent may revoke a written declaration described in paragraph (e)(1) of this section by providing written notice of the revocation to the other parent. The parent revoking the written declaration must make reasonable efforts to provide actual notice to the other parent. The revocation may be effective no earlier than the taxable year that begins in the first calendar year after the calendar year in which the parent revoking the written declaration provides, or makes reasonable efforts to provide, the written notice.

(ii) Form of revocation. The revocation may be made on Form 8332, Release/Revocation of Release of Claim to Exemption for Child by Custodial Parent, or successor form designated by the IRS whether or not the written declaration was made on a form designated by the IRS. A revocation not on that form must conform to the substance of the form and must be a document executed for the sole purpose of serving as a revocation under this section. The revocation must specify the year or years for which the revocation is effective. A revocation that specifies all future years is treated as specifying the first taxable year after the taxable year the revocation is executed and all subsequent taxable years.

(iii) Attachment to return. The parent revoking the written declaration must attach a copy of the revocation to the parent's return for each taxable year for which the parent claims a child as a dependent as a result of the revocation. The parent revoking the written declaration must keep a copy of the revocation and evidence of delivery of the notice to the other parent, or of the reasonable efforts to provide actual notice.

(4) Ineffective declaration or revocation. A written declaration or revocation that fails to satisfy the requirements of this paragraph (e) has no effect.

(5) Written declaration executed in a taxable year beginning on or before July 2, 2008. A written declaration executed in a taxable year beginning on or before July 2, 2008, that satisfies the requirements for the form of a written declaration in effect at the time the written declaration is exe-

cuted, will be treated as meeting the requirements of paragraph (e)(1) of this section. Paragraph (e)(3) of this section applies without regard to whether a custodial parent executed the written declaration in a taxable year beginning on or before July 2, 2008.

(f) Coordination with other sections. If section 152(e) and this section apply, a child is treated as the dependent of both parents for purposes of sections 105(b), 132(h)(2)(B), and 213(d)(5).

(g) Examples. The provisions of this section are illustrated by the following examples that assume, unless otherwise provided, that each taxpayer's taxable year is the calendar year, one or both of the child's parents provide over one-half of the child's support for the calendar year, one or both parents have the right under state law to physical custody of the child for more than one-half of the calendar year, and the child otherwise meets the requirements of a qualifying child under section 152(c) or a qualifying relative under section 152(d). In addition, in each of the examples, no qualified pre-1985 instrument or multiple support agreement is in effect. The examples are as follows:

Example (1). (i) B and C are the divorced parents of Child. In 2009, Child resides with B for 210 nights and with C for 155 nights. B executes a Form 8332 for 2009 releasing B's right to claim Child as a dependent for that year, which C attaches to C's 2009 return.

(ii) Under paragraph (d) of this section, B is the custodial parent of Child in 2009 because B is the parent with whom Child resides for the greater number of nights in 2009. Because the requirements of paragraphs (b)(2) and (3) of this section are met, C may claim Child as a dependent.

Example (2). The facts are the same as in Example 1 except that B does not execute a Form 8332 or similar declaration for 2009. Therefore, section 152(e) and this section do not apply. Whether Child is the qualifying child or qualifying relative of B or C is determined under section 152(c) or (d).

Example (3). (i) D and E are the divorced parents of Child. Under a custody decree, Grandmother has the right under state law to physical custody of Child from January 1 to July 31, 2009.

(ii) Because D and E do not have the right under state law to physical custody of Child for over one-half of the 2009 calendar year, under paragraph (c) of this section, Child is not in the custody of one or both parents for over one-half of the calendar year. Therefore, section 152(e) and this section do not apply, and whether Child is the qualifying child or qualifying relative of D, E, or Grandmother is determined under section 152(c) or (d).

Example (4). (i) The facts are the same as in Example 3, except that Grandmother has the right to physical custody of Child from January 1 to March 31, 2009, and, as a result, Child resides with Grandmother during this period. D and E jointly have the right to physical custody of Child from April 1 to December 31, 2009. During this period, Child resides with D for 180 nights and with E for 95 nights. D executes a Form 8332 for 2009 releasing D's right to claim Child as a dependent for that year, which E attaches to E's 2009 return.

(ii) Under paragraph (c) of this section, Child is in the custody of D and E for over one-half of the calendar year, because D and E have the right under state law to physical custody of Child for over one-half of the calendar year.

(iii) Under paragraph (d)(3)(ii) of this section, the nights that Child resides with Grandmother are not allocated to either parent. Child resides with D for a greater number of nights than with E during the calendar year and, under paragraph (d)(1) of this section, D is the custodial parent.

(iv) Because the requirements of paragraphs (b)(2) and (3) of this section are met, section 152(e) and this section apply, and E may claim Child as a dependent.

Example (5). (i) The facts are the same as in Example 4, except that D is away on military service from April 10 to June 15, 2009, and September 6 to October 20, 2009. During these periods Child resides with Grandmother in Grandmother's residence. Child would have resided with D if D had not been away on military service. Grandmother claims Child as a dependent on Grandmother's 2009 return.

(ii) Under paragraph (d)(3)(i) of this section, Child is treated as residing with D for the nights that D is away on military service. Because the requirements of paragraphs (b)(2) and (3) of this section are met, section 152(e) and this section apply, and E, not Grandmother, may claim Child as a dependent.

Example (6). F and G are the divorced parents of Child. In May of 2009, Child turns age 18 and is emancipated under the law of the state where Child resides. Therefore, in 2009 and later years, F and G do not have the right under state law to physical custody of Child for over one-half of the calendar year, and Child is not in the custody of F and G for over one-half of the calendar year. Section 152(e) and this section do not apply, and whether Child is the qualifying child or qualifying relative of F or G is determined under section 152(c) or (d).

Example (7). (i) The facts are the same as in Example 6, except that Child turns age 18 and is emancipated under state law on August 1, 2009, resides with F from January 1, 2009, through May 31, 2009, and resides with G from June 1, 2009, through December 31, 2009. F executes a Form 8332 releasing F's right to claim Child as a dependent for 2009, which G attaches to G's 2009 return.

(ii) Under paragraph (c) of this section, Child is in the custody of F and G for over one-half of the calendar year.

(iii) Under paragraph (d)(1) of this section, Child is treated as not residing with either parent after Child's emancipation. Therefore, Child resides with F for 151 nights and with G for 61 nights. Because the requirements of paragraphs (b)(2) and (3) of this section are met, section 152(e) and this section apply, and G may claim Child as a dependent.

Example (8). H and J are the divorced parents of Child. Child generally resides with H during the week and with J every other weekend. Child resides with J in H's residence for 10 consecutive nights while H is hospitalized. Under paragraph (d)(1)(i) of this section, Child resides with H for the 10 nights.

Example (9). K and L, who are separated under a written separation agreement, are the parents of Child. In August 2009, K and Child spend 10 nights together in a hotel while on vacation. Under paragraph (d)(1)(ii) of this section, Child resides with K for the 10 nights that K and Child are on vacation.

Example (10). M and N are the divorced parents of Child. On December 31, 2009, Child attends a party at M's residence. After midnight on January 1, 2010, Child travels to N's residence, where Child sleeps. Under paragraph (d)(1) of this section, Child resides with N for the night of December

31, 2009, to January 1, 2010, because Child sleeps at N's residence that night. However, under paragraph (d)(2) of this section, the night of December 31, 2009, to January 1, 2010, is allocated to taxable year 2009 for purposes of determining whether Child resides with M or N for a greater number of nights in 2009.

Example (11). O and P, who never married, are the parents of Child. In 2009, Child spends alternate weeks residing with O and P. During a week that Child is residing with O, O gives Child permission to spend a night at the home of a friend. Under paragraph (d)(3)(i) of this section, the night Child spends at the friend's home is treated as a night that Child resides with O.

Example (12). The facts are the same as in Example 11, except that Child also resides at summer camp for 6 weeks. Because Child resides with each parent for alternate weeks, Child would have resided with O for 3 weeks and with P for 3 weeks of the period that Child is at camp. Under paragraph (d)(3)(i) of this section, Child is treated as residing with O for 3 weeks and with P for 3 weeks.

Example (13). The facts are the same as in Example 12, except that Child does not spend alternate weeks residing with O and P, and it cannot be determined whether Child would have resided with O or P for the period that Child is at camp. Under paragraph (d)(3)(ii) of this section, Child is treated as residing with neither parent for the 6 weeks.

Example (14). (i) Q and R are the divorced parents of Child. Q works from 11 PM to 7 AM Sunday through Thursday nights. Because of Q's nighttime work schedule, Child resides with R Sunday through Thursday nights and with Q Friday and Saturday nights. Therefore, in 2009, Child resides with R for 261 nights and with Q for 104 nights. Child spends all daytime hours when Child is not in school with Q and Q's address is registered with Child's school as Child's primary residence. Q executes a Form 8332 for 2009 releasing Q's right to claim Child as a dependent for that year, which R attaches to R's 2009 return.

(ii) Under paragraph (d) of this section, Q is the custodial parent of Child in 2009. Child resides with R for a greater number of nights than with Q due to Q's nighttime work schedule, and Child spends a greater number of days with Q. Therefore, paragraph (d)(5) of this section applies rather than paragraph (d)(1) of this section. Because the requirements of paragraphs (b)(2) and (3) of this section are met, R may claim Child as a dependent.

Example (15). (i) In 2009, S and T, the parents of Child, execute a written separation agreement. The agreement provides that Child will live with S and that T will make monthly child support payments to S. In 2009, Child resides with S for 335 nights and with T for 30 nights. S executes a letter declaring that S will not claim Child as a dependent in 2009 and in subsequent alternate years. The letter contains all the information requested on Form 8332, does not require the satisfaction of any condition such as T's payment of support, and has no purpose other than to serve as a written declaration under section 152(e) and this section. T attaches the letter to T's return for 2009 and 2011.

(ii) In 2010, T fails to provide support for Child, and S executes a Form 8332 revoking the release of S's right to claim Child as a dependent for 2011. S delivers a copy of the Form 8332 to T, attaches a copy of the Form 8332 to S's tax return for 2011, and keeps a copy of the Form 8332 and evidence of delivery of the written notice to T.

(iii) T may claim Child as a dependent for 2009 because S releases the right to claim Child as a dependent under paragraph (b)(3) of this section by executing the letter, which conforms to the requirements of paragraph (e)(1) of this section, and T attaches the letter to T's return in accordance with paragraph (e)(2) of this section. In 2010, S revokes the release of the claim in accordance with paragraph (e)(3) of this section, and the revocation takes effect in 2011, the taxable year that begins in the first calendar year after S provides written notice of the revocation to T. Therefore, in 2011, section 152(e) and this section do not apply, and whether Child is the qualifying child or qualifying relative of S or T is determined under section 152(c) or (d).

Example (16). The facts are the same as Example 15, except that the letter expressly states that S releases the right to claim Child as a dependent only if T is current in the payment of support for Child at the end of the calendar year. The letter does not qualify as a written declaration under paragraph (b)(3) of this section because S's agreement not to claim Child as a dependent is conditioned on T's payment of support and, under paragraph (e)(1)(i) of this section, a written declaration must be unconditional. Therefore, section 152(e) and this section do not apply, and whether Child is the qualifying child or qualifying relative of S or T for 2009 as well as 2011 is determined under section 152(c) or (d).

Example (17). (i) U and V are the divorced parents of Child. Child resides with U for more nights than with V in 2009 through 2011. In 2009, U provides a written statement to V declaring that U will not claim Child as a dependent, but the statement does not specify the year or years it is effective. V attaches the statement to V's returns for 2009 through 2011.

(ii) Because the written statement does not specify a year or years, under paragraph (e)(1) of this section, it is not a written declaration that conforms to the substance of Form 8332. Under paragraph (e)(4) of this section, the statement has no effect. Section 152(e) and this section do not apply, and whether Child is the qualifying child or qualifying relative of U or V is determined under section 152(c) or (d).

Example (18). (i) W and X are the divorced parents of Child. In 2009, Child resides solely with W. The divorce decree requires X to pay child support to W and requires W to execute a Form 8332 releasing W's right to claim Child as a dependent. W fails to sign a Form 8332 for 2009, and X attaches an unsigned Form 8332 to X's return for 2009.

(ii) The order in the divorce decree requiring W to execute a Form 8332 is ineffective to allocate the right to claim Child as a dependent to X. Furthermore, under paragraph (e)(1) of this section, the unsigned Form 8332 does not conform to the substance of Form 8332, and under paragraph (e)(4) of this section, the Form 8332 has no effect. Therefore, section 152(e) and this section do not apply, and whether Child is the qualifying child or qualifying relative of W or X is determined under section 152(c) or (d).

(iii) If, however, W executes a Form 8332 for 2009, and X attaches the Form 8332 to X's return, then X may claim Child as a dependent in 2009.

Example (19). (i) Y and Z are the divorced parents of Child. In 2003, Y and Z enter into a separation agreement, which is incorporated into a divorce decree, under which Y, the custodial parent, releases Y's right to claim Child as a dependent for all future years. The separation agreement satisfies the requirements for the form of a written declaration in effect at the time it is executed. Z attaches a copy of the separation agreement to Z's returns for 2003 through 2009.

(ii) Under paragraph (e)(1)(ii) of this section, a separation agreement may not serve as a written declaration. However, under paragraph (e)(5) of this section, a written declaration executed in a taxable year beginning on or before July 2, 2008, that satisfies the requirements for the form of a written declaration in effect at the time the written declaration is executed, will be treated as meeting the requirements of paragraph (e)(1) of this section. Therefore, the separation agreement may serve as the written declaration required by paragraph (b)(3)(i) of this section for 2009, and Z may claim Child as a dependent in 2009 and later years.

Example (20). (i) The facts are the same as in Example 19, except that in 2009 Y executes a Form 8332 revoking the release of Y's right to claim Child as a dependent for 2010. Y complies with all the requirements of paragraph (e)(3) of this section.

(ii) Although Y executes the separation agreement releasing Y's right to claim Child as a dependent in a taxable year beginning on or before July 2, 2008, under paragraph (e)(5) of this section, Y's execution of the Form 8332 in 2009 is effective to revoke the release. Therefore, section 152(e) and this section do not apply in 2010, and whether Child is the qualifying child or qualifying relative of Y or Z is determined under section 152(c) or (d).

(h) Effective/applicability date. This section applies to taxable years beginning after July 2, 2008.

T.D. 7099, 3/19/71, amend T.D. 7145, 10/14/71, T.D. 7639, 8/17/79, T.D. 9408, 7/1/2008.

§ 1.153-1 Determination of marital status.

Caution: The Treasury has not yet amended Reg § 1.153-1 to reflect changes made by P.L. 94-455.

For the purpose of determining the right of an individual to claim an exemption for his spouse under section 151(b), the determination of whether such individual is married shall be made as of the close of his taxable year, unless his spouse dies during such year, in which case the determination shall be made as of the time of such death. An individually legally separated from his spouse under decree of divorce or separate maintenance shall not be considered as married. The provisions of this section may be illustrated by the following examples:

Example (1). A, who files his returns on the basis of a calendar year, married B on December 31, 1956. B, who had never previously married, had no gross income for the calendar year 1956 nor was she the dependent of another taxpayer for such year. A may claim an exemption for B for 1956.

Example (2). C and his wife, D, were married in 1940. They remained married until July 1956 at which time D was granted a decree of divorce. C, who files his income tax returns on a calendar year basis, cannot claim an exemption for D on his 1956 return as C and D were not married on the last day of C's taxable year. Had D died instead of being divorced, C could have claimed an exemption for D for 1956 as their marital status would have been determined as of the date of D's death.

T.D. 6231, 4/25/57.

§ 1.161-1 Allowance of deductions.

Section 161 provides for the allowance as deductions, in computing taxable income under section 63(a), of the items specified in part VI (section 161 and following), subchapter B, chapter 1 of the Code, subject to the exceptions provided in part IX (section 261 and following), of such subchapter B, relating to items not deductible. Double deductions are not permitted. Amounts deducted under one provision of the Internal Revenue Code of 1954 cannot again be deducted under any other provision thereof. See also section 7852(c), relating to the taking into account, both in computing a tax under subtitle A of the Internal Revenue Code of 1954 and a tax under chapter 1 or 2 of the Internal Revenue Code of 1939, of the same item of deduction.

T.D. 6291, 4/3/58.

§ 1.162-1 Business expenses.

Caution: The Treasury has not yet amended Reg § 1.162-1 to reflect changes made by P.L. 110-246.

(a) In general. Business expenses deductible from gross income include the ordinary and necessary expenditures directly connected with or pertaining to the taxpayer's trade or business, except items which are used as the basis for a deduction or a credit under provisions of law other than section 162. The cost of goods purchased for resale, with proper adjustment for opening and closing inventories, is deducted from gross sales in computing gross income. See paragraph (a) of § 1.61-3. Among the items included in business expenses are management expenses, commissions (but see section 263 and the regulations thereunder), labor, supplies, incidental repairs, operating expenses of automobiles used in the trade or business, traveling expenses while away from home solely in the pursuit of a trade or business (see § 1.162-2), advertising and other selling expenses, together with insurance premiums against fire, storm, theft, accident, or other similar losses in the case of a business, and rental for the use of business property. No such item shall be included in business expenses, however, to the extent that it is used by the taxpayer in computing the cost of property included in its inventory or used in determining the gain or loss basis of its plant, equipment, or other property. See section 1054 and the regulations thereunder. A deduction for an expense paid or incurred after December 30, 1969, which would otherwise be allowable under section 162 shall not be denied on the grounds that allowance of such deduction would frustrate a sharply defined public policy. See section 162(c), (f), and (g) and the regulations thereunder. The full amount of the allowable deduction for ordinary and necessary expenses in carrying on a business is deductible, even though such expenses exceed the gross income derived during the taxable year from such business. In the case of any sports program to which section 114 (relating to sports programs conducted for the American National Red Cross) applies, expenses described in section 114(a)(2) shall be allowable as deductions under section 162(a) only to the extent that such expenses exceed the amount excluded from gross income under section 114(a).

(b) Cross references. *(1)* For charitable contributions by individuals and corporations not deductible under section 162, see § 1.162-15.

(2) For items not deductible, see sections 261–276, inclusive, and regulations thereunder.

(3) For research and experimental expenditures, see section 174 and regulations thereunder.

(4) For soil and water conservation expenditures, see section 175 and regulations thereunder.

(5) For expenditures attributable to grant or loan by United States for encouragement of exploration for, or development or mining of, critical and strategic minerals or metals, see section 621 and regulations thereunder.

(6) For treatment of certain rental payments with respect to public utility property, see section 167(1) and § 1.167(1)-3.

(7) For limitations on the deductibility of miscellaneous itemized deductions, see section 67 and §§ 1.67-1T through 1.67-4T.

(8) For the timing of deductions with respect to notional principal contracts, see § 1.446-3.

T.D. 6291, 4/3/58, amend T.D. 6690, 11/18/63, T.D. 6996, 1/17/69, T.D. 7345, 2/19/75, T.D. 8189, 3/25/88, T.D. 8491, 10/8/93.

§ 1.162-2 Traveling expenses.

Caution: The Treasury has not yet amended Reg § 1.162-2 to reflect changes made by P.L. 108-121, P.L. 103-66, P.L. 100-647, P.L. 99-514, P.L. 99-272, P.L. 98-573, P.L. 97-248.

(a) Traveling expenses include travel fares, meals and lodging, and expenses incident to travel such as expenses for sample rooms, telephone and telegraph, public stenographers, etc. Only such traveling expenses as are reasonable and necessary in the conduct of the taxpayer's business and directly attributable to it may be deducted. If the trip is undertaken for other than business purposes, the travel fares and expenses incident to travel are personal expenses and the meals and lodging are living expenses. If the trip is solely on business, the reasonable and necessary traveling expenses, including travel fares, meals and lodging, and expenses incident to travel, are business expenses. For the allowance of traveling expenses as deductions in determining adjusted gross income, see section 62(2)(B) and the regulations thereunder.

(b) *(1)* If a taxpayer travels to a destination and while at such destination engages in both business and personal activities, traveling expenses to and from such destination are deductible only if the trip is related primarily to the taxpayer's trade or business. If the trip is primarily personal in nature, the traveling expenses to and from the destination are not deductible even though the taxpayer engages in business activities while at such destination. However, expenses while at the destination which are properly allocable to the taxpayer's trade or business are deductible even though the traveling expenses to and from the destination are not deductible.

(2) Whether a trip is related primarily to the taxpayer's trade or business or is primarily personal in nature depends on the facts and circumstances in each case. The amount of time during the period of the trip which is spent on personal activity compared to the amount of time spent on activities directly relating to the taxpayer's trade or business is an important factor in determining whether the trip is primarily personal. If, for example, a taxpayer spends one week while at a destination on activities which are directly related to his trade or business and subsequently spends an additional five weeks for vacation or other personal activities, the trip will be considered primarily personal in nature in the absence of a clear showing to the contrary.

(c) Where a taxpayer's wife accompanies him on a business trip, expenses attributable to her travel are not deductible unless it can be adequately shown that the wife's presence on the trip has a bona fide business purpose. The wife's performance of some incidental service does not cause her expenses to qualify as deductible business expenses. The same rules apply to any other members of the taxpayer's family who accompany him on such a trip.

(d) Expenses paid or incurred by a taxpayer in attending a convention or other meeting may constitute an ordinary and necessary business expense under section 162 depending upon the facts and circumstances of each case. No distinction will be made between self-employed persons and employees. The fact that an employee uses vacation or leave time or that his attendance at the convention is voluntary will not necessarily prohibit the allowance of the deduction. The allowance of deductions for such expenses will depend upon whether there is a sufficient relationship between the taxpayer's trade or business and his attendance at the convention or other meeting so that he is benefiting or advancing the interests of his trade or business by such attendance. If the convention is for political, social or other purposes unrelated to the taxpayer's trade or business, the expenses are not deductible.

(e) Commuters' fares are not considered as business expenses and are not deductible.

(f) For rules with respect to the reporting and substantiation of traveling and other business expenses of employees for taxable years beginning after December 31, 1957, see § 1.162-17.

T.D. 6291, 4/3/58, amend T.D. 6306, 8/27/58.

§ 1.162-3 Cost of materials.

Taxpayers carrying materials and supplies on hand should include in expenses the charges for materials and supplies only in the amount that they are actually consumed and used in operation during the taxable year for which the return is made, provided that the costs of such materials and supplies have not been deducted in determining the net income or loss or taxable income for any previous year. If a taxpayer carries incidental materials or supplies on hand for which no record of consumption is kept or of which physical inventories at the beginning and end of the year are not taken, it will be permissible for the taxpayer to include in his expenses and to deduct from gross income the total cost of such supplies and materials as were purchased during the taxable year for which the return is made, provided the taxable income is clearly reflected by this method.

T.D. 6291, 4/3/58.

PAR. 2.

Section 1.162-3 is revised to read as follows:

Proposed § 1.162-3 Materials and supplies. [*For Preamble, see ¶ 152,973*]

(a) In general. *(1) Non-incidental materials and supplies.* Amounts paid to acquire or produce materials and supplies are deductible in the taxable year in which the materials and supplies are used or consumed in the taxpayer's operations.

(2) Incidental materials and supplies. Amounts paid to acquire or produce incidental materials and supplies that are carried on hand and for which no record of consumption is kept or physical inventories at the beginning and end of the year are not taken, are deductible in the taxable year in which these amounts are paid, provided taxable income is clearly reflected.

(b) Rotable and temporary spare parts. For purposes of this section, rotable spare parts are parts that are removable from the unit of property, generally repaired or improved, and either reinstalled on other property, or stored for later installation. Temporary spare parts are parts that are used temporarily until a new or repaired part can be installed, and then removed and stored for later (emergency or temporary) installation. For purposes of paragraph (a)(1) of this section, rotable and temporary spare parts are used or consumed in the taxpayer's business in the taxable year in which the taxpayer disposes of the parts.

(c) Coordination with other provisions of the Internal Revenue Code. Nothing in this section changes the treatment of any amount that is specifically provided for under any provision of the Internal Revenue Code (Code) or regulations other than section 162(a) or section 212 and the regulations under those sections. For example, see § 1.263(a)-3, which requires taxpayers to capitalize amounts paid to improve units of property and section 263A and the regulations under section 263A, which require taxpayers to capitalize the direct and allocable indirect costs, including the cost of materials and supplies, to property produced or to property acquired for resale.

(d) Definitions. *(1) Materials and supplies.* For purposes of this section, materials and supplies means tangible property that is used or consumed in the taxpayer's operations and that—

(i) Is not a unit of property (as determined under § 1.263(a)-3(d)(2)) and is not acquired as part of a single unit of property;

(ii) Is a unit of property (as determined under § 1.263(a)-3(d)(2)) that has an economic useful life of 12 months or less, beginning when the property is used or consumed in the taxpayer's operations;

(iii) Is a unit of property (as determined under § 1.263(a)-3(d)(2)) that has an acquisition cost or production cost (as determined under section 263A) of $100 or less; or

(iv) Is identified in published guidance in the Federal Register or in the Internal Revenue Bulletin (see § 601.601(d)(2)(ii)(b) of this chapter) as materials and supplies for which treatment is permitted under this section.

(2) Economic useful life. (i) General rule. The economic useful life of a unit of property is not necessarily the useful life inherent in the property but is the period over which the property may reasonably be expected to be useful to the taxpayer or, if the taxpayer is engaged in a trade or business or an activity for the production of income, the period over which the property may reasonably be expected to be useful to the taxpayer in its trade or business or for the production of income, as applicable. See § 1.167(a)-1(b) for the factors to be considered in determining this period.

(ii) Taxpayers with an applicable financial statement. For taxpayers with an applicable financial statement (as defined in paragraph (d)(2)(iii) of this section), the economic useful life of a unit of property, solely for the purposes of applying the provisions of paragraph (d)(1)(ii) of this section, is the useful life initially used by the taxpayer for purposes of determining depreciation in its applicable financial statement, regardless of any salvage value of the property. If a taxpayer does not have an applicable financial statement for the taxable year in which the property was originally acquired or produced, the economic useful life of the unit of property must be determined under paragraph (d)(2)(i) of this section. Further, if a taxpayer treats amounts paid for a unit of property as an expense in its applicable financial statement on a basis other than the useful life of the property or if a taxpayer does not depreciate the unit of property on its applicable financial statement, the economic useful life of the unit of property must be determined under paragraph (d)(2)(i) of this section. For example, if a taxpayer has a policy of treating as an expense on its applicable financial statement amounts paid for property costing less than a certain dollar amount, notwithstanding that the property has a useful life of more than one year, the economic useful life of the property must be determined under paragraph (d)(2)(i) of this section.

(iii) Definition of applicable financial statement. The taxpayer's applicable financial statement is the taxpayer's financial statement listed in paragraphs (d)(2)(iii)(A) through (C) of this section that has the highest priority (including within paragraph (d)(2)(iii)(B) of this section). The financial statements are, in descending priority—

(A) A financial statement required to be filed with the Securities and Exchange Commission (SEC) (the 10-K or the Annual Statement to Shareholders);

(B) A certified audited financial statement that is accompanied by the report of an independent CPA (or in the case of a foreign entity, by the report of a similarly qualified independent professional), that is used for—

(1) Credit purposes;

(2) Reporting to shareholders, partners, or similar persons; or

(3) Any other substantial non-tax purpose; or

(C) A financial statement (other than a tax return) required to be provided to the Federal or a state government or any Federal or state agencies (other than the SEC or the Internal Revenue Service).

(3) Amount paid. For purposes of this section, in the case of a taxpayer using an accrual method of accounting, the terms amount paid and payment mean a liability incurred (within the meaning of § 1.446-1(c)(1)(ii)). A liability may not be taken into account under this section prior to the taxable year during which the liability is incurred.

(4) Produce. For purposes of this section, produce means construct, build, install, manufacture, develop, create, raise or grow. See also § 1.263(a)-2(b)(4). This definition is intended to have the same meaning as the definition used for purposes of section 263A(g)(1) and § 1.263A-2(a)(1)(i), except that improvements are excluded from the definition in this paragraph (d)(4) and are separately defined and addressed in § 1.263(a)-3. Amounts paid to produce materials and supplies must be capitalized under section 263A.

(e) Election to capitalize. A taxpayer may elect to treat as a capital expenditure the cost of any material or supply as defined in paragraph (d)(1) of this section, unless the material or supply is a component of a unit of property as described in paragraph (d)(1)(i) of this section, and the unit of property is a material or supply under paragraph (d)(1)(ii)-(iv) of this section, rather than a capital expenditure. An election made under this paragraph (e) applies to amounts paid during the taxable year to acquire or produce any material or supply to which paragraph (a) of this section would apply (but for the election under this paragraph (e)). A taxpayer makes the election by capitalizing the amounts paid to acquire or produce a material or supply in the taxable year the amounts are paid and by recovering the costs when the material or supply is placed in service by the taxpayer for the purposes of determining depreciation under the applicable Code and regulation provisions. A taxpayer must make this election in its timely filed original Federal income tax return (including extensions) for the taxable year the material or supply is placed in service by the taxpayer for purposes of determining depreciation. See § 1.263(a)-2 for the treatment of amounts paid to acquire or produce real or personal tangible property. In the case of a pass-through entity, the election is made by the pass-through entity, and not by the shareholders, partners, etc. An election must be made for each material and/or supply. A taxpayer may revoke an election made under this paragraph (e) with respect to a material or supply only by filing a request for a private letter ruling and obtaining the Commissioner's consent to revoke the election. An election may not be made or revoked through the filing of an application for change in accounting method or by an amended Federal income tax return. A taxpayer that revokes an election may not re-elect to capitalize the material or supply for a period of at least 60 months, beginning with the taxable year of revocation.

(f) Examples. The rules of this section are illustrated by the following examples, in which it is assumed (unless otherwise stated) that the property is not an incidental material or supply, that the taxpayer is a calendar year, accrual method taxpayer, and that the taxpayer has not elected to capitalize under paragraph (e) of this section.

Example (1). Not a unit of property; component of personal property. X operates a fleet of aircraft. In 2008, X purchases a stock of spare parts, which it uses to maintain and repair its aircraft. The spare parts are not units of property as determined under § 1.263(a)-3(d)(2) and are not rotable or temporary spare parts. In 2009, X uses the spare parts in a repair and maintenance activity that does not improve the property under § 1.263(a)-3. Under paragraph (a)(1) of this section, the amounts paid for the spare parts are deductible as materials and supplies in 2009, the taxable year in which the spare parts are used to repair and maintain the aircraft.

Example (2). Not a unit of property; rotable spare parts. X operates a fleet of specialized vehicles that it uses in its service business. At the time that it acquires a new type of vehicle, X also acquires a substantial number of rotable spare parts that will be kept on hand to quickly replace similar parts in X's vehicles as those parts break down or wear out. These rotable replacement parts are not units of property as determined under § 1.263(a)-3(d)(2), are removable from the vehicles, and are repaired or reconditioned, so that they can be reinstalled on the same or similar vehicles. In 2008, X acquires several vehicles and associated rotable spare parts. In 2009, X makes repairs to several vehicles by using these rotable spare parts to replace worn or damaged parts. In 2010, X removes these rotable spare parts from its vehicles, repairs them and reinstalls them on other similar vehicles. In 2012, X can no longer use the rotable parts it acquired in 2008 and disposes of them as scrap. Under paragraph (d)(1) of this section, the rotable spare parts acquired in 2008 are materials and supplies. However, under paragraph (b) of this section, these parts are not used or consumed until the taxable year in which X disposes of the parts. Therefore, under paragraph (a)(1) of this section, X may deduct the amounts paid for the rotable spare parts in 2012, the taxable year in which X disposes of the parts.

Example (3). Not a unit of property; part of a single unit of real property. X owns an apartment building and discovers that a window in one of the apartments is broken. In 2008, X pays for the acquisition, delivery, and installation of a new window to replace the broken window. In the same year, the new window is installed. The window is not a unit of property as determined under § 1.263(a)-3(d)(2), and the replacement of the window does not improve the property under § 1.263(a)-3. Under paragraph (a)(1) of this section, the amounts paid for the acquisition, delivery, and installation of the window are deductible as materials and supplies in 2008, the taxable year in which the window is installed in the apartment building.

Example (4). Economic useful life of 12 months or less. X operates a fleet of aircraft that carries freight for its customers. X owns a storage tank on its premises, which can hold a one-month supply of jet fuel for its aircraft. On December 31, 2008, X purchases a one-month supply of jet fuel. In 2009, X uses the jet fuel purchased on December 31, 2008, to fuel the aircraft used in its business. Under paragraph (a)(1) of this section, the amounts paid for the jet fuel are deductible as materials and supplies in 2009, the taxable year in which the jet fuel is used or consumed in the operation of X's aircraft.

Example (5). Unit of property that costs $100 or less. X operates a rental business that rents out a variety of small individual items to customers (rental items). X maintains a supply of rental items on hand to replace worn or damaged items. In 2008, X purchases a large quantity of rental items to use in its rental business. Each of these rental items is a unit of property that costs $100 or less. In 2009, X begins using all of the rental items purchased in 2008 by providing them to customers of its rental business. X does not sell or exchange these items on established retail markets at any time after the items are used in the rental business. Under paragraph (a)(1) of this section, the amounts paid for the rental items are deductible as materials and supplies in 2009, the taxable year in which the rental items are used in X's business.

Example (6). Unit of property that costs $100 or less. X provides billing services to its customers. In 2008, X incurs costs to purchase 50 facsimile machines to be used by its employees. Each facsimile machine is a unit of property that costs less than $100. In 2008, X's employees begin using 35 of the facsimile machines, and X stores the remaining 15 machines for use in a later taxable year. Under paragraph (a)(1) of this section, the amounts paid for 35 of the facsimile machines are deductible as materials and supplies in 2008, the taxable year in which X uses those machines. The amounts paid for each of the remaining 15 machines are deductible in the taxable year in which each machine is used.

Example (7). Materials and supplies used in improvements; coordination with § 1.263(a)-3. X owns various machines that are used in its business. In 2008, X purchases a supply of spare parts for its machines. The spare parts are not units of property as determined under § 1.263(a)-3(d)(2) and are not rotable or temporary spare parts. The spare parts may be used by X in the repair or maintenance of a machine under § 1.162-4 or in the improvement of a machine under § 1.263(a)-3. In 2009, X uses all of these spare parts in an activity that improves the unit of property under § 1.263(a)-3. Under paragraph (d)(1)(i) of this section, the spare parts purchased by X in 2008 are materials and supplies. Under paragraph (a)(1) of this section, the amounts paid for the spare parts are otherwise deductible as materials and supplies in 2009, the taxable year in which X uses those parts. However, because these materials and supplies are used to improve X's property, X is required to capitalize the amounts paid for those spare parts under § 1.263(a)-3. See also section 263A requiring taxpayers to capitalize the direct and allocable indirect costs of property produced or acquired for resale.

Example (8). Cost of producing materials and supplies; coordination with section 263A. X is a manufacturer that produces liquid waste as part of its operations. X determines that its current liquid waste disposal process is inadequate. To remedy the problem, in 2008, X constructs a leaching pit to provide a draining area for the liquid waste. The leaching pit has an economic useful life of less than 12 months, starting on the date that X begins to use the leaching pit as a draining area. At the end of this period, X's factory will be connected to the local sewer system. In 2009, X starts using the leaching pit in its operations. The amounts paid to construct the leaching pit (including the direct and allocable indirect costs of property produced under section 263A) are amounts paid for a material or supply under paragraph (d)(1)(ii) of this section. Under paragraph (a)(1) of this section, the amounts paid for the leaching pit are otherwise deductible as materials and supplies in 2009, the taxable year in which X uses the leaching pit. However, because the amounts paid to construct the leaching pit are incurred by reason of X's manufacturing operations, X is required to capitalize the amounts paid to construct the leaching pit to X's property produced. See § 1.263A-1(e)(3)(ii)(E).

Example (9). Costs of acquiring materials and supplies for production of property; coordination with section 263A. In 2008, X purchases jigs, dies, molds, and patterns for use in the manufacture of X's products. The economic useful life of each jig, die, mold, and pattern is 12 months or less, beginning when each item is used in the manufacturing process. X begins using the purchased items in 2009 to manufacture its products. These items are materials and supplies under paragraph (d)(1)(ii) of this section. Under paragraph (a)(1) of this section, the amounts paid for the items are otherwise deductible as materials and supplies in 2009, the taxable year in which X uses those items. However, because the amounts paid for these materials and supplies directly benefit or are incurred by reason of the taxpayer's production activities, X is required to capitalize the amounts paid for these items to X's property produced. See § 1.263A-1(e)(3)(ii)(E).

Example (10). Election to capitalize. X operates a rental business that rents out a variety of items (rental items) to its customers, each of which is a separate unit of property as determined under § 1.263(a)-3(d)(2). X does not sell or exchange these items on established retail markets at any time after the items are used in the rental business. In 2008, X incurs costs to purchase various rental items, all of which cost less than $100 or have an economic useful life of less than 12 months, beginning when used or consumed. X begins using the rental items in its business in 2008. Under paragraph (a)(1) of this section, the amounts paid for each rental item purchased in 2008 are deductible as a material or supply in the taxable year in which the item is used. However, for administrative reasons, X would prefer to treat all of its rental items as capital expenditures subject to depreciation. Under paragraph (e) of this section, X may elect not to apply the rule contained in paragraph (a)(1) of this section to the rental items. X makes this election by capitalizing the amounts paid for each rental item in the taxable year the costs are incurred and by beginning to recover the costs of each item on its timely filed Federal income tax return for the taxable year that the item is placed in service by X for purposes of determining depreciation under the applicable Code and regulation provisions. See § 1.263(a)-2(e) for the treatment of capital expenditures.

Example (11). Election to capitalize. X is an electric utility. In 2008, X acquires certain temporary spare parts, which it keeps on hand to avoid operational time loss in the event it must make emergency repairs to a unit of property that is subject to depreciation. These parts are not units of property as determined under § 1.263(a)-3(d)(2) and are not used to improve property under § 1.263(a)-3(d)(1). These temporary spare parts are used until a new or repaired part can be installed, and then removed and stored for later emergency installation. Under paragraphs (a)(1) and (b) of this section, the amounts paid for the temporary spare parts are deductible as materials and supplies in the taxable year in which they are disposed of by the taxpayer. However, because it is unlikely that the temporary spare parts will be disposed of in the near future, X would prefer to treat the spare parts as capital expenditures subject to depreciation. Accordingly, X may elect under paragraph (e) of this section not to apply the rule contained in paragraph (a)(1) of this section to each of its temporary spare parts. X makes this election by capitalizing the amounts paid for each spare part in the taxable year the costs are incurred and by beginning to recover the costs of each part on its timely filed Federal income tax return for the taxable year that the part is placed in service by X for purposes of determining depreciation under the applicable Code and regulation provisions. See § 1.263(a)-2(e) for the treatment of capital expenditures and section 263A requiring taxpayers to capitalize the direct and allocable indirect costs of property produced or acquired for resale.

§ 1.162-4 Repairs.

The cost of incidental repairs which neither materially add to the value of the property nor appreciably prolong its life, but keep it in an ordinarily efficient operating condition, may be deducted as an expense, provided the cost of acquisition or production or the gain or loss basis of the taxpayer's plant, equipment, or other property, as the case may be, is not increased by the amount of such expenditures. Repairs in the nature of replacements, to the extent that they arrest deterioration and appreciably prolong the life of the property, shall either be capitalized and depreciated in accordance with section 167 or charged against the depreciation reserve if such an account is kept.

T.D. 6291, 4/3/58.

PAR. 3.

Section 1.162-4 is revised to read as follows:

Proposed § 1.162-4 Repairs. [*For Preamble, see ¶ 152,973*]

Amounts paid for repairs and maintenance to tangible property are deductible if the amounts paid are not required to be capitalized under § 1.263(a)-3.

§ 1.162-5 Expenses for education.

(a) General rule. Expenditures made by an individual for education (including research undertaken as part of his educational program) which are not expenditures of a type described in paragraph (b)(2) or (3) of this section are deductible as ordinary and necessary business expenses (even though the education may lead to a degree) if the education—

(1) Maintains or improves skills required by the individual in his employment or other trade or business, or

(2) Meets the express requirements of the individual's employer, or the requirements of applicable law or regulations, imposed as a condition to the retention by the individual of an established employment relationship, status, or rate of compensation.

(b) Nondeductible educational expenditures. *(1) In general.* Educational expenditures described in subparagraphs (2) and (3) of this paragraph are personal expenditures or constitute an inseparable aggregate of personal and capital expenditures and, therefore, are not deductible as ordinary and necessary business expenses even though the education may maintain or improve skills required by the individual in his employment or other trade or business or may meet the express requirements of the individual's employer or of applicable law or regulations.

(2) Minimum educational requirements. (i) The first category of nondeductible educational expenses within the scope of subparagraph (1) of this paragraph are expenditures made by an individual for education which is required of him in order to meet the minimum educational requirements for qualification in his employment or other trade or business. The minimum education necessary to qualify for a position or other trade or business must be determined from a consideration of such factors as the requirements of the employer, the applicable law and regulations, and the standards of the profession, trade, or business involved. The fact that an individual is already performing service in an employment status does not establish that he has met the minimum educational requirements for qualification in that employment. Once an individual has met the minimum educational requirements for qualification in his employment or other trade or business (as in effect when he enters the employment or trade or business), he shall be treated as continuing to meet those requirements even though they are changed.

(ii) The minimum educational requirements for qualification of a particular individual in a position in an educational institution is the minimum level of education (in terms of aggregate college hours or degree) which under the applicable laws or regulations, in effect at the time this individual is first employed in such position, is normally required of an individual initially being employed in such a position. If there are no normal requirements as to the minimum level of education required for a position in an educational institution, then an individual in such a position shall be considered to have met the minimum educational requirements for qualification in that position when he becomes a member of the faculty of the educational institution. The determination of whether an individual is a member of the faculty of an educational institution must be made on the basis of the particular practices of the institution. However, an individual will ordinarily be considered to be a member of the faculty of an institution if (a) he has tenure or his years of service are being counted toward obtaining tenure; (b) the institution is making contributions to a retirement plan (other than Social Security or a similar program) in respect of his employment; or (c) he has a vote in faculty affairs.

(iii) The application of this subparagraph may be illustrated by the following examples:

Example (1). General facts: State X requires a bachelor's degree for beginning secondary school teachers which must include 30 credit hours of professional educational courses. In addition, in order to retain his position, a secondary school teacher must complete a fifth year of preparation within 10 years after beginning his employment. If an employing school official certifies to the State Department of Education that applicants having a bachelor's degree and the required courses in professional education cannot be found, he may hire individuals as secondary school teachers if they have completed a minimum of 90 semester hours of college work. However, to be retained in his position, such an individual must obtain his bachelor's degree and complete the required professional educational courses within 3 years after his employment commences. Under these facts, a bachelor's degree, without regard to whether it includes 30 credit hours of professional educational courses, is considered to be the minimum educational requirement for qualification as a secondary school teacher in State X. This is the case notwithstanding the number of teachers who are actually hired without such a degree. The following are examples of the application of these facts in particular situations:

Situation 1. A, at the time he is employed as a secondary school teacher in State X, has a bachelor's degree including 30 credit hours of professional educational courses. After his employment, A completes a fifth college year of education and, as a result, is issued a standard certificate. The fifth college year of education undertaken by A is not education required to meet the minimum educational requirements for qualification as a secondary school teacher. Accordingly, the expenditures for such education are deductible unless the expenditures are for education which is part of a program of study being pursued by A which will lead to qualifying him in a new trade or business.

Situation 2. Because of a shortage of applicants meeting the stated requirements, B, who has a bachelor's degree, is employed as a secondary school teacher in State X even though he has only 20 credit hours of professional educational courses. After his employment, B takes an additional 10 credit hours of professional educational courses. Since these courses do not constitute education required to meet the minimum educational requirements for qualification as a secondary school teacher which is a bachelor's degree and will not lead to qualifying B in a new trade or business, the expenditures for such courses are deductible.

Situation 3. Because of a shortage of applicants meeting the stated requirements, C is employed as a secondary school teacher in State X although he has only 90 semester hours of college work toward his bachelor's degree. After his employment, C undertakes courses leading to a bachelor's degree. These courses (including any courses in professional education) constitute education required to meet the minimum educational requirements for qualification as a secondary school teacher. Accordingly, the expenditures for such education are not deductible.

Situation 4. Subsequent to the employment of A, B, and C, but before they have completed a fifth college year of education, State X changes its requirements affecting secondary school teachers to provide that beginning teachers must have completed 5 college years of preparation. In the cases of A, B, and C, a fifth college year of education is not considered to be education undertaken to meet the minimum educational requirements for qualification as a secondary school teacher. Accordingly, expenditures for a fifth year of college will be deductible unless the expenditures are for education which is part of a program being pursued by A, B, or C which will lead to qualifying him in a new trade or business.

Example (2). D, who holds a bachelor's degree, obtains temporary employment as an instructor at University Y and undertakes graduate courses as a candidate for a graduate degree. D may become a faculty member only if he obtains a graduate degree and may continue to hold a position as instructor only so long as he shows satisfactory progress towards obtaining his graduate degree. The graduate courses taken by D constitute education required to meet the minimum educational requirements for qualification in D's trade or business and, thus, the expenditures for such courses are not deductible.

Example (3). E, who has completed 2 years of a normal 3-year law school course leading to a bachelor of laws degree (LL.B.), is hired by a law firm to do legal research and perform other functions on a full-time basis. As a condition to continued employment, E is required to obtain an LL.B. and pass the State bar examination. E completes his law school education by attending night law school, and he takes a bar review course in order to prepare for the State bar examination. The law courses and bar review course constitute education required to meet the minimum educational requirements for qualification in E's trade or business and, thus, the expenditures for such courses are not deductible.

(3) Qualification for new trade or business. (i) The second category of nondeductible educational expenses within the scope of subparagraph (1) of this paragraph are expenditures made by an individual for education which is part of a program of study being pursued by him which will lead to qualifying him in a new trade or business. In the case of an employee, a change of duties does not constitute a new trade or business if the new duties involve the same general type of work as is involved in the individual's present employment. For this purpose, all teaching and related duties shall be considered to involve the same general type of work. The following are examples of changes in duties which do not constitute new trades or businesses:

(a) Elementary to secondary school classroom teacher.

(b) Classroom teacher in one subject (such as mathematics) to classroom teacher in another subject (such as science).

(c) Classroom teacher to guidance counselor.

(d) Classroom teacher to principal.

(ii) The application of this subparagraph to individuals other than teachers may be illustrated by the following examples:

Example (1). A, a self-employed individual practicing a profession other than law, for example, engineering, accounting, etc., attends law school at night and after completing his law school studies receives a bachelor of laws degree. The expenditures made by A in attending law school are nondeductible because this course of study qualifies him for a new trade or business.

Example (2). Assume the same facts as in example (1) except that A has the status of an employee rather than a self-employed individual, and that his employer requires him to obtain a bachelor of laws degree. A intends to continue practicing his nonlegal profession as an employee of such employer. Nevertheless, the expenditures made by A in attending law school are not deductible since this course of study qualifies him for a new trade or business.

Example (3). B, a general practitioner of medicine, takes a 2-week course reviewing new developments in several specialized fields of medicine. B's expenses for the course are deductible because the course maintains or improves skills required by him in his trade or business and does not qualify him for a new trade or business.

Example (4). C, while engaged in the private practice of psychiatry, undertakes a program of study and training at an accredited psychoanalytic institute which will lead to qualifying him to practice psychoanalysis. C's expenditures for such study and training are deductible because the study and training maintains or improves skills required by him in his trade or business and does not qualify him for a new trade or business.

(c) Deductible educational expenditures. *(1) Maintaining or improving skills.* The deduction under the category of expenditures for education which maintains or improves skills required by the individual in his employment or other trade or business includes refresher courses or courses dealing with current developments as well as academic or vocational courses provided the expenditures for the courses are not within either category of nondeductible expenditures described in paragraph (b)(2) or (3) of this section.

(2) Meeting requirements of employer. An individual is considered to have undertaken education in order to meet the express requirements of his employer, or the requirements of applicable law or regulations, imposed as a condition to the retention by the taxpayer of his established employment relationship, status, or rate of compensation only if such requirements are imposed for a bona fide business purpose of the individual's employer. Only the minimum education necessary to the retention by the individual of his established employment relationship, status, or rate of compensation may be considered as undertaken to meet the express requirements of the taxpayer's employer. However, education in excess of such minimum education may qualify as education undertaken in order to maintain or improve the skills required by the taxpayer in his employment or other trade or business (see subparagraph (1) of this paragraph). In no event, however, is a deduction allowable for expenditures for education which, even though for education required by the employer or applicable law or regulations, are within one of the categories of nondeductible expenditures described in paragraph (b)(2) and (3) of this section.

(d) Travel as a form or education. Subject to the provisions of paragraph (b) and (e) of this section, expenditures for travel (including travel while on sabbatical leave) as a form of education are deductible only to the extent such expenditures are attributable to a period of travel that is directly related to the duties of the individual in his employment or other trade or business. For this purpose, a period of travel shall be considered directly related to the duties of an individual in his employment or other trade or business only if the major portion of the activities during such period is of a nature which directly maintains or improves skills required by the individual in such employment or other trade or business. The approval of a travel program by an employer or the fact that travel is accepted by an employer in the fulfillment of its requirements for retention of rate of compensation, status or employment, is not determinative that the required relationship exists between the travel involved and the duties of the individual in his particular position.

(e) Travel away from home. *(1)* If an individual travels away from home primarily to obtain education the expenses of which are deductible under this section, his expenditures for travel, meals, and lodging while away from home are deductible. However, if as an incident of such trip the individual engages in some personal activity such as sightseeing, social visiting, or entertaining, or other recreation, the portion of the expenses attributable to such personal activity constitutes nondeductible personal or living expenses and is not allowable as a deduction. If the individual's travel away from home is primarily personal, the individual's expenditures for travel, meals and lodging (other than meals and lodging during the time spent in participating in deductible education pursuits) are not deductible.

Whether a particular trip is primarily personal or primarily to obtain education the expenses of which are deductible under this section depends upon all the facts and circumstances of each case. An important factor to be taken into consideration in making the determination is the relative amount of time devoted to personal activity as compared with the time devoted to educational pursuits. The rules set forth in this paragraph are subject to the provisions of section 162(a)(2), relating to deductibility of certain traveling expenses, and section 274(c) and (d), relating to allocation of certain foreign travel expenses and substantiation required, respectively, and the regulations thereunder.

(2) Examples. The application of this subsection may be illustrated by the following examples:

Example (1). A, a self-employed tax practitioner, decides to take a 1-week course in new developments in taxation, which is offered in City X, 500 miles away from his home. His primary purpose in going to X is to take the course, but he also takes a side trip to City Y (50 miles from X) for 1 day, takes a sightseeing trip while in X, and entertains some personal friends. A's transportation expenses to City X and return to his home are deductible but his transportation expenses to City Y are not deductible. A's expenses for meals and lodging while away from home will be allocated between his educational pursuits and his personal activities. Those expenses which are entirely personal, such as sightseeing and entertaining friends, are not deductible to any extent.

Example (2). The facts are the same as in example (1) except that A's primary purpose in going to City X is to take a vacation. This purpose is indicated by several factors, one of which is the fact that he spends only 1 week attending the tax course and devotes 5 weeks entirely to personal activities. None of A's transportation expenses are deductible and his expenses for meals and lodging while away from home are not deductible to the extent attributable to personal activities. His expenses for meals and lodging allocable to the week attending the tax course are, however, deductible.

Example (3). B, a high school mathematics teacher in New York City, in the summertime travels to a university in California in order to take a mathematics course the expense of which is deductible under this section. B pursues only one-fourth of a full course of study and the remainder of her time is devoted to personal activities the expense of which is not deductible. Absent a showing by B of a substantial nonpersonal reason for taking the course in the university in California, the trip is considered taken primarily for personal reasons and the cost of traveling from New York City to California and return would not be deductible. However, one-fourth of the cost of B's meals and lodging while attending the university in California may be considered properly allocable to deductible educational pursuits and, therefore, is deductible.

T.D. 6291, 4/3/58, amend T.D. 6918, 5/1/67.

§ 1.162-6 Professional expenses.

A professional man may claim as deductions the cost of supplies used by him in the practice of his profession, expenses paid or accrued in the operation and repair of an automobile used in making professional calls, dues to professional societies and subscriptions to professional journals, the rent paid or accrued for office rooms, the cost of the fuel, light, water, telephone, etc., used in such offices, and the hire of office assistance. Amounts currently paid or accrued for books, furniture, and professional instruments and equipment, the useful life of which is short, may be deducted.

T.D. 6291, 4/3/58.

PAR. 4.

Section 1.162-6 is removed.

Proposed § 1.162-6 [Removed] [*For Preamble, see ¶ 152,973*]

§ 1.162-7 Compensation for personal services.

Caution: The Treasury has not yet amended Reg § 1.162-7 to reflect changes made by P.L. 103-66.

(a) There may be included among the ordinary and necessary expenses paid or incurred in carrying on any trade or business a reasonable allowance for salaries or other compensation for personal services actually rendered. The test of deductibility in the case of compensation payments is whether they are reasonable and are in fact payments purely for services.

(b) The test set forth in paragraph (a) of this section and its practical application may be further stated and illustrated as follows:

(1) Any amount paid in the form of compensation, but not in fact as the purchase price of services, is not deductible. An ostensible salary paid by a corporation may be a distribution of a dividend on stock. This is likely to occur in the case of a corporation having few shareholders, practically all of whom draw salaries. If in such a case the salaries are in excess of those ordinarily paid for similar services and the excessive payments correspond or bear a close relationship to the stockholdings of the officers or employees, it would seem likely that the salaries are not paid wholly for services rendered, but that the excessive payments are a distribution of earnings upon the stock. An ostensible salary may be in part payment for property. This may occur, for example, where a partnership sells out to a corporation, the former partners agreeing to continue in the service of the corporation. In such a case it may be found that the salaries of the former partners are not merely for services, but in part constitute payment for the transfer of their business.

(2) The form or method of fixing compensation is not decisive as to deductibility. While any form of contingent compensation invites scrutiny as a possible distribution of earnings of the enterprise, it does not follow that payments on a contingent basis are to be treated fundamentally on any basis different from that applying to compensation at a flat rate. Generally speaking, if contingent compensation is paid pursuant to a free bargain between the employer and the individual made before the services are rendered, not influenced by any consideration on the part of the employer other than that of securing on fair and advantageous terms the services of the individual, it should be allowed as a deduction even though in the actual working out of the contract it may prove to be greater than the amount which would ordinarily be paid.

(3) In any event the allowance for the compensation paid may not exceed what is reasonable under all the circumstances. It is, in general, just to assume that reasonable and true compensation is only such amount as would ordinarily be paid for like services by like enterprises under like circumstances. The circumstances to be taken into consideration are those existing at the date when the contract for services was made, not those existing at the date when the contract is questioned.

(4) For disallowance of deduction in the case of certain transfers of stock pursuant to employees stock options, see section 421 and the regulations thereunder.

T.D. 6291, 4/3/58.

§ 1.162-8 Treatment of excessive compensation.

The income tax liability of the recipient in respect of an amount ostensibly paid to him as compensation, but not allowed to be deducted as such by the payor, will depend upon the circumstances of each case. Thus, in the case of excessive payments by corporations, if such payments correspond or bear a close relationship to stockholdings, and are found to be a distribution of earnings or profits, the excessive payments will be treated as a dividend. If such payments constitute payment for property, they should be treated by the payor as a capital expenditure and by the recipient as part of the purchase price. In the absence of evidence to justify other treatment, excessive payments for salaries or other compensation for personal services will be included in gross income of the recipient.

T.D. 6291, 4/3/58.

§ 1.162-9 Bonuses to employees.

Bonuses to employees will constitute allowable deductions from gross income when such payments are made in good faith and as additional compensation for the services actually rendered by the employees, provided such payments, when added to the stipulated salaries, do not exceed a reasonable compensation for the services rendered. It is immaterial whether such bonuses are paid in cash or in kind or partly in cash and partly in kind. Donations made to employees and others, which do not have in them the element of compensation or which are in excess of reasonable compensation for services, are not deductible from gross income.

T.D. 6291, 4/3/58.

§ 1.162-10 Certain employee benefits.

Caution: The Treasury has not yet amended Reg § 1.162-10 to reflect changes made by P.L. 100-647, P.L. 99-514, P.L. 99-272, P.L. 98-573, P.L. 97-248.

(a) In general. Amounts paid or accrued by a taxpayer on account of injuries received by employees and lump-sum amounts paid or accrued as compensation for injuries are proper deductions as ordinary and necessary expenses. Such deductions are limited to the amount not compensated for by insurance or otherwise. Amounts paid or accrued within the taxable year for dismissal wages, unemployment benefits, guaranteed annual wages, vacations, or a sickness, accident, hospitalization, medical expense, recreational, welfare, or similar benefit plan are deductible under section 162(a) if they are ordinary and necessary expenses of the trade or business. However, except as provided in paragraph (b) of this section, such amounts shall not be deductible under section 162(a) if, under any circumstances, they may be used to provide benefits under a stock bonus, pension, annuity, profit-sharing, or other deferred compensation plan of the type referred to in section 404(a). In such an event, the extent to which these amounts are deductible from gross income shall be governed by the provisions of section 404 and the regulations issued thereunder.

(b) Certain negotiated plans. *(1)* Subject to the limitations set forth in subparagraphs (2) and (3) of this paragraph, contributions paid by an employer under a plan under which such contributions are held in a welfare trust for the purpose of paying (either from principal or income or both) for the benefit of employees, their families, and dependents, at least medical or hospital care, and pensions on retirement or death of employees, are deductible when paid as business expenses under section 162(a).

(2) For the purpose of subparagraph (1) of this paragraph, the word "plan" means any plan established prior to January 1, 1954, as a result of an agreement between employee representatives and the Government of the United States, during a period of Government operation, under seizure powers, of a major part of the productive facilities of the industry in which the employer claiming the deduction is engaged. The phrase "plan established prior to January 1, 1954, as a result of an agreement" is intended primarily to cover a trust established under the terms of such an agreement. It also includes a trust established under a plan of an employer, or group of employers, who, by reason of producing the same commodity, are in competition with the employers whose facilities were seized and who would therefore be expected to establish such a trust as a reasonable measure to maintain a sound position in the labor market producing the commodity. For example, if a trust was established under such an agreement in the bituminous coal industry, a similar trust established in the anthracite coal industry within a reasonable time, but before January 1, 1954, would qualify under subparagraph (1) of this paragraph.

(3) If any trust described in subparagraph (2) of this paragraph becomes qualified for exemption from tax under the provisions of section 501(a), the deductibility of contributions by an employer to such trust on or after any date of such qualification shall no longer be governed by the provisions of section 162, even though the trust may later lose its exemption from tax under section 501(a).

(c) Other plans providing deferred compensation. For rules relating to the deduction of amounts paid to or under a stock bonus, pension, annuity, or profit-sharing plan or amounts paid or accrued under any other plan deferring the receipt of compensation, see section 404 and the regulations thereunder.

T.D. 6291, 4/3/58.

§ 1.162-10T Questions and answers relating to the deduction of employee benefits under the Tax Reform Act of 1984; certain limits on amounts deductible (temporary).

Q-1. How does the amendment of section 404(b) by the Tax Reform Act of 1984 affect the deduction of employee benefits under section 162 of the Internal Revenue Code?

A-1. As amended by the Tax Reform Act of 1984, section 404(b) clarifies that section 404(a) and (d) (in the case of employees and nonemployees, respectively) shall govern the deduction of contributions paid or compensation paid or incurred under a plan, or method or arrangement, deferring the receipt of compensation or providing for deferred benefits. Section 404(a) and (d) requires that such a contribution or compensation be paid or incurred for purposes of section 162 or 212 and satisfy the requirements for deductibility under either of these sections. However, notwithstanding the above, section 404 does not apply to contributions paid or accrued with respect to a "welfare benefit fund" (as defined in section 419(e) after July 18, 1984, in taxable years of employers (and payors) ending after that date.

Also, section 463 shall govern the deduction of vacation pay by a taxpayer that has elected the application of such section. Section 404(b), as amended, generally applies to contributions paid and compensation paid or incurred after July 18, 1984, in taxable years of employers (and payors) ending after that date. See Q&A 3 of § 1.404(b)-1T. For rules relating to the deduction of contributions attributable to the provision of deferred benefits, see section 404(a), (b) and (d) and § 1.404(a)-1T, § 1.404(b)-1T and § 1.404(d)-1T. For rules relating to the deduction of contributions paid or accrued with respect to a welfare benefit fund, see section 419,

§ 1.419-1T and § 1.419A-2T. For rules relating to the deduction of vacation pay for which an election is made under section 463, see § 301.9100-16T of this chapter and § 1.463-1T.

Q-2. How does the enactment of section 419 by the Tax Reform Act of 1984 affect the deduction of employee benefits under section 162?

A-2. As enacted by the Tax Reform Act of 1984, section 419 shall govern the deduction of contributions paid or accrued by an employer (or a person receiving services under section 419(g)) with respect to a "welfare benefit fund" (within the meaning of section 419(e)) after December 31, 1985, in taxable years of the employer (or person receiving the services) ending after that date. Section 419(a) requires that such a contribution be paid or accrued for purposes of section 162 or 212 and satisfy the requirements for deductibility under either of those sections. Generally, subject to a binding contract exception (as described in section 511(e)(5) of the Tax Reform Act of 1984), section 419 shall also govern the deduction of the contribution of a facility) or other contribution used to acquire or improve a facility) to a welfare benefit fund after June 22, 1984. See Q&A-11 of § 1.419-1T. In the case of a welfare benefit fund maintained pursuant to a collective bargaining agreement, section 419 applies to the extent provided under the special effective date rule described in Q&A-2 of § 1.419-1T and the special rules of § 1.419A-2T. For rules relating to the deduction of contributions paid or accrued with respect to a welfare benefit fund, see section 419 and § 1.419-1T.

T.D. 8073, 1/29/86, amend T.D. 8435, 9/18/92.

§ 1.162-11 Rentals.

(a) Acquisition of a leasehold. If a leasehold is acquired for business purposes for a specified sum, the purchaser may take as a deduction in his return an aliquot part of such sum each year, based on the number of years the lease has to run. Taxes paid by a tenant to or for a landlord for business property are additional rent and constitute a deductible item to the tenant and taxable income to the landlord, the amount of the tax being deductible by the latter. For disallowance of deduction for income taxes paid by a lessee corporation pursuant to a lease arrangement with the lessor corporation, see section 110 and the regulations thereunder. See section 178 and the regulations thereunder for rules governing the effect to be given renewal options in amortizing the costs incurred after July 28, 1958, of acquiring a lease. See § 1.197-2 for rules governing the amortization of costs to acquire limited interests in section 197 intangibles.

(b) Improvements by lessee on lessor's property. *(1)* The cost to a lessee of erecting buildings or making permanent improvements on property of which he is the lessee is a capital investment, and is not deductible as a business expense. If the estimated useful life in the hands of the taxpayer of the building erected or of the improvements made, determined without regard to the terms of the lease, is longer than the remaining period of the lease, an annual deduction may be made from gross income of an amount equal to the total cost of such improvements divided by the number of years remaining in the term of the lease, and such deduction shall be in lieu of a deduction for depreciation. If, on the other hand, the useful life of such buildings or improvements in the hands of the taxpayer is equal to or shorter than the remaining period of the lease, this deduction shall be computed under the provisions of section 167 (relating to depreciation).

(2) If the lessee began improvements on leased property before July 28, 1958, or if the lessee was on such date and at all times thereafter under a binding legal obligation to make such improvements, the matter of spreading the cost of erecting buildings or making permanent improvements over the term of the original lease, together with the renewal period or periods depends upon the facts in the particular case, including the presence or absence of an obligation of renewal and the relationship between the parties. As a general rule, unless the lease has been renewed or the facts show with reasonable certainty that the lease will be renewed, the cost or other basis of the lease, or the cost of improvements shall be spread only over the number of years the lease has to run without taking into account any right of renewal. The provisions of this subparagraph may be illustrated by the following examples:

Example (1). A subsidiary corporation leases land from its parent at a fair rental for a 25-year period. The subsidiary erects on the land valuable factory buildings having an estimated useful life of 50 years. These facts show with reasonable certainty that the lease will be renewed, even though the lease contains no option of renewal. Therefore, the cost of the buildings shall be depreciated over the estimated useful life of the buildings in accordance with section 167 and the regulations thereunder.

Example (2). A retail merchandising corporation leases land at a fair rental from an unrelated lessor for the longest period that the lessor is willing to lease the land (30 years). The lessee erects on the land a department store having an estimated useful life of 40 years. These facts do not show with reasonable certainty that the lease will be renewed. Therefore, the cost of the building shall be spread over the remaining term of the lease. An annual deduction may be made of an amount equal to the cost of the building divided by the number of years remaining in the term of the lease, and such deduction shall be in lieu of a deduction for depreciation.

(3) See section 178 and the regulations thereunder for rules governing the effect to be given renewal options where a lessee begins improvements on leased property after July 28, 1958, other than improvements which on such date and at all times thereafter, the lessee was under a binding legal obligation to make.

T.D. 6291, 4/3/58, amend T.D. 6520, 12/23/60, T.D. 8865, 1/20/2000.

§ 1.162-12 Expenses of farmers.

Caution: The Treasury has not yet amended Reg § 1.162-12 to reflect changes made by P.L. 110-246.

(a) Farms engaged in for profit. A farmer who operates a farm for profit is entitled to deduct from gross income as necessary expenses all amounts actually expended in the carrying on of the business of farming. The cost of ordinary tools of short life or small cost, such as hand tools, including shovels, rakes, etc., may be deducted. The purchase of feed and other costs connected with raising livestock may be treated as expense deductions insofar as such costs represent actual outlay, but not including the value of farm produce grown upon the farm or the labor of the taxpayer. For rules regarding the capitalization of expenses of producing property in the trade or business of farming, see section 263A and the regulations thereunder. after the third sentence. For taxable years beginning after July 12, 1972 where a farmer is engaged in producing crops which take more than a year from the time of planting to the process of gathering and disposal, expenses deducted may, with the consent of the Commissioner (see section 446 and the regulations thereunder), be determined upon the crop method, and such deductions must be taken in the taxable year in which the gross income from the crop has been realized. If a farmer does not compute income upon the crop method, the cost of seeds and young plants which are purchased for further development and cultivation prior to sale in later years may be deducted as an expense for the year of purchase, provided the farmer follows a consistent practice of deducting such costs as an expense from year to year. The preceding sentence does not apply to the cost of seeds and young plants connected with the planting of timber (see section 611 and the regulations thereunder). For rules regarding the capitalization of expenses of producing property in the trade or business of farming, see section 263A of the Internal Revenue Code and § 1.263A-4. The cost of farm machinery, equipment, and farm buildings represents a capital investment and is not an allowable deduction as an item of expense. Amounts expended in the development of farms, orchards, and ranches prior to the time when the productive state is reached may, at the election of the taxpayer, be regarded as investments of capital. For the treatment of soil and water conservation expenditures as expenses which are not chargeable to capital account, see section 175 and the regulations thereunder. For taxable years beginning after December 31, 1959, in the case of expenditures paid or incurred by farmers for fertilizer, lime, etc., see section 180 and the regulations thereunder. Amounts expended in purchasing work, breeding, or dairy animals are regarded as investments of capital, and shall be depreciated unless such animals are included in an inventory in accordance with § 1.61-4. The purchase price of an automobile, even when wholly used in carrying on farming operations, is not deductible, but is regarded as an investment of capital. The cost of gasoline, repairs, and upkeep of an automobile if used wholly in the business of farming is deductible as an expense; if used partly for business purposes and partly for the pleasure or convenience of the taxpayer or his family, such cost may be apportioned according to the extent of the use for purposes of business and pleasure or convenience, and only the proportion of such cost justly attributable to business purposes is deductible as a necessary expense.

(b) Farms not engaged in for profit; taxable years beginning before January 1, 1970. *(1) In general.* If a farm is operated for recreation or pleasure and not on a commercial basis, and if the expenses incurred in connection with the farm are in excess of the receipts therefrom, the entire receipts from the sale of farm products may be ignored in rendering a return of income, and the expenses incurred, being regarded as personal expenses, will not constitute allowable deductions.

(2) Effective date. The provisions of this paragraph shall apply with respect to taxable years beginning before January 1, 1970.

(3) Cross reference. For provisions relating to activities not engaged in for profit, applicable to taxable years beginning after December 31, 1969, see section 183 and the regulations thereunder.

T.D. 6291, 4/3/58, amend T.D. 6548, 2/21/61, T.D. 7198, 7/12/72, T.D. 8729, 8/21/97, T.D. 8897, 8/18/2000.

§ 1.162-13 Depositors guaranty fund.

Banking corporations which pursuant to the laws of the State in which they are doing business are required to set apart, keep, and maintain in their banks the amount levied and assessed against them by the State authorities as a "Depositors' guaranty fund," may deduct from their gross income the amount so set apart each year to this fund provided that such fund, when set aside and carried to the credit of the State banking board or duly authorized State officer, ceases to be an asset of the bank and may be withdrawn in whole or in part upon demand by such board or State officer to meet the needs of these officers in reimbursing depositors in insolvent banks, and provided further that no portion of the amount thus set aside and credited is returnable under the laws of the State to the assets of the banking corporation. If, however, such amount is simply set up on the books of the bank as a reserve to meet a contingent liability and remains an asset of the bank, it will not be deductible except as it is actually paid out as required by law and upon demand of the proper State officers.

T.D. 6291, 4/3/58.

§ 1.162-14 Expenditures for advertising or promotion of good will.

A corporation which has, for the purpose of computing its excess profits tax credit under subchapter E, chapter 2, or subchapter D, chapter 1 of the Internal Revenue Code of 1939, elected under section 733 or section 451 (applicable to the excess profits tax imposed by subchapter E of chapter 2, and subchapter D of chapter 1, respectively) to charge to capital account for taxable years in its base period expenditures for advertising or the promotion of good will which may be regarded as capital investments, may not deduct similar expenditures for the taxable year. See section 263(b). Such a taxpayer has the burden of proving that expenditures for advertising or the promotion of good will which it seeks to deduct in the taxable year may not be regarded as capital investments under the provisions of the regulations prescribed under section 733 or section 451 of the Internal Revenue Code of 1939. See 26 CFR, 1938 ed., 35.733-2 (Regulations 112) and 26 CFR (1939) 40.451-2 (Regulations 130). For the disallowance of deductions for the cost of advertising in programs of certain conventions of political parties, or in publications part of the proceeds of which directly or indirectly insures (or is intended to insure) to or for the use of a political party or political candidate, see § 1.276-1.

T.D. 6291, 4/3/58, amend T.D. 6996, 1/17/69.

§ 1.162-15 Contributions, dues, etc.

(a) Contributions to organizations described in section 170. *(1) In general.* No deduction is allowable under section 162(a) for a contribution or gift by an individual or a corporation if any part thereof is deductible under section 170. For example, if a taxpayer makes a contribution of $5,000 and only $4,000 of this amount is deductible under section 170(a) (whether because of the percentage limitation under either section 170(b)(1) or (2), the requirement as to time of payment, or both) no deduction is allowable under section 162(a) for the remaining $1,000.

(2) Scope of limitations. The limitations provided in section 162(b) and this paragraph apply only to payments which are in fact contributions or gifts to organizations described in section 170. For example, payments by a transit company to a local hospital (which is a charitable organization within the

meaning of section 170) in consideration of a binding obligation on the part of the hospital to provide hospital services and facilities for the company's employees are not contributions or gifts within the meaning of section 170 and may be deductible under section 162(a) if the requirements of section 162(a) are otherwise satisfied.

(b) Other contributions. Donations to organizations other than those described in section 170 which bear a direct relationship to the taxpayer's business and are made with a reasonable expectation of a financial return commensurate with the amount of the donation may constitute allowable deductions as business expenses, provided the donation is not made for a purpose for which a deduction is not allowable by reason of the provisions of paragraph (b)(1)(i) or (c) of § 1.162-20. For example, a transit company may donate a sum of money to an organization (of a class not referred to in section 170) intending to hold a convention in the city in which it operates, with a reasonable expectation that the holding of such convention will augment its income through a greater number of people using its transportation facilities.

(c) Dues. Dues and other payments to an organization, such as a labor union or a trade association, which otherwise meet the requirements of the regulations under section 162, are deductible in full. For limitations on the deductibility of dues and other payments, see paragraph (b) and (c) of § 1.162-20.

(d) Cross reference. For provisions dealing with expenditures for institutional or "good will" advertising, see § 1.162-20.

T.D. 6291, 4/3/58, amend T.D. 6435, 12/28/59, T.D. 6819, 4/19/65.

§ 1.162-16 Cross reference.

For special rules relating to expenses in connection with subdividing real property for sale, see section 1237 and the regulations thereunder.

T.D. 6291, 4/3/58.

§ 1.162-17 Reporting and substantiation of certain business expenses of employees.

(a) Introductory. The purpose of the regulations in this section is to provide rules for the reporting of information on income tax returns by taxpayers who pay or incur ordinary and necessary business expenses in connection with the performance of services as an employee and to furnish guidance as to the type of records which will be useful in compiling such information and in its substantiation, if required. The rules prescribed in this section do not apply to expenses paid or incurred for incidentals, such as office supplies for the employer or local transportation in connection with an errand. Employees incurring such incidental expenses are not required to provide substantiation for such amounts. The term "ordinary and necessary business expenses" means only those expenses which are ordinary and necessary in the conduct of the taxpayer's business and are directly attributable to such business. The term does not include nondeductible personal, living or family expenses.

(b) Expenses for which the employee is required to account to his employer. *(1) Reimbursements equal to expenses.* The employee need not report on his tax return (either itemized or in total amount) expenses for travel, transportation, entertainment, and similar purposes paid or incurred by him solely for the benefit of his employer for which he is required to account and does account to his employer and which are charged directly or indirectly to the employer (for example, through credit cards) or for which the employee is paid through advances, reimbursements, or otherwise, provided the total amount of such advances, reimbursements, and charges is equal to such expenses. In such a case the taxpayer need only state in his return that the total of amounts charged directly or indirectly to his employer through credit cards or otherwise and received from the employer as advances or reimbursements did not exceed the ordinary and necessary business expenses paid or incurred by the employee.

(2) Reimbursements in excess of expenses. In case the total of amounts charged directly or indirectly to the employer and received from the employer as advances, reimbursements, or otherwise, exceeds the ordinary and necessary business expenses paid or incurred by the employee and the employee is required to and does account to his employer for such expenses, the taxpayer must include such excess in income and state on his return that he has done so.

(3) Expenses in excess of reimbursements. If the employee's ordinary and necessary business expenses exceed the total of the amounts charged directly or indirectly to the employer and received from the employer as advances, reimbursements, or otherwise, and the employee is required to and does account to his employer for such expenses, the taxpayer may make the statement in his return required by subparagraph (1) of this paragraph unless he wishes to claim a deduction for such excess. If, however, he wishes to secure a deduction for such excess, he must submit a statement showing the following information as part of his tax return:

(i) The total of any charges paid or borne by the employer and of any other amounts received from the employer for payment of expenses whether by means of advances, reimbursements or otherwise; and

(ii) The nature of his occupation, the number of days away from home on business, and the total amount of ordinary and necessary business expenses paid or incurred by him (including those charged directly or indirectly to the employer through credit cards or otherwise) broken down into such broad categories as transportation, meals and lodging while away from home overnight, entertainment expenses, and other business expenses.

(4) To "account" to his employer as used in this section means to submit an expense account or other required written statement to the employer showing the business nature and the amount of all the employee's expenses (including those charged directly or indirectly to the employer through credit cards or otherwise) broken down into such broad categories as transportation, meals and lodging while away from home overnight, entertainment expenses, and other business expenses. For this purpose, the Commissioner in his discretion may approve reasonable business practices under which mileage, per diem in lieu of subsistence, and similar allowances providing for ordinary and necessary business expenses in accordance with a fixed scale may be regarded as equivalent to an accounting to the employer.

(c) Expenses for which the employee is not required to account to his employer. If the employee is not required to account to his employer for his ordinary and necessary business expenses, e.g., travel, transportation, entertainment, and similar items, or, though required, fails to account for such expenses, he must submit, as a part of his tax return, a statement showing the following information:

(1) The total of all amounts received as advances or reimbursements from his employer in connection with the ordinary and necessary business expenses of the employee, in-

cluding amounts charged directly or indirectly to the employer through credit cards or otherwise; and

(2) The nature of his occupation, the number of days away from home on business, and the total amount of ordinary and necessary business expenses paid or incurred by him (including those charged directly or indirectly to the employer through credit cards or otherwise) broken down into such broad categories as transportation, meals and lodging while away from home overnight, entertainment expenses, and other business expenses.

(d) Substantiation of items of expense. *(1)* Although the Commissioner may require any taxpayer to substantiate such information concerning expense accounts as may appear to be pertinent in determining tax liability, taxpayers ordinarily will not be called upon to substantiate expense account information except those in the following categories:

(i) A taxpayer who is not required to account to his employer, or who does not account;

(ii) A taxpayer whose expenses exceed the total of amounts charged to his employer and amounts received through advances, reimbursements or otherwise and who claims a deduction on his return for such excess; thru advances, reimbursements or otherwise and who claims a deduction on his return for such excess;

(iii) A taxpayer who is related to his employer within the meaning of section 267 (b); and

(iv) Other taxpayers in cases where it is determined that the accounting procedures used by the employer for the reporting and substantiation of expenses by employees are not adequate.

(2) The Code contemplates that taxpayers keep such records as will be sufficient to enable the Commissioner to correctly determine income tax liability. Accordingly, it is to the advantage of taxpayers who may be called upon to substantiate expense account information to maintain as adequate and detailed records of travel, transportation, entertainment, and similar business expenses as practical since the burden of proof is upon the taxpayer to show that such expenses were not only paid or incurred but also that they constitute ordinary and necessary business expenses. One method for substantiating expenses incurred by an employee in connection with his employment is through the preparation of a daily diary or record of expenditures, maintained in sufficient detail to enable him to readily identify the amount and nature of any expenditure, and the preservation of supporting documents, especially in connection with large or exceptional expenditures. Nevertheless, it is recognized that by reason of the nature of certain expenses or the circumstances under which they are incurred, it is often difficult for an employee to maintain detailed records or to preserve supporting documents for all his expenses. Detailed records of small expenditures incurred in traveling or for transportation, as for example, tips, will not be required.

(3) Where records are incomplete or documentary proof is unavailable, it may be possible to establish the amount of the expenditures by approximations based upon reliable secondary sources of information and collateral evidence. For example, in connection with an item of traveling expense a taxpayer might establish that he was in a travel status a certain number of days but that is was impracticable for him to establish the details of all his various items of travel expense. In such a case rail fares or plane fares can usually be ascertained with exactness and automobile costs approximated on the basis of mileage covered. A reasonable approximation of meals and lodging might be based upon receipted hotel bills or upon average daily rates for such accommodations and meals prevailing in the particular community for comparable accommodations. Since detailed records of incidental items are not required, deductions for these items may be based upon a reasonable approximation. In cases where a taxpayer is called upon to substantiate expense account information, the burden is on the taxpayer to establish that the amounts claimed as a deduction are reasonably accurate and constitute ordinary and necessary business expenses paid or incurred by him in connection with his trade or business. In connection with the determination of factual matters of this type, due consideration will be given to the reasonableness of the stated expenditures for the claimed purposes in relation to the taxpayer's circumstances (such as his income and the nature of his occupation), to the reliability and accuracy of records in connection with other items more readily lending themselves to detailed record-keeping, and to all of the facts and circumstances in the particular case.

(e) Applicability. *(1)* Except as provided in subparagraph (2) of this paragraph, the provisions of the regulations in this section are supplemental to existing regulations relating to information required to be submitted with income tax returns, and shall be applicable with respect to taxable years beginning after December 31, 1957, notwithstanding any existing regulation to the contrary.

(2) With respect to taxable years ending after December 31, 1962, but only in respect of periods after such date, the provisions of the regulations in this section are superseded by the regulations under section 274(d) to the extent inconsistent therewith. See § 1.274-5.

(3) For taxable years beginning on or after January 1, 1989, the provisions of this section are superseded by the regulations under section 62(c) to the extent this section is inconsistent with those regulations. See § 1.62-2.

T.D. 6306, 8/27/58, amend T.D. 6630, 12/27/62, T.D. 8276, 12/7/89, T.D. 8324, 12/14/90.

---

§ 1.162-18 Illegal bribes and kickbacks.

Caution: The Treasury has not yet amended Reg § 1.162-18 to reflect changes made by P.L. 100-647, P.L. 99-514, P.L. 99-272, P.L. 98-573, P.L. 97-248.

(a) Illegal payments to government officials or employees. *(1) In general.* No deduction shall be allowed under section 162(a) for any amount paid or incurred, directly or indirectly, to an official or employee of any government, or of any agency or other instrumentality of any government, if—

(i) In the case of a payment made to an official or employee of a government other than a foreign government described in subparagraph (3)(ii) or (iii) of this paragraph, the payment constitutes an illegal bribe or kickback, or

(ii) In the case of a payment made to an official or employee of a foreign government described in subparagraph (3)(ii) or (iii) of this paragraph, the making of the payment would be unlawful under the laws of the United States (if such laws were applicable to the payment and to the official or employee at the time the expenses were paid or incurred).

No deduction shall be allowed for an accrued expense if the eventual payment thereof would fall within the prohibition of this section. The place where the expenses are paid or incurred is immaterial. For purposes of subdivision (ii) of this subparagraph, lawfulness or unlawfulness of the payment under the laws of the foreign country is immaterial.

(2) Indirect payment. For purposes of this paragraph, an indirect payment to an individual shall include any payment which inures to his benefit or promotes his interests, regardless of the medium in which the payment is made and regardless of the identity of the immediate recipient or payor. Thus, for example, payment made to an agent, relative, or independent contractor of an official or employee, or even directly into the general treasury of a foreign country of which the beneficiary is an official or employee, may be treated as an indirect payment to the official or employee, if in fact such payment inures or will inure to his benefit or promotes or will promote his financial or other interests. A payment made by an agent or independent contractor of the taxpayer which benefits the taxpayer shall be treated as an indirect payment by the taxpayer to the official or employee.

(3) Official or employee of a government. Any individual officially connected with—

(i) The Government of the United States, a State, a territory or possession of the United States, the District of Columbia, or the Commonwealth of Puerto Rico,

(ii) The government of a foreign country, or

(iii) A political subdivision of, or a corporation or other entity serving as an agency or instrumentality of, any of the above,

in whatever capacity, whether on a permanent or temporary basis, and whether or not serving for compensation, shall be included within the term "official or employee of a government", regardless of the place of residence or post of duty of such individual. An independent contractor would not ordinarily be considered to be an official or employee. For purposes of section 162(c) and this paragraph, the term "foreign country" shall include any foreign nation, whether or not such nation has been accorded diplomatic recognition by the United States. Individuals who purport to act on behalf of or as the government of a foreign nation, or an agency or instrumentality thereof, shall be treated under this section as officials or employees of a foreign government, whether or not such individuals in fact control such foreign nation, agency, or instrumentality, and whether or not such individuals are accorded diplomatic recognition. Accordingly, a group in rebellion against an established government shall be treated as officials or employees of a foreign government, as shall officials or employees of the government against which the group is in rebellion.

(4) Laws of the United States. The term "laws of the United States", to which reference is made in paragraph (a)(1)(ii) of this section, shall be deemed to include only Federal statutes, including State laws which are assimilated into Federal law by Federal statute, and legislative and interpretative regulations thereunder. The term shall also be limited to statutes which prohibit some act or acts, for the violation of which there is a civil or criminal penalty.

(5) Burden of proof. In any proceeding involving the issue of whether, for purposes of section 162(c)(1), a payment made to a government official or employee constitutes an illegal bribe or kickback (or would be unlawful under the laws of the United States) the burden of proof in respect of such issue shall be upon the Commissioner to the same extent as he bears the burden of proof in civil fraud cases under section 7454 (i.e., he must prove the illegality of the payment by clear and convincing evidence).

(6) Example. The application of this paragraph may be illustrated by the following example:

Example. X Corp. is in the business of selling hospital equipment in State Y. During 1970, X Corp. employed A who at the time was employed full time by State Y as Superintendent of Hospitals. The purpose of A's employment by X Corp. was to procure for it an improper advantage over other concerns in the making of sales to hospitals in respect of which A, as Superintendent, had authority. X Corp. paid A $5,000 during 1970. The making of this payment was illegal under the laws of State Y. Under section 162(c)(1), X Corp. is precluded from deducting as a trade or business expense the $5,000 paid to A.

(b) Other illegal payments. *(1) In general.* No deduction shall be allowed under section 162(a) for any payment (other than a payment described in paragraph (a) of this section) made, directly or indirectly, to any person, if the payment constitutes an illegal bribe, illegal kickback, or other illegal payment under the laws of the United States (as defined in paragraph (a)(4) of this section), or under any State law (but only if such State law is generally enforced), which subjects the payor to a criminal penalty or the loss (including a suspension) of license or privilege to engage in a trade or business (whether or not such penalty or loss is actually imposed upon the taxpayer). For purposes of this paragraph, a kickback includes a payment in consideration of the referral of a client, patient, or customer. This paragraph applies only to payments made after December 30, 1969.

(2) State law. For purposes of this paragraph, State law, means a statute of a State or the District of Columbia.

(3) Generally enforced. For purposes of this paragraph, a State law shall be considered to be generally enforced unless it is never enforced or the only persons normally charged with violations thereof in the State (or the District of Columbia) enacting the law are infamous or those whose violations are extraordinarily flagrant. For example, a criminal statute of a State shall be considered to be generally enforced unless violations of the statute which are brought to the attention of appropriate enforcement authorities do not result in any enforcement action in the absence of unusual circumstances.

(4) Burden of proof. In any proceeding involving the issue of whether, for purposes of section 162(c)(2), a payment constitutes an illegal bribe, illegal kickback, or other illegal payment the burden of proof in respect of such issue shall be upon the Commissioner to the same extent as he bears the burden of proof in civil fraud cases under section 7454 (i.e., he must prove the illegality of the payment by clear and convincing evidence).

(5) Example. The application of this paragraph may be illustrated by the following example:

Example. X Corp., a calendar-year taxpayer, is engaged in the ship repair business in State Y. During 1970, repairs on foreign ships accounted for a substantial part of its total business. It was X Corp.'s practice to kick back approximately 10 percent of the repair bill to the captain and chief engineer of all foreign-owned vessels, which kickbacks are illegal under a law of State Y (which is generally enforced) and potentially subject X Corp. to fines. During 1970, X Corp. paid $50,000 in such kickbacks. On X Corp.'s return for 1970, a deduction under section 162 was taken for the $50,000. The deduction of the $50,000 of illegal kickbacks during 1970 is disallowed under section 162(c)(2), whether or not X Corp. is prosecuted with respect to the kickbacks.

(c) Kickbacks, rebates, and bribes under medicare and medicaid. No deduction shall be allowed under section 162(a) for any kickback, rebate, or bribe (whether or not illegal) made on or after December 10, 1971, by any provider of services, supplier, physician, or other person who furnishes items or services for which payment is or may be made under the Social Security Act, as amended, or in whole or in part out of Federal funds under a State plan approved under such Act, if such kickback, rebate, or bribe is made in connection with the furnishing of such items or services or the making or receipt of such payments. For purposes of this paragraph, a kickback includes a payment in consideration of the referral of a client, patient, or customer.

T.D. 6448, 1/26/60, amend T.D. 7345, 2/19/75.

§ 1.162-19 Capital contributions to Federal National Mortgage Association.

(a) In general. The initial holder of stock of the Federal National Mortgage Association (FNMA) which is issued pursuant to section 303(c) of the Federal National Mortgage Association Charter Act (12 U.S.C., sec. 1718) in a taxable year beginning after December 31, 1959, shall treat the excess, if any, of the issuance price (the amount of capital contributions evidenced by a share of stock) over the fair market value of the stock as of the issue date of such stock as an ordinary and necessary business expense paid or incurred during the year in which occurs the date of issuance of the stock. To the extent that a sale to FNMA of mortgage paper gives rise to the issuance of a share of FNMA stock during a taxable year beginning after December 31, 1959, such sale is to be treated in a manner consistent with the purpose for, and the legislative intent underlying the enactment of, the provisions of section 8, Act of September 14, 1960 (Public Law 86-779, 74 Stat. 1003). Thus, for the purpose of determining an initial holder's gain or loss from the sale to FNMA of mortgage paper, with respect to which a share of FNMA stock is issued in a taxable year beginning after December 31, 1959 (irrespective of when the sale is made), the amount realized by the initial holder from the sale of the mortgage paper is the amount of the "FNMA purchase price". The "FNMA purchase price" is the gross amount of the consideration agreed upon between FNMA and the initial holder for the purchase of the mortgage paper, without regard to any deduction therefrom as, for example, a deduction representing a capital contribution or a purchase or marketing fee. The date of issuance of the stock is the date which appears on the stock certificates of the initial holder as the date of issue. The initial holder is the original purchaser who is issued stock of the Federal National Mortgage Association pursuant to section 303(c) of the Act, and who appears on the books of FNMA as the initial holder. In determining the period for which the initial holder has held such stock, such period shall begin with the date of issuance.

(b) Examples. The provisions of paragraph (a) of this section may be illustrated by the following examples:

Example (1). A, a banking institution which reports its income on a calendar year basis, sold mortgage paper with an outstanding principal balance of $12,500 to FNMA on October 17, 1960. The FNMA purchase price was $11,500. A's basis for the mortgage paper was $10,500. In accordance with the terms of the contract, FNMA deducted $375 ($250 representing capital contribution and $125 representing purchase and marketing fee) from the amount of the purchase price. FNMA credited A's account with the amount of the capital contribution. A stock certificate evidencing two shares of FNMA common stock of $100 par value was mailed to A and FNMA deducted $200 from A's account, leaving a net balance of $50 in such account. The stock certificate, bearing an issue date of November 1, 1960, was received by A on November 7, 1960. The fair market value of a share of FNMA stock on October 17, 1960, was $65, on November 1, 1960, was $67, and on November 7, 1960, was $68. A may deduct $66 the difference between the issuance price ($200) and the fair market value ($134) of the two shares of stock on the date of issuance (November 1, 1960), as a business expense for the taxable year 1960. The basis of each share of stock issued as of November 1, 1960 will be $67. See section 1054 and § 1.1054-1. A's gain from the sale of the mortgage paper is $875 computed as follows:

Amount realized (FNMA purchase price)		$11,500
A's basis in mortgage paper	$10,500	
Purchase and marketing fee	125	10,625
Gain on sale		875

Example (2). Assume the same facts as in example (1), and, in addition, that A sold to FNMA on December 15, 1960, additional mortgage paper having an outstanding principal balance of $12,500. FNMA deducted from the FNMA purchase price $250 representing capital contribution and credited A's account with this amount. A then had a total credit of $300 to his account consisting of the $50 balance from the transaction described in Example (1) and $250 from the December 15th transaction. A stock certificate evidencing three shares of FNMA common stock of $100 par value was mailed to A and FNMA deducted $300 from A's account. The stock certificate, bearing an issue date of January 1, 1961, was received by A on January 9, 1961. The fair market value of a share of FNMA stock on January 1, 1961, was $69. A may deduct $93, the difference between the issuance price ($300) and the fair market value ($207) of the three shares of stock on the date of issuance (January 1, 1961), as a business expense for the taxable year 1961. The gain or loss on the sale of mortgage paper on December 15, 1960, is reportable for the taxable year 1960.

T.D. 6690, 11/18/63.

§ 1.162-20 Expenditures attributable to lobbying, political campaigns, attempts to influence legislation, etc., and certain advertising.

(a) In general. *(1) Scope of section.* This section contains rules governing deductibility or nondeductibility of expenditures for lobbying purposes, for the promotion or defeat of legislation, for political campaign purposes (including the support of or opposition to any candidate for public office) or for carrying on propaganda (including advertising) related to any of the foregoing purposes. For rules applicable to such expenditures in respect of taxable years beginning before January 1, 1963, and for taxable years beginning after December 31, 1962, see paragraphs (b) and (c), respectively, of this section. This section also deals with expenditures for institutional or "good will" advertising.

(2) Institutional or "good will" advertising. Expenditures for institutional or "good will" advertising which keeps the taxpayer's name before the public are generally deductible as ordinary and necessary business expenses provided the expenditures are related to the patronage the taxpayer might reasonably expect in the future. For example, a deduction will ordinarily be allowed for the cost of advertising which keeps the taxpayer's name before the public in connection with encouraging contributions to such organizations as the Red Cross, the purchase of United States Savings Bonds, or participation in similar causes. In like fashion, expenditures for advertising which presents views on economic, financial, social, or other subjects of a general nature, but which does not involve any of the activities specified in paragraph (b) or (c) of this section for which a deduction is not allowable, are

deductible if they otherwise meet the requirements of the regulations under section 162.

(b) Taxable years beginning before January 1, 1963. *(1) In general.* (i) For taxable years beginning before January 1, 1963, expenditures for lobbying purposes, for the promotion or defeat of legislation, for political campaign purposes (including the support of or opposition to any candidate for public office), or for carrying on propaganda (including advertising) related to any of the foregoing purposes are not deductible from gross income. For example, the cost of advertising to promote or defeat legislation or to influence the public with respect to the desirability or undesirability of proposed legislation is not deductible as a business expense, even though the legislation may directly affect the taxpayer's business.

(ii) If a substantial part of the activities of an organization, such as a labor union or a trade association, consists of one or more of the activities specified in the first sentence of this subparagraph, deduction will be allowed only for such portion of the dues or other payments to the organization as the taxpayer can clearly establish is attributable to activities other than those so specified. The determination of whether such specified activities constitute a substantial part of an organization's activities shall be based on all the facts and circumstances. In no event shall special assessments or similar payments (including an in- crease in dues) made to any organization for any such specified purposes be deductible. For other provisions relating to the deductibility of dues and other payments to an organization, such as a labor union or a trade association, see paragraph (c) of § 1.162-15.

(2) Expenditures for promotion or defeat of legislation. For purposes of this paragraph, expenditures for the promotion or the defeat of legislation include, but shall not be limited to, expenditures for the purpose of attempting to—

(i) Influence members of a legislative body directly, or indirectly by urging or encouraging the public to contact such members for the purpose of proposing, supporting, or opposing legislation, or

(ii) Influence the public to approve or reject a measure in a referendum, initiative, vote on a constitutional amendment, or similar procedure.

(c) Taxable years beginning after December 31, 1962. *(1) In general.* For taxable years beginning after December 31, 1962, certain types of expenses incurred with respect to legislative matters are deductible under section 162(a) if they otherwise meet the requirements of the regulations under section 162. These deductible expenses are described in subparagraph (2) of this paragraph. All other expenditures for lobbying purposes, for the promotion or defeat of legislation (see paragraph (b)(2) of this section), for political campaign purposes (including the support of or opposition to any candidate for public office), or for carrying on propaganda (including advertising) relating to any of the foregoing purposes are not deductible from gross income for such taxable years. For the disallowance of deductions for bad debts and worthless securities of a political party, see § 1.271-1. For the disallowance of deductions for certain indirect political contributions, such as the cost of certain advertising and the cost of admission to certain dinners, programs, and inaugural events, see § 1.276-1.

(2) Appearance, etc., with respect to legislation. (i) General rule. Pursuant to the provisions of section 162(e), expenses incurred with respect to legislative matters which may be deductible are those ordinary and necessary expenses (including, but not limited to, traveling expenses described in section 162(a)(2) and the cost of preparing testimony) paid or incurred by the taxpayer during a taxable year beginning after December 31, 1962, in carrying on any trade or business which are in direct connection with—

(a) Appearances before, submission of statements to, or sending communications to, the committees, or individual members of the Congress or of any legislative body of a State, a possession of the United States, or a political subdivision of any of the foregoing with respect to legislation or proposed legislation of direct interest to the taxpayer, or

(b) Communication of information between the taxpayer and an organization of which he is a member with respect to legislation or proposed legislation of direct interest to the taxpayer and to such organization.

For provisions relating to dues paid or incurred with respect to an organization of which the taxpayer is a member, see subparagraph (3) of this paragraph.

(ii) Legislation or proposed legislation of direct interest to the taxpayer. (a) Legislation or proposed legislation. The term "legislation or proposed legislation" includes bills and resolutions introduced by a member of Congress or other legislative body referred to in subdivision (i)(a) of this subparagraph for consideration by such body as well as oral or written proposals for legislative action submitted to the legislative body or to a committee or member of such body.

(b) Direct interest. (1) In general. (i) Legislation or proposed legislation is of direct interest to a taxpayer if the legislation or proposed legislation is of such a nature that it will, or may reasonably be expected to, affect the trade or business of the taxpayer. It is immaterial whether the effect, or expected effect, on the trade or business will be beneficial or detrimental to the trade or business or whether it will be immediate. If legislation or proposed legislation has such a relationship to a trade or business that the expenses of any appearance or communication in connection with the legislation meets the ordinary and necessary test of section 162(a), then such legislation ordinarily meets the direct interest test of section 162(e). However, if the nature of the legislation or proposed legislation is such that the likelihood of its having an effect on the trade or business of the taxpayer is remote or speculative, the legislation or proposed legislation is not of direct interest to the taxpayer. Legislation or proposed legislation which will not affect the trade or business of the taxpayer is not of direct interest to the taxpayer even though such legislation will affect the personal, living, or family activities or expenses of the taxpayer. Legislation or proposed legislation is not of direct interest to a taxpayer merely because it may affect business in general; however, if the legislation or proposed legislation will, or may reasonably be expected to, affect the taxpayer's trade or business it will be of direct interest to the taxpayer even though it also will affect the trade or business of other taxpayers or business in general. To meet the direct interest test, it is not necessary that all the provisions of the legislation or proposed legislation have an effect, or expected effect, on the taxpayer's trade or business. The test will be met if one of the provisions of the legislation has the specified effect. Legislation or proposed legislation will be considered to be of direct interest to a membership organization if it is of direct interest to the organization, as such, or if it is of direct interest to one or more of its members.

(ii) Legislation which would increase or decrease the taxes applicable to the trade or business, increase or decrease the operating costs or earnings of the trade or business, or increase or decrease the administrative burdens connected with the trade or business meets the direct interest test. Legislation which would increase the social security benefits or liberalize the right to such benefits meets the direct interest test because such changes in the social security benefits may reasonably be expected to affect the retirement benefits which the employer will be asked to provide his employees or to increase his taxes. Legislation which would impose a retailer's sales tax is of direct interest to a retailer because, although the tax may be passed on to his customers, collection of the tax will impose additional burdens on the retailer, and because the increased cost of his products to the consumer may reduce the demand for them. Legislation which would provide an income tax credit or exclusion for shareholders is of direct interest to a corporation, because those tax benefits may increase the sources of capital available to the corporation. Legislation which would favorably or adversely affect the business of a competitor so as to affect the taxpayer's competitive position is of direct interest to the taxpayer. Legislation which would improve the school system of a community is of direct interest to a membership organization comprised of employers in the community because the improved school system is likely to make the community more attractive to prospective employees of such employers. On the other hand, proposed legislation relating to Presidential succession in the event of the death of the President has only a remote and speculative effect on any trade or business and therefore does not meet the direct interest test. Similarly, if a corporation is represented before a congressional committee to oppose an appropriation bill merely because of a desire to bring increased Government economy with the hope that such economy will eventually cause a reduction in the Federal income tax, the legislation does not meet the direct interest test because any effect it may have upon the corporation's trade or business is highly speculative.

(2) Appearances, etc., by expert witnesses. (i) An appearance or communication (of a type described in paragraph (c)(2)(i)(a) of this section) by an individual in connection with legislation or proposed legislation shall be considered to be with respect to legislation of direct interest to such individual if the legislation is in a field in which he specializes as an employee, if the appearance or communication is not on behalf of his employer, and if it is customary for individuals in his type of employment to publicly express their views in respect of matters in their field of competence. Expenses incurred by such an individual in connection with such an appearance or communication, including traveling expenses properly allocable thereto, represent ordinary and necessary business expenses and are, therefore, deductible under section 162. For example, if a university professor who teaches in the field of money and banking appears, on his own behalf, before a legislative committee to testify on proposed legislation regarding the banking system, his expenses incurred in connection with such appearance are deductible under section 162 since university professors customarily take an active part in the development of the law in their field of competence and publicly communicate the results of their work.

(ii) An appearance or communication (of a type described in paragraph (c)(2)(i)(a) of this section) by an employee or self-employed individual in connection with legislation or proposed legislation shall be considered to be with respect to legislation of direct interest to such person if the legislation is in the field in which he specializes in his business (or as an employee) and if the appearance or communication is made pursuant to an invitation extended to him individually for the purpose of receiving his expert testimony. Expenses incurred by an employee or self-employed individual in connection with such an appearance or communication, including traveling expenses properly allocable thereto, represent ordinary and necessary business expenses and are, therefore, deductible under section 162. For example, if a self-employed individual is personally invited by a congressional committee to testify on proposed legislation in the field in which he specializes in his business, his expenses incurred in connection with such appearance are deductible under section 162. If a self-employed individual makes an appearance, on his own behalf, before a legislative committee without having been extended an invitation his expenses will be deductible to the extent otherwise provided in this paragraph.

(3) Nominations, etc. A taxpayer does not have a direct interest in matters such as nominations, appointments, or the operation of the legislative body.

(iii) Allowable expenses. To be deductible under section 162(a), expenditures which meet the tests of deductibility under the provisions of this paragraph must also qualify as ordinary and necessary business expenses under section 162(a) and, in addition, be in direct connection with the carrying on of the activities specified in subdivision (i)(a) or (i)(b) of this subparagraph. For example, a taxpayer appearing before a committee of the Congress to present testimony concerning legislation or proposed legislation in which he has a direct interest may deduct the ordinary and necessary expenses directly connected with his appearance, such as traveling expenses described in section 162(a)(2), and the cost of preparing testimony.

(3) Deductibility of dues and other payments to an organization. If a substantial part of the activities of an organization, such as a labor union or a trade association, consists of one or more of the activities to which this paragraph relates (legislative matters, political campaigns, etc.,) exclusive of any activity constituting an appearance or communication with respect to legislation or proposed legislation of direct interest to the organization (see subparagraph (2)(ii)(b)(1)), a deduction will be allowed only for such portion of the dues or other payments to the organization as the taxpayer can clearly establish is attributable to activities to which this paragraph does not relate and to any activity constituting an appearance or communication with respect to legislation or proposed legislation of direct interest to the organization. The determination of whether a substantial part of an organization's activities consists of one or more of the activities to which this paragraph relates (exclusive of appearances or communications with respect to legislation or proposed legislation of direct interest to the organization) shall be based on all the facts and circumstances. In no event shall a deduction be allowed for that portion of a special assessment or similar payment (including an increase in dues) made to any organization for any activity to which this paragraph relates if the activity does not constitute an appearance or communication with respect to legislation or proposed legislation of direct interest to the organization. If an organization pays or incurs expenses allocable to legislative activities which meet the tests of subdivisions (i) and (ii) of subparagraph (2) of this paragraph (appearances or communications with respect to legislation or proposed legislation of direct interest to the organization), on behalf of its members, the dues paid by a taxpayer are deductible to the extent used for such activities. Dues paid by a taxpayer will be considered to be used for such an activity, and thus deductible, although the legislation or proposed legislation involved is not of direct interest to the taxpayer, if, pursuant to the provisions of subparagraph (2)(ii)(b)(1) of this paragraph, the legislation or proposed legislation is of direct interest to the organization, as such, or

is of direct interest to one or more members of the organization. For other provisions relating to the deductibility of dues and other payments to an organization, such as a labor union or a trade association, see paragraph (c) of § 1.162-15.

(4) Limitations. No deduction shall be allowed under section 162(a) for any amount paid or incurred (whether by way of contribution, gift, or otherwise) in connection with any attempt to influence the general public, or segments thereof, with respect to legislative matters, elections, or referendums. For example, no deduction shall be allowed for any expenses incurred in connection with "grassroot" campaigns or any other attempts to urge or encourage the public to contact members of a legislative body for the purpose of proposing, supporting, or opposing legislation.

(5) Expenses paid or incurred after December 31, 1993, in connection with influencing legislation other than certain local legislation. The provisions of paragraphs (c)(1) through (3) of this section are superseded for expenses paid or incurred after December 31, 1993, in connection with influencing legislation (other than certain local legislation) to the extent inconsistent with section 162(e)(1)(A) (as limited by section 162(e)(2)) and §§ 1.162-20(d) and 1.162-29.

(d) Dues allocable to expenditures after 1993. No deduction is allowed under section 162(a) for the portion of dues or other similar amounts paid by the taxpayer to an organization exempt from tax (other than an organization described in section 501(c)(3)) which the organization notifies the taxpayer under section 6033(e)(1)(A)(ii) is allocable to expenditures to which section 162(e)(1) applies. The first sentence of this paragraph (d) applies to dues or other similar amounts whether or not paid on or before December 31, 1993. Section 1.162-20(c)(3) is superseded to the extent inconsistent with this paragraph (d).

T.D. 6819, 4/19/65, amend T.D. 6996, 1/17/69, T.D. 8602, 7/20/95.

§ 1.162-21 Fines and penalties.

(a) In general. No deduction shall be allowed under section 162(a) for any fine or similar penalty paid to—

(1) The government of the United States, a State, a territory or possession of the United States, the District of Columbia, or the Commonwealth of Puerto Rico;

(2) The government of a foreign country; or

(3) A political subdivision of, or corporation or other entity serving as an agency or instrumentality of, any of the above.

(b) Definition. *(1)* For purposes of this section a fine or similar penalty includes an amount—

(i) Paid pursuant to conviction or a plea of guilty or *nolo contendere* for a crime (felony or misdemeanor) in a criminal proceeding;

(ii) Paid as a civil penalty imposed by Federal, State, or local law, including additions to tax and additional amounts and assessable penalties imposed by chapter 68 of the Internal Revenue Code of 1954;

(iii) Paid in settlement of the taxpayer's actual or potential liability for a fine or penalty (civil or criminal); or

(iv) Forfeited as collateral posted in connection with a proceeding which could result in imposition of such a fine or penalty.

(2) The amount of a fine or penalty does not include legal fees and related expenses paid or incurred in the defense of a prosecution or civil action arising from a violation of the law imposing the fine or civil penalty, nor court costs assessed against the taxpayer, or stenographic and printing charges. Compensatory damages (including damages under section 4A of the Clayton Act (15 U.S.C. 15a), as amended) paid to a government do not constitute a fine or penalty.

(c) Examples. The application of this section may be illustrated by the following examples:

Example (1). M Corp. was indicted under section 1 of the Sherman Anti-Trust Act (15 U.S.C. 1) for fixing and maintaining prices of certain electrical products. M Corp. was convicted and was fined $50,000. The United States sued M Corp. under section 4A of the Clayton Act (15 U.S.C. 15a) for $100,000, the amount of the actual damages resulting from the price fixing of which M Corp. was convicted. Pursuant to a final judgment entered in the civil action, M Corp. paid the United States $100,000 in damages. Section 162(f) precludes M Corp. from deducting the fine of $50,000 as a trade or business expense. Section 162(f) does not preclude it from deducting the $100,000 paid to the United States as actual damages.

Example (2). N Corp. was found to have violated 33 U.S.C. 1321(b)(3) when a vessel it operated discharged oil in harmful quantities into the navigable waters of the United States. A civil penalty under 33 U.S.C. 1321(b)(6) of $5,000 was assessed against N Corp. with respect to the discharge. N Corp. paid $5,000 to the Coast Guard in payment of the civil penalty. Section 162(f) precludes N Corp. from deducting the $5,000 penalty.

Example (3). O Corp., a manufacturer of motor vehicles, was found to have violated 42 U.S.C. 1857f-2(a)(1) by selling a new motor vehicle which was not covered by the required certificate of conformity. Pursuant to 42 U.S.C. 1857f-4, O Corp. was required to pay, and did pay, a civil penalty of $10,000. In addition, pursuant to 42 U.S.C. 1857f-5a(c)(1), O Corp. was required to expend, and did expend, $500 in order to remedy the nonconformity of that motor vehicle. Section 162(f) precludes O Corp. from deducting the $10,000 penalty as a trade or business expense, but does not preclude it from deducting the $500 which it expended to remedy the nonconformity.

Example (4). P Corp. was the operator of a coal mine in which occurred a violation of a mandatory safety standard prescribed by the Federal Coal Mine Health and Safety Act of 1969 (30 U.S.C. 801 *et seq.*). Pursuant to 30 U.S.C. 819(a), a civil penalty of $10,000 was assessed against P Corp., and P Corp. paid the penalty. Section 162(f) precludes P Corp. from deducting the $10,000 penalty.

Example (5). Q Corp., a common carrier engaged in interstate commerce by railroad, hauled a railroad car which was not equipped with efficient hand brakes in violation of 45 U.S.C. 11. Q Corp. was found to be liable for a penalty of $250 pursuant to 45 U.S.C. 13. Q Corp. paid that penalty. Section 162(f) precludes Q Corp. from deducting the $250 penalty.

Example (6). R Corp. owned and operated on the highways of State X a truck weighing in excess of the amount permitted under the law of State X. R Corp. was found to have violated the law and was assessed a fine of $85 which it paid to State X. Section 162(f) precludes R Corp. from deducting the amount so paid.

Example (7). S Corp. was found to have violated a law of State Y which prohibited the emission into the air of particulate matter in excess of a limit set forth in a regulation promulgated under that law. The Environmental Quality Hearing Board of State Y assessed a fine of $500 against S Corp. The fine was payable to State Y, and S Corp. paid it.

Section 162(f) precludes S Corp. from deducting the $500 fine.

Example (8). T Corp. was found by a magistrate of City Z to be operating in such city an apartment building which did not conform to a provision of the city housing code requiring operable fire escapes on apartment buildings of that type. Upon the basis of the magistrate's finding, T Corp. was required to pay, and did pay, a fine of $200 to City Z. Section 162(f) precludes T Corp. from deducting the $200 fine.

T.D. 7345, 2/19/75, amend T.D. 7366, 7/10/75.

§ 1.162-22 Treble damage payments under the antitrust laws.

(a) In general. In the case of a taxpayer who after December 31, 1969, either is convicted in a criminal action of a violation of the Federal antitrust laws or enters a plea of guilty or *nolo contendere* to an indictment or information charging such a violation, and whose conviction or plea does not occur in a new trial following an appeal of a conviction on or before such date, no deduction shall be allowed under section 162(a) for two-thirds of any amount paid or incurred after December 31, 1969, with respect to—

(1) Any judgment for damages entered against the taxpayer under section 4 of the Clayton Act (15 U.S.C. 15), as amended, on account of such violation or any related violation of the Federal antitrust laws, provided such related violation occurred prior to the date of the final judgment of such conviction, or

(2) Settlement of any action brought under such section 4 on account of such violation or related violation.

For the purposes of this section, where a civil judgment has been entered or a settlement made with respect to a violation of the antitrust laws and a criminal proceeding is based upon the same violation, the criminal proceeding need not have been brought prior to the civil judgment or settlement. If, in his return for any taxable year, a taxpayer claims a deduction for an amount paid or incurred with respect to a judgment or settlement described in the first sentence of this paragraph and is subsequently convicted of a violation of the antitrust laws which makes a portion of such amount unallowable, then the taxpayer shall file an amended return for such taxable year on which the amount of the deduction is appropriately reduced. Attorney's fees, court costs, and other amounts paid or incurred in connection with a controversy under such section 4 which meet the requirements of section 162 are deductible under that section. For purposes of subparagraph (2) of this paragraph, the amount paid or incurred in settlement shall not include amounts attributable to the plaintiff's costs of suit and attorney's fees, to the extent that such costs or fees have actually been paid.

(b) Conviction. For purposes of paragraph (a) of this section, a taxpayer is convicted of a violation of the antitrust laws if a judgment of conviction (whether or not a final judgment) with respect to such violation has been entered against him, provided a subsequent final judgment of acquittal has not been entered or criminal prosecution with respect to such violation terminated without a final judgment of conviction. During the pendency of an appeal or other action directly contesting a judgment of conviction, the taxpayer should file a protective claim for credit or refund to avoid being barred by the period of limitations on credit or refund under section 6511.

(c) Related violation. For purposes of this section, a violation of the Federal antitrust laws is related to a subsequent violation if (1) with respect to the subsequent violation the United States obtains both a judgment in a criminal proceeding and an injunction against the taxpayer, and (2) the taxpayer's actions which constituted the prior violation would have contravened such injunction if such injunction were applicable at the time of the prior violation.

(d) Settlement following a dismissal of an action or amendment of the complaint. For purposes of paragraph (a)(2) of this section, an amount may be considered as paid in settlement of an action even though the action is dismissed or otherwise disposed of prior to such settlement or the complaint is amended to eliminate the claim with respect to the violation or related violation.

(e) Antitrust laws. The term "antitrust laws" as used in section 162(g) and this section shall include the Federal acts enumerated in paragraph (1) of section 1 of the Clayton Act (15 U.S.C. 12), as amended.

(f) Examples. The application of this section may be illustrated by the following examples:

Example (1). In 1970, the United States instituted a criminal prosecution against X Co., Y Co., A, the president of X Co., and B, the president of Y Co., under section 1 of the Sherman Anti-Trust Act, 15 U.S.C. 1. In the indictment, the defendants were charged with conspiring to fix and maintain prices of electrical transformers from 1965 to 1970. All defendants entered pleas of nolo contendere to these charges. These pleas were accepted and judgments of conviction entered. In a companion civil suit, the United States obtained an injunction prohibiting the defendants from conspiring to fix and maintain prices in the electrical transformer market. Thereafter, Z Co. sued X Co. and Y Co. for $300,000 in treble damages under section 4 of the Clayton Act. Z Co.'s complaint alleged that the criminal conspiracy between X Co. and Y Co. forced Z Co. to pay excessive prices for electrical transformers. X Co. and Y Co. each paid Z Co. $85,000 in full settlement of Z Co.'s action. Of each $85,000 paid, $10,000 was attributable to court costs and attorney's fees actually paid by Z Co. Under section 162(g), X Co. and Y Co. are each precluded from deducting as a trade or business expense more than $35,000 of the $85,000 paid to Z Co. in settlement.

$$\left(\$10{,}000 + \frac{\$85{,}000 - \$10{,}000}{3}\right)$$

Example (2). Assume the same facts as in example (1) except that Z Co.'s claim for treble damages was based on a conspiracy to fix and maintain prices in the sale of electrical transformers during 1963. Although the criminal prosecution of the defendants did not involve 1963 (a year barred by the applicable criminal statute of limitations when the prosecution was instituted), Z Co.'s pleadings alleged that the civil statute of limitations had been tolled by the defendants' fraudulent concealment of their conspiracy. Since the United States has obtained both a judgment in a criminal proceeding and an injunction against the defendants in connection with their activities from 1965 to 1970, and the alleged actions of the defendants in 1963 would have contravened such injunction if it were applicable in 1963, the alleged violation in 1963 is related to the violation from 1965 to 1970. Accordingly, the tax consequences to X Co. and Y Co. of the payments of $85,000 in settlement of Z Co.'s claim against X Co. and Y Co. are the same as in example (1).

Example (3). Assume the same facts as in example (1) except that Z Co.'s claim for treble damages was based on a conspiracy to fix and maintain prices with respect to electrical insulators for high-tension power poles. Since the civil action was not based on the same violation of the Federal antitrust laws as the criminal action, or on a related violation (a violation which would have contravened the injunction if it were applicable), X Co. and Y Co. are not precluded by section 162(g) from deducting as a trade or business expense the entire $85,000 paid by each in settlement of the civil action.

T.D. 7217, 11/9/72.

Proposed § 1.162-24 Travel expenses of state legislators. [*For Preamble, see ¶ 152,983*]

(a) In general. For purposes of section 162(a), in the case of any taxpayer who is a state legislator at any time during the taxable year and who makes an election under section 162(h) for the taxable year—

(1) The taxpayer's place of residence within the legislative district represented by the taxpayer is the taxpayer's home for that taxable year;

(2) The taxpayer is deemed to have expended for living expenses (in connection with the taxpayer's trade or business as a legislator) an amount equal to the sum of the amounts determined by multiplying each legislative day of the taxpayer during the taxable year by the greater of—

(i) The amount generally allowable with respect to that day to employees of the state of which the taxpayer is a legislator for per diem while away from home, to the extent the amount does not exceed 110 percent of the amount described in paragraph (a)(2)(ii) of this section; or

(ii) The Federal per diem with respect to that day for the taxpayer's state capital; and

(3) The taxpayer is deemed to be away from home in the pursuit of a trade or business on each legislative day.

(b) Legislative day. For purposes of section 162(h)(1) and this section, for any taxpayer who makes an election under section 162(h), a legislative day is any day on which the taxpayer is a state legislator and—

(1) The legislature is in session;

(2) The legislature is not in session for a period that is not longer than 4 consecutive days, without extension for Saturdays, Sundays, or holidays;

(3) The taxpayer's attendance at a meeting of a committee of the legislature is formally recorded; or

(4) The taxpayer's attendance at any session of the legislature that only a limited number of members are expected to attend (such as a "pro forma" session), on any day not described in paragraph (b)(1) or (b)(2) of this section, is formally recorded.

(c) Fifty mile rule. Section 162(h) and this section do not apply to any taxpayer who is a state legislator and whose place of residence within the legislative district represented by the taxpayer is 50 or fewer miles from the capitol building of the state. For purposes of this paragraph (c), the distance between the taxpayer's place of residence within the legislative district represented by the taxpayer and the capitol building of the state is the shortest of the more commonly traveled routes between the two points.

(d) Definitions and special rules. The following definitions apply for purposes of section 162(h) and this section.

(1) State legislator. A taxpayer becomes a state legislator on the day the taxpayer is sworn into office and ceases to be a state legislator on the day following the day on which the taxpayer's term in office ends.

(2) Living expenses. Living expenses include lodging, meals, and incidental expenses. Incidental expenses has the same meaning as in 41 CFR 300-3.1.

(3) In session. (i) In general. For purposes of this section, the legislature of which a taxpayer is a member is in session on any day if, at any time during that day, the members of the legislature are expected to attend and participate as an assembled body of the legislature.

(ii) Examples. The following examples illustrate the rules of this paragraph (d)(3):

Example (1). B is a member of the legislature of State X. On Day 1, the State X legislature is convened and the members of the legislature generally are expected to attend and participate. On Day 1, the State X legislature is in session within the meaning of paragraph (d)(3)(i) of this section. B does not attend the session of the State X legislature on Day 1. However, Day 1 is a legislative day for B for purposes of section 162(h)(2)(A) and paragraph (b)(1) of this section.

Example (2). C, D, and E are members of the legislature of State X. On Day 2, the State X legislature is convened for a limited session in which not all members of the legislature are expected to attend and participate. C and D are the only members who are called to, and do, attend the limited session on Day 2, and their attendance at the session is formally recorded. E is not called and does not attend. Day 2 is not a day described in paragraph (b)(2) of this section. On Day 2, the State X legislature is not in session within the meaning of paragraph (d)(3)(i) of this section. Day 2 is a legislative day as to C and D under section 162(h)(2)(B) and paragraph (b)(4) of this section. Day 2 is not a legislative day as to C and D under section 162(h)(2)(A) and paragraph (b)(1) of this section. Day 2 is not a legislative day as to E under sections 162(h)(2)(A) and (h)(2)(B) and paragraphs (b)(1) and (b)(4) of this section.

(4) Committee of the legislature. A committee of the legislature is any group consisting solely of legislators charged with conducting business of the legislature. Committees of the legislature include, but are not limited to, committees to which the legislature refers bills for consideration, committees that the legislature has authorized to conduct inquiries into matters of public concern, and committees charged with the internal administration of the legislature. For purposes of this section, groups that are not considered committees of the legislature include, but are not limited to, groups that promote particular issues, raise campaign funds, or are caucuses of members of a political party.

(5) Federal per diem. The Federal per diem for any city and day is the maximum amount allowable to employees of the executive branch of the Federal government for living expenses while away from home in pursuit of a trade or business in that city on that day. See 5 U.S.C. 5702 and the regulations under that section.

(e) Election. *(1) Time for making election.* A taxpayer's election under section 162(h) must be made for each taxable year for which the election is to be in effect and must be made no later than the due date (including extensions) of the taxpayer's Federal income tax return for the taxable year.

(2) Manner of making election. A taxpayer makes an election under section 162(h) by attaching a statement to the taxpayer's income tax return for the taxable year for which the election is made. The statement must include—

(i) The taxpayer's name, address, and taxpayer identification number;

(ii) A statement that the taxpayer is making an election under section 162(h); and

(iii) Information establishing that the taxpayer is a state legislator entitled to make the election, for example, a statement identifying the taxpayer's state and legislative district and representing that the taxpayer's place of residence in the legislative district is not 50 or fewer miles from the state capitol building.

(3) Revocation of election. An election under section 162(h) may be revoked only with the consent of the Commissioner. An application for consent to revoke an election must be signed by the taxpayer and filed with the submission processing center with which the election was filed, and must include—

(i) The taxpayer's name, address, and taxpayer identification number;

(ii) A statement that the taxpayer is revoking an election under section 162(h) for a specified year; and

(iii) A statement explaining why the taxpayer seeks to revoke the election.

(f) Effect of election on otherwise deductible expenses for travel away from home. *(1) Legislative days.* (i) Living expenses. For any legislative day for which an election under section 162(h) and this section is in effect, the amount of an electing taxpayer's living expenses while away from home is the greater of the amount of the living expenses—

(A) Specified in paragraph (a)(2) of this section in connection with the trade or business of being a legislator; or

(B) Otherwise allowable under section 162(a)(2) in the pursuit of any other trade or business of the taxpayer.

(ii) Other expenses. For any legislative day for which an election under section 162(h) and this section is in effect, the amount of an electing taxpayer's expenses (other than living expenses) for travel away from home is the sum of the substantiated expenses, such as expenses for travel fares, telephone calls, and local transportation, that are otherwise deductible under section 162(a)(2) in the pursuit of any trade or business of the taxpayer.

(2) Non-legislative days. For any day that is not a legislative day, the amount of an electing taxpayer's expenses (including amounts for living expenses) for travel away from home is the sum of the substantiated expenses that are otherwise deductible under section 162(a)(2) in the pursuit of any trade or business of the taxpayer.

(g) Cross references. See Sec. 1.62-1T(e)(4) for rules regarding allocation of unreimbursed expenses of state legislators and section 274(n) for limitations on the amount allowable as a deduction for expenses for or allocable to meals.

(h) Effective/applicability date. his section applies to expenses deemed expended under section 162(h) after the date these regulations are published as final regulations in the Federal Register.

§ 1.162-25 Deductions with respect to noncash fringe benefits.

(a) [Reserved]

(b) Employee. If an employer provides the use of a vehicle (as defined in § 1.61-21(e)(2)) to an employee as a noncash fringe benefit and includes the entire value of the benefit in the employee's gross income without taking into account any exclusion for a working condition fringe allowable under section 132 and the regulations thereunder, the employee may deduct that value multiplied by the percentage of the total use of the vehicle that is in connection with the employer's trade or business (business value). For taxable years beginning before January 1, 1990, the employee may deduct the business value from gross income in determining adjusted gross income. For taxable years beginning on or after January 1, 1990, the employee may deduct the business value only as a miscellaneous itemized deduction in determining taxable income, subject to the 2-percent floor provided in section 67. If the employer determines the value of the noncash fringe benefit under a special accounting rule that allows the employer to treat the value of benefits provided during the last two months of the calendar year or any shorter period as paid during the subsequent calendar year, then the employee must determine the deduction allowable under this paragraph (b) without regard to any use of the benefit during those last two months or any shorter period. The employee may not use a cents-per-mile valuation method to determine the deduction allowable under this paragraph (b).

T.D. 8451, 12/4/92.

§ 1.162-25T Deductions with respect to noncash fringe benefits (temporary).

(a) Employer. If an employer includes the value of a noncash fringe benefit in an employee's gross income, the employer may not deduct this amount as compensation for services, but rather may deduct only the costs incurred by the employer in providing the benefit to the employee. The employer may be allowed a cost recovery deduction under section 168 or a deduction under section 179 for an expense not chargeable to capital account, or, if the noncash fringe benefit is property leased by the employer, a deduction for the ordinary and necessary business expense of leasing the property.

(b) [Reserved]

(c) Examples. The following examples illustrate the provisions of this section.

Example (1). On January 1, 1986, X Company owns and provides the use of an automobile with a fair market value of $20,000 to E, an employee, for the entire calendar year. Both X and E compute taxable income on the basis of the calendar year. Seventy percent of the use of the automobile by E is in connection with X's trade or business. If X uses the special rule provided in § 1.61-2T for valuing the availability of the automobile and takes into account the amount excludable as a working condition fringe, X would include $1,680 ($5,600, the Annual Lease Value, less 70 percent of $5,600) in E's gross income for 1986. X may not deduct the amount included in E's income as compensation for services. X may, however, determine a cost recovery deduction under section 168, subject to the limitations under section 280F, for taxable year 1986.

Example (2). The facts are the same as in example (1), except that X includes $5,600 in E's gross income, the value of the noncash fringe benefit without taking into account the amount excludable as a working condition fringe. X may not deduct that amount as compensation for services, but may determine a cost recovery deduction under section 168, subject to the limitations under section 280F. For purposes of determining adjusted gross income, E may deduct $3,920 ($5,600 multiplied by the percent of business use).

T.D. 8004, 1/2/85, amend T.D. 8061, 11/1/85, T.D. 8063, 12/18/85, T.D. 8276, 12/7/89, T.D. 8451, 12/4/92.

Proposed § 1.162-26 Continuation coverage requirements of group health plans. [*For Preamble, see ¶ 151,085*]

Caution: The Treasury has not yet amended Reg § 1.162-26 to reflect changes made by P.L. 101-508, P.L. 100-647, P.L. 99-514.

Table of Contents

COBRA in general: Q&A-1 to Q&A-6

Which plans must comply and when: Q&A-7 to Q&A-14

Qualified beneficiaries: Q&A-15 to Q&A-17

Qualifying events: Q&A-18 to Q&A-21

COBRA continuation coverage: Q&A-22 to Q&A-31

Electing COBRA continuation coverage: Q&A-32 to Q&A-37

Duration of COBRA continuation coverage: Q&A-38 to Q&A-43

Paying for COBRA continuation coverage: Q&A-44 to Q&A-48

LIST OF QUESTIONS

COBRA in General

Question 1: What are the new health care continuation coverage requirements added to the Internal Revenue Code by the Consolidated Omnibus Budget Reconciliation Act of 1985 ("COBRA")?

Question 2: What is the effect of a group health plan's failure to comply with section 162(k)?

Question 3: How are employer deductions affected by a group health plan's failure to comply with section 162(k)?

Question 4: How is the gross income of certain individuals affected by a group health plan's failure to comply with section 162(k)?

Question 5: What is the employer?

Question 6: How does COBRA apply to a group health plan before the effective date of this section?

Which Plans Must Comply and When

Question 7: What is a group health plan?

Question 8: What group health plans are subject to COBRA?

Question 9: What is a small-employer plan?

Question 10: When is an arrangement considered to be two or more separate group health plans rather than a single group health plan?

Question 11: When must group health plans comply with section 162(k)?

Question 12: What is a collectively bargained group health plan?

Question 13: What is the plan year of a group health plan?

Question 14: How do the COBRA continuation coverage requirements apply to cafeteria plans and other flexible benefit arrangements?

Qualified Beneficiaries

Question 15: Who is a qualified beneficiary?

Question 16: Who is a covered employee?

Question 17: Other than those individuals who are qualified beneficiaries as of the day before a qualifying event, can any other person (such as a newborn or adopted child or a new spouse) obtain qualified beneficiary status for COBRA continuation coverage purposes?

Qualifying Events

Question 18: What is a qualifying event?

Question 19: Can a qualifying event result from a voluntary termination of employment?

Question 20: Can a qualifying event occur before the effective date of section 162(k) (as described in Q&A-11 of this section)?

Question 21: Can a qualifying event occur while a group health plan is excepted from COBRA (see Q&A-8 of this section)?

COBRA Continuation Coverage

Question 22: What is COBRA continuation coverage?

Question 23: How is COBRA continuation coverage affected by changes in the coverage that is provided to similarly situated beneficiaries with respect to whom a qualifying event has not occurred?

Question 24: Can a group health plan require a qualified beneficiary who wishes to receive COBRA continuation coverage to elect to receive a continuation of all of the coverage that he or she was receiving under the plan immediately before the qualifying event?

Question 25: What is core coverage?

Question 26: Must a qualified beneficiary be given an opportunity to elect core coverage plus only one of two non-core coverages that the qualified beneficiary had under the plan immediately before the qualifying event?

Question 27: Must a qualified beneficiary who is covered under a single plan providing both core coverage and non-core coverage be offered the opportunity to elect non-core coverage only?

Question 28: What deductibles apply if COBRA continuation coverage is elected?

Question 29: How do a plan's limits apply to COBRA continuation coverage?

Question 30: Can a qualified beneficiary who elects COBRA continuation coverage ever change from the coverage received by that individual immediately before the qualifying event?

Question 31: Aside from open enrollment periods, can a qualified beneficiary who has elected COBRA continuation coverage choose to cover individuals (such as newborn children, adopted children, or new spouses) who join the qualified beneficiary's family on or after the date of the qualifying event?

Electing COBRA Continuation Coverage

Question 32: What is the minimum period during which a group health plan must allow a qualified beneficiary to elect COBRA continuation coverage (i.e., the election period)?

Question 33: Must a covered employee or qualified beneficiary inform the employer or plan administrator of the occurrence of a qualifying event?

Question 34: During the election period and before the qualified beneficiary has made an election, must coverage be provided?

Question 35: Is a waiver before the end of the election period effective to end a qualified beneficiary's election rights?

Question 36: Can an employer withhold money or other benefits owed to a qualified beneficiary until the qualified beneficiary either waives COBRA continuation coverage, elects and pays for such coverage, or allows the election period to expire?

Question 37: Can each qualified beneficiary make an independent election under COBRA?

Duration of Cobra Continuation Coverage

Question 38: How long must COBRA continuation coverage be available to a qualified beneficiary?

Question 39: When does the maximum coverage period end?

Question 40: Can the maximum coverage period ever be expanded?

Question 41: If coverage is provided to a qualified beneficiary after a qualifying event without regard to COBRA continuation coverage (e.g., as a result of State or local law, industry practice, a collective bargaining agreement, or plan procedure), will such alternative coverage extend the maximum coverage period?

Question 42: How can an event that occurs before a group health plan becomes subject to section 162(k) affect the maximum coverage period when a later, qualifying event occurs?

Question 43: Must a qualified beneficiary be given the right to enroll in a conversion health plan at the end of the maximum coverage period for COBRA continuation coverage?

Paying for COBRA Continuation Coverage

Question 44: Can a qualified beneficiary be required to pay for COBRA continuation coverage?

Question 45: After a qualified beneficiary has elected COBRA continuation coverage under a group health plan, can the plan increase the amount that the qualified beneficiary must pay for COBRA continuation coverage?

Question 46: Must a qualified beneficiary be allowed to pay for COBRA continuation coverage in installments?

Question 47: Can a qualified beneficiary choose to have the first payment for COBRA continuation coverage applied prospectively only?

Question 48: What is timely payment for COBRA continuation coverage?

Cobra in General

Q-1. What are the new health care continuation coverage requirements added to the Internal Revenue Code by the Consolidated Omnibus Budget Reconciliation Act of 1985 ("COBRA")?

A-1. Section 10001 of COBRA added a new section 162(k) to the Code to provide generally that a group health plan must offer each qualified beneficiary who would otherwise lose coverage under the plan as a result of a qualifying event an opportunity to elect, within the applicable election period, continuation coverage under the plan. That continuation coverage is referred to in this section as "COBRA continuation coverage" and a group health plan that is subject to section 162(k) is referred to as being "subject to COBRA" (see Q&A-8 of this section). A qualified beneficiary can be required to pay for COBRA continuation coverage. A qualified beneficiary is defined in Q&A-15 of this section. A qualifying event is defined in Q&A-18 of this section. The election procedures are described in Q&A-32 through Q&A-37 of this section. COBRA continuation coverage is described in Q&A-22 through Q&A-31 of this section. Payment for COBRA continuation coverage is addressed in Q&A-44 through Q&A-48 of this section. Unless otherwise specified, any reference in this section to "COBRA" refers to section 10001 of COBRA and to section 162(k) of the Code as added by COBRA (as amended).

Q-2. What is the effect of a group health plan's failure to comply with section 162(k)?

A-2. If a group health plan subject to COBRA fails to comply with section 162(k), certain deductions are disallowed to the employer under section 162(i)(2) (see Q&A-3 of this section) and the income exclusion under section 106(a) is denied to certain highly compensated employees of the employer under section 106(b)(1) (see Q& A-4 of this section). There may be additional non-tax consequences if the plan fails to comply with parallel requirements that were added by section 10002 of COBRA to Title I of the Employee Retirement Income Security Act of 1974 (ERISA), which is administered by the Department of Labor. Although governmental plans are not subject to section 162(k) because they are not "subject to COBRA" (see Q&A-8 of this section), certain governmental plans are subject to parallel requirements that were added by section 10003 of COBRA to the Public Health Service Act, which is administered by the Department of Health and Human Services.

Q-3. How are employer deductions affected by a group health plan's failure to comply with section 162(k)?

A-3. (a) Under section 162(i)(2), if a group health plan subject to COBRA fails to comply with section 162(k), each employer maintaining the plan is denied a deduction for any contributions or other expenses paid or incurred in connection with any group health plan that it maintains. The deduction is denied for any taxable year of the taxpayer during which there are one or more days on which plan is not in compliance with section 162(k). Thus, if a failure to comply with section 162(k) arises in one taxable year of a taxpayer and is not corrected until after the beginning of the following taxable year, the deduction for contributions or expenses for both of those taxable years is denied. Section 162(i)(2) operates each taxable year to permanently deny a deduction for amounts paid or incurred in that year, and is applied before applying any provision of the Code that governs the timing of an otherwise available deduction. Examples of such provisions include sections 263A (capitalization and inclusion in inventory costs), 419 (treatment of funded welfare benefit plans), and 460 (special rules for long-term contracts). In addition, section 162(i)(2) operates with respect to each employer maintaining the group health plan, without regard to whether the employers are treated as a single employer (see Q&A-5 of this section) and without regard to whether the failure to satisfy section 162(k) occurs with respect to only an employee of one of the employers. See Q&A-10 of this section regarding when an arrangement is treated as two or more separate group health plans.

(b) A failure of a group health plan to comply with section 162(k) that occurs before, and is not corrected by, the date that an employer maintaining the plan and another entity are first treated as a single employer under Q& A-5 of this section ("the combination date") will not result in a denial of a deduction to the other entity under paragraph (a) of this Q&A-3, so long as (1) the other entity did not also maintain the plan before the combination date, and (2) the failure is corrected before the end of the first taxable year of the other entity that begins after the combination date.

(c) The rules of this Q&A-3 are illustrated by the following examples:

Example (1). Plan A is a group health plan subject to COBRA that is maintained by two unrelated employers, X and Y. Section 162(k) became effective with respect to plan A before April 1, 1988. The taxable year of employer X ends on March 31, and the taxable year of employer Y ends on April 30. If Plan A fails to comply with section 162(k) on April 1, 1988, by not offering COBRA continuation coverage to a qualified beneficiary of an employee of employer X, and the failure is not corrected until June 1, 1988, both employers X and Y are disallowed deductions for their contributions and other expenses relating to all their group health plans (including any group health plan that is maintained only by employer X or only by employer Y) for each taxable year that includes one or more days of noncompliance. Thus, the disallowance applies to employer X for its taxable year ending March 31, 1989, and to employer Y for both its taxable year ending April 30, 1988, and its taxable year ending April 30, 1989. (However, see Q&A-10 of this section regarding when an arrangement is considered to be two or more separate group health plans.)

Example (2). Assume that companies Z and W are treated as a single employer under section 414(b) at all relevant times (see Q&A-5 of this section), that Z maintains group health plans P and Q, that W maintains group health plans R and S, and that none of these plans is excepted from COBRA (see Q&A-8 of this section). Assume further that the taxable year of company Z ends on May 31, that the taxable year of company W ends on July 31, and that section 162(k) becomes effective with respect to the group health plans as follows: for plan P on February 1, 1987; for plan Q on April 1, 1987; and for plans R and S on July 1, 1987. If at any time during February through May of 1987 plan P is not in compliance with section 162(k), then company Z is disallowed all deductions with respect to plans P and Q for its taxable year ending May 31, 1987, and company W is disallowed all deductions with respect to plans R and S for its taxable year ending July 31, 1987.

Example (3). Assume that a group health plan maintained only by M, a calendar year employer, is subject to COBRA and fails to comply with section 162(k) during February of 1988, that the failure is corrected during April of 1988, and that on June 1, 1988 employer M becomes a wholly-owned subsidiary of N, a previously unrelated corporation with a taxable year ending July 31. For 1988, M is disallowed a deduction for all its contributions with respect to any group health plan. Because M and N were not treated as a single employer (see Q&A-5 of this section) during the period of noncompliance by M's plan (i.e., February to April of 1988), the failure of M's plan to comply with section 162(k) during that period will not result in a disallowance of any deductions to N, the new parent corporation. Even if the failure to comply that arises in February of 1988 is not corrected until after June 1, 1988, it will not result in a disallowance of any deductions to N, so long as the failure to comply is corrected by July 31, 1989 (the end of N's first taxable year that begins after June 1, 1988). However, if the failure is not corrected until August of 1989, N will be disallowed a deduction for all its contributions with respect to any group health plan for its taxable years ending on July 31 of 1988, 1989, and 1990. Also, if another failure of M's plan to comply with section 162(k) arises on or after June 1, 1988, that second failure will result in a disallowance of deductions to N.

Example (4). Assume that a calendar year employer maintaining a group health plan through a welfare benefit fund contributes $800,000 to the fund in 1988 and $500,000 in 1989. Assume further that only $600,000 of the 1988 contribution would be deductible under section 419 for 1988, and that the remaining $200,000 would be deemed to be contributed in 1989 and deductible under section 419 for 1989 along with the $500,000 actually contributed in that year. However, the deduction under section 419 is only available if these amounts are otherwise deductible under section 162. Therefore, if at any time during 1988 the group health plan is not in compliance with section 162(k), the $800,000 contributed in 1988 is disallowed in full as a deduction for 1988 and for all later years. However, if the plan does comply with section 162(k) throughout 1988 but at some time during 1989 is not in compliance, the $600,000 deduction for 1988 is unaffected while the $700,000 otherwise deductible for 1989 is permanently disallowed.

Q-4. How is the gross income of certain individuals affected by a group health plan's failure to comply with section 162(k)?

A-4. (a) Under section 106(a), employer-provided coverage under an accident or health plan is generally excluded from the gross income of an employee. Under section 106(b), however, if a group health plan that is subject to COBRA fails to comply with section 162(k), certain individuals shall have certain employer-provided coverage included in their gross income for each of their taxable years during which the plan is not in compliance, even if the coverage would otherwise be excludable from income under section 106(a). The individuals referred to in the preceding sentence consist of each person who is, at any time during which the plan is not in compliance with section 162(k), a highly compensated employee (within the meaning of section 414(q) and the regulations under that section) of any employer maintaining the plan. The coverage included in the individual's gross income for each such taxable year shall consist of all coverage provided by the employer to the individual and his or her spouse and dependent children during that taxable year under any group health plan (other than a plan that is excepted from COBRA—see Q&A-8 of this section). For purposes of section 106(b) and this Q&A-4, whether an individual is a highly compensated employee shall be determined on the basis of plan years or any alternative period permitted under section 414(q) and the regulations under that section. As used in the preceding sentence, "plan year" means the plan year as defined in Q&A-13 of this section.

(b) A failure of a group health plan to comply with section 162(k) that occurs before, and is not corrected by, the date that an employer maintaining the plan and another entity are first treated as a single employer under Q& A-5 of this section ("the combination date") will not result in an income inclusion for highly compensated employees of the other entity under paragraph (a) of this Q&A-4, so long as (1) the other entity did not also maintain the plan before the combination date, and (2) the failure is corrected before the end of the first taxable year of the other entity that begins after the combination date.

(c) The rules of this Q&A-4 are illustrated by the following examples, in which it is assumed that all individuals are calendar year taxpayers:

Example (1). Employer Z maintains group health plan T, and maintains no other group health plans. If plan T fails to comply with section 162(k) on November 10, 1988, and the failure is not corrected until February 15, 1989, each individual who is a highly compensated employee of Z at any time from November 10, 1988, through February 15, 1989, shall have coverage included in gross income for that individual's 1988 and 1989 taxable years. If the individual was covered under plan T throughout those years, the coverage included in 1988 is all coverage provided by employer Z under plan T on behalf of the individual and the individual's family during 1988, and the coverage included in 1989 is all coverage provided by employer Z under plan T on behalf of the individual and the individual's family during 1989.

Example (2). The facts are the same as in Example 1, except that employer Z's highly compensated employees are covered under plan U. Even if plan U complies with section 162(k) at all times, each individual who is a highly compensated employee of Z at any time for November 10, 1988, through February 15, 1989 (the period of plan T's noncompliance), shall have coverage included in gross income for that individual's 1988 and 1989 taxable years. If the individual was covered under plan U throughout those years, the coverage included in 1988 is all coverage provided by employer Z under plan U on behalf of the individual and the individual's family during 1988, and the coverage included in 1989 is all coverage provided by employer Z under plan U on behalf of the individual and the individual's family during 1989.

Example (3). The facts are the same as in Example 1, except that the failure to comply with section 162(k) is corrected on December 20, 1988, rather than on February 15, 1989. The income inclusion for highly compensated employees applies only for the 1988 taxable year and only to those individuals who are highly compensated employees of Z at some time from November 10 to December 20, 1988.

Example (4). The facts are the same as in Example 1. In addition, employer W maintains group health plan V, and maintains no other group health plans. Employer W's taxable year ends on May 31. Employer W becomes a wholly-owned subsidiary of employer Z on December 1, 1988. Plan T's failure to comply with section 162(k) that arises on November 10, 1988, does not result in an income inclusion to any of employer W's highly compensated employees because the failure is corrected on February 15, 1989, which is before May 31, 1990 (the end of employer W's first taxable year that begins after December 1, 1988). However, if another failure of Plan T to comply with section 162(k) arises on December 15, 1988, and that failure to comply is also corrected on February 15, 1989, each employee of employer W who is a highly compensated employee at any time from December 15, 1988, through February 15, 1989, is also subject to the income inclusion set forth in this Q& A-4.

Q-5. What is the employer?

A-5. For purposes of this § 1.162-26 and sections 106(b), 162(i), and 162(k), the term "employer" refers to the employer and any entity that is a member of a group described in section 414(b), (c), (m), or (o) that includes the employer, and to any successor of either the employer or such an entity. However, the rule of this Q&A-5 does not apply for purposes of determining whether a group health plan is a small-employer plan (see Q&A-9 of this section).

Q-6. How does COBRA apply to a group health plan before the effective date of this section?

A-6. This section is proposed to be effective when final regulations that include it are published in the Federal Register as a Treasury decision. Group health plans become subject to the COBRA continuation coverage requirements at different times, however, as set forth in Q&A-11 of this section. With respect to qualifying events that occur on or after the date that a plan became or becomes subject to those requirements and before the effective date of final regulations, the plan and the employer must operate in good faith compliance with a reasonable interpretation of the statutory requirements (i.e., title X of COBRA). For the period before the effective date of final regulations, the Internal Revenue Service will consider compliance with the terms of these proposed regulations to constitute good faith compliance with a reasonable interpretation of the statutory requirements (other than the statutory requirements regarding the computation of the applicable premium or the treatment, under section 9501 of the Omnibus Budget Reconciliation Act of 1986, of certain bankruptcies as qualifying events, which are not addressed in these proposed regulations). Moreover, plans and employers will be considered to be in compliance with the terms of these proposed regulations if, between June 15, 1987 and September 14, 1987, they operate in good faith compliance with a reasonable interpretation of the statutory requirements and, from September 15, 1987 until the effective date of final regulations, they operate in compliance with the terms of these proposed regulations. In addition, the Internal Revenue Service will not consider actions inconsistent with the terms of these proposed regulations necessarily to constitute a lack of good faith compliance with a reasonable interpretation of the statutory requirements; whether there has been good faith compliance with a reasonable interpretation of the statutory requirements will depend on all the facts and circumstances of each case.

Which Plans Must Comply and When

Q-7. What is a group health plan?

A-7. (a) A group health plan is any plan maintained by an employer to provide medical care (as defined in section 213(d)) to the employer's employees, former employees, or the families of such employees or former employees, whether directly or through insurance, reimbursement, or otherwise, and whether or not provided through an on-site facility (except as set forth in paragraph (e) of this Q&A-7), or through a cafeteria plan (as defined in section 125) or other flexible benefit arrangement. For purposes of this Q&A-7, insurance includes not only group insurance policies but also one or more individual insurance policies in any arrangement that involves the provision of medical care to two or more employees. A plan "maintained by an employer" is any plan of, or contributed to (directly or indirectly) by, an employer. Thus, a group health plan is "maintained by an employer," regardless of whether the employer contributes to it, if coverage under the plan would not be available at the same cost to an employee in the event that he or she were not employed by the employer. However, a plan that is maintained by an employee representative is not "maintained by an employer" if the employer does not contribute to the plan and has no involvement (e.g., payroll checkoff) in the operation of the plan. See Q&A-10 of this section for rules governing when a single arrangement is considered to be two or more separate group health plans.

(b) Medical care (as defined in section 213(d)) includes the diagnosis, cure, mitigation, treatment, or prevention of disease, and any other undertaking for the purpose of affecting any structure or function of the body. Medical care also includes transportation primarily for and essential to medical care as described in the preceding sentence. However, medical care does not include anything that is merely beneficial to the general health of an individual, such as a vacation. Thus, if an employer maintains a program that furthers general good health, but the program does not relate to the relief or alleviation of health or medical problems and is generally accessible to and used by employees without regard to their physical condition or state of health, that program is not considered a program that provides medical care and so is not a group health plan for purposes of this section.

(c) For example, if an employer maintains a spa, swimming pool, or exercise/fitness program that is normally accessible to and used by employees for reasons other than relief of health or medical problems, such a facility would not constitute medical care. In contrast, if the employer maintains a drug or alcohol treatment program or a health clinic, or any other facility or program that is intended to relieve or alleviate a physical condition or health problem (whether the condition or problem is chronic or acute), the facility or program is considered to be the provision of medical care and so is considered a group health plan for purposes of this section.

(d) Whether a benefit provided to employees constitutes medical care is not affected by whether the benefit is excludable from income under section 132 (relating to certain fringe benefits). For example, if a department store provides its employees discounted prices on all merchandise, including health care items such as drugs or eyeglasses, the mere fact that the discounted prices also apply to health care items will not cause the program to be a plan providing medical care, so long as the discount program would normally be accessible to and used by employees without regard to health needs or physical condition. If, however, the employer maintaining the discount program is a health clinic, so that the program is used exclusively by employees with health or medical needs, the program is considered as a plan providing medical care and so is considered a group health plan for purposes of this section.

(e) The provision of medical care at a facility that is located on the premises of an employer does not constitute a group health plan if (1) the medical care consists primarily of first aid that is provided during the employer's working hours for treatment of a health condition, illness, or injury that occurs during those working hours, (2) the medical care is available only to the employer's current employees, and (3) employees are not charged for the use of the facility.

Q-8. What group health plans are subject to COBRA?

A-8. (a) All group health plans are subject to COBRA (i.e., subject to section 162(k)) except group health plans described in section 106(b)(2). However, a group health plan is not subject to COBRA before the effective date prescribed for that plan in Q&A-11 of this section.

(b) The following group health plans are described in section 106(b)(2): (1) Small-employer plans (see Q&A-9 of this section), (2) church plans (within the meaning of section 414(e)), and (3) governmental plans (within the meaning of section 414(d)). Plans that are described in section 106(b)(2) are referred to in this § 1.162-26 as "excepted from COBRA." The income inclusion rule of section 106(b)(1), the deduction denial rule of section 162(i), and the continuation coverage requirements of section 162(k) do not apply with respect to group health plans that are excepted from COBRA. Certain governmental plans, however, are governed by parallel requirements that were added by section 10003 of COBRA to the Public Health Service Act, which is administered by the Department of Health and Human Services.

Q-9. What is a small-employer plan?

A-9. (a) A "small-employer plan" is a group health plan maintained by one or more employers where each of the employers maintaining the plan for a calendar year normally employed fewer than 20 employees during the preceding calendar year. For purposes of this definition, each employer maintaining the plan shall, in combination with all other entities under common control with that employer (as determined under section 52(a) and (b)), be considered a single employer. See Q&A-10 of this section for rules governing when a single arrangement is considered to be two or more separate group health plans.

(b) An employer is considered as having normally employed fewer that 20 employees during a particular calendar year if, and only if, it had fewer than 20 employees on at least 50 percent of its working days during that year.

(c) In determining the number of its employees, an employer shall treat as employees all full-time and part-time employees, and all employees within the meaning of section 401(c)(1). For example, partners in a law firm are treated as employees for this purpose. An employer shall also treat as employees for this purpose all agents and independent contractors (and their employees, agents, and independent contractors, if any), and all directors (in the case of a corporation), but only if such individuals are eligible to participate in a group health plan maintained by the employer.

(d) The determination of whether a plan is a small-employer plan on any particular date depends on which employers are maintaining the plan on that date and on the workforce of those employers during the preceding calendar year. If a plan that is otherwise subject to COBRA ceases to be a small-employer plan because of the addition during a calendar year of an employer that did not normally employ fewer than 20 employees on a typical business day during the preceding calendar year, the plan ceases to be excepted from COBRA and section 162(k) becomes effective with respect to it immediately upon the addition of the new employer. In contrast, if the plan ceases to be a small-employer plan by reason of an increase during a calendar year in the workforce of an employer maintaining the plan, the plan ceases to be excepted from COBRA and section 162(k) becomes effective with respect to it on the January 1 immediately following the calendar year in which the employer's workforce increased. However, a plan described in the preceding sentence will be treated as not having become subject to section 162(k) on that January 1 (i.e., still excepted from COBRA) if all the employers who did not normally employ fewer than 20 employees in the preceding calendar year have ceased to maintain the plan by February 1 immediately following that January 1. For example, if each employer maintaining a group health plan normally employs fewer than 20 employees during each of 1986 and 1987 but two of the employers do not normally employ fewer than 20 employees during 1988, the entire plan becomes subject to COBRA and must begin to comply with section 162(k) on January 1, 1989, even if the plan year is not a calendar year, unless those two employers depart from the plan before February 1, 1989.

Q-10. When is an arrangement considered to be two or more separate group health plans rather than a single group health plan?

A-10. (a) The rules below in paragraphs (b) through (g) of this Q&A-10 determine when an arrangement is considered to be two or more separate group health plans. If more than one of those paragraphs applies to a particular arrangement, the paragraphs are applied in succession to break the arrangement into the smallest possible group health plans. For example, if an arrangement offers high option and low option benefit schedules (see paragraph (c)) and constitutes a multiple employer welfare arrangement maintained by three different employers (see paragraph (d)), the arrangement consists of six separate group health plans: Three high-option plans (one for each employer) and three low-option plans (one for each employer).

(b) The rules in this Q&A-10 apply without regard to whether the arrangement is maintained by one or more than one employer. Moveover, the fact that a particular arrangement has been traditionally referred to as a single plan or has reported as a single plan (e.g., by filing a single Form 5500) is not controlling in the determination of whether the arrangement will be considered as two or more separate plans for purposes of section 162(k). All references elsewhere in this section to a "group health plan" are references to a separate group health plan as determined under this Q&A-10. The identification of separate group health plans is relevant to determinations such as those involving which coverage must be separately electable, the effective date of section 162(k), which employers will be denied deductions in the event of a failure to comply with section 162(k), the cost of continuation coverage, and the availability of the exception for small-employer plans (see Q&A-9 of this section). The relevance of treating an arrangement as two or more separate group health plans is illustrated by the following examples:

Example (1). If an employee is covered under more than one group health plan at the time of a qualifying event, the qualified beneficiaries must be offered an opportunity to elect COBRA continuation coverage with respect to each of the plans. In contrast, if the arrangement in which the employee participates is treated as a single group health plan with several features, no individual features of the plan would have to be made available to a qualified beneficiary unless the qualified beneficiary elects coverage under the entire plan. (But see Q&A-24 of this section regarding the election to receive only core coverage.)

Example (2). If an arrangement that involves many employers is considered to be a single group health plan, that plan will fail to qualify for the small-employer plan exception if any one of those employers had too many employees during the preceding calendar year. However, if the arrangement is considered to be a separate plan with respect to each employer, then the exception would be available for each of those particular employers that normally employed fewer than 20 employees during the preceding calendar year.

Example (3). An arrangement covering the employees of unrelated employers A and B fails to comply with section 162(k) by failing to offer COBRA continuation coverage to an employee of employer A, but complies with section 162(k) in all other respects. If the arrangement consists of two separate group health plans, one covering the employees of A and one covering the employees of B, employer A will lose deductions under section 162(i) and A's highly compensated employees will lose the benefit of the section 106(a) exclusion, but employer B and its employees will be unaffected. In contrast, if the arrangement consists of a single group health plan, the consequences of failing to comply with section 162(k) will apply to both employers A and B.

(c) Each different benefit package or option offered under an arrangement is treated as a separate group health plan. For this purpose, self-only coverage and self-and-family coverage are not considered to be separate packages or options. The rule of this paragraph (c) is illustrated by the following examples:

Example (1). If an arrangement offers "high option" and "low option" benefit schedules and the alternatives of self-only and self-and-family coverage, the arrangement is considered to be two separate plans: One offering high option coverage (whether self-only or self-and-family), and one offering low option coverage (whether self-only or self-and-family).

Example (2). If two types of coverage differ only because one has a $100 deductible and the other has a $250 deductible, or because one has a $1500 catastrophic limit and the other has a $2500 catastrophic limit, each type of coverage is a different benefit package and so is treated as a separate group health plan.

Example (3). An arrangement has a deductible equal to 1 percent of compensation, but consists of a single plan in all other respects. The fact that employees with different levels of compensation will have different deductibles will not cause the arrangement to be treated as separate group health plans for each resulting deductible.

Example (4). If an arrangement consists of a single plan in all respects except that an employee can choose to have either hospital benefits or hospital benefits combined with mental health benefits, there are two separate plans: One providing hospital coverage, and one providing hospital-and-mental-health coverage. If an employee could instead choose independently whether to have hospital benefits and whether to have mental-health benefits, there would also be two separate plans: One providing hospital-only coverage and one providing mental-health-only coverage. In such a case an employee receiving both hospital and mental-health benefits would be covered under two separate group health plans and would have separate COBRA election rights under each plan.

(d) An arrangement that constitutes a multiple employer welfare arrangement as defined in section 3(40) of the Employee Retirement Income Security Act of 1974 (ERISA), is considered a separate group health plan with respect to each employer maintaining the arrangement. Solely for purposes of this paragraph (d), the rules of section 3(40)(B) of ERISA (regarding trades or businesses under common control) shall apply in determining whether two or more employers are treated as a single employer.

(e) In the case of an insured arrangement, if two or more groups of employees are covered under separate contracts between a participating employer or employers and an insurer or insurers, each separate contract is considered a separate group health plan, even if the coverage under the separate contracts is identical.

(f) In the case of a self-funded arrangement, each segregated portion of the arrangement shall be considered a separate group health plan. A portion of an arrangement is a segregated portion if and only if (1) assets available to pay benefits under that portion are unavailable to pay benefits under any other portion, and (2) assets available to pay benefits under any other portion are unavailable to pay benefits out of that portion. For example, if several employers contribute to a trust that provides medical benefits but each employee's benefits are payable only out of contributions (and earnings on contributions) made by that employee's employer, each employer's portion of the arrangement is considered a separate group health plan. The rule of this paragraph (f) shall apply whether or not a trust is used, and whether or not the arrangement is partially insured through stop-loss insurance, insurance for some but not all benefits, or some other method.

(g) Arrangements providing medical benefits are broken down as described in Q&A-12 of this section into their collectively bargained portion (if any) and non-collectively-bargained portion (if any), each of which is considered a separate group health plan.

Q-11. When must group health plans comply with section 162(k)?

A-11. (a) Non-collectively bargained plans: For plans that are not excepted from COBRA (see Q&A-8 of this section) and that do not constitute collectively bargained group health plans (see Q&A-12 of this section), the requirements of section 162(k) apply as of the first day of the first plan year beginning on or after July 1, 1986. For example, if such a plan has a February 1 to January 31 plan year, it must begin to comply with section 162(k) by February 1, 1987.

(b) Collectively bargained plans: For plans that are not excepted from COBRA and that constitute collectively bargained group health plans (see Q&A-12 of this section), the requirements of section 162(k) apply as of the first day of the first plan year beginning on or after the later of (1) January 1, 1987, or (2) the date on which the last of the collective bargaining agreements relating to the plan terminates (determined without regard to any extension thereof agreed to after April 7, 1986). This rule is illustrated by the following example:

Example. Assume that the plan year of a collectively bargained group health plan is the calendar year and that, as of April 7, 1986, the plan is maintained pursuant to three collective bargaining agreements having expiration dates in October 1987, February 1988, and July 1988. The plan must comply with section 162(k) beginning on January 1, 1989. Of course, the plan must begin to comply by January 1, 1987, with respect to a collective bargaining unit that was not, as of April 7, 1986, covered by one of those three agreements.

Q-12. What is a collectively bargained group health plan?

A-12. (a) A collectively bargained group health plan is a group health plan covering only employees and former employees (and their families) who are covered by an agreement that is a collective bargaining agreement entered into between employee representatives and one or more employers (as determined under section 7701(a)(46)). Thus, if an arrangement that would otherwise be considered to be a single group health plan under the standards set out in Q&A-10 of this section covers both (1) employees and former employees (and their families) who are covered by a collective bargaining agreement described in the preceding sentence and (2) employees and former employees (and their families) who are not covered by such an agreement, the arrangement consists of two separate group health plans: one plan that is a collectively bargained group health plan and one that is not. The plan that is collectively bargained will have an effective date determined under paragraph (b) of Q&A-11 of this section, and the other plan will have an effective date determined under paragraph (a) of Q& A-11 of this section. For example, if the plan year is the calendar year and the only collective bargaining agreement in effect as of April 7, 1986, expires March 31, 1988, the effective date of section 162(k) is January 1, 1989, for the plan covering bargaining-unit employees and their families, and January 1, 1987, for the plan covering the other employees and their families.

(b) For purposes of this Q&A-12, employees of an employee representative that is a party to a collective bargaining agreement described in paragraph (a) of this Q&A-12, and employees of a trust or fund maintained to pay benefits to individuals covered by the collective bargaining agreement, are considered to be employees covered by that collective bargaining agreement. Thus, a plan that is otherwise considered a single, collectively bargained plan will not fail to be a single, collectively bargained plan merely because it also covers employees or former employees (and their families) of the employee representative or of a trust or fund from which the benefits are paid.

Q-13. What is the plan year of a group health plan?

A-13. (a) For purposes of determining when a group health plan must begin to comply with section 162(k) (see Q&A-11 of this section), the plan year of a group health plan is the year that is designated as the plan year in the plan document. However, if the plan document does not designate a plan year, or if there is no plan document, the plan year is determined under paragraph (b) of this Q& A-13. The designation of a plan year on a Form 5500 filed by a group health plan is not controlling in the determination of the plan year under this Q&A-13.

(b) If the plan year of a group health plan is determined under this paragraph (b), the plan year is the plan's limit/deductible year except that (1) in the case of an insured group health plan, the plan year is the policy year if that is later than the limit/deductible year or if the plan has no limit/deductible year, and (2) in the case of a self-funded group health plan having no limit/deductible year, the plan year is the later of the calendar year or the employer's taxable year. For purposes of this paragraph (b), a plan's "limit/deductible year" means the year that is used by the plan in applying benefit limits and deductibles, except that if different years are used for benefit limits and for deductibles, it means the later of those years. For purposes of this paragraph (b), one year is "later" than another if it begins later in relation to the underlying date from which the effective date of section 162(k) is determined for the plan under Q&A-11 of this section. Compare, for example, a year that begins on March 1 with a year that begins on December 1. The March 1 year is later than a December 1 year in the case of a non-collectively-bargained plan, because the first March 1 occurring on or after July 1, 1986, is March 1, 1987, which is later than December 1, 1986 (the first December 1 occurring on or after July 1, 1986). If, however, the plan is a collectively-bargained plan and becomes subject to section 162(k) for the first plan year beginning on or after February 1, 1987, a December 1 year is later than a March 1 year.

Q-14. How do the COBRA continuation coverage requirements apply to cafeteria plans and other flexible benefit arrangements?

A-14. The provision of medical care through a cafeteria plan (as defined in section 125) or other flexible benefit arrangement constitutes a group health plan. However, the COBRA continuation coverage requirements of section 162(k) apply only to those medical benefits under the cafeteria plan or other arrangement that a covered employee has actually chosen to receive (if any). The application of this rule to a cafeteria plan is illustrated by the following examples:

Example (1). Under the terms of a cafeteria plan, employees can choose among life insurance coverage, membership in a Health Maintenance Organization (HMO), coverage for medical expenses under an indemnity arrangement, and cash compensation. Of these available choices, the HMO and the indemnity arrangement constitute separate group health plans. Assume that these group health plans are subject to COBRA (see Q&A-8 of this section) and that the employer does not provide any group health plan outside of the cafeteria plan. Assume further that B and C are unmarried employees, that B has chosen the life insurance coverage, and that C has chosen the indemnity arrangement. B does not have to be offered COBRA continuation coverage upon terminating employment, nor must a subsequent open enrollment period for active employees be made available to B. However, if C terminates employment and the termination constitutes a qualifying event, C must be offered an opportunity to elect COBRA continuation coverage under the indemnity arrangement. If C makes such an election and an open enrollment period for active employees occurs while C is still receiving the COBRA continuation coverage. C must be offered the opportunity to switch from the indemnity arrangement to the HMO (but not to the life insurance coverage because that does not constitute a group health plan).

Example (2). An employer maintains a group health plan under which all employees receive employer-paid coverage. Employees can arrange to cover their families by paying an additional amount. The employer also maintains a cafeteria plan, under which one of the options is to pay part or all of the charge for family coverage under the group health plan. Thus, an employee might pay for family coverage under the group health plan partly with before-tax dollars and partly with after-tax dollars. If an employee's family is receiving coverage under the group health plan when a qualifying event occurs, each of the qualified beneficiaries must be offered an opportunity to elect COBRA continuation coverage, regardless of how that qualified beneficiary's coverage was paid for before the qualifying event.

Example (3). One of the choices available under a cafeteria plan is an individual medical expense reimbursement arrangement. At the beginning of each calendar year, an employee can choose, instead of being paid a specified dollar amount of compensation, to have that amount placed in an account to be used for reimbursement of medical expenses incurred during the year by the employee or the employee's spouse or dependent children. Any amount remaining in the account as of the end of the year is forfeited. The reimbursement of medical expenses through these arrangements constitutes a group health plan.

Qualified Beneficiaries

Q-15. Who is a qualified beneficiary?

A-15. (a) Except as set forth in paragraphs (b) through (d) of this Q&A-15, a qualified beneficiary is any individual who, on the day before a qualifying event, is covered under a group health plan maintained by the employer of a covered employee by virtue of being on that day either (1) the covered employee, (2) the spouse of the covered employee, or (3) the dependent child of the covered employee.

(b) An individual is not a qualified beneficiary if, on the day before the qualifying event referred to in paragraph (a) of this Q&A-15, the individual (1) is covered under the group health plan by reason of another individual's election of COBRA continuation coverage and is not already a qualified beneficiary by reason of a prior qualifying event, or (2) is entitled to Medicare benefits under Title XVIII of the Social Security Act.

(c) A covered employee can be a qualified beneficiary only in connection with a qualifying event that consists of the termination (other than by reason of the covered employee's gross misconduct), or reduction of hours, of the covered employee's employment.

(d) An individual is not a qualified beneficiary if the individual's status as a covered employee is attributable to a period in which the individual was a nonresident alien who received no earned income (within the meaning of section 911(d)(2)) from the individual's employer that constituted income from sources within the United States (within the meaning of section 861(a)(3)). If, pursuant to the preceding sentence, an individual is not a qualified beneficiary, then a spouse or dependent child of the individual shall not be considered a qualified beneficiary by virtue of the relationship to the individual.

Q-16. Who is a covered employee?

A-16. (a) A covered employee is any individual who is (or was) provided coverage under a group health plan (other than a plan that is excepted from COBRA on the date of the qualifying event; see Q&A-8 of this section) by virtue of the individual's employment or previous employment with an employer. For example, a retiree or former employee who is covered by such a group health plan is a covered employee if the coverage results in whole or in part from his or her previous employment. An individual (whether a present or former employee) who is merely eligible for coverage under a group health plan is not a covered employee if the individual is not and has not been actually covered under the plan. The reason for an individual's lack of actual coverage (such as the individual's having declined participation in the plan or failed to satisfy the plan's conditions for participation) is not relevant for this purpose.

(b) The following individuals are also covered employees, but only if they are (or were) actually covered under a group health plan by virtue of their relationship to an employer maintaining the plan, and only if that plan or some other group health plan maintained by the employer covers one or more common-law employees of the employer: (1) Employees within the meaning of section 401(c)(1), (2) agents and independent contractors (and their employees, agents, and independent contractors), and (3) directors (in the case of a corporation). The rule of this paragraph (b) is illustrated by the following example:

Example. A law firm maintains a group health plan for its common-law employees. If the firm also provides group health coverage for its partners, the partners are covered employees regardless of whether their coverage is provided under the same group health plan as the common-law employees or under a separate plan. In contrast, if the partners are the only individuals who receive any health coverage, they are not covered employees.

Q-17. Other than those individuals who are qualified beneficiaries as of the day before a qualifying event, can any other person (such as a newborn or adopted child or a new spouse) obtain qualified beneficiary status for COBRA continuation coverage purposes?

A-17. (a) No. The group of qualified beneficiaries entitled to elect COBRA continuation coverage as a result of a qualifying event is closed as of the day before the qualifying event. Thus, newborn children, adopted children, and spouses who join the family of a qualified beneficiary after that day do not become qualified beneficiaries. The new family members do not themselves become qualified beneficiaries even if they become covered under the plan. (For situations in which a plan is required to make coverage available to new family members of a qualified beneficiary who is receiving COBRA continuation coverage, see Q&A-31 of this section and paragraph (c) of Q&A-30 of this section.)

(b) A qualified beneficiary who fails to elect COBRA continuation coverage in connection with a qualifying event ceases to be a qualified beneficiary at the end of the election period (see Q&A-32 of this section). Thus, for example, if such a former qualified beneficiary is later added to a covered employee's coverage (e.g., during an open enrollment period) and then another qualifying event occurs with respect to the covered employee, the former qualified beneficiary will not be treated as a qualified beneficiary

(c) The rules of this Q&A-17 are illustrated by the following examples:

Example (1). Assume that A is a single employee who voluntarily terminates employment and properly elects COBRA continuation coverage under a group health plan. Under the terms of the plan, a covered employee who marries can choose to have his or her spouse covered under the plan as of the date of marriage. One month after electing COBRA continuation coverage, A marries and chooses, to cover A's spouse under the plan. A's spouse is not a qualified beneficiary. Thus, if A dies during the period of COBRA continuation coverage, the plan does not have to offer A's surviving spouse an opportunity to elect COBRA continuation coverage.

Example (2). Assume that B is a married employee who terminates employment, B properly elects COBRA continuation coverage for B but not B's spouse, and B's spouse declines to elect such coverage. B's spouse thus ceases to be a qualified beneficiary. Later, at the next open enrollment period, B adds the spouse as a beneficiary under the plan. The addition of the spouse during the open enrollment period does not make the spouse a qualified beneficiary. The plan will thus not have to offer the spouse an opportunity to elect COBRA continuation coverage upon a later divorce from or death of B.

Example (3). Assume that, under the terms of a group health plan, a covered employee's child ceases to be a dependent eligible for coverage upon attaining age 18. At that time, the child must be offered an opportunity to elect COBRA continuation coverage. If the child elects COBRA continuation coverage, the child marries during the period of the COBRA continuation coverage, and the child's spouse becomes covered under the group health plan, the child's spouse would not become a qualified beneficiary upon a later qualifying event as a result of that coverage.

Example (4). Assume that C is a single employee who, upon retirement, is given the opportunity to elect COBRA continuation coverage but declines it in favor of an alternative offer of 12 months of employer-paid retiree health benefits. C ceases to be a qualified beneficiary and will not have to be given another opportunity to elect COBRA continuation coverage at the end of those 12 months. Assume further that C marries D during the period of retiree health coverage and, under the terms of that coverage, D becomes covered under the plan. If a divorce from or death of C will result in D's losing coverage, D will be a qualified beneficiary because D's coverage under the plan on the day before the qualifying event (i.e., the divorce) will have been by reason of C's acceptance of 12 months of employer-paid coverage after the prior qualifying event (C's retirement) rather than by reason of an election of COBRA continuation coverage.

Example (5). Assume the same facts as in Example 4 except that, under the terms of the plan, the divorce or death does not cause D to lose coverage so that D continues to be covered for the balance of the original 12-month period. D does not have to be allowed to elect COBRA continuation coverage because the divorce or death does not constitute a qualifying event. See Q&A-18 of this section.

Qualifying Events

Q-18. What is a qualifying event?

A-18. (a) A qualifying event is an event that satisfies paragraphs (b), (c), and (d) of this Q&A-18.

(b) An event satisfies this paragraph (b) if the event is either (1) the death of a covered employee, (2) the termination (other than by reason of the employee's gross misconduct), or reduction of hours, of a covered employee's employment, (3) the divorce or legal separation of a covered employee from the employee's spouse, (4) a covered employee becoming entitled to Medicare benefits under Title XVIII of the Social Security Act, or (5) a dependent child ceasing to be a dependent child of the covered employee under the generally applicable requirements of the plan. In the case of a covered employee who is not a common law employee, termination of "employment" for this purpose means termination of the relationship (e.g., directorship of a corporation or membership in a partnership) giving rise to the individual's treatment as a covered employee under paragraph (b) of Q&A-16 of this section.

(c) An event satisfies this paragraph (c) if, under the terms of the group health plan, the event causes the covered employee, or the spouse or a dependent child of the covered employee, to lose coverage under the plan. For this purpose, to "lose coverage" means to cease to be covered under the same terms and conditions as in effect immediately before the qualifying event. If coverage is reduced or eliminated in anticipation of an event, the reduction or elimination is disregarded in determining whether the event causes a loss of coverage. Moreover, for purposes of this paragraph (c), a loss of coverage need not occur immediately after the event, so long as the loss of coverage will occur before the end of the maximum coverage period (see Q& A-39 and Q&A-40 of this section). However, if neither the covered employee nor the spouse or a dependent child of the covered employee will lose coverage before the end of what would be the maximum coverage period, the event does not satisfy this paragraph (c).

(d) An event satisfies this paragraph (d) if it occurs while the plan is subject to COBRA. Thus, an event will not satisfy this paragraph (d) if it occurs before the plan becomes subject to section 162(k) (see Q&A-11 of this section) or while the plan is excepted from COBRA (see Q& A-8). See Q&A-20 and Q&A-21 of this section.

(e) The rules of this Q&A-18 are illustrated by the following examples, each of which assumes that paragraph (d) is satisfied:

Example (1). If an employee who is covered by a group health plan terminates employment (other than by reason of the employee's gross misconduct) and, as of the date of separation, is given 3 months of employer-paid coverage under the same terms and conditions as before that date, the termination is a qualifying event because it satisfies both paragraphs (b) and (c) of this Q& A-18.

Example (2). Upon the retirement of an employee who, along with the employee's spouse, has been covered under a group health plan, the employee is given identical coverage for life but the spousal coverage will not be continued beyond 6 months unless premiums are then paid by the employee or spouse. The spouse will "lose coverage" 6 months after the employee's retirement when the premium requirement takes effect, so the retirement is a qualifying event and the spouse must be given an opportunity to elect COBRA continuation coverage.

Example (3). F is a covered employee who is married to G, and both are covered under a group health plan maintained by F's employer. F and G are divorced and, under the terms of the plan, the divorce will cause G to lose coverage. The divorce is a qualifying event. If G elects COBRA continuation coverage and then remarries during the period of COBRA continuation coverage, G's new spouse might become covered under the plan. (See Q&A-31 of this section and paragraph (c) of Q&A-30 of this section.) However, G's later death or divorce from G's new spouse will not be a qualifying event because G is not a covered employee.

Q-19. Can a qualifying event result from a voluntary termination of employment?

A-19. Yes. Apart from gross misconduct, the facts surrounding a termination or reduction of hours are irrelevant. It does not matter whether the employee voluntarily terminated or was discharged. For example, a strike or walkout is a termination or reduction of hours that constitutes a qualifying event if the strike or walkout results in a loss of coverage as described in paragraph (c) of Q&A-18 of this section. Similarly, a layoff that results in such a loss of coverage is a qualifying event.

Q-20. Can a qualifying event occur before the effective date of section 162(k) (as described in Q&A-11 of this section)?

A-20. No. An event that occurs before section 162(k) becomes effective for a group health plan does not satisfy paragraph (d) of the definition of qualifying event in Q&A-18 of this section. A group health plan does not have to offer individuals whose coverage ends as a result of such an event the opportunity to elect COBRA continuation coverage. For example, if an employee terminated employment on July 15, 1986, and the plan covering the employee had a November 1 to October 31 plan year (so that the plan became subject to section 162(k) on November 1, 1986), the plan does not have to permit the employee to elect COBRA continuation coverage. Even if that employee is given 6 months of additional coverage from the July 15, 1986, termination date (whether merely as a result of the terms of the plan, or pursuant to state or local law or otherwise) so that the coverage extends beyond the November 1 effective date, the employee does not have to be given the opportunity to elect COBRA continuation coverage at the end of the 6 months' coverage because there will be no qualifying event at that time. In contrast, if the employee's spouse is covered by the 6 months' coverage and, as a result of the employee's death after the November 1 effective date and before the end of the 6-month period, the spouse will lose coverage for the balance of the 6-month period, the death will constitute a qualifying event and the spouse will be a qualified beneficiary entitled to elect COBRA continuation coverage. See Q&A-42 of this section regarding the maximum coverage period in such a case.

Q-21. Can a qualifying event occur while a group health plan is excepted from COBRA (see Q&A-8 of this section)?

A-21. No. An event that occurs while a group health plan is excepted from COBRA does not satisfy paragraph (d) of the definition of qualifying event in Q& A/18 of this section. Even if the plan later becomes subject to COBRA, it does not have to provide COBRA election rights to anyone whose coverage ends as a result of such an event. For example, if a group health plan is excepted from COBRA as a small-employer plan during 1988 (see Q&A-9 of this section) and an employee terminates employment on December 31, 1988, the termination is not a qualifying event and the plan does not have to permit the employee to elect COBRA continuation coverage. This is the case even if the plan ceases to be a small-employer plan as of January 1, 1989. Also, the same result will follow even if the employee is given 3 months of coverage beyond December 31 (i.e., through March of 1989), because there will be no qualifying event as of the termination of coverage in March. However, if the employee's spouse is initially provided with the 3-month coverage through March 1989, but the spouse divorces the employee before the end of the 3 months and loses coverage as a result of the divorce, the divorce will constitute a qualifying event during 1989 and so entitle the spouse to elect COBRA continuation coverage. See Q&A-42 of this section regarding the maximum coverage period in such a case.

COBRA Continuation Coverage

Q-22. What is COBRA continuation coverage?

A-22. If a qualifying event occurs, each qualified beneficiary (other than a qualified beneficiary for whom the qualifying event will not result in any immediate or deferred loss of coverage) must be offered an opportunity to elect to continue to receive the group health plan coverage that he or she received immediately before the qualifying event. This continued coverage is "COBRA continuation coverage." Except as set forth in Q&A-23 through Q&A-31 of this section, if the continuation coverage offered differs in any way from the coverage enjoyed immediately before the qualifying event, the coverage offered does not constitute COBRA continuation coverage and the group health plan is not in compliance with section 162(k) unless other coverage that does constitute COBRA continuation coverage is also offered. Any elimination or reduction of coverage in anticipation of a qualifying event is disregarded for purposes of this Q&A-22 and for purposes of any other reference in this section to coverage in effect immediately before (or on the day before) a qualifying event. COBRA continuation coverage must not be conditioned upon, or discriminate on the basis of lack of, evidence of insurability.

Q-23. How is COBRA continuation coverage affected by changes in the coverage that is provided to similarly situated beneficiaries with respect to whom a qualifying event has not occurred?

A-23. COBRA continuation coverage must generally be the same as the group health plan coverage enjoyed by the qualified beneficiary immediately before the qualifying event. However, if the coverage provided to similarly situated active employees is changed or eliminated but the employer continues to maintain one or more group health plans (so that the qualified beneficiary's COBRA continuation coverage cannot be terminated at that time—see Q&A-37 of this section), the employer must permit the qualified beneficiary receiving COBRA continuation coverage to elect to be covered under any of the remaining group health plans maintained by the employer or similarly situated active employees. If the coverage of the qualified beneficiary was subject to deductibles and the change in coverage occurs before the end of the prescribed period for accumulating such deductibles, the new coverage selected by the qualified beneficiary must credit him or her with the amounts incurred under the original coverage. The rule in the preceding sentence also applies to those limits that are in the nature of deductibles, such as copayment limits or catastrophic limits on a covered individual's out-of-pocket expenses. The qualified beneficiary can be charged the amount determined under Q&A-44 of this section for the coverage selected.

Q-24. Can a group health plan require a qualified beneficiary who wishes to receive COBRA continuation coverage to elect to receive a continuation of all of the coverage that he or she was receiving under the plan immediately before the qualifying event?

A-24. (a) In general, no. A qualified beneficiary who, immediately before the qualifying event, is covered by a plan that provides both core coverage and non-core coverage must be able to elect to receive either (1) the coverage that he or she had immediately before the qualifying event (including the core coverage and any non-core coverage), or (2) the core coverage only. However, there are two exceptions to this rule, as set forth in paragraphs (b) and (c) of this Q&A-24.

(b) If the applicable premium for core coverage would be at least 95 percent of the applicable premium for core coverage and non-core coverage combined, the plan does not have to offer qualified beneficiaries the opportunity to elect core coverage only. (See Q&A-44 of this section regarding the applicable premium.)

(c) If an employer maintaining a group health plan that includes non-core coverage also maintains at least one other group health plan for similarly situated active employees that does not provide any non-core coverage, the plan that includes non-core coverage does not have to offer a qualified beneficiary an opportunity to elect core coverage only. However, the qualified beneficiary must instead be offered the opportunity to elect coverage under any other group health plan maintained by the employer for similarly situated active employees.

Q-25. What is core coverage?

A-25. (a) "Core coverage" means all of the coverage that a qualified beneficiary was receiving under the group health plan immediately before a qualifying event that gives rise to the qualified beneficiary's COBRA election rights, other than "non-core coverage." "Non-core coverage" means coverage for vision benefits and dental benefits. However, coverage for vision benefits or dental benefits that must be provided under applicable law is core coverage.

(b) For purposes of this Q&A-25, vision benefits include only those benefits related to vision care of a type that is not required under local law to be performed by a physician.

(c) For purposes of this Q&A-25, dental benefits does not include any benefits for dental care or oral surgery in connection with an accidental injury.

(d) The definitions in this Q&A-25 apply only for purposes of this § 1.162-26 and sections 106, 162(i)(2), and 162(k) of the Code.

Q-26. Must a qualified beneficiary be given an opportunity to elect core coverage plus only one of two non-core coverages that the qualified beneficiary had under the plan immediately before the qualifying event?

A-26. No. A group health plan is required only to offer qualified beneficiaries the right to elect (a) core coverage, or (b) core coverage plus all non-core coverages that the qualified beneficiary had immediately before the qualifying event. Thus, a qualified beneficiary who has core coverage plus vision and dental coverage upon the occurrence of a qualifying event must be offered the opportunity to continue either the core coverage or the core coverage and both dental and vision coverage. Such a qualified beneficiary would not have to be offered the opportunity to elect core coverage plus vision coverage only or core coverage plus dental coverage only. Of course, if the vision and dental coverage are provided under two separate plans that are independent of the core plan, a qualified beneficiary would be able to continue one or both of the coverages. Assume, for example, that an employer maintains three group health plans—a core plan, a vision plan, and a dental plan—and that each active employee can elect to be covered under one or more of the three plans. (Thus, an employee could have vision-only, dental-only, or core-only coverage, or any combination of the three.) A qualified beneficiary who is covered under all three plans at the time of a qualifying event would have separate election rights with respect to each plan, and so would be able to elect coverage under the dental-only and core-only plans.

Q-27. Must a qualified beneficiary who is covered under a single plan providing both core coverage and non-core coverage be offered the opportunity to elect non-core coverage only?

A-27. No. A qualified beneficiary who is covered by a single plan providing both core coverage and non-core coverage need not be offered the opportunity to elect only non-core coverage. Of course, if immediately before the qualifying event the qualified beneficiary is covered by a group health plan that provides non-core coverage but no core coverage, the qualified beneficiary must be offered the opportunity to continue that non-core coverage. Moreover, such an individual generally would not have to be given the opportunity to elect core coverage. (But see Q&A-30 of this section regarding open enrollment periods.)

Q-28. What deductibles apply if COBRA continuation coverage is elected?

A-28. (a) Qualified beneficiaries electing COBRA continuation coverage are generally subject to the same deductibles as similarly situated employees for whom a qualifying event has not occurred. If a qualified beneficiary's COBRA continuation coverage begins before the end of the prescribed period for accumulating amounts toward deductibles, the qualified beneficiary must retain credit for expenses incurred toward those deductibles before the beginning of COBRA continuation coverage as though the qualifying event had not occurred. The specific application of this rule depends on the type of deductible, as set forth in paragraphs (b) through (d) of this Q&A-28. Special rules are set forth in paragraphs (e) and (f), and examples appear in paragraph (g).

(b) If a deductible is computed separately for each individual receiving coverage under the plan, each individual's remaining deductible amount (if any) on the date that COBRA continuation coverage begins is equal to that individual's remaining deductible amount immediately before that date.

(c) If a deductible is computed on a family basis, the deductible for each new family unit after the beginning of COBRA continuation coverage (or the existing family unit, in the case of a qualifying event that does not result in there being more than one family unit) is computed as follows: On the date that COBRA continuation coverage begins, the remaining deductible amount for each new family unit (or the remaining number of individual deductibles, in the case of a family deductible that is satisfied by completing a specified number of individual deductibles) is equal to the preexisting family unit's remaining deductible amount (or remaining number of individual deductibles, as applicable) immediately before that date. This rule applies regardless of whether the plan provides that the family deductible is an alternative to individual deductibles or an additional requirement.

(d) Deductibles that are not described in paragraphs (b) or (c) of this Q&A-28 must be treated in a manner consistent with the principles set forth in those paragraphs.

(e) If a deductible is computed on the basis of a covered employee's compensation instead of being a fixed dollar amount, the plan can treat the employee's compensation as frozen for the duration of the COBRA continuation coverage at the level that was used to compute the deductible in effect immediately before the COBRA continuation coverage began.

(f) If a single deductible is prescribed for core coverage and non-core coverage and a qualified beneficiary electing

COBRA continuation coverage elects to receive core coverage only, the treatment of expenses for non-core coverage depends on when the expenses were incurred, as follows: If the expenses were incurred before the beginning of COBRA continuation coverage, they must continue to be counted toward satisfaction of the deductible, but they need not be counted if they were incurred after the beginning of COBRA continuation coverage.

(g) The rules of the Q&A-28 are illustrated by the following examples; in each example it is assumed that deductibles are determined on a calendar year basis:

Example (1). A group health plan applies a separate $100 annual deductible to each individual whom it covers. The plan provides that the spouse and dependent children of a covered employee will lose coverage on the last day of the month after the month of the covered employee's death. A covered employee dies on June 11, 1988. The spouse and the two dependent children elect COBRA continuation coverage, which will begin on August 1, 1988. As of July 31, 1988, the spouse has incurred $80 of covered expenses, the older child has incurred no covered expenses, and the younger one has incurred $120 (i.e., already satisfied the deductible). At the beginning of COBRA continuation coverage on August 1, the spouse has a remaining deductible of $20, the older child still has the full $100 deductible, and the younger one has no further deductible.

Example (2). A group health plan applies a separate $200 annual deductible to each individual whom it covers, except that each family member will be treated as having satisfied the individual deductible once the family has incurred $500 of covered expenses during the year. The plan provides that upon the divorce of a covered employee, coverage will end immediately for the employee's spouse and any children who do not remain in the employee's custody. Assume that a covered employee with four dependent children is divorced, that the spouse obtains custody of the two oldest children, and that the spouse and those children all elect COBRA continuation coverage to begin immediately. Assume also that the family had accumulated $420 of covered expenses before the divorce, as follows: $70 by each parent, $200 by the oldest child, $80 by the youngest child, and none by the other two children. Each new family unit after the divorce (i.e., the employee plus two children, still receiving regular coverage under the plan, and the spouse plus two children, receiving COBRA continuation coverage) has a remaining family deductible amount of $80 ($500 minus $420).

Example (3). The facts are the same as in Example 2, except that the family deductible is defined as two individual $200 deductibles instead of a $500 aggregate (i.e., the plan disregards all remaining individual deductibles after the satisfaction of any two individual deductibles). Before the divorce, the family has satisfied one individual deductible (the oldest child's). At the beginning of COBRA continuation coverage, therefore, each new family unit is treated as having already satisfied one individual deductible even though the oldest child is included in only one of the new family units.

Example (4). Each year a group health plan pays 70 percent of the cost of an individual's psychotherapy after that individual's first three visits. A qualified beneficiary who elects COBRA continuation coverage beginning August 1, 1988, and has already made two visits as of that date need only pay for one more visit before the plan must begin to pay 70 percent of the cost of the remaining visits during 1988.

Example (5). A group health plan has a $250 annual deductible per covered individual. The plan provides that if the deductible is not satisfied in a particular year, expenses incurred during October through December of that year are credited toward satisfaction of the deductible in the next year. A qualified beneficiary who has incurred covered expenses of $150 from January through September of 1988 and $40 during October elects COBRA continuation coverage beginning November 1, 1988. The remaining deductible amount for this qualified beneficiary is $60 at the beginning of the COBRA continuation coverage. If this individual incurs covered expenses of $50 in November and December of 1988 combined (so that the $250 deductible for 1988 is not satisfied), the $90 incurred from October through December of 1988 are credited toward satisfaction of the deductible amount for 1989.

Q-29. How do a plan's limits apply to COBRA continuation coverage?

A-29. (a) Limits are treated in the same way as deductibles (see Q&A-28 of this section). This rule applies both to limits on plan benefits (e.g., a maximum number of hospital days or dollar amount of reimbursable expenses) and limits that are in the nature of deductibles (e.g., a copayment limit, or a catastrophic limit on a covered employee's out-of-pocket expenses). This rule applies equally to annual and lifetime limits.

(b) The rule of this Q&A-29 is illustrated by the following examples; in each example it is assumed that limits are determined on a calendar year basis:

Example (1). A group health plan pays for a maximum of 150 days of hospital confinement per individual per year. A covered employee who has had 20 days of hospital confinement as of May 1, 1989, terminates employment and elects COBRA continuation coverage as of that date. During the remainder of 1989 the plan need only pay for a maximum of 130 days of hospital confinement for this individual.

Example (2). A group health plan reimburses a maximum of $20,000 of covered expenses per family per year, and the same $20,000 limit applies to unmarried covered employees. A covered employee and spouse who have no children divorce on May 1, 1989, and the spouse elects COBRA continuation coverage as of that date. If the employee and spouse together incurred $15,000 of reimbursable expenses during January through April of 1989, each of these individuals has a $5,000 maximum benefit for the remainder of 1989, regardless who incurred what portion of the $15,000.

Example (3). A group health plan pays for 80 percent of covered expenses after satisfaction of a $100-per-individual deductible, and 100 percent of them after a family has incurred out-of-pocket costs of $2,000. An employee and spouse with three dependent children divorce on June 1, 1989, and one of the children remains with the employee. The spouse elects COBRA continuation coverage as of that date for the spouse and the other two children. During January through May of 1989, all five individual deductibles were satisfied and the family incurred $4,000 of covered expenses, resulting in out-of-pocket expenses totalling $1,200 (five $100 deductibles, plus the non-reimbursed 20 percent of the other $3,500, or $700). For the remainder of 1989, each new family unit has an out-of-pocket limit of $800.

Q-30. Can a qualified beneficiary who elects COBRA continuation coverage ever change from the coverage received by that individual immediately before the qualifying event?

A-30. (a) In general, a qualified beneficiary need only be given an opportunity to continue the coverage that he or she was receiving immediately before the qualifying event. This is true regardless of whether the coverage received by the qualified beneficiary before the qualifying event ceases to be of value to the qualified beneficiary, such as in the case of a qualified beneficiary covered under a region-specific Health Maintenance Organization (HMO) who leaves the HMO's service region. The only situations in which a qualified beneficiary must be allowed to change from the coverage received immediately before the qualifying event are as set forth in paragraphs (b) and (c) of this Q&A-30, in Q&A-24 of this section (regarding core coverage), and in Q&A-23 of this section (regarding changes to or elimination of the coverage provided to similarly situated active employees).

(b) If a qualified beneficiary participates in a region-specific plan (such as an HMO or an on-site clinic) that will not service his or her health needs in the area to which he or she is relocating (regardless of the reason for the relocation) and the employer has employees in the area to which the qualified beneficiary relocates, the qualified beneficiary must be given an opportunity to elect alternative coverage if (and on the same basis as) a similarly situated active employee who transfers to that new location while continuing to work for the employer would be given the opportunity to elect alternative coverage at the time of transfer.

(c) If an employer maintains more than one group health plan and an open enrollment period is available to similarly situated active employees with respect to whom a qualifying event has not occurred, the same open enrollment period rights must be available to each qualified beneficiary receiving COBRA continuation coverage. An open enrollment period means a period during which an employee covered under a plan can choose to be covered under another group health plan, or to add or eliminate coverage of family members.

(d) The rules of this Q&A-30 are illustrated by the following examples:

Example (1). Assume that (1) E is an employee who works for an employer that maintains several group health plans; (2) under the terms of the plans, if an employee chooses to cover any family members under a plan, all family members must be covered by the same plan and that plan must be the same as the plan covering the employee; (3) immediately before E's termination of employment (for reasons other than gross misconduct), E is covered along with E's spouse and children by a plan that provides only core coverage, and (4) the coverage under that plan will end as a result of the termination of employment. Upon E's termination of employment, each of the four family members is a qualified beneficiary. Even though the employer maintains various other plans and options, it is not necessary for the qualified beneficiaries to be allowed to switch to a new plan when E terminates employment. Assume further that none of the four family members declines to elect COBRA continuation coverage, and that 3 months after E's termination of employment there is an open enrollment period during which similarly situated active employees are offered an opportunity to choose to be covered under a new plan or to add or eliminate family coverage. During the open enrollment period, each of the four qualified beneficiaries must be offered the opportunity to switch to another plan (as though each beneficiary were an individual employee). For example, each member of E's family could choose coverage under a separate plan, even though the family members of employed individuals could not choose coverage under separate plans. Of course, if each family member chooses COBRA continuation coverage under a separate plan, each family member can be required to pay an amount for that coverage that is based on the applicable premium for individual coverage under that separate plan. See Q&A-44 of this section.

Example (2). The facts are the same as in Example 1, except that E's family members are not covered under E's group health plan when E terminates employment. Although the family members do not have to be given an opportunity to elect COBRA continuation coverage, E must be allowed to add them to E's COBRA continuation coverage during the open enrollment period. This is true even though the family members are not, and cannot become, qualified beneficiaries (see Q&A-17 of this section).

Q-31. Aside from open enrollment periods, can a qualified beneficiary who has elected COBRA continuation coverage choose to cover individuals (such as newborn children, adopted children, or new spouses) who join the qualified beneficiary's family on or after the date of the qualifying event?

A-31. If the plan covering the qualified beneficiary provides that such new family members of active employees can become covered (either automatically or upon an appropriate election) before the next open enrollment period, then the same right must be extended to the new family members of a qualified beneficiary. Of course, if the addition of a new family member will result in a higher applicable premium (e.g., if the qualified beneficiary was previously receiving COBRA continuation coverage as an individual, or if the applicable premium for family coverage depends on family size), the plan can require the qualified beneficiary to pay a correspondingly higher amount for the COBRA continuation coverage. See Q&A-44 of this section.

Electing COBRA Continuation Coverage

Q-32. What is the minimum period during which a group health plan must allow a qualified beneficiary to elect COBRA continuation coverage (i.e., the election period)?

A-32. A group health plan can condition the availability of COBRA continuation coverage upon a qualified beneficiary's timely election of such coverage. An election of COBRA continuation coverage is a timely election if it is made during the election period. The election period must begin on or before the date that the qualified beneficiary would lose coverage on account of the qualifying event. (See paragraph (c) of Q&A-18 of this section for the meaning of "lose coverage.") The election period must not end before the date that is 60 days after the later of (a) the date that the qualified beneficiary would lose coverage on account of the qualifying event, or (b) the date that the qualified beneficiary is sent notice of his or her right to elect COBRA continuation coverage. An election is considered to be made on the date that it is sent to the employer or plan administrator. The rules of this Q&A-32 are illustrated by the following example:

Example. An unmarried employee who is receiving employer-paid coverage under a group health plan voluntarily terminates employment on June 1, 1988. Case 1: If the plan provides that the employer-paid coverage ends immediately upon the termination of employment, the election period must begin on or before June 1, 1988, and must not end earlier than July 31, 1988. If the notice of the right to elect COBRA continuation coverage is not sent to the employee until June 15, 1988, the election period must not end earlier than August 14, 1988. Case 2: If the plan provides that the employer-paid coverage does not end until 6 months after the termination of employment, the employee does not lose coverage until December 1, 1988. The election period can therefore begin as late as December 1, 1988, and must not end before January 30, 1989. Case 3: If employer-paid coverage for 6 months after the termination of employment is offered only to those qualified beneficiaries who waive COBRA continuation coverage, the employee "loses coverage" on June 1, 1988, so the election period is the same as in Case 1. The difference between Case 2 and Case 3 is that in Case 2 the employee can receive 6 months of employer-paid coverage and then elect to pay for up to an additional 12 months of COBRA continuation coverage, while in Case 3 the employee must choose between 6 months of employer-paid coverage and paying for up to 18 months of COBRA continuation coverage. In all three cases, COBRA continuation coverage need not be provided for more than 18 months after the termination of employment (see Q&A-39 of this section), and in certain circumstances might be provided for a shorter period (see Q&A-38 of this section).

Q-33. Must a covered employee or qualified beneficiary inform the employer or plan administrator of the occurrence of a qualifying event?

A-33. In general, the employer or plan administrator must determine when a qualifying event has occurred. However, each covered employee or qualified beneficiary is responsible for notifying the employer or other plan administrator of the occurrence of a qualifying event that is either a dependent child ceasing to be a dependent child of the covered employee or a divorce or legal separation of a covered employee. If the notice is not sent to the employer or other plan administrator within 60 days after the later of (a) the date of the qualifying event, or (b) the date that the qualified beneficiary would lose coverage on account of the qualifying event, the group health plan does not have to offer the qualified beneficiary an opportunity to elect COBRA continuation coverage. For purposes of this Q&A-33, if more than one qualified beneficiary would lose coverage on account of a divorce or legal separation of a covered employee, a timely notice of the divorce or legal separation that is sent by the covered employee or any one of those qualified beneficiaries will be sufficient to preserve the election rights of all of the qualified beneficiaries.

Q-34. During the election period and before the qualified beneficiary has made an election, must coverage be provided?

A-34. (a) In general, each qualified beneficiary has until at least 60 days after the date that the qualifying event would cause him or her to lose coverage to decide whether to elect COBRA continuation coverage. If the election is made during that period, coverage must be provided from the date that coverage would otherwise have been lost (but see Q&A-35 of this section). This can be accomplished as described in paragraph (b) or (c) of this Q&A-34.

(b) In the case of an indemnity or reimbursement arrangement, the employer can provide for plan coverage during the election period or, if the plan allows retroactive reinstatement, the employer can drop the qualified beneficiary from the plan and reinstate him or her when the election is made. Of course, claims incurred by a qualified beneficiary during the election period do not have to be paid before the election (and, if applicable, payment for the coverage) is made.

(c) In the case of a group health plan that provides health services (such as a Health Maintenance Organization or a walk-in clinic), the plan can require that a qualified beneficiary who has not yet elected and paid for COBRA continuation coverage choose between (1) electing and paying for the coverage or (2) paying the reasonable and customary charge for the plan's services, but only if a qualified beneficiary who chooses to pay for the services will be reimbursed for that payment within 30 days after electing COBRA continuation coverage (and, if applicable, paying any balance due for the coverage). In the alternative, the plan can provide continued coverage and treat the qualified beneficiary's use of the facility as a constructive election. In such a case, the qualified beneficiary is obligated to pay any applicable charge for the coverage, but only if the qualified beneficiary is informed of the meaning of the constructive election before using the facility.

Q-35. Is a waiver before the end of the election period effective to end a qualified beneficiary's election rights?

A-35. A qualified beneficiary who, during the election period, waives COBRA continuation coverage can revoke the waiver at any time before the end of the election period. However, if a qualified beneficiary who waives COBRA continuation coverage later revokes the waiver, coverage need not be provided retroactively (i.e., from the date of the loss of coverage until the waiver is revoked). Waivers and revocations of waivers are considered made on the date that they are sent to the employer or plan administrator, as applicable.

Q-36. Can an employer withhold money or other benefits owed to a qualified beneficiary until the qualified beneficiary either waives COBRA continuation coverage, elects and pays for such coverage, or allows the election period to expire?

A-36. No. An employer must not withhold anything to which a qualified beneficiary is otherwise entitled (by operation of law or other agreement) in order to compel payment for COBRA continuation coverage or to coerce the qualified beneficiary to give up rights to COBRA continuation coverage (including the right to use the full election period to decide whether to elect such coverage). Such a withholding constitutes a failure to comply with section 162(k), and any purported waiver obtained by means of such a withholding is invalid.

Q-37. Can each qualified beneficiary make an independent election under COBRA?

A-37. Yes. Each qualified beneficiary must be offered the opportunity to make an independent election to receive COBRA continuation coverage and, if applicable, an independent election (a) to receive COBRA continuation coverage that is limited to core coverage and (b) to switch to another group health plan during an open enrollment period. However, if a qualified beneficiary who is either a covered employee or the spouse of a covered employee makes an election to provide any other qualified beneficiary with COBRA continuation coverage (whether for core coverage only or core plus non-core coverage), the election shall be binding on that other qualified beneficiary. An election on behalf of a minor child can be made by the child's parent or legal guardian. An election on behalf of a qualified beneficiary who is incapacitated or dies can be made by the legal representative of the qualified beneficiary's estate, as determined under applicable state law, or by the spouse of the qualified beneficiary. The rules of this Q&A-37 are illustrated by the following examples:

Example (1). Assume that employee H and H's spouse are covered under a group health plan immediately before H's termination of employment (for reasons other than gross misconduct), the plan provides only core coverage, and the coverage under the plan will end as a result of the termination of employment. Upon H's termination of employment both H and H's spouse are qualified beneficiaries and each must be allowed to elect COBRA continuation coverage. Thus, H might elect COBRA continuation coverage while the spouse declines to elect such coverage. However, if H elects to provide COBRA continuation coverage for both of them, that election is binding on the spouse, and the spouse cannot decline COBRA continuation coverage. In contrast, H cannot decline COBRA continuation coverage on behalf of H's spouse. Thus, if H does not elect COBRA continuation coverage on behalf of the spouse, the spouse must still be allowed to elect COBRA continuation coverage.

Example (2). The facts are the same as in Example 1, except that coverage under the plan includes both core coverage and non-core coverage, and H and H's spouse have two dependent children who are also covered under the plan immediately before H's termination of employment. All four family members are qualified beneficiaries, each of whom must be offered the opportunity to elect COBRA continuation coverage either with or without non-core coverage. One possible result, therefore, is for the children to continue their full coverage while the parents continue only core coverage. This result can be achieved in a variety of ways, including separate elections by each family member, or a single election by H that binds the entire family.

Duration of COBRA Continuation Coverage

Q-38. How long must COBRA continuation coverage be available to a qualified beneficiary?

A-38. Except for an interruption of coverage in connection with a waiver as described in Q&A-35 of this section, COBRA continuation coverage that has been elected by a qualified beneficiary must extend for at least the period beginning on the date of the qualifying event and ending not before the earliest of the following dates: (a) The last day of the maximum coverage period (see Q&A-39 of this section); (b) the first day for which timely payment is not made to the plan with respect to the qualified beneficiary (see Q&A-48 of this section); (c) the date upon which the employer ceases to maintain any group health plan (including successor plans); (d) the first date after the date of the election upon which the qualified beneficiary is covered (i.e., actually covered, rather than merely eligible to be covered) under any other group health plan that is not maintained by the employer, even if that other coverage is less valuable to the qualified beneficiary than COBRA continuation coverage (e.g., if the other coverage provides no benefits for preexisting conditions); or (e) the date the qualified beneficiary is entitled to Medicare benefits under Title XVIII of the Social Security Act. However, a group health plan can terminate for cause the coverage of a qualified beneficiary receiving COBRA continuation coverage on the same basis that the plan terminates for cause the coverage of similarly situated active employees with respect to whom a qualifying event has not occurred. For purposes of the preceding sentence, termination for cause does not include termination based on a failure to make timely payment to the plan. (See Q& A-48 of this section regarding timely payment.)

Q-39. When does the maximum coverage period end?

A-39. The maximum coverage period ends (a) 18 months after the qualifying event, if the qualifying event that gives rise to COBRA continuation coverage election rights is a termination or reduction of hours; and (b) 36 months after the qualifying event, for any other type of qualifying event. The end of the maximum coverage period is measured from the date of the qualifying event even if the qualifying event does not result in a loss of coverage under the plan until some later date. See also Q&A-40 of this section in the case of multiple qualifying events. Nothing in section 162(k) or this section prohibits a group health plan from providing coverage that continues beyond the end of the maximum coverage period.

Q-40. Can the maximum coverage period ever be expanded?

A-40. No, with one exception. The exception involves a qualifying event that gives rise to an 18-month maximum coverage period and is followed, within that 18-month period, by a second qualifying event (e.g., a death or divorce). In such a case, the original 18-month period is expanded to 36 months, but only for those individuals who were qualified beneficiaries under the group health plan as of the first qualifying event and were covered under the plan at the time of the second qualifying event. No qualifying event can give rise to a maximum coverage period that ends more than 36 months after the date of the first qualifying event. For example, if an employee covered by a group health plan that is subject to COBRA terminates employment (for reasons other than gross misconduct) on December 31, 1987, the termination is a qualifying event giving rise to a maximum coverage period that extends for 18 months to June 30, 1989. If the employee dies after the employee and the employee's spouse and dependent children have elected COBRA continuation coverage and before June 30, 1989, the spouse and children (except anyone among them whose COBRA continuation coverage had already ended for some other reason) will be able to elect COBRA continuation coverage through December 31, 1990.

Q-41. If coverage is provided to a qualified beneficiary after a qualifying event without regard to COBRA continuation coverage (e.g., as a result of state or local law, industry practice, a collective bargaining agreement, or plan procedure), will such alternative coverage extend the maximum coverage period?

A-41. (a) The alternative coverage will not extend the maximum coverage period. The end of the maximum coverage period is measured solely from the date of the qualifying event, as described in Q&A-39 and Q&A-40 of this section.

(b) If the alternative coverage does not satisfy all the requirements for COBRA continuation coverage, the group health plan covering the qualified beneficiary immediately before the qualifying event is not in compliance with section 162(k) unless the qualified beneficiary receiving the alternative coverage was also offered the opportunity to elect COBRA continuation coverage and rejected COBRA continuation coverage in favor of the alternative coverage. At the end of that alternative coverage, the individual need not be offered a COBRA election. However, if the individual is a covered employee and the spouse or a dependent child of the individual would lose that alternative coverage as a result of a qualifying event (such as the death of the covered employee), the spouse or dependent child must be given an opportunity to elect to continue that alternative coverage, with a maximum coverage period of 36 months measured from the date of that qualifying event.

(c) If the alternative coverage does satisfy the requirements for COBRA continuation coverage, it can be credited toward satisfaction of the 18- or 36-month maximum coverage period. Moreover, in the case of a covered employee who receives more than 18 months of alternative coverage that satisfies the requirements for COBRA continuation coverage, if the spouse or a dependent child of the covered employee loses coverage as a result of a second qualifying event (such as the death of the covered employee) that occurs after the 18-month period, that spouse or dependent child need not be given an election to continue coverage.

Q-42. How can an event that occurs before a group health plan becomes subject to section 162(k) affect the maximum coverage period when a later, qualifying event occurs?

A-42. (a) If there are two events that satisfy the conditions set forth in paragraph (b) of this Q&A-42, then the first event is treated as though it were a qualifying event that occurred on the date that the plan became subject to section 162(k) (i.e., with a maximum coverage period that began on that date), so that the second event is not merely a qualifying event but a second qualifying event. This treatment applies solely for purposes of determining the maximum coverage period under Q&A-39 through Q&A-41 of this section in connection with that second qualifying event. It does not give rise to any right to elect COBRA continuation coverage in connection with the first event.

(b) The conditions referred to in paragraph (a) of this Q&A-42 are as follows: (1) The first event is listed in paragraph (b) of Q&A-18 of this section (regarding what is a qualifying event) but occurs before the date that the plan becomes subject to section 162(k), (2) the plan provides coverage to a qualified beneficiary after the first event that continues to or beyond the date that the plan becomes subject to section 162(k), and (3) a second event then occurs and is a qualifying event.

(c) The rule of this Q&A-42 is illustrated by the following examples:

Example (1). Assume that a group health plan became subject to section 162(k) on January 1, 1987. Employee F, who was covered by the plan, voluntarily terminated employment on January 1, 1986, and was given employer-paid coverage that would continue for 5 more years. F's spouse was also to be covered for the 5 years, except that the spouse's coverage would terminate upon divorce or F's death. F dies on January 1, 1988. F's death is a qualifying event, so F's spouse can elect COBRA continuation coverage (unless the election is precluded for some independent reason, such as the spouse's entitlement to Medicare benefits). F's termination of employment on January 1, 1986, is treated as though it were a qualifying event that occurred on January 1, 1987. F's death is thus a second qualifying event, for which the spouse's maximum coverage period ends on January 1, 1990 (i.e., 36 months after the first qualifying event). The spouse can thus elect up to 24 months of COBRA continuation coverage.

Example (2). Assume the same facts as in Example 1, except that F's death occurs after January 1, 1990. The plan does not have to give F's spouse an opportunity to elect COBRA continuation coverage.

Q-43. Must a qualified beneficiary be given the right to enroll in a conversion health plan at the end of the maximum coverage period for COBRA continuation coverage?

A-43. If a qualified beneficiary's COBRA continuation coverage under a group health plan ends as a result of the expiration of the maximum coverage period, the group health plan must, during the 180-day period that ends on that expiration date, provide the qualified beneficiary the option of enrolling under a conversion health plan if such an option is otherwise generally available to similarly situated active employees under the group health plan. If such a conversion option is not otherwise generally available, COBRA does not require that it be made available to qualified beneficiaries.

Paying for COBRA Continuation Coverage

Q-44. Can a qualified beneficiary be required to pay for COBRA continuation coverage?

A-44. Yes. For any period of COBRA continuation coverage, a group health plan can require a qualified beneficiary to pay an amount that does not exceed 102 percent of the applicable premium for that period. The "applicable premium" is defined in section 162(k)(4) of the Code. A group health plan can terminate a qualified beneficiary's COBRA continuation coverage as of the first day of any period for which timely payment is not made to the plan with respect to that qualified beneficiary (see Q&A-38 of this section). For the meaning of "timely payment," see Q&A-48 of this section.

Q-45. After a qualified beneficiary has elected COBRA continuation coverage under a group health plan, can the plan increase the amount that the qualified beneficiary must pay for COBRA continuation coverage?

A-45. Yes, if the applicable premium increases. However, the applicable premium for each determination period must be computed and fixed by the plan before the determination period begins. A determination period is any 12-month period selected by the plan, but it must be applied consistently from year to year. Thus, each qualified beneficiary does not have a separate determination period beginning on the date (or anniversaries of the date) that COBRA continuation coverage begins for that qualified beneficiary.

Q-46. Must a qualified beneficiary be allowed to pay for COBRA continuation coverage in installments?

A-46. Yes. A group health plan must allow a qualified beneficiary to pay for COBRA continuation coverage in monthly installments. A group health plan can also allow qualified beneficiaries the alternative of paying for COBRA continuation coverage at other intervals (e.g., quarterly or semiannually).

Q-47. Can a qualified beneficiary choose to have the first payment for COBRA continuation coverage applied prospectively only?

A-47. No. The first payment for COBRA continuation coverage is applied to the period of coverage beginning immediately after the date that coverage under the plan would have been lost on account of the qualifying event. Of course, if the group health plan allows a qualified beneficiary to waive COBRA continuation coverage for any period before electing to receive COBRA continuation coverage, the first payment is not applied to period of the waiver.

Q-48. What is timely payment for COBRA continuation coverage?

A-48. (a) If a qualified beneficiary's election of COBRA continuation coverage is made after the date of the qualifying event, timely payment for any COBRA continuation coverage during the period before the date of the election means payment that is made to the plan within 45 days after the date of the election. Timely payment for any other period of COBRA continuation coverage is governed by paragraph (b) of this Q&A-48.

(b) In general, timely payment for a period of COBRA continuation coverage under a group health plan means payment that is made to the plan by the date that is 30 days after the first day of that period. However, payment that is made to the plan by a later date is also considered timely payment if either (1) under the terms of the plan, covered employees or qualified beneficiaries are allowed until that later date to pay for their coverage during the period, or (2) under the terms of an arrangement between the employer and an insurance company, Health Maintenance Organization, or other entity that provides plan benefits on the employer's behalf, the employer is allowed until that later date to pay for coverage of similarly situated employees during the period.

§ 1.162-27 Certain employee remuneration in excess of $1,000,000.

(a) Scope. This section provides rules for the application of the $1 million deduction limit under section 162(m) of the Internal Revenue Code. Paragraph (b) of this section provides the general rule limiting deductions under section 162(m). Paragraph (c) of this section provides definitions of generally applicable terms. Paragraph (d) of this section provides an exception from the deduction limit for compensation payable on a commission basis. Paragraph (e) of this section provides an exception for qualified performance-based compensation. Paragraphs (f) and (g) of this section provide special rules for corporations that become publicly held corporations and payments that are subject to section 280G, respectively. Paragraph (h) of this section provides transition rules, including the rules for contracts that are grandfathered and not subject to section 162(m). Paragraph (j) of this section contains the effective date provisions. For rules concerning the deductibility of compensation for services that are not covered by section 162(m) and this section, see section 162(a)(1) and § 1.162-7. This section is not determinative as to whether compensation meets the requirements of section 162(a)(1).

(b) Limitation on deduction. Section 162(m) precludes a deduction under chapter 1 of the Internal Revenue Code by any publicly held corporation for compensation paid to any covered employee to the extent that the compensation for the taxable year exceeds $1,000,000.

(c) Definitions. *(1) Publicly held corporation.* (i) General rule. A publicly held corporation means any corporation issuing any class of common equity securities required to be registered under section 12 of the Exchange Act. A corporation is not considered publicly held if the registration of its equity securities is voluntary. For purposes of this section, whether a corporation is publicly held is determined based solely on whether, as of the last day of its taxable year, the corporation is subject to the reporting obligations of section 12 of the Exchange Act.

(ii) Affiliated groups. A publicly held corporation includes an affiliated group of corporations, as defined in section 1504 (determined without regard to section 1504(b)). For purposes of this section, however, an affiliated group of corporations does not include any subsidiary that is itself a publicly held corporation. Such a publicly held subsidiary, and its subsidiaries (if any), are separately subject to this section. If a covered employee is paid compensation in a taxable year by more than one member of an affiliated group, compensation paid by each member of the affiliated group is aggregated with compensation paid to the covered employee by all other members of the group. Any amount disallowed as a deduction by this section must be prorated among the payor corporations in proportion to the amount of compensation paid to the covered employee by each such corporation in the taxable year.

(2) Covered employee. (i) General rule. A covered employee means any individual who, on the last day of the taxable year, is—

(A) The chief executive officer of the corporation or is acting in such capacity; or

(B) Among the four highest compensated officers (other than the chief executive officer).

(ii) Application of rules of the Securities and Exchange Commission. Whether an individual is the chief executive officer described in paragraph (c)(2)(i)(A) of this section or an officer described in paragraph (c)(2)(i)(B) of this section is determined pursuant to the executive compensation disclosure rules under the Exchange Act.

(3) Compensation. (i) In general. For purposes of the deduction limitation described in paragraph (b) of this section, compensation means the aggregate amount allowable as a deduction under chapter 1 of the Internal Revenue Code for the taxable year (determined without regard to section 162(m)) for remuneration for services performed by a covered employee, whether or not the services were performed during the taxable year.

(ii) Exceptions. Compensation does not include—

(A) Remuneration covered in section 3121(a)(5)(A) through section 3121(a)(5)(D) (concerning remuneration that is not treated as wages for purposes of the Federal Insurance Contributions Act); and

(B) Remuneration consisting of any benefit provided to or on behalf of an employee if, at the time the benefit is provided, it is reasonable to believe that the employee will be able to exclude it from gross income. In addition, compensation does not include salary reduction contributions described in section 3121(v)(1).

(4) Compensation committee. The compensation committee means the committee of directors (including any subcommittee of directors) of the publicly held corporation that has the authority to establish and administer performance goals described in paragraph (e)(2) of this section, and to certify that performance goals are attained, as described in paragraph (e)(5) of this section. A committee of directors is not treated as failing to have the authority to establish performance goals merely because the goals are ratified by the board of directors of the publicly held corporation or, if applicable, any other committee of the board of directors. See paragraph (e)(3) of this section for rules concerning the composition of the compensation committee.

(5) Exchange Act. The Exchange Act means the Securities Exchange Act of 1934.

(6) Examples. This paragraph (c) may be illustrated by the following examples:

Example (1). Corporation X is a publicly held corporation with a July 1 to June 30 fiscal year. For Corporation X's taxable year ending on June 30, 1995, Corporation X pays compensation of $2,000,000 to A, an employee. However, A's compensation is not required to be reported to shareholders under the executive compensation disclosure rules of the Exchange Act because A is neither the chief executive officer nor one of the four highest compensated officers employed on the last day of the taxable year. A's compensation is not subject to the deduction limitation of paragraph (b) of this section.

Example (2). C, a covered employee, performs services and receives compensation from Corporations X, Y, and Z, members of an affiliated group of corporations. Corporation X, the parent corporation, is a publicly held corporation. The total compensation paid to C from all affiliated group members is $3,000,000 for the taxable year, of which Corporation X pays $1,500,000; Corporation Y pays $900,000; and Corporation Z pays $600,000. Because the compensation paid by all affiliated group members is aggregated for purposes of section 162(m), $2,000,000 of the aggregate compensation paid is nondeductible. Corporations X, Y, and Z each are treated as paying a ratable portion of the nondeductible compensation. Thus, two thirds of each corporation's payment will be nondeductible. Corporation X has a nondeductible compensation expense of $1,000,000 ($1,500,000 × $2,000,000/$3,000,000). Corporation Y has a nondeductible compensation expense of $600,000 ($900,000 × $2,000,000/$3,000,000). Corporation Z has a nondeductible compensation expense of $400,000 ($600,000 × $2,000,000/$3,000,000).

Example (3). Corporation W, a calendar year taxpayer, has total assets equal to or exceeding $5 million and a class of equity security held of record by 500 or more persons on December 31, 1994. However, under the Exchange Act, Corporation W is not required to file a registration statement with respect to that security until April 30, 1995. Thus, Corporation W is not a publicly held corporation on December 31, 1994, but is a publicly held corporation on December 31, 1995.

Example (4). The facts are the same as in Example 3, except that on December 15, 1996, Corporation W files with the Securities and Exchange Commission to disclose that Corporation W is no longer required to be registered under section 12 of the Exchange Act and to terminate its registration of securities under that provision. Because Corporation W is no longer subject to Exchange Act reporting obligations as of December 31, 1996, Corporation W is not a publicly held corporation for taxable year 1996, even though the registration of Corporation W's securities does not terminate until 90 days after Corporation W files with the Securities and Exchange Commission.

(d) Exception for compensation paid on a commission basis. The deduction limit in paragraph (b) of this section shall not apply to any compensation paid on a commission basis. For this purpose, compensation is paid on a commission basis if the facts and circumstances show that it is paid solely on account of income generated directly by the individual performance of the individual to whom the compensation is paid. Compensation does not fail to be attributable directly to the individual merely because support services, such as secretarial or research services, are utilized in generating the income. However, if compensation is paid on account of broader performance standards, such as income produced by a business unit of the corporation, the compensation does not qualify for the exception provided under this paragraph (d).

(e) Exception for qualified performance-based compensation. *(1) In general.* The deduction limit in paragraph (b) of this section does not apply to qualified performance-based compensation. Qualified performance-based compensation is compensation that meets all of the requirements of paragraphs (e)(2) through (e)(5) of this section.

(2) Performance goal requirement. (i) Preestablished goal. Qualified performance-based compensation must be paid solely on account of the attainment of one or more preestablished, objective performance goals. A performance goal is considered preestablished if it is established in writing by the compensation committee not later than 90 days after the commencement of the period of service to which the performance goal relates, provided that the outcome is substantially uncertain at the time the compensation committee actually establishes the goal. However, in no event will a performance goal be considered to be preestablished if it is established after 25 percent of the period of service (as scheduled in good faith at the time the goal is established) has elapsed. A performance goal is objective if a third party having knowledge of the relevant facts could determine whether the goal is met. Performance goals can be based on one or more business criteria that apply to the individual, a business unit, or the corporation as a whole. Such business criteria could include, for example, stock price, market share, sales, earnings per share, return on equity, or costs. A performance goal need not, however, be based upon an increase or positive result under a business criterion and could include, for example, maintaining the status quo or limiting economic losses (measured, in each case, by reference to a specific business criterion). A performance goal does not include the mere continued employment of the covered employee. Thus, a vesting provision based solely on continued employment would not constitute a performance goal. See paragraph (e)(2)(vi) of this section for rules on compensation that is based on an increase in the price of stock.

(ii) Objective compensation formula. A preestablished performance goal must state, in terms of an objective formula or standard, the method for computing the amount of compensation payable to the employee if the goal is attained. A formula or standard is objective if a third party having knowledge of the relevant performance results could calculate the amount to be paid to the employee. In addition, a formula or standard must specify the individual employees or class of employees to which it applies.

(iii) Discretion. (A) The terms of an objective formula or standard must preclude discretion to increase the amount of compensation payable that would otherwise be due upon attainment of the goal. A performance goal is not discretionary for purposes of this paragraph (e)(2)(iii) merely because the compensation committee reduces or eliminates the compensation or other economic benefit that was due upon attainment of the goal. However, the exercise of negative discretion with respect to one employee is not permitted to result in an increase in the amount payable to another employee. Thus, for example, in the case of a bonus pool, if the amount payable to each employee is stated in terms of a percentage of the pool, the sum of these individual percentages of the pool is not permitted to exceed 100 percent. If the terms of an objective formula or standard fail to preclude discretion to increase the amount of compensation merely because the amount of compensation to be paid upon attainment of the performance goal is based, in whole or in part, on a percentage of salary or base pay and the dollar amount of the salary or base pay is not fixed at the time the performance goal is established, then the objective formula or standard will not be considered discretionary for purposes of this paragraph (e)(2)(iii) if the maximum dollar amount to be paid is fixed at that time.

(B) If compensation is payable upon or after the attainment of a performance goal, and a change is made to accelerate the payment of compensation to an earlier date after the attainment of the goal, the change will be treated as an increase in the amount of compensation, unless the amount of compensation paid is discounted to reasonably reflect the time value of money. If compensation is payable upon or after the attainment of a performance goal, and a change is made to defer the payment of compensation to a later date, any amount paid in excess of the amount that was originally owed to the employee will not be treated as an increase in the amount of compensation if the additional amount is based either on a reasonable rate of interest or on one or more predetermined actual investments (whether or not assets associated with the amount originally owed are actually invested therein) such that the amount payable by the employer at the later date will be based on the actual rate of return of a specific investment (including any decrease as well as any increase in the value of an investment). If compensation is payable in the form of property, a change in the timing of the transfer of that property after the attainment of the goal will not be treated as an increase in the amount of compensation for purposes of this paragraph (e)(2)(iii). Thus, for example, if the terms of a stock grant provide for stock to be transferred after the attainment of a performance goal and the transfer of the stock also is subject to a vesting schedule, a change in the vesting schedule that either accelerates or defers the transfer of stock will not be treated as an increase in the amount of compensation payable under the performance goal.

(C) Compensation attributable to a stock option, stock appreciation right, or other stock-based compensation does not fail to satisfy the requirements of this paragraph (e)(2) to the extent that a change in the grant or award is made to reflect a change in corporate capitalization, such as a stock split or dividend, or a corporate transaction, such as any merger of a corporation into another corporation, any consolidation of two or more corporations into another corporation, any separation of a corporation (including a spinoff or other distribution of stock or property by a corporation), any reorganization of a corporation (whether or not such reorganization comes within the definition of such term in section 368), or any partial or complete liquidation by a corporation.

(iv) Grant-by-grant determination. The determination of whether compensation satisfies the requirements of this paragraph (e)(2) generally shall be made on a grant-by-grant basis. Thus, for example, whether compensation attributable to a stock option grant satisfies the requirements of this paragraph (e)(2) generally is determined on the basis of the particular grant made and without regard to the terms of any other option grant, or other grant of compensation, to the same or another employee. As a further example, except as provided in paragraph (e)(2)(vi), whether a grant of restricted stock or other stock-based compensation satisfies the requirements of this paragraph (e)(2) is determined without regard to whether dividends, dividend equivalents, or other similar distributions with respect to stock, on such stock-based compensation are payable prior to the attainment of the performance goal. Dividends, dividend equivalents, or other similar distributions with respect to stock that are treated as separate grants under this paragraph (e)(2)(iv) are not performance-based compensation unless they separately satisfy the requirements of this paragraph (e)(2).

(v) Compensation contingent upon attainment of performance goal. Compensation does not satisfy the requirements of this paragraph (e)(2) if the facts and circumstances indicate that the employee would receive all or part of the compensation regardless of whether the performance goal is attained. Thus, if the payment of compensation under a grant or award is only nominally or partially contingent on attaining a performance goal, none of the compensation payable under the grant or award will be considered performance-based. For example, if an employee is entitled to a bonus under either of two arrangements, where payment under a nonperformance-based arrangement is contingent upon the failure to attain the performance goals under an otherwise performance-based arrangement, then neither arrangement provides for compensation that satisfies the requirements of this paragraph (e)(2). Compensation does not fail to be qualified performance-based compensation merely because the plan allows the compensation to be payable upon death, disability, or change of ownership or control, although compensation actually paid on account of those events prior to the attainment of the performance goal would not satisfy the requirements of this paragraph (e)(2). As an exception to the general rule set forth in the first sentence of paragraph (e)(2)(iv) of this section, the facts-and-circumstances determination referred to in the first sentence of this paragraph (e)(2)(v) is made taking into account all plans, arrangements, and agreements that provide for compensation to the employee.

(vi) Application of requirements to stock options and stock appreciation rights. (A) In general. Compensation attributable to a stock option or a stock appreciation right is deemed to satisfy the requirements of this paragraph (e)(2) if the grant or award is made by the compensation committee; the plan under which the option or right is granted states the maximum number of shares with respect to which options or rights may be granted during a specified period to any employee; and, under the terms of the option or right, the amount of compensation the employee could receive is based solely on an increase in the value of the stock after the date of the grant or award. Conversely, if the amount of compensation the employee will receive under the grant or award is not based solely on an increase in the value of the stock after the date of grant or award (e.g., in the case of restricted stock, or an option that is granted with an exercise price that is less than the fair market value of the stock as of the date of grant), none of the compensation attributable to the grant or award is qualified performance-based compensation because it does not satisfy the requirement of this paragraph (e)(2)(vi)(A). Whether a stock option grant is based solely on an increase in the value of the stock after the date of grant is determined without regard to any dividend equivalent that may be payable, provided that payment of the dividend equivalent is not made contingent on the exercise of the option. The rule that the compensation attributable to a stock option or stock appreciation right must be based solely on an increase in the value of the stock after the date of grant or award does not apply if the grant or award is made on account of, or if the vesting or exercisability of the grant or award is contingent on, the attainment of a performance goal that satisfies the requirements of this paragraph (e)(2).

(B) Cancellation and repricing. Compensation attributable to a stock option or stock appreciation right does not satisfy the requirements of this paragraph (e)(2) to the extent that the number of options granted exceeds the maximum number of shares for which options may be granted to the employee as specified in the plan. If an option is canceled, the canceled option continues to be counted against the maximum number of shares for which options may be granted to the employee under the plan. If, after grant, the exercise price of an option is reduced, the transaction is treated as a cancellation of the option and a grant of a new option. In such case, both the option that is deemed to be canceled and the option that is deemed to be granted reduce the maximum number of shares for which options may be granted to the employee under the plan. This paragraph (e)(2)(vi)(B) also applies in the case of a stock appreciation right where, after the award is made, the base amount on which stock appreciation is calculated is reduced to reflect a reduction in the fair market value of stock.

(vii) Examples. This paragraph (e)(2) may be illustrated by the following examples:

Example (1). No later than 90 days after the start of a fiscal year, but while the outcome is substantially uncertain, Corporation S establishes a bonus plan under which A, the chief executive officer, will receive a cash bonus of

$500,000, if year-end corporate sales are increased by at least 5 percent. The compensation committee retains the right, if the performance goal is met, to reduce the bonus payment to A if, in its judgment, other subjective factors warrant a reduction. The bonus will meet the requirements of this paragraph (e)(2).

Example (2). The facts are the same as in Example 1, except that the bonus is based on a percentage of Corporation S's total sales for the fiscal year. Because Corporation S is virtually certain to have some sales for the fiscal year, the outcome of the performance goal is not substantially uncertain, and therefore the bonus does not meet the requirements of this paragraph (e)(2).

Example (3). The facts are the same as in Example 1, except that the bonus is based on a percentage of Corporation S's total profits for the fiscal year. Although some sales are virtually certain for virtually all public companies, it is substantially uncertain whether a company will have profits for a specified future period even if the company has a history of profitability. Therefore, the bonus will meet the requirements of this paragraph (e)(2).

Example (4). B is the general counsel of Corporation R, which is engaged in patent litigation with Corporation S. Representatives of Corporation S have informally indicated to Corporation R a willingness to settle the litigation for $50,000,000. Subsequently, the compensation committee of Corporation R agrees to pay B a bonus if B obtains a formal settlement for at least $50,000,000. The bonus to B does not meet the requirement of this paragraph (e)(2) because the performance goal was not established at a time when the outcome was substantially uncertain.

Example (5). Corporation S, a public utility, adopts a bonus plan for selected salaried employees that will pay a bonus at the end of a 3-year period of $750,000 each if, at the end of the 3 years, the price of S stock has increased by 10 percent. The plan also provides that the 10-percent goal will automatically adjust upward or downward by the percentage change in a published utilities index. Thus, for example, if the published utilities index shows a net increase of 5 percent over a 3-year period, then the salaried employees would receive a bonus only if Corporation S stock has increased by 15 percent. Conversely, if the published utilities index shows a net decrease of 5 percent over a 3-year period, then the salaried employees would receive a bonus if Corporation S stock has increased by 5 percent. Because these automatic adjustments in the performance goal are preestablished, the bonus meets the requirement of this paragraph (e)(2), notwithstanding the potential changes in the performance goal.

Example (6). The facts are the same as in Example 5, except that the bonus plan provides that, at the end of the 3-year period, a bonus of $750,000 will be paid to each salaried employee if either the price of Corporation S stock has increased by 10 percent or the earnings per share on Corporation S stock have increased by 5 percent. If both the earnings-per-share goal and the stock-price goal are preestablished, the compensation committee's discretion to choose to pay a bonus under either of the two goals does not cause any bonus paid under the plan to fail to meet the requirement of this paragraph (e)(2) because each goal independently meets the requirements of this paragraph (e)(2). The choice to pay under either of the two goals is tantamount to the discretion to choose not to pay under one of the goals, as provided in paragraph (e)(2)(iii) of this section.

Example (7). Corporation U establishes a bonus plan under which a specified class of employees will participate in a bonus pool if certain preestablished performance goals are attained. The amount of the bonus pool is determined under an objective formula. Under the terms of the bonus plan, the compensation committee retains the discretion to determine the fraction of the bonus pool that each employee may receive. The bonus plan does not satisfy the requirements of this paragraph (e)(2). Although the aggregate amount of the bonus plan is determined under an objective formula, a third party could not determine the amount that any individual could receive under the plan.

Example (8). The facts are the same as in Example 7, except that the bonus plan provides that a specified share of the bonus pool is payable to each employee, and the total of these shares does not exceed 100% of the pool. The bonus plan satisfies the requirements of this paragraph (e)(2). In addition, the bonus plan will satisfy the requirements of this paragraph (e)(2) even if the compensation committee retains the discretion to reduce the compensation payable to any individual employee, provided that a reduction in the amount of one employee's bonus does not result in an increase in the amount of any other employee's bonus.

Example (9). Corporation V establishes a stock option plan for salaried employees. The terms of the stock option plan specify that no salaried employee shall receive options for more than 100,000 shares over any 3-year period. The compensation committee grants options for 50,000 shares to each of several salaried employees. The exercise price of each option is equal to or greater than the fair market value at the time of each grant. Compensation attributable to the exercise of the options satisfies the requirements of this paragraph (e)(2). If, however, the terms of the options provide that the exercise price is less than fair market value at the date of grant, no compensation attributable to the exercise of those options satisfies the requirements of this paragraph (e)(2) unless issuance or exercise of the options was contingent upon the attainment of a preestablished performance goal that satisfies this paragraph (e)(2).

Example (10). The facts are the same as in Example 9, except that, within the same 3-year grant period, the fair market value of Corporation V stock is significantly less than the exercise price of the options. The compensation committee reprices those options to that lower current fair market value of Corporation V stock. The repricing of the options for 50,000 shares held by each salaried employee is treated as the grant of new options for an additional 50,000 shares to each employee. Thus, each of the salaried employees is treated as having received grants for 100,000 shares. Consequently, if any additional options are granted to those employees during the 3-year period, compensation attributable to the exercise of those additional options would not satisfy the requirements of this paragraph (e)(2). The results would be the same if the compensation committee canceled the outstanding options and issued new options to the same employees that were exercisable at the fair market value of Corporation V stock on the date of reissue.

Example (11). Corporation W maintains a plan under which each participating employee may receive incentive stock options, nonqualified stock options, stock appreciation rights, or grants of restricted Corporation W stock. The plan specifies that each participating employee may receive options, stock appreciation rights, restricted stock, or any combination of each, for no more than 20,000 shares over the life of the plan. The plan provides that stock options may be granted with an exercise price of less than, equal to, or greater than fair market value on the date of grant. Options granted with an exercise price equal to, or greater than, fair market value on the date of grant do not fail to meet the requirements of this paragraph (e)(2) merely because the compensation committee has the discretion to determine the types of awards (i.e., options, rights, or restricted stock) to be granted to each employee or the discretion to issue options or make other compensation awards under the plan that would not meet the requirements of this paragraph (e)(2). Whether an option granted under the plan satisfies the requirements of this paragraph (e)(2) is determined on the basis of the specific terms of the option and without regard to other options or awards under the plan.

Example (12). Corporation X maintains a plan under which stock appreciation rights may be awarded to key employees. The plan permits the compensation committee to make awards under which the amount of compensation payable to the employee is equal to the increase in the stock price plus a percentage "gross up" intended to offset the tax liability of the employee. In addition, the plan permits the compensation committee to make awards under which the amount of compensation payable to the employee is equal to the increase in the stock price, based on the highest price, which is defined as the highest price paid for Corporation X stock (or offered in a tender offer or other arms-length offer) during the 90 days preceding exercise. Compensation attributable to awards under the plan satisfies the requirements of paragraph (e)(2)(vi) of this section, provided that the terms of the plan specify the maximum number of shares for which awards may be made.

Example (13). Corporation W adopts a plan under which a bonus will be paid to the CEO only if there is a 10% increase in earnings per share during the performance period. The plan provides that earnings per share will be calculated without regard to any change in accounting standards that may be required by the Financial Accounting Standards Board after the goal is established. After the goal is established, such a change in accounting standards occurs. Corporation W's reported earnings, for purposes of determining earnings per share under the plan, are adjusted pursuant to this plan provision to factor out this change in standards. This adjustment will not be considered an exercise of impermissible discretion because it is made pursuant to the plan provision.

Example (14). Corporation x adopts a performance-based incentive pay plan with a four-year performance period. Bonuses under the plan are scheduled to be paid in the first year after the end of the performance period (year 5). However, in the second year of the performance period, the compensation committee determines that any bonuses payable in year 5 will instead, for bona fide business reasons, be paid in year 10. The compensation committee also determines that any compensation that would have been payable in year 5 will be adjusted to reflect the delay in payment. The adjustment will be based on the greater of the future rate of return of a specified mutual fund that invests in blue chip stocks or of a specified venture capital investment over the five-year deferral period. Each of these investments, considered by itself, is a predetermined actual investment because it is based on the future rate of return of an actual investment. However, the adjustment in this case is not based on predetermined actual investments within the meaning of paragraph (e)(2)(iii)(B) of this section because the amount payable by Corporation X in year 10 will be based on the greater of the two investment returns and, thus, will not be based on the actual rate of return on either specific investment.

Example (15). The facts are the same as in Example 14, except that the increase will be based on Moody's average corporate bond yield over the five-year deferral period. Because this index reflects a reasonable rate of interest, the increase in the compensation payable that is based on the index's rate of return is not considered an impermissible increase in the amount of compensation payable under the formula.

Example (16). The facts are the same as in Example 14, except that the increase will be based on the rate of return for the Standard & Poor's 500 Index. This index does not measure interest rates and thus does not represent a reasonable rate of interest. In addition, this index does not represent an actual investment. Therefore, any additional compensation payable based on the rate of return of this index will result in an impermissible increase in the amount payable under the formula. If, in contrast, the increase were based on the rate of return of an existing mutual fund that is invested in a manner that seeks to approximate the Standard & Poor's 500 Index, the increase would be based on a predetermined actual investment within the meaning of paragraph (e)(2)(iii)(B) of this section and thus would not result in an impermissible increase in the amount payable under the formula.

(3) Outside directors. (i) General rule. The performance goal under which compensation is paid must be established by a compensation committee comprised solely of two or more outside directors. A director is an outside director if the director—

(A) Is not a current employee of the publicly held corporation;

(B) Is not a former employee of the publicly held corporation who receives compensation for prior services (other than benefits under a tax-qualified retirement plan) during the taxable year;

(C) Has not been an officer of the publicly held corporation; and

(D) Does not receive remuneration from the publicly held corporation, either directly or indirectly, in any capacity other than as a director. For this purpose, remuneration includes any payment in exchange for goods or services.

(ii) Remuneration received. For purposes of this paragraph (e)(3), remuneration is received, directly or indirectly, by a director in each of the following circumstances:

(A) If remuneration is paid, directly or indirectly, to the director personally or to an entity in which the director has a beneficial ownership interest of greater than 50 percent. For this purpose, remuneration is considered paid when actually paid (and throughout the remainder of that taxable year of the corporation) and, if earlier, throughout the period when a contract or agreement to pay remuneration is outstanding.

(B) If remuneration, other than de minimis remuneration, was paid by the publicly held corporation in its preceding taxable year to an entity in which the director has a beneficial ownership interest of at least 5 percent but not more than 50 percent. For this purpose, remuneration is considered paid when actually paid or, if earlier, when the publicly held corporation becomes liable to pay it.

(C) If remuneration, other than de minimis remuneration, was paid by the publicly held corporation in its preceding taxable year to an entity by which the director is employed or self-employed other than as a director. For this purpose, remuneration is considered paid when actually paid or, if earlier, when the publicly held corporation becomes liable to pay it.

(iii) De minimis remuneration. (A) In general. For purposes of paragraphs (e)(3)(ii)(B) and (C) of this section, remuneration that was paid by the publicly held corporation in its preceding taxable year to an entity is de minimis if payments to the entity did not exceed 5 percent of the gross revenue of the entity for its taxable year ending with or within that preceding taxable year of the publicly held corporation.

(B) Remuneration for personal services and substantial owners. Notwithstanding paragraph (e)(3)(iii)(A) of this section, remuneration in excess of $60,000 is not de minimis if the remuneration is paid to an entity described in paragraph (e)(3)(ii)(B) of this section, or is paid for personal services to an entity described in paragraph (e)(3)(ii)(C) of this section.

(iv) Remuneration for personal services. For purposes of paragraph (e)(3)(iii)(B) of this section, remuneration from a publicly held corporation is for personal services if—

(A) The remuneration is paid to an entity for personal or professional services, consisting of legal, accounting, investment banking, and management consulting services (and other similar services that may be specified by the Commissioner in revenue rulings, notices, or other guidance published in the Internal Revenue Bulletin), performed for the publicly held corporation, and the remuneration is not for services that are incidental to the purchase of goods or to the purchase of services that are not personal services; and

(B) The director performs significant services (whether or not as an employee) for the corporation, division, or similar organization (within the entity) that actually provides the services described in paragraph (e)(3)(iv)(A) of this section to the publicly held corporation, or more than 50 percent of the entity's gross revenues (for the entity's preceding taxable year) are derived from that corporation, subsidiary, or similar organization.

(v) Entity defined. For purposes of this paragraph (e)(3), entity means an organization that is a sole proprietorship, trust, estate, partnership, or corporation. The term also includes an affiliated group of corporations as defined in section 1504 (determined without regard to section 1504(b)) and a group of organizations that would be an affiliated group but for the fact that one or more of the organizations are not incorporated. However, the aggregation rules referred to in the preceding sentence do not apply for purposes of determining whether a director has a beneficial ownership interest of at least 5 percent or greater than 50 percent.

(vi) Employees and former officers. Whether a director is an employee or a former officer is determined on the basis of the facts at the time that the individual is serving as a director on the compensation committee. Thus, a director is not precluded from being an outside director solely because the director is a former officer of a corporation that previously was an affiliated corporation of the publicly held corporation. For example, a director of a parent corporation of an affiliated group is not precluded from being an outside director solely because that director is a former officer of an affiliated subsidiary that was spun off or liquidated. However, an outside director would no longer be an outside director if a corporation in which the director was previously an officer became an affiliated corporation of the publicly held corporation.

(vii) Officer. Solely for purposes of this paragraph (e)(3), officer means an administrative executive who is or was in regular and continued service. The term implies continuity of service and excludes those employed for a special and single transaction. An individual who merely has (or had) the title of officer but not the authority of an officer is not considered an officer. The determination of whether an individual is or was an officer is based on all the of facts and circumstances in the particular case, including without limitation the source of the individual's authority, the term for which the individual is elected or appointed, and the nature and extent of the individual's duties.

(viii) Members of affiliated groups. For purposes of this paragraph (e)(3), the outside directors of the publicly held member of an affiliated group are treated as the outside directors of all members of the affiliated group.

(ix) Examples. This paragraph (e)(3) may be illustrated by the following examples:

Example (1). Corporations X and Y are members of an affiliated group of corporations as defined in section 1504, until July 1, 1994, when Y is sold to another group. Prior to the sale, A served as an officer of Corporation Y. After July 1, 1994, A is not treated as a former officer of Corporation X by reason of having been an officer of Y.

Example (2). Corporation Z, a calendar-year taxpayer, uses the services of a law firm by which B is employed, but in which B has a less-than-5-percent ownership interest. The law firm reports income on a July 1 to June 30 basis. Corporation Z appoints B to serve on its compensation committee for calendar year 1998 after determining that, in calendar year 1997, it did not become liable to the law firm for remuneration exceeding the lesser of $60,000 or five percent of the law firm's gross revenue (calculated for the year ending June 30, 1997). On October 1, 1998, Corporation Z becomes liable to pay remuneration of $50,000 to the law firm on June 30, 1999. For the year ending June 30, 1998, the law firm's gross revenue was less than $1 million. Thus, in calendar year 1999, B is not an outside director. However, B may satisfy the requirements for an outside director in calendar year 2000, if, in calendar year 1999, Corporation Z does not become liable to the law firm for additional remuneration. This is because the remuneration actually paid on June 30, 1999 was considered paid on October 1, 1998 under paragraph (e)(3)(ii)(C) of this section.

Example (3). Corporation Z, a publicly held corporation, purchases goods from Corporation A. D, an executive and less-than-5-percent owner of Corporation A, sits on the board of directors of Corporation Z and on its compensation committee. For 1997, Corporation Z obtains representations to the effect that D is not eligible for any commission for D's sales to Corporation Z and that, for purposes of determining D's compensation for 1997, Corporation A's sales to Corporation Z are not otherwise treated differently than sales to other customers of Corporation A (including its affiliates, if any) or are irrelevant. In addition, Corporation Z has no reason to believe that these representations are inaccurate or that it is otherwise paying remuneration indirectly to D personally. Thus, in 1997, no remuneration is considered paid by Corporation Z indirectly to D personally under paragraph (e)(3)(ii)(A) of this section.

Example (4). (i) Corporation W, a publicly held corporation, purchases goods from Corporation T. C, an executive and less-than-5-percent owner of Corporation T, sits on the board of directors of Corporation W and on its compensation committee. Corporation T develops a new product and agrees on January 1, 1998 to pay C a bonus of $500,000 if Corporation W contracts to purchase the product. Even if Corporation W purchases the new product, sales to Corporation W will represent less than 5 percent of Corporation T's gross revenues. In 1999, Corporation W contracts to purchase the new product and, in 2000, C receives the

$500,000 bonus from Corporation T. In 1998, 1999, and 2000, Corporation W does not obtain any representations relating to indirect remuneration to C personally (such as the representations described in Example 3).

(ii) Thus, in 1998, 1999, and 2000, remuneration is considered paid by Corporation W indirectly to C personally under paragraph (e)(3)(ii)(A) of this section. Accordingly, in 1998, 1999, and 2000, C is not an outside director of Corporation W. The result would have been the same if Corporation W had obtained appropriate representations but nevertheless had reason to believe that it was paying remuneration indirectly to C personally.

Example (5). Corporation R, a publicly held corporation, purchases utility service from Corporation Q, a public utility. The chief executive officer, and less-than-5-percent owner, of Corporation Q is a director of Corporation R. Corporation R pays Corporation Q more than $60,000 per year for the utility service, but less than 5 percent of Corporation Q's gross revenues. Because utility services are not personal services, the fees paid are not subject to the $60,000 de minimis rule for remuneration for personal services within the meaning of paragraph (e)(3)(iii)(B) of this section. Thus, the chief executive officer qualifies as an outside director of Corporation R, unless disqualified on some other basis.

Example (6). Corporation A, a publicly held corporation, purchases management consulting services from Division S of Conglomerate P. The chief financial officer of Division S is a director of Corporation A. Corporation A pays more than $60,000 per year for the management consulting services, but less than 5 percent of Conglomerate P's gross revenues. Because management consulting services are personal services within the meaning of paragraph (e)(3)(iv)(A) of this section, and the chief financial officer performs significant services for Division S, the fees paid are subject to the $60,000 de minimis rule as remuneration for personal services. Thus, the chief financial officer does not qualify as an outside director of Corporation A.

Example (7). The facts are the same as in Example 6, except that the chief executive officer, and less-than-5-percent owner, of the parent company of Conglomerate P is a director of Corporation A and does not perform significant services for Division S. If the gross revenues of Division S do not constitute more than 50 percent of the gross revenues of Conglomerate P for P's preceding taxable year, the chief executive officer will qualify as an outside director of Corporation A, unless disqualified on some other basis.

(4) Shareholder approval requirement. (i) General rule. The material terms of the performance goal under which the compensation is to be paid must be disclosed to and subsequently approved by the shareholders of the publicly held corporation before the compensation is paid. The requirements of this paragraph (e)(4) are not satisfied if the compensation would be paid regardless of whether the material terms are approved by shareholders. The material terms include the employees eligible to receive compensation; a description of the business criteria on which the performance goal is based; and either the maximum amount of compensation that could be paid to any employee or the formula used to calculate the amount of compensation to be paid to the employee if the performance goal is attained (except that, in the case of a formula based, in whole or in part, on a percentage of salary or base pay, the maximum dollar amount of compensation that could be paid to the employee must be disclosed).

(ii) Eligible employees. Disclosure of the employees eligible to receive compensation need not be so specific as to identify the particular individuals by name. A general description of the class of eligible employees by title or class is sufficient, such as the chief executive officer and vice presidents, or all salaried employees, all executive officers, or all key employees.

(iii) Description of business criteria. (A) In general. Disclosure of the business criteria on which the performance goal is based need not include the specific targets that must be satisfied under the performance goal. For example, if a bonus plan provides that a bonus will be paid if earnings per share increase by 10 percent, the 10-percent figure is a target that need not be disclosed to shareholders. However, in that case, disclosure must be made that the bonus plan is based on an earnings-per-share business criterion. In the case of a plan under which employees may be granted stock options or stock appreciation rights, no specific description of the business criteria is required if the grants or awards are based on a stock price that is no less than current fair market value.

(B) Disclosure of confidential information. The requirements of this paragraph (e)(4) may be satisfied even though information that otherwise would be a material term of a performance goal is not disclosed to shareholders, provided that the compensation committee determines that the information is confidential commercial or business information, the disclosure of which would have an adverse effect on the publicly held corporation. Whether disclosure would adversely affect the corporation is determined on the basis of the facts and circumstances. If the compensation committee makes such a determination, the disclosure to shareholders must state the compensation committee's belief that the information is confidential commercial or business information, the disclosure of which would adversely affect the company. In addition, the ability not to disclose confidential information does not eliminate the requirement that disclosure be made of the maximum amount of compensation that is payable to an individual under a performance goal. Confidential information does not include the identity of an executive or the class of executives to which a performance goal applies or the amount of compensation that is payable if the goal is satisfied.

(iv) Description of compensation. Disclosure as to the compensation payable under a performance goal must be specific enough so that shareholders can determine the maximum amount of compensation that could be paid to any employee during a specified period. If the terms of the performance goal do not provide for a maximum dollar amount, the disclosure must include the formula under which the compensation would be calculated. Thus, for example, if compensation attributable to the exercise of stock options is equal to the difference in the exercise price and the current value of the stock, disclosure would be required of the maximum number of shares for which grants may be made to any employee and the exercise price of those options (e.g., fair market value on date of grant). In that case, shareholders could calculate the maximum amount of compensation that would be attributable to the exercise of options on the basis of their assumptions as to the future stock price.

(v) Disclosure requirements of the securities and exchange commission. To the extent not otherwise specifically provided in this paragraph (e)(4), whether the material terms of a performance goal are adequately disclosed to shareholders is determined under the same standards as apply under the Exchange Act.

(vi) Frequency of disclosure. Once the material terms of a performance goal are disclosed to and approved by shareholders, no additional disclosure or approval is required unless the compensation committee changes the material terms of the performance goal. If, however, the compensation committee has authority to change the targets under a performance goal after shareholder approval of the goal, material terms of the performance goal must be disclosed to and reapproved by shareholders no later than the first shareholder meeting that occurs in the fifth year following the year in which shareholders previously approved the performance goal.

(vii) Shareholder vote. For purposes of this paragraph (e)(4), the material terms of a performance goal are approved by shareholders if, in a separate vote, a majority of the votes cast on the issue (including abstentions to the extent abstentions are counted as voting under applicable state law) are cast in favor of approval.

(viii) Members of affiliated group. For purposes of this paragraph (e)(4), the shareholders of the publicly held member of the affiliated group are treated as the shareholders of all members of the affiliated group.

(ix) Examples. This paragraph (e)(4) may be illustrated by the following examples:

Example (1). Corporation X adopts a plan that will pay a specified class of its executives an annual cash bonus based on the overall increase in corporate sales during the year. Under the terms of the plan, the cash bonus of each executive equals $100,000 multiplied by the number of percentage points by which sales increase in the current year when compared to the prior year. Corporation X discloses to its shareholders prior to the vote both the class of executives eligible to receive awards and the annual formula of $100,000 multiplied by the percentage increase in sales. This disclosure meets the requirements of this paragraph (e)(4). Because the compensation committee does not have the authority to establish a different target under the plan, Corporation X need not redisclose to its shareholders and obtain their reapproval of the material terms of the plan until those material terms are changed.

Example (2). The facts are the same as in Example 1 except that Corporation X discloses only that bonuses will be paid on the basis of the annual increase in sales. This disclosure does not meet the requirements of this paragraph (e)(4) because it does not include the formula for calculating the compensation or a maximum amount of compensation to be paid if the performance goal is satisfied.

Example (3). Corporation Y adopts an incentive compensation plan in 1995 that will pay a specified class of its executives a bonus every 3 years based on the following 3 factors: increases in earnings per share, reduction in costs for specified divisions, and increases in sales by specified divisions. The bonus is payable in cash or in Corporation Y stock, at the option of the executive. Under the terms of the plan, prior to the beginning of each 3-year period, the compensation committee determines the specific targets under each of the three factors (i.e., the amount of the increase in earnings per share, the reduction in costs, and the amount of sales) that must be met in order for the executives to receive a bonus. Under the terms of the plan, the compensation committee retains the discretion to determine whether a bonus will be paid under any one of the goals. The terms of the plan also specify that no executive may receive a bonus in excess of $1,500,000 for any 3-year period. To satisfy the requirements of this paragraph (e)(4), Corporation Y obtains shareholder approval of the plan at its 1995 annual shareholder meeting. In the proxy statement issued to shareholders, Corporation Y need not disclose to shareholders the specific targets that are set by the compensation committee. However, Corporation Y must disclose that bonuses are paid on the basis of earnings per share, reductions in costs, and increases in sales of specified divisions. Corporation Y also must disclose the maximum amount of compensation that any executive may receive under the plan is $1,500,000 per 3-year period. Unless changes in the material terms of the plan are made earlier, Corporation Y need not disclose the material terms of the plan to the shareholders and obtain their reapproval until the first shareholders' meeting held in 2000.

Example (4). The same facts as in Example 3, except that prior to the beginning of the second 3-year period, the compensation committee determines that different targets will be set under the plan for that period with regard to all three of the performance criteria (i.e., earnings per share, reductions in costs, and increases in sales). In addition, the compensation committee raises the maximum dollar amount that can be paid under the plan for a 3-year period to $2,000,000. The increase in the maximum dollar amount of compensation under the plan is a changed material term. Thus, to satisfy the requirements of this paragraph (e)(4), Corporation Y must disclose to and obtain approval by the shareholders of the plan as amended.

Example (5). In 1998, Corporation Z establishes a plan under which a specified group of executives will receive a cash bonus not to exceed $750,000 each if a new product that has been in development is completed and ready for sale to customers by January 1, 2000. Although the completion of the new product is a material term of the performance goal under this paragraph (e)(4), the compensation committee determines that the disclosure to shareholders of the performance goal would adversely affect Corporation Z because its competitors would be made aware of the existence and timing of its new product. In this case, the requirements of this paragraph (e)(4) are satisfied if all other material terms, including the maximum amount of compensation, are disclosed and the disclosure affirmatively states that the terms of the performance goal are not being disclosed because the compensation committee has determined that those terms include confidential information, the disclosure of which would adversely affect Corporation Z.

(5) Compensation committee certification. The compensation committee must certify in writing prior to payment of the compensation that the performance goals and any other material terms were in fact satisfied. For this purpose, approved minutes of the compensation committee meeting in which the certification is made are treated as a written certification. Certification by the compensation committee is not required for compensation that is attributable solely to the increase in the value of the stock of the publicly held corporation.

(f) Companies that become publicly held, spinoffs, and similar transactions. *(1) In general.* In the case of a corporation that was not a publicly held corporation and then becomes a publicly held corporation, the deduction limit of paragraph (b) of this section does not apply to any remuneration paid pursuant to a compensation plan or agreement that existed during the period in which the corporation was not publicly held. However, in the case of such a corporation that becomes publicly held in connection with an initial public offering, this relief applies only to the extent that the prospectus accompanying the initial public offering disclosed information concerning those plans or agreements that satisfied all applicable securities laws then in effect. In accordance with paragraph (c)(1)(ii) of this section, a corporation that is a member of an affiliated group that includes a publicly held corporation is considered publicly held and, therefore, cannot rely on this paragraph (f)(1).

(2) Reliance period. Paragraph (f)(1) of this section may be relied upon until the earliest of—

(i) The expiration of the plan or agreement;

(ii) The material modification of the plan or agreement, within the meaning of paragraph (h)(1)(iii) of this section;

(iii) The issuance of all employer stock and other compensation that has been allocated under the plan; or

(iv) The first meeting of shareholders at which directors are to be elected that occurs after the close of the third calendar year following the calendar year in which the initial public offering occurs or, in the case of a privately held corporation that becomes publicly held without an initial public offering, the first calendar year following the calendar year in which the corporation becomes publicly held.

(3) Stock-based compensation. Paragraph (f)(1) of this section will apply to any compensation received pursuant to the exercise of a stock option or stock appreciation right, or the substantial vesting of restricted property, granted under a plan or agreement described in paragraph (f)(1) of this section if the grant occurs on or before the earliest of the events specified in paragraph (f)(2) of this section.

(4) Subsidiaries that become separate publicly held corporations. (i) In general. If a subsidiary that is a member of the affiliated group described in paragraph (c)(1)(ii) of this section becomes a separate publicly held corporation (whether by spinoff or otherwise), any remuneration paid to covered employees of the new publicly held corporation will satisfy the exception for performance-based compensation described in paragraph (e) of this section if the conditions in either paragraph (f)(4)(ii) or (f)(4)(iii) of this section are satisfied.

(ii) Prior establishment and approval. Remuneration satisfies the requirements of this paragraph (f)(4)(ii) if the remuneration satisfies the requirements for performance-based compensation set forth in paragraphs (e)(2), (e)(3), and (e)(4) of this section (by application of paragraphs (e)(3)(viii) and (e)(4)(viii) of this section) before the corporation becomes a separate publicly held corporation, and the certification required by paragraph (e)(5) of this section is made by the compensation committee of the new publicly held corporation (but if the performance goals are attained before the corporation becomes a separate publicly held corporation, the certification may be made by the compensation committee referred to in paragraph (e)(3)(viii) of this section before it becomes a separate publicly held corporation). Thus, this paragraph (f)(4)(ii) requires that the outside directors and shareholders (within the meaning of paragraphs (e)(3)(viii) and (e)(4)(viii) of this section) of the corporation before it becomes a separate publicly held corporation establish and approve, respectively, the performance-based compensation for the covered employees of the new publicly held corporation in accordance with paragraphs (e)(3) and (e)(4) of this section.

(iii) Transition period. Remuneration satisfies the requirements of this paragraph (f)(4)(iii) if the remuneration satisfies all of the requirements of paragraphs (e)(2), (e)(3), and (e)(5) of this section. The outside directors (within the meaning of paragraph (e)(3)(viii) of this section) of the corporation before it becomes a separate publicly held corporation, or the outside directors of the new publicly held corporation, may establish and administer the performance goals for the covered employees of the new publicly held corporation for purposes of satisfying the requirements of paragraphs (e)(2) and (e)(3) of this section. The certification required by paragraph (e)(5) of this section must be made by the compensation committee of the new publicly held corporation. However, a taxpayer may rely on this paragraph (f)(4)(iii) to satisfy the requirements of paragraph (e) of this section only for compensation paid, or stock options, stock appreciation rights, or restricted property granted, prior to the first regularly scheduled meeting of the shareholders of the new publicly held corporation that occurs more than 12 months after the date the corporation becomes a separate publicly held corporation. Compensation paid, or stock options, stock appreciation rights, or restricted property granted, on or after the date of that meeting of shareholders must satisfy all requirements of paragraph (e) of this section, including the shareholder approval requirement of paragraph (e)(4) of this section, in order to satisfy the requirements for performance-based compensation.

(5) Example. The following example illustrates the application of paragraph (f)(4)(ii) of this section:

Example. Corporation P, which is publicly held, decides to spin off Corporation S, a wholly owned subsidiary of Corporation P. After the spinoff, Corporation S will be a separate publicly held corporation. Before the spinoff, the compensation committee of Corporation P, pursuant to paragraph (e)(3)(viii) of this section, establishes a bonus plan for the executives of Corporation S that provides for bonuses payable after the spinoff and that satisfies the requirements of paragraph (e)(2) of this section. If, pursuant to paragraph (e)(4)(viii) of this section, the shareholders of Corporation P approve the plan prior to the spinoff, that approval will satisfy the requirements of paragraph (e)(4) of this section with respect to compensation paid pursuant to the bonus plan after the spinoff. However, the compensation committee of Corporation S will be required to certify that the goals are satisfied prior to the payment of the bonuses in order for the bonuses to be considered performance-based compensation.

(g) Coordination with disallowed excess parachute payments. The $1,000,000 limitation in paragraph (b) of this section is reduced (but not below zero) by the amount (if any) that would have been included in the compensation of the covered employee for the taxable year but for being disallowed by reason of section 280G. For example, assume that during a taxable year a corporation pays $1,500,000 to a covered employee and no portion satisfies the exception in paragraph (d) of this section for commissions or paragraph (e) of this section for qualified performance-based compensation. Of the $1,500,000, $600,000 is an excess parachute payment, as defined in section 280G(b)(1) and is disallowed by reason of that section. Because the excess parachute payment reduces the limitation of paragraph (b) of this section, the corporation can deduct $400,000, and $500,000 of the otherwise deductible amount is nondeductible by reason of section 162(m).

(h) Transition rules. *(1) Compensation payable under a written binding contract which was in effect on February 17, 1993.* (i) General rule. The deduction limit of paragraph (b) of this section does not apply to any compensation payable under a written binding contract that was in effect on February 17, 1993. The preceding sentence does not apply unless, under applicable state law, the corporation is obligated to pay the compensation if the employee performs services. However, the deduction limit of paragraph (b) of this section does apply to a contract that is renewed after February 17, 1993. A written binding contract that is terminable or cancelable by the corporation after February 17, 1993, without the employee's consent is treated as a new contract as of the date that any such termination or cancellation, if made, would be effective. Thus, for example, if the terms of a contract provide that it will be automatically renewed as of a certain date unless either the corporation or the employee gives notice of termination of the contract at least 30 days before that date, the contract is treated as a new contract as of the date that termination would be effective if that notice were given. Similarly, for example, if the terms of a contract provide that the contract will be terminated or canceled as of a certain date unless either the corporation or the employee elects to renew within 30 days of that date, the contract is treated as renewed by the corporation as of that date. Alternatively, if the corporation will remain legally obligated by the terms of a contract beyond a certain date at the sole discretion of the employee, the contract will not be treated as a new contract as of that date if the employee exercises the discretion to keep the corporation bound to the contract. A contract is not treated as terminable or cancelable if it can be terminated or canceled only by terminating the employment relationship of the employee.

(ii) Compensation payable under a plan or arrangement. If a compensation plan or arrangement meets the requirements of paragraph (h)(1)(i) of this section, the compensation paid to an employee pursuant to the plan or arrangement will not be subject to the deduction limit of paragraph (b) of this section even though the employee was not eligible to participate in the plan as of February 17, 1993. However, the preceding sentence does not apply unless the employee was employed on February 17, 1993, by the corporation that maintained the plan or arrangement, or the employee had the right to participate in the plan or arrangement under a written binding contract as of that date.

(iii) Material modifications. (A) Paragraph (h)(1)(i) of this section will not apply to any written binding contract that is materially modified. A material modification occurs when the contract is amended to increase the amount of compensation payable to the employee. If a binding written contract is materially modified, it is treated as a new contract entered into as of the date of the material modification. Thus, amounts received by an employee under the contract prior to a material modification are not affected, but amounts received subsequent to the material modification are not treated as paid under a binding, written contract described in paragraph (h)(1)(i) of this section.

(B) A modification of the contract that accelerates the payment of compensation will be treated as a material modification unless the amount of compensation paid is discounted to reasonably reflect the time value of money. If the contract is modified to defer the payment of compensation, any compensation paid in excess of the amount that was originally payable to the employee under the contract will not be treated as a material modification if the additional amount is based on either a reasonable rate of interest or one or more predetermined actual investments (whether or not assets associated with the amount originally owed are actually invested therein) such that the amount payable by the employer at the later date will be based on the actual rate of return of the specific investment (including any decrease as well as any increase in the value of the investment).

(C) The adoption of a supplemental contract or agreement that provides for increased compensation, or the payment of additional compensation, is a material modification of a binding, written contract where the facts and circumstances show that the additional compensation is paid on the basis of substantially the same elements or conditions as the compensation that is otherwise paid under the written binding contract. However, a material modification of a written binding contract does not include a supplemental payment that is equal to or less than a reasonable cost-of-living increase over the payment made in the preceding year under that written binding contract. In addition, a supplemental payment of compensation that satisfies the requirements of qualified performance-based compensation in paragraph (e) of this section will not be treated as a material modification.

(iv) Examples. The following examples illustrate the exception of this paragraph (h)(1):

Example (1). Corporation X executed a 3-year compensation arrangement with C on February 15, 1993, that constitutes a written binding contract under applicable state law. The terms of the arrangement provide for automatic extension after the 3-year term for additional 1-year periods, unless the corporation exercises its option to terminate the arrangement within 30 days of the end of the 3-year term or, thereafter, within 30 days before each anniversary date. Termination of the compensation arrangement does not require the termination of C's employment relationship with Corporation X. Unless terminated, the arrangement is treated as renewed on February 15, 1996, and the deduction limit of paragraph (b) of this section applies to payments under the arrangement after that date.

Example (2). Corporation Y executed a 5-year employment agreement with B on January 1, 1992, providing for a salary of $900,000 per year. Assume that this agreement constitutes a written binding contract under applicable state law. In 1992 and 1993, B receives the salary of $900,000 per year. In 1994, Corporation Y increases B's salary with a payment of $20,000. The $20,000 supplemental payment does not constitute a material modification of the written binding contract because the $20,000 payment is less than or equal to a reasonable cost-of-living increase from 1993. However, the $20,000 supplemental payment is subject to the limitation in paragraph (b) of this section. On January 1, 1995, Corporation Y increases B's salary to $1,200,000. The $280,000 supplemental payment is a material modification of the written binding contract because the additional compensation is paid on the basis of substantially the same elements or conditions as the compensation that is otherwise paid under the written binding contract and it is greater than a reasonable, annual cost-of-living increase. Because the written binding contract is materially modified as of January 1, 1995, all compensation paid to B in 1995 and thereafter is subject to the deduction limitation of section 162(m).

Example (3). Assume the same facts as in Example 2, except that instead of an increase in salary, B receives a restricted stock grant subject to B's continued employment for the balance of the contract. The restricted stock grant is not a material modification of the binding written contract because any additional compensation paid to B under the grant is not paid on the basis of substantially the same elements and conditions as B's salary because it is based both on the stock price and B's continued service. However, compensation attributable to the restricted stock grant is subject to the deduction limitation of section 162(m).

(2) Special transition rule for outside directors. A director who is a disinterested director is treated as satisfying the requirements of an outside director under paragraph (e)(3) of this section until the first meeting of shareholders at which directors are to be elected that occurs on or after January 1, 1996. For purposes of this paragraph (h)(2) and paragraph (h)(3) of this section, a director is a disinterested director if the director is disinterested within the meaning of Rule 16b-3(c)(2)(i), 17 CFR 240.16b-3(c)(2)(i), under the Exchange

Act (including the provisions of Rule 16b-3(d)(3), as in effect on April 30, 1991).

(3) Special transition rule for previously-approved plans. (i) In general. Any compensation paid under a plan or agreement approved by shareholders before December 20, 1993, is treated as satisfying the requirements of paragraphs (e)(3) and (e)(4) of this section, provided that the directors administering the plan or agreement are disinterested directors and the plan was approved by shareholders in a manner consistent with Rule 16b-3(b), 17 CFR 240.16b-3(b), under the Exchange Act or Rule 16b-3(a), 17 CFR 240.16b-3(a) (as contained in 17 CFR part 240 revised April 1, 1990). In addition, for purposes of satisfying the requirements of paragraph (e)(2)(vi) of this section, a plan or agreement is treated as stating a maximum number of shares with respect to which an option or right may be granted to any employee if the plan or agreement that was approved by the shareholders provided for an aggregate limit, consistent with Rule 16b-3(b), 17 CFR 250.16b-3(b), on the shares of employer stock with respect to which awards may be made under the plan or agreement.

(ii) Reliance period. The transition rule provided in this paragraph (h)(3) shall continue and may be relied upon until the earliest of—

(A) The expiration or material modification of the plan or agreement;

(B) The issuance of all employer stock and other compensation that has been allocated under the plan; or

(C) The first meeting of shareholders at which directors are to be elected that occurs after December 31, 1996.

(iii) Stock-based compensation.This paragraph (h)(3) will apply to any compensation received pursuant to the exercise of a stock option or stock appreciation right, or the substantial vesting of restricted property, granted under a plan or agreement described in paragraph (h)(3)(i) of this section if the grant occurs on or before the earliest of the events specified in paragraph (h)(3)(ii) of this section.

(iv) Example. The following example illustrates the application of this paragraph (h)(3):

Example. Corporation Z adopted a stock option plan in 1991. Pursuant to Rule 16b-3 under the Exchange Act, the stock option plan has been administered by disinterested directors and was approved by Corporation Z shareholders. Under the terms of the plan, shareholder approval is not required again until 2001. In addition, the terms of the stock option plan include an aggregate limit on the number of shares available under the plan. Option grants under the Corporation Z plan are made with an exercise price equal to or greater than the fair market value of Corporation Z stock. Compensation attributable to the exercise of options that are granted under the plan before the earliest of the dates specified in paragraph (h)(3)(ii) of this section will be treated as satisfying the requirements of paragraph (e) of this section for qualified performance-based compensation, regardless of when the options are exercised.

(i) [Reserved]

(j) Effective date. *(1) In general.* Section 162(m) and this section apply to compensation that is otherwise deductible by the corporation in a taxable year beginning on or after January 1, 1994.

(2) Delayed effective date for certain provisions. (i) Date on which remuneration is considered paid. Notwithstanding paragraph (j)(1) of this section, the rules in the second sentence of each of paragraphs (e)(3)(ii)(A), (e)(3)(ii)(B), and (e)(3)(ii)(C) of this section for determining the date or dates on which remuneration is considered paid to a director are effective for taxable years beginning on or after January 1, 1995. Prior to those taxable years, taxpayers must follow the rules in paragraphs (e)(3)(ii)(A), (e)(3)(ii)(B), and (e)(3)(ii)(C) of this section or another reasonable, good faith interpretation of section 162(m) with respect to the date or dates on which remuneration is considered paid to a director.

(ii) Separate treatment of publicly held subsidiaries. Notwithstanding paragraph (j)(1) of this section, the rule in paragraph (c)(1)(ii) of this section that treats publicly held subsidiaries as separately subject to section 162(m) is effective as of the first regularly scheduled meeting of the shareholders of the publicly held subsidiary that occurs more than 12 months after December 2, 1994. The rule for stock-based compensation set forth in paragraph (f)(3) of this section will apply for this purpose, except that the grant must occur before the shareholder meeting specified in this paragraph (j)(2)(ii). Taxpayers may choose to rely on the rule referred to in the first sentence of this paragraph (j)(2)(ii) for the period prior to the effective date of the rule.

(iii) Subsidiaries that become separate publicly held corporations. Notwithstanding paragraph (j)(1) of this section, if a subsidiary of a publicly held corporation becomes a separate publicly held corporation as described in paragraph (f)(4)(i) of this section, then, for the duration of the reliance period described in paragraph (f)(2) of this section, the rules of paragraph (f)(1) of this section are treated as applying (and the rules of paragraph (f)(4) of this section do not apply) to remuneration paid to covered employees of that new publicly held corporation pursuant to a plan or agreement that existed prior to December 2, 1994, provided that the treatment of that remuneration as performance-based is in accordance with a reasonable, good faith interpretation of section 162(m). However, if remuneration is paid to covered employees of that new publicly held corporation pursuant to a plan or agreement that existed prior to December 2, 1994, but that remuneration is not performance-based under a reasonable, good faith interpretation of section 162(m), the rules of paragraph (f)(1) of this section will be treated as applying only until the first regularly scheduled meeting of shareholders that occurs more than 12 months after December 2, 1994. The rules of paragraph (f)(4) of this section will apply as of that first regularly scheduled meeting. The rule for stock-based compensation set forth in paragraph (f)(3) of this section will apply for purposes of this paragraph (j)(2)(iii), except that the grant must occur before the shareholder meeting specified in the preceding sentence if the remuneration is not performance-based under a reasonable, good faith interpretation of section 162(m). Taxpayers may choose to rely on the rules of paragraph (f)(4) of this section for the period prior to the applicable effective date referred to in the first or second sentence of this paragraph (j)(2)(iii).

(iv) Bonus pools. Notwithstanding paragraph (j)(1) of this section, the rules in paragraph (e)(2)(iii)(A) that limit the sum of individual percentages of a bonus pool to 100 percent will not apply to remuneration paid before January 1, 2001, based on performance in any performance period that began prior to December 20, 1995.

(v) Compensation based on a percentage of salary or base pay. Notwithstanding paragraph (j)(1) of this section, the requirement in paragraph (e)(4)(i) of this section that, in the case of certain formulas based on a percentage of salary or base pay, a corporation disclose to shareholders the maximum dollar amount of compensation that could be paid to the employee, will apply only to plans approved by shareholders after April 30, 1995.

T.D. 8650, 12/19/95.

---

§ 1.162-28 Allocation of costs to lobbying activities.

(a) Introduction. *(1) In general.* Section 162(e)(1) denies a deduction for certain amounts paid or incurred in connection with activities described in section 162(e)(1)(A) and (D) (lobbying activities). To determine the nondeductible amount, a taxpayer must allocate costs to lobbying activities. This section describes costs that must be allocated to lobbying activities and prescribes rules permitting a taxpayer to use a reasonable method to allocate those costs. This section does not apply to taxpayers subject to section 162(e)(5)(A). In addition, this section does not apply for purposes of sections 4911 and 4945 and the regulations thereunder.

(2) Recordkeeping. For recordkeeping requirements, see section 6001 and the regulations thereunder.

(b) Reasonable method of allocating costs. *(1) In general.* A taxpayer must use a reasonable method to allocate the costs described in paragraph (c) of this section to lobbying activities. A method is not reasonable unless it is applied consistently and is consistent with the special rules in paragraph (g) of this section. Except as provided in paragraph (b)(2) of this section, reasonable methods of allocating costs to lobbying activities include (but are not limited to)—

(i) The ratio method described in paragraph (d) of this section;

(ii) The gross-up method described in paragraph (e) of this section; and

(iii) A method that applies the principles of section 263A and the regulations thereunder (see paragraph (f) of this section).

(2) Taxpayers not permitted to use certain methods. A taxpayer (other than one subject to section 6033(e)) that does not pay or incur reasonable labor costs for persons engaged in lobbying activities may not use the gross-up method. For example, a partnership or sole proprietorship in which the lobbying activities are performed by the owners who do not receive a salary or guaranteed payment for services does not pay or incur reasonable labor costs for persons engaged in those activities and may not use the gross-up method.

(c) Costs allocable to lobbying activities. *(1) In general.* Costs properly allocable to lobbying activities include labor costs and general and administrative costs.

(2) Labor costs. For each taxable year, labor costs include costs attributable to full-time, part-time, and contract employees. Labor costs include all elements of compensation, such as basic compensation, overtime pay, vacation pay, holiday pay, sick leave pay, payroll taxes, pension costs, employee benefits, and payments to a supplemental unemployment benefit plan.

(3) General and administrative costs. For each taxable year, general and administrative costs include depreciation, rent, utilities, insurance, maintenance costs, security costs, and other administrative department costs (for example, payroll, personnel, and accounting).

(d) Ratio method. *(1) In general.* Under the ratio method described in this paragraph (d), a taxpayer allocates to lobbying activities the sum of its third-party costs (as defined in paragraph (d)(5) of this section) allocable to lobbying activities and the costs determined by using the following formula:

$$\frac{\text{Lobbying labor hours.}}{\text{Total labor hours}} \times \text{Total costs of operations.}$$

(2) Lobbying labor hours. Lobbying labor hours are the hours that a taxpayer's personnel spend ôn lobbying activities during the taxable year. A taxpayer may use any reasonable method to determine the number of labor hours spent on lobbying activities and may use the de minimis rule of paragraph (g)(1) of this section. A taxpayer may treat as zero the lobbying labor hours of personnel engaged in secretarial, clerical, support, and other administrative activities (as opposed to activities involving significant judgment with respect to lobbying activities). Thus, for example, the hours spent on lobbying activities by para-professionals and analysts may not be treated as zero.

(3) Total labor hours. Total labor hours means the total number of hours that a taxpayer's personnel spend on a taxpayer's trade or business during the taxable year. A taxpayer may make reasonable assumptions concerning total hours spent by personnel on the taxpayer's trade or business. For example, it may be reasonable, based on all the facts and circumstances, to assume that all full-time personnel spend 1,800 hours per year on a taxpayer's trade or business. If, under paragraph (d)(2) of this section, a taxpayer treats as zero the lobbying labor hours of personnel engaged in secretarial, clerical, support, and other administrative activities, the taxpayer must also treat as zero the total labor hours of all personnel engaged in those activities.

(4) Total costs of operations. A taxpayer's total costs of operations means the total costs of the taxpayer's trade or business for a taxable year, excluding third-party costs (as defined in paragraph (d)(5) of this section).

(5) Third-party costs. Third-party costs are amounts paid or incurred in whole or in part for lobbying activities conducted by third parties (such as amounts paid to taxpayers subject to section 162(e)(5)(A) or dues or other similar amounts that are not deductible in whole or in part under section 162(e)(3)) and amounts paid or incurred for travel (including meals and lodging while away from home) and entertainment relating in whole or in part to lobbying activities.

(6) Example. The provisions of this paragraph (d) are illustrated by the following example.

Example. (i) In 1996, three full-time employees, A, B, and C, of Taxpayer W engage in both lobbying activities and nonlobbying activities. A spends 300 hours, B spends 1,700 hours, and C spends 1,000 hours on lobbying activities, for a total of 3,000 hours spent on lobbying activities for W. W reasonably assumes that each of its three employees spends 2,000 hours a year on W's business.

(ii) W's total costs of operations are $300,000. W has no third-party costs.

(iii) Under the ratio method, X allocates $150,000 to its lobbying activities for 1996, as follows:

$$\frac{\text{Lobbying labor hours}}{\text{Total labor hours}} \times \text{Total costs of operations} + \text{Allocable third-party costs} = \text{Costs allocable to lobbying activities}$$

$$\left[\frac{300 + 1{,}700 + 1{,}000}{6{,}000} \times \$300{,}000\right] + [0] = \$150{,}000.$$

(e) Gross-up method. *(1) In general.* Under the gross-up method described in this paragraph (e)(1), the taxpayer allocates to lobbying activities the sum of its third-party costs (as defined in paragraph (d)(5) of this section) allocable to lobbying activities and 175 percent of its basic lobbying labor costs (as defined in paragraph (e)(3) of this section) of all personnel.

(2) Alternative gross-up method. Under the alternative gross-up method described in this paragraph (e)(2), the taxpayer allocates to lobbying activities the sum of its third-party costs (as defined in paragraph (d)(5) of this section) allocable to lobbying activities and 225 percent of its basic lobbying labor costs (as defined in paragraph (e)(3)), excluding the costs of personnel who engage in secretarial, clerical, support, and other administrative activities (as opposed to activities involving significant judgment with respect to lobbying activities).

(3) Basic lobbying labor costs. For purposes of this paragraph (e), basic lobbying labor costs are the basic costs of lobbying labor hours (as defined in paragraph (d)(2) of this section) determined for the appropriate personnel. For purposes of this paragraph (e), basic costs of lobbying labor hours are wages or other similar costs of labor, including, for example, guaranteed payments for services. Basic costs do not include pension, profit-sharing, employee benefits, and supplemental unemployment benefit plan costs, or other similar costs.

(4) Example. The provisions of this paragraph (e) are illustrated by the following example.

Example. (i) In 1996, three employees, A, B, and C, of Taxpayer X engage in both lobbying activities and nonlobbying activities. A spends 300 hours, B spends 1,700 hours, and C spends 1,000 hours on lobbying activities.

(ii) X has no third-party costs.

(iii) For purposes of the gross-up method, X determines that its basic labor costs are \$20 per hour for A, \$30 per hour for B, and \$25 per hour for C. Thus, its basic lobbying labor costs are (\$20 × 300) + (\$30 × 1,700) + (\$25 × 1,000), or (\$6,000 + \$51,000 + \$25,000), for total basic lobbying labor costs for 1996 of \$82,000.

(iv) Under the gross-up method, X allocates \$143,500 to its lobbying activities for 1996, as follows:

$$175\% \times \text{Basic lobbying labor costs of all personnel} + \text{Allocable third-party costs} = \text{Costs allocable to lobbying activities}$$

$$[175\% \times \$82{,}000] + [0] = \$143{,}500.$$

(f) Section 263A cost allocation methods. *(1) In general.* A taxpayer may allocate its costs to lobbying activities under the principles set forth in section 263A and the regulations thereunder, except to the extent inconsistent with paragraph (g) of this section. For this purpose, lobbying activities are considered a service department or function. Therefore, a taxpayer may allocate costs to lobbying activities by applying the methods provided in §§ 1.263A-1 through 1.263A-3. See § 1.263A-1(e)(4), which describes service costs generally; § 1.263A-1(f), which sets forth cost allocation methods available under section 263A; and § 1.263A-1(g)(4), which provides methods of allocating service costs.

(2) Example. The provisions of this paragraph (f) are illustrated by the following example.

Example. (i) Three full-time employees, A, B, and C, work in the Washington office of Taxpayer Y, a manufacturing concern. They each engage in lobbying activities and nonlobbying activities. In 1996, A spends 75 hours, B spends 1,750 hours, and C spends 2,000 hours on lobbying activities. A's hours are not spent on direct contact lobbying as defined in paragraph (g)(2) of this section. All three work 2,000 hours during 1996. The Washington office also employs one secretary, D, who works exclusively for A, B, and C.

(ii) In addition, three departments in the corporate headquarters in Chicago benefit the Washington office: public affairs, human resources, and insurance.

(iii) Y is subject to section 263A and uses the step-allocation method to allocate its service costs. Prior to the amendments to section 162(e), the Washington office was treated as an overall management function for purposes of section 263A. As such, its costs were fully deductible and no further allocations were made under Y's step allocation. Following the amendments to section 162(e), Y adopts its 263A step-allocation methodology to allocate costs to lobbying activities. Y adds a lobbying department to its step-allocation program, which results in an allocation of costs to the lobbying department from both the Washington office and the Chicago office.

(iv) Y develops a labor ratio to allocate its Washington office costs between the newly defined lobbying department and the overall management department. To determine the hours allocable to lobbying activities, Y uses the de minimis rule of paragraph (g)(1) of this section. Under this rule, A's hours spent on lobbying activities are treated as zero because less than 5 percent of A's time is spent on lobbying (75/2,000 = 3.75%). In addition, because D works exclusively for personnel engaged in lobbying activities, D's hours are not used to develop the allocation ratio. Y assumes that D's allocation of time follows the average time of all the personnel engaged in lobbying activities. Thus, Y's labor ratio is determined as follows:

Departments

Employee	Lobbying hours	Overall management hours	Total hours
A	0	2,000	2,000
B	1,750	250	2,000
C	2,000	0	2,000
Totals	3,750	2,250	6,000

Lobbying Department Ratio = 3,750 ÷ 6,000 = 62.5%

Overall Management Department Ratio = 2,250 ÷ 6,000 = 37.5%

(v) In 1996, the Washington office has the following costs:

Account	Amount
Professional Salaries and Benefits	\$660,000
Clerical Salaries and Benefits	50,000
Rent Expense	100,000
Depreciation on Furniture and Equip.	40,000
Utilities	15,000
Outside Payroll Service	5,000

Miscellaneous	10,000
Third-Party Lobbying (Law Firm)	90,000
Total Washington Costs	$970,000

(vi) In addition, $233,800 of costs from the public affairs department, $30,000 of costs from the insurance department, and $5,000 of costs from the human resources department are allocable to the Washington office from departments in Chicago. Therefore, the Washington office costs are allocated to the Lobbying and Overall Management departments as follows:

Total Washington department costs from above	$ 970,000
Plus Costs Allocated From Other Departments	268,800
Less third-party costs directly allocable to lobbying	(90,000)
Total Washington office costs	$1,148,800

	Lobbying department	Overall mgmt. department
Department Allocation Ratios	62.5%	37.5%
× Washington Office Costs	$1,148,800	$1,148,800
= Costs Allocated to Departments	$ 718,000	$ 430,800

(vii) Y's step-allocation for its Lobbying Department is determined as follows:

Y's Step-Allocation	Lobbying Department
Washington costs allocated to lobbying department	$718,000
Plus third-party costs	90,000
Total costs of lobbying activities	$808,000

(g) Special rules. The following rules apply to any reasonable method of allocating costs to lobbying activities. *(1) De minimis rule for labor hours.* Subject to the exception provided in paragraph (g)(2) of this section, a taxpayer may treat time spent by an individual on lobbying activities as zero if less than five percent of the person's time is spent on lobbying activities. Reasonable methods must be used to determine if less than five percent of a person's time is spent on lobbying activities.

(2) Direct contact lobbying labor hours. Notwithstanding paragraph (g)(1) of this section, a taxpayer must treat all hours spent by a person on direct contact lobbying (as well as the hours that person spends in connection with direct contact lobbying, including time spent traveling that is allocable to the direct contact lobbying) as labor hours allocable to lobbying activities. An activity is direct contact lobbying if it is a meeting, telephone conversation, letter, or other similar means of communication with a legislator (other than a local legislator) or covered executive branch official (as defined in section 162(e)(6)) and otherwise qualifies as a lobbying activity. A person who engages in research, preparation, and other background activities related to direct contact lobbying but who does not make direct contact with a legislator or covered executive branch official is not engaged in direct contact lobbying.

(3) Taxpayer defined. For purposes of this section, a taxpayer includes a tax-exempt organization subject to section 6033(e).

(h) Effective date. This section is effective for amounts paid or incurred on or after July 21, 1995. Taxpayers must adopt a reasonable interpretation of sections 162(e)(1)(A) and (D) for amounts paid or incurred before this date.

T.D. 8602, 7/20/95.

§ 1.162-29 Influencing legislation.

(a) Scope. This section provides rules for determining whether an activity is influencing legislation for purposes of section 162 (e)(1)(A). This section does not apply for purposes of sections 4911 and 4945 and the regulations thereunder.

(b) Definitions. For purposes of this section—

(1) Influencing legislation. Influencing legislation means—

(i) Any attempt to influence any legislation through a lobbying communication; and

(ii) All activities, such as research, preparation, planning, and coordination, including deciding whether to make a lobbying communication, engaged in for a purpose of making or supporting a lobbying communication, even if not yet made. See paragraph (c) of this section for rules for determining the purposes for engaging in an activity.

(2) Attempt to influence legislation. An attempt to influence any legislation through a lobbying communication is making the lobbying communication.

(3) Lobbying communication. A lobbying communication is any communication (other than any communication compelled by subpoena, or otherwise compelled by Federal or State law) with any member or employee of a legislative body or any other government official or employee who may participate in the formulation of the legislation that—

(i) Refers to specific legislation and reflects a view on that legislation; or

(ii) Clarifies, amplifies, modifies, or provides support for views reflected in a prior lobbying communication.

(4) Legislation. Legislation includes any action with respect to Acts, bills, resolutions, or other similar items by a legislative body. Legislation includes a proposed treaty required to be submitted by the President to the Senate for its advice and consent from the time the President's representative begins to negotiate its position with the prospective parties to the proposed treaty.

(5) Specific legislation. Specific legislation includes a specific legislative proposal that has not been introduced in a legislative body.

(6) Legislative bodies. Legislative bodies are Congress, state legislatures, and other similar governing bodies, excluding local councils (and similar governing bodies), and executive, judicial, or administrative bodies. For this purpose, administrative bodies include school boards, housing authorities, sewer and water districts, zoning boards, and other similar Federal, State, or local special purpose bodies, whether elective or appointive.

(7) Examples. The provisions of this paragraph (b) are illustrated by the following examples.

Example (1). Taxpayer P's employee, A, is assigned to approach members of Congress to gain their support for a pending bill. A drafts and P prints a position letter on the bill. P distributes the letter to members of Congress. Additionally, A personally contacts several members of Congress or their staffs to seek support for P's position on the bill.

The letter and the personal contacts are lobbying communications. Therefore, P is influencing legislation.

Example (2). Taxpayer R is invited to provide testimony at a congressional oversight hearing concerning the implementation of The Financial Institutions Reform, Recovery, and Enforcement Act of 1989. Specifically, the hearing concerns a proposed regulation increasing the threshold value of commercial and residential real estate transactions for which an appraisal by a state licensed or certified appraiser is required. In its testimony, R states that it is in favor of the proposed regulation. Because R does not refer to any specific legislation or reflect a view on any such legislation, R has not made a lobbying communication. Therefore, R is not influencing legislation.

Example (3). State X enacts a statute that requires the licensing of all day-care providers. Agency B in State X is charged with writing rules to implement the statute. After the enactment of the statute, Taxpayer S sends a letter to Agency B providing detailed proposed rules that S recommends Agency B adopt to implement the statute on licensing of day-care providers. Because the letter to Agency B neither refers to nor reflects a view on any specific legislation, it is not a lobbying communication. Therefore, S is not influencing legislation.

Example (4). Taxpayer T proposes to a State Park Authority that it purchase a particular tract of land for a new park. Even if T's proposal would necessarily require the State Park Authority eventually to seek appropriations to acquire the land and develop the new park, T has not made a lobbying communication because there has been no reference to, nor any view reflected on, any specific legislation. Therefore, T's proposal is not influencing legislation.

Example (5). (i) Taxpayer U prepares a paper that asserts that lack of new capital is hurting State X's economy. The paper indicates that State X residents either should invest more in local businesses or increase their savings so that funds will be available to others interested in making investments. U forwards a summary of the unpublished paper to legislators in State X with a cover letter that states in part: You must take action to improve the availability of new capital in the state.

(ii) Because neither the summary nor the cover letter refers to any specific legislative proposal and no other facts or circumstances indicate that they refer to an existing legislative proposal, forwarding the summary to legislators in State X is not a lobbying communication. Therefore, U is not influencing legislation.

(iii) Q, a member of the legislature of State X, calls U to request a copy of the unpublished paper from which the summary was prepared. U forwards the paper with a cover letter that simply refers to the enclosed materials. Because U's letter to Q and the unpublished paper do not refer to any specific legislation or reflect a view on any such legislation, the letter is not a lobbying communication. Therefore, U is not influencing legislation.

Example (6). (i) Taxpayer V prepares a paper that asserts that lack of new capital is hurting the national economy. The paper indicates that lowering the capital gains rate would increase the availability of capital and increase tax receipts from the capital gains tax. V forwards the paper to its representatives in Congress with a cover letter that says, in part: I urge you to support a reduction in the capital gains tax rate.

(ii) V's communication is a lobbying communication because it refers to and reflects a view on a specific legislative proposal (i.e., lowering the capital gains rate). Therefore, V is influencing legislation.

Example (7). Taxpayer W, based in State A, notes in a letter to a legislator of State A that State X has passed a bill that accomplishes a stated purpose and then says that State A should pass such a bill. No such bill has been introduced into the State A legislature. The communication is a lobbying communication because it refers to and reflects a view on a specific legislative proposal. Therefore, W is influencing legislation.

Example (8). (i) Taxpayer Y represents citrus fruit growers. Y writes a letter to a United States senator discussing how pesticide O has benefited citrus fruit growers and disputing problems linked to its use. The letter discusses a bill pending in Congress and states in part: This bill would prohibit the use of pesticide O. If citrus growers are unable to use this pesticide, their crop yields will be severely reduced, leading to higher prices for consumers and lower profits, even bankruptcy, for growers.

(ii) Y's views on the bill are reflected in this statement. Thus, the communication is a lobbying communication, and Y is influencing legislation.

Example (9). (i) B, the president of Taxpayer Z, an insurance company, meets with Q, who chairs the X state legislature's committee with jurisdiction over laws regulating insurance companies, to discuss the possibility of legislation to address current problems with surplus-line companies. B recommends that legislation be introduced that would create minimum capital and surplus requirements for surplus-line companies and create clearer guidelines concerning the risks that surplus-line companies can insure. B's discussion with Q is a lobbying communication because B refers to and reflects a view on a specific legislative proposal. Therefore, Z is influencing legislation.

(ii) Q is not convinced that the market for surplus-line companies is substantial enough to warrant such legislation and requests that B provide information on the amount and types of risks covered by surplus-line companies. After the meeting, B has employees of Z prepare estimates of the percentage of property and casualty insurance risks handled by surplus-line companies. B sends the estimates with a cover letter that simply refers to the enclosed materials. Although B's follow-up letter to Q does not refer to specific legislation or reflect a view on such legislation, B's letter supports the views reflected in the earlier communication. Therefore, the letter is a lobbying communication and Z is influencing legislation.

(c) Purpose for engaging in an activity. *(1) In general.* The purposes for engaging in an activity are determined based on all the facts and circumstances. Facts and circumstances include, but are not limited to—

(i) Whether the activity and the lobbying communication are proximate in time;

(ii) Whether the activity and the lobbying communication relate to similar subject matter;

(iii) Whether the activity is performed at the request of, under the direction of, or on behalf of a person making the lobbying communication;

(iv) Whether the results of the activity are also used for a nonlobbying purpose; and

(v) Whether, at the time the taxpayer engages in the activity, there is specific legislation to which the activity relates.

(2) Multiple purposes. If a taxpayer engages in an activity both for the purpose of making or supporting a lobbying

communication and for some nonlobbying purpose, the taxpayer must treat the activity as engaged in partially for a lobbying purpose and partially for a nonlobbying purpose. This division of the activity must result in a reasonable allocation of costs to influencing legislation. See § 1.162-28 (allocation rules for certain expenditures to which section 162(e)(1) applies). A taxpayer's treatment of these multiple-purpose activities will, in general, not result in a reasonable allocation if it allocates to influencing legislation—

(i) Only the incremental amount of costs that would not have been incurred but for the lobbying purpose; or

(ii) An amount based solely on the number of purposes for engaging in that activity without regard to the relative importance of those purposes.

(3) Activities treated as having no purpose to influence legislation. A taxpayer that engages in any of the following activities is treated as having done so without a purpose of making or supporting a lobbying communication—

(i) Before evidencing a purpose to influence any specific legislation referred to in paragraph (c)(3)(i)(A) or (B) of this section (or similar legislation)—

(A) Determining the existence or procedural status of specific legislation, or the time, place, and subject of any hearing to be held by a legislative body with respect to specific legislation; or

(B) Preparing routine, brief summaries of the provisions of specific legislation;

(ii) Performing an activity for purposes of complying with the requirements of any law (for example, satisfying state or federal securities law filing requirements);

(iii) Reading any publications available to the general public or viewing or listening to other mass media communications; and

(iv) Merely attending a widely attended speech.

(4) Examples. The provisions of this paragraph (c) are illustrated by the following examples.

Example (1). (i) Facts. In 1997, Agency F issues proposed regulations relating to the business of Taxpayer W. There is no specific legislation during 1997 that is similar to the regulatory proposal. W undertakes a study of the impact of the proposed regulations on its business. W incorporates the results of that study in comments sent to Agency F in 1997. In 1998, legislation is introduced in Congress that is similar to the regulatory proposal. Also in 1998, W writes a letter to Senator P stating that it opposes the proposed legislation. W encloses with the letter a copy of the comments it sent to Agency F.

(ii) Analysis. W's letter to Senator P refers to and reflects a view on specific legislation and therefore is a lobbying communication. Although W's study of the impact of the proposed regulations is proximate in time and similar in subject matter to its lobbying communication, W performed the study and incorporated the results in comments sent to Agency F when no legislation with a similar subject matter was pending (a nonlobbying use). On these facts, W engaged in the study solely for a nonlobbying purpose.

Example (2). (i) Facts. The governor of State Q proposes a budget that includes a proposed sales tax on electricity. Using its records of electricity consumption, Taxpayer Y estimates the additional costs that the budget proposal would impose upon its business. In the same year, Y writes to members of the state legislature and explains that it opposes the proposed sales tax. In its letter, Y includes its estimate of the costs that the sales tax would impose on its business. Y does not demonstrate any other use of its estimates.

(ii) Analysis. The letter is a lobbying communication (because it refers to and reflects a view on specific legislation, the governor's proposed budget). Y's estimate of additional costs under the proposal supports the lobbying communication, is proximate in time and similar in subject matter to a specific legislative proposal then in existence, and is not used for a nonlobbying purpose. Based on these facts, Y estimated its additional costs under the budget proposal solely to support the lobbying communication.

Example (3). (i) Facts. A senator in the State Q legislature announces her intention to introduce legislation to require health insurers to cover a particular medical procedure in all policies sold in the state. Taxpayer Y has different policies for two groups of employees, one of which covers the procedure and one of which does not. After the bill is introduced, Y's legislative affairs staff asks Y's human resources staff to estimate the additional cost to cover the procedure for both groups of employees. Y's human resources staff prepares a study estimating Y's increased costs and forwards it to the legislative affairs staff. Y's legislative staff then writes to members of the state legislature and explains that it opposes the proposed change in insurance coverage based on the study. Y's legislative affairs staff thereafter forwards the study, prepared for its use in opposing the statutory proposal, to its labor relations staff for use in negotiations with employees scheduled to begin later in the year.

(ii) Analysis. The letter to legislators is a lobbying communication (because it refers to and reflects a view on specific legislation). The activity of estimating Y's additional costs under the proposed legislation relate to the same subject as the lobbying communication, occurs close in time to the lobbying communication, is conducted at the request of a person making a lobbying communication, and relates to specific legislation then in existence. Although Y used the study in its labor negotiations, mere use for that purpose does not establish that Y estimated its additional costs under the proposed legislation in part for a nonlobbying purpose. Thus, based on all the facts and circumstances, Y estimated the additional costs it would incur under the proposal solely to make or support the lobbying communication.

Example (4). (i) Facts. After several years of developmental work under various contracts, in 1996, Taxpayer A contracts with the Department of Defense (DOD) to produce a prototype of a new generation military aircraft. A is aware that DOD will be able to fund the contract only if Congress appropriates an amount for that purpose in the upcoming appropriations process. In 1997, A conducts simulation tests of the aircraft and revises the specifications of the aircraft's expected performance capabilities, as required under the contract. A submits the results of the tests and the revised specifications to DOD. In 1998, Congress considers legislation to appropriate funds for the contract. In that connection, A summarizes the results of the simulation tests and of the aircraft's expected performance capabilities, and submits the summary to interested members of Congress with a cover letter that encourages them to support appropriations of funds for the contract.

(ii) Analysis. The letter is a lobbying communication (because it refers to specific legislation (i.e., appropriations) and requests passage). The described activities in 1996, 1997, and 1998 relate to the same subject as the lobbying communication. The summary was prepared specifically for, and close in time to, that communication. Based on these facts, the summary was prepared solely for a lobbying purpose. In contrast, A conducted the tests and revised the specifications to comply with its production contract with DOD. A conducted the tests and revised the specifications solely for a nonlobbying purpose.

Example (5). (i) Facts. C, president of Taxpayer W, travels to the state capital to attend a two-day conference on new manufacturing processes. C plans to spend a third day in the capital meeting with state legislators to explain why W opposes a pending bill unrelated to the subject of the conference. At the meetings with the legislators, C makes lobbying communications by referring to and reflecting a view on the pending bill.

(ii) Analysis. C's traveling expenses (transportation and meals and lodging) are partially for the purpose of making or supporting the lobbying communications and partially for a nonlobbying purpose. As a result, under paragraph (c)(2) of this section, W must reasonably allocate C's traveling expenses between these two purposes. Allocating to influencing legislation only C's incremental transportation expenses (i.e., the taxi fare to meet with the state legislators) does not result in a reasonable allocation of traveling expenses.

Example (6). (i) Facts. On February 1, 1997, a bill is introduced in Congress that would affect Company E. Employees in E's legislative affairs department, as is customary, prepare a brief summary of the bill and periodically confirm the procedural status of the bill through conversations with employees and members of Congress. On March 31, 1997, the head of E's legislative affairs department meets with E's President to request that B, a chemist, temporarily help the legislative affairs department analyze the bill. The President agrees, and suggests that B also be assigned to draft a position letter in opposition to the bill. Employees of the legislative affairs department continue to confirm periodically the procedural status of the bill. On October 31, 1997, B's position letter in opposition to the bill is delivered to members of Congress.

(ii) Analysis. B's letter is a lobbying communication because it refers to and reflects a view on specific legislation. Under paragraph (c)(3)(i) of this section, the assignment of B to assist the legislative affairs department in analyzing the bill and in drafting a position letter in opposition to the bill evidences a purpose to influence legislation. Neither the activity of periodically confirming the procedural status of the bill nor the activity of preparing the routine, brief summary of the bill before March 31 constitutes influencing legislation. In contrast, periodically confirming the procedural status of the bill on or after March 31 relates to the same subject as, and is close in time to, the lobbying communication and is used for no nonlobbying purpose. Consequently, after March 31, E determined the procedural status of the bill for the purpose of supporting the lobbying communication by B.

(d) Lobbying communication made by another. If a taxpayer engages in activities for a purpose of supporting a lobbying communication to be made by another person (or by a group of persons), the taxpayer's activities are treated under paragraph (b) of this section as influencing legislation. For example, if a taxpayer or an employee of the taxpayer (as a volunteer or otherwise) engages in an activity to assist a trade association in preparing its lobbying communication, the taxpayer's activities are influencing legislation even if the lobbying communication is made by the trade association and not the taxpayer. If, however, the taxpayer's employee, acting outside the employee's scope of employment, volunteers to engage in those activities, then the taxpayer is not influencing legislation.

(e) No lobbying communication. Paragraph (e) of this section applies if a taxpayer engages in an activity for a purpose of making or supporting a lobbying communication, but no lobbying communication that the activity supports has yet been made.

(1) Before the filing date. Under this paragraph (e)(1), if on the filing date of the return for any taxable year the taxpayer no longer expects, under any reasonably foreseeable circumstances, that a lobbying communication will be made that is supported by the activity, then the taxpayer will be treated as if it did not engage in the activity for a purpose of making or supporting a lobbying communication. Thus, the taxpayer need not treat any amount allocated to that activity for that year under § 1.162-28 as an amount to which section 162 (e)(1)(A) applies. The filing date for purposes of paragraph (e) of this section is the earlier of the time the taxpayer files its timely return for the year or the due date of the timely return.

(2) After the filing date. (i) In general. If, at any time after the filing date, the taxpayer no longer expects, under any reasonably foreseeable circumstances, that a lobbying communication will be made that is supported by the activity, then any amount previously allocated under § 1.162-28 to the activity and disallowed under section 162 (e)(1)(A) is treated as an amount that is not subject to section 162(e)(1)(A) and that is paid or incurred only at the time the taxpayer no longer expects that a lobbying communication will be made.

(ii) Special rule for certain tax-exempt organizations. For a tax-exempt organization subject to section 6033(e), the amounts described in paragraph (e)(2)(i) of this section are treated as reducing (but not below zero) its expenditures to which section 162(e)(1) applies beginning with that year and continuing for subsequent years to the extent not treated in prior years as reducing those expenditures.

(f) Anti-avoidance rule. If a taxpayer, alone or with others, structures its activities with a principal purpose of achieving results that are unreasonable in light of the purposes of section 162(e)(1)(A) and section 6033(e), the Commissioner can recast the taxpayer's activities for federal tax purposes as appropriate to achieve tax results that are consistent with the intent of section 162(e)(1)(A), section 6033(e) (if applicable), and this section, and the pertinent facts and circumstances.

(g) Taxpayer defined. For purposes of this section, a taxpayer includes a tax-exempt organization subject to section 6033(e).

(h) Effective date. This section is effective for amounts paid or incurred on or after July 21, 1995. Taxpayers must adopt a reasonable interpretation of section 162 (e)(1)(A) for amounts paid or incurred before this date.

T.D. 8602, 7/20/95.

Proposed § 1.162-30 Notional principal contract payments. [*For Preamble, see ¶ 152,497*]

(a) In general. Amounts taken into account by a taxpayer pursuant to § 1.446-3(d)(1) (including mark-to-market deductions) with respect to a notional principal contract as defined in § 1.446-3(c)(1)(i), are deductible as ordinary and necessary business expenses. However, this section will not apply to any amount representing interest expense on the deemed loan component of a significant nonperiodic payment as described in § 1.446-3(g)(4). For any loss arising from a termination payment as defined in § 1.446-3(h)(1), see section 1234A and the regulations thereunder. For the timing of deductions with respect to notional principal contracts, see § 1.446-3.

(b) Effective date. Paragraph (a) of this section is applicable to notional principal contracts entered into on or after 30 days after the date a Treasury decision based on these proposed regulations is published in the Federal Register.

§ 1.162(k)-1 Disallowance of deduction for reacquisition payments.

(a) In general. Except as provided in paragraph (b) of this section, no deduction otherwise allowable is allowed under Chapter 1 of the Internal Revenue Code for any amount paid or incurred by a corporation in connection with the reacquisition of its stock or the stock of any related person (as defined in section 465(b)(3)(C)). Amounts paid or incurred in connection with the reacquisition of stock include amounts paid by a corporation to reacquire its stock from an ESOP that are used in a manner described in section 404(k)(2)(A). See § 1.404(k)-3.

(b) Exceptions. Paragraph (a) of this section does not apply to any—

(1) Deduction allowable under section 163 (relating to interest);

(2) Deduction for amounts that are properly allocable to indebtedness and amortized over the term of such indebtedness;

(3) Deduction for dividends paid (within the meaning of section 561); or

(4) Amount paid or incurred in connection with the redemption of any stock in a regulated investment company that issues only stock which is redeemable upon the demand of the shareholder.

(c) Effective date. This section applies with respect to amounts paid or incurred on or after August 30, 2006.

T.D. 9282, 8/29/2006.

§ 1.163-1 Interest deduction in general.

Caution: The Treasury has not yet amended Reg § 1.163-1 to reflect changes made by P.L. 105-34, P.L. 103-66, P.L. 101-508, P.L. 101-239.

(a) Except as otherwise provided in sections 264 to 267, inclusive, interest paid or accrued within the taxable year on indebtedness shall be allowed as a deduction in computing taxable income. For rules relating to interest on certain deferred payments, see section 483 and the regulations thereunder.

(b) Interest paid by the taxpayer on a mortgage upon real estate of which he is the legal or equitable owner, even though the taxpayer is not directly liable upon the bond or note secured by such mortgage, may be deducted as interest on his indebtedness. Pursuant to the provisions of section 163(c), any annual or periodic rental payment made by a taxpayer on or after January 1, 1962, under a redeemable ground rent, as defined in section 1055(c) and paragraph (b) of § 1.1055-1, is required to be treated as interest on an indebtedness secured by a mortgage and, accordingly, may be deducted by the taxpayer as interest on his indebtedness. Section 163(c) has no application in respect of any annual or periodic rental payment made prior to January 1, 1962, or pursuant to an arrangement which does not constitute a "redeemable ground rent" as defined in section 1055(c) and paragraph (b) of § 1.1055-1. Accordingly, annual or periodic payments of Pennsylvania ground rents made before, on, or after January 1, 1962, are deductible as interest if the ground rent is redeemable. An annual or periodic rental payment under a Maryland redeemable ground rent made prior to January 1, 1962, is deductible in accordance with the rules and regulations applicable at the time such payment was made. Any annual or periodic rental payment under a Maryland redeemable ground rent made by the taxpayer on or after January 1, 1962, is, pursuant to the provisions of section 163(c), treated as interest on an indebtedness secured by a mortgage and, accordingly, is deductible by the taxpayer as interest on his indebtedness. In any case where the ground rent is irredeemable, any annual or periodic ground rent payment shall be treated as rent and shall be deductible only to the extent that the payment constitutes a proper business expense. Amounts paid in redemption of a ground rent shall not be treated as interest. For treatment of redeemable ground rents and real property held subject to liabilities under redeemable ground rents, see section 1055 and the regulations thereunder.

(c) Interest calculated for costkeeping or other purposes on account of capital or surplus invested in the business which does not represent a charge arising under an interest-bearing obligation, is not an allowable deduction from gross income. Interest paid by a corporation on scrip dividends is an allowable deduction. So-called interest on preferred stock, which is in reality a dividend thereon, cannot be deducted in computing taxable income. (See, however, section 583.) In the case of banks and loan or trust companies, interest paid within the year on deposits, such as interest paid on moneys received for investment and secured by interest-bearing certificates of indebtedness issued by such bank or loan or trust company, may be deducted from gross income.

(d) To the extent of assistance payments made in respect of an indebtedness of the taxpayer during the taxable year by the Department of Housing and Urban Development under section 235 of the National Housing Act (12 USC § 1715z), as amended, no deduction shall be allowed under section 163 and this section for interest paid or accrued with respect to such indebtedness. However, such payments shall not affect the amount of any deduction under any section of the Code other than section 163. The provisions of this paragraph shall apply to taxable years beginning after December 31, 1974.

T.D. 6223, 1/23/57, amend T.D. 6593, 2/28/62, T.D. 6821, 5/3/65, T.D. 6873, 1/24/66, T.D. 7408, 3/4/76.

§ 5f.163-1 Denial of interest deduction on certain obligations issued after December 31, 1982, unless issued in registered form.

Caution: The Treasury has not yet amended Reg § 5f.163-1 to reflect changes made by P.L. 99-514.

(a) Denial of deduction generally. Interest paid or accrued on a registration-required obligation (as defined in paragraph (b) of this section) shall not be allowed as a deduction under section 163 or any other provision of law unless such obligation is issued in registered form (as defined in § 5f.103-1(c)).

(b) Registration-required obligation. For purposes of this section, the term "registration-required obligation" means any obligation except any one of the following:

(1) An obligation issued by a natural person.

(2) An obligation not of a type offered to the public. The determination as to whether an obligation is not of a type offered to the public shall be based on whether similar obligations are in fact publicly offered or traded.

(3) An obligation that has a maturity at the date of issue of not more than 1 year.

(4) An obligation issued before January 1, 1983. An obligation first issued before January 1, 1983, shall not be considered to have been issued on or after such date merely as a result of the existence of a right on the part of the holder of such obligation to convert such obligation from registered form into bearer form, or as result of the exercise of such a right.

(5) An obligation described in subparagraph (1) of paragraph (c) (relating to certain obligations issued to foreign persons).

(c) [Removed]

(d) Effective date. The provisions of this section shall apply to obligations issued after December 31, 1982, unless issued on an exercise of a warrant for the conversion of a convertible obligation if such warrant or obligation was offered or sold outside the United States without registration under the Securities Act of 1933 and was issued before August 10, 1982.

(e) Obligations first issued after December 31, 1982, where the right exists for the holder to convert such obligation from registered form into bearer form. [Reserved]

(f) Examples. The application of this section may be illustrated by the following examples:

Example (1). All of the shares of Corporation X are owned by two individuals, A and B. X desires to sell all of its assets to Corporation Y, all of the shares of which are owned by individual C. Following the sale, Corporation X will be completely liquidated. As partial consideration for the Corporation X assets, Corporation Y delivers a promissory note to X, secured by a security interest and mortgage on the acquired assets. The note given by Y to X is not of a type offered to the public.

Example (2). Corporation Z has a credit agreement with Bank M pursuant to which Corporation Z may borrow amounts not exceeding $10X upon delivery of Z's note to Bank M. The note Z delivers to M is not of a type offered to the public.

Example (3). Individuals D and E operate a retail business through partnership DE. D wishes to loan partnership DE $5X. DE's note evidencing the loan from D is not of a type offered to the public.

Example (4). Individual F owns one-third of the shares of Corporation W. F makes a cash advance to W. W's note evidencing F's cash advance is not of a type offered to the public.

Example (5). Closely-held Corporation R places its convertible debentures with 30 individuals who are United States persons. The offering is not required to be registered under the Securities Act of 1933. Similar debentures are publicly offered and traded. The obligations are not considered of a type not offered to the public.

Example (6). In 1980, Corporation V issued its bonds due in 1986 through an offering registered with the Securities and Exchange Commission. Although the bonds were initially issued in registered form, the terms of the bonds permit a holder, at his option, to convert a bond into bearer form at any time prior to maturity. Similarly, a person who holds a bond in bearer form may, at any time, have the bond converted into registered form.

(i) Assume G bought one of Corporation V's bonds upon the original issuance in 1980. In 1983, G requests that V convert the bond into bearer form. Except for the change from registered to bearer form, the terms of the bond are unchanged. The bond held by G is not considered issued after December 31, 1982, under § 5f.163-1(b)(4).

(ii) Assume H buys one of Corporation V's bonds in the secondary market in 1983. The bond H receives is in registered form, but H requests that V convert the obligation into bearer form. There is no other change in the terms of the instrument. The bond held by H is not considered issued after December 31, 1982, under § 5f.163-1(b)(4).

(iii) Assume the same facts as in (ii) except that in 1984 I purchases H's V Corporation bond, which is in bearer form. I requests V to convert the bond into registered form. There is no other change in the terms of the instrument. In 1985, I requests V to convert the bond back into bearer form. Again, there is no other change in the terms of the instrument. The bond purchased by I is not considered issued after December 31, 1982, under § 5f.163-1(b)(4).

Example (7). Corporation U wishes to make a public offering of its debentures to United States persons. U issues a master note to Bank N. The terms of the note require that any person who acquires an interest in the note must have such interest reflected in a book entry. Bank N offers for sale interests in the Corporation U note. Ownership interests in the note are reflected on the books of Bank N. Corporation U's debenture is considered issued in registered form.

Example (8). Issuer S wishes to make a public offering of its debt obligations to United States persons. The obligations will have a maturity in excess of one year. On November 1, 1982, the closing on the debt offering occurs. At the closing, the net cash proceeds of the offering are delivered to S, and S delivers a master note to the underwriter of the offering. On January 2, 1983, S delivers the debt obligations to the purchasers in definitive form and the master note is cancelled. The obligations are not registration-required because they are considered issued before January 1, 1983.

Example (9). In July 1983, Corporation T sells an issue of debt obligations maturing in 1985 to the public in the United States. Three of the obligations of the issue are issued to J in bearer form. The balance of the obligations of the issue are issued in registered form. The terms of the registered and bearer obligations are identical. The obligations issued to J are of a type offered to the public and are registration-required obligations. Since the three obligations are issued in bearer form, T is subject to the tax imposed under section 4701 with respect to the three bearer obligations. In addition, interest paid or accrued on the three bearer obligations is not deductible by T. Moreover, since the issuance of the three bearer obligations is subject to tax under section 4701, J is not prohibited from deducting losses on the obligations under section 165(j) or from treating gain on the obligations as capital gain under section 1232(d). The balance of the obligations in the issue do not give rise to liability for the tax under section 4701, and the deductibility of interest on such obligations is not affected by section 163(f).

Example (10). Broker K acquires a bond issued in 1980 by the United States Treasury through the Bureau of Public Debt. Broker K sells interests in the bond to the public after December 31, 1982. A purchaser may acquire an interest in any interest payment falling due under the bond or an interest in the principal of the bond. The bond is held by Custodian L for the benefit of the persons acquiring these interests. On receipt of interest and principal payments under the bond, Custodian L transfers the amount received to the person whose ownership interest corresponds to the bond component giving rise to the payment. Under section 1232B, each bond component is treated as an obligation issued with original issue discount equal to the excess of the state redemption price at maturity over the purchase price of the bond component. The interests sold by K are obligations of a type offered to the public. Further, the interests are, in accordance with section 1232B, considered issued after December 31, 1982. Accordingly, the interests are registration-required obligations under § 5f.163-1(b).

T.D. 7852, 11/9/82, amend T.D. 7965, 8/17/84.

PAR. 2. Section 5f.163-1 is amended by revising paragraph (b)(2) to read as set forth below.

Proposed § 5f.163-1 Denial of interest deduction on certain obligations issued after December 31, 1982, unless issued in registered form. [*For Preamble, see ¶ 151,499*]

* * * * *

(b) * * *

(2) An obligation not of a type offered to the public. (i) Readily tradeable obligations. For purposes of section 163(f)(2)(A)(ii) and this section, an obligation shall be considered to be of a type offered to the public if it either—

(A) Is treated as in a form designed to render such obligation readily tradeable in an established securities market under § 15a.453-1(e)(4) of this chapter; or

(B) Would be treated as in a form designed to render such obligation readily tradeable in an established securities market under § 15a.453-1(e)(4) of this chapter if § 15a.453-1(e)(4)(ii)(B) of this chapter provided for comparison of the obligation to obligations of other issuers (as well as other obligations of the same issuer) and the term "established securities market" were defined to include any exchange or market described in either § 151.453-1(e)(4)(iv) or § 1.897-1(m) of this chapter.

(ii) Other Obligations. When necessary to carry out the purposes of section 163(f), an obligation that is not described in paragraph (b)(2)(i) of this section may nevertheless be considered to be of a type offered to the public. The determination as to whether an obligation that is not described in paragraph (b)(2)(i) of this section is of a type offered to the public shall be based on whether similar obligations are in fact publicly offered or traded.

(iii) Effective date. Except as otherwise provided in this paragraph (b)(2)(iii), paragraph (b)(2) of this section applies with respect to obligations issued after January 21, 1993. Paragraph (b)(2) of this section shall not apply with respect to obligations issued after January 21, 1993 where substantially all of the financial terms of such obligations were agreed upon by the obligor in writing on or before January 21, 1993.

* * * * *

PAR. 39. Paragraph (f) of § 5f.163-1 is amended by removing the word "1232(d)" from each place that it appears and adding in its place the word "1287", and by removing the phrase "section 1232B" from each place that it appears and adding in its place the phrase "section 1286".

Proposed § 5f.163-1 [Amended] [*For Preamble, see ¶ 151,065*]

• ***Caution:*** Prop reg § 1.482-2 was finalized by T.D. 8204, 5/20/88. Prop regs §§ 1.163-7, 1.446-2, 1.483-1 through -5, 1.1001-1, 1.1012-1, 1.1271 through -3, 1.1272-1, 1.1273-1, 1.1273-2, 1.1274-1 throught -7, 1.1274A-1, 1.1275-1 through -3, and 1.1275-5 were withdrawn by the Treasury on 12/22/92, 57 Fed. Reg. 67050. Prop reg § 1.1275-4 was superseded by the Treasury on 12/16/94, Fed. Reg. 59, 64884, which was finalized by T.D. 8674, 6/11/96.

§ 1.163-2 Installment purchases where interest charge is not separately stated.

Caution: The Treasury has not yet amended Reg § 1.163-2 to reflect changes made by P.L. 99-514.

(a) In general. *(1)* Whenever there is a contract with a seller for the purchase of personal property providing for payment of part or all of the purchase price in installments and there is a separately stated carrying charge (including a finance charge, service charge, and the like) but the actual interest charge cannot be ascertained, a portion of the payments made during the taxable year under the contract shall be treated as interest and is deductible under section 163 and this section. Section 163(b) contains a formula, described in paragraph (b) of this section, in accordance with which the amount of interest deductible in the taxable year must be computed. This formula is designed to operate automatically in the case of any installment purchase, without regard to whether payments under the contract are made when due or are in default. For applicable limitations when an obligation to pay is terminated, see paragraph (c) of this section.

(2) Whenever there is a contract with an educational institution for the purchase of educational services providing for payment of part or all of the purchase price in installments and there is a separately stated carrying charge (including a finance charge, service charge, and the like) but the actual interest charge cannot be ascertained, a portion of the payments made during the taxable year under the contract shall be treated as interest and is deductible under section 163 and this section. See paragraphs (b) and (c) of this section for the applicable computation and limitations rules. For purposes of section 163(b) and this section, the term "educational services" means any service (including lodging) which is purchased from an educational institution (as defined in section 151(e)(4) and paragraph (c) of § 1.151-3) and which is provided for a student of such institution.

(3) Section 163(b) and this section do not apply to a contract for the loan of money, even if the loan is to be repaid in installments and even if the borrowed amount is used to purchase personal property or educational services. In cases to which the preceding sentence applies, the portion of the installment payment which constitutes interest (as distinguished from payments of principal and charges such as payments for credit life insurance) is deductible under section 163(a) and § 1.163-1.

(b) Computation. The portion of any such payments to be treated as interest shall be equal to 6 percent of the average unpaid balance under the contract during the taxable year. For purposes of this computation, the average unpaid balance under the contract is the sum of the unpaid balance outstanding on the first day of each month beginning during the taxable year, divided by 12.

(c) **Limitations.** The amount treated as interest under section 163(b) and this section for any taxable year shall not exceed the amount of the payments made under the contract during the taxable year nor the aggregate carrying charges properly attributable to each contract for such taxable year. In computing the amount to be treated as interest if the obligation to pay is terminated as, for example, in the case of a repossession of the property, the unpaid balance on the first day of the month during which the obligation is terminated shall be zero.

(d) **Illustrations.** The provisions of this section may be illustrated by the following examples:

Example (1). On January 20, 1955, A purchased a television set for $400, including a stated carrying charge of $25. The down payment was $50, and the balance was paid in 14 monthly installments of $25 each, on the 20th day of each month commencing with February. Assuming that A is a cash method, calendar year taxpayer and that no other installment purchases were made, the amount to be treated as interest in 1955 is $12.38, computed as follows:

Year 1955

First day of:	Unpaid balance outstanding
January	$ 0
February	350
March	325
April	300
May	275
June	250
July	225
August	200
September	175
October	150
November	125
December	100
	2,475

Sum of unpaid balances $2,475 ÷ 12 = $206.25; 6 percent thereof = $12.38.

Example (2). On November 20, 1955, B purchased a furniture set for $1,250, including a stated carrying charge of $48. The down payment was $50 and the balance was payable in 12 monthly installments of $100 each, on the first day of each month commencing with December 1955. Assume that B is a cash method, calendar year taxpayer and that no other installment purchases were made. Assume further that B made the first payment when due, but made only one other payment on June 1, 1956. The amount to be treated as interest in 1955 is $4, and the amount to be treated as interest in 1956 is $33, computed as follows:

Year 1955

First day of:	Unpaid balance outstanding:
December	$1,200

Sum of unpaid balances $1,200 ÷ 12 = $100; 6 percent thereof = $6.
Carrying charges attributable to 1955 = $4.

Year 1956

First day of:	Unpaid balance outstanding:
January	$1,100
February	1,000
March	900
April	800
May	700
June	600
July	500
August	400
September	300
October	200
November	100
	6,600

Sum of unpaid balances $6,600 ÷ 12 = $550; 6 percent thereof = $33.
Carrying charges attributable to 1956 = $44 ($4 × 11).
Sum of unpaid balances $6,600 ÷ 12 = $550; 6 percent thereof = $33.
Carrying charges attributable to 1956 = $44 ($4 × 11).

Example (3). Assume the same facts as in example (2), except that the furniture was repossessed and B's obligation to pay terminated as of July 15, 1956. The amount to be treated as interest in 1955 is $4, computed as in example (2) above. The amount to be treated as interest in 1956 is $25.50, computed as follows:

Year 1956

First day of:	Unpaid balance outstanding:
January	$1,100
February	1,000
March	900
April	800
May	700
June	600
July-November	0
	5,100

Sum of unpaid balances $5,100 ÷ 12 = $425; six percent thereof = $25.50.
Carrying charges attributable to 1956 = $44 ($4 × 11).

Example (4). (i) On September 15, 1968, O registered at X University for the 1968-69 academic year, C entered into an agreement with the X University for the purchase during such academic year of educational services (including lodging and tuition) for a total fee of $1,000, including a separately stated carrying charge of $50. Under the terms of the agreement, an initial payment of $200 was to be made by C on September 15, 1968, and the balance was to be paid in 6 monthly installments of $100 each, on the 15th day of each month commencing with October 1968. C made all of the required 1968 payments. Assuming that C is a cash method, calendar year taxpayer and that no other installment purchases of services or property were made, the amount to be treated as interest in 1968 is $10.50, computed as follows:

Year 1968

First day of:	Unpaid balance outstanding
January-September	$ 0
October	800
November	700
December	600
	2,100

The sum of unpaid balances ($2,100) divided by 12 is $175; 6 percent thereof is $10.50. The carrying charges attributable to 1968 are $18.75 (i.e., the total carrying charges ($50), divided by the total number of payments (8), multiplied by the number of payments made in 1968 (3)). Since the amount to be treated as interest in 1968 ($10.50) does not exceed the carrying charges attributable to 1968 ($18.75), the limitations set forth in paragraph (c) of this section is not applicable.

(ii) The result in this example would be the same even if the X University assigned the agreement to a bank or other financial institution and C made his payments directly to the bank or other financial institution.

Example (5). On September 15, 1968, D registered at Y University for the 1968-69 academic year. The tuition for such year was $1,500. In order to pay his tuition, D borrowed $1,500 from the M Corporation, a lending institution, and remitted that sum to the Y University. The loan agreement between M Corporation and D provided that D was to repay the loan, plus a service charge, in 10 equal monthly installments, on the first day of each month commencing with October 1968. The service charge consisted of interest and the cost of credit life insurance on D's life. Since section 163(b) and this section do not apply to a contract for the loan of money, D is not entitled to compute his interest deduction with respect to his loan from M Corporation under such sections. D may deduct that portion of each installment payment which constitutes interest (as distinguished from payments of principal and the charge for credit life insurance) under section 163(a) and § 1.163-1, provided that the amount of such interest can be ascertained.

(e) Effective date. Except in the case of payments made under a contract for educational services, the rule provided in section 163(b) and this section applies to payments made during taxable years beginning after December 31, 1953, and ending after August 16, 1954, regardless of when the contract of sale was made. In the case of payments made under a contract for educational services, the rule provided in section 163(b) and this section applies to payments made during taxable years beginning after December 31, 1963, regardless of when the contract for educational services was made.

T.D. 6223, 1/23/57, amend T.D. 6991, 1/16/69.

§ 1.163-3 Deduction for discount on bonds issued on or before May 27, 1969.

(a) Discount upon issuance. *(1)* If bonds are issued by a corporation at a discount, the net amount of such discount is deductible and should be prorated or amortized over the life of the bonds. For purposes of this section, the amortizable bond discount equals the excess of the amount payable at maturity (or, in the case of a callable bond, at the earlier call date) over the issue price of the bond (as defined in paragraph (b)(2) of § 1.1232-3).

(2) In the case of a bond issued by a corporation after December 31, 1954, as part of an investment unit consisting of an obligation and an option, the issue price of the bond is determined by allocating the amount received for the investment unit to the individual elements of the unit in the manner set forth in subdivision (ii)(a) of § 1.1232-3(b)(2). Discount with respect to bonds issued by a corporation as part of investment units consisting of obligations and options after December 31, 1954, and before [12/24/68]

(i) Increased by any amount treated as bond premium which has been included in gross income with respect to such bonds prior to [12/24/68], or

(ii) Decreased by any amount which has been deducted by the issuer as discount attributable to such bonds prior to [12/24/68], or

(iii) Decreased by any amount which has been deducted by the issuer prior to [12/24/68] upon the exercise or sale by investors of options issued in investment units with such bonds,

should be amortized, starting with the first taxable year ending on or after [12/24/68] over the remaining life of such bonds.

(b) Examples. The rules in paragraph (a) of this section are illustrated by the following examples:

Example (1). M Corporation, on January 1, 1960, the beginning of its taxable year, issued for $95,000, 3 percent bonds, maturing 10 years from the date of issue, with a stated redemption price at maturity of $100,000. M Corporation should treat $5,000 ($100,000 − $95,000) as the total amount to be amortized over the life of the bonds.

Example (2). Assume the same facts as example (1), except that the bonds are convertible into common stock of M Corporation. Since the issue price of the bonds includes any amount attributable to the conversion privilege, the result is the same as in example (1).

Example (3). Assume the same facts as example (1), except that the bonds are issued as part of an investment unit consisting of an obligation and an option. Assume further that the issue price of the bonds as determined under the rules of allocation set forth in subdivision (ii) *(a)* of § 1.1232-3(b)(2) is $94,000. Accordingly, M Corporation should treat $6,000 (100,000 − $94,000) as the total amount to be amortized over the life of the bonds.

Example (4). Assume in example (3), that prior to [date of publication of Treasury decision] M Corporation had only treated $5,000 as the bond discount to be amortized and deducted only $4,000 of this amount. Starting with the first taxable year ending on or after [date of publication of Treasury decision], M Corporation should amortize $2,000 ($6,000 discount, less $4,000 previously deducted) over the remaining life of the bonds.

Example (5). N Corporation, on January 1, 1956, for a consideration of $102,000, issued 20-year bonds in the face amount of $100,000, together with options to purchase stock of N Corporation. The issue price of the bonds as determined under the rules of allocation set forth in subdivision (ii)(a) of § 1.232-2(b)(2) is $99,000. Until [12/24/68], N Corporation has treated as bond premium, $2,000, representing the excess of the consideration received for the bond-option investment units over the maturity value of the bonds, and has accordingly prorated and included in income $1,200 of such amount. Starting with the first taxable year beginning on or after [12/24/68], N Corporation may amortize as a deduction over the remaining life of the bonds the amount of $2,200 ($1,000 discount, plus $1,200 previously included in income).

Example (6). O Corporation, on January 1, 1956, for a consideration of $100,000, issued 20-year bonds with a $100,000 face value, together with options to purchase stock of O Corporation, which could be exercised at any time up to 5 years from the date of issue. The issue price of the bonds as determined under the rules of allocation set forth in subdivision (ii)(a) of § 1.1232-3(b)(2) is $98,000. O Corporation, upon the exercise of the options prior to [12/24/68], had deducted from income their fair market value at the time of exercise, which is assumed for purposes of this example to have been $3,000. Even though the bonds are considered to have been issued at a discount under paragraph (a)(1) of this section, O Corporation would have no deduction over the remaining life of the bonds, inasmuch as O Corporation, in computing the amount of such deduction, is required under paragraph (a)(2)(iii) of this section to reduce the amount which would otherwise be treated as bond discount, $2,000 ($100,000 – $98,000), by the amount deducted from income upon the exercise of the options, in this case, $3,000.

(c) Deduction upon repurchase. *(1)* Except as provided in subparagraph (3) of this paragraph, if bonds are issued by a corporation and are subsequently repurchased by the corporation at a price in excess of the issue price plus any amount of discount deducted prior to repurchase, or (in the case of bonds issued subsequent to Feb. 28, 1913) minus any amount of premium returned as income prior to repurchase, the excess of the purchase price over the issue price adjusted for amortized premium or discount is a deductible expense for the taxable year.

(2) In the case of a convertible bond (except a bond which the corporation, before Sept. 5, 1968, has obligated itself to repurchase at a specified price), the deduction allowable under subparagraph (1) of this paragraph may not exceed an amount equal to 1 year's interest at the rate specified in the bond, except to the extent that the corporation can demonstrate to the satisfaction of the Commissioner or his delegate that an amount in excess of 1 year's interest does not include any amount attributable to the conversion feature.

(3) No deduction shall be allowed under subparagraph (1) of this paragraph to the extent a deduction is disallowed under subparagraph (2) of this paragraph or to the extent a deduction is disallowed by section 249 (relating to limitation on deduction of bond premium on repurchase of convertible obligation) and the regulations thereunder. See paragraph (f) of § 1.249-1 for effective date limitation on section 249.

(d) Definition. For purposes of this section, a debenture, note, certificate or other evidence of indebtedness, issued by a corporation and bearing interest shall be given the same treatment as a bond.

(e) Effective date. The provisions of this section shall not apply in respect of a bond issued after May 27, 1969, unless issued pursuant to a written commitment which was binding on that date and at all times thereafter.

T.D. 6984, 12/23/68, amend T.D. 7154, 12/27/71, T.D. 7259, 2/9/73.

---

§ 1.163-4 Deduction for original issue discount on certain obligations issued after May 27, 1969.

Caution: The Treasury has not yet amended Reg § 1.163-4 to reflect changes made by P.L. 100-647, P.L. 99-514, P.L. 98-369, P.L. 97-248.

(a) In general. *(1)* If an obligation is issued by a corporation with original issue discount, the amount of such discount is deductible as interest and shall be prorated or amortized over the life of the obligation. For purposes of this section the term "obligation" shall have the same meaning as in § 1.1232-1 (without regard to whether the obligation is a capital asset in the hands of the holder) and the term "original issue discount" shall have the same meaning as in section 1232(b)(1) (without regard to the one-fourth-of-1-percent limitation in the second sentence thereof). Thus, in general, the amount of original issue discount equals the excess of the amount payable at maturity over the issue price of the bond (as defined in paragraph (b)(2) of § 1.1232-3), regardless of whether that amount is less than one-fourth of 1 percent of the redemption price at maturity multiplied by the number of complete years to maturity. For the rule as to whether there is original issue discount in the case of an obligation issued in an exchange for property other than money, and the amount thereof, see paragraph (b)(2)(iii) of § 1.1232-3. In any case in which original issue discount is carried over from one corporation to another corporation under section 381(c)(9) or from an obligation exchanged to an obligation received in any exchange under paragraph (b)(1)(iv) of § 1.1232-3, such discount shall be carried over for purposes of this section. The amount of original issue discount carried over in an exchange of obligations under the preceding sentence shall be prorated or amortized over the life of the obligation issued in such exchange. For computation of issue price and the amount of original issue discount in the case of serial obligations, see paragraph (b)(2)(iv) of § 1.1232-3.

(2) In the case of an obligation issued by a corporation as part of an investment unit (as defined in paragraph (b)(2)(ii) *(a)* of § 1.1232-3) consisting of an obligation and other property, the issue price of the obligation is determined by allocating the amount received for the investment unit to the individual elements of the unit in the manner set forth in paragraph (b)(2)(ii) of § 1.1232-3.

(3) Recovery or retention of amounts previously deducted. In any taxable year in which an amount of original issue discount which was deducted as interest under this section is retained or recovered by the taxpayer, such as, for example, by reason of a fine, penalty, forfeiture, or other withdrawal fee, such amount shall be includible in the gross income of such taxpayer for such taxable year.

(b) Examples. The rules in paragraph (a) of this section are illustrated by the following examples:

Example (1). N Corporation, which uses the calendar year as its taxable year, on January 1, 1970, issued for $99,000 9 percent bonds maturing 10 years from the date of issue, with a stated redemption price at maturity of $100,000. The original issue discount on each bond (as determined under section 1232(b)(1) without regard to the one-fourth-of-1-percent limitation in the second sentence thereof) is $1,000, i.e., redemption price, $100,000 minus issue price, $99,000. N shall treat $1,000 as the total amount to be amortized over the life of the bonds.

Example (2). Assume the same facts as example (1), except that the bonds are convertible into common stock of N Corporation. Since the issue price of the bonds includes any amount attributable to the conversion privilege, the result is the same as in example (1).

Example (3). Assume the same facts as example (1), except that the bonds are issued as part of an investment unit consisting of an obligation and an option. Assume further that the issue price of the bonds as determined under the rules of allocation set forth in paragraph (b)(2)(ii) of § 1.1232-3 is $94,000. The original issue discount on the bond (as determined under section 1232(b)(1) without regard to the one-fourth-of-1-percent limitation in the second sentence thereof) is $6,000, i.e., redemption price, $100,000, minus issue price, $94,000. N shall treat $6,000 as the total amount to be amortized over the life of the bonds.

Example (4). On January 1, 1971, a commercial bank which uses the calendar year as its taxable year, issued a certificate of deposit for $10,000. The certificate of deposit is not redeemable until December 31, 1975, except in an emergency as defined in, and subject to the qualifications provided by, Regulations Q of the Board of Governors of the Federal Reserve. See 12 CFR § 217.4(d). The stated redemption price at maturity is $13,382.26. The certificate is an obligation to which section 1232(a)(3)(A) applies (see paragraph (d) of § 1.1232-1), and the original issue discount with respect to the certificate (as determined under section 1232(b)(1) without regard to the one-fourth-of-1-percent limitation in the second sentence thereof) is $3,382.26 (i.e., redemption price, $13,382.26, minus issued price, $10,000). Y shall treat $3,382.26 as the total amount to be amortized over the life of the certificate.

(c) Deduction upon repurchase. *(1)* Except as provided in subparagraph (2) of this paragraph, if bonds are issued by a corporation and are subsequently repurchased by the corporation at a price in excess of the issue price plus any amount of original issue discount deducted prior to repurchase, or minus any amount of premium returned as income prior to repurchase, the excess of the repurchase price over the issue price adjusted for amortized premium or deducted discount is deductible as interest for the taxable year.

(2) The provisions of subparagraph (1) of this paragraph shall not apply to the extent a deduction is disallowed by section 249 (relating to limitation on deduction of bond premium on repurchase of convertible obligation) and the regulations thereunder.

(d) Effective date. The provisions of this section shall apply in respect of obligations issued after May 27, 1969, other than—

(1) Obligations issued pursuant to a written commitment which was binding on May 27, 1969, and at all times thereafter, and

(2) Deposits made before January 1, 1971, in the case of certificates of deposit, time deposits, bonus plans, and other deposit arrangements with banks, domestic building and loan associations, and similar financial institutions.

T.D. 7154, 12/27/71, amend T.D. 7213, 10/17/72, T.D. 7259, 2/9/73.

PAR. 4. Section 1.163-4 is amended as follows:

1. The heading is revised by adding a comma and the phrase "and before July 2, 1982." after the word "1969".

2. In paragraph (a)(1), the second sentence is amended by removing the phrase "section 1232(b)(1)" and adding in its place the phrase "section 1273(a)(1)", and the second sentence is further amended by removing the phrase "the second sentence thereof" in the parenthetical and adding in its place the phrase "section 1273(a)(3)".

3. Paragraph (b) is amended by removing the phrase "section 1232(b)(1)" from each place that it appears in the paragraph and adding its place the phrase "section 1273(a)(1)", by removing the phrase "the second sentence thereof" from each place it appears in the paragraph and adding in its place the phrase "section 1273(a)(3)", and by removing the phrase "section 1232(a)(3)(A)" from *Example (4)* and adding in its place the phrase "section 1271(a)(3)(A)".

4. Paragraph (d) is amended by adding the phrase "and before July 2, 1982," after the word "1969," each place that it appears.

Proposed § 1.163-4 [Amended] [*For Preamble, see ¶ 151,065*]

• ***Caution:*** Prop reg § 1.482-2 was finalized by T.D. 8204, 5/20/88. Prop regs §§ 1.163-7, 1.446-2, 1.483-1 through -5, 1.1001-1, 1.1012-1, 1.1271 through -3, 1.1272-1, 1.1273-1, 1.1273-2, 1.1274-1 throught -7, 1.1274A-1, 1.1275-1 through -3, and 1.1275-5 were withdrawn by the Treasury on 12/22/92, 57 Fed. Reg. 67050. Prop reg § 1.1275-4 was superseded by the Treasury on 12/16/94, Fed. Reg. 59, 64884, which was finalized by T.D. 8674, 6/11/96.

§ 1.163-5 Denial of interest deduction on certain obligations issued after December 31, 1982, unless issued in registered form.

(a) [Reserved]

(b) [Reserved]

(c) Obligations issued to foreign persons after September 21, 1984. *(1) In general.* A determination of whether an obligation satisfies each of the requirements of this paragraph shall be made on an obligation-by-obligation basis. An obligation issued directly (or through affiliated entities) in bearer form by, or guaranteed by, a United States Government-owned agency or a United States Government-sponsored enterprise, such as the Federal National Mortgage Association, the Federal Home Loan Banks, the Federal Loan Mortgage Corporation, the Farm Credit Administration, and the Student Loan Marketing Association, may not satisfy this paragraph (c). An obligation issued after September 21, 1984 is described in this paragraph if—

(i) There are arrangements reasonably designed to ensure that such obligation will be sold (or resold in connection with its original issuance) only to a person who is not a United States person or who is a United States person that is a financial institution (as defined in § 1.165-12(c)(1)(v)) purchasing for its own account or for the account of a customer and that agrees to comply with the requirements of section 165(j)(3)(A), (B), or (C) and the regulations thereunder, and

(ii) In the case of an obligation which is not in registered form—

(A) Interest on such obligation is payable only outside the United States and its possessions, and

(B) Unless the obligation is described in subparagraph (2)(i)(C) of this paragraph or is a temporary global security, the following statement in English either appears on the face of the obligation and on any interest coupons which may be detached therefrom or, if the obligation is evidenced by a book entry, appears in the book or record in which the book entry is made: "Any United States person who holds this obligation will be subject to limitations under the United States income tax laws, including the limitations provided in sections 165(j) and 1287(a) of the Internal Revenue Code." For purposes of this paragraph, the term "temporary global security" means a security which is held for the benefit of the purchasers of the obligations of the issuer and interests in which are exchangeable for securities in definitive registered or bearer form prior to its stated maturity.

(2) Rules for the application of this paragraph. (i) Arrangements reasonably designed to ensure sale to non-United States persons. An obligation will be considered to satisfy paragraph (c)(1)(i) of this section if the conditions of paragraph (c)(2)(i)(A), (B), (C), or (D) of this section are met in connection with the original issuance of the obligation. However, an exchange of one obligation for another will not be considered a new issuance if the obligation received is identical in all respects to the obligation surrendered in exchange therefor, except that the obligor of the obligation received need not be the same obligor as the obligor of the obligation surrendered. An exchange of one obligation for another is considered an original issuance if and only if the exchange constitutes a disposition of property for purposes of section 1001 of the Code. Obligations that meet the conditions of paragraph (c)(2)(i)(A), (B), (C) or (D) of this section may be issued in a single public offering. The preceding sentence does not apply to certificates of deposit issued under the conditions of paragraph (c)(2)(i)(C) of this section by a United States person or by a controlled foreign corporation within the meaning of section 957(a) that is engaged in the active conduct of a banking business within the meaning of section 954(c)(3)(B) as in effect prior to the Tax Reform Act of 1986, and the regulations thereunder. A temporary global security need not satisfy the conditions of paragraph (c)(2)(i)(A), (B) or (C) of this section, but must satisfy the applicable requirements of paragraph (c)(2)(i)(D) of this section.

(A) In connection with the original issuance of an obligation, the obligation is offered for sale or resale only outside of the United States and its possessions, is delivered only outside the United States and its possessions and is not registered under the Securities Act of 1933 because it is intended for distribution to persons who are not United States persons. An obligation will not be considered to be required to be registered under the Securities Act of 1933 if the issuer, in reliance on the written opinion of counsel received prior to the issuance thereof, determines in good faith that the obligation need not be registered under the Securities Act of 1933 for the reason that it is intended for distribution to persons who are not United States persons. Solely for purposes of this subdivision (i)(A), the term "United States person" has the same meaning as it has for purposes of determining whether an obligation is intended for distribution to persons under the Securities Act of 1933. Except as provided in paragraph (c)(3) of this section, this paragraph (c)(2)(i)(A) applies only to obligations issued on or before September 7, 1990.

(B) The obligation is registered under the Securities Act of 1933, is exempt from registration by reason of section 3 or section 4 of such Act, or does not qualify as a security under the Securities Act of 1933; all of the conditions set forth in paragraph (c)(2)(i)(B)(1), (2), (3), (4), and (5) of this section are met with respect to such obligations; and, except as provided in paragraph (c)(3) of this section, the obligation is issued on or before September 7, 1990.

(1) In connection with the original issuance of an obligation in bearer form, the obligation is offered for sale or resale only outside the United States and its possessions.

(2) the issuer does not, and each underwriter and each member of the selling group, if any, covenants that it will not, in connection with the original issuance of the obligation, offer to sell or resell the obligation in bearer form to any person inside the United States or to a United States person unless such United States person is a financial institution as defined in § 1.165-12(c)(v) purchasing for its own account or for the account of a customer, which financial institution, as a condition of the purchase, agrees to provide on delivery of the obligation (or on issuance, if the obligation is not in definitive form) the certificate required under paragraph (c)(2)(i)(B)(4).

(3) In connection with its sale or resale during the original issuance of the obligation in bearer form, each underwriter and each member of the selling group, if any, or the issuer, if there is no underwriter or selling group, sends a confirmation to the purchaser of the bearer obligation stating that the purchaser represents that it is not a United States person or, if it is a United States person, it is a financial institution as defined in § 1.165-12(c)(v) purchasing for its own account or for the account of a customer and that the financial institution will comply with the requirements of section 165(j)(3)(A), (B), or (C) and the regulations thereunder. The confirmation must also state that, if the purchaser is a dealer, it will send similar confirmations to whomever purchases from it.

(4) In connection with the original issuance of the obligation in bearer form it is delivered in definite form (or issued, if the obligation is not in definitive form) to the person entitled to physical delivery thereof only outside the United States and its possessions and only upon presentation of a certificate signed by such person to the issuer, underwriter, or member of the selling group, which certificate states that the obligation is not being acquired by or on behalf of a United States person, or for offer to resell, or for resale to a United States person or any person inside the United States, or, if a beneficial interest in the obligation is being acquired by a United States person, that such person is a financial institution as defined in § 1.165.12(c)(1)(v) or is acquiring through a financial institution and that the obligation is held by a financial institution that has agreed to comply with the requirements of section 165(j)(3)(A), (B), or (C) and the regulations thereunder and that is not purchasing for offer to resell or for resale inside the United States. When a certificate is provided by a clearing organization, it must be based on statements provided to it by its member organizations. A clearing organization is an entity which is in the business of holding obligations for member organizations and transferring obligations among such members by credit or debit to the account of a member without the necessity or physical delivery of the obligation. For purposes of paragraph (c)(2)(i)(B), the term "delivery" does not include the delivery of an obligation to an underwriter or member of the selling group, if any.

(5) The issuer, underwriter, or member of the selling group does not have actual knowledge that the certificate described in paragraph (c)(2)(i)(B)(4) of this section is false. The issuer, underwriter, or member of the selling group shall be deemed to have actual knowledge that the certificate described in paragraph (c)(2)(i)(B)(4) of this section is false if the issuer, underwriter, or member of the selling group has a United States address for the beneficial owner (other than a financial institution as defined in § 1.165-12(c)(v) that represents that it will comply with the requirements of section 165(j)(3)(A), (B), or (C) and the regulations thereunder) and does not have documentary evidence as described in § 1.6049-5(c)(1) that the beneficial owner is not a United States person.

(C) The obligation is issued only outside the United States and its possessions by an issuer that does not significantly engage in interstate commerce with respect to the issuance of such obligation either directly or through its agent, an underwriter, or a member of the selling group. In the case of an issuer that is a United States person, such issuer may only satisfy the test set forth in this paragraph (c)(2)(i)(C) if—

(1) It is engaged through a branch in the active conduct of a banking business, within the meaning of section 954(c)(3)(B) as in effect before the Tax Reform Act of 1986, and the regulations thereunder, outside the United States;

(2) The obligation is issued outside of the United States by the branch in connection with that trade or business;

(3) The obligation that is so issued is sold directly to the public and is not issued as a part of a larger issuance made by means of a public offering; and

(4) The issuer either maintains documentary evidence as described in subdivision (iii) of A-5 of § 35a.9999-4T that the purchaser is not a United States person (provided that the issuer has no actual knowledge that the documentary evidence is false) or on delivery of the obligation the issuer receives a statement signed by the person entitled to physical delivery thereof and stating either that the obligation is not being acquired by or on behalf of a United States person or that, if a beneficial interest in the obligation is being acquired by a United States person, such person is a financial institution as defined in § 1.165-12(c)(v) or is acquiring through a financial institution and the obligation is held by a financial institution that has agreed to comply with the requirements of 165(j)(3)(A), (B) or (C) and the regulations thereunder and that it is not purchasing for offer to resell or for resale inside the United States (provided that the issuer has no actual knowledge that the statement is false).

In addition, an issuer that is a controlled foreign corporation within the meaning of section 957(a) that is engaged in the active conduct of a banking business outside the United States within the meaning of section 954(c)(3)(B) as in effect before the Tax Reform Act of 1986, and the regulations thereunder, can only satisfy the provisions of this paragraph (c)(2)(i)(C), if it meets the requirements of this paragraph (c)(2)(i)(C)(2), (3) and (4).

(D) The obligation is issued after September 7, 1990, and all of the conditions set forth in this paragraph (c)(2)(i)(D) are met with respect to such obligation.

(1) Offers and sales. (i) Issuer. The issuer does not offer or sell the obligation during the restricted period to a person who is within the United States or its possessions or to a United States person.

(ii) Distributors. (A) The distributor of the obligation does not offer or sell the obligation during the restricted period to a person who is within the United States or its possessions or to a United States person.

(B) The distributor of the obligation will be deemed to satisfy the requirements of paragraph (c)(2)(i)(D)(1)(ii)(A) of this section if the distributor of the obligation convenants that it will not offer or sell the obligation during the restricted period to a person who is within the United States or its possessions or to a United States person; and the distributor of the obligation has in effect, in connection with the offer and sale of the obligation during the restricted period, procedures reasonably designed to ensure that its employees or agents who are directly engaged in selling the obligation are aware that the obligation cannot be offered or sold during the restricted period to a person who is within the United States or its possessions or is a United States person.

(iii) Certain rules. For purposes of paragraph (c)(2)(i)(D)(1)(i) and (ii) of this section:

(A) An offer or sale will be considered to be made to a person who is within the United States or its possessions if the offeror or seller of the obligation has an address within the United States or its possessions for the offeree or buyer of the obligation with respect to the offer or sale.

(B) An offer or sale of an obligation will not be treated as made to a person within the United States or its possessions or to a United States person if the person to whom the offer or sale is made is: An exempt distributor, as defined in paragraph (c)(2)(i)(D)(5) of this section; An international organization as defined in section 7701(a)(18) and the regulations thereunder, or a foreign central bank as defined in section 895 and the regulations thereunder; or The foreign branch of a United States financial institution as described in paragraph (c)(2)(i)(D)(6)(i) of this section.

Paragraph (c)(2)(i)(D)(1)(iii)(B) regarding an exempt distributor will only apply to an offer to the United States office of an exempt distributor, and paragraph (c)(2)(i)(D)(1)(iii)(B) regarding an international organization or foreign central bank will only apply to an offer to an international organization or foreign central bank, if such offer is made directly and specifically to the United States office, organization or bank.

(C) A sale of an obligation will not be treated as made to a person within the United States or its possessions or to a United States person if the person to whom the sale is made is a person described in paragraph (c)(2)(i)(D)(6)(ii) of this section.

(2) Delivery. In connection with the sale of the obligation during the restricted period, neither the issuer nor any distributor delivers the obligation in definitive form within the United States or its possessions.

(3) Certification. (i) In general. On the earlier of the date of the first actual payment of interest by the issuer on the obligation or the date of delivery by the issuer of the obligation in definitive form, a certificate is provided to the issuer of the obligation stating that on such date:

(A) The obligation is owned by a person that is not a United States person:

(B) The obligation is owned by a United States person described in paragraph (c)(2)(i)(D)(6) of this section; or

(C) The obligation is owned by a financial institution for purposes of resale during the restricted period, and such financial institution certifies in addition that it has not acquired the obligation for purposes of resale directly or indirectly to a United States person or to a person within the United States or its possessions. A certificate described in paragraph (c)(2)(i)(D)(3)(i)(A) or (B) of this section may not be given with respect to an obligation that is owned by a financial institution for purposes of resale during the restricted period. For purposes of paragraph (c)(2)(i)(D)(2) and (3) of this section, a temporary global security (as defined in § 1.163-5(c)(1)(ii)(B)) is not considered to be an obligation in definitive form. If the issuer does not make the obligation available for delivery in definitive form within a reasonable period of time after the end of the restricted period, then the obligation shall be treated as not satisfying the requirements of this paragraph (c)(2)(i)(D)(3). The certificate must be signed (or sent, as provided in paragraph (c)(2)(i)(D)(3)(ii) of this section) either by the owner of the obligation or by a financial institution or clearing organization through which the owner holds the obligation, directly or indirectly. For purposes of this paragraph (c)(2)(i)(D)(3), the term "financial institution" means a financial institution described in § 1.165-12(c)(i)(v). When a certificate is provided by a clearing organization, the certificate must be based on statements provided to it by its member organizations. The requirement of this paragraph (c)(1)(D)(3) shall be deemed not to be satisfied with respect to an obligation if the issuer knows or has reason to know that the certificate with respect to such obligation is false. The certificate must be retained by the issuer (and statements by member organizations must be retained by the clearing organization, in the case of certificates based on such statements) for a period of four calendar years following the year in which the certificate is received.

(ii) Electronic certification. The certificate required by paragraph (c)(2)(i)(D)(3)(i) of this section (including a statement provided to a clearing organization by a member organization) may be provided electronically, but only if the person receiving such electronic certificate maintains adequate records, for the retention period described in paragraph (c)(2)(i)(D)(3)(i) of this section, establishing that such certificate was received in respect of the subject obligation, and only if there is a written agreement entered into prior to the time of certification (including the written membership rules of a clearing organization) to which the sender and recipient are subject, providing that the electronic certificate shall have the effect of a signed certificate described in paragraph (c)(2)(i)(D)(3)(i) of this section.

(iii) Exception for certain obligations. This paragraph (c)(2)(i)(D)(3) shall not apply, and no certificate shall be required, in the case of an obligation that is sold during the restricted period and that satisfies all of the following requirements:

(A) The interest and principal with respect to the obligation are denominated only in the currency of a single foreign country.

(B) The interest and principal with respect to the obligation are payable only within that foreign country (according to rules similar to those set forth in § 1.163-5(c)(2)(v)).

(C) The obligation is offered and sold in accordance with practices and documentation customary in that foreign country.

(D) The distributor covenants to use reasonable efforts to sell the obligation within that foreign country.

(E) The obligation is not listed, or the subject of an application for listing, on an exchange located outside that foreign country.

(F) The Commissioner has designated that foreign country as a foreign country in which certification under paragraph (c)(2)(i)(D)(3)(i) of this section is not permissible.

(G) The issuance of the obligation is subject to guidelines or restrictions imposed by governmental, banking or securities authorities in that foreign country.

(H) More then 80 percent by value of the obligations included in the offering of which the obligation is a part are offered and sold to non-distributors by distributors maintaining an office located in that foreign country. Foreign currency denominated obligations that are convertible into U.S. dollar denominated obligations or that by their terms are linked to the U.S. dollar in a way which effectively converts the obligations to U.S. dollar denominated obligations do not satisfy the requirements of this paragraph (c)(2)(i)(D)(3)(iii). A foreign currency denominated obligation will not be treated as linked, by its terms, to the U.S. dollar solely because the obligation is the subject of a swap transaction.

(4) Distributor. For purposes of this paragraph (c)(2)(i)(D), the term "distributor" means:

(i) a person that offers or sells the obligation during the restricted period pursuant to a written contract with the issuer;

(ii) any person that offers or sells the obligation during the restricted period pursuant to a written contract with a person described in paragraph (c)(2)(i)(D)(4)(i); and

(iii) any affiliate that acquires the obligation from another member of its affiliated group for the purpose of offering or selling the obligation during the restricted period, but only if the transferor member of the group is the issuer or a person described in paragraph (c)(2)(i)(D)(4)(i) or (ii) of this section. The terms "affiliate" and "affiliated group" have the same meanings as in section 1504(a) of the Code, but without regard to the exceptions contained in section 1504(b) and substituting "50 percent" for "80 percent" each time it appears.

For purposes of this paragraph (c)(2)(i)(D)(4), a written contract does not include a confirmation or other notice of the transaction.

(5) Exempt distributor. For purposes of this paragraph (c)(2)(i)(D), the term "exempt distributor" means a distributor that covenants in its contract with the issuer or with a distributor described in paragraph (c)(2)(i)(D)(4)(i) that it is buying the obligation for the purpose of resale in connection with the original issuance of the obligation, and that if it retains the obligation for its own account, it will only do so in accordance with the requirements of paragraph (c)(2)(i)(D)(6) of this section. In the latter case, the covenant will constitute the certificate required under paragraph (c)(2)(i)(D)(6). The provisions of paragraph (c)(2)(i)(D)(7) governing the restricted period for unsold allotments or subscriptions shall apply to any obligation retained for investment by an exempt distributor.

(6) Certain United States persons. A person is described in this paragraph (c)(2)(i)(D)(6) if the requirements of this paragraph are satisfied and the person is:

(i) The foreign branch of a United States financial institution purchasing for its own account or for resale, or

(ii) A United States person who acquired the obligation through the foreign branch of a United States financial institution and who, for purposes of the certification required in paragraph (c)(2)(i)(D)(3) of this section, holds the obligation through such financial institution on the date of certification.

For purposes of paragraph (c)(2)(i)(D)(6)(ii) of this section, a United States person will be considered to acquire and hold an obligation through the foreign branch of a United States financial institution if the United States person has an account with the United States office of a financial institution, and the transaction is executed by a foreign office of that financial institution, or by the foreign office of another financial institution acting on behalf of that financial institution. This paragraph (c)(2)(i)(D)(6) will apply, however, only if the United States financial institution (or the United States office of a foreign financial institution) holding the obligation provides a certificate to the issuer or distributor selling the obligation within a reasonable time stating that it agrees to comply with the requirements of section 165(j)(3)(A), (B), or (C) and the regulations thereunder. For purposes of this paragraph (c)(2)(i)(D)(6), the term "financial institution" means a financial institution as defined in § 1.165-12(c)(1)(v). As an alternative to the certification required above, a financial institution may provide a blanket certificate to the issuer or distributor selling the obligation stating that the financial institution will comply with the requirements of section 165(j)(3)(A), (B) or (C) and the regulations thereunder. A blanket certificate must be received by the issuer or the distributor in the year of the issuance of the obligation or in either of the preceding two calendar years, and must be retained by the issuer or distributor for at least four years after the end of the last calendar year to which it relates.

(7) Restricted period. For purposes of this paragraph (c)(2)(i)(D), the restricted period with respect to an obligation begins on the earlier of the closing date (or the date on which the issuer receives the loan proceeds, if there is no closing with respect to the obligation), or the first date on which the obligation is offered to persons other than a distributor. The restricted period with respect to an obligation ends on the expiration of the forty day period beginning on the closing date (or the date on which the issuer receives the loan proceeds, if there is no closing with respect to the obligation). Notwithstanding the preceding sentence, any offer or sale of the obligation by the issuer or a distributor shall be deemed to be during the restricted period if the issuer or distributor holds the obligation as part of an unsold allotment or subscription.

(8) Clearing organization. For purposes of this paragraph (c)(2)(i)(D), a "clearing organization" is an entity which is in the business of holding obligations for member organizations and transferring obligations among such members by credit or debit to the account of a member without the necessity of physical delivery of the obligation.

(ii) Special rules. An obligation shall not be considered to be described in paragraph (c)(2)(i)(C) of this section if it is—

(A) Guaranteed by a United States shareholder of the issuer;

(B) Convertible into a debt or equity interest in a United States shareholder of the issuer; or

(C) Substantially identical to an obligation issued by a United States shareholder of the issuer.

For purposes of this paragraph (c)(2)(ii), the term "United States shareholder" is defined as it is defined in section 951 (b) and the regulations thereunder. For purposes of this paragraph (c)(2)(ii)(C), obligations are substantially identical if the face amount, interest rate, term of the issue, due dates for payments, and maturity date of each is substantially identical to the other.

(iii) Interstate commerce. For purposes of this paragraph, the term "interstate commerce" means trade or commerce in obligations or any transportation or communication relating thereto between any foreign country and the United States or its possessions.

(A) An issuer will not be considered to engage significantly in interstate commerce with respect to the issuance of an obligation if the only activities with respect to which the issuer uses the means or instrumentalities of interstate commerce are activities of a preparatory or auxiliary character that do not involve communication between a prospective purchaser and an issuer, its agent, an underwriter, or member of the selling group if either is inside the United States or its possessions. Activities of a preparatory or auxiliary character include, but are not limited to, the following activities:

(1) Establishment or participation in establishment of policies concerning the issuance of obligations and the allocation of funding by a United States shareholder with respect to obligations issued by a foreign corporation or by a United States office with respect to obligations issued by a foreign branch;

(2) Negotiation between the issuer and underwriters as to the terms and pricing of an issue;

(3) Transfer of funds to an office of an issuer in the United States or its possessions by a foreign branch or to a United States shareholder by a foreign corporation;

(4) Consultation by an issuer with accountants and lawyers or other financial advisors in the United States or its possessions regarding the issuance of an obligation;

(5) Document drafting and printing;

(6) Provision of payment or delivery instructions to members of the selling group by an issuer's office or agent that is located in the United States or its possessions.

(B) Activities that will not be considered to be of a preparatory or auxiliary character include, but are not limited to, any of the following activities:

(1) Negotiation or communication between a prospective purchaser and an issuer, its agent, an underwriter, or a member of the selling group concerning the sale of an obligation if either is inside the United States or its possessions;

(2) Involvement of an issuer's office, its agent, an underwriter, or a member of the selling group in the United States or its possessions in the offer or sale of a particular obligation, either directly with the prospective purchaser, or through the issuer in a foreign country;

(3) Delivery of an obligation in the United States or its possessions; or

(4) Advertising or otherwise promoting an obligation in the United States or its possessions.

(C) The following examples illustrate the application of this subdivision (iii) of § 1.163-5(c)(2).

Example (1). Foreign corporation A, a corporation organized in and doing business in foreign country Z, and not a controlled foreign corporation within the meaning of section 957(a) that is engaged in the conduct of a banking business within the meaning of section 954(c)(3)(B) as in effect before the Tax Reform Act of 1986, issues its debentures outside the United States. The debentures are not guaranteed by a United States shareholder of A, nor are they convertible into a debt or equity interest of a United States shareholder of A, nor are they substantially identical to an obligation issued by a United States shareholder of A. A consults its accountants and lawyers in the United States for certain securities and tax advice regarding the debt offering. The underwriting and selling group in respect to A's offering is composed entirely of foreign securities firms, some of which are foreign subsidiaries of United States securities firms. A U.S. affiliate of the foreign underwriter communicates payment and delivery instructions to the selling group. All offering circulars for the offering are mailed and delivered outside the United States and its possessions. All debentures are delivered and paid for outside the United States and its possessions. No office located in the United States or in a United States possession is involved in the sale of debentures. Interest on the debentures is payable only outside the United States and its possessions. A is not significantly engaged in interstate commerce with respect to the offering.

Example (2). B, a United States bank, does business in foreign country X through a branch located in X. The branch is a staffed and operating unit engaged in the active conduct of a banking business consisting of one or more of the activities set forth in § 1.954-2(d)(2)(ii). As part of its ongoing business, the branch in X issues negotiable certificates of deposit with a maturity in excess of one year to customers upon request. The certificates of deposit are not guaranteed by a United States shareholder of B, nor are they convertible into a debt or equity interest of a United States shareholder of B, nor are they substantially identical to an obligation issued by a United States shareholder of B. Policies regarding the issuance of negotiable certificates of deposit and funding allocations for foreign branches are set in the United States at B's main office. Branch personnel decide whether to issue a negotiable certificate of deposit based on the guidelines established by the United States offices of B, but without communicating with the United States offices of B with respect to the issuance of a particular obligation. Negotiable certificates of deposits are delivered and paid for outside the United States and its possessions. Interest on the negotiable certificates of deposit is payable only outside the United States and its possessions. B maintains documentary evidence described in § 1.163-5(c)(2)(i)(C)(4). After the issuance of negotiable certificates of deposit by the foreign branch of B, the foreign branch sends the funds to a United States branch of B for use in domestic operations. B is not significantly engaged in interstate commerce with respect to the issuance of such obligation.

Example (3). The facts in Example (2) apply except that the foreign branch of B consulted, by telephone, the main office in the United States to request approval of the issuance of the certificate of deposit at a particular rate of interest. The main office granted permission to issue the negotiable certificate of deposit to the customer by a telex sent from the main office of B to the branch in X. B is significantly engaged in interstate commerce with respect to the issuance of the obligation as a result of involvement of B's United States office in the issuance of the obligation.

Example (4). The facts in Example (2) apply with the additional fact that a customer contacted the foreign branch of B through a telex originating in the United States or its possessions. Subsequent to the telex, the foreign branch issued the negotiable certificate of deposit and recorded it on the books. B is significantly engaged in interstate commerce with respect to the issuance of the obligation as a result of its communication by telex with a customer in the United States.

(iv) Possessions. For purposes of this section, the term "possessions" includes Puerto Rico, the U.S. Virgin Islands, Guam, American Samoa, Wake Island, and Northern Mariana Islands.

(v) Interest payable outside of the United States. Interest will be considered payable only outside the United States and its possessions if payment of such interest can be made only upon presentation of a coupon, or upon making of any other demand for payment, outside of the United States and its possessions to the issuer or a paying agent. The fact that payment is made by a draft drawn on a United States bank account or by a wire or other electronic transfer from a United States account does not affect this result. Interest payments will be considered to be made within the United States if the payments are made by a transfer of funds into an account maintained by the payee in the United States or mailed to an address in the United States, if—

(A) The interest is paid on an obligation issued by either a United States person, a controlled foreign corporation as defined in section 957 (a), or a foreign corporation if 50 percent or more of the gross income of the foreign corporation from all sources of the 3-year period ending with the close of its taxable year preceding the original issuance of the obligation (or for such part of the period that the foreign corporation has been in existence) was effectively connected with the conduct of a trade or business within the United States; and

(B) The interest is paid to a person other than—

(1) A person who may satisfy the requirements of section 165(j)(3)(A), (B), or (C) and the regulations thereunder;

(2) A financial institution as a step in the clearance of funds and such interest is promptly credited to an account maintained outside the United States for such financial institution or for persons for which the financial institution has collected such interest.

Interest is considered to be paid within the United States and its possessions if a coupon is presented, or a demand for payment is otherwise made, to the issuer or a paying agent (whether a United States or foreign person) in the United States and its possessions even if the funds paid are credited to an account maintained by the payee outside the United States and its possessions. Interest will be considered payable only outside the United States and its possessions notwithstanding that such interest may become payable at the office of the issuer or its United States paying agent under the following conditions: the issuer has appointed paying agents located outside the United States and its possessions with the reasonable expectation that such paying agents will be able to pay the interest in United States dollars, and the full amount of such payment at the offices of all such paying agents is illegal or effectively precluded because of the imposition of exchange controls or other similar restrictions on the full payment or receipt of interest in United States dollars. A lawsuit brought in the United States or its possessions for payment of the obligation or interest thereon as a result of a default shall not be considered to be a demand for payment. For purposes of this subdivision (v), interest includes original issue discount as defined in section 1273(a). Therefore, an amount equal to the original issue discount as defined in section 1273(a) is payable only outside the United States and its possessions. The amount of market discount as defined in section 1278(a) does not affect the amount of interest to be considered payable only outside the United States and its possessions.

(vi) Rules relating to obligations issued after December 31, 1982 and on or before September 21, 1984. Whether an obligation originally issued after December 31, 1982 and on or before September 21, 1984, or an obligation originally issued after September 21, 1984 pursuant to the exercise of a warrant or the conversion of a convertible obligation, which warrant or obligation (including conversion privilege) was issued after December 31, 1982 and on or before September 21, 1984, is described in section 163(f)(2)(B) shall be determined under the rules provided in § 5f.163-1(c) as in effect prior to its removal. Notwithstanding the preceding sentence, an issuer will be considered to satisfy the requirements of section 163(f)(2)(B) with respect to an obligation issued after December 31, 1982 and on or before September 21, 1984 or after September 21, 1984 pursuant to the exercise of a warrant or the conversion of a convertible obligation, which warrant or obligation (including conversion privilege) was issued after December 31, 1982 and on or before September 21, 1984, if the issuer substantially complied with the proposed regulations provided in § 1.163-5(c), which were published in the Federal Register on September 2, 1983 (48 FR

39953) and superseded by temporary regulations published in the Federal Register on August 22, 1984 (49 FR 33228).

(3) Effective date. (i) In general. These regulations apply generally to obligations issued after January 20, 1987. A taxpayer may choose to apply the rules of § 1.163-5(c) with respect to an obligation issued after December 31, 1982 and on or before January 20, 1987.

If this choice is made, the rules of § 1.163-5(c) will apply in lieu of § 1.163-5T(c) except that the legend requirement under § 1.163-5(c)(1)(ii)(B) does not apply with respect to a bearer obligation evidenced exclusively by a book entry and that the certification requirement under § 1.163-5T(c)(2)(i)(B)(4) applies in lieu of the certification under § 1.163-5(c)(2)(i)(B)(4).

(ii) Special rules. If an obligation is originally issued after September 7, 1990, pursuant to the exercise of a warrant or the conversion of a convertible obligation, which warrant or obligation (including conversion privilege) was issued on or before May 10, 1990, then the issuer may choose to apply either the rules of § 1.163-5(c)(2)(i)(A) or § 1.163-5(c)(2)(i)(B), or the rules of § 1.163-5(c)(2)(i)(D). The issuer of an obligation may choose to apply either the rules of § 1.163-5(c)(2)(i)(A) or (B), or the rules of § 1.163-5(c)(2)(i)(D), to an obligation that is originally issued after May 10, 1990, and on or before September 7, 1990. However, any issuer choosing to apply the rules of § 1.163-5(c)(2)(i)(A) must apply the definition of United States person used for such purposes on December 31, 1989, and must obtain any certificates that would have been required under applicable law on December 31, 1989.

T.D. 8110, 12/16/86, amend T.D. 8203, 5/18/88, T.D. 8300, 5/9/90, T.D. 8734, 10/6/97.

---

§ 1.163-5T Denial of interest deduction on certain obligations issued after December 31, 1982, unless issued in registered form (temporary).

(a) – (c) [Reserved]

(d) Pass-through certificates. *(1)* A pass-through or participation certificate evidencing an interest in a pool of mortgage loans which under Subpart E of Subchapter J of the Code is treated as a trust of which the grantor is the owner (or similar evidence of interest in a similar pooled fund or pooled trust treated as a grantor trust) ("pass-through certificate") is considered to be a "registration-required obligation" under section 163(f)(2)(A) and § 1.163-5(c) if the pass-through certificate is described in section 163(f)(2)(A) and § 1.163-5(c) without regard to whether any obligation held by the fund or trust to which the pass-through certificate relates is described in section 163(f)(2)(A) and § 1.163-5(c). A pass-through certificate is considered to be described in section 163(f)(2)(B) and § 1.163-5(c) if the pass-through certificate is described in section 163(f)(2)(B) and § 1.163-5(c) without regard to whether any obligation held by the fund or trust to which the pass-through certificate relates is described in section 163(f)(2)(B) and § 1.163-5(c).

(2) An obligation held by a fund or trust in which ownership interests are represented by pass-through certificates is considered to be in registered form under section 149(a) and the regulations thereunder or to be described in section 163(f)(2)(A) or (B), if the obligation held by the fund or trust is in registered form under section 149(a) and the regulations thereunder or is described in section 163(f)(2)(A) or (B), respectively, without regard to whether the pass-through certificates are so considered.

(3) For purposes of section 4701, a pass-through certificate is considered to be issued solely by the recipient of the proceeds from the issuance of the pass-through certificate (hereinafter the "sponsor"). The sponsor is therefore liable for any excise tax under section 4701 that may be imposed with reference to the principal amount of the pass-through certificate.

(4) In order to implement the purpose of section 163, § 1.163-5(c) and this section, the Commissioner may characterize a certificate or other evidence of interest in a fund or trust which under Subpart E of Subchapter J of the Code is treated as a trust of which the grantor is the owner and any obligation held by such fund or trust in accordance with the substance of the arrangement they represent and may impose the penalties provided under sections 163(f)(1) and 4701 in the appropriate amounts and on the appropriate persons. This provision may be applied, for example, where a corporation issues obligations purportedly in registered form, contributes them to a grantor trust as its only assets, and arranges for the sale to investors of bearer certificates of interest in the trust which do not meet the requirements of section 163(f)(2)(B). If this provision is applied, the obligations held by the fund or trust will not be considered to be issued in registered form or to meet the requirements of section 163(f)(2)(B). The corporation will not be allowed a deduction for the payment of interest on the obligations held by the trust, and the excise tax under section 4701, calculated with reference to the principal amount of the obligations held by the trust will be imposed on the corporation may be collected from the corporation and its agents. This paragraph (d)(4) will not be applied so as to alter the tax consequences of transactions as to which rulings have been issued by the Internal Revenue Service prior to September 19, 1985.

(5) The rules set forth in this paragraph (d) apply solely for purposes of sections 4701, 163(f)(2)(A), 163(f)(2)(B), § 1.163-5(c), and any other section that refers to this section for the definition of the term "registration-required obligation" (such as the regulations under sections 871(h) and 881(c)). The treatment of obligations described in this paragraph (d) for purposes of section 163(f)(2)(A) and (B) does not affect the determination of whether bearer obligations that are issued or guaranteed by the United States Government, a United States Government-owned agency, a United States Government sponsored enterprise (within the meaning of § 1.163-5(c)(1)) or that are backed (as described in the Treasury Department News Release R-2835 of September 10, 1984 and Treasury Department News Release R-2847 of September 14, 1984) by obligations issued by the United States Government, a United States Government-owned agency, or a United States Government sponsored enterprise comply with the requirements of section 163(f)(2)(B) and the regulations thereunder.

(6) The provisions of this paragraph (d)(1) through (5) may be illustrated by the following example:

Commercial Bank K forms a pool of 1000 residential mortgage loans, each made to a different individual homeowner, by assigning them to Commercial Bank L, an unrelated entity serving as trustee of the pool. Commercial Bank L immediately sells in a public offering certificates of interest in the trust of a maturity of 10 years in registered form. Commercial Bank L transfers the cash proceeds of the offering to Commercial Bank K. The certificates of interest in the trust are of a type offered to the public and are not described in section 163(f)(2)(B). Pursuant to paragraph (d)(1), the certificates of interest in the pool are registration-required obligations without regard to the fact that the obligations held by the trust are not registration-required obligations.

(e) Regular interests in REMICS. *(1)* A regular interest in a REMIC, as defined in sections 860D and 860G and the regulations thereunder, is considered to be a "registration-required obligation" under section 163(f)(2)(A) and § 1.163-5(c) if the regular interest is described in section 163(f)(2)(A) and § 1.163-5(c), without regard to whether any obligation held by the REMIC to which the regular interest relates is described in section 163(f)(2)(A) and § 1.163-5(c). A regular interest in a REMIC is considered to be described in section 163(f)(2)(B) and § 1.163-5(c), if the regular interest is described in section 163(f)(2)(B) and § 1.163-5(c), without regard to whether any obligation held by the REMIC to which the regular interest relates is described in section 163(f)(2)(B) and § 1.163-5(c).

(2) An obligation held by a REMIC is considered to be described in section 163(f)(2)(A) or (B) if such obligation is described in section 163(f)(2)(A) or (B), respectively, without regard to whether the regular interests in the REMIC are so considered.

(3) For purposes of section 4701, a regular interest is considered to be issued solely by the recipient of the proceeds from the issuance of the regular interest (hereinafter the "sponsor"). The sponsor is therefore liable for any excise tax under section 4701 that may be imposed with reference to the principal amount of the regular interest.

(4) In order to implement the purpose of section 163, § 1.163-5(c), and this section, the Commissioner may characterize a regular interest in a REMIC and any obligation held by such REMIC in accordance with the substance of the arrangement they represent and may impose the penalties provided under sections 163(f)(1) and 4701 in the appropriate amounts and on the appropriate persons. This provision may be applied, for example, where a corporation issues an obligation that is purportedly in registered form and that will qualify as a "qualified mortgage" within the meaning of section 860G(a)(3) in the hands of a REMIC, contributes the obligation to a REMIC as its only asset, and arranges for the sale to investors of regular interests in the REMIC in bearer form that do not meet the requirements of section 163(f)(2)(B). If this provision is applied, the obligation held by the REMIC will not be considered to be issued in registered form or to meet the requirements of section 163(f)(2)(B). The corporation will not be allowed a deduction for the payment of interest on the obligation held by the REMIC, and the excise tax under section 4701, calculated with reference to the principal amount of the obligation held by the REMIC, will be imposed on the corporation and may be collected from the corporation and its agents.

T.D. 8202, 5/18/88, amend T.D. 8300, 5/9/90.

PAR. 2. Paragraph (d)(7) is added immediately after paragraph (d)(6) of § 1.163-5T. The added paragraph reads as follows:

Proposed § 1.163-5T Denial of interest deduction on certain obligations issued after December 31, 1982, unless issued in registered form (temporary). [*For Preamble, see ¶ 151,117*]

(d) Pass-through certificates.

* * * * *

(7) (i) For purposes of section 4701, any person who holds a registration-required obligation that is in registered form within the meaning of § 5f.103-1(c)(1) and transfers the obligation through a method not described in § 5f.103-1(c)(1) is considered to have issued the obligation so transferred on the date of the transfer in the principal amount of the obligation received by the transferee. Such person is therefore liable for any excise tax under section 4701 that may be imposed. This paragraph (d)(7) applies to transfers of obligations occurring after August 17, 1988.

(ii) The provisions of this paragraph (d)(7) may be illustrated by the following examples:

Example (1). X, a corporation, holds a registration required obligation in registered form in the principal amount of 10x with a maturity date of December 31, 1999. X transfers the obligation through a method not described in § 5f.103-1(c)(1) on June 30, 1999. For purposes of section 4701, X is considered to have issued an obligation on June 30, 1990 in the principal amount of 10x with a maturity date of December 31, 1999. Because X has issued a registration required obligation not in registered form, X is liable for the tax imposed by section 4701 in an amount computed with reference to the principal amount of 10x and the period beginning on June 30, 1990 and ending on December 31, 1999.

Example (2). X, a corporation, holds a registration required obligation in registered form as nominee of Y, a corporation. The principal amount of the obligation is 10x and the maturity date of the obligation is December 31, 1999. On June 30, 1990, X issued a bearer receipt to Y for the obligation. For purposes of section 4701, X is considered to have issued an obligation on June 1990 in the principal amount of 10x with a maturity date of December 31, 1999. Because X has issued a registration required obligation not in registered form, X is liable for the tax imposed by section 4701 in an amount computed with reference to the principal amount of 10x and the period beginning June 30, 1990 and ending December 31, 1999.

Example (3). The facts are the same as in Example (1) except that X transfers 5x of the 10x obligation held by X. X is considered to have issued an obligation on June 30, 1990 in the principal amount of 5x with a maturity date of December 31, 1999. Because X has issued a registration required-obligation not in registered form, X is liable for the tax imposed by section 4701 in an amount computed with reference to the principal amount of 5x and the period beginning on June 30, 1990 and ending on December 31, 1999.

Example (4). The facts are the same as in Example (1) except that X is a natural person. X is considered to have issued an obligation on June 30, 1990 in the principal amount of 10x with a maturity date of December 31, 1999. Because X is a natural person, the obligation is not a registration-required obligation and, therefore, X is not subject to the tax imposed under section 4701.

§ 1.163-6T Reduction of deduction where section 25 credit taken (Temporary).

Caution: The Treasury has not yet amended Reg § 1.163-6T to reflect changes made by P.L. 100-647.

(a) In general. The amount of the deduction under section 163 for interest paid or accrued during any taxable year on a certified indebtedness amount with respect to a mortgage credit certificate which has been issued under section 25 shall be reduced by the amount of the credit allowable with respect to such interest under section 25 (determined without regard to section 26).

(b) Cross reference. See §§ 1.25-1T through 1.25-8T with respect to rules relating to mortgage credit certificates.

T.D. 8023, 5/3/85.

§ 1.163-7 Deduction for OID on certain debt instruments.

(a) General rule. Except as otherwise provided in paragraph (b) of this section, an issuer (including a transferee) determines the amount of OID that is deductible each year under section 163(e)(1) by using the constant yield method described in § 1.1272-1(b). This determination, however, is made without regard to section 1272(a)(7) (relating to acquisition premium) and § 1.1273-1(d) (relating to de minimis OID). An issuer is permitted a deduction under section 163(e)(1) only to the extent the issuer is primarily liable on the debt instrument. For certain limitations on the deductibility of OID, see sections 163(e) and 1275(b)(2). To determine the amount of interest (OID) that is deductible each year on a debt instrument that provides for contingent payments, see § 1.1275-4.

(b) Special rules for de minimis OID. *(1) Stated interest.* If a debt instrument has a de minimis amount of OID (within the meaning of § 1.1273-1(d)), the issuer treats all stated interest on the debt instrument as qualified stated interest. See §§ 1.446-2(b) and 1.461-1 for the treatment of qualified stated interest.

(2) Deduction of de minimis OID on other than a constant yield basis. In lieu of deducting de minimis OID under the general rule of paragraph (a) of this section, an issuer of a debt instrument with a de minimis amount of OID (other than a de minimis amount treated as qualified stated interest under paragraph (b)(1) of this section) may choose to deduct the OID at maturity, on a straight-line basis over the term of the debt instrument, or in proportion to stated interest payments. The issuer makes this choice by reporting the minimis OID in a manner consistent with the method chosen on the issuer's timely filed Federal income tax return for the taxable year in which the debt instrument is issued.

(c) Deduction upon repurchase. Except to the extent disallowed by any other section of the Internal Revenue Code (e.g., section 249) or this paragraph (c), if a debt instrument is repurchased by the issuer for a price in excess of its adjusted issue price (as defined in § 1.1275.1(b), the excess (repurchase premium) is deductible as interest for the taxable year in which the repurchase occurs. If the issuer repurchases a debt instrument in a debt-for-debt exchange, the repurchase price is the issue price of the newly issued debt instrument (reduced by any unstated interest within the meaning of section 483). However, if the issue price of the newly issued debt instrument is determined under either section 1273(b)(4) or section 1274, any repurchase premium is not deductible in the year of the repurchase, but is amortized over the term of the newly issued debt instrument in the same manner as if it were OID.

(d) Choice of accrual periods to determine whether a debt instrument is an applicable high yield discount obligation (AHYDO). Section 163(e)(5) affects an issuer's OID deductions for certain high yield debt instruments that have significant OID. For purposes of section 163(i)(2), which defines significant OID, the issuer's choice of accrual periods to determine OID accruals is used to determine whether a debt instrument has significant OID. See § 1.1275-2(e) for rules relating to the issuer's obligation to disclose certain information to holders.

(e) Qualified reopening. *(1) In general.* In a qualified reopening of an issue of debt instruments, if a holder pays more or less than the adjusted issue price of the original debt instruments to acquire an additional debt instrument, the issuer treats this difference as an adjustment to the issuer's interest expense for the original and additional debt instruments. As provided by paragraphs (e)(2) through (5) of this section, the adjustment is taken into account over the term of the instrument using constant yield principles.

(2) Positive adjustment. If the difference is positive (that is, the holder pays more than the adjusted issue price of the original debt instrument), then, with respect to the issuer but not the holder, the difference increases the aggregate adjusted issue prices of all of the debt instruments in the issue, both original and additional.

(3) Negative adjustment. If the difference is negative (that is, the holder pays less than the adjusted issue price of the original debt instrument), then, with respect to the issuer but not the holder, the difference reduces the aggregate adjusted issue prices of all of the debt instruments in the issue, both original and additional.

(4) Determination of issuer's interest accruals. As of the reopening date, the issuer must redetermine the yield of the debt instruments in the issue for purposes of applying the constant yield method described in § 1.1272-1(b) to determine the issuer's accruals of interest expense over the remaining term of the debt instruments in the issue. This redetermined yield is based on the aggregate adjusted issue prices of the debt instruments in the issue (as determined under this paragraph (e)) and the remaining payment schedule of the debt instruments in the issue. If the aggregate adjusted issue prices of the debt instruments in the issue (as determined under this paragraph (e)) are less than the aggregate stated redemption price at maturity of the instruments (determined as of the reopening date) by a de minimis amount (within the meaning of § 1.1273-1(d)), the issuer may use the rules in paragraph (b) of this section to determine the issuer's accruals of interest expense.

(5) Effect of adjustments on issuer's adjusted issue price. The adjustments made under this paragraph (e) are taken into account for purposes of determining the issuer's adjusted issue price under § 1.1275-1(b).

(6) Definitions. The terms additional debt instrument, original debt instrument, qualified reopening, and reopening date have the same meanings as in § 1.1275-2(k).

(f) Effective dates. This section (other than paragraph (e) of this section) applies to debt instruments issued on or after April 4, 1994. Taxpayers, however, may rely on this section (other than paragraph (e) of this section) for debt instruments issued after December 21, 1992, and before April 4, 1994. Paragraph (e) of this section applies to qualified reopenings where the reopening date is on or after March 13, 2001.

T.D. 8517, 1/27/94, amend T.D. 8674, 6/11/96, T.D. 8934, 1/11/2001.

§ 1.163-8T Allocation of interest expense among expenditures (temporary).

(a) In general. *(1) Application.* This section prescribes rules for allocating interest expense for purposes of applying sections 469 (the "passive loss limitation") and 163(d) and (h) (the "nonbusiness interest limitations").

(2) Cross-references. This paragraph provides an overview of the manner in which interest expense is allocated for the purposes of applying the passive loss limitation and nonbusi-

ness interest limitations and the manner in which interest expense allocated under this section is treated. See paragraph (b) of this section for definitions of certain terms, paragraph (c) for the rules for allocating debt and interest expense among expenditures, paragraphs (d) and (e) for the treatment of debt repayments and refinancings, paragraph (j) for the rules for reallocating debt upon the occurrence of certain events, paragraph (m) for the coordination of the rules in this section with other limitations on the deductibility of interest expense, and paragraph (n) of this section for effective date and transitional rules.

(3) Manner of allocation. In general, interest expense on a debt is allocated in the same manner as the debt to which such interest expense relates is allocated. Debt is allocated by tracing disbursements of the debt proceeds to specific expenditures. This section prescribes rules for tracing debt proceeds to specific expenditures.

(4) Treatment of interest expense. (i) General rule. Except as otherwise provided in paragraph (m) of this section (relating to limitations on interest expense other than the passive loss and nonbusiness interest limitations), interest expense allocated under the rules of this section is treated in the following manner:

(A) Interest expense allocated to a trade or business expenditure (as defined in paragraph (b)(7) of this section) is taken into account under section 163 (h)(2)(A):

(B) Interest expense allocated to a passive activity expenditure (as defined in paragraph (b)(4) of this section) or a former passive activity expenditure (as defined in paragraph (b)(2) of this section) is taken into account for purposes of section 469 in determining the income or loss from the activity to which such expenditure relates;

(C) Interest expense allocated to an investment expenditure (as defined in paragraph (b)(3) of this section) is treated for purposes of section 163(d) as investment interest;

(D) Interest expense allocated to a personal expenditure (as defined in paragraph (b)(5) of this section) is treated for purposes of section 163(h) as personal interest; and

(E) Interest expense allocated to a portfolio expenditure (as defined in paragraph (b)(6) of this section) is treated for purposes of section 469(e)(2)(B)(ii) as interest expense described in section 469(e)(1)(A)(i)(III).

(ii) Examples. The following examples illustrate the application of this paragraph (a)(4):

Example (1). Taxpayer A, an individual, incurs interest expense allocated under the rules of this section to the following expenditures:

$6,000	Passive activity expenditure
$4,000	Personal expenditure

The $6,000 interest expense allocated to the passive activity expenditure is taken into account for purposes of section 469 in computing A's income or loss from the activity to which such interest relates. Pursuant to section 163(h), A may not deduct the $4,000 interest expense allocated to the personal expenditure (except to the extent such interest is qualified residence interest, within the meaning of section 163(h)(3)).

Example (2). (i) Corporation M, a closely held C corporation (within the meaning of section 469(j)(1)) has $10,000 of interest expense for a taxable year. Under the rules of this section, M's interest expense is allocated to the following expenditures:

$2,000	Passive activity expenditure
$3,000	Portfolio expenditure
$5,000	Other expenditures

(ii) Under section 163(d)(3)(D) and this paragraph (a)(4), the $2,000 interest expense allocated to the passive activity expenditure is taken into account in computing M's passive activity loss for the taxable year, but, pursuant to section 469(e)(1) and this paragraph (a)(4), the interest expense allocated to the portfolio expenditure and the other expenditures is not taken into account for such purposes.

(iii) Since M is a closely held C corporation, its passive activity loss is allowable under section 469(e)(2)(A) as a deduction from net active income. Under section 469(e)(2)(B) and this paragraph (a)(4), the $5,000 interest expense allocated to other expenditures is taken into account in computing M's net active income, but the interest expense allocated to the passive activity expenditure and the portfolio expenditure is not taken into account for such purposes.

(iv) Since M is a corporation, the $3,000 interest expense allocated to the portfolio expenditure is allowable without regard to section 163(d). If M were an individual, however, the interest expense allocated to the portfolio expenditure would be treated as investment interest for purposes of applying the limitation of section 163(d).

(b) Definitions. For purposes of this section—

(1) "Former passive activity" means an activity described in section 469(f)(3), but only if an unused deduction or credit (within the meaning of section 469(f)(1)(A) or (B)) is allocable to the activity under section 469(b) for the taxable year.

(2) "Former passive activity expenditure" means an expenditure that is taken into account under section 469 in computing the income or loss from a former passive activity of the taxpayer or an expenditure (including an expenditure properly chargeable to capital account) that would be so taken into account if such expenditure were otherwise deductible.

(3) "Investment expenditure" means an expenditure (other than a passive activity expenditure) properly chargeable to capital account with respect to property held for investment (within the meaning of section 163(d)(5)(A)) or an expenditure in connection with the holding of such property.

(4) "Passive activity expenditure" means an expenditure that is taken into account under section 469 in computing income or loss from a passive activity of the taxpayer or an expenditure (including an expenditure properly chargeable to capital account) that would be so taken into account if such expenditure were otherwise deductible. For purposes of this section, the term passive activity expenditure does not include any expenditure with respect to any low-income housing project in any taxable year in which any benefit is allowed with respect to such project under section 502 of the Tax Reform Act of 1986.

(5) "Personal expenditure" means an expenditure that is not a trade or business expenditure, a passive activity expenditure, or an investment expenditure.

(6) "Portfolio expenditure" means an investment expenditure properly chargeable to capital account with respect to property producing income of a type described in section 469(e)(1)(A) or an investment expenditure for an expense clearly and directly allocable to such income.

(7) "Trade or business expenditure" means an expenditure (other than a passive activity expenditure or an investment expenditure) in connection with the conduct of any trade or business other than the trade or business of performing services as an employee.

(c) Allocation of debt and interest expense. *(1) Allocation in accordance with use of proceeds.* Debt is allocated to expenditures in accordance with the use of the debt proceeds and, except as provided in paragraph (m) of this section, interest expense accruing on a debt during any period is allocated to expenditures in the same manner as the debt is allocated from time to time during such period. Except as provided in paragraph (m) of this section, debt proceeds and related interest expense are allocated solely by reference to the use of such proceeds, and the allocation is not affected by the use of an interest in any property to secure the repayment of such debt or interest. The following example illustrates the principles of this paragraph (c)(1):

Example. Taxpayer A, an individual, pledges corporate stock held for investment as security for a loan and uses the debt proceeds to purchase an automobile for personal use. Interest expense accruing on the debt is allocated to the personal expenditure to purchase the automobile even though the debt is secured by investment property.

(2) Allocation period. (i) Allocation of debt. Debt is allocated to an expenditure for the period beginning on the date the proceeds of the debt are used or treated as used under the rules of this section to make the expenditure and ending on the earlier of—

(A) The date the debt is repaid; or

(B) The date the debt is reallocated in accordance with the rules in paragraphs (c)(4) and (j) of this section.

(ii) Allocation of interest expense. (A) In general. Except as otherwise provided in paragraph (m) of this section, interest expense accruing on a debt for any period is allocated in the same manner as the debt is allocated from time to time, regardless of when the interest is paid.

(B) Effect of compounding. Accrued interest is treated as a debt until it is paid and any interest accruing on unpaid interest is allocated in the same manner as the unpaid interest is allocated. For the taxable year in which a debt is reallocated under the rules in paragraphs (c)(4) and (j) of this section, however, compound interest accruing on such debt (other than compound interest accruing on interest that accrued before the beginning of the year) may be allocated between the original expenditure and the new expenditure on a straight-line basis (i.e., by allocating an equal amount of such interest expense to each day during the taxable year). In addition, a taxpayer may treat a year as consisting of 12 30-day months for purposes of allocating interest on a straight-line basis.

(C) Accrual of interest expense. For purposes of this paragraph (c)(2)(ii), the amount of interest expense that accrues during any period is determined by taking into account relevant provisions of the loan agreement and any applicable law such as sections 163(e), 483, and 1271 through 1275.

(iii) Examples. The following examples illustrate the principles of this paragraph (c)(2):

Example (1). (i) On January 1, taxpayer B, a calendar year taxpayer, borrows $1,000 at an interest rate of 11 percent, compounded semiannually. B immediately uses the debt proceeds to purchase an investment security. On July 1, B sells the investment security for $1,000 and uses the sales proceeds to make a passive activity expenditure. On December 31, B pays accrued interest on the $1,000 debt for the entire year.

(ii) Under this paragraph (c)(2) and paragraph (j) of this section, the $1,000 debt is allocated to the investment expenditure for the period from January 1 through June 30, and to the passive activity expenditure from July 1 through December 31. Interest expense accruing on the $1,000 debt is allocated in accordance with the allocation of the debt from time to time during the year even though the debt was allocated to the passive activity expenditure on the date the interest was paid. Thus, the $55 interest expense for the period from January 1 through June 30 is allocated to the investment expenditure. In addition, during the period from July 1 through December 31, the interest expense allocated to the investment expenditure is a debt, the proceeds of which are treated as used to make an investment expenditure. Accordingly, an additional $3 of interest expense for the period from July 1 through December 31 ($55 × .055) is allocated to the investment expenditure. The remaining $55 of interest expense for the period from July 1 through December 31 ($1,000 × .055) is allocated to the passive activity expenditure.

(iii) Alternatively, under the rule in paragraph (c)(2)(ii)(B) of this section, B may allocate the interest expense on a straight-line basis and may also treat the year as consisting of 12 30-day months for this purpose. In that case, $56.50 of interest expense (180/360 and the remaining $56.50 of interest expense would be allocated to the passive activity expenditure.

Example (2). On January 1, 1988, taxpayer C borrows $10,000 at an interest rate of 11 percent, compounded annually. All interest and principal on the debt is payable in a lump sum on December 31, 1992. C immediately uses the debt proceeds to make a passive activity expenditure. C materially participates in the activity in 1990, 1991, and 1992. Therefore, under paragraphs (c)(2)(i) and (j) of this section, the debt is allocated to a passive activity expenditure from January 1, 1988, through December 31, 1989, and to a former passive activity expenditure from January 1, 1990, through December 31, 1992. In accordance with the loan agreement (and consistent with § 1.1272-1(d)(1) of the proposed regulations), interest expense accruing during any period is determined on the basis of annual compounding. Accordingly, the interest expense on the debt is allocated as follows:

Year	Amount		Expenditure
1988	$10,000 × .11	$1,100	Passive activity
1989	11,100 × .11	1,221	Passive activity
1990	12,321 × .11 = 1,355		
	1,355 × 2,321/12,321	255	Passive activity
	1,355 × 10,000/12,321	1,100	Former passive activity
		1,355	
1991	13,676 × .11 = 1,504		
	1,504 × 2,576/13,676	283	Passive activity
	1,504 × 11,100/13,676	1,221	Former passive activity
		1,504	
1992	15,180 × .11 = 1,670		
	1,670 × 2,859/15,180	315	Passive activity
	1,670 × 12,321/15,180	1,355	Former passive activity
		1,670	

(3) Allocation of debt; proceeds not disbursed to borrower. (i) Third-party financing. If a lender disburses debt proceeds to a person other than the borrower in consideration for the sale or use of property, for services, or for any

other purpose, the debt is treated for purposes of this section as if the borrower used an amount of the debt proceeds equal to such disbursement to make an expenditure for such property, services, or other purpose.

(ii) Debt assumptions not involving cash disbursements. If a taxpayer incurs or assumes a debt in consideration for the sale or use of property, for services, or for any other purpose, or takes property subject to a debt, and no debt proceeds are disbursed to the taxpayer, the debt is treated for purposes of this section as if the taxpayer used an amount of the debt proceeds equal to the balance of the debt outstanding at such time to make an expenditure for such property, services, or other purpose.

(4) Allocation of debt; proceeds deposited in borrower's account. (i) Treatment of deposit. For purposes of this section, a deposit of debt proceeds in an account is treated as an investment expenditure, and amounts held in an account (whether or not interest bearing) are treated as property held for investment. Debt allocated to an account under this paragraph (c)(4)(i) must be reallocated as required by paragraph (j) of this section whenever debt proceeds held in the account are used for another expenditure. This paragraph (c)(4) provides rules for determining when debt proceeds are expended from the account. The following example illustrates the principles of this paragraph (c)(4)(i):

Example. Taxpayer C, a calendar year taxpayer, borrows $100,000 on January 1 and immediately uses the proceeds to open a noninterest-bearing checking account. No other amounts are deposited in the account during the year, and no portion of the principal amount of the debt is repaid during the year. On April 1, C uses $20,000 of the debt proceeds held in the account for a passive activity expenditure. On September 1, C uses an additional $40,000 of the debt proceeds held in the account for a personal expenditure. Under this paragraph (c)(4)(i), from January 1 through March 31 the entire $100,000 debt is allocated to an investment expenditure for the account. From April 1 through August 31, $20,000 of the debt is allocated to the passive activity expenditure, and $80,000 of the debt is allocated to the investment expenditure for the account. From September 1 through December 31, $40,000 of the debt is allocated to the personal expenditure, $20,000 is allocated to the passive activity expenditure, and $40,000 is allocated to an investment expenditure for the account.

(ii) Expenditures from account; general ordering rule. Except as provided in paragraph (c)(4)(iii)(B) or (C) of this section, debt proceeds deposited in an account are treated as expended before—

(A) Any unborrowed amounts held in the account at the time such debt proceeds are deposited; and

(B) Any amounts (borrowed or unborrowed) that are deposited in the account after such debt proceeds are deposited.

The following example illustrates the application of this paragraph (c)(4)(ii):

Example. On January 10, taxpayer E opens a checking account, depositing $500 of proceeds of Debt A and $1,000 of unborrowed funds. The following chart summarizes the transactions which occur during the year with respect to the account:

Date		Transaction
January 10	$ 500	proceeds of Debt A and $1,000 unborrowed funds deposited
January 11	$ 500	proceeds of Debt B deposited
February 17	$ 800	personal expenditure
February 26	$ 700	passive activity expenditure
June 21	$1,000	proceeds of Debt C deposited
November 24	$ 800	investment expenditure
December 20	$ 600	personal expenditure

The $800 personal expenditure is treated as made from the $500 proceeds of Debt A and $300 of the proceeds of Debt B. The $700 passive activity expenditure is treated as made from the remaining $200 proceeds of Debt B and $500 of unborrowed funds. The $800 investment expenditure is treated as made entirely from the proceeds of Debt C. The $600 personal expenditure is treated as made from the remaining $200 proceeds of Debt C and $400 of unborrowed funds. Under paragraph (c)(4)(i) of this section, debt is allocated to an investment expenditure for periods during which debt proceeds are held in the account.

(iii) Expenditures from account; supplemental ordering rules. (A) Checking or similar accounts. Except as otherwise provided in this paragraph (c)(4)(iii), an expenditure from a checking or similar account is treated as made at the time the check is written on the account, provided the check is delivered or mailed to the payee within a reasonable period after the writing of the check. For this purpose, the taxpayer may treat checks written on the same day as written in any order. In the absence of evidence to the contrary, a check is presumed to be written on the date appearing on the check and to be delivered or mailed to the payee within a reasonable period thereafter. Evidence to the contrary may include the fact that a check does not clear within a reasonable period after the date appearing on the check.

(B) Expenditures within 15 days after deposit of borrowed funds. The taxpayer may treat any expenditure made from an account within 15 days after debt proceeds are deposited in such account as made from such proceeds to the extent thereof even if under paragraph (c)(4)(ii) of this section the debt proceeds would be treated as used to make one or more other expenditures. Any such expenditures and the debt proceeds from which such expenditures are treated as made are disregarded in applying paragraph (c)(4)(ii) of this section. The following examples illustrate the application of this paragraph (c)(4)(iii)(B):

Example (1). Taxpayer D incurs a $1,000 debt on June 5 and immediately deposits the proceeds in an account ("Account A"). On June 17, D transfers $2,000 from Account A to another account ("Account B"). On June 30, D writes a $1,500 check on Account B for a passive activity expenditure. In addition, numerous deposits of borrowed and unborrowed amounts and expenditures occur with respect to both accounts throughout the month of June. Notwithstanding these other transactions, D may treat $1,000 of the deposit to Account B on June 17 as an expenditure from the debt proceeds deposited in Account A on June 5. In addition, D may similarly treat $1,000 of the passive activity expenditure on June 30 as made from debt proceeds treated as deposited in Account B on June 17.

Example (2). The facts are the same as in the example in paragraph (c)(4)(ii) of this section, except that the proceeds of Debt B are deposited on February 11 rather than on January 11. Since the $700 passive activity expenditure occurs within 15 days after the proceeds of Debt B are deposited in the account, E may treat such expenditure as being made from the proceeds of Debt B to the extent thereof. If E treats the passive activity expenditure in this manner, the expenditures from the account are treated as follows: The $800 personal expenditure is treated as made from the $500 proceeds of Debt A and $300 of unborrowed funds. The $700 passive activity expenditure is treated as made from the $500 proceeds of Debt B and $200 of unborrowed funds. The remaining expenditures are treated as in the example in paragraph (c)(4)(ii) of this section.

(C) Interest on segregated account. In the case of an account consisting solely of the proceeds of a debt and interest earned on such account, the taxpayer may treat any expenditure from such account as made first from amounts constituting interest (rather than debt proceeds) to the extent of the balance of such interest in the account at the time of the expenditure, determined by applying the rules in this paragraph (c)(4). To the extent any expenditure is treated as made from interest under this paragraph (c)(4)(iii)(C), the expenditure is disregarded in applying paragraph (c)(4)(ii) of this section.

(iv) Optional method for determining date of reallocation. Solely for the purpose of determining the date on which debt allocated to an account under paragraph (c)(4)(i) of this section is reallocated, the taxpayer may treat all expenditures made during any calendar month from debt proceeds in the account as occurring on the later of the first day of such month or the date on which such debt proceeds are deposited in the account. This paragraph (c)(4)(iv) applies only if all expenditures from an account during the same calendar month are similarly treated. The following example illustrates the application of this paragraph (c)(4)(iv):

Example. On January 10, taxpayer G opens a checking account, depositing $500 of proceeds of Debt A and $1,000 of unborrowed funds. The following chart summarizes the transactions which occur during the year with respect to the account (note that these facts are the same as the facts of the example in paragraph (c)(4)(ii) of this section):

Date	Transaction	
January 10	$ 500	proceeds of Debt A and $1,000 unborrowed funds deposited
January 11	$ 500	proceeds of Debt B deposited
February 17	$ 800	personal expenditure
February 26	$ 700	passive activity expenditure
June 21	$1,000	proceeds of Debt C deposited
November 24	$ 800	investment expenditure
December 20	$ 600	personal expenditure

Assume that G chooses to apply the optional rule of this paragraph (c)(4)(iv) to all expenditures. For purposes of determining the date on which debt is allocated to the $800 personal expenditure made on February 17, the $500 treated as made from the proceeds of Debt A and the $300 treated as made from the proceeds of Debt B are treated as expenditures occurring on February 1. Accordingly, Debt A is allocated to an investment expenditure for the account from January 10 through January 31 and to the personal expenditure from February 1 through December 31, and $300 of Debt B is allocated to an investment expenditure for the account from January 11 through January 31 and to the personal expenditure from February 1 through December 31. The remaining $200 of Debt B is allocated to an investment expenditure for the account from January 11 through January 31 and to the passive activity expenditure from February 1 through December 31. The $800 of Debt C used to make the investment expenditure on November 24 is allocated to an investment expenditure for the account from June 21 through October 31 and to an investment expenditure from November 1 through December 31. The remaining $200 of Debt C is allocated to an investment expenditure for the account from June 21 through November 30 and to a personal expenditure from December 1 through December 31.

(v) Simultaneous deposits. (A) In general. If the proceeds of two or more debts are deposited in an account simultaneously, such proceeds are treated for purposes of this paragraph (c)(4) as deposited in the order in which the debts were incurred.

(B) Order in which debts incurred. If two or more debts are incurred simultaneously or are treated under applicable law as incurred simultaneously, the debts are treated for purposes of this paragraph (c)(4)(v) as incurred in any order the taxpayer selects.

(C) Borrowings on which interest accrues at different rates. If interest does not accrue at the same fixed or variable rate on the entire amount of a borrowing, each portion of the borrowing on which interest accrues at a different fixed or variable rate is treated as a separate debt for purposes of this paragraph (c)(4)(v).

(vi) Multiple accounts. The rules in this paragraph (c)(4) apply separately to each account of a taxpayer.

(5) Allocation of debt; proceeds received in cash. (i) Expenditure within 15 days of receiving debt proceeds. If a taxpayer receives the proceeds of a debt in cash, the taxpayer may treat any cash expenditure made within 15 days after receiving the cash as made from such debt proceeds to the extent thereof and may treat such expenditure as made on the date the taxpayer received the cash. The following example illustrates the rule in this paragraph (c)(5)(i):

Example. Taxpayer F incurs a $1,000 debt on August 4 and receives the debt proceeds in cash. F deposits $1,500 cash in an account on August 15 and on August 27 writes a check on the account for a passive activity expenditure. In addition, F engages in numerous other cash transactions throughout the month of August, and numerous deposits of borrowed and unborrowed amounts and expenditures occur with respect to the account during the same period. Notwithstanding these other transactions, F may treat $1,000 of the deposit on August 15 as an expenditure made from the debt proceeds on August 4. In addition, under the rule in paragraph (c)(4)(v)(B) of this section, F may treat the passive activity expenditure on August 27 as made from the $1,000 debt proceeds treated as deposited in the account.

(ii) Other expenditures. Except as provided in paragraphs (c)(5)(i) and (iii) of this section, any debt proceeds a taxpayer (other than a corporation) receives in cash are treated as used to make personal expenditures. For purposes of this paragraph (c)(5), debt proceeds are received in cash if, for example, a withdrawal of cash from an account is treated under the rules of this section as an expenditure of debt proceeds.

(iii) Special rules for certain taxpayers. [Reserved]

(6) Special rules. (i) Qualified residence debt. [Reserved]

(ii) Debt used to pay interest. To the extent proceeds of a debt are used to pay interest, such debt is allocated in the same manner as the debt on which such interest accrued is allocated from time to time. The following example illustrates the application of this paragraph (c)(6)(ii):

Example. On January 1, taxpayer H incurs a debt of $1,000, bearing interest at an annual rate of 10 percent, compounded annually, payable at the end of each year ("Debt A"). H immediately opens a checking account, in which H deposits the proceeds of Debt A. No other amounts are deposited in the account during the year. On April 1, H writes a check for a personal expenditure in the amount of $1,000.

On December 31, H borrows $100 ("Debt B") and immediately uses the proceeds of Debt B to pay the accrued interest of $100 on Debt A. From January 1 through March 31, Debt A is allocated, under the rule in paragraph (c)(4)(i) of this section, to the investment expenditure for the account. From April 1 through December 31, Debt A is allocated to the personal expenditure. Under the rule in paragraph (c)(2)(ii) of this section, $25 of the interest on Debt A for the year is allocated to the investment expenditure, and $75 of the interest on Debt A for the year is allocated to the personal expenditure. Accordingly, for the purpose of allocating the interest on Debt B for all periods until Debt B is repaid, $25 of Debt B is allocated to the investment expenditure, and $75 of Debt B is allocated to the personal expenditure.

(iii) Debt used to pay borrowing costs. (A) Borrowing costs with respect to different debt. To the extent the proceeds of a debt (the "ancillary debt") are used to pay borrowing costs (other than interest) with respect to another debt (the "primary debt"), the ancillary debt is allocated in the same manner as the primary debt is allocated from time to time. To the extent the primary debt is repaid, the ancillary debt will continue to be allocated in the same manner as the primary debt was allocated immediately before its repayment. The following example illustrates the rule in this paragraph (c)(6)(iii)(A):

Example. Taxpayer I incurs debts of $60,000 ("Debt A") and $10,000 ("Debt B"). I immediately uses $30,000 of the proceeds of Debt A to make a trade or business expenditure, $20,000 to make a passive activity expenditure, and $10,000 to make an investment expenditure. I immediately uses $3,000 of the proceeds of Debt B to pay borrowing costs (other than interest) with respect to Debt A (such as loan origination, loan commitment, abstract, and recording fees) and deposits the remaining $7,000 in an account. Under the rule in this paragraph (c)(6)(iii)(A), the $3,000 of Debt B used to pay expenses of incurring Debt A is allocated $1,500 to the trade or business expenditure ($3,000 × $30,000/$60,000), $1,000 to the passive activity expenditure ($3,000 × $20,000/$60,000), and $500 ($3,000 × $10,000/$60,000) to the investment expenditure. The manner in which the $3,000 of Debt B used to pay expenses of incurring Debt A is allocated may change if the allocation of Debt A changes, but such allocation will be unaffected by any repayment of Debt A. The remaining $7,000 of Debt B is allocated to an investment expenditure for the account until such time, if any, as this amount is used for a different expenditure.

(B) Borrowing costs with respect to same debt. To the extent the proceeds of a debt are used to pay borrowing costs (other than interest) with respect to such debt, such debt is allocated in the same manner as the remaining debt is allocated from time to time. The remaining debt for this purpose is the portion of the debt that is not used to pay borrowing costs (other than interest) with respect to such debt. Any repayment of the debt is treated as a repayment of the debt allocated under this paragraph (c)(6)(iii)(B) and the remaining debt in the same proportion as such amounts bear to each other. The following example illustrates the application of this paragraph (c)(6)(iii)(B):

Example. (i) Taxpayer J borrows $85,000. The lender disburses $80,000 of this amount to J, retaining $5,000 for borrowing costs (other than interest) with respect to the loan. J immediately uses $40,000 of the debt proceeds to make a personal expenditure, $20,000 to make a passive activity expenditure, and $20,000 to make an investment expenditure. Under the rule in this paragraph (c)(6)(iii)(B), the $5,000 used to pay borrowing costs is allocated $2,500 ($5,000 × $40,000/$80,000) to the personal expenditure, $1,250 ($5,000 × $20,000/$80,000) to the passive activity expenditure, and $1,250 ($5,000 × $20,000/$80,000) to the investment expenditure. The manner in which this $5,000 is allocated may change if the allocation of the remaining $80,000 of debt is changed.

(ii) Assume that J repays $50,000 of the debt. The repayment is treated as a repayment of $2,941 ($50,000 × $5,000/$85,000) of the debt used to pay borrowing costs and a repayment of $47,059 ($50,000 × $80,000/$85,000) of the remaining debt. Under paragraph (d) of this section, J is treated as repaying the $42,500 of debt allocated to the personal expenditure ($2,500 of debt used to pay borrowing costs and $40,000 of remaining debt). In addition, assuming that under paragraph (d)(2) J chooses to treat the allocation to the passive activity expenditure as having occurred before the allocation to the investment expenditure, J is treated as repaying $7,500 of debt allocated to the passive activity expenditure ($441 of debt used to pay borrowing costs and $7,059 of remaining debt).

(iv) Allocation of debt before actual receipt of debt proceeds. If interest properly accrues on a debt during any period before the debt proceeds are actually received or used to make an expenditure, the debt is allocated to an investment expenditure for such period.

(7) Antiabuse rules. [Reserved]

(d) Debt repayments. *(1) General ordering rule.* If, at the time any portion of a debt is repaid, such debt is allocated to more than one expenditure, the debt is treated for purposes of this section as repaid in the following order:

(i) Amounts allocated to personal expenditures;

(ii) Amounts allocated to investment expenditures and passive activity expenditures (other than passive activity expenditures described in paragraph (d)(1)(iii) of this section).

(iii) Amounts allocated to passive activity expenditures in connection with a rental real estate activity with respect to which the taxpayer actively participates (within the meaning of section 469(i));

(iv) Amounts allocated to former passive activity expenditures; and

(v) Amounts allocated to trade or business expenditures and to expenditures described in the last sentence of paragraph (b)(4) of this section.

(2) Supplemental ordering rules for expenditures in same class. Amounts allocated to two or more expenditures that are described in the same subdivision of paragraph (d)(1) of this section (e.g., amounts allocated to different personal expenditures) are treated as repaid in the order in which the amounts were allocated (or reallocated) to such expenditures. For purposes of this paragraph (d)(2), the taxpayer may treat allocations and reallocations that occur on the same day as occurring in any order (without regard to the order in which expenditures are treated as made under paragraph (c)(4)(iii)(A) of this section).

(3) Continuous borrowings. In the case of borrowings pursuant to a line of credit or similar account or arrangement that allows a taxpayer to borrow funds periodically under a single loan agreement—

(i) All borrowings on which interest accrues at the same fixed or variable rate are treated as a single debt; and

(ii) Borrowings or portions of borrowings on which interest accrues at different fixed or variable rates are treated as different debts, and such debts are treated as repaid for purposes of this paragraph (d) in the order in which such borrowings are treated as repaid under the loan agreement.

(4) Examples. The following examples illustrate the application of this paragraph (d):

Example (1). Taxpayer B borrows $100,000 ("Debt A") on July 12, immediately deposits the proceeds in an account, and uses the debt proceeds to make the following expenditures on the following dates:

August 31	$40,000 passive activity expenditure #1
October 5	$20,000 passive activity expenditure #2
December 24	$40,000 personal expenditure

On January 19 of the following year, B repays $90,000 of Debt A (leaving $10,000 of Debt A outstanding). The $40,000 of Debt A allocated to the personal expenditure, the $40,000 allocated to passive activity expenditure #1, and $10,000 of the $20,000 allocated to passive activity expenditure #2 are treated as repaid.

Example (2). (i) Taxpayer A obtains a line of credit. Interest on any borrowing on the line of credit accrues at the lender's "prime lending rate" on the date of the borrowing plus two percentage points. The loan documents provide that borrowings on the line of credit are treated as repaid in the order the borrowings were made. A borrows $30,000 ("Borrowing #1") on the line of credit and immediately uses $20,000 of the debt proceeds to make a personal expenditure ("personal expenditure #1") and $10,000 to make a trade or business expenditure ("trade or business expenditure #1"). A subsequently borrows another $20,000 ("Borrowing #2") on the line of credit and immediately uses $15,000 of the debt proceeds to make a personal expenditure ("personal expenditure #2") and $5,000 to make a trade or business expenditure ("trade or business expenditure #2"). A then repays $40,000 of the borrowings.

(ii) If the prime lending rate plus two percentage points was the same on both the date of Borrowing #1 and the date of Borrowing #2, the borrowings are treated for purposes of this paragraph (d) as a single debt, and A is treated as having repaid $35,000 of debt allocated to personal expenditure #1 and personal expenditure #2, and $5,000 of debt allocated to trade or business expenditure #1.

(iii) If the prime lending rate plus two percentage points was different on the date of Borrowing #1 and Borrowing #2, the borrowings are treated as two debts, and, in accordance with the loan agreement, the $40,000 repaid amount is treated as a repayment of Borrowing #1 and $10,000 of Borrowing #2. Accordingly, A is treated as having repaid $20,000 of debt allocated to personal expenditure #1, $10,000 of debt allocated to trade or business expenditure #1, and $10,000 of debt allocated to personal expenditure #2.

(e) Debt refinancings. *(1) In general.* To the extent proceeds of any debt (the "replacement debt") are used to repay any portion of a debt, the replacement debt is allocated to the expenditures to which the repaid debt was allocated. The amount of replacement debt allocated to any such expenditure is equal to the amount of debt allocated to such expenditure that was repaid with proceeds of the replacement debt. To the extent proceeds of the replacement debt are used for expenditures other than repayment of a debt, the replacement debt is allocated to expenditures in accordance with the rules of this section.

(2) Example. The following example illustrates the application of this paragraph (e):

Example. Taxpayer C borrows $100,000 ("Debt A") on July 12, immediately deposits the debt proceeds in an account, and uses the proceeds to make the following expenditures on the following dates (note that the facts of this example are the same as the facts of example (1) in paragraph (d)(4) of this section):

August 31	$40,000 passive activity expenditure #1
October 5	$20,000 passive activity expenditure #2
December 24	$40,000 personal expenditure #1

On January 19 of the following year, C borrows $120,000 ("Debt B") and uses $90,000 of the proceeds to repay $90,000 of Debt A (leaving $10,000 of Debt A outstanding). In addition, C uses $30,000 of the proceeds of Debt B to make a personal expenditure ("personal expenditure #2"). Debt B is allocated $40,000 to personal expenditure #1, $40,000 to passive activity expenditure #1, $10,000 to passive activity expenditure #2, and $30,000 to personal expenditure #2. Under paragraph (d)(1) of this section, Debt B will be treated as repaid in the following order: (1) amounts allocated to personal expenditure #1, (2) amounts allocated to personal expenditure #2, (3) amounts allocated to passive activity expenditure #1, and (4) amounts allocated to passive activity expenditure #2.

(f) Debt allocated to distributions by passthrough entities. [Reserved]

(g) Repayment of passthrough entity debt. [Reserved]

(h) Debt allocated to expenditures for interests in passthrough entities. [Reserved]

(i) Allocation of debt to loans between passthrough entities and interest holders. [Reserved]

(j) Reallocation of debt. *(1) Debt allocated to capital expenditures.* (i) Time of reallocation. Except as provided in paragraph (j)(2) of this section, debt allocated to an expenditure properly chargeable to capital account with respect to an asset (the "first expenditure") is reallocated to another expenditure on the earlier of—

(A) The date on which proceeds from a disposition of such asset are used for another expenditure; or

(B) The date on which the character of the first expenditure changes (e.g., from a passive activity expenditure to an expenditure that is not a passive activity expenditure) by reason of a change in the use of the asset with respect to which the first expenditure was capitalized.

(ii) Limitation on amount reallocated. The amount of debt reallocated under paragraph (j)(1)(i)(A) of this section may not exceed the proceeds from the disposition of the asset. The amount of debt reallocated under paragraph (j)(1)(i)(B) of this section may not exceed the fair market value of the asset on the date of the change in use. In applying this paragraph (j)(1)(ii) with respect to a debt in any case in which two or more debts are allocable to expenditures properly chargeable to capital account with respect to the same asset, only a ratable portion (determined with respect to any such debt by dividing the amount of such debt by the aggregate amount of all such debts) of the fair market value or proceeds from the disposition of such asset shall be taken into account.

(iii) Treatment of loans made by the taxpayer. Except as provided in paragraph (j)(1)(iv) of this section, an expenditure to make a loan is treated as an expenditure properly chargeable to capital account with respect to an asset, and for purposes of paragraph (j)(1)(i)(A) of this section any repayment of the loan is treated as a disposition of the asset.

Paragraph (j)(3) of this section applies to any repayment of a loan in installments.

(iv) Treatment of accounts. Debt allocated to an account under paragraph (c)(4)(i) of this section is treated as allocated to an expenditure properly chargeable to capital account with respect to an asset, and any expenditure from the account is treated as a disposition of the asset. See paragraph (c)(4) of this section for rules under which debt proceeds allocated to an account are treated as used for another expenditure.

(2) Disposition proceeds in excess of debt. If the proceeds from the disposition of an asset exceed the amount of debt reallocated by reason of such disposition, or two or more debts are reallocated by reason of the disposition of an asset, the proceeds of the disposition are treated as an account to which the rules in paragraph (c)(4) of this section apply.

(3) Special rule for deferred payment sales. If any portion of the proceeds of a disposition of an asset are received subsequent to the disposition—

(i) The portion of the proceeds to be received subsequent to the disposition is treated for periods prior to the receipt as used to make an investment expenditure; and

(ii) Debt reallocated by reason of the disposition is allocated to such investment expenditure to the extent such debt exceeds the proceeds of the disposition previously received (other than proceeds used to repay such debt).

(4) Examples. The following examples illustrate the application of this paragraph (j):

Example (1). On January 1, 1988, taxpayer D sells an asset for $25,000. Immediately before the sale, the amount of debt allocated to expenditures properly chargeable to capital account with respect to the asset was $15,000. The proceeds of the disposition are treated as an account consisting of $15,000 of debt proceeds and $10,000 of unborrowed funds to which paragraph (c)(4) of this section applies. Thus, if D immediately makes a $10,000 personal expenditure from the proceeds and within 15 days deposits the remaining proceeds in an account, D may, pursuant to paragraph (c)(4)(iii)(B) of this section, treat the entire $15,000 deposited in the account as proceeds of a debt.

Example (2). The facts are the same as in example (1) except that, instead of receiving all $25,000 of the sale proceeds on January 1, 1988, D receives $5,000 on that date, $10,000 on January 1, 1989, and $10,000 on January 1, 1990. D does not use any portion of the sale proceeds to repay the debt. Between January 1, 1988, and December 31, 1988, D is treated under paragraph (j)(3) of this section as making an investment expenditure of $20,000 to which $10,000 of debt is allocated. In addition, the remaining $5,000 of debt is reallocated on January 1, 1988, in accordance with D's use of the sales proceeds received on that date. Between January 1, 1989, and December 31, 1989, D is treated as making an investment expenditure of $10,000 to which no debt is allocated. In addition, as of January 1, 1989, $10,000 of debt is reallocated in accordance with D's use of the sales proceeds received on that date.

Example (3). The facts are the same as in example (2), except that D immediately uses the $5,000 sale proceeds received on January 1, 1988, to repay $5,000 of the $15,000 debt. Between January 1, 1988, and December 31, 1988, D is treated as making an investment expenditure of $20,000 to which the remaining balance ($10,000) of the debt is reallocated. The results in 1989 are as described in example (2).

(k) Modification of rules in the case of interest expense allocated to foreign source income. [Reserved]

(l) [Reserved]

(m) Coordination with other provisions. *(1) Effect of other limitations.* (i) In general. All debt is allocated among expenditures pursuant to the rules in this section, without regard to any limitations on the deductibility of interest expense on such debt. The applicability of the passive loss and nonbusiness interest limitations to interest on such debt, however, may be affected by other limitations on the deductibility of interest expense.

(ii) Disallowance provisions. Interest expense that is not allowable as a deduction by reason of a disallowance provision (within the meaning of paragraph (m)(7)(ii) of this section) is not taken into account for any taxable year for purposes of applying the passive loss and nonbusiness interest limitations.

(iii) Deferral provisions. Interest expense that is not allowable as a deduction for the taxable year in which paid or accrued by reason of a deferral provision (within the meaning of paragraph (m)(7)(iii) of this section) is allocated in the same manner as the debt giving rise to the interest expense is allocated for such taxable year. Such interest expense is taken into account for purposes of applying the passive loss and nonbusiness interest limitations for the taxable year in which such interest expense is allowable under such deferral provision.

(iv) Capitalization provisions. Interest expense that is capitalized pursuant to a capitalization provision (within the meaning of paragraph (m)(7)(i) of this section) is not taken into account as interest for any taxable year for purposes of applying the passive loss and nonbusiness interest limitations.

(2) Effect on other limitations. (i) General rule. Except as provided in paragraph (m)(2)(ii) of this section, any limitation on the deductibility of an item (other than the passive loss and nonbusiness interest limitations) applies without regard to the manner in which debt is allocated under this section. Thus, for example, interest expense treated under section 265(a)(2) as interest on indebtedness incurred or continued to purchase or carry obligations the interest on which is wholly exempt from Federal income tax is not deductible regardless of the expenditure to which the underlying debt is allocated under this section.

(ii) Exception. Capitalization provisions (within the meaning of paragraph (m)(7)(i) of this section) do not apply to interest expense allocated to any personal expenditure under the rules of this section.

(3) Qualified residence interest. Qualified residence interest (within the meaning of section 163(h)(3)) is allowable as a deduction without regard to the manner in which such interest expense is allocated under the rules of this section. In addition, qualified residence interest is not taken into account in determining the income or loss from any activity for purposes of section 469 or in determining the amount of investment interest for purposes of section 163 (d). The following example illustrates the rule in this paragraph (m)(3):

Example. Taxpayer E, an individual, incurs a $20,000 debt secured by a residence and immediately uses the proceeds to purchase an automobile exclusively for E's personal use. Under the rules in this section, the debt and interest expense on the debt are allocated to a personal expenditure. If, however, the interest on the debt is qualified residence interest within the meaning of section 163(h)(3), the interest is not treated as personal interest for purposes of section 163 (h).

(4) Interest described in section 163(h)(2)(E). Interest described in section 163(h)(2)(E) is allowable as a deduction without regard to the rules of this section.

(5) Interest on deemed distributee debt. [Reserved]

(6) Examples. The following examples illustrate the relationship between the passive loss and nonbusiness interest limitations and other limitations on the deductibility of interest expense:

Example (1). Debt is allocated pursuant to the rules in this section to an investment expenditure for the purchase of taxable investment securities. Pursuant to section 265(a)(2), the debt is treated as indebtedness incurred or continued to purchase or carry obligations the interest on which is wholly exempt from Federal income tax, and, accordingly, interest on the debt is disallowed. If section 265(a)(2) subsequently ceases to apply (because, for example, the taxpayer ceases to hold any tax-exempt obligations), and the debt at such time continues to be allocated to an investment expenditure, interest on the debt that accrues after such time is subject to section 163 (d).

Example (2). An accrual method taxpayer incurs a debt payable to a cash method lender who is related to the taxpayer within the meaning of section 267(b). During the period in which interest on the debt is not deductible by reason of section 267(a)(2), the debt is allocated to a passive activity expenditure. Thus, interest that accrues on the debt for such period is also allocated to the passive activity expenditure. When such interest expense becomes deductible under section 267(a)(2), it will be allocated to the passive activity expenditure, regardless of how the debt is allocated at such time.

Example (3). A taxpayer incurs debt that is allocated under the rules of this section to an investment expenditure. Under section 263A(f), however, interest expense on such debt is capitalized during the production period (within the meaning of section 263A(f)(4)(B)) of property used in a passive activity of the taxpayer. The capitalized interest expense is not allocated to the investment expenditure, and depreciation deductions attributable to the capitalized interest expense are subject to the passive loss limitation as long as the property is used in a passive activity. However, interest expense on the debt for periods after the production period is allocated to the investment expenditure as long as the debt remains allocated to the investment expenditure.

(7) Other limitations on interest expense. (i) Capitalization provisions. A capitalization provision is any provision that requires or allows interest expense to be capitalized. Capitalization provisions include sections 263 (g), 263A (f), and 266.

(ii) Disallowance provisions. A disallowance provision is any provision (other than the passive loss and nonbusiness interest limitations) that disallows a deduction for interest expense for all taxable years and is not a capitalization provision. Disallowance provisions include sections 163(f)(2), 264(a)(2), 264(a)(4), 265(a)(2), 265(b)(2), 279(a), 291(e)(1)(B)(ii), 805(b)(1), and 834(c)(5).

(iii) Deferral provisions. A deferral provision is any provision (other than the passive loss and nonbusiness interest limitations) that disallows a deduction for interest expense for any taxable year and is not a capitalization or disallowance provision. Deferral provisions include sections 267(a)(2), 465, 1277, and 1282.

(n) Effective date. *(1) In general.* This section applies to interest expense paid or accrued in taxable years beginning after December 31, 1986.

(2) Transitional rule for certain expenditures. For purposes of determining whether debt is allocated to expenditures made on or before August 3, 1987, paragraphs (c)(4)(iii)(B) and (c)(5)(i) of this section are applied by substituting "90 days" for "15 days."

(3) Transitional rule for certain debt. (i) General rule. Except as provided in paragraph (n)(3)(ii) of this section, any debt outstanding on December 31, 1986, that is properly attributable to a business or rental activity is treated for purposes of this section as debt allocated to expenditures properly chargeable to capital account with respect to the assets held for use or for sale to customers in such business or rental activity. Debt is properly attributable to a business or rental activity for purposes of this section (regardless of whether such debt otherwise would be allocable under this section to expenditures in connection with such activity) if the taxpayer has properly and consistently deducted interest expense (including interest subject to limitation under section 163 (d) as in effect prior to the Tax Reform Act of 1986) on such debt on Schedule C, E, or F of Form 1040 in computing income or loss from such business or rental activity for taxable years beginning before January 1, 1987. For purposes of this paragraph (n)(3), amended returns filed after July 2, 1987, are disregarded in determining whether a taxpayer has consistently deducted interest expense on Schedule C, E, or F of Form 1040 in computing income or loss from a business or rental activity.

(ii) Exceptions. (A) Debt financed distributions by passthrough entities. [Reserved]

(B) Election out. This paragraph (n)(3) does not apply with respect to debt of a taxpayer who elects under paragraph (n)(3)(viii) of this section to allocate debt outstanding on December 31, 1986, in accordance with the provisions of this section other than this paragraph (n)(3) (i.e., in accordance with the use of the debt proceeds).

(iii) Business or rental activity. For purposes of this paragraph (n)(3), a business or rental activity is any trade or business or rental activity of the taxpayer. For this purpose—

(A) A trade or business includes a business or profession the income and deductions of which (or, in the case of a partner or S corporation shareholder, the taxpayer's share thereof) are properly reported on Schedule C, E, or F of Form 1040; and

(B) A rental activity includes an activity of renting property the income and deductions of which (or, in the case of a partner or S corporation shareholder, the taxpayer's share thereof) are properly reported on Schedule E of Form 1040.

(iv) Example. The following example illustrates the circumstances in which debt is properly attributable to a business or rental activity:

Example. Taxpayer H incurred a debt in 1979 and properly deducted the interest expense on the debt on Schedule C of Form 1040 for each year from 1979 through 1986. Under this paragraph (n)(3), the debt is properly attributable to the business the results of which are reported on Schedule C.

(v) Allocation requirement. (A) In general. Debt outstanding on December 31, 1986, that is properly attributable (within the meaning of paragraph (n)(3)(i) of this section) to a business or rental activity must be allocated in a reasonable and consistent manner among the assets held for use or for sale to customers in such activity on the last day of the taxable year that includes December 31, 1986. The taxpayer shall specify the manner in which such debt is allocated by filing a statement in accordance with paragraph (n)(3)(vii) of this section. If the taxpayer does not file such a statement or fails to allocate such debt in a reasonable and consistent manner, the Commissioner shall allocate the debt.

(B) Reasonable and consistent manner—examples of improper allocation. For purposes of this paragraph (n)(3)(v), debt is not treated as allocated in a reasonable and consistent manner if—

(1) The amount of debt allocated to goodwill exceeds the basis of the goodwill; or

(2) The amount of debt allocated to an asset exceeds the fair market value of the asset, and the amount of debt allocated to any other asset is less than the fair market value (lesser of basis or fair market value in the case of goodwill) of such other asset.

(vi) Coordination with other provisions. The effect of any events occurring after the last day of the taxable year that includes December 31, 1986, shall be determined under the rules of this section, applied by treating the debt allocated to an asset under paragraph (n)(3)(v) of this section as if proceeds of such debt were used to make an expenditure properly chargeable to capital account with respect to such asset on the last day of the taxable year that includes December 31, 1986. Thus, debt that is allocated to an asset in accordance with this paragraph (n)(3) must be reallocated in accordance with paragraph (j) of this section upon the occurrence with respect to such asset of any event described in such paragraph (j). Similarly, such debt is treated as repaid in the order prescribed in paragraph (d) of this section. In addition, a replacement debt (within the meaning of paragraph (e) of this section) is allocated to an expenditure properly chargeable to capital account with respect to an asset to the extent the proceeds of such debt are used to repay the portion of a debt allocated to such asset under this paragraph (n)(3).

(vii) Form for allocation of debt. A taxpayer shall allocate debt for purposes of this paragraph (n)(3) by attaching to the taxpayer's return for the first taxable year beginning after December 31, 1986, a statement that is prominently identified as a TRANSITIONAL ALLOCATION STATEMENT UNDER § 1.163-8T(n)(3) and includes the following information:

(A) A description of the business or rental activity to which the debt is properly attributable;

(B) The amount of debt allocated;

(C) The assets among which the debt is allocated;

(D) The manner in which the debt is allocated;

(E) The amount of debt allocated to each asset; and

(F) Such other information as the Commissioner may require.

(viii) Form for election out. A taxpayer shall elect to allocate debt outstanding on December 31, 1986, in accordance with the provisions of this section other than this paragraph (n)(3) by attaching to the taxpayer's return (or amended return) for the first taxable year beginning after December 31, 1986, a statement to that effect, prominently identified as an ELECTION OUT UNDER § 1.163-8T(n)(3).

(ix) Special rule for partnerships and S corporations. For purposes of paragraph (n)(3)(ii)(B), (v), (vii) and (viii) of this section (relating to the allocation of debt and election out), a partnership or S corporation shall be treated as the taxpayer with respect to the debt of the partnership or S corporation.

(x) Irrevocability. An allocation or election filed in accordance with paragraph (n)(3)(vii) or (viii) of this section may not be revoked or modified except with the consent of the Commissioner.

T.D. 8145, 7/1/87.

---

§ 1.163-9T Personal interest (temporary).

(a) In general. No deduction under any provision of Chapter 1 of the Internal Revenue Code shall be allowed for personal interest paid or accrued during the taxable year by a taxpayer other than a corporation.

(b) Personal interest. *(1) Definition.* For purposes of this section, personal interest is any interest expense other than—

(i) Interest paid or accrued on indebtedness properly allocable (within the meaning of § 1.163-8T) to the conduct of trade or business (other than the trade or business of performing services as an employee),

(ii) Any investment interest (within the meaning of section 163(d)(3)),

(iii) Any interest that is taken into account under section 469 in computing income or loss from a passive activity of the taxpayer,

(iv) Any qualified residence interest (within the meaning of section 163(h)(3) and § 1.163-10T), and

(v) Any interest payable under section 6601 with respect to the unpaid portion of the tax imposed by section 2001 for the period during which an extension of time for payment of such tax is in effect under section 6163, 6166, or 6166A (as in effect before its repeal by the Economic Recovery Tax Act of 1981).

(2) Interest relating to taxes. (i) In general. Except as provided in paragraph (b)(2)(iii) of this section, personal interest includes interest—

(A) Paid on underpayments of individual Federal, State or local income taxes and on indebtedness used to pay such taxes (within the meaning of § 1.163-8T), regardless of the source of the income generating the tax liability;

(B) Paid under section 453(e)(4)(B) [sic 453C(e)(4)(B)] (interest on deferred tax resulting from certain installment sales) and section 1291(c) (interest on deferred tax attributable to passive foreign investment companies); or

(C) Paid by a trust, S corporation, or other pass-through entity on underpayments of State or local income taxes and on indebtedness used to pay such taxes.

(ii) Example. A, an individual, owns stock of an S corporation. On its return for 1987, the corporation underreports its taxable income. Consequently, A underreports A's share of that income on A's tax return. In 1989, A pays the resulting deficiency plus interest to the Internal Revenue Service. The interest paid by A in 1989 on the tax deficiency is personal interest, notwithstanding the fact that the additional tax liability may have arisen out of income from a trade or business. The result would be the same if A's business had been operated as a sole proprietorship.

(iii) Certain other taxes. Personal interest does not include interest—

(A) Paid with respect to sales, excise and similar taxes that are incurred in connection with a trade or business or an investment activity;

(B) Paid by an S corporation with respect to an underpayment of income tax from a year in which the S corporation was a C corporation or with respect to an underpayment of the taxes imposed by sections 1374 or 1375, or similar provision of State law; or

(C) Paid by a transferee under section 6901 (tax liability resulting from transferred assets), or a similar provision of State law, with respect to a C corporation's underpayment of income tax.

(3) Cross references. See § 1.163-8T for rules for determining the allocation of interest expense to various activities. See § 1.163-10T for rules concerning qualified residence interest.

(c) Effective date. *(1) In general.* The provisions of this section are effective for taxable years beginning after December 31, 1986. In the case of any taxable year beginning in calendar years 1987 through 1990, the amount of personal interest that is nondeductible under this section is limited to the applicable percentage of such amount.

(2) Applicable percentages. The applicable percentage for taxable years beginning in 1987 through 1990 are as follows:

1987: 35 percent

1988: 60 percent

1989: 80 percent

1990: 90 percent

T.D. 8168, 12/21/87.

---

§ 1.163-10T Qualified residence interest (temporary).

Caution: The Treasury has not yet amended Reg § 1.163-10T to reflect changes made by P.L. 100-647, P.L. 100-203.

(a) Table of contents. This paragraph (a) lists the major paragraphs that appear in this section 1.163-10T.

(a) Table of contents.

(b) Treatment of qualified residence interest.

(c) Determination of qualified residence interest when secured debt does not exceed the adjusted purchase price.

(1) In general.

(2) Examples.

(d) Determination of qualified residence interest when secured debt exceeds adjusted purchase price. Simplified method.

(1) In general.

(2) Treatment of interest paid or accrued on secured debt that is not qualified residence interest.

(3) Example.

(e) Determination of qualified residence interest when secured debt exceeds adjusted purchase price. Exact method.

(1) In general.

(2) Determination of applicable debt limit.

(3) Example.

(4) Treatment of interest paid or accrued with respect to secured debt that is not qualified residence interest.

(i) In general.

(ii) Example.

(iii) Special rule of debt is allocated to more than one expenditure.

(iv) Example.

(f) Special rules.

(1) Special rules for personal property.

(i) In general.

(ii) Example.

(2) Special rule for real property.

(i) In general.

(ii) Example.

(g) Selection of method.

(h) Average balance.

(1) Average balance defined.

(2) Average balance reported by lender.

(3) Average balance computed on a daily basis.

(i) In general.

(ii) Example.

(4) Average balance computed using the interest rate.

(i) In general.

(ii) Points and prepaid interest.

(iii) Examples.

(5) Average balance computed using average of beginning and ending balance.

(i) In general.

(ii) Example.

(6) Highest principal balance.

(7) Other methods provided by the Commissioner.

(8) Anti-abuse rule.

(i) [Reserved]

(j) Determination of interest paid or accrued during the taxable year.

(1) In general.

(2) Special rules for cash-basis taxpayers.

(i) Points deductible in year paid under section 461(g)(2).

(ii) Points and other prepaid interest described in section 461(g)(1).

(3) Examples.

(k) Determination of adjusted purchase price and fair market value.

(1) Adjusted purchase price.

(i) In general.

(ii) Adjusted purchase price of a qualified residence acquired incident to divorce.

(iii) Examples.

(2) Fair market value.

(i) In general.

(ii) Examples.

(3) Allocation of adjusted purchase price and fair market value.

(l) [Reserved]

(m) Grandfathered amount.

(1) Substitution for adjusted purchase price.

(2) Determination of grandfathered amount.

(i) In general.

(ii) Special rule for lines of credit and certain other debt.

(iii) Fair market value limitation.

(iv) Examples.

(3) Refinancing of grandfathered debt.

(i) In general.

(ii) Determination of grandfathered amount.

(4) Limitation on terms of grandfathered debt.

(i) In general.

(ii) Special rule for nonamortizing debt.

(iii) Example.

(n) Qualified indebtedness (secured debt used for medical and educational purposes).

(1) In general.

(i) Treatment of qualified indebtedness.

(ii) Determination of amount of qualified indebtedness.

(iii) Determination of amount of qualified indebtedness for mixed-use debt.

(iv) Example.

(v) Prevention of double counting in year of refinancing.

(vi) Special rule for principal payments in excess of qualified expenses.

(2) Debt used to pay for qualified medical or educational expenses.

(i) In general.

(ii) Special rule for refinancing.

(iii) Other special rules.

(iv) Examples.

(3) Qualified medical expenses.

(4) Qualified educational expenses.

(o) Secured debt.

(1) In general.

(2) Special rule for debt in certain States.

(3) Time at which debt is treated as secured.

(4) Partially secured debt.

(i) In general.

(ii) Example.

(5) Election to treat debt as not secured by a qualified residence.

(i) In general.

(ii) Example.

(iii) Allocation of debt secured by two qualified residences.

(p) Definition of qualified residence.

(1) In general.

(2) Principal residence.

(3) Second residence.

(i) In general.

(ii) Definition of residence.

(iii) Use as a residence.

(iv) Election of second residence.

(4) Allocations between residence and other property.

(i) In general.

(ii) Special rule for rental of residence.

(iii) Examples.

(5) Residence under construction.

(i) In general.

(ii) Example.

(6) Special rule for the time-sharing arrangements.

(q) Special rules for tenant-stockholders in cooperative housing corporations.

(1) In general.

(2) Special rule where stock may not be used to secure debt.

(3) Treatment of interest expense of the cooperative described in section 216(a)(2).

(4) Special rule to prevent tax avoidance.

(5) Other definitions.

(r) Effective date.

(b) Treatment of qualified residence interest. Except as provided below, qualified residence interest is deductible under section 163(a). Qualified residence interest is not subject to limitation or otherwise taken into account under section 163(d) (limitation on investment interest), section 163(h)(1) (disallowance of deduction for personal interest), section 263A (capitalization and inclusion in inventory costs of certain expenses) or section 469 (limitations on losses from passive activities). Qualified residence interest is subject to the limitation imposed by section 263(g) (certain interest in the case of straddles), section 264(a)(2) and (4) (interest paid in connection with certain insurance), section 265(a)(2) (interest relating to tax-exempt income), section 266 (carrying charges), section 267(a)(2) (interest with respect to transactions between related taxpayers) section 465 (deductions limited to amount at risk), section 1277 (deferral of interest deduction allocable to accrued market discount), and section 1282 (deferral of interest deduction allocable to accrued discount).

(c) Determination of qualified residence interest when secured debt does not exceed adjusted purchase price. *(1) In general.* If the sum of the average balances for the taxable year of all secured debts on a qualified residence does not exceed the adjusted purchase price (determined as of the end of the taxable year) of the qualified residence, all of the interest paid or accrued during the taxable year with respect to the secured debts is qualified residence interest. If the sum of the average balances for the taxable year of all secured debts exceeds the adjusted purchase price of the qualified residences (determined as of the end of the taxable year), the taxpayer must use either the simplified method (see paragraph (d) of this section) or the exact method (see paragraph (e) of this section) to determine the amount of interest that is qualified residence interest.

(2) Examples.

Example (1). T purchases a qualified residence in 1987 for $65,000. T pays $6,500 in cash and finances the remainder of the purchase with a mortgage of $58,500. In 1988, the average balance of the mortgage is $58,000. Because the average balance of the mortgage is less than the adjusted purchase price of the residence ($65,000), all of the interest paid or accrued during 1988 on the mortgage is qualified residence interest.

Example (2). The facts are the same as in example (1), except that T incurs a second mortgage on January 1, 1988, with an initial principal balance of $2,000. The average balance of the second mortgage in 1988 is $1,900. Because the sum of the average balance of the first and second mortgages ($59,900) is less than the adjusted purchase price of the residence ($65,000), all of the interest paid or accrued during 1988 on both the first and second mortgages is qualified residence interest.

Example (3). P borrows $50,000 on January 1, 1988 and secures the debt by a qualified residence. P pays the interest on the debt monthly, but makes no principal payments in 1988. There are no other debts secured by the residence during 1988. On December 31, 1988, the adjusted purchase price of the residence is $40,000. The average balance of the debt in 1988 is $50,000. Because the average balance of the debt exceeds the adjusted purchase price ($10,000), some of the interest on the debt is not qualified residence interest. The portion of the total interest that is qualified residence interest must be determined in accordance with the rules of paragraph (d) or paragraph (e) of this section.

(d) Determination of qualified residence interest when secured debt exceeds adjusted purchase price. Simplified method. *(1) In general.* Under the simplified method, the amount of qualified residence interest for the taxable year is equal to the total interest paid or accrued during the taxable year with respect to all secured debts multiplied by a fraction (not in excess of one), the numerator of which is the adjusted purchase price (determined as of the end of the taxable year) of the qualified residence and the denominator of which is the sum of the average balances of all secured debts.

(2) Treatment of interest paid or accrued on secured debt that is not qualified residence interest. Under the simplified method, the excess of the total interest paid or accrued during the taxable year with respect to all secured debts over the amount of qualified residence interest is personal interest.

(3) Example. R's principal residence has an adjusted purchase price on December 31, 1988, of $105,000. R has two debts secured by the residence, with the following average balances and interest payments:

Debt	Date secured	Average balance	Interest
Debt 1	June 1983	$ 80,000	$ 8,000
Debt 2	May 1987	40,000	4,800
Total		120,000	12,800

The amount of qualified residence interest is determined under the simplified method by multiplying the total interest ($12,800) by a fraction (expressed as a decimal amount) equal to the adjusted purchase price ($105,000) of the residence divided by the combined average balances ($120,000). For 1988, this fraction is equal to 0.875 ($105,000/$120,000). Therefore, $11,200 ($12,800 × 0.875) of the total interest is qualified residence interest. The remaining $1,600 in interest ($12,800 − $11,200) is personal interest, even if (under the rules of § 1.163-8T) such remaining interest would be allocated to some other category of interest.

(e) Determination of qualified residence interest when secured debt exceeds adjusted purchase price. Exact method. *(1) In general.* Under the exact method, the amount of qualified residence interest for the taxable year is determined on a debt-by-debt basis by computing the applicable debt limit for each secured debt and comparing each such applicable debt limit to the average balance of the corresponding debt. If, for the taxable year, the average balance of a secured debt does not exceed the applicable debt limit for that debt, all of the interest paid or accrued during the taxable year with respect to the debt is qualified residence interest. If the average balance of the secured debt exceeds the applicable debt limit for that debt, the amount of qualified residence interest with respect to the debt is determined by multiplying the interest paid or accrued with respect to the debt by a fraction, the numerator of which is the applicable debt limit for that debt and the denominator of which is the average balance of the debt.

(2) Determination of applicable debt limit. For each secured debt, the applicable debt limit for the taxable year is equal to

(i) The lesser of—

(A) The fair market value of the qualified residence as of the date the debt is first secured, and

(B) The adjusted purchase price of the qualified residence as of the end of the taxable year.

(ii) Reduced by the average balance of each debt previously secured by the qualified residence.

For purposes of paragraph (e)(2)(ii) of this section, the average balance of a debt shall be treated as not exceeding the applicable debt limit of such debt. See paragraph (n)(1)(i) of this section for the rule that increases the adjusted purchase price in paragraph (e)(2)(i)(B) of this section by the amount of any qualified indebtedness (certain medical and educational debt). See paragraph (f) of this section for special rules relating to the determination of the fair market value of the qualified residence.

(3) Example. (i) R's principal residence has an adjusted purchase price on December 31, 1988, of $105,000. R has two debts secured by the residence. The average balances and interest payments on each debt during 1988 and fair market value of the residence on the date each debt was secured are as follows:

Debt	Date secured	Fair market value	Average balance	Interest
Debt 1	June 1983	$100,000	$ 80,000	$ 8,000
Debt 2	May 1987	140,000	40,000	4,800
Total			120,000	12,800

(ii) The amount of qualified residence interest for 1988 under the exact method is determined as follows. Because there are no debts previously secured by the residence, the applicable debt limit for Debt 1 is $100,000 (the lesser of the adjusted purchase price as of the end of the taxable year and the fair market value of the residence at the time the debt was secured). Because the average balance of Debt 1 ($80,000) does not exceed its applicable debt limit ($100,000), all of the interest paid on the debt during 1988 ($8,000) is qualified residence interest.

(iii) The applicable debt limit for Debt 2 is $25,000 ($105,000 (the lesser of $140,000 fair market value and $105,000 adjusted purchase price) reduced by $80,000 (the average balance of Debt 1)). Because the average balance of Debt 2 ($40,000) exceeds its applicable debt limit, the amount of qualified residence interest on Debt 2 is determined by multiplying the amount of interest paid on the debt during the year ($4,800) by a fraction equal to its applicable debt limit divided by its average balance ($25,000/$40,000 = 0.625). Accordingly, $3,000 ($4,800 × 0.625) of the interest paid in 1988 on Debt 2 is qualified residence interest. The character of the remaining $1,800 of interest paid on Debt 2 is determined under the rules of paragraph (e)(4) of this section.

(4) Treatment of interest paid or accrued with respect to secured debt that is not qualified residence interest—

(i) In general. Under the exact method, the excess of the interest paid or accrued during the taxable year with respect to a secured debt over the amount of qualified residence interest with respect to the debt is allocated under the rules of § 1.163-8T.

(ii) Example. T borrows $20,000 and the entire proceeds of the debt are disbursed by the lender to T's broker to purchase securities held for investment. T secures the debt with T's principal residence. In 1990, T pays $2,000 of interest on the debt. Assume that under the rules of paragraph (e) of this section, $1,500 of the interest is qualified residence interest. The remaining $500 in interest expense would be allocated under the rules of § 1.163-8T. Section 1.163-8T generally allocates debt (and the associated interest expense) by tracing disbursements of the debt proceeds to specific expenditures. Accordingly, the $500 interest expense on the debt that is not qualified residence interest is investment interest subject to section 163(d).

(iii) Special rule if debt is allocated to more than one expenditure. If—

(A) The average balance of a secured debt exceeds the applicable debt limit for that debt, and

(B) Under the rules of § 1.163-8T, interest paid or accrued with respect to such debt is allocated to more than one expenditure,

the interest expense that is not qualified residence interest may be allocated among such expenditures, to the extent of such expenditures, in any manner selected by the taxpayer.

(iv) Example.

Example. (i) C borrows $60,000 secured by a qualified residence. C uses (within the meaning of § 1.163-8T) $20,000 of the proceeds in C's trade or business, $20,000 to purchase stock held for investment and $20,000 for personal purposes. In 1990, C pays $6,000 in interest on the debt and, under the rules of § 1.163-8T, $2,000 in interest is allocable to trade or business expenses, $2,000 to investment expenses and $2,000 to personal expenses. Assume that under paragraph (e) of this section, $2,500 of the interest is qualified residence interest and $3,500 of the interest is not qualified residence interest.

(ii) Under paragraph (e)(4)(iii) of this section, C may allocate up to $2,000 of the interest that is not qualified residence interest to any of the three categories of expenditures up to a total of $3,500 for all three categories. Therefore, for example, C may allocate $2,000 of such interest to C's trade or business and $1,500 of such interest to the purchase of stock.

(f) Special rules. *(1) Special rules for personal property.* (i) In general. If a qualified residence is personal property under State law (e.g., a boat or motorized vehicle)—

(A) For purposes of paragraphs (c)(1) and (d)(1) of this section, if the fair market value of the residence as of the date that any secured debt (outstanding during the taxable year) is first secured by the residence is less than the adjusted purchase price as of the end of the taxable year, the lowest such fair market value shall be substituted for the adjusted purchase price.

(B) For purposes of paragraphs (e)(2)(i)(A) and (f)(1)(i)(A) of this section, the fair market value of the residence as of the date the debt is first secured by the residence shall not exceed the fair market value as of any date on which the taxpayer borrows any additional amount with respect to the debt.

(ii) Example. D owns a recreational vehicle that is a qualified residence under paragraph (p)(4) of this section. The adjusted purchase price and fair market value of the recreational vehicle is $20,000 in 1989. In 1989, D establishes a line of credit secured by the recreational vehicle. As of June 1, 1992, the fair market value of the vehicle has decreased to $10,000. On that day, D borrows an additional amount on the debt by using the line of credit. Although under paragraphs (e)(2)(i) and (f)(1)(i)(A) of this section, fair market value is determined at the time the debt is first secured, under paragraph (f)(1)(i)(B) of this section, the fair market value is the lesser of that amount or the fair market value on the most recent date that D borrows any additional amount with respect to the line of credit. Therefore, the fair market value with respect to the debt is $10,000.

(2) Special rule for real property. (i) In general. For purposes of paragraph (e)(2)(i)(A) of this section, the fair market value of a qualified residence that is real property under State law is presumed irrebuttably to be not less than the adjusted purchase price of the residence as of the last day of the taxable year.

(ii) Example.

Example. (i) C purchases a residence on August 11, 1987, for $50,000, incurring a first mortgage. The residence is real property under State law. During 1987, C makes $10,000 in home improvements. Accordingly, the adjusted purchase price of the residence as of December 31, 1988, is $60,000. C incurs a second mortgage on May 19, 1988, as of which time the fair market value of the residence is $55,000.

(ii) For purposes of determining the applicable debt limit for each debt, the fair market value of the residence is generally determined as of the time the debt is first secured. Accordingly, the fair market value would be $50,000 and $55,000 with respect to the first and second mortgage, respectively. Under the special rule of paragraph (f)(2)(i) of this section, however, the fair market value with respect to both debts in 1988 is $60,000, the adjusted purchase price on December 31, 1988.

(g) Selection of method. For any taxable year, a taxpayer may use the simplified method (described in paragraph (d) of this section) or the exact method (described in paragraph (e) of this section) by completing the appropriate portion of Form 8598. A taxpayer with two qualified residences may use the simplified method for one residence and the exact method for the other residence.

(h) Average balance. *(1) Average balance defined.* For purposes of this section, the term "average balance" means the amount determined under this paragraph (h). A taxpayer is not required to use the same method to determine the average balance of all secured debts during a taxable year or of any particular secured debt from one year to the next.

(2) Average balance reported by lender. If a lender that is subject to section 6050H (returns relating to mortgage interest received in trade or business from individuals) reports the average balance of a secured debt on Form 1098, the taxpayer may use the average balance so reported.

(3) Average balance computed on a daily basis. (i) In general. The average balance may be determined by—

(A) Adding the outstanding balance of a debt on each day during the taxable year that the debt is secured by a qualified residence, and

(B) Dividing the sum by the number of days during the taxable year that the residence is a qualified residence.

(ii) Example. Taxpayer A incurs a debt of $10,000 on September 1, 1989, securing the debt with A's principal residence. The residence is A's principal residence during the entire taxable year. A pays current interest on the debt monthly, but makes no principal payments. The debt is, therefore, outstanding for 122 days with a balance each day of $10,000. The residence is a qualified residence for 365 days. The average balance of the debt for 1989 is $3,342 (122 × $10,000/365).

(4) Average balance computed using the interest rate. (i) In general. If all accrued interest on a secured debt is paid at least monthly, the average balance of the secured debt may be determined by dividing the interest paid or accrued during the taxable year while the debt is secured by a qualified residence by the annual interest rate on the debt. If the interest rate on a debt varies during the taxable year, the lowest annual interest rate that applies to the debt during the taxable year must be used for purposes of this paragraph (h)(4). If the residence securing the debt is a qualified residence for less than the entire taxable year, the average balance of any secured debt may be determined by dividing the average balance determined under the preceding sentence by the percentage of the taxable year that the debt is secured by a qualified residence.

(ii) Points and prepaid interest. For purposes of paragraph (h)(4)(i) of this section, the amount of interest paid during the taxable year does not include any amount paid as points and includes prepaid interest only in the year accrued.

(iii) Examples.

Example (1). B has a line of credit secured by a qualified residence for the entire taxable year. The interest rate on the debt is 10 percent throughout the taxable year. The principal balance on the debt changes throughout the year. B pays the accrued interest on the debt monthly. B pays $2,500 in interest on the debt during the taxable year. The average balance of the debt ($25,000) may be computed by dividing the total interest paid by the interest rate ($25,000

Example (2). Assume the same facts as in example 1, except that the residence is a qualified residence, and the debt is outstanding, for only one-half of the taxable year and B pays only $1,250 in interest on the debt during the taxable year. The average balance of the debt may be computed by first dividing the total interest paid by the interest rate ($12,500 = $1,250/0.10). Second, because the residence is not a qualified residence for the entire taxable year, the average balance must be determined by dividing this amount ($12,500) by the portion of the year that the residence is qualified (0.50). The average balance is therefore $25,000 ($12,500/0.50).

(5) Average balance computed using average of beginning and ending balances. (i) In general. If—

(A) A debt requires level payments at fixed equal intervals (e.g., monthly, quarterly) no less often than semi-annually during the taxable year,

(B) The taxpayer prepays no more than one month's principal on the debt during the taxable year, and

(C) No new amounts are borrowed on the debt during the taxable year,

the average balance of the debt may be determined by adding the principal balance as of the first day of the taxable year that the debt is secured by the qualified residence and the principal balance as of the last day of the taxable year that the debt is secured by the qualified residence and dividing the sum by 2. If the debt is secured by a qualified residence for less than the entire period during the taxable year that the residence is a qualified residence, the average balance may be determined by multiplying the average balance determined under the preceding sentence by a fraction, the numerator of which is the number of days during the taxable year that the debt is secured by the qualified residence and the denominator of which is the number of days during the taxable year that the residence is a qualified residence. For purposes of this paragraph (h)(5)(i), the determination of whether payments are level shall disregard the fact that the amount of the payments may be adjusted from time to time to take into account changes in the applicable interest rate.

(ii) Example. C borrows $10,000 in 1988, securing the debt with a second mortgage on a principal residence. The terms of the loan require C to make equal monthly payments of principal and interest so as to amortize the entire loan balance over 20 years. The balance of the debt is $9,652 on January 1, 1990, and is $9,450 on December 31, 1990. The average balance of the debt during 1990 may be computed as follows:

Balance on first day of the year: $9,652

Balance on last day of the year: $9,450

$$\text{Average balance: } \frac{\$9{,}652 + \$9{,}450}{2} = \$9{,}551$$

(6) Highest principal balance. The average balance of a debt may be determined by taking the highest principal balance of the debt during the taxable year.

(7) Other methods provided by the Commissioner. The average balance may be determined using any other method provided by the Commissioner by form, publication, revenue ruling, or revenue procedure. Such methods may include methods similar to (but with restrictions different from) those provided in paragraph (h) of this section.

(8) Anti-abuse rule. If, as a result of the determination of the average balance of a debt using any of the methods specified in paragraphs (h)(4), (5), or (6) of this section, there is a significant overstatement of the amount of qualified residence interest and a principal purpose of the pattern of payments and borrowing on the debt is to cause the amount of such qualified residence interest to be overstated, the district director may redetermine the average balance using the method specified under paragraph (h)(3) of this section.

(i) [Reserved]

(j) Determination of interest paid or accrued during the taxable year. *(1) In general.* For purposes of determining the amount of qualified residence interest with respect to a secured debt, the amount of interest paid or accrued during the taxable year includes only interest paid or accrued while the debt is secured by a qualified residence.

(2) Special rules for cash-basis taxpayers. (i) Points deductible in year paid under section 461(g)(2). If points described in section 461(g)(2) (certain points paid in respect of debt incurred in connection with the purchase or improvement of a principal residence) are paid with respect to a debt, the amount of such points is qualified residence interest.

(ii) Points and other prepaid interest described in section 461(g)(1). The amount of points or other prepaid interest charged to capital account under section 461(g)(1) (prepaid interest) that is qualified residence interest shall be determined under the rules of paragraphs (c) through (e) of this section in the same manner as any other interest paid with respect to the debt in the taxable year to which such payments are allocable under section 461(g)(1).

(3) Examples.

Example (1). T designates a vacation home as a qualified residence as of October 1, 1987. The home is encumbered by a mortgage during the entire taxable year. For purposes of determining the amount of qualified residence interest for 1987, T may take into account the interest paid or accrued on the secured debt from October 1, 1987, through December 31, 1987.

Example (2). R purchases a principal residence on June 17, 1987. As part of the purchase price, R obtains a conventional 30-year mortgage, secured by the residence. At closing, R pays 2½ points on the mortgage and interest on the mortgage for the period June 17, 1987 through June 30, 1987. The points are actually paid by R and are not merely withheld from the loan proceeds. R incurs no additional secured debt during 1987. Assuming that the points satisfy the requirements of section 461(g)(2), the entire amount of points and the interest paid at closing are qualified residence interest.

Example (3). (i) On July 1, 1987, W borrows $120,000 to purchase a residence to use as a vacation home. W secures the debt with the residence. W pays 2 points, or $2,400. The debt has a term of 10 years and requires monthly payments of principal and interest. W is permitted to amortize the points at the rate of $20 per month over 120 months. W elects to treat the residence as a second residence. W has no other debt secured by the residence. The average balance of the debt in each taxable year is less than the adjusted purchase price of the residence. W sells the residence on June 30, 1990, and pays off the remaining balance of the debt.

(ii) W is entitled to treat the following amounts of the points as interest paid on a debt secured by a qualified residence—

1987	$120 = $20 × 6 months
1988	$240 = $20 × 12 months
1989	$120 = $20 × 6 months
Total	$ 480

All of the interest paid on the debt, including the allocable points, is qualified residence interest. Upon repaying the debt, the remaining $1,920 ($2,400 − $480) in unamortized points is treated as interest paid in 1990 and, because the average balance of the secured debt in 1990 is less than the adjusted purchase price, is also qualified residence interest.

(k) Determination of adjusted purchase price and fair market value. *(1) Adjusted purchase price.* (i) In general. For purposes of this section, the adjusted purchase price of a qualified residence is equal to the taxpayer's basis in the residence as initially determined under section 1012 or other applicable sections of the Internal Revenue Code, increased by the cost of any improvements to the residence that have been added to the taxpayer's basis in the residence under section 1016(a)(1). Any other adjustments to basis, including those required under section 1033(b) (involuntary conversions), and 1034(e) (rollover of gain or sale of principal residence) are disregarded in determining the taxpayer's adjusted purchase price. If, for example, a taxpayer's second residence is rented for a portion of the year and its basis is reduced by depreciation allowed in connection with the rental use of the property, the amount of the taxpayer's adjusted purchase price in the residence is not reduced. See paragraph (m) of this section for a rule that treats the sum of the grandfathered amounts of all secured debts as the adjusted purchase price of the residence.

(ii) Adjusted purchase price of a qualified residence acquired incident to divorce. [Reserved]

(iii) Examples.

Example (1). X purchases a residence for $120,000. X's basis, as determined under section 1012, is the cost of the property, or $120,000. Accordingly, the adjusted purchase price of the residence is initially $120,000.

Example (2). Y owns a principal residence that has a basis of $30,000. Y sells the residence for $100,000 and purchases a new principal residence for $120,000. Under section 1034, Y does not recognize gain on the sale of the former residence. Under section 1034(e), Y's basis in the new residence is reduced by the amount of gain not recognized. Therefore, under section 1034(e), Y's basis in the new residence is $50,000 ($120,000 − $70,000). For purposes of section 163(h), however, the adjusted purchase price of the residence is not adjusted under section 1034(e). Therefore, the adjusted purchase price of the residence is initially $120,000.

Example (3). Z acquires a residence by gift. The donor's basis in the residence was $30,000. Z's basis in the residence, determined under section 1015, is $30,000. Accordingly, the adjusted purchase price of the residence is initially $30,000.

(2) Fair market value. (i) In general. For purposes of this section, the fair market value of a qualified residence on any date is the fair market value of the taxpayer's interest in the residence on such date. In addition, the fair market value determined under this paragraph (k)(2)(i) shall be determined by taking into account the cost of improvements to the residence reasonably expected to be made with the proceeds of the debt.

(ii) Example. In 1988, the adjusted purchase price of P's second residence is $65,000 and the fair market value of the residence is $70,000. At that time, P incurs an additional debt of $10,000, the proceeds of which P reasonably expects to use to add two bedrooms to the residence. Because the fair market value is determined by taking into account the cost of improvements to the residence that are reasonably expected to be made with the proceeds of the debt, the fair market value of the residence with respect to the debt incurred in 1988 is $80,000 ($70,000 + $10,000).

(3) Allocation of adjusted purchase price and fair market value. If a property includes both a qualified residence and other property, the adjusted purchase price and the fair market value of such property must be allocated between the qualified residence and the other property. See paragraph (p)(4) of this section for rules governing such an allocation.

(l) [Reserved]

(m) Grandfathered amount. *(1) Substitution for adjusted purchase price.* If, for the taxable year, the sum of the grandfathered amounts, if any, of all secured debts exceeds the adjusted purchase price of the qualified residence, such sum may be treated as the adjusted purchase price of the residence under paragraphs (c), (d) and (e) of this section.

(2) Determination of grandfathered amount. (i) In general. For any taxable year, the grandfathered amount of any secured debt that was incurred on or before August 16, 1986, and was secured by the residence continuously from August 16, 1986, through the end of the taxable year, is the average balance of the debt for the taxable year. A secured debt that was not incurred and secured on or before August 16, 1986, has no grandfathered amount.

(ii) Special rule for lines of credit and certain other debt. If, with respect to a debt described in paragraph (m)(2)(i) of this section, a taxpayer has borrowed any additional amounts after August 16, 1986, the grandfathered amount of such debt is equal to the lesser of—

(A) The average balance of the debt for the taxable year, or

(B) The principal balance of the debt as of August 16, 1986, reduced (but not below zero) by all principal payments after August 16, 1986, and before the first day of the current taxable year.

For purposes of this paragraph (m)(2)(ii), a taxpayer shall not be considered to have borrowed any additional amount with respect to a debt merely because accrued interest is added to the principal balance of the debt, so long as such accrued interest is paid by the taxpayer no less often than quarterly.

(iii) Fair market value limitation. The grandfathered amount of any debt for any taxable year may not exceed the fair market value of the residence on August 16, 1986, reduced by the principal balance on that day of all previously secured debt.

(iv) Examples.

Example (1). As of August 16, 1986, T has one debt secured by T's principal residence. The debt is a conventional self-amortizing mortgage and, on August 16, 1986, it has an outstanding principal balance of $75,000. In 1987, the average balance of the mortgage is $73,000. The adjusted purchase price of the residence as of the end of 1987 is $50,000. Because the mortgage was incurred and secured on or before August 16, 1986 and T has not borrowed any additional amounts with respect to the mortgage, the grandfathered amount is the average balance, $73,000. Because the grandfathered amount exceeds the adjusted purchase price ($50,000), T may treat the grandfathered amount as the adjusted purchase price in determining the amount of qualified residence interest.

Example (2). (i) The facts are the same as in example (1), except that in May 1986, T also obtains a home equity line of credit that, on August 16, 1986, has a principal balance of $40,000. In November 1986, T borrows an additional $10,000 on the home equity line, increasing the balance to $50,000. In December 1986, T repays $5,000 of principal on the home equity line. The average balance of the home equity line in 1987 is $45,000.

(ii) Because T has borrowed additional amounts on the line of credit after August 16, 1986, the grandfathered amount for that debt must be determined under the rules of paragraph (m)(2)(ii) of this section. Accordingly, the grandfathered amount for the line of credit is equal to the lesser of $45,000, the average balance of the debt in 1987, and $35,000, the principal balance on August 16, 1986, reduced by all principal payments between August 17, 1986, and December 31, 1986 ($40,000 – $5,000). The sum of the grandfathered amounts with respect to the residence is $108,000 ($73,000 exceeds the adjusted purchase price ($50,000), T may treat the sum as the adjusted purchase price in determining the qualified residence interest for 1987.

(3) Refinancing of grandfathered debt. (i) In general. A debt incurred and secured on or before August 16, 1986, is refinanced if some or all of the outstanding balance of such a debt (the "original debt") is repaid out of the proceeds of a second debt secured by the same qualified residence (the "replacement debt"). In the case of a refinancing, the replacement debt is treated as a debt incurred and secured on or before August 16, 1986, and the grandfathered amount of such debt is the amount (but not less than zero) determined pursuant to paragraph (m)(3)(ii) of this section.

(ii) Determination of grandfathered amount. (A) Exact refinancing. If—

(1) The entire proceeds of a replacement debt are used to refinance one or more original debts, and

(2) The taxpayer has not borrowed any additional amounts after August 16, 1986, with respect to the original debt or debts,

the grandfathered amount of the replacement debt is the average balance of the replacement debt. For purposes of the preceding sentence, the fact that proceeds of a replacement debt are used to pay costs of obtaining the replacement debt (including points or other closing costs) shall be disregarded in determining whether the entire proceeds of the replacement debt have been used to refinance one or more original debts.

(B) Refinancing other than exact refinancings. (1) Year of refinancing. In the taxable year in which an original debt is refinanced, the grandfathered amount of the original and replacement debts is equal to the lesser of—

(i) The sum of the average balances of the original debt and the replacement debt, and

(ii) The principal balance of the original debt as of August 16, 1986, reduced by all principal payments on the original debt after August 16, 1986, and before the first day of the current taxable year.

(2) In subsequent years. In any taxable year after the taxable year in which an original debt is refinanced, the grandfathered amount of the replacement debt is equal to the least of—

(i) The average balance of the replacement debt for the taxable year,

(ii) The amount of the replacement debt used to repay the principal balance of the original debt, reduced by all principal payments on the replacement debt after the date of the refinancing and before the first day of the current taxable year, or

(iii) The principal balance of the original debt on August 16, 1986, reduced by all principal payments on the original debt after August 16, 1986, and before the date of the refinancing, and further reduced by all principal payments on the replacement debt after the date of the refinancing and before the first day of the current taxable year.

(C) Example.

Example. (i) Facts. On August 16, 1986, T has a single debt secured by a principal residence with a balance of $150,000. On July 1, 1988, T refinances the debt, which still has a principal balance of $150,000, with a new secured debt. The principal balance of the replacement debt throughout 1988 and 1989 is $150,000. The adjusted purchase price of the residence is $100,000 throughout 1987, 1988 and 1989. The average balance of the original debt was $150,000 in 1987 and $75,000 in 1988. The average balance of the replacement debt is $75,000 in 1988 and $150,000 in 1989.

(ii) Grandfathered amount in 1987. The original debt was incurred and secured on or before August 16, 1986 and T has not borrowed any additional amounts with respect to the debt. Therefore, its grandfathered amount in 1987 is its average balance ($150,000). This amount is treated as the adjusted purchase price for 1987 and all of the interest paid on the debt is qualified residence interest.

(iii) Grandfathered amount in 1988. Because the replacement debt was used to refinance a debt incurred and secured on or before August 16, 1986, the replacement debt is treated as a grandfathered debt. Because all of the proceeds of the replacement debt were used in the refinancing and because no amounts have been borrowed after August 16, 1986, on the original debt, the grandfathered amount for the original debt is its average balance ($75,000) and the grandfathered amount for the replacement debt is its average balance ($75,000). Since the sum of the grandfathered amounts ($150,000) exceeds the adjusted purchase price of the residence, the sum of the grandfathered amounts may be substituted for the adjusted purchase price for 1988 and all of the interest paid on the debt is qualified residence interest.

(iv) Grandfathered amount in 1989. The grandfathered amount for the placement debt is its average balance ($150,000). This amount is treated as the adjusted purchase price for 1989 and all of the interest paid on the mortgage is qualified residence interest.

(4) Limitation on term of grandfathered debt. (i) In general. An original debt or replacement debt shall not have any grandfathered amount in any taxable year that begins after the date, as determined on August 16, 1986, that the original debt was required to be repaid in full (the "maturity date"). If a replacement debt is used to refinance more than one original debt, the maturity date is determined by reference to the original debt that, as of August 16, 1986, had the latest maturity date.

(ii) Special rule for nonamortizing debt. If an original debt was actually incurred and secured on or before August 16, 1986, and if as of such date the terms of such debt did not require the amortization of its principal over its original term, the maturity date of the replacement debt is the earlier of the maturity date of the replacement debt or the date 30 years after the date the original debt is first refinanced.

(iii) Example. C incurs a debt on May 10, 1986, the final payment of which is due May 1, 2006. C incurs a second debt on August 11, 1990, with a term of 20 years and uses the proceeds of the second debt to refinance the first debt. Because, under paragraph (m)(4)(i) of this section, a replacement debt will not have any grandfathered amount in any taxable year that begins after the maturity date of the original debt (May 1, 2006), the second debt has no grandfathered amount in any taxable year after 2006.

(n) Qualified indebtedness (secured debt used for medical and educational purposes). *(1) In general.* (i) Treatment of qualified indebtedness. The amount of any qualified indebtedness resulting from a secured debt may be added to the adjusted purchase price under paragraph (e)(2)(i)(B) of this section to determine the applicable debt limit for that secured debt and any other debt subsequently secured by the qualified residence.

(ii) Determination of amount of qualified indebtedness. If, as of the end of the taxable year (or the last day in the taxable year that the debt is secured), at least 90 percent of the proceeds of a secured debt are used (within the meaning of paragraph (n)(2) of this section) to pay for qualified medical and educational expenses (within the meaning of paragraphs (n)(3) and (n)(4) of this section), the amount of qualified indebtedness resulting from that debt for the taxable year is equal to the average balance of such debt for the taxable year.

(iii) Determination of amount of qualified indebtedness for mixed-use debt. If, as of the end of the taxable year (or the last day in the taxable year that the debt is secured), more than ten percent of the proceeds of a secured debt are used to pay for expenses other than qualified medical and educational expenses, the amount of qualified indebtedness resulting from that debt for the taxable year shall equal the lesser of—

(A) The average balance of the debt, or

(B) The amount of the proceeds of the debt used to pay for qualified medical and educational expenses through the end of the taxable year, reduced by any principal payments on the debt before the first day of the current taxable year.

(iv) Example. (i) C incurs a $10,000 debt on April 20, 1987, which is secured on that date by C's principal residence. C immediately uses (within the meaning of paragraph (n)(2) of this section) $4,000 of the proceeds of the debt to pay for a qualified medical expense. C makes no principal payments on the debt during 1987. During 1988 and 1989, C makes principal payments of $1,000 per year. The average balance of the debt during 1988 is $9,500 and the average balance during 1989 is $8,500.

(ii) Under paragraph (n)(1)(iii) of this section, C determines the amount of qualified indebtedness for 1988 as follows:

Average balance		$9,500
Amount of debt used to pay for qualified medical expenses	$4,000	
Less payments of principal before 1988	$0	
Net qualified expenses	$4,000	

The amount of qualified indebtedness for 1988 is, therefore, $4,000 (lesser of $9,500 average balance or $4,000 net qualified expenses). This amount may be added to the adjusted purchase price of C's principal residence under paragraph (e)(2)(i)(B) of this section for purposes of computing the applicable debt limit for this debt and any other debt subsequently secured by the principal residence.

(iii) C determines the amount of qualified indebtedness for 1989 as follows:

Average balance		$8,500
Amount of debt used to pay for qualified medical expenses	$4,000	
Less payments of principal before 1988	$1,000	
Net qualified expenses	$3,000	

The amount of qualified indebtedness for 1989 is, therefore, $3,000 (lesser of $8,500 average balance or $3,000 net qualified expenses).

(v) Prevention of double counting in year of refinancing. (A) In general. A debt used to pay for qualified medical or educational expenses is refinanced if some or all of the outstanding balance of the debt (the "original debt") is repaid out of the proceeds of a second debt (the "replacement debt"). If, in the year of a refinancing, the combined qualified indebtedness of the original debt and the replacement debt exceeds the combined qualified expenses of such debts, the amount of qualified indebtedness for each such debt shall be determined by multiplying the amount of qualified indebtedness for each such debt by a fraction, the numerator of which is the combined qualified expenses and the denominator of which is the combined qualified indebtedness.

(B) Definitions. For purposes of paragraph (n)(1)(v)(A) of this section—

(1) The term "combined qualified indebtedness" means the sum of the qualified indebtedness (determined without regard to paragraph (n)(1)(v) of this section) for the original debt and the replacement debt.

(2) The term "combined qualified expenses" means the amount of the proceeds of the original debt used to pay for qualified medical and educational expenses through the end of the current taxable year, reduced by any principal payments on the debt before the first day of the current taxable year, and increased by the amount, if any, of the proceeds of the replacement debt used to pay such expenses through the end of the current taxable year other than as part of the refinancing.

(C) Example. (i) On August 11, 1987, C incurs a $8,000 debt secured by a principal residence. C uses (within the meaning of paragraph (n)(2)(i) of this section) $5,000 of the proceeds of the debt to pay for qualified educational expenses. C makes no principal payments on the debt. On July 1, 1988, C incurs a new debt in the amount of $8,000 secured by C's principal residence and uses all of the proceeds of the new debt to repay the original debt. Under paragraph (n)(2)(ii) of this section $5,000 of the new debt is treated as being used to pay for qualified educational expenses. C makes no principal payments (other than the refinancing) during 1987 or 1988 on either debt and pays all accrued interest monthly. The average balance of each debt in 1988 is $4,000.

(ii) Under paragraph (n)(1)(iii) of this section, the amount of qualified indebtedness for 1988 with respect to the original debt is $4,000 (the lesser of its average balance ($4,000) and the amount of the debt used to pay for qualified medical and educational expenses ($5,000)). Similarly, the amount of qualified indebtedness for 1988 with respect to the replacement debt is also $4,000. Both debts, however, are subject in 1988 to the limitation in paragraph (n)(1)(v)(A) of this section. The combined qualified indebtedness, determined without regard to the limitation, is $8,000 ($4,000 of qualified indebtedness from each debt). The combined qualified expenses are $5,000 ($5,000 from the original debt and $0 from the replacement debt). The amount of qualified indebtedness from each debt must, therefore, be reduced by a fraction, the numerator of which is $5,000 (the combined qualified expenses) and the denominator of which is $8,000 (the combined qualified indebtedness). After application of the limitation, the amount of qualified indebtedness for the original debt is $2,500 ($4,000 × 5/8). Similarly, the amount of qualified indebtedness for the replacement debt is $2,500. Note that the total qualified indebtedness for both the original and the replacement debt is $5,000 ($2,500 + $2,500). Therefore, C is entitled to the same amount of qualified indebtedness as C would have been entitled to if C had not refinanced the debt.

(vi) Special rule for principal payments in excess of qualified expenses. For purposes of paragraph (n)(1)(iii)(B), (n)(1)(v)(B)(2) and (n)(2)(ii) of this section, a principal payment is taken into account only to the extent that the payment, when added to all prior payments, does not exceed the amount used on or before the date of the payment to pay for qualified medical and educational expenses.

(2) Debt used to pay for qualified medical or educational expenses. (i) In general. For purposes of this section, the proceeds of a debt are used to pay for qualified medical or educational expenses to the extent that—

(A) The taxpayer pays qualified medical or educational expenses within 90 days before or after the date that amounts are actually borrowed with respect to the debt, the proceeds of the debt are not directly allocable to another expense under § 1.163-8T(c)(3) (allocation of debt; proceeds not disbursed to borrower) and the proceeds of any other debt are not allocable to the medical or educational expenses under § 1.163-8T(c)(3), or

(B) The proceeds of the debt are otherwise allocated to such expenditures under § 1.163-8T.

(ii) Special rule for refinancings. For purposes of this section, the proceeds of a debt are used to pay for qualified medical and educational expenses to the extent that the proceeds of the debt are allocated under § 1.163-8T to the repayment of another debt (the "original debt"), but only to the extent of the amount of the original debt used to pay for qualified medical and educational expenses, reduced by any principal payments on such debt up to the time of the refinancing.

(iii) Other special rules. The following special rules apply for purposes of this section.

(A) Proceeds of a debt are used to pay for qualified medical or educational expenses as of the later of the taxable year in which such proceeds are borrowed or the taxable year in which such expenses are paid.

(B) The amount of debt which may be treated as being used to pay for qualified medical or educational expenses may not exceed the amount of such expenses.

(C) Proceeds of a debt may not be treated as being used to pay for qualified medical or educational expenses to the extent that:

(1) The proceeds have been repaid as of the time the expense is paid;

(2) The proceeds are actually borrowed before August 17, 1986; or

(3) The medical or educational expenses are paid before August 17, 1986.

(iv) Examples.

Example (1). A pays a $5,000 qualified educational expense from a checking account that A maintains at Bank 1 on November 9, 1987. On January 1, 1988, A incurs a $20,000 debt that is secured by A's residence and places the proceeds of the debt in a savings account that A also maintains at Bank 1. A pays another $5,000 qualified educations expense on March 15 from a checking account that A maintains at Bank 2. Under paragraph (n)(2) of this section, the debt proceeds are used to pay for both educational expenses, regardless of other deposits to, or expenditures from, the accounts, because both expenditures are made within 90 days before or after the debt was incurred.

Example (2). B pays a $5,000 qualified educational expense from a checking account on November 1, 1987. On November 30, 1987, B incurs a debt secured by B's residence, and the lender disburses the debt proceeds directly to a person who sells B a new car. Although the educational expense is paid within 90 days of the date the debt is incurred, the proceeds of the debt are not used to pay for the educational expense because the proceeds are directly allocable to the purchase of the new car under § 1.163-8T(c)(3).

Example (3). On November 1, 1987, C borrows $5,000 from C's college. The proceeds of this debt are not disbursed to C, but rather are used to pay tuition fees for C's attendance at the college. On November 30, 1987, C incurs a second debt and secures the debt by C's residence. Although the $5,000 educational expense is paid within 90 days before the second debt is incurred, the proceeds of the second debt are not used to pay for the educational expense, because the proceeds of the first debt are directly allocable to the educational expense under § 1.163-8T(c)(3).

Example (4). On January 1, 1988, D incurs a $20,000 debt secured by a qualified residence. D places the proceeds of the debt in a separate account (*i.e.,* the proceeds of the debt are the only deposit in the account). D makes payments of $5,000 each for qualified educational expenses on September 1, 1988, September 1, 1989, September 1, 1990, and September 1, 1991. Because the debt proceeds are allocated to educational expenses as of the date the expenses are paid, under the rules of § 1.163-8T(c)(4), the following amounts of the debt proceeds are used to pay for qualified educational expenses as of the end of each year:

1988: $5,000

1989: $10,000

1990: $15,000

1991: $20,000

Example (5). During 1987 E incurs a $10,000 debt secured by a principal residence. E uses (within the meaning of paragraph (n)(2)(i) of this section) all of the proceeds of the debt to pay for qualified educational expenses. On August 20, 1988, at which time the balance of the debt is $9,500, E incurs a new debt in the amount of $9,500 secured by E's principal residence and uses all of the proceeds of the new debt to repay the original debt. Under paragraph (n)(2)(ii) of this section, all of the proceeds of the new debt are used to pay for qualified educational expenses.

(3) Qualified medical expenses. Qualified medical expenses are amounts that are paid for medical care (within the meaning of section 213(d)(1)(A) and (B)) for the taxpayer, the taxpayer's spouse, or a dependent of the taxpayer (within the meaning of section 152), and that are not compensated for by insurance or otherwise.

(4) Qualified educational expenses. Qualified educational expenses are amounts that are paid for tuition, fees, books, supplies and equipment required for enrollment, attendance or courses of instruction at an educational organization described in section 170(b)(1)(A)(ii) and for any reasonable living expenses while away from home while in attendance at such an institution, for the taxpayer, the taxpayer's spouse or a dependent of the taxpayer (within the meaning of section 152) and that are not reimbursed by scholarship or otherwise.

(o) Secured debt. *(1) In general.* For purposes of this section, the term "secured debt" means a debt that is on the security of any instrument (such as a mortgage, deed of trust, or land contract)—

(i) That makes the interest of the debtor in the qualified residence specific security for the payment of the debt,

(ii) Under which, in the event of default, the residence could be subjected to the satisfaction of the debt with the same priority as a mortgage or deed of trust in the jurisdiction in which the property is situated, and

(iii) That is recorded, where permitted, or is otherwise perfected in accordance with applicable State law.

A debt will not be considered to be secured by a qualified residence if it is secured solely by virtue of a lien upon the general assets of the taxpayer or by a security interest, such as a mechanic's lien or judgment lien, that attaches to the property without the consent of the debtor.

(2) Special rule for debt in certain States. Debt will not fail to be treated as secured solely because, under an applicable State or local homestead law or other debtor protection law in effect on August 16, 1986, the security interest is ineffective or the enforceability of the security interest is restricted.

(3) Times at which debt is treated as secured. For purposes of this section, a debt is treated as secured as of the date on which each of the requirements of paragraph (o)(1) of this section are satisfied, regardless of when amounts are actually borrowed with respect to the debt. For purposes of this paragraph (o)(3), if the instrument is recorded within a commercially reasonable time after the security interest is granted, the instrument will be treated as recorded on the date that the security interest was granted.

(4) Partially secured debt. (i) In general. If the security interest is limited to a prescribed maximum amount or portion of the residence, and the average balance of the debt exceeds such amount or the value of such portion, such excess shall not be treated as secured debt for purposes of this section.

(ii) Example. T borrows $80,000 on January 1, 1991. T secures the debt with a principal residence. The security in the residence for the debt, however, is limited to $20,000. T pays $8,000 in interest on the debt in 1991 and the average balance of the debt in that year is $80,000. Because the average balance of the debt exceeds the maximum amount of the security interest, such excess is not treated as secured debt. Therefore, for purposes of applying the limitation on qualified residence interest, the average balance of the secured debt is $20,000 (the maximum amount of the security interest) and the interest paid or accrued on the secured debt is $2,000 (the total interest paid on the debt multiplied by the ratio of the average balance of the secured debt ($20,000) and the average balance of the total debt ($80,000)).

(5) Election to treat debt as not secured by a qualified residence. (i) In general. For purposes of this section, a taxpayer may elect to treat any debt that is secured by a qualified residence as not secured by the qualified residence. An election made under this paragraph shall be effective for the taxable year for which the election is made and for all subsequent taxable years unless revoked with the consent of the Commissioner.

(ii) Example. T owns a principal residence with a fair market value of $75,000 and an adjusted purchase price of $40,000. In 1988, debt A, the proceeds of which were used to purchase the residence, has an average balance of $15,000. The proceeds of debt B, which is secured by a second mortgage on the property, are allocable to T's trade or business under § 1.163-8T and has an average balance of $25,000. In 1988, T incurs debt C, which is also secured by T's principal residence and which has an average balance in 1988 of $5,000. In the absence of an election to treat debt B as unsecured, the applicable debt limit for debt C in 1988 under paragraph (e) of this section would be zero dollars ($40,000 − $15,000 − $25,000) and none of the interest paid on debt C would be qualified residence interest. If, however, T makes or has previously made an election pursuant to paragraph (o)(5)(i) of this section to treat debt B as not secured by the residence, the applicable debt limit for debt C would be $25,000 ($40,000 − $15,000), and all of the interest paid on debt C during the taxable year would be qualified residence interest. Since the proceeds of debt B are allocable to T's trade or business under § 1.163-8T, interest on debt B may be deductible under other sections of the Internal Revenue Code.

(iii) Allocation of debt secured by two qualified residences. [Reserved]

(p) Definition of qualified residence. *(1) In general.* The term "qualified residence" means the taxpayer's principal residence (as defined in paragraph (p)(2) of this section), or the taxpayer's second residence (as defined in paragraph (p)(3) of this section).

(2) Principal residence. The term "principal residence" means the taxpayer's principal residence within the meaning of section 1034. For purposes of this section, a taxpayer cannot have more than one principal residence at any one time.

(3) Second residence. (i) In general. The term "second residence" means—

(A) A residence within the meaning of paragraph (p)(3)(ii) of this section,

(B) That the taxpayer uses as a residence within the meaning of paragraph (p)(3)(iii) of this section, and

(C) That the taxpayer elects to treat as a second residence pursuant to paragraph (p)(3)(iv) of this section.

A taxpayer cannot have more than one second residence at any time.

(ii) Definition of residence. Whether property is a residence shall be determined based on all the facts and circumstances, including the good faith of the taxpayer. A residence generally includes a house, condominium, mobile home, boat, or house trailer, that contains sleeping space and toilet and cooking facilities. A residence does not include personal property, such as furniture or a television, that, in accordance with the applicable local law, is not a fixture.

(iii) Use as a residence. If a residence is rented at any time during the taxable year, it is considered to be used as a residence only if the taxpayer uses it during the taxable year as a residence within the meaning of section 280A(d). If a residence is not rented at any time during the taxable year, it shall be considered to be used as a residence. For purposes of the preceding sentence, a residence will be deemed to be rented during any period that the taxpayer holds the residence out for rental or resale or repairs or renovates the residence with the intention of holding it out for rental or resale.

(iv) Election of second residence. A taxpayer may elect a different residence (other than the taxpayer's principal residence) to be the taxpayer's second residence for each taxable year. A taxpayer may not elect different residences as second residences at different times of the same taxable year except as provided below—

(A) If the taxpayer acquires a new residence during the taxable year, the taxpayer may elect the new residence as a taxpayer's second residence as of the date acquired;

(B) If property that was the taxpayer's principal residence during the taxable year ceases to qualify as the taxpayer's principal residence, the taxpayer may elect that property as the taxpayer's second residence as of the date that the property ceases to be the taxpayer's principal residence; or

(C) If property that was the taxpayer's second residence is sold during the taxable year or becomes the taxpayer's principal residence, the taxpayer may elect a new second residence as of such day.

(4) Allocations between residence and other property. (i) In general. For purposes of this section, the adjusted purchase price and fair market value of property must be allocated between the portion of the property that is a qualified residence and the portion that is not a qualified residence. Neither the average balance of the secured debt nor the interest paid or accrued on secured debt is so allocated. Property that is not used for residential purposes does not qualify as a residence. For example, if a portion of the property is used as an office in the taxpayer's trade or business, that portion of the property does not qualify as a residence.

(ii) Special rule for rental of residence. If a taxpayer rents a portion of his or her principal or second residence to another person (a "tenant"), such portion may be treated as used by the taxpayer for residential purposes if, but only if—

(A) Such rented portion is used by the tenant primarily for residential purposes,

(B) The rented portion is not a self-contained residential unit containing separate sleeping space and toilet and cooking facilities, and

(C) The total number of tenants renting (directly or by sublease) the same or different portions of the residence at any time during the taxable year does not exceed two. For this purpose, if two persons (and the dependents, as defined by section 152, of either of them) share the same sleeping quarters, they shall be treated as a single tenant.

(iii) Examples.

Example (1). D, a dentist, uses a room in D's principal residence as an office which qualifies under section 280A(c)(1)(B) as a portion of the dwelling unit used exclusively on a regular basis as a place of business for meeting with patients in the normal course of D's trade or business. D's adjusted purchase price of the property is $65,000; $10,000 of which is allocable under paragraph (o)(4)(i) of this section to the room used as an office. For purposes of this section, D's residence does not include the room used as an office. The adjusted purchase price of the residence is, accordingly, $55,000. Similarly, the fair market value of D's residence must be allocated between the office and the remainder of the property.

Example (2). J rents out the basement of property that is otherwise used as J's principal residence. The basement is a self-contained residential unit, with sleeping space and toilet and cooking facilities. The adjusted purchase price of the property is $100,000; $15,000 of which is allocable under paragraph (o)(4)(i) of this section to the basement. For purposes of this section, J's residence does not include the basement and the adjusted purchase price of the residence is $85,000. Similarly, the fair market value of the residence must be allocated between the basement unit and the remainder of the property.

(5) Residence under construction. (i) In general. A taxpayer may treat a residence under construction as a qualified residence for a period of up to 24 months, but only if the residence becomes a qualified residence, without regard to this paragraph (p)(5)(i), as of the time that the residence is ready for occupancy.

(ii) Example. X owns a residential lot suitable for the construction of a vacation home. On April 20, 1987, X obtains a mortgage secured by the lot and any property to be constructed on the lot. On August 9, 1987, X begins construction of a residence on the lot. The residence is ready for occupancy on November 9, 1989. The residence is used as a residence within the meaning of paragraph (p)(3)(iii) of this section during 1989 and X elects to treat the residence as his second residence for the period November 9, 1989, through December 31, 1989. Since the residence under construction is a qualified residence as of the first day that the residence is ready for occupancy (November 9, 1987), X may treat the residence as his second residence under paragraph (p)(5)(i) of this section for up to 24 months of the period during which the residence is under construction, commencing on or after the date that construction is begun (August 9, 1987). If X treats the residence under construction as X's second residence beginning on August 9, 1987, the residence under construction would cease to qualify as a qualified residence under paragraph (p)(5)(i) on August 8, 1989. The residence's status as a qualified residence for future periods would be determined without regard to paragraph (p)(5)(i) of this section.

(6) Special rule for time-sharing arrangements. Property that is otherwise a qualified residence will not fail to qualify as such solely because the taxpayer's interest in or right to use the property is restricted by an arrangement whereby two or more persons with interests in the property agree to exercise control over the property for different periods during the taxable year. For purposes of determining the use of a residence under paragraph (p)(3)(iii) of this section, a taxpayer will not be considered to have used or rented a residence during any period that the taxpayer does not have the right to use the property or to receive any benefits from the rental of the property.

(q) Special rules for tenant-stockholders in cooperative housing corporations. *(1) In general.* For purposes of this section, a residence includes stock in a cooperative housing corporation owned by a tenant-stockholder if the house or apartment which the tenant-stockholder is entitled to occupy by virtue of owning such stock is a residence within the meaning of paragraph (p)(3)(ii) of this section.

(2) Special rule where stock may not be used to secure debt. For purposes of this section, if stock described in paragraph (q)(1) of this section may not be used to secure debt because of restrictions under local or State law or because of restrictions in the cooperative agreement (other than restrictions the principal purpose of which is to permit the tenant-stockholder to treat unsecured debt as secured debt under this paragraph (q)(2)), debt may be treated as secured by such stock to the extent that the proceeds of the debt are allocated to the purchase of the stock under the rules of § 1.163-8T. For purposes of this paragraph (q)(2), proceeds of debt incurred prior to January 1, 1987, may be treated as allocated to the purchase of such stock to the extent that the tenant-stockholder has properly and consistently deducted interest expense on such debt as home mortgage interest attributable to such stock on Schedule A of Form 1040 in determining his taxable income for taxable years beginning before January 1, 1987. For purposes of this paragraph (q)(2), amended returns file after December 22, 1987, are disregarded.

(3) Treatment of interest expense of the cooperative described in section 216(a)(2). For purposes of section 163(h) and § 1.163-9T (disallowance of deduction for personal interest) and section 163(d) (limitation on investment interest), any amount allowable as a deduction to a tenant-stockholder under section 216(a)(2) shall be treated as interest paid or accrued by the tenant-stockholder. If a tenant-stockholder's stock in a cooperative housing corporation is a qualified residence of the tenant-shareholder, any amount allowable as a deduction to the tenant-stockholder under section 216(a)(2) is qualified residence interest.

(4) Special rule to prevent tax avoidance. If the amount treated as qualified residence interest under this section exceeds the amount which would be so treated if the tenant-stockholder were treated as directly owning his proportionate share of the assets and liabilities of the cooperative and one of the principal purposes of the cooperative arrangement is to permit the tenant-stockholder to increase the amount of qualified residence interest, the district director may determine that such excess is not qualified residence interest.

(5) Other definitions. For purpose of this section, the terms "tenant-stockholder," "cooperative housing corporation" and "proportionate share" shall have the meaning given by section 216 and the regulations thereunder.

(r) Effective date. The provisions of this section are effective for taxable years beginning after December 31, 1986.

T.D. 8168, 12/21/87.

§ 1.163-12 Deduction of original issue discount on instrument held by related foreign person.

Caution: The Treasury has not yet amended Reg § 1.163-12 to reflect changes made by P.L. 108-357.

(a) General rules. *(1) Deferral of deduction.* Except as provided in paragraph (b) of this section, section 163(e)(3) requires a taxpayer to use the cash method of accounting with respect to the deduction of original issue discount owed to a related foreign person. A deduction for an otherwise deductible portion of original issue discount with respect to a debt instrument will not be allowable as a deduction to the issuer until paid if, at the close of the issuer's taxable year in which such amount would otherwise be deductible, the person holding the debt instrument is a related foreign person. For purposes of this section, a related foreign person is any person that is not a United States person within the meaning of section 7701(a)(30), and that is related (within the meaning of section 267(b)) to the issuer at the close of the taxable year in which the amount incurred by the taxpayer would otherwise be deductible. Section 267(f) defines "controlled group" for purposes of section 267(b) without regard to the limitations of section 1563(b). An amount is treated as paid for purposes of this section if the amount is considered paid for purposes of section 1441 or section 1442 (including an amount taken into account pursuant to section 871(a)(1)(C), section 881(a)(3), or section 884(f)). The rules of this paragraph (a) apply even if the original issue discount is not subject to United States tax, or is subject to a reduced rate of tax, pursuant to a provision of the Internal Revenue Code or a treaty obligation of the United States. For purposes of this section, original issue discount is an amount described in section 1273, whether from sources inside or outside the United States.

(2) Change in method of accounting. A taxpayer that uses a method of accounting other than that required by the rules of this section must change its method of accounting to conform its method to the rules of this section. The taxpayer's change in method must be made pursuant to the rules of section 446(e), the regulations thereunder, and any applicable administrative procedures prescribed by the Commissioner. Because the rules of this section prescribe a method of accounting, these rules apply in the determination of a taxpayer's earnings and profits pursuant to § 1.312-6(a).

(b) Exceptions and special rules. *(1) Effectively connected income.* The provisions of section 267(a)(2) and the regulations thereunder, and not the provisions of paragraph (a) of this section, apply to an amount of original issue discount that is income of the related foreign person that is effectively connected with the conduct of a United States trade or business of such related foreign person. An amount described in this paragraph (b)(1) thus is allowable as a deduction as of the day on which the amount is includible in the gross income of the related foreign person as effectively connected income under sections 872(a)(2) or 882(b) (or, if later, as of the day on which the deduction would be so allowable but for section 267(a)(2)). However, this paragraph (b)(1) does not apply if the related foreign person is exempt from United States income tax on the amount owed, or is subject to a reduced rate of tax, pursuant to a treaty obligation of the United States (such as under an article relating to the taxation of business profits).

(2) Certain obligations issued by natural persons. This section does not apply to any debt instrument described in section 163(e)(4) (relating to obligations issued by natural persons before March 2, 1984, and to loans between natural persons).

(3) Amounts owed to a foreign personal holding company, controlled foreign corporation, or passive foreign investment company. (i) Foreign personal holding companies. If an amount to which paragraph (a) of this section otherwise applies is owed to a related foreign person that is a foreign personal holding company within the meaning of section 552, then the amount is allowable as a deduction as of the day on which the amount is includible in the income of the foreign personal holding company. The day on which the amount is includible income is determined with reference to the method of accounting under which the foreign personal holding company computes its taxable income and earnings and profits for purposes of sections 551 through 558. See section 551(c) and the regulations thereunder for the reporting requirements of the foreign personal holding company provisions (sections 551 through 558).

(ii) Controlled foreign corporations. If an amount to which paragraph (a) of this section otherwise applies is owed to a related foreign person that is a controlled foreign corporation within the meaning of section 957, then the amount is allowable as a deduction as of the day on which the amount is includible in the income of the controlled foreign corporation. The day on which the amount is includible in income is determined with reference to the method of accounting under which the controlled foreign corporation computes its taxable income and earnings and profits for purposes of sections 951 through 964. See section 6038 and the regulations thereunder for the reporting requirements of the controlled foreign corporation provisions (sections 951 through 964).

(iii) Passive foreign investment companies. If an amount to which paragraph (a) of this section otherwise applies is owed to a related foreign person that is a passive foreign investment company within the meaning of section 1296, then the amount is allowable as a deduction as of the day on which amount is includible in the income of the passive foreign investment company. The day on which the amount is includible in income is determined with reference to the method of accounting under which the earnings and profits of the passive foreign investment company are computed for purposes of sections 1291 through 1297. See sections 1291 through 1297 and the regulations thereunder for the reporting requirements of the passive foreign investment company provisions. This exception shall apply, however, only if the person that owes the amount at issue has made and has in effect an election pursuant to section 1295 with respect to the passive foreign investment company to which the amount at issue is owed.

(c) Application of section 267. Except as limited in paragraph (b)(1) of this section, the provisions of section 267 and the regulations thereunder shall apply to any amount of original issue discount to which the provisions of this section do not apply.

(d) Effective date. The rules of this section are effective with respect to all original issue discount on debt instruments issued after June 9, 1984.

T.D. 8465, 12/31/92.

---

§ 1.163-13 Treatment of bond issuance premium.

(a) General rule. If a debt instrument is issued with bond issuance premium, this section limits the amount of the issuer's interest deduction otherwise allowable under section 163(a). In general, the issuer determines its interest deduction by offsetting the interest allocable to an accrual period with the bond issuance premium allocable to that period. Bond issuance premium is allocable to an accrual period based on a constant yield. The use of a constant yield to amortize bond issuance premium is intended to generally conform the treatment of debt instruments having bond issuance premium with those having original issue discount. Unless otherwise provided, the terms used in this section have the same meaning as those terms in section 163(e), sections 1271 through 1275, and the corresponding regulations. Moreover, unless otherwise provided, the provisions of this section apply in a manner consistent with those of section 163(e), sections 1271 through 1275, and the corresponding regulations. In addition, the anti-abuse rule in § 1.1275-2(g) applies for purposes of this section. For rules dealing with the treatment of bond premium by a holder, see §§ 1.171-1 through 1.171-5.

(b) Exceptions. This section does not apply to—

(1) A debt instrument described in section 1272(a)(6)(C) (regular interests in a REMIC, qualified mortgages held by a REMIC, and certain other debt instruments, or pools of debt instruments, with payments subject to acceleration); or

(2) A debt instrument to which § 1.1275-4 applies (relating to certain debt instruments that provide for contingent payments).

(c) Bond issuance premium. Bond issuance premium is the excess, if any, of the issue price of a debt instrument over its stated redemption price at maturity. For purposes of this section, the issue price of a convertible bond (as defined in § 1.171-1(e)(1)(iii)(C)) does not include an amount equal to the value of the conversion option (as determined under § 1.171-1(e)(1)(iii)(A)).

(d) Offsetting qualified stated interest with bond issuance premium. *(1) In general.* An issuer amortizes bond issuance premium by offsetting the qualified stated interest allocable to an accrual period with the bond issuance premium allocable to the accrual period. This offset occurs when the issuer takes the qualified stated interest into account under its regular method of accounting.

(2) Qualified stated interest allocable to an accrual period. See § 1.446-2(b) to determine the accrual period to which qualified stated interest is allocable and to determine the accrual of qualified stated interest within an accrual period.

(3) Bond issuance premium allocable to an accrual period. The bond issuance premium allocable to an accrual period is determined under this paragraph (d)(3). Within an accrual period, the bond issuance premium allocable to the period accrues ratably.

(i) Step one: Determine the debt instrument's yield to maturity. The yield to maturity of a debt instrument is determined under the rules of § 1.1272-1(b)(1)(i).

(ii) Step two: Determine the accrual periods. The accrual periods are determined under the rules of § 1.1272-1(b)(1)(ii).

(iii) Step three: Determine the bond issuance premium allocable to the accrual period. The bond issuance premium allocable to an accrual period is the excess of the qualified stated interest allocable to the accrual period over the product of the adjusted issue price at the beginning of the accrual period and the yield. In performing this calculation, the yield must be stated appropriately taking into account the length of the particular accrual period. Principles similar to those in § 1.1272-1(b)(4) apply in determining the bond issuance premium allocable to an accrual period.

(4) Bond issuance premium in excess of qualified stated interest. (i) Ordinary income. If the bond issuance premium allocable to an accrual period exceeds the qualified stated interest allocable to the accrual period, the excess is treated as ordinary income by the issuer for the accrual period. However, the amount treated as ordinary income is limited to the amount by which the issuer's total interest deductions on the debt instrument in prior accrual periods exceed the total amount treated by the issuer as ordinary income on the debt instrument in prior accrual periods.

(ii) Carryforward. If the bond issuance premium allocable to an accrual period exceeds the sum of the qualified stated interest allocable to the accrual period and the amount treated as ordinary income for the accrual period under paragraph (d)(4)(i) of this section, the excess is carried forward to the next accrual period and is treated as bond issuance premium allocable to that period. If a carryforward exists on the date the debt instrument is retired, the carryforward is treated as ordinary income on that date.

(e) Special rules. *(1) Variable rate debt instruments.* An issuer determines bond issuance premium on a variable rate debt instrument by reference to the stated redemption price at maturity of the equivalent fixed rate debt instrument constructed for the variable rate debt instrument. The issuer also allocates any bond issuance premium among the accrual periods by reference to the equivalent fixed rate debt instrument. The issuer constructs the equivalent fixed rate debt instrument, as of the issue date, by using the principles of § 1.1275-5(e).

(2) Inflation-indexed debt instruments. An issuer determines bond issuance premium on an inflation-indexed debt instrument by assuming that there will be no inflation or deflation over the term of the instrument. The issuer also allocates any bond issuance premium among the accrual periods by assuming that there will be no inflation or deflation over the term of the instrument. The bond issuance premium allocable to an accrual period offsets qualified stated interest allocable to the period. Notwithstanding paragraph (d)(4) of this section, if the bond issuance premium allocable to an accrual period exceeds the qualified stated interest allocable to the period, the excess is treated as a deflation adjustment under § 1.1275-7(f)(1)(ii). See § 1.1275-7 for other rules relating to inflation-indexed debt instruments.

(3) Certain debt instruments subject to contingencies. (i) In general. Except as provided in paragraph (e)(3)(ii) of this section, the rules of § 1.1272-1(c) apply to determine a debt instrument's payment schedule for purposes of this section. For example, an issuer uses the payment schedule determined under § 1.1272-1(c) to determine the amount, if any, of bond issuance premium on the debt instrument, the yield and maturity of the debt instrument, and the allocation of bond issuance premium to an accrual period.

(ii) Mandatory sinking fund provision. Notwithstanding paragraph (e)(3)(i) of this section, if a debt instrument is subject to a mandatory sinking fund provision described in § 1.1272-1(c)(3), the issuer must determine the payment schedule by assuming that a pro rata portion of the debt instrument will be called under the sinking fund provision.

(4) Remote and incidental contingencies. For purposes of determining the amount of bond issuance premium and allocating bond issuance premium among accrual periods, if a bond provides for a contingency that is remote or incidental (within the meaning of § 1.1275-2(h)), the issuer takes the contingency into account under the rules for remote and incidental contingencies in § 1.1275-2(h).

(f) Example. The following example illustrates the rules of this section:

Example. (i) Facts. On February 1, 1999, X issues for $110,000 a debt instrument maturing on February 1, 2006, with a stated principal amount of $100,000, payable at maturity. The debt instrument provides for unconditional payments of interest of $10,000, payable on February 1 of each year. X uses the calendar year as its taxable year, X uses the cash receipts and disbursements method of accounting, and X decides to use annual accrual periods ending on February 1 of each year. X's calculations assume a 30-day month and 360-day year.

(ii) Amount of bond issuance premium. The issue price of the debt instrument is $110,000. Because the interest payments on the debt instrument are qualified stated interest, the stated redemption price at maturity of the debt instrument is $100,000. Therefore, the amount of bond issuance premium is $10,000 ($110,000 – $100,000).

(iii) Bond issuance premium allocable to the first accrual period. Based on the payment schedule and the issue price of the debt instrument, the yield of the debt instrument is 8.07 percent, compounded annually. (Although, for purposes of simplicity, the yield as stated is rounded to two decimal places, the computations do not reflect this rounding convention.) The bond issuance premium allocable to the accrual period ending on February 1, 2000, is the excess of the qualified stated interest allocable to the period ($10,000) over the product of the adjusted issue price at the beginning of the period ($110,000) and the yield (8.07 percent, compounded annually). Therefore, the bond issuance premium allocable to the accrual period is $1,118.17 ($10,000 – $8,881.83).

(iv) Premium used to offset interest. Although X makes an interest payment of $10,000 on February 1, 2000, X only deducts interest of $8,881.83, the qualified stated interest allocable to the period ($10,000) offset with the bond issuance premium allocable to the period ($1,118.17).

(g) Effective date. This section applies to debt instruments issued on or after March 2, 1998.

(h) Accounting method changes. *(1) Consent to change.* An issuer required to change its method of accounting for bond issuance premium to comply with this section must secure the consent of the Commissioner in accordance with the requirements of § 1.446-1(e). Paragraph (h)(2) of this section provides the Commissioner's automatic consent for certain changes.

(2) Automatic consent. The Commissioner grants consent for an issuer to change its method of accounting for bond issuance premium on debt instruments issued on or after March 2, 1998. Because this change is made on a cut-off basis, no items of income or deduction are omitted or duplicated and, therefore, no adjustment under section 481 is allowed. The consent granted by this paragraph (h)(2) applies provided—

(i) The change is made to comply with this section;

(ii) The change is made for the first taxable year for which the issuer must account for a debt instrument under this section; and

(iii) The issuer attaches to its federal income tax return for the taxable year containing the change a statement that it has changed its method of accounting under this section.

T.D. 8746, 12/30/97, amend T.D. 8838, 9/3/99.

§ 1.163(d)-1 Time and manner for making elections under the Omnibus Budget Reconciliation Act of 1993 and the Jobs and Growth Tax Relief Reconciliation Act of 2003.

(a) Description. Section 163(d)(4)(B)(iii), as added by section 13206(d) of the Omnibus Budget Reconciliation Act of 1993 (Pub. L. 103-66, 107 Stat. 467), allows an electing taxpayer to take all or a portion of certain net capital gain attributable to dispositions of property held for investment into account as investment income. Section 163(d)(4)(B), as amended by section 302(b) of the Jobs and Growth Tax Relief Reconciliation Act of 2003 (Pub. L. 108-27, 117 Stat. 762), allows an electing taxpayer to take all or a portion of qualified dividend income, as defined in section 1(h)(11)(B), into account as investment income. As a consequence, the net capital gain and qualified dividend income taken into account as investment income under these elections are not eligible to be taxed at the capital gains rates. An election may be made for net capital gain recognized by noncorporate taxpayers during any taxable year beginning after December 31, 1992. An election may be made for qualified dividend income received by noncorporate taxpayers during any taxable year beginning after December 31, 2002, but before January 1, 2009.

(b) Time and manner for making the elections. The elections for net capital gain and qualified dividend income must be made on or before the due date (including extensions) of the income tax return for the taxable year in which the net capital gain is recognized or the qualified dividend income is received. The elections are to be made on Form 4952, "Investment Interest Expense Deduction," in accordance with the form and its instructions.

(c) Revocability of elections. The elections described in this section are revocable with the consent of the Commissioner.

(d) Effective date. The rules set forth in this section regarding the net capital gain election apply beginning December 12, 1996. The rules set forth in this section regarding the qualified dividend income election apply to any taxable year beginning after December 31, 2002, but before January 1, 2009.

T.D. 8688, 12/11/96, amend T.D. 9147, 8/4/2004, T.D. 9191, 3/17/2005.

Proposed § 1.163(j)-0 Table of contents. [*For Preamble, see ¶ 151,279*]

This section contains a listing of the major headings of §§ 1.163(j)-1 through 1.163(j)-10.

§ 1.163(j)-1 Limitation on deduction for certain interest paid or accrued by a corporation to related persons.

(a) In general.

(1) Deduction for exempt related person interest expense disallowed.

(2) Limitation on disallowance of deduction.

(3) Disallowed interest expense carrryforward.

(b) Debt-equity ratio safe harbor test.

(c) Treatment of disallowed interest expense carryforward.

(1) In general.

(2) Effect of debt-equity safe harbor.

(d) Carryforward of excess limitation.

(e) Effect on earnings and profits.

(f) Anti-avoidance rule.

(g) Examples.

(h) Cross-references.

§ 1.163(j)-2 Definitions.

(a) Exempt related person interest expense.

(b) Excess interest expense.

(c) Excess limitation.

(d) Net interest expense.

(e) Interest income and expense.

(1) In general.

(2) Treatment of bond premium and market discount.

(3) Interest equivalents. [Reserved]

(4) Interest income of partnerships.

(5) Interest expense of partnerships.

(6) Certain substitute payments.

(f) Adjusted taxable income.

(1) In general.

(2) Additions.

(3) Subtractions.

(4) Effect of adjusted taxable loss.

(g) Related persons.

(1) In general.

(2) Anti-abuse rule.

(3) When related person status is tested.

(4) Special rule for certain partnerships.

(5) Examples.

§ 1.163(j)-3 Computation of debt-equity ratio.

(a) In general.

(b) Debt.

(1) In general.

(2) Exclusions.

(3) Liabilities of a partnership.

(4) Anti-rollover rule.

(c) Equity.

(1) In general.

(2) Treatment of stock of certain nonincludible corporations.

(3) Reduction in assets for excluded liabilities.

(4) Partnership interests owned by a corporation.

(5) Anti-avoidance rule.

(d) Determining the debt and equity of a non-dollar functional currency QBU.

§ 1.163(j)-4 Interest not subject to tax.

(a) In general.

(b) Partially exempt interest.

(c) Date for determining whether interest is subject to U.S. tax.

(d) Certain interest paid to special entities.

(1) Controlled foreign corporations.

(2) Passive foreign investment companies.

(3) Foreign personal holding companies.

(4) Producer's loan interest paid to a DISC.
§ 1.163(j)-5 Affiliated group rules.
(a) Certain related corporations treated as one taxpayer.
(1) Scope.
(2) Affiliated corporations.
(3) Certain unaffiliated corporations.
(4) Tie-breaker rules.
(b) Operative rules for consolidated groups.
(1) In general.
(2) Items determined on a consolidated basis.
(3) Exempt related person interest expense.
(4) Deferred intercompany gain.
(5) Carryforwards to current taxable year.
(6) Members leaving the group.
(7) Examples.
(c) Operative rules for other groups.
(1) In general.
(2) Determination and allocation of group items.
(3) Examples.
(d) Debt-equity ratio of related corporations treated as one taxpayer.
(1) In general.
(2) Adjustments to group members' debt.
(3) Adjustments to group members' assets.
(e) Election to use fixed stock write-off method for certain stock acquisitions.
(1) In general.
(2) Post-acquisition adjustments to special basis.
(3) Election out of fixed stock write-off method.
(4) Method for making elections.
(5) Definitions.
(6) Inclusion of target debt notwithstanding use of fixed stock write-off method.
§ 1.163(j)-6 Limitation on carryforward of tax attributes.
(a) Disallowed interest expense carryforward.
(1) Affiliated groups.
(2) Section 381(a) transactions.
(3) Section 382 and SRLY.
(4) Example.
(b) Excess limitation carryforward.
(1) Affiliated groups.
(2) Section 551(a) transactions.
(3) Anti-avoidance rules.
(c) Affiliation and non-affiliation years.
(1) In general.
(2) Predecessors and successors.
(3) Formation of affiliated groups.
(d) Anti-duplication rule.
§ 1.163(j)-7 Relationship to other provisions affecting the deductibility of interest.
(a) Paid or accrued.
(b) Coordination of section 163(j) and certain other provisions.
(1) Disallowed interest provisions.
(2) Deferred interest provisions.
(3) At risk rules and passive activity loss provisions.
(4) Capitalized interest expense.
(5) Reductions under section 246A.
(c) Examples.
§ 1.163(j)-8 Application of section 163(j) to certain foreign corporations.
(a) Scope.
(b) Disallowed interest expense.
(c) Definitions.
(1) In general.
(2) Net interest expense.
(3) Adjusted taxable income.
(4) Excess interest expense.
(5) Excess limitation.
(d) Determination of interest paid to a related person.
(e) Debt-equity ratio.
(f) Example.
(g) Coordination with branch profits tax.
(1) Effect on effectively connected earnings and profits.
(2) Effect on U.S. net equity.
(3) Example.
§ 1.163(j)-9 Guarantees and back-to-back loans. [Reserved]
§ 1.163(j)-10 Effective dates.
(a) In general.
(b) Exceptions.
(1) Interest paid on certain fixed-term obligations outstanding on July 10, 1989.
(2) Demand loans.
(c) Carryforward of excess limitation from pre-effective date taxable years to post-effective date taxable years.
(d) Examples.

Proposed § 1.163(j)-1 Limitation on deduction for certain interest paid or accrued by a corporation to related persons. [*For Preamble, see ¶ 151,279*]

Caution: The Treasury has not yet amended Reg § 1.163(j)-1 to reflect changes made by P.L. 104-188, P.L. 103-66.

(a) In general. *(1) Deduction for exempt related person interest expense disallowed.* Except as provided in this section, no deduction shall be allowed for exempt related person interest expense (as defined in § 1.163(j)-2(a)) paid or accrued during the taxable year directly or indirectly by—

(i) A domestic corporation (other than an S corporation as defined in section 1361), or

(ii) Under the special rules described in § 1.163(j)-8, a foreign corporation with income, gain, or loss that is effectively connected (or treated as effectively connected) with the conduct of a trade or business in the United States.

(2) Limitation on disallowance of deduction. The amount of exempt related person interest expense disallowed as a deduction in any taxable year (described hereafter as the year's "disallowed interest expense") shall not exceed the payor corporation's excess interest expense (as defined in § 1.163(j)-2(b)) for that year.

(3) Disallowed interest expense carryforward. Disallowed interest expense shall be carried forward to the succeeding taxable year (hereafter, a "disallowed interest expense carryforward"). A deduction for disallowed interest expense car-

ryforward may be allowed as provided in paragraph (c) of this section.

(b) Debt-equity ratio safe harbor test. No deduction shall be disallowed under paragraph (a) of this section for exempt related person interest expense paid or accrued in any taxable year in which the payor corporation's debt-equity ratio (determined as provided in § 1.163(j)-3) is less than or equal to 1.5 to 1 on the last day of the taxable year.

(c) Treatment of disallowed interest expense carryforward. *(1) In general.* A deduction for disallowed interest expense carryforward is allowed in a carryforward year if and to the extent that there is excess limitation (as defined in 1.163(j)-2(c)) for such year. Any disallowed interest expense carryforward not so deductible shall be carried forward to the succeeding taxable year.

(2) Effect of debt-equity safe harbor. The debt-equity ratio in a carryforward year is not relevant in determining whether disallowed interest expense carryforward is deductible in such year. Rather, disallowed interest expense carryforward is deductible only to the extent of the excess limitation for such year.

(d) Carryforward of excess limitation. If a corporation has excess limitation (as defined in § 1.163(j)-2(c)) for any taxable year, the amount of such excess limitation, reduced by disallowed interest expense carryforward to that year, shall be carried forward to each of the three succeeding taxable years. In each of those years, such carryforward shall reduce, and be reduced by, the amount, if any, of the corporation's excess interest expense for such year computed without regard to the carryforward. The excess limitation carryforward shall reduce, and be reduced by, excess interest expense in a carryforward year without regard to whether the corporation pays or accrues any exempt related person interest expense in that year, or whether the corporation satisfies the debt-equity ratio safe harbor test described in paragraph (b) of this section for that year. If a corporation has carryforwards from more than one taxable year, such carryforwards shall reduce, and be reduced by, excess interest expense in the order in which they arose. For purposes of all the reductions described in this paragraph, excess limitation, excess limitation carryforward, and excess interest expense shall not be reduced below zero. For rules regarding the effect of an adjusted taxable loss with respect to excess limitation carryforward, see § 1.163(j)-2(f)(4)(ii).

(e) Effect on earnings and profits. The disallowance and carryforward of a deduction for interest expense under this section shall not affect whether or when such interest expense reduces earnings and profits of the payor corporation.

(f) Anti-avoidance rule. Arrangements, including the use of partnerships or trusts, entered into with a principal purpose of avoiding the rules of section 163(j) and these regulations shall be disregarded or recharacterized to the extent necessary to carry out the purposes of section 163(j).

(g) Examples. The following examples illustrate the rules of this section.

Example (1). (i) A, a domestic corporation, is a wholly owned subsidiary of F, a foreign corporation. During its taxable year ending December 31, 1990, A has adjusted taxable income of $100, which includes $20 of interest income, and $90 of interest expense, of which $60 is paid or accrued to F. The balance of the interest expense is paid to unrelated persons. Interest paid to F by A is not subject to U.S. tax due to a tax treaty. A does not satisfy the debt-equity ratio safe harbor test in 1990, and has no excess limitation carried forward to that year.

(ii) A's excess interest expense for 1990 is $20, which is the difference between its net interest expense and 50 percent of its adjusted taxable income ($70 – $50 = $20). Since for 1990, the amount of A's exempt related person interest expense ($60) is greater than its excess interest expense ($20), a deduction for $20 of A's exempt related person interest expense is disallowed under paragraph (a) of this section. A's 1990 disallowed interest expense is carried forward to A's succeeding taxable year.

Example (2). (i) The facts are the same as in paragraph (i) of Example 1. In 1991, A has $120 of adjusted taxable income, net interest expense of $50, and $20 of disallowed interest expense carried forward from 1990. All of A's interest expense for 1991 is paid to unrelated persons. A does not satisfy the debt-equity ratio safe harbor test in 1991.

(ii) A has excess limitation (as defined in § 1.163(j)-2(c)) of $10 ($60 (50% of adjusted taxable income) – $50 (net interest expense)) in 1991. In 1991, A may deduct the interest expense paid or accrued in that year to unrelated persons, plus $10 of disallowed interest expense carryforward from 1990. The balance of A's disallowed interest expense carryforward from 1990 ($10) is carried forward to A's 1992 taxable year.

Example (3). (i) The facts are the same as in paragraph (i) of Example 2. In 1992, A satisfies the debt-equity ratio safe harbor test, has adjusted taxable income of $210, and net interest expense of $100. All A's interest expense for 1992 is paid or accrued to F.

(ii) In 1992, A has excess limitation of $105 (50% of adjusted taxable income) – $100 (net interest expense)). Applying the principles of paragraph (c) of this section, A's $10 of disallowed interest expense carryforward from 1991 (see Example 2, paragraph (ii)) is allowed in 1992 only to the extent of the $5 of excess limitation for that year. The remaining $5 of disallowed interest expense carried forward from 1991 is carried forward to A's 1993 taxable year.

Example (4). (i) The facts are the same as in paragraph (i) of Example 3. In 1993, A satisfies the debt-equity ratio safe harbor test, has adjusted taxable income of $100, and has net interest expense of $75, all of which is paid or accrued to F.

(ii) A's excess interest expense for 1993 is $25 ($75 (A's net interest expense – $50 (50% of its adjusted taxable income)). Applying the principles of paragraphs (a) and (b) of this section, section 163(j) does not disallow a deduction in 1993 for any of A's excess interest expense that is exempt related person interest expense. Under paragraph of this section, A's $5 of disallowed interest expense carryforward from 1992 (see Example 3, paragraph (ii)) is not deductible in 1993, and is carried forward to A's 1991 taxable year.

(h) Cross-references. For rules regarding affiliated groups for purposes of section 163(j), see § 1.163(j)-5. For rules limiting the deductibility of disallowed interest expense carryforward and restricting the use of excess limitation carried forward to taxable years after the occurrence of certain corporate transactions, see § 1.163(j)-6.

Proposed § 1.163(j)-2 Definitions. [*For Preamble, see ¶ 151,279*]

Caution: The Treasury has not yet amended Reg § 1.163(j)-2 to reflect changes made by P.L. 104-188, P.L. 103-66.

(a) Exempt related person interest expense. The term "exempt related person interest expense" means interest expense that is (or is treated as) paid or accrued by a corporation described in § 1.163(j)-1(a) to a related person (within the meaning of paragraph (g) of this section) if no tax is imposed with respect to such interest under rules provided in § 1.163(j)-4.

(b) Excess interest expense. The term "excess interest expense" means the excess, if any, of a corporation's net interest expense (as defined in paragraph (d) of this section) over the sum of 50 percent of its adjusted taxable income (as defined in paragraph (f) of this section) plus any excess limitation carried forward to the taxable year (under the rules of § 1.163(j)-1(d)). See paragraph (f)(4)(ii) of this section for rules regarding the effect of an adjusted taxable loss on the computation of excess interest expense.

(c) Excess limitation. The term "excess limitation" means the excess, if any, of 50 percent of a corporation's adjusted taxable income (as defined in paragraph (f) of this section) over its net interest expense (as defined in paragraph (d) of this section).

(d) Net interest expense. The term "net interest expense" means the excess, if any, of the amount of interest expense paid or accrued (directly or indirectly) by a corporation during the taxable year over the amount of interest includible (directly or indirectly) in its gross income for such year.

(e) Interest income and expense. *(1) In general.* Interest income shall generally be determined under section 61 and shall include original issue discount as provided in sections 1272 through 1275 (adjusted, under section 1272(a)(7), for any acquisition premium paid by a subsequent holder), acquisition discount as provided in sections 1281 through 1283, and amounts that are treated as original issue discount under section 1286 (pertaining to stripped bonds). Interest expense shall generally be determined under section 163(a) and shall include original issue discount as provided in section 163(e). Interest expense for a taxable year does not take into account any disallowed interest expense carried forward to that year under the rules of § 1.163(j)-1. Interest income or expense with respect to a debt instrument denominated in a nonfunctional currency (or the payments of which are determined with reference to a nonfunctional currency) shall be determined in accordance with section 988 and the regulations thereunder. For rules regarding the relationship of section 163(j) to other Code provisions under which a deduction for interest expense may be disallowed or deferred, see § 1.163(j)-7.

(2) Treatment of bond premium and market discount. (i) Bond premium. In the case of any bond with respect to which an election made under section 171(c) is in effect, amortizable bond premium (as defined in section 171(b)) shall reduce interest income. Bond premium included in income by the issuer under the principles of § 1.61-12 (or the successor provision thereof) shall reduce interest expense.

(ii) Market discount. Gain treated as ordinary income on the disposition of a market discount bond under section 1276(a) shall be treated as interest income.

(3) Interest equivalents. [Reserved]

(4) Interest income of partnerships. Interest paid or accrued to a partnership shall be treated under section 163(j) and these regulations (other than paragraph (g) of this section) as paid or accrued to the partners of the partnership in proportion to each partner's distributive share (as defined in section 704) of the partnership's interest income for the taxable year.

(5) Interest expense of partnerships. Interest expense paid or accrued by a partnership and the tax exempt interest expense of a partnership (within the meaning of § 1.163(j)-4) shall be treated for all purposes under section 163(j) and these regulations as paid or accrued by the partners of the partnership in proportion to each partner's distributive share (as defined in section 704) of the partnership's interest expense and tax exempt interest expense, respectively, for the taxable year. Thus, a corporation which is a partner in a partnership shall be treated as paying or accruing its share of the partnership's interest expense, and is treated as the payor of such interest expense.

(6) Certain substitute payments. (i) In general. If pursuant to an agreement meeting the requirements of section 1058 (b), there is a transfer of securities (as defined in section 1236(c)) between related persons (within the meaning of paragraph (g) of this section), payments described in section 1058(b)(2) with respect to such transferred securities ("substitute payments") shall be treated as interest expense for purposes of section 163(j) and these regulations.

(ii) Effective date. This paragraph (e)(6) shall be effective with respect to substitute payments paid or accrued after July 18, 1991.

(f) Adjusted taxable income. *(1) In general.* The term "adjusted taxable income" means a corporation's taxable income for the taxable year, computed without regard to any carryforwards or disallowances under section 163(j), and determined with the modifications described in paragraphs (f)(2) and (f)(3) of this section. A corporation's adjusted taxable income may be a negative amount (i.e. an adjusted taxable loss). See paragraph (f)(4) of this section for rules regarding the effect of an adjusted taxable loss.

(2) Additions. The following amounts shall be added to a corporation's taxable income to determine its adjusted taxable income:

(i) The net interest expense (as defined in paragraph (d) of this section) for the taxable year;

(ii) The net operating loss deduction under section 172;

(iii) Deductions for depreciation under sections 167 and 168;

(iv) Deductions for the amortization of intangibles and other amortized expenditures (e.g., start-up expenditures under section 195 and organizational expenditures under section 248);

(v) Deductions for depletion under section 611;

(vi) Carryovers of excess charitable contributions (within the meaning of section 170(d)(2)), to the extent allowable as a deduction in the taxable year;

(vii) The increase, if any, between the end of the preceding year and the end of the current year in accounts payable (other than interest payable) that are included in the computation of taxable income;

(viii) The decrease, if any, between the end of the preceding taxable year and the end of the current taxable year in accounts receivable (other than interest receivable) that are included in the computation of taxable income;

(ix) Interest which is excluded from gross income under section 103;

(x) The dividends received deduction as provided under section 243 (other than deductions under section 243(a)(3));

(xi) The increase, if any, in the LIFO recapture amount (as defined in section 312(n)(4)(B)) between the end of the preceding taxable year and the end of the current taxable year; and

(xii) Any deduction in the taxable year for capital loss carrybacks or carryovers.

(3) Subtractions. The following amounts shall be subtracted from taxable income to determine adjusted taxable income:

(i) With respect to the sale or disposition of property (including a sale or disposition of property by a partnership), any depreciation, amortization, or depletion deductions which were allowed or allowable for the taxpayer's taxable years beginning after July 10, 1986, with respect to such property;

(ii) With respect to the sale or disposition of stock of a member of a consolidated group that includes the selling corporation, an amount equal to the investment adjustments (as defined under §§ 1.1502-32 and 1.1502-32T) with respect to such stock that are attributable to deductions described in paragraph (f)(3)(i) of this section;

(iii) With respect to the sale or other disposition of an interest in a partnership, an amount equal to the taxpayer's distributive share of deductions described in paragraph (f)(3)(i) of this section with respect to property held by the partnership at the time of such sale or other disposition;

(iv) The decrease, if any, between the end of the preceding taxable year and the end of the current taxable year in accounts payable (other than interest payable) which are included in the computation of the corporation's taxable income;

(v) The increase, if any, between the end of the preceding taxable year and the end of the current taxable year in accounts receivable (other than interest receivable) which are included in the computation of the corporation's taxable income;

(vi) Amounts that would be deductible but for section 265 (regarding expenses and interest relating to tax-exempt income) or 279 (regarding interest on indebtedness incurred by a corporation to acquire stock or assets of another corporation);

(vii) The amount of any charitable contribution (as defined in section 170(c)) made during the taxable year that exceeds the amount deductible in that year by reason of section 170(b)(2);

(viii) The decrease, if any, in the LIFO recapture amount (as defined in section 312(n)(4)(B)) between the end of the preceding taxable year and the end of the current taxable year; and

(ix) The amount of any net capital loss (as defined in section 1222(10)) for the taxable year.

(4) Effect of adjusted taxable loss. (i) In general. If a payor corporation has an adjusted taxable loss for the taxable year, then its adjusted taxable income shall be treated as zero.

(ii) Effect on excess limitation carryforward. The amount of an adjusted taxable loss reduces excess limitation carryforward for the purpose of determining whether there is excess interest expense for a taxable year.

(iii) Adjusted taxable loss not carried forward. An adjusted taxable loss in one taxable year shall not affect the determination of a corporation's adjusted taxable income for any other taxable year.

(g) Related persons. *(1) In general.* The term "related person" means any person who is related to the taxpayer within the meaning of sections 267(b) or 707(b)(1). For this purpose, the constructive ownership and attribution rules of section 267(c) shall apply.

(2) Anti-abuse rule. In determining whether persons are related, the substance, rather than the form, of ownership is controlling. Thus, for example, the principles of § 1.957-1(b)(2) shall apply to determine whether an arrangement to shift formal voting power or formal ownership of shares away from any person for the purpose of avoiding the application of section 163(j) shall be given effect.

(3) When related person status is tested. Whether a person is related to a payor corporation under section 163(j) is determined with respect to an item of interest expense when such interest expense accrues. For this purpose (notwithstanding the rules in § 1.163(j)-7), interest expense (including amounts treated as interest under this section) shall be treated as accruing daily under principles similar to section 1272(a). Also for this purpose, interest described in paragraph (e)(5) of this section shall be treated as accrued by a partner as it is accrued, under the principles of the preceding sentence, by the partnership. Changes in the relationship between the payor corporation and the payee after an item of interest expense accrues shall not be taken into account.

(4) Special rule for certain partnerships. (i) Less than 10 percent of partnership held by tax exempt persons. Any interest expense pad or accrued to a partnership directly or indirectly by a payor corporation that (without regard to this paragraph (g)(4)) is related to the partnership within the meaning of this paragraph (g) shall not be treated as paid or accrued to a related person if less than 10 percent of the capital and profits interests in such partnership are held by persons with respect to whom no tax is imposed on such interest by subtitle A of the Internal Revenue Code under rules provided in § 1.163(j)-4. However, the preceding sentence shall not apply to treat as interest paid to an unrelated person any interest that (under rules described in this section) is includible in the gross income of a partner in such a partnership who is itself a related person with respect to the payor of such interest.

(ii) Reduction of tax by treaty. If a treaty between the United States and a foreign country reduces the rate of tax imposed by subtitle A of the Code on a partner's distributive share of any interest paid or accrued to a partnership, such partner's interest in the partnership shall, for purposes of § 1.163(j)-2(g)(4)(i), be treated as held in part by a taxable person and in part by a tax exempt person in accordance with the rules described in § 1.163(j)-4(b).

(5) Examples. The principles of this paragraph (g) are illustrated by the following examples.

Example (1). (i) Fifty-one percent of the total combined voting power and value of domestic corporation A is owned by a domestic tax-exempt corporation, D1; the remainder is owned by foreign corporation F1. F1 is organized under the laws of country 2. Under a U.S. tax treaty with country Z, interest paid by A to F1 is exempt from U.S. tax under the rules of § 1.163(j)-4.

(ii) Under these facts, D1 is related to A under section 267(b)(3) (because D1 and A are members of the same controlled group of corporations, as defined in section 267(f)), and interest payments made by A to D1 are exempt related person interest expense, a deduction for which may be disallowed under section 163(j). F1 is not related to A within the meaning of sections 267(b) or 707(b)(1). Deductions for interest paid by A to F1 are not subject to disallowance under section 163(j).

Example (2). (i) The facts are the same as in paragraph (i) of Example 1, except that D1 and F1 each own 50 percent of the vote and value of X's stock.

(ii) Unless the substance of D1's and F1's ownership differs from its form, so that paragraph (g)(2) of this section (regarding abusive ownership structures) applies, none of the interest paid by A to D1 or F1 is subject to disallowance under section 163(j).

Example (3). (i) A, a domestic corporation whose taxable year is the calendar year, is a wholly owned subsidiary of F, a foreign corporation. A is a partner, with a one-third share in the capital and profits interests, of P, a domestic partnership whose taxable year is the calendar year. During its taxable year ending December 31, 1990, and taking into account its interest in P, A has adjusted taxable income of $126.67. A's directly incurred interest income and expense for the taxable year are $20 and $90. Of the $90 of interest expense, $60 is paid or accrued to F.

(ii) P's interest income and interest expense for the taxable year of the partnership ending December 31, 1990, are $20 and $50, respectively. A's share of these amounts (determined under rules described in § 1.163(j)-2) are $6.67 and $16.67, respectively. Of P's $50 interest expense for the taxable year, $20 is paid or accrued to F, and the balance is paid or accrued to persons unrelated to A or to any of the other partners of P.

(iii) Interest paid or treated as paid to F by A is not subject to U.S. tax due to a tax treaty. Taking into account A's investment in the partnership (under rules described in § 1.163(j)-3), A does not satisfy the debt-equity ratio safe harbor test in 1990.

(iv) Under § 1.163(j)-1(a) and paragraphs (e)(4) and (3) of this section, in its taxable year ending December 31, 1990, A is required to take into account the interest income and interest expense it directly incurs, plus its share of P's interest income and interest expense. Thus, A's interest income for 1990 is $26.67, and its interest expense is $106.67. A's excess interest expense for 1990 is $16.67, which is the difference between its net interest expense ($106.67 (interest expense) − $26.67 (interest income) = $80) and 50 percent of its adjusted taxable income (($126.67 × 50% = $63.33).

(v) For 1990, under the rule described in paragraph (e)(5) of this section, the amount of A's exempt related person interest expense is $66.67 ($60 + $6.67 = $66.67). Since that amount is greater than its excess interest expense ($16.67), section 163(j) disallows a deduction for $16.67 of A's interest expense for the taxable year. That disallowed interest expense is carried forward to A's 1991 taxable year.

Example (4). (i) X, a domestic corporation, is wholly owned by Y, a partnership. A treaty between the United States and foreign country U reduces the rate of tax on interest paid to residents of country U from 30 percent (the applicable rate for related person interest under sections 871 and 881 in the absence of a treaty) to 15 percent. Nineteen percent of the capital and profits interests of partnership Y are held by Z, a country U corporation entitled to claim the reduced (treaty) rate of tax on interest income; the balance is held by unrelated persons not exempt from U.S. tax on their distributive shares of interest paid by the corporation to the partnership.

(ii) Under paragraph (g)(4) of this section, less than ten percent (19 percent divided by two (30/15)) of Y's capital and profits interests are treated as held by persons who are tax exempt. Accordingly, all interest paid to partnership Y by corporation X is treated as paid to an unrelated person.

Proposed § 1.163(j)-3 Computation of debt-equity ratio.
[For Preamble, see ¶ 151,279]

(a) In general. For purposes of section 163(j), the term "debt-equity ratio" means the ratio that the debt of the corporation bears to the equity of the corporation. For rules defining debt and equity, see paragraphs (b) and (c) of this section. For rules regarding the computation of the debt and equity of an affiliated group or a foreign corporation, see §§ 1.163(j)-5 or 1.163(j)-8, respectively.

(b) Debt. *(1) In general.* The debt of a corporation means its liabilities determined according to generally applicable tax principles. Thus, the amount taken into account on the issue date with respect to a debt instrument which is not issued at a discount or a premium shall be the issue price. The amount taken into account with respect to any debt with original issue discount shall be its issue price plus the portion of the original issue discount previously accrued as determined under the rules of section 1272 (determined without regard to section 1272(a)(7) or (b)(4)). In addition, with respect to the issuer, unamortized bond premium shall be treated as debt.

(2) Exclusions. Short-term liabilities as defined in paragraph (b)(2)(i) of this section and commercial financing liabilities as defined in paragraph (b)(2)(ii) of this section shall be excluded from characterization as debt.

(i) Short-term liabilities. The term "short-term liabilities" means accrued operating expenses, accrued taxes payable, and any account payable for the first 90 days of its existence provided that no interest is accrued with respect to any portion of such 90 day period.

(ii) Commercial financing liabilities. The term "commercial financing liabilities" means any liability if it—

(A) Is incurred by the obligor under a commercial financing agreement (such as an automobile "floorplan" agreement) to buy an item of inventory;

(B) Is secured by the item;

(C) Is due on or before sale of the item; and

(D) If entered into between related parties, has terms that are comparable to the terms of such financing agreements between unrelated parties in the same (or a similar) industry.

(3) Liabilities of a partnership. In determining the debt of a corporation that owns an interest in a partnership (directly or indirectly through one or more pass-through entities), liabilities of the partnership shall be treated as liabilities incurred directly by each partner in the same manner and proportions that the liabilities of the partnership are treated as shared by its partners under section 752.

(4) Anti-rollover rule. Decreases in a corporation's aggregate debt during the last 90 days of its taxable year shall be disregarded to the extent that the corporation's aggregate debt is increased during the first 90 days of the succeeding taxable year.

(c) Equity. *(1) In general.* Equity means the sum of money and the adjusted basis of all other assets of the corporation reduced (but not below zero) by the taxpayer's debt (as defined in paragraph (b) of this section). Whether an item constitutes an asset shall be determined according to generally applicable tax principles.

(2) Treatment of stock of certain nonincludible corporations. Under the general rule of paragraph (c)(1) of this section, assets include the adjusted basis of stock of any corporation which is not an includible corporation (as defined under section 1504(b)). The adjusted basis of stock held in a corporation which is not an includible corporation shall be further adjusted under principles similar to those in section 864(e)(4) if the taxpayer (or the members of an affiliated group of which the taxpayer is a member) owns stock in the

corporation satisfying the requirements of section 864(e)(4)(B)(ii). Cf. § 1.861-12T(c)(2).

(3) Reduction in assets for excluded liabilities. The amount of a taxpayer's equity under paragraph (c)(1) and (2) of this section shall be reduced (but not below zero) by an amount equal to the amount of liabilities excluded under paragraph (b)(2) of this section.

(4) Partnership interests owned by a corporation. In determining the assets of a corporation that owns an interest in a partnership, the corporation shall treat as an asset the adjusted basis of its partnership interest.

(5) Anti-avoidance rules. (i) In general. An asset of the taxpayer shall be disregarded in computing the taxpayer's debt-equity ratio if the principal purpose for acquiring the asset was to reduce the taxpayer's debt-equity ratio.

(ii) Anti-stuffing rule. In determining a corporation's equity, any transfer of assets made by a related person to the corporation during the last 90 days of its taxable year shall be disregarded to the extent that there is a transfer of the same or similar assets by the corporation to a related person during the first 90 days of the corporation's succeeding taxable year. However, this rule shall not apply to the extent that there is full consideration for a transfer in money or property (as that term is defined in section 317(a)).

(d) Determining the debt and equity of a non-dollar functional currency QBU. In determining the dollar value of liabilities and assets on the books of a qualified business unit that has a functional currency other than the dollar, such liabilities and assets shall be translated at the spot rate on the last day of the taxable year.

Proposed § 1.163(j)-4 Interest not subject to tax. [*For Preamble, see ¶ 151,279*]

Caution: The Treasury has not yet amended Reg § 1.163(j)-4 to reflect changes made by P.L. 103-66.

(a) In general. Interest paid or accrued by a corporation under the rules of § 1.163(j)-1 is not subject to tax for purposes of section 163(j) if no U.S. tax is imposed with respect to such interest under subtitle A of the Internal Revenue Code (determined without regard to net operating losses or net operating loss carryovers), taking into account any applicable treaty obligation of the United States. For this purpose, whether interest paid or accrued to a partnership is subject to tax is determined at the partner level.

(b) Partially exempt interest. Interest that is subject to a reduced rate of tax under any treaty obligation of the United States applicable to the recipient shall be treated as in part subject to the statutory tax rate under sections 871 or 881 and in part not subject to tax, based on the proportion that the rate of tax under the treaty bears to the statutory tax rate. Thus, for purposes of section 163(j), if the statutory tax rate is 30 percent, and pursuant to a treaty U.S. tax is instead limited to a rate of 10 percent, two-thirds of such interest shall be considered interest not subject to tax.

(c) Date for determining whether interest is subject to U.S. tax. The determination of whether interest is subject to U.S. tax is made on the date the interest is received or accrued by the payee, whichever is relevant under normally applicable U.S. tax principles for purposes of determining the tax, if any, on the payee.

(d) Certain interest paid to special entities. *(1) Controlled foreign corporations.* (i) In general. Interest that is paid or accrued to a foreign corporation described in section 957(a) (a "controlled foreign corporation") and that is not otherwise subject to tax under paragraph (a) of this section shall be deemed subject to tax to the extent that such interest is included in the foreign corporation's net foreign personal holding company income under § 1.954-1T(c) and results in an inclusion in the gross income of a United States shareholder under section 951(a)(1)(A)(i) (or would have been included in a United States shareholder's gross income but for an election under § 1.954-1T(d)).

(ii) Effect of section 952(c)(1)(A) (earnings and profits) limitation. For purposes of paragraph (d)(1) of this section, if a controlled foreign corporation's subpart F income for the taxable year is limited under section 952(c)(1)(A), each category of subpart F income described in section 952(a), and, within each such category, each component thereof shall be treated as reduced ratably.

(iii) Net foreign personal holding company income. To determine whether an item of interest income is included in a controlled foreign corporation's net foreign personal holding company income for the taxable year, the expenses allocable to such interest shall be deemed to bear the same ratio to the total expenses allocable to the controlled foreign corporation's net foreign personal holding company income (determined pursuant to 1.954-1T(c)) as the amount of such interest bears to the controlled foreign corporation's gross foreign personal holding company income (determined under § 1.954-1T(a)(2)(i)).

(iv) Related person interest. If related person interest is allocated to the item of interest under the provisions of § 1.904-5(c)(2) and paragraph (d)(1)(iii) of this section, and if the United States shareholder receiving such related person interest is subject to United States tax, then, for purposes of paragraph (d)(1)(i) of this section, such allocable related person interest shall be deemed to be net foreign personal holding company income that results in an inclusion under section 951(a)(1)(A)(i).

(v) Section 78 amount. Any foreign taxes that are allocable to an item of interest income satisfying the requirements of paragraph (d)(1)(i) of this section and that are included in a United States shareholder's income under section 78 (or would have been included, but for an election under 1.954-1T(d)) shall, for purposes of paragraph (d)(1)(i) of this section, be deemed to be net foreign personal holding company income that results in an inclusion under section 951(a)(1)(A)(i).

(2) Passive foreign investment companies. (i) In general. Interest that is not otherwise subject to tax under paragraph (a) of this section, and that is paid or accrued to a passive foreign investment company (as defined in section 1296) that is not a controlled foreign corporation, and which a U.S. person has elected under section 1295 to treat as a qualified electing fund ("QEF"), shall be treated as subject to tax to the extent that such interest is included in the QEF's ordinary earnings (as defined in section 1293(e)(1)) and results in an inclusion in income of such U.S. person under section 1293(a)(1)(A).

(ii) Ordinary earnings. In determining whether an item of interest income is included in the ordinary earnings of a passive foreign investment company, the item shall be reduced by deductions allocable and apportionable to that item under §§ 1.861-8 through 1.861-14T.

(iii) Section 78 amount. Any foreign taxes that are allocable to an item of interest income satisfying the requirements of paragraph (d)(2)(i) of this section and that are included in a U.S. person's income under section 78 pursuant to section 1293(f) shall, for purposes of paragraph (d)(2)(i) of this section, be deemed to be ordinary earnings that are included in the income of a U.S. person under section 1293(a)(1)(A).

(3) Foreign personal holding companies. (i) In general. Interest that is not otherwise subject to tax under paragraph (a) of this section, and that is paid or accrued to a foreign personal holding company (as defined in section 552) that is neither a passive foreign investment company nor a controlled foreign corporation, shall be treated as subject to tax to the extent that such interest is included in the company's undistributed foreign personal holding company income (as defined in section 556) and results in an inclusion in income of a U.S. person under section 551(a).

(ii) Undistributed foreign personal company income. In determining whether an item of interest income is included in the undistributed foreign personal holding company income of a foreign personal holding company, the item shall be reduced by deductions allocable and apportionable to that item under § 1.861-8 through 1.861-14T.

(iii) Effect of distributions. Any amount that would be treated as subject to tax by virtue of this paragraph (d)(3) but for a dividends paid deduction under section 561 shall be treated subject to tax.

(4) Producer's loan interest paid to a DISC. Interest paid or accrued with respect to a DISC (as defined in section 992) that is treated as interest with respect to a producer's loan (as defined in section 993(d)) is treated as subject to U.S. tax if such interest is taxed to the shareholders of the DISC under section 995(b)(1)(A).

Proposed § 1.163(j)-5 Affiliated group rules. [*For Preamble, see ¶ 151,279*]

(a) Certain related corporations treated as one taxpayer. *(1) Scope.* This section applies section 163(j) to certain related corporations which are (or are treated as) members of an affiliated group and which under section 163(j)(6)(C) and (7) are treated as a single taxpayer. Paragraphs (a)(2) and (a)(3) of this section describe the corporations that are subject to such treatment. (For purposes of section 163(j) and these regulations, the rules in regulations under section 1502 apply, but unless the context otherwise requires, the term "member" means a corporation that is, or is treated as, a member of an affiliated group under this paragraph (a), and the term "group" refers collectively to the member and the other corporations that are so treated.) Paragraph (a)(4) of this section provides rules that treat a corporation as a member of a single affiliated group if the rules of this paragraph (a) would otherwise cause it to be treated as a member of more than one affiliated group. Paragraph (b) of this section provides rules regarding the computation of items of income, expense, and carryovers under section 163(j) for an affiliated group of corporations if all of the members of such group join in the filing of a single consolidated return for the taxable year under section 1501. Paragraph (c) of this section provides rules for corporations that are not members of consolidated groups which are subject to the rules of § 1.163(j)-5(b). Paragraph (d) of this section provides rules regarding the computation of the debt-equity ratio for purposes of applying the debt-equity ratio safe harbor test described in § 1.163(j)-1(b). Paragraph (e) of this section provides rules regarding the treatment of, and an election pertaining to, assets of certain acquired corporations.

(2) Affiliated corporations. To the extent provided in this section, all the members of an affiliated group (as defined in section 1504(a)) of which a corporation is a member on the last day of its taxable year shall be treated as one taxpayer for purposes of section 163(j) and this section, without regard to whether such affiliated group files a consolidated return pursuant to section 1501.

(3) Certain unaffiliated corporations. (i) In general. If at least 80 percent of the total voting power and total value of the stock of an includible corporation (as defined in section 1504(b)) is owned, directly or indirectly, by another includible corporation, the first corporation shall be treated as a member of an affiliated group that includes the other corporation and its affiliates. The attribution rules of section 318 shall apply for purposes of determining indirect stock ownership under this paragraph (a)(3).

(ii) Example. The principles of this paragraph (a)(3) are illustrated by the following example.

Example. X and Y are wholly owned domestic subsidiaries of F, a foreign corporation. X and Y are not members of an affiliated group under section 1504(a) because F is not itself an includible corporation under section 1504(b)(3). However, under paragraph (a)(3) of this section, X and Y are treated as members of an affiliated group, since, under section 318(a)(3)(C), X is treated as owning indirectly 100 percent of Y, and Y is treated as owning indirectly 100 percent of X.

(4) Tie-breaker rules. If the rules of this paragraph (a) would treat a corporation as a member of more than one affiliated group, then the principles of section 1563(b)(4) and the regulations thereunder shall determine the group of which such corporation shall be treated as a member.

(b) Operative rules for consolidated groups. *(1) In general.* If all of the members of the affiliated group are members of a single consolidated group for the taxable year, the computations required by section 163(j) and these regulations (other than the computation of the group's debt-equity ratio under paragraph (d) of this section) shall be made in accordance with the rules of this paragraph (b). See paragraph (c) of this section for rules applicable to affiliated groups not described in the preceding sentence.

(2) Items determined on a consolidated basis. The computations required by section 163(j) and these regulations shall be determined for the group on a consolidated basis. For example, the group's taxable income shall be the consolidated taxable income determined under § 1.1502-11 (without regard to any carryforwards or disallowances under section 163(j)), and the group's net interest expense shall be the excess, if any, of the group's aggregate interest expense over the group's aggregate interest income (as provided in §§ 1.163(j)-2(d) and (e)). Similarly, the group's excess interest expense shall be determined by reference to the group's net interest expense, adjusted taxable income, and excess limitation carryforward (as determined under paragraph (b)(5) of this section). Except as provided in paragraphs (b)(5) and (6) of this section, disallowed interest expense carryforwards and excess limitation carryforwards shall also be determined on a consolidated basis.

(3) Exempt related person interest expense. In determining the group's exempt related person interest expense, interest expense shall be treated as paid or accrued to a related person (within the meaning of § 1.163(j)-2(g)) if it would be so treated if paid or accrued to the same payee by any member of the group.

(4) Deferred intercompany gain. For purposes of determining the adjusted taxable income of the group, the following special rules shall apply—

(i) Any gain on a deferred intercompany transaction (including any gain described in § 1.1502-14T(a)) that is restored in accordance with the rules under §§ 1.1502-13(d) or

1.1502-13T(1) shall be subtracted from the group's consolidated taxable income.

(ii) If property is disposed of under § 1.1502-13(e)(2) or (f) or § 1.1502-13T(m), any amount subtracted from the group's consolidated taxable income in a previous taxable year with respect to such property under paragraph (b)(4)(i) of this section shall be added to the group's consolidated taxable income.

(iii) Example. The principles of this paragraph (b)(4) are illustrated by the following example.

Example. (i) On January 1, 1991, X, a member of an affiliated group which files a consolidated return for the calendar year, purchases property for $200 from an unrelated person. X depreciates the property over a 5-year period. On January 1, 1996, when X's basis in the property is $0, X sells the property to Y, another member of the group, for $200, which is the property's fair market value at such time. The sale is a deferred intercompany transaction under § 1.1502-13, and X's gain of $200 is deferred under § 1.1502-13(c). In the hands of Y the property is once again depreciable over a 5-year period. The group claims a depreciation deduction with respect to the property of $40 in 1996, which results, in the restoration of $40 of X's deferred gain under § 1.1502-13T(1) for such year.

(ii) As provided in paragraph (b)(3)(1) of this section, the group's taxable income for 1996 is reduced by $40, the amount of restored gain under § 1.1502-13T(1) with respect to the transferred property. In addition, as provided in § 1.163(j)-2(f)(2)(iii) and paragraph (b)(2) of this section, the group's taxable income for 1996 is increased by $40, the amount of the group's depreciation deduction with respect to the transferred property for such year.

(iii) On January 1, 1997, Y sells the property for $200 to an unrelated person and recognizes gain of $40. The sale results in restoration of $160 of gain under § 1.1502-13T(m) with respect to the earlier transfer of property from X to Y. Thus, Y's sale results in the group's 1997 consolidated taxable income increasing by $200 prior to any adjustment under section 163(j). Under § 1.163(j)-2(f)(3)(i), the consolidated taxable income is reduced by $240 to reflect previous depreciation deductions with respect to such property. In addition, as provided in paragraph (b)(4)(ii) of this section, the consolidated taxable income is increased by $40, the amount subtracted from the group's 1996 consolidated taxable income by virtue of the restoration of $40 of deferred gain in that year.

(5) Carryforwards to current taxable year. The group's disallowed interest expense carryforward or excess limitation carryforwards to the current taxable year shall be the relevant carryforwards from the group's prior taxable years, plus any disallowed interest expense carryforward or excess limitation carryforwards from separate return years permitted to be used by the group under the rules of § 1.163(j)-6.

(6) Members leaving the group. (i) Disallowed interest expense carryforward. A member leaving the group shall carry forward to its separate return years a portion of the group disallowed interest expense carryforward determined as of the end of the last consolidated return year during which the corporation was a member of the group. Such portion shall equal the amount of the group's disallowed interest expense carryforward multiplied by a fraction, the numerator of which is the aggregate amount of exempt related person interest expense paid or accrued by such member during the period when it was a member of the group, and the denominator of which is the aggregate amount of exempt related person interest expense paid or accrued by all members of the group. If a member has pre-affiliation disallowed interest expense carryforward upon entering the group, the amount of such member's disallowed interest expense carryforward shall be treated as exempt related person interest expense of both the member and the group. Further, the group's disallowed interest expense carryforward shall be reduced by the amount allocated to the member. If the member leaves the group during the consolidated return year, rules similar to the rules of § 1.1502-21(b)(2) shall apply.

(ii) Excess limitation carryforward. A member leaving the group shall not carry forward to its separate return years any portion of the group's excess limitation carryforward, and the group's excess limitation carryforward shall not be reduced by virtue of such member's departure from the group. However, if all the members of a consolidated group become members of another consolidated group, the acquired group's excess limitation carryforward shall become excess limitation carryforward of the corporation that was the common parent of the acquired group. For purposes of determining the extent to which this excess limitation carryforward becomes excess limitation carryforward of the acquiring group under paragraph (b)(5) of this section, see § 1.163(j)-6(b).

(7) Examples. The following examples illustrate the principles of this paragraph (b).

Example (1). (i) X, Y, and Z are domestic corporations that are members of a newly formed consolidated group described in paragraph (b) of this section. X owns 100 percent of the stock of Y, and Y owns 80 percent of the stock of Z. F1, a foreign corporation, owns 60 percent of the stock of X. Any interest paid or accrued by X, Y, or Z to F1 is exempt under section 163(j) because it is exempt from U.S. withholding tax under a treaty with F1's country of residence. Such interest, (including interest paid by Z) is also paid or accrued to a related person within the meaning of 1.163(j)-2(g) and paragraph (b)(3) of this section.

(ii) For 1991, the group's first taxable year, X, Y, and Z have the following relevant items of income and expense—

Company	Interest income	Interest expense	Exempt related person interest expense
X	$600	$ 500	......
Y	200	900	$600
Z	......	200	150
Total	800	1,600	750

(iii) Under § 1.1502-11, the group's consolidated taxable income for the 1991 year is $150. Adjustments to consolidated taxable income total $50, resulting in consolidated adjusted taxable income of $200. The group's net interest expense for 1991 is $800 ($1,600 – $800), and its excess interest expense is $300 ($800 – ($1,000/2)). The group's exempt related person interest expense for 1991 is $750. The group's disallowed interest expense for 1991 is the lesser of its excess interest expense or its exempt related person interest expense, or $300. This $300 is a group disallowed interest expense carryforward to the group's 1992 taxable year.

Example (2). (i) The facts are the same as in Example 1. In the group's 1992 taxable year, the members have the following relevant items of income and expense—

Company	Interest income	Interest expense	Exempt related person interest expense
X	$600	$500	$ 50
Y	200	900	600
Z	......	200	150
Total	800	1600	800

(ii) Under § 1.1502-11, the group's consolidated taxable income for 1992 is $1,100. Adjustments to consolidated taxable income total $200, resulting in consolidated adjusted taxable income of $1,300. The group's net interest expense for 1992 is $800 ($1,600 – $800), its excess interest expense is $0 ($800 – ($2,100/2)), and it has excess limitation for the year of $250 ($2,100/2-$800). The group is permitted to deduct all of its current exempt related person interest expense ($800), plus an amount of its disallowed interest expense carryforward from 1991 equal to its 1992 excess limitation, or $250. This leaves a disallowed interest expense carryforward to the group's 1993 taxable year of $50.

Example (3). The facts are the same as in Example 2, except that Z leaves the group on December 31, 1992. Under the rules of paragraph (b)(6)(i) of this section, Z's disallowed interest expense carryforward to its 1993 separate return year is equal to the group's remaining carryforward at the end of 1992 ($50), multiplied by a fraction, the numerator of which is $300 (the total amount of exempt related person interest expense paid or accrued by Z while it was a member of the group) and the denominator of which is $1,550 (the total amount of exempt related person interest expense paid or accrued by all members of the group). Thus, Z's carryforward to its 1993 separate return year is $9.68. The XY group's carryforward to its consolidated 1993 taxable year is reduced by that amount, and is therefore $40.32.

(c) Operative rules for other groups. *(1) In general.* (i) Group members computation years. This paragraph (c) provides rules for the application of section 163(j) and these regulations to corporations that are members of a group not governed by paragraph (b) of this section. Under this paragraph (c), a corporation that is a group member is required to take into account the items of income, expense, and carryovers that are pertinent under section 163(j) for all group members whose taxable years end with or within the taxable year of the member with respect to which computations are required (hereafter, a "computation year").

(ii) Treatment of consolidated subgroup. If some of the members of a group subject to this paragraph (c) join in filing a consolidated return under section 1501 for a taxable year ("consolidated subgroup"), such consolidated subgroup shall be treated as a single member of the group for purposes of applying this paragraph (c). The consolidated subgroup's items of income, expense and carrryover that are pertinent under section 163(j) and these regulations shall be determined on a consolidated group basis, as if the consolidated subgroup were described in paragraph (b) of this section.

(2) Determination and allocation of group items. The computations required to be made under this paragraph (c) shall be made as follows—

(i) Step 1. Certain items determined separately. The exempt related person interest expense, interest income, interest expense, taxable income, and adjustments to taxable income required by § 1.163(j)-2(f), other than the adjustment for net interest expense described in § 1.163(j)-2(f)(2)(i), shall be determined separately for each member of the group.

(ii) Step 2. Computation of certain group items. (A) Net interest expense. The separately determined amounts of interest income and interest expense for each member shall be aggregated and then netted to determine the group's net interest expense.

(B) Adjusted taxable income. To determine the group's adjusted taxable income, the separately determined taxable income of each member and adjustments thereto (other than net interest expense) shall be aggregated, and the amount of the group's net interest expense (as determined under paragraph (c)(2)(ii)(A) of this section) shall be added to such amount.

(C) Exempt related person interest expense. To determine the amount of the group's exempt related person interest expense, the separately determined amounts of exempt related person interest expense for each member shall be aggregated. In making this determination, interest expense shall be treated as paid or accrued to a related person (within the meaning of § 1.163(j)-2(g)) if it would be so treated if paid or accrued to the same payee by any member of the group.

(D) Excess limitation carryforward. To determine the amount of the group's excess limitation carryforward from each of the three prior computation years, the amount of each member's excess limitation carryforward from each of such prior years shall be aggregated.

(E) Disallowed interest expense carryforward. To determine the amount of the group's disallowed interest expense carryforward, the amounts of disallowed interest expense carryforward of each member shall be aggregated.

(iii) Step 3. Determination of the group's interest deduction. (A) Excess interest expense of the group. The group's excess interest expense for the computation year shall be determined by reference to its net interest expense, adjusted taxable income, and excess limitation carryforward (as determined in Step 2). The ordering rule of § 1.163(j)-1(d) shall apply in determining which, if any, of the group's excess limitation carryforwards from prior years are absorbed in this computation.

(B) Disallowed interest expense of the group. The group's disallowed interest expense for the computation year shall be determined by reference to its exempt related person interest expense and excess interest expense as determined in Step 2 and Step 3. respectively. Disallowed interest expense of the group arising in the computation year shall be allocated to each member based on the following ratio:

$$\frac{\text{Exempt related person interest expense of the member for the computation year}}{\text{Exempt related person interest expense of the group for the computation year}}$$

(C) Excess limitation and deduction of disallowed interest expense carryforward. (1) Excess limitation. The group's excess limitation for the computation year shall be determined by reference to its net interest expense and adjusted taxable income (as determined in Step 2).

(2) Deduction of disallowed interest expense carryforward. The amount of the group's disallowed interest expense carried forward to the current computation year (as determined in Step 2) that is deductible therein under § 1.163(j)-1(c) shall be determined by reference to the excess limitation of the group. The deduction for such carryforward shall be allo-

cated to each member of the group based on the following ratio:

$$\frac{\text{Disallowed interest expense carryforward of the member from the preceding computation year}}{\text{Disallowed interest expense carryforward of the group from the preceding computation year}}$$

(iv) Step 4. Carryforwards to next computation year. (A) Amounts not deductible in the current computation year. Each member's disallowed interest expense carryforward to the next computation year shall consist of such member's allocable share of the group's disallowed interest expense for the current year (as determined in Step 3), plus such member's allocable share of the group's disallowed interest expense carryforward to the current year that is not deductible in the current year (because such amount exceeds any excess limitation of the group for that year). The group's unused disallowed interest expense carryforward to the current year shall be allocated to each member of the group based on the following ratio:

$$\frac{\text{Disallowed interest expense carryforward of the member from the preceding computation year}}{\text{Disallowed interest expense carryforward of the group from the preceding computation year}}$$

(B) Excess limitation carryforward. The excess limitation carryforward of the group, if any, from each of the two prior computation years that is not absorbed in the current computation year (as provided in Step 3) shall be allocated, by year, to each member of the group (succeeding computation years) based on the following ratio:

$$\frac{\text{Excess limitation carryforward of the member from the specific prior computation year}}{\text{Excess limitation carryforward of the group from the same prior computation year}}$$

(The group's excess limitation carryforward from the third prior computation year expires after the current computation year and therefore cannot be carried forward to the next year. See § 1.163(j)-1 (d).)

(C) Allocation of remaining excess limitation of the group for the computation year. (1) In general. Excess limitation of the group for the computation year remaining after the deduction of disallowed interest expense carryforward to such year is allocated to each member of the group based on the following ratio:

$$\frac{\text{Separate excess limitation for each member of the group for the computation year}}{\text{Total of the separate excess limitations of each member of the group for the computation year}}$$

(2) Separate excess limitation. The separate excess limitation of each member shall be computed as if the member was not a member of an affiliated group for the computation year. The separate excess limitation of each member shall be determined under the rules of § 1.163(j)-2(c) and before reduction for the amount of any disallowed interest expense carried forward to that year by such member. For purposes of these computations, a member that has net interest income for the computation year has net interest expense of zero, and a member that has excess interest expense for the computation year has separate excess limitation of zero.

(D) Members leaving a group. A member leaving a group shall carry forward to succeeding taxable years any excess limitation or disallowed interest expense allocated to it under this paragraph (c). For rules limiting the use of such carryforwards when such member becomes a member of another affiliated group, or has transferred its assets in a transaction to which section 381(a) applies, see § 1.163(j)-6.

(3) Examples. The following examples illustrate the principles of this paragraph (c).

Example (1). A, B, and C are calendar-year domestic corporations that are members of an affiliated group. Table 1 depicts amounts determined in Step 1 for these corporations for their taxable years ending December 31, 1991. Under rules described in paragraph (d) of this section, this group does not satisfy the debt-equity ratio safe harbor test for 1991. Assume, for purposes of this example, that there are no excess limitation carryforwards and no disallowed interest expense carryforwards to the 1991 taxable year for any member of the group.

Table 1

	Interest income	Interest expense	Taxable income before applying § 163 (j)	Adjustments to taxable income (not including net interest expense)	Exempt related person interest expense
A	$600.00	$ 500.00	$ 50.00	$ 25.00	
B	200.00	900.00	200.00	75.00	$600.00
C	—	200.00	50.00	—	150.00
Total	800.00	1,600.00	300.00	100.00	750.00

(a) Step 2 determinations. The group's Step 2 determinations are as follows:

(1) Net interest expense. The separately determined interest income and interest expense of A, B, and C are aggregated. Thus, the net interest expense of the group is $800 ($1,600 − $800).

(2) Adjusted taxable income. The separately determined taxable income and the separately determined adjustments (other than net interest expense) of A, B, and C are aggregated and added to the group's net interest expense to determine the group's adjusted taxable income of $1,200 ($300 + $100 + $800 = $1,200).

(3) Exempt related person interest expense. The separately determined amounts of exempt related person interest expense of A, B, and C are aggregated to determine the group's exempt related person interest expense of $750 ($600 + $150).

(b) Step 3 determinations. The group's Step 3 determinations are as follows:

(1) Excess interest expense. The group's excess interest expense is equal to its net interest expense less one-half of its adjusted taxable income (each as determined to Step 2) ($800 – (½ × $1,200) = $200).

(2) Disallowed interest expense. The group's disallowed interest is $200, which is the lesser of its exempt related person interest expense (as determined in Step 2 ($750)) or its excess interest expense (as determined in this Step 3 ($200)).

(3) Disallowed interest expense allocations. Disallowed interest expense for the computation year shall be allocated among A, B, and C under Step 3 based on the ratio of each member's exempt related person interest expense to the group's exempt related person interest expense. Since A has no exempt related person interest expense, no disallowed interest expense is allocated to it. Disallowed interest expense of $160 is allocated to B (($600/$750) × $200). Disallowed interest expense of $40 is allocated to C (($150/$750) × $200). Thus, B and C have $160 and $40, respectively, of disallowed interest expense which shall be carried forward to their succeeding taxable years under Step 4.

Example (2). The facts are the same as in Example 1, and thus B and C have $160 and $40, respectively, of disallowed interest expense carried forward to the computation year ending December 31, 1992. Table 2 depicts the separately determined items as determined in Step 1 for the taxable years of A, B, and C ending December 31, 1992. Under rules described in paragraph (d) of this section, this group does not satisfy the debt equity ratio safe harbor test for 1992.

Table 2

	Interest income	Interest expense	Taxable income before applying § 163 (j)	Adjustments to taxable income (not including net interest expense)	Exempt related person interest expense
A	$200.00	$ 800.00	$ 400.00	$ 50.00	$300.00
B	100.00	500.00	600.00	100.00	300.00
C	300.00	200.00	500.00	50.00	100.00
Total	600.00	1,500.00	1,500.00	200.00	700.00

(a) Step 2 determinations. For the 1992 computation year, the Step 2 determinations of A, B, and C are as follows:

(1) Net interest expense. The separately determined interest income and interest expense of A, B, and C are aggregated to determine the group's net interest expense of $900 ($1,500 – $600).

(2) Adjusted taxable income. The separately determined taxable income and adjustments to taxable income (other than net interest expense) of A, B, and C are aggregated and added to the group's net interest expense to yield the group's adjusted taxable income of $2,600 ($1,500 + $200 + $900 = $2,600).

(3) Exempt related person interest expense. Each member's separately determined amounts of exempt related person interest expense are aggregated to determine the group's exempt related person interest expense of $700 ($300 + $300 + $100).

(b) Step 3 determinations. The group has excess limitation of $400 in 1992 ((½ × $2,600) (adjusted taxable income) – $900 (net interest expense)). All $200 of the group's disallowed interest expense carried forward to 1992 is deductible by B and C (in accordance with the allocation described in Step 3) and reduces the group's excess limitation arising in 1992 to $200 ($400 – $200).

(c) Step 4 determinations. Under Step 4, A, B, and C must allocate the $200 of remaining excess limitation among themselves based on the ratio that each member's separate excess limitation bears to the sum of the member's separate excess limitations.

(1) Computation of each member's separate excess limitation. The separate excess limitation for each member shall be determined separately, as if each member was not a member of an affiliated group. Accordingly, the separate excess limitations of A, B, and C are determined as follows. A has separate excess interest expense of $75 ($600 – (½ × $1,050)). B has a separate excess limitation of $150 (½ × $1,100) – $400). C has separate excess limitation of $275 (½ × $500).

(2) Allocation of group excess limitation. Since A has separate excess interest expense rather than separate excess limitation, no excess limitation is allocated to A. The group's excess limitation of $200 is allocated between B and C as follows. B is allocated $70.59 ($200 × ($150/$425)) and C is allocated $129.41 ($200 × ($275/$425)). Thus, B and C will carry forward $70.59 and $129.41 of excess limitation, respectively, to their succeeding taxable years.

Example (3). A, B, and C are domestic corporations that are members of the same affiliated group under the rules of paragraph (a) of this section. Table 3 depicts their Step 1 determinations for A's taxable year ending September 30, 1990, B's taxable year ending December 31, 1990, and C's taxable year ending January 31, 1991. Assume, for the taxable years illustrated in Table 3, that there is no pre-effective date excess limitation carryforward, that (under the rules described in paragraph (d) of this section) the group does not satisfy the debt-equity ratio safe harbor test described in § 1.163 (j)-1 (b), and that all interest expense paid by A, B, and C is exempt related person interest expense.

Table 3

	Interest income	Interest expense	Taxable income before applying § 163 (j)	Adjustments to taxable income (not including net interest expense)	Exempt related person interest expense
A	$100.00	$ 500.00	$ 150.00	$ 50.00	$ 500.00
B	200.00	600.00	350.00	50.00	600.00
C		600.00	300.00	100.00	600.00
Total	300.00	1,700.00	800.00	200.00	1,700.00

(a) A's determinations. With respect to A's computation year ending September 30, 1990, only A is treated as a member of the affiliated group (since for B and C these are pre-effective date years). Therefore, A's disallowed interest expense is $100, which is the lesser of its excess interest expense of $100 ($400 – (½ × $600)) or its exempt related person interest expense ($500). As disallowed interest expense of $100, is carried forward to A's next computation year.

(b) B's Step 2 determinations. For purposes of computing B's disallowed interest expense for its taxable year ending December 31, 1990, only A and B are treated as affiliated group members (since for C this is a pre-effective date year). B's Step 2 determinations are as follows:

(1) Net interest expense. The separately determined interest income and interest expense of A and B are aggregated to determine their net interest expense of $800 ((500 + $600) – ($100 + $200)).

(2) Adjusted taxable income. The separately determined taxable income of A and B ($150 + $350) and the separately determined adjustments to their taxable income (other than net interest expense) ($50 + $50) are aggregated and added to their net interest expense (as provided in Step 2) ($800) to yield the adjusted taxable income of A and B of $1,400 ($500 + $100 + $800).

(3) Exempt related person interest expense. The separately determined amounts of exempt related person interest expense of A and B are aggregated to determine their exempt related person interest expense of $1,000 ($500 + $600).

(c) B's Step 3 determinations. B's Step 3 determinations are as follows:

(1) Excess interest expense. The excess interest expense of A and B is $100, which is equal to their net interest expense less one-half of their adjusted taxable income, each as determined in Step 2 ($800 – (½ × $1,400)).

(2) Disallowed interest expense. The disallowed interest expense of A and B is $100, which is the lesser of the exempt related person interest expense of A and B (as determined in Step 2 ($1,100)) or their excess interest expense (as determined in Step 3 ($100)).

(3) Disallowed interest expense allocations. Disallowed interest expense for the computation year is allocated to B under Step 3 based on the ratio of B's separate exempt related person interest expense ($600) to the sum of A and B's exempt related person interest expense ($1,100). Thus, the amount of disallowed interest expense allocated to B with respect to its computation year ending December 31, 1990, is $54.55 (($600/$1,100) × $100), which is carried forward to B's next computation year under Step 4. Because this is B's computation year, no allocation of disallowed interest expense for the computation year is made to A.

(d) C's Step 2 determinations. To compute its disallowed interest for its computation year ending January 31, 1991, C's Step 2 determinations are as follows:

(1) Net interest expense. The separately determined interest income and interest expense of A, B, and C are aggregated. Thus, the net interest expense of A, B, and C is $1,400 ($1,700 – $300).

(2) Adjusted taxable income. The separately determined taxable income of A, B, and C ($150 + $350 + 300) and the separately determined adjustments (other than net interest expense) of A, B, and C ($50 + $50 + $100) are aggregated and combined with the net interest expense of A, B, and C ($1,400, as determined in Step 2) to yield the adjusted taxable income of A, B, and C of $2,400 ($800 + $200 + $1,400).

(3) Exempt related person interest expense. The separately determined amounts of exempt related person interest expense of A, B, and C are aggregated to determine their exempt related person interest expense of $1,700 ($500 + $600 + $600).

(e) C's Step 3 determination. C's Step 3 determinations for its computation year ending January 31, 1991 are as follows:

(1) Excess interest expense. The excess interest expense of A, B, and C is equal to $200, which is the net interest expense of A, B, and C less one-half of their adjusted taxable incomes, each as determined in Step 2 ($1,400 – (½ × $2,400)).

(2) Disallowed interest expense. The disallowed interest expense of A, B, and C is $200, which is the lesser of the sum of the exempt related person interest expense of A, B, and C as determined in Step 2 ($1,700) or their excess interest expense as determined in this Step 3 ($200).

(3) Disallowed interest expense allocations. For C's computation year ending January 31, 1991, C is allocated disallowed interest expense under Step 3 based on the ratio that its exempt related person interest expense ($600) bears to the sum of the exempt related person interest expense of A, B, and C ($500 + $600 + $600 = $1,700). The amount of disallowed interest expense allocated to C with respect to that computation year is $70.59 (($600/$1,700) × $200), which is carried forward to C's next computation year under Step 4. Because this is C's computation year, no allocation of disallowed interest expense for the computation year is made to A or B.

(d) Debt-equity ratio of related corporations treated as one taxpayer. *(1) In general.* In the case of an affiliated § 1.163(j)-1(b) shall be applied on a group basis. In the case of a consolidated group subject to paragraph (b) of this section, the debt-equity ratio of the group shall be determined by aggregating the separately determined debt and assets (adjusted as described in paragraphs (d)(2) and (3) of this section) of each member of the group as of the last day of the consolidated return year. In the case of an affiliated group subject to the rules of paragraph (c) of this section, the debt-equity ratio of the group shall be determined, with respect to any member's computation year, by aggregating the separately determined debt and assets (adjusted as described in paragraphs (d)(2) and (3) of this section) of each member of the group as of the last day of its taxable year that is included in the computing member's computation year. For rules regarding the special treatment of, and an election pertaining to, assets of certain acquired corporations, see paragraph (e) of this section.

(2) Adjustments to group member's debt. A member's debt shall be reduced by the amount of its liabilities to another member, and by the amount of any other liability which, if included, would result in duplication of amounts in the group's aggregate debt.

(3) Adjustments to group member's assets. The assets of a member of a group shall be adjusted as follows—

(i) Any amount which represents direct or indirect stock ownership if any member of the affiliated group shall be eliminated from total assets of the affiliated group;

(ii) A note or other evidence of indebtedness between members of an affiliated group shall be eliminated as an asset;

(iii) With respect to transactions between members of an affiliated group in which gain or loss is deferred under §§ 1.1502-13, 1.1502-13T, 1.1502-14, or 1.1502-14T, the adjusted basis of any asset involved in such transaction shall be decreased to the extent of deferred intercompany gain, if any, that has not been taken into account; and

(iv) There shall be eliminated from the assets of the affiliated group any other amount which, if included, would result in duplication of the assets of the affiliated group.

(e) Election to use fixed stock write-off method for certain stock acquisitions. *(1) In general.* Notwithstanding paragraph (d)(3) of this section, in the case of a qualified stock purchase, an election may be made, in the manner described in paragraph (e)(4) of this section, to determine the group's assets in accordance with the following rules—

(i) The stock of the target corporation and target affiliates (other than stock that is described in paragraph (d)(1)(ii) of this section) shall be treated as an asset of the purchasing corporation. The basis of such stock shall be determined under section 1012, and shall be increased by the amount of the liabilities of the target corporation and target affiliates as of the close of the acquisition date. Solely for purposes of this section, these amounts (together, the "special basis") shall be amortized ratably, on a monthly basis, over the applicable fixed stock write-off period (as described in paragraph (e)(5)(vi) of this section), beginning with the first day of the month in which the acquisition date occurs.

(ii) All assets of the target corporation, target affiliates, and any other members of the affiliated group, the stock of which is owned directly or indirectly by the target or a target affiliate, shall be disregarded.

(iii) Adjustments shall be made to the special basis of the stock of the target corporation and target affiliates solely as provided in paragraphs (e)(1)(i) and (e)(2) of this section. Thus, for example, the special basis shall not be adjusted under the rules of § 1.1502-32.

(2) Post-acquisition adjustments to special basis. The following adjustments shall be made to the special basis of the target corporation and target affiliates—

(i) The special basis of the stock of the target corporation and target affiliates shall be increased under the rules of section 358 for any property contributed to such corporations following the acquisition date;

(ii) The special basis of the stock of the target corporation and target affiliates shall be reduced by the fair market value of any property distributed by such corporations. Solely for purposes of the preceding sentence, any transfer of assets by the target corporation, by any target affiliate, or by any corporation that would be a target affiliate but for the fact that it is not an includible corporation, to any member of the affiliated group other than such corporations, shall be deemed to be a distribution that reduces special basis, but only if such transfer qualifies for nonrecognition under any provision of the Code or is an interaffiliate loan; and

(iii) Where an adjustment is made pursuant to paragraphs (e)(2)(i) or (ii) of this section, the special basis shall be adjusted as of the last day of the month which includes the date of the transaction (or the last day of the shareholder's taxable year, whichever comes first), and the adjusted amount shall be amortized over the remaining amortization period.

(3) Election out affixed stock write-off method. A taxpayer may elect out of the fixed stock write-off method for any year during the amortization period and use the adjusted tax basis of the assets of the target corporation and its target affiliates to determine its debt-equity ratio for that year and all future years.

(4) Method for making elections. (i) Election to use method. An election to use the fixed stock write-off method is made by attaching a statement to the return of the purchasing corporation (including a consolidated return, where appropriate) for the taxable year that includes the acquisition date for the qualified stock purchase. The election must be signed by an authorized official of, and is effective for, each member of the purchasing corporation's affiliated group.

(ii) Election to cease to use method. An election to cease to use the fixed stock write-off method is made by attaching a statement to the return of the purchasing corporation (including a consolidated return, where appropriate) for the taxable year in which the election is to become effective. The election must be signed by an authorized official of, and is effective for, each member of the purchasing corporation's affiliated group.

(5) Definitions. (i) Qualified stock purchase. For purposes of this paragraph (e), the term "qualified stock purchase" means a qualified stock purchase (as defined under section 338(d)(3)) with respect to which no election has been made under section 338(g), but only if the purchase is made by a corporation which is an includible corporation (as defined in section 1504(b)).

(ii) Target corporation. For purposes of this paragraph (e), the term "target corporation" shall mean a target corporation as defined under section 338(d)(2), but only if such corporation is includible within the purchasing corporation's affiliated group for purposes of this section.

(iii) Target affiliate. For purposes of this paragraph (e), the term "target affiliate" shall mean a target affiliate as defined under section 338(h)(6), but only if such corporation is includible within the purchasing corporation's affiliated group for purposes of this section.

(iv) Purchasing corporation. For purposes of this paragraph (e), the term "purchasing corporation" shall mean a purchasing corporation as defined under section 338(d)(1).

(v) Acquisition date. For purposes of this paragraph (e), the term "acquisition date" shall mean the acquisition date as defined under section 338(h)(2).

(vi) Fixed stock write-off period (A) In general. Except as provided in paragraph (e)(5)(vi)(B) of this section, the applicable "fixed stock write-off period" means 96 months.

(B) Acquired corporations owning long-lived assets. If more than fifty percent, by value, of the assets of the target corporation and any target affiliates on the acquisition date are described in this paragraph (e)(5)(vi)(B), then the applicable "fixed stock write-off period means 180 months. An asset is described in this paragraph (e)(5)(vi)(B) if—

(1) It is inventory or a non-wasting tangible or intangible asset (e.g., land or goodwill);

(2) In the case of a depreciable asset, it has a recovery period in excess of 25 years;

(3) In the case of a depletable asset, it has a recovery period for purposes of cost depletion in excess of 25 years;

(4) In the case of an amortizable asset, it has an amortization period in excess of 25 years. Determinations for purposes of this paragraph (e)(5)(vi)(B) shall be made as if the asset were sold on the acquisition date, and cash, cash items, and marketable securities shall be disregarded for all purposes. A purchasing corporation is only entitled to the benefit of the paragraph (e)(5)(vi)(B) if it demonstrates that it satisfies the requirements of this paragraph in a statement attached to its return accompanying its election to use the fixed stock write-off method. Such statement must provide all necessary information, including all appropriate computations.

(6) Inclusion of target debt notwithstanding use affixed stock write-off method. Debt of the affiliated group includes the liabilities of a target corporation and any target affiliates notwithstanding that the assets of such corporations are determined using the fixed stock write-off method.

Proposed § 1.163(j)-6 Limitation on carryforward of tax attributes. [*For Preamble, see ¶ 151,279*]

(a) Disallowed interest expense carryforward. *(1) Affiliated groups.* If a corporation becomes a member of an affiliated group, the amount of any disallowed interest expense carryforward from a non-affiliation year that may be deducted by the members of an affiliated group under § 1.163(j)-5(b) or (c) may not exceed the amount, if any, of the current year's excess limitation of the affiliated group (determined under §§ 1.163(j)-2(c) and 1.163(j)-5(b) or (c).

(2) Section 381(a) transactions. The amount of any disallowed interest expense carryforward from a non-affiliation year of a transferor or distributor corporation that may be deducted by the transferee or distributee corporation (or the consolidated group of which it is a member) following a transaction described in section 381(a) may not exceed the amount, if any, of the current year's excess limitation (determined under § 1.163(j)-2(c)).

(3) Section 382 and SRLY. For the application of additional limitations governing disallowed interest expense carryovers, see section 382(h) (relating to built-in deductions of loss corporations) and the regulations thereunder (including § 1.1502-91, relating to section 382(h) rule for built-in deductions of consolidated groups) and § 1.1502-15 (relating to separate return limitation year rules for built-in deductions of consolidated groups)).

(4) Example. The provisions of this paragraph (a) are illustrated by the following example.

Example. In 1992, Z, a non-affiliated corporation, becomes a member of a consolidated group. There is no section 382 ownership change. Under § 1.163(j)-1, Z has $3,000 of disallowed interest expense carryforward from separate return limitation years. Under § 1.163(j)-5(b), the consolidated group (including Z) has excess limitation of $2,000 for 1992 (computed without regard to any disallowed interest expense carryforward). In addition, the consolidated group has excess limitation carryforward of $1,000 from 1991. Under paragraph (a)(1) of this section, only $2,000 (the amount of the consolidated group's excess limitation for 1992) of S's separate return limitation year disallowed interest expense carryforward is deductible in 1992. The remaining $1,000 of S's disallowed interest expense carryforward is carried forward to subsequent years and remains subject to the limitations described in paragraph (a) of this section.

(b) Excess limitation carryforward. *(1) Affiliated groups.* (i) General rule. If a corporation becomes a member of an affiliated group, the amount of any excess limitation carryforward from a non-affiliation year that may be used by members of the group under § 1.163(j)-5(b) or (c) may not exceed the excess, if any, of the corporation's separately computed net interest expense over 50 percent of the corporation's separately computed adjusted taxable income.

(ii) Special rule for acquired groups. If all the members of a group, whether or not consolidated, become members of a consolidated group, the amount of the acquired group's excess limitation carryforward (if any) from non-affiliation years that may be used by the consolidated group may not exceed the acquired group's excess interest expense (if any) for the taxable year. For this purpose, the acquired group's excess interest expense for any taxable year equals the excess interest expense of the former members of the acquired group for the taxable year computed as if they were members of a separate affiliated group making computations under § 1.163(i)-5(c).

(2) Section 381(a) transactions. If a corporation transfers or distributes its assets to another corporation in a transaction described in section 381(a) (other than a transaction described in section 368(a)(1)(F)), the excess limitation carryforward, if any, of the transferor or distributor from a non-affiliation year is reduced to zero immediately after the transaction.

(3) Anti-avoidance rules. Solely for purposes of paragraph (b)(1) of this section, in determining the net interest expense of a member or a group, interest expense paid or accrued with respect to loans incurred or assumed by such member in connection with or after becoming a member of the group are disregarded unless the loan proceeds are actually utilized by the member in its pre-affiliation business. For example, if a loan is incurred by one member of the affiliated group with excess limitation carryforward from non-affiliation years, but the proceeds of the loan are actually utilized by another member of the group, the interest expense with respect to the loan is disregarded for purposes of applying paragraph (b)(1) of this section. In addition, interest on a loan used for the acquisition of the stock of a corporation which is incurred by the acquired corporation may be disregarded for purposes of paragraph (b)(1) of this section if the facts indicate that one of the purposes for the acquired corporation's incurring the loan was to avoid the limitation of such paragraph.

(c) Affiliation and non-affiliation years. *(1) In general.* For purposes of this section, the taxable year of a member of an affiliated group (as defined in § 1.163(j)-5(a)) is an "affiliation year" with respect to another member if the members were members of an affiliated group (whether or not the same affiliated group as the current affiliated group) with each other on the last day of the taxable year. A "non-affiliated year" is any taxable year that is not an affiliation year,

(2) Predecessors and successors. For purposes of this section, any reference to a corporation or member or the years of a corporation or member includes, as the context may require, a reference to a successor or predecessor (as defined in § 1.1502-1(f)(4)) or to the years of a successor or predecessor.

(3) Formation of affiliated groups. For purposes of determining whether a corporation has become a member of another corporation's affiliated group solely by reason of § 1.163(j)-5(a). corporations (or affiliated groups) with greater value are deemed to acquire corporations (or affiliated groups) with lesser value and the principles of § 1.1502-75(d)(3) (governing "reverse acquisitions") shall apply.

(d) Anti-duplication rule. The same item of income, expense, or carryforward may not be taken into account more than once if inconsistent with the principles of section 163(j) or these regulations.

Proposed § 1.163(j)-7 Relationship to other provisions affecting the deductibility of interest. [*For Preamble, see ¶ 151,279*]

Caution: The Treasury has not yet amended Reg § 1.163(j)-7 to reflect changes made by P.L. 104-188.

(a) Paid or accrued. For purposes of section 163(j), interest expense is not considered "paid or accrued" until such interest would be deductible but for such section.

(b) Coordination of section 163(j) and certain other provisions. *(1) Disallowed interest provisions.* Except as provided under § 1.163(j)-2(f)(3)(vi), interest expense which is permanently disallowed as a deduction (e.g. under sections 265 or 279) is not taken into account under section 163(j).

(2) Deferred interest provisions. Provisions which defer the deductibility of interest (such as sections 163(e)(3) and 267(a)(3)) apply before the application of section 163(j).

(3) At risk rules and passive activity loss provisions. Sections 465 and 469 shall be applied before applying section 163(j). There shall be no recomputation of deductions under section 469.

(4) Capitalized interest expenses. Provisions that require the capitalization of interest shall be applied before section 163(j). Capitalized interest is not treated as interest for any purpose under section 163(j). See regulations under section 263A(f) for ordering rules that determine whether exempt related person interest expense is capitalized under section 263A(f).

(5) Reductions under section 216A. Section 246A shall be applied before section 163(j). Any reduction in the dividends received deduction under section 246A shall reduce interest expense taken into account under section 163(j).

(c) Examples. The provisions of this section are illustrated by the following examples.

Example (1). (i) In 1990, Z, a domestic corporation that does not satisfy the debt-equity ratio safe harbor test, has $30,000 of interest expense, all of which is paid to related persons, and no interest income. Of Z's interest expense, $10.000 is permanently disallowed under section 265. The remaining $20,000 of interest expense is exempt from tax under the rules of § 1.163(j)-4. Z's adjusted taxable income for the year is $42,000.

(ii) Under paragraph (b)(1) of this section, the $10.000 interest expense that is permanently disallowed is not taken into consideration for purposes of section 163(j) Therefore, in 1990, none of Z's $20,000 interest expense is disallowed under section 163(j) since that amount is less than 50 percent of Z's 1990 adjusted taxable income ($21,000).

Example (2). (i) In 1990, Q, a domestic corporation that does not satisfy the debt-equity ratio safe harbor test, has $80,000 of adjusted taxable income and $60,000 of interest expense, of which $50,000 is exempt related person interest expense. Q has no interest income. Of Q's exempt related person interest expense, $20,000 is not currently deductible under section 267(a)(2). Assume that the $20,000 expense will be allowed as a deduction under section 267(a)(2) in 1991.

(ii) Under paragraph (b)(2) of this section, section 267(a)(2) is applied before section 163(i). Thus, in computing Q's excess interest expense for 1990, the $20,000 is not taken into account. Accordingly, in 1990, Q has no excess interest expense, since its net interest expense of $40,000 ($60,000 – $20,000) is equal to 50 percent of its adjusted taxable income for the taxable year. The $20,000 of interest expense not allowed as a deduction in 1990 under section 267(a)(2) is taken into account under section 163(j) in 1991, the year in which it is allowed as a deduction under section 267(a)(2).

Example (3). (i) for 1990, H, a closely held domestic corporation that does not satisfy the debt-equity ratio safe harbor test, has $2,000 of rental income and $3,000 of deductions consisting of $1,500 of interest expense, all of which is exempt related person interest expense, $600 of rental expense, and of depreciation expense. Under the passive activity loss provisions of section 469, only $2,000 of H's total expenses are allowable as deductions. These consist of $1,000 ($2,000/$3,000 × $1,500) of interest expense, $400 (2,000/$3,000 × $600) of rental expense, and $500 of depreciation expense ($2,000/$3,600 × $900). No deduction is allowed in 1990 for H's passive activity loss of $1,000, which consists of $500 of interest expense, $200 of rental expense, and $300 of depreciation expense.

(ii) Under paragraph (b)(3) of this section, section 469 is first applied to determine the amount of interest expense allowable as a deduction ($1,000), after which the rules of section 163(j) are applied. Under section 163(j), H's $1.000 of interest expense is allowable to the extent of 50 percent of its adjusted taxable income ($1.600, determined by adding to H's taxable income (zero) its allowable deductions for interest expense ($1,000) and depreciation deductions ($600). Since H's interest expense of $1,600 (determined after applying section 469) exceeds 50 percent of its adjusted taxable income for 1990 ($800), H's excess Interest expense of $200 is disallowed under section 163(j). There is no recomputation of deductions under section 469.

Proposed § 1.163(j)-8 Application of section 163(j) to certain foreign corporations. [*For Preamble, see ¶ 151,279*]

(a) Scope. A foreign corporation that has income, gain or loss that is effectively connected (or is treated as effectively connected) with the conduct of a trade or business in the United States for the taxable year will be subject to the rules of this section for the taxable year, provided that it has a debt-equity ratio that exceeds 1.5 to 1 on the last day of the taxable year, computed using the definitions of debt and equity under paragraph (e) of this section.

(b) Disallowed interest expense. In computing its effectively connected taxable income for a taxable year, a foreign corporation described in paragraph (a) of this section will not be allowed to deduct interest expense allocated to Its effectively connected income that it has paid, or is deemed to have paid, to a related person (as determined under paragraph (d) of this section) if no tax is imposed with respect to such interest as determined under § 1.163(j)-4. The amount of interest expense disallowed under this paragraph (b), however, shall not exceed the corporation's excess interest expense (as defined in paragraph (c)(2) of this section). Any interest expense that is disallowed under this section may be carried forward to a subsequent taxable year of the foreign corporation and allowed in such year to the extent provided in §§ 1.163 (j)-1(c) and 1.163(j)-6 (a)(2) and (3). See § 1.163(j)-7 for rules relating to the coordination of this section with other provisions of the Code affecting the deductibility of interest.

(c) Definitions. *(1) In general.* The terms "net interest expense", "adjusted taxable income", "excess interest expense", and "excess limitation" shall have the same meanings as provided elsewhere in these regulations under section 163(j), with the following additions and modifications. All other terms used in this section shall have the same meanings as provided elsewhere in these regulations under section 163(j).

(2) Net interest expense. The net interest expense of a foreign corporation means the excess, if any, of interest expense that is allocated to the effectively connected income of the foreign corporation for the taxable year and that is taken into account under section 163(j) as provided in § 1.163(j)-7, over the amount of interest includible in its effectively connected gross income for the taxable year.

(3) Adjust taxable income. The adjusted taxable income of a foreign corporation is its effectively connected taxable income that is not exempt from tax by reason of a U.S. income tax treaty, modified by the additions, and subtractions provided in § 1.163(j)-2(f) that are attributable to such effectively connected income.

(4) Excess interest expense. The excess interest expense of a foreign corporation is the excess of its net interest expense determined under paragraph (c)(2) of this section over the sum of 50 percent of its adjusted taxable income determined under paragraph (c)(3) of this section plus any excess limitation carryforward determined under §§ 1.163 (j)-1 (d) and 1.163 (j)-6 (b)(2).

(5) Excess limitation. The excess limitation of a foreign corporation means the excess, if any, of 50 percent of the adjusted taxable income of the foreign corporation (determined under paragraph (c)(3) of this section), over its net interest expense (determined under paragraph (c)(2) of this section). For rules regarding the carryforward of any excess limitation of a foreign corporation, see §§ 1.163(j)-1(d) and 1.63(j)-6(b)(2).

(d) Determination of interest paid to a related person. For purposes of this section, the amount of interest that is paid, or deemed paid, by a foreign corporation to a related person, as defined in § 1.163(j)-2(g), shall equal the sum of the amount of interest paid by a U.S. trade or business of the foreign corporation under section 884(f)(1)(A) to a person that is related to the foreign corporation and the amount of interest described in section 884(f)(1)(B) ("excess interest" within the meaning of § 1.884-4T(a)).

(e) Debt-equity ratio. For purposes of computing the debt-equity ratio of a foreign corporation subject to the rules of this section, the debt of the foreign corporation shall equal the amount of its worldwide liabilities for purposes of Step 2 of § 1.882-5, adjusted in accordance with the rules in § 1.163(j)-3(b) without regard to 1.163(j)-(b)(3). The equity of the foreign corporation shall equal the amount of its worldwide assets for purposes of Step 2 of § 1.882-5, adjusted in accordance with the rules in § 1.163(j)-3(c) without regard to § 1.163(j)-3(c)(4), less its worldwide liabilities as determined in the preceding sentence.

(f) Example. The rules of paragraphs (b) through (e) of this section may be illustrated with the following example.

Example. FC, a country X corporation, is engaged in the active conduct of a trade or business in the United States. FP, a country X corporation, owns all the stock of FC. The debt-equity ratio of FC under paragraph (e) of this section is 3:1. FC has $700 of adjusted taxable income under paragraph (c)(3) of this section, and net interest expense of $600 ($600 of Interest expense allocated under § 1.882-5 over $0 of effectively connected interest income) under paragraph (c)(2) of this section. Under § 1.884-4T, $600 of FC's allocated interest expense is treated as interest paid by the U.S. trade or business of FC to FP, and $100 of FC's allocated interest expense is treated as if it were paid by a wholly owned domestic corporation to FC. FC and FP are both qualified residents of country X. Under the treaty, the rate of tax on the $500 of interest paid to FP and on FC's $100 of excess interest is reduced from 30 percent to 10 percent. Thus, of the $600 of interest paid or deemed paid by FC to related persons, two-thirds of the interest is treated as tax-exempt, or $400. The excess interest expense of FC is the excess of FC's net interest exense ($600) over 50 percent of FC's adjusted taxable income ($350) or $250. Thus, $250 of the $400 of interest paid by FC to tax-exempt related persons will be disallowed in computing FC's effectively connected taxable income for the taxable year but may be carried over by FC to a subsequent taxable year.

(g) Coordination with branch profits tax. *(1) Effect on effectively connected earnings and profits.* The disallowance and carryforward of interest expense under this section shall not affect when such interest expense reduces the effectively connected earnings and profits of a foreign corporation, as defined in § 1.884-1T(f).

(2) Effect on U.S. net equity. The disallowance and carryforward of interest expense under this section shall not affect the computation of the U.S. net equity of a foreign corporation, as defined in § 1.884-1T (c).

(3) Example. The principles of this § 1.163(j)-8(g) are illustrated by the following example.

Example. Assume foreign corporation FC uses money that is treated as a U.S. asset under § 1.884-1T(d)(6) in order to pay interest described in paragraph (d) of this section, and that under this section a deduction for such interest expense is disallowed. Assuming that FC's U.S. assets otherwise remain constant during the year, the U.S. assets of FC will have decreased by the amount of money used to pay the interest expense, and the U.S. net equity of FC will be computed accordingly.

Proposed § 1.163(j)-9 Guarantees and back-to-back loans. [Reserved] [*For Preamble, see ¶ 151,279*]

Proposed § 1.163(j)-10 Effective dates. [*For Preamble, see ¶ 151,279*]

(a) In general. Section 163(j) generally applies to interest paid or accrued directly or indirectly by the payor corporation in its taxable years beginning after July 10, 1989.

(b) Exceptions. *(1) Interest paid on certain fixed-term obligations outstanding on July 10, 1989.* (i) In general. Interest paid or accrued with respect to a fixed-term debt obligation outstanding on July 10, 1989, shall not be treated as disallowed interest expense, even though such interest is paid or accrued in a taxable year of the payor corporation beginning after July 10, 1989. Such interest expense is, however, taken into account under section 163(j) for all other purposes (e.g. determining whether other interest expense paid or accrued during the taxable year is treated as excess interest expense).

(ii) Certain obligations issued pursuant to written contracts binding on July 10, 1989. (A) In general. Interest paid or accrued with respect to a fixed-term obligation that is issued after July 10, 1989, pursuant to a written contract binding on that date and at all times thereafter until the issuance of the obligation, shall be treated in the same manner as interest paid or accrued with respect to a fixed-term debt obligation outstanding on July 10, 1959 [sic 1989].

(B) Whether a contract is binding. In determining whether a contract is a binding contract, the following rules apply:

(1) A written contract between related persons (as defined in § 1.163(j)-2(g)) shall only be treated as binding on a particular date if it was enforceable on that date (whether on the basis of reliance or otherwise) by an unrelated third party.

(2) A written contract duly executed by authorized individuals on or before July 10, 1989, will not be considered non-binding solely because it is subject to a condition outside the control of the parties; insubstantial contract terms remain to be negotiated by the parties; or it is subject to approval by the board of directors of a corporate party where, prior to July 11, 1989, the board had authorized or been apprised of the status of negotiations and formal board approval occurred reasonably promptly following execution of the written contract without further change to the agreement (except for insubstantial contract terms).

(iii) Modification of certain fixed-term obligations outstanding on July 10, 1989. (A) In general. If an obligation described in paragraphs (b)(1)(i) or (b)(1)(ii) of this section is modified after July 10, 1989, it shall be treated thereafter as a new obligation for purposes of section 163(j).

(B) Modification defined. (1) In general. Except as provided in this paragraph (b)(1)(ii)(B), an obligation described in paragraphs (b)(1)(i) or (b)(1)(ii) of this section shall be treated as modified for purposes of paragraph (b)(1)(iii)(A) of this section if it is revised (whether by renegotiation, assumption, reissuance, or otherwise) in a manner that would give rise to a deemed exchange of debt instruments by the obligee under section 1001. In any case, an obligation shall not be treated as modified under this paragraph (b)(1)(iii)(A) solely because a new obligor is substituted for the original obligor to reflect the terms of a reorganization described in section 368(a) or incident to a liquidation described in section 332(a).

(2) Extension of maturity date. An obligation shall be treated as modified if its maturity date is extended even if such extension would not give rise to a deemed exchange of debt instruments under section 1001.

(3) Anti-abuse rule. If a fixed-term debt obligation outstanding on July 10, 1989, or an obligation described in paragraph (b)(1)(ii)(A) of this section, is acquired by a person related to the obligor (within the meaning of § 1.183(j)-2(g)) from an obligee that is not so related, and the obligor (or any member of its affiliated group) issues new debt that has the effect of replacing the acquired debt (whether or not such issuance is to the original obligee), the acquired obligation shall be treated as modified for purposes of paragraph (b)(1)(iii) of this section.

(2) Demand loans. Interest paid or accrued prior to September 1, 1989, on a demand loan (or other obligation with no fixed term) outstanding on July 10, 1989, shall not be treated as disallowed by section 183(j) even though it is paid or accrued in a taxable year beginning after the latter date. Such interest expense is, however, taken into account under section 183(j) for all other purposes.

(c) Carryforward of excess limitation from pre-effective date taxable years to post-effective date taxable years. In computing a corporation's excess limitation carryforwards for its first, second, and third taxable years beginning after July 10, 1989, a corporation shall take into account amounts that would have been treated as excess limitation carryforwards to those years as if section 163(j) had been in effect throughout the corporation's taxable years beginning after July 10, 1986. For this purpose, such corporation shall be treated as having had zero excess limitation or disallowed interest expense carried forward to its first taxable year beginning after July 10, 1986.

(d) Examples. The following examples illustrate the operation of this section.

Example (1). (i) S is a calendar year domestic corporation. In each of 1987, 1988, 1969, and 1990, S's adjusted taxable income is $100. In 1987, 1988, 1989, and 1990, S's net interest expense is $40, $54, $55, and $50, respectively. All of S's interest expense for these years is exempt related person interest expense incurred with respect to demand loans. S does not satisfy the debt-equity ratio safe harbor test in 1990.

(ii) Pursuant to § 1.1630(j)-2(c) and this section, S has excess limitation of $10 n 1967 which (subject to the limitations described in § 1.163(j)-1(d)) can be carried forward to its next three succeeding taxable years. In 1988, C's excess limitation carryforward from 1987 is reduced by $4 (its excess interest expense ($54) over 50 percent of its adjusted taxable income ($50)).

(iii) In 1989, $5 of S's $6 excess limitation carryforward from 1988 is applied against, and reduced by, S's $5 excess interest expense.

(iv) In 1990, the $1 balance of S's excess limitation carryforward from 1987 expires without tax benefit to S.

Example (2). (i) The facts are the same as in Example 1, except as follows: In 1988, S's net interest expense is $49. S's net interest expense is $55 in 1989, $50 in 1990, and $55 in 1991. S does not satisfy the debt-equity ratio safe harbor test in 1991.

(ii) In 1988, S has excess limitation carried forward from 1987 of $10, none of which is used or expires in 1988, and has excess limitation of $1 for 1988. In 1989, $5 of S's excess limitation carryforward from 1987 reduces to zero the amount of S's excess interest expense in that year. Thus, in 1990, S has total available excess limitation carryforward of $6, of which $5 is from 1987 and $1 from 1988. All $5 of S's remaining excess limitation carryforward from 1987 expires without tax benefit to S in 1990. In 1991, the $1 of excess limitation carryforward from 1988 reduces S's disallowed interest expense to $4.

Example (3). (i) D is a calendar-year domestic corporation. In 1987 and 1988, D's adjusted taxable income is $120 and its net interest expense is $60. In 1989, D's adjusted taxable income is $100 and its net interest expense is $30. In 1990, D has negative adjusted taxable income (i.e. an adjusted taxable loss) of $100 and $50 of net interest expense. In each year, all of D's net interest expense is exempt related person interest expense incurred with respect to demand loans.

(ii) D has neither excess limitation nor excess interest expense from 1987 and 1998. In 1989, D has $20 ($50-$30) of excess limitation which (subject to the limitations described in § 1.163(j)-1(d)) can be carried forward to its next three succeeding taxable years. In 1990, D's first taxable year in which its interest expense may be disallowed as a deduction under section 163(j) the $20 of excess limitation D carried forward from 1989 is reduced (but not below zero) by its $100 adjusted taxable loss for that year under § 1.163(j)-2(f)(4). Therefore, none of D's excess limitation carryforward from 1989 can be applied to reduce D's $50 excess interest expense in 1990.

§ 1.164-1 Deduction for taxes.

> ***Caution:*** The Treasury has not yet amended Reg § 1.164-1 to reflect changes made by P.L. 110-343, P.L. 99-514, P.L. 98-21, P.L. 96-223.

(a) In general. Only the following taxes shall be allowed as a deduction under this section for the taxable year within which paid or accrued, according to the method of accounting used in computing taxable income:

(1) State and local, and foreign, real property taxes.

(2) State and local personal property taxes.

(3) State and local, and foreign, income, war profits, and excess profits taxes.

(4) State and local general sales taxes.

(5) State and local taxes on the sale of gasoline, diesel fuel, and other motor fuels. In addition, there shall be allowed as a deduction under this section State and local, and foreign, taxes not described in subparagraphs (1) through (5) of this paragraph which are paid or accrued within the taxable year in carrying on a trade or business or an activity described in section 212 (relating to expenses for production of income). For example, dealers or investors in securities and dealers or investors in real estate may deduct State stock transfer and real estate transfer taxes, respectively, under section 164, to the extent they are expenses incurred in carrying on a trade or business or an activity for the production of income. In general, taxes are deductible only by the person upon whom they are imposed. However, see § 1.164-5 in the case of certain taxes paid by the consumer.

In addition, there shall be allowed as a deduction under this section State and local, and foreign, taxes not described in subparagraphs (1) through (5) of this paragraph which are paid or accrued within the taxable year in carrying on a trade or business or an activity described in section 212 (relating to expenses for production of income). For example, dealers or investors in securities and dealers or investors in real estate may deduct State stock transfer and real estate transfer taxes, respectively, under section 164, to the extent they are expenses incurred in carrying on a trade or business or an activity for the production of income. In general, taxes are deductible only by the person upon whom they are imposed. However, see § 1.164-5 in the case of certain taxes paid by the consumer. Also, in the case of a qualified State individual income tax (as defined in section 6362 and the regulations thereunder) which is determined by reference to a percentage of the Federal income tax (pursuant to section 6362(c)), an accrual method taxpayer shall use the cash receipts and disbursements method to compute the amount of his deduction therefor. Thus, the deduction under section 164 is in the amount actually paid with respect to the qualified tax, rather than the amount accrued with respect thereto, during the taxable year even though the taxpayer uses the accrual method of accounting for other purposes. In addition, see paragraph (f)(1) of § 301.6361-1 of this chapter (Regulations on Procedure and Administration) with respect to rules relating to allocation and reallocation of amounts collected on account of the Federal income tax and qualified taxes.

(b) Taxable years beginning before January 1, 1964. For taxable years beginning before January 1, 1964, except as otherwise provided in §§ 1.164-2 through 1.164-8, inclusive, taxes imposed by the United States, any State, territory, possession of the United States, or a political subdivision of any of the foregoing, or by any foreign country, are deductible from gross income for the taxable year in which paid or accrued, according to the method of accounting used in computing taxable income. For this purpose, postage is not a tax and automobile license or registration fees are ordinarily taxes.

(c) Cross references. For the definition of the term "real property taxes", see paragraph (b) of § 1.164-3. For the definition of the term "foreign taxes", see paragraph (d) of § 1.164-4. For the definition of the term "general sales taxes", see paragraph (f) of § 1.164-3. For the treatment of gasoline, diesel fuel, and other motor fuel taxes, see § 1.164-5. For apportionment of taxes on real property between seller and purchaser, see section 164(d) and § 1.164-6. For the general rule for taxable year of deduction, see section 461. For provisions disallowing any deduction for the tax paid at the source on interest from tax-free covenant bonds, see section 1451(f).

T.D. 6256, 10/7/57, amend T.D. 6406, 8/14/59, T.D. 6780, 12/21/64, T.D. 7577, 12/19/78.

---

§ 1.164-2 Deduction denied in case of certain taxes.

> ***Caution:*** The Treasury has not yet amended Reg § 1.164-2 to reflect changes made by P.L. 99-514, P.L. 98-21.

This section and § 1.275 describe certain taxes for which no deduction is allowed. In the case of taxable years beginning before January 1, 1964, the denial is provided for by section 164(b) (prior to being amended by section 207 of the Revenue Act of 1964 (78 Stat. 40)). In the case of taxable years beginning after December 31, 1963, the denial is governed by sections 164 and 275. No deduction is allowed for the following taxes:

(a) Federal income taxes. Federal income taxes, including the taxes imposed by section 3101, relating to the tax on employees under the Federal Insurance Contributions Act (chapter 21 of the Code); sections 3201 and 3211, relating to the taxes on railroad employees and railroad employee representatives; section 3402, relating to the tax withheld at source on wages; and by corresponding provisions of prior internal revenue laws.

(b) Federal war profits and excess profits taxes. Federal war profits and excess profits taxes including those imposed by Title II of the Revenue Act of 1917 (39 Stat. 1000), Title III of the Revenue Act of 1918 (40 Stat. 1088), Title III of the Revenue Act of 1921 (42 Stat. 271), section 216 of the National Industrial Recovery Act (48 Stat. 208), section 702 of the Revenue Act of 1934 (48 Stat. 770), subchapter D, chapter 1 of the Internal Revenue Code of 1939, and subchapter E, chapter 2 of the Internal Revenue Code of 1939.

(c) Estate and gift taxes. Estate, inheritance, legacy, succession, and gift taxes.

(d) Foreign income, war profits, and excess profits taxes. Income, war profits, and excess profits taxes imposed by the authority of any foreign country or possession of the United States, if the taxpayer chooses to take to any extent the benefits of section 901, relating to the credit for taxes of foreign countries and possessions of the United States.

(e) Real property taxes. Taxes on real property, to the extent that section 164(d) and § 1.164-6 require such taxes to be treated as imposed on another taxpayer.

(f) Federal duties and excise taxes. Federal import or tariff duties, business, license, privilege, excise, and stamp taxes (not described in paragraphs (a), (b), (c) or (h) of this section, or § 1.164-4) paid or accrued within the taxable year. The fact that any such tax is not deductible as a tax under section 164 does not prevent (1) its deduction under section 162 or section 212, provided it represents an ordinary and necessary expense paid or incurred during the taxable year by a corporation or an individual in the conduct of any trade or business or, in the case of an individual for the production or collection of income, for the management, conservation, or maintenance of property held for the production of income, or in connection with the determination, collection, or refund of any tax, or (2) its being taken into account during the taxable year by a corporation or an individual as a part of the cost of acquiring or producing property in the trade or business or, in the case of an individual, as a part of the cost of property held for the production of income with respect to which it relates.

(g) Taxes for local benefits. Except as provided in § 1.164-4, taxes assessed against local benefits of a kind tending to increase the value of the property assessed.

(h) Excise tax on real estate investment trusts. The excise tax imposed on certain real estate investment trusts by section 4981.

T.D. 6256, 10/7/57, amend T.D. 6780, 12/21/64, T.D. 7767, 2/3/81.

---

§ 1.164-3 Definitions and special rules.

Caution: The Treasury has not yet amended Reg § 1.164-3 to reflect changes made by P.L. 99-514.

For purposes of section 164 and § 1.164-1 to § 1.164-8, inclusive—

(a) State or local taxes. A State or local tax includes only a tax imposed by a State, a possession of the United States, or a political subdivision of any of the foregoing, or by the District of Columbia.

(b) Real property taxes. The term "real property taxes" means taxes imposed on interests in real property and levied for the general public welfare, but it does not include taxes assessed against local benefits. See § 1.164-4.

(c) Personal property taxes. The term "personal property tax" means an ad valorem tax which is imposed on an annual basis in respect of personal property. To qualify as a personal property tax, a tax must meet the following three tests:

(1) The tax must be ad valorem, that is, substantially in proportion to the value of the personal property. A tax which is based on criteria other than value does not qualify as ad valorem. For example, a motor vehicle tax based on weight, model year, and horsepower, or any of these characteristics is not an ad valorem tax. However, a tax which is partly based on value and partly based on other criteria may qualify in part. For example, in the case of a motor vehicle tax of 1 percent of value plus 40 cents per hundredweight, the part of the tax equal to 1 percent of value qualifies as an ad valorem tax and the balance does not qualify.

(2) The tax must be imposed on an annual basis, even if collected more frequently or less frequently.

(3) The tax must be imposed in respect of personal property. A tax may be considered to be imposed in respect of personal property even if in form it is imposed on the exercise of a privilege. Thus, for taxable years beginning after December 31, 1963, State and local taxes on the registration or licensing of highway motor vehicles are not deductible as personal property taxes unless and to the extent that the tests prescribed in this subparagraph are met. For example, an annual ad valorem tax qualifies as a personal property tax although it is denominated a registration fee imposed for the privilege of registering motor vehicles or of using them on the highways.

(d) Foreign taxes. The term "foreign tax" includes only a tax imposed by the authority of a foreign country. A tax imposed by a political subdivision of a foreign country is considered to be imposed by the authority of that foreign country.

(e) Sales tax. *(1)* The term "sales tax" means a tax imposed upon persons engaged in selling tangible personal property, or upon the consumers of such property, including persons selling gasoline or other motor vehicle fuels at wholesale or retail, which is a stated sum per unit of property sold or which is measured by the gross sales price or the gross receipts from the sale. The term also includes a tax imposed upon persons engaged in furnishing services which is measured by the gross receipts for furnishing such services.

(2) In general, the term "consumer" means the ultimate user or purchaser; it does not include a purchaser such as a retailer, who acquires the property for resale.

(f) General sales tax. A "general sales tax" is a sales tax which is imposed at one rate in respect of the sale at retail of a broad range of classes of items. No foreign sales tax is deductible under section 164(a) and paragraph (a)(4) of § 1.164-1. To qualify as a general sales tax, a tax must meet the following two tests:

(1) The tax must be a tax in respect of sales at retail. This may include a tax imposed on persons engaged in selling property at retail or furnishing services at retail, for example, if the tax is measured by gross sales price or by gross receipts from sales or services. Rentals qualify as sales at retail if so treated under applicable State sales tax laws.

(2) The tax must be general, that is, it must be imposed at one rate in respect of the retail sales of a broad range of classes of items. A sales tax is considered to be general although imposed on sales of various classes of items at more than one rate provided that one rate applies to the retail sales of a broad range of classes of items. The term "items" includes both commodities and services.

(g) Special rules relating to general sales taxes. *(1)* A sales tax which is general is usually imposed at one rate in respect of the retail sales of all tangible personal property (with exceptions and additions). However, a sales tax which is selective, that is, a tax which applies at one rate with respect to retail sales of specified classes of items also qualifies as general if the specified classes represent a broad range of classes of items. A selective sales tax which does not apply at one rate to the retail sales of a broad range of classes of items is not general. For example, a tax which applies only to sales of alcoholic beverages, tobacco, admissions, luxury items, and a few other items is not general. Similarly, a tax imposed solely on services is not general. However, a selective sales tax may be deemed to be part of the general sales tax and hence may be deductible, even if imposed by a separate Title, etc., of the State or local law, if imposed at the same rate as the general rate of tax (as defined in subparagraph (4) of this paragraph) which qualifies a tax in the taxing jurisdiction as a general sales tax. For example, if a State has a 5 percent general sales tax and a separate selective sales tax of 5 percent on transient accommodations, the tax on transient accommodations is deductible.

(2) A tax is imposed at one rate only if it is imposed at that rate on generally the same base for all items subject to tax. For example, a sales tax imposed at a 3 percent rate on 100 percent of the sales price of some classes of items and at a 3 percent rate on 50 percent of the sales price of other classes of items would not be imposed at one rate with respect to all such classes. However, a tax is considered to be imposed at one rate although it allows dollar exemptions, if the exemptions are designed to exclude all sales under a certain dollar amount. For example, a tax may be imposed at one rate although it applies to all sales of tangible personal property but applies only to sales amounting to more than 10 cents.

(3) The fact that a sales tax exempts food, clothing, medical supplies, and motor vehicles, or any of them, shall not be taken into account in determining whether the tax applies to a broad range of classes of items. The fact that a sales tax applies to food, clothing, medical supplies, and motor vehicles, or any of them, at a rate which is lower than the general rate of tax (as defined in subparagraph (4) of this paragraph) is not taken into account in determining whether the tax is imposed at one rate on the retail sales of a broad range of classes of items. For purposes of this section, the term "food" means food for human consumption off the premises where sold, and the term "medical supplies" includes drugs, medicines, and medical devices.

(4) Except in the case of a lower rate of tax applicable in respect of food, clothing, medical supplies, and motor vehicles, or any of them, no deduction is allowed for a general sales tax in respect of any item if the tax is imposed on such item at a rate other than the general rate of tax. The general rate of tax is the one rate which qualifies a tax in a taxing jurisdiction as a general sales tax because the tax is imposed at such one rate on a broad range of classes of items. There can be only one general rate of tax in any one taxing jurisdiction. However, a general sales tax imposed at a lower rate or rates on food, clothing, motor vehicles, and medical supplies, or any of them, may nonetheless be deductible with respect to such items. For example, a sales tax which is imposed at 1 percent with respect to food, imposed at 3 percent with respect to a broad range of classes of tangible personal property, and imposed at 4 percent with respect to transient accommodations would qualify as a general sales tax. Taxes paid at the 1 percent and the 3 percent rates are deductible, but tax paid at the 4 percent rate is not deductible. The fact that a sales tax provides for the adjustment of the general rate of tax to reflect the sales tax rate in another taxing jurisdiction shall not be taken into account in determining whether the tax is imposed at one rate on the retail sales of a broad range of classes of items. Moreover, a general sales tax imposed at a lower rate with respect to an item in order to reflect the tax rate in another jurisdiction is also deductible at such lower rate. For example, State E imposes a general sales tax whose general rate is 3 percent. The State E sales tax law provides that in areas bordering on States with general sales taxes, selective sales taxes, or special excise taxes, the rate applied in the adjoining State will be used if such rate is under 3 percent. State F imposes a 2 percent sales tax. The 2 percent sales tax paid by residents of State E in areas bordering on State F is deductible.

(h) Compensating use taxes. A compensating use tax in respect of any item is treated as a general sales tax. The term "compensating use tax" means, in respect of any item, a tax which is imposed on the use, storage, or consumption of such item and which is complementary to a general sales tax which is deductible with respect to sales of similar items.

(i) Special rules relating to compensating use taxes. *(1)* In general, a use tax on an item is complementary to a general sales tax on similar items if the use tax is imposed on an item which was not subject to such general sales tax but which would have been subject to such general sales tax if the sale of the item had taken place within the jurisdiction imposing the use tax. For example, a tax imposed by State A on the use of a motor vehicle purchased in State B is complementary to the general sales tax of State A on similar items, if the latter tax applies to motor vehicles sold in State A.

(2) Since a compensating use tax is treated as a general sales tax, it is subject to the rule of subparagraph (C) of section 164(b)(2) and paragraph (g)(4) of this section that no deduction is allowed for a general sales tax imposed in respect of an item at a rate other than the general rate of tax (except in the case of lower rates on the sale of food, clothing, medical supplies, and motor vehicles). The fact that a compensating use tax in respect of any item provides for an adjustment in the rate of the compensating use tax or the amount of such tax to be paid on account of a sales tax on such item imposed by another taxing jurisdiction is not taken into account in determining whether the compensating use tax is imposed in respect of the item at a rate other than the general rate of tax. For example, a compensating use tax imposed by State C on the use of an item purchased in State D is considered to be imposed at the general rate of tax even though the tax imposed by State C allows a credit for any sales tax paid on such item in State D, or the rate of such compensating use tax is adjusted to reflect the rate of sales tax imposed by State D.

T.D. 6256, 10/7/57, amend T.D. 6780, 12/21/64.

§ 1.164-4 Taxes for local benefits.

(a) So-called taxes for local benefits referred to in paragraph (g) of § 1.164-2, more properly assessments, paid for local benefits such as street, sidewalk, and other like improvements, imposed because of and measured by some benefit inuring directly to the property against which the assessment is levied are not deductible as taxes. A tax is considered assessed against local benefits when the property subject to the tax is limited to property benefited. Special assessments are not deductible, even though an incidental benefit may inure to the public welfare. The real property taxes deductible are those levied for the general public welfare by the proper taxing authorities at a like rate against all property in the territory over which such authorities have jurisdiction. Assessments under the statutes of California relating to irrigation, and of Iowa relating to drainage, and under certain statutes of Tennessee relating to levees, are limited to property benefited, and if the assessments are so limited, the amounts paid thereunder are not deductible as taxes. For treatment of assessments for local benefits as adjustments to the basis of property, see section 1016(a)(1) and the regulations thereunder.

(b) *(1)* Insofar as assessments against local benefits are made for the purpose of maintenance or repair or for the purpose of meeting interest charges with respect to such benefits, they are deductible. In such cases, the burden is on the taxpayer to show the allocation of the amounts assessed to the different purposes. If the allocation cannot be made, none of the amount so paid is deductible.

(2) Taxes levied by a special taxing district which was in existence on December 31, 1963, for the purpose of retiring indebtedness existing on such date, are deductible, to the extent levied for such purpose, if (i) the district covers the whole of at least one county, (ii) if at least 1,000 persons are subject to the taxes levied by the district, and (iii) if the district levies its assessments annually at a uniform rate on the same assessed value of real property, including improvements, as is used for purposes of the real property tax generally.

T.D. 6256, 10/7/57, amend T.D. 6780, 12/21/64.

§ 1.164-5 Certain retails sales taxes and gasoline taxes.

Caution: The Treasury has not yet amended Reg § 1.164-5 to reflect changes made by P.L. 99-514, P.L. 98-21, P.L. 95-600.

For taxable years beginning before January 1, 1964, any amount representing a State or local sales tax paid by a consumer of services or tangible personal property is deductible by such consumer as a tax, provided it is separately stated and not paid in connection with his trade or business. For taxable years beginning after December 31, 1963, only the amount of any separately stated State and local general sales tax (as defined in paragraph (g) of § 1.164-3) and tax on the sale of gasoline, diesel fuel or other motor fuel paid by the consumer (other than in connection with his trade or business) is deductible by the consumer as tax. The fact that, under the law imposing it, the incidence of such State or local tax does not fall on the consumer is immaterial. The requirement that the amount of tax must be separately stated will be deemed complied with where it clearly appears that at the time of sale to the consumer, the tax was added to the sales price and collected or charged as a separate item. It is not necessary, for the purpose of this section, that the consumer be furnished with a sales slip, bill, invoice, or other statement on which the tax is separately stated. For example, where the law imposing the State or local tax for which the taxpayer seeks a deduction contains a prohibition against the seller absorbing the tax, or a provision requiring a posted notice stating that the tax will be added to the quoted price, or a requirement that the tax be separately shown in advertisements or separately stated on all bills and invoices, it is presumed that the amount of the State or local tax was separately stated at the time paid by the consumer; except that such presumption shall have no application to a tax on the sale of gasoline, diesel fuel or other motor fuel imposed upon a wholesaler unless such provisions of law apply with respect to both the sale at wholesale and the sale at retail.

T.D. 6256, 10/7/57, amend T.D. 6780, 12/21/64.

§ 1.164-6 Apportionment of taxes on real property between seller and purchaser.

(a) Scope. Except as provided otherwise in section 164(f) and § 1.164-8, when real property is sold, section 164(d)(1) governs the deduction by the seller and the purchaser of current real property taxes. Section 164(d)(1) performs two functions: (1) It provides a method by which a portion of the taxes for the real property tax year in which the property is sold may be deducted by the seller and a portion by the purchaser; and (2) it limits the deduction of the seller and the purchaser to the portion of the taxes corresponding to the part of the real property tax year during which each was the owner of the property. These functions are accomplished by treating a portion of the taxes for the real property tax year in which the property is sold as imposed on the seller and a portion as imposed on the purchaser. To the extent that the taxes are treated as imposed on the seller and the purchaser, each shall be allowed a deduction, under section 164(a), in the taxable year such tax is paid or accrued, or treated as paid or accrued under section 164(d)(2)(A) or (D) and this section. No deduction is allowed for taxes on real property to the extent that they are imposed on another taxpayer, or are treated as imposed on another taxpayer under section 164(d). For the election to accrue real property taxes ratably see section 461(c) and the regulations thereunder.

(b) Application of rule of apportionment. *(1)* (i) For purposes of the deduction provided by section 164(a), if real property is sold during any real property tax year, the portion of the real property tax properly allocable to that part of the real property tax year which ends on the day before the date of the sale shall be treated as a tax imposed on the seller, and the portion of such tax properly allocable to that part of such real property tax year which begins on the date of the sale shall be treated as a tax imposed on the purchaser. For definition of "real property tax year" see paragraph (c) of this section. This rule shall apply whether or not the seller and the purchaser apportion such tax. The rule of apportionment contained in section 164(d)(1) applies even though the same real property is sold more than once during the real property tax year. (See paragraph (d)(5) of this section for rule requiring inclusion in gross income of excess deductions.)

(ii) Where the real property tax becomes a personal liability or a lien before the beginning of the real property tax year to which it relates and the real property is sold subsequent to the time the tax becomes a personal liability or a lien but prior to the beginning of the related real property tax year—

(a) The seller may not deduct any amount for real property taxes for the related real property tax year, and

(b) To the extent that he holds the property for such real property tax year, the purchaser may deduct the amount of such taxes for the taxable year they are paid (or amounts representing such taxes are paid to the seller, mortgagee, trustee or other person having an interest in the property as security) or accrued by him according to his method of accounting.

(iii) Similarly, where the real property tax becomes a personal liability or a lien after the end of the real property tax year to which it relates and the real property is sold prior to the time the tax becomes a personal liability or a lien but after the end of the related real property tax year—

(a) The purchaser may not deduct any amount for real property taxes for the related real property tax year, and

(b) To the extent that he holds the property for such real property tax year, the seller may deduct the amount of such taxes for the taxable year they are paid (or amounts representing such taxes are paid to the purchaser, mortgagee, trustee, or other person having an interest in the property as security) or accrued by him according to his method of accounting.

(iv) Where the real property is sold (or purchased) during the related real property tax year the real property taxes for such year are apportioned between the parties to such sale and may be deducted by such parties in accordance with the provisions of paragraph (d) of this section.

(2) Section 164(d) does not apply to delinquent real property taxes for any real property tax year prior to the real property tax year in which the property is sold.

(3) The provisions of this paragraph may be illustrated by the following examples:

Example (1). The real property tax year in County R is April 1 to March 31. A, the owner on April 1, 1954, of real property located in County R sells the real property to B on June 30, 1954. B owns the real property from June 30, 1954, through March 31, 1955. The real property tax for the real property tax year April 1, 1954–March 31, 1955 is $365. For purposes of section 164(a), $90 (90/365 × $365, April 1, 1954–June 29, 1954) of the real property tax is treated as imposed on A, the seller, and $275 (275/365 × $365, June 30, 1954–March 31, 1955) of such real property tax is treated as imposed on B, the purchaser.

Example (2). In County S the real property tax year is the calendar year. The real property tax becomes a lien on June 1 and is payable on July 1 of the current real property tax year, but there is no personal liability for such tax. On April 30, 1955, C, the owner of real property in County S on January 1, 1955, sells the real property to D. On July 1, 1955, D pays the 1955 real property tax. On August 31, 1955, D sells the same real property to E. C, D, and E use the cash receipts and disbursements method of accounting. Under the provisions of section 164(d)(1), 119/365 (January 1–April 29, 1955) of the real property tax payable on July 1, 1955, for the 1955 real property tax year is treated as imposed on C, and, under the provisions of section 164(d)(2)(A), such portion is treated as having been paid by him on the date of sale. Under the provisions of section 164(d)(1), 123/365 (April 30– August 30, 1955) of the real property tax paid July 1, 1955, for the 1955 real property tax year is treated as imposed on D and may be deducted by him. Under the provisions of section 164(d)(1), 123/365 (August 31–December 31, 1955) of the real property tax due and paid on July 1, 1955, for the 1955 real property tax year is treated as imposed on E and, under the provisions of section 164(d)(2)(A) such portion is treated as having been paid by him on the date of sale.

Example (3). In State X the real property tax year is the calendar year. The real property tax becomes a lien on November 1 of the proceeding calendar year. On November 15, 1955, F sells real property in State X to G. G owns the real property through December 31, 1956. Under section 164(d)(1), the real property tax (which became a lien on November 1, 1954) for the 1955 real property tax year is apportioned between F and G. No part of the real property tax for the 1956 real property tax year may be deducted by F. The entire real property tax for the 1956 real property tax year may be deducted by G when paid or accrued, depending upon the method of accounting used by him. See subparagraph (6) of paragraph (d) and section 461(c) and the regulations thereunder.

(c) Real property tax year. As used in section 164(d), the term "real property tax year" refers to the period which, under the law imposing the tax, is regarded as the period to which the tax imposed relates. Where the State and one or more local governmental units each imposes a tax on real property, the real property tax year for each tax must be determined for purposes of applying the rule of apportionment of section 164(d)(1) to each tax. The time when the tax rate is determined, the time when the assessment is made, the time when the tax becomes a lien, or the time when the tax becomes due or delinquent does not necessarily determine the real property tax year. The real property tax year may or may not correspond to the fiscal year of the governmental unit imposing the tax. In each case the State or local law determines what constitutes the real property tax year. Although the seller and the purchaser may or may not make an allocation of real property taxes, the meaning of "real property tax year" in section 164(d) and the application of section 164(d) do not depend upon what real property taxes were allocated nor the method of allocation used by the parties.

(d) Special rules. *(1) Seller using cash receipts and disbursements method of accounting.* Under the provisions of section 164(d), if the seller by reason of his method of accounting may not deduct any amount for taxes unless paid, and—

(i) The purchaser (under the law imposing the real property tax) is liable for the real property tax for the real property tax year, or

(ii) The seller (under the law imposing the real property tax) is liable for the real property tax for the real property tax year and the tax is not payable until after the date of sale.

then the portion of the tax treated under section 164(d)(1) as imposed upon the seller (whether or not actually paid by him in the taxable year in which the sale occurs) shall be considered as having been paid by him in such taxable year. Such portion may be deducted by him for the taxable year in which the sale occurs, or, if at a later time, for the taxable year (which would be proper under the taxpayer's method of accounting) in which the tax is actually paid, or an amount representing such tax is paid to the purchaser, mortgagee, trustee, or other person having an interest in the property as security.

(2) Purchasers using the cash receipts and disbursements method of accounting. Under the provisions of section 164(d), if the purchaser by reason of his method of accounting may not deduct any amount for taxes unless paid and the seller (under the law imposing the real property tax) is liable for the real property tax for the real property tax year, the portion of the tax treated under section 164(d)(1) as imposed upon the purchaser (whether or not actually paid by him in the taxable year in which the sale occurs) shall be considered as having been paid by him in such taxable year. Such portion may be deducted by him for the taxable year in which the sale occurs, or, if at a later time, for the taxable year (which would be proper under the taxpayer's method of accounting) in which the tax is actually paid, or an amount representing such tax is paid to the seller, mortgagee, trustee, or other person having an interest in the property as security.

(3) Persons considered liable for tax. Where the tax is not a liability of any person, the person who holds the property at the time the tax becomes a lien on the property shall be

considered liable for the tax. As to a particular sale, in determining:

(i) Whether the other party to the sale is liable for the tax or,

(ii) The person who holds the property at the time the tax becomes a lien on the property (where the tax is not a liability of any person), prior or subsequent sales of the property during the real property tax year shall be disregarded.

(4) Examples. The provisions of subparagraphs (1), (2), and (3) of this paragraph may be illustrated as follows:

Example (1). In County X the real property tax year is the calendar year. The real property tax is a personal liability of the owner of the real property on June 30 of the current real property tax year, but is not payable until February 28 of the following real property tax year. A, the owner of real property in County X on January 1, 1955, uses the cash receipts and disbursements method of accounting. On May 30, 1955, A sells the real property to B, who also uses the cash receipts and disbursements method of accounting. B retains ownership of the real property for the balance of the 1955 calendar year. Under the provisions of section 164(d)(1), 149/365 (January 1–May 29, 1955) of the real property tax payable on February 28, 1956, for the 1955 real property tax year is treated as imposed on A, the seller, and under the provisions of section 164(d)(2)(A) such portion is treated as having been paid by him on the date of sale and may be deducted by him for his taxable year in which the sale occurs (whether or not such portion is actually paid by him in that year) or for his taxable year in which the tax is actually paid or an amount representing such tax is paid. Under the provisions of section 164(d)(1), 216/365 (May 30–December 31, 1955) of the real property tax payable on February 28, 1956, for the 1955 real property tax year is treated as imposed on B, the purchaser, and may be deducted by him for his taxable year in which the tax is actually paid, or an amount representing such tax is paid.

Example (2). In County Y, the real property tax year is the calendar year. The real property tax becomes a lien on January 1, 1955, and is payable on April 30, 1955. There is no personal liability for the real property tax imposed by County Y. On April 30, 1955, C, the owner of real property in County Y on January 1, 1955, pays the real property tax for the 1955 real property tax year. On May 1, 1955, C sells the real property to D. On September 1, 1955, D sells the real property to E. C, D, and E use the cash receipts and disbursements method of accounting. Under the provisions of section 164(d)(1), 120/365 (January 1– April 30, 1955) of the real property tax is treated as imposed upon C and may be deducted by him for his taxable year in which the tax is actually paid. Under section 164(d)(1), 123/365 (May 1–August 31, 1955) of the real property tax is treated as imposed upon D and, under the provisions of section 164(d)(2)(A), is treated as having been paid by him on May 1, 1955, and may be deducted by D for his taxable year in which the sale from C to him occurs (whether or not such portion is actually paid by him in that year), or for his taxable year in which an amount representing such tax is paid. Since, according to paragraph (d)(3) of this section, the prior sale by C to D is disregarded, under the provisions of section 164(d)(1), 122/365 (September 1–December 31, 1955) of the real property tax is treated as imposed on E and, under the provisions of section 164(d)(2)(A), is treated as having been paid by him on September 1, 1955, and may be deducted by E for his taxable year in which the sale from D to him occurs (whether or not such portion is actually paid by him in that year), or for his taxable year in which an amount representing such tax is paid.

Example (3). In County X the real property tax year is the calendar year and the real property taxes are assessed and become a lien on June 30 of the current real property tax year, but are not payable until September 1 of that year. There is no personal liability for the real property tax imposed by County X. A, the owner on January 1, 1955, of real property in County X, uses the cash receipts and disbursements method of accounting. On July 15, 1955, A sells the real property to B. Under the provisions of section 164(d)(1), 195/365 (January 1–July 14, 1955) of the real property tax payable on September 1, 1955, for the 1955 real property tax year is treated as imposed on A, and may be deducted by him for his taxable year in which the sale occurs (whether or not such portion is actually paid by him in that year) or for his taxable year in which the tax is actually paid or an amount representing such tax is paid. Under the provisions of section 164(d)(1), 170/365 (July 15–December 31, 1955) of the real property tax is treated as imposed on B and may be deducted by him for his taxable year in which the sale occurs (whether or not such portion is actually paid by him in that year), or for his taxable year in which the tax is actually paid or an amount representing such tax is paid.

(5) Treatment of excess deduction. If, for a taxable year prior to the taxable year of sale of real property, a taxpayer has deducted an amount for real property tax in excess of the portion of such real property tax treated as imposed on him under the provisions of section 164(d), the excess of the amount deducted over the portion treated as imposed on him shall be included in his gross income for the taxable year of the sale, subject to the provisions of section 111, relating to the recovery of bad debts, prior taxes, and delinquency amounts. The provisions of this subparagraph may be illustrated as follows:

Example (1). In Borough Y the real property tax is due and payable on November 30 for the succeeding calendar year, which is also the real property tax year. On November 30, 1954, taxpayer A, who reports his income on a calendar year under the cash receipts and disbursements method of accounting, pays the real property tax on real property owned by him in Borough Y for the 1955 real property tax year. On June 30, 1955, A sells the real property. Under the provisions of section 164(d), only 180/365 (January 1–June 29, 1955) of the real property tax for the 1955 real property tax year is treated as imposed on A, and the excess of the amount of real property tax for 1955 deducted by A, on his 1954 income tax return, over the 180/365 portion of such tax treated as imposed on him under section 164(d), must be included in gross income in A's 1955 income tax return, subject to the provisions of section 111.

Example (2). In County Z the real property tax year is the calendar year. The real property tax becomes a personal liability of the owner of real property on January 1 of the current real property tax year, and is payable on July 1 of the current real property tax year. On May 1, 1955, A, the owner of real property in County Z on January 1, 1955, sells the real property to B. On November 1, 1955, B sells the same real property to C. B uses the cash receipts and disbursements method of accounting and reports his income on the basis of a fiscal year ending July 31. B, on July 1, 1955, pays the entire real property tax for the real property tax year ending December 31, 1955. Under the provisions of section 164(d), only 184/365 (May 1– October 31, 1955) of the real property tax for the 1955 real property tax year is treated as imposed on B, and the excess of the amount of real property tax for 1955 deducted by B on his income tax return for the fiscal year ending July 31, 1955, over the 184/365 portion of such tax treated as imposed on him under section 164(d), must be included in gross income in B's income tax return for his fiscal year ending July 31, 1956, subject to the provisions of section 111.

(6) Persons using an accrual method of accounting. Where real property is sold and the seller or the purchaser computes his taxable income (for the taxable year during which the sale occurs) on an accrual method of accounting, then, if the seller or the purchaser has not made the election provided in section 461(c) (relating to the accrual of real property taxes), the portion of any real property tax which is treated as imposed on him and which may not be deducted by him for any taxable year by reason of his method of accounting shall be treated as having accrued on the date of sale. The provisions of this subparagraph may be illustrated as follows:

Example. In County X the real property tax becomes a lien on property and is assessed on November 30 for the current calendar year, which is also the real property tax year. There is no personal liability for the real property tax imposed by County X. A owns, on January 1, 1955, real property in County X. A uses an accrual method of accounting and has not made any election under section 461(c) to accrue ratably real property taxes. A sells real property on June 30, 1955. By reason of A's method of accounting, he could not deduct any part of the real property tax for 1955 on the real property since he sold the real property prior to November 30, 1955, the accrual date. Under section 164(d)(1), 180/365 (January 1–June 29, 1955) of the real property tax for the 1955 real property tax year is treated as imposed on A, and under section 164(d)(2)(D) that portion is treated as having accrued on June 30, 1955, and may be deducted by A for his taxable year in which such date falls. B, the purchaser from A, who uses an accrual method of accounting, has likewise not made an election under section 461(c) to accrue real property taxes ratably. Under section 164(d)(1), 185/365 of the real property taxes may be accrued by B on November 30, 1955, and deducted for his taxable year in which such date falls.

(7) Cross references. For determination of amount realized on a sale of real property, see section 1001(b) and the regulations thereunder. For determination of basis of real property acquired by purchase, see section 1012 and the regulations thereunder.

(8) Effective dates. Section 164(d) applies to taxable years ending after December 31, 1953, but only in the case of sales made after December 31, 1953. However, section 164(d) does not apply to any real property tax to the extent that such tax was allowable as a deduction under the Internal Revenue Code of 1939 to the seller for any taxable year which ended before January 1, 1954.

T.D. 6256, 10/7/57, amend T.D. 6293, 5/20/58, T.D. 6406, 8/14/59.

§ 1.164-7 Taxes of shareholder paid by corporation.

Banks and other corporations paying taxes assessed against their shareholders on account of their ownership of the shares of stock issued by such corporations without reimbursement from such shareholders may deduct the amount of taxes so paid. In such cases no deduction shall be allowed to the shareholders for such taxes. The amount so paid should not be included in the gross income of the shareholder.

T.D. 6256, 10/7/57.

§ 1.164-8 Payments for municipal services in atomic energy communities.

Caution: The Treasury has not yet amended Reg § 1.164-8 to reflect changes made by P.L. 94-455.

(a) General. For taxable years beginning after December 31, 1957, amounts paid or accrued by any owner of real property within any community (as defined in section 21b of the Atomic Energy Community Act of 1955 (42 USC 2304)) to compensate the Atomic Energy Commission for municipal-type services (or any agent or contractor authorized by the Atomic Energy Commission to charge for such services) shall be treated as State real property taxes paid or accrued for purposes of section 164. Such amounts shall be deductible as taxes to the extent provided in section 164, §§ 1.164-1 through 1.164-7, and this section. See paragraph (b) of this section for definition of the term "Atomic Energy Commission"; paragraph (c) of this section for the definition of the term "municipal-type services"; and paragraph (d) of this section for the definition of the term "owner".

(b) Atomic Energy Commission. For purposes of paragraph (a) of this section, the term "Atomic Energy Commission" shall mean—

(1) The Atomic Energy Commission, and

(2) Any other agency of the United States Government to which the duties and responsibilities of providing municipal-type services are delegated under the authority of section 101 of the Atomic Energy Community Act of 1955 (42 USC 2313).

(c) Municipal-type services. For purposes of paragraph (a) of this section, the term "municipal-type services" includes services usually rendered by a municipality and usually paid for by taxes. Examples of municipal-type services are police protection, fire protection, public recreational facilities, public libraries, public schools, public health, public welfare, and the maintenance of roads and streets. The term shall include sewage and refuse disposal which are maintained out of revenues derived from a general charge of municipal-type services; however, the term shall not include sewage and refuse disposal if a separate charge for such services is made. Charges assessed against local benefits of a kind tending to increase the value of the property assessed are not charges for municipal-type services. See section 164(c)(1) and § 1.164-4.

(d) Owner. For purposes of paragraph (a) of this section, the term "owner" includes a person who holds the real property under a leasehold of 40 or more years from the Atomic Energy Commission (or any agency of the United States Government to which the duties and responsibilities of leasing real property are delegated under section 101 of the Atomic Energy Community Act of 1955), and a person who has entered into a contract to purchase under section 61 of the Atomic Energy Community Act of 1955 (42 USC 2361). An assignee (either immediate or more remote) of a lessee referred to in the preceding sentence will also qualify as an owner for purposes of paragraph (a) of this section.

(e) Nonapplication of section 164(d). Section 164(d) and § 1.164-6, relating to apportionment of taxes on real property between seller and purchaser, do not apply to a sale by the United States or any of its agencies of real property to which section 164(f) and this section apply. Thus, amounts paid or accrued which qualify under paragraph (a) of this section will continue to be deductible as taxes to the extent provided in this section, even in the taxable year in which the owner actually purchases the real property from the United States or any of its agencies. However, the provisions of section

164(d) and § 1.164-6 shall apply to a sale of real property to which section 164(f) and this section apply, if the seller is other than the United States or any of its agencies.

T.D. 6406, 8/14/59, amend T.D. 6780, 12/21/64.

§ 1.165-1 Losses.

(a) Allowance of deduction. Section 165(a) provides that, in computing taxable income under section 63, any loss actually sustained during the taxable year and not made good by insurance or some other form of compensation shall be allowed as a deduction subject to any provision of the internal revenue laws which prohibits or limits the amount of deduction. This deduction for losses sustained shall be taken in accordance with section 165 and the regulations thereunder. For the disallowance of deductions for worthless securities issued by a political party, see § 1.271-1.

(b) Nature of loss allowable. To be allowable as a deduction under section 165(a), a loss must be evidenced by closed and completed transactions, fixed by identifiable events, and, except as otherwise provided in section 165(h) and § 1.165-11, relating to disaster losses, actually sustained during the taxable year. Only a bona fide loss is allowable. Substance and not mere form shall govern in determining a deductible loss.

(c) Amount deductible. *(1)* The amount of loss allowable as a deduction under section 165(a) shall not exceed the amount prescribed by § 1.1011-1 as the adjusted basis for determining the loss from the sale or other disposition of the property involved. In the case of each such deduction claimed, therefore, the basis of the property must be properly adjusted as prescribed by § 1.1011-1 for such items as expenditures, receipts, or losses, properly chargeable to capital account, and for such items as depreciation, obsolescence, amortization, and depletion, in order to determine the amount of loss allowable as a deduction. To determine the allowable loss in the case of property acquired before March 1, 1913, see also paragraph (b) of § 1.1053-1.

(2) The amount of loss recognized upon the sale or exchange of property shall be determined for purposes of section 165(a) in accordance with § 1.1002-1.

(3) A loss from the sale or exchange of a capital asset shall be allowed as a deduction under section 165(a) but only to the extent allowed in section 1211 (relating to limitation on capital losses) and section 1212 (relating to capital loss carrybacks and carryovers), and in the regulations under those sections.

(4) In determining the amount of loss actually sustained for purposes of section 165(a), proper adjustment shall be made for any salvage value and for any insurance or other compensation received.

(d) Year of deduction. *(1)* A loss shall be allowed as a deduction under section 165(a) only for the taxable year in which the loss is sustained. For this purpose, a loss shall be treated as sustained during the taxable year in which the loss occurs as evidenced by closed and completed transactions and as fixed by identifiable events occurring in such taxable year. For provisions relating to situations where a loss attributable to a disaster will be treated as sustained in the taxable year immediately preceding the taxable year in which the disaster actually occurred, see section 165(h) and § 1.165-11.

(2) (i) If a casualty or other event occurs which may result in a loss and, in the year of such casualty or event, there exists a claim for reimbursement with respect to which there is a reasonable prospect of recovery, no portion of the loss with respect to which reimbursement may be received is sustained, for purposes of section 165, until it can be ascertained with reasonable certainty whether or not such reimbursement will be received. Whether a reasonable prospect of recovery exists with respect to a claim for reimbursement of a loss is a question of fact to be determined upon an examination of all facts and circumstances. Whether or not such reimbursement will be received may be ascertained with reasonable certainty, for example, by a settlement of the claim, by an adjudication of the claim, or by an abandonment of the claim. When a taxpayer claims that the taxable year in which a loss is sustained is fixed by his abandonment of the claim for reimbursement, he must be able to produce objective evidence of his having abandoned the claim, such as the execution of a release.

(ii) If in the year of the casualty or other event a portion of the loss is not covered by a claim for reimbursement with respect to which there is a reasonable prospect of recovery, then such portion of the loss is sustained during the taxable year in which the casualty or other event occurs. For example, if property having an adjusted basis of $10,000 is completely destroyed by fire in 1961, and if the taxpayer's only claim for reimbursement consists of an insurance claim for $8,000 which is settled in 1962, the taxpayer sustains a loss of $2,000 in 1961. However, if the taxpayer's automobile is completely destroyed in 1961 as a result of the negligence of another person and there exists a reasonable prospect of recovery on a claim for the full value of the automobile against such person, the taxpayer does not sustain any loss until the taxable year in which the claim is adjudicated or otherwise settled. If the automobile had an adjusted basis of $5,000 and the taxpayer secures a judgment of $4,000 in 1962, $1,000 is deductible for the taxable year 1962.

If in 1963 it becomes reasonably certain that only $3,500 can ever be collected on such judgment, $500 is deductible for the taxable year 1963.

(iii) If the taxpayer deducted a loss in accordance with the provisions of this paragraph and in a subsequent taxable year receives reimbursement for such loss, he does not recompute the tax for the taxable year in which the deduction was taken but includes the amount of such reimbursement in his gross income for the taxable year in which received, subject to the provisions of section 111, relating to recovery of amounts previously deducted.

(3) Any loss arising from theft shall be treated as sustained during the taxable year in which the taxpayer discovers the loss (see § 1.165-8, relating to theft losses). However, if in the year of discovery there exists a claim for reimbursement with respect to which there is a reasonable prospect of recovery, no portion of the loss with respect to which reimbursement may be received is sustained, for purposes of section 165, until the taxable year in which it can be ascertained with reasonable certainty whether or not such reimbursement will be received.

(4) The rules of this paragraph are applicable with respect to a casualty or other event which may result in a loss and which occurs after January 16, 1960. If the casualty or other event occurs on or before such date, a taxpayer may treat any loss resulting therefrom in accordance with the rules then applicable, or, if he so desires, in accordance with the provisions of this paragraph; but no provision of this paragraph shall be construed to permit a deduction of the same loss or any part thereof in more than one taxable year or to extend the period of limitations within which a claim for credit or refund may filed under section 6511.

(e) Limitation on losses of individuals. In the case of an individual, the deduction for losses granted by section 165(a) shall, subject to the provisions of section 165(c) and paragraph (a) of this section, be limited to:

(1) Losses incurred in a trade or business;

(2) Losses incurred in any transaction entered into for profit, though not connected with a trade or business; and

(3) Losses of property not connected with a trade or business and not incurred in any transaction entered into for profit, if such losses arise from fire, storm, shipwreck, or other casualty, or from theft, and if the loss involved has not been allowed for estate tax purposes in the estate tax return. For additional provisions pertaining to the allowance of casualty and theft losses, see §§ 1.165-7 and 1.165-8, respectively.

For special rules relating to an election by a taxpayer to deduct disaster losses in the taxable year immediately preceding the taxable year in which the disaster occurred, see section 165(h) and § 1.165-11.

T.D. 6445, 1/15/60, amend T.D. 6735, 5/18/64, T.D. 6996, 1/17/69, T.D. 7301, 1/3/74, T.D. 7522, 12/13/77.

§ 1.165-2 Obsolescence of nondepreciable property.

(a) Allowance of deduction. A loss incurred in a business or in a transaction entered into for profit and arising from the sudden termination of the usefulness in such business or transaction of any nondepreciable property, in a case where such business or transaction is discontinued or where such property is permanently discarded from use therein, shall be allowed as a deduction under section 165(a) for the taxable year in which the loss is actually sustained. For this purpose, the taxable year in which the loss is sustained is not necessarily the taxable year in which the overt act of abandonment, or the loss of title to the property, occurs.

(b) Exceptions. This section does not apply to losses sustained upon the sale or exchange of property, losses sustained upon the obsolescence or worthlessness of depreciable property, casualty losses, or losses reflected in inventories required to be taken under section 471. The limitations contained in sections 1211 and 1212 upon losses from the sale or exchange of capital assets do not apply to losses allowable under this section.

(c) Cross references. For the allowance under section 165(a) of losses arising from the permanent withdrawal of depreciable property from use in the trade or business or in the production of income, see § 1.167(a)-8. For provisions respecting the obsolescence of depreciable property, see § 1.167(a)-9. For the allowance of casualty losses, see § 1.165-7.

T.D. 6445, 1/15/60.

§ 1.165-3 Demolition of buildings.

Caution: The Treasury has not yet amended Reg § 1.165-3 to reflect changes made by P.L. 98-369.

(a) Intent to demolish formed at time of purchase. *(1)* Except as provided in subparagraph (2) of this paragraph, the following rule shall apply when, in the course of a trade or business or in a transaction entered into for profit, real property is purchased with the intention of demolishing either immediately or subsequently the buildings situated thereon: No deduction shall be allowed under section 165(a) on account of the demolition of the old buildings even though any demolition originally planned is subsequently deferred or abandoned. The entire basis of the property so purchased shall, notwithstanding the provisions of § 1.167(a)-5, be allocated to the land only. Such basis shall be increased by the net cost of demolition or decreased by the net proceeds from demolition.

(2) (i) If the property is purchased with the intention of demolishing the buildings and the buildings are used in a trade or business or held for the production of income before their demolition, a portion of the basis of the property may be allocated to such buildings and depreciated over the period during which they are so used or held. The fact that the taxpayer intends to demolish the buildings shall be taken into account in making the apportionment of basis between the land and buildings under § 1.167(a)-5. In any event, the portion of the purchase price which may be allocated to the buildings shall not exceed the present value of the right to receive rentals from the buildings over the period of their intended use. The present value of such right shall be determined at the time that the buildings are first used in the trade or business or first held for the production of income. If the taxpayer does not rent the buildings, but uses them in his own trade or business or in the production of his income, the present value of such right shall be determined by reference to the rentals which could be realized during such period of intended use. The fact that the taxpayer intends to rent or use the buildings for a limited period before their demolition shall also be taken into account in computing the useful life in accordance with paragraph (b) of § 1.167(a)-1.

(ii) Any portion of the purchase price which is allocated to the buildings in accordance with this subparagraph shall not be included in the basis of the land computed under subparagraph (1) of this paragraph, and any portion of the basis of the buildings which has not been recovered through depreciation or otherwise at the time of the demolition of the buildings is allowable as a deduction under section 165.

(iii) The application of this subparagraph may be illustrated by the following example:

Example. In January 1958, A purchased land and a building for $60,000 with the intention of demolishing the building. In the following April, A concludes that he will be unable to commence the construction of a proposed new building for a period of more than 3 years. Accordingly, on June 1, 1958, he leased the building for a period of 3 years at an annual rental of $1,200. A intends to demolish the building upon expiration of the lease. A may allocate a portion of the $60,000 basis of the property to the building to be depreciated over the 3-year period. That portion is equal to the present value of the right to receive $3,600 (3 times $1,200). Assuming that the present value of that right determined as of June 1, 1958, is $2,850, A may allocate that amount to the building and, if A files his return on the basis of a taxable year ending May 31, 1959, A may take a depreciation deduction with respect to such building of $950 for such taxable year. The basis of the land to A as determined under subparagraph (1) of this paragraph is reduced by $2,850. If on June 1, 1960, A ceases to rent the building and demolishes it, the balance of the undepreciated portion allocated to the buildings, $950, may be deducted from gross income under section 165.

(3) The basis of any building acquired in replacement of the old buildings shall not include any part of the basis of the property originally purchased even though such part was, at the time of purchase, allocated to the buildings to be demolished for purposes of determining allowable depreciation for the period before demolition.

(b) Intent to demolish formed subsequent to the time of acquisition. *(1)* Except as provided in subparagraph (2) of this paragraph, the loss incurred in a trade or business or in a transaction entered into for profit and arising from a demolition of old buildings shall be allowed as a deduction under section 165(a) if the demolition occurs as a result of a plan formed subsequent to the acquisition of the buildings demolished. The amount of the loss shall be the adjusted basis of the buildings demolished increased by the net cost of demolition or decreased by the net proceeds from demolition. See paragraph (c) of § 1.165-1 relating to amount deductible under section 165. The basis of any building acquired in replacement of the old buildings shall not include any part of the basis of the property demolished.

(2) If a lessor or lessee of real property demolishes the buildings situated thereon pursuant to a lease or an agreement which resulted in a lease, under which either the lessor was required or the lessee was required or permitted to demolish such buildings, no deduction shall be allowed to the lessor under section 165(a) on account of the demolition of the old buildings. However, the adjusted basis of the demolished buildings, increased by the net cost of demolition or decreased by the net proceeds from demolition, shall be considered as a part of the cost of the lease to be amortized over the remaining term thereof.

(c) Evidence of intention. *(1)* Whether real property has been purchased with the intention of demolishing the buildings thereon or whether the demolition of the buildings occurs as a result of a plan formed subsequent to their acquisition is a question of fact, and the answer depends upon an examination of all the surrounding facts and circumstances. The answer to the question does not depend solely upon the statements of the taxpayer at the time he acquired the property or demolished the buildings, but such statements, if made, are relevant and will be considered. Certain other relevant facts and circumstances that exist in some cases and the inferences that might reasonably be drawn from them are described in subparagraphs (2) and (3) of this paragraph. The question as to the taxpayer's intention is not answered by any inference that is drawn from any one fact or circumstance but can be answered only by a consideration of all relevant facts and circumstances and the reasonable inferences to be drawn therefrom.

(2) An intention at the time of acquisition to demolish may be suggested by:

(i) A short delay between the date of acquisition and the date of demolition;

(ii) Evidence of prohibitive remodeling costs determined at the time of acquisition;

(iii) Existence of municipal regulations at the time of acquisition which would prohibit the continued use of the buildings for profit purposes;

(iv) Unsuitability of the buildings for the taxpayer's trade or business at the time of acquisition; or

(v) Inability at the time of acquisition to realize a reasonable income from the buildings.

(3) The fact that the demolition occurred pursuant to a plan formed subsequent to the acquisition of the property may be suggested by:

(i) Substantial improvement of the buildings immediately after their acquisition;

(ii) Prolonged use of the buildings for business purposes after their acquisition;

(iii) Suitability of the buildings for investment purposes at the time of acquisition;

(iv) Substantial change in economic or business conditions after the date of acquisition;

(v) Loss of useful value occurring after the date of acquisition;

(vi) Substantial damage to the buildings occurring after their acquisition;

(vii) Discovery of latent structural defects in the buildings after their acquisition;

(viii) Decline in the taxpayer's business after the date of acquisition;

(ix) Condemnation of the property by municipal authorities after the date of acquisition; or

(x) Inability after acquisition to obtain building material necessary for the improvement of the property.

T.D. 6445, 1/15/60, amend T.D. 7447, 12/21/76.

§ 1.165-4 Decline in value of stock.

(a) Deduction disallowed. No deduction shall be allowed under section 165(a) solely on account of a decline in the value of stock owned by the taxpayer when the decline is due to a fluctuation in the market price of the stock or to other similar cause. A mere shrinkage in the value of stock owned by the taxpayer, even though extensive, does not give rise to a deduction under section 165(a) if the stock has any recognizable value on the date claimed as the date of loss. No loss for a decline in the value of stock owned by the taxpayer shall be allowed as a deduction under section 165(a) except insofar as the loss is recognized under § 1.1002-1 upon the sale or exchange of the stock and except as otherwise provided in § 1.165-5 with respect to stock which becomes worthless during the taxable year.

(b) Stock owned by banks. *(1)* In the regulation of banks and certain other corporations, Federal and State authorities may require that stock owned by such organizations be charged off as worthless or written down to a nominal value. If, in any such case, this requirement is premised upon the worthlessness of the stock, the charging off or writing down will be considered prima facie evidence of worthlessness for purposes of section 165(a); but, if the charging off or writing down is due to a fluctuation in the market price of the stock or if no reasonable attempt to determine the worthlessness of the stock has been made, then no deduction shall be allowed under section 165(a) for the amount so charged off or written down.

(2) This paragraph shall not be construed, however, to permit a deduction under section 165(a) unless the stock owned by the bank or other corporation actually becomes worthless in the taxable year. Such a taxpayer owning stock which becomes worthless during the taxable year is not precluded from deducting the loss under section 165(a) merely because, in obedience to the specific orders or general policy of such supervisory authorities, the value of the stock is written down to a nominal amount instead of being charged off completely.

(c) Application to inventories. This section does not apply to a decline in the value of corporate stock reflected in inventories required to be taken by a dealer in securities under section 471. See § 1.471-5.

(d) Definition. As used in this section, the term "stock" means a share of stock in a corporation or a right to subscribe for, or to receive, a share of stock in a corporation.

T.D. 6445, 1/15/60.

§ 1.165-5 Worthless securities.

Caution: The Treasury has not yet amended Reg § 1.165-5 to reflect changes made by P.L. 106-554.

(a) Definition of security. As used in section 165(g) and this section, the term "security" means:

(1) A share of stock in a corporation;

(2) A right to subscribe for, or to receive, a share of stock in a corporation; or

(3) A bond, debenture, note, or certificate, or other evidence of indebtedness to pay a fixed or determinable sum of money, which has been issued with interest coupons or in registered form by a domestic or foreign corporation or by any government or political subdivision thereof.

(b) Ordinary loss. If any security which is not a capital asset becomes wholly worthless during the taxable year, the loss resulting therefrom may be deducted under section 165(a) as an ordinary loss.

(c) Capital loss. If any security which is a capital asset becomes wholly worthless at any time during the taxable year, the loss resulting therefrom may be deducted under section 165(a) but only as though it were a loss from a sale or exchange, on the last day of the taxable year, of a capital asset. See section 165(g)(1). The amount so allowed as a deduction shall be subject to the limitations upon capital losses described in paragraph (c)(3) of § 1.165-1.

(d) Loss on worthless securities of an affiliated corporation. *(1) Deductible as an ordinary loss.* If a taxpayer which is a domestic corporation owns any security of a domestic or foreign corporation which is affiliated with the taxpayer within the meaning of subparagraph (2) of this paragraph and such security becomes wholly worthless during the taxable year, the loss resulting therefrom may be deducted under section 165(a) as an ordinary loss in accordance with paragraph (b) of this section. The fact that the security is in fact a capital asset of the taxpayer is immaterial for this purpose, since section 165(g)(3) provides that such security shall be treated as though it were not a capital asset for the purposes of section 165(g)(1). A debt which becomes wholly worthless during the taxable year shall be allowed as an ordinary loss in accordance with the provisions of this subparagraph, to the extent that such debt is a security within the meaning of paragraph (a)(3) of this section.

(2) Affiliated corporation defined. For purposes of this paragraph, a corporation shall be treated as affiliated with the taxpayer owning the security if—

(i) (a) In the case of a taxable year beginning on or after January 1, 1970, the taxpayer owns directly—

(1) Stock possessing at least 80 percent of the voting power of all classes of such corporation's stock, and

(2) At least 80 percent of each class of such corporation's nonvoting stock excluding for purposes of this subdivision (i)*(a)* nonvoting stock which is limited and preferred as to dividends (see section 1504(a)), or

(b) In the case of a taxable year beginning before January 1, 1970, the taxpayer owns directly at least 95 percent of each class of the stock of such corporation;

(ii) None of the stock of such corporation was acquired by the taxpayer solely for the purpose of converting a capital loss sustained by reason of the worthlessness of any such stock into an ordinary loss under section 165(g)(3), and

(iii) More than 90 percent of the aggregate of the gross receipts of such corporation for all the taxable years during which it has been in existence has been from sources other than royalties, rents (except rents derived from rental of properties to employees of such corporation in the ordinary course of its operating business), dividends, interest (except interest received on the deferred purchase price of operating assets sold), annuities, and gains from sales or exchanges of stocks and securities. For this purpose, the term "gross receipts" means total receipts determined without any deduction for cost of goods sold, and gross receipts from sales or exchanges of stocks and securities shall be taken into account only to the extent of gains from such sales or exchanges.

(e) Bonds issued by an insolvent corporation. A bond of an insolvent corporation secured only by a mortgage from which nothing is realized for the bondholders on foreclosure shall be regarded as having become worthless not later than the year of the foreclosure sale, and no deduction in respect of the loss shall be allowed under section 165(a) in computing a bondholder's taxable income for a subsequent year. See also paragraph (d) of § 1.165-1.

(f) Decline in market value. A taxpayer possessing a security to which this section relates shall not be allowed any deduction under section 165(a) on account of mere market fluctuation in the value of such security. See also § 1.165-4.

(g) Application to inventories. This section does not apply to any loss upon the worthlessness of any security reflected in inventories required to be taken by a dealer in securities under section 471. See § 1.471-5.

(h) Special rules for banks. For special rules applicable under this section to worthless securities of a bank, including securities issued by an affiliated bank, see § 1.582-1.

(i) Abandonment of securities. *(1) In general.* For purposes of section 165 and this section, a security that becomes wholly worthless includes a security described in paragraph (a) of this section that is abandoned and otherwise satisfies the requirements for a deductible loss under section 165. If the abandoned security is a capital asset and is not described in section 165(g)(3) and paragraph (d) of this section (concerning worthless securities of certain affiliated corporations), the resulting loss is treated as a loss from the sale or exchange, on the last day of the taxable year, of a capital asset. See section 165(g)(1) and paragraph (c) of this section. To abandon a security, a taxpayer must permanently surrender and relinquish all rights in the security and receive no consideration in exchange for the security. For purposes of this section, all the facts and circumstances determine whether the transaction is properly characterized as an abandonment or other type of transaction, such as an actual sale or exchange, contribution to capital, dividend, or gift.

(2) Effective/applicability date. This paragraph (i) applies to any abandonment of stock or other securities after March 12, 2008.

(j) Examples. The provisions of this section may be illustrated by the following examples:

Example (1). (i) X Corporation, a domestic manufacturing corporation which makes its return on the basis of the calendar year, owns 100 percent of each class of the stock of Y Corporation; and, in addition, 19 percent of the common stock (the only class of stock) of Z Corporation, which it acquired in 1948. Y Corporation, a domestic manufacturing corporation which makes its return on the basis of the calendar year, owns 81 percent of the common stock of Z Corporation, which it acquired in 1946. It is established that the stock of Z Corporation, which has from its inception derived all its gross receipts from manufacturing operations, became worthless during 1971.

(ii) Since the stock of Z Corporation which is owned by X Corporation is a capital asset and since X Corporation does not directly own at least 80 percent of the stock of Z Corporation, any loss sustained by X Corporation upon the worthlessness of such stock shall be deducted under section 165(g)(1) and paragraph (c) of this section as a loss from a sale or exchange on December 31, 1971, of a capital asset. The loss so sustained by X Corporation shall be considered a long-term capital loss under the provisions of section 1222(4), since the stock was held by that corporation for more than 6 months.

(iii) Since Z Corporation is considered to be affiliated with Y Corporation under the provisions of paragraph (d)(2) of this section, any loss sustained by Y Corporation upon the worthlessness of the stock of Z Corporation shall be deducted in 1971 under section 165(g)(3) and paragraph (d)(1) of this section as an ordinary loss.

Example (2). (i) On January 1, 1971, X Corporation, a domestic manufacturing corporation which makes its return on the basis of the calendar year, owns 60 percent of each class of the stock of Y Corporation, a foreign corporation, which it acquired in 1950. Y Corporation has, from the date of its incorporation, derived all of its gross receipts from manufacturing operations. It is established that the stock of Y Corporation became worthless on June 30, 1971. On August 1, 1971, X Corporation acquires the balance of the stock of Y Corporation for the purpose of obtaining the benefit of section 165(g)(3) with respect to the loss it has sustained on the worthlessness of the stock of Y Corporation.

(ii) Since the stock of Y Corporation which is owned by X Corporation is a capital asset and since Y Corporation is not to be treated as affiliated with X Corporation under the provisions of paragraph (d)(2) of this section, notwithstanding the fact that, at the close of 1971, X Corporation owns 100 percent of each class of stock of Y Corporation, any loss sustained by X Corporation upon the worthlessness of such stock shall be deducted under the provisions of section 165(g)(1) and paragraph (c) of this section as a loss from a sale or exchange on December 31, 1971, of a capital asset.

Example (3). (i) X Corporation, a domestic manufacturing corporation which makes its return on the basis of the calendar year, owns 80 percent of each class of the stock of Y Corporation, which from its inception has derived all of its gross receipts from manufacturing operations. As one of its capital assets, X Corporation owns $100,000 in registered bonds issued by Y Corporation payable at maturity on December 31, 1974. It is established that these bonds became worthless during 1971.

(ii) Since Y Corporation is considered to be affiliated with X Corporation under the provisions of paragraph (d)(2) of this section, any loss sustained by X Corporation upon the worthlessness of these bonds may be deducted in 1971 under section 165(g)(3) and paragraph (d)(1) of this section as an ordinary loss. The loss may not be deducted under section 166 as a bad debt. See section 166(e).

T.D. 6445, 1/15/60, amend T.D. 7224, 12/5/72, T.D. 9386, 3/11/2008.

§ 1.165-6 Farming losses.

(a) Allowance of losses. *(1)* Except as otherwise provided in this section, any loss incurred in the operation of a farm as a trade or business shall be allowed as a deduction under section 165(a) or as a net operating loss deduction in accordance with the provisions of section 172. See § 1.172-1.

(2) If the taxpayer owns and operates a farm for profit in addition to being engaged in another trade or business, but sustains a loss from the operation of the farming business, then the amount of loss sustained in the operation of the farm may be deducted from gross income, if any, from all other sources.

(3) Loss incurred in the operation of a farm for recreation or pleasure shall not be allowed as a deduction from gross income. See § 1.162-12.

(b) Loss from shrinkage. If, in the course of the business of farming, farm products are held for a favorable market, no deduction shall be allowed under section 165(a) in respect of such products merely because of shrinkage in weight, decline in value, or deterioration in storage.

(c) Loss of prospective crop. The total loss by frost, storm, flood, or fire of a prospective crop being grown in the business of farming shall not be allowed as a deduction under section 165(a).

(d) Loss of livestock. *(1) Raised stock.* A taxpayer engaged in the business of raising and selling livestock, such as cattle, sheep, or horses, may not deduct as a loss under section 165(a) the value of animals that perish from among those which were raised on the farm.

(2) Purchased stock. The loss sustained upon the death by disease, exposure, or injury of any livestock purchased and used in the trade or business of farming shall be allowed as a deduction under section 165(a). See, also, paragraph (e) of this section.

(e) Loss due to compliance with orders of governmental authority. The loss sustained upon the destruction by order of the United States, a State, or any other governmental authority, of any livestock, or other property, purchased and used in the trade or business of farming shall be allowed as a deduction under section 165(a).

(f) Amount deductible. *(1) Expenses of operation.* The cost of any feed, pasture, or care which is allowed under section 162 as an expense of operating a farm for profit shall not be included as a part of the cost of livestock for purposes of determining the amount of loss deductible under section 165(a) and this section. For the deduction of farming expenses, see § 1.162-12.

(2) Losses reflected in inventories. If inventories are taken into account in determining the income from the trade or business of farming, no deduction shall be allowed under this section for losses sustained during the taxable year upon livestock or other products, whether purchased for resale or produce on the farm, to the extent such losses are reflected in the inventory on hand at the close of the taxable year. Nothing in this section shall be construed to disallow the deduction of any loss reflected in the inventories of the taxpayer. For provisions relating to inventories of farmers, see section 471 and the regulations thereunder.

(3) Other limitations. For other provisions relating to the amount deductible under this section, see paragraph (c) of § 1.165-1, relating to the amount deductible under section 165(a); § 1.165-7, relating to casualty losses; and § 1.1231-1, relating to gains and losses from the sale or exchange of certain property used in the trade or business.

(g) Other provisions applicable to farmers. For other provisions relating to farmers, see § 1.61-4, relating to gross income of farmers; paragraph (b) of § 1.167(a)-6, relating to depreciation in the case of farmers; and § 1.175-1, relating to soil and water conservation expenditures.

T.D. 6445, 1/15/60.

§ 1.165-7 Casualty losses.

Caution: The Treasury has not yet amended Reg § 1.165-7 to reflect changes made by P.L. 97-248.

(a) In general. *(1) Allowance of deduction.* Except as otherwise provided in paragraphs (b)(4) and (c) of this section, any loss arising from fire, storm, shipwreck, or other casualty is allowable as a deduction under section 165(a) for the taxable year in which the loss is sustained. However, see § 1.165-6, relating to farming losses, and § 1.165-11, relating to an election by a taxpayer to deduct disaster losses in the taxable year immediately preceding the taxable year in which the disaster occurred. The manner of determining the amount of a casualty loss allowable as a deduction in computing taxable income under section 63 is the same whether the loss has been incurred in a trade or business or in any transaction entered into for profit, or whether it has been a loss of property not connected with a trade or business and not incurred in any transaction entered into for profit. The amount of a casualty loss shall be determined in accordance with paragraph (b) of this section. For other rules relating to the treatment of deductible casualty losses, see § 1.1231-1, relating to the involuntary conversion of property.

(2) Method of valuation. (i) In determining the amount of loss deductible under this section, the fair market value of the property immediately before and immediately after the casualty shall generally be ascertained by competent appraisal. This appraisal must recognize the effects of any general market decline affecting undamaged as well as damaged property which may occur simultaneously with the casualty, in order that any deduction under this section shall be limited to the actual loss resulting from damage to the property.

(ii) The cost of repairs to the property damaged is acceptable as evidence of the loss of value if the taxpayer shows that (a) the repairs are necessary to restore the property to its condition immediately before the casualty, (b) the amount spent for such repairs is not excessive, (c) the repairs do not care for more than the damage suffered, and (d) the value of the property after the repairs does not as a result of the repairs exceed the value of the property immediately before the casualty.

(3) Damage to automobiles. An automobile owned by the taxpayer, whether used for business purposes or maintained for recreation or pleasure, may be the subject of a casualty loss, including those losses specifically referred to in subparagraph (1) of this paragraph. In addition, a casualty loss occurs when an automobile owned by the taxpayer is damaged and when:

(i) The damage results from the faulty driving of the taxpayer or other person operating the automobile but is not due to the willful act or willful negligence of the taxpayer or of one acting in his behalf, or

(ii) The damage results from the faulty driving of the operator of the vehicle with which the automobile of the taxpayer collides.

(4) Application to inventories. This section does not apply to a casualty loss reflected in the inventories of the taxpayer. For provisions relating to inventories, see section 471 and the regulations thereunder.

(5) Property converted from personal use. In the case of property which originally was not used in the trade or business or for income-producing purposes and which is thereafter converted to either of such uses, the fair market value of the property on the date of conversion, if less than the adjusted basis of the property at such time, shall be used, after making proper adjustments in respect of basis, as the basis for determining the amount of loss under paragraph (b)(1) of this section. See paragraph (b) of § 1.165-9, and § 1.167(g)-1.

(6) Theft losses. A loss which arises from theft is not considered a casualty loss for purposes of this section. See § 1.165-8, relating to theft losses.

(b) Amount deductible. *(1) General rule.* In the case of any casualty loss whether or not incurred in a trade or business or in any transaction entered into for profit, the amount of loss to be taken into account for purposes of section 165(a) shall be the lesser of either—

(i) The amount which is equal to the fair market value of the property immediately before the casualty reduced by the fair market value of the property immediately after the casualty; or

(ii) The amount of the adjusted basis prescribed in § 1.1011-1 for determining the loss from the sale or other disposition of the property involved. However, if property used in a trade or business or held for the production of income is totally destroyed by casualty, and if the fair market value of such property immediately before the casualty is less than the adjusted basis of such property, the amount of the adjusted basis of such property shall be treated as the amount of the loss for purposes of section 165(a).

(2) Aggregation of property for computing loss. (i) A loss incurred in a trade or business or in any transaction entered into for profit shall be determined under subparagraph (1) of this paragraph by reference to the single, identifiable property damaged or destroyed. Thus, for example, in determining the fair market value of the property before and after the casualty in a case where damage by casualty has occurred to a building and ornamental or fruit trees used in a trade or business, the decrease in value shall be measured by taking the building and trees into account separately, and not together as an integral part of the realty, and separate losses shall be determined for such building and trees.

(ii) In determining a casualty loss involving real property and improvements thereon not used in a trade or business or in any transaction entered into for profit, the improvements (such as buildings and ornamental trees and shrubbery) to the property damaged or destroyed shall be considered an integral part of the property, for purposes of subparagraph (1) of this paragraph, and no separate basis need be apportioned to such improvements.

(3) Examples. The application of this paragraph may be illustrated by the following examples:

Example (1). In 1956 B purchases for $3,600 an automobile which he uses for nonbusiness purposes. In 1959 the automobile is damaged in an accidental collision with another automobile. The fair market value of B's automobile is $2,000 immediately before the collision and $1,500 immediately after the collision. B receives insurance proceeds of $300 to cover the loss. The amount of the deduction allowable under section 165(a) for the taxable year 1959 is $200, computed as follows:

Value of automobile immediately before casualty	$2,000
Less: Value of automobile immediately after casualty	1,500
Value of property actually destroyed	500
Loss to be taken into account for purposes of section 165(a): Lesser amount of property actually destroyed ($500) or adjusted basis of property ($3,600)	$ 500
Less: Insurance received	300
Deduction allowable	$ 200

Example (2). In 1958 A purchases land containing an office building for the lump sum of $90,000. The purchase price is allocated between the land ($18,000) and the building ($72,000) for purposes of determining basis. After the purchase A planted trees and ornamental shrubs on the grounds surrounding the building. In 1961 the land, building, trees, and shrubs are damaged by hurricane. At the time of the casualty the adjusted basis of the land is $18,000 and the adjusted basis of the building is $66,000. At that time the trees and shrubs have an adjusted basis of $1,200. The fair market value of the land and building immediately before the casualty is $18,000 and $70,000, respectively, and immediately after the casualty is $18,000 and $52,000, respectively. The fair market value of the trees and shrubs immediately before the casualty is $2,000 and immediately after the casualty is $400. In 1961 insurance of $5,000 is received to cover the loss to the building. A has no other gains or losses in 1961 subject to section 1231 and § 1.1231-1. The amount of the deduction allowable under section 165(a) with respect to the building for the taxable year 1961 is $13,000, computed as follows:

Value of property immediately before casualty	$70,000
Less: Value of property immediately after casualty	52,000
Value of property actually destroyed	18,000
Loss to be taken into account for purposes of section 165(a): Lesser amount of property actually destroyed ($18,000) or adjusted basis of property ($66,000)	$18,000
Less: Insurance received	5,000
Deduction allowable	13,000

The amount of the deduction allowable under section 165(a) with respect to the trees and shrubs for the taxable year 1961 is $1,200, computed as follows:

Value of property immediately before casualty	$2,000
Less: Value of property immediately after casualty	400
Value of property actually destroyed	1,600
Loss to be taken into account for purposes of section 165(a): Lesser amount of property actually destroyed ($1,600) or adjusted basis of property ($1,200)	1,200

Example (3). Assume the same facts as in example (2) except that A purchases land containing a house instead of an office building. The house is used as his private residence. Since the property is used for personal purposes, no allocation of the purchase price is necessary for the land and house. Likewise, no individual determination of the fair market values of the land, house, trees, and shrubs is necessary. The amount of the deduction allowable under section 165(a) with respect to the land, house, trees, and shrubs for the taxable year 1961 is $14,600, computed as follows:

Value of property immediately before casualty	$90,000
Less: Value of property immediately after casualty	70,400
Value of property actually destroyed	19,600
Loss to be taken into account for purposes of section 165(a): Lesser amount of property actually destroyed ($19,600) or adjusted basis of property ($91,200)	19,600
Less: Insurance received	5,000
Deduction allowable	14,600

(4) Limitation on certain losses sustained by individuals after December 31, 1963. (i) Pursuant to section 165(c)(3), the deduction allowable under section 165(a) in respect of a loss sustained—

(a) After December 31, 1963, in a taxable year ending after such date,

(b) In respect of property not used in a trade or business or for income producing purposes, and

(c) From a single casualty

shall be limited to that portion of the loss which is in excess of $100. The nondeductibility of the first $100 of loss applies to a loss sustained after December 31, 1963, without regard to when the casualty occurred. Thus, if property not used in a trade or business or for income producing purposes is damaged or destroyed by a casualty which occurred prior to January 1, 1964, and loss resulting therefrom is sustained after December 31, 1963, the $100 limitation applies.

(ii) The $100 limitation applies separately in respect of each casualty and applies to the entire loss sustained from each casualty. Thus, if as a result of a particular casualty occurring in 1964, a taxpayer sustains in 1964 a loss of $40 and in 1965 a loss of $250, no deduction is allowable for the loss sustained in 1964 and the loss sustained in 1965 must be reduced by $60 ($100 – $40). The determination of whether damage to, or destruction of, property resulted from a single casualty or from two or more separate casualties will be made upon the basis of the particular facts of each case. However, events which are closely related in origin generally give rise to a single casualty. For example, if a storm damages a taxpayer's residence and his automobile parked in his driveway, any loss sustained results from a single casualty. Similarly, if a hurricane causes high waves, all wind and flood damage to a taxpayer's property caused by the hurricane and the waves results from a single casualty.

(iii) Except as otherwise provided in this subdivision, the $100 limitation applies separately to each individual taxpayer who sustains a loss even though the property damaged or destroyed is owned by two or more individuals. Thus, if a house occupied by two sisters and jointly owned by them is damaged or destroyed, the $100 limitation applies separately to each sister in respect of any loss sustained by her. However, for purposes of applying the $100 limitation, a husband and wife who file a joint return for the first taxable year in which the loss is allowable as a deduction are treated as one individual taxpayer. Accordingly, if property jointly owned by a husband and wife, or property separately owned by the husband or by the wife, is damaged or destroyed by a single casualty in 1964, and a loss is sustained in that year by either or both the husband or wife, only one $100 limitation applies of a joint return is filed for 1964. If, however, the husband and wife file separate returns for 1964, the $100 limitation applies separately in respect of any loss sustained by the husband and in respect of any loss sustained by the wife. Where losses from a single casualty are sustained in two or more separate tax years, the husband and wife shall, for purposes of applying the $100 limitation to such losses, be treated as one individual for all such years if they file a joint return for the first year in which a loss is sustained from the casualty; they shall be treated as separate individuals for all such years if they file separate returns for the first such year. If a joint return is filed in the first loss year but separate returns are filed in a subsequent year, any unused portion of the $100 limitation shall be allocated equally between the husband and wife in the latter year.

(iv) If a loss is sustained in respect of property used partially for business and partially for nonbusiness purposes, the $100 limitation applies only to that portion of the loss properly attributable to the nonbusiness use. For example, if a taxpayer sustains a $1,000 loss in respect of an automobile which he uses 60 percent for business and 40 percent for nonbusiness, the loss is allocated 60 percent to business use and 40 percent to nonbusiness use. The $100 limitation applies to the portion of the loss allocable to the nonbusiness loss.

(c) Loss sustained by an estate. A casualty loss of property not connected with a trade or business and not incurred in any transaction entered into for profit which is sustained during the settlement of an estate shall be allowed as a deduction under sections 165(a) and 641(b) in computing the taxable income of the estate if the loss has not been allowed under section 2054 in computing the taxable estate of the decedent and if the statement has been filed in accordance with § 1.642(g)-1. See section 165(c)(3).

(d) Loss treated as though attributable to a trade or business. For the rule treating a casualty loss not connected with a trade or business as though it were a deduction attributable to a trade or business for purposes of computing a net operating loss, see paragraph (a)(3)(iii) of § 1.172-3.

(e) Effective date. The rules of this section are applicable to any taxable year beginning after January 16, 1960. If, for any taxable year beginning on or before such date, a taxpayer computed the amount of any casualty loss in accordance with the rules then applicable, such taxpayer is not required to change the amount of the casualty loss allowable for any such prior taxable year. On the other hand, the taxpayer may, if he so desires, amend his income tax return for such year to compute the amount of a casualty loss in accordance with the provisions of this section, but no provision in this section shall be construed as extending the period of limitations within which a claim for credit or refund may be filed under section 6511.

T.D. 6445, 1/15/60, amend T.D. 6712, 3/23/64, T.D. 6735, 5/18/64, T.D. 6786, 12/28/64, T.D. 7522, 12/13/77.

---

§ 1.165-8 Theft losses.

(a) Allowance of deduction. *(1)* Except as otherwise provided in paragraphs (b) and (c) of this section, any loss arising from theft is allowable as a deduction under section 165(a) for the taxable year in which the loss is sustained. See section 165(c)(3).

(2) A loss arising from theft shall be treated under section 165(a) as sustained during the taxable year in which the taxpayer discovers the loss. See section 165(e). Thus, a theft loss is not deductible under section 165(a) for the taxable year in which the theft actually occurs unless that is also the year in which the taxpayer discovers the loss. However, if in the year of discovery there exists a claim for reimbursement with respect to which there is a reasonable prospect of recovery, see paragraph (d) of § 1.165-1.

(3) The same theft loss shall not be taken into account both in computing a tax under chapter 1, relating to the income tax, or chapter 2, relating to additional income taxes, of the Internal Revenue Code of 1939 and in computing the income tax under the Internal Revenue Code of 1954. See section 7852(c), relating to items not to be twice deducted from income.

(b) Loss sustained by an estate. A theft loss of property not connected with a trade or business and not incurred in any transaction entered into for profit which is discovered during the settlement of an estate, even though the theft actually occurred during a taxable year of the decedent, shall be allowed as a deduction under sections 165(a) and 641(b) in computing the taxable income of the estate if the loss has not been allowed under section 2054 in computing the taxable estate of the decedent and if the statement has been filed in accordance with § 1.642(g)-1. See section 165(c)(3). For purposes of determining the year of deduction, see paragraph (a)(2) of this section.

(c) Amount deductible. The amount deductible under this section in respect of a theft loss shall be determined consistently with the manner prescribed in § 1.165-7 for determining the amount of casualty loss allowable as a deduction under section 165(a). In applying the provisions of paragraph (b) of § 1.165-7 for this purpose, the fair market value of the property immediately after the theft shall be considered to be zero. In the case of a loss sustained after December 31, 1963, in a taxable year ending after such date, in respect of property not used in a trade or business or for income producing purposes, the amount deductible shall be limited to that portion of the loss which is in excess of $100. For rules applicable in applying the $100 limitation, see paragraph (b)(4) of § 1.165-7. For other rules relating to the treatment of deductible theft losses, see § 1.1231-1, relating to the involuntary conversion of property.

(d) Definition. For purposes of this section the term "theft" shall be deemed to include, but shall not necessarily be limited to, larceny, embezzlement, and robbery.

(e) Application to inventories. This section does not apply to a theft loss reflected in the inventories of the taxpayer. For provisions relating to inventories, see section 471 and the regulations thereunder.

(f) Example. The application of this section may be illustrated by the following example:

Example. In 1955 B, who makes her return on the basis of the calendar year, purchases for personal use a diamond brooch costing $4,000. On November 30, 1961, at which time it has a fair market value of $3,500, the brooch is stolen; but B does not discover the loss until January 1962. The brooch was fully insured against theft. A controversy develops with the insurance company over its liability in respect of the loss. However, in 1962, B has a reasonable prospect of recovery of the fair market value of the brooch from the insurance company. The controversy is settled in March 1963, at which time B receives $2,000 in insurance proceeds to cover the loss from theft. No deduction for the loss is allowable for 1961 or 1962; but the amount of the deduction allowable under section 165(a) for the taxable year 1963 is $1,500, computed as follows:

Value of property immediately before theft	$3,500
Less: Value of property immediately after the theft	0
Balance	3,500
Loss to be taken into account for purposes of section 165(a): ($3,500 but not to exceed adjusted basis of $4,000 at time of theft)	$3,500
Less: Insurance received in 1963	2,000
Deduction allowable for 1963	1,500

T.D. 6445, 1/15/60, amend T.D. 6786, 12/28/64.

§ 1.165-9 Sale of residential property.

(a) Losses not allowed. A loss sustained on the sale of residential property purchased or constructed by the taxpayer for use as his personal residence and so used by him up to the time of the sale is not deductible under section 165(a).

(b) Property converted from personal use. *(1)* If property purchased or constructed by the taxpayer for use as his personal residence is, prior to its sale, rented or otherwise appropriated to income-producing purposes and is used for such purposes up to the time of its sale, a loss sustained on the sale of the property shall be allowed as a deduction under section 165(a).

(2) The loss allowed under this paragraph upon the sale of the property shall be the excess of the adjusted basis prescribed in § 1.1011-1 for determining loss over the amount realized from the sale. For this purpose, the adjusted basis for determining loss shall be the lesser of either of the following amounts, adjusted as prescribed in § 1.1011-1 for the period subsequent to the conversion of the property to income-producing purposes:

(i) The fair market value of the property at the time of conversion, or

(ii) The adjusted basis for loss, at the time of conversion, determined under § 1.1011-1 but without reference to the fair market value.

(3) For rules relating to casualty losses of property converted from personal use, see paragraph (a)(5) of § 1.165-7. To determine the basis for depreciation in the case of such property, see § 1.167(g)-1. For limitations on the loss from the sale of a capital asset, see paragraph (c)(3) of § 1.165-1.

(c) Examples. The application of paragraph (b) of this section may be illustrated by the following examples:

Example (1). Residential property is purchased by the taxpayer in 1943 for use as his personal residence at a cost of $25,000, of which $15,000 is allocable to the building. The taxpayer uses the property as his personal residence until January 1, 1952, at which time its fair market value is $22,000, of which $12,000 is allocable to the building. The taxpayer rents the property from January 1, 1952, until January 1, 1955, at which time it is sold for $16,000. On January 1, 1952, the building has an estimated useful life of 20 years. It is assumed that the building has no estimated salvage value and that there are no adjustments in respect of basis other than depreciation, which is computed on the straight-line method. The loss to be taken into account for purposes of section 165(a) for the taxable year 1955 is $4,200, computed as follows:

Basis of property at time of conversion for purposes of this section (that is, the lesser of $25,000 cost or $22,000 fair market value)	$22,000
Less: Depreciation allowable from January 1, 1952, to January 1, 1955 (3 years at 5 percent based on $12,000, the value of the building at time of conversion as prescribed by § 1.167(g)-1	1,800
Adjusted basis prescribed in § 1.1011-1 for determining loss on sale of the property	20,200
Less: Amount realized on sale	16,000
Loss to be taken into account for purposes of section 165(a)	4,200

In this example the value of the building at the time of conversion is used as the basis for computing depreciation. See example (2) of this paragraph wherein the adjusted basis of the building is required to be used for such purpose.

Example (2). Residential property is purchased by the taxpayer in 1940 for use as his personal residence at a cost of $23,000, of which $10,000 is allocable to the building. The taxpayer uses the property as his personal residence until January 1, 1953, at which time its fair market value is $20,000, of which $12,000 is allocable to the building. The taxpayer rents the property from January 1, 1953, until January 1, 1957, at which time it is sold for $17,000. On January 1, 1953, the building has an estimated useful life of 20 years. It is assumed that the building has no estimated salvage value and that there are no adjustments in respect of basis other than depreciation, which is computed on the straight-line method. The loss to be taken into account for purposes of section 165(a) for the taxable year 1957 is $1,000, computed as follows:

Basis of property at time of conversion for purposes of this section (that is, the lesser of $23,000 cost or $20,000 fair market value)	$20,000
Less, Depreciation allowable from January 1, 1953, to January 1, 1957 (4 years at 5 percent based on $10,000, the cost of the building, as prescribed by § 1.167(g)-1)	2,000
Adjusted basis prescribed in § 1.1011-1 for determining loss on sale of the property	18,000
Less: Amount realized on sale	17,000
Loss to be taken into account for purposes of section 165(a)	1,000

T.D. 6445, 1/15/60, amend T.D. 6712, 3/23/64.

§ 1.165-10 Wagering losses.

Losses sustained during the taxable year on wagering transactions shall be allowed as a deduction but only to the extent of the gains during the taxable year from such transactions. In the case of a husband and wife making a joint return for the taxable year, the combined losses of the spouses from wagering transactions shall be allowed to the extent of the combined gains of the spouses from wagering transactions.

T.D. 6445, 1/15/60.

§ 1.165-11 Election in respect of losses attributable to a disaster.

Caution: The Treasury has not yet amended Reg § 1.165-11 to reflect changes made by P.L. 108-311, P.L. 98-369.

(a) In general. Section 165(h) provides that a taxpayer who has sustained a disaster loss which is allowable as a deduction under section 165(a) may, under certain circumstances, elect to deduct such loss for the taxable year immediately preceding the taxable year in which the disaster actually occurred.

(b) Loss subject to election. The election provided by section 165(h) and paragraph (a) of this section applies only to a loss:

(1) Arising from a disaster resulting in a determination referred to in subparagraph (2) of this paragraph and occurring—

(i) After December 31, 1971, or

(ii) After December 31, 1961, and before January 1, 1972, and during the period following the close of a particular taxable year of the taxpayer and on or before the due date for filing the income tax return for that taxable year (determined without regard to any extension of time granted the taxpayer for filing such return);

(2) Occurring in an area subsequently determined by the President of the United States to warrant assistance by the Federal Government under the Disaster Relief Act of 1974; and

(3) Constituting a loss otherwise allowable as a deduction for the year in which the loss occurred under section 165(a) and the provisions of §§ 1.165-1 through 1.165-10 which are applicable to such losses.

(c) Amount of loss to which election applies. The amount of the loss to which section 165(h) and this section apply shall be the amount of the loss sustained during the period specified in paragraph (b)(1) of this section computed in accordance with the provisions of section 165 and those provisions of §§ 1.165-1 through 1.165-10 which are applicable to such losses. However, for purposes of making such computation, the period specified in paragraph (b)(1) of this section shall be deemed to be a taxable year.

(d) Scope and effect of election. An election made pursuant to section 165(h) and this section in respect of a loss arising from a particular disaster shall apply to the entire loss sustained by the taxpayer from such disaster during the period specified in paragraph (b)(1) of this section in the area specified in paragraph (b)(2) of this section. If such an election is made, the disaster to which the election relates will be deemed to have occurred in the taxable year immediately preceding the taxable year in which the disaster actually occurred, and the loss to which the election applies will be deemed to have been sustained in such preceding taxable year.

(e) Time and manner of making election. An election to claim a deduction with respect to a disaster loss described in paragraph (b) of this section for the taxable year immediately preceding the taxable year in which the disaster actually occurred must be made by filing a return, an amended return, or a claim for refund clearly showing that the election provided by section 165(h) has been made. In general, the return or claim should specify the date or dates of the disaster which gave rise to the loss, and the city, town, county, and State in which the property which was damaged or destroyed was located at the time of the disaster. An election in respect of a loss arising from a particular disaster occurring after December 31, 1971, must be made on or before the later of (1) the due date for filing the income tax return (determined without regard to any extension of time granted the taxpayer for filing such return) for the taxable year in which the disaster actually occurred, or (2) the due date of filing the income tax return (determined with regard to any extension of time granted the taxpayer for filing such return) for the taxable year immediately preceding the taxable year in which the disaster actually occurred. Such election shall be irrevocable after the later of (1) 90 days after the date on which the election was made, or (2) March 6, 1973. No revocation of such election shall be effective unless the amount of any credit or refund which resulted from such election is paid to the Internal Revenue Service within the revocation period described in the preceding sentence. However, in the case of a revocation made before receipt by the taxpayer of a refund claimed pursuant to such election, the revocation shall be effective if the refund is repaid within 30 calendar days after such receipt. An election in respect of a loss arising from a particular disaster occurring after December 31, 1961, and before January 1, 1972, must be made on or before the later of (1) the 15th day of the third month following the month in which falls the date prescribed for the filing of the income tax return (determined without regard to any extension of time granted the taxpayer for filing such return) for the taxable year immediately preceding the taxable year in which the disaster actually occurred, or (2) the due date for filing the income tax return (determined with regard to any extension of time granted the taxpayer for filing such return) for the taxable year immediately preceding the taxable year in which the disaster actually occurred. Such election shall be irrevocable after the date by which it must be made.

T.D. 6735, 5/18/64, amend T.D. 7224, 12/5/72, T.D. 7522, 12/13/77.

---

§ 1.165-12 Denial of deduction for losses on registration-required obligations not in registered form.

(a) In general. Except as provided in paragraph (c) of this section, nothing in section 165(a) and the regulations thereunder, or in any other provision of law, shall be construed to provide a deduction for any loss sustained on any registration-required obligation held after December 31, 1982, unless the obligation is in registered form or the issuance of the obligation was subject to tax under section 4701. The term "registration-required obligation" has the meaning given to that term in section 163(f)(2), except that clause (iv) of subparagraph (A) thereof shall not apply. Therefore, although an obligation that is not in registered form is described in § 1.163-5(c)(1), the holder of such an obligation shall not be allowed a deduction for any loss sustained on such obligation unless paragraph (c) of this section applies. The term "holder" means the person that would be denied a loss deduction under section 165(j)(1) or denied capital gain treatment under section 1287(a). For purposes of this section, the term *United States* means the United States and its possessions within the meaning of § 1.163-5(c)(2)(iv).

(b) Registered form. *(1) Obligations issued after September 21, 1984.* With respect to any obligation originally issued after September 21, 1984, the term "registered form" has the meaning given that term in section 103(j)(3) and the regulations thereunder. Therefore, an obligation that would otherwise be in registered form is not considered to be in registered form if it can be transferred at that time or at any time until its maturity by any means not described in § 5f.103-1(c). An obligation that, as of a particular time, is not considered to be in registered form because it can be transferred by any means not described in § 5f.103-1(c) is considered to be in registered form at all times during the period beginning with a later time and ending with the maturity of the obligation in which the obligation can be transferred only by a means described in § 5f.103-1(c).

(2) Obligations issued after December 31, 1982 and on or before September 21, 1984. With respect to any obligation originally issued after December 31, 1982 and on or before

September 21, 1984 or an obligation originally issued after September 21, 1984 pursuant to the exercise of a warrant or the conversion of a convertible obligation, which warrant or obligation [including conversion privilege] was issued after December 31, 1982 and on or before September 21, 1984, that obligation will be considered in registered form if it satisfied § 5f.163-1 or the proposed regulations provided in § 1.163-5(c) and published in the Federal Register on September 2, 1983 (48 FR 39953).

(c) Registration-required obligations not in registered form which are not subject to section 165(j)(1). Notwithstanding the fact that an obligation is a registration-required obligation that is not in registered form, the holder will not be subject to section 165(j)(1) if the holder meets the conditions of any one of the following subparagraphs (1), (2), (3), or (4) of this paragraph (c).

(1) Persons permitted to hold in connection with the conduct of a trade or business. (i) The holder is an underwriter, broker, dealer, bank, or other financial institution (defined in paragraph (c)(1)(iv)) that holds such obligation in connection with its trade or business conducted outside the United States; or the holder is a broker-dealer (registered under Federal or State law or exempted from registration by the provisions of such law because it is a bank) that holds such obligation for sale to customers in the ordinary course of its trade or business.

(ii) The holder must offer to sell, sell and deliver the obligation in bearer form only outside of the United States except that a holder that is a registered broker-dealer as described in paragraph (c)(1)(i) of this section may offer to sell and sell the obligation in bearer form inside the United States to a financial institution as defined in paragraph (c)(1)(iv) of this section for its own account or for the account of another financial institution or of an exempt organization as defined in section 501(c)(3).

(iii) The holder may deliver an obligation in bearer form that is offered or sold inside the United States only if the holder delivers it to a financial institution that is purchasing for its own account, or for the account of another financial institution or of an exempt organization, and the financial institution or organization that purchases the obligation for its own account or for whose account the obligation is purchased represents that it will comply with the requirements of section 165(j)(3)(A), (B), or (C). Absent actual knowledge that the representation is false, the holder may rely on a written statement provided by the financial institution or exempt organization, including a statement that is delivered in electronic form. The holder may deliver a registration-required obligation in bearer form that is offered and sold outside the United States to a person other than a financial institution only if the holder has evidence in its records that such person is not a U.S. citizen or resident and does not have actual knowledge that such evidence is false. Such evidence may include a written statement by that person, including a statement that is delivered electronically. For purposes of this paragraph (c), the term *deliver* includes a transfer of an obligation evidenced by a book entry including a book entry notation by a clearing organization evidencing transfer of the obligation from one member of the organization to another member. For purposes of this paragraph (c), the term *deliver* does not include a transfer of an obligation to the issuer or its agent for cancellation or extinguishment. The record-retention provisions in § 1.1441-1(e)(4)(iii) shall apply to any statement that a holder receives pursuant to this paragraph (c)(1)(iii).

(iv) For purposes of paragraph (c) of this section, the term "financial institution" means a person which itself is, or more than 50 percent of the total combined voting power of all classes of whose stock entitled to vote is owned by a person which is—

(A) Engaged in the conduct of a banking, financing, or similar business within the meaning of section 954(c)(3)(B) as in effect before the Tax Reform Act of 1986, and the regulations thereunder;

(B) Engaged in business as a broker or dealer in securities;

(C) An insurance company;

(D) A person that provides pensions or other similar benefits to retired employees;

(E) Primarily engaged in the business of rendering investment advice;

(F) A regulated investment company or other mutual fund; or

(G) A finance corporation a substantial part of the business of which consists of making loans (including the acquisition of obligations under a lease which is entered into primarily as a financing transaction), acquiring accounts receivable, notes or installment obligations arising out of the sale of tangible personal property or the performing of services, or servicing debt obligations.

(2) Persons permitted to hold obligations for their own investment account. The holder is a financial institution holding the obligation for its own investment account that satisfies the conditions set forth in subdivisions (i), (ii), (iii), and (iv) of his paragraph (c)(2).

(i) The holder reports on its Federal income tax return for the taxable year any interest payments received (including original issue discount includable in gross income for such taxable year) with respect to such obligation and gain or loss on the sale or other disposition of such obligation;

(ii) The holder indicates on its Federal income tax return that income, gain or loss described in paragraph (c)(2)(i) is attributable to registration-required obligations held in bearer form for its own account;

(iii) The holder of a bearer obligation that resells the obligation inside the United States resells the obligation only to another financial institution for its own account or for the account of another financial institution or exempt organization; and

(iv) The holder delivers such obligation in bearer form to any other person in accordance with paragraph (c)(1)(ii) and (iii) of this section.

(3) Persons permitted to hold through financial institutions. The holder is any person that purchases and holds a registration-required obligation in bearer form through a financial institution with which the holder maintains a customer, custodial or nominee relationship and such institution agrees to satisfy, and does in fact satisfy, the conditions set forth in subdivisions (i), (ii), (iii), (iv) and (v) of this paragraph (c)(3).

(i) The financial institution makes a return of information of the Internal Revenue Service with respect to any interest payments received. The financial institution must report original issue discount includable in the holder's gross income for the taxable year on any obligation so held, but only if the obligation appears in an Internal Revenue Service publication of obligations issued at an original issue discount and only in an amount determined in accordance with information contained in that publication. An information return for any interest payment shall be made on a Form 1099 for the calendar year. It shall indicate the aggregate amount of the payment received, the name, address and taxpayer identification number of the holder, and such other information as is required by the form. No return of information is required under this subdivision if the financial institution reports payments under section 6041 or 6049.

(ii) The financial institution makes a return of information on Form 1099B with respect to any disposition by the holder of such obligation. The return shall show the name, address, and taxpayer identification number of the holder of the obligation, Committee on Uniform Security Information Procedures (CUSIP), gross proceeds, sale date, and such other information as may be required by the form. No return of information is required under this subdivision if such financial institution reports with respect to the disposition under section 6045.

(iii) In the case of a bearer obligation offered for resale or resold in the United States, the financial institution may resell the obligation only to another financial institution for its own account or for the account of an exempt organization.

(iv) The financial institution covenants with the holder that the financial institution will deliver the obligation in bearer form in accordance with the requirements set forth in paragraph (c)(1)(ii) and (iii).

(v) The financial institution delivers the obligation in bearer form in accordance with paragraph (c)(1)(ii) and (iv) as if the financial institution delivering the obligation were the holder referred to in such paragraph.

(4) Conversion of obligations into registered form. The holder is not a person described in paragraph (c)(1), (2), or (3) of this section, and within thirty days of the date when the seller or other transferor is reasonably able to make the bearer obligation available to the holder, the holder surrenders the obligation to a transfer agent or the issuer for conversion of the obligation into registered form. If such obligation is not registered within such 30 day period, the holder shall be subject to sections 165(j) and 1287(a).

(d) Effective date. These regulations apply generally to obligations issued after January 20, 1987. However, a taxpayer may choose to apply the rules of § 1.165-12 with respect to an obligation issued after December 31, 1982 and on or before January 20, 1987, which obligation is held after January 20, 1987.

T.D. 8110, 12/16/86, amend T.D. 8734, 10/6/97.

§ 1.165-13T Questions and answers relating to the treatment of losses on certain straddle transactions entered into before the effective date of the Economic Recovery Tax Act of 1981, under section 108 of the Tax Reform Act of 1984 (temporary).

The following questions and answers concern the treatment of losses on certain straddle transactions entered into before the effective date of the Economic Recovery Tax Act of 1981, under the Tax Reform Act of 1984 (98 Stat. 494).

Q-1. What is the scope of section 108 of the Tax Reform Act of 1984 (Act)?

A-1. Section 108 of the Act provides that in the case of any disposition of one or more positions, which were entered into before 1982 and form part of a straddle, and to which the provisions of Title V of The Economic Recovery Act of 1981 (ERTA) do not apply, any loss from such disposition shall be allowed for the taxable year of the disposition if such position is part of a transaction entered into for profit. For purposes of section 108 of the Act, the term "straddle" has the meaning given to such term by section 1092(c) of the Internal Revenue Code of 1954 as in effect on the day after the date of enactment of ERTA; including a straddle all the positions of which are regulated futures contracts (as defined in Q&A-6 of this section). Straddles in certain listed stock options were not covered by ERTA and are not affected by this provision.

Q-2. What transactions are considered entered into for profit?

A-2. A transaction is considered entered into for profit if the transaction is entered into for profit within the meaning of section 165(c)(2) of the Code. In this respect, section 108 of the Act restates existing law applicable to straddle transactions. All the circumstances surrounding the transaction, including the magnitude and timing for entry into, and disposition of, the positions comprising the transaction are relevant in making the determination whether a transaction is considered entered into for profit. Moreover, in order for section 108 of the Act to apply, the transaction must have sufficient substance to be recognized for Federal income tax purposes. Thus, for example, since a "sham" transaction would not be recognized for tax purposes, section 106 of the Act would not apply to such a transaction.

Q-3. If a loss is disallowed in a taxable year (year 1) because the transaction was not entered into for profit, is the entire gain from the straddle occurring in a later taxable year taxed?

A-3. No. Under section 108(c) of the Act the taxpayer is allowed to offset the gain in the subsequent taxable year by the amount of loss (including expenses) disallowed in year 1.

Q-4. In what manner does the for-profit test of Q&A-2 apply to losses from straddle transactions sustained by commodities dealers and persons regularly engaged in investing in regulated futures contracts?

A-4. In general, for a loss to be allowable with respect to positions that form part of a straddle, the for-profit test of Q&A-2 must be satisfied. However, certain positions (see Q&A-6) held by a commodities dealer or person regularly engaged in investing in regulated futures contracts are rebuttably presumed to be part of a transaction entered into for profit. Thus, the for profit test is applied to commodities dealers and persons regularly engaged in investing in regulated futures contracts in light of the factors relating to the applicability and rebuttal of the profit presumption, including, for example, the nature and extent of the taxpayer's trading activities.

Q-5. Under what circumstances is the presumption considered rebutted?

A-5. All the facts and circumstances of each case are to be considered in determining if the presumption is rebutted. The following factors are significant in making this determination: (1) The level of transaction costs; (2) the extent to which the transaction results from trading patterns different from the taxpayer's regular patterns; and (3) the extent of straddle transactions having tax results disproportionate to economic consequences. Factors other than the ones described above may be taken into account in making the determination. Moreover, a determination is not to be made solely on the basis of the number of factors indicating that the presumption is rebutted.

Q-6. Does a commodities dealer or person regularly engaged in investing in regulated futures contracts qualify for the profit presumption for all transactions?

A-6. No. The presumption is only applicable to regulated futures contract transactions in property that is the subject of the person's regular trading activity. For example, a commodities dealer who regularly trades only in agricultural futures will not qualify for the presumption for a silver futures straddle transaction. For purposes of this section, the term "regulated futures contracts" has the meaning given to such term by section 1256(b) of the Code as in effect before the enactment of the Tax Reform Act of 1984.

Q-7. Who qualifies as a commodities dealer or as a person regularly engaged in investing in regulated futures contracts for purposes of the profit presumption?

A-7. For purposes of this section, the term "commodities dealer" has the meaning given to such term by section 1402(i)(2)(B) of the Code. Section 1402(i)(2)(B) defines a commodities dealer as a person who is actively engaged in trading section 1256 contracts (which includes regulated futures contracts as defined in Q& A-6) and is registered with a domestic board of trade which is designated as a contract market by the Commodity Futures Trading Commission. To determine if a person is regularly engaged in investing in regulated futures contracts all the facts and circumstances should be considered including, but not limited to, the following factors: (1) Regularity of trading at all times throughout the year; (2) the level of transaction costs; (3) substantial volume and economic consequences of trading at all times throughout the year; (4) percentage of time dedicated to commodity trading activities as compared to other activities; and (5) the person's knowledge of the regulated futures contract market.

Q-8. If a commodities dealer or a person regularly engaged in investing in regulated futures contracts participates in a syndicate, as defined in section 1256(e)(3)(B) of the Code, does the rebuttable presumption of "entered into for profit" apply to the transactions entered into through the syndicate?

A-8. No. A participant in a syndicate does not qualify for the rebuttable presumption of "entered into for profit" with respect to transactions entered into by or for the syndicate. A syndicate is defined in section 1256(e)(3)(B) of the Code as any partnership or other entity (other than a corporation which is not an S corporation) if more than 35 percent of the losses of such entity during the taxable year are allocable to limited partners or limited entrepreneurs (within the meaning of section 464(e)(2)).

Q-9. Will the Service continue to make the closed and completed transaction argument set forth in Rev. Rul. 77-185, 1977-1 C.B. 48, with respect to transactions covered by section 108 of the Act?

A-9. No. The closed and completed transaction argument will not be made regarding transactions subject to section 108 of the Act. In general, losses in such transactions will be allowed for the taxable year of disposition if the transaction is not viewed as a sham and satisfies the "entered into for profit" test described in Q&A-2. Nevertheless, for certain positions covered by section 108 of the Act, various Code sections may apply without regard to whether such position constitutes a straddle to disallow or limit the loss otherwise allowable in the year of the disposition. For example, dispositions of certain positions held by a partnership which resulted in a loss to a partner may be limited or disallowed under section 465 of 704(d).

T.D. 7968, 8/21/84.

§ 1.9200-2 Manner of taking deduction.

(a) In general. The deduction provided by § 1.9200-1 shall be taken by multiplying the amount of the monthly deduction determined under § 1.9200-1(c)(2) for each motor carrier operating authority by the number of months in the taxable year for which the deduction is allowable, and entering the resulting amount at the appropriate place on the taxpayer's return for each year in which the deduction is properly claimed. Additionally, any taxpayer who has claimed the deduction provided by § 1.9200-1 must (unless it has already filed a statement containing the required information) attach a statement to the next income tax return of the taxpayer which has a filing due date on or after June 4, 1984. The statement shall provide, in addition to the taxpayer's name, address, and taxpayer identification number, the following information for each motor carrier operating authority for which a deduction was claimed:

(1) the taxable year of the taxpayer for which the deduction was first claimed;

(2) whether the taxpayer's deduction was determined using the adjusted basis of the authority under section 1012 or an allocated stock basis under § 1.9200-1(e)(2); and

(3) if an allocation of stock basis has been made under § 1.9200-1(e)(2), the calculations made in determining the amount of basis to be allocated to the authority.

(b) Filing and amendment of returns. A taxpayer who has filed its return for the taxable year that includes July 1, 1980, claiming the deduction allowed under § 1.9200-1, may amend its return for such year in order to elect under § 1.9200-1(c)(1)(ii) to begin the 60-month period in the subsequent taxable year. A taxpayer eligible to take the deduction under § 1.9200-1 who has filed its returns for both the taxable year that includes July 1, 1980, and the following taxable year without claiming the deduction, may claim the deduction by filing amended returns or claims for refund for the taxable year in which the taxpayer elects to begin the 60-month period, and for subsequent taxable years. If a taxpayer first claims the deduction on an amended return under the preceding sentence, the statement required by paragraph (a) of this section must be attached to such amended return.

(c) Deduction taken for operating authority other than under § 1.9200-1. If a deduction other than the deduction allowed under § 1.9200-1 was taken in any taxable year for the reduction in value of a motor carrier operating authority caused by administrative or legislative actions to decrease restrictions on entry into the interstate motor carrier business, the taxpayer should file an amended return for such taxable year which computes taxable income without regard to such deduction.

T.D. 7947, 3/5/84.

§ 1.166-1 Bad debts.

Caution: The Treasury has not yet amended Reg § 1.166-1 to reflect changes made by P.L. 99-514.

(a) Allowance of deduction. Section 166 provides that, in computing taxable income under section 63, a deduction shall be allowed in respect of bad debts owed to the taxpayer. For this purpose, bad debts shall, subject to the provisions of section 166 and the regulations thereunder, be taken into account either as—

(1) A deduction in respect of debts which become worthless in whole or in part; or as

(2) A deduction for a reasonable addition to a reserve for bad debts.

(b) Manner of selecting method. *(1)* A taxpayer filing a return of income for the first taxable year for which he is entitled to a bad debt deduction may select either of the two methods prescribed by paragraph (a) of this section for treating bad debts, but such selection is subject to the approval of the district director upon examination of the return. If the method so selected is approved, it shall be used in returns for all subsequent taxable years unless the Commissioner grants permission to use the other method. A statement of facts substantiating any deduction claimed under section 166 on account of bad debts shall accompany each return of income.

(2) Taxpayers who have properly selected one of the two methods for treating bad debts under provisions of prior law corresponding to section 166 shall continue to use that method for all subsequent taxable years unless the Commissioner grants permission to use the other method.

(3) (i) For taxable years beginning after December 31, 1959, application for permission to change the method of treating bad debts shall be made in accordance with section 446(e) and paragraph (e)(3) of § 1.446-1.

(ii) For taxable years beginning before January 1, 1960, application for permission to change the method of treating bad debts shall be made at least 30 days before the close of the taxable year for which the change is effective.

(4) Notwithstanding paragraphs (b)(1), (2), and (3) of this section, a dealer in property currently employing the accrual method of accounting and currently maintaining a reserve for bad debts under section 166(c) (which may have included guaranteed debt obligations described in section 166(f)(1)(A)) may establish a reserve for section 166(f)(1)(A) guaranteed debt obligations for a taxable year ending after October 21, 1965 under section 166(f) and § 1.166-10 by filing on or before April 17, 1986 an amended return indicating that such a reserve has been established. The establishment of such a reserve will not be considered a change in method of accounting for purposes of section 446(e). However, an election by a taxpayer to establish a reserve for bad debts under section 166(c) shall be treated as a change in method of accounting. See also § 1.166-4, relating to reserve for bad debts, and § 1.166-10, relating to reserve for guaranteed debt obligations.

(c) Bona fide debt required. Only a bona fide debt qualifies for purposes of section 166. A bona fide debt is a debt which arises from a debtor-creditor relationship based upon a valid and enforceable obligation to pay a fixed or determinable sum of money. A debt arising out of the receivables of an accrual method taxpayer is deemed to be an enforceable obligation for purposes of the preceding sentence to the extent that the income such debt represents have been included in the return of income for the year for which the deduction as a bad debt is claimed or for a prior taxable year. For example, a debt arising out of gambling receivables that are unenforceable under state or local law, which an accrual method taxpayer includes in income under section 61, is an enforceable obligation for purposes of this paragraph. A gift or contribution to capital shall not be considered a debt for purposes of section 166. The fact that a bad debt its not due at the time of deduction shall not of itself prevent is allowance under section 166. For the disallowance of deductions for bad debts owed by a political party, see § 1.271-1.

(d) Amount deductible. *(1) General rule.* Except in the case of a deduction for a reasonable addition to a reserve for bad debts, the basis for determining the amount of deduction under section 166 in respect of a bad debt shall be the same as the adjusted basis prescribed by § 1.1011-1 for determining the loss from the sale or other disposition of property. To determine the allowable deduction in the case of obligations acquired before March 1, 1913, see also paragraph (b) of § 1.1053-1.

(2) Specific cases. Subject to any provision of section 166 and the regulations thereunder which provides to the contrary, the following amounts are deductible as bad debts:

(i) Notes or accounts receivable. (a) If, in computing taxable income, a taxpayer values his notes or accounts receivable at their fair market value when received, the amount deductible as a bad debt under section 166 in respect of such receivables shall be limited to such fair market value even though it is less than their face value.

(b) A purchaser of accounts receivable which become worthless during the taxable year shall be entitled under section 166 to a deduction which is based upon the price he paid for such receivables but not upon their face value.

(ii) Bankruptcy claim. Only the difference between the amount received in distribution of the assets of an bankrupt and the amount of the claim may be deducted under section 166 as a bad debt.

(iii) Claim against decedent's estate. The excess of the amount of the claim over the amount received by a creditor of a decedent in distribution of the assets of the decedent's estate may be considered a worthless debt under section 166.

(e) Prior inclusion in income required. Worthless debts arising from unpaid wages, salaries, fees, rents, and similar items of taxable income shall not be allowed as a deduction under section 166 unless the income such items represent has been included in the return of income for the year for which the deduction as a bad debt is claimed or for a prior taxable year.

(f) Recovery of bad debts. Any amount attributable to the recovery during the taxable year of a bad debt, or of a part of a bad debt, which was allowed as a deduction from gross income in a prior taxable year shall be included in gross income for the taxable year of recovery, except to the extent that the recovery is excluded from gross income under the provisions of § 1.111-1, relating to the recovery of certain items previously deducted or credited. This paragraph shall not apply, however, to a bad debt which was previously charged against a reserve by a taxpayer on the reserve method of treating bad debts.

(g) Worthless securities. *(1)* Section 166 and the regulations thereunder do not apply to a debt which is evidenced by a bond, debenture, note, or certificate, or other evidence of indebtedness, issued by a corporation or by a government or political subdivision thereof, with interest coupons or in registered form. See section 166(e). For provisions allowing the deduction of a loss resulting from the worthlessness of such a debt, see § 1.165-5.

(2) The provisions of subparagraph (1) of this paragraph do not apply to any loss sustained by a bank and resulting from the worthlessness of a security described in section 165(g)(2)(C). See paragraph (a) of § 1.582-1.

T.D. 6403, 7/30/59, amend T.D. 6996, 1/17/69, T.D. 7902, 7/20/83, T.D. 8071, 1/16/86.

---

§ 1.166-2 Evidence of worthlessness.

(a) General rule. In determining whether a debt is worthless in whole or in part the district director will consider all pertinent evidence, including the value of the collateral, if any, securing the debt and the financial condition of the debtor.

(b) Legal action not required. Where the surrounding circumstances indicate that a debt is worthless and uncollectible and that legal action to enforce payment would in all probability not result in the satisfaction of execution on a judgment, a showing of these facts will be sufficient evidence of the worthlessness of the debt for purposes of the deduction under section 166.

(c) Bankruptcy. *(1) General rule.* Bankruptcy is generally an indication of the worthlessness of at least a part of an unsecured and unpreferred debt.

(2) Year of deduction. In bankruptcy cases a debt may become worthless before settlement in some instances; and in others, only when a settlement in bankruptcy has been reached. In either case, the mere fact that bankruptcy proceedings instituted against the debtor are terminated in a later year, thereby confirming the conclusion that the debt is worthless, shall not authorize the shifting of the deduction under section 166 to such later year.

(d) Banks and other regulated corporations. *(1) Worthlessness presumed in year of charge-off.* If a bank or other corporation which is subject to supervision by Federal authorities, or by State authorities maintaining substantially equivalent standards, charges off a debt in whole or in part, either—

(i) In obedience to the specific orders of such authorities, or

(ii) In accordance with established policies of such authorities, and, upon their first audit of the bank or other corporation subsequent to the charge-off, such authorities confirm in writing that the charge-off would have been subject to such specific orders if the audit had been made on the date of the charge-off, then the debt shall, to the extent charged off during the taxable year, be conclusively presumed to have become worthless, or worthless only in part, as the case may be, during such taxable year. But no such debt shall be so conclusively presumed to be worthless, or worthless only in part, as the case may be, if the amount so charged off is not claimed as a deduction by the taxpayer at the time of filing the return for the taxable year in which the charge-off takes place.

(2) Evidence of worthlessness in later taxable year. If such a bank or other corporation does not claim a deduction for such a totally or partially worthless debt in its return for the taxable year in which the charge-off takes place, but claims the deduction for a later taxable year, then the charge-off in the prior taxable year shall be deemed to have been involuntary and the deduction under section 166 shall be allowed for the taxable year for which claimed, provided that the taxpayer produces sufficient evidence to show that—

(i) The debt became wholly worthless in the later taxable year, or became recoverable only in part subsequent to the taxable year of the involuntary charge-off, as the case may be; and,

(ii) To the extent that the deduction claimed in the later taxable year for a debt partially worthless was not involuntarily charged off in prior taxable years, it was charged off in the later taxable year.

(3) Conformity election. (i) Eligibility for election. In lieu of applying paragraphs (d)(1) and (2) of this section, a bank (as defined in paragraph (d)(4)(i) of this section) that is subject to supervision by Federal authorities, or by state authorities maintaining substantially equivalent standards, may elect under this paragraph (d)(3) to use a method of accounting that establishes a conclusive presumption of worthlessness for debts, provided that the bank meets the express determination requirement of paragraph (d)(3)(iii)(D) of this section for the taxable year of the election.

(ii) Conclusive presumption. (A) In general. If a bank satisfies the express determination requirement of paragraph (d)(3)(iii)(D) of this section and elects to use the method of accounting under this paragraph (d)(3)—

(1) Debts charged off, in whole or in part, for regulatory purposes during a taxable year are conclusively presumed to have become worthless, or worthless only in part, as the case may be, during that year, but only if the charge-off results from a specific order of the bank's supervisory authority or corresponds to the bank's classification of the debt, in whole or in part, as a loss asset, as described in paragraph (d)(3)(ii)(C) of this section; and

(2) a bad debt deduction for a debt that is subject to regulatory loss classification standards is allowed for a taxable year only to the extent that the debt is conclusively presumed to have become worthless under paragraph (d)(3)(ii)(A)(1) of this section during that year.

(B) Charge-off should have been made in earlier year. The conclusive presumption that a debt is worthless in the year that it is charged off for regulatory purposes applies even if the bank's supervisory authority determines in a subsequent year that the charge-off should have been made in an earlier year. A pattern of charge-offs in the wrong year, however, may result in revocation of the bank's election by the Commissioner pursuant to paragraph (d)(3)(iv)(D) of this section.

(C) Loss asset defined. A debt is classified as a loss asset by a bank if the bank assigns the debt to a class that corresponds to a loss asset classification under the standards set forth in the "Uniform Agreement on the Classification of Assets and Securities Held by Banks" (See Attachment to Comptroller of the Currency Banking Circular No. 127, Rev. 4-26-91, Comptroller of the Currency, Communications Department, Washington, DC 20219) or similar guidance issued by the Office of the Comptroller of the Currency, the Federal Deposit Insurance Corporation, the Board of Governors of the Federal Reserve, or the Farm Credit Administration; or for institutions under the supervision of the Office of Thrift Supervision, 12 CFR 563.160(b)(3).

(iii) Election. (A) In general. An election under this paragraph (d)(3) is to be made on bank-by-bank basis and constitutes either the adoption of or a change in method of accounting, depending on the particular bank's facts. A change in method of accounting that results from the making of an election under this paragraph (d)(3) has the effects described in paragraph (d)(3)(iii)(B) of this section.

(B) Effect of change in method of accounting. A change in method of accounting resulting from an election under this paragraph (d)(3) does not require or permit an adjustment under section 481(a). Under this cut-off approach—

(1) There is no change in the § 1.1011-1 adjusted basis of the bank's existing debts (as determined under the bank's former method of accounting for bad debts) as a result of the change in method of accounting;

(2) With respect to debts that are subject to regulatory loss classification standards and are held by the bank at the beginning of the year of change (to the extent that they have not been charged off for regulatory purposes), and with respect to debts subject to regulatory loss classification standards that are originated or acquired subsequent to the beginning of the year of change, bad debt deductions in the year of change and thereafter are determined under the method of accounting for bad debts prescribed by this paragraph (d)(3);

(3) With respect to debts that are not subject to regulatory loss classification standards or that have been totally charged off prior to the year of change, bad debt deductions are determined under the general rules of section 166; and

(4) If there was any partial charge-off of a debt in a prechange year, any portion of which was not claimed as a deduction, the deduction reflecting that partial charge-off must be taken in the first year in which there is any further charge-off of the debt for regulatory purposes.

(C) Procedures. (1) In general. A new bank adopts the method of accounting under this paragraph (d)(3) for any taxable year ending on or after December 31, 1991 (and for all subsequent taxable years) when it adopts its overall method of accounting for bad debts, by attaching a statement to this effect to its income tax return for that year. Any other bank makes an election for any taxable year ending on or after December 31, 1991 (and for all subsequent taxable years) by filing a completed Form 3115 (Application for Change in Accounting Method) in accordance with the rules of paragraph (d)(3)(iii)(C)(2) or (3) of this section. The statement or Form 3115 must include the name, address, and taxpayer identification number of the electing bank and contain a declaration that the express determination requirement of paragraph (d)(3)(iii)(D) of this section is satisfied for the taxable year of the election. When a Form 3115 is used, the declaration must be made in the space provided on the form for "Other changes in method of accounting." The words "ELECTION UNDER § 1.166-2(d)(3)" must be typed or legibly printed at the top of the statement or page 1 of the Form 3115.

(2) First election. The first time a bank makes this election, the statement or Form 3115 must be attached to the bank's timely filed return (taking into account extensions of time to file) for the first taxable year covered by the election. The consent of the Commissioner to make a change in method of accounting under this paragraph (d)(3) is granted, pursuant to section 446(e), to any bank that makes the election in accordance with this paragraph (d)(3)(iii)(C), provided the bank has not made a prior election under this paragraph (d)(3).

(3) Subsequent elections. The advance consent of the Commissioner is required to make any election under this paragraph (d)(3) after a previous election has been revoked pursuant to paragraph (d)(3)(iv) of this section. This consent must be requested under the procedures, terms, and conditions prescribed under the authority of section 446(e) and § 1.446-1(e) for requesting a change in method of accounting.

(D) Express determination requirement. In connection with its most recent examination involving the bank's loan review process, the bank's supervisory authority must have made an express determination (in accordance with any applicable administrative procedure prescribed hereunder) that the bank maintains and applies loan loss classification standards that are consistent with the regulatory standards of that supervisory authority. For purposes of this paragraph (d)(3)(iii)(D), the supervisory authority of a bank is the appropriate Federal banking agency for the bank, as that term is defined in 12 U.S.C. 1813(q), or, in the case of an institution in the Farm Credit System, the Farm Credit Administration.

(E) Transition period election. For taxable years ending before completion of the first examination of the bank by its supervisory authority (as defined in paragraph (d)(3)(iii)(D) of this section) that is after October 1, 1992, and that involves the bank's loan review process, the statement or Form 3115 filed by the bank must include a declaration that the bank maintains and applies loan loss classification standards that are consistent with the regulatory standards of that supervisory authority. A bank that makes this declaration is deemed to satisfy the express determination requirement of paragraph (d)(3)(iii)(D) of this section for those years, even though an express determination has not yet been made.

(iv) Revocation of election. (A) In general. Revocation of an election under this paragraph (d)(3) constitutes a change in method of accounting that has the effects described in paragraph (d)(3)(iv)(B) of this section. If an election under this paragraph (d)(3) has been revoked, a bank may make a subsequent election only under the provisions of paragraph (d)(3)(iii)(C)(3) of this section.

(B) Effect of change in method of accounting. A change in method of accounting resulting from revocation of an election under this paragraph (d)(3) does not require or permit an adjustment under section 481(a). Under this cut-off approach—

(1) There is no change in the § 1.1011-1 adjusted basis of the bank's existing debts (as determined under this paragraph (d)(3) method or any other former method of accounting used by the bank with respect to its bad debts) as a result of the change in method of accounting; and

(2) Bad debt deductions in the year of change and thereafter with respect to all debts held by the bank, whether in existence at the beginning of the year of change or subsequently originated or acquired, are determined under the new method of accounting.

(C) Automatic revocation. (1) In general. A bank's election under this paragraph (d)(3) is revoked automatically if, in connection with any examination involving the bank's loan review process by the bank's supervisory authority as defined in paragraph (d)(3)(iii)(D) of this section, the bank does not obtain the express determination required by that paragraph.

(2) Year of revocation. If a bank makes the conformity election under the transition rules of paragraph (d)(3)(iii)(E) of this section and does not obtain the express determination in connection with the first examination involving the bank's loan review process that is after October 1, 1992, the election is revoked as of the beginning of the taxable year of the election or, if later, the earliest taxable year for which tax may be assessed. In other cases in which a bank does not obtain an express determination in connection with an examination of its loan review process, the election is revoked as of the beginning of the taxable year that includes the date as of which the supervisory authority conducts the examination even if the examination is completed in the following taxable year.

(3) Consent granted. Under the Commissioner's authority in section 446(e) and § 1.446-1(e), the bank is directed to and is granted consent to change from this paragraph (3)(1) method as of the year of revocation (year of change) prescribed by paragraph (d)(3)(iv)(C)(2) of this section.

(4) Requirements. A bank changing its method of accounting under the automatic revocation rules of this paragraph (d)(3)(iv)(C) must attach a completed Form 3115 to its income tax return for the year of revocation prescribed by paragraph (d)(3)(iv)(C)(2) of this section. The words "REVOCATION OF § 1.166-2(d)(3) ELECTION" must be typed or legibly printed at the top of page 1 of the Form 3115. If the year of revocation is a year for which the bank has already filed its income tax return, the bank must file an amended return for that year reflecting its change in method of accounting and must attach the completed Form 3115 to that

amended return. The bank also must file amended returns reflecting the new method of accounting for all subsequent taxable years for which returns have been filed and tax may be assessed.

(D) Revocation by Commissioner. An election under this paragraph (d)(3) may be revoked by the Commissioner as of the beginning of any taxable year for which a bank fails to follow the method of accounting prescribed by this paragraph. In addition, the Commissioner may revoke an election as of the beginning of any taxable year for which the Commissioner determines that a bank has taken charge-offs and deductions that, under all facts and circumstances existing at the time, were substantially in excess of those warranted by the exercise of reasonable business judgment in applying the regulatory standards of the bank's supervisory authority as defined in paragraph (d)(3)(III)(D) of this section.

(E) Voluntary revocation. A bank may apply for revocation of its election made under this paragraph (d)(3) by timely filing a completed Form 3115 for the appropriate year and obtaining the consent of the Commissioner in accordance with section 446(e) and § 1.446-1(e) (including any applicable administrative procedures prescribed thereunder). The words "REVOCATION OF § 1.166-2(d)(3) ELECTION" must be typed or legibly printed at the top of page 1 of the Form 3115. If any bank has had its election automatically revoked pursuant to paragraph (d)(3)(iv)(C) of this section and has not changed its method of accounting in accordance with the requirements of that paragraph, the Commissioner will require that any voluntary change in method of accounting under this paragraph (d)(3)(iv)(E) be implemented retroactively pursuant to the same amended return terms and conditions as are prescribed by paragraph (d)(3)(iv)(C) of this section.

(4) Definitions. For purposes of this paragraph (d)—

(i) Bank. The term "bank" has the meaning assigned to it by section 581. The term "bank" also includes any corporation that would be a bank within the meaning of section 581 except for the fact that it is a foreign corporation, but this paragraph (d) applies only with respect to loans the interest on which is effectively connected with the conduct of a banking business within the United States. In addition, the term "bank" includes a Farm Credit System institution that is subject to supervision by the Farm Credit Administration.

(ii) Charge-off. For banks regulated by the Office of Thrift Supervision, the term "charge-off" includes the establishment of specific allowances for loan losses in the amount of 100 percent of the portion of the debt classified as loss.

T.D. 6403, 7/30/59, amend T.D. 7254, 1/24/73, T.D. 8396, 2/21/92, T.D. 8441, 10/1/92, T.D. 8492, 10/15/93.

§ 1.166-3 Partial or total worthlessness.

(a) Partial worthlessness. *(1) Applicable to specific debts only.* A deduction under section 166(a)(2) on account of partially worthless debts shall be allowed with respect to specific debts only.

(2) Charge-off required. (i) If, from all the surrounding and attending circumstances, the district director is satisfied that a debt is partially worthless, the amount which has become worthless shall be allowed as a deduction under section 166(a)(2) but only to the extent charged off during the taxable year.

(ii) If a taxpayer claims a deduction for a part of a debt for the taxable year within which that part of the debt is charged off and the deduction is disallowed for that taxable year, then, in a case where the debt becomes partially worthless after the close of that taxable year, a deduction under section 166(a)(2) shall be allowed for a subsequent taxable year but not in excess of the amount charged off in the prior taxable year plus any amount charged off in the subsequent taxable year. In such instance, the charge-off in the prior taxable year shall, if consistently maintained as such, be sufficient to that extent to meet the charge-off requirement of section 166(a)(2) with respect to the subsequent taxable year.

(iii) Before a taxpayer may deduct a debt in part, he must be able to demonstrate to the satisfaction of the district director the amount thereof which is worthless and the part thereof which has been charged off.

(3) Significantly modified debt. (i) Deemed charge-off. If a significant modification of a debt instrument (within the meaning of § 1.1001-3) during a taxable year results in the recognition of gain by a taxpayer under § 1.1001-1(a), and if the requirements of paragraph (a)(3)(ii) of this section are met, there is a deemed charge-off of the debt during that taxable year in the amount specified in paragraph (a)(3)(iii) of this section.

(ii) Requirements for deemed charge-off. A debt is deemed to have been charged off only if—

(A) The taxpayer (or, in the case of a debt that constitutes transferred basis property within the meaning of section 7701(a)(43), a transferor taxpayer) has claimed a deduction for partial worthlessness of the debt in any prior taxable year; and

(B) Each prior charge-off and deduction for partial worthlessness satisfied the requirements of paragraphs (a)(1) and (2) of this section.

(iii) Amount of deemed charge-off. The amount of the deemed charge-off, if any, is the amount by which the tax basis of the debt exceeds the greater of the fair market value of the debt or the amount of the debt recorded on the taxpayer's books and records reduced as appropriate for a specific allowance for loan losses. The amount of the deemed charge-off, however, may not exceed the amount of recognized gain described in paragraph (a)(3)(i) of this section.

(iv) Effective date. This paragraph (a)(3) applies to significant modifications of debt instruments occurring on or after September 23, 1996.

(b) Total worthlessness. If a debt becomes wholly worthless during the taxable year, the amount thereof which has not been allowed as a deduction from gross income for any prior taxable year shall be allowed as a deduction for the current taxable year.

T.D. 6403, 7/30/59, amend T.D. 8763, 1/28/98.

§ 1.166-4 Reserve for bad debts.

Caution: The Treasury has not yet amended Reg § 1.166-4 to reflect changes made by P.L. 99-514.

(a) Allowance of deduction. A taxpayer who has established the reserve method of treating bad debts and has maintained proper reserve accounts for bad debts or who, in accordance with paragraph (b) of § 1.166-1, adopts the reserve method of treating bad debts may deduct from gross income a reasonable addition to a reserve for bad debts in lieu of deducting specific bad debt items. This paragraph applies both to bad debts owed to the taxpayer and to bad debts arising out of section 166(f)(1)(A) guaranteed debt obligations. If a reserve is maintained for bad debts arising out of section 166(f)(1)(A) guaranteed debt obligations, then a separate reserve must also be maintained for all other debt obligations of the taxpayer in the same trade or business, if any. A taxpayer may not maintain a reserve for bad debts arising out of section 166(f)(1)(A) guaranteed debt obligations if with respect to direct debt obligations in the same trade or business the taxpayer takes deductions when the debts become worthless in whole or in part rather than maintaining a reserve for such obligations. See § 1.166-10 for rules concerning section 166(f)(1)(A) guaranteed debt obligations.

(b) Reasonableness of addition to reserve. *(1) Relevant factors.* What constitutes a reasonable addition to a reserve for bad debts shall be determined in the light of the facts existing at the close of the taxable year of the proposed addition. The reasonableness of the addition will vary as between classes of business and with conditions of business prosperity. It will depend primarily upon the total amount of debts outstanding as of the close of the taxable year, including those arising currently as well as those arising in prior taxable years, and the total amount of the existing reserve.

(2) Correction of errors in prior estimates. In the event that subsequent realizations upon outstanding debts prove to be more or less than estimated at the time of the creation of the existing reserve, the amount of the excess or inadequacy in the existing reserve shall be reflected in the determination of the reasonable addition necessary in the current taxable year.

(c) Statement required. A taxpayer using the reserve method shall file with his return a statement showing—

(1) The volume of his charge sales or other business transactions for the taxable year and the percentage of the reserve to such amount;

(2) The total amount of notes and accounts receivable at the beginning and close of the taxable year;

(3) The amount of the debts which have become wholly or partially worthless and have been charged against the reserve account; and

(4) The computation of the addition to the reserve for bad debts.

(d) Special rules applicable to financial institutions. *(1)* For special rules for the addition to the bad debt reserves of certain banks, see §§ 1.585-1 through 1.585-3.

(2) For special rules for the addition to the bad debt reserves of small business investment companies and business development corporations, see §§ 1.586-1 and 1.586-2.

(3) For special rules for the addition to the bad debts reserves of certain mutual savings banks, domestic building and loan associations, and cooperative banks, see §§ 1.593-1 through 1.593-11.

T.D. 6403, 7/30/59, amend T.D. 6728, 5/4/64, T.D. 7444, 12/6/76, T.D. 8071, 1/16/86.

PARAGRAPH 1. Paragraph (d)(3) of § 1.166-4 is amended by removing "§§ 1.593-1 through 1.593-11" and inserting "§§ 1.593-1 through 1.593-8" in lieu thereof.

Proposed § 1.166-4 [Amended] [*For Preamble, see ¶ 150,911*]

§ 1.166-5 Nonbusiness debts.

(a) Allowance of deduction as capital loss. *(1)* The loss resulting from any nonbusiness debt's becoming partially or wholly worthless within the taxable year shall not be allowed as a deduction under either section 166(a) or section 166(c) in determining the taxable income of a taxpayer other than a corporation. See section 166(d)(1)(A).

(2) If, in the case of a taxpayer other than a corporation, a nonbusiness debt becomes wholly worthless within the taxable year, the loss resulting therefrom shall be treated as a loss from the sale or exchange, during the taxable year, of a capital asset held for not more than 1 year (6 months for taxable years beginning before 1977; 9 months for taxable years beginning in 1977). Such a loss is subject to the limitations provided in section 1211, relating to the limitation on capital losses, and section 1212, relating to the capital loss carryover, and in the regulations under those sections. A loss on a nonbusiness debt shall be treated as sustained only if and when the debt has become totally worthless, and no deduction shall be allowed for a nonbusiness debt which is recoverable in part during the taxable year.

(b) Nonbusiness debt defined. For purposes of section 166 and this section, a nonbusiness debt is any debt other than—

(1) A debt which is created, or acquired, in the course of a trade or business of the taxpayer, determined without regard to the relationship of the debt to a trade or business of the taxpayer at the time when the debt becomes worthless; or

(2) A debt the loss from the worthlessness of which is incurred in the taxpayer's trade or business.

The question whether a debt is a nonbusiness debt is a question of fact in each particular case. The determination of whether the loss on a debt's becoming worthless has been incurred in a trade or business of the taxpayer shall, for this purpose, be made in substantially the same manner for determining whether a loss has been incurred in a trade or business for purposes of section 165(c)(1). For purposes of subparagraph (2) of this paragraph, the character of the debt is to be determined by the relation which the loss resulting from the debt's becoming worthless bears to the trade or business of the taxpayer. If that relation is a proximate one in the conduct of the trade or business in which the taxpayer is engaged at the time the debt becomes worthless, the debt comes within the exception provided by that subparagraph. The use to which the borrowed funds are put by the debtor is of no consequence in making a determination under this paragraph. For purposes of section 166 and this section, a nonbusiness debt does not include a debt described in section 165(g)(2)(C). See § 1.165-5, relating to losses on worthless securities.

(c) Guaranty of corporate obligations. For provisions treating a loss sustained by a guarantor of obligations as a loss resulting from the worthlessness of a debt, see §§ 1.166-8 and 1.66-9.

(d) Examples. The application of this section may be illustrated by the following examples involving a case where A, an individual who is engaged in the grocery business and who makes his return on the basis of the calendar year, extends credit to B in 1955 on an open account:

Example (1). In 1956 A sells the business but retains the claim against B. The claim becomes worthless in A's hands in 1957. A's loss is not controlled by the nonbusiness debt provisions, since the original consideration has been advanced by A in his trade or business.

Example (2). In 1956 A sells the business to C but sells the claim against B to the taxpayer, D. The claim becomes worthless in D's hands in 1957. During 1956 and 1957, D is not engaged in any trade or business. D's loss is controlled by the nonbusiness debt provisions even though the original consideration has been advanced by A in his trade or business, since the debt has not been created or acquired in connection with a trade or business of D and since in 1957 D is not engaged in a trade or business incident to the conduct of which a loss from the worthlessness of such claim is a proximate result.

Example (3). In 1956 A dies, leaving the business, including the accounts receivable, to his son, C, the taxpayer. The claim against B becomes worthless in C's hands in 1957. C's loss is not controlled by the nonbusiness debt provisions. While C does not advance any consideration for the claim, or create or acquire it in connection with his trade or business, the loss is sustained as a proximate incident to the conduct of the trade or business in which he is engaged at the time the debt becomes worthless.

Example (4). In 1956 A dies, leaving the business to his son, C, but leaving the claim against B to his son, D, the taxpayer. The claim against B becomes worthless in D's hands in 1957. During 1956 and 1957, D is not engaged in any trade or business. D's loss is controlled by the nonbusiness debt provisions even though the original consideration has been advanced by A in his trade or business, since the debt has not been created or acquired in connection with a trade or business of D and since in 1957 D is not engaged in a trade or business incident to the conduct of which a loss from the worthlessness of such claim is a proximate result.

Example (5). In 1956 A dies; and, while his executor, C, is carrying on the business, the claim against B becomes worthless in 1957. The loss sustained by A's estate is not controlled by the nonbusiness debt provisions. While C does not advance any consideration for the claim on behalf of the estate, or create or acquire it in connection with a trade or business in which the estate is engaged, the loss is sustained as a proximate incident to the conduct of the trade or business in which the estate is engaged at the time the debt becomes worthless.

Example (6). In 1956, A, in liquidating the business, attempts to collect the claim against B but finds that it has become worthless. A's loss is not controlled by the nonbusiness debt provisions, since the original consideration has been advanced by A in his trade or business and since a loss incurred in liquidating a trade or business is a proximate incident to the conduct thereof.

T.D. 6403, 7/30/59,amend T.D. 7657, 11/28/79, T.D. 7728, 10/31/80.

§ 1.166-6 Sale of mortgaged or pledged property.

Caution: The Treasury has not yet amended Reg § 1.166-6 to reflect changes made by P.L. 104-188.

(a) Deficiency deductible as bad debt. *(1) Principal amount.* If mortgaged or pledged property is lawfully sold (whether to the creditor or another purchaser) for less than the amount of the debt, and the portion of the indebtedness remaining unsatisfied after the sale is wholly or partially uncollectible, the mortgagee or pledgee may deduct such amount under section 166(a) (to the extent that it constitutes capital or represents an item the income from which has been returned by him) as a bad debt for the taxable year in which it becomes wholly worthless or is charged off as partially worthless. See § 1.166-3.

(2) Accrued interest. Accrued interest may be included as part of the deduction allowable under this paragraph, but only if it has previously been returned as income.

(b) Realization of gain or loss. *(1) Determination of amount.* If, in the case of a sale described in paragraph (a) of this section, the creditor buys in the mortgaged or pledged property, loss or gain is also realized, measured by the difference between the amount of those obligations of the debtor which are applied to the purchase or bid price of the property (to the extent that such obligations constitute capital or represent an item the income from which has been returned by the creditor) and the fair market value of the property.

(2) Fair market value defined. The fair market value of the property for this purpose shall, in the absence of clear and convincing proof to the contrary, be presumed to be the amount for which it is bid in by the taxpayer.

(c) Basis of property purchased. If the creditor subsequently sells the property so acquired, the basis for determining gain or loss upon the subsequent sale is the fair market value of the property at the date of its acquisition by the creditor.

(d) Special rules applicable to certain banking organizations. For special rules relating to the treatment of mortgaged or pledged property by certain mutual savings banks, domestic building and loan associations, and cooperative banks, see section 595 and the regulations thereunder.

(e) Special rules applicable to certain reacquisitions of real property. Notwithstanding this section, special rules apply for taxable years beginning after September 2, 1964 (and for certain taxable years beginning after December 31, 1957), to the gain or loss on certain reacquisitions of real property, to indebtedness remaining unsatisfied as a result of such reacquisitions, and to the basis of the reacquired real property. See §§ 1.1038 through 1.1038-3.

T.D. 6403, 7/30/59, amend T.D. 6814, 4/6/65, T.D. 6916, 4/12/67.

§ 1.166-7 Worthless bonds issued by an individual.

(a) Allowance of deduction. A bond or other similar obligation issued by an individual, if it becomes worthless in whole or in part, is subject to the bad debt provisions of section 166. The loss from the worthlessness of any such bond or obligation is deductible in accordance with section 166(a), unless such bond or obligation is a nonbusiness debt as defined in section 166(d)(2). If the bond or obligation is a nonbusiness debt, it is subject to section 166(d) and § 1.166-5.

(b) Decline in market value. A taxpayer possessing debts evidenced by bonds or other similar obligations issued by an individual shall not be allowed any deduction under section 166 on account of mere market fluctuation in the value of such obligations.

(c) Worthless bonds issued by corporation. For provisions allowing the deduction under section 165(a) of the loss sustained upon the worthlessness of any bond or similar obligation issued by a corporation or a government, see § 1.165-5.

(d) Application to inventories. This section does not apply to any loss upon the worthlessness of any bond or similar obligation reflected in inventories required to be taken by a dealer in securities under section 471. See § 1.471-5.

T.D. 6403, 7/30/59.

§ 1.166-8 Losses of guarantors, endorsers, and indemnitors incurred on agreements made before January 1, 1976.

(a) Noncorporate obligations. *(1) Deductible as bad debt.* A payment during the taxable year by a taxpayer other than a corporation in discharge of part or all of his obligation as a guarantor, endorser, or indemnitor of an obligation issued by a person other than a corporation shall, for purposes of section 166 and the regulations thereunder, be treated as a debt's becoming worthless within the taxable year, if—

(i) The proceeds of the obligation so issued have been used in the trade or business of the borrower, and

(ii) The borrower's obligation to the person to whom the taxpayer's payment is made is worthless at the time of payment except for the existence of the guaranty, endorsement, or indemnity, whether or not such obligation has in fact become worthless within the taxable year in which payment is made.

(2) Nonbusiness debt rule not applicable. If a payment is treated as a loss in accordance with the provisions of subparagraph (1) of this paragraph, section 166(d), relating to the special rule for losses sustained on the worthlessness of a nonbusiness debt, shall not apply. Accordingly, in each instance the loss shall be deducted under section 166(a)(1) as a wholly worthless debt even though there has been a discharge of only a part of the taxpayer's obligation. Thus, if the taxpayer makes a payment during the taxable year in discharge of only part of his obligation as a guarantor, endorser, or indemnitor, he may treat such payment under section 166(a)(1) as a debt's becoming wholly worthless within the taxable year, provided that he can establish that such part of the borrower's obligation to the person to whom the taxpayer's payment is made is worthless at the time of payment and the conditions of subparagraph (1) of this paragraph have otherwise been satisfied.

(3) Other applicable provisions. Other provisions of the internal revenue laws relating to bad debts, such as section 111, relating to the recovery of bad debts, shall be deemed to apply to any payment which, under the provisions of this paragraph, is treated as a bad debt. If the requirements of section 166(f) are not met, any loss sustained by a guarantor, endorser, or indemnitor upon the worthlessness of the debtor's obligation shall be treated under the provisions of law applicable thereto. See, for example, paragraph (b) of this section.

(b) Corporate obligations. The loss sustained during the taxable year by a taxpayer other than a corporation in discharge of all of his obligation as a guarantor of an obligation issued by a corporation shall be treated, in accordance with section 166(d) and the regulations thereunder, as a loss sustained on the worthlessness of a nonbusiness debt if the debt created in the guarantor's favor as a result of the payment does not come within the exceptions prescribed by section 166(d)(2)(A) or (B). See paragraph (a)(2) of § 1.166-5.

(c) Examples. The application of this section may be illustrated by the following examples:

Example (1). During 1955, A, an individual who makes his return on the basis of the calendar year, guarantees payment of an obligation of B, an individual, to the X Bank, the proceeds of the obligation being used in B's business. B defaults on his obligation in 1956. A makes payment to the X Bank during 1957 in discharge of his entire obligation as a guarantor, the obligation of B to the X Bank being wholly worthless. For his taxable year 1957, A is entitled to a deduction under section 166(a)(1) as a result of his payment during that year.

Example (2). During 1955, A, an individual who makes his return on the basis of the calendar year, guarantees payment of an obligation of B, an individual, to the X Bank, the proceeds of the obligation being used in B's business. In 1956, B pays a part of his obligation to the X Bank but defaults on the remaining part. In 1957, A makes payment to the X Bank, in discharge of part of his obligation as a guarantor, of the remaining unpaid part of B's obligation to the bank, such part of B's obligation then being worthless. For his taxable year 1957, A is entitled to a deduction under section 166(a)(1) as a result of his payment of the remaining unpaid part of B's obligation.

Example (3). During 1955, A, an individual who makes his return on the basis of the calendar year, guarantees payment of an obligation of B, an individual, to the X Bank, the proceeds of the obligation being used for B's personal use. B defaults on his obligation in 1956. A makes payment to the X Bank during 1957 in discharge of his entire obligation as a guarantor, the obligation of B to X Bank being wholly worthless. A may not apply the benefit of section 166(f) to his loss, since the proceeds of B's obligation have not been used in B's trade or business.

Example (4). During 1955, A, an individual who makes his return on the basis of the calendar year, guarantees payment of an obligation of Y Corporation to the X Bank, the proceeds of the obligation being used in Y Corporation's business. Y Corporation defaults on its obligation in 1956. A makes payment to the X Bank during 1957 in discharge of his entire obligation as a guarantor, the obligation of Y Corporation to the X Bank being wholly worthless. At no time during 1955 or 1957 is A engaged in a trade or business. For his taxable year 1957, A is entitled to deduct a capital loss in accordance with the provisions of section 166(d) and paragraph (a)(2) of § 1.166-5. He may not apply the benefit of section 166(f) to his loss, since his payment is in discharge of an obligation issued by a corporation.

(d) Effective date. This section applies only to losses, regardless of the taxable year in which incurred, on agreements made before January 1, 1976.

T.D. 6403, 7/30/59, amend T.D. 7657, 11/28/79.

§ 1.166-9 Losses of guarantors, endorsers, and indemnitors incurred, on agreements made after December 31, 1975, in taxable years beginning after such date.

(a) Payment treated as worthless business debt. This paragraph applies to taxpayers who, after December 31, 1975, enter into an agreement in the course of their trade or business to act as (or in a manner essentially equivalent to) a guarantor, endorser, or indemnitor of (or other secondary obligor upon) a debt obligation. Subject to the provisions of paragraphs (c), (d), and (e) of this section, a payment of principal or interest made during a taxable year beginning after December 31, 1975, by the taxpayer in discharge of part or all of the taxpayer's obligation as a guarantor, endorser, or indemnitor is treated as a business debt becoming worthless in the taxable year in which the payment is made or in the taxable year described in paragraph (e)(2) of this section. Neither section 163 (Relating to interest) nor section 165 (relating to losses) shall apply with respect to such a payment.

(b) Payment treated as worthless nonbusiness debt. This paragraph applies to taxpayers (other than corporations) who, after December 31, 1975, enter into a transaction for profit, but not in the course of their trade or business, to act as (or in a manner essentially equivalent to) a guarantor, endorser, or indemnitor of (or other secondary obligor upon) a debt obligation. Subject to the provisions of paragraphs (c), (d), and (e) of this section, a payment of principal or interest made during a taxable year beginning after December 31, 1975, by the taxpayer in discharge of part or all of the taxpayer's obligation as a guarantor, endorser, or indemnitor is treated as a worthless nonbusiness debt in the taxable year in which the payment is made or in the taxable year described in paragraph (e)(2) of this section. Neither section 163 nor section 165 shall apply with respect to such a payment.

(c) Obligations issued by corporations. No treatment as a worthless debt is allowed with respect to a payment made by the taxpayer in discharge of part or all of the taxpayer's obligation as a guarantor, endorser, or indemnitor of an obligation issued by a corporation if, on the basis of the facts and circumstances at the time the obligation was entered into, the payment constitutes a contribution to capital by a shareholder. The rule of this paragraph (c) applies to payments whenever made (see paragraph (f) of this section).

(d) Certain payments treated as worthless debts. A payment in discharge of part of all of taxpayer's agreement to act as guarantor, endorser, or indemnitor of an obligation is to be treated as a worthless debt only if—

(1) The agreement was entered into in the course of the taxpayer's trade or business or a transaction for profit;

(2) There was an enforceable legal duty upon the taxpayer to make the payment (except that legal action need not have been brought against the taxpayer); and

(3) The agreement was entered into before the obligation became worthless (or partially worthless in the case of an agreement entered into in the course of the taxpayer's trade or business). See §§ 1.166-2 and 1.166-3 for rules on worthless and partially worthless debts. For purposes of this paragraph (d)(3), an agreement is considered as entered into before the obligation became worthless (or partially worthless) if there was a reasonable expectation on the part of the taxpayer at the time the agreement was entered into that the taxpayer would not be called upon to pay the debt (subject to such agreement) without full reimbursement from the issuer of the obligation.

(e) Special rules. *(1) Reasonable consideration required.* Treatment as a worthless debt of a payment made by a taxpayer in discharge of part or all of the taxpayer's agreement to act as a guarantor, endorser, or indemnitor of an obligation is allowed only if the taxpayer demonstrates that reasonable consideration was received for entering into the agreement. For purposes of this paragraph (e)(1), reasonable consideration is not limited to direct consideration in the form of cash or property. Thus, where a taxpayer can demonstrate that the agreement was given without direct consideration in the form of cash or property but in accordance with normal business practice or for a good faith business purpose, worthless debt treatment is allowed with respect to a payment in discharge of part or all of the agreement if the conditions of this section are met. However, consideration received from a taxpayer's spouse or any individual listed in section 152(a) must be direct consideration in the form of cash or property.

(2) Right of subrogation. With respect to a payment made by a taxpayer in discharge of part or all the taxpayer's agreement to act as a guarantor, endorser, or indemnitor where the agreement provides for a right of subrogation or other similar right against the issuer, treatment as a worthless debt is not allowed until the taxable year in which the right of subrogation or other similar right becomes totally worthless (or partially worthless in the case of an agreement which arose in the course of the taxpayer's trade or business).

(3) Other applicable provisions. Unless inconsistent with this section, other Internal Revenue laws concerning worthless debts, such as section 111 relating to the recovery of bad debts, apply to any payment which, under the provisions of this section, is treated as giving rise to a worthless debt.

(4) Taxpayer defined. For purposes of this section, except as otherwise provided, the term "taxpayer" means any taxpayer and includes individuals, corporations, partnerships, trusts and estates.

(f) Effective date. This section applies to losses incurred on agreements made after December 31, 1975, in taxable years beginning after such date. However, paragraph (c) of this section also applies to payments, regardless of the taxable year in which made, under agreements made before January 1, 1976.

T.D. 7657, 11/28/79, amend T.D. 7747, 12/29/80, T.D. 7920, 11/2/83.

---

§ 1.166-10 Reserve for guaranteed debt obligations.

(a) Definitions. The following provisions apply for purposes of this section and section 166(f):

(1) Dealer in property. A dealer in property is a person who regularly sells property in the ordinary course of the persons's trade or business.

(2) Guaranteed debt obligation. A guaranteed debt obligation is a legal duty of one person as a guarantor, endorser or indemnitor of a second person to pay a third person. It does not include duties based solely on moral or good public relations considerations that are not legally binding. A guaranteed debt obligation typically arises where a seller receives in payment for property or services the debt obligation of a purchaser and sells that obligation to a third party with recourse. However, a guaranteed debt obligation also may arise out of a sale in respect of which there is no direct debtor-creditor relationship between the debtor purchaser and the seller. For example, it arises where a purchaser borrows money from a third party to make payment to the seller and the seller guarantees the payment of the purchaser's debt. Generally, debt obligations which are sold without recourse do not result in any obligation of the seller as a guarantor, endorser, or indemnitor. However, there are certain without-recourse transactions which may give rise to a seller's liability as a guarantor or indemnitor. For example, such a liability may arise where a holder of a debt obligation holds money or other property of a seller which the holder may apply, without seeking permission of the seller, against any uncollectible debt obligations transferred to the holder by the seller without recourse, or where the seller is under a legal obligation to reacquire the real or tangible personal property from the holder of the debt obligation who repossessed property in satisfaction of the debt obligations.

(3) Real or tangible personal property. Real or tangible personal property generally does not include other forms of property, such as securities. However, if the sale of other property is related to the sale of actual real or tangible personal property, the other property will be considered to be real or tangible personal property. In order for the sale of other property to be related, it must be—

(i) Incidental to the sale of the actual real or tangible personal property; and

(ii) Made under an agreement, entered into at the same time as the sale of actual real or tangible personal property, between the dealer in that property and the customer with respect to that property.

The other property may be charged for as a part of, or in addition to, the sales price of the actual real or tangible personal property. If the value of the other property is not greater than 20 percent of the total sales price, including the value of all related services other than financing services, the sale of the other property is related to the sale of actual real or tangible personal property.

(4) Related services. In the case of a sale of both property and services a determination must be made as to whether the services are related to the property. Related services include only those services which are—

(i) Incidental to the sale of the real or tangible personal property; and

(ii) To be performed under an agreement, entered into at the same time as the sale of the property, between the dealer in property and the customer with respect to the property. Delivery, financing installation, maintenance, repair, or instructional services generally qualify as related services. The services may be charged for as a part of, or in addition to, the sales price of the property. Where the value of all services other than financing services is not greater than 20 percent of the total of the sales price of the property, including the value of all the services other than financing services, all of the services are considered to be incidental to the sale of the property. Where the value of the services is greater than 20 percent, the determination as to whether a service is a related service in a particular case is to be made on the basis of all relevant facts and circumstances.

(5) Examples. The following examples apply to paragraph (a)(4) of this section:

Example (1). A, a dealer in television sets sells a television set to B, his customer. If at the time of the sale A, for a separate charge which is added to the sales price of the set and which is not greater than 20 percent of the total sales price, provides a 3-year service contract on only that television set, the service contract is a related service agreement. However, if A does not sell the service contract to B contemporaneously with the sale of the television set, as would be the case if the service agreement were entered into after the sale of the set were completed, or if the service contract includes services for a television set in addition to the one then sold by A to B, the service contract is not an agreement for a related service.

Example (2). C, an automobile dealer, at the time of the sale by C of an automobile to D, agrees to made available to D driving instructions furnished by the M driving school, the cost of which is included in the sale price of the automobile and is not greater than 20 percent of the total sales price. C also agrees to pay M for the driving instructions furnished to D. Since C's agreement with D to make available driving instructions is incidental to the sale of the automobile, is made contemporaneously with the sale, and is charged for as part of the sales price of the automobile, it is an agreement for a related service. In contrast, however, because M's agreement with C is not an agreement between the dealer in property and the customer, M's agreement with C to provide driving instructions to C's customers is not an agreement for a related service.

(b) Incorporation of section 166(c) rules. A reserve for section 166(f)(1)(A) guaranteed debt obligations must be established and maintained under the rules applicable to the reserve for bad debts under section 166(c) (with the exception of the statement requirement under § 1.166-4(c)). For example, the rules in § 1.166-4(b), relating to what constitutes a reasonable addition to a reserve for bad debts and to correction of errors in prior estimates, apply to a reserve for section 166(f)(1)(A) guaranteed debt obligations as well.

(c) Special requirements. Any reserve for section 166(f)(1)(A) guaranteed debt obligations must be established and maintained separately from any reserve for other debt obligations. In addition, a taxpayer who charges off direct debts when they become worthless in whole or in part rather than maintaining a reserve for such obligations may not maintain a reserve for section 166(f)(1)(A) guaranteed debt obligations in the same trade or business.

(d) Requirement of statement. A taxpayer who uses the reserve method of treating section 166(f)(1)(A) guaranteed debt obligations must attach to his return for each taxable year, returns for which are filed after April 17, 1986, and for each trade or business for which the reserve is maintained a statement showing—

(1) The total amount of these obligations at the beginning of the taxable year;

(2) The total amount of these obligations incurred during the taxable year;

(3) The amount of the initial balance of the suspense account, if any, established with respect to these obligations;

(4) The balance of the suspense account, if any, at the beginning of the taxable year,

(5) The adjustment, if any, to that account;

(6) The adjusted balance, if any, at the close of the taxable year;

(7) The reconciliation of the beginning and closing balances of the reserve for these obligations and the computation of the addition to the reserve; and

(8) The taxable year for which the reserve for these obligations was established.

(e) Computation of opening balance. *(1) In general.* The opening balance of a reserve for section 166(f)(1)(A) guaranteed debt obligations established for the first taxable year for which a taxpayer maintains such a reserve shall be determined as if the taxpayer had maintained such a reserve for the taxable years preceding that taxable year. The amount of the opening balance may be determined under the following formula:

$$OB = CG \times \frac{SNL}{SG}$$

where—

OB = the opening balance at the beginning of the first taxable year

CG = the amount of these obligations at the close of the last preceding taxable year

SG = the sum of the amounts of these obligations at the close of the five preceding taxable years

SNL = the sum of the amounts of net losses arising from these obligations for the five preceding taxable years

(2) Example. The following example applies to paragraph (e)(1) of this section.

Example. For 1977, A, a dealer in automobiles who uses the calendar year as the taxable year, adopts in accordance with this section the reserve method of treating section 166(f)(1)(A) guaranteed debt obligations. A's first year in business as an automobile dealer is 1973. For 1972, 1973, 1974, 1975, and 1976, A's records disclose the following information with respect to these obligations:

Year	Obligations outstanding at close of year	Gross losses from these obligations	Recoveries from these obligations	Net losses from these obligations
1972	$ 0	$ 0	$ 0	$ 0
1973	780,000	9,700	1,000	8,700
1974	795,000	8,900	1,050	7,850
1975	850,000	8,850	850	8,000
1976	820,000	8,300	1,400	7,900
Total	3,245,000	36,750	4,300	32,450

The opening balance for 1977 of A's reserve for these obligations is $8,200, determined as follows:

$$\$8{,}200 = \$820{,}000 \times \frac{\$32{,}450}{\$3{,}245{,}000}$$

(3) More appropriate balance. A taxpayer may select a balance other than the one produced under paragraph (e)(1) of this section if it is more appropriate, based upon the taxpayer's actual experience, and in the event the taxpayer's return is examined, if the balance is approved by the district director.

(4) No losses in the five preceding taxable years. If a taxpayer is in the taxpayer's first taxable year of a particular trade or business, or if the taxpayer has no losses arising from section 166(f)(1)(A) guaranteed debt obligations in a particular trade or business for any other reason in the five preceding taxable years, then the taxpayer's opening balance is zero for that particular trade or business.

(5) Where reserve method was used before October 22, 1965. If for a taxable year ending before October 22, 1965, the taxpayer maintained a reserve for bad debts under section 166(c) which included guaranteed debt obligations described in section 166(f)(1)(A), and if the taxpayer is allowed a deduction referred to in paragraph (g)(2) of this section on account of those obligations, the amount of the opening balance of the reserve for section 166(f)(1)(A) guaranteed debt obligations for the taxpayer's first taxable year ending after October 21, 1965, shall be an amount equal to that portion of the section 166(c) reserve at the close of the last taxable year which is attributable to those debt obligations. The amount of the balance of the section 166(c) reserve for the taxable year shall be reduced by the amount of the opening balance of the reserve for those guaranteed debt obligations.

(f) Suspense account. *(1) Zero opening balance cases.* No suspense account shall be maintained if the opening balance of the reserve for section 166(f)(1)(A) guaranteed debt obligations under section 166(f)(3) is zero

(2) Example. The following example applies to section 166(f)(4)(B), relating to adjustments to the suspense account:

Example. In 1977, A, an individual who operates an appliance store and uses the calendar year as the taxable year, adopts the reserve method of treating section 166(f)(1)(A) guaranteed debt obligations. The initial balance of A's suspense account is $8,200. At the close of 1977, 1978, 1979, and 1980, the balance of A's reserve for these obligations is $8,400, $8,250, $8,150, and $8,175, respectively, after making the addition to the reserve for each year. The adjustments under section 166(f)(4)(B) to the suspense account at the close of each of the years involved are as follows:

(1) Taxable year	1977	1978	1979	1980
(2) Closing reserve account balance	$8,400	$8,250	$8,150	$8,175
(3) Opening suspense account balance	8,200	8,200	8,200	8,150
(4) Line (2) less line (3)	200	50	(50)	25
(5) Adjustment to suspense account balance	0	0	(50)	25
(6) Closing suspense account balance (line 3 plus line 5)	8,200	8,200	8,150	8,175

(g) Effective date. *(1) In general.* This section is generally effective for taxable years ending after October 21, 1965.

(2) Transitional rule. Section 2(b) of the Act of November 2, 1966 (Pub. L. 89-722, 80 Stat. 1151) allows additions to section 166(c) bad debt reserves in earlier taxable years on account of section 166(f)(1)(A) guaranteed debt obligations to be deducted for those earlier taxable years. Paragraphs (c), (d), (e), and (f) of this section do not apply in determining whether a deduction is allowed under section 2(b) of the Act. See Rev. Rul. 68-313 (1968-1C.B. 75) for rules relating to that deduction.

T.D. 8071, 1/16/86.

§ 1.167(a)-1 Depreciation in general.

(a) Reasonable allowance. Section 167(a) provides that a reasonable allowance for the exhaustion, wear and tear, and obsolescence of property used in the trade or business or of property held by the taxpayer for the production of income shall be allowed as a depreciation deduction. The allowance is that amount which should be set aside for the taxable year in accordance with a reasonably consistent plan (not necessarily at a uniform rate), so that the aggregate of the amounts set aside, plus the salvage value, will, at the end of the estimated useful life of the depreciable property, equal the cost or other basis of the property as provided in section 167(g) and § 1.167(g)-1. An asset shall not be depreciated below a reasonable salvage value under any method of computing depreciation. However, see section 167(f) and § 1.167(f)-1 for rules which permit a reduction in the amount of salvage value to be taken into account for certain personal property acquired after October 16, 1962. See also paragraph (c) of this section for definition of salvage. The allowance shall not reflect amounts representing a mere reduction in market value. See section 179 and § 1.179-1 for a further description of the term "reasonable allowance."

(b) Useful life. For the purpose of section 167 the estimated useful life of an asset is not necessarily the useful life inherent in the asset but is the period over which the asset may reasonably be expected to be useful to the taxpayer in his trade or business or in the production of his income. This period shall be determined by reference to his experience with similar property taking into account present conditions and probable future developments. Some of the factors to be considered in determining this period are (1) wear and tear and decay or decline from natural causes, (2) the normal progress of the art, economic changes, inventions, and current developments within the industry and the taxpayer's trade or business, (3) the climatic and other local conditions peculiar to the taxpayer's trade or business, and (4) the taxpayer's policy as to repairs, renewals, and replacements. Salvage value is not a factor for the purpose of determining useful life. If the taxpayer's experience is inadequate, the general experience in the industry may be used until such time as the taxpayer's own experience forms an adequate basis for making the determination. The estimated remaining useful life may be subject to modification by reason of conditions known to exist at the end of the taxable year and shall be redetermined when necessary regardless of the method of computing depreciation. However, estimated remaining useful life shall be redetermined only when the change in the useful life is significant and there is a clear and convincing basis for the redetermination. For rules covering agreements with respect to useful life, see section 167(d) and § 1.167(d)-1. If a taxpayer claims an investment credit with respect to an asset for a taxable year preceding the taxable year in which the asset is considered as placed in service under § 1.167(a)-10(b) or § 1.167(a)-11(e), the useful life of the asset under this paragraph shall be the same useful life assigned to the asset under § 1.46-3(e).

(c) Salvage. *(1)* Salvage value is the amount (determined at the time of acquisition) which is estimated will be realizable upon sale or other disposition of an asset when it is no longer useful in the taxpayer's trade or business or in the production of his income and is to be retired from service by the taxpayer. Salvage value shall not be changed at any time after the determination made at the time of acquisition merely because of changes in price levels. However, if there is a redetermination of useful life under the rules of paragraph (b) of this section, salvage value may be redetermined based upon facts known at the time of such redetermination of useful life. Salvage, when reduced by the cost of removal, is referred to as net salvage. The time at which an asset is retired from service may vary according to the policy of the taxpayer. If the taxpayer's policy is to dispose of assets which are still in good operating condition, the salvage value may represent a relatively large proportion of the original basis of the asset. However, if the taxpayer customarily uses an asset until its inherent useful life has been substantially exhausted, salvage value may represent no more than junk value. Salvage value must be taken into account in determining the depreciation deduction either by a reduction of the amount subject to depreciation or by a reduction in the rate of depreciation, but in no event shall an asset (or an account) be depreciated below a reasonable salvage value. See, however, paragraph (a) of § 1.167(b)-2 for the treatment of salvage under the declining balance method, and § 1.179-1 for the treatment of salvage in computing the additional first-year depreciation allowance. The taxpayer may use either salvage or net salvage in determining depreciation allowances but such practice must be consistently followed and the treatment of the costs of removal must be consistent with the practice adopted. For specific treatment of salvage value, see §§ 1.167(b)-1, 1.167(b)-2, and 1.167(b)-3. When an asset is retired or disposed of, appropriate adjustments shall be made in the asset and depreciation reserve accounts. For example, the amount of the salvage adjusted for the costs of removal may be credited to the depreciation reserve.

(2) For taxable years beginning after December 31, 1961, and ending after October 16, 1962, see section 167(f) and § 1.167(f)-1 for rules applicable to the reduction of salvage value taken into account for certain personal property acquired after October 16, 1962.

T.D. 6182, 6/11/56, amend T.D. 6507, 12/1/60, T.D. 6712, 3/23/64, T.D. 7203, 8/24/72.

§ 1.167(a)-2 Tangible property.

The depreciation allowance in the case of tangible property applies only to that part of the property which is subject to wear and tear, to decay or decline from natural causes, to exhaustion, and to obsolescence. The allowance does not apply to inventories or stock in trade, or to land apart from the improvements or physical development added to it. The allowance does not apply to natural resources which are subject to the allowance for depletion provided in section 611. No deduction for depreciation shall be allowed on automobiles or other vehicles used solely for pleasure, on a building used by the taxpayer solely as his residence, or on furniture or furnishings therein, personal effects, or clothing; but properties and costumes used exclusively in a business, such as a theatrical business, may be depreciated.

T.D. 6182, 6/11/56.

§ 1.167(a)-3 Intangibles.

Caution: The Treasury has not yet amended Reg § 1.167(a)-3 to reflect changes made by P.L. 103-66, P.L. 101-508, P.L. 100-647.

(a) In general. If an intangible asset is known from experience or other factors to be of use in the business or in the production of income for only a limited period, the length of which can be estimated with reasonable accuracy, such an intangible asset may be the subject of a depreciation allowance. Examples are patents and copyrights. An intangible asset, the useful life of which is not limited, is not subject to the allowance for depreciation. No allowance will be permitted merely because, in the unsupported opinion of the taxpayer, the intangible asset has a limited useful life. No deduction for depreciation is allowable with respect to goodwill. For rules with respect to organizational expenditures, see section 248 and the regulations thereunder. For rules with respect to trademark and trade name expenditures, see section 177 and the regulations thereunder. See sections 197 and 167(f) and, to the extent applicable, §§ 1.197-2 and 1.167(a)-14 for amortization of goodwill and certain other intangibles acquired after August 10, 1993, or after July 25, 1991, if a valid retroactive election under § 1.197-1T has been made.

(b) Safe harbor amortization for certain intangible assets. *(1) Useful life.* Solely for purposes of determining the depreciation allowance referred to in paragraph (a) of this section, a taxpayer may treat an intangible asset as having a useful life equal to 15 years unless—

(i) An amortization period or useful life for the intangible asset is specifically prescribed or prohibited by the Internal Revenue Code, the regulations thereunder (other than by this paragraph (b)), or other published guidance in the Internal Revenue Bulletin (see § 601.601(d)(2) of this chapter);

(ii) The intangible asset is described in § 1.263(a)-4(c) (relating to intangibles acquired from another person) or § 1.263(a)-4(d)(2) (relating to created financial interests);

(iii) The intangible asset has a useful life the length of which can be estimated with reasonable accuracy; or

(iv) The intangible asset is described in § 1.263(a)-4(d)(8) (relating to certain benefits arising from the provision, production, or improvement of real property), in which case the taxpayer may treat the intangible asset as having a useful life equal to 25 years solely for purposes of determining the depreciation allowance referred to in paragraph (a) of this section.

(2) Applicability to acquisitions of a trade or business, changes in the capital structure of a business entity, and certain other transactions. The safe harbor useful life provided by paragraph (b)(1) of this section does not apply to an amount required to be capitalized by § 1.263(a)-5 (relating to amounts paid to facilitate an acquisition of a trade or business, a change in the capital structure of a business entity, and certain other transactions).

(3) Depreciation method. A taxpayer that determines its depreciation allowance for an intangible asset using the 15-year useful life prescribed by paragraph (b)(1) of this section (or the 25-year useful life in the case of an intangible asset described in § 1.263(a)-4(d)(8)) must determine the allowance by amortizing the basis of the intangible asset (as determined under section 167(c) and without regard to salvage value) ratably over the useful life beginning on the first day of the month in which the intangible asset is placed in service by the taxpayer. The intangible asset is not eligible for amortization in the month of disposition.

(4) Effective date. This paragraph (b) applies to intangible assets created on or after December 31, 2003.

T.D. 6182, 6/11/56, amend T.D. 6452, 2/3/60, T.D. 8865, 1/20/2000, T.D. 9107, 12/31/2003.

§ 1.167(a)-4 Leased property.

Capital expenditures made by a lessee for the permanent improvements on leased property are recoverable through allowances for depreciation or amortization. If the useful life of such improvements in the hands of the taxpayer is equal to or shorter than the remaining period of the lease, the allowances shall take the form of depreciation under section 167. See §§ 1.167(b)-0, 1.167(b)-1, 1.167(b)-2, 1.167(b)-3, and 1.167(b)-4 for methods of computing such depreciation allowances. If, on the other hand, the estimated useful life of such property in the hands of the taxpayer, determined without regard to the terms of the lease, would be longer than the remaining period of such lease, the allowances shall take the form of annual deductions from gross income in an amount equal to the unrecovered cost of such capital expenditures divided by the number of years remaining of the term of the lease. Such deductions shall be in lieu of allowances for depreciation. See section 162 and the regulations thereunder. See section 178 and the regulations thereunder for rules governing the effect to be given renewal options in determining whether the useful life of the improvement exceeds the remaining term of the lease where a lessee begins improvements on leased property after July 28, 1958, other than improvements which on such date and at all times thereafter, the lessee was under a binding legal obligation to make. Capital expenditures made by a lessor for the erection of buildings or other improvements shall, if subject to depreciation allowances, be recovered by him over the estimated life of the improvements without regard to the period of the lease.

T.D. 6182, 6/11/56, amend T.D. 6520, 12/23/60.

§ 1.167(a)-5 Appointment of basis.

In the case of the acquisition on or after March 1, 1913, of a combination of depreciable and nondepreciable property for a lump sum, as for example, buildings and land, the basis for depreciation cannot exceed an amount which bears the same proportion to the lump sum as the value of the depreciable property at the time of acquisition bears to the value of the entire property at that time. In the case of property which is subject to both the allowance for depreciation and amortization, depreciation is allowable only with respect to the portion of the depreciable property which is not subject to the allowance for amortization and may be taken concurrently with the allowance for amortization. After the close of the amortization period or after amortization deductions have been discontinued with respect to any such property, the unrecovered cost or other basis of the depreciable portion of such property will be subject to depreciation. For adjustments to basis, see section 1016 and other applicable provisions of law. For the adjustment to the basis of a structure in the case of a donation of a qualified conservation contribution under section 170(h), see § 1.170A-14(h)(3)(iii).

T.D. 6182, 6/11/56, amend T.D. 8069, 1/13/86.

§ 1.167(a)-5T Application of section 1060 to section 167 (temporary).

In the case of an acquisition of a combination of depreciable and nondepreciable property for a lump sum in an applicable asset acquisition to which section 1060 applies, the basis for depreciation of the depreciable property cannot exceed the amount of consideration allocated to that property under section 1060 and § 1.1060-1T.

T.D. 8215, 7/15/88.

§ 1.167(a)-6 Depreciation in special cases.

Caution: The Treasury has not yet amended Reg § 1.167(a)-6 to reflect changes made by P.L. 110-246.

(a) Depreciation of patents or copyrights. The cost or other basis of a patent or copyright shall be depreciated over its remaining useful life. Its cost to the patentee includes the various Government fees, cost of drawings, models, attorneys' fees, and similar expenditures. For rules applicable to research and experimental expenditures, see sections 174 and 1016 and the regulations thereunder. If a patent or copyright becomes valueless in any year before its expiration the unrecovered cost or other basis may be deducted in that year. See § 1.167(a)-14(c)(4) for depreciation of a separately acquired interest in a patent or copyright described in section 167(f)(2) acquired after January 25, 2000. See § 1.197-2 for amortization of interests in patents and copyrights that constitute amortizable section 197 intangibles.

(b) Depreciation in case of farmers. A reasonable allowance for depreciation may be claimed on farm buildings (except a dwelling occupied by the owner), farm machinery, and other physical property but not including land. Livestock acquired for work, breeding, or dairy purposes may be depreciated unless included in an inventory used to determine profits in accordance with section 61 and the regulations thereunder. Such depreciation should be determined with reference to the cost or other basis, salvage value, and the estimated useful life of the livestock. See also section 162 and the regulations thereunder relating to trade or business expenses, section 165 and the regulations thereunder relating to losses of farmers, and section 175 and the regulations thereunder relating to soil or water conservation expenditures.

T.D. 6182, 6/11/56, amend T.D. 8865, 1/20/2000.

§ 1.167(a)-7 Accounting for depreciable property.

(a) Depreciable property may be accounted for by treating each individual item as an account, or by combining two or more assets in a single account. Assets may be grouped in an account in a variety of ways. For example, assets similar in kind with approximately the same useful lives may be grouped together. Such an account is commonly known as a group account. Another appropriate grouping might consist of assets segregated according to use without regard to useful life, for example, machinery and equipment, furniture and fixtures, or transportation equipment. Such an account is commonly known as a classified account. A broader grouping, where assets are included in the same account regardless of their character or useful lives, is commonly referred to as a composite account. For example, all the assets used in a business may be included in a single account. Group, classified, or composite accounts may be further broken down on the basis of location, dates of acquisition, cost, character, use, etc.

(b) When group, classified, or composite accounts are used with average useful lives and a normal retirement occurs, the full cost or other basis of the asset retired, unadjusted for depreciation or salvage, shall be removed from the asset account and shall be charged to the depreciation reserve. Amounts representing salvage ordinarily are credited to the depreciation reserve. Where an asset is disposed of for reasons other than normal retirement, the full cost or other basis of the asset shall be removed from the asset account, and the depreciation reserve shall be charged with the depreciation applicable to the retired asset. For rules with respect to losses on normal retirements, see § 1.167(a)-8.

(c) A taxpayer may establish as many accounts for depreciable property as he desires. Depreciation allowances shall be computed separately for each account. Such depreciation preferably should be recorded in a depreciation reserve account; however, in appropriate cases it may be recorded directly in the asset account. Where depreciation reserves are maintained, a separate reserve account shall be maintained for each asset account. The regular books of account or permanent auxiliary records shall show for each account the basis of the property, including adjustments necessary to conform to the requirements of section 1016 and other provisions of law relating to adjustments to basis, and the depreciation allowances for tax purposes. In the event that reserves for book purposes do not correspond with reserves maintained for tax purposes, permanent auxiliary records shall be maintained with the regular books of accounts reconciling the differences in depreciation for tax and book purposes because of different methods of depreciation, bases, rates, salvage, or other factors. Depreciation schedules filed with the income tax return shall show the accumulated reserves computed in accordance with the allowances for income tax purposes.

(d) In classified or composite accounts, the average useful life and rate shall be redetermined whenever additions, retirements, or replacements substantially alter the relative proportion of types of assets in the accounts. See example (2) paragraph (b) of § 1.167(b)-1 for method of determining the depreciation rate for a classified or composite account.

T.D. 6182, 6/11/56.

§ 1.167(a)-8 Retirements.

(a) Gains and losses on retirements. For the purposes of this section the term "retirement" means the permanent withdrawal of depreciable property from use in the trade or business or in the production of income. The withdrawal may be made in one of several ways. For example, the withdrawal may be made by selling or exchanging the asset, or by actual abandonment. In addition, the asset may be withdrawn from such productive use without disposition as, for example, by being placed in a supplies or scrap account. The tax consequences of a retirement depend upon the form of the transaction, the reason therefor, the timing of the retirement, the estimated useful life used in computing depreciation, and whether the asset is accounted for in a separate or multiple asset account. Upon the retirement of assets, the rules in this section apply in determining whether gain or loss will be recognized, the amount of such gain or loss, and the basis for determining gain or loss:

(1) Where an asset is retired by sale at arm's length, recognition of gain or loss will be subject to the provisions of sections 1002, 1231, and other applicable provisions of law.

(2) Where an asset is retired by exchange, the recognition of gain or loss will be subject to the provisions of sections 1002, 1031, 1231, and other applicable provisions of law.

(3) Where an asset is permanently retired from use in the trade or business or in the production of income but is not disposed of by the taxpayer or physically abandoned (as, for example, when the asset is transferred to a supplies or scrap account), gain will not be recognized. In such a case loss will be recognized measured by the excess of the adjusted basis of the asset at the time of retirement over the estimated salvage value or over the fair market value at the time of such retirement if greater, but only if—

(i) The retirement is an abnormal retirement, or

(ii) The retirement is a normal retirement from a single asset account (but see paragraph (d) of this section for special rule for item accounts), or

(iii) The retirement is a normal retirement from a multiple asset account in which the depreciation rate was based on the maximum expected life of the longest lived asset contained in the account.

(4) Where an asset is retired by actual physical abandonment (as, for example, in the case of a building condemned as unfit for further occupancy or other use), loss will be recognized measured by the amount of the adjusted basis of the asset abandoned at the time of such abandonment. In order to qualify for the recognition of loss from physical abandonment, the intent of the taxpayer must be irrevocably to discard the asset so that it will neither be used again by him nor retrieved by him for sale, exchange, or other disposition.

Experience with assets which have attained an exceptional or unusual age shall, with respect to similar assets, be disregarded in determining the maximum expected useful life of the longest lived asset in a multiple asset account. For example, if a manufacturer establishes a proper multiple asset account for 50 assets which are expected to have an average life of 30 years but which will remain useful to him for varying periods between 20 and 40 years, the maximum expected useful life will be 40 years, even though an occasional asset of this kind may last 60 years.

(b) Definition of normal and abnormal retirements. For the purpose of this section the determination of whether a retirement is normal or abnormal shall be made in the light of all the facts and circumstances. In general, a retirement shall be considered a normal retirement unless the taxpayer can show that the withdrawal of the asset was due to a cause not contemplated in setting the applicable depreciation rate. For example, a retirement is considered normal if made within the range of years taken into consideration in fixing the depreciation rate and if the asset has reached a condition at which, in the normal course of events, the taxpayer customarily retires similar assets from use in his business. On the other hand, a retirement may be abnormal if the asset is withdrawn at an earlier time or under other circumstances, as, for example, when the asset has been damaged by casualty or has lost its usefulness suddenly as the result of extraordinary obsolescence.

(c) Basis of assets retired. The basis of an asset at the time of retirement for computing gain or loss shall be its adjusted basis for determining gain or loss upon a sale or other disposition as determined in accordance with the provisions of section 1011 and the following rules:

(1) In the case of a normal retirement of an asset from a multiple asset account where the depreciation rate is based on average expected useful life, the term "adjusted basis" means the salvage value estimated in determining the depreciation deduction in accordance with the provisions in paragraph (c) of § 1.167(a)-1.

(2) In the case of a normal retirement of an asset from a multiple asset account in which the depreciation rate was based on the maximum expected life of the longest lived asset in the account, the adjustment for depreciation allowed or allowable shall be made at the rate which would have been proper if the asset had been depreciated in a single asset account (under the method of depreciation used for the multiple asset account) using a rate based upon the maximum expected useful life of that asset, and

(3) In the case of an abnormal retirement from a multiple asset account the adjustment for depreciation allowed or allowable shall be made at the rate which would have been proper had the asset been depreciated in a single asset account (under the method of depreciation used for the multiple asset account) and using a rate based upon either the average expected useful life or the maximum expected useful life of the asset, depending upon the method of determining the rate of depreciation used in connection with the multiple asset account.

(d) Special rule for item accounts. *(1)* As indicated in paragraph (a)(3)(ii) and (iii) of this section, a loss is recognized upon the normal retirement of an asset from a single asset account but a loss on the normal retirement of an asset in a multiple asset account is not allowable where the depreciation rate is based upon the average useful life of the assets in the account. Where a taxpayer with more than one depreciable asset chooses to set up a separate account for each such asset and the depreciation rate is based on the average useful life of such assets (so that he uses the same life for each account), the question arises whether his depreciation deductions in substance are the equivalent of those which would result from the use of multiple asset accounts and, therefore, he should be subject to the rules governing losses on retirements of assets from multiple asset accounts. Where a taxpayer has only a few depreciable assets which he chooses to account for in single asset accounts, particularly where such assets cover a relatively narrow range of lives, it cannot be said in the usual case that the allowance of losses on retirements from such accounts clearly will distort income. This results from the fact that where a taxpayer has only a few depreciable assets it is usually not possible clearly to determine that the depreciation rate is based upon the average useful life of such assets. Accordingly, it cannot be said that the taxpayer is in effect clearly operating with a multiple asset account using an average life rate so that losses should not be allowed on normal retirements. Therefore, losses normally will be allowed upon retirement of assets from single asset accounts where the taxpayer has only a few depreciable assets. On the other hand, when a taxpayer who has only a few depreciable assets chooses to account for them in single asset accounts, using for each account a depreciation rate based on the average useful life of such assets, and the assets cover a wide range of lives, the likelihood that income will be distorted is greater than where the group of assets covers a relatively narrow range of lives. In those cases where the allowance of losses would distort income, the rules with respect to the allowance of losses on normal retirement shall be applied to such assets in the same manner as though the assets had been accounted for in multiple asset accounts using a rate based upon average expected useful life.

(2) Where a taxpayer has a large number of depreciable assets and depreciation is based on the average useful life of such assets, then, whether such assets are similar or dissimilar and regardless of whether they are accounted for in individual asset accounts or multiple asset accounts the allowance of losses on the normal retirement of such assets would distort income. Such distortion would result from the fact that the use of average useful life (and, accordingly, average rate) assumes that while some assets normally will be retired before the expiration of the average life, others normally will be retired after expiration of the average life. Accordingly, if instead of accounting for a large number of similar or dissimilar depreciable assets in multiple asset accounts, the taxpayer chooses to account separately for such assets, using a rate based upon the average life of such assets, the rules with respect to the allowances of losses on normal retirements will be applied to such assets in the same manner as though the assets were accounted for in multiple asset accounts using a rate based upon average expected useful life.

(3) Where a taxpayer who does not have a large number of depreciable assets (and who therefore is not subject to subparagraph (2) of this paragraph) chooses to set up a separate account for each such asset, and has sought to compute an average life for such assets on which to base his depreciation deductions (so that he uses the same life for each account), the allowance of losses on normal retirements from such accounts may in some situations substantially distort income. Such distortion would result from the fact that the use of average useful life (and, accordingly, average rate) assumes that while some assets normally will be retired before expiration of the average life, others normally will be retired after expiration of the average life. Accordingly, where a taxpayer chooses to account separately for such assets instead of accounting for them in multiple asset accounts, and the result is to substantially distort his income, the rules with respect to the allowance of losses on normal retirements shall be applied to such assets in the same manner as though the assets had been accounted for in multiple asset accounts using a rate based upon average expected useful life.

(4) Whenever a taxpayer is treated under this paragraph as though his assets were accounted for in a multiple asset account using an average life rate, and, therefore, he is denied a loss on retirements, the unrecovered cost less salvage of

each asset which was accounted for separately may be amortized in accordance with the regulation stated in paragraph (e)(1)(ii) of this section.

(e) Accounting treatment of asset retirements. *(1)* In the case of a normal retirement where under the foregoing rules no loss is recognized and where the asset is retired without disposition or abandonment, (i) if the asset was contained in a multiple asset account, the full cost of such asset, reduced by estimated salvage, shall be charged to the depreciation reserve, or (ii) if the asset was accounted for separately, the unrecovered cost or other basis, less salvage, of the asset may be amortized through annual deductions from gross income in amounts equal to the unrecovered cost or other basis of such asset, divided by the average expected useful life (not the remaining useful life) applicable to the asset at the time of retirement. For example, if an asset is retired after six years of use and at the time of retirement depreciation was being claimed on the basis of an average expected useful life of ten years, the unrecovered cost or other basis less salvage would be amortized through equal annual deductions over a period of ten years from the time of retirement.

(2) Where multiple asset accounts are used and acquisitions and retirements are numerous, if a taxpayer, in order to avoid unnecessarily detailed accounting for individual retirements, consistently follows the practice of charging the reserve with the full cost or other basis of assets retired and of crediting it with all receipts from salvage, the practice may be continued so long as, in the opinion of the Commissioner, it clearly reflects income. Conversely, where the taxpayer customarily follows a practice of reporting all receipts from salvage as ordinary taxable income such practice may be continued so long as, in the opinion of the Commissioner, it clearly reflects income.

(f) Cross reference. For special rules in connection with the retirement of the last assets of a given year's acquisitions under the declining balance method, see example (2) in paragraph (b) of § 1.167(b)-2.

T.D. 6182, 6/11/56.

§ 1.167(a)-9 Obsolescence.

The depreciation allowance includes an allowance for normal obsolescence which should be taken into account to the extent that the expected useful life of property will be shortened by reason thereof. Obsolescence may render an asset economically useless to the taxpayer regardless of its physical condition. Obsolescence is attributable to many causes, including technological improvements and reasonably foreseeable economic changes. Among these causes are normal progress of the arts and sciences, supersession or inadequacy brought about by developments in the industry, products, methods, markets, sources of supply, and other like changes, and legislative or regulatory action. In any case in which the taxpayer shows that the estimated useful life previously used should be shortened by reason of obsolescence greater than had been assumed in computing such estimated useful life, a change to a new and shorter estimated useful life computed in accordance with such showing will be permitted. No such change will be permitted merely because in the unsupported opinion of the taxpayer the property may become obsolete. For rules governing the allowance of a loss when the usefulness of depreciable property is suddenly terminated, see § 1.167(a)-8. If the estimated useful life and the depreciation rates have been the subject of a previous agreement, see section 167(d) and § 1.167(d)-1.

T.D. 6182, 6/11/56, amend T.D. 6445, 1/15/60.

§ 1.167(a)-10 When depreciation deduction is allowable.

(a) A taxpayer should deduct the proper depreciation allowance each year and may not increase his depreciation allowances in later years by reason of his failure to deduct any depreciation allowance or of his action in deducting an allowance plainly inadequate under the known facts in prior years. The inadequacy of the depreciation allowance for property in prior years shall be determined on the basis of the allowable method of depreciation used by the taxpayer for such property or under the straight line method if no allowance has ever been claimed for such property. The preceding sentence shall not be construed as precluding application of any method provided in section 167(b) if taxpayer's failure to claim any allowance for depreciation was due solely to erroneously treating as a deductible expense an item properly chargeable to capital account. For rules relating to adjustments to basis, see section 1016 and the regulations thereunder.

(b) The period for depreciation of an asset shall begin when the asset is placed in service and shall end when the asset is retired from service. A proportionate part of one year's depreciation is allowable for that part of the first and last year during which the asset was in service. However, in the case of a multiple asset account, the amount of depreciation may be determined by using what is commonly described as an "averaging convention," that is, by using an assumed timing of additions and retirements. For example, it might be assumed that all additions and retirements to the asset account occur uniformly throughout the taxable year, in which case depreciation is computed on the average of the beginning and ending balances on the asset account for the taxable year. See example (3) under paragraph (b) of § 1.167(b)-1. Among still other averaging conventions which may be used is the one under which it is assumed that all additions and retirements during the first half of a given year were made on the first day of that year and that all additions and retirements during the second half of the year were made on the first day of the following year. Thus, a full year's depreciation would be taken on additions in the first half of the year and no depreciation would be taken on additions in the second half. Moreover, under this convention, no depreciation would be taken on retirements in the first half of the year and a full year's depreciation would be taken on the retirements in the second half. An averaging convention, if used, must be consistently followed as to the account or accounts for which it is adopted, and must be applied to both additions and retirements. In any year in which an averaging convention substantially distorts the depreciation allowance for the taxable year, it may not be used.

T.D. 6182, 6/11/56.

§ 1.167(a)-11 Depreciation based on class lives and asset depreciation ranges for property placed in service after December 31, 1970.

(a) In general. *(1) Summary.* This section provides an asset depreciation range and class life system for determining the reasonable allowance for depreciation of designated classes of assets placed in service after December 31, 1970. The system is designed to minimize disputes between taxpayers and the Internal Revenue Service as to the useful life of property, and as to salvage value, repairs, and other matters. The system is optional with the taxpayer. The taxpayer has an annual election. Generally, an election for a taxable year must apply to all additions of eligible property during the taxable year of election, but does not apply to additions of eligible property in any other taxable year. The taxpayer's election, made with the return for the taxable year, may not be revoked or modified for any property included in the election. Generally, the taxpayer must establish vintage accounts for all eligible property included in the election, must determine the allowance for depreciation of such property in the taxable year of election, and in subsequent taxable years, on the basis of the asset depreciation period selected, and must apply the first-year convention specified in the election to determine the allowance for depreciation of such property. This section also contains special provisions for the treatment of salvage value, retirements, and the costs of the repair, maintenance, rehabilitation or improvement of property. In general, a taxpayer may not apply any provision of this section unless he makes an election and thereby consents to, and agrees to apply, all the provisions of this section. A taxpayer who elects to apply this section does, however, have certain options as to the application of specified provisions of this section. A taxpayer may elect to apply this section for a taxable year only if for such taxable year he complies with the requirements of paragraph (f)(4) of this section.

(2) Definitions. For the meaning of certain terms used in this section, see paragraphs (b)(2) ("eligible property"), (b)(3) ("vintage account" and "vintage"), (b)(4) ("asset depreciation range", "asset guideline class", "asset guideline period", and "asset depreciation period"), (b)(5)(iii) *(c)* ("used property"), (b)(6)(i) ("public utility property"), (c)(1)(iv) ("original use"), (c)(1)(v) ("unadjusted basis" and "adjusted basis"), (c)(2)(ii) ("modified half-year convention"), (c)(2)(iii) ("half-year convention"), (d)(1)(i) ("gross salvage value"), (d)(1)(ii) ("salvage value"), (d)(2)(iii) ("repair allowance", "repair allowance percentage", and "repair allowance property"), (d)(2)(vi) ("excluded addition"), (d)(2)(vii) ("property improvement"), (d)(3)(ii) ("ordinary retirement" and "extraordinary retirement"), (d)(3)(vi) ("special basis vintage account"), and (e)(1) ("first placed in service") of this section.

(b) Reasonable allowance using asset depreciation ranges. *(1) In general.* The allowance for depreciation of eligible property (as defined in subparagraph (2) of this paragraph) to which the taxpayer elects to apply this section shall be determined as provided in paragraph (c) of this section and shall constitute the reasonable allowance for depreciation of such property under section 167(a).

(2) Definition of eligible property. For purposes of this section, the term "eligible property" means tangible property which is subject to the allowance for depreciation provided by section 167(a) but only if—

(i) An asset guideline class and asset guideline period are in effect for such property for the taxable year of election (see subparagraph (4) of this paragraph);

(ii) The property is first placed in service (as described in paragraph (e)(1) of this section) by the taxpayer after December 31, 1970 (but see subparagraph (7) of this paragraph for special rule where there is a mere change in the form of conducting a trade or business); and

(iii) The property is either—

(a) Section 1245 property as defined in section 1245(a)(3), or

(b) Section 1250 property as defined in section 1250(c).

See, however, subparagraph (6) of this paragraph for special rule for certain public utility property as defined in section 167(l)(3)(A). Property which meets the requirements of this subparagraph is eligible property even if depreciation with respect to such property, determined in accordance with this section, is allocated to or otherwise required to be reflected in the cost of a capitalized item. The term "eligible property" includes any property which meets the requirements of this subparagraph, whether such property is new property, "used property" (as described in subparagraph (5)(iii)(c) of this paragraph), a "property improvement" (as described in paragraph (d)(2)(vii) of this section), or an "excluded addition" (as described in paragraph (d)(2)(vi) of this section). For the treatment of expenditures for the repair, maintenance, rehabilitation or improvement of certain property, see paragraph (d)(2) of this section.

(3) Requirement of vintage accounts. (i) In general. For purposes of this section, a "vintage account" is a closed-end depreciation account containing eligible property to which the taxpayer elects to apply this section, first placed in service by the taxpayer during the taxable year of election. The "vintage" of an account refers to the taxable year during which the eligible property in the account is first placed in service by the taxpayer. Such an account will consist of an asset, or a group of assets, within a single asset guideline class established pursuant to subparagraph (4) of this paragraph and may contain only eligible property. Each item of eligible property to which the taxpayer elects to apply this section, first placed in service by the taxpayer during the taxable year of election (determined without regard to a convention described in paragraph (c)(2) of this section) shall be placed in a vintage account of the taxable year of election. For rule regarding "special basis vintage accounts" for certain property improvements, see paragraph (d)(2)(viii) and (3)(vi) of this section. Any number of vintage accounts of a taxable year may be established. More than one account of the same vintage may be established for different assets of the same asset guideline class. See paragraph (d)(3)(xi) of this section for special rule for treatment of certain multiple asset and item accounts.

(ii) Special rule. Section 1245 property may not be placed in a vintage account with section 1250 property. Property the original use of which does not commence with the taxpayer may not be placed in a vintage account with property the original use of which commences with the taxpayer. Property described in section 167(f)(2) may not be placed in a vintage account with property not described in section 167(f)(2). Property described in section 179(d)(1) for which the taxpayer elects the allowance for the first taxable year in accordance with section 179(c) may not be placed in a vintage account with property not described in section 179(d)(1) or for which the taxpayer does not elect such allowance for the first taxable year. For special rule for property acquired in a transaction to which section 381(a) applies, see paragraph (e)(3)(i) of this section. For additional rules with respect to accounting for eligible property, see paragraph (e) of this section.

(4) Asset depreciation ranges and periods. (i) Selection of asset depreciation period. The taxpayer's books and records specify for each vintage account of the taxable year of election—

(a) In the case of vintage account for property in an asset guideline class for which no asset depreciation range is in effect for the taxable year, the asset depreciation period (which shall be equal to the asset guideline period for the assets in such account), or

(b) In the case of a vintage account for property in an asset guideline class for which an asset depreciation range is in effect for the taxable year, the asset depreciation period selected by the taxpayer from the asset depreciation range for the assets in such account.

Unless otherwise expressly provided in the establishment thereof, for purposes of this section, the term "asset guideline class" means a category of assets (including "subsidiary assets") for which a separate asset guideline period is in effect for the taxable year as provided in subdivision (ii) of this subparagraph. The "asset depreciation range" is a period of years which extends from 80 percent of the asset guideline period to 120 percent of such period, determined in each case by rounding any fractional part of a year to the nearer of the nearest whole or half year. Except as provided in paragraph (e)(3)(iv) of this section, in the case of an asset guideline class for which an asset depreciation range is in effect, any period within the asset depreciation range for the assets in a vintage account which is a whole number of years or a whole number of years plus a half year, may be selected. The term "asset depreciation period" means the period selected from the asset depreciation range, or if no asset depreciation range is in effect for the class, the asset guideline period. The "asset guideline period" is established in accordance with subdivision (ii) of this subparagraph and is the class life under section 167(m). See Revenue Procedure 72-10 for special rules for section 1250 property and property predominately used outside the United States. In general, an asset guideline period, but no asset depreciation range, is in effect for such property.

(ii) Establishment of asset guideline classes and periods. The asset guideline classes and the asset guideline periods, and the asset depreciation ranges determined from such periods, in effect, for taxable years ending before the effective date of the first supplemental asset guideline classes, asset guideline periods, and asset depreciation ranges, established pursuant to this section are set forth in Revenue Procedure 72-10. Asset guideline classes and periods, and asset depreciation ranges, will from time to time be established, supplemented, and revised with express reference to this section, and will be published in the Internal Revenue Bulletin. The asset guideline classes, the asset guideline periods, and the asset depreciation ranges determined from such periods in effect as of the last day of a taxable year of election shall apply to all vintage accounts of such taxable year, except that neither the asset guideline period not the lower limit of the asset depreciation range for any such account shall be longer than the asset guideline period or the lower limit of the asset depreciation range, as the case may be, for such account in effect as of the first day of the taxable year (or as of such later time in such year as an asset guideline class first established during such year becomes effective). Generally, the reasonable allowance for depreciation of property for any taxable year in a vintage account shall not be changed to reflect any supplement or revision of the asset guideline classes or periods, and asset depreciation ranges, for the taxable year in which the account is established, which occurs after the end of such taxable year. However, if expressly provided in such a supplement or revision, the taxpayer may, at his option in the manner specified therein, apply the revised or supplemented asset guideline classes or periods and asset depreciation ranges to such property for such taxable year and succeeding taxable years.

(iii) Applicable guideline classes and periods in special situations. (a) An electric or gas utility which would in accordance with Revenue Procedure 64-21 be entitled to use a composite guideline class basis for applying Revenue Procedure 62-21 may, solely with respect to property for which an asset depreciation range is in effect for the taxable year, elect to apply this section on the basis of a composite asset guideline class and asset guideline period determined by applying the provisions of Revenue Procedure 64-21 to such property. The asset depreciation range for such a composite asset guideline class shall be determined by reference to the composite asset guideline period at the beginning of the first taxable year to which the taxpayer elects to apply this section and shall not be changed until such time as major variations in the asset mix or the asset guideline classes or periods justify some other composite asset guideline period. Except as provided in paragraph (d)(2)(iii) of this section with respect to buildings and other structures, for the purposes of this section, all property in the composite asset guideline class shall be treated as included in a single asset guideline class. If the taxpayer elects to apply this subdivision, the election shall be made on the tax return filed for the first taxable year for which the taxpayer elects to apply this section. An election to apply this subdivision for any taxable year shall apply to all succeeding taxable years to which the taxpayer elects to apply this section, except to the extent the election to apply this subdivision is with the consent of the Commissioner terminated with respect to a succeeding taxable year and all taxable years thereafter.

(b) For purposes of this section, property shall be included in the asset guideline class for the activity in which the property is primarily used. See paragraph (e)(3)(iii) of this section for rule for leased property. Property shall be classified according to primary use even though the activity in which such property is primarily used is insubstantial in relation to all the taxpayer's activities. No change in the classification of property shall be made because of a change in primary use after the end of the taxable year in which property is first placed in service, including a change in use which results in section 1250 property becoming section 1245 property.

(c) An incorrect classification or characterization by the taxpayer of property for the purposes of this section (such as under (b) of this subdivision or under subparagraph (2) or (3)(ii) of this paragraph) shall not cause or permit a revocation of the election to apply this section for the taxable year in which such property was first placed in service. The classification or characterization of such property shall be corrected. All adjustments necessary to the correction shall be made, including adjustments of unadjusted basis, adjusted basis, salvage value, the reserve for depreciation of all vintage accounts affected, and the amount of depreciation allowable for all taxable years for which the period for assessment of tax prescribed in section 6501 has not expired. If because of incorrect classification or characterization property included in an election to apply this section was not placed in a vintage account and no asset depreciation period was selected for the property or the property was placed in a vintage account but an asset depreciation period was selected from an incorrect asset depreciation range, the taxpayer shall place the property in a vintage account and select an asset depreciation period for the account from the correct asset depreciation range.

(d) Generally, except as provided in subparagraph (5)(v)(a) of this paragraph, a taxpayer may not compute depreciation for eligible property first placed in service during the taxable year under a method of depreciation not described in section 167(b)(1), (2), or (3). (If the taxpayer computes depreciation with respect to such property under section 167(k), or amortizes such property, the property must be excluded from the election to apply this section.) (See subparagraph (5)(v)(b) of this paragraph.) However, if the taxpayer establishes to the satisfaction of the Commissioner that a method of depreciation not described in section 167(b) (1), (2), (3), or (k) was adopted for property in the asset guideline class on the basis of a good faith mistake as to the proper asset guideline class for the property, then, unless the requirements of subparagraph (5)(v)(a) of this paragraph are met, the taxpayer must terminate (as of the beginning of the taxable year) such method of depreciation with respect to all eligible property in the asset guideline class which was first placed in service during the taxable year. In such event, the taxpayer's election to apply this section shall include eligible property in the asset guideline class without regard to subparagraph (5)(v)(a) of this paragraph. The provisions of (c) of this subdivision shall apply to the correction in the classification of the property.

(e) If the provisions of section 167(j) apply to require a change in the method of depreciation with respect to an item of section 1250 property in a multiple asset vintage account, the asset shall be removed from the account and placed in a separate item vintage account. The unadjusted basis of the asset shall be removed from the unadjusted basis of the vintage account as of the first day of the taxable year in which the change in method of depreciation is required and the depreciation reserve established for the account shall be reduced by the depreciation allowable for the property computed in the manner prescribed in paragraph (c)(1)(v)(b) of this section for determination of the adjusted basis of property. See paragraph (d)(3)(vii)(e) of this section for treatment of salvage value when property is removed from a vintage account.

(iv) Examples. The principles of this subparagraph may be illustrated by the following examples:

Example (1). Corporation X purchases a bulldozer for the use in its construction business. The bulldozer is first placed in service in 1972. Since the bulldozer is tangible property for which an asset guideline class and period have been established, the bulldozer is eligible property. The bulldozer is in asset guideline class 15.1 of Revenue Procedure 72-10, and the asset depreciation range is 4–6 years.

Example (2). In 1972, corporation Y first places in service a factory building. Since the factory building is tangible property for which an asset guideline class and period have been established, it is eligible property. The factory building is in asset guideline class 65.11 of Revenue Procedure 72-10. Since no asset depreciation range is in effect for the asset guideline class, the asset depreciation period is the asset guideline period of 45 years. (See subparagraph (5)(vi) of this paragraph for election to exclude certain section 1250 property during transition period.)

Example (3). In January of 1971, corporation Y, a calendar year taxpayer, pays or incurs $2,000 for the rehabilitation and improvement of machine A which was first placed in service in 1969. On January 1, 1971, corporation Y first placed in service machines B and C, each with an unadjusted basis of $10,000. Machines B and C are eligible property. Machine A would be eligible property but for the fact it was first placed in service prior to January 1, 1971 (that is, machine A is eligible property determined without regard to subparagraph (2)(ii) of this paragraph). Corporation Y elects to apply this section for the taxable year, and adopts the modified half-year convention described in paragraph (c)(2)(ii) of this section, but does not elect to apply the asset guideline class repair allowance described in paragraph (d)(2)(iii) of this section. Machines A, B, and C are in asset guideline class 24.4 under Revenue Procedure 72-10 for which the asset depreciation range is 8 to 12 years. The $2,000 expended on machine A substantially increases its capacity and is a capital expenditure under sections 162 and 263. The $2,000 is a property improvement (as defined in paragraph (d)(2)(vii)(b) of this section) which is eligible property. However, corporation Y by mistake treats the property improvement of $2,000 as a deductible repair. Also by mistake, corporation Y includes machine B in asset guideline class 24.3 under Revenue Procedure 72-10 for which the asset depreciation range is 5 to 7 years. Corporation Y establishes vintage accounts for 1971, and computes depreciation for 1971 and 1972 as follows:

	Dec. 31, 1972 reserve for depreciation	Dec. 31, 1972 adjusted basis
Vintage account for machine B, with an asset depreciation period of 5 years and an unadjusted basis of $10,000 for which corporation Y adopts the straight line method	$4,000	$6,000
Vintage account for machine C, with an asset depreciation period of 8 years and an unadjusted basis of $10,000 for which corporation Y adopts the straight line method	2,500	7,500

After audit in 1973 of corporation Y's taxable years 1971 and 1972, it is determined that the $2,000 paid in 1971 for the rehabilitation and improvement of machine A is a capital expenditure and that machine B is in asset guideline class 24.4. The incorrect classification is corrected. Corporation Y places machine B and the property improvement in a vintage account of 1971 and on its tax return filed for 1973 selects an asset depreciation period of 8 years for that account. Giving effect to the correction in classification of the property in accordance with subdivision (iii)(c) of this subparagraph, at the end of 1972 the unadjusted basis reserve for depreciation, and adjusted basis of the vintage account for machine B and the property improvement with respect to machine A are $12,000, $3,000, and $9,000 respectively. Corporation Y's deduction of the $2,000 property improvement in 1971 as a repair expense under section 162 is disallowed. For 1971 and 1972 depreciation deductions are disallowed in the amount of $500 each year (that is, $750 excess annual depreciation on machine B minus $250 annual depreciation on the property improvement).

Example (4). (a) In 1971, Corporation X, a calendar year taxpayer, first places in service machines A through M, all of which are eligible property. All the machines except machine A are in asset guideline class 24.3 under Revenue Procedure 72-10. Machine A is in asset guideline class 24.4 under Revenue Procedure 72-10. Machine B has an unadjusted basis equal to 80 percent of the total unadjusted basis of machines B through M. By good faith mistake as to proper classification, corporation X includes both machine A and machine B in asset guideline class 24.4. Corporation X consistently uses the machine hour method of depreciation on all property in asset guideline class 24.4, and for 1971 computes depreciation for machines A and B under that method. Corporation X elects to apply this section for 1971 on the assumption that the election includes machines C through M which are in asset guideline class 24.3. In 1973, upon audit of corporation X's taxable years 1971 and 1972, it is determined that machine B is included in asset guideline class 24.3 and that since for 1971 corporation X computed depreciation on machine B under the machine hour method, in accordance with subparagraph (5)(v)(a) of this paragraph, all property in asset guideline class 24.3 (machines B through M) is excluded from corporation X's election to apply this section for 1971. Although corporation X has consistently used the machine hour method for asset guideline class 24.4, corporation X has not in the past used the machine hour method for machines of the type and function of machines C through M which are in asset guideline class 24.3. Both machine A and machine B are used in connection with the manufacture of wood products. There is reasonable basis for corporation X having assumed that machine B is in asset guideline class 24.4 along with machine A to which it is similar. Corporation X establishes to the satisfaction of the Commissioner that it used the machine hour method for machine B on the basis of a good faith mistake as to the proper classification of the machine. Corporation X may, at its option (see subparagraph (5)(v) of this paragraph), terminate the machine hour method of depreciation for machine B as of the beginning of 1971, and in that event corporation X's election to apply this section for 1971 will apply to machines B through M without regard to subparagraph (5)(v)(a) of this paragraph. The adjustments provided in subdivision (iii)(c) of this subparagraph will be made as a result of the correction in classification of property. If corporation X does not terminate the machine hour method with respect to machine B, machines B through M must be excluded from the election to apply this section (see subparagraph (5)(v) of this paragraph).

(b) The facts are the same as in (a) of this example except that machine B has an unadjusted basis equal to only 65 percent of the total unadjusted basis of machines B through M. In this case, corporation X must either terminate the machine hour method of depreciation with respect to asset B (since the provisions of subparagraph (5)(v) of this paragraph do not permit the exclusion of the property from the election to apply this section) or otherwise comply with the provisions of subparagraph (5)(v) of this paragraph. (See paragraph (c)(1)(iv) for limitation on methods which may be adopted for property included in the election to apply this section.)

(5) Requirements of election. (i) In general. Except as otherwise provided in paragraph (d)(2) of this section dealing with expenditures for the repair, maintenance, rehabilitation or improvement of certain property, no provision of this section shall apply to any property other than eligible property to which the taxpayer elects in accordance with this section, to apply this section. For the time and manner of election, and certain conditions to an election, see paragraph (f) of this section. Except as otherwise provided in subparagraph (4)(iii) of this paragraph, subdivision (v) of this subparagraph and in subparagraph (6)(iii) of this paragraph, a taxpayer's election to apply this section may not be revoked or modified after the last day prescribed for filing the election. Thus, for example, after such day, a taxpayer may not cease to apply this section to property included in the election, establish different vintage accounts for the taxable year of election, select a different period from the asset depreciation range for any such account, or adopt a different first-year convention for any such account.

(ii) Property required to be included in election. Except as otherwise provided in subdivision (iii) of this subparagraph dealing with certain "used property", in subdivision (iv) of this subparagraph dealing with "section 38 property", in subdivision (v) of this subparagraph dealing with property subject to special depreciation or amortization, in subdivision (vi) of this subparagraph dealing with certain section 1250 property, in subdivision (vii) of this subparagraph dealing with certain subsidiary assets, and in paragraph (e)(3) (i) and (iv) of this section dealing with transactions to which section 381(a) applies, if the taxpayer elects to apply this section to any eligible property first placed in service by the taxpayer during the taxable year of election, the election shall apply to all such eligible property, whether placed in service in a trade or business or held for production of income.

(iii) Special 10 percent used property rule. (a) If (1) the unadjusted basis of eligible used section 1245 property (as defined in (c) of this subdivision) first placed in service by the taxpayer during the taxable year of election, for which no specific used property asset guideline class (as defined in (c) of this subdivision) is in effect for the taxable year, exceeds (2) 10 percent of the unadjusted basis of all eligible section 1245 property first placed in service during the taxable year of election, the taxpayer may exclude all (but not less than all) the property described in (a)(1) of this subdivision from the election to apply this section.

(b) If (i) the unadjusted basis of eligible used section 1250 property first placed in service by the taxpayer during the taxable year of election, for which no specific used property asset guideline class is in effect for the taxable year, exceeds (2) 10 percent of the unadjusted basis of all eligible section 1250 property first placed in service during the taxable year of election, the taxpayer may exclude all (but not less than all) the property described in (b)(1) of this subdivision from the election to apply this section.

(c) For the purposes of this section, the term "used property" means property the original use of which does not commence with the taxpayer. Solely for the purpose of determining whether the 10 percent rule of this subdivision is satisfied, (1) eligible used property first placed in service during the taxable year and excluded from the election to apply this section pursuant to subdivision (v)(a) of this subparagraph and *(2)* eligible property acquired during the taxable year in a transaction to which section 381(a) applies, shall all be treated as used property regardless of whether such property would be treated as new property under section 167(c) and the regulations thereunder. The term "specific used property asset guideline class" means a class established in accordance with subparagraph (4) of this paragraph solely for used property primarily used in connection with the activity to which the class relates.

(iv) Property subject to investment tax credit. The taxpayer may exclude from an election to apply this section all, or less than all, units of eligible property first placed in service during the taxable year which is—

(a) "Section 38 property" as defined in section 48(a) which meets the requirements of section 49 and which is not property described in section 50, or

(b) Property to which section 47(a)(5)(B) applies which would be section 38 property but for section 49 and which is placed in service to replace section 38 property (other than property described in section 50) disposed of prior to August 15, 1971.

(v) Property subject to special method of depreciation or amortization. (a) In the case of eligible property first placed in service in a taxable year of election (and not otherwise properly excluded from an election to apply this section) the taxpayer may not compute depreciation for any of such property in the asset guideline class under a method not described in section 167(b)(1), (2), (3), or (k) unless he (1) computes depreciation under a method or methods not so described for eligible property first placed in service in the taxable year in the asset guideline class with an unadjusted basis at least equal to 75 percent of the unadjusted basis of all eligible property first placed in service in the taxable year in the asset guideline class and (2) agrees to continue to depreciate such property under such method or methods until the consent of the Commissioner is obtained to a change in method. The consent of the Commissioner must be obtained by filing Form 3115 with the Commissioner of Internal Revenue, Washington, D.C. 20224, within the first 180 days of the taxable year for which the change is desired. If for the taxable year of election the taxpayer computes depreciation under any method not described in section 167(b)(1), (2), (3), or (k) for any eligible property (other than property otherwise properly excluded from an election to apply this section) first placed in service during the taxable year, an election to apply this section for the taxable year shall not include such property or any other eligible property in the same asset guideline class as such property. With respect to a taxable year beginning before January 1, 1973, if the taxpayer has adopted a method of depreciation which is not permitted under this subdivision, the taxpayer may under this section adopt a method of depreciation permitted under this subdivision or otherwise comply with the provisions of this subdivision.

(b) An election to apply this section shall not include eligible property for which, for the taxable year of election, the taxpayer computes depreciation under section 167(k), or computes amortization under section 169, 184, 185, 187, 188, or paragraph (b) of § 1.162-11. If the taxpayer has elected to apply this section to eligible property described in section 167(k), 169, 184, 185, or 187 and the taxpayer thereafter computes depreciation or amortization for such property for any taxable year in accordance with section 167(k), 169, 184, 185, or 187, then the election to apply this section to such property shall terminate as of the beginning of the taxable year for which depreciation or amortization is computed under such section. Application of this section to the property for any period prior to the termination date will not be affected by the termination. The unadjusted basis of the property shall be removed as of the termination date from the unadjusted basis of the vintage account. The depreciation reserve established for the account shall be reduced by the depreciation allowable for the property, computed in the manner prescribed in paragraph (c)(1)(v)(b) of this section for determination of the adjusted basis of the property. See paragraph (d)(3)(vii)(e) of this section for treatment of salvage value when property is removed from a vintage account.

(vi) Certain section 1250 property. (a) The taxpayer may exclude from an election to apply this section all, or less than all, items of eligible section 1250 property first placed in service during the taxable year of election provided that—

(1) The item is first placed in service before the earlier of the effective date of the first supplemental asset guideline class including such property established in accordance with subparagraph (4)(ii) of this paragraph, or January 1, 1974, and

(2) The taxpayer establishes that a useful life shorter than the asset guideline period in effect on January 1, 1971, for such item of property is justified for such taxable year.

A useful life shorter than the asset guideline period in effect on January 1, 1971, will be considered justified only if such life is justified in accordance with the provisions of Revenue Procedure 62-21 (including all modifications, amendments or supplements thereto as of January 1, 1971), determined without application of the minimal adjustment rule in section 4, part II, of Revenue Procedure 65-13. If an item of section 1250 property is excluded from an election to apply this section pursuant to this subdivision, any elevator or escalator which is a part of such item shall also be excluded from the election.

(b) If the taxpayer excludes an item of section 1250 property from an election to apply this section in accordance with this subdivision, the useful life justified under Revenue Procedure 62-21 in accordance with this subdivision for the taxable year of exclusion will be treated as justified for such item of section 1250 property for the taxable year of the exclusion and all subsequent taxable years.

(vii) Subsidiary assets. The taxpayer may exclude from an election to apply this section all (but not less than all) subsidiary assets first placed in service during the taxable year of election in an asset guideline class, provided that—

(a) The unadjusted basis of eligible subsidiary assets first placed in service during the taxable year in the class is as much as 3 percent of the unadjusted basis of all eligible property first placed in service during the taxable year in the class, and

(b) Such subsidiary assets are first placed in service by the taxpayer before the earlier of (1) the effective date of the first supplemental asset guideline class including such subsidiary assets established in accordance with subparagraph (4)(ii) of this paragraph, or (2) January 1, 1974.

For purposes of this subdivision the term "subsidiary assets" includes jigs, dies, molds, returnable containers, glassware, silverware, textile mill cam assemblies, and other equipment included in group 1, class 5, of Revenue Procedure 62-21, which is usually and properly accounted for separately from other property and under a method of depreciation not expressed in terms of years.

(6) Special rule for certain public utility property. (i) Requirement of normalization in certain cases. Under section 167(1), in the case of public utility property (as defined in section 167(1)(3)(A)), if the taxpayer—

(a) Is entitled to use a method of depreciation other than a "subsection (1) method" of depreciation (as defined in section 167(1)(3)(F)) only if it uses the "normalization method of accounting" (as defined in section 167(1)(3)(G)) with respect to such property, or

(b) Is entitled for the taxable year to use only a "subsection (1) method" of depreciation,

such property shall be eligible property (as defined in subparagraph (2) of this paragraph) only if the taxpayer normalizes the tax deferral resulting from the election to apply this section.

(ii) Normalization. The taxpayer will be considered to normalize the tax deferral resulting from the election to apply this section only if it computes its tax expense for purposes of establishing its cost of service for ratemaking purposes and for reflecting operating results in its regulated books of account using a period for depreciation no less than the lesser of—

(a) 100 percent of the asset guideline period in effect in accordance with subparagraph (4)(ii) of this paragraph for the first taxable year to which this section applies, or

(b) The period for computing its depreciation expense for ratemaking purposes and for reflecting operating results in its regulated books of account, and makes adjustments to a reserve to reflect the deferral of taxes resulting from the use of a period for depreciation under section 167 in accordance with an election to apply this section different from the lesser of the periods described in (a) and (b) of this subdivision. In the case of public utility property described in section 167(1)(3)(A)(iii) for which no guideline life was prescribed in revenue procedure 62-21 (or for which reference was made in revenue procedure 62-21 to lives or rates established by governmental regulatory agencies), for the purpose of (a) of this subdivision, the asset guideline period shall be deemed to be the period for computing the taxpayer's depreciation expense for ratemaking purposes and for reflecting operating results in its regulated books of account instead of the asset guideline period in effect in accordance with subparagraph (4)(ii) of this paragraph for the first taxable year to which this section applies. A determination whether the taxpayer is considered to normalize under this subdivision the tax deferral resulting from the election to apply this section shall be made in a manner consistent with the principles for determining whether a taxpayer is using the "normalization" method of accounting (within the meaning of section 167(l)(3)(G)). See § 1.167(l)-1(h).

(iii) Failure to normalize. If a taxpayer, which has elected to apply this section to any eligible public utility property and is required under subdivision (i) of this subparagraph to normalize the tax deferral resulting from the election to apply this section to such property, fails to normalize such tax deferral, the election to apply this section to such property shall terminate as of the beginning of the taxable year for which the taxpayer fails to normalize such tax deferral. Application of this section to such property for any period prior to the termination date will not be affected by the termination. The unadjusted basis of the property shall be removed as of the termination date from the unadjusted basis of the vintage account. The depreciation reserve established for the account shall be reduced by the depreciation allowable for the property, computed in the manner prescribed in paragraph (c)(1)(v)(b) of this section for determination of the adjusted basis of the property. See paragraph (d)(3)(vii)(e) of this section for treatment of salvage value when property is removed from a vintage account.

(iv) Examples. The principles of this subparagraph may be illustrated by the following examples:

Example (1). Corporation A is a gas pipeline company, subject to the jurisdiction of the Federal Power Commission, which is entitled under section 167(1) to use a method of depreciation other than a "subsection (1) method" of depreciation (as defined in section 167(1)(3)(F)) only if it uses the "normalization method of accounting" (as defined in section 167(1)(3)(G)). Corporation A elects to apply this section for 1972 with respect to all eligible property. In 1972, corporation A places in service eligible property with an unadjusted basis of $2 million. One hundred percent of the asset guideline period for such property is 22 years and the asset depreciation range is from 17.5 years to 26.5 years. The taxpayer uses the double declining balance method of depreciation, selects an asset depreciation period of 17.5 years and applies the half-year convention (described in paragraph (c)(2)(iii) of this section). The depreciation allowable under this section with respect to such property in 1972 is $114,235. The taxpayer will be considered to normalize the tax deferral resulting from the election to apply this section and to use the "normalization method of accounting" (within the meaning of section 167(1)(3)(G)) if it computes its tax expense for purposes of determining its cost of service for rate making purposes and for reflecting operating results in its regulated books of account using a "subsection (1) method" of depreciation, such as the straight line method, determined by using a depreciation period of 22 years (that is, 100 percent of the asset guideline period). A depreciation allowance computed in this manner is $45,454. The difference in the amount determined under this section ($114,285) and the amount used in computing its tax expense for purposes of estimating its cost of service for rate making purposes and for reflecting operating results in its regulated books of account ($45,454) is $68,831. Assuming a tax rate of 48 percent, the deferral of taxes resulting from an election to apply this section and using a different method of depreciation for tax purposes from that used for establishing its cost of service for rate making purposes and for reflecting operating results in its regulated books of account is 48 percent of $68,831, or $33,039, which amount should be added to a reserve to reflect the deferral of taxes resulting from the election to apply this section and from the use of a different method of depreciation in computing the allowance for depreciation under section 167 from that used in computing its depreciation expense for purposes of establishing its cost of service for rate making purposes and for reflecting operating results in its regulated books of account.

Example (2). Corporation B, a telephone company subject to the jurisdiction of the Federal Communications Commission used a "flow-through method of accounting" (as defined in section 167(1)(3)(H)) for its "July 1969 accounting period" (as defined in section 167(1)(3)(I)) with respect to all of its pre-1970 public utility property and did not make an election under section 167(1)(4)(A). Thus, corporation B is entitled under section 167(1) to use a method of depreciation other than a "subsection (1) method" with respect to certain property without using the "normalization method of accounting." In 1972, corporation B makes an election to apply this section with respect to all eligible property. Corporation B is not required to normalize the tax deferral resulting from the election to apply this section in the case of property for which it is not required to use the "normalization method of accounting" under section 167(1).

Example (3). Assume the same facts as in example (2) except that corporation B made a timely election under section 167(1)(4)(A) that section 167(1)(2)(C) not apply with respect to property which increases the productive or operational capacity of the taxpayer. Corporation B must normalize the tax deferral resulting from the election to apply this section with respect to such property.

(7) Mere change in form of conducting a trade or business. Property which was first placed in service by the transferor before January 1, 1971, shall not be eligible property if such property is first placed in service by the transferee after December 31, 1970, by reason of a mere change in the form of conducting a trade or business in which such property is used. A mere change in the form of conducting a trade or business in which such property is used will be considered to have occurred if—

(i) The transferor (or in a case where the transferor is a partnership, estate, trust, or corporation, the partners, beneficiaries, or shareholders) of such property retains a substantial interest in such trade or business, or

(ii) The basis of such property in the hands of the transferee is determined in whole or in part by reference to the basis of such property in the hands of the transferor.

For purposes of this subparagraph, a transferor (or in a case where the transferor is a partnership, estate, trust, or corporation, the partners, beneficiaries, or shareholders) shall be considered as having retained a substantial interest in the trade or business only if, after the change in form, his (or their) interest in such trade or business is substantial in relation to the total interest of all persons in such trade or business. This subparagraph shall apply to property first placed in service prior to January 1, 1971, held for the production of income (within the meaning of section 167(a)(2)) as well as to property used in a trade or business. The principles of this subdivision may be illustrated by the following examples:

Example (1). Corporation X and corporation Y are includible corporations in an affiliated group as defined in section 1504(a). In 1971 corporation X sells property to corporation Y for cash. The property would meet the requirements of subparagraph (2) of this paragraph for eligible property except that it was first placed in service by corporation X in 1970. After the transfer, the property is first placed in service by corporation Y in 1971. The property is not eligible property because of the mere change in the form of conducting a trade or business.

Example (2). In 1971, in a transaction to which section 351 applies, taxpayer B transfers to corporation W property which would meet the requirements of subparagraph (2) of this paragraph for eligible property except that the property was first placed in service by B in 1969. Corporation W first places the property in service in 1971. The property is not eligible property because of the mere change in the form of conducting a trade or business.

(c) Manner of determining allowance. *(1) In general.* (i) Computation of allowance. (a) The allowance for depreciation of property in a vintage account shall be determined in the manner specified in this paragraph by using the method of depreciation adopted by the taxpayer for the account and a rate based upon the asset depreciation period for the account. (For limitations on methods of depreciation permitted with respect to property, see section 167 (c) and (j) and subdivision (iv) of this subparagraph.) In applying the method of depreciation adopted by the taxpayer, the annual allowance for depreciation of a vintage account shall be determined without adjustment for the salvage value of the property in such account except that no account may be depreciated below the reasonable salvage value of the account. (For rules regarding estimation and treatment of salvage value, see paragraph (d) (1) and (3) (vii) and (viii) of this section.) Regardless of the method of depreciation adopted by the taxpayer, the depreciation allowable for a taxable year with respect to a vintage account may not exceed the amount by which (as of the beginning of the taxable year) the unadjusted basis of the account exceeds (1) the reserve for depreciation established for the account plus (2) the salvage value of the account. The unadjusted basis of a vintage account is defined in subdivision (v) of this subparagraph. The adjustments to the depreciation reserve are described in subdivision (ii) of this subparagraph.

(b) The annual allowance for depreciation of a vintage account using the straight line method of depreciation shall be determined by dividing the unadjusted basis of the vintage account (without reduction for salvage value) by the number of years in the asset depreciation period selected for the account. See subdivision (iii)(b) of this subparagraph for the manner of computing the depreciation allowance following a change from the declining balance method or the sum of the years-digits method to the straight line method.

(c) In the case of the sum of the years-digits method, the annual allowance for depreciation of a vintage account shall be computed by multiplying the unadjusted basis of the vintage account (without reduction for salvage value) by a fraction, the numerator of which changes each year to a number which corresponds to the years remaining in the asset depreciation period for the account (including the year for which the allowance is being computed) and the denominator of which is the sum of all the year's digits corresponding to the asset depreciation period for the account. See subdivision (iii)*(c)* of this subparagraph for the manner of computing the depreciation allowance following a change from the declining balance method to the sum of the years-digits method.

(d) The annual allowance for depreciation of a vintage account using a declining balance method is determined by applying a uniform rate to the excess of the unadjusted basis of the vintage account over the depreciation reserve established for that account. The rate under the declining balance method may not exceed twice the straight line rate based upon the asset depreciation period for the vintage account.

(e) The allowance for depreciation under this paragraph shall constitute the amount of depreciation allowable under section 167. See section 179 for additional first-year allowance for certain property.

(ii) Establishment of depreciation reserve. The taxpayer must establish a depreciation reserve for each vintage account. The amount of the reserve for a guideline class must be stated on each income tax return on which depreciation with respect to such class is determined under this section. The depreciation reserve for a vintage account consists of the accumulated depreciation allowable under this section with respect to the vintage account, increased by the adjustments for ordinary retirements prescribed by paragraph (d)(3)(iii) of this section, by the adjustments for reduction of the salvage value of a vintage account prescribed by paragraph (d)(3)(vii)(d) of this section, and by the adjustments for transfers to supplies or scrap prescribed by paragraph (d)(3)(viii)(b) of this section, and decreased by the adjustments for extraordinary retirements and certain special retirements as prescribed by paragraph (d)(3) (iv) and (v) of this section, by the adjustments for the amount of the reserve in excess of the unadjusted basis of a vintage account prescribed by paragraph (d)(3)(ix)(a) of this section, and by the adjustments for property removed from a vintage account prescribed by paragraph (b)(4)(iii)(e), (5)(v)(b) and (6)(iii) of this section. The adjustments to the depreciation reserve for ordinary retirements during the taxable year shall be made as of the beginning of the taxable year. The adjustments to the depreciation reserve for extraordinary retirements shall be made as of the date the retirement is treated as having occurred in accordance with the first-year convention (described in subparagraph (2) of this paragraph) adopted by the taxpayer for the vintage account. The adjustment to the depreciation reserve for reduction of salvage value and for transfers to supplies or scrap shall, in the case of an ordinary retirement, be made as of the beginning of the taxable year, and in the case of an extraordinary retirement the adjustment for reduction of salvage value shall be made as of the date the retirement is treated as having occurred in accordance with the first-year convention (described in subparagraph *(2)* of this paragraph) adopted by the taxpayer for the vintage account. The adjustment to the depreciation reserve for property removed from a vintage account in accordance with paragraph (b)(4)(iii)(e), (5)(v)(b) and (6)(iii) of this section shall be made as of the beginning of the taxable year. The depreciation reserve of a vintage account may not be decreased below zero.

(iii) Consent to change in method of depreciation. (a) During the asset depreciation period for a vintage account, the taxpayer is permitted to change under this section from a declining balance method of depreciation to the sum of the years-digits method of depreciation and from a declining balance method of depreciation or the sum of the years-digits method of depreciation to the straight line method of depreciation with respect to such account. Except as provided in section 167(j)(2)(1), and paragraph (e)(3)(i) of this section, no other changes in the method of depreciation adopted for a vintage account will be permitted. The provisions of § 1.167(e)-1 shall not apply to any change in depreciation method permitted under this section. The change in method applies to all property in the vintage account and must be adhered to for the entire taxable year of the change.

(b) When a change is made to the straight line method of depreciation, the annual allowance for depreciation of the vintage account shall be determined by dividing the adjusted basis of the vintage account (without reduction for salvage value) by the number of years remaining (at the time as of which the change is made) in the asset depreciation period selected for the account. However, the depreciation allowable for any taxable year following a change to the straight line method may not exceed an amount determined by dividing the unadjusted basis of the vintage account (without reduction for salvage value) by the number of years in the asset depreciation period selected for the account.

(c) When a change is made from the declining balance method of depreciation to the sum of the years-digits method of depreciation, the annual allowance for depreciation of a vintage account shall be determined by multiplying the adjusted basis of the account (without reduction for salvage value) at the time as of which the change is made by a fraction, the numerator of which changes each year to a number which corresponds to the number of years remaining in the asset depreciation period selected for the account (including the year for which the allowance is being computed), and the denominator of which is the sum of all the year's digits corresponding to the number of years remaining in the asset depreciation period at the time as of which the change is made.

(d) The number of years remaining in the asset depreciation period selected for an account is equal to the asset depreciation period less the number of years of depreciation previously allowed. For this purpose, regardless of the first year convention adopted by the taxpayer, it will be assumed that depreciation was allowed for one-half of a year in the first year.

(e) The taxpayer shall furnish a statement setting forth the vintage accounts for which the change is made with the income tax return filed for the taxable year of the change.

(f) The principles of this subdivision may be illustrated by the following examples:

Example (1). A, a calendar year taxpayer, places new section 1245 property in service in a trade or business as follows:

Asset	Placed in service	Unadjusted basis	Estimated salvage
X	Mar. 15, 1971	$400	$20
Y	June 13, 1971	500	50
Z...............	July 30, 1971	100	0

The property is eligible property and is properly included in a single vintage account. The asset depreciation range for such property is 5 to 7 years and the taxpayer selects an asset depreciation period of 5½ years and adopts the 200-percent declining balance method of depreciation. The taxpayer adopts the half-year convention described in subparagraph (2)(iii) of this paragraph. After 3 years, A changes from the 200-percent declining balance method to the straight line method of depreciation. Depreciation allowances would be as follows:

Year	Unadjusted basis	Rate	Depreciation	Reserve	Adjusted basis
1971	$1,000	0.18182	$181.82	$181.82	$818.18
1972	1,000	.36363	297.52	479.34	520.66
1973	1,000	.36363	189.33	668.67	331.33
1974	1,000	.33333[1]	110.44	779.11	220.89
1975	1,000	.33333	110.44	889.56	110.41
1976	1,000	.33333	40.44[2]	930.00	70.00

[1] Rate applied to adjusted basis of the account (without reduction by salvage) at the time as of which the change is made to the straight line method.

[2] The allowable depreciation is limited by estimated salvage.

Example (2). The facts are the same as in example (1) except that A elects to use the modified half-year convention described in subparagraph (2)(ii) of this paragraph. The depreciation allowances would be as follows:

Year	Unadjusted basis	Rate	Depreciation	Reserve	Adjusted basis
1971	$1,000	0.36363[1]	$328.27	$327.27	$672.73
1972	1,000	.36363	244.63	571.90	428.10
1973	1,000	.36363	155.67	727.57	272.43
1974	1,000	.33333	90.81	818.33	181.62
1975	1,000	.33333	90.81	909.19	90.81
1976	1,000	.33333	20.81[2]	930.00	70.00

[1] Rate applied to $900, the amount of assets placed in service during the first half of the taxable year.

[2] The allowable depreciation is limited by estimated salvage.

Example (3). The facts are the same as in example (1) except that A adopted the sum of the years-digits method of depreciation and does not change to the straight line method of depreciation. The depreciation allowances would be as follows:

Year	Unadjusted basis	Rate	Depreciation	Reserve	Adjusted basis
1971	$1,000	2.75/18[1]	$152.78	$152.78	$847.22
1972	1,000	5/18	277.78	430.56	569.44
1973	1,000	4/18	222.22	652.78	347.22
1974	1,000	3/18	166.67	819.45	180.55
1975	1,000	2/18	110.55[2]	930.00	70.00
1976	1,000	1/18	930.00	70.00	
1977	1,000	0.25/18	0.00	930.00	70.00

[1] Rate is equal to one-half of 5.5/18. The denominator is equal to 5.5 + 4.5 + 3.5 + 2.5 + 1.5 + 0.5.
[2] The allowable depreciation is limited by estimated salvage.

Example (4). The facts are the same as in example (3) except that A elects to use the modified half-year convention described in subparagraph (2)(ii) of this paragraph. The depreciation allowances would be as follows:

Year	Unadjusted basis	Rate	Depreciation	Reserve	Adjusted basis
1971	$1,000	5.5/18[1]	$275.00	$275.00	$725.00
1972	1,000	5/18	277.78	552.78	447.22
1973	1,000	4/18	222.22	775.00	225.00
1974	1,000	3/18	155.00[2]	930.00	70.00
1975	1,000	2/18	0.00	930.00	70.00
1976	1,000	1/18	0.00	930.00	70.00
1977	1,000	0.25/18	0.00	930.00	70.00

[1] Rate applied to $900, the amount of assets placed in service during the first half of the taxable year.
[2] The allowable depreciation is limited by estimated salvage.

Example (5). The facts are the same as in example (2) except that after 2 years A changes from the 200-percent declining balance method to the sum of the years-digits method of depreciation. The depreciation allowances would be as follows:

Year	Unadjusted basis	Rate	Depreciation	Reserve	Adjusted basis
1971	$1,000	0.36363	$327.27	$327.27	$672.73
1972	1,000	.36363	244.63	571.90	428.10
1973	1,000	4/10	171.24	743.14	256.86
1974	1,000	3/10	128.43	871.57	128.43
1975	1,000	2/10	58.43[1]	930.00	70.00
1976	1,000	1/10	0.00	930.00	70.00

[1] The allowable depreciation is limited by estimated salvage.

(iv) Limitation on methods. (a) The same method of depreciation must be adopted for all property in a single vintage account. Generally, the method of depreciation which may be adopted is subject to the limitations contained in section 167 (c) and (j).

(b) Except as otherwise provided in section 167(j) with respect to certain eligible section 1250 property—

(1) In the case of a vintage account for which the taxpayer has selected an asset depreciation period of 3 years or more and which only contains property the original use of which commences with the taxpayer, any method of depreciation described in section 167(b)(1), (2), or (3) may be adopted, but if the vintage account contains property the original use of which does not commence with the taxpayer, or if the asset depreciation period for the account is less than 3 years, a method of depreciation described in section 167(b) (2) or (3) may not be adopted for the account, and

(2) The declining balance method using a rate not in excess of 150 percent of the straight line rate based upon the asset depreciation period for the vintage account may be adopted for the account even if the original use of the property does not commence with the taxpayer provided the asset depreciation period for the account is at least 3 years.

(c) The term "original use" means the first use to which the property is put, whether or not such use corresponds to the use of such property by the taxpayer. (See § 1.167(c)-1).

(v) Unadjusted and adjusted basis. (a) For purposes of this section, the unadjusted basis of an asset (including an "excluded addition" and a "property improvement" as described, respectively, in paragraph (d)(2) (vi) and (vii) of this section) is its cost or other basis without any adjustment for depreciation or amortization (other than depreciation under section 179) but with other adjustments required under section 1016 or other applicable provisions of law. The unadjusted basis of a vintage account is the total of the unadjusted bases of all the assets in the account. The unadjusted basis of a "special basis vintage account" as described in paragraph (d)(3)(vi) of this section is the amount of the property improvement determined in paragraph (d)(2)(vii) (a) of this section.

(b) The adjusted basis of a vintage account is the amount by which the unadjusted basis of the account exceeds the reserve for depreciation for the account. The adjusted basis of an asset in a vintage account is the amount by which the unadjusted basis of the asset exceeds the amount of depreciation allowable for the asset under this section computed by using the method of depreciation and the rate applicable to the account. For purposes of this subdivision, the depreciation allowable for an asset shall include, to the extent identifiable, the amount of proceeds previously added to the depreciation reserve in accordance with paragraph (d)(3)(iii) of this section upon the retirement of any portion of such asset. (See paragraph (d)(3)(vi) of this section for election under certain circumstances to allocate adjusted basis of an amount of property improvement determined under paragraph (d)(2)(vii) *(a)* of this section.)

(2) Conventions applied to additions and retirements. (i) In general. The allowance for depreciation of a vintage account (whether an item account or a multiple asset account) shall be determined by applying one of the conventions described in subdivisions (ii) and (iii) of this subparagraph. (For the manner of applying a convention in the case of taxable years beginning before and ending after December 31, 1970, see subparagraph (3) of this paragraph.) The same convention must be adopted for all vintage accounts of a taxable year, but the same convention need not be adopted for the vintage accounts of another taxable year. An election to apply this section must specify the convention adopted. (See paragraph (f) of this section for information required in making the election.) The convention adopted by the taxpayer is a method of accounting for purposes of section 446, but the consent of the Commissioner will be deemed granted to make an annual adoption of either of the conventions described in subdivisions (ii) and (iii) of this subparagraph.

(ii) Modified half-year convention. The depreciation allowance for a vintage account for which the taxpayer adopts the "modified half-year convention" shall be determined by treating:*(a)* All property in such account which is placed in service during the first half of the taxable year as placed in service on the first day of the taxable year; and (b) all property in such account which is placed in service during the second half of the taxable year as placed in service on the first day of the succeeding taxable year. The depreciation allowance for a vintage account for a taxable year in which there is an extraordinary retirement (as defined in paragraph (d)(3)(ii) of this section) of property first placed in service during the first half of the taxable year is determined by treating all such retirements from such account during the first half of the taxable year as occurring on the first day of the taxable year and all such retirements from such account during the second half of the taxable year as occurring on the first day of the second half of the taxable year. The depreciation allowance for a vintage account for a taxable year in which there is an extraordinary retirement (as defined in paragraph (d)(3)(ii) of this section) of property first placed in service during the second half of the taxable year is determined by treating all such retirements from such account during the first half of the taxable year as occurring on the first day of the second half of the taxable year and all such retirements in the second half of the taxable year as occurring on the first day of the succeeding taxable year.

(iii) Half-year convention. The depreciation allowance for a vintage account for which the taxpayer adopts the "half-year convention" shall be determined by treating all property in the account as placed in service on the first day of the second half of the taxable year and by treating all extraordinary retirements (as defined in paragraph (d)(3)(ii) of this section) from the account as occurring on the first day of the second half of the taxable year.

(iv) Rules of application. (a) The first-year convention adopted for a vintage account must be consistently applied to all additions to and all extraordinary retirements from such account. See paragraph (d)(3) (ii) and (iii) of this section for definition and treatment of ordinary retirements.

(b) If the actual number of months in a taxable year is other than 12 full calendar months, depreciation is allowed only for such actual number of months and the term "taxable year", for purposes of this subparagraph, shall mean only such number of months. In such event, the first half of such taxable year shall be deemed to expire at the close of the last day of a calendar month which is the closest such last day to the middle of such taxable year and the second half of such taxable year shall be deemed to begin the day after the expiration of the first half of such taxable year. If a taxable year consists of a period which includes only 1 calendar month, the first half of the taxable year shall be deemed to expire on the first day which is nearest to the midpoint of the month, and the second half of the taxable year shall begin the day after the expiration of the first half of the month.

(c) For purposes of this subparagraph, for property placed in service after November 14, 1979, other than depreciable property described in paragraph (c)(2)(iv)(e) of this section, the taxable year of the person placing such property in service does not include any month before the month in which the person begins engaging in a trade or business or holding depreciable property for the production of income.

(d) For purposes of paragraph (c)(2)(iv)(c) of this section,

(1) For property placed in service after February 21, 1981, an employee is not considered engaged in a trade or business by virtue of employment.

(2) If a person engages in a small amount of trade or business activity after February 21, 1981, for the purpose of obtaining a disproportionately large depreciation deduction for assets for the taxable year in which they are placed in service, and placing those assets in service represents a substantial increase in the person's level of business activity, then for purposes of depreciating those assets the person will not be treated as beginning a trade or business until the increased amount of business activity begins. For property held for the production of income, the principle of the preceding sentence applies.

(3) A person may elect to apply the rules of § 1.167(a)-11(c)(2)(iv)(d) as set forth in T.D. 7763 ("(d) rules T.D. 7763"). This election shall be made by reflecting it under paragraph (f)(4) of this section in the books and records. If necessary, amended returns shall be filed.

(4) If an averaging convention was adopted in reliance on or in anticipation of the (d) rules in T.D. 7763, that convention may be changed without regard to paragraph (f)(3) of this section. Similarly, if an election is made under paragraph (c)(2)(iv)(d)(3) of this section to apply to the (d) rules in T.D. 7763, the averaging convention adopted for the taxable years for which the election is made may be changed. The change shall be made by filing a timely amended return for the taxable year for which the convention was adopted. Notwithstanding the three preceding sentences, if an averaging convention was adopted in reliance on or in anticipation of the (d) rules in T.D. 7763, and if an election is made to apply those rules, the averaging convention adopted cannot be changed except as provided in paragraph (f) of this section.

(e) The rules in paragraph (c)(2)(iv)(c) of this section do not apply to depreciable property placed in service after November 14, 1979, and the rules in paragraph (c)(2)(iv)(d) of this section do not apply to depreciable property placed in service after February 21, 1981, with respect to which substantial expenditures were paid or incurred prior to November 15, 1979. For purposes of the preceding sentence, expenditures will not be considered substantial unless they exceed the lesser of 30 percent of the final cost of the property or $10 million. Expenditures that are not includible in the basis of the depreciable property will be considered expenditures with respect to property if they are directly related to a specific project involving such property. For purposes of determining whether expenditures were paid or incurred prior to November 15, 1979, expenditures made by a person (transferor) other than the person placing the property in service (transferee) will be taken into account only if the basis of the property in the hands of the transferee is determined in whole or in part by reference to the basis in the hands of the transferor. The principle of the preceding sentence also applies if there are multiple transfers.

(v) Mass assets. In the case of mass assets, if extraordinary retirements of such assets in a guideline class during the first half of the taxable year are allocated to a particular vintage year for which the taxpayer applied the modified half-year convention, then that portion of the mass assets so allocated which bears the same ratio to the total number of mass assets so allocated as the mass assets in the same vintage and assets guideline class placed in service during the first half of that vintage year bear to the total mass assets in the same vintage and asset guideline class shall be treated as retired on the first day of the taxable year. The remaining mass assets which are subject to extraordinary retirement during the first half of the taxable year and which are allocated to that vintage year and assets guideline class shall be treated as retired on the first days of the second half of the taxable year. If extraordinary retirements of mass assets in a guideline class occur in the second half of the taxable year and are allocated to a particular vintage year for which the taxpayer applied the modified half-year convention, then that portion of the mass assets so allocated which bears the same ratio to the total number of mass assets so allocated as the mass assets in the same vintage and asset guideline class first placed in service during the first half of that vintage year bear to the total mass assets in the same vintage and asset guideline class shall be treated as retired on the first day of the second half of the taxable year. The remaining mass assets which are subject to extraordinary retirement during the second half of the taxable year and which are allocated to that same vintage and asset guideline class shall be treated as retired on the first day of the succeeding taxable year. If the taxpayer has applied the half-year convention for the vintage year to which the extraordinary retirements are allocated, the mass assets shall be treated as retired on the first day of the second half of the taxable year.

(3) Taxable years beginning before and ending after December 31, 1970. In the case of a taxable year which begins before January 1, 1971, and ends after December 31, 1970, property first placed in service after December 31, 1970, but treated as first placed in service before January 1, 1971, by application of a convention described in subparagraph (2) of this paragraph shall be treated as provided in this subparagraph. The depreciation allowed (or allowable) for the taxable year shall consist of the depreciation allowed (or allowable) for the period before January 1, 1971, determined without regard to this section plus the amount allowable for the period after December 31, 1970, determined under this section. However, neither the modified half-year convention described in subparagraph (2)(ii) of this paragraph, nor the half-year convention described in subparagraph (2)(iii) of this paragraph may for any such taxable year be applied with respect to property placed in service after December 31, 1970, to allow depreciation for any period prior to January 1, 1971, unless such convention is consistent with the convention applied by the taxpayer with respect to property placed in service in such taxable year prior to January 1, 1971.

(4) Examples. The principles of this paragraph may be illustrated by the following examples:

Example (1). Taxpayer A, a calendar year taxpayer, places new property in service in a trade or business as follows:

Asset	Placed in service	Unadjusted basis
W	Apr. 1, 1971	$ 5,000
X	June 30, 1971	8,000
Y	July 15, 1971	12,000

Taxpayer A adopts the modified half-year convention described in subparagraph (2)(ii) of this paragraph. Assets W, X, and Y are placed in a multiple asset account for which the asset depreciation range is 8 to 12 years. A selects 8 years, the minimum asset depreciation period with respect to such assets, and adopts the declining balance method of depreciation using a rate twice the straight line rate (computed without reduction for salvage). The annual rate under this method using a period of 8 years is 25 percent. The depreciation allowance for assets W and X for 1971 is $3,250, a full year's depreciation under the modified half-year convention (that is, basis of $13,000 (unreduced by salvage) multiplied by 25 percent). The depreciation allowance for asset Y for 1971 is zero under the modified half-year convention.

Example (2). The facts are the same as in example (1), except that the taxpayer adopts the half-year convention described in subparagraph (2)(iii) of this paragraph. The depreciation allowance with respect to asset Y is $1,500 (that is the basis of $12,000 multiplied by 25 percent, then multiplied by ½). Assets W and X are also entitled to a depreciation allowance for only a half year. Thus, the depreciation allowance for assets W and X for 1971 is $1,625 (that is, ½ of the $3,250 allowance computed in example (1)).

Example (3). Asset Z is placed in service by a calendar year taxpayer on December 1, 1971. The taxpayer places asset Z in an item account and adopts the sum of the years-digits method and the half year convention described in subparagraph (2)(iii) of this paragraph. The asset depreciation range for such asset is 4 to 6 years and the taxpayer selects an asset depreciation period of 5 years. The depreciation allowance for asset Z in 1971 is $10,000 (that is, basis of $60,000 (unreduced by salvage) multiplied by $^5/_{15}$, the appropriate fraction using the sum of the years-digits method then multiplied by ½, since only one half year's depreciation is allowable under the convention).

Example (4). A is a calendar year taxpayer. All taxpayer A's assets are placed in service in the first half of 1971. If the taxpayer selects the modified half-year convention described in subparagraph (2)(ii) of this paragraph, a full year's depreciation is allowable for all assets.

Example (5). (i) The taxpayer during his taxable year which begins April 1, 1970, and ends March 31, 1971, places new property in service in a trade or business as follows:

Asset	Placed in service	Unadjusted basis
A	Apr.30, 1970	$10,000
B....................	Dec.15, 1970	10,000
C....................	Jan. 1, 1971	10,000

The taxpayer adopted a convention under § 1.167(a)-10(b) with respect to assets placed in service prior to January 1, 1971, which treats assets placed in service during the first half of the year as placed in service on the first day of such year and assets placed in service in the second half of the year as placed in service on the first day of the following year. If the taxpayer selects the half-year convention described in subparagraph (2)(iii) of this paragraph, one year's depreciation is allowable on asset A determined without regard to this section. No depreciation is allowable for asset B. No depreciation is allowable for asset C for the period prior to January 1, 1971. One-fourth year's depreciation is allowable on asset C determined under this section.

(ii) The facts are the same as in (i) of this example except that the taxpayer adopts the modified half-year convention described in subparagraph (2)(ii) of this paragraph for 1971. No depreciation is allowable for assets B and C which were placed in service in the second half of the taxable year.

Example (6). The taxpayer during his taxable year which begins August 1, 1970, and ends July 31, 1971, places new property in service in a trade or business as follows:

Assets	Placed in service
A	Aug. 1, 1970.
B	Jan. 15, 1971.
C	June 30, 1971.

The taxpayer adopted a convention under § 1.167(a)-10(b) with respect to assets placed in service prior to January 1, 1971, which treats all assets as placed in service at the midpoint of the taxable year. If the taxpayer selects the half-year convention described in subparagraph (2)(iii) of this paragraph, one-half year's depreciation is allowable for asset A determined without regard to this section. One-half year's depreciation is allowable for assets B and C determined under this section.

Example (7). X, a calendar year corporation, is incorporated on July 1, 1978, and begins engaging in a trade or business in September 1979. X purchases asset A and places it in service on November 20, 1979. Substantial expenditures were not paid or incurred by X with respect to asset A prior to November 15, 1979. For purposes of applying the conventions under this section to determine depreciation for asset A, the 1979 taxable year is treated as consisting of 4 months. The first half of the taxable year ends on October 31, 1979, and the second half begins on November 1, 1979. X adopts the half-year convention. Asset A is treated as placed in service on November 1, 1979.

Example (8). On January 20, 1982, A, B, and C enter an agreement to form partnership P for the purpose of purchasing and leasing a ship to a third party, Z. P uses the calendar year as its taxable year. On December 15, 1982, P acquires the ship and leases it to Z. For purposes of applying the conventions, P begins its leasing business in December 1982, and its taxable year begins on December 1, 1982. Assuming that P elects to apply this section and adopts the modified half-year convention, P depreciates the ship placed in service in 1982 for the 1-month period beginning December 1, 1982, and ending December 31, 1982.

Example (9). A and B form partnership P on December 15, 1981, to conduct a business of leasing small aircraft. P uses the calendar year as its taxable year. On January 15, 1982, P acquires and places in service a $25,000 aircraft. P begins engaging in business with only one aircraft for the purpose of obtaining a disproportionately large depreciation deduction for aircraft that P plans to acquire at the end of the year. On December 10, 1982, P acquires and places in service 4 aircraft, the total purchase price of which is $250,000. For purposes of applying the convention to the aircraft acquired in December, P begins its leasing business in December 1982, and P's taxable year begins December 1, 1982, and ends December 31, 1982. Assuming that P elects to apply this section and adopts the modified half-year convention, P depreciates the aircraft placed in service in December 1982, for the 1-month period beginning December 1, 1982, and ending December 31, 1982. P depreciates the aircraft placed in service in January 1982, for the 12-month period beginning January 1, 1982, and ending December 31, 1982.

(d) Special rules for salvage, repairs and retirements. *(1) Salvage value.* (i) Definition of gross salvage value. "Gross salvage" value is the amount which is estimated will be realized upon a sale or other disposition of the property in the vintage account when it is no longer useful in the taxpayer's trade or business or in the production of his income and is to be retired from service, without reduction for the cost of removal, dismantling, demolition or similar operations. If a taxpayer customarily sells or otherwise disposes of property at a time when such property is still in good operating condition, the gross salvage value of such property is the amount expected to be realized upon such sale or disposition, and under certain circumstances, as where such property is customarily sold at a time when it is still relatively new, the gross salvage value may constitute a relatively large proportion of the unadjusted basis of such property.

(ii) Definition of salvage value. "Salvage value" means gross salvage value less the amount, if any, by which the gross salvage value is reduced by application of section 167(f). Generally, as provided in section 167(f), a taxpayer may reduce the amount of gross salvage value of a vintage account by an amount which does not exceed 10 percent of the unadjusted basis of the personal property (as defined in section 167(f)(2)) in the account. See paragraph (b)(3)(ii) of this section for requirement of separate vintage accounts for personal property described in section 167(f)(2).

(iii) Estimation of salvage value. The salvage value of each vintage account of the taxable year shall be estimated by the taxpayer at the time the election to apply this section is made, upon the basis of all the facts and circumstances existing at the close of the taxable year in which the account is established. The taxpayer shall specify the amount, if any, by which gross salvage value taken into account is reduced by application of section 167(f). The salvage value estimated by the taxpayer will not be redetermined merely as a result of fluctuations in price levels or as a result of other facts and circumstances occurring after the close of the taxable year of election. Salvage value for a vintage account need not be established or increased as a result of a property improvement as described in subparagraph (2) (vii) of this paragraph. The taxpayer shall maintain records reasonably sufficient to determine facts and circumstances taken into account in estimating salvage value.

(iv) Salvage as limitation on depreciation. In no case may a vintage account be depreciated below a reasonable salvage value after taking into account any reduction in gross salvage value permitted by section 167(f).

(v) Limitation on adjustment of reasonable salvage value. The salvage value established by the taxpayer for a vintage account will not be redetermined if it is reasonable. Since the determination of salvage value is a matter of estimation, minimal adjustments will not be made. The salvage value established by the taxpayer will be deemed to be reasonable unless there is sufficient basis in the facts and circumstances existing at the close of the taxable year in which the account is established for a determination of an amount of salvage value for the account which exceeds the salvage value established by the taxpayer for the account by an amount greater than 10 percent of the unadjusted basis of the account at the close of the taxable year in which the account is established. If the salvage value established by the taxpayer for the account is not within the 10 percent range, or if the taxpayer follows the practice of understating his estimates of gross salvage value to take advantage of this subdivision, and if there is a determination of an amount of salvage value for the account which exceeds the salvage value established by the taxpayer for the account, an adjustment will be made by increasing the salvage value established by the taxpayer for the account by an amount equal to the difference between the salvage value as determined and the salvage value established by the taxpayer for the account. For the purposes of this subdivision, a determination of salvage value shall include all determinations at all levels of audit and appellate proceedings, and as well as all final determinations within the meaning of section 1313(a)(1). This subdivision shall apply to each such determination. (See example (3) of subdivision (vi) of this subparagraph.)

(vi) Examples. The principles of this subparagraph may be illustrated by the following examples in which it is assumed that the taxpayer has not followed a practice of understating his estimates of gross salvage value:

Example (1). Taxpayer B elects to apply this section to assets Y and Z, which are placed in a multiple asset vintage account of 1971 for which the taxpayer selects an asset depreciation period of 8 years. The unadjusted basis of asset Y is $50,000 and the unadjusted basis of asset Z is $30,000. B estimates a gross salvage value of $55,000. The property qualifies under section 167(f)(2) and B reduces the amount of salvage taken into account by $8,000 (that is, 10 percent of $80,000 under section 167(f)). Thus, B establishes a salvage value of $47,000 for the account. Assume that there is not sufficient basis for determining a salvage value for the account greater than $52,000 (that is, $60,000 minus the $8,000 reduction under section 167(f)). Since the salvage value of $47,000 established by B for the account is within the 10 percent range, it is reasonable. Salvage value for the account will not be redetermined.

Example (2). The facts are the same as in example (1) except that estimates a gross salvage value of $50,000 and establishes a salvage value of $42,000 for the account (that is, $50,000 minus the $8,000 reduction under section 167(f)). There is sufficient basis for determining an amount of salvage value greater than $50,000 (that is, $58,000 minus the $8,000 reduction under section 167(f)). The salvage value of $42,000 established by B for the account can be redetermined without regard to the limitation in subdivision (v) of this subparagraph, since it is not within the 10 percent range. Upon audit of B's tax return for a taxable year for which the redetermination would affect the amount of depreciation allowable for the account, salvage value is determined to be $52,000 after taking into account the reduction under section 167(f). Salvage value for the account will be adjusted to $52,000.

Example (3). The facts are the same as in example (1) except that upon audit of B's tax return for a taxable year the examining officer determines the salvage value to be $58,000 (that is, $66,000 minus the $8,000 reduction under section 167(f)), and proposes to adjust salvage value for the vintage account to $58,000 which will result in disallowing an amount of depreciation for the taxable year. B does not agree with the finding of the examining officer. After receipt of a "30-day letter", B waives a district conference and initiates proceedings before the Appellate Division. In consideration of the case by the Appellate Division it is concluded that there is not sufficient basis for determining an amount of salvage value for the account in excess of $55,000 (that is $63,000 minus the $8,000 reduction under section 167(f)). Since the salvage of $47,000 established by B for the account is within the 10 percent range, it is reasonable. Salvage value for the account will not be redetermined.

Example (4). Taxpayer C elects to apply this section to factory building X which is placed in an item vintage account of 1971. The unadjusted basis of factory building X is $90,000. C estimates a gross salvage value for the account of $10,000. The property does not qualify under section 167(f)(2). C establishes a salvage value of $10,000 for the account. Assume that there is not sufficient basis for determining a salvage value for the account greater than $18,000. Since the salvage value of 10,000 established by B for the account is within the 10 percent range, it is reasonable. Salvage value for the account will not be redetermined.

(2) Treatment of repairs. (i) In general. (a) Sections 162, 212, and 263 provide general rules for the treatment of certain expenditures for the repair, maintenance, rehabilitation or improvement of property. In general, under those sections, expenditures which substantially prolong the life of an asset, or are made to increase its value or adapt it to a different use are capital expenditures. If an expenditure is treated as a capital expenditure under section 162, 212, or 263, it is subject to the allowance for depreciation. On the other hand, in general, expenditures which do not substantially prolong the life of an asset or materially increase its value or adapt it for a substantially different use may be deducted as an expense in the taxable year in which paid or incurred. Expenditures, or a series of expenditures, may have characteristics both of deductible expenses and capital expenditures. Other expenditures may have the characteristics of capital expenditures, as in the case of an "excluded addition" (as defined in subdivision (vi) of this subparagraph). This subparagraph provides a simplified procedure for determining whether expenditures with respect to certain property are to be treated as deductible expenses or capital expenditures.

(b) [Reserved]

(ii) Election of repair allowance. In the case of an asset guideline class which consists of "repair allowance property" as defined in subdivision (iii) of this subparagraph, subject to the provisions of subdivision (v) of this subparagraph, the taxpayer may elect to apply the asset guideline class repair allowance described in subdivision (iii) of this subparagraph for any taxable year ending after December 31, 1970, for which the taxpayer elects to apply this section.

(iii) Repair allowance for an asset guideline class. For a taxable year for which the taxpayer elects to apply this section, the "repair allowance" for an asset guideline class which consists of "repair allowance property" is an amount equal to—

(a) The average of (1) the unadjusted basis of all "repair allowance property" in the asset guideline class at the beginning of the taxable year, less in the case of such property in a vintage account the unadjusted basis of all such property retired in an ordinary retirement (as described in subparagraph (3)(ii) of this paragraph) in prior taxable years, and (2) the unadjusted basis of all "repair allowance property" in the asset guideline class at the end of the taxable year, less in the case of such property in a vintage account the unadjusted basis of all such property retired in an ordinary retirement (including ordinary retirements during the taxable year), multiplied by—

(b) The repair allowance percentage in effect for the asset guideline class for the taxable year.

In applying the asset guideline class repair allowance to buildings which are section 1250 property, for the purpose of this subparagraph each building shall be treated as in a separate asset guideline class. If two or more buildings are in the same asset guideline class determined without regard to the preceding sentence and are operated as an integrated unit (as evidenced by their actual operation, management, financing and accounting), they shall be treated as a single building for this purpose. The "repair allowance percentages" in effect for taxable years ending before the effective date of the first supplemental repair allowance percentages established pursuant to this section are set forth in Revenue Procedure 72-10. Repair allowance percentages will from time to time be established, supplemented and revised with express reference to this section. These repair allowance percentages will be published in the Internal Revenue Bulletin. The repair allowance percentages in effect on the last day of the taxable year shall apply for the taxable year, except that the repair allowance percentage for a particular taxable year shall not be less than the repair allowance percentage in effect on the first day of such taxable year (or as of such later time in such year as a repair allowance percentage first established during such year becomes effective). Generally, the repair allowance percentages for a taxable year shall not be changed to reflect any supplement or revision of the repair allowance percentages after the end of such taxable year. However, if expressly provided in such a supplement or revision of the repair allowance percentages, the taxpayer may, at his option in the manner specified therein, apply the revised or supplemented repair allowance percentages for such taxable year and succeeding taxable years. For the purposes of this section, "repair allowance property" means eligible property determined without regard to paragraph (b)(2)(ii) of this section (that is, without regard to whether such property was first placed in service by the taxpayer before or after December 31, 1970) in an asset guideline class for which a repair allowance percentage is in effect for the taxable year. The determination whether property is repair allowance property shall be made without regard to whether such property is excluded, under paragraph (b)(5) of this section, from an election to apply this section. Property in an asset guideline class for which the taxpayer elects to apply the asset guideline class repair allowance described in this subdivision, which results from expenditures in the taxable year of election for the repair, maintenance, rehabilitation, or improvement of property in an asset guideline class shall not be "repair allowance property" for such taxable year but shall be for each succeeding taxable year provided such property is a property improvement as described in subdivision (vii)(a) of this subparagraph and is in an asset guideline class for which a repair allowance percentage is in effect for such succeeding taxable year.

(iv) Application of asset guideline class repair allowance. In accordance with the principles of sections 162, 212, and 263, if the taxpayer pays or incurs any expenditures during the taxable year for the repair, maintenance, rehabilitation or improvement of eligible property (determined without regard to paragraph (b)(2)(ii) of this section), the taxpayer must either—

(a) If such property is repair allowance property and if the taxpayer elects to apply the repair allowance for the asset guideline class, treat an amount of all such expenditures in such taxable year with respect to all such property in the asset guideline class which does not exceed in total the repair allowance for that asset guideline class as deductible repairs, and treat the excess of all such expenditures with respect to all such property in the asset guideline class in the manner described for a property improvement in subdivision (viii) of this subparagraph, or

(b) If such property is not repair allowance property or if the taxpayer does not elect to apply the repair allowance for the asset guideline class, treat each of such expenditures in such taxable year with respect to all such property in the asset guideline class as either a capital expenditure or as a deductible repair in accordance with the principles of sections 162, 212, and 263 (without regard to (a) of this subdivision), and treat the expenditures which are required to be capitalized under sections 162, 212, and 263 (without regard to (a) of this subdivision) in the manner described for a property improvement in subdivision (viii) of this subparagraph.

For the purposes of (a) of this subdivision, expenditures for the repair, maintenance, rehabilitation or improvement of property do not include expenditures for an excluded addition or for which a deduction is allowed under section 167(k). (See subdivision (viii) of this subparagraph for treatment of an excluded addition.) The taxpayer shall elect each taxable year whether to apply the repair allowance and treat expenditures under (a) of this subdivision, or to treat expenditures under (b) of this subdivision. The treatment of expenditures under this subdivision for a taxable year for all asset guideline classes shall be specified in the books and records of the taxpayer for the taxable year. The taxpayer may treat expenditures under (a) of this subdivision with respect to property in one asset guideline class and treat expenditures under (b) of this subdivision with respect to property in some other asset guideline class. In addition, the taxpayer may treat expenditures with respect to property in an asset guideline class under (a) of this subdivision in one taxable year, and treat expenditures with respect to property in that asset guideline class under (b) of this subdivision in another taxable year.

(v) Special rules for repair allowance. (a) The asset guideline class repair allowance described in subdivision (iii) of this subparagraph shall apply only to expenditures for the repair, maintenance, rehabilitation or improvement of repair allowance property (as described in subdivision (iii) of this subparagraph). The taxpayer may apply the asset guideline class repair allowance for the taxable year only if he maintains books and records reasonably sufficient to determine:

(1) The amount of expenditures paid or incurred during the taxable year for the repair, maintenance, rehabilitation or improvement of repair allowance property in the asset guideline class, and

(2) The expenditures (and the amount thereof) with respect to such property which are for excluded additions (such as whether the expenditure is for an additional identifiable unit of property, or substantially increases the produc-

tivity or capacity of an existing identifiable unit of property or adapts it for a substantially different use).

In general, such books and records shall be sufficient to identify the amount and nature of expenditures with respect to specific items of repair allowance property or groups of similar properties in the same asset guideline class. However, in the case of such expenditures with respect to property, part of which is in one asset guideline class and part in another, or part of which is repair allowance property and part of which is not, and in comparable circumstances involving property in the same asset guideline class, to the extent books and records are not maintained identifying such expenditures with specific items of property or groups of similar properties and it is not practicable to do so, the total amount of such expenditures which is not specifically identified may be allocated by any reasonable method consistently applied. In any case, the cost of repair, maintenance, rehabilitation or improvement of property performed by production personnel may be allocated by any reasonable method consistently applied and if performed incidental to production and not substantial in amount, no allocation to repair, maintenance, rehabilitation or improvement need be made. The types of expenditures for which specific identification would ordinarily be made include: Substantial expenditures such as for major parts or major structural materials for which a work order is or would customarily be written; expenditures for work performed by an outside contractor; or expenditures under a specific down time program. Types of expenditures for which specific identification would ordinarily be impractical include: General maintenance costs of machinery, equipment, and plant in the case of a taxpayer having assets in more than one class (or different types of assets in the same class) which are located together and generally maintained by the same work crew; small supplies which are used with respect to various classes or types of property; labor costs of personnel who work on property in different classes, or different types of property in the same class, if the work is performed on a routine, as needed, basis and the only identification of the property repaired is by the personnel. Factors which will be taken into account in determining the reasonableness of the taxpayer's allocation of expenditures include prior experience of the taxpayer; relative bases of the assets in the guideline class; types of assets involved; and relationship to specifically identified expenditures.

(b) If for the taxable year the taxpayer elects to deduct under section 263(e) expenditures with respect to repair allowance property consisting of railroad rolling stock (other than a locomotive) in a particular asset guideline class, the taxpayer may not, for such taxable year, use the asset guideline class repair allowance described in subdivision (iii) of this subparagraph for any property in such asset guideline class.

(c) (1) If the taxpayer repairs, rehabilitates or improves property for sale or resale to customers, the asset guideline class repair allowance described in subdivision (iii) of this subparagraph shall not apply to expenditures for the repair, maintenance, rehabilitation or improvement of such property, or (2) if a taxpayer follows the practice of acquiring for his own use property (in need of repair, rehabilitation or improvement to be suitable for the use intended by the taxpayer) and of making expenditures to repair, rehabilitate or improve such property in order to take advantage of this subparagraph, the asset guideline class repair allowance described in subdivision (iii) of this subparagraph shall not apply to such expenditures. In either event, such property shall not be "repair allowance property" as described in subdivision (iii) of this subparagraph.

(vi) Definition of excluded addition. The term "excluded addition" means—

(a) An expenditure which substantially increases the productivity of an existing identifiable unit of property over its productivity when first acquired by the taxpayer;

(b) An expenditure which substantially increases the capacity of an existing identifiable unit of property over its capacity when first acquired by the taxpayer;

(c) An expenditure which modifies an existing identifiable unit of property for a substantially different use;

(d) An expenditure for an identifiable unit of property if (1) such expenditure is for an additional identifiable unit of property or (2) such expenditure (other than an expenditure described in (e) of this subdivision) is for replacement of an identifiable unit of property which was retired;

(e) An expenditure for replacement of a part in or a component or portion of an existing identifiable unit of property (whether or not such part, component or portion is also an identifiable unit of property) if such part, component or portion is for replacement of a part, component or portion which was retired in a retirement upon which gain or loss is recognized (or would be recognized but for a special nonrecognition provision of the Code or § 1.1502-13).

(f) In the case of a building or other structure (in addition to (b), (c), (d), and (e) of this subdivision which also apply to such property), an expenditure for additional cubic or linear space; and

(g) In the case of those units of property of pipelines, electric utilities, telephone companies, and telegraph companies consisting of lines, cables and poles (in addition to (a) through (e) of this subdivision which also apply to such property), an expenditure for replacement of a material portion of the unit of property.

Except as provided in (d) and (e) of this subdivision, notwithstanding any other provision of this subdivision, the term "excluded addition" does not include any expenditure in connection with the repair, maintenance, rehabilitation or improvement of an identifiable unit of property which does not exceed $100. For this purpose all related expenditures with respect to the unit of property shall be treated as a single expenditure. For the purposes of (a), and (b) of this subdivision, an increase in productivity or capacity is substantial only if the increase is more than 25 percent. An expenditure which merely extends the productive life of an identifiable unit of property is not an increase in productivity within the meaning of (a) of this subdivision. Under (g) of this subdivision a replacement is material only if the portion replaced exceeds 5 percent of the unit of property with respect to which the replacement is made. For the purposes of this subdivision, a unit of property generally consists of each operating unit (that is, each separate machine or piece of equipment) which performs a discrete function and which the taxpayer customarily acquires for original installation and retires as a unit. The taxpayer's accounting classification of units of property will generally be accepted for purposes of this subdivision provided the classifications are reasonably consistent with the preceding sentence and are consistently applied. In the case of a building the unit of property generally consists of the building as well as its structural components; except that each building service system (such as an elevator, an escalator, the electrical system, or the heating and cooling system) is an identifiable unit for the purpose of (a), (b), (c), and (d) of this subdivision. However, both in the case of machinery and equipment and in the case of a building, for the purpose of applying (d)(1) of this subdivision a unit of property may consist of a part in or a component or portion of a larger unit of property. In the case of property described in (g) of this subdivision (such as a pipeline), a unit of property generally consists of each segment which performs a discrete function either as to capacity, service, transmission or distribution between identifiable points. Thus, for example, under this subdivision in the case of a vintage account of five automobiles each automobile is an identifiable unit of property (which is not merely a part in or a component or portion of larger unit of property within the meaning of (e) of this subdivision). Accordingly, the replacement of one of the automobiles (which is retired) with another automobile is an excluded addition under (d)(2) of this subdivision. Also the purchase of a sixth automobile is an expenditure for an additional identifiable unit of property and is an excluded addition under (d)(1) of this subdivision. An automobile air conditioner is also an identifiable unit of property for the purposes of (d)(1) of this subdivision, but not for the purposes of (d)(2) of this subdivision. Accordingly, the addition of an air conditioner to an automobile is an excluded addition under (d)(1) of this subdivision, but the replacement of an existing air conditioner in an automobile is not an excluded addition under (d)(2) of this subdivision (since it is merely the replacement of a part in an existing identifiable unit of property). The replacement of the air conditioner may, however, be an excluded addition under (e) of this subdivision, if the air conditioner replaced was retired in a retirement upon which gain or loss was recognized. The principles of this subdivision may be further illustrated by the following examples in which it is assumed (unless otherwise stated) that (e) of this subdivision does not apply:

Example (1). For the taxable year, B pays or incurs only the following expenditures: (1) $5,000 for general maintenance of repair allowance property (as described in subdivision (iii) of this subparagraph) such as inspection, oiling, machine adjustments, cleaning, and painting; (2) $175 for replacement of bearings and gears in an existing lathe; (3) $125 for replacement of an electric starter (of the same capacity) and certain electrical wiring in an automatic drill press; (4) $300 for modification of a metal fabricating machine (including replacement of certain parts) which substantially increases its capacity; (5) $175 for repair of the same metal fabricating machine which does not substantially increase its capacity; (6) $600 for the replacement of an existing lathe with a new lathe; and (7) $65 for the repair of a drill press. Expenditures (1) through (3) are expenditures for the repair, maintenance, rehabilitation or improvement of property to which B can elect to apply the asset guideline class repair allowance described in subdivision (iii) of this subparagraph. Expenditure (4) is an excluded addition under (b) of this subdivision. Expenditure (5) is not an excluded addition. Expenditure (6) is an excluded addition under (d)(2) of this subdivision. Without regard to (a), (b), and (c) of this subdivision, expenditure (7) is not an excluded addition since the expenditure does not exceed $100.

Example (2). Corporation M operates a steel plant which produces rails, blooms, billets, special bar sections, reinforcing bars, and large diameter line pipe. During the taxable year, corporation M: (1) relines an open hearth furnace; (2) places in service 20 new ingot molds; (3) replaces one reversing roll in the blooming mill; (4) overhauls the rail and billet mill with no increase in capacity; (5) replaces a roll stand in the 20-inch bar mill; and (6) overhauls the 11-inch bar mill and reducing stands increasing billet speed from 1,800 feet per minute to 2,300 feet per minute. Assume that each expenditure exceeds $100. Expenditure (1) is not an excluded addition. Expenditure (2) is an excluded addition under (d)(1) of this subdivision. Expenditure (3) is not an excluded addition since the expenditure for the reversing roll merely replaces a part in an existing identifiable unit of property. Expenditure (4) is not an excluded addition. Expenditure (5) is an excluded addition under (d)(2) of this subdivision since the roll stand is not merely a part of an existing identifiable unit of property. Expenditure (6) is an excluded addition under (a) of this subdivision since it increases the billet speed by more than 25 percent.

Example (3). For the taxable year, corporation X pays or incurs the following expenditures: (1) $1,000 for two new temporary partition walls in the company's offices; (2) $1,400 for repainting the exterior of a terminal building; (3) $300 for repair of the roof of a warehouse; (4) $150 for replacement of two window frames and panes in the warehouse; and (5) $100 for plumbing repair. Expenditure (1) is an excluded addition under (d)(1) of this subdivision. None of the other expenditures are excluded additions.

Example (4). For the taxable year, corporation Y pays or incurs the following expenditures: (1) $10,000 for expansion of a loading dock from 600 square feet to 750 square feet; (2) $600 for replacement of two roof girders in a factory building; and (3) $9,500 for replacement of columns and girders supporting the floor of a second story loft storage area within the factory building in order to permit storage of supplies with a gross weight 50 percent greater than the previous capacity of the loft. Expenditure (1) is an excluded addition under (f) of this subdivision. Expenditure (2) is not an excluded addition. Expenditure (3) is an excluded addition under (b) of this subdivision.

Example (5). Corporation A has an office building with an unadjusted basis of $10 million. The building has 10 elevators, five of which are manually operated and five of which are automatic. During 1971, corporation A:

(1) Replaces the five manually operated elevators with highspeed automatic elevators at a cost of $400,000;

(2) Replaces the cable in one of the existing automatic elevators at a cost of $1,700. The replacements of the elevators are excluded additions under (d)(2) of this subdivision. The replacement of the cable is not an excluded addition.

Example (6). Taxpayer W, a cement manufacturer, engages in the following modification and maintenance activities during the taxable year: (1) replaces eccentric-bearing, spindle, and wearing surface in a gyratory crusher; (2) places in service a new apron feeder and hammer mill; (3) replaces four buckets on a chain bucket elevator; (4) relines refractory surface in the burning zone of a rotary kiln; (5) installs additional new dust collectors; and (6) replaces two 16-inch x 90-foot belts on his conveyer system. Assume that there is no increase in productivity or capacity and that each expenditure exceeds $100. Expenditure (1) is not an excluded addition. Expenditure (2) an excluded addition under (d)(1) of this subdivision. Expenditures (3) and (4) are not excluded additions. Expenditures (5) is an excluded addition under (d)(1) of this subdivision. Expenditure (6) is not an excluded addition.

Example (7). Corporation X, a gas pipeline company, has, in addition to others, the following units of property: (1) A gathering pipeline for a field consisting of 25 gas wells; (2) the main transmission line between compressor stations (that is, in the case of a 500-mile main transmission line with a compressor station every 100 miles, each one hundred miles section between compressor stations is a separate unit of property); (3) a lateral transmission line from the main transmission line to a city border station; (4) a medium pressure distribution line to the northern portion of the city; and (5) a low pressure distribution line serving a group of approximately 200 residential customers off the medium pressure distribution line. In 1971, corporation (X pays or incurs the following expenditures in connection with the repair, maintenance, rehabilitation or improvement of repair allowance property: (1) replaces a meter on a gas well; (2) in connection with the repair and rehabilitation of a unit of property consisting of a 2-mile gathering pipeline, replaces a 3,000-foot section of the gathering line; (3) in connection with the repair of leaks in a unit of property consisting of a 100-mile gas transmission line (that is, the 100 miles between compressor stations), replaces a 2,000-foot section of pipeline at one point; and (4) at another point replaces a 7-mile section of the same 100-mile gas transmission line. Assume that none of these expenditures substantially increases capacity and that each expenditure exceeds $100. Expenditure (1) is an excluded addition under (d) of this subdivision. Expenditure (2) is an excluded addition under (g) of this subdivision since the portion replaced is more than 5 percent of the unit of property. Expenditure (3) is not an excluded addition. Expenditure (4) is an excluded addition under (g) of this subdivision.

Example (8). Taxpayer Y, an electric utility company, has in addition to others, the following units of property: (1) a high voltage transmission circuit from the switching station (at the generating station) to the transmission station; (2) a series of 100 poles (fully dressed) supporting the circuit in (1); (3) a high voltage circuit from the transmission station to the distribution substation; (4) a high voltage distribution circuit (either radial or looped) from the distribution substation; (5) a transformer on a distribution pole; (6) a circuit breaker on a distribution pole; and (7) all 220 (and lower) volt circuit (including customer service connections) off the distribution circuit in (4). In 1971, taxpayer Y pays or incurs the following expenditures for the repair, maintenance, rehabilitation or improvement of repair allowance property: (1) replaces 25 adjacent poles in a unit of property consisting of the 300 poles supporting a radial distribution circuit from a distribution substation; (2) replaces a transformer on one of the poles in (1); (3) replaces a cross-arm on one of the poles in (1); (4) replaces a 200-foot section of a 2-mile radial distribution circuit serving 100 residential customers, and (5) replaces a 2,000-foot section on a 10-mile high voltage circuit from a transmission station to a distribution substation which was destroyed by a casualty which taxpayer Y treated as an extraordinary retirement under paragraph (d)(3)(ii) of this section. Expenditure (1) is an excluded addition under (g) of this subdivision. Expenditure (2) is an excluded addition under (d)(2) of this subdivision. Expenditures (3) and (4) are not excluded additions. Expenditure (5) is an excluded addition under (e) of this subdivision.

Example (9). Corporation Z, a telephone company, has in addition to others, the following units of property: (1) A buried feeder cable 3 miles in length off a local switching station; (2) a buried subfeeder cable 1 mile in length off the feeder cable in (1); (3) all the distribution cable (and customer service drops) off the subfeeder cable in (2); (4) the 300 poles (fully dressed) supporting the distribution cable in (3); (5) a 10-mile local trunk cable which interconnects two local tandem switching stations; (6) a toll connecting trunk cable from a local tandem switching station to a long distance tandem switching station; (7) a toll trunk cable 50 miles in length from the access point at one city to the access point at another city. In 1971, corporation Z pays or incurs the following expenditures in connection with the repair, maintenance, rehabilitation or improvement of repair allowance property: (1) replaces 100 feet of distribution cable in a unit of property consisting of 8 miles of local distribution cable (plus customer service drops); (2) replaces an amplifier in the distribution system; and (3) replaces 10 miles of a unit of property consisting of a toll trunk cable 50 miles in length. Expenditure (1) is not an excluded addition. Expenditure (2) is an excluded addition under (d)(2) of this subdivision. Expenditure (3) is an excluded addition under (g) of this subdivision.

(vii) Definition of property improvement. The term "property improvement" means—

(a) If the taxpayer treats expenditures for the asset guideline class under subdivision (iv)(a) of this subparagraph, the amount of all expenditures paid or incurred during the taxable year for the repair, maintenance, rehabilitation or improvement of repair allowance property in the asset guideline class, which exceeds the asset guideline class repair allowance for the taxable year; and

(b) If the taxpayer treats expenditures for the asset guideline class under subdivision (iv)(b) of this subparagraph, the amount of each expenditure paid or incurred during the taxable year for the repair, maintenance, rehabilitation or improvement of property which is treated under sections 162, 212, and 263 as a capital expenditure.

The term "property improvement" does not include any expenditure for an excluded addition.

(viii) Treatment of property improvements and excluded additions. If for the taxable year there is a property improvement as described in subdivision (vii) of this subparagraph or an excluded addition as described in subdivision (vi) of this subparagraph, the following rules shall apply—

(a) The total amount of any property improvement for the asset guideline class determined under subdivision (vii)(a) of this subparagraph shall be capitalized in a single "special basis vintage account" of the taxable year in accordance with the taxpayer's election to apply this section for the taxable year (applied without regard to paragraph (b)(5)(v)(a) of this section). See subparagraph (3)(vi) of this paragraph for definition and treatment of a "special basis vintage account".

(b) Each property improvement determined under subdivision (vii)(b) of this subparagraph, if it is eligible property, shall be capitalized in a vintage account of the taxable year in accordance with the taxpayer's election to apply this section for the taxable year (applied without regard to paragraph (b)(5)(v)(a) of this section).

(c) Each excluded addition, if it is eligible property, shall be capitalized in a vintage account of the taxable year in accordance with the taxpayer's election to apply this section for the taxable year.

For rule as to date on which a property improvement or an excluded addition is first placed in service, see paragraph (e)(1)(iii) and (iv) of this section.

(ix) Examples. The principles of this subparagraph may be illustrated by the following examples:

Example (1). For the taxable year 1972, B elects to apply this section. B has repair allowance property (as described in subdivision (iii) of this subparagraph) in asset guideline class 20.2 under Revenue Procedure 72-10 with an average unadjusted basis determined as provided in subdivision (iii) *(a)* of this subparagraph of $100,000 and repair allowance property in asset guideline class 24.4 with an average unadjusted basis of $300,000. The repair allowance percentage for asset guideline class 20.2 is 4.5 percent and for asset guideline class 24.4 is 6.5 percent. The two asset guideline class repair allowances for 1972 are $4,500 and $19,500, respectively, determined as follows:

Asset Guideline Class 20.2

$100,000 average unadjusted basis multiplied by 4.5 percent	$ 4,500

Asset Guideline Class 24.4

$300,000 average unadjusted basis multiplied by 6.5 percent	$19,500

Example (2). The facts are the same as in example (1). During the taxable year 1972, B pays or incurs the following expenditures for the repair, maintenance, rehabilitation or improvement of repair allowance property in asset guideline class 20.2.

General maintenance (including primarily labor costs)	$3,000
Replacement of parts in several machines (including labor costs of $1,650)	4,000
	7,000

In addition, in connection with the rehabilitation and improvement of two other machines B pays or incurs $6,000 (including labor costs of $2,000) which is treated as an excluded addition because the capacity of the machines was substantially increased. For 1972, B elects to apply this section and to apply the asset guideline class repair allowance to asset guideline class 20.2. Since the asset guideline class repair allowance is $4,500, B can deduct $4,500 in accordance with subdivision (iv)(a) of this subparagraph. B must capitalize $2,500 in a special basis vintage account in accordance with subdivisions (vii)(a) and (viii)(a) of this subparagraph. Since the excluded addition is a capital item and is eligible property, B must also capitalize $6,000 in a vintage account in accordance with subdivision (viii)(c) of this subparagraph. B selects from the asset depreciation range an asset depreciation period of 17 years for the special basis vintage account. B includes the excluded addition in a vintage account of 1972 for which he also selects an asset depreciation period of 17 years.

(3) Treatment of retirements. (i) In general. The rules of this subparagraph specify the treatment of all retirements from vintage accounts. The rules of § 1.167(a)-8 shall not apply to any retirement from a vintage account. An asset in a vintage account is retired when such asset is permanently withdrawn from use in a trade or business or in the production of income by the taxpayer. A retirement may occur as a result of a sale or exchange, by other act of the taxpayer amounting to a permanent disposition of an asset, or by physical abandonment of an asset. A retirement may also occur by transfer of an asset to supplies or scrap.

(ii) Definitions of ordinary and extraordinary retirements. The term "ordinary retirement" means any retirement of section 1245 property from a vintage account which is not treated as an "extraordinary retirement" under this subparagraph. The retirement of an asset from a vintage account in a taxable year is an "extraordinary retirement" if—

(a) The asset is section 1250 property;

(b) The asset is section 1245 property which is retired as the direct result of fire, storm, shipwreck, or other casualty and the taxpayer, at his option consistently applied (taking into account type, frequency, and the size of such casualties) treats such retirements as extraordinary; or

(c) (1) The asset is section 1245 property which is retired (other than by transfer to supplies or scrap) in a taxable year as the direct result of a cessation, termination, curtailment, or disposition of a business, manufacturing, or other income producing process, operation, facility or unit, and (2) the unadjusted basis (determined without regard to subdivision (vi) of this subparagraph) of all such assets so retired in such taxable year from such account as a direct result of the event described in (c)(1) of this subdivision exceeds 20 percent of the unadjusted basis of such account immediately prior to such event.

For the purposes of (c) of this subdivision, all accounts (other than a special basis vintage account as described in subdivision (vi) of this subparagraph containing section 1245 property of the same vintage in the same asset guideline class, and from which a retirement as a direct result of such event occurs within the taxable year, shall be treated as a single vintage account. See subdivision (xi) of this subparagraph for special rule for item accounts. The principles of this subdivision may be illustrated by the following examples:

Example (1). Taxpayer A is a processor and distributor of dairy products. Part of taxpayer A's operation is a bottle washing facility consisting of machines X, Y, and Z, each of which is in an item vintage account of 1971. Each item vintage account has an unadjusted basis of $1,000. Taxpayer A also has a 1971 multiple asset vintage account consisting of machines E, S, and C. Machines E and S, used in processing butter, each has an unadjusted basis of $10,000. Machine C used in capping bottles has an unadjusted basis of $1,000. In 1975, taxpayer A changes to the use of paper milk cartons and disposes of all bottle washing machines (X, Y, and Z) as well as machine C which was used in capping bottles. The sales of machine C, X, Y, and Z are the direct result of the termination of a manufacturing process. However, since the total unadjusted basis of the eligible section 1245 property retired as a direct result of such event is only $4,000 (which is less than 20 percent of the total unadjusted basis of machines E, S, C, X, Y, and Z, $24,000) the sales are ordinary retirements. All the assets are in the same asset guideline class and are of the same vintage. Accordingly, machines E, S, C, X, Y, and Z are for this purpose treated as being in a single vintage account.

Example (2). The facts are the same as in example (1) except that in 1976, taxpayer A sells six of his 12 milk delivery trucks as a direct result of eliminating home deliveries to customers in the suburbs. Deliveries within the city require only six trucks. Each of the trucks has an unadjusted basis of $3,000. Six of the taxpayer's delivery trucks are in a multiple asset vintage account of 1974 and six are in a multiple asset vintage account of 1972. Neither account contains any other property. Four trucks are retired from the 1972 vintage account and two trucks are retired from the 1974 vintage account. The sales result from the curtailment of taxpayer A's home delivery operation. The unadjusted basis of the four trucks retired from the 1972 vintage exceeds 20 percent of the total unadjusted basis of the affected account. The same is true for the two trucks retired from the 1974 vintage account. The sales of the trucks are extraordinary retirements.

(d) The asset is section 1245 property which is retired after December 30, 1980 by a charitable contribution for which a deduction is allowable under section 170.

(iii) Treatment of ordinary retirements. No loss shall be recognized upon an ordinary retirement. Gain shall be recognized only to the extent specified in this subparagraph. All proceeds from ordinary retirements shall be added to the depreciation reserve of the vintage account from which the retirement occurs. See subdivision (vi) of this subparagraph for optional allocation of basis in the case of a special basis vintage account. See subdivision (ix) of this subparagraph for recognition of gain when the depreciation reserve exceeds the unadjusted basis of the vintage account. The amount of salvage value for a vintage account shall be reduced (but not below zero) as of the beginning of the taxable year by the excess of (a) the depreciation reserve for the account, after adjustment for depreciation allowable for such taxable year and all other adjustments prescribed by this section (other than the adjustment prescribed by subdivision (ix) of this subparagraph), over (b) the unadjusted basis of the account less the amount of salvage value for the account before such reduction. Thus, in the case of a vintage account with an unadjusted basis of $1,000 and a salvage value of $100, to the extent that proceeds from ordinary retirements increase the depreciation reserve above $900, the salvage value is reduced. If the proceeds increase the depreciation reserve for the account to $1,000, the salvage value is reduced to zero. The unadjusted basis of the asset retired in an ordinary retirement is not removed from the account and the depreciation reserve for the account is not reduced by the depreciation allowable for the retired asset. The previously unrecovered basis of the retired asset will be recovered through the allowance for depreciation with respect to the vintage account. See subdivision (v)(a) of this subparagraph for treatment of retirements on which gain or loss is not recognized in whole or in part. See subdivision (v)(b) of this subparagraph for treatment of retirements by disposition to a member of an affiliated group as defined in section 1504(a). See subdivision (v)(c) of this subparagraph for treatment of transfers between members of an affiliated group of corporations or other related parties as extraordinary retirements.

(iv) Treatment of extraordinary retirements (a) Unless the transaction is governed by a special nonrecognition section of the Code such as 1031 or 337 or is one to which subdivision (v)(b) of this subparagraph applies, gain or loss shall be recognized upon an extraordinary retirement in the taxable year in which such retirement occurs subject to section 1231, section 165, and all other applicable provisions of law such as sections 1245 and 1250. If the asset which is retired in an extraordinary retirement is the only or last asset in the account, the account shall terminate and no longer be an account to which this section applies. In all other cases, the unadjusted basis of the retired asset shall be removed from the unadjusted basis of the vintage account, and the depreciation reserve established for the account shall be reduced by the depreciation allowable for the retired asset computed in the manner prescribed in paragraph (c)(1)(v)(b) of this section for determination of the adjusted basis of the asset. See subdivision (ix) of this subparagraph for recognition of gain in the case of an account containing section 1245 property when the depreciation reserve exceeds the unadjusted basis of the vintage account. See subdivision (iii) of this subparagraph for reduction of salvage value for such an account when the depreciation reserve exceeds the unadjusted basis of the account minus salvage value. See subdivision (v)(b) of this subparagraph for treatment of retirements by disposition to a member of an affiliated group as defined in section 1504(a).

(b) The principles of this subdivision may be illustrated by the following examples:

Example (1). Corporation X has a multiple asset vintage account of 1971 consisting of assets K, R, A, and P all of which are section 1245 property. The unadjusted basis of the account is $40,000. The unadjusted basis of asset A is $10,000. When the reserve for depreciation for the account is $20,000, asset A is sold in an extraordinary retirement for $8,000 in cash. The $10,000 unadjusted basis of asset A is removed from the account and the $5,000 depreciation allowable for asset A is removed from the reserve for depreciation. Gain in the amount of $3,000 (to which section 1245 applies) is recognized upon the sale of asset A.

Example (2). Corporation X has an item vintage account of 1972 consisting of residential apartment unit A. Unit A is section 1250 property. It is residential rental property and meets the requirements of section 167(j)(2). Corporation X adopts the declining balance method of depreciation using a rate twice the straight line rate. The asset depreciation period is 40 years. Unit A has an unadjusted basis of $200,000. On June 30, 1974, when the reserve for depreciation for the account is $19,500, unit A is sold for $220,000. Since unit A is section 1250 property, the sale is an extraordinary retirement in accordance with subdivision (ii)(a) of this subparagraph (without regard to subdivision (ii)(b) or (c) of this subparagraph). The adjusted basis of unit A is $180,500. Gain in the amount of $39,500 is recognized. The "additional depreciation" (as defined in section 1250(b)) for unit A is $9,500. Accordingly, $9,500 is in accordance with section 1250 treated as gain from the sale or exchange of an asset which is neither a capital asset nor property described in section 1231. The $30,000 balance of the gain from the sale of unit A may be gain to which section 1231 applies.

(v) Special rule for certain retirements. (a) In the case of an ordinary retirement on which gain or loss is in whole or in part not recognized because of a special nonrecognition section of the Code, such as 1031 or 337, no part of the proceeds from such retirement shall be added to the depreciation reserve of the vintage account in accordance with subdivision (iii) of this subparagraph. Instead, such retirement shall for all purposes of this section be treated as an extraordinary retirement.

(b) The provisions of § 1.1502-13 shall apply to a retirement. In the case of an ordinary retirement to which the provisions of § 1.1502-13 apply, no part of the proceeds from such retirement shall be added to the depreciation reserve of the vintage account in accordance with subdivision (iii) of this subparagraph. Instead, such retirement shall for all purposes of this section be treated as an extraordinary retirement.

(c) In a case in which property is transferred, in a transaction which would without regard to this subdivision be treated as an ordinary retirement, during the taxable year in which first placed in service to a person who bears a relationship described in section 179(d)(2)(A) or (B), such transfer shall for all purposes of this section be treated as an extraordinary retirement.

(d) (1) If, in the case of mass assets, it is impracticable for the taxpayer to maintain records from which he can establish the vintage of such assets as retirements occur, and if he adopts other reasonable recordkeeping practices, then the vintage of mass asset retirements may be determined by use of an appropriate mortality dispersion table. Such a mortality dispersion table may be based upon an acceptable sampling of the taxpayer's actual experience or other acceptable statistical or engineering techniques. Alternatively, the taxpayer may use a standard mortality dispersion table prescribed by the Commissioner for this purpose. If the taxpayer uses such standard mortality dispersion table for any taxable year of election, it must be used for all subsequent taxable years of election unless the taxpayer obtains the consent of the Commissioner to change to another dispersion table or to actual identification of retirements. For information requirements regarding mass assets, see paragraph (f)(5) of this section.

(2) For purposes of this section, the term "mass assets" has the same meaning as when used in paragraph (e)(4) of § 1.47-1.

(e) The principles of this subdivision may be illustrated by the following examples:

Example (1). Corporation X has a vintage account of 1971 consisting of machines A, B, and C, each with an unadjusted basis of $1,000. The unadjusted basis of the account is $3,000 and at the end of 1977 the reserve for depreciation is $2,100. On January 1, 1978, machine A is transferred to corporation Y solely for stock in the amount of $1,400 in a transaction to which section 351 applies. Since the adjusted basis of machine A is $300, a gain of $1,100 is realized, but no gain is recognized under section 351. Even though machine A was transferred in an ordinary retirement in accordance with *(a)* of this subdivision the rules for an extraordinary retirement are applied. The proceeds are not added to the reserve for depreciation for the account. Machine A is removed from the account, the unadjusted basis of the account is reduced by $1,000, and the reserve for depreciation for the account is reduced by $700.

Example (2). The facts are the same as in example (1) except that the consideration received for machine A is stock of corporation Y in the amount of $1,200 and cash in the amount of $200. The result is the same as in example (1) except that gain is recognized in the amount of $200 all of which is gain to which section 1245 applies.

Example (3). The facts are the same as in example (1) except that machine A is sold for $1,400 cash in an ordinary retirement and corporation X and corporation Y are includible corporations in an affiliated group as defined in section 1504(a) which files a consolidated return for 1978. Accordingly, (b) of this subdivision applies. The retirement is treated as an extraordinary retirement. Machine A is removed from the account, the unadjusted basis of the account is reduced by $1,000, and the reserve for depreciation for the account is reduced by $700. The gain of $1,100 is deferred gain to which § 1.1502-13 applies.

(vi) Treatment of special basis vintage accounts. A "special basis vintage account" is a vintage account for an amount of property improvement determined under subparagraph (2)(vii)(a) of this paragraph. In general, reference in this section to a "vintage account" shall include a special basis vintage account. The unadjusted basis of a special basis vintage account shall be recovered through the allowance for depreciation in accordance with this section over the asset depreciation period for the account. Except as provided in this subdivision, the unadjusted basis, adjusted basis and reserve for depreciation of such account shall not be allocated to any specific asset in the asset guideline class, and the provisions of this subparagraph shall not apply to such account. However, in the event of a sale, exchange or other disposition of "repair allowance property" (as described in subparagraph (2)(iii) of this paragraph) in an extraordinary retirement as described in subdivision (ii) of this subparagraph (or if the asset is not in a vintage account, in an abnormal retirement as described in § 1.167(a)-8), the taxpayer may, if consistently applied to all such retirements in the taxable year and adequately identified in the taxpayer's books and records, elect to allocate the adjusted basis (as of the end of the taxable year) of all special basis vintage accounts for the asset guideline class to each such retired asset in the proportion that the adjusted basis of the retired asset (as of the beginning of the taxable year) bears to the adjusted basis of all repair allowance property in the asset guideline class at the beginning of the taxable year. The election to allocate basis in accordance with this subdivision shall be made on the tax return filed for the taxable year. The principles of this subdivision may be illustrated by the following example:

Example. In addition to other property, the taxpayer has machines A, B, and C all in the same asset guideline class and each with an adjusted basis on January 1, 1977, of $10,000. The adjusted basis on January 1, 1977, of all repair allowance property (as described in subparagraph (2)(iii) of this paragraph) in the asset guideline class is $90,000. The machines are sold in an extraordinary retirement in 1977. The taxpayer is entitled to and does elect to allocate basis in accordance with this subdivision. There is also a 1972 special basis vintage account for the asset guideline class, as follows:

	Unadjusted basis	Reserve for depreciation	Dec. 31, 1977 adjusted basis
1972 special basis vintage account, for which the taxpayer selected an asset depreciation period of 10 years, adopted the straight line method, and used the half-year convention	$2,000	$1,100	$900

By application of this subdivision, the adjusted basis of machines A, B, and C is increased to $10,000 each (that is

$$\frac{\$10{,}000}{\$90{,}000} \times \$900 = \$100).$$

The unadjusted basis, reserve for depreciation and adjusted basis of the special basis vintage account are reduced, respectively, by one-third (that is,

$$\frac{\$300}{\$900} = ⅓)$$

in order to reflect the allocation of basis to the special basis vintage account.

(vii) Reduction in the salvage value of a vintage account. (a) A taxpayer may apply this section without reducing the salvage value for a vintage account in accordance with this subdivision or in accordance with subdivision (viii) of this subparagraph (relating to transfers to supplies or scrap). See subdivision (iii) of this subparagraph for reduction of salvage value in certain circumstances in the amount of proceeds from ordinary retirements.

(b) However, the taxpayer may, at his option, follow the consistent practice of reducing, as retirements occur, the salvage value for a vintage account by the amount of salvage value attributable to the retired asset, or the taxpayer may consistently follow the practice of so reducing the salvage value for a vintage account as extraordinary retirements occur while not reducing the salvage value for the account as ordinary retirements occur. If the taxpayer does not reduce the salvage value for a vintage account as ordinary retirements occur, the taxpayer may be entitled to a deduction in the taxable year in which the last asset is retired from the account in accordance with subdivision (ix)(b) of this subparagraph.

(c) For purposes of this subdivision, the portion of the salvage value for a vintage account attributable to a retired asset may be determined by multiplying the salvage value for the account by a fraction, the numerator of which is the unadjusted basis of the retired asset and the denominator of which is the unadjusted basis of the account, or any other method consistently applied which reasonably reflects that portion of the salvage value for the account originally attributable to the retired asset.

(d) In the case of ordinary retirements the taxpayer may—

(1) In the case of retirements (other than by transfer to supplies or scrap) follow the consistent practice of reducing the salvage value for the account by the amount of salvage value attributable to the retired asset and not adding the same amount to the depreciation reserve for the account, and

(2) In the case of retirements by transfer to supplies or scrap, follow the consistent practice of reducing the salvage value for the account by the amount of salvage value attributable to the retired asset and not adding the same amount to the depreciation reserve for the account (in which case the basis in the supplies or scrap account of the retired asset will be zero) or follow the consistent practice of reducing the salvage value for the account by the amount of salvage value attributable to the retired asset and adding the same amount to the depreciation reserve for the account (up to an amount which does not increase the depreciation reserve to an amount in excess of the unadjusted basis of the account) in which case the basis in the supplies or scrap account of the retired asset will be the amount added to the depreciation reserve for the account.

Thus, for example, in the case of an ordinary retirement by transfer of an asset to supplies or scrap, the basis of the asset in the supplies or scrap account would either be zero or the amount added to the depreciation reserve of the vintage account from which the retirement occurred. When the depreciation reserve for the account equals the unadjusted basis of the account no further adjustment to salvage value for the account will be made. See subdivision (viii) of this subparagraph for special optional rule for reduction of salvage value in the case of an ordinary retirement by transfer of an asset to supplies or scrap.

(e) In the event of a removal of property from a vintage account in accordance with paragraph (b) (4)(iii)(e), (5)(v)(b) or (6)(iii) of this section the salvage value for the account may be reduced by the amount of salvage value attributable to the asset removed determined as provided in (c) of this subdivision.

(viii) Special optional adjustments for transfers to supplies or scrap. If the taxpayer does not follow the consistent practice of reducing, as ordinary retirements occur, the salvage value for a vintage account in accordance with subdivision (vii) of this subparagraph, the taxpayer may (in lieu of the method described in subdivision (vii)(c) and (d) of this subparagraph) follow the consistent practice of reducing salvage value as ordinary retirements occur by transfer of assets to supplies or scrap and of determining the basis (in the supplies or scrap account) as assets retired in an ordinary retirement by transfer to supplies or scrap, in the following manner—

(a) The taxpayer may determine the value of the asset (not to exceed its unadjusted basis) by any reasonable method consistently applied (such as average cost, conditioned cost, or fair market value) if such method is adequately identified in the taxpayer's books and records.

(b) The value attributable to the asset determined in accordance with (a) of this subdivision shall be subtracted from the salvage value for the account (to the extent thereof) and the greater of (1) the amount subtracted from the salvage value for the vintage account and (2) the value of the asset determined in accordance with (a) of this subdivision, shall be added to the reserve for depreciation of the vintage account.

(c) The amount added to the reserve for depreciation of the vintage account in accordance with (b) of this subdivision shall be treated as the basis of the retired asset in the supplies or scrap account.

If the taxpayer makes the adjustments in accordance with this subdivision, the reserve for depreciation of the vintage account may exceed the unadjusted basis of the account, and in that event gain will be recognized in accordance with subdivision (ix) of this subparagraph.

(ix) Recognition of gain or loss in certain situations. (a) In the case of a vintage account for section 1245 property, if at the end of any taxable year after adjustment for depreciation allowable for such taxable year and all other adjustments prescribed by this section, the depreciation reserve established for such account exceeds the unadjusted basis of the account, the entire amount of such excess shall be recognized as gain in such taxable year. Such gain—

(1) Shall constitute gain to which section 1245 applies to the extent that it does not exceed the total amount of depreciation allowances in the depreciation reserve at the end of such taxable year, reduced by gain recognized pursuant to this subdivision with respect to the account previously treated as gain to which section 1245 applies, and

(2) May constitute gain to which section 1231 applies to the extent that it exceeds such total amount as so reduced.

In such event, the depreciation reserve shall be reduced by the amount of gain recognized, so that after such reduction the amount of the depreciation reserve is equal to the unadjusted basis of the account.

(b) In the case of an account for section 1245 property, if at the time the last asset in the vintage account is retired the unadjusted basis of the account exceeds the depreciation reserve for the account (after all adjustments prescribed by this section), the entire amount of such excess shall be recognized in such taxable year as a loss under section 165 or as a deduction for depreciation under section 167. If the retirement of such asset occurs by sale or exchange on which gain or loss is recognized, the amount of such excess may constitute a loss subject to section 1231. Upon retirement of the last asset in a vintage account, the account shall terminate and no longer be an account to which this section applies. See subdivision (xi) of this subparagraph for treatment of certain multiple asset and item accounts.

(c) The principles of this subdivision may be illustrated by the following example:

Example. The taxpayer has a vintage account for section 1245 property with an unadjusted basis of $1,000 and a depreciation reserve of $700 (of which $600 represents depreciation allowances and $100 represents the proceeds of ordinary retirements from the account). If $500 is realized during the taxable year from ordinary retirements of assets from the account, the reserve is increased to $1,200, gain is recognized to the extent of $200 (the amount by which the depreciation reserve before further adjustment exceeds $1,000) and the depreciation reserve is then decreased to $1,000. The $200 of gain constitutes gain to which section 1245 applies. If the amount realized from ordinary retirements during the year had been $1,100 instead of $500, the gain of $800 would have consisted of $600 of gain to which section 1245 applies and $200 of gain to which section 1231 may apply.

(x) Dismantling cost. The cost of dismantling, demolishing, or removing an asset in the process of a retirement from the vintage account shall be treated as an expense deductible in the year paid or incurred, and such cost shall not be subtracted from the depreciation reserve for the account.

(xi) Special rule for treatment of multiple asset and item accounts. For the purposes of subdivision (ix)(b) of this subparagraph, all accounts (other than a special basis vintage account as described in subdivision (vi) of this subparagraph) of the same vintage in the same asset guideline class for which the taxpayer has selected the same asset depreciation period and adopted the same method of depreciation, and which contain only section 1245 property permitted by paragraph (b)(3)(ii) of this section to be included in the same vintage account, shall be treated as a single multiple asset vintage account.

(4) Examples. The principles of this paragraph may be illustrated by the following examples:

Example (1). (a) Taxpayer A has a multiple asset vintage account for section 1245 property with an unadjusted basis of $1,000. All the assets were first placed in service by A on January 15, 1971. This account contains all of A's assets in a single asset guideline class. A elects to apply this section for 1971 and adopts the modified half-year convention. A estimates a salvage value for the account of $100 and this estimate is determined to be reasonable. (See subparagraph (1)(v) of this paragraph for limitation on adjustment of reasonable salvage value.) A adopts the straight line method of depreciation with respect to the account and selects a 10-year asset depreciation period. A does not follow a practice of reducing the salvage value for the account in the amount of salvage value attributable to each retired asset in accordance with subparagraph (3)(vii) of this paragraph. The depreciation allowance for each of the first 4 years is $100, that is 1/10 multiplied by the unadjusted basis of $1,000, without reduction for salvage.

(b) In the fifth year of the asset depreciation period, three assets are sold in an ordinary retirement for $300. Under paragraph (c)(1)(ii) of this section and subparagraph (3)(iii) of this paragraph, the proceeds of the retirement are added to the depreciation reserve as of the beginning of the fifth year. Accordingly, the reserve as of the beginning of the fifth year is $700, that is, $400 of depreciation as of the beginning of the year plus $300 proceeds from ordinary retirements. The depreciation allowance for the fifth year is $100, that is 1/10 multiplied by the unadjusted basis of $1,000, without reduction for salvage. Accordingly, the depreciation reserve at the end of the fifth year is $800.

(c) In the sixth year, asset X is sold in an extraordinary retirement for $30 and gain or loss is recognized. Under the first-year convention used by the taxpayer, the unadjusted basis of X, $300, is removed from the unadjusted basis of the vintage account as of the beginning of the sixth year and the depreciation reserve as of the beginning of such year is reduced to $650 by removing the depreciation applicable to asset X, $150 (see subparagraph (3)(iv) of this paragraph). Since the depreciation reserve ($650) exceeds the unadjusted basis of the account ($700) minus salvage value ($100) by $50, under subparagraph (3)(iii) of this paragraph, salvage value is reduced by $50. No depreciation is allowable for the sixth year.

(d) In the seventh year, an asset is sold in an ordinary retirement for $110. This would increase the reserve as of the beginning of the seventh year to $760 and under subparagraph (3)(iii) of this paragraph the salvage value is reduced to zero. Under subparagraph (3)(ix)(a) of this paragraph the depreciation reserve is then decreased to $700 (the unadjusted basis of the account) and $60 is reported as gain, without regard to the adjusted basis of the asset. No depreciation is allowable for the seventh year since the depreciation reserve ($700) equals the unadjusted basis of the account ($700).

(e)

(1) In the eighth year, A elects to apply this section and to treat expenditures during the year for repair, maintenance, rehabilitation or improvement under subparagraph (2)(iii) and (iv)(a) of this paragraph (the "guideline class repair allowance"). This results in the treatment of $300 as a property improvement for the asset guideline class. (See subparagraph (2)(vii) of this paragraph for definition of a property improvement.) The property improvement is capitalized in a special basis vintage account of the eighth taxable year (see subparagraph (2)(viii)(a) of this paragraph). A selects an asset depreciation period of 10 years and adopts the straight line method for the special basis vintage account. A adopts the modified half-year convention for the eighth year.

(2) In the eighth year, A sells asset X in an ordinary retirement for $175. Under paragraph (c)(1)(ii) of this section and subparagraph (3)(iii) of this paragraph, $175 is added to the depreciation reserve for the account as of the beginning of the taxable year. Since the depreciation reserve for the account ($875) exceeds the unadjusted basis of the account ($700) by $175, that amount of gain is recognized under subparagraph (3)(ix) of this paragraph. Upon recognition of gain in the amount of $175, the depreciation reserve for the account is reduced to $700.

(3) No depreciation is allowable in the eighth year for the vintage account since the depreciation reserve ($700) equals the unadjusted basis of the account ($700). The depreciation allowable in the eighth year for the special basis vintage account is $15, that is, unadjusted basis of $300, multiplied by 1/10, the asset depreciation period selected for the special basis vintage account, but limited to $15 under the modified half-year convention. (See paragraph (e)(1)(iv) of this section for treatment of $150 of the property improvement as first placed in service in the first half of the taxable year and $150 of the property improvement as first placed in service in the last half of the taxable year.)

Example (2). Taxpayer B has a 1971 multiple asset vintage account for section 1245 property with an unadjusted basis of $100,000. B selects from the asset depreciation range an asset depreciation period of 10 years and adopts the straight line method of depreciation and the modified half-year convention. B establishes a salvage value for the account of $10,000. All the assets in the account are first placed in service on January 15, 1971. B follows the practice of reducing salvage value for the account as ordinary retirements occur in accordance with subparagraph (3)(vii) of this paragraph, but does not follow the optional practice of determining the basis of assets transferred to supplies or scrap in accordance with subparagraph (3)(viii) of this paragraph. No retirements occur during the first five years. The depreciation reserve at the beginning of the sixth year is $50,000. In the sixth year an asset with an unadjusted basis of $20,000 is transferred to supplies in an ordinary retirement. By application of subparagraph (3)(vii) (c) and (d)(2) of this paragraph B determines the reduction in salvage value for the account attributable to such asset to be $2,000 (that is,

$$\frac{\$20{,}000}{100{,}000} \times \$10{,}000 = \$2{,}000).$$

B reduces the salvage value for the account by $2,000 and adds $2,000 to the depreciation reserve for the account. The basis of the retired asset in the supplies account is $2,000. The depreciation allowable for the account for the sixth year is $10,000. The depreciation reserve for the account at the beginning of the seventh year is $63,000. At the mid-point of the seventh year all the remaining assets in the account are sold in an ordinary retirement for $20,000, which is added to the depreciation reserve as of the beginning of the seventh year, thus increasing the reserve to $82,000. The $5,000 depreciation allowable for the account for the seventh year (one-half of a full-year's depreciation of $10,000) increases the depreciation reserve to $87,000. Under subparagraph (3)(ix) *(b)* of this paragraph, a loss of $13,000 subject to section 1231 is realized in the seventh year (that is, the excess of the unadjusted basis of $100,000 over the depreciation reserve of $87,000). No depreciation is allowable for the account after the mid-point of the seventh year since all the assets are retired and the account has terminated.

(e) Accounting for eligible property. *(1) Definition of first placed in service.* (i) In general. The term "first placed in service" refers to the time the property is first placed in service by the taxpayer, not to the first time the property is placed in service. Property is first placed in service when first placed in a condition or state of readiness and availability for a specifically assigned function, whether in a trade or business, in the production of income, in a tax-exempt activity, or in a personal activity. In general, the provisions of paragraph (d)(1)(ii) and (d)(2) of § 1.46-3 shall apply for the purpose of determining the date on which property is placed in service, but see subdivision (ii) of this subparagraph for special rule for certain replacement parts. In the case of a building which is intended to house machinery and equipment and which is constructed, reconstructed, or erected by or for the taxpayer and for the taxpayer's use, the building will ordinarily be placed in service on the date such construction, reconstruction, or erection is substantially complete and the building is in a condition or state of readiness and availability. Thus, for example, in the case of a factory building, such readiness and availability shall be determined without regard to whether the machinery or equipment which the building houses, or is intended to house, has been placed in service. However, in an appropriate case, as for example where the building is essentially an item of machinery or equipment, or the use of the building is so closely related to the use of the machinery or equipment that it clearly can be expected to be replaced or retired when the property it initially houses is replaced or retired, the determination of readiness or availability of the building shall be made by taking into account the readiness and availability of such machinery or equipment. The date on which depreciation begins under a convention used by the taxpayer or under a particular method of depreciation, such as the unit of production method or the retirement method, shall not determine the date on which the property is first placed in service. See paragraph (c)(2) of this section for application of a first-year convention to determine the allowance for depreciation of property in a vintage account.

(ii) Certain replacement parts. Property (such as replacement parts) the cost or other basis of which is deducted as a repair expense in accordance with the asset guideline repair allowance described in paragraph (d)(2)(iii) of this section shall not be treated as placed in service.

(iii) Property improvements and excluded additions. (a) Except as provided in (b) of this subdivision, a property improvement determined under paragraph (d)(2)(vii)(b) of this section, and an excluded addition (other than an excluded addition referred to in the succeeding sentence) is first placed in service when its cost is paid or incurred. The general rule in subdivision (i) of this subparagraph applies to an excluded addition described in paragraph (d)(2)(vi)(d), (e), (f), or (g) of this section.

(b) If a property improvement or an excluded addition to which the first sentence of (a) of this subdivision applies is paid or incurred in part in one taxable year and in part in the succeeding taxable year (or in part in the first half of a taxable year and in part in the last half of the taxable year) the taxpayer may at his option consistently treat such property improvements and excluded additions under the general rule in subdivision (i) of this subparagraph.

(iv) Certain property improvements. In the case of an amount of property improvement determined under paragraph (d)(2)(vii)(a) of this section, one-half of such amount is first placed in service in the first half of the taxable year in which the cost is paid or incurred and one-half is first placed in service in the last half of such taxable year.

(v) Special rules for clearing accounts. In the case of public utilities which consistently account for certain property through "clearing accounts," the date on which such property is first placed in service shall be determined in accordance with rules to be prescribed by the Commissioner.

(2) Special rules for transferred property. If eligible property is first placed in service by the taxpayer during a taxable year of election, and the property is disposed of before the end of the taxable year, the election for such taxable year shall include such property unless such property is excluded in accordance with paragraph (b)(5)(iii), (iv), (v), (vi), or (vii) of this section.

(3) Special rules in the case of certain transfers. (i) Transaction to which section 381(a) applies. (a) In general the acquiring corporation in a transaction to which section 381(a) applies is for the purposes of this section treated as if it were the distributor or transferor corporation.

(b) If the distributor or transferor corporation (including any distributor or transferor corporation of any distributor or transferor corporation) has made an election to apply this section to eligible property transferred in a transaction to which section 381(a) applies, the acquiring corporation must segregate such eligible property (to which the distributor or transferor corporation elected to apply this section) into vintage accounts as nearly coextensive as possible with the vintage accounts created by the distributor or transferor corporation identified by reference to the year the property was first placed in service by the distributor or transferor corporation. The asset depreciation period for the vintage account in the hands of the distributor or transferor corporation must be used by the acquiring corporation. The method of depreciation adopted by the distributor or transferor corporation, shall be used by the acquiring corporation unless such corporation obtains the consent of the Commissioner to use another method of depreciation in accordance with paragraph (e) of § 1.446-1 or changes the method of depreciation under paragraph (c)(1)(iii) of this section.

(c) The acquiring corporation may apply this section to the property so acquired only if the distributor or transferor corporation elected to apply this section to such property.

(d) See paragraph (b)(7) of this section for special rule for certain property where there is a mere change in the form of conducting a trade or business.

(ii) Partnerships, trusts, estates, donees, and corporations. Except as provided in subdivision (i) of this subparagraph with respect to transactions to which section 381(a) applies and subdivision (iv) of this subparagraph with respect to certain transfers between members of an affiliated group of corporations or other related parties, if eligible property is placed in service by an individual, trust, estate, partnership or corporation, the election to apply this section shall be made by the individual, trust, estate, partnership or corporation placing such property in service. For example, if a partnership places in service property contributed to the partnership by a partner, the partnership may elect to apply this section to such property. If the partnership does not make the election, this section will not apply to such property. See paragraph (b)(7) of this section for special rule for certain property where there is mere change in the form of conducting a trade or business.

(iii) Leased property. The asset depreciation range and the asset depreciation period for eligible property subject to a lease shall be determined without regard to the period for which such property is leased, including any extensions or renewals of such period. See paragraph (b)(5)(v) of this section for exclusion of property amortized under paragraph (b) of § 1.162-11 from an election to apply this section. In the case of a lessor of property, unless there is an asset guideline class in effect for lessors of such property, the asset guideline class for such property shall be determined as if the property were owned by the lessee. However, in the case of an asset guideline class based upon the type of property (such as trucks or railroad cars) as distinguished from the activity in which used, the property shall be classified without regard to the activity of the lessee. Notwithstanding the preceding sentence, if a lease with respect to property, which would be includible in an asset guideline class based upon the type of property under the preceding sentence (such as trucks or railroad cars), is entered into after March 12, 1971, and before April 23, 1973, or a written contract to execute such a lease is entered into during such period and such contract is binding on April 23, 1973, and at all times thereafter, and if the rent or rate of return is based on a classification of such property as if it were owned by the lessee, then such property shall be classified as if it were owned by the lessee. However, the preceding sentence shall not apply if pursuant to the terms or conditions of the lease or binding contract the rent or rate of return may be adjusted to take account of a change in the period for depreciation with respect to the property resulting from inclusion of the property in an asset guideline class based upon the type of property rather than in an asset guideline class based upon the activity of the lessee. Similarly, where the terms of such a lease or contract provide that the obligation of the taxpayer to enter into the lease is subject to a condition that the property be included in an asset guideline class based upon the activity of the lessee, the contract or lease will not be considered as binding upon the taxpayer, for purposes of this subdivision. See paragraph (b)(4)(iii)(b) of this section for general rule for classification of property according to primary use.

(iv) Treatment of certain transfers between members of affiliated groups or other related persons. If section 38 property in an asset guideline class (determined without regard to whether the taxpayer elects to apply this section) is transferred by the taxpayer to a person who bears a relationship described in section 179(d)(2)(A) or (B), such property is in the same asset guideline class in the hands of transferee, and the transfer is neither described in section 381(a) nor treated as a disposition or cessation within the meaning of section 47, then the asset guideline period for such property selected by the taxpayer under this section shall not be shorter than the period used for computing the qualified investment with respect to the property under section 46(c). In a case in which the asset depreciation range for the asset guideline class which includes such property does not include the period for depreciation used by the transferor in computing the qualified investment with respect to such property, the transferee will not be permitted to include such property in an election under this section. However, in such a case, the transferor of the property may recompute the qualified investment for the year the property was placed in service using a period for depreciation which falls within the asset depreciation range.

(f) Election with respect to eligible property. *(1) Time and manner of election.* (i) In general. An election to apply this section to eligible property shall be made with the income tax return filed for the taxable year in which the property is first placed in service (see paragraph (e)(1) of this section) by the taxpayer. In the case of an affiliated group of corporations (as defined in section 1504(a) which makes a consolidated return with respect to income tax in accordance with section 1502 and the regulations thereunder, each corporation which joins in the making of such return may elect to apply this section for a taxable year. An election to compute the allowance for depreciation under this section is a method of accounting but the consent of the Commissioner will be deemed granted to make an annual election. For election by a partnership see section 703(b) and paragraph (e)(3)(ii) of this section. If the taxpayer does not file a timely return (taking into account extensions of the time for filing) for the taxable year in which the property is first placed in service, the election shall be filed at the time the taxpayer files his first return for that year. The election may be made with an amended return filed within the time prescribed by law (including extensions) for filing the original return for the taxable year of election. If an election is not made within the time and in the manner prescribed in this paragraph, no election may be made for such taxable year (by the filing of an amended return or in any other manner) with respect to any eligible property placed in service in the taxable year.

(ii) Other elections under this section. All other elections under this section may be made only within the time and in the manner prescribed by subdivision (i) of this subparagraph with respect to an election to apply this section.

(iii) Effective date. See paragraph (f)(6) of this section for the effective date of this paragraph.

(2) Information required. A taxpayer who elects to apply this section must specify in the election:

(i) That the taxpayer makes such election and consents to and agrees to apply, all the provisions of this section;

(ii) The asset guideline class for each vintage account of the taxable year;

(iii) The first-year convention adopted by the taxpayer for the taxable year of election;

(iv) Whether the special 10 percent used property rule described in paragraph (b)(5)(iii) of this section has been applied to exclude used property from the election;

(v) Whether the taxpayer elects to apply the asset guideline class repair allowance described in paragraph (d)(2)(iii) of this section;

(vi) Whether the taxpayer elects for the taxable year to allocate the adjusted basis of a special basis vintage account in accordance with paragraph (d)(3)(vi) of this section;

(vii) Whether any eligible property for which the taxpayer was not required or permitted to make an election was excluded because of the special rules of paragraph (b)(5)(v) or (6), or paragraph (e)(3)(i) or (iv) of this section;

(viii) Whether any "section 38 property" was excluded under paragraph (b)(5)(iv) of this section from the election to apply this section;

(ix) If the taxpayer is an electric or gas utility, whether the taxpayer elects to apply this section on the basis of a composite asset guideline class in accordance with paragraph (b)(4)(iii)(a) of this section; and

(x) Such other information as may reasonably be required. The information required under this subparagraph may be provided in accordance with rules prescribed by the Commissioner for reasonable grouping of assets or accounts. Form 4832 is provided for making an election and for submission of the information required. An election may be made and the information submitted only in accordance with Form 4832. An election to apply this section will not be rendered invalid under this subparagraph so long as there is substantial compliance, in good faith, with the requirements of this subparagraph.

(3) Irrevocable election. An election to apply this section to eligible property for any taxable year may not be revoked or changed after the time for filing the election prescribed under subparagraph (1) of this paragraph has expired. No other election under this section may be revoked or changed after such time unless expressly provided for under this section. (See paragraph (b)(5)(v)(b) of this section for special rule.)

(4) Special conditions to election to apply this section. (i) Maintenance of books and records. The taxpayer may not elect to apply this section for a taxable year unless the taxpayer maintains the books and records required under this section. In addition to any other information required under this section, the taxpayer's books and records must specify—

(a) The asset depreciation period selected by the taxpayer for each vintage account;

(b) If the taxpayer applies the modified half-year convention, the total cost or other basis of all eligible property first placed in service in the first half of the taxable year and the total cost or other basis of all eligible property first placed in service in the last half of the taxable year;

(c) The unadjusted basis and salvage value for each vintage account, and the amount, if any, by which gross salvage value was decreased under section 167(f);

(d) Each asset guideline class for which the taxpayer elects to apply the asset guideline class repair allowance described in paragraph (d)(2)(iii) of this section;

(e) The amount of property improvement, determined under paragraph (d)(2)(vii)(a) of this section, for each asset guideline class for which the taxpayer elects to apply the asset guideline class repair allowance;

(f) A reasonable description of property excluded from an election to apply this section and the basis for the exclusion;

(g) The total unadjusted basis of all assets retired during the taxable year from each asset guideline class, and the proceeds realized during the taxable year from such retirements; and

(h) The vintage (that is, the taxable year in which established) of the assets retired during the year from each asset guideline class.

For purposes of paragraph (f)(4)(i)(g) and (h) of this section, all accounts of the same vintage and asset guideline class may be treated as a single account. The taxpayer must specify the information required under paragraph (f)(4)(i)(g) and (h) without regard to the retirement of an asset by transfer to a supplies account for reuse.

(ii) Response to survey. Taxpayers who elect to apply this section must respond to infrequent data surveys conducted by the Treasury Department. These periodic surveys, which will be conducted on the basis of scientifically sound sampling methods, are designed to obtain data (including industry asset acquisitions and retirements) used to keep the asset guideline classes and periods up to date.

(iii) Effective of noncompliance. An election to apply this section will not be rendered invalid under this subparagraph so long as there is substantial compliance, in good faith, with the requirements of this subparagraph.

(5) Mass assets. In the case of mass assets, if the taxpayer assigns retirements to vintage accounts in the manner provided in paragraph (d)(3)(v)(d) of this section, the following information must be supplied with Form 4832:

(i) Whether the taxpayer used the standard mortality dispersion curve or a curve based upon his own experience, and

(ii) Such other reasonable information as may be required by the Commissioner.

(6) Effective date. The rules in this paragraph apply to elections for taxable years ending on or after December 31, 1978. In the case of an election for a taxable year ending before December 31, 1978, the rules in paragraph (f) of this section, in effect before the amendments made by T.D. 7593 approved January 11, 1979, shall apply. See 26 CFR § 1.167 (a)-11(f) (1977) for paragraph (f) of this section as it appeared before the amendments made by T.D. 7593.

(g) Relationship to other provisions. *(1) Useful life.* (i) In general. Except as provided in subdivision (ii) of this subparagraph, an election to apply this section to eligible property constitutes an agreement under section 167(d) and this section to treat the asset depreciation period for each vintage account as the useful life of the property in such account for all purposes of the Code, including sections 46, 47, 48, 57, 163(d), 167(c), 167(f)(2), 179, 312(m), 514(a), and 4940(c). For example, since section 167(c) requires a useful life of at least 3 years and the asset depreciation period selected is treated as the useful life for purposes of section 167(c), the taxpayer may adopt a method of depreciation described in section 167(b)(2) or (3) for an account only if the asset depreciation period selected for the account is at least 3 years.

(ii) Special rules. (a) For the purposes of paragraph (d) of this section, the anticipated period of use (estimated at the close of the taxable year in which the asset is first placed in service) on the basis of which salvage value is estimated, shall be determined without regard to the asset depreciation period for the property.

(b) For the purposes of sections 162 and 263 and the regulations thereunder, whether an expenditure prolongs the life of an asset shall be determined on the basis of the anticipated period of use of the asset (estimated at the close of the taxable year in which the asset is first placed in service) without regard to the asset depreciation period for such asset.

(c) The determination whether a transaction with respect to qualified property constitutes a sale or a lease of such property shall be made without regard to the asset depreciation period for the property.

(d) The principles of this subdivision may be illustrated by the following example:

Example. Corporation X has assets in asset guideline class 32.3 which are used in the manufacture of stone and clay products. The asset depreciation range for assets in asset guideline class 32.3 is from 12 to 18 years. Assume that corporation X selects 14 years as the asset depreciation period for all assets in asset guideline class 32.3. Under paragraph (d)(1)(i) of this section, corporation X must estimate salvage value on the basis of the anticipated period of use of the property (determined as of the close of the taxable year in which the property is first placed in service). The anticipated period of use must also be used for purposes of sections 162 and 263 in determining whether an expenditure materially prolongs the useful life of an asset. The anticipated period of use of an asset is determined without regard to the asset depreciation period of 14 years. Corporation X has, among other assets in the asset guideline class, machines A, B, and C. Corporation X estimates the anticipated period of use of machines A, B, and C as 8 years, 14 years, and 22 years, respectively. These estimates are reasonable and will be used for estimating salvage value and for purposes of sections 162 and 263.

(2) Section 167(d) agreements. If the taxpayer has, prior to January 1, 1971, entered into a section 167(d) agreement which applies to any eligible property, the taxpayer will be permitted to withdraw the eligible property from the agreement provided that an election is made to apply this section to such property. The statement of intent to withdraw eligible property from such an agreement must be made in an election filed for the taxable year in which the property is first placed in service. The withdrawal, in accordance with this subparagraph, of any eligible property from a section 167(d) agreement shall not affect any other property covered by such an agreement.

(3) Relationship to the straight line method. (i) In general. For purposes of determining the amount of depreciation which would be allowable under the straight line method of depreciation, such amount shall be computed with respect to any property in a vintage account using the straight line method in the manner described in paragraph (c)(1)(i) of this section and a rate based upon the period for the vintage account selected from the asset depreciation range. Thus, for example, section 57(a)(3) requires a taxpayer to compute an amount using the straight line method of depreciation if the taxpayer uses an accelerated method of depreciation. For purposes of section 57(a)(3), the amount for property in a vintage account shall be computed using the asset depreciation period for the vintage account selected from the asset depreciation range. In the case of property to which the taxpayer does not elect to apply this section, such amount computed by using the straight line method shall be determined under § 1.167(b)-1 without regard to this section.

(ii) Examples. The principles of this subparagraph may be illustrated by the following example:

Example. (a) Corporation X places a new asset in service to which it elects to apply this section. The cost of the asset is $200,000 and the estimated salvage value is zero. The taxpayer selects 9 years from the applicable asset depreciation range of 8 to 12 years. Corporation X adopts the double declining balance method of depreciation and thus the rate of depreciation is 22.2 percent (twice the applicable straight line rate). The depreciation allowance in the first year would be $44,400, that is, 22.2 percent of $200,000.

(b) Assume that the provisions of section 57(a)(3) apply to the property. The amount of the tax preference would be $22,200, that is, the excess of the depreciation allowed under this section ($44,400) over the depreciation which would have been allowable if the taxpayer had used the period selected from the asset depreciation range and the straight line rate ($22,200).

T.D. 7128, 6/22/71, amend T.D. 7272, 4/20/73, T.D. 7315, 6/6/74, T.D. 7593, 1/25/79, T.D. 7763, 1/16/81, T.D. 7818, 8/31/82, T.D. 7831, 9/3/82, T.D. 8597, 7/12/95.

PAR. 5. Paragraph (d)(3)(v)(d)(2) of § 1.167(a)-11 is amended by removing "paragraph (e)(4)" and inserting in its place "paragraph (g)(2)."

Proposed § 1.167(a)-11 [Amended] [*For Preamble, see ¶ 151,041*]

PARAGRAPH 1. Section 1.167(a)-11 is amended as follows:

1. Paragraph (a)(1) is amended by adding a new sentence at the beginning thereof.

2. Paragraph (d)(2) is amended as follows:

a. A caption is added to paragraph (d)(2)(i) *(a)* and new paragraph (d)(2)(i) *(b)* is added,

b. Paragraph (d)(2)(ii) is amended by adding a new sentence at the end thereof,

c. In paragraph (d)(2)(iii), the tenth sentence is amended by adding "property that is first placed in service (as provided in paragraph (e)(1)(i) and (ii) of this section) before January 1, 1981, and is" immediately after the phrase " 'repair allowance propertymeans", and

d. New paragraph (d)(2)(viii)(d) is added immediately after paragraph (d)(2)(viii) *(c)*.

The revised and added provisions read as follows:

Proposed § 1.167(a)-11 Depreciation based on class lives and asset depreciation ranges for property placed in service after December 31, 1970. [*For Preamble, see ¶ 150,941*]

(a) In general. *(1) Summary.* This section does not apply with respect to recovery property (within the meaning of section 168 and the regulations thereunder) placed in service after December 31, 1980. * * *

* * * * *

(d) Special rules for salvage, repairs and retirements. * * *

(2) Treatment of repairs. (i) In general. (a) Treatment of repair expenditures. * * *

(b) Property placed in service after December 31, 1980.

This paragraph (d)(2) does not apply to any expenditures with respect to property first placed in service after December 31, 1980, but may apply to expenditures paid or incurred after such date with respect to property first placed in service before January 1, 1981. Expenditures with respect to property first placed in service after December 31, 1980, shall be treated as capital expenditures or as deductible expenses for the taxable year in which paid or incurred in accordance with the general rules provided in sections 162, 212, and 263. Property is considered first placed in service for purposes of this paragraph (d)(2)(i)(b) under the rules of paragraph (e)(1)(i) and (ii) of this section.

(ii) Election of repair allowance. * * * For taxable years ending after December 31, 1980, and before [February 16 1984], notwithstanding paragraph (f)(1) of this section, the taxpayer may elect (in the original return or in an amended return) to apply this section and the asset guideline class repair allowance described in paragraph (d)(2)(iii) of this section on or before the later of the due date (including extensions) of the taxpayer's tax return for the taxable year or [November 16 1984].

* * * * *

(vii) Treatment of property improvements and excluded additions. * * *

(d) Paragraph (d)(2)(viii)(a), (b), and (c) of this section does not apply to a property improvement, excluded addition, or part thereof considered first placed in service by the taxpayer after December 31, 1980. Such property improvement, excluded addition, or part thereof shall generally be treated as a separate item of recovery property (as defined in section 168(c)(1)), and shall be assigned to the appropriate class of recovery property in accordance with section 168(c)(2). See § 1.168-2(e)(2). For taxable years ending after December 31, 1980, notwithstanding the succeeding sentence, for purposes of this paragraph (d)(2)(viii)(d), a property improvement, excluded addition, or part thereof is considered first placed in service under the rules provided in paragraph (e)(1)(i) and (ii) of this section and not under the rules provided in paragraph (e)(1)(iii) and (iv) of this section. * * *

§ 1.167(a)-12 Depreciation based on class lives for property first placed in service before January 1, 1971.

(a) In general. *(1) Summary.* This section provides an elective class life system for determining the reasonable allowance for depreciation of certain classes of assets for taxable years ending after December 31, 1970. The system applies only to assets placed in service before January 1, 1971. Depreciation for such assets during periods prior to January 1, 1971, may have been determined in accordance with Revenue Procedure 62-21. Accordingly, rules are provided which permit taxpayers to apply the system in taxable years ending after December 31, 1970, to such assets without the necessity of changing or regrouping their depreciation accounts other than as previously required by Revenue Procedure 62-21. The system is designed to minimize disputes between taxpayers and the Internal Revenue Service as to the useful life of assets, salvage value, and repairs. See § 1.167(a)-11 for a similar system for property placed in service after December 31, 1970. See paragraph (d)(2) of § 1.167(a)-11 for treatment of expenditures for the repair, maintenance, rehabilitation or improvement of certain property. The system provided by this section is optional with the taxpayer. An election under this section applies only to qualified property in an asset guideline class for which an election is made and only for the taxable year of election. The taxpayer's election is made with the income tax return for the taxable year. This section also revokes the reserve ratio test for taxable years ending after December 31, 1970, and provides transitional rules for taxpayers who after January 11, 1971, adopt Revenue Procedure 62-21 for a taxable year ending prior to January 1, 1971.

(2) Revocation of reserve ratio test and other matters. Except as otherwise expressly provided in this section and in paragraph (b)(5)(vi) of § 1.167(a)-11, the provisions of Revenue Procedure 62-21 shall not apply to any property for any taxable year ending after December 31, 1970, whether or not the taxpayer elects to apply this section to any property. See paragraph (f) of this section for rules for the adoption of Revenue Procedure 62-21 for taxable years ending prior to January 1, 1971.

(3) Definition of qualified property. The term "qualified property" means tangible property which is subject to the allowance for depreciation provided by section 167(a), but only if—

(i) An asset guideline class and asset guideline period are in effect for such property for the taxable year, and

(ii) The property is first placed in service by the taxpayer before January 1, 1971,

(iii) The property is placed in service before January 1, 1971, but first placed in service by the taxpayer after December 31, 1970, and is not includible in an election under § 1.167(a)-11 by reason of § 1.167(a)-11(b)(7) (property acquired as a result of a mere change in form) or § 1.167(a)-11(e)(3)(i) (certain property acquired in a transaction to which section 381(a) applies), or

(iv) The property is acquired and first placed in service by the taxpayer after December 31, 1970, pursuant to a binding written contract entered into prior to January 1, 1971, and is excluded in accordance with paragraph (b)(5)(iv) of § 1.167(a)-11 from an election to apply § 1.167(a)-11.

The provisions of paragraph (e)(1) of § 1.167(a)-11 apply in determining whether property is first placed in service before January 1, 1971. See subparagraph (4)(ii) of this paragraph for special rules for the exclusion of property from the definition of qualified property.

(4) Requirements of election. (i) In general. An election to apply this section to qualified property must be made within the time and in the manner specified in paragraph (e) of this section. The election must specify that the taxpayer consents to and agrees to apply all the provisions of this section. The election may be made separately for each asset guideline class. Thus, a taxpayer may for the taxable year elect to apply this section to one, more than one, or all asset guideline classes in which he has qualified property. An election to apply this section for a taxable year must include all qualified property in the asset guideline class for which the election is made.

(ii) Special rules for exclusion of property from application of this section. (a) If for the taxable year of election, the taxpayer computes depreciation under section 167(k) or computes amortization under sections 169, 185, 187, 188, or paragraph (b) of § 1.162-11 with respect to property, such property is not qualified property for such taxable year. If for the taxable year of election, the taxpayer computes depreciation under any method of depreciation (other than a method described in the preceding sentence) not permitted by subparagraph (5)(v) of this paragraph for any property in an asset guideline class (other than subsidiary assets excluded from an election under (b) of this subdivision), no property in such asset guideline class is qualified property for such taxable year.

(b) The taxpayer may exclude from an election to apply this section all (but not less than all) subsidiary assets. Subsidiary assets so excluded are not qualified property for such taxable year. For purposes of this subdivision the term "subsidiary assets" includes jigs, dies, molds, returnable containers, glassware, silverware, textile mill cam assemblies, and other equipment includable in Group One, Class 5, of Revenue Procedure 62-21 which is usually and properly accounted for separately from other property and under a method of depreciation not expressed in terms of years. See § 1.167(l)-1(h).

(iii) Special rule for certain public utility property. (a) In the case of public utility property described in section 167(l)(3)(A)(iii) for which no guideline life was prescribed in Revenue Procedure 62-21 (or for which reference was made in Revenue Procedure 62-21 to lives or rates established by governmental regulatory agencies) of a taxpayer which—

(1) Is entitled to use a method of depreciation other than a "subsection (l) method" of depreciation (as defined in section 167(l)(3)(F)) only if it uses the "normalization method of accounting" (as defined in section 167(l)(3)(G)) with respect to such property, or

(2) Is entitled for the taxable year to use only a "subsection (l) method" of depreciation, such property shall be qualified property (as defined in subparagraph (3) of this paragraph) only if the taxpayer normalizes the tax deferral resulting from the election to apply this section.

(b) The taxpayer will be considered to normalize the tax deferral resulting from the election to apply this section only if it computes its tax expense for purposes of establishing its cost of service for ratemaking purposes and for reflecting operating results in its regulated books of account using a period for depreciation no less than the period used for computing its depreciation expense for ratemaking purposes and for reflecting operating results in its regulated books of account for the taxable year, and the taxpayer makes adjustments to a reserve to reflect the deferral of taxes resulting from the use of a period for depreciation under section 167 in accordance with an election to apply this section different from the period used for computing its depreciation expense for ratemaking purposes and for reflecting operating results in its regulated books of account for the taxable year. A determination whether the taxpayer is considered to normalize under this subdivision the tax deferral resulting from the election to apply this section shall be made in a manner consistent with the principles for determining whether a taxpayer is using the "normalization method of accounting" (within the meaning of section 167(l)(3)(G)). See § 13.13 of the temporary regulations prescribed by T.D. 7049 approved June 25, 1970.

(c) If a taxpayer, which has elected to apply this section to any qualified public utility property and is required under (a) of this subdivision to normalize the tax deferral resulting from the election to apply this section to such property, fails to normalize such tax deferral, the election to apply this section to such property shall terminate as of the beginning of the taxable year for which the taxpayer fails to normalize such tax deferral. Application of this section to such property for any period prior to the termination date will not be affected by this termination.

(5) Determination of reasonable allowance for depreciation. (i) In general. The allowance for depreciation of qualified property to which the taxpayer elects to apply this section shall be determined in accordance with this section. The annual allowance for depreciation is determined by using the method of depreciation adopted by the taxpayer and a rate based upon a life permitted by this section. In the case of the straight-line method of depreciation, the rate of depreciation shall be based upon the class life (or individual life if the taxpayer assigns individual depreciable lives in accordance with subdivision (iii) of this subparagraph) used by the taxpayer with respect to the assets in the asset guideline class. Such rate will be applied to the unadjusted basis of the asset guideline class (individual assets or depreciation accounts if the taxpayer assigns individual depreciable lives). In the case of the sum of the years-digits method of depreciation, the rate of depreciation will be determined based upon the remaining life of the class (or individual remaining lives if the taxpayer assigns such lives in accordance with subdivision (iii) of this subparagraph) and is applied to the adjusted basis of the class (or individual accounts or assets) as of the beginning of the taxable year of election. The remaining life of a depreciation account is determined by dividing the unrecovered cost or other basis of the account, as computed by straight-line depreciation, by the gross cost or unadjusted basis of the account, and multiplying the result by the class life used with respect to the account. In the case of the declining balance method of depreciation, the rate of depreciation for the asset guideline class shall be based upon the class life (or individual life if the taxpayer assigns such lives in accordance with subdivision (iii) of this subparagraph). Such rate is applied to the adjusted basis of the class (or individual accounts or assets) as of the beginning of the taxable year of election.

(ii) Reasonable allowance by reference to class lives. The amount of depreciation for all qualified property in an asset guideline class to which the taxpayer elects to apply this section will constitute the reasonable allowance provided by section 167(a) and the depreciation for the asset guideline class will not be adjusted if—

(a) The taxpayer's qualified property is accounted for in one or more depreciation accounts which conform to the asset guideline class, and the depreciation for each such account is determined by using a rate based upon a life not less than the class life, or

(b) The taxpayer's qualified property is accounted for in one or more depreciation accounts (whether or not conforming to the asset guideline class) for which depreciation is determined at a rate based upon the taxpayer's estimate of the lives of the assets (instead of the class life) and the total amount of depreciation so determined for the asset guideline class for the taxable year of election is not more than would be permitted under (a) of this subdivision for such year using the method of depreciation adopted by the taxpayer for the property.

See subdivision (vii) of this subparagraph for determination of reasonable allowance if depreciation exceeds the amount permitted by this subdivision. See paragraph (b) of this section for rules regarding the determination of "class life". For rules for regrouping depreciation accounts to conform to the asset guideline class, see subdivision (iv) of this subparagraph.

(iii) Consistency when individual lives are used. If the taxpayer assigns individual depreciable lives to assets in accordance with subdivision (ii)(b) of this subparagraph, even though the total amount of depreciation for the asset guideline class will not be adjusted, the lives assigned to the various assets in the asset guideline class must be reasonably in proportion to their relative expected periods of use in the taxpayer's business. Thus, although the taxpayer who uses individual asset lives normally has latitude in thereby allocating the depreciation for the asset guideline class among the assets, if the lives are grossly disproportionate (as where a short life is assigned to one asset and a long life to another even though the expected periods of use are the same), the taxpayer's allocation of depreciation to particular assets or depreciation accounts may be adjusted. For example, the taxpayer's allocation may be adjusted for purposes of determining adjusted basis under section 1016(a) or in allocating depreciation to the 50-percent limitation on percentage depletion provided by section 613(a). See paragraph (d) of this section for rules regarding the use of individual asset lives for purposes of classifying retirements as normal or abnormal.

(iv) Regrouping depreciation accounts. Without the consent of the Commissioner, the taxpayer may for any taxable year for which he elects to apply this section to an asset guideline class, regroup his accounts for that and all succeeding taxable years to conform to the asset guideline class. Other changes in accounting, including a change from item accounts to multiple-asset accounting, may be made with the consent of the Commissioner. No depreciation accounts for which the straight line or sum of the years-digits method of depreciation is adopted may be combined under this section which would not be permitted to be combined under part III of Revenue Procedure 65-13, as in effect on January 1, 1971. Accordingly, whether or not the taxpayer adopted the guideline system of Revenue Procedure 62-21 for a taxable year to which part III of Revenue Procedure 65-13 is applicable, the depreciation allowance for any taxable year of election under this section may not exceed that amount which would have been allowed for such year if the taxpayer had used item accounts or year of acquisition accounts. Thus, for example, if a calendar year taxpayer acquired a $90 asset on the first day of each year from 1966 through 1970, placed such assets in a single multiple asset account, adopted the sum of the years-digits method of depreciation and used a 5-year depreciable life for such assets, and in 1971 uses the 5-year class life determined under paragraph (b) of this section, the depreciation allowance for such assets in 1971 under this section may not exceed $60, that is, the amount which would be allowed if the taxpayer had used year of acquisition accounts for the assets for the years 1966 through 1970.

For purposes of this subparagraph, a taxpayer's depreciation accounts conform to the asset guideline class if each depreciation account includes only assets of the same asset guideline class.

(v) Method of depreciation. The same method of depreciation must be applied to all property in a single depreciation account. The method of depreciation is subject to the limitations of section 167(c), (j) and (l). Except as otherwise provided in this subdivision, the taxpayer must apply a method of depreciation described in section 167(b)(1), (2), or (3) for qualified property to which the taxpayer elects to apply this section. A method of depreciation permitted under section 167(b)(4) may be used under this section if the method was used by the taxpayer with respect to the property for his last taxable year ending before January 1, 1971, the method is expressed in terms of years, the taxpayer establishes to the satisfaction of the Commissioner that the method is both a reasonable and consistent method, and if the taxpayer applies paragraph (b)(2) of this section (relating to class lives in special situations) to determine a class life, that the method of determining such class life is consistent with the principles of Revenue Procedure 62-21 as applied to such a method. If the taxpayer has applied a method of depreciation with respect to the property which is not described in section 167(b) (1), (2), (3), or (4) (as permitted under the preceding sentence), he must change under this section to a method of depreciation described in section 167(b) (1), (2), or (3) for the first taxable year for which an election is made under this section. Other changes in depreciation method may be made with the consent of the Commissioner (see sec. 446 and the regulations thereunder). (See also sec. 167(e).)

(vi) Salvage value. In applying the method of depreciation adopted by the taxpayer, the annual allowance for depreciation is determined without adjustment for the salvage value of the property, except that no depreciation account may be depreciated below a reasonable salvage value for the account. See paragraph (c) of this section for definition and treatment of salvage value.

(vii) Reasonable allowance when depreciation exceeds amount based on class life. In the event that the total amount of depreciation claimed by the taxpayer on his income tax return, in a claim for refund, or otherwise, for an asset guideline class with respect to which an election is made under this section for the taxable year, exceeds the maximum amount permitted under subdivision (ii)(a) of this subparagraph—

(a) If the excess is established to the satisfaction of the Commissioner to be the result of a good faith mistake by the taxpayer in determining the maximum amount permitted under subdivision (ii)(a) of this subparagraph, the taxpayer's election to apply this section will be treated as valid and only such excess will be disallowed, and

(b) In all other cases, the taxpayer's election to apply this section to the asset guideline class for the taxable year is invalid and the reasonable allowance for depreciation will be determined without regard to this section. (See § 1.167(a)-1(b) for rules regarding the estimated useful life of property.)

(b) Determination of class lives. *(1) Class lives in general.* The class life determined under this paragraph (without regard to any range or variance permitted with respect to class lives under § 1.167(a)-11) will be applied for purposes of determining whether the allowance for depreciation for qualified property included in an election under this section is subject to adjustment. The taxpayer is not required to use the class life determined under this paragraph for purposes of determining the allowance for depreciation. Except as provided in subparagraph (2) of this paragraph, the class life of qualified property to which the taxpayer elects to apply this section is the shorter of—

(i) The asset guideline period for the asset guideline class as set forth in Revenue Procedure 72-10 as in effect on March 1, 1972 (applied without regard to any special provision therein with respect to property predominantly used outside the United States), or

(ii) The asset guideline period for the asset guideline class as set forth in any supplement or revision of Revenue Procedure 72-10, but only if and to the extent by express reference in such supplement or revision made applicable for the purpose of changing the asset guideline period or classification of qualified property to which this section applies.

See paragraph (e)(3)(iii) of this section for requirement that the election for the taxable year specify the class life for each asset guideline class. Generally, the applicable asset guideline class and asset guideline period for qualified property to which the taxpayer has elected to apply this section will not be changed for the taxable year of election to reflect any supplement or revision thereof after the taxable year. However, if expressly provided in such a supplement or revision, the taxpayer may, at his option in the manner specified therein, apply the revised or supplemented asset guideline classes or periods to such property for such taxable year and succeeding taxable years. The principles of this subparagraph may be illustrated by the following example:

Example. (i) Corporation X, a calendar year taxpayer, has assets in asset guideline class 20.4 of Revenue Procedure 72-10 which were placed in service by corporation X in 1967, 1968, and 1970. Corporation X also has assets in asset guideline class 22.1 of Revenue Procedure 72-10 which were placed in service at various times prior to 1971. Corporation X has no other qualified property. Corporation X elects to apply this section for 1971 to both classes. Assume that the class lives are determined under this subparagraph and not under subparagraph (2) of this paragraph.

(ii) The class lives for asset guideline classes 20.4 and 22.1 are their respective asset guideline periods of 12 years and 9 years in Revenue Procedure 72-10.

(iii) Accordingly, in the election for the taxable year, in accordance with paragraph (e)(3)(iii) of this section, corporation X specifies a class life of 12 years for asset guideline class 20.4 and a class life of 9 years for asset guideline class 22.1.

(2) Class lives in special situations. Notwithstanding subparagraph (1) of this paragraph, for the purposes of this section the class life for the asset guideline class determined under this subparagraph shall be used if such class life is shorter than the class life determined under subparagraph (1) of this paragraph. If property described in paragraph (a)(2)(iii) of this section in an asset guideline class is acquired by the taxpayer in a transaction to which section 381(a) applies, for purposes of this subparagraph such property shall be segregated from other property in the class and treated as in a separate asset guideline class, and the class life for that asset guideline class under this subparagraph shall be the shortest class life the transferor was entitled to use under this section for such property on the date of such transfer. In all other cases, the class life for the asset guideline class for purposes of this subparagraph shall be the shortest class life (within the meaning of sec. 4, part II, of Revenue Procedure 62-21) which can be justified by application of §§ 3.02(a), 3.03(a), or 3.05, part II, of Revenue Procedure 62-21 (other than the portion of such § 3.05 dealing with justification of a class life by reference to facts and circumstances) for the taxpayer's last taxable year ending prior to January 1, 1971.

A class life justified by application of section 3.03(a), Part II, of Revenue Procedure 62-21 shall not be shorter than can be justified under the Adjustment Table for Class Lives in Part III of such Revenue Procedure. For purposes of this subparagraph and paragraph (f)(1)(iii) of this section, the reserve ratio test is met only if the taxpayer's reserve ratio does not exceed the upper limit of the appropriate reserve ratio range or in the alternative during the transitional period there provided does not exceed the appropriate "transitional upper limit" in section 3, Part II, of Revenue Procedure 65-13. References to Revenue Procedure 62-21 include all modifications, amendments, and supplements thereto as of January 1, 1971. The guideline form of the reserve ratio test, as described in Revenue Procedure 65-13, may be applied for purposes of this subparagraph in a manner consistent with the rules contained in section 7, Part II, of Revenue Procedure 65-13 and sections 3.02, 3.03, and 3.05, Part II, of Revenue Procedure 62-21. The principles of this subparagraph may be illustrated by the following examples:

Example (1). Corporation X, a calendar year taxpayer, has all its assets in asset guideline class 20.4 of Revenue Procedure 72-10 which were placed in service by corporation X prior to 1971. Corporation X elects to apply this section for 1971. For taxable years 1967 through 1969, corporation X had used a class life (within the meaning of section 4, Part II, of Revenue Procedure 62-21) for asset guideline class 20.4 of 12 years. The asset guideline period in Revenue Procedure 72-10 in effect for 1971 is also 12 years. Assume that for 1969 corporation X's reserve ratio was below the appropriate reserve ratio lower limit. However, corporation X could not justify a class life shorter than the asset guideline period of 12 years for 1970 since corporation X had not used the 12-year class life for a period at least equal to one-half of 12 years. (See section 3.03(a), Part II, of Revenue Procedure 62-21.) Accordingly, the class life for asset guideline class 20.4 in 1971 is the asset guideline period of 12 years in accordance with subparagraph (1) of this paragraph.

Example (2). The facts are the same as in example (1) except that corporation X had used a class life of 10 years for guideline class 20.4 since 1967. Corporation X had not used the class life of 10 years for a period at least equal to one-half of 10 years. However, in 1968 corporation X's 10-year class life was accepted on audit by the Internal Revenue Service and corporation X met the reserve ratio test in 1970 for guideline class 20.4 using a test life of 10 years. (See section 3.05, Part II, of Revenue Procedure 62-21.) Accordingly, the class life of 10 years is justified for 1970 and the class life for 1971 is 10 years in accordance with this subparagraph. If the taxpayer's class life had not been audited and accepted for 1968, and in the absence of other circumstances, the taxpayer could not justify a class life shorter than the asset guideline period of 12 years since it had not used the 10-year class life for a period at least equal to one-half of 10 years. (See section 3.02, Part II, of Revenue Procedure 62-21.)

Example (3). Corporation Y, a calendar year taxpayer, has all its assets in asset guideline class 13.3 of Revenue Procedure 72-10 which were placed in service from 1960 through 1970. Corporation Y elects to apply this section for 1971. The asset guideline period in Revenue Procedure 72-10 in effect for 1971 is 16 years. Since 1963 corporation Y had used a class life of 16 years for asset guideline 13.3. At the end of 1969 corporation Y's reserve ratio for guideline class 13.3 was 36 percent. With a growth rate of 8 percent and a test life of 16 years the appropriate reserve ratio lower limit was 37 percent. Corporation Y's reserve ratio of 36 percent was below the lower limit of the appropriate reserve ratio range. Corporation Y had used the 16-year class life for at least eight years. A class life of 13.5 years for 1970 was justified by application of section 3.03(a), Part II, of Revenue Procedure 62-21 and the Adjustment Table for Class Lives in Part III, of Revenue Procedure 62-21. The class life for 1971 is 13.5 years in accordance with this subparagraph.

(3) Classification of property. (i) In general. Property to which this section applies shall be included in the asset guideline class for the activity in which the property is primarily used in the taxable year of election. See paragraph (d)(5) of this section for rule regarding the classification of leased property.

(ii) Insubstantial activity. The provisions of Revenue Produce 62-21 with respect to classification of assets used in an activity which is insubstantial may be applied under this section.

(iii) Special rule for certain public utilities. An electric or gas utility which in accordance with Revenue Procedure 64-

21 used a composite guideline class basis for applying Revenue Procedure 62-21 for its last taxable year prior to January 1, 1971, may apply Revenue Procedure 72-10 and this section on the basis of such composite asset guideline class determined as provided in Revenue Procedure 64-21. For the purposes of this section all property in the composite guideline class shall be treated as included in a single asset guideline class.

(c) Salvage value. *(1) In general.* (i) Definition of gross salvage value. "Gross salvage" value is the amount (determined at or as of the time of acquisition but without regard to the application of Revenue Procedure 62-21) which is estimated will be realized upon a sale or other disposition of qualified property when it is no longer useful in the taxpayer's trade or business or in the production of his income and is to be retired from service, without reduction for the cost of removal, dismantling, demolition, or similar operations. "Net salvage" is gross salvage reduced by the cost of removal, dismantling, demolition, or similar operations. If a taxpayer customarily sells or otherwise disposes of property at a time when such property is still in good operating condition, the gross salvage value of such property is the amount expected to be realized upon such sale or disposition, and under certain circumstances, as where such property is customarily sold at a time when it is still relatively new, the gross salvage value may constitute a relatively large proportion of the unadjusted basis of such property.

(ii) Definition of salvage value. "Salvage value" for purposes of this section means gross or net salvage value less the amount, if any, by which reduced by application of section 167(f). Generally, as provided in section 167(f), a taxpayer may reduce the gross or net salvage value for an account by an amount which does not exceed 10 percent of the unadjusted basis of the personal property (as defined in section 167(f)(2)) in the account.

(2) Estimation of salvage value. (i) In general. For the first taxable year for which he elects to apply this section, the taxpayer must (in accordance with paragraph (e)(3)(iv)(c) of this section) establish salvage value for all qualified property to which the election applies. The taxpayer may (in accordance with subparagraph (1) of this paragraph) determine either gross or net salvage, but an election under this section does not constitute permission to change the manner of estimating salvage. Permission to change the manner of estimating salvage must be obtained by filing form 3115 with the Commissioner of Internal Revenue, Washington, D.C. 20224, within the time otherwise permitted for the taxable year or before September 6, 1973. Salvage value in succeeding taxable years of election will be determined by adjustments of such initial salvage value for the account, as retirements occur. This salvage value established by the taxpayer for the first taxable year of election will not be redetermined merely as a result of fluctuations in price levels or as a result of other circumstances occurring after the close of such taxable year. See paragraph (e)(3)(iv) of this section for requirements that the taxpayer specify in his election the aggregate amount of salvage value for an asset guideline class and that the taxpayer maintain records reasonably sufficient to identify the salvage value established for each depreciation account in the class.

(ii) Salvage as limitation on depreciation. In no case may an account be depreciated under this section below a reasonable salvage value, after taking into account any reduction in gross or net salvage value permitted by section 167(f). For example, if the salvage value of an account for 1971 is $75, the unadjusted basis of the account is $500, and the depreciation reserve is $425, no depreciation is allowable for 1971.

(iii) Special rule for first taxable year. If for a taxable year ending prior to January 1, 1971, the taxpayer had adopted Revenue Procedure 62-21 prior to January 12, 1971 (see paragraph (f)(2) of this section), no adjustment in the amount of depreciation allowable for any taxable year ending prior to January 1, 1971, shall be made solely by reason of establishing salvage value under this paragraph for any taxable year ending after December 31, 1970. The principles of this subdivision may be illustrated by the following example:

Example. Taxpayer A had adopted Revenue Procedure 62-21 prior to January 12, 1971, for taxable years prior to 1971. Taxpayer A had not taken into account any salvage value for account No. 1 which is one of four depreciation accounts A has in the class. The reserve ratio test has been met for all years prior to 1971 and in accordance with Revenue Procedure 62-21 no adjustments in depreciable lives or salvage values were made. At the end of A's taxable year 1970, the unadjusted basis of account No. 1 was $10,000 and the reserve for depreciation was $9,800. Pursuant to this paragraph. A establishes a salvage value of $400 for account No. 1 (determined at or as of the time of acquisition). This salvage value is determined to be correct. No depreciation is allowable for account No. 1 in 1971. No depreciation is disallowed for any taxable year prior to 1971, solely by reason of establishing salvage value under this paragraph.

(3) Limitation on adjustment of reasonable salvage value. The salvage value established by the taxpayer for a depreciation account will not be redetermined if it is reasonable. Since the determination of salvage value is a matter of estimation, minimal adjustments will not be made. The salvage value established by the taxpayer will be deemed to be reasonable unless there is sufficient basis for a determination of an amount of salvage value for the account which exceeds the salvage value established by the taxpayer for the account by an amount greater than 10 percent of the unadjusted basis of the account at the close of such taxable year. If the salvage value established by the taxpayer for the account is not within the 10-percent range or if the taxpayer follows the practice of understating his estimates of salvage to take advantage of this subdivision, and if there is a determination of an amount of salvage value for the account for the taxable year which exceeds the salvage value established by the taxpayer for the account for such taxable year, an adjustment will be made by increasing the salvage value established by the taxpayer for the account by an amount equal to the difference between the salvage value as determined and the salvage value established by the taxpayer for the account. For the purposes of this subdivision, a determination of salvage value shall include all determinations at all levels of audit and appellate proceedings, and as well as all final determinations within the meaning of section 1313(a)(1). This subparagraph shall apply to each such determination.

(4) Examples. The principles of this paragraph may be illustrated by the following examples in which it is assumed that the taxpayer has established salvage value in accordance with this paragraph and has not followed a practice of understating his estimates of salvage value:

Example (1). Taxpayer B elects to apply this section for 1971. Assets Y and Z are the only assets in a multiple asset account of 1967, the year in which the assets were acquired. The unadjusted basis of asset Y is $50,000 and the unadjusted basis of asset Z is $30,000. B estimated a gross salvage value of $55,000 at the time of acquisition. The property qualified under section 167(f)(2) and B reduced the amount of salvage taken into account by $8,000 (that is, 10 percent of $80,000, under sec. 167(f)). Thus, in accordance with this paragraph and paragraph (e)(3)(iv) *(c)* of this section, B establishes a salvage value of $47,000 for the account for 1971. Assume that there is not sufficient basis for determining a salvage value for the account greater $52,000 (that is $60,000 minus the $8,000 reduction under sec. 167(f)). Since the salvage value of $47,000 established by B for the account is within the 10 percent range, it is reasonable. Salvage for the account will not be redetermined.

Example (2). The facts are the same as in example (1) except that B estimated a gross salvage value of $50,000 and establishes a salvage value of $42,000 for the account (that is, $50,000 minus the $8,000 reduction under section 167(f)). There is sufficient basis for determining an amount of salvage value greater than $50,000 (that is, $58,000 minus the $8,000 reduction under section 167(f)). The salvage value of $42,000 established by B for the account can be redetermined without regard to the limitation in subparagraph (3) of this paragraph, since it is not within the 10 percent range. Upon audit of B's tax return for 1971 (a year in which the redetermination would affect the amount of depreciation allowable for the account), salvage value is determined to be $52,000 after taking into account the reduction under section 167(f). Salvage value for the account will be adjusted to $52,000.

Example (3). The facts are the same as in example (1) except that upon audit of B's tax return for 1971 the examining officer determines the salvage value to be $58,000 (that is, $66,000 minus the $8,000 reduction under section 167(f)), and proposes to adjust salvage value for the account to $58,000 which will result in disallowing an amount of depreciation for the taxable year. B does not agree with the finding of the examining officer. After receipt of a "30-day letter," B waives a district conference and initiates proceedings before the Appellate Division. In consideration of the case by the Appellate Division it is concluded that there is not sufficient basis for determining an amount of salvage value for the account in excess of $55,000 (that is, $63,000 minus the $8,000 reduction under section 167(f)). Since the salvage value of $47,000 established by B for the account is within the 10 percent range, it is reasonable. Salvage value for the account will not be redetermined.

Example (4). For 1971, taxpayer C elects to apply this section to factory building X which is in an item account of 1965, the year in which the building was acquired. The unadjusted basis of factory building X is $90,000. C estimated a gross salvage value for the account of $10,000. The property did not qualify under section 167(f)(2). Thus, C establishes a salvage value of $10,000 for the account for 1971. Assume that there is not sufficient basis for determining a salvage value for the account greater than $14,000. Since the salvage value of $10,000 established by C for the account is within the 10-percent range, it is reasonable. Salvage value for the account will not be redetermined.

(d) Accounting for qualified property. *(1) In general.* Qualified property for which the taxpayer elects to apply this section may be accounted for in any number of item or multiple asset accounts.

(2) Retirements of qualified property. (i) In general. The provisions of this subparagraph and § 1.167(a)-8 apply to retirements of qualified property to which the taxpayer elects to apply this section for the taxable year. See subdivision (iii) of this subparagraph for special rule for normal retirements.

(ii) Adjusted basis of assets retired. In the case of a taxpayer who depreciates qualified property in a multiple-asset account conforming to the asset guideline class at a rate based on the class life in accordance with paragraph (a)(5)(ii)(a) of this section, § 1.167(a)-8(c) (relating to basis of assets retired) shall be applied by assuming that the class life is the average expected useful life of the assets in the account. See § 1.167(a)-8, generally, for the basis of assets retired.

(iii) Definition of normal retirements. Notwithstanding § 1.167(a)-8(b), the determination whether a retirement of qualified property is normal or abnormal shall be made in light of all the facts and circumstances, primarily with reference to the expected period of use of the asset in the taxpayer's business without regard to paragraph (a)(5)(ii) of this section. A retirement is not abnormal unless the taxpayer can show that the withdrawal of the asset was not due to a cause which would customarily be contemplated (in light of the taxpayer's practice and experience) in setting a depreciation rate for the assets without regard to paragraph (a)(5)(ii) of this section. Thus, for example, a retirement is normal if made within the range of years which would customarily be taken into account in setting such depreciation rate and if the asset has reached a condition at which, in the normal course of events, the taxpayer customarily retires similar assets from use in his business. A retirement may be abnormal if the asset is withdrawn at an earlier time or under other circumstances, as, for example, when the asset has been damaged by casualty or has lost its usefulness suddenly as the result of extraordinary obsolescence.

(3) Special rules. (i) In general. The provisions of this subparagraph shall apply to qualified property in a taxable year for which an election to apply this section is made.

(ii) Repairs. For the purpose of sections 162 and 263 and the regulations thereunder, whether an expenditure prolongs the life of an asset shall be determined by reference to the expected period of use of the asset in the taxpayer's business without regard to paragraph (a)(5)(ii) of this section.

(iii) Sale and lease. For the purpose of comparison with the term of a lease of such property, the remaining life of qualified property shall be determined by reference to the expected period of use of the asset in the taxpayer's business without regard to paragraph (a)(5)(ii) of this section.

(4) Expected period of use. For the purposes of subparagraphs (2) and (3) of this paragraph, the determination of the expected period of use of an asset shall be made in light of all the facts and circumstances. The expected period of use of a particular asset will not necessarily coincide with the class life used for depreciation (or with the individual asset life for depreciation under the alternative method in paragraph (a)(5)(ii)(b) of this section for applying the class life). Thus, for example, if the question is whether an asset has been leased for a period less than, equal to or greater than its remaining life, the determination shall be based on the remaining expected period of use of the individual asset without regard to the fact that the asset is depreciated at a rate based on the class life in accordance with paragraph (a)(5)(ii)(a) of this section.

(5) Leased property. In the case of a lessor of qualified property, unless there is an asset guideline class in effect for such lessors, the asset guideline class for such property shall be determined by reference to the activity in which such property is primarily used by the lessee. See paragraph (b)(3) of this section for general rule for classification of qualified property according to primary use. However, in the

case of an asset guideline class based upon the type of property (such as trucks or railroad cars), as distinguished from the activity in which used, the property shall be classified without regard to the activity of the lessee.

(e) Election under this section. *(1) Consent to change in method of accounting.* An election to apply this section for a taxable year ending after December 31, 1970, is a method of accounting but the consent of the Commissioner will be deemed granted to make an annual election.

(2) Election for taxable years ending after December 31, 1976. For taxable years ending after December 31, 1976, the election to apply this section for a taxable year shall be made by attaching to the income tax return a statement that an election under this section is being made. If the taxpayer does not file a timely return (taking into account extensions of time for filing) for the taxable year, the election shall be made at the time the taxpayer files his first return for the taxable year. The election may be made with an amended return only if such amended return is filed no later than the time prescribed by law (including extensions thereof) for filing the return for the taxable year. A taxpayer who makes an election under this subparagraph must maintain books and records reflecting the information described in paragraph (e)(3)(ii) and (iii) of this section.

(3) Election for taxable years ending on or before December 31, 1976. (i) For taxable years ending on or before December 31, 1976, the election to apply this section for a taxable year may be made by filing Form 5006 with the income tax return for the taxable year. If the taxpayer does not file a timely return (taking into account extensions of time for filing) for the taxable year, the election shall be filed at the time the taxpayer files his first return for the taxable year. The election may be made with an amended return only if such amended return is filed no later that the later of (a) the time prescribed by law (including extensions thereof) for filing the return for the taxable year, or (b) November 5, 1973.

(ii) The election to apply this section for a taxable year ending on or before December 31, 1976, will be deemed to be made if the tax return (filed within the periods referred to in paragraph (e)(3)(i) of this section) contains information sufficient to establish the following:

(a) Each asset guideline class for which the election is intended to apply;

(b) The class life for each such asset guideline class and whether the class life is determined under paragraph (b)(1) or (2) of this section;

(c) For each asset guideline class, as of the end of the taxable year of election, (1) the total unadjusted basis of all qualified property, (2) the aggregate of the reserves for depreciation of accounts in the asset guideline class, and (3) the aggregate of the salvage value established for all accounts in the asset guideline class; and

(d) Whether the taxpayer is an electric or gas utility using a composite asset guideline class basis in accordance with paragraph (b)(3)(iii) of this section.

If an election is deemed to be made under this subdivision (ii), the taxpayer will be deemed to have consented to apply all the provisions of this section.

(iii) A taxpayer to whom the election applies shall maintain books and records for each asset guideline class reasonably sufficient to identify the unadjusted basis, reserve for depreciation and salvage value established for each depreciation account in such asset guidelines class.

(f) Depreciation for taxable years ending before January 1, 1971. *(1) Adoption of Revenue Procedure 62-21.* (i) In general. Except as provided in subdivision (ii) of this subparagraph, a taxpayer may elect to be examined under the provisions of Revenue Procedure 62-21 for a taxable year ending before January 1, 1971, only in accordance with the rules of this paragraph. The election must specify:

(a) That the taxpayer makes such election and consents to, and agrees to apply, all the provisions of this paragraph;

(b) Each guideline class and taxable year for which the taxpayer elects to be examined under Revenue Procedure 62-21;

(c) The class life claimed for each such guideline class;

(d) The class life and the total amount of the depreciation for the guideline class claimed on the last income tax return for such taxable year filed prior to January 12, 1971 (or in case no income tax return was filed prior to January 12, 1971, on the first income tax return filed for such taxable year);

(e) The class life claimed and the total amount of depreciation for the guideline class under the election to apply Revenue Procedure 62-21, in accordance with this paragraph, for the taxable year; and

(f) If the class life or total amount of depreciation for the guideline class is different in (d) and (e) of this subdivision, a reasonable description of the computation of the class life in (e) of this subdivision, the amount of difference in tax liability resulting therefrom, and the amount of any refund or reduction in any deficiency in tax. The election shall be made in an amended tax return or claim for refund (or by a supplement to the tax return or claim) for the taxable year, and if the class life or total amount of depreciation for the guideline class is different in accordance with (f) of this subdivision, such difference shall be reflected in the amended tax return or claim for refund. Forms may be provided for making the election and submission of the information. In the case of an election made after issuance of such forms and more than 30 days after publication of notice thereof in the Internal Revenue Bulletin, the election may be made and the information submitted only in accordance with such forms. An election will not otherwise be invalid under this paragraph so long as there is substantial compliance, in good faith, with the requirements of this paragraph.

(ii) Special rule. The provisions of this subparagraph shall not apply to a guideline class in any taxable year for which the taxpayer has prior to January 12, 1971, adopted Revenue Procedure 62-21 for such class. See subparagraph (2) of this paragraph for determination of adoption of Revenue Procedure 62-21 prior to January 12, 1971.

(iii) Justification of class life claimed and limitations on refunds. If the taxpayer elects for a taxable year to be examined under the provisions of Revenue Procedure 62-21 in accordance with subdivision (i) of this subparagraph, any of the provisions of Revenue Procedure 62-21 may be applied to justify a class life claimed on the income tax return filed for such year or to offset an increase in tax liability for such year. Unless it meets the reserve ratio test, no class life will be accepted on audit which (after all other adjustments in tax liability for such year) results in a reduction (or further reduction) in the amount of tax liability shown on the income tax return (specified in subdivision (i)(d) of this subparagraph) for such taxable year, or results in an amount of loss carryback or carryover to any taxable year, but if it is justified under Revenue Procedure 62-21 and meets the reserve ratio test, a class life will be accepted on audit without regard to the foregoing limitations and, for example, may produce a refund or credit against tax. For example, if a class life of 9 years is otherwise justified under Revenue Procedure 62-21 for 1969, but years, a class life of 9 years (or any class life justified under Revenue Procedure 62-21) will be accepted on audit under Revenue Procedure 62-21 pursuant to an election in accordance with this paragraph provided it does not result in the reduction or further reduction in tax liability or in an amount of loss carryback or carryover as described in the preceding sentence. On the other hand, for example, if a class life of 10 years is justified under Revenue Procedure 62-21 for 1969 and the taxpayer meets the reserve ratio test for 1969 using a test life of 10 years, a class life of 10 years will be accepted on audit under Revenue Procedure 62-21 pursuant to an election in accordance with this paragraph even though it results in a reduction or further reduction in tax liability or in an amount of loss carryback or carryover as described above and produces a refund of tax. For purposes of this section, the term "audit" includes examination of claims for refund or credit against tax.

(iv) Definitions. For purposes of this paragraph, the determination whether the reserve ratio test is met shall be made in accordance with that portion of paragraph (b)(2) of this section which is by express reference therein made applicable to this paragraph. In addition, the guideline form of the reserve ratio test, as described in Revenue Procedure 65-13, may be applied. . . . For purposes of this paragraph, references to Revenue Procedure 62-21 include all modifications, amendments, and supplements thereto as of January 11, 1971. The terms "class life" and "guideline class" have the same meaning as in Revenue Procedure 62-21.

(2) Determination whether Revenue Procedure 62-21 adopted prior to January 12, 1971. (i) In general. For the purposes of this paragraph, a taxpayer will be treated as having adopted prior to January 12, 1971, Revenue Procedure 62-21 for a guideline class for a taxable year ending before January 1, 1971, only if—

(a) For the guideline class and taxable year, the taxpayer adopted Revenue Procedure 62-21 by expressly so indicating on the income tax return filed for such taxable year prior to January 12, 1971;

(b) For the guideline class and taxable year, the taxpayer adopted Revenue Procedure 62-21 prior to January 12, 1971, by expressly so indicating in a proceeding before the Internal Revenue Service (such as upon examination of the income tax return for such taxable year) and there is reasonable evidence to that effect; or

(c) There is other reasonable evidence that prior to January 12, 1971, the taxpayer adopted Revenue Procedure 62-21 for the guideline class and taxable year.

If not treated under (b) or (c) of this subdivision as having done so for the last taxable year ending before January 1, 1971, and if the taxpayer files his first income tax return for such taxable year after January 11, 1971, the taxpayer will be treated as having adopted Revenue Procedure 62-21 prior to January 12, 1971, for a guideline class for such taxable year if he expressly so indicated on that return, or is treated under this subparagraph as having adopted Revenue Procedure 62-21 prior to January 12, 1971, for that guideline class for the immediately preceding taxable year.

(ii) Examples. The principles of this subparagraph may be illustrated by the following examples:

Example (1). Taxpayer A, an individual who uses the calendar year as his taxable year, has property in Group Three, Class 16(a), of Revenue Procedure 62-21. On A's income tax return for 1968, filed prior to January 12, 1971, he adopted Revenue Procedure 62-21 for the guideline class by so indicating under "Summary of Depreciation" in the appropriate schedule of Form 1040 for 1968. Under subdivision (i)(a) of this subparagraph, A is treated as having adopted Revenue Procedure 62-21 for the guideline class for 1968 prior to January 12, 1971.

Example (2). Taxpayer B, an individual who uses the calendar year as his taxable year, has property in Group Two, Class 5, of Revenue Procedure 62-21. B filed timely income tax returns for 1966 through 1968 but did not adopt Revenue Procedures 62-21 on any of such returns. In 1969 upon audit of B's taxable years 1966 through 1968, B exercised his option to be examined under the provisions of Revenue Procedure 62-21. The Revenue Agent's report shows that B was examined under Revenue Procedure 62-21 for taxable years 1966 through 1968. B will be treated under subdivision (ii)(b) of this subparagraph as having adopted Revenue Procedure 62-21 for such years prior to January 12, 1971.

Example (3). The facts are the same as in example (2) except that B did not upon examination by the Revenue Agent in 1969 exercise his option to be examined under Revenue Procedure 62-21. B has six accounts in the guideline class, Nos. 1 through 6. The Revenue Agent proposed to lengthen the depreciable lives on accounts Nos. 2 and 3 from 8 years to 12 years. In proceedings before the Appellate Division in 1970, B exercised his option to be examined under the provisions of Revenue Procedure 62-21. This is shown by correspondence between B and the Appellate Conferee as well as by other documents in the case before the Appellate Division. The case was settled on that basis before the Appellate Division without adjustment of the depreciable lives for B's accounts Nos. 2 and 3. B will be treated under subdivision (ii)(b) of this subparagraph as having adopted Revenue Procedure 62-21 for taxable years 1966 through 1968 prior to January 12, 1971.

Example (4). Corporation X uses the calendar year as its taxable year and has assets in Group Two, Class 5, of Revenue Procedure 62-21. Beginning in 1964, corporation X used the guideline life of 10 years as the depreciable life for all assets in the guideline class. In 1967, corporation X's taxable years 1964 through 1966 were examined and corporation X exercised its option to be examined under the provisions of Revenue Procedure 62-21. Corporation X did not adopt Revenue Procedure 62-21 on any of its income tax returns, for the years 1964 through 1970. Corporation X has not been examined since 1967, but has continued to use the guideline life of 10 years for all property in the guideline class including additions since 1966. Corporation X will be treated under subdivision (ii)(c) and (d) of this subparagraph as having adopted Revenue Procedure 62-21 prior to January 12, 1971, for taxable years 1964 through 1970.

Example (5). Corporation Y uses the calendar year as its taxable year and has asset in Group Two, Class 5, of Revenue Procedure 62-21. Since 1964, corporation Y has used various depreciable lives, based on the facts and circumstances, for different accounts in the guideline class. Corporation Y was examined in 1968 for taxable years 1965 through 1967. Corporation Y was also examined in 1970 for taxable years 1968 and 1969. Corporation Y did not exercise its option to be examined under the provisions of Revenue Procedure 62-21. Corporation Y has not adopted Revenue Procedure 62-21 on any income tax return. For taxable years 1964 through 1970, corporation Y's class life (within the meaning of section 4, Part II, of Revenue Procedure 62-21) was between 12 and 14 years. In August of 1971, corporation Y filed amended income tax returns for 1968 and 1969, and an income tax return for 1970, using a depreciable life of 10 years (equal to the guideline life) for all assets in the guideline class. Corporation Y will not be treated as having adopted Revenue Procedure 62-21 prior to January 12, 1971.

Example (6). Corporation Z uses the calendar year as its taxable year and has assets in group 2, class 5, of Revenue Procedure 62-21. Corporation Z adopted Revenue Procedure 62-21 for this guideline class by expressly so indicating on its tax return for 1966, which was filed before January 12, 1971. Corporation Z computed its allowable depreciation for 1966 as if it adopted Revenue Procedure 62-21 for this guideline class for its taxable years 1962 through 1965, although it had earlier filed its tax returns for those years without regard to Revenue Procedure 62-21. The depreciation thus claimed in 1966 was less than what would have been allowable if corporation Z first adopted Revenue Procedure 62-21 in 1966. This was the result of certain accounts becoming fully depreciated through use of Revenue Procedure 62-21 in computing depreciation for 1962 through 1965. In addition, in deferred tax accounting procedures employed before January 12, 1971, for financial reporting purposes, corporation Z calculated its tax deferrals on the basis that it had adopted Revenue Procedure 62-21 for the years 1962 through 1965. Corporation Z will be treated under subdivision (i)(c) of this subparagraph as having adopted Revenue Procedure 62-21 for taxable years 1962 through 1965 prior to January 12, 1971.

T.D. 7278, 6/6/73, amend T.D. 7315, 6/6/74, T.D. 7517, 11/11/77, T.D. 7593, 1/25/79.

Proposed § 1.167(a)-13 Certain elections for intangible property. [*For Preamble, see ¶ 151,563*]

For rules applying the elections under sections 13261(g)(2) and (3) of the Revenue Reconciliation Act of 1993 to intangible property described under section 167(f), see § 1.197-1.

§ 1.167(a)-13T Certain elections for intangible property (temporary).

• ***Caution:*** Under Code Sec. 7805, temporary regulations expire within three years of the date of issuance. This temporary regulation was issued on 3/10/94.

For rules applying the elections under section 13261(g)(2) and (3) of the Omnibus Budget Reconciliation Act of 1993 to intangible property described in section 167(f), see § 1.197-1T.

T.D. 8528, 3/10/94.

§ 1.167(a)-14 Treatment of certain intangible property excluded from section 197.

Caution: The Treasury has not yet amended Reg § 1.167(a)-14 to reflect changes made by P.L. 110-343.

(a) Overview. This section provides rules for the amortization of certain intangibles that are excluded from section 197 (relating to the amortization of goodwill and certain other intangibles). These excluded intangibles are specifically described in § 1.197-2(c) (4), (6), (7), (11), and (13) and include certain computer software and certain other separately acquired rights, such as rights to receive tangible property or services, patents and copyrights, certain mortgage servicing rights, and rights of fixed duration or amount. Intangibles for which an amortization amount is determined under section 167(f) and intangibles otherwise excluded from section 197 are amortizable only if they qualify as property subject to the allowance for depreciation under section 167(a).

(b) Computer software. *(1) In general.* The amount of the deduction for computer software described in section 167(f)(1) and § 1.197-2(c)(4) is determined by amortizing the cost or other basis of the computer software using the straight line method described in § 1.167(b)-1 (except that its salvage value is treated as zero) and an amortization period of 36 months beginning on the first day of the month that the computer software is placed in service. Before determining the amortization deduction allowable under this paragraph (b), the cost or other basis of computer software that is section 179 property, as defined in section 179(d)(1)(A)(ii), must be reduced for any portion of the basis the taxpayer properly elects to treat as an expense under section 179. In addition, the cost or other basis of computer software that is qualified property under section 168(k)(2) or § 1.168(k)-1, 50-percent bonus depreciation property under section 168(k)(4) or § 1.168(k)-1, or qualified New York Liberty Zone property under section 1400L(b) or § 1.1400L(b)-1, must be reduced by the amount of the additional first year depreciation deduction allowed or allowable, whichever is greater, under section 168(k) or section 1400L(b) for the computer software. If costs for developing computer software that the taxpayer properly elects to defer under section 174(b) result in the development of property subject to the allowance for depreciation under section 167, the rules of this paragraph (b) will apply to the unrecovered costs. In addition, this paragraph (b) applies to the cost of separately acquired computer software if the cost to acquire the software is separately stated and the cost is required to be capitalized under section 263(a).

(2) Exceptions. Paragraph (b)(1) of this section does not apply to the cost of computer software properly and consistently taken into account under § 1.162-11. The cost of acquiring an interest in computer software that is included, without being separately stated, in the cost of the hardware or other tangible property is treated as part of the cost of the hardware or other tangible property that is capitalized and depreciated under other applicable sections of the Internal Revenue Code.

(3) Additional rules. Rules similar to those in § 1.197-2 (f)(1)(iii), (f)(1)(iv), and (f)(2) (relating to the computation of amortization deductions and the treatment of contingent amounts) apply for purposes of this paragraph (b).

(c) Certain interests or rights not acquired as part of a purchase of a trade or business. *(1) Certain rights to receive tangible property or services.* The amount of the deduction for a right (other than a right acquired as part of a purchase of a trade or business) to receive tangible property or services under a contract or from a governmental unit (as specified in section 167(f)(2) and § 1.197-2(c)(6)) is determined as follows:

(i) Amortization of fixed amounts. The basis of a right to receive a fixed amount of tangible property or services is amortized for each taxable year by multiplying the basis of the right by a fraction, the numerator of which is the amount of tangible property or services received during the taxable year and the denominator of which is the total amount of tangible property or services received or to be received under the terms of the contract or governmental grant. For example, if a taxpayer acquires a favorable contract right to receive a fixed amount of raw materials during an unspecified period, the taxpayer must amortize the cost of acquiring the contract right by multiplying the total cost by a fraction, the numerator of which is the amount of raw materials received under the contract during the taxable year and the denominator of which is the total amount of raw materials received or to be received under the contract.

(ii) Amortization of unspecified amount over fixed period. The cost or other basis of a right to receive an unspecified amount of tangible property or services over a fixed period is amortized ratably over the period of the right. (See paragraph (c)(3) of this section regarding renewals).

(iii) Amortization in other cases. [Reserved]

(2) Rights of fixed duration or amount. The amount of the deduction for a right (other than a right acquired as part of a purchase of a trade or business) of fixed duration or amount received under a contract or granted by a governmental unit (specified in section 167(f)(2) and § 1.197-2(c)(13)) and not covered by paragraph (c)(1) of this section is determined as follows:

(i) Rights to a fixed amount. The basis of a right to a fixed amount is amortized for each taxable year by multiplying the basis by a fraction, the numerator of which is the amount received during the taxable year and the denominator of which is the total amount received or to be received under the terms of the contract or governmental grant.

(ii) Rights to an unspecified amount over fixed duration of less than 15 years. The basis of a right to an unspecified amount over a fixed duration of less than 15 years is amortized ratably over the period of the right.

(3) Application of renewals. (i) For purposes of paragraphs (c) (1) and (2) of this section, the duration of a right under a contract (or granted by a governmental unit) includes any renewal period if, based on all of the facts and circumstances in existence at any time during the taxable year in which the right is acquired, the facts clearly indicate a reasonable expectancy of renewal.

(ii) The mere fact that a taxpayer will have the opportunity to renew a contract right or other right on the same terms as are available to others, in a competitive auction or similar process that is designed to reflect fair market value and in which the taxpayer is not contractually advantaged, will generally not be taken into account in determining the duration of such right provided that the bidding produces a fair market value price comparable to the price that would be obtained if the rights were purchased immediately after renewal from a person (other than the person granting the renewal) in an arm's-length transaction.

(iii) The cost of a renewal not included in the terms of the contract or governmental grant is treated as the acquisition of a separate intangible asset.

(4) Patents and copyrights. If the purchase price of a interest (other than an interest acquired as part of a purchase of a trade or business) in a patent or copyright described in section 167(f)(2) and § 1.197-2(c)(7) is payable on at least an annual basis as either a fixed amount per use or a fixed percentage of the revenue derived from the use of the patent or copyright, the depreciation deduction for a taxable year is equal to the amount of the purchase price paid or incurred during the year. Otherwise, the basis of such patent or copyright (or an interest therein) is depreciated either ratably over its remaining useful life or under section 167(g) (income forecast method). If a patent or copyright becomes valueless in any year before its legal expiration, the adjusted basis may be deducted in that year.

(5) Additional rules. The period of amortization under paragraphs (c) (1) through (4) of this section begins when the intangible is placed in service, and rules similar to those in § 1.197-2(f)(2) apply for purposes of this paragraph (c).

(d) Mortgage servicing rights. *(1) In general.* The amount of the deduction for mortgage servicing rights described in section 167(f)(3) and § 1.197-2(c)(11) is determined by using the straight line method described in § 1.167(b)-1 (except that the salvage value is treated as zero) and an amortization period of 108 months beginning on the first day of the month that the rights are placed in service. Mortgage servicing rights are not depreciable to the extent the rights are stripped coupons under section 1286.

(2) Treatment of rights acquired as a pool. (i) In general. Except as provided in paragraph (d)(2)(ii) of this section, all mortgage servicing rights acquired in the same transaction or in a series of related transactions are treated as a single asset (the pool) for purposes of determining the depreciation deduction under this paragragh (d) and any gain or loss from the sale, exchange, or other disposition of the rights. Thus, if some (but not all) of the rights in a pool become worthless as a result of prepayments, no loss is recognized by reason of the prepayment and the adjusted basis of the pool is not affected by the unrecognized loss. Similarly, any amount realized from the sale or exchange of some (but not all) of the mortgage servicing rights is included in income and the adjusted basis of the pool is not affected by the realization.

(ii) Multiple accounts. If the taxpayer establishes multiple accounts within a pool at the time of its acquisition, gain or loss is recognized on the sale or exchange of all mortgage servicing rights within any such account.

(3) Additional rules. Rules similar to those in § 1.197-2(f)(1)(iii), (f)(1)(iv), and (f)(2) (relating to the computation of amortization deductions and the treatment of contingent amounts) apply for purposes of this paragraph (d).

(e) Effective dates. *(1) In general.* This section applies to property acquired after January 25, 2000, except that § 1.167(a)-14(c)(2) (depreciation of the cost of certain separately acquired rights) and so much of § 1.167(a)-14(c)(3) as relates to § 1.167(a)-14(c)(2) apply to property acquired after August 10, 1993 (or July 25, 1991, if a valid retroactive election has been made under § 1.197-1T).

(2) Change in method of accounting. See § 1.197-2(l)(4) for rules relating to changes in method of accounting for property to which § 1.167(a)-14 applies. However, see § 1.168(k)-1(g)(4) or 1.1400L(b)-1(g)(4) for rules relating to changes in method of accounting for computer software to which the third sentence in § 1.167(a)-14(b)(1) applies.

(3) Qualified property, 50-percent bonus depreciation property, qualified New York Liberty Zone property, or section 179 property. This section also applies to computer software that is qualified property under section 168(k)(2) or qualified New York Liberty Zone property under section 1400L(b) acquired by a taxpayer after September 10, 2001, and to computer software that is 50-percent bonus depreciation property under section 168(k)(4) acquired by a taxpayer after May 5, 2003. This section also applies to computer software that is section 179 property placed in service by a taxpayer in a taxable year beginning after 2002 and before 2010.

T.D. 8865, 1/20/2000, amend T.D. 9091, 9/5/2003, T.D. 9283, 8/28/2006.

§ 1.167(b)-0 Methods of computing depreciation.

(a) In general. Any reasonable and consistently applied method of computing depreciation may be used or continued in use under section 167. Regardless of the method used in computing depreciation, deductions for depreciation shall not exceed such amounts as may be necessary to recover the unrecovered cost or other basis less salvage during the remaining useful life of the property. The reasonableness of any claim for depreciation shall be determined upon the basis of conditions known to exist at the end of the period for which the return is made. It is the responsibility of the taxpayer to establish the reasonableness of the deduction for depreciation claimed. Generally, depreciation deductions so claimed will be changed only where there is a clear and convincing basis for a change.

(b) Certain methods. Methods previously found adequate to produce a reasonable allowance under the Internal Revenue Code of 1939 or prior revenue laws will, if used consistently by the taxpayer, continue to be acceptable under section 167(a). Examples of such methods which continue to be acceptable are the straight line method, the declining balance method with the rate limited to 150 percent of the applicable straight line rate, and under appropriate circumstances, the unit of production method. The methods described in section 167(b) and §§ 1.167(b)-1, 1.167(b)-2, 1.167(b)-3, and 1.167(b)-4 shall be deemed to produce a reasonable allowance for depreciation except as limited under section 167(c) and § 1.167(c)-1. See also § 1.167(e)-1 for rules relating to change in method of computing depreciation.

(c) Application of methods. In the case of item accounts, any method which results in a reasonable allowance for depreciation may be selected for each item of property, but such method must thereafter be applied consistently to that particular item. In the case of group, classified, or composite accounts, any method may be selected for each account. Such method must be applied to that particular account consistently thereafter but need not necessarily be applied to acquisitions of similar property in the same or subsequent years, provided such acquisitions are set up in separate accounts. See however, § 1.167(e)-1 and section 446 and the regulations thereunder, for rules relating to changes in the method of computing depreciation, and § 1.167(c)-1 for restriction on the use of certain methods. See also § 1.167(a)-7 for definition of account.

T.D. 6182, 6/11/56.

§ 1.167(b)-1 Straight line method.

(a) Application of method. Under the straight line method the cost or other basis of the property less its estimated salvage value is deductible in equal annual amounts over the period of the estimated useful life of the property. The allowance for depreciation for the taxable year is determined by dividing the adjusted basis of the property at the beginning of the taxable year, less salvage value, by the remaining useful life of the property at such time. For convenience, the allowance so determined may be reduced to a percentage or fraction. The straight line method may be used in determining a reasonable allowance for depreciation for any property which is subject to depreciation under section 167 and it shall be used in all cases where the taxpayer has not adopted a different acceptable method with respect to such property.

(b) Illustrations. The straight line method is illustrated by the following examples:

Example (1). Under the straight line method items may be depreciated separately:

Year	Item	Cost or other basis less salvage	Useful life	Depreciation allowable		
				1954	1955	1956
1954	Asset A......	$ 1,600	4	$200[1]	$400	$400
	Asset B......	12,000	40	150[1]	300	300

[1] In this example it is assumed that the assets were placed in service on July 1, 1954.

Example (2). In group, classified, or composite accounting, a number of assets with the same or different useful lives may be combined into one account, and a single rate of depreciation, i.e., the group, classified, or composite rate used for the entire account. In the case of group accounts, i.e., accounts containing assets which are similar in kind and which have approximately the same estimated useful lives, the group rate is determined from the average of the useful lives of the assets. In the case of classified or composite accounts, the classified or composite rate is generally computed by determining the amount of one year's depreciation for each item or each group of similar items, and by dividing the total depreciation thus obtained by the total cost or other basis of the assets. The average rate so obtained is to be used as long as subsequent additions, retirements, or replacements do not substantially alter the relative proportions of different types of assets in the account. An example of the computation of a classified or composite rate follows:

Cost or other basis	Estimated useful life	Annual depreciation
$10,000	5	$2,000
10,000	15	667
20,000		2,667

Average rate is 13.33 percent ($2,667 ÷ $20,000) unadjusted for salvage. Assuming the estimated salvage value is 10 percent of the cost or other basis, the rate adjusted for salvage will be 13.33 percent minus 10 percent of 13.33 percent (13.33% – 1.33%), or 12 percent.

Example (3). The use of the straight line method for group, classified, or composite accounts is illustrated by the following example: A taxpayer filing his returns on a calendar year basis maintains an asset account for which a group rate of 20 percent has been determined, before adjustment for salvage. Estimated salvage is determined to be 6⅔ percent, resulting in an adjusted rate of 18.67 percent. During the years illustrated, the initial investment, additions, retirements, and salvage recoveries, which were determined not to change the composition of the group sufficiently to require a change in rate, were assumed to have been made as follows:

1954—Initial investment of $12,000.

1957—Retirement $2,000, salvage realized $200.

1958—Retirement $2,000, salvage realized $200.

1959—Retirement $4,000, salvage realized $400.

1959—Additions $10,000.

1960—Retirement $2,000, no salvage realized.

1961—Retirement $2,000, no salvage realized.

Depreciable Asset Account and Depreciation Computation on Average Balances

Year	Asset balance Jan. 1	Current additions	Current retirements	Asset balance Dec. 31	Average balance	Rate (percent)	Allowable depreciation
1954	—	$12,000	—	$12,000	$ 6,000	18.67	$1,120
1955	$12,000	—	—	12,000	12,000	18.67	2,240
1956	12,000	—	—	12,000	12,000	18.67	2,240
1957	12,000	—	$2,000	10,000	11,000	18.67	2,054
1958	10,000	—	2,000	8,000	9,000	18.67	1,680
1959	8,000	10,000	4,000	14,000	11,000	18.67	2,054
1960	14,000	—	2,000	12,000	13,000	18.67	2,427
1961	12,000	—	2,000	10,000	11,000	18.67	2,054

Corresponding Depreciation Reserve Account

Year	Depreciation reserve Jan. 1	Depreciation allowable	Current retirements	Salvage realized	Depreciation reserve Dec. 31
1954	—	$1,120	—	—	$1,120
1955	$1,120	2,240	—	—	3,360
1956	3,360	2,240	—	—	5,600
1957	5,600	2,054	$2,000	$200	5,854
1958	5,854	1,680	2,000	200	5,734
1959	5,734	2,054	4,000	400	4,188
1960	4,188	2,427	2,000	—	4,615
1961	4,615	2,054	2,000	—	4,669

T.D. 6182, 6/11/56.

§ 1.167(b)-2 Declining balance method.

(a) Application of method. Under the declining balance method a uniform rate is applied each year to the unrecovered cost or other basis of the property. The unrecovered cost or other basis is the basis provided by section 167(g), adjusted for depreciation previously allowed or allowable, and for all other adjustments provided by section 1016 and other applicable provisions of law. The declining balance rate may be determined without resort to formula. Such rate determined under section 167(b)(2) shall not exceed twice the appropriate straight line rate computed without adjustment for salvage. While salvage is not taken into account in determining the annual allowances under this method, in no event shall an asset (or an account) be depreciated below a reasonable salvage value. However, see section 167(f) and § 1.167(f)-1 for rules which permit a reduction in the amount of salvage value to be taken into account for certain personal property acquired after October 16, 1962. Also, see section 167(c) and § 1.167(c)-1 for restrictions on the use of the declining balance method.

(b) Illustrations. The declining balance method is illustrated by the following examples:

Example (1). A new asset having an estimated useful life of 20 years was purchased on January 1, 1954, for $1,000. The normal straight line rate (without adjustment for salvage) is 5 percent, and the declining balance rate at twice the normal straight line rate is 10 percent. The annual depreciation allowances for 1954, 1955, and 1956 are as follows:

Year	Basis	Declining balance rate (percent)	Depreciation allowance
1954	$1,000	10%	$100
1955	900	10%	90
1956	810	10%	81

Example (2). A taxpayer filing his returns on a calendar year basis maintains a group account to which a 5 year life and a 40 percent declining balance rate are applicable. Original investment, additions, retirements, and salvage recoveries are the same as those set forth in example (3) of paragraph (b) of § 1.167(b)-1. Although salvage value is not taken into consideration in computing a declining balance rate, it must be recognized and accounted for when assets are retired.

Depreciable Asset Account and Depreciation Computation Using Average Asset and Reserve Balances

Year	Asset balance Jan. 1	Current additions	Current retirements	Asset balance Dec. 31	Average balance	Average reserve before depreciation	Net depreciable balance	Rate	Allowable depreciation
1954	—	$12,000	—	$12,000	$ 6,000	—	$6,000	40%	$2,400
1955	$12,000	—	—	12,000	12,000	$2,400	9,600	40%	3,840
1956	12,000	—	—	12,000	12,000	6,240	5,760	40%	2,304
1957	12,000	—	$2,000	10,000	11,000	7,644	3,356	40%	1,342
1958	10,000	—	2,000	8,000	9,000	7,186	1,814	40%	726
1959	8,000	10,000	4,000	14,000	11,000	5,212	5,788	40%	2,315
1960	14,000	—	2,000	12,000	13,000	4,727	8,273	40%	3,309

1961	12,000	—	2,000	10,000	11,000	6,036	4,964	40%	1,986

Depreciation Reserve

Year	Jan. 1 Reserve	Current retirements	Salvage realized	Reserve Dec. 31, before depreciation	Average reserve before depreciation	Allowable depreciation	Reserve Dec. 31, after depreciation
1954	—	—	—	—	—	$2,400	$2,400
1955	$2,400	—	—	$2,400	$2,400	3,840	6,240
1956	6,240	—	—	6,240	6,240	2,304	8,544
1957	8,544	$2,000	$200	6,744	7,644	1,342	8,086
1958	8,086	2,000	200	6,286	7,186	726	7,012
1959	7,012	4,000	400	3,412	5,212	2,315	5,727
1960	5,727	2,000	—	3,727	4,727	3,309	7,036
1961	7,036	2,000	—	5,036	6,036	1,986	7,022

Where separate depreciation accounts are maintained by year of acquisition and there is an unrecovered balance at the time of the last retirement, such unrecovered balance may be deducted as part of the depreciation allowance for the year of such retirement. Thus, if the taxpayer had kept separate depreciation accounts by year of acquisition and all the retirements shown in the example above were from 1954 acquisitions, depreciation would be computed on the 1954 and 1959 acquisitions as follows:

1954 Acquisitions

Year	Asset balance Jan. 1	Acquisitions	Current retirements	Asset balance Dec. 31	Average balance	Average reserve before depreciation	Net depreciable balance	Rate	Allowable depreciation
1954	—	$12,000	—	$12,000	$ 6,000	—	$6,000	40%	$2,400
1955	$12,000	—	—	12,000	12,000	$2,400	9,600	40%	3,840
1956	12,000	—	—	12,000	12,000	6,240	5,760	40%	2,304
1957	12,000	—	$2,000	10,000	11,000	7,644	3,356	40%	1,342
1958	10,000	—	2,000	8,000	9,000	7,186	1,814	40%	726
1959	8,000	—	4,000	4,000	6,000	5,212	788	40%	315
1960	4,000	—	2,000	2,000	3,000	2,727	273	40%	109
1961	2,000	—	2,000	—	1,000	836	164	—	164[1]

[1] Balance allowable as depreciation in the year of retirement of the last survivor of the 1954 acquisitions.

Depreciation Reserve for 1954 Acquisitions

Year	Reserve Jan. 1	Current retirements	Salvage realized	Reserve Dec. 31, before depreciation	Average reserve before depreciation	Allowable depreciation	Reserve Dec. 31, after depreciation
1954	—	—	—	—	—	$2,400	$2,400
1955	$2,400	—	—	$2,400	$2,400	3,840	6,240
1956	6,240	—	—	6,240	6,240	2,304	8,544
1957	8,544	$2,000	$200	6,744	7,644	1,342	8,086
1958	8,086	2,000	200	6,286	7,186	726	7,012
1959	7,012	4,000	400	3,412	5,212	315	3,727
1960	3,727	2,000	—	1,727	2,727	109	1,836
1961	1,836	2,000	—	(164)	836	164	—

1959 Acquisitions

Year	Asset balance Jan. 1	Acquisition	Asset balance Dec. 31	Average balance	Reserve Dec. 31, before depreciation	Net depreciable balance	Rate	Allowable depreciation	Reserve Dec. 31, after depreciation
1959	—	$10,000	$10,000	$ 5,000	None	$5,000	40%	$2,000	$2,000
1960	$10,000		10,000	10,000	$2,000	8,000	40%	3,200	5,200
1961	10,000		10,000	10,000	5,200	4,800	40%	1,920	7,120

In the above example, the allowable depreciation on the 1954 acquisition totals $11,200. This amount when increased by salvage realized in the amount of $800, equals the entire cost or other basis of the 1954 acquisitions ($12,000).

(c) Change in estimated useful life. In the declining balance method when a change is justified in the useful life estimated for an account, subsequent computations shall be made as though the revised useful life had been originally estimated. For example, assume that an account has an estimated useful life of ten years and that a declining balance rate of 20 percent is applicable. If, at the end of the sixth year, it is determined that the remaining useful life of the account is six years, computations shall be made as though the estimated useful life was originally determined as twelve years. Accordingly, the applicable depreciation rate will be 16⅔ percent. This rate is thereafter applied to the unrecovered cost or other basis.

T.D. 6182, 6/11/56, amend T.D. 6712, 3/23/64.

§ 1.167(b)-3 Sum of the years-digits method.

(a) Applied to a single asset. *(1) General rule.* Under the sum of the years-digits method annual allowances for depreciation are computed by applying changing fractions to the cost or other basis of the property reduced by estimated salvage. The numerator of the fraction changes each year to a number which corresponds to the remaining useful life of the asset (including the year for which the allowance is being computed), and the denominator which remains constant is the sum of all the years digits corresponding to the estimated useful life of the asset. See section 167 (c) and § 1.167 (c)-1 for restrictions on the use of the sum of the years-digits method.

(i) Illustrations. Computation of depreciation allowances on a single asset under the sum of the years-digits method is illustrated by the following examples:

Example (1). A new asset having an estimated useful life of five years was acquired on January 1, 1954, for $1,750. The estimated salvage is $250. For a taxpayer filing his returns on a calendar year basis, the annual depreciation allowances are as follows:

Year	Cost or other basis less salvage	Fraction[1]	Allowable depreciation	Depreciation reserve
1954	$1,500	5/15	$500	$ 500
1955	1,500	4/15	400	900
1956	1,500	3/15	300	1,200
1957	1,500	2/15	200	1,400
1958	1,500	1/15	100	1,500
	Unrecovered value (salvage)			250

[1] The denominator of the fraction is the sum of the digits representing the years of useful life, i.e., 5, 4, 3, 2, and 1, or 15.

Example (2). Assume in connection with an asset acquired in 1954 that three-fourths of a year's depreciation is allowable in that year. The following illustrates a reasonable method of allocating depreciation:

	Depreciation for 12 months	Allowable depreciation 1954	1955	1956
1st year	$500	(¾) $375	(¼) $125	
2nd year	400		(¾) 300	(¼) $100
3rd year	300			(¾) 225
		375	425	325

(ii) Change in useful life. Where in the case of a single asset, a change is justified in the useful life, subsequent computations shall be made as though the remaining useful life at the beginning of the taxable year of change were the useful life of a new asset acquired at such time and with a basis equal to the unrecovered cost or other basis of the asset at that time. For example, assume that a new asset with an estimated useful life of ten years is purchased in 1954. At the time of making out his return for 1959, the taxpayer finds that the asset has a remaining useful life of seven years from January 1, 1959. Depreciation for 1959 should then be computed as though 1959 were the first year of the life of an asset estimated to have a useful life of seven years, and the allowance for 1959 would be 7/28 of the unrecovered cost or other basis of the asset after adjustment for salvage.

(2) Remaining life. (i) Application. Under the sum of the years-digits method, annual allowances for depreciation may also be computed by applying changing fractions to the unrecovered cost or other basis of the asset reduced by estimated salvage. The numerator of the fraction changes each year to a number which corresponds to the remaining useful life of the asset (including the year for which the allowance is being computed), and the denominator changes each year to a number which represents the sum of the digits corresponding to the years of estimated remaining useful life of the asset. For decimal equivalents of such fractions, see Table I of subdivision (ii) of this subparagraph. For example, a new asset with an estimated useful life of 10 years is purchased January 1, 1954, for $6,000. Assuming a salvage value of $500, the depreciation allowance for 1954 is $1,000 ($5,500 × 0.1818, the applicable rate from Table I). For 1955, the unrecovered balance is $4,500, and the remaining life is 9 years. The depreciation allowance for 1955 would then be $900 ($4,500 × 0.2000, the applicable rate from Table I).

(ii) Table I. This table shows decimal equivalents of sum of the years-digits fractions corresponding to remaining lives from 1 to 100 years.

TABLE I— DECIMAL EQUIVALENTS FOR USE OF SUM OF THE YEARS-DIGITS METHOD, BASED ON REMAINING LIFE

Remaining life (years)	Decimal equivalent	Remaining life (years)	Decimal equivalent	Remaining life (years)	Decimal equivalent
100.0	0.0198	99.5	.0199	99.0	.0200
99.9	.0198	99.4	.0199	98.9	.0200
99.8	.0198	99.3	.0199	98.8	.0200
99.7	.0199	99.2	.0200	98.7	.0201
99.6	.0199	99.1	.0200	98.6	.0201

Remaining life (years)	Decimal equivalent
98.5	.0201
98.4	.0201
98.3	.0201
98.2	.0202
98.1	.0202
98.0	.0202
97.9	.0202
97.8	.0202
97.7	.0203
97.6	.0203
97.5	.0203
97.4	.0203
97.3	.0203
97.2	.0204
97.1	.0204
97.0	.0204
96.9	.0204
96.8	.0204
96.7	.0205
96.6	.0205
96.5	.0205
96.4	.0205
96.3	.0206
96.2	.0206
96.1	.0206
96.0	.0206
95.9	.0206
95.8	.0207
95.7	.0207
95.6	.0207
95.5	.0207
95.4	.0207
95.3	.0208
95.2	.0208
95.1	.0208
95.0	.0208
94.9	.0209
94.8	.0209
94.7	.0209
94.6	.0209
94.5	.0209
94.4	.0210
94.3	.0210
94.2	.0210
94.1	.0210
94.0	.0211
93.9	.0211
93.8	.0211
93.7	.0211
93.6	.0211
93.5	.0212
93.4	0212
93.3	.0212
93.2	.0212
93.1	.0213
93.0	.0213
92.9	.0213
92.8	.0213
92.7	.0213
92.8	.0213
92.7	.0213
92.6	.0214
92.5	.0214

Remaining life (years)	Decimal equivalent
92.4	.0214
92.3	.0214
92.2	.0215
92.1	.0215
92.0	.0215
91.9	.0215
91.8	.0216
91.7	.0216
91.6	.0216
91.5	.0216
91.4	.0216
91.3	.0217
91.2	.0217
91.1	.0217
91.0	.0217
90.9	.0218
90.8	.0218
90.7	.0218
90.6	.0218
90.5	.0219
90.4	.0219
90.3	.0219
90.2	.0219
90.1	.0220
90.0	.0220
89.9	.0220
89.8	.0220
89.7	.0221
89.6	.0221
89.5	.0221
89.4	.0221
89.3	.0221
89.2	.0222
89.1	.0222
89.0	.0222
88.9	.0222
88.8	.0223
88.7	.0223
88.6	.0223
88.5	.0223
88.4	.0224
88.3	.0224
88.2	.0224
88.1	.0224
88.0	.0225
87.9	.0225
87.8	.0225
87.7	.0225
87.6	.0226
87.5	.0226
87.4	.0226
87.3	.0226
87.2	.0227
87.1	.0227
87.0	.0227
86.9	.0228
86.8	.0228
86.7	.0228
86.6	.0228
86.5	.0229
86.4	.0229
86.3	.0229
86.2	.0229

Remaining life (years)	Decimal equivalent
86.1	.0230
86.0	.0230
85.9	.0230
85.8	.0230
85.7	.0231
85.6	.0231
85.4	.0231
85.3	.0232
85.2	.0232
85.1	.0232
85.0	.0233
84.9	.0233
84.8	.0233
84.7	.0233
84.6	.0234
84.5	.0234
84.4	.0234
84.3	.0234
84.2	.0235
84.1	.0235
84.0	.0235
83.9	.0236
83.8	.0236
83.7	.0236
83.6	.0236
83.5	.0237
83.4	.0237
83.3	.0237
83.2	.0238
83.1	.0238
83.0	.0238
82.9	.0238
82.8	.0239
82.7	.0239
82.6	.0239
82.5	.0240
82.4	.0240
82.3	.0240
82.2	.0240
82.1	.0241
82.0	.0241
81.9	.0241
81.8	.0242
81.7	.0242
81.6	.0242
81.5	.0242
81.4	.0243
81.3	.0243
81.2	.0243
81.1	.0244
81.0	.0244
80.9	.0244
80.8	.0244
80.7	.0245
80.6	.0245
80.5	.0245
80.4	.0246
80.3	.0246
80.2	.0246
80.1	.0247
80.0	.0247
79.9	.0247
79.8	.0248

Remaining life (years)	Decimal equivalent
79.7	.0248
79.6	.0248
79.5	.0248
79.4	.0249
79.3	.0249
79.2	.0249
79.1	.0250
79.0	.0250
78.9	.0250
78.8	.0251
78.7	.0251
78.6	.0251
78.5	.0252
78.4	.0252
78.3	.0252
78.2	.0253
78.1	.0253
78.0	.0253
77.9	.0253
77.8	.0254
77.7	.0254
77.6	.0254
77.5	.0255
77.4	.0255
77.3	.0255
77.2	.0256
77.1	.0256
77.0	.0256
76.9	.0257
76.8	.0257
76.7	.0257
76.6	.0258
76.5	.0258
76.4	.0258
76.3	.0259
76.2	.0259
76.1	.0259
76.0	.0260
75.9	.0260
75.8	.0260
75.7	.0261
75.8	.0261
75.5	.0261
76.4	.0262
75.3	.0262
75.2	.0262
75.1	.0263
75.0	.0263
74.9	.0264
74.8	.0264
74.7	.0264
74.8	.0265
74.5	.0265
74.4	.0265
74.3	.0266
74.2	.0266
74.1	.0266
74.0	.0267
73.9	.0267
73.8	.0267
73.7	.0268
73.6	.0268
73.5	.0268

Remaining life (years)	Decimal equivalent
73.4	.0269
73.3	.0269
73.2	.0270
73.1	.0270
73.0	.0270
72.9	.0271
72.8	.0271
72.7	.0271
72.6	.0272
72.5	.0272
72.4	.0272
72.3	.0273
72.2	.0273
72.1	.0274
72.0	.0274
71.9	.0274
71.8	.0275
71.7	.0275
71.6	.0275
71.5	.0276
71.4	.0276
71.3	.0277
71.2	.0277
71.1	.0277
71.0	.0278
70.9	.0278
70.8	.0279
70.7	.0279
70.6	.0279
70.5	.0280
70.4	.0280
70.3	.0280
70.2	.0281
70.1	.0281
70.0	.0282
69.9	.0282
69.8	.0282
69.7	.0283
69.6	.0283
69.5	.0284
69.4	.0284
69.3	.0284
69.2	.0285
69.1	.0285
69.0	.0286
68.9	.0286
68.8	.0287
68.7	.0287
68.6	.0287
68.5	.0288
68.4	.0288
68.3	.0289
68.2	.0289
68.1	.0289
68.0	.0290
67.9	.0290
67.8	.0291
67.7	.0291
67.6	.0292
67.5	.0292
67.4	.0292
67.3	.0293
67.2	.0293

Remaining life (years)	Decimal equivalent
67.1	.0294
67.0	.0294
68.9	.0295
66.8	.0295
66.7	.0295
66.6	.0296
66.5	.0296
66.4	.0297
66.3	.0297
66.2	.0298
66.1	.0298
65.0	.0299
65.9	.0299
65.8	.0299
65.7	.0300
65.6	.0300
63.5	.0301
65.4	.0301
65.3	.0302
65.2	.0302
65.1	.0303
65.0	.0303
64.9	.0303
64.8	.0304
64.7	.0304
64.6	.0305
64.5	.0305
64.4	.0306
64.3	.0306
64.2	.0307
64.1	.0307
64.0	.0308
63.9	.0308
63.8	.0309
63.7	.0309
63.6	.0310
63.5	.0310
63.4	.0311
63.3	.0311
63.2	.0312
63.1	.0312
63.0	.0313
62.9	.0313
62.8	.0313
62.7	.0314
62.6	.0314
62.5	.0315
62.4	.0315
62.3	.0316
62.2	.0316
62.1	.0317
62.0	.0317
61.9	.0318
61.8	.0318
61.7	.0319
61.6	.0319
61.5	.0320
61.4	.0320
61.3	.0321
61.2	.0322
61.1	.0322
61.0	.0323
60.9	.0323

Remaining life (years)	Decimal equivalent
60.8	.0324
60.7	.0324
60.6	.0325
60.5	.0325
60.4	.0326
60.3	.0326
60.2	.0327
60.1	.0327
60.0	.0328
59.9	.0328
59.8	.0329
59.7	.0329
59.6	.0330
59.5	.0331
59.4	.0331
59.3	.0332
59.2	.0332
59.1	.0333
59.0	.0333
58.9	.0334
58.8	.0334
58.7	.0335
58.6	.0336
58.5	.0336
58.4	.0337
58.3	.0337
58.2	.0338
58.1	.0338
58.0	.0339
57.9	.0340
57.8	.0840
57.7	.0341
57.8	.0341
57.5	.0342
57.4	.0342
57.3	.0343
57.2	.0344
57.1	.0344
57.0	.0345
56.9	.0345
56.8	.0346
56.7	.0347
56.6	.0347
56.5	.0248
56.4	.0348
56.3	.0349
56.2	.0350
56.1	.0350
56.0	.0351
55.9	.0351
55.8	.0352
55.7	.0352
55.6	.0353
55.5	.0354
55.4	.0355
55.3	.0355
55.2	.0356
55.1	.0356
55.0	.0357
54.9	.0358
54.3	.0358
54.7	.0359
54.6	.0360

Remaining life (years)	Decimal equivalent
54.5	.0360
54.4	.0361
54.3	.0362
54.2	.0362
54.1	.0363
54.0	.0364
53.9	.0364
53.8	.0365
53.7	.0366
53.6	.0366
53.5	.0367
53.4	.0368
53.3	.0368
53.2	.0369
53.1	.0370
53.0	.0370
52.9	.0371
52.8	.0372
52.7	.0372
52.6	.0373
52.5	.0374
52.4	.0374
52.3	.0375
52.2	.0376
52.1	.0377
52.0	.0377
51.9	.0378
51.8	.0379
51.7	.0379
51.6	.0380
51.5	.0381
51.4	.0382
51.3	.0382
51.2	.0383
51.1	.0384
51.0	.0385
50.9	.0385
50.8	.0386
50.7	.0387
50.6	.0388
50.5	.0388
50.4	.0389
50.3	.0390
50.2	.0391
50.1	.0391
50.0	.0392
49.9	.0393
49.8	.0394
49.7	.0394
49.6	.0395
49.5	.0396
49.4	.0397
40.3	.0398
49.2	.0398
49.1	.0399
49.0	.0400
48.9	.0401
48.8	.0402
48.7	.0402
46.6	.0403
48.5	.0404
48.4	.0405
48.3	.0406

Remaining life (years)	Decimal equivalent
48.2	.0406
48.1	.0407
48.0	.0408
47.9	.0409
47.8	.0410
47.7	.0411
47.6	.0411
47.5	.0412
47.4	.0413
47.3	.0414
47.2	.0415
47.1	.0416
47.0	.0417
46.9	.0418
46.8	.0418
46.7	.0419
46.6	.0420
46.5	.0421
46.4	.0422
46.3	.0423
46.2	.0424
46.1	.0425
46.0	.0426
45.9	.0426
45.8	.0427
45.7	.0428
45.6	.0429
45.5	.0430
45.4	.0431
45.3	.0432
45.2	.0433
45.1	.0434
45.0	.0435
44.9	.0436
44.8	.0437
44.7	.0438
44.6	.0439
44.5	.0440
44.4	.0440
44.3	.0441
44.2	.0442
44.1	.0443
44.0	.0444
43.9	.0445
43.8	.0446
43.7	.0447
43.6	.0448
43.5	.0449
43.4	.0450
43.3	.0451
43.2	.0452
43.1	.0453
43.0	.0455
42.9	.0456
42.8	.0457
42.7	.0458
42.6	.0459
42.5	.0460
42.4	.0461
42.3	.0462
42.2	.0463
42.1	.0464
42.0	.0465

Remaining life (years)	Decimal equivalent
41.9	.0466
41.8	.0467
41.7	.0468
41.6	.0469
41.5	.0471
41.4	.0472
41.3	.0473
41.2	.0474
41.1	.0475
41.0	.0476
40.9	.0477
40.8	.0478
40.7	.0480
40.6	.0481
40.5	.0482
40.4	.0483
40.3	.0484
40.2	.0485
40.1	.0487
40.0	.0488
39.9	.0489
39.8	.0490
39.7	.0491
39.6	.0493
39.5	.0494
39.4	.0495
39.3	.0496
39.2	.0497
39.1	.0499
39.0	.0500
38.9	.0501
38.8	.0502
38.7	.0504
38.6	.0505
38.5	.0506
38.4	.0508
38.3	.0509
38.2	.0510
38.1	.0511
38.0	.0513
37.9	.0514
37.8	.0515
37.7	.0517
37.6	.0518
37.5	.0519
37.4	.0521
37.3	.0522
37.2	.0524
37.1	.0525
37.0	.0526
36.9	.0528
36.8	.0529
36.7	.0530
36.6	.0532
36.5	.0533
36.4	.0535
36.3	.0536
36.2	.0538
36.1	.0539
36.0	.0541
35.9	.0542
35.8	.0543
35.7	.0545

Remaining life (years)	Decimal equivalent
35.6	.0546
35.5	.0548
35.4	.0549
35.3	.0551
35.2	.0552
35.1	.0554
35.0	.0556
34.9	.0557
34.8	.0559
34.7	.0560
34.6	.0562
34.5	.0563
34.4	.0565
34.3	.0566
34.2	.0568
34.1	.0570
34.0	.0571
33.9	.0573
33.8	.0575
33.7	.0576
33.6	.0578
33.5	.0580
33.4	.0581
33.3	.0583
33.2	.0585
33.1	.0586
33.0	.0588
32.9	.0590
32.8	.0592
32.7	.0593
32.6	.0595
32.5	.0597
32.4	.0599
32.3	.0600
32.2	.0602
32.1	.0604
32.0	.0606
31.9	.0608
31.8	.0610
31.7	.0611
31.6	.0613
31.5	.0615
31.4	.0617
31.3	.0619
31.2	.0621
31.1	.0623
31.0	.0625
30.9	.0627
30.8	.0629
30.7	.0631
30.6	.0633
30.5	.0635
30.4	.0637
30.3	.0639
30.2	.0641
30.1	.0643
30.0	.0645
29.9	.0647
29.8	.0649
29.7	.0651
29.6	.0653
29.5	.0656
29.4	.0658

Remaining life (years)	Decimal equivalent
29.3	.0660
29.2	.0662
29.1	.0664
29.0	.0667
28.9	.0669
28.8	.0671
28.7	.0673
28.6	.0675
28.5	.0678
28.4	.0680
28.3	.0682
28.2	.0685
28.1	.0687
28.0	.0690
27.9	.0692
27.8	.0694
27.7	.0697
27.6	.0699
27.5	.0702
27.4	.0704
27.3	.0707
27.2	.0709
27.1	.0712
27.0	.0714
26.9	.0717
26.8	.0719
26.7	.0722
26.6	.0724
26.5	.0727
26.4	.0730
26.3	.0732
26.2	.0735
26.1	.0738
26.0	.0741
25.9	.0743
25.8	.0746
25.7	.0749
25.6	.0752
25.5	.0754
25.4	.0757
25.3	.0760
25.2	.0763
25.1	.0766
25.0	.0769
24.9	.0772
24.8	.0775
24.7	.0778
24.6	.0781
24.5	.0784
24.4	.0787
24.3	.0790
24.2	.0793
24.1	.0797
24.0	.0800
23.9	.0803
23.8	.0806
23.7	.0809
23.6	.0813
23.5	.0816
23.4	.0819
23.3	.0823
23.2	.0826
23.1	.0830

Remaining life (years)	Decimal equivalent
23.0	.0833
22.9	.0837
22.8	.0840
22.7	.0844
22.6	.0847
22.5	.0851
22.4	.0854
22.3	.0858
22.2	.0862
22.1	.0866
22.0	.0870
21.9	.0873
21.8	.0877
21.7	.0881
21.6	.0885
21.5	.0888
21.4	.0892
21.3	.0896
21.2	.0901
21.1	.0905
21.0	.0909
20.9	.0913
20.8	.0917
20.7	.0921
20.6	.0925
20.5	.0930
20.4	.0934
20.3	.0939
20.2	.0943
20.1	.0948
20.0	.0952
19.9	.0957
19.8	.0961
19.7	.0966
19.6	.0970
19.5	.0975
19.4	.0980
19.3	.0985
19.2	.0990
19.1	.0995
19.0	.1000
18.9	.1005
18.8	.1010
18.7	.1015
18.6	.1020
18.5	.1025
18.4	.1030
18.3	.1036
18.2	.1041
18.1	.1047
18.0	.1053
17.9	.1058
17.8	.1063
17.7	.1069
17.6	.1074
17.5	.1080
17.4	.1086
17.3	.1092
17.2	.1098
17.1	.1105
17.0	.1111
16.9	.1117
16.8	.1123

Remaining life (years)	Decimal equivalent
16.7	.1129
16.6	.1135
16.5	.1142
16.4	.1148
16.3	.1155
16.2	.1162
16.1	.1169
16.0	.1176
15.9	.1183
15.8	.1190
15.7	.1197
15.6	.1204
15.5	.1211
15.4	.1218
15.3	.1226
15.2	.1234
15.1	.1242
15.0	.1250
14.9	.1257
14.8	.1265
14.7	.1273
14.6	.1281
14.5	.1289
14.4	.1297
14.3	.1306
14.2	.1315
14.1	.1324
14.0	.1333
13.9	.1342
13.8	.1350
13.7	.1359
13.6	.1368
13.5	.1378
13.4	.1387
13.3	.1397
13.2	.1407
13.1	.1418
13.0	.1429
12.9	.1438
12.8	.1448
12.7	.1458
12.6	.1469
12.5	.1479
12.4	.1490
12.3	.1502
12.2	.1514
12.1	.1526
12.0	.1538
11.9	.1549
11.8	.1561
11.7	.1573
11.6	.1585
11.5	.1597
11.4	.1610
11.3	.1624
11.2	.1637
11.1	.1652
11.0	.1667
10.9	.1680
10.8	.1693
10.7	.1707
10.6	.1721
10.5	.1736

Remaining life (years)	Decimal equivalent
10.4	.1751
10.3	.1767
10.2	.1783
10.1	.1800
10.0	.1818
9.9	.1833
9.8	.1849
9.7	.1865
9.6	.1882
9.5	.1900
9.4	.1918
9.3	.1938
9.2	.1957
9.1	.1978
9.0	.2000
8.9	.2018
8.8	.2037
8.7	.2057
8.6	.2077
8.5	.2099
8.4	.2121
8.3	.2145
8.2	.2169
8.1	.2195
8.0	.2222
7.9	.2244
7.8	.2267
7.7	.2292
7.6	.2317
7.5	.2344
7.4	.2372
7.3	.2401
7.2	.2432
7.1	.2465
7.0	.2500
6.9	.2527
6.8	.2556
6.7	.2587
6.6	.2619
6.5	.2653
6.4	.2689
6.3	.2727
6.2	.2768
6.1	.2811
6.0	.2857
5.9	.2892
5.8	.2929
5.7	.2969
5.6	.3011
5.5	.3056
5.4	.3103
5.3	.3155
5.2	.3210
5.1	.3269
5.0	.3333
4.9	.3379
4.8	.3429
4.7	.3481
4.6	.3538
4.5	.3600
4.4	.3667
4.3	.3739
4.2	.3818

Remaining life (years)	Decimal equivalent
4.1	.3905
4.0	.4000
3.9	.4053
3.8	.4130
3.7	.4205
3.6	.4286
3.5	.4375
3.4	.4474
3.3	.4583
3.2	.4706
3.1	.4844
3.0	.5000
2.9	.5088
2.8	.5185
2.7	.5294
2.6	.5417
2.5	.5556
2.4	.5714
2.3	.5897
2.2	.6111
2.1	.6364
2.0	.6667
1.9	.6786
1.8	.6923
1.7	.7083
1.6	.7273
1.5	.7500
1.4	.7778
1.3	.8125
1.2	.8571
1.1	.9167
1.0	1.0000

NOTE: For determination of decimal equivalents of remaining lives falling between those shown in the above table, the taxpayer may use the next longest life shown in the table, interpolate from the table, or use the following formula from which the table was derived.

$$D = \frac{2R}{(W+2F)(W+1)}$$

where:

D = Decimal equivalent.

R = Remaining life.

W = Whole number of years in remaining life.

F = Fractional part of year in remaining life.

If the taxpayer desires to carry his calculations of decimal equivalents to a greater number of decimal places than is provided in the table, he may use the formula. The procedure adopted must be consistently followed thereafter.

(b) Applied to group, classified, or composite accounts. *(1) General rule.* The sum of the years-digits method may be applied to group, classified, or composite accounts in accordance with the plan described in subparagraph (2) of this paragraph or in accordance with other plans as explained in subparagraph (3) of this paragraph.

(2) Remaining life plan. The remaining life plan as applied to a single asset is described in paragraph (a)(2) of this section. This plan may also be applied to group, classified, or composite accounts. Under this plan the allowance for depreciation is computed by applying changing fractions to the unrecovered cost or other basis of the account reduced by estimated salvage. The numerator of the fraction changes each year to a number which corresponds to the remaining useful life of the account (including the year for which the allowance is being computed), and the denominator changes each year to a number which represents the sum of the years digits corresponding to the years of estimated remaining useful life of the account. Decimal equivalents of such fractions can be obtained by use of Table I under paragraph (a)(2)(ii) of this section. The proper application of this method requires that the estimated remaining useful life of the account be determined each year. This determination, of course, may be made each year by analysis, i.e., by determining the remaining lives for each of the components in the account, and averaging them. The estimated remaining life of any account, however, may also be determined arithmetically. For example, it may be computed by dividing the unrecovered cost or other basis of the account, as computed by straight line depreciation, by the gross cost or other basis of the account, and multiplying the result by the average life of the assets in the account.

Salvage value is not a factor for the purpose of determining remaining life. Thus, if a group account with an average life of ten years had at January 1, 1958, a gross asset balance of $12,600 and a depreciation reserve computed on the straight line method of $9,450, the remaining life of the account at January 1, 1958, would be computed as follows:

$$\frac{\$12,600 - \$9,450}{\$12,600} \times 10 \text{ years} = 2.50 \text{ years}$$

Example. The use of the sum of the years-digits method with group, classified, or composite accounts under the remaining life plan is illustrated by the following example: A calendar year taxpayer maintains a group account to which a five-year life is applicable. Original investment, additions, retirements, and salvage recoveries are the same as those set forth in example (3) of paragraph (b) of § 1.167(b)-1.

						Sum of the years digits depreciation			
Straight line amount	Straight line reserve	Remaining life	Asset balance reduced by salvage	Current additions reduced by salvage	Salvage realized	Accumulated reserve Jan. 1	Unrecovered Jan. 1	Rate based on Col. (7) from Table 1	Allowable depreciation

Year	Asset balance Jan. 1	Current additions	Current retirements	Average asset balance	Col. (4) ÷ life	Col. (5)– Col. (3) accumulated Jan. 1	[Col. (1)– Col. (6)÷ Col. (1)]× average service life	Col. (1)× (100%– 6.67%)	Col. (2)× (100%– 6.67%)		Prior reserve+ Col. (14)+ Col. (10)– Col.(3)	Col. (8)– Col. (11)		Col. (12)× Col. (13)+ ½ Col. (9)×F[2]
1954		$12,000		$ 6,000	$1,200[1]		5.00		$11,200				0.3333	$1,866
1955	$12,000			12,000	2,400	$ 1,200	4.50	$11,200			$1,866	$9,334	.3600	3,360
1956	12,000			12,000	2,400	3,600	3.50	11,200			5,226	5,974	.4375	2,614
1957	12,000		$2,000	11,000	2,200	6,000	2.50	11,200		$200	7,840	3,360	.5556	1,867
1958	10,000		2,000	9,000	1,800	6,200	1.90	9,333		200	7,907	1,426	.6786	968
1959	8,000	10,000	4,000	11,000	2,200	6,000	1.25	7,466	9,333	400	7,075	391	.8125	1,874
1960	14,000		2,000	13,000	2,600	4,200	3.50	13,066			5,349	7,717	.4375	3,376
1961	12,000		2,000	11,000	2,200	4,800	3.00	11,200			6,725	4,475	.5000	2,238
1962						5,000					6,963			

[2] F=Rate based on average service life (0.3333 in this example).

[1] ½ year's amount.

(3) Other plans for application of the sum of the years-digits method. Taxpayers who wish to use the sum of the years-digits method in computing depreciation for group, classified, or composite accounts in accordance with a sum of the years digits plan other than the remaining life plan described herein may do so only with the consent of the Commissioner. Request for permission to use plans other than that described shall be addressed to the Commissioner of Internal Revenue, Washington 25, D. C.

T.D. 6182, 6/11/56.

§ 1.167(b)-4 Other methods.

(a) Under section 167(b)(4) a taxpayer may use any consistent method of computing depreciation, such as the sinking fund method, provided depreciation allowances computed in accordance with such method do not result in accumulated allowances at the end of any taxable year greater than the total of the accumulated allowances which could have resulted from the use of the declining balance method described in section 167(b)(2). This limitation applies only during the first two-thirds of the useful life of the property. For example, an asset costing $1,000 having a useful life of six years may be depreciated under the declining balance method in accordance with § 1.167(b)-2, at a rate of 33⅓ percent. During the first four years or ⅔ of its useful life, maximum depreciation allowances under the declining balance method would be as follows:

	Current depreciation	Accumulated depreciation	Balance
Cost of asset			$1,000
1st year	$333	$333	667
2nd year	222	555	445
3rd year	148	703	297
4th year	99	802	198

An annual allowance computed by any other method under section 167(b)(4) could not exceed $333 for the first year, and at the end of the second year the total allowances for the two years could not exceed $555. Likewise, the total allowances for the three years could not exceed $703 and for the four years could not exceed $802. This limitation would not apply in the fifth and sixth years. See section 167(c) and § 1.167(c)-1 for restrictions on the use of certain methods.

(b) It shall be the responsibility of the taxpayer to establish to the satisfaction of the Commissioner that a method of depreciation under section 167(b)(4) is both a reasonable and consistent method and that it does not produce depreciation allowances in excess of the amount permitted under the limitations provided in such section.

T.D. 6182, 6/11/56.

§ 1.167(c)-1 Limitations on methods of computing depreciation under section 167(b)(2), (3), and (4).

Caution: The Treasury has not yet amended Reg § 1.167(c)-1 to reflect changes made by P.L. 101-508, P.L. 97-34.

(a) In general. *(1)* Section 167(c) provides limitations on the use of the declining balance method described in section 167(b)(2), the sum of the years-digits method described in section 167(b)(3), and certain other methods authorized by section 167(b)(4). These methods are applicable only to tangible property having a useful life of three years or more. If construction, reconstruction, or erection by the taxpayer began before January 1, 1954, and was completed after December 31, 1953, these methods apply only to that portion of the basis of the property which is properly attributable to such construction, reconstruction, or erection after December 31, 1953. Property is considered as constructed, reconstructed, or erected by the taxpayer if the work is done for him in accordance with his specifications. The portion of the basis of such property attributable to construction, reconstruction, or erection after December 31, 1953, consists of all costs of the property allocable to the period after December 31, 1953, including the cost or other basis of materials entering into such work. It is not necessary that such materials be acquired after December 31, 1953, or that they be new in use. If construction or erection by the taxpayer began after December 31, 1953, the entire cost or other basis of such construction or erection qualifies for these methods of depreciation. In the case of reconstruction of property, these methods do not apply to any part of the adjusted basis of such property on December 31, 1953. For purposes of this section, construction, reconstruction, or erection by the taxpayer begins when physical work is started on such construction, reconstruction, or erection.

(2) If the property was not constructed, reconstructed, or erected by the taxpayer, these methods apply only if it was acquired after December 31, 1953, and if the original use of the property commences with the taxpayer and commences after December 31, 1953. For the purpose of the preceding sentence, property shall be deemed to be acquired when reduced to physical possession, or control. The term "original use" means the first use to which the property is put, whether or not such use corresponds to the use of such property by the taxpayer. For example, a reconditioned or rebuilt machine acquired after December 31, 1953, will not be treated as being put to original use by the taxpayer even though it is put to a different use, nor will a horse acquired for breeding purposes be treated as being put to original use by the taxpayer if prior to the purchase the horse was used for racing purposes. See §§ 1.167(b)-2, 1.167(b)-3, and 1.167(b)-4 for application of the various methods.

(3) Assets having an estimated average useful life of less than three years shall not be included in a group, classified, or composite account to which the methods described in §§ 1.167(b)-2, 1.167(b)-3, and 1.167(b)-4 are applicable. However, an incidental retirement of an asset from such an account prior to the expiration of a useful life of three years will not prevent the application of these methods to such an account.

(4) See section 381(c)(6) and the regulations thereunder for rules covering the use of depreciation methods by acquiring corporations in the case of certain corporate acquisitions.

(5) See §§ 1.1502-12(g) and 1.1502-13 for provisions dealing with depreciation of property received by a member of an affiliated group from another member of the group during a consolidated return period.

(6) Except in the cases described in subparagraphs (4) and (5) of this paragraph, the methods of depreciation described in §§ 1.167(b)-2, 1.167(b)-3, and 1.167(b)-4 are not applicable to property in the hands of a distributee, vendee, transferee, donee, or grantee unless the original use of the property begins with such person and the conditions required by section 167(c) and this section are otherwise met. For example, these methods of depreciation may not be used by a corporation with respect to property which it acquires from an individual or partnership in exchange for its stock. Similarly, if an individual or partnership receives property in a distribution upon dissolution of a corporation, these methods of depreciation may not be used with respect to property so acquired by such individual or partnership. As a further example, these methods of depreciation may not be used by a partnership with respect to contributed property, nor by a partner with respect to partnership property distributed to him. Moreover, where a partnership is entitled to use these depreciation methods, and the optional adjustment to basis of partnership property provided by section 743 is applicable, (i) in the case of an increase in the adjusted basis of the partnership property under such section, the transferee partner with respect to whom such adjustment is applicable shall not be entitled to use such methods with respect to such increase, and (ii) in the case of a decrease in the adjusted basis of the partnership property under such section, the transferee partner with respect to whom such adjustment is applicable shall include in his income an amount equal to the portion of the depreciation deducted by the partnership which is attributable to such decrease.

(b) Illustrations. *(1)* The application of these methods to property constructed, reconstructed, or erected by the taxpayer after December 31, 1953, may be illustrated by the following examples:

Example (1). If a building with a total cost of $100,000 is completed after December 31, 1953, and the portion attributable to construction after December 31, 1953, is determined by engineering estimates or by cost accounting records to be $30,000, the methods referred to in paragraph (a)(1) of this section are applicable only to the $30,000 portion of the total.

Example (2). In 1954, a taxpayer has an old machine with an unrecovered cost of $1,000. If he contracts to have it reconditioned, or reconditions it himself, at a cost of an additional $5,000, only the $5,000 may be depreciated under the methods referred to in paragraph (a)(1) of this section, whether or not the materials used for reconditioning are new in use.

Example (3). A taxpayer who acquired a building in 1940 makes major maintenance or repair expenditures in 1954 of a type which must be capitalized. For these expenditures the taxpayer may use a method of depreciation different from that used on the building (for example, the methods referred to in paragraph (a)(1) of this section) only if he accounts for such expenditures separately from the account which contained the original building. In such case, the unadjusted basis on any parts replaced shall be removed from the asset account and shall be charged to the appropriate depreciation reserve account. In the alternative he may capitalize such expenditures by charging them to the depreciation reserve account for the building.

(2) The application of these methods to property which was not constructed, reconstructed, or erected by the taxpayer but which was acquired after December 31, 1953, may be illustrated by the following examples:

Example (1). A taxpayer contracted in 1953 to purchase a new machine which he acquired in 1954 and put into first use in that year. He may use the methods referred to in paragraph (a)(1) of this section, in recovering the cost of the new machine.

Example (2). A taxpayer instead of reconditioning his old machine buys a "factory reconditioned" machine in 1954 to replace it. He cannot apply the methods referred to in paragraph (a)(1) of this section, to any part of the cost of the reconditioned machine since he is not the first user of the machine.

Example (3). In 1954, a taxpayer buys a house for $20,000 which had been used as a personal residence and thus had not been subject to depreciation allowances. He makes a capital addition of $5,000 and rents the property to another. The taxpayer may use the methods referred to in paragraph (a)(1) of this section, only with respect to the $5,000 cost of the addition.

(c) Election to use methods. Subject to the limitations set forth in paragraph (a) of this section, the methods of computing the allowance for depreciation specified in section 167(b)(2), (3), and (4) may be adopted without permission and no formal election is required. In order for a taxpayer to elect to use these methods for any property described in paragraph (a) of this section, he need only compute depreciation thereon under any of these methods for any taxable year ending after December 31, 1953, in which the property may first be depreciated by him. The election with respect to any property shall not be binding with respect to acquisitions of similar property in the same year or subsequent year which are set up in separate accounts. If a taxpayer has filed his return for a taxable year ending after December 31, 1953, for which the return is required to be filed on or before September 15, 1956, an election to compute the depreciation allowance under any of the methods specified in section 167(b) or a change in such an election may be made in an amended return or claim for refund filed on or before September 15, 1956.

T.D. 6182, 6/11/56, amend T.D. 7244, 12/29/72, T.D. 8560, 8/12/94, T.D. 8597, 7/12/95.

§ 1.167(d)-1 Agreement as to useful life and rates of depreciation.

Caution: The Treasury has not yet amended Reg § 1.167(d)-1 to reflect changes made by P.L. 97-34.

After August 16, 1954, a taxpayer may, for taxable years ending after December 31, 1953, enter into an agreement with respect to the estimated useful life, method and rate of depreciation and treatment of salvage of any property which is subject to the allowance for depreciation. An application for such agreement may be made to the district director for the internal revenue district in which the taxpayer's return is required to be filed. Such application shall be filed in quadruplicate and shall contain in such detail as may be practical the following information:

(a) The character and location of the property.

(b) The original cost or other basis and date of acquisition.

(c) Proper adjustments to the basis including depreciation accumulated to the first taxable year to be covered by the agreement.

(d) Estimated useful life and estimated salvage value.

(e) Method and rate of depreciation.

(f) Any other facts and circumstances pertinent to making a reasonable estimate of the useful life of the property and its salvage value.

The agreement must be in writing and must be signed by the taxpayer and by the district director. The agreement must be signed in quadruplicate, and two of the signed copies will be returned to the taxpayer. The agreement shall set forth its effective date, the estimated remaining useful life, the estimated salvage value, and rate and method of depreciation of the property and the facts and circumstances taken into consideration in adoption of the agreement, and shall relate only to depreciation allowances for such property on and after the effective date of the agreement. Such an agreement shall be binding on both parties until such time as facts and circumstances which were not taken into account in making the agreement are shown to exist. The party wishing to modify or change the agreement shall have the responsibility of establishing the existence of such facts and circumstances. Any change in the useful life or rate specified in such agreement shall be effective only prospectively, that is, it shall be effective beginning with the taxable year in which notice of the intention to change, including facts and circumstances warranting the adjustment of useful life and rate, is sent by the party proposing the change to the other party and is sent by registered mail, if such notice is mailed before September 3, 1958, or is sent by certified mail or registered mail, if such notice is mailed after September 2, 1958. A copy of the agreement (and any modification thereof) shall be filed with the taxpayer's return for the first taxable year which is affected by the agreement (or any modification thereof). A signed copy should be retained with the permanent records of the taxpayer. For rules relating to changes in method of depreciation, see § 1.167(e)-1 and section 446 and the regulations thereunder.

T.D. 6182, 6/11/56, amend T.D. 6426, 11/30/59.

§ 1.167(e)-1 Change in method.

Caution: The Treasury has not yet amended Reg § 1.167(e)-1 to reflect changes made by P.L. 94-455.

(a) In general. *(1)* Any change in the method of computing the depreciation allowances with respect to a particular account (other than a change in method permitted or required by reason of the operation of former section 167(j)(2) and § 1.167(j)-3(c)) is a change in method of accounting, and such a change will be permitted only with the consent of the Commissioner, except that certain changes to the straight line method of depreciation will be permitted without consent as provided in former section 167(e)(1), (2), and (3). Except as provided in paragraphs (c) and (d) of this section, a change in method of computing depreciation will be permitted only with respect to all the assets contained in a particular account as defined in § 1.167(a)-7. Any change in the percentage of the current straight line rate under the declining balance method, for example, from 200 percent of the straight line rate to any other percent of the straight line rate, or any change in the interest factor used in connection with a compound interest or sinking fund method, will constitute a change in method of depreciation. Any request for a change in method of depreciation shall be made in accordance with section 446(e) and the regulations under section 446(e). For rules covering the use of depreciation methods by acquiring corporations in the case of certain corporate acquisitions, see section 381(c)(6) and the regulations under section 381(c)(6).

(2) Paragraphs (b), (c), and (d) of this section apply to property for which depreciation is determined under section 167 (other than under section 168, section 14001, section 1400L(c), under section 168 prior to its amendment by the Tax Reform Act of 1986 (100 Stat. 2121), or under an additional first year depreciation deduction provision (for example, section 168(k), 1400L(b), or 1400N(d))) of the Internal Revenue Code.

(b) Declining balance to straight line. In the case of an account to which the method described in section 167(b)(2) is applicable, a taxpayer may change without the consent of the Commissioner, from the declining balance method of depreciation to the straight line method at any time during the useful life of the property under the following conditions. Such a change may not be made if a provision prohibiting such a change is contained in an agreement under section 167(d). When the change is made, the unrecovered cost or other basis (less a reasonable estimate for salvage) shall be recovered through annual allowances over the estimated remaining useful life determined in accordance with the circumstances existing at the time. With respect to any account, this change will be permitted only if applied to all the assets in the account as defined in § 1.167(a)-7. If the method of depreciation described in section 167(b)(2) (the declining balance method of depreciation using a rate not exceeding 200 percent of the straight line rate) is an acceptable method of depreciation with respect to a particular account, the taxpayer may elect under this paragraph to change to the straight line method of depreciation even if with respect to that particular account the declining balance method is permitted under a provision other than section 167(b)(2). Thus, for example, in the case of section 1250 property to which section 167(j)(1) is applicable, section 167(b) does not apply, but the declining balance method of depreciation using 150 percent of the straight line rate is an acceptable method of depreciation under section 167(j)(1)(B). Accordingly, the taxpayer may elect under this paragraph to change to the straight line method of depreciation with respect to such property. Similarly, if the taxpayer acquired used property before July 25, 1969, and adopted the 150 percent declining balance method of depreciation permitted with respect to such property under § 1.167(b)-0(b), the taxpayer may elect under this paragraph to change to the straight line method of depreciation with respect to such property. The taxpayer shall furnish a statement with respect to the property which is the subject of the change showing the date of acquisition, cost or other basis amounts recovered through depreciation and other allowances, the estimated salvage value, the character of the property, the remaining useful life of the property, and such other information as may be required. The statement shall be attached to the taxpayer's return for the taxable year in which the change is made. A change to the straight line method must be adhered to for the entire taxable year of the change and for all subsequent taxable years unless, with the consent of the Commissioner, a change to another method is permitted.

(c) Change with respect to section 1245 property. *(1)* In respect of his first taxable year beginning after December 31, 1962, a taxpayer may elect, without the consent of the Commissioner, to change the method of depreciation of section 1245 property (as defined in section 1245(a)(3)) from any declining balance method or sum of the years-digits method to the straight line method. With respect to any account (as defined in § 1.167(a-7), this change may be made notwithstanding any provision to the contrary in an agreement under section 167(d), but such change shall constitute (as of the first day of such taxable year) a termination of such agreement as to all property in such account. With respect to any account, this change will be permitted only if applied to all the section 1245 property in the account. The election shall be made by a statement on, or attached to, the return for such taxable year filed on or before the last day prescribed by law, including any extensions thereof, for filing such return.

(2) When an election under this paragraph is made in respect of section 1245 property in an account, the unrecovered cost or other basis (less a reasonable estimate for salvage) of all the section 1245 property in the account shall be recovered through annual allowances over the estimated remaining useful life determined in accordance with the circumstances existing at that time. If there is other property in such account, the other property shall be placed in a separate account and depreciated by using the same method as was used before the change permitted by this paragraph, but the estimated useful life of such property shall be redetermined in accordance with the § 1.167(b)-2 or 1.167(b)-3, whichever is applicable. The taxpayer shall maintain records which permit specific identification of the section 1245 property in the account with respect to which the election is made, and any other property in such account. The records shall also show for all the property in the account the date of acquisition, cost or other basis, amounts recovered through depreciation and other allowances, the estimated salvage value, the character of the property, and the remaining useful life of the property. A change to the straight line method under this paragraph must be adhered to for the entire taxable year of the change and for all subsequent taxable years unless, with the consent of the Commissioner, a change to another method is permitted.

(d) Change with respect to section 1250 property. *(1)* In respect of his first taxable year beginning after July 24, 1969, a taxpayer may elect, without the consent of the Commissioner, to change the method of depreciation of section 1250 property (as defined in section 1250(c)) from any declining balance method or sum of the years-digits method to the straight line method. With respect to any account (as defined in § 1.167(a)-7) this change may be made notwithstanding any provision to the contrary in an agreement under section 167(d), but such change will constitute (as of the first day of such taxable year) a termination of such agreement as to all property in such account. With respect to any account, this change will be permitted only if applied to all the section 1250 property in the account. The election shall be made by a statement on, or attached to, the return for such taxable year filed on or before the last day prescribed by law, including extensions thereof, for filing such return.

(2) When an election under this paragraph is made in respect of section 1250 property in an account, the unrecovered cost or other basis (less a reasonable estimate for salvage) of all the section 1250 property in the account shall be recovered through annual allowances over the estimated remaining useful life determined in accordance with the circumstances existing at that time. If there is other property in such account, the other property shall be placed in a separate account and depreciated by using the same method as was used before the change permitted by this paragraph, but the estimated useful life of such property shall be redetermined in accordance with § 1.167(b)-2 or § 1.167(b)-3, whichever is applicable. The taxpayer shall maintain records which permit specific identification of the section 1250 property in the account with respect to which the election is made and any other property in such account. The records shall also show for all the property in the account the date of the acquisition, cost or other basis, amounts recovered through depreciation and other allowances, the estimated salvage value, the character of the property, and the estimated remaining useful life of the property. A change to the straight line method under this paragraph must be adhered to for the entire taxable year of the change and for all subsequent taxable years unless, with the consent of the Commissioner, a change to another method is permitted.

(e) Effective date. This section applies on or after December 30, 2003. For the applicability of regulations before December 30, 2003, see § 1.167(e)-1 in effect prior to December 30, 2003 (§ 1.167(e)-1 as contained in 26 CFR part 1 edition revised as of April 1, 2003).

T.D. 6182, 6/11/56, amend T.D. 6832, 7/6/65, T.D. 7166, 3/10/72, T.D. 9105, 12/30/2003, T.D. 9307, 12/22/2006.

§ 1.167(f)-1 Reduction of salvage value taken into account for certain personal property.

(a) In general. For taxable years beginning after December 31, 1961, and ending after October 16, 1962, a taxpayer may reduce the amount taken into account as salvage value in computing the allowance for depreciation under section 167(a) with respect to "personal property" as defined in section 167(f)(2) and paragraph (b) of this section. The reduction may be made in an amount which does not exceed 10 percent of the basis of the property for determining depreciation, as of the time as of which salvage value is required to be determined (or when salvage value is redetermined), taking into account all adjustments under section 1016 other than (1) the adjustment under section 1016(a)(2) for depreciation allowed or allowable to the taxpayer, and (2) the adjustment under section 1016(a)(19) for a credit earned by the taxpayer under section 38, to the extent such adjustment is reflected in the basis for depreciation. See paragraph (c) of § 1.167(a)-1 for the definition of salvage value, the time for making the determination, the redetermination of salvage value, and the general rules with respect to the treatment of salvage value. See also section 167(g) and § 1.167(g)-1 for basis for depreciation. A reduction of the amount taken into account as salvage value with respect to any property shall not be binding with respect to other property. In no event shall an asset (or an account) be depreciated below a reasonable salvage value after taking into account the reduction in salvage value permitted by section 167(f) and this section.

(b) Definitions and special rules. The following definitions and special rules apply for purposes of section 167(f) and this section.

(1) Personal property. The term "personal property" shall include only depreciable—

(i) Tangible personal property (as defined in section 48 and the regulations thereunder) and

(ii) Intangible personal property which has an estimated useful life (determined at the time of acquisition) of 3 years or more and which is acquired after October 16, 1962. Such term shall not include livestock. The term "livestock" includes horses, cattle, hogs, sheep, goats, and mink and other fur-bearing animals, irrespective of the use to which they are put or the purpose for which they are held. The original use of the property need not commence with the taxpayer so long as he acquired it after October 16, 1962; thus, the property may be new or used. For purposes of determining the estimated useful life, the provisions of paragraph (b) of § 1.167(a)-1 shall be applied. For rules determining when property is acquired, see subparagraph (2) of this paragraph. For purposes of determining the types of intangible personal property which are subject to the allowance for depreciation, see § 1.167(a)-3.

(2) Acquired. In determining whether property is acquired after October 16, 1962, property shall be deemed to be acquired when reduced to physical possession, or control. Property which has not been used in the taxpayer's trade or business or held for the production of income and which is thereafter converted by the taxpayer to such use shall be deemed to be acquired on the date of such conversion. In addition, property shall be deemed to be acquired if constructed, reconstructed, or erected by the taxpayer. If construction, reconstruction, or erection by the taxpayer began before October 17, 1962, and was completed after October 16, 1962, section 167(f) and this section apply only to that portion of the basis of the property which is properly attributable to such construction, reconstruction, or erection after October 16, 1962. Property is considered as constructed, reconstructed, or erected by the taxpayer if the work is done for him in accordance with his specifications. The portion of the basis of such property attributable to construction, reconstruction, or erection after October 16, 1962, consists of all costs of the property allocable to the period after October 16, 1962, including the cost or other basis of materials entering into such work. It is not necessary that such materials be acquired after October 16, 1962, or that they be new in use. If construction or erection by the taxpayer began after October 16, 1962, the entire cost or other basis of such construction or erection qualifies for the reduction provided for by section 167(f) and this section. In the case of reconstruction of property, section 167(f) and this section do not apply to any part of the adjusted basis of such property on October 16, 1962. For purposes of this section, construction, reconstruction, or erection by the taxpayer begins when physical work is started on such construction, reconstruction, or erection.

(c) Illustrations. The provisions of paragraphs (a) and (b) of this section may be illustrated by the following examples:

Example (1). Taxpayer A purchases a new asset for use in his business on January 1, 1963, for $10,000. The asset qualifies for the investment credit under section 38 and for the additional first-year depreciation allowance under section 179. A is entitled to an investment credit of $700 (7% × $10,000) and elects to take an additional first-year depreciation allowance of $2,000 (20% × $10,000). The basis for depreciation (determined in accordance with the provisions of section 167(g) and § 1.167(g)-1 is computed as follows:

Purchase price		$10,000
Less: Adjustment required for taxable years beginning before Jan. 1, 1964, under section 1016(a)(19) for the investment credit	$ 700	
Adjustment required under section 1016(a)(2) for the additional first-year depreciation allowance	2,000	
		2,700
Basis for depreciation for the taxable year 1963		7,300

However, the basis of the property for determining depreciation as of the time as of which salvage value is required to be determined is $10,000, the purchase price of the property. A files his income tax returns on a calendar year basis and uses the straight line method of depreciation. A estimates that he will use the asset in his business for 10 years after which it will have a salvage value of $500, which is less than $1,000 (10% × $10,000, the basis of the property for determining depreciation as of the time as of which salvage value is required to be determined). For the taxable year 1963 A may deduct $730 as the depreciation allowance. As of January 1, 1964, the basis of the asset is increased by $700 in accordance with paragraph (d) of § 1.48-7. In computing his total depreciation allowance on the asset, A may reduce the amount taken into account as salvage value to zero and may claim depreciation deductions (including the additional first-year depreciation allowance) totaling $10,000. See paragraph (d) of § 1.48-7 for the computation of depreciation for taxable years beginning after December 31, 1963, where there is an increase in basis of property subject to the investment credit.

Example (2). Assume the same facts as in example (1) except that A in a subsequent taxable year redetermines the estimate of the useful life of the asset and at the same time also redetermines the estimate of salvage value. Assume also that at such time the only reductions reflected in the basis are for depreciation allowed or allowable. Accordingly, the reduction under section 167(f) and this section will be computed with regard to the purchase price and not the unrecovered basis for depreciation at the time of the redetermination.

Example (3). Assume the same facts as in example (1) except that A estimates that the asset will have a salvage value of $1,200 at the end of its useful life. In computing his depreciation for the asset, A may reduce the amount to be taken into account as salvage value to $200 ($1,200 − $1,000). Accordingly, A may claim depreciation deductions (including the additional first-year depreciation allowance) totaling $9,800, i.e., the purchase price of the property ($10,000) less the amount taken into account as salvage value ($200).

Example (4). Assume the same facts as in example (1) except that the taxpayer had taken into account salvage value of only $200 but that the estimated salvage value had actually been $700. The amount of salvage value taken into account by the taxpayer is permissible since the reduction of salvage value by $500 ($700 – $200) would be within the limit provided for in section 167(f), i.e., $1,000 (10% × $10,000).

Example (5). On January 1, 1963, taxpayer B, a taxicab operator, traded his old taxicab plus cash for a new one, which had an estimated useful life of three years, in a transaction qualifying as a nontaxable exchange. The old taxicab had an adjusted basis of $2,500. B was allowed $3,000 for his old taxicab and paid $1,000 in cash. The basis of the new taxicab for determining depreciation (as determined under section 167(g) and § 1.167(g)-1) is the adjusted basis of the old taxicab at the time of trade-in ($2,500) plus the additional cash paid out ($1,000), or $3,500. In computing his depreciation allowance on the new taxicab, B may reduce the amount taken into account as salvage value by $350 (10% of $3,500).

Example (6). Taxpayer C purchases a new asset for use in his business on January 1, 1963, for $10,000. At the time of purchase, the asset has an estimated useful life of 10 years and an estimated salvage value of $1,500. C elects to compute his depreciation allowance for the asset by the declining balance method of depreciation, using a rate of 20% which is twice the normal straight line rate of 10% (without adjustment for salvage value). C files his income tax returns on a calendar year basis. In computing his depreciation allowance for the year 1966, C changes his method of determining the depreciation allowance for the asset from the declining balance method to the straight line method (in which salvage value is accounted for in determining the annual depreciation allowances) in accordance with the provisions of section 167(e) and paragraph (b) of § 1.167(e)-1. He also wishes to reduce the amount of salvage value taken into account in accordance with the provisions of section 167(f) and this section. At the close of the year 1966, the only reductions reflected in the basis of the asset are for depreciation allowances. Thus, C may reduce the amount of salvage value taken into account by $1,000 (10% × $10,000, the basis of the asset when it was acquired), and, therefore, will account for salvage value of only $500 in computing his depreciation allowance for the asset in 1966 and subsequent years.

Example (7). Taxpayer D purchases a station wagon for his personal use on January 1, 1962, for $4,500. On January 1, 1963, D converts the use of the station wagon to his business, and at that time it has an estimated useful life of 4 years, an estimated salvage value of $500, and a basis of $3,000 (as determined under section 167(g) and § 1.167(g)-1). Thus, for purposes of section 167(f) and this section, D is deemed to have acquired the station wagon on January 1, 1963. D elects the straight line method of depreciation in computing the depreciation allowance for the station wagon and also wishes to reduce the amount of salvage value taken into account in accordance with the provisions of section 167(f) and this section. Accordingly, D may reduce the amount of salvage value taken into account by $300 (10% of $3,000). D files his income tax returns on a calendar year basis. His depreciation allowance for the year 1963 would be computed as follows:

Basis for depreciation		$3,000
Less:		
Salvage value	$500	
Reduction permitted by section 167(f)	300	
		200
Amount to be depreciated over the useful life		2,800

D's depreciation allowance on the station wagon for the year 1963 would be $700 ($2,800 divided by 4, the remaining useful life).

T.D. 6712, 3/23/64, amend T.D. 6838, 7/19/65.

§ 1.167(g)-1 Basis for depreciation.

Caution: The Treasury has not yet amended Reg § 1.167(g)-1 to reflect changes made by P.L. 103-66, P.L. 101-508.

The basis upon which the allowance for depreciation is to be computed with respect to any property shall be the adjusted basis provided in section 1011 for the purpose of determining gain on the sale or other disposition of such property. In the case of property which has not been used in the trade or business or held for the prodnction of income and which is thereafter converted to such use, the fair market value on the date of such conversion, if less than the adjusted basis of the property at that time, is the basis for computing depreciation.

T.D. 6182, 6/11/56, amend T.D. 6712, 3/23/64.

§ 1.167(h)-1 Life tenants and beneficiaries of trusts and estates.

Caution: The Treasury has not yet amended Reg § 1.167(h)-1 to reflect changes made by P.L. 101-508.

(a) Life tenants. In the case of property held by one person for life with remainder to another person, the deduction for depreciation shall be computed as if the life tenant were the absolute owner of the property so that he will be entitled to the deduction during his life, and thereafter the deduction, if any, shall be allowed to the remainderman.

(b) Trusts. If property is held in trust, the allowable deduction is to be apportioned between the income beneficiaries and the trustee on the basis of the trust income allocable to each, unless the governing instrument (or local law) requires or permits the trustee to maintain a reserve for depreciation in any amount. In the latter case, the deduction is first allocated to the trustee to the extent that income is set aside for a depreciation reserve, and any part of the deduction in excess of the income set aside for the reserve shall be apportioned between the income beneficiaries and the trustee on the basis of the trust income (in excess of the income set aside for the reserve) allocable to each. For example:

(1) If under the trust instrument or local law the income of a trust computed without regard to depreciation is to be distributed to a named beneficiary, the beneficiary is entitled to the deduction to the exclusion of the trustee.

(2) If under the trust instrument or local law the income of a trust is to be distributed to a named beneficiary, but the trustee is directed to maintain a reserve for depreciation in any amount, the deduction is allowed to the trustee (except to the extent that income set aside for the reserve is less than the allowable deduction). The same result would follow if the trustee sets aside income for a depreciation reserve pur-

suant to discretionary authority to do so in the governing instrument.

No effect shall be given to any allocation of the depreciation deduction which gives any beneficiary or the trustee a share of such deduction greater than his pro rata share of the trust income, irrespective of any provisions in the trust instrument, except as otherwise provided in this paragraph when the trust instrument or local law requires or permits the trustee to maintain a reserve for depreciation.

(c) Estates. In the case of an estate, the allowable deduction shall be apportioned between the estate and the heirs, legatees, and devisees on the basis of income of the estate which is allocable to each.

T.D. 6182, 6/11/56, amend T.D. 6712, 3/23/64.

§ 1.167(i)-1 Depreciation of improvements in the case of mines, etc.

Caution: The Treasury has not yet amended Reg § 1.167(i)-1 to reflect changes made by P.L. 101-508.

Property used in the trade or business or held for the production of income which is subject to the allowance for depreciation provided in section 611 shall be treated for all purposes of the Code as if it were property subject to the allowance for depreciation under section 167. The preceding sentence shall not limit the allowance for depreciation otherwise allowable under section 611.

T.D. 6182, 6/11/56, amend T.D. 6712, 3/23/64.

§ 1.167(l)-1 Limitations on reasonable allowance in case of property of certain public utilities.

Caution: The Treasury has not yet amended Reg § 1.167(l)-1 to reflect changes made by P.L. 101-508.

(a) In general. *(1) Scope.* Section 167(l) in general provides limitations on the use of certain methods of computing a reasonable allowance for depreciation under section 167(a) with respect to "public utility property" (see paragraph (b) of this section) for all taxable years for which a Federal income tax return was not filed before August 1, 1969. The limitations are set forth in paragraph (c) of this section for "pre-1970 public utility property" and in paragraph (d) of this section for "post-1969 public utility property." Under section 167(l), a taxpayer may always use a straight line method (or other "subsection (l) method" as defined in paragraph (f) of this section). In general, the use of a method of depreciation other than a subsection (l) method is not prohibited by section 167(1) for any taxpayer if the taxpayer uses a "normalization method of regulated accounting" (described in paragraph (h) of this section). In certain cases, the use of a method of depreciation other than a subsection (l) method is not prohibited by section 167(l) if the taxpayer used a "flow-through method of regulated accounting" described in paragraph (i) of this section) for its "July 1969 regulated accounting period" (described in paragraph (g) of this section) whether or not the taxpayer uses either a normalization or a flow-through method of regulated accounting after its July 1969 regulated accounting period. However, in no event may a method of depreciation other than a subsection (l) method be used in the case of pre-1970 public utility property unless such method of depreciation is the "applicable 1968 method" (within the meaning of paragraph (e) of this section). The normalization requirements of section 167(l) with respect to public utility property defined in section 167(l)(3)(A) pertain only to the deferral of Federal income tax liability resulting from the use of an accelerated method of depreciation for computing the allowance for depreciation under section 167 and the use of straight line depreciation for computing tax expense and depreciation expense for purposes of establishing cost of services and for reflecting operating results in regulated books of account. Regulations under section 167(l) do not pertain to other book-tax timing differences with respect to State income taxes, F.I.C.A. taxes, construction costs, or any other taxes and items. The rules provided in paragraph (h)(6) of this section are to insure that the same time period is used to determine the deferred tax reserve amount resulting from the use of an accelerated method of depreciation for cost of service purposes and the reserve amount that may be excluded from the rate base or included in no-cost capital in determining such cost of services. The formula provided in paragraph (h)(6)(ii) of this section is to be used in conjunction with the method of accounting for the reserve for deferred taxes (otherwise proper under paragraph (h)(2) of this section) in accordance with the accounting requirements prescribed or approved, if applicable, by the regulatory body having jurisdiction over the taxpayer's regulated books of account. The formula provides a method to determine the period of time during which the taxpayer will be treated as having received amounts credited or charged to the reserve account so that the disallowance of earnings with respect to such amounts through rate base exclusion or treatment as no-cost capital will take into account the factor of time for which such amounts are held by the taxpayer. The formula serves to limit the amount of such disallowance.

(2) Methods of depreciation. For purposes of section 167(l), in the case of a declining balance method each different uniform rate applied to the unrecovered cost or other basis of the property is a different method of depreciation. For purposes of section 167(l), a change in a uniform rate of depreciation due to a change in the useful life of the property or a change in the taxpayer's unrecovered cost or other basis for the property is not a change in the method of depreciation. The use of "guideline lives" or "class lives" for Federal income tax purposes and different lives on the taxpayer's regulated books of account is generally not treated for purposes of section 167(l) as a different method of depreciation. Further, the use of an unrecovered cost or other basis or salvage value for Federal income tax purposes different from the basis or salvage value used on the taxpayer's regulated books of account is not treated as a different method of depreciation.

(3) Application of certain other provisions to public utility property. For rules with respect to application of the investment credit to public utility property, see section 46(e). For rules with respect to the application of the class life asset depreciation range system, including the treatment of the use of "class lives" for Federal income tax purposes and different lives on the taxpayer's regulated books of account, see § 1.167(a)-11 and § 1.167(a)-12.

(4) Effect on agreements under section 167(d). If the taxpayer has entered into an agreement under section 167(d) as to any public utility property and such agreement requires the use of a method of depreciation prohibited by section 167(l), such agreement shall terminate as to such property. The termination, in accordance with this subparagraph, shall not affect any other property (whether or not public utility property) covered by the agreement.

(5) Effect of change in method of depreciation. If, because the method of depreciation used by the taxpayer with respect

to public utility property is prohibited by section 167(l), the taxpayer changes to a method of depreciation not prohibited by section 167(l), then when the change is made the unrecovered cost or other basis shall be recovered through annual allowances over the estimated remaining useful life determined in accordance with the circumstances existing at that time.

(b) Public utility property. *(1) In general.* Under section 167(1)(3)(A), property is "public utility property" during any period in which it is used predominantly in a "section 167(l) public utility activity." The term "section 167(l) public utility activity" means the trade or business of the furnishing or sale of—

(i) Electrical energy, water, or sewage disposal services,

(ii) Gas or steam through a local distribution system,

(iii) Telephone services,

(iv) Other communication services (whether or not telephone services) if furnished or sold by the Communications Satellite Corporation for purposes authorized by the Communications Satellite Act of 1962 (47 U.S.C. 701), or

(v) Transportation of gas or steam by pipeline,

if the rates for such furnishing or sale, as the case may be, are regulated, i.e., have been established or approved by a regulatory body described in section 167(l)(3)(A). The term "regulatory body described in section 167(l)(3)(A)" means a State (including the District of Columbia) or political subdivision thereof, any agency or instrumentality of the United States, or a public service or public utility commission or other body of any State or political subdivision thereof similar to such a commission. The term "established or approved" includes the filing of a schedule of rates with a regulatory body which has the power to approve such rates, even though such body has taken no action on the filed schedule or generally leaves undisturbed rates filed by the taxpayer involved.

(2) Classification of property. If property is not used solely in a section 167(l) public utility activity, such property shall be public utility property if its predominant use is in a section 167(l) public utility activity. The predominant use of property for any period shall be determined by reference to the proper accounts to which expenditures for such property are chargeable under the system of regulated accounts required to be used for the period for which the determination is made and in accordance with the principles of § 1.46-3(g)(4) (relating to credit for investment in certain depreciable property). Thus, for example, for purposes of determining whether property is used predominantly in the trade or business of the furnishing or sale of transportation of gas by pipeline, or furnishing or sale of gas through a local distribution system, or both, the rules prescribed in § 1.46-3(g)(4) apply, except that accounts 365 through 371, inclusive (Transmission Plant), shall be added to the accounts enumerated in subdivision (i) of such paragraph (g)(4).

(c) Pre-1970 public utility property. *(1) Definition.* (i) Under section 167(l)(3)(B), the term "pre-1970 public utility property" means property which was public utility property at any time before January 1, 1970. If a taxpayer acquires pre-1970 public utility property, such property shall be pre-1970 public utility property in the hands of the taxpayer even though such property may have been acquired by the taxpayer in an arm's-length cash sale at fair market value or in a tax-free exchange. Thus, for example, if corporation X which is a member of the same controlled group of corporations (within the meaning of section 1563(a)) as corporation Y sells pre-1970 public utility property to Y, such property is pre-1970 public utility property in the hands of Y. The result would be the same if X and Y were not members of the same controlled group of corporations.

(ii) If the basis of public utility property acquired by the taxpayer in a transaction is determined in whole or in part by reference to the basis of any of the taxpayer's pre-1970 public utility property by reason of the application of any provision of the code, and if immediately after the transaction the adjusted basis of the property acquired is less than 200 percent of the adjusted basis of such pre-1970 public utility property immediately before the transaction, the property acquired is pre-1970 public utility property.

(2) Methods of depreciation not prohibited. Under section 167(l)(1), in the case of pre-1970 public utility property, the term "reasonable allowance" as used in section 167(a) means, for a taxable year for which a Federal income tax return was not filed before August 1, 1969, and in which such property is public utility property, an allowance (allowable without regard to section 167(l)) computed under—

(i) A subsection (l) method, or

(ii) The applicable 1968 method (other than a subsection (l) method) used by the taxpayer for such property, but only if—

(a) The taxpayer uses in respect of such taxable year a normalization method of regulated accounting for such property,

(b) The taxpayer used a flow-through method of regulated accounting for such property for its July 1969 regulated accounting period, or

(c) The taxpayer's first regulated accounting period with respect to such property is after the taxpayer's July 1969 regulated accounting period and the taxpayer used a flow-through method of regulated accounting for its July 1969 regulated accounting period for public utility property of the same kind (or if there is no property of the same kind, property of the most similar kind) most recently placed in service. See paragraph (e)(5) of this section for determination of same (or similar) kind.

(3) Flow-through method of regulated accounting in certain cases. See paragraph (e)(6) of this section for treatment of certain taxpayers with pending applications for change in method of accounting as being deemed to have used a flow-through method of regulated accounting for the July 1969 regulated accounting period.

(4) Examples. The provisions of this paragraph may be illustrated by the following examples:

Example (1). Corporation X, a calendar-year taxpayer subject to the jurisdiction of a regulatory body described in section 167(l)(3)(A), used the straight line method of depreciation (a subsection (l) method) for all of its public utility property for which depreciation was allowable on its Federal income tax return for 1967 (the latest taxable year for which X, prior to August 1, 1969, filed a return). Assume that under paragraph (e) of this section, X's applicable 1968 method is a subsection (l) method with respect to all of its public utility property. Thus, with respect to its pre-1970 public utility property, X may only use a straight line method (or any other subsection (l) method) of depreciation for all taxable years after 1967.

Example (2). Corporation Y, a calendar-year taxpayer subject to the jurisdiction of the Federal Power Commission, is engaged exclusively in the transportation of gas by pipeline. On its Federal income tax return for 1967 (the latest taxable year for which Y, prior to August 1, 1969, filed a return), Y used the declining balance method of depreciation using a rate of 150 percent of the straight-line rate for all of its nonsection 1250 public utility property with respect to which depreciation was allowable. Assume that with respect to all of such property, Y's applicable 1968 method under paragraph (e) of this section is such 150 percent declining balance method. Assume that Y used a normalization method of regulated accounting for all relevant regulated accounting periods. If Y continues to use a normalization method of regulated accounting, Y may compute its reasonable allowance for purposes of section 167(a) using such 150 percent declining balance method for its nonsection 1250 pre-1970 public utility property for all taxable years beginning with 1968, provided the use of such method is allowable without regard to section 167(l). Y may also use a subsection (l) method for any of such pre- 1970 public utility property for all taxable years beginning after 1967. However, because each different uniform rate applied to the basis of the property is a different method of depreciation, Y may not use a declining balance method of depreciation using a rate of twice the straight line rate for any of such pre-1970 public utility property for any taxable year beginning after 1967.

Example (3). Assume the same facts as in example (2) except that with respect to all of its nonsection 1250 pre-1970 public utility property accounted for in its July 1969 regulated accounting period Y used a flow-through method of regulated accounting for such period. Assume further that such property is the property on the basis of which the applicable 1968 method is established for pre-1970 public utility property of the same kind, but having a first regulated accounting period after the taxpayer's July 1969 regulated accounting period. Beginning with 1968, with respect to such property Y may compute its reasonable allowance for purposes of section 167(a) using the declining balance method of depreciation and a rate of 150 percent of the straight line rate, whether it uses a normalization or flow-through method of regulated accounting after its July 1969 regulated accounting period, provided the use of such method is allowable without regard to section 167(l).

(d) Post-1969 public utility property. *(1) In general.* Under section 167(l)(3)(C), the term "post-1969 public utility property" means any public utility property which is not pre-1970 public utility property.

(2) Methods of depreciation not prohibited. Under section 167(l)(2), in the case of post-1969 public utility property, the term "reasonable allowance" as used in section 167(a) means, for a taxable year, an allowance (allowable without regard to section 167(l)) computed under—

(i) A subsection (l) method,

(ii) A method of depreciation otherwise allowable under section 167 if, with respect to the property, the taxpayer uses in respect of such taxable year a normalization method of regulated accounting, or

(iii) The taxpayer's applicable 1968 method (other than a subsection (l) method) with respect to the property in question, if the taxpayer used a flow-through method of regulated accounting for its July 1969 regulated accounting period for the property of the same (or similar) kind most recently placed in service, provided that the property in question is not property to which an election under section 167(l)(4)(A) applies. See § 1.167(l)-2 for rules with respect to an election under section 167(l)(4)(A). See paragraph (e)(5) of this section for definition of same (or similar) kind.

(3) Examples. The provisions of this paragraph may be illustrated by the following examples:

Example (1). Corporation X is engaged exclusively in the trade or business of the transportation of gas by pipeline and is subject to the jurisdiction of the Federal Power Commission. With respect to all its public utility property, X's applicable 1968 method (as determined under paragraph (e) of this section) is the straight line method of depreciation. X may determine its reasonable allowance for depreciation under section 167(a) with respect to its post-1969 public utility property under a straight line method (or other subsection (l) method) or, if X uses a normalization method of regulated accounting, any other method of depreciation, provided that the use of such other method is allowable under section 167 without regard to section 167(l).

Example (2). Assume the same facts as in example (1) except that with respect to all of X's post-1969 public utility property the applicable 1968 method (as determined under paragraph (e) of this section) is the declining balance method using a rate of 150 percent of the straight line rate. Assume further that all of X's pre-1970 public utility property was accounted for in its July 1969 regulated accounting period, and that X used a flow-through method of regulated accounting for such period. X may determine its reasonable allowance for depreciation under section 167 with respect to its post-1969 public utility property by using the straight line method of depreciation (or any other subsection (l) method), by using any method otherwise allowable under section 167 (such as a declining balance method) if X uses a normalization method of regulated accounting, or, by using the declining balance method using a rate of 150 percent of the straight line rate, whether or not X uses a normalization or a flow-through method of regulated accounting.

(e) Applicable 1968 method. *(1) In general.* Under section 167(l)(3)(D), except as provided in subparagraphs (3) and (4) of this paragraph, the term "applicable 1968 method" means with respect to any public utility property—

(i) The method of depreciation properly used by the taxpayer in its Federal income tax return with respect to such property for the latest taxable year for which a return was filed before August 1, 1969,

(ii) If subdivision (i) of this subparagraph does not apply, the method of depreciation properly used by the taxpayer in its Federal income tax return for the latest taxable year for which a return was filed before August 1, 1969, with respect to public utility property of the same kind (or if there is no property of the same kind, property of the most similar kind) most recently placed in service before the end of such latest taxable year, or

(iii) If neither subdivision (i) nor (ii) of this subparagraph applies, a subsection (l) method.

If, on or after August 1, 1969, the taxpayer files an amended return for the taxable year referred to in subdivisions (i) and (ii) of this subparagraph, such amended return shall not be taken into consideration in determining the applicable 1968 method. The term "applicable 1968 method" also means with respect to any public utility property, for the year of change and subsequent years, a method of depreciation otherwise allowable under section 167 to which the taxpayer changes from an applicable 1968 method if, such new method results in a lesser allowance for depreciation for such property under section 167 in the year of change and the taxpayer secures the Commissioner's consent to the change in accordance with the procedures of section 446(e) and § 1.446-1.

(2) *Placed in service.* For purposes of this section, property is placed in service on the date on which the period for depreciation begins under section 167. See, for example, § 1.167(a)-10(b) and § 1.167(a)-11(c)(2). If under an averaging convention property which is placed in service (as defined in § 1.46-3(d)(ii)) by the taxpayer on different dates is treated as placed in service on the same date, then for purposes of section 167(l) the property shall be treated as having been placed in service on the date the period for depreciation with respect to such property would begin under section 167 absent such averaging convention. Thus, for example, if, except for the fact that the averaging convention used assumes that all additions and retirements made during the first half of the year were made on the first day of the year, the period of depreciation for two items of public utility property would begin on January 10 and March 15, respectively, then for purposes of determining the property of the same (or similar) kind most recently placed in service, such items of property shall be treated as placed in service on January 10 and March 15, respectively.

(3) *Certain section 1250 property.* If a taxpayer is required under section 167(j) to use a method of depreciation other than its applicable 1968 method with respect to any section 1250 property, the term "applicable 1968 method" means the method of depreciation allowable under section 167(j) which is the most nearly comparable method to the applicable 1968 method determined under subparagraph (1) of this paragraph. For example, if the applicable 1968 method on new section 1250 property is the declining balance method using 200 percent of the straight line rate, the most nearly comparable method allowable for new section 1250 property under section 167(j) would be the declining balance method using 150 percent of the straight line rate. If the applicable 1968 method determined under subparagraph (1) of this paragraph is the sum of the years-digits method, the term "most nearly comparable method" refers to any method of depreciation allowable under section 167(j).

(4) *Applicable 1968 method in certain cases.* (i) (a) Under section 167(l)(3)(E), if the taxpayer evidenced within the time and manner specified in (b) of this subdivision (i) the intent to use a method of depreciation under section 167 (other than its applicable 1968 method as determined under subparagraph (1) or (3) of this paragraph or a subsection (l) method) with respect to any public utility property, such method of depreciation shall be deemed to be the taxpayer's applicable 1968 method with respect to such public utility property and public utility property of the same (or most similar) kind subsequently placed in service.

(b) Under this subdivision (i), the intent to use a method of depreciation under section 167 is evidenced—

(1) By a timely application for permission for a change in method of accounting filed by the taxpayer before August 1, 1969, or

(2) By the use of such method of depreciation in the computation by the taxpayer of its tax expense for purposes of reflecting operating results in its regulated books of account for its July 1969 regulated accounting period, as established in the manner prescribed in subparagraph (g)(1) (i), (ii), or (iii) of this section.

(ii) (a) If public utility property is acquired in a transaction in which its basis in the hands of the transferee is determined in whole or in part by reference to its basis in the hands of the transferor by reason of the application of any provision of the Code, or in a transfer (including any purchase for cash or in exchange) from a related person, then in the hands of the transferee the applicable 1968 method with respect to such property shall be determined by reference to the treatment in respect of such property in the hands of the transferor.

(b) For purposes of this subdivision (ii), the term "related person" means a person who is related to another person if either immediately before or after the transfer—

(1) The relationship between such persons would result in a disallowance of losses under section 267 (relating to disallowance of losses, etc., between related taxpayers) or section 707(b) (relating to losses disallowed, etc., between partners and controlled partnerships) and the regulations thereunder, or

(2) Such persons are members of the same controlled group of corporations, as defined in section 1563(a) (relating to definition of controlled group of corporations), except that "more than 50 percent" shall be substituted for "at least 80 percent" each place it appears in section 1563(a) and the regulations thereunder.

(5) *Same or similar.* The classification of property as being of the same (or similar) kind shall be made by reference to the function of the public utility to which the primary use of the property relates. Property which performs the identical function in the identical manner shall be treated as property of the same kind. The determination that property is of a similar kind shall be made by reference to the proper account to which expenditures for the property are chargeable under the system of regulated accounts required to be used by the taxpayer for the period in which the property in question was acquired. Property, the expenditure for which is chargeable to the same account, is property of the most similar kind. Property, the expenditure for which is chargeable to an account for property which serves the same general function, is property of a similar kind. Thus, for example, if corporation X, a natural gas company, subject to the jurisdiction of the Federal Power Commission, had property properly chargeable to account 366 (relating to transmission plant structures and improvements) acquired an additional structure properly chargeable to account 366, under the uniform system of accounts prescribed for natural gas companies (class A and class B) by the Federal Power Commission, effective September 1, 1968, the addition would constitute property of the same kind if it performed the identical function in the identical manner. If, however, the addition did not perform the identical function in the identical manner, it would be property of the most similar kind.

(6) *Regulated method of accounting in certain cases.* Under section 167(l)(4)(B), if with respect to any pre-1970 public utility property the taxpayer filed a timely application for change in method of accounting referred to in subparagraph (4)(i) *(b)(1)* of this paragraph and with respect to property of the same (or similar) kind most recently placed in service the taxpayer used a flow-through method of regulated accounting for its July 1969 regulated accounting period, then for purposes of section 167(l)(1)(B) and paragraph (c) of this section the taxpayer shall be deemed to have used a flow-through method of regulated accounting with respect to such pre-1970 public utility property.

(7) *Examples.* The provisions of this paragraph may be illustrated by the following examples:

Example (1). Corporation X is a calendar-year taxpayer. On its Federal income tax return for 1967 (the latest taxable year for which X, prior to August 1, 1969, filed a return) X used a straight line method of depreciation with respect to certain public utility property placed in service before 1965 and used the declining balance method of depreciation using

200 percent of the straight line rate (double declining balance) with respect to the same kind of public utility property placed in service after 1964. In 1968 and 1970, X placed in service additional public utility property of the same kind. The applicable 1968 method with respect to the above described public utility property is shown in the following chart:

Property held in 1970	Placed in service	Method on 1967 return	Applicable 1968 method
Group 1	Before 1965	Straight line	Straight line
Group 2	After 1964 and before 1968	Double declining balance	Double declining balance
Group 3	After 1967 and before 1969		Do
Group 4	After 1968		Do

Example (2). Corporation Y is a calendar-year taxpayer engaged exclusively in the trade or business of the furnishing of electrical energy. In 1954, Y placed in service hydroelectric generators and for all purposes Y has taken straight line depreciation with respect to such generators. In 1960, Y placed in service fossil fuel generators and for all purposes since 1960 has used the declining balance method of depreciation using a rate of 150 percent of the straight line rate (computed without reduction for salvage) with respect to such generators. After 1960 and before 1970 Y did not place in service any generators. In 1970, Y placed in service additional hydroelectric generators. The applicable 1968 method with respect to the hydroelectric generators placed in service in 1970 would be the straight line method because it was the method used by Y on its return for the latest taxable year for which Y filed a return before August 1, 1969, with respect to property of the same kind (i.e., hydroelectric generators) most recently placed in service.

Example (3). Assume the same facts as in example (2), except that the generators placed in service in 1970 were nuclear generators. The applicable 1968 method with respect to such generators is the declining balance method using a rate of 150 percent of the straight line rate because, with respect to property of the most similar kind (fossil fuel generators) most recently placed in service, Y used such declining balance method on its return for the latest taxable year for which it filed a return before August 1, 1969.

(f) Subsection (l) method. Under section 167(l)(3)(F), the term "subsection (l) method" means a reasonable and consistently applied ratable method of computing depreciation which is allowable under section 167(a), such as, for example, the straight line method or a unit of production method or machine-hour method. The term "subsection (l) method" does not include any declining balance method (regardless of the uniform rate applied), sum of the years-digits method, or method of depreciation which is allowable solely by reason of section 167(b)(4) or (j)(1)(C).

(g) July 1969 regulated accounting period. *(1) In general.* Under section 167(l)(3)(I), the term "July 1969 regulated accounting period" means the taxpayer's latest accounting period ending before August 1, 1969, for which the taxpayer regularly computed, before January 1, 1970, its tax expense for purposes of reflecting operating results in its regulated books of account. The computation by the taxpayer of such tax expense may be established by reference to the following:

(i) The most recent periodic report of a period ending before August 1, 1969, required by a regulatory body described in section 167(l)(3)(A) having jurisdiction over the taxpayer's regulated books of account which was filed with such body before January 1, 1970 (whether or not such body has jurisdiction over rates).

(ii) If subdivision (i) of this subparagraph does not apply, the taxpayer's most recent report to its shareholders for a period ending before August 1, 1969, but only if such report was distributed to the shareholders before January 1, 1970, and if the taxpayer's stocks or securities are traded in an established securities market during such period. For purposes of this subdivision, the term "established securities market" has the meaning assigned to such term in § 1.453-3(d)(4).

(iii) If subdivisions (i) and (ii) of this subparagraph do not apply, entries made to the satisfaction of the district director before January 1, 1970, in its regulated books of account for its most recent accounting period ending before August 1, 1969.

(2) July 1969 method of regulated accounting in certain acquisitions. If public utility property is acquired in a transaction in which its basis in the hands of the transferee is determined in whole or in part by reference to its basis in the hands of the transferor by reason of the application of any provision of the Code, or in a transfer (including any purchase for cash or in exchange) from a related person, then in the hands of the transferee the method of regulated accounting for such property's July 1969 regulated accounting period shall be determined by reference to the treatment in respect of such property in the hands of the transferor. See paragraph (e)(4)(ii) of this section for definition of "related person".

(3) Determination date. For purposes of section 167(l), any reference to a method of depreciation under section 167(a), or a method of regulated accounting, taken into account by the taxpayer in computing its tax expense for its July 1969 regulated accounting period shall be a reference to such tax expense as shown on the periodic report or report to share-holders to which subparagraph (1)(i) or (ii) of this paragraph applies or the entries made on the taxpayer's regulated books of account to which subparagraph (1)(iii) of this paragraph applies. Thus, for example, assume that regulatory body A having jurisdiction over public utility property with respect to X's regulated books of account requires X to reflect its tax expense in such books using the same method of depreciation which regulatory body B uses for determining X's cost of service for ratemaking purposes. If in 1971, in the course of approving a rate change for X, B retroactively determines X's cost of service for ratemaking purposes for X's July 1969 regulated accounting period using a method of depreciation different from the method reflected in X's regulated books of account as of January 1, 1970, the method of depreciation used by X for its July 1969 regulated accounting period would be determined without reference to the method retroactively used by B in 1971.

(h) Normalization method of accounting. *(1) In general.* (i) Under section 167(l), a taxpayer uses a normalization method of regulated accounting with respect to public utility property—

(a) If the same method of depreciation (whether or not a subsection (l) method) is used to compute both its tax expense and its depreciation expense for purposes of establishing cost of service for ratemaking purposes and for reflecting operating results in its regulated books of account, and

(b) If to compute its allowance for depreciation under section 167 it uses a method of depreciation other than the method it used for purposes described in *(a)* of this subdivision, the taxpayer makes adjustments consistent with subparagraph (2) of this paragraph to a reserve to reflect the total amount of the deferral of Federal income tax liability resulting from the use with respect to all of its public utility property of such different methods of depreciation.

(ii) In the case of a taxpayer described in section 167(l)(1)(B) or (2)(C), the reference in subdivision (i) of this subparagraph shall be a reference only to such taxpayer's "qualified public utility property". See § 1.167(l)-2(b) for definition of "qualified public utility property".

(iii) Except as provided in this subparagraph, the amount of Federal income tax liability deferred as a result of the use of different method of depreciation under subdivision (i) of this subparagraph is the excess (computed without regard to credits) of the amount the tax liability would have been had a subsection (l) method been used over the amount of the actual tax liability. Such amount shall be taken into account for the taxable year in which such different methods of depreciation are used. If, however, in respect of any taxable year the use of a method of depreciation other than a subsection (l) method for purposes of determining the taxpayer's reasonable allowance under section 167(a) results in a net operating loss carryover (as determined under section 172) to a year succeeding such taxable year which would not have arisen (or an increase in such carryover which would not have arisen) had the taxpayer determined his reasonable allowance under section 167(a) using a subsection (l) method, then the amount and time of the deferral of tax liability shall be taken into account in such appropriate time and manner as is satisfactory to the district director.

(2) Adjustments to reserve. (i) The taxpayer must credit the amount of deferred Federal income tax determined under subparagraph (1)(i) of this paragraph for any taxable year to a reserve for deferred taxes, a depreciation reserve, or other reserve account. The taxpayer need not establish a separate reserve account for such amount but the amount of deferred tax determined under subparagraph (1)(i) of this paragraph must be accounted for in such a manner so as to be readily identifiable. With respect to any account, the aggregate amount allocable to deferred tax under section 167(l) shall not be reduced except to reflect the amount for any taxable year by which Federal income taxes are greater by reason of the prior use of different methods of depreciation under subparagraph (1)(i) of this paragraph. An additional exception is that the aggregate amount allocable to deferred tax under section 167(l) may be properly adjusted to reflect asset retirements or the expiration of the period for depreciation used in determining the allowance for depreciation under section 167(a).

(ii) The provisions of this subparagraph may be illustrated by the following examples:

Example (1). Corporation X is exclusively engaged in the transportation of gas by pipeline subject to the jurisdiction of the Federal Power Commission. With respect to its post-1969 public utility property, X is entitled under section 167(l)(2)(B) to use a method of depreciation other than a subsection (l) method if it uses a normalization method of regulated accounting. With respect to such property, X has not made any election under § 1.167(a)-11 (relating to depreciation based on class lives and asset depreciation ranges). In 1972, X places in service public utility property with an unadjusted basis of $2 million, and an estimated useful life of 20 years. X uses the declining balance method of depreciation with a rate twice the straight line rate. If X uses a normalization method of regulated accounting, the amount of depreciation allowable under section 167(a) with respect to such property for 1972 computed under the double declining balance method would be $200,000. X computes its tax expense and depreciation expense for purposes of determining its cost of service for rate-making purposes and for reflecting operating results in its regulated books of account using the straight line method of depreciation (a subsection (l) method). A depreciation allowance computed in this manner is $100,000. The excess of the depreciation allowance determined under the double declining balance method ($200,000) over the depreciation expense computed using the straight line method ($100,000) is $100,000. Thus, assuming a tax rate of 48 percent, X used a normalization method of regulated accounting for 1972 with respect to property placed in service that year if for 1972 it added to a reserve $48,000 as taxes deferred as a result of the use by X of a method of depreciation for Federal income tax purposes different from that used for establishing its cost of service for ratemaking purposes and for reflecting operating results in its regulated books of account.

Example (2). Assume the same facts as in example (1), except that X elects to apply § 1.167(a)-11 with respect to all eligible property placed in service in 1972. Assume further that all property X placed in service in 1972 is eligible property. One hundred percent of the asset guideline period for such property is 22 years and the asset depreciation range is from 17.5 years to 26.5 years. X uses the double declining balance method of depreciation, selects an asset depreciation period of 17.5 years, and applies the half-year convention (described in § 1.167(a)-11(c)(2)(iii)). In 1972, the depreciation allowable under section 167(a) with respect to property placed in service in 1972 is $114,285 (determined without regard to the normalization requirements in § 1.167(a)-11(b)(6) and in section 167(l)). X computes its tax expense for purposes of determining its cost of service for ratemaking purposes and for reflecting operating results in its regulated books of account using the straight line method of depreciation (a subsection (l) method), an estimated useful life of 22 years (that is, 100 percent of the asset guideline period), and the half-year convention. A depreciation allowance computed in this manner is $45,454. Assuming a tax rate of 48 percent, the amount that X must add to a reserve for 1972 with respect to property placed in service that year in order to qualify as using a normalization method of regulated accounting under section 167(l)(3)(G) is $27,429 and the amount in order to satisfy the normalization requirements of § 1.167(a)-11(b)(6) is $5,610. X determined such amounts as follows:

(1) Depreciation allowance on tax return (determined without regard to section 167(l) and § 1.167(a)-11(b)(6))	$114,285
(2) Line (1), recomputed using a straight line method	57,142
(3) Difference in depreciation allowance attributable to different methods (line (1) minus line (2))	$ 57,143
(4) Amount to add to reserve under this paragraph (48 percent of line (3))	27,429
(5) Amount in line (2)	$ 57,142
(6) Line (5), recomputed by using an estimated useful life of 22 years and the half-year convention	45,454

(7) Difference in depreciation allowance attributable to difference in depreciation periods	$ 11,688
(8) Amount to add to reserve under § 1.167(a)-11(b)(6)(ii) (48 percent of line (7))	5,610

If, for its depreciation expense for purposes of determining its cost of service for rate-making purposes and for reflecting operating results in its regulated books of account, X had used a period in excess of the asset guideline period of 22 years, the total amount in lines (4) and (8) in this example would not be changed.

Example (3). Corporation Y, a calendar-year taxpayer which is engaged in furnishing electrical energy, made the election provided by section 167(l)(4)(a) with respect to its "qualified public utility property" (as defined in § 1.167(l)-2(b)). In 1971, Y placed in service qualified public utility property which had an adjusted basis of $2 million, estimated useful life of 10 years, and no salvage value. With respect to property of the same kind most recently placed in service, Y used a flow-through method of regulated accounting for its July 1969 regulated accounting period and the applicable 1968 method is the declining balance method of depreciation using 200 percent of the straight line rate. The amount of depreciation allowable under the double declining balance method with respect to the qualified public utility property would be $200,000. Y computes its tax expense and depreciation expense for purposes of determining its cost of service for ratemaking purposes and for reflecting operating results in its regulated books of account using the straight line method of depreciation. A depreciation allowance with respect to the qualified public utility property determined in this manner is $100,000. The excess of the depreciation allowance determined under the double declining balance method ($200,000) over the depreciation expense computed using the straight line method ($100,000) is $100,000. Thus, assuming a tax rate of 48 percent, Y used a normalization method of regulated accounting for 1971 if for 1971 it added to a reserve $48,000 as tax deferred as a result of the use by Y of a method of depreciation for Federal income tax purposes with respect to its qualified public utility property which method was different from that used for establishing its cost of service for ratemaking purposes and for reflecting operating results in its regulated books of account for such property.

Example (4). Corporation Z, exclusively engaged in a public utility activity did not use a flow-through method of regulated accounting for its July 1969 regulated accounting period. In 1971, a regulatory body having jurisdiction over all of Z's property issued an order applicable to all years beginning with 1968 which provided, in effect, that Z use an accelerated method of depreciation for purposes of section 167 and for determining its tax expenses for purposes of reflecting operating results in its regulated books of account. The order further provided that Z normalize 50 percent of the tax deferral resulting from the use of the accelerated method of depreciation and that Z flow-through 50 percent of the tax deferral resulting therefrom. Under section 167(l), the method of accounting provided in the order would not be a normalization method of regulated accounting because Z would not be permitted to normalize 100 percent of the tax deferral resulting from the use of an accelerated method of depreciation. Thus, with respect to its public utility property for purposes of section 167, Z may only use a subsection (l) method of depreciation.

Example (5). Assume the same facts as in example (4) except that the order of the regulatory body provided, in effect, that Z normalize 100 percent of the tax deferral with respect to 50 percent of its public utility property and flow-through the tax savings with respect to the other 50 percent of its property. Because the effect of such an order would allow Z to flow-through a portion of the tax savings resulting from the use of an accelerated method of depreciation, Z would not be using a normalization method of regulated accounting with respect to any of its properties. Thus, with respect to its public utility property for purposes of section 167, Z may only use a subsection (l) method of depreciation.

(3) Establishing compliance with normalization requirements in respect of operating books of account. The taxpayer may establish compliance with the requirement in subparagraph (1)(i) of this paragraph in respect of reflecting operating results, and adjustments to a reserve, in its operating books of account by reference to the following:

(i) The most recent periodic report for a period beginning before the end of the taxable year, required by a regulatory body described in section 167(l)(3)(A) having jurisdiction over the taxpayer's regulated operating books of account which was filed with such body before the due date (determined with regard to extensions) of the taxpayer's Federal income tax return for such taxable year (whether or not such body has jurisdiction over rates).

(ii) If subdivision (i) of this subparagraph does not apply, the taxpayer's most recent report to its shareholders for the taxable year but only if (a) such report was distributed to the shareholders before the due date (determined with regard to extensions) of the taxpayer's Federal income tax return for the taxable year and (b) the taxpayer's stocks or securities are traded in an established securities market during such taxable year. For purposes of this subdivision, the term "established securities market" has the meaning assigned to such term in § 1.453-3(d)(4).

(iii) If neither subdivision (i) nor (ii) of this subparagraph applies, entries made to the satisfaction of the district director before the due date (determined with regard to extensions) of the taxpayer's Federal income tax return for the taxable year in its regulated books of account for its most recent period beginning before the end of such taxable year.

(4) Establishing compliance with normalization requirements in computing cost of service for ratemaking purposes. (i) In the case of a taxpayer which used a flow-through method or regulated accounting for its July 1969 regulated accounting period or thereafter, with respect to all or a portion of its pre-1970 public utility property, if a regulatory body having jurisdiction to establish the rates of such taxpayer as to such property (or a court which has jurisdiction over such body) issues an order of general application (or an order of specific application to the taxpayer) which states that such regulatory body (or court) will permit a class of taxpayers of which such taxpayer is a member (or such taxpayer) to use the normalization method of regulated accounting to establish cost of service for ratemaking purposes with respect to all or a portion of its public utility property, the taxpayer will be presumed to be using the same method of depreciation to compute both its tax expense and its depreciation expense for purposes of establishing its cost of service for ratemaking purposes with respect to the public utility property to which such order applies. In the event that such order is in any way conditional, the preceding sentence shall not apply until all of the conditions contained in such order which are applicable to the taxpayer have been fulfilled. The taxpayer shall establish to the satisfaction of the Commis-

sioner or his delegate that such conditions have been fulfilled.

(ii) In the case of a taxpayer which did not use the flow-through method of regulated accounting for its July 1969 regulated accounting period or thereafter (including a taxpayer which used a subsection (l) method of depreciation to compute its allowance for depreciation under section 167(a) and to compute its tax expense for purposes of reflecting operating results in its regulated books of account), with respect to any of its public utility property, it will be presumed that such taxpayer is using the same method of depreciation to compute both its tax expense and its depreciation expense for purposes of establishing its cost of service for ratemaking purposes with respect to its post-1969 public utility property. The presumption described in the preceding sentence shall not apply in any case where there is (a) an expression of intent (regardless of the manner in which such expression of intent is indicated) by the regulatory body (or bodies), having jurisdiction to establish the rates of such taxpayer, which indicates that the policy of such regulatory body is in any way inconsistent with the use of the normalization method of regulated accounting by such taxpayer or by a class of taxpayers of which such taxpayer is a member, or (b) a decision by a court having jurisdiction over such regulatory body which decision is in any way inconsistent with the use of the normalization method of regulated accounting by such taxpayer or a class of taxpayers of which such taxpayer is a member. The presumption shall be applicable on January 1, 1970, and shall, unless rebutted, be effective until an inconsistent expression of intent is indicated by such regulatory body or by such court. An example of such an inconsistent expression of intent is the case of a regulatory body which has, after the July 1969 regulated accounting period and before January 1, 1970, directed public utilities subject to its ratemaking jurisdiction to use a flow-through method of regulated accounting, or has issued an order of general application which states that such agency will direct a class of public utilities of which the taxpayer is a member to use a flow-through method of regulated accounting. The presumption described in this subdivision may be rebutted by evidence that the flow-through method of regulated accounting is being used by the taxpayer with respect to such property.

(iii) The provisions of this subparagraph may be illustrated by the following examples:

Example (1). Corporation X is a calendar-year taxpayer and its "applicable 1968 method" is a straight line method of depreciation. Effective January 1, 1970, X began collecting rates which were based on a sum of the years-digits method of depreciation and a normalization method of regulated accounting which rates had been approved by a regulatory body having jurisdiction over X. On October 1, 1971, a court of proper jurisdiction annulled the rate order prospectively, which annulment was not appealed, on the basis that the regulatory body had abused its discretion by determining the rates on the basis of a normalization method of regulated accounting. As there was no inconsistent expression of intent during 1970 or prior to the due date of X's return for 1970, X's use of the sum of the years-digits method of depreciation for purposes of section 167 on such return was proper. For 1971, the presumption is in effect through September 30. During 1971, X may use the sum of the years-digits method of depreciation for purposes of section 167 from January 1 through September 30, 1971. After September 30, 1971, and for taxable years after 1971, X must use a straight line method of depreciation until the inconsistent court decision is no longer in effect.

Example (2). Assume the same facts as in example (1), except that pursuant to the order of annulment, X was required to refund the portion of the rates attributable to the use of the normalization method of regulated accounting. As there was no inconsistent expression of intent during 1970 or prior to the due date of X's return for 1970, X has the benefit of the presumption with respect to its use of the sum of the years-digits method of depreciation for purposes of section 167, but because of the retroactive nature of the rate order X must file an amended return for 1970 using a straight line method of depreciation. As the inconsistent decision by the court was handed down prior to the due date of X's Federal income tax return for 1971, for 1971 and thereafter the presumption of subdivision (ii) of this subparagraph does not apply. X must file its Federal income tax returns for such years using a straight line method of depreciation.

Example (3). Assume the same facts as in example (2), except that the annulment order was stayed pending appeal of the decision to a court of proper appellate jurisdiction. X has the benefit of the presumption as described in example (2) for the year 1970, but for 1971 and thereafter the presumption of subdivision (ii) of this subparagraph does not apply. Further, X must file an amended return for 1970 using a straight line method of depreciation and for 1971 and thereafter X must file its returns using a straight line method of depreciation unless X and the district director have consented in writing to extend the time for assessment of tax for 1970 and thereafter with respect to the issue of normalization method of regulated accounting for as long as may be necessary to allow for resolution of the appeal with respect to the annulment of the rate order.

(5) Change in method of regulated accounting. The taxpayer shall notify the district director of a change in its method of regulated accounting, an order by a regulatory body or court that such method be changed, or an interim or final rate determination by a regulatory body which determination is inconsistent with the method of regulated accounting used by the taxpayer immediately prior to the effective date of such rate determination. Such notification shall be made within 90 days of the date that the change in method, the order, or the determination is effective. In the case of a change in the method of regulated accounting, the taxpayer shall recompute its tax liability for any affected taxable year and such recomputation shall be made in the form of an amended return where necessary unless the taxpayer and the district director have consented in writing to extend the time for assessment of tax with respect to the issue of normalization method of regulated accounting.

(6) Exclusion of normalization reserve from rate base. (i) Notwithstanding the provisions of subparagraph (1) of this paragraph, a taxpayer does not use a normalization method of regulated accounting if, for ratemaking purposes, the amount of the reserve for deferred taxes under section 167(l) which is excluded from the base to which the taxpayer's rate of return is applied, or which is treated as no-cost capital in those rate cases in which the rate of return is based upon the cost of capital, exceeds the amount of such reserve for deferred taxes for the period used in determining the taxpayer's tax expense in computing cost of service in such ratemaking.

(ii) For the purpose of determining the maximum amount of the reserve to be excluded from the rate base (or to be included as no-cost capital) under subdivision (i) of this subparagraph, if solely an historical period is used to determine depreciation for Federal income tax expense for ratemaking purposes, then the amount of the reserve account for the period is the amount of the reserve (determined under subparagraph (2) of this paragraph) at the end of the historical period. If solely a future period is used for such determination, the amount of the reserve account for the period is the amount of the reserve at the beginning of the period and a pro rata portion of the amount of any projected increase to be credited or decrease to be charged to the account during such period. If such determination is made by reference both to an historical portion and to a future portion of a period, the amount of the reserve account for the period is the amount of the reserve at the end of the historical portion of the period and a pro rata portion of the amount of any projected increase to be credited or decrease to be charged to the account during the future portion of the period. The pro rata portion of any increase to be credited or decrease to be charged during a future period (or the future portion of a part-historical and part-future period) shall be determined by multiplying any such increase or decrease by a fraction, the numerator of which is the number of days remaining in the period at the time such increase or decrease is to be accrued, and the denominator of which is the total number of days in the period (or future portion).

(iii) The provisions of subdivision (i) of this subparagraph shall not apply in the case of a final determination of a rate case entered on or before May 31, 1973. For this purpose, a determination is final if all rights to request a review, a rehearing, or a redetermination by the regulatory body which makes such determination have been exhausted or have lapsed. The provisions of subdivision (ii) of this subparagraph shall not apply in the case of a rate case filed prior to June 7, 1974, for which a rate order is entered by a regulatory body having jurisdiction to establish the rates of the taxpayer prior to September 5, 1974, whether or not such order is final, appealable, or subject to further review or reconsideration.

(iv) The provisions of this subparagraph may be illustrated by the following examples:

Example (1). Corporation X is exclusively engaged in the transportation of gas by pipeline subject to the jurisdiction of the Z Power Commission. With respect to its post-1969 public utility property, X is entitled under section 167(l)(2)(B) to use a method of depreciation other than a subsection (l) method if it uses a normalization method of regulated accounting. With respect to X the Z Power Commission for purposes of establishing cost of service uses a recent consecutive 12-month period ending not more than 4 months prior to the date of filing a rate case adjusted for certain known changes occurring within a 9-month period subsequent to the base period. X's rate case is filed on January 1, 1975. The year 1974 is the recorded test period for X's rate case and is the period used in determining X's tax expense in computing cost of service. The rates are contemplated to be in effect for the years 1975, 1976, and 1977. The adjustments for known changes relate only to wages and salaries. X's rate base at the end of 1974 is $145,000,000. The amount of the reserve for deferred taxes under section 167(l) at the end of 1974 is $1,300,000, and the reserve is projected to be $4,400,000 at the end of 1975, $6,600,000 at the end of 1976, and $9,800,000 at the end of 1977. X does not use a normalization method of regulated accounting if the Z Power Commission excludes more than $1,300,000 from the rate base to which X's rate of return is applied. Similarly, X does not use a normalization method of regulated accounting if, instead of the above, the Z Power Commission, in determining X's rate of return which is applied to the rate base, assigns to no-cost capital an amount that represents the reserve account for deferred tax that is greater than $1,300,000.

Example (2). Assume the same facts as in example (1) except that the adjustments for known changes in cost of service made by the Z Power Commission include an additional depreciation expense that reflects the installation of new equipment put into service on January 1, 1975. Assume further that the reserve for deferred taxes under section 167(l) at the end of 1974 is $1,300,000 and that the monthly net increase for the first 9 months of 1975 are projected to be

January 1-31	$ 310,000
February 1-28	300,000
March 1-31	300,000
April 1-30	280,000
May 1-31	270,000
June 1-30	260,000
July 1-31	260,000
August 1-31	250,000
September 1-30	240,000
	$2,470,000

For its regulated books of account X accrues such increases as of the last day of the month but as a matter of convenience credits increases or charges decreases to the reserve account on the 15th day of the month following the whole month for which such increase or decrease is accrued. The maximum amount that may be excluded from the rate base is $2,470,879 (the amount in the reserve at the end of the historical portion of the period ($1,300,000) and a pro rata portion of the amount of any projected increase for the future portion of the period to be credited to the reserve ($1,170,879)). Such pro rata portion is computed (without regard to the date such increase will actually be posted to the account) as follows:

$310,000 × 243/273 =	$ 275,934
300,000 × 215/273 =	236,264
300,000 × 184/273 =	202,198
280,000 × 154/273 =	157,949
270,000 × 123/273 =	121,648
260,000 × 93/273 =	88,571
260,000 × 62/273 =	59,048
250,000 × 31/273 =	28,388
240,000 × 1/273 =	879
	$1,170,879

Example (3). Assume the same facts as in example (1) except that for purposes of establishing cost of service the Z Power Commission uses a future test year (1975). The rates are contemplated to be in effect for 1975, 1976, and 1977. Assume further that plant additions, depreciation expense, and taxes are projected to the end of 1975 and that the reserve for deferred taxes under section 167(l) is $1,300,000 for 1974 and is projected to be $4,400,000 at the end of 1975. Assume also that the Z Power Commission applies the rate of return to X's 1974 rate base of $145,000,000 X and the Z Power Commission through negotiation arrive at the level of approved rates. X uses a normalization method of regulated accounting only if the settlement agreement, the rate order, or record of the proceedings of the Z Power Commission indicates that the Z Power Commission did not exclude an amount representing the reserve for deferred taxes from X's rate base ($145,000,000) greater than $1,300,000 plus a pro rata portion of the projected increases and decreases that are to be credited or charged to the reserve account for 1975. Assume that for 1975 quarterly net increases are projected to be

1st quarter	$ 910,000
2nd quarter	810,000
3rd quarter	750,000
4th quarter	630,000
Total	$3,100,000

For its regulated books of account X will accrue such increases as of the last day of the quarter but as a matter of convenience will credit increases or charge decreases to the reserve account on the 15th day of the month following the last month of the quarter for which such increase or decrease will be accrued. The maximum amount that may be excluded from the rate base is $2,591,480 (the amount of the reserve at the beginning of the period ($1,300,000) plus a pro rata portion ($1,291,480) of the $3,100,000 projected increase to be credited to the reserve during the period). Such portion is computed (without regard to the date such increase will actually be posted to the account) as follows:

$910,000 × 276/365 =	$ 688,110
810,000 × 185/365 =	410,548
750,000 × 93/365 =	191,096
630,000 × 1/365 =	1,726
	$1,291,480

(i) Flow-through method of regulated accounting. Under section 167(l)(3)(H), a taxpayer uses a flow-through method of regulated accounting with respect to public utility property if it uses the same method of depreciation (other than a subsection (l) method) to compute its allowance for depreciation under section 167 and to compute its tax expense for purposes of reflecting operating results in its regulated books of account unless such method is the same method used by the taxpayer to determine its depreciation expense for purposes of reflecting operating results in its regulated books of account. Except as provided in the preceding sentence, the method of depreciation used by a taxpayer with respect to public utility property for purposes of determining cost of service for ratemaking purposes or rate base for ratemaking purposes shall not be considered in determining whether the taxpayer used a flow-through method of regulated accounting. A taxpayer may establish use of a flow-through method of regulated accounting in the same manner that compliance with normalization requirements in respect of operating books of account may be established under paragraph (h)(4) of this section.

T.D. 7315, 6/6/74.

§ 1.167(l)-2 Public utility property; election as to post-1969 property representing growth in capacity.

(a) In general. Section 167(l)(2) prescribes the methods of depreciation which may be used by a taxpayer with respect to its post-1969 public utility property. Under section 167(l)(2)(A) and (B) the taxpayer may use a subsection (l) method of depreciation (as defined in section 167(l)(3)(F)) or any other method of depreciation which is otherwise allowable under section 167 if, in conjunction with the use of such other method, such taxpayer uses the normalization method of accounting (as defined in section 167(l)(3)(G)). Paragraph (2)(C) of section 167(l) permits a taxpayer which used the flow-through method of accounting for its July 1969 accounting period (as these terms are defined in section 167(l)(3)(H) and (I), respectively) to use its applicable 1968 method of depreciation with respect to certain property. Section 167(l)(3)(D) describes the term "applicable 1968 method." Accordingly, a regulatory agency is not precluded by section 167(l) from requiring such a taxpayer subject to its jurisdiction to continue to use the flow-through method of accounting unless the taxpayer makes the election pursuant to section 167(l)(4)(A) and this section. Whether or not the election is made, if such regulatory agency permits the taxpayer to change from the flow-through method of accounting, subsection (l)(2)(A) or (B) would apply and such taxpayer could, subject to the provisions of section 167(e) and the regulations thereunder (relating to change in method), use a subsection (l) method of depreciation or, if the taxpayer uses the normalization method of accounting, any other method of depreciation otherwise allowable under section 167.

(1) Election. Under subparagraph (A) of section 167(l)(4), if the taxpayer so elects, the provisions of paragraph (2)(C) of section 167(l) shall not apply to its qualified public utility property (as such term is described in paragraph (b) of this section). In such case the taxpayer making the election shall use a method of depreciation prescribed by section 167(l)(2)(A) or (B) with respect to such property.

(2) Property to which election shall apply. (i) Except as provided in subdivision (ii) of this subparagraph the election provided by section 167(l)(4)(A) shall apply to all of the qualified public utility property of the taxpayer.

(ii) In the event that the taxpayer wishes the election provided by section 167(l)(4)(A) to apply to only a portion of its qualified public utility property, it must clearly identify the property to be subject to the election in the statement of election described in paragraph (e) of this section. Where all property which performs a certain function is included within the election, the election shall apply to all future acquisitions of qualified public utility property which performs the same function. Where only certain property within a functional group of property is included within the election, the election shall apply only to property which is of the same kind as the included property.

(iii) The provisions of subdivision (ii) of this subparagraph may be illustrated by the following examples:

Example (1). Corporation A, an electric utility company, wishes to have the election provided by section 167(l)(4)(A) apply only with respect to its production plant. A statement that the election shall apply only with respect to production plant will be sufficient to include within the election all of the taxpayer's qualified production plant of any kind. All public utility property of the taxpayer other than production plant will not be subject to the election.

Example (2). Corporation B, an electric utility company, wishes to have the election provided by section 167(l)(4)(A) apply only with respect to nuclear production plant. A statement which clearly indicates that only nuclear production plant will be included in the election will be sufficient to exclude from the election all public utility property other than nuclear production plant.

(b) Qualified public utility property. *(1) Definition.* For purposes of this section the term "qualified public utility property" means post-1969 public utility property to which section 167(l)(2)(C) applies, or would apply if the election described in section 167(l)(4)(A) had not been made, to the extent that such property constitutes property which increases the productive or operational capacity of the taxpayer with respect to the goods or services described in section 167(l)(3)(A) and does not represent the replacement of existing capacity. In the event that particular assets which are post-1969 public utility property both replace existing public utility property and increase the productive or operational capacity of the taxpayer, only that portion of each such asset which is properly allocable, pursuant to the provisions of subparagraph (3)(v) of this paragraph or paragraph (c)(2) of this section (as the case may be), to increasing the productive or operational capacity of the taxpayer shall be qualified public utility property.

(2) Limitation on use of formula method. A taxpayer which makes the election with respect to all of its post-1969 public utility property may determine the amount of its qualified public utility property by using the formula method described in paragraph (c) of this section or, where the taxpayer so chooses, it may use any other method based on engineering data which is satisfactory to the public utility property in the election described in paragraph (a)(1) of this section shall, in a manner satisfactory to the Commissioner and consistent with the provisions of subparagraph (3) of this paragraph, use a method based on engineering data. If a taxpayer uses the formula method described in paragraph (c) of this section, it must continue to use such method with respect to additions made in subsequent taxable years. The taxpayer may change from an engineering method to the formula method described in paragraph (c) of this section by filing a statement described in paragraph (h) of this section if it could have used such formula method for the prior taxable year.

(3) Measuring capacity under an engineering method in the case of a general election. (i) The provisions of this subparagraph apply in the case of an election made with respect to all of the post-1969 public utility property of the taxpayer.

(ii) A taxpayer which uses a method based on engineering data to determine the portion of its additions for a taxable year which constitutes qualified public utility property shall make such determination with reference to its "adjusted capacity" as of the first day of the taxable year during which such additions are placed in service. For purposes of this subparagraph, the term "adjusted capacity" means the taxpayer's capacity as of January 1, 1970, adjusted upward in the manner described in subdivision (iii) of this subparagraph for each taxable year ending after December 31, 1969, and before the first day of the taxable year during which the additions described in the preceding sentence are placed in service.

(iii) The adjustment described in this subdivision for each taxable year shall be equal to the number of units of capacity by which additions for the taxable year of public utility property with respect to which the election had been made exceed the number of units of capacity of retirements for such taxable year of public utility property with respect to which the flow-through method of accounting was being used at the time of their retirement. If for any taxable year the computation in the preceding sentence results in a negative amount, such negative amount shall be taken into account as a reduction in the amount of the adjustment (computed without regard to this sentence) in succeeding taxable years.

(iv) The provisions of this subparagraph may be illustrated by the following table which assumes that the taxpayer's adjusted capacity as of January 1, 1970, was 5,000 units.

1 Year	2 Additions	3 Flow-through Retirements	4 Net additions	5 Adjusted capacity[1]	6 Actual capacity	7 Units of qualified additions[2]
1970	1000	700	300	5000	5300	300
1971	300	500	(200)	5300	5100	....
1972	500	200	300	5300	5400	100
1973	400	800	(400)	5400	5000	....
1974	600	400	200	5400	5200	....
1975	800	300	500	5400	5700	300

[1] Capacity as of Jan. 1, 1970, plus amounts in column 7 for years prior to the year for which determination is being made.
[2] Column 6 minus column 5.

(v) The qualified portion of the basis for depreciation (as defined in section 167(g)) of each asset or group of assets (if group or composite accounting is used by the taxpayer) subject to the election shall be determined using the following ratio:

$$\frac{\text{Qualified portion of basis of asset}}{\text{Total basis of asset}} = \frac{\text{Units of qualified additions computed in column 7 on chart}}{\text{Units of capacity of additions computed in column 2 on chart}}$$

(c) Formula method of determining amount of property subject to election. *(1) In general.* The following formula method may be used to determine the amount of qualified public utility property:

Step 1. Find the total cost (within the meaning of section 1012) to the taxpayer of additions during the taxable year of all post-1969 public utility property with respect to which section 167(l)(2)(C) would apply if the election had not been made.

Step 2. Aggregate the cost (within the meaning of section 1012) to the taxpayer of all retirements during the taxable year of public utility property with respect to which the flow-through method of accounting was being used at the time of their retirement.

Step 3. Subtract the figure reached in step 2 from the figure reached in step 1.

In the event that the figure reached in step 2 exceeds the figure reached in step 1 such excess shall be carried forward to the next taxable year and shall be aggregated with the cost (within the meaning of section 1012) to the taxpayer of all retirements referred to in step 2 for such next taxable year.

(2) Allocation of bases. The amount of qualified public utility property as determined in accordance with the formula method described in subparagraph (1) of this paragraph shall be allocated to the basis for depreciation (as defined in section 167(g)) of each asset or group of assets (if group or composite accounting is used by the taxpayer) subject to the election using the following ratio:

$$\frac{\text{Amount of qualified additions computed in step 3}}{\text{Amount of total additions computed in step 1}} = \frac{\text{Qualified portion of basis of asset}}{\text{Total basis of asset}}$$

(d) Examples. The provisions of this section may be illustrated by the following examples:

Example (1). Corporation A, a telephone company subject to the jurisdiction of the Federal Communications Commission, elected, pursuant to the provisions of section 167(l)(4)(A) and this section, with respect to all of its qualified post-1969 public utility property to have the provisions of paragraph (2)(C) of section 167(l) not apply. In 1971 the Corporation added new underground cable with a cost (within the meaning of section 1012) to it of $4 million to its underground cable account. In the same year it retired public utility property with a cost (within the meaning of section 1012) to Corporation A of $1.5 million. The flow-through method of accounting was being used with respect to all of the retired property at the time of retirement. Using the formula method described in paragraph (c) of this section, the amount of qualified underground cable would be determined as follows:

	Million
Step 1. Aggregate cost of flow-through additions ..	$4.0
Step 2. Cost of all flow-through retirements	1.5
Step 3. Figure reached in step 1 less figure reached in step 2	2.5

The amount of qualified public utility property to which section 167(l)(2)(C) will not apply is $2.5 million. Pursuant to the provisions of paragraph (c)(2) of this section the amount of qualified public utility property would be allocated to the basis for depreciation (as defined in section 167(g)) of an asset with a total basis for depreciation of $2 million as follows:

$$\frac{\text{\$2.5 million (figure in step 3)}}{\text{\$4 million (figure in step 1)}} = \frac{\text{Qualified portion of basis of asset}}{\text{\$2 million}}$$

Qualified portion of basis of asset = $1.25 million

Example (2). In 1972 Corporation A (the corporation described in example (1)) added underground cable with a cost (within the meaning of section 1012) to it of $1 million. In the same year the cost (within the meaning of section 1012) to the corporation of retirements of public utility property with respect to which the flow-through method of accounting was being used was $3 million. There were no other additions or retirements. The amount of qualified public utility property would be determined as follows:

	Million
Step 1. Aggregate cost of flow-through additions ..	$1.0
Step 2. Cost of all flow-through retirements.......	3.0
Step 3. Figure reached in step 1 less figure reached in step 2	(2.0)

Since retirements of flow-through public utility property for the year 1972 exceeded additions made during such year, the excess retirements, $2.0 million, must be carried forward to be aggregated with retirements for 1973.

Example (3). Corporation B, a gas pipeline company subject to the jurisdiction of the Federal Power Commission, made the election provided by section 167(1)(4)(A) and this section with respect to all of its post-1969 public utility property. Corporation B chose to use an engineering data method of determining which property was subject to the election provided by this section. In 1970, the corporation replaced a portion of its pipeline with respect to which the flow-through method of accounting was being used at the time of its retirement which had a peak capacity on January 1, 1970, of 100,000 thousand cubic feet (M c.f.) per day at a pressure of 14.73 pounds per square inch absolute (p.s.i.a.) with pipe with a capacity of 125,000 M c.f. per day at 14.73 p.s.i.a. Assuming that there were no other additions or retirements, using an engineering data method one-fifth of the new pipeline would be property subject to the election of this section effective for its taxable year beginning on January 1, 1971.

Example (4). In 1970 Corporation C (with the same characteristics as the corporation described in example (3)) extended its pipeline 5 miles further than it extended on January 1, 1970. Assuming that there were no other additions or retirements, the entire extension would be property subject to the election provided by this section effective for its taxable year beginning on January 1, 1971.

Example (5). As a result of a change of service areas between two corporations, in 1970 Corporation D (with the same characteristics as the corporation described in example 3)) retired a pipeline running north and south and replaced it with a pipeline of equal length and capacity running east and west. No part of the pipeline running east and west is property subject to the election.

(e) Manner of making election. The election described in paragraph (a) of this section shall be made by filing, in duplicate, with the Commissioner of Internal Revenue, Washington, D.C. 20224, Attention, T:I:E, a statement of such election.

(f) Content of statement. The statement described in paragraph (e) of this section shall indicate that an election is being made under section 167(l) of the Internal Revenue Code of 1954, and it shall contain the following information:

(1) The name, address, and taxpayer identification number of the taxpayer,

(2) Whether the taxpayer will use the formula method of determining the amount of its qualified public utility property described in paragraph (c) of this section, or an engineering method, and

(3) Where the taxpayer wishes to include only a portion of its public utility property in the election pursuant to the provisions of paragraph (a)(2) of this section, a description sufficient to clearly identify the property to be included.

(g) Time for making election. The election permitted by this section shall be made by filing the statement described in paragraph (e) of this section not later than Monday, June 29, 1970.

(h) Change of method of determining amount of qualified property. Where a taxpayer which has elected pursuant to the provisions of section 167(l)(4)(A) wishes to change, pursuant to the provisions of paragraph (b)(2) of this section, from an engineering data method of determining which of its property is qualified public utility property to the formula method described in paragraph (c) of this section, it may do so by filing a statement to that effect at the time that it files its income tax return, with the district director or director of the regional service center, with whom the taxpayer's income tax return is required to be filed.

(i) Revocability of election. An election made under section 167(1) shall be irrevocable.

(j) Effective date. The election prescribed by section 167(l)(4)(A) and this section shall be effective for taxable years beginning after December 31, 1970.

T.D. 7045, 6/5/70, amend T.D. 7315, 6/6/74.

§ 1.167(l)-3 Multiple regulation, asset acquisitions, reorganizations, etc.

(a) Property not entirely subject to jurisdiction of one regulatory body. *(1) In general.* If a taxpayer which uses a method of depreciation other than a subsection (1) method of depreciation is required by a regulatory body having jurisdiction over less than all of its property to use, or not to use, a method of regulated accounting (i.e., normalization or flow-through), such taxpayer shall be considered as using, or not using, such method of regulated accounting only with respect to property subject to the jurisdiction of such regulatory body. In the case of property which is contained in a multiple asset account, the provisions of § 1.167(a)-7(c) and § 1.167(a)-11(c)(1)(iv) apply to prohibit depreciating a single account by two or more different methods.

(2) Jurisdiction of regulatory body. For purposes of this paragraph, a regulatory body is considered to have jurisdiction over property of a taxpayer if expenses with respect to the property are included in cost of service as determined by the regulatory body for ratemaking purposes or for reflecting operating results in its regulated books of account. For example, if regulatory body A, having jurisdiction over 60 percent of an item of X corporation's public utility property, required X to use the flow-through method of regulated accounting in circumstances which would bar X from using a method of depreciation under section 167(a) other than a subsection (1) method, and if regulatory body B, having jurisdiction over the remaining 40 percent of such item of property does not so require X to use the flow-through method of regulated accounting (or if the remaining 40 percent is not subject to the jurisdiction of any regulatory body), then with respect to 60 percent of the adjusted basis of the property X is prohibited from using a method of depreciation for purposes of section 167(a) other than a subsection (1) method. If in such example, A, having jurisdiction over 60 percent of X's public utility property, had jurisdiction over 100 percent of a particular generator, then with respect to the generator X would be prohibited from using a method of depreciation other than a subsection (1) method.

(3) Public utility property subject to more than one regulatory body. If a regulatory body having jurisdiction over public utility property with respect to the taxpayer's regulated books of account requires the taxpayer to reflect its tax expense in such books in the manner used by the regulatory body having jurisdiction over the public utility property for purposes of determining the taxpayer's cost of service for ratemaking purposes, the rules of subparagraphs (1) and (2) of this paragraph shall apply.

(b) Leasing transactions. *(1) Leased property.* Public utility property as defined in paragraph (b) of § 1.167(l)-1 includes property which is leased by a taxpayer where the leasing of such property is part of the lessor's section 167(l) public utility activity. Thus, such leased property qualifies as public utility property even though the predominant use of such property by the lessee is in other than a section 167(l) public utility activity. Further, leased property qualifies as public utility property under section 167(l) even though the leasing is not part of the lessor's public utility activity if the predominant use of such property by the lessee or any sublessee is in a section 167(l) public utility activity. However, the limitations of section 167(l) apply to a taxpayer only if such taxpayer is subject to the jurisdiction of a regulatory body described in section 167(l)(3)(A). For example, if a financial institution purchases property which it then leases to a lessee which uses such property predominantly in a section 167(l) public utility activity, the property qualifies as public utility property. However, because the financial institution's rates for leasing the property are not subject to the jurisdiction of a regulatory body described in section 167(l)(3)(A), the provisions of section 167(1) do not apply to the depreciation deductions taken with respect to the property by the financial institution. For possible application of section 167(l) to the lessee, see subparagraph (2) of this paragraph.

(2) Certain rental payments. Under section 167(l)(5), if a taxpayer leases property which is public utility property and the regulatory body having jurisdiction over such property for purposes of determining the taxpayer's operating results in its regulated books of account or for ratemaking purposes allows only an amount of such lessee's expenses with respect to the lease which is less than the amount which the taxpayer deducts for purposes of its Federal income tax liability, then a portion of the difference between such amounts shall not be allowed as a deduction by the taxpayer for purposes of its Federal income tax liability in such manner and time as the Commissioner or his delegate may determine consistent with the principles of § 1.167(l)-1 and this section applicable as to when a method of depreciation other than a subsection (1) method may be used for purposes of section 167(a).

(c) Certain partnership arrangements. Under section 167(l)(5), if property held by a partnership is not public utility property in the hands of the partnership but would be public utility property if an election was made under section 761 to be excluded from partnership treatment, then section 167(l) shall be applied by treating the partners as directly owning the property in proportion to their partnership interests.

(d) Cross reference. See § 1.167(l)-1(c)(1) for treatment of certain property as "pre-1970 public utility property" and § 1.167(l)-1(e)(4)(ii) for applicable 1968 method in the case of property acquired in certain transactions.

T.D. 7315, 6/6/74.

§ 1.167(l)-4 Public utility property; election to use asset depreciation range system.

(a) Application of section 167(l) to certain property subject to asset depreciation range system. If the taxpayer elects to compute depreciation under the asset depreciation range system described in § 1.167(a)-11 with respect to certain public utility property placed in service after December 31, 1970, see § 1.167(a)-11(b)(6).

T.D. 7128, 6/22/71, amend T.D. 7315, 6/6/74.

§ 1.167(m)-1 Class lives.

Caution: The Treasury has not yet amended Reg § 1.167(m)-1 to reflect changes made by P.L. 101-508.

(a) For rules regarding the election to use the class life system authorized by section 167(m), see the provisions of § 1.167(a)-11.

T.D. 7272, 4/20/73.

Proposed § 1.167(n)-0 Outline of regulation sections for section 167(g). [*For Preamble, see ¶ 152,279*]

This section lists the major captions contained in § 1.167(n)-1 through § 1.167(n)-7

§ 1.167(n)-1 Income forecast method.

(a) Overview.

(b) Method of accounting.

(1) In general.

(2) Election of the income forecast method.

§ 1.167(n)-2 Basis.

(a) Depreciable basis.

(1) In general.

(2) Timing of basis determinations and redeterminations.

(3) Separate Property.

(b) Basis redeterminations.

(c) Unrecovered depreciable basis.

(d) Example.

§ 1.167(n)-3 Income from the property.

(a) Current year income.

(1) In general.

(2) Special rule for advance payments.

(b) Forecasted total income.

(c) Revised forecasted total income.

(d) Special rules.

(1) Disposition of the property.

(2) Syndication income from television series.

(3) Apportionment of income in certain circumstances.

(4) Examples.

§ 1.167(n)-4 Computation of depreciation using the income forecast method.

(a) Computation of depreciation allowance.

(b) Revised computation.

(1) Change in estimated income.

(2) Requirement to use the revised computation.

(c) Basis redeterminations.

(1) Calculation of depreciation allowance.

(2) Example.

(d) Special rules.

(1) Final year depreciation.

(2) Certain basis redeterminations.

(3) Disposition of property.

(4) Separate property.

(e) Examples.

§ 1.167(n)-5 Property for which the income forecast method may be used.

(a) In general.

(b) Specific exclusions.

(c) Costs treated as separate property.

(1) Costs giving rise to a significant increase in income.

(2) Significant increase in income.

(3) Special rule for costs paid or incurred after the end of the final year.

(4) Time separate property is placed in service.

(5) Examples.

(d) Aggregations treated as a single income forecast property.

(1) Multiple episodes of a television series produced in the same taxable year.

(2) Multiple episodes of a television series produced in more than one taxable year.

(3) Multiple interests acquired pursuant to a single contract.

(4) Videocassettes and DVDs.

§ 1.167(n)-6 Look-back method.

(a) Application of the look-back method.

(b) Operation of the look-back method.

(1) In general.

(2) Property-by-property application.

(c) Recalculation of depreciation allowances.

(1) Computation.

(2) Revised forecasted total income from the property.

(3) Special rule for basis redeterminations.

(d) Hypothetical overpayment or underpayment of tax.

(1) In general.

(2) Hypothetical overpayment or underpayment, actual recomputation.

(3) Hypothetical overpayment or underpayment, simplified method.

(4) Definitions.

(e) Recomputation year.

(1) In general.

(2) Look-back method inapplicable in certain de minimis cases.

(f) De minimis basis exception.

(g) Treatment of look-back interest.

(1) In general.

(2) Additional interest due on interest only after tax liability due.

(3) Timing of look-back interest.

(4) Statute of limitations; compounding of interest on look-back interest.

(h) Example.

§ 1.167(n)-7 Effective date.

Proposed § 1.167(n)-1 Income forecast method. [*For Preamble, see ¶ 152,279*]

(a) Overview. This section and Secs. 1.167(n)-2 through 1.167(n)-7 provide rules for computing depreciation allowances under section 167 for property depreciated using the income forecast method. Because the income forecast method is only appropriate for property with unique income earning characteristics, only property specified in § 1.167(n)-5 may be depreciated under the income forecast method. A taxpayer using the income forecast method generally computes depreciation allowances each year based upon the ratio of current year income to forecasted total income from the property as described in § 1.167(n)-4. Current year income and forecasted total income are determined in accordance with the provisions of § 1.167(n)-3. In addition, a taxpayer must determine depreciable basis for income forecast property in accordance with the basis rules of § 1.167(n)-2. Property depreciated under the income forecast method generally is subject to the look-back rules of § 1.167(n)-6 whereby taxpayers must determine the amount of interest owed on any hypothetical underpayment of tax, or due on any hypothetical overpayment of tax, attributable to the use of estimated income in the computation of income forecast depreciation. Under these rules, look-back computations must be performed in specified recomputation years, which are generally the 3rd and 10th taxable years after the taxable year that the property is placed in service.

(b) Method of accounting. *(1) In general.* The computation of depreciation under the income forecast method is elected on a property-by-property basis, and is a method of accounting under section 446 that may not be changed without the consent of the Commissioner. However, a change in forecasted total income in accordance with the rules of § 1.167(n)-4 is not a change in method of accounting requiring the Commissioner's consent.

(2) Election of the income forecast method. A taxpayer elects the income forecast method by computing allowances for depreciation for the eligible property in accordance with the provisions of this section and § § 1.167(n)-2 through § 1.167(n)-6. See § 1.167(n)-5 for rules regarding eligible property.

Proposed § 1.167(n)-2 Basis. [*For Preamble, see ¶ 152,279*]

Caution: The Treasury has not yet amended Reg § 1.167(n)-2 to reflect changes made by P.L. 108-357.

(a) Depreciable basis. *(1) In general.* The basis upon which the allowance for depreciation is computed with respect to income forecast property is the basis of the income forecast property for purposes of section 1011 without regard to the adjustments described in section 1016(a)(2) and (3).

(2) Timing of basis determinations and redeterminations. Costs paid or incurred in or after the taxable year in which the income forecast property is placed in service are taken into account in accordance with a taxpayer's method of accounting in redetermining the basis of income forecast property in the taxable year paid or incurred (i.e., when all events have occurred that establish the fact of the liability, the amount of the liability can be determined with reasonable accuracy, and economic performance has occurred with respect to the liability). See § 1.446-1(c)(1)(i) and (ii), 1.461-1(a)(1) and (2), and 1.263A-1(c). Accordingly, contingent payments may not be included in the basis of income forecast property when the property is placed in service, but are included in the basis of income forecast property in the taxable year in which they are paid or incurred, even if the forecasted total income used in the computation of income forecast depreciation allowances is sufficient to indicate that the contingency will be satisfied.

(3) Separate property. Certain amounts paid or incurred in taxable years after income forecast property is placed in service are treated as separate property for purposes of computing depreciation allowances under the income forecast method. See § 1.167(n)-5(c).

(b) Basis redeterminations. If an amount required to be capitalized into the basis of income forecast property is paid or incurred after the income forecast property is placed in service, and if the amount required to be capitalized is not treated as separate property in accordance with § 1.167(n)-5(c), the basis of the income forecast property is redetermined and the amount required to be capitalized is the basis redetermination amount. The redetermined basis of the income forecast property is the depreciable basis of the income forecast property increased by the basis redetermination amount. In the year basis is redetermined (and in subsequent taxable years), the redetermined basis must be used to determine depreciation under the income forecast method. An additional allowance for depreciation under the income forecast method is allowed in the taxable year the basis of certain income forecast property is redetermined. See § 1.167(n)-4(c).

(c) Unrecovered depreciable basis. For any taxable year, the unrecovered depreciable basis of an income forecast property is the depreciable basis of the property less the adjustments described in section 1016(a)(2) and (3).

(d) Example. The provisions of § 1.167(n)-2 are illustrated by the following example:

Example. (i) Studio contracts with Actor to star in a motion picture film to be produced by Studio. Both Studio and Actor are calendar year taxpayers; Studio is an accrual basis taxpayer and Actor is a cash basis taxpayer. As compensation for Actor's services, the contract guarantees Actor a payment of five percent of the gross income from the film, beginning after the film has earned a total gross income (net of distribution costs) of $100x. Studio estimates that the film will earn a total gross income of $160x by the end of the 10th taxable year following the taxable year that the film is placed in service. The film is placed in service and earns $65x of gross income in year one, $30x in year two, and $25x in year three. Because the income from the film does not exceed $100x in either year one or year two, Studio pays nothing under the contract to Actor in years one and two. In year three, the cumulative income from the film reaches $120x, which exceeds the $100x threshold by $20x. Based on this excess, Studio calculates that it owes Actor $1x, calculated by multiplying $20x by Actor's contractual percentage of five percent. Studio pays $1x to Actor 20 days after the end of year three.

(ii) Studio may not include the $1x paid to Actor in the basis of the film in years one or two because Studio does not have a fixed liability to pay Actor any amount under the contract in years one and two. Furthermore, while Studio does have a fixed liability to pay Actor $1x in year three, the requirements of section 404 are not met in year three and Studio thus may not include the $1x in the basis of the film in year three. In year four, when section 404 is satisfied, Studio incurs the $1x in accordance with § 1.263A-1(c) and increases its basis in the film. The $1x is treated as a basis redetermination amount under § 1.167(n)-2(b) in year four.

Proposed § 1.167(n)-3 Income from the property. [*For Preamble, see ¶ 152,279*]

Caution: The Treasury has not yet amended Reg § 1.167(n)-3 to reflect changes made by P.L. 108-357.

(a) Current year income. *(1) In general.* Current year income is the income from an income forecast property for the current year (less the distribution costs of the income forecast property for such year), determined in accordance with the taxpayer's method of accounting. All income earned in connection with the income forecast property is included in current year income, except as provided in paragraph (d) of this section. In the case of a film, television show, or similar property, such income includes, but is not limited to—

(i) Income from foreign and domestic theatrical, television, and other releases and syndications;

(ii) Income from releases, sales, rentals, and syndications of video tape, DVD, and other media; and

(iii) Incidental income associated with the property, such as income from the financial exploitation of characters, designs, titles, scripts, and scores, but only to the extent that such incidental income is earned in connection with the ultimate use of such items by, or the ultimate sale of merchandise to, persons who are not related to the taxpayer (within the meaning of section 267(b)).

(2) Special rule for advance payments. In the year that income forecast property is placed in service, current year income for an income forecast property includes income included in gross income for any prior taxable year in connection with the property. This paragraph applies separately to any cost treated as separate property under § 1.167(n)-5(c).

(b) Forecasted total income. Forecasted total income is the sum of current year income for the year that income forecast property is placed in service, plus all income from the income forecast property that the taxpayer reasonably believes will be includible in current year income in subsequent taxable years (as adjusted for distribution costs) up to and including the 10th taxable year after the year in which the income forecast property is placed in service. Forecasted total income is based on the conditions known to exist at the end of the taxable year for which the income forecast property is placed in service.

(c) Revised forecasted total income. If information is discovered in a taxable year following the year in which income forecast property is placed in service that indicates that forecasted total income is inaccurate, a taxpayer must compute revised forecasted total income for the taxable year. Revised forecasted total income is based on the conditions known to exist at the end of the taxable year for which the revised forecast is being made. Revised forecasted total income for the taxable year is the sum of current year income for the taxable year and all prior taxable years, plus all income from the income forecast property that the taxpayer reasonably believes will be includible in current year income in taxable years after the current taxable year up to and including the 10th taxable year after the year in which the income forecast property is placed in service. Where a taxpayer computes revised forecasted total income in accordance with this § 1.167(n)-3(c), see § 1.167(n)-4(b) for the computation of the allowance for income forecast depreciation.

(d) Special rules. *(1) Disposition of the property.* In computing the depreciation allowance for an income forecast property, income from the sale or other disposition of income forecast property is not included in current year income. However, if the income forecast property is disposed of prior to the end of the 10th taxable year following the taxable year in which the property is placed in service, income from the sale or other disposition of income forecast property is taken into account in calculating revised forecasted total income both for purposes of calculating the allowance for depreciation in the year of disposition and for purposes of applying look-back. See § 1.167(n)-4(d)(3) and § 1.167(n)-6(c)(2).

(2) Syndication income from television series. (i) In the case of a television series produced for distribution on television networks, current year income and forecasted total income (or, if applicable, revised forecasted total income) used in the computation of the depreciation allowance for such property under § 1.167(n)-4 need not include income from syndication of the television series before the earlier of—

(A) The fourth taxable year beginning after the date the first episode in the series is placed in service; or

(B) The earliest taxable year in which the taxpayer has an arrangement relating to the syndication of the series.

(ii) For purposes of this paragraph (d)(2), an arrangement relating to syndication of a series of television shows means any arrangement other than the first run exhibition agreement. For example, an arrangement for exhibition of a television series by individual television stations is an arrangement for syndication if it results in an exhibition of one or more episodes of the series beginning after one or more episodes of the series have been exhibited on a television network. A first run exhibition agreement is an agreement under which any episode (including a pilot episode) of a television series is first placed in service within a particular market.

(3) Apportionment of income in certain circumstances. When income from a particular source relates to more than one income forecast property the taxpayer must make a reasonable allocation of the income among those properties based on all relevant factors. Situations where allocation is necessary include income generated by a syndication arrangement involving more than one income forecast property, incidental income described in paragraph (a)(1)(iii) of this section that relates to more than one motion picture, and income associated with income forecast property when expenditures relating to the property have given rise to separate property as defined in § 1.167(n)-5(c). For example, when a taxpayer sells or licenses merchandise that features the likeness of a character that has appeared in more than one film, relevant factors might include merchandise sales figures prior to the release of the subsequent film, specific identification of certain merchandise with one particular film, and the taxpayer's prior experience with similar situations.

(4) Examples. The provisions of this section are illustrated by the following examples:

Example (1). C produces a motion picture film featuring the adventures of a fictional character. C sells merchandise using the character's image, enters into licensing agreements with unrelated parties for the use of the image, and uses the image to promote a ride at an amusement park that is wholly owned by C. Pursuant to paragraph (a)(1) of this section, income from the sales of merchandise by C to consumers and income from the licensing agreements are included in current year income. No portion of the admission fees for the amusement park is included in current year income because the amusement part is wholly owned by C.

Example (2). Assume the same facts as in Example 1. C forecasts that the cumulative amount of current year income it will earn (net of distribution costs) from the year it places the motion picture film in service through the end of the 7th taxable year thereafter to be $345x. C also forecasts that the motion picture film will earn current year income of $155x from the beginning of the 8th taxable year through the end of the 10th taxable year after the year the income forecast property is placed in service. C anticipates the sale of the motion picture film at the end of the 7th taxable year after the year the property is placed in service and in fact sells the motion picture film for $200x on the last day of the 7th taxable year after the year the property is placed in service. C's computations of forecasted total income must reflect the fact that C forecasts that $500x will be earned by the motion picture film through the end of the 10th taxable year after the year the property is placed in service ($345x from the year the film is placed in service through the end of the 7th taxable year after the taxable year that the property was placed in service, plus $155x C forecasts from the beginning of the 8th taxable year through the end of the 10th taxable year after the year the property is placed in service). Even though C only expects to earn $345x prior to the sale of the film, C may not use $345x as forecasted total income in computing its depreciation allowance under the income forecast method. Similarly, C may not use the combination of the amounts it expects to earn prior to the sale ($345x) plus the anticipated sales proceeds ($200x) or $545x as forecasted total income, except when computing its depreciation allowance for the 7th taxable year after the year in which the income forecast property was placed in service and for purposes of computing look-back interest.

Proposed § 1.167(n)-4 Computation of depreciation using the income forecast method. [*For Preamble, see ¶ 152,279*]

(a) Computation of depreciation allowance. Generally, the depreciation allowance for an income forecast property for a given taxable year is computed by multiplying the depreciable or redetermined basis of the property (as defined in § 1.167(n)-2) by a fraction, the numerator of which is current year income (as defined in § 1.167(n)-3(a)) and the denominator of which is forecasted total income (as defined in § 1.167(n)-3(b)).

(b) Revised computation. *(1) Change in estimated income.* The depreciation allowance for an income forecast property for any taxable year following the year in which income forecast property is placed in service may be computed using the computation provided in this paragraph (b)(1) if revised forecasted total income differs from forecasted total income. Thus, for example, a taxpayer using the income forecast method for a motion picture may revise upward the forecast of total income from the motion picture (to arrive at revised forecasted total income) in a taxable year wherein the taxpayer discovers that the motion picture is more popular than originally expected, and may thereafter use the revised computation to compute the allowance for income forecast depreciation for the motion picture. Under the revised computation, the unrecovered depreciable basis of the income forecast property (as defined in § 1.167(n)-2(c)) is multiplied by a fraction, the numerator of which is current year income and the denominator of which is obtained by subtracting from revised forecasted total income the amounts of current year income from prior taxable years.

(2) Requirement to use the revised computation. The revised computation described in paragraph (b)(1) of this section must be used in any taxable year following the year in which income forecast property is placed in service if forecasted total income (as defined in § 1.167(n)-3(b)) (or, if applicable, revised forecasted total income (as defined in § 1.167(n)-3(c)) in the immediately preceding taxable year is either—

(i) Less than 90 percent of revised forecasted total income for the taxable year; or

(ii) Greater than 110 percent of revised forecasted total income for the taxable year.

(c) Basis redeterminations. *(1) Calculation of depreciation allowance.* An additional depreciation allowance is available under this paragraph in the taxable year that basis is redetermined under § 1.167(n)-2(b) when that taxable year is subsequent to the taxable year in which income forecast property is placed in service, but prior to the 10th taxable year following the taxable year in which the property is placed in service. The additional depreciation allowance is that portion of the basis redetermination amount that would have been recovered through depreciation allowances in prior taxable years if the basis redetermination amount had been included in depreciable basis in the taxable year that the property was placed in service. This § 1.167(n)-4(c) does not apply to property treated as a single income forecast property pursuant to § 1.167(n)-5(d)(1) through (4).

(2) Example. The provisions of paragraph (c)(1) of this section are illustrated by the following example:

Example. D, an accrual basis movie producer, enters into a contract with E, an author, under which D will make a film based on E's book. E performs no services for D, but merely permits D to use the book as a basis for D's film. D pays E a fixed dollar amount upon entry into the agreement and promises to pay E a contingent payment of five percent of D's income from the film, beginning after the film has earned $100,000 (net of distribution costs). D estimates that forecasted total income from the film will be $200,000. The film earns $65,000 of current year income in year one, $30,000 in year two, and $25,000 in year three. D takes allowances for depreciation in year one ($65,000 divided by $200,000, multiplied by the basis of the film) and year two ($30,000 divided by $200,000, multiplied by the basis of the film). In year three, D's liability to E becomes fixed and D pays E $1,000. The $1,000 incurred by D is a basis redetermination amount that increases the basis of the film for purposes of computing D's depreciation allowance for the film for year three. In addition to the year three allowance based on current year income ($25,000 divided by $200,000 multiplied by the basis of the film, which includes for year three the $1,000 basis redetermination amount), D is entitled to an additional allowance for depreciation for year three under paragraph (c)(1). This additional allowance is $475, the sum of the allowance of $325 that would have been allowed in year one ($65,000 divided by $200,000, multiplied by the $1,000 payment to E) and the allowance of $150 that would have been allowed in year two ($30,000 divided by $200,000, multiplied by $1,000) if the $1,000 had been included in basis in the year that the film was placed in service.

(d) Special rules. *(1) Final year depreciation.* Except as provided in paragraphs (d)(2) and (3) of this section, a taxpayer may deduct as a depreciation allowance the remaining depreciable basis of income forecast property depreciated under the income forecast method in the earlier of—

(i) The year in which the taxpayer reasonably believes, based on the conditions known to exist at the end of the taxable year, that no income from the income forecast property will be included in current year income in any subsequent taxable year up to and including the 10th taxable year following the taxable year the income forecast property is placed in service; or

(ii) The 10th taxable year following the taxable year the income forecast property is placed in service.

(2) Certain basis redeterminations. A taxpayer may deduct as a depreciation allowance the amount of any basis redetermination that occurs in a taxable year in which the taxpayer reasonably believes, based on the conditions known to exist at the end of the taxable year, that no income from the income forecast property will be included in current year income in any subsequent taxable year. In addition, a taxpayer may deduct as a depreciation allowance the amount of any basis redetermination that occurs in a taxable year following

a taxable year in which a deduction is allowable under paragraph (d)(1) of this section.

(3) Disposition of property. Paragraph (d)(1) of this section does not apply to income forecast property that is sold or otherwise disposed of before the end of the 10th taxable year following the taxable year that the property is placed in service. In the case of such a disposition, the allowance for depreciation in the year of disposition is calculated by multiplying the depreciable basis (or, if applicable, the redetermined basis) of the property by a fraction, the numerator of which is current year income and the denominator of which is the sum of the amount realized on the disposition of the property plus all amounts included in current year income in the year of disposition and in taxable years prior to the year of disposition.

(4) Separate property. The deductions provided in paragraphs (d)(1) and (2) of this section apply separately to property that is treated as separate property under § 1.167(n)-5(c).

(e) Examples. The provisions of this section are illustrated by the following examples:

Example (1). F places in service income forecast property with a depreciable basis of $100x, and estimates that forecasted total income from the property will be $200x. In taxable year one, current year income is $80x. The depreciation allowance for year one is $40x, computed by multiplying the depreciable basis of the property of $100x by the fraction obtained by dividing current year income of $80x by forecasted total income of $200x.

Example (2). Assume the same facts as in Example 1. In year two, F's current year income is $40x. In addition, F computes revised forecasted total income to be $176x. F is required to compute its depreciation allowance for this property using the revised computation of paragraph (b)(1) of this section because forecasted total income in year one of $200x is greater than 110 percent of revised forecasted total income in year two (110 percent of $176x = $193.6x). The depreciation allowance for taxable year two computed under the revised computation is $25x, computed by multiplying the unrecovered depreciable basis of $60x by the fraction obtained by dividing current year income of $40x by $96x (revised forecasted total income of $176x less current year income from prior taxable years of $80x).

Example (3). Assume the same facts as in Example 2. Because F used the revised computation in year two, the revised computation applies in year three. In year three, F's current year income is $32x. The depreciation allowance for year three computed under the revised computation is $20x, computed by multiplying the unrecovered depreciable basis of $60x by the fraction obtained by dividing current year income of $32x by $96x (revised forecasted total income of $176x less current year income from taxable years prior to the change in estimate taxable year of $80x).

Proposed § 1.167(n)-5 Property for which the income forecast method may be used. [*For Preamble, see ¶ 152,279*]

Caution: The Treasury has not yet amended Reg § 1.167(n)-5 to reflect changes made by P.L. 108-357.

(a) In general. The depreciation allowance under § 1.167(n)-4 may be computed under the income forecast method only with respect to eligible property. Eligible property is limited to an interest (including interests involving limited rights in property) in the following property—

(1) Property described in section 168(f)(3) and (4);

(2) Copyrights;

(3) Books;

(4) Patents;

(5) Theatrical productions; and

(6) Other property as designated in published guidance by the Commissioner.

(b) Specific exclusions. The income forecast method does not apply to any amortizable section 197 intangible (as defined in section 197(c) and § 1.197-2(d)).

(c) Costs treated as separate property. *(1) Costs giving rise to a significant increase in income.* (i) In general. For purposes of § 1.167(n)-1 through § 1.167(n)-6, any amount paid or incurred after the income forecast property is placed in service must be treated as a separate property if the cost is significant and gives rise to an increase in income that is significant and that was not included in either forecasted total income or revised forecasted total income in a prior taxable year.

(ii) Exception for de minimis amounts. For purposes of this paragraph, a cost that is less than the lesser of 5 percent of the depreciable basis (as of the date the amount is paid or incurred) of the income forecast property to which the amount relates or $100,000 is not significant. Such a cost is therefore not treated as separate property but is instead treated as a basis redetermination amount in accordance with § 1.167(n)-2(b).

(2) Significant increase in income. For purposes of this paragraph, whether an increase in income is significant is determined by comparing the amount that would be considered revised forecasted total income from the amounts treated as separate property to the most recent estimate of forecasted total income or revised forecasted total income used in calculating an allowance for depreciation with respect to the income forecast property.

(3) Special rule for costs paid or incurred after the end of the final year. For purposes of § 1.167(n)-1 through § 1.167(n)-6, any amount paid or incurred with respect to an income forecast property in a taxable year following the year in which the taxpayer claims a depreciation allowance in accordance with the final year depreciation rules of § 1.167(n)-4(d)(1) is treated as a basis redetermination amount under § 1.167(n)-2(b) provided the amount is not expected to give rise to a significant increase in current year income in any taxable year.

(4) Time separate property is placed in service. Separate property is treated as placed in service in the year the amount giving rise to the property is paid or incurred.

(5) Examples. The provisions of this paragraph (c) are illustrated in the following examples:

Example (1). G releases a film in 2001 and begins to recover the depreciable basis in the film using the income forecast method in the year 2001. In 2003, the film is re-edited and restored, and director's commentary is added in order to prepare the film for release on DVD. The total cost of preparing the film for the DVD release exceeds both 5 percent of the depreciable basis of the film and $100,000. G did not anticipate the income from the DVD market, and did not include any DVD release income in the income projections for the film in prior years. If G anticipates that the additional DVD release income will be significant in relation to the forecasted total income used in calculating an allowance for depreciation for 2002 (the previous taxable year), the additional amount gives rise to separate property and must be recovered over the forecasted total income from the DVD. If not, G must treat the additional amounts as additions to basis under § 1.167(n)-2(b).

Example (2). G releases a film in 2001 and recovers the depreciable basis in the film using the income forecast method in the years 2001 through 2011. In 2018, the film is re-edited and restored, and director's commentary is added in order to prepare the film for release on a newly discovered technology. If G anticipates that the additional new technology release income will be significant in relation to the revised forecasted total income used in calculating an allowance for depreciation for 2011 (the last taxable year for which an allowance was claimed), the cost of preparing the release gives rise to separate property and must be recovered over the forecasted total income from the new technology release. If not, G may deduct the cost in 2018, the year paid or incurred.

(d) Aggregations treated as a single income forecast property. Taxpayers must apply the income forecast method on a property-by-property basis, unless one of the aggregation rules provided in paragraphs (d)(1) through (4) of this section applies. If a taxpayer applies one of the aggregation rules provided in paragraphs (d)(1) through (4) of this section, costs incurred in taxable years after the initial income forecast property is placed in service are treated as basis redeterminations under § 1.167(n)-2; however, the additional allowance for depreciation provided in § 1.167(n)-4(c)(1) does not apply. The application of the provisions of paragraphs (d)(1) through (d)(4) is a method of accounting that may not be changed without the consent of the Commissioner. Permissible aggregations are limited to the following:

(1) Multiple episodes of a television series produced in the same taxable year. The producer of a television series may treat multiple episodes of a single television series produced in the same taxable year as a single unit of property for purposes of the income forecast method.

(2) Multiple episodes of a television series produced in more than one taxable year. The producer of a television series may treat multiple episodes of a single television series that are produced as a single season of episodes and placed in service over a period not in excess of twelve consecutive calendar months as a single unit of property for purposes of the income forecast method notwithstanding that the twelve-month period may span more than one taxable year.

(3) Multiple interests acquired pursuant to a single contract. Multiple interests in specifically identified income forecast properties acquired for broadcast pursuant to a single contract may be treated as a single unit of property for purposes of the income forecast method.

(4) Videocassettes and DVDs. The purchaser or licensee of videocassettes and DVDs for rental to the public may treat multiple copies of the same title purchased or licensed in the same taxable year as a single unit of property for purposes of the income forecast method.

Proposed § 1.167(n)-6 Look-back method. [*For Preamble, see ¶ 152,279*]

Caution: The Treasury has not yet amended Reg § 1.167(n)-6 to reflect changes made by P.L. 108-357.

(a) Application of the look-back method. If a taxpayer claims a depreciation deduction under the income forecast method for any eligible income forecast property, such taxpayer is required to pay (or is entitled to receive) interest computed as described in this paragraph for any year to which the look-back method applies (a recomputation year). The look-back method generally must be applied when income forecast property is disposed of or ceases to generate income. Further, the look-back method generally applies in the 3rd and 10th taxable years following the year in which income forecast property is placed in service. Under the look-back method, taxpayers must pay interest on deductions accelerated by the underestimation of either forecasted total income or revised forecasted total income from income forecast property. Conversely, taxpayers are entitled to receive interest on deductions delayed by the overestimation of either forecasted total income or revised forecasted total income from income forecast property. If either forecasted total income or revised forecasted total income are overestimated or underestimated, interest may arise from basis redeterminations. The computation of adjusted tax liability as part of the look-back method is hypothetical; application of the look-back method does not require a taxpayer to adjust tax liability as reported on the taxpayer's tax returns, on an amended return, or as adjusted on examination for prior years.

(b) Operation of the look-back method. *(1) In general.* Under the look-back method, a taxpayer must perform a series of computations to determine look-back interest that the taxpayer is either required to pay or entitled to receive. As specified in paragraph (c) of this section, a taxpayer must first recompute depreciation allowances using revised forecasted total income rather than forecasted total income from income forecast property for the recomputation year (as defined in paragraph (e) of this section) and each prior year. These recomputed depreciation amounts are then used to determine a hypothetical tax liability that would have arisen had the taxpayer used revised forecasted total income rather than forecasted total income in determining depreciation allowances. The hypothetical tax liability is compared to the taxpayer's prior tax liability and interest is calculated in accordance with paragraph (d) of this section on the resulting hypothetical overpayments or underpayments of tax for each year. Reporting requirements and special rules for the resulting amounts of interest are specified in paragraph (g) of this section.

(2) Property-by-property application. Except as provided in this section, the look-back method applies to each property for which the income forecast method is used. Aggregations properly treated as a single income forecast property pursuant to § 1.167(n)-5(d) are treated as a single property for purposes of applying the look-back method.

(c) Recalculation of depreciation allowances. *(1) Computation.* Under the look-back method, a taxpayer must compute the depreciation allowances for each income forecast property subject to the look-back method that would have been allowable under § 1.167(n)-1 through § 1.167(n)-5 for prior taxable years if the computation of the amounts so allowable had been made using revised forecasted total income as calculated at the end of the recomputation year.

(2) Revised forecasted total income from the property. (i) In general. Except as provided in this paragraph (c)(2), revised forecasted total income is determined in accordance with § 1.167(n)-3(c).

(ii) Syndication income from television series. Income excluded from forecasted total income (or, if appropriate revised forecasted total income) in any prior taxable year pursuant to § 1.167(n)-3(d)(2) is excluded from revised forecasted total income for purposes of this section for that year.

(iii) Disposition of income forecast property. For purposes of this section, income from the disposition of property must be taken into account in determining the amount of revised forecasted total income. Thus, when income forecast property is disposed of prior to the end of the 10th taxable year following the taxable year the property is placed in service, revised forecasted total income from the property for the year of disposition is deemed to be the sum of the amount realized on the disposition of the property plus all amounts included in current year income in the year of disposition and in taxable years prior to the year of disposition.

(3) Special rule for basis redeterminations. For purposes of the look-back calculation, any amount that is not treated as a separate property under § 1.167(n)-5(c) that is paid or incurred with respect to income forecast property after the property is placed in service is taken into account by discounting (using the Federal mid-term rate determined under section 1274(d) as of the time the cost is paid or incurred) the amount to its value as of the date the property is placed in service. The taxpayer may elect for the recomputation year with respect to any income forecast property to have the preceding sentence not apply to the property by taking the amount into account in the year that the amount was paid or incurred in the same manner as it was taken into account under § 1.167(n)-2.

(d) Hypothetical overpayment or underpayment of tax. *(1) In general.* (i) Years for which a hypothetical overpayment or underpayment must be computed. After recalculating depreciation allowances in accordance with paragraph (c) of this section, a taxpayer must calculate a hypothetical overpayment or underpayment of tax for each prior taxable year for which income tax liability is affected by the change in depreciation allowances. A redetermination of income tax liability is required for every tax year for which the income tax liability would have been affected by a change in the allowance for income forecast depreciation in any year. For example, if the change in depreciation allowance results in a net operating loss carryforward that affects income tax liability in a subsequent taxable year, income tax liability must be recomputed for such subsequent year.

(ii) Methods of determining a hypothetical overpayment or underpayment. Generally, the calculation of the hypothetical overpayment or underpayment of tax must be made under the method described in paragraph (d)(2) of this section. Certain taxpayers are required to use the simplified method contained in paragraph (d)(3) of this section.

(iii) Cumulative determination of hypothetical income tax liability. The redetermination of income tax liability in any prior taxable year for which income tax liability is affected by the change in depreciation allowances must take into account all previous applications of the look-back calculation. Thus, for example, in computing the amount of a hypothetical overpayment or underpayment of tax for a prior taxable year for which income tax liability is affected by the change in depreciation allowances, the hypothetical income tax liability is compared to the hypothetical income tax liability for that year determined as of the previous application of the look-back method.

(2) Hypothetical overpayment or underpayment, actual recomputation. (i) Computation of change in income tax liability. The hypothetical overpayment or underpayment is calculated first by redetermining the tax liability for each prior taxable year (either as originally reported, or as subsequently adjusted on examination or by amended return) using depreciation allowances calculated in paragraph (c) of this section for each prior taxable year in which depreciation allowances were determined under the income forecast method for the income forecast property (affected year). These recomputed depreciation allowances are then substituted for the depreciation allowances allowed (or allowable) for each affected year (whether originally reported, or as subsequently adjusted on examination or by amended return) and a revised taxable income is computed. A hypothetical income tax liability is then computed for each affected year using revised taxable income for that year. The hypothetical income tax liability for any affected year must be computed by taking into account all applicable additions to tax, credits, and net operating loss carrybacks and carryforwards. The tax, if any, imposed under section 55 (relating to alternative minimum tax) must be taken into account. Hypothetical income tax liability for each affected year is then compared to the tax liability determined as of the latest of the following dates—

(A) The original due date of the return (including extensions);

(B) The date of a subsequently amended or adjusted return; or

(C) The date of the previous application of the look-back method, in which case the hypothetical income tax liability for the affected year used in the most recent previous application of the look-back method (previous hypothetical tax liability) is used.

(ii) Determination of interest. Once the hypothetical overpayment or underpayment for each year is computed, the adjusted overpayment rate under section 460(b)(7), compounded daily, is applied to the overpayment or underpayment determined under paragraph (d)(2)(i) of this section for the period beginning with the due date of the return (determined without regard to extensions) for the year in which either an overpayment or underpayment arises, and ending on the earlier of the due date of the return (determined without regard to extensions) for the redetermination year, or the first date by which both the income tax return for the filing year is filed and the tax for that year has been paid in full. The amounts of interest on overpayments are then netted against interest on underpayments to arrive at look-back interest that must be paid by the taxpayer or that the taxpayer is entitled to receive.

(iii) Changes in the amount of a loss or credit carryback or carryforward. If a recomputation of income forecast depreciation results in an increase or decrease to a net operating loss carryback (but not a carryforward), the interest a taxpayer is entitled to receive or required to pay must be computed on the decrease or increase in tax attributable to the change to the carryback only from the due date (not including extensions) of the return for the prior taxable year that generated the carryback and not from the due date of the return for the prior taxable year in which the carryback was absorbed. In the case of a change in the amount of a carryforward as a result of applying the look-back method, interest is computed from the due date of the return for the years in which the carryforward was absorbed.

(iv) Changes in the amount of income tax liability that generated a subsequent refund. If the hypothetical income tax liability for any affected year is less than the amount of the affected year tax liability (as reported on the taxpayer's original return, as subsequently adjusted on examination, as adjusted by amended return, or as redetermined by the last previous application of the look-back method), and any portion of the affected year tax liability was refunded as a result of a loss or credit carryback arising in a year subsequent to the affected year, the look-back method applies as follows to properly reflect the time period of the use of the tax overpayment. To the extent the amount of refund because of the carryback exceeds the hypothetical income tax liability for the affected year, the taxpayer is entitled to receive interest only until the due date (not including extensions) of the return for the year in which the carryback arose.

(v) Example. The provisions of this paragraph (d)(2) are illustrated by the following example:

Example. Upon the cessation of income from an income forecast property in 2003, the taxpayer computes a hypothetical income tax liability for 2001 under the look-back method. This computation results in a hypothetical income tax liability ($1,200x) that is less than the actual income tax liability the taxpayer originally reported ($1,500x). In addition, the taxpayer had already received a refund of some or all of the actual 2001 income tax liability by carrying back a net operating loss (NOL) that arose in 2002. The time period over which interest would be computed on the hypothetical overpayment of $300x for 2001 would depend on the amount of the refund generated by the carryback, as illustrated by the following three alternative situations:

(i) If the amount refunded because of the NOL is $1,500x, interest is credited to the taxpayer on the entire hypothetical overpayment of $300x from the due date of the 2001 return, when the hypothetical overpayment occurred, until the due date of the 2002 return, when the taxpayer received a refund for the entire amount of the 2001 tax, including the hypothetical overpayment.

(ii) If the amount refunded because of the NOL is $1,000x, interest is credited to the taxpayer on the entire amount of the hypothetical overpayment of $300x from the due date of the 2001 return, when the hypothetical overpayment occurred, until the due date of the 2003 return. In this situation interest is credited until the due date of the return for the recomputation year, rather than the due date of the return for the year in which the carryback arose, because the amount refunded was less than the hypothetical income tax liability of $1,200x. Therefore, no portion of the hypothetical overpayment is treated as having been refunded to the taxpayer before the recomputation year.

(iii) If the amount refunded because of the NOL is $1,300x, interest is credited to the taxpayer on $100x ($1,300x-$1,200x) from the due date of the 2001 return until the due date of the 2002 return because only this portion of the total hypothetical overpayment is treated as having been refunded to the taxpayer before the recomputation year. However, the taxpayer did not receive a refund for the remaining $200x of the overpayment at that time and, therefore, is credited with interest on $200x through the due date of the tax return for 2003, the recomputation year.

(3) Hypothetical overpayment or underpayment, simplified method. (i) Introduction. This paragraph provides a simplified method for calculating look-back interest. A pass-through entity that is not a closely held pass-through entity is required to apply the simplified method at the entity level with respect to income forecast property and the owners of the entity do not calculate look-back interest for the property. Under the simplified method, a taxpayer calculates the hypothetical underpayments or overpayments of tax for a prior year based on an assumed marginal tax rate.

(ii) Operation of the simplified method. Under the simplified method, depreciation allowances for income forecast property are first recomputed in accordance with the procedures contained in paragraph (c) of this section. These recomputed depreciation allowances are then compared with depreciation allowances allowed (or allowable) for each prior taxable year (whether originally reported, as subsequently adjusted on examination or by amended return, or as recomputed in the most recent previous application of the look-back method) to arrive at changes in depreciation allowances for the income forecast property. When multiple properties are subject to the look-back method in any given affected year, the changes in depreciation allowances attributable to each income forecast property determined in accordance with paragraph (c) of this section for each such year are cumulated or netted against one another to arrive at a net change in income forecast depreciation for purposes of computing the hypothetical overpayment or underpayment attributable to the year. The hypothetical underpayment or overpayment of tax for each affected year is then determined by multiplying the applicable regular tax rate (as defined in paragraph (d)(3)(iv) of this section) by the increase or decrease in depreciation allowances.

(iii) Determination of interest. Interest is credited to the taxpayer on the net overpayment and is charged to the taxpayer on the net underpayment for each affected year by applying the adjusted overpayment rate under section 460(b)(7), compounded daily, to the overpayment or underpayment determined under paragraph (d)(3)(ii) of this section for the period beginning with the due date of the return (determined without regard to extensions) for the affected year, and ending on the earlier of the due date of the return (determined without regard to extensions) for the recomputation year, or the first date by which both the income tax return for the recomputation year is filed and the tax for that year has been paid in full. The resulting amounts of interest are then netted to arrive at look-back interest that must be paid by the taxpayer or that the taxpayer is entitled to receive.

(iv) Applicable tax rate. For purposes of determining hypothetical underpayments or overpayments of tax under the simplified method, the applicable regular rate is generally the highest rate of tax in effect for corporations under section 11. However, the applicable regular tax rate is the highest rate of tax imposed on individuals under section 1 if, at all times during all affected years, more than 50 percent of the interests in the entity were held by individuals directly or through 1 or more pass-through entities. The highest rate of tax imposed on individuals is determined without regard to any additional tax imposed for the purpose of phasing out multiple tax brackets or exemptions.

(4) Definitions. (i) Pass-through entity. For purposes of this section, a pass-through entity is either a partnership, an S corporation, an estate or a trust.

(ii) Closely-held pass-through entity. A closely-held pass-through entity is a pass-through entity that, at any time during any year for which allowances for depreciation are recomputed, 50 percent or more (by value) of the beneficial interests in that entity are held (directly or indirectly) by or for 5 or fewer persons. For this purpose, the term person has the same meaning as in section 7701(a)(1), except that a pass-through entity is not treated as a person. In addition, the constructive ownership rules of section 1563(e) apply by substituting the term beneficial interest for the term stock and by substituting the term pass-through entity for the term corporation used in that section, as appropriate, for purposes of determining whether a beneficial interest in a pass-through entity is indirectly owned by any person.

(e) Recomputation year. *(1) In general.* Except as provided in this paragraph (e), the term recomputation year means, with respect to any income forecast property—

(i) The earlier of—

(A) The year the income from the income forecast property ceases with respect to the taxpayer (and with respect to any person who would be treated as a single taxpayer with the taxpayer under rules similar to those in section 41(f)(1)); or

(B) The 3rd taxable year beginning after the taxable year in which the income forecast property was placed in service; and

(ii) The earlier of—

(A) The year the income from the income forecast property ceases with respect to the taxpayer (and with respect to any person who would be treated as a single taxpayer with the taxpayer under rules similar to those in section 41(f)(1)); or

(B) The 10th taxable year following the taxable year the income forecast property is placed in service.

(2) Look-back method inapplicable in certain de minimis cases. (i) De minimis difference between actual and forecasted income. A taxable year described in paragraph (e)(1) of this section is not a recomputation year if forecasted total income (as defined in § 1.167(n)-3(b)) or, where applicable, revised forecasted total income (as defined in § 1.167(n)-3(c)), for each preceding taxable years is—

(A) Greater than 90 percent of revised forecasted total income for the taxable year that would otherwise be a recomputation year; and

(B) Less than 110 percent of revised forecasted total income for the taxable year that would otherwise be a recomputation year.

(ii) Application of the de minimis rule where the look-back method was previously applied. For purposes of applying paragraph (e)(2)(i) of this section in any taxable year after a taxable year in which the look-back method has previously been applied, revised forecasted total income for the year the look-back method was applied, forecasted total income for the year the income forecast property was placed in service, and revised forecasted total income for all taxable years preceding the taxable year in which the look-back method was previously applied are deemed to be equal to the amount of revised forecasted total income that was used for purposes of applying the look-back method in the most recent taxable year for which the look-back method was applied.

(f) De minimis basis exception. The look-back method does not apply to any income forecast property with an adjusted basis, determined in accordance with section 1011 but without regard to the adjustments described in section 1016(a)(2) and (3), as of the close of any year that would otherwise be a recomputation year of $100,000 or less.

(g) Treatment of look-back interest. *(1) In general.* The amount of interest a taxpayer is required to pay is treated as an income tax under Subtitle A of the Internal Revenue Code, but only for purposes of Subtitle F of the Internal Revenue Code (other than sections 6654 and 6655), which addresses tax procedure and administration. Thus, a taxpayer that fails to report look-back interest when due is subject to any penalties under Subtitle F of the Internal Revenue Code applicable to a failure to report and pay a tax liability. However, look-back interest to be paid is treated as interest arising from an underpayment of tax under Subtitle A of the Internal Revenue Code, even though it is treated as an income tax liability for penalty purposes. Thus, look-back interest required to be paid by an individual, or by a pass-through entity on behalf of an individual owner (or beneficiary) under the simplified method, is personal interest and, therefore, is not deductible in accordance with § 1.163-9T(b)(2). Interest received under the look-back method is treated as taxable interest income for all purposes, and is not treated as a reduction in tax liability. The determination of whether interest computed under the look-back method is treated as income tax under Subtitle A of the Internal Revenue Code is determined on a net basis for each recomputation year. Thus, if a taxpayer computes both hypothetical overpayments of tax and hypothetical underpayments of tax for years prior to any given recomputation year, the taxpayer has an increase in tax only if the total interest computed on underpayments for all prior taxable years for which income tax liability is affected by the application of the look-back method exceeds the total interest computed on overpayments for such years, taking into account all income forecast property for which the look-back method is required. Interest determined at the entity level under the simplified method is allocated among the owners (or beneficiaries) for reporting purposes in the same manner that interest income and interest expense are allocated to owners (or beneficiaries) and subject to the allocation rules applicable to such entities.

(2) Additional interest due on interest only after tax liability due. For each recomputation year, taxpayers are required to file a Form 8866, "Interest Computation Under the Look-back Method for Property Depreciated Under the Income Forecast Method," at the time the return for that recomputation year is filed to report the interest a taxpayer is required to pay or entitled to receive under the look-back method. Even if the taxpayer has received an extension to file its income tax return for the recomputation year, look-back interest is computed with respect to the hypothetical increase (or decrease) in the tax liability determined under the look-back method only until the initial due date of that return (without regard to the extension). Interest is charged, unless the taxpayer otherwise has a refund that fully offsets the amount of interest due, (or credited) with respect to the amount of look-back interest due (or to be refunded) under the look-back method from the initial due date of the return through the date the return is filed. No interest is charged (or credited) after the due date of the return with respect to the amount of the hypothetical increases (or decreases) in tax liability determined under the look-back method.

(3) Timing of look-back interest. For purposes of determining taxable income under Subtitle A of the Internal Revenue Code, any amount refunded to the taxpayer as a result of the application of the look-back method is includible in gross income in accordance with the taxpayer's method of accounting for interest income. Any amount required to be paid is taken into account as interest expense arising from an underpayment of income tax in the tax year it is properly taken into account under the taxpayer's method of accounting for interest expense.

(4) Statute of limitations; compounding of interest on look-back interest. For guidance on the statute of limitations applicable to the assessment and collection of look-back interest owed by a taxpayer, see sections 6501 and 6502. A taxpayer's claim for credit or refund of look-back interest previously paid by or collected from a taxpayer is a claim for credit or refund of an overpayment of tax and is subject to the statute of limitations provided in section 6511. A taxpayer's claim for look-back interest (or interest payable on look-back interest) that is not attributable to an amount previously paid or collected from a taxpayer is a general claim against the federal government. For guidance on the statute

of limitations that applies to general claims against the federal government, see 28 U.S.C. 2401 and 2501. For guidance applicable to the compounding of interest when the look-back interest is not paid, see sections 6601 to 6622.

(h) Example. The provisions of this section are illustrated by the following example:

Example. (i) H, a calendar year corporation, creates a motion picture at a cost of $60x. H completes the motion picture in 2001 and begins exhibition of the film that same year. Assume that $60x is greater than $100,000. In 2001, H anticipates that it will earn $200x from the motion picture (net of distribution costs). H therefore uses this amount as Forecasted Total Income when computing depreciation allowances for the motion picture.

(ii) H earns current year income of $80x in 2001, $60x in 2002, and $40x in 2003. During the period from 2001 to 2004, one of the actors who appeared in H's film became more popular, and this increase in the actor's popularity increased the demand for H's film. In 2004, therefore, H revised its forecast of income from the film upward to $240x. H earns $20x in 2004 from the motion picture and $10x in 2005.

(iii) Based on these facts, H's allowances for depreciation for the motion picture for 2001 would be $24x, computed by multiplying the depreciable basis of the motion picture of $60x by current year income of $80x divided by forecasted total income of $200x under § 1.167(n)-4(a). Similarly, H's allowances for depreciation for the motion picture for 2002 would be $18x, computed by multiplying the depreciable basis of the motion picture of $60x by current year income of $60x divided by forecasted total income of $200x, and H's allowances for depreciation for the motion picture for 2003 would be $12x, computed by multiplying the depreciable basis of the motion picture of $60x by current year income of $40x divided by forecasted total income of $200x.

(iv) In 2004, H determines revised forecasted total income of $240x in accordance with § 1.167(n)-3(c). Because revised forecasted total income in 2004 of $240x is greater than 110 percent of forecasted total income used in computing the allowance for depreciation in the immediately preceding year (110 percent of $200x equals $220x), H is required under § 1.167(n)-4(b)(2) to compute the allowance for depreciation in 2004 and thereafter using the revised computation. H first computes its unrecovered depreciable basis in the motion picture under § 1.167(n)-2(c) of $6x by subtracting from the depreciable basis of $60x the depreciation allowances for 2001, 2002, and 2003 of $24x, $18x, and $12x. H then multiplies the unrecovered depreciable basis of $6x by the current year income for 2004 of $20x divided by $60x (revised forecasted total income $240x less current year income for all years prior to 2004 ($80x + $60x + $40x or $180x), resulting in a depreciation allowance for 2004 of $2x.

(v) In 2005, H is required to use the revised computation because H used it in 2004. Thus, H multiplies the unrecovered depreciable basis of $6x times current year income for 2005 of $10x divided by $60x (revised forecasted total income as computed in 2004), resulting in a depreciation allowance for 2005 of $1x.

(vi) Thus, H's allowances for depreciation may be summarized as follows:

Year	Current year income	Forecasted total income	Revised forecasted total income	Depreciable basis	Unrecovered depreciable basis	Depreciation allowance
2001	80x	200x	—	60x	—	24x
2002	60x	200x	—	60x	—	18x
2003	40x	200x	—	60x	—	12x
2004	20x	—	240x	—	6x	2x
2005	10x	—	240x	—	6x	1x

(vii) Under paragraph (e)(1)(i)(B) of this section, 2004 is a recomputation year (because 2004 is the third taxable year after the year in which the motion picture was placed in service) unless a de minimis rule applies. The de minimis rule in paragraph (e)(2) of this section does not apply in 2004 because forecasted total income of $200x used in the computation of income forecast depreciation in 2001, 2002 and 2003 is not greater than 90 percent of year 2004 revised forecasted total income of $240x (90 percent of $240x = $216x). Thus, H must apply the look-back method for 2004.

(viii) If H sells the motion picture in 2006 for $25x prior to earning any current year income from the motion picture, H would not be entitled to any allowance for depreciation in 2006. (The special rule of § 1.167(n)-3(d)(1) precludes H from including income from the sale of the motion picture in current year income, H has no other current year income, and § 1.167(n)-4(d)(3) precludes the use of the final year depreciation rule of § 1.167(n)-4(d)(1).) Under paragraph (e)(1)(ii)(A) of this section, 2006 is a recomputation year (because in 2006 the income from the property to H ceases) unless a de minimis rule applies.

(ix) To determine whether the de minimis rule applies, H is required to determine revised forecasted total income for 2006. Under paragraph (c)(2) of this section, revised forecasted total income for 2006 is deemed to be the sum of current year income for the years 2001-2006 of $210x ($80x + $60x + $40x + $20x + $10x + $0x) plus the amount realized from the sale of the motion picture of $25x or $235x. Revised forecasted total income for 2005 is $240x, and pursuant to paragraph (e)(2)(ii) of this section, revised forecasted total income for the years 2001-2004 is deemed (for purposes of determining whether 2006 is a recomputation year) to be the amount of revised forecasted total income used in the 2004 application of the look-back method of $240x. Because $240x is greater than $212x (90 percent of $235x) and less than $259x (110 percent of $235x), the de minimis rule applies and H is not required to apply the look-back method in 2006.

Proposed § 1.167(n)-7 Effective date. [*For Preamble, see ¶ 152,279*]

The regulations under § 1.167(n)-1 through § 1.167(n)-6 are applicable for property placed in service on or after the date that final regulations are published in the Federal Register.

§ 301.9100-4T Time and manner of making certain elections under the Economic Recovery Tax Act of 1981 (temporary).

(a) Miscellaneous elections. *(1) Elections to which this paragraph applies.* This paragraph applies to the following elections provided under the Economic Recovery Tax Act of 1981:

Section of act	Section of code	Description of election	Availability of election
127(a)	162(i) (originally enacted as sec 162(h); subsequently redesignated by sec 2146 of Pub. Law 97-35).	Travel expenses of state legislators	Taxable years beginning after 1975
201(a)	168(b)(3)	Different recovery period	Property placed in service after 1980
201(a)	168(d)(2)(A)	Inclusion in income of entire proceeds of disposition	Property placed in service after 1980
201(a)	168(e)(2)	Exclusion of property from recovery system	Property placed in service after 1980
201(a)	168(f)(2)(C)	Different recovery period for property used outside U.S.	Property placed in service after 1980
202(a)	179	Expensing certain depreciable property	Taxable years beginning after 1981
237	474	For small business to use one inventory pool when LIFO is elected	Taxable years beginning after 1981
266(a)		Deferral of commencement of amortization period for motor carrier operating authority.	Taxable years ending after June 30, 1980
508(c)		Application of Title V of the Act to all regulated futures contracts or positions held on June 23, 1981.	Property held on June 23, 1981.
509		Application of Code sec. 1256 and extension of time for payment of tax for all regulated futures contracts held at any time during taxable year that includes June 23, 1981.	Property held during taxable year that includes June 23, 1981.

(2) Time for making elections. (i) In general. Except as otherwise provided in this paragraph (a)(2), the elections specified in paragraph (a)(1) of this section shall be made by the later of—

(A) The due date (taking extensions into account) of the income tax return for the taxable year for which the election is to be effective, or

(B) April 15, 1982.

(ii) No extension of time for payment. Payments of tax due shall be made in accordance with chapter 62 of the Code.

(iii) Elections under section 508(c) or 509 of the Act. Elections under section 508(c) or 509 of the Act shall be made by the due date (taking extensions into account) of the income tax return for the taxable year for which the election is to be effective.

(iv) No extension of refund period with respect to travel expenses of state legislators. In no event may an election be made under this section after the expiration of the period of limitation for filing a claim for credit or refund of overpayment of tax for the taxable year to which the election relates.

(3) Manner of making elections. The elections specified in paragraph (a)(1) of this section shall be made by attaching a statement to the income tax return (or amended return) for the taxable year for which the election is made. Except as otherwise provided in the return or in the instructions accompanying the return for the taxable year, the statement shall—

(i) Contain the name, address, and taxpayer identification number of the electing taxpayer,

(ii) Identify the election,

(iii) Indicate the section of the Code (or, if the provision is not codified, the section of the Act) under which the election is being made,

(iv) Specify the period for which the election is being made and the property to which the election is to apply, and

(v) Provide any information required by the relevant statutory provisions and any information necessary to show that the taxpayer is entitled to make the election.

(b) Designation of principal campaign committee. This paragraph applies to the designation of a principal campaign committee under section 527(h) of the Code, as added by section 128 of the Act. References in this section to "elections" include designations under section 527(h). Under that provision a candidate for Congress may designate one committee as the candidate's principal campaign committee. The political organization taxable income of that committee shall be taxed at the appropriate rates under section 11(b); that income is ordinarily taxed at the highest rate specified in section 11(b). The candidate shall designate the principal campaign committee by filing a statement of designation with the income tax return of the committee for the first taxable year of the committee ending after 1981 for which the designation is to be effective. The return and the statement shall be filed by the due date (taking extensions into account) of the return. The rules of section 21 (relating to effects of changes in rates during a taxable year) shall apply in the case of any taxable year beginning before 1982 for which a designation is made. The statement of designation shall be signed by the candidate and shall—

(1) Contain the name, address, and taxpayer identification number of the candidate and of the committee,

(2) Identify the statement as a designation under section 527(y) of the Code, and

(3) Designate the committee as the principal campaign committee of the candidate.

The candidate shall attach to the statement a copy of the statement of designation filed with the Federal Election Commission.

(c) Election to be treated as a qualified fund for purposes of the research credit. This paragraph applies to the election provided under section 44F(e)(4) of the Code, as added by section 221(a) of the Act. The election to be treated as a qualified fund for purposes of the research credit may be made effective as of any date after June 30, 1981, and before January 1, 1986. An organization shall make this election by filing with the service center with which it files its annual return a statement signed by a person authorized to act on behalf of the organization. That statement shall—

(1) Contain the name, address, and taxpayer identification number of the electing organization and of the organization that established and maintains the electing organization,

(2) Identify the election as an election under section 44F(e)(4) of the Code,

(3) Specify the date on which the election is to become effective (in the case of elections filed before February 1, 1982, not earlier than the date that is 7 months before the date on which the election is filed; in the case of elections filed after January 31, 1982, not earlier than the date on which the election is filed), and

(4) Provide all information necessary to show that the organization is entitled to make the election.

(d) Election to treat qualified subchapter S trust as grantor trust. This paragraph applies to the election provided under section 1371(g)(2) of the Code, as added by section 234(b) of the Act. The election to treat a qualified subchapter S trust as a grantor trust described in section 1371(e)(1)(A) of the Code is available for taxable years beginning after 1981. The beneficiary of the trust (or the legal representative of the beneficiary) shall make this election by signing and filing with the service center with which the subchapter S corporation files its income tax return a statement that—

(1) Contains the name, address, and taxpayer identification number of the beneficiary, the trust, and the subchapter S corporation,

(2) Identifies the election as an election under section 1371(g)(2) of the Code,

(3) Specifies the date on which the election is to become effective (not earlier than 60 days before the date on which the election is filed), and

(4) Provides all information necessary to show that the beneficiary is entitled to make the election.

Note that this election does not itself constitute an election as to the status of the corporation; the corporation must make the election provided in section 1372(a) to be treated as an electing small business corporation.

(e) Election to have Code section 422A apply to options granted before 1981. This paragraph applies to the election provided under section 251(c)(1)(B) of the Act to have Code section 422A apply to certain options granted before 1981. A corporation may make only one election under this provision. Thus, a corporation that makes an election under this provision with respect to certain options granted before 1981 may not make any subsequent election under this provision with respect to other options granted before 1981. An election under this provision shall be made no later than the due date (taking extensions into account) of the income tax return of the corporation for its first taxable year during which either an option subject to the election or an option subject to the rules of section 422A of the Code is exercised. In any event, no election under this provision will be permitted after the due date (taking extensions into account) of the income tax return for the taxable year including December 31, 1982. A corporation shall make this election by attaching to its income tax return (or amended return) a statement that—

(1) Contains the name, address, and taxpayer identification number of the corporation,

(2) Identifies the election as an election under section 251(c)(1)(B) of the Economic Recovery Tax Act of 1981,

(3) Specifies the options to which the election applies, and

(4) Provides all information necessary to show that the corporation is entitled to make the election.

(f) Election to increase basis of property on which additional estate tax is imposed. This paragraph applies to the election provided under section 1016(c) of the Code, as amended by section 421(g) of the Act. The election to increase the basis of property on which additional estate tax is imposed is available with respect to the estates of decedents dying after 1981. The qualified heir shall make this election by filing with the Form 706-A (Additional Estate Tax Return) a statement that—

(1) Contains the name, address, and taxpayer identification number of the qualified heir and of the estate,

(2) Identifies the election as an election under section 1016(c) of the Code,

(3) Specifies the property with respect to which the election is made, and

(4) Provides any additional information required by the instructions accompanying Form 706-A.

A qualified heir making an election under this paragraph must pay interest on the additional estate tax from the date that is 9 months after the date of the decedent's death to the date of the payment of the additional estate tax.

(g) Revocation of elections. Elections under paragraph (f) of this section are irrevocable. Other elections made under this section may be revoked only with the consent of the Commissioner. An application for consent to revoke an election shall be signed by the applicant and filed with the service center with which the election was filed and shall—

(1) Contain the name, address, and taxpayer identification number of all parties identified in connection with the election,

(2) Identify the election being revoked by reference to the section of the Code or Act under which the election was made,

(3) Specify the scope of the election, and

(4) Explain why the applicant seeks to revoke the election.

(h) Additional information required. If later regulations issued under the section of the Code or Act under which the election was made require the furnishing of information in addition to that which was furnished with the statement of election and an office of the Internal Revenue Service requests the taxpayer to provide the additional information, the taxpayer shall furnish the additional information in a statement filed with that office of the Internal Revenue Service within 60 days after the request is made. This statement shall also—

(1) Contain the name, address, and taxpayer identification numbers of all parties identified in connection with the election,

(2) Identify the election by reference to the section of the Code or Act under which the election was made, and

(3) Specify the scope of the election.

If the additional information is not provided within 60 days after the request is made, the election may, at the discretion of the Commissioner, be held invalid.

(i) Effective date. This section applies to elections made after August 12, 1981.

T.D. 7793, 11/2/81, amend T.D. 8435, 9/18/92.

PAR. 4. Section 301.9100-4T is amended by removing from the table in paragraph (a)(1) section 127(a) and removing paragraph (a)(2)(iv).

Proposed § 301.9100-4T [*For Preamble, see ¶ 152,983*]

[Amended]

§ 301.9100-5T Time and manner of making certain elections under the Tax Equity and Fiscal Responsibility Act of 1982 (temporary).

(a) Miscellaneous elections. *(1) Elections to which this paragraph applies.* This paragraph applies to the following elections provided under the Tax Equity and Fiscal Responsibility Act of 1982.

Section of act	Section of code	Description of election	Availability of election
201(c) . . .	58(i)(1) . .	Optional 10 year write off of certain tax preferences.	Taxable years beginning after Dec. 31, 1982.
201(c)(1)	58(i)(4) . .	Intangible drilling and development costs.	Taxable years beginning after Dec. 31, 1982
205(a) . . .	48(q)	Reduced investment credit in lieu of basis adjustment.	Generally to period beginning after Dec. 31, 1982.
256(f) . . .	820	Insurance company revocation of election under section 820.	Contracts which took effect in 1980 or 1981

(2) Time for making elections. (i) In general. Except as otherwise provided in paragraph (a)(2) of this section, the elections specified in paragraph (a)(1) of this section shall be made by the later of—

(A) The due date (taking extensions into account) of the income tax return for the taxable year for which the election is to be effective, or

(B) April 15, 1983.

(ii) No extensions of time for payment. Payments of tax due shall be made in accordance with chapter 62 of the Code.

(iii) Election by insurance companies relating to repeal of section 820. Elections under section 256(f) of the Act, relating to special rule allowing reinsured insurance company to revoke an election under section 820, must be made before March 5, 1983.

(3) Manner of making elections. The elections specified in paragraph (a)(1) of this section shall be made by attaching a statement to the income tax return (or amended return) for the taxable year for which the election is made. Except as otherwise provided in the return or in the instructions accompanying the return for the taxable year, the statement shall—

(i) Contain the name, address, and taxpayer identification number of the electing taxpayer,

(ii) Identify the election,

(iii) Indicate the section of the Code (or, if the provision is not codified, the section of the Act) under which the election is being made,

(iv) Specify the period for which the election is being made and the property to which the election is to apply and

(v) Provide any information required by the relevant statutory provisions and any information necessary to show that the taxpayer is entitled to make the election.

(b) Special rules for reduced investment credit in lieu of basis adjustment. *(1) Appropriate return.* For purposes of section 48(q) of the Code and paragraph (a)(2)(i)(A) and (3) of this section the term "income tax return for the taxable year for which the election is effective" with respect to any property is the tax return for the taxable year in which such property is placed in service, or in the case of property to which an election under section 46(d) (relating to qualified progress expenditures) applies, the appropriate return is the return for the first taxable year for which qualified progress expenditures were taken into account with respect to such property.

(2) Applicability of election. In general, the election under section 48(q) is applicable to periods beginning after December 31, 1982 under rules similar to the rules of section 48(m) of the Code. However, the election does not apply to property excepted by section 205(c)(1)(B) of the Act.

(c) Election by a reinsurer to make installment payments of taxes owed resulting from the repeal of section 820. This paragraph applies to the election by an insurance company provided under section 256(e) of the Act. A reinsurer that is a calendar year taxpayer shall be considered to have made an election under section 256(e) of the Act if by March 15, 1983 it files its income tax return (or an application on Form 7004 for an automatic extension of time to file its income tax return), with the statement required to be filed under this paragraph attached and, unless the reinsurer is making a further election under section 256(e)(2)(B) of the Act, pays one-third of the amount described in section 256(e)(1) of the Act by March 15, 1983. A reinsurer making an election under section 256(e)(2)(B) of the Act must pay one-sixth of the amount described in section 256(e)(1) of the

Act by March 15, 1983 and one-sixth of such amount by June 15, 1983. The statement required to be filed under this paragraph shall—

(1) Contain the name, address, and tax-payer identification number of the corporation,

(2) Identify the election as an election under section 256(e) of the Act, and section 256(e)(2)(B) if applicable, and

(3) Provide all information necessary to show the taxpayer is entitled to make the election.

For provisions relating to the use of authorized financial institutions in depositing the taxes, see § 1.6302-1.

(d) [Reserved].

(e) Additional information required. If later regulations issued under the section of the Code or Act under which the election was made require the furnishing of information in addition to that which was furnished with the statement of election and an office of the Internal Revenue Service requests the taxpayer to provide the additional information, the taxpayer shall furnish the additional information in a statement filed with that office of the Internal Revenue Service within 60 days after the request is made. This statement shall also—

(1) Contain the name, address, and taxpayer identification numbers of all parties identified in connection with the election,

(2) Identify the election by reference to the section of the Code or Act under which the election was made, and

(3) Specify the scope of the election. If the additional information is not provided within 60 days after the request is made, the election may, at the discretion of the Commissioner, be held invalid.

(e [sic (f)]) Effective date. This section applies to elections made after September 3, 1982.

T.D. 7870, 1/21/83, amend T.D. 8435, 9/18/92, T.D. 8952, 6/25/2001.

§ 301.9100-6T Time and manner of making certain elections under the Deficit Reduction Act of 1984 (temporary).

Caution: The Treasury has not yet amended Reg § 301.9100-6T to reflect changes made by P.L. 104-188.

(a) Miscellaneous elections. *(1) Elections to which this paragraph applies.* This paragraph applies to the following elections provided under the Deficit Reduction Act of 1984 (the Act):

Section of Act	Section of Code	Description of election	Availability of election
31(a) and 31(g)(16)	168(j)(4)(E)(ii)	Election by certain 501(c)(12) organizations to be treated as taxable organizations and to have certain arbitrage profits taxed.	Generally for property placed in service after May 23, 1983 or leased after such date.
31(f)	46(e)(4)(C)	Election by section 593 organizations not to apply section 46(e)(4)(A).	Generally for property placed in service after Nov. 5, 1983 or leased after such date.
41(a)	1282(b)(2)	Election to have section 1281 apply to all short-term obligations acquired on or after the first day of the first taxable year to which the election relates (but not to obligations acquired before July 19, 1984).	Taxable years ending after July 18, 1984, with respect to obligations acquired after such date.
41(a)	1283(c)(2)	Election to have section 1283(c)(1) not apply to all obligations acquired on or after the first day of the first taxable year to which the election relates (but not to obligations acquired before July 19, 1984).	Do.
113	48(r)	Election by all persons having an ownership interest in a sound recording to treat such recording as 3-yr. recovery property.	Property placed in service after Mar. 15, 1984.
211	806(d)(4)	Election with respect to loss from operations of member of group.	Taxable years beginning after Dec. 31, 1983.
211	807(d)(4)(C)	Election to use preceding year's interest rate for nonannuity reserves.	Taxable years beginning after Dec. 31, 1983.
211	810(b)(3)	Election to forgo carryback period by life insurance companies.	Losses from operations for taxable years beginning after Dec. 31, 1983.

Section of Act	Section of Code	Description of election	Availability of election
216(c)(1)		Election not to have reserves recomputed.	First taxable year beginning after Dec. 31, 1983.
216(c)(2)		Election to use adjusted statutory reserves for certain contracts.	Generally for contracts issued after 1983 and before 1989 by certain companies that make an election under sec. 216(c)(1) of the act.
217(i)		Election to treat individual noncancellable accident and health contracts as cancellable.	First taxable year beginning after Dec. 31, 1983
217(l)(2)(B)		Treatment of losses from certain guaranteed interest contracts.	Taxable years beginning after Dec. 31, 1983, before Jan. 1, 1988.
431(e)(2)	46(c)(8) and (9), 48(d)(6), 47(d)(1) and (2).	Election to apply the investment tax credit at risk rules as modified by the Tax Reform Act of 1984 to all transactions covered by sec. 211(f) of the Economic Recovery Tax Act of 1981.	Generally to property placed in service between Feb. 18, 1981, and July 19, 1984.
712(l)(7)(B)	304	Election to apply certain technical corrections of sec. 304 to all transfers covered by the changes made to sec. 304 by the Tax Equity and Fiscal Responsibility Act of 1982.	Stock acquired after Aug. 31, 1982, and before June 19, 1984.
712(l)(7)(C)(ii)	304	Election with respect to bank holding companies to apply certain technical corrections of sec. 304 to stock acquired after June 18, 1984.	Generally to transfers to bank holding companies formed pursuant to application filed with Federal Reserve Board before June 18, 1984.
1066	163(d)	Election to treat certain income from S corporations, for purposes of sec. 163(d), as such income would have been treated prior to the Subchapter S Revision Act of 1982.	With respect to S corporation taxable years beginning in 1983 or 1984.
1078		Election to exclude from gross income payments from U.S. Forest Service as a result of restricting motorized traffic in the boundary waters canoe area.	Payments in taxable years beginning after Dec. 31, 1979.

(2) Time for making elections. (i) In general. Except as otherwise provided in this paragraph (a)(2), the elections specified in paragraph (a)(1) of this section shall be made by the later of—

(A) The due date (taking extensions into account) of the tax return for the first taxable year for which the election is to be effective, or

(B) April 15, 1985 (in which case the election generally must be made by amended return).

(ii) No extension of time for payment. Payments of tax due shall be made in accordance with chapter 62 of the Code.

(iii) Time for making certain life insurance company elections. (A) Election to use preceding year's interest rate for non-annuity reserves. The election under section 807(d)(4)(C) to use the preceding year's interest rate for non-annuity reserves applies on a contract-by-contract basis. For contracts issued before the first day of the first taxable year beginning after December 31, 1983, the election shall be made by the due date (including extensions) of the income tax return for the first taxable year beginning after December 31, 1983. For contracts issued on or after the first day of the first taxable year beginning after December 31, 1983, the election shall be made by the due date (including extensions) of the income tax return for the taxable year in which the contract is issued.

(B) Election not to have reserves recomputed. The election under section 216(c)(1) of the Act not to have reserves recomputed shall be made by the due date (including extensions) of the income tax return for the first taxable year beginning after December 31, 1983.

(C) Election to use adjusted statutory reserves for certain contracts. The election under section 216(c)(2) of the Act to use adjusted statutory reserves for certain contracts may be made only by life insurance companies that make an election under section 216(c)(1) of the Act and that meet the other requirements of section 216(c)(2). The election, if made, applies to all contracts issued on or after the first day of the first taxable year beginning after December 31, 1983, and before January 1, 1989. The election shall be made by the due date (including extensions) of the income tax return for the first taxable year beginning after December 31, 1983.

(D) Election to treat individual non-cancellable accident and health contracts as cancellable. The election under section 217(i) of the Act to treat individual non-cancellable accident and health contracts as cancellable shall be made by the due date (including extensions) of the income tax return for the first taxable year beginning after December 31, 1983.

(E) Treatment of losses from certain guaranteed interest contracts. The election under section 217(l)(2)(B) of the Act with respect to the treatment of losses from certain guaranteed interest contracts shall be made by the due date (including extensions) of the income tax return for the first taxable year beginning after December 31, 1983.

(iv) Time for making the election to exclude from gross income payments received from the U.S. Forest Service as a result of the restriction of motorized traffic in the Boundary Waters Canoe Area. Elections under section 1078 of the Act shall be made by the later of the expiration of the period for making a claim for credit or refund of the tax imposed by chapter 1 of the Code for the taxable year in which the reinvestment of the payment occurred, or July 18, 1985. Amended returns for years after the year for which the election is made must be filed if making this election affects the tax liability for such years.

(3) Manner of making elections. (i) In general. The elections specified in paragraph (a)(1) of this section shall be made by attaching a statement to the tax return for the taxable year in which the election is made. If because of paragraph (a)(2)(i)(B) the election may be filed after the due date of the tax return for the first taxable year for which the election is to be effective, such election must be attached to a tax return or amended return for the taxable year to which the election relates. Except as otherwise provided in the return or in the instructions accompanying the return for the taxable year, the statement shall—

(A) Contain the name, address, and taxpayer identification number of the electing taxpayer,

(B) Identify the election,

(C) Indicate the section of the Code (or, if the provision is not codified, the section of the Act) under which the election is made,

(D) Specify, as applicable, the period for which the election is being made and/or the property or other items to which the election is to apply, and

(E) Provide any information required by the relevant statutory provisions and any information necessary to show that the taxpayer is entitled to make the election.

(ii) Special rules for making the election with respect to sound recordings. The election under section 48(r), as amended by section 113 of the Act, shall be made separately for each sound recording and must be made by all persons having an ownership interest in the sound recording. In the case of an ownership interest held by a partnership or an S corporation, the partnership or S corporation shall make the election. Each person making the election shall do so in accordance with paragraph (a)(2) and (3) of this section, and shall identify in the statement described in paragraph (a)(3) of this section the persons with ownership interests in the sound recording, and shall state that each such person is making the election with respect to that sound recording.

(iii) Special rules for making the election with respect to redemption through use of related corporations. For either election available under section 712(l)(7) of the Act (relating to redemptions through related corporations) to be effective, such election must be made jointly by both the issuing and acquiring corporations. The election is made jointly when both the issuing and acquiring corporations make the election in accordance with paragraph (a)(2) and (3) of this section.

(iv) Special rules for making the election for investment tax credit at risk rules. The election under section 431(e)(2) of the Act is made by filing an amended return for the first taxable year ending after February 18, 1981, during which taxable year property, to which the amendments made by section 211(f) of the Economic Recovery Tax Act of 1981 apply, was placed in service. If that taxable year is a closed year, the election is made by filing an amended return for the first succeeding open taxable year, but in such event this election can be made only if the aggregate amount of the investment tax credit that would have been allowable in the closed years had the election been effective for those years is greater than or equal to the amount of the investment tax credits actually claimed in the closed years. In the case of partnerships and S corporations, the election under section 431(e) is made, respectively, at the partner or the shareholder level. Any election made under section 431(e) shall apply to all property of the taxpayer to which the amendments made by section 211(f) of the Economic Recovery Tax Act of 1981 apply. Amended returns must be filed for any year the tax liability for which is affected by making this election.

(v) Special rules for certain elections by life insurance companies. (A) Election with respect to loss from operations of member of group. Any life insurance company that makes an election under section 806(d)(4) must include on the statement described in paragraph (a)(3) of this section the name, address and taxpayer identification number of the members of the controlled group that did not file a consolidated return with the life insurance company for the taxable year to which the election applies, the amount of loss subject to the limitation provided by section 806(d)(4)(B), and a computation showing how such amount was derived.

(B) Election to use preceding year's interest rate for non-annuity reserves. If the election under section 807(d)(4)(C) is not made for all non-annuity contracts issued by the life insurance company before the end of the taxable year in which the election is made, the company must reasonably identify, in the statement described in paragraph (a)(3) of this section, the contracts or groups of contracts for which the election is made. The statement, however, need not specify each individual contract for which the election is made.

(4) Revocation. The elections under Act sections 31(a), 31(g)(16), 31(f), 113, 211 (Code section 810(b)(3)), 216(c)(1) and (2), 217(l), 431(e)(2), and 712(l)(7)(B) and (C)(ii) are irrevocable. Elections under Act sections 41(a) (Code sections 1282(b)(2) and 1283(c)(2)), 211 (Code sections 806(d)(4), and 807(d)(4)(C)), 217(i), 1066, and 1078 are revocable only with the consent of the Commissioner. A revocation under Act section 211 (Code section 807(d)(4)(C)) shall be treated as a change in basis of computing reserves that is subject to the adjustment provided in section 807(f) of the Code.

(b) Church or qualified church-controlled organization's election of exemption from social security taxes under chapter 21. *(1) In general.* This paragraph applies to the election under section 3121(w) of the Code, as added by section 2603(b) of the Act, by a church or qualified church-controlled organization (as defined in section 3121(w)(3)) that service performed in the employ of such church or organization shall be excluded from employment for purposes of title II of the Social Security Act and chapter 21 of the Internal Revenue Code. Any election made under section 3121(w) shall apply to all services performed on or after January 1, 1984, by employees of such church or organization (whether or not they were employees on that date or on the date the election is made). Employees of the electing church or organization are subject to the provisions of chapter 2 of the Code (relating to the tax on self-employment income) as amended by section 2603(c)(2) and (d)(2) of the Act for service performed for such church or organization on or after January 1, 1984.

(2) Time for making the election. Any election under section 3121(w) by a church or qualified church-controlled organization for which a quarterly employment tax return for the tax imposed under section 3111 is due (or would be due but for the election) on October 31, 1984, must be made on or before October 30, 1984. Any election under section 3121(w) by a church or organization for which the first quarterly employment tax return for the tax imposed under section 3111 is due (or would be due but for this election) after October 31, 1984, must be made on or before the day before the first date that such tax return would be due from the church or organization (disregarding any extension of such due date). A purported election filed after the date prescribed in this paragraph (b)(2) shall be void.

(3) Manner of making the election. To make an election under section 3121(w), a church or qualified church-controlled organization must certify that it is opposed for religious reasons to the payment of the tax imposed by section 3111 (relating to the employer tax) of the Code. The election and certification are made by executing and filing Form 8274 in accordance with the form and its instructions. The form shall be signed by an official authorized to sign tax returns for the church or organization. Where tax imposed by section 3111 is reported (or would be reported but for this election) with respect to more than one church or organization on a single quarterly employment tax return, and the election under section 3121(w) is made, then all of the churches and organizations covered by the last such return filed before such election was made for which the time for making the election has not expired shall be covered by the election unless specifically excluded by stating such exclusion in the election.

(4) Refunds of FICA taxes paid. Where a church or qualified church-controlled organization makes a timely election under section 3121(w), a refund, without interest, shall be made to such church or organization of any taxes paid under sections 3101 and 3111 with respect to service performed after December 31, 1983, covered by the election. However, the refund will be made only if the church or organization agrees on its claim for the refund to pay to each employee covered by the election the portion of the refund attributable to the tax imposed on the wages of the employee by section 3101. The employee may not receive any other refund of such taxes. The claim for refund shall be made by the church or organization by filing Form 843 with the service center where the Form 941 on which the taxes subject to refund was filed. Form 843 shall be executed in accordance with the form and its instructions, and also in accordance with the instructions to Form 8274 that relate to Form 843.

(5) Irrevocability of election except by Commissioner. An election under section 3121 shall be irrevocable by the electing church or organization. The Commissioner, however, shall permanently revoke the election if the church or organization fails to furnish the information required under section 6051 to the Internal Revenue Service for a period of 2 years or more and also fails to furnish such information within 60 days after a written request therefor is made by the Internal Revenue Service.

(c) Election to issue taxable student loan bonds. This paragraph applies to the election by an issuer to issue taxable student loan bonds under section 625(c) of the Act. The election is available for obligations issued after December 31, 1983, and is made by filing a statement and necessary attachments with the Internal Revenue Service Center, Philadelphia, PA 19255, prior to the issuance of such taxable bonds. The statement shall identify the election as made under section 625(c) of the Tax Reform Act of 1984 and shall contain the name, address and taxpayer identification number of the issuer, and the total purchase price, face amount and interest rate of the issue, bond issuance costs, amounts allocated to reasonably required reserve or replacement funds, and the date of issue. The issuer shall attach to the statement of election a copy of previous Internal Revenue Service correspondence relating to the tax exempt status of the issuing authority and a statement containing the total purchase price, face amount, interest rate, bond issuance costs, amounts allocated to reasonably required reserve or replacement funds, and the date of issuance of outstanding tax exempt issues of student loan bonds of the issuer. With respect to outstanding tax exempt issues of student loan bonds of the issuer issued after December 31, 1982, the issuer may alternatively attach copies of the Form 8038 filed with respect to such issues. Each taxable student loan bond must state on its face that the interest paid on such bond is subject to federal income taxation. An election with respect to an issue is irrevocable once made.

(d) Reserved.

(e) Election not to claim the credit for alcohol used as fuel. The election under section 40(f) (as added by section 474(k) of the Act) not to claim the alcohol fuels credit is available for taxable years beginning after December 31, 1983, and shall be made for the taxable year in which such credit is determined by not claiming such credit on an original return or amended return at any time before the expiration of the 3-year period beginning on the last date prescribed by law for filing the return for the taxable year (determined without regard for extensions). The election may be revoked within the 3-year period by filing an amended return and claiming the credit on the return.

(f) Protective election to adopt LIFO method. *(1) Time for making the election.* A protective election in connection with the enactment of section 95 of the Act to adopt the LIFO method of accounting for inventory under section 472 of the Code can only be made for the taxpayer's first taxable year beginning after July 18, 1984, and must be made on or before the due date (including extensions) of the tax return for such taxable year. Once made, the election is irrevocable unless the Commissioner authorizes the use of another inventory method (see § 1.472-5).

(2) Manner for making a protective election. The protective election is made by completing all line items on a current Form 970 and indicating that the election is a protective election filed in connection with the enactment of section 95

of the Tax Reform Act of 1984. The Form 970 must be attached to the taxpayer's income tax return for the taxable year for which the protective election is made. The LIFO method adopted under the protective election must be consistent in all respects with the taxpayer's LIFO method used in the taxpayer's most recently completed taxable year for which the LIFO method was used. In completing the current Form 970, the taxpayer shall specify the method of inventory valuation that the taxpayer would have used, the opening LIFO inventory for the taxable year for which the protective election is made, and the section 481 adjustment that would be required, as if the taxpayer were not on the LIFO method for the taxable year immediately preceding the taxable year for which the protective election is made.

(g) Election by an estate or trust to recognize gain or loss on the distribution of property (other than cash) to a beneficiary. This paragraph applies to the election made by a trust or estate to recognize gain or loss on the distribution of property (other than cash) to a beneficiary under section 643(d) of the Code as amended by section 81 of the Act. The election is available for distributions made after June 1, 1984, in taxable years ending after such date. The election must be made by the fiduciary who is required to make the return of the estate or trust under section 641 and § 1.641(b)-2. The election shall be made by such fiduciary on the tax return of the estate or trust for the taxable year with respect to which the distribution of property was made and must be filed by the due date (including extensions) of such return. Until the Form 1041, U.S. Fiduciary Income Tax Return is revised, the election should be made by including the gain or loss on the Schedule D (or other appropriate schedule, if applicable) of the Form 1041 and attaching the statement described in paragraph (a)(3) of this section to the tax return on which the election is made and including on that statement the name and taxpayer identification number of the distributee. For distributions made after June 1, 1984, and before July 18, 1984, the election must be filed by the later of the due date (including extensions) of the tax return of the estate or trust for the taxable year with respect to which the distribution was made or January 1, 1985. For those distributions, the fiduciary may make the election in the manner described above on a tax return, or amended return, for the year with respect to which the distribution was made. An election under section 643(d) may be revoked only with the consent of the Commissioner. The request for revocation of an election should be made by the fiduciary in the form of a ruling request and must contain the information required by regulations and revenue procedures pertaining thereto.

(h) Election to treat a stapled foreign entity as a subsidiary. This paragraph applies to the election, provided under section 136(c)(6) of the Act, to treat a foreign corporation which was a stapled entity with a domestic corporation as of June 30, 1983, as being owned (to the extent of its stapled interests) by the domestic corporation with which it is stapled. This treatment, if so elected, is in lieu of the treatment prescribed in section 269B(a)(1) of the Code, as added by the Act. This election may be made by the domestic corporation with which the foreign entity is stapled. The election may not be made by the foreign entity or by shareholders of the domestic corporation. This election must be made no later than January 14, 1985, and may be revoked only with the consent of the Commissioner. This election shall be effective after December 31, 1986. The domestic corporation shall make this election by filing with the service center with which the domestic corporation files its income tax return a statement that—

(1) Contains the name, address, and taxpayer identification number of the domestic corporation,

(2) Identifies the election as made under section 136(c)(6) of the Tax Reform Act of 1984, and,

(3) Identifies the foreign entity and the interests in the foreign entity which constitute stapled interests with respect to the stock of the domestic corporation, and specifies the date on which those interests became stapled interests. If this election is not made, the foreign corporation (interests in which were stapled interests as of June 30, 1983) will be treated as a domestic corporation, effective January 1, 1987, under section 269B(a)(1) of the Code.

(i) Election to treat certain section 1248 amounts as included in gross income under section 951(a)(1)(A). This paragraph applies to the elections, provided under section 133(d)(3) of the Act, to treat amounts included in the gross income of any person as a dividend by reason of section 1248(a) or (f) after October 9, 1975, and before July 19, 1985, as an amount included in the gross income of such person under section 951(a)(1)(A). The election with respect to transactions to which section 1248(a) applies may be made by the foreign corporation described in section 1248(a) (or its successor in interest). The election with respect to transactions to which section 1248(f) applies may be made by the domestic corporation described in section 1248(f)(1) (or its successor in interest). Neither election may be made by an affected shareholder of any such corporation (unless the shareholder is the successor in interest). This election must be made no later than January 14, 1985, and shall apply with respect to all transactions to which section 1248(a) or (f) applies that occurred after October 9, 1975, and before July 19, 1984. Once made, the election may be revoked only with the consent of the Commissioner. A foreign corporation shall make this election by filing the statement described in this paragraph with the Internal Revenue Service Center, Philadelphia, PA 19255. A domestic corporation shall make this election by filing the statement described in this paragraph with the service center with which the domestic corporation files its income tax return. In either case, the statement shall—

(1) Contain the name, address, and taxpayer identification number (if any) of the corporation making the election,

(2) Identify the election as made under section 133(d)(3) of the Tax Reform Act of 1984, and

(3) Identify all of the transactions (including the date of each transaction), shareholders involved in those transactions, and amounts to which the election applies.

(j) Special election for computing investment company taxable income. This paragraph applies to the election by a regulated investment company provided under section 1071(b) of the Act, which added section 852(b)(2)(F) to the Code. Under section 852(b)(2)(F), the taxable income of a regulated investment company shall be computed without regard to section 454(b) (relating to short-term obligations issued on a discount basis) if the company so elects. The election may be made only for taxable years beginning after December 31, 1978. A regulated investment company shall make the election by computing taxable income without regard to section 454(b) on its return for the first taxable year for which it desires the election to apply and shall attach the statement described in paragraph (a)(3) of this section to the return on which the election is made. A regulated investment company shall make the election by the time set forth in paragraph (a)(2) of this section. Once made, the election applies to the first taxable year for which it is made and to all subsequent taxable years and cannot be revoked without the consent of the Commissioner.

(k) Election of extension of time for payment of estate tax for interests in certain holding companies. An election under section 6166(b)(8), as added by section 1021(a) of the Act, or under section 1021(d)(2) of the Act, shall be made by including on the notice of election under section 6166 required by § 20.6166-1(b) a statement that an election is being made under section 6166(b)(8) or section 1021(d)(2) of the Act (whichever is applicable) and the facts which formed the basis for the executor's conclusion that the estate qualified for such election. If a taxpayer makes an election described in this paragraph (k), then the special 4-percent interest rate of section 6601(j) and the 5-year deferral of principal payments of section 6166(a)(3) are not available. Thus, the first installment of tax is due on the date prescribed by section 6151(a) and subsequent installments bear interest at the rate determined under section 6621. If the executor makes an election described in this paragraph (k) and the notice of election under section 6166 fails to state the amount of tax to be paid in installments or the number of installments, then the election is presumed to be for the maximum amount so payable and for payment thereof in 10 equal annual installments, beginning on the date prescribed in section 6151(a). The elections described under this paragraph (k) are available for estates of decedents dying after July 18, 1984.

(l) Subchapter S election by commodities dealers and options dealers. This paragraph applies to a commodities dealer or options dealer referred to in section 102(d)(3) of the Act (relating to the election by such a dealer to be an S corporation) whose taxable year is the calendar year and that was a small business corporation (as defined in section 1361(b) of the Code) as of January 1, 1984. The election by such a dealer under section 102(d)(3) of the Act shall be made in the manner prescribed by section 1362 and the regulations thereunder, except that the election under section 102(d)(3) must be made before October 2, 1984. In addition to making the election in the manner prescribed under such section 1362 and the regulations thereunder, the commodities dealer or options dealer must indicate on Form 2553 that the election is made under section 102(d)(3) of the Act. Although section 102(d)(3) of the Act applies to dealers not covered by this paragraph, and such dealers may make an election under such section 102(d)(3), guidelines for making such an election are not provided in this paragraph and are forthcoming.

(m) Election with respect to treatment of S termination year. For the election provided under section 1362(e)(3), as amended by section 721(h) of the Act, see § 18.1362-4 of this chapter.

(n) Election to be an S corporation; certain short taxable years. For the election provided under section 1362(b), as amended by section 721(l) of the Act, see § 18.1362-1(b) of this chapter.

(o) Election with respect to subchapter S passive investment income rules. For the election provided under section 721(i) of the Act which amends section 6(b) of the Subchapter S Revision Act of 1982, see § 18.1362-5 of this chapter.

(p) Election with respect to subchapter S distributions during certain post-termination transition periods. For the election provided under section 1371(e), as amended by section 721(o) of the Act, see § 18.1371-1 of this chapter.

(q) No elections for closed year. Any election under this section which is allowed to be made by filing an amended return may only be made if the period for making a claim for refund or credit with respect to the taxable year for which such election is to be effective has not expired. This paragraph shall not apply to the election under paragraph (a)(2)(iv) of this section with respect to the election under section 1078 of the Act.

(r) Additional information required. Later regulations or revenue procedures issued under provisions of the Code or Act covered by this section may require the furnishing of information in addition to that which was furnished with the statement of election described herein. In such event the later regulations or revenue procedures will provide guidance with respect to the furnishing of such additional information.

T.D. 7976, 9/5/84, amend T.D. 8062, 11/5/85, T.D. 8435, 9/18/92, T.D. 9172, 1/3/2005.

§ 301.9100-12T Various elections under the Tax Reform Act of 1976 (temporary).

(a) Elections covered by temporary rules. The sections of the Internal Revenue Code of 1954, or of the Tax Reform Act of 1976, to which this section applies and under which an election or notification may be made pursuant to the procedures described in paragraphs (b) and (d) are as follows:

Section	Description of election	Availability of election
	(1) FIRST CATEGORY	
167(o) of Code	Substantially rehabilitated historic property	Additions to capital account occurring after June 30, 1976, and before July 1, 1981.
172(b)(3)(E) of Code	Forego of carryback period	Any taxable year ending after December 31, 1975.
402(e)(4)(L) of Code	Lump sum distributions from qualified plans	Distributions and payments made after December 31, 1975, in taxable years beginning after such date.
451(e) of Code	Livestock sold on account of drought	Any taxable year beginning after December 31, 1975.
812(b)(3) of Code	Forego of carryback period by life insurance companies	Any taxable year ending after December 31, 1975.
819A of Code	Contiguous country branches of domestic life insurance companies	All taxable years beginning after December 31, 1975.
825(d)(2) of Code	Forego of carryback period by mutual insurance companies	Any taxable year ending after December 31, 1975.

911(e) of Code	Foregoing of benefits of section 911	All taxable years beginning after December 31, 1975.

(2) SECOND CATEGORY

185(d) of Code	Amortization of railroad grading and tunnel bores.	All taxable years beginning after December 31, 1974.
1057 of Code	Transfer to foreign trusts etc.	Any transfer of property after October 2, 1975.

(b) Time for making election or serving notice. *(1) Category (1).* A taxpayer may make an election under any section referred to in paragraph (a)(1) of this section for the first taxable year for which the election is required to be made or for the taxable year selected by the taxpayer when the choice of the taxable year is optional. The election must be made by the later of the time, including extensions thereof, prescribed by law for filing income tax returns for such taxable year or March 8, 1977.

(2) Category (2). A taxpayer may make an election under any section referred to in paragraph (a)(2) for the first taxable year for which the election is allowed or for the taxable year selected by the taxpayer when the choice of the taxable year is optional. The election must be made (i) for any taxable year ending before December 31, 1976, for which a return has been filed before January 31, 1977, by filing an amended return, provided that the period of limitation for filing claim for credit or refund of overpayment of tax, determined from the time the return was filed, has not expired or (ii) for all other years by filing the income tax return for the year for which the election is made not later than the time, including extensions thereof, prescribed by law for filing income tax returns for such year. However, an organization which has its exempt status under section 501(a) of the Code revoked for any taxable year and which is described in section 528 of the Code, may make an election under section 528(c)(1)(E) of the Code for such year, before the expiration of the period for filing claim for credit or refund of overpayment of tax.

(c) Certain other elections. The elections described in this paragraph shall be made in the manner and within the time prescribed herein and in paragraph (d) of this section.

(1) The following elections under the Tax Reform Act of 1976 shall be made:

(i) Sec. 207(c)(3) of Act; change from static value method of accounting; all taxable years beginning after December 31, 1976.

by filing Form 3115 with the National Office of the Internal Revenue Service before October 5, 1977.

(ii) Sec. 604 of Act; travel expenses of State legislators; all taxable years beginning before January 1, 1976.

by filing an amended return for any taxable year for which the period for assessing or collecting a deficiency has not expired before October 4, 1976, by the last day for filing a claim for refund or credit for the taxable year but in no event shall such day be earlier than October 4, 1977.

(iii) Sec. 804(e)(2) of Act; retroactive applications of amendments to property described in section 50(a) of Code; certain taxable years beginning before January 1, 1975.

by filing amended returns before October 5, 1977, for all taxable years to which applicable for which the period of limitation for filing claim for credit or refund for overpayment of tax has not expired.

(iv) Sec. 1608(d)(2) of Act; election as a result of determination as defined in section 859(c) of the Code; determinations made after October 4, 1976.

by filing a statement with the district director for the district in which the taxpayer maintains its principal place of business within 60 days after such determination.

(v) Sec. 2103 of Act; treatment of certain 1972 disaster losses. Any taxable year in which payment is received or indebtedness is forgiven.

by filing a return for the taxable year or an amended return by the last day for making a claim for credit or refund for the taxable year but in no event shall such day be earlier than October 4, 1977.

(3) The election provided for in section 167(e)(3) of the Code shall be made in accordance with § 1.167(e)-1(d) except that the election shall be applicable for the first taxable year of the taxpayer beginning after December 31, 1975.

(4) [Removed.]

(5) The election provided in section 1033(g)(3) of the Code may be made for any taxable year beginning after December 31, 1970, by filing an amendment return for any taxable year for which the period of limitation for filing a claim for credit or refund of overpayment has not expired, and for any taxable year ending on or after December 31, 1976, by filing the income tax return for the year the election is made not later than the time, including extensions thereof, prescribed by law for filing income tax returns for such taxable year.

(d) Manner of making election. Unless otherwise provided in the return or in a form accompanying a return for the taxable year, the elections described in paragraphs (a) and (c) (except paragraphs (c)(1)(i), and (c)(5)) shall be made by a statement attached to the return (or amended return) for the taxable year. The statement required when making an election pursuant to this section shall indicate the section under which the election is being made and shall set forth information to identify the election, the period for which it applies, and the taxpayer's basis or entitlement for making the election.

(e) Effect of election. *(1) Consent to revoke required.* Except where otherwise provided by statute or except as provided in subparagraph (2) of this paragraph, an election to which this section applies made in accordance with this section shall be binding unless consent to revoke the election is obtained from the Commissioner. An application for consent to revoke the election will not be accepted before the promulgation of the permanent regulations relating to the section of the Code or Act under which the election is made. Such regulations will provide a reasonable period of time within which taxpayers will be permitted to apply for consent to revoke the election.

(2) Revocation without consent. An election to which this section applies, made in accordance with this section, may be revoked without the consent of the Commissioner not later than 90 days after the permanent regulations relating to

the section of the Code or Act under which the election is made are filed with the Office of the Federal Register, provided such regulations grant taxpayers blanket permission to revoke that election within such time without the consent of the Commissioner. Such blanket permission to revoke an election will be provided by the permanent regulations in the event of a determination by the Secretary or his delegate that such regulations contain provisions that may not reasonably have been anticipated by taxpayers at the time of making such election.

(f) Furnishing of supplementary information required. If the permanent regulations which are issued under the section of the Code or Act referred to in this section to which the election relates require the furnishing of information in addition to that which was furnished with the statement of election filed pursuant to paragraph (d) of this section, the taxpayer must furnish such additional information in a statement addressed to the district director, or the director of the regional service center, with whom the election was filed. This statement must clearly identify the election and the taxable year for which it was made. If such information is not provided the election may, at the discretion of the Commissioner, be held invalid.

T.D. 7459, 1/4/77, amend T.D. 7478, 4/6/77, T.D. 7526, 12/23/77, T.D. 7670, 1/30/80, T.D. 7673, 2/7/80, T.D. 7692, 4/17/80, T.D. 7743, 12/19/80, T.D. 7758, 1/16/81, T.D. 8308, 8/30/90, T.D. 8435, 9/18/92.

§ 301.9100-17T Procedure applicable to certain elections (temporary).

(a) Elections covered by temporary rules. The sections of the Internal Revenue Code of 1954, or of the Tax Reform Act of 1969, to which paragraph (b) of this section applies and under which an election or notification may be made pursuant to the procedures prescribed in such paragraph are as follows:

Section	Description of election	Availability of election
(1) First category:		
167(e)(3) of Code	Change of depreciation method on sec. 1250 property.	First taxable year beginning after July 24, 1969.
185(c) of Code	Amortization of qualified railroad grading and tunnel bores.	Any taxable year beginning after Dec. 31, 1969.
231(d)(2) of Act	Moving expenses.	Expenses paid or incurred before July 1, 1970, if employee was notified of move by employer on or before Dec. 19, 1969.
433(d)(2) of Act	Bonds, etc., held by financial institutions.	All taxable years beginning after July 11, 1969, and before July 11, 1974.
503(c)(2) of Act	Carved-out mineral production payments.	All mineral production payments carved out of mineral properties after beginning of last taxable year ending before Aug. 7, 1969.
516(d)(3) of Act	Contingent payments by transferee of franchise, trademark, or trade name.	Payments made in taxable years ending after Dec. 31, 1969, and beginning before Jan. 1, 1980, on transfers made before Jan. 1, 1970.
642(c)(1) of Code	Charitable contributions of estates or trusts paid in following year.	Amounts paid in any taxable year beginning after Dec. 31, 1969.
1039(a) of Code	Gain from sale of low-income housing project.	Approved dispositions after Oct. 9, 1969.
1251(b)(4) of Code	No additions to excess deductions account of taxpayers electing to compute taxable income from farming in certain manner.	Any taxable year beginning after Dec. 31, 1969.
(2) Second category:		
169(b) of Code	Amortization of pollution control facilities.	Any taxable year ending after Dec. 31, 1968, in which facility is completed or acquired (or succeeding taxable year).
184(b) of Code	Amortization of qualified railroad rolling stock.	Any taxable year beginning after Dec. 31, 1969, in which rolling stock was placed in service (or succeeding taxable year).
187(b) of Code	Amortization of certified coal mine safety equipment.	Any taxable year ending after Dec. 31, 1969, in which safety equipment was placed in service (or succeeding taxable year).
(3) Third category:		
504(d)(2) of Act	Notification not to have sec. 615(e) election treated as a sec. 617(a) election.	Exploration expenditures paid or incurred after Dec. 31, 1969.

(b) Manner of making election or serving notice. *(1) In general.* (i) Except as provided in subparagraph (2) of this paragraph, a taxpayer may make an election under any section referred to in paragraph (a)(1) or (2) of this section for the first taxable year for which the election is required to be made or for the taxable year selected by the taxpayer when the choice of a taxable year is optional. The election must be made not later than (a) the time, including extensions thereof, prescribed by law for filing the income tax return for such taxable year or (b) 90 days after the date on which the regulations in this section are filed with the Office of the Federal Register, whichever is later.

(ii) The election shall be made by a statement attached to the return (or an amended return) for the taxable year, indicating the section under which the election is being made and setting forth information to identify the election, the period for which it applies, and the facility, property, or amounts to which it applies.

(2) Additional time for certain elections. An election under section 503(c)(2) of the Act or section 642(c)(1) of the Code must be made in accordance with subparagraph (1) of this paragraph but not later than (i) the time, including extensions thereof, prescribed by law for filing the income tax return for the taxable year following the taxable year for which the election is made or (ii) 90 days after the date on which the regulations in this section are filed with the Office of the Federal Register, whichever is later.

(3) Notification as to section 615(e) election. (i) The notification referred to in paragraph (a)(3) of this section in respect of an election under section 615(e) which was made before the date on which the regulations in this section are filed with the Office of the Federal Register shall be made in a statement attached to the taxpayer's income tax return for the first taxable year in which expenditures are paid or incurred after December 31, 1969, which would be deductible by the taxpayer under section 617 if he so elects. The statement shall indicate the first taxable year for which such election was effective and the district director, or the director of the regional service center, with whom the election was filed.

(ii) The notification referred to in paragraph (a)(3) of this section, in respect of an election under section 615(e) which is made on or after the date on which the regulations in this section are filed with the Office of the Federal Register, shall be made in the statement of election required by paragraph (a)(2) of § 15.1-1 of this chapter (Temporary Income Tax Regulations Relating to Exploration Expenditures in the Case of Mining).

(iii) The serving of notice pursuant to this subparagraph shall not preclude the subsequent making of an election under section 617(a). A failure to serve notice pursuant to this subparagraph shall be treated as an election under section 617(a) and paragraph (a)(1) of § 15.1-1 of this chapter with respect to exploration expenditures paid or incurred after December 31, 1969, whether or not the taxpayer subsequently revokes his election under section 615(e) with respect to exploration expenditures paid or incurred before January 1, 1970.

(iv) For rules relating to the revocation of an election under section 615(e), including such an election which is treated pursuant to this subparagraph as an election under section 617(a), see paragraph (a) of § 15.1-2 of this chapter (T.D. 6907, C.B. 1967-1, 531, 535).

(c) Effect of election. *(1) Revocations.* (i) Consent to revoke required. Except as provided in subdivision (ii) of this subparagraph, an election made in accordance with paragraph (b)(1) of this section shall be binding unless consent to revoke the election is obtained from the Commissioner. An application for consent to revoke the election will not be accepted before the promulgation of the permanent regulations relating to the section of the Code or Act under which the election is made. Such regulations will provide a reasonable period of time within which taxpayers will be permitted to apply for consent to revoke the election.

(ii) Revocation without consent. An election made in accordance with paragraph (b)(1) of this section may be revoked without the consent of the Commissioner not later than 90 days after the permanent regulations relating to the section of the Code or Act under which the election is made are filed with the Office of the Federal Register, provided such regulations grant taxpayers blanket permission to revoke that election within such time without the consent of the Commissioner. Such blanket permission to revoke an election will be provided by the permanent regulations in the event of a determination by the Secretary or his delegate that such regulations contain provisions that may not reasonably have been anticipated by taxpayers at the time of making such election.

(iii) Election treated as tentative. Until the expiration of the reasonable period referred to in subdivision (i) of this subparagraph or the 90-day period referred to in subdivision (ii), of this subparagraph, an election under section 433(d)(2) of the Act will be considered a tentative election, subject to revocation under the provisions of such subdivisions.

(iv) Place for filing revocations. A revocation under subdivision (i) or (ii) of this subparagraph shall be made by filing a statement to that effect with the district director, or the director of the regional service center, with whom the election was filed.

(2) Termination without consent. An election which is made in accordance with paragraph (b)(1) of this section under a section referred to in paragraph (a)(2) of this section and is not revoked pursuant to subparagraph (1) of this paragraph may, without the consent of the Commissioner, be terminated at any time after making the election by filing a statement to that effect with the district director, or the director of the regional service center, with whom the election was filed. This statement giving notice of termination must be filed before the beginning of the month specified in the statement for which the termination is to be effective. If pursuant to this subparagraph the taxpayer terminates an election made under any such section, he may not thereafter make a new election under that section with respect to the facility, property, or equipment to which the termination relates.

(d) Furnishing of supplementary information required. If the permanent regulations which are issued under the section of the Code or Act referred to in paragraph (a)(1) or (2) of this section to which the election relates require the furnishing of information in addition to that which was furnished with the statement of election filed pursuant to paragraph (b)(1) of this section, the taxpayer must furnish such additional information in a statement addressed to the district director, or the director of the regional service center, with whom the election was filed. This statement must clearly identify the election and the taxable year for which it was made.

(e) Other elections. Elections under the following sections of the Code may not be made pursuant to paragraph (b)(1) of this section but are to be made under regulations, whether temporary or permanent, which will be issued under amendments made by the Act. If necessary, such regulations will provide a reasonable period of time within which taxpayers will be permitted to make elections under these sections for taxable years ending before the date on which such regulations are filed with the Office of the Federal Register:

Section	Description
167(k)(1)	Expenditures to rehabilitate low-income rental housing.
167(l)(4)	Post-1969 property of certain utilities representing growth in capacity.
170(b)(1)(D)(iii) ..	Special limitation with respect to contributions of certain capital gain property.
453(c)	Revocation of election to report income on installment basis.

507(b)(1)(B)(ii) . . .	Notice of termination of private foundation status.
1564(a)(2)	Allowance of certain amounts to component member of controlled group of corporations.
4942(h)(2)	Deficient distributions of private foundations for prior taxable years.
4943(c)(4)(E)	Determination of holdings of a private foundation in a business enterprise where substantial contributors hold more than 15 percent of voting stock.

(f) Cross reference. For temporary regulations under sections 57(c) and 163(d)(7) of the code, relating to elections with respect to net leases of real property, see § 12.8 of the regulations in this part (Temporary Income Tax Regulations Under the Revenue Act of 1971).

T.D. 7032, 3/10/70, amend T.D. 7271, 4/11/73, T.D. 8435, 9/18/92.

§ 301.9100-18T Election to include in gross income in year of transfer (temporary).

(a) In general. Under section 83(b) of the Internal Revenue Code of 1954 any person who performs services in connection with which property is transferred which at the time of transfer is not transferable by the transferee and is subject to a substantial risk of forfeiture may elect to include in his gross income for the taxable year in which such property is transferred, the excess of the fair market value of such property at the time of transfer (determined without regard to any restriction other than a restriction which by its terms will never lapse) over the amount (if any) paid for such property. If this election is made section 83(a) does not apply with respect to such property, and any subsequent appreciation in the value of the property is not taxable as compensation. However, if the property is later forfeited, no deduction is allowed to any person with respect to such forfeiture. This election is not necessary in the case of property which is transferred subject only to a restriction which by its terms will never lapse.

(b) Manner of making the election. The election referred to in paragraph (a) of this section is made by filing two copies of a written statement with the internal revenue officer with whom the person who performed the services files his return.

(c) Additional copies. The person who performed the services shall also submit a copy of the statement referred to in paragraph (b) of this section to the person for whom the services are performed, and, in addition, if the person who performs the services in connection with which restricted property is transferred and the transferee of such property are not the same person, the person who performs the services shall submit a copy of such statement to the transferee of the property.

(d) Content of statement. The statement shall indicate that it is being made under section 83(b) of the Code, and shall contain the following information:

(1) The name, address, taxpayer identification number and the taxable year (For example, "Calendar year 1969" or "Fiscal year ending May 31, 1970") of the person who performed the services;

(2) A description of each property with respect to which the election is being made;

(3) The date or dates on which the property is transferred;

(4) The nature of the restriction or restrictions to which the property is subject;

(5) The fair market value at the time of transfer (determined without regard to any restriction other than a restriction which by its terms will never lapse) of each property with respect to which the election is being made; and

(6) The amount (if any) paid for such property.

(e) Time for making election. The statement referred to in paragraph (b) of this section shall be filed not later than 30 days after the date the property was transferred (or, if later, Jan. 29, 1970). Any statement filed before February 15, 1970, may be amended not later than 30 days after the publication of this Treasury decision in the *Federal Register* [Jan. 17, '70] in order to make it conform to the requirements of paragraph (d) of this section.

(f) Revocability of election. An election under section 83(b) may not be revoked except with the consent of the Commissioner.

T.D. 7021, 1/16/70, amend T.D. 8435, 9/18/92.

Proposed § 1.168-1 Accelerated Cost Recovery System; in general. [*For Preamble, see ¶ 150,941*]

Caution: The Treasury has not yet amended Reg § 1.168-1 to reflect changes made by P.L. 101-508, P.L. 101-239, P.L. 100-647, P.L. 99-514, P.L. 98-369.

(a) Cost recovery deduction allowed. Section 168 of the Internal Revenue Code of 1954 provides a system for determining cost recovery deductions for recovery property, the Accelerated Cost Recovery System ("ACRS"). The deduction allowable under section 168 is deemed to constitute the reasonable allowance for depreciation allowed as a deduction under section 167(a). Operating rules regarding determination of the allowable cost recovery deduction are provided in § 1.168-2. The definition of recovery property and the classification of recovery property into recovery categories of 3, 5, 10, and 15 years are provided in § 1.168-3. ACRS must be applied with respect to recovery property placed in service after December 31, 1980, except for certain property which does not qualify under section 168 or which may be excluded from ACRS; § 1.168-4 provides rules regarding such exclusions and nonqualifications. Special rules regarding ACRS are provided in § 1.168-5. Rules relating to the recognition of gain or loss on dispositions are provided in § 1.168-6.

(b) Cross references. See § 1.167(a)-11(d)(2) regarding the election after 1980 of the repair allowance for certain property. See § 1.178-1 regarding the availability of ACRS deductions for, or the amortization of, improvements on leased property. See § 1.1016-3(a)(3) regarding the basis adjustment for the amount allowable where no ACRS deduction is claimed.

Proposed § 1.168-2 Amount of deduction for recovery property. [*For Preamble, see ¶ 150,941*]

Caution: The Treasury has not yet amended Reg § 1.168-2 to reflect changes made by P.L. 101-508, P.L. 101-239, P.L. 100-647, P.L. 99-514, P.L. 98-369.

(a) Computation of recovery allowance. *(1) General rule.* Except as otherwise provided in section 168 and the regulations thereunder, the recovery allowance for any taxable year equals the aggregate amount determined by multiplying the unadjusted basis (as defined in § 1.168-2(d)) of recovery property (as defined in § 1.168-3) by the appropriate applicable percentage provided in paragraph (b) of this section. For purposes of determining the recovery allowance, salvage value shall be disregarded.

(2) No allowance in year of disposition. Except for 15-year real property and except as otherwise provided in § 1.168-5, no recovery allowance shall be allowed in the year of disposition of recovery property.

(3) Proration of allowance in year of disposition of 15-year real property. In the taxable year in which 15-year real property is disposed of, the recovery allowance shall be determined by multiplying the allowance (determined without regard to this subparagraph) by a fraction, the numerator of which equals the number of months in the taxable year that the property is in service in the taxpayer's trade or business or for the production of income and the denominator of which is 12. In the case of 15-year real property that is disposed of in the first recovery year, the denominator shall equal the number of months in the taxpayer's taxable year after the recovery property was placed in service by the taxpayer (including the month the property was placed in service). If the recovery allowance for the taxable year is limited by reason of the short taxable year rules of section 168(f)(5) and paragraph (f) of this section (e.g., if the taxpayer dies, or if the taxpayer is a corporation which becomes a member, or ceases being a member, of an affiliated group of corporations filing a consolidated return), then the denominator shall equal the number of months in the taxpayer's taxable year. For purposes of this subparagraph, 15-year real property shall be treated as disposed of as of the last day of the month preceding the month in which it is withdrawn from service.

(b) Applicable percentage. *(1) Property other than 15-year real property.* The applicable percentage for recovery property, other than 15-year real property, is as follows:

If the recovery year is:	And the class of property is:			
	3-year	5-year	10-year	15-year Public Utility
	The applicable percentage is:			
1	25	15	8	5
2	38	22	14	10
3	37	21	12	9
4		21	10	8
5		21	10	7
6			10	7
7			9	6
8			9	6
9			9	6
10			9	6
11				6
12				6
13				6
14				6
15				6

(2) 15-year real property. (i) The applicable percentage for 15-year real property, other than low-income housing is as follows:

If the recovery year is:	And the month in the 1st recovery year the property is placed in service is:											
	1	2	3	4	5	6	7	8	9	10	11	12
	The applicable percentage is:											
1	12	11	10	9	8	7	6	5	4	3	2	1
2	10	10	11	11	11	11	11	11	11	11	11	12
3	9	9	9	9	10	10	10	10	10	10	10	10
4	8	8	8	8	8	8	9	9	9	9	9	9
5	7	7	7	7	7	7	8	8	8	8	8	8
6	6	6	6	6	7	7	7	7	7	7	7	7
7	6	6	6	6	6	6	6	6	6	6	6	6
8	6	6	6	6	6	6	5	6	6	6	6	6
9	6	6	6	6	5	6	5	5	5	6	6	6
10	5	6	5	6	5	5	5	5	5	5	6	5
11	5	5	5	5	5	5	5	5	5	5	5	5
12	5	5	5	5	5	5	5	5	5	5	5	5
13	5	5	5	5	5	5	5	5	5	5	5	5
14	5	5	5	5	5	5	5	5	5	5	5	5
15	5	5	5	5	5	5	5	5	5	5	5	5
16	—	—	1	1	2	2	3	3	4	4	4	5

(ii) The applicable percentage for 15-year real property that is low-income housing is as follows:

If the recovery year is:	And the month in the 1st recovery year the property is placed in service is:											
	1	2	3	4	5	6	7	8	9	10	11	12
	The applicable percentage is:											
1	13	12	11	10	9	8	7	6	4	3	2	1
2	12	12	12	12	12	12	12	13	13	13	13	13
3	10	10	10	10	11	11	11	11	11	11	11	11
4	9	9	9	9	9	9	9	9	10	10	10	10
5	8	8	8	8	8	8	8	8	8	8	8	9
6	7	7	7	7	7	7	7	7	7	7	7	7
7	6	6	6	6	6	6	6	6	6	6	6	6
8	5	5	5	5	5	5	5	5	5	5	6	6
9	5	5	5	5	5	5	5	5	5	5	5	5
10	5	5	5	5	5	5	5	5	5	5	5	5
11	4	5	5	5	5	5	5	5	5	5	5	5
12	4	4	4	5	4	5	5	5	5	5	5	5
13	4	4	4	4	4	4	5	4	5	5	5	5
14	4	4	4	4	4	4	4	4	4	5	4	4
15	4	4	4	4	4	4	4	4	4	4	4	4
16	—	—	1	1	2	2	2	3	3	3	4	4

(iii) For purposes of this section, the term "Low-income housing" means property described in clause (i), (ii), (iii), or (iv) of section 1250(a)(1)(B).

(iv) For purposes of this subparagraph (2), 15-year real property placed in service on or after the first day of a month shall be treated as placed in service in that month.

(c) Election of optional recovery percentage. *(1) Straight line method.* Except as provided by section 168(f)(2) and § 1.168-2(g) (relating to property used predominantly outside the United States), in lieu of using the applicable percentages prescribed in section 168(b)(1) and (2) and § 1.168-2(b), the taxpayer may elect (in accordance with § 1.168-5(e)), for recovery property placed in service during the taxable year, to determine the recovery allowance by using the straight line method over one of the recovery periods elected by the taxpayer and set forth in the following table:

Class of property	Recovery periods
3-year property	3, 5, or 12 years
5-year property	5, 12, or 25 years
10-year property	10, 25, or 35 years
15-year real property	15, 35, or 45 years
15-year public utility property	15, 35, or 45 years

Such election is irrevocable without the consent of the Commissioner. See subparagraph (4) of this paragraph for tables containing the applicable percentages to be used in computing the recovery allowance.

(2) Election for property other than 15-year real property. Except in the case of 15-year real property, a single recovery period must be elected under this paragraph for all recovery property which is in the same recovery class and which is placed in service in the same taxable year. A different recovery period may be elected (or the tables provided in section 168(b)(1) and § 1.168-2(b)(1) may be used) for recovery property in different recovery classes placed in service during the same taxable year, or for recovery property placed in service in different taxable years, whether or not in the same recovery class.

(3) Election for 15-year real property. In the case of 15-year real property, the election provided in paragraph (c)(1) may be made separately with respect to each property.

(4) Applicable percentage. (i) For property other than 15-year real property—

If the recovery year is:	And the period elected is:							
	3	5	10	12	15	25	35	45
	The applicable percentage is:							
1	17	10	5	4	3	2	1	1.1
2	33	20	10	9	7	4	3	2.3
3	33	20	10	9	7	4	3	2.3
4	17	20	10	9	7	4	3	2.3
5		20	10	9	7	4	3	2.3
6		10	10	8	7	4	3	2.3
7			10	8	7	4	3	2.3
8			10	8	7	4	3	2.3
9			10	8	7	4	3	2.3
10			10	8	7	4	3	2.3
11			5	8	7	4	3	2.3
12				8	6	4	3	2.2

13	4	6	4	3	2.2
14		6	4	3	2.2
15		6	4	3	2.2
16		3	4	3	2.2
17			4	3	2.2
18			4	3	2.2
19			4	3	2.2
20			4	3	2.2
21			4	3	2.2
22			4	3	2.2
23			4	3	2.2
24			4	3	2.2
25			4	3	2.2
26			2	3	2.2
27				3	2.2
28				3	2.2
29				3	2.2
30				3	2.2
31				3	2.2
32				2	2.2
33				2	2.2
34				2	2.2
35				2	2.2
36				1	2.2
37					2.2
38					2.2
39					2.2
40					2.2
41					2.2
42					2.2
43					2.2
44					2.2
45					2.2
46					1.1

(ii) For 15-year real property—

(A) For which a 15-year period is elected—

If the recovery year is:	And the month in the 1st recovery year that the property is placed in service is:						
	1	2-3	4	5-6	7-8	9-10	11-12
	The applicable percentage is:						
1	7	6	5	4	3	2	1
2	7	7	7	7	7	7	7
3	7	7	7	7	7	7	7
4	7	7	7	7	7	7	7
5	7	7	7	7	7	7	7
6	7	7	7	7	7	7	7
7	7	7	7	7	7	7	7
8	7	7	7	7	7	7	7
9	7	7	7	7	7	7	7
10	7	7	7	7	7	7	7
11	6	6	6	6	6	6	6
12	6	6	6	6	6	6	6
13	6	6	6	6	6	6	6
14	6	6	6	6	6	6	6
15	6	6	6	6	6	6	6
16		1	2	3	4	6	6

(B) For which a 35-year period is elected—

If the recovery year is:	And the month in the 1st recovery year that the property is placed in service is:		
	1-2	3-6	7-12
	The applicable percentage is:		
1	3	2	1
2	3	3	3
3	3	3	3
4	3	3	3
5	3	3	3
6	3	3	3
7	3	3	3
8	3	3	3
9	3	3	3
10	3	3	3
11	3	3	3
12	3	3	3
13	3	3	3
14	3	3	3
15	3	3	3
16	3	3	3
17	3	3	3
18	3	3	3
19	3	3	3
20	3	3	3
21	3	3	3
22	3	3	3
23	3	3	3
24	3	3	3
25	3	3	3
26	3	3	3
27	3	3	3
28	3	3	3
29	3	3	3
30	3	3	3
31	2	2	2
32	2	2	2
33	2	2	2
34	2	2	2
35	2	2	2
36		1	2

(C) For which a 45-year period is elected—

If the recovery year is:	And the month in the 1st recovery year the property is placed in service is:											
	1	2	3	4	5	6	7	8	9	10	11	12
	The applicable percentage is:											
1	2.3	2.0	1.9	1.7	1.5	1.3	1.2	.9	.7	.6	.4	.2
2	2.3	2.3	2.3	2.3	2.3	2.3	2.3	2.3	2.3	2.3	2.3	2.3
3	2.3	2.3	2.3	2.3	2.3	2.3	2.3	2.3	2.3	2.3	2.3	2.3
4	2.3	2.3	2.3	2.3	2.3	2.3	2.3	2.3	2.3	2.3	2.3	2.3
5	2.3	2.3	2.3	2.3	2.3	2.3	2.3	2.3	2.3	2.3	2.3	2.3
6	2.3	2.3	2.3	2.3	2.3	2.3	2.3	2.3	2.3	2.3	2.3	2.3
7	2.3	2.3	2.3	2.3	2.3	2.3	2.3	2.3	2.3	2.3	2.3	2.3
8	2.3	2.3	2.3	2.3	2.3	2.3	2.3	2.3	2.3	2.3	2.3	2.3
9	2.3	2.3	2.3	2.3	2.3	2.3	2.3	2.3	2.3	2.3	2.3	2.3
10	2.3	2.3	2.3	2.3	2.3	2.3	2.3	2.3	2.3	2.3	2.3	2.3
11	2.2	2.2	2.2	2.2	2.2	2.2	2.2	2.2	2.2	2.2	2.2	2.2
12	2.2	2.2	2.2	2.2	2.2	2.2	2.2	2.2	2.2	2.2	2.2	2.2
13	2.2	2.2	2.2	2.2	2.2	2.2	2.2	2.2	2.2	2.2	2.2	2.2
14	2.2	2.2	2.2	2.2	2.2	2.2	2.2	2.2	2.2	2.2	2.2	2.2
15	2.2	2.2	2.2	2.2	2.2	2.2	2.2	2.2	2.2	2.2	2.2	2.2
16	2.2	2.2	2.2	2.2	2.2	2.2	2.2	2.2	2.2	2.2	2.2	2.2
17	2.2	2.2	2.2	2.2	2.2	2.2	2.2	2.2	2.2	2.2	2.2	2.2
18	2.2	2.2	2.2	2.2	2.2	2.2	2.2	2.2	2.2	2.2	2.2	2.2
19	2.2	2.2	2.2	2.2	2.2	2.2	2.2	2.2	2.2	2.2	2.2	2.2
20	2.2	2.2	2.2	2.2	2.2	2.2	2.2	2.2	2.2	2.2	2.2	2.2
21	2.2	2.2	2.2	2.2	2.2	2.2	2.2	2.2	2.2	2.2	2.2	2.2
22	2.2	2.2	2.2	2.2	2.2	2.2	2.2	2.2	2.2	2.2	2.2	2.2
23	2.2	2.2	2.2	2.2	2.2	2.2	2.2	2.2	2.2	2.2	2.2	2.2
24	2.2	2.2	2.2	2.2	2.2	2.2	2.2	2.2	2.2	2.2	2.2	2.2
25	2.2	2.2	2.2	2.2	2.2	2.2	2.2	2.2	2.2	2.2	2.2	2.2
26	2.2	2.2	2.2	2.2	2.2	2.2	2.2	2.2	2.2	2.2	2.2	2.2
27	2.2	2.2	2.2	2.2	2.2	2.2	2.2	2.2	2.2	2.2	2.2	2.2
28	2.2	2.2	2.2	2.2	2.2	2.2	2.2	2.2	2.2	2.2	2.2	2.2
29	2.2	2.2	2.2	2.2	2.2	2.2	2.2	2.2	2.2	2.2	2.2	2.2
30	2.2	2.2	2.2	2.2	2.2	2.2	2.2	2.2	2.2	2.2	2.2	2.2
31	2.2	2.2	2.2	2.2	2.2	2.2	2.2	2.2	2.2	2.2	2.2	2.2
32	2.2	2.2	2.2	2.2	2.2	2.2	2.2	2.2	2.2	2.2	2.2	2.2
33	2.2	2.2	2.2	2.2	2.2	2.2	2.2	2.2	2.2	2.2	2.2	2.2
34	2.2	2.2	2.2	2.2	2.2	2.2	2.2	2.2	2.2	2.2	2.2	2.2

35	2.2	2.2	2.2	2.2	2.2	2.2	2.2	2.2	2.2	2.2	2.2	2.2
36	2.2	2.2	2.2	2.2	2.2	2.2	2.2	2.2	2.2	2.2	2.2	2.2
37	2.2	2.2	2.2	2.2	2.2	2.2	2.2	2.2	2.2	2.2	2.2	2.2
38	2.2	2.2	2.2	2.2	2.2	2.2	2.2	2.2	2.2	2.2	2.2	2.2
39	2.2	2.2	2.2	2.2	2.2	2.2	2.2	2.2	2.2	2.2	2.2	2.2
40	2.2	2.2	2.2	2.2	2.2	2.2	2.2	2.2	2.2	2.2	2.2	2.2
41	2.2	2.2	2.2	2.2	2.2	2.2	2.2	2.2	2.2	2.2	2.2	2.2
42	2.2	2.2	2.2	2.2	2.2	2.2	2.2	2.2	2.2	2.2	2.2	2.2
43	2.2	2.2	2.2	2.2	2.2	2.2	2.2	2.2	2.2	2.2	2.2	2.2
44	2.2	2.2	2.2	2.2	2.2	2.2	2.2	2.2	2.2	2.2	2.2	2.2
45	2.2	2.2	2.2	2.2	2.2	2.2	2.2	2.2	2.2	2.2	2.2	2.2
46		.3	.4	.6	.8	1.0	1.1	1.4	1.6	1.7	1.9	2.1

(iii) For purposes of this paragraph, 15-year real property that is placed in service on or after the first day of a month shall be treated as placed in service in that month.

(5) Property financed with the proceeds of industrial development bonds. If, in accordance with section 168(f)(12) and § 1.168-2(m), the recovery allowance for property financed with the proceeds of an industrial development bond (as described in section 103(b)) is determined using the straight line method, then an election as provided in section 168(b)(3) and this paragraph shall be deemed to have been made with respect to such property.

(d) Unadjusted basis. *(1) Computation.* Except as provided in paragraph (j)(6)(ii) of this section (relating to change of status), the unadjusted basis of recovery property is equal to the difference between—

(i) The basis of the property for purposes of determining gain under sections 1011 through 1024 but without regard to any adjustments to basis described in section 1016(a)(2) and (3), and

(ii) Any portion of the basis for which the taxpayer properly elects amortization in lieu of cost recovery *(e.g., under section 167(k)) or treatment as an expense under section 179.*

The unadjusted basis of recovery property shall be first taken into account under this section for the taxable year in which the property is placed in service (as defined in paragraph (1)(2) of this § 1.168-2) as recovery property.

(2) Reduction in basis. (i) If an investment tax credit is determined under section 46(a)(2) with respect to recovery property, then, unless the taxpayer makes an election provided under section 48(q)(4), for purposes of this section the unadjusted basis shall be reduced by 50 percent of the amount of the credit so determined. In the case of a credit determined under section 46(a)(2) for any qualified rehabilitation expenditure made in connection with a qualified rehabilitated building (other than a certified historic structure), the unadjusted basis shall be reduced by 100 percent of the amount of the credit so determined. See section 48(q) and the regulations thereunder. For rules relating to the treatment of such basis adjustment upon the disposition of an asset from a mass asset account, see § 1.168-2(h)(4).

(ii) Subject to the rules of other applicable provisions of the Code *(e.g., section 280A)*, for recovery property which is used in the taxpayer's trade or business (or for the production of income) as well as in a personal or tax-exempt activity throughout a taxable year, the unadjusted basis shall be determined by multiplying the unadjusted basis (determined without regard to this subdivision) by a fraction, the numerator of which equals the taxpayer's use of the property during the taxable year in his trade or business (or for the production of income) and the denominator of which equals the taxpayer's total use of the property during the taxable year. For property converted from personal or tax-exempt use to use in the taxpayer's trade or business (or for the production of income), or for property devoted to increased use in the taxpayer's trade or business (or for the production of income), see § 1.168-2(j).

(iii) The provisions of subdivision (ii) may be illustrated by the following example:

Example. In 1981, A, a calendar year taxpayer, purchases a car for $10,000 to be used in his business as well as for his personal enjoyment. During 1981, A drives the car a total of 20,000 miles of which 8,000 miles *(i.e.,* 40 percent) is in the course of A's business. During 1982, A drives the car a total of 30,000 miles of which 21,000 miles *(i.e.,* 70 percent) is in the course of A's business. During 1983, A drives the car a total of 10,000 miles of which 3,000 miles *(i.e.,* 30 percent) is in the course of A's business. The optional straight line method provided under § 1.168-2(c) is not elected. Thus, A's recovery allowance in 1981 equals $1,000 *(i.e.,* ($10,000 × .40) × .25), in 1982 equals $2,660 *(i.e.,* ($10,000 × .70) × .38) and in 1983 equals $1,110 *(i.e.,* ($10,000 × .30) × .37). If A continues to use the car in his business after 1983, additional recovery may be allowed. See § 1.168-2(j).

(3) Redeterminations. (i) For the taxable year (and subsequent taxable years) in which the unadjusted basis of recovery property is redetermined *(e.g., due to contingent purchase price or discharge of indebtedness),* the recovery allowance shall be the amount determined by multiplying the redetermined adjusted basis by the redetermined applicable percentage. For purposes of this subparagraph, the redetermined adjusted basis is the unadjusted basis reduced by the recovery allowance previously allowed or allowable to the taxpayer with respect to the property and adjusted to reflect the redetermination. The redetermined applicable percentage is the percentage determined by dividing the applicable percentage otherwise provided in paragraph (b), (c), (g), or (m) of § 1.168-2 for the recovery year by an amount equal to the unrecovered percentage *(i.e.,* 100 percent minus the applicable percentage for recovery years prior to the year in which the basis is redetermined). Thus, the increase or decrease in basis shall be accounted for over the remaining recovery years beginning with the recovery year in which the basis is redetermined.

(ii) The following examples illustrate the provisions of this subparagraph (3):

Example (1). On July 15, 1984, A places in service 5-year recovery property with an unadjusted basis of $100,000. In order to purchase the property, A borrowed $80,000 from B. On December 1, 1984, B forgives $10,000 of the indebtedness. A makes the election provided in section 108(d)(4). The recovery allowance for the property in 1984 is $15,000.

Under section 1017(a), as of January 1, 1985, the adjusted basis of the property is $75,000. In 1985 the recovery allowance is $19,411.77 *(i.e.,* .22/(1.00 – .15) × ($100,000 – ($10,000 + $15,000))). In 1986, 1987, and 1988 the recovery allowance is $18,529.41 in each year *(i.e.,* .21/1.00 – .15) × ($100,000 – ($10,000 + $15,000))).

Example (2). On July 15, 1984, C purchases and places in service 5-year recovery property with an unadjusted basis of $100,000. In addition to the $100,000, C agrees to pay the seller 25 percent of the gross profits from the operation of the property in the first year. On July 15, 1985, C pays to the seller an additional $10,000. The recovery allowance for the property in 1984 is $15,000. In 1985 the recovery allowance is $24,588.23 *(i.e.,* .22/(1.00 × .15) × ($100,000 + ($10,000 – $15,000))). In 1986, 1987, and 1988 the recovery allowance is $23,470.59 in each year *(i.e.,* .21/(1.00 – .15) × ($100,000 + ($10,000 – $15,000))).

(e) Components and improvements. *(1) Component cost recovery not permitted.* In general, the unadjusted basis of structural components (as defined in § 1.48-1(e)(2)) of a building must be recovered as a whole. Thus, the same recovery period and method must be used for all structural components, and such components must be recovered as constituent parts of the building of which they are a part. The recovery period for a component begins on the later of the first day of the month in which the component is placed in service as recovery property or the first day of the month in which the building of which the component is a part is placed in service as recovery property. See subparagraph (3) of this paragraph for the treatment of components of a building which is made available in stages.

(2) Treatment of amounts added to capital account. (i) Sections 162, 212, and 263 provide rules for the treatment of certain expenditures for the repair, maintenance, rehabilitation, or improvement of property. An expenditure which is treated as a capital expenditure under such sections (after application of the repair allowance rules of § 1.167(a)-11(d)(2)) is treated as the purchase of recovery property if the improvement for which the expenditure is made is placed in service after December 31, 1980. The recovery of such expenditure shall begin when the improvement is placed in service. See subparagraph (3) of this paragraph for the treatment of a building which is made available in stages.

(ii) For capital expenditures (which are section 1250 class property) made with respect to an improvement of a building which is recovery property, the taxpayer must use the same recovery period and method as are used with respect to the building, unless the improvement qualifies as a substantial improvement. See subparagraph (4) of this paragraph. If capital expenditures (which are section 1250 class property) are made with respect to improvements of a building which is not recovery property under section 168(e) and § 1.168-4, then the taxpayer may select any applicable recovery period and method for the recovery of the first of such expenditures. The recovery period and method so selected shall apply to each subsequent expenditure (unless the improvement qualifies as a substantial improvement).

(iii) A capital expenditure made with respect to the improvement of property, other than a building, is assigned to the same recovery class (as defined in § 1.168-3(b)) as the property of which the improvement is a part. For such an expenditure, the taxpayer need not use the same recovery period and method as are used with respect to the property of which the improvement is a part.

(3) Recovery for a building which is made available in stages. This subparagraph (3) (and not subparagraphs (1) and (2) of this paragraph) applies to a building which is made available in stages. For purposes of this section, a building shall be considered placed in service (and, therefore, recovery will begin) only when a significant portion is made available for use in a finished condition *(e.g.,* when a certificate of occupancy is issued with respect to such portion). If less than the entire building is made available, then the unadjusted basis which is taken into account under this section shall be that amount of the unadjusted basis of the building (including capital expenditures for any components) as is properly allocable to the portion made available. If another portion of the building is subsequently made available, then that amount of the unadjusted basis (including capital expenditures for any components) as is properly allocable to the ensuring portion shall be taken into account under this section when such portion becomes available. The taxpayer must use the same recovery period and method for all portions of the building.

(4) Substantial improvements. (i) A substantial improvement to a building shall be treated as a separate building. Thus, the taxpayer may use a different period and method for computing the recovery allowance for the substantial improvement than are used for computing the allowance for the building.

(ii) An improvement is a substantial improvement if—

(A) Over 24 consecutive months the aggregate expenditures properly chargeable to the capital account for a building equal at least 25 percent of the adjusted basis of the building (disregarding adjustments provided in section 1016(a)(2) and (3)) as of the day on which the first expenditure is made, and

(B) All expenditures for the improvement are made 3 or more years after the building is placed in service by the taxpayer.

For purposes of the preceding sentence, a building acquired in a transaction to which section 1031 or 1033 applies is considered placed in service when the building that was replaced was placed in service. Similarly, a building acquired in a transaction to which section 168(f)(10)(A) applies is deemed placed in service by the transferee when such building was placed in service by the transferor. An expenditure which is allocated to a 24-month period shall not be allocated to another 24-month period. For example, an expenditure may not be part of one substantial improvement when considered together with an expenditure incurred 15 months earlier and also be part of another substantial improvement when combined with an expenditure incurred 10 months later.

(iii) It is possible that an improvement will not be part of a substantial improvement in the taxable year in which the improvement is placed in service but will become part of a substantial improvement in a subsequent taxable year. In such case, if the taxpayer uses a different method and recovery period with respect to the substantial improvement, then the tax return filed for the taxable year in which the first improvement is placed in service shall be amended accordingly.

(5) Examples. The provisions of this paragraph may be illustrated by the following examples:

Example (1). In 1985, A spends $10,000 to improve machinery used in his trade or business. The $10,000 is added to capital account under the principles of sections 162, 212, and 263. The machinery would be 5-year property if placed in service after 1980. The $10,000 expenditure is treated as the purchase of 5-year recovery property, placed in service in 1985. Any election made by A with respect to the underlying machinery will not affect the recovery allowance for the improvement.

Example (2). B, a calendar year taxpayer, begins constructing a 10-story office building in 1982. All floors will have approximately the same amount of usable floor space. By 1983, B has paid or incurred $10 million for the building's shell (and other items not directly related to any specific portion of the building), $4 million for work with respect to the first three floors, and $5 million for work directly related to other floors (including installation of components). In March 1983, B receives a certificate of occupancy for the first three floors and begins offering the floors for rental to tenants. The building is considered placed in service in March 1983. No deduction is allowable under this section with respect to the building for 1982. No election is made under § 1.168-2(c) to use the optional recovery percentages. B's recovery for 1983 is the properly allocable unadjusted basis times the applicable percentage (10 percent). The properly allocable unadjusted basis is $7 million, consisting of the amount of unadjusted directly related to the portion of the building which is made available for use ($4 million), plus that amount of the unadjusted basis which is not directly related to any specific portion of the building ($10 million) properly allocable to the portion which is made available for use *(i.e.,* 3 floors/10 floors equals 30 percent or $3 million). No deduction is allowable in 1983 for the $5 million paid or incurred for work directly related to portions of the building not made available for use. B will recover the $7 million unadjusted basis over the 15-year recovery period, beginning in March 1983.

Example (3). The facts are the same as in example (2) except that, in January 1984, B receives a certificate of occupancy for the remaining seven floors and begins offering them for rental to tenants. B has spent an additional $7 million to complete the building as of the date on which the remaining seven floors are offered for rental. In January 1984, B takes into account as unadjusted basis the $12 million not previously taken into account, plus the $7 million of later expenditures. B will recover the $19 million unadjusted basis over a 15-year recovery period beginning in January 1984. B may not use a different recovery period and method for such amount than were used for the amount taken into account in March 1983.

Example (4). The facts are the same as in examples (2) and (3) except that in 1990 B spends $1 million, which is added to capital account to rehabilitate certain portions of the building. The $1 million is treated as the purchase by B of 15-year real property in 1990. B must use the same recovery period and method with respect to that improvement as were used for the underlying building. The improvement has a 15-year recovery period, and the recovery begins when the improvement is placed in service.

Example (5). In 1983 C spends $1 million, which is added to capital account, to rehabilitate certain portions of a building placed in service by C in 1975. The $1 million is treated as the purchase by C of 15-year real property in 1983. C may use any applicable recovery period and method with respect to such expenditure, and the recovery begins when the improvement is placed in service. The recovery period and method selected with respect to such expenditure, however, will apply to all ensuing capital expenditures made by C with respect to the building, unless an expenditure qualifies as part of a substantial improvement. The result in this example would be the same if the building were placed in service by C after 1980, but did not qualify as recovery property by reason of the provisions of section 168(e)(4) and § 1.168-4(d).

(f) Short taxable years. *(1) General rule.* For any recovery year in which there are less than 12 months (hereinafter in this section referred to as a " short taxable year"), the recovery allowance shall be determined by multiplying the deduction which would have been allowable if the recovery year were not a short taxable year by a fraction the numerator of which equals the number of months and part-months in the short taxable year and the denominator of which is 12. This paragraph shall not apply to 15-year real property for the year the property is placed in service or disposed of.

(2) Subsequent years' allowance. Recovery allowances for years in a recovery period following a short taxable year shall be determined in accordance with paragraph (a), (c), (g), or (m) of this section without reference to the short taxable year.

(3) Unrecovered allowance. In the taxable year following the last year in the recovery period, a recovery allowance is permitted to the extent of any unrecovered allowance. If the optional recovery percentages are elected under § 1.168-2(c) or (g)(3) and the short taxable year is the last recovery year, then the unrecovered allowance shall be allowed in the year following the short taxable year. The term "unrecovered allowance" means the difference between—

(i) The recovery allowance properly allowed for the short taxable year, and

(ii) The recovery allowance which would have been allowable if such year were not a short taxable year.

In no event shall the recovery allowance for any taxable year following the last year in the recovery period be greater than what the recovery allowance would be for the last year in the recovery period assuming that such year consists of 12 months. Any amount in excess of such recovery allowance for the last year in the recovery period shall be taken into account in the following taxable year or years in the same manner as provided in this subparagraph (3).

(4) When a taxable year begins. For purposes of this section, a taxable year of a person placing property in service does not include any month prior to the month in which the person begins engaging in a trade or business or holding recovery or depreciable property for the production of income. For purposes of applying the preceding sentence to an employee, an employee is not considered engaged in a trade or business by virtue of his employment except that, for purposes of applying this section to recovery property used for purposes of employment, the taxable year includes any month during which a person is engaged in trade or business as an employee. In addition, if a person engages in a small amount of trade or business activity for the purpose of obtaining a disproportionately large recovery allowance for assets for the taxable year in which they are placed in service, and if placing those assets in service represents a substantial increase in the person's level of business activity, then for purposes of the recovery allowance for such assets the person will not be treated as beginning a trade or business until the increased amount of business activity begins. For property held for the production of income, the principle of the preceding sentence also applies.

(5) Successive short taxable years. In applying the rule of subparagraph (1) of this paragraph, no month shall be taken into account more than once. Thus, if a taxpayer has successive short taxable years, with one taxable year ending and

the following taxable year beginning in the same calendar month, then the recovery year which is ending shall not include the month in which the taxable year terminates.

(6) Examples. The following examples illustrate the application of this paragraph:

Example (1). On October 10, 1983, A and B enter into an agreement to form a partnership (P), for the purpose of leasing sailboats. The partnership adopts a calendar year as its taxable year pursuant to § 1.706-1(b)(1). On November 5, 1983, P purchases four sailboats for a total of $20,000 and places the sailboats in service immediately. For purposes of section 168, P's taxable year begins on November 5, 1983. Sailboats are 5-year recovery property as defined in section 168(c)(2). No straight line election is made under § 1.168-2(c). The recovery allowance for the sailboats in 1983, a short taxable year, is $500 *(i.e.,* .15 × $20,000 × 2/12. In 1984, the recovery allowance is $4,400 (.22 × $20,000). In 1985, 1986, and 1987, the recovery allowance is $4,200 annually (.21 × $20,000). In 1988, the taxable year following the last year in the recovery period, the unrecovered allowance equal to $2,500 may be deducted by A and B.

Example (2). In November 1984, Corporation L is incorporated and places in service two race horses which it acquired for a total of $18,500. The corporation adopts a calendar year as its taxable year. For purposes of section 168, the race horses are 3-year recovery property. No straight line election is made under § 1.168-2(c). In 1984, the recovery allowance permitted to L for the race horses is $770.83 *(i.e.,* (.25 × $18,500) × 2/12). At the close of business on June 30, 1985, all of the stock of L is acquired by Corporation M. M elects in accordance with section 1501 to file a consolidated return with respect to M and L. M's taxable year begins on July 1. By reason of becoming included in the consolidated return, under § 1.1502-76 L's second taxable year ending June 30, 1985, is also a short taxable year containing 6 months. In the second taxable year, L is permitted a recovery allowance equal to $3,515 *(i.e.,* .38 × $18,500 × 6/12). In the third taxable year ending June 30, 1986, L is entitled to a recovery allowance of $6,845 *(i.e.,* .37 × $18,500). Thus, the unrecovered allowance as of July 1, 1986, equals $7,369.17. Since the unrecovered allowance exceeds the recovery allowance for the third recovery year (the last year in the recovery period), the recovery allowance for the taxable year ending June 30, 1987, equals the allowance for such year, $6,845. The recovery allowance in the taxable year ending June 30, 1988, equals $524.17, the remaining unrecovered allowance.

Example (3). On August 1, 1984, Partnership M is formed and places in service a warehouse which will be leased to an unrelated person. M acquires the warehouse for $250,000. M adopts a calendar year as its taxable year pursuant to § 1.706-1(b)(1). In 1984, M has a short taxable year within the meaning of § 1.168-2(f)(1). Since the property is 15-year real property, however, the recovery allowance is computed as though 1984 were a full taxable year. Because the recovery property would have been placed in service in the eighth month of M's normal taxable year, the recovery property is deemed placed in service in the eighth month of the first recovery year. The recovery allowance in 1984 is $12,500 *(i.e.,* .05 × $250,000).

Example (4). In July 1983, D, who has been an employee of Corporation N since 1982, purchases an automobile for use in the performance of his employment for N. On June 5, 1984, D purchases a truck for use in another business. D begins the new business on June 5, 1984. In 1984, D holds no other depreciable or recovery property for the production of income. D does not have a short taxable year for the automobile purchased in 1983 since the automobile is used by D in his trade or business as an employee. Since an employee is not considered engaged in a trade or business by virtue of employment, however, for purposes of determining when a taxable year begins with respect to property not used in the trade or business of employment, D has a short taxable year in 1984 for the truck purchased in that year. The recovery allowance permitted D in 1984 with respect to the truck must be adjusted in accordance with the provisions of § 1.168-2(f).

Example (5). A has been actively engaged in the trade or business of selling used cars since 1981. On July 1, 1983, A accepts employment with Corporation M and on that same date purchases a truck for $10,000 for use in the performance of his employment for M. A does not have a short taxable year for the truck because the taxable year of a person placing property in service includes all months during which that person is engaged in a trade or business.

Example (6). In 1983, C graduates from college and on July 1, 1983, is employed by N. On that same day, C purchases an automobile for $10,000 for use in the performance of his employment for N. C has a short taxable year for the automobile purchased in 1983. Although, for recovery property used for purposes of employment, the taxable year includes any month during which a person is an employee, C does not begin that trade or business until July. In addition, C is engaged in no other trade or business (and does not hold any depreciable or recovery property for the production of income) during the taxable year. The recovery allowance permitted C in 1983 with respect to the automobile must be adjusted in accordance with the provisions of § 1.168-2(f).

Example (7). Corporation X, a calendar year taxpayer, has been in the trade or business of selling household appliances since 1979. On July 1, 1983, X purchases a restaurant. On that same day, X purchases restaurant equipment for use in its new business. X does not have a short taxable year for the restaurant equipment because the taxable year of a person placing property in service includes all months during which that person is engaged in a trade or business.

(g) Special rules for property used predominantly outside the United States. *(1) General rule.* (i) In lieu of the deduction allowed under paragraphs (a) and (c) of this § 1.168-2, except as provided in subparagraphs (3) and (4) of this paragraph, and except as otherwise provided in section 168 and the regulations thereunder, the recovery allowance for recovery property used predominantly outside the United States (as described in § 1.168-2(g)(5)) during the taxable year equals the aggregate amount determined by multiplying the unadjusted basis (as defined in § 1.168-2(d)) of such recovery property by the applicable percentage provided in paragraph (g)(2) of this section. For purposes of determining the recovery allowance, salvage value shall be disregarded.

(ii) The recovery period for recovery property used predominantly outside the United States, other than 15-year real property, shall be the present class life. For recovery property (other than 15-year real property) which is not assigned a present class life, the recovery period shall be 12 years. For 15-year real property used predominantly outside the United States, the recovery period shall be 35 years.

(iii) Except for 15-year real property and except as otherwise provided in § 1.168-5, no recovery allowance shall be allowed in the year of disposition of recovery property described in this paragraph.

(iv) For purposes of this paragraph, rules similar to the rules of paragraph (e) of this section shall apply.

(2) Applicable percentages. (i) For property other than 15-year real property—

If the recovery year is:	And the recovery period is: 2.5	3	3.5	4	5	6	6.5	7	7.5	8
	The applicable percentage is:									
1	40	33	29	25	20	17	15	14	13	13
2	48	45	41	38	32	28	26	25	23	22
3	12	15	17	19	19	18	18	17	17	16
4		7	13	12	12	12	13	13	13	12
5				6	12	10	10	9	9	9
6					5	10	9	9	9	8
7						5	9	9	8	8
8								4	8	8
9										4

If the recovery year is:	And the recovery period is: 8.5	9	9.5	10	10.5	11	11.5	12	12.5	13
	The applicable percentage is:									
1	12	11	11	10	10	9	9	8	8	8
2	21	20	19	18	17	17	16	15	15	14
3	16	15	15	14	14	13	13	13	12	12
4	12	12	12	12	11	11	11	11	10	10
5	9	9	9	9	9	9	9	9	9	9
6	8	8	7	7	7	7	7	7	7	7
7	8	7	7	7	7	7	6	6	6	6
8	7	7	7	7	7	6	6	6	6	6
9	7	7	7	7	6	6	6	6	6	5
10		4	6	6	6	6	6	6	6	5
11				3	6	6	6	5	5	5
12						3	5	5	5	5
13								3	5	5
14										3

If the recovery year is:	And the recovery period is: 13.5	14	15	16	16.5	17	18	19	20	22
	The applicable percentage is:									
1	7	7	7	6	6	6	6	5	5	5
2	14	13	12	12	11	11	10	10	10	9
3	12	11	11	10	10	10	9	9	9	8
4	10	10	9	9	9	9	8	8	8	7
5	8	8	8	8	8	8	7	7	7	6
6	7	7	7	7	7	7	7	6	6	6
7	6	6	6	6	6	6	6	6	6	5
8	6	5	5	5	5	5	5	5	5	5
9	5	5	5	5	5	5	5	5	4	4
10	5	5	5	5	5	4	4	4	4	4
11	5	5	5	5	4	4	4	4	4	4
12	5	5	5	4	4	4	4	4	4	4
13	5	5	5	4	4	4	4	4	4	4
14	5	5	4	4	4	4	4	4	4	3
15		3	4	4	4	4	4	4	3	3
16			2	4	4	4	4	4	3	3
17				2	4	3	4	3	3	3
18						2	3	3	3	3
19							2	3	3	3
20								2	3	3
21									2	3
22										3

23	2

If the recovery year is:	And the recovery period is:						
	25	26.5	28	30	35	45	50
	The applicable percentage is:						
1	4	4	4	3	3	2	2
2	8	7	7	6	6	4	4
3	7	7	6	6	5	4	4
4	6	6	6	6	5	4	4
5	6	6	6	5	5	4	3
6	6	5	5	5	4	4	3
7	5	5	5	5	4	3	3
8	5	5	4	4	4	3	3
9	4	4	4	4	4	3	3
10	4	4	4	4	3	3	3
11	4	4	4	3	3	3	3
12	3	3	3	3	3	3	3
13	3	3	3	3	3	3	2
14	3	3	3	3	3	3	2
15	3	3	3	3	3	2	2
16	3	3	3	3	3	2	2
17	3	3	3	3	2	2	2
18	3	3	3	3	2	2	2
19	3	3	3	3	2	2	2
20	3	3	3	3	2	2	2
21	3	3	3	3	2	2	2
22	3	3	2	2	2	2	2
23	3	3	2	2	2	2	2
24	2	2	2	2	2	2	2
25	2	2	2	2	2	2	2
26	1	2	2	2	2	2	2
27		1	2	2	2	2	2
28			2	2	2	2	2
29			1	2	2	2	2
30				2	2	2	2
31				1	2	2	2
32					2	2	2
33					2	2	2
34					2	2	2
35					2	2	2
36					1	2	1
37						1	1
38						1	1
39						1	1
40						1	1
41						1	1
42						1	1
43						1	1
44						1	1
45						1	1
46						1	1
47							1
48							1
49							1
50							1
51							1

(ii) For 15-year real property—

If the recovery year is:	And the month in the 1st recovery year in which the property is placed in service is:				
	1	2, 3	4, 5, 6	7, 8	9, 10, 11, 12
	The applicable percentage is:				
1	4	4	3	2	1
2	4	4	4	4	4
3	4	4	4	4	4
4	4	4	4	4	4
5	4	4	4	4	4
6	3	3	3	4	4
7	3	3	3	3	3
8	3	3	3	3	3
9	3	3	3	3	3
10	3	3	3	3	3
11	3	3	3	3	3
12	3	3	3	3	3
13	3	3	3	3	3
14	3	3	3	3	3
15	3	3	3	3	3
16	3	3	3	3	3
17	3	3	3	3	3
18	3	3	3	3	3
19	3	3	3	3	3
20	3	3	3	3	3
21	3	3	3	3	3
22	3	3	3	3	3
23	3	3	3	3	3
24	3	3	3	3	3
25	3	2	3	2	3
26	2	2	2	2	2
27	2	2	2	2	2
28	2	2	2	2	2
29	2	2	2	2	2
30	2	2	2	2	2
31	2	2	2	2	2
32	2	2	2	2	2
33	2	2	2	2	2
34	2	2	2	2	
35	2	2	2	2	2
36		1	1	2	2

(3) Election of optional recovery percentage method. (i) In lieu of the applicable percentage provided by subparagraphs (1) and (2), the taxpayer may elect (in accordance with § 1.168-5(e)), for recovery property used predominantly outside the United States that is placed in service during the taxable year, to determine the recovery allowance by using the straight line method over one of the recovery periods elected by the taxpayer and set forth in the following table:

CLASS OF PROPERTY	RECOVERY PERIOD
3-year property	5 or 12 years or present class life
5-year property	12 or 25 years or present class life
10-year property	25 or 35 years or present class life
15-year real property	35 or 45 years
15-year public utility property	35 or 45 years or present class life

Such election is irrevocable without the consent of the Commissioner. See subdivision (iv) of this subparagraph for tables containing the applicable percentages to be used in computing the recovery allowance.

(ii) Except in the case of 15-year real property, a single recovery period must be elected under this subparagraph for all recovery property placed in service in the same taxable year which is in the same recovery class and which has the same present class life. For property other than 15-year real property the recovery period elected may not be shorter than the present class life (or, if none, 12 years). A different recovery period may be elected (or the tables provided in subparagraph (2) may be used) for recovery property in different recovery classes, or with different present class lives, placed in service during the taxable year, or for recovery property placed in service in a different taxable year, whether or not in the same recovery class or with the same present class life.

(iii) In the case of 15-year real property, the election provided by this subparagraph may be made separately with respect to each property.

(iv) (A) For property other than 15-year real property—

If the recovery year is:	And the period elected is:								
	2.5	3	3.5	4	5	6	6.5	7	7.5
	The applicable percentage is:								
1	20	17	14	13	10	8	8	8	7
2	40	33	29	25	20	17	16	14	14
3	40	33	29	25	20	17	16	14	14
4		17	28	25	20	17	15	14	13
5				12	20	17	15	14	13
6					10	17	15	14	13
7						7	15	14	13
8								8	13

If the recovery year is:	And the period elected is:								
	8	8.5	9	9.5	10	10.5	11	11.5	12
	The applicable percentage is:								
1	6	6	6	5	5	5	5	4	4
2	13	12	11	11	10	10	9	9	9
3	13	12	11	11	10	10	9	9	9
4	13	12	11	11	10	10	9	9	9
5	13	12	11	11	10	10	9	9	9
6	12	12	11	11	10	10	9	9	8
7	12	12	11	10	10	9	9	9	8
8	12	11	11	10	10	9	9	9	8
9	6	11	11	10	10	9	9	9	8
10			6	10	10	9	9	8	8
11					5	9	9	8	8
12						5	8	8	8
13									4

If the recovery year is:	And the period elected is:								
	12.5	13	13.5	14	15	16	16.5	17	18
	The applicable percentage is:								
1	4	4	4	4	3	3	3	3	3
2	8	8	8	8	7	7	7	6	6
3	8	8	8	7	7	7	6	6	6
4	8	8	8	7	7	7	6	6	6
5	8	8	8	7	7	7	6	6	6
6	8	8	8	7	7	6	6	6	6
7	8	8	7	7	7	6	6	6	6
8	8	8	7	7	7	6	6	6	6
9	8	8	7	7	7	6	6	6	6
10	8	8	7	7	7	6	6	6	6
11	8	7	7	7	7	6	6	6	6
12	8	7	7	7	6	6	6	6	5
13	8	7	7	7	6	6	6	6	5
14		3	7	7	6	6	6	6	5
15				4	6	6	6	6	5
16					3	6	6	6	5
17						3	6	5	5
18								2	5
19									2

If the recovery year is:	And the period elected is:							
	19	20	22	25	26.5	28	30	35
	The applicable percentage is:							
1	3	3	2	2	2	2	2	1
2	6	5	5	4	4	4	4	3
3	6	5	5	4	4	4	4	3
4	6	5	5	4	4	4	4	3
5	6	5	5	4	4	4	4	3
6	6	5	5	4	4	4	4	3
7	5	5	5	4	4	4	4	3
8	5	5	5	4	4	4	4	3
9	5	5	5	4	4	4	4	3
10	5	5	5	4	4	4	4	3
11	5	5	5	4	4	4	3	3
12	5	5	5	4	4	4	3	3
13	5	5	5	4	4	4	3	3
14	5	5	4	4	4	4	3	3
15	5	5	4	4	4	4	3	3
16	5	5	4	4	4	4	3	3
17	5	5	4	4	4	3	3	3
18	5	5	4	4	4	3	3	3
19	5	5	4	4	4	3	3	3
20	2	5	4	4	4	3	3	3
21		2	4	4	4	3	3	3
22			4	4	3	3	3	3
23			2	4	3	3	3	3
24				4	3	3	3	3
25				4	3	3	3	3
26				2	3	3	3	3
27					3	3	3	3
28						3	3	3
29						2	3	3
30							3	3
31							2	3
32								2
33								2
34								2
35								2
36								1

If the recovery year is:	And the period elected is:	
	45	50
	The applicable percentage is:	
1	1.1	1
2	2.3	2
3	2.3	2
4	2.3	2
5	2.3	2
6	2.3	2
7	2.3	2
8	2.3	2
9	2.3	2
10	2.3	2
11	2.3	2
12	2.2	2
13	2.2	2
14	2.2	2
15	2.2	2
16	2.2	2
17	2.2	2
18	2.2	2
19	2.2	2
20	2.2	2
21	2.2	2

22	2.2	2
23	2.2	2
24	2.2	2
25	2.2	2
26	2.2	2
27	2.2	2
28	2.2	2
29	2.2	2
30	2.2	2
31	2.2	2
32	2.2	2
33	2.2	2
34	2.2	2
35	2.2	2
36	2.2	2
37	2.2	2
38	2.2	2
39	2.2	2
40	2.2	2
41	2.2	2
42	2.2	2
43	2.2	2
44	2.2	2
45	2.2	2
46	1.1	2
47		2
48		2
49		2
50		2
51		1

(B) For 15-year real property. (1) If a 35-year period is elected—

If the recovery year is:	And the month in the 1st recovery year the property is placed in service is:		
	1-2	3-6	7-12
	The applicable percentage is:		
1	3	2	1
2	3	3	3
3	3	3	3
4	3	3	3
5	3	3	3
6	3	3	3
7	3	3	3
8	3	3	3
9	3	3	3
10	3	3	3
11	3	3	3
12	3	3	3
13	3	3	3
14	3	3	3
15	3	3	3
16	3	3	3
17	3	3	3
18	3	3	3
19	3	3	3
20	3	3	3
21	3	3	3
22	3	3	3
23	3	3	3
24	3	3	3
25	3	3	3
26	3	3	3
27	3	3	3

28	3	3	3
29	3	3	3
30	3	3	3
31	2	2	2
32	2	2	2
33	2	2	2
34	2	2	2
35	2	2	2
36		1	2

(2) If a 45-year period is elected—

If the recovery year is:	And the month in the 1st recovery year the property is placed in service is											
	1	2	3	4	5	6	7	8	9	10	11	12
	The applicable percentage is:											
1	2.3	2.0	1.9	1.7	1.5	1.3	1.2	.9	.7	.6	.4	.2
2	2.3	2.3	2.3	2.3	2.3	2.3	2.3	2.3	2.3	2.3	2.3	2.3
3	2.3	2.3	2.3	2.3	2.3	2.3	2.3	2.3	2.3	2.3	2.3	2.3
4	2.3	2.3	2.3	2.3	2.3	2.3	2.3	2.3	2.3	2.3	2.3	2.3
5	2.3	2.3	2.3	2.3	2.3	2.3	2.3	2.3	2.3	2.3	2.3	2.3
6	2.3	2.3	2.3	2.3	2.3	2.3	2.3	2.3	2.3	2.3	2.3	2.3
7	2.3	2.3	2.3	2.3	2.3	2.3	2.3	2.3	2.3	2.3	2.3	2.3
8	2.3	2.3	2.3	2.3	2.3	2.3	2.3	2.3	2.3	2.3	2.3	2.3
9	2.3	2.3	2.3	2.3	2.3	2.3	2.3	2.3	2.3	2.3	2.3	2.3
10	2.3	2.3	2.3	2.3	2.3	2.3	2.3	2.3	2.3	2.3	2.3	2.3
11	2.2	2.2	2.2	2.2	2.2	2.2	2.2	2.2	2.2	2.2	2.2	2.2
12	2.2	2.2	2.2	2.2	2.2	2.2	2.2	2.2	2.2	2.2	2.2	2.2
13	2.2	2.2	2.2	2.2	2.2	2.2	2.2	2.2	2.2	2.2	2.2	2.2
14	2.2	2.2	2.2	2.2	2.2	2.2	2.2	2.2	2.2	2.2	2.2	2.2
15	2.2	2.2	2.2	2.2	2.2	2.2	2.2	2.2	2.2	2.2	2.2	2.2
16	2.2	2.2	2.2	2.2	2.2	2.2	2.2	2.2	2.2	2.2	2.2	2.2
17	2.2	2.2	2.2	2.2	2.2	2.2	2.2	2.2	2.2	2.2	2.2	2.2
18	2.2	2.2	2.2	2.2	2.2	2.2	2.2	2.2	2.2	2.2	2.2	2.2
19	2.2	2.2	2.2	2.2	2.2	2.2	2.2	2.2	2.2	2.2	2.2	2.2
20	2.2	2.2	2.2	2.2	2.2	2.2	2.2	2.2	2.2	2.2	2.2	2.2
21	2.2	2.2	2.2	2.2	2.2	2.2	2.2	2.2	2.2	2.2	2.2	2.2
22	2.2	2.2	2.2	2.2	2.2	2.2	2.2	2.2	2.2	2.2	2.2	2.2
23	2.2	2.2	2.2	2.2	2.2	2.2	2.2	2.2	2.2	2.2	2.2	2.2
24	2.2	2.2	2.2	2.2	2.2	2.2	2.2	2.2	2.2	2.2	2.2	2.2
25	2.2	2.2	2.2	2.2	2.2	2.2	2.2	2.2	2.2	2.2	2.2	2.2
26	2.2	2.2	2.2	2.2	2.2	2.2	2.2	2.2	2.2	2.2	2.2	2.2
27	2.2	2.2	2.2	2.2	2.2	2.2	2.2	2.2	2.2	2.2	2.2	2.2
28	2.2	2.2	2.2	2.2	2.2	2.2	2.2	2.2	2.2	2.2	2.2	2.2
29	2.2	2.2	2.2	2.2	2.2	2.2	2.2	2.2	2.2	2.2	2.2	2.2
30	2.2	2.2	2.2	2.2	2.2	2.2	2.2	2.2	2.2	2.2	2.2	2.2
31	2.2	2.2	2.2	2.2	2.2	2.2	2.2	2.2	2.2	2.2	2.2	2.2
32	2.2	2.2	2.2	2.2	2.2	2.2	2.2	2.2	2.2	2.2	2.2	2.2
33	2.2	2.2	2.2	2.2	2.2	2.2	2.2	2.2	2.2	2.2	2.2	2.2
34	2.2	2.2	2.2	2.2	2.2	2.2	2.2	2.2	2.2	2.2	2.2	2.2
35	2.2	2.2	2.2	2.2	2.2	2.2	2.2	2.2	2.2	2.2	2.2	2.2
36	2.2	2.2	2.2	2.2	2.2	2.2	2.2	2.2	2.2	2.2	2.2	2.2
37	2.2	2.2	2.2	2.2	2.2	2.2	2.2	2.2	2.2	2.2	2.2	2.2
38	2.2	2.2	2.2	2.2	2.2	2.2	2.2	2.2	2.2	2.2	2.2	2.2
39	2.2	2.2	2.2	2.2	2.2	2.2	2.2	2.2	2.2	2.2	2.2	2.2
40	2.2	2.2	2.2	2.2	2.2	2.2	2.2	2.2	2.2	2.2	2.2	2.2
41	2.2	2.2	2.2	2.2	2.2	2.2	2.2	2.2	2.2	2.2	2.2	2.2
42	2.2	2.2	2.2	2.2	2.2	2.2	2.2	2.2	2.2	2.2	2.2	2.2
43	2.2	2.2	2.2	2.2	2.2	2.2	2.2	2.2	2.2	2.2	2.2	2.2
44	2.2	2.2	2.2	2.2	2.2	2.2	2.2	2.2	2.2	2.2	2.2	2.2
45	2.2	2.2	2.2	2.2	2.2	2.2	2.2	2.2	2.2	2.2	2.2	2.2
46		.3	.4	.6	.8	1.0	1.1	1.4	1.6	1.7	1.9	2.1

(4) Rules for year of disposition and placement in service of 15-year real property. (i) In the taxable year in which 15-year real property is disposed of, the recovery allowance shall be determined by multiplying the allowance (deter-

mined without regard to this subdivision) by a fraction, the numerator of which equals the number of months in the taxable year that the property is in service in the taxpayer's trade or business or for the production of income and the denominator of which is 12. In the case of 15-year real property that is disposed of during the first recovery year, the denominator shall equal the number of months in the taxpayer's taxable year after the property was placed in service by the taxpayer (including the month the property was placed in service). If the recovery allowance for the taxable year is limited by reason of the short taxable year rules of section 168(f)(5) and paragraph (f) of this section *(e.g.*, if the taxpayer dies, or if the taxpayer is a corporation which becomes a member, or ceases being a member, of an affiliated group of corporations filing a consolidated return), then the denominator shall equal the number of months in the taxpayer's taxable year.

(ii) For purposes of this paragraph—

(A) 15-year real property that is placed in service on or after the first day of a month shall be treated as placed in service in that month; and

(B) 15-year real property that is disposed of during the recovery year shall be treated as disposed of as of the last day of the month preceding the month in which it is withdrawn from service.

(5) Determination of whether property is used predominantly outside the United States. (i) The determination of whether property is used predominantly outside the United States (as defined in section 7701(a)(9)) during the taxable year shall be made by comparing the period in such year during which the property is physically located outside of the United States with the period during which the property is physically located within the United States. If the property is physically located outside the United States during more than 50 percent of the taxable year, such property shall be considered used predominantly outside the United States during the year. If property is placed in service after the first day of the taxable year, the determination of whether such property is physically located outside the United States during more than 50 percent of the taxable year shall be made with respect to the period beginning on the date on which the property is placed in service and ending on the last day of such taxable year.

(ii) This paragraph applies whether recovery property is used predominantly outside the United States by the owner or by the lessee of the property. For recovery property which is leased, the determination of whether such property is physically located outside the United States during the taxable year shall be made with respect to the taxable year of the lessor.

(iii) For purposes of this § 1.168-2(g), the following property is not "property used predominantly outside the United States":

(A) Any aircraft which is registered by the Administrator of the Federal Aviation Agency, and which (1) is operated, whether on a scheduled or nonscheduled basis, to and from the United States, or (2) is operated under contract with the United States, provided that the use of the aircraft under the contract constitutes its principal use outside the United States during the taxable year. The term "to and from the United States" shall not exclude an aircraft which makes flights from one point in a foreign country to another such point, as long as such aircraft returns to the United States with some degree of frequency;

(B) Rolling stock which is used within and without the United States and which is (1) of a domestic railroad corporation subject to part I of the Interstate Commerce Act or (2) of a United States person (other than a corporation subject to part I of the Interstate Commerce Act) but only if the rolling stock is not leased to one or more foreign persons for periods totaling more than 12 months in any 24-month period. For purposes of this subdivision (iii)(B), the term "rolling stock" means locomotives, freight and passenger train cars, floating equipment, and miscellaneous transportation equipment on wheels, the expenditures for which are of the type chargeable to the equipment investment accounts in the uniform system of accounts for railroad companies prescribed by the Interstate Commerce Commission;

(C) Any vessel documented under the laws of the United States which is operated in the foreign or domestic commerce of the United States. A vessel is documented under the laws of the United States if it is registered, enrolled, or licensed under the laws of the United States by the Commandant, United States Coast Guard. Vessels operated in the foreign or domestic commerce of the United States include those documented for use in foreign trade, coastwise trade, or fisheries;

(D) Any motor vehicle of a United States person (as defined in section 7701(a)(30)) which is operated to and from the United States with some degree of frequency;

(E) Any container of a United States person which is used in the transportation of property to and from the United States;

(F) Any property (other than a vessel or an aircraft) of a United States person which is used for the purpose of exploring for, developing, removing, or transporting resources from the outer Continental Shelf (within the meaning of section 2 of the Outer Continental Shelf Lands Act, as amended and supplemented, 43 U.S.C. section 1331), *e.g.*, offshore drilling equipment;

(G) Any property which (1) is owned by a domestic corporation (other than a corporation which has an election in effect under section 936 or which is entitled to the benefits of section 934(b)), by a United States citizen (other than a citizen entitled to the benefits of section 931, 932, 933, or 934(c)), or by a domestic partnership, all of whose partners are domestic corporations (none of which has an election in effect under section 936 or is entitled to the benefits of section 934(b)) or United States citizens (none of whom is entitled to the benefits of section 931, 932, 933, or 934(c)), and (2) which is used predominantly in a possession of the United States during the taxable year by such a corporation, citizen, or partnership, or by a corporation created or organized in, or under the law of, a possession of the United States. The determination of whether property is used predominantly in a possession of the United States during the taxable year shall be made under principles similar to those described in subdivision (i) of this subparagraph. For example, if a machine is placed in service in a possession of the United States on July 1, 1981, by a calendar year taxpayer and if it is physically located in such a possession during more than 50 percent of the period beginning on July 1, 1981, and ending on December 31, 1981, then such machine shall be considered used predominantly in a possession of the United States during the taxable year 1981;

(H) Any communications satellite (as defined in section 103(3) of the Communications Satellite Act of 1962, 47 U.S.C. section 702(3)), or any interest therein, of a United States person;

(I) Any cable, or any interest therein, of a domestic corporation engaged in furnishing telephone service to which section 46(c)(3)(B)(iii) applies (or of a wholly owned domestic subsidiary of such corporation), if such cable is part of a submarine cable system which constitutes part of a communications link exclusively between the United States and one or more foreign countries;

(J) Any property (other than a vessel or an aircraft) of a United States person which is used in international or territorial waters within the northern portion of the Western Hemisphere for the purpose of exploring for, developing, removing, or transporting resources from ocean waters or deposits under such waters. The term "northern portion of the Western Hemisphere" means the area lying west of the 30th meridian west of Greenwich, east of the international dateline, and north of the Equator, but not including any foreign country which is a country of South America; and

(K) Any property described in section 48(l)(3)(A)(ix) which is owned by a United States person and which is used in international or territorial waters to generate energy for use in the United States.

(h) Mass asset accounts. *(1) In general.* In accordance with the provisions of § 1.168-5(e), a taxpayer may elect to account for mass assets (as defined in § 1.168-2(h)(2)) in the same mass asset account, as though such assets were a single asset. If such treatment is elected, the taxpayer, upon disposition of an asset in the account, shall include as ordinary income (as defined in section 64) all proceeds realized to the extent of the unadjusted basis in the account (as defined in paragraph (d) of this section), less any amounts previously so included, and shall include as capital gain any excess, unless gain on such disposition is not recognized under another provision of the Code. With respect to the recovery allowance, the account shall be treated as though the asset were not disposed of.

(2) Definition. For purposes of this section, the term "mass assets" means a mass or group of individual items of recovery property (i) not necessarily homogenous, (ii) each of which is minor in value relative to the total value of such mass or group, (iii) numerous in quantity, (iv) usually accounted for only on a total dollar or quantity basis, (v) with respect to which separate identification is impracticable, (vi) with the same present class life, and (vii) placed in service in the same taxable year.

(3) Election. The election under this paragraph shall be made for the taxable year in which the assets in the account are placed in service. The election shall apply, with respect to the account, throughout the applicable recovery period and for all subsequent taxable years. The taxpayer is not bound by such election with respect to assets placed in service in other taxable years, or with respect to other assets placed in service in the same taxable year, which may properly be included in another mass asset account *(e.g.,* assets with a different present class life).

(4) Recovery of an increase in basis. To the extent that § 1.168-2(d)(2)(i) (relating to reductions in basis) applies, if as a result of early disposition of an asset in a mass asset account (determined in accordance with the provision of subparagraph (5) of this paragraph), the investment tax credit is recaptured (in accordance with section 47 and the regulations thereunder), then the basis of the account shall be increased by an amount equal to one-half of the amount of the recapture. Such increase shall be treated in a manner similar to § 1.168-2(d)(3), relating to redeterminations. For purposes of subparagraph (1) of this paragraph, such increase will be taken into account as unadjusted basis in determining the inclusion of proceeds as ordinary income.

(5) Identification of dispositions for purposes of basis increase. For purposes of subparagraph (4) of this paragraph, disposition of assets from a mass asset account shall be determined by the use of an appropriate mortality dispersion table. If the taxpayer adopts recordkeeping practices consistent with his prior practices and consonant with good accounting and engineering practices, and supplies such reasonable information as may be required by the Commissioner, the mortality dispersion table may be based upon an acceptable sampling of the taxpayer's actual experience or other acceptable statistical or engineering techniques. Alternatively, the taxpayer may use the following standard mortality dispersion table:

Standard Mortality Dispersion Table

[Percentage of basis of mass asset account considered disposed of each 12-mo. period after the account is placed in service]

Present class life	1st	2nd	3rd	4th	5th	6th	7th	8th	9th	10th
	(1)	(2)	(3)	(4)	(5)	(6)	(7)	(8)	(9)	(10)
2.5	3.59	23.84	45.14	23.84	3.59					
3	2.8	13.59	34.13	34.13	13.59	2.28				
3.5	1.62	8.23	23.51	33.28	23.51	8.23	1.62			
4	1.22	5.46	15.98	27.34	27.34	15.98	5.46	1.22		
5	.82	2.77	7.92	15.91	22.58	22.58	15.91	7.92	2.77	.82
6	.62	1.66	4.40	9.19	14.98	19.15	19.15	14.98	9.19	4.40
6.5	.55	1.33	1.38	7.25	12.00	16.39	18.20	16.39	12.00	7.25
7	.51	1.11	2.74	5.49	9.64	13.87	16.64	16.64	13.87	9.64
7.5	.47	.92	2.20	4.49	7.79	11.55	14.65	15.86	14.65	11.55
8	.44	.78	1.85	3.61	6.46	9.52	12.91	14.43	14.43	12.91
8.5	.40	.70	1.52	2.97	5.16	8.19	10.87	13.05	14.28	13.05
9	.38	.61	1.29	2.47	4.43	6.69	9.27	11.93	12.93	12.93
9.5	.37	.52	1.13	2.07	3.69	5.57	8.13	10.44	11.72	12.72
10 and 10.5	.35	.47	.97	1.80	3.09	4.83	6.90	9.01	10.79	11.79
11 and 11.5	.32	.39	.75	1.35	2.24	3.64	5.10	6.82	8.51	10.24
12 and 12.5	.30	.32	.60	1.06	1.73	2.67	3.88	5.31	6.79	8.19
13 and 13.5	.28	.27	.49	.84	1.34	2.04	3.12	4.13	5.37	6.63
14	.27	.24	.40	.71	1.06	1.68	2.32	3.17	4.38	5.26
15	.26	.21	.35	.57	.89	1.31	1.89	2.60	3.43	4.36
16 and 16.5	.25	.18	.29	.49	.75	1.10	1.48	2.13	2.83	3.83

17	.24	.16	.28	.42	.60	.92	1.30	1.67	2.34	2.82
18	.23	.15	.24	.37	.51	.78	1.06	1.39	1.93	2.50
19	.23	.14	.20	.32	.47	.66	.92	1.15	1.61	2.08
20 to 24	.22	.13	.19	.28	.40	.57	.77	1.03	1.36	1.73
25 to 29	.20	.09	.12	.18	.23	.31	.41	.53	.67	.85
30 to 50	.19	.07	.09	.12	.15	.20	.25	.32	.40	.49

Present class life	11th	12th	13th	14th	15th	16th	17th	18th	19th	20th
	(11)	(12)	(13)	(14)	(15)	(16)	(17)	(18)	(19)	(20)
2.5										
3										
3.5										
4										
5										
6	1.66	.62								
6.5	3.36	1.33	.55							
7	5.49	2.74	1.11	.51						
7.5	7.70	4.49	2.20	.92	.47					
8	9.52	6.46	3.61	1.85	.78	.44				
8.5	10.87	8.19	5.16	2.97	1.52	.70	.40			
9	11.93	9.27	6.69	4.43	2.47	1.29	.61	.38		
9.5	11.72	10.44	8.13	5.57	3.69	2.07	1.13	.52	.37	
10 and 10.5	11.79	10.79	9.01	6.90	4.83	3.09	1.80	.97	.47	.35
11 and 11.5	10.64	10.64	10.24	8.51	6.82	5.10	3.64	2.24	1.35	.75
12 and 12.5	9.28	9.87	9.87	9.26	8.19	6.79	5.31	3.88	2.67	1.73
13 and 13.5	7.77	8.62	9.10	9.10	8.62	7.77	6.63	5.37	4.13	3.12
14	6.62	7.25	8.32	8.32	8.32	8.32	7.25	6.62	5.26	4.38
15	5.32	6.23	7.04	7.61	7.93	7.93	7.61	7.04	6.23	5.32
16 and 16.5	4.22	5.30	6.11	6.80	6.89	7.54	7.64	6.89	6.80	6.11
17	3.71	4.48	4.94	5.93	6.51	6.54	7.14	7.14	6.54	6.51
18	3.12	3.57	4.46	4.81	5.71	6.19	6.21	6.75	6.75	6.21
19	2.60	2.97	3.76	4.37	4.96	5.48	5.53	6.19	6.36	6.36
20 to 24	2.17	2.66	3.18	3.72	4.25	4.76	5.22	5.57	5.83	5.96
25 to 29	1.06	1.29	1.55	1.85	2.18	2.50	2.84	3.19	3.54	3.84
30 to 50	.59	.72	.87	1.02	1.20	1.40	1.60	1.83	2.06	2.30

For purposes of applying the standard mortality dispersion table, all assets in a mass asset account placed in service during a taxable year are considered to be placed in service on the same day. If the taxpayer uses the standard mortality dispersion table for a taxable year, such table must be used for all subsequent taxable years unless the taxpayer obtains the consent of the Commissioner.

(6) Transitional rule. Unless the taxpayer establishes to the contrary (by statistical methods or otherwise), all proceeds realized upon the disposition of assets from one or more mass asset accounts shall be considered realized with respect to accounts placed in service by the taxpayer after December 31, 1980.

(i) [Reserved]

(j) Changes in use. *(1) Conversion from personal use or use in tax-exempt activity.* If property which was previously used by the taxpayer for personal purposes or in a tax-exempt activity is converted to use in a trade or business or for the production of income during the taxable year, then the recovery allowance for the taxable year (and subsequent taxable years) shall be determined as though the property were placed in service by the taxpayer as recovery property on the date on which the conversion occurs. Thus, the recovery allowance shall be determined by multiplying the unadjusted basis (as provided in subparagraph (6)(ii) of this paragraph) by the applicable percentage.

(2) Increased business use of property. If a taxpayer uses property in a trade or business (or for the production of income) and for personal (or tax-exempt) purposes during a recovery period, and increases the business (or income-producing) use of such property after the recovery for that period is completed, then a recovery allowance shall continue to be allowed with respect to such property. The amount of the allowance shall be determined as though, to the extent of the increase in business (or income-producing) use, the property were placed in service by the taxpayer as recovery property at the beginning of the taxable year in which such increased use occurs. Thus, the recovery allowance for the taxable year shall be determined first by multiplying the unadjusted basis (as provided in subparagraph (6)(ii) of this paragraph) by the applicable percentage, and then by the excess of the percentage of the business (or income-producing) use during the taxable year over the average of such use during the prior recovery period (or periods). The combined recovery under this subparagraph and subparagraph (1) shall not exceed the original cost of the property. See Example (2) of subparagraph (7) of this paragraph.

(3) Domestic property changing recovery classes. (i) When the class of recovery property not used predominantly outside the United States changes during the taxable year, and the property continues to be used as recovery property by the taxpayer *(e.g.,* when property ceases to be used predominantly in connection with research and experimentation) the following rules apply:

(A) If the change results in the property's being assigned to a class with a shorter recovery period, then the recovery allowance for the taxable year in which the change occurs (and subsequent taxable years) shall be determined as though the property were placed in service as recovery property in the year of the change. Thus, the recovery allowance shall be determined by multiplying the unadjusted basis (as provided in subparagraph (6)(ii) of this paragraph) by the applicable percentage. Alternatively, the taxpayer may continue to treat the property as though the change had not occurred.

(B) If the change results in the property's being assigned to a class with a longer recovery period, then the recovery allowance for the taxable year of the change (and subsequent taxable years) shall be determined as though the property had originally been assigned to that longer recovery class. Proper adjustment shall be made under the principles of § 1.168-2(d)(3) (relating to redeterminations) to account for the deductions allowable to the taxpayer with respect to the property prior to the year of the change in excess of those which would have been allowable had the taxpayer used the applicable percentages for the longer recovery class for those years.

(4) Foreign property. (i) If recovery property ceases being used predominantly outside the United States during a taxable year, and the property continues to be used as recovery property by the taxpayer, then the recovery allowance for the taxable year (and subsequent taxable years) shall be determined as though the property were placed in service as recovery property in the year of the cessation. Thus, the recovery allowance shall be determined by multiplying the unadjusted basis (as provided in subparagraph (6)(ii) of this paragraph) by the applicable percentage. Alternatively, the taxpayer may continue to treat the property as though the cessation had not occurred. See §§ 1.168-5(e)(5) and 1.1016-3(a)(3)(iii) and (iv).

(ii) If the recovery property begins to be used by the taxpayer predominantly outside the United States during a taxable year after having been used otherwise by the taxpayer as recovery property in the previous taxable year, then the recovery allowance for the taxable year in which the change occurs (and subsequent years) shall be determined as though the property had originally been placed in service by the taxpayer as recovery property used predominantly outside the United States. Proper adjustment shall be made under the principles of § 1.168-2(d)(3) to account for the difference between the deductions allowable with respect to the property prior to the year of the change and those which would have been allowable had the taxpayer used the applicable percentages for property used predominantly outside the United States for those years.

(5) Low income housing. If 15-year real property begins or ceases to be low income housing (as defined in § 1.168-2(b)(2)(iii)) during a taxable year, then the recovery allowance for the taxable year in which the change occurs (and subsequent taxable years) shall be determined under the principles of paragraph (j)(3)(i)(B) and (4)(ii) of this section.

(6) Special rules. (i) For purposes of this paragraph, if, prior to a change in status, the taxpayer used the optional applicable percentages (under paragraph (c) or (g)(3) of this section) with respect to recovery property, then similar optional percentages shall be used with respect to the property after the change.

(ii) For purposes of subparagraphs (1) and (2) of this paragraph, the unadjusted basis shall be the lesser of the fair market value or the adjusted basis of the property (taking into account the adjustments described in section 1016(a)(3)) at the time of the conversion to use in the taxpayer's trade or business (or for the production of income), or at the beginning of the taxable year in which the increase in business (or income-producing) use occurs, as the case may be. For purposes of subparagraphs (3)(i)(A) and (4)(i) of this paragraph, the unadjusted basis shall be the adjusted basis of the property (taking into account the adjustments described in section 1016(a)(2) and (3)) at the beginning of the year in which the change or cessation occurs.

(7) Examples. The following examples illustrate the application of this paragraph:

Example (1). A, a calendar year taxpayer, purchases a house in 1981 which he occupies as his principal residence. In June 1985, A ceases to occupy the house and converts it to rental property. Under paragraph (j)(1) of this section, for purposes of determining the recovery allowance, A is deemed to have placed the house in service as recovery property in June 1985. A does not elect to compute the recovery allowance by use of the optional recovery method provided in § 1.168-2(c). Thus, A's recovery allowance under section 168 for 1985 is determined by multiplying the unadjusted basis of the property by .07. Under paragraph (j)(6)(ii) of this section, the unadjusted basis is the lesser of the property's basis or its fair market value in June 1985. See also section 280A and the regulations thereunder.

Example (2). In 1981, B (a calendar year taxpayer) purchases an automobile for $10,000. In taxable years 1981 through 1983, B's business use of the automobile is 60 percent of his total use. B does not elect use of the optional percentages provided in § 1.168-2(c). The fair market value of the automobile at the beginning of 1984 is $7,500. In 1984, B's business use of the automobile is 70 percent of the total. B's allowable deduction for 1984 is $187.50, computed as follows: $7,500 (lesser of basis or fair market value) × .25 (applicable percentage) × .10 (increase in the percentage business use in 1984 (70 percent) over the average business use during 1981-1983 (60 percent)). In 1985, B's business use of the automobile is 50 percent of the total. B is entitled to no recovery allowance with respect to the automobile for 1985 since B's business use of the automobile in that year does not exceed the average business use during 1981-1983 (60 percent). In 1986, B's business use of the automobile is 75 percent of the total. B's allowable deduction for 1986 is $416.25 computed as follows: $7,500 (lesser of basis or fair market value in 1984) × .37 (applicable percentage) × .15 (increase in the percentage business use in 1986 (75 percent) over the average business use during 1981-1983 (60 percent)).

Example (3). In 1981 C, a calendar year taxpayer, purchases for $20,000 and places in service section 1245 class property used predominantly in connection with research and experimentation. C does not elect to compute the recovery allowance by use of the optional method as provided in § 1.168-2(c). In 1981 C's allowable deduction is $5,000 (*i.e.*, .25 × $20,000). In 1982 C continues to use the property as recovery property, but not predominantly in connection with research and experimentation. As a result, in 1982 the property is treated as 5-year property. C's recovery allowance for 1982 (and subsequent taxable years) is determined as though C had placed the property in service in 1981 as 5-year property. The excess recovery allowance allowed in 1981 is accounted for in accordance with § 1.168-2(d)(3). Thus, the difference between the recovery allowance which would have been allowed had the applicable percentage for 5-year property been used (*i.e.*, .15 × $20,000 =

$3,000) and the recovery allowance allowed in 1981 *(i.e.,* .25 × $20,000 = $5,000) equals $2,000 and is accounted for as follows:

Unadjusted basis × applicable percentage for second recovery year ($20,000.00 × .22)	$4,400.00
Excess allowance × applicable percentage for second recovery year ÷ the sum of the remaining unused applicable percentages (($2,000.00 × .22) /.85)	– 517.65
Difference—allowable deduction for 1982	$3,882.35

Example (4). In 1981 D, a calendar year taxpayer, places in service 5-year recovery property with an unadjusted basis of $100,000 and a present class life of 8 years. D uses the property predominantly outside the United States in 1981, 1982, and 1983. D does not elect to compute the recovery allowance by use of the optional method as provided in § 1.168-2(g)(3). In 1984 D uses the property as recovery property but not predominantly outside the United States. D's allowable deduction for 1984 (and subsequent taxable years) is determined as though D placed the property in service in 1984 as recovery property not used predominantly outside the United States. The basis of the property is deemed to be the adjusted basis in 1984. Thus, D's allowable deduction for 1984 is $7,350 *(i.e.,* .15 × $49,000 (basis)) and for 1985 is $10,780 *(i.e.,* .22 × 49,000 (basis)). If D elected to use the optional method based on the present class life, D would use the optional percentages based on a 5-year recovery period. Alternatively, D may continue to treat the property as though it continued to be used predominantly outside the United States. If so treated D's allowable deductions for 1984 and 1985 would be $12,000 *(i.e.,* .12 × $100,000) and $9,000 (.09 × $100,000), respectively.

Example (5). The facts are the same as in example (4) except that the recovery property is not used predominantly outside the United States for 1981 through 1983. In 1984, however, D begins using the property predominantly outside the United States. D's allowable deduction for 1984 is determined as though D placed the property in service in 1981 as property used predominantly outside the United States. Additionally, D accounts for the difference between the recovery allowance for 1981 through 1983 ($58,000) and the allowance which would have been allowable for those years had the applicable percentages for property used predominantly outside the United States been used ($51,000) in accordance with § 1.168-2(d)(3). Thus, the recovery allowance in 1984 is $10,285.71, determined as follows:

Unadjusted basis × applicable percentage for 4th recovery year for property with an 8-year present class life ($100,000.00 × .12)	$12,000.00
Excess recovery from 1981 through 1983 × applicable percentage for 4th recovery year ÷ the sum of the remaining unused applicable percentages (($7,000.00 × .12) /.49)	– 1,714.29
Difference	$10,285.71

If, for 1981 through 1983, D elected to use the optional method based on a 5-year recovery period, then the allowable deduction for 1984 and subsequent taxable years would be determined using the optional percentages over the 8-year present class life.

(k) Ratable inclusion rule. *(1) General rule.* In general, the recovery allowance provided by section 168 and this section shall be considered as accruing ratably over the taxable year. Thus, for example, the distributive share of the recovery allowance for each partner in a partnership in which a partner's partnership interest varies so as to be subject to section 706(c)(2)(B) shall be determined by allocating to each partner a pro rata share of such allowance for the entire taxable year of the partnership. This paragraph does not apply, however, in determining the recovery allowance for the taxable year in which 15-year real property is placed in service or disposed of.

(2) Example. The provisions of this subparagraph are illustrated by the following example:

Example. In 1978 A and B each acquire 50 percent interests in partnership P which is in the business of renting and managing beach resort property. On December 1, 1983, C and D each acquire from the partnership 25 percent interests in the partnership. On December 15, 1983, the partnership acquires for rental and places in service two sailboats (5-year recovery property) for $10,000 each. No election is made to use the optional recovery percentages provided by § 1.168-2(c). The recovery allowance for P for the sailboats in 1983 equals $3,000 *(i.e.,* .15 × $20,000). The recovery allowance, however, must be allocated pro rata over the taxable year. As such, the distributive share of the recovery allowance for A and B is $1,437.50 each. The distributive share of the recovery allowance for C and D is $62.50 each.

(l) Definitions. For purposes of section 168 and §§ 1.168-1 through 1.168-6—

(1) Disposition. The term "disposition" means the permanent withdrawal of property from use in the taxpayer's trade or business or use for the production of income. Withdrawal may be made in several ways, including sale, exchange, retirement, abandonment, or destruction. A disposition does not include a transfer of property by gift or by reason of the death of the taxpayer. See § 1.168-5(f)(3) and (4). A disposition also does not include the retirement of a structural component of 15-year real property. The manner of of disposition *(e.g.,* ordinary retirement, abnormal retirement) is not a consideration. For rules relating to nonrecognition transactions see section 168(f)(7) and (10) and the regulations thereunder. For rules relating to the recognition of gain or loss on dispositions, see § 1.168-6.

(2) Placed in service. The term "placed in service" means the time that property is first placed by the taxpayer in a condition or state of readiness and availability for a specifically assigned function, whether for use in a trade or business, for the production of income, in a tax-exempt activity, or in a personal activity. In the case of a building which is intended to house machinery and equipment, such readiness and availability shall be determined without regard to whether the machinery or equipment which the building houses, or is intended to house, has been placed in service. However, in an appropriate case, as, for example, where the building is essentially an item of machinery or equipment, or the use of the building is so closely related to the use of the machinery or equipment that it clearly can be expected to be replaced or retired when the property it initially houses is replaced or retired, the determination of readiness or availability of the building shall be made by taking into account the readiness and availability of such machinery or equipment. For a building which becomes available for use in separate stages, see paragraph (e)(3) of this section.

(3) Recovery year. The term "recovery year" means the taxable year during which recovery property is placed in service by the taxpayer and each subsequent taxable year for which a deduction is allowable to the taxpayer under this section with respect to such property.

(4) Recovery period. The term "recovery period" means the actual period of years assigned, or elected by the taxpayer, for the computation under this section of the recovery allowance with respect to the unadjusted basis of the recovery property (*e.g.*, 3 years, 5 years, 12 years, present class life). The recovery period does not include any year after the end of the period assigned or elected, even though under paragraph (c), (g)(3), or (m) of this section a year following the recovery period may be a recovery year (as defined in subparagraph (3)).

(m) Limitation on property financed with proceeds of industrial development bonds. [Reserved]

• ***Caution:*** Prop Reg § 1.168-2(n) is withdrawn by the Treasury 1/29/98, 63 Fed. Reg. 4408.

(n) Application to adjustment to basis of partnership property under sections 734(b) and 743(b).

Proposed § 1.168-3 Recovery property. [*For Preamble, see ¶ 150,941*]

Caution: The Treasury has not yet amended Reg § 1.168-3 to reflect changes made by P.L. 101-508, P.L. 101-239, P.L. 100-647, P.L. 99-514, P.L. 98-369.

(a) Recovery property. *(1) In general.* Except as provided in § 1.168-4, "recovery property" to which ACRS applies means tangible property of a character subject to the allowance for depreciation which is—

(i) Used in a trade or business, or

(ii) Held for the production of income. Property is considered recovery property only if such property would have been depreciable under section 167. Thus, ACRS applies only to that part of the property which is subject to wear and tear, to decay or decline from natural causes, to exhaustion, and to obsolescence. ACRS does not apply to inventories or stock in trade, works of art, or to land apart from the improvements or physical development added to it. ACRS does not apply to natural resources which are subject to the allowance for depletion provided in section 611. No deduction shall be allowed under ACRS for automobiles or other vehicles used solely for pleasure, for a building used by the taxpayer solely as his residence, or for furniture or furnishings therein, personal effects, or clothing; but properties and costumes used exclusively in a business, such as a theatrical business, may be recovery property. For rules regarding the recovery allowance for property which is used partly for business and partly for personal purposes, or which is converted from personal to business use, see §§ 1.168-2(d)(2)(ii) and 1.168-2(j)(1) and (2).

(2) Intangible property. [Reserved]

(3) Boilers fueled by oil or gas. The term "recovery property" includes property described in section 167(p), relating to boilers fueled by oil or gas, if such property otherwise qualifies as "recovery property" under section 168 and subparagraph (1) of this paragraph.

(b) Classes of recovery property. Each item of recovery property shall be assigned to one of the following classes of property:

(1) 3-year property,

(2) 5-year property,

(3) 10-year property,

(4) 15-year real property, or

(5) 15-year public utility property.

Any property which is treated as included in a class of property by reason of paragraph (c)(1), (2), (3), (4), or (5) of this § 1.168-3 shall not be treated as property included in any other class.

(c) 3-, 5-, 10-, and 15-year recovery property; definitions. *(1) 3-year property.* The following recovery property is included in the 3-year class:

(i) Section 1245 class property (as defined in paragraph (c)(6) of this § 1.168-3) with a present class life (as defined in paragraph (c)(8)) of 4 years or less,

(ii) Section 1245 class property predominantly used in connection with research and experimentation (as described in section 174 and § 1.174-2(a)). Property is used in connection with research and experimentation if the property is used (A) by its owner to conduct research and experimentation in its owner's trade or business, (B) by its owner to conduct research and experimentation for another person, (C) by a lessee to conduct research and experimentation in its trade or business, or (D) by the lessee to conduct research and experimentation for another person, and

(iii) Any race horse which is more than 2 years old at the time the horse is placed in service and any other horse which is more than 12 years old at the time the horse is placed in service. A horse is more than 2 (or 12) years old after 24 (or 144) months after its actual birthdate.

Examples of 3-year recovery property are automobiles and light-duty trucks.

(2) 5-year property. The following recovery property is included in the 5-year class: Section 1245 class property which is not 3-year property (as defined in paragraph (c)(1)), or 10-year property (as defined in paragraph (c)(3)), or 15-year public utility property (as defined in paragraph (c)(5) and (10)). Included in the 5-year recovery property class are horses which are not included in the 3-year recovery property class, property which, prior to January 1, 1981, may have been depreciated under the retirement-replacement-betterment method (subject to the provisions of § 1.168-5(a)), single-purpose agricultural and horticultural structures, and storage facilities (other than buildings and their structural components) used in connection with the distribution of petroleum or any of its primary products. Primary products of petroleum are products described in § 1.993-3(g)(3)(i).

(3) 10-year property. The following recovery property is included in the 10-year class:

(i) Public utility property with a present class life of more than 18 years but not more than 25 years, other than section 1250 class property (as defined in paragraph (c)(7)) or 3-year property,

(ii) Section 1250 class property with a present class life of 12.5 years or less,

(iii) Railroad tank cars,

(iv) Manufactured homes (as defined in 42 U.S.C. section 5402(6)) which are section 1250 class property used as dwelling units, and

(v) Qualified coal utilization property (as defined in paragraph (c)(9)) which would otherwise be 15-year public utility property.

A building (and its structural components, if any) is not treated as having a present class life of 12.5 years or less if, in its original use (as defined in paragraph (c)(11) of this § 1.168-3), the building (and its structural components, if any) does not have a present class life of 12.5 years or less. Thus, for example, a theme park structure is considered 10-year property only if the original use of such structure is as a theme park structure.

(4) 15-year real property. Fifteen-year real property is section 1250 class property which does not have a present class life of 12.5 years or less (including section 1250 class property which does not have a present class life). Examples of 15-year real property are office buildings and elevators and escalators.

(5) 15-year public utility property. Fifteen-year public utility property is public utility property, other than section 1250 class property or 3-year property, with a present class life of more than 25 years. Examples of 15-year public utility property are: most property in electric utility steam production plants, gas utility manufactured gas production plants, water utility property, and telephone distribution plants.

(6) Section 1245 class property defined. For purposes of section 168 and §§ 1.168-1 through 1.168-6, section 1245 class property is tangible property described in section 1245(a)(3) (other than subparagraphs (C) and (D)). See § 1.168-4 for exclusion of certain "section 1245 class property" from recovery property.

(7) Section 1250 class property defined. For purposes of section 168 and §§ 1.168-1 through 1.168-6, section 1250 class property is property described in section 1250(c) and property described in section 1245(a)(3)(C). See § 1.168-4 for exclusion of certain "section 1250 class property" from recovery property.

(8) Present class life defined. (i) For purposes of section 168 and §§ 1.168-1 through 1.168-6, present class life is the asset depreciation range (ADR) class life ("midpoint" or "asset guideline period") (if any) applicable with respect to the property as of January 1, 1981, published in Rev. Proc. 83-35. No changes will be made to the classes or class lives which are set forth in Rev. Proc. 83-35.

(ii) The application of subdivision (i) may be illustrated by the following example:

Example. X purchases a light-duty truck to be used in his trade or business. The ADR midpoint life of this asset as of January 1, 1981, determined under Rev. Proc. 83-35 is 4 years. Since this truck is section 1245 class property with a present class life of 4 years or less, it is 3-year recovery property under section 168.

(9) Qualified coal utilization property. See section 168(g)(8) for the definition of "qualified coal utilization property".

(10) Public utility property. (i) For purposes of section 168 and §§ 1.168-1 through 1.168-6, the term "public utility property" means property used predominantly in the trade or business of the furnishing or sale of—

(A) Electrical energy, water, or sewage disposal services,

(B) Gas or steam through a local distribution system,

(C) Telephone services, or other communication services if furnished or sold by the Communications Satellite Corporation for purposes authorized by the Communications Satellite Act of 1962 (47 U.S.C. section 701), or

(D) Transportation of gas or steam by pipeline, if the rates for such furnishing or sale, as the case may be, are regulated, *i.e.*, are established or approved by a State (including the District of Columbia) or political subdivision thereof, by any agency or instrumentality of the United States, or by a public service or public utility commission or other similar body of any State or political subdivision thereof. A taxpayer's rates are "regulated" if they are established or approved on a rate-of-return basis. Rates regulated on a rate-of-return basis are an authorization to collect revenues that cover the taxpayer's cost of providing goods or services, including a fair return on the taxpayer's investment in providing such goods or services, where the taxpayer's costs and investment are determined by use of a uniform system of accounts prescribed by the regulatory body. A taxpayer's rates are not "regulated" if they are established or approved on the basis of maintaining competition within an industry, insuring adequate service to customers of an industry, insuring adequate security for loans, or charging " reasonable" rates within an industry since the taxpayer is not authorized to collect revenues based on the taxpayer's cost of providing goods or services. Rates are considered to be "established or approved" if a schedule of rates is filed with a regulatory body that has the power to approve such rates, even though the regulatory body takes no action on the filed schedule or generally leaves undisturbed rates filed by the taxpayer.

(ii) Public utility property includes property which is leased to others by a taxpayer, where the leasing of such property is part of the lessor's public utility activity, as described in subdivision (i). Public utility property also includes property leased to a person who uses such property predominantly in a public utility activity, as described in subdivision (i).

(11) "Original use". The term "original use" means the first use to which the property is put, whether or not such use corresponds to the use of such property by the taxpayer.

Proposed § 1.168-4 Exclusions from ACRS. [*For Preamble, see ¶ 150,941*]

Caution: The Treasury has not yet amended Reg § 1.168-4 to reflect changes made by P.L. 101-508, P.L. 101-239, P.L. 100-647, P.L. 99-514, P.L. 98-369.

(a) Property placed in service by the taxpayer before January 1, 1981. ACRS does not apply with respect to property placed in service by the taxpayer before January 1, 1981. See § 1.168-2(1)(2) for when property is placed in service. As provided in paragraph (d) of this section, ACRS does not apply with respect to property placed in service before January 1, 1981, which is transferred in certain "churning" transactions. If property is excluded from ACRS, the provisions of section 167 (and related provisions) apply in determining the allowable depreciation deduction with respect to such property.

(b) Property amortized or depreciated other than in term of years. *(1) Depreciation.* If—

(i) Property can properly be depreciated under a method not expressed in a term of years (such as unit-of-production) which, before January 1, 1981, was a recognized method within the particular industry for the type of property in question, and

(ii) The taxpayer properly elects such treatment for such property in accordance with section 168(f)(4) and § 1.168-5(e) for the first taxable year for which an ACRS deduction would (but for this election) be allowable with respect to such property in the hands of the taxpayer,

then such property shall be entirely excluded from ACRS so long as it remains in the hands of such taxpayer. A taxpayer may elect to apply a depreciation method not expressed in a term of years (and thereby exclude the property from ACRS) with respect to some or all property within the same recovery class and placed in service in the same taxable year.

(2) Amortization. If—

(i) The basis of a recovery property may be amortized, in lieu of being depreciated, under any section of the Code (such as section 167(k), relating to expenditures to rehabilitate low-income rental housing, or section 169, relating to pollution control facilities), and

(ii) The taxpayer properly elects to amortize such property in accordance with the relevant amortization provision,

then the amount subject to such amortization shall be excluded from the property's unadjusted basis as defined in section 168(d)(1)(A) and § 1.168-2(d). A taxpayer may elect amortization with respect to one property (or a portion thereof) and apply ACRS with respect to other property (or the remaining portion) within the same recovery class and placed in service in the same taxable year.

(c) Special rule for public utility property. [Reserved]

(d) Anti-churning rules for certain transactions in property placed in service before 1981. *(1) In general.* To be eligible for ACRS, property must be placed in service by the taxpayer after 1980. The anti-churning rules of section 168(e)(4) and this paragraph (d) are designed generally to deny ACRS to property in service before 1981 in the absence of a significant change in ownership or use.

(2) Section 1245 class property. (i) In general. Section 1245 class property, as defined in section 168(g)(3) and § 1.168-3(c)(6), acquired by the taxpayer after December 31, 1980, will not qualify for ACRS if—

(A) The property was owned or used at any time during 1980 by the taxpayer or a related person,

(B) The property is acquired from a person who owned such property at any time during 1980, and, as part of the transaction, the user of the property does not change,

(C) The property is leased by the taxpayer for more than 3 months to a person (or a person related to such person) who owned or used such property at any time during 1980, or

(D) The property is acquired in a transaction in which the user of such property does not change, and the property does not qualify for ACRS in the hands of the person from whom the property is so acquired due to subdivisions (B) and (C) of this paragraph (d)(2)(i).

See section 168(e)(4)(D) and subparagraph (6) of this paragraph (d) for definition of the term "related person". See subparagraph (3) of this paragraph (d) for the treatment of the acquisition of section 1245 class property acquired incidental to the acquisition of section 1250 class property. See subparagraph (4) of this paragraph (d) for other special rules.

(ii) Change in user. For purposes of subdivision (i) of this paragraph (d)(2), the user of a section 1245 class property shall not be considered to have changed as part of a transaction if the property is physically used, for more than 3 months after its transfer, by the same person (or a related person) who used such property before the transfer, or if such person, pursuant to a plan, resumes use of the property after the transfer. If the former owner (or a related person) continues to operate section 1245 class property through an arrangement such as a management contract for more than 3 months after the transfer, then all facts and circumstances will be taken into account in determining whether the user of the property has changed as part of such transaction for purposes of section 168(e)(4)(A) and subdivision (i) of this paragraph (d)(2). Among the factors which would indicate that the user of section 1245 property has changed in such case are—

(A) The arrangement in question is a customary commercial practice,

(B) The transaction in question has been arranged at arm's length, and

(C) The new owner has assumed all benefits and burdens of ownership. For purposes of this subdivision (ii)(C), the former owner will not be considered to have retained any benefits and burdens of ownership solely by reason of receiving contingent payments if such payments—

(1) Represent the real value of services rendered,

(2) Are reasonable in amount, and

(3) Are ordinary and customary in both nature and amount within the industry and region for the transaction in question.

(3) Section 1250 class property. A section 1250 class property, as defined in section 168(g)(4) and § 1.168-3(c)(7), acquired by the taxpayer after December 31, 1980, will not qualify for ACRS if—

(i) The property was owned at any time during 1980 by the taxpayer or a related person,

(ii) The property is leased by the taxpayer for more than 3 months to a person (or a person related to such person) who owned such property at any time during 1980, or

(iii) The property is acquired in an exchange described in section 1031 (relating to exchange of property held for productive use or investment), section 1033 (relating to involuntary conversions), section 1038 (relating to certain reacquisitions of real property), or section 1039 (relating to certain sales of low-income housing projects), to the extent that the basis of such property includes an amount representing the adjusted basis of other property owned by the taxpayer or a related person at any time during 1980. The excess of the basis of the property acquired over the adjusted basis of such other property shall be considered a separate item of property, eligible for ACRS, provided that the exchange is not otherwise treated as a "churning" transaction under section 168(e)(4) and this paragraph. Property which does not qualify for ACRS under this subdivision shall be considered, for purposes of this section, as owned by the taxpayer during 1980.

See section 168(e)(4)(D) and subparagraph (6) of this paragraph (d) for definition of the term "related person". If, in a transaction, section 1245 class property is acquired incidental to the acquisition of section 1250 class property, then the rules of section 168(e)(4)(B) and this subparagraph shall apply with respect to the section 1245 property acquired in such transaction instead of the rules of section 168(e)(4)(A) and paragraph (d)(2) of this section. The preceding sentence will not apply in transactions where section 1245 property constitutes a significant portion of the property acquired.

(4) Special rules. (i) Property under construction during 1980. For purposes of paragraph (d)(2) and (3) of this section, a taxpayer shall not be deemed to own property under construction during 1980 until it is placed in service, as described in § 1.168-2(l)(2).

(ii) Entire property excluded. Except as provided in paragraph (d)(3)(iii) of this section (relating to excess basis in substituted basis transactions), subdivision (iii) of this paragraph (d)(4) (relating to the lease of a portion of section 1250 class property), and paragraph (d)(6)(ii)(C) of this section (relating to transactions between persons related by reason of the application of § 1.267(b)-1(b)), if property is acquired in a transaction described in paragraph (d)(2) or (3) of this section, the entire property shall be excluded from ACRS.

(iii) Lease of portion of section 1250 class property. Paragraph (d)(3)(ii) of this section (relating to the lease of section 1250 class property) shall apply only with respect to that portion of the property (determined on a fair market value basis) that is leased to the person (or to a person related to such person) who owned the property during 1980. The portion of the property excluded from ACRS shall not exceed the portion of the property which was owned by the lessee (or a person related to the lessee) during 1980.

(iv) Undivided interests. Subject to the provisions of paragraph (d)(7) of this section (relating to avoidance), if an undivided interest in property is acquired, and the resulting arrangement is not a partnership for tax purposes, then such interest shall be treated as a separate item of property for purposes of paragraph (d)(2) and (3) of this section.

(v) Acquisition by or lease to 1980 owner or user. If recovery property is acquired by, or leased to, its 1980 owner (or, in the case of section 1245 class property, its 1980 owner or user), or a related person, then the property shall cease to qualify for ACRS.

(vi) Sale-leaseback of disqualified property. If property which does not qualify for ACRS under this section becomes the subject of a sale-leaseback transaction, then the property shall not become ACRS property by virtue of that transaction.

(5) Certain nonrecognition transactions. (i) In general. With respect to property placed in service by the transferor or distributor before January 1, 1981, and which is acquired by the taxpayer after December 31, 1980, in a nonrecognition transaction described in section 168(e)(4)(C) and in subdivision (ii) of this paragraph (d)(5), ACRS shall not apply to the extent that the property's basis in the hands of the taxpayer is determined by reference to its basis in the hands of the transferor or distributor. In such a transaction, the taxpayer shall be treated as the transferor or distributor for purposes of computing the depreciation allowance under section 167 with respect to so much of the basis of the acquired property in the hands of the taxpayer as does not exceed its adjusted basis in the hands of the transferor or distributor. However, the taxpayer shall treat the portion of the basis of the acquired property which exceeds the adjusted basis in the hands of the transferor or distributor as a separate item of property, eligible for ACRS, provided that sale or exchange of such property by the transferor or distributor to the taxpayer would not be treated as a "churning" transaction under section 168(e)(4) and this paragraph.

(ii) Nonrecognition transactions affected. Subdivision (i) of this paragraph (d)(5) applies to transactions described in any of the following provisions:

(A) Section 332 (relating to distributions in complete liquidation of an 80 percent or more controlled subsidiary corporation) except where the basis of the assets distributed is determined under section 334(b)(2) (as in effect on August 31, 1982);

(B) Section 351 (relating to transfer to a corporation controlled by transferor);

(C) Section 361 (relating to exchanges pursuant to certain corporate reorganizations);

(D) Section 371(a) (relating to exchanges pursuant to certain receivership and bankruptcy proceedings);

(E) Section 374(a) (relating to exchanges pursuant to certain railroad reorganizations);

(F) Section 721 (relating to transfers to a partnership in exchange for a partnership interest); and

(G) Section 731 (relating to distributions by a partnership to a partner).

A distribution of property by a partnership to a partner in liquidation of the partner's interest in the partnership (where the basis of the distributed property to the partner is determined under section 732(b)) is not a transaction described in section 168(e)(4)(C) and this subdivision (ii) since, in such case, the basis of the property is determined by reference to the partner's adjusted basis in his interest in the partnership and not by reference to the basis of the property in the hands of the partnership. However, such distribution may be described in paragraph (d)(2) or (3) of this section.

(iii) Successive application. Property which does not qualify for ACRS by reason of its acquisition in a nonrecognition transaction will not qualify for ACRS if it is subsequently transferred in another nonrecognition transaction. The preceding sentence shall apply to the extent that the basis of the property in the hands of the transferee does not exceed the basis that does not qualify for ACRS in the hands of the transferor.

(6) Related person defined. (i) In general. For purposes of this paragraph (d) except as provided in section 168(e)(4)(E) and in subparagraph (11) of this paragraph (d), persons are related if—

(A) They bear a relationship specified in section 267(b) or section 707(b)(1) and the regulations thereunder, or

(B) They are engaged in trades or businesses under common control (as defined by subsections (a) and (b) of section 52 and the regulations thereunder).

For purposes of applying section 267(b) and 707(b)(1) with respect to this paragraph (d)(6), "10 percent" shall be substituted for "50 percent".

(ii) Special rules. (A) In general, persons are related if they are related either immediately before or immediately after the taxpayer's acquisition of the property in question. When a partnership's acquisition of property results from the termination of another partnership under section 708(b)(1)(B), whether the acquiring partnership is related to such other partnership shall be determined by comparing the ownership of the acquiring partnership immediately after the acquisition with that of the terminated partnership as it existed immediately before the event resulting in such termination occurs. Similarly, when the acquisition of property by a partner results from the termination of a partnership under section 708(b)(1)(A), whether the acquiring person is related to the partnership shall be determined immediately before the event resulting in such termination occurs.

(B) If a person would be related to a corporation, partnership, or trust which owned (or, in the case of section 1245 class property, owned or used) property during 1980 but for the fact that such corporation, partnership, or trust is no longer in existence when the taxpayer acquires such property, the, for purposes of this subparagraph (6), such corporation, partnership, or trust is deemed to be in existence when the taxpayer acquires such property. Similarly, when a taxpayer leases property to a newly-created corporation, partnership, or trust, and a person who owned (or, in the case of section 1245 class property, owned or used) such property during 1980 would be related to the lessee but for the fact that such corporation, partnership, or trust is not in existence when the taxpayer acquires such property, then, for purposes of this subparagraph (6), such corporation, partnership, or trust is deemed to be in existence when the taxpayer acquires such property.

(C) If persons are related by reason of the application of § 1.267(b)-1(b), then only a portion of the property shall be excluded from ACRS, consistent with the principles of § 1.267(b)-1(b). See, however, paragraph (d)(7) of this section (relating to avoidance).

(D) If persons are not considered to be engaged in trades or businesses under common control (as defined by subsections (a) and (b) of section 52 and the regulations thereunder), but are considered to be related persons by substituting "10 percent" for "50 percent" within the provisions of section 267(b) or 707(b)(1), then such persons are considered to be related persons for purposes of this subparagraph (6).

(7) Avoidance purpose indicated. Property acquired by the taxpayer after December 31, 1980, does not qualify for ACRS if it is acquired in a transaction one of whose principal purposes is to avoid the operation of the effective date rule of section 168(e)(1) and the "anti-churning" rules of section 168(e)(4), and the rules of this section. A transaction will be presumed to have a principal purpose of avoidance if it does not effect a significant change in ownership or use of property in service before 1981 commensurate with that otherwise required for ACRS to apply. Among the circumstances in which a principal avoidance purpose may be indicated, and in which the property involved in the transfer may therefore be ineligible for ACRS, are—

(i) The same person owns (other than as a nominee), directly or indirectly, more than a 10 percent interest in the taxpayer (or the taxpayer's lessee) and in a person who owned (or, in the case of section 1245 class property, owned or used) the property during 1980;

(ii) There is a mere change in form of the ownership of property owned by a person during 1980 (such as from a partnership to undivided interests);

(iii) The taxpayer (or the taxpayer's lessee) and a person who owned (or, in the case of section 1245 class property, owned or used) the property during 1980 are engaged in trades or businesses under common control within the meaning of section 52(a) and (b) and the regulations thereunder, substituting a 25 percent test for the 50 percent tests of § 1.52-1, or there is a similar 25 percent common ownership in the property (or in a leasehold of the property) and in a person who owned (or, in the case of section 1245 class property, owned or used) the property during 1980;

(iv) The taxpayer (or the taxpayer's lessee) is related during 1980 to the person who owned (or, in the case of section 1245 class property, owned or used) the property during 1980;

(v) Section 1250 class property is operated by a person who owned such property during 1980 (or by a related person) under a management contract and, had such property been section 1245 class property instead of section 1250 class property, the user would be considered not to have changed as part of the transaction (see § 1.168-4(d)(2)(ii));

(vi) The taxpayer leases section 1250 class property to a person and, through one or more subleases, the property is leased to a person who owned such property during 1980 (or to a related person); or

(vii) Section 1245 class property is acquired in an exchange described in section 1031, relating to exchange of property held for productive use or investment, to the extent that the basis of such property includes an amount representing the adjusted basis of other property owned by the taxpayer or a related person at any time during 1980. In the case of property which does not qualify for ACRS under this subdivision, rules similar to those of paragraph (d)(3)(iii) of this section shall apply.

In general, the avoidance intent indicated in subdivisions (i) through (vii) may be rebutted by evidence of an overriding business purpose (or purposes) for the transaction. However, even if the taxpayer demonstrates an overriding business purpose (or purposes) for the transaction, the property will not qualify for ACRS if the Internal Revenue Service establishes that one of the principal purposes of the transaction is to avoid the operation of the effective date rule of section 168(e)(1) and the "anti-churning" rules of section 168(e)(4), and the rules of this section.

(8) Adjustment to basis of partnership property. ACRS shall not apply with respect to any adjustment to the basis of partnership property made under section 734(b) (relating to the optional adjustment to the basis of undistributed partnership property) or section 743(b) (relating to the optional adjustment to the basis of partnership property) if the partnership property itself does not qualify for ACRS because of section 168(e) and this section. If a partnership has property which qualifies for ACRS, see § 1.168-2(n) for the application of ACRS to the adjustments, pursuant to section 734(b) or 743(b), to the basis of such property.

(9) Acquisitions by reason of death. Property acquired by the taxpayer after December 31, 1980, by reason of death, for which the basis is determined under section 1014(a), is eligible for ACRS.

(10) Reduction in unadjusted basis. The unadjusted basis of property for purposes of section 168(d)(1) and § 1.168-2(d) shall be reduced to the extent that such property does not qualify for ACRS due to the application of this paragraph (d). The basis not taken into account for ACRS purposes pursuant to the preceding sentence shall be taken into account by the taxpayer for purposes of other provisions of the Code.

(11) Certain corporate transactions. For purposes of section 168(e)(4) and § 1.168-4(d)(6), a corporation is not related to a distributee (or, in the case of a transaction described in section 338, the new target corporation) if—

(i) Such corporation is a distributing corporation in a transaction to which section 334(b)(2)(B) (as in effect on August 31, 1982) applies, or is a target corporation for which an election under section 338 is made, and at least 80 percent of the stock of such corporation (as described in section 334(b)(2)(B) or 338(d)(3)) is acquired by purchase after December 31, 1980, or

(ii) Such corporation is a distributing corporation in a complete liquidation to which section 331(a) applies, or a partial liquidation to which section 331(a) (as in effect on August 31, 1982) applies, or to which section 302(b)(4) applies, and the distributee (or a related person) by himself or together with one or more persons acquires the amount of stock specified in subdivision (i) of this paragraph (d)(11) by purchase after December 31, 1980.

(e) Examples. The application of this section may be illustrated by the following examples:

Example (1). In 1978 A buys a house which he uses as his family residence. In 1983, A's family moves out, and A converts the house into rental property. A may not use ACRS with respect to the property because he placed it in service before 1981. A must depreciate the property in accordance with section 167 and the regulations thereunder, subject to the other applicable provisions of the Code.

Example (2). In 1982 X Corp. purchases and places in service two major pieces of manufacturing equipment. One is newly constructed, while the other is a used machine expected to produce only 5,000 additional units. X elects to depreciate the used machine under the unit-of-production method. Such method was properly used within X's industry before 1981. Assuming that X has met the requirements of section 168(f)(4) and § 1.168-5(e), the used machine will not be recovery property as defined in section 168(c)(1) and § 1.168-3(a). X will apply ACRS with respect to the new machine even though it properly elected to apply the unit-of-production method with respect to the used machine.

Example (3). On November 15, 1984, B, a calendar year taxpayer, places in service a 10-unit apartment building for individuals and families of low income under section 8 of the United States Housing Act of 1937. B acquired the building for $100,000 and has incurred an additional $100,000 of expenditures for its rehabilitation, which B elects to amortize under section 167(k). In 1984, B is entitled to an allowance under ACRS of $2,000 (*i.e.,* .02 × $100,000). The $100,000 which B amortizes under section 167(k) is not included in the unadjusted basis and therefore is not recovered under the provisions of ACRS.

Example (4). C is an individual engaged in the trucking business. On February 1, 1983, C purchases a new truck from a dealer. As is his normal business practice, C financed the transaction partly by trading in a truck C had used in his business for the previous 3 years. Although this transaction is described in section 1031, it does not have as one of its principal purposes avoidance of the rules of section 168(e)(1) and (4). C therefore will use ACRS with respect to the entire unadjusted basis of the truck purchased in 1983, including cash paid, indebtedness incurred, and the amount attributable to the adjusted basis of the used truck traded in.

Example (5). On June 1, 1983, in a transaction described in section 1031, Corporation M exchanges a corporate jet, acquired before 1981, for a very similar corporate jet owned and also acquired before 1981 by unrelated Corporation N. There is no significant difference to M or N in the use of the jet acquired from that of the jet exchanged, and the operations of each corporation do not change significantly as a result of the transaction. These facts and circumstances indicate that one of the principal purposes of this transaction is to avoid the principles of paragraphs (1) and (4) of section 168(e). Thus, absent evidence of an overriding business purpose (or purposes) for the transaction, neither of the jets will be treated as recovery property. Further, even if an overriding business purpose (or purposes) for the transaction is (or are) demonstrated, the property will not be eligible for ACRS if the Internal Revenue Service establishes that one of the principal purposes of the transaction is to avoid the principles of paragraphs (1) and (4) of section 168(e). The result in this example would be the same if, after the exchange, M or N sold the acquired property and leased it back, or sold the property to a related person.

Example (6). Z Corp., owner and largest occupant of the Z Building since 1965, sells this building to an institutional investor, M Corp., on May 1, 1983. After this sale, 25 percent of the Z building is leased to Z until May 1, 1985. Because 25 percent of the Z building is leased for more than 3 months by Z, which owned the building during 1980, M may not take ACRS deductions with respect to this 25 percent portion. Such portion must be depreciated in accordance with section 167. However, ACRS will apply with respect to the portion of the Z Building which is not leased by Z for more than 3 months after the above-described sale. If Z had leased the building only until July 31, 1983, then M Corp. would apply ACRS with respect to the entire building.

Example (7). During 1980 O Corp. undertakes construction of a department store which becomes available for its assigned business function on April 1, 1981. For purposes of section 168(e)(4)(B), O is not treated as owning the department store building under construction until it placed it in service on April 1, 1981. Accordingly, ACRS will apply with respect to the building, beginning on the day it is placed in service.

Example (8). On June 1, 1983, P Corp. sells an undivided 70 percent interest in a building it has owned since March 1, 1980, to Q Corp. which is not related to P. R. Corp., which is not related to P, has occupied the building as a tenant since June 1980 and will continue to occupy it after this sale. P and Q will own the building as tenants-in-common. Q, but not P, will take ACRS deductions with respect to its portion of the building. The fact that the user of the building did not change will not affect this result. However, if P and Q had formed a partnership which owned the building after the sale, no portion of the building would qualify for ACRS because the taxpayer acquiring the property after 1980 (the partnership) would be related under section 168(e)(4)(D) to a person (P) which owned the building in 1980.

Example (9). On January 1, 1984, D, a 20 percent partner in Partnership W, sells his entire partnership interest to E for $400,000. Partnership W has one asset, a building it placed in service before 1981. D's adjusted basis in his partnership interest, allocable entirely to the building, is $200,000 when it is sold. A valid election under section 754 is in effect with respect to the sale of the partnership interest. Accordingly, Partnership W makes an adjustment pursuant to section 743(b) to increase the basis of the building with respect to E from $200,000 to $400,000. Under the provisions of § 1.168-4(d)(8) no portion of the increase in the basis of the partnership property with respect to E is eligible for ACRS because the partnership property itself does not qualify for ACRS due to the provisions of section 168(e)(1) and § 1.168-4(a).

Example (10). In 1983, F, an individual, sells a piece of business equipment he placed in service in 1980 to X, a partnership in which F owns a 20 percent interest. No portion of such equipment will qualify for ACRS since it was acquired after 1980 by the taxpayer (Partnership X) and was owned during 1980 by a related person (partner F). The result in this example would not be changed if F owned no interest in X in 1980.

Example (11). G, an individual, has owned an apartment building containing furnished apartments since 1979. On June 1, 1983, G sells the building and its furnishings to unrelated Partnership Y. The furniture was purchased by G before 1981. Most of these apartments will continue to be occupied by the same tenants who occupied them before the sale. For purposes of section 168(e)(4)(I) and § 1.168-4(d)(3), the furniture is acquired incidental to the acquisition of the building. Therefore, ACRS will apply with respect to the furniture, notwithstanding that many of the tenants who used the furniture do not change as part of the transaction.

Example (12). On June 1, 1983, Partnership Z purchases a factory which has been leased by Corporation S, an unrelated person, since 1979. Corporation S continues to use this factory for more than 3 months after the sale. The pre-1981 section 1245 class property transferred in this transaction, such as machinery and equipment, represents a significant portion of the unadjusted basis of the property purchased by Z. Since the unadjusted basis of such section 1245 class property is significant in relation to the factory's unadjusted basis, for purposes of section 168(e)(4)(I) and § 1.168-4(d)(3), the machinery and equipment are not acquired incidental to the acquisition of the factory. Since the user of such machinery and equipment does not change as part of the transaction, Partnership Z may not use ACRS with respect to such section 1245 class property. However, Z will use ACRS with respect to the factory and the other section 1250 class property acquired.

Example (13). Partnership W, in which Partner E holds a 25 percent interest, has as its sole asset an office building it placed in service in 1980. On May 1, 1983, E dies, and his partnership interest, whose basis is determined under section 1014, passes to his daughter, D. ACRS is not available with respect to any increase in the basis of the partnership property with respect to D, because the partnership property itself does not qualify for ACRS due to the provisions of section 168(e)(1) and § 1.168-4(a).

Example (14). On July 1, 1983, Corporation X sells a building it had owned in 1980 to Corporation Y, an unrelated person. X retains an option to repurchase this building within 5 years. This building qualifies as recovery property in Y's hands, and Y will take ACRS deductions under section 168 with respect to it. On July 1, 1985, X exercises its option and repurchases the building. When X repurchases the building, it ceases to be recovery property because the taxpayer (X) owned the building during 1980. X may not take ACRS deductions with respect to the repurchased building. Instead, X must depreciate it under section 167 and the regulations thereunder.

Example (15). F, an individual, sells his business (including section 1245 class property owned in 1980) to G, on August 1, 1983. Under their arrangement, F continues to manage the business for G, using the same equipment he had previously used. F receives as compensation for managing the business a fixed salary plus 5 percent of the gross profits. The arrangement follows customary commercial practice and was negotiated by F and G at arm's length. In addition, the amounts received (including the 5 percent of gross profits) represent the real value of the services rendered by F and are reasonable in amount. Further, receipt of 5 percent of gross profits under these circumstances is an ordinary and customary feature in the sale of a business in the industry and region in question. This arrangement results in a sufficient change in the ownership and use of the equipment that G will recover the cost of such equipment under ACRS.

Example (16). Individuals J and K each own a 50 percent interest in Partnership X, whose only asset is a building placed in service before 1981. On August 1, 1983, H, an individual, purchases a 25 percent interest each from J and K. Partnership X is deemed under section 708(b)(1)(B) to have terminated when H purchases the 50 percent interest. The building is not eligible for ACRS because the taxpayer acquiring the property after 1980 (the new partnership formed by H, J, and K) is related to the person who owned the property during 1980 (the old partnership), since J and K own more than a 10 percent interest in each of the two partnerships.

Example (17). In 1980, individual A owns all of the stock of Corporation T, which in turn owns depreciable property. In 1982, A sells the stock of T to unrelated Corporation V. Shortly thereafter, T sells some of the depreciable property it owned in 1980 to A. Under section 168(e)(4)(D), the property is not owned during 1980 by a person related to the taxpayer (A) since A is not related to the 1980 owner (T) when A acquires the property. However, an avoidance purpose is indicated under § 1.168-4(d)(7)(iv) since A was related in 1980 to the 1980 owner (T). Also, A broke the relationship with T shortly before acquiring the property. Accordingly, A may not use ACRS with respect to the property acquired, unless he can demonstrate an overriding business purpose (or purposes) for the transaction. Further, even if an overriding business purpose (or purposes) for the transaction is (or are) demonstrated, the property will not be eligible for ACRS if the Internal Revenue Service establishes that one of the principal purposes of the transaction is to avoid the principles of paragraphs (1) and (4) of section 168(e).

Example (18). In 1980, individual B owns all of the stock of Corporations X and Y. In 1980, X owns depreciable property. In 1981, X liquidates. In 1982, B sells to Y property owned by X in 1980. Y may not use ACRS with respect to the acquired property. Since the taxpayer (Y) would be related to the 1980 owner (X) but for the fact that X is no longer in existence when Y acquires the property, then, under § 1.168-4(d)(6)(ii)(B), X is considered to be in existence for purposes of determining whether the property was owned (or used) by a related person during 1980.

Example (19). In 1980, individual C owns all of the stock of Corporation M, which in turn owns all of the stock of Corporation N. In 1980, N owns depreciable property. In 1981, N distributes such 1980 property to M. In 1982, M sells the N stock to an unrelated person. In 1983, M distributes to C the property it received from N. Under section 168(e)(4)(D), the property is not owned during 1980 by a person related to the taxpayer (C), since C is not related to the 1980 owner (N) when C acquires the property. However, under § 1.168-4(d)(7)(iv) an avoidance purpose is indicated since the taxpayer (C) is related in 1980 to the 1980 owner (N). Also, upon acquisition, C is related to the person from whom the property is acquired (M). Therefore, C may not use ACRS with respect to the property unless he demonstrates an overriding business purpose (or purposes) for the transaction. Further, even if an overriding business purpose (or purposes) for the transaction is (or are) demonstrated, the property will not be eligible for ACRS if the Internal Revenue Service establishes that one of the principal purposes of the transaction is to avoid the principles of paragraphs (1) and (4) of section 168(e).

Example (20). D owns 20 percent of Corporation X and a 20 percent interest in Partnership P. X owns depreciable property in 1980. In 1981, X sells the property to P. Under § 1.267(b)-1(b), the sale is considered as occurring between X and the members of the partnership (including D) separately. Accordingly, under the principles of § 1.267(b)-1(b), 20 percent of the unadjusted basis of the property is excluded from ACRS. In addition, under § 1.168-4(d)(7)(i) an avoidance purpose is indicated since D owns more than a 10 percent interest in the taxpayer (P) and the person who owned the property during 1980 (X). Therefore, ACRS is not available with respect to the remainder of the unadjusted basis of the property unless an overriding business purpose (or purposes) for the transaction is (or are) demonstrated. Further, even if an overriding business purpose (or purposes) for the transaction is (or are) demonstrated, the property will not be eligible for ACRS if the Internal Revenue Service establishes that one of the principal purposes of the transaction is to avoid the principles of paragraphs (1) and (4) of section 168(e).

Example (21). In 1980, E leases section 1245 class property to F. In 1982, at the termination of the lease, F purchases the property from E and continues to use it for more than 3 months after the sale. F is not entitled to use ACRS with respect to the property since, as part of the transaction, the user of the property did not change. The result in this example would be the same if, instead of selling the property to F, E sold the property to G, subject to F's lease, with F's use continuing for more than 3 months after the sale.

Example (22). In 1980, H and I each own section 1245 class property which they use in their respective businesses. In 1981, H and I swap titles to the property, with the parties continuing to use the same property as before the exchange. Neither H nor I is entitled to use ACRS with respect to the acquired property, since the user of the property does not change as part of the transaction.

Example (23). A owns section 1250 class property in 1980. In 1981, A sells the property to B who leases it back to A. B later sells the property to C, subject to A's lease. ACRS is not available with respect to the property in the hands of C since the taxpayer (C) leases the property to a person who owned it during 1980 (A).

Example (24). D owns section 1250 class property in 1980. In 1981, D transfers the property to E (an unrelated person) in exchange for property of a like kind in a transaction described in section 1031. Subsequently, D sells to and leases back from F the property acquired from E. Under § 1.168-4(d)(3)(iii), the property acquired from E is considered to have been owned by D in 1980. Therefore, ACRS is not available with respect to such property in the hands of F since the taxpayer (F) leases the property to a person who owned it during 1980 (D). The result in this example would be the same if, instead of selling the property to F, D sold it to G (regardless of whether G leased it back to D), a person related to D under section 168(e)(4)(D) and § 1.168-4(d)(6).

Example (25). In 1980, Corporation X places in service section 1245 class property. In 1981, X merges into Corporation Y in a transaction described in section 368(a)(1)(A). Subsequently, Y sells to and leases back from Z the 1980 section 1245 class property acquired from X in the merger. Under § 1.168-4(d)(4)(vi), ACRS is not available with respect to the property in the hands of Z.

§ 1.168-5 Special rules.

(a) Retirement-replacement-betterment (RRB) property. *(1) RRB replacement property placed in service before January 1, 1985.* (i) Except as provided in paragraph (a)(1)(ii) of this section, the recovery deduction for the taxable year for retirement-replacement-betterment (RRB) replacement property (as defined in paragraph (a)(3) of this section) placed in service before January 1, 1985, shall be (in lieu of the amount determined under section 168(b)) an amount determined by applying to the unadjusted basis (as defined in section 168(d)(1) and the regulations thereunder) of such property the applicable percentage determined in accordance with the following table:

If the recovery year is:	And the year the property is placed in service is:			
	1981	1982	1983	1984
	The applicable percentage is:			
1	100	50	33	25
2		50	45	38
3			22	25
4				12

(ii) The provisions of paragraph (a)(1)(i) of this section do not apply to any taxpayer who did not use the RRB method of depreciation under section 167 as of December 31, 1980. In such case, RRB replacement property placed in service by the taxpayer after December 31, 1980, shall be treated as other 5-year recovery property under section 168.

(2) RRB replacement property placed in service after December 31, 1984. RRB replacement property placed in service after December 31, 1984, is treated as other 5-year recovery property under section 168.

(3) RRB replacement property defined. RRB replacement property, for purposes of section 168, means replacement track material (including rail, ties, other track material, and ballast) installed by a railroad (including a railroad switching or terminal company) if—

(i) The replacement is made pursuant to a scheduled program for replacement.

(ii) The replacement is made pursuant to observations by maintenance-of-way personnel of specific track material needing replacement.

(iii) The replacement is made pursuant to the detection by a rail-test car of specific track material needing replacement, or

(iv) The replacement is made as a result of a casualty. Replacements made as a result of a casualty shall be RRB replacement property only to the extent that, in the case of each casualty, the replacement cost with respect to the replacement track material exceeds $50,000.

(4) Recovery of adjusted basis of RRB property as of December 31, 1980. The taxpayer shall recover the adjusted basis of RRB property (as defined in section 168(g)(6)) as of December 31, 1980, over a period of not less than 5 years and not more than 50 years, using a rate of recovery consistent with any method described in section 167(b), including the method described in section 167(b)(2), switching to the method described in section 167(b)(3) at a time to maximize the deduction. For purposes of determining the recovery allowance under this subparagraph, salvage value shall be disregarded and, in the case of a taxpayer that depreciated RRB property placed in service before January 1, 1981, using the RRB method consistently for all periods after February 28, 1913, the adjusted basis of RRB property is the adjusted basis for purposes of determining the deduction for retirements under the RRB method, with no adjustment for depreciation sustained prior to March 1, 1913.

(5) RRB property (which is not RRB replacement property) placed in service after December 31, 1980. Property placed in service by the taxpayer after December 31, 1980, which is not RRB replacement property and which, under the taxpayer's method of depreciation as of December 31, 1980, would have been depreciated by the taxpayer under the RRB method, is treated as other property under section 168.

(b) - (f) [Reserved]

T.D. 8166, 12/23/86.

Proposed § 1.168-5 Special rules. [*For Preamble, see ¶ 150,941*]

Caution: The Treasury has not yet amended Reg § 1.168-5 to reflect changes made by P.L. 101-508, P.L. 101-239, P.L. 100-647, P.L. 99-514, P.L. 98-369.

* * * * *

(b) Transferee bound by transferor's period and method in certain transactions. *(1) In general.* In the case of recovery property which is transferred in a transaction described in section 168(f)(10)(B) and subparagraph (2) of this § 1.168-5(b), the transferee shall be treated as the transferor for purposes of computing the recovery allowance under section 168(a) and § 1.168-2 with respect to so much of the basis of such property in the hands of the transferee as does not exceed its adjusted basis (determined before the application of the section 48(q)(2) adjustment, if any) in the hands of the transferor immediately before the transfer.

(2) Transactions covered. The provisions of subparagraph (1) of this paragraph (b) apply to the following transactions:

(i) A transaction described in—

(A) Section 332 (relating to distributions in complete liquidation of an 80 percent or more controlled subsidiary corporation) except where the basis of the assets distributed is determined under section 334(b)(2) (as in effect on August 31, 1982);

(B) Section 351 (relating to transfer to a corporation controlled by transferor);

(C) Section 361 (relating to exchanges pursuant to certain corporate reorganizations);

(D) Section 371(a) (relating to exchanges pursuant to certain receivership and bankruptcy proceedings);

(E) Section 374(a) (relating to exchanges pursuant to certain railroad reorganizations);

(F) Section 721 (relating to transfers to a partnership in exchange for a partnership interest); and

(G) Section 731 (relating to distributions by a partnership to a partner);

(ii) An acquisition (other than one described in subdivision (i) of this paragraph (2)) from a related person (as defined in section 168(e)(4)(D) and § 1.168-4(d)(6)). Property acquired from a decedent is not property acquired in a transaction included in this subdivision (ii); and

(iii) An acquisition followed by a leaseback to the person from whom the property is acquired. A leaseback does not exist for purposes of this subdivision (iii) if the former owner in turn subleases the property to another person.

(3) Transactions excluded. The provisions of section 168(f)(10)(A) and paragraph (b)(1) of this section do not apply—

(i) To recovery property which is transferred within 12 months after the property is placed in service by the transferor. The exception of this subdivision (i) shall not apply in the case of a transaction also described in section 168(f)(7) (i.e., a transaction in which gain or loss is not recognized in whole or in part); or

(ii) To any transaction described in section 168(e)(4) and § 1.168-4(d).

(4) Allowable deduction when transferor and transferee are calendar year taxpayers or have the same fiscal year. When the transferor and transferee are calendar year taxpayers or when both the transferee and transferor have the same fiscal year—

(i) Allowable deduction in year of transfer. The allowable deduction for the recovery year in which the property is transferred shall be prorated between the transferor and the transferee on a monthly basis. For property other than 15-year real property, the transferor's deduction for such year is the deduction allowable to the transferor (determined without regard to this subdivision) multiplied by a fraction, the numerator of which is the number of months in the transferor's taxable year before the month in which the transfer occurs, and the denominator of which is the total number of months in the transferor's taxable year. The remaining portion of the transferor's allowable deduction for the taxable year of the transfer (determined without regard to this subdivision) shall be allocated to the transferee. For property transferred in a transaction described in section 332, 361, 371(a), 374(a), or 731, the two preceding sentences shall be applied by disregarding that the taxable year of the transferor may end on the date of the transfer. In the case of 15-year real property, the transferor's deduction for the year of the transfer is the deduction allowable to the transferor under the disposition rules of § 1.168-2(a)(3) or (g)(4) (as the case may be). The remaining portion of the transferor's allowable deduction for the taxable year of the transfer (determined as if the transfer had not occurred) shall be allocated to the transferee. See subdivision (ii) of this paragraph (4) for a special rule applicable to certain nonrecognition transactions.

(ii) Special rule for certain nonrecognition transactions occurring as of the close of business on the last day of any calendar month. For purposes of this paragraph (b), in the case of a transaction described in section 168(f)(10)(B)(i) and paragraph (b)(2)(i) of this section, if the transfer occurs as of the close of business on the last day of any calendar month, such transfer is deemed to occur on the first day of the next calendar month.

(iii) Transferee's allowable deduction for a taxable year subsequent to the year of transfer. The allowable deduction to the transferee for taxable years subsequent to the year of transfer shall be determined as if the cost of the property were being recovered in the transferor's hands (i.e., by multiplying the transferor's applicable recovery percentage for the current recovery year by the transferor's unadjusted basis in the transferred property).

Thus, for example, A, a calendar year taxpayer, purchases for $30,000 and places in service 15-year real property (other than low income housing) on February 15, 1981, and transfers the property to partnership B, a calendar year partnership, on March 15, 1981, in a transaction described in section 721. A does not elect to use the optional recovery percentages provided in § 1.168-2(c). For 1981, A's allowable deduction is $300 (i.e., $30,000 × .11 × 1/11). B's allowable deductions for 1981 and 1982 are $3,000 (i.e., $3,300 − $300) and $3,000 (i.e., .10 × $30,000), respectively.

(5) Allowable deduction when transferor and transferee have different taxable years. When the transferor and the transferee have different taxable years—

(i) Transferor's allowable deduction. The allowable deduction to the transferor for any taxable year in which the property is transferred shall be determined as under paragraph (b)(4)(i) and (ii) of this section.

(ii) Transferee's allowable deduction. In computing the transferee's allowable deduction for the year of transfer and for subsequent taxable years, the property shall similarly be treated as if its cost were being recovered by the transferor. However, the allowable deduction for any taxable year shall be allocated to the transferee based on the transferee's taxable year.

Thus, for example, B, a calendar year taxpayer, purchases for $30,000 and places in service 15-year real property (other than low income housing) on February 15, 1981. B's allowable deduction for 1981 is $3,300 (i.e., .11 × $30,000). B transfers the property to C on March 15, 1982. C's taxable year is a fiscal year ending June 30. For 1982, B's allowable deduction is $500 (i.e., $30,000 × .10 × 2/12). For fiscal year 1982, C's allowable deduction is $1,000 (i.e., the remainder of B's 1982 deduction ($2,500), allocated to the period

March 1 through June 30, 1982 (4 months/10 months)). For fiscal year 1983, C's allowable deduction is $2,850 (i.e., the remainder of B's allowable 1982 deduction ($1,500), plus $1,350 which is B's allowable 1983 deduction of $2,700 ($30,000 × .09) allocated to the period January 1 through June 30, 1983 (i.e., $2,700 × 6 months/12 months).

(6) Transferee's basis lower than transferor's. If the adjusted basis of the property in the hands of the transferee is lower than the adjusted basis of the property in the hands of the transferor immediately before the transfer, see § 1.168-2(d)(3) for rules relating to redeterminations of basis.

(7) Portion of basis in hands of transferee which exceeds transferor's adjusted basis. The transferee shall treat as newly purchased ACRS property that portion of the basis of the property in the hands of the transferee that exceeds the adjusted basis (determined before the application of the section 48(q)(2) adjustment, if any) of the property in the hands of the transferor immediately before the transfer. Thus, such excess shall be treated as recovery property placed in service by the transferee in the year of the transfer. The transferee may choose any applicable recovery period and recovery method with respect to such excess and need not use the transferor's recovery period and recovery method.

(8) Examples. The application of this paragraph (b) may be illustrated by the following examples:

Example (1). In 1981, A, a calendar year taxpayer, purchases for $12,000 and places in service 3-year recovery property. Under section 168(b)(1) and § 1.168-2(b)(1), the recovery allowances for the first and second recovery years are $3,000 (i.e., .25 × $12,000) and $4,560 (i.e., .38 × $12,000), respectively. On February 15, 1983, A transfers the property to M Corporation, a calendar year taxpayer, in exchange for M's stock and $2,000 cash in a transaction described in section 351. A's recovery allowance for 1983 is $370 (i.e., (1/12 × .37) × $12,000). A's adjusted basis immediately before the exchange is $4,070 (i.e., $12,000 − $7,930). Assume A recognizes gain of $2,000 on the transaction. The basis attributable to the property under section 362 is determined to be $6,070 in the hands of M Corporation. Under the provisions of section 168(f)(10)(A) and this paragraph (b), M, the transferee, is treated the same as A, the transferor, with respect to $4,070, which is so much of M's basis as does not exceed A's adjusted basis. However, in computing the deduction allowable with respect to such basis, A's unadjusted basis ($12,000) is used. Thus, in the third recovery year, M may deduct $4,070 (i.e., (11/12 × .37) × $12,000) under section 168(f)(10)(A) and § 1.168-5(b)(1) and (4). The remaining $2,000 of basis in the property is treated as newly purchased ACRS property placed in service in 1983. M may choose any applicable recovery period and recovery method with respect to such $2,000 and need not use A's recovery period and recovery method.

Example (2). In 1983, B, a calendar year taxpayer, purchases for $12,000 and places in service 5-year recovery property. Under section 46, B's investment tax credit for such property is $1,200. Under section 48(q)(1) and § 1.168-2(d)(2), B reduces his basis of $600 (i.e., .50 × $1,200). Therefore, B's unadjusted basis for purposes of section 168 is $11,400 (i.e., $12,000 − $600). Under section 168(b)(1) and § 1.168-2(b)(1), the recovery allowances for the first and second recovery years are $1,710 (i.e., .15 × $11,400) and $2,508 (i.e., .22 × $11,400), respectively. On February 15, 1985, B sells the property for $13,000 to C, a related party (as defined in section 168(e)(4)(D) and § 1.168-4(d)(6)) who is a calendar year taxpayer. B's recovery allowance for 1985 is $199.50 (i.e., (1/12 × .21) × $11,400). B's adjusted basis (determined without regard to the section 48(q)(2) adjustment), immediately before the sale is $6,982.50 (i.e., $11,400 − $4,417.50). The basis of the property under section 1012 is $13,000 in C's hands. Under the provisions of section 168(f)(10)(A) and this paragraph (b), C, the transferee, is treated the same as B, the transferor, with respect to $6,982.50, which is so much of C's basis as does not exceed B's adjusted basis. However, in computing the deduction allowable with respect to such basis, B's unadjusted basis ($11,400) is used. Thus, in the third recovery year, C may deduct $2,194.50 (i.e., (11/12 × .21) × $11,400) under section 168(f)(10)(A) and § 1.168-5(b)(1) and (4). In the fourth and fifth recovery years, C may deduct $2,394 (i.e., .21 × $11,400) each year. The remaining basis of $6,017.50 (i.e., $13,000 − $6,982.50) in property is treated as newly purchased ACRS property placed in service in 1985. C may choose any applicable period and recovery method with respect to such amount and need not use B's recovery period and recovery method.

Example (3). In 1981, D, a calendar year taxpayer, purchases for $12,000 and places in service 5-year recovery property. Under section 168(b)(1) and § 1.168-2(b)(1), the recovery allowances for the first and second recovery years are $1,800 (i.e., .15 × $12,000) and $2,640 (i.e., .22 × $12,000), respectively. On March 15, 1983, D transfers the property to N Corporation, a taxpayer having a fiscal year ending June 30, in exchange for N's stock and $2,000 cash in a transaction described in section 351. D's recovery allowance for 1983 is $420 (i.e., (2/12 × .21) × $12,000). D's adjusted basis in the property immediately before the exchange is $7,140 (i.e., $12,000 − $4,860). Assume D recognizes gain of $2,000 on the transaction. The basis attributable to the property under section 362 is determined to be $9,140 in the hands of N Corporation. Under the provisions of section 168(f)(10)(A) and this paragraph (b), N, the transferee, is treated the same as D, the transferor, with respect to $7,140, which is so much of N's basis as does not exceed D's adjusted basis. However, in computing the deduction allowable with respect to such basis, D's unadjusted basis ($12,000) is used. Thus, for fiscal year 1983, N Corporation's allowable deduction with respect to the carryover basis is $840 (i.e., (4/12 × .21) × $12,000). For fiscal years 1984 and 1985, N Corporation's allowable deduction is $2,520 (i.e., [(6/12 × .21) + (6/12 × .21)] × $12,000). For fiscal year 1986, N Corporation's allowable deduction is $1,260 (i.e., (6/12 × .21) × $12,000). The remaining $2,000 of basis in the property is treated as newly purchased ACRS property. N may choose any applicable recovery period and recovery method with respect to such basis and need not use D's recovery period and recovery method. N elects to use the optional recovery percentage based on a 5-year recovery period with respect to the $2,000 of basis which is treated as newly purchased ACRS property. For fiscal years 1983, 1984, 1985, 1986, 1987, and 1988, N's recovery allowance with respect to such $2,000 basis are $200, $400, $400, $400, $400, and $200, respectively. If N's fiscal year ending June 30, 1983, were a short taxable year, the provisions of § 1.168-2(f) would apply with respect to the $2,000 considered newly purchased ACRS property, but not with respect to N's basis carried over from D.

Example (4). On May 1, 1981, E, a calendar year taxpayer, purchases for $100,000 and places in service 5-year recovery property. On April 1, 1982, E sells the property for $100,000 to F who leases it back to E. Under the provisions of paragraph (b)(3), section 168(f)(10)(A) and § 1.168-5(b)(1) do not apply. Thus, F may choose any applicable recovery period and recovery method with respect to its unadjusted basis of $100,000, with recovery beginning in 1982.

Example (5). Assume the same facts as in example (4) except that the property is sold to F and leased back to E on June 15, 1982. Assume further that F's fiscal year ends on July 31, 1982. For 1981, E's allowable deduction is $15,000 (i.e., .15 × $100,000), and for 1982 is $9,166.67 (i.e., $100,000 × .22 × 5/12). E's adjusted basis in the property immediately before the transfer is $75,833.33 (i.e., $100,000 – $24,166.67). Under the provisions of section 168(f)(10)(A) and this paragraph (b), F, the transferee, is treated the same as E, the transferor, with respect to $75,833.33 which is so much of F's basis as does not exceed E's adjusted basis. However, in computing the deduction allowable with respect to such basis, E's unadjusted basis ($100,000) is used. Thus, for the fiscal year ending July 31, 1982, F's allowable deduction with respect to the carryover basis is $3,666.66 (i.e., 2/12 × .22 × $100,000). For fiscal year 1983, F's allowable deduction is $21,416.67 (i.e., (5/12 × .22 × $100,000) + (7/12 × .21 × $100,000)). For fiscal years 1984 and 1985, F's allowable deductions are $21,000 (i.e., (.21 × 5/12 × $100,000) + (.21 × 7/12 × $100,000)). For the fiscal year ending July 31, 1986, F's allowable deduction is $8,750 (i.e., 5/12 × .21 × $100,000). The remaining $24,166.67 of basis is treated as newly-purchased property, placed in service by F in 1981. F may choose any applicable recovery period and method for such amount and need not use E's recovery period and method.

Example (6). On January 1, 1981, G, a calendar year taxpayer, purchases for $1 million and places in service 15-year real property (other than low income housing). On July 15, 1988, G sells the property to H for $1.5 million, who leases it back to G. H's taxable year is a fiscal year ending September 30. G does not elect use of the optional percentages provided by § 1.168-2(c). For 1988, G's allowable deduction is $30,000 (i.e., .06 × $1,000,000 × 6/12). H is treated the same as G with respect to $390,000, which is so much of the basis of the property in the hands of H as does not exceed its adjusted basis to G immediately before the transfer (i.e., $1,000,000 – $610,000). H's allowable deduction for its fiscal year ending September 30, 1988, with respect to such basis is $15,000 (i.e., the remainder of G's allowable deduction for 1988 ($30,000) allocated to the period July 1 through September 30, 1988 (3 months/6 months)). For H's fiscal year ending September 30, 1989, H's allowable deduction is $60,000 (i.e., the remainder of G's allowable 1988 deduction ($15,000) plus G's allowable 1989 deduction ($60,000) allocated to the period January 1 through September 30, 1989 (9 months/12 months) or $45,000). For H's fiscal year ending September 30, 1990, H's allowable deduction is $52,500 (i.e., the remainder of G's allowable deduction for 1989 ($15,000), plus G's allowable deduction for 1990 ($50,000), allocated to the period January 1 through September 30, 1990 (9 months/12 months), or $37,500). For H's fiscal year ending September 30, 1996, H is entitled to G's allowable deduction for 1995 ($50,000), allocated to the period October 1 through December 31, 1995 (3 months/12 months), or $12,500. The amount of H's basis in excess of G's adjusted basis (i.e., $1,500,000 less $390,000, or $1,110,000) is treated as newly purchased ACRS property placed in service by H on July 15, 1988. H may use any applicable recovery period and method with respect to such basis. Thus, assuming H does not elect the optional percentages provided by § 1.168-2(c), H has an additional allowable deduction for its year ending September 30, 1988, of $33,300 (i.e., .03 × $1,110,000). For its fiscal year ending September 30, 1989, H's allowable deduction with respect to such basis is $122,100 (i.e., .11 × $1,110,000).

Example (7). On January 1, 1981, partnership P, a calendar year taxpayer, purchases for $1,000,000 and places in service 15-year real property (other than low income housing) which is the only asset of the partnership. At no time does the partnership have an election under section 754 in effect. P is owned equally by partners A, B, and C. On April 18, 1985, individual D purchases the interests of B and C for $1,500,000, thereby terminating the partnership under section 708(b)(1)(B). The deduction allowable with respect to the property for 1985 prior to the termination is $17,500 (i.e., $1,000,000 × .07 × 3/12). The partnership's adjusted basis in the property immediately before the termination is $592,500 (i.e., $1,000,000 – $407,500). Under the provisions of section 168(f)(10)(A) and § 1.168-5(b)(1), the new partnership which is created by A and D is treated the same as the old partnership with respect to $592,500, which is so much of the adjusted basis of the property to the new partnership as does not exceed its adjusted basis to the old partnership. However, in computing the allowable deduction with respect to such basis the old partnership's unadjusted basis ($1,000,000) is used. Thus, for 1985, the deduction allowable to the new partnership with respect to such basis is $52,500 (i.e., $1,000,000 × .07 × 9/12) and for 1986 is $60,000 (i.e., $1,000,000 × .06). This result would be the same if D purchased a 95 percent interest in the partnership. Recovery of such basis will be completed in 1995. The new partnership's basis in the property in excess of that of the old partnership is taken into account under ACRS as if it were newly-purchased recovery property placed in service in 1985. Any applicable period and method may be used with respect to such basis.

Example (8). In 1981, Corporation X, a calendar year taxpayer, purchases for $100,000 and places in service 5-year recovery property. Under section 168(b)(1) and § 1.168-2(b)(1), X's recovery allowance for 1981 is $15,000. On March 15, 1982, X merges into Corporation Y in a transaction described in section 368(a)(1)(A) solely in exchange for Y stock. Y's taxable year is a fiscal year ending August 31. X's recovery allowance for 1982 is $3,666.66 (i.e., 2/12 × .22 × $100,000). Under section 362, Y's basis in the property is the same as the property's adjusted basis in the hands of X immediately before the transfer. Therefore, for fiscal year 1982, Y's allowable deduction is $11,000 which is the remainder of X's allowable deduction for 1982, $18,333.34 (i.e., $22,000 – $3,666.66) allocated to the period March 1, 1982, through August 31, 1982 (i.e., 6 months/10 months). For fiscal year 1983, Y's allowable deduction is $21,333.34 which is the remainder of X's allowable deduction for 1982 ($7,333.34) plus the deduction which would be allowable to X in 1983 (i.e., $100,000 × .21, or $21,000) allocated to the period January 1 through August 31, 1983 (i.e., $21,000 × 8 months/12 months or $14,000). In computing the deductions allowable to X and Y, the fact that X's taxable year ends on the date of the merger is disregarded.

(c) Recovery property reacquired by the taxpayer. *(1) In general.* Recovery property which is disposed of and then reacquired by the taxpayer shall be treated (for purposes of computing the allowable deduction under section 168(a) and § 1.168-2) as if such property had not been disposed of by the taxpayer. This paragraph (c)(1) generally applies only to so much of the taxpayer's adjusted basis in the reacquired property as does not exceed his adjusted basis at the time he disposed of the property.

(2) Taxpayers to whom provisions apply. The provisions of section 168(f)(10)(C) and paragraph (c)(1) of this section apply only to a taxpayer who, at the time of the disposition of the property, anticipates a reacquisition of the same property.

(3) Exceptions. Section 168(f)(10)(C) and paragraph (c)(1) of this section shall not apply—

(i) To recovery property which is disposed of during the same taxable year that the property is placed in service by the taxpayer, or

(ii) To any transaction described in section 168(e)(4) and § 1.168-4(d).

(4) Taxpayer resumes prior recovery. For purposes of paragraph (c)(1) of this § 1.168-5, the reacquiring taxpayer shall resume the recovery under § 1.168-2 applicable at the time of the disposition. For example, if the taxpayer originally uses a 3-year recovery period and the applicable percentages prescribed in section 168(b)(1) and § 1.168-2(b)(1), in the year of reacquisition the recovery allowance is computed by applying the applicable percentage for the year of disposition to the original unadjusted basis (i.e., the unadjusted basis at the time the taxpayer originally placed the recovery property in service).

(5) Portion of unadjusted basis in reacquired property which exceeds taxpayer's adjusted basis at the time of disposition. That part of the unadjusted basis in the reacquired property which exceeds the taxpayer's adjusted basis in the property at the time of disposition shall be treated generally as newly purchased ACRS property. For property other than a building, any appropriate recovery period and method may be used with respect to such excess. For a building, the taxpayer must use the same recovery period and method with respect to such excess as are used for the building, unless such excess would qualify as a substantial improvement under § 1.168-2(e)(4) if paid or incurred by the taxpayer for an improvement if he had continued to own the building.

(6) Unadjusted basis in reacquired property lower than taxpayer's adjusted basis at time of disposition. If the unadjusted basis in the reacquired property is lower than the taxpayer's adjusted basis in the property at the time of disposition, see § 1.168-2(d)(3) for rules relating to redetermination of basis.

(7) Examples. The provisions of this paragraph may be illustrated by the following examples:

Example (1). In 1981 A, a calendar year taxpayer, purchases for $6,000 and places in service 3-year recovery property. A does not elect an optional recovery percentage under § 1.168-2(c). Under section 168(b)(1) and § 1.168-2(b)(1), A's recovery allowance for 1981 is $1,500 (i.e., .25 × $6,000). A wants to change his method of cost recovery from the use of the accelerated percentages to the use of the optional straight line percentages. To effectuate this change, A sells the property to B in 1982 for $7,000 anticipating that B will sell the property back to A. B does not elect to use an optional recovery percentage. B's recovery deduction for 1982 is $1,750 (i.e., .25 × $7,000). In 1983 A reacquires the property from B for $9,000. With respect to that portion of A's unadjusted basis in the reacquired property which does not exceed the adjusted basis at the time of disposition (i.e., $4,500), A's recovery allowance for 1983 is determined as if A had not disposed of the property, that is, by applying the percentage (38 percent) applicable for the second recovery year (i.e., 1982, the year of disposition) to the original unadjusted basis ($6,000). Thus, A's allowable deduction is $2,280 (i.e., .38 × $6,000). That portion of the unadjusted basis in the reacquired property which exceeds A's adjusted basis at the time of disposition (i.e., $4,500) is treated as newly purchased ACRS property placed in service in 1983. A may use any appropriate recovery period and method for such excess. Thus, if A uses the tables under § 1.168-2(b)(1), A's recovery allowance for 1983 also includes $1,125 (i.e., .25 × $4,500). A's recovery allowances for 1984 are $2,220 (i.e., .37 × $6,000) plus $1,710 (i.e., .38 × $4,500). A's recovery allowance for 1985 is $1,665 (i.e., .37 × $4,500).

Example (2). In 1981 C, a calendar year taxpayer, purchases for $15,000 and places in service 3-year recovery property and elects under § 1.168-2(c) the optional 5-year recovery period using the straight line method.

Under § 1.168-2(c)(4), C's recovery allowance for 1981 is $1,500 (i.e., .10 × $15,000). C wants to change his method of cost recovery from the use of the optional straight line percentages to the use of the accelerated percentages. Consent to change is not granted to C under section 168(f)(4). Therefore, C tries to effectuate this change by selling the property to D in 1982 for $16,000 anticipating that D will sell the property back to C. D does not elect to use the optional recovery percentages. D's recovery allowance for 1982 is $4,000 (i.e., .25 × $16,000). In 1983, C reacquires the property from D for $17,000. With respect to that portion of C's unadjusted basis in the reacquired property that does not exceed the adjusted basis at the time of disposition (i.e., $13,500), C must use the option recovery percentages originally elected. C's recovery allowances for 1983, 1984, 1985, 1986, and 1987 are determined as if C had not disposed of the property, that is, by applying the applicable percentages beginning in the second recovery year to the original unadjusted basis ($15,000). Thus, C's allowable deductions are $3,000, $3,000, $3,000, $3,000, and $1,500, respectively. With respect to that portion of the unadjusted basis in the reacquired property which exceeds C's adjusted basis at the time of disposition (i.e., $3,500), C may use any appropriate recovery period and method. Cost recovery for this portion of the reacquired property begins in 1983 as if C placed the property in service in that year.

Example (3). On February 15, 1981, E, a calendar year taxpayer, purchases for $30,000 and places in service 15-year real property (other than low income housing) and does not elect the optional straight line percentages under § 1.168-2(c). Under § 1.168-2(b)(2), E's recovery allowance for 1981 is $3,300 (i.e., .11 × $30,000). E wants to change his method of cost recovery from the use of the accelerated percentages to the use of the optional straight line percentages. To effectuate this change, E sells the property to F on February 15, 1983, anticipating that F will sell the property back to E. E's recovery allowance for 1982 is $3,000 (i.e., .10 × $30,000) and for 1983 is $225 (i.e., .09 × $1/12$ × $30,000). In 1985 E reacquires the property from F for $28,000. With respect to that portion of E's unadjusted basis in the reacquired property which does not exceed the adjusted basis at the time of disposition (i.e., $23,475) E's recovery allowance for 1985 is determined as if E had not disposed of the property, that is, by applying the percentage (9 percent) applicable for the third recovery year to the original unadjusted basis ($30,000). The recovery for the year of reacquisition must be adjusted to reflect the number of months the property is used by the taxpayer in that year as recovery property. Thus, if E reacquired the property in July, E's recovery allowance for 1985 would be $1,350 (i.e., .09 × $6/12$ × $30,000). The unrecovered allowance for the third recovery year, $1,125 ($30,000 × .09 × $5/12$), must be recovered in the year following the last recovery year. With respect to that portion of the unadjusted basis in the reacquired property which exceeds E's adjusted basis at the time of disposition (i.e., $4,525), E may not elect an optional recovery period. Cost recovery for this portion of the reacquired property will begin in 1985. Thus, if the reacquisition occurred in July, E's allowable deduction for 1985 with respect to this portion would be $271.50 (i.e., .06 × $4,525).

(d) Treatment of leasehold improvements. *(1) In general.* Capital expenditures made by a lessee for the erection of buildings or the construction of other permanent improvements on leased property are recoverable through ACRS deductions or amortization deductions. If the recovery period of such improvements in the hands of the taxpayer is equal to or shorter than the remaining period of the lease, the allowances shall take the form of ACRS deductions under section 168. If, on the other hand, the recovery period of such property in the hands of the taxpayer would be longer than the remaining period of such lease, the allowances shall take the form of annual deductions from gross income in an amount equal to the unrecovered cost of such capital expenditures divided by the number of years remaining on the term of the lease. Such deductions shall be in lieu of ACRS deductions. See section 162 and the regulations thereunder.

(2) Determination of recovery period. For purposes of determining whether the recovery period is longer than the lease term, an election of an optional recovery period under section 168(b)(3) or (f)(2)(C) shall be taken into account.

(3) Determination of the effect given to lease renewal options; related lessee and lessor. Section 178 governs the effect to be given renewal options in determining whether the recovery period of the improvements exceeds the remaining period of the lease. Section 178 also provides rules for determining the period of a lease when the lessee and lessor are related. In making any determination under section 178, the "recovery period" of the improvement shall be taken into account in lieu of its useful life. See § 1.178-1.

(4) Improvements made by lessor. If a lessor makes an improvement to the leased property, the cost of the improvement must be recovered under the general provisions of section 168. The provisions of 168(f)(6) and this paragraph (d) do not apply to improvements made by the lessor.

(5) Example. The application of this paragraph may be illustrated by the following example:

Example. In 1981, A leases B's land for a term of 99 years. The lease provisions do not include any options to renew the lease. In 2034, A places in service 15-year real property which he built on the leased premises. Since the remaining term of the lease (46 years) is longer than any recovery period which A could select under section 168 (i.e., 15, 35, or 45 years), A must recover the costs of the improvement under section 168.

(e) Manner and time for making election. *(1) Elections to which this paragraph applies.* The rules in this paragraph apply to the following elections provided under section 168:

(i) Section 168(b)(3)(A) and (B)(i) and § 1.168-2(c)(1) and (2), relating to election of optional recovery percentage with respect to property in the same recovery class (i.e., all 3-year recovery property);

(ii) Section 168(b)(3)(A) and (B)(ii) and § 1.168-2(c)(1) and (3), relating to election of optional recovery percentage on a property-by-property basis for 15-year real property;

(iii) Section 168(d)(2)(A) and § 1.168-2(h), relating to election to account for mass assets in the same mass asset account and to include in income all proceeds realized on disposition;

(iv) Section 168(e)(2) and § 1.168-4(b), relating to election to exclude property from ACRS by use of a method of depreciation not expressed in a term of years;

(v) Section 168(f)(2)(C)(i) and (ii)(I) and § 1.168-2(g)(3)(i) and (ii), relating to election of optional recovery percentage for property used predominantly outside the United States in the same recovery class and with the same present class life (e.g., 3-year recovery property with a present class life of 4 years); and

(vi) Section 168(f)(2)(C)(i) and (ii)(II) and § 1.168-2(g)(3)(i) and (iii), relating to election of optional recovery percentage on a property-by-property basis for 15-year real property used predominantly outside the United States.

Use by a taxpayer of a method of cost recovery described in section 168(b)(1) and (2) and § 1.168-2(b)(1) and (2) or section 168(f)(2)(A) and (B) and § 1.168-2(g)(1) and (2) (relating to the use of the accelerated percentages) is not an election for purposes of section 168 and this paragraph (e). Thus, no consent will be granted to change from such a method to another method described in section 168. The provisions of section 168(f)(4) and this paragraph (e) do not apply to elections which must be made under another section of the Code. Thus, for example, if a taxpayer wants to amortize property under section 167(k), the rules under section 167(k) apply with respect to such election and the revocation of such election.

(2) Time for making elections. Except as provided in subparagraph (4) or (5), the elections specified in subparagraph (1) of this paragraph (e) shall be made on the taxpayer's income tax return filed for the taxable year in which the property is placed in service as recovery property (as defined in § 1.168-3(a)) by the taxpayer. If the taxpayer does not file a timely return (taking into account extensions of the time for filing) for such taxable year, the election shall be made at the time the taxpayer files his first return for such year. The election may be made on a return, as amended, filed within the time prescribed by law (including extensions) for filing the return for such taxable year. A separate election may be made for each corporation which is a member of an affiliated group (as defined in section 1504) and which joins in the making of a consolidated return in accordance with section 1502 and the regulations thereunder. See § 1.1502-77.

(3) Manner of making elections. Except as provided in subparagraph (5), Form 4562 is provided for making an election under this paragraph and for submitting the information required. The taxpayer must specify in the election—

(i) The name of the taxpayer;

(ii) The taxpayer's identification number;

(iii) The year the recovery property was placed in service (or, in the case of 15-year real property, the month the property was placed in service);

(iv) The unadjusted basis of the recovery property; and

(v) Such other information as may be required.

An election will not be rendered invalid so long as there is substantial compliance, in good faith, with the requirements of this subparagraph (3).

(4) Special rule for qualified rehabilitated buildings. In the case of any qualified rehabilitated building (as defined in section 48(g)(1)), an election under section 168(b)(3) and § 1.168-2(c) (relating to election of optional recovery percentage) may be made at any time before the date 3 years after the building was placed in service by the taxpayer.

(5) Special rule for foreign taxpayers. (i) Foreign corporations subject to section 964. In the case of a foreign corporation whose earnings and profits are determined under section 964, the elections specified in subparagraph (1) of this paragraph (e) shall be made at the time and in the manner provided in § 1.964-1(c). Except as provided in the regulations under section 952 and section 1248, any election made under this subdivision (i) shall apply with respect to the recovery property affected by the election from the taxable year in which such property is placed in service. Such election may be revoked only as provided in § 1.964-1(c)(7) and subparagraph (9) of this paragraph.

(ii) Foreign taxpayers other than corporations subject to section 964. In the case of a foreign taxpayer other than a corporation described in subdivision (i) of this subparagraph (5), the elections specified in subparagraph (1) of this paragraph (e) shall be made at the time and in the manner provided in subparagraphs (2) and (3) of this paragraph, except that the election shall be made on the taxpayer's income tax return for the later of the taxable year in which the property is placed in service as recovery property by the taxpayer or the first taxable year in which the taxpayer is subject to United States tax. Any election made under this subdivision (ii) shall apply with respect to the recovery property affected by the election from the taxable year in which such property is placed in service. Such election may be revoked only as provided in subparagraph (9) of this paragraph. No election may be made under this subdivision (ii) by a taxpayer who was required to, but did not make the election at the time and in the manner prescribed under subdivision (i). For purposes of this subdivision (ii)—

(A) "Foreign taxpayer" means a taxpayer that is not a United States person as defined in section 7701(a)(30), and

(B) "United States tax" means tax under subtitle A of the Code (relating to income taxes) other than sections 871(a)(1) and 881 thereof.

(6) Failure to elect optional recovery percentages. If a taxpayer does not elect to use the optional recovery percentages within the time and in the manner prescribed in subparagraphs (2), (3), (4), and (5) (or is not considered to have elected under § 1.168-2(c)(5)), the amount allowable under section 168 must be determined under section 168(b)(1) or (2) (or under section 168(f)(2)(A) or (B), where applicable) for the year in which the recovery property is placed in service and for all subsequent recovery years. Thus, no election to use such optional percentages may be made by the taxpayer in any other manner (e.g., through a request under section 446(e) to change the taxpayer's method of accounting).

(7) Individuals, partnerships, trusts, estates, and corporations. Except as provided in subparagraph (8) of this paragraph with respect to transactions to which section 168(f)(10)(A) and (B) applies, and subject to other applicable provisions of the Code and regulations, if recovery property is placed in service by an individual, trust, estate, partnership, or corporation, an election under this paragraph shall be made by the individual, trust, estate, partnership, or corporation placing such property in service.

(8) Transactions to which section 168(f)(10)(A) and (B) applies. In a transaction to which section 168(f)(10)(A) and (B) and paragraph (b) of this § 1.168-5 apply, the transferee is bound by the transferor's election (or nonelection) under this paragraph with respect to the property so acquired. The rule of the preceding sentence shall apply only with respect to so much of the basis of the property in the hands of the transferee as does not exceed the adjusted basis of the property in the hands of the transferor immediately before the transfer.

(9) Revocation of election. An election under this paragraph, once made, may be revoked only with the consent of the Commissioner. Such consent will be granted only in extraordinary circumstances. Requests for consent must be filed with the Commissioner of Internal Revenue, Washington, D. C. 20224.

(f) Treatment of certain nonrecognition transactions. *(1) Section 1033 transactions.* (i) Allowable deduction for section 1033 converted property. For any taxable year in which a transaction described in section 1033 occurs, the full year's allowable deduction shall be prorated on a monthly basis under the principles of paragraph (b)(4)(i) of this section. Thus, for example, on March 3, 1981, A, a calendar year taxpayer, purchases for $25,000 and places in service 3-year recovery property. On August 14, 1981, the property is converted. A's 1981 allowable deduction for the converted property is $3,645.83 (i.e., $25,000 × .25 × 7/12). If the property were 15-year real property (other than low income housing) A's 1981 allowable deduction for the converted property would be $1,250 (i.e., $25,000 × .10 × 5/10).

(ii) Allowable deduction for section 1033 replacement property in year of replacement and subsequent taxable years. (A) Replacement property acquired in a transaction to which section 1033 applies, which qualifies as recovery property, shall be treated the same as the converted property. Thus, the replacement property shall be recovered over the remaining recovery period using the same recovery method as the converted property. The preceding sentence applies only with respect to so much of the basis (as determined under section 1033(b)) in the replacement property as does not exceed the adjusted basis in the converted property. Any excess of the unadjusted basis of the replacement property over the adjusted basis of the converted property shall be treated as newly purchased ACRS property. Any excess of the adjusted basis of the converted property over the unadjusted basis of the replacement property shall be recovered under the principles of § 1.168-2(d)(3) (relating to redeterminations).

(B) The allowable deduction for the replacement property in the year of replacement (whether such replacement year is the same as the year of conversion or a later year) shall be based on the number of months the replacement property is in service as recovery property during the replacement year.

(1) If the number of months in the conversion year after the property is converted (including the month of conversion) is greater than or equal to the number of months the replacement property is in service during the replacement year, the allowable deduction for the replacement year shall equal—

$(a/b \times c) \times d$

where

a = number of months replacement property is in service as recovery property during replacement year,

b = 12 or, in the case of 15-year real property converted in the first recovery year, the number of months in the taxpayer's taxable year after the converted property was placed in service by the taxpayer (including the month the property was placed in service),

c = applicable recovery percentage for converted property in year of conversion, and

d = unadjusted basis of converted property.

An allowance is permitted to the extent of any unrecovered allowance in the taxable year following the final recovery year. The term "unrecovered allowance" means the difference between—

(i) The sum of recovery allowances for the year of the conversion and the year of the replacement, and

(ii) The recovery allowance which would have been allowable in the year of conversion had such conversion not occurred.

In a year following the year of replacement, the allowable deduction shall be computed by multiplying the applicable recovery percentage for the next recovery year to the unadjusted basis of the converted property.

(2) If the number of months in the conversion year after the property is converted (including the month of conversion) is less than the number of months the replacement property is in service during the replacement year, the allowable deduction for the replacement year shall equal—

[(a/b × c) + (d/12 × e)] × f where

a = number of months in conversion year after the property is converted (including the month of conversion),

b = 12 or, in the case of 15-year real property converted in the first recovery year, the number of months in the taxpayer's taxable year after the converted property was placed in service by the taxpayer (including the month the property was placed in service),

c = applicable recovery percentage for converted property in the year of conversion,

d = number of months replacement property is in service as recovery property during replacement year minus a,

e = applicable recovery percentage for the next recovery year, and

f = unadjusted basis of converted property.

An allowance is permitted to the extent of any unrecovered allowance in the taxable year following the final recovery year. The term "unrecovered allowance" means the difference between—

(i) The sum of the recovery allowances for the year of conversion and the year of replacement, and

(ii) The sum of the recovery allowances which would have been allowable in the year of conversion and the next recovery year had such conversion not occurred.

In a year following the year of replacement, the allowable deduction shall be computed by multiplying the unadjusted basis of the converted property by the applicable recovery percentage for the second recovery year after the year of conversion.

(iii) Examples. The provisions of paragraph (f)(1)(i) and (ii) may be illustrated by the following examples:

Example (1). On January 1, 1981, A, a calendar year taxpayer, purchases for $40,000 and places in service recovery property which is 15-year real property (other than low income housing). Under section 168(b)(2) and § 1.168-2(b)(2), the allowable deductions for the first and second recovery years are $4,800 (i.e., .12 × $40,000) and $4,000 (i.e., .10 × $40,000). On March 3, 1983, A's property is involuntarily converted. Under the provisions of subdivision (i), A's 1983 allowable deduction for the converted property is $600 (i.e., 2/12 × .09 × $40,000). On May 15, 1984, A acquires replacement property. A's unadjusted basis in the replacement property is the same as his adjusted basis in the converted property (i.e., $30,600). Under the provisions of subdivision (ii), the replacement property is treated the same as the converted property with respect to such $30,600 of basis. However, in computing the allowable deduction with respect to such basis, A's unadjusted basis in the converted property ($40,000) is used. Thus, A's allowable deduction for 1984 is $2,400 (i.e., 8/12 × .09 × $40,000). Under the provisions of subdivision (ii)(B)(1), the unrecovered allowance is $600 (i.e., $3,600 − $3,000), and it must be recovered in the taxable year following the final recovery year, that is, in the taxable year following the fifteenth recovery year. A's allowable deduction for 1985 is $3,200 (i.e., .08 × $40,000).

Example (2). Assume the same facts as in example (1) except that A acquires the replacement property on January 1, 1984. A's allowable deduction for 1984 is $3,533.33 (i.e., [(10/12 × .09) + (2/12 × .08)] × $40,000). Under the provisions of subdivision (ii)(B)(2), the unrecovered allowance is $2,666.67 (i.e., $6,800 − $4,133.33), and it must be recovered in the taxable year following the final recovery year, that is, in the taxable year following the fifteenth recovery year. A's allowable deduction for 1985 is $2,800 (i.e., .07 × $40,000).

Example (3). Assume the same facts as in example (1) except that A acquires the replacement property on the same day as the conversion (March 3, 1983). A's allowable deduction for 1983 for the converted property is $600 (i.e., (2/12 × .09) × $40,000). A's allowable deduction for 1983 for the replacement property is $3,000 (i.e., (10/12 × .09) × $40,000). A's allowable deduction for 1984 is $3,200 (i.e., $40,000 × .08).

Example (4). On February 3, 1981, B, a calendar year taxpayer, purchases for $100,000 and places in service recovery property which is 15-year real property (other than low income housing). On June 25, 1981, B's property is involuntarily converted. On that same day B acquires replacement property with the same basis as the converted property. B's allowable deduction for 1981 for the converted property is $4,000 (i.e., 4/11 × .11 × $100,000). B's allowable deduction for 1981 for the replacement property is $7,000 (i.e., 7/11 × .11 × $100,000). B's allowable deduction for 1982 is $10,000 (i.e., $100,000 × .10).

(2) Section 1031 transactions. (i) Allowable deductions. In a transaction to which section 1031 applies, the allowable deduction for the exchanged and acquired properties shall be determined under the principles of subparagraph (1) of this paragraph. Similarly, any excess of the unadjusted basis of the acquired property over the adjusted basis of the exchanged property shall be treated as newly purchased ACRS property, and any excess of the adjusted basis of the exchanged property over the unadjusted basis of the acquired property shall be recovered under the principles of § 1.168-2(d)(3) (relating to redeterminations).

(ii) Examples. The provisions of paragraph (f)(2)(i) may be illustrated by the following examples:

Example (1). In 1981 A, a calendar year taxpayer, purchases for $12,000 and places in service recovery property which is 3-year recovery property. Under section 168(b)(1) and § 1.168-2(b)(1), the allowable deductions for the first and second recovery years are $3,000 (i.e., .25 × $12,000) and $4,560 (i.e., .38 × $12,000), respectively. On March 3, 1983, A exchanges this property and $1,000 cash for property of a "like kind." A's 1983 allowable deduction for the exchanged property is $740 (i.e., 2/12 × .37 × $12,000). A's basis in the acquired property is $4,700. The acquired property is treated the same as the exchanged property with respect to $3,700, which is so much of the basis in the acquired property as does not exceed the adjusted basis in the exchanged property. However, in computing the allowable deduction with respect to such basis, A's unadjusted basis in the exchanged property ($12,000) is used. Therefore, A's 1983 allowable deduction for the acquired property with respect to the substituted basis is $3,700 (i.e., 10/12 × .37 × $12,000). The remaining $1,000 of basis in the acquired property is treated as newly purchased ACRS property placed in service in 1983. A may choose any applicable recovery period and recovery method for such basis and need not use the same recovery period and recovery method used for the exchanged property. If A uses the tables provided in section 168(b)(1) and § 1.168-2(b)(1), for 1983, 1984, and 1985, A is entitled to additional allowable deductions of $250, $380, and $370, respectively.

Example (2). On February 8, 1981, B, a calendar year taxpayer, purchases for $80,000 and places in service 15-year real property (other than low income housing). Under the provisions of section 168(b)(2) and § 1.168-2(b)(2), the allowable deduction for 1981 is $8,800 (i.e., .11 × $80,000). On March 3, 1982, B exchanges this property and $20,000 cash for property of a "like kind." B's 1982 allowable deduction for the exchanged property is $1,333.33 (i.e., 2/12 × .10 × $80,000). B's basis in the acquired property is $89,866.67. The acquired property is treated the same as the exchanged property with respect to $69,866.67, which is so much of the basis in the acquired property as does not exceed the adjusted basis in the exchanged property. However, in computing the allowable deduction with respect to such basis, B's unadjusted basis in the exchanged property ($80,000) is used. Therefore, B's 1982 and 1983 allowable deductions for the acquired property with respect to the substituted basis are $6,666.66 (i.e., 10/12 × .10 × $80,000) and $7,200 (i.e., .09 × $80,000), respectively. The remaining $20,000 of basis in the acquired property is treated as newly purchased ACRS property placed in service in March 1982. B may choose any applicable recovery period and recovery method for this basis and need not use the same period and method used for the exchanged property. If B uses the tables prescribed in § 1.168-2(b)(2), B's 1982 allowable deduction for this basis is $2,000 (i.e., $20,000 × .10).

(3) Transfers of property by gift. (i) Allowable deductions. With respect to recovery property which is transferred by gift (where the donee's basis is determined under section 1015), the allowable deduction for the taxable year of the gift shall be apportioned between the donor and donee under the principles of paragraphs (b) (including paragraph (b)(4)(ii)) and (f)(1) of this section, and the donee shall be treated as the donor for subsequent taxable years to the extent that the donee's basis is carried over from the donor. That portion of the donee's basis (as determined under section 1015) in the property that exceeds the donor's adjusted basis immediately preceding the gift shall be treated as newly purchased ACRS property. The donee may choose any applicable recovery period and recovery method with respect to such excess and need not use the donor's recovery period and recovery method.

(ii) Example. The provisions of paragraph (f)(3)(i) may be illustrated by the following example:

Example. In 1981 A, a calendar year taxpayer, purchases for $12,000 and places in service 5-year recovery property. Under section 168(b)(1) and § 1.168-2(b)(1), the allowable deduction for 1981 is $1,800 (i.e., .15 × $12,000). On March 15, 1982, A transfers the property by gift to B (another calendar year taxpayer) who continues to use it as recovery property. A's 1982 allowable deduction is $440 (i.e., 2/12 × .22 × $12,000). Under section 1015, B's basis in the property is determined to be $11,000. In the hands of B, the donee, the property is treated the same as in the hands of the donor with respect to $9,760, which is so much of the carryover basis as does not exceed the donor's adjusted basis in the property immediately preceding the gift. However, in computing the allowable deduction with respect to such basis, the donor's unadjusted basis ($12,000) is used. Therefore, B's 1982 allowable deduction with respect to such basis is $2,200 (i.e., 10/12 × .22 × $12,000). The remaining $1,240 (i.e., $11,000 − $9,760) of basis is treated as newly purchased ACRS property. B may choose any applicable recovery period and recovery method for such basis and need not use the donor's recovery period and recovery method.

(4) Transfers of property by reason of death. Where recovery property is transferred by reason of the death of the taxpayer, the allowable deduction for the taxpayer's taxable year which ends upon his death shall be governed by the rules applicable to short taxable years. See § 1.168-2(f).

Proposed § 1.168-6 Gain or loss on dispositions. [*For Preamble, see ¶ 150,941*]

Caution: The Treasury has not yet amended Reg § 1.168-6 to reflect changes made by P.L. 101-508, P.L. 101-239, P.L. 100-647, P.L. 99-514, P.L. 98-369.

(a) General rule. Except as provided in § 1.168-2(h) (relating to mass assets), where recovery property is disposed of during a taxable year, the following rules shall apply:

(1) If the asset is disposed of by sale or exchange, gain or loss shall be recognized as provided under the applicable provisions of the Code.

(2) If the asset is disposed of by physical abandonment, loss shall be recognized in the amount of the adjusted basis of the asset at the time of the abandonment. For a loss to qualify for recognition under this subparagraph (2), the taxpayer must intend to discard the asset irrevocably so that he will neither use the asset again, nor retrieve it for sale, exchange, or other disposition.

(3) If the asset is disposed of other than by sale or exchange or physical abandonment (as, for example, where the asset is transferred to a supplies or scrap account), gain shall not be recognized. Loss shall be recognized in the amount of the excess of the adjusted basis of the asset over its fair market value at the time of the disposition. No loss shall be recognized upon the conversion of property to personal use.

(b) Definitions. *(1)* See § 1.168-2(l)(1) for the definition of "disposition," which excludes the retirement of a structural component of 15-year real property. Thus, no loss shall be recognized on such retirement, and the unadjusted basis of the property under § 1.168-2(d) shall not be reduced. For example, if a taxpayer replaces the roof on 15-year real property, no loss is recognized upon the retirement of the replaced roof, and the unadjusted basis of the property continues to be recovered over the remaining period. For determination of the deductions allowable under section 168 with respect to the expenditures paid or incurred to replace the roof, see § 1.168-2(e).

(2) The adjusted basis of an asset at the time of its disposition is its unadjusted basis, as provided in § 1.168-2, adjusted as prescribed in § 1.1011-1.

§ 1.168(a)-1 Modified accelerated cost recovery system.

(a) Section 168 determines the depreciation allowance for tangible property that is of a character subject to the allowance for depreciation provided in section 167(a) and that is placed in service after December 31, 1986 (or after July 31,

1986, if the taxpayer made an election under section 203(a)(1)(B) of the Tax Reform Act of 1986; 100 Stat. 2143). Except for property excluded from the application of section 168 as a result of section 168(f) or as a result of a transitional rule, the provisions of section 168 are mandatory for all eligible property. The allowance for depreciation under section 168 constitutes the amount of depreciation allowable under section 167(a). The determination of whether tangible property is property of a character subject to the allowance for depreciation is made under section 167 and the regulations under section 167.

(b) This section is applicable on and after February 27, 2004.

T.D. 9314, 2/26/2007.

§ 1.168(b)-1 Definitions.

(a) Definitions. For purposes of section 168 and the regulations under section 168, the following definitions apply:

(1) Depreciable property is property that is of a character subject to the allowance for depreciation as determined under section 167 and the regulations under section 167.

(2) MACRS property is tangible, depreciable property that is placed in service after December 31, 1986 (or after July 31, 1986, if the taxpayer made an election under section 203(a)(1)(B) of the Tax Reform Act of 1986; 100 Stat. 2143) and subject to section 168, except for property excluded from the application of section 168 as a result of section 168(f) or as a result of a transitional rule.

(3) Unadjusted depreciable basis is the basis of property for purposes of section 1011 without regard to any adjustments described in section 1016(a)(2) and (3). This basis reflects the reduction in basis for the percentage of the taxpayer's use of property for the taxable year other than in the taxpayer's trade or business (or for the production of income), for any portion of the basis the taxpayer properly elects to treat as an expense under section 179, section 179C, or any similar provision, and for any adjustments to basis provided by other provisions of the Internal Revenue Code and the regulations under the Code (other than section 1016(a)(2) and (3)) (for example, a reduction in basis by the amount of the disabled access credit pursuant to section 44(d)(7)). For property subject to a lease, see section 167(c)(2).

(4) Adjusted depreciable basis is the unadjusted depreciable basis of the property, as defined in § 1.168(b)-1(a)(3), less the adjustments described in section 1016(a)(2) and (3).

(b) Effective date. This section is applicable on or after February 27, 2004.

T.D. 9314, 2/26/2007.

§ 1.168(d)-0 Table of contents for the applicable convention rules.

This section lists the major paragraphs in § 1.168(d)-1.

§ 1.168(d)-1 Applicable conventions. Half-year and mid-quarter conventions.

(a) In general.

(b) Additional rules for determining whether the mid-quarter convention applies and for applying the applicable convention.

(1) Property described in section 168(f).

(2) Listed property.

(3) Property placed in service and disposed of in the same taxable year.

(4) Aggregate basis of property.

(5) Special rules for affiliated groups.

(6) Special rule for partnerships and S corporations.

(7) Certain nonrecognition transactions.

(c) Disposition of property subject to the half-year or mid-quarter convention.

(1) In general.

(2) Example.

(d) Effective date.

T.D. 8444, 10/28/92.

§ 1.168(d)-1 Applicable conventions--half-year and mid-quarter conventions.

Caution: The Treasury has not yet amended Reg § 1.168(d)-1 to reflect changes made by P.L. 110-343.

(a) In general. Under section 168(d), the half-year convention applies to depreciable property (other than certain real property described in section 168(d)(2)) placed in service during a taxable year, unless the mid-quarter convention applies to the property. Under section 168(d)(3)(A), the mid-quarter convention applies to depreciable property (other than certain real property described in section 168(d)(2)) placed in service during a taxable year if the aggregate basis of property placed in service during the last three months of the taxable year exceeds 40 percent of the aggregate basis of property placed in service during the taxable year (" the 40-percent test"). Thus, if the depreciable property is placed in service during a taxable year that consists of three months or less, the mid-quarter convention applies to the property. Under section 168(d)(3)(B)(i), the depreciable basis of nonresidential real property, residential rental property, and any railroad grading or tunnel bore is disregarded in applying the 40-percent test. For rules regarding property that is placed in service and disposed of in the same taxable year, see paragraph (b)(3) of this section. For the definition of "aggregate basis of property," see paragraph (b)(4) of this section.

(b) Additional rules for determining whether the mid-quarter convention applies and for applying the applicable convention. *(1) Property described in section 168(f).* In determining whether the 40-percent test is satisfied for a taxable year, the depreciable basis of property described in section 168(f) (property to which section 168 does not apply) is not taken into account.

(2) Listed property. The depreciable basis of listed property (as defined in section 280F(d)(4) and the regulations thereunder) placed in service during a taxable year is taken into account (unless otherwise excluded) in applying the 40-percent test.

(3) Property placed in service and disposed of in the same taxable year.

(i) Under section 168(d)(3)(B)(ii), the depreciable basis of property placed in service and disposed of in the same taxable year is not taken into account in determining whether the 40-percent test is satisfied. However, the depreciable basis of property placed in service, disposed of, subsequently reacquired, and again placed in service, by the taxpayer in the same taxable year must be taken into account in applying the 40-percent test, but the basis of the property is only taken into account on the later of the dates that the property is placed in service by the taxpayer during the taxable year. Further, see §§ 1.168(i)-6(c)(4)(v)(B) and 1.168(i)-6(f) for rules relating to property placed in service and exchanged or involuntarily converted during the same taxable year.

(ii) The applicable convention, as determined under this section, applies to all depreciable property (except nonresidential real property, residential rental property, and any railroad grading or tunnel bore) placed in service by the taxpayer during the taxable year, excluding property placed in service and disposed of in the same taxable year. However, see §§ 1.168(i)-6(c)(4)(v)(A) and 1.168(i)-6(f) for rules relating to MACRS property that has a basis determined under section 1031(d) or section 1033(b). No depreciation deduction is allowed for property placed in service and disposed of during the same taxable year. However, see § 1.168(k)-1(f)(1) for rules relating to qualified property or 50-percent bonus depreciation property, and § 1.1400L(b)-1(f)(1) for rules relating to qualified New York Liberty Zone property, that is placed in service by the taxpayer in the same taxable year in which either a partnership is terminated as a result of a technical termination under section 708(b)(1)(B) or the property is transferred in a transaction described in section 168(i)(7).

(4) Aggregate basis of property. For purposes of the 40-percent test, the term "aggregate basis of property" means the sum of the depreciable bases of all items of depreciable property that are taken into account in applying the 40-percent test. "Depreciable basis" means the basis of depreciable property for purposes of determining gain under sections 1011 through 1024. The depreciable basis for the taxable year the property is placed in service reflects the reduction in basis for—

(i) Any portion of the basis the taxpayer properly elects to treat as an expense under section 179;

(ii) Any adjustment to basis under section 48(q); and

(iii) The percentage of the taxpayer's use of property for the taxable year other than in the taxpayer's trade or business (or for the production of income), but is determined before any reduction for depreciation under section 167(a) for that taxable year.

(5) Special rules for affiliated groups. (i) In the case of a consolidated group (as defined in § 1.1502-1(h)), all members of the group that are included on the consolidated return are treated as one taxpayer for purposes of applying the 40-percent test, Thus, the depreciable bases of all property placed in service by members of a consolidated group during a consolidated return year are taken into account (unless otherwise excluded) in applying the 40-percent test to determine whether the mid-quarter convention applies to property placed in service by the members during the consolidated return year. The 40-percent test is applied separately to the depreciable bases of property placed in service by any member of an affiliated group that is not included in a consolidated return for the taxable year in which the property is placed in service.

(ii) In the case of a corporation formed by a member or members of a consolidated group and that is itself a member of the consolidated group ("newly-formed subsidiary"), the depreciable bases of property placed in service by the newly-formed subsidiary in the consolidated return year in which it is formed is included with the depreciable bases of property placed in service during the consolidated return year by the other members of the consolidated group in applying the 40-percent test. If depreciable property is placed in service by a newly-formed subsidiary during the consolidated return year in which it was formed, the newly-formed subsidiary is considered as being in existence for the entire consolidated return year for purposes of applying the applicable convention to determine when the recovery period begins.

(iii) The provisions of paragraph (b)(5)(ii) of this section are illustrated by the following example.

Example. Assume a member of a consolidated group that files its return on a calendar-year basis forms a subsidiary on August 1. The subsidiary places depreciable property in service on August 5. If the mid-quarter convention applies to property placed in service by the members of the consolidated group (including the newly-formed subsidiary), the property placed in service by the subsidiary on August 5 is deemed placed in service on the mid-point of the third quarter of the consolidated return year (i.e., August 15). If the mid-quarter convention does not apply, the property is deemed placed in service on the mid-point of the consolidated return year (i.e., July 1).

(iv) In the case of a corporation that joins or leaves a consolidated group, the depreciable bases of property placed in service by the corporation joining or leaving the group during the portion of the consolidated return year that the corporation is a member of the consolidated group is included with the depreciable bases of property placed in service during the consolidated return year by the other members in applying the 40-percent test. The depreciable bases of property placed in service by the joining or leaving member in the taxable year before it joins or after it leaves the consolidated group is not taken into account by the consolidated group in applying the 40-percent test for the consolidated return year. If a corporation leaves a consolidated group and joins another consolidated group, each consolidated group takes into account, in applying the 40-percent test, the depreciable bases of property placed in service by the corporation while a member of the group.

(v) The provisions of paragraph (b)(5)(iv) of this section are illustrated by the following example.

Example. Assume Corporations A and B file a consolidated return on a calendar-year basis. Corporation C, also a calendar-year taxpayer, enters the consolidated group on July 1 and is included on the consolidated return for that taxable year. The depreciable bases of property placed in service by C during the period of July 1 to December 31 is included with the depreciable bases of property placed in service by A and B during the entire consolidated return year in applying the 40-percent test. The depreciable bases of property placed in service by C from January 1 to June 30 is not taken into account by the consolidated group in applying the 40-percent test. If C was a member of another consolidated group during the period from January 1 to June 30, that consolidated group would include the depreciable bases of property placed in service by C during that period.

(vi) A corporation that joins or leaves a consolidated group during a consolidated year is considered as being a member of the consolidated group for the entire consolidated return year for purposes of applying the applicable convention to determine when the recovery period begins for depreciable property placed in service by the corporation during the portion of the consolidated return year that the corporation is a member of the group.

(vii) If depreciable property is placed in service by a corporation in the taxable year ending immediately before it joins a consolidated group or beginning immediately after it leaves a consolidated group, the applicable convention is applied to the property under either the full taxable year rules or the short taxable year rules, as applicable.

(viii) The provisions of paragraphs (d)(5)(vi) and (vii) of this section are illustrated by the following example.

Example. Assume that on July 1, C, a calendar-year corporation, joins a consolidated group that files a return on a calendar-year basis. The short taxable year rules apply to C for the period of January 1 to June 30. However, in applying the applicable convention to determine when the recovery period begins for depreciable property placed in service for the period of July 1 to December 31, C is considered as being a member of the consolidated group for the entire consolidated return year. Thus, if the half-year convention applies to depreciable property placed in service by the consolidated group (taking into account the depreciable bases of property placed in service by C after June 30), the property is deemed placed in service on the mid-point of the consolidated return year (i.e., July 1, if the group did not have a short taxable year).

(ix) In the case of a transfer of depreciable property between members of a consolidated group, the following special rules apply for purposes of applying the 40-percent test. Property that is placed in service by one member of a consolidated group and transferred to another member of the same group is considered as placed in service on the date that it is placed in service by the transferor member, and the date it is placed in service by the transferee member is disregarded. In the case of multiple transfers of property between members of a consolidated group, the property is considered as placed in service on the date that the first member places the property in service, and the dates it is placed in service by other members are disregarded. The depreciable basis of the transferred property that is taken into account in applying the 40-percent test is the depreciable basis of the property in the hands of the transferor member (as determined under paragraph (b)(4) of this section), or, in the case of multiple transfers of property between members, the depreciable basis in the hands of the first member that placed the property in service.

(x) The provisions of paragraph (b)(5)(ix) of this section are illustrated by the following example.

Example. Assume the ABC consolidated group files its return on a calendar-year basis. A, a member of the consolidated group, purchases depreciable property costing $50,000 and places the property in service on January 5, 1991. On December 1, 1991, the property is transferred for $75,000 to B, another member of the consolidated group. In applying the 40-percent test to the members of the consolidated group for 1991, the property is considered as placed in service on January 5, the date that A placed the property in service, and the depreciable basis of the property that is taken into account is $50,000.

(6) Special rule for partnerships and S corporations. In the case of property placed in service by a partnership or an S corporation, the 40-percent test is generally applied at the partnership or corporate level. However, if a partnership or an S corporation is formed or availed of for the principal purpose of either avoiding the application of the mid-quarter convention or having the mid-quarter convention apply where it otherwise would not, the 40-percent test is applied at the partner, shareholder, or other appropriate level.

(7) Certain nonrecognition transactions. (i) Except as provided in paragraph (b)(6) of this section, if depreciable property is transferred in a transaction described in section 168(i)(7)(B)(i) (other than in a transaction between members of a consolidated group) in the same taxable year that the property is placed in service by the transferor, the 40-percent test is applied by treating the transferred property as placed in service by the transferee on the date of transfer. Thus, if the aggregate basis of property (including the transferred property) placed in service by the transferee during the last three months of its taxable year exceeds 40 percent of the aggregate basis of property (including the transferred property) placed in service by the transferee during the taxable year, the mid-quarter convention applies to the transferee's depreciable property, including the transferred property. The depreciable basis of the transferred property is not taken into account by the transferor in applying the 40-percent test for the taxable year that the transferor placed the property in service.

(ii) In applying the applicable convention to determine when the recovery period for the transferred property begins, the date on which the transferor placed the property in service must be used. Thus, for example, if the mid-quarter convention applies, the recovery period for the transferred property begins on the mid-point of the quarter of the taxable year that the transferor placed the property in service. If the transferor placed the transferred property in service in a short taxable year, then for purposes of applying the applicable convention and allocating the depreciation deduction between the transferor and the transferee, the transferor is treated as having a full 12-month taxable year commencing on the first day of the short taxable year. The depreciation deduction for the transferor's taxable year in which the property was placed in service is allocated between the transferor and the transferee based on the number of months in the transferor's taxable year that each party held the property in service. For purposes of allocating the depreciation deduction, the transferor takes into account the month in which the property was placed in service but does not take into account the month in which the property was transferred. The transferee is allocated the remaining portion of the depreciation deduction for the transferor's taxable year in which the property was transferred. For the remainder of the transferee's current taxable year (if the transferee has a different taxable year than the transferor) and for subsequent taxable years, the depreciation deduction for the transferee is calculated by allocating to the transferee's taxable year the depreciation attributable to each recovery year, or portion thereof, that falls within the transferee's taxable year.

(iii) If the applicable convention for the transferred property has not been determined by the time the transferor files its income tax return for the year of transfer because the transferee's taxable year has not ended, the transferor may use either the mid-quarter or the half-year convention in determining the depreciation deduction for the property. However, the transferor must specify on the depreciation form filed for the taxable year that the applicable convention has not been determined for the property. If the transferee determines that a different convention applies to the transferred property, the transferor should redetermine the depreciation deduction on the property, and, within the period of limitation, should file an amended income tax return for the taxable year and pay any additional tax due plus interest.

(iv) The provisions of this paragraph (b)(7) are illustrated by the following example.

Example. (i) During 1991, C, a calendar-year taxpayer, purchases satellite equipment costing $100,000, and computer equipment costing $15,000. The satellite equipment is placed in service in January, and the computer equipment in February. On October 1, C transfers the computer equipment to Z Partnership in a transaction described in section 721. During 1991, Z, a calendar-year partnership, purchases 30 office desks for a total of $15,000. The desks are placed in service in June. These are the only items of depreciable property placed in service by C and Z during 1991.

(ii) In applying the 40-percent test, because C transferred the computer equipment in a transaction described in section 168(i)(7)(B)(i) in the same taxable year that C placed it in service, the computer equipment is treated as placed in service by the transferee, Z, on the date of transfer, October 1. The 40-percent test is satisfied with respect to Z, because the computer equipment is placed in service during the last three months of Z's taxable year and its basis ($15,000) exceeds 40 percent of the aggregate basis of property placed in service by Z during the taxable year (desks and computer equipment with an aggregate basis of $30,000).

(iii) In applying the mid-quarter convention to determine when the computer equipment is deemed to be placed in service, the date on which C placed the property in service is used. Accordingly, because C placed the computer equipment in service during the first quarter of its taxable year, the computer equipment is deemed placed in service on February 15, 1991, the mid-point of the first quarter of C's taxable year. The depreciation deduction allowable for C's 1991 taxable year, $5,250 ($15,000 × 40 percent × 10.5/12), is allocated between C and Z based on the number of months in C's taxable year that C and Z held the property in service. Thus, because the property was in service for 11 months during C's 1991 taxable year and C held it for 8 of those 11 months, C is allocated $3,818 (8/11 × $5,250). Z is allocated $1,432, the remaining 3/11 of the $5,250 depreciation deduction for C's 1991 taxable year. For 1992, Z's depreciation deduction for the computer equipment is $3,900, the sum of the remaining 1.5 months of depreciation deduction for the first recovery year and 10.5 months of depreciation deduction for the second recovery year (($15,000 × 40 percent × 1.5/12) + ($9,000 × 40 percent × 10.5/12)).

(c) Disposition of property subject to the half-year or mid-quarter convention. *(1) In general.* If depreciable property is subject to the half-year (or mid-quarter) convention in the taxable year in which it is placed in service, it also is subject to the half-year (or mid-quarter) convention in the taxable year in which it is disposed of.

(2) Example. The provisions of paragraph (c)(1) of this section are illustrated by the following example.

Example. In October 1991, B, a calendar-year taxpayer, purchases and places in service a light general purpose truck costing $10,000. B does not elect to expense any part of the cost of the truck, and this is the only item of depreciable property placed in service by B during 1991. The 40-percent test is satisfied and the mid-quarter convention applies, because the truck is placed in service during the last three months of the taxable year and no other assets are placed in service in that year. In April 1993 (prior to the end of the truck's recovery period), B sells the truck. The mid-quarter convention applies in determining the depreciation deduction for the truck in 1993, the year of disposition.

(d) Effective dates. *(1) In general.* This section applies to depreciable property placed in service in taxable years ending after January 30, 1991. For depreciable property placed in service after December 31, 1986, in taxable years ending on or before January 30, 1991, a taxpayer may use a method other than the method provided in this section in applying the 40-percent test and the applicable convention, provided the method is reasonable and is consistently applied to the taxpayer's property.

(2) Qualified property, 50-percent bonus depreciation property, or qualified New York Liberty Zone property. This section also applies to qualified property under section 168(k)(2) or qualified New York Liberty Zone property under section 1400L(b) acquired by a taxpayer after September 10, 2001, and to 50-percent bonus depreciation property under section 168(k)(4) acquired by a taxpayer after May 5, 2003.

(3) Like-kind exchanges and involuntary conversions. The last sentence in paragraph (b)(3)(i) and the second sentence in paragraph (b)(3)(ii) of this section apply to exchanges to which section 1031 applies, and involuntary conversions to which section 1033 applies, of MACRS property for which the time of disposition and the time of replacement both occur after February 27, 2004.

T.D. 8444, 10/28/92, amend T.D. 9091, 9/5/2003, T.D. 9115, 2/27/2004, T.D. 9283, 8/28/2006, T.D. 9314, 2/26/2007.

§ 5c.168(f)(8)-1 Special rules for leases.

Caution: The Treasury has not yet amended Reg § 5c.168(f)(8)-1 to reflect changes made by P.L. 100-647, P.L. 99-514, P.L. 98-369, P.L. 97-248.

(a) In general. Section 168(f)(8) of the Internal Revenue Code of 1954 provides special rules for characterizing certain agreements as leases and characterizing the parties to the agreement as lessors and lessees for Federal tax law purposes. These rules apply only with respect to qualified leased property. If all the requirements of section 168(f)(8) and §§ 5c.168(f)(8)-2 through 5c.168(f)(8)-11 are met, then the agreement shall be treated as a lease, and the party characterized as the lessor shall be treated as the owner of the property. In such case, the lessor shall be deemed to have entered into the lease in the course of carrying on a trade or business and shall be allowed accelerated cost recovery system (ACRS) deductions under section 168 and the investment tax credit under section 38 with respect to the leased property.

(b) Exception for qualified research expenditures. For purposes of section 44F(b)(2)(A)(iii), the determination of whether any amount is paid or incurred to another person for the right to use personal property in the conduct of qualified research shall be made without regard to the characterization of the transaction as a lease under section 168(f)(8). Thus, if a lessee would be considered the owner of the property without regard to section 168(f)(8), any amounts paid by the lessee under the lease shall not be considered amounts paid or incurred for the right to use the property.

(c) Other factors disregarded. If an agreement meets the requirements of section 168(f)(8) and §§ 5c.168(f)(8)-2 through 5c.168(f)(8)-11, the following factors will not be taken into account in determining whether the transaction is a lease:

(1) Whether the lessor or lessee must take the tax benefits into account in order to determine that a profit is made from the transaction;

(2) The fact that the lessee is the nominal owner of the property for State or local law purposes *(e.g.,* has legal title to the property) and retains the burdens, benefits, and incidents of ownership (such as payment of taxes and maintenance charges with respect to the property);

(3) Whether or not a person other than the lessee may be able to use the property after the lease term;

(4) The fact that the property may (or must) be bought or sold at the end of the lease term at a fixed or determinable price that is more or less than its fair market value at that time;

(5) The fact that the lessee or related party has provided financing or has guaranteed financing for the transaction (other than for the lessor's minimum 10 percent investment); and

(6) The fact that the obligation of any person is subject to any contingency or offset agreement. See, for example, the rent and debt service offset in Example (2) of paragraph (e).

An agreement that meets the requirements of section 168(f)(8) and §§ 5c.168(f)(8)-2 through 5c.168(f)(8)-11 may be treated by the parties as a lease for Federal Tax law purposes only. Similarly, a sale by the lessee of the leased property to the lessor in a transaction where the property is leased back under an agreement that meets the requirements of section 168(f)(8) may be treated by the parties as a sale for Federal tax law purposes only. The agreements need not comply with State law requirements concerning transfer of title, recording, etc.

(d) Ownership in one of the parties. Notwithstanding any other section, if neither the lessor nor the lessee would be the owner of the property without regard to section 168(f)(8), or, if any party with an economic interest in the property (other than the lessor or lessee or any subsequent transferee of their interests) claims ACRS deductions or any investment tax credit with respect to the leased property, an election under section 168(f)(8) with respect to such property shall be void as of the date of the execution of the lease agreement.

(e) Examples. The application of section 168(f)(8) and §§ 5c.168(f)(8)-2 through 5c.168(f)(8)-11 may be illustrated by the following examples:

Example (1). X Corp. wishes to acquire a $1 million piece of equipment which is "qualified leased property" as defined in section 168(f)(8)(D). The equipment has a 10-year economic life and falls within the 5-year ACRS class. Y Corp. is a person meeting the qualifications set forth in section 168(f)(8)(B)(i) and § 5c.168(f)(8)-3 and wishes to be the owner of the property for Federal tax law purposes. Y therefore purchases the equipment from the manufacturer for $1 million, paying $200,000 in cash and borrowing $800,000 from a bank (payable over 9 years and requiring nine equal annual payments of principal and interest of $168,000). Y then leases the equipment to X under an agreement providing for nine annual rental payments of $168,000, and the parties elect in accordance with the provisions of § 5c.168(f)(8)-2 to have the provisions of section 168(f)(8) apply. The time and amount of the rental payments required to be made by X (the "lessee-user") under the lease will be exactly equal to the timing and amount of the principal and interest payments that Y (the "lessor") will be required to make to the bank under its purchase money note. Under these circumstances, Y is treated as the owner and lessor of the property for Federal tax law purposes; it therefore is entitled to the investment tax credit and the ACRS deductions with respect to the property. Y's basis in the property is $1 million. Y must report the rent as income and will be entitled to deduct the interest on the purchase money note. The aggregate payments required to be made by X under the lease are treated as rent in accordance with § 5c.168(f)(8)-7 and are deductible as such.

Example (2). The facts are the same as in example (1) except that X purchases the equipment for $1 million and wishes to transfer ownership of the property for Federal tax law purposes to Y under a sale and leaseback arrangement. Accordingly, X sells the property to Y for $200,000 in cash (which represents the agreed upon compensation for the tax benefits to be enjoyed by Y as lessor) plus a 9-year, $800,000 note calling for nine $168,000 annual payments of principal and interest. Y then leases the property back to X under an agreement providing for nine annual rental payments of $168,000. The parties elect in accordance with the provisions of § 5c.168(f)(8)-2 to have the provisions of section 168(f)(8) apply. The timing and amount of the rental payments required to be made by X (as the lessee-user) under the lease will be exactly equal to the timing and amount of the principal and interest payments that Y will be required to make to X under Y's purchase money note, so that the only cash transferred between X and Y is the $200,000 down payment. Y's obligation to make debt service payments on the note is contingent on X's obligation to make rental payments under the lease. Under these circumstances, Y is treated as the owner and lessor of the property for Federal tax law purposes; it therefore is entitled to the investment tax credit and ACRS deductions with respect to the property. Y's basis in the property is $1 million. Y must report the rent as income and will be entitled to deduct the interest on the purchase money note. No gain or loss will be recognized by X on the sale of the property since the sale price equals X's basis in the property. X must report as income the interest paid by Y on the note and will be entitled to a deduction for the rental payments it makes under the lease in accordance with § 5c.168(f)(8)-7.

Example (3). Assume that in both examples (1) and (2) X has an option to purchase the equipment at the end of the lease term for $1.00. The fact that the property may (or must) be bought or sold at the end of the lease term at a fixed or determinable price that is more or less than its fair market value is not taken into account in determining the status of the transactions as leases under section 168(f)(8).

T.D. 7791, 10/20/81, amend T.D. 7795, 11/10/81.

§ 5f.168(f)(8)-1 Questions and answers concerning transitional rules and related matters regarding certain safe harbor leases.

Caution: The Treasury has not yet amended Reg § 5f.168(f)(8)-1 to reflect changes made by P.L. 100-647, P.L. 99-514, P.L. 98-369.

The following questions and answers concern the transitional rules and related matters regarding certain safe harbor leases under section 208(d) of the Tax Equity and Fiscal Responsibility Act of 1982 (Pub. L. 97-248) ("TEFRA"):

Q-1. If a lessee, prior to the period beginning after December 31, 1980, and ending before July 2, 1982 (the "window period"), enters into a binding contract to acquire property and the property is delivered to the lessee during the window period, is the property eligible for the transitional rule provided in section 208(d)(3) of TEFRA which applies the safe harbor leasing rules of section 168(f)(8) of the Internal Revenue Code of 1954 as in effect before the enactment of TEFRA?

A-1. Yes, assuming all other requirements of the TEFRA transitional rules are met. Section 208(d)(3)(A)(i) and (ii) of TEFRA provide alternative tests under which an item of property may constitute "transitional safe harbor lease property" for purposes of the transitional rules under the modifications to the safe harbor lease provisions of section 168(f)(8). The tests are:

(i) The lease entered into a binding contract to acquire the property;

(ii) The lessee entered into a binding contract to construct the property;

(iii) The property was acquired by the lessee; or

(iv) Construction of the property was commenced by or for the lessee.

These tests are stated in the alternative, and, accordingly, property may be eligible for pre-TEFRA safe harbor leasing if any one of the tests is satisfied. Thus, if a lessee acquired property during the window period, the property may be eligible for pre-TEFRA safe harbor leasing even though a binding contract to acquire the property was executed before the window period. Similarly, if construction of property commences during the window period, the property may be eligible for pre-TEFRA safe harbor leasing even though a binding contract to construct the property was executed before the window period.

Q-2. How do the transitional rules apply to components of an integrated manufacturing, production, or extraction process, none of which would be considered "placed in service" until all of the components are placed in service?

A-2. (i) The transitional rules regarding acquisition, binding contracts, and commencement of construction are applied to each separate item of property which is part of a manufacturing, production, or extraction process. What constitutes a separate item will be determined on a case-by-case basis, taking into account all relevant factors. In general, a discrete component capable of performing a function which is separate from or in addition to the function of other components to which it may be related is a separate item of property; but an item that is integrated into a component which performs a function separate from other components to which it is related is not itself a separate item of property. For example, a bolt or a nut that is used to construct a machine does not constitute a separate item of property. On the other hand, the transitional rules will not be applied to an entire facility as a whole, as was the case under the investment tax credit transition rule of section 50 in *Hawaiian Independent Refinery, Inc. v. United States,* 49 AFTR 2d 675 (Ct. Cl. Tr. Judge 1982), where the taxpayer was held to have constructed a property which consisted of an entire refinery complex. Thus, for example, for purposes of these transitional rules, an oil or gas well, storage tanks, and pipeline located on a lease would not be considered a single item of property. Although each item is related to the production of oil or gas, each is discrete and each is capable of performing a separate function from the other. In addition, in the case of an integrated manufacturing, production, or extraction process, commencement of construction of one item of property within the process would not be considered construction of any other item of property that is part of the process.

(ii) If property qualifies as transitional safe harbor lease property, all direct and indirect costs allocable to the property (except for those described in § 5c.168(f)(8)-6(a)(2)(ii)) and required to be capitalized for Federal income tax purposes will also qualify as transitional safe harbor lease property to the extent such costs are incurred on or before the date on which the property is leased under section 168(f)(8).

(iii) The adjusted basis to the lessor of property leased on or prior to December 1, 1982, under a transitional safe harbor lease shall be deemed to include all direct and indirect costs (including installation costs) described in subdivision (ii) allocable to such property that were incurred before it was leased despite the fact that such costs were not included in the lessor's adjusted basis of such property under the terms of the lease agreement, provided that the parties to such agreement reasonably believed that they had leased the whole of such property. Such costs will be treated as having been included in the lessor's adjusted basis of such safe harbor lease property on the date the lease agreement was executed without regard to any provisions in the lease agreement that limits the dollar amount of the permissible adjustment of the lessor's adjusted basis to such property. To qualify for inclusion of such direct and indirect costs within the basis of such property, the parties to such agreement must file an amended Form 6793, the Safe Harbor Lease Information Return, no later than April 21, 1983, which reflects the parties intent to include installation and other such costs within the basis of such property. For purposes of this subdivision, a transitional safe harbor lease is a lease either which was executed after July 1, 1982, and on or prior to December 1, 1982, or which includes some transitional safe harbor lease property, as defined in TEFRA section 208(d)(3), that was placed in service after July 1, 1982, and on or prior to December 1, 1982.

Q-3. What test will be applied in determining whether an item of property is constructed or acquired by the lessee?

A-3. Except as expressly provided in section 208(d)(3)(D) or (E) of TEFRA, the determination of whether and when any such events occurred with respect to an item of property will generally be made in accordance with the principles and precedents prior to TEFRA under the investment tax credit and depreciation allowance transitional provisions. See §§ 1.48-2(b)(6) and 1.167(c)-1(a)(2), which provide definitions of the term "acquired", and §§ 1.48-2(b)(1) and 1.167(c)-1(a)(1), which provide definitions of the term "constructed by". Also see Rev. Rul. 80-312, 1980-2 C.B. 21, which discusses the factors to be considered in determining when a taxpayer has control over a project being constructed.

In general, for purposes of TEFRA section 208(d)(3), construction of an item of property is considered to have commenced when physical work of a significant nature has begun with respect to the property. Thus, construction does not begin when parts or components which enter into construction are acquired. If property is assembled from purchased parts or components, the commencement of construction occurs when actual assembly of the property begins. If a taxpayer manufactures a major part or component of an item of property for itself, construction will be considered to have begun when the manufacturing of that part or component commences. However, construction of an item of property will not be considered as begun if physical work by the taxpayer relates to minor parts or components. Clearing and grading of land will be considered in determining when construction begins on an item of property only if they are directly associated with the construction of the property.

Q-4. Under section 168(f)(8)(J), the at-risk rules are liberalized for closely held lessors that engage in safe harbor leasing. These rules apply "in the case of property placed in service after the date of enactment of this subparagraph," namely, after September 3, 1982.

Do the liberalized at-risk rules apply in the case where otherwise qualified property is placed in service by a lessee in August of 1982 but is leased by a corporate lessor subject to the at-risk rules after September 3, 1982?

A-4. The liberalized at-risk rule in section 168(f)(8)(J) is applicable in this case because, in determining whether property is placed in service before or after the date of enactment of section 168(f)(8)(J), the relevant date is the date the property is placed in service by the lessor. Additionally, a closely held corporate lessor, which is not a personal service corporation, may lease transitional safe harbor lease property placed in service after September 3, 1982, under the liberalized at-risk rule.

Q-5. Is it necessary for property placed in service by a lessee in December of 1982 to be leased before January 1, 1983, in order to qualify under the general transitional rule of section 208(d)(3)(A) of TEFRA, which requires that the property be placed in service before January 1, 1983?

A-5. The legislative intent of this transitional rule was to provide a 3-month period after property is placed in service by a lessee in which a safe harbor lease could be entered into. *Cf.* section 209(c) of TEFRA (3-month window applies to true leases entered into after 1983). The legislative intent further was to permit property to qualify as transitional safe harbor lease property if it was placed in service by the end of 1982 by a lessee. Accordingly, transitional safe harbor lease property placed in service in 1982 by a lessee may be leased in a safe harbor lease transaction within 3 months after it is placed in service by the lessee without losing its status as transitional safe harbor lease property.

However, for all other purposes of the Code other than section 168(f)(8)(D)(i), section 168(f)(8)(D)(viii)(II) will apply and the property will be treated as originally placed in service not earlier than the date that the property is used under the lease. Thus, for example, if transitional safe harbor lease property is placed in service in December of 1982 and leased under section 168(f)(8) in January of 1983, the property will not lose its status as transitional safe harbor lease property, but the basis adjustment rules of section 48(g) will apply with respect to the property.

Q-6. Will a contract to acquire property be considered "binding" for purposes of section 208(d)(3)(A)(i) of TEFRA if the contract contains no liquidated damages clause?

A-6. Generally, an irrevocable contract which contains no provision for liquidated damages in the event of breach or cancellation would be considered binding. Moreover, in determining the amount of the lessee's potential liability, the fair market value of the property will not be taken into account. For example, if a lessee entered into an irrevocable contract to purchase an asset for $100 and the contract contained no provision for liquidated damages, the contract would be considered binding notwithstanding the fact that the property at all times after July 1, 1982, had a value of $99 and under local law the seller could only recover the difference in the event the lessee failed to perform. On the other hand, if the contract by its terms provided for liquidated damages of less than 5 percent of the purchase price which is in lieu of any damages allowable by law, in the event of breach or cancellation, the contract would not be considered binding.

Q-7. How does the 50-percent limitation on lessors in section 168(i)(1) and the 45-percent limitation on lessees in section 168(f)(8)(D)(ii) apply to corporations which are part of an affiliated group filing consolidated returns?

A-7. Both the 50-percent limitation on lessors and the 45-percent limitation on lessees will be applied on a consolidated basis for corporations filing consolidated returns.

Q-8. Section 168(f)(8)(J) liberalized the at-risk rules for safe harbor leasing and provides that in cases where the safe harbor lessee would be considered the owner of the property without regard to the safe harbor lease, the lessor is considered to be at risk with respect to the property in an amount equal to the amount the lessee is considered at risk with respect to such property as determined under section 465.

Will a corporate lessor that would ordinarily be subject to the at-risk rules under section 465 be exempt from such rules under section 168(f)(8)(J) in a situation where acquisition of the leased property is financed with nonrecourse debt by a lessee that is not subject to the at-risk rules?

A-8. Yes. The liberalized at-risk rules of section 168(f)(8)(J) will apply in cases where the lessee's ACRS deductions and investment tax credit with respect to the property would not have been limited under the at-risk rules had the parties not elected treatment under section 168(f)(8).

Q-9. Section 168(f)(8)(J)(ii) excepts certain service corporations from the liberalized at-risk rules of section 168(f)(8)(J)(i). Does the exception in subdivision (ii) also extend to subsidiaries of such service corporations that file consolidated returns?

A-9. Yes. The liberalized at-risk rules of section 168(f)(8)(J)(i) will not apply to any subsidiary filing a consolidated return with a service organization described in section 168(f)(8)(J)(ii).

Q-10. Will property lose its status as transitional safe harbor lease property under section 208(d)(3) of TEFRA solely by reason of the fact that the person who is a party to a binding contract to acquire the property assigns his rights in the contract to another person?

A-10. When a person who is a party to a binding contract transfers his rights in the contract (or the property covered by the contract) to another person and the transferor (or a corporation which is a member of the same affiliated group as the transferor) will use the property under a lease for a period not less than 50 percent of the appropriate recovery period for the leased property under section 168(c), then to the extent of the transferred rights, this other person will succeed to the position of the transferor with respect to the binding contract and the property. Accordingly, under these circumstances, property will not lose its status as transitional safe harbor lease property.

In addition, property will not be disqualified as transitional safe harbor lease property solely by reason of a transfer by a person of his rights in a contract (or the property covered by the contract) in a transaction in which the basis of the property in the hands of the transferee is determined by reference to its basis in the hands of the transferor *(e.g.,* transfers governed by sections 332, 351, 361, 721, 731). Thus, for example, if a corporation entered into a binding contract for the construction or acquisition of property prior to July 1, 1982, and after such date assigned the contract to a corporation within the same affiliated group which files consolidated returns, the assignee will be entitled to treat the property acquired pursuant to the contract as transitional safe harbor lease property, assuming the property would have so qualified in the hands of the transferor. Similarly, if a joint venture or partnership between two corporations entered into a binding contract or commenced construction of property before July 2, 1982, but dissolved and distributed its assets to the partners or joint venturers after July 2, 1982, the joint venturers or partners may treat the assets as transitional safe harbor lease property, assuming the property would have so qualified had the joint venture or partnership remained in existence.

Q-11. During 1982, Corporation Y placed in service section 38 property with a total cost of $100X. On August 15, 1982, Corporation Y placed in service the last component of an entire facility within the meaning of § 5c.168(f)(8)-

6(b)(2). The facility had a total cost basis of $40X, of which $30X was transitional safe harbor lease property within the meaning of section 208(d)(3) of TEFRA and $10X was not transitional safe harbor lease property. On November 1, 1982, Corporation Y sold and leased back under a section 168(f)(8) lease the $30X of transitional safe harbor lease property in the facility.

Will the entire facility rule in § 5c.168(f)(8)-6(b)(2) apply in this situation where the taxpayer has not leased all of the section 38 property in the facility?

A-11. No. The placed in service date, for purposes of the rule requiring that property be leased within 3 months after such property was placed in service by the lessee, would be determined under the entire facility rule in § 5c.168(f)(8)-6(b)(2) only if Corporation Y had leased all the qualified leased property in the facility. Since Corporation Y leased only the $30X of transitional section 38 property, of the facility and did not lease the $10X of nontransitional property, Corporation Y may not rely on the entire facility rule of § 5c.168(f)(8)-6(b) (2) for purposes of determining the placed in service date for the property under the section 168(f)(8) lease.

Q-12. Assume the same facts as in Q-11, except that Corporation Y had also placed in service by August 15, 1982, $30X of miscellaneous machinery and equipment all of which was transitional safe harbor lease property within the meaning of section 208(d)(3) of TEFRA. On November 1, 1982, in addition to the $30X of transitional property in the facility, Corporation Y also sold and leased back under a separate section 168(f)(8) lease the $30X of miscellaneous machinery and equipment.

Will the entire facility rule in § 5c.168(f)(8)-6(b)(2) apply in this situation to the $30X of transitional property in the facility?

A-12. Yes. Since Corporation Y leased $30X of transitional machinery and equipment and the $30X of the facility which consisted of transitional property, Corporation Y can lease none of the nontransitional property in the facility because, by reason of the 45-percent cap on lessees contained in section 168(f)(8)(D)(ii) and (iii) and (I), it is not qualified leased property for purposes of section 168(f)(8). Thus, on the facts, Corporation Y has leased all the qualified leased property in the facility.

Q-13. Corporation X constructed a manufacturing complex consisting of three integrated operational components, each with a different ADR present class life midpoint, which together constitute an "entire facility" within the meaning of § 5c.168(f)(8)-6(b)(2). The last components of the facility were placed in service on August 15, 1982. On October 1, 1982, Corporation X sold to Corporation Z and leased back under section 168(f)(8) all the qualified leased property of the facility.

For purposes of the rule requiring that property be leased within 3 months after such property was placed in service by the lessee, will the leased components of the entire facility be considered placed in service by the lessee on August 15, 1982, the date the last components were placed in service, if the components are leased at one time pursuant to documents consisting of three section 168(f)(8) leases with different terms to reflect the different ADR midpoint lives of the qualified leased property in the facility?

A-13. Yes. If the entire facility rule in § 5c.168(f)(8)-6(b)(2) applies, the facility components which were placed in service prior to August 15, 1982, will be treated as placed in service by the lessee on August 15, 1982, for purposes of the 3-month rule. This rule will apply if all the qualified leased property of the facility is leased at one time. The documentation may be in the form of multiple, simultaneously executed agreements or maybe in the form of an agreement comprised of one or more parts or schedules. Each of the multiple agreements, or each of the parts or schedules of an agreement, may have different lease terms for property with different ADR midpoint lives, so long as each such agreement or part of schedule individually would be treated as a lease under section 168(f)(8), taking into account the entire facility rule, with lease terms commencing on the same date. A single transaction effected by multiple agreements or by an agreement with one or more parts or schedules will meet the maximum lease term requirement of § 5c.168(f)(8)-5(b) so long as each agreement or each part or schedule of an agreement meets the maximum lease term requirement.

Q-14. Under § 5c.168(f)(8)-6(b)(2), the special rule for facilities applies only if the entire facility is leased under a section 168(f)(8) lease.

Will a transaction not qualify under section 168(f)(8) if the parties, acting in good faith, omit an insubstantial portion of the qualified lease property from the lease?

A-14. No. The facility rule of § 5c.168(f)(8)-6(b)(2) will apply if the parties, acting in good faith, substantially comply with its terms.

Q-15. When will construction of an aircraft be considered to have been begun after June 25, 1981, and before February 20, 1982, for purposes of TEFRA Section 208(d)(3)(D)?

A-15. Construction of an aircraft will be considered to have been begun after June 25, 1981, and before February 20, 1982, if during such period any of the following events occurred:

(i) Construction or reconstruction of a subassembly designated for the aircraft was commenced;

(ii) Construction of a lot increment of subassemblies (one or more of which was designated for the aircraft) was commenced; or

(iii) The stub wing join occurred.

Q-16. Does the definition of assets used in the manufacture or production of steel for purposes of TEFRA section 208(d)(2)(F) include all assets used in this function (such as electrical and steam generators and distribution equipment, coke oven by-product equipment) although not necessarily includible in the former ADR guideline class for primary steel mill products?

A-16. Yes, all assets that are used, in their primary function, as an integral part of the steel manufacturing or production process are included. *Cf.* § 1.48-1(d)(4). However, the steel manufacturing or production process does not include processing beyond the production of primary ferrous metals (as defined by the ADR Class for Manufacture of Primary Ferrous Metals).

Q-17. Where a qualified mass commuting vehicle meets the requirements for both the TEFRA section 208(d)(2) transitional rule and the TEFRA section 208(d)(5) special rule for mass commuting vehicles, which provision will control?

A-17. The general transitional rule of TEFRA section 208(d)(2) will apply. Thus, pursuant to TEFRA section 208(d)(2)(B), the provisions of section 168(f)(8)(J), but not the provisions of section 168(i)(1), will apply only to such property. If the general transitional rule does not apply to a specific mass commuting vehicle, the provision of section 168(i)(1) applies to the lessor who leases such vehicle.

Q-18. Does the definition of a qualified mass commuting vehicle include component parts of a qualified mass commuting vehicle—such as an undercarriage of a subway car or the costs of rehabilitation or reconstruction of a mass commuting vehicle (or component part thereof)?

A-18. Yes.

T.D. 7850, 11/5/92, amend T.D. 7879, 3/21/83.

§ 1.168(f)(8)-1T Safe-harbor lease information returns concerning qualified mass commuting vehicles (temporary).

In general. Form 6793, Safe Harbor Lease Information Return, is obsolete for safe harbor lease agreements executed after June 30, 1985. The parties to a safe harbor lease agreement under section 168(f)(8) executed after June 30, 1985 must file with their timely filed (including extensions) Federal income tax returns for the taxable year during which the lease term begins a statement containing the following information:

(a) The name, address, and taxpayer identification number of the lessor and the lessee;

(b) A description of the property with respect to which safe-harbor lease treatment is claimed;

(c) The date on which the lessee places the property in service, the date on which the lease begins, and the term of the lease;

(d) The recovery property class of the leased property under section 168(c)(2) (for example, 5-year);

(e) The terms of the payments between the parties to the lease transaction;

(f) The unadjusted basis of the property as defined in section 168(d)(1) and its adjusted basis as determined under § 5c.168(f)(8)-6(b)(3); and

(g) If the lessor is a partnership or grantor trust, the name, address, and taxpayer identification number of the partners or beneficiaries and the service center at which the income tax return of each partner or beneficiary is filed. The lessor's failure to file the above-described statement shall void such agreement as a safe-harbor lease under section 168(f)(8) as of the date of the execution of the lease agreement. For rules regarding extensions of time for filing elections, see § 1.9100-1.

T.D. 8033, 6/28/85.

§ 5c.168(f)(8)-2 Election to characterize transaction as a section 168(f)(8) lease.

Caution: The Treasury has not yet amended Reg § 5c.168(f)(8)-2 to reflect changes made by P.L. 100-647, P.L. 99-514, P.L. 98-369, P.L. 97-248.

(a) Election. *(1) In general.* The election to characterize a transaction as a lease qualifying under section 168(f)(8) shall be made within the time and manner as set forth in this section without regard to section 168(f)(4).

(2) Lease agreement. For an agreement to be treated as a lease under section 168(f)(8) and this section, the lease agreement must be executed not later than 3 months after the property was first placed in service, as defined in § 5c.168(f)(8)-6(b)(2)(i) (or prior to November 14, 1981, if the property was first placed in service by the lessee after December 31, 1980, and before August 14, 1981). The agreement must be in writing and must state that all of the parties to the agreement agree to characterize it as a lease for purposes of Federal tax law and elect to have the provisions of section 168(f)(8) apply to the transaction. The agreement must also name the party who will be treated as the lessor and the party who will be treated as the lessee.

(3) Information return concerning the election. (i) Except as provided in subdivision (ii), for each lease agreement, the lessor and lessee must jointly file Form 6793, Safe Harbor Lease Information Return, concerning their election under section 168(f)(8). The information return must be signed by both the lessor and the lessee and filed not later than the 30th day after the agreement is executed with the Commissioner of Internal Revenue, 1111 Constitution Avenue, N.W., Washington, D.C. 20224 (Attn: Form 6793). Unless the failure to file timely is shown to be due to reasonable cause, the failure to file the information return timely shall void the section 168(f)(8) election as of the date of the execution of the lease agreement. The information return shall include the following items:

(A) The name, address, and taxpayer identifying number of the lessor and the lessee (and the common parent company if a consolidated return is filed);

(B) The service center with which the income tax returns of the lessor and lessee are filed;

(C) A description of each property with respect to which the election is made;

(D) The date on which the lessee places the property in service (determined as defined in § 5c.168(f)(8)-6(b)(2)(i)), the date on which the lease begins, and the term of the lease;

(E) the recovery property class of the leased property under section 168(c)(2) (for example, 5 years) and the ADR midpoint life of the leased property;

(F) The terms of the payments between the parties to the lease transaction;

(G) Whether the ACRS deductions and the investment tax credit are allowable to the same taxpayer;

(H) The aggregate amount paid to outside parties to arrange or carry out the transaction, such as, for example, legal and investment banking fees;

(I) For the lessor only: The unadjusted basis of the property as defined in section 168(d)(1);

(J) For the lessor only: If the lessor is a partnership or a grantor trust, the name, address, and taxpayer identifying number of the partners or the beneficiaries, and the Service Center with which the income tax return of each partner or beneficiary is filed; and

(K) Such other information as may be required by the return or its instructions. The aggregate amount paid to outside parties which is described in paragraph (a)(3)(i)(H) of this section need not be disclosed unless it is reasonable to estimate that either the lessor or the lessee will lease property under section 168(f)(8) for the calendar year which has an aggregate adjusted basis to such person of more than $1,000,000. If either the lessor or the lessee reasonably expects to lease property with an aggregate basis of more than $1,000,000, then both parties must disclose their transaction costs.

(ii) In the case of an agreement executed before January 1, 1982, only the lessor is required to file the information return described in paragraph (a)(3)(i) of this section and the return must be postmarked not later than January 31, 1982. Unless the failure to file timely is shown to be due to reasonable cause, or unless the lessee files the information return postmarked by January 31, 1982, the lessor's failure to file the information return timely shall be a disqualifying event as of February 1, 1982, which shall cause an agreement to cease to be treated as a lease under section 168(f)(8). For the Federal income tax consequences of a disqualifying event, see § 5c.168(f)(8)-8.

(iii) A copy of the information return described in paragraph (a)(3)(i) and (ii) shall be filed by each party with its timely filed Federal income tax return for its taxable year during which the lease term begins. However, for taxable years ending in 1981 with respect to lease agreements executed during calendar year 1981, such statement shall be filed by the later of (A) the due date (taking extensions into account) of the party's 1981 Federal income tax return, or (B) where the filing of an amended return is required, with the amended return within 3 months following the execution of the lease agreement. For the requirement to file an amended return within 3 months and the consequences of the failure to so file, see § 5c.168(f)(8)-6(b)(2)(ii). A taxpayer that is required to file the information return with its Federal income tax return before an information return form is available shall file, in lieu of the required information return, a statement which contains the information set forth in subparagraphs (A) through (J) of paragraph (a)(3)(i). The failure by the lessor to file the information return (or, if applicable, the statement referred to in the preceding sentence) with its timely filed Federal income tax return shall be a disqualifying event which shall cause an agreement to cease to be treated as a lease under section 168(f)(8). For the Federal income tax consequences of a disqualifying event, see § 5c.168(f)(8)-8.

(4) Election is irrevocable. An agreement made pursuant to paragraph (a)(2) of this section shall be irrevocable as of the later of the date such agreement was executed or November 23, 1981.

(5) Disposition by lessee. Except in the case of transactions described in subparagraph (6), of this paragraph, if the lessee (or any transferee of the lessee's interest) sells or assigns its interest in the lease or in the property, the agreement will cease to be characterized as a lease under section 168(f)(8) as of the time of the sale or assignment unless the transferee furnishes to the lessor within 60 days following the transfer the transferee's written consent to take the property subject to the lease, and the transferee and lessor file a statement with their timely filed Federal income tax returns for the taxable year in which the transfer occurs containing the following information:

(i) The name, address, and taxpayer identifying number of the lessor and the transferee;

(ii) The district director's office with which the income tax returns of the lessor and transferee are filed;

(iii) A description of the property; and

(iv) Confirmation of the transferee's consent.

See § 5c.168(f)(8)-8 for the Federal income tax consequence where an agreement ceases to be characterized as a lease under section 168(f)(8).

(6) Disposition of lessee's interest in bankruptcy, etc., or similar proceeding. In the case of an agreement executed after May 31, 1982, where the lessee's interest in the lease or in the property is sold or assigned in a bankruptcy, liquidation, receivership, a court-supervised foreclosure, or in any similar proceeding for the relief or protection of insolvent debtors in Federal or State court, the agreement will continue to be characterized as a lease under section 168(f)(8) and the purchaser or assignee shall take the property subject to the lease if—

(i) Prior to the consummation of the sale or assignment, the lessor gives written notice of its Federal income tax ownership to the judicial or administrative body having jurisdiction over the proceeding and to the debtor in possession of the interest or, if at such time a trustee, receiver or similar person has been appointed by the court, to the person appointed. The notice must contain a request that the court and the debtor or the person appointed provide a copy of the notice to the purchaser or assignee prior to the consummation of the sale or assignment. Within 60 days following the sale or assignment, the lessor must provide notice of its Federal income tax ownership and copies of the lease agreement, and, in the case of a sale and leaseback transaction, the lessor's purchase money obligation, to the purchaser or assignee;

(ii) The lessor files a statement with its timely filed Federal income tax return for the taxable year in which the sale or assignment occurs containing the following information:

(A) The name, address, and taxpayer identifying number of the lessor and the purchaser or assignee;

(B) The district director's office with which the Federal income tax returns of the lessor and purchaser or assignee are filed;

(C) A description of the property; and

(iii) Prior to the consummation of the sale or assignment, all secured lenders of the lessee with interests in the property, which interests arose not later than the time the lessee first used the property under the lease (and which were perfected in accordance with applicable local law), specifically either exclude or release in writing the Federal income tax ownership of the property from their interests.

The purchaser or assignee of the interest with respect to which this paragraph applies shall file a statement with its timely filed Federal income tax return for the taxable year in which the sale or assignment occurs containing the information described in subdivision (ii) of this Subparagraph. If the interest is subsequently transferred (other than in a bankruptcy, liquidation, receivership, court-supervised foreclosure, or similar proceeding) during the term of the lease, the agreement will continue to be characterized as a lease under section 168(f)(8) and the transferee will take the property subject to the lease if either (A) the lessor gives the transferee, prior to the transfer, a copy of the lease, written notice of its Federal income tax ownership, and, in the case of a sale and leaseback transaction, a copy of the lessor's purchase money obligation, and the lessor files a statement with its timely filed Federal income tax return as described in subdivision (ii) of this subparagraph, or (B) within 60 days following the transfer, the transferee agrees in writing to take the property subject to the lease and the lessor and transferee file a statement with their timely filed Federal income tax returns within the time and in the manner described in paragraph (a)(5) of this section. However, an agreement will not continue to be characterized as a lease under this subparagraph, if, under another applicable provision, it would cease to be characterized as a lease. See § 5c.168(f)(8)-8 for the Federal income tax consequences where an agreement ceased to be characterized as a lease under section 168(f)(8).

(7) Consequences of taking the property subject to the lease agreement. For purposes of § 5c.168(f)(8)-1 through 5c168(f)(8)-11, in a situation where a transferee of a lessee's interest acquires the property subject to the lease, the transferee shall be deemed to have acquired a leasehold interest in the property equal to the remaining lease term, any unpaid

obligation of the lessor arising in connection with the sale of the property by the original lessee in a sale and leaseback transaction, and any option of the lessee to purchase the property. Any consideration paid by the transferee for the property shall be allocated to the lessor's obligation to the extent of the unpaid balance of the obligation. Any excess over the unpaid balance shall be allocated between the leasehold interest and the purchase option in proportion to their relative fair market values. As the new lessee, the transferee shall not be entitled to claim any ACRS deduction with respect to the property while the lease remains in effect and shall not be entitled to any investment tax credit with respect to the property. The transferee shall report interest income on the lessor's obligation, and shall be entitled to deduct the rent paid under the lease, in accordance with § 5c.168(f)(8)-7. In addition, the transferee shall be entitled to amortize the portion of its cost allocable to the leasehold interest. Conversely, as long as the lease remains in effect, the lessor will continue to be recognized as the owner of the property for Federal income tax purposes, shall be required to report rents due under the lease, and shall be entitled to deduct interest on its obligation.

(8) Election to treat certain leases under subparagraph (6) rules. The lessor under a section 168(f)(8) lease executed on or before May 31, 1982, may elect to have the provisions of paragraph (a)(6) of this section apply in the case of a sale or assignment of the lessee's interest in the lease or in the property in a bankruptcy, receivership, liquidation, court-supervised foreclosure, or similar proceeding. The election of the lessor with respect to any leased property may be made at any time prior to the consummation of any sale or assignment of such property in a bankruptcy, etc., or similar proceeding, by complying with the provisions of subparagraph (6) of this paragraph.

(b) Examples. The application of the provisions of this section may be illustrated by the following examples:

Example (1). X Corp. maintains its books and records for Federal tax law purposes on a calendar year basis. On February 1, 1981, X acquires certain equipment for use in its business, and the equipment is deemed to be placed in service on that date within the meaning of § 5c.163(f)(8)-6(b)(2)(i). On November 1, 1981, X sells the equipment to Y and leases it back under a lease in which the parties elect to have the provisions of section 168(f)(8) apply. The election is considered timely for purposes of making Y the owner of the property under section 168(f)(8) since the lease agreement was executed before November 14, 1981.

Example (2). The facts are the same as in example (1) except that X Corp.'s taxable year ends on February 28, 1981. X claimed the investment tax credit and depreciation deductions with respect to the property in its return filed April 1, 1981. The lease will qualify for safe harbor treatment under section 168(f)(8) provided X, within 3 months after the lease agreement was executed, files an amended return pursuant to § 5c.168(f)(8)-6(b)(2)(ii) for its taxable year ending February 28, 1981, in which X foregoes its right to claim any investment tax credit or ACRS deductions with respect to the property subject to the lease.

Example (3). X Corp. (as lessee) sells certain new equipment to Y Corp. (as lessor) and leases it back under a section 168(f)(8) lease. During the term of the lease X sells its interest in the property to T Corp. (other than in a bankruptcy or similar proceeding), and T does not give Y a written consent to take the property subject to the leased. The agreement ceases to be treated as a lease under section 168(f)(8) as of the date of the sale.

Example (4). The facts are the same as in example (3) except that the sale of the property takes place while X is under the jurisdiction of a court in a bankruptcy proceeding. All lenders of X having perfected interests in the property that arose by the time the property was first used under the lease have specifically either excluded or released the ownership of the property for Federal income tax purposes from their interests. Within the required time periods, Y gives appropriate notification to the court, the bankruptcy trustee, and T that the property is subject to the lease and files the required statement with its Federal income tax return for the taxable year in which the sale occurs. The agreement continues to be treated as a lease under section 168(f)(8). T will take the property subject to the lease. T must allocate the purchase price among the lessor's note, the leasehold interest, and the option (if any) to purchase the property.

Example (5). The facts are the same as in example (4), except that one lender of X having a perfected and timely interest in the property does not specifically exclude or release the Federal income tax ownership of the property from its interest. The agreement will cease to be treated as a lease under section 168(f)(8) as of the date of the transfer to T. The result would be the same if Y failed to furnish any of the notices required by subdivision (i) of paragraph (a) and (6) or failed to file a statement as required by subdivision (ii) of paragraph (a)(6).

Example (6). The facts are the same as in example (4). In addition, during the term of the lease T transfers the property to U Corp. and Y fails to furnish U with written notice that the property is subject to the lease prior to the sale and U refuses to agree to consent to the lease agreement. The agreement will cease to be treated as a lease under section 168(f)(8) as of the date of the transfer to U. The result would be the same if Y furnished U with timely written notice of its tax ownership but failed to file the required statement with its tax return for its taxable year in which the sale occurred.

T.D. 7791, 10/20/81, amend T.D. 7795, 11/10/81, T.D. 7800, 12/28/81.

---

§ 5c.168(f)(8)-3 Requirements for lessor.

Caution: The Treasury has not yet amended Reg § 5c.168(f)(8)-3 to reflect changes made by P.L. 100-647, P.L. 99-514, P.L. 98-369, P.L. 97-248.

(a) Qualified lessor. In order for an agreement to be treated as a lease under section 168(f)(8), the party characterized in the agreement as the lessor must be a qualified lessor. The term "qualified lessor" means—

(1) A corporation which is neither an electing small business corporation under section 1371(b) nor a personal holding company under section 542(a), or

(2) A partnership all of whose partners are corporations described in subparagraph (1), or

(3) A grantor trust whose grantor and beneficiaries are all corporations described in paragraph (a)(1) or partnerships described in paragraph (a)(2).

(b) Effect of disqualification of lessor. If at any time during the term of the agreement the lessor ceases to be a qualified lessor, the agreement will lose its characterization as a lease under section 168(f)(8) as of the date of the event causing such disqualification. If any partner of a partnership described in paragraph (a)(2) ceases to be a corporation described in paragraph (a)(1), the partnership entity shall cease to be a qualified lessor. Similarly, if any beneficiary of a trust described in paragraph (a)(3) ceases to be a corporation described in paragraph (a)(1), the trust shall cease to be a qualified lessor. See § 5c.168(f)(8)-8 for the Federal income tax consequences of such a disqualification.

(c) One tax owner per property. Only one person may be a qualified lessor under section 168(f)(8) with respect to leased property. Thus, property that is subject to a lease under section 168(f)(8) may not be subleased under a lease for which a section 168(f)(8) election is made. In addition, if a lessor sells or assigns in a taxable transaction its interest in a section 168(f)(8) lease or in the underlying property, the lease shall cease to qualify under section 168(f)(8) and no other lease may be executed under section 168(f)(8) with respect to the property. The preceding sentence applies to a sale or assignment of its interest by a partner of a lessor that is a partnership described in paragraph (a)(2) of this section or by a beneficiary of a lessor that is a trust described in paragraph (a)(3) of this section. See § 5c.168(f)(8)-8 for the Federal income tax consequences where a lease ceases to qualify under section 168(f)(8). However, lease brokers, agents, etc., may, for example, prepare executory contracts with the lessee whereby the broker's assignee may execute a lease as lessor, and, if the requirements of section 168(f)(8) and §§ 5c.168(f)(8)-1 through 5c.168(f)(8)-11 are met, the lease will qualify under section 168(f)(8).

(d) Examples. The application of paragraph (c) may be illustrated by the following examples:

Example (1). X Corp. (as lessee) sells certain new equipment to Y Corp. (as lessor) and leases it back under a section 168(f)(8) lease. Within 3 months after the property was placed in service, Y assigns its interest in the lease to Z. Upon the transfer to Z, the lease will no longer qualify for treatment under section 168(f)(8). The property may not thereafter be the subject of a section 168(f)(8) lease.

Example (2). X Corp., which wishes to acquire certain equipment for use in its business and to transfer ownership of the property for Federal income tax law purposes, purchases the equipment and enters into an executory contract with LB, a lease broker, under which X agrees to execute a section 168(f)(8) lease as lessee with a third party lessor. At a later date (but within the prescribed 3-month period), LB arranges for X and T Corp. (which wishes to secure Federal income tax law ownership) to execute a lease agreement in accordance with § 5c.168(f)(8)-2. The lease will qualify for treatment under section 168(f)(8).

T.D. 7791, 10/20/81, amend T.D. 7795, 11/10/81.

§ 5c.168(f)(8)-4 Minimum investment of lessor.

Caution: The Treasury has not yet amended Reg § 5c.168(f)(8)-4 to reflect changes made by P.L. 100-647, P.L. 99-514, P.L. 98-369, P.L. 97-248.

(a) Minimum investment. Under section 168(f)(8)(B)(ii), an agreement will not be characterized as a lease for purposes of section 168(f)(8) unless the qualified lessor has a minimum at risk investment which, at the time the property is placed in service under the lease and at all times during the term of the lease, is not less than 10 percent of the adjusted basis of the leased property. As the adjusted basis of the leased property is reduced by capital cost recovery deductions, the minimum investment required will also be reduced to 10 percent of the revised adjusted basis, until the adjusted basis has been completely recovered, at which time no minimum investment will be required. Financing provided by the lessee or a party related to the lessee, such as a recourse note given by the lessor to the lessee, will not be taken into account in determining the lessor's minimum investment.

(b) At risk amount. The minimum investment which the lessor has at risk with respect to the leased property for purposes of paragraph (a) of this section includes only consideration paid and recourse indebtedness incurred by the lessor to purchase the property. The lessor must have sufficient net worth (without regard to the value of any leases which qualify under section 168(f)(8)) to satisfy any personal liability incurred. Any tax benefits which the lessor derives from the leased property shall not be taken into account to reduce the amount the lessor has at risk. An agreement between the lessor and the lessee requiring either or both parties to purchase or sell the qualified leased property at some price (whether or not fixed in the agreement) at the end of the lease term shall not affect the amount the lessor has at risk with respect to the property. However, an option held by the lessor to sell the property that is exercisable before the end of the period prescribed under section 168(c)(2) for the recovery property class of the leased property (taking into account any election by the lessor or lessee under section 168(b)(3)) shall reduce the amount the lessor is considered to have at risk by the amount of the option price at the time the option becomes exercisable.

T.D. 7791, 10/20/81.

§ 5c.168(f)(8)-5 Term of lease.

Caution: The Treasury has not yet amended Reg § 5c.168(f)(8)-5 to reflect changes made by P.L. 100-647, P.L. 99-514, P.L. 98-369, P.L. 97-248.

(a) Term of lease. *(1) Basic rules.* To qualify as a lease under section 168(f)(8) and § 5c.168(f)(8)-1(a), the lease agreement must provide for a term that does not exceed the maximum term described in paragraph (b) of this section; such term must also at least equal the minimum term described in paragraph (c).

(b) Maximum term. For purposes of section 168(f)(8)(B)(iii) and this section, the term of the lease may not exceed the greater of—

(1) 90 percent of the useful life of the property under section 167, or

(2) 150 percent of the asset depreciation range (ADR) present class life ("midpoint") of such property, applicable as of January 1, 1981 (without regard to section 167(m)(4)), published in Rev. Proc. 77-10, 1977-1 C.B. 548, and revisions thereto.

Solely for purposes of this paragraph (b), "useful life" means the period when the leased asset can reasonably be expected to be economically useful in anyone's trade or business; such term does not mean the period during which the lessor expects to lease the property. Any option to extend the term of the lease, whether or not at fair market value rent, must be included in the term of the lease for purposes of this paragraph. If several different pieces of property are the subject of a single lease, the maximum allowable term for such lease will be measured with respect to the property with the shortest life. In no case, however, will the lease term qualify under this section if such term with respect to any piece of property is less than the minimum term described in paragraph (c).

(c) Minimum term. For purposes of this section, the term of the lease must at least equal the period prescribed under section 168(c)(2) for the recovery property class of the leased property. For example, if a piece of leased equipment is in the 5-year recovery property class, the lease agreement must have a minimum term of 5 years. In general, the determination of whether property is 3-year recovery property, 5-year recovery property, etc., in the hands of the lessor will be based on the characterization of the property in the hands of the owner as determined without regard to the section 168(f)(8) lease. Thus, for example, property which is public utility property or RRB replacement property absent the section 168(f)(8) lease will be characterized as such in the hands of the lessor for purposes of section 168(f)(8). However, with respect to RRB replacement property, the transitional rule of section 168(f)(3) shall be inapplicable to the lessor. In addition, any election under section 168(b)(3) by the lessor with respect to the class of recovery property to which the qualified leased property is assigned shall apply to the leased property in determining the term of the lease. A lease term that does not exceed the term required to satisfy the minimum lease term of this paragraph will be deemed to comply with the maximum lease term described in paragraph (b) if such minimum lease term exceeds such maximum lease term.

(d) Examples. The application of this section may be illustrated by the following examples:

Example (1). X Corp. (as lessee) and Y Corp. (as lessor) enter into a lease which they elect to be treated under section 168(f)(8) with respect to a chemical manufacturing facility that will also generate steam for use in the production of electricity. The assets comprising the chemical plant are described in ADR guideline class 28.0 (midpoint life of 9.5 years), and the assets comprising the steam plant are described in ADR class 00.4 (midpoint life of 22 years). To satisfy the maximum lease term requirement of section 168(f)(8)(B)(iii)(II) and § 5c.168 (f)(8)-5(b), the lease term may not exceed 14.25 years (150 percent of the 9.5 year midpoint life of the chemical plant).

Example (2). The facts are the same as in example (1) except that the chemical plant and the steam plant are the subject of separate leases. For purposes of section 168(f)(8)(B)(iii)(II) and § 5c.168(f)(8)-5(b), the maximum term of the lease with respect to the chemical plant is 14.25 years (150 percent of 9.5 years) and the maximum term of the lease with respect to the steam plant is 33 years (150 percent of 22 years).

T.D. 7791, 10/20/81.

§ 5c.168(f)(8)-6 Qualified leased property.

Caution: The Treasury has not yet amended Reg § 5c.168(f)(8)-6 to reflect changes made by P.L. 100-647, P.L. 99-514, P.L. 98-369, P.L. 97-248.

(a) Basic rules. *(1) In general.* An agreement shall be treated as a section 168(f)(8) lease only if the property which is leased is qualified leased property. Qualified leased property is recovery property as defined in section 168(c) and is either—

(i) Except as provided in subparagraph (2), new section 38 property of the lessor which is leased no later than 3 months after the date the property was placed in service (or prior to November 14, 1981, if the property was placed in service after December 31, 1980, and before August 14, 1981) and which, if acquired by the lessee, would have been new section 38 property of the lessee, or

(ii) Property which is a qualified mass commuting vehicle (as defined in section 103(b)(9)) and which is financed in whole or in part by proceeds from an issue of obligations the interest on which is excludable from income under section 103(a).

(2) Sale and leaseback arrangement. (i) Where the leased property is purchased, directly or indirectly, by the lessor from the lessee (or a party related to the lessee), the property will not be qualified leased property unless the property was (or would have been) new section 38 property of the lessee and was purchased and leased no later than 3 months after the date the property was placed in service by the lessee (or prior to November 14, 1981, if the property was placed in service by the lessee after December 31, 1980 and before August 14, 1981) and with respect to which the lessor's adjusted basis does not exceed the adjusted basis of the lessee (or a party related to the lessee) at the time of the lease. If the lessor's adjusted basis in the property exceeds the seller's adjusted basis with respect to the property at the beginning of the lease, the property will not be qualified leased property.

(ii) For purposes of this paragraph (a)(2) and paragraph (b)(3)(ii) of this section, transactional costs with respect to a sale and leaseback arrangement that are not currently deductible shall be allocated to the lease agreement (and not included in the lessor's adjusted basis with respect to the property) and amortized over the term of the lease. These costs include legal and investment banking fees and printing costs.

(iii) The application of this paragraph (a)(2) may be illustrated by the following examples:

Example (1). X, an airline, contracts to have an airplane constructed for a fixed price of $10 million. Prior to completion of construction of the airplane, the value of the airplane increases to $11 million. X buys the airplane at the contract price of $10 million and, before it is placed in service, sells the airplane at its fair market value of $11 million to Y and then leases it back. The lease will not qualify for safe harbor protection under section 168(f)(8) because the lessor's adjusted basis in the airplane exceeds the lessee's adjusted basis. This result obtains even though the airplane qualifies as new section 38 property of X airline.

Example (2). Assume the same facts as in example (1) except that, prior to completion of the construction of the airplane, X assigns its contract to Y for $1 million, and Y thereafter buys the airplane at the contract price of $10 million. The acquisition by Y is treated as an indirect purchase from the lessee. Because Y's adjusted basis in the airplane would exceed the lessee's adjusted basis, the lease will not qualify under section 168(f)(8).

(b) Special rules. *(1) New section 38 property.* (i) new section 38 property is section 38 property described in subsection (b) of section 48 and the regulations thereunder other than a qualified rehabilitated building (within the meaning of section 48(g)(1)). Qualified leased property must be new section 38 property at the beginning of the lease and must continue to be section 38 property in the hands of the lessor and the lessee throughout the lease term. The fact that the lessee used the property within the 3-month period prior to the lease will not disqualify the property as new section 38 property of the lessee.

(ii) The application of this paragraph (b)(1) may be illustrated by the following examples:

Example (1). N is a hospital exempt from Federal income tax and wishes to purchase certain equipment for use in furtherance of its exempt functions *(i.e.,* other than for use in an unrelated trade or business). O, a qualified lessor as defined in § 5c.168(f)(8)-3(a), acquires the property and leases it to N. Since the equipment would not be new section 38 property of N if N had acquired it by virtue of section 48(a)(4) (relating to exception from definition of section 38 property for certain property used by certain tax-exempt organizations), the equipment is not qualified leased property and the lease does not qualify under section 168(f)(8). Whether O is considered the owner of the property for Federal tax law purposes will be determined without regard to the provisions of section 166(f)(8).

Example (2). P Corp. is constructing progress expenditure property as defined in section 46(d)(2) for R Corp. Progress expenditure property is property which it is reasonable to believe will be section 38 property in the hands of the taxpayer when it is placed in service. Before the date that the property is placed in service (as defined in § 5c.168(f)(8)-6(b)(2)(i)), the property is not new section 38 property. Accordingly, progress expenditure property cannot be qualified leased property.

Example (3). R Corp., a foreign railroad, acquires new rolling stock and enters into a sale and leaseback transaction with B Corp., a domestic corporation. R uses the rolling stock within and without the United States, but predominantly outside the United States within the meaning of section 48(a)(2)(A). Section 48(a)(2)(B)(ii) is inapplicable to R because R is neither a domestic railroad corporation nor a United States person; therefore, the rolling stock cannot be section 38 property to R. The property is not qualified leased property.

(2) Placed in service. (i) Property shall be considered as placed in service at the time the property is placed in a condition or state of readiness and availability for a specifically assigned function. If an entire facility is leased under one lease, property which is part of the facility will not be considered placed in service under this rule until the entire facility is placed in service. If the lessee claims any investment tax credit or ACRS deductions with respect to any component which is part of an entire facility that is subsequently leased, the lessee must file an amended return within the time prescribed in paragraph (b)(2)(ii) of this section in which it foregoes its claim to the investment tax credit and ACRS deductions. If such amended return may not be filed because the time for filing a claim for refund with respect to any component under section 6511 has expired, each component of the facility will be considered as placed in service at the time the individual component is placed in a condition or state of readiness and availability for a specifically assigned function and not when the entire facility is placed in service.

(ii) For purposes other than determining whether property is qualified leased property, property subject to a lease under section 168(f)(8) will be deemed to have been placed in service not earlier than the date such property is used under the lease. If the lessee claims any investment tax credit or ACRS deductions with respect to property placed in service under a lease, the lessee must file an amended return within 3 months following the execution of the lease agreement in which the lessee foregoes its claim to the investment tax credit and ACRS deductions with respect to the leased property or the election under section 168(f)(8) will be void.

(iii) The application of this paragraph (b)(2) may be illustrated by the following examples:

Example (1). X Corp. acquires equipment on December 31, 1982, and places the equipment in service. X's taxable year ends December 31. On March 20, 1983, X sells the equipment to Y Corp. and leases it back in a transaction that qualifies under section 168(f)(8). The property is considered to be new section 38 property to X under paragraph (b)(1). X is not allowed any investment tax credit or ACRS deductions with respect to the property in 1982 because the property is not considered to have been placed in service for purposes other than determining whether it is qualified leased property until it is used under the lease under subdivision (ii) of this subparagraph (2). If X has claimed credits or deductions on its 1982 return, it must file an amended return for 1982 within 3 months following the execution of the lease agreement or the election will be void.

Example (2). In March 1985, K Corp. completes reconditioning of a machine, which it constructed and placed in service in 1982 and which has an adjusted basis in 1985 of $10,000. The cost of reconditioning amounts to an additional $20,000. K would be entitled to a basis of $20,000 in computing its qualified investment in new section 38 property for 1985. In May 1985, K enters into a sale and leaseback transaction with L Corp. with respect to the reconditioned parts of the machine that are new section 38 property to K. K and L elect to have section 168(f)(8) apply. Assuming that the adjusted basis of the leased property is the same to L as it is to K, the property qualifies as qualified leased property under section 168(f)(8)(D)(ii) and L is considered the tax owner of the property. Since, for purposes other than determining whether property is qualified leased property, the property is deemed originally placed in service not earlier than the date the property is used under the lease, the property is new section 38 property to L and L may claim the investment tax credit (and ACRS deductions) with respect to the leased property.

(3) Qualified mass commuting vehicle. (i) A qualified mass commuting vehicle as defined in section 103(b)(9) will constitute qualified leased property for purposes of section 168(f)(8)(D)(iii) and this section provided all of the following requirements are met:

(A) At least part (as, for example, 5 percent) of the financing for the purchase of such vehicle must be derived from proceeds of obligations the interest on which is excludable from income under section 103(a)(1) (whether or not such obligations are described in section 103(b)(4)(I));

(B) The vehicle must be recovery property (i.e., it must have been first placed in service by the lessee after December 31, 1980); and

(C) the vehicle must not have been previously leased under a section 168(f)(8) lease by the lessee.

A qualified mass commuting vehicle that is qualified leased property may be leased under section 168(f)(8) at any time after December 31, 1980. The requirement of paragraph (b)(3)(i)(A) of this section may be satisfied where the vehicles leased under a section 168(f)(8) lease are refinanced with proceeds of an obligation the interest on which is excludable from income under section 103(a)(1).

(ii) Where the leased property is purchased, directly or indirectly, by the lessor from the lessee (or a party related to the lessee), the property will not qualify under this subsection unless the lessor's adjusted basis in the property does not exceed the adjusted basis of the lessee (or related party) at the time of the execution of the lease. The adjusted basis of property to a lessee (or related party) shall be determined under part II of subchapter O of chapter 1 of the Code for purposes of determining gain, except that the adjustment described in section 1016(a)(3) and § 1.1016-4 need not be made for property acquired during calendar year 1981 and leased no later than March 1, 1982.

(iii) In a transaction characterized as a lease under section 168(f)(8), the lessor's adjusted basis may not include that portion, if any, of the cost of the vehicle to the lessee (or related party) that is financed, directly or indirectly, with an Urban Mass Transportation Administration (UMTA) grant (excluding a grant under the interstate transfer provision of the Federal-Aid Highway Act (FAHA)), a FAHA grant, or any other Federal grant. Where a vehicle is included as part of an UMTA-funded project, 80 percent of the vehicle's cost will be deemed to be financed with an UMTA grant and 20 percent will be deemed to be financed from non-Federal sources without regard to whether the UMTA funds or the non-Federal funds are traceable to any particular vehicle included within the project. For purposes of this subparagraph and paragraph (b)(3)(ii) of this section, amounts originating from non-Federal sources which are paid or incurred with respect to leased property by a State or political subdivision of the State (or political subdivision created by the joint authorization of two or more States) shall be taken into account in computing the lessee's adjusted basis in the leased property as if the lessee had paid or incurred such amounts.

(iv) If a vehicle is purchased pending approval of an UMTA grant, the lessor's unadjusted basis in the vehicle may equal the lessee's unadjusted basis unreduced by any subsequently approved UMTA grant; however, if an UMTA grant is later approved and the vehicle is included as part of an UMTA-funded project, except as provided hereinafter in this subparagraph, the lease shall terminate with respect to an undivided 80 percent interest in the vehicle. For the Federal income tax consequences of the termination of a lease, see § 5c.168(f)(8)-8. If such a subsequently approved UMTA grant is used to purchase additional qualified mass commuting vehicles, the portion of each vehicle deemed to be allocable to non-UMTA financing (i.e., 20 percent) may be leased under section 168(f)(8). If a vehicle is purchased pending approval of an UMTA grant and leased under section 168(f)(8), the lease will not be deemed to have terminated with respect to 80 percent of the vehicle when the UMTA grant is later approved if the total interest leased before the grant is approved did not exceed 20 percent of the lessee's adjusted basis in the vehicle (unadjusted basis prior to March 1, 1982) unreduced by any subsequently approved UMTA grant. For purposes of this subparagraph and paragraph (b)(3)(iii) of this section, the allocation principles applicable to UMTA grants shall apply in the case of FAHA grants except that 85 percent and 15 percent shall be substituted for 80 percent and 20 percent, respectively. Similar allocation rules shall also apply to other Federal grants used to finance the acquisition of qualified mass commuting vehicles.

(v) (A) Notwithstanding the provisions of § 5c.168(f)(8)-2(a)(3)(iii), the lessee in a transaction to which this paragraph (b)(3) applies is not required to file an information return or a statement concerning its election under section 168(f)(8).

(B) Notwithstanding the provisions of § 5c.168(f)(8)-2(a)(5), if the transfer of a qualified mass commuting vehicle is not otherwise a disqualifying event, the transferee is not required to file the statement mentioned therein.

(C) The fact that a qualified mass commuting vehicle is not section 38 property because it is used by an exempt entity will not disqualify the lease under § 5c.168(f)(8)-8(b)(4); however, a disqualifying event will occur, and the agreement will cease to be characterized as a lease under section 168(f)(8), with respect to a vehicle which (1) ceases to be a qualified mass commuting vehicle or (2) would cease to be section 38 property if used by a taxable entity as, for example, a vehicle used predominantly outside the United States. For the Federal income tax consequences of a disqualifying event, see § 5c.168(f)(8)-8.

(vi) The lessor of a qualified vehicle will not be allowed an investment tax credit with respect to it under section 38.

(vii) The application of this paragraph (b)(3) may be illustrated by the following examples:

Example (1). On July 1, 1981, a unit of city X, X Transit Authority (XTA), purchases 100 buses after receiving an UMTA grant for 80 percent of their purchase price. Fifteen percent of the purchase price is financed with a combination of State and local governmental grants and 5 percent is financed with proceeds from an issue of tax-exempt obligations described in section 103(b)(4)(I). Because UMTA financed an 80 percent interest in the 100 buses, XTA may lease under section 168(f)(8) only a 20 percent interest in each bus. If XTA were to lease 100 percent of 20 buses, only 20 percent of such buses would be deemed to be leased under a safe harbor lease.

Example (2). The facts are the same as in example (1) except that UMTA has not yet approved XTA's application in 1981. Pending the UMTA approval, XTA purchases and places in service 20 buses in July 1981. The 20 buses are financed with tax-exempt obligations described in section 103(b)(4)(I). On December 15, 1981, XTA sells a 100 percent interest in these 20 buses to Corporation M and leases them back under a lease in which the parties elect to have the provisions of section 168(f)(8) apply. M is a calendar-year taxpayer and claims an ACRS deduction with respect to the buses on its return for taxable year 1981. On July 1, 1982, UMTA approves XTA's grant application, thus enabling XTA to purchase an additional 80 buses. Because 80 percent of the original 20 buses are deemed to have been financed by UMTA beginning on July 1, 1982, the safe harbor lease terminates with respect to an undivided 80 percent interest in the 20 buses. If XTA would be considered the owner of the buses without regard to section 168(f)(8), the termination will result in a deemed sale of an undivided 80 percent interest in the 20 buses by M to XTA. The amount realized by M on the sale will include a proportionate part of the outstanding amount of M's debt plus the sum of any other consideration received by M. M will realize gain or loss, depending upon its basis, with applicable section 1245 recapture. However, XTA may lease the 20 percent interest in the 80 new buses it purchased in 1982 which is deemed to have been financed with non-Federal funds.

Example (3). The facts are the same as in example (2) except that the grant approved by UMTA is used to purchase and renovate a bus garage facility. Eighty percent of the original 20 buses are deemed to have been financed by UMTA beginning on July 1, 1982. The lease would still terminate with respect to an undivided 80 percent interest in the vehicles. XTA cannot lease the garage facility under 168(f)(8) because it does not constitute a qualified mass commuting vehicle.

Example (4). The facts are the same as in example (2) except that on December 15, 1981, XTA sells and leases back only a 20 percent interest in the 20 buses acquired in July 1981. When the UMTA grant is later approved, the lease will not terminate with respect to any portion of the 20 buses. In addition, XTA may lease the 20 percent interest in the 80 new buses purchased in 1982 and deemed to have been financed with non-Federal funds.

Example (5). On August 1, 1982, UMTA approves a grant for a major 5-year capital expenditure program to improve city Y's rapid rail transit system. None of the funds relating to this UMTA-funded project, provided either by UMTA or by city Y, will be used to purchase qualified mass commuting vehicles. Instead, a number of rapid rail cars and buses will be purchased entirely with funds provided with a combination of grants by the State and city governments and of proceeds from an issue of tax-exempt obligations described in section 103(a). Because none of the rapid rail cars and buses are included as part of the UMTA-funded project, no part of them is deemed to be financed by UMTA. If at least 5 percent of the cost of the qualified mass commuting vehicles is provided by tax exempt obligations under section 103(a), the vehicles will be qualified leased property in their entirety.

Example (6). City Z has a mass transit agency (ZTA) which purchases on July 1, 1982, 10 buses for which it pays $1,000,000, 95 percent of which is derived from grants from city Z and 5 percent from tax exempt obligations described in section 103(a). The buses have a useful life within the meaning of § 1.167(a)-1(b) of 10 years and their salvage value is zero. On July 1, 1983, ZTA sells these buses to corporation P and leases them back in a transaction which the parties elect to have treated as a lease under section 168(f)(8). At the time of the sale and leaseback, ZTA's adjusted basis in the 10 buses under section 1016(a)(3) and § 1.1016-4 is $900,000 ($1,000,000 cost less $100,000 of depreciation sustained, computed on a straight-line basis). Before the transaction will qualify under section 168(f)(8) and § 5c.168(f)(8)-6(b)(3)(ii), P's adjusted basis in the vehicles may not exceed ZTA's basis, or $900,000.

Assuming that the transaction qualifies under section 168(f)(8) and that corporation P is a calendar year taxpayer, P may claim ACRS deductions for 1982 of $135,000 (15 percent of $900,000).

Example (7). The facts are the same as in example (6) except that the sale and leaseback transaction is closed on December 31, 1982. P's adjusted basis in the vehicles may not exceed ZTA's basis, or $950,000 ($1,000,000 cost less $50,000 of depreciation sustained, computed on a straight-line basis).

Example (8). The facts are the same as in example (6) except that ZTA purchases the buses on June 1, 1981, and enters into the sale and leaseback transaction with corporation P on December 31, 1981. Under § 5c.168(f)(8)-6(b)(3)(ii), no adjustment is made to ZTA's basis in the buses for depreciation sustained. Therefore, P's basis in the buses may equal ZTA's cost of $1,000,000.

Example (9). On July 1, 1981, a unit of city W, W Transit Authority (WTA), purchases 100 buses with local grants derived entirely from a city W sales tax. The buses do not constitute qualified leased property under 5c.168(f)(8)-6(b)(3) because no part of the financing for their purchase was derived from the proceeds of tax exempt obligations.

Example (10). The facts are the same as in example (9) except that on November 1, 1981, WTA borrows 5 percent of the cost of the buses and pledges them as security. The interest on WTA's obligation is excludable from income under section 103(a)(1). On December 31, 1981, WTA sells to T Corp. all 100 buses and leases them back. Under § 5c.168(f)(8)-6(b)(3)(i), each bus is deemed to be financed with the proceeds of tax exempt obligations. Therefore, if the vehicles otherwise meet the definition of qualified leased property, all the vehicles will be qualified leased property under this section.

(4) Foreign lessees. In addition to the other provisions of this section, property which is leased under a section 168(f)(8) lease to a foreign person shall not be qualified leased property unless the gross income attributable to the property from all sources (determined without regard to section 872(a) or 882(b)) is effectively connected with a trade or business within the United States, and the taxable income, if any, attributable to the property is subject to tax under section 871(b)(1) or 882(a)(1).

(5) Other rules. (i) Qualified leased property may include undivided interests in property or property regardless of whether or not it is considered separate property under State or local law. If property subject to a section 168(f)(8) lease is later determined not to be qualified leased property, disqualification of the lease under section 168(f)(8) will apply only as to that property.

(ii) The application of this paragraph (b)(5) may be illustrated by the following examples:

Example (1). On July 1, 1981, X Corp. contracts to have a manufacturing facility constructed for use in its business. Construction of the facility is completed on July 1, 1982, and the facility is deemed to be placed in service as of that date under § 5c.168(f)(8)-6(b)(2)(i). The facility is comprised of a mixture of new section 38 property and buildings that do not qualify as section 38 property. On August 1, 1982, X sells the new section 38 property in the facility to Y and leases it back under an agreement in which the parties elect to be treated as a lease described in section 168(f)(8). Assuming that the other requirements of this paragraph are met, the new section 38 property contained in the facility will be qualified leased property. If it is later determined that property subject to the section 168(f)(8) lease is not new section 38 property (and thus not qualified leased property), the safe harbor protection will be lost only as to that property.

Example (2). X Corp. acquires a certain piece of equipment (which is new section 38 property) for use in its business. Within 3 months, X sells a 70 percent undivided interest in the property to lessor A and a 10 percent undivided interest in the property to lessor B and leases both portions back under separate section 168(f)(8) leases. The investment tax credit and ACRS deductions associated with the property will be divided among X, lessor A, and lessor B, on a basis of 20 percent, 70 percent, and 10 percent, respectively.

T.D. 7791, 10/20/81, amend T.D. 7795, 11/10/81, T.D. 7800, 12/28/81.

§ 5c.168(f)(8)-7 Reporting of income, deductions and investment tax credit; at risk rules.

Caution: The Treasury has not yet amended Reg § 5c.168(f)(8)-7 to reflect changes made by P.L. 100-647, P.L. 99-514, P.L. 98-369, P.L. 97-248.

(a) In general. The fact that the lessor's payments of interest and principal and the lessee's rental payments under the lease are not equal in amount will not prevent the lease from qualifying under section 168(f)(8). However, see paragraph (b) for special requirements in sale and leaseback transactions. In determining the parties' income, deductions, and investment tax credit under the lease, the rules in paragraphs (c) through (g) of this section shall apply regardless of the overall method of accounting otherwise used by the parties.

(b) Requirements for sale and leaseback transaction. If the property leased is financed by the lessee (or a related party of the leasee) in a sale and leaseback transaction, the lease will not qualify under section 168(f)(8) unless—

(1) The term of the lessor's purchase money obligation is conterminous with the term of the lease, and

(2) The lessor's obligation bears a reasonable rate of interest. For this purpose, a rate of interest shall be presumed to be reasonable if, on the date the agreement is executed, it is within 3 percentage points of (i) the rate in effect under section 6621, the prime rate in effect at any local commercial bank, or the most recent applicable rate determined by the Secretary under § 1.385-6(e)(2)(i), or (ii) an arm's-length rate as defined in § 1.482-2, or (iii) any rate between any two of the rates described by subdivisions (i) and (ii) of this paragraph(b)(2).

(c) Interest deductions and income. *(1) Deductibility from income.* In determining the amount of interest that a lessor may deduct in a taxable year with respect to its purchase money obligation given to the lessee or to a third party creditor, the lessor may not claim a deduction that would be—

(i) Greater than a deduction that would be allowed to an accrual basis taxpayer under a level-payment mortgage, amortized over a period equal to the term of the lessor's obligation, or

(ii) Less than a deduction that would be allowed to an accrual basis taxpayer under a straight line amortization of the principal over the term of the lessor's obligation.

In cases in which the property is not financed by the lessee or a party related to the lessee, the computation of the interest deduction may take into account fluctuations in the interest rate which are dependent on adjustments in the prime rate or events outside the control of the lessor and the third party creditor.

(2) Includibility in income. The lessee shall include interest on the lessor's purchase money obligation in income at the same time and in the same amount as the lessor's interest deductions, as determined under paragraph (c)(1).

(d) Rental income and deductions. *(1) Deductibility from income.* The amount of the lessee's rent deduction under a section 168(f)(8) lease with respect to any taxable year shall be a pro rata portion of the aggregate amount required to be paid by the lessee to the lessor under the terms of the lease agreement. If the lessee is required to purchase the leased property at the end of the lease term, or if the lessor has an option to sell the property to the lessee, rent shall not include the lesser of—

(i) The amount of the lessee's purchase obligation, whether fixed by the terms of the lease agreement or conditioned on the exercise of the lessor's option to sell the property to the lessee, or

(ii) The fair market value of the property at the end of the lease term determined at the beginning of the lease term.

For this purpose, fair market value shall be determined without taking into account any increase or decrease for inflation or deflation during the lease term. Rent deductions may be adjusted pursuant to the terms of the lease agreement to account for fluctuations which are dependent on events outside the control of the lessor and lessee, such as a change in the interest rate charged by a third party creditor of the lessor on the debt incurred to finance the purchase of the leased property.

(2) Includibility in income. The lessor shall include rent in income as follows:

(i) In the case of prepayments of rent, the earlier of when such rent is paid by the lessee or accrued under the lease, and

(ii) In the case of other rent, at the same time and in the same amount as the lessee's rent deductions, as determined under paragraph (d)(1).

(e) ACRS deductions. The deductions that the lessor is allowed under section 168(a) with respect to property subject to a section 168(f)(8) lease shall be determined without regard to the limitation in section 168(f)(10)(B)(iii). The recovery class of qualified leased property in the hands of the lessor shall be determined by the character of the property in the hands of the owner of the property without regard to section 168(f)(8). Any elections under section 168(b)(3) by the lessor with respect to the class of recovery property to which the qualified leased property is assigned shall apply to the leased property. However, with respect to RRB replacement property, the transitional rule of section 168(f)(3) shall be inapplicable to the lessor.

(f) At risk requirements. The amount of the investment credit and ACRS deductions that a lessor shall be allowed with respect to the leased property shall be limited to the extent the at risk rules under the investment tax credit provisions and section 465 apply to the lessee or to the lessor. In determining the amount the lessee would be at risk, the at risk rules will be applied as if the lessee had not elected to have section 168(f)(8) apply. Thus, for example, if, without regard to section 168(f)(8), an individual lessee would be treated as the owner of the leased property for Federal tax law purposes, the lessor under a section 168(f)(8) lease would be allowed ACRS deductions or investment tax credits with respect to the property only to the extent that the lessee may have claimed them had the parties not elected treatment under section 168(f)(8). In addition, the ACRS deductions and investment tax credits that a lessor is allowed with respect to the property are further limited to the extent that the at risk rules apply to the lessor as owner of the property under the section 168(f)(8) lease. If the lessor and the lessee are subject to the at risk rules, the lessor is allowed only the lesser of the ACRS deductions and investment tax credits allowable to the lessor and the lessee.

(g) Limitation on section 48(d) amount. If in a sale and leaseback transaction the lessor elects pursuant to section 48(d) to treat the lessee (which is the user of the property) as having acquired the property for purposes of claiming the investment tax credit, the lessee shall be treated as acquiring the property for an amount equal to the basis of the property to the lessor (and not for an amount equal to its fair market value). The investment tax credit allowable to the lessee is further limited to the extent the at risk rules apply to either the lessor or to the lessee. See paragraph (f) of this section.

(h) Examples. The application of the provisions of this section may be illustrated by the following examples.

Example (1). Y, a qualified lessor, acquires a piece of equipment which is qualified leased property for $1 million and leases it to X under a lease which the parties properly elect to have characterized as a lease described in section 168(f)(8). The equipment has a 10-year economic life and falls within the 5-year ACRS class. Under the terms of the lease, X, the lessee-user, is obligated to pay Y nine annual payments of $10,000 and, at the end of the lease term, Y has the option to sell the property to X for $2,160,000. Under § 5c.168(f)(8)-7(d), the aggregate payments required to be made by X under the lease are $2,250,000 ($90,000 rent plus $2,160,000 option price) and are treated as rent to Y (less a reasonable estimate for the residual value of the property) and taxable as such. Assuming a reasonable estimate of the residual value is zero, the full $2,250,000 will be treated as rent, and under § 5c.168(f)(8)-7(d), such amount is deductible by X and includible in Y's income ratably over the term of the lease, *i.e.*, at a rate of $250,000 per year ($2,250,000 divided by 9).

Example (2). The facts are the same as in example (1) except that under the terms of the lease X is obligated to make rental payments of $100,000 for each of the first 5 years of the lease and $300,000 for each of the 4 remaining years under the lease. Further, X has an option to purchase the equipment for $1.00 at the end of the lease term. Pursuant to § 5c.168(f)(8)-7(d), X's aggregate rental payments are deductible by X and are includible in Y's income ratably over the term of the lease. Thus, the annual rental payments are deemed to be $188,000 per year ($1,700,000 divided by 9).

T.D. 7791, 10/20/81, amend T.D. 7795, 11/10/81.

§ 5c.168(f)(8)-8 Loss of section 168(f)(8) protection; recapture.

Caution: The Treasury has not yet amended Reg § 5c.168(f)(8)-8 to reflect changes made by P.L. 100-647, P.L. 99-514, P.L. 98-369, P.L. 97-248.

(a) In general. Upon the occurrence of an event that causes an agreement to cease to be characterized as a lease under section 168(f)(8), the characterization of the lessor and the lessee shall be determined without regard to section 168(f)(8).

(b) Events which cause an agreement to cease to be characterized as a lease. A disqualifying event shall cause an agreement to cease to be treated as a lease under section 168(f)(8) as of the date of the disqualifying event. A disqualifying event shall include the following:

(1) The lessor sells or assigns its interest in the lease or in the qualified leased property in a taxable transaction.

(2) The failure by the lessor to file a copy of the information return (or applicable statement) with its income tax return as required in § 5c.168(f)(8)-2(a)(3)(iii).

(3) The lessee (or any transferee of the lessee's interest) sells or assigns its interest in the lease or in the qualified leased property in a transaction not described in § 5c.168(f)(8)-2(a)(6) and the transferee fails to execute, within the prescribed time, the consent described in § 5c.168(f)(8)-2(a)(5), or either the lessor or the transferee fail to file statements with their income tax returns as required by that paragraph.

(4) The property ceases to be section 38 property as defined in § 1.48-1 in the hands of the lessor or lessee, for example, due to its conversion to personal use or to use predominantly outside the United States, or to use by a lessee exempt from Federal income taxation.

(5) The lessor ceases to be a qualified lessor by becoming an electing small business corporation or a personal holding company (within the meaning of section 542(a)).

(6) The minimum investment of the lessor becomes less than 10 percent of the adjusted basis of the qualified leased property as described in section 168(f)(8)(B)(ii) and § 5c.168(f)(8)-4.

(7) The lease terminates.

(8) The property becomes subject to more than one lease for which an election is made under section 168(f)(8).

(9) Retirements and casualties. [Reserved]

(10) The property is transferred in a bankruptcy or similar proceeding and the lessor fails either to furnish the appropriate notification or to file a statement with its income tax return as required by § 5c.168(f)(8)-2(a)(6).

(11) The property is transferred in a bankruptcy or similar proceeding and not all lenders with perfected and timely interests in the property specifically exclude or release the Federal income tax ownership of the property as required under § 5c.168(f)(8)-2(a)(6)(iii.)

(12) The property is transferred subsequent to a bankruptcy or similar proceeding and the lessor fails to furnish notice to the transferee prior to the transfer or fails to file a statement with its income tax return, and either the lessor fails to secure the transferee's consent or the lessor or the transferee fail to file statements with their returns.

(13) The property is leased under the provisions of section 168(f)(8)(D)(iii) and § 5c.168(f)(8)-6(b)(3) and ceases to be a qualified mass commuting vehicle.

(14) The failure by the lessor to file the required information return described in § 5c.168(f)(8)-2(a)(3)(ii) by January 31, 1982, unless the lessee files such return by January 31, 1982.

(c) Recapture. The required amount of recapture of the investment tax credit and of accelerated cost recovery deductions after a disqualifying event shall be determined under sections 47 and 1245, respectively.

(d) Consequences of loss of safe harbor protection. The tax consequences of a disqualifying event depend upon the characterization of the parties without regard to section 168(f)(8). If the lessee would be the owner of the property without regard to section 168(f)(8), the disqualifying event will be deemed to be a sale of the qualified leased property by the lessor to the lessee. The amount realized by the lessor on the sale will include the outstanding amount (if any) of the lessor's debt on the property plus the sum of any other consideration received by the lessor. A disposition that results from a disqualifying event shall not be treated as an installment sale under section 453.

(e) Examples. The application of the provisions of this section may be illustrated by the following examples:

Example (1). M Corp. and N Corp. enter into a sale and leaseback transaction in which the leaseback agreement is characterized as a lease under section 168(f)(8) and M is treated as the lessor. In the second year of the lease, M becomes an electing small business corporation under subchapter S. The agreement ceases to be treated as a lease under section 168(f)(8) as of the date of the subchapter S election. Without respect to section 168(f)(8), N would be considered the owner of the property. The disqualification of M will be treated as a sale of the qualified leased property from M to N for the amount of the purchase money debt on the property then outstanding. M will realize gain or loss, depending upon its basis, with applicable investment tax credit and section 1245 recapture. N will acquire the property with a basis equal to the amount of the outstanding obligation. The property will not be used section 38 property to N under § 1.48-3(a)(2).

Example (2). Q Corp. (as lessor) and P Corp. (as lessee) enter into a lease that is characterized as a lease under section 168(f)(8). The lease has a 6-year term. P has no option to renew the lease or to purchase the property. At the end of

6 years, if P would be considered the owner of the property without regard to section 168(f)(8), upon the termination of the lease the property will be deemed to be sold by Q to P for the amount of the purchase money debt outstanding with respect to the property.

T.D. 7791, 10/20/81, amend T.D. 7795, 11/10/81, T.D. 7800, 12/28/81.

---

§ 5c.168(f)(8)-9 [Reserved]

§ 5c.168(f)(8)-10 [Reserved]

§ 5c.168(f)(8)-11 [Reserved]

§ 1.168(h)-1 Like-kind exchanges involving tax-exempt use property.

(a) Scope. *(1)* This section applies with respect to a direct or indirect transfer of property among related persons, including transfers made through a qualified intermediary (as defined in § 1.1031(k)-1(g)(4)) or other unrelated person, (a transfer) if—

(i) Section 1031 applies to any party to the transfer or to any related transaction; and

(ii) A principal purpose of the transfer or any related transaction is to avoid or limit the application of the alternative depreciation system (within the meaning of section 168(g)).

(2) For purposes of this section, a person is related to another person if they bear a relationship specified in section 267(b) or section 707(b)(1).

(b) Allowable depreciation deduction for property subject to this section. *(1) In general.* Property (tainted property) transferred directly or indirectly to a taxpayer by a related person (related party) as part of, or in connection with, a transaction in which the related party receives tax-exempt use property (related tax-exempt use property) will, if the tainted property is subject to an allowance for depreciation, be treated in the same manner as the related tax-exempt use property for purposes of determining the allowable depreciation deduction under section 167(a). Under this paragraph (b), the tainted property is depreciated by the taxpayer over the remaining recovery period of, and using the same depreciation method and convention as that of, the related tax-exempt use property.

(2) Limitations. (i) Taxpayer's basis in related tax-exempt use property. The rules of this paragraph (b) apply only with respect to so much of the taxpayer's basis in the tainted property as does not exceed the taxpayer's adjusted basis in the related tax-exempt use property prior to the transfer. Any excess of the taxpayer's basis in the tainted property over its adjusted basis in the related tax-exempt use property prior to the transfer is treated as property to which this section does not apply. This paragraph (b)(2)(i) does not apply if the related tax-exempt use property is not acquired from the taxpayer (e.g., if the taxpayer acquires the tainted property for cash but section 1031 nevertheless applies to the related party because the transfer involves a qualified intermediary).

(ii) Application of section 168(i)(7). This section does not apply to so much of the taxpayer's basis in the tainted property as is subject to section 168(i)(7).

(c) Related tax-exempt use property. *(1)* For purposes of paragraph (b) of this section, related tax-exempt use property includes—

(i) Property that is tax-exempt use property (as defined in section 168(h)) at the time of the transfer; and

(ii) Property that does not become tax-exempt use property until after the transfer if, at the time of the transfer, it was intended that the property become tax-exempt use property.

(2) For purposes of determining the remaining recovery period of the related tax-exempt use property in the circumstances described in paragraph (c)(1)(ii) of this section, the related tax-exempt use property will be treated as having, prior to the transfer, a lease term equal to the term of any lease that causes such property to become tax-exempt use property.

(d) Examples. The following examples illustrate the application of this section. The examples do not address common law doctrines or other authorities that may apply to recharacterize or alter the effects of the transactions described therein. Unless otherwise indicated, parties to the transactions are not related to one another.

Example (1). (i) X owns all of the stock of two subsidiaries, B and Z. X, B and Z do not file a consolidated federal income tax return. On May 5, 1995, B purchases an aircraft (FA) for $1 million and leases it to a foreign airline whose income is not subject to United States taxation and which is a tax-exempt entity as defined in section 168(h)(2). On the same date, Z owns an aircraft (FA) with a fair market value of $1 million, which has been, and continues to be, leased to an airline that is a United States taxpayer. Z's adjusted basis in DA is $0. The next day, at a time when each aircraft is still worth $1 million, B transfers FA to Z (subject to the lease to the foreign airline) in exchange for DA (subject to the lease to the airline that is a United States taxpayer). Z realizes gain of $1 million on the exchange, but that gain is not recognized pursuant to section 1031(a) because the exchange is of like-kind properties. Assume that a principal purpose of the transfer of DA to B or of FA to Z is to avoid the application of the alternative depreciation system. Following the exchange, Z has a $0 basis in FA pursuant to section 1031(d). B has a $1 million basis in DA.

(ii) B has acquired property from Z, a related person; Z's gain is not recognized pursuant to section 1031(a); Z has received tax-exempt use property as part of the transaction; and a principal purpose of the transfer of DA to B or of FA to Z is to avoid the application of the alternative depreciation system. Accordingly, the transaction is within the scope of this section. Pursuant to paragraph (b) of this section, B must recover its $1 million basis in DA over the remaining recovery period of, and using the same depreciation method and convention as that of, FA, the related tax-exempt use property.

(iii) If FA did not become tax-exempt use property until after the exchange, it would still be related tax-exempt use property and paragraph (b) of this section would apply if, at the time of the exchange, it was intended that FA become tax-exempt use property.

Example (2). (i) X owns all of the stock of two subsidiaries, B and Z. X, B and Z do not file a consolidated federal income tax return. B and Z each own identical aircraft. B's aircraft (FA) is leased to a tax-exempt entity as defined in section 168(h)(2) and has a fair market value of $1 million and an adjusted basis of $500,000. Z's aircraft (DA) is leased to a United States taxpayer and has a fair market value of $1 million and an adjusted basis of $10,000. On Nay l, 1995, B and Z exchange aircraft, subject to their respective leases. B realizes gain of $500,000 and Z realizes gain of $990,000, but neither person recognizes gain because of the operation of section 1031(a). Moreover, assume that a principal purpose of the transfer of DA to B or of FA to Z is to avoid the application of the alternative depreciation system.

(ii) As in Example 1, B has acquired property from Z, a related person; Z's gain is not recognized pursuant to section 1031(a); Z has received tax-exempt use property as part of the transaction; and a principal purpose of the transfer of DA to B or of FA to Z is to avoid the application of the alternative depreciation system. Thus, the transaction is within the scope of this section even though B has held tax-exempt use property for a period of time and, during that time, has used the alternative depreciation system with respect to such property. Pursuant to paragraph (b) of this section, B, which has a substituted basis determined pursuant to section 1031(d) of $500,000 in DA, must depreciate the aircraft over the remaining recovery period of FA, using the same depreciation method and convention. Z holds tax-exempt use property with a basis of $10,000, which must be depreciated under the alternative depreciation system.

(iii) Assume the same facts as in paragraph (i) of this Example 2, except that B and Z are members of an affiliated group that files a consolidated federal income tax return. Of B's $500,000 basis in DA, $10,000 is subject to section 168(i)(7) and therefore not subject to this section. The remaining $490,000 of basis is subject to this section. But see § 1.1502-80(f) making section 1031 inapplicable to intercompany transactions occurring in consolidated return years beginning on or after July 12, 1995.

(e) Effective date. This section applies to transfers made on or after April 20, 1995.

T.D. 8667, 4/26/96.

§ 1.168(i)-0 Table of contents for the general asset account rules.

This section lists the major paragraphs contained in section 1.168(i)-1.

§ 1.168(i)-1 General asset accounts.

(a) Scope.

(b) Definitions.

(1) Unadjusted depreciable basis.

(2) Unadjusted depreciable basis of the general asset account.

(3) Adjusted depreciable basis of the general asset account.

(4) Expensed cost.

(c) Establishment of general asset accounts.

(1) Assets eligible for general asset accounts.

(i) General rules.

(ii) Special rules for assets generating foreign source income.

(2) Grouping assets in general asset accounts.

(i) General rules.

(ii) Special rules.

(d) Determination of depreciation allowance.

(1) In general.

(2) Special rule for passenger automobiles.

(e) Disposition of an asset from a general asset account.

(1) Scope.

(2) General rules for a disposition.

(i) No immediate recovery of basis.

(ii) Treatment of amount realized.

(iii) Effect of disposition on a general asset account.

(iv) Coordination with nonrecognition provisions.

(v) and (vi) [Reserved]. For further guidance see the entries for § 1.168(i)-1T(e)(3)(v) and (vi).

(3) Special rules.

(i) In general.

(ii) Disposition of all assets remaining in a general asset account.

(iii) Disposition of an asset in a qualifying disposition.

(iv) Transactions subject to section 168(i)(7).

(v) Transactions subject to section 1031 or 1033.

(vi) Anti-abuse rule.

(f) Assets generating foreign source income.

(1) In general.

(2) Source of ordinary income, gain, or loss.

(i) Source determined by allocation and apportionment of depreciation allowed.

(ii) Formula for determining foreign source income, gain, or loss.

(3) Section 904(d) separate categories.

(g) Assets subject to recapture.

(h) Changes in use.

(1) Conversion to personal use.

(2) Change in use results in a different recovery period and/or depreciation method.

(i) No effect on general asset account election.

(ii) Asset is removed from the general asset account.

(iii) New general asset account is established.

(i) Identification of disposed or converted asset.

(j) Effect of adjustments on prior dispositions.

(k) Election.

(1) Irrevocable election.

(2) Time for making election.

(3) Manner of making election.

(l) Effective date.

(1) In general.

(2) Exceptions.

(3) Like-kind exchanges and involuntary conversions.

T.D. 8566, 10/7/94, amend T.D. 9115, 2/27/2004, T.D. 9132, 6/16/2004, T.D. 9314, 2/26/2007.

§ 1.168(i)-1 General asset accounts.

Caution: The Treasury has not yet amended Reg § 1.168(i)-1 to reflect changes made by P.L. 108-27, P.L. 107-147, P.L. 105-34.

(a) Scope. This section provides rules for general asset accounts under section 168(i)(4). The provisions of this section apply only to assets for which an election has been made under paragraph (k) of this section.

(b) Definitions. For purposes of this section, the following definitions apply:

(1) Unadjusted depreciable basis is the basis of an asset for purposes of section 1011 without regard to any adjustments described in section 1016(a)(2) and (3). This basis reflects the reduction in basis for the percentage of the taxpayer's use of property for the taxable year other than in the taxpayer's trade or business (or for the production of in-

come), for any portion of the basis the taxpayer properly elects to treat as an expense under section 179, and for any adjustments to basis provided by other provisions of the Internal Revenue Code and the regulations under the Internal Revenue Code (other than section 1016(a)(2) and (3)) (for example, a reduction in basis by the amount of the disabled access credit pursuant to section 44(d)(7)). For property subject to a lease, see section 167(c)(2).

(2) Unadjusted depreciable basis of the general asset account is the sum of the unadjusted depreciable bases of all assets included in the general asset account.

(3) Adjusted depreciable basis of the general asset account is the unadjusted depreciable basis of the general asset account less the adjustments to basis described in sections 1016(a)(2) and (3).

(4) Expensed cost is the amount of any allowable credit or deduction treated as a deduction allowable for depreciation or amortization for purposes of section 1245 (for example, a credit allowable under section 30 or a deduction allowable under section 179, 179A, or 190).

(c) Establishment of general asset accounts. *(1) Assets eligible for general asset accounts.* (i) General rules. Assets that are subject to either the general depreciation system of section 168(a) or the alternative depreciation system of section 168(g) may be accounted for in one or more general asset accounts. An asset may be included in a general asset account only to the extent of the asset's unadjusted depreciable basis (for example, if, in 1995, a taxpayer places in service an asset that costs $20,000 and elects under section 179 to expense $17,500 of that asset's cost, the unadjusted depreciable basis of the asset is $2,500 and, therefore, only $2,500 of the asset's cost may be included in a general asset account). However, an asset is not to be included in a general asset account if the asset is used both in a trade or business (or for the production of income) and in a personal activity at any time during the taxable year in which the asset is first placed in service by the taxpayer.

(ii) Special rules for assets generating foreign source income. (A) Assets that generate foreign source income, both United States and foreign source income, or combined gross income of a FSC (as defined in section 922), DISC (as defined in section 992(a)), or possessions corporation (as defined in section 936) and its related supplier, may be included in a general asset account if the requirements of paragraph (c)(2)(i) of this section are satisfied. If, however, the inclusion of these assets in a general asset account results in a substantial distortion of income, the Commissioner may disregard the general asset account election and make any reallocations of income or expense necessary to clearly reflect income.

(B) A general asset account shall be treated as a single asset for purposes of applying the rules in § 1.861-9T(g)(3) (relating to allocation and apportionment of interest expense under the asset method). A general asset account that generates income in more than one grouping of income (statutory and residual) is a multiple category asset (as defined in § 1.861-9T(g)(3)(ii)), and the income yield from the general asset account must be determined by applying the rules for multiple category assets as if the general asset account were a single asset.

(2) Grouping assets in general asset accounts. (i) General rules. If a taxpayer makes the election under paragraph (k) of this section, assets that are subject to the election are grouped into one or more general asset accounts. Assets that are eligible to be grouped into a single general asset account may be divided into more than one general asset account. Each general asset account must include only assets that—

(A) Have the same asset class (for further guidance, see Rev. Proc. 87-56, 1987-2 C.B. 674, and § 601.601(d)(2)(ii)(b) of this chapter);

(B) Have the same applicable depreciation method;

(C) Have the same applicable recovery period;

(D) Have the same applicable convention; and

(E) Are placed in service by the taxpayer in the same taxable year.

(ii) Special rules. In addition to the general rules in paragraph (c)(2)(i) of this section, the following rules apply when establishing general asset accounts—

(A) Assets without an asset class, but with the same characteristics described in paragraphs (c)(2)(i)(B), (C), (D), and (E) of this section, may be grouped into a general asset account;

(B) Assets subject to the mid-quarter convention may only be grouped into a general asset account with assets that are placed in service in the same quarter of the taxable year;

(C) Assets subject to the mid-month convention may only be grouped into a general asset account with assets that are placed in service in the same month of the taxable year;

(D) Passenger automobiles for which the depreciation allowance is limited under section 280F(a) must be grouped into a separate general asset account; and

(E) Assets subject to paragraph (h)(2)(iii)(A) of this section (change in use results in a shorter recovery period and/or a more accelerated depreciation method) for which the depreciation allowance for the year of change (as defined in § 1.168(i)-4(a)) is not determined by using an optional depreciation table must be grouped into a separate general asset account.

(d) Determination of depreciation allowance. *(1) In general.* Depreciation allowances are determined for each general asset account by using the applicable depreciation method, recovery period, and convention for the assets in the account. The depreciation allowances are recorded in a depreciation reserve account for each general asset account. The allowance for depreciation under this section constitutes the amount of depreciation allowable under section 167(a).

(2) Special rule for passenger automobiles. For purposes of applying section 280F(a), the depreciation allowance for a general asset account established for passenger automobiles is limited for each taxable year to the amount prescribed in section 280F(a) multiplied by the excess of the number of automobiles originally included in the account over the number of automobiles disposed of during the taxable year or in any prior taxable year in a transaction described in paragraph (e)(3)(iii) (disposition of an asset in a qualifying disposition), (e)(3)(iv) (transactions subject to section 168(i)(7)), (e)(3)(v) (transactions subject to section 1031 or 1033), (e)(3)(vi) (anti-abuse rule), (g) (assets subject to recapture), or (h)(1) (conversion to personal use) of this section.

(e) Disposition of an asset from a general asset account. *(1) Scope.* This paragraph (e) provides rules applicable to dispositions of assets included in a general asset account. For purposes of this paragraph (e), an asset in a general asset account is disposed of when ownership of the asset is transferred or when the asset is permanently withdrawn from use either in the taxpayer's trade or business or in the production of income. A disposition includes the sale, exchange, retirement, physical abandonment, or destruction of an asset. A disposition also occurs when an asset is transferred to a supplies, scrap, or similar account. A disposition does not include, however, the retirement of a structural component of real property.

(2) General rules for a disposition. (i) No immediate recovery of basis. Immediately before a disposition of any asset in a general asset account, the asset is treated as having an adjusted basis of zero for purposes of section 1011. Therefore, no loss is realized upon the disposition of an asset from the general asset account. Similarly, where an asset is disposed of by transfer to a supplies, scrap, or similar account, the basis of the asset in the supplies, scrap, or similar account will be zero.

(ii) Treatment of amount realized. Any amount realized on a disposition is recognized as ordinary income (notwithstanding any other provision of subtitle A of the Internal Revenue Code (Code)) to the extent the sum of the unadjusted depreciable basis of the general asset account and any expensed cost (as defined in paragraph (b)(4) of this section) for assets in the account exceeds any amounts previously recognized as ordinary income upon the disposition of other assets in the account. The recognition and character of any excess amount realized are determined under other applicable provisions of the Code (other than sections 1245 and 1250 or provisions of the Code that treat gain on a disposition as subject to section 1245 or 1250).

(iii) Effect of disposition on a general asset account. The unadjusted depreciable basis and the depreciation reserve of the general asset account are not affected as a result of a disposition of an asset from the general asset account.

(iv) Coordination with nonrecognition provisions. For purposes of determining the basis of an asset acquired in a transaction described in paragraph (e)(3)(iii)(B)(4) of this section (relating to certain nonrecognition provisions), the amount of ordinary income recognized under this paragraph (e)(2) is treated as the amount of gain recognized on the disposition.

(v) Examples. The following examples illustrate the application of this paragraph (e)(2).

Example (1). (i) R, a calendar-year corporation, maintains one general asset account for ten machines. The machines cost a total of $10,000 and were placed in service in June 1995. Of the ten machines, one machine costs $8,200 and nine machines cost a total of $1,800. Assume this general asset account has a depreciation method of 200 percent declining balance, a recovery period of 5 years, and a half-year convention. R does not make a section 179 election for any of the machines. As of January 1, 1996, the depreciation reserve of the account is $2,000 [(($10,000 – $0) × 40%) / 2].

(ii) On February 8, 1996, R sells the machine that cost $8,200 to an unrelated party for $9,000. Under paragraph (e)(2)(i) of this section, this machine has an adjusted basis of zero.

(iii) On its 1996 tax return, R recognizes the amount realized of $9,000 as ordinary income because such amount does not exceed the unadjusted depreciable basis of the general asset account ($10,000), plus any expensed cost for assets in the account ($0), less amounts previously recognized as ordinary income ($0). Moreover, the unadjusted depreciable basis and depreciation reserve of the account are not affected by the disposition of the machine. Thus, the depreciation allowance for the account in 1996 is $3,200 (($10,000 – $2,000) × 40%).

Example (2). (i) The facts are the same as in Example 1. In addition, on June 4, 1997, R sells seven machines to an unrelated party for a total of $1,100. In accordance with paragraph (e)(2)(i) of this section, these machines have an adjusted basis of zero.

(ii) On its 1997 tax return, R recognizes $1,000 as ordinary income (the unadjusted depreciable basis of $10,000, plus the expensed cost of $0, less the amount of $9,000 previously recognized as ordinary income). The recognition and character of the excess amount realized of $100 ($1,100 – $1,000) are determined under applicable provisions of the Code other than section 1245 (such as section 1231). Moreover, the unadjusted depreciable basis and depreciation reserve of the account are not affected by the disposition of the machines. Thus, the depreciation allowance for the account in 1997 is $1,920 (($10,000 – $5,200) × 40%).

(3) Special rules. (i) In general. This paragraph (e)(3) provides the rules for terminating general asset account treatment upon certain dispositions. While the rules under paragraphs (e)(3)(ii) and (iii) of this section are optional rules, the rules under paragraphs (e)(3)(iv), (v), and (vi) of this section are mandatory rules. A taxpayer applies paragraph (e)(3)(ii) or (iii) of this section by reporting the gain, loss, or other deduction on the taxpayer's timely filed Federal income tax return (including extensions) for the taxable year in which the disposition occurs. For purposes of applying paragraph (e)(3)(iii) through (vi) of this section, see paragraph (i) of this section for identifying the unadjusted depreciable basis of a disposed asset.

(ii) Disposition of all assets remaining in a general asset account. (A) Optional termination of a general asset account. Upon the disposition of all of the assets, or the last asset, in a general asset account, a taxpayer may apply this paragraph (e)(3)(ii) to recover the adjusted depreciable basis of the general asset account (rather than having paragraph (e)(2) of this section apply). Under this paragraph (e)(3)(ii), the general asset account terminates and the amount of gain or loss for the general asset account is determined under section 1001(a) by taking into account the adjusted depreciable basis of the general asset account at the time of the disposition. The recognition and character of the gain or loss are determined under other applicable provisions of the Code, except that the amount of gain subject to section 1245 (or section 1250) is limited to the excess of the depreciation allowed or allowable for the general asset account, including any expensed cost (or the excess of the additional depreciation allowed or allowable for the general asset account), over any amounts previously recognized as ordinary income under paragraph (e)(2) of this section.

(B) Example. The following example illustrates the application of this paragraph (e)(3)(ii).

Example. (i) T, a calendar-year corporation, maintains a general asset account for 1,000 calculators. The calculators cost a total of $60,000 and were placed in service in 1995. Assume this general asset account has a depreciation method of 200 percent declining balance, a recovery period of 5 years, and a half-year convention. T does not make a section 179 election for any of the calculators. In 1996, T sells 200 of the calculators to an unrelated party for a total of $10,000 and recognizes the $10,000 as ordinary income in accordance with paragraph (e)(2) of this section.

(ii) On March 26, 1997, T sells the remaining calculators in the general asset account to an unrelated party for $35,000. T chooses to apply paragraph (e)(3)(ii) of this section. As a result, the account terminates and gain or loss is determined for the account.

(iii) On the date of disposition, the adjusted depreciable basis of the account is $23,040 (unadjusted depreciable basis of $60,000 less the depreciation allowed or allowable of $36,960). Thus, in 1997, T recognizes gain of $11,960 (amount realized of $35,000 less the adjusted depreciable basis of $23,040). The gain of $11,960 is subject to section 1245 to the extent of the depreciation allowed or allowable for the account (plus the expensed cost for assets in the account) less the amounts previously recognized as ordinary income ($36,960 + $0 – $10,000 = $26,960). As a result, the entire gain of $11,960 is subject to section 1245.

(iii) Disposition of an asset in a qualifying disposition. (A) Optional determination of the amount of gain, loss, or other deduction. In the case of a qualifying disposition of an asset (described in paragraph (e)(3)(iii)(B) of this section), a taxpayer may apply this paragraph (e)(3)(iii) (rather than having paragraph (e)(2) of this section apply). Under this paragraph (e)(3)(iii), general asset account treatment for the asset terminates as of the first day of the taxable year in which the qualifying disposition occurs, and the amount of gain, loss, or other deduction for the asset is determined by taking into account the asset's adjusted basis. The adjusted basis of the asset at the time of the disposition equals the unadjusted depreciable basis of the asset less the depreciation allowed or allowable for the asset, computed by using the depreciation method, recovery period, and convention applicable to the general asset account in which the asset was included. The recognition and character of the gain, loss, or other deduction are determined under other applicable provisions of the Code, except that the amount of gain subject to section 1245 (or section 1250) is limited to the lesser of—

(1) The depreciation allowed or allowable for the asset, including any expensed cost (or the additional depreciation allowed or allowable for the asset); or

(2) The excess of—

(i) The original unadjusted depreciable basis of the general asset account plus, in the case of section 1245 property originally included in the general asset account, any expensed cost; over

(ii) The cumulative amounts of gain previously recognized as ordinary income under either paragraph (e)(2) of this section or section 1245 (or section 1250).

(B) Qualifying dispositions. A qualifying disposition is a disposition that does not involve all the assets, or the last asset, remaining in a general asset account and that is—

(1) A direct result of a fire, storm, shipwreck, or other casualty, or from theft;

(2) A charitable contribution for which a deduction is allowable under section 170;

(3) A direct result of a cessation, termination, or disposition of a business, manufacturing or other income producing process, operation, facility, plant, or other unit (other than by transfer to a supplies, scrap, or similar account); or

(4) A transaction, other than a transaction described in paragraphs (e)(3)(iv) (pertaining to transactions subject to section 168(i)(7)) and (e)(3)(v) (pertaining to transactions subject to section 1031 or 1033) of this section, to which a nonrecognition section of the Code applies (determined without regard to this section).

(C) Effect of a qualifying disposition on a general asset account. If the taxpayer applies this paragraph (e)(3)(iii) to a qualifying disposition of an asset, then—

(1) The asset is removed from the general asset account as of the first day of the taxable year in which the qualifying disposition occurs;

(2) The unadjusted depreciable basis of the general asset account is reduced by the unadjusted depreciable basis of the asset as of the first day of the taxable year in which the disposition occurs;

(3) The depreciation reserve of the general asset account is reduced by the depreciation allowed or allowable for the asset as of the end of the taxable year immediately preceding the year of disposition, computed by using the depreciation method, recovery period, and convention applicable to the general asset account in which the asset was included; and

(4) For purposes of determining the amount of gain realized on subsequent dispositions that is subject to ordinary income treatment under paragraph (e)(2)(ii) of this section, the amount of any expensed cost with respect to the asset is disregarded.

(D) Example. The provisions of this paragraph (e)(3)(iii) are illustrated by the following example.

Example. (i) Z, a calendar-year corporation, maintains one general asset account for 12 machines. Each machine costs $15,000 and was placed in service in 1995. Of the 12 machines, nine machines that cost a total of $135,000 are used in Z's Kentucky plant, and three machines that cost a total of $45,000 are used in Z's Ohio plant. Assume this general asset account has a depreciation method of 200 percent declining balance, a recovery period of 5 years, and a half-year convention. Z does not make a section 179 election for any of the machines. As of January 1, 1997, the depreciation reserve for the account is $93,600.

(ii) On May 27, 1997, Z sells its entire manufacturing plant in Ohio to an unrelated party. The sales proceeds allocated to each of the three machines at the Ohio plant is $5,000. Because this transaction is a qualifying disposition under paragraph (e)(3)(iii)(B)(3) of this section, Z chooses to apply paragraph (e)(3)(iii) of this section.

(iii) For Z's 1997 return, the depreciation allowance for the account is computed as follows. As of December 31, 1996, the depreciation allowed or allowable for the three machines at the Ohio plant is $23,400. Thus, as of January 1, 1997, the unadjusted depreciable basis of the account is reduced from $180,000 to $135,000 ($180,000 less the unadjusted depreciable basis of $45,000 for the three machines), and the depreciation reserve of the account is decreased from $93,600 to $70,200 ($93,600 less the depreciation allowed or allowable of $23,400 for the three machines as of December 31, 1996). Consequently, the depreciation allowance for the account in 1997 is $25,920 (($135,000 – $70,200) × 40%).

(iv) For Z's 1997 return, gain or loss for each of the three machines at the Ohio plant is determined as follows. The depreciation allowed or allowable in 1997 for each machine is $1,440 [(($15,000 – $7,800) × 40%) / 2]. Thus, the adjusted basis of each machine under section 1011 is $5,760 (the adjusted depreciable basis of $7,200 removed from the account less the depreciation allowed or allowable of $1,440 in 1997). As a result, the loss recognized in 1997 for each machine is $760 ($5,000 – $5,760), which is subject to section 1231.

(iv) Transactions subject to section 168(i)(7). If an asset in a general asset account is transferred in a transaction described in section 168(i)(7)(B) (pertaining to treatment of transferees in certain nonrecognition transactions), the transferor must remove the transferred asset from the general asset account as of the first day of the taxable year in which the transaction occurs. In addition, the adjustments to the general asset account described in paragraph (e)(3)(iii)(C)(2) through (4) of this section must be made. The transferee is bound by the transferor's election under paragraph (k) of this section with respect to so much of the asset's basis in the hands of the transferee as does not exceed the asset's adjusted basis in the hands of the transferor. If all of the assets, or the last asset, in a general asset account are transferred, the transferee's basis in the assets or asset transferred is equal to the adjusted depreciable basis of the general asset account as of the beginning of the transferor's taxable year in which the transaction occurs, decreased by the amount of depreciation allocable to the transferor for the year of the transfer.

(v) Transactions subject to section 1031 or section 1033. (A) Like-kind exchange or involuntary conversion of all assets remaining in a general asset account. If all the assets, or the last asset, in a general asset account are transferred by a taxpayer in a like-kind exchange (as defined under § 1.168-6(b)(11)) or in an involuntary conversion (as defined under § 1.168-6(b)(12)), the taxpayer must apply this paragraph (e)(3)(v)(A) (instead of applying paragraph (e)(2), (e)(3)(ii), or (e)(3)(iii) of this section). Under this paragraph (e)(3)(v)(A), the general asset account terminates as of the first day of the year of disposition (as defined in § 1.168(i)-6(b)(5)) and—

(1) The amount of gain or loss for the general asset account is determined under section 1001(a) by taking into account the adjusted depreciable basis of the general asset account at the time of disposition (as defined in § 1.168(i)-6(b)(3)). The depreciation allowance for the general asset account in the year of disposition is determined in the same manner as the depreciation allowance for the relinquished MACRS property (as defined in § 1.168(i)-6(b)(2)) in the year of disposition is determined under § 1.168(i)-6. The recognition and character of gain or loss are determined in accordance with paragraph (e)(3)(ii)(A) of this section (notwithstanding that paragraph (e)(3)(ii) of this section is an optional rule); and

(2) The adjusted depreciable basis of the general asset account at the time of disposition is treated as the adjusted depreciable basis of the relinquished MACRS property.

(B) Like-kind exchange or involuntary conversion of less than all assets remaining in a general asset account. If an asset in a general asset account is transferred by a taxpayer in a like-kind exchange or in an involuntary conversion and if paragraph (e)(3)(v)(A) of this section does not apply to this asset, the taxpayer must apply this paragraph (e)(3)(v)(B) (instead of applying paragraph (e)(2), (e)(3)(ii), or (e)(3)(iii) of this section). Under this paragraph (e)(3)(v)(B), general asset account treatment for the asset terminates as of the first day of the year of disposition (as defined in § 1.168(i)-6(b)(5)), and—

(1) The amount of gain or loss for the asset is determined by taking into account the asset's adjusted basis at the time of disposition (as defined in § 1.168(i)-6(b)(3)). The adjusted basis of the asset at the time of disposition equals the unadjusted depreciable basis of the asset less the depreciation allowed or allowable for the asset, computed by using the depreciation method, recovery period, and convention applicable to the general asset account in which the asset was included. The depreciation allowance for the asset in the year of disposition is determined in the same manner as the depreciation allowance for the relinquished MACRS property (as defined in § 1.168(i)-6(b)(2)) in the year of disposition is determined under § 1.168(i)-6. The recognition and character of the gain or loss are determined in accordance with paragraph (e)(3)(iii)(A) of this section (notwithstanding that paragraph (e)(3)(iii) of this section is an optional rule); and

(2) As of the first day of the year of disposition, the taxpayer must remove the relinquished asset from the general asset account and make the adjustments to the general asset account described in paragraph (e)(3)(iii)(C)(2) through (4) of this section.

(vi) Anti-abuse rule. (A) In general. If an asset in a general asset account is disposed of by a taxpayer in a transaction described in paragraph (e)(3)(vi)(B) of this section, general asset account treatment for the asset terminates as of the first day of the taxable year in which the disposition occurs. Consequently, the taxpayer must determine the amount of gain, loss, or other deduction attributable to the disposition in the manner described in paragraph (e)(3)(iii)(A) of this section (notwithstanding that paragraph (e)(3)(iii)(A) of this section is an optional rule) and must make the adjustments to the general asset account described in paragraph (e)(3)(iii)(C)(1) through (4) of this section.

(B) Abusive transactions. A transaction is described in this paragraph (e)(3)(vi)(B) if the transaction is not described in paragraph (e)(3)(iv) or (e)(3)(v) of this section and the transaction is entered into, or made, with a principal purpose of achieving a tax benefit or result that would not be available absent an election under this section. Examples of these types of transactions include—

(1) A transaction entered into with a principal purpose of shifting income or deductions among taxpayers in a manner that would not be possible absent an election under this section in order to take advantage of differing effective tax rates among the taxpayers; or

(2) An election made under this section with a principal purpose of disposing of an asset from a general asset account in order to utilize an expiring net operating loss or credit. The fact that a taxpayer with a net operating loss carryover or a credit carryover transfers an asset to a related person or transfers an asset pursuant to an arrangement where the asset continues to be used (or is available for use) by the taxpayer pursuant to a lease (or otherwise) indicates, absent strong evidence to the contrary, that the transaction is described in this paragraph (e)(3)(vi)(B).

(f) Assets generating foreign source income. *(1) In general.* This paragraph (f) provides the rules for determining the source of any income, gain, or loss recognized, and the appropriate section 904(d) separate limitation category or categories for any foreign source income, gain, or loss recognized, on a disposition (within the meaning of paragraph (e)(1) of this section) of an asset in a general asset account that consists of assets generating both United States and foreign source income. These rules apply only to a disposition to which paragraph (e)(2) (general disposition rules), (e)(3)(ii) (disposition of all assets remaining in a general asset account), (e)(3)(iii) (disposition of an asset in a qualifying disposition), (e)(3)(v) (transactions subject to section 1031 or 1033), or (e)(3)(vi) (anti-abuse rule) of this section applies.

(2) Source of ordinary income, gain, or loss. (i) Source determined by allocation and apportionment of depreciation allowed. The amount of any ordinary income, gain, or loss that is recognized on the disposition of an asset in a general asset account must be apportioned between United States and foreign sources based on the allocation and apportionment of the--

(A) Depreciation allowed for the general asset account as of the end of the taxable year in which the disposition occurs if paragraph (e)(2) of this section applies to the disposition;

(B) Depreciation allowed for the general asset account as of the time of disposition if the taxpayer applies paragraph (e)(3)(ii) of this section to the disposition of all assets, or the last asset, in the general asset account, or if all the assets, or the last asset, in the general asset account are disposed of in a transaction described in paragraph (e)(3)(v)(A) of this section; or

(C) Depreciation allowed for the disposed asset for only the taxable year in which the disposition occurs if the taxpayer applies paragraph (e)(3)(iii) of this section to the disposition of the asset in a qualifying disposition, if the asset is disposed of in a transaction described in paragraph (e)(3)(v)(B) of this section (like-kind exchange or involuntary conversion), or if the asset is disposed in a transaction described in paragraph (e)(3)(vi) of this section (anti-abuse rule).

(ii) Formula for determining foreign source income, gain, or loss. The amount of ordinary income, gain, or loss recognized on the disposition that shall be treated as foreign source income, gain, or loss must be determined under the formula in this paragraph (f)(2)(ii). For purposes of this formula, the allowed depreciation deductions are determined for the applicable time period provided in paragraph (f)(2)(i) of this section. The formula is:

$$\text{Foreign Source Income, Gain, or Loss from the Disposition of an Asset} = \text{Total Ordinary Income, Gain, or Loss from Disposition of an Asset} \times \frac{\text{Allowed Depreciation Deductions Allocated and Apportioned to Foreign Source Income}}{\text{Total Allowed Depreciation Deductions for the General Asset Account or for the Disposed Asset (as applicable)}}$$

(3) Section 904(d) separate categories. If the assets in the general asset account generate foreign source income in more than one separate category under section 904(d)(1) or another section of the Code (for example, income treated as foreign source income under section 904(g)(10)), or under a United States income tax treaty that requires the foreign tax credit limitation to be determined separately for specified types of income, the amount of "foreign source income, gain, or loss from the disposition of an asset" (as determined under the formula in paragraph (f)(2)(ii) of this section) must be allocated and apportioned to the applicable separate category or categories under the formula in this paragraph (f)(3). For purposes of this formula, the allowed depreciation deductions are determined for the applicable time period provided in paragraph (f)(2)(i) of this section. The formula is:

$$\text{Foreign Source Income, Gain, or Loss In a Separate Category} = \text{Foreign Source Income, Gain, or Loss from the Disposition of an Asset} \times \frac{\text{Allowed Depreciation Deductions Allocated and Apportioned to a Separate Category}}{\text{Total Allowed Depreciation Deductions Allocated and Apportioned to Foreign Source Income}}$$

(g) Assets subject to recapture. If the basis of an asset in a general asset account is increased as a result of the recapture of any allowable credit or deduction (for example, the basis adjustment for the recapture amount under section 30(d)(2), 50(c)(2), 179(d)(10), or 179A(e)(4)), general asset account treatment for the asset terminates as of the first day of the taxable year in which the recapture event occurs. Consequently, the taxpayer must remove the asset from the general asset account as of that day and must make the adjustments to the general asset account described in paragraph (e)(3)(iii)(C)(2) through (4) of this section.

(h) Changes in use. *(1) Conversion to personal use.* An asset in a general asset account becomes ineligible for general asset account treatment if a taxpayer uses the asset in a personal activity during a taxable year. Upon a conversion to personal use, the taxpayer must remove the asset from the general asset account as of the first day of the taxable year in which the change in use occurs (the year of change) and must make the adjustments to the general asset account described in paragraph (e)(3)(iii)(C)(2) through (4) of this section.

(2) Change in use results in a different recovery period and/or depreciation method. (i) No effect on general asset account election. A change in the use described in § 1.168(i)-4(d) (change in use results in a different recovery period and/or depreciation method) of an asset in a general asset account shall not cause or permit the revocation of the election made under this section.

(ii) Asset is removed from the general asset account. Upon a change in the use described in § 1.168(i)-4(d), the taxpayer must remove the asset from the general asset account as of the first day of the year of change and must make the adjustments to the general asset account described in paragraphs (e)(3)(iii)(C)(2) through (4) of this section. If, however, the result of the change in use is described in § 1.168(i)-4(d)(3) (change in use results in a shorter recovery period and/or a more accelerated depreciation method) and the taxpayer elects to treat the asset as though the change in use had not occurred pursuant to § 1.168(i)-4(d)(3)(ii), no adjustment is made to the general asset account upon the change in use.

(iii) New general asset account is established. (A) Change in use results in a shorter recovery period and/or a more accelerated depreciation method. If the result of the change in use is described in § 1.168(i)-4(d)(3) (change in use results in a shorter recovery period and/or a more accelerated depreciation method) and adjustments to the general asset account are made pursuant to paragraph (h)(2)(ii) of this section, the taxpayer must establish a new general asset account for the asset in the year of change in accordance with the rules in paragraph (c) of this section, except that the adjusted depreciable basis of the asset as of the first day of the year of change is included in the general asset account. For purposes of paragraph (c)(2) of this section, the applicable depreciation method, recovery period, and convention are determined under § 1.168(i)-4(d)(3)(i).

(B) Change in use results in a longer recovery period and/or a slower depreciation method. If the result of the change in use is described in § 1.168(i)-4(d)(4) (change in use results in a longer recovery period and/or a slower depreciation method), the taxpayer must establish a separate general asset account for the asset in the year of change in accordance with the rules in paragraph (c) of this section, except that the unadjusted depreciable basis of the asset, and the greater of the depreciation of the asset allowed or allowable in accordance with section 1016(a)(2), as of the first day of the year of change are included in the newly established general asset account. Consequently, this general asset account as of the first day of the year of change will have a beginning balance for both the unadjusted depreciable basis and the depreciation reserve of the general asset account. For purposes of paragraph (c)(2) of this section, the applicable depreciation method, recovery period, and convention are determined under § 1.168(i)-4(d)(4)(ii).

(i) Identification of disposed or converted asset. A taxpayer may use any reasonable method that is consistently applied to the taxpayer's general asset accounts for purposes of determining the unadjusted depreciable basis of a disposed or converted asset in a transaction described in paragraph (e)(3)(iii) (disposition of an asset in a qualifying disposition), (e)(3)(iv) (transactions subject to section 168(i)(7)), (e)(3)(v) (transactions subject to section 1031 or 1033), (e)(3)(vi) (anti-abuse rule), (g) (assets subject to recapture), or (h)(1) (conversion to personal use) of this section.

(j) Effect of adjustments on prior dispositions. The adjustments to a general asset account under paragraph (e)(3)(iii), (e)(3)(iv), (e)(3)(v), (e)(3)(vi), (g), or (h)(1) of this section have no effect on the recognition and character of prior dispositions subject to paragraph (e)(2) of this section.

(k) Election. *(1) Irrevocable election.* If a taxpayer makes an election under this paragraph (k), the taxpayer consents to, and agrees to apply, all of the provisions of this section to the assets included in a general asset account. Except as provided in paragraph (c)(1)(ii)(A), (e)(3), (g), or (h) of this section, an election made under this section is irrevocable and will be binding on the taxpayer for computing taxable income for the taxable year for which the election is made and for all subsequent taxable years. An election under this paragraph (k) is made separately by each person owning an asset to which this section applies (for example, by each member of a consolidated group, at the partnership level (and not by the partner separately), or at the S corporation level (and not by the shareholder separately)).

(2) Time for making election. The election to apply this section shall be made on the taxpayer's timely filed (including extensions) income tax return for the taxable year in which the assets included in the general asset account are placed in service by the taxpayer.

(3) Manner of making election. In the year of election, a taxpayer makes the election under this section by typing or legibly printing at the top of the Form 4562, "GENERAL ASSET ACCOUNT ELECTION MADE UNDER SECTION 168(i)(4)," or in the manner provided for on Form 4562 and its instructions. The taxpayer shall maintain records (for example, "General Asset Account #1 - all 1995 additions in asset class 00.11 for Salt Lake City, Utah facility") that identify the assets included in each general asset account, that establish the unadjusted depreciable basis and depreciation reserve of the general asset account, and that reflect the amount realized during the taxable year upon dispositions from each general asset account. (But see section 179(c) and § 1.179-5 for the recordkeeping requirements for section 179 property.) The taxpayer's recordkeeping practices should be consistently applied to the general asset accounts. If Form 4562 is revised or renumbered, any reference in this section to that form shall be treated as a reference to the revised or renumbered form.

(l) Effective dates. *(1) In general.* Except as provided in paragraphs (l)(2) and (l)(3) of this section, this section applies to depreciable assets placed in service in taxable years ending on or after October 11, 1994. For depreciable assets placed in service after December 31, 1986, in taxable years ending before October 11, 1994, the Internal Revenue Service will allow any reasonable method that is consistently applied to the taxpayer's general asset accounts.

(2) Exceptions. (i) In general. (A) Paragraph (b)(1) of this section applies on or after June 17, 2004. For the applicability of § 1.168(i)-1(b)(1) before June 17, 2004, see § 1.168(i)-1(b)(1) in effect prior to June 17, 2004 (§ 1.168(i)-1(b)(1) as contained in 26 CFR part 1 edition revised as of April 1, 2004).

(B) Paragraphs (c)(2)(ii)(E) and (h)(2) of this section apply to any change in the use of depreciable assets pursuant to § 1.168(i)-4(d) in a taxable year ending on or after June 17, 2004. For any change in the use of depreciable assets as described in § 1.168(i)-4(d) after December 31, 1986, in a taxable year ending before June 17, 2004, the Internal Revenue Service will allow any reasonable method that is consistently applied to the taxpayer's general asset accounts or the taxpayer may choose, on an asset-by-asset basis, to apply paragraphs (c)(2)(ii)(E) and (h)(2) of this section.

(ii) Change in method of accounting. (A) In general. If a taxpayer adopted a method of accounting for general asset account treatment due to a change in the use of depreciable assets pursuant to § 1.168(i)-4(d) in a taxable year ending on or after December 30, 2003, and the method adopted is not in accordance with the method of accounting provided in paragraphs (c)(2)(ii)(E) and (h)(2) of this section, a change to the method of accounting provided in paragraphs (c)(2)(ii)(E) and (h)(2) of this section is a change in method of accounting to which the provisions of section 446(e) and the regulations under section 446(e) apply. However, if a taxpayer adopted a method of accounting for general asset account treatment due to a change in the use of depreciable assets pursuant to § 1.168(i)-4(d) after December 31, 1986, in a taxable year ending before December 30, 2003, and the method adopted is not in accordance with the method of accounting provided in paragraphs (c)(2)(ii)(E) and (h)(2) of this section, the taxpayer may treat the change to the method of accounting provided in paragraphs (c)(2)(ii)(E) and (h)(2) of this section as a change in method of accounting to which the provisions of section 446(e) and the regulations under section 446(e) apply.

(B) Automatic consent to change method of accounting. A taxpayer changing its method of accounting in accordance with this paragraph (l)(2)(ii) must follow the applicable administrative procedures issued under § 1.446-1(e)(3)(ii) for obtaining the Commissioner's automatic consent to a change in method of accounting (for further guidance, for example, see Rev. Proc. 2002-9 (2002-1 C.B. 327), (see § 601.601(d)(2)(ii)(b) of this chapter)). Because this change does not change the adjusted depreciable basis of the asset, the method change is made on a cut-off basis and, therefore, no adjustment under section 481(a) is required or allowed. For purposes of Form 3115, Application for Change in Accounting Method, the designated number for the automatic accounting method change authorized by this paragraph (l)(2)(ii) is "87." If Form 3115 is revised or renumbered, any reference in this section to that form is treated as a reference to the revised or renumbered form.

(3) Like-kind exchanges and involuntary conversions. This section applies for an asset transferred by a taxpayer in a like-kind exchange (as defined under § 1.168-6(b)(11)) or in an involuntary conversion (as defined under § 1.168-6(b)(12)) for which the time of disposition (as defined in § 1.168(i)-6(b)(3)) and the time of replacement (as defined in § 1.168(i)-6(b)(4)) both occur after February 27, 2004. For an asset transferred by a taxpayer in a like-kind exchange or in an involuntary conversion for which the time of disposition, the time of replacement, or both occur on or before February 27, 2004, see § 1.168(i)-1 in effect prior to February 27, 2004 (§ 1.168(i)-1 as contained in 26 CFR part 1 edition revised as of April 1, 2003).

T.D. 8566, 10/7/94, amend T.D. 9115, 2/27/2004, T.D. 9132, 6/16/2004, T.D. 9314, 2/26/2007.

---

§ 1.168(i)-2 Lease term.

(a) In general. For purposes of section 168, a lease term is determined under all the facts and circumstances. Paragraph (b) of this section and § 1.168(j)-1T, Q&A 17, describe certain circumstances that will result in a period of time not included in the stated duration of an original lease (additional period) nevertheless being included in the lease term. These rules do not prevent the inclusion of an additional period in the lease term in other circumstances.

(b) Lessee retains financial obligation. *(1) In general.* An additional period of time during which a lessee may not continue to be the lessee will nevertheless be included in the lease term if the lessee (or a related person)—

(i) Has agreed that one or both of them will or could be obligated to make a payment of rent or a payment in the nature of rent with respect to such period; or

(ii) Has assumed or retained any risk of loss with respect to the property for such period (including, for example, by holding a note secured by the property).

(2) Payments in the nature of rent. For purposes of paragraph (b)(1)(i) of this section, a payment in the nature of rent includes a payment intended to substitute for rent or to fund or supplement the rental payments of another. For example, a payment in the nature of rent includes a payment of any kind (whether denominated as supplemental rent, as liquidated damages, or otherwise) that is required to be made in the event that—

(i) The leased property is not leased for the additional period;

(ii) The leased property is leased for the additional period under terms that do not satisfy specified terms and conditions;

(iii) There is a failure to make a payment of rent with respect to such additional period; or

(iv) Circumstances similar to those described in paragraph (b)(2)(i), (ii), or (iii) of this section occur.

(3) De minimis rule. For the purposes of this paragraph (b), obligations to make de minimis payments will be disregarded.

(c) Multiple leases or subleases. If property is subject to more than one lease (including any sublease) entered into as part of a single transaction (or a series of related transactions), the lease term includes all periods described in one or more of such leases. For example, if one taxable corporation leases property to another taxable corporation for a 20-year term and, as part of the same transaction, the lessee subleases the property to a tax-exempt entity for a 10-year term, then the lease term of the property for purposes of section 168 is 20 years. During the period of tax-exempt use, the property must be depreciated under the alternative depreciation system using the straight line method over the greater of its class life or 25 years (125 percent of the 20-year lease term).

(d) Related person. For purposes of paragraph (b) of this section, a person is related to the lessee if such person is described in section 168(h)(4).

(e) Changes in status. Section 168(i)(5) (changes in status) applies if an additional period is included in a lease term under this section and the leased property ceases to be tax-exempt use property for such additional period.

(f) Example. The following example illustrates the principles of this section. The example does not address common law doctrines or other authorities that may apply to cause an additional period to be included in the lease term or to recharacterize a lease as a conditional sale or otherwise for federal income tax purposes. Unless otherwise indicated, parties to the transactions are not related to one another.

Example. Financial obligation with respect to an additional period.

(i) Facts. X, a taxable corporation, and Y, a foreign airline whose income is not subject to United States taxation, enter into a lease agreement under which X agrees to lease an aircraft to Y for a period of 10 years. The lease agreement provides that, at the end of the lease period, Y is obligated to find a subsequent lessee (replacement lessee) to enter into a subsequent lease (replacement lease) of the aircraft from X for an additional 10-year period. The provisions of the lease agreement require that any replacement lessee be unrelated to Y and that it not be a tax-exempt entity as defined in section 168(h)(2). The provisions of the lease agreement also set forth the basic terms and conditions of the replacement lease, including its duration and the required rental payments. In the event Y fails to secure a replacement lease, the lease agreement requires Y to make a payment to X in an amount determined under the lease agreement.

(ii) Application of this section. The lease agreement between X and Y obligates Y to make a payment in the event the aircraft is not leased for the period commencing after the initial 10-year lease period and ending on the date the replacement lease is scheduled to end. Accordingly, pursuant to paragraph (b) of this section, the term of the lease between X and Y includes such additional period, and the lease term is 20 years for purposes of section 168.

(iii) Facts modified. Assume the same facts as in paragraph (i) of this Example, except that Y is required to guarantee the payment of rentals under the 10-year replacement lease and to make a payment to X equal to the present value of any excess of the replacement lease rental payments specified in the lease agreement between X and Y, over the rental payments actually agreed to be paid by the replacement lessee. Pursuant to paragraph (b) of this section, the term of the lease between X and Y includes the additional period, and the lease term is 20 years for purposes of section 168.

(iv) Changes in status. If, upon the conclusion of the stated duration of the lease between X and Y, the aircraft either is returned to X or leased to a replacement lessee that is not a tax-exempt entity as defined in section 168(h)(2), the subsequent method of depreciation will be determined pursuant to section 168(i)(5)

(g) Effective date. *(1) In general.* Except as provided in paragraph (g)(2) of this section, this section applies to leases entered into on or after April 20, 1995.

(2) Special rules. Paragraphs (b)(1)(ii) and (c) of this section apply to leases entered into after April 29, 1996.

T.D. 8667, 4/26/96.

§ 1.168(i)-3 Treatment of excess deferred income tax reserve upon disposition of deregulated public utility property.

(a) Scope. *(1) In general.* This section provides rules for the application of section 203(e) of the Tax Reform Act of 1986, Public Law 99-514 (100 Stat. 2146) to a taxpayer with respect to public utility property (within the meaning of section 168(i)(10)) that ceases, whether by disposition, deregulation, or otherwise, to be public utility property with respect to the taxpayer and that is not described in paragraph (a)(2) of this section (deregulated public utility property).

(2) Exceptions. This section does not apply to the following property:

(i) Property that ceases to be public utility property with respect to the taxpayer on account of an ordinary retirement within the meaning of § 1.167(a)-11(d)(3)(ii).

(ii) Property transferred by the taxpayer if after the transfer the property is public utility property of the transferee and the taxpayer's excess tax reserve with respect to the property (within the meaning of section 203(e) of the Tax Reform Act of 1986) is treated as an excess tax reserve of the transferee with respect to the property.

(b) Amount of reduction. If public utility property of a taxpayer becomes deregulated public utility property to which this section applies, the reduction in the taxpayer's excess tax reserve permitted under section 203(e) of the Tax Reform Act of 1986 is equal to the amount by which the reserve could be reduced under that provision if all such property had remained public utility property of the taxpayer and the taxpayer had continued use of its normalization method of accounting with respect to such property.

(c) Cross reference. See § 1.46-6(k) for rules relating to the treatment of accumulated deferred investment tax credits when utilities dispose of regulated public utility property.

(d) Effective/applicability dates. *(1) In general.* Except as provided in paragraph (d)(2) of this section, this section applies to public utility property that becomes deregulated public utility property after December 21, 2005.

(2) Property that becomes public utility property of the transferee. This section does not apply to property that becomes deregulated public utility property with respect to a taxpayer on account of a transfer on or before March 20, 2008 if after the transfer the property is public utility property of the transferee.

(3) Application of regulation project (REG-104385-01). A reduction in the taxpayer's excess deferred income tax reserve will be treated as ratable if it is consistent with the proposed rules in regulation project (REG-104385-01) (68 FR 10190) March 4, 2003, and occurs during the period beginning on March 5, 2003, and ending on the earlier of—

(i) The last date on which the utility's rates are determined under the rate order in effect on December 21, 2005; or

(ii) December 21, 2007.

T.D. 9387, 3/19/2008.

§ 1.168(i)-4 Changes in use.

Caution: The Treasury has not yet amended Reg § 1.168(i)-4 to reflect changes made by P.L. 110-343.

(a) Scope. This section provides the rules for determining the depreciation allowance for MACRS property (as defined in § 1.168(b)-1T(a)(2)) for which the use changes in the hands of the same taxpayer (change in the use). The allowance for depreciation under this section constitutes the amount of depreciation allowable under section 167(a) for the year of change and any subsequent taxable year. For purposes of this section, the year of change is the taxable year in which a change in the use occurs.

(b) Conversion to business or income-producing use. *(1) Depreciation deduction allowable.* This paragraph (b) applies to property that is converted from personal use to use in a taxpayer's trade or business, or for the production of income, during a taxable year. This conversion includes property that was previously used by the taxpayer for personal purposes, including real property (other than land) that is acquired before 1987 and converted from personal use to business or income-producing use after 1986, and depreciable property that was previously used by a tax-exempt entity before the entity changed to a taxable entity. Except as otherwise provided by the Internal Revenue Code or regulations under the Internal Revenue Code, upon a conversion to business or income-producing use, the depreciation allowance for the year of change and any subsequent taxable year is determined as though the property is placed in service by the taxpayer on the date on which the conversion occurs. Thus, except as otherwise provided by the Internal Revenue Code or regulations under the Internal Revenue Code, the taxpayer must use any applicable depreciation method, recovery period, and convention prescribed under section 168 for the property in the year of change, consistent with any election made under section 168 by the taxpayer for that year (see, for example, section 168(b)(5)). See §§ 1.168(k)-1T(f)(6)(iii) and 1.1400L(b)-1T(f)(6) for the additional first year depreciation deduction rules applicable to a conversion to business or income-producing use. The depreciable basis of the property for the year of change is the lesser of its fair market value or its adjusted depreciable basis (as defined in § 1.168(b)-1T(a)(4)), as applicable, at the time of the conversion to business or income-producing use.

(2) Example. The application of this paragraph (b) is illustrated by the following example:

Example. A, a calendar-year taxpayer, purchases a house in 1985 that she occupies as her principal residence. In February 2004, A ceases to occupy the house and converts it to residential rental property. At the time of the conversion to residential rental property, the house's fair market value (excluding land) is $130,000 and adjusted depreciable basis attributable to the house (excluding land) is $150,000. Pursuant to this paragraph (b), A is considered to have placed in service residential rental property in February 2004 with a depreciable basis of $130,000. A depreciates the residential rental property under the general depreciation system by using the straight-line method, a 27.5-year recovery period, and the mid-month convention. Pursuant to §§ 1.168(k)-1T(f)(6)(iii)(B) or 1.1400L(b)-1T(f)(6), this property is not eligible for the additional first year depreciation deduction provided by section 168(k) or section 1400L(b). Thus, the depreciation allowance for the house for 2004 is $4,137, after taking into account the mid-month convention (($130,000 adjusted depreciable basis multiplied by the applicable depreciation rate of 3.636% (1/27.5)) multiplied by the mid-month convention fraction of 10.5/12). The amount of depreciation computed under section 168, however, may be limited under other provisions of the Internal Revenue Code, such as, section 280A.

(c) Conversion to personal use. The conversion of MACRS property from business or income-producing use to personal use during a taxable year is treated as a disposition of the property in that taxable year. The depreciation allowance for MACRS property for the year of change in which the property is treated as being disposed of is determined by first multiplying the adjusted depreciable basis of the property as of the first day of the year of change by the applicable depreciation rate for that taxable year (for further guidance, for example, see section 6 of Rev. Proc. 87-57 (1987-2 C. B. 687, 692) (see § 601.601(d)(2)(ii)(b) of this chapter)). This amount is then multiplied by a fraction, the numerator of which is the number of months (including fractions of months) the property is deemed to be placed in service during the year of change (taking into account the applicable convention) and the denominator of which is 12. No depreciation deduction is allowable for MACRS property placed in service and disposed of in the same taxable year. See §§ 1.168(k)-1T(f)(6)(ii) and 1.1400L(b)-1T(f)(6) for the additional first year depreciation deduction rules applicable to property placed in service and converted to personal use in the same taxable year. Upon the conversion to personal use, no gain, loss, or depreciation recapture under section 1245 or section 1250 is recognized. However, the provisions of section 1245 or section 1250 apply to any disposition of the converted property by the taxpayer at a later date. For listed property (as defined in section 280F(d)(4)), see section 280F(b)(2) for the recapture of excess depreciation upon the conversion to personal use.

(d) Change in the use results in a different recovery period and/or depreciation method. *(1) In general.* This paragraph (d) applies to a change in the use of MACRS property during a taxable year subsequent to the placed-in-service year, if the property continues to be MACRS property owned by the same taxpayer and, as a result of the change in the use, has a different recovery period, a different depreciation method, or both. For example, this paragraph (d) applies to MACRS property that—

(i) Begins or ceases to be used predominantly outside the United States;

(ii) Results in a reclassification of the property under section 168(e) due to a change in the use of the property; or

(iii) Begins or ceases to be tax-exempt use property (as defined in section 168(h)).

(2) Determination of change in the use. (i) In general. Except as provided in paragraph (d)(2)(ii) of this section, a change in the use of MACRS property occurs when the primary use of the MACRS property in the taxable year is different from its primary use in the immediately preceding taxable year. The primary use of MACRS property may be determined in any reasonable manner that is consistently applied to the taxpayer's MACRS property.

(ii) Alternative depreciation system property. (A) Property used within or outside the United States. A change in the use of MACRS property occurs when a taxpayer begins or ceases to use MACRS property predominantly outside the United States during the taxable year. The determination of whether MACRS property is used predominantly outside the United States is made in accordance with the test in § 1.48-1(g)(1)(i) for determining predominant use.

(B) Tax-exempt bond financed property. A change in the use of MACRS property occurs when the property changes to tax-exempt bond financed property, as described in section 168(g)(1)(C) and (g)(5), during the taxable year. For purposes of this paragraph (d), MACRS property changes to tax-exempt bond financed property when a tax-exempt bond is first issued after the MACRS property is placed in service. MACRS property continues to be tax-exempt bond financed property in the hands of the taxpayer even if the tax-exempt bond (including any refunding issue) is no longer outstanding or is redeemed.

(C) Other mandatory alternative depreciation system property. A change in the use of MACRS property occurs when the property changes to, or changes from, property described in section 168(g)(1)(B) (tax-exempt use property) or (D) (imported property covered by an Executive order) during the taxable year.

(iii) Change in the use deemed to occur on first day of the year of change. If a change in the use of MACRS property occurs under this paragraph (d)(2), the depreciation allowance for that MACRS property for the year of change is determined as though the use of the MACRS property changed on the first day of the year of change.

(3) Change in the use results in a shorter recovery period and/or a more accelerated depreciation method. (i) Treated as placed in service in the year of change. (A) In general. If a change in the use results in the MACRS property changing to a shorter recovery period and/or a depreciation method that is more accelerated than the method used for the MACRS property before the change in the use, the depreciation allowances beginning in the year of change are determined as though the MACRS property is placed in service by the taxpayer in the year of change.

(B) Computation of depreciation allowance. The depreciation allowances for the MACRS property for any 12-month taxable year beginning with the year of change are determined by multiplying the adjusted depreciable basis of the MACRS property as of the first day of each taxable year by the applicable depreciation rate for each taxable year. In determining the applicable depreciation rate for the year of change and subsequent taxable years, the taxpayer must use any applicable depreciation method and recovery period prescribed under section 168 for the MACRS property in the year of change, consistent with any election made under section 168 by the taxpayer for that year (see, for example, section 168(b)(5)). If there is a change in the use of MACRS property, the applicable convention that applies to the

MACRS property is the same as the convention that applied before the change in the use of the MACRS property. However, the depreciation allowance for the year of change for the MACRS property is determined without applying the applicable convention, unless the MACRS property is disposed of during the year of change. See paragraph (d)(5) of this section for the rules relating to the computation of the depreciation allowance under the optional depreciation tables. If the year of change or any subsequent taxable year is less than 12 months, the depreciation allowance determined under this paragraph (d)(3)(i) must be adjusted for a short taxable year (for further guidance, for example, see Rev. Proc. 89-15 (1989-1 C.B. 816) (see § 601.601(d)(2)(ii)(b) of this chapter)).

(C) Special rules. MACRS property affected by this paragraph (d)(3)(i) is not eligible in the year of change for the election provided under section 168(f)(1), 179, or 1400L(f), or for the additional first year depreciation deduction provided in section 168(k) or 1400L(b). See §§ 1.168(k)-1T(f)(6)(iv) and 1.1400L(b)-1T(f)(6) for other additional first year depreciation deduction rules applicable to a change in the use of MACRS property subsequent to its placed-in-service year. For purposes of determining whether the mid-quarter convention applies to other MACRS property placed in service during the year of change, the unadjusted depreciable basis (as defined in § 1.168(b)-1T(a)(3)) or the adjusted depreciable basis of MACRS property affected by this paragraph (d)(3)(i) is not taken into account.

(ii) Option to disregard the change in the use. In lieu of applying paragraph (d)(3)(i) of this section, the taxpayer may elect to determine the depreciation allowance as though the change in the use had not occurred. The taxpayer elects this option by claiming on the taxpayer's timely filed (including extensions) Federal income tax return for the year of change the depreciation allowance for the property as though the change in the use had not occurred. See paragraph (g)(2) of this section for the manner for revoking this election.

(4) Change in the use results in a longer recovery period and/or a slower depreciation method. (i) Treated as originally placed in service with longer recovery period and/or slower depreciation method. If a change in the use results in a longer recovery period and/or a depreciation method for the MACRS property that is less accelerated than the method used for the MACRS property before the change in the use, the depreciation allowances beginning with the year of change are determined as though the MACRS property had been originally placed in service by the taxpayer with the longer recovery period and/or the slower depreciation method. MACRS property affected by this paragraph (d)(4) is not eligible in the year of change for the election provided under section 168(f)(1), 179, or 1400L(f), or for the additional first year depreciation deduction provided in section 168(k) or 1400L(b). See §§ 1.168(k)-1T(f)(6)(iv) and 1.1400L(b)-1T(f)(6) for other additional first year depreciation deduction rules applicable to a change in the use of MACRS property subsequent to its placed-in-service year.

(ii) Computation of the depreciation allowance. The depreciation allowances for the MACRS property for any 12-month taxable year beginning with the year of change are determined by multiplying the adjusted depreciable basis of the MACRS property as of the first day of each taxable year by the applicable depreciation rate for each taxable year. If there is a change in the use of MACRS property, the applicable convention that applies to the MACRS property is the same as the convention that applied before the change in the use of the MACRS property. If the year of change or any subsequent taxable year is less than 12 months, the depreciation allowance determined under this paragraph (d)(4)(ii) must be adjusted for a short taxable year (for further guidance, for example, see Rev. Proc. 89-15 (1989-1 C.B. 816) (see § 601.601(d)(2)(ii)(b) of this chapter)). See paragraph (d)(5) of this section for the rules relating to the computation of the depreciation allowance under the optional depreciation tables. In determining the applicable depreciation rate for the year of change and any subsequent taxable year—

(A) The applicable depreciation method is the depreciation method that would apply in the year of change and any subsequent taxable year for the MACRS property had the taxpayer used the longer recovery period and/or the slower depreciation method in the placed-in-service year of the property. If the 200-or 150-percent declining balance method would have applied in the placed-in-service year but the method would have switched to the straight line method in the year of change or any prior taxable year, the applicable depreciation method beginning with the year of change is the straight line method; and

(B) The applicable recovery period is either—

(1) The longer recovery period resulting from the change in the use if the applicable depreciation method is the 200-or 150-percent declining balance method (as determined under paragraph (d)(4)(ii)(A) of this section) unless the recovery period did not change as a result of the change in the use, in which case the applicable recovery period is the same recovery period that applied before the change in the use; or

(2) The number of years remaining as of the beginning of each taxable year (taking into account the applicable convention) had the taxpayer used the longer recovery period in the placed-in-service year of the property if the applicable depreciation method is the straight line method (as determined under paragraph (d)(4)(ii)(A) of this section) unless the recovery period did not change as a result of the change in the use, in which case the applicable recovery period is the number of years remaining as of the beginning of each taxable year (taking into account the applicable convention) based on the recovery period that applied before the change in the use.

(5) Using optional depreciation tables. (i) Taxpayer not bound by prior use of table. If a taxpayer used an optional depreciation table for the MACRS property before a change in the use, the taxpayer is not bound to use the appropriate new table for that MACRS property beginning in the year of change (for further guidance, for example, see section 8 of Rev. Proc. 87-57 (1987-2 C.B. 687, 693) (see § 601.601(d)(2)(ii)(b) of this chapter)). If a taxpayer did not use an optional depreciation table for MACRS property before a change in the use and the change in the use results in a shorter recovery period and/ or a more accelerated depreciation method (as described in paragraph (d)(3)(i) of this section), the taxpayer may use the appropriate new table for that MACRS property beginning in the year of change. If a taxpayer chooses not to use the optional depreciation table, the depreciation allowances for the MACRS property beginning in the year of change are determined under paragraph (d)(3)(i) or (4) of this section, as applicable.

(ii) Taxpayer chooses to use optional depreciation table after a change in the use. If a taxpayer chooses to use an optional depreciation table for the MACRS property after a change in the use, the depreciation allowances for the MACRS property for any 12-month taxable year beginning with the year of change are determined as follows:

(A) Change in the use results in a shorter recovery period and/or a more accelerated depreciation method. If a change in the use results in a shorter recovery period and/or a more accelerated depreciation method (as described in paragraph (d)(3)(i) of this section), the depreciation allowances for the MACRS property for any 12-month taxable year beginning with the year of change are determined by multiplying the adjusted depreciable basis of the MACRS property as of the first day of the year of change by the annual depreciation rate for each recovery year (expressed as a decimal equivalent) specified in the appropriate optional depreciation table. The appropriate optional depreciation table for the MACRS property is based on the depreciation system, depreciation method, recovery period, and convention applicable to the MACRS property in the year of change as determined under paragraph (d)(3)(i) of this section. The depreciation allowance for the year of change for the MACRS property is determined by taking into account the applicable convention (which is already factored into the optional depreciation tables). If the year of change or any subsequent taxable year is less than 12 months, the depreciation allowance determined under this paragraph (d)(5)(ii)(A) must be adjusted for a short taxable year (for further guidance, for example, see Rev. Proc. 89-15 (1989-1 C.B. 816) (see § 601.601(d)(2)(ii)(b) of this chapter)).

(B) Change in the use results in a longer recovery period and/or a slower depreciation method. (1) Determination of the appropriate optional depreciation table. If a change in the use results in a longer recovery period and/or a slower depreciation method (as described in paragraph (d)(4)(i) of this section), the depreciation allowances for the MACRS property for any 12-month taxable year beginning with the year of change are determined by choosing the optional depreciation table that corresponds to the depreciation system, depreciation method, recovery period, and convention that would have applied to the MACRS property in the placed-in-service year had that property been originally placed in service by the taxpayer with the longer recovery period and/or the slower depreciation method. If there is a change in the use of MACRS property, the applicable convention that applies to the MACRS property is the same as the convention that applied before the change in the use of the MACRS property. If the year of change or any subsequent taxable year is less than 12 months, the depreciation allowance determined under this paragraph (d)(5)(ii)(B) must be adjusted for a short taxable year (for further guidance, for example, see Rev. Proc. 89-15 (1989-1 C.B. 816) (see § 601.601(d)(2)(ii)(b) of this chapter)).

(2) Computation of the depreciation allowance. The depreciation allowances for the MACRS property for any 12-month taxable year beginning with the year of change are computed by first determining the appropriate recovery year in the table identified under paragraph (d)(5)(ii)(B)(1) of this section. The appropriate recovery year for the year of change is the year that corresponds to the year of change. For example, if the recovery year for the year of change would have been Year 4 in the table that applied before the change in the use of the MACRS property, then the recovery year for the year of change is Year 4 in the table identified under paragraph (d)(5)(ii)(B)(1) of this section. Next, the annual depreciation rate (expressed as a decimal equivalent) for each recovery year is multiplied by a transaction coefficient. The transaction coefficient is the formula (1 / (1-x)) where x equals the sum of the annual depreciation rates from the table identified under paragraph (d)(5)(ii)(B)(1) of this section (expressed as a decimal equivalent) for the taxable years beginning with the placed-in-service year of the MACRS property through the taxable year immediately prior to the year of change. The product of the annual depreciation rate and the transaction coefficient is multiplied by the adjusted depreciable basis of the MACRS property as of the beginning of the year of change.

(6) Examples. The application of this paragraph (d) is illustrated by the following examples:

Example (1). Change in the use results in a shorter recovery period and/or a more accelerated depreciation method and optional depreciation table is not used. (i) X, a calendar-year corporation, places in service in 1999 equipment at a cost of $100,000 and uses this equipment from 1999 through 2003 primarily in its A business. X depreciates the equipment for 1999 through 2003 under the general depreciation system as 7-year property by using the 200-percent declining balance method (which switched to the straight-line method in 2003), a 7-year recovery period, and a half-year convention. Beginning in 2004, X primarily uses the equipment in its B business. As a result, the classification of the equipment under section 168(e) changes from 7-year property to 5-year property and the recovery period of the equipment under the general depreciation system changes from 7 years to 5 years. The depreciation method does not change. On January 1, 2004, the adjusted depreciable basis of the equipment is $22,311. X depreciates its 5-year recovery property placed in service in 2004 under the general depreciation system by using the 200-percent declining balance method and a 5-year recovery period. X does not use the optional depreciation tables.

(ii) Under paragraph (d)(3)(i) of this section, X's allowable depreciation deduction for the equipment for 2004 and subsequent taxable years is determined as though X placed the equipment in service in 2004 for use primarily in its B business. The depreciable basis of the equipment as of January 1, 2004, is $22,311 (the adjusted depreciable basis at January 1, 2004). Because X does not use the optional depreciation tables, the depreciation allowance for 2004 (the deemed placed-in-service year) for this equipment only is computed without taking into account the half-year convention. Pursuant to paragraph (d)(3)(i)(C) of this section, this equipment is not eligible for the additional first year depreciation deduction provided by section 168(k) or section 1400L(b). Thus, X's allowable depreciation deduction for the equipment for 2004 is $8,924 ($22,311 adjusted depreciable basis at January 1, 2004, multiplied by the applicable depreciation rate of 40% (200/5)). X's allowable depreciation deduction for the equipment for 2005 is $5,355 ($13,387 adjusted depreciable basis at January 1, 2005, multiplied by the applicable depreciation rate of 40% (200/5)).

(iii) Alternatively, under paragraph (d)(3)(ii) of this section, X may elect to disregard the change in the use and, as a result, may continue to treat the equipment as though it is used primarily in its A business. If the election is made, X's allowable depreciation deduction for the equipment for 2004 is $8,924 ($22,311 adjusted depreciable basis at January 1, 2004, multiplied by the applicable depreciation rate of 40% (1/2.5 years remaining at January 1, 2004)). X's allowable depreciation deduction for the equipment for 2005 is $8,925 ($13,387 adjusted depreciable basis at January 1, 2005, multiplied by the applicable depreciation rate of 66.67% (1/ 1.5 years remaining at January 1, 2005)).

Example (2). Change in the use results in a shorter recovery period and/or a more accelerated depreciation method and optional depreciation table is used. (i) Same facts as in Example 1, except that X used the optional depreciation tables for computing depreciation for 1999 through 2003. Pursuant to paragraph (d)(5) of this section, X chooses to continue to use the optional depreciation table for the equipment. X does not make the election provided in paragraph (d)(3)(ii) of this section to disregard the change in use.

(ii) In accordance with paragraph (d)(5)(ii)(A) of this section, X must first identify the appropriate optional depreciation table for the equipment. This table is table 1 in Rev. Proc. 87-57 because the equipment will be depreciated in the year of change (2004) under the general depreciation system using the 200-percent declining balance method, a 5-year recovery period, and the half-year convention (which is the convention that applied to the equipment in 1999). Pursuant to paragraph (d)(3)(i)(C) of this section, this equipment is not eligible for the additional first year depreciation deduction provided by section 168(k) or section 1400L(b). For 2004, X multiplies its adjusted depreciable basis in the equipment as of January 1, 2004, of $22,311, by the annual depreciation rate in table 1 for recovery year 1 for a 5-year recovery period (.20), to determine the depreciation allowance of $4,462. For 2005, X multiplies its adjusted depreciable basis in the equipment as of January 1, 2004, of $22,311, by the annual depreciation rate in table 1 for recovery year 2 for a 5-year recovery period (.32), to determine the depreciation allowance of $7,140.

Example (3). Change in the use results in a longer recovery period and/or a slower depreciation method. (i) Y, a calendar-year corporation, places in service in January 2002, equipment at a cost of $100,000 and uses this equipment in 2002 and 2003 only within the United States. Y elects not to deduct the additional first year depreciation under section 168(k). Y depreciates the equipment for 2002 and 2003 under the general depreciation system by using the 200-percent declining balance method, a 5-year recovery period, and a half-year convention. Beginning in 2004, Y uses the equipment predominantly outside the United States. As a result of this change in the use, the equipment is subject to the alternative depreciation system beginning in 2004. Under the alternative depreciation system, the equipment is depreciated by using the straight line method and a 9-year recovery period. The adjusted depreciable basis of the equipment at January 1, 2004, is $48,000.

(ii) Pursuant to paragraph (d)(4) of this section, Y's allowable depreciation deduction for 2004 and subsequent taxable years is determined as though the equipment had been placed in service in January 2002, as property used predominantly outside the United States. Further, pursuant to paragraph (d)(4)(i) of this section, the equipment is not eligible in 2004 for the additional first year depreciation deduction provided by section 168(k) or section 1400L(b). In determining the applicable depreciation rate for 2004, the applicable depreciation method is the straight line method and the applicable recovery period is 7.5 years, which is the number of years remaining at January 1, 2004, for property placed in service in 2002 with a 9-year recovery period (taking into account the half-year convention). Thus, the depreciation allowance for 2004 is $6,398 ($48,000 adjusted depreciable basis at January 1, 2004, multiplied by the applicable depreciation rate of 13.33% (1/7.5 years)). The depreciation allowance for 2005 is $6,398 ($41,602 adjusted depreciable basis at January 1, 2005, multiplied by the applicable depreciation rate of 15.38% (1/6.5 years remaining at January 1, 2005)).

Example (4). Change in the use results in a longer recovery period and/or a slower depreciation method and optional depreciation table is used. (i) Same facts as in Example 3, except that Y used the optional depreciation tables for computing depreciation in 2002 and 2003. Pursuant to paragraph (d)(5) of this section, Y chooses to continue to use the optional depreciation table for the equipment. Further, pursuant to paragraph (d)(4)(i) of this section, the equipment is not eligible in 2004 for the additional first year depreciation deduction provided by section 168(k) or section 1400L(b).

(ii) In accordance with paragraph (d)(5)(ii)(B) of this section, Y must first determine the appropriate optional depreciation table for the equipment pursuant to paragraph (d)(5)(ii)(B)(1) of this section. This table is table 8 in Rev. Proc. 87-57, which corresponds to the alternative depreciation system, the straight line method, a 9-year recovery period, and the half-year convention (because Y depreciated 5-year property in 2002 using a half-year convention). Next, Y must determine the appropriate recovery year in table 8. Because the year of change is 2004, the depreciation allowance for the equipment for 2004 is determined using recovery year 3 of table 8. For 2004, Y multiplies its adjusted depreciable basis in the equipment as of January 1, 2004, of $48,000, by the product of the annual depreciation rate in table 8 for recovery year 3 for a 9-year recovery period (.1111) and the transaction coefficient of 1.200 [1/(1-(.0556 (table 8 for recovery year 1 for a 9-year recovery period) + .1111 (table 8 for recovery year 2 for a 9-year recovery period)))], to determine the depreciation allowance of $6,399. For 2005, Y multiplies its adjusted depreciable basis in the equipment as of January 1, 2004, of $48,000, by the product of the annual depreciation rate in table 8 for recovery year 4 for a 9-year recovery period (.1111) and the transaction coefficient (1.200), to determine the depreciation allowance of $6,399.

(e) Change in the use of MACRS property during the placed-in-service year. *(1) In general.* Except as provided in paragraph (e)(2) of this section, if a change in the use of MACRS property occurs during the placed-in-service year and the property continues to be MACRS property owned by the same taxpayer, the depreciation allowance for that property for the placed-in-service year is determined by its primary use during that year. The primary use of MACRS property may be determined in any reasonable manner that is consistently applied to the taxpayer's MACRS property. For purposes of this paragraph (e), the determination of whether the mid-quarter convention applies to any MACRS property placed in service during the year of change is made in accordance with § 1.168(d)-1.

(2) Alternative depreciation system property. (i) Property used within and outside the United States. The depreciation allowance for the placed-in-service year for MACRS property that is used within and outside the United States is determined by its predominant use during that year. The determination of whether MACRS property is used predominantly outside the United States during the placed-in-service year shall be made in accordance with the test in § 1.48-1(g)(1)(i) for determining predominant use.

(ii) Tax-exempt bond financed property. The depreciation allowance for the placed-in-service year for MACRS property that changes to tax-exempt bond financed property, as described in section 168(g)(1)(C) and (g)(5), during that taxable year is determined under the alternative depreciation system. For purposes of this paragraph (e), MACRS property changes to tax-exempt bond financed property when a tax-exempt bond is first issued after the MACRS property is placed in service. MACRS property continues to be tax-exempt bond financed property in the hands of the taxpayer even if the tax-exempt bond (including any refunding issue) is not outstanding at, or is redeemed by, the end of the placed-in-service year.

(iii) Other mandatory alternative depreciation system property. The depreciation allowance for the placed-in-service year for MACRS property that changes to, or changes from, property described in section 168(g)(1)(B) (tax-exempt use property) or (D) (imported property covered by an Executive order) during that taxable year is determined under—

(A) The alternative depreciation system if the MACRS property is described in section 168(g)(1)(B) or (D) at the end of the placed-in-service year; or

(B) The general depreciation system if the MACRS property is not described in section 168(g)(1)(B) or (D) at the end of the placed-in-service year, unless other provisions of the Internal Revenue Code or regulations under the Internal Revenue Code require the depreciation allowance for that MACRS property to be determined under the alternative depreciation system (for example, section 168(g)(7)).

(3) Examples. The application of this paragraph (e) is illustrated by the following examples:

Example (1). (i) Z, a utility and calendar-year corporation, acquires and places in service on January 1, 2004, equipment at a cost of $100,000. Z uses this equipment in its combustion turbine production plant for 4 months and then uses the equipment in its steam production plant for the remainder of 2004. Z's combustion turbine production plant assets are classified as 15-year property and are depreciated by Z under the general depreciation system using a 15-year recovery period and the 150-percent declining balance method of depreciation. Z's steam production plant assets are classified as 20-year property and are depreciated by Z under the general depreciation system using a 20-year recovery period and the 150-percent declining balance method of depreciation. Z uses the optional depreciation tables. The equipment is 50-percent bonus depreciation property for purposes of section 168(k).

(ii) Pursuant to this paragraph (e), Z must determine depreciation based on the primary use of the equipment during the placed-in-service year. Z has consistently determined the primary use of all of its MACRS properties by comparing the number of full months in the taxable year during which a MACRS property is used in one manner with the number of full months in that taxable year during which that MACRS property is used in another manner. Applying this approach, Z determines the depreciation allowance for the equipment for 2004 is based on the equipment being classified as 20-year property because the equipment was used by Z in its steam production plant for 8 months in 2004. If the half-year convention applies in 2004, the appropriate optional depreciation table is table 1 in Rev. Proc. 87-57, which is the table for MACRS property subject to the general depreciation system, the 150-percent declining balance method, a 20-year recovery period, and the half-year convention. Thus, the depreciation allowance for the equipment for 2004 is $51,875, which is the total of $50,000 for the 50-percent additional first year depreciation deduction allowable (the unadjusted depreciable basis of $100,000 multiplied by .50), plus $1,875 for the 2004 depreciation allowance on the remaining adjusted depreciable basis of $50,000 [(the unadjusted depreciable basis of $100,000 less the additional first year depreciation deduction of $50,000) multiplied by the annual depreciation rate of .0375 in table 1 for recovery year 1 for a 20-year recovery period].

Example (2). T, a calendar year corporation, places in service on January 1, 2004, several computers at a total cost of $100,000. T uses these computers within the United States for 3 months in 2004 and then moves and uses the computers outside the United States for the remainder of 2004. Pursuant to § 1.48-1(g)(1)(i), the computers are considered as used predominantly outside the United States in 2004. As a result, for 2004, the computers are required to be depreciated under the alternative depreciation system of section 168(g) with a recovery period of 5 years pursuant to section 168(g)(3)(C). T uses the optional depreciation tables. If the half-year convention applies in 2004, the appropriate optional depreciation table is table 8 in Rev. Proc. 87-57, which is the table for MACRS property subject to the alternative depreciation system, the straight line method, a 5-year recovery period, and the half-year convention. Thus, the depreciation allowance for the computers for 2004 is $10,000, which is equal to the unadjusted depreciable basis of $100,000 multiplied by the annual depreciation rate of .10 in table 8 for recovery year 1 for a 5-year recovery period. Because the computers are required to be depreciated under the alternative depreciation system in their placed-in-service year, pursuant to section 168(k)(2)(C)(i) and § 1.168(k)-1T(b)(2)(ii), the computers are not eligible for the additional first year depreciation deduction provided by section 168(k).

(f) No change in accounting method. A change in computing the depreciation allowance in the year of change for property subject to this section is not a change in method of accounting under section 446(e). See § 1.446-1(e)(2)(ii)(d)(3)(ii).

(g) Effective dates. *(1) In general.* This section applies to any change in the use of MACRS property in a taxable year ending on or after June 17, 2004. For any change in the use of MACRS property after December 31, 1986, in a taxable year ending before June 17, 2004, the Internal Revenue Service will allow any reasonable method of depreciating the property under section 168 in the year of change and the subsequent taxable years that is consistently applied to any property for which the use changes in the hands of the same taxpayer or the taxpayer may choose, on a property-by-property basis, to apply the provisions of this section.

(2) Change in method of accounting. (i) In general. If a taxpayer adopted a method of accounting for depreciation due to a change in the use of MACRS property in a taxable year ending on or after December 30, 2003, and the method adopted is not in accordance with the method of accounting for depreciation provided in this section, a change to the method of accounting for depreciation provided in this section is a change in the method of accounting to which the provisions of sections 446(e) and 481 and the regulations under sections 446(e) and 481 apply. Also, a revocation of the election provided in paragraph (d)(3)(ii) of this section to disregard a change in the use is a change in method of accounting to which the provisions of sections 446(e) and 481 and the regulations under sections 446(e) and 481 apply. However, if a taxpayer adopted a method of accounting for depreciation due to a change in the use of MACRS property after December 31, 1986, in a taxable year ending before December 30, 2003, and the method adopted is not in accordance with the method of accounting for depreciation provided in this section, the taxpayer may treat the change to the method of accounting for depreciation provided in this section as a change in method of accounting to which the provisions of sections 446(e) and 481 and the regulations under sections 446(e) and 481 apply.

(ii) Automatic consent to change method of accounting. A taxpayer changing its method of accounting in accordance with this paragraph (g)(2) must follow the applicable administrative procedures issued under § 1.446-1(e)(3)(ii) for obtaining the Commissioner's automatic consent to a change in method of accounting (for further guidance, for example, see Rev. Proc. 2002-9 (2002-1 C.B. 327), (see § 601.601(d)(2)(ii)(b) of this chapter)). Any change in method of accounting made under this paragraph (g)(2) must be made using an adjustment under section 481(a). For purposes of Form 3115, Application for Change in Accounting Method, the designated number for the automatic accounting method change authorized by this paragraph (g)(2) is "88." If Form 3115 is revised or renumbered, any reference in this section to that form is treated as a reference to the revised or renumbered form.

T.D. 9132, 6/16/2004, amend T.D. 9307, 12/22/2006.

§ 1.168(i)-5 Table of contents.

This section lists the major paragraphs contained in Sec. 1.168(i)-6.

§ 1.168(i)-6 Like-kind exchanges and involuntary conversions.

(a) Scope.

(b) Definitions.

(1) Replacement MACRS property.

(2) Relinquished MACRS property.

(3) Time of disposition.

(4) Time of replacement.

(5) Year of disposition.

(6) Year of replacement.

(7) Exchanged basis.

(8) Excess basis.

(9) Depreciable exchanged basis.

(10) Depreciable excess basis.

(11) Like-kind exchange.

(12) Involuntary conversion.

(c) Determination of depreciation allowance.

(1) Computation of the depreciation allowance for depreciable exchanged basis beginning in the year of replacement.

(i) In general.

(ii) Applicable recovery period, depreciation method, and convention.

(2) Effect of depreciation treatment of the replacement MACRS property by previous owners of the acquired property.

(3) Recovery period and/or depreciation method of the properties are the same, or both are not the same.

(i) In general.

(ii) Both the recovery period and the depreciation method are the same.

(iii) Either the recovery period or the depreciation method is the same, or both are not the same.

(4) Recovery period or depreciation method of the properties is not the same.

(i) Longer recovery period.

(ii) Shorter recovery period.

(iii) Less accelerated depreciation method.

(iv) More accelerated depreciation method.

(v) Convention.

(A) Either the relinquished MACRS property or the replacement MACRS property is mid-month property.

(B) Neither the relinquished MACRS property nor the replacement MACRS property is mid-month property.

(5) Year of disposition and year of replacement.

(i) Relinquished MACRS property.

(A) General rule.

(B) Special rule.

(ii) Replacement MACRS property.

(A) Remaining recovery period of the replacement MACRS property.

(B) Year of replacement is 12 months.

(iii) Year of disposition or year of replacement is less than 12 months.

(iv) Deferred transactions.

(A) In general.

(B) Allowable depreciation for a qualified intermediary.

(v) Remaining recovery period.

(6) Examples.

(d) Special rules for determining depreciation allowances.

(1) Excess basis.

(i) In general.

(ii) Example.

(2) Depreciable and nondepreciable property.

(3) Depreciation limitations for automobiles.

(i) In general.

(ii) Order in which limitations on depreciation under section 280F(a) are applied.

(iii) Examples.

(4) Involuntary conversion for which the replacement MACRS property is acquired and placed in service before disposition of relinquished MACRS property.

(e) Use of optional depreciation tables.

(1) Taxpayer not bound by prior use of table.

(2) Determination of the depreciation deduction.

(i) Relinquished MACRS property.

(ii) Replacement MACRS property.

(A) Determination of the appropriate optional depreciation table.

(B) Calculating the depreciation deduction for the replacement MACRS property.

(iii) Unrecovered basis.

(3) Excess basis.

(4) Examples.

(f) Mid-quarter convention.

(1) Exchanged basis.

(2) Excess basis.

(3) Depreciable property acquired for nondepreciable property.

(g) Section 179 election.

(h) Additional first year depreciation deduction.

(i) Elections.

(1) Election not to apply this section.

(2) Election to treat certain replacement property as MACRS property.

(j) Time and manner of making election under paragraph (i)(1) of this section.

(1) In general.

(2) Time for making election.

(3) Manner of making election.

(4) Revocation.

(k) Effective date.

(1) In general.

(2) Application to pre-effective date like-kind exchanges and involuntary conversions.

(3) Like-kind exchanges and involuntary conversions where the taxpayer made the election under section 168(f)(1) for the relinquished property.

T.D. 9314, 2/26/2007.

§ 1.168(i)-6 Like-kind exchanges and involuntary conversions.

Caution: The Treasury has not yet amended Reg § 1.168(i)-6 to reflect changes made by P.L. 110-343.

(a) Scope. This section provides the rules for determining the depreciation allowance for MACRS property acquired in a like-kind exchange or an involuntary conversion, including a like-kind exchange or an involuntary conversion of MACRS property that is exchanged or replaced with other MACRS property in a transaction between members of the same affiliated group. The allowance for depreciation under this section constitutes the amount of depreciation allowable under section 167(a) for the year of replacement and any subsequent taxable year for the replacement MACRS property and for the year of disposition of the relinquished MACRS property. The provisions of this section apply only to MACRS property to which § 1.168(h)-1 (like-kind exchanges of tax-exempt use property) does not apply. Additionally, paragraphs (c) through (f) of this section apply only to MACRS property for which an election under paragraph (i) of this section has not been made.

(b) Definitions. For purposes of this section, the following definitions apply:

(1) Replacement MACRS property is MACRS property (as defined in § 1.168(b)-1(a)(2)) in the hands of the acquiring taxpayer that is acquired for other MACRS property in a like-kind exchange or an involuntary conversion.

(2) Relinquished MACRS property is MACRS property that is transferred by the taxpayer in a like-kind exchange, or in an involuntary conversion.

(3) Time of disposition is when the disposition of the relinquished MACRS property takes place under the convention, as determined under § 1.168(d)-1, that applies to the relinquished MACRS property.

(4) Time of replacement is the later of—

(i) When the replacement MACRS property is placed in service under the convention, as determined under this section, that applies to the replacement MACRS property; or

(ii) The time of disposition of the exchanged or involuntarily converted property.

(5) Year of disposition is the taxable year that includes the time of disposition.

(6) Year of replacement is the taxable year that includes the time of replacement.

(7) Exchanged basis is determined after the depreciation deductions for the year of disposition are determined under paragraph (c)(5)(i) of this section and is the lesser of—

(i) The basis in the replacement MACRS property, as determined under section 1031(d) and the regulations under section 1031(d) or section 1033(b) and the regulations under section 1033(b); or

(ii) The adjusted depreciable basis (as defined in § 1.168(b)-1(a)(4)) of the relinquished MACRS property.

(8) Excess basis is any excess of the basis in the replacement MACRS property, as determined under section 1031(d) and the regulations under section 1031(d) or section 1033(b) and the regulations under section 1033(b), over the exchanged basis as determined under paragraph (b)(7) of this section.

(9) Depreciable exchanged basis is the exchanged basis as determined under paragraph (b)(7) of this section reduced by—

(i) The percentage of such basis attributable to the taxpayer's use of property for the taxable year other than in the taxpayer's trade or business (or for the production of income); and

(ii) Any adjustments to basis provided by other provisions of the Internal Revenue Code (Code) and the regulations under the Code (including section 1016(a)(2) and (3), for example, depreciation deductions in the year of replacement allowable under section 168(k) or 1400L(b)).

(10) Depreciable excess basis is the excess basis as determined under paragraph (b)(8) of this section reduced by—

(i) The percentage of such basis attributable to the taxpayer's use of property for the taxable year other than in the taxpayer's trade or business (or for the production of income);

(ii) Any portion of the basis the taxpayer properly elects to treat as an expense under section 179; and

(iii) Any adjustments to basis provided by other provisions of the Code and the regulations under the Code (including section 1016(a)(2) and (3), for example, depreciation deductions in the year of replacement allowable under section 168(k) or 1400L(b)).

(11) Like-kind exchange is an exchange of property in a transaction to which section 1031(a)(1), (b), or (c) applies.

(12) Involuntary conversion is a transaction described in section 1033(a)(1) or (2) that resulted in the nonrecognition of any part of the gain realized as the result of the conversion.

(c) Determination of depreciation allowance.

(1) Computation of the depreciation allowance for depreciable exchanged basis beginning in the year of replacement.

(i) In general. This paragraph (c) provides rules for determining the applicable recovery period, the applicable depreciation method, and the applicable convention used to determine the depreciation allowances for the depreciable exchanged basis beginning in the year of replacement. See paragraph (c)(5) of this section for rules relating to the computation of the depreciation allowance for the year of disposition and for the year of replacement. See paragraph (d)(1) of this section for rules relating to the computation of the depreciation allowance for depreciable excess basis. See paragraph (d)(4) of this section if the replacement MACRS property is acquired before disposition of the relinquished MACRS property in a transaction to which section 1033 applies. See paragraph (e) of this section for rules relating to the computation of the depreciation allowance using the optional depreciation tables.

(ii) Applicable recovery period, depreciation method, and convention. The recovery period, depreciation method, and convention determined under this paragraph (c) are the only permissible methods of accounting for MACRS property within the scope of this section unless the taxpayer makes the election under paragraph (i) of this section not to apply this section.

(2) Effect of depreciation treatment of the replacement MACRS property by previous owners of the acquired property. If replacement MACRS property is acquired by a taxpayer in a like-kind exchange or an involuntary conversion, the depreciation treatment of the replacement MACRS property by previous owners has no effect on the determination of depreciation allowances for the replacement MACRS property in the hands of the acquiring taxpayer. For example, a taxpayer exchanging, in a like-kind exchange, MACRS property for property that was depreciated under section 168 of the Internal Revenue Code of 1954 (ACRS) by the previous owner must use this section because the replacement property will become MACRS property in the hands of the acquiring taxpayer. In addition, elections made by previous owners in determining depreciation allowances for the replacement MACRS property have no effect on the acquiring taxpayer. For example, a taxpayer exchanging, in a like-kind exchange, MACRS property that the taxpayer depreciates under the general depreciation system of section 168(a) for other MACRS property that the previous owner elected to depreciate under the alternative depreciation system pursuant to section 168(g)(7) does not have to continue using the alternative depreciation system for the replacement MACRS property.

(3) Recovery period and/or depreciation method of the properties are the same, or both are not the same. (i) In general. For purposes of paragraphs (c)(3) and (c)(4) of this section in determining whether the recovery period and the depreciation method prescribed under section 168 for the replacement MACRS property are the same as the recovery period and the depreciation method prescribed under section 168 for the relinquished MACRS property, the recovery period and the depreciation method for the replacement MACRS property are considered to be the recovery period and the depreciation method that would have applied under section 168, taking into account any elections made by the acquiring taxpayer under section 168(b)(5) or 168(g)(7), had the replacement MACRS property been placed in service by the acquiring taxpayer at the same time as the relinquished MACRS property.

(ii) Both the recovery period and the depreciation method are the same. If both the recovery period and the depreciation method prescribed under section 168 for the replacement MACRS property are the same as the recovery period and the depreciation method prescribed under section 168 for the relinquished MACRS property, the depreciation allowances for the replacement MACRS property beginning in the year of replacement are determined by using the same recovery period and depreciation method that were used for the relinquished MACRS property. Thus, the replacement MACRS property is depreciated over the remaining recovery period (taking into account the applicable convention), and by using the depreciation method, of the relinquished MACRS property. Except as provided in paragraph (c)(5) of this section, the depreciation allowances for the depreciable exchanged basis for any 12-month taxable year beginning with the year of replacement are determined by multiplying the depreciable exchanged basis by the applicable depreciation rate for each taxable year (for further guidance, for example, see section 6 of Rev. Proc. 87-57 (1987-2 CB 687, 692) and § 601.601(d)(2)(ii)(b) of this chapter).

(iii) Either the recovery period or the depreciation method is the same, or both are not the same. If either the recovery period or the depreciation method prescribed under section 168 for the replacement MACRS property is the same as the recovery period or the depreciation method prescribed under section 168 for the relinquished MACRS property, the depreciation allowances for the depreciable exchanged basis beginning in the year of replacement are determined using the recovery period or the depreciation method that is the same as the relinquished MACRS property. See paragraph (c)(4) of this section to determine the depreciation allowances when the recovery period or the depreciation method of the replacement MACRS property is not the same as that of the relinquished MACRS property.

(4) Recovery period or depreciation method of the properties is not the same. If the recovery period prescribed under section 168 for the replacement MACRS property (as determined under paragraph (c)(3)(i) of this section) is not the same as the recovery period prescribed under section 168 for the relinquished MACRS property, the depreciation allowances for the depreciable exchanged basis beginning in the year of replacement are determined under this paragraph (c)(4). Similarly, if the depreciation method prescribed under section 168 for the replacement MACRS property (as determined under paragraph (c)(3)(i) of this section) is not the same as the depreciation method prescribed under section 168 for the relinquished MACRS property, the depreciation method used to determine the depreciation allowances for the depreciable exchanged basis beginning in the year of replacement is determined under this paragraph (c)(4).

(i) Longer recovery period. If the recovery period prescribed under section 168 for the replacement MACRS property (as determined under paragraph (c)(3)(i) of this section) is longer than that prescribed for the relinquished MACRS property, the depreciation allowances for the depreciable exchanged basis beginning in the year of replacement are determined as though the replacement MACRS property had originally been placed in service by the acquiring taxpayer in the same taxable year the relinquished MACRS property was placed in service by the acquiring taxpayer, but using the longer recovery period of the replacement MACRS property (as determined under paragraph (c)(3)(i) of this section) and the convention determined under paragraph (c)(4)(v) of this section. Thus, the depreciable exchanged basis is depreciated over the remaining recovery period (taking into account the applicable convention) of the replacement MACRS property.

(ii) Shorter recovery period. If the recovery period prescribed under section 168 for the replacement MACRS property (as determined under paragraph (c)(3)(i) of this section) is shorter than that of the relinquished MACRS property, the depreciation allowances for the depreciable exchanged basis beginning in the year of replacement are determined using the same recovery period as that of the relinquished MACRS property. Thus, the depreciable exchanged basis is depreciated over the remaining recovery period (taking into account the applicable convention) of the relinquished MACRS property.

(iii) Less accelerated depreciation method.

(A) If the depreciation method prescribed under section 168 for the replacement MACRS property (as determined under paragraph (c)(3)(i) of this section) is less accelerated than that of the relinquished MACRS property at the time of disposition, the depreciation allowances for the depreciable exchanged basis beginning in the year of replacement are determined as though the replacement MACRS property had originally been placed in service by the acquiring taxpayer at the same time the relinquished MACRS property was placed in service by the acquiring taxpayer, but using the less accelerated depreciation method. Thus, the depreciable exchanged basis is depreciated using the less accelerated depreciation method.

(B) Except as provided in paragraph (c)(5) of this section, the depreciation allowances for the depreciable exchanged basis for any 12-month taxable year beginning in the year of replacement are determined by multiplying the adjusted depreciable basis by the applicable depreciation rate for each taxable year. If, for example, the depreciation method of the replacement MACRS property in the year of replacement is the 150-percent declining balance method and the depreciation method of the relinquished MACRS property in the year of replacement is the 200-percent declining balance method, and neither method had been switched to the straight line method in the year of replacement or any prior taxable year, the applicable depreciation rate for the year of replacement and subsequent taxable years is determined by using the depreciation rate of the replacement MACRS property as if the replacement MACRS property was placed in service by the acquiring taxpayer at the same time the relinquished MACRS property was placed in service by the acquiring taxpayer, until the 150-percent declining balance method has been switched to the straight line method. If, for example, the depreciation method of the replacement MACRS property is the straight line method, the applicable depreciation rate for the year of replacement is determined by using the remaining recovery period at the beginning of the year of disposition (as determined under this paragraph (c)(4) and taking into account the applicable convention).

(iv) More accelerated depreciation method. (A) If the depreciation method prescribed under section 168 for the replacement MACRS property (as determined under paragraph (c)(3)(i) of this section) is more accelerated than that of the relinquished MACRS property at the time of disposition, the depreciation allowances for the replacement MACRS property beginning in the year of replacement are determined using the same depreciation method as the relinquished MACRS property.

(B) Except as provided in paragraph (c)(5) of this section, the depreciation allowances for the depreciable exchanged basis for any 12-month taxable year beginning in the year of replacement are determined by multiplying the adjusted depreciable basis by the applicable depreciation rate for each taxable year. If, for example, the depreciation method of the relinquished MACRS property in the year of replacement is the 150-percent declining balance method and the depreciation method of the replacement MACRS property in the year of replacement is the 200-percent declining balance method, and neither method had been switched to the straight line method in the year of replacement or any prior taxable year, the applicable depreciation rate for the year of replacement and subsequent taxable years is the same depreciation rate that applied to the relinquished MACRS property in the year of replacement, until the 150-percent declining balance method has been switched to the straight line method. If, for example, the depreciation method is the straight line method, the applicable depreciation rate for the year of replacement is determined by using the remaining recovery period at the beginning of the year of disposition (as determined under this paragraph (c)(4) and taking into account the applicable convention).

(v) Convention. The applicable convention for the exchanged basis is determined under this paragraph (c)(4)(v).

(A) Either the relinquished MACRS property or the replacement MACRS property is mid-month property. If either the relinquished MACRS property or the replacement MACRS property is property for which the applicable convention (as determined under section 168(d)) is the mid-month convention, the exchanged basis must be depreciated using the mid-month convention.

(B) Neither the relinquished MACRS property nor the replacement MACRS property is mid-month property. If neither the relinquished MACRS property nor the replacement MACRS property is property for which the applicable convention (as determined under section 168(d)) is the mid-month convention, the applicable convention for the exchanged basis is the same convention that applied to the relinquished MACRS property. If the relinquished MACRS property is placed in service in the year of disposition, and the time of replacement is also in the year of disposition, the convention that applies to the relinquished MACRS property is determined under paragraph (f)(1)(i) of this section. If, however, relinquished MACRS property was placed in service in the year of disposition and the time of replacement is in a taxable year subsequent to the year of disposition, the convention that applies to the exchanged basis is the convention that applies in that subsequent taxable year (see paragraph (f)(1)(ii) of this section).

(5) Year of disposition and year of replacement. No depreciation deduction is allowable for MACRS property disposed of by a taxpayer in a like-kind exchange or involuntary conversion in the same taxable year that such property was placed in service by the taxpayer. If replacement MACRS property is disposed of by a taxpayer during the same taxable year that the relinquished MACRS property is placed in service by the taxpayer, no depreciation deduction is allowable for either MACRS property. Otherwise, the depreciation allowances for the year of disposition and for the year of replacement are determined as follows:

(i) Relinquished MACRS property. (A) General rule. Except as provided in paragraphs (c)(5)(i)(B), (c)(5)(iii), (e), and (i) of this section, the depreciation allowance in the year of disposition for the relinquished MACRS property is computed by multiplying the allowable depreciation deduction for the property for that year by a fraction, the numerator of which is the number of months (including fractions of months) the property is deemed to be placed in service during the year of disposition (taking into account the applicable convention of the relinquished MACRS property), and the denominator of which is 12. In the case of termination under § 1.168(i)-1(e)(3)(v) of general asset account treatment of an asset, or of all the assets remaining, in a general asset account, the allowable depreciation deduction in the year of disposition for the asset or assets for which general asset account treatment is terminated is determined using the depreciation method, recovery period, and convention of the general asset account. This allowable depreciation deduction is adjusted to account for the period the asset or assets is deemed to be in service in accordance with this paragraph (c)(5)(i).

(B) Special rule. If, at the beginning of the year of disposition, the remaining recovery period of the relinquished MACRS property, taking into account the applicable convention of such property, is less than the period between the beginning of the year of disposition and the time of disposition, the depreciation deduction for the relinquished MACRS property for the year of disposition is equal to the adjusted depreciable basis of the relinquished MACRS property at the beginning of the year of disposition. If this paragraph applies, the exchanged basis is zero and no depreciation is allowable for the exchanged basis in the replacement MACRS property.

(ii) Replacement MACRS property. (A) Remaining recovery period of the replacement MACRS property. The replacement MACRS property is treated as placed in service at the time of replacement under the convention that applies to the replacement MACRS property as determined under this paragraph (c)(5)(ii). The remaining recovery period of the replacement MACRS property at the time of replacement is the excess of the recovery period for the replacement MACRS property, as determined under paragraph (c) of this section, over the period of time that the replacement MACRS property would have been in service if it had been placed in service when the relinquished MACRS property was placed in service and removed from service at the time of disposition of the relinquished MACRS property. This period is determined by using the convention that applied to the relinquished MACRS property to determine the date that the relinquished MACRS property is deemed to have been placed in service and the date that it is deemed to have been disposed of. The length of time the replacement MACRS property would have been in service is determined by using these dates and the convention that applies to the replacement MACRS property.

(B) Year of replacement is 12 months. Except as provided in paragraphs (c)(5)(iii), (e), and (i) of this section, the depreciation allowance in the year of replacement for the depreciable exchanged basis is determined by—

(1) Calculating the applicable depreciation rate for the replacement MACRS property as of the beginning of the year of replacement taking into account the depreciation method prescribed for the replacement MACRS property under paragraph (c)(3) of this section and the remaining recovery period of the replacement MACRS property as of the beginning of the year of disposition as determined under this paragraph (c)(5)(ii);

(2) Calculating the depreciable exchanged basis of the replacement MACRS property, and adding to that amount the amount determined under paragraph (c)(5)(i) of this section for the year of disposition; and

(3) Multiplying the product of the amounts determined under paragraphs (c)(5)(ii)(B)(1) and (B)(2) of this section by a fraction, the numerator of which is the number of months (including fractions of months) the property is deemed to be in service during the year of replacement (in the year of replacement the replacement MACRS property is deemed to be placed in service by the acquiring taxpayer at the time of replacement under the convention determined under paragraph (c)(4)(v) of this section), and the denominator of which is 12.

(iii) Year of disposition or year of replacement is less than 12 months. If the year of disposition or the year of replacement is less than 12 months, the depreciation allowance determined under paragraph (c)(5)(ii)(A) of this section must be adjusted for a short taxable year (for further guidance, for example, see Rev. Proc. 89-15 (1989-1 CB 816) and § 601.601(d)(2)(ii)(b) of this chapter).

(iv) Deferred transactions. (A) In general. If the replacement MACRS property is not acquired until after the disposition of the relinquished MACRS property, taking into account the applicable convention of the relinquished MACRS property and replacement MACRS property, depreciation is not allowable during the period between the disposition of the relinquished MACRS property and the acquisition of the replacement MACRS property. The recovery period for the replacement MACRS property is suspended during this period. For purposes of paragraph (c)(5)(ii) of this section, only the depreciable exchanged basis of the replacement MACRS property is taken into account for calculating the amount in paragraph (c)(5)(ii)(B)(2) of this section if the year of replacement is a taxable year subsequent to the year of disposition.

(B) Allowable depreciation for a qualified intermediary. [Reserved].

(v) Remaining recovery period. The remaining recovery period of the replacement MACRS property is determined as of the beginning of the year of disposition of the relinquished MACRS property. For purposes of determining the remaining recovery period of the replacement MACRS property, the replacement MACRS property is deemed to have been originally placed in service under the convention determined under paragraph (c)(4)(v) of this section, but at the time the relinquished MACRS property was deemed to be placed in service under the convention that applied to it when it was placed in service.

(6) Examples. The application of this paragraph (c) is illustrated by the following examples:

Example (1). A1, a calendar-year taxpayer, exchanges Building M, an office building, for Building N, a warehouse in a like-kind exchange. Building M is relinquished in July 2004 and Building N is acquired and placed in service in October 2004. A1 did not make any elections under section 168 for either Building M or Building N. The unadjusted depreciable basis of Building M was $4,680,000 when placed in service in July 1997. Since the recovery period and depreciation method prescribed under section 168 for Building N (39 years, straight line method) are the same as the recovery period and depreciation method prescribed under section 168 for Building M (39 years, straight line method), Building N is depreciated over the remaining recovery period of, and using the same depreciation method and convention as that of, Building M. Applying the applicable convention, Building M is deemed disposed of on July 15, 2004, and Building N is placed in service on October 15, 2004. Thus, Building N will be depreciated using the straight line method over a remaining recovery period of 32 years beginning in October 2004 (the remaining recovery period of 32 years and 6.5 months at the beginning of 2004, less the 6.5 months of depreciation taken prior to the disposition of the exchanged MACRS property (Building M) in 2004). For 2004, the year in which the transaction takes place, the depreciation allowance for Building M is ($120,000)(6.5/12) which equals $65,000. The depreciation allowance for Building N for 2004 is ($120,000)(2.5/12) which equals $25,000. For 2005 and subsequent years, Building N is depreciated over the remaining recovery period of, and using the same depreciation method and convention as that of, Building M. Thus, the depreciation allowance for Building N is the same as Building M, namely $10,000 per month.

Example (2). B, a calendar-year taxpayer, placed in service Bridge P in January 1998. Bridge P is depreciated using the half-year convention. In January 2004, B exchanges Bridge P for Building Q, an apartment building, in a like-kind exchange. Pursuant to paragraph (k)(2)(i) of this section, B decided to apply § 1.168(i)-6 to the exchange of Bridge P for Building Q, the replacement MACRS property.

B did not make any elections under section 168 for either Bridge P or Building Q. Since the recovery period prescribed under section 168 for Building Q (27.5 years) is longer than that of Bridge P (15 years), Building Q is depreciated as if it had originally been placed in service in July 1998 and disposed of in July 2004 using a 27.5 year recovery period. Additionally, since the depreciation method prescribed under section 168 for Building Q (straight line method) is less accelerated than that of Bridge P (150-percent declining balance method), then the depreciation allowance for Building Q is computed using the straight line method. Thus, when Building Q is acquired and placed in service in 2004, its basis is depreciated over the remaining 21.5 year recovery period using the straight line method of depreciation and the mid-month convention beginning in July 2004.

Example (3). C, a calendar-year taxpayer, placed in service Building R, a restaurant, in January 1996. In January 2004, C exchanges Building R for Tower S, a radio transmitting tower, in a like-kind exchange. Pursuant to paragraph (k)(2)(i) of this section, C decided to apply § 1.168(i)-6 to the exchange of Building R for Tower S, the replacement MACRS property. C did not make any elections under section 168 for either Building R or Tower S. Since the recovery period prescribed under section 168 for Tower S (15 years) is shorter than that of Building R (39 years), Tower S is depreciated over the remaining recovery period of Building R. Additionally, since the depreciation method prescribed under section 168 for Tower S (150% declining balance method) is more accelerated than that of Building R (straight line method), then the depreciation allowance for Tower S is also computed using the same depreciation method as Building R. Thus, Tower S is depreciated over the remaining 31 year recovery period of Building R using the straight line method of depreciation and the mid-month convention. Alternatively, C may elect under paragraph (i) of this section to treat Tower S as though it is placed in service in January 2004. In such case, C uses the applicable recovery period, depreciation method, and convention prescribed under section 168 for Tower S.

Example (4). (i) In February 2002, D, a calendar-year taxpayer and manufacturer of rubber products, acquired for $60,000 and placed in service Asset T (a special tool) and depreciated Asset T using the straight line method election under section 168(b)(5) and the mid-quarter convention over its 3-year recovery period. D elected not to deduct the additional first year depreciation for 3-year property placed in service in 2002. In June 2004, D exchanges Asset T for Asset U (not a special tool) in a like-kind exchange. D elected not to deduct the additional first year depreciation for 7-year property placed in service in 2004. Since the recovery period prescribed under section 168 for Asset U (7 years) is longer than that of Asset T (3 years), Asset U is depreciated as if it had originally been placed in service in February 2002 using a 7-year recovery period. Additionally, since the depreciation method prescribed under section 168 for Asset U (200-percent declining balance method) is more accelerated than that of Asset T (straight line method) at the time of disposition, the depreciation allowance for Asset U is computed using the straight line method. Asset U is depreciated over its remaining recovery period of 4.75 years using the straight line method of depreciation and the mid-quarter convention.

(ii) The 2004 depreciation allowance for Asset T is $7,500 ($20,000 allowable depreciation deduction for 2004) x 4.5 months / 12).

(iii) The depreciation rate in 2004 for Asset U is 0.1951 (1 / 5.125 years (the length of the applicable recovery period remaining as of the beginning of 2004)). Therefore, the depreciation allowance for Asset U in 2004 is $2,744 (0.1951 x $22,500 (the sum of the $15,000 depreciable exchanged basis of Asset U ($22,500 adjusted depreciable basis at the beginning of 2004 for Asset T, less the $7,500 depreciation allowable for Asset T for 2004) and the $7,500 depreciation allowable for Asset T for 2004) x 7.5 months / 12).

Example (5). The facts are the same as in Example 4 except that D exchanges Asset T for Asset U in June 2005, in a like-kind exchange. Under these facts, the remaining recovery period of Asset T at the beginning of 2005 is 1.5 months and, as a result, is less than the 5-month period between the beginning of 2005 (year of disposition) and June 2005 (time of disposition). Accordingly, pursuant to paragraph (c)(5)(i)(B) of this section, the 2005 depreciation allowance for Asset T is $2,500 ($2,500 adjusted depreciable basis at the beginning of 2005 ($60,000 original basis minus $17,500 depreciation deduction for 2002 minus $20,000 depreciation deduction for 2003 minus $20,000 depreciation deduction for 2004)). Because the exchanged basis of asset U is $0.00, no depreciation is allowable for asset U.

Example (6). On January 1, 2004, E, a calendar-year taxpayer, acquired and placed in service Canopy V, a gas station canopy. The purchase price of Canopy V was $60,000. On August 1, 2004, Canopy V was destroyed in a hurricane and was therefore no longer usable in E's business. On October 1, 2004, as part of the involuntary conversion, E acquired and placed in service new Canopy W with the insurance proceeds E received due to the loss of Canopy V. E elected not to deduct the additional first year depreciation for 5-year property placed in service in 2004. E depreciates both canopies under the general depreciation system of section 168(a) by using the 200-percent declining balance method of depreciation, a 5-year recovery period, and the half-year convention. No depreciation deduction is allowable for Canopy V. The depreciation deduction allowable for Canopy W for 2004 is $12,000 ($60,000 x the annual depreciation rate of .40 x ½ year). For 2005, the depreciation deduction for Canopy W is $19,200 ($48,000 adjusted basis x the annual depreciation rate of .40).

Example (7). The facts are the same as in Example 6, except that E did not make the election out of the additional first year depreciation for 5-year property placed in service in 2004. E depreciates both canopies under the general depreciation system of section 168(a) by using the 200-percent declining balance method of depreciation, a 5-year recovery period, and the half-year convention. No depreciation deduction is allowable for Canopy V. For 2004, E is allowed a 50-percent additional first year depreciation deduction of $30,000 for Canopy W (the unadjusted depreciable basis of $60,000 multiplied by .50), and a regular MACRS depreciation deduction of $6,000 for Canopy W (the depreciable exchanged basis of $30,000 multiplied by the annual depreciation rate of .40 x ½ year). For 2005, E is allowed a regular MACRS depreciation deduction of $9,600 for Canopy W (the depreciable exchanged basis of $24,000 ($30,000 minus regular 2003 depreciation of $6,000) multiplied by the annual depreciation rate of .40).

Example (8). In January 2001, F, a calendar-year taxpayer, places in service a paved parking lot, Lot W, and begins depreciating Lot W over its 15-year recovery period. F's unadjusted depreciable basis in Lot W is $1,000x. On April 1, 2004, F disposes of Lot W in a like-kind exchange for Building X, which is nonresidential real property. Lot W is depreciated using the 150 percent declining balance method and the half-year convention. Building X is depreciated using the straight-line method with a 39-year recovery period and using the mid-month convention. Both Lot W and Building X were in service at the time of the exchange. Because Lot W was depreciated using the half-year convention, it is deemed to have been placed in service on July 1, 2001, the first day of the second half of 2001, and to have been disposed of on July 1, 2004, the first day of the second half of 2004. To determine the remaining recovery period of Building X at the time of replacement, Building X is deemed to have been placed in service on July 1, 2001, and removed from service on July 1, 2004. Thus, Building X is deemed to have been in service, at the time of replacement, for 3 years (36 months = 5.5 months in 2001 + 12 months in 2002 + 12 months in 2003 + 6.5 months in 2004) and its remaining recovery period is 36 years (39 - 3). Because Building X is deemed to be placed in service at the time of replacement, July 1, 2004, the first day of the second half of 2004, Building X is depreciated for 5.5 months in 2004. However, at the beginning of the year of replacement the remaining recovery period for Building X is 36 years and 6.5 months (39 years - 2 years and 5.5 months (5.5 months in 2001 + 12 months in 2002 + 12 months in 2003)). The depreciation rate for building X for 2004 is 0.02737 (= 1/(39-2-5.5/12)). For 2005, the depreciation rate for Building X is 0.02814 (= 1/(39-3-5.5/12)).

Example (9). The facts are the same as in Example 8. F did not make the election under paragraph (i) of this section for Building Y in the initial exchange. In January 2006, F exchanges Building Y for Building Z, an office building, in a like-kind exchange. F did not make any elections under section 168 for either Building Y or Building Z. Since the recovery period prescribed for Building Y as a result of the initial exchange (39 years) is longer than that of Building Z (27.5 years), Building Z is depreciated over the remaining 33 years of the recovery period of Building Y. The depreciation methods are the same for both Building Y and Building Z so F's exchanged basis in Building Z is depreciated over 33 years, using the straight-line method and the mid-month convention, beginning in January 2006. Alternatively, F could have made the election under paragraph (i) of this section. If F makes such election, Building Z is treated as placed in service by F when acquired in January 2006 and F would recover its exchanged basis in Building Z over 27.5 years, using the straight line method and the mid-month convention, beginning in January 2006.

(d) Special rules for determining depreciation allowances. *(1) Excess basis.* (i) In general. Any excess basis in the replacement MACRS property is treated as property that is placed in service by the acquiring taxpayer in the year of replacement. Thus, the depreciation allowances for the depreciable excess basis are determined by using the applicable recovery period, depreciation method, and convention prescribed under section 168 for the property at the time of replacement. However, if replacement MACRS property is disposed of during the same taxable year the relinquished MACRS property is placed in service by the acquiring taxpayer, no depreciation deduction is allowable for either MACRS property. See paragraph (g) of this section regarding the application of section 179. See paragraph (h) of this section regarding the application of section 168(k) or 1400L(b).

(ii) Example. The application of this paragraph (d)(1) is illustrated by the following example:

Example. In 1989, G placed in service a hospital. On January 16, 2004, G exchanges this hospital plus $2,000,000 cash for an office building in a like-kind exchange. On January 16, 2004, the hospital has an adjusted depreciable basis of $1,500,000. After the exchange, the basis of the office building is $3,500,000. Pursuant to paragraph (k)(2)(i) of this section, G decided to apply § 1.168(i)-6 to the exchange of the hospital for the office building, the replacement MACRS property. The depreciable exchanged basis of the office building is depreciated in accordance with paragraph (c) of this section. The depreciable excess basis of $2,000,000 is treated as being placed in service by G in 2004 and, as a result, is depreciated using the applicable depreciation method, recovery period, and convention prescribed for the office building under section 168 at the time of replacement.

(2) Depreciable and nondepreciable property. (i) If land or other nondepreciable property is acquired in a like-kind exchange for, or as a result of an involuntary conversion of, depreciable property, the land or other nondepreciable property is not depreciated. If both MACRS and nondepreciable property are acquired in a like-kind exchange for, or as part of an involuntary conversion of, MACRS property, the basis allocated to the nondepreciable property (as determined under section 1031(d) and the regulations under section 1031(d) or section 1033(b) and the regulations under section 1033(b)) is not depreciated and the basis allocated to the replacement MACRS property (as determined under section 1031(d) and the regulations under section 1031(d) or section 1033(b) and the regulations under section 1033(b)) is depreciated in accordance with this section.

(ii) If MACRS property is acquired, or if both MACRS and nondepreciable property are acquired, in a like-kind exchange for, or as part of an involuntary conversion of, land or other nondepreciable property, the basis in the replacement MACRS property that is attributable to the relinquished nondepreciable property is treated as though the replacement MACRS property is placed in service by the acquiring taxpayer in the year of replacement. Thus, the depreciation allowances for the replacement MACRS property are determined by using the applicable recovery period, depreciation method, and convention prescribed under section 168 for the replacement MACRS property at the time of replacement. See paragraph (g) of this section regarding the application of section 179. See paragraph (h) of this section regarding the application of section 168(k) or 1400L(b).

(3) Depreciation limitations for automobiles. (i) In general. Depreciation allowances under section 179 and section 167 (including allowances under sections 168 and 1400L(b)) for a passenger automobile, as defined in section 280F(d)(5), are subject to the limitations of section 280F(a). The depreciation allowances for a passenger automobile that is replacement MACRS property (replacement MACRS passenger automobile) generally are limited in any taxable year to the replacement automobile section 280F limit for the taxable year. The taxpayer's basis in the replacement MACRS passenger automobile is treated as being comprised of two separate components. The first component is the exchanged basis and the second component is the excess basis, if any. The depreciation allowances for a passenger automobile that is relinquished MACRS property (relinquished MACRS passenger automobile) for the taxable year generally are limited to the relinquished automobile section 280F limit for that taxable year. In the year of disposition the sum of the depreciation deductions for the relinquished MACRS passenger automobile and the replacement MACRS passenger automo-

bile may not exceed the replacement automobile section 280F limit unless the taxpayer makes the election under § 1.168(i)-6(i). For purposes of this paragraph (d)(3), the following definitions apply:

(A) Replacement automobile section 280F limit is the limit on depreciation deductions under section 280F(a) for the taxable year based on the time of replacement of the replacement MACRS passenger automobile (including the effect of any elections under section 168(k) or section 1400L(b), as applicable).

(B) Relinquished automobile section 280F limit is the limit on depreciation deductions under section 280F(a) for the taxable year based on when the relinquished MACRS passenger automobile was placed in service by the taxpayer.

(ii) Order in which limitations on depreciation under section 280F(a) are applied. Generally, depreciation deductions allowable under section 280F(a) reduce the basis in the relinquished MACRS passenger automobile and the exchanged basis of the replacement MACRS passenger automobile, before the excess basis of the replacement MACRS passenger automobile is reduced. The depreciation deductions for the relinquished MACRS passenger automobile in the year of disposition and the replacement MACRS passenger automobile in the year of replacement and each subsequent taxable year are allowable in the following order:

(A) The depreciation deduction allowable for the relinquished MACRS passenger automobile as determined under paragraph (c)(5)(i) of this section for the year of disposition to the extent of the smaller of the replacement automobile section 280F limit and the relinquished automobile section 280F limit, if the year of disposition is the year of replacement. If the year of replacement is a taxable year subsequent to the year of disposition, the depreciation deduction allowable for the relinquished MACRS passenger automobile for the year of disposition is limited to the relinquished automobile section 280F limit.

(B) The additional first year depreciation allowable on the remaining exchanged basis (remaining carryover basis as determined under § 1.168(k)-1(f)(5) or § 1.1400L(b)-1(f)(5), as applicable) of the replacement MACRS passenger automobile, as determined under § 1.168(k)-1(f)(5) or § 1.1400L(b)-1(f)(5), as applicable, to the extent of the excess of the replacement automobile section 280F limit over the amount allowable under paragraph (d)(3)(ii)(A) of this section.

(C) The depreciation deduction allowable for the taxable year on the depreciable exchanged basis of the replacement MACRS passenger automobile determined under paragraph (c) of this section to the extent of any excess over the sum of the amounts allowable under paragraphs (d)(3)(ii)(A) and (B) of this section of the smaller of the replacement automobile section 280F limit and the relinquished automobile section 280F limit.

(D) Any section 179 deduction allowable in the year of replacement on the excess basis of the replacement MACRS passenger automobile to the extent of the excess of the replacement automobile section 280F limit over the sum of the amounts allowable under paragraphs (d)(3)(ii)(A), (B), and (C) of this section.

(E) The additional first year depreciation allowable on the remaining excess basis of the replacement MACRS passenger automobile, as determined under § 1.168(k)-1(f)(5) or § 1.1400L(b)-1(f)(5), as applicable, to the extent of the excess of the replacement automobile section 280F limit over the sum of the amounts allowable under paragraphs (d)(3)(ii)(A), (B), (C), and (D) of this section.

(F) The depreciation deduction allowable under paragraph (d) of this section for the depreciable excess basis of the replacement MACRS passenger automobile to the extent of the excess of the replacement automobile section 280F limit over the sum of the amounts allowable under paragraphs (d)(3)(ii)(A), (B), (C), (D), and (E) of this section.

(iii) Examples. The application of this paragraph (d)(3) is illustrated by the following examples:

Example (1). H, a calendar-year taxpayer, acquired and placed in service Automobile X in January 2000 for $30,000 to be used solely for H's business. In December 2003, H exchanges, in a like-kind exchange, Automobile X plus $15,000 cash for new Automobile Y that will also be used solely in H's business. Automobile Y is 50-percent bonus depreciation property for purposes of section 168(k)(4). Both automobiles are depreciated using the double declining balance method, the half-year convention, and a 5-year recovery period. Pursuant to § 1.168(k)-1(g)(3)(ii) and paragraph (k)(2)(i) of this section, H decided to apply § 1.168(i)-6 to the exchange of Automobile X for Automobile Y, the replacement MACRS property. The relinquished automobile section 280F limit for 2003 for Automobile X is $1,775. The replacement automobile section 280F limit for Automobile Y is $10,710. The exchanged basis for Automobile Y is $17,315 ($30,000 less total depreciation allowable of $12,685 (($3,060 for 2000, $4,900 for 2001, $2,950 for 2002, and $1,775 for 2003)). Without taking section 280F into account, the additional first year depreciation deduction for the remaining exchanged basis is $8,658 ($17,315 x 0.5). Because this amount is less than $8,935 ($10,710 (the replacement automobile section 280F limit for 2003 for Automobile Y) - $1,775 (the depreciation allowable for Automobile X for 2003)), the additional first year depreciation deduction for the exchanged basis is $8,658. No depreciation deduction is allowable in 2003 for the depreciable exchanged basis because the depreciation deductions taken for Automobile X and the remaining exchanged basis exceed the exchanged automobile section 280F limit. An additional first year depreciation deduction of $277 is allowable for the excess basis of $15,000 in Automobile Y. Thus, at the end of 2003 the adjusted depreciable basis in Automobile Y is $23,379 comprised of adjusted depreciable exchanged basis of $8,657 ($17,315 (exchanged basis) - $8,658 (additional first year depreciation for exchanged basis)) and of an adjusted depreciable excess basis of $14,723 ($15,000 (excess basis) - $277 (additional first year depreciation for 2003)).

Example (2). The facts are the same as in Example 1, except that H used Automobile X only 75 percent for business use. As such, the total allowable depreciation for Automobile X is reduced to reflect that the automobile is only used 75 percent for business. The total allowable depreciation of Automobile X is $9,513.75 ($2,295 for 2000 ($3,060 limit x .75), $3,675 for 2001 ($4,900 limit x .75), $2,212.50 for 2002 ($2,950 limit x .75), and $1,331.25 for 2003 ($1,775 limit x .75). However, under § 1.280F-2T(g)(2)(ii)(A), the exchanged basis is reduced by the excess (if any) of the depreciation that would have been allowable if the exchanged automobile had been used solely for business over the depreciation that was allowable in those years. Thus, the exchanged basis, for purposes of computing depreciation, for Automobile Y is $17,315.

Example (3). The facts are the same as in Example 1, except that H placed in service Automobile X in January 2002, and H elected not to claim the additional first year depreciation deduction for 5-year property placed in service in 2002 and 2003. The relinquished automobile section 280F limit for Automobile X for 2003 is $4,900. Because the replacement automobile section 280F limit for 2003 for Automobile Y ($3,060) is less than the relinquished automobile section 280F limit for Automobile X for 2003 and is less than $5,388 (($30,000 (cost) - $3,060 (depreciation allowable for 2002)) x 0.4 x 6/12), the depreciation that would be allowable for Automobile X (determined without regard to section 280F) in the year of disposition, the depreciation for Automobile X in the year of disposition is limited to $3,060. For 2003 no depreciation is allowable for the excess basis and the exchanged basis in Automobile Y.

Example (4). AB, a calendar-year taxpayer, purchased and placed in service Automobile X1 in February 2000 for $10,000. X1 is a passenger automobile subject to section 280F(a) and is used solely for AB's business. AB depreciated X1 using a 5-year recovery period, the double declining balance method, and the half-year convention. As of January 1, 2003, the adjusted depreciable basis of X1 was $2,880 ($10,000 original cost minus $2,000 depreciation deduction for 2000, minus $3,200 depreciation deduction for 2001, and $1,920 depreciation deduction for 2002). In November 2003, AB exchanges, in a like-kind exchange, Automobile X1 plus $14,000 cash for new Automobile Y1 that will be used solely in AB's business. Automobile Y1 is 50-percent bonus depreciation property for purposes of section 168(k)(4) and qualifies for the expensing election under section 179. Pursuant to paragraph § 1.168(k)-1(g)(3)(ii) and paragraph (k)(2)(i) of this section, AB decided to apply § 1.168(i)-6 to the exchange of Automobile X1 for Automobile Y1, the replacement MACRS property. AB also makes the election under section 179 for the excess basis of Automobile Y1. AB depreciates Y1 using a five-year recovery period, the double declining balance method and the half-year convention. For 2003, the relinquished automobile section 280F limit for Automobile X1 is $1,775 and the replacement automobile section 280F limit for 2003 for Automobile Y1 is $10,710.

(i) The 2003 depreciation deduction for Automobile X1 is $576. The depreciation deduction calculated for X1 is $576 (the adjusted depreciable basis of Automobile X1 at the beginning of 2003 of $2,880 x 40% x ½ year), which is less than the relinquished automobile section 280F limit and the replacement automobile section 280F limit.

(ii) The additional first year depreciation deduction for the exchanged basis is $1,152. The additional first year depreciation deduction of $1,152 (remaining exchanged basis of $2,304 ($2,880 adjusted basis of Automobile X1 at the beginning of 2003 minus $576) - 0.5)) is less than the replacement automobile section 280F limit minus $576.

(iii) AB's MACRS depreciation deduction allowable in 2003 for the remaining exchanged basis of $1,152 is $47 (the relinquished automobile section 280F limit of $1,775 less the depreciation deduction of $576 taken for Automobile X1 less the additional first year depreciation deduction of $1,152 taken for the exchanged basis) which is less than the depreciation deduction calculated for the depreciable exchanged basis.

(iv) For 2003, AB takes a $1,400 section 179 deduction for the excess basis of Automobile Y1. AB must reduce the excess basis of $14,000 by the section 179 deduction of $1,400 to determine the remaining excess basis of $12,600.

(v) For 2003, AB is allowed a 50-percent additional first year depreciation deduction of $6,300 (the remaining excess basis of $12,600 multiplied by .50).

(vi) For 2003, AB's depreciation deduction for the depreciable excess basis is limited to $1,235. The depreciation deduction computed without regard to the replacement automobile section 280F limit is $1,260 ($6,300 depreciable excess basis x 0.4 x 6/12). However the depreciation deduction for the depreciable excess basis is limited to $1,235 ($10,710 (replacement automobile section 280F limit) - $576 (depreciation deduction for Automobile X1) - $1,152 (additional first year depreciation deduction for the exchanged basis) - $47 (depreciation deduction for exchanged basis) - 1,400 (section 179 deduction) - $6,300 (additional first year depreciation deduction for remaining excess basis)).

(4) Involuntary conversion for which the replacement MACRS property is acquired and placed in service before disposition of relinquished MACRS property. If, in an involuntary conversion, a taxpayer acquires and places in service the replacement MACRS property before the date of disposition of the relinquished MACRS property, the taxpayer depreciates the unadjusted depreciable basis of the replacement MACRS property under section 168 beginning in the taxable year when the replacement MACRS property is placed in service by the taxpayer and by using the applicable depreciation method, recovery period, and convention prescribed under section 168 for the replacement MACRS property at the placed-in-service date. However, at the time of disposition of the relinquished MACRS property, the taxpayer determines the exchanged basis and the excess basis of the replacement MACRS property and begins to depreciate the depreciable exchanged basis of the replacement MACRS property in accordance with paragraph (c) of this section. The depreciable excess basis of the replacement MACRS property continues to be depreciated by the taxpayer in accordance with the first sentence of this paragraph (d)(4). Further, in the year of disposition of the relinquished MACRS property, the taxpayer must include in taxable income the excess of the depreciation deductions allowable on the unadjusted depreciable basis of the replacement MACRS property over the depreciation deductions that would have been allowable to the taxpayer on the depreciable excess basis of the replacement MACRS property from the date the replacement MACRS property was placed in service by the taxpayer (taking into account the applicable convention) to the time of disposition of the relinquished MACRS property. However, see § 1.168(k)-1(f)(5)(v) for replacement MACRS property that is qualified property or 50-percent bonus depreciation property and § 1.1400L(b)-1(f)(5) for replacement MACRS property that is qualified New York Liberty Zone property.

(e) Use of optional depreciation tables. *(1) Taxpayer not bound by prior use of table.* If a taxpayer used an optional depreciation table for the relinquished MACRS property, the taxpayer is not required to use an optional table for the depreciable exchanged basis of the replacement MACRS property. Conversely, if a taxpayer did not use an optional depreciation table for the relinquished MACRS property, the taxpayer may use the appropriate table for the depreciable exchanged basis of the replacement MACRS property. If a taxpayer decides not to use the table for the depreciable exchanged basis of the replacement MACRS property, the depreciation allowance for this property for the year of replacement and subsequent taxable years is determined under paragraph (c) of this section. If a taxpayer decides to use the optional depreciation tables, no depreciation deduction is allowable for MACRS property placed in service by the acquiring taxpayer and subsequently exchanged or involuntarily converted by such taxpayer in the same taxable year, and, if, during the same taxable year, MACRS property is placed in service by the acquiring taxpayer, exchanged or involuntarily converted by such taxpayer, and the replacement MACRS property is disposed of by such taxpayer, no depreciation deduction is allowable for either MACRS property.

(2) Determination of the depreciation deduction. (i) Relinquished MACRS property. In the year of disposition, the depreciation allowance for the relinquished MACRS property is computed by multiplying the unadjusted depreciable basis (less the amount of the additional first year depreciation deduction allowed or allowable, whichever is greater, under section 168(k) or section 1400L(b), as applicable) of the relinquished MACRS property by the annual depreciation rate (expressed as a decimal equivalent) specified in the appropriate table for the recovery year corresponding to the year of disposition. This product is then multiplied by a fraction, the numerator of which is the number of months (including fractions of months) the property is deemed to be placed in service during the year of the exchange or involuntary conversion (taking into account the applicable convention) and the denominator of which is 12. However, if the year of disposition is less than 12 months, the depreciation allowance determined under this paragraph (e)(2)(i) must be adjusted for a short taxable year (for further guidance, for example, see Rev. Proc. 89-15 (1989-1 CB 816) and § 601.601(d)(2)(ii)(b) of this chapter).

(ii) Replacement MACRS property. (A) Determination of the appropriate optional depreciation table. If a taxpayer chooses to use the appropriate optional depreciation table for the depreciable exchanged basis, the depreciation allowances for the depreciable exchanged basis beginning in the year of replacement are determined by choosing the optional depreciation table that corresponds to the recovery period, depreciation method, and convention of the replacement MACRS property determined under paragraph (c) of this section.

(B) Calculating the depreciation deduction for the replacement MACRS property. (1) The depreciation deduction for the taxable year is computed by first determining the appropriate recovery year in the table identified under paragraph (e)(2)(ii)(A) of this section. The appropriate recovery year for the year of replacement is the same as the recovery year for the year of disposition, regardless of the taxable year in which the replacement property is acquired. For example, if the recovery year for the year of disposition would have been year 4 in the table that applied before the disposition of the relinquished MACRS property, then the recovery year for the year of replacement is Year 4 in the table identified under paragraph (e)(2)(ii)(A) of this section.

(2) Next, the annual depreciation rate (expressed as a decimal equivalent) for each recovery year is multiplied by a transaction coefficient. The transaction coefficient is the formula (1 / (1 - x)) where x equals the sum of the annual depreciation rates from the table identified under paragraph (e)(2)(ii)(A) of this section (expressed as a decimal equivalent) corresponding to the replacement MACRS property (as determined under paragraph (e)(2)(ii)(A) of this section) for the taxable years beginning with the placed-in-service year of the relinquished MACRS property through the taxable year immediately prior to the year of disposition. The product of the annual depreciation rate and the transaction coefficient is multiplied by the depreciable exchanged basis (taking into account paragraph (e)(2)(i) of this section). In the year of replacement, this product is then multiplied by a fraction, the numerator of which is the number of months (including fractions of months) the property is deemed to be placed in service by the acquiring taxpayer during the year of replacement (taking into account the applicable convention) and the denominator of which is 12. However, if the year of replacement is the year the relinquished MACRS property is placed in service by the acquiring taxpayer, the preceding sentence does not apply. In addition, if the year of replacement is less than 12 months, the depreciation allowance determined under paragraph (e)(2)(ii) of this section must be adjusted for a short taxable year (for further guidance, for example, see Rev. Proc. 89-15 (1989-1 CB 816) and § 601.601(d)(2)(ii)(b) of this chapter).

(iii) Unrecovered basis. If the replacement MACRS property would have unrecovered depreciable basis after the final recovery year (for example, due to a deferred exchange), the unrecovered basis is an allowable depreciation deduction in the taxable year that corresponds to the final recovery year unless the unrecovered basis is subject to a depreciation limitation such as section 280F.

(3) Excess basis. As provided in paragraph (d)(1) of this section, any excess basis in the replacement MACRS property is treated as property that is placed in service by the acquiring taxpayer at the time of replacement. Thus, if the taxpayer chooses to use the appropriate optional depreciation table for the depreciable excess basis in the replacement MACRS property, the depreciation allowances for the depreciable excess basis are determined by multiplying the depreciable excess basis by the annual depreciation rate (expressed as a decimal equivalent) specified in the appropriate table for each taxable year. The appropriate table for the depreciable excess basis is based on the depreciation method, recovery period, and convention applicable to the depreciable excess basis under section 168 at the time of replacement. However, If the year of replacement is less than 12 months, the depreciation allowance determined under this paragraph (e)(3) must be adjusted for a short taxable year (for further guidance, for example, see Rev. Proc. 89-15 (1989-1 CB 816) and § 601.601(d)(2)(ii)(b) of this chapter).

(4) Examples. The application of this paragraph (e) is illustrated by the following examples:

Example (1). J, a calendar-year taxpayer, acquired 5-year property for $10,000 and placed it in service in January 2001. J uses the optional tables to depreciate the property. J uses the half-year convention and did not make any elections for the property. In December 2003, J exchanges the 5-year property for used 7-year property in a like-kind exchange. Pursuant to paragraph (k)(2)(i) of this section, J decided to apply § 1.168(i)-6 to the exchange of the 5-year property for the 7-year property, the replacement MACRS property. The depreciable exchanged basis of the 7-year property equals the adjusted depreciable basis of the 5-year property at the time of disposition of the relinquished MACRS property, namely $3,840 ($10,000 less $2,000 depreciation in 2001, $3,200 depreciation in 2002, and $960 depreciation in 2003). J must first determine the appropriate optional depreciation table pursuant to paragraph (c) of this section. Since the replacement MACRS property has a longer recovery period and the same depreciation method as the relinquished MACRS property, J uses the optional depreciation table corresponding to a 7-year recovery period, the 200% declining balance method, and the half-year convention (because the 5-year property was depreciated using a half-year convention). Had the replacement MACRS property been placed in service in the same taxable year as the placed-in-service year of the relinquished MACRS property, the depreciation allowance for the replacement MACRS property for the year of replacement would be determined using recovery year 3 of the optional table. The depreciation allowance equals the depreciable exchanged basis ($3,840) multiplied by the annual depreciation rate for the current taxable year (.1749 for recovery year 3) as modified by the transaction coefficient [1 / (1 - (.1429 + .2449))] which equals 1.6335. Thus, J multiplies $3,840, its depreciable exchanged basis in the replacement MACRS property, by the product of .1749 and 1.6335, and then by one-half, to determine the depreciation allowance for 2003, $549. For 2004, J multiples its depreciable exchanged basis in the replacement MACRS property determined at the time of replacement of $3,840 by the product of the modified annual depreciation rate for the current taxable year (.1249 for recovery year 4) and the transaction coefficient (1.6335) to determine its depreciation allowance of $783.

Example (2). K, a calendar-year taxpayer, acquired used Asset V for $100,000 and placed it in service in January 1999. K depreciated Asset V under the general depreciation system of section 168(a) by using a 5-year recovery period, the 200-percent declining balance method of depreciation, and the half-year convention. In December 2003, as part of the involuntary conversion, Asset V is involuntarily converted due to an earthquake. In October 2005, K purchases used Asset W with the insurance proceeds from the destruction of Asset V and places Asset W in service to replace Asset V. Pursuant to paragraph (k)(2)(i) of this section, K decided to apply § 1.168(i)-6 to the involuntary conversion of Asset V with the replacement of Asset W, the replacement MACRS property. If Asset W had been placed in service when Asset V was placed in service, it would have been depreciated using a 7-year recovery period, the 200-percent declining balance method, and the half-year convention. K uses the optional depreciation tables to depreciate Asset V and Asset W. For 2003 (recovery year 5 on the optional table), the depreciation deduction for Asset V is $5,760 ((0.1152)($100,000)(1/2)). Thus, the adjusted depreciable basis of Asset V at the time of replacement is $11,520 ($100,000 less $20,000 depreciation in 1999, $32,000 depreciation in 2000, $19,200 depreciation in 2001, $11,520 depreciation in 2002, and $5,760 depreciation in 2003). Under the table that applied to Asset V, the year of disposition was recovery year 5 and the depreciation deduction was determined under the straight line method. The table that applies for Asset W is the table that applies the straight line depreciation method, the half-year convention, and a 7-year recovery period. The appropriate recovery year under this table is recovery year 5. The depreciation deduction for Asset W for 2005 is $1,646 (($11,520)(0.1429)(1/(1-0.5))(1/2)). Thus, the depreciation deduction for Asset W in 2006 (recovery year 6) is $3,290 ($11,520)(0.1428)(1/(1-0.5)). The depreciation deduction for 2007 (recovery year 7) is $3,292 (($11,520)(.1429)(1/(1-.5))). The depreciation deduction for 2008 (recovery year 8) is $3292 ($11,520 less allowable depreciation for Asset W for 2005 through 2007 ($1,646 + $3,290 + $3,292)).

Example (3). L, a calendar-year taxpayer, placed in service used Computer X in January 2002 for $5,000. L depreciated Computer X under the general depreciation system of section 168(a) by using the 200-percent declining balance method of depreciation, a 5-year recovery period, and the half-year convention. Computer X is destroyed in a fire in March 2004. For 2004, the depreciation deduction allowable for Computer X equals $480 ([($5,000)(.1920)] x (1/2)). Thus, the adjusted depreciable basis of Computer X was $1,920 when it was destroyed ($5,000 unadjusted depreciable basis less $1,000 depreciation for 2002, $1,600 depreciation for 2003, and $480 depreciation for 2004). In April 2004, as part of the involuntary conversion, L acquired and placed in service used Computer Y with insurance proceeds received due to the loss of Computer X. Computer Y will be depreciated using the same depreciation method, recovery period, and convention as Computer X. L elected to use the optional depreciation tables to compute the depreciation allowance for Computer X and Computer Y. The depreciation deduction allowable for 2004 for Computer Y equals $384 ([$1,920 x (.1920)(1/(1-.52))] x (1/2)).

(f) Mid-quarter convention. For purposes of applying the 40-percent test under section 168(d) and the regulations under section 168(d), the following rules apply:

(1) Exchanged basis. If, in a taxable year, MACRS property is placed in service by the acquiring taxpayer (but not as a result of a like-kind exchange or involuntary conversion) and—

(i) In the same taxable year, is disposed of by the acquiring taxpayer in a like-kind exchange or an involuntary conversion and replaced by the acquiring taxpayer with replacement MACRS property, the exchanged basis (determined without any adjustments for depreciation deductions during the taxable year) of the replacement MACRS property is taken into account in the year of replacement in the quarter the relinquished MACRS property was placed in service by the acquiring taxpayer; or

(ii) In the same taxable year, is disposed of by the acquiring taxpayer in a like-kind exchange or an involuntary conversion, and in a subsequent taxable year is replaced by the acquiring taxpayer with replacement MACRS property, the exchanged basis (determined without any adjustments for depreciation deductions during the taxable year) of the replacement MACRS property is taken into account in the year of replacement in the quarter the replacement MACRS property was placed in service by the acquiring taxpayer; or

(iii) In a subsequent taxable year, disposed of by the acquiring taxpayer in a like-kind exchange or involuntary conversion, the exchanged basis of the replacement MACRS property is not taken into account in the year of replacement.

(2) Excess basis. Any excess basis is taken into account in the quarter the replacement MACRS property is placed in service by the acquiring taxpayer.

(3) Depreciable property acquired for nondepreciable property. Both the exchanged basis and excess basis of the replacement MACRS property described in paragraph (d)(2)(ii) of this section (depreciable property acquired for nondepreciable property), are taken into account for determining whether the mid-quarter convention applies in the year of replacement.

(g) Section 179 election. In applying the section 179 election, only the excess basis, if any, in the replacement MACRS property is taken into account. If the replacement MACRS property is described in paragraph (d)(2)(ii) of this section (depreciable property acquired for nondepreciable property), only the excess basis in the replacement MACRS property is taken into account.

(h) Additional first year depreciation deduction. See § 1.168(k)-1(f)(5) (for qualified property or 50-percent bonus depreciation property) and § 1.1400L(b)-1(f)(5) (for qualified New York Liberty Zone property).

(i) Elections. *(1) Election not to apply this section.* A taxpayer may elect not to apply this section for any MACRS property involved in a like-kind exchange or involuntary conversion. An election under this paragraph (i)(1) applies only to the taxpayer making the election and the election applies to both the relinquished MACRS property and the replacement MACRS property. If an election is made under this paragraph (i)(1), the depreciation allowances for the replacement MACRS property beginning in the year of replacement and for the relinquished MACRS property in the year of disposition are not determined under this section (except as otherwise provided in this paragraph). Instead, for depreciation purposes only, the sum of the exchanged basis and excess basis, if any, in the replacement MACRS property is treated as property placed in service by the taxpayer at the time of replacement and the adjusted depreciable basis of the relinquished MACRS property is treated as being disposed of by the taxpayer at the time of disposition. While the relinquished MACRS property is treated as being disposed of at the time of disposition for depreciation purposes, the election not to apply this section does not affect the application of sections 1031 and 1033 (for example, if a taxpayer does not make the election under this paragraph (i)(1) and does not recognize gain or loss under section 1031, this result would not change if the taxpayer chose to make the election under this paragraph (i)(1)). In addition, the election not to apply this section does not affect the application of sections 1245 and 1250 to the relinquished MACRS property. Paragraphs (c)(5)(i) (determination of depreciation for relinquished MACRS property in the year of disposition), (c)(5)(iii) (rules for deferred transactions), (g) (section 179 election), and (h) (additional first year depreciation deduction) of this section apply to property to which this paragraph (i)(1) applies. See paragraph (j) of this section for the time and manner of making the election under this paragraph (i)(1).

(2) Election to treat certain replacement property as MACRS property. If the tangible depreciable property acquired by a taxpayer in a like-kind exchange or involuntary conversion (the replacement property) replaces tangible depreciable property for which the taxpayer made a valid election under section 168(f)(1) to exclude it from the application of MACRS (the relinquished property), the taxpayer may elect to treat, for depreciation purposes only, the sum of the exchanged basis and excess basis, if any, of the replacement property as MACRS property that is placed in service by the taxpayer at the time of replacement. An election under this paragraph (i)(2) applies only to the taxpayer making the election and the election applies to both the relinquished property and the replacement property. If an election is made under this paragraph (i)(2), the adjusted depreciable basis of the relinquished property is treated as being disposed of by the taxpayer at the time of disposition. Rules similar to those provided in §§ 1.168(i)-6(b)(3) and (4) apply for purposes of determining the time of disposition and time of replacement under this paragraph (i)(2). While the relinquished property is treated as being disposed of at the time of disposition for depreciation purposes, the election under this paragraph (i)(2) does not affect the application of sections 1031 and 1033, and the application of sections 1245 and 1250 to the relinquished property. If an election is made under this paragraph (i)(2), rules similar to those provided in paragraphs (c)(5)(iii) (rules for deferred transactions), (g) (section 179 election), and (h) (additional first year depreciation deduction) of this section apply to property. Except as provided in paragraph (k)(3)(ii) of this section, a taxpayer makes the election under this paragraph (i)(2) by claiming the depreciation allowance as determined under MACRS for the replacement property on the taxpayer's timely filed (including extensions) original Federal tax return for the placed-in-service year of the replacement property as determined under this paragraph (i)(2).

(j) Time and manner of making election under paragraph (i)(1) of this section. *(1) In general.* The election provided in paragraph (i)(1) of this section is made separately by each person acquiring replacement MACRS property. The election is made for each member of a consolidated group by the common parent of the group, by the partnership (and not by the partners separately) in the case of a partnership, or by the S corporation (and not by the shareholders separately) in the case of an S corporation. A separate election under paragraph (i)(1) of this section is required for each like-kind exchange or involuntary conversion. The election provided in paragraph (i)(1) of this section must be made within the time and manner provided in paragraph (j)(2) and (3) of this section and may not be made by the taxpayer in any other manner (for example, the election cannot be made through a request under section 446(e) to change the taxpayer's method of accounting), except as provided in paragraph (k)(2) of this section.

(2) Time for making election. The election provided in paragraph (i)(1) of this section must be made by the due date (including extensions) of the taxpayer's Federal tax return for the year of replacement.

(3) Manner of making election. The election provided in paragraph (i)(1) of this section is made in the manner provided for on Form 4562, Depreciation and Amortization, and its instructions. If Form 4562 is revised or renumbered, any reference in this section to that form is treated as a reference to the revised or renumbered form.

(4) Revocation. The election provided in paragraph (i)(1) of this section, once made, may be revoked only with the consent of the Commissioner of Internal Revenue. Such consent will be granted only in extraordinary circumstances. Requests for consent are requests for a letter ruling and must be filed with the Commissioner of Internal Revenue, Washington, DC 20224. Requests for consent may not be made in any other manner (for example, through a request under section 446(e) to change the taxpayer's method of accounting).

(k) Effective date. *(1) In general.* Except as provided in paragraph (k)(3) of this section, this section applies to a like-kind exchange or an involuntary conversion of MACRS property for which the time of disposition and the time of replacement both occur after February 27, 2004.

(2) Application to pre-effective date like-kind exchanges and involuntary conversions. For a like-kind exchange or an involuntary conversion of MACRS property for which the time of disposition, the time of replacement, or both occur on or before February 27, 2004, a taxpayer may—

(i) Apply the provisions of this section. If a taxpayer's applicable Federal tax return has been filed on or before February 27, 2004, and the taxpayer has treated the replacement MACRS property as acquired, and the relinquished MACRS property as disposed of, in a like-kind exchange or an involuntary conversion, the taxpayer changes its method of accounting for depreciation of the replacement MACRS property and relinquished MACRS property in accordance with this paragraph (k)(2)(i) by following the applicable administrative procedures issued under § 1.446-1(e)(3)(ii) for obtaining the Commissioner's automatic consent to a change in method of accounting (for further guidance, see Rev. Proc. 2002-9 (2002-1 CB 327) and § 601.601(d)(2)(ii)(b) of this chapter); or

(ii) Rely on prior guidance issued by the Internal Revenue Service for determining the depreciation deductions of replacement MACRS property and relinquished MACRS property (for further guidance, for example, see Notice 2000-4

(2001-1 CB 313) and § 601.601(d)(2)(ii)(b) of this chapter). In relying on such guidance, a taxpayer may use any reasonable, consistent method of determining depreciation in the year of disposition and the year of replacement. If a taxpayer's applicable Federal tax return has been filed on or before February 27, 2004, and the taxpayer has treated the replacement MACRS property as acquired, and the relinquished MACRS property as disposed of, in a like-kind exchange or an involuntary conversion, the taxpayer changes its method of accounting for depreciation of the replacement MACRS property and relinquished MACRS property in accordance with this paragraph (k)(2)(ii) by following the applicable administrative procedures issued under § 1.446-1(e)(3)(ii) for obtaining the Commissioner's automatic consent to a change in method of accounting (for further guidance, see Rev. Proc. 2002-9 (2002-1 CB 327) and § 601.601(d)(2)(ii)(b) of this chapter).

(3) Like-kind exchanges and involuntary conversions where the taxpayer made the election under section 168(f)(1) for the relinquished property. (i) In general. If the tangible depreciable property acquired by a taxpayer in a like-kind exchange or involuntary conversion (the replacement property) replaces tangible depreciable property for which the taxpayer made a valid election under section 168(f)(1) to exclude it from the application of MACRS (the relinquished property), paragraph (i)(2) of this section applies to such relinquished property and replacement property for which the time of disposition and the time of replacement (both as determined under paragraph (i)(2) of this section) both occur after February 26, 2007.

(ii) Application of paragraph (i)(2) of this section to pre-February 26, 2007 like-kind exchanges and involuntary conversions. If the tangible depreciable property acquired by a taxpayer in a like-kind exchange or involuntary conversion (the replacement property) replaces tangible depreciable property for which the taxpayer made a valid election under section 168(f)(1) to exclude it from the application of MACRS (the relinquished property), the taxpayer may apply paragraph (i)(2) of this section to the relinquished property and the replacement property for which the time of disposition, the time of replacement (both as determined under paragraph (i)(2) of this section), or both occur on or before February 26, 2007. If the taxpayer wants to apply paragraph (i)(2) of this section and the taxpayer's applicable Federal tax return has been filed on or before February 26, 2007, the taxpayer must change its method of accounting for depreciation of the replacement property and relinquished property in accordance with this paragraph (k)(3)(ii) by following the applicable administrative procedures issued under § 1.446-1(e)(3)(ii) for obtaining the Commissioner's automatic consent to a change in method of accounting (for further guidance, see Rev. Proc. 2002-9 (2002-1 CB 327) and § 601.601(d)(2)(ii)(b) of this chapter).

T.D. 9314, 2/26/2007.

§ 1.168(j)-1T Questions and answers concerning tax-exempt entity leasing rules (temporary).

Caution: The Treasury has not yet amended Reg § 1.168(j)-1T to reflect changes made by P.L. 107-147.

The following questions and answers concern tax-exempt entity leasing under section 168(j) of the Internal Revenue Code of 1954, as enacted by section 31 of the Tax Reform Act of 1984 ("TRA") (Pub. L. 98-369):

Consequences of Tax-Exempt Use Status

Q-1. If recovery property is subject to the tax-exempt entity leasing provisions of section 168(j), how must the taxpayer compute the property's recovery deductions?

A-1. The taxpayer must compute the property's recovery deductions in accordance with section 168(j)(1) and (2); that is, the taxpayer must use the straight line method and the specified recovery period. For property other than 18-year real property, the applicable recovery percentages for the specified recovery period are to be determined with reference to the tables contained in Prop. Treas. Reg. § 1.168-2(g)(3)(iv)(A). For 18-year real property for which a 40-year recovery period is required, the applicable recovery percentages are to be determined under the following table:

40-Year Straight Line Method (Assuming Mid-Month Convention)

If the recovery year is—	And the month in the first recovery year the property is placed in service is—											
	1	2	3	4	5	6	7	8	9	10	11	12
	The applicable recovery percentage is—											
1	2.4	2.2	2.0	1.8	1.6	1.4	1.1	0.9	0.7	0.5	0.3	0.1
2	2.5	2.5	2.5	2.5	2.5	2.5	2.5	2.5	2.5	2.5	2.5	2.5
3	2.5	2.5	2.5	2.5	2.5	2.5	2.5	2.5	2.5	2.5	2.5	2.5
4	2.5	2.5	2.5	2.5	2.5	2.5	2.5	2.5	2.5	2.5	2.5	2.5
5	2.5	2.5	2.5	2.5	2.5	2.5	2.5	2.5	2.5	2.5	2.5	2.5
6	2.5	2.5	2.5	2.5	2.5	2.5	2.5	2.5	2.5	2.5	2.5	2.5
7	2.5	2.5	2.5	2.5	2.5	2.5	2.5	2.5	2.5	2.5	2.5	2.5
8	2.5	2.5	2.5	2.5	2.5	2.5	2.5	2.5	2.5	2.5	2.5	2.5
9	2.5	2.5	2.5	2.5	2.5	2.5	2.5	2.5	2.5	2.5	2.5	2.5
10	2.5	2.5	2.5	2.5	2.5	2.5	2.5	2.5	2.5	2.5	2.5	2.5
11	2.5	2.5	2.5	2.5	2.5	2.5	2.5	2.5	2.5	2.5	2.5	2.5
12	2.5	2.5	2.5	2.5	2.5	2.5	2.5	2.5	2.5	2.5	2.5	2.5
13	2.5	2.5	2.5	2.5	2.5	2.5	2.5	2.5	2.5	2.5	2.5	2.5
14	2.5	2.5	2.5	2.5	2.5	2.5	2.5	2.5	2.5	2.5	2.5	2.5
15	2.5	2.5	2.5	2.5	2.5	2.5	2.5	2.5	2.5	2.5	2.5	2.5
16	2.5	2.5	2.5	2.5	2.5	2.5	2.5	2.5	2.5	2.5	2.5	2.5
17	2.5	2.5	2.5	2.5	2.5	2.5	2.5	2.5	2.5	2.5	2.5	2.5
18	2.5	2.5	2.5	2.5	2.5	2.5	2.5	2.5	2.5	2.5	2.5	2.5
19	2.5	2.5	2.5	2.5	2.5	2.5	2.5	2.5	2.5	2.5	2.5	2.5
20	2.5	2.5	2.5	2.5	2.5	2.5	2.5	2.5	2.5	2.5	2.5	2.5

21	2.5	2.5	2.5	2.5	2.5	2.5	2.5	2.5	2.5	2.5	2.5	2.5
22	2.5	2.5	2.5	2.5	2.5	2.5	2.5	2.5	2.5	2.5	2.5	2.5
23	2.5	2.5	2.5	2.5	2.5	2.5	2.5	2.5	2.5	2.5	2.5	2.5
24	2.5	2.5	2.5	2.5	2.5	2.5	2.5	2.5	2.5	2.5	2.5	2.5
25	2.5	2.5	2.5	2.5	2.5	2.5	2.5	2.5	2.5	2.5	2.5	2.5
26	2.5	2.5	2.5	2.5	2.5	2.5	2.5	2.5	2.5	2.5	2.5	2.5
27	2.5	2.5	2.5	2.5	2.5	2.5	2.5	2.5	2.5	2.5	2.5	2.5
28	2.5	2.5	2.5	2.5	2.5	2.5	2.5	2.5	2.5	2.5	2.5	2.5
29	2.5	2.5	2.5	2.5	2.5	2.5	2.5	2.5	2.5	2.5	2.5	2.5
30	2.5	2.5	2.5	2.5	2.5	2.5	2.5	2.5	2.5	2.5	2.5	2.5
31	2.5	2.5	2.5	2.5	2.5	2.5	2.5	2.5	2.5	2.5	2.5	2.5
32	2.5	2.5	2.5	2.5	2.5	2.5	2.5	2.5	2.5	2.5	2.5	2.5
33	2.5	2.5	2.5	2.5	2.5	2.5	2.5	2.5	2.5	2.5	2.5	2.5
34	2.5	2.5	2.5	2.5	2.5	2.5	2.5	2.5	2.5	2.5	2.5	2.5
35	2.5	2.5	2.5	2.5	2.5	2.5	2.5	2.5	2.5	2.5	2.5	2.5
36	2.5	2.5	2.5	2.5	2.5	2.5	2.5	2.5	2.5	2.5	2.5	2.5
37	2.5	2.5	2.5	2.5	2.5	2.5	2.5	2.5	2.5	2.5	2.5	2.5
38	2.5	2.5	2.5	2.5	2.5	2.5	2.5	2.5	2.5	2.5	2.5	2.5
39	2.5	2.5	2.5	2.5	2.5	2.5	2.5	2.5	2.5	2.5	2.5	2.5
40	2.5	2.5	2.5	2.5	2.5	2.5	2.5	2.5	2.5	2.5	2.5	2.5
41	0.1	0.3	0.5	0.7	0.9	1.1	1.4	1.6	1.8	2.0	2.2	2.4

Q-2. If recovery property that was placed in service after December 31, 1980 by a taxable entity subsequently becomes tax-exempt use property, how are such property's cost recovery deductions under section 168 affected?

A-2. A change to tax-exempt use property, as defined in section 168(j)(3), will cause the cost recovery deductions under the accelerated cost recovery system (ACRS) to be recomputed. The allowable recovery deduction for the taxable year in which the change occurs (and for subsequent taxable years) must be determined as if the property had originally been tax-exempt use property. Proper adjustment must be made under the principles of Prop. Treas. Reg. § 1.168-2(j)(3)(i)(B) to account for the difference between the deductions allowable with respect to the property prior to the year of change and those which would have been allowable had the taxpayer used the recovery period and method for tax-exempt use property under section 168(j)(1) and (2). However, no adjustment is made pursuant to the provisions of this A-2 if section 168(j)(2)(C) applies, that is, if the taxpayer had selected a longer recovery period in the year the property was placed in service than the recovery period prescribed for such property under section 168(j)(1).

Example (1). On July 1, 1983, X, a calendar year taxpayer, places in service 5-year recovery property with an unadjusted basis of $100. For 1983, X's allowable deduction is $15 (i.e., .15 × $100). In 1984, the property becomes tax-exempt use property. Under section 168(j), assume the prescribed recovery period is 12 years. For 1984 (and subsequent taxable years), X's allowable deduction is determined as if the property had been tax-exempt use property since 1983, that is, the year it was placed in service. Thus, taxable year 1984 is the property's second recovery year of its 12-year recovery period. Additionally, X must account for the excess allowable recovery deduction of $11 (i.e., the difference between the recovery allowance for 1983 ($15) and the allowance for that year had the property been tax-exempt use property ($4)) in accordance with the principles of Prop. Treas. Reg. § 1.168-2(j)(3)(i)(B). Thus, the recovery allowances in 1984 and 1985 are $7.97, determined as follows:

Unadjusted basis multiplied by the applicable recovery percentage for second recovery year ($100 × .09)	$ 9.00
Excess allowable recovery deduction multiplied by the applicable recovery percentage for second recovery year divided by the sum of the remaining unused applicable percentages for tax-exempt use property existing as of the taxable year of change (1984) (($11 × .09)/.96)	− 1.03
Difference—allowable deduction for 1984	$ 7.97
Unadjusted basis multiplied by the applicable recovery percentage for third recovery year ($100 × .09)	$ 9.00
Excess allowable recovery deduction multiplied by the applicable recovery percentage for third recovery year divided by the sum of the remaining unused applicable percentages for tax-exempt use property existing as of the taxable year of change (1984) (($11 × .09)/.96)	− 1.03
Difference—allowable deduction for 1985	$ 7.97

Additionally, X must make a similar adjustment for the taxable years 1986 through 1995, that is, his fourth through thirteenth recovery years.

Example (2). Assume the same facts as in Example (1) except that in 1983, X elected under section 168(b)(3) with respect to the 5-year property to use the optional recovery percentages over a 25-year recovery period. Based on these facts, the provisions of this A-2 do not apply.

Definition of Tax-Exempt Use Property

Mixed Leases of Real and Personal Property

Q-3. How is a mixed lease of real property and personal property (e.g., a building with furniture) to be treated for purposes of applying the rules of section 168(j)(3) defining which property constitutes tax-exempt use property?

A-3. The general rule is that 18-year real property and property other than 18-year real property are tested separately to determine whether each constitutes tax-exempt use property. However, if a lease of section 1245 class property is incidental to a lease of 18-year real property, and the 18-year real property is not tax-exempt use property, then the section 1245 class property also does not constitute tax-exempt use property. A lease of section 1245 class property will be considered incidental if the adjusted basis of all section 1245 class property leased in the same transaction is 1 percent or less of the adjusted basis of all 18-year real property leased in such transaction.

Buildings Which Are Partially Tax-Exempt Use Property

Q-4. If part of a building is leased to a tax-exempt entity in a disqualified lease and part of the building is leased other than to a tax-exempt entity in a disqualified lease, to what extent do the tax-exempt entity leasing rules apply to such building?

A-4. The taxpayer must determine the amount of the building's unadjusted basis that is properly allocable to the portion of the building that is tax-exempt use property; the section 168(j) rules apply to the allocated amount. Solely for purposes of determining what percentage of the building's basis is subject to the tax-exempt entity leasing rules, no part of the basis is allocated to common areas.

Example. A constructs a 3-story building in 1984 at a cost of $900,000. Each floor consists of 30,000 square feet. The only common area (10,000 square feet) in the building is on the first floor. A leases the first floor (other than the common areas) to a firm that is not a tax-exempt entity. A leases the top two floors to a tax-exempt entity in a 25-year lease. The top two floors constitute tax-exempt use property. Assume that square footage is the appropriate method for allocating basis in this case. Thus, A must allocate $675,000 of the $900,000 basis to the tax-exempt use portion, determined as follows:

square footage of building which is tax-exempt use property (excluding common areas) / total square footage in the building (excluding common areas)	=	60,000 sq. feet / 80,000 sq. feet	=	¾

¾ × $900,000 = $675,000

A must compute his recovery deductions on this portion of the basis ($675,000) in accordance with the rules of section 168(j)(1) and (2).

Requirement of a Lease

Q-5. Can the use of property by a party other than a tax-exempt entity result in the property being treated as tax-exempt use property within the meaning of section 168(j)(3)?

A-5. Yes, if based on all the facts and circumstances it is more appropriate to characterize the transaction as a lease to a tax-exempt entity. A transaction can be characterized as a lease to a tax-exempt entity under section 168(j)(6)(A), which provides that "the termlease includes any grant of a right to use property"; or under the service contract rules of section 7701(e). See Q&A #18 for rules regarding service contracts.

Example. A trust is executed on January 1, 1984, to create a pooled income fund (P) that meets the requirements of section 642(c)(5). A university (U) that is tax-exempt under section 501(c)(3) is the remainderman of the pooled income fund. P's purpose is to construct and operate an athletic center on land adjacent to U's campus. Construction of the athletic center, which has a 50-year useful life, was completed and the center was placed in service on February 1, 1985. The athletic center is managed for a fee by M, an unrelated taxable organization which operates athletic facilities open to the public. Office space at the facility is occupied rent-free by both the U athletic department and M. Scheduling of activities at the center is handled jointly by members of U's athletic department and M. General operating expenses of the athletic center are paid by P. Although the athletic center is open to the public for a membership fee, the majority of members are U's students who pay membership fees as part of their tuition. These fees are remitted by U to P. This arrangement is in substance a grant to U of a right to use the facility, and therefore a lease to U under section 168(j)(6)(A). U, as remainderman, will have obtained title to the entire building when the last pooled income fund donor dies. This arrangement is a disqualified lease because either (1) U has the equivalent of a fixed price purchase option under section 168(j)(3)(B)(ii)(II) (if U receives title as remainderman before the end of the useful life of the building), or (2) the lease has a term in excess of 20 years under section 168(j)(3)(B)(ii)(III) (if U does not receive title as remainderman until 20 years have elapsed), or both. Therefore, the allowable recovery deductions (without regard to salvage value) must be computed in accordance with section 168(j)(1) and (2). In addition, because this arrangement is treated as a lease under section 168(j), the facility is used by U for purposes of section 48(a)(4), and thus no investment tax credit is permitted with respect to any portion of the facility. This arrangement also may be treated as a lease to U for all purposes of chapter 1 of the Internal Revenue Code under section 7701(e).

"More Than 35 Percent of the Property" Test

Q-6. How is the percentage of 18-year real property leased to a tax-exempt entity in a disqualified lease to be determined for purposes of the "more than 35 percent of the property" test of section 168(j)(3)(B)(iii)?

A-6. The phrase "more than 35 percent of the property" means more than 35 percent of the net rentable floor space of the property. The net rentable floor space in a building does not include the common areas of the building, regardless of the terms of the lease. For purposes of the "more than 35 percent of the property" rule, two or more buildings will be treated as separate properties unless they are part of the same project, in which case they will be treated as one property. Two or more buildings will be treated as part of the same project if the buildings are constructed, under a common plan, within a reasonable time of each other on the same site and will be used in an integrated manner.

Q-7. Are disqualified leases to different tax-exempt entities (regardless of whether they are related) aggregated in determining whether 18-year real property is tax-exempt use property?

A-7. Yes.

Example. A tax-exempt entity participates in industrial development bond financing for the acquisition of a new building by a taxable entity. The tax-exempt entity leases 60 percent of the net rentable floor space in the building for 5 years. Sixty percent of the building is tax-exempt use property. If the same tax-exempt entity leased only 19 percent of the net rentable floor space in the building for 5 years, no portion of the building would be tax-exempt use property because not more than 35 percent of the property is leased to a tax-exempt entity pursuant to a disqualified lease. If such tax-exempt entity leased only 19 percent of the net rentable floor space in the building for 5 years and another tax-exempt entity leased 20 percent of the net rentable floor space in the building for a term in excess of 20 years (or a related entity leased 20 percent of the building for 5 years), 39 percent of the building would be tax-exempt use property. See A-4 regarding the determination of the amount of the building's unadjusted basis that is properly allocable to the portion of the building that is tax-exempt use property.

"Predominantly Used" Test

Q-8. What does the term "predominantly used" mean for purposes of the section 168(j)(3)(D) exception to the tax-exempt use property rules?

A-8. "Predominantly used" means that for more than 50 percent of the time used, as determined for each taxable year, the real or personal property is used in an unrelated trade or business the income of which is subject to tax under section 511 (determined without regard to the debt-financed income rules of section 514). If only a portion of property is predominantly used in an unrelated trade or business, the remainder may nevertheless be tax-exempt use property.

Q-9. How is the "predominantly used" test of section 168(j)(3)(D) to be applied to a building?

A-9. The "predominantly used" test is to be applied to a building in the following manner:

(i) Identify the discrete portions (excluding common areas) of the building which are leased to a tax-exempt entity in a disqualified lease under section 168(j)(3)(B)(ii). A discrete portion of a building is an area physically separated from other areas. An area is physically separated from other areas if separated by permanent walls or by partitions serving as room dividers if such partitions remain in place throughout the taxable year. A discrete portion can be the entire building, floors, wings, offices, rooms, or a combination thereof. For example, a building whose entire internal space consists of a single large room used as a gymnasium has only one discrete portion. On the other hand, if the building has 3 stories with 10 offices on each floor, each of the 30 offices is a discrete portion.

(ii) Determine whether each discrete portion is predominantly used in an unrelated trade or business subject to tax under section 511. See A-8 for the rules regarding how to make this determination.

(iii) Once the discrete portions of the building that constitute tax-exempt use property have been identified, an appropriate allocation of basis must be made to such discrete portions. See A-4 for rules regarding how to make such allocation.

(iv) The application of these rules is illustrated by the following example:

Example. A building, constructed in 1985, is leased in its entirety to a tax-exempt entity (E) pursuant to a 25-year lease. The building has 25,000 square feet of net rentable floor space and consists of an auditorium (15,000 square feet), a retail shop (10,000 square feet), plus common area of 5,000 square feet. E uses the auditorium 80 percent of the time in its exempt activity and 20 percent of the time in an unrelated trade or business subject to tax under section 511. The retail shop is used 90 percent of the time in an unrelated trade or business subject to tax under section 511 and 10 percent of the time in an exempt activity. Thus, the auditorium is tax-exempt use property; the retail shop is not. An appropriate allocation of basis to the auditorium must be made. See A-4.

Definition of Tax-Exempt Entity

Q-10. What elections must be made in order to avoid the "5-year lookback" rule of section 168(j)(4)(E)(i)?

A-10. Only organizations which were exempt from tax under section 501(a) as organizations described in section 501(c)(12) (and which are no longer tax-exempt) may avoid the 5-year lookback rule of section 168(j)(4)(E)(i). In order to avoid the 5-year lookback rule with respect to any property, two elections are required. First, the organization must elect not to be exempt from tax under section 501(a) during the tax-exempt use period (as defined in section 168(j)(4)(E)(ii)(II)) with respect to the property. Second, the organization must elect to be taxed on the exempt arbitrage profits as provided in section 31(g)(16) of the Tax Reform Act of 1984. See Temp. Treas. Reg. § 301.9100-6T(a) for the time and manner of making these elections. These elections, once made, are irrevocable.

Q-11. Does the term "tax-exempt entity" include tax-exempt plans of deferred compensation and similar arrangements?

A-11. Yes. For purposes of section 168(j), the term "tax-exempt entity" includes trusts or other entities that are tax-qualified under section 401(a), individual retirement accounts, simplified employee pensions, and other tax-exempt arrangements described in subchapter D of chapter 1 of the Internal Revenue Code.

Special Rules for High Technology Equipment

Q-12. What effect do the tax-exempt entity leasing provisions have on "qualified technological equipment" ?

A-12. "Qualified technological equipment" which is leased to a tax-exempt entity for a term of 5 years or less shall not constitute tax-exempt use property. If "qualified technological equipment" which is leased to a tax-exempt entity for a term of more than 5 years constitutes tax-exempt use property (as defined in section 168(j)(3)) and is not used predominantly outside the United States, the rules of section 168(j)(1) and (2) apply except that the recovery period to be used for such equipment shall be 5 years regardless of the length of the lease term. For purposes of section 168(j)(5), "qualified technological equipment" means (1) any computer or peripheral equipment, (2) any high technology telephone station equipment installed on the customer's premises, and (3) any high technology medical equipment. For definitions of these terms, see A-13 through A-16.

Q-13. What is a "computer" as that term is used in section 168(j)(5)(C)(i)(I)?

A-13. Computers are electronically activated devices that are programmable by the user and that are capable of accepting information, applying prescribed processes to it, and supplying the results of those processes with or without human intervention. Computers consist of a central processing unit containing extensive storage, logic, arithmetic, and control capabilities. A computer does not include any equipment which is an integral part of property that is not a user-programmable device, any video games or other devices used by the user primarily for amusement or entertainment purposes, or any typewriters, calculators, adding or accounting machines, copiers, duplicating equipment, or similar equipment. A computer does not include any equipment that is not tangible personal property.

Q-14. What is "peripheral equipment" as that term is used in section 168(j)(5)(C)(i)(I)?

A-14. Peripheral equipment means tangible personal property such as auxiliary machines, whether on-line or off-line, that are designed to be placed under the control of the central processing unit of the computer. Some examples of peripheral equipment are: card readers, card punches, magnetic tape feeds, high speed printers, optical character readers, tape cassettes, mass storage units, paper tape equipment, keypunches, data entry devices, teleprinters, terminals, tape drives, disc drives, disc files, disc packs, visual image projector tubes, card sorters, plotters, and collators. Peripheral equipment does not include equipment not included in Asset Depreciation Range (ADR) 00.12 listed in section 3 of Rev. Proc. 83-35, 1983-1 C.B. 745, 746. Peripheral equipment also does not include any equipment that is an integral part of property that is not a user-programmable device, any video games or other devices used by the user primarily for amusement or entertainment purposes, or any typewriters, calculators, adding or accounting machines, copiers, duplicating equipment, or similar equipment.

Q-15. What does "high technology telephone station equipment" mean as that term is used in section 168(j)(5)(C)(i)(II)?

A-15. High technology telephone station equipment includes only tangible personal property described in asset depreciation range (ADR) class 48.13 listed in section 3 of Rev. Proc. 83-35, 1983-1 C.B. 745, 758 that has a high technology content and which, because of such high technology content, can reasonably be expected to become obsolete before the expiration of its physical useful life. For example, telephone booths and telephones which include only a standard dialing feature are not high technology equipment. However, telephones with features such as an abbreviated dialing short program, an automatic callback, or conference call feature may qualify as high technology equipment. High technology telephone station equipment may include terminal equipment including such extra features but not terminal equipment used in conjunction with features offered through central office capacity. There are no current plans to utilize the regulatory authority provided in section 168(j)(5)(C)(iv).

Q-16. What is "high technology medical equipment" as that term is used in section 168(j)(5)(C)(i)(III)?

A-16. High technology medical equipment is any electronic, electromechanical, or computer-based high technology equipment which is tangible personal property used in the screening, monitoring, observation, diagnosis, or treatment of human patients in a laboratory, medical, or hospital environment. High technology medical equipment includes only equipment that has a high technology content and which, because of such high technology content, can reasonably be expected to become obsolete before the expiration of its physical useful life. High technology medical equipment may include computer axial tomography (C.A.T.) scanners, nuclear magnetic resonance equipment, clinical chemistry analyzers, drug monitors, diagnostic ultrasound scanners, nuclear cameras, radiographic and fluoroscopic systems, Holter monitors, and bedside monitors. Incidental use of any such equipment for other purposes, such as research, will not prevent it from qualifying as high technology medical equipment. There are no current plans to utilize the regulatory authority provided in section 168(j)(5)(C)(iv).

Lease Term

Q-17. What is included in determining the length of a lease term?

A-17. (i) The lease term starts when the property is first made available to the lessee under the lease. The lease term includes not only the stated duration, but also any additional period of time which is within the "realistic contemplation of the parties at the time the property is first put into service. Hokanson v. Commissioner, 730 F.2d 1245, 1248 (9th Cir. 1984). A subsequent period of time is included in the term of the original lease if the circumstances indicate that the parties, upon entering into the original lease, had informally agreed that there would be an extension of the original lease.

(ii) With respect to personal property, the lease term includes all periods for which the tax-exempt lessee or a related party (as defined under section 168(j)(7)) has a legally enforceable option to renew the lease, or the lessor has a legally enforceable option to compel its renewal by the tax-exempt entity or a related party. This is true regardless of the renewal terms of the lease agreement or whether the lease is in fact renewed.

(iii) With respect to real property, the lease term includes all periods for which the tax-exempt lessee or a related party (as defined under section 168(j)(7)) has a legally enforceable option to renew the lease, or the lessor has a legally enforceable option to compel its renewal by the tax-exempt entity or a related party, unless the option to renew is at fair market value, determined at the time of renewal. The Hokanson facts and circumstances test (see (i) above) may cause the term of a fair market value renewal option to be treated as part of the original lease term.

(iv) Successive leases that are part of the same transaction or a series of related transactions concerning the same or substantially similar property shall be treated as one lease. This rule applies if at substantially the same time or as part of one arrangement the parties enter into multiple leases covering the same or substantially similar property, each having a different term. If so, then the original lease term will be treated as running through the term of the lease that has the last expiration date of the multiple leases. The multiple lease rule will not apply merely because the parties enter into a new lease at fair market rental value at the end of the original lease term.

(v) The application of the above rules is illustrated by the following examples:

Example (1). On December 30, 1984, X, a taxable corporation, and Y, a tax-exempt entity, enter into a requirements contract for a period of 3 years. The requirements contract sets the terms and conditions under which X and Y will do business on those occasions when X actually leases items of personal property to Y. The requirements contract imposes no obligation on either party to actually enter into a lease agreement. Pursuant to this requirements contract, on January 1, 1985, X and Y enter into three separate leases. Under the leases, Y obtained the use of three identical items of personal property, each for a term of six months beginning on January 1, 1985. On March 1, 1985, Y entered into a fourth lease for the use of a fourth item of personal property substantially similar to the other three items for a term of 20 months beginning on that date. The mere fact that all 4 leases were entered into pursuant to the same requirements contract and involved the same or substantially similar property does not require aggregation of the terms of such leases under section 168(j)(6)(B).

Example (2). Assume the same facts as in Example (1) except that, instead of the 4 leases entered into in Example (1), on January 1, 1985, pursuant to the requirements contract, X and Y enter into a lease for an item of personal property for one year. On January 10, 1986, after the end of the one-year lease term, X and Y enter into a second lease with respect to the same or substantially similar equipment. Assuming that the requirements contract itself is not a lease and assuming that the parties did not have any informal or implicit understanding (other than the general expectation of doing some business in the future) to enter into the second lease when the first lease was entered into, these two leases are not aggregated. The mere fact that the parties entered into two leases under the requirements contract does not result in the application of the section 168(j)(6)(B) rules for successive leases.

Example (3). The facts are the same as in Example (2) except that the parties did have an understanding, informal or otherwise, at the time of the first lease that they would enter into a second lease of the same personal property. The terms of the leases are aggregated.

Example (4). The facts are the same as in Example (2) except that, instead of the leases entered into in Example (2), on January 1, 1985, X and Y enter into two separate leases, each for a term of one year. One lease is for the period beginning on January 1, 1985 and ending on December 31, 1985. The other lease is for the period beginning on January 1, 1986 and ending on December 31, 1986. Both leases involve the same or substantially similar personal property. Under the successive lease rule, the terms of both leases are aggregated for purposes of determining the term of either lease under section 168(j)(6)(B). This result occurs because the two leases were entered into as part of the same transaction, and they relate to the same or substantially similar personal property.

Service Contract Issues

Q-18. How is the treatment of service contracts affected by the service contract rules set forth in section 7701(e)?

A-18. If a contract which purports to be a service contract is treated as a lease under section 7701(e), such contract is to be treated as a lease for all purposes of Chapter 1 of the Internal Revenue Code (including, for example, section 168(j) and section 48(a)(4) and (5)).

Q-19. Does a contract to provide heating, maintenance, etc. services in low-income housing come within the low-income housing exception in section 7701(e)(5) to the service contract rules set forth in section 7701(e)?

A-19. No. Although certain low-income housing operated by or for an organization described in paragraphs (3) or (4) of section 501(c) is not subject to the service contract rules in section 7701(e), a contract, for instance, to provide heating services to low-income housing units, such as by installing and operating a furnace, does not constitute "low-income housing" within the meaning of section 7701(e)(5). Thus, the rules of section 7701(e) apply to such contracts in determining whether they are properly treated as leases.

Partnership Issues

Q-20. Do the provisions applicable to property leased to partnerships, set forth in section 168(j)(8), and the provisions applicable to property owned by partnerships, set forth in section 168(j)(9), apply to pass-through entities other than partnerships?

A-20. Yes. Rules similar to those provided in paragraphs (8), (9)(A), (9)(B), and (9)(C) of section 168(j) and those provided in Q & A's 21-26 apply to pass-through entities other than partnerships.

Q-21. What rules apply to property owned by a partnership in which one or more partners is a tax-exempt entity?

A-21. If property is owned by a partnership having both taxable and tax-exempt entities as partners, and any allocation to a tax-exempt entity partner is not a "qualified allocation" under section 168(j)(9)(B), then such entity's proportionate share of the property is to be treated as tax-exempt use property for all purposes. However, the property will not be tax-exempt use property if it is predominantly used by the partnership in an activity which, with respect to the tax-exempt entity, is an unrelated trade or business. An activity is an unrelated trade or business with respect to a tax-exempt entity if such entity's distributive share of the partnership's gross income from the activity is includible in computing its unrelated business taxable income under section 512(c) (determined without regard to the debt-financed income rules of section 514). A tax-exempt entity partner's proportionate share of property of a partnership equals such partner's share of that item of the partnership's income or gain (excluding income or gain allocated under section 704(c)) in which the tax-exempt entity has the highest share. If the tax-exempt entity partner's share of any item of income or gain (excluding income or gain allocated under section 704(c)) may vary during the period it is a partner, the previous sentence shall be applied with reference to the highest share of any such item that it may receive at any time during such period. The application of these rules is illustrated by the following example:

Example. A partnership (P) operates a factory, which consists of a building and various items of machinery. P has one tax-exempt entity (E) as a partner, and E's proportionate share is 10 percent (i.e., 10 percent is the largest share of any item of income or gain that E may receive during the time E is a partner). Unless P's allocations to E are qualified under section 168(j)(9)(B), 10 percent of each item of partnership property (including the building) is tax-exempt use property, notwithstanding the 35 percent threshold test of section 168(j)(3)(B)(iii) that is otherwise applicable to 18-year real property. However, the property will not be tax-exempt use property if it is predominantly used by the partnership in an activity which, with respect to E, is an unrelated trade or business (determined without regard to the debt-financed income rules of section 514).

Q-22. What constitutes a "qualified allocation" under section 168(j)(9)(B)?

A-22. (i) A "qualified allocation" means any allocation to a tax-exempt entity which is consistent with such entity's being allocated the same share (i.e., the identical percentage) of each and every item of partnership income, gain, loss, deduction, credit, and basis during the entire period such entity is a partner. Except as provided in A-23, an allocation is not qualified if it does not have substantial economic effect under section 704(b). However, for purposes of the two preceding sentences, items allocated under section 704(c) (relating to contributed property) are not taken into account. An allocation is not a "qualified allocation" under section 168(j)(9)(B) if the partnership agreement provides for, or the partners have otherwise formally or informally agreed to, any change (regardless of whether such change is contingent upon the happening of one or more events) in the tax-exempt entity's distributive share of income, gain, loss, deduction, credit, or basis at any time during the entire period the tax-exempt entity is a partner.

(ii) A change in a tax-exempt entity's distributive share of income, gain, loss, deduction, credit, or basis which occurs as a result of a sale or redemption of a partnership interest (or portion thereof) or a contribution of cash or property to the partnership shall be disregarded in determining whether the partnership allocations are qualified, provided that such transaction is based on fair market value at the time of the transaction and that the allocations are qualified after the change. For this purpose, the consideration determined by the parties dealing at arm's length and with adverse interests normally will be deemed to satisfy the fair market value requirement. In addition, a change in a tax-exempt entity's distributive share which occurs as a result of a partner's default (other than a prearranged default) under the terms of the partnership agreement will be disregarded, provided that the allocations are qualified after the change, and that the change does not have the effect of avoiding the restrictions of section 168(j)(9). Any of the above-described transactions between existing partners (and parties related to them) will be closely scrutinized.

Example (1). A, a taxable entity, and B, a tax-exempt entity, form a partnership in 1985. A contributes $800,000 to the partnership; B contributes $200,000. The partnership agreement allocates 95 percent of each item of income, gain, loss, deduction, credit, and basis to A; B's share of each of these items is 5 percent. Liquidation proceeds are, throughout the term of the partnership, to be distributed in accordance with the partner's capital account balances, and any partner with a deficit in his capital account following the distribution of liquidation proceeds is required to restore the amount of such deficit to the partnership. Assuming that these allocations have substantial economic effect within the meaning of section 704(b)(2), they are qualified because B's distributive share of each item of income, gain, loss, deduction, credit, and basis will remain the same during the entire period that B is a partner. The fact that the liquidation proceeds may be distributed in a ratio other than 95 percent/5 percent does not cause the allocations not to be qualified.

Example (2). A, B, and E are members of a partnership formed on July 1, 1984. On that date the partnership places in service a building and section 1245 class property. A and B are taxable entities; E is a tax-exempt entity. The partnership agreement provides that during the first 5 years of the partnership, A and B are each allocated 40 percent of each item of income, gain, loss, deduction, credit, and basis; E is allocated 20 percent. Thereafter, A, B, and E are each allocated 33⅓ percent of each item of income, gain, loss, deduction, credit, and basis. Assume that these allocations meet the substantial economic effect test of section 704(b)(2) and E's distributive share of the partnership's income is not unrelated trade or business income subject to tax under section 511. The allocations to E are not qualified allocations under section 168(j)(9)(B) because E's distributive share of partnership items does not remain the same during the entire period that E is a partner in the partnership. Thus, 33⅓ percent of the building and 33⅓ percent of the section 1245 class property are tax-exempt use property from the time each is placed in service by the partnership and are thus subject to the cost recovery rules of section 168(j)(1) and (2). In addition, no investment tax credit is allowed for 33⅓ percent of the section 1245 class property because of section 48(a)(4).

Q-23. In determining whether allocations constitute qualified allocations, what rules are applied to test allocations that are not governed by the substantial economic effect rules?

A-23. A-22 provides the general rules to be used in determining whether an allocation is a qualified allocation, including the rule that the allocation must have substantial economic effect. However, certain allocations are not governed by the substantial economic effect rules (e.g., an allocation of basis of an oil and gas property is generally governed by section 613A(c)(7)(D), rather than section 704(b)), and other allocations cannot satisfy the substantial economic effect rules (e.g., allocations of credits, allocations of deduction and loss attributable to nonrecourse debt, and allocations of percentage depletion in excess of basis). Since allocations in either of these categories cannot be tested under the substantial economic effect test, these allocations, in order to be qualified, must comply with the relevant Code or regulation section that governs the particular allocation (e.g., in the case of an allocation of basis of an oil and gas property, section 613A(c)(7)(D)).

Q-24. Will the Internal Revenue Service issue letter rulings on the issue of whether an allocation is a "qualified allocation" for purposes of section 168(j)(9)?

A-24. The Internal Revenue Service will accept requests for rulings on the question of whether an allocation is a "qualified allocation" for purposes of section 168(j)(9). Such requests should be submitted in accordance with the appropriate revenue procedure. One requirement of a qualified allocation is that such allocation must have substantial economic effect under section 704(b)(2). Currently, the Service will not rule on the question of whether an allocation has substantial economic effect under section 704(b)(2). Therefore, unless and until this policy is changed, a ruling request regarding a qualified allocation must contain a representation that the subject allocation has substantial economic effect (or complies with A-23, if applicable).

Q-25. Do priority cash distributions which constitute guaranteed payments under section 707(c) disqualify an otherwise qualified allocation?

A-25. Priority cash distributions to partners which constitute guaranteed payments will not disqualify an otherwise qualified allocation if the priority cash distributions are reasonable in amount (e.g., equal to the Federal short-term rate described in section 1274(d)) and are made in equal priorities to all partners in proportion to their capital in the partnership. Other guaranteed payments will be closely scrutinized and, in appropriate cases, will disqualify an otherwise qualified allocation.

Example. A and B form Partnership AB to operate a manufacturing business. A is a tax-exempt entity; B is a taxable person. A contributes $500,000 to the partnership; B contributes $100,000. The partnership agreement provides that A and B are each entitled to cash distributions each year, in equal priority, in an amount equal to 8 percent of their capital contribution. Assume that these payments are reasonable in amount and constitute guaranteed payments under section 707(c). Without taking into consideration the guaranteed payments, all allocations constitute qualified allocations under section 168(j)(9)(B) and A-22. These guaranteed payments will not disqualify such allocations.

Q-26. Can property be treated as tax-exempt use property under both the general rule of section 168(j)(3) and the partnership provisions of section 168(j)(9)?

A-26. Yes. For example, a tax-exempt entity may be a partner in a partnership that owns a building 60 percent of which is tax-exempt use property because it is leased to an unrelated tax-exempt entity under a 25-year lease. The status of the remaining 40 percent depends on whether or not allocations under the partnership agreement are qualified under section 168(j)(9). If the allocations are not qualified under section 168(j)(9), the tax-exempt entity's proportionate share (as determined under section 168(j)(9)(C)) of the remaining 40 percent will be tax-exempt use property. For example, if the tax-exempt entity's proportionate share is 30 percent, then 12 percent of the remaining 40 percent (i.e., .30 times .40) is tax-exempt use property and a total of 72 percent of the property (60 percent + 12 percent) is tax-exempt use property.

Effective Date Questions

Q-27. Does an amendment to a lease (or sublease) to a tax-exempt entity of property which, pursuant to the effective date provisions of section 31(g) of TRA, is not subject to section 168(j) cause such property to be subject to the provisions of section 168(j)?

A-27. An amendment to such a lease (or sublease) does not cause such property to be subject to the provisions of section 168(j) unless the amendment increases the term of the lease (or sublease). However, if the amendment increases the amount of property subject to the lease, the additional property must be tested independently under the effective date provisions of section 31(g) of TRA. See A-31 for special rules regarding improvements to property.

Example. On May 1, 1983, X, a taxable entity, and E, a tax-exempt entity, enter into a lease whereby X will lease to E the top 4 floors of a ten-story building for a lease term of 25 years. In 1985, the lease is amended to provide that E will lease an additional floor for the balance of the lease term. At that time the annual rent due under the lease is increased. Pursuant to the provisions of section 31(g)(2)(A) of TRA, section 168(j) does not apply to the lease to E of the top 4 floors of the building. Assuming that no other provision of section 31(g) of TRA provides otherwise, the floor added to the lease in 1985 is subject to the provisions of section 168(j).

Q-28. If property which is not subject to section 168(j) by virtue of the effective date provisions of section 31(g) of TRA is sold, subject to the lease to the tax-exempt entity, what are the consequences?

A-28. Property to which section 168(j) does not apply by virtue of the effective date provisions set forth in section 31(g)(2), (3), and (4) of TRA will not become subject to section 168(j) merely by reason of a transfer of the property subject to the lease by the lessor (or a transfer of the contract to acquire, construct, reconstruct, or rehabilitate the property), so long as the lessee (or party obligated to lease) does not change. For purposes of the preceding sentence, the term "transfer" includes the sale-leaseback by a taxable lessor of its interest in the property, subject to the underlying lease to the tax-exempt entity. However, if property is transferred to a partnership or other pass-through entity after the effective date of section 168(j)(9) (see section 31(g) of TRA), such property is subject to the provisions of section 168(j)(9).

Q-29. Can property which was leased to a tax-exempt entity after May 23, 1983 and acquired by a partnership before October 22, 1983 be tax-exempt use property?

A-29. Yes. Because the property was leased to a tax-exempt entity after May 23, 1983, it may be tax-exempt use property under section 168(j)(3) and section 31(g)(1) of TRA. However, if the partnership included a tax-exempt entity as a partner, section 168(j)(9) would be inapplicable under section 31(g)(3)(B) of TRA because the partnership acquired the property before October 22, 1983.

Q-30. What is a binding contract for purposes of the transitional rules in section 31(g) of TRA?

A-30. (i) A contract is binding only if it is enforceable under State law against the taxpayer or a predecessor and does not limit damages to a specified amount, as for example, by a liquidated damages provision. A contract that limits damages to an amount equal to at least 5 percent of the total contract price will not be treated as limiting damages for this purpose. In determining whether a contract limits damages, the fact that there may be little or no damages because the contract price does not significantly differ from fair market value will not be taken into account. For example, if a taxpayer entered into an irrevocable contract to purchase an asset for $100 and the contract contained no provision for liquidated damages, the contract is considered binding notwithstanding the fact that the property had a fair market value of $99 and under local law the seller would only recover the difference in the event the purchaser failed to perform. If the contract provided for a refund of the purchase price in lieu of any damages allowable by law in the event of breach or cancellation, the contract is not considered binding.

(ii) A contract is binding even if subject to a condition, so long as the condition is not within the control of either party or a predecessor in interest. A contract will not be treated as ceasing to be binding merely because the parties make insubstantial changes in its terms or because any term is to be determined by a standard beyond the control of either party. A contract which imposes significant obligations on the taxpayer (or a predecessor) will be treated as binding notwithstanding the fact that insubstantial terms remain to be negotiated by the parties to the contract.

(iii) A binding contract to acquire a component part of a larger piece of property will not be treated as a binding contract to acquire the larger piece of property. For example, if a tax-exempt entity entered into a binding contract on May 1, 1983 to acquire a new aircraft engine, there would be a binding contract to acquire only the engine, not the entire aircraft.

Q-31. If an improvement is made to a property that is "grandfathered" (i.e., property that is not subject to section 168(j) because of the effective date provisions of section 31(g) of TRA), to what extent will such improvement be grandfathered?

A-31. Section 31(g)(20)(B) provides that a "substantial improvement" to property is treated as a separate property for purposes of the effective date provisions of section 31(g) of TRA. As a result, a "substantial improvement" will not be grandfathered unless such "substantial improvement" is grandfathered under a provision other than section 31(g)(20)(B). A property that is grandfathered will not become subject to section 168(j) merely because an improvement is made to such property, regardless of whether the improvement is a "substantial improvement". If an improvement other than a "substantial improvement" is made to property (other than land) that is grandfathered, that improvement also will be grandfathered. The determination of whether new construction constitutes an improvement to property or the creation of a new separate property will be based on all facts and circumstances. Furthermore, any improvement to land will be treated as a separate property.

Example. On January 3, 1983, T, a taxable entity, entered into a lease of a parking lot to E, a tax-exempt entity. On January 1, 1985, T begins construction of a building for use by E on the site of the parking lot. The building is completed and placed in service in November 1985. The building is treated as a separate property, and is thus subject to the provisions of section 168(j), unless the building is grandfathered under a provision other than section 31(g)(20)(B) of TRA.

Q-32. What is "significant official governmental action" for purposes of the section 31(g)(4) transitional rule of TRA?

A-32. (i) "Significant official governmental action" involves three separate requirements. First, the action must be an official action. Second, the action must be specific action with respect to a particular project. Third, the action must be taken by a governmental entity having authority to commit the tax-exempt entity to the project, to provide funds for it, or to approve the project under State or local law.

(ii) The first requirement of official action means that the governing body must adopt a resolution or ordinance, or take similar official action, on or before November 1, 1983. The action qualifies only if it conforms with Federal, State, and local law (as applicable) and is a proper exercise of the powers of the governing body. Moreover, the action must not have been withdrawn. There must be satisfactory written evidence of the action that was in existence on or before November 1, 1983. Satisfactory written evidence includes a formal resolution or ordinance, minutes of meetings, and binding contracts with third parties pursuant to which third parties are to render services in furtherance of the project.

(iii) The second requirement of specific action is directed at the substance of the action taken. The action must be a specific action with respect to a particular project in which the governing body indicates an intent to have the project (or the design work for it) proceed. This requires that a specific project have been formulated and that the significant official action be a step toward consummation of the project. If the action does not relate to a specific project or merely directs that a proposal or recommendation be formulated, it will not qualify. The following set of actions with respect to a particular project constitute specific action: the hiring of bond counsel or bond underwriters necessary to assist in the issuance and sale of bonds to finance a particular project or the adoption of an inducement resolution relating to bonds to be issued for such a project; applying for an Urban Development Action Grant on behalf of the project described in the application, receiving such a grant concerning the project, or the recommendation of a city planning authority to proceed with a project; the enactment of a State law authorizing the sale, lease, or construction of the property; the appropriation of funds for the property or authorization of a feasibility study or a development services contract with respect to it; the approval of financing arrangements by a regulatory agency; the enactment of a State law designed to provide funding for a project; the certification of a building as a historic structure by a State agency and the Department of the Interior; or the endorsement of the application for a certification of need with respect to a medical facility by a regulatory agency other than the agency empowered to issue such a certificate.

(iv) The third requirement for significant official governmental action is that the action must be taken by a Federal, State, or local governing body having authority to commit the tax-exempt entity to the project, to provide funds for it, or to approve the project under applicable law.

If the chief executive or another representative of a governing body has such authority, action by such representative would satisfy the requirement of this (iv). A governing body may have the authority to commit the tax-exempt entity to a project notwithstanding the fact that the project cannot be consummated without other governmental action being taken. For example, a city council will be treated as having authority to commit a city to do a sale-leaseback of its city hall notwithstanding the fact that State law needs to be amended to permit such a transaction. Similarly, if a local project cannot be completed without Federal approval, either legislative or administrative, the obtaining of such approval satisfies the requirements of this (iv).

(v) Routine governmental action at a local level will not qualify as significant official governmental action. Routine governmental action includes the granting of building permits or zoning changes and the issuance of environmental impact statements.

(vi) In order to qualify under the transitional rule of TRA section 31(g)(4), a sale and leaseback pursuant to a binding contract entered into before January 1, 1985 must be part of the project as to which there was significant official governmental action. Except as provided in the following sentence, where there has been significant official governmental action on or before November 1, 1983 with respect to the construction, reconstruction or rehabilitation of a property, the sale and leaseback of such property pursuant to a binding contract entered into before January 1, 1985 will be treated as part of the project which was the subject of the significant official governmental action. However, if the construction, reconstruction or rehabilitation was substantially completed prior to January 1, 1983, the sale and leaseback of such property will be treated as a separate project, unless the sale and leaseback was contemplated at the time of the significant official governmental action. Nevertheless, where the sale and leaseback is treated as a separate project, section 31(g)(4) may apply if there was significant official governmental action on or before November 1, 1983, with respect to such sale and leaseback. The application of this provision is illustrated by the following example:

Example. In the summer of 1927, the Board of Aldermen of City C passed a resolution authorizing the design and construction of a new city hall and appropriated the funds necessary for such project. Construction was completed in 1928. At the time of the significant official governmental action, City C had no plan to enter into a sale-leaseback arrangement with respect to the facility. On December 15, 1984, City C entered into a binding sale-leaseback arrangement concerning the city hall. This transaction will not qualify for exclusion from section 168(j) under the section 31(g)(4) of TRA since construction of the facility in question was substantially completed before January 1, 1983. If, however, there had been significant official governmental action on or before November 1, 1983 with respect to the sale-leaseback project, then the transitional rule of section 31(g)(4) of TRA would apply.

T.D. 8033, 6/28/85, amend T.D. 8435, 9/18/92.

§ 1.168(k)-0 Table of contents.

This section lists the headings that appear in Sec. 1.168(k)-1.

§ 1.168(k)-1 Additional first year depreciation deduction (temporary).

(a) Scope and definitions.

(1) Scope.

(2) Definitions.

(b) Qualified property or 50-percent bonus depreciation property.

(1) In general.

(2) Description of qualified property or 50-percent bonus depreciation property.

(i) In general.

(ii) Property not eligible for additional first year depreciation deduction.

(A) Property that is not qualified property.

(B) Property that is not 50-percent bonus depreciation property.

(3) Original use.

(i) In general.

(ii) Conversion to business or income-producing use.

(A) Personal use to business or income-producing use.
(B) Inventory to business or income-producing use.
(iii) Sale-leaseback, syndication, and certain other transactions.
(A) Sale-leaseback transaction.
(B) Syndication transaction and certain other transactions.
(C) Sale-leaseback transaction followed by a syndication transaction and certain other transactions.
(iv) Fractional interests in property.
(v) Examples.
(4) Acquisition of property.
(i) In general.
(A) Qualified property.
(B) 50-percent bonus depreciation property.
(ii) Definition of binding contract.
(A) In general.
(B) Conditions.
(C) Options.
(D) Supply agreements.
(E) Components.
(iii) Self-constructed property.
(A) In general.
(B) When does manufacture, construction, or production begin.
(1) In general.
(2) Safe harbor.
(C) Components of self-constructed property.
(1) Acquired components.
(2) Self-constructed components.
(iv) Disqualified transactions.
(A) In general.
(B) Related party defined.
(v) Examples.
(5) Placed-in-service date.
(i) In general.
(ii) Sale-leaseback, syndication, and certain other transactions.
(A) Sale-leaseback transaction.
(B) Syndication transaction and certain other transactions.
(C) Sale-leaseback transaction followed by a syndication transaction and certain other transactions.
(iii) Technical termination of a partnership.
(iv) Section 168(i)(7) transactions.
(v) Example.
(c) Qualified leasehold improvement property.
(1) In general.
(2) Certain improvements not included.
(3) Definitions.
(d) Computation of depreciation deduction for qualified property or 50-percent bonus depreciation property.
(1) Additional first year depreciation deduction.
(i) In general.
(ii) Property having a longer production period.
(iii) Alternative minimum tax.
(2) Otherwise allowable depreciation deduction.
(i) In general.
(ii) Alternative minimum tax.
(3) Examples.
(e) Election not to deduct additional first year depreciation.
(1) In general.
(i) Qualified property.
(ii) 50-percent bonus depreciation property.
(2) Definition of class of property.
(3) Time and manner for making election.
(i) Time for making election.
(ii) Manner of making election.
(4) Special rules for 2000 or 2001 returns.
(5) Failure to make election.
(6) Alternative minimum tax.
(7) Revocation.
(i) In general.
(ii) Automatic 6-month extension.
(f) Special rules.
(1) Property placed in service and disposed of in the same taxable year.
(i) In general.
(ii) Technical termination of a partnership.
(iii) Section 168(i)(7) transactions.
(iv) Examples.
(2) Redetermination of basis.
(i) Increase in basis.
(ii) Decrease in basis.
(iii) Definition.
(iv) Examples.
(3) Section 1245 and 1250 depreciation recapture.
(4) Coordination with section 169.
(5) Like-kind exchanges and involuntary conversions.
(i) Scope.
(ii) Definitions.
(iii) Computation.
(A) In general.
(B) Year of disposition and year of replacement.
(C) Property having a longer production period.
(D) Alternative minimum tax.
(iv) Sale-leasebacks.
(v) Acquired MACRS property or acquired computer software that is acquired and placed in service before disposition of involuntarily converted MACRS property or involuntarily converted computer software.
(A) Time of replacement.
(B) Depreciation of acquired MACRS property or acquired computer software.
(vi) Examples.
(6) Change in use.
(i) Change in use of depreciable property.
(ii) Conversion to personal use.
(iii) Conversion to business or income-producing use.
(A) During the same taxable year.
(B) Subsequent to the acquisition year.

(iv) Depreciable property changes use subsequent to the placed-in-service year.

(v) Examples.

(7) Earnings and profits.

(8) Limitation of amount of depreciation for certain passenger automobiles.

(9) Section 754 election.

(10) Coordination with section 47.

(11) Coordination with section 514(a)(3).

(g) Effective date.

(1) In general.

(2) Technical termination of a partnership or section 168(i)(7) transactions.

(3) Like-kind exchanges and involuntary conversions.

(4) Change in method of accounting.

(i) Special rules for 2000 or 2001 returns.

(ii) Like-kind exchanges and involuntary conversions.

(5) Revisions to paragraphs (b)(3)(ii)(B) and (b)(5)(ii)(B).

(6) Rehabilitation credit.

T.D. 9091, 9/5/2003, amend T.D. 9283, 8/28/2006.

---

§ 1.168(k)-1 Additional first year depreciation deduction.

(a) Scope and definitions. *(1) Scope.* This section provides the rules for determining the 30-percent additional first year depreciation deduction allowable under section 168(k)(1) for qualified property and the 50-percent additional first year depreciation deduction allowable under section 168(k)(4) for 50-percent bonus depreciation property.

(2) Definitions. For purposes of section 168(k) and this section, the following definitions apply:

(i) Depreciable property is property that is of a character subject to the allowance for depreciation as determined under section 167 and the regulations thereunder.

(ii) MACRS property is tangible, depreciable property that is placed in service after December 31, 1986 (or after July 31, 1986, if the taxpayer made an election under section 203(a)(1)(B) of the Tax Reform Act of 1986; 100 Stat. 2143) and subject to section 168, except for property excluded from the application of section 168 as a result of section 168(f) or as a result of a transitional rule.

(iii) Unadjusted depreciable basis is the basis of property for purposes of section 1011 without regard to any adjustments described in section 1016(a)(2) and (3). This basis reflects the reduction in basis for the percentage of the taxpayer's use of property for the taxable year other than in the taxpayer's trade or business (or for the production of income), for any portion of the basis the taxpayer properly elects to treat as an expense under section 179 or section 179C, and for any adjustments to basis provided by other provisions of the Internal Revenue Code and the regulations thereunder (other than section 1016(a)(2) and (3)) (for example, a reduction in basis by the amount of the disabled access credit pursuant to section 44(d)(7)). For property subject to a lease, see section 167(c)(2).

(iv) Adjusted depreciable basis is the unadjusted depreciable basis of the property, as defined in § 1.168(k)-1(a)(2)(iii), less the adjustments described in section 1016(a)(2) and (3).

(b) Qualified property or 50-percent bonus depreciation property. *(1) In general.* Qualified property or 50-percent bonus depreciation property is depreciable property that meets all the following requirements in the first taxable year in which the property is subject to depreciation by the taxpayer whether or not depreciation deductions for the property are allowable:

(i) The requirements in § 1.168(k)-1(b)(2) (description of property);

(ii) The requirements in § 1.168(k)-1(b)(3) (original use);

(iii) The requirements in § 1.168(k)-1(b)(4) (acquisition of property); and

(iv) The requirements in § 1.168(k)-1(b)(5)' (placed-in-service date).

(2) Description of qualified property or 50-percent bonus depreciation property. (i) In general. Depreciable property will meet the requirements of this paragraph (b)(2) if the property is—

(A) MACRS property (as defined in § 1.168(k)-T(a)(2)(ii)) that has a recovery period of 20 years or less. For purposes of this paragraph (b)(2)(i)(A) and section 168(k)(2)(B)(i)(II) and 168(k)(4)(C), the recovery period is determined in accordance with section 168(c) regardless of any election made by the taxpayer under section 168(g)(7);

(B) Computer software as defined in, and depreciated under, section 167(f)(1) and the regulations thereunder;

(C) Water utility property as defined in section 168(e)(5) and depreciated under section 168; or

(D) Qualified leasehold improvement property as defined in paragraph (c) of this section and depreciated under section 168.

(ii) Property not eligible for additional first year depreciation deduction. (A) Property that is not qualified property. For purposes of the 30-percent additional first year depreciation deduction, depreciable property will not meet the requirements of this paragraph (b)(2) if the property is—

(1) Described in section 168(f);

(2) Required to be depreciated under the alternative depreciation system of section 168(g) pursuant to section 168(g)(1)(A) through (D) or other provisions of the Internal Revenue Code (for example, property described in section 263A(e)(2)(A) if the taxpayer (or any related person as defined in section 263A(e)(2)(B)) has made an election under section 263A(d)(3), or property described in section 280F(b)(1)).

(3) Included in any class of property for which the taxpayer elects not to deduct the 30-percent additional first year depreciation (for further guidance, see paragraph (e) of this section); or

(4) Qualified New York Liberty Zone leasehold improvement property as defined in section 1400L(c)(2).

(B) Property that is not 50-percent bonus depreciation property. For purposes of the 50-percent additional first year depreciation deduction, depreciable property will not meet the requirements of this paragraph (b)(2) if the property is—

(1) Described in paragraph (b)(2)(ii)(A)(1), (2), or (4) of this section; or

(2) Included in any class of property for which the taxpayer elects the 30-percent, instead of the 50-percent, additional first year depreciation deduction or elects not to deduct any additional first year depreciation (for further guidance, see paragraph (e) of this section).

(3) Original use. (i) In general. For purposes of the 30-percent additional first year depreciation deduction, depreciable property will meet the requirements of this paragraph (b)(3) if the original use of the property commences with the

taxpayer after September 10, 2001. For purposes of the 50-percent additional first year depreciation deduction, depreciable property will meet the requirements of this paragraph (b)(3) if the original use of the property commences with the taxpayer after May 5, 2003. Except as provided in paragraphs (b)(3)(iii) and (iv) of this section, original use means the first use to which the property is put, whether or not that use corresponds to the use of the property by the taxpayer. Thus, additional capital expenditures incurred by a taxpayer to recondition or rebuild property acquired or owned by the taxpayer satisfies the original use requirement. However, the cost of reconditioned or rebuilt property does not satisfy the original use requirement. The question of whether property is reconditioned or rebuilt property is a question of fact. For purposes of this paragraph (b)(3)(i), property that contains used parts will not be treated as reconditioned or rebuilt if the cost of the used parts is not more than 20 percent of the total cost of the property, whether acquired or self-constructed.

(ii) Conversion to business or income-producing use. (A) Personal use to business or income-producing use. If a taxpayer initially acquires new property for personal use and subsequently uses the property in the taxpayer's trade or business or for the taxpayer's production of income, the taxpayer is considered the original user of the property. If a person initially acquires new property for personal use and a taxpayer subsequently acquires the property from the person for use in the taxpayer's trade or business or for the taxpayer's production of income, the taxpayer is not considered the original user of the property.

(B) Inventory to business or income-producing use. If a taxpayer initially acquires new property and holds the property primarily for sale to customers in the ordinary course of the taxpayer's business and subsequently withdraws the property from inventory and uses the property primarily in the taxpayer's trade or business or primarily for the taxpayer's production of income, the taxpayer is considered the original user of the property. If a person initially acquires new property and holds the property primarily for sale to customers in the ordinary course of the person's business and a taxpayer subsequently acquires the property from the person for use primarily in the taxpayer's trade or business or primarily for the taxpayer's production of income, the taxpayer is considered the original user of the property. For purposes of this paragraph (b)(3)(ii)(B), the original use of the property by the taxpayer commences on the date on which the taxpayer uses the property primarily in the taxpayer's trade or business or primarily for the taxpayer's production of income.

(iii) Sale-leaseback, syndication, and certain other transactions. (A) Sale-leaseback transaction. If new property is originally placed in service by a person after September 10, 2001 (for qualified property), or after May 5, 2003 (for 50-percent bonus depreciation property), and is sold to a taxpayer and leased back to the person by the taxpayer within three months after the date the property was originally placed in service by the person, the taxpayer-lessor is considered the original user of the property.

(B) Syndication transaction and certain other transactions. If new property is originally placed in service by a lessor (including by operation of paragraph (b)(5)(ii)(A) of this section) after September 10, 2001 (for qualified property), or after May 5, 2003 (for 50-percent bonus depreciation property), and is sold by the lessor or any subsequent purchaser within three months after the date the property was originally placed in service by the lessor (or, in the case of multiple units of property subject to the same lease, within three months after the date the final unit is placed in service, so long as the period between the time the first unit is placed in service and the time the last unit is placed in service does not exceed 12 months), and the user of the property after the last sale during the three-month period remains the same as when the property was originally placed in service by the lessor, the purchaser of the property in the last sale during the three-month period is considered the original user of the property.

(C) Sale-leaseback transaction followed by a syndication transaction and certain other transactions. If a sale-leaseback transaction that satisfies the requirements in paragraph (b)(3)(iii)(A) of this section is followed by a transaction that satisfies the requirements in paragraph (b)(3)(iii)(B) of this section, the original user of the property is determined in accordance with paragraph (b)(3)(iii)(B) of this section.

(iv) Fractional interests in property. If, in the ordinary course of its business, a taxpayer sells fractional interests in property to third parties unrelated to the taxpayer, each first fractional owner of the property is considered as the original user of its proportionate share of the property. Furthermore, if the taxpayer uses the property before all of the fractional interests of the property are sold but the property continues to be held primarily for sale by the taxpayer, the original use of any fractional interest sold to a third party unrelated to the taxpayer subsequent to the taxpayer's use of the property begins with the first purchaser of that fractional interest. For purposes of this paragraph (b)(3)(iv), persons are not related if they do not have a relationship described in section 267(b) or 707(b) and the regulations thereunder.

(v) Examples. The application of this paragraph (b)(3) is illustrated by the following examples:

Example (1). On August 1, 2002, A buys from B for $20,000 a machine that has been previously used by B in B's trade or business. On March 1, 2003, A makes a $5,000 capital expenditure to recondition the machine. The $20,000 purchase price does not qualify for the additional first year depreciation deduction because the original use requirement of this paragraph (b)(3) is not met. However, the $5,000 expenditure satisfies the original use requirement of this paragraph (b)(3) and, assuming all other requirements are met, qualifies for the 30-percent additional first year depreciation deduction, regardless of whether the $5,000 is added to the basis of the machine or is capitalized as a separate asset.

Example (2). C, an automobile dealer, uses some of its automobiles as demonstrators in order to show them to prospective customers. The automobiles that are used as demonstrators by C are held by C primarily for sale to customers in the ordinary course of its business. On September 1, 2002, D buys from C an automobile that was previously used as a demonstrator by C. D will use the automobile solely for business purposes. The use of the automobile by C as a demonstrator does not constitute a "use" for purposes of the original use requirement and, therefore, D will be considered the original user of the automobile for purposes of this paragraph (b)(3). Assuming all other requirements are met, D's purchase price of the automobile qualifies for the 30-percent additional first year depreciation deduction for D, subject to any limitation under section 280F.

Example (3). On April 1, 2000, E acquires a horse to be used in E's thoroughbred racing business. On October 1, 2003, F buys the horse from E and will use the horse in F's horse breeding business. The use of the horse by E in its racing business prevents the original use of the horse from commencing with F. Thus, F's purchase price of the horse does not qualify for the additional first year depreciation deduction.

Example (4). In the ordinary course of its business, G sells fractional interests in its aircraft to unrelated parties. G holds out for sale eight equal fractional interests in an aircraft. On January 1, 2003, G sells five of the eight fractional interests in the aircraft to H, an unrelated party, and H begins to use its proportionate share of the aircraft immediately upon purchase. On June 1, 2003, G sells to I, an unrelated party to G, the remaining unsold ⅜ fractional interests in the aircraft. H is considered the original user as to its ⅝ fractional interest in the aircraft and I is considered the original user as to its ⅜ fractional interest in the aircraft. Thus, assuming all other requirements are met, H's purchase price for its ⅝ fractional interest in the aircraft qualifies for the 30-percent additional first year depreciation deduction and I's purchase price for its ⅜ fractional interest in the aircraft qualifies for the 50-percent additional first year depreciation deduction.

Example (5). On September 1, 2001, JJ, an equipment dealer, buys new tractors that are held by JJ primarily for sale to customers in the ordinary course of its business. On October 15, 2001, JJ withdraws the tractors from inventory and begins to use the tractors primarily for producing rental income. The holding of the tractors by JJ as inventory does not constitute a ''use'' for purposes of the original use requirement and, therefore, the original use of the tractors commences with JJ on October 15, 2001, for purposes of paragraph (b)(3) of this section. However, the tractors are not eligible for the additional first year depreciation deduction because JJ acquired the tractors before September 11, 2001.

(4) Acquisition of property. (i) In general. (A) Qualified property. For purposes of the 30-percent additional first year depreciation deduction, depreciable property will meet the requirements of this paragraph (b)(4) if the property is—

(1) Acquired by the taxpayer after September 10, 2001, and before January 1, 2005, but only if no written binding contract for the acquisition of the property was in effect before September 11, 2001; or

(2) Acquired by the taxpayer pursuant to a written binding contract that was entered into after September 10, 2001, and before January 1, 2005.

(B) 50-percent bonus depreciation property. For purposes of the 50-percent additional first year depreciation deduction, depreciable property will meet the requirements of this paragraph (b)(4) if the property is—

(1) Acquired by the taxpayer after May 5, 2003, and before January 1, 2005, but only if no written binding contract for the acquisition of the property was in effect before May 6, 2003; or

(2) Acquired by the taxpayer pursuant to a written binding contract that was entered into after May 5, 2003, and before January 1, 2005.

(ii) Definition of binding contract. (A) In general. A contract is binding only if it is enforceable under State law against the taxpayer or a predecessor, and does not limit damages to a specified amount (for example, by use of a liquidated damages provision). For this purpose, a contractual provision that limits damages to an amount equal to at least 5 percent of the total contract price will not be treated as limiting damages to a specified amount. In determining whether a contract limits damages, the fact that there may be little or no damages because the contract price does not significantly differ from fair market value will not be taken into account. For example, if a taxpayer entered into an irrevocable written contract to purchase an asset for $100 and the contract contained no provision for liquidated damages, the contract is considered binding notwithstanding the fact that the asset had a fair market value of $99 and under local law the seller would only recover the difference in the event the purchaser failed to perform. If the contract provided for a full refund of the purchase price in lieu of any damages allowable by law in the event of breach or cancellation, the contract is not considered binding.

(B) Conditions. A contract is binding even if subject to a condition, as long as the condition is not within the control of either party or a predecessor. A contract will continue to be binding if the parties make insubstantial changes in its terms and conditions or because any term is to be determined by a standard beyond the control of either party. A contract that imposes significant obligations on the taxpayer or a predecessor will be treated as binding notwithstanding the fact that certain terms remain to be negotiated by the parties to the contract.

(C) Options. An option to either acquire or sell property is not a binding contract.

(D) Supply agreements. A binding contract does not include a supply or similar agreement if the amount and design specifications of the property to be purchased have not been specified. The contract will not be a binding contract for the property to be purchased until both the amount and the design specifications are specified. For example, if the provisions of a supply or similar agreement state the design specifications of the property to be purchased, a purchase order under the agreement for a specific number of assets is treated as a binding contract.

(E) Components. A binding contract to acquire one or more components of a larger property will not be treated as a binding contract to acquire the larger property. If a binding contract to acquire the component does not satisfy the requirements of this paragraph (b)(4), the component does not qualify for the 30-percent or 50-percent additional first year depreciation deduction, as applicable.

(iii) Self-constructed property. (A) In general. If a taxpayer manufactures, constructs, or produces property for use by the taxpayer in its trade or business (or for its production of income), the acquisition rules in paragraph (b)(4)(i) of this section are treated as met for qualified property if the taxpayer begins manufacturing, constructing, or producing the property after September 10, 2001, and before January 1, 2005, and for 50-percent bonus depreciation property if the taxpayer begins manufacturing, constructing, or producing the property after May 5, 2003, and before January 1, 2005. Property that is manufactured, constructed, or produced for the taxpayer by another person under a written binding contract (as defined in paragraph (b)(4)(ii) of this section) that is entered into prior to the manufacture, construction, or production of the property for use by the taxpayer in its trade or business (or for its production of income) is considered to be manufactured, constructed, or produced by the taxpayer. If a taxpayer enters into a written binding contract (as defined in paragraph (b)(4)(ii) of this section) after September 10, 2001, and before January 1, 2005, with another person to manufacture, construct, or produce property described in section 168(k)(2)(B) (longer production period property) or section 168(k)(2)(C) (certain aircraft) and the manufacture, construction, or production of this property begins after December 31, 2004, the acquisition rule in paragraph (b)(4)(i)(A)(2) or (b)(4)(i)(B)(2) of this section is met.

(B) When does manufacture, construction, or production begin. (1) In general. For purposes of paragraph (b)(4)(iii) of this section, manufacture, construction, or production of property begins when physical work of a significant nature begins. Physical work does not include preliminary activities such as planning or designing, securing financing, exploring, or researching. The determination of when physical work of a significant nature begins depends on the facts and circumstances. For example, if a retail motor fuels outlet or other facility is to be constructed on-site, construction begins when physical work of a significant nature commences at the site; that is, when work begins on the excavation for footings, pouring the pads for the outlet, or the driving of foundation pilings into the ground. Preliminary work, such as clearing a site, test drilling to determine soil condition, or excavation to change the contour of the land (as distinguished from excavation for footings) does not constitute the beginning of construction. However, if a retail motor fuels outlet or other facility is to be assembled on-site from modular units manufactured off-site and delivered to the site where the outlet will be used, manufacturing begins when physical work of a significant nature commences at the off-site location.

(2) Safe harbor. For purposes of paragraph (b)(4)(iii)(B)(1) of this section, a taxpayer may choose to determine when physical work of a significant nature begins in accordance with this paragraph (b)(4)(iii)(B)(2). Physical work of a significant nature will not be considered to begin before the taxpayer incurs (in the case of an accrual basis taxpayer) or pays (in the case of a cash basis taxpayer) more than 10 percent of the total cost of the property (excluding the cost of any land and preliminary activities such as planning or designing, securing financing, exploring, or researching). When property is manufactured, constructed, or produced for the taxpayer by another person, this safe harbor test must be satisfied by the taxpayer. For example, if a retail motor fuels outlet or other facility is to be constructed for an accrual basis taxpayer by another person for the total cost of $200,000 (excluding the cost of any land and preliminary activities such as planning or designing, securing financing, exploring, or researching), construction is deemed to begin for purposes of this paragraph (b)(4)(iii)(B)(2) when the taxpayer has incurred more than 10 percent (more than $20,000) of the total cost of the property. A taxpayer chooses to apply this paragraph (b)(4)(iii)(B)(2) by filing an income tax return for the placed-in-service year of the property that determines when physical work of a significant nature begins consistent with this paragraph (b)(4)(iii)(B)(2).

(C) Components of self-constructed property. (1) Acquired components. If a binding contract (as defined in paragraph (b)(4)(ii) of this section) to acquire a component does not satisfy the requirements of paragraph (b)(4)(i) of this section, the component does not qualify for the 30-percent or 50-percent additional first year depreciation deduction, as applicable. A binding contract (as defined in paragraph (b)(4)(ii) of this section) to acquire one or more components of a larger self-constructed property will not preclude the larger self-constructed property from satisfying the acquisition rules in paragraph (b)(4)(iii)(A) of this section. Accordingly, the unadjusted depreciable basis of the larger self-constructed property that is eligible for the 30-percent or 50-percent additional first year depreciation deduction, as applicable (assuming all other requirements are met), must not include the unadjusted depreciable basis of any component that does not satisfy the requirements of paragraph (b)(4)(i) of this section. If the manufacture, construction, or production of the larger self-constructed property begins before September 11, 2001, for qualified property, or before May 6, 2003, for 50-percent bonus depreciation property, the larger self-constructed property and any acquired components related to the larger self-constructed property do not qualify for the 30-percent or 50-percent additional first year depreciation deduction, as applicable. If a binding contract to acquire the component is entered into after September 10, 2001, for qualified property, or after May 5, 2003, for 50-percent bonus depreciation property, and before January 1, 2005, but the manufacture, construction, or production of the larger self-constructed property does not begin before January 1, 2005, the component qualifies for the additional first year depreciation deduction (assuming all other requirements are met) but the larger self-constructed property does not.

(2) Self-constructed components. If the manufacture, construction, or production of a component does not satisfy the requirements of paragraph (b)(4)(iii)(A) of this section, the component does not qualify for the 30-percent or 50-percent additional first year depreciation deduction, as applicable. However, if the manufacture, construction, or production of a component does not satisfy the requirements of paragraph (b)(4)(iii)(A) of this section, but the manufacture, construction, or production of the larger self-constructed property satisfies the requirements of paragraph (b)(4)(iii)(A) of this section, the larger self-constructed property qualifies for the 30-percent or 50-percent additional first year depreciation deduction, as applicable (assuming all other requirements are met) even though the component does not qualify for the 30-percent or 50-percent additional first year depreciation deduction. Accordingly, the unadjusted depreciable basis of the larger self-constructed property that is eligible for the 30-percent or 50-percent additional first year depreciation deduction, as applicable (assuming all other requirements are met), must not include the unadjusted depreciable basis of any component that does not qualify for the 30-percent or 50-percent additional first year depreciation deduction. If the manufacture, construction, or production of the larger self-constructed property began before September 11, 2001, for qualified property, or before May 6, 2003, for 50-percent bonus depreciation property, the larger self-constructed property and any self-constructed components related to the larger self-constructed property do not qualify for the 30-percent or 50-percent additional first year depreciation deduction, as applicable. If the manufacture, construction, or production of a component begins after September 10, 2001, for qualified property, or after May 5, 2003, for 50-percent bonus depreciation property, and before January 1, 2005, but the manufacture, construction, or production of the larger self-constructed property does not begin before January 1, 2005, the component qualifies for the additional first year depreciation deduction (assuming all other requirements are met) but the larger self-constructed property does not.

(iv) Disqualified transactions. (A) In general. Property does not satisfy the requirements of this paragraph (b)(4) if the user of the property as of the date on which the property was originally placed in service (including by operation of paragraphs (b)(5)(ii), (iii), and (iv) of this section), or a related party to the user or to the taxpayer, acquired, or had a written binding contract (as defined in paragraph (b)(4)(ii) of this section) in effect for the acquisition of the property at any time before September 11, 2001 (for qualified property), or before May 6, 2003 (for 50-percent bonus depreciation property). In addition, property manufactured, constructed, or produced for the use by the user of the property or by a related party to the user or to the taxpayer does not satisfy the requirements of this paragraph (b)(4) if the manufacture, construction, or production of the property for the user or the related party began at any time before September 11, 2001 (for qualified property), or before May 6, 2003 (for 50-percent bonus depreciation property).

(B) Related party defined. For purposes of this paragraph (b)(4)(iv), persons are related if they have a relationship specified in section 267(b) or 707(b) and the regulations thereunder.

(v) Examples. The application of this paragraph (b)(4) is illustrated by the following examples:

Example (1). On September 1, 2001, J, a corporation, entered into a written agreement with K, a manufacturer, to purchase 20 new lamps for $100 each within the next two years. Although the agreement specifies the number of lamps to be purchased, the agreement does not specify the design of the lamps to be purchased. Accordingly, the agreement is not a binding contract pursuant to paragraph (b)(4)(ii)(D) of this section.

Example (2). Same facts as Example 1. On December 1, 2001, J placed a purchase order with K to purchase 20 new model XPC5 lamps for $100 each for a total amount of $2,000. Because the agreement specifies the number of lamps to be purchased and the purchase order specifies the design of the lamps to be purchased, the purchase order placed by J with K on December 1, 2001, is a binding contract pursuant to paragraph (b)(4)(ii)(D) of this section. Accordingly, the cost of the 20 lamps qualifies for the 30-percent additional first year depreciation deduction.

Example (3). Same facts as Example 1 except that the written agreement between J and K is to purchase 100 model XPC5 lamps for $100 each within the next two years. Because this agreement specifies the amount and design of the lamps to be purchased, the agreement is a binding contract pursuant to paragraph (b)(4)(ii)(D) of this section. Accordingly, because the agreement was entered into before September 11, 2001, any lamp acquired by J under this contract does not qualify for the additional first year depreciation deduction.

Example (4). On September 1, 2001, L began constructing an electric generation power plant for its own use. On November 1, 2002, L ceases construction of the power plant prior to its completion. Between September 1, 2001, and November 1, 2002, L incurred $3,000,000 for the construction of the power plant. On May 6, 2003, L resumed construction of the power plant and completed its construction on August 31, 2003. Between May 6, 2003, and August 31, 2003, L incurred another $1,600,000 to complete the construction of the power plant and, on September 1, 2003, L placed the power plant in service. None of L's total expenditures of $4,600,000 qualify for the additional first year depreciation deduction because, pursuant to paragraph (b)(4)(iii)(A) of this section, L began constructing the power plant before September 11, 2001.

Example (5). Same facts as Example 4 except that L began constructing the electric generation power plant for its own use on October 1, 2001. L's total expenditures of $4,600,000 qualify for the additional first year depreciation deduction because, pursuant to paragraph (b)(4)(iii)(A) of this section, L began constructing the power plant after September 10, 2001, and placed the power plant in service before January 1, 2005. Accordingly, the additional first year depreciation deduction for the power plant will be $1,380,000, computed as $4,600,000 multiplied by 30 percent.

Example (6). On August 1, 2001, M entered into a written binding contract to acquire a new turbine. The new turbine is a component part of a new electric generation power plant that is being constructed on M's behalf. The construction of the new electric generation power plant commenced in November 2001, and the new electric generation power plant was completed in November 2002. Because M entered into a written binding contract to acquire a component part (the new turbine) prior to September 11, 2001, pursuant to paragraph (b)(4)(iii)(C) of this section, the component part does not qualify for the additional first year depreciation deduction. However, pursuant to paragraphs (b)(4)(iii)(A) and (C) of this section, the new plant constructed for M will qualify for the 30-percent additional first year depreciation deduction because construction of the new plant began after September 10, 2001, and before May 6, 2003. Accordingly, the unadjusted depreciable basis of the new plant that is eligible for the 30-percent additional first year depreciation deduction must not include the unadjusted depreciable basis of the new turbine.

Example (7). Same facts as Example 6 except that M entered into the written binding contract to acquire the new turbine on September 30, 2002, and construction of the new plant commenced on August 1, 2001. Because M began construction of the new plant prior to September 11, 2001, pursuant to paragraphs (b)(4)(iii)(A) and (C) of this section, neither the new plant constructed for M nor the turbine will qualify for the additional first year depreciation deduction because self-construction of the new plant began prior to September 11, 2001.

Example (8). On September 1, 2001, N began constructing property for its own use. On October 1, 2001, N sold its rights to the property to O, a related party under section 267(b). Pursuant to paragraph (b)(4)(iv) of this section, the property is not eligible for the additional first year depreciation deduction because N and O are related parties and construction of the property by N began prior to September 11, 2001.

Example (9). On September 1, 2001, P entered into a written binding contract to acquire property. On October 1, 2001, P sold its rights to the property to Q, a related party under section 267(b). Pursuant to paragraph (b)(4)(iv) of this section, the property is not eligible for the additional first year depreciation deduction because P and Q are related parties and a written binding contract for the acquisition of the property was in effect prior to September 11, 2001.

Example (10). Prior to September 11, 2001, R began constructing an electric generation power plant for its own use. On May 1, 2003, prior to the completion of the power plant, R transferred the rights to own and use this power plant to S, an unrelated party, for $6,000,000. Between May 6, 2003, and June 30, 2003, S, a calendar-year taxpayer, began construction, and incurred another $1,200,000 to complete the construction, of the power plant and, on August 1, 2003, S placed the power plant in service. Because R and S are not related parties, the transaction between R and S will not be a disqualified transaction pursuant to paragraph (b)(4)(iv) of this section. Accordingly, S's total expenditures of $7,200,000 for the power plant qualify for the additional first year depreciation deduction. S's additional first year depreciation deduction for the power plant will be $2,400,000, computed as $6,000,000 multiplied by 30 percent, plus $1,200,000 multiplied by 50 percent. The $6,000,000 portion of the total $7,200,000 unadjusted depreciable basis qualifies for the 30-percent additional first year depreciation deduction because that portion of the total unadjusted depreciable basis was acquired by S after September 10, 2001, and before May 6, 2003. However, because S began construction to complete the power plant after May 5, 2003, the $1,200,000 portion of the total $7,200,000 unadjusted depreciable basis qualifies for the 50-percent additional first year depreciation deduction.

Example (11). On September 1, 2001, T acquired and placed in service equipment. On October 15, 2001, T sells the equipment to U, an unrelated party, and leases the property back from U in a sale-leaseback transaction. Pursuant to paragraph (b)(4)(iv) of this section, the equipment does not qualify for the additional first year depreciation deduction because T, the user of the equipment, acquired the equipment prior to September 11, 2001. In addition, the sale-leaseback rules in paragraphs (b)(3)(iii)(A) and (b)(5)(ii)(A) of this section do not apply because the equipment was originally placed in service by T before September 11, 2001.

Example (12). On July 1, 2001, KK began constructing property for its own use. KK placed this property in service on September 15, 2001. On October 15, 2001, KK sells the property to LL, an unrelated party, and leases the property back from LL in a sale-leaseback transaction. Pursuant to paragraph (b)(4)(iv) of this section, the property does not qualify for the additional first year depreciation deduction because the property was constructed for KK, the user of the property, and that construction began prior to September 11, 2001.

Example (13). On June 1, 2004, MM decided to construct property described in section 168(k)(2)(B) for its own use. However, one of the component parts of the property had to be manufactured by another person for MM. On August 15, 2004, MM entered into a written binding contract with NN to acquire this component part of the property for $100,000. The manufacture of the component part commenced on September 1, 2004, and MM received the completed component part on February 1, 2005. The cost of this component part is 9 percent of the total cost of the property to be constructed by MM. MM began constructing the property described in section 168(k)(2)(B) on January 15, 2005, and placed this property (including all component parts) in service on November 1, 2005. Pursuant to paragraph (b)(4)(iii)(C)(2) of this section, the self-constructed component part of $100,000 manufactured by NN for MM is eligible for the additional first year depreciation deduction (assuming all other requirements are met) because the manufacturing of the component part began after September 10, 2001, and before January 1, 2005, and the property described in section 168(k)(2)(B), the larger self-constructed property, was placed in service by MM before January 1, 2006. However, pursuant to paragraph (b)(4)(iii)(A) of this section, the cost of the property described in section 168(k)(2)(B) (excluding the cost of the self-constructed component part of $100,000 manufactured by NN for MM) is not eligible for the additional first year depreciation deduction because construction of the property began after December 31, 2004.

Example (14). On December 1, 2004, OO entered into a written binding contract (as defined in paragraph (b)(4)(ii) of this section) with PP to manufacture an aircraft described in section 168(k)(2)(C) for use in OO's trade or business. PP begins to manufacture the aircraft on February 1, 2005. OO places the aircraft in service on August 1, 2005. Pursuant to paragraph (b)(4)(iii)(A) of this section, the aircraft meets the requirements of paragraph (b)(4)(i)(B)(2) of this section because the aircraft was acquired by OO pursuant to a written binding contract entered into after May 5, 2003, and before January 1, 2005.

(5) Placed-in-service date. (i) In general. Depreciable property will meet the requirements of this paragraph (b)(5) if the property is placed in service by the taxpayer for use in its trade or business or for production of income before January 1, 2005, or, in the case of property described in section 168(k)(2)(B) or (C), is placed in service by the taxpayer for use in its trade or business or for production of income before January 1, 2006 (or placed in service by the taxpayer for use in its trade or business or for production of income before January 1, 2007, in the case of property described in section 168(k)(2)(B) or (C) to which section 105 of the Gulf Opportunity Zone Act of 2005 (Pub. L. 109-135, 119 Stat. 2577) applies (for further guidance, see Announcement 2006-29 (2006-19 I.R.B. 879) and § 601.601(d)(2)(ii)(b) of this chapter)).

(ii) Sale-leaseback, syndication, and certain other transactions. (A) Sale-leaseback transaction. If qualified property is originally placed in service after September 10, 2001, or 50-percent bonus depreciation property is originally placed in service after May 5, 2003, by a person and sold to a taxpayer and leased back to the person by the taxpayer within three months after the date the property was originally placed in service by the person, the property is treated as originally placed in service by the taxpayer-lessor not earlier than the date on which the property is used by the lessee under the leaseback.

(B) Syndication transaction and certain other transactions. If qualified property is originally placed in service after September 10, 2001, or 50-percent bonus depreciation property is originally placed in service after May 5, 2003, by a lessor (including by operation of paragraph (b)(5)(ii)(A) of this section) and is sold by the lessor or any subsequent purchaser within three months after the date the property was originally placed in service by the lessor (or, in the case of multiple units of property subject to the same lease, within three months after the date the final unit is placed in service, so long as the period between the time the first unit is placed in service and the time the last unit is placed in service does not exceed 12 months), and the user of the property after the last sale during this three-month period remains the same as when the property was originally placed in service by the lessor, the property is treated as originally placed in service by the purchaser of the property in the last sale during the three-month period but not earlier than the date of the last sale.

(C) Sale-leaseback transaction followed by a syndication transaction and certain other transactions. If a sale-leaseback transaction that satisfies the requirements in paragraph (b)(5)(ii)(A) of this section is followed by a transaction that satisfies the requirements in paragraph (b)(5)(ii)(B) of this section, the placed-in-service date of the property is determined in accordance with paragraph (b)(5)(ii)(B) of this section.

(iii) Technical termination of a partnership. For purposes of this paragraph (b)(5), in the case of a technical termination of a partnership under section 708(b)(1)(B), qualified property or 50-percent bonus depreciation property placed in service by the terminated partnership during the taxable year of termination is treated as originally placed in service by the new partnership on the date the qualified property or the 50-percent bonus depreciation property is contributed by the terminated partnership to the new partnership.

(iv) Section 168(i)(7) transactions. For purposes of this paragraph (b)(5), if qualified property or 50-percent bonus depreciation property is transferred in a transaction described in section 168(i)(7) in the same taxable year that the qualified property or the 50-percent bonus depreciation property is placed in service by the transferor, the transferred property is treated as originally placed in service on the date the transferor placed in service the qualified property or the 50-percent bonus depreciation property, as applicable. In the case of multiple transfers of qualified property or 50-percent bonus depreciation property in multiple transactions described in section 168(i)(7) in the same taxable year, the placed in service date of the transferred property is deemed to be the date on which the first transferor placed in service the qualified property or the 50-percent bonus depreciation property, as applicable.

(v) Example. The application of this paragraph (b)(5) is illustrated by the following example:

Example. On September 15, 2004, QQ acquired and placed in service new equipment. This equipment is not described in section 168(k)(2)(B) or (C). On December 1, 2004, QQ sells the equipment to RR and leases the equipment back from RR in a sale-leaseback transaction. On February 15, 2005, RR sells the equipment to TT subject to the lease with QQ. As of February 15, 2005, QQ is still the user of the equipment. The sale-leaseback transaction of December 1, 2004, between QQ and RR satisfies the requirements of paragraph (b)(5)(ii)(A) of this section. The sale transaction of February 15, 2005, between RR and TT satisfies the requirements of paragraph (b)(5)(ii)(B) of this section. Consequently, pursuant to paragraph (b)(5)(ii)(C) of this section, the equipment is treated as originally placed in service by TT on February 15, 2005. Further, pursuant to paragraph (b)(3)(iii)(C) of this section, TT is considered the original user of the equipment. Accordingly, the equipment is not eligible for the additional first year depreciation deduction.

(c) Qualified leasehold improvement property. *(1) In general.* For purposes of section 168(k), qualified leasehold improvement property means any improvement, which is section 1250 property, to an interior portion of a building that is nonresidential real property if—

(i) The improvement is made under or pursuant to a lease by the lessee (or any sublessee) of the interior portion, or by the lessor of that interior portion;

(ii) The interior portion of the building is to be occupied exclusively by the lessee (or any sublessee) of that interior portion; and

(iii) The improvement is placed in service more than 3 years after the date the building was first placed in service by any person.

(2) Certain improvements not included. Qualified leasehold improvement property does not include any improvement for which the expenditure is attributable to:

(i) The enlargement of the building;

(ii) Any elevator or escalator;

(iii) Any structural component benefiting a common area; or

(iv) The internal structural framework of the building.

(3) Definitions. For purposes of this paragraph (c), the following definitions apply:

(i) Building has the same meaning as that term is defined in § 1.48-1(e)(1).

(ii) Common area means any portion of a building that is equally available to all users of the building on the same basis for uses that are incidental to the primary use of the building. For example, stairways, hallways, lobbies, common seating areas, interior and exterior pedestrian walkways and pedestrian bridges, loading docks and areas, and rest rooms generally are treated as common areas if they are used by different lessees of a building.

(iii) Elevator and escalator have the same meanings as those terms are defined in § 1.48-1(m)(2).

(iv) Enlargement has the same meaning as that term is defined in § 1.48-12(c)(10).

(v) Internal structural framework has the same meaning as that term is defined in § 1.48-12(b)(3)(i)(D)(iii).

(vi) Lease has the same meaning as that term is defined in section 168(h)(7). In addition, a commitment to enter into a lease is treated as a lease, and the parties to the commitment are treated as lessor and lessee. However, a lease between related persons is not considered a lease. For purposes of the preceding sentence, related persons are—

(A) Members of an affiliated group (as defined in section 1504 and the regulations thereunder); and

(B) Persons having a relationship described in section 267(b) and the regulations thereunder. For purposes of applying section 267(b), the language "80 percent or more" is used instead of "more than 50 percent."

(vii) Nonresidential real property has the same meaning as that term is defined in section 168(e)(2)(B).

(viii) Structural component has the same meaning as that term is defined in § 1.48-1(e)(2).

(d) Computation of depreciation deduction for qualified property or 50-percent bonus depreciation property. *(1) Additional first year depreciation deduction.* (i) In general. Except as provided in paragraph (f) of this section, the additional first year depreciation deduction is allowable in the first taxable year in which the qualified property or 50-percent bonus depreciation property is placed in service by the taxpayer for use in its trade or business or for the production of income. Except as provided in paragraph (f)(5) of this section, the allowable additional first year depreciation deduction for qualified property is determined by multiplying the unadjusted depreciable basis (as defined in § 1.168(k)-1(a)(2)(iii)) of the qualified property by 30 percent. Except as provided in paragraph (f)(5) of this section, the allowable additional first year depreciation deduction for 50-percent bonus depreciation property is determined by multiplying the unadjusted depreciable basis (as defined in § 1.168(k)-1(a)(2)(iii)) of the 50-percent bonus depreciation property by 50 percent. Except as provided in paragraph (f)(1) of this section, the 30-percent or 50-percent additional first year depreciation deduction is not affected by a taxable year of less than 12 months. See paragraph (f)(1) of this section for qualified property or 50-percent bonus depreciation property placed in service and disposed of in the same taxable year. See paragraph (f)(5) of this section for qualified property or 50-percent bonus depreciation property acquired in a like-kind exchange or as a result of an involuntary conversion.

(ii) Property having a longer production period. For purposes of paragraph (d)(1)(i) of this section, the unadjusted depreciable basis (as defined in § 1.168(k)-T(a)(2)(iii)) of qualified property or 50-percent bonus depreciation property described in section 168(k)(2)(B) is limited to the property's unadjusted depreciable basis attributable to the property's manufacture, construction, or production after September 10, 2001 (for qualified property), or May 5, 2003 (for 50-percent bonus depreciation property), and before January 1, 2005.

(iii) Alternative minimum tax. The 30-percent or 50-percent additional first year depreciation deduction is allowed for alternative minimum tax purposes for the taxable year in which the qualified property or the 50-percent bonus depreciation property is placed in service by the taxpayer. In general, the 30-percent or 50-percent additional first year depreciation deduction for alternative minimum tax purposes is based on the unadjusted depreciable basis of the property for alternative minimum tax purposes. However, see paragraph (f)(5)(iii)(D) of this section for qualified property or 50-percent bonus depreciation property acquired in a like-kind exchange or as a result of an involuntary conversion.

(2) Otherwise allowable depreciation deduction. (i) In general. Before determining the amount otherwise allowable as a depreciation deduction for the qualified property or the 50-percent bonus depreciation property for the placed-in-service year and any subsequent taxable year, the taxpayer must determine the remaining adjusted depreciable basis of the qualified property or the 50-percent bonus depreciation property. This remaining adjusted depreciable basis is equal to the unadjusted depreciable basis of the qualified property or the 50-percent bonus depreciation property reduced by the amount of the additional first year depreciation allowed or allowable, whichever is greater. The remaining adjusted depreciable basis of the qualified property or the 50-percent bonus depreciation property is then depreciated using the applicable depreciation provisions under the Internal Revenue Code for the qualified property or the 50-percent bonus depreciation property. The remaining adjusted depreciable basis of the qualified property or the 50-percent bonus depreciation property that is MACRS property is also the basis to which the annual depreciation rates in the optional depreciation tables apply (for further guidance, see section 8 of Rev. Proc. 87-57 (1987-2 C.B. 687) and § 601.601(d)(2)(ii)(b) of this chapter). The depreciation deduction allowable for the remaining adjusted depreciable basis of the qualified property or the 50-percent bonus depreciation property is affected by a taxable year of less than 12 months.

(ii) Alternative minimum tax. For alternative minimum tax purposes, the depreciation deduction allowable for the remaining adjusted depreciable basis of the qualified property or the 50-percent bonus depreciation property is based on the remaining adjusted depreciable basis for alternative minimum tax purposes. The remaining adjusted depreciable basis of the qualified property or the 50-percent bonus depreciable property for alternative minimum tax purposes is depreciated using the same depreciation method, recovery period (or useful life in the case of computer software), and convention that apply to the qualified property or the 50-percent bonus depreciation property for regular tax purposes.

(3) Examples. This paragraph (d) is illustrated by the following examples:

Example (1). On March 1, 2003, V, a calendar-year taxpayer, purchased and placed in service qualified property that costs $1 million and is 5-year property under section 168(e). V depreciates its 5-year property placed in service in 2003 using the optional depreciation table that corresponds with the general depreciation system, the 200-percent declining balance method, a 5-year recovery period, and the half-year convention. For 2003, V is allowed a 30-percent additional first year depreciation deduction of $300,000 (the unadjusted depreciable basis of $1 million multiplied by .30). Next, V must reduce the unadjusted depreciable basis of $1 million by the additional first year depreciation deduction of $300,000 to determine the remaining adjusted depreciable basis of $700,000. Then, V's depreciation deduction allowable in 2003 for the remaining adjusted depreciable basis of $700,000 is $140,000 (the remaining adjusted depreciable basis of $700,000 multiplied by the annual depreciation rate of .20 for recovery year 1).

Example (2). On June 1, 2003, W, a calendar-year taxpayer, purchased and placed in service 50-percent bonus depreciation property that costs $126,000. The property qualifies for the expensing election under section 179 and is 5-year property under section 168(e). W did not purchase any other section 179 property in 2003. W makes the election under section 179 for the property and depreciates its 5-year property placed in service in 2003 using the optional depreciation table that corresponds with the general depreciation system, the 200-percent declining balance method, a 5-year recovery period, and the half-year convention. For 2003, W is first allowed a $100,000 deduction under section 179. Next, W must reduce the cost of $126,000 by the section 179 deduction of $100,000 to determine the unadjusted depreciable basis of $26,000. Then, for 2003, W is allowed a 50-percent additional first year depreciation deduction of $13,000 (the unadjusted depreciable basis of $26,000 multiplied by .50). Next, W must reduce the unadjusted depreciable basis of $26,000 by the additional first year depreciation deduction of $13,000 to determine the remaining adjusted depreciable basis of $13,000. Then, W's depreciation deduction allowable in 2003 for the remaining adjusted depreciable basis of $13,000 is $2,600 (the remaining adjusted depreciable basis of $13,000 multiplied by the annual depreciation rate of .20 for recovery year 1).

(e) Election not to deduct additional first year depreciation. *(1) In general.* If a taxpayer makes an election under this paragraph (e), the election applies to all qualified property or 50-percent bonus depreciation property, as applicable, that is in the same class of property and placed in service in the same taxable year. The rules of this paragraph (e) apply to the following elections provided under section 168(k):

(i) Qualified property. A taxpayer may make an election not to deduct the 30-percent additional first year depreciation for any class of property that is qualified property placed in service during the taxable year. If this election is made, no additional first year depreciation deduction is allowable for the property placed in service during the taxable year in the class of property.

(ii) 50-percent bonus depreciation property. For any class of property that is 50-percent bonus depreciation property placed in service during the taxable year, a taxpayer may make an election—

(A) To deduct the 30-percent, instead of the 50-percent, additional first year depreciation. If this election is made, the allowable additional first year depreciation deduction is determined as though the class of property is qualified property under section 168(k)(2); or

(B) Not to deduct both the 30-percent and the 50-percent additional first year depreciation. If this election is made, no additional first year depreciation deduction is allowable for the class of property.

(2) Definition of class of property. For purposes of this paragraph (e), the term class of property means:

(i) Except for the property described in paragraphs (e)(2)(ii) and (iv) of this section, each class of property described in section 168(e) (for example, 5-year property);

(ii) Water utility property as defined in section 168(e)(5) and depreciated under section 168;

(iii) Computer software as defined in, and depreciated under, section 167(f)(1) and the regulations thereunder; or

(iv) Qualified leasehold improvement property as defined in paragraph (c) of this section and depreciated under section 168.

(3) Time and manner for making election. (i) Time for making election. Except as provided in paragraph (e)(4) of this section, any election specified in paragraph (e)(1) of this section must be made by the due date (including extensions) of the Federal tax return for the taxable year in which the qualified property or the 50-percent bonus depreciation property, as applicable, is placed in service by the taxpayer.

(ii) Manner of making election. Except as provided in paragraph (e)(4) of this section, any election specified in paragraph (e)(1) of this section must be made in the manner prescribed on Form 4562, "Depreciation and Amortization," and its instructions. The election is made separately by each person owning qualified property or 50-percent bonus depreciation property (for example, for each member of a consolidated group by the common parent of the group, by the partnership, or by the S corporation). If Form 4562 is revised or renumbered, any reference in this section to that form shall be treated as a reference to the revised or renumbered form.

(4) Special rules for 2000 or 2001 returns. For the election specified in paragraph (e)(1)(i) of this section for qualified property placed in service by the taxpayer during the taxable year that included September 11, 2001, the taxpayer should refer to the guidance provided by the Internal Revenue Service for the time and manner of making this election on the 2000 or 2001 Federal tax return for the taxable year that included September 11, 2001 (for further guidance, see sections 3.03(3) and 4 of Rev. Proc. 2002-33 (2002-1 C.B. 963), Rev. Proc. 2003-50 (2003-29 I.R.B. 119), and § 601.601(d)(2)(ii)(b) of this chapter).

(5) Failure to make election. If a taxpayer does not make the applicable election specified in paragraph (e)(1) of this section within the time and in the manner prescribed in paragraph (e)(3) or (4) of this section, the amount of depreciation allowable for that property under section 167(f)(1) or under section 168, as applicable, must be determined for the placed-in-service year and for all subsequent taxable years by taking into account the additional first year depreciation deduction. Thus, any election specified in paragraph (e)(1) of this section shall not be made by the taxpayer in any other manner (for example, the election cannot be made through a request under section 446(e) to change the taxpayer's method of accounting).

(6) Alternative minimum tax. If a taxpayer makes an election specified in paragraph (e)(1) of this section for a class of property, the depreciation adjustments under section 56 and the regulations under section 56 apply to the property to which that election applies for purposes of computing the taxpayer's alternative minimum taxable income.

(7) Revocation of election. (i) In general. Except as provided in paragraph (e)(7)(ii) of this section, an election specified in paragraph (e)(1) of this section, once made, may be revoked only with the written consent of the Commissioner of Internal Revenue. To seek the Commissioner's consent, the taxpayer must submit a request for a letter ruling.

(ii) Automatic 6-month extension. If a taxpayer made an election specified in paragraph (e)(1) of this section for a class of property, an automatic extension of 6 months from the due date of the taxpayer's Federal tax return (excluding extensions) for the placed-in-service year of the class of property is granted to revoke that election, provided the taxpayer timely filed the taxpayer's Federal tax return for the placed-in-service year of the class of property and, within this 6-month extension period, the taxpayer (and all taxpayers whose tax liability would be affected by the election) files an amended Federal tax return for the placed-in-service year of the class of property in a manner that is consistent with the revocation of the election.

(f) Special rules. *(1) Property placed in service and disposed of in the same taxable year.* (i) In general. Except as provided in paragraphs (f)(1)(ii) and (iii) of this section, the additional first year depreciation deduction is not allowed for qualified property or 50-percent bonus depreciation property placed in service and disposed of during the same taxable year. Also if qualified property or 50-percent bonus depreciation property is placed in service and disposed of during the same taxable year and then reacquired and again placed in service in a subsequent taxable year, the additional first year depreciation deduction is not allowable for the property in the subsequent taxable year.

(ii) Technical termination of a partnership. In the case of a technical termination of a partnership under section 708(b)(1)(B), the additional first year depreciation deduction is allowable for any qualified property or 50-percent bonus depreciation property placed in service by the terminated partnership during the taxable year of termination and contributed by the terminated partnership to the new partnership. The allowable additional first year depreciation deduction for the qualified property or the 50-percent bonus depreciation property shall not be claimed by the terminated partnership but instead shall be claimed by the new partnership for the new partnership's taxable year in which the qualified property or the 50-percent bonus depreciation property was contributed by the terminated partnership to the new partnership. However, if qualified property or 50-percent bonus depreciation property is both placed in service and contributed to a new partnership in a transaction described in section 708(b)(1)(B) by the terminated partnership during the taxable year of termination, and if such property is disposed of by the new partnership in the same taxable year the new partnership received such property from the terminated partnership, then no additional first year depreciation deduction is allowable to either partnership.

(iii) Section 168(i)(7) transactions. If any qualified property or 50-percent bonus depreciation property is transferred in a transaction described in section 168(i)(7) in the same taxable year that the qualified property or the 50-percent bonus depreciation property is placed in service by the transferor, the additional first year depreciation deduction is allowable for the qualified property or the 50-percent bonus depreciation property. The allowable additional first year depreciation deduction for the qualified property or the 50-percent bonus depreciation property for the transferor's taxable year in which the property is placed in service is allocated between the transferor and the transferee on a monthly basis. This allocation shall be made in accordance with the rules in § 1.168(d)-1(b)(7)(ii) for allocating the depreciation deduction between the transferor and the transferee. However, if qualified property or 50-percent bonus depreciation property is both placed in service and transferred in a transaction described in section 168(i)(7) by the transferor during the same taxable year, and if such property is disposed of by the transferee (other than by a transaction described in section 168(i)(7)) during the same taxable year the transferee received such property from the transferor, then no additional first year depreciation deduction is allowable to either party.

(iv) Examples. The application of this paragraph (f)(1) is illustrated by the following examples:

Example (1). X and Y are equal partners in Partnership XY, a general partnership. On February 1, 2002, Partnership XY purchased and placed in service new equipment at a cost of $30,000. On March 1, 2002, X sells its entire 50 percent interest to Z in a transfer that terminates the partnership under section 708(b)(1)(B). As a result, terminated Partnership XY is deemed to have contributed the equipment to new Partnership XY. Pursuant to paragraph (f)(1)(ii) of this section, new Partnership XY, not terminated Partnership XY, is eligible to claim the 30-percent additional first year depreciation deduction allowable for the equipment for the taxable year 2002 (assuming all other requirements are met).

Example (2). On January 5, 2002, BB purchased and placed in service new office desks for a total amount of $8,000. On August 20, 2002, BB transferred the office desks to Partnership BC in a transaction described in section 721. BB and Partnership BC are calendar-year taxpayers. Because the transaction between BB and Partnership BC is a transaction described in section 168(i)(7), pursuant to paragraph (f)(1)(iii) of this section the 30-percent additional first year depreciation deduction allowable for the desks is allocated between BB and Partnership BC in accordance with the rules in § 1.168(d)-1(b)(7)(ii) for allocating the depreciation deduction between the transferor and the transferee. Accordingly, the 30-percent additional first year depreciation deduction allowable for the desks for 2002 of $2,400 (the unadjusted depreciable basis of $8,000 multiplied by .30) is allocated between BB and Partnership BC based on the number of months that BB and Partnership BC held the desks in service. Thus, because the desks were held in service by BB for 7 of 12 months, which includes the month in which BB placed the desks in service but does not include the month in which the desks were transferred, BB is allocated $1,400 (7/12 x $2,400 additional first year depreciation deduction). Partnership BC is allocated $1,000, the remaining 5/12 of the $2,400 additional first year depreciation deduction allowable for the desks.

(2) Redetermination of basis. Redetermination of basis. If the unadjusted depreciable basis (as defined in § 1.168(k)-1(a)(2)(iii)) of qualified property or 50-percent bonus depreciation property is redetermined (for example, due to contingent purchase price or discharge of indebtedness) before January 1, 2005, or, in the case of property described in section 168(k)(2)(B) or (C), is redetermined before January 1, 2006 (or redetermined before January 1, 2007, in the case of property described in section 168(k)(2)(B) or (C) to which section 105 of the Gulf Opportunity Zone Act of 2005 (Pub. L. 109-135, 119 Stat. 2577) applies (for further guidance, see Announcement 2006-29 (2006-19 I.R.B. 879) and § 601.601(d)(2)(ii)(b) of this chapter)), the additional first year depreciation deduction allowable for the qualified property or the 50-percent bonus depreciation property is redetermined as follows:

(i) Increase in basis. For the taxable year in which an increase in basis of qualified property or 50-percent bonus depreciation property occurs, the taxpayer shall claim an additional first year depreciation deduction for qualified property by multiplying the amount of the increase in basis for this property by 30 percent or, for 50-percent bonus depreciation property, by multiplying the amount of the increase in basis for this property by 50 percent. For purposes of this paragraph (f)(2)(i), the 30-percent additional first year depreciation deduction applies to the increase in basis if the underlying property is qualified property and the 50-percent additional first year depreciation deduction applies to the increase in basis if the underlying property is 50-percent bonus depreciation property. To determine the amount otherwise allowable as a depreciation deduction for the increase in basis of qualified property or 50-percent bonus depreciation property, the amount of the increase in basis of the qualified property or the 50-percent bonus depreciation property must be reduced by the additional first year depreciation deduction allowed or allowable, whichever is greater, for the increase in basis and the remaining increase in basis of—

(A) Qualified property or 50-percent bonus depreciation property (except for computer software described in paragraph (b)(2)(i)(B) of this section) is depreciated over the recovery period of the qualified property or the 50-percent bonus depreciation property, as applicable, remaining as of the beginning of the taxable year in which the increase in basis occurs, and using the same depreciation method and convention applicable to the qualified property or 50-percent bonus depreciation property, as applicable, that applies for the taxable year in which the increase in basis occurs; and

(B) Computer software (as defined in paragraph (b)(2)(i)(B) of this section) that is qualified property or 50-percent bonus depreciation property is depreciated ratably over the remainder of the 36-month period (the useful life under section 167(f)(1)) as of the beginning of the first day of the month in which the increase in basis occurs.

(ii) Decrease in basis. For the taxable year in which a decrease in basis of qualified property or 50-percent bonus depreciation property occurs, the taxpayer shall reduce the total amount otherwise allowable as a depreciation deduction for all of the taxpayer's depreciable property by the excess additional first year depreciation deduction previously claimed for the qualified property or the 50-percent bonus depreciation property. If, for such taxable year, the excess additional first year depreciation deduction exceeds the total amount otherwise allowable as a depreciation deduction for all of the taxpayer's depreciable property, the taxpayer shall take into account a negative depreciation deduction in computing taxable income. The excess additional first year depreciation deduction for qualified property is determined by multiplying the amount of the decrease in basis for this property by 30 percent. The excess additional first year depreciation deduction for 50-percent bonus depreciation property is determined by multiplying the amount of the decrease in basis for this property by 50 percent. For purposes of this paragraph (f)(2)(ii), the 30-percent additional first year depreciation deduction applies to the decrease in basis if the underlying property is qualified property and the 50-percent additional first year depreciation deduction applies to the decrease in basis if the underlying property is 50-percent bonus depreciation property. Also, if the taxpayer establishes by adequate records or other sufficient evidence that the taxpayer claimed less than the additional first year depreciation deduction allowable for the qualified property or the 50-percent bonus depreciation property before the decrease in basis or if the taxpayer claimed more than the additional first year depreciation deduction allowable for the qualified property or the 50-percent bonus depreciation property before the decrease in basis, the excess additional first year depreciation deduction is determined by multiplying the amount of the decrease in basis by the additional first year depreciation deduction percentage actually claimed by the taxpayer for the qualified property or the 50-percent bonus depreciation property, as applicable, before the decrease in basis. To determine the amount to reduce the total amount otherwise allowable as a depreciation deduction for all of the taxpayer's depreciable property for the excess depreciation previously claimed (other than the additional first year depreciation deduction) resulting from the decrease in basis of the qualified property or the 50-percent bonus depreciation property, the amount of the decrease in basis of the qualified property or the 50-percent bonus depreciation property must be adjusted by the excess additional first year depreciation deduction that reduced the total amount otherwise allowable as a depreciation deduction (as determined under this paragraph) and the remaining decrease in basis of—

(A) Qualified property or 50-percent bonus depreciation property (except for computer software described in paragraph (b)(2)(i)(B) of this section) reduces the amount otherwise allowable as a depreciation deduction over the recovery period of the qualified property or the 50-percent bonus depreciation property, as applicable, remaining as of the beginning of the taxable year in which the decrease in basis occurs, and using the same depreciation method and convention of the qualified property or 50-percent bonus depreciation property, as applicable, that applies in the taxable year in which the decrease in basis occurs. If, for any taxable year, the reduction to the amount otherwise allowable as a depreciation deduction (as determined under this paragraph (f)(2)(ii)(A)) exceeds the total amount otherwise allowable as a depreciation deduction for all of the taxpayer's depreciable property, the taxpayer shall take into account a negative depreciation deduction in computing taxable income; and

(B) Computer software (as defined in paragraph (b)(2)(i)(B) of this section) that is qualified property or 50-percent bonus depreciation property reduces the amount otherwise allowable as a depreciation deduction over the remainder of the 36-month period (the useful life under section 167(f)(1)) as of the beginning of the first day of the month in which the decrease in basis occurs. If, for any taxable year, the reduction to the amount otherwise allowable as a depreciation deduction (as determined under this paragraph (f)(2)(ii)(B)) exceeds the total amount otherwise allowable as a depreciation deduction for all of the taxpayer's depreciable property, the taxpayer shall take into account a negative depreciation deduction in computing taxable income.

(iii) Definition. Except as otherwise expressly provided by the Internal Revenue Code (for example, section 1017(a)), the regulations under the Internal Revenue Code, or other guidance published in the Internal Revenue Bulletin (see § 601.601(d)(2)(ii)(b) of this chapter), for purposes of this paragraph (f)(2):

(A) An increase in basis occurs in the taxable year an amount is taken into account under section 461; and

(B) A decrease in basis occurs in the taxable year an amount would be taken into account under section 451.

(iv) Examples. The application of this paragraph (f)(2) is illustrated by the following examples:

Example (1). (i) On May 15, 2002, CC, a cash-basis taxpayer, purchased and placed in service qualified property that is 5-year property at a cost of $200,000. In addition to the $200,000, CC agrees to pay the seller 25 percent of the gross profits from the operation of the property in 2002. On May 15, 2003, CC paid to the seller an additional $10,000. CC depreciates the 5-year property placed in service in 2002 using the optional depreciation table that corresponds with the general depreciation system, the 200-percent declining balance method, a 5-year recovery period, and the half-year convention.

(ii) For 2002, CC is allowed a 30-percent additional first year depreciation deduction of $60,000 (the unadjusted depreciable basis of $200,000 multiplied by .30). In addition, CC's depreciation deduction for 2002 for the remaining adjusted depreciable basis of $140,000 (the unadjusted depreciable basis of $200,000 reduced by the additional first year depreciation deduction of $60,000) is $28,000 (the remaining adjusted depreciable basis of $140,000 multiplied by the annual depreciation rate of .20 for recovery year 1).

(iii) For 2003, CC's depreciation deduction for the remaining adjusted depreciable basis of $140,000 is $44,800 (the remaining adjusted depreciable basis of $140,000 multiplied by the annual depreciation rate of .32 for recovery year 2). In addition, pursuant to paragraph (f)(2)(i) of this section, CC is allowed an additional first year depreciation deduction for 2003 for the $10,000 increase in basis of the qualified property. Consequently, CC is allowed an additional first year depreciation deduction of $3,000 (the increase in basis of $10,000 multiplied by .30). Also, CC is allowed a depreciation deduction for 2003 attributable to the remaining increase in basis of $7,000 (the increase in basis of $10,000 reduced by the additional first year depreciation deduction of $3,000). The depreciation deduction allowable for 2003 attributable to the remaining increase in basis of $7,000 is $3,111 (the remaining increase in basis of $7,000 multiplied by .4444, which is equal to 1/remaining recovery period of 4.5 years at January 1, 2003, multiplied by 2). Accordingly, for 2003, CC's total depreciation deduction allowable for the qualified property is $50,911.

Example (2). (i) On May 15, 2002, DD, a calendar-year taxpayer, purchased and placed in service qualified property that is 5-year property at a cost of $400,000. To purchase the property, DD borrowed $250,000 from Bank2. On May 15, 2003, Bank2 forgives $50,000 of the indebtedness. DD makes the election provided in section 108(b)(5) to apply any portion of the reduction under section 1017 to the basis of the depreciable property of the taxpayer. DD depreciates the 5-year property placed in service in 2002 using the optional depreciation table that corresponds with the general depreciation system, the 200-percent declining balance method, a 5-year recovery period, and the half-year convention.

(ii) For 2002, DD is allowed a 30-percent additional first year depreciation deduction of $120,000 (the unadjusted depreciable basis of $400,000 multiplied by .30). In addition, DD's depreciation deduction allowable for 2002 for the remaining adjusted depreciable basis of $280,000 (the unadjusted depreciable basis of $400,000 reduced by the additional first year depreciation deduction of $120,000) is $56,000 (the remaining adjusted depreciable basis of $280,000 multiplied by the annual depreciation rate of .20 for recovery year 1).

(iii) For 2003, DD's deduction for the remaining adjusted depreciable basis of $280,000 is $89,600 (the remaining adjusted depreciable basis of $280,000 multiplied by the annual depreciation rate .32 for recovery year 2). Although Bank2 forgave the indebtedness in 2003, the basis of the property is reduced on January 1, 2004, pursuant to sections 108(b)(5) and 1017(a) under which basis is reduced at the beginning of the taxable year following the taxable year in which the discharge of indebtedness occurs.

(iv) For 2004, DD's deduction for the remaining adjusted depreciable basis of $280,000 is $53,760 (the remaining adjusted depreciable basis of $280,000 multiplied by the annual depreciation rate .192 for recovery year 3). However, pursuant to paragraph (f)(2)(ii) of this section, DD must reduce the amount otherwise allowable as a depreciation deduction for 2004 by the excess depreciation previously claimed for the $50,000 decrease in basis of the qualified property. Consequently, DD must reduce the amount of depreciation otherwise allowable for 2004 by the excess additional first year depreciation of $15,000 (the decrease in basis of $50,000 multiplied by .30). Also, DD must reduce the amount of depreciation otherwise allowable for 2004 by the excess depreciation attributable to the remaining decrease in basis of $35,000 (the decrease in basis of $50,000 reduced by the excess additional first year depreciation of $15,000). The reduction in the amount of depreciation otherwise allowable for 2004 for the remaining decrease in basis of $35,000 is $19,999 (the remaining decrease in basis of $35,000 multiplied by .5714, which is equal to 1/remaining recovery period of 3.5 years at January 1, 2004, multiplied by 2). Accordingly, assuming the qualified property is the only depreciable property owned by DD, for 2004, DD's total depreciation deduction allowable for the qualified property is $18,761 ($53,760 minus $15,000 minus $19,999).

(3) Section 1245 and 1250 depreciation recapture. For purposes of section 1245 and the regulations thereunder, the additional first year depreciation deduction is an amount allowed or allowable for depreciation. Further, for purposes of section 1250(b) and the regulations thereunder, the additional first year depreciation deduction is not a straight line method.

(4) Coordination with section 169. The additional first year depreciation deduction is allowable in the placed-in-service year of a certified pollution control facility (as defined in § 1.169-2(a)) that is qualified property or 50-percent bonus depreciation property, even if the taxpayer makes the election to amortize the certified pollution control facility under section 169 and the regulations thereunder in the certified pollution control facility's placed-in-service year.

(5) Like-kind exchanges and involuntary conversions. (i) Scope. The rules of this paragraph (f)(5) apply to acquired MACRS property or acquired computer software that is qualified property or 50-percent bonus depreciation property at the time of replacement provided the time of replacement is after September 10, 2001, and before January 1, 2005, or, in the case of acquired MACRS property or acquired computer software that is qualified property, or 50-percent bonus depreciation property, described in section 168(k)(2)(B) or (C), the time of replacement is after September 10, 2001, and before January 1, 2006 (or the time of replacement is after September 10, 2001, and before January 1, 2007, in the case of property described in section 168(k)(2)(B) or (C) to which section 105 of the Gulf Opportunity Zone Act of 2005 (Pub. L. 109-135, 119 Stat. 2577) applies (for further guidance, see Announcement 2006-29 (2006-19 I.R.B. 879) and § 601.601(d)(2)(ii)(b) of this chapter)).

(ii) Definitions. For purposes of this paragraph (f)(5), the following definitions apply:

(A) Acquired MACRS property is MACRS property in the hands of the acquiring taxpayer that is acquired in a transaction described in section 1031(a), (b), or (c) for other MACRS property or that is acquired in connection with an involuntary conversion of other MACRS property in a transaction to which section 1033 applies.

(B) Exchanged or involuntarily converted MACRS property is MACRS property that is transferred by the taxpayer in a transaction described in section 1031(a), (b), or (c), or that is converted as a result of an involuntary conversion to which section 1033 applies.

(C) Acquired computer software is computer software (as defined in paragraph (b)(2)(i)(B) of this section) in the hands of the acquiring taxpayer that is acquired in a like-kind exchange under section 1031 or as a result of an involuntary conversion under section 1033.

(D) Exchanged or involuntarily converted computer software is computer software (as defined in paragraph (b)(2)(i)(B) of this section) that is transferred by the taxpayer in a like-kind exchange under section 1031 or that is converted as a result of an involuntary conversion under section 1033.

(E) Time of disposition is when the disposition of the exchanged or involuntarily converted MACRS property or the exchanged or involuntarily converted computer software, as applicable, takes place.

(F) Except as provided in paragraph (f)(5)(v) of this section, the time of replacement is the later of—

(1) When the acquired MACRS property or acquired computer software is placed in service; or

(2) The time of disposition of the exchanged or involuntarily converted property.

(G) Carryover basis is the lesser of:

(1) The basis in the acquired MACRS property or acquired computer software, as applicable and as determined under section 1031(d) or 1033(b) and the regulations thereunder; or

(2) The adjusted depreciable basis of the exchanged or involuntarily converted MACRS property or the exchanged or involuntarily converted computer software, as applicable.

(H) Excess basis is any excess of the basis in the acquired MACRS property or acquired computer software, as applicable and as determined under section 1031(d) or 1033(b) and the regulations thereunder, over the carryover basis as determined under paragraph (f)(5)(ii)(G) of this section.

(I) Remaining carryover basis is the carryover basis as determined under paragraph (f)(5)(ii)(G) of this section reduced by—

(1) The percentage of the taxpayer's use of property for the taxable year other than in the taxpayer's trade or business (or for the production of income); and

(2) Any adjustments to basis provided by other provisions of the Code and the regulations thereunder (including section 1016(a)(2) and (3)) for periods prior to the disposition of the exchanged or involuntarily converted property.

(J) Remaining excess basis is the excess basis as determined under paragraph (f)(5)(ii)(H) of this section reduced by—

(1) The percentage of the taxpayer's use of property for the taxable year other than in the taxpayer's trade or business (or for the production of income);

(2) Any portion of the basis the taxpayer properly elects to treat as an expense under section 179 or section 179C;

(3) Any adjustments to basis provided by other provisions of the Code and the regulations thereunder.

(K) Year of disposition is the taxable year that includes the time of disposition.

(L) Year of replacement is the taxable year that includes the time of replacement.

(iii) Computation. (A) In general. Assuming all other requirements of section 168(k) and this section are met, the remaining carryover basis for the year of replacement and the remaining excess basis, if any, for the year of replacement for the acquired MACRS property or the acquired computer software, as applicable, are eligible for the additional first year depreciation deduction. The 30-percent additional first year depreciation deduction applies to the remaining carryover basis and the remaining excess basis, if any, of the acquired MACRS property or the acquired computer software if the time of replacement is after September 10, 2001, and before May 6, 2003, or if the taxpayer made the election provided in paragraph (e)(1)(ii)(A) of this section. The 50-percent additional first year depreciation deduction applies to the remaining carryover basis and the remaining excess basis, if any, of the acquired MACRS property or the acquired computer software if the time of replacement is after May 5, 2003, and before January 1, 2005, or, in the case of acquired MACRS property or acquired computer software that is 50-percent bonus depreciation property described in section 168(k)(2)(B) or (C), the time of replacement is after May 5, 2003, and before January 1, 2006 (or the time of replacement is after May 5, 2003, and before January 1, 2007, in the case of 50-percent bonus depreciation property described in section 168(k)(2)(B) or (C) to which section 105 of the Gulf Opportunity Zone Act of 2005 (Pub. L. 109-135, 119 Stat. 2577) applies (for further guidance, see Announcement 2006-29 (2006-19 I.R.B. 879) and § 601.601(d)(2)(ii)(b) of this chapter)). The additional first year depreciation deduction is computed separately for the remaining carryover basis and the remaining excess basis.

(B) Year of disposition and year of replacement. The additional first year depreciation deduction is allowable for the acquired MACRS property or acquired computer software in the year of replacement. However, the additional first year depreciation deduction is not allowable for the exchanged or involuntarily converted MACRS property or the exchanged or involuntarily converted computer software if the exchanged or involuntarily converted MACRS property or the exchanged or involuntarily converted computer software, as applicable, is placed in service and disposed of in an exchange or involuntary conversion in the same taxable year.

(C) Property having a longer production period. For purposes of paragraph (f)(5)(iii)(A) of this section, the total of the remaining carryover basis and the remaining excess basis, if any, of the acquired MACRS property that is qualified property or 50-percent bonus depreciation property described in section 168(k)(2)(B) is limited to the total of the property's remaining carryover basis and remaining excess basis, if any, attributable to the property's manufacture, construction, or production after September 10, 2001 (for qualified property), or May 5, 2003 (for 50-percent bonus depreciation property), and before January 1, 2005.

(D) Alternative minimum tax. The 30-percent or 50-percent additional first year depreciation deduction is allowed for alternative minimum tax purposes for the year of replacement of acquired MACRS property or acquired computer software that is qualified property or 50-percent bonus depreciation property. The 30-percent or 50-percent additional first year depreciation deduction for alternative minimum tax purposes is based on the remaining carryover basis and the remaining excess basis, if any, of the acquired MACRS property or the acquired computer software for alternative minimum tax purposes.

(iv) Sale-leaseback transaction. For purposes of this paragraph (f)(5), if MACRS property or computer software is sold to a taxpayer and leased back to a person by the taxpayer within three months after the time of disposition of the MACRS property or computer software, as applicable, the time of replacement for this MACRS property or computer software, as applicable, shall not be earlier than the date on which the MACRS property or computer software, as applicable, is used by the lessee under the leaseback.

(v) Acquired MACRS property or acquired computer software that is acquired and placed in service before disposition of involuntarily converted MACRS property or involuntarily converted computer software. If, in an involuntary conversion, a taxpayer acquires and places in service the acquired MACRS property or the acquired computer software before the time of disposition of the involuntarily converted MACRS property or the involuntarily converted computer software and the time of disposition of the involuntarily converted MACRS property or the involuntarily converted computer software is after December 31, 2004, or, in the case of property described in section 168(k)(2)(B) or (C), after December 31, 2005 (or after December 31, 2006, in the case of property described in section 168(k)(2)(B) or (C) to which section 105 of the Gulf Opportunity Zone Act of 2005 (Pub. L. 109-135, 119 Stat. 2577) applies (for further guidance, see Announcement 2006-29 (2006-19 I.R.B. 879) and § 601.601(d)(2)(ii)(b) of this chapter)), then—

(A) Time of replacement. The time of replacement for purposes of this paragraph (f)(5) is when the acquired MACRS property or acquired computer software is placed in service by the taxpayer, provided the threat or imminence of requisition or condemnation of the involuntarily converted MACRS property or involuntarily converted computer software existed before January 1, 2005, or, in the case of property described in section 168(k)(2)(B) or (C), existed before January 1, 2006 (or existed before January 1, 2007, in the case of property described in section 168(k)(2)(B) or (C) to which section 105 of the Gulf Opportunity Zone Act of 2005 (Pub. L. 109-135, 119 Stat. 2577) applies (for further guidance, see Announcement 2006-29 (2006-19 I.R.B. 879) and § 601.601(d)(2)(ii)(b) of this chapter)); and

(B) Depreciation of acquired MACRS property or acquired computer software. The taxpayer depreciates the acquired MACRS property or acquired computer software in accordance with paragraph (d) of this section. However, at the time of disposition of the involuntarily converted MACRS property, the taxpayer determines the exchanged basis (as defined in § 1.168(i)-6(b)(7)) and the excess basis (as defined in § 1.168(i)-6(b)(8)) of the acquired MACRS property and begins to depreciate the depreciable exchanged basis (as defined in § 1.168(i)-6(b)(9) of the acquired MACRS property in accordance with § 1.168(i)-6(c). The depreciable excess basis (as defined in § 1.168(i)-6(b)(10)) of the acquired MACRS property continues to be depreciated by the taxpayer in accordance with the first sentence of this paragraph (f)(5)(v)(B). Further, in the year of disposition of the involuntarily converted MACRS property, the taxpayer must include in taxable income the excess of the depreciation deductions allowable, including the additional first year depreciation deduction allowable, on the unadjusted depreciable basis of the acquired MACRS property over the additional first year depreciation deduction that would have been allowable to the taxpayer on the remaining carryover basis of the acquired MACRS property at the time of replacement (as defined in paragraph (f)(5)(v)(A) of this section) plus the depreciation deductions that would have been allowable, including the additional first year depreciation deduction allowable, to the taxpayer on the depreciable excess basis of the acquired MACRS property from the date the acquired MACRS property was placed in service by the taxpayer (taking into account the applicable convention) to the time of disposition of the involuntarily converted MACRS property. Similar rules apply to acquired computer software.

(vi) Examples. The application of this paragraph (f)(5) is illustrated by the following examples:

Example (1). (i) In December 2002, EE, a calendar-year corporation, acquired for $200,000 and placed in service Canopy V1, a gas station canopy. Canopy V1 is qualified property under section 168(k)(1) and is 5-year property under section 168(e). EE depreciated Canopy V1 under the general depreciation system of section 168(a) by using the 200-percent declining balance method of depreciation, a 5-year recovery period, and the half-year convention. EE elected to use the optional depreciation tables to compute the depreciation allowance for Canopy V1. On January 1, 2003, Canopy V1 was destroyed in a fire and was no longer usable in EE's business. On June 1, 2003, in an involuntary conversion, EE acquired and placed in service new Canopy W1 with all of the $160,000 of insurance proceeds EE received due to the loss of Canopy V1. Canopy W1 is 50-percent bonus depreciation property under section 168(k)(4) and is 5-year property under section 168(e). Pursuant to paragraph (g)(3)(ii) of this section and § 1.168(i)-6(k)(2)(i), EE decided to apply § 1.168(i)-6 to the involuntary conversion of Canopy V1 with the replacement of Canopy W1, the acquired MACRS property.

(ii) For 2002, EE is allowed a 30-percent additional first year depreciation deduction of $60,000 for Canopy V1 (the unadjusted depreciable basis of $200,000 multiplied by .30), and a regular MACRS depreciation deduction of $28,000 for Canopy V1 (the remaining adjusted depreciable basis of $140,000 multiplied by the annual depreciation rate of .20 for recovery year 1).

(iii) For 2003, EE is allowed a regular MACRS depreciation deduction of $22,400 for Canopy V1 (the remaining adjusted depreciable basis of $140,000 multiplied by the annual depreciation rate of .32 for recovery year 2 x ½ year).

(iv) Pursuant to paragraph (f)(5)(iii)(A) of this section, the additional first year depreciation deduction allowable for Canopy W1 equals $44,800 (.50 of Canopy W1's remaining carryover basis at the time of replacement of $89,600 (Canopy V1's remaining adjusted depreciable basis of $140,000 minus 2002 regular MACRS depreciation deduction of $28,000 minus 2003 regular MACRS depreciation deduction of $22,400).

Example (2). (i) Same facts as in Example 1, except EE elected not to deduct the additional first year depreciation for 5-year property placed in service in 2002. EE deducted the additional first year depreciation for 5-year property placed in service in 2003.

(ii) For 2002, EE is allowed a regular MACRS depreciation deduction of $40,000 for Canopy V1 (the unadjusted depreciable basis of $200,000 multiplied by the annual depreciation rate of .20 for recovery year 1).

(iii) For 2003, EE is allowed a regular MACRS depreciation deduction of $32,000 for Canopy V1 (the unadjusted depreciable basis of $200,000 multiplied by the annual depreciation rate of .32 for recovery year 2 x ½ year).

(iv) Pursuant to paragraph (f)(5)(iii)(A) of this section, the additional first year depreciation deduction allowable for Canopy W1 equals $64,000 (.50 of Canopy W1's remaining carryover basis at the time of replacement of $128,000 (Canopy V1's unadjusted depreciable basis of $200,000 minus 2002 regular MACRS depreciation deduction of $40,000 minus 2003 regular MACRS depreciation deduction of $32,000)).

Example (3). (i) In December 2001, FF, a calendar-year corporation, acquired for $10,000 and placed in service Computer X2. Computer X2 is qualified property under section 168(k)(1) and is 5-year property under section 168(e). FF depreciated Computer X2 under the general depreciation system of section 168(a) by using the 200-percent declining balance method of depreciation, a 5-year recovery period, and the half-year convention. FF elected to use the optional depreciation tables to compute the depreciation allowance for Computer X2. On January 1, 2002, FF acquired new Computer Y2 by exchanging Computer X2 and $1,000 cash in a like-kind exchange. Computer Y2 is qualified property under section 168(k)(1) and is 5-year property under section 168(e). Pursuant to paragraph (g)(3)(ii) of this section and § 1.168(i)-6(k)(2)(i), FF decided to apply § 1.168(i)-6 to the exchange of Computer X2 for Computer Y2, the acquired MACRS property.

(ii) For 2001, FF is allowed a 30-percent additional first year depreciation deduction of $3,000 for Computer X2 (unadjusted basis of $10,000 multiplied by .30), and a regular MACRS depreciation deduction of $1,400 for Computer X2 (the remaining adjusted depreciable basis of $7,000 multiplied by the annual depreciation rate of .20 for recovery year 1).

(iii) For 2002, FF is allowed a regular MACRS depreciation deduction of $1,120 for Computer X2 (the remaining adjusted depreciable basis of $7,000 multiplied by the annual depreciation rate of .32 for recovery year 2 x ½ year).

(iv) Pursuant to paragraph (f)(5)(iii)(A) of this section, the 30-percent additional first year depreciation deduction for Computer Y2 is allowable for the remaining carryover basis at the time of replacement of $4,480 (Computer X2's unadjusted depreciable basis of $10,000 minus additional first year depreciation deduction allowable of $3,000 minus 2001 regular MACRS depreciation deduction of $1,400 minus 2002 regular MACRS depreciation deduction of $1,120) and for the remaining excess basis at the time of replacement of $1,000 (cash paid for Computer Y2). Thus, the 30-percent additional first year depreciation deduction for the remaining carryover basis at the time of replacement equals $1,344 ($4,480 multiplied by .30) and for the remaining excess basis at the time of replacement equals $300 ($1,000 multiplied by .30), which totals $1,644.

Example (4). (i) In September 2002, GG, a June 30 year-end corporation, acquired for $20,000 and placed in service Equipment X3. Equipment X3 is qualified property under section 168(k)(1) and is 5-year property under section 168(e). GG depreciated Equipment X3 under the general depreciation system of section 168(a) by using the 200-percent declining balance method of depreciation, a 5-year recovery period, and the half-year convention. GG elected to use the optional depreciation tables to compute the depreciation allowance for Equipment X3. In December 2002, GG acquired new Equipment Y3 by exchanging Equipment X3 and $5,000 cash in a like-kind exchange. Equipment Y3 is qualified property under section 168(k)(1) and is 5-year property under section 168(e). Pursuant to paragraph (g)(3)(ii) of this section and § 1.168(i)-6(k)(2)(i), GG decided to apply § 1.168(i)-6 to the exchange of Equipment X3 for Equipment Y3, the acquired MACRS property.

(ii) Pursuant to paragraph (f)(5)(iii)(B) of this section, no additional first year depreciation deduction is allowable for Equipment X3 and, pursuant to § 1.168(d)-1T(b)(3)(ii), no regular depreciation deduction is allowable for Equipment X3, for the taxable year ended June 30, 2003.

(iii) Pursuant to paragraph (f)(5)(iii)(A) of this section, the 30-percent additional first year depreciation deduction for Equipment Y3 is allowable for the remaining carryover basis at the time of replacement of $20,000 (Equipment X3's unadjusted depreciable basis of $20,000) and for the remaining excess basis at the time of replacement of $5,000 (cash paid for Equipment Y3). Thus, the 30-percent additional first year depreciation deduction for the remaining carryover basis at the time of replacement equals $6,000 ($20,000 multiplied by .30) and for the remaining excess basis at the time of replacement equals $1,500 ($5,000 multiplied by .30), which totals $7,500.

Example (5). (i) Same facts as in Example 4. GG depreciated Equipment Y3 under the general depreciation system of section 168(a) by using the 200-percent declining balance method of depreciation, a 5-year recovery period, and the half-year convention. GG elected to use the optional depreciation tables to compute the depreciation allowance for Equipment Y3. On July 1, 2003, GG acquired new Equipment Z1 by exchanging Equipment Y3 in a like-kind exchange. Equipment Z1 is 50-percent bonus depreciation property under section 168(k)(4) and is 5-year property under section 168(e). Pursuant to paragraph (g)(3)(ii) of this section and § 1.168(i)-6(k)(2)(i), GG decided to apply § 1.168(i)-6 to the exchange of Equipment Y3 for Equipment Z1, the acquired MACRS property.

(ii) For the taxable year ending June 30, 2003, the regular MACRS depreciation deduction allowable for the remaining carryover basis at the time of replacement (after taking into account the additional first year depreciation deduction) of Equipment Y3 is $2,800 (the remaining carryover basis at the time of replacement of $20,000 minus the additional first year depreciation deduction of $6,000, multiplied by the annual depreciation rate of .20 for recovery year 1) and for the remaining excess basis at the time of replacement (after taking into account the additional first year depreciation deduction) of Equipment Y3 is $700 (the remaining excess basis at the time of replacement of $5,000 minus the additional first year depreciation deduction of $1,500, multiplied by the annual depreciation rate of .20 for recovery year 1), which totals $3,500.

(iii) For the taxable year ending June 30, 2004, the regular MACRS depreciation deduction allowable for the remaining carryover basis (after taking into account the additional first year depreciation deduction) of Equipment Y3 is $2,240 (the remaining carryover basis at the time of replacement of $20,000 minus the additional first year depreciation deduction of $6,000, multiplied by the annual depreciation rate of .32 for recovery year 2 x ½ year) and for the remaining excess basis (after taking into account the additional first year depreciation deduction) of Equipment Y3 is $560 (the remaining excess basis at the time of replacement of $5,000 minus the additional first year depreciation deduction of $1,500, multiplied by the annual depreciation rate of .32 for recovery year 2 x ½ year), which totals $2,800.

(iv) For the taxable year ending June 30, 2004, pursuant to paragraph (f)(5)(iii)(A) of this section, the 50-percent additional first year depreciation deduction for Equipment Z1 is allowable for the remaining carryover basis at the time of replacement of $11,200 (Equipment Y3's unadjusted depreciable basis of $25,000 minus the total additional first year depreciation deduction of $7,500 minus the total 2003 regular MACRS depreciation deduction of $3,500 minus the total 2004 regular depreciation deduction (taking into account the half-year convention) of $2,800). Thus, the 50-percent additional first year depreciation deduction for the remaining carryover basis at the time of replacement equals $5,600 ($11,200 multiplied by .50).

Example (6). (i) In April 2004, SS, a calendar year-end corporation, acquired and placed in service Equipment K89. Equipment K89 is 50-percent bonus depreciation property under section 168(k)(4). In November 2004, SS acquired and placed in service used Equipment N78 by exchanging Equipment K89 in a like-kind exchange.

(ii) Pursuant to paragraph (f)(5)(iii)(B) of this section, no additional first year deduction is allowable for Equipment K89 and, pursuant to § 1.168(d)-1T(b)(3)(ii), no regular depreciation deduction is allowable for Equipment K89, for the taxable year ended December 31, 2004.

(iii) Equipment N78 is not qualified property under section 168(k)(1) or 50-percent bonus depreciation property under section 168(k)(4) because the original use requirement of paragraph (b)(3) of this section is not met. Accordingly, no additional first year depreciation deduction is allowable for Equipment N78.

(6) Change in use. (i) Change in use of depreciable property. The determination of whether the use of depreciable property changes is made in accordance with section 168(i)(5) and regulations thereunder.

(ii) Conversion to personal use. If qualified property or 50-percent bonus depreciation property is converted from business or income-producing use to personal use in the same taxable year in which the property is placed in service by a taxpayer, the additional first year depreciation deduction is not allowable for the property.

(iii) Conversion to business or income-producing use. (A) During the same taxable year. If, during the same taxable year, property is acquired by a taxpayer for personal use and is converted by the taxpayer from personal use to business or income-producing use, the additional first year depreciation deduction is allowable for the property in the taxable year the property is converted to business or income-producing use (assuming all of the requirements in paragraph (b) of this section are met). See paragraph (b)(3)(ii) of this section relating to the original use rules for a conversion of property to business or income-producing use.

(B) Subsequent to the acquisition year. If property is acquired by a taxpayer for personal use and, during a subsequent taxable year, is converted by the taxpayer from personal use to business or income-producing use, the additional first year depreciation deduction is allowable for the property in the taxable year the property is converted to business or income-producing use (assuming all of the requirements in paragraph (b) of this section are met). For purposes of paragraphs (b)(4) and (5) of this section, the property must be acquired by the taxpayer for personal use after September 10, 2001 (for qualified property), or after May 5, 2003 (for 50-percent bonus depreciation property), and converted by the taxpayer from personal use to business or income-producing use by January 1, 2005. See paragraph (b)(3)(ii) of this section relating to the original use rules for a conversion of property to business or income-producing use.

(iv) Depreciable property changes use subsequent to the placed-in-service year. (A) If the use of qualified property or 50-percent bonus depreciation property changes in the hands of the same taxpayer subsequent to the taxable year the qualified property or the 50-percent bonus depreciation property, as applicable, is placed in service and, as a result of the change in use, the property is no longer qualified property or 50-percent bonus depreciation property, as applicable, the additional first year depreciation deduction allowable for the qualified property or the 50-percent bonus depreciation property, as applicable, is not redetermined.

(B) If depreciable property is not qualified property or 50-percent bonus depreciation property in the taxable year the property is placed in service by the taxpayer, the additional first year depreciation deduction is not allowable for the property even if a change in the use of the property subsequent to the taxable year the property is placed in service results in the property being qualified property or 50-percent bonus depreciation property in the taxable year of the change in use.

(v) Examples. The application of this paragraph (f)(6) is illustrated by the following examples:

Example (1). (i) On January 1, 2002, HH, a calendar year corporation, purchased and placed in service several new computers at a total cost of $100,000. HH used these computers within the United States for 3 months in 2002 and then moved and used the computers outside the United States for the remainder of 2002. On January 1, 2003, HH permanently returns the computers to the United States for use in its business.

(ii) For 2002, the computers are considered as used predominantly outside the United States in 2002 pursuant to § 1.48-1(g)(1)(i). As a result, the computers are required to be depreciated under the alternative depreciation system of section 168(g). Pursuant to paragraph (b)(2)(ii)(A)2) of this section, the computers are not qualified property in 2002, the placed-in-service year. Thus, pursuant to (f)(6)(iv)(B) of this section, no additional first year depreciation deduction is allowed for these computers, regardless of the fact that the computers are permanently returned to the United States in 2003.

Example (2). (i) On February 8, 2002, II, a calendar year corporation, purchased and placed in service new equipment at a cost of $1,000,000 for use in its California plant. The equipment is 5-year property under section 168(e) and is qualified property under section 168(k). II depreciates its 5-year property placed in service in 2002 using the optional depreciation table that corresponds with the general depreciation system, the 200-percent declining balance method, a 5-year recovery period, and the half-year convention. On June 4, 2003, due to changes in II's business circumstances, II permanently moves the equipment to its plant in Mexico.

(ii) For 2002, II is allowed a 30-percent additional first year depreciation deduction of $300,000 (the adjusted depreciable basis of $1,000,000 multiplied by .30). In addition, II's depreciation deduction allowable in 2002 for the remaining adjusted depreciable basis of $700,000 (the unadjusted depreciable basis of $1,000,000 reduced by the additional first year depreciation deduction of $300,000) is $140,000 (the remaining adjusted depreciable basis of $700,000 multiplied by the annual depreciation rate of .20 for recovery year 1).

(iii) For 2003, the equipment is considered as used predominantly outside the United States pursuant to § 1.48-1(g)(1)(i). As a result of this change in use, the adjusted depreciable basis of $560,000 for the equipment is required to be depreciated under the alternative depreciation system of section 168(g) beginning in 2003. However, the additional first year depreciation deduction of $300,000 allowed for the equipment in 2002 is not redetermined.

(7) Earnings and profits. The additional first year depreciation deduction is not allowable for purposes of computing earnings and profits.

(8) Limitation of amount of depreciation for certain passenger automobiles. For a passenger automobile as defined in section 280F(d)(5), the limitation under section 280F(a)(1)(A)(i) is increased by—

(i) $4,600 for qualified property acquired by a taxpayer after September 10, 2001, and before May 6, 2003; and

(ii) $7,650 for qualified property or 50-percent bonus depreciation property acquired by a taxpayer after May 5, 2003.

(9) Section 754 election. In general, for purposes of section 168(k) any increase in basis of qualified property or 50-percent bonus depreciation property due to a section 754 election is not eligible for the additional first year depreciation deduction. However, if qualified property or 50-percent bonus depreciation property is placed in service by a partnership in the taxable year the partnership terminates under section 708(b)(1)(B), any increase in basis of the qualified property or the 50-percent bonus depreciation property due to a section 754 election is eligible for the additional first year depreciation deduction.

(10) Coordination with section 47. (i) In general. If qualified rehabilitation expenditures (as defined in section 47(c)(2) and § 1.48-12(c)) incurred by a taxpayer with respect to a qualified rehabilitated building (as defined in section 47(c)(1) and § 1.48-12(b)) are qualified property or 50-percent bonus depreciation property, the taxpayer may claim the rehabilitation credit provided by section 47(a) (provided the requirements of section 47 are met)—

(A) With respect to the portion of the basis of the qualified rehabilitated building that is attributable to the qualified rehabilitation expenditures if the taxpayer makes the applicable election under paragraph (e)(1)(i) or (e)(1)(ii)(B) of this section not to deduct any additional first year depreciation for the class of property that includes the qualified rehabilitation expenditures; or

(B) With respect to the portion of the remaining rehabilitated basis of the qualified rehabilitated building that is attributable to the qualified rehabilitation expenditures if the taxpayer claims the additional first year depreciation deduction on the unadjusted depreciable basis (as defined in paragraph (a)(2)(iii) of this section but before the reduction in basis for the amount of the rehabilitation credit) of the qualified rehabilitation expenditures and the taxpayer depreciates the remaining adjusted depreciable basis (as defined in paragraph (d)(2)(i) of this section) of such expenditures using straight line cost recovery in accordance with section 47(c)(2)(B)(i) and § 1.48-12(c)(7)(i). For purposes of this paragraph (f)(10)(i)(B), the remaining rehabilitated basis is equal to the unadjusted depreciable basis (as defined in paragraph (a)(2)(iii) of this section but before the reduction in basis for the amount of the rehabilitation credit) of the qualified rehabilitation expenditures that are qualified property or 50-percent bonus depreciation property reduced by the additional first year depreciation allowed or allowable, whichever is greater.

(ii) Example. The application of this paragraph (f)(10) is illustrated by the following example.

Example. (i) Between February 8, 2004, and June 4, 2004, UU, a calendar-year taxpayer, incurred qualified rehabilitation expenditures of $200,000 with respect to a qualified rehabilitated building that is nonresidential real property under section 168(e). These qualified rehabilitation expenditures are 50-percent bonus depreciation property and qualify for the 10-percent rehabilitation credit under section 47(a)(1). UU's basis in the qualified rehabilitated building is zero before incurring the qualified rehabilitation expenditures and UU placed the qualified rehabilitated building in service in July 2004. UU depreciates its nonresidential real property placed in service in 2004 under the general depreciation system of section 168(a) by using the straight line method of depreciation, a 39-year recovery period, and the mid-month convention. UU elected to use the optional depreciation tables to compute the depreciation allowance for its depreciable property placed in service in 2004. Further, for 2004, UU did not make any election under paragraph (e) of this section.

(ii) Because UU did not make any election under paragraph (e) of this section, UU is allowed a 50-percent additional first year depreciation deduction of $100,000 for the qualified rehabilitation expenditures for 2004 (the unadjusted depreciable basis of $200,000 (before reduction in basis for the rehabilitation credit) multiplied by .50). For 2004, UU also is allowed to claim a rehabilitation credit of $10,000 for the remaining rehabilitated basis of $100,000 (the unadjusted depreciable basis (before reduction in basis for the rehabilitation credit) of $200,000 less the additional first year depreciation deduction of $100,000). Further, UU's depreciation deduction for 2004 for the remaining adjusted depreciable basis of $90,000 (the unadjusted depreciable basis (before reduction in basis for the rehabilitation credit) of $200,000 less the additional first year depreciation deduction of $100,000 less the rehabilitation credit of $10,000) is $1,059.30 (the remaining adjusted depreciable basis of $90,000 multiplied by the depreciation rate of .01177 for recovery year 1, placed in service in month 7).

(11) Coordination with section 514(a)(3). The additional first year depreciation deduction is not allowable for purposes of section 514(a)(3).

(g) Effective date.

(1) In general. Except as provided in paragraphs (g)(2), (3), and (5) of this section, this section applies to qualified property under section 168(k)(2) acquired by a taxpayer after September 10, 2001, and to 50-percent bonus depreciation property under section 168(k)(4) acquired by a taxpayer after May 5, 2003.

(2) Technical termination of a partnership or section 168(i)(7) transactions. If qualified property or 50 percent bonus depreciation property is transferred in a technical termination of a partnership under section 708(b)(1)(B) or in a transaction described in section 168(i)(7) for a taxable year ending on or before September 8, 2003, and the additional first year depreciation deduction allowable for the property was not determined in accordance with paragraph (f)(1)(ii) or (iii) of this section, as applicable, the Internal Revenue Service will allow any reasonable method of determining the additional first year depreciation deduction allowable for the property in the year of the transaction that is consistently applied to the property by all parties to the transaction.

(3) (i) Like-kind exchanges and involuntary conversions. If a taxpayer did not claim on a federal tax return for a taxable year ending on or before September 8, 2003, the additional first year depreciation deduction for the remaining carryover basis of qualified property or 50-percent bonus depreciation property acquired in a transaction described in section 1031(a), (b), or (c), or in a transaction to which section 1033 applies and the taxpayer did not make an election not to deduct the additional first year depreciation deduction for the class of property applicable to the remaining carryover basis, the Internal Revenue Service will treat the taxpayer's method of not claiming the additional first year depreciation deduction for the remaining carryover basis as a permissible method of accounting and will treat the amount of the additional first year depreciation deduction allowable for the remaining carryover basis as being equal to zero, provided the taxpayer does not claim the additional first year depreciation deduction for the remaining carryover basis in accordance with paragraph (g)(4)(ii) of this section.

(ii) Paragraphs (f)(5)(ii)(F)(2) and (f)(5)(v) of this section apply to a like-kind exchange or an involuntary conversion of MACRS property and computer software for which the time of disposition and the time of replacement both occur after February 27, 2004. For a like-kind exchange or an involuntary conversion of MACRS property for which the time of disposition, the time of replacement, or both occur on or before February 27, 2004, see § 1.168(i)-6(k)(2)(ii). For a like-kind exchange or involuntary conversion of computer software for which the time of disposition, the time of replacement, or both occur on or before February 27, 2004, a taxpayer may rely on prior guidance issued by the Internal Revenue Service for determining the depreciation deductions of the acquired computer software and the exchanged or involuntarily converted computer software (for further guidance, see § 1.168(k)-1T(f)(5) published in the Federal Register on September 8, 2003 (68 FR 53000)). In relying on such guidance, a taxpayer may use any reasonable, consistent method of determining depreciation in the year of disposition and the year of replacement.

(4) Change in method of accounting. (i) Special rules for 2000 or 2001 returns. If a taxpayer did not claim on the Federal tax return for the taxable year that included September 11, 2001, any additional first year depreciation deduction for a class of property that is qualified property and did not make an election not to deduct the additional first year depreciation deduction for that class of property, the taxpayer should refer to the guidance provided by the Internal Revenue Service for the time and manner of claiming the additional first year depreciation deduction for the class of property (for further guidance, see section 4 of Rev. Proc. 2002-33 (2002-1 C.B. 963), Rev. Proc. 2003-50 (2003-29 I.R.B. 119), and § 601.601(d)(2)(ii)(b) of this chapter).

(ii) Like-kind exchanges and involuntary conversions. If a taxpayer did not claim on a federal tax return for any taxable year ending on or before September 8, 2003, the additional first year depreciation deduction allowable for the remaining carryover basis of qualified property or 50-percent bonus depreciation property acquired in a transaction described in section 1031(a), (b), or (c), or in a transaction to which section 1033 applies and the taxpayer did not make an election not to deduct the additional first year depreciation deduction for the class of property applicable to the remaining carryover basis, the taxpayer may claim the additional first year depreciation deduction allowable for the remaining carryover basis in accordance with paragraph (f)(5) of this section either:

(A) By filing an amended return (or a qualified amended return, if applicable (for further guidance, see Rev. Proc. 94-69 (1994-2 C.B. 804) and § 601.601(d)(2)(ii)(b) of this chapter)) on or before December 31, 2003, for the year of replacement and any affected subsequent taxable year; or,

(B) By following the applicable administrative procedures issued under § 1.446-1(e)(3)(ii) for obtaining the Commissioner's automatic consent to a change in method of accounting (for further guidance, see Rev. Proc. 2002-9 (2002-1 C.B. 327) and § 601.601(d)(2)(ii)(b) of this chapter).

(5) Revision to paragraphs (b)(3)(iii)(B) and (b)(5)(ii)(B) of this section. The addition of "(or, in the case of multiple units of property subject to the same lease, within three months after the date the final unit is placed in service, so long as the period between the time the first unit is placed in service and the time the last unit is placed in service does not exceed 12 months)" to paragraphs (b)(3)(iii)(B) and

(b)(5)(ii)(B) of this section applies to property sold after June 4, 2004.

(6) Rehabilitation credit. If a taxpayer did not claim on a Federal tax return for any taxable year ending on or before September 1, 2006, the rehabilitation credit provided by section 47(a) with respect to the portion of the basis of a qualified rehabilitated building that is attributable to qualified rehabilitation expenditures and the qualified rehabilitation expenditures are qualified property or 50-percent bonus depreciation property, and the taxpayer did not make the applicable election specified in paragraph (e)(1)(i) or (e)(1)(ii)(B) of this section for the class of property that includes the qualified rehabilitation expenditures, the taxpayer may claim the rehabilitation credit for the remaining rehabilitated basis (as defined in paragraph (f)(10)(i)(B) of this section) of the qualified rehabilitated building that is attributable to the qualified rehabilitation expenditures (assuming all the requirements of section 47 are met) in accordance with paragraph (f)(10)(i)(B) of this section by filing an amended Federal tax return for the taxable year for which the rehabilitation credit is to be claimed. The amended Federal tax return must include the adjustment to the tax liability for the rehabilitation credit and any collateral adjustments to taxable income or to the tax liability (for example, the amount of depreciation allowed or allowable in that taxable year for the qualified rehabilitated building). Such adjustments must also be made on amended Federal tax returns for any affected succeeding taxable years.

T.D. 9091, 9/5/2003, amend T.D. 9115, 2/27/2004, T.D. 9283, 8/28/2006, T.D. 9314, 2/26/2007.

§ 1.168A-1 Amortization of emergency facilities; general rule.

(a) A person (including an estate or trust (see section 642(f) and § 1.642(f)-1) and a partnership (see section 703 and § 1.703-1)) is entitled, by election, to a deduction with respect to the amortization of the adjusted basis (for determining gain) of an emergency facility, such amortization to be based on a period of 60 months. As to the adjusted basis of an emergency facility, see § 1.168A-5. The taxpayer may elect to begin the 60-month amortization period with (1) the month following the month in which such facility was completed or acquired, or (2) the taxable year succeeding that in which such facility was completed or acquired (see § 1.168A-2). The date on which, or the month within which, an emergency facility is completed or acquired is to be determined upon the facts in the particular case. Ordinarily, the taxpayer is in possession of all the facts and, therefore, in a position to ascertain such date. A statement of the date ascertained by the taxpayer, together with a statement of the pertinent facts relied upon, should be filed with the taxpayer's election to take amortization deductions with respect to such facility.

(b) Generally, an amortization deduction will not be allowed with respect to an emergency facility for any taxable year unless such facility has been certified before the date of filing of the taxpayer's income tax return for such taxable year. However, this limitation does not apply in the case of a certificate made after August 22, 1957, for an emergency facility to provide primary processing for uranium ore or uranium concentrate under a program of the Atomic Energy Commission for the development of any sources of uranium ore or uranium concentrate, if application for such certificate was filed either (1) before September 2, 1958, and before the expiration of six months after the beginning of construction, reconstruction, erection, or installation or the date of acquisition of the facility, or (2) after September 1, 1958, and on or before December 2, 1958.

(c) In general, with respect to each month of the 60-month period which falls within the taxable year, the amortization deduction is an amount equal to the adjusted basis of the facility at the end of each month divided by the number of months (including the particular month for which the deduction is computed) remaining in the 60-month period. The adjusted basis at the end of any month shall be computed without regard to the amortization deduction for such month. The total amortization deduction with respect to an emergency facility for a particular taxable year is the sum of the amortization deductions allowable for each month of the 60-month period which falls within such taxable year. The amortization deduction taken for any month is in lieu of the deduction for depreciation which would otherwise be allowable under section 167. See, however, § 1.168A-6, relating to depreciation with respect to any portion of the emergency facility not subject to amortization.

(d) This section may be illustrated by the following examples:

Example (1). On July 1, 1954, the X Corporation, which makes its income tax returns on the calendar year basis, begins the construction of an emergency facility which is completed on September 30, 1954, at a cost of $240,000. The certificate covers the entire construction. The X Corporation elects to take amortization deductions with respect to the facility and to begin the 60-month amortization period with October, the month following its completion. The adjusted basis of the facility at the end of October is $240,000. The allowable amortization deduction with respect to such facility for the taxable year 1954 is $12,000, computed as follows:

Monthly amortization deductions:	
October: $240,000 divided by 60	$ 4,000
November: $236,000 ($240,000 minus $4,000) divided by 50	4,000
December: $232,000 ($236,000 minus $4,000) divided by 58	4,000
Total amortization deduction for 1954	12,000

Example (2). The Y Corporation, which makes its income tax returns on the basis of a fiscal year ending November 30, purchases an emergency facility (No. 1) on July 29, 1955. On June 15, 1955, it begins the construction of an emergency facility (No. 2) which is completed on August 2, 1955. The entire acquisition and construction of such facilities are covered by the certificate. The Y Corporation elects to take amortization deductions with respect to both facilities and to begin the 60-month amortization period in each case with the month following the month of acquisition or completion. At the end of the first month of the amortization period the adjusted basis of facility No. 1 is $300,000 and the adjusted basis of facility No. 2 is $54,000. In September 1955, facility No. 1 is damaged by fire, as a result of which its adjusted basis is properly reduced by $25,370. The allowable amortization deduction with respect to such facilities for the taxable year ending November 30, 1955, is $21,410, computed as follows:

Facility No. 1

Monthly amortization deductions:

August: $300,000 divided by 60	$ 5,000
September: $269,630 ($300,000 minus $5,000 and $25,370) divided by 59	4,570
October: $265,060 ($269,630 minus $4,570) divided by 58	4,570
November: $260,490 ($265,060 minus $4,570) divided by 57	4,570
Amortization deduction for 1955	18,710

Facility No. 2

Monthly amortization deductions:

September: $54,000 divided by 60	$ 900
October: $53,100 divided by 50	900
November: $52,200 divided by 58	900
Amortization deduction for 1955	2,700
Total amortization deduction for 1955	21,410

Example (3). On June 15, 1954, the Z Corporation, which makes its income tax returns on the calendar year basis, completes the construction of an emergency facility at a cost of $110,000. In its income tax return for 1954, filed on March 15, 1955, the Z Corporation elects to take amortization deductions with respect to such facility and to begin the 60-month amortization period with July 1954, the month following its completion. No certificate with respect to such facility is made until April 10, 1955, and therefore no amortization deduction with respect to such facility is allowable for any month in the taxable year 1954. The Z Corporation is entitled, however, to take a deduction for depreciation of such facility for the taxable year 1954, such deduction being assumed, for the purposes of this example, to be $2,000. Accordingly, the adjusted basis of such facility at the end of January 1955 (without regard to the amortization deduction for such month) is $108,000 ($110,000 minus $2,000). For the taxable year 1955, the Z Corporation is, with respect to such facility, entitled to an amortization deduction of $24,000, computed as follows:

Monthly amortization deductions:

January: $108,000 divided by 54	$ 2,000
February: $106,000 ($108,000 minus $2,000) divided by 53	2,000
March: $104,000 ($106,000 minus $2,000) divided by 52	2,000
For the remaining nine months (annually computed)	18,000
Total amortization deduction for 1955	24,000

Since the Z Corporation elected in its return for 1954 to take amortization deductions with respect to such facility and to begin the 60-month amortization period with July 1954, it must compute its amortization deductions for the 12 months in the taxable year 1955 on the basis of the remaining months of the established 60-month amortization period, as indicated in the above computation.

T.D. 6500, 11/25/60, amend T.D. 8116, 12/23/86.

§ 1.168A-2 Election of amortization.

(a) General rule. An election by the taxpayer to take amortization deductions with respect to an emergency facility and to begin the 60-month amortization period either with the month following the month in which such facility was completed or acquired, or with the taxable year succeeding the taxable year in which such facility was completed or acquired, shall be made by a statement to that effect in its return for the taxable year in which falls the first month of the 60-month amortization period so elected. However, if the facility is described in section 168(e)(2)(C) and an application for a certificate is filed within the period prescribed by section 9(c) of the Technical Amendments Act of 1958 (72 Stat. 1609) and paragraph (b) of § 1.168A-1, the election may be made by a statement in an amended income tax return for the taxable year in which falls the first month of the 60-month amortization period so elected. The statement and amended return in such case must be filed not later than 90 days after the date the certificate is made or not later than April 4, 1960, whichever is later. Amended income tax returns or claims for credit or refund should also be filed for other taxable years which are within such amortization period and which precede the taxable year in which the election is made. Nothing in this paragraph should be construed as extending the time specified in section 6511 within which a claim for credit or refund may be filed.

(b) Election not made, in prescribed manner. If the statement of election is not made by the taxpayer as prescribed in paragraph (a) of this section, it may, in the discretion of the Commissioner and for good cause shown, be made in such manner and form and within such time as may be approved by the Commissioner.

(c) Other requirements and considerations. No method of making such election other than those prescribed in this section and corresponding sections of prior regulations is permitted. Any statement of election should contain a description clearly identifying each emergency facility for which an amortization deduction is claimed. A taxpayer which does not elect, in the manner prescribed in this section or corresponding sections of prior regulations, to take amortization deductions with respect to an emergency facility shall not be entitled to such deductions.

T.D. 6500, 11/25/60, amend T.D. 8116, 12/23/86.

§ 1.168A-3 Election to discontinue amortization.

(a) If a taxpayer has elected to take amortization deductions with respect to an emergency facility, it may, after such election and prior to the expiration of the 60-month amortization period, discontinue the amortization deductions for the remainder of the 60-month period. An election to discontinue the amortization deductions shall be made by a notice in writing filed with the district director for the internal revenue district in which the return of the taxpayer is required to be filed, specifying the month as of the beginning of which the taxpayer elects to discontinue such deductions. Such notice shall be filed before the beginning of the month specified therein, and shall contain a description clearly identifying the emergency facility with respect to which the taxpayer elects to discontinue the amortization deductions. If the taxpayer so elects to discontinue the amortization deductions, it shall not be entitled to any further amortization deductions with respect to such facility.

(b) A taxpayer which thus elects to discontinue amortization deductions with respect to an emergency facility is entitled, if such facility is depreciable property under section 167 and the regulations thereunder, to a deduction for depreciation with respect to such facility. The deduction for depreciation shall begin with the first month as to which the amortization deduction is not applicable, and shall be computed on the adjusted basis of the property as of the beginning of such month (see section 1011 and the regulations thereunder).

(c) This section may be illustrated by the following example:

Example. On July 1, 1954, the X Corporation, which makes its income tax returns on the calendar year basis, purchases an emergency facility, consisting of land with a building thereon, at a cost of $306,000 of which $60,000 is allocable to the land and $246,000 to the building. The certificate covers the entire acquisition. The corporation elects to take amortization deductions with respect to the facility and to begin the 60-month amortization period with the taxable year 1955. Depreciation of the building in the amount of $6,000 is deducted and allowed for the taxable year 1954. On March 25, 1956, the corporation files notice with the district director of its election to discontinue the amortization deductions beginning with the month of April 1956. The adjusted basis of the facility on January 31, 1955, is $300,000, or the cost of the facility ($306,000) less the depreciation allowed for 1954 ($6,000). The amortization deductions for the taxable year 1955 and the months of January, February, and March 1956, amount to $75,000, or $5,000 per month for 15 months. Since, at the beginning of the amortization period (January 1, 1955), the adjusted basis of the land ($60,000) is one-fifth of the adjusted basis of the entire facility ($300,000) and since there are no adjustments to basis other than on account of amortization during the period, the adjusted basis of the land should be reduced by $15,000, or one-fifth of the entire amortization deduction, and the adjusted basis of the building should be reduced by $60,000, or four-fifths of the entire amortization deduction. Accordingly, the adjusted basis of the facility as of April 1, 1956, is $225,000, of which $180,000 is allocable to the building for the purpose of depreciation deductions under section 167, and $45,000 is allocable to the land.

T.D. 6500, 11/25/60, amend T.D. 8116, 12/23/86.

§ 1.168A-4 Definitions.

As used in the regulations under section 168, the term—

(a) "Certifying authority" means the certifying authority designated by the President by Executive order.

(b) "Emergency facility" means any facility, land, building, machinery, or equipment, or any part thereof, the acquisition of which occurred after December 31, 1949, or the construction, reconstruction, erection, or installation of which was completed after such date, and with respect to which a certificate under section 168(e) has been made. In the case of an application for a certificate under section 168(e) which is filed after March 23, 1951, only the part of any such facility which is constructed, reconstructed, erected, or installed by any person not earlier than six months prior to the filing of such application, and which is certified in accordance with section 168(e), shall be deemed to be an emergency facility, notwithstanding that the other part of such facility was constructed, reconstructed, erected, or installed earlier than six months prior to the filing of such application. However, if the facility is one described in section 168(e)(2)(C) and the application was filed after September 1, 1958, and on or before December 2, 1958, the preceding sentence shall not apply. The term "emergency facility," as so defined, may include, among other things, improvements of land, such as the construction of roads, bridges, and airstrips, and the dredging of channels.

(c) "Emergency period" means the period beginning on January 1, 1950, and ending on the date on which the President proclaims that the utilization of a substantial portion of the certified emergency facilities is no longer required in the interest of national defense.

T.D. 6500, 11/25/60, amend T.D. 8116, 12/23/86.

§ 1.168A-5 Adjusted basis of emergency facility.

(a) In general. *(1)* The adjusted basis of an emergency facility for the purpose of computing the amortization deduction may differ from what would otherwise constitute the adjusted basis of such emergency facility in that it shall be the adjusted basis for determining gain (see Part II (section 1011 and following), Subchapter 0, Chapter 1 of the Code) and in that it may be only a portion of what would otherwise constitute the adjusted basis. It will be only a portion of such other adjusted basis if only a portion of the basis (unadjusted) is attributable to certified construction, reconstruction, erection, installation, or acquisition taking place after December 31, 1949. Also, it will be only a portion of what would otherwise constitute the adjusted basis of the emergency facility if only a portion of the basis (unadjusted) is certified as attributable to defense purposes or, in the case of a certification after August 22, 1957, if only a portion of the basis (unadjusted) is certified as attributable to the national defense program. It is therefore necessary first to determine the unadjusted basis of the emergency facility from which the adjusted basis for amortization purposes is derived.

(2) The unadjusted basis for amortization purposes is the same as the unadjusted basis otherwise determined only when the entire construction, reconstruction, erection, installation, or acquisition takes place after December 31, 1949, and is certified in its entirety by the certifying authority.

(3) In cases in which only a portion of the construction, reconstruction, erection, installation, or acquisition takes place after December 31, 1949, and that portion is certified in its entirety by the certifying authority, the unadjusted basis for the purpose of amortization is so much of the entire unadjusted basis as is attributable to the certified construction, reconstruction, erection, installation, or acquisition which takes place after December 31, 1949. For example, the X Corporation begins the construction of a facility on November 15, 1949, and such facility is completed on April 1, 1952, at a cost of $5,000,000, of which $4,600,000 is attributable to construction after December 31, 1949. The entire construction after December 31, 1949, is certified by the certifying authority. The unadjusted basis of the emergency facility for amortization purposes is therefore $4,600,000. For depreciation of the remaining portion ($400,000) of the cost see § 1.168A-6.

(4) If the certifying authority certifies only a portion of the construction, reconstruction, erection, installation, or acquisition of property which takes place after December 31, 1949, the unadjusted basis for amortization purposes is limited to such portion so certified. Assuming the same facts as in the example in subparagraph (3) of this paragraph, except that only 50 percent of the construction, reconstruction, erection, installation, or acquisition after December 31, 1949, is certified, the unadjusted basis for amortization purposes is 50 percent of $4,600,000, or $2,300,000.

(5) The adjusted basis of an emergency facility for amortization purposes is the unadjusted basis for amortization purposes less the adjustments properly applicable thereto. Such adjustments are those specified in sections 1016 and 1017, except that no adjustments are to be taken into account which increase the adjusted basis. (See paragraph (b) of this section.) If the taxpayer constructs, reconstructs, erects, installs, or acquires an emergency facility pursuant to a cost

reimbursement contract with an obligation for reimbursement by the United States of all or a part of the cost of such facility, the unadjusted basis of such facility for amortization purposes shall not include that part of the cost for which the taxpayer is entitled to reimbursement, and the amount received as reimbursement shall be treated as a capital receipt. However, amounts received by a taxpayer which represent in fact compensation by reason of termination of a government contract or payment for articles under such a contract, though denominated reimbursements for all or a part of the cost of an emergency facility, are not to be treated as capital receipts but are to be taken into account in computing income, and are therefore not to be applied in reduction of the basis of such facility.

(6) The following examples will illustrate the computation of the adjusted basis of an emergency facility for amortization purposes:

Example (1). The X Corporation completes an emergency facility on July 1, 1954, the entire unadjusted basis of which is $500,000, and the unadjusted basis of which for the purpose of amortization is $300,000. The X Corporation elects to begin amortization as of January 1, 1955. The only adjustment to basis for the period July 1, 1954, to January 31, 1955, other than depreciation or amortization for January 1955, is $5,000 for depreciation for the last six months of 1954. The adjusted basis for the purpose of amortization is therefore $300,000 less $3,000 (300,000/500,000 × $5,000), or $297,000.

Example (2). On July 31, 1956, the Y Corporation has an emergency facility (a building) which was completed on July 1, 1952, the entire basis of which is $500,000 and the unadjusted basis of which for the purpose of amortization is $300,000. The corporation elected to begin amortization as of January 1, 1953, at which time it was entitled to $5,000 depreciation for the last six months of 1952. On July 1, 1956, the facility was damaged by fire, as the result of which its adjusted basis is properly reduced by $200,000. The adjusted basis of the emergency facility as of July 1956 for the purpose of amortization and depreciation, and the adjusted basis for other purposes, are $23,849.18, $49,250.82, and $73,100.00, respectively, computed as follows:

	For amortization	For depreciation	For other purposes
Unadjusted basis	$300,000.00	$200,000.00	$500,000
Less depreciation to Jan 1, 1953	3,000.00	2,000.00	5,000
Adjusted basis January 1953	297,000.00	196,000.00	495,000
Less amortization for 42 months	207,900.00		207,900
Less depreciation for 42 months		14,000.00	14,000
Adjusted basis at time of fire	89,100.00	184,000.00	273,100
Less fire loss (apportioned as explained below)	65,250.82	134,749.18	200,000
Adjusted basis after fire loss	23,849.18	49,250.82	73,100

The $200,000 fire loss is applied against the adjusted basis for the purpose of amortization and the adjusted basis for the purpose of depreciation in the proportion that each such adjusted basis at the time of the fire bears to their sum, i.e., 89,100/273,100 and 184,000/273,100 × $200,000, or $134,749.18 against the depreciation basis.

(b) Capital additions. *(1)* If, after the completion or acquisition of an emergency facility which has been certified by the certifying authority, further expenditures are made for construction, reconstruction, erection, installation, or acquisition attributable to such facility but not covered by such certification, such expenditures shall not be added to the adjusted basis of the emergency facility for amortization purposes under such certification. If such further expenditures are separately certified in accordance with the provisions of section 168(e)(1) or (2) and this section, they are treated as certified expenditures in connection with a new and separate emergency facility and, if proper election is made, will be taken into account in computing the adjusted basis of such new and separate emergency facility for the purpose of amortization.

(2) The application of subparagraph (1) of this paragraph may be illustrated by the following example:

Example. On March 1, 1954, the certifying authority certifies as an emergency facility a heating plant proposed to be constructed by the Z Corporation. Such facility is completed on July 1, 1954. The Z Corporation, on August 1, 1954, begins the installation in the plant of an additional boiler, which is not included in the certification for the plant but is certified as a new and separate emergency facility. For amortization purposes, the adjusted basis of the heating plant is determined without including the cost of the additional boiler. Such cost is taken into account in computing the adjusted basis of the new and separate emergency facility (the boiler), as to which the taxpayer has a separate election for amortization purposes and a separate amortization period.

T.D. 6500, 11/25/60, amend T.D. 8116, 12/23/86.

§ 1.168A-6 Depreciation of portion of emergency facility not subject to amortization.

(a) The rule that an amortization deduction with respect to an emergency facility is in lieu of any deduction for depreciation which would otherwise be allowable under section 167 is subject to the exception provided in section 168(f). Under this exception, if the property constituting such facility is depreciable property under section 167 and the regulations thereunder and if the adjusted basis of such facility as computed under section 1011 for purposes other than the amortization deductions is in excess of the adjusted basis computed for the purpose of the amortization deductions, then the excess shall be charged off over the useful life of the facility and recovered through depreciation deductions. Thus, if the construction of an emergency facility is begun on or before December 31, 1949, and completed after such date, no amortization deductions are allowable with respect to the amount attributable to such construction on or before such date (see § 1.168A-5). However, if the property constituting such facility is depreciable property under section 167 and the regulations thereunder, then the depreciation deduction provided by such section and regulations is allowable with respect to the amount attributable to such construction on or before December 31, 1949.

(b) Similarly, if only a portion of the construction, reconstruction, erection, installation, or acquisition after December 31, 1949, of an emergency facility has been certified by the certifying authority, and if such facility is depreciable property under section 167 and the regulations thereunder, then the depreciation deduction provided by such section and regulations is allowable with respect to the portion which has not been so certified.

(c) For illustration of the treatment of a depreciable portion of an emergency facility, see example (2) in paragraph (a)(6) of § 1.168A-5.

T.D. 6500, 11/25/60, amend T.D. 8116, 12/23/86.

§ 1.168A-7 Payment by United States of unamortized cost of facility.

(a) Section 168(g) contemplates that certain payments may be made by the United States to a taxpayer as compensation for the unamortized cost of an emergency facility. If any such payment is properly includible in gross income and has been certified, as provided in section 168(g), as having been paid under the circumstances described therein, a taxpayer which is recovering the adjusted basis of an emergency facility through amortization rather than depreciation may elect to take an amount equal to such payment as an amortization deduction with respect to such facility for the month in which such payment is so includible. Such amortization deduction shall be in lieu of the amortization deduction otherwise allowable with respect to such facility for such month, but it shall not in any case exceed the adjusted basis of such facility (see § 1.168A-5) as of the end of such month (computed without regard to any amortization deduction for such month). The election referred to in this paragraph shall be made in the return for the taxable year in which the amount of such payment is includible in gross income.

(b) If a taxpayer is recovering the adjusted basis of an emergency facility through depreciation rather than amortization, the depreciation deduction allowable under section 167 for the month in which the amount of any such payment is includible in gross income shall, at the taxpayer's election, be increased by such amount; but the total deduction with respect to the certified portion of such facility shall not in any case exceed the adjusted basis of such facility (computed as provided in section 168(e) and § 1.168A-5 for amortization purposes) as of the end of such month (computed without regard to any amount allowable for such month under section 167 or 168(g)(2)). The election referred to in this paragraph shall be made in the return for the taxable year in which the amount of such payment is includible in gross income.

(c) This section may be illustrated by the following examples:

Example (1). On January 31, 1954, the X Corporation purchases an emergency facility at a cost of $600,000. The certificate covers the entire acquisition. The X Corporation elects to take amortization deductions with respect to such facility and to begin the 60-month amortization period with February 1954, the month following the month of acquisition. On July 15, 1955, as a result of the cancellation of certain contracts with the X Corporation, the United States makes a payment of $300,000 to the corporation as compensation for the unamortized cost of such facility. The $300,000 payment is includible in the X Corporation's gross income for July 1955. The adjusted basis of such facility for amortization purposes as of the end of July 1955, computed without regard to any amortization deduction for such month, is $430,000. Accordingly, the corporation is entitled to take an amortization deduction of $300,000 for such month, in lieu of the $10,000 amortization deduction which is otherwise allowable.

Example (2). On November 30, 1954, the Y Corporation purchases an emergency facility, consisting of land with a building thereon, at a cost of $500,000, of which $200,000 is allocable to the land and $300,000 to the building. The certificate covers the entire acquisition. The Y Corporation does not elect to take amortization deductions with respect to such facility, but is entitled to a depreciation deduction with respect to the building at the rate of 3 percent per annum, or $750 per month. On August 12, 1956, as a result of cancellation of certain contracts, the United States makes a payment of $400,000 to the corporation as compensation for the unrecovered cost of such facility. The $400,000 is includible in the Y Corporation's gross income for August 1956. The adjusted basis of the facility as of the end of August 1956, computed without regard to depreciation for such month, is $485,000, of which amount $200,000 is allocable to the land and $285,000 to the building. Accordingly, the corporation is entitled to increase the $750 depreciation deduction for August 1956 by the full amount of the $400,000 payment.

T.D. 6500, 11/25/60, amend T.D. 8116, 12/23/86.

§ 301.9100-7T Time and manner of making the elections under the Tax Reform Act of 1986 (temporary).

(a) Miscellaneous elections. *(1) Elections to which this paragraph applies.* This paragraph applies to the elections set forth below provided under the Tax Reform Act of 1986 (the Act). General rules regarding the time for making the elections are provided in paragraph (a)(2) of this section. General rules regarding the manner for making certain elections are provided in paragraph (a)(3) of this section. Special rules regarding the time and manner for making certain elections are contained in paragraphs (a)-(i) of this section. If a special rule applies to one of the elections listed below, a cross-reference to the special rule is shown in brackets at the end of the description of the "Availability of Election." Paragraph (j) of this section provides that additional information with respect to elections may be required by future regulations or revenue procedures.

Section of Act	Section of Code	Description of election	Availability of election
201(a)	168(b)(5)	Election to depreciate property using the straight line method of recovery with respect to one or more classes of property for any taxable year.	Property placed in service after 12-31-86. Election must be made for taxable year in which property is placed in service. Election shall apply to all property in the class placed in service during the taxable year for which the election is made.
201(a)	168(f)(1)	Election to exclude certain property from the accelerated cost recovery system	Property placed in service after 12-31-86. Election must be made for taxable year in which property is placed in service
201(a)	168(g)(7)	Election to use alternative depreciation system with respect to one or more classes of property for any taxable year (except for residential rental or non-residential real property where the election may be made separately with respect to each property).	Property placed in service after 12-31-86. Election must be made for taxable year in which property is placed in service. Except for residential rental or non-residential real property, election shall apply to all property in the class placed in service during the taxable year for which the election is made.
201(a), 1802(a)	168(h)(6)(F)(iii), 168(j) (as in effect before October 22, 1986.	Election by a tax-exempt controlled entity to treat any gain recognized by the tax-exempt parent on any disposition of an interest in the tax-exempt controlled entity (and to treat any dividends or interest received or accrued from the tax-exempt controlled entity) as unrelated business taxable income under Code section 511 in order for the tax-exempt controlled entity to not be treated as a tax-exempt entity (or as a successor to a tax-exempt entity)	Property placed in service after 9-27-85, but can apply to property placed in service before such date if the tax-exempt controlled entity so elects. [See paragraph (a)(3)(ii) of this section.]
203(a)(1)(B)		Election to apply Act section 201 (including all elections within section 201)	Property placed in service after 7-31-86 and before 1-1-87.
204(e)		Election to have Act section 201 either (i) not apply to any property placed in service during the 1987 or 1988 which is replacement property for property lost damaged or destroyed in a flood which occurred 11-3-85 through 11-7-85 and which was declared a natural disaster area by the President of the United States, or (ii) apply to all such replacement property placed in service during 1985 or 1986	(i) Property placed in service during 1987 or 1988; or (ii) property placed in service during 1985 or 1986.
243(a)		Election to begin the 60 month amortization period with the first month of the taxpayer's first taxable year beginning after 11-19-82 in lieu of the 11-19-82 date or the bus operating authority acquisition date	Bus operating authorities held on 11/19/82, or acquired after that date under a written contract that was binding on that date
243(b)		Election to begin the 60 month amortization period on the first month of the taxpayer's first taxable year beginning after the Deregulation month in lieu of the deregulation month.	Freight forwarder operating authorities held at the beginning of the 60 month period applicable to the taxpayer (i.e. the deregulation date or the first taxable year beginning after the deregulation date).

Section of Act	Section of Code	Description of election	Availability of election
243(a), (b)		Election by a qualified corporate taxpayer to allocate a portion of the cost basis of a qualified acquiring corporation in the stock of an acqtired corporation to the basis of the authority	For bus operating authorities: authorities held on 11/19/82, or acquired after that date under a written contract that was binding on that date. For freight forwarders: authorities held at the beginning of the 60 month period applicable to the taxpayer.
252(a)	42(f)(1)	Election concerning beginning of credit period for low-income housing credit	Buildings placed in service after 12-31-86 and before 1-1-90 (before 1-1-91 for buildings described in Code section 42(n)(2)(B)). [See paragraph (b) of this section.]
252(a)	42(g)(1)	Election concerning qualified low-income housing project to either satisfy the 20-50 or the 40-60 occupancy test	Buildings placed in service after 12-31-86 and before 1-1-90 (before 1-1-91 for buildings described in Code section 42(n)(2)(B)). [See paragraph (b) of this section]
252(a)	42(i)(2)	Election to reduce eligible basis by outstanding balance of Federal loan subsidy	Buildings placed in service after 12-31-86 and before 1-1-90 (before 1-1-91 for buildings described in Code section 42(n)(2)(B)). [See paragraph (b) of this section.]
252(a)	42(j)(5)	Election to have certain partnerships treated as the taxpayer eligible for low-income housing credit	Buildings placed in service after 12-31-86 and before 1-1-90 (before 1-1-91 for buildings described in Code section 42(n)(2)(B) [See paragraph (b) of this section.]
311(d)(2)		Revocation of prior election under Code section 631(a)	Election for taxable years beginning before 1-1-87 may be revoked for taxable years ending after 12-31-86
411(b)(1)	263(i)	For intangible drilling and development costs paid or incurred with respect to an oil, gas, or geothermal well located outside the United States, election to include such costs in adjusted basis for purposes of computing the amount of any deduction under Code section 611 (without regard to section 613).	Costs paid or incurred after 12-31-86 in taxable years ending after such date. [See paragraph (a)(2)(iii) of this section.]
411(b)(2)	616(d)	For expenditures paid or incurred with respect to the development of a mine or other natural deposit (other than an oil, gas, or geothermal well) located outside the United States, election to include such expenditures paid or incurred during the taxable year for which made in adjusted basis for purposes of computing the amount of any deduction under Code section 611 (without regard to section 613)	Costs paid or incurred after 12-31-86 in taxable years ending after such date. [See paragraph (a)(2)(iv) of this section.]
411(b)(2)	617(h)	For expenditures paid or incurred before the development stage for the purpose of ascertaining the existence, location, extent or quality of any deposit or ore or other mineral deposit (other than an oil, gas or geothermal well) located outside the United States, election to include all such expenditures, paid or incurred during the taxable year with respect to any such deposit, in adjusted basis for purposes of computing the amount of any deduction under Code section 611 (without regard to section 613)	Costs paid or incurred after 12-31-86 in taxable years ending after such date. [See paragraph (a)(2)(v) of this section.]

Section of Act	Section of Code	Description of election	Availability of election
501(a)	469(j)(9)	Election to increase basis of property by amount of disallowed credit for purposes of determining gain or loss from a disposition of property used in a passive activity	Taxable years beginning after 12-31-86. [See paragraph (a)(3)(iii) of this section.]
614(b)	1059(c)(4)	Election to determine whether a dividend is extraordinary by reference to the fair market value of the share of stock with respect to which the dividend was received	Dividends declared after July 18, 1986 in taxable years ending after such date.
644(d)	216(b)(3)	Election by a corporative housing corporation to allocate real estate or interest or both to each tenant-stockholder's dwelling unit in a manner which reasonably reflects the costs to the corporation of the tenant-stockholder's dwelling unit.	Taxable years beginning after 12-31-86. [See paragraph (a)(3)(iv) of this section.]
646		Election by an entity to be treated as a trust under the Internal Revenue Code if such entity was created in 1906 as a common law trust and governed by the trust laws of the State of Minnesota, receives royalties from iron ore leases, and income interests in the entity are publicly traded on a national stock exchange.	The election is effective beginning on the first day of the first taxable year beginning after October 22, 1986 and following the year in which the election is made. Such election must be accompanied by a written agreement signed by the board of trustees of the entity.
651	4982(e)(4)	Election by a regulated investment company to use taxable years ending on 11-30 or 12-31 for purposes of computing capital gain net income under Code section 4982.	Calendar years beginning after 12-31-86. [See paragraph (a)(2)(vi) of this section.]
701(a)	56(f)(3)(B)	Election to have amount of net book income be equal to amount earnings and profits.	Taxable years beginning after 12-31-86.
801(a)	448(d)(4)	Election of common parent of an affiliated group that all members of such group be treated as one taxpayer if substantially all the activities of all members of the affiliated group involve performance of services in the same field.	Taxable years beginning after 12-31-86.
801(d)(2)		Election to continue using the cash method of accounting for loans, leases and related party transactions.	Loans, leases, and related party transactions entered into before 9-26-85.
802	474	Election by certain small businesses to use the simplified dollar-value LIFO method	Taxable years beginning after 12-31-86. [See paragraph (a)(3)(v) of this section.]
803(a)	263A(d)(3)	Election to have rules of Code section 236A (relating to capitalization and inclusion in inventory costs of certain expenses) not apply to any plant or animal produced in any farming business conducted by the electing taxpayer.	Unless consent is obtained from the Commissioner, the first taxable year beginning after 12-31-86 during which the taxpayer engages in a farming business. [See paragraph (c) of this section.]

Section of Act	Section of Code	Description of election	Availability of election
806(e)(2)(C)		Election to have net income for the short taxable year of a partnership or S corporation which results from the required change in accounting period included entirely in income for such short taxable year	Partner and shareholder taxable years beginning after 12-31-86 with or within which the short taxable year created under section 806 of the Act ends. [See paragraph (d) of this section.]
		Election to reduce partnership or S corporation income for the short taxable year resulting from a required change in accounting period under section 806 of the Act by an unamortized adjustment amount existing as of October 22, 1986, where such adjustment was required to effectuate a previous accounting period change under Rev. Proc. 72-51, 1972-2 C.B. 832 or Rev. Proc. 83-25, 1983-1 C. B. 689.	Short taxable years of partnerships or S corporations beginning after 12-31-86. [See paragraph (e) of this section.]
811(a)	453C(b)(2)(B)	Election to compute adjusted bases using depreciation deduction used under Code section 312(k)	Taxable years ending after 12-31-86 with respect to dispositions made after 2-26-86.
811(a)	453C(e)(4)	Election to have Code section 453C not apply to obligations arising from sales of timeshares and unimproved residential lots to individuals.	Taxable years ending after 12-31-86 with respect to dispositions made after 2-28-86. [See paragraph (a)(3)(vi) of this section.]
905(a)	165(l)(1)	Election to treat amount of reasonably estimated loss on a deposit in insolvent or bankrupt qualified financial institution as a loss described in Code section 165(c)(3) and incurred in the taxable year.	Taxable years beginning after 12-31-81. [See paragraph (f) of this section.]
905(c)		Election to apply Code section 451(f) (relating to treatment of interest on frozen deposits in certain financial institutions).	Taxable years beginning after 12-31-82 and before 1-1-87.
1301(b)	141(b)(9)	Election by issuer of tax-exempt bonds to treat a portion of an issue as a qualified 501(c)(3) bond if such portion would have qualified as a 501(c)(3) bond had it been issued separately.	Bonds issued after 8-15-86. [See paragraph (g) of this section.]
1301(b)	142(d)(1)	Election by issuer of tax-exempt bonds for residential rental property to satisfy either the 20-50 or the 40-60 occupancy test.	Bonds issued after 8-15-86. [See paragraph (g) of this section.]
1301(b)	142(d)(4)(B)	Election by issuer of tax-exempt bonds for residential rental property to treat the project as a deep rent skewed project.	Bonds issued after 8-15-86. [See paragraph (g) of this section.]
1301(b)	143(k)(9)(D)(iii)	Election to test limited equity cooperative housing as residential real property and not as owner-occupied housing.	Bonds issued after 8-15-86 and before 1-1-89. [See paragraph (g) of this section.]
1301(b)	145(d)	Election by issuer of tax-exempt bonds to have Code section 145 not apply to the issue if the issue is an issue of exempt facility bonds or qualified redevelopment bonds to which the volume cap applies.	Bonds issued after 8-15-86. [See paragraph (g) of this See paragraph (g) of section.]

Section of Act	Section of Code	Description of election	Availability of election
1301(b)	147(b)(4)(A)	Election by issuer of qualified 501(c)(3) to have such bonds treated as meeting the limitation on maturity requirements of Code section 147(b)(1) if the requirements of section 147(b)(4)(B) are met.	Bonds issued after 8-15-86. [See paragraph (g) of this section.]
1704(b)		Election to revoke prior election under Code section 1402(e) (relating to exemption from social security taxes for certain clergy).	Remuneration received in taxable years ending on or after October 22, 1986. [See paragraph (h) of this section.]
1801(a)	168(i) (as in effect before October 22, 1986).	Election to make finance leasing rules inapplicable to property which would otherwise be subject to them under the transitional rule of section 12(c)(1) of the Tax Reform Act of 1984.	Personal property leased under certain lease agreements effective on or after 1-1-84. [See paragraph (a)(3)(vii) of this section.]
1804(e)(4)		Election by a common parent of an affiliated group to apply amendments made the Tax Reform Act of 1984 for taxable years beginning 12-31-83.	Groups which include a corporation which on 6-22-84 is a member of the group which files a consolidated return for such corporation's taxable year which includes 6-22-84.
1807(a)(7)	468B	Election to treat a qualified payment made to a court-ordered fund as a payment to a designated settlement fund.	Generally, liabilities arising out of personal injury, death or property damage that are incurred after 7-18-84 under law in effect before the enactment of Code section 461(h). Election is made for the taxable year in which qualified payments are made to a designated settlement fund.
1809(e)(2)	48(b)(2)	Election by lessee and lessor not to apply the rule of Code section 48(b)(2) concerning the date leased property is treated as originally placed in service	Property originally placed in service after 4-11-84 (as determined under Code section 48(b) prior to its amendment by section 114(a) of the Tax Reform Act of 1984. [see paragraph (a)(3)(vii) of this section.]
1810(l)(4)	7701(b)	Election to be treated as a resident alien.	Taxable years beginning after December 31, 1984. [See paragraph (a)(3)(ix) of this section.]
1879(p)(1)	83(c)(3)	Election to treat certain stock acquired upon the exercise of nonqualified stock options as subject to a substantial risk of forfeiture by reason of Code section 83(c)(3) even though the transfer of stock pursuant to such exercise occurred before 1-1-82, the effective date of section 83(c)(3).	Transfers of stock described in section 1879(p)(1) of the Act. [See paragraph (a)(2)(vii) and (a)(3)(x) of this section.]
1882(c)	3121(w)(2)	Election to revoke prior election under Code section 3121(w) (relating to exemption from social security taxes for certain churches and qualified church-controlled organizations)	Remuneration paid after 12-31-86 unless such electing church or church-controlled organization had withheld and paid over all employment taxes due, as if such election had never been in effect during the period from the stated effective date of the election being being reworked through 12-31-86. [See paragraph (i) of this section.]

(2) Time for making elections. (i) In general. Except as otherwise provided in this section, the elections specified in paragraph (a)(1) of this section shall be made by the later of—

(A) The due date (taking extensions into account) of the tax return for the first taxable year for which the election is to be effective, or

(B) April 15, 1987 (in which case the election generally must be made by amended return).

(ii) No extension of time for payment. Payments of tax due shall be made in accordance with chapter 62 of the Code.

(iii) Time for making the election with respect to foreign intangible drilling costs. With respect to the election under

Act section 411(b)(1) (Code section 263(i)(2)(A)), the election shall be made on a property-by-property basis for each oil, gas, or geothermal property (as defined in Code section 614). The election shall be made by the due date (taking extensions into account) of the income tax return for the first taxable year in which the taxpayer pays or incurs any cost with respect to the development of such property for which the election is available.

(iv) Time for making the election with respect to foreign development expenditures. With respect to the election under Act section 411(b)(2) (Code section 616(d)(2)(A)), the election shall be made for each mineral or other natural deposit not later than the time prescribed by law for filing the income tax return (taking extensions into account) for the taxable year to which such election is applicable.

(v) Time for making the election with respect to foreign exploration expenditures. With respect to the election under Act section 411(b)(2) (Code section 617(h)(2)(A)), the election may be made at any time before the expiration of the period prescribed for filing a claim for credit or refund of the tax imposed by chapter 1 of the Code for the first taxable year for which the taxpayer desires the election to be applicable.

(vi) Time for making certain elections by regulated investment companies. The election under Act section 651 (Code section 4982(e)(4)) shall be made on a statement attached to the form prescribed by the Internal Revenue Service which is used to report and pay the excise tax liability under section 4982. The election shall be filed on or before the later of—

(A) March 15 of the first calendar year beginning after the end of the first excise tax period for which the election is to be effective, or

(B) If the regulated investment company has been granted an extension of time to file a return for the excise tax under Code section 4982 for such excise tax period, the due date (including extensions thereof) for such return. The statement of election under section 4982(e)(4) shall be attached to the prescribed form regardless of whether the regulated investment company is liable for the excise tax imposed by section 4982 for the excise tax period in question.

(vii) Time for making the election with respect to certain nonqualified stock options. The election under section 1879(p)(1) of the Act (Code section 83(c)(3)) shall be made—

(A) By April 21, 1987, in any case in which the operation of any law or rule of law on or before such date would prevent the credit or refund of any overpayment of tax resulting from such election, and

(B) By no later than any date after April 21, 1987 on which the operation of any law or rule of law would prevent the credit or refund of any overpayment of tax resulting from such election.

(3) Manner of making elections. (i) In general. Except as otherwise provided in this section, the elections specified in paragraph (a)(1) of this section shall be made by attaching a statement to the tax return for the taxable year for which the election is to be effective. If because of paragraph (a)(2)(i)(B) of this section the election may be filed after the due date of the tax return for the first taxable year for which the election is to be effective, such statement must be attached to a tax return or amended return for the taxable year to which the election relates. Except as otherwise provided in the return or in the instructions accompanying the return for the taxable year, the statement shall—

(A) Contain the name, address and taxpayer identification number of the electing taxpayer,

(B) Identify the election,

(C) Indicate the section of the Code (or, if the provision is not codified, the section of the Act) under which the election is made,

(D) Specify, as applicable, the period for which the election is being made and/or the property or other items to which the election is to apply, and

(E) Provide any information required by the relevant statutory provisions and any information necessary to show that the taxpayer is entitled to make the election.

(ii) Special rules for making the transitional rule elections with respect to certain tax-exempt controlled entities. The irrevocable election under Act sections 201(a) and 1802(a) (Code sections 168(h)(6)(F)(ii) and 168(j), as in effect before October 22, 1986), shall be made by the tax-exempt controlled entity at the time and in the manner described in paragraphs (a)(2) and (a)(3)(i) of this section. A copy of the election statement filed by the tax-exempt controlled entity shall also be attached to the Federal tax returns (e.g., Form 990 or 5500) of each of the tax-exempt shareholders or beneficiaries of the controlled entity.

(iii) Special rule for making the election with respect to gain or loss from a disposition of property used in a passive activity. The election under Act section 501(a) (Code section 469(j)(9)) shall be made on the form prescribed by the Internal Revenue Service for computing the taxpayer's passive activity loss and credit for the taxable year in which the property is disposed.

(iv) Special rules for making the election with respect to cooperative housing corporations. The election under Act section 644(d) (Code section 216(b)(3)(B)(ii)) may be made by a cooperative housing corporation with respect to its real estate taxes or interest or both. The election is available for any taxable year beginning after December 31, 1986, if the cooperative housing corporation has, by January 31 of the year following the first calendar year that includes any period to which the election applies, furnished to each tenant-stockholder during that period a written statement showing the amount of the allocation (or allocations) under section 216(b)(3)(B)(i) attributable to such tenant-stockholder's dwelling unit (or units) for that period. Any cooperative housing corporation making the election shall do so in accordance with paragraphs (a)(2) and (3) of this section and shall identify in the statement described in paragraph (a)(3) of this section whether the election is for real estate taxes or interest or both.

(v) Special rules for making the election with respect to the simplified dollar-value LIFO method. The election under Act section 802 (Code section 474) may be made only if the taxpayer files with the taxpayer's income tax return for the taxable year as of the close of which the method is first to be used a statement of the taxpayer's election to use the simplified dollar-value LIFO inventory method. The statement shall be on Form 970 pursuant to the instructions to the form and to the requirements of the regulations under section 474, or in such other manner as may be acceptable to the Commissioner.

(vi) Special rules for making the election to have section 453C not apply to obligations arising from sales of timeshares and unimproved residential lots to individuals. The election under Act section 811(a) (Code section 453C(e)(4)) to have section 453C not apply to obligations arising from sales of timeshares and unimproved residential lots to individuals may be made with respect to any obligation, or with respect to a class of such obligations. In the case of an election made with respect to a class of obligations, such election shall describe the class of obligations with such specificity as to make the class readily identifiable.

(vii) Special rules for making certain finance leasing transitional rule elections. The election relating to finance leases under Act section 1801(a)(1) (Code section 168(i) as in effect before October 22, 1986) shall be made by the lessor under a lease agreement subject to the finance lease rules of section 168(i) of the Code, as in effect before October 22, 1986, by noting this election in the books and records relating to the lease agreement within 12 months after February 5, 1987.

(viii) Special rules for making the election relating to the date leased property is treated as originally placed in service. The election under Act section 1809(e)(2) (Code section 48(b)(2)) must be made jointly by the lessee and the lessor. The election is made jointly when both the lessee and the lessor make the election in accordance with paragraphs (a)(2) and (a)(3)(i) of this section. In addition to the other information required to be provided under paragraph (a)(3)(i) of this section, the statement described therein shall include a copy of the lease agreement and shall be signed by both the lessee and the lessor.

(ix) Special rules for making the election to be treated as a resident alien. The election under Act section 1810(l)(4) (Code section 7701(b)) to the treated as a resident under Code section 7701(b) shall be made by an alien individual by attaching a statement to the individual's income tax return (Form 1040), for the taxable year for which the election is to be in effect (the election year). The alien individual may not make this election until such time as he has satisfied the substantial presence test of Code section 7701(b)(1)(A)(ii) for the year following the election year. If an alien individual has not satisfied the substantial presence test for the year following the election year as of the due date (without regard to extensions) of the tax return for the election year, the alien individual may request an extension of time for filing the return until after he has satisfied such test, provided that he pays with his extension application the amount of tax he expects to owe for the election year, computed as if he were a non-resident alien throughout the election year. The statement shall include the name and address of the alien individual and contain a signed declaration that the election is being made. It must specify—

(A) That the alien individual was not a resident in the year immediately preceding the election year;

(B) That the alien individual is a resident in the year immediately following the election year under the substantial presence test and the individual's number of days of presence in the United States during such year;

(C) The date or dates of the alien individual's 31 consecutive day period of presence and continuous presence in the United States during the election year; and

(D) The date or dates of absence from the United States during the election year that are deemed to be days of presence.

(x) Special rules for making the election with respect to the treatment of the exercise of certain nonqualified stock options. The election under Act section 1879(p)(1) (Code section 83(c)(3)) is made by filing on Form 1040X a claim for credit or refund of the overpayment of tax resulting from the election. In order to satisfy the requirements of § 301.6402-2(b)(1) (relating to grounds set forth in claim), the claim for credit or refund must set forth)—

(A) The date on which the option was granted,

(B) The name of the corporation which granted the option,

(C) The date on which the stock was transferred pursuant to the exercise of the option,

(D) The fair market value of such stock on December 4, 1973,

(E) The fair market value on July 1, 1974 of the stock received upon the reorganization of the corporation which granted the option, and

(F) The date on which the taxpayer sold substantially all of the stock received in such reorganization. The taxpayer shall file a single claim for credit or refund of the entire overpayment of tax resulting from the election under Act section 1879(p)(1).

(4) Revocation. (i) Irrevocable elections. The elections described in this section under Act sections 201(a) (Code sections 168(b)(5), 168(f)(1), 168(g)(7), and 168(h)(6)(F)(ii)), 203(a)(1)(B), 252(a) (Code sections 42(f)(1), 42(g)(1), 42(i)(2), and 42(j)(5)), 411(b)(1) (Code section 263(i)), 411(b)(2)(A) (Code section 616(d)(2)(A)), 501(a) (Code section 469(j)(9)), 801(d)(2), 905(c), 1301(b) (Code sections 141(b)(9), 142(d)(1), 142(d)(4)(B), 143(k)(9)(D)(iii), 145(d), and 147(b)(4)(A)), (Code section 2652(a)(3)), 1704(b), 1802(a) (Code section 168(j) as in effect before October 22, 1986), 1804(e)(4), 1879(p)(1) (Code section 83(c)(3)), and 1882(C) (Code section 3121(w)(2)) are irrevocable.

(ii) Elections revocable with the consent of the Commissioner. The elections described in this section under Act sections 204(e), 243(a), 243(b), 243(a)(b), 411(b)(2)(B) (Code section 617(h)(2)(A)), 614(b) (Code section 1059(c)(4)), 644(d) (Code section 216(b)(3)), 646, 651 (Code section 4982(e)(4)(B)), 701(a) (Code section 56(f)(3)(B)), 801(a) (Code section 448(d)(4)), 802 (Code section 474), 803(a) (Code section 263A(d)(3)), 806(e)(2)(C) (and the election described in H.R. Rep. No. 99-841 at II-320), 811(a) (Code sections 453C(b)(2)(B)(i) and 453C(e)(4)), 905(a) (Code section 165(l)(1)), 1801(a) (Code section 168(i) as in effect before October 22, 1986), 1807(a)(7) (Code section 468B), 1809(e)(2) (Code section 48(b)(2)), and 1810(l)(4) (Code section 7701(b)) are revocable only with the consent of the Commissioner.

(iii) Freely revocable elections. The election described in this section under Act section 311(d)(2) is freely revocable.

(b) Elections with respect to the low-income housing credit. The elections under Act section 252(a) (Code sections 42(f)(1), 42(g)(1), 42(i)(2), and 42(j)(5)) must be made for the taxable year in which the project is placed in service and shall be made in the certification required to be filed pursuant to section 42(l)(1).

(c) Election to have the rules of section 263A (relating to capitalization and inclusion in inventory costs of certain expenses) not apply to any plant or animal produced in any farming business conducted by the electing taxpayer. *(1) In general.* This paragraph applies to the election under Act section 803(a) (Code section 263A(d)(3)) to have the rules of section 263A (relating to capitalization and inclusion in inventory costs of certain expenses) not apply to any plant or animal produced in any farming business conducted by the electing taxpayer. The election is available to taxpayers engaged in the business of farming, including producers of agricultural crops, livestock, nursery stock, sod, trees bearing fruit, nuts or other crops, and ornamental trees (for purposes of section 263A, an evergreen tree that is more than 6 years old at the time it is severed from the roots shall not be treated as an ornamental tree). The election is not available to a corporation, partnership, or tax shelter that is required to use the accrual method of accounting under section 447 or section 448(a)(3), or farming syndicates (as defined in section 464(c)), or with respect to the planting, cultivation, maintenance or development of pistachio trees. In addition, the election does not apply with respect to costs incurred for the planting, cultivation, maintenance or development of any citrus or almond grove incurred during the 4-taxable-year period beginning with the taxable year in which such grove was planted. If a citrus or almond grove is planted in more than one taxable year, the portion of the grove planted in one taxable year is treated as a separate grove for this purpose.

(2) Time and manner of making the election. Unless consent is obtained from the Commissioner, the election may only be made for the taxpayer's first taxable hear that begins after December 31, 1966, and during which the taxpayer engages in a farming business. The election shall be made on the Schedule E, F or other schedule required to be attached to the income tax return for the first taxable year for which the election is effective. In the case of a partnership or S corporation, the election must be made at the partner or shareholder level.

(3) Election treated as if made if certain requirements satisfied. A taxpayer eligible to make the election under section 263A(d)(3) shall be treated as having made the election if such taxpayer reports income and expense in accordance with the rules under the election on a timely filed income tax return.

(4) Revocation. Once the election is made, it is revocable only with the consent of the Commissioner.

(5) Special rules for treatment of expenses. If the election is made, the plant or animal produced is treated as section 1245 property and gain is recaptured (treated as ordinary income) in the amount of deductions which, but for the election, would have been required to be capitalized with respect to the plant or animal. If the taxpayer or a related person makes the election, a non-accelerated method of depreciation (as defined in section 168(g)(2)) shall be applied to all property used predominantly in any farming business of the taxpayer or related person and placed in service in any taxable year during which the election is in effect. For purposes of this election, related party means: (i) the members of the taxpayer's family (defined for this purpose to include the spouse of the taxpayer and any of this or her children who have not reached the age of 18 as of the last day of the taxable year); (ii) any corporation (including an S corporation) 50 percent or more of the value of which is owned directly or indirectly (through the application of section 318) by the taxpayer or members of the taxpayer's family; (iii) any corporation that is a member of the same controlled group (within the meaning of section 1563) as the taxpayer; and (iv) any partnership if 50 percent or more of the value of the interests in such partnership is owned directly or indirectly (through the application of section 318) by the taxpayer or members of the taxpayer's family.

(d) Election with respect to the treatment of net income for the short taxable year resulting from a required change in accounting period. This paragraph applies to the election under section 806(e)(2)(C) of the Act. Net income for the short taxable year resulting form a required change in accounting period under the provisions of section 806 of the Act which is to be included ratably in the partners' and S corporation shareholders' income for the first four taxable years (including the short taxable year) beginning after December 31, 1986, or included entirely in income for the short taxable year at the election of the partner or shareholder, shall be taken into account in accordance with section 702 (with respect to partners) and section 1366 (with respect to S corporation shareholders).

(e) Election with respect to reducing partnership or S corporation income for the short taxable year resulting from a required change in accounting period under section 806 of the Act by an unamortized adjustment amount existing as of October 22, 1986. *(1) In general.* This paragraph applies to the election described in H.R. Rep. No. 99-841 at II-320.

(2) Partnerships or S corporations that make the election to reduce income for the short taxable year by an unamortized adjustment amount existing as of October 22, 1986. Where a partnership or S corporation elects to reduce its income for the short taxable year required under the provisions of section 806 of the Act by the unamortized adjustment amount existing as of October 22, 1986, in accordance with paragraph (a) of this section, the income for the short taxable year (reduced by the unamortized adjustment amount) may then be subject to the election, under section 806(e)(2)(C) of the Act, by partners and S corporation shareholders to include all the net income for the short taxable year entirely in income for the partners' or shareholders' taxable year with or within which the short taxable year ends.

(3) Partnerships or S corporations that do not make the election to reduce income for the short taxable year by an unamortized adjustment amount existing as of October 22, 1986. Where a partnership or S corporation does not elect to reduce its income for the short taxable year created by the provisions of section 806 of the Act by the unamortized adjustment amount existing as of October 22, 1986, as provided in paragraph (a) of this section, the short taxable year required under the provisions of section 806 of the Act shall be considered one taxable year for purposes of amortizing the adjustment amount under the requirements of Rev. Proc. 72-51, 1972-2 C.B. 832, or Rev. Proc. 83-25, 1983-1 C.B 689. The net income of the partnership or S corporation after reduction by the adjustment amount for the short taxable year may then be subject to the election under section 806(e)(2)(C) of the Act by partners or S corporation shareholders to include all the net income for the short taxable year entirely in income for the partners' or shareholders' taxable year with or within which the short taxable year of the partnership or S corporation ends.

(f) Cross-reference. See § 301.9100-8(d) for rules on both the election under section 950(a) of the Act, relating to section 165(l)(1), and the related election under section 165(l)(5), added by section 1009(d) of the Technical and Miscellaneous Revenue Act of 1988, 102 Stat. 3342. An election under section 165(l) is available only to qualified individuals and, in general, applies to reasonably estimated losses on deposits in an insolvent or bankrupt financial institution.

(g) Elections with respect to certain bonds. The elections under Act section 1301(b) (Code sections 141(b)(9), 142(d)(1), 142(d)(4)(B), 143(k)(9)(D)(iii), 145(d), and 147(b)(4)(A)) must be made in the § 5h.5(g) bond indenture or a related document (as defined in § 1.103-13(b)(8)) on or before the date of issue. With respect to obligations issued on or before March 9, 1987 these elections must be made on or before March 9, 1987 and need not be made in the bond indenture or a related document, but must be made in writing and retained as part of the issuer's books and records.

(h) Revocation of the election for exemption from social security taxes by certain clergy. *(1) In general.* This paragraph applies to the election under Act section 1704(b) to revoke an election under section 1402(e)(1) of the Code by a duly ordained, commissioned, or licensed minister of a church, a member of a religious order (other than a member of a religious order who has taken a vow of poverty as a member of such order), or a Christian Science practitioner. Only elections which are effective for the taxable year containing October 22, 1986 may be revoked under this paragraph.

(2) Time for revoking the election. The election shall be revoked by filing Form 2031 before the date on which the individual becomes entitled to benefits under sections 202(a) or 223 of the Social Security Act (without regard to sections 202(j)(1) or 223(b) of such Act), and not later than the due date of the Federal income tax return (including any extension thereof) for the individual's first taxable year beginning after October 22, 1986.

(3) Manner of revoking the election. To revoke an election under section 1402(a)(1), the individual shall file Form 2031 in accordance with the instructions accompanying that form. The revocation shall be made effective, as designated by the individual on the form, either with respect to the individual's first taxable year beginning after October 22, 1986.

(4) Special rules for payment of self-employment taxes with respect to certain taxable years ending on or after October 22, 1986. (i) Elections filed after the due date of the Federal income tax return. In Form 2031 is filed on or after the due date of the Federal income tax return (including any extension thereof) for the individual's first taxable year ending on or after October 22, 1986, and the election made therein is effective with respect to that taxable year, Form 2031 shall be accompanied by an amended Federal income tax return for such taxable year together with payment in full of an amount equal to the total of the taxes that would have been imposed by section 1401 of the Code with respect to all of the individual's income derived in that taxable year which would have constituted net earnings from self-employment for purposes of chapter 2 of subtitle A of the Code (notwithstanding paragraph (4) or (5) of section 1402(c)) but for the exemption under section 1402(e)(1).

(ii) Elections filed before the due date of the Federal income tax return. If Form 2031 is filed before the due date of the Federal income tax return (including any extension thereof) for the individual's first taxable year ending on or after October 22, 1986, and the election is effective with respect to that taxable year, payment in full of an amount equal to the total of the taxes that would have been imposed by section 1401 of the Code with respect to all of the individual's income derived in that taxable year which would have constituted net earnings from self-employment for purposes of chapter 2 of the subtitle A of the Code (notwithstanding paragraph (4) or (5) of section 1402(c)) but for the exemption under section 1402(e)(1) shall be made:

(A) In the case of Forms 2031 that are filed on or before the date on which the individual's Federal income tax return for such first taxable year is filed, with the individual's Federal income tax return for such taxable year; and

(B) In the case of Forms 2031 that are filed after the date on which the individual's Federal income tax return for such first taxable year is filed, with an amended Federal income tax return for that taxable year filed on or before the due date for the individual's Federal income tax return (including any extension thereof) for such taxable year.

(iii) Interest on amounts paid after the due date of the Federal income tax return. If any amount of tax imposed by section 1401 for an individual's taxable year with respect to which an election under this paragraph (h) is effective is paid after the due date of the individual's Federal income tax return (without regard to extensions) for such taxable year, interest will be assessed on such tax from the due date of such return (without regard to extensions) to the date on which such tax is paid.

(5) Revocability of the revocation of the election. Once having filed Form 2031, the individual may not thereafter file an application for an exemption under section 1402(e)(1).

(6) Effective date of this provision. This provision shall apply with respect to remuneration received in the taxable years for which the individual designates the revocation to be effective, as described in paragraph (h)(3) of this section, and with respect to monthly insurance benefits payable under title II of the Social Security Act on the basis of the wages and self-employment income of any individual for months in or after the calendar year in which such individual's application for revocation is effective (and lump-sum death payments payable under such title on the basis of such wages and self-employment income in the case of deaths occurring in or after such calendar year).

(i) Revocation of the election for exemption from social security taxes by certain churches on qualified church-controlled organizations. *(1) In general.* This paragraph applies to the election under Act section 1882 (Code section 3121(w)(2)) to revoke an election under section 3121(w) by a church or qualified church-controlled organization (as defined in section 3121(w)(3)).

(2) Time and manner of revoking the election. The revocation described in this paragraph (i) shall be made by filing a Form 941 on or before the due date for filing Form 941 (without regard to extensions) for the first quarter for which the revocation is to be effective, accompanied by payment in full of the taxes that would be due for that quarter had there been no election under section 3121(w). See paragraph (i)(4) of this section for the effective date of revocation made under this paragraph (i).

(3) Revocability of the revocation of the election. Once an election under section 3121(w) is revoked under this paragraph (i), a new election under section 3121(w) may not be made.

(4) Effective date of this paragraph. A revocation made under this paragraph (i) shall be effective for the quarter of the calendar year covered by the Form 941 on which the revocation is made in accordance with paragraph (i)(2) of this section and all subsequent quarters. However, no revocation shall be effective prior to January 1, 1987 unless such electing church or church-controlled organization had withheld and paid over all employment taxes due, as if such election had never been in effect, during the period from the effective date of the election being revoked through December 31, 1986.

(j) Additional information required. Later regulations or revenue procedures issued under provisions of the Code or Act covered by this section may require the furnishing of information in addition to that which was furnished with the statement of election described in this section. In such event, the later regulations or revenue procedures will provide guidance with respect to the furnishing of such additional information. (26 U.S.C. 7805).

T.D. 8124, 2/4/87, amend T.D. 8180, 2/29/88, T.D. 8267, 9/21/89, T.D. 8435, 9/18/92, T.D. 8513, 12/28/93, T.D. 8530, 3/17/94, T.D. 8644, 12/16/95.

§ 1.169-1 Amortization of pollution control facilities.

Caution: The Treasury has not yet amended Reg § 1.169-1 to reflect changes made by P.L. 94-455.

(a) Allowance of deduction. *(1) In general.* Under section 169(a), every person, at his election, shall be entitled to a deduction with respect to the amortization of the amortizable basis (as defined in § 1.169-3) of any certified pollution control facility (as defined in § 1.169-2), based on a period of 60 months. Under section 169(b) and paragraph (a) of § 1.169-4, the taxpayer may further elect to begin such 60-month period either with the month following the month in which the facility is completed or acquired or with the first month of the taxable year succeeding the taxable year in which such facility is completed or acquired. Under section 169(c), a taxpayer who has elected under section 169(b) to take the amortization deduction provided by section 169(a) may, at any time after making such election and prior to the expiration of the 60-month amortization period, elect to discontinue the amortization deduction for the remainder of the 60-month period in the manner prescribed in paragraph (b)(1) of § 1.169-4. In addition, if on or before May 18, 1971, an election under section 169(a) has been made, consent is hereby given to revoke such election without the consent of the Commissioner in the manner prescribed in (b)(2) of § 1.169-4.

(2) Amount of deduction. With respect to each month of such 60-month period which falls within the taxable year, the amortization deduction shall be an amount equal to the amortizable basis of the certified pollution control facility at the end of such month divided by the number of months (including the month for which the deduction is computed) remaining in such 60-month period. The amortizable basis at the end of any month shall be computed without regard to the amortization deduction for such month. The total amortization deduction with respect to a certified pollution control facility for a taxable year is the sum of the amortization deductions allowable for each month of the 60-month period which falls within such taxable year. If a certified pollution control facility is sold or exchanged or otherwise disposed of during 1 month, the amortization deduction (if any) allowable to the original holder in respect of such month shall be that portion of the amount to which such person would be entitled for a full month which the number of days in such month during which the facility was held by such person bears to the total number of days in such month.

(3) Effect on other deductions. (i) The amortization deduction provided by section 169 with respect to any month shall be in lieu of the depreciation deduction which would otherwise be allowable under section 167 or a deduction in lieu of depreciation which would otherwise be allowable under paragraph (b) of § 1.162-11 for such month.

(ii) If the adjusted basis of such facility as computed under section 1011 for purposes other than the amortization deduction provided by section 169 is in excess of the amortizable basis, as computed under § 1.169-3, such excess shall be recovered through depreciation deductions under the rules of section 167. See section 169(g).

(iii) See section 179 and paragraph (e)(1)(ii) of § 1.179-1 and paragraph (b)(2) of § 1.169-3 for additional first-year depreciation in respect of a certified pollution control facility.

(4) [Removed]

(5) Special rules. (i) In the case of a certified pollution control facility held by one person for life with the remainder to another person, the amortization deduction under section 169(a) shall be computed as if the life tenant were the absolute owner of the property and shall be allowable to the life tenant during his life.

(ii) If the assets of a corporation which has elected to take the amortization deduction under section 169(a) are acquired by another corporation in a transaction to which section 381 (relating to carryovers in certain corporate acquisitions) applies, the acquiring corporation is to be treated as if it were the distributor or transferor corporation for purposes of this section.

(iii) For the right of estates and trusts to amortize pollution control facilities see section 642(f) and § 1.642(f)-1. For the allowance of the amortization deduction in the case of pollution control facilities of partnerships, see section 703 and § 1.703-1.

(6) Depreciation subsequent to discontinuance or in the case of revocation of amortization. A taxpayer which elects in the manner prescribed under paragraph (b)(1) of § 1.169-4 to discontinue amortization deductions or under paragraph (b)(2) of § 1.169-4 to revoke an election under section 169(a) with respect to a certified pollution control facility is entitled, if such facility is of a character subject to the allowance for depreciation provided in section 167, to a deduction for depreciation (to the extent allowable) with respect to such facility. In the case of an election to discontinue an amortization deduction, the deduction for depreciation shall begin with the first month as to which such amortization deduction is not applicable and shall be computed on the adjusted basis of the property as of the beginning of such month (see section 1011 and the regulations thereunder). Such depreciation deduction shall be based upon the remaining portion of the period authorized under section 167 for the facility as determined, as of the first day of the first month as of which the amortization deduction is not applicable. If the taxpayer so elects to discontinue the amortization deduction under section 169(a), such taxpayer shall not be entitled to any further amortization deduction under this section and section 169(a) with respect to such pollution control facility. In the case of a revocation of an election under section 169(a), the deduction for depreciation shall begin as of the time such depreciation deduction would have been taken but for the election under section 169(a). See paragraph (b)(2) of § 1.169-4 for rules as to filing amended returns for years for which amortization deductions have been taken.

(7) Definitions. Except as otherwise provided in § 1.169-2, all terms used in section 169 and the regulations thereunder shall have the meaning provided by this section and §§ 1.169-2 through 1.169-4.

(b) Examples. This section may be illustrated by the following examples:

Example (1). On September 30, 1970, the X Corporation, which uses the calendar year as its taxable year, completes the installation of a facility all of which qualifies as a certified pollution control facility within the meaning of paragraph (a) of § 1.169-2. The cost of the facility is $120,000 and the period referred to in paragraph (a)(6) of § 1.169-2 is 10 years in accordance with the rules set forth in paragraph (a) of § 1.169-4, on its income tax return filed for 1970, X elects to take amortization deductions under section 169(a) with respect to the facility and to begin the 60-month amortization period with October 1970, the month following the month in which it was completed. The amortizable basis at the end of October 1970 (determined without regard to the amortization deduction under section 169(a) for that month) is $120,000. The allowable amortization deduction with respect to such facility for the taxable year 1970 is $6,000, computed as follows:

Monthly amortization deductions:	
October: $120,000 divided by 60	$2,000
November: $118,000 (that is, $120,000 minus $2,000) divided by 59	2,000
December: $116,000 (that is, $118,000 minus $2,000) divided by 59	2,000
Total amortization deduction for 1970	6,000

Example (2). Assume the same facts as in example (1). Assume further that on May 20, 1972, X properly files notice of its election to discontinue the amortization deductions with the month of June 1972. The adjusted basis of the facility as of June 1, 1972, is $80,000, computed as follows:

Yearly amortization deductions:	
1970 (as computed in example (1))	$ 6,000
1971 (computed in accordance with example (1))	24,000
1972 (for the first 5 months of 1972 computed in accordance with example (1))	10,000
Total amortization deductions for 20 months	40,000
Adjusted basis as beginning of amortization period	120,000
Less: Amortization deductions	40,000
Adjusted basis as of June 1, 1972	80,000

Beginning as of June 1, 1972, the deduction for depreciation under section 167 is allowable with respect to the property on its adjusted basis of $80,000.

T.D. 7116, 5/17/71, amend T.D. 7203, 8/24/72.

§ 1.169-2 Definitions.

Caution: The Treasury has not yet amended Reg § 1.169-2 to reflect changes made by P.L. 94-455, P.L. 92-178.

(a) Certified pollution control facility. *(1) In general.* Under section 169(d), the term "certified pollution control facility" means a facility which—

(i) The Federal certifying authority certifies, in accordance with the rules prescribed in paragraph (c) of this section, is a "treatment facility" described in subparagraph (2) of this paragraph, and

(ii) Is "a new identifiable facility" (as defined in paragraph (b) of this section).

For profitmaking abatement works limitation, see paragraph (d) of this section.

(2) Treatment facility. For purposes of subparagraph (1)(i) of this paragraph, a "treatment facility" is a facility which (i) is used to abate or control water or atmospheric pollution or contamination by removing, altering, disposing, or storing of pollutants, contaminants, wastes, or heat and (ii) is used in connection with a plant or other property in operation before January 1, 1969. Determinations under subdivision (i) of this subparagraph shall be made solely by the Federal certifying authority. See subparagraph (3) of this paragraph. For meaning of the phrases "plant or other property" and "in operation before January 1, 1969," see subparagraphs (4) and (5), respectively, of this paragraph.

(3) Facilities performing multiple functions or used in connection with several plants, etc. (i) If a facility is designed to perform or does perform a function in addition to abating or controlling water or atmospheric pollution or contamination by removing, altering, disposing or storing pollutants, contaminants, wastes, or heat, such facility shall be a treatment facility only with respect to that part of the cost thereof which is certified by the Federal certifying authority as attributable to abating of controlling water or atmospheric pollution or contamination. For example, if a machine which performs a function in addition to abating water pollution is installed at a cost of $100,000 in, and is used only in connection with, a plant which was in operation before January 1, 1969, and if the Federal certifying authority certifies that $30,000 of the cost of such machine is allocable to its function of abating water pollution, such $30,000 will be deemed to be the adjusted basis for purposes of determining gain for purposes of paragraph (a) of § 1.169-3.

(ii) If a facility is used in connection with more than one plant or other property, and at least one such plant or other property was not in operation before January 1, 1969, such facility shall be a treatment facility only to the extent of that part of the cost thereof certified by the Federal certifying authority as attributable to abating or controlling water or atmospheric pollution in connection with plants or other property in operation before January 1, 1969. For example, if a machine is constructed after December 31, 1968, at a cost of $100,000 and is used in connection with a number of plants only some of which were in operation before January 1, 1969, and if the Federal certifying authority certifies that $20,000 of the cost of such machine is allocable to its function of abating or controlling water pollution in connection with the plants or other property in operation before January 1, 1969, such $20,000 will be deemed to be the adjusted basis for purposes of determining gain for purposes of paragraph (a) of § 1.169-3. In a case in which the Federal certifying authority certifies the percentage of a facility which is used in connection with plants or other property in operation before January 1, 1969, the adjusted basis for the purposes of determining gain for purposes of paragraph (a) of § 1.169-3 of the portion of the facility so used shall be the adjusted basis for determining gain of the entire facility multiplied by such percentage.

(4) Plant or other property. As used in subparagraph (2) of this paragraph, the phrase "plant or other property" means any tangible property whether or not such property is used in the trade or business or held for the production of income. Such term includes, for example, a papermill, a motor vehicle, or a furnace in an apartment house.

(5) In operation before January 1, 1969. (i) For purposes of subparagraph (2) of this paragraph and section 169(d), a plant or other property will be considered to be in operation before January 1, 1969, if prior to that date such plant or other property was actually performing the function for which it was constructed or acquired. For example, a papermill which is completed in July 1968, but which is not actually used to produce paper until 1969 would not be considered to be in operation before January 1, 1969. The fact that such plant or other property was only operating at partial capacity prior to January 1, 1969, or was being used as a

standby facility prior to such date, shall not prevent its being considered to be in operation before such date.

(ii) (a) A piece of machinery which replaces one which was in operation prior to January 1, 1969, and which was a part of the manufacturing operation carried on by the plant but which does not substantially increase the capacity of the plant will be considered to be in operation prior to January 1, 1969. However, an additional machine that is added to a plant which was in operation before January 1, 1969, and which represents a substantial increase in the plant's capacity will not be considered to have been in operation before such date. There shall be deemed to be a substantial increase in the capacity of a plant or other property as of the time its capacity exceeds by more than 20 percent its capacity on December 31, 1968.

(b) In addition, if the total replacements of equipment in any single taxable year beginning after December 31, 1968, represent the replacement of a substantial portion of a manufacturing plant which had been in operation before such date, such replacement shall be considered to result in a new plant which was not in operation before such date. Thus, if a substantial portion of a plant which was in existence before January 1, 1969, is subsequently destroyed by fire and such substantial portion is replaced in a taxable year beginning after that date, such replacement property shall not be considered to have been in operation before January 1, 1969. The replacement of a substantial portion of a plant or other property shall be deemed to have occurred if, during a single taxable year, the taxpayer replaces manufacturing or production facilities or equipment which comprises such plant or other property and which has an adjusted basis (determined without regard to the adjustments provided in section 1016(a) (2) and (3)) in excess of 20 percent of the adjusted basis (so determined) of such plant or other property determined as of the first day of such taxable year.

(6) Useful life. For purposes of section 169 and the regulations thereunder, the terms "useful life" and "actual life" shall mean the shortest period authorized under section 167 and the regulations thereunder if an election were not made under section 169.

(b) New identifiable facility. *(1) In general.* For purposes of paragraph (a)(1)(ii) of this section, the term "new identifiable facility" includes only tangible property (not including a building and its structural components referred to in subparagraph (2)(i) of this paragraph, other than a building and its structural components which under subparagraph (2)(ii) of this paragraph is exclusively a treatment facility) which—

(i) Is of a character subject to the allowance for depreciation provided in section 167.

(ii) (a) Is property the construction, reconstruction, or erection (as defined in subparagraph (2)(ii) of this paragraph) of which is completed by the taxpayer after December 31, 1968, or

(b) Is property acquired by the taxpayer after December 31, 1968, if the original use of the property commences with the taxpayer and commences after such date (see subparagraph (2)(iii) of this paragraph), and

(iii) Is placed in service (as defined in subparagraph (2)(v) of this paragraph) prior to January 1, 1975.

(2) Meaning of terms. (i) For purposes of subparagraph (1) of this paragraph, the terms "building" and "structural component" shall be construed in a manner consistent with the principles set forth in paragraph (e) of § 1.48-1. Thus, for example, the following rules are applicable:

(a) The term "building" generally means any structure or edifice enclosing a space within its walls, and usually covered by a roof, the purpose of which is, for example, to provide shelter or housing, or to provide working, office, parking, display, or sales space. The term includes, for example, structures such as apartment houses, factory and office buildings, warehouses, barns, garages, railway or bus stations, and stores. Such term includes any such structure constructed by, or for, a lessee even if such structure must be removed, or ownership of such structure reverts to the lessor, at the termination of the lease. Such term does not include (1) a structure which is essentially an item of machinery or equipment, or (2) an enclosure which is so closely combined with the machinery or equipment which it supports, houses, or serves that it must be replaced, retired, or abandoned contemporaneously with such machinery or equipment, and which is depreciated over the life of such machinery or equipment. Thus, the term "building" does not include such structures as oil and gas storage tanks, grain storage bins, silos, fractioning towers, blast furnaces, coke ovens, brick kilns, and coal tipples.

(b) The term "structural components" includes, for example, chimneys, and other components relating to the operating or maintenance of a building. However, the term "structural components" does not include machinery or a device which serves no function other than the abatement or control of water or atmospheric pollution.

(ii) For purposes of subparagraph (1) of this paragraph, a building and its structural components will be considered to be exclusively a treatment facility if its only function is the abatement or control of air or water pollution. However, the incidental recovery of profits from wastes or otherwise shall not be deemed to be a function other than the abatement or control of air or water pollution. A building and its structural components which serve no function other than the treatment of wastes will be considered to be exclusively a treatment facility even if it contains areas for employees to operate the treatment facility, rest rooms for such workers, and an office for the management of such treatment facility. However, for example, if a portion of a building is used for the treatment of sewage and another portion of the building is used for the manufacture of machinery, the building is not exclusively a treatment facility. The Federal certifying authority will not certify as to what is a building and its structural components within the meaning of subdivision (i) of this subparagraph.

(iii) For purposes of subparagraph (1)(ii)(a) and (b) of this paragraph (relating to construction, reconstruction, or erection after December 31, 1968, and original use after December 31, 1968) and paragraph (b)(1) of § 1.169-3 (relating to definition of amortizable basis), the principles set forth in paragraph (a)(1) and (2) of § 1.167(c)-1 and in paragraphs (b) and (c) of § 1.48-2 shall be applied. Thus, for example, the following rules are applicable:

(a) Property is considered as constructed, reconstructed, or erected by the taxpayer if the work is done for him in accordance with his specifications.

(b) The portion of the basis of property attributable to construction, reconstruction, or erection after December 31, 1968, consists of all costs of construction, reconstruction, or erection allocable to the period after December 31, 1968, including the cost or other basis of materials entering into such work (but not including, in the case of reconstruction of property, the adjusted basis of the property as of the time such reconstruction is commenced).

(c) It is not necessary that materials entering into construction, reconstruction or erection be acquired after December 31, 1968, or that they be new in use.

(d) If construction or erection by the taxpayer began after December 31, 1968, the entire cost or other basis of such construction or erection may be taken into account for purposes of determining the amortizable basis under section 169.

(e) Construction, reconstruction, or erection by the taxpayer begins when physical work is started on such construction, reconstruction, or erection.

(f) Property shall be deemed to be acquired when reduced to physical possession or control.

(g) The term "original use" means the first use to which the property is put, whether or not such use corresponds to the use of such property by the taxpayer. For example, a reconditioned or rebuilt machine acquired by the taxpayer after December 31, 1968, for pollution control purposes will not be treated as being put to original use by the taxpayer regardless of whether it was used for purposes other than pollution control by its previous owner. Whether property is reconditioned or rebuilt property is a question of fact. Property will not be treated as reconditioned or rebuilt merely because it contains some used parts.

(iv) For purposes of subparagraph (1)(iii) of this paragraph (relating to property placed in service prior to January 1, 1975), the principles set forth in paragraph (d) of § 1.46-3 are applicable. Thus, property shall be considered placed in service in the earlier of the following taxable years:

(a) The taxable year in which, under the taxpayer's depreciation practice, the period for depreciation with respect to such property begins or would have begun; or

(b) The taxable year in which the property is placed in a condition or state of readiness and availability for the abatement or control of water or atmospheric pollution.

Thus, if property meets the conditions of (b) of this subdivision in a taxable year, it shall be considered placed in service in such year notwithstanding that the period for depreciation with respect to such property begins or would have begun in a succeeding taxable year because, for example, under the taxpayer's depreciation practice such property is or would have been accounted for in a multiple asset account and depreciation is or would have been computed under an "averaging convention" (§ 1.167(a)-10), or depreciation with respect to such property would have been computed under the completed contract method, the unit of production method, or the retirement method. In the case of property acquired by a taxpayer for use in his trade or business (or in the production of income), property shall be considered in a condition or state of readiness and availability for the abatement or control of water or atmospheric pollution if, for example, equipment is acquired for the abatement or control of water or atmospheric pollution and is operational but is undergoing testing to eliminate any defects. However, materials and parts acquired to be used in the construction of an item of equipment shall not be considered in a condition or state of readiness and availability for the abatement or control of water or atmospheric pollution.

(c) Certification. *(1) In general.* For purposes of paragraph (a)(1) of this section, a facility is certified in accordance with the rules prescribed in this paragraph if—

(i) The State certifying authority (as defined in subparagraph (2) of this paragraph) having jurisdiction with respect to such facility has certified to the Federal certifying authority (as defined in subparagraph (3) of this paragraph) that the facility was constructed, reconstructed, erected, or acquired in conformity with the State program or requirements for the abatement or control of water or atmosphere pollution or contamination applicable at the time of such certification, and

(ii) The Federal certifying authority has certified such facility to the Secretary or his delegate as (a) being in compliance with the applicable regulations of Federal agencies (such as, for example, the Atomic Energy Commission's regulations pertaining to radiological discharge (190 CFR Part 20)) and (b) being in furtherance of the general policy of the United States for cooperation with the States in the prevention and abatement of water pollution under the Federal Water Pollution Control Act, as amended (33 U.S.C. 1151– 1175) or in the prevention and abatement of atmospheric pollution and contamination under the Clean Air Act, as amended (42 U.S.C. 1857 *et seq.*).

(2) State certifying authority. The term "state certifying authority" means—

(i) In the case of water pollution, the State water pollution control agency as defined in section 23(a) of the Federal Water Pollution Control Act, as amended (33 U.S.C. 1173(a)),

(ii) In the case of air pollution, the air pollution control agency designated pursuant to section 302(b)(1) of the Clean Air Act, as amended (42 U.S.C. 1857h(b)), and

(iii) Any interstate agency authorized to act in place of a certifying authority of a State. See section 23(a) of the Federal Water Pollution Control Act, as amended (33 U.S.C. 1173(b)) and section 302(c) of the Clean Air Act, as amended (42 U.S.C. 1857h(c)).

(3) Federal certifying authority. The term "Federal certifying authority" means the Administrator of the Environmental Protection Agency (see Reorganization Plan No. 3 of 1970, 35 F.R. 15623).

(d) Profitmaking abatement works, etc. *(1) In general.* Section 169(e) provides that the Federal certifying authority shall not certify any property to the extent it appears that by reason of estimated profits to be derived through the recovery of wastes or otherwise in the operation of such property its costs will be recovered over the period referred to in paragraph (a)(6) of this section for such property. The Federal certifying authority need not certify the amount of estimated profits to be derived from such recovery of wastes or otherwise with respect to such facility. Such estimated profits shall be determined pursuant to subparagraph (2) of this paragraph. However, the Federal certifying authority shall certify—

(i) Whether, in connection with any treatment facility so certified, there is potential cost recovery through the recovery of wastes or otherwise, and

(ii) A specific description of the wastes which will be recovered, or the nature of such cost recovery if otherwise than through the recovery of wastes.

For effect on computation of amortizable basis, see paragraph (c) of § 1.169-3.

(2) Estimated profits. For purpose of this paragraph, the term "estimated profits" means the estimated gross receipts from the sale of recovered wastes reduced by the sum of the (i) estimated average annual maintenance and operating expenses, including utilities and labor, allocable to that portion of the facility which is certified as a treatment facility pursuant to paragraph (a)(1)(i) of this section which produces the recovered waste from which the gross receipts are derived

and (ii) estimated selling expenses. However, in determining expenses to be subtracted neither depreciation nor amortization of the facility is to be taken into account. Estimated profits shall not include any estimated savings to the taxpayer by reason of the taxpayer's reuse or recycling of wastes or other items recovered in connection with the operation of the plant or other property served by the treatment facility.

(3) Special rules. The estimates of cost recovery required by subparagraph (2) of this paragraph shall be based on the period referred to in paragraph (a)(6) of this section. Such estimates shall be made at the time the election provided for by section 169 is made and shall also be set out in the application for certification made to the Federal certifying authority. There shall be no redetermination of estimated profits due to unanticipated fluctuations in the market price for wastes or other items, to an unanticipated increase or decrease in the costs of extracting them from the gas or liquid released, or to other unanticipated factors or events occurring after certification.

T.D. 7116, 5/17/71.

---

§ 1.169-3 Amortizable basis.

Caution: The Treasury has not yet amended Reg § 1.169-3 to reflect changes made by P.L. 110-343, P.L. 92-178.

(a) In general. The amortizable basis of a certified pollution control facility for the purpose of computing the amortization deduction under section 169 is the adjusted basis of the facility for purposes of determining gain (see part II (section 1011 and following), subchapter O, chapter 1 of the Internal Revenue Code), in conjunction with paragraphs (b), (c), and (d) of this section. The adjusted basis for purposes of determining gain (computed without regard to paragraphs (b), (c), and (d) of this section) of a facility that performs a function in addition to pollution control, or that is used in connection with more than one plant or other property, or both, is determined under § 1.169-2(a)(3). For rules as to additions and improvements to such a facility, see paragraph (f) of this section. Before computing the amortization deduction allowable under section 169, the adjusted basis for purposes of determining gain for a facility that is placed in service by a taxpayer after September 10, 2001, and that is qualified property under section 168(k)(2) or § 1.168(k)-1, 50-percent bonus depreciation property under section 168(k)(4) or § 1.168(k)-1, or qualified New York Liberty Zone property under section 1400L(b) or § 1.1400L(b)-1 must be reduced by the amount of the additional first year depreciation deduction allowed or allowable, whichever is greater, under section 168(k) or section 1400L(b), as applicable, for the facility.

(b) Limitation to post-1968 construction, reconstruction, or erection. *(1)* If the construction, reconstruction, or erection was begun before January 1, 1969, there shall be included in the amortizable basis only so much of the adjusted basis of such facility for purposes of determining gain (referred to in paragraph (a) of this section) as is properly attributable under the rules set forth in paragraph (b)(2)(iii) of § 1.169-2 to construction, reconstruction, or erection after December 31, 1968. See section 169(d)(4). For example, assume a certified pollution control facility for which the shortest period authorized under section 167 is 10 years has a cost of $500,000, of which $450,000 is attributable to construction after December 31, 1968. Further, assume such facility does not perform a function in addition to pollution control and is used only in connection with a plant in operation before January 1, 1969. The facility would have an amortizable basis of $450,000 (computed without regard to paragraphs (c) and (d) of this section). For depreciation of the remaining portion ($50,000) of the cost, see section 169(g) and paragraph (a)(3)(ii) of § 1.169-1. For the definition of the term "certified pollution control facility" see paragraph (a) of § 1.169-2.

(2) the taxpayer elects to begin the 60-month amortization period with the first month of the taxable year succeeding the taxable year in which the facility is completed or acquired and a depreciation deduction is allowable under section 167 (including an additional first-year depreciation allowance under former section 179; for a facility that is acquired by the taxpayer after September 10, 2001, and that is qualified property under section 168(k)(2) or § 1.168(k)-1 or qualified New York Liberty Zone property under section 1400L(b) or § 1.1400L(b)-1, the additional first year depreciation deduction under section 168(k)(1) or 1400L(b), as applicable; and for a facility that is acquired by the taxpayer after May 5, 2003, and that is 50-percent bonus depreciation property under section 168(k)(4) or § 1.168(k)-1, the additional first year depreciation deduction under section 168(k)(4)) with respect to the facility for the taxable year in which it is completed or acquired, the amount determined under paragraph (b)(1) of this section shall be reduced by an amount equal to the amount of the depreciation deduction allowed or allowable, whichever is greater, multiplied by a fraction the numerator of which is the amount determined under paragraph (b)(1) of this section, and the denominator of which is the facility's total cost. The additional first-year allowance for depreciation under former section 179 will be allowable only for the taxable year in which the facility is completed or acquired and only if the taxpayer elects to begin the amortization deduction under section 169 with the taxable year succeeding the taxable year in which such facility is completed or acquired. For a facility that is acquired by a taxpayer after September 10, 2001, and that is qualified property under section 168(k)(2) or § 1.168(k)-1 or qualified New York Liberty Zone property under section 1400L(b) or § 1.1400L(b)-1, see § 1.168(k)-1(f)(4) or § 1.1400L(b)-1(f)(4), as applicable, with respect to when the additional first year depreciation deduction under section 168(k)(1) or 1400L(b) is allowable. For a facility that is acquired by a taxpayer after May 5, 2003, and that is 50-percent bonus depreciation property under section 168(k)(4) or § 1.168(k)-1, see § 1.168(k)-1(f)(4) with respect to when the additional first year depreciation deduction under section 168(k)(4) is allowable.

(c) Modification for profitmaking abatement works, etc. If it appears that by reason of estimated profits to be derived through the recovery of wastes, or otherwise (as determined by applying the rules prescribed in paragraph (d) of § 1.169-2) a portion or all of the total costs of the certified pollution control facility will be recovered over the period referred to in paragraph (a)(b) of § 1.169-2, its amortizable basis (computed without regard to this paragraph and paragraph (d) of this section) shall be reduced by an amount equal to (1) its amortizable basis (so computed) multiplied by (2) a fraction the numerator of which is such estimated profits and the denominator of which is its adjusted basis for purposes of determining gain. See section 169(e).

(d) Cases in which the period referred to in paragraph (a)(6) of § 1.169-2 exceeds 15 years. If as to a certified pollution control facility the period referred to in paragraph (a)(6) of § 1.169-2 exceeds 15 years (determined as of the first day of the first month for which a deduction is allowable under the election made under the section 169(b) and paragraph (a) of § 1.169-4), the amortizable basis of such facility shall be an amount equal to (1) its amortizable basis (computed without regard to this paragraph) multiplied by (2) a fraction the numerator of which is 15 years and the denominator of which is the number of years of such period. See section 169(f)(2)(A).

(e) **Examples.** This section may be illustrated by the following example:

Example (1). The X Corporation, which uses the calendar year as its taxable year, began the installation of a facility on November 1, 1968, and completed the installation on June 30, 1970, at a cost of $400,000. All of the facility qualifies as a certified pollution control facility within the meaning of paragraph (a) of § 1.169-2. $40,000 of such cost is attributable to construction prior to January 1, 1969. The X Corporation elects to take amortization deductions under section 169(a) with respect to the facility and to begin the 60-month amortization period with January 1, 1971. The corporation takes a depreciation deduction under sections 167 and 179 of $10,000 (the amount allowable, of which $2,000 is for additional first year depreciation under section 179) for the last 6 months of 1970. It is estimated that over the period referred to in paragraph (a)(6) of § 1.169-2 (20 years) as to such facility, $80,000 in profits will be realized from the sale of wastes recovered in its operation. The amortizable basis of the facility for purposes of computing the amortization deduction as of January 1, 1971, is $210,000, computed as follows:

(1) Portion of $400,000 cost attributable to post-1968 construction, reconstruction, or erection		$360,000
(2) Reduction for portion of depreciation deduction taken for the taxable year in which the facility was completed:		
(a) $10,000 depreciation deduction taken for last 6 months of 1970 including $2,000 for additional first year depreciation under section 179	$10,000	
(b) Multiplied by the amount in line (1) and divided by the total cost of the facility $360,000/$400,000)	0.9	$ 9,000
(3) Subtotal		$351,000
(4) Modification for profit making abatement works: Multiply line (3) by estimated profits through waste recovery ($80,000) and divide by the adjusted basis for determining gain of the facility ($400,000)		
(5) Reduction		$ 70,200
(6) Subtotal		$280,800
(7) Modification for period referred to in paragraph (a)(6) of § 1.169-2 exceeding 15 years: Multiply by 15 years and divide by such period (determined in accordance with paragraph (d) of this section)(20 years)......		0.75
(8) Amortizable basis........................		$210,600

Example (2). Assume the same facts as in example (1) except that the facility is used in connection with a number of separate plants some of which were in operation before January 1, 1969, that the Federal certifying authority certifies that 80 percent of the capacity of the facility is allocable to the plants which were in operation before such date, and that all of the waste recovery is allocable to the portion of the facility used in connection with the plants in operation before January 1, 1969. The amortizable basis of such facility, for purposes of computing the amortization deduction as of January 1, 1971, is $157,950 computed as follows:

(1) Adjusted basis for purposes of determining gain: Multiply percent certified as allocable to plants in operation before January 1, 1969 (80 percent) by cost of entire facility ($400,000)		$320,000
(2) Portion of adjusted basis for determining gain attributable to post-1968 construction, reconstruction, or erection: Multiply line (1) by portion of total cost of facility attributable to post-1968 construction, reconstruction, or erection ($360,000) and divide by the total cost of the facility ($400,000)		$288,000
(3) Reduction for portion of depreciation deduction taken for the taxable year in which the facility was completed:		
(a) $10,000 depreciation deduction taken for the last 6 months of 1970 including $2,000 for additional first year depreciation under section 170	$10,000	
(b) Multiplied by the amount in line (2) and divided by the total cost of the facility ($288,000/$400,000)..........	0.72	$ 7,200
(4) Subtotal		$280,000
(5) Modification for profit making abatement works: Multiply line (4) by estimated profits through waste recovery ($80,000) and divide by the amount in line (1) ($320,000):		
(6) Reduction		$ 70,200
(7) Subtotal		$210,600
(8) Modification for period referred to in paragraph (a)(6) of Sec. 1.169-2 exceeding 15 years: Multiply by 15 years and divide by such period (determined in accordance with paragraph (d) of this section) (20 years)		0.75
(9) Amortizable basis........................		$157,950

(f) **Additions or improvements.** *(1)* If after the completion or acquisition of a certified pollution control facility further expenditures are made for additional construction, reconstruction, or improvements, the cost of such additions or improvements made prior to the beginning of the amortization period shall increase the amortizable basis of such facility, but the cost of additions or improvements made after the amortization period has begun, shall not increase the amortizable basis. See section 169(f)(2)(B).

(2) If expenditures for such additional construction, reconstruction, or improvements result in a facility which is new and is separately certified as a certified pollution control facility as defined in section 169(d)(1) and paragraph (a) of § 1.169-2, and, if proper election is made, such expenditures shall be taken into account in computing under paragraph (a) of this section the amortizable basis of such new and separately certified pollution control facility.

(g) **Effective date for qualified property, 50-percent bonus depreciation property, and qualified New York Liberty Zone property.** This section applies to a certified pollution control facility. This section also applies to a certified pollution control facility that is qualified property under section 168(k)(2) or qualified New York Liberty Zone property under section 1400L(b) acquired by a taxpayer after September 10, 2001, and to a certified pollution control facility that is 50-percent bonus depreciation property under section 168(k)(4) acquired by a taxpayer after May 5, 2003.

T.D. 7116, 5/17/71, amend T.D. 9091, 9/5/2003, T.D. 9283, 8/28/2006.

§ 1.169-4 Time and manner of making elections.

(a) Election of amortization. *(1) In general.* Under section 169(b), an election by the taxpayer to take an amortization deduction with respect to a certified pollution control facility and to begin the 60-month amortization period (either with the month following the month in which the facility is completed or acquired, or with the first month of the taxable year succeeding the taxable year in which such facility is completed or acquired) shall be made by a statement to that effect attached to its return for the taxable year in which falls the first month of the 60-month amortization period so elected. Such statement shall include the following information (if not otherwise included in the documents referred to in subdivision (ix) of this subparagraph):

(i) A description clearly identifying each certified pollution control facility for which an amortization deduction is claimed;

(ii) The date on which such facility was completed or acquired (see paragraph (z)(2)(iii) of § 1.169-2);

(iii) The period referred to in paragraph (a)(6) of § 1.169-2 for the facility as of the date the property is placed in service;

(iv) The date as of which the amortization period is to begin;

(v) The date the plant or other property to which the facility is connected began operating (see paragraph (a)(5) of § 1.169-2);

(vi) The total costs and expenditures paid or incurred in the acquisition, construction, and installation of such facility;

(vii) A description of any wastes which the facility will recover during the course of its operation, and a reasonable estimate of the profits which will be realized by the sale of such wastes whether pollutants or otherwise, over the period referred to in paragraph (a)(6) of § 1.169-2 as to the facility. Such estimate shall include a schedule setting forth a detailed computation illustrating how the estimate was arrived at including every element prescribed in the definition of estimated profits in paragraph (d)(2) of § 1.169-2;

(viii) A computation showing the amortizable basis (as defined in § 1.169-3) of the facility as of the first month for which the amortization deduction provided for by section 169(a) is elected; and

(ix) (a) A statement that the facility has been certified by the Federal certifying authority, together with a copy of such certification, and a copy of the application for certification which was filed with and approved by the Federal certifying authority or (b), if the facility has not been certified by the Federal certifying authority, a statement that application has been made to the proper State certifying authority (see paragraph (c)(2) of § 1.169-2) together with a copy of such application and (except in the case of an election to which subparagraph (4) of this paragraph applies) a copy of the application filed or to be filed with the Federal certifying authority.

If subdivision (ix)(b) of this subparagraph applies, within 90 days after receipt by the taxpayer, the certification from the Federal certifying authority shall be filed by the taxpayer with the district director, or with the director of the internal revenue service center, with whom the return referred to in this subparagraph was filed.

(2) Special rule. If the return for the taxable year in which falls the first month of the 60-month amortization period to be elected was filed before November 16, 1971, without making the election for such year, then on or before December 31, 1971 (or if there is no State certifying authority in existence on November 16, 1971, on or before the 90th day after such authority is established), the election may be made by a statement attached to an amended income tax return for the taxable year in which falls the first month of the 60-month amortization period so elected. Amended income tax returns or claims for credit or refund must also be filed at this time for other taxable years which are within the amortization period and which are subsequent to the taxable year for which the election is made. Nothing in this paragraph should be construed as extending the time specified in section 6511 within which a claim for credit or refund may be filed.

(3) Other requirements and considerations. No method of making the election provided for in section 169(a) other than that prescribed in this section shall be permitted on or after May 18, 1971. A taxpayer which does not elect in the manner prescribed in this section to take amortization deductions with respect to a certified pollution control facility shall not be entitled to such deductions. In the case of a taxpayer which elects prior to May 18, 1971, the statement required by subparagraph (1) of this paragraph shall be attached to its income tax return for its taxable year in which December 31, 1971, occurs or its taxable year preceding such year.

(4) Elections filed before February 29, 1972. If a statement of election required by subparagraph (1) of this paragraph is attached to a return (including an amended return referred to in subparagraph (2) of this paragraph) filed before February 29, 1972, such statement of election need not include a copy of the Federal application to be filed with the Federal certifying authority but a copy of such application must be filed no later than February 29, 1972, by the taxpayer with the district director, or with the director of the internal revenue service center, with whom the return or amended return referred to in this subparagraph was filed.

(b) Election to discontinue or revoke amortization. *(1) Election to discontinue.* An election to discontinue the amortization deduction provided by section 169(c) and paragraph (a)(1) of § 1.169-1 shall be made by a statement in writing filed with the district director, or with the director of the internal revenue service center, with whom the return of the taxpayer is required to be filed for its taxable year in which falls the first month for which the election terminates. Such statement shall specify the month as of the beginning of which the taxpayer elects to discontinue such deductions. Unless the election to discontinue amortization is one to which subparagraph (2) of this paragraph applies, such statement shall be filed before the beginning of the month specified therein. In addition, such statement shall contain a description clearly identifying the certified pollution control facility with respect to which the taxpayer elects to discontinue the amortization deduction, and, if a certification has previously been issued, a copy of the certification by the Federal certifying authority. If at the time of such election a certification has not been issued (or if one has been issued it has not been filed as provided in paragraph (a)(1) of this section), the taxpayer shall file, with respect to any taxable year or years for which a deduction under section 169 has been taken, a copy of such certification within 90 days after receipt thereof. For purposes of this paragraph, notification to the Secretary or his delegate from the Federal certifying authority that the facility no longer meets the requirements under which certification was originally granted by the State or Federal certifying authority shall have the same effect as a notice from the taxpayer electing to terminate amortization as of the month following the month such facility ceased functioning in accordance with such requirements.

(2) Revocation of elections made prior to May 18, 1971. If on or before May 18, 1971, an election under section 169(a) has been made, such election may be revoked (see paragraph (a)(1) of § 1.169-1) by filing on or before August 16, 1971, a statement of revocation of an election under section 169(a) in accordance with the requirements in subparagraph (1) of this paragraph for filing a notice to discontinue an election. If such election to revoke is for a period which falls within one or more taxable years for which an income tax return has been filed, amended income tax returns shall be filed for any such taxable years in which deductions were taken under section 169 on or before August 16, 1971.

T.D. 7116, 5/17/71, amend T.D. 7135, 7/30/71, T.D. 7153, 12/27/71.

§ 1.170-0 Effective dates.

Except as otherwise provided in this section, the provisions of § 1.170 and §§ 1.170-1 through 1.170-3 are applicable to contributions paid in taxable years beginning before January 1, 1970, and all references therein to sections of the Code are to sections of the Internal Revenue Code of 1954 prior to the amendments made by section 201(a) of the Tax Reform Act of 1969 (83 Stat. 549). Except as otherwise provided therein, §§ 1.170A through 1.170A-11 are applicable to contributions paid in taxable years beginning after December 31, 1969. In a case where a provision in §§ 1.170A through 1.170A-11 is applicable to a contribution paid in a taxable year beginning before January 1, 1970, such provision shall apply to the contribution and §§ 1.170-1 through 1.170-3, shall not apply to the contribution.

T.D. 7207, 10/3/72.

PAR. 2.

Sections 1.170-0 and 1.170-2 are removed.

PAR. 2.

Sections 1.170-0 and 1.170-2 are removed.

Proposed § 1.170-0 - [*For Preamble, see ¶ 153,047*]

[Removed]

§ 1.170-2 Charitable deductions by individuals; limitations (before amendment by Tax Reform Act of 1969).

(a) In general. *(1)* A deduction is allowable to an individual under section 170 only for charitable contributions actually paid during the taxable year, regardless of when pledged and regardless of the method of accounting employed by the taxpayer in keeping his books and records. A contribution to an organization described in section 170(c) is deductible even though some portion of the funds of the organization may be used in foreign countries for charitable or educational purposes. The deduction by an individual for charitable contributions under section 170 is limited generally to 20 percent of the taxpayer's adjusted gross income (computed without regard to any net operating loss carryback to the taxable year under section 172). If a husband and wife make a joint return, the deduction for contributions is the aggregate of the contributions made by the spouses, and the limitation in section 170(b) is based on the aggregate adjusted gross income of the spouses. The 20-percent limitation applies to amounts contributed during the taxable year "to or for the use of" those recipients described in section 170(c), including amounts treated under section 170(d) as paid for the use of an organization described in section 170(c) (2), (3), or (4). See paragraph (f) of this section. The limitation is computed without regard to contributions qualifying for the additional 10-percent deduction. For examples of the application of the 10- and 20-percent limitation, see paragraph (b)(5) of this section. For special rules reducing amount of certain charitable deductions, see paragraph (c)(2) of § 1.170-1.

(2) No deduction is allowable for contribution of services. However, unreimbursed expenditures made incident to the rendition of services to an organization contributions to which are deductible may constitute a deductible contribution. For example, the cost of a uniform without general utility which is required to be worn in performing donated services is deductible. Similarly, out-of-pocket transportation expenses necessarily incurred in rendering donated services are deductible. Reasonable expenditures for meals and lodging necessarily incurred while away from home in the course of rendering donated services also are deductible. For the purposes of this section, the phrase "while away from home" has the same meaning as that phrase is used for purposes of section 162.

(3) (i) In the case of an annuity or portion thereof purchased from an organization described in section 170(c), there shall be allowed as a deduction the excess of the amount paid over the value at the time of purchase of the annuity or portion purchased.

(ii) The value of the annuity or portion is the value of the annuity determined in accordance with section 101(b) and the regulations thereunder.

(b) Additional 10-percent deduction. *(1) In general.* In addition to the deduction which may be allowed for contributions subject to the general 20-percent limitation, an individual may deduct charitable contributions made during the taxable year to the organizations specified in section 170(b)(1)(A) to the extent that such contributions in the aggregate do not exceed 10 percent of his adjusted gross income (computed without regard to any net operating loss carryback to the taxable year under section 172). The additional 10-percent deduction may be allowed with respect to contributions to—

(i) A church or a convention or association of churches,

(ii) An educational organization referred to in section 503(b)(2) and defined in subparagraph (3)(i) of this paragraph.

(iii) A hospital referred to in section 503(b)(5) and defined in subparagraph (4)(i) of this paragraph,

(iv) Subject to certain conditions and limitations set forth in subparagraph (4)(ii) of this paragraph, and for taxable years beginning after December 31, 1955, a medical research organization referred to in section 503(b)(5),

(v) Subject to certain limitations and conditions set forth in subparagraph (3)(ii) of this paragraph, and for taxable years beginning after December 31, 1960, an organization referred to in section 503(b)(3) which is organized and operated for the benefit of certain State and municipal colleges and universities,

(vi) For taxable years beginning after December 31, 1963, a governmental unit referred to in section 170(c)(1), and

(vii) Subject to certain limitations and conditions set forth in subparagraph (5) of this paragraph, and for taxable years beginning after December 31, 1963, an organization referred to in section 170(c)(2).

To qualify for the additional 10-percent deduction the contributions must be made "to", and not merely "for the use of", one of the specified organizations. A contribution to an organization referred to in section 170(c)(2) (other than an organization specified in subdivisions (i) through (vi) of this subparagraph) which, for taxable years beginning after December 31, 1963, is not "publicly supported" under the rules of subparagraph (5) of this paragraph will not qualify for the additional 10-percent deduction even though such organization makes the contribution available to an organization which is specified in section 170(b)(1)(A). The computation of this additional deduction is not necessary unless the total contributions paid during the taxable year are in excess of the general 20-percent limitation. Where the total contributions exceed the 20-percent limitation, the taxpayer should first ascertain the amount of charitable contributions subject to the 10-percent limitation, and any excess over the 10-percent limitation should then be added to all other contributions and limited by the 20-percent limitation. For provisions relating to a carryover of certain charitable contributions made by individuals, see paragraph (g) of this section.

(2) Church. For definition of "church", see the regulations under section 511.

(3) Educational organization and organizations for the benefit of certain State and municipal colleges and universities. (i) Education organization. An "educational organization" within the meaning of section 170(b)(1)(A) is one whose primary function is the presentation of formal instruction and which normally maintains a regular faculty and curriculum and normally has a regularly enrolled body of pupils or students in attendance at the place where its educational activities are regularly carried on. The term, therefore, includes institutions such as primary, secondary, preparatory, or high schools, and colleges and universities. It includes Federal, State, and other public-supported schools which otherwise come within the definition. It does not include organizations engaged in both educational and noneducational activities unless the latter are merely incidental to and growing out of the educational activities. A recognized university which incidentally operates a museum or sponsors concerts is an educational organization. However, the operation of a school by a museum does not necessarily qualify the museum as an educational organization. A gift to an educational institution through an alumni association or a class organization, which acts simply as a fund-raising or collection agency through which gifts may be made currently to the institution, is a gift to the entire educational organization if the entire gift inures to its benefit, but not if any part of it inures to the general or operating fund of the agency. Similarly, a gift to one or more educational institutions through an association of educational institutions will be considered a gift to the institutions if it inures entirely to their benefit.

(ii) Organizations for the benefit of certain State and municipal colleges and universities. (a) For taxable years beginning after December 31, 1960, gifts made to an organization referred to in section 503(b)(3) organized and operated exclusively to receive, hold, invest, and administer property and to make expenditures to or for the benefit of certain colleges and universities, may be taken into account in computing the additional 10-percent limitation. The phrase "expenditures to or for the benefit of certain colleges and universities" includes expenditures made for any one or more of the normally accepted functions of colleges and universities, for example, for the acquisition and maintenance of real property comprising part of the campus area, the erection of or participation in the erection of college or university buildings, scholarships, libraries, student loans, and the acquisition and maintenance of equipment and furnishings used for or in conjunction with normally accepted functions of colleges and universities.

(b) The recipient organization must be one which normally receives a substantial portion of its support from the United States or any State or political subdivision thereof or from direct or indirect contributions from the general public, or from a combination of two or more of such sources. An example of an indirect contribution from the public would be the receipt by the organization of its share of the proceeds of an annual collection campaign of a community chest, community fund, or united fund.

(c) The college or university (including land grant colleges and universities) to be benefited must be an educational organization referred to in section 170(b)(1)(A)(ii) and subdivision (i) of this subparagraph; and must be an agency or instrumentality of a State or political subdivision thereof, or must be owned or operated by a State or political subdivision thereof or by an agency or instrumentality of one or more States of political subdivisions.

(4) Hospital and medical research organization. (i) Hospital. The term "hospital", as used in section 170(b)(1)(A), means an organization the principal purposes or functions of which are the providing of hospital or medical care. The term includes Federal and State hospitals otherwise coming within the definition but does not include medical education organizations, or medical research organizations. See, however, subdivision (ii) of this subparagraph, relating to contributions to certain medical research organizations for taxable years beginning after December 31, 1955. A rehabilitation institution or an out-patient clinic may qualify as a hospital if its principal purposes or functions are the providing of hospital or medical care. The term "hospital" does not include convalescent homes or homes for children or the aged, nor does the term include institutions whose principal purposes or functions are to train handicapped individuals to pursue some vocation.

(ii) Certain medical research organizations. (a) For taxable years beginning after December 31, 1955, certain charitable contributions made to certain medical research organizations may be taken into account in computing the additional 10-percent limitation. To be so taken into account the charitable contribution must be made to a medical research organization that is directly engaged in the continuous active conduct of medical research in conjunction with a hospital (as defined in subdivision (i) of this subparagraph), and, during the calendar year in which the contribution is made, the organization must be committed to spend the contribution for such active conduct of medical research before January 1 of the fifth calendar year beginning after the date the contribution is made.

(b) As used in section 170(b)(1)(A) and this subparagraph, the term "medical research organization" means an organization the principal purpose or function of which is to engage in medical research. Medical research may be defined as the conduct of investigations, experiments, and studies to discover, develop, or verify knowledge relating to the causes, diagnosis, treatment, prevention, or control of physical or mental diseases and impairments of man. To qualify as a medical research organization, the organization must have the appropriate equipment and professional personnel necessary to carry out its principal function.

(c) The organization must, at the time of the contribution, be directly engaged in the continuous active conduct of medical research in conjunction with a hospital described in subdivision (i) of this paragraph. The organization need not be formally affiliated with a hospital to be considered engaged in the active conduct of medical research in conjunction with a hospital, but it must be physically connected, or closely associated, with a hospital. In any case, there must be a joint effort on the part of the research organization and the hospital pursuant to an understanding that the two organizations shall maintain continuing close cooperation in the active conduct of medical research. For example, the necessary joint effort will normally be found to exist if the activities of the medical research organization are carried on in space located within or adjacent to a hospital provided that the organization is permitted to utilize the facilities (including equipment, case studies, etc.) of the hospital on a continuing basis in the active conduct of medical research. A medical research organization which is closely associated, in the manner described above, with a particular hospital or particular hospitals, may be considered to be pursuing research in conjunction with a hospital if the necessary joint effort is supported by substantial evidence of the close cooperation of the members of the research organization and the staff of the particular hospital or hospitals. The active participation in medical research by the staff of the particular hospital or hospitals will be considered as evidence of the requisite joint effort. If the organization's primary purpose is to disburse funds to other organizations for the conduct of research by them, or, if the organization's primary purpose is to extend research grants or scholarships to others, it is not directly engaged in the active conduct of medical research, and contributions to such an organization may not be taken into account for purposes of the additional 10-percent limitation.

(d) A charitable contribution to a medical research organization may be taken into account in computing the additional 10-percent limitation only if the organization is committed to spend such contribution for medical research in conjunction with a hospital on or before the first day of the fifth calendar year which begins after the date the contribution is made. The organization's commitment that the contribution will be spent within the prescribed time only for the prescribed purposes must be legally enforceable. A promise in writing to the donor in consideration of his making a contribution that such contribution will be so spent within the prescribed time will constitute a commitment. The expenditure of contributions received for plant, facilities, or equipment, used solely for medical research purposes shall ordinarily be considered to be an expenditure for medical research for purposes of section 170(b) and this section. If a contribution is made in other than money, it shall be considered spent for medical research if the funds from the proceeds of a disposition thereof are spent by the organization within the five-year period for medical research; or, if such property is of such a kind that it is used in a continuing basis directly in connection with such research, it shall be considered spent for medical research in the year in which it is first so used.

(5) Corporation, trust, or community chest, fund, or foundation. (i) In general. (a) For taxable years beginning after December 31, 1963, gifts made to a corporation, trust, or community chest, fund, or foundation, referred to in section 170(c)(2) (other than an organization specified in subparagraph (1)(i) through (vi) of this paragraph), may be taken into account in computing the additional 10-percent limitation, provided the organization is a "publicly supported" organization. For purposes of this subparagraph, an organization is "publicly supported" if it normally receives a substantial part of its support from a governmental unit referred to in section 170(c)(1) or from direct or indirect contributions from the general public.

(b) An important factor in determining whether an organization normally receives a substantial part of its support from "direct or indirect contributions from the general public" is the extent to which the organization derives its support from or through voluntary contributions made by persons representing the general public. Except in unusual situations (particularly in the case of newly created organizations), an organization is not "publicly supported" if it receives contributions only from the members of a single family or from a few individuals.

(ii) Special rules and meaning of terms (a) For purposes of this subparagraph, the term "support", except as otherwise provided in (b) of this subdivision (ii), means all forms of support including (but not limited to) contributions received by the organization, investment income (such as, interest, rents, royalties, and dividends), and net income from unrelated business activities whether or not such activities are carried on regularly as a trade or business.

(b) The term "support" does not include—

(1) Any amounts received from the exercise or performance by an organization of its charitable, educational, or other purpose or function constituting the basis for its exemption under section 501(a). In general, such amounts include amounts received from any activity the conduct of which is substantially related to the furtherance of such purpose or function (other than through the production of income).

(2) Any gain upon the sale or exchange of property which would be considered under any section of the Code as gain from the sale or exchange of a capital asset.

(3) Contributions of services for which a deduction is not allowable.

(c) The term "support from a governmental unit" includes—

(1) Any amounts received from a governmental unit including donations or contributions and amounts received in connection with a contract entered into with a governmental unit for the performance of services or in connection with a government research grant, provided such amounts are not excluded from the term "support" under (b) of this subdivision (ii). For purposes of (b)(1) of this subdivision (ii), an amount paid by a governmental unit to an organization is not received from the exercise or performance of its charitable, educational, or other purpose or function constituting the basis for its exemption under section 501(a) if the purpose of the payment is to enable the organization to provide a service to, or maintain a facility for, the direct benefit of the public, as, for example, the maintenance of library facilities which are open to the public.

(2) Tax revenues levied for the benefit of the organization and either paid to or expended on behalf of the organization.

(3) The value of services or facilities (exclusive of services or facilities generally furnished, without charge, to the public) furnished by a governmental unit to the organization without charge, as, for example, where a city pays the salaries of personnel used to guard a museum, art gallery, etc., or provides, rent free, the use of a building. However, the

term does not include the value of any exemption from Federal, State, or local tax or any similar benefit.

(d) The term "indirect contributions from the general public" includes contributions received by the organization from organizations which normally receive a substantial part of their support from direct contributions from the general public.

(iii) Determination of whether organization is "publicly supported" (a) In general. No single test which would be appropriate in every case may be prescribed for determining whether a corporation, trust, or community chest, fund, or foundation, referred to in section 170(c)(2), is "publicly supported". For example, since the statutory test is whether the organization normally receives a substantial part of its support from the prescribed sources, a test which would be appropriate in the case of an organization which has been in operation for a number of years would not necessarily be appropriate in the case of a newly established organization. The determination of whether an organization is "publicly supported" depends on the facts and circumstances in each case. Thus, although a "mechanical test" is set forth in (b) of this subdivision (iii), such test is not an exclusive test. Accordingly, an organization which does not qualify as a "publicly supported" organization by application of the "mechanical test" may qualify as a "publicly supported" organization on the basis of the facts and circumstances in its case. For provisions relating to the facts and circumstances test, see (c) of this subdivision (iii).

(b) Mechanical test. An organization will be considered to be a "publicly supported" organization for its current taxable year and the taxable year immediately succeeding its current year, if, for the four taxable years immediately preceding the current taxable year, the total amount of the support which the organization receives from governmental units, from donations made directly or indirectly by the general public, or from a combination of these sources equals 33⅓ percent or more of the total support of the organization for such four taxable years. The rule in the preceding sentence does not apply if there are substantial changes in the organization's character, purposes, or methods of operation in the current year, and does not apply in respect of the immediately succeeding taxable year if such changes occur in such year. In determining whether the 33⅓-percent-of-support test is met, contributions by an individual, trust, or corporation shall be taken into account only to the extent that the total amount of the contributions by any such individual, trust, or corporation during the four-taxable-year period does not exceed 1 percent of the organization's total support for such four taxable years. In applying the 1-percent limitation, all contributions made by a donor and by any person or persons standing in a relationship to the donor which is described in section 267(b) and the regulations thereunder shall be treated as made by one person. The 1-percent limitation shall not apply to support from governmental units referred to in section 170(c)(1) or to contributions from "publicly supported" organizations. A national organization which carries out its purposes through local chapters with which it has an identity of aims and purposes may, for purposes of determining whether the organization and the local chapters meet the mechanical test, make the computation on an aggregate basis.

Example. For the years 1964 through 1967, X, an organization referred to in section 170(c)(2), received support (as defined in subdivision (ii) of this subparagraph) of $600,000 from the following sources:

Investment income	$300,000
City Y (a governmental unit referred to in section 170(c)(1))	40,000
United Fund (an organization referred to in section 170(c)(2) which is "publicly supported")	40,000
Contributions	220,000
Total support	$600,000

For the years 1964 through 1967, X received in excess of 33⅓ percent of its support from a governmental unit referred to in section 170(c)(1) and from direct and indirect contributions from the general public computed as follows:

33⅓ percent of total support	$200,000
Support from a governmental unit referred to in section 170(c)(1)	40,000
Indirect contributions from the general public (United Fund)	40,000
Contributions by various donors (no one donor having made contributions which total in excess of $6,000—1 percent of total support)	50,000
12 contributions (each in excess of $6,000—1 percent of total support) 12 × $6,000	72,000
	$202,000

Since the amount of X's support from governmental units referred to in section 170(c)(1) and from direct and indirect contributions from the general public in the years 1964 through 1967 is in excess of 33⅓ percent of X's total support for such four taxable years, X is considered a "publicly supported" organization with respect to contributions made to it during 1968 and 1969 without regard to whether X receives 33⅓ percent of its support during 1968 or 1969 from such sources (assuming that there are no substantial changes in X's character, purposes, or methods of operation).

(c) Facts and circumstances test. (1) A corporation, trust, or community chest, fund or foundation referred to in section 170(c)(2) which does not qualify as a "publicly supported" organization under the mechanical test described in (b) of this subdivision (iii) (including an organization which has not been in existence for a sufficient length of time to make such test applicable) may be a "publicly supported" organization on the basis of the facts and circumstances in its case.

(2) The facts and circumstances which are relevant and the weight to be accorded such facts and circumstances may differ in certain cases depending, for example, on the nature of the organization and the period of time it has been in existence. However, under no circumstances will an organization which normally receives substantially all of its contributions (directly or indirectly) from the members of a single family or from a few individuals qualify as a "publicly supported" organization.

(3) For purposes of the facts and circumstances test the most important consideration is the organization's source of support. An organization will be considered a "publicly supported" organization if it is constituted so as to attract substantial support from contributions, directly or indirectly, from a representative number of persons in the community or area in which it operates. In determining what is a "representative number of persons," consideration must be given to the type of organization and whether or not the organization limits its activities to a special field which can be expected to appeal to a limited number of persons. An organization is so constituted if, for example, it establishes that it does in fact receive substantial support from contributions

from a representative number of persons; that pursuant to its organizational structure and method of operation it makes bona fide solicitations for broad based public support, or, in the case of a newly created organization, that its organizational structure and method of operation are such as to require bona fide solicitations for broad based public support; that it receives substantial support from a community chest or similar public federated fund raising organization, such as a United Fund or United Appeal; or that it has a substantial number of members (in relation to the community it serves, the nature of its activities, and its total support) who pay annual membership dues.

(4) Although primary consideration will be given to the source of an organization's support, other relevant factors may be taken into account in determining whether or not the organization is of a public nature, such as:

(i) Whether the organization has a governing body (whether designated in the organization's bylaws, certificate of incorporation, deed of trust, etc., as a Board of Directors, Board of Trustees, etc.) which is comprised of public officials, of individuals chosen by public officials acting in their capacity as such, or of citizens broadly representative of the interests and views of the public. This characteristic does not exist if the membership of an organization's governing body is such as to indicate that it represents the personal or private interests of a limited number of donors to the organization (or persons standing in a relationship to such donors which is described in section 267(b) and the regulations thereunder), rather than the interests of the community or the general public.

(ii) Whether the organization annually or more frequently makes available to the public financial reports or, in the case of a newly created organization, is constituted so as to require such reporting. For this purpose an information or other return made pursuant to a requirement of a governmental unit shall not be considered a financial report. An organization shall be considered as making financial reports of its operations available to the public if it publishes a financial report in a newspaper which is widely circulated in the community in which the organization operates or if it makes a bona fide dissemination of a brochure containing a financial report.

(iii) If the organization is of type which generally holds open to the public its buildings (as in the case of a museum) or performances conducted by it (as in the case of a symphonic orchestra), whether the organization actually follows such practice, or, in the case of a newly created organization, is so organized as to require that its facilities be open to the public.

(5) The application of this subdivision (c) may be illustrated by the following examples:

Example (1). M, a community trust, is an organization referred to in section 170(c)(2). In 1950, M was organized in the X Community by several leading trusts and financial institutions with the purpose of serving permanently the educational and charitable needs of the X Community by providing a means by which the public may establish funds or make gifts of various amounts to established funds which are administered as an aggregate fund with provision for distribution of income and, in certain cases, principal for educational or charitable purposes by a single impartial committee. The M Organization, by distribution of pamphlets to the public through participating trustee banks, actively solicits members of the X Community and other concerned parties to establish funds within the trust or to contribute to established funds within the trust. Under the declaration of trust, a contributor to a fund may suggest or request (but not require) that his contribution be used in respect of his preferred charitable, educational, or other benevolent purpose, and distributions of the income from the fund, and in certain cases the principal, will be made by the Distribution Committee with regard to such request unless changing conditions make such purpose unnecessary, undesirable, impractical, or impossible in which case income and (where the contributor has so specified) principal will be distributed by the Distribution Committee in order to promote the public welfare more effectively. Where a contributor has not expressed a desire as to a charitable, educational, or other benevolent purpose, the Distribution Committee will distribute the entire annual income from the fund to such a purpose agreed upon by such committee. The Distribution Committee is composed of representatives of the community chosen one each by the X Bar Association, the X Medical Society, the mayor of X Community, the judge of the highest X Court, and the president of the X College, and two representatives chosen by the participating trustee banks. There are a number of separate funds within the trust administered by several participating banks. M has consistently distributed or used its entire annual income for projects with purposes described in section 170(c)(2)(B) from which members of the public may benefit or to other organizations described in section 170(b)(1)(A) which so distribute or use such income. Through its participating trustee banks, M annually makes available to the public a brochure containing a financial statement of its operations including a list of all receipts and disbursements. Under the facts and circumstances, M is a "publicly supported" organization.

Example (2). Assume the same facts as in example (1) except that M has been in existence for only one year and only two contributors have established funds within the trust. The Distribution Committee has been chosen and is required by the governing declaration of trust to make annual distribution of the entire income of the trust to projects with purposes described in section 170(c)(2)(B) from which members of the public may benefit or to other organizations described in section 170(b)(1)(A) which so distribute or use such income. The declaration of trust and other governing instruments require (1) that the M Community Trust actively solicit contributions from members of the X Community through dissemination of literature and other public appeals, and (2) that it make available to the members of the X Community, annual financial reports of its operations. Under the facts and circumstances, M is a "publicly supported" organization.

Example (3). N, an art museum, is an organization referred to in section 170(c)(2). In 1930, N was founded in Y City by the members of a single family to collect, preserve, interpret, and display to the public important works of art. N is governed by a self-perpetuating Board of Trustees limited by the governing instruments to a maximum membership of 20 individuals. The original board consisted almost entirely of members of the founding family. Since 1945, members of the founding family or persons standing in a relationship to the members of such family described in section 267(b) have annually constituted less than one-fifth of the Board of Trustees. The remaining board members are citizens of Y City from a variety of professions and occupations who represent the interests and views of the people of Y City in the activities carried on by the organization rather than the personal or private interests of the founding family. N solicits contributions from the general public and for each of its four most recent taxable years has received total contributions in small sums (less than $100) in excess of $10,000. For N's four most recent taxable years, investment income from several large endowment funds has constituted 75 percent of its total support. N normally expends a substantial part of its annual income for purposes described in section 170(c)(2)(B). N has, for the entire period of its existence, been open to the public and more than 300,000 people (from the Y City and elsewhere) have visited the museum in each of its four most recent taxable years. N annually publishes a financial report of its operation in the Y City newspaper. Under the facts and circumstances, N museum is a "publicly supported" organization.

Example (4). In 1960, the O Philharmonic Orchestra was organized in Z City through the combined efforts of a local music society and a local women's club to present to the public a wide variety of musical programs intended to foster music appreciation in the community. O is an organization referred to in section 170(c)(2). The orchestra is composed of professional musicians who are paid by the association. Twelve performances, open to the public, are scheduled each year. The admission charge for each of these performances is $3. In addition, several performances are staged annually without charge. In each of its four most recent taxable years, O has received separate contributions of $10,000 from A, B, C, and D (not members of a single family) and support of $5,000 from the Z Community Chest, a public federated fund raising organization operating in Z City. O is governed by a Board of Directors comprised of five individuals. A faculty member of a local college, the president of a local music society, the head of a local banking institution, a prominent doctor, and a member of the governing body of the local Chamber of Commerce currently serve on the Board and represent the interests and views of the community in the activities carried on by O. O annually files a financial report with Z City which makes such report available for public inspection. Under the facts and circumstances, O is a "publicly supported" organization.

Example (5). P is a newly created organization of a type referred to in section 170(c)(2). P's charter requires that its governing body be selected by public officials and by public organizations representing the community in which it operates. Pursuant to P's charter, a continuing fund raising campaign which will encompass the entire community has been planned. P's charter requires that its entire annual income be distributed to or used for projects with purposes described in section 170(c)(2)(B) and that it make available to the public annual financial reports of its operations. By reason of the express provisions of P's charter relating to its organizational structure and prescribed methods of operation, P is a "publicly supported" organization.

(6) Examples. The application of the special 10-percent limitation and the general 20-percent limitation on contributions by individuals may be illustrated by the following examples:

Example (1). A, an individual, reports his income on the calendar year basis and for the year 1957 has an adjusted gross income of $10,000. During 1957 he made the following charitable contributions:

		Deductible contributions
1. Contributions qualifying for the additional 10-percent deduction under section 170(b)(1)(A)	$2,400	
2. Other charitable contributions	700	
3. Total contributions paid	3,100	
4. Contributions qualifying for the additional 10-percent deduction under section 170(b)(1)(A)	$2,400	
5. Special limitation under section 170(b)(1)(A): 10 percent of adjusted gross income	1,000	
6. Deductible amount: line 4 or line 5, whichever is the lesser		$1,000
7. Excess of line 4 over line 5	1,400	
8. Add: Other charitable contributions	700	
9. Contributions subject to the general 20-percent limitation under section 170(b)(1)(B)	2,100	
10. Limitation under section 170(b)(1)(B): 20-percent of the adjusted gross income	2,000	
11. Deductible amount: line 9 or line 10, whichever is the lesser		2,000
12. Contributions not deductible	100	
13. Total deduction for contributions		3,000

Example (2). B, an individual, reports his income on the calendar year basis and for the year 1957 has an adjusted gross income of $10,000. calendar year basis and for the year 1957 has an adjusted gross income of $10,000. During 1957 he made the following charitable contributions:

1. Contributions qualifying for the additional 10-percent deduction under section 170(b)(1)(A)	$ 700	
2. Other charitable contributions	2,400	
3. Total contributions paid	3,100	
4. Contributions qualifying for the additional 10-percent deduction under section 170(b)(1)(A)	$ 700	
5. Limitation described in section 170(b)(1)(A): 10 percent of the adjusted gross income	1,000	
6. Deductible amount: line 4 or line 5, whichever is the lesser		$ 700
7. Excess of line 4 over line 5	0	
8. Add: Other charitable contributions	2,400	
9. Contributions subject to the general 20-percent limitation under section 170(b)(1)(B)	$2,400	
10. Limitation under section 170(b)(1)(B): 20 percent of the adjusted gross income	2,000	

11. Deductible amount: line 9 or line 10, whichever is the lesser		2,000
12. Contributions not deductible	400	
13. Total deduction for contributions		2,700

(c) Unlimited deduction for individuals. *(1) In general.* (1) The deduction for charitable contributions made by an individual is not subject to the 10- and 20-percent limitations of section 170(b) if in the taxable year and each of 8 of the 10 preceding taxable years the sum of his charitable contributions paid during the year, plus his payments during the year on account of Federal income taxes, is more than 90 percent of his taxable income for the year (or net income, in years governed by the Internal Revenue Code of 1939). In determining the applicability of the 10- and 20-percent limitations of section 170(b) for taxable years beginning after December 31, 1957, there may be substituted, in lieu of the amount of income tax paid during any year, the amount of income tax paid in respect of such year, provided that any amount so included for the year in respect of which payment was made shall not be included for any other year. For the purpose of the first sentence of this paragraph, taxable income under the 1954 Code is determined without regard to the deductions for charitable contributions under section 170, for personal exemptions under section 151, or for a net operating loss carryback under section 172. On the other hand, for this purpose net income under the 1939 Code is computed without the benefit only of the deduction for charitable contributions. See section 120 of the Internal Revenue Code of 1939. The term "income tax" as used in section 170(b)(1)(C) means only Federal income taxes, and does not include the taxes imposed on self-employment income, on employees under the Federal Insurance Contributions Act, and on railroad employees and their representatives under the Railroad Retirement Tax Act by chapters 2, 21, and 22, respectively, or corresponding provisions of the Internal Revenue Code of 1939. For purposes of section 170(b)(1)(C) and this paragraph, the amount of income tax paid during a taxable year shall be determined (except as provided in subdivision (ii) of this subparagraph) by including all payments made by the taxpayer during such taxable year on account of his Federal income taxes (whether for the taxable year or for preceding taxable years). Such payments would include any amount paid during the taxable year as estimated tax (exclusive of any portion of such amount for taxable years beginning after December 31, 1966, which is attributable to the self-employment tax imposed by chapter (2) for that year, payment of the final installment of estimated tax (exclusive of any portion of such installment, for taxable years beginning after December 31, 1966, which is attributable to the self-employment tax imposed by chapter 2) for the preceding taxable year, final payment for the preceding taxable year, and any payment of a deficiency for an earlier taxable year, to the extent that such payments do not exceed the tax for the taxable year for which payment is made. Any payment of income tax with respect to which the taxpayer receives a refund or credit shall be reduced by the amount of such refund or credit. Any such refund or credit shall be applied against the most recent payments for the taxable year in respect of which the refund or credit arose.

(ii) For any taxable year beginning after December 31, 1957, the applicability of the 10- and 20-percent limitations of section 170(b) may be determined either with reference to the income tax paid during the year or any prior year, or with reference to the income tax paid in respect of any such year or prior years. The 90-percent test of section 170(b)(1)(C) may be applied for the taxable year, or for any one or more of the preceding 10 taxable years, by taking into account the income taxes paid in respect of that year or years, and for the balance of the 10 years by taking into account the income tax payments made during those years. Thus, a taxable year which qualifies under either of the two permissible methods shall be considered as a qualifying year irrespective of whether the taxable year begins before or after December 31, 1957. However, a particular income tax payment may only be taken into account once, either with respect to the year of liability or for the year of payment.

(2) Joint Returns. (i) Joint return for current taxable year. If a husband and wife make a joint return for any taxable year, their deduction for charitable contributions is not subject to the 10- and 20-percent limitations of section 170(b), if, under the rules of subparagraph (1) of this paragraph, in the taxable year and in each of 8 of the 10 preceding taxable years (regardless of whether separate or joint returns were filed), the aggregate charitable contributions of both spouses paid during the year, plus their aggregate payments during the year on account of Federal income taxes (or, if the taxable year begins after December 31, 1957, the aggregate tax paid in respect of such taxable year or any preceding taxable year) exceed 90 percent of their aggregate taxable incomes for the year.

(ii) Separate return by spouse or by unremarried widow or widower. If a spouse, or the unremarried widow or widower of a deceased spouse, makes a separate return for any taxable year, his deduction for charitable contributions is not subject to the 10- and 20-percent limitations of section 170(b), if, under the rules of subparagraph (1) of this paragraph, in the taxable year and each of 8 of the 10 preceding taxable years—

(a) For which the taxpayer filed a joint return with his spouse, either their aggregate charitable contributions and payments of Federal income taxes made during the taxable year (or if the taxable year) exceed 90 percent of their aggregate in respect of such taxable year or any preceding taxable year) exceed 90 percent of the aggregate taxable income for that year, or the taxpayer's separate charitable contributions and payments of Federal income taxes allocable to his separate income and made during the taxable year (or if the taxable year begins after December 31, 1957, made in respect of such taxable year or any preceding taxable year) exceed 90 percent of his separate taxable income for that year, and

(b) For which the taxpayer did not file a joint return with his spouse, the aggregate of his charitable contributions and payments of Federal income taxes made during the taxable year (or, if the taxable year begins after December 31, 1957, the payments of income taxes made in respect of such taxable year or any preceding taxable year) exceeds 90 percent of his taxable income for that year.

For the purpose of the preceding sentence, the word "spouse" does not include a spouse from whom the taxpayer has been divorced.

(iii) Joint return with former spouse for prior taxable year. A divorced or remarried taxpayer who filed a joint return for a prior taxable year with a former spouse shall, for purposes of applying this paragraph, be treated in the same manner as if he had filed a separate return for such prior taxable year, and as if his Federal income tax liability and taxable income for such prior taxable year were his allocable portions of the joint tax liability and combined taxable income, respectively, for such year.

(iv) Allocation. Whenever it is necessary to allocate the joint tax liability or the combined taxable income, or both, for a taxable year for which a joint return was filed, a computation shall be made for the taxpayer and for his spouse or former spouse showing for each of them the Federal income taxes and taxable income which would be determined if separate returns had been filed by them for such taxable year. The joint tax liability and combined taxable income for such taxable year shall then be allocated proportionately to the income taxes and taxable income, respectively, so computed. Whenever it is necessary to determine the separate payments made by a taxpayer in respect of a joint tax liability, the amount paid by him during the taxable year as estimated tax (exclusive of any portion of such amount for taxable years beginning after December 31, 1966, which is attributable to the self-employment tax imposed by chapter 2) for that year shall be included to the extent it does not exceed his allocable portion of the joint tax under chapter 1 (exclusive of tax under section 56) for the taxable year, and any amount paid by him for a prior year (whether as the final installment of estimated tax—exclusive of any portion of such installment, for taxable years beginning after December 31, 1966, which is attributable to the self-employment tax imposed by chapter 2—for the preceding taxable year, or a final payment for the preceding year, or the payment of a deficiency for an earlier year) shall be included to the extent such amount, when added to amounts previously paid by him for such prior year, does not exceed his allocable portion of the joint tax liability for the prior year.

(d) Denial of deduction in case of certain transfers in trust. *(1) Reversionary interest in grantor.* No charitable deduction will be allowed for the value of any interest in property transferred to a trust after March 9, 1954, if the grantor at the time of the transfer has a reversionary interest in the corpus or income and the value of such reversionary interest exceeds 5 percent of the total value on which the charitable deduction would, but for section 170(b)(1)(D), be determined. For purposes of this paragraph, the term "reversionary interest" means a possibility that after the possession or enjoyment of property or its income has been obtained by a charitable donee, the property or its income may revest in the grantor or his estate, or may be subject to a power exercisable by the grantor or a nonadverse party (within the meaning of section 672(b)), or both, to revest in, or return to or for the benefit of, the grantor or his estate the property or income therefrom. An interest of the grantor which, in any event, will terminate before the ripening of the assured charitable gift for which a deduction is claimed is not considered a reversionary interest for purposes of this section. For example, assume that a taxpayer conveyed property to a trust under the terms of which the income is payable to the taxpayer's wife for her life, and, if she predeceases him, to him for his life, and after the death of both the property is to be transferred to a charitable organization.

(2) Valuation of interests. The present value of the remainder interest in the property, taking into account the value of the life estates reserved to the taxpayer and his wife, may be allowed as a charitable deduction. Where the corpus of the trust is to return to the grantor after a number of years certain, the value of the reversionary interest at the time of the transfer may be computed by the use of tables showing the present value at 3½ percent a year, compounded annually, of $1 payable at the end of a number of years certain. See paragraph (f), Table II, of § 20.2031-7 of this chapter (Estate Tax Regulations). Where the value of a reversionary interest is dependent upon the continuation or termination of the life of one or more persons, it must be determined on the basis of Table 38 of United States Life Tables and Actuarial Tables 1939–1941, published by the United States Department of Commerce, Bureau of the Census, and interest at the rate of 3½ percent a year, compounded annually. See paragraph (f), Table I, of § 20.2031-7 of this chapter (Estate Tax Regulations) for valuations based on one life, and "Actuarial Values for Estate and Gift Tax" (Internal Revenue Service Publication No. 11, Rev. 5–59) for values based on more than one life. In an actual case (not merely hypothetical), the grantor or his legal representative may, upon request, obtain the information necessary to determine such a value from the district director with whom the grantor files his return. The request must be accompanied by a statement showing the date of birth of each person the duration of whose life may affect the value of the reversionary interest and by copies of the instruments relevant to the transfer.

(e) Fiscal years and short taxable years ending after March 9, 1954, subject to the Internal Revenue Code of 1939. Pursuant to section 7851(a)(1)(C) of the Internal Revenue Code of 1954, the regulations prescribed in paragraph (d) of this section, to the extent that they relate to transfers in trust occurring after March 9, 1954, shall apply to all taxable years ending after March 9, 1954, even though those years may be subject to the Internal Revenue Code of 1939.

(f) Amounts paid to maintain certain students as members of the taxpayer's household. *(1) In general.* (i) For taxable years beginning after December 31, 1959, the term "charitable contribution" includes amounts paid by the taxpayer during the taxable year to maintain certain students as members of his household which, under the provisions of section 170(d) and this paragraph, are treated as amounts paid for the use of an organization described in section 170(c) (2), (3), or (4), and such amounts, to the extent they do not exceed the limitations under section 170(d)(2) and subparagraph (2) of this paragraph, are deductible contributions under section 170. In order for such amounts to be so treated, the student must be an individual who is neither a dependent (as defined in section 152) of the taxpayer nor related to the taxpayer in a manner described in any of the paragraphs (1) through (8) of section 152(a), and such individual must be a member of the taxpayer's household pursuant to a written agreement between the taxpayer and an organization described in section 170(c) (2), (3), or (4) to implement a program of the organization to provide educational opportunities for pupils or students placed in private homes by such organization. Furthermore, such amounts must be paid to maintain such individual during the period in the taxable year he is a member of the taxpayer's household and is a full-time pupil or student in the twelfth or any lower grade at an educational institution (as defined in section 151(e)(4)) located in the United States. Amounts paid outside of the period (but within the taxable year) for expenses necessary for the maintenance of the student during the period will qualify for the charitable deduction if the other limitation requirements of the section are met.

(ii) For purposes of subdivision (i) of this subparagraph, amounts treated as charitable contributions include only those amounts actually paid by the taxpayer during the taxable year which are directly attributable to the maintenance of the student while he is a member of the taxpayer's household and is attending school on a full-time basis. This would include amounts paid to ensure the well-being of the individual and to carry out the purpose for which the individual was placed in the taxpayer's home. For example, a deduction would be allowed for amounts paid for books, tuition, food, clothing, transportation, medical and dental care, and recreation for the individual. Amounts treated as charitable contributions under this paragraph do not include amounts which the taxpayer would have expended had the student not been in the household. They would not include, for example, amounts paid in connection with the taxpayer's home for taxes, insurance, interest on a mortgage, repairs, etc. Moreover, such amounts do not include any depreciation sustained by the taxpayer in maintaining such student or students in his household, nor do they include the value of any services rendered on behalf of such student or students by the taxpayer or any member of the taxpayer's household.

(iii) For purposes of section 170(d) and this paragraph, an individual will be considered to be a full-time pupil or student at an educational institution only if he is enrolled for a course of study (prescribed for a full-time student) at such institution and is attending classes on a full-time basis. Nevertheless, such individual may be absent from school due to special circumstances and still be considered to be in full-time attendance. Periods during the regular school term when the school is closed for holidays, such as Christmas and Easter, and for periods between semesters are treated as periods during which the pupil or student is in full-time attendance at the school. Also, absences during the regular school term due to illness of such individual shall not prevent him from being considered as a full-time pupil or student. Similarly, absences from the taxpayer's household due to special circumstances will not disqualify the student as a member of the household. Summer vacations between regular school terms are not considered periods of school attendance.

(iv) As in the case of other charitable deductions, any deduction claimed for amounts described in section 170(d) and this paragraph which are treated as charitable contributions under section 170(c) is subject to verification by the district director. When claiming a deduction for such amounts, the taxpayer should submit a copy of his agreement with the organization sponsoring the individual placed in the taxpayer's household together with a summary of the various items for which amounts were paid to maintain such individual, and a statement as to the date the individual became a member of the household and the period of his attendance at school and the name and location of such school. Substantiation of amounts claimed must be supported by adequate records of the amounts actually paid. Due to the nature of certain items, such as food, a record of amounts spent for all members of the household, with an equal portion thereof allocated to each member, will be acceptable.

(2) Limitations. Section 170(d) and this paragraph shall apply to amounts paid during the taxable year only to the extent that the amounts paid in maintaining each pupil or student do not exceed $50 multiplied by the number of full calendar months in the taxable year that the pupil or student is maintained in accordance with the provisions of this paragraph. For purposes of such limitation, if 15 or more days of a calendar month fall within the period to which the maintenance of such pupil or student relates, such month is considered as a full calendar month. To the extent that such amounts qualify as charitable contributions under section 170(c), the aggregate of such amounts plus other contributions made during the taxable year is deductible under section 170, subject to the 20-percent limitation provided in section 170(b)(1)(B). Also, see § 1.170-2(a)(1).

(3) Compensation or reimbursement. Amounts paid during the taxable year to maintain a pupil or student as a member of the taxpayer's household, as provided in subparagraph (1) of this paragraph, shall not be taken into account under section 170(d) of this paragraph, if the taxpayer receives any money or other property as compensation or reimbursement for any portion of such amounts. The taxpayer will not be denied the benefits of section 170(d) if he prepays an extraordinary or nonrecurring expense, such as a hospital bill or vacation trip, at the request of the individual's parents or the sponsoring organization and is reimbursed for such prepayment. The value of services performed by the pupil or student in attending to ordinary chores of the household will not generally be considered to constitute compensation or reimbursement. However, if the pupil or student is taken into the taxpayer's household to replace a former employee of the taxpayer or gratuitously to perform substantial services for the taxpayer, the facts and circumstances may warrant a conclusion that the taxpayer received reimbursement for maintaining the pupil or student.

(4) No other amount allowed as deduction. Except to the extent that amounts described in section 170(d) and this paragraph are treated as charitable contributions under section 170(c) and, therefore, deductible under section 170(a), no deduction is allowed for any amount paid to maintain an individual, as a member of the taxpayer's household, in accordance with the provisions of section 170(d) and this paragraph.

(5) Examples. Application of the provisions of this paragraph may be illustrated by the following examples:

Example (1). The X organization is an organization described in section 170(c)(2) and is engaged in a program under which a number of European children are placed in the homes of United States residents in order to further the children's high school education. In accordance with the provisions of subparagraph (1) of this paragraph, the taxpayer, A, who reports his income on the calendar year basis, agreed with X to take two of the children, and they were placed in the taxpayer's home on January 2, 1960, where they remained until January 21, 1961, during which time they were fully maintained by the taxpayer. The children enrolled at the local high school for the full course of study prescribed for tenth grade students and attended the school on a full-time basis for the spring semester starting January 18, 1960, and ending June 3, 1960, and for the fall semester starting September 1, 1960, and ending January 13, 1961. The total cost of food paid by A in 1960 for himself, his wife, and the two children amounted to $1,920, or $40 per month for each member of the household. Since the children were actually full-time students for only 8½ months during 1960, the amount paid for food for each child during that period amounted to $340. Other amounts paid during the 8½ month period for each child for laundry, lights, water, recreation, and school supplies amounted to $160. Thus, the amounts treated under section 170(d) and this paragraph as paid for the use of X would, with respect to each child, total $500 ($340 + $160), or a total for both children of $1,000, subject to the limitations of subparagraph (2) of this paragraph. Since, for purposes of such limitations, the children were full-time students for only 8 full calendar months during 1960 (less than 15 days in January 1960), the taxpayer may treat only $800 as a charitable contribution made in 1960, that is, $50 multiplied by the 8 full calendar months, or $400 paid for the maintenance of each child. Neither the excess payments nor amounts paid to maintain the children during the period before school opened and for the period in summer between regular school terms is taken into account by reason of section 170(d). Also, because the children were full-time students for less than 15 days in January 1961 (although maintained in the taxpayer's household for 21 days), amounts paid to maintain the children during 1961 would not qualify as a charitable contribution.

Example (2). A religious organization described in section 170(c)(2) has a program for providing educational opportunities for children it places in private homes. In order to implement the program, the taxpayer, H, who resides with his wife, son, and daughter of high school age in a town in the United States, signs an agreement with the organization to maintain a girl sponsored by the organization as a member of his household while the child attends the local high school for the regular 1960–61 school year. The child is a full-time student at the school during the school year starting September 6, 1960, and ending June 6, 1961, and is a member of the taxpayer's household during that period. Although the taxpayer pays $200 during the school period falling in 1960, and $240 during the school period falling in 1961, to maintain the child, he cannot claim either amount as a charitable contribution because the child's parents, from time to time during the school year, send butter, eggs, meat, and vegetables to H to help defray the expenses of maintaining the child. This is considered property received as reimbursement under subparagraph (3) of this paragraph. Had her parents not contributed the food, the fact that the child, in addition to the normal chores she shared with the taxpayer's daughter, such as cleaning their own rooms and helping with the shopping and cooking, was responsible for the family laundry and for the heavy cleaning of the entire house while the taxpayer's daughter had no comparable responsibilities would also preclude a claim for a charitable deduction. These substantial gratuitous services are considered property received as reimbursement under subparagraph (3) of this paragraph.

Example (3). A taxpayer resides with his wife in a city in the eastern United States. He agrees, in writing, with a fraternal society described in section 170(c)(4) to accept a child selected by the society for maintenance by him as a member of his household during 1961 in order that the child may attend the local grammar school as a part of the society's program to provide elementary education for certain children selected by it. The taxpayer maintains the child, who has as his principal place of abode the home of the taxpayer, and is a member of the taxpayer's household, during the entire year 1961. The child is a full-time student at the local grammar school for 9 full calendar months during the year. Under the agreement, the society pays the taxpayer $30 per month to help maintain the child. Since the $30 per month is considered as compensation or reimbursement to the taxpayer for some portion of the maintenance paid on behalf of the child, no amounts paid with respect to such maintenance can be treated as amounts paid in accordance with section 170(d). In the absence of the $30 per month payments, if the child qualifies as a dependent of the taxpayer under section 152(a)(9), that fact would also prevent the maintenance payments from being treated as charitable contributions paid for the use of the fraternal society.

(g) Charitable contributions carryover of individuals. *(1) Computation of excess charitable contributions made in contribution year.* Subject to certain conditions and limitations, the excess of—

(i) The amount of the charitable contributions made by an individual in a taxable year beginning after December 31, 1963 (hereinafter in this paragraph referred to as the "contribution year"), to organizations specified in section 170(b)(1)(A) (see paragraph (b) of this section), over

(ii) Thirty percent of his adjusted gross income (computed without regard to any net operating loss carryback to such year under section 172) for such contribution year,

shall be treated as a charitable contribution paid by him to an organization specified in section 170(b)(1)(A) and paragraph (b) of this section, relating to the additional 10-percent deduction, in each of the 5 taxable years immediately succeeding the contribution year in order of time. (For provisions requiring a reduction of such excess, see subparagraph (5) of this paragraph.) The provisions of this subparagraph apply even though the taxpayer elects under section 144 to take the standard deduction in the contribution year instead of itemizing the deductions (other than those specified in sections 62 and 151) allowable in computing taxable income for the contribution year. No excess charitable contribution carryover shall be allowed with respect to contributions "for the use of" rather than "to" organizations described in section 170(b)(1)(A) and paragraph (b) of this section or with respect to contributions made "to" or "for the use of" organizations which are not described in such sections. The provisions of section 170(b)(5) and this paragraph are not applicable in the case of estates or trusts, see section 642(c), relating to deductions for amounts paid or permanently set aside for a charitable purpose, and the regulations thereunder. The provisions of this subparagraph may be illustrated by the following examples:

Example (1). Assume that H and W (husband and wife) have adjusted gross income for 1964 of $50,000 and for 1965 of $40,000 and file a joint return for each year. Assume further that in 1964 they contribute $16,500 to a church and $1,000 to X (an organization not referred to in section 170(b)(1)(A)) and in 1965 contribute $11,000 to the church and $400 to X. They may claim a charitable contribution deduction of $15,000 in 1964, and the excess of $16,500 (contribution to the church) over $15,000 (30 percent of adjusted gross income) or $1,500 constitutes a charitable contribution carryover which shall be treated as a charitable contribution paid by them to an organization referred to in section 170(b)(1)(A) in each of the 5 succeeding taxable years in order of time. No carryover is allowed with respect to the $1,000 contribution made to X in 1964. Since 30 percent of their adjusted gross income for 1965 ($12,000) exceeds the charitable contributions of $11,000 made by them in 1965 to organizations referred to in section 170(b)(1)(A) (computed without regard to section 170(b)(5) and this paragraph) the portion of the 1964 carryover equal to such excess of $1,000 ($12,000 minus $11,000) is treated, pursuant to the provisions of subparagraph (2) of this paragraph, as paid to a section 170(b)(1)(A) organization in 1965; the remaining $500 constitutes an unused charitable contribution carryover. No carryover is allowed with respect to the $400 contribution made to X in 1965.

Example (2). Assume the same facts as in example (1) except that H and W have adjusted gross income, for 1965 of $42,000. Since 30 percent of their adjusted gross income for 1965 ($12,600) exceeds by $1,600 the charitable contribution of $11,000 made by them in 1965 to organizations referred to in section 170(b)(1)(A) (computed without regard to section 170(b)(5) and this paragraph), the full amount of the 1964 carryover of $1,500 is treated, pursuant to the provisions of subparagraph (2) of this paragraph, as paid to a section 170(b)(1)(A) organization in 1965. They may also claim a charitable contribution of $100 ($12,600—$12,500 ($11,000 × $1,500)) with respect to the gift to X in 1965. No carryover is allowed with respect to the $300 ($400—$100) of the contribution to X which is not deductible in 1965.

(2) Determination of amount treated as paid in taxable years succeeding contribution year. Notwithstanding the provisions of subparagraph (1) of this paragraph, the amount of the excess computed in accordance with the provisions of subparagraphs (1) and (5) of this paragraph which is to be treated as paid in any one of the 5 taxable years immediately succeeding the contribution year to an organization specified in section 170(b)(1)(A) shall not exceed the lesser of the amount computed under subdivision (i) or (ii) of this subparagraph:

(i) The amount by which (a) 30 percent of the taxpayer's adjusted gross income for such succeeding taxable year (computed without regard to any net operating loss carryback to such succeeding taxable year under section 172) exceeds (b) the sum of (1) the charitable contributions actually made (computed without regard to the provisions of section 170(b)(5) and this paragraph) by the taxpayer in such succeeding taxable year to organizations referred to in section 170(b)(1)(A), and (2) the charitable contributions made to organizations referred to in section 170(b)(1)(A) in taxable years (excluding any taxable year beginning before January 1, 1964) preceding the contribution year which, pursuant to the provision of section 170(b)(5) and this paragraph, are treated as having been paid to an organization referred to in section 170(b)(1)(A) in such succeeding year.

(ii) In the case of the first taxable year succeeding the contribution year, the amount of the excess charitable contribution in the contribution year, computed under subparagraphs (1) and (5) of this paragraph. In the case of the second, third, fourth, and fifth succeeding taxable years, the portion of the excess charitable contribution in the contribution year (computed under subparagraphs (1) and (5) of this paragraph) which has not been treated as paid to a section 170(b)(1)(A) organization in a year intervening between the contribution year and such succeeding taxable year.

If a taxpayer, in any one of the four taxable years succeeding a contribution year, elects under section 144 to take the standard deduction in the amount provided for in section 141 instead of itemizing the deductions (other than those specified in sections 62 and 151) allowable in computing taxable income, there shall be treated as paid (but not allowable as a deduction) in the standard deduction year the amount determined under subdivision (i) or (ii) of this subparagraph, whichever is the lesser. The provisions of this subparagraph may be illustrated by the following examples:

Example (1). Assume that B has adjusted gross income for 1966 of $20,000 and for 1967 of $30,000. Assume further that in 1966 B contributed $8,000 to a church and in 1967 he contributes $7,500 to the church. B may claim a charitable contribution deduction of $6,000 in 1966, and the excess of $8,000 (contribution to the church) over $6,000 (30 percent of B's adjusted gross income) or $2,000 constitutes a charitable contribution carryover which shall be treated as a charitable contribution paid by B to an organization referred to in section 170(b)(1)(A) in the 5 taxable years succeeding 1966 in order of time. (B made no excess contributions in 1964 or 1965 which should be treated as paid in years succeeding 1964 or 1965.) B may claim a charitable contribution deduction of $9,000 in 1967. Such $9,000 consists of the $7,500 contribution to the church in 1967 and $1,500 carried over from 1966 and treated as a charitable contribution paid to a section 170(b)(1)(A) organization in 1967. The $1,500 contribution treated as paid in 1967 is computed as follows:

1966 excess contributions		$2,000
30 percent of B's adjusted gross income for 1967		9,000
Less:		
Contributions actually made in 1967 to section 170(b)(1)(A) organizations	$7,500	
Contributions made to section 170(b)(1)(A) organizations in taxable years prior to 1966 treated as having been paid in 1967	0	7,500
		1,500
Amount of 1966 excess treated as paid in 1967—the lesser of $2,000 (1966 excess contributions) or $1,500 (30 percent of adjusted gross income for 1967 ($9,000) over the section 170(b)(1)(A) contributions actually made in 1967 ($7,500) and the section 170(b)(1)(A) contributions made in years prior to 1966 treated as having been paid in 1967 (0))		1,500

If the excess contributions made by B in 1966 had been $1,000 instead of $2,000, then, for purposes of this example, the amount of the 1966 excess treated as paid in 1967 would be $1,000 rather than $1,500.

Example (2). Assume the same facts as in example (1), and, in addition, that B has adjusted gross income for 1968 of $10,000 and for 1969 of $20,000. Assume further with respect to 1968 that B elects under section 144 to take the standard deduction in computing taxable income and that his actual contributions to organizations specified in section 170(b)(1)(A) are $300. Assume further with respect to 1969, that B itemizes his deductions which include a $5,000 contribution to a church. B's deductions for 1968 are not increased by reason of the $500 available as a charitable contribution carryover from 1966 (excess contributions made in 1966 ($2,000) less the amount of such excess treated as paid in 1967 ($1,500)) since B elected to take the standard deduction in 1968. However, for purposes of determining the amount of the excess charitable contributions made in 1966 which is available as a carryover to 1969, B is required to treat such $500 as a charitable contribution paid in 1968—the lessor of $500 or $2,700 (30 percent of adjusted gross income ($3,000) over contributions actually made in 1968 to section 170(b)(1)(A) organizations ($300). Therefore, even though the $5,000 contribution made by B in 1969 to a church does not amount to 30 percent of B's adjusted gross income for 1969 (30 percent of $20,000 = $6,000), B may claim a charitable contribution deduction of only the $5,000 actually paid in 1969 since the entire excess charitable contribution made in 1966 ($2,000) has been treated as paid in 1967 ($1,500) and 1968 ($500).

Example (3). Assume the following factual situation for C who itemizes his deductions in computing taxable income for each of the years set forth in the example:

	1964	1965	1966	1967	1968
Adjusted gross income	$10,000	$7,000	$15,000	$10,000	$9,000
Contributions to section 170(b)(1)(A) organizations (no other contributions)	4,000	3,000	5,000	1,000	1,500
Allowable charitable contributions deductions computed without regard to carryover of contributions	3,000	2,100	4,500	1,000	1,500
Excess contributions for taxable year to be treated as paid in 5 succeeding taxable years	1,000	900	500	0	0

Since C's contributions in 1967 and 1968 to section 170(b)(1)(A) organizations are less than 30 percent of his adjusted gross income for such years, the excess contributions for 1964, 1965, and 1966 are treated as having been paid to section 170(b)(1)(A) organizations in 1967 and 1968 as follows:

1967

Contribution year	Total excess	Less: Amount treated as paid in year prior to 1967	Available charitable contribution carryovers
1964	$1,000	0	$1,000
1965	900	0	900
1966	500	0	500
			2,400

30 percent of B's adjusted gross income for 1967	3,000
Less: Charitable contributions made in 1967 to section 170(b)(1)(A) organizations	1,000
	2,000
Amount of excess contributions treated as paid in 1967—the lesser of $2,400 (available carryovers to 1967) or $2,000 (excess of 30 percent of adjusted gross income ($3,000) over contributions actually made in 1967 to section 170(b)(1)(A) organizations ($1,000))	2,000

1968

Contribution year	Total excess	Less: Amount treated as paid in year prior to 1968	Available charitable contribution carryovers
1964	$1,000	$1,000	0
1965	900	900	0
1966	500	100	$ 400
1967	0	0	0
			400

30 percent of B's adjusted gross income for 1968	2,700
Less: Charitable contributions made in 1968 to section 170(b)(1)(A) organizations	1,500
	1,200
Amount of excess contributions treated as paid in 1968—the lesser of $400 (available carryovers to 1968) or $1,200 (30 percent of adjusted gross income $2,700) over contributions actually made in 1968 to section 170(b)(1)(A) organizations ($1,500)	400

(3) Effect of net operation loss carryback to contribution year. The amount of the excess contribution for a contribution year (computed as provided in subparagraphs (1) and (5) of this paragraph) shall not be increased because a net operating loss carryback is available as a deduction in the contribution year. In addition, in determining (under the provisions of section 172(b)(2)) the amount of the net operating loss for any year subsequent to the contribution year which is a carryback or carryover to taxable years succeeding the contribution year, the amount of contributions made to organizations referred to in section 170(b)(1)(A) shall be limited to the amount of such contributions which did not exceed 30 percent of the donor's adjusted gross income (computed without regard to any net operating loss carryback or any of the modifications referred to in section 172(d) for the contribution year.

(4) Effect of net operating loss carryback to taxable years succeeding the contribution year. The amount of the charitable contribution from a preceding taxable year which is treated as paid (as provided in subparagraph (2) of this paragraph) in a current taxable year (hereinafter referred to in this subparagraph as the "deduction year") shall not be reduced because a net operating loss carryback is available as a deduction in the deduction year. In addition, in determining (under the provisions of section 172(b)(2)) the amount of the net operating loss for any year subsequent to the deduction year which is a carryback or carryover to taxable years succeeding the deduction year, the amount of contributions made to organizations referred to in section 170(b)(1)(A) in the deduction year shall be limited to the amount of such contributions which were actually made in such year and those which were treated as paid in such year which did not exceed 30 percent of the donor's adjusted gross income (computed without regard to any net operating loss carryback or any of the modifications referred to in section 172(d)) for the deduction year.

(5) Reduction of excess contributions. An individual having a net operating loss carryover from a prior taxable year

which is available as a deduction in a contribution year must apply the special rule of section 170(b)(5)(B) and this subparagraph in computing the excess described in subparagraph (1) of this paragraph for such contribution year. In determining the amount of excess charitable contributions that shall be treated as paid in each of the 5 taxable years succeeding the contribution year, the excess charitable contributions described in such subparagraph (1) must be reduced by the amount by which such excess reduces taxable income (for purposes of determining the portion of a net operating loss which shall be carried to taxable years succeeding the contribution year under the second sentence of section 172(b)(2)) and increases the net operating loss which is carried to a succeeding taxable year. In reducing taxable income under the second sentence of section 172(b)(2), an individual who has made charitable contributions in the contribution year to both organizations specified in section 170(b)(1)(A) (see paragraph (b) of this section) and to organizations not so specified must first deduct contributions made to the section 170(b)(1)(A) organizations from his adjusted gross income computed without regard to his net operating loss deduction before any of the contributions made to organizations not specified in section 170(b)(1)(A) may be deducted from such adjusted gross income. Thus, if the excess of the contributions made in the contribution year to organizations specified in section 170(b)(1)(A) over the amount deductible in such contribution year is utilized to reduce taxable income (under the provisions of section 172(b)(2)) for such year, thereby serving to increase the amount of the net operating loss carryover to a succeeding year or years, no part of the excess charitable contributions made in such contribution year shall be treated as paid in any of the 5 immediately succeeding taxable years. If only a portion of the excess charitable contributions is so used, the excess charitable contributions will be reduced only to that extent. The provisions of this subparagraph may be illustrated by the following examples:

Example (1). B, an individual, reports his income on the calendar year basis and for the year 1964 has adjusted gross income (computed without regard to any net operating loss deduction) of $50,000. During 1964 he made charitable contributions in the amount of $20,000 all of which were to organizations specified in section 170(b)(1)(A). B has a net operating loss carryover from 1963 of $50,000. In the absence of the net operating loss deduction B would have been allowed a deduction for charitable contributions of $15,000. After the application of the net operating loss deduction, B is allowed no deduction for charitable contributions, and there is (before applying the special rule of section 170(b)(5)(B) and this subparagraph) a tentative excess charitable contribution of $20,000. For purposes of determining the net operating loss which remains to be carried over to 1965, B computes his taxable income for his prior taxable year, 1964, under section 172(b)(2) by deducting the $15,000 charitable contribution. After the $50,000 net operating loss carryover is applied against the $35,000 of taxable income for 1964 (computed in accordance with section 172(b)(2), assuming no deductions other than the charitable contribution deduction are applicable in making such computation), there remains a $15,000 net operating loss carryover to 1965. Since the application of the net operating loss carryover of $50,000 from 1963 reduces the 1964 adjusted gross income (for purposes of determining 1964 tax liability) to zero, no part of the $20,000 of charitable contributions in that year is deductible under section 170(b)(1). However, in determining the amount of the excess charitable contributions which shall be treated as paid in taxable years 1965, 1966, 1967, 1968, 1969, the $20,000 must be reduced by the portion thereof ($15,000) which was used to reduce taxable income for 1964 (as computed for purposes of the second sentence of section 172(b)(2)) and which thereby served to increase the net operating loss carryover to 1965 from zero to $15,000.

Example (2). Assume the same facts as in example (1), except that B's total contributions of $20,000 made during 1964 consisted of $15,000 to organizations specified in section 170(b)(1)(A) and $5,000 to organizations not so specified. Under these facts there is a tentative excess charitable contribution of $15,000, rather than $20,000 as in example (1). For purposes of determining the net operating loss which remains to be carried over to 1965, B computes his taxable income for his prior taxable year, 1964, under section 172(b)(2) by deducting the $15,000 of charitable contributions made to organizations specified in section 170(b)(1)(A). Since the excess charitable contribution of $15,000 determined in accordance with subparagraph (1) of this paragraph was used to reduce taxable income for 1964 (as computed for purposes of the second sentence of section 172(b)(2)) and thereby served to increase the net operating loss carryover to 1965 from zero to $15,000, no part of such excess charitable contributions made in the contribution year shall be treated as paid in any of the five immediately succeeding taxable years. No carryover is allowed with respect to the $5,000 of charitable contributions made in 1964 to organizations not specified in section 170(b)(1)(A).

(6) Change in type of return filed. (i) From joint return to separate returns. If a husband and wife—

(a) Make a joint return for a contribution year and compute an excess charitable contribution for such year in accordance with the provisions of subparagraphs (1) and (5) of this paragraph, and

(b) Make separate returns for one or more of the 5 taxable years immediately succeeding such contribution year,

any excess charitable contribution for the contribution year which is unused at the beginning of the first such taxable year for which separate returns are filed shall be allocated between the husband and wife. For purposes of the allocation, a computation shall be made of the amount of any excess charitable contribution which each spouse would have computed in accordance with subparagraphs (1) and (5) of this paragraph if separate returns (rather than a joint return) had been filed for the contribution year. The portion of the total unused excess charitable contribution for the contribution year allocated to each spouse shall be an amount which bears the same ratio to such unused excess charitable contribution as such spouse's excess contribution (based on the separate return computation) bears to the total excess contributions of both spouses (based on the separate return computation). To the extent that a portion of the amount allocated to either spouse in accordance with the foregoing provisions of this subdivision is not treated in accordance with the provisions of subparagraph (2) of this paragraph as a charitable contribution paid to an organization specified in section 170(b)(1)(A) in the taxable year in which a separate return or separate returns are filed, each spouse shall for purposes of subparagraph (2) of this paragraph treat his respective unused portion as the available charitable contributions carryover to the next succeeding taxable year in which the joint excess charitable contribution may be treated as paid in accordance with subparagraph (1) of this paragraph. If such husband and wife make a joint return in one of the five taxable years immediately succeeding the contribution year with respect to which a joint excess charitable contribution is computed and following the first succeeding year in which such husband and wife filed a separate return or separate returns, the amounts allocated to each spouse in accordance with this subdivision for such first year reduced by the portion of such amounts treated as paid to an organization specified in section 170(b)(1)(A) in such first year and in any taxable year intervening between such first year and the succeeding taxable year in which the joint return is filed shall be aggregated for purposes of determining the amount of the available charitable contributions carryover to such succeeding taxable year. The provisions of this subdivision (i) may be illustrated by the following example:

Example. H and W file joint returns for 1964, 1965, and 1966, and in 1967 they file separate returns. In each such year H and W itemize their deductions in computing taxable income. Assume the following factual situation with respect to H and W for 1964:

1964

	H	W	Joint return
Adjusted gross income	$50,000	$40,000	$90,000
Contributions to section 170(b)(1)(A) organization (no other contributions)	27,000	20,000	47,000
Allowable charitable contribution deductions	15,000	12,000	27,000
Excess contributions for taxable year to be treated as paid in 5 succeeding taxable years	12,000	8,000	20,000

The joint excess charitable contribution of $20,000 is to be treated as having been paid to a section 170(b)(1)(A) organization in the five succeeding taxable years. Assume that in 1965, the portion of such excess treated as paid by H and W is $3,000 and that in 1966, the portion of such excess treated as paid is $7,000. Thus, the unused portion of the excess charitable contribution made in the contribution year is $10,000 ($20,000 less $3,000 (amount treated as paid in 1965) and $7,000 (amount treated as paid in 1966)). Since H and W file separate returns in 1967, $6,000 of such $10,000 is allocable to H and $4,000 is allocable to W. Such allocation is computed as follows:

$$\frac{\text{\$12,000 (excess charitable contributions made by H (based on separate return computation) in 1964)}}{\text{\$20,000 (total excess charitable contributions made by H and W (based on separate return computation) in 1964)}} \times \$10,000 = \$6,000$$

$$\frac{\text{\$8,000 (excess charitable contributions made by W (based on separate return computation) in 1964)}}{\text{\$20,000 (total excess charitable contributions made by H and W (based on separate return computation) in 1964)}} \times \$10,000 = \$4,000$$

In 1967 H has adjusted gross income of $70,000 and he contributes $14,000 to an organization specified in section 170(b)(1)(A). In 1967 W has adjusted gross income of $50,000, and she contributes $10,000 to an organization specified in section 170(b)(1)(A). H may claim a charitable contribution deduction of $20,000 in 1967, and W may claim a charitable contribution deduction of $14,000 in 1967. H's $20,000 deduction consists of the $14,000 contribution to the section 170(b)(1)(A) organization in 1967 and $6,000 carried over from 1964 and treated as a charitable contribution paid to a section 170(b)(1)(A) organization in 1967. W's $14,000 deduction consists of the $10,000 contribution made to a section 170(b)(1)(A) organization in 1967 and $4,000 carried over from 1964 and treated as a charitable contribution paid to a section 170(b)(1)(A) organization in 1967. The $6,000 contribution treated as paid in 1967 by H, and the $4,000 contribution treated as paid in 1967 by W are computed as follows:

	H	W
Available charitable contribution carryover (see computations above)	$ 6,000	$ 4,000
30-percent of adjusted gross income	21,000	15,000
Contributions made in 1967 to section 170(b)(1)(A) organization (no other contributions)	14,000	10,000
Amount of allowable deduction unused	7,000	5,000
Amount of excess contributions treated as paid in 1967—the lesser of $6,000 (available carryover of H to 1967) or $7,000 (excess of 30 percent of adjusted gross income ($21,000) over contributions actually made in 1967 to section 170(b)(1)(A) organizations ($14,000)	6,000	
The lesser of $4,000 (available carryover of W to 1967) or $5,000 (excess of 30 percent of adjusted gross income ($15,000) over contributions actually made in 1967 to section 170(b)(1)(A) organizations ($10,000))	—	4,000

(ii) From separate returns to joint return and remarried taxpayers. If in the case of a husband and wife—

(a) Either or both of the spouses make a separate return for a contribution year and compute an excess charitable contribution for such year in accordance with the provisions of subparagraphs (1) and (5) of this paragraph, and

(b) Such husband and wife make a joint return for one or more of the taxable years immediately succeeding such contribution year, the excess charitable contribution of the husband and wife for the contribution year which is unused at the beginning of the first taxable year for which a joint return is filed shall be aggregated for purposes of determining the portion of such unused charitable contribution which shall be treated in accordance with subparagraph (2) of this paragraph as a charitable contribution paid to an organization specified in section 170(b)(1)(A). The provisions of this subdivision are also applicable in the case of two single individuals who are subsequently married and file a joint return. A remarried taxpayer who filed a joint return with a former spouse in a contribution year with respect to which an excess charitable contribution was computed and who in any one of the five taxable years immediately succeeding such contribution year files a joint return with his (or her) present spouse shall treat the unused portion of such excess charitable contribution allocated to him (or her) in accordance with subdivision (i) of this subparagraph in the same manner as the unused portion of an excess charitable contribution computed in a contribution year in which he filed a separate return for purposes of determining the amount which in accordance with subparagraph (2) of this paragraph shall be treated as paid to an organization specified in section 170(b)(1)(A) in such succeeding year.

(iii) Unused excess charitable contribution of deceased spouse. In case of the death of one spouse, any unused portion of an excess charitable contribution which is allocable (in accordance with subdivision (i) of this subparagraph) to such spouse shall not be treated as paid in the taxable year in which such death occurs or in any subsequent taxable year except on a separate return made for the deceased spouse by a fiduciary for the taxable year which ends with the date of death or on a joint return for the taxable year in which such death occurs. The application of this subdivision may be illustrated by the following example:

Example. Assume the same facts as in the example in subdivision (i) of this subparagraph except that H dies in 1966 and W files a separate return for 1967. W made a joint return for herself and H for 1966. In that example, the unused excess charitable contribution as of January 1, 1967, was $10,000, $6,000 of which was allocable to H and $4,000 to W. No portion of the $6,000 allocable to H may be treated as paid by W or any other person in 1967 or any subsequent year.

(7) Information required in support of a deduction of an amount treated as paid. If, in a taxable year, a deduction is claimed in respect of an excess charitable contribution which, in accordance with the provisions of subparagraph (2) of this paragraph, is treated (in whole or in part) as paid in such taxable year, the taxpayer shall attach to his return a statement showing:

(i) The year (or years) in which the excess charitable contributions were made (the contribution year or years),

(ii) The excess charitable contributions made in each contribution year,

(iii) The portion of such excess (or each such excess) treated as paid in accordance with subparagraph (2) of this paragraph in any taxable year intervening between the contribution year and the taxable year for which the return is made, and

(iv) Such other information as the return or the instructions relating thereto may require.

T.D. 6285, 3/13/58, amend T.D. 6605, 8/14/62, T.D. 6639, 2/25/63, T.D. 6732, 5/12/64, T.D. 6900, 11/16/66, T.D. 7207, 10/3/72, T.D. 7427, 8/9/76.

PAR. 2. Sections 1.170-0 and 1.170-2 are removed.

PAR. 2. Sections 1.170-0 and 1.170-2 are removed.

Proposed § 1.170-2 [*For Preamble, see ¶ 153,047*]

[Removed]

§ 1.170A-1 Charitable, etc., contributions and gifts; allowance of deduction.

Caution: The Treasury has not yet amended Reg § 1.170A-1 to reflect changes made by P.L. 109-280, P.L. 105-277.

(a) Allowance of deduction. Any charitable contribution, as defined in section 170(c), actually paid during the taxable year is allowable as a deduction in computing taxable income irrespective of the method of accounting employed or of the date on which the contribution is pledged. However, charitable contributions by corporations may under certain circumstances be deductible even though not paid during the taxable year as provided in section 170(a)(2) and § 1.170A-11. For rules relating to record keeping and return requirements in support of deductions for charitable contributions (whether by an itemizing or nonitemizing taxpayer) see § 1.170A-13. The deduction is subject to the limitations of section 170(b) and § 1.170A-8 or § 1.170A-11. Subject to the provisions of section 170(d) and §§ 1.170A-10 and 1.170A-11, certain excess charitable contributions made by individuals and corporations shall be treated as paid in certain succeeding taxable years. For provisions relating to direct charitable deductions under section 63 by nonitemizers, see section 63(b)(1)(C) and (i) and section 170(i). For rules relating to the determination of, and the deduction for, amounts paid to maintain certain students as members of the taxpayer's household and treated under section 170(g) as paid for the use of an organization described in section 170(c)(2), (3), or (4), see § 1.170A-2. For the reduction of any charitable contributions for interest on certain indebtedness, see section 170(f)(5) and § 1.170A-3. For a special rule relating to the computation of the amount of the deduction with respect to a charitable contribution of certain ordinary income or capital gain property, see section 170(e) and § 1.170A-4 and § 1.170A-4A. For rules for postponing the time for deduction of a charitable contribution of a future interest in tangible personal property, see section 170(a)(3) and § 1.170A-5. For rules with respect to transfers in trust and of partial interests in property, see section 170(e), section 170(f)(2) and (3), § 1.170A-4, § 1.170A-6, and § 1.170A-7. For definition of the term "section 170(b)(1)(A) organization," see § 1.170A-9. For valuation of a remainder interest in real property, see section 170(f)(4) and the regulations thereunder. The deduction for charitable contributions is subject to verification by the district director.

(b) Time of making contribution. Ordinarily, a contribution is made at the time delivery is effected. The unconditional delivery or mailing of a check which subsequently clears in due course will constitute an effective contribution on the date of delivery or mailing. If a taxpayer unconditionally delivers or mails a properly endorsed stock certificate to a charitable donee or the donee's agent, the gift is completed on the date of delivery or, if such certificate is received in the ordinary course of the mails, on the date of mailing. If the donor delivers the stock certificate to his bank or broker as the donor's agent, or to the issuing corporation or its agent, for transfer into the name of the donee, the gift is completed on the date the stock is transferred on the books of the corporation. For rules relating to the date of payment of a contribution consisting of a future interest in tangible personal property, see section 170(a)(3) and § 1.170A-5.

(c) Value of a contribution in property. *(1)* If a charitable contribution is made in property other than money, the amount of the contribution is the fair market value of the property at the time of the contribution reduced as provided in section 170(e)(1) and paragraph (a) of § 1.170A-4, or section 170(e)(3) and paragraph (c) of § 1.170A-4A.

(2) The fair market value is the price at which the property would change hands between a willing buyer and a willing seller, neither being under any compulsion to buy or sell and both having reasonable knowledge of relevant facts. If the contribution is made in property of a type which the taxpayer sells in the course of his business, the fair market value is the price which the taxpayer would have received if he had sold the contributed property in the usual market in which he customarily sells, at the time and place of the contribution and, in the case of a contribution of goods in quantity, in the quantity contributed. The usual market of a manufacturer or other producer consists of the wholesalers or other distributors to or through whom he customarily sells, but if he sells only at retail the usual market consists of his retail customers.

(3) If a donor makes a charitable contribution of property, such as stock in trade, at a time when he could not reasonably have been expected to realize its usual selling price, the value of the gift is not the usual selling price but is the amount for which the quantity of property contributed would have been sold by the donor at the time of the contribution.

(4) Any costs and expenses pertaining to the contributed property which were incurred in taxable years preceding the year of contribution and are properly reflected in the opening inventory for the year of contribution must be removed from inventory and are not a part of the cost of goods sold for purposes of determining gross income for the year of contribution. Any costs and expenses pertaining to the contributed property which are incurred in the year of contribution and would, under the method of accounting used, be properly reflected in the cost of goods sold for such year are to be treated as part of the cost of goods sold for such year. If costs and expenses incurred in producing or acquiring the contributed property are, under the method of accounting used, properly deducted under section 162 or other section of the Code, such costs and expenses will be allowed as deductions for the taxable year in which they are paid or incurred, whether or not such year is the year of the contribution. Any such costs and expenses which are treated as part of the cost of goods sold for the year of contribution, and any such costs and expenses which are properly deducted under section 162 or other section of the Code, are not to be treated under any section of the Code as resulting in any basis for the contributed property. Thus, for example, the contributed property has no basis for purposes of determining under section 170(e)(1)(A) and paragraph (a) of § 1.170A-4 the amount of gain which would have been recognized if such property had been sold by the donor at its fair market value at the time of its contribution. The amount of any charitable contribution for the taxable year is not to be reduced by the amount of any costs or expenses pertaining to the contributed property which was properly deducted under section 162 or other section of the Code for any taxable year preceding the year of the contribution. This subparagraph applies only to property which was held by the taxpayer for sale in the course of a trade or business. The application of this subparagraph may be illustrated by the following examples:

Example (1). In 1970, A, an individual using the calendar year as the taxable year and the accrual method of accounting, contributed to a church property from inventory having a fair market value of $600. The closing inventory at the end of 1969 properly included $400 of costs attributable to the acquisition of such property, and in 1969 A properly deducted under section 162 $50 of administrative and other expenses attributable to such property. Under section 170(e)(1)(A) and paragraph (a) of § 1.170A-4, the amount of the charitable contribution allowed for 1970 is $400 ($600 – [$600 – $400]). Pursuant to this subparagraph, the cost of goods sold to be used in determining gross income for 1970 may not include the $400 which was included in opening inventory for that year.

Example (2). The facts are the same as in example (1) except that the contributed property was acquired in 1970 at a cost of $400. The $400 cost of the property is included in determining the cost of goods sold for 1970, and $50 is allowed as a deduction for that year under section 162. A is not allowed any deduction under section 170 for the contributed property, since under section 170(e)(1)(A) and paragraph (a) of § 1.170A-4 the amount of the charitable contribution is reduced to zero ($600 – [$600 – $0]).

Example (3). In 1970, B, an individual using the calendar year as the taxable year and the accrual method of accounting, contributed to a church property from inventory having a fair market value of $600. Under § 1.471-3(c), the closing inventory at the end of 1969 properly included $450 costs attributable to the production of such property, including $50 of administrative and other indirect expenses which, under his method of accounting, was properly added to inventory rather than deducted as a business expense. Under section 170(e)(1)(A) and paragraph (a) of § 1.170A-4, the amount of the charitable contribution allowed for 1970 is $450 ($600 – [$600 – $450]). Pursuant to this subparagraph, the cost of goods sold to be used in determining gross income for 1970 may not include the $450 which was included in opening inventory for that year.

Example (4). The facts are the same as in example (3) except that the contributed property was produced in 1970 at a cost of $450, including $50 of administrative and other indirect expenses. The $450 cost of the property is included in determining the cost of goods sold for 1970. B is not allowed any deduction under section 170 for the contributed property, since under section 170(e)(1)(A) and paragraph (a) of § 1.170A-4 the amount of the charitable contribution is reduced to zero ($600 – [$600 – $0]).

Example (5). In 1970, C, a farmer using the cash method of accounting and the calendar year as the taxable year, contributed to a church a quantity of grain which he had raised having a fair market value of $600. In 1969, C paid expenses of $450 in raising the property which he properly deducted for such year under section 162. Under section 170(e)(1)(A) and paragraph (a) of § 1.170A-4, the amount of the charitable contribution in 1970 is reduced to zero ($600 – [$600 – $0]). Accordingly, C is not allowed any deduction under section 170 for the contributed property.

Example (6). The facts are the same as in example (5) except that the $450 expenses incurred in raising the contributed property were paid in 1970. The result in the same as in example (5), except the amount of $450 is deductible under section 162 for 1970.

(5) Transfers of property to an organization described in section 170(c) which bear a direct relationship to the taxpayer's trade or business and which are made with a reasonable expectation of financial return commensurate with the amount of the transfer may constitute allowable deductions as trade or business expenses rather than as charitable contributions. See section 162 and the regulations thereunder.

(d) Purchase of an annuity. *(1)* In the case of an annuity or portion thereof purchased from an organization described in section 170(c), there shall be allowed as a deduction the excess of the amount paid over the value at the time of purchase of the annuity or portion purchased.

(2) The value of the annuity or portion is the value of the annuity determined in accordance with paragraph (e)(1)(iii)(b)(2) of § 1.101-2.

(3) For determining gain on any such transaction constituting a bargain sale, see section 1011(b) and § 1.1011-2.

(e) Transfers subject to a condition or power. If as of the date of a gift a transfer for charitable purposes is dependent upon the performance of some act or the happening of a precedent event in order that it might become effective, no deduction is allowable unless the possibility that the charitable transfer will not become effective is so remote as to be negligible. If an interest in property passes to, or is vested in, charity on the date of the gift and the interest would be defeated by the subsequent performance of some act or the happening of some event, the possibility of occurrence of which appears on the date of the gift to be so remote as to be negligible, the deduction is allowable. For example, A transfers land to a city government for as long as the land is used by the city for a public park. If on the date of the gift the city does plan to use the land for a park and the possibility that the city will not use the land for a public park is so remote as to be negligible. A is entitled to a deduction under section 170 for his charitable contribution.

(f) Special rules applicable to certain contributions. *(1)* See section 14 of the Wild and Scenic Rivers Act (Public Law 90-542, 82 Stat. 918) for provisions relating to the claim and allowance of the value of certain easements as a charitable contribution under section 170.

(2) For treatment of gifts accepted by the Secretary of State or the Secretary of Commerce, for the purpose of organizing and holding an international conference to negotiate a Patent Corporation Treaty, as gifts to or for the use of the United States, see section 3 of joint resolution of December 24, 1969 (Public Law 91-160, 83 Stat. 443).

(3) For treatment of gifts accepted by the Secretary of the Department of Housing and Urban Development, for the purpose of aiding or facilitating the work of the Department, as gifts to or for the use of the United States, see section 7(k) of the Department of Housing and Urban Development Act (42 U.S.C. 3535), as added by section 905 of Public Law 91-609 (84 Stat. 1809).

(g) Contributions of services. No deduction is allowable under section 170 for a contribution of services. However, unreimbursed expenditures made incident to the rendition of services to an organization, contributions to which are deductible may constitute a deductible contribution. For example, the cost of a uniform without general utility which is required to be worn in performing donated services is deductible. Similarly, out-of-pocket transportation expenses necessarily incurred in performing donated services are deductible. Reasonable expenditures for meals and lodging necessarily incurred while away from home in the course of performing donated services also are deductible. For the purposes of this paragraph, the phrase "while away from home" has the same meaning as that phrase is used for purposes of section 162 and the regulations thereunder.

(h) Payment in exchange for consideration. *(1) Burden on taxpayer to show that all or part of payment is a charitable contribution or gift.* No part of a payment that a taxpayer makes to or for the use of an organization described in section 170(c) that is in consideration for (as defined in § 1.170A-13(f)(6)) goods or services (as defined in § 1.170A-13(f)(5)) is a contribution or gift within the meaning of section 170(c) unless the taxpayer—

(i) Intends to make a payment in an amount that exceeds the fair market value of the goods or services; and

(ii) Makes a payment in an amount that exceeds the fair market value of the goods or services.

(2) Limitation on amount deductible. (i) In general. The charitable contribution deduction under section 170(a) for a payment a taxpayer makes partly in consideration for goods or services may not exceed the excess of—

(A) The amount of any cash paid and the fair market value of any property (other than cash) transferred by the taxpayer to an organization described in section 170(c); over

(B) The fair market value of the goods or services the organization provides in return.

(ii) Special rules. For special limits on the deduction for charitable contributions of ordinary income and capital gain property, see section 170(e) and §§ 1.170A-4 and 1.170A-4A.

(3) Certain goods or services disregarded. For purposes of section 170(a) and paragraphs (h)(1) and (h)(2) of this section, goods or services described in § 1.170A-13(f)(8)(i) or § 1.170A13(f)(9)(i) are disregarded.

(4) Donee estimates of the value of goods or services may be treated as fair market value. (i) In general. For purposes of section 170(a), a taxpayer may rely on either a contemporaneous written acknowledgment provided under section 170(f)(8) and § 1.170A-13(f) or a written disclosure statement provided under section 6115 for the fair market value of any goods or services provided to the taxpayer by the donee organization.

(ii) Exception. A taxpayer may not treat an estimate of the value of goods or services as their fair market value if the taxpayer knows, or has reason to know, that such treatment is unreasonable. For example, if a taxpayer knows, or has reason to know, that there is an error in an estimate provided by an organization described in section 170(c) pertaining to goods or services that have a readily ascertainable value, it is unreasonable for the taxpayer to treat the estimate as the fair market value of the goods or services. Similarly, if a taxpayer is a dealer in the type of goods or services provided in consideration for the taxpayer's payment and knows, or has reason to know, that the estimate is in error, it is unreasonable for the taxpayer to treat the estimate as the fair market value of the goods or services.

(5) Examples. The following examples illustrate the rules of this paragraph (h).

Example (1). Certain goods or services disregarded. Taxpayer makes a $50 payment to Charity B, an organization described in section 170(c), in exchange for a family membership. The family membership entitles Taxpayer and members of Taxpayer's family to certain benefits. These benefits include free admission to weekly poetry readings, discounts on merchandise sold by B in its gift shop or by mail order, and invitations to special events for members only, such as lectures or informal receptions. When B first offers its membership package for the year, B reasonably projects that each special event for members will have a cost to B, excluding any allocable overhead, of $5 or less per person attending the event. Because the family membership benefits are disregarded pursuant to § 1.170A-13(f)(8)(i), Taxpayer may treat the $50 payment as a contribution or gift within the meaning of section 170(c), regardless of Taxpayer's intent and whether or not the payment exceeds the fair market value of the goods or services. Furthermore, any charitable contribution deduction available to Taxpayer may be calculated without regard to the membership benefits.

Example (2). Treatment of good faith estimate at auction as the fair market value. Taxpayer attends an auction held by Charity C, an organization described in section 170(c). Prior to the auction, C publishes a catalog that meets the requirements for a written disclosure statement under section 6115(a) (including C's good faith estimate of the value of items that will be available for bidding). A representative of C gives a copy of the catalog to each individual (including Taxpayer) who attends the auction. Taxpayer notes that in the catalog C's estimate of the value of a vase is $100. Taxpayer has no reason to doubt the accuracy of this estimate. Taxpayer successfully bids and pays $500 for the vase. Because Taxpayer knew, prior to making her payment, that the estimate in the catalog was less than the amount of her payment, Taxpayer satisfies the requirement of paragraph (h)(1)(i) of this section. Because Taxpayer makes a payment in an amount that exceeds that estimate, Taxpayer satisfies the requirements of paragraph (h)(1)(ii) of this section. Taxpayer may treat C's estimate of the value of the vase as its fair market value in determining the amount of her charitable contribution deduction.

Example (3). Good faith estimate not in error. Taxpayer makes a $200 payment to Charity D, an organization described in section 170(c). In return for Taxpayer's payment, D gives Taxpayer a book that Taxpayer could buy at retail prices typically ranging from $18 to $25. D provides Taxpayer with a good faith estimate, in a written disclosure statement under section 6115(a), of $20 for the value of the book. Because the estimate is within the range of typical retail prices for the book, the estimate contained in the written disclosure statement is not in error. Although Taxpayer knows that the book is sold for as much as $25, Taxpayer may treat the estimate of $20 as the fair market value of the book in determining the amount of his charitable contribution deduction.

(i) [Reserved]

(j) Exceptions and other rules. *(1)* The provisions of section 170 do not apply to contributions by an estate; nor do they apply to a trust unless the trust is a private foundation which, pursuant to section 642(c)(6) and § 1.642(c)-4, is allowed a deduction under section 170 subject to the provisions applicable to individuals.

(2) No deduction shall be allowed under section 170 for a charitable contribution to or for the use of an organization or trust described in section 508(d) or 4948(c)(4), subject to the conditions specified in such sections and the regulations thereunder.

(3) For disallowance of deductions for contributions to or for the use of communist controlled organizations, see section 11(a) of the Internal Security Act of 1950, as amended (50 U.S.C. 790).

(4) For denial of deductions for charitable contributions as trade or business expenses and rules with respect to treatment of payments to organizations other than those described in section 170(c), see section 162 and the regulations thereunder.

(5) No deduction shall be allowed under section 170 for amounts paid to an organization:

(i) Which is disqualified for tax exemption under section 501(c)(3) by reason of attempting to influence legislation, or

(ii) Which participates in or intervenes in (including the publishing or distributing of statements), any political campaign on behalf of or in opposition to any candidate for public office.

For purposes of determining whether an organization is attempting to influence legislation or is engaging in political activities, see sections 501(c)(3), 501(h), 4911 and the regulations thereunder.

(6) No deduction shall be allowed under section 170 for expenditures for lobbying purposes, the promotion or defeat of legislation, etc. See also the regulations under sections 162 and 4945.

(7) No deduction for charitable contributions is allowed in computing the taxable income of a common trust fund or of a partnership. See sections 584(d)(3) and 703(a)(2)(D). However, a partner's distributive share of charitable contributions actually paid by a partnership during its taxable year may be allowed as a deduction in the partner's separate return for his taxable year with or within which the taxable year of the partnership ends, to the extent that the aggregate of his share of the partnership contributions and his own contributions does not exceed the limitations in section 170(b).

(8) For charitable contributions paid by a nonresident alien individual or a foreign corporation, see § 1.170A-4(b)(5) and sections 873, 876, 877, and 882(c), and the regulations thereunder.

(9) Charitable contributions paid by bona fide residents of a section 931 possession as defined in § 1.931-1(c)(1) or Puerto Rico are deductible only to the extent allocable to income that is not excluded under section 931 or 933. For the rules for allocating deductions for charitable contributions, see the regulations under section 861.

(10) For carryover of excess charitable contributions in certain corporate acquisitions, see section 381(c)(19) and the regulations thereunder.

(11) No deduction shall be allowed under section 170 for out-of-pocket expenditures on behalf of an eligible organization (within the meaning of § 1.501(h)-2(b)(1)) if the expenditure is made in connection with influencing legislation (within the meaning of section 501(c)(3) or § 56.4911-2), or in connection with the payment of the organization's tax liability under section 4911. For the treatment of similar expenditures on behalf of other organizations see paragraph (h)(6) of this section.

(k) Effective/applicability date. In general this section applies to contributions paid in taxable years beginning after December 31, 1969. Paragraph (j)(11) of this section, however, applies only to out-of-pocket expenditures made in taxable years beginning after December 31, 1976. In addition, paragraph (h) of this section applies only to payments made on or after December 16, 1996. However, taxpayers may rely on the rules of paragraph (h) of this section for payments made on or after January 1, 1994. Paragraph (j)(9) of this section is applicable for taxable years ending after April 9, 2008.

T.D. 7207, 10/3/72, amend T.D. 7340, 1/6/75, T.D. 7807, 1/29/82, T.D. 8002, 12/26/84, T.D. 8308, 8/30/90, T.D. 8690, 12/13/96, T.D. 9194, 4/6/2005, T.D. 9391, 4/4/2008.

§ 1.170A-2 Amounts paid to maintain certain students as members of the taxpayer's household.

(a) In general. *(1)* The term "charitable contributions" includes amounts paid by the taxpayer during the taxable year to maintain certain students as members of his household which, under the provisions of section 170(h) and this section, are treated as amounts paid for the use of an organization described in section 170(c)(2), (3), or (4), and such amounts, to the extent they do not exceed the limitations under section 170(h)(2) and paragraph (b) of this section, are contributions deductible under section 170. In order for such amounts to be so treated, the student must be an individual who is neither a dependent (as defined in section 152) of the taxpayer nor related to the taxpayer in a manner described in any of the paragraphs (1) through (8) of section 152(a), and such individual must be a member of the taxpayer's household pursuant to a written agreement between the taxpayer and an organization described in section 170(c)(2), (3), or (4) to implement a program of the organization to provide educational opportunities for pupils or students placed in private homes by such organization. Furthermore, such amounts must be paid to maintain such individual during the period in the taxable year he is a member of the taxpayer's household and is a full-time pupil or student in the 12th or any lower grade at an educational institution, as defined in section 151(e)(4) and § 1.151-3, located in the United States. Amounts paid outside of such period, but within the taxable year, for expenses necessary for the maintenance of the student during the period will qualify for the charitable contributions deduction if the other limitation requirements of the section are met.

(2) For purposes of subparagraph (1) of this paragraph, amounts treated as charitable contributions include only those amounts actually paid by the taxpayer during the taxable year which are directly attributable to the maintenance of the student while he is a member of the taxpayer's household and is attending an educational institution on a full-time basis. This would include amounts paid to insure the well-being of the individual and to carry out the purpose for which the individual was placed in the taxpayer's home. For example, a deduction under section 170 would be allowed for amounts paid for books, tuition, food, clothing, transportation, medical and dental care, and recreation for the individual. Amounts treated as charitable contributions under this section do not include amounts which the taxpayer would have expended had the student not been in the household. They would not include, for example, amounts paid in connection with the taxpayer's home for taxes, insurance, interest on a mortgage, repairs, etc. Moreover, such amounts do not include any depreciation sustained by the taxpayer in maintaining such student or students in his household, nor do they include the value of any services rendered on behalf of such student or students by the taxpayer or any member of the taxpayer's household.

(3) For purposes of section 170(h) and this section, an individual will be considered to be a full-time pupil or student at an educational institution only if he is enrolled for a course of study prescribed for a full-time student at such institution and is attending classes on a full-time basis. Nevertheless, such individual may be absent from school due to special circumstances and still be considered to be in full-time attendance. Periods during the regular school term when the school is closed for holidays, such as Christmas and Easter, and for periods between semesters are treated as periods during which the pupil or student is in full-time attendance at the school. Also, absences during the regular school term due to illness of such individual shall not prevent him from being considered as a full-time pupil or student. Similarly, absences from the taxpayer's household due to special circumstances will not disqualify the student as a member of the household. Summer vacations between regular school terms are not considered periods of school attendance.

(4) When claiming a deduction for amounts described in section 170(h) and this section, the taxpayer must submit with his return a copy of his agreement with the organization sponsoring the individual placed in the taxpayer's household, together with a summary of the various items for which amounts were paid to maintain such individual, and a statement as to the date the individual became a member of the household and the period of his full-time attendance at school and the name and location of such school. Substantiation of amounts claimed must be supported by adequate records of the amounts actually paid. Due to the nature of certain items, such as food, a record of amount spent for all members of the household, with an equal portion thereof allocated to each member, will be acceptable.

(b) Limitations. Section 170(h) and this section shall apply to amounts paid during the taxable year only to the extent that the amounts paid in maintaining each pupil or student do not exceed $50 multiplied by the number of full calendar months in the taxable year that the pupil or student is maintained in accordance with the provisions of this section. For purposes of such limitation if 15 or more days of a calendar month fall within the period to which the maintenance of such pupil or student relates, such month is considered as a full calendar month. To the extent that such amounts qualify as charitable contributions under section 170(c), the aggregate of such amounts plus other contributions made during the taxable year for the use of an organization described in section 170(c) is deductible under section 170 subject to the limitation provided in section 170(b)(1)(B) and paragraph (c) of § 1.170-A-8.

(c) Compensation or reimbursement. Amounts paid during the taxable year to maintain a pupil or student as a member of the taxpayer's household as provided in paragraph (a) of this section, shall not be taken into account under section 170(h) and this section, if the taxpayer receives any money or other property as compensation or reimbursement for any portion of such amounts. The taxpayer will not be denied the benefits of section 170(h) if he prepays an extraordinary or nonrecurring expense, such as a hospital bill or vacation trip, at the request of the individual's parents or the sponsoring organization and is reimbursed for such prepayment. The value of services performed by the pupil or student in attending to ordinary chores of the household will generally not be considered to constitute compensation or reimbursement. However, if the pupil or student is taken into the taxpayer's household to replace a former employee of the taxpayer or gratuitously to perform substantial services for the taxpayer, the facts and circumstances may warrant a conclusion that the taxpayer received reimbursement for maintaining the pupil or student.

(d) No other amount allowed as deduction. Except to the extent that amounts described in section 170(h) and this section are treated as charitable contributions under section 170(c) and, therefore, deductible under section 170(a), no deduction is allowed for any amount paid to maintain an individual, as a member of the taxpayers household, in accordance with the provisions of section 170(h) and this section.

(e) Illustrations. The application of this section may be illustrated by the following examples:

Example (1). The X organization is an organization described in section 170(c)(2) and is engaged in a program under which a number of European children are placed in the homes of U.S. residents in order to further the children's high school education. In accordance with paragraph (a) of this section, the taxpayer, A, who reports his income on the calendar year basis, agreed with X to take two of the children, and they were placed in the taxpayer's home on January 2, 1970, where they remained until January 21, 1971, during which time they were fully maintained by the taxpayer. The children enrolled at the local high school for the full course of study prescribed for 10th grade students and attended the school on a full-time basis for the spring semester starting January 18, 1970, and ending June 3, 1970, and for the fall semester starting September 1, 1970, and ending January 13, 1971. The total cost of food paid by A in 1970 for himself, his wife, and the two children amounted to $1,920, or $40 per month for each member of the household. Since, the children were actually full-time students for only 8½ months during 1970, the amount paid for food for each child during that period amounted to $340. Other amounts paid during the 8½ month period for each child for laundry, lights, water, recreation, and school supplies amounted to $160. Thus, the amounts treated under section 170(h) and this section as paid for the use of X would, with respect to each child, total $500 ($340 + $160), or a total for both children of $1,000, subject to the limitations of paragraph (b) of this section. Since, for purposes of such limitations, the children were full-time students for only 8 full calendar months during 1970 (less than 15 days in January 1970), the taxpayer may treat only $800 as a charitable contribution made in 1970, that is, $50 multiplied by the 8 full calendar months, or $400 paid for the maintenance of each child. Neither the excess payments nor amounts paid to maintain the children during the period before school opened and for the period in summer between regular school terms is taken into account by reason of section 170(h). Also, because the children were full-time students for less than 15 days in January 1971 (although maintained in the taxpayer's household for 21 days), amounts paid to maintain the children during 1971 would not qualify as a charitable contribution.

Example (2). A religious organization described in section 170(c)(2) has a program for providing educational opportunities for children it places in private homes. In order to implement the program, the taxpayer, H, who resides with his wife, son, and daughter of high school age in a town in the United States, signs an agreement with the organization to maintain a girl sponsored by the organization as a member of his household while the child attends the local high school for the regular 1970-71 school year. The child is a full-time student at the school during the school year starting September 6, 1970, and ending June 6, 1971, and is a member of the taxpayer's household during that period. Although the taxpayer pays $200 during the school period falling in 1970, and $240 during the school period falling in 1971, to maintain the child, he cannot claim either amount as a charitable contribution because the child's parents, from time to time during the school year, sent butter, eggs, meat, and vegetables to H to help defray the expenses of maintaining the child. This is considered property received as reimbursement under paragraph (c) of this section. Had her parents not contributed the food, the fact that the child, in addition to the normal chores she shared with the taxpayer's daughter, such as cleaning their own rooms and helping with the shopping and cooking, was responsible for the family laundry and for the heavy cleaning of the entire house while the taxpayer's daughter had no comparable responsibilities would also preclude a claim for a charitable contributions deduction. These substantial gratuitous services are considered property received as reimbursement under paragraph (c) of this section.

Example (3). A taxpayer resides with his wife in a city in the eastern United States. He agrees, in writing, with a fraternal society described in section 170(c)(4) to accept a child selected by the society for maintenance by him as a member of his household during 1971 in order that the child may attend the local grammar school as a part of the society's program to provide elementary education for certain children selected by it. The taxpayer maintains the child, who has as his principal place of abode the home of the taxpayer, and is a member of the taxpayer's household, during the entire year 1971. The child is a full-time student at a local grammar school for 9 full calendar months during the year. Under the agreement, the society pays the taxpayer $30 per month to help maintain the child. Since the $30 per month is considered as compensation or reimbursement to the taxpayer for some portion of the maintenance paid on behalf of the child, no amounts paid with respect to such maintenance can be treated as amounts paid in accordance with section 170(h). In the absence of the $30 per month payments, if the child qualifies as a dependent of the taxpayer under section 152(a)(9), that fact would also prevent the maintenance payments from being treated as charitable contributions paid for the use of the fraternal society.

(f) Effective date. This section applies only to contributions paid in taxable years beginning after December 31, 1969.

T.D. 7207, 10/3/72.

§ 1.170A-3 Reduction of charitable contribution for interest on certain indebtedness.

(a) In general. Section 170(f)(5) requires that the amount of a charitable contribution be reduced for certain interest to the extent necessary to avoid the deduction of the same amount both as an interest deduction under section 163 and as a deduction for charitable contributions under section 170. The reduction is to be determined in accordance with paragraphs (b) and (c) of this section.

(b) Interest attributable to postcontribution period. In determining the amount to be taken into account as a charitable contribution for purposes of section 170, the amount determined without regard to section 170(f)(5) or this section shall be reduced by the amount of interest which has been paid, or is to be paid, by the taxpayer, which is attributable to any liability connected with the contribution and which is attributable to any period of time after the making of the contribution. The deduction otherwise allowable for charitable contributions under section 170 is required to be reduced pursuant to section 170(f)(5) and this section only if, in connection with a charitable contribution, a liability is assumed by the recipient of the contribution or by any other person or if the charitable contribution is of property which is subject to a liability. Thus, if a charitable contribution is made in property and the transfer is conditioned upon the assumption of a liability by the donee or by some other person, the contribution must be reduced by the amount of any interest which has ben paid, or will be paid, by the taxpayer, which is attributable to the liability, and which is attributable to any period after the making of the contribution. The adjustment referred to in this paragraph must also be made where the contributed property is subject to a liability and the value of the property reflects the payment by the donor of interest with respect to a period of time after the making of the contribution.

(c) Interest attributable to precontribution period. If, in connection with the charitable contribution of a bond, a liability is assumed by the recipient or by any other person, or if the bond is subject to a liability, then, in determining the amount to be taken into account as a charitable contribution under section 170, the amount determined without regard to section 170(f)(5) and this section shall, without regard to whether any reduction may be required by paragraph (b) of this section, also be reduced for interest which has been paid, or is to be paid, by the taxpayer on indebtedness incurred or continued to purchase or carry such bond, and which is attributable to any period before the making of the contribution. However, the reduction referred to in this paragraph shall be made only to the extent that such reduction does not exceed the interest (including bond discount and other interest equivalent) receivable on the bond, and attributable to any period before the making of the contribution which is not, by reason of the taxpayer's method of accounting, includible in the taxpayer's gross income for any taxable year. For purposes of section 170(f)(5) and this section the term "bond" means any bond, debenture, note, or certificate or other evidence of indebtedness.

(d) Illustrations. The application of this section may be illustrated by the following examples:

Example (1). On January 1, 1970, A, a cash basis taxpayer using the calendar year as the taxable year, contributed to a charitable organization real estate having a fair market value and adjusted basis of $10,000. In connection with the contribution the charitable organization assumed an indebtedness of $8,000 which A had incurred. On December 31, 1969, A prepaid one year's interest on that indebtedness for 1970, amounting to $960, and took an interest deduction of $960 for such amount. The amount of the gift, determined without regard to this section, is $2,960 ($10,000 less $8,000, the outstanding indebtedness, plus $960, the amount of prepaid interest). In determining the amount of the deduction for the charitable contribution, the value of the gift ($2,960) must be reduced by $960 to eliminate from computation of such deduction that portion thereof for which A has been allowed an interest deduction.

Example (2). (a) On January 1, 1970, B, an individual using the cash receipts and disbursements method of accounting, purchased for $9,950 a 5½ percent $10,000, 20-year M Corporation bond, the interest on which was payable semiannually on June 30 and December 31. The M Corporation had issued the bond on January 1, 1960, at a discount of $720 from the principal amount. On December 1, 1970, B donated the bond to a charitable organization, and, in connection with the contribution, the charitable organization assumed an indebtedness of $7,000 which B had incurred to purchase and carry the bond.

(b) During the calendar year 1970 B paid accrued interest of $330 on the indebtedness for the period from January 1, 1970, to December 1, 1970, and has taken an interest deduction of $330 for such amount. No portion of the bond discount of $36 a year ($720 divided by 20 years) has been included in B's income, and of the $550 of annual interest receivable on the bond, he included in income only the June 30, 1970, payment of $275.

(c) The market value of the bond on December 1, 1970, was $9,902. Such value includes $229 of interest receivable which had accrued from July 1 to December 1, 1970.

(d) The amount of the charitable contribution determined without regard to this section is $2,902 ($9,902, the value of the property on the date of gift, less $7,000, the amount of the liability assumed by the charitable organization). In determining the amount of the allowance deduction for charitable contributions, the value of the gift ($2,902) must be reduced to eliminate from the deduction that portion thereof for which B has been allowed an interest deduction. Although the amount of such interest deduction was $330, the reduction required by this section is limited to $262, since the reduction is not in excess of the amount of interest income on the bond ($229 of accrued interest plus $33, the amount of bond discount attributable to the 11-month period B held the bond).

(e) Effective date. This section applies only to contributions paid in taxable years beginning after December 31, 1969.

T.D. 7207, 10/3/72.

§ 1.170A-4 Reduction in amount of charitable contributions of certain appreciated property.

Caution: The Treasury has not yet amended Reg § 1.170A-4 to reflect changes made by P.L. 109-280, P.L. 108-357, P.L. 108-27, P.L. 107-16, P.L. 105-277.

(a) Amount of reduction. Section 170(e)(1) requires that the amount of the charitable contribution which would be taken into account under section 170(a) without regard to section 170(e) shall be reduced before applying the percentage limitations under section 170(b):

(1) In the case of a contribution by an individual or by a corporation of ordinary income property, as defined in paragraph (b)(1) of this section, by the amount of gain (hereinafter in this section referred to as ordinary income) which would have been recognized as gain which is not long-term capital gain if the property had been sold by the donor at its fair market value at the time of its contribution to the charitable organization,

(2) In the case of a contribution by an individual of section 170(e) capital gain property, as defined in paragraph (b)(2) of this section, by 50 percent of the amount of gain (hereinafter in this section referred to as long-term capital gain) which would have been recognized as long-term capital gain if the property has been sold by the donor at its fair market value at the time of its contribution to the charitable organization, and

(3) In the case of a contribution by a corporation of section 170(e) capital gain property, as defined in paragraph (b)(2) of this section, by 62½ percent of the amount of gain (hereinafter in this section referred to as long-term capital gain) which would have been recognized as long-term capital gain if the property had been sold by the donor at its fair market value at the time of its contribution to the charitable organization.

Section 170(e)(1) and this paragraph do not apply to reduce the amount of the charitable contribution where, by reason of the transfer of the contributed property, ordinary income or capital gain is recognized by the donor in the same taxable year in which the contribution is made. Thus, where income or gain is recognized under section 453(d) upon the transfer of an installment obligation to a charitable organization, or under section 454(b) upon the transfer of an obligation issued at a discount to such an organization, or upon the assignment of income to such an organization, section 170(e)(1) and this paragraph do not apply if recognition of the income or gain occurs in the same taxable year in which the contribution is made. Section 170(e)(1) and this paragraph apply to a charitable contribution of an interest in ordinary income property or section 170(e) capital gain property which is described in paragraph (b) of § 1.170A-6, or paragraph (b) of § 1.170A-7. For purposes of applying section 170(e)(1) and this paragraph it is immaterial whether the charitable contribution is made "to" the charitable organization or whether it is made "for the use of" the charitable organization. See § 1.170A-8(a)(2).

(b) Definitions and other rules. For purposes of this section. *(1) Ordinary income property.* The term "ordinary income property" means property any portion of the gain on which would not have been long term capital gain if the property had been sold by the donor at its fair market value at the time of its contribution to the charitable organization. Such term includes, for example, property held by the donor primarily for sale to customers in the ordinary course of his trade or business, a work of art created by the donor, a manuscript prepared by the donor, letters and memorandums prepared by or for the donor, a capital asset held by the donor for not more than 1 year (6 months for taxable years beginning before 1977; 9 months for taxable years beginning in 1977), and stock described in section 306(a), 341(a), or 1248(a) to the extent that, after applying such section, gain on its disposition would not have been long term capital gain. The term does not include an income interest in respect of which a deduction is allowed under section 170(f)(2)(B) and paragraph (c) of § 1.170A-6.

(2) Section 170(e) capital gain property. The term "section 170(e) capital gain property" means property any portion of the gain on which would have been treated as long-term capital gain if the property had been sold by the donor at its fair market value at the time of its contribution to the charitable organization and which:

(i) Is contributed to or for the use of a private foundation, as defined in section 509(a) and the regulations thereunder, other than a private foundation described in section 170(b)(1)(E),

(ii) Constitutes tangible personal property contributed to or for the use of a charitable organization, other than a private foundation to which subdivision (i) of this subparagraph applies, which is put to an unrelated use by the charitable organization within the meaning of subparagraph (3) of this paragraph, or

(iii) Constitutes property not described in subdivision (i) or (ii) of this subparagraph which is 30-percent capital gain property to which an election under paragraph (d)(2) of § 1.170A-8 applies.

For purposes of this subparagraph a fixture which is intended to be severed from real property shall be treated as tangible personal property.

(3) Unrelated use. (i) In general. The term "unrelated use" means a use which is unrelated to the purpose or function constituting the basis of the charitable organization's exemption under section 501 or, in the case of a contribution of property to a governmental unit, the use of such property by such unit for other than exclusively public purposes. For example, if a painting contributed to an educational institution is used by that organization for educational purposes by being placed in its library for display and study by art students, the use is not an unrelated use; but if the painting is sold and the proceeds used by the organization for educational purposes, the use of the property is an unrelated use. If furnishings contributed to a charitable organization are used by it in its offices and buildings in the course of carrying out its functions, the use of the property is not an unrelated use. If a set or collection of items of tangible personal property is contributed to a charitable organization or governmental unit, the use of the set or collection is not an unrelated use if the donee sells or otherwise disposes of only an insubstantial portion of the set or collection. The use by a trust of tangible personal property contributed to it for the benefit of a charitable organization is an unrelated use if the use by the trust is one which would have been unrelated if made by the charitable organization.

(ii) Proof of use. For purposes of applying subparagraph (2)(ii) of this paragraph, a taxpayer who makes a charitable contribution of tangible personal property to or for the use of a charitable organization or governmental unit may treat such property as not being put to an unrelated use by the donee if:

(a) He establishes that the property is not in fact put to an unrelated use by the donee, or

(b) At the time of the contribution or at the time the contribution is treated as made, it is reasonable to anticipate that the property will not be put to an unrelated use by the donee. In the case of a contribution of tangible personal property to or for the use of a museum, if the object donated is of a general type normally retained by such museum or other museums for museum purposes, it will be reasonable for the donor to anticipate, unless he has actual knowledge to the contrary, that the object will not be put to an unrelated use by the donee, whether or not the object is later sold or exchanged by the donee.

(4) Property used in trade or business. For purposes of applying subparagraphs (1) and (2) of this paragraph, property which is used in the trade or business, as defined in section 1231(b), shall be treated as a capital asset, except that any gain in respect of such property which would have been recognized if the property had been sold by the donor at its fair market value at the time of its contribution to the charitable organization shall be treated as ordinary income to the extent that such gains would have constituted ordinary income by reason of the application of section 617(d)(1), 1245(a), 1250(a), 1251(c), 1252(a), or 1254(a).

(5) Nonresident alien individuals and foreign corporations. The reduction in the case of a nonresident alien individual or a foreign corporation shall be determined by taking into account the gain which would have been recognized and subject to tax under chapter 1 of the Code if the property had been sold or disposed of within the United States by the donor at its fair market value at the time of its contribution to the charitable organization. However, the amount of such gain which would have been subject to tax under section 871(a) or 881 (relating to gain not effectively connected with the conduct of a trade or business within the United States) if there had been a sale or other disposition within the United States shall be treated as long-term capital gain. Thus, a charitable contribution by a nonresident alien individual or a foreign corporation of property the sale or other disposition of which within the United States would have resulted in gain subject to tax under section 871(a) or 881 will be reduced only as provided in section 170(e)(1)(B) and paragraph (a)(2) or (3) of this section, but only if the property contributed is described in subdivision (i), (ii), or (iii) of subparagraph (2) of this paragraph. A charitable contribution by a nonresident alien individual or a foreign corporation of property the sale or other disposition of which within the United States would have resulted in gain subject to tax under section 871(a) or 881 will in no case be reduced under section 170(e)(1)(A) and paragraph (a)(1) of this section.

(c) Allocation of basis and gain. *(1) In general.* Except as provided in subparagraph (2) of this paragraph:

(i) If a taxpayer makes a charitable contribution of less than his entire interest in appreciated property, whether or not the transfer is made in trust, as, for example, in the case of a transfer of appreciated property to a pooled income fund described in section 642(c)(5) and § 1.642(c)-5, and is allowed a deduction under section 170 for a portion of the fair market value of such property, then for purposes of applying the reduction rules of section 170(e)(1) and this section to the contributed portion of the property the taxpayer's adjusted basis in such property at the time of the contribution shall be allocated under section 170(e)(2) between the contributed portion of the property and the noncontributed portion.

(ii) The adjusted basis of the contributed portion of the property shall be that portion of the adjusted basis of the entire property which bears the same ratio to the total adjusted basis as the fair market value of the contributed portion of the property bears to the fair market value of the entire property.

(iii) The ordinary income and the long-term capital gain which shall be taken into account in applying section 170(e)(1) and paragraph (a) of this section to the contributed portion of the property shall be the amount of gain which would have been recognized as ordinary income and long-term capital gain if such contributed portion had been sold by the donor at its fair market value at the time of its contribution to the charitable organization.

(2) Bargain sale. (i) Section 1011(b) and § 1.1011-2 apply to bargain sales of property to charitable organizations. For purposes of applying the reduction rules of section 170(e)(1) and this section to the contributed portion of the property in the case of a bargain sale, there shall be allocated under section 1011(b) to the contributed portion of the property that portion of the adjusted basis of the entire property that bears the same ratio to the total adjusted basis as the fair market value of the contributed portion of the property bears to the fair market value of the entire property. For purposes of applying section 170(e)(1) and paragraph (a) of this section to the contributed portion of the property in such a case, there shall be allocated to the contributed portion the amount of gain that is not recognized on the bargain sale but that would have been recognized if such contributed portion had been sold by the donor at its fair market value at the time of its contribution to the charitable organization.

(ii) The term "bargain sale", as used in this subparagraph, means a transfer of property which is in part a sale or exchange of property and in part a charitable contribution, as defined in section 170(c), of the property.

(3) Ratio of ordinary income and capital gain. For purposes of applying subparagraphs (1)(iii) and (2)(i) of this paragraph, the amount of ordinary income (or long-term capital gain) which would have been recognized if the contributed portion of the property had been sold by the donor at its fair market value at the time of its contribution shall be that amount which bears the same ratio to the ordinary income (or long-term capital gain) which would have been recognized if the entire property had been sold by the donor at its fair market value at the time of its contribution as (i) the fair market value of the contributed portion at such time bears to (ii) the fair market value of the entire property at such time. In the case of a bargain sale, the fair market value of the contributed portion for purposes of subdivision (i) is the amount determined by subtracting from the fair market value of the entire property the amount realized on the sale.

(4) Donee's basis of property acquired. The adjusted basis of the contributed portion of the property, as determined under subparagraph (1) or (2) of this paragraph, shall be used by the donee in applying to the contributed portion such provisions as section 514(a)(1), relating to adjusted basis of debt-financed property; section 1015(a), relating to basis of property acquired by gift; section 4940(c)(4), relating to capital gains and losses in determination of net investment income; and section 4942(f)(2)(B), relating to net short-term capital gain in determination of tax on failure to distribute income. The fair market value of the contributed portion of the property at the time of the contribution shall not be used by the donee as the basis of such contributed portion.

(d) Illustrations. The application of this section may be illustrated by the following examples:

Example (1). (a) On July 1, 1970, C, an individual, makes the following charitable contributions, all of which are made to a church except in the case of the stock (as indicated):

Property	Fair market value	Adjusted basis	Recognized gain if sold
Ordinary income property	$50,000	$35,000	$15,000
Property which, if sold, would produce long-term capital gain:			
(1) Stock held more than 6 months contributed to—			
(i) A church	25,000	21,000	4,000
(ii) A private foundation not described in section 170(b)(1)(E)	15,000	10,000	5,000
(2) Tangible personal property held more than 6 months (put to unrelated use by church)	12,000	6,000	6,000
Total	102,000	72,000	30,000

(b) After making the reductions required by paragraph (a) of this section, the amount of charitable contributions allowed (before application of section 170(b) limitations) is as follows:

Property	Fair market value	Reduction	Contribution allowed
Ordinary income property	$50,000	$15,000	$35,000
Property which, if sold, would produce long-term capital gain:			
(1) Stock contributed to—			
(i) The church	25,000	—	25,000
(ii) The private foundation	15,000	3,125	11,875
(2) Tangible personal property	12,000	3,750	8,250
Total	102,000	21,875	80,125

(c) If C were a corporation, rather than an individual, the amount of charitable contributions allowed (before application of section 170(b) limitation) would be as follows:

Property	Fair market value	Reduction	Contribution allowed
Ordinary income property	$50,000	$15,000	$35,000
Property which, if sold, would produce long-term capital gain:			
(1) Stock contributed to—			
(i) The church	25,000	—	25,000
(ii) The private foundation	15,000	3,125	11,875
(2) Tangible personal property	12,000	3,750	8,250
Total	102,000	21,875	80,125

Example (2). On March 1, 1970, D, an individual, contributes to a church intangible property to which section 1245 applies which has a fair market value of $60,000 and an adjusted basis of $10,000. At the time of the contribution D has used the property in his business for more than 6 months. If the property had been sold by D at its fair market value at the time of its contribution, it is assumed that under section 1245 $20,000 of the gain of $50,000 would have been treated as ordinary income and $30,000 would have been long-term capital gain. Under paragraph (a)(1) of this section, D's contribution of $60,000 is reduced by $20,000.

Example (3). The facts are the same as in *example (2)* except that the property is contributed to a private foundation not described in section 170(b)(1)(E). Under paragraph (a)(1) and (2) of this section, D's contribution is reduced by $35,000 (100 percent of the ordinary income of $20,000 and 50 percent of the long-term capital gain of $30,000).

Example (4). (a) In 1971, E, an individual calendar-year taxpayer, contributes to a church stock held for more than 6 months which has a fair market value of $90,000 and an adjusted basis of $10,000. In 1972, E also contributes to a church stock held for more than 6 months which has a fair market value of $20,000 and an adjusted basis of $10,000. E's contribution base for 1971 is $200,000; and for 1972, is $150,000. E makes no other charitable contributions for these 2 taxable years.

(b) For 1971 the amount of the contribution which may be taken into account under section 170(a) is limited by section 170(b)(1)(D)(i) to $60,000 ($200,000 × 30%), and A is allowed a deduction for $60,000. Under section 170(b)(1)(D)(ii), E has a $30,000 carryover to 1972 of 30-percent capital gain property, as defined in paragraph (d)(3) of § 1.170A-8. For 1972 the amount of the charitable contributions deduction is $45,000 (total contributions of $50,000 [$30,000 + $20,000] but not to exceed 30% of $150,000).

(c) Assuming, however, that in 1972 E elects under section 170(b)(1)(D)(iii) and paragraph (d)(2) of § 1.170A-8 to have section 170(e)(1)(B) apply to his contributions and carryovers of 30-percent capital gain property, he must apply section 170(d)(1) as if section 170(e)(1)(B) had applied to the contribution for 1971. If section 170(e)(1)(B) had applied in 1971 to his contributions of 30-percent capital gain property, E's contribution would have been reduced from $90,000 to $50,000, the reduction of $40,000 being 50 percent of the gain of $80,000 ($90,000 − $10,000) which would have been recognized as long-term capital gain if the property had been sold by E at its fair market value at the time of its contribution to the church. Accordingly, by taking the election into account, E has no carryover of 30-percent capital gain property to 1972 since the charitable contributions deduction of $60,000 allowed for 1971 in respect of that property exceeds the reduced contribution of $50,000 for 1971 which may be taken into account by reason of the election. The charitable contributions deduction of $60,000 allowed for 1971 is not reduced by reason of the election.

(d) Since by reason of the election E is allowed under paragraph (a)(2) of this section a charitable contributions deduction for 1972 of $15,000 ($20,000 − [$20,000 − $10,000) × 50%]) and since the $30,000 carryover from 1971 is eliminated, it would not be to E's advantage to make the election under section 170(b)(1)(D)(iii) in 1972.

Example (5). In 1970, F, an individual calendar-year taxpayer, sells to a church for $4,000 ordinary income property with a fair market value of $10,000 and an adjusted basis of $4,000. F's contribution base for 1970 is $20,000, and F makes no other charitable contributions in 1970. Thus, F makes a charitable contribution to the church of $6,000 ($10,000 − $4,000 amount realized), which is 60% of the value of the property. The amount realized on the bargain sale is 40% ($4,000/$10,000) of the value of the property. In applying section 1011(b) to the bargain sale, adjusted basis in the amount of $1,600 ($4,000 adjusted basis × 40%) is allocated under § 1.1011-2(b) to the noncontributed portion of the property, and F recognizes $2,400 ($4,000 amount realized less $1,600 adjusted basis) of ordinary income. Under paragraphs (a)(1) and (c)(2)(i) of this section, F's contribution of $6,000 is reduced by $3,600 ($6,000 − [$4,000 adjusted basis × 60%]) (i.e, the amount of ordinary income that would have been recognized on the contributed portion had the property been sold). The reduced contribution of $2,400 consists of the portion ($4,000×60%) of the adjusted basis not allocated to the noncontributed portion of the property. That is, the reduced contribution consists of the portion of the adjusted basis allocated to the contributed portion. Under sections 1012 and 1015(a) the basis of the property to the church is $6,400 ($4,000 + $2,400).

Example (6). In 1970, G, an individual calendar-year taxpayer, sells to a church for $6,000 ordinary income property with a fair market value of $10,000 and an adjusted basis of $4,000. G's contribution base for 1970 is $20,000 and G makes no other charitable contributions in 1970. Thus, G makes a charitable contribution to the church of $4,000 ($10,000 − $6,000 amount realized), which is 40% of the value of the property. The amount realized on the bargain sale is 60% ($6,000/$10,000) of the value of the property. In applying section 1011(b) to the bargain sale, adjusted basis in the amount of $2,400 ($4,000 adjusted basis × 60%) is allocated under § 1.1011-2(b) to the noncontributed portion of the property, and G recognizes $3,600 ($6,000 amount realized less $2,400 adjusted basis) of ordinary income. Under paragraphs (a)(1) and (c)(2)(i) of this section, G's contribution of $4,000 is reduced by $2,400 [($4,000 − ($4,000 adjusted basis × 40%]) (i.e., the amount of ordinary income that would have been recognized on the contributed portion had the property been sold). The reduced contribution of $1,600 consist of the portion ($4,000 × 40%) of the adjusted basis not allocated to the noncontributed portion of the property. That is, the reduced contribution consists of the portion of the adjusted basis allocated to the contributed portion.

Under sections 1012 and 1015(a) the basis of the property to the church is $7,600 ($6,000 + $1,600).

Example (7). In 1970, H, an individual calendar-year taxpayer, sells to a church for $2,000 stock held for not more than 6 months which has an adjusted basis of $4,000 and a fair market value of $10,000. H's contribution base for 1970 is $20,000, and H makes no other charitable contributions in 1970. Thus, H makes a charitable contribution to the church of $8,000 ($10,000 – $2,000 amount realized), which is 80% of the value of the property. The amount realized on the bargain sale is 20% ($2,000/$10,000) of the value of the property. In applying section 1011(b) to the bargain sale, adjusted basis in the amount of $800 ($4,000 adjusted basis × 20%) is allocated under § 1.1011-2(b) to the noncontributed portion of the property, and H recognizes $1,200 ($2,000 amount realized less $800 adjusted basis) of ordinary income. Under paragraphs (a)(1) and (c)(2)(i) of this section, H's contribution of $8,000 is reduced by $4,800 ($8,000 – [$4,000 adjusted basis × 80%]) (i.e., the amount of ordinary income that would have been recognized on the contributed portion had the property been sold). The reduced contribution of $3,200 consists of the portion ($4,000 × 80%) of the adjusted basis not allocated to the noncontributed portion of the property. That is, the reduced contribution consists of the portion of the adjusted basis allocated to the contributed portion. Under sections 1012 and 1015(a) the basis of the property to the church is $5,200 ($2,000 + 3,200).

Example (8). In 1970, F, an individual calendar-year taxpayer, sells for $4,000 to a private foundation not described in section 170(b)(1)(E) property to which section 1245 applies which has a fair market value of $10,000 and an adjusted basis of $4,000. F's contribution base for 1970 is $20,000, and F makes no other charitable contributions in 1970. At the time of the bargain sale, F has used the property in his business for more than 6 months. Thus F makes a charitable contribution of $6,000 ($10,000 – $4,000 amount realized), which is 60% of the value of the property. The amount realized on the bargain sale is 40% ($4,000/$10,000) of the value of the property. If the property had been sold by F at its fair market value at the time of its contribution, it is assumed that under section 1245 $4,000 of the gain of $6,000 ($10,000 – $4,000 adjusted basis) would have been treated as ordinary income and $2,000 would have been long-term capital gain. In applying section 1011(b) to the bargain sale, adjusted basis in the amount of $1,600 ($4,000 adjusted basis × 40%) is allocated under § 1.1011-2(b) to the noncontributed portion of the property, and F's recognized gain of $2,400 ($4,000 amount realized less $1,600 adjusted basis) consists of $1,600 ($4,000 × 40%) of ordinary income and $800 ($2,000 × 40% of long-term capital gain. Under paragraph's (a) and (c)(2)(i) of this section, F's contribution of $6,000 is reduced by $3,000 (the sum of $2,400 ($4,000 × 60%) of ordinary income and $600 ([$2,000 × 60%] × 50%) of long-term capital gain) (i.e., the amount of gain that would have been recognized on the contributed portion had the property been sold). The reduced contribution of $3,000 consists of $2,400 ($4,000 × 60%) of adjusted basis and $600 ([$2,000 × 60%] × 50%) of long-term capital gain not used as a reduction under paragraph (a)(2) of this section. Under sections 1012 and 1015(a) the basis of the property to the private foundation is $6,400 ($4,000 + $2,400).

Example (9). On January 1, 1970, A, an individual, transfers to a charitable remainder annuity trust described in section 664(d)(1) stock which he has held for more than 6 months and which has a fair market value of $250,000 and an adjusted basis of $50,000, an irrevocable remainder interest in the property being contributed to a private foundation not described in section 170(b)(1)(E). The trusts provides that an annuity of $12,500 a year is payable to A at the end of each year for 20 years. By reference to § 20.2031-7A(c) of this chapter (Estate Tax Regulations) the figure in column (2) opposite 20 years in 11.4699. Therefore, under § 1.664-2 the fair market value of the gift of the remainder interest to charity is $106,626.25 ($250,000 – [$12,500 × 11.4699]). Under paragraph (c)(1)(ii) of this section, the adjusted basis allocated to the contributed portion of the property is $21,325.25 ($50,000 × $106,626.25/$250,000). Under paragraphs (a)(2) and (c)(1) of this section, A's contribution is reduced by $42,650.50 (50 percent × [$106,626.25 – $21,325.25]) to $63,975.75 ($106,626.25 – $42,650.50). If, however, the irrevocable remainder interest in the property had been contributed to a section 170(b)(1)(A) organization, A's contribution of $106,626.25 would not be reduced under paragraph (a) of this section.

Example (10). (a) On July 1, 1970, B, a calendar-year individual taxpayer, sells to a church for $75,000 intangible property to which section 1245 applies which has a fair market value of $250,000 and an adjusted basis of $75,000. Thus, B makes a charitable contribution to the church of $175,000 ($250,000 – $75,000 amount realized), which is 70% ($175,000/$250,000) of the value of the property, the amount realized on the bargain sale is 30% ($75,000/$250,000) of the value of the property. At the time of the bargain sale, B has used the property in his business for more than 6 months. B's contribution base for 1970 is $500,000, and B makes no other charitable contributions in 1970. If the property had been sold by B at its fair market value at the time of its contribution, it is assumed that under section 1245 $105,000 of the gain of $175,000 ($250,000 – $75,000 adjusted basis) would have been treated as ordinary income and $70,000 would have been long-term capital gain. In applying section 1011(b) to the bargain sale, adjusted basis in the amount of $22,500 ($75,000 adjusted basis × 30%) is allocated under § 1.1011-2(b) to the noncontributed portion of the property and B's recognized gain of $52,500 ($75,000 amount realized less $22,500 adjusted basis) consists of $31,500 ($105,000 × 30%) of ordinary income and $21,000 ($70,000 × 30%) of long term capital gain.

(b) Under paragraphs (a)(1) and (c)(2)(i) of this section B's contribution of $175,000 is reduced by $73,500 ($105,000 × 70%) (i.e., the amount of ordinary income that would have been recognized on the contributed portion had the property been sold). The reduced contribution of $101,500 consists of $52,500 ($75,000 × 70%) of adjusted basis allocated to the contributed portion of the property and $49,000 ($70,000 × 70%) of long-term capital gain allocated to the contributed portion. Under sections 1012 and 1015(a) the basis of the property to the church is $127,500 ($75,000 + $52,500).

(e) Effective date. This section applies only to contributions paid after December 31, 1969, except that, in the case of a charitable contribution of a letter, memorandum, or property similar to a letter or memorandum, it applies to contributions paid after July 25, 1969.

T.D. 7207, 10/3/72, amend T.D. 7728, 10/31/80, T.D. 7807, 1/29/82, T.D. 8176, 2/24/88, T.D. 8540, 6/9/94.

---

§ 1.170A-4A Special rule for the deduction of certain charitable contributions of inventory and other property.

Caution: The Treasury has not yet amended Reg § 1.170A-4A to reflect changes made by 109-73, P.L. 100-647, P.L. 100-203, P.L. 99-514, P.L. 98-369.

(a) Introduction. Section 170(e)(3) provides a special rule for the deduction of certain qualified contributions of inventory and certain other property. To be treated as a "qualified contribution", a contribution must meet the restrictions and requirements of section 170(e)(3)(A) and paragraph (b) of this section. Paragraph (b)(1) of this section describes the corporations whose contributions may be subject to this section, the exempt organizations to which these contributions may be made, and the kinds of property which may be contributed. Under paragraph (b)(2) of this section, the use of the property must be related to the purpose or function constituting the ground for the exemption of the organization to which the contribution is made. Also, the property must be used for the care of the ill, needy, or infants. Under paragraph (b)(3) of this section, the recipient organization may not, except as there provided, require or receive in exchange money, property, or services for the transfer or use of property contributed under section 170(e)(3). Under paragraph (b)(4) of this section, the recipient organization must provide the contributing taxpayer with a written statement representing that the organization intends to comply with the restrictions set forth in paragraph (b)(2) and (3) of this section on the use and transfer of the property. Under paragraph (b)(5) of this section, the contributed property must conform to any applicable provisions of the Federal Food, Drug, and Cosmetic Act (as amended), and the regulations thereunder, at the date of contribution and for the immediately preceding 180 days. Paragraph (c) of this section provides the rules for determining the amount of reduction of the charitable contribution under section 170(e)(3). In general, the amount of the reduction is equal to one-half of the amount of gain (other than gain described in paragraph (d) of this section) which would not have been long-term capital gain if the property had been sold by the donor-taxpayer at fair market value at the date of contribution. If, after this reduction, the amount of the deduction would be more than twice the basis of the contributed property, the amount of the deduction is accordingly further reduced under paragraph (c)(1) of this section. The basis of contributed property which is inventory is determined under paragraph (c)(2) of this section, and the donor's cost of goods sold for the year of contribution must be adjusted under paragraph (c)(3) of this section. Under paragraph (d) of this section, a deduction is not allowed for any amount which, if the property had been sold by the donor-taxpayer, would have been gain to which the recapture provisions of section 617, 1245, 1250, 1251, or 1252 would have applied. For purposes of section 170(e)(3) the rules of § 1.170A-4 apply where not inconsistent with the rules of this section.

(b) Qualified contributions. *(1) In general.* A contribution of property qualifies under section 170(e)(3) of this section only if it is a charitable contribution—

(i) By a corporation, other than a corporation which is an electing small business corporation within the meaning of section 1371(b);

(ii) To an organization described in section 501(c)(3) and exempt under section 501(a), other than a private foundation, as defined in section 509(a), which is not an operating foundation, as defined in section 4942(j)(e);

(iii) Of property described in section 1221 (1) or (2);

(iv) Which contribution meets the restrictions and requirements of paragraph (b)(2) through (5) of this section.

(2) Restrictions on use of contributed property. In order for the contribution to qualify under this section, the contributed property is subject to the following restrictions in use. If the transferred property is used or transferred by the donee organization (or by any subsequent transferee that furnished to the donee organization the written statement described in paragraph (b)(4)(ii) of this section) in a manner inconsistent with the requirements of subdivision (i) or (ii) of this paragraph (b)(2) or the requirements of paragraph (b)(3) of this section, the donor's deduction is reduced to the amount allowable under section 170 of the regulations thereunder, determined without regard to section 170(e)(3) of this section. If, however, the donor establishes that, at the time of the contribution, the donor reasonably anticipated that the property would be used in a manner consistent with those requirements, then the donor's deduction is not reduced.

(i) Requirement of use for exempt purpose. The use of the property must be related to the purpose or function constituting the ground for exemption under section 501(c)(3) of the organization to which the contribution is made. The property may not be used in connection with any activity which gives rise to unrelated trade or business income, as defined in sections 512 and 513 and the regulations thereunder.

(ii) Requirement of use for care of the ill, needy, or infants. (A) In general. The property must be used for the care of the ill, needy, or infants, as defined in this subdivision (ii). The property itself must ultimately either be transferred to (or for the use of) the ill, needy, or infants for their care or be retained for their care. No other person may use the contributed property except as incidental to primary use in the care of the ill, needy, or infants. The organization may satisfy the requirement of this subdivision by transferring the property to a relative, custodian, parent or guardian of the ill or needy individual or infant, or to any other individual if it makes a reasonable effort to ascertain that the property will ultimately be used primarily for the care of the ill or needy individual, or infant, and not for the primary benefit of any other person. The recipient organization may transfer the property to another exempt organization within the jurisdiction of the United States which meets the description contained in paragraph (b)(1)(ii) of this section, or to an organization not within the jurisdiction of the United States that, but for the fact that it is not within the jurisdiction of the United States, would be described in paragraph (b)(1)(ii) of this section. If an organization transfers the property to another organization, the transferring organization must obtain a written statement from the transferee organization as set forth in paragraph (b)(4) of this section. If the property is ultimately transferred to, or used for the benefit of, ill or needy persons, or infants, not within the jurisdiction of the United States, the organization which so transfers the property outside the jurisdiction of the United States must necessarily be a corporation. See section 170(c)(2) and § 1.170A-11(a). For purposes of this subdivision, if the donee-organization charges for its transfer of contributed property (other than a fee allowed by paragraph (b)(3)(ii) of this section), the requirement of this subdivision is not met. See paragraph (b)(3) of this section.

(B) Definition of the ill. An ill person is a person who requires medical care within the meaning of § 1.213-1(e). Examples of ill persons include a person suffering from physical injury, a person with a significant impairment of a bodily organ, a person with an existing handicap, whether from birth or later injury, a person suffering from malnutrition, a person with a disease, sickness, or infection which significantly impairs physical health, a person partially or totally incapable of self-care (including incapacity due to old age). A person suffering from mental illness is included if the person is hospitalized or institutionalized for the mental disorder, or, although the person is nonhospitalized or noninstitutionalized, if the person's mental illness constitutes a significant health impairment.

(C) Definition of care of the ill. Care of the ill means alleviation or cure of an existing illness and includes care of the physical, mental, or emotional needs of the ill.

(D) Definition of the needy. A needy person is a person who lacks the necessities of life, involving physical, mental, or emotional well-being, as a result of poverty or temporary distress. Examples of needy persons include a person who is financially impoverished as a result of low income and lack of financial resources, a person who temporarily lacks food or shelter (and the means to provide for it), a person who is the victim of a natural disaster (such as fire or flood), a person who is the victim of a civil disaster (such as a civil disturbance), a person who is temporarily not self-sufficient as a result of a sudden and severe personal or family crisis (such as a person who is the victim of a crime of violence or who has been physically abused), a person who is a refugee or immigrant and who is experiencing language, cultural, or financial difficulties, a minor child who is not self-sufficient and who is not cared for by a parent or guardian, and a person who is not self-sufficient as a result of previous institutionalization (such as a former prisoner or a former patient in a mental institution).

(E) Definition of care of the needy. Care of the needy means alleviation or satisfaction of an existing need. Since a person may be needy in some respects and not needy in other respects, care of the needy must relate to the particular need which causes the person to be needy. For example, a person whose temporary need arises from a natural disaster may need temporary shelter and food but not recreational facilities.

(F) Definition of infant. An infant is a minor child (as determined under the laws of the jurisdiction in which the child resides).

(G) Definition of care of an infant. Care of an infant means performance of parental functions and provision for the physical, mental, and emotional needs of the infant.

(3) Restrictions on Transfer of contributed property. (i) In general. Except as otherwise provided in subdivision (ii) of this paragraph (b)(3), a contribution will not qualify under this section, if the donee-organization or any transferee of the donee-organization requires or receives any money, property, or services for the transfer or use of property contributed under section 170(e)(3). For example, if an organization provides temporary shelter for a fee, and also provides free meals to ill or needy individuals, or infants using food contributed under this section the contribution of food is subject to this section (if the other requirements of this section are met). However, the fee charged by the organization for the shelter may not be increased merely because meals are served to the ill or needy individuals or infants.

(ii) Exception. A contribution may qualify under this section if the donee-organization charges a fee to another organization in connection with its transfer of the donated property, if—

(A) The fee is small or nominal in relation to the value of the transferred property and is not determined by this value; and

(B) The fee is designed to reimburse the donee-organization for its administrative, warehousing, or other similar costs.

For example, if a charitable organization (such as a food bank) accepts surplus food to distribute to other charities which give the food to needy persons, a small fee may be charged to cover administrative, warehousing, and other similar costs. This fee may be charged on the basis of the total number of pounds of food distributed to the transferee charity but not on the basis of the value of the food distributed. The provisions of this subdivision (ii) do not apply to a transfer of donated property directly from an organization to ill or needy individuals, or infants.

(4) Requirement of a written statement. (i) Furnished to taxpayer. In the case of any contribution made on or after [Date which is 30 days after the issuance of these regulations by Treasury decision], the donee-organization must furnish to the taxpayer a written statement which—

(A) Describes the contributed property, stating the date of its receipt;

(B) Represents that the property will be used in compliance with section 170(e)(3) and paragraphs (b)(2) and (3) of this section;

(C) Represents that the donee-organization meets the requirements of paragraph (b)(1)(ii) of this section; and

(D) Represents that adequate books and records will be maintained, and made available to the Internal Revenue Service upon request.

The written statement must be furnished within a reasonable period after the contribution, but not later than the date (including extensions) by which the donor is required to file a United States corporate income tax return for the year in which the contribution was made. The books and records described in (D) of this subdivision (i) need not trace the receipt and disposition of specific items of donated property if they disclose compliance with the requirements by reference to aggregate quantities of donated property. The books and records are adequate if they reflect total amounts received and distributed (or used), and outline the procedure used for determining that the ultimate recipient of the property is an ill or needy individual, or infant. However, the books and records need not reflect the names of the ultimate individual recipients or the property distributed to (or used by) each one.

(ii) Furnished to transferring organization. If an organization that received a contribution under this section transfers the contributed property to another organization on or after [Date which is 30 days after the issuance of these regulations by Treasury decision], the transferee organization must furnish to the transferring organization a written statement which contains the information required in paragraph (b)(4)(i)(A), (B) and (D) of this section. The statement must also represent that the transferee organization meets the requirements of paragraph (b)(1)(ii) of this section (or, in the case of a transferee organization which is a foreign organization not within the jurisdiction of the United States, that, but for such fact, the organization would meet the requirements of paragraph (b)(1)(ii) of this section). The written statement must be furnished within a reasonable period after the transfer.

(5) Requirement of compliance with the Federal Food, Drug, and Cosmetic Act. (i) In general. With respect to property contributed under this section which is subject to the Federal Food, Drug, and Cosmetic Act (as amended), and regulations thereunder, the contributed property must comply with the applicable provisions of that Act and regulations thereunder at the date of the contribution and for the immediately preceding 180 days. In the case of specific items of contributed property not in existence for the entire period of 180 days immediately preceding the date of contribution, the requirement of this paragraph (b)(5) is considered met if the contributed property complied with that Act and the regulations thereunder during the period of its existence and at the date of contribution and if, for the 180 day period prior to contribution other property (if any) held by the taxpayer at any time during that period, which property was fungible with the contributed property, complied with that Act and the regulations thereunder during the period held by the taxpayer.

(ii) Example. The rule of this paragraph (b)(5) may be illustrated by the following example.

Example. Corporation X a grocery store, contributes 12 crates of navel oranges. The oranges were picked and placed in the grocery store's stock two weeks prior to the date of contribution. The contribution satisfies the requirements of this paragraph (b)(5) if X complied with the Act and regulations thereunder for 180 days prior to the date of contribution with respect to all navel oranges in stock during that period.

(c) Amount of reduction. *(1) In general.* Section 170(e)(3)(B) requires that the amount of the charitable contribution subject to this section which would be taken into account under section 170(a), without regard to section 170(e), must be reduced before applying the percentage limitations under section 170(b). The amount of the first reduction is equal to one-half of the amount of gain which would not have been long-term capital gain if the property had been sold by the donor-taxpayer at its fair market value on the date of its contribution, excluding, however, any amount described in paragraph (d) of this section. If the amount of the charitable contribution which remains after this reduction exceeds twice the basis of the contributed property, then the amount of the charitable contribution is reduced a second time to an amount which is equal to twice the amount of the basis of the property.

(2) Basis of contributed property which is inventory. For the purposes of this section, notwithstanding the rules of § 1.170A-1(c)(4), the basis of contributed property which is inventory must be determined under the donor's method of accounting for inventory for purposes of United States income tax. The donor must use as the basis of the contributed item the inventoriable carrying cost assigned to any similar item not included in closing inventory. For example, under the LIFO dollar value method of accounting for inventory, where there has been an invasion of a prior year's layer, the donor may choose to treat the item contributed as having a basis of the unit's cost with reference to the layer(s) of prior year(s) cost or with reference to the current year cost.

(3) Adjustment to cost of goods sold. Notwithstanding the rules of § 1.170A-1(c)(4), the donor of the property which is inventory contributed under this section must make a corresponding adjustment to cost of goods sold by decreasing the cost of goods sold by the lesser of the fair market value of the contributed item or the amount of basis determined under paragraph (c)(2) of this section.

(4) Examples. The rules of this paragraph (c) may be illustrated by the following examples:

Example (1). During 1978 corporation X, a calendar year taxpayer, makes a qualified contribution of women's coats which were section 1221(1) property. The fair market value of the property at the date of contribution is $1,000, and the basis of the property is $200. The amount of the charitable contribution which would be taken into account under section 170(a) is the fair market value ($1,000). The amount of gain which would not have been long-term capital gain if the property had been sold is $800 ($1,000 – $200). The amount of the contribution is reduced by one-half the amount which would not have been capital gain if the property had been sold ($800/2 = $400).

After this reduction, the amount of the contribution which may be taken into account is $600 ($1,000 – $400). A second reduction is made in the amount of the charitable contribution because this amount (as first reduced to $600) is more than $400 which is an amount equal to twice the basis of the property. The amount of the further reduction is $200 [$600 – (2 × $200)], and the amount of the contribution as finally reduced is $400 [$1,00 – ($400 + $200)] . X would also have to decrease its cost of goods sold for the year of contribution by $200.

Example (2). Assume the same facts as set forth in example (1) except that the basis of the property is $600. The amount of the first reduction is $200 (($1,000 – $600)/2).

As reduced, the amount of the contribution which may be taken into account is $800 ($1,000 – $200). There is no second reduction because $800 is less than $1,200 which is twice the basis of the property. However, X would have to decrease its cost of goods sold for the year of contribution by $600.

(d) Recapture excluded. A deduction is not allowed under section 170(e)(3) or this section for any amount which, if the property had been sold by the donor-taxpayer on the date of its contribution for an amount equal to its fair market value, would have been treated as ordinary income under section 617, 1245, 1250, 1251, or 1252. Thus, before making either reduction required by section 170(e)(3)(B) and paragraph (c) of this section, the fair market value of the contributed property must be reduced by the amount of gain that would have been recognized (if the property had been sold) as ordinary income under section 617, 1245, 1250, 1251, or 1252.

(e) Effective date. This section applies to qualified contributions made after October 4, 1976.

T.D. 7807, 1/29/82, amend T.D. 7962, 6/28/84.

§ 1.170A-5 Future interests in tangible personal property.

Caution: The Treasury has not yet amended Reg § 1.170A-5 to reflect changes made by P.L. 100-203, P.L. 99-514, P.L. 98-369.

(a) In general. *(1)* A contribution consisting of a transfer of a future interest in tangible personal property shall be treated as made only when all intervening interests in, and rights to the actual possession or enjoyment of the property—

(i) Have expired, or

(ii) Are held by persons other than the taxpayer or those standing in a relationship to the taxpayer described in section 267(b) and the regulations thereunder, relating to losses, expenses, and interest with respect to transactions between related taxpayers.

(2) Section 170(a)(3) and this section have no application in respect of a transfer of an undivided present interest in property. For example, a contribution of an undivided one-quarter interest in a painting with respect to which the donee is entitled to possession during 3 months of each year shall be treated as made upon the receipt by the donee of a formally executed and acknowledged deed of gift. However, the period of initial possession by the donee may not be deferred in time for more than 1 year.

(3) Section 170(a)(3) and this section have no application in respect of a transfer of a future interest in intangible personal property or in real property. However, a fixture which is intended to be severed from real property shall be treated as tangible personal property. For example, a contribution of a future interest in a chandelier which is attached to a building is considered a contribution which consists of a future interest in tangible personal property if the transferor intends that it be detached from the building at or prior to the time when the charitable organization's right to possession or enjoyment of the chandelier is to commence.

(4) For purposes of section 170(a)(3) and this section, the term "future interest" has generally the same meaning as it has when used in section 2503 and § 25.2503-3 of this chapter (Gift Tax Regulations); it includes reversions, remainders, and other interests or estates, whether vested or contingent, and whether or not supported by a particular interest or estate, which are limited to commence in use, possession, or enjoyment at some future date or time. The term "future interest" includes situations in which a donor purports to give tangible personal property to a charitable organization, but has an understanding, arrangement, agreement, etc., whether written or oral, with the charitable organization which has the effect of reserving to, or retaining in, such donor a right to the use, possession, or enjoyment of the property.

(5) In the case of a charitable contribution of a future interest to which section 170(a)(3) and this section apply, the other provisions of section 170 and the regulations thereunder are inapplicable to the contribution until such time as the contribution is treated as made under section 170(a)(3).

(b) Illustrations. The application of this section may be illustrated by the following examples:

Example (1). On December 31, 1970, A, an individual who reports his income on the calendar year basis, conveys by deed of gift to a museum title to a painting, but reserves to himself the right to the use, possession, and enjoyment of the painting during his lifetime. It is assumed that there was no intention to avoid the application of section 170(f)(3)(A) by the conveyance. At the time of the gift the value of the painting is $90,000. Since the contribution consists of a future interest in tangible personal property in which the donor has retained an intervening interest, no contribution is considered to have been made in 1970.

Example (2). Assume the same facts as in example (1) except that on December 31, 1971, A relinquishes all of his right to the use, possession, and enjoyment of the painting and delivers the painting to the museum. Assuming that the value of the painting has increased to $95,000, A is treated as having made a charitable contribution of $95,000 in 1971 for which a deduction is allowable without regard to section 170(f)(3)(A).

Example (3). Assume the same facts as in example (1) except A dies without relinquishing his right to the use, possession, and enjoyment of the painting. Since A did not relinquish his right to the use, possession, and enjoyment of the property during his life, A is treated as not having made a charitable contribution of the painting for income tax purposes.

Example (4). Assume the same facts as in example (1) except A, on December 31, 1971, transfers his interest in the painting to his son, B, who reports his income on the calendar year basis. Since the relationship between A and B is one described in section 267(b), no contribution of the remainder interest in the painting is considered to have been made in 1971.

Example (5). Assume the same facts as in example (4). Also assume that on December 31, 1972, B conveys to the museum the interest measured by A's life. B has made a charitable contribution of the present interest in the painting conveyed to the museum. In addition, since all intervening interests in, and rights to the actual possession or enjoyment of the property, have expired, a charitable contribution of the remainder interest is treated as having been made by A in 1972 for which a deduction is allowable without regard to section 170(f)(3)(A). Such remainder interest is valued according to § 20.2031-7A(c) of this chapter (estate tax regulations), determined by subtracting the value of B's interest measured by A's life expectancy in 1972, and B receives a deduction in 1972 for the life interest measured by A's life expectancy and valued according to Table A(1) in such section.

Example (6). On December 31, 1970, C, an individual who reports his income on the calendar year basis, transfers a valuable painting to a pooled income fund described in section 642(c)(5), which is maintained by a university. C retains for himself for life an income interest in the painting, the remainder interest in the painting being contributed to the university. Since the contribution consists of a future interest in tangible personal property in which the donor has retained an intervening interest, no charitable contribution is considered to have been made in 1970.

Example (7). On January 15, 1972, D, an individual who reports his income on the calendar year basis, transfers a capital asset held for more than 6 months consisting of a valuable painting to a pooled income fund described in section 642 (c)(5), which is maintained by a university, and creates an income interest in such painting for E for life. E is an individual not standing in a relationship to D described in section 267(b). The remainder interest in the property is contributed by D to the university. The trustee of the pooled income fund puts the painting to an unrelated use within the meaning of paragraph (b)(3) of § 1.170A-4. Accordingly, D is allowed a deduction under section 170 in 1972 for the present value of the remainder interest in the painting, after reducing such amount under section 170(e)(1)(B)(i) and paragraph (a)(2) of § 1.170A-4. This reduction in the amount of the contribution is required since under paragraph (b)(3) of that section the use by the pooled income fund of the painting is a use which would have been an unrelated use if it had been made by the university.

(c) Effective date. This section applies only to contributions paid in taxable years beginning after December 31, 1969.

T.D. 7207, 10/3/72, amend T.D. 8540, 6/9/94.

§ 1.170A-6 Charitable contribution in trust.

Caution: The Treasury has not yet amended Reg § 1.170A-6 to reflect changes made by P.L. 100-203, P.L. 99-514, P.L. 98-369.

(a) In general. *(1)* No deduction is allowed under section 170 for the fair market value of a charitable contribution of any interest in property which is less than the donor's entire interest in the property and which is transferred in trust unless the transfer meets the requirements of paragraph (b) or (c) of this section. If the donor's entire interest in the property is transferred in trust and is contributed to a charitable organization described in section 170(c), a deduction is allowed under section 170. Thus, if on July 1, 1972, property is transferred in trust with the requirement that the income of the trust be paid for a term of 20 years to a church and thereafter the remainder be paid to an educational organization described in section 170(b)(1)(A), a deduction is allowed for the value of such property. See section 170(f)(2) and (3)(B), and paragraph (b)(1) § 1.170A-7.

(2) A deduction is allowed without regard to this section for a contribution of a partial interest in property if such interest is the taxpayer's entire interest in the property, such as an income interest or a remainder interest. If, however, the property in which such partial interest exists was divided in order to create such interest and thus avoid section 170(f)(2), the deduction will not be allowed. Thus, for example, assume that a taxpayer desires to contribute to a charitable organization the reversionary interest in certain stocks and bonds which he owns. If the taxpayer transfers such property in trust with the requirement that the income of the trust be paid to his son for life and that the reversionary interest to a charitable organization, no deduction will be allowed under section 170 for the contribution of the taxpayer's entire interest consisting of the reversionary interest in the trust.

(b) Charitable contribution of a remainder interest in trust. *(1) In general.* No deduction is allowed under section 170 for the fair market value of a charitable contribution of a remainder interest in property which is less than the donor's entire interest in the property and which the donor transfers in trust unless the trust is—

(i) A pooled income fund described in section 642(c)(5) and § 1.642(c)-5,

(ii) A charitable remainder annuity trust described in section 664(d)(1) and § 1.664-2, or

(iii) A charitable remainder unitrust described in section 664(d)(2) and § 1.664-3.

(2) Value of a remainder interest. The fair market value of a remainder interest in a pooled income fund shall be computed under § 1.642(c)-6. The fair market value of a remainder interest in a charitable remainder annuity trust shall be computed under § 1.664-2. The fair market value of a remainder interest in a charitable remainder unitrust shall be computed under § 1.664-4. However, in some cases a reduction in the amount of a charitable contribution of the remainder interest may be required. See section 170(e) and § 1.170A-4.

(c) Charitable contribution of an income interest in trust. *(1) In general.* No deduction is allowed under section 170 for the fair market value of a charitable contribution of an income interest in property which is less than the donor's entire interest in the property and which the donor transfers in trust unless the income interest is either a guaranteed annuity interest or a unitrust interest, as defined in paragraph (c)(2) of this section, and the grantor is treated as the owner of such interest for purposes of applying section 671, relating to grantors and others treated as substantial owners. See section 4947(a)(2) for the application to such income interests in trust of the provisions relating to private foundations and section 508(e) for rules relating to provisions required in the governing instruments.

(2) Definitions. For purposes of this paragraph—

(i) Guaranteed annuity interest. (A) An income interest is a "guaranteed annuity interest" only if it is an irrevocable right pursuant to the governing instrument of the trust to receive a guaranteed annuity. A guaranteed annuity is an arrangement under which a determinable amount is paid periodically, but not less often than annually, for a specified term of years or for the life or lives of certain individuals, each of whom must be living at the date of transfer and can be ascertained at such date. Only one or more of the following individuals may be used as measuring lives: the donor, the donor's spouse, and an individual who, with respect to all remainder beneficiaries (other than charitable organizations described in section 170, 2055, or 2522), is either a lineal ancestor or the spouse of a lineal ancestor of those beneficiaries. A trust will satisfy the requirement that all noncharitable remainder beneficiaries are lineal descendants of the individual who is the measuring life, or that individual's spouse, if there is less than a 15% probability that individuals who are not lineal descendants will receive any trust corpus. This probability must be computed, based on the current applicable Life Table contained in § 20.2031-7, at the time property is transferred to the trust taking into account the interests of all primary and contingent remainder beneficiaries who are living at that time. An interest payable for a specified term of years can qualify as a guaranteed annuity interest even if the governing instrument contains a savings clause intended to ensure compliance with a rule against perpetuities. The savings clause must utilize a period for vesting of 21 years after the deaths of measuring lives who are selected to maximize, rather than limit, the term of the trust. The rule in this paragraph that a charitable interest may be payable for the life or lives of only certain specified individuals does not apply in the case of a charitable guaranteed annuity interest payable under a charitable remainder trust described in section 664. An amount is determinable if the exact amount which must be paid under the conditions specified in the governing instrument of the trust can be ascertained as of the date of transfer. For example, the amount to be paid may be a stated sum for a term of years, or for the life of the donor, at the expiration of which it may be changed by a specified amount, but it may not be redetermined by reference to a fluctuating index such as the cost of living index. In further illustration, the amount to be paid may be expressed in terms of a fraction or percentage of the cost of living index on the date of transfer.

(B) An income interest is a guaranteed annuity interest only if it is a guaranteed annuity interest in every respect. For example, if the income interest is the right to receive from a trust each year a payment equal to the lesser of a sum certain or a fixed percentage of the net fair market value of the trust assets, determined annually, such interest is not a guaranteed annuity interest.

(C) Where a charitable interest is in the form of a guaranteed annuity interest, the governing instrument of the trust may provide that income of the trust which is in excess of the amount required to pay the guaranteed annuity interest shall be paid to or for the use of a charitable organization. Nevertheless, the amount of the deduction under section 170(f)(2)(B) shall be limited to the fair market value of the guaranteed annuity interest as determined under paragraph (c)(3) of this section. For a rule relating to treatment by the grantor of any contribution made by the trust in excess of the amount required to pay the guaranteed annuity interest, see paragraph (d)(2)(ii) of this section.

(D) If the present value on the date of transfer of all the income interests for a charitable purpose exceeds 60 percent of the aggregate fair market value of all amounts in the trust (after the payment of liabilities), the income interest will not be considered a guaranteed annuity interest unless the governing instrument of the trust prohibits both the acquisition and the retention of assets which would give rise to a tax under section 4944 if the trustee had acquired such assets. The requirement in this subdivision (D) for a prohibition in the governing instrument against the retention of assets which would give rise to a tax under section 4944 if the trustee had acquired the assets shall not apply to a transfer in trust made on or before May 21, 1972.

(E) Where a charitable interest in the form of a guaranteed annuity interest is transferred after May 21, 1972, the charitable interest generally is not a guaranteed annuity interest if any amount may be paid by the trust for a private purpose before the expiration of all the charitable annuity interests. There are two exceptions to this general rule. First, the charitable interest is a guaranteed annuity interest if the amount payable for a private purpose is in the form of a guaranteed annuity interest and the trust's governing instrument does not provide for any preference or priority in the payment of the private annuity as opposed to the charitable annuity. Second, the charitable interest is a guaranteed annuity interest if under the trust's governing instrument the amount that may be paid for a private purpose is payable only from a group of assets that are devoted exclusively to private purposes and to which section 4947(a)(2) is inapplicable by reason of section 4947(a)(2)(B). For purposes of this paragraph (c)(2)(i)(E), an amount is not paid for a private purpose if it is paid for an adequate and full consideration in money or money's worth. See § 53.4947-1(c) of this chapter for rules relating to the inapplicability of section 4947(a)(2) to segregated amounts in a split-interest trust.

(F) For rules relating to certain governing instrument requirements and to the imposition of certain excise taxes where the guaranteed annuity interest is in trust and for rules governing payment of private income interests by a split-interest trust, see section 4947(a)(2) and (b)(3)(A), and the regulations thereunder.

(ii) Unitrust interest. (A) An income interest is a "unitrust interest" only if it is an irrevocable right pursuant to the governing instrument of the trust to receive payment, not less often than annually, of a fixed percentage of the net fair market value of the trust assets, determined annually. In computing the net fair market value of the trust assets, all assets and liabilities shall be taken into account without regard to whether particular items are taken into account in determining the income of the trust. The net fair market value of the trust assets may be determined on any one date during the year or by taking the average of valuations made on more than one date during the year, provided that the same valuation date or dates and valuation methods are used each year. Where the governing instrument of the trust does not specify the valuation date or dates, the trustee shall select such date or dates and shall indicate his selection on the first return on Form 1041 which the trust is required to file. Payments under a unitrust interest may be paid for a specified term of years or for the life or lives of certain individuals, each of whom must be living at the date of transfer and can be ascertained at such date. Only one or more of the following individuals may be used as measuring lives: the donor, the donor's spouse, and an individual who, with respect to all remainder beneficiaries (other than charitable organizations described in section 170, 2055, or 2522), is either a lineal ancestor or the spouse of a lineal ancestor of those beneficiaries. A trust will satisfy the requirement that all noncharitable remainder beneficiaries are lineal descendants of the individual who is the measuring life, or that individual's spouse, if there is less than a 15% probability that individuals who are not lineal descendants will receive any trust corpus. This probability must be computed, based on the current applicable Life Table contained in § 20.2031-7, at the time property is transferred to the trust taking into account the interests of all primary and contingent remainder beneficiaries who are living at that time. An interest payable for a specified term of years can qualify as a unitrust interest even if the governing instrument contains a savings clause intended to ensure compliance with a rule against perpetuities. The savings clause must utilize a period for vesting of 21 years after the deaths of measuring lives who are selected to maximize, rather than limit, the term of the trust. The rule in this paragraph that a charitable interest may be payable for the life or lives of only certain specified individuals does not apply in the case of a charitable unitrust interest payable under a charitable remainder trust described in section 664.

(B) An income interest is a unitrust interest only if it is a unitrust interest in every respect. For example, if the income interest is the right to receive from a trust each year a payment equal to the lesser of a sum certain or a fixed percentage of the net fair market value of the trust assets, determined annually, such interest is not a unitrust interest.

(C) Where a charitable interest is in the form of a unitrust interest, the governing instrument of the trust may provide that income of the trust which is in excess of the amount required to pay the unitrust interest shall be paid to or for the use of a charitable organization. Nevertheless, the amount of the deduction under section 170(f)(2)(B) shall be limited to the fair market value of the unitrust interest as determined under paragraph (c)(3) of this section. For a rule relating to treatment by the grantor of any contribution made by the trust in excess of the amount required to pay the unitrust interest, see paragraph (d)(2)(ii) of this section.

(D) Where a charitable interest is in the form of a unitrust interest, the charitable interest generally is not a unitrust interest if any amount may be paid by the trust for a private purpose before the expiration of all the charitable unitrust interests. There are two exceptions to this general rule. First, the charitable interest is a unitrust interest if the amount payable for a private purpose is in the form of a unitrust interest and the trust's governing instrument does not provide for any preference or priority in the payment of the private unitrust interest as opposed to the charitable unitrust interest. Second, the charitable interest is a unitrust interest if under the trust's governing instrument the amount that may be paid for a private purpose is payable only from a group of assets that are devoted exclusively to private purposes and to which section 4947(a)(2) is inapplicable by reason of section 4947(a)(2)(B). For purposes of this paragraph (c)(2)(ii)(D), an amount is not paid for a private purpose if it is paid for an adequate and full consideration in money or money's worth. See § 53.4947-1(c) of this chapter for rules relating to the inapplicability of section 4947(a)(2) to segregated amounts in a split-interest trust.

(E) For rules relating to certain governing instrument requirements and to the imposition of certain excise taxes where the unitrust interest is in trust and for rules governing payment of private income interests by a split-interest trust, see section 4947(a)(2) and (b)(3)(A), and the regulations thereunder.

(3) Valuation of income interest. (i) The deduction allowed by section 170(f)(2)(B) for a charitable contribution of a guaranteed annuity interest is limited to the fair market value of such interest on the date of contribution, as computed under § 20.2031-7 or, for certain prior periods, 20.2031-7A of this chapter (Estate Tax Regulations).

(ii) The deduction allowed under section 170(f)(2)(B) for a charitable contribution of a unitrust interest is limited to the fair market value of the unitrust interest on the date of contribution. The fair market value of the unitrust interest shall be determined by subtracting the present value of all interests in the transferred property other than the unitrust interest from the fair market value of the transferred property.

(iii) If by reason of all the conditions and circumstances surrounding a transfer of an income interest in property in trust it appears that the charity may not receive the beneficial enjoyment of the interest, a deduction will be allowed under paragraph (c)(1) of this section only for the minimum amount it is evident the charity will receive. The application of this subdivision may be illustrated by the following examples:

Example (1). In 1972, B transfers $20,000 in trust with the requirement that M Church be paid a guaranteed annuity interest (as defined in subparagraph (2)(i) of this paragraph) of $4,000, payable annually at the end of each year for 9 years, and that the residue revert to himself. Since the fair market value of an annuity of $4,000 a year for a period of 9 years, as determined under § 20.2031-7A(c) of this chapter, is $27,206.80 ($4,000 × 6.8017), it appears that M will not receive the beneficial enjoyment of the income interest. Accordingly, even though B is treated as the owner of the trust under section 673, he is allowed a deduction under subparagraph (1) of this paragraph for only $20,000, which is the minimum amount it is evident M will receive.

Example (2). In 1975, C transfers $40,000 in trust with the requirement that D, an individual, and X Charity be paid simultaneously guaranteed annuity interests (as defined in subparagraph (2)(i) of this paragraph) of $5,000 a year each, payable annually at the end of each year, for a period of 5 years and that the remainder be paid to C's children. The fair market value of two annuities of $5,000 each a year for a period of 5 years is $42,124 ([$5,000 × 4.2124] × 2), as determined under § 20.2031-7A(c) of this chapter. The trust instrument provides that in the event the trust fund is insufficient to pay both annuities in a given year, the trust fund will be evenly divided between the charitable and private annuitants. The deduction under subparagraph (1) of this paragraph with respect to the charitable annuity will be limited to $20,000, which is the minimum amount it is evident X will receive.

Example (3). In 1975, D transfers $65,000 in trust with the requirement that a guaranteed annuity interest (as defined in subparagraph (2)(i) of this paragraph) of $5,000 a year, payable annually at the end of each year, be paid to Y Charity for a period of 10 years and that a guaranteed annuity interest (as defined in subparagraph (2)(i) of this paragraph) of $5,000 a year, payable annually at the end of each year, be paid to W, his wife, aged 62, for 10 years or until her prior death. The annuities are to be paid simultaneously, and the remainder is to be paid to D's children. The fair market value of the private annuity is $33,877 ($5,000 × 6.7754), as determined pursuant to § 20.2031-7A(c) of this chapter and by the use of factors involving one life and a term of years as published in Publication 723A (12-70). The fair market value of the charitable annuity is $36,800.50 ($5,000 × 7.3601), as determined under § 20.2031-7A(c) of this chapter. It is not evident from the governing instrument of the trust or from local law that the trustee would be required to apportion the trust fund between the wife and charity in the event the fund were insufficient to pay both annuities in a given year. Accordingly, the deduction under subparagraph (1) of this paragraph with respect to the charitable annuity will be limited to $31,123 ($65,000 less $33,877 [the value of the private annuity]), which is the minimum amount it is evident Y will receive.

(iv) See paragraph (b)(1) of § 1.170A-4 for rule that the term "ordinary income property" for purposes of section 170(e) does not include an income interest in respect of which a deduction is allowed under section 170(f)(2)(B) and this paragraph.

(4) Recapture upon termination of treatment as owner. If for any reason the donor of an income interest in property ceases at any time before the termination of such interest to be treated as the owner of such interest for purposes of applying section 671, as for example, where he dies before the termination of such interest, he shall for purposes of this chapter be considered as having received, on the date he ceases to be so treated, an amount of income equal to (i) the amount of any deduction he was allowed under section 170 for the contribution of such interest reduced by (ii) the discounted value of all amounts which were required to be, and actually were, paid with respect to such interest under the terms of trust to the charitable organization before the time at which he ceases to be treated as the owner of the interest. The discounted value of the amounts described in subdivision (ii) of this subparagraph shall be computed by treating each such amount as a contribution of a remainder interest after a term of years and valuing such amount as of the date of contribution of the income interest by the donor, such value to be determined under § 20.2031-7 of this chapter consistently with the manner in which the fair market value of the income interest was determined pursuant to subparagraph (3)(i) of this paragraph. The application of this subparagraph will not be construed to disallow a deduction to the trust for amounts paid by the trust to the charitable organization after the time at which the donor ceased to be treated as the owner of the trust.

(5) Illustrations. The application of this paragraph may be illustrated by the following examples:

Example (1). On January 1, 1971, A contributes to a church in trust a 9-year irrevocable income interest in property. Both A and the trust report income on a calendar year basis. The fair market value of the property placed in trust is $10,000. The trust instrument provides that the church will receive an annuity of $500, payable annually at the end of each year for 9 years. The income interest is a guaranteed annuity interest as defined in subparagraph (2)(i) of this paragraph; upon termination of such interest the residue of the trust is to revert to A. By reference to § 20.2031-7A(c) of this chapter, it is found that the figure in column (2) opposite 9 years is 6.8017. The present value of the annuity is therefore $3,400.85 ($500 × 6.8017). The present value of the income interest and A's charitable contribution for 1971 is $3,400.85.

Example (2). (a) On January 1, 1971, B contributes to a church in trust a 9-year irrevocable income interest in property. Both B and the trust report income on a calendar year basis. The fair market value of the property placed in trust is

$10,000. The trust instrument provides that the trust will pay to the church at the end of each year for 9 years, 5 percent of the fair market value of all property in the trust at the beginning of the year. The income interest is a unitrust interest as defined in subparagraph (2)(ii) of this paragraph; upon termination of such interest the residue of the trust is to revert to B.

(b) The section 7520 rate at the time of the transfer was 6.0 percent. By reference to Table F(6.0) in § 1.664-4(e)(6), the adjusted payout rate is 4.717% (5% × 0.943396). The present value of the reversion is $6,473.75, computed by reference to Table D in § 1.664-4(e)(6), as follows:

Factor at 4.6 percent for 9 years	0.654539
Factor at 4.8 percent for 9 years	.642292
Difference	.012247

Interpolation adjustment:

$$\frac{4.717\% - 4.6\%}{0.2\%} = \frac{X}{0.012247}$$

$$X = 0.007164$$

Factor at 4.6 percent for 9 years	.654539
Less: Interpolation adjustment	.007164
Interpolated factor	.647375
Present value of reversion ($10,000 × 0.647375)	$6,473.75

(c) The present value of the income interest and B's charitable contribution is $3,526.25 ($10,000 – $6,473.75).

Example (3). (a) On January 1, 1971, C contributes to a church in trust a 9-year irrevocable income interest in property. Both C and the trust report income on a calendar year basis. The fair market value of the property placed in trust is $10,000. The trust instrument provides that the church will receive an annuity of $500, payable annually at the end of each year for 9 years. The income interest is a guaranteed annuity interest as defined in subparagraph (2)(i) of this paragraph; upon termination of such interest the residue of the trust is to revert to C. C's charitable contribution for 1971 is $3,400.85, determined as provided in example (1). The trust earns income of $600 in 1971, $400 in 1972, and $500 in 1973, all of which is taxable to C under section 671. The church is paid $500 at the end of 1971, 1972, and 1973, respectively. On December 31, 1972, C dies and ceases to be treated as the owner of the income interest under section 673.

(b) Pursuant to subparagraph (4) of this paragraph, the discounted value as of January 1, 1971, of the amounts paid to the church by the trust is $1,336.51, determined by reference to column (4) of Table B in § 20-2031-7A(c) of this chapter, as follows:

Annuity — Payment date	Amount paid	Years from Jan. 1, 1971, to payment date	Discount factor	Discounted value as of Jan. 1, 1971
Dec. 31, 1971	$500	1	0.943396	$471.70
Dec. 31, 1972	500	2	.889996	445.00
Dec. 31, 1973	500	3	.839619	419.81
Total discounted value				1,336.51

(c) Pursuant to subparagraph (4) of this paragraph, there must be included in C's gross income for 1973 the amount of $2,064.34 ($3,400.85 less $1,336.51).

(d) For deduction by the trust for amounts paid to the church after December 31, 1973, see section 642(c)(1) and the regulations thereunder.

(d) Denial of deduction for certain contributions by a trust. *(1)* If by reason of section 170(f)(2)(B) and paragraph (c) of this section a charitable contributions deduction is allowed under section 170 for the fair market value of an income interest transferred in trust, neither the grantor of the income interest, the trust, nor any other person shall be allowed a deduction under section 170 or any other section for the amount of any charitable contribution made by the trust with respect to, or in fulfillment of, such income interest.

(2) Section 170(f)(2)(C) and subparagraph (1) of this paragraph shall not be construed, however, to—

(i) Disallow a deduction to the trust, pursuant to section 642(c)(1) and the regulations thereunder for amounts paid by the trust after the grantor ceases to be treated as the owner of the income interest for purposes of applying section 671 and which are not taken into account in determining the amount of recapture under paragraph (c)(4) of this section, or

(ii) Disallow a deduction to the grantor under section 671 and § 1.671-2(c) for a charitable contribution made by the trust in excess of the contribution required to be made by the trust under the terms of the trust instrument with respect to, or in fulfillment of, the income interest.

(3) Although a deduction for the fair market value of an income interest in property which is less than the donor's entire interest in the property and which the donor transfers in trust is disallowed under section 170 because such interest is not a guaranteed annuity interest, or a unitrust interest, as defined in paragraph (c)(2) of this section, the donor may be entitled to a deduction under section 671 and § 1.671-2(c) for any charitable contributions made by the trust if he is treated as the owner of such interest for purposes of applying section 671.

(e) Effective date. This section applies only to transfers in trust made after July 31, 1969. In addition, the rule in paragraphs (c)(2)(i)(A) and (ii)(A) of this section that guaranteed annuity interests and unitrust interests, respectively, may be payable for a specified term of years or for the life or lives of only certain individuals applies to transfers made on or after April 4, 2000. If a transfer is made to a trust on or after April 4, 2000 that uses an individual other than one permitted in paragraphs (c)(2)(i)(A) and (ii)(A) of this section, the trust may be reformed to satisfy this rule. As an alternative to reformation, rescission may be available for a transfer made on or before March 6, 2001. See § 25.2522(c)-3(e) of this chapter for the requirements concerning reformation or possible rescission of these interests.

T.D. 7207, 10/3/72, amend T.D. 7340, 1/6/75, T.D. 7955, 5/10/84, T.D. 8540, 6/9/94, T.D. 8819, 4/29/99, T.D. 8923, 1/4/2001, T.D. 9068, 7/3/2003.

§ 1.170A-7 Contributions not in trust of partial interests in property.

(a) In general. *(1)* In the case of a charitable contribution, not made by a transfer in trust, of any interest in property which consists of less than the donor's entire interest in such property, no deduction is allowed under section 170 for the value of such interest unless the interest is an interest described in paragraph (b) of this section. See section 170(f)(3)(A). For purposes of this section, a contribution of the right to use property which the donor owns, for example, a rent-free lease, shall be treated as a contribution of less than the taxpayer's entire interest in such property.

(2) (i) A deduction is allowed without regard to this section for a contribution of a partial interest in property if such interest is the taxpayer's entire interest in the property, such as an income interest or a remainder interest. Thus, if securities are given to A for life, with the remainder over to B, and B makes a charitable contribution of his remainder interest to an organization described in section 170(c), a deduction is allowed under section 170 for the present value of B's remainder interest in the securities. If, however, the property in which such partial interest exists was divided in order to create such interest and thus avoid section 170(f)(3)(A), the deduction will not be allowed. Thus, for example, assume that a taxpayer desires to contribute to a charitable organization an income interest in property held by him, which is not of a type described in paragraph (b)(2) of this section. If the taxpayer transfers the remainder interest in such property to his son and immediately thereafter contributes the income interest to a charitable organization, no deduction shall be allowed under section 170 for the contribution of the taxpayer's entire interest consisting of the retained income interest. In further illustration, assume that a taxpayer desires to contribute to a charitable organization the reversionary interest in certain stocks and bonds held by him, which is not of a type described in paragraph (b)(2) of this section. If the taxpayer grants a life estate in such property to his son and immediately thereafter contributes the reversionary interest to a charitable organization, no deduction will be allowed under section 170 for the contribution of the taxpayer's entire interest consisting of the reversionary interest.

(ii) A deduction is allowed without regard to this section for a contribution of a partial interest in property if such contribution constitutes part of a charitable contribution not in trust in which all interests of the taxpayer in the property are given to a charitable organization described in section 170(c). Thus, if on March 1, 1971, an income interest in property is given not in trust to a church and the remainder interest in the property is given not in trust to an educational organization described in section 170(b)(1)(A), a deduction is allowed for the value of such property.

(3) A deduction shall not be disallowed under section 170(f)(3)(A) and this section merely because the interest which passes to, or is vested in, the charity may be defeated by the performance of some act or the happening or some event, if on the date of the gift it appears that the possibility that such act or event will occur is so remote as to be negligible. See paragraph (e) of § 1.170A-1.

(b) Contributions of certain partial interests in property for which a deduction is allowed. A deduction is allowed under section 170 for a contribution not in trust of a partial interest which is less than the donor's entire interest in property and which qualifies under one of the following subparagraphs:

(1) Undivided portion of donor's entire interest. (i) A deduction is allowed under section 170 for the value of a charitable contribution not in trust of an undivided portion of a donor's entire interest in property. An undivided portion of a donor's entire interest in property must consist of a fraction or percentage of each and every substantial interest or right owned by the donor in such property and must extend over the entire term of the donor's interest in such property and in other property into which such property is converted. For example, assuming that in 1967 B has been given a life estate in an office building for the life of A and that B has no other interest in the office building, B will be allowed a deduction under section 170 for his contribution in 1972 to charity of a one-half interest in such life estate in a transfer which is not made in trust. Such contribution by B will be considered a contribution of an undivided portion of the donor's entire interest in property. In further illustration, assuming that in 1968 C has been given the remainder interest in a trust created under the will of his father and C has no other interest in the trust, C will be allowed a deduction under section 170 for his contribution in 1972 to charity of a 20-percent interest in such remainder interest in a transfer which is not made in trust. Such contribution by C will be considered a contribution of an undivided portion of the donor's entire interest in property. If a taxpayer owns 100 acres of land and makes a contribution of 50 acres to a charitable organization, the charitable contribution is allowed as a deduction under section 170. A deduction is allowed under section 170 for a contribution of property to a charitable organization whereby such organization is given the right, as a tenant in common with the donor, to possession, dominion, and control of the property for a portion of each year appropriate to its interest in such property. However, for purposes of this subparagraph a charitable contribution in perpetuity of an interest in property not in trust where the donor transfers some specific rights and retains other substantial rights will not be considered a contribution of an undivided portion of the donor's entire interest in property to which section 170(f)(3)(A) does not apply. Thus, for example, a deduction is not allowable for the value of an immediate and perpetual gift not in trust of an interest in original historic motion picture films to a charitable organization where the donor retains the exclusive right to make reproductions of such films and to exploit such reproductions commercially.

(ii) With respect to contributions made on or before December 17, 1980. For purposes of this subparagraph a charitable contribution of an open space easement in gross in perpetuity shall be considered a contribution of an undivided portion of the donor's entire interest in property to which section 170(f) (3)(A) does not apply. For this purpose an easement in gross is a mere personal interest in, or right to use, the land of another; it is not supported by a dominant estate but is attached to, and vested in, the person to whom it is granted. Thus, for example, a deduction is allowed under section 170 for the value of a restrictive easement gratuitously conveyed to the United States in perpetuity whereby the donor agrees to certain restrictions on the use of his property, such as, restrictions on the type and height of buildings that may be erected, the removal of trees, the erection of utility lines, the dumping of trash, and the use of signs. For the deductibility of a qualified conservation contribution, see § 1.170A-14.

(2) Partial interests in property which would be deductible in trust. A deduction is allowed under section 170 for the value of a charitable contribution not in trust of a partial interest in property which is less than the donor's entire interest in the property and which would be deductible under section 170(f)(2) and § 1.170A-6 if such interest had been transferred in trust.

(3) Contribution of a remainder interest in a personal residence. A deduction is allowed under section 170 for the value of a charitable contribution not in trust of an irrevocable remainder interest in a personal residence which is not the donor's entire interest in such property. Thus, for example, if a taxpayer contributes not in trust to an organization described in section 170(c) a remainder interest in a personal residence and retains an estate in such property for life or for a term of years, a deduction is allowed under section 170 for the value of such remainder interest not transferred in trust. For purposes of section 170(f)(3)(B)(i) and this subparagraph, the term "personal residence" means any property used by the taxpayer as his personal residence even though it is not used as his principal residence. For example, the taxpayer's vacation home may be a personal residence for purposes of this subparagraph. The term "personal residence" also includes stock owned by a taxpayer as a tenant-stockholder in a cooperative housing corporation (as those terms are defined in section 216(b)(1) and (2) if the dwelling which the taxpayer is entitled to occupy as such stockholder is used by him as his personal residence.

(4) Contribution of a remainder interest in a farm. A deduction is allowed under section 170 for the value of a charitable contribution not in trust of an irrevocable remainder interest in a farm which is not the donor's entire interest in such property. Thus, for example, if a taxpayer contributes not in trust to an organization described in section 170(c) a remainder interest in a farm and retains an estate in such farm for life or for a term of years, a deduction is allowed under section 170 for the value of such remainder interest not transferred in trust. For purposes of section 170(f)(3)(B)(i) and this subparagraph, the term "farm" means any land used by the taxpayer or his tenant for the production of crops, fruits, or other agricultural products or for the sustenance of livestock. The term "livestock" includes cattle, hogs, horses, mules, donkeys, sheep, goats, captive fur-bearing animals, chickens, turkeys, pigeons, and other poultry. A farm includes the improvement thereon.

(5) Qualified conservation contribution. A deduction is allowed under section 170 for the value of a qualified conservation contribution. For the definition of a qualified conservation contribution, see § 1.170A-14.

(c) Valuation of a partial interest in property. Except as provided in § 1.170A-14, the amount of the deduction under section 170 in the case of a charitable contribution of a partial interest in property to which paragraph (b) of this section applies is the fair market value of the partial interest at the time of the contribution. See § 1.170A-1(c). The fair market value of such partial interest must be determined in accordance with § 20.2031-7 of this chapter (Estate Tax Regulations), except that, in the case of a charitable contribution of a remainder interest in real property which is not transferred in trust, the fair market value of such interest must be determined in accordance with section 170(f)(4) and § 1.170A-12. In the case of a charitable contribution of a remainder interest in the form of a remainder interest in a pooled income fund, a charitable remainder annuity trust, or a charitable remainder unitrust, the fair market value of the remainder interest must be determined as provided in paragraph (b)(2) of § 1.170A-6. However, in some cases a reduction in the amount of a charitable contribution of the remainder interest may be required. See section 170(e) and paragraph (a) of § 1.170A-4.

(d) Illustrations. The application of this section may be illustrated by the following examples:

Example (1). A, an individual owning a 10-story office building, donates the rent-free use of the top floor of the building for the year 1971 to a charitable organization. Since A's contribution consists of a partial interest to which section 170(f)(3)(A) applies, he is not entitled to a charitable contributions deduction for the contribution of such partial interest.

Example (2). In 1971, B contributes to a charitable organization an undivided one-half interest in 100 acres of land, whereby as tenants in common they share in the economic benefits from the property. The present value of the contributed property is $50,000. Since B's contribution consists of an undivided portion of his entire interest in the property to which section 170(f)(3)(B) applies, he is allowed a deduction in 1971 for his charitable contribution of $50,000.

Example (3). In 1971, D loans $10,000 in cash to a charitable organization and does not require the organization to pay any interest for the use of the money. Since D's contribution consists of a partial interest to which section 170(f)(3)(A) applies, he is not entitled to a charitable contributions deduction for the contribution of such partial interest.

(e) Effective date. This section applies only to contributions made after July 31, 1969. The deduction allowable under § 1.170A-7(b)(1)(ii) shall be available only for contributions made on or before December 17, 1980. Except as otherwise provided in § 1.170A-14(g)(4)(ii), the deduction allowable under § 1.170A-7(b)(5) shall be available for contributions made on or after December 18, 1980.

T.D. 7207, 10/3/72, amend T.D. 7955, 5/11/84, T.D. 8069, 1/13/86, T.D. 8540, 6/9/94.

§ 1.170A-8 Limitations on charitable deductions by individuals.

Caution: The Treasury has not yet amended Reg § 1.170A-8 to reflect changes made by P.L. 109-280, P.L. 100-647, P.L. 100-203, P.L. 99-514, P.L. 98-369, P.L. 97-34, P.L. 94-455.

(a) Percentage limitations. *(1) In general.* An individual's charitable contributions deduction is subject to 20-, 30-, and 50-percent limitations unless the individual qualifies for the unlimited charitable contributions deduction under section 170(b)(1)(C). For a discussion of these limitations and examples of their application, see paragraphs (b) through (f) of this section. If a husband and wife make a joint return, the deduction for contributions is the aggregate of the contributions made by the spouses, and the limitations in section 170(b) and this section are based on the aggregate contribution base of the spouses. A charitable contribution by an individual to or for the use of an organization described in section 170(c) may be deductible even though all, or some portion, of the funds of the organization may be used in foreign countries for charitable or educational purposes.

(2) "To" or "for the use of" defined. For purposes of section 170, a contribution of an income interest in property, whether or not such contributed interest is transferred in trust, for which a deduction is allowed under section 170(f)(2)(B) or (3)(A) shall be considered as made "for the use

of" rather than "to" the charitable organization. A contribution of a remainder interest in property, whether or not such contributed interest is transferred in trust, for which a deduction is allowed under section 170(f) (2)(A) or (3)(A), shall be considered as made "to" the charitable organization except that, if such interest is transferred in trust and, pursuant to the terms of the trust instrument, the interest contributed is, upon termination of the predecessor estate, to be held in trust for the benefit of such organization, the contribution shall be considered as made "for the use of" such organization. Thus, for example, assume that A transfers property to a charitable remainder annuity trust described in section 664(d)(1) which is required to pay to B for life an annuity equal to 5 percent of the initial fair market value of the property transferred in trust. The trust instrument provides that after B's death the remainder interest in the trust is to be transferred to M Church or, in the event M Church is not an organization described in section 170(c) when the amount is to be irrevocably transferred to such church, to an organization which is described in section 170(c) at that time. The contribution by A of the remainder interest shall be considered as made "to" M Church. However, if in the trust instrument A had directed that after B's death the remainder interest is to be held in trust for the benefit of M Church, the contribution shall be considered as made "for the use of" M Church. This subparagraph does not apply to the contribution of a partial interest in property, or of an undivided portion of such partial interest, if such partial interest is the donor's entire interest in the property and such entire interest was not created to avoid section 170(f)(2) or (3)(A). See paragraph (a)(2) of § 1.170A-6 and paragraphs (a)(2)(i) and (b)(1) of § 1.170A-7.

(b) 50-percent limitation. An individual may deduct charitable contributions made during a taxable year to any one or more section 170(b)(1) (A) organizations, as defined in § 1.170A-9, to the extent that such contributions in the aggregate do not exceed 50 percent of his contribution base, as defined in section 170(b)(1)(F) and paragraph (e) of this section, for the taxable year. However, see paragraph (d) of this section for a limitation on the amount of charitable contributions of 30-percent capital gain property. To qualify for the 50-percent limitation the contributions must be made "to," and not merely "for the use of," one of the specified organizations. A contribution to an organization referred to in section 170(c)(2), other than a section 170(b)(1)(A) organization, will not qualify for the 50-percent limitation even though such organization makes the contribution available to an organization which is a section 170(b)(1)(A) organization. For provisions relating to the carryover of contributions in excess of 50-percent of an individual's contribution base see section 170(d)(1) and paragraph (b) of § 1.170A-10.

(c) 20-percent limitation. *(1)* An individual may deduct charitable contributions made during a taxable year—

(i) To any one or more charitable organizations described in section 170(c) other than section 170(b)(1)(A) organizations, as defined in § 1.170A-9, and,

(ii) For the use of any charitable organization described in section 170(c), to the extent that such contributions in the aggregate do not exceed the lesser of the limitations under subparagraph (2) of this paragraph.

(2) For purposes of subparagraph (1) of this paragraph the limitations are—

(i) 20 percent of the individual's contribution base, as defined in paragraph (e) of this section, for the taxable year, or

(ii) The excess of 50 percent of the individual's contribution base, as so defined, for the taxable year over the total amount of the charitable contributions allowed under section 170(b)(1)(A) and paragraph (b) of this section, determined by first reducing the amount of such contributions under section 170(e) (1) and paragraph (a) of § 1.170A-4 but without applying the 30-percent limitation under section 170(b)(1)(D)(i) and paragraph (d)(1) of this section.

However, see paragraph (d) of this section for a limitation on the amount of charitable contributions of 30-percent capital gain property. If an election under section 170(b)(1)(D)(iii) and paragraph (d)(2) of this section applies to any contributions of 30-percent capital gain property made during the taxable year or carried over to the taxable year, the amount allowed for the taxable year under paragraph (b) of this section with respect to such contributions for purposes of applying subdivision (ii) of this subparagraph shall be the reduced amount of such contributions determined by applying paragraph (d)(2) of this section.

(d) 30-percent limitation. *(1) In general.* An individual may deduct charitable contributions of 30-percent capital gain property, as defined in subparagraph (3) of this paragraph, made during a taxable year to or for the use of any charitable organization described in section 170(c) to the extent that such contributions in the aggregate do not exceed 30-percent of his contribution base, as defined in paragraph (e) of this section, subject, however, to the 50- and 20-percent limitations prescribed by paragraphs (b) and (c) of this section. For purposes of applying the 50-percent and 20-percent limitations described in paragraphs (b) and (c) of this section, charitable contributions of 30-percent capital gain property paid during the taxable year, and limited as provided by this subparagraph, shall be taken into account after all other charitable contributions paid during the taxable year. For provisions relating to the carryover of certain contributions of 30-percent capital gain property in excess of 30-percent of an individual's contribution base, see section 170(b)(1)(D) (ii) and paragraph (c) of § 1.170A-10.

(2) Election by an individual to have section 170(e)(1)(B) apply to contributions. (i) In general. (a) An individual may elect under section 170(b)(1)(D)(iii) for any taxable year to have the reduction rule of section 170(e)(1)(B) and paragraph (a) of § 1.170A-4 apply to all his charitable contributions of 30-percent capital gain property made during such taxable year or carried over to such taxable year from a taxable year beginning after December 31, 1969. If such election is made such contributions shall be treated as contributions of section 170(e) capital gain property in accordance with paragraph (b)(2)(iii) of § 1.170A-4. The election may be made with respect to contributions of 30-percent capital gain property carried over to the taxable year even though the individual has not made any contribution of 30-percent capital gain property in such year. If such an election is made, section 170(b)(1)(D)(i) and (ii) and subparagraph (1) of this paragraph shall not apply to such contributions made during such year. However, such contributions must be reduced as required under section 170(e)(1)(B) and paragraph (a) of § 1.170A-4.

(b) If there are carryovers to such taxable year of charitable contributions of 30-percent capital gain property made in preceding taxable years beginning after December 31, 1969, the amount of such contributions in each such preceding year shall be reduced as if section 170(e)(1)(B) had applied to them in the preceding year and shall be carried over to the taxable year and succeeding taxable years under section 170(d) (1) and paragraph (b) of § 1.170A-10 as contributions of property other than 30-percent capital gain property. For purposes of applying the immediately preceding sentence, the percentage limitations under section 170(b) for the preceding taxable year and for any taxable years intervening between such year and the year of the election shall not be redetermined and the amount of any deduction allowed for such years under section 170 in respect of the charitable contributions of 30-percent capital gain property in the preceding taxable year shall not be redetermined. However, the amount of the deduction so allowed under section 170 in the preceding taxable year must be subtracted from the reduced amount of the charitable contributions made in such year in order to determine the excess amount which is carried over from such year under section 170(d)(1). If the amount of the deduction so allowed in the preceding taxable year equals or exceeds the reduced amount of the charitable contributions, there shall be no carryover from such year to the year of the election.

(c) An election under this subparagraph may be made for each taxable year in which charitable contributions of 30-percent capital gain property are made or to which they are carried over under section 170(b)(1)(D)(ii). If there are also carryovers under section 170(d)(1) to the year of the election by reason of an election made under this subparagraph for a previous taxable year, such carryovers under section 170(d)(1) shall not be redetermined by reason of the subsequent election.

(ii) Husband and wife making joint return. If a husband and wife make a joint return of income for a contribution year and one of the spouses elects under this subparagraph in a later year when he files a separate return, or if a spouse dies after a contribution year for which a joint return is made, any excess contribution of 30 percent capital gain property which is carried over to the election year from the contribution year shall be allocated between the husband and wife as provided in paragraph (d)(4)(i) and (iii) of § 1.170A-10. If a husband and wife file separate returns in a contribution year, any election under this subparagraph in a later year when a joint return is filed shall be applicable to any excess contributions of 30-percent capital gain property of either taxpayer carried over from the contribution year to the election year. The immediately preceding sentence shall also apply where two single individuals are subsequently married and file a joint return. A remarried individual who filed a joint return with his former spouse for a contribution year and thereafter files a joint return with his present spouse shall treat the carryover to the election year as provided in paragraph (d)(4)(ii) of § 1.170A-10.

(iii) Manner of making election. The election under subdivision (i) of this subparagraph shall be made by attaching to the income tax return for the election year a statement indicating that the election under section 170(b)(1)(D)(iii) and this subparagraph is being made. If there is a carryover to the taxable year of any charitable contributions of 30-percent capital gain property from a previous taxable year or years, the statement shall show a recomputation, in accordance with this subparagraph and § 1.170A-4, of such carryover, setting forth sufficient information with respect to the previous taxable year or any intervening year to show the basis of the recomputation. The statement shall indicate the district director, or the director of the internal revenue service center, with whom the return for the previous taxable year or years was filed, the name or names in which such return or returns were filed, and whether each such return was a joint or separate return.

(3) 30-percent capital gain property defined. If there is a charitable contribution of a capital asset which, if it were sold by the donor at its fair market value at the time of its contribution, would result in the recognition of gain all, or any portion, of which would be long-term capital gain and if the amount of such contribution is not required to be reduced under section 170(e)(1)(B) and § 1.170A-4(a)(2), such capital asset shall be treated as "30-percent capital gain property" for purposes of section 170 and the regulations thereunder. For such purposes any property which is property used in the trade or business, as defined in section 1231(b), shall be treated as a capital asset. However, see paragraph (b)(4) of § 1.170A-4. For the treatment of such property as section 170(e) capital gain property, see paragraph (b)(2)(iii) of § 1.170A-4.

(e) Contribution base defined. For purposes of section 170 the term "contribution base" means adjusted gross income under section 62, computed without regard to any net operating loss carryback to the taxable year under section 172. See section 170(b)(1)(F).

(f) Illustrations. The application of this section may be illustrated by the following examples:

Example (1). B, an individual, reports his income on the calendar-year basis and for 1970 has a contribution base of $100,000. During 1970 he makes charitable contributions of $70,000 in cash, of which $40,000 is given to section 170(b)(1)(A) organizations and $30,000 is given to other organizations described in section 170(c). Accordingly, B is allowed a charitable contributions deduction of $50,000 (50% of $100,000), which consists of the $40,000 contributed to section 170(b)(1)(A) organizations and $10,000 of the $30,000 contributed to the other organizations. Under paragraph (c) of this section, only $10,000 of the $30,000 contributed to the other organizations is allowed as a deduction since such contribution of $30,000 is allowed to the extent of the lesser of $20,000 (20% of $100,000) or $10,000 ([50% of $100,000] – $40,000 (contributions allowed under section 170(b)(1)(A) and paragraph (b) of this section)). Under section 170(b)(1)(D)(ii) and (d)(1) and § 1. 170A-10,B is not allowed a carryover to 1971 or to any other taxable year for any of the $20,000 ($30,000 – $10,000) not deductible under section 170(b)(1)(B) and paragraph (c) of this section.

Example (2). C, an individual, reports his income on the calendar-year basis and for 1970 has a contribution base of $100,000. During 1970 he makes charitable contributions of $40,000 in 30-percent capital gain property to section 170(b)(1)(A) organizations and of $30,000 in cash to other organizations described in section 170(c). The 20-percent limitation in section 170(b)(1)(B) and paragraph (c) of this section is applied before the 30-percent limitation in section 170(b)(1)(D)(i) and paragraph (d) of this section; accordingly section 170(b)(1)(B)(ii) limits the deduction for the $30,000 cash contribution to $10,000 ([%50% of $100,000] – $40,000). The amount of the contribution of 30-percent capital gain property is limited by section 170(b)(1)(D) (i) and paragraph (d) of this section to $30,000 (30% of $100,000). Accordingly, C's charitable contributions deduction for 1970 is limited to $40,000 ($10,000 + $30,000). Under section 170(b)(1)(D)(ii) and paragraph (c) of § 1.170A-10, C is allowed a carryover to 1971 of $10,000 ($40,000 – $30,000) in respect of his contributions of 30-percent capital gain property. C is not allowed a carryover to 1971 or to any other taxable year for any of the $20,000 cash ($30,000 – $10,000) not deductible under section 170(b)(1)(B) and paragraph (c) of this section.

Example (3). (a) D, an individual, reports his income on the calendar-year basis and for 1970 has a contribution base of $100,000. During 1970 he makes charitable contributions of $70,000 in cash, of which $40,000 is given to section 170(b)(1)(A) organizations and $30,000 is given to other organizations described in section 170(c). During 1971 D makes charitable contributions to a section 170(b)(1)(A) organization of $12,000 consisting of cash of $1,000 and $11,000 in 30-percent capital gain property. His contribution base for 1971 is $10,000.

(b) For 1970, D is allowed a charitable contributions deduction of $50,000 (50% of $100,000), which consists of the $40,000 contributed to section 170(b)(1)(A) organizations and $10,000 of the $30,000 contributed to the other organizations. Under paragraph (c) of this section, only $10,000 of the $30,000 contributed to the other organizations is allowed as a deduction since such contribution of $30,000 is allowed to the extent of the lesser of $20,000 (20% of $100,000) or $10,000 ([50% of $100,000]) – $40,000 (contributions allowed under section 170(b)(1)(A) and paragraph (b) of this section)). D is not allowed a carryover to 1971 or to any other taxable year for any of the $20,000 ($30,000 – $10,000) not deductible under section 170(b)(1)(B) and paragraph (c) of this section.

(c) For 1971, D is allowed a charitable contributions deduction of $4,000, consisting of $1,000 cash and $3,000 of the 30-percent capital gain property (30% of $10,000). Under section 170(b)(1)(D)(ii) and paragraph (c) of § 1.170A-10, D is allowed a carryover to 1972 of $8,000 ($11,000 – $3,000) in respect of his contribution of 30-percent capital gain property in 1971.

Example (4). (a) E, an individual, reports his income on the calendar-year basis and for 1970 has a contribution base of $100,000. During 1970 he makes charitable contributions of $70,000 in cash, of which $40,000 is given to section 170(b)(1)(A) organizations and $30,000 is given to other organizations described in section 170(c). During 1971 E makes charitable contributions to a section 170(b)(1)(A) organization of $14,000 consisting of cash of $3,000 and $11,000 in 30-percent capital gain property. His contribution base for 1971 is $10,000.

(b) For 1970, E is allowed a charitable contributions deduction of $50,000 (50% of $100,000), which consists of the $40,000 contributed to section 170(b)(1)(A) organizations and $10,000 of the $30,000 contributed to the other organizations. Under paragraph (c) of this section, only $10,000 of the $30,000 contributed to the other organizations is allowed as a deduction since such contribution of $30,000 is allowed to the extent of the lesser of $20,000 (20% of $100,000) or ($10,000 ([50% of $100,000] – $40,000 (contributions allowed under section 170(b)(1)(A) and paragraph (b) of this section)). E is not allowed a carryover to 1971 or to any other taxable year for any of the $20,000 ($30,000 – $10,000) not deductible under section 170(b)(1)(B) and paragraph (c) of this section.

(c) For 1971, E is allowed a charitable contributions deduction of $5,000 (50% of $10,000), consisting of $3,000 cash and $2,000 of the $3,000 (30% of $10,000) 30-percent capital gain property which is taken into account. This result is reached because, as provided in section 170(b)(1)(D)(i) and paragraph (d)(1) of this section, cash contributions are taken into account before charitable contributions of 30-percent capital gain property. Under section 170(b)(1)(D)(ii) and (d)(1) and paragraphs (b) and (c) of § 1.170A-10, E is allowed a carryover of $9,000 ([$11,000 – $3,000] plus [$6,000 – $5,000]) to 1972 in respect of this contribution of 30-percent capital gain property in 1971.

Example (5). In 1970, C, a calendar-year individual taxpayer, contributes to section 170(b)(1)(A) organizations the amount of $8,000, consisting of $3,000 in cash and $5,000 in 30-percent capital gain property. In 1970, C also makes charitable contributions of $8,500 in 30 percent capital gain property to other organizations described in section 170(c). C's contribution base for 1970 is $20,000. The 20-percent limitation in section 170(b)(1)(B) and paragraph (c) of this section is applied before the 30-percent limitation in section 170(b)(1)(D)(i) and paragraph (d) of this section; accordingly, section 170(b)(1)(B)(ii) limits the deduction for the $8,500 of contributions to the other organizations described in section 170(c) to $2,000 ([50% of $20,000] – [$3,000 + $5,000]). However, the total amounts of contributions of 30-percent capital gain property which is allowed as a deduction for 1970 is limited by section 170(b)(1)(D)(i) and paragraph (d) of this section to $6,000 (30% of $20,000), consisting of the $5,000 contribution to the section 170(b)(1)(A) organizations and $1,000 of the contributions to the other organizations described in section 170(c). Accordingly, C is allowed a charitable contributions deduction for 1970 of $9,000, which consists of $3,000 cash and $6,000 of the $13,500 of 30-percent capital gain property. C is not allowed to carry over to 1971 or any other year the remaining $7,500 because his contributions of 30-percent capital gain property for 1970 to section 170(b)(1)(A) organizations amount only to $5,000 and do not exceed $6,000 (30% of $20,000). Thus, the requirement of section 170(b)(1)(D)(ii) is not satisfied.

Example (6). During 1971, D, a calendar-year individual taxpayer, makes a charitable contribution to a church of $8,000, consisting of $5,000 in cash and $3,000 in 30-percent capital gain property. For such year, D's contribution base is $10,000. Accordingly, D is allowed a charitable contributions deduction for 1971 of $5,000 (50% of $10,000) of cash. Under section 170(d)(1) and paragraph (b) of § 1.170A-10, D is allowed a carryover to 1972 of his $3,000 contribution of 30-percent capital gain property, even though such amount does not exceed 30 percent of his contribution base for 1971.

Example (7). In 1970, E, a calendar-year individual taxpayer, makes a charitable contribution to a section 170(b)(1)(A) organization in the amount of $10,000, consisting of $8,000 in 30-percent capital gain property and of $2,000 (after reduction under section 170(e)) in other property. E's contribution base of 1970 is $20,000. Accordingly, E is allowed a charitable contributions deduction for 1970 of $8,000, consisting of the $2,000 of property the amount of which was reduced under section 170(e) and $6,000 (30% of $20,000) of the 30-percent capital gain property. Under section 170(b)(1)(D)(ii) and paragraph (c) of § 1.170A-10, E is allowed to carry over to 1971 $2,000 ($8,000 – $6,000) of his contribution of 30-percent capital gain property.

Example (8). (a) In 1972, F, a calendar-year individual taxpayer, makes a charitable contribution to a church of $4,000, consisting of $1,000 in cash and $3,000 in 30-percent capital gain property. In addition, F makes a charitable contribution in 1972 of $2,000 in cash to an organization described in section 170(c)(4). F also has a carryover from 1971 under section 170(d)(1) of $5,000 (none of which consists of contributions of 30-percent capital gain property) and a carryover from 1971 under section 170(b)(1)(D)(ii) of $6,000 of contributions of 30-percent capital gain property. F's contribution base for 1972 is $11,000. Accordingly, F is allowed a charitable contributions deduction for 1972 of

$5,500 (50% of $11,000), which consists of $1,000 cash contributed in 1972 to the church, $3,000 of 30-percent capital gain property contributed in 1972 to the church, and $1,500 (carryover of $5,000 but not to exceed [$5,500 – ($1,000 + $3,000)]) of the carryover from 1971 under section 170(d)(1).

(b) No deduction is allowed for 1972 for the contribution in that year of $2,000 cash to the section 170(c)(4) organization since section 170(b)(1)(B)(ii) and paragraph (c) of this section limit the deduction for such contribution to $0 ([50% of $11,000] – [$1,000 + $1,500 + $3,000]). Moreover, F is not allowed a carryover to 1973 or to any other year for any of such $2,000 cash contributed to the section 170(c)(4) organization.

(c) Under section 170(d)(1) and paragraph (b) of § 1.170A-10, F is allowed a carryover to 1973 from 1971 of $3,500 ($5,000 – $1,500) of contributions of other than 30-percent capital gain property. Under section 170(b)(1)(D)(ii) and paragraph (c) of § 1.170A-10, F is allowed a carryover to 1973 from 1971 of $6,000 ($6,000 – $0 of such carryover treated as paid in 1972) of contributions of 30-percent capital gain property. The portion of such $6,000 carryover from 1971 which is treated as paid in 1972 is $0 ([50% of $11,000] – [$4,000 contributions to the church in 1972 plus $1,500 of section 170(d)(1) carryover treated as paid in 1972]).

Example (9). (a) In 1970, A, a calendar-year individual taxpayer, makes a charitable contribution to a church of 30-percent capital gain property having a fair market value of $60,000 and an adjusted basis of $10,000. A's contribution base for 1970 is $50,000, and he makes no other charitable contributions in that year. A does not elect for 1970 under paragraph (d)(2) of this section to have section 170(e)(1)(B) apply to such contribution. Accordingly, under section 170(b)(1)(D)(i) and paragraph (d) of this section, A is allowed a charitable contributions deduction for 1970 of $15,000 (30% of $50,000). Under section 170(b)(1)(D)(ii) and paragraph (c) of § 1.170A-10, A is allowed a carryover to 1971 of $45,000 ($60,000 – $15,000) for his contribution of 30-percent capital gain property.

(b) In 1971, A makes a charitable contribution to a church of 30-percent capital gain property having a fair market value of $11,000 and an adjusted basis of $10,000. A's contribution base for 1971 is $60,000, and he makes no other charitable contributions in that year. A elects for 1971 under paragraph (d)(2) of this section to have section 170(e)(1)(B) and § 1.170A-4 apply to his contribution of $11,000 in that year and to his carryover of $45,000 from 1970. Accordingly, he is required to recompute his carryover from 1970 as if section 170(e)(1)(B) had applied to his contribution of 30-percent capital gain property in that year.

(c) If section 170(e)(1)(B) had applied in 1970 to his contribution of 30-percent capital gain property, A's contribution would have been reduced from $60,000 to $35,000, the reduction of $25,000 being 50 percent of the gain of $50,000 ($60,000 – $10,000) which would have been recognized as long-term capital gain if the property had been sold by A at its fair market value at the time of the contribution in 1970. Accordingly, by taking the election under paragraph (d)(2) of this section into account, A has a recomputed carryover to 1971 of $20,000 ($35,000 – $15,000) of his contribution of 30-percent capital gain property in 1970. However, A's charitable contributions deduction of $15,000 allowed for 1970 is not recomputed by reason of the election.

(d) Pursuant to the election for 1971, the contribution of 30-percent capital gain property for 1971 is reduced from $11,000 to $10,500, the reduction of $500 being 50 percent of the gain of $1,000 ($11,000 – $10,000) which would have been recognized as long-term capital gain if the property had been sold by A at its fair market value at the time of its contribution in 1971.

(e) Accordingly, A is allowed a charitable contributions deduction for 1971 of $30,000 (total contributions of $30,500 [$20,000 – $10,500] but not to exceed 50% of $60,000).

(f) Under section 170(d)(1) and paragraph (b) of § 1.170A-10, A is allowed a carryover of $500 ($30,500 – $30,000) to 1972 and the 3 succeeding taxable years. The $500 carryover, which by reason of the election is no longer treated as a contribution of 30-percent capital gain property, is treated as carried over under paragraph (b) of § 1.170A-10 from 1970 since in 1971 current year contributions are deducted before contributions which are carried over from preceding taxable years.

Example (10). The facts are the same as in example (9) except that A also makes a charitable contribution in 1971 of $2,000 cash to a private foundation not described in section 170(b)(1)(E) and that A's contribution base for that year is $62,000 instead of $60,000. Accordingly, A is allowed a charitable contributions deduction for 1971 of $31,000, determined in the following manner. Under section 170(b)(1)(A) and paragraph (b) of this section, A is allowed a charitable contributions deduction for 1971 of $30,500, consisting of $10,500 of property contributed to the church in 1971 and $20,000 (carryover of $20,000 but not to exceed [($62,000 × 50%) – $10,500]) of contributions of property carried over to 1971 under section 170(d)(1) and paragraph (b) of § 1.170A-10. Under section 170(b)(1)(B) and paragraph (c) of this section, A is allowed a charitable contributions deduction for 1971 of $500 ([50% of $62,000] – [$10,500 + $20,000]) of cash contributed to the private foundation in that year. A is not allowed a carryover to 1972 or to any other taxable year for any of the $1,500 ($2,000 – $500) cash not deductible in 1971 under section 170(b)(1)(B) and paragraph (c) of this section.

Example (11). The facts are the same as in example (9) except that A's contribution base for 1970 is $120,000. Thus, before making the election under paragraph (d)(2) of this section for 1971, A is allowed a charitable contributions deduction for 1970 of $36,000 (30% of $120,000) and is allowed a carryover to 1971 of $24,000 ($60,000 – $36,000). By making the election for 1971, A is required to recompute the carryover from 1970, which is reduced from $24,000 to zero, since the charitable contributions deduction of $36,000 allowed for 1970 exceeds the reduced $35,000 contribution for 1970 which may be taken into account by reason of the election for 1971. Accordingly, A is allowed a deduction for 1971 of $10,500 and is allowed no carryover to 1972, since the reduced contribution for 1971 ($10,500) does not exceed the limitation of $30,000 (50% of $60,000) for 1971 which applies under section 170(d)(1) and paragraph (b) of § 1.170A-10. A's charitable contributions deduction of $36,000 allowed for 1970 is not recomputed by reason of the election. Thus, it is not to A's advantage to make the election under paragraph (d)(2) of this section.

Example (12). (a) B, an individual, reports his income on the calendar-year basis and for 1970 has a contribution base of $100,000. During 1970 he makes charitable contributions of $70,000, consisting of $50,000 in 30-percent capital gain property contributed to a church and $20,000 in cash contributed to a private foundation not described in section 170(b)(1)(E). For 1971, B's contribution base is $40,000, and in that year he makes a charitable contribution of $5,000 in cash to such private foundation. During the years involved B makes no other charitable contributions.

(b) The amount of the contribution of 30-percent capital gain property which may be taken into account for 1970 is limited by section 170(b)(1)(D)(i) and paragraph (d) of this section to $30,000 (30% of $100,000). Accordingly, under section 170(b)(1)(A) and paragraph (b) of this section B is allowed a deduction for 1970 of $30,000 of 30-percent capital gain property (contribution of $30,000 but not to exceed $50,000 [50% of $100,000]). No deduction is allowed for 1970 for the contribution in that year of $20,000 of cash to the private foundation since section 170(b)(1)(B)(ii) and paragraph (c) of this section limit the deduction for such contribution to $0 ([50% of $100,000] – $50,000, the amount of the contribution of 30-percent capital gain property).

(c) Under section 170(b)(1)(D)(ii) and paragraph (c) of § 1.170A-10, B is allowed a carryover to 1971 of $20,000 ($50,000 – [30% of $100,000]) of his contribution in 1970 of 30-percent capital gain property. B is not allowed a carryover to 1971 or to any other taxable year for any of the $20,000 cash contribution in 1970 which is not deductible under section 170(b)(1)(B) and paragraph (c) of this section.

(d) The amount of the contribution of 30-percent capital gain property which may be taken into account for 1971 is limited by section 170(b)(1)(D)(i) and paragraph (d) of this section to $12,000 (30% of $40,000). Accordingly, under section 170(b)(1)(A) and paragraph (b) of this section B is allowed a deduction for 1971 of $12,000 of 30-percent capital gain property (contribution of $12,000 but not to exceed $20,000 [50% of $40,000]). No deduction is allowed for 1971 for the contribution in that year of $5,000 of cash to the private foundation, since section 170(b)(1)(B)(ii) and paragraph (c) of this section limit the deduction for such contribution of $0 [50% of $40,000 – $20,000 carryover of 30-percent capital gain property from 1970).

(e) Under section 170(b)(1)(D)(ii) and paragraph (c) of § 1.170A-10, B is allowed a carryover to 1972 of $8,000 ($20,000 – 30% of $40,000]) of his contribution in 1970 of 30-percent capital gain property. B is not allowed a carryover to 1972 or to any other taxable year for any of the $5,000 cash contribution for 1971 which is not deductible under section 170(b)(1)(B) and paragraph (c) of this section.

Example (13). D, an individual, reports his income on the calendar-year basis and for 1970 has a contribution base of $100,000. On March 1, 1970, he contributes to a church intangible property to which section 1245 applies which has a fair market value of $60,000 and an adjusted basis of $10,000. At the time of the contribution D has used the property in his business for more than 6 months. If the property had been sold by D at its fair market value at the time of its contribution, it is assumed that under section 1245 $20,000 of the gain of $50,000 would have been treated as ordinary income and $30,000 would have been long-term capital gain. Since the property contributed is ordinary income property within the meaning of paragraph (b)(1) of § 1.170A-4, D's contribution of $60,000 is reduced under paragraph (a)(1) of such section to $40,000 ($60,000 – $20,000 ordinary income). However, since the property contributed is also 30-percent capital gain property within the meaning of paragraph (d)(3) of this section. D's deduction for 1970 is limited by section 170(b)(1)(D)(i) and paragraph (d) of this section to $30,000 (30% of $100,000). Under section 170(b)(1)(D)(ii) and paragraph (c) of § 1.170A-10, D is allowed to carry over to 1971 $10,000 ($40,000 – $30,000) of his contribution of 30-percent capital gain property.

Example (14). C, an individual, reports his income on the calendar-year basis and for 1970 has a contribution base of $50,000. During 1970 he makes charitable contributions to a church of $57,000, consisting of $2,000 cash and of 30-percent capital gain property with a fair market value of $55,000 and an adjusted basis of $15,000. In addition, C contributes $3,000 cash in 1970 to a private foundation not described in section 170(b)(1)(E). For 1970, C elects under paragraph (d)(2) of this section to have section 170(e)(1)(E) and § 1.170A-4(a) apply to his contribution of property to the church. Accordingly, for 1970 C's contribution of property to the church is reduced from $55,000 to $35,000, the reduction of $20,000 being 50 percent of the gain of $40,000 ($55,000 – $15,000) which would have been recognized as long term capital gain if the property had been sold by C at its fair market value at the time of its contribution to the church. Under section 170(b)(1)(A) and paragraph (b) of this section, C is allowed a charitable contributions deduction for 1970 of $25,000 ([$2,000 + $35,000] but not to exceed [$50,000 × 50%]). Under section 170(d)(1) and paragraph (b) of § 1.170A-10, C is allowed a carryover from 1970 to 1971 of $12,000 ($37,000 – $25,000). No deduction is allowed for 1970 for the contribution in that year of $3,000 cash to the private foundation since section 170(b)(1)(B) and paragraph (c) of this section limit the deduction for such contribution to the smaller of $10,000 ($50,000 × 20%) or $0 ([$50,000 × 50%] – $25,000). C is not allowed a carryover from 1970 for any of the $3,000 cash contribution in that year which is not deductible under section 170(b)(1)(B) and paragraph (c) of this section.

Example (15). (a) D, an individual, reports his income on the calendar-year basis and for 1970 has a contribution base of $100,000. During 1970 he makes a charitable contribution to a church of 30-percent capital gain property with a fair market value of $40,000 and an adjusted basis of $21,000. In addition, he contributes $23,000 cash in 1970 to a private foundation not described in section 170(b)(1)(E). For 1970, D elects under paragraph (d)(2) of this section to have section 170(e)(1)(B) and § 1.170A-4(a) apply to his contribution of property to the church. Accordingly, for 1970 D's contribution of property to the church is reduced from $40,000 to $30,500, the reduction of $9,500 being 50 percent of the gain of $19,000 ($40,000 – $21,000) which would have been recognized as long-term capital gain if the property had been sold by D at its fair market value at the time of its contribution to the church. Under section 170(b)(1)(A) and paragraph (b) of this section, D is allowed a charitable contributions deduction for 1970 of $30,500 for the property contributed to the church. In addition, under section 170(b)(1)(B) and paragraph (c) of this section D is allowed a deduction of $19,500 for the cash contributed to the private foundation, since such contribution of $23,000 is allowed to the extent of the lesser of $20,000 (20% of $100,000) or $19,500 ([$100,000 × 50%] – $30,500). D is not allowed a carryover to 1971 or to any other taxable year for any of the $3,500 ($23,000 – $19,500) of cash not deductible under section 170(b)(1)(B) and paragraph (c) of this section.

(b) If D had not made the election under paragraph (d)(2) of this section for 1970, his deduction for 1970 under section 170(a) for the $40,000 contribution of property to the church would have been limited by section 170(b)(1)(D)(i) and paragraph (d) of this section to $30,000 (30% of $100,000), and under section 170(b)(1)(D)(ii) and paragraph (c) of § 1.170A-10 he would have been allowed a carryover to 1971 of $10,000 ($40,000 – $30,000) for his contribution of such property. In addition, he would have been allowed under section 170(b)(1)(B)(ii) and paragraph (c) of this section for 1970 a charitable contributions deduction of $10,000 ([$100,000 × 50%] – $40,000) for the cash contributed to the private foundation. In such case, D would not have been allowed a carryover to 1971 or to any other taxable year for any of the $13,000 ($23,000 – $10,000) of cash not deductible under section 170(b)(1)(B) and paragraph (c) of this section.

(g) Effective date. This section applies only to contributions paid in taxable years beginning after December 31, 1969.

T.D. 7207, 10/3/72.

---

§ 1.170A-9 Definition of section 170(b)(1)(A) organization.

Caution: The Treasury has not yet amended Reg § 1.170A-9 to reflect changes made by P.L. 108-357.

(a) The term section 170(b)(1)(A) organization as used in the regulations under section 170 means any organization described in paragraphs (b) through (j) of this section, effective with respect to taxable years beginning after December 31, 1969, except as otherwise provided. Section 1.170-2(b) shall continue to be applicable with respect to taxable years beginning prior to January 1, 1970. The term one or more organizations described in section 170(b)(1)(A) (other than clauses (vii) and (viii)) as used in sections 507 and 509 of the Internal Revenue Code (Code) and the regulations means one or more organizations described in paragraphs (b) through (f) of this section, except as modified by the regulations under part II of subchapter F of chapter 1 or under chapter 42.

(b) Church or a convention or association of churches. An organization is described in section 170(b)(1)(A)(i) if it is a church or a convention or association of churches.

(c) Educational organization and organizations for the benefit of certain State and municipal colleges and universities. *(1) Educational organization.* An educational organization is described in section 170(b)(1)(A)(ii) if its primary function is the presentation of formal instruction and it normally maintains a regular faculty and curriculum and normally has a regularly enrolled body of pupils or students in attendance at the place where its educational activities are regularly carried on. The term includes institutions such as primary, secondary, preparatory, or high schools, and colleges and universities. It includes Federal, State, and other public-supported schools which otherwise come within the definition. It does not include organizations engaged in both educational and noneducational activities unless the latter are merely incidental to the educational activities. A recognized university which incidentally operates a museum or sponsors concerts is an educational organization within the meaning of section 170(b)(1)(A)(ii). However, the operation of a school by a museum does not necessarily qualify the museum as an educational organization within the meaning of this subparagraph.

(2) Organizations for the benefit of certain State and municipal colleges and universities. (i) An organization is described in section 170(b)(1)(A)(iv) if it meets the support requirements of subdivision (ii) of this subparagraph and is organized and operated exclusively to receive, hold, invest, and administer property and to make expenditures to or for the benefit of a college or university which is an organization described in subdivision (iii) of this subparagraph. The phrase "expenditures to or for the benefit of a college or university" includes expenditures made for any one or more of the normal functions of colleges and universities such as the acquisition and maintenance of real property comprising part of the campus area; the erection of, or participation in the erection of, college or university buildings; the acquisition and maintenance of equipment and furnishings used for, or in conjunction with, normal functions of colleges and universities; or expenditures for scholarships, libraries and student loans.

(ii) To qualify under section 170(b)(1)(A)(iv), the organization receiving the contribution must normally receive a substantial part of its support from the United States or any State or political subdivision thereof or from direct or indirect contributions from the general public, or from a combination of two or more of such sources. For such purposes, the term "support" does not include income received in the exercise or performance by the organization of its charitable, educational, or other purpose or function constituting the basis for its exemption under section 501(a). An example of an indirect contribution from the public is the receipt by the organization of its share of the proceeds of an annual collection campaign of a community chest, community fund, or united fund. In determining the amount of support received by such organization with respect to a contribution of property which is subject to reduction under section 170(e), the fair market value of the property shall be taken into account.

(iii) The college or university (including a land grant college or university) to be benefited must be an educational organization referred to in section 170(b)(1)(A)(ii) and subparagraph (1) of this paragraph which is an agency or instrumentality of a State or political subdivision thereof, or which is owned or operated by a State or political subdivision thereof or by an agency or instrumentality of one or more States or political subdivisions.

(d) Hospitals and medical research organizations. *(1) Hospitals.* An organization (other than one described in paragraph (d)(2) of this section) is described in section 170(b)(1)(A)(iii) if—

(i) It is a hospital; and

(ii) Its principal purpose or function is the providing of medical or hospital care or medical education or medical research.

(A) The term hospital includes—

(*1*) Federal hospitals; and

(*2*) State, county, and municipal hospitals which are instrumentalities of governmental units referred to in section 170(c)(1) and otherwise come within the definition. A rehabilitation institution, outpatient clinic, or community mental health or drug treatment center may qualify as a "hospital" within the meaning of paragraph (d)(1)(i) of this section if its principal purpose or function is the providing of hospital or medical care. For purposes of this paragraph (d)(1)(ii), the term medical care shall include the treatment of any physical or mental disability or condition, whether on an inpatient or outpatient basis, provided the cost of such treatment is deductible under section 213 by the person treated. An organization, all the accommodations of which qualify as being part of a "skilled nursing facility" within the meaning of 42 U.S.C. 1395x(j), may qualify as a "hospital" within the meaning of paragraph (d)(1)(i) of this section if its principal purpose or function is the providing of hospital or medical care. For taxable years ending after June 28, 1968, the term hospital also includes cooperative hospital service organizations which meet the requirements of section 501(e) and § 1.501(e)-1.

(B) The term hospital does not, however, include convalescent homes or homes for children or the aged, nor does the term include institutions whose principal purpose or function is to train handicapped individuals to pursue some vocation. An organization whose principal purpose or function is the providing of medical education or medical research will not be considered a "hospital" within the meaning of paragraph (d)(1)(i) of this section, unless it is also actively engaged in providing medical or hospital care to patients on its premises or in its facilities, on an inpatient or outpatient basis, as an integral part of its medical education or medical research functions. See, however, paragraph (d)(2) of this section with respect to certain medical research organizations.

(2) Certain medical research organizations. (i) Introduction. A medical research organization is described in section 170(b)(1)(A)(iii) if the principal purpose or functions of such organization are medical research and if it is directly engaged in the continuous active conduct of medical research in conjunction with a hospital. In addition, for purposes of the 50 percent limitation of section 170(b)(1)(A) with respect to a contribution, during the calendar year in which the contribution is made such organization must be committed to spend such contribution for such research before January 1 of the fifth calendar year which begins after the date such contribution is made. An organization need not receive contributions deductible under section 170 to qualify as a medical research organization and such organization need not be committed to spend amounts to which the limitation of section 170(b)(1)(A) does not apply within the 5-year period referred to in this paragraph (d)(2)(i). However, the requirement of continuous active conduct of medical research indicates that the type of organization contemplated in this paragraph (d)(2) is one which is primarily engaged directly in the continuous active conduct of medical research, as compared to an inactive medical research organization or an organization primarily engaged in funding the programs of other medical research organizations. As in the case of a hospital, since an organization is ordinarily not described in section 170(b)(1)(A)(iii) as a hospital unless it functions primarily as a hospital, similarly a medical research organization is not so described unless it is primarily engaged directly in the continuous active conduct of medical research in conjunction with a hospital. Accordingly, the rules of this paragraph (d)(2) shall only apply with respect to such medical research organizations.

(ii) General rule. An organization (other than a hospital described in paragraph (d)(1) of this section) is described in section 170(b)(1)(A)(iii) only if within the meaning of this paragraph (d)(2):

(A) The principal purpose or functions of such organization are to engage primarily in the conduct of medical research; and

(B) It is primarily engaged directly in the continuous active conduct of medical research in conjunction with a hospital which is—

(1) Described in section 501(c)(3);

(2) A Federal hospital; or

(3) An instrumentality of a governmental unit referred to in section 170(c)(1).

(C) In order for a contribution to such organization to qualify for purposes of the 50 percent limitation of section 170(b)(1)(A), during the calendar year in which such contribution is made or treated as made, such organization must be committed (within the meaning of paragraph (d)(2)(viii) of this section) to spend such contribution for such active conduct of medical research before January 1 of the fifth calendar year beginning after the date such contribution is made. For the meaning of the term "medical research" see paragraph (d)(2)(iii) of this section. For the meaning of the term "principal purpose or functions" see paragraph (d)(2)(iv) of this section. For the meaning of the term "primarily engaged directly in the continuous active conduct of medical research" see paragraph (d)(2)(v) of this section. For the meaning of the term "medical research in conjunction with a hospital" see paragraph (d)(2)(vii) of this section.

(iii) Definition of medical research. Medical research means the conduct of investigations, experiments, and studies to discover, develop, or verify knowledge relating to the causes, diagnosis, treatment, prevention, or control of physical or mental diseases and impairments of man. To qualify as a medical research organization, the organization must have or must have continuously available for its regular use the appropriate equipment and professional personnel necessary to carry out its principal function. Medical research encompasses the associated disciplines spanning the biological, social and behavioral sciences. Such disciplines include chemistry (biochemistry, physical chemistry, bioorganic chemistry, etc.), behavioral sciences (psychiatry, physiological psychology, neurophysiology, neurology, neurobiology, and social psychology, etc.), biomedical engineering (applied biophysics, medical physics, and medical electronics, for example, developing pacemakers and other medically related electrical equipment), virology, immunology, biophysics, cell biology, molecular biology, pharmacology, toxicology, genetics, pathology, physiology, microbiology, parasitology, endocrinology, bacteriology, and epidemiology.

(iv) Principal purpose or functions. An organization must be organized for the principal purpose of engaging primarily in the conduct of medical research in order to be an organization meeting the requirements of this paragraph (d)(2). An organization will normally be considered to be so organized if it is expressly organized for the purpose of conducting medical research and is actually engaged primarily in the conduct of medical research. Other facts and circumstances, however, may indicate that an organization does not meet the principal purpose requirement of this paragraph (d)(2)(iv) even where its governing instrument so expressly provides. An organization that otherwise meets all of the requirements of this paragraph (d)(2) (including this paragraph (d)(2)(iv)) to qualify as a medical research organization will not fail to so qualify solely because its governing instrument does not specifically state that its principal purpose is to conduct medical research.

(v) Primarily engaged directly in the continuous active conduct of medical research. (A) In order for an organization to be primarily engaged directly in the continuous active conduct of medical research, the organization must either devote a substantial part of its assets to, or expend a significant percentage of its endowment for, such purposes, or both. Whether an organization devotes a substantial part of its assets to, or makes significant expenditures for, such continuous active conduct depends upon the facts and circumstances existing in each specific case. An organization will be treated as devoting a substantial part of its assets to, or expending a significant percentage of its endowment for, such purposes if it meets the appropriate test contained in paragraph (d)(2)(v)(B) of this section. If an organization fails to satisfy both of such tests, in evaluating the facts and circumstances, the factor given most weight is the margin by which the organization failed to meet such tests. Some of the other facts and circumstances to be considered in making such a determination are—

(1) If the organization fails to satisfy the tests because it failed to properly value its assets or endowment, then upon determination of the improper valuation it devotes additional assets to, or makes additional expenditures for, such purposes, so that it satisfies such tests on an aggregate basis for the prior year in addition to such tests for the current year;

(2) The organization acquires new assets or has a significant increase in the value of its securities after it had developed a budget in a prior year based on the assets then owned and the then current values;

(3) The organization fails to make expenditures in any given year because of the interrelated aspects of its budget and long-term planning requirements, for example, where an organization prematurely terminates an unsuccessful program and because of long-term planning requirements it will not be able to establish a fully operational replacement program immediately; and

(4) The organization has as its objective to spend less than a significant percentage in a particular year but make up the difference in the subsequent few years, or to budget a greater percentage in an earlier year and a lower percentage in a later year.

(B) For purposes of this section, an organization which devotes more than one half of its assets to the continuous active conduct of medical research will be considered to be devoting a substantial part of its assets to such conduct within the meaning of paragraph (d)(2)(v)(A) of this section. An organization which expends funds equaling 3.5 percent or more of the fair market value of its endowment for the continuous active conduct of medical research will be considered to have expended a significant percentage of its endowment for such purposes within the meaning of paragraph (d)(2)(v)(A) of this section.

(C) Engaging directly in the continuous active conduct of medical research does not include the disbursing of funds to other organizations for the conduct of research by them or the extending of grants or scholarships to others. Therefore, if an organization's primary purpose is to disburse funds to other organizations for the conduct of research by them or to extend grants or scholarships to others, it is not primarily engaged directly in the continuous active conduct of medical research.

(vi) Special rules. The following rules shall apply in determining whether a substantial part of an organization's assets are devoted to, or its endowment is expended for, the continuous active conduct of medical research activities:

(A) An organization may satisfy the tests of paragraph (d)(2)(v)(B) of this section by meeting such tests either for a computation period consisting of the immediately preceding taxable year, or for the computation period consisting of the immediately preceding four taxable years. In addition, for taxable years beginning in 1970, 1971, 1972, 1973, and 1974, if an organization meets such tests for the computation period consisting of the first four taxable years beginning after December 31, 1969, an organization will be treated as meeting such tests, not only for the taxable year beginning in 1974, but also for the preceding four taxable years. Thus, for example, if a calendar year organization failed to satisfy such tests for a computation period consisting of 1969, 1970, 1971, and 1972, but on the basis of a computation period consisting of the years 1970 through 1973, it expended funds equaling 3.5 percent or more of the fair market value of its endowment for the continuous active conduct of medical research, such organization will be considered to have expended a significant percentage of its endowment for such purposes for the taxable years 1970 through 1974. In applying such tests for a four-year computation period, although the organization's expenditures for the entire four-year period shall be aggregated, the fair market value of its endowment for each year shall be summed, even though, in the case of an asset held throughout the four-year period, the fair market value of such an asset will be counted four times. Similarly, the fair market value of an organization's assets for each year of a four-year computation period shall be summed.

(B) Any property substantially all the use of which is "substantially related" (within the meaning of section 514(b)(1)(A)) to the exercise or performance of the organization's medical research activities will not be treated as part of its endowment.

(C) The valuation of assets must be made with commonly accepted methods of valuation. A method of valuation made in accordance with the principles stated in the regulations under section 2031 constitutes an acceptable method of valuation. Assets may be valued as of any day in the organization's taxable year to which such valuation applies, provided the organization follows a consistent practice of valuing such asset as of such date in all taxable years. For purposes of paragraph (d)(2)(v) of this section, an asset held by the organization for part of a taxable year shall be taken into account by multiplying the fair market value of such asset by a fraction, the numerator of which is the number of days in such taxable year that the organization held such asset and the denominator of which is the number of days in such taxable year.

(vii) Medical research in conjunction with a hospital. The organization need not be formally affiliated with a hospital to be considered primarily engaged directly in the continuous active conduct of medical research in conjunction with a hospital, but in any event there must be a joint effort on the part of the research organization and the hospital pursuant to an understanding that the two organizations will maintain continuing close cooperation in the active conduct of medical research. For example, the necessary joint effort will normally be found to exist if the activities of the medical research organization are carried on in space located within or adjacent to a hospital, the organization is permitted to utilize the facilities (including equipment, case studies, etc.) of the hospital on a continuing basis directly in the active conduct of medical research, and there is substantial evidence of the close cooperation of the members of the staff of the research organization and members of the staff of the particular hospital or hospitals. The active participation in medical research by members of the staff of the particular hospital or hospitals will be considered to be evidence of such close cooperation. Because medical research may involve substantial investigation, experimentation and study not immediately connected with hospital or medical care, the requisite joint effort will also normally be found to exist if there is an established relationship between the research organization and the hospital which provides that the cooperation of appropriate personnel and the use of facilities of the particular hospital or hospitals will be required whenever it would aid such research.

(viii) Commitment to spend contributions. The organization's commitment that the contribution will be spent within the prescribed time only for the prescribed purposes must be legally enforceable. A promise in writing to the donor in consideration of his making a contribution that such contribution will be so spent within the prescribed time will constitute a commitment. The expenditure of contributions received for plant, facilities, or equipment, used solely for medical research purposes (within the meaning of paragraph (d)(2)(ii) of this section), shall ordinarily be considered to be an expenditure for medical research. If a contribution is made in other than money, it shall be considered spent for medical research if the funds from the proceeds of a disposition thereof are spent by the organization within the five-year period for medical research; or, if such property is of such a kind that it is used on a continuing basis directly in connection with such research, it shall be considered spent for medical research in the year in which it is first so used. A medical research organization will be presumed to have made the commitment required under this paragraph (d)(2)(viii) with respect to any contribution if its governing instrument or by-laws require that every contribution be spent for medical research before January 1 of the fifth year which begins after the date such contribution is made.

(ix) Organizational period for new organizations. A newly created organization, for its "organizational" period, shall be considered to be primarily engaged directly in the continuous active conduct of medical research in conjunction with a hospital within the meaning of paragraphs (d)(2)(v) and (d)(2)(vii) of this section if during such period the organization establishes to the satisfaction of the Commissioner that it reasonably can be expected to be so engaged by the end of such period. The information to be submitted shall include detailed plans showing the proposed initial medical research program, architectural drawings for the erection of buildings and facilities to be used for medical research in accordance with such plans, plans to assemble a professional staff and detailed projections showing the timetable for the expected accomplishment of the foregoing. The "organizational" period shall be that period which is appropriate to implement the proposed plans, giving effect to the proposed amounts involved and the magnitude and complexity of the projected medical research program, but in no event in excess of three years following organization.

(x) Examples. The application of this paragraph (d)(2) may be illustrated by the following examples:

Example (1). N, an organization referred to in section 170(c)(2), was created to promote human knowledge within the field of medical research and medical education. All of N's assets were contributed to it by A and consist of a diversified portfolio of stocks and bonds. N's endowment earns 3.5 percent annually, which N expends in the conduct of various medical research programs in conjunction with Y hospital. N is located adjacent to Y hospital, makes substantial use of Y's facilities, and there is close cooperation between the staffs of N and Y. N is directly engaged in the continuous active conduct of medical research in conjunction with a hospital, meets the principal purpose test described in paragraph (d)(2)(iv) of this section, and is therefore an organization described in section 170(b)(1)(A)(iii).

Example (2). O, an organization referred to in section 170(c)(2), was created to promote human knowledge within the field of medical research and medical education. All of O's assets consist of a diversified portfolio of stocks and bonds. O's endowment earns 3.5 percent annually, which O expends in the conduct of various medical research programs in conjunction with certain hospitals. However, in 1974, O receives a substantial bequest of additional stocks and bonds. O's budget for 1974 does not take into account the bequest and as a result O expends only 3.1 percent of its endowment in 1974. However, O establishes that it will expend at least 3.5 percent of its endowment for the active conduct of medical research for taxable years 1975 through 1978. O is therefore directly engaged in the continuous active conduct of medical research in conjunction with a hospital for taxable year 1975. Since O also meets the principal purpose test described in paragraph (d)(2)(iv) of this section, it is therefore an organization described in section 170(b)(1)(A)(iii) for taxable year 1975.

Example (3). M, an organization referred to in section 170(c)(2), was created to promote human knowledge within the field of medical research and medical education. M's activities consist of the conduct of medical research programs in conjunction with various hospitals. Under such programs, researchers employed by M engage in research at laboratories set aside for M within the various hospitals. Substantially all of M's assets consist of 100 percent of the stock of X corporation, which has a fair market value of approximately 100 million dollars. X pays M approximately 3.3 million dollars in dividends annually, which M expends in the conduct of its medical research programs. Since M expends only 3.3 percent of its endowment, which does not constitute a significant percentage, in the active conduct of medical research, M is not an organization described in section 170(b)(1)(A)(iii) because M is not engaged in the continuous active conduct of medical research.

(xi) Special rule for organizations with existing ruling. This paragraph (d)(2)(xi) shall apply to an organization that prior to January 1, 1970, had received a ruling or determination letter which has not been expressly revoked holding the organization to be a medical research organization described in section 170(b)(1)(A)(iii) and with respect to which the facts and circumstances on which the ruling was based have not substantially changed. An organization to which this paragraph (d)(2)(xi) applies shall be treated as an organization described in section 170(b)(1)(A)(iii) for a period not ending prior to 90 days after February 13, 1976 (or where appropriate, for taxable years beginning before such 90th day). In addition, with respect to a grantor or contributor under sections 170, 507, 545(b)(2), 556(b)(2), 642(c), 4942, 4945, 2055, 2106(a)(2), and 2522, the status of an organization to which this paragraph (d)(2)(xi) applies will not be affected until notice of change of status under section 170(b)(1)(A)(iii) is made to the public (such as by publication in the Internal Revenue Bulletin). The preceding sentence shall not apply if the grantor or contributor had previously acquired knowledge that the Internal Revenue Service had given notice to such organization that it would be deleted from classification as a section 170(b)(1)(A)(iii) organization.

(e) Governmental unit. A governmental unit is described in section 170(b)(1)(A)(v) if it is referred to in section 170(c)(1).

(f) Definition of section 170(b)(1)(A)(vi) organization. *(1) In general.* An organization is described in section 170(b)(1)(A)(vi) if it is:

(i) A corporation, trust, or community chest, fund, or foundation, referred to in section 170(c)(2) (other than an organization specifically described in paragraphs (a) through (d) of this section), and

(ii) A "publicly supported" organization. For purposes of this paragraph, an organization is "publicly supported" if it normally receives a substantial part of its support from a governmental unit referred to in section 170(c)(1) or from direct or indirect contributions from the general public. An organization will be treated as being "public supported" if it meets the requirements of either subparagraph (2) or subparagraph (3) of this paragraph. Types of organizations which, subject to the provisions of this paragraph, generally qualify under section 170(b)(1)(A)(vi) as "publicly supported" are publicly or governmentally supported museums of history, art, or science, libraries, community centers to promote the arts, organizations providing facilities for the support of an opera, symphony orchestra, ballet, or repertory drama or for some other direct service to the general public, and organizations such as the American Red Cross or the United Givers Fund.

(2) Determination whether an organization is "publicly supported"; 33⅓ percent-of-support test. An organization will be treated as a "publicly supported" organization if the total amount of support which the organization "normally" (as defined in subparagraph (4) of this paragraph) receives from governmental units referred to in section 170(c)(1), from contributions made directly or indirectly by the general public, or from a combination or these sources, equals at least 33⅓ percent of the total support "normally" received by the organization. See subparagraphs (6), (7), and (8) of this paragraph for the definition of "support." The application of this test is illustrated by Example (1) of subparagraph (9) of this paragraph.

(3) Determination whether an organization is "publicly supported;" facts and circumstances test for organizations failing to meet 33⅓ percent-of-support test. Even if an organization fails to meet the 33⅓ percent-of-support test described in subparagraph (2) of this paragraph, it will be treated as a "publicly supported" organization if it normally receives a substantial part of its support from governmental units, from direct or indirect contributions from the general public, or from a combination of these sources, and meets the other requirements of this subparagraph. In order to satisfy this subparagraph, an organization must meet the requirements of subdivisions (i) and (ii) of this subparagraph in order to establish, under all the facts and circumstances, that it normally receives a substantial part of its support from governmental units or from direct or indirect contributions from the general public, and it must be in the nature of a "publicly supported" organization, taking into account the factors described in subdivisions (iii) through (vii) of this subparagraph. The requirements and factors referred to in the preceding sentence with respect to a "publicly supported" organization (other than one described in subparagraph (2) of this paragraph) are:

(i) Ten percent-of-support limitation. The percentage of support "normally" (as defined in subparagraph (4) of this paragraph) received by an organization from governmental units, from contributions made directly or indirectly by the general public, or from a combination of these sources, must be "substantial." For purposes of this subparagraph, an organization will not be treated as "normally" receiving a "substantial" amount of governmental or public support unless the total amount of governmental and public support "normally" received equals at least 10 percent of the total support "normally" received by such organization. See subparagraphs (6), (7), and (8) of this paragraph for the definition of "support."

(ii) Attraction of public support. An organization must be so organized and operated as to attract new and additional public or governmental support on a continuous basis. An organization will be considered to meet this requirement if it maintains a continuous and bona fide program for solicitation of funds from the general public, community, or membership group involved, or if it carries on activities designed to attract support from governmental units or other organizations described in section 170(b)(1)(A)(i) through (vi). In determining whether an organization maintains a continuous and bona fide program for solicitation of funds from the general public or community, consideration will be given to whether the scope of its fund-raising activities is reasonable in light of its charitable activities. Consideration will also be given to the fact that an organization may, in its early years of existence, limit the scope of its solicitation to persons deemed most likely to provide seed money in an amount sufficient to enable it to commence its charitable activities and expand its solicitation program.

In addition to the requirements set forth in subdivisions (i) and (ii) of this subparagraph which must be satisfied, all pertinent facts and circumstances, including the following factors, will be taken into consideration in determining whether an organization is "publicly supported" within the meaning of subparagraph (1) of this paragraph. However, an organization is not generally required to satisfy all of the factors in subdivisions (iii) through (vii) of this subparagraph. The factors relevant to each case and the weight accorded to any one of them may differ depending upon the nature and purpose of the organization and the length of time it has been in existence.

(iii) Percentage of financial support. The percentage of support received by an organization from public or governmental sources will be taken into consideration in determining whether an organization is "publicly supported." The higher the percentage of support above the 10 percent requirement of subdivision (i) of this subparagraph from public or governmental sources, the lesser will be the burden of establishing the publicly supported nature of the organization through other factors described in this subparagraph, while the lower the percentage, the greater will be the burden. If the percentage of the organization's support from public or governmental sources is low because it receives a high percentage of its total support from investment income on its endowment funds, such fact will be treated as evidence of compliance with this subdivision if such endowment funds were originally contributed by a governmental unit or by the general public. However, if such endowment funds were originally contributed by a few individuals or members of their families, such fact will increase the burden on the organization of establishing compliance with the other factors described in this subparagraph.

(iv) Sources of support. The fact that an organization meets the requirement of subdivision (i) of this subparagraph through support from governmental units or directly or indirectly from a representative number of persons, rather than receiving almost all of its support from the members of a single family, will be taken into consideration in determining whether an organization is "publicly supported." In determining what is a "representative number of persons," consideration will be given to the type of organization involved, the length of time it has been in existence, and whether it limits its activities to a particular community or region or to a special field which can be expected to appeal to a limited number of persons.

(v) Representative governing body. The fact that an organization has a governing body which represents the broad interests of the public, rather than the personal or private interests of a limited number of donors (or persons standing in a relationship to such donors which is described in section 4946(a)(1) (C) through (G)) will be taken into account in determining whether an organization is "publicly supported." An organization will be treated as meeting this requirement if it has a governing body (whether designated in the organization's governing instrument or bylaws as a Board of Directors, Board of Trustees, etc.) which is comprised of public officials acting in their capacities as such; of individuals selected by public officials acting in their capacities as such; of persons having special knowledge or expertise in the particular field or discipline in which the organization is operating; of community leaders, such as elected or appointed officials, clergymen, educators, civic leaders, or other such persons representing a broad cross-section of the views and interests of the community; or, in the case of a membership organization, of individuals elected pursuant to the organization's governing instrument or bylaws by a broadly based membership.

(vi) Availability of public facilities or services; public participation in programs or policies. (a) The fact that an organization is of the type which generally provides facilities or services directly for the benefit of the general public on a continuing basis (such as a museum or library which holds open its building and facilities to the public, a symphony orchestra which gives public performances, a conservation organization which provides educational services to the public through the distribution of educational materials, or an old age home which provides domiciliary or nursing services for members of the general public) will be considered evidence that such organization is "publicly supported."

(b) The fact that an organization is an educational or research institution which regularly publishes scholarly studies that are widely used by colleges and universities or by members of the general public will also be considered evidence that such organization is "publicly supported."

(c) Similarly, the following factors will also be considered evidence that an organization is "publicly supported:"

(1) The participation in, or sponsorship of, the programs of the organization by members of the public having special knowledge or expertise, public officials, or civic or community leaders;

(2) The maintenance of a definitive program by an organization to accomplish its charitable work in the community, such as slum clearance or developing employment opportunities; and

(3) The receipt of a significant part of its funds from a public charity or governmental agency to which it is in some way held accountable as a condition of the grant, contract, or contribution.

(vii) Additional factors pertinent to membership organizations. The following are additional factors to be considered in determining whether a membership organization is "publicly supported":

(a) Whether the solicitation for dues-paying members is designed to enroll a substantial number of persons in the community or area, or in a particular profession or field of special interest (taking into account the size of the area and the nature of the organization's activities);

(b) Whether membership dues for individual (rather than institutional) members have been fixed at rates designed to make membership available to a broad cross section of the interested public, rather than to restrict membership to a limited number of persons; and

(c) Whether the activities of the organization will be likely to appeal to persons having some broad common interest or purpose, such as educational activities in the case of alumni associations, musical activities in the case of symphony societies, or civic affairs in the case of parent-teacher associations.

See examples (2) through (5) contained in subparagraph (9) of this paragraph for illustrations of this subparagraph.

(4) Definition of "normally"; general rule. (i) Normally; one-third support test. For purposes of subparagraph (2) of this paragraph, an organization will be considered as "normally" meeting the 33⅓ percent-of-support test for its current taxable year and the taxable year immediately succeeding its current year, if, for the 4 taxable years immediately preceding the current taxable year, the organization meets the 33⅓ percent-of-support test described in subparagraph (2) of this paragraph on an aggregate basis.

(ii) Normally; facts and circumstances test. For purposes of subparagraph (3) of this paragraph, an organization will be considered as "normally" meeting the requirements of subparagraph (3) of this paragraph for its current taxable year and the taxable year immediately succeeding its current year, if, for the 4 taxable years immediately preceding the current taxable year, the organization meets the requirements of subparagraph (3) (i) and (ii) of this paragraph on an aggregate basis and satisfies a sufficient combination of the factors set forth in subparagraph (3) (iii) through (vii) of this paragraph. In the case of subparagraph (3) (iii) and (iv) of this paragraph, facts pertinent to years preceding 4 taxable years immediately preceding the current taxable year may also be taken into consideration. The combination of factors set forth in subparagraph (3) (iii) through (vii) of this paragraph which an organization "normally" must meet does not have to be the same for each 4-year period so long as there exists a sufficient combination of factors to show compliance with subparagraph (3) of this paragraph.

(iii) Special rule. The fact that an organization has "normally" met the requirements of subparagraph (2) of this paragraph for a current taxable year, but is unable "normally" to meet such requirements for a succeeding taxable year, will not in itself prevent such organization from meeting the requirements of subparagraph (3) of this paragraph for such succeeding taxable year.

(iv) Illustration. The application of subdivisions (i), (ii), and (iii) of this subparagraph may be illustrated by the following example:

Example. X, an organization described in section 170(c)(2), meets the 33⅓ percent-of-support test described in subparagraph (2) of this paragraph in taxable year 1975 on the basis of support received during taxable years 1971, 1972, 1973, and 1974. It therefore "normally" meets the requirements of subparagraph (2) of this paragraph for 1975 and 1976, the taxable year immediately succeeding 1975 (the current taxable year). For the taxable year 1976, X is unable to meet the 33⅓ percent-of-support test described in subparagraph (2) of this paragraph on the basis of support received during taxable years 1972, 1973, 1974, and 1975. If X can meet the requirements of subparagraph (3) of this paragraph on the basis of taxable years 1972, 1973, 1974, and 1975, X will meet the requirements of subparagraph (3) of this paragraph for 1977 (the taxable year immediately succeeding 1976, the current taxable year) under subdivision (ii) of this subparagraph. However, if on the basis of both the taxable years 1972 through 1975 and 1973 through 1976, X, fails to meet the requirements of both subparagraphs (2) and (3) of this paragraph, X will not be described in section 170(b)(1)(A)(vi) for 1977. However, X will not be disqualified as a section 170(b)(1)(A)(vi) organization for taxable year 1976, because it "normally" met the requirements of subparagraph (2) of this paragraph on the basis of the taxable years 1971 through 1974, unless the provisions of subdivision (v) of this subparagraph become applicable.

(v) Exception for material changes in sources of support. (a) In general. If for the current taxable year there are substantial and material changes in an organization's sources of support other than changes arising from unusual grants excluded under subparagraph (6)(ii) of this paragraph, then in applying subparagraph (2) or (3) of this paragraph, neither the 4-year computation period applicable to such year as an immediately succeeding taxable year or as a current taxable year shall apply, and in lieu of such computation periods there shall be applied a computation period consisting of the taxable year of substantial and material changes and the 4 taxable years immediately preceding such year. Thus, for example, if there are substantial and material changes in an organization's sources of support for taxable year 1976, then even though such organization meets the requirements of subparagraph (2) or (3) of this paragraph based on a computation period of taxable years 1971–74 or 1972–75, such an organization will not meet the requirements of section 170(b)(1)(A)(vi) unless it meets the requirements of subparagraph (2) or (3) of this paragraph for a computation period consisting of the taxable years 1972–76. See Example (3) in § 1.509(a)-3(c)(6) for an illustration of a similar rule. An example of a substantial and material change is the receipt of an unusually large contribution or bequest which does not qualify as an unusual grant under subparagraph (6)(ii) of this paragraph. See subparagraph (6)(iv)(b) of this paragraph as to the procedure for obtaining a ruling whether an unusually large grant may be excluded as an unusual grant.

(b) Status of grantors and contributors. If as a result of (a) of this subdivision, an organization is not able to meet the requirements of either the 33⅓ percent-of-support test described in subparagraph (2) of this paragraph, or the facts and circumstances test described in subparagraph (3) of this paragraph for its current taxable year, its status (with respect to a grantor or contributor under sections 170, 507, 545(b)(2), 556(b)(2), 642(c), 4942, 4945, 2055, 2106(a)(2), and 2522) will not be affected until notice of change of status under section 170(b)(1)(A)(vi) is made to the public (such as by publication in the Internal Revenue Bulletin). The preceding sentence shall not apply, however, if the grantor or contributor was responsible for, or was aware of, the substantial and material change referred to in (a) of this subdivision, or acquired knowledge that the Internal Revenue Service had given notice to such organization that it would be deleted from classification as a section 170(b)(1)(A)(vi) organization.

(c) Reliance by grantors and contributors. A grantor or contributor, other than one of the organization's founders, creators, or foundation managers (within the meaning of section 4946(b)) will not be considered to be responsible for, or aware of, the substantial and material change referred to in *(a)* of this subdivision, if such grantor or contributor has made such grant or contribution in reliance upon a written statement by the grantee organization that such grant or contribution will not result in the loss of such organization's classification as a publicly supported organization as described in section 170(b)(1)(A)(vi). Such statement must be signed by a responsible officer of the grantee organization and must set forth sufficient information, including a summary of the pertinent financial data for the 4 preceding years, to assure a reasonably prudent man that his grant or contribution will not result in the loss of the grantee organization's classification as a publicly supported organization as described in section 170(b)(1)(A)(vi). If a reasonable doubt exists as to the effect of such grant or contribution, or if the grantor or contributor is one of the organizations' founders, creators, or foundation managers, the procedure set forth in subparagraph (6)(iv)(b) of this paragraph may be followed by the grantee organization for the protection of the grantor or contributor.

(vi) Special rule for new organizations. If an organization has)) been in existence for at least 1 taxable year consisting of at least 8 months, but for fewer than 5 taxable years, the number of years for which the organization has been in existence immediately preceding each current taxable year being tested will be substituted for the 4-year period described in subdivision (i) or (ii) of this subparagraph to determine whether the organization "normally" meets the requirements of subparagraph (2) or (3) of this paragraph. However, if subdivision (v)(a) of this subparagraph applies, then the period consisting of the number of years for which the organization has been in existence (up to and including the current year) will be substituted for the 4-year period described in subdivision (i) or (ii) of this subparagraph. An organization which has been in existence for at least 1 taxable year, consisting of 8 or more months, may be issued a ruling or determination letter if it "normally" meets the requirements of subparagraph (2) or (3) of this paragraph for the number of years described in this subdivision. Such an organization may apply for a ruling or determination letter under the provisions of this subparagraph, rather than under the provisions of subparagraph (5) of this paragraph. The issuance of a ruling or determination letter will be discretionary with the Commissioner. See subparagraph (5)(v) of this paragraph as to the initial determination of the status of a newly created organization. This subdivision shall not apply to those organizations receiving an extended advance ruling under subparagraph (5)(iv) of this paragraph.

(vii) Special rule for organizations with existing ruling. This subdivision shall apply to an organization that prior to January 1, 1970, had received a ruling or determination letter which has not been expressly revoked holding the organization to be a publicly supported organization described in section 170(b)(1)(A)(vi) and with respect to which the facts and circumstances on which the ruling was based have not substantially changed. An organization to which this subdivision applies shall be treated as an organization described in section 170(b)(1)(A)(vi) for a period not ending prior to 90 days after December 29, 1972. In addition, with respect to a grantor or contributor under sections 170, 507, 545(b)(2), 556(b)(2), 642(c), 4942, 4945, 2055, 2106(a)(2), and 2522, the status of an organization to which this subdivision applies will not be affected until notice of change of status under section 170(b)(1)(A)(vi) is made to the public (such as by publication in the Internal Revenue Bulletin). The preceding sentence shall not apply if the grantor or contributor had previously acquired knowledge that the Internal Revenue Service had given notice to such organization that it would be deleted from classification as a section 170(b)(1)(A)(vi) organization.

(viii) Termination of status. For the transitional rules applicable to an organization that is unable to meet the requirements of this paragraph for its first taxable year beginning after December 31, 1969 (as extended by § 1.507-2(j)) and wishes to terminate its private foundation status, see § 1.507-2(c) (2) and (3).

(ix) Status of ruling. The provisions of this subparagraph do not require an organization to file a new application with the Internal Revenue Service every 2 years in order to maintain or reaffirm its status as a "publicly supported" organization described in section 170(b)(1)(A)(vi).

(5) Advance rulings to newly created organizations. (i) In general. A ruling or determination letter that an organization is described in section 170(b)(1)(A)(vi) will not be issued to a newly created organization prior to the close of its first taxable year consisting of at least 8 months. However, such organization may request a ruling or determination letter that it will be treated as a section 170(b)(1)(A)(vi) organization for its first 2 taxable years (or its first 3 taxable years, if its first taxable year consists of less than 8 months). For purposes of this section, such 2- or 3-year period, whichever is applicable, shall be referred to as the advance ruling period. Such an advance ruling or determination letter may be issued if the organization can reasonably be expected to meet the requirements of subparagraph (2) or (3) of this paragraph during the advance ruling period. The issuance of a ruling or determination letter will be discretionary with the Commissioner.

(ii) Basic consideration. In determining whether an organization can reasonably be expected (within the meaning of subdivision (i) of this subparagraph) to meet the requirements of subparagraph (2) or (3) of this paragraph for its advance ruling period or extended advance ruling period as provided in subdivision (iv) of this subparagraph, if applicable, the basic consideration is whether its organizational structure, proposed programs or activities, and intended method of operation are such as to attract the type of broadly based support from the general public, public charities, and governmental units which is necessary to meet such tests. The information to be considered for this purpose shall consist of all pertinent facts and circumstances relating to the requirements set forth in subparagraph (3) of this paragraph.

(iii) Status of newly created organizations. (a) Advance ruling. This subdivision shall apply to a newly created organization which has received an advance ruling or determination letter under subdivision (i) of this subparagraph, or an extended advance ruling or determination letter under subdivision (iv) of this subparagraph, that it will be treated as a section 170(b)(1)(A)(vi) organization for its advance or extended advance ruling period. So long as such an organization's ruling or determination letter has not been terminated by the Commissioner before the expiration of the advance or extended advance ruling period, then whether or not such organization has satisfied the requirements of subparagraph (2) or (3) of this paragraph during such advance or extended advance ruling period, such an organization will be treated as an organization described in section 170(b)(1)(A)(vi) in accordance with (b) and (c) of this subdivision, both for purposes of the organization and any grantor or contributor to such organization.

(b) Reliance period. Except as provided in (a) and (c) of this subdivision, an organization described in (a) of this subdivision will be treated as an organization described in section 170(b)(1)(A)(vi) for all purposes other than sections 507(d) and 4940 for the period beginning with its inception and ending 90 days after its advance or extended advance ruling period. Such period will be extended until a final determination is made of such an organization's status only if the organization submits, within the 90-day period, information needed to determine whether it meets the requirements of subparagraph (2) or (3) of this paragraph for its advance or extended advance ruling period (even if such organization fails to meet the requirements of such subparagraph (2) or (3)). However, since this subparagraph does not apply to the tax imposed by section 4940, if it is subsequently determined that the organization was a private foundation from its inception, then the tax imposed by section 4940 shall be due without regard to the advance or extended advance ruling or determination letter. Consequently, if any amount of tax under section 4940 in such a case is not paid on or before the last date prescribed for payment, the organization is liable for interest in accordance with section 6601. However, since any failure to pay such tax during the period referred to in this subparagraph is due to reasonable cause, the penalty under section 6651 with respect to the tax imposed by section 4940 shall not apply.

(c) Grantors or contributors. If a ruling or determination letter is terminated by the Commissioner prior to the expiration of the period described in (b) of this subdivision, for purposes of sections 170, 507, 545(b)(2), 556(b)(2), 642(c), 4942, 4945, 2055, 2106(a)(2), and 2522, the status of grants or contributions with respect to grantors or contributors to such organizations will not be affected until notice of change of status of such organization is made to the public (such as by publication of the Internal Revenue Bulletin). The preceding sentence shall not apply however, if the grantor or contributor was responsible for, or aware of, the act or failure to act that resulted in the organization's loss of classification under section 170(b)(1)(A)(vi) or acquired knowledge that the Internal Revenue Service had given notice to such organization that it would be deleted from such classification. Prior to the making of any grant or contribution which allegedly will not result in the grantee's loss of classification under section 170(b)(1)(A)(vi), a potential grantee organization may request a ruling whether such grant or contribution may be made without such loss of classification. A request for such ruling may be filed by the grantee organization with the district director. The issuance of such ruling will be at the sole discretion of the Commissioner. The organization must submit all information necessary to make a determination on the factors referred to in subparagraph (6)(iii) of this paragraph. If a favorable ruling is issued, such ruling may be relied upon by the grantor or contributor of the particular contribution in question for purposes of sections 170, 507, 545(b)(2), 556(b)(2), 642(c), 4942, 4945, 2055, 2106(a)(2), and 2522 and by the grantee organization for purposes of subparagraph (6)(ii) of this paragraph.

(iv) Extension of advance ruling period. (a) The advance ruling period described in subdivision (i) of this subparagraph shall be extended for a period of 3 taxable years after the close of the unextended advance ruling period if the organization so requests, but only if such organization's request accompanies its request for an advance ruling and is filed with a consent under section 6501(c)(4) to the effect that the period of limitation upon assessment under section 4940 for any taxable year within the extended advance ruling period shall not expire prior to 1 year after the date of the expiration of the time prescribed by law for the assessment of a deficiency for the last taxable year within the extended advance ruling period. An organization's extended advance ruling period is 5 taxable years if its first taxable year consists of at least 8 months, or is 6 years if its first taxable year is less than 8 months.

(b) Notwithstanding (a) of this subdivision, an organization which has received or applied for an advance ruling prior to January 29, 1973, may file its request for the 3-year extension within 90 days from such date, but only if it files the consents required in this section.

(c) See subdivision (v) of this subparagraph for the effect upon the initial determination of status of an organization which receives a ruling for an extended advance ruling period.

(v) Initial determination of status. (a) The initial determination of status of a newly created organization is the first determination (other than by issuance of an advance ruling or determination letter under subdivision (i) of this subparagraph or an extended advance ruling or determination letter under subdivision (iv) of this subparagraph) that the organization will be considered as "normally" meeting the requirements of subparagraphs (2) or (3) of this paragraph for a period beginning with its first taxable year.

(b) In the case of a new organization whose first taxable year is at least 8 months, except as provided for in subdivision (v)(d) of this subparagraph, the initial determination of status shall be based on a computation period of either the first taxable year or the first and second taxable years.

(c) In the case of a new organization whose first taxable year is less than 8 taxable months, except as provided for in subdivision (v) (d) of this subparagraph, the initial determination of status shall be based on a computation period of either the first and second taxable years or the first, second, and third taxable years.

(d) In the case of an organization which has received a ruling or determination letter for an extended advance ruling period under subdivision (iv) of this subparagraph, the initial determination of status shall be based on a computation period of all of the taxable years in the extended advance ruling period. However, where the ruling or determination letter for an extended advance ruling period under subdivision (iv) of this subparagraph is terminated by the Commissioner prior to the expiration of the relevant period described in subdivision (iii)(b) of this subparagraph, the initial determination of status shall be based on a computation period of the period provided in (b) or (c) of this subdivision or, if greater, the number of years to which the advance ruling applies.

(e) An initial determination that an organization will be considered as "normally" meeting the requirements of subparagraph (2) or (3) of this paragraph shall be effective for each taxable year in the computation period plus (except as provided by subparagraph (4)(v)(a) of this paragraph, relating to material changes in sources of support) the 2 taxable years immediately succeeding the computation period. Therefore, in the case of an organization referred to in (b) of this subdivision to which subparagraph (4)(v)(a) of this paragraph does not apply, with respect to its first, second, and third taxable years, such an organization shall be described in section 170(b)(1)(A)(vi) if it meets the requirements of subparagraph (2) or (3) of this paragraph for either its first taxable year or for its first and second taxable years on an aggregate basis. In addition, if it meets the requirements of subparagraph (2) or (3) of this paragraph for its first and second taxable years, it shall be described in section 170(b)(1)(A)(vi) for its fourth taxable year. Once an organization is considered as "normally" meeting the requirements of subparagraph (2) or (3) of this paragraph for a period specified under this subdivision, subparagraph (4) (i), (ii), (v), or (vi) of this paragraph shall apply.

(f) The provisions of this subdivision may be illustrated by the following examples:

Example (1). X, a calendar year organization described in section 501(c)(3), is created in February 1972. The support received from the public in 1972 by X will satisfy the one-third support test described in subparagraph (4)(i) of this paragraph over its first taxable year, 1972. X may therefore get an initial determination that it meets the requirements of subparagraph (2) of this paragraph for its first taxable year beginning in February 1972 and ending on December 31, 1972. This determination will be effective for taxable years 1972, 1973, and 1974.

Example (2). Assume the same facts as in example (1) except that X also receives a substantial contribution from one individual in 1972 which is not excluded from the denominator of the one-third support fraction described in subparagraph (4)(i) of this paragraph by reason of the unusual grant provision of subparagraph (6)(ii) of this paragraph. Because of this substantial contribution, X fails to satisfy the one-third support test over its first taxable year, 1972. X also fails to satisfy the "facts and circumstances" test described in subparagraph (4)(ii) of this paragraph for its first taxable year, 1972. However, the support received from the public over X's first and second taxable years in the aggregate will satisfy the one-third support test. X may therefore get an initial determination that it meets the requirements of subparagraph (2) of this paragraph for its first and second taxable years in the aggregate beginning in February 1972 and ending on December 31, 1973. This determination will be effective for taxable years 1972, 1973, 1974, and 1975.

Example (3). Y, a calendar year organization described in section 501(c)(3), is created in July 1972. Y requests and receives an extended advance ruling period of 5 full taxable years plus its initial short taxable year of 6 months under subparagraph (5)(iv) of this paragraph. The extended advance ruling period begins in July 1972 and ends on December 31, 1977. The support received from the public over Y's first through sixth taxable years in the aggregate will satisfy the one-third support test described in subparagraph (4)(i) of this paragraph. Therefore, Y in 1978 may get an initial determination that it meets the requirements of subparagraph (2) of this paragraph in the aggregate over all the taxable years in its extended advance ruling period beginning in July 1972 and ending on December 31, 1977. This determination will be effective for taxable years 1973 through 1979.

Example (4). Assume the same facts as in example (3) except that the ruling for the extended advance ruling period is terminated prospectively at the end of 1975, so that Y may not rely upon such ruling for 1976 or any succeeding year. The support received from the public over Y's first through fourth taxable years (1972 through 1975) will not satisfy either the one-third support test described in subparagraph (4)(i) of this paragraph, or the "facts and circumstances" test described in subparagraph (4)(ii) of this paragraph. Because the ruling was terminated the computation period for Y's initial determination of status is the period 1972 through 1975. Since Y has not met the requirements of either subparagraph (2) or (3) of this paragraph for such computation period, Y is not described in section 170(b)(1)(A)(vi) for purposes of its initial determination of status. If Y is not described in section 170(b)(1)(A)(i) through (v) or section 509(a) (2), (3), or (4), then Y is a private foundation. As of 1976, Y shall be treated as a private foundation for all purposes (except as provided in subdivision (iii) (c) of this subparagraph with respect to grantors and contributors), and as of July 1972 for purposes of the tax imposed by section 4940 and for purposes of section 507(d) (relating to aggregate tax benefit).

(vi) Failure to obtain advance ruling. (a) Unless a newly created organization has obtained an advance ruling or determination letter under subdivision (i) of this subparagraph, or an extended advance ruling or determination letter under subdivision (iv) of this subparagraph, that it will be treated as a section 170(b)(1)(A)(vi) organization for its advance or extended advance ruling period, it cannot rely upon the possibility it will meet the requirements of subparagraph (2) or (3) of this paragraph for a taxable year which begins before the close of either applicable computation period provided for in subdivision (v) (b) or (c) of this subparagraph. Therefore, such an organization, in order to avoid the risk of subsequently being determined to be a private foundation because of failure to qualify under section 170(b)(1)(A)(vi) and therefore under section 509(a)(1), may comply with the rules applicable to private foundations and may pay, for example, the tax imposed by section 4940. In that event, if the organization subsequently meets the requirements of subparagraph (2) or (3) of this paragraph for either applicable computation period, it shall be treated as a section 170(b)(1)(A)(vi) organization from its inception and, therefore, any tax imposed under chapter 42 shall be refunded and section 509(b) shall not apply.

(b) If a newly created organization fails to obtain an advance ruling or determination letter under subdivision (i) of this subparagraph, or an extended advance ruling or determination letter under subdivision (iv) of this subparagraph, and fails to meet the requirements of subparagraph (2) or (3) of this paragraph for the first applicable computation period provided for in subdivision (v) (b) or (c) of this subparagraph, see section 6651 for penalty for failure to file return and pay tax.

(6) Definition of support; meaning of general public. (i) In general. In determining whether the 33⅓ percent-of-support test described in subparagraph (2) of this paragraph or the 10 percent-of-support limitation described in subparagraph (3)(i) of this paragraph is "normally" met, contributions by an individual, trust; or corporation shall be taken into account as "support" from direct or indirect contributions from the general public only to the extent that the total amount of the contributions by any such individual, trust, or corporation during the period described in subparagraph (4) (i), (ii), (v), or (vi) or (5) (v) of this paragraph does not exceed 2 percent of the organization's total support for such period, except as provided in subdivision (ii) of this subparagraph. Therefore, any contribution by one individual will be included in full in the denominator of the fraction determining the 33⅓ percent-of-support or the 10 percent-of-support limitation, but will only be includible in the numerator of such fraction to the extent that such amount does not exceed 2 percent of the denominator. In applying the 2 percent limitation, all contributions made by a donor and by any person or persons standing in a relationship to the donor which is described in section 4946(a)(1)(C) through (G) and the regulations thereunder shall be treated as made by one person. The 2 percent limitation shall not apply to support received from governmental units referred to in section 170(c)(1) or to contributions from organizations described in section 170(b)(1)(A)(vi), except as provided in subdivision (v) of this subparagraph. For purposes of subparagraphs (2), (3)(i) and (7)(ii)(b) of this paragraph, the term "indirect contributions from the general public" includes contributions received by the organization from organizations (such as section 170(b)(1)(A)(vi) organizations) which normally receive a substantial part of their support from direct contributions from the general public, except as provided in subdivision (v) of this subparagraph. See the examples in subparagraph (9) of this paragraph for the application of this subdivision. For purposes of this paragraph (e), the term contributions includes qualified sponsorship payments (as defined in § 1.513-4) in the form of money or property (but not services).

(ii) Exclusion of unusual grants. For purposes of applying the 2 percent limitation described in subdivision (i) of this subparagraph to determine whether the 33⅓ percent-of-support test in subparagraph (2) of this paragraph or the 10 percent-of-support limitation in subparagraph (3)(i) of this paragraph is satisfied, one or more contributions may be excluded from both the numerator and the denominator of the applicable percent-of-support fraction if such contributions meet the requirements of subdivision (iii) of this subparagraph. The exclusion provided by this subdivision is generally intended to apply to substantial contributions or bequests from disinterested parties which contributions or bequests:

(a) Are attracted by reason of the publicly supported nature of the organization;

(b) Are unusual or unexpected with respect to the amount thereof; and

(c) Would, by reason of their size, adversely affect the status of the organization as normally being publicly supported for the applicable period described in subparagraph (4) or (5) of this paragraph.

In the case of a grant (as defined in § 1.509(a)-3(g)) which meets the requirements of this subdivision, if the terms of the granting instrument (whether executed before or after 1969) require that the funds be paid to the recipient organization over a period of years, the amount received by the organization each year pursuant to the terms of such grant may be excluded for such year. However, no item of gross investment income may be excluded under this subparagraph. The provisions of this subparagraph shall apply to exclude unusual grants made during any of the applicable periods described in subparagraph (4), (5), or (6) of this paragraph. See subdivision (iv) of this subparagraph as to reliance by a grantee organization upon an unusual grant ruling under this subparagraph.

(iii) Determining factors. In determining whether a particular contribution may be excluded under subdivision (ii) of this subparagraph all pertinent facts and circumstances will be taken into consideration. No single factor will necessarily be determinative. For some of the factors similar to the factors to be considered, see § 1.509(a)-3(c)(4).

(iv) Grantors and contributors. (a) As to the status of grants and contributions which result in substantial and material changes in the organization (as described in subparagraph (4)(v) (a) of this paragraph) and which fail to meet the requirements for exclusion under subdivision (ii) of this subparagraph, see the rules prescribed in subparagraph (4)(v) (b) and (c) of this paragraph.

(b) Prior to the making of any grant or contribution which will allegedly meet the requirements for exclusion under subdivision (ii) of this subparagraph, a potential grantee organization may request a ruling whether such grant or contribution may be so excluded. Requests for such ruling may be filed by the grantee organization with the district director. The issuance of such ruling will be at the sole discretion of the Commissioner. The organization must submit all information necessary to make a determination on the factors referred to in subdivision (iii) of this subparagraph. If a favorable ruling is issued, such ruling may be relied upon by the grantor or contributor of the particular contribution in question for purposes of sections 170, 507, 545(b)(2), 556(b)(2), 642(c), 4942, 4945, 2055, 2106(a)(2), and 2522 and by the grantee organization for purposes of subdivision (ii) of this subparagraph.

(v) Grants from public charities. Pursuant to subdivision (i) of this subparagraph, contributions received from a governmental unit or from a section 170(b)(1)(A)(vi) organization are not subject to the 2 percent limitation described in that subdivision unless such contributions represent amounts which have been expressly or impliedly earmarked by a donor to such governmental unit or section 170(b)(1)(A)(vi) organization as being for, or for the benefit of, the particular organization claiming section 170(b)(1)(A)(vi) status. See § 1.509(a)-3(j)(3) for examples illustrating the rules of this subdivision.

(7) Definition of support; special rules and meaning of terms. (i) Definition of support. For purposes of this paragraph, the term "support" shall be as defined in section 509(d) (without regard to section 509(d)(2)). The term "support" does not include:

(a) Any amounts received from the exercise or performance by an organization of its charitable, educational, or other purpose or function constituting the basis for its exemption under section 501(a). In general, such amounts include amounts received from any activity the conduct of which is substantially related to the furtherance of such purpose or function (other than through the production of income), or

(b) Contributions of services for which a deduction is not allowable.

For purposes of the 33⅓ percent-of-support test in subparagraph (2) of this paragraph and the 10 percent-of-support limitation in subparagraph (3)(i) of this paragraph, all amounts received which are described in (a) or (b) of this division are to be excluded from both the numerator and the denominator of the fractions determining compliance with such tests, except as provided in subdivision (ii) of this subparagraph.

(ii) Organizations dependent primarily on gross receipts from related activities. Notwithstanding the provisions of subdivision (i) of this subparagraph, an organization will not be treated as satisfying the 33⅓ percent-of-support test in subparagraph (2) of this paragraph or the 10 percent-of-support limitation in subparagraph (3)(i) of this paragraph if it receives:

(a) Almost all of its support (as defined in section 509(d)) from gross receipts from related activities; and

(b) An insignificant amount of its support from governmental units (without regard to amounts referred to in subdivision (i) (a) of this subparagraph) and contributions made directly or indirectly by the general public.

For example X, an organization described in section 501(c)(3), is controlled by A, its president. X received $500,000 during the 4 taxable years immediately preceding its current taxable year under a contract with the Department of Transportation, pursuant to which X has engaged in research to improve a particular vehicle used primarily by the Federal Government. During this same period, the only other support received by X consisted of $5,000 in small contributions primarily from X's employees and business associates. The $500,000 amount constitutes support under section 509(d)(2) and 509(d)(2)(a) of this subdivision. Under these circumstances, X meets the conditions of (a) and (b) of this subdivision and will not be treated as meeting the requirements of either subparagraph (2) or subparagraph (3) of this paragraph. As to the rules applicable to organizations which fail to qualify under section 170(b)(1)(A)(vi) because of the provisions of this subdivision, see section 509(a)(2) and the regulations thereunder. For the distinction between gross receipts (as referred to in section 509(d)(2)) and gross investment income (as referred to in section 509(d)(4)), see § 1.509(a)-3(m).

(iii) Membership fees. For purposes of this subparagraph, the term "support" shall include "membership fees" within the meaning of § 1.509(a)-3(h) (that is, if the basic purpose for making a payment is to provide support for the organization rather than to purchase admissions, merchandise, services, or the use of facilities).

(8) Support from a governmental unit. (i) For purposes of subparagraphs (2) and (3)(i) of this paragraph, the term "support from a governmental unit" includes any amounts received from a governmental unit, including donations or contributions and amounts received in connection with a contract entered into with a governmental unit for the performance of services or in connection with a Government research grant. However, such amounts will not constitute "support from a governmental unit" for such purposes if they constitute amounts received from the exercise or performance of the organization's exempt functions as provided in subparagraph (7)(i)(a) of this paragraph.

(ii) For purposes of subdivision (i) of this subparagraph, any amount paid by a governmental unit to an organization is not to be treated as received from the exercise or performance of its charitable, educational, or other purpose or function constituting the basis for its exemption under section 501(a) (within the meaning of subparagraph (7)(i)(a) of this paragraph) if the purpose of the payment is primarily to enable the organization to provide a service to, or maintain a facility for, the direct benefit of the public (regardless of whether part of the expense of providing such service or facility is paid for by the public), rather than to serve the direct and immediate needs of the payor. For example:

(a) Amounts paid for the maintenance of library facilities which are open to the public,

(b) Amounts paid under Government programs to nursing homes or homes for the aged in order to provide health care or domiciliary services to residents of such facilities, and

(c) Amounts paid to child placement or child guidance organizations under Government programs for services rendered to children in the community, are considered payments the purpose of which is primarily to enable the recipient organization to provide a service or maintain a facility for the direct benefit of the public, rather than to serve the direct and immediate needs of the payor. Furthermore, any amount received from a governmental unit under circumstances such that the amount would be treated as a "grant" within the meaning of § 1.509(a)-3(g) will generally constitute "support from a governmental unit" described in this subdivision, rather than an amount described in subparagraph (7)(i)(a) of this paragraph.

(9) Examples. The application of subparagraphs (1) through (8) of this paragraph may be illustrated by the following examples:

Example (1). (a) M is an organization referred to in section 170(c)(2). For the years 1970 through 1973 (the applicable period with respect to the taxable year 1974 under subparagraph (4) of this paragraph), M received support (as defined in subparagraphs (6) through (8) of this paragraph) of $600,000 from the following sources:

Investment Income	$300,000
City Y (a governmental unit referred to in section 170(c)(1))	40,000
United Fund (an organization referred to in section 170(b)(1)(A)(vi)	40,000
Contributions	220,000
Total Support	600,000

(b) With respect to the taxable year 1974, M "normally" received in excess of 33⅓ percent of its support from a governmental unit referred to in section 170(c)(1) and from direct and indirect contributions from the general public (as defined in subparagraph (6) of this paragraph) computed as follows:

33⅓ percent of total support	$200,000
Support from a governmental unit referred to in section 170(c)(1)	40,000
Indirect contributions from the general public (United Fund)	40,000
Contributions by various donors (no one having made contributions which total in excess of $12,000—2 percent of total support)	50,000
Six contributions (each in excess of $12,000—2 percent total support) 6 × $12,000	72,000
	202,000

(c) Since the amount of X's support from governmental units referred to in section 170(c)(1) and from direct and indirect contributions from the general public with respect to the taxable year 1974 "normally" exceeds 33⅓ percent of M's total support for the applicable period (1970–73), X meets the 33⅓ percent-of-support test under subparagraph (2) of this paragraph and is therefore treated as satisfying the requirements for classification as a "publicly supported" organization under subparagraph (2) of this paragraph for the taxable years 1974 and 1975 (there being no substantial and material changes in the organization's character, purposes, methods of operation, or sources of support in these years).

Example (2). N is an organization referred to in section 170(c)(2). It was created to maintain public gardens containing botanical specimens and displaying statuary and other art objects. The facilities, works of art, and a large endowment were all contributed by a single contributor. The members of the governing body of the organization are unrelated to its creator. The gardens are open to the public without charge and attract a substantial number of visitors each year. For the 4 taxable years immediately preceding the current taxable year, 95 percent of the organization's total support was received from investment income from its original endowment. N also maintains a membership society which is supported by members of the general public who wish to contribute to the upkeep of the gardens by paying a small annual membership fee. Over the 4-year period in question, these fees from the general public constituted the remaining 5 percent of the organization's total support for such period. Under these circumstances, N does not meet the 33⅓ percent-of-support test under subparagraph (2) of this paragraph for its current taxable year. Furthermore, since only 5 percent of its total support is, with respect to the current taxable year, normally received from the general public, N does not satisfy the 10 percent-of-support limitation described in subparagraph (3)(i) of this paragraph and cannot therefore be classified as "publicly supported" under subparagraph (3) of this paragraph. For its current taxable year, N therefore, is not an organization described in section 170(b)(1)(A)(vi). Since N has failed to satisfy the 10 percent-of-support limitation under subparagraph (3)(i) of this paragraph, none of the other requirements or factors set forth in subparagraph (3)(iii) through (vii) of this paragraph can be considered in determining whether N qualifies as a "publicly supported" organization.

Example (3). (a) O, an art museum, is an organization referred to in section 170(c)(2). In 1930, O was founded in Y City by the members of a single family to collect, preserve, interpret, and display to the public important works of art. O is governed by a Board of Trustees which originally consisted almost entirely of members of the founding family. However, since 1945, members of the founding family or persons standing in a relationship to the members of such family described in section 4946(a)(1) (C) through (G) have annually constituted less than one-fifth of the Board of Trustees. The remaining board members are citizens of Y City from a variety of professions and occupations who represent the interests and views of the people of Y City in the activities carried on by the organization rather than the personal or private interests of the founding family. O solicits contributions from the general public and for each of its 4 most recent taxable years has received total contributions (in small sums of less than $100, none of which exceeds 2 percent of O's total support for such period) in excess of $10,000. These contributions from the general public (as defined in subparagraph (6) of this paragraph) represent 25 percent of the organization's total support for such 4-year period. For this same period, investment income from several large endowment funds has constituted 75 percent of its total support. O expends substantially all of its annual income for its exempt purposes and thus depends upon the funds it annually solicits from the public as well as its investment income in order to carry out its activities on a normal and continuing basis and to acquire new works of art. O has, for the entire period of its existence, been open to the public and more than 300,000 people (from Y City and elsewhere) have visited the museum in each of its four most recent taxable years.

(b) Under these circumstances, O does not meet the 33⅓ percent-of-support test under subparagraph (2) of this paragraph for its current year since it has received only 25 percent of its total support for the applicable 4-year period from the general public. However, under the facts set forth above, O has met the 10 percent-of-support limitation under subparagraph (3)(1), as well as the requirements of subparagraph (3)(ii), of this paragraph. Under all of the facts set forth in this example, O is considered as meeting the requirements of subparagraph (3) of this paragraph on the basis of satisfying subparagraph (3) (i) and (ii) of this paragraph and the factors set forth in subparagraph (3) (iii), (iv), (v), and (vi) of this paragraph, and is therefore classified as a "publicly supported organization" under subparagraph (1) of this paragraph for its current taxable year and the immediately succeeding taxable year (there being no substantial and material changes in the organization's character, purposes, methods of operation, or sources of support in these years).

Example (4). (a) In 1960, the P Philharmonic Orchestra was organized in Z City through the combined efforts of a local music society and a local women's club to present to the public a wide variety of musical programs intended to foster music appreciation in the community. P is an organization referred to in section 170(c)(2). The orchestra is composed of professional musicians who are paid by the association. Twelve performances open to the public are scheduled each year. A small admission charge is made for each of these performances. In addition, several performances are staged annually without charge. During its 4 most recent taxable years, P has received separate contributions of $200,000 each from A and B (not members of a single family) and support of $120,000 from the Z Community Chest, a public federated fundraising organization operating in Z City. P depends on these funds in order to carry out its activities and will continue to depend on contributions of this type to be made in the future. P has also begun a fundraising campaign in an attempt to expand its activities for the coming years. P is governed by a Board of Directors comprised of five individuals. A faculty member of a local college, the president of a local music society, the head of a local banking institution, a prominent doctor, and a member of the governing body of the local chamber of commerce currently serve on the Board and represent the interests and views of the community in the activities carried on by P.

(b) With respect to P's current taxable year, P's sources of support are computed on the basis of the 4 immediately preceding years, as follows:

Contributions	$520,000
Receipts from performances	100,000
Total support	620,000
Less:	
Receipts from performances (excluded under subparagraph (7)(i)*(a)* of this paragraph)	100,000
Total support for purposes of subparagraphs (2) and (3)(i) of this paragraph	520,000

(c) For purposes of subparagraphs (2) and (3)(i) of this paragraph, P's support is computed as follows:

Z Community Chest (indirect support from the general public)	120,000
Two contributions (each in excess of $10,400—2 percent of total support) 2 × $10,400	20,800
Total	140,800

(d) P's support from the general public, directly and indirectly, does not meet the 33⅓ percent-of-support test under subparagraph (2) of this paragraph ($140,800/$520,000 = 27 percent of total support). However, since P receives 27 percent of its total support from the general public, it meets the 10 percent-of-support limitation under subparagraph (3)(i) of this paragraph. P also meets the requirements of subparagraph (3)(ii) of this paragraph. As a result of satisfying these requirements and the factors set forth in subparagraph (3)(iii), (iv), (v), and (vi) of this paragraph, P is considered as meeting the requirements of subparagraph (3) of this paragraph and is therefore considered to be a "publicly supported" organization under subparagraph (1) of this paragraph.

(e) If, instead of the above facts, P were a newly created organization, P could obtain a ruling pursuant to subparagraph (5) of this paragraph by reason of its purposes, organizational structure and proposed method of operation. Even if P had initially been founded by the contributions of a few individuals, such fact would not, in and of itself, disqualify P from receiving a ruling under subparagraph (5) of this paragraph.

Example (5). (a) Q is an organization referred to in section 170(c)(2). It is a philanthropic organization founded in 1965 by A for the purpose of making annual contributions to worthy charities. A created Q as a charitable trust by the transfer of $500,000 worth of appreciated securities to Q. Pursuant to the trust agreement, A and two other members of his family are the sole trustees and are vested with the right to appoint successor trustees. In each of its four most recent taxable years, Q received $15,000 in investment income from its original endowment. Each year Q makes a solicitation for funds by operating a charity ball at A's residence. Guests are invited and requested to make contributions of $100 per couple. During the 4-year period involved, $15,000 was received from the proceeds of these events. A and his family have also made contributions to Q of $25,000 over the course of the organization's 4 most recent taxable years. Q makes disbursements each year of substantially all of its net income to the public charities chosen by the trustees.

(b) With respect to Q's current taxable year, Q's sources of support are computed on the basis of the 4 immediately preceding years as follows:

Investment income	$ 60,000
Contributions	40,000
Total support	$100,000

(c) For purposes of subparagraphs (2) and (3)(i) of this paragraph, Q's support is computed as follows:

Contributions from the general public	$15,000
One contribution (in excess of $2,000—2 percent of total support) 1 × $2,000	2,000
Total	$17,000

(d) Q's support from the general public does not meet the 33⅓ percent-of-support test under subparagraph (2) of this paragraph ($17,000/$100,000 = 17 percent of total support). Thus, Q's classification as a "publicly supported" organization depends on whether it meets the requirements of subparagraph (3) of this paragraph. Even though it satisfies the 10 percent-of-support limitation under subparagraph (3)(i) of this paragraph, its method of solicitation makes it questionable whether Q satisfies the requirements of subparagraph (3)(ii) of this paragraph. Because of its method of operating, Q also has a greater burden of establishing its publicly supported nature under subparagraph (3)(iii) of this paragraph. Based upon the foregoing and upon Q's failure to receive favorable consideration under the factors set forth in subparagraph (3)(iv), (v), and (vi) of this paragraph, Q does not satisfy the requirements of subparagraph (3) of this paragraph as a "publicly supported" organization.

(e) If, instead of the above facts, Q were a newly created organization, Q would not be able to receive a ruling pursuant to subparagraph (5) of this paragraph. Its purposes, organizational structure, and method of operation would be insufficient to establish that Q could reasonably be expected to meet the requirements of subparagraph (2) or (3) of this paragraph for its first 2 or its first 5 taxable years.

(10) Community trust; introduction. Community trusts have often been established to attract large contributions of a capital or endowment nature for the benefit of a particular community or area, and often such contributions have come initially from a small number of donors. While the community trust generally has a governing body comprised or representatives of the particular community or area, its contributions are often received and maintained in the form of separate trusts or funds, which are subject to varying degrees of control by the governing body. To qualify as a "publicly supported" organization, a community trust must meet the 33⅓ percent-of-support test of paragraph (e)(2) of this section, or, if it cannot meet that test, be organized and operated so as to attract new and additional public or governmental support on a continuous basis sufficient to meet the

facts and circumstances test of paragraph (e)(3) of this section. Such facts and circumstances test includes a requirement of attraction of public support in paragraph (e)(3)(ii) of this section which, as applied to community trusts will generally be satisfied, if they seek gifts and bequests from a wide range of potential donors in the community or area served, through banks or trust companies, through attorneys or other professional persons, or in other appropriate ways which call attention to the community trust as a potential recipient of gifts and bequests made for the benefit of the community or area served. A community trust is not required to engage in periodic, community-wide, fund-raising campaigns directed toward attracting a large number of small contributions in a manner similar to campaigns conducted by a community chest or united fund. Paragraph (e)(12) and (13) of this section provide a transitional ruling period for certain community trusts in existence before November 11, 1976 that had irregular public support, so that they can meet the requirements of paragraph (e)(2) or (3) of this section based on the 4-year computation period described in paragraph (e)(4) of this section. Paragraph (e)(11) of this section provides rules for determining the extent to which separate trusts or funds may be treated as component parts of a community trust, fund or foundation (herein collectively referred to as a "community trust", and sometimes referred to as an "organization") for purposes of meeting the requirements of this paragraph for classification as a "publicly supported" organization. Paragraph (e)(14) of this section contains rules for trusts or funds which are prevented from qualifying as component parts of a community trust by paragraph (e)(11) of this section.

(11) Community trusts; requirements for treatment as a single entity. (i) General rule. For purposes of sections 170, 501, 507, 508, 509, and chapter 42, any organization that meets the requirements contained in paragraph (e)(11)(iii) through (vi) of this section will be treated as a single entity, rather than as an aggregation of separate funds, and except as otherwise provided, all funds associated with such organization (whether a trust, not-for-profit corporation, unincorporated association, or a combination thereof) which meet the requirements of paragraph (e)(11)(ii) of this section will be treated as component parts of such organization.

(ii) Component part of a community trust. In order to be treated as a component part of a community trust referred to in paragraph (e)(11) of this section (rather than as a separate trust or not-for-profit corporation or association) a trust or fund:

(A) Must be created by a gift, bequest, legacy, devise, or other transfer to a community trust which is treated as a single entity under paragraph (e)(11) of this section; and

(B) May not be directly or indirectly subjected by the transferor to any material restriction or condition (within the meaning of § 1.507-2(a)(8)) with respect to the transferred assets.

For purposes of paragraph (e)(11)(ii)(B) of this section, if the transferor is not a private foundation, the provisions of § 1.507-2(a)(8) shall be applied to the trust or fund as if the transferor were a private foundation established and funded by the person establishing the trust or fund and such foundation transferred all its assets to the trust or fund. Any transfer made to a fund or trust which is treated as a component part of a community trust under paragraph (e)(11)(ii) of this section will be treated as a transfer made "to" a "publicly supported" community trust for purposes of section 170(b)(1)(A) and 507(b)(1)(A) if such community trust meets the requirements of section 170(b)(1)(A)(vi) as a "publicly supported" organization at the time of the transfer, except as provided in § 1.170A-9(e)(4)(v)(b) or § 1.508-1(b)(4) and (6) relating, generally, to reliance by grantors and contributors. See, also, paragraph (e)(14)(ii) and (iii) of this section for special provisions relating to split-interest trusts and certain private foundations described in section 170(b)(1)(E)(iii).

(iii) Name. The organization must be commonly known as a community trust, fund, foundation or other similar name conveying the concept of a capital or endowment fund to support charitable activities (within the meaning of section 170(c)(1) or (2)(B)) in the community or area it serves.

(iv) Common instrument. All funds of the organization must be subject to a common governing instrument or a master trust or agency agreement (herein referred to as the "governing instrument"), which may be embodied in a single document or several documents containing common language. Language in an instrument of transfer to the community trust making a fund subject to the community trust's governing instrument or master trust or agency agreement will satisfy the requirements of paragraph (e)(11)(iv) of this section. In addition, if a community trust adopts a new governing instrument (or creates a corporation) to put into effect new provisions (applying to future transfers to the community trust), the adoption of such new governing instrument (or creation of a corporation with a governing instrument) which contains common language with the existing governing instrument shall not preclude the community trust from meeting the requirements of such paragraph (e)(11)(iv).

(v) Common governing body. (A) In general. The organization must have a common governing body or distribution committee (herein referred to as the "governing body") which either directs or, in the case of a fund designated for specified beneficiaries, monitors the distribution of all of the funds exclusively for charitable purposes (within the meaning of section 170(c)(1) or (2)(B)).

For purposes of this (v) a fund is designated for specified beneficiaries only if no person is left with the discretion to direct the distribution of the fund.

(B) Powers of modification and removal. Except as provided in paragraph (e)(11)(v)(C) of this section, the governing body must have the power in the governing instrument, the instrument of transfer, the resolutions or by-laws of the governing body, a written agreement, or otherwise—

(1) To modify any restriction or condition on the distribution of funds for any specified charitable purposes or to specified organizations if in the sole judgment of the governing body (without the necessity of the approval of any participating trustee, custodian, or agent), such restriction or condition becomes, in effect, unnecessary, incapable of fulfillment, or inconsistent with the charitable needs of the community or area served;

(2) To replace any participating trustee, custodian, or agent for breach of fiduciary duty under State law; and

(3) To replace any participating trustee, custodian, or agent for failure to produce a reasonable (as determined by the governing body) return of net income (within the meaning of paragraph (e)(11)(v)(F) of this section) over a reasonable period of time (as determined by the governing body).

The fact that the exercise of any such power in paragraph (e)(11)(v)(B)(1), (2) or (3) of this section is reviewable by an appropriate State authority will not preclude the community trust from meeting the requirements of paragraph (e)(11)(v)(B) of this section.

(C) Transitional rule. (1) Notwithstanding paragraph (e)(11)(v)(B) of this section, if a community trust meets the requirements of paragraph (e)(11)(v)(C)(2) of this section, then in the case of any instrument of transfer which is executed before July 19, 1977 and is not revoked or amended thereafter (with respect to any dispositive provision affecting the transfer to the community trust), and in the case of any instrument of transfer which is irrevocable on January 19, 1982, the governing body must have the power to cause proceedings to be instituted (by request to the appropriate State authority)—

(i) To modify any restriction or condition on the distribution of funds for any specified charitable purposes or to specified organizations if in the judgment of the governing body such restriction or condition becomes, in effect, unnecessary, incapable of fulfillment, or inconsistent with the charitable needs of the community or area served; and

(ii) To remove any participating trustee, custodian, or agent for breach of fiduciary duty under State law.

The necessity for the governing body to obtain the approval of a participating trustee to exercise such a power shall be treated as not preventing the governing body from having such power, unless (and until) such approval has been (or is) requested by the governing body and has been (or is) denied.

(2) Paragraph (e)(11)(v)(C)(1) of this section shall not apply unless the community trust meets the requirements of paragraph (e)(11)(v)(B) of this section, with respect to funds other than those under instruments of transfer described in the first sentence of such paragraph (e)(11)(v)(C)(1), by January 19, 1978, or such later date as the Commissioner may provide for such community trust, and unless the community trust does not, once it so complies, thereafter solicit for funds that will not qualify under the requirements of such paragraph (e)(11)(v)(B).

(D) Inconsistent State law. (1) For purposes of paragraph (e)(11)(v)(B)(1), (2), or (3) or (C)(1)(i) or (ii) or (E) of this section, if a power described in such a provision is inconsistent with State law even if such power were expressly granted to the governing body by the governing instrument and were accepted without limitation under an instrument of transfer, then the community trust will be treated as meeting the requirements of such a provision if it meets such requirements to the fullest extent possible consistent with State law (if such power is or had been so expressly granted).

(2) For example, if under the conditions of paragraph (e)(11)(v)(D)(1) of this section, the power to modify is inconsistent with State law, but the power to institute proceedings to modify, if so expressly granted, would be consistent with State law, the community trust will be treated as meeting such requirements to the fullest extent possible if the governing body has the power (in the governing instrument or otherwise) to institute proceedings to modify a condition or restriction. On the other hand, if in such a case the community trust has only the power to cause proceedings to be instituted to modify a condition or restriction, it will not be treated as meeting such requirements to the fullest extent possible.

(3) In addition, if, for example, under the conditions of paragraph (e)(11)(v)(D)(1) of this section, the power to modify and the power to institute proceedings to modify a condition or restriction is inconsistent with State law, but the power to cause such proceedings to be instituted would be consistent with State law, if it were expressly granted in the governing instrument and if the approval of the State Attorney General were obtained, then the community trust will be treated as meeting such requirements to the fullest extent possible if it has the power (in the governing instrument or otherwise) to cause such proceedings to be instituted, even if such proceedings can be instituted only with the approval of the State Attorney General.

(E) Exercise of powers. The governing body shall (by resolution or otherwise) commit itself to exercise the powers described in paragraph (e)(11)(v)(B), (C) and (D) of this section in the best interests of the community trust. The governing body will be considered not to be so committed where it has grounds to exercise such a power and fails to exercise it by taking appropriate action. Such appropriate action may include, for example, consulting with the appropriate State authority prior to taking action to replace a participating trustee.

(F) Reasonable return. In addition to the requirements of paragraph (e)(11)(v)(B), (C), (D) or (E) of this section, the governing body shall (by resolution or otherwise) commit itself to obtain information and take other appropriate steps with the view to seeing that each participating trustee, custodian, or agent, with respect to each restricted (within the meaning of paragraph (e)(13)(x) of this section) trust or fund that is, and with respect to the aggregate of the unrestricted trusts or funds that are, a component part of the community trust, administers such trust or fund in accordance with the terms of its governing instrument and accepted standards of fiduciary conduct to produce a reasonable return of net income (or appreciation where not inconsistent with the community trust's need for current income), with due regard to safety of principal, in furtherance of the exempt purposes of the community trust (except for assets held for the active conduct of the community trust's exempt activities). In the case of a low return of net income (and, where appropriate, appreciation), the Internal Revenue Service will examine carefully whether the governing body has, in fact, committed itself to take the appropriate steps.

(vi) Common reports. The organization must prepare periodic financial reports treating all of the funds which are held by the community trust, either directly or in component parts, as funds of the organization.

(vii) Transitional rule. If the governing instrument of a community trust (or an instrument of transfer) is inconsistent with the requirements of paragraph (e)(11)(iv) or (v) of this section but with respect to gifts or bequests acquired before January 1, 1982, the community trust changes its governing instrument (or instrument of transfer) by the later of November 11, 1977, or one year after the gift or bequest is acquired, in order to conform such instruments to such provisions, then such an instrument shall be treated as consistent with paragraph (e)(11)(iv) or (v) of this section for taxable years beginning after December 31, 1969. In addition, if prior to the later of such dates, the organization has instituted court proceedings in order to conform such an instrument, then it may apply (prior to the later of such dates) for an extension of the period to conform such instrument to such provisions. Such application shall be made the the Commissioner of Internal Revenue, Attention: E:EO, Washington, D.C. 20224. The Commissioner, at the Commissioner's discretion, may grant such an extension, if in the Commissioner's opinion such a change will conform the instrument to such provisions and will be made within a reasonable time.

(12) Community trusts qualifying for 5-year transitional ruling period. (i) In general. Paragraph (e)(12) and (13) of this section contain transitional rules for certain community trusts in existence before November 11, 1976 which are una-

ble to meet the requirements of paragraph (e)(2) or (3) of this section based upon a 4-year computation period under paragraph (e)(4) of this section. A community trust that satisfies the requirements of paragraph (e)(12)(ii) of this section will be eligible for a transitional ruling or determination letter that it will be treated as a section 170(b)(1)(A)(vi) organization for a 5-year transitional ruling period (referred to in this section as "transitional ruling or determination letter"). These transitional rules apply to—

(A) A community trust which has been in existence less than 9 taxable years before November 11, 1976; and

(B) Other community trusts that for each taxable year beginning after December 31, 1969, and before January 1, 1978, qualify as "publicly supported" under paragraph (e)(2) or (3) of this section based upon a computation period of either—

(1) 10 taxable year, or

(2) The number of taxable years (but not more than 20 nor less than 10) preceding such taxable year that the organization was in existence.

For special rules in applying the requirements of paragraph (e)(2) or (3) of this section based upon such computation periods, see paragraph (e)(12)(v) of this section. For purposes of paragraph (e)(12) of this section the initial taxable year of the 5-year transitional ruling period (hereinafter referred to as the "transitional ruling period") shall be the organization's taxable year beginning in 1977, and (unless terminated earlier) the last year of the transitional ruling period is the organization's taxable year which begins in 1981.

(ii) Transitional 5-year ruling. (A) If a community trust meets the requirements of paragraph (e)(11), (12) and (13) of this section and can reasonably be expected to meet the requirements of paragraph (e)(2) or (3) of this section—

(1) For each of its taxable years (if such a year begins after its tenth taxable year) beginning in 1978, 1979, 1980 and 1981 based upon a 10-year computation period, and

(2) For its taxable year beginning in 1982 based upon a 4-year computation period under paragraph (e)(4) of this section;

it may, at the discretion of the Commissioner, receive a transitional ruling or determination letter for a 5-year transitional ruling period.

(B) (1) However, if for the taxable year beginning in 1977, a community trust can meet the requirements of paragraph (e)(12)(i)(B) of this section only by using the computation period of its existence described in paragraph (e)(12)(i)(B)(2) of this section, then the community trust may meet the requirements of paragraph (e)(12)(ii)(A)(1) of this section if it is reasonably expected to meet the requirements of paragraph (e)(2) or (3) of this section for each of its taxable years beginning in 1978, 1979, 1980 and 1981 based upon a computation period consisting of the number of taxable years (but not more than 20 nor less than 10) preceding such taxable year that the organization was in existence.

(2) In the case of a community trust that will not have been in existence more than ten taxable years as of its taxable year beginning in 1981, a transitional ruling or determination letter for the transitional ruling period will not be granted unless the community trust can reasonably be expected to meet the requirements of paragraph (e)(2) or (3) of this section for its taxable year beginning in 1982 based upon a 4-year computation period under paragraph (e)(4) of this section and also a computation period consisting of the taxable years the organization has been in existence (other than the organization's taxable year beginning in 1982).

(C) A community trust that is eligible for a transitional ruling or determination letter must apply with the district director for such ruling or determination letter within one year after November 11, 1976. A transitional ruling or determination letter will be granted only if the requesting organization files with its request for such ruling or determination letter a consent letter under section 6501(c)(4) to the effect that the period of limitation upon assessment under section 4940 for all taxable years beginning before January 1, 1982 during the transitional ruling period shall not expire prior to 1 year after the date of the expiration of the time prescribed by law for the assessment of a deficiency for its taxable year beginning in 1981. The provisions of paragraph (e)(5)(iii) of this section (relating to reliance upon ruling) shall apply with respect to a community trust which receives a transitional ruling or determination letter and with respect to its grantors and contributors, except that the transitional ruling period described in paragraph (e)(12)(ii) of this section shall be substituted for the advance ruling period described in paragraph (e)(5)(i) or (iv) of this section.

(D) A community trust does not have to meet the requirements of paragraph (e)(13) of this section for taxable years beginning prior to the date of its application for a transitional ruling or determination letter or for any taxable year beginning after the expiration or termination of its transitional ruling or determination letter. In applying paragraph (e)(13) of this section to organizations applying for a transitional ruling or determination letter, paragraph (e)(13)(x) and (xii) of this section (relating to unrestricted gifts and excess holdings, respectively) shall be applied without regard to assets acquired prior to November 11, 1976. In addition, if within 1 year from acquiring any asset, the community trust removes any restriction inconsistent with paragraph (e)(13) of this section, such asset shall be treated as if it were not subject to such restriction as of the time it was acquired. Since under paragraph (e)(12)(ii)(D) of this section, a community trust does not have to meet the requirements of paragraph (e)(13) of this section for taxable years beginning prior to the date of its application for the transitional ruling or determination letter, then if the community trust makes such application in its taxable year beginning in 1977 and it terminates such ruling or determination letter in such year as well, such a community trust does not have to meet such requirements for any taxable year.

(E) After the transitional ruling or determination letter of an organization has expired or been terminated under paragraph (e)(12)(iii) of this section, the organization must qualify as a "publicly supported" organization pursuant to the rules set forth in paragraph (e)(1) through (11) of this section. Thus, since the transitional ruling period of a community trust expires with its taxable year beginning in 1981, for its taxable year beginning in 1982 and thereafter, the community trust must meet the requirements of paragraph (e)(2) or (3) of this section based upon the 4-year computation period under paragraph (e)(4) of this section.

(iii) Termination of transitional ruling. (A) The transitional ruling or determination letter issued under this paragraph is subject to termination under paragraph (e)(12)(iii)(B) or (D) of this section without a request from the organization. In addition, such a ruling or determination letter is subject to termination under paragraph (e)(12)(iii)(E) of this section at the request of the organization. A transitional ruling or determination letter is subject to termination for any taxable year beginning after December 31, 1976, and before January 1, 1982, under paragraph (e)(12)(iii)(B), (D) or (E) of this section.

(B) The transitional ruling or determination letter issued under this paragraph shall be terminated for any taxable year (if such a year begins after its tenth taxable year) beginning in 1978, 1979, 1980 or 1981 for which a community trust receiving such a ruling or determination letter fails to meet the requirements of paragraph (e)(2) or (3) of this section for a 10-year computation period, except as provided in paragraph (e)(12)(iii)(C) of this section.

(C) In applying paragraph (e)(12)(iii)(B) of this section to a community trust described in paragraph (e)(12)(ii)(B)*(1)* of this section, a computation period consisting of the number of taxable years (but not more than 20 nor less than 10) preceding such taxable year that the organization was in existence shall be substituted for the 10-year computation period until the first taxable year beginning in 1978, 1979, 1980 or 1981 that the community trust can meet the requirements of paragraph (e)(2) or (3) of this section based upon a 10-year computation period.

(D) The Commissioner may, at the discretion of the Commissioner, terminate the transitional ruling or determination only if the community trust for any taxable year beginning prior to January 1, 1982, for which the organization fails to meet the requirements of paragraph (e)(11), (12) or (13) of this section as provided in paragraph (e)(12)(ii) of this section.

(E) A community trust may request an immediate termination of the community trust's transitional ruling or determination letter in order that, for the current taxable year, it may be determined if such community trust meets the requirements of paragraph (e)(2) or (3) of this section based upon a 4-year computation period under paragraph (e)(4) of this section. Such a request shall be granted and the transitional ruling or determination letter only if the community trust meets such requirements, and in the case of an organization that has been in existence less than 11 taxable years at the time of such request, the organization also meets the requirements of paragraph (e)(2) or (3) of this section for the computation period consisting of the taxable years that the organization has been in existence.

(iv) Initial determination of status. (A) The initial determination of status of a community trust is the first determination (other than by issuance of an advance ruling or determination letter under paragraph (e)(5) or a transitional ruling or determination letter under paragraph (e)(12)(ii) of this section) that the community trust will be considered as "normally" meeting the requirements of paragraph (e)(2) or (3) of this section for a period beginning with its first taxable year.

(B) (1) In the case of a community trust described in paragraph (e)(12)(i)(B) of this section, the initial determination of status shall be made for the community trust's taxable year beginning in 1977 if such community trust has met the requirements of paragraph (e)(2) or (3) of this section for its taxable year beginning in 1977, based upon a 10-year computation period.

(2) In the case of any other community trust described in paragraph (e)(12)(i)(B) of this section (but not described in paragraph (e)(12)(iv)(B)(1) of this section), the initial determination of status shall be made for its first taxable year beginning after December 31, 1976 and before January 1, 1982, for which it meets the requirements of paragraph (e)(2) or (3) of this section based upon a 10-year computation period (if the community trust has received a transitional ruling or determination letter that has not been terminated before such taxable year).

(C) In the case of a community trust described in paragraph (e)(12)(i)(A) of this section (relating to an organization in existence less than 9 taxable years) that reaches its 11th taxable year before its taxable year beginning in 1982, its initial determination of status shall be for its 11th taxable year based upon a 10-year computation period (if it has received a transitional ruling or determination letter that has not been terminated before such taxable year).

(D) If a community trust has not received an initial determination of status prior to the expiration or termination of its transitional ruling period, the initial determination of status shall be made—

(1) In the case of an expiration, for the taxable year beginning in 1982, or

(2) In the case of a termination, for the last taxable year of the terminated transitional period, based upon a 4-year computation period under paragraph (e)(4) of this section. In the case of an organization that has been in existence less than 11 taxable years at such time, the initial determination of status shall also be based upon a computation period consisting of the taxable years it has been in existence.

For example, if the initial determination of status (for an organization that has been in existence for at least 11 taxable years) is made for its taxable year beginning in 1982, then, except as provided in paragraph (e)(4)(v) of this section (relating to exception for material changes of support), such determination shall be based upon a 4-year computation period ending with the taxable year beginning in 1980 or 1981 (treating the taxable year beginning in 1982, as the subsequent year or current year, respectively).
On the other hand, if, for example, the transitional ruling or determination letter is terminated in the taxable year beginning in 1980, then, except as provided in such paragraph (e)(4)(v), the initial determination of status shall be made for the taxable year beginning in 1980 based upon the 4-year computation period ending with the taxable year beginning in 1978 or 1979.

(v) Special rules. (A) Consequences of organization failing to meet requirements at end of transitional period. If upon the expiration (or termination) of the transitional period an organization with a transitional ruling or determination letter fails to meet the requirements of paragraph (e)(2) or (3) of this section based upon the 4-year computation period of paragraph (e)(4) of this section, it shall not be treated as an organization described in section 170(b)(1)(A)(vi) for its taxable year beginning in 1982 (or for the last taxable year of its terminated transitional period, as the case may be). If, by reason of failing to qualify as an organization described in section 170(b)(1)(A)(vi), such organization becomes a private foundation, then the organization will be a private foundation for its taxable year beginning in 1982 (or the last taxable year of its terminated transitional period, as the case may be) and all subsequent taxable years, unless and until it terminates its status under section 507. In addition, such an organization is a private foundation for all taxable years beginning prior to its taxable year beginning in 1982 (or for the last taxable year of the terminated transition period, as the case may be), except—

(1) That if the organization had received an initial determination of status that it met the requirements of paragraph (e)(2) or (3) of this section, then the organization will be treated as "publicly supported" for the taxable years to which the initial determination of status is effective, as well

as for all taxable years beginning after the last of such years and before January 1, 1982, for which the organization consecutively meets the requirements of paragraph (e)(2) or (3) of this section based upon a 10-year computation period,

(2) That in the case of an organization that has reached its tenth taxable year of existence before January 1, 1970, if the organization has not received an initial determination of status prior to its taxable year beginning in 1982, then the organization will be treated as "publicly supported" for each taxable year beginning before January 1, 1977, that the organization, beginning with the taxable year beginning in 1970, consecutively met the requirements of paragraph (e)(2) or (3) of this section based upon a 10-year computation period, or

(3) That in the case of an organization whose 11th taxable year of its existence began after December 31, 1970 and before January 1, 1977, if the organization has not received an initial determination of status prior to its taxable year beginning in 1982, but the organization for its 11th taxable year of existence met the requirements of paragraph (e)(2) or (3) of this section based upon a 10-year computation period, then the organization will be treated as "publicly supported" for the first 12 taxable years of its existence. In addition, such an organization will be so treated for its 13th taxable year and each subsequent taxable year (if such a year begins before January 1, 1977) that the organization, beginning with its 12th taxable year, consecutively met the requirements of paragraph (e)(2) or (3) of this section based upon a 10-year computation period.

(4) To the extent provided in paragraph (e)(4)(vii) of this section (relating to special rule for organization with existing rulings), § 1.508-1(b) (relating to notice that an organization is not a private foundation) or § 1.509(a)-7 (relating to reliance by grantors and contributors to section 509(a)(1), (2), and (3) organizations).

(B) Computation period. In applying the requirements of paragraph (e)(2) or (3) of this section to a 10-year or other computation period under paragraph (e)(12) or (13) of this section, such 10-year or other computation period shall be substituted for the 4-year computation period of paragraph (e)(4) of this section. Thus, for example, an organization will (except as provided in paragraph (e)(4)(v) of this section relating to exemption for material changes in sources of support) meet the "publicly supported" test of this paragraph for the taxable year beginning in 1977 based upon a 10-year computation period, if it met the requirements of paragraph (e)(2) or (3) of this section for a computation period consisting of either the taxable years beginning in the years 1966 through 1975 or the years 1967 through 1976, since under paragraph (e)(4) of this section, meeting the requirements for a computation period is effective for the current taxable year and the immediately succeeding taxable year. However, in substituting a 10-year or other computation period for the 4-year computation period of paragraph (e)(4) of this section, the rules of such paragraph (e)(4) and (6) apply, including the 2-percent limitation under paragraph (e)(6)(i) of this section and the exclusion for unusual grants under paragraph (e)(6)(ii) of this section. In applying such provisions, the fact that the computation period is other than a 4-year computation period shall be taken into account, so that, for example, the 2-percent limitation shall be applied, in the case of a 10-year computation period, with reference to 2 percent of the organization's total support for the 10-year computation period rather than a 4-year computation period.

In addition, in substituting a 10-year or other computation period for purposes of paragraph (e)(3) of this section, all of the facts and circumstances referred to in such paragraph (e)(3) shall be considered with respect to such period, viewing such period as a whole. See, also, paragraph (e)(10) of this section with respect to the organization being organized and operated to attract public support.

(C) First taxable year of less than 8 months. In the case of an organization whose first taxable year consisted of less than 8 months, in order to coordinate the rules of paragraph (e)(12) of this section with the rules of paragraph (e)(5) of this section, in applying the rules of paragraph (e)(12) of this section, such an organization shall be treated as organized at the beginning of its succeeding taxable year, so that such succeeding taxable year shall be treated as its first taxable year of existence. However, the support received for the period preceding such succeeding taxable year shall be taken into account with the support received in such succeeding taxable year.

(13) Community trusts; requirements for 5-year transitional ruling period. (i) In general. In order for a community trust to be eligible for a transitional ruling or determination letter for the transitional ruling period under paragraph (e)(12) of this section, it must establish that it is organized, and will be operated, in such manner that it can reasonably be expected to meet the requirements of paragraph (e)(13) of this section, and can reasonably be expected to meet the requirements of paragraph (e)(2) or (3) of this section, for each taxable year during and immediately following the transitional ruling period, as provided in paragraph (e)(12)(ii) of this section. In determining whether an organization can reasonably be expected to meet the requirements of paragraph (e)(2) or (3) of this section for each such taxable year, the basic consideration is whether its organizational structure, proposed programs or activities, and intended method of operation are such as to attract the type of broadly based support from the general public, public charities, and governmental units which is necessary to meet such tests. The information to be considered for this purpose shall consist of all pertinent facts and circumstances relating to the requirements set forth in paragraph (e)(3) of this section. For purposes of meeting the requirements of paragraph (e)(13) of this section, a community trust may, prior to its application for a transitional ruling or determination letter under paragraph (e)(12)(i)(C) of this section, adopt a resolution stating that, as a matter of policy, it will attempt to meet the conditions set forth in paragraph (e)(13) of this section during the transitional ruling period. A community trust will not be treated as failing to satisfy the requirements of paragraph (e)(13) of this section merely because the governing body, or any of its trustees, agents, or custodians, fails to meet one or more of the requirements contained in paragraph (e)(13)(ii) through (xiii) of this section by reason of isolated and nonrepetitive acts. However, any continuing pattern on the part of the governing body, or its trustees, agents or custodians, indicating a continued and repetitive failure to comply with a policy of meeting such requirements will result in termination of the transitional ruling or determination letter under paragraph (e)(12)(iii)(D) of this section.

(ii) Area. The community trust is organized and operated exclusively to carry out charitable purposes (within the meeting of section 170(c)(1) or (2)(B)) primarily within a broad geographical area which it serves, such as a municipality, county, metropolitan area, State or region.

(iii) General composition of governing body. The governing body must represent the broad interests of the public rather than the personal or private interests of a limited number of donors. An organization will be treated as meeting this requirement if it has a governing body comprised of public officials acting in their capacities as such; individuals selected by public officials acting in their capacities as such; persons having special knowledge or expertise in a particular field or discipline in which the community trust operates; community leaders, such as elected or appointed officials, clergymen, educators, civic leaders; or other such persons representing a broad cross-section of the views and interests of the area served.

(iv) Rules for governing body. With respect to terms of office beginning after the date of the application of the community trust for a transitional ruling or determination letter—

(A) Its governing body is comprised of members who may serve a period of not more than ten consecutive years;

(B) Upon completion of a period of service (beginning before or after such date) no person may serve within a period consisting of the lesser of 5 years or the number of consecutive years the member has immediately completed serving;

(C) Persons who would be described in section 4946(a)(1)(A) or (C) through (G) if the community trust were a private foundation do not constitute more than one-third of its governing body; and

(D) Representatives of banks or trust companies which serve as trustees, investment managers, custodians, or agents, plus persons described in paragraph (e)(13)(iv)(C) of this section, do not constitute a majority of the governing body.

No term of office beginning on or before the date of such application may continue for more than 10 years from such date.

(v) Fiduciary responsibility. Fiduciary responsibility with respect to the funds of the community trust is imposed, either by the master trust or agency agreement or by State law, on either its governing body or its trustee banks or trust companies or both.

(vi) Ultimate control of assets. Neither its governing body, nor any of its trustees, investment managers, custodians or agents may be subjected by any donor to the community trust to any material condition or restriction within the meaning of § 1.507-2(a)(8) which would prevent it from exercising ultimate control over its assets.

(vii) Administration. Administration and investment of all gifts and bequests are accomplished through:

(A) A governing body which directly holds, administers or invests such gifts and bequests exclusively for charitable purposes;

(B) Banks or trust companies (acting or appointed as trustees), investment managers, custodians or agents of the community trust or one or more components thereof; or

(C) A combination of such persons.

(viii) Annual distributions. It makes annual distributions for purposes described in section 170(c)(1) or (2)(B), including administrative expenses and amounts paid to acquire an asset used (or held for use) directly in carrying out one or more of such purposes, in an amount not less than its adjusted net income (as defined in section 4942(f)). For purposes of paragraph (e)(13)(viii) of this section, the term "distributions" shall include amounts set aside for a specific project, but only if prior to making the set-aside the organization has, pursuant to a request for a ruling, established to the satisfaction of the Commissioner that—

(A) the amount will be paid for the specific project within 5 years; and

(B) The project is one which can be better accomplished by such set-aside than by immediate distribution of funds.

All annual distributions required to be made pursuant to paragraph (e)(13)(viii) of this section, except for set-asides, must be made no later than the close of the organization's first taxable year after the taxable year for which the adjusted net income is computed. Thus, in the case of a calendar year community trust which has received a transitional ruling or determination letter upon an application made in 1977, it must make distributions under paragraph (e)(13)(vii) of this section for 1978, 1979, 1980 and 1981 based upon its adjusted net income for 1977, 1978, 1979 and 1980, respectively, unless its transitional ruling or determination letter is terminated. If such a community trust's transitional ruling or determination letter is terminated in 1979, it must make distributions under paragraph (e)(13)(viii) of this section only for 1978 based upon its adjusted net income for 1977.

On the other hand, if such ruling or letter is terminated in 1977 or 1978, no distribution under paragraph (e)(13)(viii) of this section need be made.

(ix) Net income. The community trust's funds must, on an aggregate basis, be invested to produce an annual adjusted net income (as defined in section 4942(f)) of not less than two-thirds of what would be its minimum investment return (within the meaning of section 4942(e)) if such organization were a private foundation.

(x) Unrestricted gifts. At least one-half of the total income which the community trust derives from the investment of gifts and bequests received must be unrestricted (within the meaning of this (x)) with respect to its availability for distribution by the governing body. For purposes of this (x), any income which has been designated by the donor of the gift or bequest to which such income is attributable as being available only for the use or benefit of a broad charitable purpose, such as the encouragement of higher education or the promotion of better health care in the community, will be treated as unrestricted. However, any income which has been designated for the use or benefit of a named charitable organization or agency or for the use or benefit of a particular class of charitable organizations or agencies, the members of which are readily ascertainable and are less than five in number, will be treated as restricted.

(xi) Self-dealing. The community trust may not engage in any act with any person (other than a foundation manager acting only in such capacity) which would constitute self-dealing within the meaning of section 4941 if such community trust were a private foundation.

(xii) Excess holdings. The community trust must dispose of any holdings which would constitute excess business holdings (within the meaning of section 4943—applied on a component-by-component basis as if each component were a private foundation, except that components will be combined for purposes of this paragraph if such components would have been described in section 4946(a)(1)(H)(ii)).

(xiii) Expenditure responsibility. The community trust must exercise expenditure responsibility (within the meaning of section 4945(h)) through either its governing body, trustees, investment managers, custodians, or agents with respect to any grant which would otherwise constitute a taxable expenditure under section 4945(d)(4) if the community trust were a private foundation, except that it need not make the reports required of private foundations by section 4945(h)(3).

(14) Community trusts; treatment of trusts and not-for-profit corporations and associations not included as components. (i) For purposes of sections 170, 501, 507, 508, 509

and chapter 42, any trust or not-for-profit corporation or association which is alleged to be a component part of a community trust, but which fails to meet the requirements of paragraph (e)(11)(ii) of this section, shall not be treated as a component part of a community trust and, if a trust, shall be treated as a separate trust and be subject to the provisions of section 501 or section 4947(a)(1) or (2), as the case may be. If such organization is a not-for-profit corporation or association, it will be treated as a separate entity, and, if it is described in section 501(c)(3), it will be treated as a private foundation unless it is described in section 509(a)(1), (2), (3), or (4). Any transfer made in connection with the creation of such separate trust or not-for-profit organization, or to such entity, will not be treated as being made "to" the community trust or one of its components for purposes of sections 170(b)(1)(A) and 507(b)(1)(A) even though a deduction with respect to such transfer is allowable under § 1.170-1(e), § 20.2055-2(b), or § 25.2522(a)-2(b), unless such treatment is permitted under § 1.170A-9(e)(4)(v)(b) or § 1.508-1(b)(4). In the case of a fund which is ultimately treated as not being a component part of a community trust pursuant to paragraph (e)(14) of this section, if the Form 990 filed annually by the community trust included financial information with respect to such fund and treated such fund in the same manner as other component parts thereof, such returns filed by the community trust prior to the taxable year in which the Commissioner notifies such fund that it will not be treated as a component part will be treated as its separate return for purpose of subchapter A of chapter 61 of Subtitle F, and the first such return filed by the community trust will be treated as the notification required of the separate entity for purposes of section 508(a).

(ii) If a transfer is made in trust to a community trust to make income or other payments for a period of a life or lives in being or a term of years to any individual or for any noncharitable purpose, followed by payments to or for the use of the community trust (such as in the case of a charitable remainder annuity trust or a charitable remainder unitrust described in section 664 or a pooled income fund described in section 642(c)(5)), such trust will be treated as a component part of the community trust upon the termination of all intervening noncharitable interests and rights to the actual possession or enjoyment of the property if such trust satisfies the requirements of paragraph (e)(11) of this section at such time. Until such time, the trust will be treated as a separate trust. If a transfer is made in trust to a community trust to make income or other payments to or for the use of the community trust, followed by payments to any individual or for any noncharitable purpose, such trust will be treated as a separate trust rather than as a component part of the community trust. See section 4947(a)(2) and the regulations thereunder for the treatment of such split-interest trusts. The provisions of this (ii) only provide rules for determining when a charitable remainder trust or pooled income fund may be treated as a component part of a community trust and are not intended to preclude a community trust from maintaining a charitable remainder trust or pooled income fund. Thus, for purposes of grantors and contributors, a pooled income fund of a "publicly supported" community trust shall be treated no differently than a polled income fund of any other "publicly supported" organization.

(iii) An organization described in section 170(b)(1)(E)(iii) will not ordinarily satisfy the requirements of paragraph (e)(11)(ii) of this section because of the unqualified right of the donor to designate the recipients of the income and principal of the trust. Such organization will therefore ordinarily be treated as other than a component part of a community trust under paragraph (e)(14)(i) of this section. However, see section 170(b)(1)(E)(iii) and the regulations thereunder with respect to the treatment of contributions to such organizations.

(g) Private operating foundation. An organization is described in section 170(b)(1) (A)(vii) and (E)(i) if it is a private "operating foundation" as defined in section 4942(j)(3) and the regulations thereunder.

(h) Private nonoperating foundation distributing amount equal to all contributions received. *(1) In general.* (i) An organization is described in section 170(b)(1) (A)(vii) and (E)(ii) if it is a private foundation which, not later than the 15th day of the third month after the close of its taxable year in which any contributions are received, distributes an amount equal in value to 100 percent of all contributions received in such year. Such distributions must be qualifying distributions (as defined in section 4942(g) without regard to paragraph (3) thereof) which are treated, after the application of section 4942(g)(3), as distributions out of corpus in accordance with section 4942(h). Qualifying distributions, as defined in section 4942(g) without regard to paragraph (3) thereof, cannot be made to (i) an organization controlled directly or indirectly by the foundation or by one or more disqualified persons (as defined in section 4946) with respect to the foundation or (ii) a private foundation which is not an operating foundation (as defined in section 4942(j)(3)). The phrase "after the application of section 4942(g)(3)" means that every contribution described in section 4942(g)(3) received by a private foundation described in this subparagraph in a particular taxable year must be distributed (within the meaning of section 4942(g)(3)(A)) by such foundation not later than the 15th day of the third month after the close of such taxable year in order for any other distribution by such foundation to be counted toward the 100-percent requirement described in this subparagraph.

(ii) In order for an organization to meet the distribution requirements of subdivision (i) of this subparagraph, it must, not later than the 15th day of the third month after the close of its taxable year in which any contributions are received, distribute (within the meaning of subdivision (i) of this subparagraph) an amount equal in value to 100 percent of all contributions received in such year and have no remaining undistributed income for such year.

(iii) The provisions of this subparagraph may be illustrated by the following examples:

Example (1). X is a private foundation on a calendar year basis. As of January 1, 1971, X had no undistributed income for 1970. X's distributable amount for 1971 was $600,000. In July 1971, A, an individual, contributed $500,000 (fair market value determined at the time of the contribution) of appreciated property to X (which, if sold, would give rise to long-term capital gain). X did not receive any other contribution in either 1970 or 1971. During 1971, X made qualifying distributions of $700,000 which were treated as made out of the undistributed income for 1971 and $100,000 out of corpus. X will meet the requirements of section 170(b)(1)(E)(ii) for 1971 if it makes additional qualifying distributions of $400,000 out of corpus by March 15, 1972.

Example (2). Assume of January 1, 1971, X had $100,000 of undistributed income for 1970. Under these circumstances, the $700,000 distributed by X in 1971 would be treated as made out of the undistributed income for 1970 and 1971. X would therefore have to make additional qualifying distributions of $500,000 out of corpus between January 1,

1972, and March 15, 1972, in order to meet the requirements of section 170(b)(1)(E)(ii) for 1971.

(2) Special rules. In applying subparagraph (1) of this paragraph—

(i) For purposes of section 170(b)(1)(A)(vii), an organization described in section 170(b)(1)(E)(ii) must distribute all contributions received in any year, whether of cash or property. However, solely for purposes of section 170(e)(1)(B)(ii), an organization described in section 170(b)(1)(E)(ii) is required to distribute all contributions of property only received in any year. Contributions for purposes of this paragraph do not include bequests, legacies, devises, or transfers within the meaning of section 2055 or 2106(a)(2) with respect to which a deduction was not allowed under section 170.

(ii) Any distributions made by a private foundation pursuant to subparagraph (1) of this paragraph with respect to a particular taxable year shall be treated as made first out of contributions of property and then out of contributions of cash received by such foundation in such year.

(iii) A private foundation is not required to trace specific contributions of property, or amounts into which such contributions are converted, to specific distributions.

(iv) For purposes of satisfying the requirements of section 170(b)(1)(D)(ii), except as provided to the contrary in this subdivision (iv), the fair market value of contributed property, determined on the date of contribution, is required to be used for purposes of determining whether an amount equal in value to 100 percent of the contributions received has been distributed. However, reasonable selling expenses, if any, incurred by the foundation in the sale of the contributed property may be deducted from the fair market value of the contributed property on the date of contribution, and distribution of the balance of the fair market value will satisfy the 100 percent distribution requirement. If a private foundation receives a contribution of property and, within 30 days thereafter, either sells the property or makes an in kind distribution of the property to a public charity, then at the choice of the private foundation the gross amount received on the sale (less reasonable selling expenses incurred) or the fair market value of the contributed property at the date of its distribution to the public charity, and not the fair market value of the contributed property on the date of contribution (less reasonable selling expenses, if any), is considered to be the amount of the fair market value of the contributed property for purposes of the requirements of section 170(b)(1)(D)(ii).

(v) A private foundation may satisfy the requirements of subparagraph (1) of this paragraph for a particular taxable year by electing (pursuant to section 4942(h)(2) and the regulations thereunder) to treat a portion or all of one or more distributions, made not later than the 15th day of the third month after the close of such year, as made out of corpus.

(3) Transitional rules. (i) Taxable years beginning before January 1, 1970, and ending after December 31, 1969. In order for an organization to meet the distribution requirements of subparagraph (1)(i) of this paragraph for a taxable year which begins before January 1, 1970, and ends after December 31, 1969, it must, not later than the 15th day of the third month after the close of such taxable year, distribute (within the meaning of subparagraph (1)(i) of this paragraph) an amount equal in value to 100 percent of all contributions (other than contributions described in section 4942(g)(3)) which were received between January 1, 1970, and the last day of such taxable year. Because the organization is not subject to the provisions of section 4942 for such year, the organization need not satisfy subparagraph (1)(ii) of this paragraph or the phrase "after the application of section 4942(g)(3)" for such year.

(ii) Extension of period. For purposes of section 170(b)(1)(A)(vii) and 170(e)(1)(B)(ii), in the case of a taxable year ending in either 1970, 1971 or 1972, the period referred to in section 170(b)(1)(E)(ii) for making distributions shall not expire before April 2, 1973.

(4) Adequate records required. A taxpayer claiming a deduction under section 170 for a charitable contribution to a foundation described in subparagraph (1) of this paragraph must obtain adequate records or other sufficient evidence from such foundation showing that the foundation made the required qualifying distributions within the time prescribed. Such records or other evidence must be attached to the taxpayer's return for the taxable year for which the charitable contribution deduction is claimed. If necessary, an amended income tax return or claim for refund may be filed in accordance with § 301.6402-2 and § 301.6402-3 of this chapter (procedure and administration regulations).

(i) Private foundation maintaining a common fund. *(1) Designation by substantial contributors.* An organization is described in section 170(b)(1)(A)(vii) and (E)(iii) if it is a private foundation all of the contributions to which are pooled in a common fund and which would be described in section 509(a)(3) but for the right of any donor who is a substantial contributor or his spouse to designate annually the recipients, from among public charities, of the income attributable to the donor's contribution to the fund and to direct (by deed or by will) the payment, to public charities, of the corpus in the common fund attributable to the donor's contribution. For purposes of this paragraph, the private foundation is to be treated as meeting the requirements of section 509(a)(3)(A) and (B) even though donors to the foundation, or their spouses, retain the right to, and in fact do, designate public charities to receive income or corpus from the fund.

(2) Distribution requirements. To qualify under subparagraph (1) of this paragraph, the private foundation described therein must be required by its governing instrument to distribute, and it must in fact distribute (including administrative expenses)—

(i) All of the adjusted net income (as defined in section 4942(f)) of the common fund to one or more public charities not later than the 15th day of the third month after the close of the taxable year in which such income is realized by the fund, and

(ii) All the corpus attributable to any donor's contribution to the fund to one or more public charities not later than 1 year after the donor's death or after the death of the donor's surviving spouse if such surviving spouse has the right to designate the recipients of such corpus.

(3) Failure to designate. A private foundation will not fail to qualify under this paragraph merely because a substantial contributor or his spouse fails to exercise his right to designate the recipients of income or corpus of the fund, provided that the income and corpus attributable to his contribution are distributed as required by subparagraph (2) of this paragraph.

(4) Definitions. For purposes of this paragraph—

(i) The term "substantial contributor" is as defined in section 507(d)(2) and the regulations thereunder.

(ii) The term "public charity" means an organization described in section 170(b)(1)(A)(i) through (vi). If an organization is described in section 170(b)(1)(A)(i) through (vi), and is also described in section 170(b)(1)(A)(viii), it shall be treated as a public charity for purposes of this paragraph.

(iii) The term "income attributable to" means the income earned by the fund which is properly allocable to the contributed amount by any reasonable and consistently applied method. See, for example, § 1.642(c)-5(c).

(iv) The term "corpus attributable to" means the portion of the corpus of the fund attributable to the contributed amount. Such portion may be determined by any reasonable and consistently applied method.

(v) The term "donor" means any individual who makes a contribution (whether of cash or property) to the private foundation, whether or not such individual is a substantial contributor.

(j) Section 509(a)(2) or (3) organization. An organization is described in section 170(b)(1)(A)(viii) if it is described in section 509(a)(2) or (3) and the regulations thereunder.

(k) Effective/applicability date. This section shall apply to taxable years beginning after December 31, 1969. The applicability of paragraph (f) of this section shall be limited to taxable years beginning before January 1, 2008.

T.D. 7242, 12/29/72, amend T.D. 7406, 2/13/76, T.D. 7440, 11/11/76, T.D. 7465, 1/19/77, T.D. 7679, 2/28/80, T.D. 8100, 9/3/86, T.D. 8991, 4/24/2002, T.D. 9423, 9/8/2008.

PAR. 2. Section 1.170A-9 is amended by revising paragraphs (f) and (k) to read as follows:

Proposed § 1.170A-9 Definition of section 170(b)(1)(A) organization. [*For Preamble, see ¶ 153,055*]

* * * * *

(f) [The text of this proposed amendment to § 1.170A-9(f) is the same as the text of § 1.170A-9T(f) published elsewhere in this issue of the Federal Register.] [*See T.D. 9423, 09/09/2008, 73 Fed. Reg. 175.*]

* * * * *

(k) [The text of this proposed amendment to § 1.170A-9(k) is the same as the text of § 1.170A-9T(k)(1) and (k)(2) published elsewhere in this issue of the Federal Register.] [*See T.D. 9423, 09/09/2008, 73 Fed. Reg. 175.*]

§ 1.170A-9T Definition of section 170(b)(1)(A) organization (temporary).

(a) through (e) [Reserved]. For further guidance, see § 1.170A-9(a) through (e).

(f) Definition of section 170(b)(1)(A)(vi) organization. *(1) In general.* An organization is described in section 170(b)(1)(A)(vi) if it—

(i) Is referred to in section 170(c)(2) (other than an organization specifically described in paragraphs (b) through (e) of this section); and

(ii) Normally receives a substantial part of its support from a governmental unit referred to in section 170(c)(1) or from direct or indirect contributions from the general public ("publicly supported"). For purposes of this paragraph (f)(1)(ii), an organization is publicly supported if it meets the requirements of either paragraph (f)(2) of this section (33⅓ percent support test) or paragraph (f)(3) of this section (facts and circumstances test). Paragraph (f)(4) of this section defines normally for purposes of the 33⅓ percent support test, the facts and circumstances test and for new organizations in the first 5 years of the organization's existence as a section 501(c)(3) organization. Paragraph (f)(5) of this section provides for determinations of foundation classification and rules for reliance by donors and contributors. Paragraphs (f)(6), (7), and (8) of this section list the items that are included and excluded from the term support. Paragraph (f)(9) of this section provides examples of the application of this paragraph. Types of organizations that, subject to the provisions of this paragraph, generally qualify under section 170(b)(1)(A)(vi) as "publicly supported" are publicly or governmentally supported museums of history, art, or science, libraries, community centers to promote the arts, organizations providing facilities for the support of an opera, symphony orchestra, ballet, or repertory drama or for some other direct service to the general public.

(2) Determination whether an organization is "publicly supported"; 33⅓ percent support test. An organization is publicly supported if the total amount of support (see paragraphs (f)(6), (7), and (8) of this section) that the organization normally (see paragraph (f)(4)(i) of this section) receives from governmental units referred to in section 170(c)(1), from contributions made directly or indirectly by the general public, or from a combination of these sources, equals at least 33⅓ percent of the total support normally received by the organization. See paragraph (f)(9) Example 1 of this section.

(3) Determination whether an organization is "publicly supported"; facts and circumstances test. Even if an organization fails to meet the 33⅓ percent support test, it is publicly supported if it normally receives a substantial part of its support from governmental units, from contributions made directly or indirectly by the general public, or from a combination of these sources, and meets the other requirements of this paragraph (f)(3). In order to satisfy the facts and circumstances test, an organization must meet the requirements of paragraphs (f)(3)(i) and (f)(3)(ii) of this section. In addition, the organization must be in the nature of an organization that is publicly supported, taking into account all relevant facts and circumstances, including the factors listed in paragraphs (f)(3)(iii)(A) through (E) of this section.

(i) Ten percent support limitation. The percentage of support (see paragraphs (f)(6), (7) and (8) of this section) normally (see paragraph (f)(4) of this section) received by an organization from governmental units, from contributions made directly or indirectly by the general public, or from a combination of these sources, must be substantial. For purposes of this paragraph (f)(3), an organization will not be treated as normally receiving a substantial amount of governmental or public support unless the total amount of governmental and public support normally received equals at least 10 percent of the total support normally received by such organization.

(ii) Attraction of public support. An organization must be so organized and operated as to attract new and additional public or governmental support on a continuous basis. An organization will be considered to meet this requirement if it maintains a continuous and bona fide program for solicitation of funds from the general public, community, or membership group involved, or if it carries on activities designed to attract support from governmental units or other organizations described in section 170(b)(1)(A)(i) through (vi). In determining whether an organization maintains a continuous and bona fide program for solicitation of funds from the general public or community, consideration will be given to whether the scope of its fundraising activities is reasonable in light of its charitable activities. Consideration will also be given to the fact that an organization may, in its early years of existence, limit the scope of its solicitation to persons deemed most likely to provide seed money in an amount sufficient to enable it to commence its charitable activities and expand its solicitation program.

(iii) In addition to the requirements set forth in paragraphs (f)(3)(i) and (ii) of this section that must be satisfied, all pertinent facts and circumstances, including the following factors, will be taken into consideration in determining whether an organization is "publicly supported" within the meaning of paragraph (f)(1) of this section. However, an organization is not generally required to satisfy all of the factors in paragraphs (f)(3)(iii)(A) through (E) of this section. The factors relevant to each case and the weight accorded to any one of them may differ depending upon the nature and purpose of the organization and the length of time it has been in existence.

(A) Percentage of financial support. The percentage of support received by an organization from public or governmental sources will be taken into consideration in determining whether an organization is "publicly supported." The higher the percentage of support above the 10 percent requirement of paragraph (f)(3)(i) of this section from public or governmental sources, the lesser will be the burden of establishing the publicly supported nature of the organization through other factors described in this paragraph (f)(3), while the lower the percentage, the greater will be the burden. If the percentage of the organization's support from public or governmental sources is low because it receives a high percentage of its total support from investment income on its endowment funds, such fact will be treated as evidence of compliance with this subdivision if such endowment funds were originally contributed by a governmental unit or by the general public. However, if such endowment funds were originally contributed by a few individuals or members of their families, such fact will increase the burden on the organization of establishing compliance with the other factors described in paragraph (f)(3)(iii) of this section.

(B) Sources of support. The fact that an organization meets the requirement of paragraph (f)(3)(i) of this section through support from governmental units or directly or indirectly from a representative number of persons, rather than receiving almost all of its support from the members of a single family, will be taken into consideration in determining whether an organization is "publicly supported." In determining what is a "representative number of persons," consideration will be given to the type of organization involved, the length of time it has been in existence, and whether it limits its activities to a particular community or region or to a special field which can be expected to appeal to a limited number of persons.

(C) Representative governing body. The fact that an organization has a governing body which represents the broad interests of the public, rather than the personal or private interests of a limited number of donors (or persons standing in a relationship to such donors which is described in section 4946(a)(1)(C) through (G)), will be taken into account in determining whether an organization is "publicly supported." An organization will be treated as meeting this requirement if it has a governing body (whether designated in the organization's governing instrument or bylaws as a Board of Directors, Board of Trustees, etc.) which is comprised of public officials acting in their capacities as such; of individuals selected by public officials acting in their capacities as such; of persons having special knowledge or expertise in the particular field or discipline in which the organization is operating; of community leaders, such as elected or appointed officials, clergymen, educators, civic leaders, or other such persons representing a broad cross-section of the views and interests of the community; or, in the case of a membership organization, of individuals elected pursuant to the organization's governing instrument or bylaws by a broadly based membership.

(D) Availability of public facilities or services; public participation in programs or policies. (1) The fact that an organization is of the type which generally provides facilities or services directly for the benefit of the general public on a continuing basis (such as a museum or library which holds open its building or facilities to the public, a symphony orchestra which gives public performances, a conservation organization which provides educational services to the public through the distribution of educational materials, or an old age home which provides domiciliary or nursing services for members of the general public) will be considered evidence that such organization is "publicly supported."

(2) The fact that an organization is an educational or research institution which regularly publishes scholarly studies that are widely used by colleges and universities or by members of the general public will also be considered evidence that such organization is "publicly supported."

(3) Similarly, the following factors will also be considered evidence that an organization is "publicly supported":

(i) The participation in, or sponsorship of, the programs of the organization by members of the public having special knowledge or expertise, public officials, or civic or community leaders.

(ii) The maintenance of a definitive program by an organization to accomplish its charitable work in the community, such as combating community deterioration in an economically depressed area that has suffered a major loss of population and jobs.

(iii) The receipt of a significant part of its funds from a public charity or governmental agency to which it is in some way held accountable as a condition of the grant, contract, or contribution.

(E) Additional factors pertinent to membership organizations. The following are additional factors to be considered in determining whether a membership organization is "publicly supported":

(1) Whether the solicitation for dues-paying members is designed to enroll a substantial number of persons in the community or area, or in a particular profession or field of special interest (taking into account the size of the area and the nature of the organization's activities).

(2) Whether membership dues for individual (rather than institutional) members have been fixed at rates designed to make membership available to a broad cross section of the interested public, rather than to restrict membership to a limited number of persons.

(3) Whether the activities of the organization will be likely to appeal to persons having some broad common interest or purpose, such as educational activities in the case of alumni associations, musical activities in the case of symphony societies, or civic affairs in the case of parent-teacher associations. See Examples 2 through 5 contained in paragraph (f)(9) of this section for illustrations of this paragraph (f)(3).

(4) Definition of normally; general rule. (i) Normally; 33⅓ percent support test. An organization meets the 33⅓ percent support test for its current taxable year and the taxable year immediately succeeding its current year, if, for the

current taxable year and the 4 taxable years immediately preceding the current taxable year, the organization meets the 33⅓ percent support test on an aggregate basis.

(ii) Normally; facts and circumstances test. An organization meets the facts and circumstances test for its current taxable year and the taxable year immediately succeeding its current year, if, for the current taxable year and the 4 taxable years immediately preceding the current taxable year, the organization meets the facts and circumstances test on an aggregate basis. In the case of paragraphs (f)(3)(iii)(A) and (B) of this section, facts pertinent to the 5-year period may also be taken into consideration. The combination of factors set forth in paragraphs (f)(3)(iii)(A) through (E) of this section that an organization "normally" must meet does not have to be the same for each 5-year period so long as there exists a sufficient combination of factors to show compliance with the facts and circumstances test.

(iii) Special rule. The fact that an organization has normally met the requirements of the 33⅓ percent support test for a current taxable year, but is unable normally to meet such requirements for a succeeding taxable year, will not in itself prevent such organization from meeting the facts and circumstances test for such succeeding taxable year.

(iv) Example. The application of paragraphs (f)(4)(i), (ii), and (iii) of this section may be illustrated by the following example:

Example. (i) X is recognized as an organization described in section 501(c)(3). On the basis of support received during taxable years 2008, 2009, 2010, 2011 and 2012, it meets the 33⅓ percent support test for taxable year 2012 (the current taxable year). X also meets the 33⅓ support test for 2013, as the immediately succeeding taxable year.

(ii) In taxable years 2009, 2010, 2011, 2012 and 2013, in the aggregate, X does not receive at least 33⅓ percent of its support from governmental units referred to in section 170(c)(1), from contributions made directly or indirectly by the general public, or from a combination of these sources. X still meets the 33⅓ percent support test for taxable year 2013 based on the aggregate support received for taxable years 2008 through 2012.

(iii) In taxable years 2010, 2011, 2012, 2013 and 2014, in the aggregate, X does not receive at least 33⅓ percent of its support from governmental units referred to in section 170(c)(1), from contributions made directly or indirectly by the general public, or from a combination of these sources. X does not meet the 33⅓ percent support test for taxable year 2014.

(iv) Based on the aggregate support and other factors listed in paragraphs (f)(3)(iii)(A) through (E) of this section for taxable years 2009, 2010, 2011, 2012, and 2013, X meets the facts and circumstances test for taxable year 2013 and for taxable year 2014 (as the immediately succeeding taxable year). Therefore, X is still an organization described in section 170(b)(1)(A)(vi) for taxable year 2014, even though X did not meet the 33⅓ percent support test for that year.

(v) Normally; first five years of an organization's existence.

(A) An organization meets the 33⅓ public support test or the facts and circumstances test during its first five taxable years as a section 501(c)(3) organization if the organization can reasonably be expected to meet the requirements of the 33⅓ percent support test or the facts and circumstances test during that period. With respect to such organization's sixth taxable year, the organization shall be described in section 170(b)(1)(A)(vi) if it meets the 33⅓ percent support test or the facts and circumstances test under the definitions of normally set forth in paragraphs (f)(4)(i) through (iii) of this section for its sixth taxable year (based on support received in its second through sixth taxable years), or for its fifth taxable year (based on support received in its first through fifth taxable years).

(B) Basic consideration. In determining whether an organization can reasonably be expected (within the meaning of paragraph (f)(4)(v)(A) of this section) to meet the requirements of the 33⅓ percent support test or the facts and circumstances test during its first five taxable years, the basic consideration is whether its organizational structure, current or proposed programs or activities, and actual or intended method of operation are such as can reasonably be expected to attract the type of broadly based support from the general public, public charities, and governmental units that is necessary to meet such tests. The factors that are relevant to this determination, and the weight accorded to each of them, may differ from case to case, depending on the nature and functions of the organization. The information to be considered for this purpose shall consist of all pertinent facts and circumstances relating to the requirements set forth in paragraph (f)(3) of this section.

(vi) Example. The application of paragraph (f)(4)(v) of this section may be illustrated by the following example:

Example. (i) Organization Y was formed in January 2008, and uses a December 31 taxable year. After September 9, 2008, and before December 31, 2008, Organization Y filed Form 1023 requesting recognition of exemption as an organization described in section 501(c)(3) and in sections 170(b)(1)(A)(vi) and 509(a)(1). In its application, Organization Y established that it can reasonably be expected to operate as a public charity under paragraph (f)(4)(v) of this section. Subsequently, Organization Y received a ruling or determination letter that it is an organization described in section 501(c)(3) and sections 170(b)(1)(A)(vi) and 509(a)(1) effective as of the date of its formation.

(ii) Organization Y is described in sections 170(b)(1)(A)(vi) and 509(a)(1) for its first 5 taxable years (the taxable years ending December 31, 2008, through December 31, 2012).

(iii) Organization Y can qualify as a public charity beginning with the taxable year ending December 31, 2013, if Organization Y can meet the requirements of paragraphs (f)(2) through (3) of this section or § 1.509(a)-3T(a) through (b) for the taxable years ending December 31, 2009, through December 31, 2013, or for the taxable years ending December 31, 2008, through December 31, 2012.

(5) Determinations on foundation classification and reliance. (i) A ruling or determination letter that an organization is described in section 170(b)(1)(A)(vi) may be issued to an organization. Such determination may be made in conjunction with the recognition of the organization's tax-exempt status or at such other time as the organization believes it is described in section 170(b)(1)(A)(vi). The ruling or determination letter that the organization is described in section 170(b)(1)(A)(vi) may be revoked if, upon examination, the organization has not met the requirements of paragraph (f) of this section. The ruling or determination letter that the organization is described in section 170(b)(1)(A)(vi) also may be revoked if the organization's application for a ruling or determination contained one or more material misstatements of fact or if such application was part of a scheme or plan to avoid or evade any provision of the Internal Revenue Code. The revocation of the determination that an organization is

described in section 170(b)(1)(A)(vi) does not preclude revocation of the determination that the organization is described in section 501(c)(3).

(ii) Status of grantors or contributors. For purposes of sections 170, 507, 545(b)(2), 642(c), 4942, 4945, 2055, 2106(a)(2), and 2522, grantors or contributors may rely upon a determination letter or ruling that an organization is described in section 170(b)(1)(A)(vi) until the Internal Revenue Service publishes notice of a change of status (for example, in the Internal Revenue Bulletin or Publication 78, "Cumulative List of Organizations described in Section 170(c) of the Internal Revenue Code of 1986," which can be searched at www.irs.gov). For this purpose, grantors or contributors also may rely on an advance ruling that expires on or after June 9, 2008. However, a grantor or contributor may not rely on such an advance ruling or any determination letter or ruling if the grantor or contributor was responsible for, or aware of, the act or failure to act that resulted in the organization's loss of classification under section 170(b)(1)(A)(vi) or acquired knowledge that the Internal Revenue Service had given notice to such organization that it would be deleted from such classification.

(6) Definition of support; meaning of general public. (i) In general. In determining whether the 33⅓ percent support test or the 10 percent support limitation described in paragraph (f)(3)(i) of this section is met, contributions by an individual, trust, or corporation shall be taken into account as support from direct or indirect contributions from the general public only to the extent that the total amount of the contributions by any such individual, trust, or corporation during the period described in paragraphs (f)(4)(i) or (ii) of this section does not exceed 2 percent of the organization's total support for such period, except as provided in paragraph (f)(6)(ii) of this section. Therefore, any contribution by one individual will be included in full in the denominator of the fraction determining the 33⅓ percent support or the 10 percent support limitation, but will be includible in the numerator of such fraction only to the extent that such amount does not exceed 2 percent of the denominator. In applying the 2 percent limitation, all contributions made by a donor and by any person or persons standing in a relationship to the donor that is described in section 4946(a)(1)(C) through (G) and the regulations relating to section 4946(a)(1)(C) through (G) shall be treated as made by one person. The 2 percent limitation shall not apply to support received from governmental units referred to in section 170(c)(1) or to contributions from organizations described in section 170(b)(1)(A)(vi), except as provided in paragraph (f)(6)(v) of this section. For purposes of paragraphs (f)(2), (f)(3)(i) and (f)(7)(iii)(A)(2) of this section, the term indirect contributions from the general public includes contributions received by the organization from organizations (such as section 170(b)(1)(A)(vi) organizations) that normally receive a substantial part of their support from direct contributions from the general public, except as provided in paragraph (f)(6)(v) of this section. See the examples in paragraph (f)(9) of this section for the application of this paragraph (f)(6)(i). For purposes of this paragraph (f), the term contributions includes qualified sponsorship payments (as defined in § 1.513-4) in the form of money or property (but not services).

(ii) Exclusion of unusual grants. (A) For purposes of applying the 2 percent limitation described in paragraph (f)(6)(i) of this section to determine whether the 33⅓ percent support test or the 10 percent support limitation in paragraph (f)(3)(i) of this section is satisfied, one or more contributions may be excluded from both the numerator and the denominator of the applicable support fraction if such contributions meet the requirements of paragraph (f)(6)(iii) of this section. The exclusion provided by this paragraph (f)(6)(ii) is generally intended to apply to substantial contributions or bequests from disinterested parties, which contributions or bequests—

(1) Are attracted by reason of the publicly supported nature of the organization;

(2) Are unusual or unexpected with respect to the amount thereof; and

(3) Would, by reason of their size, adversely affect the status of the organization as normally being publicly supported for the applicable period described in paragraph (f)(4) of this section.

(B) In the case of a grant (as defined in § 1.509(a)-3(g)) that meets the requirements of this paragraph (f)(6)(ii), if the terms of the granting instrument (whether executed before or after 1969) require that the funds be paid to the recipient organization over a period of years, the amount received by the organization each year pursuant to the terms of such grant may be excluded for such year. However, no item of gross investment income may be excluded under this paragraph (f)(6). The provisions of this paragraph (f)(6) shall apply to exclude unusual grants made during any of the applicable periods described in paragraph (f)(4) or (f)(6) of this section. See paragraph (f)(6)(iv) of this section as to reliance by a grantee organization upon an unusual grant ruling under this paragraph (f)(6).

(iii) Determining factors. In determining whether a particular contribution may be excluded under paragraph (f)(6)(ii) of this section all pertinent facts and circumstances will be taken into consideration. No single factor will necessarily be determinative. For some of the factors similar to the factors to be considered, see § 1.509(a)-3T(c)(4).

(iv) Grantors and contributors. Prior to the making of any grant or contribution that will allegedly meet the requirements for exclusion under paragraph (f)(6)(ii) of this section, a potential grantee organization may request a determination whether such grant or contribution may be so excluded. Requests for such determination may be filed by the grantee organization. The issuance of such determination will be at the sole discretion of the Commissioner. The organization must submit all information necessary to make a determination on the factors referred to in paragraph (f)(6)(iii) of this section. If a favorable ruling is issued, such ruling may be relied upon by the grantor or contributor of the particular contribution in question for purposes of sections 170, 507, 545(b)(2), 642(c), 4942, 4945, 2055, 2106(a)(2), and 2522 and by the grantee organization for purposes of paragraph (f)(6)(ii) of this section.

(v) Grants from public charities. Pursuant to paragraph (f)(6)(i) of this section, contributions received from a governmental unit or from a section 170(b)(1)(A)(vi) organization are not subject to the 2 percent limitation described in paragraph (f)(6)(i) of this section unless such contributions represent amounts which have been expressly or impliedly earmarked by a donor to such governmental unit or section 170(b)(1)(A)(vi) organization as being for, or for the benefit of, the particular organization claiming section 170(b)(1)(A)(vi) status. See § 1.509(a)-3(j)(3) for examples illustrating the rules of this paragraph (f)(6)(v).

(7) Definition of support; special rules and meaning of terms. (i) Definition of support. For purposes of this paragraph (f)(7), the term "support" shall be as defined in sec-

tion 509(d) (without regard to section 509(d)(2)). The term "support" does not include—

(A) Any amounts received from the exercise or performance by an organization of its charitable, educational, or other purpose or function constituting the basis for its exemption under section 501(a). In general, such amounts include amounts received from any activity the conduct of which is substantially related to the furtherance of such purpose or function (other than through the production of income); or

(B) Contributions of services for which a deduction is not allowable.

(ii) For purposes of the 33⅓ percent support test and the 10 percent support limitation in paragraph (f)(3)(i) of this section, all amounts received that are described in paragraphs (f)(7)(i)(A) or (B) of this section are to be excluded from both the numerator and the denominator of the fractions determining compliance with such tests, except as provided in paragraph (f)(7)(iii) of this section.

(iii) Organizations dependent primarily on gross receipts from related activities. (A) Notwithstanding the provisions of paragraph (f)(7)(i) of this section, an organization will not be treated as satisfying the 33⅓ percent support test or the 10 percent support limitation in paragraph (f)(3)(i) of this section if it receives—

(1) Almost all of its support (as defined in section 509(d)) from gross receipts from related activities; and

(2) An insignificant amount of its support from governmental units (without regard to amounts referred to in paragraph (f)(7)(i)(A) of this section) and contributions made directly or indirectly by the general public.

(B) Example. The application of this paragraph (f)(7)(iii) may be illustrated by the following example:

Example. Z, an organization described in section 501(c)(3), is controlled by A, its president. Z received $500,000 during the period consisting of the current taxable year and the four immediately preceding taxable years under a contract with the Department of Transportation, pursuant to which Z has engaged in research to improve a particular vehicle used primarily by the Federal government. During this same period, the only other support received by Z consisted of $5,000 in small contributions primarily from Z's employees and business associates. The $500,000 amount constitutes support under sections 509(d)(2) and 509(a)(2)(A). Under these circumstances, Z meets the conditions of paragraphs (f)(7)(iii)(A)(1) and (2) of this section and will not be treated as meeting the requirements of either the 33⅓ percent support test or the facts and circumstances test. As to the rules applicable to organizations that fail to qualify under section 170(b)(1)(A)(vi) because of the provisions of this paragraph (f)(7)(ii), see section 509(a)(2) and the accompanying regulations. For the distinction between gross receipts (as referred to in section 509(d)(2)) and gross investment income (as referred to in section 509(d)(4)), see § 1.509(a)-3(m).

(iv) Membership fees. For purposes of this paragraph (f)(7), the term support shall include "membership fees" within the meaning of § 1.509(a)-3(h) (that is, if the basic purpose for making a payment is to provide support for the organization rather than to purchase admissions, merchandise, services, or the use of facilities).

(8) Support from a governmental unit. (i) For purposes of the 33⅓ percent support test and the 10 percent support limitation described in paragraph (f)(3)(i) of this section, the term support from a governmental unit includes any amounts received from a governmental unit, including donations or contributions and amounts received in connection with a contract entered into with a governmental unit for the performance of services or in connection with a government research grant. However, such amounts will not constitute support from a governmental unit for such purposes if they constitute amounts received from the exercise or performance of the organization's exempt functions as provided in paragraph (f)(7)(i)(A) of this section.

(ii) For purposes of paragraph (f)(8)(i) of this section, any amount paid by a governmental unit to an organization is not to be treated as received from the exercise or performance of its charitable, educational, or other purpose or function constituting the basis for its exemption under section 501(a) (within the meaning of paragraph (f)(7)(i)(A) of this section) if the purpose of the payment is primarily to enable the organization to provide a service to, or maintain a facility for, the direct benefit of the public (regardless of whether part of the expense of providing such service or facility is paid for by the public), rather than to serve the direct and immediate needs of the payor. For example—

(A) Amounts paid for the maintenance of library facilities which are open to the public;

(B) Amounts paid under government programs to nursing homes or homes for the aged in order to provide health care or domiciliary services to residents of such facilities; and

(C) Amounts paid to child placement or child guidance organizations under government programs for services rendered to children in the community, are considered payments the purpose of which is primarily to enable the recipient organization to provide a service or maintain a facility for the direct benefit of the public, rather than to serve the direct and immediate needs of the payor. Furthermore, any amount received from a governmental unit under circumstances such that the amount would be treated as a "grant" within the meaning of § 1.509(a)-3(g) will generally constitute "support from a governmental unit" described in this paragraph (f)(8), rather than an amount described in paragraph (f)(7)(i)(A) of this section.

(9) Examples. The application of paragraphs (f)(1) through (8) of this section may be illustrated by the following examples:

Example (1). (i) M is recognized as an organization described in section 501(c)(3). For the years 2008 through 2012 (the applicable period with respect to the taxable year 2012 under paragraph (f)(4) of this section), M received support (as defined in paragraphs (f)(6) through (8) of this section) of $600,000 from the following sources:

Investment Income	$300,000
City R (a governmental unit described in section 170(c)(1))	40,000
United Fund (an organization described in section 170(b)(1)(A)(vi))	40,000
Contributions	220,000
Total Support	$600,000

(ii) With respect to the taxable year 2012, M's public support is computed as follows:

Support from a governmental unit described in section 170(c)(1)	40,000
Indirect contributions from the general public (United Fund)	40,000
Contributions by various donors (no one having made contributions that total in excess of $12,000--2 percent of total support)	50,000
Six contributions (each in excess of $12,000--2 percent total support) 6 x $12,000	72,000
	202,000

(iii) M's support from governmental units referred to in section 170(c)(1) and from direct and indirect contributions from the general public (as defined in paragraph (f)(6) of this section) with respect to the taxable year 2012 normally exceeds 33⅓ percent of M's total support ($202,000/$600,000 = 33.67 percent) for the applicable period (2008 through 2012). M meets the 33⅓ percent support test with respect to 2012 and is therefore publicly supported for the taxable years 2012 and 2013.

Example (2). N is recognized as an organization described in section 501(c)(3). It was created to maintain public gardens containing botanical specimens and displaying statuary and other art objects. The facilities, works of art, and a large endowment were all contributed by a single contributor. The members of the governing body of the organization are unrelated to its creator. The gardens are open to the public without charge and attract a substantial number of visitors each year. For the current taxable year and the four taxable years immediately preceding the current taxable year, 95 percent of the organization's total support was received from investment income from its original endowment. N also maintains a membership society that is supported by members of the general public who wish to contribute to the upkeep of the gardens by paying a small annual membership fee. Over the 5-year period in question, these fees from the general public constituted the remaining 5 percent of the organization's total support for such period. Under these circumstances, N does not meet the 33⅓ percent support test for its current taxable year. Furthermore, because only 5 percent of its total support is, with respect to the current taxable year, normally received from the general public, N does not satisfy the 10 percent support limitation described in paragraph (f)(3)(i) of this section and therefore does not qualify as publicly supported under the facts and circumstances test. Because N has failed to satisfy the 10 percent support limitation under paragraph (f)(3)(i) of this section, none of the other requirements or factors set forth in paragraphs (f)(3)(iii)(A) through (E) of this section can be considered in determining whether N qualifies as a publicly supported organization. For its current taxable year, N therefore is not an organization described in section 170(b)(1)(A)(vi).

Example (3). (i) O, an art museum, is recognized as an organization described in section 501(c)(3). In 1930, O was founded in S City by the members of a single family to collect, preserve, interpret, and display to the public important works of art. O is governed by a Board of Trustees that originally consisted almost entirely of members of the founding family. However, since 1945, members of the founding family or persons standing in a relationship to the members of such family described in section 4946(a)(1)(C) through (G) have annually constituted less than one-fifth of the Board of Trustees. The remaining board members are citizens of S City from a variety of professions and occupations who represent the interests and views of the people of S City in the activities carried on by the organization rather than the personal or private interests of the founding family. O solicits contributions from the general public and for the current taxable year and each of the four taxable years immediately preceding the current taxable year, O has received total contributions (in small sums of less than $100, none of which exceeds 2 percent of O's total support for such period) in excess of $10,000. These contributions from the general public (as defined in paragraph (f)(6) of this section) represent 25 percent of the organization's total support for such 5-year period. For this same period, investment income from several large endowment funds has constituted 75 percent of O's total support. O expends substantially all of its annual income for its exempt purposes and thus depends upon the funds it annually solicits from the public as well as its investment income in order to carry out its activities on a normal and continuing basis and to acquire new works of art. O has, for the entire period of its existence, been open to the public and more than 300,000 people (from S City and elsewhere) have visited the museum in each of the current taxable year and the four most recent taxable years.

(ii) Under these circumstances, O does not meet the 33⅓ percent support test for its current year because it has received only 25 percent of its total support for the applicable 5-year period from the general public. However, under the facts set forth above, O has met the 10 percent support limitation under paragraph (f)(3)(i) of this section, as well as the requirements of paragraph (f)(3)(ii) of this section. Under all of the facts set forth in this example, O is considered as meeting the requirements of the facts and circumstances test on the basis of satisfying paragraphs (f)(3)(i) and (ii) of this section and the factors set forth in paragraphs (f)(3)(iii)(A) through (D) of this section. O is therefore publicly supported for its current taxable year and the immediately succeeding taxable year.

Example (4). (i) In 1960, the P Philharmonic Orchestra was organized in T City through the combined efforts of a local music society and a local women's club to present to the public a wide variety of musical programs intended to foster music appreciation in the community. P is recognized as an organization described in section 501(c)(3). The orchestra is composed of professional musicians who are paid by the association. Twelve performances open to the public are scheduled each year. A small admission fee is charged for each of these performances. In addition, several performances are staged annually without charge. During the current taxable year and the four taxable years immediately preceding the current taxable year, P has received separate contributions of $200,000 each from A and B (not members of a single family) and support of $120,000 from the T Community Chest, a public federated fundraising organization operating in T City. P depends on these funds in order to carry out its activities and will continue to depend on contributions of this type to be made in the future. P has also begun a fundraising campaign in an attempt to expand its activities for the coming years. P is governed by a Board of Directors comprised of 5 individuals. A faculty member of a local college, the president of a local music society, the head of a local banking institution, a prominent doctor, and a member of the governing body of the local chamber of commerce currently serve on P's Board and represent the interests and views of the community in the activities carried on by P.

(ii) With respect to P's current taxable year, P's sources of support are computed on the basis of the current taxable year and the four taxable years immediately preceding the current taxable year, as follows:

Contributions	$520,000
Receipts from performances	100,000
Total support	620,000
Less:	
Receipts from performances (excluded under paragraph (f)(7)(i)(A) of this section)	100,000
Total support for purposes of paragraphs (f)(2) and (f)(3)(i) of this section	S520,000

(iii) For purposes of paragraphs (f)(2) and (f)(3)(i) of this section, P's support is computed as follows:

T Community Chest (indirect support from the general public)	120,000
Two contributions (each in excess of $10,400--2 percent of total support) 2 x $10,400	20,800
Total	140,800

(iv) P's support from the direct and indirect contributions from the general public does not meet the 33⅓ percent support test ($140,800/$520,000 = 27 percent of total support). However, because P receives 27 percent of its total support from the general public, it meets the 10 percent support limitation under paragraph (f)(3)(i) of this section. P also meets the requirements of paragraph (f)(3)(ii) of this section. As a result of satisfying these requirements and the factors set forth in paragraphs (f)(3)(iii)(A) through (D) of this section, P is considered to meet the facts and circumstances test and therefore qualifies as a publicly supported organization under paragraph (f)(1) of this section for its current taxable year and the immediately succeeding taxable year.

Example (5). (i) Q is recognized as an organization described in section 501(c)(3). It is a philanthropic organization founded in 1965 by C for the purpose of making annual contributions to worthy charities. C created Q as a charitable trust by the transfer of appreciated securities worth $500,000 to Q. Pursuant to the trust agreement, C and two other members of his family are the sole trustees of Q and are vested with the right to appoint successor trustees. In each of the current taxable year and the four taxable years immediately preceding the current taxable year, Q received $15,000 in investment income from its original endowment. Each year Q makes a solicitation for funds by operating a charity ball at C's residence. Guests are invited and requested to make contributions of $100 per couple. During the 5-year period at issue, $15,000 was received from the proceeds of these events. C and his family have also made contributions to Q of $25,000 over the 5-year period at issue. Q makes disbursements each year of substantially all of its net income to the public charities chosen by the trustees.

(ii) Q's sources of support for the current taxable year and the four taxable years immediately preceding the current taxable year as follows:

Investment income	$ 60,000
Contributions	40,000
Total support	$100,000

(iii) For purposes of paragraphs (f)(2) and (f)(3)(i) of this section, Q's support is computed as follows:

Contributions from the general public	$15,000
One contribution (in excess of $2,000--2 percent of total support) 1 x $2,000	2,000
Total	$17,000

(iv) Q's support from the general public does not meet the 33⅓ percent support test ($17,000/$100,000 = 17 percent of total support). Thus, Q's classification as a "publicly supported" organization depends on whether it meets the requirements of the facts and circumstances test. Even though it satisfies the 10 percent support limitation under paragraph (f)(3)(i) of this section, its method of solicitation makes it questionable whether Q satisfies the requirements of paragraph (f)(3)(ii) of this section. Because of its method of operating, Q also has a greater burden of establishing its publicly supported nature under paragraph (f)(3)(iii)(A) of this section. Based upon the foregoing and upon Q's failure to receive favorable consideration under the remaining factors set forth in paragraphs (f)(3)(iii)(B), (C) and (D) of this section, Q does not satisfy the facts and circumstances test.

(10) Community trust; introduction. Community trusts have often been established to attract large contributions of a capital or endowment nature for the benefit of a particular community or area, and often such contributions have come initially from a small number of donors. While the community trust generally has a governing body comprised of representatives of the particular community or area, its contributions are often received and maintained in the form of separate trusts or funds, which are subject to varying degrees of control by the governing body. To qualify as a "publicly supported" organization, a community trust must meet the 33⅓ percent support test, or, if it cannot meet that test, be organized and operated so as to attract new and additional public or governmental support on a continuous basis sufficient to meet the facts and circumstances test. Such facts and circumstances test includes a requirement of attraction of public support in paragraph (f)(3)(ii) of this section which, as applied to community trusts, generally will be satisfied if they seek gifts and bequests from a wide range of potential donors in the community or area served, through banks or trust companies, through attorneys or other professional persons, or in other appropriate ways that call attention to the community trust as a potential recipient of gifts and bequests made for the benefit of the community or area served. A community trust is not required to engage in periodic, community-wide, fundraising campaigns directed toward attracting a large number of small contributions in a manner similar to campaigns conducted by a community chest or united fund. Paragraph (f)(11) of this section provides rules for determining the extent to which separate trusts or funds may be treated as component parts of a community trust, fund or foundation (herein collectively referred to as a "community trust", and sometimes referred to as an "organization") for purposes of meeting the requirements of this paragraph for classification as a publicly supported organization. Paragraph (f)(12) of this section contains rules for trusts or funds that are prevented from qualifying as component parts of a community trust by paragraph (f)(11) of this section.

(11) Community trusts; requirements for treatment as a single entity. (i) General rule. For purposes of sections 170, 501, 507, 508, 509, and Chapter 42, any organization that meets the requirements contained in paragraphs (f)(11)(iii) through (iv) of this section will be treated as a single entity, rather than as an aggregation of separate funds, and except as otherwise provided, all funds associated with such organization (whether a trust, not-for-profit corporation, unincorporated association, or a combination thereof) which meet the requirements of paragraph (f)(11)(ii) of this section will be treated as component parts of such organization.

(ii) Component part of a community trust. In order to be treated as a component part of a community trust referred to in this paragraph (f)(11) (rather than as a separate trust or not-for-profit corporation or association), a trust or fund:

(A) Must be created by a gift, bequest, legacy, devise, or other transfer to a community trust which is treated as a single entity under this paragraph (f)(11); and

(B) May not be directly or indirectly subjected by the transferor to any material restriction or condition (within the meaning of § 1.507-2T(a)(7)) with respect to the transferred assets. For purposes of this paragraph (f)(11)(ii)(B), if the transferor is not a private foundation, the provisions of § 1.507-2T(a)(7) shall be applied to the trust or fund as if the transferor were a private foundation established and funded by the person establishing the trust or fund and such foundation transferred all its assets to the trust or fund. Any transfer made to a fund or trust which is treated as a component part of a community trust under this paragraph (f)(11)(ii) will be treated as a transfer made "to" a "publicly supported" community trust for purposes of section 170(b)(1)(A) and 507(b)(1)(A) if such community trust meets the requirements of section 170(b)(1)(A)(vi) as a "publicly supported" organization at the time of the transfer, except as provided in paragraph (f)(4)(v)(B) of this section or § 1.508-1(b)(4) and (6) (relating, generally, to reliance by grantors and contributors). See also paragraphs (f)(12)(ii) and (iii) of this section for special provisions relating to split-interest trusts and certain private foundations described in section 170(b)(1)(F)(iii).

(iii) Name. The organization must be commonly known as a community trust, fund, foundation or other similar name conveying the concept of a capital or endowment fund to support charitable activities (within the meaning of section 170(c)(1) or (2)(B)) in the community or area it serves.

(iv) Common instrument. All funds of the organization must be subject to a common governing instrument or a master trust or agency agreement (herein referred to as the "governing instrument"), which may be embodied in a single document or several documents containing common language. Language in an instrument of transfer to the community trust making a fund subject to the community trust's governing instrument or master trust or agency agreement will satisfy the requirements of this paragraph (f)(11)(iv). In addition, if a community trust adopts a new governing instrument (or creates a corporation) to put into effect new provisions (applying to future transfers to the community trust), the adoption of such new governing instrument (or creation of a corporation with a governing instrument) which contains common language with the existing governing instrument shall not preclude the community trust from meeting the requirements of this paragraph (f)(11)(iv).

(v) Common governing body. (A) The organization must have a common governing body or distribution committee (herein referred to as the "governing body") which either directs or, in the case of a fund designated for specified beneficiaries, monitors the distribution of all of the funds exclusively for charitable purposes (within the meaning of section 170(c)(1) or (2)(B)). For purposes of this paragraph (f)(11)(v), a fund is designated for specified beneficiaries only if no person is left with the discretion to direct the distribution of the fund.

(B) Powers of modification and removal. The fact that the exercise of any power described in this paragraph (f)(11)(v)(B) is reviewable by an appropriate State authority will not preclude the community trust from meeting the requirements of this paragraph (f)(11)(v)(B). Except as provided in paragraph (f)(11)(v)(C) of this section, the governing body must have the power in the governing instrument, the instrument of transfer, the resolutions or bylaws of the governing body, a written agreement, or otherwise—

(1) To modify any restriction or condition on the distribution of funds for any specified charitable purposes or to specified organizations if in the sole judgment of the governing body (without the necessity of the approval of any participating trustee, custodian, or agent), such restriction or condition becomes, in effect, unnecessary, incapable of fulfillment, or inconsistent with the charitable needs of the community or area served;

(2) To replace any participating trustee, custodian, or agent for breach of fiduciary duty under State law; and

(3) To replace any participating trustee, custodian, or agent for failure to produce a reasonable (as determined by the governing body) return of net income (within the meaning of paragraph (f)(11)(v)(F) of this section) over a reasonable period of time (as determined by the governing body).

(C) Transitional rule. (1) Notwithstanding paragraph (f)(11)(v)(B) of this section, if a community trust meets the requirements of paragraph (f)(11)(v)(C)(3) of this section, then in the case of any instrument of transfer which is executed before July 19, 1977, and is not revoked or amended thereafter (with respect to any dispositive provision affecting the transfer to the community trust), and in the case of any instrument of transfer which is irrevocable on January 19, 1982, the governing body must have the power to cause proceedings to be instituted (by request to the appropriate State authority):

(i) To modify any restriction or condition on the distribution of funds for any specified charitable purposes or to specified organizations if in the judgment of the governing body such restriction or condition becomes, in effect, unnecessary, incapable of fulfillment, or inconsistent with the charitable needs of the community or area served; and

(ii) To remove any participating trustee, custodian, or agent for breach of fiduciary duty under State law.

(2) The necessity for the governing body to obtain the approval of a participating trustee to exercise the powers described in paragraph (f)(11)(v)(C)(1) of this section shall be treated as not preventing the governing body from having such power, unless (and until) such approval has been (or is) requested by the governing body and has been (or is) denied.

(3) Paragraph (f)(11)(v)(C)(1) of this section shall not apply unless the community trust meets the requirements of paragraph (f)(11)(v)(B) of this section, with respect to funds other than those under instruments of transfer described in the first sentence of such paragraph (f)(11)(v)(C)(1) of this section, by January 19, 1978, or such later date as the Commissioner may provide for such community trust, and unless the community trust does not, once it so complies, thereafter solicit for funds that will not qualify under the requirements of paragraph (f)(11)(v)(B) of this section.

(D) Inconsistent State law. (1) For purposes of paragraphs (f)(11)(v)(B)(1), (2), or (3), (f)(11)(v)(C)(1)(i) or (ii) or (f)(11)(v)(E) of this section, if a power described in such a provision is inconsistent with State law even if such power were expressly granted to the governing body by the governing instrument and were accepted without limitation under an instrument of transfer, then the community trust will be treated as meeting the requirements of such a provision if it meets such requirements to the fullest extent possible consistent with State law (if such power is or had been so expressly granted).

(2) For example, if, under the conditions of paragraph (f)(11)(v)(D)(1) of this section, the power to modify is inconsistent with State law, but the power to institute proceedings to modify, if so expressly granted, would be consistent with State law, the community trust will be treated as meeting such requirements to the fullest extent possible if the governing body has the power (in the governing instrument or otherwise) to institute proceedings to modify a condition or restriction. On the other hand, if in such a case the community trust has only the power to cause proceedings to be instituted to modify a condition or restriction, it will not be treated as meeting such requirements to the fullest extent possible.

(3) In addition, if, for example, under the conditions of paragraph (f)(11)(v)(D)(1) of this section, the power to modify and the power to institute proceedings to modify a condition or restriction is inconsistent with State law, but the power to cause such proceedings to be instituted would be consistent with State law, if it were expressly granted in the governing instrument and if the approval of the State Attorney General were obtained, then the community trust will be treated as meeting such requirements to the fullest extent possible if it has the power (in the governing instrument or otherwise) to cause such proceedings to be instituted, even if such proceedings can be instituted only with the approval of the State Attorney General.

(E) Exercise of powers. The governing body shall (by resolution or otherwise) commit itself to exercise the powers described in paragraphs (f)(11)(v)(B), (C) and (D) of this section in the best interests of the community trust. The governing body will be considered not to be so committed where it has grounds to exercise such a power and fails to exercise it by taking appropriate action. Such appropriate action may include, for example, consulting with the appropriate State authority prior to taking action to replace a participating trustee.

(F) Reasonable return. In addition to the requirements of paragraphs (f)(11)(v)(B), (C), (D) or (E) of this section, the governing body shall (by resolution or otherwise) commit itself to obtain information and take other appropriate steps with the view to seeing that each participating trustee, custodian, or agent, with respect to each restricted trust or fund that is, and with respect to the aggregate of the unrestricted trusts or funds that are, a component part of the community trust, administers such trust or fund in accordance with the terms of its governing instrument and accepted standards of fiduciary conduct to produce a reasonable return of net income (or appreciation where not inconsistent with the community trust's need for current income), with due regard to safety of principal, in furtherance of the exempt purposes of the community trust (except for assets held for the active conduct of the community trust's exempt activities). In the case of a low return of net income (and, where appropriate, appreciation), the Internal Revenue Service will examine carefully whether the governing body has, in fact, committed itself to take the appropriate steps. For purposes of this paragraph (f)(11)(v)(F), any income that has been designated by the donor of the gift or bequest to which such income is attributable as being available only for the use or benefit of a broad charitable purpose, such as the encouragement of higher education or the promotion of better health care in the community, will be treated as unrestricted. However, any income that has been designated for the use or benefit of a named charitable organization or agency or for the use or benefit of a particular class of charitable organizations or agencies, the members of which are readily ascertainable and are less than five in number, will be treated as restricted.

(vi) Common reports. The organization must prepare periodic financial reports treating all of the funds which are held by the community trust, either directly or in component parts, as funds of the organization.

(12) Community trusts; treatment of trusts and not-for-profit corporations and associations not included as components. (i) For purposes of sections 170, 501, 507, 508, 509 and Chapter 42, any trust or not-for-profit corporation or association that is alleged to be a component part of a community trust, but that fails to meet the requirements of paragraph (f)(11)(ii) of this section, shall not be treated as a component part of a community trust and, if a trust, shall be treated as a separate trust and be subject to the provisions of section 501 or section 4947(a)(1) or (2), as the case may be. If such organization is a not-for-profit corporation or association, it will be treated as a separate entity, and, if it is described in section 501(c)(3), it will be treated as a private foundation unless it is described in section 509(a)(1), (2), (3), or (4). In the case of a fund that is ultimately treated as not being a component part of a community trust pursuant to this paragraph (f)(12), if the Forms 990 filed annually by the community trust included financial information with respect to such fund and treated such fund in the same manner as other component parts thereof, such returns filed by the community trust prior to the taxable year in which the Commissioner notifies such fund that it will not be treated as a component part will be treated as its separate return for purpose of Subchapter A of Chapter 61 of Subtitle F, and the first such return filed by the community trust will be treated as the notification required of the separate entity for purposes of section 508(a).

(ii) If a transfer is made in trust to a community trust to make income or other payments for a period of a life or lives in being or a term of years to any individual or for any noncharitable purpose, followed by payments to or for the use of the community trust (such as in the case of a charitable remainder annuity trust or a charitable remainder unitrust described in section 664 or a pooled income fund described in section 642(c)(5)), such trust will be treated as a component part of the community trust upon the termination of all intervening noncharitable interests and rights to the actual possession or enjoyment of the property if such trust satisfies the requirements of paragraph (f)(11) of this section at such time. Until such time, the trust will be treated as a separate trust. If a transfer is made in trust to a community trust to make income or other payments to or for the use of the community trust, followed by payments to any individual or for any noncharitable purpose, such trust will be treated as a separate trust rather than as a component part of the community trust. See section 4947(a)(2) and the regulations relating to section 4947(a)(2) for the treatment of such split-interest trusts. The provisions of this paragraph (f)(12)(ii) provide rules only for determining when a charitable remainder trust or pooled income fund may be treated as a component part of a community trust and are not intended to preclude a community trust from maintaining a charitable remainder trust or pooled income fund. For purposes of grantors and contributors, a pooled income fund of a publicly supported community trust shall be treated no differently than a pooled income fund of any other publicly supported organization.

(iii) An organization described in section 170(b)(1)(F)(iii) will not ordinarily satisfy the requirements of paragraph (f)(11)(ii) of this section because of the unqualified right of the donor to designate the recipients of the income and principal of the trust. Such organization will therefore ordinarily be treated as other than a component part of a community trust under paragraph (f)(12)(i) of this section. However, see section 170(b)(1)(F)(iii) and the regulations relating to section 170(b)(1)(F)(iii) with respect to the treatment of contributions to such organizations.

(13) Method of accounting. For purposes of section 170(b)(1)(A)(vi), an organization's support will be determined under the method of accounting on the basis of which the organization regularly computes its income in keeping its books under section 446. For example, if a grantor makes a grant to an organization payable over a term of years, such grant will be includible in the support fraction of the grantee organization under the method of accounting on the basis of which the grantee organization regularly computes its income in keeping its books under section 446.

(14) Transition rules. (i) An organization that received an advance ruling, that expires on or after June 9, 2008, that it will be treated as an organization described in sections 170(b)(1)(A)(vi) and 509(a)(1) or in section 509(a)(2) will be treated as meeting the requirements of paragraph (f)(4)(v) of this section for the first five taxable years of its existence as a section 501(c)(3) organization unless the Internal Revenue Service issued the organization a proposed determination prior to September 9, 2008, that the organization is not described in sections 170(b)(1)(A)(vi) and 509(a)(1) or in section 509(a)(2).

(ii) Paragraph (f)(4)(v) of this section shall not apply to an organization that received an advance ruling that expired prior to June 9, 2008, and that did not timely file with the Internal Revenue Service the required information to establish that it is an organization described in sections 170(b)(1)(A)(vi) and 509(a)(1) or in section 509(a)(2).

(iii) An organization that fails to meet a public support test for its first taxable year beginning on or after January 1, 2008, under the regulations in this section may use the prior test set forth in § 1.170A-9(e)(4)(i) and (ii) or § 1.509(a)-3(c)(1) as in effect before September 9, 2008, (as contained in 26 CFR part 1 revised April 1, 2008) to determine whether the organization may be publicly supported for its 2008 taxable year based on its satisfaction of a public support test for taxable year 2007, computed over the period 2003 through 2006.

(ii) Examples. The application of this paragraph (f)(14) may be illustrated by the following examples:

Example (1). (i) Organization X was formed in January 2004 and uses a June 30 taxable year. Organization X received an advance ruling letter that it is recognized as an organization described in section 501(c)(3) effective as of the date of its formation and that it is treated as a public charity under sections 170(b)(1)(A)(vi) and 509(a)(1) during the five-year advance ruling period that will end on June 30, 2008. This date is within 90 days before September 9, 2008.

(ii) Under the transition rule, Organization X is a public charity described in sections 170(b)(1)(A)(vi) and 509(a)(1) for the taxable years ending June 30, 2004, through June 30, 2008. Organization X does not need to establish within 90 days after June 30, 2008, that it met a public support test under § 1.170A-9(e) or § 1.509(a)-3, as in effect prior September 9, 2008, (as contained in 26 CFR part 1 revised April 1, 2008), for its advance ruling period.

(iii) Organization X can qualify as a public charity beginning with the taxable year ending June 30, 2009, if Organization X can meet the requirements of paragraphs (f)(4)(i) or (ii) of this section or § 1.509(a)-3T(c)(1) for the taxable years ending June 30, 2005, through June 30, 2009, or for the taxable years ending June 30, 2004, through June 30, 2008. In addition, for its taxable year ending June 30, 2009, Organization X may qualify as a public charity by availing itself of the transition rule contained in paragraph (f)(14)(iii) of this section, which looks to support received by X in the taxable years ending June 30, 2004, through June 30, 2007.

Example (2). (i) Organization Y was formed in January 2000, and uses a December 31 taxable year. Organization Y received a final determination that it was recognized as tax-exempt under section 501(c)(3) and as a public charity prior to September 9, 2008.

(ii) For taxable year 2008, Organization Y will qualify as publicly supported if it meets the requirements under either paragraphs (f)(4)(i) or (ii) of this section or § 1.509(a)-3T(c)(1) for the five-year period January 1, 2004, through December 31, 2008. Organization Y will also qualify as publicly supported for taxable year 2008 if it meets the requirements under either § 1.170A-9(e)(4)(i) or (ii) or § 1.509(a)-3(c)(1) as in effect prior to September 9, 2008, (as contained in 26 CFR part 1 revised April 1, 2008) for taxable year 2007, using the four-year period from January 1, 2003, through December 31, 2006.

(g) through (j) [Reserved]. For further guidance, see § 1.170A-9(g) through (j).

(k) Effective/applicability date. *(1) Effective date.* These regulations are effective on September 9, 2008.

(2) Applicability date. The regulations in paragraph (f) of this section shall apply to tax years beginning on or after January 1, 2008.

(3) Expiration date. The applicability of this section expires on September 8, 2011.

T.D. 9423, 9/8/2008.

§ 1.170A-10 Charitable contributions carryovers of individuals.

Caution: The Treasury has not yet amended Reg § 1.170A-10 to reflect changes made by P.L. 100-647, P.L. 100-203, P.L. 99-514, P.L. 98-369, P.L. 97-34.

(a) In general. *(1)* Section 170(d)(1), relating to carryover of charitable contributions in excess of 50 percent of contribution base, and section 170(b)(1)(D)(ii), relating to carryover of charitable contributions in excess of 30 percent of contribution base, provide for excess charitable contributions carryovers by individuals of charitable contributions to section 170(b)(1)(A) organizations described in § 1.170A-9. These carryovers shall be determined as provided in paragraphs (b) and (c) of this section. No excess charitable contributions carryover shall be allowed with respect to contributions "for the use of," rather than "to," section 170(b)(1)(A) organizations or with respect to contributions "to" or "for the use of" organizations which are not section 170(b)(1)(A) organizations. See § 1.170A-8(a)(2) for definitions of "to" or "for the use of" a charitable organization.

(2) The carryover provisions apply with respect to contributions made during a taxable year in excess of the applicable percentage limitation even though the taxpayer elects under section 144 to take the standard deduction in that year instead of itemizing the deduction allowable in computing taxable income for that year.

(3) For provisions requiring a reduction of the excess charitable contribution computed under paragraph (b)(1) or (c)(1) of this section when there is a net operating loss car-

ryover to the taxable year, see paragraph (d)(1) of this section.

(4) The provisions of section 170(b)(1)(D)(ii) and (d)(1) and this section do not apply to contributions by an estate; nor do they apply to a trust unless the trust is a private foundation which, pursuant to § 1.642(c)-4, is allowed a deduction under section 170 subject to the provisions applicable to individuals.

(b) 50-percent charitable contributions carryover of individuals. *(1) Computations of excess of charitable contributions made in a contribution year.* Under section 170(d)(1), subject to certain conditions and limitations, the excess of—

(i) The amount of the charitable contributions made by an individual in a taxable year (hereinafter in this paragraph referred to as the "contribution year") to section 170(b)(1)(A) organizations described in § 1.170A-9, over

(ii) 50 percent of his contribution base, as defined in section 170(b)(1)(F), for such contribution year,

shall be treated as a charitable contribution paid by him to a section 170(b)(1)(A) organization in each of the 5 taxable years immediately succeeding the contribution year in order of time. However, such excess to the extent it consists of contributions of 30-percent capital gain property, as defined in § 1.170A-8(d)(3), shall be subject to the rules of section 170(b)(1)(D)(ii) and paragraph (c) of this section in the years to which it is carried over. A charitable contribution made in a taxable year beginning before January 1, 1970, to a section 170(b)(1)(A) organization and carried over to a taxable year beginning after December 31, 1969, under section 170(b)(5) (before its amendment by the Tax Reform Act of 1969) shall be treated in such taxable year beginning after December 31, 1969, as a charitable contribution of cash subject to the limitations of this paragraph, whether or not such carryover consists of contributions of 30-percent capital gain property or of ordinary income property described in § 1.170A-4(b)(1). For purposes of applying this paragraph and paragraph (c) of this section such a carryover from a taxable year beginning before January 1, 1970, which is so treated as paid to a section 170(b)(1)(A) organization in a taxable year beginning after December 31, 1969, shall be treated as paid to such an organization under section 170(d)(1) and this section. The provisions of this subparagraph may be illustrated by the following examples:

Example (1). Assume that H and W (husband and wife) have a contribution base for 1970 of $50,000 and for 1971 of $40,000 and file a joint return for each year. Assume further that in 1970 they make a charitable contribution in cash of $26,500 to a church and $1,000 to X (not a section 170(b)(1)(A) organization) and in 1971 they make a charitable contribution in cash of $19,000 to a church and $600 to X. They may claim a charitable contributions deduction of $25,000 in 1970, and the excess of $26,500 (contribution to the church) over $25,000 (50 percent of contribution base), or $1,500, constitutes a charitable contributions carryover which shall be treated as a charitable contribution paid by them to a section 170(b)(1)(A) organization in each of the 5 succeeding taxable years in order of time. No carryover is allowed with respect to the $1,000 contribution made to X in 1970. Since 50 percent of their contribution base for 1971 ($20,000) exceeds the charitable contributions of $19,000 made by them in 1971 to section 170(b)(1)(A) organizations (computed without regard to section 170(b)(1)(D)(ii) and (d)(1) and this section), the portion of the 1970 carryover equal to such excess of $1,000 ($20,000 minus $19,000) is treated, pursuant to the provisions of subparagraph (2) of this paragraph, as paid to a section 170(b)(1)(A) organization in 1971; the remaining $500 constitutes an unused charitable contributions carryover. No deduction for 1971, and no carryover, are allowed with respect to the $600 contribution made to X in 1971.

Example (2). Assume the same facts as in example (1) except that H and W have a contribution base for 1971 of $42,000. Since 50 percent of their contribution base for 1971 ($21,000) exceeds by $2,000 the charitable contribution of $19,000 made by them in 1971 to the section 170(b)(1)(A) organization (computed without regard to section 170(b)(1)(D)(ii) and (d)(1) and this section, the full amount of the 1970 carryover of $1,500 is treated, pursuant to the provisions of section 170(b)(1)(A) organization in 1971. They may also claim a charitable contribution of $500 ($21,000 − $20,500[$19,000 + $1,500]) with respect to the gift to X in 1971. No carryover is allowed with respect to the $100 ($600 − $500) of the contribution to X which is not deductible in 1971.

(2) Determination of amount treated as paid in taxable years succeeding contribution year. In applying the provisions of subparagraph (1) of this paragraph, the amount of the excess computed in accordance with the provisions of such subparagraph and paragraph (d)(1) of this section which is to be treated as paid in any one of the 5 taxable years immediately succeeding the contribution year to a section 170(b)(1)(A) organization shall not exceed the lesser of the amounts computed under subdivisions (i) to (iii), inclusive, of this subparagraph:

(i) The amount by which 50 percent of the taxpayer's contribution base for such succeeding taxable year exceeds the sum of—

(a) The charitable contributions actually made (computed without regard to the provisions of section 170(b)(1)(D)(ii) and (d)(1) and this section) by the taxpayer in such succeeding taxable year to section 170(b)(1)(A) organizations, and

(b) The charitable contributions, other than contributions of 30-percent capital gain property, made to section 170(b)(1)(A) organizations in taxable years preceding the contribution year which, pursuant to the provisions of section 170(d)(1) and this section, are treated as having been paid to a section 170(b)(1)(A) organization in such succeeding year.

(ii) In the case of the first taxable year succeeding the contribution year, the amount of the excess charitable contribution in the contribution year, computed under subparagraph (1) of this paragraph and paragraph (d)(1) of this section.

(iii) In the case of the second, third, fourth, and fifth taxable years succeeding the contribution year, the portion of the excess charitable contribution in the contribution year, computed under subparagraph (1) of this paragraph and paragraph (d)(1) of this section, which has not been treated as paid to a section 170(b)(1)(A) organization in a year intervening between the contribution year and such succeeding taxable year.

For purposes of applying subdivision (i)(a) of this subparagraph, the amount of charitable contributions of 30-percent capital gain property actually made in a taxable year succeeding the contribution year shall be determined by first applying the 30-percent limitation of section 170(b)(1)(D)(i) and paragraph (d) of § 1.170A-8. If a taxpayer, in any one of the 4 taxable years succeeding a contribution year, elects under section 144 to take the standard deduction instead of itemizing the deductions allowable in computing taxable income, there shall be treated as paid (but not allowable as a deduction) in such standard deduction year the lesser of the amounts determined under subdivisions (i) to (iii), inclusive, of this subparagraph. The provisions of this subparagraph may be illustrated by the following examples:

Example (1). Assume that B has a contribution base for 1970 of $20,000 and for 1971 of $30,000. Assume further that in 1970 B contributed $12,000 in cash to a church and in 1971 he contributed $13,500 in cash to the church. B may claim a charitable contributions deduction of $10,000 in 1970, and the excess of $12,000 (contribution to the church) over $10,000 (50 percent of B's contribution base), or $2,000, constitutes a charitable contributions carryover which shall be treated as a charitable contribution paid by B to a section 170(b)(1)(A) organization in the 5 taxable years succeeding 1970 in order of time. B may claim a charitable contributions deduction of $15,000 in 1971. Such $15,000 consists of the $13,500 contribution to the church in 1971 and $1,500 carried over from 1970 and treated as a charitable contribution paid to a section 170(b)(1)(A) organization in 1971. The $1,500 contribution treated as paid in 1971 is computed as follows:

1970 excess contributions		$ 2,000
50 percent of B's contribution base for 1971		15,000
Less:		
Contributions actually made in 1971 to section 170(b)(1)(A) organizations	$13,500	
Contributions made to section 170(b)(1)(A) organizations in taxable years prior to 1970 treated as having been paid in 1971	0	13,500
Balance		1,500
Amount of 1970 excess treated as paid in 1971—the lesser of $2,000 (1970 excess contributions) or $1,500 (excess of 50 percent of contribution base for 1971 ($15,000) over the sum of the section 170(b)(1)(A) contributions actually made in 1971 ($13,500) and the section 170(b)(1)(A) contributions made in years prior to 1970 treated as having been paid in 1971 ($0)		1,500

If the excess contributions made by B in 1970 had been $1,000 instead of $2,000, then, for purposes of this example, the amount of the 1970 excess treated as paid in 1971 would be $1,000 rather than $1,500.

Example (2). Assume the same facts as in example (1), and, in addition, that B has a contribution base for 1972 of $10,000 and for 1973 of $20,000. Assume further with respect to 1972 that B elects under section 144 to take the standard deduction in computing taxable income and that his actual contributions to section 170(b)(1)(A) organizations in that year are $300 in cash. Assume further with respect to 1973 that B itemizes his deductions, which include a $5,000 cash contribution to a church. B's deductions for 1972 are not increased by reason of the $500 available as a charitable contributions carryover from 1970 (excess) contributions made in 1970 ($2,000) less the amount of such excess treated as paid in 1971 ($1,500)), since B elected to take the standard deduction in 1972. However, for purposes of determining the amount of the excess charitable contributions made in 1970 which is available as a carryover to 1973, B is required to treat such $500 as a charitable contribution paid in 1972—the lesser of $500 or $4,700 (50 percent of contribution base ($5,000) over contributions actually made in 1972 to section 170(b)(1)(A) organizations ($300)). Therefore, even though the $5,000 contribution made by B in 1973 to a church does not amount to 50 percent of B's contribution base for 1973 (50 percent of $20,000), B may claim a charitable contributions deduction of only the $5,000 actually paid in 1973 since the entire excess charitable contribution made in 1970 ($2,000) has been treated as paid in 1971 ($1,500) and 1972 ($500).

Example (3). Assume the following factual situation for C who itemizes his deductions in computing taxable income for each of the years set forth in the example:

	1970	1971	1972	1973	1974
Contribution base	$10,000	$7,000	$15,000	$10,000	$9,000
Contributions of cash to section 170(b)(1)(A) organizations (no other contributions)	6,000	4,400	8,000	3,000	1,500
Allowable charitable contributions deductions com-puted without regard to carryover of contributions	5,000	3,500	7,500	3,000	1,500
Excess contributions for taxable year to be treated as paid in 5 succeeding taxable years	1,000	900	500	0	0

Since C's contributions in 1973 and 1974 to section 170(b)(1)(A) organizations are less than 50 percent of his contribution base for such years, the excess contributions for 1970, 1971, and 1972 are treated as having been paid to section 170(b)(1)(A) organizations in 1973 and 1974 as follows:

1973

Contribution year	Total excess	Less: Amount treated as paid in year prior to 1973	Available charitable contributions carryovers
1970	$1,000	0	$1,000
1971	900	0	900
1972	500	0	500
Total			2,400
50 percent of B's contribution base for 1973			$5,000
Less: Charitable contributions made in 1973 to section 170(b)(1)(A) organizations			3,000
			2,000

Amount of excess contributions treated as paid in 1973—lesser of $2,400 (available carryovers to 1973) or $2,000 (excess of 50 percent of contribution base ($5,000) over contributions actually made in 1973 to section 170(b)(1)(A) organizations ($3,000)	2,000

1974

Contribution year	Total excess	Less: Amount treated as paid in year prior to 1974	Available charitable contributions carryovers
1970	$1,000	$1,000	0
1971	900	900	0
1972	500	100	$ 400
1973	0	0	0
Total			400

50 percent of B's contribution base for 1974	$4,500
Less: Charitable contributions made in 1974 to section 170(b)(1)(A) organizations	1,500
	3,000
Amount of excess contributions treated as paid in 1974—the lesser of $400 (available carryovers to 1974) or $3,000 (excess of 50 percent of contribution base ($4,500) over contributions actually made in 1974 to section 170(b)(1)(A) organizations ($1,500))	400

(c) 30-percent charitable contributions carryover of individuals. *(1) Computation of excess of charitable contributions made in a contribution year.* Under section 170(b)(1)(D)(ii), subject to certain conditions and limitations, the excess of—

(i) The amount of the charitable contributions of 30-percent capital gain property, as defined in § 1.170A-8(d)(3) made by an individual in a taxable year (hereinafter in this paragraph referred to as the "contribution year") to section 170(b)(1)(A) organizations described in § 1.170A-9, over

(ii) 30 percent of his contribution base for such contribution year,

shall, subject to section 170(b)(1)(A) and paragraph (b) of § 1.170A-8, be treated as a charitable contribution of 30-percent capital gain property paid by him to a section 170(b)(1)(A) organization in each of the 5 taxable years immediately succeeding the contribution year in order of time. In addition, any charitable contribution of 30-percent capital gain property which is carried over to such years under section 170(d)(1) and paragraph (b) of this section shall also be treated as though it were a carryover of 30-percent capital gain property under section 170(b)(1)(D)(ii) and this paragraph. The provisions of this subparagraph may be illustrated by the following examples:

Example (1). Assume that H and W (husband and wife) have a contribution base for 1970 of $50,000 and for 1971 of $40,000 and file a joint return for each year. Assume further that in 1970 they contribute $20,000 cash and $13,000 of 30-percent capital gain property to a church, and that in 1971 they contribute $5,000 cash and $10,000 of 30-percent capital gain property to a church. They may claim a charitable contributions deduction of $25,000 in 1970 and the excess of $33,000 (contributed to the church) over $25,000 (50 percent of contribution base), or $8,000, constitutes a charitable contributions carryover which shall be treated as a charitable contribution of 30-percent capital gain property paid by them to a section 170(b)(1)(A) organization in each of the 5 succeeding taxable years in order of time. Since 30 percent of their contribution base for 1971 ($12,000) exceeds the charitable contributions of 30-percent capital gain property ($10,000) made by them in 1971 to section 170(b)(1)(A) organizations (computed without regard to section 170(b)(1)(D)(ii) and (d)(1) and this section), the portion of the 1970 carryover equal to such excess of $2,000 ($12,000 – $10,000) is treated, pursuant to the provisions of subparagraph (2) of this paragraph, as paid to a section 170(b)(1)(A) organization in 1971; the remaining $6,000 constitutes an unused charitable contributions carryover in respect of 30-percent capital gain property from 1970.

Example (2). Assume the same facts as in example (1) except the $33,000 of charitable contributions in 1970 are all 30-percent capital gain property. Since their charitable contributions in 1970 exceed 30 percent of their contribution base ($15,000) by $18,000 ($33,000 – $15,000), they may claim a charitable contribution deduction of $15,000 in 1970, and the excess of $33,000 over $15,000, or $18,000, constitutes a charitable contributions carryover which shall be treated as a charitable contribution of 30-percent capital gain property paid by them to a section 170(b)(1)(A) organization in each of the 5 succeeding taxable years in order of time. Since they are allowed to treat only $2,000 of their 1970 contribution as paid in 1971, they have a remaining unused charitable contributions carryover of $16,000 in respect of 30-percent capital gain property from 1970.

(2) Determination of amount treated as paid in taxable years succeeding contribution year. In applying the provisions of subparagraph (1) of this paragraph, the amount of the excess computed in accordance with the provisions of such subparagraph and paragraph (d)(1) of this section which is to be treated as paid in any one of the 5 taxable years immediately succeeding the contribution year to a section 170(b)(1)(A) organization shall not exceed the least of the amounts computed under subdivisions (i) to (iv), inclusive of this subparagraph:

(i) The amount by which 30 percent of the taxpayer's contribution base for such succeeding taxable year exceeds the sum of—

(a) The charitable contributions of 30-percent capital gain property actually made (computed without regard to the provisions of section 170(b)(1)(D)(ii) and (d)(1) and this section) by the taxpayer in such succeeding taxable year to section 170(b)(1)(A) organizations, and

(b) The charitable contributions of 30-percent capital gain property made to section 170(b)(1)(A) organizations in taxable years preceding the contribution year, which, pursuant to the provisions of section 170(b)(1)(D)(ii) and (d)(1) and this section, are treated as having been paid to a section 170(b)(1)(A) organization in such succeeding year.

(ii) The amount by which 50 percent of the taxpayer's contribution base for such succeeding taxable year exceeds the sum of—

(a) The charitable contributions actually made (computed without regard to the provisions of section 170(b)(1)(D)(ii) and (d)(1) of this section) by the taxpayer in such succeeding taxable year to section 170(b)(1)(A) organizations,

(b) The charitable contributions of 30-percent capital gain property made to section 170(b)(1)(A) organizations in taxable years preceding the contribution year which, pursuant to the provisions of section 170(b)(1)(D)(ii) and (d)(1) and this section, are treated as having been paid to a section 170(b)(1)(A) organization in such succeeding year, and

(c) The charitable contributions, other than contributions of 30-percent capital gain property, made to section 170(b)(1)(A) organizations which, pursuant to the provisions of section 170(d)(1) and paragraph (b) of this section, are treated as having been paid to a section 170(b)(1)(A) organization in such succeeding year.

(iii) In the case of the first taxable year succeeding the contribution year, the amount of the excess charitable contribution of 30-percent capital gain property in the contribution year, computed under subparagraph (1) of this paragraph and paragraph (d)(1) of this section.

(iv) In the case of the second, third, fourth, and fifth succeeding taxable years succeeding the contribution year, the portion of the excess charitable contribution of 30-percent capital gain property in the contribution year (computed under subparagraph (1) of this paragraph and paragraph (d)(1) of this section) which has not been treated as paid to a section 170(b)(1)(A) organization in a year intervening between the contribution year and such succeeding taxable year.

For purposes of applying subdivisions (i) and (ii) of this subparagraph, the amount of charitable contributions of 30-percent capital gain property actually made in a taxable year succeeding the contribution year shall be determined by first applying the 30-percent limitation of section 170(b)(1)(D)(i) and paragraph (d) of § 1.170A-8. If a taxpayer, in any one of the four taxable years succeeding a contribution year, elects under section 144 to take the standard deduction instead of itemizing the deductions allowable in computing taxable income, there shall be treated as paid (but not allowable as a deduction) in the standard deduction year the least of the amounts determined under subdivisions (i) to (iv), inclusive, of this subparagraph. The provisions of this subparagraph may be illustrated by the following example:

Example. Assume the following factual situation for C who itemizes his deductions in computing taxable income for each of the years set forth in the example:

	1970	1971	1972	1973	1974
Contribution base	$10,000	$15,000	$20,000	$15,000	$33,000
Contributions of cash to section 170(b)(1)(A) organizations	2,000	8,500	0	14,000	700
Contributions of 30 percent capital gain property to section 170(b)(1)(A) organizations	5,000	0	7,800	0	6,400
Allowable charitable contributions deductions (computed without regard to carryover of contributions) subject to limitations of:					
50 percent	2,000	7,500	0	7,500	700
30 percent	3,000	0	6,000	0	6,400
Total	5,000	7,500	6,000	7,500	7,100
Excess of contributions for taxable year to be treated as paid in 5 succeeding taxable years:					
Carryover of contributions of property other than 30-percent capital gain property	0	1,000	0	6,500	
Carryover of contributions of 30-percent capital gain property	2,000	0	1,800	0	0

C's excess contributions for 1970, 1971, 1972, and 1973 which are treated as having been paid to section 170(b)(1)(A) organizations in 1972, 1973, and 1974 are indicated below. The portion of the excess charitable contribution for 1972 of 30-percent capital gain property which is not treated as paid in 1974 ($1,800−$900) is available as a carryover to 1975.

1971

Contribution year	Less Total excess 50%	Less Total excess 30%	Amount treated as paid in years prior to 1971	Available charitable contributions carryovers 50%	Available charitable contributions carryovers 30%
1970	0	$2,000	0	0	$2,000

	50%	30%
50 percent of C's contribution base for 1971	$7,500	
30 percent of C's contribution base for 1971		4,500
Less: Charitable contributions actually made in 1971 to section 170(b)(1)(A) organizations ($8,500, but not to exceed 50% of contribution base)	7,500	0
Excess	0	4,500

The amount of excess contributions for 1970 of 30-percent capital gain property which is treated as paid in 1971 is the least of—

(i) Available carryover from 1970 to 1971 of contributions of 30-percent capital gain property	2,000	
(ii) Excess of 50 percent of contribution base for 1971 ($7,500) over sum of contributions actually made in 1971 to section 170(b)(1)(A) organizations ($7,500)	0	
(iii) Excess of 30 percent of contribution base for 1971 ($4,500) over contributions of 30 percent capital gain property actually made in 1971 to section 170(b)(1)(A) organizations ($0)	4,500	
Amount treated as paid		0

1972

Contribution year	Total excess 50%	Total excess 30%	Less: Amount treated as paid in years prior to 1972	Available charitable contributions carryovers 50%	Available charitable contributions carryovers 30%
1970	0	$2,000	0	0	$2,000
1971	$1,000	0	0	$ 1,000	0
				1,000	2,000

50 percent of C's contribution base for 1972	10,000	
30 percent of C's contribution base for 1972		6,000
Less: Charitable contributions actually made in 1972 to section 170(b)(1)(A) organizations ($7,800, but not to exceed 30% of contribution base)	0	6,000
Excess	10,000	0

(1) The amount of excess contributions for 1971 of property other than 30-percent capital gain property which is treated as paid in 1972 is the lesser of—		
(i) Available carryover from 1971 to 1972 of contributions of property other than 30-percent capital gain property		1,000
(ii) Excess of 50 percent of contribution base for 1972 ($10,000) over contributions actually made in 1972 to section 170(b)(1)(A) organizations ($6,000)		4,000
Amount treated as paid		1,000
(2) The amount of excess contributions for 1970 of 30-percent capital gain property which is treated as paid in 1972 is the least of—		
(i) Available carryover from 1970 to 1972 of contributions of 30-percent capital gain property	2,000	
(ii) Excess of 50 percent of contribution base for 1972 ($10,000) over sum of contributions actually made in 1972 to section 170(b)(1)(A) organizations ($6,000) and excess contributions for 1971 treated under item (1) above as paid in 1972 ($1,000)	3,000	
(iii) Excess of 30 percent of contribution base for 1972 ($6,000) over contributions of 30-percent capital gain property actually made in 1972 to section 170(b)(1)(A) organizations ($6,000)	0	
Amount treated as paid		0

1973

Contribution year	Total excess 50%	Total excess 30%	Less: Amount treated as paid in years prior to 1973	Available charitable contributions carryovers 50%	Available charitable contributions carryovers 30%
1970	0	$2,000	0	0	$2,000
1971	$1,000	0	$1,000	0	0
1972	0	1,800	0	0	1,800
				0	3,800

50 percent of C's contribution base for 1973	$7,500	
50 percent of C's contribution base for 1973		4,500
Less: Charitable contributions actually made in 1973 to section 170(b)(1)(A) organizations ($14,000, but not to exceed 50% of contribution base)	7,500	0
Excess	0	4,500

(1) The amount of excess contributions for 1970 of 30-percent capital gain property which is treated as paid in 1973 is the least of—

(i) Available carryover from 1970 to 1973 of contributions of 30-percent capital gain property	2,000	
(ii) Excess of 50 percent of contribution base for 1973 ($7,500) over contributions actually made in 1973 to section 170(b)(1)(A) organizations ($7,500)	0	
(iii) Excess of 30 percent of contribution base for 1973 ($4,500) over contributions of 30-percent capital gain property actually made in 1973 to section 170(b)(1)(A) organizations ($0)	4,500	
Amount treated as paid		0
(2) The amount of excess contributions for 1972 of 30-percent capital gain property which is treated as paid in 1973 is the least of—		
(i) Available carryover from 1972 to 1973 of contributions of 30-percent capital gain property	1,800	
(ii) Excess of 50 percent of contribution base for 1973 ($7,500) over contributions actually made in 1973 to section 170(b)(1)(A) organizations ($7,500)	0	
(iii) Excess of 30 percent of contribution base for 1973 ($4,500) over sum of contributions of 30-percent capital gain property actually made in 1973 to section 170(b)(1)(A) organizations ($0) and excess contributions for 1970 treated under item (1) above as paid in 1973 ($0)	4,500	
Amount treated as paid		0

1974

Contribution year	Total excess 50%	Total excess 30%	Less: Amount treated as paid in years prior to 1974	Available charitable contributions carryovers 50%	Available charitable contributions carryovers 30%
1970	0	$2,000	0	0	$2,000
1971	$1,000	0	$1,000	0	0
1972	0	1,800	0	0	$1,800
1973	6,500	0	0	$ 6,500	0
Excess				6,500	3,800
50 percent of C's contribution base for 1974				16,500	
20 percent of C's contribution base for 1974					9,900
Less: Charitable contributions actually made in 1974 to section 170(b)(1)(A) organizations				700	6,400
Excess				15,800	3,500
(1) The amount of excess contributions for 1973 of property other than 30 percent capital gain property which is treated as paid in 1974 is the lesser of—					
(i) Available carryover from 1973 to 1974 of contributions of property other than 30-percent capital gain property				6,500	
(ii) Excess of 50 percent of contribution base for 1974 ($16,500) over contributions actually made in 1974 to section 170(b)(1)(A) organizations ($7,100)				9,400	
Amount treated as paid					6,500
(2) The amount of excess contributions for 1970 of 30-percent capital gain property which is treated as paid in 1974 is the least of—					
(i) Available carryover from 1970 to 1974 of contributions of 30-percent capital gain property				$ 2,000	
(ii) Excess of 50 percent of contribution base for 1974 ($16,500) over sum of contributions actually made in 1974 to section 170(b)(1)(A) organizations ($7,100) and excess contributions for 1973 of property other than 30-percent capital gain property treated under item (1) above as paid in 1974 ($6,500)				2,900	
(iii) Excess of 30 percent of contribution base for 1974 ($9,900) over contributions of 30-percent capital gain property actually made in 1974 to section 170(b)(1)(A) organizations ($6,400)				3,500	
Amount treated as paid					$2,000
(3) The amount of excess contributions for 1972 of 30-percent capital gain property which is treated as paid in 1974 is the least of—					
(i) Available carryover from 1972 to 1974 of contributions of 30-percent capital gain property				1,800	

(ii) Excess of 50 percent of contribution base for 1974 ($16,500) over sum of contributions actually made in 1974 to section 170(b)(1)(A) organizations ($7,100) and excess contributions for 1973 and 1970 treated under items (1) and (2) above as paid in 1974 ($8,500)	900	
(iii) Excess of 30 percent of contribution base for 1974 ($9,000) over sum of contributions of 30-percent capital gain property actually made in 1974 to section 170(b)(1)(A) organizations ($6,400) and excess contributions for 1970 of 30-percent capital gain property treated under item (2) above as paid in 1974 ($2,000)	1,500	
Amount treated as paid		900

(d) Adjustments. *(1)* Effect of net operating loss carryovers on carryover of excess contributions. An individual having a net operating loss carryover from a prior taxable year which is available as a deduction in a contribution year must apply the special rule of section 170(d)(1)(B) and this subparagraph in computing the excess described in paragraph (b)(1) or (c)(1) of this section for such contribution year. In determining the amount of excess charitable contributions that shall be treated as paid in each of the 5 taxable years succeeding the contribution year, the excess charitable contributions described in paragraph (b)(1) or (c)(1) of this section must be reduced by the amount by which such excess reduces taxable income (for purposes of determining the portion of a net operating loss which shall be carried to taxable years succeeding the contribution year under the second sentence of section 172(b)(2)) and increases the net operating loss which is carried to a succeeding taxable year. In reducing taxable income under the second sentence of section 172(b)(2), an individual who has made charitable contributions in the contribution year to both section 170(b)(1)(A) organizations, as defined in § 1.170A-9, and to organizations which are not section 170(b)(1)(A) organizations must first deduct contributions made to the section 170(b)(1)(A) organizations from his adjusted gross income computed without regard to his net operating loss deduction before any of the contributions made to organizations which are not section 170(b)(1)(A) organizations may be deducted from such adjusted gross income. Thus, if the excess of the contributions made in the contribution year to section 170(b)(1)(A) organizations over the amount deductible in such contribution year is utilized to reduce taxable income (under the provisions of section 172(b)(2)) for such year, thereby serving to increase the amount of the net operating loss carryover to a succeeding year or years, no part of the excess charitable contributions made in such contribution year shall be treated as paid in any of the 5 immediately succeeding taxable years. If only a portion of the excess charitable contributions is so used, the excess charitable contributions shall be reduced only to that extent. The provisions of this subparagraph may be illustrated by the following examples:

Example (1). B, an individual, reports his income on the calendar year basis and for the year 1970 has adjusted gross income (computed without regard to any net operating loss deduction) of $50,000. During 1970 he made charitable contributions of cash in the amount of $30,000 all of which were to section 170(b)(1)(A) organizations. B has a net operating loss carryover from 1969 of $50,000. In the absence of the net operating loss deduction B would have been allowed a deduction for charitable contributions of $25,000. After the application of the net operating loss deduction, B is allowed no deduction for charitable contributions, and there is (before applying the special rule of section 170(d)(1)(B) and this subparagraph) a tentative excess charitable contribution of $30,000. For purposes of determining the net operating loss which remains to be carried over to 1971, B computes his taxable income for 1970 under section 172(b)(2) by deducting the $25,000 charitable contribution. After the $50,000 net operating loss carryover is applied against the $25,000 of taxable income for 1970 (computed in accordance with section 172(b)(2), assuming no deductions other than the charitable contributions deduction are applicable in making such computation), there remains a $25,000 net operating loss carryover to 1971. Since the application of the net operating loss carryover of $50,000 from 1969 reduces the 1970 adjusted gross income (for purposes of determining 1970 tax liability) to zero, no part of the $25,000 of charitable contributions in that year is deductible under section 170(b)(1). However, in determining the amount of the excess charitable contributions which shall be treated as paid in taxable years 1971, 1972, 1973, 1974, and 1975, the $30,000 must be reduced to $5,000 by the portion of the excess charitable contributions ($25,000) which was used to reduce taxable income for 1970 (as computed for purposes of the second sentence of section 172(b)(2)) and which thereby served to increase the net operating loss carryover to 1971 from zero to $25,000.

Example (2). Assume the same facts as in example (1), except that B's total charitable contributions of $30,000 in cash made during 1970 consisted of $25,000 to section 170(b)(1)(A) organizations and $5,000 to organizations other than section 170(b)(1)(A) organizations. Under these facts there is a tentative excess charitable contribution of $25,000, rather than $30,000 as in example (1). For purposes of determining the net operating loss which remains to be carried over to 1971, B computes his taxable income for 1970 under section 172(b)(2) by deducting the $25,000 of charitable contributions made to section 170(b)(1)(A) organizations. Since the excess charitable contribution of $25,000 determined in accordance with paragraph (b)(1) of this section was used to reduce taxable income for 1970 (as computed for purposes of the second sentence of section 172(b)(2)) and thereby served to increase the net operating loss carryover to 1971 from zero to $25,000, no part of such excess charitable contributions made in the contribution year shall be treated as paid in any of the five immediately succeeding taxable years. No carryover is allowed with respect to the $5,000 of charitable contributions made in 1970 to organizations other than section 170(b)(1)(A) organizations.

Example (3). Assume the same facts as in example (1), except that B's total contributions of $30,000 made during 1970 were of 30-percent capital gain property. Under these facts there is a tentative excess charitable contribution of $30,000. For purposes of determining the net operating loss which remains to be carried over to 1971, B computes his taxable income for 1970 under section 172(b)(2)(B) by deducting the $15,000 (30% of $50,000) contribution of 30-percent capital gain property which would have been deductible in 1970 absent the net operating loss deduction. Since

$15,000 of the excess charitable contribution of $30,000 determined in accordance with paragraph (c)(1) of this section was used to reduce taxable income for 1970 (as computed for purposes of the second sentence of section 172(b)(2)) and thereby served to increase the net operating loss carryover to 1971 from zero to $15,000, only $15,000 ($30,000 − $15,000) of such excess shall be treated as paid in taxable years 1971, 1972, 1973, 1974, and 1975.

(2) Effect of net operating loss carryback to contribution year. The amount of the excess contribution for a contribution year computed as provided in paragraph (b)(1) or (c)(1) of this section and subparagraph (1) of this paragraph shall not be increased because a net operating loss carryback is available as a deduction in the contribution year. Thus, for example, assuming that in 1970 there is an excess contribution of $50,000 (determined as provided in paragraph (b)(1) of this section) which is to be carried to the 5 succeeding taxable years and that in 1973 the taxpayer has a net operating loss which may be carried back to 1970, the excess contribution of $50,000 for 1970 is not increased by reason of the fact that the adjusted gross income for 1970 (on which such excess contribution was based) is subsequently decreased by the carryback of the net operating loss from 1973. In addition, in determining under the provisions of section 172(b)(2) the amount of the net operating loss for any year subsequent to the contribution year which is a carryback or carryover to taxable years succeeding the contribution year, the amount of contributions made to section 170(b)(1)(A) organizations shall be limited to the amount of such contributions which did not exceed 50 percent or, in the case of 30-percent capital gain property, 30 percent of the donor's contribution base, computed without regard to any of the modifications referred to in section 172(d), for the contribution year. Thus, for example, assume that the taxpayer has a net operating loss in 1973 which is carried back to 1970 and in turn to 1971 and that he has made charitable contributions in 1970 to section 170(b)(1)(A) organizations. In determining the maximum amount of such charitable contributions which may be deducted in 1970 for purposes of determining the taxable income for 1970 which is deducted under section 172(b)(2) from the 1973 loss in order to ascertain the amount of such loss which is carried back to 1971, the 50-percent limitation of section 170(b)(1)(A) is based upon the adjusted gross income for 1970 computed without taking into account the net operating loss carryback from 1973 and without making any of the modifications specified in section 172(d).

(3) Effect of net operating loss carryback to taxable years succeeding the contribution year. The amount of the charitable contribution from a preceding taxable year which is treated as paid, as provided in paragraph (b)(2) or (c)(2) of this section, in a current taxable year (hereinafter referred to in this subparagraph as the "deduction year") shall not be reduced because a net operating loss carryback is available as a deduction in the deduction year. In addition, in determining under the provisions of section 172(b)(2) the amount of the net operating loss for any taxable year subsequent to the deduction year which is a carryback or carryover to taxable years succeeding the deduction year shall be limited to the amount of such contributions, which were actually made in such year and those which were treated as paid in such year, which did not exceed 50 percent or, in the case of 30-percent capital gain property, 30 percent of the donor's contribution base, computed without regard to any of the modifications referred to in section 172(d), for the deduction year.

(4) Husband and wife filing joint returns. (i) Change from joint return to separate returns. If a husband and wife—

(a) Make a joint return for a contribution year and compute an excess charitable contribution for such year in accordance with the provisions of paragraph (b)(1) or (c)(1) of this section and subparagraph (1) of this paragraph, and

(b) Make separate returns for one or more of the 5 taxable years immediately succeeding such contribution year,

any excess charitable contribution for the contribution year which is unused at the beginning of the first such taxable year for which separate returns are filed shall be allocated between the husband and wife. For purposes of the allocation, a computation shall be made of the amount of any excess charitable contribution which each spouse would have computed in accordance with paragraph (b)(1) or (c)(1) of this section and subparagraph (1) of this paragraph if separate returns (rather than a joint return) had been filed for the contribution year. The portion of the total unused excess charitable contribution for the contribution year allocated to each spouse shall be an amount which bears the same ratio to such unused excess charitable contribution as such spouse's excess contribution, based on the separate return computation, bears to the total excess contributions of both spouses, based on the separate return computation. To the extent that a portion of the amount allocated to either spouse in accordance with the foregoing provisions of this subdivision is not treated in accordance with the provisions of paragraph (b)(2) or (c)(2) of this section as a charitable contribution paid to a section 170(b)(1)(A) organization in the taxable year in which a separate return or separate returns are filed, each spouse shall for purposes of paragraph (b)(2) or (c)(2) of this section treat his respective unused portion as the available charitable contributions carryover to the next succeeding taxable year in which the joint excess charitable contribution may be treated as paid in accordance with paragraph (b)(1) or (c)(1) of this section. If such husband and wife make a joint return in one of the 5 taxable years immediately succeeding the contribution year with respect to which a joint excess charitable contribution is computed and following such first taxable year for which such husband and wife filed a separate return, the amounts allocated to each spouse in accordance with this subdivision for such first year reduced by the portion of such amounts treated as paid to a section 170(b)(1)(A) organization in such first year and in any taxable year intervening between such first year and the succeeding taxable year in which the joint return is filed shall be aggregated for purposes of determining the amount of the available charitable contributions carryover to such succeeding taxable year. The provisions of this subdivision may be illustrated by the following example:

Example. (a) H and W file joint returns for 1970, 1971, and 1972, and in 1973 they file separate returns. In each such year H and W itemize their deductions in computing taxable income. Assume the following factual situation with respect to H and W for 1970;

1970

	H	W	Joint return
Contribution base	$50,000	$40,000	$90,000
Contributions of cash to section 170(b)(1)(A) organizations (no other contributions)	37,000	28,000	65,000

Allowable charitable contributions deductions	25,000	20,000	45,000
Excess contributions for taxable year to be treated as paid in 5 succeeding taxable years.....	12,000	8,000	20,000

(b) The joint excess charitable contribution of $20,000 is to be treated as having been paid to a section 170(b)(1)(A) organization in the 5 succeeding taxable years. Assume that in 1971 the portion of such excess treated as paid by H and W is $3,000, and that in 1972 the portion of such excess treated as paid is $7,000. Thus, the unused portion of the excess charitable contribution made in the contribution year is $10,000 ($20,000 less $3,000 [amount treated as paid in 1971] and $7,000 [amount treated as paid in 1972]). Since H and W file separate returns in 1973, $6,000 of such $10,000 is allocable to H, and $4,000 is allocable to W. Such allocation is computed as follows:

$$\frac{\text{\$12,000 (excess charitable contributions made by H (based on separate return computation) in 1970)}}{\text{\$20,000 (total excess charitable contributions made by H and W (based on separate return computation) in 1970)}} \times \$10{,}000 = \$6{,}000$$

$$\frac{\text{\$8,000 (excess charitable contributions made by W (based on separate return computation) in 1970)}}{\text{\$20,000 (total excess charitable contributions made by H and W (based on separate return computation) in 1970)}} \times \$10{,}000 = \$4{,}000$$

(c) In 1973 H had a contribution base of $70,000, and he contributes $14,000 in cash to a section 170(b)(1)(A) organization. In 1973 W has a contribution base of $50,000, and she contributes $10,000 in cash to a section 170(b)(1)(A) organization. Accordingly, H may claim a charitable contributions deduction of $20,000 in 1973, and W may claim a charitable contributions deduction of $14,000 in 1973. H's $20,000 deduction consists of the $14,000 contribution made to the section 170(b)(1)(A) organization in 1973 and the $6,000 carried over from 1970 and treated as a charitable contribution paid by him to a section 170(b)(1)(A) organization in 1973. W's $14,000 deduction consists of the $10,000 contribution made to a section 170(b)(1)(A) organization in 1973 and the $4,000 carried over from 1970 and treated as a charitable contribution paid by her to a section 170(b)(1)(A) organization in 1973.

(d) The $6,000 contribution treated as paid in 1973 by H, and the $4,000 contribution treated as paid in 1973, by W, are computed as follows:

	H	W
Available charitable contribution carryover (see computations in (b)). ...	$ 6,000	$ 4,000
50 percent of contribution base	35,000	25,000
Contributions of cash made in 1973 to section 170(b)(1)(A) organizations (no other contributions)................	14,000	10,000
	21,000	15,000
Amount of excess contributions treated as paid in 1973:		
The lesser of $6,000 (available carryover of H to 1973) or $21,000 (excess of 50 percent of contribution base ($35,000) over contributions actually made in 1973 to section 170(b)(1)(A) organizations ($14,000))	$ 6,000	
The lesser of $4,000 (available carryover of W to 1973) or $15,000 (excess of 50 percent of contribution base ($25,000) over contributions actually made in 1973 to section 170(b)(1)(A) organizations ($10,000))		$ 4,000

(e) It is assumed that H and W made no contributions of 30-percent capital gain property during these years. If they had made such contributions, there would have been similar adjustments based on 30 percent of the contribution base.

(ii) Change from separate returns to joint return. If in the case of a husband and wife—

(a) Either or both of the spouses make a separate return for a contribution year and compute an excess charitable contribution for such year in accordance with the provisions of paragraph (b)(1) or (c)(1) of this section and subparagraph (1) of this paragraph, and

(b) Such husband and wife make a joint return for one or more of the taxable years succeeding such contribution year.

the excess charitable contribution of the husband and wife for the contribution year which is unused at the beginning of the first taxable year for which a joint return is filed shall be aggregated for purposes of determining the portion of such unused charitable contribution which shall be treated in accordance with paragraph (b)(2) or (c)(2) of this section as a charitable contribution paid to a section 170(b)(1)(A) organization. The provisions of this subdivision also apply in the case of two single individuals who are subsequently married and file a joint return. A remarried taxpayer who filed a joint return with a former spouse in a contribution year with respect to which an excess charitable contribution was computed and who in any one of the 5 taxable years succeeding such contribution year files a joint return with his or her present spouse shall treat the unused portion of such excess charitable contribution allocated to him or her in accordance with subdivision (i) of this subparagraph in the same manner as the unused portion of an excess charitable contribution computed in a contribution year in which he filed a separate return, for purposes of determining the amount which in accordance with paragraph (b)(2) or (c)(2) of this section shall be treated as paid to an organization specified in section 170(b)(1)(A) in such succeeding year.

(iii) Unused excess charitable contribution of deceased spouse. In case of the death of one spouse, any unused portion of an excess charitable contribution which is allocable in accordance with subdivision (i) of this subparagraph to such spouse shall not be treated as paid in the taxable year in which such death occurs or in any subsequent taxable year except on a separate return made for the deceased spouse by a fiduciary for the taxable year which ends with the date of death or on a joint return for the taxable year in which such death occurs. The application of this subdivision may be illustrated by the following example:

Example. Assume the same facts as in the example in subdivision (i) of this subparagraph except that H dies in 1972 and W files a separate return for 1973. W made a joint return for herself and H for 1972. In that example, the unused excess charitable contribution as of January 1, 1973, was $10,000, $6,000 of which was allocable to H and $4,000 to W. No portion of the $6,000 allocable to H may be treated as paid by W or any other person in 1973 or any subsequent year.

(e) Information required in support of a deduction of an amount carried over and treated as paid. If, in a taxable year, a deduction is claimed in respect of an excess charitable contribution which, in accordance with the provisions of paragraph (b)(2) or (c)(2) of this section, is treated (in whole or in part) as paid in such taxable year, the taxpayer shall attach to his return a statement showing:

(1) The contribution year (or years) in which the excess charitable contributions were made,

(2) The excess charitable contributions made in each contribution year, and the amount of such excess charitable contributions consisting of 30-percent capital gain property.

(3) The portion of such excess, or of each such excess, treated as paid in accordance with paragraph (b)(2) or (c)(2) of this section in any taxable year intervening between the contribution year and the taxable year for which the return is made, and the portion of such excess which consists of 30-percent capital gain property.

(4) Whether or not an election under section 170(b)(1)(D)(iii) has been made which affects any of such excess contributions of 30-percent capital gain property, and

(5) Such other information as the return or the instructions relating thereto may require.

(f) Effective date. This section applies only to contributions paid in taxable years beginning after December 31, 1969. For purposes of applying section 170(d)(1) with respect to contributions paid in a taxable year beginning before January 1, 1970, subsection (b)(1)(D), subsection (e), and paragraphs (1), (2), (3), and (4) of subsection (f) of section 170 shall not apply. See section 201(g)(1)(D) of the Tax Reform Act of 1969 (83 Stat. 564).

T.D. 7207, 10/3/72, amend T.D. 7340, 1/6/75.

§ 1.170A-11 Limitation on, and carryover of, contributions by corporations.

Caution: The Treasury has not yet amended Reg § 1.170A-11 to reflect changes made by P.L. 100-647, P.L. 100-203, P.L. 99-514, P.L. 98-369, P.L. 97-34.

(a) In general. The deduction by a corporation in any taxable year for charitable contributions, as defined in section 170(c), is limited to 5 percent of its taxable income for the year, computed without regard to—

(1) The deduction under section 170 for charitable contributions,

(2) The special deductions for corporations allowed under part VIII (except section 248), subchapter B, chapter 1 of the Code,

(3) Any net operating loss carryback to the taxable year under section 172, and

(4) Any capital loss carryback to the taxable year under section 1212(a)(1).

A charitable contribution by a corporation to a trust, chest, fund, or foundation described in section 170(c)(2) is deductible under section 170 only if the contribution is to be used in the United States or its possessions exclusively for religious, charitable, scientific, literary, or educational purposes or for the prevention of cruelty to children or animals. For the purposes of section 170, amounts excluded from the gross income of a corporation under section 114, relating to sports programs conducted for the American National Red Cross, are not to be considered contributions or gifts.

(b) Election by corporations on an accrual method. *(1)* A Corporation reporting its taxable income on an accrual method may elect to have a charitable contribution treated as paid during the taxable year, if payment is actually made on or before the 15th day of the third month following the close of such year and if, during such year, its board of directors authorizes the charitable contribution. If by reason of such an election a charitable contribution (other than a contribution of a letter, memorandum, or property similar to a letter or memorandum) paid in a taxable year beginning after December 31, 1969, is treated as paid during a taxable year beginning before January 1, 1970, the provisions of § 1.170A-4 shall not be applied to reduce the amount of such contribution. However, see section 170(e) before its amendment by the Tax Reform Act of 1969.

(2) The election must be made at the time the return for the taxable year is filed, by reporting the contribution on the return. There shall be attached to the return when filed a written declaration stating that the resolution authorizing the contribution was adopted by the board of directors during the taxable year. For taxable years beginning before January 1, 2003, the declaration shall be verified by a statement signed by an officer authorized to sign the return that it is made under penalties of perjury, and there shall also be attached to the return when filed a copy of the resolution of the board of directors authorizing the contribution. For taxable years beginning after December 31, 2002, the declaration must also include the date of the resolution, the declaration shall be verified by signing the return, and a copy of the resolution of the board of directors authorizing the contribution is a record that the taxpayer must retain and keep available for inspection in the manner required by § 1.6001-1(e).

(c) Charitable contributions carryover of corporations. *(1) In general.* Subject to the reduction provided in subparagraph (2) of this paragraph, any charitable contributions made by a corporation in a taxable year (hereinafter in this paragraph referred to as the "contribution year") in excess of the amount deductible in such contribution year under the 5-percent limitation of section 170(b)(2) are deductible in each of the five succeeding taxable years in order of time, but only to the extent of the lesser of the following amounts:

(i) The excess of the maximum amount deductible for such succeeding taxable year under the 5-percent limitation of section 170(b)(2) over the sum of the charitable contributions made in that year plus the aggregate of the excess contributions which were made in taxable years before the contribution year and which are deductible under this paragraph in such succeeding taxable year; or

(ii) In the case of the first taxable year succeeding the contribution year, the amount of the excess charitable contributions, and in the case of the second, third, fourth, and fifth taxable years succeeding the contribution year, the portion of the excess charitable contributions not deductible under this subparagraph for any taxable year intervening between the contribution year and such succeeding taxable year.

This paragraph applies to excess charitable contributions by a corporation, whether or not such contributions are made to, or for the use of, the donee organization and whether or not such organization is a section 170(b)(1)(A) organization, as defined in § 1.170A-9. For purposes of applying this paragraph, a charitable contribution made in a taxable year beginning before January 1, 1970, which is carried over to taxable year beginning after December 31, 1969, under section 170(b)(2) (before its amendment by the Tax Reform Act of 1969) and is deductible in such taxable year beginning after December 31, 1969, shall be treated as deductible under section 170(d)(1) and this paragraph. The application of this subparagraph may be illustrated by the following example:

Example. A corporation which reports its income on the calendar year basis makes a charitable contribution of $20,000 in 1970. Its taxable income (determined without regard to any deduction for charitable contributions) for 1970 is $100,000. Accordingly, the charitable contributions deduction for that year is limited to $5,000 (5 percent of $100,000). The excess charitable contribution not deductible in 1970 ($15,000) is a carryover to 1971. The corporation has taxable income (determined without regard to any deduction for charitable contributions) of $150,000 in 1971 and makes a charitable contribution of $5,000 in that year. For 1971 the corporation may deduct as a charitable contribution the amount of $7,500 (5 percent of $150,000). This amount consists of the $5,000 contribution made in 1971 and of the $2,500 carried over from 1970. The remaining $12,500 carried over from 1970 and not allowable as a deduction for 1971 because of the 5-percent limitation may be carried over to 1972. The corporation has taxable income (determined without regard to any deduction for charitable contributions) of $200,000 in 1972 and makes a charitable contribution of $5,000 in that year. For 1972 the corporation may deduct the amount of $10,000 (5 percent of $200,000). This amount consists of the $5,000 contributed in 1972, and $5,000 of the $12,500 carried over from 1970 to 1972. The remaining $7,500 of the carryover from 1970 is available for purposes of computing the charitable contributions carryover from 1970 to 1973, 1974, and 1975.

(2) Effect of net operating loss carryovers on carryover of excess contributions. A corporation having a net operating loss carryover from any taxable year must apply the special rule of section 170(d)(2)(B) and this subparagraph before computing under subparagraph (1) of this paragraph the excess charitable contributions carryover from any taxable year. In determining the amount of excess charitable contributions that may be deducted in accordance with subparagraph (1) of this paragraph in taxable years succeeding the contribution year, the excess of the charitable contributions made by a corporation in the contributions year over the amount deductible in such year must be reduced by the amount by which such excess reduces taxable income for purposes of determining the net operating loss carryover under the second sentence of section 172(b)(2) and increases a net operating loss carryover to a succeeding taxable year. Thus, if the excess of the contributions made in a taxable year over the amount deductible in the taxable year is utilized to reduce taxable income (under the provisions of section 172(b)(2)) for such year, thereby serving to increase the amount of the net operating loss carryover to a succeeding taxable year or years, no charitable contributions carryover will be allowed. If only a portion of the excess charitable contributions is so used, the charitable contributions carryover will be reduced only to that extent. The application of this subparagraph may be illustrated by the following example:

Example. A corporation, which reports its income on the calendar year basis, makes a charitable contribution of $10,000 during 1971. Its taxable income for 1971 is $80,000 (computed without regard to any net operating loss deduction and computed in accordance with section 170(b)(2) without regard to any deduction for charitable contributions). The corporation has a net operating loss carryover from 1970 of $80,000. In the absence of the net operating loss deduction the corporation would have been allowed a deduction for charitable contributions of $4,000 (5 percent of $80,000). After the application of the net operating loss deduction the corporation is allowed no deduction for charitable contributions, and there is a tentative charitable contribution carryover from 1971 of $10,000. For purposes of determining the net operating loss carryover to 1972 the corporation computes its taxable income for 1971 under section 172(b)(2) by deducting the $4,000 charitable contribution. Thus, after the $80,000 net operating loss carryover is applied against the $76,000 of taxable income for 1971 (computed in accordance with section 172(b)(2)), there remains a $4,000 net operating loss carryover to 1972. Since the application of the net operating loss carryover of $80,000 from 1970 reduces the taxable income for 1971 to zero, no part of the $10,000 of charitable contributions in that year is deductible under section 170(b)(2). However, in determining the amount of the allowable charitable contributions carryover from 1971 to 1972, 1973, 1974, 1975, and 1976, the $10,000 must be reduced by the portion thereof ($4,000) which was used to reduce taxable income for 1971 (as computed for purposes of the second sentence of section 172(b)(2)) and which thereby served to increase the net operating loss carryover from 1970 to 1972 from zero to $4,000.

(3) Effect of net operating loss carryback to contribution year. The amount of the excess contribution for a contribution year computed as provided in subparagraph (1) of this paragraph shall not be increased because a net operating loss carryback is available as a deduction in the contribution year. In addition, in determining under the provisions of section 172(b)(2) the amount of the net operating loss for any year subsequent to the contribution year which is a carryback or carryover to taxable years succeeding the contribution year, the amount of any charitable contributions shall be limited to the amount of such contributions which did not exceed 5 percent of the donor's taxable income, computed as provided in paragraph (a) of this section and without regard to any of the modifications referred to in section 172(d), for the contribution year. For illustrations, see paragraph (d)(2) of § 1.170A-10.

(4) Effect of net operating loss carryback to taxable year succeeding the contribution year. The amount of the charitable contribution from a preceding taxable year which is deductible (as provided in this paragraph) in a current taxable year (hereinafter referred to in this subparagraph as the "deduction year") shall not be reduced because a net operating loss carryback is available as a deduction in the deduction year. In addition, in determining under the provisions of section 172(b)(2) the amount of the net operating loss for any taxable year subsequent to the deduction year which is a carryback or a carryover to taxable years succeeding the deduction year, the amount of contributions made in the deduction year shall be limited to the amount of such contributions, which were actually made in such year and those which were deductible in such year under section 170(d)(2), which

did not exceed 5 percent of the donor's taxable income, computed as provided in paragraph (a) of this section and without regard to any of the modifications referred to in section 172(d), for the deduction year.

(5) Year contribution is made. For purposes of this paragraph, contributions made by a corporation in a contribution year include contributions which, in accordance with the provisions of section 170(a)(2) and paragraph (b) of this section, are considered as paid during such contribution year.

(d) Effective date. This section applies only to contributions paid in taxable years beginning after December 31, 1969. For purposes of applying section 170(d)(2) with respect to contributions paid, or treated under section 170(a)(2) as paid, in a taxable year beginning before January 1, 1970, subsection (e), and paragraphs (1), (2), (3), and (4) of subsection (f) of section 170 shall not apply. See section 201(g)(1)(D) of the Tax Reform Act of 1969 (83 Stat. 564).

T.D. 7207, 10/3/72, amend T.D. 7807, 1/29/82, T.D. 9100, 12/18/2003, T.D. 9300, 12/7/2006.

§ 1.170A-12 Valuation of a remainder interest in real property for contributions made after July 31, 1969.

(a) In general. *(1)* Section 170(f)(4) provides that, in determining the value of a remainder interest in real property for purposes of section 170, depreciation and depletion of such property shall be taken into account. Depreciation shall be computed by the straight line method and depletion shall be computed by the cost depletion method. Section 170(f)(4) and this section apply only in the case of a contribution, not made in trust, of a remainder interest in real property made after July 31, 1969, for which a deduction is otherwise allowable under section 170.

(2) In the case of the contribution of a remainder interest in real property consisting of a combination of both depreciable and nondepreciable property, or of both depletable and nondepletable property, and allocation of the fair market value of the property at the time of the contribution shall be made between the depreciable and nondepreciable property, or the depletable and nondepletable property, and depreciation or depletion shall be taken into account only with respect to the depreciable or depletable property. The expected value at the end of its "estimated useful life" (as defined in paragraph (d) of this section) of that part of the remainder interest consisting of depreciable property shall be considered to be nondepreciable property for purposes of the required allocation. In the case of the contribution of a remainder interest in stock in a cooperative housing corporation (as defined in section 216(b)(1)), an allocation of the fair market value of the stock at the time of the contribution shall be made to reflect the respective values of the depreciable and nondepreciable property underlying such stock, and depreciation on the depreciable part shall be taken into account for purposes of valuing the remainder interest in such stock.

(3) If the remainder interest that has been contributed follows only one life, the value of the remainder interest shall be computed under the rules contained in paragraph (b) of this section. If the remainder interest that has been contributed follows a term for years, the value of the remainder interest shall be computed under the rules contained in paragraph (c) of this section. If the remainder interest that has been contributed is dependent upon the continuation or the termination of more than one life or upon a term certain concurrent with one or more lives, the provisions of paragraph (e) of this section shall apply. In every case where it is provided in this section that the rules contained in § 25.2512-5 (or, for certain prior periods, § 25.2512-5A) of this chapter (Gift Tax Regulations) apply, such rules shall apply notwithstanding the general effective date for such rules contained in paragraph (a) of such section. Except as provided in § 1.7520-3(b) of this chapter, for transfers of remainder interests after April 30, 1989, the present value of the remainder interest is determined under § 25.2512-5 of this chapter by use of the interest rate component on the date the interest is transferred unless an election is made under section 7520 and § 1.7520-2 of this chapter to compute the present value of the interest transferred by use of the interest rate component for either of the 2 months preceding the month in which the interest is transferred. In some cases, a reduction in the amount of a charitable contribution of a remainder interest, after the computation of its value under section 170(f)(4) and this section, may be required. See section 170(e) and § 1.170A-4.

(b) Valuation of a remainder interest following only one life. *(1) General rule.* The value of a remainder interest in real property following only one life is determined under the rules provided in § 20.2031-7 (or for certain prior periods, § 20.2031-7A) of this chapter (Estate Tax Regulations), using the interest rate and life contingencies prescribed for the date of the gift. See, however, § 1.7520-3(b) (relating to exceptions to the use of prescribed tables under certain circumstances). However, if any part of the real property is subject to exhaustion, wear and tear, or obsolescence, the special factor determined under paragraph (b)(2) of this section shall be used in valuing the remainder interest in that part. Further, if any part of the property is subject to depletion of its natural resources, such depletion is taken into account in determining the value of the remainder interest.

(2) Computation of depreciation factor. If the valuation of the remainder interest in depreciable property is dependent upon the continuation of one life, a special factor must be used. The factor determined under this paragraph (b)(2) is carried to the fifth decimal place. The special factor is to be computed on the basis of the interest rate and life contingencies prescribed in § 20.2031-7 of this chapter (or for periods before May 1, 1999, § 20.2031-7A) and on the assumption that the property depreciates on a straight-line basis over its estimated useful life. For transfers for which the valuation date is after April 30, 1999, special factors for determining the present value of a remainder interest following one life and an example describing the computation is contained in Internal Revenue Service Publication 1459, "Actuarial Values, Book Gimel," (7-1999). A copy of this publication is available for purchase from the Superintendent of Documents, United States Government Printing Office, Washington, DC 20402. For transfers for which the valuation date is after April 30, 1989, and before May 1, 1999, special factors for determining the present value of a remainder interest following one life and an example describing the computation is contained in Internal Revenue Service Publication 1459, "Actuarial Values, Gamma Volume," (8-89). This publication is no longer available for purchase from the Superintendent of Documents. However, it may be obtained by requesting a copy from: CC:DOM:CORP:R (IRS Publication 1459), room 5226, Internal Revenue Service, POB 7604, Ben Franklin Station, Washington, DC 20044. See, however, § 1.7520-3(b) (relating to exceptions to the use of prescribed tables under certain circumstances). Otherwise, in the case of the valuation of a remainder interest following one life, the special factor may be obtained through use of the following formula:

$$\left(1+\frac{i}{2}\right)\sum_{t=0}^{n-1} v^{(t+1)}\left[\left(1-\frac{l_{x+t+1}}{l_x}\right)-\left(1-\frac{l_{x+t}}{l_x}\right)\right]\left(1-\frac{1}{2n}-\frac{t}{n}\right)$$

Where:

n=the estimated number of years of useful life,

i=the applicable interest rate under section 7520 of the Internal Revenue Code,

v=1 divided by the sum of 1 plus the applicable interest rate under section 7520 of the Internal Revenue Code,

x=the age of the life tenant, and

lx=number of persons living at age x as set forth in Table 90CM of § 20.2031-7 (or, for periods before May 1, 1999, the tables set forth under § 20.2031-7A) of this chapter.

(3) Example. The following example illustrates the provisions of this paragraph (b):

Example. A, who is 62, donates to Y University a remainder interest in a personal residence, consisting of a house and land, subject to a reserved life estate in A. At the time of the gift, the land has a value of $30,000 and the house has a value of $100,000 with an estimated useful life of 45 years, at the end of which the value of the house is expected to be $20,000. The portion of the property considered to be depreciable is $80,000 (the value of the house ($100,000) less its expected value at the end of 45 years ($20,000)). The portion of the property considered to be nondepreciable is $50,000 (the value of the land at the time of the gift ($30,000) plus the expected value of the house at the end of 45 years ($20,000)). At the time of the gift, the interest rate prescribed under section 7520 is 8.4 percent. Based on an interest rate of 8.4 percent, the remainder factor for $1.00 prescribed in § 20.2031-7(d) of this chapter for a person age 62 is 0.27925. The value of the nondepreciable remainder interest is $13,962.50 (0.27925 times $50,000). The value of the depreciable remainder interest is $16,148.80 (0.20186, computed under the formula described in paragraph (b)(2) of this section, times $80,000). Therefore, the value of the remainder interest is $30,111.30.

(c) Valuation of a remainder interest following a term for years. The value of a remainder interest in real property following a term for years shall be determined under the rules provided in § 25.2512-5 (or, for certain prior periods, § 25.2512-5A) of this chapter (Gift Tax Regulations) using Table B provided in § 20.2031-7(d) of this chapter. However, if any part of the real property is subject to exhaustion, wear and tear, or obsolescence, in valuing the remainder interest in that part the value of such part is adjusted by subtracting from the value of such part the amount determined by multiplying such value by a fraction, the numerator of which is the number of years in the term or, if less, the estimated useful life of the property, and the denominator of which is the estimated useful life of the property. The resultant figure is the value of the property to be used in § 25.2512-5 (or, for certain prior periods, § 25.2512-5A) of this chapter (Gift Tax Regulations). Further, if any part of the property is subject to depletion of its natural resources, such depletion shall be taken into account in determining the value of the remainder interest. The provisions of this paragraph as it relates to depreciation are illustrated by the following example:

Example. In 1972, B donates to Z University a remainder interest in his personal residence, consisting of a house and land, subject to a 20 year term interest provided for his sister. At such time the house has a value of $60,000, and an expected useful life of 45 years, at the end of which time it is expected to have a value of $10,000, and the land has a value of $8,000. The value of the portion of the property considered to be depreciable is $50,000 (the value of the house ($60,000) less its expected value at the end of 45 years ($10,000)), and this is multiplied by the fraction 20/45. The product, $22,222.22, is subtracted from $68,000, the value of the entire property, and the balance, $45,777.78, is multiplied by the factor .311805 (see § 25.2512-5A(c)). The result, $14,273.74, is the value of the remainder interest in the property.

(d) Definition of estimated useful life. For the purposes of this section, the determination of the estimated useful life of depreciable property shall take account of the expected use of such property during the period of the life estate or term for years. The term "estimated useful life" means the estimated period (beginning with the date of the contribution) over which such property may reasonably be expected to be useful for such expected use. This period shall be determined by reference to the experience based on any prior use of the property for such purposes if such prior experience is adequate. If such prior experience is inadequate or if the property has not been previously used for such purposes, the estimated useful life shall be determined by reference to the general experience of persons normally holding similar property for such expected use, taking into account present conditions and probable future developments. The estimated useful life of such depreciable property is not limited to the period of the life estate or term for years preceding the remainder interest. In determining the expected use and the estimated useful life of the property, consideration is to be given to the provisions of the governing instrument creating the life estate or term for years or applicable local law, if any, relating to use, preservation, and maintenance of the property during the life estate or term for years. In arriving at the estimated useful life of the property, estimates, if available, of engineers or other persons skilled in estimating the useful life of similar property may be taken into account. At the option of the taxpayer, the estimated useful life of property contributed after December 31, 1970, for purposes of this section, shall be an asset depreciation period selected by the taxpayer that is within the permissible asset depreciation range for the relevant asset guideline class established pursuant to § 1.167(a)-11(b)(4)(ii). For purposes of the preceding sentence, such period, range, and class shall be those which are in effect at the time that the contribution of the remainder interest was made. At the option of the taxpayer, in the case of property contributed before January 1, 1971, the estimated useful life, for purposes of this section, shall be the guideline life provided in Revenue Procedure 62-21 for the relevant asset guideline class.

(e) Valuation of a remainder interest following more than one life or a term certain concurrent with one or

more lives. *(1)* (i) If the valuation of the remainder interest in the real property is dependent upon the continuation or the termination of more than one life or upon a term certain concurrent with one or more lives, a special factor must be used.

(ii) The special factor is to be computed on the basis of—

(A) Interest at the rate prescribed under § 25.2512-5 (or, for certain prior periods, § 25.2512-5A) of this chapter, compounded annually;

(B) Life contingencies determined from the values that are set forth in the mortality table in § 20.2031-7 (or, for certain prior periods, § 20.2031-7A) of this chapter; and

(C) If depreciation is involved, the assumption that the property depreciates on a straight-line basis over its estimated useful life.

(iii) If any part of the property is subject to depletion of its natural resources, such depletion must be taken into account in determining the value of the remainder interest.

(2) In the case of the valuation of a remainder interest following two lives, the special factor may be obtained through use of the following formula:

$$\left(1+\frac{i}{2}\right)\sum_{t=0}^{n-1} v^{(t+1)}\left[\left(1-\frac{l_{x+t+1}}{l_x}\right)\left(1-\frac{l_{y+t+1}}{l_y}\right)-\left(1-\frac{l_{x+t}}{l_x}\right)\left(1-\frac{l_{y+t}}{l_y}\right)\right]\left(1-\frac{1}{2n}-\frac{t}{n}\right)$$

Where:

n =the estimated number of years of useful life
i =the applicable interest rate under section 7520 of the Internal Revenue Code,
v =1 divided by the sum of 1 plus the applicable interest rate under section 7520 of the Internal Revenue Code,
x and y =the ages of the life tenants, and
lx and ly =the number of persons living at ages x and y set forth in Table 90CNSMT in § 20.2031-7 (or, for prior periods, in § 20.2031-7A) of this chapter.

(3) Notwithstanding that the taxpayer may be able to compute the special factor in certain cases under paragraph (2), if a special factor is required in the case of an actual contribution, the Commissioner will furnish the factor to the donor upon request. The request must be accompanied by a statement of the sex and date of birth of each person the duration of whose life may affect the value of the remainder interest, copies of the relevant instruments, and, if depreciation is involved, a statement of the estimated useful life of the depreciable property. However, since remainder interests in that part of any property which is depletable cannot be valued on a purely actuarial basis, special factors will not be furnished with respect to such part. Requests should be forwarded to the Commissioner of Internal Revenue, Attention: OP:E:EP:A:1, Washington, D.C. 20224.

T.D. 7370, 8/14/75, amend T.D. 7955, 5/10/84, T.D. 8540, 6/9/94, T.D. 8819, 4/29/99, T.D. 8886, 6/9/2000.

§ 1.170A-13 Recordkeeping and return requirements for deductions for charitable contributions.

Caution: The Treasury has not yet amended Reg § 1.170A-13 to reflect changes made by P.L. 109-280, P.L. 108-357, P.L. 100-647.

(a) Charitable contributions of money made in taxable years beginning after December 31, 1982. *(1) In general.* If a taxpayer makes a charitable contribution of money in a taxable year beginning after December 31, 1982, the taxpayer shall maintain for each contribution one of the following.

(i) A cancelled check.

(ii) A receipt from the donee charitable organization showing the name of the donee, the date of the contribution, and the amount of the contribution. A letter or other communication from the donee charitable organization acknowledging receipt of a contribution and showing the date and amount of the contribution constitutes a receipt for purposes of this paragraph (a).

(iii) In the absence of a canceled check or receipt from the donee charitable organization, other reliable written records showing the name of the donee, the date of the contribution, and the amount of the contribution.

(2) Special rules. (i) Reliability of records. The reliability of the written records described in paragraph (a)(1)(iii) of this section is to be determined on the basis of all of the facts and circumstances of a particular case. In all events, however, the burden shall be on the taxpayer to establish reliability. Factors indicating that the written records are reliable include, but are not limited to:

(A) The contemporaneous nature of the writing evidencing the contribution.

(B) The regularity of the taxpayer's recordkeeping procedures. For example, a contemporaneous diary entry stating the amount and date of the donation and the name of the donee charitable organization made by a taxpayer who regularly makes such diary entries would generally be considered reliable.

(C) In the case of a contribution of a small amount, the existence of any written or other evidence from the donee charitable organization evidencing receipt of a donation that would not otherwise constitute a receipt under paragraph (a)(1)(ii) of this section (including an emblem, button, or other token traditionally associated with a charitable organization and regularly given by the organization to persons making cash donations).

(ii) Information stated in income tax return. The information required by paragraph (a)(1)(iii) of this section shall be stated in the taxpayer's income tax return if required by the return form or its instructions.

(3) Taxpayer option to apply paragraph (d)(1) to pre-1985 contribution. See paragraph (d)(1) of this section with regard to contributions of money made on or before December 31, 1984.

(b) Charitable contributions of property other than money made in taxable years beginning after December 31, 1982. *(1) In general.* Except in the case of certain charitable contributions of property made after December 31, 1984, to which paragraph (c) of this section applies, any taxpayer who makes a charitable contribution of property other than money in a taxable year beginning after December 31,

1982, shall maintain for each contribution a receipt from the donee showing the following information:

(i) The name of the donee.

(ii) The date and location of the contribution.

(iii) A description of the property in detail reasonably sufficient under the circumstances. Although the fair market value of the property is one of the circumstances to be taken into account in determining the amount of detail to be included on the receipt, such value need not be stated on the receipt.

A letter or other written communication from the donee acknowledging receipt of the contribution, showing the date of the contribution, and containing the required description of the property contributed constitutes a receipt for purposes of this paragraph. A receipt is not required if the contribution is made in circumstances where it is impractical to obtain a receipt (e.g., by depositing property at a charity's unattended drop site). In such cases, however, the taxpayer shall maintain reliable written records with respect to each item of donated property that include the information required by paragraph (b)(2)(ii) of this section.

(2) Special rules. (i) Reliability of records. The rules described in paragraph (a)(2)(i) of this section also apply to this paragraph (b) for determining the reliability of the written records described in paragraph (b)(1) of this section.

(ii) Content of records. The written records described in paragraph (b)(1) of this section shall include the following information and such information shall be stated in the taxpayers income tax return if required by the return form or its instructions:

(A) The name and address of the donee organization to which the contribution was made.

(B) The date and location of the contribution.

(C) A description of the property in detail reasonable under the circumstances (including the value of the property), and, in the case of securities, the name of the issuer, the type of security, and whether or not such security is regularly traded on a stock exchange or in an over-the-counter market.

(D) The fair market value of the property at the time the contribution was made, the method utilized in determining the fair market value, and, if the valuation was determined by appraisal, a copy of the signed report of the appraiser.

(E) In the case of property to which section 170(e) applies, the cost or other basis, adjusted as provided by section 1016, the reduction by reason of section 170(e)(1) in the amount of the charitable contribution otherwise taken into account, and the manner in which such reduction was determined. A taxpayer who elects under paragraph (d)(2) of § 1.170A-8 to apply section 170(e)(1) to contributions and carryovers of 30 percent capital gain property shall maintain a written record indicating the years for which the election was made and showing the contributions in the current year and carryovers from preceding years to which it applies. For the definition of the term "30-percent capital gain property," see paragraph (d)(3) of § 1.170A-8.

(F) If less than the entire interest in the property is contributed during the taxable year, the total amount claimed as a deduction for the taxable year due to the contribution of the property, and the amount claimed as a deduction in any prior year or years for contributions of other interests in such property, the name and address of each organization to which any such contribution was made, the place where any such property which is tangible property is located or kept, and the name of any person, other than the organization to which the property giving rise to the deduction was contributed, having actual possession of the property.

(G) The terms of any agreement or understanding entered into by or on behalf of the taxpayer which relates to the use, sale, or other disposition of the property contributed, including for example, the terms of any agreement or understanding which—

(1) Restricts temporarily or permanently the donee's right to use or dispose of the donated property,

(2) Reserves to, or confers upon, anyone (other than the donee organization or an organization participating with the donee organization in cooperative fundraising) any right to the income from the donated property or to the possession of the property, including the right to vote donated securities, to acquire the property by purchase or otherwise, or to designate the person having such income, possession, or right to acquire, or

(3) Earmarks donated property for a particular use.

(3) Deductions in excess of $500 claimed for a charitable contribution of property other than money. (i) In general. In addition to the information required under paragraph (b)(2)(ii) of this section, if a taxpayer makes a charitable contribution of property other than money in a taxable year beginning after December 31, 1982, and claims a deduction in excess of $500 in respect of the contribution of such item, the taxpayer shall maintain written records that include the following information with respect to such item of donated property, and shall state such information in his or her income tax return if required by the return form or its instructions:

(A) The manner of acquisition, as for example by purchase, gift bequest, inheritance, or exchange, and the approximate date of acquisition of the property by the taxpayer or, if the property was created, produced, or manufactured by or for the taxpayer, the approximate date the property was substantially completed.

(B) The cost or other basis, adjusted as provided by section 1016, of property, other than publicly traded securities, held by the taxpayer for a period of less than 12 months (6 months for property contributed in taxable years beginning after December 31, 1982, and on or before June 6, 1988) immediately preceding the date on which the contribution was made and, when the information is available, of property, other than publicly traded securities, held for a period of 12 months or more (6 months or more for property contributed in taxable years beginning after December 31, 1982, and on or before June 6, 1988) preceding the date on which the contribution was made.

(ii) Information on acquisition date or cost basis no available. If the return form or its instructions require the taxpayer to provide information on either the acquisition date of the property or the cost basis as described it paragraph (b)(3)(i)(A) and (B), respectively, of this section, and the taxpayer has reasonable cause for not being able to provide such information, the taxpayer shall attach an explanatory statement to the return. If a taxpayer has reasonable cause for not being able to provide such information, the taxpayer shall not be disallowed a charitable contribution deduction under section 170 for failure to comply with paragraph (b)(3)(i)(A) and (B) of the section.

(4) Taxpayer option to apply paragraph (d)(1) and (2) to pre-1985 contributions. See paragraph (d)(1) and (2) of this section with regard to contributions of property made on or before December 31, 1984.

(c) Deductions in excess of $5,000 for certain charitable contributions of property made after December 31, 1984. *(1) General rule.* (i) In general. This paragraph applies to any charitable contribution made after December 31, 1984, by an individual, closely held corporation, personal service corporation, partnership, or S corporation of an item of property (other than money and publicly traded securities to which § 1.170A-13(c)(7)(xi)(B) does not apply if the amount claimed or reported as a deduction under section 170 with respect to such item exceeds $5,000. This paragraph also applies to charitable contributions by C corporations (as defined in section 1361(a)(2) of the Code) to the extent described in paragraph (c)(2)(ii) of this section. No deduction under section 170 shall be allowed with respect to a charitable contribution to which this paragraph applies unless the substantiation requirements described in paragraph (c)(2) of this section are met. For purposes of this paragraph (c), the amount claimed or reported as a deduction for an item of property is the aggregate amount claimed or reported as a deduction for a charitable contribution under section 170 for such items of property and all similar items of property (as defined in paragraph (c)(7)(iii) of this section) by the same donor for the same taxable year (whether or not donated to the same donee).

(ii) Special rule for property to which section 170(e)(3) or (4) applies. For purposes of this paragraph (c), in computing the amount claimed or reported as a deduction for donated property to which section 170(e)(3) or (4) applies (pertaining to certain contributions of inventory and scientific equipment) there shall be taken into account only the amount claimed or reported as a deduction in excess of the amount which would have been taken into account for tax purposes by the donor as costs of goods sold if the donor had sold the contributed property to the donee. For example, assume that a donor makes a contribution from inventory of clothing for the care of the needy to which section 170(e)(3) applies. The cost of the property to the donor was $5,000, and, pursuant to section 170(e)(3)(B), the donor claims a charitable contribution deduction of $8,000 with respect to the property. Therefore, $3,000 ($8,000 − $5,000) is the amount taken into account for purposes of determining whether the $5,000 threshold of this paragraph (c)(1) is met.

(2) Substantiation requirements. (i) In general. Except as provided in paragraph (c)(2)(ii) of this section, a donor who claims or reports a deduction with respect to a charitable contribution to which this paragraph (c) applies must comply with the following three requirements:

(A) Obtain a qualified appraisal (as defined in paragraph (c)(3) of this section) for such property contributed. If the contributed property is a partial interest, the appraisal shall be of the partial interest.

(B) Attach a fully completed appraisal summary (as defined in paragraph (c)(4) of this section) to the tax return (or, in the case of a donor that is a partnership or S corporation, the information return) on which the deduction for the contribution is first claimed (or reported) by the donor.

(C) Maintain records containing the information required by paragraph (b)(2)(ii) of this section.

(ii) Special rules for certain nonpublicly traded stock, certain publicly traded securities, and contributions by certain C corporations. (A) In cases described in paragraph (c)(2)(ii)(B) of this section, a qualified appraisal is not required, and only a partially completed appraisal summary form (as described in paragraph (c)(4)(iv)(A) of this section) is required to be attached to the tax or information return specified in paragraph (c)(2)(i)(B) of this section. However, in all cases donors must maintain records containing the information required by paragraph (b)(2)(ii) of this section.

(B) This paragraph (c)(2)(ii) applies in each of the following cases:

(1) The contribution of nonpublicly traded stock, if the amount claimed or reported as a deduct ion for the charitable contribution of such stock is greater than $5,000 but does not exceed $ 10,000;

(2) The contribution of a security to which paragraph (c)(7)(xi)(B) of this section applies; and

(3) The contribution of an item of property or of similar items of property described in paragraph (c)(1) of this section made after June 6, 1988, by a C corporation (as defined in section 1861(a)(2) of the Code), other than a closely held corporation or a personal service corporation.

(3) Qualified appraisal. (i) In general. For purposes of this paragraph (c), the term "qualified appraisal" means an appraisal document that—

(A) Relates to an appraisal that is made not earlier than 60 days prior to the date of contribution of the appraised property nor later than the date specified in paragraph (c)(3)(iv)(B) of this section;

(B) Is prepared, signed, and dated by a qualified appraiser (within the meaning of paragraph (c)(5) of this section);

(C) Includes the information required by paragraph (c)(3)(ii) of this section; and

(D) Does not involve an appraisal fee prohibited by paragraph (c)(6) of this section.

(ii) Information included in qualified appraisal. A qualified appraisal shall include the following information:

(A) A description of the property in sufficient detail for a person who is not generally familiar with the type of property to ascertain that the property that was appraised is the property that was (or will be) contributed;

(B) In the case of tangible property, the physical condition of the property;

(C) The date (or expected date) of contribution to the donee;

(D) The terms of any agreement or understanding entered into (or expected to be entered into) by or on behalf of the donor or donee that relates to the use, sale, or other disposition of the property contributed, including, for example, the terms of any agreement or understanding that—

(1) Restricts temporarily or permanently a donee's right to use or dispose of the donated property,

(2) Reserves to, or confers upon, anyone (other than a donee organization or an organization participating with a donee organization in cooperative fundraising) any right to the income from the contributed property or to the possession of the property, including the right to vote donated securities, to acquire the property by purchase or otherwise, or to designate the person having such income, possession, or right to acquire, or

(3) Earmarks donated property for a particular use;

(E) The name, address, and (if a taxpayer identification number is otherwise required by section 6109 and the regulations thereunder) the identifying number of the qualified appraiser; and, if the qualified appraiser is acting in his or her capacity as a partner in a partnership, an employee of any person (whether an individual, corporation, or partnerships), or an independent contractor engaged by a person other than the donor; the name, address, and taxpayer identification number (if a number is otherwise required by section 6109 and the regulations thereunder) of the partnership or the person who employs or engages the qualified appraiser;

(F) The qualifications of the qualified appraiser who signs the appraisal, including the appraiser's background, experience, education, and membership, if any, in professional appraisal associations;

(G) A statement that the appraisal was prepared for income tax purposes;

(H) The date (or dates) on which the property was appraised;

(I) The appraised fair market value (within the meaning of § 1.170A-1(c)(2)) of the property on the date (or expected date) of contribution;

(J) The method of valuation to determine the fair market value, such as the income approach, the market-data approach, and the replacement-cost-less-depreciation approach; and

(K) The specific basis for the valuation, such as specific comparable sales transactions or statistical sampling, including a justification for using sampling and an explanation of the sampling procedure employed.

(iii) Effect of signature of the qualified appraiser. Any appraiser who falsely or fraudulently overstates the value of the contributed property referred to in a qualified appraisal or appraisal summary (as defined in paragraphs (c)(3) and (4), respectively, of this section) that the appraiser has signed may be subject to a civil penalty under section 6701 for aiding and abetting an understatement of tax liability and, moreover, may have appraisals disregarded pursuant to 31 U.S.C. 330(c).

(iv) Special rules. (A) Number of qualified appraisals. For purposes of paragraph (c)(2)(i)(A) of this section, a separate qualified appraisal is required for each item of property that is not included in a group of similar items of property. See paragraph (c)(7)(iii) of this section for the definition of similar items of property. Only one qualified appraisal is required for a group of similar items of property contributed in the same taxable year of the donor, although a donor may obtain separate qualified appraisals for each item of property. A qualified appraisal prepared with respect to a group of similar items of property shall provide all the information required by paragraph (c)(3)(ii) of this section for each item of similar property, except that the appraiser may select any items whose aggregate value is appraised at $100 or less and provide a group description of such items.

(B) Time of receipt of qualified appraisal. The qualified appraisal must be received by the donor before the due date (including extensions) of the return on which a deduction is first claimed (or reported in the case of a donor that is a partnership or S corporation) under section 170 with respect to the donated property, or, in the case of a deduction first claimed (or reported) on an amended return, the date on which the return is filed.

(C) Retention of qualified appraisal. The donor must retain the qualified appraisal in the donor's records for so long as it may be relevant in the administration of any internal revenue law.

(D) Appraisal disregarded pursuant to 31 U.S.C. 330(c). If an appraisal is disregarded pursuant to 31 U.S.C. 330(c) it shall have no probative effect as to the value of the appraised property. Such appraisal will, however, otherwise constitute a "qualified appraisal" for purposes of this paragraph (c) if the appraisal summary includes the declaration described in paragraph (c)(4)(ii)(L)(2) and the taxpayer had no knowledge that such declaration was false as of the time described in paragraph (c)(4)(i)(B) of this section.

(4) Appraisal summary. (i) In general. For purposes of this paragraph (c), except as provided in paragraph (c)(4)(iv)(A) of this section, the term "appraisal summary" means a summary of a qualified appraisal that—

(A) Is made on the form prescribed by the Internal Revenue Service;

(B) Is signed and dated (as described in paragraph (c)(4)(iii) of this section) by the donee (or presented to the donee for signature in cases described in paragraph (c)(4)(iv)(C)(2) of this section);

(C) Is signed and dated by the qualified appraiser (within the meaning of paragraph (c)(5) of this section) who prepared the qualified appraisal (within the meaning of paragraph (c)(3) of this section); and

(D) Includes the information required by paragraph (c)(4)(ii) of this section.

(ii) Information included in an appraisal summary. An appraisal summary shall include the following information:

(A) The name and taxpayer identification number of the donor (social security number if the donor is an individual or, employer identification number if the donor is a partnership or corporation);

(B) A description of the property in sufficient detail for a person who is not generally familiar with the type of property to ascertain that the property that was appraised is the property that was contributed;

(C) In the case of tangible property, a brief summary of the overall physical condition of the property at the time of the contribution;

(D) The manner of acquisition (e.g., purchase, exchange, gift, or bequest) and the date of acquisition of the property by the donor, or, if the property was created, produced, or manufactured by or for the donor, a statement to that effect and the approximate date the property was substantially completed;

(E) The cost or other basis of the property adjusted as provided by section 1016;

(F) The name, address, and taxpayer identification number of the donee;

(G) The date the donee received the property;

(H) For charitable contributions made after June 6 1988, a statement explaining whether or not the charitable contribution was made by means of a bargain sale and the amount of any consideration received from the donee for the contribution;

(I) The name, ad, dress, and (if a taxpayer identification number is otherwise required by section 6109 and the regulations thereunder) the identifying number of the qualified appraiser who signs the appraisal summary and of other persons as required by paragraph (c)(3)(ii)(E) of this section;

(J) The appraised fair market value of the property on the date of contribution;

(K) The declaration by the appraiser described in paragraph (c)(5)(i) of this section;

(L) A declaration by the appraiser stating that—

(1) The fee charged for the appraisal is not of a type prohibited by paragraph (e)(6) of this section; and

(2) Appraisals prepared by the appraiser are not being disregarded pursuant to 31 U.S.C. 330(c) on the date the appraisal summary is signed by the appraiser; and

(M) Such other information as may be specified by the form.

(iii) Signature of the original donee. The person who signs the appraisal summary for the donee shall be an official authorized to sign the tax or information returns of the donee, or a person specifically authorized to sign appraisal summaries by an official authorized to sign the tax or information returns of such done. In the case of a donee that is a governmental unit, the person who signs the appraisal summary for such donee shall be the official authorized by such donee to sign appraisal summaries. The signature of the donee on the appraisal summary does not represent concurrence in the appraised value of the contributed property. Rather, it represents acknowledgment of receipt of the property described in the appraisal summary on the date specified in the appraisal summary and that the donee understands the information reporting requirements imposed by section 6050L and § 1.6050L-1. In general, § 1.6050L-1 requires the donee to file an information return with the Internal Revenue Service in the event the donee sells, exchanges, consumes, or otherwise disposes of the property (or any portion thereof) described inn the appraisal summary within 2 years after the date of the donor's contribution of such property.

(iv) Special rules. (A) Content of appraisal summary required in certain cases. With respect to contributions of nonpublicly traded stock described in paragraph (c)(2)(ii)(B)(1) of this section, contributions of securities described in paragraph (c)(7)(xi)(B) of this section, and contributions by C corporations described in paragraph (c)(2)(ii)(B)(3) of this section, the term "appraisal summary" means a document that—

(1) Complies with the requirements of paragraph (c)(4)(i)(A) and (B) of this section,

(2) Includes the information required by paragraph (c)(4)(ii)(A) through (H) of this section,

(3) Includes the amount claimed or reported as a charitable contribution deduction, and

(4) In the case of securities described in paragraph (c)(7)(xi)(B) of this section, also includes the pertinent average trading price (as described in paragraph (c)(7)(xi)(B)(2)(iii) of this section).

(B) Number of appraisal summaries. A separate appraisal summary for each item of property described in paragraph (c)(1) of this section must be attached to the donor's return. If, during the donor's taxable year, the donor contributes similar items of property described in paragraph (c)(1) of this section to more than one donee, the donor shall attach to the donor's return a separate appraisal summary for each donee. See paragraph (c)(7)(iii) of this section for the definition of similar items of property. If, however, during the donor's taxable year, a donor contributes similar items of property described in paragraph (c)(1) of this section to the same donee, the donor may attach to the donor's return a single appraisal summary with respect to all similar items of property contributed to the same donee. Such an appraisal summary shall provide all the information required by paragraph (c)(4)(ii) of this section for each item of property, except that the appraiser may select any items whose aggregate value is appraised at $100 or less and provide a group description for such items.

(C) Manner of acquisition, cost basis and donee's signature. (1) If a taxpayer has reasonable cause for being unable to provide the information required by paragraph (c)(4)(ii)(D) and (E) of this section (relating to the manner of acquisition and basis of the contributed property), an appropriate explanation should be attached to the appraisal summary. The taxpayer's deduction will not be disallowed simply because of the inability (for reasonable cause) to provide these items of information.

(2) In rare and unusual circumstances in which it is impossible for the taxpayer to obtain the signature of the donee on the appraisal summary as required by paragraph (c)(4)(i)(B) of this section, the taxpayer's deduction will not be disallowed for that reason provided that the taxpayer attaches a statement to the appraisal summary explaining, in detail, why it was not possible to obtain the donee's signature. For example, if the donee ceases to exist as an entity subsequent to the date of the contribution and prior to the date when the appraisal summary must be signed, and the donor acted reasonably in not obtaining the donee's signature at the time of the contribution, relief under this paragraph (c)(4)(iv)(C)(2) would generally be appropriate.

(D) Information excluded from certain appraisal summaries. The information required by paragraph (c)(4)(i)(C), paragraph (c)(4)(ii)(D), (E), (H) through (M), and paragraph (c)(4)(iv)(A)(3), and the average trading price referred to in paragraph (c)(4)(iv)(A)(4) of this section do not have to be included on the appraisal summary at the time it is signed by the donee or a copy is provided to the donee pursuant to paragraph (c)(4)(iv)(E) of this section.

(E) Statement to be furnished by donors to donees. Every donor who presents an appraisal summary to a donee for signature after June 6, 1988, in order to comply with paragraph (c)(4)(i)(B) of this section shall furnish a copy of the appraisal summary to such donee.

(F) Appraisal summary required to be provided to partners and S corporation shareholders. If the donor is a partnership or S corporation, the donor shall provide a copy of the appraisal summary to every partner or shareholder, respectively, who receives an allocation of a charitable contribution deduction under section 170 with respect to the property described in the appraisal summary.

(G) Partners and S corporation shareholders. A partner of a partnership or shareholder of an S corporation who receives an allocation of a deduction under section 170 for a charitable contribution of property to which this paragraph (c) applies must attach a copy of the partnership's or S corporation's appraisal summary to the tax return on which the deduction for the contribution is first claimed. If such appraisal summary is not attached, the partner's or shareholder's deduction shall not be allowed except as provided for in paragraph (c)(4)(iv)(H) of this section.

(H) Failure to attach appraisal summary. In the event that a donor fails to attach to the donor's return an appraisal summary as required by paragraph (c)(2)(i)(B) of this section, the Internal Revenue Service may request that the donor submit the appraisal summary within 90 days of the request. If such a request is made and the donor complies with the request within the 90-day period, the deduction under section 170 shall not be disallowed for failure to attach the appraisal summary, provided that the donor's failure to attach the appraisal summary was a good faith omission and the requirements of paragraph (c)(3) and (4) of this section are met (including the completion of the qualified appraisal prior to the date specified in paragraph (c)(3)(iv)(B) of this section).

(5) Qualified appraiser. (i) In general. The term "qualified appraiser" means an individual (other than a person described in paragraph (c)(5)(iv) of this section) who includes on the appraisal summary (described in paragraph (c)(4) of this section), a declaration that—

(A) The individual either holds himself or herself out to the public as an appraiser or performs appraisals on a regular basis;

(B) Because of the appraiser's qualifications as described in the appraisal (pursuant to paragraph (c)(3)(ii)(F) of this section), the appraiser is qualified to make appraisals of the type of property being valued;

(C) The appraiser is not one of the persons described in paragraph (c)(5)(iv) of this section; and

(D) The appraiser understands that an intentionally false or fraudulent overstatement of the value of the property described in the qualified appraisal or appraisal summary may subject the appraiser to a civil penalty under section 6701 for aiding and abetting an understatement of tax liability, and, moreover, the appraiser may have appraisals disregarded pursuant to 31 U.S.C. 330(c) (see paragraph (c)(3)(iii) of this section).

(ii) Exception. An individual is not a qualified appraiser with respect to a particular donation, even if the declaration specified in paragraph (c)(5)(i) of this section is provided in the appraisal summary, if the donor had knowledge of facts that would cause a reasonable person to expect the appraiser falsely to overstate the value of the donated property (e.g., the donor and the appraiser make an agreement concerning the amount at which the property will be valued and the donor knows that such amount exceeds the fair market value of the property).

(iii) Numbers of appraisers. More than one appraiser may appraise the donated property. If more than one appraiser appraises the property, the donor does not have to use each appraiser's appraisal for purposes of substantiating the charitable contribution deduction pursuant to this paragraph (c). If the donor uses the appraisal of more than one appraiser, or if two or more appraisers contribute to a single appraisal, each appraiser shall comply with the requirements of this paragraph (c), including signing the qualified appraisal and appraisal summary as required by paragraphs (c)(3)(i)(B) and (c)(4)(i)(C) of this section, respectively.

(iv) Qualified appraiser exclusions. The following persons cannot be qualified appraisers with respect to particular property:

(A) The donor or the taxpayer who claims or reports a deductions under section 170 for the contribution of the property that is being appraised.

(B) A party to the transaction in which the donor acquired the property being appraised (i.e., the person who sold, exchanged, or gave the property to the donor, or any person who acted as an agent for the transferor or for the donor with respect to such sale, exchange, or gift), unless the property is donated within 2 months of the date of acquisition and its appraised value does not exceed its acquisition price.

(C) The donee of the property.

(D) Any person employed by any of the foregoing persons (e.g., if the donor acquired a painting from an art dealer, neither the art dealer nor persons employed by the dealer can be qualified appraisers with respect to that painting).

(E) Any person related to any of the foregoing persons under section 267(b), or, with respect to appraisals made after June 6, 1988, married to a person who is in a relationship described in section 267(b) with any of the foregoing persons.

(F) An appraiser who is regularly used by any person described in paragraph (c)(5)(iv)(A), (B), or (C) of this section and who does not perform a majority of his or her appraisals made during his or her taxable year for other persons.

(6) Appraisal fees. (i) In general. Except as otherwise provided in paragraph (c)(6)(ii) of this section, no pan of the fee arrangement for a qualified appraisal can be based, in effect, on a percentage (or set of percentages) of the appraised value of the property. If a fee arrangement for an appraisal is based in whole or in part on the amount of the appraised value of the property, if any, that is allowed as a deduction under section 170, after Internal Revenue Service a examination or otherwise, it shall be treated as a fee based on a percentage of the appraised value of the property. For example, an appraiser's fee that is subject to reduction by the same percentage as the appraised value may be reduced by the Internal Revenue Service would be treated as a fee that violates this paragraph (c)(6).

(ii) Exception. Paragraph (c)(6)(i) of this section does not apply to a fee paid to a generally recognized association that regulates appraisers provided all of the following requirements are met:

(A) The association is not organized for profit and no part of the net earnings of the association inures to the benefit of any private shareholder or individual (these terms have the same meaning as in section 501(c)),

(B) The appraiser does not receive any compensation from the association or any other persons for making the appraisal, and

(C) The fee arrangement is not based in whole or in part on the amount of the appraised value of the donated property, if any, that is allowed as a deduction under section 170 after Internal Revenue Service examination or otherwise.

(7) Meaning of terms. For purposes of this paragraph (c)—

(i) Closely held corporation. The term "closely held corporation" means any corporation (other than an S corporation) with respect to which the stock ownership requirement of paragraph (2) of section 542(a) of the Code is met.

(ii) Personal service corporation. The term "personal service corporation" means any corporation (other than an S corporation) which is a service organization (within the meaning of section 414(m)(3) of the Code).

(iii) Similar items of property. The phrase "similar items of property" means property of the same generic category or type, such as stamp collections (including philatelic supplies and books on stamp collecting), coin collections (including numismatic supplies and books on coin collecting), lithographs, paintings, photographs, books, nonpublicly traded stock, nonpublicly traded securities other than nonpublicly trade stock, land, buildings, clothing, jewelry, furniture, electronic equipment, household appliances, toys, everyday kitchenware, china, crystal, or silver. For example, if a donor claims on her return for the year deductions of $2,000 for books given by her to College A $2,500 for books given by her to College B, and $900 for books given by her to College C, the $5,000 threshold of paragraph (c)(1) of this section is exceeded. Therefore, the donor must obtain a qualified appraisal for the books and attach to her return three appraisal summaries for the books donated to A, B, and C. For rules regarding the number of qualified appraisals and appraisal summaries required when similar items of property are contributed, see paragraphs (c)(3)(iv)(A) and (c)(4)(iv)(B), respectively, of this section.

(iv) Donor. The term "donor" means a person or entity (other than an organization described in section 170(c) to which the donated property was previously contributed) that makes a charitable contribution of property.

(v) Donee. The term "donee" means—

(A) Except as provided in paragraph (c)(7)(v)(B) and (C) of this section, an organization described in section 170(c) to which property is contributed,

(B) Except as provided in paragraph (c)(7)(v)(C) of this section, in the case of a charitable contribution of property placed in trust for the benefit of an organization described in section 170(c), the trust, or

(C) In the case of a charitable contribution of property placed in trust for the benefit of an organization described in section 170(c) made on or before June 6, 1988, the beneficiary that is an organization described in section 170(c), or if the trust has assumed the duties of a donee by signing the appraisal summary pursuant to paragraph (c)(4)(i)(B) of this section, the trust.

In general, the term, refers only to the original donee. However, with respect to paragraph (c)(3)(ii)(D), the last sentence of paragraph (c)(4)(iii), and paragraph (c)(5)(iv)(C) of this section, the term "donee" means the original donee and all successor donees in cases where the original donee transfers the contributed property to a successor donee after July 5, 1988.

(vi) Original donee. The term "original donee" means the donee to or for which property is initially donated by a donor.

(vii) Successor donee. The term "successor donee" means any donee of property other than its original donee (i.e., a transferee of property for less than fair market value from an original donee or another successor donee).

(viii) Fair market value. For the meaning of the term "fair market value," see § 1.170A-1(c)(2).

(ix) Nonpublicly traded securities. The term "nonpublicly traded securities" means securities (within the meaning of section 165(g)(2) of the Code) which are not publicly traded securities as defined in paragraph (c)(7)(xi) of this section.

(x) Nonpublicly traded stock. The term "nonpublicly traded stock" means any stock of a corporation (evidence by a, stock certificate) which is not a publicly traded security. The term stock does not include a debenture or any other evidence of indebtedness.

(xi) Publicly traded securities. (A) In general. Except as provided in paragraph (c)(7)(xi)(C) of this section, the term "publicly traded securities" means securities (within the meaning of section 165(g)(2) of the Code) for which (as of the date of the contribution) market quotations are readily available on an established securities market. For purposes of this section, market quotations are readily available on an established securities market with respect to a security if:

(1) The security is listed on the New York Stock Exchange, the American Stock Exchange, or any city or regional exchange in which quotations are published on a daily basis, including foreign securities listed on a recognized foreign, national, or regional exchange in which quotations are published on a daily basis;

(2) The security is regularly traded in the national or regional over-the-counter market, for which published quotations are available; or

(3) The security is a share of an open-end investment company (commonly known as a mutual fund) registered under the Investment Company Act of 1940, as amended (15 U.S.C. 80a-1 to 80b-2), for which quotations are published on a daily basis in a newspaper of general circulation throughout the United States.

(If the market value of an issue of a security is reflected only on an interdealer quotation system, the issue shall not be considered to be publicly traded unless the special rule described in paragraph (c)(7)(xi)(B) of this section is satisfied.)

(B) Special rule. (1) In general. An issue of a security that does not satisfy the requirements of paragraph (c)(7)(xi)(A)(1), (2), or (3) of this section shall nonetheless be considered to have market quotations readily available on an established securities market for purposes of paragraph (c)(7)(xi)(A) of this section if all of the following five requirements are met:

(i) The issue is regularly traded during the computational period (as defined in paragraph (c)(7)(xi)(B)(2)(iv) of this section) in a market that is reflected by the existence of an interdealer quotation system for the issue,

(ii) The issuer or an agent of the issuer computes the average trading price (as defined in paragraph (c)(7)(xi)(B)(2)(iii) of this section) for the issue for the computational period,

(iii) The average trading price and total volume of the issue during the computational period are published in a newspaper of general circulation throughout the United States not later than the last day of the month following the end of the calendar quarter in which the computational period ends,

(iv) The issuer or its agent keeps books and records that list for each transaction during the computational period involving each issue covered by this procedure the date of the settlement of the transaction, the name and address of the broker or dealer making the market in which the transaction occurred, and the trading price and volume, and

(v) The issuer or its agent permits the Internal Revenue Service to review the books and records described in paragraph (c)(7)(xi)(B)(1)(iv) of this section with respect to transactions during the computational period upon giving reasonable notice to the issuer or agent.

(2) Definitions. For purposes of this paragraph (c)(7)(xi)(B)—

(i) Issue of a security. The term "issue of a security" means a class of debt securities with the same obligor and identical terms except as to their relative denominations (amounts) or a class of stock having identical rights.

(ii) Interdealer quotation system. The term "interdealer quotation system" means any system of general circulation to brokers and dealers that regularly disseminates quotations of obligations by two or more identified brokers or dealers, who are not related to either the issuer of the security or to the issuer's agent, who compute the average trading price of the security. A quotation sheet prepared and distributed by a broker or dealer in the regular course of its business and containing only quotations of such broker or dealer is not an interdealer quotation system.

(iii) Average trading price. The term "average trading price" means the mean price of all transactions (weighted by volume), other than original issue or redemption transactions, conducted through a United States office of a broker or dealer who maintains a market in the issue of the security during the computational period. For this purpose, bid and asked quotations are not taken into account.

(iv) Computational period. For calendar quarters beginning on or after June 6, 1988, the term "computational period" means weekly during October through December (beginning with the first Monday in October and ending with the first Sunday following the last Monday in December) and monthly during January through September (beginning January 1). For calendar quarters beginning before June 6, 1988, the term "computational period" means weekly during October through December and monthly during January through September.

(C) Exception. Securities described m paragraph (c)(7)(xi)(A) or (B) of this section shall not be considered publicly traded securities if—

(1) The securities are subject to any restrictions that materially affect the value of the securities to the donor or prevent the securities from being freely traded, or

(2) If the amount claimed or reported as a deduction with respect to the contribution of the securities is different than the amount listed in the market quotations that are readily available on an established securities market pursuant to paragraph (c)(7)(xi)(A) or (B) of this section.

(D) Market quotations and fair market value. The fair market value of a publicly traded security, as defined in this paragraph (c)(7)(xi), is not necessarily equal to its market quotation, its average trading price (as defined in paragraph (c)(7)(xi)(B)(2)(iii) of this section), or its face value, if any. See § 1.170A-1(c)(2) for the definition of "fair market value."

(d) Charitable contributions; information required in support of deductions for taxable years beginning before January 1, 1983. *(1) In general.* This paragraph (d)(1) shall apply to deductions for charitable contributions made in taxable years beginning before January 1, 1983. At the option of the taxpayer the requirements of this paragraph (d)(1) shall also apply to all charitable contributions made on or before December 31, 1984 (in lieu of the requirements of paragraphs (a) and (b) of this section). In connection with claims for deductions for charitable contributions, taxpayers shall state in their income tax returns the name of each organization to which a contribution was made and the amount and date of the actual payment of each contribution. If a contribution is made in property other than money, the taxpayer shall state the kind of property contributed, for example, used clothing, paintings, or securities, the method utilized in determining the fair market value of the property at the time the contribution was made, and whether or not the amount of the contribution was reduced under section 170(e). If a taxpayer makes more than one cash contribution to an organization during the taxable year, then in lieu of listing each cash contribution and the date of payment the taxpayer may state the total cash payments made to such organization during the taxable year. A taxpayer who elects under paragraph (d)(2) of § 1.170A-8 to apply section 170(e)(1) to his contributions and carryovers of 30-percent capital gain property must file a statement with his return indicating that he has made the election and showing the contributions in the current year and carryovers from preceding years to which it applies. For the definition of the term "30-percent capital gains property", see paragraph (d)(3) of § 1.170A-8.

(2) Contribution by individual of property other than money. This paragraph (d)(2) shall apply to deductions for charitable contributions made in taxable years beginning before January 1, 1983. At the option of the taxpayer, the requirements of this paragraph (d)(2) shall also apply to contributions of property made on or before December 31, 1984 (in lieu of the requirements of paragraph (b) of this section). If an individual taxpayer makes a charitable contribution of an item of property other than money and claims a deduction in excess of $200 in respect of his contribution of such item, he shall attach to his income tax return the following information with respect to such item:

(i) The name and address of the organization to which the contribution was made.

(ii) The date of the actual contribution.

(iii) A description of the property in sufficient detail to identify the particular property contributed, including in the case of tangible property the physical condition of the property at the time of contribution, and, in the case of securities, the name of the issuer, the type of security, and whether or not such security is regularly traded on a stock exchange or in an over-the-counter market.

(iv) The manner of acquisition, as, for example, by purchase, gift, bequest, inheritance, or exchange, and the approximate date of acquisition of the property by the taxpayer or if the property was created, produced, or manufactured by or for the taxpayer, the approximate date the property was substantially completed.

(v) The fair market value of the property at the time the contribution was made, the method utilized in determining the fair market value, and, if the valuation was determined by appraisal, a copy of the signed report of the appraiser.

(vi) The cost or other basis, adjusted as provided by section 1016, of property, other than securities, held by the taxpayer for a period of less than 5 years immediately preceding the date on which the contribution was made and, when the information is available, of property, other than securities, held for a period of 5 years or more preceding the date on which the contribution was made.

(vii) In the case of property to which section 170(e) applies, the cost or other basis, adjusted as provided by section 1016, the reduction by reason of section 170(e)(1) in the amount of the charitable contribution otherwise taken into account, and the manner in which such reduction was determined.

(viii) The terms of any agreement or understanding entered into by or on behalf of the taxpayer which relates to the use, sale, or disposition of the property contributed, as, for example, the terms of any agreement or understanding which

(A) Restricts temporarily or permanently the donee's right to dispose of the donated property,

(B) Reserves to, or confers upon, anyone other than the donee organization or other than an organization participating with such organization in cooperative fund raising, any right to the income from such property, to the possession of the property, including the right to vote securities, to acquire such property by purchase or otherwise, or to designate the person to have such income, possession, or right to acquire, or

(C) Earmarks contributed property for a particular charitable use, such as the use of donated furniture in the reading room of the donee organization's library.

(ix) The total amount claimed as a deduction for the taxable year due to the contribution of the property and, if less than the entire interest in the property is contributed during the taxable year, the amount claimed as a deduction in any prior year or years for contributions of other interests in such property, the name and address of each organization to which any such contribution was made, the place where any such property which is tangible property is located or kept, and the name of any person, other than the organization to which the property giving rise to the deduction was contributed, having actual possession of the property.

(3) Statement from donee organization. Any deduction for a charitable contribution must be substantiated, when required by the district director, by a statement from the organization to which the contribution was made indicating whether the organization is a domestic organization, the name and address of the contributor, the amount of the contribution, the date of actual receipt of the contribution, and such other information as the district director may deem necessary. If the contribution includes an item of property, other than money or securities which are regularly traded on a stock exchange or in an over-the-counter market, which the donee deems to have a fair market value in excess of $500 ($200 in the case of a charitable contribution made in a taxable year beginning before January 1, 1983) at the time of receipt, such statement shall also indicate for each such item its location if it is retained by the organization, the amount received by the organization on any sale of the property and the date of sale or, in case of any other disposition of the property, the method of disposition. In the case of any contribution of tangible personal property, the statement shall indicate the use of the property by the organization and whether or not it is used for a purpose or function constituting the basis for the donee organization's exemption from income tax under section 501 or, in the case of a governmental unit, whether or not it is used for exclusively public purposes.

(e) [Reserved]

(f) Substantiation of charitable contributions of $250 or more. *(1) In general.* No deduction is allowed under section 170(a) for all or part of any contribution of $250 or more unless the taxpayer substantiates the contribution with a contemporaneous written acknowledgment from the donee organization. A taxpayer who makes more than one contribution of $250 or more to a donee organization in a taxable year may substantiate the contributions with one or more contemporaneous written acknowledgments. Section 170(f)(8) does not apply to a payment of $250 or more if the amount contributed (as determined under § 1.170A-1(h)) is less than $250. Separate contributions of less than $250 are not subject to the requirements of section 170(f)(8), regardless of whether the sum of the contributions made by a taxpayer to a donee organization during a taxable year equals $250 or more.

(2) Written acknowledgment. Except as otherwise provided in paragraphs (f)(8) through (f)(11) and (f)(13) of this section, a written acknowledgment from a donee organization must provide the following information—

(i) The amount of any cash the taxpayer paid and a description (but not necessarily the value) of any property other than cash the taxpayer transferred to the donee organization;

(ii) A statement of whether or not the donee organization provides any goods or services in consideration, in whole or in part, for any of the cash or other property transferred to the donee organization;

(iii) If the donee organization provides any goods or services other than intangible religious benefits (as described in section 170(f)(8)), a description and good faith estimate of the value of those goods or services; and

(iv) If the donee organization provides any intangible religious benefits, a statement to that effect.

(3) Contemporaneous. A written acknowledgment is contemporaneous if it is obtained by the taxpayer on or before the earlier of—

(i) The date the taxpayer files the original return for the taxable year in which the contribution was made; or

(ii) The due date (including extensions) for filing the taxpayer's original return for that year.

(4) Donee organization. For purposes of this paragraph (f), a donee organization is an organization described in section 170(c).

(5) Goods or services. Goods or services means cash, property, services, benefits, and privileges.

(6) In consideration for. A donee organization provides goods or services in consideration for a taxpayer's payment if, at the time the taxpayer makes the payment to the donee organization, the taxpayer receives or expects to receive goods or services in exchange for that payment. Goods or services a donee organization provides in consideration for a payment by a taxpayer include goods or services provided in a year other than the year in which the taxpayer makes the payment to the donee organization.

(7) Good faith estimate. For purposes of this section, good faith estimate means a donee organization's estimate of the fair market value of any goods or services, without regard to the manner in which the organization in fact made that estimate. See § 1.170A-1(h)(4) for rules regarding when a taxpayer may treat a donee organization's estimate of the value of goods or services as the fair market value.

(8) Certain goods or services disregarded. (i) In general. For purposes of section 170(f)(8), the following goods or services are disregarded—

(A) Goods or services that have insubstantial value under the guidelines provided in Revenue Procedures 90-12, 1990-1 C.B. 471, 92-49, 1992-1 C.B. 987, and any successor documents. (See § 601.601(d)(2)(ii) of the Statement of Procedural Rules, 26 CFR part 601.); and

(B) Annual membership benefits offered to a taxpayer in exchange for a payment of $75 or less per year that consist of—

(1) Any rights or privileges, other than those described in section 170(l), that the taxpayer can exercise frequently during the membership period. Examples of such rights and privileges may include, but are not limited to, free or discounted admission to the organization's facilities or events, free or discounted parking, preferred access to goods or services, and discounts on the purchase of goods or services; and

(2) Admission to events during the membership period that are open only to members of a donee organization and for which the donee organization reasonably projects that the cost per person (excluding any allocable overhead) attending each such event is within the limits established for "low cost articles" under section 513(h)(2). The projected cost to the donee organization is determined at the time the organization first offers its membership package for the year (using section 3.07 of Revenue Procedure 90-12, or any successor documents, to determine the cost of any items or services that are donated).

(ii) Examples. The following examples illustrate the rules of this paragraph (f)(8).

Example (1). Membership benefits disregarded. Performing Arts Center E is an organization described in section 170(c). In return for a payment of $75, E offers a package of basic membership benefits that includes the right to purchase tickets to performances one week before they go on sale to the general public, free parking in E's garage during evening and weekend performances, and a 10% discount on merchandise sold in E's gift shop. In return for a payment of $150, E offers a package of preferred membership benefits that includes all of the benefits in the $75 package as well as a poster that is sold in E's gift shop for $20. The basic membership and the preferred membership are each valid for twelve months, and there are approximately 50 performances of various productions at E during a twelve-month period. E's gift shop is open for several hours each week and at performance times. F, a patron of the arts, is solicited by E to make a contribution. E offers F the preferred membership benefits in return for a payment of $150 or more. F makes a payment of $300 to E. F can satisfy the substantiation requirement of section 170(f)(8) by obtaining a contemporaneous written acknowledgment from E that includes a description of the poster and a good faith estimate of its fair market value ($20) and disregards the remaining membership benefits.

Example (2). Contemporaneous written acknowledgment need not mention rights or privileges that can be disregarded. The facts are the same as in Example 1, except that F made a payment of $300 and received only a basic membership. F can satisfy the section 170(f)(8) substantiation requirement with a contemporaneous written acknowledgment stating that no goods or services were provided.

Example (3). Rights or privileges that cannot be exercised frequently. Community Theater Group G is an organization described in section 170(c). Every summer, G performs four different plays. Each play is performed two times. In return for a membership fee of $60, G offers its members free admission to any of its performances. Non-members may purchase tickets on a performance by performance basis for $15 a ticket. H, an individual who is a sponsor of the theater, is solicited by G to make a contribution. G tells H that the membership benefit will be provided in return for any payment of $60 or more. H chooses to make a payment of $350 to G and receives in return the membership benefit. G's membership benefit of free admission is not described in paragraph (f)(8)(i)(B) of this section because it is not a privilege that can be exercised frequently (due to the limited number of performances offered by G). Therefore, to meet the requirements of section 170(f)(8), a contemporaneous written acknowledgment of H's $350 payment must include a description of the free admission benefit and a good faith estimate of its value.

Example (4). Multiple memberships. In December of each year, K, an individual, gives each of her six grandchildren a junior membership in Dinosaur Museum, an organization described in section 170(c). Each junior membership costs $50, and K makes a single payment of $300 for all six memberships. A junior member is entitled to free admission to the museum and to weekly films, slide shows, and lectures about dinosaurs. In addition, each junior member receives a bi-monthly, non-commercial quality newsletter with information about dinosaurs and upcoming events. K's contemporaneous written acknowledgment from Dinosaur Museum may state that no goods or services were provided in exchange for K's payment.

(9) Goods or services provided to employees or partners of donors. (i) Certain goods or services disregarded. For purposes of section 170(f)(8), goods or services provided by a donee organization to employees of a donor, or to partners of a partnership that is a donor, in return for a payment to the organization may be disregarded to the extent that the goods or services provided to each employee or partner are the same as those described in paragraph (f)(8)(i) of this section.

(ii) No good faith estimate required for other goods or services. If a taxpayer makes a contribution of $250 or more to a donee organization and, in return, the donee organization offers the taxpayer's employees or partners goods or services other than those described in paragraph (f)(9)(i) of this section, the contemporaneous written acknowledgment of the taxpayer's contribution is not required to include a good faith estimate of the value of such goods or services but must include a description of those goods or services.

(iii) Example. The following example illustrates the rules of this paragraph (f)(9).

Example. Museum J is an organization described in section 170(c). For a payment of $40, J offers a package of basic membership benefits that includes free admission and a 10% discount on merchandise sold in J's gift shop. J's other membership categories are for supporters who contribute $100 or more. Corporation K makes a payment of $50,000 to J and, in return, J offers K's employees free admission for one year, a tee-shirt with J's logo that costs J $4.50, and a gift shop discount of 25% for one year. The free admission for K's employees is the same as the benefit made available to holders of the $40 membership and is otherwise described in paragraph (f)(8)(i)(B) of this section. The tee-shirt given to each of K's employees is described in paragraph (f)(8)(i)(A) of this section. Therefore, the contemporaneous written acknowledgment of K's payment is not required to include a description or good faith estimate of the value of the free admission or the tee-shirts. However, because the gift shop discount offered to K's employees is different than that offered to those who purchase the $40 membership, the discount is not described in paragraph (f)(8)(i) of this section. Therefore, the contemporaneous written acknowledgment of K's payment is required to include a description of the 25% discount offered to K's employees.

(10) Substantiation of out-of-pocket expenses. A taxpayer who incurs unreimbursed expenditures incident to the rendition of services, within the meaning of § 1.170A-1(g), is treated as having obtained a contemporaneous written acknowledgment of those expenditures if the taxpayer—

(i) Has adequate records under paragraph (a) of this section to substantiate the amount of the expenditures; and

(ii) Obtains by the date prescribed in paragraph (f)(3) of this section a statement prepared by the donee organization containing—

(A) A description of the services provided by the taxpayer;

(B) A statement of whether or not the donee organization provides any goods or services in consideration, in whole or in part, for the unreimbursed expenditures; and

(C) The information required by paragraphs (f)(2)(iii) and (iv) of this section.

(11) Contributions made by payroll deduction. (i) Form of substantiation. A contribution made by means of withholding from a taxpayer's wages and payment by the taxpayer's employer to a donee organization may be substantiated, for purposes of section 170(f)(8), by both—

(A) A pay stub, Form W-2, or other document furnished by the employer that sets forth the amount withheld by the employer for the purpose of payment to a donee organization; and

(B) A pledge card or other document prepared by or at the direction of the donee organization that includes a statement to the effect that the organization does not provide goods or services in whole or partial consideration for any contributions made to the organization by payroll deduction.

(ii) Application of $250 threshold. For the purpose of applying the $250 threshold provided in section 170(f)(8)(A) to contributions made by the means described in paragraph (f)(11)(i) of this section, the amount withheld from each payment of wages to a taxpayer is treated as a separate contribution.

(12) Distributing organizations as donees. An organization described in section 170(c), or an organization described in 5 CFR 950.105 (a Principal Combined Fund Organization for purposes of the Combined Federal Campaign) and acting in that capacity, that receives a payment made as a contribution is treated as a donee organization solely for purposes of section 170(f)(8), even if the organization (pursuant to the donor's instructions or otherwise) distributes the amount received to one or more organizations described in section 170(c). This paragraph (f)(12) does not apply, however, to a case in which the distributee organization provides goods or services as part of a transaction structured with a view to avoid taking the goods or services into account in determining the amount of the deduction to which the donor is entitled under section 170.

(13) Transfers to certain trusts. Section 170(f)(8) does not apply to a transfer of property to a trust described in section 170(f)(2)(B), a charitable remainder annuity trust (as defined in section 664(d)(1)), or a charitable remainder unitrust (as defined in section 664(d)(2) or (d)(3) or § 1.664-3(a)(1)(i)(b)). Section 170(f)(8) does apply, however, to a transfer to a pooled income fund (as defined in section 642(c)(5)); for such a transfer, the contemporaneous written acknowledgment must state that the contribution was transferred to the donee organization's pooled income fund and indicate whether any goods or services (in addition to an income interest in the fund) were provided in exchange for the transfer. The contemporaneous written acknowledgment is not required to include a good faith estimate of the income interest.

(14) Substantiation of payments to a college or university for the right to purchase tickets to athletic events. For purposes of paragraph (f)(2)(iii) of this section, the right to purchase tickets for seating at an athletic event in exchange for a payment described in section 170(l) is treated as having a value equal to twenty percent of such payment. For example, when a taxpayer makes a payment of $312.50 for the right to purchase tickets for seating at an athletic event, the right to purchase tickets is treated as having a value of $62.50. The remaining $250 is treated as a charitable contribution, which the taxpayer must substantiate in accordance with the requirements of this section.

(15) Substantiation of charitable contributions made by a partnership or an S corporation. If a partnership or an S corporation makes a charitable contribution of $250 or more, the partnership or S corporation will be treated as the taxpayer for purposes of section 170(f)(8). Therefore, the partnership or S corporation must substantiate the contribution with a contemporaneous written acknowledgment from the donee organization before reporting the contribution on its income tax return for the year in which the contribution was made and must maintain the contemporaneous written acknowledgment in its records. A partner of a partnership or a shareholder of an S corporation is not required to obtain any additional substantiation for his or her share of the partnership's or S corporation's charitable contribution.

(16) Purchase of an annuity. If a taxpayer purchases an annuity from a charitable organization and claims a charitable contribution deduction of $250 or more for the excess of the amount paid over the value of the annuity, the contemporaneous written acknowledgment must state whether any goods or services in addition to the annuity were provided to the taxpayer. The contemporaneous written acknowledgment is not required to include a good faith estimate of the value of the annuity. See § 1.170A1(d)(2) for guidance in determining the value of the annuity.

(17) Substantiation of matched payments. (i) In general. For purposes of section 170, if a taxpayer's payment to a donee organization is matched, in whole or in part, by another payor, and the taxpayer receives goods or services in consideration for its payment and some or all of the matching payment, those goods or services will be treated as provided in consideration for the taxpayer's payment and not in consideration for the matching payment.

(ii) Example. The following example illustrates the rules of this paragraph (f)(17).

Example. Taxpayer makes a $400 payment to Charity L, a donee organization. Pursuant to a matching payment plan, Taxpayer's employer matches Taxpayer's $400 payment with an additional payment of $400. In consideration for the combined payments of $800, L gives Taxpayer an item that it estimates has a fair market value of $100. L does not give the employer any goods or services in consideration for its contribution. The contemporaneous written acknowledgment provided to the employer must include a statement that no goods or services were provided in consideration for the employer's $400 payment. The contemporaneous written acknowledgment provided to Taxpayer must include a statement of the amount of Taxpayer's payment, a description of the item received by Taxpayer, and a statement that L's good faith estimate of the value of the item received by Taxpayer is $100.

(18) Effective date. This paragraph (f) applies to contributions made on or after December 16, 1996. However, taxpayers may rely on the rules of this paragraph (f) for contributions made on or after January 1, 1994.

T.D. 8002, 12/26/84, amend T.D. 8003, 12/26/84, T.D. 8199, 5/4/88, T.D. 8623, 10/11/95, T.D. 8690, 12/13/96.

PAR. 3. In § 1.170A-13, paragraphs (a)(3), (b)(3)(i)(B), (b)(4), and (d) are removed.

Proposed § 1.170A-13 [*For Preamble, see ¶ 153,047*]

[Amended]

PAR. 4. Section 1.170A-13 is amended as follows:

1. The heading for paragraph (c) is revised to read as set forth below.

2. Paragraph (c)(1)(i) is revised to read as set forth below.

3. Paragraph (c)(1)(ii) is redesignated as paragraph (c)(1)(iii) and a new paragraph (c)(1)(ii) is inserted after paragraph (c)(1)(i) to read as set forth below.

4. Paragraph (c)(2)(ii)(B)(3) is revised to read as set forth below.

5. Paragraph (c)(4)(iv)(A) is revised to read as set forth below.

Proposed § 1.170A-13 Recordkeeping and return requirements for deductions for charitable contributions. [*For Preamble, see ¶ 151,114*]

Caution: The Treasury has not yet amended Reg § 1.170A-13 to reflect changes made by P.L. 103-66.

* * * * *

(c) Deductions in excess of $5,000 for charitable contributions of certain property. *(1) General rule.* (i) In general. No deduction under section 170 shall be allowed with respect to a charitable contribution to which this paragraph (c) applies unless the substantiation requirements described in paragraph (c)(2) of this section are met. This paragraph (c) applies to any charitable contribution described in paragraph (c)(1)(ii) of this section made by any donor after [THE DATE THAT IS 30 DAYS AFTER TREASURY DECISION ON THE SUBJECT OF THIS NOTICE OF PROPOSED RULEMAKING IS PUBLISHED IN THE FEDERAL REGISTER]. It also applies to any such contribution made before that date as follows:

(A) In the case of an individual, closely held corporation, personal service corporation, partnership, or S corporation if made after December 31, 1984, and

(B) In the case of a C corporation (as defined in section 1361(a)(2) of the Code) if made after June 6, 1988. (See paragraph (c)(2)(ii) of this section for special rules with respect to contributions made by C corporations on or before [THE DATE THAT IS 30 DAYS AFTER A TREASURY DECISION ON THE SUBJECT OF THIS NOTICE OF PROPOSED RULEMAKING IS PUBLISHED IN THE FEDERAL REGISTER].)

(ii) Charitable contribution. Paragraph (c)(1)(i) of this section applies to a charitable contribution of an item of property (other than money and publicly traded securities to which paragraph (c)(7)(xi)(B) of this section does not apply) if the amount claimed or reported as a deduction under section 170 with respect to such item exceeds $5,000. For purposes of this paragraph (c), the amount claimed or reported as a deduction for an item of property is the aggregate amount claimed or reported as a deduction for a charitable contribution under section 170 for such item of property and all similar items of property (as defined in paragraph (c)(7)(iii) of this section) by the same donor for the same taxable year (whether or not donated to the same donee).

* * * * *

(2) Substantiation requirements. * * *

(ii) Special rules for certain nonpublicly traded stock, certain publicly traded securities, and contributions by certain C corporations. * * *

(B) * * *

(3) The contribution by a C corporation (as defined in section 1361(a)(2)), other than a closely held corporation or a personal service corporation, of an item of property or of similar items of property described in paragraph (c)(1) of this section made after June 6, 1988, and on or before [THE DATE THAT IS 30 DAYS AFTER A TREASURY DECISION ON THE SUBJECT OF THIS NOTICE OF PROPOSED RULEMAKING IS PUBLISHED IN THE FEDERAL REGISTER].

* * * * *

(4) Appraisal summary. * * *

(iv) Special rules. (A) Content of appraisal summary required in certain cases. With respect to contributions of nonpublicly traded stock described in paragraph (c)(2)(ii)(B)(1) of this section contributions of securities described in paragraph (c)(7)(xi)(B) of this section, and contributions described in paragraph (c)(2)(ii)(B)(3) of this section made after June 6, 1988 and on or before [THE DATE THAT IS 30 DAYS AFTER A TREASURY DECISION ON THE SUBJECT OF THIS NOTICE OF PROPOSED RULEMAKING IS PUBLISHED IN THE FEDERAL REGISTER] by a C corporation, the term "appraisal summary" means a document that—

(1) Complies with the requirements of paragraph (c)(4)(i)(A) and (B) of this section,

(2) Includes the information required by paragraph (c)(4)(ii)(A) and through (H) of this section,

(3) Includes the amount claimed or reported as a charitable contribution deduction, and

(4) In the case of securities described in paragraph (c)(7)(xi)(B) of this section, also includes the pertinent average trading price (as described in paragraph (c)(7)(xi)(B)(2)(iii) of this section).

* * * * *

§ 1.170A-14 Qualified conservation contributions.

(a) Qualified conservation contributions. A deduction under section 170 is generally not allowed for a charitable contribution of any interest in property that consists of less than the donor's entire interest in the property other than certain transfers in trust (see § 1.170A-6 relating to charitable contributions in trust and § 1.170A-7 relating to contributions not in trust of partial interests in property). However, a deduction may be allowed under section 170(f)(3)(B)(iii) for the value of a qualified conservation contribution if the requirements of this section are met. A qualified conservation contribution is the contribution of a qualified real property interest to a qualified organization exclusively for conservation purposes. To be eligible for a deduction under this section, the conservation purpose must be protected in perpetuity.

(b) Qualified real property interest. *(1) Entire interest of donor other than qualified mineral interest.* (i) The entire interest of the donor other than a qualified mineral interest is a qualified real property interest. A qualified mineral interest is the donor's interest in subsurface oil, gas, or other minerals and the right of access to such minerals.

(ii) A real property interest shall not be treated as an entire interest other than a qualified mineral interest by reason of section 170(h)(2)(A) and this paragraph (b)(1) if the property in which the donor's interest exists was divided prior to the contribution in order to enable the donor to retain control of more than a qualified mineral interest or to reduce the real property interest donated. See Treasury regulations § 1.170A-7(a)(2)(i). An entire interest in real property may consist of an undivided interest in the property. But see section 170(h)(5)(A) and the regulations thereunder (relating to the requirement that the conservation purpose which is the subject of the donation must be protected in perpetuity). Minor interests, such as rights-of-way, that will not interfere with the conservation purposes of the donation, may be transferred prior to the conservation contribution without affecting the treatment of a property interest as a qualified real property interest under this paragraph (b)(1).

(2) Perpetual conservation restriction. A perpetual conservation restriction is a qualified real property interest. A "perpetual conservation restriction" is a restriction granted in perpetuity on the use which may be made of real property—

including, an easement or other interest in real property that under state law has attributes similar to an easement (e.g., a restrictive covenant or equitable servitude). For purposes of this section, the terms "easement", "conservation restriction", and "perpetual conservation restriction" have the same meaning. The definition of "perpetual conservation restriction" under this paragraph (b)(2) is not intended to preclude the deductibility of a donation of affirmative rights to use a land or water area under § 1.170A-13(d)(2). Any rights reserved by the donor in the donation of a perpetual conservation restriction must conform to the requirements of this section. See e.g., paragraph (d)(4)(ii), (d)(5)(i), (e)(3), and (g)(4) of this section.

(c) Qualified organization. *(1) Eligible donee.* To be considered an eligible donee under this section, an organization must be a qualified organization, have a commitment to protect the conservation purposes of the donation, and have the resources to enforce the restrictions. A conservation group organized or operated primarily or substantially for one of the conservation purposes specified in section 170(h)(4)(A) will be considered to have the commitment required by the preceding sentence. A qualified organization need not set aside funds to enforce the restrictions that are the subject of the contribution. For purposes of this section, the term "qualified organization" means:

(i) A governmental unit described in section 170(b)(1)(A)(v);

(ii) An organization described in section 170(b)(1)(A)(vi);

(iii) A charitable organization described in section 501(c)(3) that meets the public support test of section 509(a)(2);

(iv) A charitable organization described in section 501(c)(3) that meets the requirements of section 509(a)(3) and is controlled by an organization described in paragraphs (c)(1)(i), (ii), or (iii) of this section.

(2) Transfers by donee. A deduction shall be allowed for a contribution under this section only if in the instrument of conveyance the donor prohibits the donee from subsequently transferring the easement (or, in the case of a remainder interest or the reservation of a qualified mineral interest, the property), whether or not for consideration, unless the donee organization, as a condition of the subsequent transfer, requires that the conservation purposes which the contribution was originally intended to advance continue to be carried out. Moreover, subsequent transfers must be restricted to organizations qualifying, at the time of the subsequent transfer, as an eligible donee under paragraph (c)(1) of this section. When a later unexpected change in the conditions surrounding the property that is the subject of a donation under paragraph (b)(1), (2), or (3) of this section makes impossible or impractical the continued use of the property for conservation purposes, the requirement of this paragraph will be met if the property is sold or exchanged and any proceeds are used by the donee organization in a manner consistent with the conservation purposes of the original contribution. In the case of a donation under paragraph (b)(3) of this section to which the preceding sentence applies, see also paragraph (g)(5)(ii) of this section.

(d) Conservation purposes. *(1) In general.* For purposes of section 170(h) and this section, the term "conservation purposes" means—

(i) The preservation of land areas for outdoor recreation by, or the education of, the general public, within the meaning of paragraph (d)(2) of this section,

(ii) The protection of a relatively natural habitat of fish, wildlife, or plants, or similar ecosystem, within the meaning of paragraph (d)(3) of this section.

(iii) The preservation of certain open space (including farmland and forest land) within the meaning of paragraph (d)(4) of this section, or

(iv) The preservation of a historically important land area or a certified historic structure, within the meaning of paragraph (d)(5) of this section.

(2) Recreation or education. (i) In general. The donation of a qualified real property interest to preserve land areas for the outdoor recreation of the general public or for the education of the general public will meet the conservation purposes test of this section. Thus, conservation purposes would include, for example, the preservation of a water area for the use of the public for boating or fishing, or a nature or hiking trail for the use of the public.

(ii) Access. The preservation of land areas for recreation or education will not meet the test of this section unless the recreation or education is for the substantial and regular use of the general public.

(3) Protection of environmental system. (i) In general. The donation of a qualified real property interest to protect a significant relatively natural habitat in which a fish, wildlife, or plant community, or similar ecosystem normally lives will meet the conservation purposes test of this section. The fact that the habitat or environment has been altered to some extent by human activity will not result in a deduction being denied under this section if the fish, wildlife, or plants continue to exist there in a relatively natural state. For example, the preservation of a lake formed by a man-made dam or a salt pond formed by a man-made dike would meet the conservation purposes test if the lake or pond were a nature feeding area for a wildlife community that included rare, endangered, or threatened native species.

(ii) Significant habitat or ecosystem. Significant habitats and ecosystems include, but are not limited to, habitats for rare, endangered, or threatened species of animal, fish, or plants; natural areas that represent high quality examples of a terrestrial community or aquatic community, such as islands that are undeveloped or not intensely developed where the coastal ecosystem is relatively intact; and natural areas which are included in, or which contribute to, the ecological viability of a local, state, or national park, nature preserve, wildlife refuge, wilderness area, or other similar conservation area.

(iii) Access. Limitations on public access to property that is the subject of a donation under this paragraph (d)(3) shall not render the donation nondeductible. For example, a restriction on all public access to the habitat of a threatened native animal species protected by a donation under this paragraph (d)(3) would not cause the donation to be nondeductible.

(4) Preservation of open space. (i) In general. The donation of a qualified real property interest to preserve open space (including farmland and forest land) will meet the conservation purposes test of this section if such preservation is—

(A) Pursuant to a clearly delineated Federal, state, or local governmental conservation policy and will yield a significant public benefit, or

(B) For the scenic enjoyment of the general public and will yield a significant public benefit.

An open space easement donated on or after December 18, 1980, must meet the requirements of section 170(h) in order to be deductible.

(ii) Scenic enjoyment. (A) Factors. A contribution made for the preservation of open space may be for the scenic enjoyment of the general public. Preservation of land may be for the scenic enjoyment of the general public if development of the property would impair the scenic character of the local rural or urban landscape or would interfere with a scenic panorama that can be enjoyed from a park, nature preserve, road, waterbody, trail, or historic structure or land area, and such area or transportation way is open to, or utilized by, the public. "Scenic enjoyment" will be evaluated by considering all pertinent facts and circumstances germane to the contribution. Regional variations in topography, geology, biology, and cultural and economic conditions require flexibility in the application of this test, but do not lessen the burden on the taxpayer to demonstrate the scenic characteristics of a donation under this paragraph. The application of a particular objective factor to help define a view as "scenic" in one setting may in fact be entirely inappropriate in another setting. Among the factors to be considered are:

(1) The compatibility of the land use with other land in the vicinity;

(2) The degree of contrast and variety provided by the visual scene;

(3) The openness of the land (which would be a more significant factor in an urban or densely populated setting or in a heavily wooded area);

(4) Relief from urban closeness;

(5) The harmonious variety of shapes and textures;

(6) The degree to which the land use maintains the scale and character of the urban landscape to preserve open space, visual enjoyment, and sunlight for the surrounding area;

(7) The consistency of the proposed scenic view with a methodical state scenic identification program, such as a state landscape inventory; and

(8) The consistency of the proposed scenic view with a regional or local landscape inventory made pursuant to a sufficiently rigorous review process, especially if the donation is endorsed by an appropriate state or local governmental agency.

(B) Access. To satisfy the requirement of scenic enjoyment by the general public, visual (rather than physical) access to or across the property by the general public is sufficient. Under the terms of an open space easement on scenic property, the entire property need not be visible to the public for a donation to qualify under this section, although the public benefit from the donation may be insufficient to qualify for a deduction if only a small portion of the property is visible to the public.

(iii) Governmental conservation policy. (A) In general. The requirement that the preservation of open space be pursuant to a clearly delineated Federal, state, or local governmental policy is intended to protect the types of property identified by representatives of the general public as worthy of preservation or conservation. A general declaration of conservation goals by a single official or legislative body is not sufficient. However, a governmental conservation policy need not be a certification program that identifies particular lots or small parcels of individually owned property. This requirement will be met by donations that further a specific, identified conservation project, such as the preservation of land within a state or local landmark district that is locally recognized as being significant to that district; the preservation of a wild or scenic river, the preservation of farmland pursuant to a state program for flood prevention and control; or the protection of the scenic, ecological, or historic character of land that is contiguous to, or an integral part of, the surroundings of existing recreation or conservation sites. For example, the donation of a perpetual conservation restriction to a qualified organization pursuant to a formal resolution or certification by a local governmental agency established under state law specifically identifying the subject properly as worthy of protection for conservation purposes will meet the requirement of this paragraph. A program need not be funded to satisfy this requirement, but the program must involve a significant commitment by the government with respect to the conservation project. For example, a governmental program according preferential tax assessment or preferential zoning for certain property deemed worthy of protection for conservation purposes would constitute a significant commitment by the government.

(B) Effect of acceptance by governmental agency. Acceptance of an easement by an agency of the Federal Government or by an agency of a state or local government (or by a commission, authority, or similar body duly constituted by the state or local government and acting on behalf of the state or local government) tends to establish the requisite clearly delineated governmental policy, although such acceptance, without more, is not sufficient. The more rigorous the review process by the governmental agency, the more the acceptance of the easement tends to establish the requisite clearly delineated governmental policy. For example, in a state where the legislature has established an Environmental Trust to accept gifts to the state which meet certain conservation purposes and to submit the gifts to a review that requires the approval of the state's highest officials, acceptance of a gift by the Trust tends to establish the requisite clearly delineated governmental policy. However, if the Trust merely accepts such gifts without a review process, the requisite clearly delineated governmental policy is not established.

(C) Access. A limitation on public access to property subject to a donation under this paragraph (d)(4)(iii) shall not render the deduction nondeductible unless the conservation purpose of the donation would be undermined or frustrated without public access. For example, a donation pursuant to a governmental policy to protect the scenic character of land near a river requires visual access to the same extent as would a donation under paragraph (d)(4)(ii) of this section.

(iv) Significant public benefit. (A) Factors. All contributions made for the preservation of open space must yield a significant public benefit. Public benefit will be evaluated by considering all pertinent facts and circumstances germane to the contribution. Factors germane to the evaluation of public benefit from one contribution may be irrelevant in determining public benefit from another contribution. No single factor will necessarily be determinative. Among the factors to be considered are:

(1) The uniqueness of the property to the area;

(2) The intensity of land development in the vicinity of the property (both existing development and foreseeable trends of development);

(3) The consistency of the proposed open space use with public programs (whether Federal, state or local) for conservation in the region, including programs for outdoor recreation, irrigation or water supply protection, water quality maintenance or enhancement, flood prevention and control, erosion control, shoreline protection, and protection of land

areas included in, or related to, a government approved master plan or land management area;

(4) The consistency of the proposed open space use with existing private conservation programs in the area, as evidenced by other land, protected by easement or fee ownership by organizations referred to in § 1.170A-14(c)(1), in close proximity to the property;

(5) The likelihood that development of the property would lead to or contribute to degradation of the scenic, natural, or historic character of the area;

(6) The opportunity for the general public to use the property or to appreciate its scenic values;

(7) The importance of the property in preserving a local or regional landscape or resource that attracts tourism or commerce to the area;

(8) The likelihood that the donee will acquire equally desirable and valuable substitute property or property rights;

(9) The cost to the donee of enforcing the terms of the conservation restriction;

(10) The population density in the area of the property; and

(11) The consistency of the proposed open space use with a legislatively mandated program identifying particular parcels of land for future protection.

(B) Illustrations. The preservation of an ordinary tract of land would not in and of itself yield a significant public benefit, but the preservation of ordinary land areas in conjunction with other factors that demonstrate significant public benefit or the preservation of a unique land area for public employment would yield a significant public benefit.

For example, the preservation of a vacant downtown lot would not by itself yield a significant public benefit, but the preservation of the downtown lot as a public garden would, absent countervailing factors, yield a significant public benefit. The following are other examples of contributions which would, absent countervailing factors, yield a significant public benefit: The preservation of farmland pursuant to a state program for flood prevention and control; the preservation of a unique natural land formation for the enjoyment of the general public; the preservation of woodland along a public highway pursuant to a government program to preserve the appearance of the area so as to maintain the scenic view from the highway; and the preservation of a stretch of undeveloped property located between a public highway and the ocean in order to maintain the scenic ocean view from the highway.

(v) Limitation. A deduction will not be allowed for the preservation of open space under section 170(h)(4)(A)(iii), if the terms of the easement permit a degree of intrusion or future development that would interfere with the essential scenic quality of the land or with the governmental conservation policy that is being furthered by the donation. See § 1.170A-14(e)(2) for rules relating to inconsistent use.

(vi) Relationship of requirements. (A) Clearly delineated governmental policy and significant public benefit. Although the requirements of "clearly delineated governmental policy" and "significant public benefit" must be met independently, for purposes of this section the two requirements may also be related. The more specific the governmental policy with respect to the particular site to be protected, the more likely the governmental decision, by itself, will tend to establish the significant public benefit associated with the donation. For example, while a statute in State X permitting preferential assessment for farmland is, by definition, governmental policy, it is distinguishable from a s state statute, accompanied by appropriations, naming the X River as a valuable resource and articulating the legislative policy that the X River and the relatively natural quality of its surrounding be protected. On these facts, an open space easement on farmland in State X would have to demonstrate additional factors to establish "significant public benefit." The specificity of the legislative mandate to protect the X River, however, would by itself tend to establish the significant public benefit associated with an open space easement on land fronting the X River.

(B) Scenic enjoyment and significant public benefit. With respect to the relationship between the requirements of "scenic enjoyment" and "significant public benefit," since the degrees of scenic enjoyment offered by a variety of open space easements are subjective and not as easily delineated as are increasingly specific levels of governmental policy, the significant public benefit of preserving a scenic view must be independently established in all cases.

(C) Donations may satisfy more than one test. In some cases, open space easements may be both for scenic enjoyment and pursuant to a clearly delineated governmental policy. For example, the preservation of a particular scenic view identified as part of a scenic landscape inventory by a rigorous governmental review process will meet the tests of both paragraphs (d)(4)(i)(A) and (d)(4)(i)(B) of this section.

(5) Historic preservation. (i) In general. The donation of a qualified real property interest to preserve an historically important land area or a certified historic structure will meet the conservation purposes test of this section. When restrictions to preserve a building or land area within a registered historic district permit future development on the site, a deduction will be allowed under this section only if the terms of the restrictions require that such development conform with appropriate local, state, or Federal standards for construction or rehabilitation within the district. See also, § 1.170A-14(h)(3)(ii).

(ii) Historically important land area. The term "historically important land area" includes:

(A) An independently significant land area including any related historic resources (for example, an archaeological site or a Civil War battlefield with related monuments, bridges, cannons, or houses) that meets the National Register Criteria for Evaluation in 36 CFR 60.4 (Pub. L. 89-665, 80 Stat. 915);

(B) Any land area within a registered historic district including any buildings on the land area that can reasonably be considered as contributing to the significance of the district; and

(C) Any land area (including related historic resources) adjacent to a property listed individually in the National Register of Historic Places (but not within a registered historic district) in a case where the physical or environmental features of the land area contribute to the historic or cultural integrity of the property.

(iii) Certified historic structure. The term "certified historic structure," for purposes of this section, means any building, structure or land area which is—

(A) Listed in the National Register, or

(B) Located in a registered historic district (as defined in section 48(g)(3)(B)) and is certified by the Secretary of the Interior (pursuant to 36 CFR 67.4) to the Secretary of the Treasury as being of historic significance to the district.

A "structure" for purposes of this section means any structure, whether or not it is depreciable. Accordingly easements on private residences may qualify under this section. In addition, a structure would be considered to be a certified historic structure if it were certified either at the time the transfer was made or at the due date (including extensions) for filing the donor's return for the taxable year in which the contribution was made.

(iv) Access. (A) In order for a conservation contribution described in section 170(h)(4)(A)(iv) and this paragraph (d)(5) to be deductible, some visual public access to the donated property is required. In the case of an historically important land area, the entire property need not be visible to the public for a donation to qualify under this section. However, the public benefit from the donation may be insufficient to qualify for a deduction if only a small portion of the property is so visible. Where the historic land area or certified historic structure which is the subject of the donation is not visible from a public way (e.g., the structure is hidden from view by a wall or shrubbery, the structure is too far from the public way, or interior characteristics and features of the structure are the subject of the easement), the terms of the easement must be such that the general public is given the opportunity on a regular basis to view the characteristics and features of the property which are preserved by the easement to the extent consistent with the nature and condition of the property.

(B) Factors to be considered in determining the type and amount of public access required under paragraph (d)(5)(iv)(A) of this section include the historical significance of the donated property, the nature of the features that are the subject of the easement, the remoteness or accessibility of the site of the donated property, the possibility of physical hazards to the public visiting the property (for example, an unoccupied structure in a dilapidated condition), the extent to which public access would be an unreasonable intrusion on any privacy interests of individuals living on the property, the degree to which public access would impair the preservation interests which are the subject of the donation, and the availability of opportunities for the public to view the property by means other than visits to the site.

(C) The amount of access afforded the public by the donation of an easement shall be determined with reference to the amount of access permitted by the terms of the easement which are established by the donor, rather than the amount of access actually provided by the donee organization. However, if the donor is aware of any facts indicating that the amount of access that the donee organization will provide is significantly less than the amount of access permitted under the terms of the easement, then the amount of access afforded the public shall be determined with reference to this lesser amount.

(v) Examples. The provisions of paragraph (d)(5)(iv) of this section may be illustrated by the following examples:

Example (1). A and his family live in a house in a certified historic district in the State of X. The entire house, including its interior, has architectural features representing classic Victorian period architecture. A donates an exterior and interior easement on the property to a qualified organization but continues to live in the house with his family. A's house is surrounded by a high stone wall which obscures the public's view of it from the street. Pursuant to the terms of the easement, the house may be opened to the public from 10:00 a.m. to 4:00 p.m. on one Sunday in May and one Sunday in November each year for house and garden tours. These tours are to be under the supervision of the donee and open to members of the general public upon payment of a small fee. In addition, under the terms of the easement, the donee organization is given the right to photograph the interior and exterior of the house and distribute such photographs to magazines, newsletters, or other publicly available publications. The terms of the easement also permit persons affiliated with educational organizations, professional architectural associations, and historical societies to make an appointment through the donee organization to study the property. The donor is not aware of any facts indicating that the public access to be provided by the donee organization will be significantly less than that permitted by the terms of the easement. The 2 opportunities for public visits per year, when combined with the ability of the general public to view the architectural characteristics and features that are the subject of the easement through photographs, the opportunity for scholarly study of the property, and the fact that the house is used as an occupied residence, will enable the donation to satisfy the requirement of public access.

Example (2). B owns an unoccupied farmhouse built in the 1840's and located on a property that is adjacent to a Civil War battlefield. During the Civil War the farmhouse was used as quarters for Union troops. The battlefield is visited year round by the general public. The condition of the farmhouse is such that the safety of visitors will not be jeopardized and opening it to the public will not result in significant deterioration. The farmhouse is not visible from the battlefield or any public way. It is accessible only by way of a private road owned by B. B donates a conservation easement on the farmhouse to a qualified organization. The terms of the easement provide that the donee organization may open the property (via B's road) to the general public on four weekends each year from 8:30 a.m. to 4:00 p.m. The donation does not meet the public access requirement because the farmhouse is safe, unoccupied, and easily accessible to the general public who have come to the site to visit Civil War historic land areas (and related resources), but will only be open to the public on four weekends each year. However, the donation would meet the public access requirement if the terms of the easement permitted the donee organization to open the property to the public every other weekend during the year and the donor is not aware of any facts indicating that the donee organization will provide significantly less access than that permitted.

(e) Exclusively for conservation purposes. *(1) In general.* To meet the requirements of this section, a donation must be exclusively for conservation purposes. See paragraphs (c)(1) and (g)(1) through (g)(6)(ii) of this section. A deduction will not be denied under this section when incidental benefit inures to the donor merely as a result of conservation restrictions limiting the uses to which the donor's property may be put.

(2) Inconsistent use. Except as provided in paragraph (e)(4) of this section, a deduction will not be allowed if the contribution would accomplish one of the enumerated conservation purposes but would permit destruction of other significant conservation interests. For example, the preservation of farmland pursuant to a State program for flood prevention and control would not qualify under paragraph (d)(4) of this section if under the terms of the contribution a significant naturally occurring ecosystem could be injured or destroyed by the use of pesticides in the operation of the farm. However, this requirement is not intended to prohibit uses of the property, such as selective timber harvesting or selective farming if, under the circumstances, those uses do not impair significant conservation interests.

(3) Inconsistent use permitted. A use that is destructive of conservation interests will be permitted only if such use is necessary for the protection of the conservation interests that are the subject of the contribution. For example, a deduction for the donation of an easement to preserve an archaeological site that is listed on the National Register of Historic Places will not be disallowed if site excavation consistent with sound archaeological practices may impair a scenic view of which the land is a part. A donor may continue a pre-existing use of the property that does not conflict with the conservation purposes of the gift.

(f) Examples. The provisions of this section relating to conservation purposes may be illustrated by the following examples.

Example (1). State S contains many large tract forests that are desirable recreation and scenic areas for the general public. The forests' scenic values attract millions of people to the State. However, due to the increasing intensity of land development in State S, the continued existence of forestland parcels greater than 45 acres is threatened. J grants a perpetual easement on a 100-acre parcel of forestland that is part of one of the State's scenic areas to a qualifying organization. The easement imposes restrictions on the use of the parcel for the purpose of maintaining its scenic values. The restrictions include a requirement that the parcel be maintained forever as open space devoted exclusively to conservation purposes and wildlife protection, and that there be no commercial, industrial, residential, or other development use of such parcel. The law of State S recognizes a limited public right to enter private land, particularly for recreational pursuits, unless such land is posted or the landowner objects. The easement specifically restricts the landowner from posting the parcel, or from objecting, thereby maintaining public access to the parcel according to the custom of the State. J's parcel provides the opportunity for the public to enjoy the use of the property and appreciate its scenic values. Accordingly, J's donation qualifies for a deduction under this section.

Example (2). A qualified conservation organization owns Greenacre in fee as a nature preserve. Greenacre contains a high quality example of a tall grass prairie ecosystem. Farmacre, an operating farm, adjoins Greenacre and is a compatible buffer to the nature preserve. Conversion of Farmacre to a more intense use, such as a housing development, would adversely affect the continued use of Greenacre as a nature preserve because of human traffic generated by the development. The owner of Farmacre donates an easement preventing any future development on Farmacre to the qualified conservation organization for conservation purposes. Normal agricultural uses will be allowed on Farmacre. Accordingly, the donation qualifies for a deduction under this section.

Example (3). H owns Greenacre, a 900-acre parcel of woodland, rolling pasture, and orchards on the crest of a mountain. All of Greenacre is clearly visible from a nearby national park. Because of the strict enforcement of an applicable zoning plan, the highest and best use of Greenacre is as a subdivision of 40-acre tracts. H wishes to donate a scenic easement on Greenacre to a qualifying conservation organization, but H would like to reserve the right to subdivide Greenacre into 90-acre parcels with no more than one single-family home allowable on each parcel. Random building on the property, even as little as one home for each 90 acres, would destroy the scenic character of the view. Accordingly, no deduction would be allowable under this section.

Example (4). Assume the same facts as in example (3), except that not all of Greenacre is visible from the park and the deed of easement allows for limited cluster development of no more than five nine-acre clusters (with four houses on each cluster) located in areas generally not visible from the national park and subject to site and building plan approval by the donee organization in order to preserve the scenic view from the park. The donor and the donee have already identified sites where limited cluster development would not be visible from the park or would not impair the view. Owners of homes in the clusters will not have any rights with respect to the surrounding Greenacre property that are not also available to the general public. Accordingly, the donation qualifies for a deduction under this section.

Example (5). In order to protect State S's declining open space that is suited for agricultural use from increasing development pressure that has led to a marked decline in such open space, the Legislature of State S passed a statute authorizing the purchase of "agricultural land development rights" on open acreage. Agricultural land development rights allow the State to place agricultural preservation restrictions on land designated as worthy of protection in order to preserve open space and farm resources. Agricultural preservation restrictions prohibit or limit construction or placement of buildings except those used for agricultural purposes or dwellings used for family living by the farmer and his family and employees; removal of mineral substances in any manner that adversely affects the land's agricultural potential; or other uses detrimental to retention of the land for agricultural use. Money has been appropriated for this program and some landowners have in fact sold their "agricultural land development rights" to State S. K owns and operates a small dairy farm in State S located in an area designated by the Legislature as worthy of protection. K desires to preserve his farm for agricultural purposes in perpetuity. Rather than selling the development rights to State S, K grants to a qualified organization an agricultural preservation restriction on his property in the form of a conservation easement. K reserves to himself, his heirs and assigns the right to manage the farm consistent with sound agricultural and management practices. The preservation of K's land is pursuant to a clearly delineated governmental policy of preserving open space available for agricultural use, and will yield a significant public benefit by preserving open space against increasing development pressures.

(g) Enforceable in perpetuity. *(1) In general.* In the case of any donation under this section, any interest in the property retained by the donor (and the donor's successors in interest) must be subject to legally enforceable restrictions (for example, by recordation in the land records of the jurisdiction in which the property is located) that will prevent uses of the retained interest inconsistent with the conservation purposes of the donation. In the case of a contribution of a remainder interest, the contribution will not qualify if the tenants, whether they are tenants for life or a term of years, can use the property in a manner that diminishes the conservation values which are intended to be protected by the contribution.

(2) Protection of a conservation purpose in case of donation of property subject to a mortgage. In the case of conservation contributions made after February 13, 1986, no deduction will be permitted under this section for an interest in property which is subject to a mortgage unless the mortgagee subordinates its rights in the property to the right of the qualified organization to enforce the conservation purposes of the gift in perpetuity. For conservation contributions made

prior to February 14, 1986, the requirement of section 170(h)(5)(A) is satisfied in the case of mortgaged property (with respect to which the mortgagee has not subordinated its rights) only if the donor can demonstrate that the conservation purpose is protected in perpetuity without subordination of the mortgagee's rights.

(3) Remote future event. A deduction shall not be disallowed under section 170(f)(3)(B)(iii) and this section merely because the interest which passes to, or is vested in, the donee organization may be defeated by the performance of some act or the happening of some event, if on the date of the gift it appears that the possibility that such act or event will occur is so remote as to be negligible. See paragraph (e) of § 1.170A-1. For example, a state's statutory requirement that use restrictions must be rerecorded every 30 years to remain enforceable shall not, by itself, render an easement nonperpetual.

(4) Retention of qualified mineral interest. (i) In general. Except as otherwise provided in paragraph (g)(4)(ii) of this section, the requirements of this section are not met and no deduction shall be allowed in the case of a contribution of any interest when there is a retention by any person of a qualified mineral interest (as defined in paragraph (b)(1)(i) of this section) if at any time there may be extractions or removal of minerals by any surface mining method. Moreover, in the case of a qualified mineral interest gift, the requirement that the conservation purposes be protected in perpetuity is not satisfied if any method of mining that is inconsistent with the particular conservation purposes of a contribution is permitted at any time. See also § 1.170A-14(e)(2). However, a deduction under this section will not be denied in the case of certain methods of mining that may have limited, localized impact on the real property but that are not irremediably destructive of significant conservation interests. For example, a deduction will not be denied in a case where production facilities are concealed or compatible with existing topography and landscape and when surface alteration is to be restored to its original state.

(ii) Exception for qualified conservation contributions after July 1984 (A) A contribution made after July 18, 1984, of a qualified real property interest described in section 170(h)(2)(A) shall not be disqualified under the first sentence of paragraph (g)(4)(i) of this section if the following requirements are satisfied.

(1) The ownership of the surface estate and mineral interest were separated before June 13, 1976, and remain so separated up to and including the time of the contribution.

(2) The present owner of the mineral interest is not a person whose relationship to the owner of the surface estate is described at the time of the contribution in section 267(b) or section 707(b), and

(3) The probability of extraction or removal of minerals by any surface mining method is so remote as to be negligible.

Whether the probability of extraction or removal of minerals by surface mining is so remote as to be negligible is a question of fact and is to be made on a case by case basis. Relevant factors to be considered in determining if the probability of extraction or removal of minerals by surface mining is so remote as to be negligible include: Geological, geophysical or economic data showing the absence of mineral reserves on the property, or the lack of commercial feasibility at the time of the contribution of surface mining the mineral interest.

(B) If the ownership of the surface estate and mineral interest first became separated after June 12, 1976, no deduction is permitted for a contribution under this section unless surface mining on the property is completely prohibited.

(iii) Examples. The provisions of paragraph (g)(4)(i) and (ii) of this section may be illustrated by the following examples:

Example (1). K owns 5,000 acres of bottomland hardwood property along a major watershed system in the southern part of the United States. Agencies within the Department of the Interior have determined that southern bottomland hardwoods are a rapidly diminishing resource and a critical ecosystem in the south because of the intense pressure to cut the trees and convert the land to agricultural use. These agencies have further determined (and have indicated in correspondence with K) that bottomland hardwoods provide a superb habitat for numerous species and play an important role in controlling floods and purifying rivers. K donates to a qualified organization his entire interest in this property other than his interest in the gas and oil deposits that have been identified under K's property. K covenants and can ensure that, although drilling for gas and oil on the property may have some temporary localized impact on the real property, the drilling will not interfere with the overall conservation purpose of the gift, which is to protect the unique bottomland hardwood ecosystem. Accordingly, the donation qualifies for a deduction under this section.

Example (2). Assume the same facts as in example (1), except that in 1979, K sells the mineral interest to A, an unrelated person, in an arm's-length transaction, subject to a recorded prohibition on the removal of any minerals by any surface mining method and a recorded prohibition against any mining technique that will harm the bottomland hardwood ecosystem. After the sale to A, K donates a qualified real property interest to a qualified organization to protect the bottomland hardwood ecosystem. Since at the time of the transfer, surface mining and any mining technique that will harm the bottomland hardwood ecosystem are completely prohibited, the donation qualifies for a deduction under this section.

(5) Protection of conservation purpose where taxpayer reserves certain rights. (i) Documentation. In the case of a donation made after February 13, 1986, of any qualified real property interest when the donor reserves rights the exercise of which may impair the conservation interests associated with the property, for a deduction to be allowable under this section the donor must make available to the donee, prior to the time the donation is made, documentation sufficient to establish the condition of the property at the time of the gift.

Such documentation is designed to protect the conservation interests associated with the property, which although protected in perpetuity by the easement, could be adversely affected by the exercise of the reserved rights. Such documentation may include:

(A) The appropriate survey maps from the United States Geological Survey, showing the property line and other contiguous or nearby protected areas;

(B) A map of the area drawn to scale showing all existing man-made improvements or incursions (such as roads, buildings, fences, or gravel pits), vegetation and identification of flora and fauna (including, for example, rare species locations, animal breeding and roosting areas, and migration routes), land use history (including present uses and recent past disturbances), and distinct natural features (such as large trees and aquatic areas);

(C) An aerial photograph of the property at an appropriate scale taken as close as possible to the date the donation is made; and

(D) On-site photographs taken at appropriate locations on the property. If the terms of the donation contain restrictions with regard to a particular natural resource to be protected, such as water quality or air quality, the condition of the resource at or near the time of the gift must be established. The documentation, including the maps and photographs, must be accompanied by a statement signed by the donor and a representative of the donee clearly referencing the documentation and in substance saying "This natural resources inventory is an accurate representation of [the protected property] at the time of the transfer.".

(ii) Donee's right to inspection and legal remedies. In the case of any donation referred to in paragraph (g)(5)(i) of this section, the donor must agree to notify the donee, in writing, before exercising any reserved right, e.g. the right to extract certain minerals which may have an adverse impact on the conservation interests associated with the qualified real property interest. The terms of the donation must provide a right of the donee to enter the property at reasonable times for the purpose of inspection the property to determine if there is compliance with the terms of the donation. Additionally, the terms of the donation must provide a right of the donee to enforce the conservation restrictions by appropriate legal proceedings, including but not limited to, the right to require the restoration of the property to its condition at the time of the donation.

(6) Extinguishment. (i) In general. If a subsequent unexpected change in the conditions surrounding the property that is the subject of a donation under this paragraph can make impossible or impractical the continued use of the property for conservation purposes, the conservation purpose can nonetheless be treated as protected in perpetuity if the restrictions are extinguished by judicial proceeding and all of the donee's proceeds (determined under paragraph (g)(6)(ii) of this section) from a subsequent sale or exchange of the property are used by the donee organization in a manner consistent with the conservation purposes of the original contribution.

(ii) Proceeds. In case of a donation made after February 13, 1986, for a deduction to be allowed under this section, at the time of the gift the donor must agree that the donation of the perpetual conservation restriction gives rise to a property right, immediately vested in the donee organization, with a fair market value that is at least equal to the proportionate value that the perpetual conservation restriction at the time of the gift, bears to the value of the property as a whole at that time. See § 1.170A-14(h)(3)(iii) relating to the allocation of basis. For purposes of this paragraph (g)(6)(ii), that proportionate value of the donee's property rights shall remain constant. Accordingly, when a change in conditions give rise to the extinguishment of a perpetual conservation restriction under paragraph (g)(6)(i) of this section, the donee organization, on a subsequent sale, exchange, or involuntary conversion of the subject property, must be entitled to a portion of the proceeds at least equal to that proportionate value of the perpetual conservation restriction, unless state law provides that the donor is entitled to the full proceeds from the conversion without regard to the terms of the prior perpetual conservation restriction.

(h) Valuation. *(1) Entire interest of donor other than qualified mineral interest.* The value of the contribution under section 170 in the case of a contribution of a taxpayer's entire interest in property other than a qualified mineral interest is the fair market value of the surface rights in the property contributed. The value of the contribution shall be computed without regard to the mineral rights. See paragraph (h)(4), example (1), of this section.

(2) Remainder interest in real property. In the case of a contribution of any remainder interest in real property, section 170(f)(4) provides that in determining the value of such interest for purposes of section 170, depreciation and depletion of such property shall be taken into account. See § 1.170A-12. In the case of the contribution of a remainder interest for conservation purposes, the current fair market value of the property (against which the limitations of § 1.170A-12 are applied) must take into account any pre-existing or contemporaneously recorded rights limiting, for conservation purposes, the use to which the subject property may be put.

(3) Perpetual conservation restriction. (i) In general. The value of the contribution under section 170 in the case of a charitable contribution of a perpetual conservation restriction is the fair market value of the perpetual conservation restriction at the time of the contribution. See § 1.170A-7(c). If there is a substantial record of sales of easements comparable to the donated easement (such as purchases pursuant to a governmental program), the fair market value of the donated easement is based on the sales prices of such comparable easements. If no substantial record of market-place sales is available to use as a meaningful or valid comparison, as a general rule (but not necessarily in all cases) the fair market value of a perpetual conservation restriction is equal to the difference between the fair market value of the property it encumbers before the granting of the restriction and the fair market value of the encumbered property after the granting of the restriction. The amount of the deduction in the case of a charitable contribution of a perpetual conservation restriction covering a portion of the contiguous property owned by a donor and the donor's family (as defined in section 267(c)(4)) is the difference between the fair market value of the entire contiguous parcel of property before and after the granting of the restriction. If the granting of a perpetual conservation restriction after January 14, 1986, has the effect of increasing the value of any other property owned by the donor or a related person, the amount of the deduction for the conservation contribution shall be reduced by the amount of the increase in the value of the other property, whether or not such property is contiguous. If, as a result of the donation of a perpetual conservation restriction, the donor or a related person receives, or can reasonably expect to receive, financial or economic benefits that are greater than those that will inure to the general public from the transfer, no deduction is allowable under this section. However, if the donor or a related person receives, or can reasonably expect to receive, a financial or economic benefit that is substantial, but it is clearly shown that the benefit is less than the amount of the transfer, then a deduction under this section is allowable for the excess of the amount transferred over the amount of the financial or economic benefit received or reasonably expected to be received by the donor or the related person. For purposes of this paragraph (h)(3)(i), related person shall have the same meaning as in either section 267(b) or section 707(b). (See example (10) of paragraph (h)(4) of this section.)

(ii) Fair market value of property before and after restriction. If before and after valuation is used, the fair market value of the property before contribution of the conservation restriction must take into account not only the current use of the property but also an objective assessment of how immediate or remote the likelihood is that the property, absent the restriction, would in fact be developed, as well as any effect from zoning, conservation, or historic preservation laws that already restrict the property's potential highest and best use. Further, there may be instances where the grant of a conservation restriction may have no material effect on the value of the property or may in fact serve to enhance, rather than reduce, the value of property. In such instances no deduction would be allowable. In the case of a conservation restriction that allows for any development, however limited, on the property to be protected, the fair market value of the property after contribution of the restriction must take into account the effect of the development. In the case of a conservation easement such as an easement on a certified historic structure, the fair market value of the property after contribution of the restriction must take into account the amount of access permitted by the terms of the easement. Additionally, if before and after valuation is used, an appraisal of the property after contribution of the restriction must take into account the effect of restrictions that will result in a reduction of the potential fair market value represented by highest and best use but will, nevertheless, permit uses of the property that will increase its fair market value above that represented by the property's current use. The value of a perpetual conservation restriction shall not be reduced by reason of the existence of restrictions on transfer designed solely to ensure that the conservation restriction will be dedicated to conservation purposes. See § 1.170A-14(c)(3).

(iii) Allocation of basis. In the case of the donation of a qualified real property interest for conservation purposes, the basis of the property retained by the donor must be adjusted by the elimination of that part of the total basis of the property that is properly allocable to the qualified real property interest granted. The amount of the basis that is allocable to the qualified real property interest shall bear the same ratio to the total basis of the property as the fair market value of the qualified real property interest bears to the fair market value of the property before the granting of the qualified real property interest. When a taxpayer donates to a qualifying conservation organization an easement on a structure with respect to which deductions are taken for depreciation, the reduction required by this paragraph (h)(3)(ii) in the basis of the property retained by the taxpayer must be allocated between the structure and the underlying land.

(4) Examples. The provisions of this section may be illustrated by the following examples. In examples illustrating the value or deductibility of donations, the applicable restrictions and limitations of § 1.170A-4, with respect to reduction in amount of charitable contributions of certain appreciated property, and § 1.170A-8, with respect to limitations on charitable deductions by individuals must also be taken into account.

Example (1). A owns Goldacre, a property adjacent to a state park. A wants to donate Goldacre to the state to be used as part of the park, but A wants to reserve a qualified mineral interest in the property, to exploit currently and to devise at death. The fair market value of the surface rights in Goldacre is $200,000 and the fair market value of the mineral rights in $100.000. In order to ensure that the quality of the park will not be degraded, restrictions must be imposed on the right to extract the minerals that reduce the fair market value of the mineral rights to $80,000. Under this section, the value of the contribution is $200,000 (the value of the surface rights).

Example (2). In 1984 B, who is 62, donates a remainder interest in Greenacre to a qualifying organization for conservation purposes. Greenacre is a tract of 200 acres of undeveloped woodland that is valued at $200,000 at its highest and best use. Under § 1.170A-12(b), the value of a remainder interest in real property following one life is determined under § 25.2512-5 of this chapter (Gift Tax Regulations). (See § 25.2512-5A of this chapter with respect to the valuation of annuities, interests for life or term of years, and remainder or reversionary interests transferred before May 1, 1999). Accordingly, the value of the remainder interest, and thus the amount eligible for an income tax deduction under sections 170(f), is $55,996 ($200,000 × .27998).

Example (3). Assume the same facts as in example (2), except that Greenacre is B's 200-acre estate with a home built during the colonial period. Some of the acreage around the home is cleared; the balance of Greenacre, except for access roads, is wooded and undeveloped. See section 170(f)(3)(B)(i). However, B would like Greenacre to be maintained in its current state after his death, so he donates a remainder interest in Greenacre to a qualifying organization for conservation purposes pursuant to section 170(f)(3)(B)(iii) and (h)(2)(B). At the time of the gift the land has a value of $200,000 and the house has a value of $100,000. The value of the remainder interest, and thus the amount eligible for an income tax deduction under section 170(f), is computed pursuant to § 1.170A-12. See § 1.170A-12(b)(3).

Example (4). Assume the same facts as in example (2), except that at age 62 instead of donating a remainder interest B donates an easement in Greenacre to a qualifying organization for conservation purposes. The fair market value of Greenacre after the donation is reduced to $110,000. Accordingly, the value of the easement, and thus the amount eligible for a deduction under section 170(f), is $90,000 ($200,000 less $110,000).

Example (5). Assume the same facts as in example (4), and assume that three years later, at age 65, B decides to donate a remainder interest in Greenacre to a qualifying organization for conservation purposes. Increasing real estate values in the area have raised the fair market value of Greenacre (subject to the easement) to $130,000. Accordingly, the value of the remainder interest, and thus the amount eligible for a deduction under section 170(f), is $41,639 ($130,000 × .32030).

Example (6). Assume the same facts as in example (2), except that at the time of the donation of a remainder interest in Greenacre, B also donates an easement to a different qualifying organization for conservation purposes. Based on all the facts and circumstances, the value of the easement is determined to be $100,000. Therefore, the value of the property after the easement is $100,000 and the value of the remainder interest, and thus the amount eligible for deduction under section 170(f), is $27,998 ($100,000 × .27998).

Example (7). C owns Greenacre, a 200-acre estate containing a house built during the colonial period. At its highest and best use, for home development, the fair market value of Greenacre is $300,000. C donates an easement (to maintain the house and Greenacre in their current state) to a qualifying organization for conservation purposes. The fair market value of Greenacre after the donation is reduced to $125,000. Accordingly, the value of the easement and the amount eligible for a deduction under section 170(f) is $175,000 ($300,000 less $125,000).

Example (8). Assume the same facts as in example (7) and assume that three years later, C decides to donate a remainder interest in Greenacre to a qualifying organization for conservation purposes. Increasing real estate values in the area have raised the fair market value of Greenacre to $180,000. Assume that because of the perpetual easement prohibiting any development of the land, the value of the house is $120,000 and the value of the land is $60,000. The value of the remainder interest, and thus the amount eligible for an income tax deduction under section 170(f), is computed pursuant to § 1.170A-12. See § 1.170A-12(b)(3).

Example (9). D owns property with a basis of $20,000 and a fair market value of $80,000. D donates to a qualifying organization an easement for conservation purposes that is determined under this section to have a fair market value of $60,000. The amount of basis allocable to the easement is $15,000 ($60,000/$80,000 is reduced to $5,000 ($20,000 minus $15,000).

Example (10). E owns 10 one-acre lots that are currently woods and parkland. The fair market value of each of E's lots is $15,000 and the basis of each lot is $3,000. E grants to the county a perpetual easement for conservation purposes to use and maintain eight of the acres as a public park and to restrict any future development on those eight acres. As a result of the restrictions, the value of the eight acres is reduced to $1,000 an acre. However, by perpetually restricting development on this portion of the land, E has ensured that the two remaining acres will always be bordered by parkland, thus increasing their fair market value to $22,500 each. If the eight acres represented all of E's land, the fair market value of the easement would be $112,000, an amount equal to the fair market value of the land before the granting of the easement (8 x $15,000 = $120,000) minus the fair market value of the encumbered land after the granting of the easement (8 x $1,000 = $8,000). However, because the easement only covered a portion of the taxpayer's contiguous land, the amount of the deduction under section 170 is reduced to $97,000 ($150,000 - $53,000), that is, the difference between the fair market value of the entire tract of land before ($150,000) and after ((8 x $1,000) + (2 x $22,500)) the granting of the easement.

Example (11). Assume the same facts as in example (10). Since the easement covers a portion of E's land, only the basis of that portion is adjusted. Therefore, the amount of basis allocable to the easement is $22,400 ((8 × $3,000) × ($112,000/$120,000)). Accordingly, the basis of the eight acres encumbered by the easement is reduced to $1,600 ($24,000 − $22,400), or $200 for each acre. The basis of the two remaining acres is not affected by the donation.

Example (12). F owns and uses as professional offices a two-story building that lies within a registered historic district F's building is an outstanding example of period architecture with a fair market value of $125,000. Restricted to its current use, which is the highest and best use of the property without making changes to the facade, the building and lot would have a fair market value of $100,000, of which $80,000 would be allocable to the building and $20,000 would be allocable to the lot. F's basis in the property is $50,000, of which $40,000 is allocable to the building and $10,000 is allocable to the lot. F's neighborhood is a mix of residential and commercial uses, and it is possible that F (or another owner) could enlarge the building for more extensive commercial use, which is its highest and best use. However, this would require changes to the facade. F would like to donate to a qualifying preservation organization an easement restricting any changes to the facade and promising to maintain the facade in perpetuity, the donation would qualify for a deduction under this section. The fair market value of the easement is $25,000 (the fair market value of the property before the easement, $125,000, minus the fair market value of the property after the easement, $100,000). Pursuant to § 1.170A-14(h)(3)(iii), the basis allocable to the easement is $10,000 and the basis of the underlying property (building and lot) is reduced to $40,000.

(i) Substantiation requirement. If a taxpayer makes a qualified conservation contribution and claims a deduction, the taxpayer must maintain written records of the fair market value of the underlying property before and after the donation and the conservation purpose furthered by the donation and such information shall be stated in the taxpayer's income tax return if required by the return or its instructions. See also § 1.170A-13(c) (relating to substantiation requirements for deductions in excess of $5,000 for charitable contributions made after 1984), and section 6659 (relating to additions to tax in the case of valuation overstatements).

(j) Effective date. Except as otherwise provided in § 1.170A-14(g)(4)(ii), this section applies only to contributions made on or after December 18, 1980.

T.D. 8069, 1/13/86, amend T.D. 8199, 5/4/88, T.D. 8540, 6/9/94, T.D. 8819, 4/29/99.

Proposed § 1.170A-15 Substantiation requirements for charitable contribution of a cash, check, or other monetary gift. [*For Preamble, see ¶ 153,047*]

(a) In general. *(1) Bank record or written communication required.* No deduction is allowed under section 170(a) for a charitable contribution in the form of a cash, check, or other monetary gift (as described in paragraph (b)(1) of this section) unless the donor substantiates the deduction with a bank record (as described in paragraph (b)(2) of this section) or a written communication (as described in paragraph (b)(3) of this section) from the donee showing the name of the donee, the date of the contribution, and the amount of the contribution.

(2) Additional substantiation required for contributions of $250 or more. No deduction is allowed under section 170(a) for any contribution of $250 or more unless the donor substantiates the contribution with a contemporaneous written acknowledgment (as described in section 170(f)(8) and § 1.170A-13(f)) from the donee.

(3) Single document may be used. The requirements of paragraphs (a)(1) and (a)(2) of this section may be met by a single document that contains all the information required by paragraphs (a)(1) and (a)(2) of this section, if the single document is obtained by the donor no later than the date prescribed by paragraph (c) of this section.

(b) Terms. *(1)* Monetary gift includes a transfer of a gift card redeemable for cash, and a payment made by credit card, electronic fund transfer (as described in section 5061(e)(2)), an online payment service, or payroll deduction.

(2) Bank record includes a statement from a financial institution, an electronic fund transfer receipt, a canceled check, a scanned image of both sides of a canceled check obtained from a bank Web site, or a credit card statement.

(3) Written communication includes electronic mail correspondence.

(c) Deadline for receipt of substantiation. The substantiation described in paragraph (a) of this section must be received by the donor on or before the earlier of—

(1) The date the donor files the original return for the taxable year in which the contribution was made; or

(2) The due date (including extensions) for filing the donor's original return for that year.

(d) Distributing organizations as donees. *(1) In general.* The following organizations are treated as donees for purposes of section 170(f)(17) and paragraph (a) of this section, even if the organization (pursuant to the donor's instructions or otherwise) distributes the amount received to one or more organizations described in section 170(c):

(i) An organization described in section 170(c).

(ii) An organization described in 5 CFR 950.105 (a Principal Combined Fund Organization for purposes of the Combined Federal Campaign) and acting in that capacity.

(2) Contributions made by payroll deduction. In the case of a charitable contribution made by payroll deduction, a donor is treated as meeting the requirements of section 170(f)(17) and paragraph (a) of this section if, no later than the date described in paragraph (c) of this section, the donor obtains—

(i) A pay stub, Form W-2, "Wage and Tax Statement," or other employer-furnished document that sets forth the amount withheld during the taxable year for payment to a donee; and

(ii) A pledge card or other document prepared by or at the direction of the donee that shows the name of the donee.

(e) Substantiation of out-of-pocket expenses. Paragraph (a)(1) of this section does not apply to a donor who incurs unreimbursed expenses of less than $250 incident to the rendition of services, within the meaning of § 1.170A-1(g). For substantiation of unreimbursed out-of-pocket expenses of $250 or more, see § 1.170A-13(f)(10).

(f) Charitable contributions made by partnership or S corporation. If a partnership or an S corporation makes a charitable contribution, the partnership or S corporation is treated as the donor for purposes of section 170(f)(17) and paragraph (a) of this section.

(g) Transfers to certain trusts. The requirements of section 170(f)(17) and paragraph (a)(1) of this section do not apply to a transfer of a cash, check, or other monetary gift to a trust described in section 170(f)(2)(B), a charitable remainder annuity trust (as defined in section 664(d)(1)), or a charitable remainder unitrust (as defined in section 664(d)(2) or (d)(3) or § 1.664-3(a)(1)(i)(b)). The requirements of section 170(f)(17) and paragraphs (a)(1) and (a)(2) of this section do apply, however, to a transfer to a pooled income fund (as defined in section 642(c)(5)). For contributions of $250 or more, see section 170(f)(8) and § 1.170A-13(f)(13).

(h) Effective/applicability date. This section applies to contributions made after the date these regulations are published as final regulations in the Federal Register.

Proposed § 1.170A-16 Substantiation and reporting requirements for noncash charitable contributions. [*For Preamble, see ¶ 153,047*]

(a) Substantiation of charitable contributions of less than $250. *(1) Individuals, partnerships, and certain corporations required to obtain receipt.* Except as provided in paragraph (a)(2) of this section, no deduction is allowed under section 170(a) for a noncash charitable contribution of less than $250 by an individual, partnership, S corporation, or C corporation that is a personal service corporation or closely held corporation unless the donor maintains for each contribution a receipt from the donee showing the following information:

(i) The name and address of the donee;

(ii) The date of the contribution;

(iii) A description of the property in sufficient detail under the circumstances (taking into account the value of the property) for a person who is not generally familiar with the type of property to ascertain that the described property is the contributed property; and

(iv) In the case of securities, the name of the issuer, the type of security, and whether the securities are publicly traded securities within the meaning of § 1.170A-13(c)(7)(xi).

(2) Substitution of reliable written records. (i) In general. If it is impractical to obtain a receipt (for example, a donor deposits canned food at a donee's unattended drop site), the donor may satisfy the recordkeeping rules of this paragraph (a)(2)(i) by maintaining reliable written records (as described in paragraphs (a)(2)(ii) and (a)(2)(iii) of this section) for the contributed property.

(ii) Reliable written records. The reliability of written records is to be determined on the basis of all of the facts and circumstances of a particular case, including the contemporaneous nature of the writing evidencing the contribution.

(iii) Contents of reliable written records. Reliable written records must include—

(A) The information required by paragraph (a)(1) of this section;

(B) The fair market value of the property on the date the contribution was made;

(C) The method used in determining the fair market value; and

(D) In the case of a contribution of clothing or a household item as defined in § 1.170A-18(c), the condition of the item.

(3) Additional substantiation rules may apply. For additional substantiation rules, see paragraph (f) of this section.

(b) Substantiation of charitable contributions of $250 or more but not more than $500. No deduction is allowed under section 170(a) for a noncash charitable contribution of $250 or more but not more than $500 unless the donor substantiates the contribution with a contemporaneous written acknowledgment (as described in section 170(f)(8) and § 1.170A-13(f)).

(c) Substantiation of charitable contributions of more than $500 but not more than $5,000. *(1) In general.* No deduction is allowed under section 170(a) for a noncash charitable contribution of more than $500 but not more than $5,000 unless the donor substantiates the contribution with a contemporaneous written acknowledgment (as described in section 170(f)(8) and § 1.170A-13(f)) and meets the applicable requirements of this section.

(2) Individuals, partnerships, and certain corporations also required to file Form 8283 (Section A). No deduction is allowed under section 170(a) for a noncash charitable contribution of more than $500 but not more than $5,000 by an individual, partnership, S corporation, or C corporation that is a personal service corporation or closely held corporation unless the donor—

(i) Substantiates the contribution with a contemporaneous written acknowledgment (as described in section 170(f)(8) and § 1.170A-13(f)); and

(ii) Completes Form 8283 (Section A), "Noncash Charitable Contributions" (as provided in paragraph (c)(3) of this section), or a successor form, and files it with the return on which the deduction is claimed.

(3) Completion of Form 8283 (Section A). A completed Form 8283 (Section A) includes—

(i) The donor's name and taxpayer identification number (social security number if the donor is an individual or employer identification number if the donor is a partnership or corporation);

(ii) The name and address of the donee;

(iii) The date of the contribution;

(iv) The following information about the contributed property:

(A) A description of the property in sufficient detail under the circumstances (taking into account the value of the property) for a person who is not generally familiar with the type of property to ascertain that the described property is the contributed property;

(B) In the case of real or personal property, the condition of the property;

(C) In the case of securities, the name of the issuer, the type of security, and whether the securities are publicly traded securities within the meaning of § 1.170A-13(c)(7)(xi); and

(D) The fair market value of the property on the date the contribution was made and the method used in determining the fair market value;

(v) The manner of acquisition (for example, by purchase, gift, bequest, inheritance, or exchange), and the approximate date of acquisition of the property by the donor (except that in the case of a contribution of publicly traded securities as defined in § 1.170A-13(c)(7)(xi), a representation that the donor held the securities for more than one year is sufficient) or, if the property was created, produced, or manufactured by or for the donor, the approximate date the property was substantially completed;

(vi) The cost or other basis, adjusted as provided by section 1016, of the property (except that the cost or basis is not required for contributions of publicly traded securities (as defined in § 1.170A-13(c)(7)(xi)) that if sold on the contribution date would have resulted in long term capital gain);

(vii) In the case of tangible personal property, whether the donee has certified it for a use related to the purpose or function constituting the donee's basis for exemption under section 501 (or in the case of a governmental unit, an exclusively public purpose); and

(viii) Any other information required by Form 8283 (Section A) or the instructions to Form 8283 (Section A).

(4) Additional requirement for certain motor vehicle contributions. In the case of a contribution of a qualified vehicle described in section 170(f)(12)(A)(ii) for which an acknowledgment under section 170(f)(12)(B)(iii) is provided to the IRS by the donee organization, the donor must attach a copy of the acknowledgment to the Form 8283 (Section A) for the return on which the deduction is claimed.

(5) Additional substantiation rules may apply. For additional substantiation rules, see paragraph (f) of this section.

(d) Substantiation of charitable contributions of more than $5,000. *(1) In general.* Except as provided in paragraph (d)(2) of this section, no deduction is allowed under section 170(a) for a noncash charitable contribution of more than $5,000 unless the donor—

(i) Substantiates the contribution with a contemporaneous written acknowledgment (as described in section 170(f)(8) and § 1.170A-13(f));

(ii) Obtains a qualified appraisal (as defined in § 1.170A-17(a)(1)) prepared by a qualified appraiser (as defined in § 1.170A-17(b)(1)); and

(iii) Completes Form 8283 (Section B) (as provided in paragraph (d)(3) of this section), or a successor form, and files it with the return on which the deduction is claimed.

(2) Exception for certain noncash contributions. A qualified appraisal is not required, and a completed Form 8283 (Section A) (containing the information required in paragraph (c)(3) of this section) meets the requirements of paragraph (d)(1)(iii) of this section for contributions of—

(i) Publicly traded securities as defined in § 1.170A-13(c)(7)(xi);

(ii) Property described in section 170(e)(1)(B)(iii)(certain intellectual property);

(iii) A qualified vehicle described in section 170(f)(12)(A)(ii) for which an acknowledgment under section 170(f)(12)(B)(iii) is provided to the IRS by the donee organization and attached to the Form 8283 (Section A) by the donor; and

(iv) Property described in section 1221(a)(1) (inventory and property held by the donor primarily for sale to customers in the ordinary course of the donor's trade or business).

(3) Completed Form 8283 (Section B). A completed Form 8283 (Section B) includes—

(i) The donor's name and taxpayer identification number (social security number if the donor is an individual or employer identification number if the donor is a partnership or corporation);

(ii) The donee's name, address, taxpayer identification number, and signature, the date signed by the donee, and the date the donee received the property;

(iii) The appraiser's name, address, taxpayer identification number, appraiser declaration (as described in paragraph (d)(4) of this section), signature, and the date signed by the appraiser;

(iv) The following information about the contributed property:

(A) The fair market value on the valuation effective date (as defined in § 1.170A-17(a)(5)(i)).

(B) A description in sufficient detail under the circumstances (taking into account the value of the property) for a person who is not generally familiar with the type of property to ascertain that the described property is the contributed property.

(C) In the case of real or tangible personal property, the condition of the property;

(v) The manner of acquisition (for example, by purchase, gift, bequest, inheritance, or exchange), and the approximate date of acquisition of the property by the donor, or, if the property was created, produced, or manufactured by or for the donor, the approximate date the property was substantially completed;

(vi) The cost or other basis, adjusted as provided by section 1016;

(vii) A statement explaining whether the charitable contribution was made by means of a bargain sale and, if so, the amount of any consideration received from the donee for the contribution; and

(viii) Any other information required by Form 8283 (Section B) or the instructions to Form 8283 (Section B).

(4) Appraiser declaration. The appraiser declaration referred to in paragraph (d)(3)(iii) of this section must include the following statement: "I understand that my appraisal will be used in connection with a return or claim for refund. I also understand that, if a substantial or gross valuation misstatement of the value of the property claimed on the return or claim for refund results from my appraisal, I may be subject to a penalty under section 6695A of the Internal Revenue Code, as well as other applicable penalties. I affirm that I have not been barred from presenting evidence or testimony before the Department of the Treasury or the Internal Revenue Service pursuant to 31 U.S.C. section 330(c)."

(5) Donee signature. (i) Person authorized to sign. The person who signs Form 8283 for the donee must be either an official authorized to sign the tax or information returns of the donee, or a person specifically authorized to sign Forms 8283 by that official. In the case of a donee that is a governmental unit, the person who signs Form 8283 for the donee must be an official of the governmental unit.

(ii) Effect of donee signature. The signature of the donee on Form 8283 does not represent concurrence in the appraised value of the contributed property. Rather, it represents acknowledgment of receipt of the property described in Form 8283 on the date specified in Form 8283 and that the donee understands the information reporting requirements imposed by section 6050L and § 1.6050L-1.

(iii) Certain information not required on Form 8283 before donee signs. Before Form 8283 is signed by the donee, Form 8283 must be completed (as described in paragraph (d)(3) of this section), except that it is not required to contain the following:

(A) Information about the qualified appraiser or the appraiser declaration.

(B) The manner or date of acquisition.

(C) The cost or other basis of the property.

(D) The appraised fair market value of the contributed property.

(E) The amount claimed as a charitable contribution.

(6) Additional substantiation rules may apply. For additional substantiation rules, see paragraph (f) of this section.

(e) Substantiation of noncash charitable contributions of more than $500,000. *(1) In general.* Except as provided in paragraph (e)(2) of this section, no deduction is allowed under section 170(a) for a noncash charitable contribution of more than $500,000 unless the donor—

(i) Substantiates the contribution with a contemporaneous written acknowledgment (as described in section 170(f)(8) and § 1.170A-13(f));

(ii) Obtains a qualified appraisal (as defined in § 1.170A-17(a)(1)) prepared by a qualified appraiser (as defined in § 1.170A-17(b)(1));

(iii) Completes (as described in paragraph (d)(3) of this section) Form 8283 (Section B) and files it with the return on which the deduction is claimed; and

(iv) Attaches the qualified appraisal of the property to the return on which the deduction is claimed.

(2) Exception for certain noncash contributions. For contributions of property described in paragraph (d)(2) of this section, a qualified appraisal is not required, and a completed Form 8283 (Section A) (containing the information required in paragraph (c)(3) of this section) meets the requirements of paragraph (e)(1)(iii) of this section.

(3) Additional substantiation rules may apply. For additional substantiation rules, see paragraph (f) of this section.

(f) Additional substantiation requirements that may be applicable to any noncash contribution. *(1) Signed Form 8283 furnished by donor to donee.* A donor who presents a Form 8283 to a donee for signature must furnish to the donee a copy of Form 8283 as signed by the donee.

(2) Number of Forms 8283. (i) In general. For each item of contributed property for which a Form 8283 is required under paragraphs (c), (d), or (e) of this section, a donor must attach a separate Form 8283 to the return on which the deduction for the item is claimed.

(ii) Exception for similar items. The donor may attach a single Form 8283 for all similar items of property (as defined in § 1.170A-13(c)(7)(iii)) contributed to the same donee during the donor's taxable year, if the donor includes on Form 8283 the information required by paragraph (c)(3) or (d)(3) of this section for each item of property.

(3) Substantiation requirements for carryovers of noncash contribution deductions. The rules in paragraphs (c)(2)(ii), (d)(1)(iii), (d)(2), (e)(1)(iii) and (e)(1)(iv) of this section (regarding substantiation that must be submitted with a return) apply to the return for any carryover year under section 170(d).

(4) Partners and S corporation shareholders. (i) Form 8283 must be provided to partners and S corporation shareholders. If the donor is a partnership or S corporation, the donor must provide a copy of the completed Form 8283 to every partner or shareholder who receives an allocation of a charitable contribution deduction under section 170 for the property described in Form 8283.

(ii) Partners and S corporation shareholders must attach Form 8283 to return. A partner of a partnership or shareholder of an S corporation who receives an allocation of a deduction under section 170 for a charitable contribution of property to which paragraphs (c), (d), or (e) of this section applies must attach a copy of the partnership's or S corporation's completed Form 8283 to the return on which the deduction is claimed.

(5) Determination of deduction amount for purposes of substantiation rules. (i) In general. In determining whether the amount of a donor's deduction exceeds the amounts set forth in section 170(f)(11)(B) (noncash contributions exceeding $500), 170(f)(11)(C) (noncash contributions exceeding $5,000), or 170(f)(11)(D) (noncash contributions exceeding $500,000), the rules of paragraphs (f)(5)(ii) and (f)(5)(iii) of this section apply.

(ii) Similar items of property must be aggregated. Under section 170(f)(11)(F), the donor must aggregate the amount claimed as a deduction for all similar items of property (as defined in § 1.170A-13(c)(7)(iii)) contributed during the taxable year. For rules regarding the number of qualified appraisals and Forms 8283 required if similar items of property are contributed, see §§ 1.170A-13(c)(3)(iv)(A) and 1.170A-13(c)(4)(iv)(B).

(iii) For contributions of certain inventory and scientific property, excess of amount claimed over cost of goods sold taken into account. (A) In general. In determining the amount of a donor's contribution of property to which section 170(e)(3) or (4) applies, the donor must take into account only the excess of the amount claimed as a deduction over the amount that would have been treated as the cost of goods sold if the donor had sold the contributed property to the donee.

(B) Example. The following example illustrates the rule of this paragraph (f)(5)(iii):

Example. X Corporation makes a contribution to which section 170(e)(3) applies of clothing for the care of the needy. The cost of the property to X Corporation is $5,000, and, pursuant to section 170(e)(3)(B), X Corporation claims a charitable contribution deduction of $8,000. The amount taken into account for purposes of determining the $5,000 threshold of paragraph (d) of this section is $3,000 ($8,000 - $5,000).

(6) Failure due to reasonable cause. If a donor fails to meet the requirements of paragraphs (c), (d), or (e) of this section, the donor's deduction will be disallowed unless the donor establishes that the failure was due to reasonable cause and not to willful neglect. The donor may establish that the failure was due to reasonable cause and not to willful neglect only if the donor—

(i) Submits with the return a detailed explanation that the failure to meet the requirements of this section was due to reasonable cause and not to willful neglect;

(ii) Obtained a contemporaneous written acknowledgment (as required by section 170(f)(8) and § 1.170A-13(f)(3)); and

(iii) Obtained a qualified appraisal (as defined by section 170(f)(11)(E)(i) and § 1.170A-17(a)(1)) prepared by a qualified appraiser (as defined by section 170(f)(11)(E)(ii) and § 1.170A-17(b)(1)) within the dates specified in § 1.170A-17(a)(4), if required.

(7) Additional requirement for returns claiming conservation easements for buildings in registered historic districts. [Reserved]

(g) Effective/applicability date. This section applies to contributions made after the date these regulations are published as final regulations in the Federal Register.

Proposed § 1.170A-17 Qualified appraisal and qualified appraiser. [*For Preamble, see ¶ 153,047*]

(a) Qualified appraisal. *(1) Definition.* For purposes of section 170(f)(11) and §§ 1.170A-16(d)(1)(ii) and 1.170A-16(e)(1)(ii), the term qualified appraisal means an appraisal document that is prepared by a qualified appraiser (as defined in paragraph (b)(1) of this section) in accordance with generally accepted appraisal standards (as defined in paragraph (a)(2) of this section) and otherwise complies with the requirements of this paragraph (a).

(2) Generally accepted appraisal standards defined. For purposes of paragraph (a)(1) of this section, generally accepted appraisal standards means the substance and principles of the Uniform Standards of Professional Appraisal Practice, as developed by the Appraisal Standards Board of the Appraisal Foundation.

(3) Contents of qualified appraisal. A qualified appraisal must include—

(i) The following information about the contributed property:

(A) A description in sufficient detail under the circumstances (taking into account the value of the property) for a person who is not generally familiar with the type of property to ascertain that the appraised property is the contributed property.

(B) In the case of real or personal tangible property, the condition of the property.

(C) The valuation effective date (as defined in paragraph (a)(5)(i) of this section).

(D) The fair market value (within the meaning of § 1.170A-1(c)(2)) of the contributed property on the valuation effective date;

(ii) The terms of any agreement or understanding by or on behalf of the donor and donee that relates to the use, sale, or other disposition of the contributed property, including, for example, the terms of any agreement or understanding that—

(A) Restricts temporarily or permanently a donee's right to use or dispose of the contributed property;

(B) Reserves to, or confers upon, anyone (other than a donee or an organization participating with a donee in cooperative fundraising) any right to the income from the contributed property or to the possession of the property, including the right to vote contributed securities, to acquire the property by purchase or otherwise, or to designate the person having income, possession, or right to acquire; or

(C) Earmarks contributed property for a particular use;

(iii) The date (or expected date) of the contribution to the donee;

(iv) The following information about the appraiser:

(A) Name, address, and taxpayer identification number.

(B) Qualifications to value the type of property being valued, including the appraiser's education and experience.

(C) If the appraiser is acting in his or her capacity as a partner in a partnership, an employee of any person (whether an individual, corporation, or partnership), or an independent contractor engaged by a person other than the donor, the name, address, and taxpayer identification number of the partnership or the person who employs or engages the qualified appraiser;

(v) The signature of the appraiser and the date signed by the appraiser (appraisal report date);

(vi) The following declaration by the appraiser: "I understand that my appraisal will be used in connection with a return or claim for refund. I also understand that, if a substantial or gross valuation misstatement of the value of the property claimed on the return or claim for refund results from my appraisal, I may be subject to a penalty under section 6695A of the Internal Revenue Code, as well as other applicable penalties. I affirm that I have not been barred from presenting evidence or testimony before the Department of the Treasury or the Internal Revenue Service pursuant to 31 U.S.C. section 330(c);"

(vii) A statement that the appraisal was prepared for income tax purposes;

(viii) The method of valuation used to determine the fair market value, such as the income approach, the market-data approach, or the replacement-cost-less-depreciation approach; and

(ix) The specific basis for the valuation, such as specific comparable sales transactions or statistical sampling, including a justification for using sampling and an explanation of the sampling procedure employed.

(4) Timely appraisal report. A qualified appraisal must be signed and dated by the qualified appraiser no earlier than 60 days before the date of the contribution and no later than—

(i) The due date (including extensions) of the return on which the deduction for the contribution is first claimed;

(ii) In the case of a donor that is a partnership or S corporation, the due date (including extensions) of the return on which the deduction for the contribution is first reported; or

(iii) In the case of a deduction first claimed on an amended return, the date on which the amended return is filed.

(5) Valuation effective date. (i) Definition. The valuation effective date is the date to which the value opinion applies.

(ii) Timely valuation effective date. For an appraisal report dated before the date of the contribution (as described in § 1.170A-1(b)), the valuation effective date must be no earlier than 60 days before the date of the contribution and no later than the date of the contribution. For an appraisal report dated on or after the date of the contribution, the valuation effective date must be the date of the contribution.

(6) Exclusion for donor knowledge of falsity. An appraisal is not a qualified appraisal for a particular contribution, even if the requirements of this paragraph (a) are met, if a reasonable person would conclude that the donor failed to disclose or misrepresented facts that would cause the appraiser to overstate the value of the contributed property.

(7) Number of appraisals required. A donor must obtain a separate qualified appraisal for each item of property for which an appraisal is required under paragraphs (c), (d), or (e) of this section and that is not included in a group of similar items of property (as defined in § 1.170A-13(c)(7)(iii)). For rules regarding the number of appraisals required if similar items of property are contributed, see § 1.170A-13(c)(3)(iv)(A).

(8) Prohibited appraisal fees. The fee for a qualified appraisal cannot be based to any extent on the appraised value of the property. For example, a fee for an appraisal will be treated as based on the appraised value of the property if any part of the fee depends on the amount of the appraised value that is allowed by the IRS after an examination.

(9) Retention of qualified appraisal. The donor must retain the qualified appraisal for so long as it may be relevant in the administration of any internal revenue law.

(10) Appraisal disregarded pursuant to 31 U.S.C. 330(c). If an appraisal is disregarded pursuant to 31 U.S.C. 330(c), it has no probative effect as to the value of the appraised property and does not satisfy the appraisal requirements of paragraphs (d) and (e) of this section, unless the appraisal and Form 8283 include the appraiser signature, the date signed by the appraiser, and the appraiser declaration described in paragraphs (a)(3)(v) and (a)(3)(vi) of this section and §§ 1.170A-16(d)(3)(iii) and (d)(4), and the donor had no knowledge that the signature, date, or declaration was false when the appraisal and Form 8283 were signed by the appraiser.

(11) Partial interest. If the contributed property is a partial interest, the appraisal must be of the partial interest.

(b) Qualified appraiser. *(1) Definition.* For purposes of section 170(f)(11) and §§ 1.170A-16(d)(1)(ii) and 1.170A-16(e)(1)(ii), the term qualified appraiser means an individual with verifiable education and experience in valuing the relevant type of property for which the appraisal is performed (as described in paragraphs (b)(2) through (b)(4) of this section).

(2) Education and experience in valuing relevant type of property. (i) In general. An individual is treated as having education and experience in valuing the relevant type of property within the meaning of paragraph (b)(1) of this section if, as of the date the individual signs the appraisal, the individual has—

(A) Successfully completed (for example, received a passing grade on a final examination) professional or college-level coursework (as described in paragraph (b)(2)(ii) of this section) in valuing the relevant type of property (as described in paragraph (b)(3) of this section), and has two or more years of experience in valuing the relevant type of property (as described in paragraph (b)(3) of this section); or

(B) Earned a recognized appraisal designation (as described in paragraph (b)(2)(iii) of this section) for the relevant type of property (as described in paragraph (b)(3) of this section).

(ii) Coursework must be obtained from professional or college-level educational institution, appraisal organization, or employer educational program. For purposes of paragraph (b)(2)(i)(A) of this section, the coursework must be obtained from—

(A) A professional or college-level educational organization described in section 170(b)(1)(A)(ii);

(B) A generally recognized professional appraisal organization that regularly offers educational programs in the principles of valuation; or

(C) An employer as part of an employee apprenticeship or educational program substantially similar to the educational programs described in paragraphs (b)(2)(ii)(A) and (B) of this section.

(iii) Recognized appraisal designation defined. A recognized appraisal designation means a designation awarded by a recognized professional appraiser organization on the basis of demonstrated competency. For example, an appraiser who has earned a designation similar to the Member of the Appraisal Institute (MAI), Senior Residential Appraiser (SRA), Senior Real Estate Appraiser (SREA), or Senior Real Property Appraiser (SRPA) membership designation has earned a recognized appraisal designation.

(3) Relevant type of property defined. (i) In general. The relevant type of property means the category of property customary in the appraisal field for an appraiser to value.

(ii) Examples. The following examples illustrate the rule of paragraph (b)(3)(i) of this section:

Example (1). Coursework in valuing relevant type of property. There are very few professional-level courses offered in widget appraising, and it is customary in the appraisal field for personal property appraisers to appraise widgets. Appraiser A has successfully completed professional-level coursework in valuing personal property generally but has completed no coursework in valuing widgets. The coursework completed by Appraiser A is for the relevant type of property under paragraphs (b)(2)(i) and (b)(3)(i) of this section.

Example (2). Experience in valuing relevant type of property. It is customary for professional antique appraisers to appraise antique widgets. Appraiser A has 2 years of experience in valuing antiques generally and is asked to appraise an antique widget. Appraiser A has obtained experience in valuing the relevant type of property under paragraphs (b)(2)(i) and (b)(3)(i) of this section.

Example (3). No experience in valuing relevant type of property. It is not customary for professional antique appraisers to appraise new widgets. Appraiser A has experience in appraising antiques generally but no experience in appraising new widgets. Appraiser A is asked to appraise a new widget. Appraiser A does not have experience in valuing the relevant type of property under paragraphs (b)(2)(i) and (b)(3)(i) of this section.

(4) Verifiable. For purposes of paragraph (b)(1) of this section, education and experience in valuing the relevant

type of property are verifiable if the appraiser specifies in the appraisal the appraiser's education and experience in valuing the relevant type of property (as described in paragraphs (b)(2) and (b)(3) of this section), and the appraiser makes a declaration in the appraisal that, because of the appraiser's education and experience described in this paragraph (b)(4), the appraiser is qualified to make appraisals of the relevant type of property being valued.

(5) Individuals who are not qualified appraisers. The following individuals cannot be qualified appraisers for the appraised property:

(i) An individual who receives a fee prohibited by paragraph (a)(8) of this section.

(ii) The donor of the property.

(iii) A party to the transaction in which the donor acquired the property (for example, the individual who sold, exchanged, or gave the property to the donor, or any individual who acted as an agent for the transferor or for the donor for the sale, exchange, or gift), unless the property is contributed within 2 months of the date of acquisition and its appraised value does not exceed its acquisition price.

(iv) The donee of the property.

(v) Any individual who is either—

(A) Related (within the meaning of section 267(b)) to, or an employee of, any of the individuals described in paragraphs (b)(5)(ii), (b)(5)(iii), or (b)(5)(iv) of this section, or married to an individual who is in a relationship described in section 267(b) with any of the foregoing individuals; or

(B) An independent contractor who is regularly used as an appraiser by any of the individuals described in paragraphs (b)(5)(ii), (b)(5)(iii), or (b)(5)(iv) of this section, and who does not perform a majority of his or her appraisals for others during the taxable year.

(vi) An individual who is prohibited from practicing before the Internal Revenue Service by the Secretary under 31 U.S.C. section 330(c) at any time during the 3-year period ending on the date the appraisal is signed by the individual.

(c) Effective/applicability date. This section applies to contributions made after the date these regulations are published as final regulations in the Federal Register.

Proposed § 1.170A-18 Contributions of clothing and household items. (a) In general. Except as provided in paragraph (b) of this section, no deduction is allowed under section 170(a) for a contribution of clothing or a household item (as described in paragraph (c) of this section) unless—

(1) The item is in good used condition or better at the time of the contribution; and

(2) The donor meets the substantiation requirements of § 1.170A-16.

(b) Certain contributions of clothing or household items with claimed value of more than $500. The rule described in paragraph (a)(1) of this section does not apply to a contribution of a single item of clothing or a household item for which a deduction of more than $500 is claimed, if the donor submits with the return on which the deduction is claimed a qualified appraisal (as defined in § 1.170A-17(a)(1)) of the property prepared by a qualified appraiser (as defined in § 1.170A-17(b)(1)) and a completed Form 8283 (Section B) (as described in § 1.170A-16(d)(3)).

(c) Definition of household items. For purposes of section 170(f)(16) and this section, the term household items includes furniture, furnishings, electronics, appliances, linens, and other similar items. Food, paintings, antiques, and other objects of art, jewelry, gems, and collections are not household items.

(d) Effective/applicability date. This section applies to contributions made after the date these regulations are published as final regulations in the Federal Register.

§ 1.171-1 Bond premium.

(a) Overview. *(1) In general.* This section and §§ 1.171-2 through 1.171-5 provide rules for the determination and amortization of bond premium by a holder. In general, a holder amortizes bond premium by offsetting the interest allocable to an accrual period with the premium allocable to that period. Bond premium is allocable to an accrual period based on a constant yield. The use of a constant yield to amortize bond premium is intended to generally conform the treatment of bond premium to the treatment of original issue discount under sections 1271 through 1275. Unless otherwise provided, the terms used in this section and §§ 1.171-2 through 1.171-5 have the same meaning as those terms in sections 1271 through 1275 and the corresponding regulations. Moreover, unless otherwise provided, the provisions of this section and §§ 1.171-2 through 1.171-5 apply in a manner consistent with those of sections 1271 through 1275 and the corresponding regulations. In addition, the anti-abuse rule in § 1.1275-2(g) applies for purposes of this section and §§ 1.171-2 through 1.171-5.

(2) Cross-references. For rules dealing with the adjustments to a holder's basis to reflect the amortization of bond premium, see § 1.1016-5(b). For rules dealing with the treatment of bond issuance premium by an issuer, see § 1.163-13.

(b) Scope. *(1) In general.* Except as provided in paragraph (b)(2) of this section and § 1.171-5, this section and §§ 1.171-2 through 1.171-4 apply to any bond that, upon its acquisition by the holder, is held with bond premium. For purposes of this section and §§ 1.171-2 through 1.171-5, the term *bond* has the same meaning as the *term debt instrument* in § 1.1275-1(d).

(2) Exceptions. This section and §§ 1.171-2 through 1.171-5 do not apply to—

(i) A bond described in section 1272(a)(6)(C) (regular interests in a REMIC, qualified mortgages held by a REMIC, and certain other debt instruments, or pools of debt instruments, with payments subject to acceleration);

(ii) A bond to which § 1.1275-4 applies (relating to certain debt instruments that provide for contingent payments);

(iii) A bond held by a holder that has made a § 1.1272-3 election with respect to the bond;

(iv) A bond that is stock in trade of the holder, a bond of a kind that would properly be included in the inventory of the holder if on hand at the close of the taxable year, or a bond held primarily for sale to customers in the ordinary course of the holder's trade or business; or

(v) A bond issued before September 28, 1985, unless the bond bears interest and was issued by a corporation or by a government or political subdivision thereof.

(c) General rule. *(1) Tax-exempt obligations.* A holder must amortize bond premium on a bond that is a tax-exempt obligation. See § 1.171-2(c) Example 4.

(2) Taxable bonds. A holder may elect to amortize bond premium on a taxable bond. Except as provided in paragraph (c)(3) of this section, a taxable bond is any bond other than a tax-exempt obligation. See § 1.171-4 for rules relating to the election to amortize bond premium on a taxable bond.

(3) Bonds the interest on which is partially excludable. For purposes of this section and §§ 1.171-2 through 1.171-5, a bond the interest on which is partially excludable from gross income is treated as two instruments, a tax-exempt obligation and a taxable bond. The holder's basis in the bond and each payment on the bond are allocated between the two instruments based on a reasonable method.

(d) Determination of bond premium. *(1) In general.* A holder acquires a bond at a premium if the holder's basis in the bond immediately after its acquisition by the holder exceeds the sum of all amounts payable on the bond after the acquisition date (other than payments of qualified stated interest). This excess is bond premium, which is amortizable under § 1.171-2.

(2) Additional rules for amounts payable on certain bonds. Additional rules apply to determine the amounts payable on a variable rate debt instrument, an inflation-indexed debt instrument, a bond that provides for certain alternative payment schedules, and a bond that provides for remote or incidental contingencies. See § 1.171-3.

(e) Basis. A holder determines its basis in a bond under this paragraph (e). This determination of basis applies only for purposes of this section and §§ 1.171-2 through 1.171-5. Because of the application of this paragraph (e), the holder's basis in the bond for purposes of these sections may differ from the holder's basis for determining gain or loss on the sale or exchange of the bond.

(1) Determination of basis. (i) In general. In general, the holder's basis in the bond is the holder's basis for determining loss on the sale or exchange of the bond.

(ii) Bonds acquired in certain exchanges. If the holder acquired the bond in exchange for other property (other than in a reorganization defined in section 368) and the holder's basis in the bond is determined in whole or in part by reference to the holder's basis in the other property, the holder's basis in the bond may not exceed its fair market value immediately after the exchange. See paragraph (f) Example 1 of this section. If the bond is acquired in a reorganization, see section 171(b)(4)(B).

(iii) Convertible bonds. (A) General rule. If the bond is a convertible bond, the holder's basis in the bond is reduced by an amount equal to the value of the conversion option. The value of the conversion option may be determined under any reasonable method. For example, the holder may determine the value of the conversion option by comparing the market price of the convertible bond to the market prices of similar bonds that do not have conversion options. See paragraph (f) Example 2 of this section.

(B) Convertible bonds acquired in certain exchanges. If the bond is a convertible bond acquired in a transaction described in paragraph (e)(1)(ii) of this section, the holder's basis in the bond may not exceed its fair market value immediately after the exchange reduced by the value of the conversion option.

(C) Definition of convertible bond. A convertible bond is a bond that provides the holder with an option to convert the bond into stock of the issuer, stock or debt of a related party (within the meaning of section 267(b) or 707(b)(1)), or into cash or other property in an amount equal to the approximate value of such stock or debt.

(2) Basis in bonds held by certain transferees. Notwithstanding paragraph (e)(1) of this section, if the bond is transferred basis property (as defined in section 7701(a)(43)) and the transferor had acquired the bond at a premium, the holder's basis in the bond is—

(i) The holder's basis for determining loss on the sale or exchange of the bond; reduced by

(ii) Any amounts that the transferor could not have amortized under this paragraph (e) or under § 1.171-4(c), except to the extent that the holder's basis already reflects a reduction attributable to such nonamortizable amounts.

(f) Examples. The following examples illustrate the rules of this section:

Example (1). Bond received in liquidation of a partnership interest.

(i) Facts. PR is a partner in partnership PRS. PRS does not have any unrealized receivables or inventory items as defined in section 751. On January 1, 1998, PRS distributes to PR a taxable bond, issued by an unrelated corporation, in liquidation of PR's partnership interest. At that time, the fair market value of PR's partnership interest is $40,000 and the basis is $100,000. The fair market value of the bond is $40,000.

(ii) Determination of basis. Under section 732(b), PR's basis in the bond is equal to PR's basis in the partnership interest. Therefore, PR's basis for determining loss on the sale or exchange of the bond is $100,000. However, because the distribution is treated as an exchange for purposes of section 171(b)(4), PR's basis in the bond is $40,000 for purposes of this section and §§ 1.171-2 through 1.171-5. See paragraph (e)(1)(ii) of this section.

Example (2). Convertible bond.

(i) Facts. On January 11, 1998, A purchases for $1,100 B corporation's bond maturing on January 1, 2001, with a stated principal amount of $1,000, payable at maturity. The bond provides for unconditional payments of interest of $30 on January 1 and July 1 of each year. In addition, the bond is convertible into 15 shares of B corporation stock at the option of the holder. On January 1, 1998, B corporation's nonconvertible, publicly-traded, three-year debt with a similar credit rating trades at a price that reflects a yield of 6.75 percent, compounded semiannually.

(ii) Determination of basis. A's basis for determining loss on the sale or exchange of the bond is $1,100. As of January 1, 1998, discounting the remaining payments on the bond at the yield at which B's similar nonconvertible bonds trade (6.75 percent, compounded semiannually) results in a present value of $980. Thus, the value of the conversion option is $120. Under paragraph (e)(1)(iii)(A) of this section, A's basis is $980 ($1,100 – $120) for purposes of this section and §§ 1.171-2 through 1.171-5. The sum of all amounts payable on the bond other than qualified stated interest is $1,000. Because A's basis (as determined under paragraph (e)(1)(iii)(A) of this section) does not exceed $1,000, A does not acquire the bond at a premium.

T.D. 6278, 12/10/57, amend T.D. 8746, 12/30/97.

§ 1.171-2 Amortization of bond premium.

(a) Offsetting qualified stated interest with premium. *(1) In general.* A holder amortizes bond premium by offsetting the qualified stated interest allocable to an accrual period with the bond premium allocable to the accrual period. This offset occurs when the holder takes the qualified stated interest into account under the holder's regular method of accounting.

(2) Qualified stated interest allocable to an accrual period. See § 1.446-2(b) to determine the accrual period to which qualified stated interest is allocable and to determine the accrual of qualified stated interest within an accrual period.

(3) Bond premium allocable to an accrual period. The bond premium allocable to an accrual period is determined under this paragraph (a)(3). Within an accrual period, the bond premium allocable to the period accrues ratably.

(i) Step one: Determine the holder's yield. The holder's yield is the discount rate that, when used in computing the present value of all remaining payments to be made on the bond (including payments of qualified stated interest), produces an amount equal to the holder's basis in the bond as determined under § 1.171-1(e). For this purpose, the remaining payments include only payments to be made after the date the holder acquires the bond. The yield is calculated as of the date the holder acquires the bond, must be constant over the term of the bond, and must be calculated to at least two decimal places when expressed as a percentage.

(ii) Step two: Determine the accrual periods. A holder determines the accrual periods for the bond under the rules of § 1.1272-1(b)(1)(ii).

(iii) Step three: Determine the bond premium allocable to the accrual period. The bond premium allocable to an accrual period is the excess of the qualified stated interest allocable to the accrual period over the product of the holder's adjusted acquisition price (as defined in paragraph (b) of this section) at the beginning of the accrual period and the holder's yield. In performing this calculation, the yield must be stated appropriately taking into account the length of the particular accrual period. Principles similar to those in § 1.1272-1(b)(4) apply in determining the bond premium allocable to an accrual period.

(4) Bond premium in excess of qualified stated interest. (i) Taxable bonds. (A) Bond premium deduction. In the case of a taxable bond, if the bond premium allocable to an accrual period exceeds the qualified stated interest allocable to the accrual period, the excess is treated by the holder as a bond premium deduction under section 171(a)(1) for the accrual period. However, the amount treated as a bond premium deduction is limited to the amount by which the holder's total interest inclusions on the bond in prior accrual periods exceed the total amount treated by the holder as a bond premium deduction on the bond in prior accrual periods. A deduction determined under this paragraph (a)(4)(i)(A) is not subject to section 67 (the 2-percent floor on miscellaneous itemized deductions). See Example 1 of § 1.171-3(e).

(B) Carryforward. If the bond premium allocable to an accrual period exceeds the sum of the qualified stated interest allocable to the accrual period and the amount treated as a deduction for the accrual period under paragraph (a)(4)(i)(A) of this section, the excess is carried forward to the next accrual period and is treated as bond premium allocable to that period.

(ii) Tax-exempt obligations. In the case of a tax-exempt obligation, if the bond premium allocable to an accrual period exceeds the qualified stated interest allocable to the accrual period, the excess is a nondeductible loss. If a regulated investment company (RIC) within the meaning of section 851 has excess bond premium for an accrual period that would be a nondeductible loss under the prior sentence, the RIC must use this excess bond premium to reduce its tax-exempt interest income on other tax-exempt obligations held during the accrual period.

(5) Additional rules for certain bonds. Additional rules apply to determine the amortization of bond premium on a variable rate debt instrument, an inflation-indexed debt instrument, a bond that provides for certain alternative payment schedules, and a bond that provides for remote or incidental contingencies. See § 1.171-3.

(b) Adjusted acquisition price. The adjusted acquisition price of a bond at the beginning of the first accrual period is the holder's basis as determined under § 1.171-1(e). Thereafter, the adjusted acquisition price is the holder's basis in the bond decreased by—

(1) The amount of bond premium previously allocable under paragraph (a)(3) of this section; and

(2) The amount of any payment previously made on the bond other than a payment of qualified stated interest.

(c) Examples. The following examples illustrate the rules of this section. Each example assumes the holder uses the calendar year as its taxable year and has elected to amortize bond premium, effective for all relevant taxable years. In addition, each example assumes a 30-day month and 360-day year. Although, for purposes of simplicity, the yield as stated is rounded to two decimal places, the computations do not reflect this rounding convention. The examples are as follows:

Example (1). Taxable bond.

(i) Facts. On February 1, 1999, A purchases for $110,000 a taxable bond maturing on February 1, 2006, with a stated principal amount of $100,000, payable at maturity. The bond provides for unconditional payments of interest of $10,000, payable on February 1 of each year. A uses the cash receipts and disbursements method of accounting, and A decides to use annual accrual periods ending on February 1 of each year.

(ii) Amount of bond premium. The interest payments on the bond are qualified stated interest. Therefore, the sum of all amounts payable on the bond (other than the interest payments) is $100,000. Under § 1.171-1, the amount of bond premium is $10,000 ($110,000 – $100,000).

(iii) Bond premium allocable to the first accrual period. Based on the remaining payment schedule of the bond and A's basis in the bond, A's yield is 8.07 percent, compounded annually. The bond premium allocable to the accrual period ending on February 1, 2000, is the excess of the qualified stated interest allocable to the period ($10,000) over the product of the adjusted acquisition price at the beginning of the period ($110,000) and A's yield (8.07 percent, compounded annually). Therefore, the bond premium allocable to the accrual period is $1,118.17 ($10,000 – $8,881.83).

(iv) Premium used to offset interest. Although A receives an interest payment of $10,000 on February 1, 2000, A only includes in income $8,881.83, the qualified stated interest allocable to the period ($10,000) offset with bond premium allocable to the period ($1,118.17). Under § 1.1016-5(b), A's basis in the bond is reduced by $1,118.17 on February 1, 2000.

Example (2). Alternative accrual periods.

(i) Facts. The facts are the same as in Example 1 of this paragraph (c) except that A decides to use semiannual accrual periods ending on February 1 and August 1 of each year.

(ii) Bond premium allocable to the first accrual period. Based on the remaining payment schedule of the bond and A's basis in the bond, A's yield is 7.92 percent, compounded semiannually. The bond premium allocable to the accrual period ending on August 1, 1999, is the excess of the qualified stated interest allocable to the period ($5,000) over the product of the adjusted acquisition price at the beginning of the period ($110,000) and A's yield, stated appropriately taking into account the length of the accrual period (7.92 percent/2). Therefore, the bond premium allocable to the accrual period is $645.29 ($5,000 – $4,354.71). Although the accrual period ends on August 1, 1999, the qualified stated interest of $5,000 is not taken into income until February 1, 2000, the date it is received. Likewise, the bond premium of $645.29 is not taken into account until February 1, 2000. The adjusted acquisition price of the bond on August 1, 1999, is $109,354.71 (the adjusted acquisition price at the beginning of the period ($110,000) less the bond premium allocable to the period ($645.29)).

(iii) Bond premium allocable to the second accrual period. Because the interval between payments of qualified stated interest contains more than one accrual period, the adjusted acquisition price at the beginning of the second accrual period must be adjusted for the accrued but unpaid qualified stated interest. See paragraph (a)(3)(iii) of this section and § 1.1272-1(b)(4)(i)(B). Therefore, the adjusted acquisition price on August 1, 1999, is $114,354.71 ($109,354.71 + $5,000). The bond premium allocable to the accrual period ending on February 1, 2000, is the excess of the qualified stated interest allocable to the period ($5,000) over the product of the adjusted acquisition price at the beginning of the period ($114,354.71) and A's yield, stated appropriately taking into account the length of the accrual period (7.92 percent/2). Therefore, the bond premium allocable to the accrual period is $472.88 ($5,000 – $4,527.12).

(iv) Premium used to offset interest. Although A receives an interest payment of $10,000 on February 1, 2000, A only includes in income $8,881.83, the qualified stated interest of $10,000 ($5,000 allocable to the accrual period ending on August 1, 1999, and $5,000 allocable to the accrual period ending on February 1, 2000) offset with bond premium of $1,118.17 ($645.29 allocable to the accrual period ending on August 1, 1999, and $472.88 allocable to the accrual period ending on February 1, 2000). As indicated in Example 1 of this paragraph (c), this same amount would be taken into income at the same time had A used annual accrual periods.

Example (3). Holder uses accrual method of accounting.

(i) Facts. The facts are the same as in Example 1 of this paragraph (c) except that A uses an accrual method of accounting. Thus, for the accrual period ending on February 1, 2000, the qualified stated interest allocable to the period is $10,000, and the bond premium allocable to the period is $1,118.17. Because the accrual period extends beyond the end of A's taxable year, A must allocate these amounts between the two taxable years.

(ii) Amounts allocable to the first taxable year. The qualified stated interest allocable to the first taxable year is $9,166.67 ($10,000 × 11/12). The bond premium allocable to the first taxable year is $1,024.99 ($1,118.17 × 11/12).

(iii) Premium used to offset interest. For 1999, A includes in income $8,141.68, the qualified stated interest allocable to the period ($9,166.67) offset with bond premium allocable to the period ($1,024.99). Under § 1.1016-5(b), A's basis in the bond is reduced by $1,024.99 in 1999.

(iv) Amounts allocable to the next taxable year. The remaining amounts of qualified stated interest and bond premium allocable to the accrual period ending on February 1, 2000, are taken into account for the taxable year ending on December 31, 2000.

Example (4). Tax-exempt obligation.

(i) Facts. On January 15, 1999, C purchases for $120,000 a tax-exempt obligation maturing on January 15, 2006, with a stated principal amount of $100,000, payable at maturity. The obligation provides for unconditional payments of interest of $9,000, payable on January 15 of each year. C uses the cash receipts and disbursements method of accounting, and C decides to use annual accrual periods ending on January 15 of each year.

(ii) Amount of bond premium. The interest payments on the obligation are qualified stated interest. Therefore, the sum of all amounts payable on the obligation (other than the interest payments) is $100,000. Under § 1.171-1, the amount of bond premium is $20,000 ($120,000 – $100,000).

(iii) Bond premium allocable to the first accrual period. Based on the remaining payment schedule of the obligation and C's basis in the obligation, C's yield is 5.48 percent, compounded annually. The bond premium allocable to the accrual period ending on January 15, 2000, is the excess of the qualified stated interest allocable to the period ($9,000) over the product of the adjusted acquisition price at the beginning of the period ($120,000) and C's yield (5.48 percent, compounded annually). Therefore, the bond premium allocable to the accrual period is $2,420.55 ($9,000 – $6,579.45).

(iv) Premium used to offset interest. Although C receives an interest payment of $9,000 on January 15, 2000, C only receives tax-exempt interest income of $6,579.45, the qualified stated interest allocable to the period ($9,000) offset with bond premium allocable to the period ($2,420.55). Under § 1.1016-5(b), C's basis in the obligation is reduced by $2,420.55 on January 15, 2000.

T.D. 6278, 12/10/57, amend T.D. 6647, 4/10/63, T.D. 6984, 12/23/68, T.D. 8746, 12/30/97.

---

§ 1.171-3 Special rules for certain bonds.

(a) Variable rate debt instruments. A holder determines bond premium on a variable rate debt instrument by reference to the stated redemption price at maturity of the equivalent fixed rate debt instrument constructed for the variable rate debt instrument. The holder also allocates any bond premium among the accrual periods by reference to the equivalent fixed rate debt instrument. The holder constructs the equivalent fixed rate debt instrument, as of the date the holder acquires the variable rate debt instrument, by using the principles of § 1.1275-5(e). See paragraph (e) Example 1 of this section.

(b) Inflation-indexed debt instruments. A holder determines bond premium on an inflation-indexed debt instrument by assuming that there will be no inflation or deflation over the remaining term of the instrument. The holder also allocates any bond premium among the accrual periods by assuming that there will be no inflation or deflation over the remaining term of the instrument. The bond premium allocable to an accrual period offsets qualified stated interest allocable to the period. Notwithstanding § 1.171-2(a)(4), if the bond premium allocable to an accrual period exceeds the qualified stated interest allocable to the period, the excess is treated as a deflation adjustment under § 1.1275-7(f)(1)(i). See § 1.1275-7 for other rules relating to inflation-indexed debt instruments.

(c) Yield and remaining payment schedule of certain bonds subject to contingencies. *(1) Applicability*. This paragraph (c) provides rules that apply in determining the yield and remaining payment schedule of certain bonds that provide for an alternative payment schedule (or schedules) applicable upon the occurrence of a contingency (or contingencies). This paragraph (c) applies, however, only if the timing and amounts of the payments that comprise each payment schedule are known as of the date the holder acquires the bond (the acquisition date) and the bond is subject to paragraph (c)(2), (3), or (4) of this section. A bond does not provide for an alternative payment schedule merely because there is a possibility of impairment of a payment (or payments) by insolvency, default, or similar circumstances. See § 1.1275-4 for the treatment of a bond that provides for a contingency that is not described in this paragraph (c).

(2) Remaining payment schedule that is significantly more likely than not to occur. If, based on all the facts and circumstances as of the acquisition date, a single remaining payment schedule for a bond is significantly more likely than not to occur, this remaining payment schedule is used to determine and amortize bond premium under §§ 1.171-1 and 1.171-2.

(3) Mandatory sinking fund provision. Notwithstanding paragraph (c)(2) of this section, if a bond is subject to a mandatory sinking fund provision described in § 1.1272-1(c)(3), the provision is ignored for purposes of determining and amortizing bond premium under §§ 1.171-1 and 1.171-2.

(4) Treatment of certain options. (i) Applicability. Notwithstanding paragraphs (c)(2) and (3) of this section, the rules of this paragraph (c)(4) determine the remaining payment schedule of a bond that provides the holder or issuer with an unconditional option or options, exercisable on one or more dates during the remaining term of the bond, to alter the bond's remaining payment schedule.

(ii) Operating rules. A holder determines the remaining payment schedule of a bond by assuming that each option will (or will not) be exercised under the following rules:

(A) Issuer options. In general, the issuer is deemed to exercise or not exercise an option or combination of options in the manner that minimizes the holder's yield on the obligation. However, the issuer of a taxable bond is deemed to exercise or not exercise a call option or combination of call options in the manner that maximizes the holder's yield on the bond.

(B) Holder options. A holder is deemed to exercise or not exercise an option or combination of options in the manner that maximizes the holder's yield on the bond.

(C) Multiple options. If both the issuer and the holder have options, the rules of paragraphs (c)(4)(ii)(A) and (B) of this section are applied to the options in the order that they may be exercised. Thus, the deemed exercise of one option may eliminate other options that are later in time.

(5) Subsequent adjustments. (i) In general. Except as provided in paragraph (c)(5)(ii) of this section, if a contingency described in this paragraph (c) (including the exercise of an option described in paragraph (c)(4) of this section) actually occurs or does not occur, contrary to the assumption made pursuant to paragraph (c) of this section (a change in circumstances), then solely for purposes of section 171, the bond is treated as retired and reacquired by the holder on the date of the change in circumstances for an amount equal to the adjusted acquisition price of the bond as of that date. If, however, the change in circumstances results in a substantially contemporaneous pro-rata prepayment as defined in § 1.1275-2(f)(2), the pro-rata prepayment is treated as a payment in retirement of a portion of the bond. See paragraph (e) Example 2 of this section.

(ii) Bond premium deduction on the issuer's call of a taxable bond. If a change in circumstances results from an issuer's call of a taxable bond or a partial call that is a pro-rata prepayment, the holder may deduct as bond premium an amount equal to the excess, if any, of the holder's adjusted acquisition price of the bond over the greater of—

(A) The amount received on redemption; and

(B) The amounts that would have been payable under the bond (other than payments of qualified stated interest) if no change in circumstances had occurred.

(d) Remote and incidental contingencies. For purposes of determining and amortizing bond premium, if a bond provides for a contingency that is remote or incidental (within the meaning of § 1.1275-2(h)), the holder takes the contingency into account under the rules for remote and incidental contingencies in § 1.1275-2(h).

(e) Examples. The following examples illustrate the rules of this section. Each example assumes the holder uses the calendar year as its taxable year and has elected to amortize bond premium, effective for all relevant taxable years. In addition, each example assumes a 30-day month and 360-day year. Although, for purposes of simplicity, the yield as stated is rounded to two decimal places, the computations do not reflect this rounding convention. The examples are as follows:

Example (1). Variable rate debt instrument.

(i) Facts. On March 1, 1999, E purchases for $110,000 a taxable bond maturing on March 1, 2007, with a stated principal amount of $100,000, payable at maturity. The bond provides for unconditional payments of interest on March 1 of each year based on the percentage appreciation of a nationally-known commodity index. On March 1, 1999, it is reasonably expected that the bond will yield 12 percent, compounded annually. E uses the cash receipts and disbursements method of accounting, and E decides to use annual accrual periods ending on March 1 of each year. Assume that the bond is a variable rate debt instrument under § 1.1275-5.

(ii) Amount of bond premium. Because the bond is a variable rate debt instrument, E determines and amortizes its bond premium by reference to the equivalent fixed rate debt instrument constructed for the bond as of March 1, 1999. Because the bond provides for interest at a single objective rate that is reasonably expected to yield 12 percent, compounded annually, the equivalent fixed rate debt instrument for the bond is an eight-year bond with a principal amount of $100,000, payable at maturity. It provides for annual payments of interest of $12,000. E's basis in the equivalent fixed rate debt instrument is $110,000. The sum of all amounts payable on the equivalent fixed rate debt instrument (other than payments of qualified stated interest) is $100,000. Under § 1.171-1, the amount of bond premium is $10,000 ($110,000 – $100,000).

(iii) Bond premium allocable to each accrual period. E allocates bond premium to the remaining accrual periods by reference to the payment schedule on the equivalent fixed rate debt instrument. Based on the payment schedule of the equivalent fixed rate debt instrument and E's basis in the bond, E's yield is 10.12 percent, compounded annually. The bond premium allocable to the accrual period ending on March 1, 2000, is the excess of the qualified stated interest allocable to the period for the equivalent fixed rate debt instrument ($12,000) over the product of the adjusted acquisition price at the beginning of the period ($110,000) and E's yield (10.12 percent, compounded annually). Therefore, the bond premium allocable to the accrual period is $870.71 ($12,000 – $11,129.29). The bond premium allocable to all the accrual periods is listed in the following schedule:

Accrual period ending	Adjusted acquisition price at beginning of accrual period	Premium allocable to accruable period
3/1/00	$110,000.00	$ 870.71
3/1/01	109,129.29	958.81
3/1/02	108,170.48	1,055.82
3/1/03	107,114.66	1,162.64
3/1/04	105,952.02	1,280.27
3/1/05	104,671.75	1,409.80
3/1/06	103,261.95	1,552.44
3/1/07	101,709.51	1,709.51
		10,000.00

(iv) Qualified stated interest for each accrual period. Assume the bond actually pays the following amounts of qualified stated interest:

Accrual period ending	Qualified stated interest
3/1/00	$ 2,000.00
3/1/01	0.00
3/1/02	0.00
3/1/03	10,000.00
3/1/04	8,000.00
3/1/05	12,000.00
3/1/06	15,000.00
3/1/07	8,500.00

(v) Premium used to offset interest. E's interest income for each accrual period is determined by offsetting the qualified stated interest allocable to the period with the bond premium allocable to the period. For the accrual period ending on March 1, 2000, E includes in income $1,129.29, the qualified stated interest allocable to the period ($2,000) offset with the bond premium allocable to the period ($870.71). For the accrual period ending on March 1, 2001, the bond premium allocable to the accrual period ($958.81) exceeds the qualified stated interest allocable to the period ($0) and, therefore, E does not have interest income for this accrual period. However, under § 1.171-2(a)(4)(i)(A), E may deduct as bond premium $958.81, the excess of the bond premium allocable to the accrual period ($958.81) over the qualified stated interest allocable to the accrual period ($0). For the accrual period ending on March 1, 2002, the bond premium allocable to the accrual period ($1,055.82) exceeds the qualified stated interest allocable to the accrual period ($0) and, therefore, E does not have interest income for the accrual period. Under § 1.171-2(a)(4)(i)(A), E's deduction for bond premium for the accrual period is limited to $170.48, the excess of E's total interest inclusions on the bond in prior accrual periods ($1,129.29) over the total amount treated by E as a bond premium deduction in prior accrual periods ($958.81). Under § 1.171-2(a)(4)(i)(B), E must carry forward the remaining $885.34 of bond premium allocable to the period ending March 1, 2002, and treat it as bond premium allocable to the period ending March 1, 2003. The amount E includes in income for each accrual period is shown in the following schedule:

Accrual period ending	Qualified stated interest	Premium allocable to accrual period	Interest income	Premium deduction	Premium carryforward
3/1/00	$ 2,000.00	$ 870.71	$ 1,129.29		
3/1/01	0.00	958.81	0.00	$ 958.81	
3/1/02	0.00	1,055.82	0.00	170.48	$885.34
3/1/03	10,000.00	1,162.64	7,951.93		
3/1/04	8,000.00	1,280.27	6,719.73		
3/1/05	12,000.00	1,409.80	10,590.20		
3/1/06	15,000.00	1,552.44	13,447.56		
3/1/07	8,500.00	1,709.51	6,790.49		
		10,000.00			

Example (2). Partial call that results in a pro-rata prepayment.

(i) Facts. On April 1, 1999, M purchases for $110,000 N's taxable bond maturing on April 1, 2006, with a stated principal amount of $100,000, payable at maturity. The bond provides for unconditional payments of interest of $10,000, payable on April 1 of each year. N has the option to call all or part of the bond on April 1, 2001, at a 5 percent premium over the principal amount. M uses the cash receipts and disbursements method of accounting.

(ii) Determination of yield and the remaining payment schedule. M's yield determined without regard to the call option is 8.07 percent, compounded annually. M's yield determined by assuming N exercises its call option is 6.89 percent, compounded annually. Under paragraph (c)(4)(ii)(A) of this section, it is assumed N will not exercise the call option because exercising the option would minimize M's yield. Thus, for purposes of determining and amortizing bond premium, the bond is assumed to be a seven-year bond with a single principal payment at maturity of $100,000.

(iii) Amount of bond premium. The interest payments on the bond are qualified stated interest. Therefore, the sum of all amounts payable on the bond (other than the interest payments) is $100,000. Under § 1.171-1, the amount of bond premium is $10,000 ($110,000 – $100,000).

(iv) Bond premium allocable to the first two accrual periods. For the accrual period ending on April 1, 2000, M includes in income $8,881.83, the qualified stated interest allocable to the period ($10,000) offset with bond premium allocable to the period ($1,118.17). The adjusted acquisition price on April 1, 2000, is $108,881.83 ($110,000 – $1,118.17). For the accrual period ending on April 1, 2001, M includes in income $8,791.54, the qualified stated interest allocable to the period ($10,000) offset with bond premium allocable to the period ($1,208.46). The adjusted acquisition price on April 1, 2001, is $107,673.37 ($108,881.83 – $1,208.46).

(v) Partial call. Assume N calls one-half of M's bond for $52,500 on April 1, 2001. Because it was assumed the call would not be exercised, the call is a change in circumstances. However, the partial call is also a pro-rata prepayment within the meaning of § 1.1275-2(f)(2). As a result, the call is treated as a retirement of one-half of the bond. Under paragraph (c)(5)(ii) of this section, M may deduct $1,336.68, the excess of its adjusted acquisition price in the retired portion of the bond ($107,673.37/2, or $53,836.68) over the amount received on redemption ($52,500). M's adjusted basis in the portion of the bond that remains outstanding is $53,836.68 ($107,673.37 – $53,836.68).

T.D. 6278, 12/10/57, amend T.D. 8746, 12/30/97, T.D. 8838, 9/3/99.

§ 1.171-4 Election to amortize bond premium on taxable bonds.

(a) Time and manner of making the election. *(1) In general.* A holder makes the election to amortize bond premium by offsetting interest income with bond premium in the holder's timely filed federal income tax return for the first taxable year to which the holder desires the election to apply. The holder should attach to the return a statement that the holder is making the election under this section.

(2) Coordination with OID election. If a holder makes an election under § 1.1272-3 for a bond with bond premium, the holder is deemed to have made the election under this section.

(b) Scope of election. The election under this section applies to all taxable bonds held during or after the taxable year for which the election is made.

(c) Election to amortize made in a subsequent taxable year. *(1) In general.* If a holder elects to amortize bond premium and holds a taxable bond acquired before the taxable year for which the election is made, the holder may not amortize amounts that would have been amortized in prior taxable years had an election been in effect for those prior years.

(2) Example. The following example illustrates the rule of this paragraph (c):

Example. (i) Facts. On May 1, 1999, C purchases for $130,000 a taxable bond maturing on May 1, 2006, with a stated principal amount of $100,000, payable at maturity. The bond provides for unconditional payments of interest of $15,000, payable on May 1 of each year. C uses the cash receipts and disbursements method of accounting and the calendar year as its taxable year. C has not previously elected to amortize bond premium, but does so for 2002.

(ii) Amount to amortize. C's basis for determining loss on the sale or exchange of the bond is $130,000. Thus, under § 1.171-1, the amount of bond premium is $30,000. Under § 1.171-2, if a bond premium election were in effect for the prior taxable years, C would have amortized $3,257.44 of bond premium on May 1, 2000, and $3,551.68 of bond premium on May 1, 2001, based on annual accrual periods ending on May 1. Thus, for 2002 and future years to which the election applies, C may amortize only $23,190.88 ($30,000 – $3,257.44 – $3,551.68).

(d) Revocation of election. The election under this section may not be revoked unless approved by the Commissioner. Because a revocation of the election is a change in accounting method, a taxpayer must follow the rules under § 1.446-1(e)(3)(i) to request the Commissioner's consent to revoke the election. A revocation of the election applies to all taxable bonds held during or after the taxable year for which the revocation is effective. The holder may not amortize any remaining bond premium on bonds held at the beginning of the taxable year for which the revocation is effective. Therefore, no adjustment under section 481 is allowed upon the revocation of the election because no items of income or deduction are omitted or duplicated.

T.D. 6278, 12/10/57, amend T.D. 8746, 12/30/97.

§ 1.171-5 Effective date and transition rules.

(a) Effective date. *(1) In general.* Sections 1.171-1 through 1.171-4 apply to bonds acquired on or after March 2, 1998. However, if a holder makes the election under § 1.171-4 for the taxable year containing March 2, 1998, or any subsequent taxable year, §§ 1.171-1 through 1.171-4 apply to bonds held on or after the first day of the taxable year in which the election is made.

(2) Transition rule for use of constant yield. Notwithstanding paragraph (a)(1) of this section, § 1.171-2(a)(3) (providing that the bond premium allocable to an accrual period is determined with reference to a constant yield) does not apply to a bond issued before September 28, 1985.

(b) Coordination with existing election. A holder is deemed to have made the election under § 1.171-4 for the taxable year containing March 2, 1998, if the holder elected to amortize bond premium under section 171 and that election is effective on March 2, 1998. If the holder is deemed to have made the election under § 1.171-4 for the taxable year containing March 2, 1998, §§ 1.171-1 through 1.171-4 apply to bonds acquired on or after the first day of that taxable year. See § 1.171-4(d) for rules relating to a revocation of an election under section 171.

(c) Accounting method changes. *(1) Consent to change.* A holder required to change its method of accounting for bond premium to comply with §§ 1.171-1 through 1.171-3 must secure the consent of the Commissioner in accordance with the requirements of § 1.446-1(e). Paragraph (c)(2) of this section provides the Commissioner's automatic consent for certain changes. A holder making the election under § 1.171-4 does not need the Commissioner's consent to make the election.

(2) Automatic consent. The Commissioner grants consent for a holder to change its method of accounting for bond premium with respect to taxable bonds to which §§ 1.171-1 through 1.171-3 apply. Because this change is made on a cut-off basis, no items of income or deduction are omitted or duplicated and, therefore, no adjustment under section 481 is allowed. The consent granted by this paragraph (c)(2) applies provided—

(i) The holder elected to amortize bond premium under section 171 for a taxable year prior to the taxable year containing March 2, 1998, and that election has not been revoked;

(ii) The change is made for the first taxable year for which the holder must account for a bond under §§ 1.171-1 through 1.171-3; and

(iii) The holder attaches to its return for the taxable year containing the change a statement that it has changed its method of accounting under this section.

T.D. 8746, 12/30/97.

§ 1.172-1 Net operating loss deduction.

(a) Allowance of deduction. Section 172(a) allows as a deduction in computing taxable income for any taxable year subject to the Code the aggregate of the net operating loss carryovers and net operating loss carrybacks to such taxable year. This deduction is referred to as the net operating loss deduction. The net operating loss is the basis for the computation of the net operating loss carryovers and net operating loss carrybacks and ultimately for the net operating loss deduction itself. The net operating loss deduction shall not be disallowed for any taxable year merely because the taxpayer has no income from a trade or business for the taxable year.

(b) Steps in computation of net operating loss deduction. The three steps to be taken in the ascertainment of the net operating loss deduction for any taxable year subject to the Code are as follows:

(1) Compute the net operating loss for any preceding or succeeding taxable year from which a net operating loss may be carried over or carried back to such taxable year.

(2) Compute the net operating loss carryovers to such taxable year from such preceding taxable years and the net operating loss carrybacks to such taxable year from such succeeding taxable years.

(3) Add such net operating loss carryovers and carrybacks in order to determine the net operating loss deduction for such taxable year.

(c) Statement with tax return. Every taxpayer claiming a net operating loss deduction for any taxable year shall file with his return for such year a concise statement setting forth the amount of the net operating loss deduction claimed and all material and pertinent facts relative thereto, including a detailed schedule showing the computation of the net operating loss deduction.

(d) Ascertainment of deduction dependent upon net operating loss carryback. If the taxpayer is entitled in computing his net operating loss deduction to a carryback which he is not able to ascertain at the time his return is due, he shall compute the net operating loss deduction on his return without regard to such net operating loss carryback. When the taxpayer ascertains the net operating loss carryback, he may within the applicable period of limitations file a claim for credit or refund of the overpayment, if any, resulting from the failure to compute the net operating loss deduction for the taxable year with the inclusion of such carryback; or he may file an application under the provisions of section 6411 for a tentative carryback adjustment.

(e) Law applicable to computations. *(1)* In determining the amount of any net operating loss carryback or carryover to any taxable year, the necessary computations involving any other taxable year shall be made under the law applicable to such other taxable year.

(2) The net operating loss for any taxable year shall be determined under the law applicable to that year without regard to the year to which it is to be carried and in which, in effect, it is to be deducted as part of the net operating loss deduction.

(3) The amount of the net operating loss deduction which shall be allowed for any taxable year shall be determined under the law applicable to that year.

(f) Electing small business corporations. In determining the amount of the net operating loss deduction of any corporation, there shall be disregarded the net operating loss of such corporation for any taxable year for which such corporation was an electing small business corporation under subchapter S (section 1371 and following), chapter 1 of the Code. In applying section 172(b)(1) and (2) to a net operating loss sustained in a taxable year in which the corporation was not an electing small business corporation, a taxable year in which the corporation was an electing small business corporation is counted as a taxable year to which such net operating loss is carried back or over. However, the taxable income for such year as determined under section 172(b)(2) is treated as if it were zero for purposes of computing the balance of the loss available to the corporation as a carryback or carryover to other taxable years in which the corporation is not an electing small business corporation. See section 1374 and the regulations thereunder for allowance of a deduction to shareholders for a net operating loss sustained by an electing small business corporation.

(g) Husband and wife. The net operating loss deduction of a husband and wife shall be determined in accordance with this section, but subject also to the provisions of § 1.172-7.

T.D. 6192, 7/23/56, amend T.D. 6486, 8/12/60, T.D. 8107, 12/1/86.

§ 1.172-2 Net operating loss in case of a corporation.

Caution: The Treasury has not yet amended Reg § 1.172-2 to reflect changes made by P.L. 101-508, P.L. 101-239.

(a) Modification of deductions. A net operating loss is sustained by a corporation in any taxable year if and to the extent that, for such year, there is an excess of deductions allowed by chapter 1 of the Code over gross income computed thereunder. In determining the excess of deductions over gross income for such purpose—

(1) Items not deductible. No deduction shall be allowed under—

(i) Section 172 for the net operating loss deduction, and

(ii) Section 922 in respect of Western Hemisphere trade corporations;

(2) Dividends received. The 85-percent limitation provided by section 246(b) shall not apply to the deductions otherwise allowed under—

(i) Section 243(a) in respect of dividends received from domestic corporations.

(ii) Section 244 in respect of dividends received on preferred stock of public utilities, and

(iii) Section 245 in respect of dividends received from foreign corporations; and

(3) Dividends paid. The deduction granted by section 247 in respect of dividends paid on the preferred stock of public utilities shall be computed without regard to subsection (a)(1)(B) of Section 247.

(b) Example. The following example illustrates the application of paragraph (a):

Example. For the calendar year 1981, the X corporation has a gross income of $400,000 and total deductions allowed by chapter 1 of the Code of $375,000 exclusive of any net operating loss deduction and exclusive of any deduction for dividends received or paid. Corporation X in 1981 received $100,000 of dividends entitled to the benefits of section 243(a). These dividends are included in Corporation X's $400,000 gross income. Corporation X has no other deductions to which section 172(d) applies. On the basis of these facts, Corporation X has a net operating loss for the year 1981 of $60,000, computed as follows:

Deductions for 1981	$375,000
Plus: Deduction for dividends received, computed without regard to the limitation provided in section 246(b) (85% of $100,000)	85,000
Total	460,000
Less: Gross income for 1981 (including $100,000 dividends)	400,000
Net operating loss for 1981	60,000

(c) **Qualified real estate investment trusts.** For taxable years ending after October 4, 1976, the net operating loss of a qualified real estate investment trust (as defined in § 1.172-10(b)) is computed by taking into account the adjustments described in section 857(b)(2) (other than the deduction for dividends paid, as defined in section 561), as well as the modifications required by paragraph (a)(1) of this section. Thus, for example, the special deductions for dividends received, etc., provided in part VIII of subchapter B (other than section 248), as well as the net operating loss deduction under section 172, are not allowed in computing the net operating loss of a qualified real estate investment trust.

T.D. 6192, 7/23/56, amend T.D. 6486, 8/12/60, T.D. 7767, 2/3/81, T.D. 8107, 12/1/86.

§ 1.172-3 Net operating loss in case of a taxpayer other than a corporation.

Caution: The Treasury has not yet amended Reg § 1.172-3 to reflect changes made by P.L. 105-277, P.L. 103-66.

(a) **Modification of deductions.** A net operating loss is sustained by a taxpayer other than a corporation in any taxable year if and to the extent that, for such year there is an excess of deductions allowed by chapter 1 of the Internal Revenue Code over gross income computed thereunder. In determining the excess of deductions over gross income for such purpose—

(1) Items not deductible. No deduction shall be allowed under—

(i) Section 151 for the personal exemptions or under any other section which grants a deduction in lieu of the deductions allowed by section 151,

(ii) Section 172 for the net operating loss deduction, and

(iii) Section 1202 in respect of the net long-term capital gain.

(2) Capital losses. (i) The amount deductible on account of business capital losses shall not exceed the sum of the amount includible on account of business capital gains and that portion of nonbusiness capital gains which is computed in accordance with paragraph (a) of this section.

(ii) The amount deductible on account of nonbusiness capital losses shall not exceed the amount includible on account of nonbusiness capital gains.

(3) Nonbusiness deductions. (i) Ordinary deductions. Ordinary nonbusiness deductions shall be taken into account without regard to the amount of business deductions and shall be allowed in full to the extent, but not in excess, of that amount which is the sum of the ordinary nonbusiness gross income and the excess of nonbusiness capital gains over nonbusiness capital losses. See paragraph (c) of this section. For purposes of section 172, nonbusiness deductions and income are those deductions and that income which are not attributable to, or derived from, a taxpayer's trade or business. Wages and salary constitute income attributable to the taxpayer's trade or business for such purposes.

(ii) Sale of business property. Any gain or loss on the sale or other disposition of property which is used in the taxpayer's trade or business and which is of a character that is subject to the allowance for depreciation provided in section 167, or of real property used in the taxpayer's trade or business, shall be considered, for purposes of section 172(d)(4), as attributable to, or derived from, the taxpayer's trade or business. Such gains and losses are to be taken into account fully in computing a net operating loss without regard to the limitation on nonbusiness deductions. Thus a farmer who sells at a loss land used in the business of farming may, in computing a net operating loss, include in full the deduction otherwise allowable with respect to such loss, without regard to the amount of his nonbusiness income and without regard to whether he is engaged in the trade or business of selling farms. Similarly, an individual who sells at a loss machinery which is used in his trade or business and which is of a character that is subject to the allowance for depreciation may, in computing the net operating loss, include in full the deduction otherwise allowable with respect to such loss.

(iii) Casualty losses. Any deduction allowable under section 165(c)(3) for losses of property not connected with a trade or business shall not be considered, for purposes of section 172(d)(4), to be a nonbusiness deduction but shall be treated as a deduction attributable to the taxpayer's trade or business.

(iv) Self-employed retirement plans. Any deduction allowed under section 404, relating to contributions of an employer to an employees' trust or annuity plan, or under section 405(c), relating to contributions to a bond purchase plan, to the extent attributable to contributions made on behalf of an individual while he is an employee within the meaning of section 401(c)(1), shall not be treated, for purposes of section 172(d)(4), as attributable to, or derived from, the taxpayer's trade or business, but shall be treated as a nonbusiness deduction.

(v) Limitation. The provisions of this subparagraph shall not be construed to permit the deduction of items disallowed by subparagraph (1) of this paragraph.

(b) **Treatment of capital loss carryovers.** Because of the distinction between business and nonbusiness capital gains and losses, a taxpayer who has a capital loss carryover from a preceding taxable year, includible by virtue of section 1212 among the capital losses for the taxable year in issue, is required to determine how much of such capital loss carryover is a business capital loss and how much is a nonbusiness capital loss. In order to make this determination, the taxpayer shall first ascertain what proportion of the net capital loss for such preceding taxable year was attributable to an excess of business capital losses over business capital gains for such year, and what proportion was attributable to an excess of nonbusiness capital losses over nonbusiness capital gains. The same proportion of the capital loss carryover from such preceding taxable year shall be treated as a business capital loss and a nonbusiness capital loss, respectively. In order to determine the composition (business—nonbusiness) of a net capital loss for a taxable year, for purposes of this paragraph, if such net capital loss is computed under paragraph (b) of § 1.1212-1 and takes into account a capital loss carryover from a preceding taxable year, the composition (business—nonbusiness) of the net capital loss for such preceding taxable year must also be determined. For purposes of this paragraph, the term "capital loss carryover" means the sum of the short-term and long-term capital loss carryovers from such year. This paragraph may be illustrated by the following examples:

Example (1). (i) A, an individual, has $5,000 ordinary taxable income (computed without regard to the deductions for personal exemptions) for the calendar year 1954 and also has the following capital gains and losses for such year: Business capital gains of $2,000; business capital losses of $3,200; nonbusiness capital gains of $1,000; and nonbusiness capital losses of $1,200.

(ii) A's net capital loss for the taxable year 1954 is $400, computed as follows:

Capital losses	$4,400
Capital gains	3,000
Excess of capital losses over capital gains	1,400
Less: $1,000 of such ordinary taxable income	1,000
Net capital loss for 1954	400

(iii) A's capital losses for 1954 exceeded his capital gains for such year by $1,400. Since A's business capital losses for 1954 exceeded his business capital gains for such year by $1,200, 6/7ths ($1,200/$1,400) of A's net capital loss for 1954 is attributable to an excess of his business capital losses over his business capital gains for such year. Similarly, 1/7th of the net capital loss is attributable to the excess of nonbusiness capital losses over nonbusiness capital gains. Since the capital loss carryover for 1954 to 1955 is $400, 6/7ths of $400, or $342.86, shall be treated as a business capital loss in 1955; and 1/7th of $400, or $57.14, as a nonbusiness capital loss.

Example (2). (i) A, an individual who is computing a net operating loss for the calendar year 1966, has a capital loss carryover from 1965 of $8,000. In order to apply the provisions of this paragraph, A must determine what portion of the $8,000 carryover is attributable to the excess of business capital losses over business capital gains and what portion thereof is attributable to the excess of nonbusiness capital losses over nonbusiness capital gains. For 1965, A had $10,000 ordinary taxable income (computed without regard to the deductions for personal exemptions), and a short-term capital loss carryover of $6,000 from 1964. In order to determine the composition (business—nonbusiness) of the $8,000 carryover from 1965, A first determines that of the $6,000 carryover from 1964, $5,000 is a business capital loss and $1,000 is a nonbusiness capital loss. This must be done since, under paragraph (b) of § 1.1212-1, the net capital loss for 1965 is computed by taking into account the capital loss carryover from 1964. A's capital gains and losses for 1965 are as follows:

	1965	Carried over from 1964
Business capital gains	$2,000	
Business capital losses	3,000	$5,000
Nonbusiness capital gains	4,000	
Nonbusiness capital losses	6,000	1,000

(ii) A's net capital loss for the taxable year 1965 is $8,000, computed as follows:

Capital losses (including carryovers)	$15,000
Capital gains	6,000
Excess of capital losses over capital gains	9,000
Less: $1,000 of such ordinary taxable income	1,000
Net capital loss for 1965	8,000

(iii) A's capital losses, including carryovers, for 1965 exceeded his capital gains for such year by $9,000. Since A's business capital losses for 1965 exceeded his business capital gains for such year by $6,000, 2/3rds ($6,000/$9,000) of A's net capital loss for 1965 is attributable to an excess of his business capital losses over his business capital gains for such year. Similarly, 1/3rd of the net capital loss is attributable to the excess of nonbusiness capital losses over nonbusiness capital gains. Since the total capital loss carryover from 1965 to 1966 is $8,000, 2/3rds of $8,000, or $5,333.33, shall be treated as a business capital loss in 1966; and 1/3rd of $8,000, or $2,666.67, as a nonbusiness capital loss.

(c) Determination of portion of nonbusiness capital gains available for the deduction of business capital losses. In the computation of a net operating loss a taxpayer other than a corporation must use his nonbusiness capital gains for the deduction of his nonbusiness capital losses. Any amount not necessary for this purpose shall then be used for the deduction of any excess of ordinary nonbusiness deductions over ordinary nonbusiness gross income. The remainder, computed by applying the excess nonbusiness capital gains, shall be treated as nonbusiness capital gains and used for the purpose of determining the deductibility of business capital losses under paragraph (a)(2)(i) of this section. This principle may be illustrated by the following example:

Example (1). A, an individual, has a total nonbusiness gross income of $20,500, computed as follows:

Ordinary gross income	$ 7,500
Capital gains	13,000
Total gross income	20,500

Example (2). A also has total nonbusiness deductions of $16,000, computed as follows:

Ordinary deductions	$ 9,000
Capital loss	7,000
Total deductions	16,000

Example (3). The portion of nonbusiness capital gains to be used for the purpose of determining the deductibility of business capital losses is $4,500, computed as follows:

Nonbusiness capital gains		$13,000
Less: Nonbusiness capital loss		7,000
Excess to be taken into account for purposes of paragraph (a)(3)(i) of this section		6,000
Ordinary nonbusiness deductions	$9,000	
Less: Ordinary nonbusiness gross income	7,500	
		1,500
Portion of nonbusiness capital gains to be used for purposes of paragraph (a)(2)(i) of this section		4,500

(d) Joint net operating loss of husband and wife. In the case of a husband and wife, the joint net operating loss for any taxable year for which a joint return is filed is to be computed on the basis of the combined income and deductions of both spouses, and the modifications prescribed in paragraph (a) of this section are to be computed as if the combined income and deductions of both spouses were the income and deductions of one individual.

(e) Illustration of computation of net operating loss of a taxpayer other than a corporation. *(1) Facts.* For the calendar year 1954 A, an individual, has gross income of $483,000 and allowable deductions of $540,000. The latter amount does not include the net operating loss deduction or any deduction on account of the sale or exchange of capital assets. Included in gross income are business capital gains of $50,000 and ordinary nonbusiness income of $10,000. Included among the deductions are ordinary nonbusiness deductions of $12,000 and a deduction of $600 for his personal exemption. A has a business capital loss of $60,000 in 1964. A has no other items of income or deductions to which section 172(d) applies.

(2) Computation. On the basis of these facts, A has a net operating loss for 1954 of $104,400, computed as follows:

Deductions for 1954 (as specified in first sentence of subparagraph (1))		$540,000
Plus: Amount of business capital loss ($60,000) to extent such amount does not exceed business capital gains ($50,000)		50,000
Total		$590,000
Less: Excess of ordinary nonbusiness deductions over ordinary nonbusiness gross income ($12,000 minus $10,000)	$2,000	
Deduction for personal exemption	600	
		$ 2,600
Deductions for 1954 adjusted as required by section 172(d)		$587,400
Gross income for 1954		483,000
Net operating loss for 1954		$104,400

T.D. 6192, 7/23/56, amend T.D. 6828, 6/16/65, T.D. 6862, 11/17/65, T.D. 8107, 12/1/86.

§ 1.172-4 Net operating loss carrybacks and net operating loss carryovers.

Caution: The Treasury has not yet amended Reg § 1.172-4 to reflect changes made by P.L. 109-135, P.L. 105-277, P.L. 105-34, P.L. 104-188, P.L. 101-508.

(a) General provisions. *(1) Years to which loss may be carried.* (i) In general. In order to compute the net operating loss deduction the taxpayer must first determine the part of any net operating losses for any preceding or succeeding taxable years which are carrybacks or carryovers to the taxable year in issue.

(ii) General rule for carrybacks and carryovers. Except as provided in section 172 (b)(1)(C), (D), (E), (F), (G), (H), (I), and (J), paragraphs (a)(1)(iii), (iv), (v), and (vi) of this section, and § 1.172-10(a), a net operating loss shall be carried back to the 3 preceding taxable years and carried over to the 15 succeeding taxable years (5 succeeding taxable years for a loss sustained in a taxable year ending before January 1, 1976).

(iii) Loss of a regulated transportation corporation. Except as provided in subdivision (iv) of this subparagraph and § 1.172-10(a), a net operating loss sustained by a taxpayer which is a regulated transportation corporation (as defined in section 172(g)(1)) in a taxable year ending before January 1, 1976, shall, subject to the provisions of section 172(g) and § 1.172-8, be carried back to the taxable years specified in paragraph (a)(1)(ii) of this section and shall be carried over to the 7 succeeding taxable years.

(iv) Loss attributable to foreign expropriation. If the provisions of section 172(b)(3)(A) and § 1.172-9 are satisfied, the portion of a net operating loss attributable to a foreign expropriation loss (as defined in section 172(h)) shall not be a net operating loss carryback to any taxable year preceding the taxable year of such loss and shall be a net operating loss carryover to each of the 10 taxable years following the taxable year of such loss.

(v) Loss of a financial institution. A net operating loss sustained in a taxable year beginning after December 31, 1975, by a taxpayer to which section 585, 586, or 593 applies shall be carried back (except as provided in § 1.172-10(a)) to the 10 preceding taxable years and shall be carried over to the 5 succeeding taxable years.

(vi) Loss of a Bank for Cooperatives. A net operating loss sustained by a taxpayer which is a Bank for Cooperatives (organized and chartered pursuant to section 2 of the Farm Credit Act of 1933 (12 U.S.C. 1134)) shall be carried back (except as provided in § 1.172-10(a)) to the 10 preceding taxable years and shall be carried over to the 5 succeeding taxable years.

(2) Periods of less than 12 months. A fractional part of a year which is a taxable year under sections 441(b) and 7701(a)(23) is a preceding or a succeeding taxable year for the purpose of determining under section 172 the first, second, etc., preceding or succeeding taxable year.

(3) Amount of loss to be carried. The amount which is carried back or carried over to any taxable year is the net operating loss to the extent it was not absorbed in the computation of the taxable (or net) income for other taxable years, preceding such taxable year, to which it may be carried back or carried over. For the purpose of determining the taxable (or net) income for any such preceding taxable year, the various net operating loss carryovers and carrybacks to such taxable year are considered to be applied in reduction of the taxable (or net) income in the order of the taxable years from which such losses are carried over or carried back, beginning with the loss for the earliest taxable year.

(4) Husband and wife. The net operating loss carryovers and carrybacks of a husband and wife shall be determined in accordance with this section, but subject also to the provisions of § 1.172-7.

(5) Corporate acquisitions. For the computation of the net operating loss carryovers in the case of certain acquisitions of the assets of a corporation by another corporation, see section 381 and the regulations thereunder.

(6) Special limitations. For special limitations on the net operating loss carryovers in certain cases of change in both the ownership and the trade or business of a corporation and in certain cases of corporate reorganization lacking specified continuity of ownership, see section 382 and the regulations thereunder.

(7) Electing small business corporations. For special rule applicable to corporations which were electing small business corporations under subchapter S (section 1361 and following), chapter 1 of the Code, during one or more of the taxable years described in section 172(b)(1), see paragraph (f) of § 1.172-1.

(b) Portion of net operating loss which is a carryback or a carryover to the taxable year in issue. *(1)* A net operating loss shall first be carried to the earliest of the several taxable years for which such loss is allowable as a carryback or a carryover, and shall then be carried to the next earliest of such several taxable years, etc. Except as provided in § 1.172-9, the entire net operating loss shall be carried back to such earliest year.

(2) The portion of the loss which shall be carried to any of such several taxable years subsequent to the earliest taxable year is the excess of such net operating loss over the sum of the taxable incomes (computed as provided in § 1.172-5) for all of such several taxable years preceding such subsequent taxable year.

(3) If a portion of the net operating loss for a taxable year is attributable to a foreign expropriation loss (as defined in section 172(h)) and if an election under paragraph (c) of § 1.172-9 is made with respect to such portion of the net operating loss, then see § 1.172-9 for the separate treatment of such portion of the net operating loss.

(c) Illustration. The principles of this section are illustrated in § 1.172-6.

T.D. 6192, 7/23/56, amend T.D. 6486, 8/12/60, T.D. 6862, 11/17/65, T.D. 7444, 12/6/76, T.D. 7767, 2/3/81, T.D. 8096, 8/26/86, T.D. 8107, 12/1/86.

§ 1.172-5 Taxable income which is subtracted from net operating loss to determine carryback or carryover.

Caution: The Treasury has not yet amended Reg § 1.172-5 to reflect changes made by P.L. 105-34.

(a) Taxable year subject to the Internal Revenue Code of 1954. The taxable income for any taxable year subject to the Internal Revenue Code of 1954 which is subtracted from the net operating loss for any other taxable year to determine the portion of such net operating loss which is a carryback or a carryover to a particular taxable year is computed with the modifications prescribed in this paragraph. These modifications shall be made independently of, and without reference to, the modifications required by §§ 1.172-2(a) and 1.172-3(a) for purposes of computing the net operating loss itself.

(1) Modifications applicable to unincorporated taxpayers only. In the case of a taxpayer other than a corporation, in computing taxable income and adjusted gross income—

(i) No deduction shall be allowed under section 151 for the personal exemptions (or under any other section which grants a deduction in lieu of the deductions allowed by section 151) and under section 1202 in respect of the net long-term capital gain.

(ii) The amount deductible on account of losses from sales or exchanges of capital assets shall not exceed the amount includible on account of gains from sales or exchanges of capital assets.

(2) Modifications applicable to all taxpayers. In the case either of a corporation or of a taxpayer other than a corporation—

(i) Net operating loss deduction. The net operating loss deduction for such taxable year shall be computed by taking into account only such net operating losses otherwise allowable as carrybacks or carryovers to such taxable year as were sustained in taxable years preceding the taxable year in which the taxpayer sustained the net operating loss from which the taxable income is to be deducted. Thus, for such purposes, the net operating loss for the loss year or any taxable year thereafter shall not be taken into account.

Example. The taxpayer's income tax returns are made on the basis of the calendar year. In computing the net operating loss deduction for 1954, the taxpayer has a carryover from 1952 of $9,000, a carryover from 1953 of $6,000, a carryback from 1955 of $18,000, and a carryback from 1956 of $10,000, or an aggregate of $43,000 in carryovers and carrybacks. Thus, the net operating loss deduction for 1954, for purposes of determining the tax liability for 1954, is $43,000. However, in computing the taxable income for 1954 which is subtracted from the net operating loss for 1955 for the purpose of determining the portion of such loss which may be carried over to subsequent taxable years, the net operating loss deduction for 1954 is $15,000, that is, the aggregate of the $9,000 carryover from 1952 and the $6,000 carryover from 1953. In computing the net operating loss deduction for such purpose, the $18,000 carryback from 1955 and the $10,000 carryback from 1956 are disregarded. In computing the taxable income for 1954, however, which is subtracted from the net operating loss for 1956 for the purpose of determining the portion of such loss which may be carried over to subsequent taxable years, the net operating loss deduction for 1954 is $33,000, that is, the aggregate of the $9,000 carryover from 1952, the $6,000 carryover from 1953, and the $18,000 carryback from 1955. In computing the net operating loss deduction for such purpose, the $10,000 carryback from 1956 is disregarded.

(ii) Recomputation of percentage limitations. Unless otherwise specifically provided in this subchapter, any deduction which is limited in amount to a percentage of the taxpayer's taxable income or adjusted gross income shall be recomputed upon the basis of the taxable income or adjusted gross income, as the case may be, determined with the modifications prescribed in this paragraph. Thus, in the case of an individual the deduction for medical expenses would be recomputed after making all of the modifications prescribed in this paragraph, whereas the deduction for charitable contributions would be determined without regard to any net operating loss carryback but with regard to any other modifications so prescribed. See, however, the regulations under paragraph (g) of § 1.170-2 (relating to charitable contributions carryover of individuals) and paragraph (c) of § 1.170-3 (relating to charitable contributions carryover of corporations) for special rules regarding charitable contributions in excess of the percentage limitations which may be treated as paid in succeeding taxable years.

Example (1). For the calendar year 1954 the taxpayer, an individual, files a return showing taxable income of $4,800, computed as follows:

Salary		$5,000
Net long-term capital gain		4,000
Total gross income		9,000
Less: Deduction allowed by section 1202 in respect of net long-term capital gain		2,000
Adjusted gross income		7,000
Less:		
Deduction for personal exemption	$600	
Deduction for medical expense ($410 actually paid but allowable only to extent in excess of 3 percent of adjusted gross income)	200	
Deduction for charitable contributions ($2,000 actually paid but allowable only to extent not in excess of 20 percent of adjusted gross income)	1,400	
		$2,200
Taxable income		4,800

In 1955 the taxpayer undertakes the operation of a trade or business and sustains therein a net operating loss of $3,000. Under section 172(b)(2), it is determined that the entire $3,000 is a carryback to 1954. In 1956 he sustains a net operating loss of $10,000 in the operation of the business. In determining the amount of the carryover of the 1956 loss to 1957, the taxable income for 1954 as computed under this paragraph is $3,970, determined as follows:

Salary		$5,000
Net long-term capital gain		4,000
Total gross income		9,000
Less: Deduction for carryback of 1955 net operating loss		3,000
Adjusted gross income		6,000
Less:		
Deduction for medical expense ($410 actually paid but allowable only to extent in excess of 3 percent of adjusted gross income as modified under this paragraph)	$230	
Deduction for charitable contributions ($2,000 actually paid but allowable only to extent not in excess of 20 percent of adjusted gross income determined with all the modifications prescribed in this paragraph other than the net operating loss carryback)	1,800	
		2,030
Taxable income		3,970

Example (2). For the calendar year 1959 the taxpayer, an individual, files a return showing taxable income of $5,700, computed as follows:

Salary		$5,000
Net long-term capital gain		4,000
Total gross income		9,000
Less: Deduction allowed by section 1202 in respect of net long-term capital gain		2,000
Adjusted gross income		7,000
Less:		
Deduction for personal exemption	$600	
Standard deduction allowed by section 141	700	
		1,300
Taxable income		5,700

In 1960 the taxpayer undertakes the operation of a trade or business and sustains therein a net operating loss of $4,700. In 1961 he sustains a net operating loss of $10,000 in the operation of the business. Under section 172(b)(2), it is determined that the entire amount of each loss, $4,700 and $10,000, is a carryback to 1959. In determining the amount of the carryover of the 1961 loss to 1962, the taxable income for 1959 as computed under this paragraph is $3,870, determined as follows:

Salary	$5,000
Net long-term capital gain	4,000
Total gross income	9,000
Less: Deduction for carryback of 1960 net operating loss	4,700
Adjusted gross income	4,300
Less: Standard deduction	430
Taxable income	3,870

(iii) Minimum limitation. The taxable income, as modified under this paragraph, shall in no case be considered less than zero.

(3) Electing small business corporations. For special rule applicable to corporations which were electing small business corporations under subchapter S (section 1361 and following), chapter 1 of the Code, during one or more of the taxable years described in section 172(b)(1), see paragraph (f) of § 1.172-1.

(4) Qualified real estate investment trust. Where a net operating loss is carried over to a qualified taxable year (as defined in § 1.172-10(b)) ending after October 4, 1976, the real estate investment trust taxable income (as defined in section 857(b)(2)) shall be used as the "taxable income" for that taxable year to determine, under section 172(b)(2), the balance of the net operating loss available as a carryover to a subsequent taxable year. The real estate investment trust taxable income, however, is computed by applying the rules applicable to corporations in paragraph (a)(2) of this section. Thus, in computing real estate investment trust taxable income for purposes of section 172(b)(2), the net operating loss deduction for the taxable year shall be computed in accordance with paragraph (a)(2)(i) of this section. The principles of this subparagraph may be illustrated by the following examples:

Example (1). Corporation X, a calendar year taxpayer, is formed on January 1, 1977. X incurs a net operating loss of $100,000 for its taxable year 1977, which under section 172(b)(2), is a carryover to 1978. For 1978 X is a qualified real estate investment trust (as defined in § 1.172-10(b)) and has real estate investment trust taxable income (determined without regard to the deduction for dividends paid or the net operating loss deduction) of $150,000, all of which consists of ordinary income, X pays dividends in 1978 totaling $120,000 that qualify for the deduction for dividends paid under section 857(b)(2)(B). The portion of the 1977 net operating loss available as a carryover to 1979 and subsequent years is $70,000 (i.e., the excess of the amount of the net operating loss ($100,000) over the amount of the real estate investment trust taxable income for 1978 ($30,000), determined by taking into account the deduction for dividends paid allowable under section 857(b)(2)(B) and without taking into account the net operating loss of 1977).

Example (2). (i) Assume the same facts as in example (1), except that the $150,000 of real estate investment trust taxable income (determined without the net operating loss deduction or the dividends paid deduction) consists of $80,000 of ordinary income and $70,000 of net capital gain. The amount of capital gain dividends which may be paid for 1978 is limited to $50,000, that is, the amount of the real estate investment trust taxable income for 1978, determined by taking into account the net operating loss deduction for the taxable year, but not the deduction for dividends paid ($150,000 minus $100,000). See § 1.857-6(e)(1)(ii).

(ii) X designated $50,000 of the $120,000 of dividends paid as capital gains dividends (as defined in section 857(b)(3)(C) and § 1.857-6(e)). Thus, $70,000 is an ordinary dividend. Since both ordinary dividends and capital gains dividends are taken into account in computing the deduction for dividends paid under section 857(b)(2)(B), the result will be the same as in example (1); that is, the portion of the 1977 net operating loss available as a carryover to 1979 and subsequent years is $70,000.

(b) Reserved

T.D. 6192, 7/23/56, amend T.D. 6486, 8/12/60, T.D. 6862, 11/17/65, T.D. 6900, 11/16/66, T.D. 7767, 2/3/81, T.D. 8107, 12/1/86.

§ 1.172-6 Illustration of net operating loss carrybacks and carryovers.

Caution: The Treasury has not yet amended Reg § 1.172-6 to reflect changes made by P.L. 105-34.

The application of § 1.172-4 may be illustrated by the following example:

(a) Facts. The books of the taxpayer, whose return is made on the basis of the calendar year, reveal the following facts:

Taxable year	Taxable income	Net operating loss
1954	$15,000	—
1955	30,000	—
1956	—	($75,000)
1957	20,000	—
1958	—	($150,000)
1959	30,000	—
1960	35,000	—
1961	75,000	—
1962	17,000	—
1963	53,000	—

The taxable income thus shown is computed without any net operating loss deduction. The assumption is also made that none of the other modifications prescribed in § 1.172-5 apply. There are no net operating losses for 1950, 1951, 1952, 1953, 1964, 1965, or 1966.

(b) Loss sustained in 1956. The portions of the $75,000 net operating loss for 1956 which shall be used as carrybacks to 1954 and 1955 and as carryovers to 1957, 1958, 1959, 1960, and 1961 are computed as follows:

(1) Carryback to 1954. The carryback to this year is $75,000, that is, the amount of the net operating loss.

(2) Carryback to 1955. The carryback to this year is $60,000, computed as follows:

Net operating loss		$75,000
Less:		
Taxable income for 1954 (computed without the deduction of the carryback from 1956)		15,000
Carryback		60,000

(3) Carryover to 1957. The carryover to this year is $30,000, computed as follows:

Net operating loss		$75,000
Less:		
Taxable income for 1954 (computed without the deduction of the carryback from 1956)	$15,000	
Taxable income for 1955 (computed without the deduction of the carryback from 1956 or the carryback from 1958)	30,000	
		45,000
Carryover		30,000

(4) Carryover to 1958. The carryover to this year is $10,000, computed as follows:

Net operating loss		$75,000
Less:		
Taxable income for 1954 (computed without the deduction of the carryback from 1956)	$15,000	
Taxable income for 1955 (computed without the deduction of the carryback from 1956 or the carryback from 1958)	30,000	
Taxable income for 1957 (computed without the deduction of the carryover from 1956 or the carryback from 1958)	20,000	
		65,000
Carryover		10,000

(5) Carryover to 1959. The carryover to this year is $10,000, computed as follows:

Net operating loss		$75,000
Less:		
Taxable income for 1954 (computed without the deduction of the carryback from 1956)	$15,000	
Taxable income for 1955 (computed without the deduction of the carryback from 1956 or the carryback from 1958)	30,000	
Taxable income for 1957 (computed without the deduction of the carryover from 1956 or the carryback from 1958)	20,000	
Taxable income for 1958 (a year in which a net operating loss was sustained)	0	
		65,000
Carryover		10,000

(6) Carryover to 1960. The carryover to this year is $0, computed as follows:

Net operating loss		$75,000
Less:		
Taxable income for 1954 (computed without the deduction of the carryback from 1956)	$15,000	
Taxable income for 1955 (computed without the deduction of the carryback from 1956 or the carryback from 1958)	30,000	
Taxable income for 1957 (computed without the deduction of the carryover from 1956 or the carryback from 1958)	20,000	
Taxable income for 1958 (a year in which a net operating loss was sustained)	0	
Taxable income for 1959 (computed without the deduction of the carryover from 1956 or the carryover from 1958)	30,000	
		95,000
Carryover		0

(7) Carryover to 1961. The carryover to this year is $0, computed as follows:

Net operating loss		$ 75,000
Less:		
Taxable income for 1954 (computed without the deduction of the carryback from 1956)	$15,000	
Taxable income for 1955 (computed without the deduction of the carryback from 1956 or the carryback from 1958)	$30,000	
Taxable income for 1957 (computed without the deduction of the carryover from 1956 or the carryback from 1958)	20,000	
Taxable income for 1958 (a year in which a net operating loss was sustained)	0	
Taxable income for 1959 (computed without the deduction of the carryover from 1956 or the carryover from 1958)	30,000	
Taxable income for 1960 (computed without the deduction of the carryover from 1956 or the carryover from 1958)	35,000	
		$130,000
Carryover		0

(c) Loss sustained in 1958. The portions of the $150,000 net operating loss for 1958 which shall be used as carrybacks to 1955, 1956, and 1957 and as carryovers to 1959, 1960, 1961, 1962, and 1963 are computed as follows:

(1) Carryback to 1955. The carryback to this year is $150,000, that is, the amount of the net operating loss.

(2) Carryback to 1956. The carryback to this year is $150,000, computed as follows:

Net operating loss		$150,000
Less:		
Taxable income for 1955 (the $30,000 taxable income for such year reduced by the carryback to such year of $60,000 from 1956, the carryback from 1958 to 1955 not being taken into account)		0
Carryback		150,000

(3) Carryback to 1957. The carryback to this year is $150,000, computed as follows:

Net operating loss		$150,000
Less:		
Taxable income for 1955 (the $30,000 taxable income for such year reduced by the carryback to such year of $60,000 from 1956, the carryback from 1958 to 1955 not being taken into account)	$0	
Taxable income for 1956 (a year in which a net operating loss was sustained)	0	
		0
Carryback		150,000

(4) Carryover to 1959. The carryover to this year is $150,000, computed as follows:

Net operating loss		$150,000
Less:		
Taxable income for 1955 (the $30,000 taxable income for such year reduced by the carryback to such year of $60,000 from 1956, the carryback from 1958 to 1955 not being taken into account)	$0	
Taxable income for 1956 (a year in which a net operating loss was sustained)	0	
Taxable income for 1957 (the $20,000 taxable income for such year reduced by the carryover to such year of $30,000 from 1956, the carryback from 1958 to 1957 not being taken into account)	0	
		0
Carryover		150,000

(5) Carryover to 1960. The carryover to this year is $130,000, computed as follows:

Net operating loss		$150,000
Less:		
Taxable income for 1955 (the $30,000 taxable income for such year reduced by the carryback to such year of $60,000 from 1956, the carryback from 1958 to 1955 not being taken into account)	$ 0	
Taxable income for 1956 (a year in which a net operating loss was sustained)	0	
Taxable income for 1957 (the $20,000 taxable income for such year reduced by the carryover to such year of $30,000 from 1956, the carryback from 1958 to 1957 not being taken into account)	0	
Taxable income for 1959 (the $30,000 taxable income for such year reduced by the carryover to such year of $10,000 from 1956, the carryover from 1958 to 1959 not being taken into account)	$20,000	
		20,000
Carryover		130,000

(6) Carryover to 1961. The carryover to this year is $95,000, computed as follows:

Net operating loss		$150,000
Less:		
Taxable income for 1955 (the $30,000 taxable income for such year reduced by the carryback to such year of $60,000 from 1956, the carryback from 1958 to 1955 not being taken into account)	$0	
Taxable income for 1956 (a year in which a net operating loss was sustained)	0	
Taxable income for 1957 (the $20,000 taxable income for such year reduced by the carryover to such year of $30,000 from 1956, the carryback from 1958 to 1957 not being taken into account)	0	

Taxable income for 1959 (the $30,000 taxable income for such year reduced by the carryover to such year of $10,000 from 1956, the carryover from 1958 to 1959 not being taken into account) 20,000

Taxable income for 1960 (the $35,000 taxable income for such year reduced by the carryover to such year of $0 from 1956, the carryover from 1958 to 1960 not being taken into account) 35,000

55,000

Carryover 95,000

(7) Carryover to 1962. The carryover to this year is $20,000, computed as follows:

Net operating loss $150,000

Less:

Taxable income for 1955 (the $30,000 taxable income for such year reduced by the carryback to such year of $60,000 from 1956, the carryback from 1958 to 1955 not being taken into account ..... $ 0

Taxable income for 1956 (a year in which a net operating loss was sustained) 0

Taxable income for 1957 (the $20,000 taxable income for such year reduced by the carryover to such year of $30,000 from 1956, the carryback from 1958 to 1957 not being taken into account) 0

Taxable income for 1959 (the $30,000 taxable income for such year reduced by the carryover to such year of $10,000 from 1956, the carryover from 1958 to 1959 not being taken into account) 20,000

Taxable income for 1960 (the $35,000 taxable income for such year reduced by the carryover to such year of $0 from 1956, the carryover from 1958 to 1960 not being taken into account) 35,000

Taxable income for 1961 (the $75,000 taxable income for such year reduced by the carryover to such year of $0 from 1956, the carryover from 1958 to 1961 not being taken into account) 75,000

$130,000

Carryover 20,000

(8) Carryover to 1963. The carryover to this year is $3,000, computed as follows:

Net operating loss $150,000

Less:

Taxable income for 1955 (the $30,000 taxable income for such year reduced by the carryback to such year of $60,000 from 1956, the carryback from 1958 to 1955 not being taken into account) $0

Taxable income for 1956 (a year in which a net operating loss was sustained) 0

Taxable income for 1957 (the $20,000 taxable income for such year reduced by the carryover to such year of $30,000 from 1956, the carryback from 1958 to 1957 not being taken into account) 0

Taxable income for 1959 (the $30,000 taxable income for such year reduced by the carryover to such year of $10,000 from 1956, the carryover from 1958 to 1959 not being taken into account) 20,000

Taxable income for 1960 (the $35,000 taxable income for such year reduced by the carryover to such year of $0 from 1956, the carryover from 1958 to 1960 not being taken into account) 35,000

Taxable income for 1961 (the $75,000 taxable income for such year reduced by the carryover to such year of $0 from 1956, the carryover from 1958 to 1961 not being taken into account) 75,000

Taxable income for 1962 (computed without the deduction of the carryover from 1958) 17,000

147,000

Carryover 3,000

(d) Determination of net operating loss deduction for each year. The carryovers and carrybacks computed under paragraphs (b) and (c) of this section are used as a basis for the computation of the net operating loss deduction in the following manner:

Taxable year	Carryover From 1956	Carryover From 1958	Carryback From 1956	Carryback From 1958	Net operating loss deduction
1954	—	—	$75,000	—	$ 75,000
1955	—	—	60,000	$150,000	210,000
1957	$30,000	—	—	150,000	180,000
1959	10,000	$150,000	—	—	160,000
1960	—	130,000	—	—	130,000
1961	—	95,000	—	—	95,000
1962	—	20,000	—	—	20,000
1963	—	3,000	—	—	3,000

T.D. 6192, 7/23/56, amend T.D. 6486, 8/12/60.

§ 1.172-7 Joint return by husband and wife.

Caution: The Treasury has not yet amended Reg § 1.172-7 to reflect changes made by P.L. 105-34.

(a) In general. This section prescribes additional rules for computing the net operating loss carrybacks and carryovers of a husband and wife making a joint return for one or more of the taxable years involved in the computation of the net operating loss deduction.

(b) From separate to joint return. If a husband and wife, making a joint return for any taxable year, did not make a joint return for any of the taxable years involved in the computation of a net operating loss carryover or a net operating loss carryback to the taxable year for which the joint return is made, such separate net operating loss carryover or separate net operating loss carryback is a joint net operating loss carryover or joint net operating loss carryback to such taxable year.

(c) **Continuous use of joint return.** If a husband and wife making a joint return for a taxable year made a joint return for each of the taxable years involved in the computation of a net operating loss carryover or net operating loss carryback to such taxable year, the joint net operating loss carryover or joint net operating loss carryback to such taxable year is computed in the same manner as the net operating loss carryover or net operating loss carryback of an individual under § 1.172-4 but upon the basis of the joint net operating losses and the combined taxable income of both spouses.

(d) **From joint to separate return.** If a husband and wife making separate returns for a taxable year made a joint return for any, or all, of the taxable years involved in the computation of a net operating loss carryover or net operating loss carryback to such taxable year, the separate net operating loss carryover or separate net operating loss carryback of each spouse to the taxable year is computed in the manner set forth in § 1.172-4 but with the following modifications:

(1) Net operating loss. The net operating loss of each spouse for a taxable year for which a joint return was made shall be deemed to be that portion of the joint net operating loss (computed in accordance with paragraph (d) of § 1.172-3) which is attributable to the gross income and deductions of such spouse, gross income and deductions being taken into account to the same extent that they are taken into account in computing the joint net operating loss.

(2) Taxable income to be subtracted. (i) Net operating loss of other spouse. The taxable income of a particular spouse for any taxable year which is subtracted from the net operating loss of such spouse for another taxable year in order to determine the amount of such loss which may be carried back or carried over to still another taxable year is deemed to be, in a case in which such taxable income was reported in a joint return, the sum of the following:

(a) That portion of the combined taxable income of both spouses for such year for which the joint return was made which is attributable to the gross income and deductions of the particular spouse, gross income and deductions being taken into account to the same extent that they are taken into account in computing such combined taxable income, and

(b) That portion of such combined taxable income which is attributable to the other spouse; but, if such other spouse sustained a net operating loss in a taxable year beginning on the same date as the taxable year in which the particular spouse sustained the net operating loss from which the taxable income is subtracted, then such portion shall first be reduced by such net operating loss of such other spouse.

(ii) Modifications. For purposes of this subparagraph, the combined taxable income shall be computed as though the combined income and deductions of both spouses were those of one individual. The provisions of § 1.172-5 shall apply in computing the combined taxable income for such purposes except that the net operating loss deduction shall be determined without taking into account any separate net operating loss of either spouse, or any joint net operating loss of both spouses, which was sustained in a taxable year beginning on or after the date of the beginning of the taxable year in which the particular spouse sustained the net operating loss from which the taxable income is subtracted.

(e) **Recurrent use of joint return.** If a husband and wife making a joint return for any taxable year made a joint return for one or more, but not all, of the taxable years involved in the computation of a net operating loss carryover or net operating loss carryback to such taxable year, such net operating loss carryover or net operating loss carryback to the taxable year is computed in the manner set forth in paragraph (d) of this section. Such net operating loss carryover or net operating loss carryback is considered a joint net operating loss carryover or joint net operating loss carryback to such taxable year.

(f) **Joint carryovers and carrybacks.** The joint net operating loss carryovers and the joint net operating loss carrybacks to any taxable year for which a joint return is made are all the net operating loss carryovers and net operating loss carrybacks of both spouses to such taxable year. For example, a husband and wife file a joint return for the calendar year 1956, having a joint taxable income for such year. The wife filed a separate return for the calendar years 1954 and 1955, in which years she sustained net operating losses. The husband filed separate returns for his fiscal year ending June 30, 1955, and, having received permission to change his accounting period to a calendar year basis, for the 6-month period ending December 31, 1955. The husband sustained net operating losses in both such taxable years. Since the husband and wife did not file a joint return for any taxable year involved in the computation of the net operating loss carryovers to 1956 from 1954 and 1955, the joint net operating loss carryovers to 1956 are the separate net operating loss carryovers of the wife from the calendar years 1954 and 1955 and the separate net operating loss carryovers of the husband from the fiscal year ending June 30, 1955, and from the short taxable year ending December 31, 1955. If the husband and wife also file joint returns for the calendar years 1957, 1958, and 1959, having joint taxable income in 1957 and 1958 and a joint net operating loss in 1959, the joint net operating loss carrybacks to 1956, 1957, and 1958 from 1959 are computed on the basis of the joint net operating loss for 1959, since separate returns were not made for any taxable year involved in the computation of such carrybacks.

(g) **Illustration of principles.** In the following examples, which illustrate the application of this section, it is assumed that there are no items of adjustment under section 172(b)(2)(A) and that the taxable income or loss in each case is the taxable income or loss determined without any net operating loss deduction. The taxpayers in each example, H, a husband, and W, his wife, report their income on the calendar-year basis.

Example (1). H and W filed joint returns for 1954 and 1955. They sustained a joint net operating loss of $1,000 for 1954 and a joint net operating loss of $2,000 for 1955. For 1954 the deductions of H exceeded his gross income by $700, and the deductions of W exceeded her gross income by $300, the total of such amounts being $1,000. Therefore, $700 of the $1,000 joint net operating loss for 1954 is considered the net operating loss of H for 1954, and $300 of such joint net operating loss is considered the net operating loss of W for 1954. For 1955 the gross income of H exceeded his deductions, so that his separate taxable income would be $1,500, and the deductions of W exceeded her gross income by $3,500. Therefore, all of the $2,000 joint net operating loss for 1955 is considered the separate net operating loss of W for 1955.

Example (2). (i) H and W filed joint returns for 1954 and 1956, and separate returns for 1955 and 1957. For the years 1954, 1955, 1956, and 1957 they had taxable incomes and net operating losses as follows, losses being indicated in parentheses:

	1954	1955	1956	1957
H	($5,000)	($2,500)	$6,500	($4,000)
W	(3,000)	2,000	3,000	(1,500)
Total	($8,000)	—	9,500	—

(ii) The net operating loss carryover of H from 1957 to 1958 is $4,000, that is, his $4,000 net operating loss for 1957 which is not reduced by any part of the taxable income for 1956, since none of such taxable income is attributable to H and the portion attributable to W is entirely offset by her separate net operating loss for her taxable year 1957, which taxable year begins on the same date as H's taxable year 1957. H's $4,000 net operating loss for 1957 likewise is not reduced by reference to 1955 since H sustained a loss in 1955. The $0 taxable income for 1956 which reduces H's net operating loss for 1957 is computed as follows:

(iii) The combined taxable income of $9,500 for 1956 is reduced to $1,000 by the net operating loss deduction for such year of $8,500. This net operating loss deduction is computed without taking into account any net operating loss of either H or W sustained in a taxable year beginning on or after January 1, 1957, the date of the beginning of the taxable year in which H sustained the net operating loss from which the taxable income is subtracted. This $8,500 is composed of H's carryovers of $5,000 from 1954 and $2,500 from 1955, and of W's carryover of $1,000 from 1954 (the excess of W's $3,000 loss for 1954 over her $2,000 income for 1955). None of the $1,000 combined taxable income for 1956 (computed with the net operating loss deduction described above) is attributable to H since it is caused by W's income (computed after deducting her separate carryover) offsetting H's loss (computed by deducting from his income his separate carryovers). No part of the $1,000 combined taxable income for 1956 which is attributable to W is used to reduce H's net operating loss for 1957 since such taxable income attributable to W must first be reduced by W's $1,500 net operating loss for 1957, her taxable year beginning on the same date as the taxable year of H in which he sustained the net operating loss from which the taxable income is subtracted.

(iv) The net operating loss carryover of W from 1957 to 1958 is $500, her $1,500 loss reduced by the sum of her $0 taxable income for 1955 (computed by taking into account her $3,000 carryover from 1954) and her $1,000 taxable income for 1956, that is, the portion of the combined taxable income for 1956 which is attributable to her.

Example (3). (i) Assume the same facts as in example (2) except that for 1957 the net operating loss of W is $200 instead of $1,500.

(ii) The net operating loss carryover of H from 1957 to 1958 is $3,200, that is, his $4,000 net operating loss for 1957 reduced by the sum of his $0 taxable income for 1955 (a year in which he sustained a loss) and his $800 taxable income for 1956. Such $800 is computed as follows:

(iii) The combined taxable income for 1956, computed with the net operating loss deduction in the manner described in example (2), remains $1,000, no part of which is attributable to H. To the $0 taxable income attributable to H for 1956 there is added $800, the excess of the $1,000 taxable income for such year attributable to W over her $200 net operating loss sustained in 1957, a taxable year beginning on the same date as the taxable year of H in which he sustained the $4,000 net operating loss from which the taxable income is subtracted.

(iv) W has no net operating loss carryover from 1957 to 1958 since her net operating loss of $200 for 1957 does not exceed the $1,000 taxable income for 1956 attributable to her.

Example (4). (i) Assume the same facts as in example (2), except that W changes her accounting period in 1957 to a fiscal year ending on January 31, and has neither income nor losses for the taxable year January 1, 1957, to January 31, 1957, or for the fiscal year February 1, 1957, to January 31, 1958, but has a net operating loss of $200 for the fiscal year February 1, 1958, to January 31, 1959.

(ii) The net operating loss carryover of H from 1957 to 1958 is $3,000, that is, his net operating loss of $4,000 for 1957 reduced by the sum of his $0 taxable income for 1955 (a year in which he sustained a loss) and his $1,000 taxable income for 1956. Such $1,000 is computed as follows:

(iii) The combined taxable income for 1956, computed with the net operating loss deduction in the manner described in example (2), remains $1,000, no part of which is attributable to H. To the $0 taxable income attributable to H for 1956 there is added the $1,000 taxable income attributable to W for such year. The taxable income attributable to W is not reduced by any amount since she does not have a net operating loss for her taxable year beginning on January 1, 1957, the date of the beginning of the taxable year of H in which he sustained the $4,000 net operating loss from which his taxable income is subtracted.

(iv) The net operating loss carryover of W from the fiscal year beginning February 1, 1958, to her next fiscal year is $200, that is, her net operating loss of $200 for the fiscal year beginning February 1, 1958, reduced by the sum of her $0 taxable income for 1956, her $0 taxable income for the taxable year January 1, 1957, to January 31, 1957 (a year in which she had neither income nor loss), and her $0 taxable income for the fiscal year February 1, 1957, to January 31, 1958 (also a year in which she had neither income nor loss). The $0 taxable income for 1956 is computed as follows:

(v) The combined taxable income of $9,500 for 1956 is reduced to $0 amount by the net operating loss deduction for such year of $12,500. This net operating loss deduction is computed by taking into account the net operating loss of H for 1957 since it was sustained in a taxable year beginning before February 1, 1958, the date of the beginning of the taxable year of W in which she sustained the $200 net operating loss from which her taxable income is subtracted. This $12,500 is composed of H's carryovers of $5,000 from 1954 and $2,500 from 1955 and of his carryback of $4,000 from 1957, plus W's carryover of $1,000 from 1954 (the excess of W's $3,000 loss for 1954 over her $2,000 income for 1955). Since there is no combined taxable income for 1956, there is no taxable income attributable to W for such year.

T.D. 6192, 7/23/56, amend T.D. 6486, 8/12/60, T.D. 8107, 12/1/86.

§ 1.172-8 Net operating loss carryovers for regulated transportation corporations.

Caution: The Treasury has not yet amended Reg § 1.172-8 to reflect changes made by P.L. 101-508.

(a) In general. A net operating loss sustained in a taxable year ending before January 1, 1976, shall be a carryover to the 7 succeeding taxable years if the taxpayer is a regulated transportation corporation (as defined in paragraph (b) of this section) for the loss year and for the 6th and 7th succeeding taxable years. If, however, the taxpayer is a regulated transportation corporation for the loss year and for the 6th succeeding taxable year, but not for the 7th succeeding taxable year, then the loss shall be a carryover to the 6 succeeding taxable years. If the taxpayer is not a regulated transportation corporation for the 6th succeeding taxable year then this section shall not apply. A net operating loss sustained in a taxable year ending after December 31, 1975, shall be a carryover to the 15 succeeding taxable years.

(b) Regulated transportation corporations. A corporation is a "regulated transportation corporation" for a taxable year if it is included within one or more of the following categories:

(1) Eighty percent or more of the corporation's gross income (computed without regard to dividends and capital gains and losses) for such taxable year is income from transportation sources described in paragraph (c) of this section.

(2) The corporation is a railroad corporation, subject to Part I of the Interstate Commerce Act, which is either a lessor railroad corporation described in section 7701(a)(33)(G) or a common parent railroad corporation described in section 7701(a)(33)(H).

(3) The corporation is a member of a regulated transportation system for the taxable year. For purposes of this section, a member of a regulated transportation system for a taxable year means a member of an affiliated group of corporations making a consolidated return for such year, if 80 percent or more of the sum of the gross incomes of the members of the affiliated group for such year (computed without regard to dividends, capital gains and losses, or eliminations for intercompany transactions) is derived from transportation sources described in paragraph (c) of this section. For purposes of this subparagraph, income derived by a corporation described in subparagraph (2) of this paragraph from leases described in section 7701(a)(33)(G) shall be considered as income from transportation sources described in paragraph (c) of this section.

(c) Transportation sources. For purposes of this section, income from "transportation sources" means income received directly in consideration for transportation services, and income from the furnishing or sale of essential facilities, products, and other services which are directly necessary and incidental to the furnishing of transportation services. For purposes of the preceding sentence, the term "transportation services" means—

(1) Transportation by railroad as a common carrier subject to the jurisdiction of the Interstate Commerce Commission;

(2) (i) Transportation, which is not included in subparagraph (1) of this paragraph—

(a) On an intrastate, suburban, municipal, or interurban electric railroad,

(b) On an intrastate, municipal, or suburban trackless trolley system,

(c) On a municipal or suburban bus system, or

(d) By motor vehicle not otherwise included in this subparagraph,

if the rates for the furnishing or sale of such transportation are established or approved by a regulatory body described in section 7701(a)(33)(A);

(ii) In the case of a corporation which establishes to the satisfaction of the district director that—

(a) Its revenue from regulated rates from transportation services described in subdivision (i) of this subparagraph and its revenue derived from unregulated rates are derived from its operation of a single interconnected and coordinated system or from the operation of more than one such system, and

(b) The unregulated rates have been and are substantially as favorable to users and consumers as are the regulated rates, transportation, which is not included in subparagraph (1) of this paragraph, from which such revenue from unregulated rates is derived.

(3) Transportation by air as a common carrier subject to the jurisdiction of the Civil Aeronautics Board; and

(4) Transportation by water by common carrier subject to the jurisdiction of either the Interstate Commerce Commission under Part III of the Interstate Commerce Act (54 Stat. 929), or the Federal Maritime Board under the Intercoastal Shipping Act, 1933 (52 Stat. 965).

(d) Corporate acquisitions. This section shall apply to a carryover of a net operating loss sustained by a regulated transportation corporation (as defined in paragraph (b) of this section) to which an acquiring corporation succeeds under section 381(a) only if the acquiring corporation is a regulated transportation corporation (as defined in paragraph (b) of this section)—

(1) For the sixth succeeding taxable year in the case of a carryover to the sixth succeeding taxable year, and

(2) For the sixth and seventh succeeding taxable years in the case of a carryover to the seventh succeeding taxable year.

T.D. 6862, 11/17/65, amend T.D. 8107, 12/1/86.

§ 1.172-9 Election with respect to portion of net operating loss attributable to foreign expropriation loss.

Caution: The Treasury has not yet amended Reg § 1.172-9 to reflect changes made by P.L. 101-508.

(a) In general. If a taxpayer has a net operating loss for a taxable year ending after December 31, 1958, and if the foreign expropriation loss for such year (as defined in paragraph (b)(1) of this section) equals or exceeds 50 percent of the net operating loss for such year, then the taxpayer may elect (at the time and in the manner provided in paragraph (c)(1) or (2) of this section, whichever is applicable) to have the provisions of this section apply. If the taxpayer so elects, the portion of the net operating loss for such taxable year attributable (under paragraph (b)(2) of this section) to such foreign expropriation loss shall not be a net operating loss carryback to any taxable year preceding the taxable year of such loss and shall be a net operating loss carryover to each of the ten taxable years following the taxable year of such loss. In such case, the portion, if any, of the net operating loss not attributable to a foreign expropriation loss shall be carried back or carried over as provided in paragraph (a)(1)(ii) of § 1.172-4.

(b) Determination of "foreign expropriation loss". *(1) Definition of "foreign expropriation loss".* The term "foreign expropriation loss" means, for any taxable year, the sum of the losses allowable as deductions under section 165 (other than losses from, or which under section 165(g) or 1231(a) are treated or considered as losses from, sales or exchanges of capital assets and other than losses described in section 165(i)(1)) sustained by reason of the expropriation, intervention, seizure, or similar taking of property by the government of any foreign country, any political subdivision thereof, or any agency or instrumentality of the foregoing. For purposes of the preceding sentence, a debt which becomes worthless in whole or in part, shall, to the extent of any deduction allowed under section 166(a), be treated as a loss allowable as a deduction under section 165.

(2) Portion of the net operating loss attributable to a foreign expropriation loss. (i) Except as provided in subdivision (ii) of this subparagraph, the portion of the net operating loss for any taxable year attributable to a foreign expropriation loss is the amount of the foreign expropriation loss for such taxable year (determined under subparagraph (1) of this paragraph).

(ii) The portion of the net operating loss for a taxable year attributable to a foreign expropriation loss shall not exceed the amount of the net operating loss, computed under section 172(c), for such year.

(3) Examples. The application of this paragraph may be illustrated by the following examples:

Example (1). M Corporation, a domestic calendar year corporation manufacturing cigars in the United States, owns, in country X, a tobacco plantation having an adjusted basis of $400,000 and farm equipment having an adjusted basis of $300,000. On January 15, 1961, country X expropriates the plantation and equipment without any allowance for compensation. For the taxable year 1961, M Corporation sustains a loss from the operation of its business (not including losses from the seizure of its plantation and equipment in country X) of $200,000, which loss would not have been sustained in the absence of the seizure. Accordingly, M has a net operating loss of $900,000 (the sum of $400,000, $300,000, and $200,000). For purposes of section 172(k)(1), M Corporation has a foreign expropriation loss for 1961 of $700,000 (the sum of $400,000 and $300,000, the losses directly sustained by reason of the seizure of its property by country X). Since the foreign expropriation loss for 1961, $700,000, equals or exceeds 50 percent of the net operating loss for such year, or $450,000 (i.e., 50 percent of $900,000), M Corporation may make the election under paragraph (c)(2) of this section with respect to $700,000, the portion of the net operating loss attributable to the foreign expropriation loss.

Example (2). Assume the same facts as in example (1) except that for 1961, M Corporation has operating profits of $300,000 (not including losses from the seizure of its plantation and equipment in country X) so that its net operating loss (as defined in section 172(c)) is only $400,000. Under the provisions of section 172(k)(2) and paragraph (b)(2) of this section, the portion of the net operating loss for 1961 attributable to a foreign expropriation loss is limited to $400,000, the amount of the net operating loss.

(c) Time and manner of making election. *(1) Taxable years ending after December 31, 1963.* In the case of a taxpayer who has a foreign expropriation loss for a taxable year ending after December 31, 1963, the election referred to in paragraph (a) of this section shall be made by attaching to the taxpayer's income tax return (filed within the time prescribed by law, including extensions of time) for the taxable year of such foreign expropriation loss a statement containing the information required by subparagraph (3) of this paragraph. Such election shall be irrevocable after the due date (including extensions of time) of such return.

(2) Information required. The statement referred to in subparagraph (1) of this paragraph shall contain the following information:

(i) The name, address, and taxpayer account number of the taxpayer;

(ii) A statement that the taxpayer elects under section 172(b)(3)(A)(ii) or (iii), whichever is applicable, to have section 172(b)(1)(D) of the Code apply;

(iii) The amount of the net operating loss for the taxable year; and

(iv) The amount of the foreign expropriation loss for the taxable year, including a schedule showing the computation of such foreign expropriation loss.

(d) Amount of foreign expropriation loss which is a carryover to the taxable year in issue. *(1) General.* If a portion of a net operating loss for the taxable year is attributable to a foreign expropriation loss and if an election under paragraph (a) of this section has been made with respect to such portion of the net operating loss, then such portion shall be considered to be a separate net operating loss for such year, and, for the purpose of determining the amount of such separate loss which may be carried over to other taxable years, such portion shall be applied after the other portion (if any) of such net operating loss. Such separate loss shall be carried to the earliest of the several taxable years to which such separate loss is allowable as a carryover under the provisions of paragraph (a)(1)(iv) of § 1.172-4, and the amount of such separate loss which shall be carried over to any taxable year subsequent to such earliest year is an amount (not exceeding such separate loss) equal to the excess of—

(i) The sum of (a) such separate loss and (b) the other portion (if any) of the net operating loss (i.e., that portion not attributable to a foreign expropriation loss) to the extent such other portion is a carryover to such earliest taxable year, over

(ii) The sum of the aggregate of the taxable incomes (computed as provided in § 1.172-5) for all of such several taxable years preceding such subsequent taxable year.

(2) Cross reference. The portion of a net operating loss which is not attributable to a foreign expropriation loss shall be carried back or carried over, in accordance with the rules provided in paragraph (b)(1) of § 1.172-4, as if such portion were the only net operating loss for such year.

(3) Examples. The application of this paragraph may be illustrated by the following examples:

Example (1). Corporation A, organized in 1960 and whose return is made on the basis of the calendar year, incurs for 1960 a net operating loss of $10,000, of which $7,500 is attributable to a foreign expropriation loss. With respect to such $7,500, A makes the election described in paragraph (a) of this section. In each of the years 1961, 1962, 1963, 1964, and 1965, A has taxable income in the amount of $600 (computed without any net operating loss deduction). The assumption is made that none of the other modifications prescribed in § 1.172-5 apply. The portion of the net operating loss attributable to the foreign expropriation loss which is a carryover to the year 1966 is $7,000, which is the sum of $7,500 (the portion of the net operating loss attributable to the foreign expropriation loss) and $2,500 (the other portion of the net operating loss available as a carryover to 1961), minus $3,000 (the aggregate of the taxable incomes for taxable years 1961 through 1965).

Example (2). Assume the same facts as in example (1) except that taxable income for each of the years 1961 through 1965 is $400 (computed without any net operating loss deduction). The carryover to the year 1966 is $7,500, that is, the sum of $7,500 (the portion of the net operating loss attributable to the foreign expropriation loss) and $2,500 (the other portion of the net operating loss available as a carryover to 1961), minus $2,000 (the aggregate of the taxable incomes for taxable years 1961 through 1965), but limited to $7,500 (the portion of the net operating loss attributable to the foreign expropriation loss).

(e) Taxable income which is subtracted from net operating loss to determine carryback or carryover. In computing taxable income for a taxable year (hereinafter called a "prior taxable year") for the purpose of determining the portion of a net operating loss for another taxable year which shall be carried to each of the several taxable years subsequent to the earliest taxable year to which such loss may be carried, the net operating loss deduction for any such prior taxable year shall be determined without regard to that portion, if any, of a net operating loss for a taxable year attributable to a foreign expropriation loss, if such portion may not, under the provisions of section 172(b)(1)(D) and paragraph (a)(1)(iv) of § 1.172-4, be carried back to such prior taxable year. Thus, if the taxpayer has a foreign expropriation loss for 1962 and elects the 10-year carryover with respect to the portion of his net operating loss for 1962 attributable to the foreign expropriation loss, then in computing taxable income for the year 1960 for the purpose of determining the portion of a net operating loss for 1963 which is carried to years subsequent to 1960, the net operating loss deduction for 1960 is determined without regard to the portion of the net operating loss for 1962 attributable to the foreign expropriation loss, since under the provisions of section 172(b)(1)(D) and paragraph (a)(1)(iv) of § 1.172-4 such portion of the net operating loss for 1962 may not be carried back to 1960.

T.D. 6862, 11/17/65, amend T.D. 8107, 12/1/86.

§ 1.172-10 Net operating losses of real estate investment trusts.

(a) Taxable years to which a loss may be carried. *(1)* A net operating loss sustained by a qualified real estate investment trust (as defined in paragraph (b)(1) of this section) in a qualified taxable year (as defined in paragraph (b)(2) of this section) ending after October 4, 1976, shall not be carried back to a preceding taxable year.

(2) A net operating loss sustained by a qualified real estate investment trust in a qualified taxable year ending before October 5, 1976, shall be carried back to the 3 preceding taxable years. However, see § 1.857-2(a)(5), which does not allow the net operating loss deduction in computing real estate investment trust taxable income for taxable years ending before October 5, 1976.

(3) A net operating loss sustained by a qualified real estate investment trust in a qualified taxable year ending after December 31, 1972, shall be carried over to the 15 succeeding taxable years. However, see § 1.857-2(a)(5).

(4) A net operating loss sustained by a qualified real estate investment trust in a qualified taxable year ending before January 1, 1973, shall be carried over to 8 succeeding taxable years. However, see § 1.857-2(a)(5).

(5) A net operating loss sustained in a taxable year for which the taxpayer is not a qualified real estate investment trust generally may be carried back to the 3 preceding taxable years; however, a net operating loss sustained in a taxable year ending after December 31, 1975, shall not be carried back to any qualified taxable year. However, see § 1.857-2(a)(5), with respect to a net operating loss sustained in a taxable year ending before January 1, 1976.

(6) A net operating loss sustained in a taxable year ending after December 31, 1975, for which the taxpayer is not a qualified real estate investment trust generally may be carried over to the 15 succeeding taxable years.

(7) (i) A net operating loss sustained in a taxable year ending before January 1, 1986, for which the taxpayer is not a qualified real estate investment trust generally may be a net operating loss carryover to each of the 5 succeeding taxable years. However, where the loss was a net operating loss carryback to one or more qualified taxable years, the net operating loss, in accordance with paragraph (a)(7)(ii) of this section shall be—

(A) Carried over to the 15 succeeding taxable years if the loss could be a net operating loss carryover to a taxable year ending in 1981, or

(B) Carried over to the 5, 6, 7, or 8 succeeding taxable years if paragraph (a)(7)(i)(A) of this section does not apply.

(ii) For purposes of determining whether a net operating loss could be a carryover to a taxable year ending in 1981 under paragraph (a)(7)(i)(A) of this section or, where paragraph (a)(7)(i)(A) of this section does not apply, to determine the actual carryover period under paragraph (a)(7)(i)(B) of this section, the net operating loss shall have a carryover period of 5 years, and such period shall be increased (to a number not greater than 8) by the number of qualified taxable years to which such loss was a net operating loss carryback; however, where the taxpayer acted so as to cause itself to cease to be a qualified real estate investment trust and the principal purpose for such action was to secure the benefit of the allowance of a net operating loss carryover under section 172(b)(1)(B), the net operating loss carryover period shall be limited to 5 years. However, see § 1.857-2(a)(5).

(8) A qualified taxable year is a taxable year preceding or following the taxable year of the net operating loss, for purposes of section 172(b)(1), even though the loss may not be carried to, or allowed as a reduction in, such qualified taxable year. Thus, a qualified taxable year ending before October 5, 1976 (for which no net operating loss deduction is allowable) is nevertheless a preceding or following taxable year for purposes of section 172(b)(1). Moreover, a qualified taxable year ending after October 4, 1976 (to which a net operating loss cannot be carried back because of section 172(b)(1)(E)) is nevertheless a preceding taxable year for purposes of section 172(b)(1). For purposes of determining, under section 172(b)(2), the balance of the loss available as a carryback or carryover to other taxable years, however, the net operating loss is not reduced on account of such qualified taxable year being a preceding or following taxable year.

(b) Definitions. For purposes of this section §§ 1.172-2 and 1.172-5—

(1) The terms "qualified real estate investment trust" means, with respect to any taxable year, a real estate investment trust within the meaning of part II of subchapter M which is taxable for such year under that part as a real estate investment trust, and

(2) The term "qualified taxable year" means a taxable year for which the taxpayer is a qualified real estate investment trust.

(c) Examples. The provisions of this section may be illustrated by the following examples:

Example (1). (i) Facts. X was a qualified real estate investment trust for the taxable years ending on December 31, 1972, and December 31, 1973. X was not a qualified real estate investment trust for the taxable years ending on December 31, 1971, and December 31, 1974. X sustained a net operating loss for the taxable year ending on December 31, 1974.

(ii) Applicable carryback and carryover periods. The net operating loss must be carried back to the 3 preceding taxable years. Under § 1.857-2(a)(5) the net operating loss deduction shall not be allowed in computing real estate investment trust taxable income for the years ending December 31, 1972, and December 31, 1973. Where a net operating loss is sustained in a taxable year ending before January 1, 1976, for which the taxpayer is not a qualified real estate investment trust and the loss is a net operating loss carryback to one or more qualified taxable years, the carryover period is determined under § 1.172-10(a)(7); the carryover period is determined by first applying the rule provided in paragraph (a)(7)(ii) of this section to obtain the carryover period for purposes of determining whether the net operating loss could have been a net operating loss carryover to a taxable year ending in 1981. Under these facts, paragraph (a)(7)(ii) of this section provides for a 7-year carryover period (5 years increased by the 2 qualified taxable years to which the loss was a net operating loss carryback); therefore, since the carryover period provided for by paragraph (a)(7)(ii) of this section would allow the net operating loss to be a net operating loss carryover to a taxable year ending in 1981, under paragraph (a)(7)(ii)(A) of this section the applicable carryover period is 15 years (provided that X did not act so as to cause itself to cease to qualify as a real estate investment trust for the principal purpose of securing the benefit of a net operating loss carryover under section 172(b)(1)(B)).

Example (2). (i) Facts. The facts are the same as in *example* (1) except that the taxable year ending December 31, 1973, was not a qualified taxable year for X.

(ii) Applicable carryback and carryover periods. The net operating loss must be carried back to the 3 preceding taxable years. Section 1.857-2(a)(5) provides that the net operating loss deduction shall not be allowed in computing real estate investment trust taxable income for the year ending December 31, 1972. Under these facts the carryover period is determined under § 1.172-10(a)(7). Paragraph (a)(7)(ii) of this section provides for a 6 year carryover period (5 years increased by the 1 qualified taxable year to which the loss was a net operating loss carryback); therefore, since a 6 year carryover period would not allow the net operating loss to be a net operating loss carryover to a taxable year ending in 1981, paragraph (a)(7)(i)(A) of this section does not apply. Where the rule stated in paragraph (a)(7)(i)(A) of this section does not apply, paragraph (a)(7)(i)(B) of this section provides that the applicable carryover period is the carryover period determined under paragraph (a)(7)(ii) of this section, which, in this case, is 6 years (provided that the principal purpose for X acting so as to cause itself to cease to qualify as a real estate investment trust was not to secure the benefit of the allowance of a net operating loss carryover under section 172(b)(1)(B)).

(d) Cross references. See §§ 1.172-2(c) and 1.172-5(a)(5) for the computation of the net operating loss of a qualified real estate investment trust for a taxable year ending after October 4, 1976, and the amount of a net operating loss which is absorbed when carried over to a qualified taxable year ending after October 4, 1976. See § 1.857-2(a)(5), which provides that for a taxable year ending before October 5, 1976, the net operating loss deduction is not allowed in computing the real estate investment trust taxable income of a qualified real estate investment trust.

T.D. 7767, 2/3/81, amend T.D. 8107, 12/1/86.

§ 1.172-13 Product liability losses.

(a) Entitlement to 10-year carryback. *(1) In general.* Unless an election is made pursuant to paragraph (c) of this section, in the case of a taxpayer which has a product liability loss (as defined in section 172(j) and paragraph (b)(1) of this section) for a taxable year beginning after September 30, 1979 (hereinafter "loss year"), the product liability loss shall be a net operating loss carryback to each of the 10 taxable years preceding the loss year.

(2) Years to which loss may be carried. A product liability loss shall first be carried to the earliest of the taxable years to which such loss is allowable as a carryback and shall then be carried to the next earliest of such taxable years, etc.

(3) Example. The application of this paragraph may be illustrated as follows:

Example. Taxpayer A incurs a net operating loss for taxable year 1980 of $80,000, of which $60,000 is a product liability loss. A's taxable income for each of the 10 years immediately preceding taxable year 1980 was $5,000. The product liability loss of $60,000 is first carried back to the 10th through the 4th preceding taxable years $5,000 per year), thus offsetting $35,000 of the loss. The remaining $25,000 of product liability loss is added to the remaining portion of the total net operating loss for taxable year 1980 which was not a product liability loss ($20,000), and the total is then carried back to the 3rd through 1st years preceding taxable year 1980, which offsets $15,000 of this loss. The remaining loss ($30,000) is carried forward pursuant to section 172(b)(1) and the regulations thereunder without regard to whether all or any portion thereof originated as a product liability loss.

(b) Definitions. *(1) Product liability loss.* The term "product liability loss" means, for any taxable year, the lesser of—

(i) The net operating loss for the current taxable year (not including the portion of such net operating loss attributable to foreign expropriation losses, as defined in § 1.172-11), or

(ii) The total of the amounts allowable as deductions under sections 162 and 165 directly attributable to—

(A) Product liability (as defined in paragraph (b)(2) of this section), and

(B) Expenses (including settlement payments) incurred in connection with the investigation or settlement of or opposition to claims against the taxpayer on account of alleged product liability.

Indirect corporate expense, or overhead, is not to be allocated to product liability claims so as to become a product liability loss.

(2) Product liability. (i) The term "product liability" means the liability of a taxpayer for damages resulting from physical injury or emotional harm to individuals, or damage to or loss of the use of property, on account of any defect in any product which is manufactured, leased, or sold by the taxpayer. The preceding sentence applies only to the extent that the injury, harm, or damage occurs after the taxpayer has completed or terminated operations with respect to the

product, including, but not limited to the manufacture, installation, delivery, or testing of the product, and has relinquished possession of such product.

(ii) The term "product liability" does not include liabilities arising under warranty theories relating to repair or replacement of the property that are essentially contract liabilities. For example, the costs incurred by a taxpayer in repairing or replacing defective products under the terms of a warranty, express or implied, are not product liability losses. On the other hand, the taxpayer's liability for damage done to other property or for harm done to persons that is attributable to a defective product may be product liability losses regardless of whether the claim sounds in tort or contract. Further, liability incurred as a result of services performed by a taxpayer is not product liability. For purposes of the preceding sentence, where both a product and services are integral parts of a transaction, product liability does not arise until all operations with respect to the product are completed and the taxpayer has relinquished possession of it. On the other hand, any liability that arises after completion of the initial delivery, installation, servicing, testing, etc., is considered "product liability" even if such liability arises during the subsequent servicing of the product pursuant to a service agreement or otherwise.

(iii) Liability for injury, harm, or damage due to a defective product as described in this subparagraph shall be "product liability" notwithstanding that the liability is not considered product liability under the law of the State in which such liability arose.

(iv) Amounts paid for insurance against product liability risks are not paid on account of product liability.

(v) Notwithstanding subparagraph (iv), an amount is paid on account of product liability (even if such amount is paid to an insurance company) if the amount satisfies the provisions of paragraph (b)(2)(i) through (iii) of this section and the amount—

(A) Is paid on account of specific claims against the taxpayer (or on account of expenses incurred in connection with the investigation or settlement of or opposition to such claims, subsequent to the events giving rise to the claims and pursuant to a contract entered into before those events,

(B) Is not refundable, and

(C) Is not applicable to other claims, other expenses or to subsequent coverage.

(3) Examples. Paragraph (b)(2) of this section is illustrated by the following examples:

Example (1). X, a manufacturer of heating equipment, sells a boiler to A, a homeowner. Subsequent to the sale and installation of the boiler, the boiler explodes due to a defect causing physical injury to A. A sues X for damages for the injuries sustained in the explosion and is awarded $250,000, which X pays. The payment was made on account of product liability.

Example (2). Assume the same facts as in example (1) and that A also sues under the contract with X to recover for the cost of the boiler and recovers $1,000, the boiler's replacement cost. The $1,000 payment is not a payment on account of product liability. Similarly, if X agrees to repair the destroyed boiler, any amount expended by X for such repair is not payment made on account of product liability.

Example (3). Y, a professional medical association, is sued by B, a patient, in an action based on the malpractice of one of its doctors. B recovers $25,000. Because the suit was based on the service of B, the payment is not made on account of product liability.

Example (4). R, a retailer of communications equipment, sells a telecommunication device to C. R also contracts with C to service the equipment for 3 years. While R is installing the equipment, the unit catches on fire due to faulty wiring within the unit and destroys C's office. Because R had not relinquished possession of this equipment when the fire started, any amount paid to C by R for the damage to C's property on account of the defective product is not payment on account of product liability.

Example (5). Assume the same facts as in example (4) except that the fire and resulting property damages occurred after R had installed the equipment and relinquished possession of it. Any amount paid for the property damages sustained on account of the defective product is payment on account of product liability.

Example (6). Assume the same facts as in example (4) except that the equipment catches on fire during the subsequent servicing of the unit. Because C is in possession of the unit during the servicing, any amount paid for the property damage sustained on account of the defective product would be payment on account of product liability.

Example (7). X, a manufacturer of computers, sells a computer to A. X also has its employees periodically service the computer for A from time to time after it is placed in service. After the initial delivery, installation, servicing, and testing of the computer is completed, the computer catches on fire while X's employee is servicing the equipment. This fire causes property damage to A's office and physical injury to A. Any amount paid for the property or physical damage sustained on account of the defective product is payment on account of product liability.

(c) Election. *(1) In general.* The 10-year carryback provision of this section applies, except as provided in this paragraph, to any taxpayer who, for a taxable year beginning after September 30, 1979, incurs a product liability loss. Any taxpayer entitled to a 10-year carryback under paragraph (a) of this section in any loss year may elect (at the time and in the manner provided in paragraph (c)(2) of this section) to have the carryback period with respect to the product liability loss determined without regard to the carryback rules provided by paragraph (a) of this section. If the taxpayer so elects, the product liability loss shall not be carried back to the 10th through the 4th taxable years preceding the loss year. In such case, the product liability loss shall be carried back or carried over as provided by section 172(b) (except subparagraph (1)(I) thereof) and the regulations thereunder.

(2) Time and manner of making election. An election by any taxpayer entitled to the 10-year carryback for the product liability loss to have the carryback with respect to such loss determined without regard to the 10-year carryback provision of paragraph (a) of this section must be made by attaching to the taxpayer's tax return (filed within the time prescribed by law, including extensions of time) for the taxable year in which such product liability loss is sustained, a statement containing the information required by paragraph (c)(3) of this section. Such election, once made for any taxable year, shall be irrevocable after the due date (including extensions of time) of the taxpayer's tax return for that taxable year.

(3) Information required. In the case of a statement filed after April 25, 1983, the statement referred to in paragraph (c)(2) of this section shall contain the following information:

(i) The name, address, and taxpayer identifying number of the taxpayer; and

(ii) A statement that the taxpayer elects under section 172(j)(3) not to have section 172(b)(1)(I) apply.

(4) Relationship with section 172(b)(3)(C) election. If a taxpayer sustains during the taxable year both a net operating loss not attributable to product liability and a product liability loss (as defined in section 172(j)(1) and paragraph (b)(1) of this section), an election pursuant to section 172(b)(3)(C) (relating to election to relinquish the entire carryback period) does not preclude the product liability loss from being carried back 10 years under section 172(b)(1)(I) and paragraph (a)(1) of this section.

T.D. 8096, 8/26/86.

§ 1.173-1 Circulation expenditures.

Caution: The Treasury has not yet amended Reg § 1.173-1 to reflect changes made by P.L. 97-248.

(a) Allowance of deduction. Section 173 provides for the deduction from gross income of all expenditures to establish, maintain, or increase the circulation of a newspaper, magazine, or other periodical, subject to the following limitations:

(1) No deduction shall be allowed for expenditures for the purchase of land or depreciable property or for the acquisition of circulation through the purchase of any part of the business of another publisher of a newspaper, magazine, or other periodical;

(2) The deduction shall be allowed only to the publisher making the circulation expenditure; and

(3) The deduction shall be allowed only for the taxable year in which such expenditures are paid or incurred.

Subject to the provisions of paragraph (c) of this section, the deduction permitted under section 173 and this paragraph shall be allowed without regard to the method of accounting used by the taxpayer and notwithstanding the provisions of section 263 and the regulations thereunder, relating to capital expenditures.

(b) Deferred expenditures. Notwithstanding the provisions of paragraph (a)(3) of this section, expenditures paid or incurred in a taxable year subject to the Internal Revenue Code of 1939 which are deferrable pursuant to I.T. 3369 (C.B. 1940-1, 46), as modified by Rev. Rul., 57-87 C.B. 1957-1, 507), may be deducted in the taxable year subject to the Internal Revenue Code of 1954 to which so deferred.

(c) Election to capitalize. *(1)* A taxpayer entitled to the deduction for circulation expenditures provided in section 173 and paragraph (a) of this section may, in lieu of taking such deduction, elect to capitalize the portion of such circulation expenditures which is properly chargeable to capital account. As a general rule, expenditures normally made from year to year in an effort to maintain circulation are not properly chargeable to capital account; conversely, expenditures made in an effort to establish or to increase circulation are properly chargeable to capital account. For example, if a newspaper normally employs five persons to obtain renewals of subscriptions by telephone, the expenditures in connection therewith would not be properly chargeable to capital account. However, if such newspaper, in a special effort to increase its circulation, hires for a limited period 20 additional employees to obtain new subscriptions by means of telephone calls to the general public, the expenditures in connection therewith would be properly chargeable to capital account. If an election is made by a taxpayer to treat any portion of his circulation expenditures as chargeable to capital account, the election must apply to all such expenditures which are properly so chargeable. In such case, no deduction shall be allowed under section 173 for any such expenditures. In particular cases, the extent to which any deductions attributable to the amortization of capital expenditures are allowed may be determined under sections 162, 263, and 461.

(2) A taxpayer may make the election referred to in subparagraph (1) of this paragraph by attaching a statement to his return for the first taxable year to which the election is applicable. Once an election is made, the taxpayer must continue in subsequent taxable years to charge to capital account all circulation expenditures properly so chargeable, unless the Commissioner, on application made to him in writing by the taxpayer, permits a revocation of such election for any subsequent taxable year or years. Permission to revoke such election may be granted subject to such conditions as the Commissioner deems necessary.

(3) Elections filed under section 23(bb) of the Internal Revenue Code of 1939 shall be given the same effect as if they were filed under section 173. (See section 7807(b)(2).)

T.D. 6254, 9/27/57.

§ 1.174-1 Research and experimental expenditures; in general.

Section 174 provides two methods for treating research or experimental expenditures paid or incurred by the taxpayer in connection with his trade or business. These expenditures may be treated as expenses not chargeable to capital account and deducted in the year in which they are paid or incurred (see § 1.174-3), or they may be deferred and amortized (see § 1.174-4). Research or experimental expenditures which are neither treated as expenses nor deferred and amortized under section 174 must be charged to capital account. The expenditures to which section 174 applies may relate either to a general research program or to a particular project. See § 1.174-2 for the definition of research and experimental expenditures. The term "paid or incurred", as used in section 174 and in §§ 1.174-1 to 1.174-4, inclusive, is to be construed according to the method of accounting used by the taxpayer in computing taxable income. See section 7701(a)(25).

T.D. 6255, 10/3/57.

§ 1.174-2 Definition of research and experimental expenditures.

(a) In general. *(1)* The term *research or experimental expenditures,* as used in section 174, means expenditures incurred in connection with the taxpayer's trade or business which represent research and development costs in the experimental or laboratory sense. The term generally includes all such costs incident to the development or improvement of a product. The term includes the costs of obtaining a patent, such as attorneys' fees expended in making and perfecting a patent application. Expenditures represent research and development costs in the experimental or laboratory sense if they are for activities intended to discover information that would eliminate uncertainty concerning the development or improvement of a product. Uncertainty exists if the information available to the taxpayer does not establish the capability or method for developing or improving the product or the appropriate design of the product. Whether expenditures qualify as research or experimental expenditures depends on the nature of the activity to which the expenditures relate, not the nature of the product or improvement being developed or the level of technological advancement the product or improvement represents.

(2) For purposes of this section, the term *product* includes any pilot model, process, formula, invention, technique, patent, or similar property, and includes products to be used by the taxpayer in its trade or business as well as products to be held for sale, lease, or license.

(3) The term *research or experimental expenditures* does not include expenditures for—

(i) The ordinary testing or inspection of materials or products for quality control (quality control testing);

(ii) Efficiency surveys;

(iii) Management studies;

(iv) Consumer surveys;

(v) Advertising or promotions;

(vi) The acquisition of another's patent, model, production or process; or

(vii) Research in connection with literary, historical, or similar projects.

(4) For purposes of paragraph (a)(3)(i) of this section, testing or inspection to determine whether particular units of materials or products conform to specified parameters is quality control testing. However, quality control testing does not include testing to determine if the design of the product is appropriate.

(5) See section 263A and the regulations thereunder for cost capitalization rules which apply to expenditures paid or incurred for research in connection with literary, historical, or similar projects involving the production of property, including the production of films, sound recordings, video tapes, books, or similar properties.

(6) Section 174 applies to a research or experimental expenditure only to the extent that the amount of the expenditure is reasonable under the circumstances. In general, the amount of an expenditure for research or experimental activities is reasonable if the amount would ordinarily be paid for like activities by like enterprises under like circumstances. Amounts supposedly paid for research that are not reasonable under the circumstances may be characterized as disguised dividends, gifts, loans, or similar payments. The reasonableness requirement of this paragraph (a)(6) does not apply to the reasonableness of the type or nature of the activities themselves.

(7) This paragraph (a) applies to taxable years beginning after October 3, 1994.

(8) The provisions of this section apply not only to costs paid or incurred by the taxpayer for research or experimentation undertaken directly by him but also to expenditures paid or incurred for research or experimentation carried on in his behalf by another person or organization (such as a research institute, foundation, engineering company, or similar contractor). However, any expenditures for research or experimentation carried on in the taxpayer's behalf by another person are not expenditures to which section 174 relates, to the extent that they represent expenditures for the acquisition or improvement of land or depreciable property, used in connection with the research or experimentation, to which the taxpayer acquires rights of ownership.

(9) The application of subparagraph (2) of this paragraph may be illustrated by the following examples:

Example (1). A engages B to undertake research and experimental work in order to create a particular product. B will be paid annually a fixed sum plus an amount equivalent to his actual expenditures. In 1957, A pays to B in respect of the project the sum of $150,000 of which $25,000 represents an addition to B's laboratory and the balance represents charges for research and experimentation on the project. It is agreed between the parties that A will absorb the entire cost of this addition to B's laboratory which will be retained by B. A may treat the entire $150,000 as expenditures under section 174.

Example (2). X Corporation, a manufacturer of explosives, contracts with the Y research organization to attempt through research and experimentation the creation of a new process for making certain explosives. Because of the danger involved in such an undertaking, Y is compelled to acquire an isolated tract of land on which to conduct the research and experimentation. It is agreed that upon completion of the project Y will transfer this tract, including any improvements thereon, to X. Section 174 does not apply to the amount paid to Y representing the costs of the tract of land and improvements.

(b) Certain expenditures with respect to land and other property. *(1)* Expenditures by the taxpayer for the acquisition or improvement of land, or for the acquisition or improvement of property which is subject to an allowance for depreciation under section 167 or depletion under section 611, are not deductible under section 174, irrespective of the fact that the property or improvements may be used by the taxpayer in connection with research or experimentation. However, allowances for depreciation or depletion of property are considered as research or experimental expenditures, for purposes of section 174, to the extent that the property to which the allowances relate is used in connection with research or experimentation. If any part of the cost of acquisition or improvement of depreciable property is attributable to research or experimentation (whether made by the taxpayer or another), see subparagraphs (2), (3), and (4) of this paragraph.

(2) Expenditures for research or experimentation which result, as an end product of the research or experimentation, in depreciable property to be used in the taxpayer's trade or business may, subject to the limitations of subparagraph (4) of this paragraph, be allowable as a current expense deduction under section 174 (a). Such expenditures cannot be amortized under section 174 (b) except to the extent provided in paragraph (a)(4) of § 1.174-4.

(3) If expenditures for research or experimentation are incurred in connection with the construction or manufacture of depreciable property by another, they are deductible under section 174(a) only if made upon the taxpayer's order and at his risk. No deduction will be allowed (i) if the taxpayer purchases another's product under a performance guarantee (whether express, implied, or imposed by local law) unless the guarantee is limited, to engineering specifications or otherwise, in such a way that economic utility is not taken into account; or (ii) for any part of the purchase price of a product in regular production. For example, if a taxpayer orders a specially-built automatic milling machine under a guarantee that the machine will be capable of producing a given number of units per hour, no portion of the expenditure is deductible since none of it is made at the taxpayer's risk. Similarly, no deductible expense is incurred if a taxpayer enters into a contract for the construction of a new type of chemical processing plant under a turn-key contract guaranteeing a given annual production and a given consumption of raw material and fuel per unit. On the other hand if the contract contained no guarantee of quality of production and of quan-

tity of units in relation to consumption of raw material and fuel, and if real doubt existed as to the capabilities of the process, expenses for research or experimentation under the contract are at the taxpayer's risk and are deductible under section 174(a). However, see subparagraph (4) of this paragraph.

(4) The deductions referred to in subparagraphs (2) and (3) of this paragraph for expenditures in connection with the acquisition or production of depreciable property to be used in the taxpayer's trade or business are limited to amounts expended for research or experimentation. For the purpose of the preceding sentence, amounts expended for research or experimentation do not include the costs of the component materials of the depreciable property, the costs of labor or other elements involved in its construction and installation, or costs attributable to the acquisition or improvement of the property. For example, a taxpayer undertakes to develop a new machine for use in his business. He expends $30,000 on the project of which $10,000 represents the actual costs of material, labor, etc., to construct the machine, and $20,000 represents research costs which are not attributable to the machine itself. Under section 174(a) the taxpayer would be permitted to deduct the $20,000 as expenses not chargeable to capital account, but the $10,000 must be charged to the asset account (the machine).

(c) Exploration expenditures. The provisions of section 174 are not applicable to any expenditures paid or incurred for the purpose of ascertaining the existence, location, extent, or quality of any deposit of ore, oil, gas or other mineral. See sections 617 and 263.

T.D. 6255, 10/3/57, amend T.D. 8131, 3/24/87, T.D. 8562, 9/30/94.

§ 1.174-3 Treatment as expenses.

(a) In general. Research or experimental expenditures paid or incurred by a taxpayer during the taxable year in connection with his trade or business are deductible as expenses, and are not chargeable to capital account, if the taxpayer adopts the method provided in section 174(a). See paragraph (b) of this section. If adopted, the method shall apply to all research and experimental expenditures paid or incurred in the taxable year of adoption and all subsequent taxable years, unless a different method is authorized by the Commissioner under section 174(a)(3) with respect to part or all of the expenditures. See paragraph (b)(3) of this section. Thus, if a change to the deferred expense method under section 174(b) is authorized by the Commissioner with respect to research or experimental expenditures attributable to a particular project or projects, the taxpayer, for the taxable year of the change and for subsequent taxable years, must apply the deferred expense method to all such expenditures paid or incurred during any of those taxable years in connection with the particular project or projects, even though all other research and experimental expenditures are required to be deducted as current expenses under this section. In no event will the taxpayer be permitted to adopt the method described in this section as to part of the expenditures relative to a particular project and adopt for the same taxable year a different method of treating the balance of the expenditures relating to the same project.

(b) Adoption and change of method. *(1) Adoption without consent.* The method described in this section may be adopted for any taxable year beginning after December 31, 1953, and ending after August 16, 1954. The consent of the Commissioner is not required if the taxpayer adopts the method for the first such taxable year in which he pays or incurs research or experimental expenditures. The taxpayer may do so by claiming in his income tax return for such year a deduction for his research or experimental expenditures. If the taxpayer fails to adopt the method for the first taxable year in which he incurs such expenditures, he cannot do so in subsequent taxable years unless he obtains the consent of the Commissioner under section 174(a)(2)(B) and subparagraph (2) of this paragraph. See, however, subparagraph (4) of this paragraph, relating to extensions of time.

(2) Adoption with consent. A taxpayer may, with the consent of the Commissioner, adopt at any time the method provided in section 174(a). The method adopted in this manner shall be applicable only to expenditures paid or incurred during the taxable year for which the request is made and in subsequent taxable years. A request to adopt this method shall be in writing and shall be addressed to the Commissioner of Internal Revenue, Attention: T:R, Washington 25, D.C. The request shall set forth the name and address of the taxpayer, the first taxable year for which the adoption of the method is requested, and a description of the project or projects with respect to which research or experimental expenditures are to be, or have already been, paid or incurred. The request shall be signed by the taxpayer (or his duly authorized representative) and shall be filed not later than the last day of the first taxable year for which the adoption of the method is requested. See, however, subparagraph (4) of this paragraph, relating to extensions of time.

(3) Change of method. An application for permission to change to a different method of treating research or experimental expenditures shall be in writing and shall be addressed to the Commissioner of Internal Revenue, Attention: T:R, Washington 25, D.C. The application shall include the name and address of the taxpayer, shall be signed by the taxpayer (or his duly authorized representative), and shall be filed not later than the last day of the first taxable year for which the change in method is to apply. See, however, subparagraph (4) of this paragraph, relating to extensions of time. The application shall—

(i) State the first year to which the requested change is to be applicable;

(ii) State whether the change is to apply to all research or experimental expenditures paid or incurred by the taxpayer, or only to expenditures attributable to a particular project or projects;

(iii) Include such information as will identify the project or projects to which the change is applicable;

(iv) Indicate the number of months (not less than 60) selected for amortization of the expenditures, if any, which are to be treated as deferred expenses under section 174(b);

(v) State that, upon approval of the application, the taxpayer will make an accounting segregation on his books and records of the research or experimental expenditures to which the change in method is to apply; and

(vi) State the reasons for the change. If permission is granted to make the change, the taxpayer shall attach a copy of the letter granting permission to his income tax return for the first taxable year in which the different method is effective.

(4) Special rules. If the last day prescribed by law for filing a return for any taxable year (including extensions thereof) to which section 174(a) is applicable falls before January 2, 1958, consent is hereby given for the taxpayer to adopt the expense method or to change from the expense method to a different method. In the case of a change from the expense method to a different method, the taxpayer, on

or before January 2, 1958, must submit to the district director for the internal revenue district in which the return was filed the information required by subparagraph (3) of this paragraph. For any taxable year for which the expense method or a different method is adopted pursuant to this subparagraph, an amended return reflecting such method shall be filed on or before January 2, 1958, if such return is necessary.

T.D. 6255, 10/3/57.

---

§ 1.174-4 Treatment as deferred expenses.

Caution: The Treasury has not yet amended Reg § 1.174-4 to reflect changes made by P.L. 97-248.

(a) In general. *(1)* If a taxpayer has not adopted the method provided in section 174(a) of treating research or experimental expenditures paid or incurred by him in connection with his trade or business as currently deductible expenses, he may, for any taxable year beginning after December 31, 1953, elect to treat such expenditures as deferred expenses under section 174(b), subject to the limitations of subparagraph (2) of this paragraph. If a taxpayer has adopted the method of treating such expenditures as expenses under section 174(a), he may not elect to defer and amortize any such expenditures unless permission to do so is granted under section 174(a)(3). See paragraph (b) of this section.

(2) The election to treat research or experimental expenditures as deferred expenses under section 174(b) applies only to those expenditures which are chargeable to capital account but which are not chargeable to property of a character subject to an allowance for depreciation or depletion under section 167 or 611, respectively. Thus, the election under section 174(b) applies only if the property resulting from the research or experimental expenditures has no determinable useful life. If the property resulting from the expenditures has a determinable useful life, section 174(b) is not applicable, and the capitalized expenditures must be amortized or depreciated over the determinable useful life. Amounts treated as deferred expenses are properly chargeable to capital account for purposes of section 1016(a)(1), relating to adjustments to basis of property. See section 1016(a)(14). See section 174(c) and paragraph (b)(1) of § 1.174-2 for treatment of expenditures for the acquisition or improvement of land or of depreciable or depletable property to be used in connection with the research or experimentation.

(3) Expenditures which are treated as deferred expenses under section 174(b) are allowable as a deduction ratably over a period of not less than 60 consecutive months beginning with the month in which the taxpayer first realizes benefits from the expenditures. The length of the period shall be selected by the taxpayer at the time he makes the election to defer the expenditures. If a taxpayer has two or more separate projects, he may select a different amortization period for each project. In absence of a showing to the contrary, the taxpayer will be deemed to have begun to realize benefits from the deferred expenditures in the month in which the taxpayer first puts the process, formula, invention, or similar property to which the expenditures relate to an income-producing use. See section 1016(a)(14) for adjustments to basis of property for amounts allowed as deductions under section 174(b) and this section. See section 165 and the regulations thereunder for rules relating to the treatment of losses resulting from abandonment.

(4) If expenditures which the taxpayer has elected to defer and deduct ratably over a period of time in accordance with section 174(b) result in the development of depreciable property, deductions for the unrecovered expenditures, beginning with the time the asset becomes depreciable in character, shall be determined under section 167 (relating to depreciation) and the regulations thereunder. For example, for the taxable year 1954, A, who reports his income on the basis of a calendar year, elects to defer and deduct ratably over a period of 60 months research and experimental expenditures made in connection with a particular project. In 1956, the total of the deferred expenditures amounts to $60,000. At that time, A has developed a process which he seeks to patent. On July 1, 1956, A first realized benefits from the marketing of products resulting from this process. Therefore, the expenditures deferred are deductible ratably over the 60-month period beginning with July 1, 1956 (when A first realized benefits from the project). In his return for the year 1956, A deducted $6,000; in 1957, A deducted $12,000 ($1,000 per month). On July 1, 1958, a patent protecting his process is obtained by A. In his return for 1958, A is entitled to a deduction of $6,000, representing the amortizable portion of the deferred expenses attributable to the period prior to July 1, 1958. The balance of the unrecovered expenditures ($60,000 minus $24,000, or $36,000) is to be recovered as a depreciation deduction over the life of the patent commencing with July 1, 1958. Thus, one-half of the annual depreciation deduction based upon the useful life of the patent is also deductible for 1958 (from July 1 to December 31).

(5) The election shall be applicable to all research and experimental expenditures paid or incurred by the taxpayer or, if so limited by the taxpayer's election, to all such expenditures with respect to the particular project, subject to the limitations of subparagraph (2) of this paragraph. The election shall apply for the taxable year for which the election is made and for all subsequent taxable years, unless a change to a different treatment is authorized by the Commissioner under section 174(b)(2). See paragraph (b)(2) of this section. Likewise, the taxpayer shall adhere to the amortization period selected at the time of the election unless a different period of amortization with respect to a part or all of the expenditures is similarly authorized. However, no change in method will be permitted with respect to expenditures paid or incurred before the taxable year to which the change is to apply. In no event will the taxpayer be permitted to treat part of the expenditures with respect to a particular project as deferred expenses under section 174(b) and to adopt a different method of treating the balance of the expenditures relating to the same project for the same taxable year. The election under this section shall not apply to any expenditures paid or incurred before the taxable year for which the taxpayer makes the election.

(b) Election and change of method. *(1) Election.* The election under section 174(b) shall be made not later than the time (including extensions) prescribed by law for filing the return for the taxable year for which the method is to be adopted. The election shall be made by attaching a statement to the taxpayer's return for the first taxable year to which the election is applicable. The statement shall be signed by the taxpayer (or his duly authorized representative), and shall—

(i) Set forth the name and address of the taxpayer;

(ii) Designate the first taxable year to which the election is to apply;

(iii) State whether the election is intended to apply to all expenditures within the permissible scope of the election, or only to a particular project or projects, and, if the latter, include such information as will identify the project or projects as to which the election is to apply;

(iv) Set forth the amount of all research or experimental expenditures paid or incurred during the taxable year for which the election is made;

(v) Indicate the number of months (not less than 60) selected for amortization of the deferred expenses for each project; and

(vi) State that the taxpayer will make an accounting segregation in his books and records of the expenditures to which the election relates.

(2) Change to a different method or period. Application for permission to change to a different method of treating research or experimental expenditures or to a different period of amortization for deferred expenses shall be in writing and shall be addressed to the Commissioner of Internal Revenue, Attention: T:R, Washington 25, D.C. The application shall include the name and address of the taxpayer, shall be signed by the taxpayer (or his duly authorized representative), and shall be filed not later than the end of the first taxable year in which the different method or different amortization period is to be used (unless subparagraph (3) of this paragraph, relating to extensions of time, is applicable). The application shall set forth the following information with regard to the research or experimental expenditures which are being treated under section 174(b) as deferred expenses:

(i) Total amount of research or experimental expenditures attributable to each project;

(ii) Amortization period applicable to each project; and

(iii) Unamortized expenditures attributable to each project at the beginning of the taxable year in which the application is filed. In addition, the application shall set forth the length of the new period or periods proposed, or the new method of treatment proposed, the reasons for the proposed change, and such information as will identify the project or projects to which the expenditures affected by the change relate. If permission is granted to make the change, the taxpayer shall attach a copy of the letter granting the permission to his income tax return for the first taxable year in which the different method or period is to be effective.

(3) Special rules. If the last day prescribed by law for filing a return for any taxable year for which the deferred method provided in section 174(b) has been adopted falls before January 2, 1958, consent is hereby given for the taxpayer to change from such method and adopt a different method of treating research or experimental expenditures, provided that on or before January 2, 1958, he submits to the district director for the district in which the return was filed the information required by subparagraph (2) of this paragraph, relating to a change to a different method or period. For any taxable year for which the different method is adopted pursuant to this subparagraph, an amended return reflecting such method shall be filed on or before January 2, 1958.

(c) Example. The application of this section is illustrated by the following example:

Example. N Corporation is engaged in the business of manufacturing chemical products. On January 1, 1955, work is begun on a special research project. N Corporation elects, pursuant to section 174(b), to defer the expenditures relating to the special project and to amortize the expenditures over a period of 72 months beginning with the month in which benefits from the expenditures are first realized. On January 1, 1955, N Corporation also purchased for $57,600 a building having a remaining useful life of 12 years as of the date of purchase and no salvage value at the end of the period. Fifty percent of the building's facilities are to be used in connection with the special research project. During 1955, N Corporation pays or incurs the following expenditures relating to the special research project:

Salaries	$15,000
Heat, light and power	700
Drawings	2,000
Models	6,500
Laboratory materials	8,000
Attorneys' fees	1,400
Depreciation on building attributable to project (50 percent of $4,800 allowable depreciation)	2,400
Total research and development expenditures	36,000

The above expenditures result in a process which is marketable but not patentable and which has no determinable useful life. N Corporation first realizes benefits from the process in January 1956. N Corporation is entitled to deduct the amount of $6,000

$$\left(\frac{\$36,000 \times 12 \text{ months}}{72 \text{ months}}\right)$$

as deferred expenses under section 174(b) in computing taxable income for 1956.

T.D. 6255, 10/3/57.

§ 1.175-1 Soil and water conservation expenditures; in general.

Caution: The Treasury has not yet amended Reg § 1.175-1 to reflect changes made by P.L. 110-246, P.L. 99-514, P.L. 90-630.

Under section 175, a farmer may deduct his soil or water conservation expenditures which do not give rise to a deduction for depreciation and which are not otherwise deductible. The amount of the deduction is limited annually to 25 percent of the taxpayer's gross income from farming. Any excess may be carried over and deducted in succeeding taxable years. As a general rule, once a farmer has adopted this method of treating soil and water conservation expenditures, he must deduct all such expenditures (subject to the 25-percent limitation) for the current and subsequent taxable years. If a farmer does not adopt this method, such expenditures increase the basis of the property to which they relate.

T.D. 6235, 5/31/57.

§ 1.175-2 Definition of soil and water conservation expenditures.

Caution: The Treasury has not yet amended Reg § 1.175-2 to reflect changes made by P.L. 110-246, P.L. 99-514.

(a) Expenditures treated as a deduction. *(1)* The method described in section 175 applies to expenditures paid or incurred for the purpose of soil or water conservation in respect of land used in farming, or for the prevention of erosion of land used in farming, but only if such expenditures are made in the furtherance of the business of farming. More specifically, a farmer may deduct expenditures made for these purposes which are for (i) the treatment or moving of earth, (ii) the construction, control, and protection of diversion channels, drainage ditches, irrigation ditches, earthen dams, watercourses, outlets, and ponds, (iii) the eradication of brush, and (iv) the planting of windbreaks. Expenditures for the treatment or moving of earth include but are not limited to expenditures for leveling, conditioning, grading, terracing, contour furrowing, and restoration of soil fertility. For rules relating to the allocation of expenditures that benefit both land used in farming and other land of the taxpayer, see § 1.175-7.

(2) The following are examples of soil and water conservation: (i) Constructing terraces, or the like, to detain or control the flow of water, to check soil erosion on sloping land, to intercept runoff, and to divert excess water to protected outlets; (ii) constructing water detention or sediment retention dams to prevent or fill gullies, to retard or reduce runoff of water, or to collect stock water; and (iii) constructing earthen floodways, levies, or dikes, to prevent flood damage to farmland.

(b) Expenditures not subject to section 175 treatment. *(1)* The method described in section 175 applies only to expenditures for nondepreciable items. Accordingly, a taxpayer may not deduct expenditures for the purchase, construction, installation, or improvement of structures, appliances, or facilities subject to the allowance for depreciation. Thus, the method does not apply to depreciable nonearthen items such as those made of masonry or concrete (see section 167). For example, expenditures in respect of depreciable property include those for materials, supplies, wages, fuel, hauling, and dirt moving for making structures such as tanks, reservoirs, pipes, conduits, canals, dams, wells, or pumps composed of masonry, concrete, tile, metal, or wood. However, the method applies to expenditures for earthen items which are not subject to a depreciation allowance. For example, expenditures for earthen terraces and dams which are nondepreciable are deductible under section 175. For taxable years beginning after December 31, 1959, in the case of expenditures paid or incurred by farmers for fertilizer, lime, etc., for purposes other than soil or water conservation, see section 180 and the regulations thereunder.

(2) The method does not apply to expenses deductible apart from section 175. Adoption of the method is not necessary in order to deduct such expenses in full without limitation. Thus, the method does not apply to interest (deductible under section 163), not to taxes (deductible under section 164). It does not apply to expenses for the repair of completed soil or water conservation structures, such as costs of annual removal of sediment from a drainage ditch. It does not apply to expenditures paid or incurred primarily to produce an agricultural crop even though they incidentally conserve soil. Thus, the cost of fertilizing (the effectiveness of which does not last beyond one year) used to produce hay is deductible without adoption of the method prescribed in section 175. For taxable years beginning after December 31, 1959, in the case of expenditures paid or incurred by farmers for fertilizer, lime, etc., for purposes other than soil or water conservation, see section 180 and the regulations thereunder. However, the method would apply to expenses incurred to produce vegetation primarily to conserve soil or water or to prevent erosion. Thus, for example, the method would apply to such expenditures as the cost of dirt moving, lime, fertilizer, seed and planting stock used in gulley stabilization, or in stabilizing severely eroded areas, in order to obtain a soil binding stand of vegetation on raw or infertile land.

(c) Assessments. The method applies also to that part of assessments levied by a soil or water conservation or drainage district to reimburse it for its expenditures which, if actually paid or incurred during the taxable year by the taxpayer directly, would be deductible under section 175. Depending upon the farmer's method of accounting, the time when the farmer pays or incurs the assessment, and not the time when the expenditures are paid or incurred by the district, controls the time the deduction must be taken. The provisions of this paragraph may be illustrated by the following example:

Example. In 1955 a soil and water conservation district levies an assessment of $700 upon a farmer on the cash method of accounting. The assessment is to reimburse the district for its expenditures in 1954. The farmer's share of such expenditures is as follows: $400 for digging drainage ditches for soil conservation and $300 for assets subject to the allowance for depreciation. If the farmer pays the assessment in 1955 and has adopted the method of treating expenditures for soil or water conservation as current expenses under section 175, he may deduct in 1955 the $400 attributable to the digging of drainage ditches as a soil conservation expenditure subject to the 25-percent limitation.

T.D. 6235, 5/31/57, amend T.D. 6548, 2/21/61, T.D. 7740, 11/21/80.

§ 1.175-3 Definition of "the business of farming."

The method described in section 175 is available only to a taxpayer engaged in "the business of farming". A taxpayer is engaged in the business of farming if he cultivates, operates, or manages a farm for gain or profit, either as owner or tenant. For the purpose of section 175, a taxpayer who receives a rental (either in cash or in kind) which is based upon farm production is engaged in the business of farming. However, a taxpayer who receives a fixed rental (without reference to production) is engaged in the business of farming only if he participates to a material extent in the operation or management of the farm. A taxpayer engaged in forestry or the growing of timber is not thereby engaged in the business of farming. A person cultivating or operating a farm for recreation or pleasure rather than a profit is not engaged in the business of farming. For the purpose of this section, the term "farm" is used in its ordinary, accepted sense and includes stock, dairy, poultry, fish, fruit, and truck farms, and also plantations, ranches, ranges, and orchards. A fish farm is an area where fish are grown or raised, as opposed to merely caught or harvested; that is, an area where they are artificially fed, protected, cared for, etc. A taxpayer is engaged in "the business of farming" if he is a member of a partnership engaged in the business of farming. See paragraphs (a)(8)(i) and (c)(1)(iv) of § 1.702-1.

T.D. 6235, 5/31/57, amend T.D. 6649, 4/17/63.

§ 1.175-4 Definition of "land used in farming."

(a) Requirements. For purposes of section 175, the term "land used in farming" means land which is used in the business of farming and which meets both of the following requirements:

(1) The land must be used for the production of crops, fruits, or other agricultural products, including fish, or for the sustenance of livestock. The term "livestock" includes cattle, hogs, horses, mules, donkeys, sheep, goats, captive fur-bearing animals, chickens, turkeys, pigeons, and other poultry. Land used for the sustenance of livestock includes land used for grazing such livestock.

(2) The land must be or have been so used either by the taxpayer or his tenant at some time before or at the same time as, the taxpayer makes the expenditures for soil or water conservation or for the prevention of the erosion of

land. The taxpayer will be considered to have used the land in farming before making such expenditure if he or his tenant has employed the land in a farming use in the past. If the expenditures are made by the taxpayer in respect of land newly acquired from one who immediately prior to the acquisition was using it in farming, the taxpayer will be considered to be using the land in farming at the time that such expenditures are made, if the use which is made by the taxpayer of the land from the time of its acquisition by him is substantially a continuation of its use in farming, whether for the same farming use as that of the taxpayer's predecessor or for one of the other uses specified in paragraph (a)(1) of this section.

(b) Examples. The provisions of paragraph (a) of this section may be illustrated by the following examples:

Example (1). A purchases an operating farm from B in the autumn after B has harvested his crops. Prior to spring plowing and planting when the land is idle because of the season, A makes certain soil and water conservation expenditures on this farm. At the time such expenditures are made the land is considered to be used by A in farming, and A may deduct such expenditures under section 175, subject to the other requisite conditions of such section.

Example (2). C acquires uncultivated land, not previously used in farming, which he intends to develop for farming. Prior to putting this land into production it is necessary for C to clear brush, construct earthen terraces and ponds, and make other soil and water conservation expenditures. The land is not used in farming at the same time that such expenditures are made. Therefore, C may not deduct such expenditures under section 175.

Example (3). D acquires several tracts of land from persons who had used such land immediately prior to D's acquisition for grazing cattle. D intends to use the land for growing grapes. In order to make the land suitable for this use, D constructs earthen terraces, builds drainage ditches and irrigation ditches, extensively treats the soil, and makes other soil and water conservation expenditures. The land is considered to be used in farming by D at the time he makes such expenditures, even though it is being prepared for a different type of farming activity than that engaged in by D's predecessors. Therefore, D may deduct such expenditures under section 175, subject to the other requisite conditions of such section.

(c) Cross reference. For rules relating to the allocation of expenditures that benefit both land used in farming and other land of the taxpayer, see § 1.175-7.

T.D. 6235, 5/31/57, amend T.D. 6649, 4/17/63, T.D. 7740, 11/21/80.

§ 1.175-5 Percentage limitation and carryover.

(a) The limitation. *(1) General rule.* The amount of soil and water conservation expenditures which the taxpayer may deduct under section 175 in any one taxable year is limited to 25 percent of his "gross income from farming".

(2) Definition of "gross income from farming." For the purpose of section 175, the term "gross income from farming" means the gross income of the taxpayer, derived in "the business of farming" as defined in § 1.175-3 from the production of crops, fruits, or other agricultural products, including fish, or from livestock (including livestock held for draft, breeding, or dairy purposes). It includes such income from land used in farming other than that upon which expenditures are made for soil or water conservation or for the prevention of erosion of land. It does not include gains from sales of assets such as farm machinery or gains from the disposition of land. A taxpayer shall compute his "gross income from farming" in accordance with his accounting method used in determining gross income. (See the regulations under section 61 relating to accounting methods used by farmers in determining gross income.) The provisions of this subparagraph may be illustrated by the following example.

Example. A, who uses the cash receipts and disbursements method of accounting, includes in his "gross income from farming" for purposes of determining the 25-percent limitation the following items:

Proceeds from sale of his 1955 yield of corn	$10,000
Gain from disposition of old breeding cows replaced by younger cows	500
Total gross income from farming	$10,500

A must exclude from "gross income from farming" the following items which are included in his gross income:

Gain from sale of tractor	$ 100
Gain from sale of 40 acres of taxpayer's farm	8,000
Interest on loan to neighboring farmer	100

(3) Deduction qualifies for net operating loss deduction. Any amount allowed as a deduction under section 175, either for the year in which the expenditure is paid or incurred or for the year to which it is carried, is taken into account in computing a net operating loss for such taxable year. If a deduction for soil or water conservation expenditures has been taken into account in computing a net operating loss carryback or carryover, it shall not be considered a soil or water conservation expenditure for the year to which the loss is carried, and therefore, is not subject to the 25-percent limitation for that year. The provisions of this subparagraph may be illustrated by the following example:

Example. Assume that in 1956 A has gross income from farming of $4,000, soil and water conservation expenditures of $1,600, and deductible farm expenses of $3,500. Of the soil and water conservation expenditures, $1,000 is deductible in 1956. The $600 in excess of 25 percent of A's gross income from farming is carried over into 1957. Assuming that A has no other income, his deductions of $4,500 ($1,000 plus $3,500) exceed his gross income of $4,000 by $500. This $500 will constitute a net operating loss which he must carry back two years and carry forward five years, until it has offset $500 of taxable income. No part of this $500 net operating loss carryback or carryover will be taken into account in determining the amount of soil and water conservation expenditures in the years to which it is carried.

(b) Carryover of expenditures in excess of deduction. The deduction for soil and water conservation expenditures in any one taxable year is limited to 25 percent of the taxpayer's gross income from farming. The taxpayer may carry over the excess of such expenditures over 25 percent of his gross income from farming into his next taxable year, and, if not deductible in that year, into the next year, and so on without limit as to time. In determining the deductible amount of such expenditures for any taxable year, the actual expenditures of that year shall be added to any such expenditures carried over from prior years, before applying the 25-percent limitation. Any such expenditures in excess of the deductible amount may be carried over during the taxpayer's entire existence. For this purpose in a farm partnership, since the 25-percent limitation is applied to each partner, not the partnership, the carryover may be carried forward during the life of the partner. The provisions of this paragraph may be illustrated by the following example:

Example. Assume the expenditures and income shown in the following table:

	Deductible soil and water conservation expenditures				
Year	Paid or incurred during taxable year	Carried forward from prior year	Total	25% of gross income from farming	Excess to be carried forward
1954	$ 900	None	$ 900	$ 800	$100
1955	1,000	100	1,100	900	200
1956	None	200	200	1,000	None

The deduction for 1954 is limited to $800. The remainder, $100 ($900 minus $800), not being deductible for 1954, is a carryover to 1955. For 1955, accordingly, the total of the expenditures to be taken into account is $1,100 (the $100 carryover and the $1,000 actually paid in that year). The deduction for 1955 is limited to $900, and the remainder of the $1,100 total, or $200, is a carryover to 1956. The deduction for 1956 consists solely of this carryover of $200. Since the total expenditures, actual and carried-over, for 1956 are less than 25 percent of gross income from farming, there is no carryover into 1957.

T.D. 6235, 5/31/57, amend T.D. 6649, 4/17/63.

§ 1.175-6 Adoption or change of method.

Caution: The Treasury has not yet amended Reg § 1.175-6 to reflect changes made by P.L. 110-246.

(a) Adoption without consent. A taxpayer may, without consent, adopt the method of treating expenditures for soil or water conservation as expenses for the first taxable year:

(1) Which begins after December 31, 1953, and ends after August 16, 1954, and

(2) For which soil or water conservation expenditures described in section 175(a) are paid or incurred.

Such adoption shall be made by claiming the deduction on his income tax return. For a taxable year ending prior to May 31, 1957, the adoption of the method described in section 175 shall be made by claiming the deduction on such return for that year, or by claiming the deduction on an amended return filed for that year on or before August 30, 1957.

(b) Adoption with consent. A taxpayer may adopt the method of treating soil and water conservation expenditures as provided by section 175 for any taxable year to which the section is applicable if consent is obtained from the district director for the internal revenue district in which the taxpayer's return is required to be filed.

(c) Change of method. A taxpayer who has adopted the method of treating expenditures for soil or water conservation, as provided by section 175, may change from this method and capitalize such expenditures made after the effective date of the change, if he obtains the consent of the district director for the internal revenue district in which his return is required to be filed.

(d) Request for consent to adopt or change method. Where the consent of the district director is required under paragraph (b) or (c) of this section, the request for his consent shall be in writing, signed by the taxpayer or his authorized representative, and shall be filed not later than the date prescribed by law for filing the income tax return for the first taxable year to which the adoption of, or change of, method is to apply, or not later than August 20, 1957, following their adoption, whichever is later. The request shall:

(1) Set forth the name and address of the taxpayer;

(2) Designate the first taxable year to which the method or change of method is to apply;

(3) State whether the method or change of method is intended to apply to all expenditures within the permissible scope of section 175, or only to a particular project or farm and, if the latter, include such information as will identify the project or farm as to which the method or change of method is to apply;

(4) Set forth the amount of all soil and water conservation expenditures paid or incurred during the first taxable year for which the method or change of method is to apply; and

(5) State that the taxpayer will make an accounting segregation in his books and records of the expenditures to which the election relates.

(e) Scope of method. Except with the consent of the district director as provided in paragraph (b) or (c) of this section, the taxpayer's method of treating soil and water conservation expenditures described in section 175 shall apply to all such expenditures for the taxable year of adoption and all subsequent taxable years. Although a taxpayer may have elected to deduct soil and water conservation expenditures, he may request an authorization to capitalize his soil and water conservation expenditures attributable to a special project or single farm. Similarly, a taxpayer who has not elected to deduct such expenditures may request an authorization to deduct his soil and water conservation expenditures attributable to a special project or single farm. The authorization with respect to the special project or single farm will not affect the method adopted with respect to the taxpayer's regularly incurred soil and water conservation expenditures. No adoption of, or change of, the method under section 175 will be permitted as to expenditures actually paid or incurred before the taxable year to which the method or change of method is to apply. Thus, if a taxpayer adopts such method for 1956, he cannot deduct any part of such expenditures which he capitalized, or should have capitalized, in 1955. Likewise, if a taxpayer who has adopted such method has an unused carryover of such expenditures in excess of the 25-percent limitation, and is granted consent to capitalize soil and water conservation expenditures beginning in 1956, he cannot capitalize any part of the unused carryover. The excess expenditures carried over continue to be deductible to the extent of 25 percent of the taxpayer's gross income from farming. No adjustment to the basis of land shall be made under section 1016 for expenditures to which the method under section 175 applies. For example, A has an unused carryover of soil and water conservation expenditures amounting to $5,000 as of December 31, 1956. On January 1, 1957, A sells his farm and goes out of the business of farming. The unused carryover of $5,000 cannot be added to the basis of the farm for purposes of determining gain or loss on its sale. In 1959, A purchases another farm and resumes the business of farming. In such year, A may deduct the amount of the unused carryover to the extent of 25 percent of his gross income from farming and may carry over any excess to subsequent years.

T.D. 6235, 5/31/57.

§ 1.175-7 Allocation of expenditures in certain circumstances.

Caution: The Treasury has not yet amended Reg § 1.175-7 to reflect changes made by P.L. 110-246.

(a) General rule. If at the time the taxpayer paid or incurred expenditures for the purpose of soil or water conservation, or for the prevention of erosion of land, it was reasonable to believe that such expenditures would directly and substantially benefit land of the taxpayer which does not qualify as "land used in farming," as defined in § 1.175-4, as well as land of the taxpayer which does so qualify, then, for purposes of section 175, only a part of the taxpayer's total expenditures is in respect of "land used in farming."

(b) Method of allocation. The part of expenditures allocable to "land used in farming" generally equals the amount which bears the same proportion to the total amount of such expenditures as the area of land of the taxpayer used in farming which it was reasonable to believe would be directly and substantially benefited as a result of the expenditures bears to the total area of land of the taxpayer which it was reasonable to believe would be so benefited. If it is established by clear and convincing evidence that, in the light of all the facts and circumstances, another method of allocation is more reasonable than the method provided in the preceding sentence, the taxpayer may allocate the expenditures under that other method. For purposes of this section, the term "land of the taxpayer" means land with respect to which the taxpayer has title, leasehold, or some other substantial interest.

(c) Examples. The provisions of this section may be illustrated by the following examples:

Example (1). A owns a 200-acre tract of land, 80 acres of which qualify as "land used in farming." A makes expenditures for the purpose of soil and water conservation which can reasonably be expected to directly and substantially benefit the entire 200-acre tract. In the absence of clear and convincing evidence that a different allocation is more reasonable, A may deduct 40 percent (80/200) of such expenditures under section 175. The same result would obtain if A had made the expenditures after newly acquiring the tract from a person who had used 80 of the 200 acres in farming immediately prior to A's acquisition.

Example (2). Assume the same facts as in example (1), except that A's expenditures for the purpose of soil and water conservation can reasonably be expected to directly and substantially benefit only the 80 acres which qualify as land used in farming; any benefit to the other 120 acres would be minor and incidental. A may deduct all of such expenditures under section 175.

Example (3). Assume the same facts as in example (1), except that A's expenditures for the purpose of soil and water conservation can reasonably be expected to directly and substantially benefit only the 120 acres which did not qualify as land used in farming. A may not deduct any of such expenditures under section 175. The same result would obtain even if A had leased the 200-acre tract to B in the expectation that B would farm the entire tract.

T.D. 7740, 11/21/80.

§ 1.177-1 Election to amortize trademark and trade name expenditures.

Caution: The Treasury has not yet amended Reg § 1.177-1 to reflect changes made by P.L. 99-514.

(a) In general. *(1)* Section 177 provides that a taxpayer may elect to treat any trademark or trade name expenditure (defined in section 177(b) and paragraph (b) of this section) paid or incurred during a taxable year beginning after December 31, 1955, as a deferred expense. Any expenditure so treated shall be allowed as a deduction ratably over the number of continuous months (not less than 60) selected by the taxpayer, beginning with the first month of the taxable year in which the expenditures is paid or incurred. The term "paid or incurred", as used in section 177 and this section, is to be construed according to the method of accounting used by the taxpayer in computing taxable income. See section 7701(a)(25). An election under section 177 is irrevocable insofar as it applies to a particular trademark or trade name expenditure, but separate elections may be made with respect to other trademark or trade name expenditures. See subparagraph (3) of this paragraph. See also paragraph (c) of this section for time and manner of making election.

(2) The number of continuous months selected by the taxpayer may be equal to or greater, but not less, than 60, but in any event the deduction must begin with the first month of the taxable year in which the expenditure is paid or incurred. The number of months selected by the taxpayer at the time he makes the election may not be subsequently changed but shall be adhered to in computing taxable income for the taxable year for which the election is made and all subsequent taxable years.

(3) Section 177 permits an election by the taxpayer for each separate trademark or trade name expenditure. Thus, a taxpayer who has several trademark or trade name expenditures in a taxable year may elect under section 177 with respect to some of such expenditures and not elect with respect to the other expenditures. Also, a taxpayer may choose different amortization periods for different trademark or trade name expenditures with respect to which he has made the election under section 177.

(4) All trademark and trade name expenditures are properly chargeable to capital account for purposes of section 1016(a)(1), relating to adjustments to basis of property, whether or not they are to be amortized under section 177. However, the trademark and trade name expenditures with respect to which the taxpayer has made an election under section 177 must be kept in a separate account in the taxpayer's books and records. See paragraph (c) of this section. See also section 1016(a)(16) and paragraph (m) of § 1.1016-5 for adjustments to basis of property for amounts allowed as deductions under section 177 and this section.

(b) Trademark and trade name expenditures defined. *(1)* The term "trademark and trade name expenditure", as used in section 177 and this section, means any expenditure which—

(i) Is directly connected with the acquisition, protection, expansion, registration (Federal, State, or foreign), or defense of a trademark or trade name;

(ii) Is chargeable to capital account; and

(iii) Is not part of the consideration or purchase price paid for a trademark, trade name, or a business (including goodwill) already in existence.

An expenditure which fails to meet one or more of these tests is not a trademark or trade name expenditure for purposes of section 177 and this section. Amounts paid in connection with the acquisition of an existing trademark or trade name may not be amortized under section 177 even though such amounts may be paid to protect or expand a previously owned trademark or trade name through purchase of a competitive trademark. Similarly, the provisions of section 177 and this section are not applicable to expenditures paid or incurred for an agreement to discontinue the use of a trademark or trade name (if the effect of the agreement is the purchase of a trademark or trade name) nor to expenditures paid or incurred in acquiring franchises or rights to the use of a trademark or trade name. Generally, section 177 will apply to expenditures such as legal fees and other costs in connection with the acquisition of a certificate of registration of a trademark from the United States or other government, artists' fees and similar expenses connected with the design of a distinctive mark for a product or service, litigation expenses connected with infringement proceedings, and costs in connection with the preparation and filing of an application for renewal of registration and continued use of a trademark.

(2) Expenditures for a trademark or trade name which has a determinable useful life and which would otherwise be depreciable under section 167 must be deferred and amortized under section 177 if an election under section 177 is made with respect to such expenditures.

(3) The following examples illustrate the application of section 177:

Example (1). X Corporation engages an artist to design a distinctive trademark for its product. At the same time it retains an attorney to prepare the papers necessary for registration of this trademark with the Federal Government. The fees of both the artist and the attorney may be amortized under section 177 over a period of not less than 60 continuous months.

Example (2). Y Corporation wishes to expand the market served by its product. It acquires a competing firm in a neighboring State. The contract of sale provides for a purchase price of $250,000 of which $225,000 shall constitute payment for physical assets and $25,000 for the trademark and goodwill. No part of the purchase price may be amortized under section 177.

Example (3). M Corporation brings suit against N Corporation for infringement of M's trademark. The costs of this litigation may be amortized under section 177.

(c) Time and manner of making election. *(1)* A taxpayer who elects to defer and amortize any trademark or trade name expenditure paid or incurred during a taxable year beginning after December 31, 1955, shall, within the time prescribed by law (including extensions thereof) for filing his income tax return for that year, attach to his income tax return a statement signifying his election under section 177 and setting forth the following:

(i) Name and address of the taxpayer, and the taxable year involved;

(ii) An identification of the character and amount of each expenditure to which the election applies and the number of continuous months (not less than 60) during which the expenditures are to be ratably deducted; and

(iii) A declaration by the taxpayer that he will make an accounting segregation on his books and records of the trademark and trade name expenditures for which the election has been made, sufficient to permit an identification of the character and amount of each such expenditure and the amortization period selected for each expenditure.

(2) The provisions of subparagraph (1) of this paragraph shall apply to income tax returns and statements required to be filed after May 4, 1960. Elections properly made in accordance with the provisions of Treasury Decision 6209, approved October 26, 1956 (21 F.R. 8319, C.B. 1956-2, 1370), continue in effect.

T.D. 6452, 2/3/60.

§ 1.178-1 Depreciation or amortization of improvements on leased property and cost of acquiring a lease.

Caution: The Treasury has not yet amended Reg § 1.178-1 to reflect changes made by P.L. 99-514.

(a) In general. Section 178 provides rules for determining the amount of the deduction allowable for any taxable year to a lessee for depreciation or amortization of improvements made on leased property and as amortization of the cost of acquiring a lease. For purposes of section 178 the term "depreciation" means the deduction allowable for exhaustion, wear and tear, or obsolescence under provisions of the Code such as section 167 or 611 and the regulations thereunder and the term "amortization" means the deduction allowable for amortization of buildings or other improvements made on leased property or for amortization of the cost of acquiring a lease under provisions of the Code such as section 162 or 212 and the regulations thereunder. The provisions of section 178 are applicable with respect to costs of acquiring a lease incurred, and improvements begun, after July 28, 1958, other than improvements which, on July 28, 1958, and at all times thereafter, the lessee was under a binding legal obligation to make.

(b) Determination of amount of deduction. *(1)* In determining the amount of the deduction allowable to a lessee (other than a lessee who is related to the lessor within the meaning of § 1.178-2) for any taxable year for depreciation or amortization of improvements made on leased property, or for amortization in respect of the cost of acquiring a lease, the term of the lease shall, except as provided in subparagraph (2) of this paragraph, be treated as including all periods for which the lease may be renewed, extended, or continued pursuant to an option or options exercisable by the lessee (whether or not specifically provided for in the lease) if—

(i) In the case of any building erected, or other improvements made, by the lessee on the leased property, the portion of the term of the lease (excluding all periods for which the lease may subsequently be renewed, extended, or continued pursuant to an option or options exercisable by the lessee) remaining upon the completion of such building or other improvements is less than 60 percent of the estimated useful life of such building or other improvements; or

(ii) In the case of any cost of acquiring the lease, less than 75 percent of such cost is attributable to the portion of the term of the lease (excluding all periods for which the lease may be renewed, extended, or continued pursuant to an option or options exercisable by the lessee) remaining on the date of its acquisition.

(2) The rules provided in subparagraph (1) of this paragraph shall not apply if the lessee establishes that, as of the close of the taxable year, it is more probable that the lease will not be renewed, extended, or continued than that the lease will be renewed, extended, or continued. In such case, the cost of improvements made on leased property or the cost of acquiring a lease shall be amortized over the remaining term of the lease without regard to any options exercisa-

ble by the lessee to renew, extend, or continue the lease. The probability test referred to in the first sentence of this paragraph shall be applicable to each option period to which the lease may be renewed, extended, or continued. The establishment by a lessee as of the close of the taxable year that it is more probable that the lease will not be renewed, extended, or continued will ordinarily be effective as of the close of such taxable year and any subsequent taxable year, and the deduction for amortization will be based on the term of the lease without regard to any periods for which the lease may be renewed, extended, or continued pursuant to an option or options exercisable by the lessee. However, in appropriate cases, if the facts as of the close of any subsequent taxable year indicate that it is more probable that the lease will be renewed, extended, or continued, the deduction for amortization (or depreciation) shall, beginning with the first day of such subsequent taxable year, be determined by including in the remaining term of the lease all periods for which it is more probable that the lease will be renewed, extended, or continued.

(3) If at any time the remaining term of the lease determined in accordance with section 178 and this section is equal to or of longer duration than the then estimated useful life of the improvements made on the leased property by the lessee, the cost of such improvements shall be depreciated over the estimated useful life of such improvements under the provisions of section 167 and the regulations thereunder.

(4) For purposes of section 178(a)(1) and this section, the date on which the building erected or other improvements made are completed is the date on which the building or improvements are usable, whether or not used.

(5) (i) For purposes of section 178(a)(2) and this section, the portion of the cost of acquiring a lease which is attributable to the term of the lease remaining on the date of its acquisition without regard to options exercisable by the lessee to renew, or continue the lease shall be determined on the basis of the facts and circumstances of each case. In some cases, it may be appropriate to determine such portion of the cost of acquiring a lease by applying the principles used to measure the present value of an annuity. Where that method is used, such portion shall be determined by multiplying the cost of the lease by a fraction, the numerator comprised of a factor representing the present value of an annually recurring savings of $1 per year for the period of the remaining term of the lease (without regard to options to renew, extend, or continue the lease) at an appropriate rate of interest (determined on the basis of all the facts and circumstances in each case), and the denominator comprised of a factor representing the present value of $1 per year for the period of the remaining term of the lease including the options to renew, extend, or continue the lease at an appropriate rate of interest.

(ii) The provisions of this subparagraph may be illustrated by the following example:

Example. Lessee A acquires a lease with respect to unimproved property at a cost of $100,000 at which time there are 21 years remaining in the original term of the lease with two renewal options of 21 years each. The lease provides for a uniform annual rental for the remaining term of the lease and the renewal periods. It has been determined that this is an appropriate case for the application of the principles used to measure the present value of an annuity. Assume that in this case the appropriate rate of interest is 5 percent. By applying the tables (Inwood) used to measure the present value of an annuity of $1 per year, the factor representing the present value of $1 per annum for 21 years at 5% is ascertained to be 12.821, and the factor representing the present value of $1 per annum for 63 years at 5% is 19.075. The portion of the cost of the lease ($100,000) attributable to the remaining term of the original lease (21 years) is 67.21% or $67,210 determined as follows:

$$\frac{12.821}{19.075} \text{ or } 67.21\%$$

(6) The provisions of this paragraph may be illustrated by the following examples:

Example (1). Lessee A constructs a building on land leased from lessor B. The construction is commenced on August 1, 1958, and is completed and placed in service on December 31, 1958, at which time A has 15 years remaining on his lease with an option to renew for an additional 20 years. Lessee A computes his taxable income on a calendar year basis. Lessee A was not, on July 28, 1958, under a binding legal obligation to erect the building. The building has an estimated useful life of 30 years. A is not related to B. Since the portion of the term of the lease (without regard to any renewals) remaining upon completion of the building (15 years) is less than 60 percent of the estimated useful life of the building (60 percent of 30 years, or 18 years), the term of the lease shall be treated as including the remaining portion of the original lease period and the renewal period, or 35 years. Since the estimated useful life of the building (30 years) is less than 35 years, the cost of the building shall, in accord with paragraph (b)(3) of this section, be depreciated under the provisions of section 167, over its estimated useful life. If, however, lessee A establishes, as of the close of the taxable year 1958, it is more probable that the lease will not be renewed than that it will be renewed, then in such case the remaining term of the lease shall be treated as including only the 15-year period remaining in the original lease. Since this is less than the estimated useful life of the building, the remaining cost of the building would be amortized over such 15-year period under the provisions of section 162 and the regulations thereunder.

Example (2). Assume the same facts as in example (1), except that A has 21 years remaining on his lease with an option to renew for an additional 10 years. Section 178(a) and paragraph (b)(1) of this section do not apply since the term of the lease remaining on the date of completion of the building (21 years) is not less than 60 percent of the estimated useful life of the building (60 percent of 30 years, or 18 years).

Example (3). Assume the same facts as in example (1), except that A has no renewal option until July 1, 1961, when lessor B grants A an option to renew the lease for a 10-year period. Because there is no option to renew the lease, the term of the lease is, for the taxable years 1959 and 1960 and for the first six months of the taxable year 1961, determined without regard to section 178(a). However, as of July 1, 1961, the date the renewal option is granted, section 178(a) and paragraph (b)(1) of this section become applicable since the portion of the term of the lease remaining upon completion of the building (15 years) was less than 60 percent of the estimated useful life of the building (60 percent of 30 years, or 18 years). As of July 1, 1961, the term of the lease shall be treated as including the remaining portion of the original lease period (12½ years) and the 10-year renewal period, or 22½ years, unless lessee A can establish that, as of the close of 1961, it is more probable that the lease will not be renewed than that it will be.

Example (4). On January 1, 1959, lessee A pays $10,000 to acquire a lease for 20 years with two options exercisable by him to renew for periods of 5 years each. Of the total

$10,000 cost to acquire the lease, $7,000 was paid for the original 20-year lease period and the balance of $3,000 was paid for the renewal options. Since the $7,000 cost of acquiring the initial lease is less than 75 percent of the $10,000 cost of the lease ($7,500), the term of the lease shall be treated as including the original lease period and the 2 renewal periods, or 30 years. However, if lessee A establishes that, as of the close of the taxable year 1959, it is more probable that the lease will not be renewed than that it will be renewed, the term of the lease shall be treated as including only the original lease period, or 20 years.

Example (5). Assume the same facts as in example (4), except that the portion of the total cost ($10,000) paid for the 20-year original lease period is $8,000. Since the $8,000 cost of acquiring the original lease is not less than 75 percent of the $10,000 cost of the lease ($7,500), section 178(a) and paragraph (b)(1) of this section do not apply.

(c) Application of section 178(a) where lessee gives notice to lessor of intention to exercise option. *(1)* If the lessee has given notice to the lessor of his intention to renew, extend, or continue a lease, the lessee shall, for purposes of applying the provisions of section 178(a) and paragraph (b)(1) of this section, take into account such renewal or extension in determining the portion of the term of the lease remaining upon the completion of the improvements or on the date of the acquisition of the lease.

(2) The application of the provisions of this paragraph may be illustrated by the following examples:

Example (1). Lessee A constructs a building on land leased from lessor B. The construction was commenced on September 1, 1958, and was completed and placed in service on December 31, 1958. Lessee A was not, on July 28, 1958, under a binding legal obligation to erect the building. A and B are not related. At the time the building was completed (December 31, 1958), lessee A had 3 years remaining on his lease with 2 options to renew for periods of 20 years each. The estimated useful life of the building is 50 years. Prior to completion of the building, lessee A gives notice to lessor B of his intention to exercise the first 20-year option. Therefore, the portion of the term of the lease remaining on January 1, 1959, shall be the 3 years remaining in the original lease period plus the 20-year renewal period, or 23 years. Since the term of the lease remaining upon completion of the building (23 years) is less than 60 percent of the estimated useful life of the building (60 percent of 50 years, or 30 years), the provisions of section 178(a) and paragraph (b)(1) of this section are applicable. Accordingly, the term of the lease shall be treated as including the aggregate of the remaining term of the original lease (23 years) and the second 20-year renewal period or 43 years, unless lessee A establishes that it is more probable that the lease will not be renewed, extended, or continued under the second 20-year option than that it will be so renewed, extended, or continued under such option. If this is established by lessee A, then the term of the lease shall be treated as including only the remaining portion of the original lease period and the first 20-year renewal period, or 23 years.

Example (2). Assume the same facts as in example (1), except that the estimated useful life of the building is 30 years. Since the term of the lease remaining upon completion of the building (23 years) is not less than 60 percent of the estimated life of the building (60 percent of 30 years, or 18 years), the provisions of section 178(a) and paragraph (b)(1) of this section do not apply.

Example (3). If in examples (1) and (2), the lessee failed to give notice of his intention to exercise the renewal option, the renewal period would not be taken into account in computing the percentage requirements under section 178(a) and paragraph (b)(1) of this section. Thus, unless lessee A establishes the required probability, the provisions of section 178(a) and paragraph (b)(1) of this section would apply in both examples since the term of the lease remaining upon completion of the building (3 years) is less than 60 percent of the estimated useful life of the building in either example (60 percent of 50 years, or 30 years; 60 percent of 30 years, or 18 years).

(d) Application of section 178 where lessee is related to lessor. *(1)* (i) If the lessee and lessor are related persons within the meaning of section 178(b)(2) and § 1.178-2 at any time during the taxable year, the lease shall be treated as including a period of not less duration than the remaining estimated useful life of improvements made by the lessee on leased property for purposes of determining the amount of deduction allowable to the lessee for such taxable year for depreciation or amortization in respect of any building erected or other improvements made on leased property. If the lessee and lessor cease to be related persons during any taxable year, then for the immediately following and subsequent taxable years during which they continue to be unrelated, the amount allowable to the lessee as a deduction shall be determined without reference to section 178(b) and in accordance with section 178(a) or section 178(c), whichever is applicable.

(ii) Although the related lessee and lessor rule of section 178(b) and § 1.178-2 does not apply in determining the period over which the cost of acquiring a lease may be amortized, the relationship between a lessee and lessor will be a significant factor in applying section 178 (a) and (c) in cases in which the lease may be renewed, extended, or continued pursuant to an option or options exercisable by the lessee.

(2) The application of the provisions of this paragraph may be illustrated by the following examples:

Example (1). Lessee A constructs a building on land leased from lessor B. The construction was commenced on August 1, 1958, and was completed and put in service on December 31, 1958. Lessee A was not on July 28, 1958, under a binding legal obligation to erect the building. On the completion date of the building, lessee A had 20 years remaining in his original lease period with an option to renew for an additional 20 years. The building has an estimated useful life of 50 years. During the taxable years 1959 and 1960, A and B are related persons within the meaning of section 178(b)(2) and § 1.178-2, but they are not related persons at any time during the taxable year 1961 or during any subsequent taxable year. Since A and B are related persons during the taxable years 1959 and 1960, the term of the lease shall, for each of those years, be treated as 50 years. Section 178(a) and paragraph (b)(1) of this section become applicable in the taxable year 1961 since A and B are not related persons at any time during that year and because the portion of the original lease period remaining at the time the building was completed (20 years) is less than 60 percent of the estimated useful life of the building (60 percent of 50 years, or 30 years). Thus, the term of the lease shall, beginning on January 1, 1961, be treated as including the remaining portion of the original lease period (18 years) and the renewal period (20 years), or 38 years, unless lessee A can establish that, as of the close of the taxable year 1961 or any subsequent taxable year, it is more probable that the lease will not be renewed than that it will be renewed.

Example (2). Assume the same facts as in example (1), except that the estimated useful life of the building is 30 years. During the taxable years 1959 and 1960, the term of the lease shall be treated as 30 years. For the taxable year 1961, however, neither section 178(a) nor section 178(b) apply since the percentage requirement of section 178(a) and paragraph (b) of this section are not satisfied and A and B are not related persons within the meaning of section 178(b)(2) and § 1.178-2.

T.D. 6520, 12/23/60.

PAR. 3. Section 1.178-1 is amended as follows:

1. Paragraph (a) is amended by removing the term "section 167 or 611" and inserting "section 167, 168, or 611" in its place.

2. Paragraph (b)(1)(i) and (3) is amended by removing the term "estimated useful life" in each of the three places it appears and removing the term "section 167" in the one place it appears and by inserting "estimated useful life or, in the case of recovery property (as defined in section 168), the recovery period (including, where applicable, any optional recovery period under section 168(b)(3) or (f)(2)(C))" and by inserting "section 167 or 168", respectively, in its place.

3. Paragraph (b)(2) is amended by removing the term "(or depreciation)" and by inserting "(or depreciation under section 167 or accelerated cost recovery under section 168)" in lieu thereof.

4. Paragraph (d)(1)(i) is amended by removing the term "remaining estimated useful life" and by inserting "remaining estimated useful life or, in the case of recovery property (as defined in section 168), the recovery period (including, where applicable, any optional recovery period under section 168(b)(3) or (f)(2)(C)) in its place.

5. Paragraph (b)(6) is amended by adding two examples immediately after example (5), which read as follows:

Proposed § 1.178-1 Depreciation or amortization of improvements on leased property and cost of acquiring a lease. [*For Preamble, see ¶ 150,941*]

* * * * *

(b) Determination of amount of deduction. * * *

(6) * * *

Example (6). Lessee C, a calendar year taxpayer, constructs a building on land leased from lessor D. The construction is completed and the building is placed in service on January 1, 1984, at which time C has 8 years remaining on the lease with no options to renew. On January 1, 1988, D grants C an option to renew the lease for a 10-year period. As of January 1, 1988, the date the renewal option is granted, section 178(a) and paragraph (b)(1) of this section become applicable, since the portion of the term of the lease remaining upon completion of the building (8 years) is less than 60 percent of any recovery period applicable to the building (60 percent of the shortest recovery period (15 years) is 9 years). As of January 1, 1988, the term of the lease shall be treated as including the remaining portion of the original lease (4 years) and the 10-year renewal, or 14 years, unless C can establish that, as of the close of 1988, it is more probable that the lease will not be renewed than that it will be. In such case, since the term of the lease as of January 1, 1988 (14 years), is less than the ACRS recovery period, a deduction is not allowed under section 168 with respect to such building.

Example (7). The facts are the same as in example (6), except that the option to renew is for 15 years. If, as of the close of 1988, C cannot establish that it is more probable that the lease will not be renewed than that it will be, the term of the lease as of January 1, 1988, will be 19 years. Since the term of the lease would be longer than the ACRS recovery period (unless a 35- or 45-year optional recovery period were desired), the provisions of section 168 will be applicable with respect to this building. For purposes of section 168, C is considered as having placed the building in service on January 1, 1988, with a 15-year recovery period extending from that time. C's unadjusted basis for purposes of section 168 is the adjusted basis in the building as of January 1, 1988.

§ 1.178-2 Related lessee and lessor.

Caution: The Treasury has not yet amended Reg § 1.178-2 to reflect changes made by P.L. 99-514.

(a) For purposes of section 178 and § 1.178-1, a lessor and lessee shall be considered to be related persons if—

(1) The lessor and lessee are members of an affiliated group, as defined in section 1504 and the regulations thereunder; or

(2) The relationship between the lessor and lessee is one described in section 267(b), except that the phrase "80 percent or more" shall be substituted for the phrase "more than 50 percent" wherever such phrase appears in section 267(b).

(b) In the application of section 267(b) for purposes of section 178, the rules provided in section 267(c) shall apply, except that the family of an individual shall include only his spouse, ancestors, and lineal descendants. Thus, if the lessee is the brother or sister of the lessor, the lessee and lessor will not be considered to be related persons for purposes of section 178 and § 1.178-1. If the lessor leases property to a corporation of which he owns 80 percent or more in value of the outstanding stock, the lessor and lessee shall be considered to be related persons. On the other hand, if the lessor leases property to a corporation of which he owns less than 80 percent in value of the outstanding stock and his brother owns the remaining stock, the lessor and lessee will not be considered to be related persons.

(c) If a relationship described in section 267(b) exists independently of family status, the brother-sister exception does not apply. For example, if the lessor leases property to the fiduciary of a trust of which he is the grantor, the lessor and lessee will be considered to be related persons for purposes of section 178. This result obtains whether or not the fiduciary is the brother or sister of the lessor since the disqualifying relationship exists because of the grantor-fiduciary status and not because of family status.

T.D. 6520, 12/23/60.

§ 1.178-3 Reasonable certainty test.

Caution: The Treasury has not yet amended Reg § 1.178-3 to reflect changes made by P.L. 99-514.

(a) In any case in which neither section 178(a) nor (b) applies, the determination as to the amount of the deduction allowable to a lessee for any taxable year for depreciation or amortization in respect of any building erected, or other improvements made, on leased property, or in respect of any cost of acquiring a lease, shall be made with reference to the original term of the lease (excluding any period for which the lease may subsequently be renewed, extended, or continued pursuant to an option exercisable by the lessee) unless the lease has been renewed, extended, or continued, or the facts show with reasonable certainty that the lease will be renewed, extended, or continued. In a case in which the facts show with reasonable certainty that the lease will be renewed, extended, or continued, the term of the lease shall, beginning with the taxable year in which such reasonable certainty is shown, be treated as including the period or periods for which it is reasonably certain that the lease will be renewed, extended, or continued. If the lessee has given notice to the lessor of his intention to renew, extend, or continue a lease, the lease shall be considered as renewed, extended, or continued for the periods specified in the notice. See paragraph (c) of § 1.178-1.

(b) The reasonable certainty test is applicable to each option to which the lease is subject. Thus, in a case of two successive options, the facts in a particular taxable year may show with reasonable certainty that the lease will be renewed pursuant to an exercise of only the first option; and, beginning with such year, the term of the lease will be treated as including the first option, but not the second. If in a subsequent taxable year the facts show with reasonable certainty that the second option will also be exercised, the term of the lease shall, beginning with such subsequent taxable year, be treated as including both options. Although the related lessee and lessor rule of section 178(b) and paragraph (d) of § 1.178-1 does not apply in determining the period over which the cost of acquiring a lease may be amortized, the relationship between the lessee and lessor will be a significant factor in determining whether the "reasonable certainty" rule of section 178(c) and this section applies.

(c) The application of the provisions of this section may be illustrated by the following examples:

Example (1). Corporation A leases land from lessor B for a period of 30 years beginning with January 1, 1958. Corporation A and lessor B are not related persons. The lease provides that Corporation A will have two renewal options of 5 years each at the same annual rental as specified in the lease for the initial 30 years. Corporation A constructs a factory building on the leased land at a cost of $100,000. Corporation A was not, on July 28, 1958, under a binding legal obligation to erect the building. The construction was commenced on August 1, 1958, and was completed and placed in service on December 31, 1958. On January 1, 1959, Corporation A has 29 years remaining in the initial term of the lease. The estimated useful life of the building on January 1, 1959, is 40 years. The location of the leased property is particularly suitable for Corporation A's business and the annual rental of the property is lower than A would have to pay for other suitable property. No factors are present which establish that these conditions will not continue to exist beyond the initial term of the lease. Since the period remaining in the initial term of the lease on January 1, 1959 (29 years) is not less than 60 percent of the estimated useful life of the building (60 percent of 40 years, or 24 years), the provisions of section 178(a) and paragraph (b)(1) of § 1.178-1 do not apply, and since Corporation A and lessor B are not related, section 178(b) and paragraph (d) of § 1.178-1 do not apply. However, since the facts show with reasonable certainty that Corporation A will renew the lease for the period of the two options (10 years), the cost of the building shall be amortized over the term of the lease, including the two renewal options, or 39 years.

Example (2). Assume the same facts as in example (1), except that a term of 30 years is the longest period that lessor B is willing to lease the unimproved property; that there was no agreement that Corporation A will have any renewal options; and that any other location would be as suitable for Corporation A's business as the leased property. Since the facts do not show with reasonable certainty that the initial term of the lease will be renewed, extended, or continued, Corporation A shall amortize the cost of the building over the remaining term of the lease, or 29 years.

T.D. 6520, 12/23/60.

---

§ 1.179-0 Table of contents for section 179 expensing rules.

This section lists captioned paragraphs contained in §§ 1.179-1 through 1.179-6.

§ 1.179-1 Election to expense certain depreciable assets.

(a) In general.

(b) Cost subject to expense.

(c) Proration not required.

(1) In general.

(2) Example.

(d) Partial business use.

(1) In general.

(2) Example.

(3) Additional rules that may apply.

(e) Change in use; recapture.

(1) In general.

(2) Predominant use.

(3) Basis; application with section 1245.

(4) Carryover of disallowed deduction.

(5) Example.

(f) Basis.

(1) In general.

(2) Special rules for partnerships and S corporations.

(3) Special rules with respect to trusts and estates which are partners or S corporation shareholders.

(g) Disallowance of the section 38 credit.

(h) Partnerships and S corporations.

(1) In general.

(2) Example.

(i) Leasing of section 179 property.

(1) In general.

(2) Noncorporate lessor.

(j) Application of sections 263 and 263A.

(k) Cross references.

§ 1.179-2 Limitations on amount subject to section 179 election.

(a) In general.

(b) Dollar limitation.

(1) In general.

(2) Excess section 179 property.

(3) Application to partnerships.

(i) In general.

(ii) Example.

(iii) Partner's share of section 179 expenses.

(iv) Taxable year.

(v) Example.

(4) S corporations.

(5) Joint returns.

(i) In general.
(ii) Joint returns filed after separate returns.
(iii) Example.
(6) Married individuals filing separately.
(i) In general.
(ii) Example.
(7) Component members of a controlled group.
(i) In general.
(ii) Statement to be filed.
(iii) Revocation.
(c) Taxable income limitation.
(1) In general.
(2) Application to partnerships and partners.
(i) In general.
(ii) Taxable year.
(iii) Example.
(iv) Taxable income of a partnership.
(v) Partner's share of partnership taxable income.
(3) S corporations and S corporation shareholders.
(i) In general.
(ii) Taxable income of an S corporation.
(iii) Shareholder's share of S corporation taxable income.
(4) Taxable income of a corporation other than an S corporation.
(5) Ordering rule for certain circular problems.
(i) In general.
(ii) Example.
(6) Active conduct by the taxpayer of a trade or business.
(i) Trade or business.
(ii) Active conduct.
(iii) Example.
(iv) Employees.
(7) Joint returns.
(i) In general.
(ii) Joint returns filed after separate returns.
(8) Married individuals filing separately.
(d) Examples.
§ 1.179-3 Carryover of disallowed deduction.
(a) In general.
(b) Deduction of carryover of disallowed deduction.
(1) In general.
(2) Cross references.
(c) Unused section 179 expense allowance.
(d) Example.
(e) Recordkeeping requirement and ordering rule.
(f) Dispositions and other transfers of section 179 property.
(1) In general.
(2) Recapture under section 179(d) (10).
(g) Special rules for partnerships and S corporations.
(1) In general.
(2) Basis adjustment.
(3) Dispositions and other transfers of section 179 property by a partnership or an S corporation.
(4) Example.
(h) Special rules for partners and S corporation shareholders.
(1) In general.
(2) Dispositions and other transfers of a partner's interest in a partnership or a shareholder's interest in an S corporation.
(3) Examples.
§ 1.179-4 Definitions.
(a) Section 179 property.
(b) Section 38 property.
(c) Purchase.
(d) Cost.
(e) Placed in service.
(f) Controlled group of corporations and component member of controlled group.
§ 1.179-5 Time and manner of making election.
(a) Election.
(b) Revocation.
(c) Section 179 property placed in service by the taxpayer in a taxable year beginning after 2002 and before 2008.
(d) Election or revocation must not be made in any other manner.
§ 1.179-6 Effective dates.
(a) In general.
(b) Section 179 property placed in service by the taxpayer in a taxable year beginning after 2002 and before 2008.
(c) Application of § 1.179-5(d).

T.D. 8455, 12/23/92, amend T.D. 9146, 8/3/2004, T.D. 9209, 7/12/2005.

§ 1.179-1 Election to expense certain depreciable assets.

Caution: The Treasury has not yet amended Reg § 1.179-1 to reflect changes made by P.L. 109-135.

(a) In general. Section 179(a) allows a taxpayer to elect to expense the cost (as defined in § 1.179-4(d)), or a portion of the cost, of section 179 property (as defined in § 1.179-4(a)) for the taxable year in which the property is placed in service (as defined in § 1.179-4(e)). The election is not available for trusts, estates, and certain noncorporate lessors. See paragraph (i)(2) of this section for rules concerning noncorporate lessors. However, section 179(b) provides certain limitations on the amount that a taxpayer may elect to expense in any one taxable year. See §§ 1.179-2 and 1.179-3 for rules relating to the dollar and taxable income limitations and the carryover of disallowed deduction rules. For rules describing the time and manner of making an election under section 179, see § 1.179-5. For the effective date, see § 1.179-6.

(b) Cost subject to expense. The expense deduction under section 179 is allowed for the entire cost or a portion of the cost of one or more items of section 179 property. This expense deduction is subject to the limitations of section 179(b) and § 1.179-2. The taxpayer may select the properties that are subject to the election as well as the portion of each property's cost to expense.

(c) Proration not required. *(1) In general.* The expense deduction under section 179 is determined without any proration based on—

(i) The period of time the section 179 property has been in service during the taxable year; or

(ii) The length of the taxable year in which the property is placed in service.

(2) Example. The following example illustrates the provisions of paragraph (c)(1) of this section.

Example. On December 1, 1991, X, a calendar-year corporation, purchases and places in service section 179 property costing $20,000. For the taxable year ending December 31, 1991, X may elect to claim a section 179 expense deduction on the property (subject to the limitations imposed under section 179(b)) without proration of its cost for the number of days in 1991 during which the property was in service.

(d) Partial business use. *(1) In general.* If a taxpayer uses section 179 property for trade or business as well as other purposes, the portion of the cost of the property attributable to the trade or business use is eligible for expensing under section 179 provided that more than 50 percent of the property's use in the taxable year is for trade or business purposes. The limitations of section 179(b) and § 1.179-2 are applied to the portion of the cost attributable to the trade or business use.

(2) Example. The following example illustrates the provisions of paragraph (d)(1) of this section.

Example. A purchases section 179 property costing $10,000 in 1991 for which 80 percent of its use will be in A's trade or business. The cost of the property adjusted to reflect the business use of the property is $8,000 (80 percent × $10,000). Thus, A may elect to expense up to $8,000 of the cost of the property (subject to the limitations imposed under section 179(b) and § 1.179-2).

(3) Additional rules that may apply. If a section 179 election is made for "listed property" within the meaning of section 280F(d)(4) and there is personal use of the property, section 280F(d)(1), which provides rules that coordinate section 179 with the section 280F limitation on the amount of depreciation, may apply. If section 179 property is no longer predominantly used in the taxpayer's trade or business, paragraphs (e)(1) through (4) of this section, relating to recapture of the section 179 deduction, may apply.

(e) Change in use; recapture. *(1) In general.* If a taxpayer's section 179 property is not used predominantly in a trade or business of the taxpayer at any time before the end of the property's recovery period, the taxpayer must recapture in the taxable year in which the section 179 property is not used predominantly in a trade or business any benefit derived from expensing such property. The benefit derived from expensing the property is equal to the excess of the amount expensed under this section over the total amount that would have been allowable for prior taxable years and the taxable year of recapture as a deduction under section 168 (had section 179 not been elected) for the portion of the cost of the property to which the expensing relates (regardless of whether such excess reduced the taxpayer's tax liability). For purposes of the preceding sentence (i) the "amount expensed under this section" shall not include any amount that was not allowed as a deduction to a taxpayer because the taxpayer's aggregate amount of allowable section 179 expenses exceeded the section 179(b) dollar limitation, and (ii) in the case of an individual who does not elect to itemize deductions under section 63(g) in the taxable year of recapture, the amount allowable as a deduction under section 168 in the taxable year of recapture shall be determined by treating property used in the production of income other than rents or royalties as being property used for personal purposes. The amount to be recaptured shall be treated as ordinary income for the taxable year in which the property is no longer used predominantly in a trade or business of the taxpayer. For taxable years following the year of recapture, the taxpayer's deductions under section 1688(a) shall be determined as if no section 179 election with respect to the property had been made. However, see section 280F(d)(1) relating to the coordination of section 179 with the limitation on the amount of depreciation for luxury automobiles and where certain property is used for personal purposes. If the recapture rules of both section 280F(b)(2) and this paragraph (e)(1) apply to an item of section 179 property, the amount of recapture for such property shall be determined only under the rules of section 280F(b)(2).

(2) Predominant use. Property will be treated as not used predominantly in a trade or business of the taxpayer if 50 percent or more of the use of such property during any taxable year within the recapture period is for a use other than in a trade or business of the taxpayer. If during any taxable year of the recapture period the taxpayer disposes of the property (other than in a disposition to which section 1245(a) applies) or ceases to use the property in a trade or business in a manner that had the taxpayer claimed a credit under section 38 for such property such disposition or cessation in use would cause recapture under section 47, the property will be treated as not used in a trade or business of the taxpayer. However, for purposes of applying the recapture rules of section 47 pursuant to the preceding sentence, converting the use of the property from use in trade or business to use in the production of income will be treated as a conversion to personal use.

(3) Basis; application with section 1245. The basis of property with respect to which there is recapture under paragraph (e)(1) of this section shall be increased immediately before the event resulting in such recapture by the amount recaptured. If section 1245(a) applies to a disposition of property, there is no recapture under paragraph (e)(1) of this section.

(4) Carryover of disallowed deduction. See § 1.179-3 for rules on applying the recapture provisions of this paragraph (e) when a taxpayer has a carryover of disallowed deduction.

(5) Example. The following example illustrates the provisions of paragraphs (e)(1) through (e)(4) of this section.

Example. A, a calendar-year taxpayer, purchases and places in service on January 1, 1991, section 179 property costing $15,000. The property is 5-year property for section 168 purposes and is the only item of depreciable property placed in service by A during 1991. A properly elects to expense $10,000 of the cost and elects under section 168(b)(5) to depreciate the remaining cost under the straight-line method. On January 1, 1992, A converts the property from use in A's business to use for the production of income, and A uses the property in the latter capacity for the entire year. A elects to itemize deductions for 1992. Because the property was predominantly used in A's trade or business in 1992, A must recapture any benefit derived from expensing the property under section 179. Had A not elected to expense the $10,000 in 1991, A would have been entitled to deduct, under section 168, 10 percent of the $10,000 in 1991, and 20 percent of the $10,000 in 1992. Therefore, A must include $7,000 in ordinary income for the 1992 taxable year, the excess of $10,000 (the section 179 expense amount) over $3,000 (30 percent of $10,000).

(f) Basis. *(1) In general.* A taxpayer who elects to expense under section 179 must reduce the depreciable basis of the section 179 property by the amount of the section 179 expense deduction.

(2) Special rules for partnerships and S corporations. Generally, the basis of a partnership or S corporation's section 179 property must be reduced to reflect the amount of section 179 expense elected by the partnership or S corporation. This reduction must be made in the basis of partnership or S corporation property even if the limitations of section 179(b) and § 1.179-2 prevent a partner in a partnership or a shareholder in an S corporation from deducting all or a portion of the amount of the section 179 expense allocated by the partnership or S corporation. See § 1.179-3 for rules on applying the basis provisions of this paragraph (f) when a person has a carryover of disallowed deduction.

(3) Special rules with respect to trusts and estates which are partners or S corporation shareholders. Since the section 179 election is not available for trusts or estates, a partner or S corporation shareholder that is a trust or estate may not deduct its allocable share of the section 179 expense elected by the partnership or S corporation. The partnership or S corporation's basis in section 179 property shall not be reduced to reflect any portion of the section 179 expense that is allocable to the trust or estate. Accordingly, the partnership or S corporation may claim a depreciation deduction under section 168 or a section 38 credit (if available) with respect to any depreciable basis resulting from the trust or estate's inability to claim its allocable portion of the section 179 expense.

(g) Disallowance of the section 38 credit. If a taxpayer elects to expense under section 179, no section 38 credit is allowable for the portion of the cost expensed. In addition, no section 38 credit shall be allowed under section 48(d) to a lessee of property for the portion of the cost of the property that the lessor expensed under section 179.

(h) Partnerships and S corporations. *(1) In general.* In the case of property purchased and placed in service by a partnership or an S corporation, the determination of whether the property is section 179 property is made at the partnership or S corporation level. The election to expense the cost of section 179 property is made by the partnership or the S corporation. See sections 703(b), 1363(c), 6221, 6231(a)(3), 6241, and 6245.

(2) Example. The following example illustrates the provisions of paragraph (h)(1) of this section.

Example. A owns certain residential rental property as an investment. A and others form ABC partnership whose function is to rent and manage such property. A and ABC partnership file their income tax returns on a calendar-year basis. In 1991, ABC partnership purchases and places in service office furniture costing $20,000 to be used in the active conduct of ABC's business. Although the office furniture is used with respect to an investment activity of A, the furniture is being used in the active conduct of ABC's trade or business. Therefore, because the determination of whether property is section 179 property is made at the partnership level, the office furniture is section 179 property and ABC may elect to expense a portion of its cost under section 179.

(i) Leasing of section 179 property. *(1) In general.* A lessor of section 179 property who is treated as the owner of the property for Federal tax purposes will be entitled to the section 179 expense deduction if the requirements of section 179 and the regulations thereunder are met. These requirements will not be met if the lessor merely holds the property for the production of income. For certain leases entered into prior to January 1, 1984, the safe harbor provisions of section 168(f)(8) apply in determining whether an agreement is treated as a lease for Federal tax purposes.

(2) Noncorporate lessor. In determining the class of taxpayers (other than an estate or trust) for which section 179 is applicable, section 179(d)(5) provides that if a taxpayer is a noncorporate lessor (i.e., a person who is not a corporation and is a lessor), the taxpayer shall not be entitled to claim a section 179 expense for section 179 property purchased and leased by the taxpayer unless the taxpayer has satisfied all of the requirements of sections 179(d)(5)(A) or (B).

(j) Application of sections 263 and 263A. Under section 263(a)(1)(G), expenditures for which a deduction is allowed under section 179 and this section are excluded from capitalization under section 263(a). Under this paragraph (j), amounts allowed as a deduction under section 179 and this section are excluded from the application of the uniform capitalization rules of section 263A.

(k) Cross references. See section 453(i) and the regulations thereunder with respect to installment sales of section 179 property. See section 1033(g)(3) and the regulations thereunder relating to condemnation of outdoor advertising displays. See section 1245(a) and the regulations thereunder with respect to recapture rules for section 179 property.

T.D. 6507, 12/1/60, amend T.D. 6712, 3/23/64, T.D. 7116, 5/17/71, T.D. 7137, 8/10/71, T.D. 8121, 1/5/87, T.D. 8455, 12/23/92.

§ 1.179-2 Limitations on amount subject to section 179 election.

Caution: The Treasury has not yet amended Reg § 1.179-2 to reflect changes made by P.L. 110-28, P.L. 109-222, P.L. 104-188, P.L. 103-66.

(a) In general. Sections 179(b)(1) and (2) limit the aggregate cost of section 179 property that a taxpayer may elect to expense under section 179 for any one taxable year (dollar limitation). See paragraph (b) of this section. Section 179(b)(3)(A) limits the aggregate cost of section 179 property that a taxpayer may deduct in any taxable year (taxable income limitation). See paragraph (c) of this section. Any cost that is elected to be expensed but that is not currently deductible because of the taxable income limitation may be carried forward to the next taxable year (carryover of disallowed deduction). See § 1.179-3 for rules relating to carryovers of disallowed deductions. See also sections 280F(a), (b), and (d)(1) relating to the coordination of section 179 with the limitations on the amount of depreciation for luxury automobiles and other listed property. The dollar and taxable income limitations apply to each taxpayer and not to each trade or business in which the taxpayer has an interest.

(b) Dollar limitation. *(1) In general.* The aggregate cost of section 179 property that a taxpayer may elect to expense under section 179 for any taxable year beginning in 2003 and thereafter is $25,000 ($100,000 in the case of taxable years beginning after 2002 and before 2008 under section 179(b)(1), indexed annually for inflation under section 179(b)(5) for taxable years beginning after 2003 and before 2008), reduced (but not below zero) by the amount of any excess section 179 property (described in paragraph (b)(2) of this section) placed in service during the taxable year.

(2) Excess section 179 property. The amount of any excess section 179 property for a taxable year equals the excess (if any) of—

(i) The cost of section 179 property placed in service by the taxpayer in the taxable year; over

(ii) $200,000 ($400,000 in the case of taxable years beginning after 2002 and before 2008 under section 179(b)(2), indexed annually for inflation under section 179(b)(5) for taxable years beginning after 2003 and before 2008).

(3) Application to partnerships. (i) In general. The dollar limitation of this paragraph (b) applies to the partnership as well as to each partner. In applying the dollar limitation to a taxpayer that is a partner in one or more partnerships, the partner's share of section 179 expenses allocated to the partner from each partnership is aggregated with any nonpartnership section 179 expenses of the taxpayer for the taxable year. However, in determining the excess section 179 property placed in service by a partner in a taxable year, the cost of section 179 property placed in service by the partnership is not attributed to any partner.

(ii) Example. The following example illustrates the provisions of paragraph (b)(3)(i) of this section.

Example. Example. During 1991, CD, a calendar-year partnership, purchases and places in service section 179 property costing $150,000 and elects under section 179(c) and § 1.179-5 to expense $10,000 of the cost of that property. CD properly allocates to C, a calendar-year taxpayer and a partner in CD, $5,000 of section 179 expenses (C's distributive share of CD's section 179 expenses for 1991). In applying the dollar limitation to C for 1991, C must include the $5,000 of section 179 expenses allocated from CD. However, in determining the amount of any excess section 179 property C placed in service during 1991, C does not include any of the cost of section 179 property placed in service by CD, including the $5,000 of cost represented by the $5,000 of section 179 expenses allocated to C by the partnership.

(iii) Partner's share of section 179 expenses. Section 704 and the regulations thereunder govern the determination of a partner's share of a partnership's section 179 expenses for any taxable year. However, no allocation among partners of the section 179 expenses may be modified after the due date of the partnership return (without regard to extensions of time) for the taxable year for which the election under section 179 is made.

(iv) Taxable year. If the taxable years of a partner and the partnership do not coincide, then for purposes of section 179, the amount of the partnership's section 179 expenses attributable to a partner for a taxable year is determined under section 706 and the regulations thereunder (generally the partner's distributive share of partnership section 179 expenses for the partnership year that ends with or within the partner's taxable year).

(v) Example. The following example illustrates the provisions of paragraph (b)(3)(iv) of this section.

Example. AB partnership has a taxable year ending January 31. A, a partner of AB, has a taxable year ending December 31. AB purchases and places in service section 179 property on March 10, 1991, and elects to expense a portion of the cost of that property under section 179. Under section 706 and § 1.706-1(a)(1), A will be unable to claim A's distributive share of any of AB's section 179 expenses attributable to the property placed in service on March 10, 1991, until A's taxable year ending December 31, 1992.

(4) S Corporations. Rules similar to those contained in paragraph (b)(3) of this section apply in the case of S corporations (as defined in section 1361(a)) and their shareholders. Each shareholder's share of the section 179 expenses of an S corporation is determined under section 1366.

(5) Joint returns. (i) In general. A husband and wife who file a joint income tax return under section 6013(a) are treated as one taxpayer in determining the amount of the dollar limitation under paragraph (b)(1) of this section, regardless of which spouse purchased the property or placed it in service.

(ii) Joint returns filed after separate returns. In the case of a husband and wife who elect under section 6013(b) to file a joint income tax return for a taxable year after the time prescribed by law for filing the return for such taxable year has expired, the dollar limitation under paragraph (b)(1) of this section is the lesser of—

(A) The dollar limitation (as determined under paragraph (b)(5)(i) of this section); or

(B) The aggregate cost of section 179 property elected to be expensed by the husband and wife on their separate returns.

(iii) Example. The following example illustrates the provisions of paragraph (b)(5)(ii) of this section.

Example. During 1991, Mr. and Mrs. B, both calendar-year taxpayers, purchase and place in service section 179 property costing $100,000. On their separate returns for 1991, Mr. B elects to expense $3,000 of section 179 property as an expense and Mrs. B elects to expense $4,000. After the due date of the return they elect under section 6013(b) to file a joint income tax return for 1991. The dollar limitation for their joint income tax return is $7,000, the lesser of the dollar limitation ($10,000) or the aggregate cost elected to be expensed under section 179 on their separate returns ($3,000 elected by Mr. B plus $4,000 elected by Mrs. B, or $7,000).

(6) Married individuals filing separately. (i) In general. In the case of an individual who is married but files a separate income tax return for a taxable year, the dollar limitation of this paragraph (b) for such taxable year is the amount that would be determined under paragraph (b)(5)(i) of this section if the individual filed a joint income tax return under section 6013(a) multiplied by either the percentage elected by the individual under this paragraph (b)(6) or 50 percent. The election in the preceding sentence is made in accordance with the requirements of section 179(c) and § 1.179-5. However, the amount determined under paragraph (b)(5)(i) of this section must be multiplied by 50 percent if either the individual or the individual's spouse does not elect a percentage under this paragraph (b)(6) or the sum of the percentages elected by the individual and the individual's spouse does not equal 100 percent. For purposes of this paragraph (b)(6), marital status is determined under section 7703 and the regulations thereunder.

(ii) Example. The following example illustrates the provisions of paragraph (b)(6)(i) of this section.

Example. Mr. and Mrs. D, both calendar-year taxpayers, file separate income tax returns for 1991. During 1991, Mr. D places $195,000 of section 179 property in service and Mrs. D places $9,000 of section 179 property in service. Neither of them elects a percentage under paragraph (b)(6)(i) of this section. The 1991 dollar limitation for both Mr. D and Mrs. D is determined by multiplying by 50 percent the dollar limitation that would apply had they filed a joint income tax return. Had Mr. and Mrs. D filed a joint return for 1991, the dollar limitation would have been $6,000, $10,000 reduced by the excess section 179 property they placed in service during 1991 ($195,000 placed in service by Mr. D plus $9,000 placed in service by Mrs. D less $200,000, or

$4,000). Thus, the 1991 dollar limitation for Mr. and Mrs. D is $3,000 each ($6,000 multiplied by 50 percent).

(7) Component members of a controlled group. (i) In general. Component members of a controlled group (as defined in § 1.179-4(f)) on a December 31 are treated as one taxpayer in applying the dollar limitation of sections 179(b)(1) and (2) of this paragraph (b). The expense deduction may be taken by any one component member or allocated (for the taxable year of each member that includes that December 31) among the several members in any manner. Any allocation of the expense deduction must be pursuant to an allocation by the common parent corporation if a consolidated return is filed for all component members of the group, or in accordance with an agreement entered into by the members of the group if separate returns are filed. If a consolidated return is filed by some component members of the group and separate returns are filed by other component members, the common parent of the group filing the consolidated return must enter into an agreement with those members that do not join in filing the consolidated return allocating the amount between the group filing the consolidated return and the other component members of the controlled group that do not join in filing the consolidated return. The amount of the expense allocated to any component member, however, may not exceed the cost of section 179 property actually purchased and placed in service by the member in the taxable year. If the component members have different taxable years, the term "taxable year" in sections 179(b)(1) and (2) means the taxable year of the member whose taxable year begins on the earliest date.

(ii) Statement to be filed. If a consolidated return is filed, the common parent corporation must file a separate statement attached to the income tax return on which the election is made to claim an expense deduction under section 179. See § 1.179-5. If separate returns are filed by some or all component members of the group, each component member not included in a consolidated return must file a separate statement attached to the income tax return on which an election is made to claim a deduction under section 179. The statement must include the name, address, employer identification number, and the taxable year of each component member of the controlled group, a copy of the allocation agreement signed by persons duly authorized to act on behalf of the component members, and a description of the manner in which the deduction under section 179 has been divided among the component members.

(iii) Revocation. If a consolidated return is filed for all component members of the group, an allocation among such members of the expense deduction under section 179 may not be revoked after the due date of the return (including extensions of time) of the common parent corporation for the taxable year for which an election to take an expense deduction is made. If some or all of the component members of the controlled group file separate returns for taxable years including a particular December 31 for which an election to take the expense deduction is made, the allocation as to all members of the group may not be revoked after the due date of the return (including extensions of time) of the component member of the controlled group whose taxable year that includes such December 31 ends on the latest date.

(c) Taxable income limitation. *(1) In general.* The aggregate cost of section 179 property elected to be expensed under section 179 that may be deducted for any taxable year may not exceed the aggregate amount of taxable income of the taxpayer for such taxable year that is derived from the active conduct by the taxpayer of any trade or business during the taxable year. For purposes of section 179(b)(3) and this paragraph (c), the aggregate amount of taxable income derived from the active conduct by an individual, a partnership, or an S corporation of any trade or business is computed by aggregating the net income (or loss) from all of the trades or businesses actively conducted by the individual, partnership, or S corporation during the taxable year. Items of income that are derived from the active conduct of a trade or business include section 1231 gains (or losses) from the trade or business and interest from working capital of the trade or business. Taxable income derived from the active conduct of a trade or business is computed without regard to the deduction allowable under section 179, any section 164(f) deduction, any net operating loss carryback or carryforward, and deductions suspended under any section of the Code. See paragraph (c)(6) of this section for rules on determining whether a taxpayer is engaged in the active conduct of a trade or business for this purpose.

(2) Application to partnerships and partners. (i) In general. The taxable income limitation of this paragraph (c) applies to the partnership as well as to each partner. Thus, the partnership may not allocate to its partners as a section 179 expense deduction for any taxable year more than the partnership's taxable income limitation for that taxable year, and a partner may not deduct as a section 179 expense deduction for any taxable year more than the partner's taxable income limitation for that taxable year.

(ii) Taxable year. If the taxable year of a partner and the partnership do not coincide, then for purposes of section 179, the amount of the partnership's taxable income attributable to a partner for a taxable year is determined under section 706 and the regulations thereunder (generally the partner's distributive share of partnership taxable income for the partnership year that ends with or within the partner's taxable year).

(iii) Example. The following example illustrates the provisions of paragraph (c)(2)(ii) of this section.

Example. AB partnership has a taxable year ending January 31. A, a partner of AB, has a taxable year ending December 31. For AB's taxable year ending January 31, 1992, AB has taxable income from the active conduct of its trade or business of $100,000, $90,000 of which was earned during 1991. Under section 706 and § 1.706-1(a)(1), A includes A's entire share of partnership taxable income in computing A's taxable income limitation for A's taxable year ending December 31, 1992.

(iv) Taxable income of a partnership. The taxable income (or loss) derived from the active conduct by a partnership of any trade or business is computed by aggregating the net income (or loss) from all of the trades or businesses actively conducted by the partnership during the taxable year. The net income (or loss) from a trade or business actively conducted by the partnership is determined by taking into account the aggregate amount of the partnership's items described in section 702(a) (other than credits, tax-exempt income, and guaranteed payments under section 707(c)) derived from that trade or business. For purposes of determining the aggregate amount of partnership items, deductions and losses are treated as negative income. Any limitation on the amount of a partnership item described in section 702(a) which may be taken into account for purposes of computing the taxable income of a partner shall be disregarded in computing the taxable income of the partnership.

(v) Partner's share of partnership taxable income. A taxpayer who is a partner in a partnership and is engaged in the active conduct of at least one of the partnership's trades or businesses includes as taxable income derived from the active conduct of a trade or business the amount of the taxpayer's allocable share of taxable income derived from the active conduct by the partnership of any trade or business (as determined under paragraph (c)(2)(iv) of this section).

(3) S corporations and S corporation shareholders. (i) In general. Rules similar to those contained in paragraphs (c)(2)(i) and (ii) of this section apply in the case of S corporations (as defined in section 1361(a)) and their shareholders. Each shareholder's share of the taxable income of an S corporation is determined under section 1366.

(ii) Taxable income of an S corporation. The taxable income (or loss) derived from the active conduct by an S corporation of any trade or business is computed by aggregating the net income (or loss) from all of the trades or businesses actively conducted by the S corporation during the taxable year. The net income (or loss) from a trade or business actively conducted by an S corporation is determined by taking into account the aggregate amount of the S corporation's items described in section 1366(a) (other than credits, tax-exempt income, and deductions for compensation paid to an S corporation's shareholder-employees) derived from that trade or business. For purposes of determining the aggregate amount of S corporation items, deductions and losses are treated as negative income. Any limitation on the amount of an S corporation item described in section 1366(a) which may be taken into account for purposes of computing the taxable income of a shareholder shall be disregarded in computing the taxable income of the S corporation.

(iii) Shareholder's share of S corporation taxable income. Rules similar to those contained in paragraph (c)(2)(v) and (c)(6)(ii) of this section apply to a taxpayer who is a shareholder in an S corporation and is engaged in the active conduct of the S corporation's trades or businesses.

(4) Taxable income of a corporation other than an S corporation. The aggregate amount of taxable income derived from the active conduct by a corporation other than an S corporation of any trade or business is the amount of the corporation's taxable income before deducting its net operating loss deduction and special deductions (as reported on the corporation's income tax return), adjusted to reflect those items of income or deduction included in that amount that were not derived by the corporation from a trade or business actively conducted by the corporation during the taxable year.

(5) Ordering rule for certain circular problems. (i) In general. A taxpayer who elects to expense the cost of section 179 property (the deduction of which is subject to the taxable income limitation) also may have to apply another Internal Revenue Code section that has a limitation based on the taxpayer's taxable income. Except as provided in paragraph (c)(1) of this section, this section provides rules for applying the taxable income limitation under section 179 in such a case. First, taxable income is computed for the other section of the Internal Revenue Code. In computing the taxable income of the taxpayer for the other section of the Internal Revenue Code, the taxpayer's section 179 deduction is computed by assuming that the taxpayer's taxable income is determined without regard to the deduction under the other Internal Revenue Code section. Next, after reducing taxable income by the amount of the section 179 deduction so computed, a hypothetical amount of deduction is determined for the other section of the Internal Revenue Code. The taxable income limitation of the taxpayer under section 179(b)(3) and this paragraph (c) then is computed by including the hypothetical amount in determining taxable income.

(ii) Example. The following example illustrates the ordering rule described in paragraph (c)(5)(i) of this section.

Example. X, a calendar-year corporation, elects to expense $10,000 of the cost of section 179 property purchased and placed in service during 1991. Assume X's dollar limitation is $10,000. X also gives a charitable contribution of $5,000 during the taxable year. X's taxable income for purposes of both sections 179 and 170(b)(2), but without regard to any deduction allowable under either section 179 or section 170, is $11,000. In determining X's taxable income limitation under section 179(b)(3) and this paragraph (c), X must first compute its section 170 deduction. However, section 170(b)(2) limits X's charitable contribution to 10 percent of its taxable income determined by taking into account its section 179 deduction. Paragraph (c)(5)(i) of this section provides that in determining X's section 179 deduction for 1991, X first computes a hypothetical section 170 deduction by assuming that its section 179 deduction is not affected by the section 170 deduction. Thus, in computing X's hypothetical section 170 deduction, X's taxable income limitation under section 179 is $11,000 and its section 179 deduction is $10,000. X's hypothetical section 170 deduction is $100 (10 percent of $1,000 ($11,000 less $10,000 section 179 deduction)). X's taxable income limitation for section 179 purposes is then computed by deducting the hypothetical charitable contribution of $100 for 1991. Thus, X's section 179 taxable income limitation is $10,900 ($11,000 less hypothetical $100 section 170 deduction), and its section 179 deduction for 1991 is $10,000. X's section 179 deduction so calculated applies for all purposes of the Code, including the computation of its actual section 170 deduction.

(6) Active conduct by the taxpayer of a trade or business. (i) Trade or business. For purposes of this section and § 1.179-4(a), the term "trade or business" has the same meaning as in section 162 and the regulations thereunder. Thus, property held merely for the production of income or used in an activity not engaged in for profit (as described in section 183) does not qualify as section 179 property and taxable income derived from property held for the production of income or from an activity not engaged in for profit is not taken into account in determining the taxable income limitation.

(ii) Active conduct. For purposes of this section, the determination of whether a trade or business is actively conducted by the taxpayer is to be made from all the facts and circumstances and is to be applied in light of the purpose of the active conduct requirement of section 179(b)(3)(A). In the context of section 179, the purpose of the active conduct requirement is to prevent a passive investor in a trade or business from deducting section 179 expenses against taxable income derived from that trade or business. Consistent with this purpose, a taxpayer generally is considered to actively conduct a trade or business if the taxpayer meaningfully participates in the management or operations of the trade or business. Generally, a partner is considered to actively conduct a trade or business of the partnership if the partner meaningfully participates in the management or operations of the trade or business. A mere passive investor in a trade or business does not actively conduct the trade or business.

(iii) Example. The following example illustrates the provisions of paragraph (c)(6)(ii) of this section.

Example. A owns a salon as a sole proprietorship and employs B to operate it. A periodically meets with B to review developments relating to the business. A also approves the salon's annual budget that is prepared by B. B performs all the necessary operating functions, including hiring beauticians, acquiring the necessary beauty supplies, and writing the checks to pay all bills and the beauticians' salaries. In 1991, B purchased, as provided for in the salon's annual budget, equipment costing $9,500 for use in the active conduct of the salon. There were no other purchases of section 179 property during 1991. A's net income from the salon, before any section 179 deduction, totaled $8,000. A also is a partner in PRS, a calendar-year partnership, which owns a grocery store. C, a partner in PRS, runs the grocery store for the partnership, making all the management and operating decisions. PRS did not purchase any section 179 property during 1991. A's allocable share of partnership net income was $6,000. Based on the facts and circumstances, A meaningfully participates in the management of the salon. However, A does not meaningfully participate in the management or operations of the trade or business of PRS. Under section 179(b)(3)(A) and this paragraph (c), A's aggregate taxable income derived from the active conduct by A of any trade or business is $8,000, the net income from the salon.

(iv) Employees. For purposes of this section, employees are considered to be engaged in the active conduct of the trade or business of their employment. Thus, wages, salaries, tips, and other compensation (not reduced by unreimbursed employee business expenses) derived by a taxpayer as an employee are included in the aggregate amount of taxable income of the taxpayer under paragraph (c)(1) of this section.

(7) Joint returns. (i) In general. The taxable income limitation of this paragraph (c) is applied to a husband and wife who file a joint income tax return under section 6013(a) by aggregating the taxable income of each spouse (as determined under paragraph (c)(1) of this section).

(ii) Joint returns filed after separate returns. In the case of a husband and wife who elect under section 6013(b) to file a joint income tax return for a taxable year after the time prescribed by law for filing the return for such taxable year, the taxable income limitation of this paragraph (c) for the taxable year for which the joint return is filed is determined under paragraph (c)(7)(i) of this section.

(8) Married individuals filing separately. In the case of an individual who is married but files a separate tax return for a taxable year, the taxable income limitation for that individual is determined under paragraph (c)(1) of this section by treating the husband and wife as separate taxpayers.

(d) Examples. The following examples illustrate the provisions of paragraphs (b) and (c) of this section.

Example (1). (i) During 1991, PRS, a calendar-year partnership, purchases and places in service $50,000 of section 179 property. The taxable income of PRS derived from the active conduct of all its trades or businesses (as determined under paragraph (c)(1) of this section) is $8,000.

(ii) Under the dollar limitation of paragraph (b) of this section, PRS may elect to expense $10,000 of the cost of section 179 property purchased in 1991. Assume PRS elects under section 179(c) and § 1.179-5 to expense $10,000 of the cost of section 179 property purchased in 1991.

(iii) Under the taxable income limitation of paragraph (c) of this section, PRS may allocate to its partners as a deduction only $8,000 of the cost of section 179 property in 1991. Under section 179(b)(3)(B) and § 1.179-3(a), PRS may carry forward the remaining $2,000 it elected to expense, which would have been deductible under section 179(a) for 1991 absent the taxable income limitation.

Example (2). (i) The facts are the same as in Example 1, except that on December 31, 1991, PRS allocates to A, a calendar-year taxpayer and a partner in PRS, $7,000 of section 179 expenses and $2,000 of taxable income. A was engaged in the active conduct of a trade or business of PRS during 1991.

(ii) In addition to being a partner in PRS, A conducts a business as a sole proprietor. During 1991, A purchases and places in service $201,000 of section 179 property in connection with the sole proprietorship. A's 1991 taxable income derived from the active conduct of this business is $6,000.

(iii) Under the dollar limitation, A may elect to expense only $9,000 of the cost of section 179 property purchased in 1991, the $10,000 limit reduced by $1,000 (the amount by which the cost of section 179 property placed in service during 1991 ($201,000) exceeds $200,000). Under paragraph (b)(3)(i) of this section, the $7,000 of section 179 expenses allocated from PRS is subject to the $9,000 limit. Assume that A elects to expense $2,000 of the cost of section 179 property purchased by A's sole proprietorship in 1991. Thus, A has elected to expense under section 179 an amount equal to the dollar limitation for 1991 ($2,000 elected to be expensed by A's sole proprietorship plus $7,000, the amount of PRS's section 179 expenses allocated to A in 1991).

(iv) Under the taxable income limitation, A may only deduct $8,000 of the cost of section 179 property elected to be expensed in 1991, the aggregate taxable income derived from the active conduct of A's trades or businesses in 1991 ($2,000 from PRS and $6,000 from A's sole proprietorship). The entire $2,000 of taxable income allocated from PRS is included by A as taxable income derived from the active conduct by A of a trade or business because it was derived from the active conduct of a trade or business by PRS and A was engaged in the active conduct of a trade or business of PRS during 1991. Under section 179(b)(3)(B) and § 1.179-3(a), A may carry forward the remaining $1,000 A elected to expense, which would have been deductible under section 179(a) for 1991 absent the taxable income limitation.

T.D. 6507, 12/1/60, amend T.D. 6579, 11/6/61, T.D. 7181, 4/24/72, T.D. 8121, 1/5/87, T.D. 8455, 12/23/92, T.D. 9146, 8/3/2004, T.D. 9209, 7/12/2005.

§ 1.179-3 Carryover of disallowed deduction.

Caution: The Treasury has not yet amended Reg § 1.179-3 to reflect changes made by P.L. 104-188.

(a) In general. Under section 179(b)(3)(B), a taxpayer may carry forward for an unlimited number of years the amount of any cost of section 179 property elected to be expensed in a taxable year but disallowed as a deduction in that taxable year because of the taxable income limitation of section 179(b)(3)(A) and § 1.179-2(c) ("carryover of disallowed deduction"). This carryover of disallowed deduction may be deducted under section 179(a) and § 1.179-1(a) in a future taxable year as provided in paragraph (b) of this section.

(b) Deduction of carryover of disallowed deduction. *(1) In general.* The amount allowable as a deduction under section 179(a) and § 1.179-1(a) for any taxable year is increased by the lesser of—

(i) The aggregate amount disallowed under section 179(b)(3)(A) and § 1.179-2(c) for all prior taxable years (to the extent not previously allowed as a deduction by reason of this section); or

(ii) The amount of any unused section 179 expense allowance for the taxable year (as described in paragraph (c) of this section).

(2) Cross references. See paragraph (f) of this section for rules that apply when a taxpayer disposes of or otherwise transfers section 179 property for which a carryover of disallowed deduction is outstanding. See paragraph (g) of this section for special rules that apply to partnerships and S corporations and paragraph (h) of this section for special rules that apply to partners and S corporation shareholders.

(c) Unused section 179 expense allowance. The amount of any unused section 179 expense allowance for a taxable year equals the excess (if any) of—

(1) The maximum cost of section 179 property that the taxpayer may deduct under section 179 and § 1.179-1 for the taxable year after applying the limitations of section 179(b) and § 1.179-2; over

(2) The amount of section 179 property that the taxpayer actually elected to expense under section 179 and § 1.179-1(a) for the taxable year.

(d) Example. The following example illustrates the provisions of paragraphs (b) and (c) of this section.

Example. A, a calendar-year taxpayer, has a $3,000 carryover of disallowed deduction for an item of section 179 property purchased and placed in service in 1991. In 1992, A purchases and places in service an item of section 179 property costing $25,000. A's 1992 taxable income from the active conduct of all A's trades or businesses is $100,000. A elects, under section 179(c) and § 1.179-5, to expense $8,000 of the cost of the item of section 179 property purchased in 1992. Under paragraph (b) of this section, A may deduct $2,000 of A's carryover of disallowed deduction from 1991 (the lesser of A's total outstanding carryover of disallowed deductions ($3,000), or the amount of any unused section 179 expense allowance for 1992 ($10,000 limit less $8,000 elected to be expensed, or $2,000)). For 1993, A has a $1,000 carryover of disallowed deduction for the item of section 179 property purchased and placed in service in 1991.

(e) Recordkeeping requirement and ordering rule. The properties and the apportionment of cost that will be subject to a carryover of disallowed deduction are selected by the taxpayer in the year the properties are placed in service. This selection must be evidenced on the taxpayer's books and records and be applied consistently in subsequent years. If no selection is made, the total carryover of disallowed deduction is apportioned equally over the items of section 179 property elected to be expensed for the taxable year. For this purpose, the taxpayer treats any section 179 expense amount allocated from a partnership (or an S corporation) for a taxable year as one item of section 179 property. If the taxpayer is allowed to deduct a portion of the total carryover of disallowed deduction under paragraph (b) of this section, the taxpayer must deduct the cost of section 179 property carried forward from the earliest taxable year.

(f) Dispositions and other transfers of section 179 property. *(1) In general.* Upon a sale or other disposition of section 179 property, or a transfer of section 179 property in a transaction in which gain or loss is not recognized in whole or in part (including transfers at death), immediately before the transfer the adjusted basis of the section 179 property is increased by the amount of any outstanding carryover of disallowed deduction with respect to the property. This carryover of disallowed deduction is not available as a deduction to the transferor or the transferee of the section 179 property.

(2) Recapture under section 179(d)(10). Under § 1.179-1(e), if a taxpayer's section 179 property is subject to recapture under section 179(d)(10), the taxpayer must recapture the benefit derived from expensing the property. Upon recapture, any outstanding carryover of disallowed deduction with respect to the property is no longer available for expensing. In determining the amount subject to recapture under section 179(d)(10) and § 1.179-1(e), any outstanding carryover of disallowed deduction with respect to that property is not treated as an amount expensed under section 179.

(g) Special rules for partnerships and S corporations. *(1) In general.* Under section 179(d)(8) and § 1.179-2(c), the taxable income limitation applies at the partnership level as well as at the partner level. Therefore, a partnership may have a carryover of disallowed deduction with respect to the cost of its section 179 property. Similar rules apply to S corporations. This paragraph (g) provides special rules that apply when a partnership or an S corporation has a carryover of disallowed deduction.

(2) Basis adjustment. Under § 1.179-1(f)(2), the basis of a partnership's section 179 property must be reduced to reflect the amount of section 179 expense elected by the partnership. This reduction must be made for the taxable year for which the election is made even if the section 179 expense amount, or a portion thereof, must be carried forward by the partnership. Similar rules apply to S corporations.

(3) Dispositions and other transfers of section 179 property by a partnership or an S corporation. The provisions of paragraph (f) of this section apply in determining the treatment of any outstanding carryover of disallowed deduction with respect to section 179 property disposed of, or transferred in a nonrecognition transaction, by a partnership or an S corporation.

(4) Example. The following example illustrates the provisions of this paragraph (g).

Example. ABC, a calendar-year partnership, owns and operates a restaurant business. During 1992, ABC purchases and places in service two items of section 179 property—a cash register costing $4,000 and office furniture costing $6,000. ABC elects to expense under section 179(c) the full cost of the cash register and the office furniture. For 1992, ABC has $6,000 of taxable income derived from the active conduct of its restaurant business. Therefore, ABC may deduct only $6,000 of section 179 expenses and must carry forward the remaining $4,000 of section 179 expenses at the partnership level. ABC must reduce the adjusted basis of the section 179 property by the full amount elected to be expensed. However, ABC may not allocate to its partners any portion of the carryover of disallowed deduction until ABC is able to deduct it under paragraph (b) of this section.

(h) Special rules for partners and S corporation shareholders. *(1) In general.* Under section 179(d)(8) and § 1.179-2(c), a partner may have a carryover of disallowed deduction with respect to the cost of section 179 property elected to be expensed by the partnership and allocated to the partner. A partner who is allocated section 179 expenses from a partnership must reduce the basis of his or her partnership interest by the full amount allocated regardless of whether the partner may deduct for the taxable year the allocated section 179 expenses or is required to carry forward all or a portion of the expenses. Similar rules apply to S corporation shareholders.

(2) Dispositions and other transfers of a partner's interest in a partnership or a shareholder's interest in an S corporation. A partner who disposes of a partnership interest, or transfers a partnership interest in a transaction in which gain or loss is not recognized in whole or in part (including transfers of a partnership interest at death), may have an outstanding carryover of disallowed deduction of section 179 expenses allocated from the partnership. In such a case, immediately before the transfer the partner's basis in the partnership interest is increased by the amount of the partner's outstanding carryover of disallowed deduction with respect to the partnership interest. This carryover of disallowed deduction is not available as a deduction to the transferor or transferee partner of the section 179 property. Similar rules apply to S corporation shareholders.

(3) Examples. The following examples illustrate the provisions of this paragraph (h).

Example (1). (i) G is a general partner in GD, a calendar-year partnership, and is engaged in the active conduct of GD's business. During 1991, GD purchases and places section 179 property in service and elects to expense a portion of the cost of the property under section 179. GD allocates $2,500 of section 179 expenses and $15,000 of taxable income (determined without regard to the section 179 deduction) to G. The income was derived from the active conduct by GD of a trade or business.

(ii) In addition to being a partner in GD, G conducts a business as a sole proprietor. During 1991, G purchases and places in service office equipment costing $25,000 and a computer costing $10,000 in connection with the sole proprietorship. G elects under section 179(c) and § 1.179-5 to expense $7,500 of the cost of the office equipment. G has a taxable loss (determined without regard to the section 179 deduction) derived from the active conduct of this business of $12,500.

(iii) G has no other taxable income (or loss) derived from the active conduct of a trade or business during 1991. G's taxable income limitation for 1991 is $2,500 ($15,000 taxable income allocated from GD less $12,500 taxable loss from the sole proprietorship). Therefore, G may deduct during 1991 only $2,500 of the $10,000 of section 179 expenses. G notes on the appropriate books and records that G expenses the $2,500 of section 179 expenses allocated from GD and carries forward the $7,500 of section 179 expenses with respect to the office equipment purchased by G's sole proprietorship.

(iv) On January 1, 1992, G sells the office equipment G's sole proprietorship purchased and placed in service in 1991. Under paragraph (f) of this section, immediately before the sale G increases the adjusted basis of the office equipment by $7,500, the amount of the outstanding carryover of disallowed deduction with respect to the office equipment.

Example (2). (i) Assume the same facts as in Example 1, except that G notes on the appropriate books and records that G expenses $2,500 of section 179 expenses relating to G's sole proprietorship and carries forward the remaining $5,000 of section 179 expenses relating to G's sole proprietorship and $2,500 of section 179 expenses allocated from GD.

(ii) On January 1, 1992, G sells G's partnership interest to A. Under paragraph (h)(2) of this section, immediately before the sale G increases the adjusted basis of G's partnership interest by $2,500, the amount of the outstanding carryover of disallowed deduction with respect to the partnership interest.

T.D. 8455, 12/23/92.

§ 1.179-4 Definitions.

Caution: The Treasury has not yet amended Reg § 1.179-4 to reflect changes made by P.L. 110-28, P.L. 109-222, P.L. 104-188.

The following definitions apply for purposes of section 179 and §§ 1.179-1 through 1.179-6:

(a) Section 179 property. The term section 179 property means any tangible property described in section 179(d)(1) that is acquired by purchase for use in the active conduct of the taxpayer's trade or business (as described in § 1.179-2(c)(6)). For taxable years beginning after 2002 and before 2008, the term section 179 property includes computer software described in section 179(d)(1) that is placed in service by the taxpayer in a taxable year beginning after 2002 and before 2008 and is acquired by purchase for use in the active conduct of the taxpayer's trade or business (as described in 1.179-2(c)(6)). For purposes of this paragraph (a), the term trade or business has the same meaning as in section 162 and the regulations under section 162.

(b) Section 38 property. The term "section 38 property" shall have the same meaning assigned to it in section 48(a) and the regulations thereunder.

(c) Purchase. *(1)* (i) Except as otherwise provided in paragraph (d)(2) of this section, the term "purchase" means any acquisition of the property, but only if all the requirements of paragraphs (c)(1)(ii), (iii), and (iv) of this section are satisfied.

(ii) Property is not acquired by purchase if it is acquired from a person whose relationship to the person acquiring it would result in the disallowance of losses under section 267 or 707(b). The property is considered not acquired by purchase only to the extent that losses would be disallowed under section 267 or 707(b). Thus, for example, if property is purchased by a husband and wife jointly from the husband's father, the property will be treated as not acquired by purchase only to the extent of the husband's interest in the property. However, in applying the rules of section 267 (b) and (c) for this purpose, section 267(c)(4) shall be treated as providing that the family of an individual will include only his spouse, ancestors, and lineal descendants. For example, a purchase of property from a corporation by a taxpayer who owns, directly or indirectly, more than 50 percent in value of the outstanding stock of such corporation does not qualify as a purchase under section 179(d)(2); nor does the purchase of property by a husband from his wife. However, the purchase of section 179 property by a taxpayer from his brother or sister does qualify as a purchase for purposes of section 179(d)(2).

(iii) The property is not acquired by purchase if acquired from a component member of a controlled group of corporations (as defined in paragraph (g) of this section) by another component member of the same group.

(iv) The property is not acquired by purchase if the basis of the property in the hands of the person acquiring it is determined in whole or in part by reference to the adjusted basis of such property in the hands of the person from whom acquired, or is determined under section 1014(a), relating to property acquired from a decedent. For example, property acquired by gift or bequest does not qualify as property acquired by purchase for purposes of section 179(d)(2); nor does property received in a corporate distribution the basis of which is determined under section 301(d)(2)(B), property acquired by a corporation in a transaction to which section 351 applies, property acquired by a partnership through contribution (section 723), or property received in a partnership distribution which has a carryover basis under section 732(a)(1).

(2) Property deemed to have been acquired by a new target corporation as a result of a section 338 election (relating to certain stock purchases treated as asset acquisitions) will be considered acquired by purchase.

(d) Cost. The cost of section 179 property does not include so much of the basis of such property as is determined by reference to the basis of other property held at any time by the taxpayer. For example, X Corporation purchases a new drill press costing $10,000 in November 1984 which qualifies as section 179 property, and is granted a trade-in allowance of $2,000 on its old drill press. The old drill press had a basis of $1,200. Under the provisions of sections 1012 and 1031(d), the basis of the new drill press is $9,200 ($1,200 basis of oil drill press plus cash expended of $8,000). However, only $8,000 of the basis of the new drill press qualifies as cost for purposes of the section 179 expense deduction; the remaining $1,200 is not part of the cost because it is determined by reference to the basis of the old drill press.

(e) Placed in service. The term "placed in service" means the time that property is first placed by the taxpayer in a condition or state of readiness and availability for a specifically assigned function, whether for use in a trade or business, for the production of income, in a tax-exempt activity, or in a personal activity. See § 1.46-3(d)(2) for examples regarding when property shall be considered in a condition or state of readiness and availability for a specifically assigned function.

(f) Controlled group of corporations and component member of controlled group. The terms "controlled group of corporations" and "component member" of a controlled group of corporations shall have the same meaning assigned to those terms in section 1563(a) and (b), except that the phrase "more than 50 percent" shall be substituted for the phrase "at least 80 percent" each place it appears in section 1563(a)(1).

T.D. 6507, 12/1/60, amend T.D. 7180, 4/24/72, T.D. 8121, 1/5/87, T.D. 8455, 12/23/92, T.D. 9146, 8/3/2004, T.D. 9209, 7/12/2005.

§ 1.179-5 Time and manner of making election.

Caution: The Treasury has not yet amended Reg § 1.179-5 to reflect changes made by P.L. 110-28, P.L. 109-222, P.L. 108-357.

(a) Election. A separate election must be made for each taxable year in which a section 179 expense deduction is claimed with respect to section 179 property. However, for this purpose a partner (or an S corporation shareholder) treats partnership (or S corporation) section 179 property for which section 179 expenses are allocated from a partnership (or an S corporation) as one item of section property. The election under section 179 and § 1.179-1 to claim a section 179 expense deduction for section 179 property shall be made on the taxpayer's first income tax return for the taxable year to which the election applies (whether or not the return is timely) or on an amended return filed within the time prescribed by law (including extensions) for filing the return for such taxable year. The election shall be made by showing as a separate item on the taxpayer's income tax return the following items:

(1) The total section 179 expense deduction claimed with respect to all section 179 property selected, and

(2) The portion of that deduction allocable to each specific item. The person shall maintain records which permit specific identification of each piece of section 179 property and reflect how and from whom such property was acquired and when such property was placed in service. The election to claim a section 179 expense deduction under this section, with respect to any property, is irrevocable and will be binding on the taxpayer with respect to such property for the taxable year for which the election is made and for all subsequent taxable years, unless the Commissioner consents to the revocation of the election. Similarly, the selection of section 179 property by the taxpayer to be subject to the expense deduction and apportionment scheme must be adhered to in computing the taxpayer's taxable income for the taxable year for which the election is made and for all subsequent taxable years, unless consent to change is given by the Commissioner.

(b) Revocation. Any election made under section 179, and any specification contained in such election, may not be revoked except with the consent of the Commissioner. Such consent will be granted only in extraordinary circumstances. Requests for consent must be filed with the Commissioner of Internal Revenue, Washington, D.C., 20224. The request must include the name, address, and taxpayer identification number of the taxpayer and must be signed by the taxpayer or his duly authorized representative. It must be accompanied by a statement showing the year and property involved, and must set forth in detail the reasons for the request.

(c) Section 179 property placed in service by the taxpayer in a taxable year beginning after 2002 and before 2008. *(1) In general.* For any taxable year beginning after 2002 and before 2008, a taxpayer is permitted to make or revoke an election under section 179 without the consent of the Commissioner on an amended Federal tax return for that taxable year. This amended return must be filed within the time prescribed by law for filing an amended return for such taxable year.

(2) Election. (i) In general. For any taxable year beginning after 2002 and before 2008, a taxpayer is permitted to make an election under section 179 on an amended Federal tax return for that taxable year without the consent of the Commissioner. Thus, the election under section 179 and § 1.179-1 to claim a section 179 expense deduction for section 179 property may be made on an amended Federal tax return for the taxable year to which the election applies. The amended Federal tax return must include the adjustment to taxable income for the section 179 election and any collateral adjustments to taxable income or to the tax liability (for example, the amount of depreciation allowed or allowable in that taxable year for the item of section 179 property to which the election pertains). Such adjustments must also be made on amended Federal tax returns for any affected succeeding taxable years.

(ii) Specifications of elections. Any election under section 179 must specify the items of section 179 property and the portion of the cost of each such item to be taken into account under section 179(a). Any election under section 179 must comply with the specification requirements of section 179(c)(1)(A), § 1.179-1(b), and § 1.179-5(a). If a taxpayer elects to expense only a portion of the cost basis of an item of section 179 property for a taxable year beginning after

2002 and before 2008 (or did not elect to expense any portion of the cost basis of the item of section 179 property), the taxpayer is permitted to file an amended Federal tax return for that particular taxable year and increase the portion of the cost of the item of section 179 property to be taken into account under section 179(a) (or elect to expense any portion of the cost basis of the item of section 179 property if no prior election was made) without the consent of the Commissioner. Any such increase in the amount expensed under section 179 is not deemed to be a revocation of the prior election for that particular taxable year.

(3) Revocation. (i) In general. Section 179(c)(2) permits the revocation of an entire election or specification, or a portion of the selected dollar amount of a specification. The term specification in section 179(c)(2) refers to both the selected specific item of section 179 property subject to a section 179 election and the selected dollar amount allocable to the specific item of section 179 property. Any portion of the cost basis of an item of section 179 property subject to an election under section 179 for a taxable year beginning after 2002 and before 2008 may be revoked by the taxpayer without the consent of the Commissioner by filing an amended Federal tax return for that particular taxable year. The amended Federal tax return must include the adjustment to taxable income for the section 179 revocation and any collateral adjustments to taxable income or to the tax liability (for example, allowable depreciation in that taxable year for the item of section 179 property to which the revocation pertains). Such adjustments must also be made on amended Federal tax returns for any affected succeeding taxable years. Reducing or eliminating a specified dollar amount for any item of section 179 property with respect to any taxable year beginning after 2002 and before 2008 results in a revocation of that specified dollar amount.

(ii) Effect of revocation. Such revocation, once made, shall be irrevocable. If the selected dollar amount reflects the entire cost of the item of section 179 property subject to the section 179 election, a revocation of the entire selected dollar amount is treated as a revocation of the section 179 election for that item of section 179 property and the taxpayer is unable to make a new section 179 election with respect to that item of property. If the selected dollar amount is a portion of the cost of the item of section 179 property, revocation of a selected dollar amount shall be treated as a revocation of only that selected dollar amount. The revoked dollars cannot be the subject of a new section 179 election for the same item of property.

(4) Examples. The following examples illustrate the rules of this paragraph (c):

Example (1). Taxpayer, a sole proprietor, owns and operates a jewelry store. During 2003, Taxpayer purchased and placed in service two items of section 179 property—a cash register costing $4,000 (5-year MACRS property) and office furniture costing $10,000 (7-year MACRS property). On his 2003 Federal tax return filed on April 15, 2004, Taxpayer elected to expense under section 179 the full cost of the cash register and, with respect to the office furniture, claimed the depreciation allowable. In November 2004, Taxpayer determines it would have been more advantageous to have made an election under section 179 to expense the full cost of the office furniture rather than the cash register. Pursuant to paragraph (c)(1) of this section, Taxpayer is permitted to file an amended Federal tax return for 2003 revoking the section 179 election for the cash register, claiming the depreciation allowable in 2003 for the cash register, and making an election to expense under section 179 the cost of the office furniture. The amended return must include an adjustment for the depreciation previously claimed in 2003 for the office furniture, an adjustment for the depreciation allowable in 2003 for the cash register, and any other collateral adjustments to taxable income or to the tax liability. In addition, once Taxpayer revokes the section 179 election for the entire cost basis of the cash register, Taxpayer can no longer expense under section 179 any portion of the cost of the cash register.

Example (2). Taxpayer, a sole proprietor, owns and operates a machine shop that does specialized repair work on industrial equipment. During 2003, Taxpayer purchased and placed in service one item of section 179 property—a milling machine costing $135,000. On Taxpayer's 2003 Federal tax return filed on April 15, 2004, Taxpayer elected to expense under section 179 $5,000 of the cost of the milling machine and claimed allowable depreciation on the remaining cost. Subsequently, Taxpayer determines it would have been to Taxpayer's advantage to have elected to expense $100,000 of the cost of the milling machine on Taxpayer's 2003 Federal tax return. In November 2004, Taxpayer files an amended Federal tax return for 2003, increasing the amount of the cost of the milling machine that is to be taken into account under section 179(a) to $100,000, decreasing the depreciation allowable in 2003 for the milling machine, and making any other collateral adjustments to taxable income or to the tax liability. Pursuant to paragraph (c)(2)(ii) of this section, increasing the amount of the cost of the milling machine to be taken into account under section 179(a) supplements the portion of the cost of the milling machine that was already taken into account by the original section 179 election made on the 2003 Federal tax return and no revocation of any specification with respect to the milling machine has occurred.

Example (3). Taxpayer, a sole proprietor, owns and operates a real estate brokerage business located in a rented storefront office. During 2003, Taxpayer purchases and places in service two items of section 179 property—a laptop computer costing $2,500 and a desktop computer costing $1,500. On Taxpayer's 2003 Federal tax return filed on April 15, 2004, Taxpayer elected to expense under section 179 the full cost of the laptop computer and the full cost of the desktop computer. Subsequently, Taxpayer determines it would have been to Taxpayer's advantage to have originally elected to expense under section 179 only $1,500 of the cost of the laptop computer on Taxpayer's 2003 Federal tax return. In November 2004, Taxpayer files an amended Federal tax return for 2003 reducing the amount of the cost of the laptop computer that was taken into account under section 179(a) to $1,500, claiming the depreciation allowable in 2003 on the remaining cost of $1,000 for that item, and making any other collateral adjustments to taxable income or to the tax liability. Pursuant to paragraph (c)(3)(ii) of this section, the $1,000 reduction represents a revocation of a portion of the selected dollar amount and no portion of those revoked dollars may be the subject of a new section 179 election for the laptop computer.

Example (4). Taxpayer, a sole proprietor, owns and operates a furniture making business. During 2003, Taxpayer purchases and places in service one item of section 179 property—an industrial-grade cabinet table saw costing $5,000. On Taxpayer's 2003 Federal tax return filed on April 15, 2004, Taxpayer elected to expense under section 179 $3,000 of the cost of the saw and, with respect to the remaining $2,000 of the cost of the saw, claimed the depreciation allowable. In November 2004, Taxpayer files an amended Federal tax return for 2003 revoking the selected $3,000 amount for the saw, claiming the depreciation allowable in 2003 on the $3,000 cost of the saw, and making any other collateral adjustments to taxable income or to the tax liability. Subsequently, in December 2004, Taxpayer files a second amended Federal tax return for 2003 selecting a new dollar amount of $2,000 for the saw, including an adjustment for the depreciation previously claimed in 2003 on the $2,000, and making any other collateral adjustments to taxable income or to the tax liability. Pursuant to paragraph (c)(2)(ii) of this section, Taxpayer is permitted to select a new selected dollar amount to expense under section 179 encompassing all or a part of the initially non-elected portion of the cost of the elected item of section 179 property. However, no portion of the revoked $3,000 may be the subject of a new section 179 dollar amount selection for the saw. In December 2005, Taxpayer files a third amended Federal tax return for 2003 revoking the entire selected $2,000 amount with respect to the saw, claiming the depreciation allowable in 2003 for the $2,000, and making any other collateral adjustments to taxable income or to the tax liability. Because Taxpayer elected to expense, and subsequently revoke, the entire cost basis of the saw, the section 179 election for the saw has been revoked and Taxpayer is unable to make a new section 179 election with respect to the saw.

(d) Election or revocation must not be made in any other manner. Any election or revocation specified in this section must be made in the manner prescribed in paragraphs (a), (b), and (c) of this section. Thus, this election or revocation must not be made by the taxpayer in any other manner (for example, an election or a revocation of an election cannot be made through a request under section 446(e) to change the taxpayer's method of accounting), except as otherwise expressly provided by the Internal Revenue Code, the regulations under the Code, or other guidance published in the Internal Revenue Bulletin.

T.D. 6507, 12/1/60, amend T.D. 6579, 11/7/61, T.D. 6737, 6/9/64, T.D. 8121, 1/5/87, T.D. 8455, 12/23/92, T.D. 9146, 8/3/2004, T.D. 9209, 7/12/2005.

§ 1.179-6 Effective dates.

Caution: The Treasury has not yet amended Reg § 1.179-6 to reflect changes made by P.L. 110-28, P.L. 109-222, P.L. 108-357.

(a) In general. Except as provided in paragraphs (b) and (c) of this section, the provisions of §§ 1.179-1 through 1.179-5 apply for property placed in service by the taxpayer in taxable years ending after January 25, 1993. However, a taxpayer may apply the provisions of §§ 1.179-1 through 1.179-5 to property placed in service by the taxpayer after December 31, 1986, in taxable years ending on or before January 25, 1993. Otherwise, for property placed in service by the taxpayer after December 31, 1986, in taxable years ending on or before January 25, 1993, the final regulations under section 179 as in effect for the year the property was placed in service apply, except to the extent modified by the changes made to section 179 by the Tax Reform Act of 1986 (100 Stat. 2085), the Technical and Miscellaneous Revenue Act of 1988 (102 Stat. 3342) and the Revenue Reconciliation Act of 1990 (104 Stat. 1388-400). For that property, a taxpayer may apply any reasonable method that clearly reflects income in applying the changes to section 179, provided the taxpayer consistently applies the method to the property.

(b) Section 179 property placed in service by the taxpayer in a taxable year beginning after 2002 and before 2008. The provisions of § 1.179-2(b)(1) and (b)(2)(ii), the second sentence of § 1.179-4(a), and the provisions of § 1.179-5(c), reflecting changes made to section 179 by the Jobs and Growth Tax Relief Reconciliation Act of 2003 (117 Stat. 752) and the American Jobs Creation Act of 2004 (118 Stat. 1418), apply for property placed in service in taxable years beginning after 2002 and before 2008.

(c) Application of § 1.179-5(d). Section 1.179-5(d) applies on or after July 12, 2005.

T.D. 9146, 8/3/2004, amend T.D. 9209, 7/12/2005.

§ 1.179A-1 Recapture of deduction for qualified clean-fuel vehicle property and qualified clean-fuel vehicle refueling property.

Caution: The Treasury has not yet amended Reg § 1.179A-1 to reflect changes made by P.L. 107-147.

(a) In general. If a recapture event occurs with respect to a taxpayer's qualified clean-fuel vehicle property or qualified clean-fuel vehicle refueling property, the taxpayer must include the recapture amount in taxable income for the taxable year in which the recapture event occurs.

(b) Recapture event. *(1) Qualified clean-fuel vehicle property.* (i) In general. A recapture event occurs if, within 3 full years from the date a vehicle of which qualified clean-fuel vehicle property is a part is placed in service, the property ceases to be qualified clean-fuel vehicle property. Property ceases to be qualified clean-fuel vehicle property if—

(A) The vehicle is modified by the taxpayer so that it may no longer be propelled by a clean-burning fuel;

(B) The vehicle is used by the taxpayer in a manner described in section 50(b);

(C) The vehicle otherwise ceases to qualify as property defined in section 179A(c); or

(D) The taxpayer receiving the deduction under section 179A sells or disposes of the vehicle and knows or has reason to know that the vehicle will be used in a manner described in paragraph (b)(1)(i)(A), (B), or (C) of this section.

(ii) Exception for disposition. Except as provided in paragraph (b)(1)(i)(D) of this section, a sale or other disposition (including a disposition by reason of an accident or other casualty) of qualified clean-fuel vehicle property is not a recapture event.

(2) Qualified clean-fuel vehicle refueling property. (i) In general. A recapture event occurs if, at any time before the end of its recovery period, the property ceases to be qualified clean-fuel vehicle refueling property. Property ceases to be qualified clean-fuel vehicle refueling property if—

(A) The property no longer qualifies as property described in section 179A(d);

(B) The property is no longer used predominantly in a trade or business (property will be treated as no longer used predominantly in a trade or business if 50 percent or more of the use of the property in a taxable year is for use other than in a trade or business);

(C) The property is used by the taxpayer in a manner described in section 50(b); or

(D) The taxpayer receiving the deduction under section 179A sells or disposes of the property and knows or has reason to know that the property will be used in a manner described in paragraph (b)(2)(i)(A), (B), or (C) of this section.

(ii) Exception for disposition. Except as provided in paragraph (b)(2)(i)(D) of this section, a sale or other disposition (including a disposition by reason of an accident or other casualty) of qualified clean-fuel vehicle refueling property is not a recapture event.

(c) Recapture date. *(1) Qualified clean-fuel vehicle property.* The recapture date is the actual date of the recapture event unless an event described in paragraph (b)(1)(i)(B) of this section occurs, in which case the recapture date is the first day of the recapture year.

(2) Qualified clean-fuel vehicle refueling property. The recapture date is the actual date of the recapture event unless the recapture occurs as a result of an event described in paragraph (b)(2)(i)(B) or (C) of this section, in which case the recapture date is the first day of the recapture year.

(d) Recapture amount. *(1) Qualified clean-fuel vehicle property.* The recapture amount is equal to the benefit of the section 179A deduction allowable multiplied by the recapture percentage. The recapture percentage is—

(i) 100, if the recapture date is within the first full year after the date the vehicle is placed in service;

(ii) 66⅔, if the recapture date is within the second full year after the date the vehicle is placed in service; or

(iii) 33⅓, if the recapture date is within the third full year after the date the vehicle is placed in service.

(2) Qualified clean-fuel vehicle refueling property. The recapture amount is equal to the benefit of the section 179A deduction allowable multiplied by the following fraction. The numerator of the fraction equals the total recovery period for the property minus the number of recovery years prior to, but not including, the recapture year. The denominator of the fraction equals the total recovery period.

(e) Basis adjustment. As of the first day of the taxable year in which the recapture event occurs, the basis of the vehicle of which qualified clean-fuel vehicle property is a part or the basis of qualified clean-fuel vehicle refueling property is increased by the recapture amount. For a vehicle or refueling property that is of a character that is subject to an allowance for depreciation, this increase in basis is recoverable over its remaining recovery period beginning as of the first day of the taxable year in which the recapture event occurs.

(f) Application of section 1245 for sales and other dispositions. For purposes of section 1245, the amount of the deduction allowable under section 179A(a) with respect to any property that is (or has been) of a character subject to an allowance for depreciation is treated as a deduction allowed for depreciation under section 167. Therefore, upon a sale or other disposition of depreciable qualified clean-fuel vehicle refueling property or a depreciable vehicle of which qualified clean-fuel vehicle property is a part, section 1245 will apply to any gain recognized to the extent the basis of the depreciable property or vehicle was reduced under section 179A(e)(6) net of any basis increase described in paragraph (e) of this section.

(g) Examples. The following examples illustrate the provisions of this section:

Example (1). A, a calendar-year taxpayer, purchases and places in service for personal use on January 1, 1995, a clean-fuel vehicle, a portion of which is qualified clean-fuel vehicle property, costing $25,000. The qualified clean-fuel vehicle property costs $11,000. On A's 1995 federal income tax return, A claims a section 179A deduction of $2,000. On January 2, 1996, A sells the vehicle to an unrelated third party who subsequently converts the vehicle into a gasoline-propelled vehicle on October 15, 1996. There is no recapture upon the sale of the vehicle by A provided A did not know or have reason to know that the purchaser intended to convert the vehicle to a gasoline-propelled vehicle.

Example (2). B, a calendar-year taxpayer, purchases and places in service for personal use on October 11, 1994, a clean-fuel vehicle costing $20,000, a portion of which is qualified clean-fuel vehicle property. The qualified clean-fuel vehicle property costs $10,000. On B's 1994 federal income tax return, B claims a deduction of $2,000, which reduces B's gross income by $2,000. The basis of the vehicle is reduced to $18,000 ($20,000 – $2,000). On January 31, 1996, B sells the vehicle to a tax-exempt entity. Because B knowingly sold the vehicle to a tax-exempt entity described in section 50(b) in the second full year from the date the vehicle was placed in service, B must recapture $1,333 ($2,000 × 66⅔ percent). This recapture amount increases B's gross income by $1,333 on B's 1996 federal income tax return and is added to the basis of the motor vehicle as of January 1, 1996, the beginning of the taxable year of recapture.

Example (3). X, a calendar-year taxpayer, purchases and places in service for its business use on January 1, 1994, qualified clean-fuel vehicle refueling property costing $400,000. Assume this property has a 5-year recovery period. On X's 1994 federal income tax return, X claims a deduction of $100,000, which reduces X's gross income by $100,000. The basis of the property is reduced to $300,000 ($400,000 – $100,000) prior to any adjustments for depreciation. In 1996, more than 50 percent of the use of the property is other than in X's trade or business. Because the property is no longer used predominantly in X's business, X must recapture three-fifths of the section 179A deduction or $60,000 ($100,000 × (5 – 2)/5 = $60,000) and include that amount in gross income on its 1996 federal income tax return. The recapture amount of $60,000 is added to the basis of the property as of January 1, 1996, the beginning of the taxable year of recapture, and to the extent the property remains depreciable, the adjusted basis is recoverable over the remaining recovery period.

Example (4). X, a calendar-year taxpayer, purchases and places in service for business use on January 1, 1994, qualified clean-fuel vehicle refueling property costing $350,000. Assume this property has a 5-year recovery period. On X's 1994 federal income tax return, X claims a deduction of $100,000, which reduces X's gross income by $100,000. The basis of the property is reduced to $250,000 ($350,000 – $100,000) prior to any adjustments for depreciation. In 1995, X converts the property to store and dispense gasoline. Because the property is no longer used as qualified clean-fuel vehicle refueling property in 1995, X must recapture four-fifths of the section 179A deduction or $80,000 ($100,000 × (5 – 1)/5 = $80,000) and include that amount in gross income on its 1995 federal income tax return. The recapture amount of $80,000 is added to the basis of the property as of January 1, 1995, the beginning of the taxable year of recapture, and to the extent the property remains depreciable, the adjusted basis is recoverable over the remaining recovery period.

Example (5). The facts are the same as in Example 4. In 1996, X sells the refueling property for $351,000, recognizing a gain from this sale. Under paragraph (f) of this section, section 1245 will apply to any gain recognized on the sale of depreciable property to the extent the basis of the property was reduced by the section 179A deduction net of any basis increase from recapture of the section 179A deduction. Accordingly, the gain from the sale of the property is subject to section 1245 to the extent of the depreciation allowance for the property plus the deduction allowed under section 179A ($100,000), less the previous recapture amount ($80,000). Any remaining amount of gain may be subject to other applicable provisions of the Internal Revenue Code.

(h) Effective date. This section is effective on October 14, 1994. If the recapture date is before the effective date of this section, a taxpayer may use any reasonable method to recapture the benefit of any deduction allowable under section 179A(a) consistent with section 179A and its legislative history. For this purpose, the recapture date is defined in paragraph (c) of this section.

T.D. 8606, 8/2/95.

Proposed § 1.179B-1 Deduction for capital costs incurred in complying with Environmental Protection Agency sulfur regulations. [*For Preamble, see ¶ 153,015*]

[The text of this proposed § 1.179B-1 is the same as the text of § 1.179B-1T published elsewhere in this issue of the Federal Register]. [*See T.D. 9404, 06/27/2008, 73 Fed. Reg. 125.*]

§ 1.179B-1T Deduction for capital costs incurred in complying with Environmental Protection Agency sulfur regulations (temporary).

(a) Scope and definitions. *(1) Scope.* This section provides the rules for determining the amount of the deduction allowable under section 179B(a) for qualified capital costs paid or incurred by a small business refiner to comply with the highway diesel fuel sulfur control requirements of the Environmental Protection Agency (EPA). This section also provides rules for making elections under section 179B.

(2) Definitions. For purposes of section 179B and this section, the following definitions apply:

(i) The applicable EPA regulations are the EPA regulations establishing the highway diesel fuel sulfur control program (40 CFR part 80, subpart I).

(ii) The average daily domestic refinery run for a refinery is the lesser of—

(A) The total amount of crude oil input (in barrels) to the refinery's domestic processing units during the 1-year period ending on December 31, 2002, divided by 365; or

(B) The total amount of refined petroleum product (in barrels) produced by the refinery's domestic processing units during such 1-year period divided by 365.

(iii) The aggregate average domestic daily refinery run for a refiner is the sum of the average daily domestic refinery runs for all refineries that were owned by the refiner or a related person on April 1, 2003.

(iv) Cooperative owner is a person that—

(A) Directly holds an ownership interest in a cooperative small business refiner, as defined in paragraph (a)(2)(v) of this section; and

(B) Is a cooperative to which part 1 of subchapter T of the Internal Revenue Code (Code) applies.

(v) Cooperative small business refiner is a small business refiner that is a cooperative to which part 1 of subchapter T of the Code applies.

(vi) Low sulfur diesel fuel has the meaning prescribed in section 45H(c)(5).

(vii) Qualified capital costs are qualified costs as defined in section 45H(c)(2) that are properly chargeable to capital account.

(viii) Related person has the meaning prescribed in section 613A(d)(3) and the regulations under section 613A(d)(3).

(ix) Small business refiner has the meaning prescribed in section 45H(c)(1).

(b) Section 179B deduction. *(1) In general.* Section 179B(a) allows a deduction with respect to the qualified capital costs paid or incurred by a small business refiner (the section 179B deduction). The deduction is allowable with respect to the qualified capital costs paid or incurred during a taxable year only if the small business refiner makes an election under paragraph (d) of this section for the taxable year. The certification requirement in section 45H(e) (relating to the certification required to support a credit under section 45H) does not apply for purposes of the section 179B deduction. Accordingly, the section 179B deduction is allowable with respect to the qualified capital costs of an electing small business refiner even if the refiner never obtains a certification under section 45H(e) with respect to those costs.

(2) Computation of section 179B deduction. (i) In general. Except as provided in paragraphs (b)(2)(ii) and (c)(3) of this section, a small business refiner that makes an election under paragraph (d) of this section for a taxable year is allowed a section 179B deduction in an amount equal to 75 percent of qualified capital costs that are paid or incurred by the small business refiner during the taxable year.

(ii) Reduced percentage. A small business refiner's section 179B deduction is reduced if the refiner's aggregate average daily domestic refinery run is in excess of 155,000 barrels. In that case, the number of percentage points used in computing the deduction under paragraph (b)(2)(i) of this section (75) is reduced (not below zero) by the product of 75 and the ratio of the excess barrels to 50,000 barrels.

(3) Example. The application of this paragraph (b) is illustrated by the following example:

Example. (i) A, an accrual method taxpayer, is a small business refiner with a taxable year ending December 31. On April 1, 2003, A owns a refinery with an average daily domestic refinery run (that is, an average daily run during calendar year 2002) of 100,000 barrels and a person related to A owns a refinery with an average daily domestic refinery run of 85,000 barrels. These are the only domestic refineries owned by A and persons related to A. A's aggregate average daily domestic refinery run for the two refineries is 185,000 barrels. A incurs qualified capital costs of $10 million in the taxable year ended December 31, 2007. The costs are incurred with respect to property that is placed in service in year 2008. A makes the election under paragraph (d) of this section for the 2007 taxable year.

(ii) Because A's aggregate average daily domestic refinery run is 185,000 barrels, the percentage of the qualified capital costs that is deductible under section 179B(a) is reduced from 75 percent to 30 percent (75 percent reduced by 75 percent multiplied by 0.6 ((185,000 barrels minus 155,000 barrels)/50,000 barrels)). Thus, for 2007, A's deduction under section 179B(a) is $3,000,000 ($10,000,000 qualified capital costs multiplied by .30).

(c) Effect on basis. *(1) In general.* If qualified capital costs are included in the basis of property, the basis of the property is reduced by the amount of the section 179B deduction allowed with respect to such costs.

(2) Treatment as depreciation. If qualified capital costs are included in the basis of depreciable property, the amount of the section 179B deduction allowed with respect to such costs is treated as a depreciation deduction for purposes of section 1245.

(d) Election to deduct qualified capital costs. *(1) In general.* (i) Section 179B election. This paragraph (d) prescribes rules for the election to deduct the qualified capital costs paid or incurred by a small business refiner during a taxable year (the section 179B election). A small business refiner making the section 179B election for a taxable year consents to, and agrees to apply, all of the provisions of section 179B and this section to qualified capital costs paid or incurred by the refiner during the taxable year. The section 179B election for a taxable year applies with respect to all qualified capital costs paid or incurred by the small business refiner during that taxable year.

(ii) Year-by-year election. A separate section 179B election must be made for each taxable year in which the taxpayer seeks to deduct qualified capital costs under section 179B. A small business refiner may make the section 179B election for some taxable years and not for other taxable years.

(iii) Elections for cooperative small business refiners. See paragraph (e) of this section for the rules applicable to the election provided under section 179B(e), relating to the election to allocate the section 179B deduction to cooperative owners of a cooperative small business refiner (the section 179B(e) election).

(2) Time and manner for making section 179B election. (i) Time for making election. Except as provided in paragraph (d)(2)(iii) of this section, a taxpayer's section 179B election for a taxable year must be made by the due date (including extensions) for filing the taxpayer's Federal income tax return for the taxable year.

(ii) Manner of making election. (A) In general. Except as provided in paragraph (d)(2)(iii) of this section, the section 179B election for a taxable year is made by claiming a section 179B deduction on the taxpayer's original Federal income tax return for the taxable year and attaching the statement described in paragraph (d)(2)(ii)(B) of this section to the return. The section 179B election with respect to qualified capital costs paid or incurred by a partnership is made by the partnership and the section 179B election with respect to qualified capital costs paid or incurred by an S corporation is made by the S corporation. In the case of qualified capital costs paid or incurred by the members of a consolidated group (within the meaning of § 1.1502-1(h)), the section 179B election with respect to such costs is made for each member by the common parent of the group.

(B) Information required in election statement. The election statement attached to the taxpayer's return must contain the following information:

(1) The name and identification number of the small business refiner.

(2) The amount of the qualified capital costs paid or incurred during the taxable year for which the election is made.

(3) The aggregate average daily domestic refinery run (as determined under paragraph (a)(2)(iii) of this section).

(4) The date by which the small business refiner must comply with the applicable EPA regulations. If this date is not June 1, 2006, the statement also must explain why compliance is not required by June 1, 2006.

(5) The calculation of the section 179B deduction for the taxable year.

(6) For each property that will have its basis reduced on account of the section 179B deduction for the taxable year, a description of the property, the amount included in the basis of the property on account of qualified capital costs paid or incurred during the taxable year, and the amount of the basis reduction to that property on account of the section 179B deduction for the taxable year.

(iii) Except as otherwise expressly provided by the Code, the regulations under the Code, or other guidance published in the Internal Revenue Bulletin, a section 179B election is valid only if made at the time and in the manner prescribed in this paragraph (d)(2). For example, except as otherwise expressly provided, the 179B election cannot be made for a taxable year to which this section applies through a request under section 446(e) to change the taxpayer's method of accounting.

(3) Revocation of election. An election made under this paragraph (d) may not be revoked without the prior written consent of the Commissioner of Internal Revenue. To seek the Commissioner's consent, the taxpayer must submit a request for a private letter ruling (for further guidance, see, for example, Rev. Proc. 2008-1 (2008-1 IRB 1) and § 601.601(d)(2)(ii)(b) of this chapter).

(4) Failure to make election. If a small business refiner does not make the section 179B election for a taxable year at the time and in the manner prescribed in paragraph (d)(2) of this section, no deduction is allowed for the qualified capital costs that the refiner paid or incurred during the year. Instead these qualified capital costs are chargeable to a capital account in that taxable year, the basis of the property to which these costs are capitalized is not reduced on account of section 179B, and the amount of depreciation allowable for the property attributable to these costs is determined by reference to these costs unreduced by section 179B.

(5) Elections for taxable years ending before June 26, 2008. This section does not apply to section 179B elections for taxable years ending before June 26, 2008. The rules for making the section 179B election for a taxable year ending before June 26, 2008 are provided in Notice 2006-47 (2006-20 IRB 892). See § 601.601(d)(2)(ii)(b) of this chapter.

(e) Election under section 179B(e) to allocate section 179B deduction to cooperative owners. *(1) In general.* A cooperative small business refiner may elect to allocate part or all of its cooperative owners' ratable shares of the section 179B deduction for a taxable year to the cooperative owners (the section 179B(e) election). The section 179B deduction allocated to a cooperative owner is equal to the cooperative owner's ratable share of the total section 179B deduction allocated. A cooperative owner's ratable share is determined for this purpose on the basis of the cooperative owner's ownership interest in the cooperative small business refiner during the cooperative small business refiner's taxable year. If the cooperative owners' interests vary during the year, the cooperative small business refiner shall determine the owners' ratable shares under a consistently applied method that reasonably takes into account the owners' varying interests during the taxable year.

(2) Cooperative small business refiner denied section 1382 deduction for allocated portion. In computing taxable income under section 1382, a cooperative small business refiner must reduce its section 179B deduction for the taxable year by an amount equal to the section 179B deduction allocated

under this paragraph (e) to the refiner's cooperative owners for the taxable year.

(3) Time and manner for making election. (i) Time for making election. The section 179B(e) election for a taxable year must be made by the due date (including extensions) for filing the cooperative small business refiner's Federal income tax return for the taxable year.

(ii) Manner of making election. The section 179B(e) election for a taxable year is made by attaching a statement to the cooperative small business refiner's Federal income tax return for the taxable year. The election statement must contain the following information:

(A) The name and identification number of the cooperative small business refiner.

(B) The amount of the section 179B deduction allowable to the cooperative small business refiner for the taxable year (determined before the application of section 179B(e) and this paragraph (e)).

(C) The name and identification number of each cooperative owner to which the cooperative small business refiner is allocating all or some of the section 179B deduction.

(D) The amount of the section 179B deduction that is allocated to each cooperative owner listed in response to paragraph (e)(3)(ii)(C) of this section.

(4) Irrevocable election. A section 179B(e) election for a taxable year, once made, is irrevocable for that taxable year.

(5) Written notice to owners. A cooperative small business refiner that makes a section 179B(e) election for a taxable year must notify each cooperative owner of the amount of the section 179B deduction that is allocated to that cooperative owner. This notification must be provided in a written notice that is mailed by the cooperative small business refiner to its cooperative owner before the due date (including extensions) of the cooperative small business refiner's Federal income tax return for the election year. In addition, the cooperative small business refiner must report the amount of the cooperative owner's section 179B deduction on Form 1099-PATR, "Taxable Distributions Received From Cooperatives," issued to the cooperative owner. If Form 1099-PATR is revised or renumbered, the amount of the cooperative owner's section 179B deduction must be reported on the revised or renumbered form.

(f) Effective/applicability date. *(1) In general.* This section applies to taxable years ending on or after June 26, 2008.

(2) Application to taxable years ending before June 26, 2008. A small business refiner may apply this section to a taxable year ending before June 26, 2008, provided that the small business refiner applies all provisions in this section, with the modifications described in paragraph (f)(3) of this section, to the taxable year.

(3) Modifications applicable to taxable years ending before June 26, 2008. The following modifications to the rules of this section apply to a small business refiner that applies those rules to a taxable year ending before June 26, 2008:

(i) Rules relating to section 179B election. The section 179B election for a taxable year ending before June 26, 2008 may be made under the rules provided in Notice 2006-47, rather than under the rules set forth in paragraph (d) of this section.

(ii) Rules relating to section 179B(e) election. A section 179B(e) election for a taxable year ending before June 26, 2008 will be treated as satisfying the requirements of paragraph (f) if the cooperative small business refiner has calculated its tax liability in a manner consistent with the election and has used any reasonable method consistent with the principles of section 179B(e) to inform the Internal Revenue Service that an election has been made under section 179B(e) and to inform cooperative owners of the amount of the section 179B deduction they have been allocated.

(4) Expiration date. The applicability of § 179B-1T expires on June 24, 2011.

T.D. 9404, 6/26/2008.

PAR. 2. Section 1.179C-1 is added to read as follows:

Proposed § 1.179C-1 Election to expense certain refineries. [*For Preamble, see ¶ 153,025*]

[The text of proposed § 1.79C-1 is the same as the text of § 1.179C-1T (a) through (g) published elsewhere in this issue of the Federal Register]. [*See T.D. 9412, 07/09/2008, 73 Fed. Reg. 132.*]

§ 1.179C-1T Election to expense certain refineries (temporary).

(a) Scope and definitions. *(1) Scope.* This section provides the rules for determining the deduction allowable under section 179C(a) for the cost of any qualified refinery property. The provisions of this section apply only to a taxpayer that elects to apply section 179C in the manner prescribed under paragraph (d) of this section.

(2) Definitions. For purposes of section 179C and this section, the following definitions apply:

(i) Applicable environmental laws are any applicable Federal, state, or local environmental laws.

(ii) Qualified fuels has the meaning set forth in section 45K(c).

(iii) Cost is the unadjusted depreciable basis (as defined in § 1.168(b)-1(a)(3), but without regard to the reduction in basis for any portion of the basis the taxpayer properly elects to treat as an expense under section 179C and this section) of the property.

(iv) Throughput is a volumetric rate measuring the flow of crude oil or qualified fuels processed over a given period of time, typically referenced on the basis of barrels per calendar day.

(v) Barrels per calendar day is the amount of fuels that a facility can process under usual operating conditions, expressed in terms of capacity during a 24-hour period and reduced to account for down time and other limitations.

(vi) United States has the same meaning as that term is defined in section 7701(a)(9).

(b) Qualified refinery property. *(1) In general.* Qualified refinery property is any property that meets the requirements set forth in paragraphs (b)(2) through (b)(7) of this section.

(2) Description of qualified refinery property. (i) In general. Property that comprises any portion of a qualified refinery may be qualified refinery property. For purposes of section 179C and this section, a qualified refinery is any refinery located in the United States that is designed to serve the primary purpose of processing crude oil or qualified fuels.

(ii) Nonqualified refinery property. Refinery property is not qualified refinery property for purposes of this paragraph (b)(2) if—

(A) The primary purpose of the refinery property is for use as a topping plant, asphalt plant, lube oil facility, crude or product terminal, or blending facility; or

(B) The refinery property is built solely to comply with consent decrees or projects mandated by Federal, state or local governments.

(3) Original use. (i) In general. For purposes of the deduction allowable under section 179C(a), refinery property will meet the requirements of this paragraph (b)(3) if the original use of the property commences with the taxpayer. Except as provided in paragraph (b)(3)(ii) of this section, original use means the first use to which the property is put, whether or not that use corresponds to the use of the property by the taxpayer. Thus, if a taxpayer incurs capital expenditures to recondition or rebuild property acquired or owned by the taxpayer, only the capital expenditures incurred by the taxpayer to recondition or rebuild the property acquired or owned by the taxpayer satisfy the original use requirement. However, the cost of reconditioned or rebuilt property acquired by a taxpayer does not satisfy the original use requirement. Whether property is reconditioned or rebuilt property is a question of fact. For purposes of this paragraph (b)(3)(i), acquired or self-constructed property that contains used parts will be treated as reconditioned or rebuilt only if the cost of the used parts is more than 20 percent of the total cost of the property.

(ii) Sale-leaseback. If any new portion of a qualified refinery is originally placed in service by a person after August 8, 2005, and is sold to a taxpayer and leased back to the person by the taxpayer within three months after the date the property was originally placed in service by the person, the taxpayer-lessor is considered the original user of the property.

(4) Placed-in-service date. (i) In general. Refinery property will meet the requirements of this paragraph (b)(4) if the property is placed in service by the taxpayer after August 8, 2005, and before January 1, 2012.

(ii) Sale-leaseback. If a new portion of refinery property is originally placed in service by a person after August 8, 2005, and is sold to a taxpayer and leased back to the person by the taxpayer within three months after the date the property was originally placed in service by the person, the property is treated as originally placed in service by the taxpayer-lessor not earlier than the date on which the property is used by the lessee under the leaseback.

(5) Production capacity. (i) In general. Refinery property is considered qualified refinery property if—

(A) It enables the existing qualified refinery to increase the total volume output, determined without regard to asphalt or lube oil, by at least five percent on an average daily basis; or

(B) It enables the existing qualified refinery to increase the percentage of total throughput attributable to processing qualified fuels to a rate that is at least 25 percent of total throughput on an average daily basis.

(ii) When production capacity is tested. The production capacity requirement of this paragraph (b)(5) is determined as of the date the property is placed in service by the taxpayer. Any reasonable method may be used to determine the appropriate baseline for measuring capacity increases and to demonstrate and substantiate that the capacity of the existing qualified refinery has been sufficiently increased.

(iii) Multi-stage projects. In the case of multi-stage projects, a taxpayer must satisfy the reporting requirements of paragraph (f)(2) of this section, sufficient to establish that the production capacity requirements of this paragraph (b)(5) will be met as a result of the taxpayer's overall plan.

(6) Applicable environmental laws. (i) In general. The environmental compliance requirement applies only with respect to refinery property, or any portion of refinery property, that is placed in service after August 8, 2005. A refinery's failure to meet applicable environmental laws with respect to a portion of the refinery that was in service prior to August 8, 2005 will not disqualify a taxpayer from making the election under section 179C(a) with respect to otherwise qualifying refinery property.

(ii) Waiver under the Clean Air Act. Refinery property must comply with the Clean Air Act, notwithstanding any waiver received by the taxpayer under that Act.

(7) Construction of property. (i) In general. Qualified property will meet the requirements of this paragraph (b)(7) if—

(A) The property is placed in service by the taxpayer after August 8, 2005, and before January 1, 2012; and

(B) No written binding contract for the construction of the property was in effect before June 14, 2005.

(ii) Definition of binding contract. (A) In general. A contract is binding only if it is enforceable under state law against the taxpayer or a predecessor, and does not limit damages to a specified amount (for example, by use of a liquidated damages provision). For this purpose, a contractual provision that limits damages to an amount equal to at least 5 percent of the total contract price will not be treated as limiting damages to a specified amount. In determining whether a contract limits damages, the fact that there may be little or no damages because the contract price does not significantly differ from fair market value will not be taken into account.

(B) Conditions. A contract is binding even if subject to a condition, as long as the condition is not within the control of either party or the predecessor of either party. A contract will continue to be binding if the parties make insubstantial changes in its terms and conditions, or if any term is to be determined by a standard beyond the control of either party. A contract that imposes significant obligations on the taxpayer or a predecessor will be treated as binding, notwithstanding the fact that insubstantial terms remain to be negotiated by the parties to the contract.

(C) Options. An option to either acquire or sell property is not a binding contract.

(D) Supply agreements. A binding contract does not include a supply or similar agreement if the payment amount and design specification of the property to be purchased have not been specified.

(E) Components. A binding contract to acquire one or more components of a larger property will not be treated as a binding contract to acquire the larger property. If a binding contract to acquire a component does not satisfy the requirements of this paragraph (b)(7), the component is not qualified refinery property.

(iii) Self-constructed property. (A) In general. Except as provided in paragraph (b)(7)(iii)(B) of this section, if a taxpayer manufactures, constructs, or produces property for use by the taxpayer in its trade or business (or for the production of income by the taxpayer), the construction of property rules in this paragraph (b)(7) are treated as met for qualified refinery property if the taxpayer began manufacturing, constructing, or producing the property after June 14, 2005, and before January 1, 2008. Property that is manufactured, constructed or produced for the taxpayer by another person under a written binding contract (as defined in paragraph (b)(7)(ii) of this section) that is entered into prior to the manufacture, construction, or production of the property for use by the taxpayer in its trade or business (or for the production of income) is considered to be manufactured, constructed, or produced by the taxpayer.

(B) When construction begins. For purposes of this paragraph (b)(7)(iii), construction of property generally begins when physical work of a significant nature begins. Physical work does not include preliminary activities such as planning or designing, securing financing, exploring, or researching. The determination of when physical work of a significant nature begins depends on the facts and circumstances. Nevertheless, physical work of a significant nature will be deemed to have begun for purposes of this paragraph (b)(7)(iii)(B), and the construction of the property will be deemed to have met the requirements of paragraph (b)(7)(iii)(A) of this section, if the taxpayer performed some physical work before January 1, 2008 (such as clearing a site or excavation) and has performed physical work of a significant nature (as defined in Treas. Regs. § 1.168(k)-1(b)(4)(iii)(B)) before October 7, 2008.

(C) Components of self-constructed property. (1) Acquired components. If a binding contract (as defined in paragraph (b)(7)(ii) of this section) to acquire a component of self-constructed property is in effect on or before June 14, 2005, the component does not satisfy the requirements of paragraph (b)(7)(i) of this section, and is not qualified refinery property. However, if construction of the self-constructed property begins after June 14, 2005, the self-constructed property may be qualified refinery property if it meets all other requirements of section 179C and this section (including paragraph (b)(7)(i) of this section), even though the component is not qualified refinery property. If the construction of self-constructed property begins before June 14, 2005, neither the self-constructed property nor any component related to the self-constructed property is qualified refinery property. If the component was acquired before January 1, 2008, but the construction of the self-constructed property begins after December 31, 2007, the component may qualify as qualified refinery property even if the self-constructed property is not qualified refinery property.

(2) Self-constructed components. If the manufacture, construction, or production of a component fails to meet any of the requirements of paragraph (b)(7)(iii) of this section, the component is not qualified refinery property. However, if the manufacture, construction, or production of a component fails to meet any of the requirements provided in paragraph (b)(7)(iii) of this section, but the construction of the self-constructed property begins after June 14, 2005, the self-constructed property may qualify as qualified refinery property if it meets all other requirements of section 179C and this section (including paragraph (b)(7)(i) of this section). If the construction of the self-constructed property begins before June 14, 2005, neither the self-constructed property nor any components related to the self-constructed property are qualified refinery property. If the component was self-constructed before January 1, 2008, but the construction of the self-constructed property begins after December 31, 2007, the component may qualify as qualified refinery property, although the self-constructed property is not qualified refinery property.

(c) Computation of expense deduction for qualified refinery property. In general, the allowable deduction under paragraph (d) of this section for qualified refinery property is determined by multiplying by 50 percent the cost of the qualified refinery property paid or incurred by the taxpayer.

(d) Election. *(1) In general.* A taxpayer may make an election to deduct as an expense 50 percent of the cost of any qualified refinery property. A taxpayer making this election takes the 50 percent deduction for the taxable year in which the qualified refinery property is placed in service.

(2) Time and manner for making election. (i) Time for making election. An election specified in this paragraph (d) generally must be made not later than the due date (including extensions) for filing the original Federal income tax return for the taxable year in which the qualified refinery property is placed in service by the taxpayer. However, a taxpayer that did not claim the section 179C(a) deduction on a Federal income tax return filed for a taxable year ending prior to July 9, 2008 but wishes to claim the deduction for that taxable year may do so by properly making a section 179C(a) election under this paragraph (d) on an amended return filed by December 31, 2008.

(ii) Manner of making election. The taxpayer makes an election under section 179C(a) and this paragraph (d) by entering the amount of the deduction at the appropriate place on the taxpayer's timely filed original Federal income tax return for the taxable year in which the qualified refinery property is placed in service (or on the amended return, as provided in paragraph (d)(2)(i) of this section), and attaching a report as specified in paragraph (f) of this section to the taxpayer's timely filed original Federal income tax return for the taxable year in which the qualified refinery property is placed in service (or on the amended return, as provided in paragraph (d)(2)(i) of this section).

(3) Revocation of election. (i) In general. An election made under section 179C(a) and this paragraph (d), and any specification contained in such election, may not be revoked except with the consent of the Commissioner of Internal Revenue.

(ii) Revocation prior to the revocation deadline. A taxpayer is deemed to have requested, and to have been granted, consent of the Commissioner to revoke an election under section 179C(a) and this paragraph (d) if the taxpayer revokes the election before the revocation deadline. The revocation deadline is the later of December 31, 2008, or 24 months after the due date (including extensions) for filing the taxpayer's Federal income tax return for the taxable year for which the election applies. An election under section 179C(a) and this paragraph (d) is revoked by attaching a statement to an amended return for the taxable year for which the election applies. The statement must specify the name and address of the refinery for which the election applies and the amount deducted on the taxpayer's original Federal income tax return for the taxable year for which the election applies.

(iii) Revocation after the revocation deadline. An election under section 179C(a) and this paragraph (d) may not be revoked after the revocation deadline. The revocation deadline may not be extended under § 301.9100-1.

(iv) Revocation by cooperative taxpayer. A taxpayer that has made an election to allocate the section 179C deduction to cooperative owners under section 179C(g) and paragraph (e) of this section may not revoke its election under section 179C(a).

(e) Election to allocate section 179C deduction to cooperative owners. *(1) In general.* If a cooperative taxpayer makes an election under section 179C(g) and this paragraph (e), the cooperative taxpayer may elect to allocate all, some, or none of the deduction allowable under section 179C(a) for that taxable year to the cooperative owner(s). This allocation is equal to the cooperative owner(s)' ratable share of the total amount allocated, determined on the basis of each cooperative owner's ownership interest in the cooperative taxpayer. For purposes of this section, a cooperative taxpayer is an organization to which part I of subchapter T applies, and in which another organization to which part I of subchapter T applies (cooperative owner) directly holds an ownership interest. No deduction shall be allowed under section 1382 for any amount allocated under this paragraph (e).

(2) Time and manner for making election. (i) Time for making election. A cooperative taxpayer must make the election under section 179(g) and this paragraph (e) by the due date (including extensions) for filing the cooperative taxpayer's original Federal income tax return for the taxable year to which the cooperative taxpayer's election under section 179C(a) and paragraph (d) of this section applies.

(ii) Manner of making election. An election under this paragraph (e) is made by attaching to the cooperative taxpayer's timely filed Federal income tax return for the taxable year (including extensions) to which the cooperative taxpayer's election under section 179C(a) and paragraph (d) of this section applies a statement providing the following information:

(A) The name and taxpayer identification number of the cooperative taxpayer.

(B) The amount of the deduction allowable to the cooperative taxpayer for the taxable year to which the election under section 179C(a) and paragraph (d) of this section applies.

(C) The name and taxpayer identification number of each cooperative owner to which the cooperative taxpayer is allocating all or some of the deduction allowable.

(D) The amount of the allowable deduction that is allocated to each cooperative owner listed in paragraph (e)(2)(ii)(C) of this section.

(3) Written notice to owners. If any portion of the deduction allowable under section 179C(a) is allocated to a cooperative owner, the cooperative taxpayer must notify the cooperative owner of the amount of the deduction allocated to the cooperative owner in a written notice, and on Form 1099-PATR, ''Taxable Distributions Received from Cooperatives.'' This notice must be provided on or before the due date (including extensions) of the cooperative taxpayer's original Federal income tax return for the taxable year for which the cooperative taxpayer's election under section 179C(a) and paragraph (d) of this section applies.

(4) Irrevocable election. A section 179C(g) election, once made, is irrevocable.

(f) Reporting requirement. *(1) In general.* A taxpayer may not claim a deduction under section 179C(a) for any taxable year unless the taxpayer files a report with the Secretary containing information with respect to the operation of the taxpayer's refineries.

(2) Information to be included in the report. The taxpayer must specify—

(i) The name and address of the refinery;

(ii) Under which production capacity requirement under section 179C(e) and paragraph (b)(5)(i)(A) and (B) of this section the taxpayer's qualified refinery qualifies;

(iii) Whether the refinery is qualified refinery property under section 179C(d) and paragraph (b)(2) of this section, sufficient to establish that the primary purpose of the refinery is to process liquid fuel from crude oil or qualified fuels.

(iv) The total cost basis of the qualified refinery property at issue for the taxpayer's current taxable year; and

(v) The depreciation treatment of the capitalized portion of the qualified refinery property.

(3) Time and manner for submitting report. (i) Time for submitting report. The taxpayer is required to submit the report specified in this paragraph (f) not later than the due date (including extensions) of the taxpayer's Federal income tax return for the taxable year in which the qualified refinery property is placed in service. A taxpayer that has made a section 179C(a) election for a prior taxable year by claiming the section 179C(a) deduction on a Federal income tax return filed prior to July 23, 2008, but has not already filed a report for that year, must attach a report to its next Federal income tax return for each taxable year the taxpayer claimed the deduction but did not file a report.

(ii) Manner of submitting report. The taxpayer must attach the report specified in this paragraph (f) to the taxpayer's timely filed original Federal income tax return for the taxable year in which the qualified refinery property is placed in service.

(g) Effective/applicability date. This section is applicable for taxable years ending on or after July 9, 2008.

(h) Expiration date. The applicability of this section expires on or before July 1, 2011.

T.D. 9412, 7/3/2008.

Proposed § 1.181-0 Table of contents. [*For Preamble, see ¶ 152,835*]

[The text of this proposed section is the same as the text of § 1.181-0T published elsewhere in this issue of the Federal Register.] [*See T.D. 9312, 2/9/2007, 72 Fed. Reg. 27.*]

§ 1.181-0T Table of contents (temporary).

This section lists the table of contents for §§ 1.181-1T through 1.181-6T.

§ 1.181-1T Deduction for qualified film and television production costs (temporary).

(a) Deduction.

(1) In general.

(2) Owner.

(3) Production costs.

(b) Limit on amount of production costs and amount of deduction.

(1) In general.

(2) Higher limit for productions in certain areas.

(i) In general.

(ii) Significantly incurred.

(iii) Animated film and television productions.

(iv) Productions incorporating both live action and animation.

(v) Records required.

(c) No other depreciation or amortization deduction allowed.

§ 1.181-2T Election (temporary).

(a) Time and manner of making election.

(b) Election by entity.

(c) Information required.

(1) Initial election.

(2) Subsequent taxable years.

(3) Deductions by more than one owner.

(d) Revocation of election.

(1) In general.

(2) Consent granted.

(e) Transition rules.

(1) Costs first paid or incurred prior to October 23, 2004.

(2) Returns filed after June 14, 2006, and before March 12, 2007.

(3) Information required.

§ 1.181-3T Qualified film or television production (temporary).

(a) In general.

(b) Production.

(1) In general.

(2) Special rules for television productions.

(3) Exception for certain sexually explicit productions.

(c) Compensation.

(d) Qualified compensation.

(e) Special rule for acquired productions.

(f) Other definitions.

(1) Actors.

(2) Production personnel.

(3) United States.

§ 1.181-4T Special rules (temporary).

(a) Recapture.

(1) Applicability.

(2) Principal photography not commencing prior to January 1, 2009.

(3) Amount of recapture.

(b) Recapture under section 1245.

§ 1.181-5T Examples (temporary).

§ 1.181-6T Effective date (temporary).

(a) In general.

(b) Application of regulation project REG-115403-05 to pre-effective date productions.

(c) Special rules for returns filed for prior taxable years.

T.D. 9312, 2/8/2007.

§ 1.180-1 Expenditures by farmers for fertilizer, etc.

(a) In general. A taxpayer engaged in the business of farming may elect, for any taxable year beginning after December 31, 1959, to treat as deductible expenses those expenditures otherwise chargeable to capital account which are paid or incurred by him during the taxable year for the purchase or acquisition of fertilizer, lime, ground limestone, marl, or other materials to enrich, neutralize, or condition land used in farming, and those expenditures otherwise chargeable to capital account paid or incurred for the application of such items and materials to such land. No election is required to be made for those expenditures which are not capital in nature. Section 180, § 1.180-2, and this section are not applicable to those expenses which are deductible under section 162 and the regulations thereunder or which are subject to the method described in section 175 and the regulations thereunder.

(b) Land used in farming. For purposes of section 180(a) and of paragraph (a) of this section, the term "land used in farming" means land used (before or simultaneously with the expenditures described in such section and such paragraph) by the taxpayer or his tenant for the production of crops, fruits, or other agricultural products or for the sustenance of livestock. See section 180(b). Expenditures for the initial preparation of land never previously used for farming purposes by the taxpayer or his tenant (although chargeable to capital account) are not subject to the election. The principles stated in §§ 1.175-3 and 1.175-4 are equally applicable under this section in determining whether the taxpayer is engaged in the business of farming and whether the land is used in farming.

T.D. 6548, 2/21/61.

Proposed § 1.181-1 Deduction for qualified film and television production costs. [*For Preamble, see ¶ 152,835*]

[The text of this proposed section is the same as the text of § 1.181-1T published elsewhere in this issue of the Federal Register.] [*See T.D. 9312, 2/9/2007, 72 Fed. Reg. 27.*]

§ 1.181-1T Deduction for qualified film and television production costs (temporary).

Caution: The Treasury has not yet amended Reg § 1.181-1T to reflect changes made by P.L. 110-343.

(a) Deduction.

(1) In general. The owner (as defined in paragraph (a)(2) of this section) of any film or television production (as defined in § 1.181-3T(b)) that the owner reasonably expects will be, upon completion, a qualified film or television production (as defined in § 1.181-3T(a)) for which the production costs (as defined in paragraph (a)(3) of this section) will not be in excess of the production cost limit of paragraph (b) of this section may elect to treat all production costs incurred by the owner as an expense that is deductible in the taxable year in which the costs are paid (in the case of a taxpayer who uses the cash method of accounting) or incurred (in the case of a taxpayer who uses the accrual method of accounting). This deduction is subject to recapture if the owner's expectations prove to be inaccurate. This section provides rules for determining who is the owner of a production, what is a production cost, and the maximum production cost that may be incurred for a production for which an election is made under section 181 of the Internal Revenue Code (Code). Section 1.181-2T provides rules for making the election under section 181. Section 1.181-3T provides definitions and rules concerning qualified film and television productions. Section 1.181-4T provides special rules, including rules for recapture of the deduction. Section 1.181-5T provides examples of the application of §§ 1.181-1T through 1.181-4T, while § 1.181-6T provides the effective date of §§ 1.181-1T through 1.181-5T.

(2) Owner. For purposes of this section and §§ 1.181-2T through 1.181-6T, the owner of a production is any taxpayer that is required under section 263A to capitalize costs paid or incurred in producing the production into the cost basis of the production, or that would be required to do so if section 263A applied to that taxpayer. A taxpayer that obtains only a limited license or right to exploit a production, or receives an interest or profit participation in a production as compensation for services, generally is not an owner of the production for purposes of this section and §§ 1.181-2T through 1.181-6T.

(3) Production costs. (i) The term production costs means all costs paid or incurred by the owner in producing or acquiring a production that are required, absent the provisions of section 181, to be capitalized under section 263A, or that would be required to be capitalized if section 263A applied to the owner. These production costs specifically include, but are not limited to, participations and residuals, compensation paid for services, compensation paid for property rights, non-compensation costs, and costs paid or incurred in connection with obtaining financing for the production (for example, premiums paid or incurred to obtain a completion bond for the production).

(ii) Production costs do not include costs paid or incurred to distribute or exploit a production (including advertising and print costs).

(iii) Production costs do not include the costs to prepare a new release or new broadcast of an existing film or video after the initial release or initial broadcast of the film or video (for instance, the preparation of a DVD release of a theatrically-released film, or the preparation of an edited version of a theatrically-released film for television broadcast). Costs paid or incurred to prepare a new release or a new broadcast of a film or video that has previously been released or broadcast, therefore, are not taken into account for purposes of paragraph (b) of this section, and may not be deducted under this paragraph (a).

(iv) If a production (or any right or interest in a production) is acquired from any person bearing a relationship to the taxpayer described in section 267(b) or section 707(b)(1), and the costs paid or incurred to acquire the production are less than the seller's production cost, the purchaser must treat the seller's production cost as a production cost of the acquired production for purposes of determining whether the aggregate production cost paid or incurred with respect to the production exceeds the applicable production cost limit imposed under paragraphs (b)(1) and (b)(2) of this section. Notwithstanding this paragraph (a)(3)(iv), the taxpayer's deduction under section 181 is limited to the taxpayer's acquisition cost of the production plus any further production costs incurred by the taxpayer.

(v) The provisions of this paragraph (a) apply notwithstanding the provisions of section 167(g)(7)(D).

(b) Limit on amount of production cost and amount of deduction. *(1) In general.* Except as provided under paragraph (b)(2) of this section, the deduction permitted under section 181 does not apply in the case of any production, the production cost of which exceeds $15,000,000.

(2) Higher limit for productions in certain areas. (i) In general. This section is applied by substituting $20,000,000 for $15,000,000 in the case of any production the aggregate production cost of which is significantly incurred in an area eligible for designation as—

(A) A low income community under section 45D; or

(B) A distressed county or isolated area of distress by the Delta Regional Authority established under 7 U.S.C section 2009aa-1.

(ii) Significantly incurred. The aggregate production cost of a production is significantly incurred within one or more areas specified in paragraph (b)(2)(i) of this section if—

(A) At least 20 percent of the total production cost incurred in connection with first-unit principal photography for the production is incurred in connection with first-unit principal photography that takes place in such areas; or

(B) At least 50 percent of the total number of days of first-unit principal photography for the production consists of days during which first-unit principal photography takes place in such areas.

(iii) Animated film and television productions. For purposes of an animated film or television production, the aggregate production cost of the production is significantly incurred within one or more areas specified in paragraph (b)(2)(i) of this section if—

(A) At least 20 percent of the total production cost incurred in connection with keyframe animation, in-between animation, animation photography, and the recording of voice acting performances for the production is incurred in connection with such activities that take place in such areas; or

(B) At least 50 percent of the total number of days of keyframe animation, in-between animation, animation photography, and the recording of voice acting performances for the production consists of days during which such activities take place in such areas.

(iv) Productions incorporating both live action and animation. For purposes of a production incorporating both live action and animation, the aggregate production cost of the production is significantly incurred within one or more areas specified in paragraph (b)(2)(i) of this section if—

(A) At least 20 percent of the total production cost incurred in connection with first-unit principal photography, keyframe animation, in-between animation, animation photography, and the recording of voice acting performances for the production is incurred in connection with such activities that take place in such areas; or

(B) At least 50 percent of the total number of days of first unit principal photography, keyframe animation, in-between animation, animation photography, and the recording of voice acting performances for the production consists of days during which such activities take place in such areas.

(v) Records required. A taxpayer intending to utilize the higher production cost limit under paragraph (b)(2)(i) of this section must maintain records adequate to demonstrate qualification under this paragraph (b)(2).

(c) No other depreciation or amortization deduction allowed. *(1)* Except as provided in paragraph (c)(2) of this section, an owner that elects to deduct production costs under section 181 with respect to a production may not deduct production costs for that production under any provision of the Code other than section 181 unless § 1.181-4T(a) applies to the production. In addition, except as provided in paragraph (c)(2) of this section, an owner that has, in a previous taxable year, deducted any production cost of a production under a provision of the Code other than section 181 is ineligible to make an election with respect to that production under section 181.

(2) An owner may make an election under section 181 despite prior deductions claimed for amortization of the cost of acquiring or developing screenplays, scripts, story outlines, motion picture production rights to books and plays, and other similar properties for purposes of potential future development or production of a production under any provision of the Code if such costs were incurred before the first taxable year in which an election could be made under § 1.181-2T(a). However, the production cost of the production does not include costs that a taxpayer has begun to amortize prior to the time that the production is set for production (for further guidance, see Rev. Proc. 2004-36 (2004-1 CB 1063) and § 601.601(d)(2)(ii)(b) of this chapter).

T.D. 9312, 2/8/2007.

§ 1.180-2 Time and manner of making election and revocation.

(a) Election. The claiming of a deduction on the taxpayer's return for an amount to which section 180 applies for amounts (otherwise chargeable to capital account) expended for fertilizer, lime, etc., shall constitute an election under section 180 and paragraph (a) of § 1.180-1. Such election shall be effective only for the taxable year for which the deduction is claimed.

(b) Revocation. Once the election is made for any taxable year such election may not be revoked without the consent of the district director for the district in which the taxpayer's return is required to be filed. Such requests for consent shall be in writing and signed by the taxpayer or his authorized representative and shall set forth—

(1) The name and address of the taxpayer;

(2) The taxable year to which the revocation of the election is to apply;

(3) The amount of expenditures paid or incurred during the taxable year, or portions thereof (where applicable), previously taken as a deduction on the return in respect of which the revocation of the election is to be applicable; and

(4) The reasons for the request to revoke the election.

T.D. 6548, 2/21/61.

Proposed § 1.181-2 Election. [*For Preamble, see ¶ 152,835*]

[The text of this proposed section is the same as the text of § 1.181-2T published elsewhere in this issue of the Federal Register.] [*See T.D. 9312, 2/9/2007, 72 Fed. Reg. 27.*]

§ 1.181-2T Election (temporary).

Caution: The Treasury has not yet amended Reg § 1.181-2T to reflect changes made by P.L. 110-343.

(a) Time and manner of making election. *(1)* Except as provided in paragraph (e) of this section, a taxpayer electing to deduct the production cost of a production under section 181 must do so in the time and manner described in this paragraph (a). Except as provided in paragraphs (a)(2) and (e) of this section, the election must be made by the due date (including extensions) for filing the taxpayer's Federal income tax return for the first taxable year in which production costs (as defined in § 1.181-1T(a)(3)) have been paid or incurred. See § 301.9100-2 of this chapter for a six-month extension of this period in certain circumstances. The election under section 181 is made separately for each production produced by the owner.

(2) An owner may not make an election under paragraph (a)(1) of this section until the first taxable year in which the owner reasonably expects (based on all of the facts and circumstances) that—

(i) The production will be set for production and will, upon completion, be a qualified film or television production; and

(ii) The aggregate production cost paid or incurred with respect to the production will, at no time, exceed the applicable production cost limit set forth under § 1.181-1T(b) of the regulations.

(3) If the election under this paragraph (a) is made in a taxable year subsequent to the taxable year in which production costs were first paid or incurred because paragraph (a)(2) of this section was not satisfied until such subsequent taxable year, the election must be made in the first such taxable year, and any production costs incurred prior to the taxable year in which the taxpayer makes the election are treated as production costs (except as provided in § 1.181-1T(c)(2)) that are deductible under § 1.181-1T(a) in the taxable year paragraph (a)(2) of this section is first satisfied and the election is made.

(b) Election by entity. In the case of a production owned by an entity, the election is made by the entity. For example, the election is made for each member of a consolidated group by the common parent of the group, for each partner by the partnership, or for each shareholder by the S corporation. The election must be made by the due date (including extensions) for filing the return for the later of the taxable year of the entity in which production costs are first paid or incurred or the first taxable year in which § 1.181-2T(a)(2) is satisfied.

(c) Information required. *(1) Initial election.* For each production to which the election applies, the taxpayer must attach a statement to the return stating that the taxpayer is making an election under section 181 and providing—

(i) The name (or other unique identifying designation) of the production;

(ii) The date production costs were first paid or incurred with respect to the production;

(iii) The amount of production costs (as defined in § 1.181-1T(a)(3)) paid or incurred with respect to the production during the taxable year (including costs described in § 1.181-2T(a)(3));

(iv) The aggregate amount of qualified compensation (as defined in § 1.181-3T(d)) paid or incurred with respect to the production during the taxable year (including costs described in § 1.181-2T(a)(3));

(v) The aggregate amount of compensation (as defined in § 1.181-3T(c)) paid or incurred with respect to the production during the taxable year (including costs described in § 1.181-2T(a)(3));

(vi) If the owner expects that the total production cost of the production will be significantly paid or incurred in (or, if applicable, if a significant portion of the total number of days of principal photography will occur in) one or more of the areas specified in § 1.181-1T(b)(2)(i), the identity of the area or areas, the amount of production costs paid or incurred (or the number of days of principal photography engaged in) for the applicable activities described in § 1.181-1T(b)(2)(ii), (iii), or (iv), as applicable, that take place within such areas (including costs described in § 1.181-2T(a)(3)), and the total production cost paid or incurred (or the total number of days of principal photography engaged in) for such activities (whether or not they take place in such areas), for the taxable year (including costs described in § 1.181-2T(a)(3)); and

(vii) A declaration that the owner reasonably expects (based on all of the facts and circumstances at the time the election was filed) both that the production will be set for production (or has been set for production) and will be a qualified film or television production, and that the aggregate production cost of the production paid or incurred will not, at any time, exceed the applicable dollar amount set forth under § 1.181-1T(b).

(2) Subsequent taxable years. If the owner pays or incurs additional production costs in any taxable year subsequent to the taxable year in which production costs are first deducted under section 181, the owner must attach a statement to its Federal income tax return for that subsequent taxable year providing—

(i) The name (or other unique identifying designation) of the production;

(ii) The date the production costs were first paid or incurred;

(iii) The amount of production costs paid or incurred by the owner with respect to the production during the taxable year;

(iv) The amount of qualified compensation paid or incurred with respect to the production during the taxable year;

(v) The aggregate amount of compensation paid or incurred with respect to the production during the taxable year, and the aggregate amount of compensation paid or incurred with respect to the production in all prior taxable years;

(vi) If the owner expects that the total production cost of the production will be significantly paid or incurred in (or, if applicable, if a significant portion of the total number of days of principal photography will occur in) one or more of the areas specified in § 1.181-1T(b)(2)(i), the identity of the area or areas, the amount of production costs paid or incurred (or the number of days of principal photography engaged in) for the applicable activities described in § 1.181-1T(b)(2)(ii), (iii), or (iv), as applicable, that take place within such areas, and the total production cost paid or incurred (or the number of days of principal photography engaged in) for such activities (whether or not they take place in such areas), for the taxable year; and

(vii) A declaration that the owner continues to reasonably expect (based on all of the facts and circumstances at the time the election was filed) both that the production will be set for production (or has been set for production) and will be a qualified film or television production, and that the aggregate production cost of the production paid or incurred will not, at any time, exceed the applicable dollar amount set forth under § 1.181-1T(b).

(3) Deductions by more than one owner. If more than one taxpayer will claim deductions under section 181 with respect to the production for the taxable year, each owner (but not the members of an entity who are issued a Schedule K-1 by the entity with respect to their interest in the production) must provide a list of the names and taxpayer identification numbers of all such taxpayers, the dollar amount that each such taxpayer is entitled to deduct under section 181, and the information required by paragraphs (c)(1)(iii) through (vi) and (c)(2)(iii) through (vi) of this section for all owners.

(d) Revocation of election. *(1) In general.* An election made under this section may not be revoked without the consent of the Secretary.

(2) Consent granted. The Secretary's consent to revoke an election under this section with respect to a particular production will be granted if the owner—

(i) Files a Federal income tax return in which the owner complies with the recapture provisions of § 1.181-4T(a) to recapture the amount described in § 1.181-4T(a)(3); and

(ii) Attaches a statement to the owner's return clearly indicating the name (or other unique identifying designation) of the production, and stating that the election under section 181 with respect to that production is being revoked pursuant to § 1.181-2T(d)(2).

(e) Transition rules. *(1) Costs first paid or incurred prior to October 23, 2004.* If a taxpayer begins principal photography of a production after October 22, 2004, but first paid or incurred production costs before October 23, 2004, the taxpayer is entitled to make an election under this section with respect to those costs. If, before June 15, 2006, the taxpayer filed its Federal tax return for the taxable year in which production costs were first paid or incurred, and if the taxpayer wants to make a section 181 election for that taxable year, the taxpayer may make the election either by—

(i) Filing an amended Federal tax return for the taxable year in which production costs were first paid or incurred, and for all subsequent affected taxable year(s), on or before November 15, 2006, provided that all of these years are open under the period of limitations for assessment under section 6501(a); or

(ii) Filing a Form 3115, "Application For Change in Accounting Method," for the first or second taxable year ending on or after December 31, 2005, in accordance with the administrative procedures issued under § 1.446-1(e)(3)(ii) for obtaining the Commissioner's automatic consent to a change in accounting method (for further guidance, for example, see Rev. Proc. 2002-9, 2002-1 CB 327, and § 601.601(d)(2)(ii)(b) of this chapter). This change in method of accounting results in a section 481 adjustment. Further, any limitations on obtaining the automatic consent of the Commissioner do not apply to a taxpayer seeking to change its method of accounting under this paragraph (e)(1). Moreover, the taxpayer must include on line 1a of the Form 3115 the designated automatic accounting method change number "100".

(2) Returns filed after June 14, 2006, and before March 12, 2007. If, after June 14, 2006, and before March 12, 2007, the owner of a film or television production filed its original Federal income tax return for a taxable year ending after October 22, 2004, without making an election under section 181 for production costs first paid or incurred after October 22, 2004, and if the taxpayer wants to make an election under section 181 for production costs first paid or incurred during that taxable year, the taxpayer must make the election within the time provided by paragraph (a) of this section and in the manner provided in paragraph (c)(1) of this section, except that the election statement attached to the return must include the information required in paragraphs (c)(1)(i) through (vi) of this section.

(3) Information required. If, in accordance with paragraph (e)(1) of this section, the taxpayer is making an election for a prior taxable year by filing amended Federal tax return(s), the statement and information required by paragraphs (c)(1) and (c)(2) of this section must be attached to each amended return. If, in accordance with paragraph (e)(1) of this section, the taxpayer is making a section 181 election for a prior taxable year by filing a Form 3115 for the first or second taxable year ending on or after December 31, 2005, the statement and information required by paragraphs (c)(1) and (c)(2) of this section must be attached to the Form 3115. For purposes of the preceding sentence, the amount of the cost or compensation paid or incurred for the production must only include the amount paid or incurred in taxable years prior to the year of change (for further guidance on year of change, see section 5.02 of Rev. Proc. 2002-9 and § 601.601(d)(2)(ii)(b) of this chapter).

T.D. 9312, 2/8/2007.

Proposed § 1.181-3 Qualified film or television production. [*For Preamble, see ¶ 152,835*]

[The text of this proposed section is the same as the text of § 1.181-3T published elsewhere in this issue of the Federal Register.] [*See T.D. 9312, 2/9/2007, 72 Fed. Reg. 27.*]

§ 1.181-3T Qualified film or television production (temporary).

Caution: The Treasury has not yet amended Reg § 1.181-3T to reflect changes made by P.L. 110-343.

(a) In general. The term qualified film or television production means any production (as defined in paragraph (b) of this section) if not less than 75 percent of the total amount of compensation (as defined in paragraph (c) of this section) paid with respect to the production is qualified compensation (as defined in paragraph (d) of this section).

(b) Production. *(1) In general.* Except as provided in paragraph (b)(3) of this section, for purposes of this section and §§ 1.181-1T, 1.181-2T, 1.181-4T, 1.181-5T, and 1.181-6T, a film or television production (or production) means any film or video (including digital video) production the production cost of which is subject to capitalization under section 263A, or that would be would be subject to capitalization if section 263A applied to the owner of the production.

(2) Special rules for television productions. Each episode of a television series is a separate production to which the rules, limitations, and election requirements of this section and §§ 1.181-1T, 1.181-2T, 1.181-4T, 1.181-5T, and 1.181-6T apply. A taxpayer may elect to deduct production costs under section 181 only for the first 44 episodes of a television series (including pilot episodes). A television series may include more than one season of programming.

(3) Exception for certain sexually explicit productions. A production does not include property with respect to which records are required to be maintained under 18 U.S.C. 2257. Section 2257 of Title 18 requires maintenance of certain records with respect to any book, magazine, periodical, film, videotape, or other matter that—

(i) Contains one or more visual depictions made after November 1, 1990, of active sexually explicit conduct; and

(ii) is produced in whole or in part with materials that have been mailed or shipped in interstate or foreign commerce, or is shipped or transported or is intended for shipment or transportation in interstate or foreign commerce.

(c) Compensation. The term compensation means, for purposes of this section and § 1.181-2T(c), all payments made by the owner (whether paid directly by the owner or paid indirectly on the owner's behalf) for services performed by actors (as defined in paragraph (f)(1) of this section), directors, producers, and other relevant production personnel (as defined in paragraph (f)(2) of this section) with respect to the production. Indirect payments on the owner's behalf include, for example, payments by a partner on behalf of an owner that is a partnership, payments by a shareholder on behalf of an owner that is a corporation, and payments by a contract producer on behalf of an owner. Payments for services include all elements of compensation as provided for in § 1.263A-1(e)(2)(i)(B) and (3)(ii)(D). Compensation is not limited to wages reported on Form W-2, "Wage and Tax Statement," and includes compensation paid to independent contractors. However, solely for purposes of paragraph (a) of this section, the term "compensation" does not include participations and residuals (as defined in section 167(g)(7)(B)). See § 1.181-1T(a)(3) for additional rules concerning participations and residuals.

(d) Qualified compensation. The term qualified compensation means, for purposes of this section and § 1.181-2T(c), all payments made by the owner (whether paid directly by the owner or paid indirectly on the owner's behalf) paid for services performed in the United States (as defined in paragraph (f)(3) of this section) by actors, directors, producers, and other relevant production personnel with respect to the production. A service is performed in the United States for purposes of this paragraph (d) if the principal photography to which the compensated service relates occurs within the United States and the person performing the service is physically present in the United States. For purposes of an animated film or animated television production, the location where production activities such as keyframe animation, in-between animation, animation photography, and the recording of voice acting performances are performed is considered in lieu of the location of principal photography. For purposes of a production incorporating both live action and animation, the location where production activities such as keyframe animation, in-between animation, animation photography, and the recording of voice acting performances for the production is considered in addition to the location of principal photography.

(e) Special rule for acquired productions. A taxpayer who acquires an unfinished production from a prior owner must take into account all compensation paid by or on behalf of the seller and any previous owners in determining if the production is a qualified film or television production as defined in paragraph (a) of this section. Any owner seeking to deduct as a production cost either the cost of acquiring a production or any subsequent production costs should obtain from the seller detailed records concerning the compensation paid with respect to the production in order to demonstrate the eligibility of the production under section 181.

(f) Other definitions. The following definitions apply for purposes of this section and §§ 1.181-1T, 1.181-2T, 1.181-4T, 1.181-5T, and 1.181-6T:

(1) Actors. The term actors includes players, newscasters, or any other persons who are compensated for their performance or appearance in a production.

(2) Production personnel. The term production personnel includes, for example, writers, choreographers, and composers providing services during production, casting agents, camera operators, set designers, lighting technicians, makeup artists, and others who are compensated for providing services directly related to producing the production.

(3) United States. The term United States includes the 50 states, the District of Columbia, the territorial waters of the continental United States, the airspace or space over the continental United States and its territorial waters, and the seabed and subsoil of those submarine areas that are adjacent to the territorial waters of the continental United States and over which the United States has exclusive rights, in accordance with international law, with respect to the exploration and exploitation of natural resources. The term United States does not include possessions and territories of the United States (or the airspace or space over these areas).

T.D. 9312, 2/8/2007.

Proposed § 1.181-4 Special rules. [*For Preamble, see ¶ 152,835*]

[The text of this proposed section is the same as the text of § 1.181-4T published elsewhere in this issue of the Federal Register.] [*See T.D. 9312, 2/9/2007, 72 Fed. Reg. 27.*]

§ 1.181-4T Special rules (temporary).

Caution: The Treasury has not yet amended Reg § 1.181-4T to reflect changes made by P.L. 110-343.

(a) Recapture. *(1) Applicability.* The rules of this paragraph (a) apply notwithstanding whether a taxpayer has satisfied the requirements of § 1.181-2T(d). A taxpayer that, with respect to a production, claimed a deduction under section 181 in any taxable year in an amount in excess of the amount that would be allowable as a deduction for that year in the absence of section 181 must recapture deductions as provided for in paragraph (a)(3) of this section for the production in the first taxable year in which—

(i) The aggregate production cost of the production exceeds the applicable production cost limit under § 1.181-1T(b);

(ii) The owner no longer reasonably expects (based on all of the facts and circumstances at the time the election was filed) both that the production will be set for production (or has been set for production) and will be a qualified film or television production, and that the aggregate production cost of the production paid or incurred will not, at any time, exceed the applicable dollar amount set forth under § 1.181-1T(b); or

(iii) the taxpayer revokes the election pursuant to § 1.181-2T(d).

(2) Principal photography not commencing prior to January 1, 2009. If a taxpayer claims a deduction under section 181 with respect to a production for which principal photography does not commence prior to January 1, 2009, the taxpayer must recapture deductions as provided for in paragraph (a)(3) of this section in the taxpayer's taxable year that includes December 31, 2008.

(3) Amount of recapture. A taxpayer subject to recapture under this triggered, include in the taxpayer's gross income and add to the taxpayer's adjusted basis in the property—

(i) For a production that is placed in service in a taxable year prior to the taxable year in which recapture is triggered, the difference between the aggregate amount claimed as a deduction under section 181 with respect to the production in all such prior taxable years and the aggregate depreciation deductions that would have been allowable with respect to the property for such prior taxable years (or that the taxpayer could have elected to deduct in the taxable year that the property was placed in service) with respect to the production under the taxpayer's method of accounting; or

(ii) For a production that has not been placed in service, the aggregate amount claimed as a deduction under section 181 with respect to the production in all such prior taxable years.

(b) Recapture under section 1245. For purposes of recapture under section 1245, any deduction allowed under section 181 is treated as a deduction allowable for amortization.

T.D. 9312, 2/8/2007.

Proposed § 1.181-5 Examples. [*For Preamble, see ¶ 152,835*]

[The text of this proposed section is the same as the text of § 1.181-5T published elsewhere in this issue of the Federal Register.] [*See T.D. 9312, 2/9/2007, 72 Fed. Reg. 27.*]

§ 1.181-5T Examples (temporary).

Caution: The Treasury has not yet amended Reg § 1.181-5T to reflect changes made by P.L. 110-343.

The following examples illustrate the application of §§ 1.181-1T through 1.181-4T:

Example (1). X, a corporation using a calendar taxable year, is a producer of films. X is the owner (within the meaning of § 1.181-1T(a)(2)) of film ABC. X incurs production costs in year 1, but does not commence principal photography for film ABC until year 2. In year 1, X reasonably expects, based on all of the facts and circumstances, that film ABC will be set for production and will be a qualified film or television production, and that at no time will the production cost of film ABC exceed the applicable production cost limit of § 1.181-1T(b). Provided that X satisfies all other requirements of §§ 1.181-1T through 1.181-4T and § 1.181-6T, X may deduct in year 1 the production costs for film ABC that X incurred in year 1.

Example (2). The facts are the same as in Example 1. In year 2, X begins, but does not complete, principal photography for film ABC. Most of the scenes that X films in year 2 are shot outside the United States and, as of December 31, year 2, less than 75 percent of the total compensation paid with respect to film ABC is qualified compensation. Nevertheless, X still reasonably expects, based on all of the facts and circumstances, that film ABC will be a qualified film or television production, and that at no time will the production cost of film ABC exceed the applicable production cost limit of § 1.181-1T(b). Provided that X satisfies all other requirements of §§ 1.181-1T through 1.181-4T and § 1.181-6T, X may deduct in year 2 the production costs for film ABC that X incurred in year 2.

Example (3). The facts are the same as in Example 2. In year 3, X continues, but does not complete, production of film ABC. Due to changes in the expected production cost of film ABC, X no longer expects film ABC to qualify under section 181. X files a statement with its return for year 3 identifying the film and stating that X revokes its election under section 181. X includes in income in year 3 the deductions claimed in year 1 and in year 2 as provided for in § 1.181-4T. X has successfully revoked its election pursuant to § 1.181-2T(d).

Example (4). The facts are the same as in Example 2. In year 3, X completes production of film ABC at a cost of $14.5 million and places it into service. ABC is an unexpected success in year 4, causing participation payments to drive the total production cost of film ABC above $15 million in year 4. X includes in income in year 4 as recapture under § 1.181-4T(a) the difference between the deductions claimed in year 1, year 2, and year 3, and the deductions that it would have claimed under the income forecast method described in section 167(g) of the Internal Revenue Code, a method that was allowable for the film in year 3 (the year the film was placed in service). Because X calculated the recapture amount by comparing actual deductions to deductions under the income forecast method, X must use this method to calculate deductions for film ABC for year 4 and in subsequent taxable years.

T.D. 9312, 2/8/2007.

Proposed § 1.181-6 Effective date. [*For Preamble, see ¶ 152,835*]

[The text of this proposed section is the same as the text of § 1.181-6T published elsewhere in this issue of the Federal Register.] [*See T.D. 9312, 2/9/2007, 72 Fed. Reg. 27.*]

§ 1.181-6T Effective date (temporary).

Caution: The Treasury has not yet amended Reg § 1.181-6T to reflect changes made by P.L. 110-343.

(a) In general.

(1) Section 181 applies to productions commencing after October 22, 2004, and shall not apply to productions commencing after December 31, 2008. Except as provided in paragraphs (b) and (c) of this section, §§ 1.181-1T through 1.181-5T apply to productions, the first day of principal photography for which occurs on or after February 9, 2007, and before January 1, 2009. In the case of an animated production, this paragraph (a) should be applied by substituting "in-between animation" in place of "principal photography". Productions involving both animation and live-action photography may use either standard.

(2) The applicability of §§ 1.181-1T through 1.181-5T expires on February 8, 2010.

(b) Application of regulation project REG-115403-05 to pre-effective date productions. A taxpayer may apply §§ 1.181-1T through 1.181-5T to productions, the first day of principal photography (or "in-between" animation) for which occurs after October 22, 2004, and before February 9, 2007, provided that the taxpayer applies all provisions in §§ 1.181-1T through 1.181-5T to the productions.

(c) Special rules for returns filed for prior taxable years. If before March 12, 2007, an owner of a film or television production began principal photography (or "in-between" animation) for the production after October 22, 2004, and filed its original Federal income tax return for the year such costs were first paid or incurred without making an election under section 181 for the costs of the production, and if the taxpayer wants to make an election under section 181 for such taxable year, see § 1.181-2T(e) for the time and manner of making the election.

T.D. 9312, 2/8/2007.

§ 12.9 Election to postpone determination with respect to the presumption described in section 183(d).

(a) In general. An individual, electing small business corporation, trust or estate may elect in accordance with the rules set forth in this section to postpone a determination whether the presumption described in section 183(d) applies with respect to any activity in which the taxpayer engages until after the close of the fourth taxable year (sixth taxable year, in the case of an activity described in § 1.183-1(c)(3)) following the taxable year in which the taxpayer first engages in such activity. The election must be made in accordance with the applicable requirements of paragraphs (b), (c) and (d) of this section. Except as otherwise provided in paragraphs (c) and (e) of this section, an election made pursuant to this section shall be binding for the first taxable year in which the taxpayer first engages in the activity and for all subsequent taxable years in the five (or seven) year period referred to in the first sentence of this paragraph. For purposes of this section, a taxpayer shall be treated as not having engaged in an activity during any taxable year beginning before January 1, 1970.

(b) Period to which an election applies. An individual, trust, estate, or small business corporation may make the election. The five year presumption period (seven year presumption period in the case of an activity described in § 1.183-1(c)(3)) to which the election shall apply shall be the five (or seven) consecutive taxable years of such taxpayer beginning with the taxable year in which such taxpayer first engages in the activity. For purposes of this section, a taxpayer who engages in an activity as a partner, engages in it in each of his taxable years with or within which ends a partnership year during which the activity was carried on by the partnership.

(c) Time for making an election. A taxpayer who is an individual, trust estate or small business corporation may make the election provided in § 183(e) by filing the statement and consents required by paragraph (d) of this section within—

(1) 3 years after the due date of such taxpayer's return (determined without extensions) for the taxable year in which such taxpayer first engages in the activity, but not later than

(2) 60 days after such taxpayer receives a written notice (if any) from a district director that the district director proposes to disallow deductions attributable to an activity not engaged in for profit under section 183.

The provisions of paragraph (c)(2) of this section shall in no event be construed to extend the period described in (c)(1) of this section for making such election. Notwithstanding the time periods prescribed in paragraph (c)(1) and (2) of this section, if no election has been made before a suit or proceeding described in section 7422(a) is maintained or a petition is filed in the Tax Court for a redetermination of a deficiency for any taxable year within the presumption period to which the election would apply, no election may be made except with the consent of the Commissioner which will not be given unless no appreciable delay in the suit or proceeding will be caused.

(d) Manner of making election. *(1)* The election shall be made by the individual, trust, estate, or electing small business corporation, as the case may be, engaged in the activity, by filing a statement which sets forth the following information—

(i) The name, address, and taxpayer identification number of such taxpayer, and, if applicable, of the partnership in which he engages in the activity,

(ii) A declaration stating that the taxpayer elects to postpone a determination as to whether the presumption described in section 183(d) applies until after the close of the taxpayer's fourth taxable year (sixth taxable year, in the case of an activity described in § 1.183-1(c)(3)) following the taxable year in which the taxpayer first engaged in such activity and identifying that first such taxable year, and,

(iii) A description of each activity (as defined in § 1.183-1(d)(1)) with respect to which the election is being made.

(2) For an election to be effective, there must be attached to the statement properly executed consents, in the form prescribed by Commissioner, extending the period prescribed by section 6501 for the assessment of any tax to a date which is not earlier than 18 months after the due date of the return (determined without extensions) for the final year in the presumption period to which the election applies, as follows:

(i) Consents for each of the taxpayer's taxable years in the presumption period to which the election applies.

(ii) If the election is made by an electing small business corporation, a consent of each person who is a shareholder during any taxable year to which the election applies, for each of such shareholder's taxable years with or within which end each of the corporation's taxable years in the presumption period.

(iii) If a taxpayer referred to in paragraph (d)(2)(i) of this section or shareholder referred to in paragraph (d)(2)(ii) of this section is married at the time of the election, in the case of his present spouse, a consent for each of such spouse's taxable years which correspond to the taxable years (other than prior years of the shareholder during no part of which he was a shareholder) for which consents are required by paragraph (d)(2)(i) or (ii) of this section as the case may be. Such consents shall not be construed to shorten the period described in section 6501 for any taxable year within the presumption period to which the election applies.

(3) The statement, with the required consents attached, shall be filed—

(i) With the service center at which the taxpayer making the election is required to file his return, or

(ii) If the taxpayer is notified by a district director that, pursuant to section 183 he is proposing to disallow deductions with respect to an activity not engaged in for profit, with such district director.

(e) Subsequent invalidations. If, after a timely election has been made, but still within the presumption period, a suit or proceeding (as described in section 7422(a)) is maintained by the electing taxpayer, a shareholder referred to in paragraph (d)(2)(ii) of this section, or spouse referred to in paragraph (d)(2)(iii) of this section for any taxable year for which a consent is required by this section and the taxpayer, shareholder, or spouse has not been issued a notice of deficiency (as described in section 6212(a)) with respect to such taxable year such election shall not be effective to postpone the determination whether the presumption applies, for such taxable year, but the consents extending the statute of limitations filed with the election shall not thereby be invalidated. The immediately preceding sentence shall not apply to a suit or proceeding maintained by the spouse of an electing taxpayer for a taxable year for which such spouse has filed a separate return, or a suit or proceeding maintained by a shareholder for a taxable year in which he was not such a shareholder. An election by an individual taxpayer or electing small business corporation, shall be subsequently invalidated for all years in the presumption period to which it had applied if—

(1) The electing taxpayer or shareholder taxpayer files a joint return for one of the first three (five, in the case of an activity described in § 1.183-1(c)(3)) taxable years in such presumption period, and

(2) The spouse with whom he files such joint return has not previously executed a consent described in paragraph (d)(2)(iii) of this section, and

(3) Within one year after the filing of such joint return (or, if later, 90 days after March 14, 1974), such spouse has not filed a consent described in paragraph (d)(2) of this section.

An election by an electing small business corporation shall be invalidated for all years in the presumption period to which it applies if a person who was not a shareholder on the date of election becomes a shareholder during the first three (or five) years of the presumption period to which election applies and does not, within 90 days after the date on which he becomes a shareholder (or, if later, 90 days after March 14, 1974), a consent required by paragraph (d)(2) of this section. Invalidation of the election by operation of this paragraph will in no case affect the validity of the consents filed with such election.

(f) Extension of time for filing election in hardship cases. The Commissioner may upon application by a taxpayer, consent to an extension of time prescribed in this section for making an election if he finds that such an extension would be justified by hardship incurred by reason of the time at which this section is published. The burden will be on the taxpayer to establish that under the relevant facts the Commissioner should so consent.

Because of the need for immediate guidance with respect to the provisions contained in this Treasury decision, it is found impracticable to issue it with notice and public procedure thereon under subsection (b) of section 553 of title 5 of the United States Code or subject to the effective date limitation of subsection (d) of that section.

T.D. 7308, 3/14/74.

---

§ 1.183-1 Activities not engaged in for profit.

Caution: The Treasury has not yet amended Reg § 1.183-1 to reflect changes made by P.L. 100-647, P.L. 99-514.

(a) In general. Section 183 provides rules relating to the allowance of deductions in the case of activities (whether active or passive in character) not engaged in for profit by individuals and electing small business corporations, creates a presumption that an activity is engaged in for profit if certain requirements are met, and permits the taxpayer to elect to postpone determination of whether such presumption applies until he has engaged in the activity for at least 5 taxable years, or, in certain cases, 7 taxable years. Whether an activity is engaged in for profit is determined under section 162 and section 212(1) and (2) except insofar as section 183(d) creates a presumption that the activity is engaged in for profit. If deductions are not allowable under sections 162 and 212(1) and (2), the deduction allowance rules of section 183(b) and this section apply. Pursuant to section 641(b), the taxable income of an estate or trust is computed in the same manner as in the case of an individual, with certain exceptions not here relevant. Accordingly, where an estate or trust engages in an activity or activities which are not for profit, the rules of section 183 and this section apply in computing the allowable deductions of such trust or estate. No inference is to be drawn from the provisions of section 183 and the regulations thereunder that any activity of a corporation (other than an electing small business corporation) is or is not a business or engaged in for profit. For rules relating to the deductions that may be taken into account by taxable membership organizations which are operated primarily to furnish services, facilities, or goods to members, see section 277 and the regulations thereunder. For the definition of an activity not engaged in for profit, see § 1.183-2. For rules relating to the election contained in section 183(e), see § 1.183-3.

(b) Deductions allowable. *(1) Manner and extent.* If an activity is not engaged in for profit, deductions are allowable under section 183(b) in the following order and only to the following extent:

(i) Amounts allowable as deductions during the taxable year under chapter 1 of the Code without regard to whether the activity giving rise to such amounts was engaged in for profit are allowable to the full extent allowed by the relevant sections of the Code, determined after taking into account any limitations or exceptions with respect to the allowability of such amounts. For example, the allowability-of-interest expenses incurred with respect to activities not engaged in for profit is limited by the rules contained in section 163(d).

(ii) Amounts otherwise allowable as deductions during the taxable year under chapter 1 of the Code, but only if such allowance does not result in an adjustment to the basis of property, determined as if the activity giving rise to such amounts was engaged in for profit, are allowed only to the extent the gross income attributable to such activity exceeds the deductions allowed or allowable under subdivision (i) of this subparagraph.

(iii) Amounts otherwise allowable as deductions for the taxable year under chapter 1 of the Code which result in (or if otherwise allowed would have resulted in) an adjustment to the basis of property, determined as if the activity giving rise to such deductions was engaged in for profit, are allowed only to the extent the gross income attributable to such activity exceeds the deductions allowed or allowable under subdivisions (i) and (ii) of this subparagraph. Deductions falling within this subdivision include such items as depreciation, partial losses with respect to property, partially worthless debts, amortization, and amortizable bond premium.

(2) Rule for deductions involving basis adjustments. (i) In general. If deductions are allowed under subparagraph (1)(iii) of this paragraph, and such deductions are allowed with respect to more than one asset, the deduction allowed with respect to each asset shall be determined separately in accordance with the computation set forth in subdivision (ii) of this subparagraph.

(ii) Basis adjustment fraction. The deduction allowed under subparagraph (1)(iii) of this paragraph is computed by multiplying the amount which would have been allowed, had the activity been engaged in for profit, as a deduction with respect to each particular asset which involves a basis adjustment, by the basis adjustment fraction—

(a) The numerator of which is the total of deductions allowable under subparagraph (1)(iii) of this paragraph, and

(b) The denominator of which is the total of deductions which involve basis adjustments which would have been allowed with respect to the activity had the activity been engaged in for profit. The amount resulting from this computation is the deduction allowed under subparagraph (1)(iii) of this paragraph with respect to the particular asset. The basis of such asset is adjusted only to the extent of such deduction.

(3) Examples. The provisions of subparagraphs (1) and (2) of this paragraph may be illustrated by the following examples:

Example (1). A, an individual, maintains a herd of dairy cattle, which is an "activity not engaged in for profit" within the meaning of section 183(c). A sold milk for $1,000 during the year. During the year A paid $300 State taxes on gasoline used to transport the cows, milk, etc., and paid $1,200 for feed for the cows. For the year A also had a casualty loss attributable to this activity of $500. A determines the amount of his allowable deductions under section 183 as follows:

(i) First, A computes his deductions allowable under subparagraph (1)(i) of this paragraph as follows:

State gasoline taxes specifically allowed under section 164(a)(5) without regard to whether the activity is engaged in for profit	$300
Casualty loss specifically allowed under section 165(c)(3) without regard to whether the activity is engaged in for profit ($500 less $100 limitation)	400
Deductions allowable under subparagraph (1)(i) of this paragraph	700

(ii) Second, A computes his deductions allowable under subparagraph (1)(ii) of this paragraph (deductions which would be allowed under chapter 1 of the Code if the activity were engaged in for profit and which do not involve basis adjustments) as follows: Maximum amount of deductions allowable under subparagraph (1)(ii) of this paragraph:

Income from milk sales	$1,000
Gross income from activity	1,000
Less: deductions allowable under subparagraph (1)(i) of this paragraph	700
Maximum amount of deductions allowable under subparagraph (1)(ii) of this paragraph	300
Feed for cows	1,200
Deduction allowed under subparagraph (1)(ii) of this paragraph	300

$900 of the feed expense is not allowed as a deduction under section 183 because the total feed expense ($1,200) exceeds the maximum amount of deductions allowable under subparagraph (1)(ii) of this paragraph ($300). In view of these circumstances, it is not necessary to determine deductions allowable under subparagraph (1)(iii) of this paragraph which would be allowable under chapter 1 of the Code if the activity were engaged in for profit and which involve basis adjustment (the $100 of casualty loss not allowable under subparagraph (1)(i) of this paragraph because of the limitation in section 165(c)(3)) because none of such amount will be allowed as a deduction under section 183.

Example (2). Assume the same facts as in example (1), except that A also had income from sales of hay grown on the farm of $1,200 and that depreciation of $750 with respect to a barn, and $650 with respect to a tractor would have been allowed with respect to the activity had it been engaged in for profit. A determines the amount of his allowable deductions under section 183 as follows:

(i) First, A computes his deductions allowable under subparagraph (1)(i) of this paragraph as follows:

State gasoline taxes specifically allowed under section 164(a)(5) without regard to whether the activity is engaged in for profit	$300
Casualty loss specifically allowed under section 165(c)(3) without regard to whether the activity is engaged in for profit ($500 less $100 limitation)	400
Deductions allowable under subparagraph (1)(i) of this paragraph	700

(ii) Second, A computes his deductions allowable under subparagraph (1)(ii) of this paragraph (deductions which would be allowable under chapter 1 of the Code if the activity were engaged in for profit and which do not involve basis adjustments) as follows: Maximum amount of deductions allowable under subparagraph (1)(ii) of this paragraph:

Income from milk sales	$1,000
Income from hay sales	1,200
Gross income from activity	2,200
Less: deductions allowable under subparagraph (1)(i) of this paragraph	700
Maximum amount of deductions allowable under subparagraph (1)(ii) of this paragraph	1,500
Feed for cows	1,200

The entire $1,200 of expenses relating to feed for cows is allowable as a deduction under subparagraph (1)(ii) of this paragraph, since it does not exceed the maximum amount of deductions allowable under such subparagraph.

(iii) Last, A computes the deductions allowable under subparagraph (1)(iii) of this paragraph (deductions which would be allowable under chapter 1 of the Code if the activity were engaged in for profit and which involve basis adjustments) as follows:

Maximum amount of deductions allowable under subparagraph (1)(iii) of this paragraph:

Gross income from farming		$2,200
Less: Deductions allowed under subparagraph (1)(i) of this paragraph	$ 700	
Deductions allowed under subparagraph (1)(ii) of this paragraph	$1,200	1,900
Maximum amount of deductions allowable under subparagraph (1)(iii) of this paragraph		300

(iv) Since the total of A's deductions under chapter 1 of the Code (determined as if the activity was engaged in for profit) which involve basis adjustments ($750 with respect to barn, $650 with respect to tractor, and $100 with respect to limitation on casualty loss) exceeds the maximum amount of the deductions allowable under subparagraph (1)(iii) of this paragraph ($300), A computes his allowable deductions with respect to such assets as follows:

A first computes his basis adjustment fraction under subparagraph (2)(ii) of this paragraph as follows:

The numerator of the fraction is the maximum of deductions allowable under subparagraph (1)(iii) of this paragraph which involve basis adjustments	$ 300
The denominator of the fraction is the total of deductions that involve basis adjustments which would have been allowed with respect to the activity had the activity been engaged in for profit	$1,500

The basis adjustment fraction is then applied to the amount of each deduction which would have been allowable if the activity were engaged in for profit and which involves a basis adjustment as follows:

Depreciation allowed with respect to barn ($^{300}/_{1,500}$ × $750)	$150
Depreciation allowed with respect to tractor ($^{300}/_{1,500}$ × $650)	$130
Deduction allowed with respect to limitation on casualty loss ($^{300}/_{1,500}$ × $100)	$ 20

The basis of the barn and of the tractor are adjusted only by the amount of depreciation actually allowed under section 183 with respect to each (as determined by the above computation). The basis of the asset with regard to which the casualty loss was suffered is adjusted only to the extent of the amount of the casualty loss actually allowed as a deduction under subparagraph (1)(i) and (iii) of this paragraph.

(4) Rule for capital gains and losses. (i) In general. For purposes of section 183 and the regulations thereunder, the gross income from any activity not engaged in for profit includes the total of all capital gains attributable to such activity determined without regard to the section 1202 deduction. Amounts attributable to an activity not engaged in for profit which would be allowable as a deduction under section 1202, without regard to section 183, shall be allowable as a deduction under section 183(b)(1) in accordance with the rules stated in this subparagraph.

(ii) Cases where deduction not allowed under section 183. No deduction is allowable under section 183(b)(1) with respect to capital gains attributable to an activity not engaged in for profit if—

(a) Without regard to section 183 and the regulations thereunder, there is no excess of net long-term capital gain over net short-term capital loss for the year, or

(b) There is no excess of net long-term capital gain attributable to the activity over net short-term capital loss attributable to the activity.

(iii) Allocation of deduction. If there is—

(a) An excess of net long-term capital gain over net short-term capital loss attributable to an activity not engaged in for profit, and

(b) Such an excess attributable to all activities, determined without regard to section 183 and the regulations thereunder, the deduction allowable under section 183(b)(1) attributable to capital gains with respect to each activity not engaged in for profit (with respect to which there is an excess of net long-term capital gain over net short-term capital loss for the year) shall be an amount equal to the deduction allowable under section 1202 for the taxable year (determined without regard to section 183) multiplied by a fraction the numerator of which is the excess of the net long-term capital gain attributable to the activity over the net short-term capital loss attributable to the activity and the denominator of which is an amount equal to the total excess of net long-term capital gain over net short-term capital loss for all activities with respect to which there is such excess. The amount of the total section 1202 deduction allowable for the year shall be reduced by the amount determined to be allocable to activities not engaged in for profit and accordingly allowed as a deduction under section 183(b)(1).

(iv) Example. The provisions of this subparagraph may be illustrated by the following example:

Example. A, an individual who uses the cash receipts and disbursement method of accounting and the calendar year as the taxable year, has three activities not engaged in for profit. For his taxable year ending on December 31, 1973, A has a $200 net long-term capital gain from activity No. 1, a $100 net short-term capital loss from activity No. 2, and a $300 net long-term capital gain from activity No. 3. In addition, A has a $500 net long-term capital gain from another activity which he engages in for profit. A computes his deductions for capital gains for calendar year 1973 as follows:

Section 1202 deduction without regard to section 183 is determined as follows:

Net long-term capital gain from activity No. 1	$ 200
Net long-term capital gain from activity No. 3	300
Net long-term capital gain from activity engaged in for profit	500
Total net long-term capital gain from all activities	1,000
Less: Net short-term capital loss attributable to activity No. 2	100
Aggregate net long-term capital gain over net short-term capital loss from all activities	900
Section 1202 deduction determined without regard to section 183 (one-half of $900)	$ 450

Allocation of the total section 1202 deduction among A's various activities:

Portion allocable to activity No. 1 which is deductible under section 183(b)(1) (Excess net long-term capital gain attributable to activity No. 1 ($200) over total excess net long-term capital gain attributable to all of A's activities with respect to which there is such an excess ($1,000) times amount of section 1202 deduction ($450)	90
Portion allocable to activity No. 3 which is deductible under section 183(b)(1) (Excess net long-term capital gain attributable to activity No. 3 ($300) over total excess net long-term capital gain attributable to all of A's activities with respect to which there is such an excess ($1,000) times amount of section 1202 deduction ($450)	135
Portion allocable to all activities engaged in for profit (total section 1202 deduction ($450) less section 1202 deduction allowable to activities Nos. 1 and 3 ($225))	225
Total section 1202 deduction deductible under sections 1202 and 183(b)(1)	450

(c) Presumption that activity is engaged in for profit. *(1) In general.* If for—

(i) Any 2 of 7 consecutive taxable years, in the case of an activity which consists in major part of the breeding, training, showing, or racing of horses, or

(ii) Any 2 of 5 consecutive taxable years, in the case of any other activity, the gross income derived from an activity exceeds the deductions attributable to such activity which would be allowed or allowable if the activity were engaged in for profit, such activity is presumed, unless the Commissioner establishes to the contrary, to be engaged in for profit. For purposes of this determination the deduction permitted by section 1202 shall not be taken into account. Such presumption applies with respect to the second profit year and all years subsequent to the second profit year within the 5- or 7-year period beginning with the first profit year. This presumption arises only if the activity is substantially the same activity for each of the relevant taxable years, including the taxable year in question. If the taxpayer does not meet the requirements of section 183(d) and this paragraph, no inference that the activity is not engaged in for profit shall arise by reason of the provisions of section 183. For purposes of this paragraph, a net operating loss deduction is not taken into account as a deduction. For purposes of this subparagraph a short taxable year constitutes a taxable year.

(2) Examples. The provisions of subparagraph (1) of this paragraph may be illustrated by the following examples, in each of which it is assumed that the taxpayer has not elected, in accordance with section 183(e), to postpone determination of whether the presumption described in section 183(d) and this paragraph is applicable.

Example (1). For taxable years 1970-74, A, an individual who uses the cash receipts and disbursement method of accounting and the calendar year as the taxable year, is engaged in the activity of farming. In taxable years 1971, 1973, and 1974, A's deductible expenditures with respect to such activity exceed his gross income from the activity. In taxable years 1970 and 1972 A has income from the sale of farm produce of $30,000 for each year. In each of such years A had expenses for feed for his livestock of $10,000, depreciation of equipment of $10,000, and fertilizer cost of $5,000 which he elects to take as a deduction. A also has a net operating loss carryover to taxable year 1970 of $6,000. A is presumed, for taxable years 1972, 1973, and 1974, to have engaged in the activity of farming for profit, since for 2 years of a 5-consecutive-year period the gross income from the activity ($30,000 for each year) exceeded the deductions (computed without regard to the net operating loss) which are allowable in the case of the activity ($25,000 for each year).

Example (2). For the taxable years 1970 and 1971, B, an individual who uses the cash receipts and disbursement method of accounting and the calendar year as the taxable year, engaged in raising pure-bred Charolais cattle for breeding purposes. The operation showed a loss during 1970. At the end of 1971, B sold a substantial portion of his herd and the cattle operation showed a profit for that year. For all subsequent relevant taxable years B continued to keep a few Charolais bulls at stud. In 1972, B started to raise Tennessee Walking Horses for breeding and show purposes, utilizing substantially the same pasture land, barns, and (with structural modifications) the same stalls. The Walking Horse operations showed a small profit in 1973 and losses in 1972 and 1974 through 1976.

(i) Assuming that under paragraph (d)(1) of this section the raising of cattle and raising of horses are determined to be separate activities, no presumption that the Walking Horse operation was carried on for profit arises under section 183(d) and this paragraph since this activity was not the same activity that generated the profit in 1971 and there are not, therefore, 2 profit years attributable to the horse activity.

(ii) Assuming the same facts as in (i) above, if there were no stud fees received in 1972 with respect to Charolais bulls, but for 1973 stud fees with respect to such bulls exceed deductions attributable to maintenance of the bulls in that year, the presumption will arise under section 183(d) and this paragraph with respect to the activity of raising and maintaining Charolais cattle for 1973 and for all subsequent years within the 5-year period beginning with taxable year 1971, since the activity of raising and maintaining Charolais cattle is the same activity in 1971 and in 1973, although carried on by B on a much reduced basis and in a different manner. Since it has been assumed that the horse and cattle operations are separate activities, no presumption will arise with respect to the Walking Horse operation because there are not 2 profit years attributable to such horse operation during the period in question.

(iii) Assuming, alternatively, that the raising of cattle and raising of horses would be considered a single activity under paragraph (d)(1) of this section, B would receive the benefit of the presumption beginning in 1973 with respect to both the cattle and horses since there were profits in 1971 and 1973. The presumption would be effective though 1977 (and longer if there is an excess of income over deductions in this activity in 1974, 1975, 1976, or 1977 which would extend the presumption) if, under section 183(d) and subparagraph (3) of this paragraph, it was determined that the activity consists in major part of the breeding, training, showing, or racing of horses. Otherwise, the presumption would be effective only through 19/5 (assuming no excess of income over deductions in this activity in 1974 or 1975 which would extend the presumption).

(3) Activity which consists in major part of the breeding, training, showing, or racing of horses. For purposes of this paragraph an activity consists in major part of the breeding, training, showing, or racing of horses for the taxable year if the average of the portion of expenditures attributable to breeding, training, showing, and racing of horses for the 3

taxable years preceding the taxable year (or, in the case of an activity which has not been conducted by the taxpayer for 3 years, for so long as it has been carried on by him) was at least 50 percent of the total expenditures attributable to the activity for such prior taxable years.

(4) Transitional rule. In applying the presumption described in section 183(d) and this paragraph, only taxable years beginning after December 31, 1969, shall be taken into account. Accordingly, in the case of an activity referred to in subparagraph (1)(i) or (ii) of this paragraph, section 183(d) does not apply prior to the second profitable taxable year beginning after December 31, 1969, since taxable years prior to such date are not taken into account.

(5) Cross reference. For rules relating to section 183(e) which permits a taxpayer to elect to postpone determination of whether any activity shall be presumed to be "an activity engaged in for profit" by operation of the presumption described in section 183(d) and this paragraph until after the close of the fourth taxable year (sixth taxable year, in the case of activity which consists in major part of breeding, training, showing, or racing of horses) following the taxable year in which the taxpayer first engages in the activity, see § 1.183-3.

(d) Activity defined. *(1) Ascertainment of activity.* In order to determine whether, and to what extent, section 183 and the regulations thereunder apply, the activity or activities of the taxpayer must be ascertained. For instance, where the taxpayer is engaged in several undertakings, each of these may be a separate activity, or several undertakings may constitute one activity. In ascertaining the activity or activities of the taxpayer, all the facts and circumstances of the case must be taken into account. Generally, the most significant facts and circumstances in making this determination are the degree of organizational and economic interrelationship of various undertakings, the business purpose which is (or might be) served by carrying on the various undertakings separately or together in a trade or business or in an investment setting, and the similarity of various undertakings. Generally, the Commissioner will accept the characterization by the taxpayer of several undertakings either as a single activity or as separate activities. The taxpayer's characterization will not be accepted, however, when it appears that his characterization is artificial and cannot be reasonably supported under the facts and circumstances of the case. If the taxpayer engages in two or more separate activities, deductions and income from each separate activity are not aggregated either in determining whether a particular activity is engaged in for profit or in applying section 183. Where land is purchased or held primarily with the intent to profit from increase in its value, and the taxpayer also engages in farming on such land, the farming and the holding of the land will ordinarily be considered a single activity only if the farming activity reduces the net cost of carrying the land for its appreciation in value. Thus, the farming and holding of the land will be considered a single activity only if the income derived from farming exceeds the deductions attributable to the farming activity which are not directly attributable to the holding of the land (that is, deductions other than those directly attributable to the holding of the land such as interest on a mortgage secured by the land, annual property taxes attributable to the land and improvements, and depreciation of improvements to the land).

(2) Rules for allocation of expenses. If the taxpayer is engaged in more than one activity, an item of deduction or income may be allocated between two or more of these activities. Where property is used in several activities, and one or more of such activities is determined not to be engaged in for profit, deductions relating to such property must be allocated between the various activities on a reasonable and consistently applied basis.

(3) Example. The provisions of this paragraph may be illustrated by the following example:

Example. (i) A, an individual, owns a small house located near the beach in a resort community. Visitors come to the area for recreational purposes during only 3 months of the year. During the remaining 9 months of the year houses such as A's are not rented. Customarily, A arranges that the house will be leased for 2 months of 3-month recreational season to vacationers and reserves the house for his own vacation during the remaining month of the recreational season. In 1971, A leases the house for 2 months for $1,000 per month and actually uses the house for his own vacation during the other months of the recreational season. For 1971, the expenses attributable to the house are $1,200 interest, $600 real estate taxes, $600 maintenance, $300 utilities, and $1,200 which would have been allowed as depreciation had the activity been engaged in for profit. Under these facts and circumstances, A is engaged in a single activity, holding the beach house primarily for personal purposes, which is an "activity not engaged in for profit" within the meaning of section 183(c). See paragraph (b)(9) of § 1.183-2.

(ii) Since the $1,200 of interest and the $600 of real estate taxes are specifically allowable as deductions under sections 163 and 164(a) without regard to whether the beach house activity is engaged in for profit, no allocation of these expenses between the uses of the beach house is necessary. However, since section 262 specifically disallows personal, living, and family expenses as deductions, the maintenance and utilities expenses and the depreciation from the activity must be allocated between the rental use and the personal use of the beach house. Under the particular facts and circumstances, ⅔ (2 months of rental use over 3 months of total use) of each of these expenses are allocated to the rental use, and ⅓ (1 month of personal use over 3 months of total use) of each of these expenses are allocated to the personal use as follows:

	Rental use⅔—expenses allocable to section 183(b)(2)	Personal use⅓—expenses allocable to section 262
Maintenance expense $600	$ 400	$200
Utilities expense $300	200	100
Depreciation $1,200	800	400
Total	1,400	700

The $700 of expenses and depreciation allocated to the personal use of the beach house are disallowed as a deduction under section 262. In addition, the allowability of each of the expenses and the depreciation allocated to section 183(b)(2) is determined under paragraph (b)(1)(ii) and (iii) of this section. Thus, the maximum amount allowable as a deduction under section 183(b)(2) is $200 ($2,000 gross income from activity, less $1,800 deductions under section 183(b)(1)). Since the amounts described in section 183(b)(2) ($1,400) exceed the maximum amount allowable ($200), and since the amounts described in paragraph (b)(1)(ii) of this section ($600) exceed such maximum amount allowable ($200), none of the depreciation (an amount described in paragraph (b)(1)(iii) of this section) is allowable as a deduction.

(e) Gross income from activity not engaged in for profit defined. For purposes of section 183 and the regulations thereunder, gross income derived from an activity not engaged in for profit includes the total of all gains from the sale, exchange, or other disposition of property, and all other gross receipts derived from such activity. Such gross income shall include, for instance, capital gains, and rents received for the use of property which is held in connection with the activity. The taxpayer may determine gross income from any activity by subtracting the cost of goods sold from the gross receipts so long as he consistently does so and follows generally accepted methods of accounting in determining such gross income.

(f) Rule for electing small business corporations. Section 183 and this section shall be applied at the corporate level in determining the allowable deductions of an electing small business corporation.

T.D. 7198, 7/12/72.

PARAGRAPH 1. Section 1.183-1 is amended by adding at the end thereof the following new paragraph:

Proposed § 1.183-1 Activities not engaged in for profit.
[*For Preamble, see ¶ 150,615*]

* * * * *

(g) Coordination with section 280A. If section 280A(a) (relating to disallowance of deductions for certain expenses with respect to the use of a dwelling unit used as a residence) applies with respect to any dwelling unit (or portion thereof) for the taxable year—

(1) Section 183 and this section shall not apply to that unit (or portion thereof) for that year, but

(2) That year shall be taken into account as a taxable year for purposes of applying section 183(d).

See section 280A and the regulations thereunder for definitions and rules relating to use of dwelling units. Note that the limitation of section 280A(e) and § 1.280A-3(c) applies in any case where an individual or an electing small business corporation uses a dwelling unit for personal purposes on any day during the taxable year.

§ 1.183-2 Activity not engaged in for profit defined.

(a) In general. For purposes of section 183 and the regulations thereunder, the term "activity not engaged in for profit" means any activity other than one with respect to which deductions are allowable for the taxable year under section 162 or under paragraph (1) or (2) of section 212. Deductions are allowable under section 162 for expenses of carrying on activities which constitute a trade or business of the taxpayer and under section 212 for expenses incurred in connection with activities engaged in for the production or collection of income or for the management, conservation, or maintenance of property held for the production of income. Except as provided in section 183 and § 1.183-1, no deductions are allowable for expenses incurred in connection with activities which are not engaged in for profit. Thus, for example, deductions are not allowable under section 162 or 212 for activities which are carried on primarily as a sport, hobby, or for recreation. The determination whether an activity is engaged in for profit is to be made by reference to objective standards, taking into account all of the facts and circumstances of each case. Although a reasonable expectation of profit is not required, the facts and circumstances must indicate that the taxpayer entered into the activity, or continued the activity, with the objective of making a profit. In determining whether such an objective exists, it may be sufficient that there is a small chance of making a large profit. Thus it may be found that an investor in a wildcat oil well who incurs very substantial expenditures is in the venture for profit even though the expectation of a profit might be considered unreasonable. In determining whether an activity is engaged in for profit, greater weight is given to objective facts than to the taxpayer's mere statement of his intent.

(b) Relevant factors. In determining whether an activity is engaged in for profit, all facts and circumstances with respect to the activity are to be taken into account. No one factor is determinative in making this determination. In addition, it is not intended that only the factors described in this paragraph are to be taken into account in making the determination, or that a determination is to be made on the basis that the number of factors (whether or not listed in this paragraph) indicating a lack of profit objective exceeds the number of factors indicating a profit objective, or vice versa. Among the factors which should normally be taken into account are the following:

(1) Manner in which the taxpayer carries on the activity. The fact that the taxpayer carries on the activity in a businesslike manner and maintains complete and accurate books and records may indicate that the activity is engaged in for profit. Similarly, where an activity is carried on in a manner substantially similar to other activities of the same nature which are profitable, a profit motive may be indicated. A change of operating methods, adoption of new techniques or abandonment of unprofitable methods in a manner consistent with an intent to improve profitability may also indicate a profit motive.

(2) The expertise of the taxpayer or his advisors. Preparation for the activity by extensive study of its accepted business, economic, and scientific practices, or consultation with those who are expert therein, may indicate that the taxpayer has a profit motive where the taxpayer carries on the activity in accordance with such practices. Where a taxpayer has such preparation or procures such expert advice, but does not carry on the activity in accordance with such practices, a lack of intent to derive profit may be indicated unless it appears that the taxpayer is attempting to develop new or superior techniques which may result in profits from the activity.

(3) The time and effort expended by the taxpayer in carrying on the activity. The fact that the taxpayer devotes much of his personal time and effort to carrying on an activity, particularly if the activity does not have substantial personal or recreational aspects, may indicate an intention to derive a profit. A taxpayer's withdrawal from another occupation to devote most of his energies to the activity may also be evidence that the activity is engaged in for profit. The fact that the taxpayer devotes a limited amount of time to an activity does not necessarily indicate a lack of profit motive where the taxpayer employs competent and qualified persons to carry on such activity.

(4) Expectation that assets used in activity may appreciate in value. The term "profit" encompasses appreciation in the value of assets, such as land, used in the activity. Thus, the taxpayer may intend to derive a profit from the operation of the activity, and may also intend that, even if no profit from current operations is derived, an overall profit will result when appreciation in the value of land used in the activity is realized since income from the activity together with the appreciation of land will exceed expenses of operation. See,

however, paragraph (d) of § 1.183-1 for definition of an activity in this connection.

(5) The success of the taxpayer in carrying on other similar or dissimilar activities. The fact that the taxpayer has engaged in similar activities in the past and converted them from unprofitable to profitable enterprises may indicate that he is engaged in the present activity for profit, even though the activity is presently unprofitable.

(6) The taxpayer's history of income or losses with respect to the activity. A series of losses during the initial or start-up stage of an activity may not necessarily be an indication that the activity is not engaged in for profit. However, where losses continue to be sustained beyond the period which customarily is necessary to bring the operation to profitable status such continued losses, if not explainable, as due to customary business risks or reverses, may be indicative that the activity is not being engaged in for profit. If losses are sustained because of unforeseen or fortuitous circumstances which are beyond the control of the taxpayer, such as drought, disease, fire, theft, weather damages, other involuntary conversions, or depressed market conditions, such losses would not be an indication that the activity is not engaged in for profit. A series of years in which net income was realized would of course be strong evidence that the activity is engaged in for profit.

(7) The amount of occasional profits, if any, which are earned. The amount of profits in relation to the amount of losses incurred, and in relation to the amount of the taxpayer's investment and the value of the assets used in the activity, may provide useful criteria in determining the taxpayer's intent. An occasional small profit from an activity generating large losses, or from an activity in which the taxpayer has made a large investment, would not generally be determinative that the activity is engaged in for profit. However, substantial profit, though only occasional, would generally be indicative that an activity is engaged in for profit, where the investment or losses are comparatively small. Moreover an opportunity to earn a substantial ultimate profit in a highly speculative venture is ordinarily sufficient to indicate that the activity is engaged in for profit even though losses or only occasional small profits are actually generated.

(8) The financial status of the taxpayer. The fact that the taxpayer does not have substantial income or capital from sources other than the activity may indicate that an activity is engaged in for profit. Substantial income from sources other than the activity (particularly if the losses from the activity generate substantial tax benefits) may indicate that the activity is not engaged in for profit especially if there are personal or recreational elements involved.

(9) Elements of personal pleasure or recreation. The presence of personal motives in carrying on of an activity may indicate that the activity is not engaged in for profit, especially where there are recreational or personal elements involved. On the other hand, a profit motivation may be indicated where an activity lacks any appeal other than profit. It is not, however, necessary that an activity be engaged in with the exclusive intention of deriving a profit or with the intention of maximizing profits. For example, the availability of other investments which would yield a higher return, or which would be more likely to be profitable, is not evidence that an activity is not engaged in for profit. An activity will not be treated as not engaged in for profit merely because the taxpayer has purposes or motivations other than solely to make a profit. Also, the fact that the taxpayer derives personal pleasure from engaging in the activity is not sufficient to cause the activity to be classified as not engaged in for profit if the activity is in fact engaged in for profit as evidenced by other factors whether or not listed in this paragraph.

(c) Examples. The provisions of this section may be illustrated by the following examples:

Example (1). The taxpayer inherited a farm from her husband in an area which was becoming largely residential, and is now nearly all so. The farm had never made a profit before the taxpayer inherited it, and the farm has since had substantial losses in each year. The decedent from whom the taxpayer inherited the farm was a stockbroker, and he also left the taxpayer substantial stock holdings which yield large income from dividends. The taxpayer lives on an area of the farm which is set aside exclusively for living purposes. A farm manager is employed to operate the farm, but modern methods are not used in operating the farm. The taxpayer was born and raised on a farm, and expresses a strong preference for living on a farm. The taxpayer's activity of farming, based on all the facts and circumstances, could be found not to be engaged in for profit.

Example (2). The taxpayer is a wealthy individual who is greatly interested in philosophy. During the past 30 years he has written and published at his own expense several pamphlets, and he has engaged in extensive lecturing activity, advocating and disseminating his ideas. He has made a profit from these activities in only occasional years, and the profits in those years were small in relation to the amount of the losses in all other years. The taxpayer has very sizable income from securities (dividends and capital gains) which constitutes the principal source of his livelihood. The activity of lecturing, publishing pamphlets, and disseminating his ideas is not an activity engaged in by the taxpayer for profit.

Example (3). The taxpayer, very successful in the business of retailing soft drinks, raise dogs and horses. He began raising a particular breed of dog many years ago in the belief that the breed was in danger of declining, and he has raised and sold the dogs in each year since. The taxpayer recently began raising and racing thoroughbred horses. The losses from the taxpayer's dog and horse activities have increased in magnitude over the years, and he has not made a profit on these operations during any of the last 15 years. The taxpayer generally sells the dogs only to friends, does not advertise the dogs for sale, and shows the dogs only infrequently. The taxpayer races his horses only at the "prestige" tracks at which he combines his racing activities with social and recreational activities. The horse and dog operations are conducted at a large residential property on which the taxpayer also lives, which includes substantial living quarters and attractive recreational facilities for the taxpayer and his family. Since (i) the activity of raising dogs and horses and racing the horses is of a sporting and recreational nature, (ii) the taxpayer has substantial income from his business activities of retailing soft drinks, (iii) the horse and dog operations are not conducted in a businesslike manner, and (iv) such operations have a continuous record of losses, it could be determined that the horse and dog activities of the taxpayer are not engaged in for profit.

Example (4). The taxpayer inherited a farm of 65 acres from his parents when they died 6 years ago. The taxpayer moved to the farm from his house in a small nearby town, and he operates it in the same manner as his parents operated the farm before they died. The taxpayer is employed as a skilled machine operator in a nearby factory, for which he is paid approximately $8,500 per year. The farm has not been profitable for the past 15 years because of rising costs of operating farms in general, and because of the decline in the price of the produce of this farm in particular. The taxpayer consults the local agent of the State agricultural service from time-to-time, and the suggestions of the agent have generally been followed. The manner in which the farm is operated by the taxpayer is substantially similar to the manner in which farms of similar size, and which grow similar crops in the area are operated. Many of these other farms do not make profits. The taxpayer does much of the required labor around the farm himself, such as fixing fences, planting, crops, etc. The activity of farming could be found, based on all the facts and circumstances, to be engaged in by the taxpayer for profit.

Example (5). A, an independent oil and gas operator, frequently engages in the activity of searching for oil on undeveloped and unexplored land which is not near proven fields. He does so in a manner substantially similar to that of others who engage in the same activity. The changes, based on the experience of A and others who engaged in this activity, are strong that A will not find a commercially profitable oil deposit when he drills on land not established geologically to be proven oil bearing land. However, on the rare occasions that these activities do result in discovering a well, the operator generally realizes a very large return from such activity. Thus, there is a small chance that A will make a large profit from his oil exploration activity. Under these circumstances, A is engaged in the activity of oil drilling for profit.

Example (6). C, a chemist, is employed by a large chemical company and is engaged in a wide variety of basic research projects for his employer. Although he does no work for his employer with respect to the development of new plastics, he has always been interested in such development and has outfitted a workshop in his home at his own expense which he uses to experiment in the field. He has patented several developments at his own expense but as yet has realized no income from his inventions or from such patents. C conducts his research on a regular, systematic basis, incurs fees to secure consultation on his projects from time to time, and makes extensive efforts to "market" his developments. C has devoted substantial time and expense in an effort to develop a plastic sufficiently hard, durable, and malleable that it could be used in lieu of sheet steel in many major applications, such as automobile bodies. Although there may be only a small chance that C will invent new plastics, the return from any such development would be so large that it induces C to incur the costs of his experimental work. C is sufficiently qualified by his background that there is some reasonable basis for his experimental activities. C's experimental work does not involve substantial personal or recreational aspects and is conducted in an effort to find practical applications for his work. Under these circumstances, C may be found to be engaged in the experimental activities for profit.

T.D. 7198, 7/12/72.

§ 1.183-3 Election to postpone determination with respect to the presumption described in section 183(d). [Reserved]

§ 1.183-4 Taxable years affected.

The provisions of section 183 and the regulations thereunder shall apply only with respect to taxable years beginning after December 31, 1969. For provisions applicable to prior taxable years, see section 270 and § 1.270-1.

T.D. 7198, 7/12/72.

§ 1.186-1 Recoveries of damages for antitrust violations, etc.

(a) Allowance of deduction. Under section 186, when a compensatory amount which is included in gross income is received or accrued during a taxable year for a compensable injury, a deduction is allowed in an amount equal to the lesser of (1) such compensatory amount, or (2) the unrecovered losses sustained as a result of such compensable injury.

(b) Compensable injury. *(1) In general.* for purposes of this section, the term "compensable injury" means any of the injuries described in subparagraph (2), (3), or (4) of this paragraph.

(2) Patent infringement. An injury sustained as a result of an infringement of a patent issued by the United States (whether or not issued to the taxpayer or another person or persons) constitutes a compensable injury. The term "patent issued by the United States" means any patent issued or granted by the United States under the authority of the Commissioner of Patents pursuant to 35 U.S.C. 153.

(3) Breach of contract or of fiduciary duty or relationship. An injury sustained as a result of a breach of contract (including an injury sustained by a third party beneficiary) or a breach of fiduciary duty or relationship constitutes a compensable injury.

(4) Injury suffered under certain antitrust law violations. An injury sustained in business, or to property, by reason of any conduct forbidden in the antitrust laws for which a civil action may be brought under section 4 of the Act of October 15, 1914 (15 U.S.C. 15), commonly known as the Clayton Act, constitutes a compensable injury.

(c) Compensatory amount. *(1) In general.* For purposes of this section, the term, "compensatory amount" means any amount received or accrued during the taxable year as damages as a result of an award in, or in settlement of, a civil action for recovery for a compensable injury, reduced by any amounts paid or incurred in the taxable year in securing such award or settlement. The term "compensatory amount" includes only amounts compensating for actual economic injury. Thus, additional amounts representing punitive, exemplary, or treble damages are not included within the term. Where, for example, a taxpayer recovers treble damages under section 4 of the Clayton Act, only one-third of the recovery representing economic injury constitutes a compensatory amount. In the absence of any indication to the contrary, amounts received in settlement of an action shall be deemed to be a recovery for an actual economic injury except to the extent such settlement amounts exceed actual damages claimed by the taxpayer in such action.

(2) Interest on a compensatory amount. Interest attributable to a compensatory amount shall not be included within the term "compensatory amount."

(3) Settlement of a civil action for damages. (i) Necessity for an action. The term "compensatory amount" does not include an amount received or accrued in settlement of a claim for a compensable injury if the amount is received or accrued prior to institution of an action. An action shall be considered as instituted upon completion of service of process, in accordance with the laws and rules of the court in which the action has been commenced or to which the action has been commenced or to which the action has been removed, upon all defendants who pay or incur an obligation to pay a compensatory amount.

(ii) Specifications of the parties. If an action for a compensable injury is settled, the specifications of the parties will generally determine compensatory amounts unless such specifications are not reasonably supported by the facts and circumstances of the case. For example, the parties may provide that the sum of $1,000 represents actual damages sustained as the result of antitrust violations and that the total amount of the settlement after the trebling of damages is $3,000. In such case, only the sum of $1,000 would be a compensatory amount. In the absence of specifications of the parties, the complaint filed by the taxpayer may be considered in determining what portion of the amount of the settlement is a compensatory amount.

(4) Amounts paid or incurred in securing the award or settlement. For purposes of this section, the term "amounts paid or incurred in the taxable year in securing such award or settlement" shall include legal expenses such as attorney's fees, witness fees, accountant fees, and court costs. Expenses incurred in securing a recovery of both a compensatory amount and other amounts from the same action shall be allocated among such amounts in the ratio each of such amounts bears to the total recovery. For instance, where a taxpayer incurs attorney's fees and other expenses of $3,000 in recovering $10,000 as a compensatory amount, $5,000 as a return of capital, and $25,000 as punitive damages from the same action, the taxpayer shall allocate $750 of the expenses to the compensatory amount (10,000/40,000 × 3,000), $375 to the return of capital (5,000/40,000 × 3,000), and $1,875 to the punitive damages (25,000/40,000 × 3,000).

(d) Unrecovered losses. *(1) In general.* For purposes of this section, the term "unrecovered losses sustained as a result of such compensable injury" means the sum of the amounts of the net operating losses for each taxable year in whole or in part within the injury period, to the extent that such net operating losses are attributable to such compensable injury, reduced by (i) the sum of any amounts of such net operating losses which were allowed as a net operating loss carryback or carryover for any prior taxable year under the provisions of section 172, and (ii) the sum of any amounts allowed as deductions under section 186(a) and this section for all prior taxable years with respect to the same compensable injury. Accordingly, a deduction is permitted under section 186(a) and this section with respect to net operating losses whether or not the period for carryover under section 172 has expired.

(2) Injury period. For purposes of this section, the term "injury period" means (i) with respect to an infringement of a patent, the period during which the infringement of the patent continued, (ii) with respect to a breach of contract or breach of fiduciary duty or relationship, the period during which amounts would have been received or accrued but for such breach of contract of fiduciary duty or relationship, or (iii) with respect to injuries sustained by reason of a violation of section 4 of the Clayton Act, the period during which such injuries were sustained. The injury period will be determined on the basis of the facts and circumstances of the taxpayer's situation. The injury period may include periods before and after the period covered by the civil action instituted.

(3) Net operating losses attributable to compensable injuries. A net operating loss for any taxable year shall be treated as attributable (whether actually attributable or not) to a compensable injury to the extent the compensable injury is sustained during the taxable year. For purposes of determining the extent of the compensable injury sustained during a taxable year, a judgment for a compensable injury apportioning the amount of the recovery (not reduced by any amounts paid or incurred in securing such recovery) to specific taxable years within the injury period will be conclusive. If a judgment for a compensable injury does not apportion the amount of the recovery to specific taxable years within the injury period, the amount of the recovery will be prorated among the years within the injury period in the proportion that the net operating loss sustained in each of such years bear to the total net operating losses sustained for all such years. If an action is settled, the specifications of the parties will generally determine the apportionment of the amount of the recovery unless such specifications are not reasonably supported by the facts and circumstances of the case. In the absence of specifications of the parties, the amount of the recovery will be prorated among the years within the injury period in the proportion that the net operating loss sustained in each of the years bears to the total net operating losses sustained for all such years.

(4) Application of losses attributable to a compensable injury. If only a portion of a net operating loss for any taxable year is attributable to a compensable injury, such portion shall (in applying section 172 for purposes of this section) be considered to be a separate net operating loss for such year to be applied after the other portion of such net operating loss. If, for example, in the year of the compensable injury the net operating loss was $1,000 and the amount of the compensable injury was $600, the amount of $400 not attributable to the compensable injury would be used first to offset profits in the carryover or carryback periods as prescribed by section 172. After the amount not attributable to the compensable injury is used to offset profits in other years, then the amount attributable to the compensable injury will be applied against profits in the carryback or carryback periods.

(e) Effect on net operating loss carryovers. *(1) In general.* Under section 186(e) if for the taxable year in which a compensatory amount is received of accrued any portion of the net operating loss carryovers to such year is attributable to the compensable injury for which such amount is received or accrued, such portion of the net operating loss carryovers must be reduced by the excess, if any, of (i) the amount computed under section 186(e)(1) with respect to such compensatory amount, over (ii) the amount computed under section 186(e)(2) with respect to such compensable injury.

(2) Amount computed under section 186(e)(1). The amount computed under section 186(e)(1) is equal to the deduction allowed under section 186(a) with respect to the compensatory amount received or accrued for the taxable year.

(3) Amount computed under section 186(e)(2). The amount computed under section 186(e)(2) is equal to that portion of the unrecovered losses sustained as a result of the compensable injury with respect to which, as of the beginning of the taxable year, the period for carryover under section 172 has expired without benefit to the taxpayer, but only to the extent that such portion of the unrecovered losses did not reduce an amount computed under section 186(e)(1) for any prior taxable year.

(4) Increase in income under section 172(b)(2). If there is a reduction for any taxable year under subparagraph (1) of this paragraph in the portion of the net operating loss carryovers to such year attributable to a compensable injury, then, solely for purposes of determining the amount of such portion which may be carried to subsequent taxable years, the income of such taxable year, as computed by the amount of the reduction computed under subparagraph (1) of this paragraph, for such year.

(f) Illustration. The provisions of section 186 and this section may be illustrated by the following example:

Example. (i) As of the beginning of his taxable year 1969, taxpayer A has a net operating loss carryover from his taxable year 1966 of $550 of which $250 is attributable to a compensable injury. In addition, he has a net operating loss attributable to the compensable injury of $150 with respect to which the period for carryover under section 172 has expired without benefit to the taxpayer. In 1969, he receives a $100 compensatory amount with respect to that injury and he has $75 in other income. Thus, A has gross income of $175 and he is entitled to a $100 deduction (the compensatory amount received) under section 186(a) and this section since this amount is less than the uncovered losses sustained as a result of the compensable injury ($250 + $150 = $400). No portion of the net operating loss carryover to the current taxable year attributable to the compensable injury is reduced under section 186(e) since the amount determined under section 186(e)(2) ($150). Therefore, A applies a net operating loss carryover of $550 against his remaining income of $75 and retains a net operating loss carryover of $475 to following years of which amount $250 remains attributable to the compensable injury. In addition, he retains $50 of net operating losses attributable to the compensable injury with respect to which the period for carryover under section 172 has expired without benefit to the taxpayer.

(ii) In 1970, A receives a $200 compensatory amount with respect to the same compensable injury and has $75 of other income. Thus, A has gross income of $275 and he is entitled to a $200 deduction (the compensatory amount received) under section 186(a) and this section since this amount is less than the remaining unrecovered loss sustained as a result of the compensable injury ($250 + $50 = $300). The net operating loss carryover to the current taxable year of $250 attributable to the compensable injury is reduced under section 186(e) by $150, which is the excess of the amount determined under section 186(e)(1) ($200) over the amount determined under section 186(e)(2) ($50). Therefore, A applies net operating loss carryovers of $325 ($225 not attributable to the compensable injury, + $100 attributable to such injury) against his remaining income of $75. A retains net operating loss carryovers of $250 for following years, of which amount $100 is attributable to the compensable injury. A has used all of his net operating losses attributable to the compensable injury with respect to which the period for carryover under section 172 has expired without benefit to the taxpayer.

(iii) In 1971, A receives a $200 compensatory amount with respect to the same compensable injury and has $75 of other income. Thus, A has gross income of $275 and he is entitled to a $100 deduction (the amount of unrecovered losses) under section 186(a) and this section since this amount is less than the compensatory amount received ($200). The net operating loss carryover to the current taxable year of $100 attributable to the compensable injury is reduced under section 186(e) by $100, which is the excess of the amount determined under section 186(e)(1) ($100) over the amount determined under section 186(e)(2) ($0). Therefore, A applies net operating loss carryovers of $150 against his remaining income of $175 ($100 compensatory amount plus $75 other income) which leaves $25 taxable income. No net operating loss carryover remains for following years.

(g) Effective date. The provisions of this section are applicable as to compensatory amounts received or accrued in taxable years beginning after December 31, 1968, even though the compensable injury was sustained in taxable years beginning before such date.

T.D. 7220, 11/20/72.

---

§ 1.188-1 Amortization of certain expenditures for qualified on-the-job training and child care facilities.

Caution: The Treasury has not yet amended Reg § 1.188-1 to reflect changes made by P.L. 101-508.

(a) Allowance of deduction. *(1) In general.* Under section 188, at the election of the taxpayer, any eligible expenditure (as defined in paragraph (d)(1) of this section) made by such taxpayer to acquire, construct, reconstruct, or rehabilitate section 188 property (as defined in paragraph (d)(2) of this section) shall be allowable as a deduction ratably over a period of 60 months. Such 60-month period shall begin with the month in which such property is placed in service. For rules for making the election, see paragraph (b) of this section. For rules relating to the termination of an election, see paragraph (c) of this section.

(2) Amount of deduction. (i) In general. For each eligible expenditure attributable to an item of section 188 property the amortization deduction shall be an amount, with respect to each month of the 60-month amortization period which falls within the taxable year, equal to the eligible expenditure divided by 60. The total amortization deduction with respect to each item of section 188 property for a particular taxable year is the sum of the amortization deductions allowable for each month of the 60-month period which falls within such taxable year. The total amortization deduction under section 188 for a particular taxable year is the sum of the amortization deductions allowable with respect to each item of section 188 property for that taxable year.

(ii) Separate amortization period for each expenditure. Each eligible expenditure attributable to an item of section 188 property to which an election relates shall be amortized over a 60-month period beginning with the month in which the item of section 188 property is placed in service. Thus, if a taxpayer makes an eligible expenditure for an addition to, or improvement of, section 188 property, such expenditure must be amortized over a separate 60-month period beginning with the month in which the section 188 property is placed in service.

(iii) Separate items. The determination of what constitutes a separate item of section 188 property is to be made on the basis of the facts and circumstances of each individual case. Additions or improvements to an existing item of section 188 property are treated as a separate item of section 188 property. In general, each item of personal property is a separate item of property and each building, or separate element or structural component thereof, is a separate item of property. For purposes of subdivisions (i) and (ii) of this subparagraph, two or more items of property may be treated as a single item of property if such items (A) are placed in service within the same month of the taxable year, (B) have the same estimated useful life, and (C) are to be used in a functionally related manner in the operation of a qualified on-the-job training or child care facility, or are integrally related facilities (described in paragraph (d)(3) or (4) of this section).

(iv) Disposition of property or termination of election. If an item of section 188 property is sold or exchanged or otherwise disposed of (or if the item of property ceases to be used as section 188 property by the taxpayer) during a particular month, then the amortization deduction (if any) allowable to the taxpayer in respect of that item for that month shall be an amount which bears the same ratio to the amount to which the taxpayer would be entitled for a full month as the number of days in such month during which the property was held by him (or used by him as section 188 property) bears to the total number of days in such month.

(3) Effect on other deductions. The amortization deduction provided by section 188(a) with respect to any month shall be in lieu of any depreciation deduction which would otherwise be allowable under section 167 or 179 with respect to that portion of the adjusted basis of the property attributable to an adjustment under section 1016(a)(1) made on account of an eligible expenditure.

(4) Depreciation with respect to property ceasing to be used as section 188 property. A taxpayer is entitled to a deduction for the depreciation (to the extent allowable under section 167) of property with respect to which the election under section 188 is terminated under the provisions of paragraph (c) of this section. The deduction for depreciation shall begin with the date of such termination and shall be computed on the adjusted basis of the property as of such date. The depreciation deduction shall be based upon the estimated remaining useful life and salvage value authorized under section 167 for the property as of the termination date.

(5) Investment credit not to be allowed. Any property with respect to which an election has been made under section 188(a) shall not be treated as section 38 property within the meaning of section 48(a).

(6) Special rules. (i) Life estates. In the case of section 188 property held by one person for life with the remainder to another person, the amortization deduction under section 188(a) shall be computed as if the life tenant were the absolute owner of the property and shall be allowable to the life tenant during his life.

(ii) Certain corporate acquisitions. If the assets of a corporation which has elected to take the amortization deduction under section 188(a) are acquired by another corporation in a transaction to which section 381(a) (relating to carryovers in certain corporate acquisitions) applies, the acquiring corporation is to be treated as if it were the distributor or transferor corporation for purposes of this section.

(iii) Estates and trusts. For the allowance of the amortization deduction in the case of estates and trusts, see section 642(f) and § 1.642(f)-1.

(iv) Partnerships. For the allowance of the amortization deduction in the case of partnerships, see section 703 and § 1.703-1.

(b) Time and manner of making election. *(1) In general.* Except as otherwise provided in subparagraph (2) of this paragraph, and election to amortize an eligible expenditure under section 188 shall be made by attaching, to the taxpayer's income tax return for the taxable period for which the deduction if first allowable to such taxpayer, a written statement containing:

(i) A description clearly identifying each item of property (or two or more items of property treated as a single item) forming a part of a qualified on-the-job training or child care facility to which the election relates, e.g., building, classroom equipment, etc.;

(ii) The date on which the eligible expenditure was made for such item of property (or the period during which eligible expenditures were made for two or more items of property treated as a single item of property);

(iii) The date on which such item of property was "placed in service" (see paragraph (d)(5) of this section);

(iv) The amount of the eligible expenditure for such item of property (or the total amount of expenditures for two or more items of property treated as a single item); and

(v) The annual amortization deduction claimed with respect to such item of property.

If the taxpayer does not file a timely return (taking into account extensions of the time for filing) for the taxable year for which the election is first to be made, the election shall be filed at the time the taxpayer files his first return for that year. The election may be made with an amended return only if such amended return is filed no later than the time prescribed by law (including extensions thereof) for filing the return for the taxable year of election.

(2) Special rule. With respect to any return filed before (90 days after the date on which final regulations are filed with the Office of the Federal Register), the election to amortize an eligible expenditure for section 188 property shall be made by a statement on, or attached to, the income tax return (or an amended return) for the taxable year, indicating that an election is being made under section 188 and setting forth information to identify the election and the facility or facilities to which it applies. An election made under the provisions of this subparagraph, must be made not later than (i) the time, including extensions thereof, prescribed by law for filing the income tax return for the first taxable year for which the election is being made or (ii) before (90 days after the date on which final regulations under section 188 are filed with the Office of the Federal Register), whichever is later. Nothing in this subparagraph shall be construed as extending the time specified in section 6511 within which a claim for credit or refund may be filed.

(3) No other method of making election. No method for making the election under section 188(a) other than the method prescribed in this paragraph shall be permitted. If an election to amortize section 188 property is not made within the time and in the manner prescribed in this paragraph, no election may be made (by the filing of an amended return or in any other manner) with respect to such section 188 property.

(4) Effect of election. An election once made may not be revoked by a taxpayer with respect to any item of section 188 property to which the election relates. The election of the amortization deducted for an item of section 188 property shall not affect the taxpayer's right to elect or not to elect the amortization deduction as to other items of section 188 property even though the items are part of the same facility. For rules relating to the termination of an election other than by revocation by the taxpayer, see paragraph (c) of this section.

(c) Termination of election. If the specific use of an item of section 188 property in connection with a qualified on-the-job training or child care facility is discontinued, the election made with respect to that item of property shall be terminated. The termination shall be effective with respect to such item of property as of the earliest date on which the taxpayer's specific use of the item is no longer in connection with the operation of a qualified on-the-job training or child care facility. If a facility ceases to meet the applicable requirements of paragraph (d)(3) of this section, relating to qualified on-the-job training facilities, or paragraph (d)(4) of this section, relating to qualified child care facilities, the election or elections made with respect to the items of section 188 property comprising such facility shall be terminated. The termination shall be effective with respect to such items of property as of the earliest date on which the facility is no longer qualified under the applicable rules. For rules relating to depreciation with respect to property ceasing to be used as section 188 property, see paragraph (a)(4) of this section.

(d) Definitions and special requirements. *(1) Eligible expenditure.* For purposes of this section, the term "eligible expenditure" means an expenditure—

(i) Chargeable to capital account;

(ii) Made after December 31, 1971, and before January 1, 1982, to acquire, construct, reconstruct, or rehabilitate section 188 property which is a qualified child care center facility; (or, made after December 31, 1971, and before January 1, 1977, to acquire, construct, reconstruct, or rehabilitate section 188 property which is a qualified on-the-job training facility); and

(iii) For which, but only to the extent that, a grant or other reimbursement excludable from gross income is not, directly or indirectly, payable to, or for the benefit of, the taxpayer with respect to such expenditure under any job training or child care program established or funded by the United States, a State, or any instrumentality of the foregoing, or the District of Columbia.

For purposes of this subparagraph, an expenditure is considered to be made when actually paid by a taxpayer who computes his taxable income under the cash receipts and disbursements method or when the obligation therefor is incurred by a taxpayer who computes his taxable income under the accrual method. See subparagraph (5) of this paragraph for the determination of when section 188 property is placed in service for purposes of beginning the 60-month amortization period.

(2) Section 188 property. Section 188 property is tangible property which is—

(i) Of a character subject to depreciation;

(ii) Located within the United States; and

(iii) Specifically used as an integral part of a qualified on-the-job training facility (as defined in subparagraph (3) of this paragraph) or as an integral part of a qualified child care center facility (as defined in subparagraph (4) of this paragraph).

(3) Qualified on-the-job training facility. A "qualified on-the-job training facility" is a facility specifically used by an employer as an on-the-job training facility in connection with an occupational training program for his employees or prospective employees provided that with respect to such program—

(i) All of the following requirements are met—

(A) There is offered at the training facility a systematic program comprised of work and training and related instruction;

(B) The occupation, together with a listing of its basic skills, and the estimated schedule of time for accomplishments of such skills, are clearly identified;

(C) The content of the training is adequate to qualify the employee, or prospective employee, for the occupation for which the individual is being trained;

(D) The skills are to be imparted by competent instructors;

(E) Upon completion of the training, placement is to be based primarily upon the skills learned through the training program;

(F) The period of training is not less than the time necessary to acquire minimum job skills nor longer than the usual period of training for the same occupation; and

(G) There is reasonable certainty that employment will be available with the employer in the occupation for which the training is provided; or

(ii) The employer has entered into an agreement with the United States, or a State agency, under the provisions of the Manpower Development and Training Act of 1962, as amended and supplemented (42 U.S.C. 2571 *et seq.*), the Economic Opportunity Act of 1964, as amended and supplemented (42 U.S.C. 2701 *et seq.*), section 432(b)(1) of the Social Security Act, as amended and supplemented (42 U.S.C. 632(b)(1)), the National Apprenticeship Act of 1937, as amended and supplemented (29 U.S.C. 50 *et seq.*), or other similar Federal statute.

A "facility" consists of a building or any portion of a building and its structural components in which training is conducted, and equipment or other personal property necessary to teach a trainee the basic skills required for satisfactory performance in the occupation for which the training is being given. A facility also includes a building or portion of a building which provides essential services for trainees during the course of the training program, such as a dormitory or dining hall. For purposes of this section, a facility is considered to be specifically used as an on-the-job training facility if such facility is actually used for such purposes and is not used in a significant manner for any purpose other than job training or the furnishing of essential services for trainees such as meals and lodging. For purposes of the preceding sentence if a facility is used 20 percent of the time for a purpose other than on-the-job training or providing trainees with essential services, it would not satisfy the significant use test. Thus, a production facility is not an on-the-job training facility for purposes of section 188 simply because new employees receive training on the machines they will be using as fully productive employees. A facility is considered to be used by an employer in connection with an occupational training program for his employees or prospective employees if at least 80 percent of the trainees participating in the program are employees or prospective employees. For purposes of this section, a prospective employee is a trainee with respect to whom it is reasonably expected that the trainee will be employed by the employer upon successful completion of the training program.

(4) Qualified child care facility. A "qualified child care facility" is a facility which is—

(i) Particularly suited to provide child care services and specifically used by an employer to provide such services primarily for his employees' children;

(ii) Operated as a licensed or approved facility under applicable local law, if any, relating to the day care of children; and

(iii) If directly or indirectly funded to any extent by the United States, established and operated in compliance with the requirements contained in Part 71 of title 45 of the Code of Federal Regulations, relating to Federal Interagency Day Care Requirements.

For purposes of this subparagraph, a "facility" consists of the buildings, or portions or structural components thereof, in which children receive such personal care, protection, and supervision in the absence of their parents as may be required to meet their needs, and the equipment or other personal property necessary to render such services. Whether or not a facility, or any component property thereof, is particularly suited for the needs of the children being cared for depends upon the facts and circumstances of each individual case. Generally, a building and its structural components, or a room therein, and equipment are particularly suitable for furnishing child care service if they are designed or adapted for such use or satisfy requirements under local law for such use as a condition to granting a license for the operation of the facility. For example, such property includes special kitchen or toilet facilities connected to the building or room in which the services are rendered and equipment such as children's desks, chairs, and play or instructional equipment. Such property would not include general purpose rooms used for many purposes (for example, a room used as an employee recreation center during the evening) nor would it include a room or a part of a room which is simply screened off for use by children during the day. For purposes of this section, a facility is considered to be specifically used as a child care facility if such facility is actually used for such purpose and is not used in a significant manner for any purpose other than child care. For purposes of this subparagraph, a child care facility is used by an employer to provide child care services primarily for children of employees of the employer if, for any month, no more than 20 percent of the average daily enrolled or attending children for such month are other than children of such employees.

(5) Placed in service. For purposes of section 188 and this section, the term "placed in service" shall have the meaning assigned to such term in paragraph (d) of § 1.46-3.

(6) Employees. For purposes of section 188 and this section, the terms "employees" and "prospective employees" include employees and prospective employees of a member of a controlled group of corporations (within the meaning of section 1563) of which the taxpayer is a member.

(e) Effective date. The provisions of section 188 and this section apply to taxable years ending after December 31, 1971.

T.D. 7599, 3/12/79.

§ 1.190-1 Expenditures to remove architectural and transportation barriers to the handicapped and elderly.

Caution: The Treasury has not yet amended Reg § 1.190-1 to reflect changes made by P.L. 101-508, P.L. 99-514, P.L. 98-369, P.L. 96-167.

(a) In general. Under section 190 of the Internal Revenue Code of 1954, a taxpayer may elect, in the manner provided in § 1.190-3 of this chapter, to deduct certain amounts paid or incurred by him in any taxable year beginning after December 31, 1976, and before January 1, 1980, for qualified architectural and transportation barrier removal expenses (as defined in § 1.190-2(b) of this chapter). In the case of a partnership, the election shall be made by the partnership. The election applies to expenditures paid or incurred during the taxable year which (but for the election) are chargeable to capital account.

(b) Limitation. The maximum deduction for a taxpayer (including an affiliated group of corporations filing a consolidated return) for any taxable year is $25,000. The $25,000 limitation applies to a partnership and to each partner. Expenditures paid or incurred in a taxable year in excess of the amount deductible under section 190 for such taxable year are capital expenditures and are adjustments to basis under section 1016(a). A partner must combine his distributive share of the partnership's deductible expenditures (after application of the $25,000 limitation at the partnership level) with that partner's distributive share of deductible expenditures from any other partnership plus that partner's own section 190 expenditures, if any (if he makes the election with respect to his own expenditures), and apply the partner's $25,000 limitation to the combined total to determine the aggregate amount deductible by that partner. In so doing, the partner may allocate the partner's $25,000 limitation among the partner's own section 190 expenditures and the partner's distributive share of partnership deductible expenditures in any manner. If such allocation results in all or a portion of the partner's distributive share of a partnership's deductible expenditures not being an allowable deduction by the partner, the partnership may capitalize such unallowable portion by an appropriate adjustment to the basis of the relevant partnership property under section 1016. For purposes of adjustments to the basis of properties held by a partnership, however, it shall be presumed that each partner's distributive share of partnership deductible expenditures (after application of the $25,000 limitation at the partnership level) was allowable in full to the partner. This presumption can be rebutted only by clear and convincing evidence that all or any portion of a partner's distributive share of the partnership section 190 deduction was not allowable as a deduction to the partner because it exceeded that partner's $25,000 limitation as allocated by him. For example, suppose for 1978 A's distributive share of the ABC partnership's deductible section 190 expenditures (after application of the $25,000 limitation at the partnership level) is $15,000. A also made section 190 expenditures of $20,000 in 1978 which he elects to deduct. A allocates $10,000 of his $25,000 limitation to his distributive share of the ABC expenditures and $15,000 to his own expenditures. A may capitalize the excess $5,000 of his own expenditures. In addition, if ABC obtains from A evidence which meets the requisite burden of proof, it may capitalize the $5,000 of A's distributive share which is not allowable as a deduction to A.

T.D. 7634, 7/23/79.

§ 1.190-2 Definitions.

For purposes of section 190 and the regulations thereunder—

(a) Architectural and transportation barrier removal expenses. The term "architectural and transportation barrier removal expenses" means expenditures for the purpose of making any facility, or public transportation vehicle, owned or leased by the taxpayer for use in connection with his trade or business more accessible to, or usable by, handicapped individuals or elderly individuals. For purposes of this section—

(1) The term "facility" means all or any portion of buildings, structures, equipment, roads, walks, parking lots, or similar real or personal property.

(2) The term "public transportation vehicle" means a vehicle, such as a bus, a railroad car, or other conveyance, which provides to the public general or special transportation service (including such service rendered to the customers of a taxpayer who is not in the trade or business of rendering transportation services).

(3) The term "handicapped individual" means any individual who has—

(i) A physical or mental disability (including, but not limited to, blindness or deafness) which for such individual constitutes or results in a functional limitation to employment, or

(ii) A physical or mental impairment (including, but not limited to, a sight or hearing impairment) which substantially limits one or more of such individual's major life activities, such as performing manual tasks, walking, speaking, breathing, learning, or working.

(4) The term "elderly individual" means an individual age 65 or over.

(b) Qualified architectural and transportation barrier removal expense. *(1) In general.* The term "qualified architectural and transportation barrier removal expense" means an architectural or transportation barrier removal expenses (as defined in paragraph (a) of this section) with respect to which the taxpayer establishes, to the satisfaction of the Commissioner or his delegate, that the resulting removal of any such barrier conforms a facility or public transportation vehicle to all the requirements set forth in one or more of paragraphs (b) (2) through (22) of this section or in one or more of the subdivisions of paragraph (b)(20) or (21). Such term includes only expenses specifically attributable to the removal of an existing architectural or transportation barrier. It does not include any part of any expense paid or incurred in connection with the construction or comprehensive renovation of a facility or public transportation vehicle or the normal replacement of depreciable property. Such term may include expenses of construction, as, for example, the construction of a ramp to remove the barrier posed for wheelchair users by steps. Major portions of the standards set forth in this paragraph were adapted from "American National Standard Specifications for Making Buildings and Facilities Accessible to, and Usable by the Physically Handicapped" (1971), the copyright for which is held by the American National Standards Institute, 1430 Broadway, New York, New York 10018.

(2) Grading. The grading of ground, even contrary to existing topography, shall attain a level with a normal entrance to make a facility accessible to individuals with physical disabilities.

(3) Walks. (i) A public walk shall be at least 48 inches wide and shall have a gradient not greater than 5 percent. A walk of maximum or near maximum grade and of considerable length shall have level areas at regular intervals. A walk or driveway shall have a nonslip surface.

(ii) A walk shall be of a continuing common surface and shall not be interrupted by steps or abrupt changes in level.

(iii) Where a walk crosses a walk, a driveway, or a parking lot, they shall blend to a common level. However, the preceding sentence does not require the elimination of those curbs which are a safety feature for the handicapped, particularly the blind (iv) An inclined walk shall have a level platform at the top and at the bottom. If a door swings out onto the platform toward the walk, such platform shall be at least 5 feet deep and 5 feet wide. If a door does not swing onto the platform or toward the walk, such platform shall be at least 3 feet deep and 5 feet wide. A platform shall extend at least 1 foot beyond the strike jamb side of any doorway.

(4) Parking lots. (i) At least one parking space that is accessible and approximate to a facility shall be set aside and identified for use by the handicapped.

(ii) A parking space shall be open on one side to allow room for individuals in wheelchairs and individuals on braces or crutches to get in and out of an automobile onto a level surface which is suitable for wheeling and walking.

(iii) A parking space for the handicapped, when placed between two conventional diagonal or head-on parking spaces, shall be at least 12 feet wide.

(iv) A parking space shall be positioned so that individuals in wheelchairs and individuals on braces or crutches need not wheel or walk behind parked cars.

(5) Ramps. (i) A ramp shall not have a slope greater than 1 inch rise in 12 inches.

(ii) A ramp shall have at least one handrail that is 32 inches in height, measured from the surface of the ramp, that is smooth, and that extends 1 foot beyond the top and bottom of the ramp. However, the preceding sentence does not require a handrail extension which is itself a hazard.

(iii) A ramp shall have a nonslip surface.

(iv) A ramp shall have a level platform at the top and at the bottom. If a door swings out onto the platform or toward the ramp, such platform shall be at least 5 feet deep and 5 feet wide. If a door does not swing onto the platform or toward the ramp, such platform shall be at least 3 feet deep and 5 feet wide. A platform shall extend at least 1 foot beyond the strike jamb side of any doorway.

(v) A ramp shall have level platforms at not more than 30-foot intervals and at any turn.

(vi) A curb ramp shall be provided at an intersection. The curb ramp shall not be less than 4 feet wide; it shall not have a slope greater than 1 inch rise in 12 inches. The transition between the two surfaces shall be smooth. A curb ramp shall have a nonslip surface.

(6) Entrances. A building shall have at least one primary entrance which is usable by individuals in wheelchairs and which is on a level accessible to an elevator.

(7) Doors and doorways. (i) A door shall have a clear opening of no less than 32 inches and shall be operable by a single effort.

(ii) The floor on the inside and outside of a doorway shall be level for a distance of at least 5 feet from the door in the direction the door swings and shall extend at least 1 foot beyond the strike jamb side of the doorway.

(iii) There shall be no sharp inclines or abrupt changes in level at a doorway. The threshold shall be flush with the floor. The door closer shall be selected, placed, and set so as not to impair the use of the door by the handicapped.

(8) Stairs. (i) Stairsteps shall have round nosing of between 1 and 1½-inch radius.

(ii) Stairs shall have a handrail 32 inches high as measured from the tread at the face of the riser.

(iii) Stairs shall have at least one handrail that extends at least 18 inches beyond the top step and beyond the bottom step. The preceding sentence does not require a handrail extension which is itself a hazard.

(iv) Steps shall have risers which do not exceed 7 inches.

(9) Floors. (i) Floors shall have a nonslip surface.

(ii) Floors on a given story of a building shall be of a common level or shall be connected by a ramp in accordance with subparagraph (5) of this paragraph.

(10) Toilet rooms. (i) A toilet room shall have sufficient space to allow traffic of individuals in wheelchairs.

(ii) A toilet room shall have at least one toilet stall that—

(A) Is at least 36 inches wide;

(B) Is at least 56 inches deep;

(C) Has a door, if any, that is at least 32 inches wide and swings out;

(D) Has handrails on each side, 33 inches high and parallel to the floor, 1½ inches in outside diameter, 1½ inches clearance between rail and wall, and fastened securely at ends and center; and

(E) Has a water closet with a seat 19 to 20 inches from the finished floor.

(iii) A toilet room shall have, in addition to or in lieu of a toilet stall described in (ii), at least one toilet stall that—

(A) Is at least 66 inches wide;

(B) Is at least 60 inches deep;

(C) Has a door, if any, that is at least 32 inches wide and swings out;

(D) Has a handrail on one side, 33 inches high and parallel to the floor, 1½ inches in outside diameter, 1½ inches clearance between rail and wall, and fastened securely at ends and center; and

(E) Has a water closet with a seat 19 to 20 inches from the finished floor, centerline located 18 inches from the side wall on which the handrail is located.

(iv) A toilet room shall have lavatories with narrow aprons. Drain pipes and hot water pipes under a lavatory shall be covered or insulated.

(v) A mirror and a shelf above a lavatory shall be no higher than 40 inches above the floor, measured from the top of the shelf and the bottom of the mirror.

(vi) A toilet room for men shall have wall-mounted urinals with the opening of the basin 15 to 19 inches from the finished floor or shall have floor-mounted urinals that are level with the main floor of the toilet room.

(vii) Towel racks, towel dispensers, and other dispensers and disposal units shall be mounted no higher than 40 inches from the floor.

(11) Water fountains. (i) A water fountain and a cooler shall have upfront spouts and controls.

(ii) A water fountain and a cooler shall be hand-operated or hand-and-foot-operated.

(iii) A water fountain mounted on the side of a floor-mounted cooler shall not be more than 30 inches above the floor.

(iv) A wall-mounted, hand-operated water cooler shall be mounted with the basin 36 inches from the floor.

(v) A water fountain shall not be fully recessed and shall not be set into an alcove unless the alcove is at least 36 inches wide.

(12) Public telephones. (i) A public telephone shall be placed so that the dial and the headset can be reached by individuals in wheelchairs.

(ii) A public telephone shall be equipped for those with hearing disabilities and so identified with instructions for use.

(iii) Coin slots of public telephones shall be not more than 48 inches from the floor.

(13) Elevators. (i) An elevator shall be accessible to, and usable by, the handicapped or the elderly on the levels they use to enter the building and all levels and areas normally used.

(ii) Cab size shall allow for the turning of a wheelchair. It shall measure at least 54 by 68 inches.

(iii) Door clear opening width shall be at least 32 inches.

(iv) All essential controls shall be within 48 to 54 inches from cab floor. Such controls shall be usable by the blind and shall be tactilely identifiable.

(14) Controls. Switches and controls for light, heat, ventilation, windows, draperies, fire alarms, and all similar controls of frequent or essential use, shall be placed within the reach of individuals in wheelchairs. Such switches and controls shall be no higher than 48 inches from the floor.

(15) Identification. (i) Raised letters or numbers shall be used to identify a room or an office. Such identification shall be placed on the wall to the right or left of the door at a height of 54 inches to 66 inches, measured from the finished floor.

(ii) A door that might prove dangerous if a blind person were to exit or enter by it (such as a door leading to a loading platform, boiler room, stage, or fire escape) shall be tactilely identifiable.

(16) Warning signals. (i) An audible warning signal shall be accompanied by a simultaneous visual signal for the benefit of those with hearing disabilities.

(ii) A visual warning signal shall be accompanied by a simultaneous audible signal for the benefit of the blind.

(17) Hazards. Hanging signs, ceiling lights, and similar objects and fixtures shall be placed at a minimum height of 7 feet, measured from the floor.

(18) International accessibility symbol. The international accessibility symbol (see illustration) shall be displayed on routes to and at wheelchair-accessible entrances to facilities and public transportation vehicles.

(19) Additional standards for rail facilities. (i) A rail facility shall contain a fare control area with at least one entrance with a clear opening at least 36 inches wide.

(ii) A boarding platform edge bordering a drop-off or other dangerous condition shall be marked with a warning device consisting of a strip of floor material differing in color and texture from the remaining floor surface. The gap between boarding platform and vehicle doorway shall be minimized.

(20) Standards for buses. (i) A bus shall have a level change mechanism (e.g., lift or ramp) to enter the bus and sufficient clearance to permit a wheelchair user to reach a secure location.

(ii) A bus shall have a wheelchair securement device. However, the preceding sentence does not require a wheelchair securement device which is itself a barrier or hazard.

(iii) The vertical distance from a curb or from street level to the first front door step shall not exceed 8 inches; the riser height for each front doorstep after the first step up from the curb or street level shall also not exceed 8 inches; and the tread depth of steps at front and rear doors shall be no less than 12 inches.

(iv) A bus shall contain clearly legible signs that indicate that seats in the front of the bus are priority seats for handicapped or elderly persons, and that encourage other passengers to make such seats available to handicapped and elderly persons who wish to use them.

(v) Handrails and stanchions shall be provided in the entranceway to the bus in a configuration that allows handicapped and elderly persons to grasp such assists from outside the bus while starting to board and to continue to use such assists throughout the boarding and fare collection processes. The configuration of the passenger assist system shall include a rail across the front of the interior of the bus located to allow passengers to lean against it while paying fares. Overhead handrails shall be continuous except for a gap at the rear doorway.

(vi) Floors and steps shall have nonslip surfaces. Step edges shall have a band of bright contrasting color running the full width of the step.

(vii) A stepwell immediately adjacent to the driver shall have, when the door is open, at least 2 foot-candles of illumination measured on the step tread. Other stepwells shall have, at all times, at least 2 foot-candles of illumination measured on the step tread.

(viii) The doorways of the bus shall have outside lighting that provides at least 1 foot-candle of illumination on the street surface for a distance of 3 feet from all points on the bottom step tread edge. Such lighting shall be located below window level and shall be shielded to protect the eyes of entering and exiting passengers.

(ix) The fare box shall be located as far forward as practicable and shall not obstruct traffic in the vestibule.

(21) Standards for rapid and light rail vehicles. (i) Passenger doorways on the vehicle sides shall have clear openings at least 32 inches wide.

(ii) Audible or visual warning signals shall be provided to alert handicapped and elderly persons of closing doors.

(iii) Handrails and stanchions shall be sufficient to permit safe boarding, on-board circulation, seating and standing assistance, and unboarding by handicapped and elderly persons. On a level-entry vehicle, handrails, stanchions, and seats shall be located so as to allow a wheelchair user to enter the vehicle and position the wheelchair in a location which does not obstruct the movement of other passengers. On a vehicle that requires the use of steps in the boarding process, handrails and stanchions shall be provided in the entranceway to the vehicle in a configuration that allows handicapped and elderly persons to grasp such assists from outside the vehicle while starting to board, and to continue using such assists throughout the boarding process.

(iv) Floors shall have nonslip surfaces. Step edges on a light rail vehicle shall have a band of bright contrasting color running the full width of the step.

(v) A stepwell immediately adjacent to the driver shall have, when the door is open, at least 2 foot-candles of illumination measured on the step tread. Other stepwells shall have, at all times, at least 2 foot-candles of illumination measured on the step tread.

(vi) Doorways on a light rail vehicle shall have outside lighting that provides at least 1 foot-candle of illumination on the street surface for a distance of 3 feet from all points on the bottom step tread edge. Such lighting shall be located below window level and shall be shielded to protect the eyes of entering and exiting passengers.

(22) Other barrier removals. The provisions of this subparagraph apply to any barrier which would not be removed by compliance with paragraphs (b)(2) through (21) of this section. The requirements of this subparagraph are:

(i) A substantial barrier to the access to or use of a facility or public transportation vehicle by handicapped or elderly individuals is removed;

(ii) The barrier which is removed had been a barrier for one or more major classes of such individuals (such as the blind, deaf, or wheelchair users); and

(iii) The removal of that barrier is accomplished without creating any new barrier that significantly impairs access to or use of the facility or vehicle by such class or classes.

T.D. 7634, 7/23/79.

§ 1.190-3 Election to deduct architectural and transportation barrier removal expenses.

(a) Manner of making election. The election to deduct expenditures for removal of architectural and transportation barriers provided by section 190(a) shall be made by claiming the deduction as a separate item identified as such on the taxpayer's income tax return for the taxable year for which such election is to apply (or, in the case of a partnership, to the return of partnership income for such year). For the election to be valid, the return must be filed not later than the time prescribed by law for filing the return (including extensions thereof) for the taxable year for which the election is to apply.

(b) Scope of election. An election under section 190(a) shall apply to all expenditures described in § 1.190-2 (or, in the case of a taxpayer whose architectural and transportation barrier removal expenses exceed $25,000 for the taxable year, to the $25,000 of such expenses with respect to which the deduction is claimed) paid or incurred during the taxable year for which made and shall be irrevocable after the date by which any such election must have been made.

(c) Records to be kept. In any case in which an election is made under section 190(a), the taxpayer shall have available, for the period prescribed by paragraph (e) of § 1.6001-1 of this chapter (Income Tax Regulations), records and documentation, including architectural plans and blueprints, contracts, and any building permits, of all the facts necessary to determine the amount of any deduction to which he is entitled by reason of the election, as well as the amount of any adjustment to basis made for expenditures in excess of the amount deductible under section 190.

T.D. 7634, 7/23/79.

§ 1.193-1 Deduction for tertiary injectant expenses.

(a) In general. Subject to the limitations and restrictions of paragraphs (c) and (d) of this section, there shall be allowed as a deduction from gross income an amount equal to the qualified tertiary injectant expenses of the taxpayer. This deduction is allowed for the later of—

(1) The taxable year in which the injectant is injected, or

(2) The taxable year in which the expenses are paid or incurred.

(b) Definitions. *(1) Qualified tertiary injectant expenses.* Except as otherwise provided in this section, the term "qualified tertiary injectant expense" means any cost paid or incurred for any tertiary injectant which is used as part of a tertiary recovery method.

(2) Tertiary recovery method. "Tertiary recovery method" means—

(i) Any method which is described in subparagraphs (1) through (9) of section 212.78(c) of the June 1979 energy regulations (as defined by section 4996(b)(8)(C)),

(ii) Any method for which the taxpayer has obtained the approval of the Associate Chief Counsel (Technical), under section 4993(d)(1)(B) for purposes of Chapter 45 of the Internal Revenue Code,

(iii) Any method which is approved in the regulations under section 4993(d)(1)(B), or

(iv) Any other method to provide tertiary enhanced recovery for which the taxpayer obtains the approval of the Associate Chief Counsel (Technical) for purposes of section 193.

(c) Special rules for hydrocarbons. *(1) In general.* If an injectant contains more than an insignificant amount of recoverable hydrocarbons, the amount deductible under section 193 and paragraph (a) of this section shall be limited to the cost of the injectant reduced by the lesser of—

(i) The fair market value of the hydrocarbon component in the form in which it is recovered, or

(ii) The cost to the taxpayer of the hydrocarbon component of the injectant.

Price levels at the time of injection are to be used in determining the fair market value of the recoverable hydrocarbons.

(2) Presumption of recoverability. Except to the extent that the taxpayer can demonstrate otherwise, all hydrocarbons shall be presumed recoverable and shall be presumed to have the same value on recovery that they would have if separated from the other components of the injectant before injection. Estimates based on generally accepted engineering practices may provide evidence of limitations on the amount or value of recoverable hydrocarbons.

(3) Significant amount. For purposes of section 193 and this section, an injectant contains more than an insignificant amount of recoverable hydrocarbons if the fair market value of the recoverable hydrocarbon component of the injectant, in the form in which it is recovered, equals or exceeds 25 percent of the cost of the injectant.

(4) Hydrocarbon defined. For purposes of section 193 and this section, the term hydrocarbon means all forms of natural gas and crude oil (which includes oil recovered from sources such as oil shale and condensate).

(5) Injectant defined. For purposes of applying this paragraph (c), an injectant is the substance or mixture of substances injected at a particular time. Substances injected at different times are not treated as components of a single injectant even if the injections are part of a single tertiary recovery process.

(d) Application with other deductions. No deduction shall be allowed under section 193 and this section for any expenditure—

(1) With respect to which the taxpayer has made an election under section 263(c) or

(2) With respect to which a deduction is allowed or allowable under any other provision of chapter 1 of the Code.

(e) Examples. The application of this section may be illustrated by the following examples:

Example (1). B, a calendar year taxpayer why uses the cash receipts and disbursements method of accounting, uses an approved tertiary recovery method for the enhanced recovery of crude oil from one of B's oil properties. During 1980, B pays $100x for a tertiary injectant which contains 1,000y units of hydrocarbon; if separated from the other components of the injectant before injection, the hydrocarbons would have a fair market value of $80x. B uses this injectant during the recovery effort during 1981. B has not made any election under section 263(c) with respect to the expenditures for the injectant, and no section of chapter 1 of the Code other than section 193 allows a deduction for the expenditure. B is unable to demonstrate that the value of the injected hydrocarbons recovered during production will be less than $80x. B's deduction under section 193 is limited to the excess of the cost for the injectant over the fair market value of the hydrocarbon component expected to be recovered ($100x − $80x = $20x). B may claim the deduction only for 1981, the year of the injection.

Example (2). Assume the same facts as in example (1) except that through engineering studies B has shown that 700y units or 70 percent of the hydrocarbon injected is nonrecoverable. The recoverable hydrocarbons have a fair market value of $24x (30 percent of $80x). The recoverable hydrocarbon portion of the injectant is 24 percent of the cost of the injectant ($24x divided by $100x). The injectant does not contain a significant amount of recoverable hydrocarbons. B may claim a deduction for $100x, the entire cost of the injectant.

Example (3). Assume the same facts as in example (1) except that through laboratory studies B has shown that because of chemical changes in the course of production the injected hydrocarbons that are recovered will have a fair market value of only $40x. B may claim a deduction for $60x, the excess of the cost of the injectant ($100x) over the fair market value of the recoverable hydrocarbons ($40x).

Example (4). B prepares an injectant from crude oil and certain non-hydrocarbon materials purchased by B. The total cost of the injectant to B is $100x, of which $24x is attributable to the crude oil. The fair market value of the crude oil used in the injectant is $27x. B is unable to demonstrate that the value of the crude oil from the injectant that will be recovered is less than $27x. The injectant contains more than an insignificant amount of recoverable hydrocarbons because the value of the recoverable crude oil ($27x) exceeds $25x (25 percent of $100x, the cost of the injectant). Because the cost to B of the hydrocarbon component of the injectant ($24x) is less than the fair market value of the hydrocarbon component in the form in which it is recovered ($27x), the cost rather than the value is taken into account in the adjustment required under paragraph (c)(1) of this section. B's deduction under section 193 is limited to the excess of the cost of the injectant over the cost of the hydrocarbon component ($100x − $24x = $76x).

T.D. 7980, 10/2/84.

§ 1.194-1 Amortization of reforestation expenditures.

Caution: The Treasury has not yet amended Reg § 1.194-1 to reflect changes made by P.L. 109-135, P.L. 108-357.

(a) In general. Section 194 allows a taxpayer to elect to amortize over an 84-month period, up to $10,000 of reforestation expenditures as defined in § 1.194-3(c)) incurred by the taxpayer in a taxable year in connection with qualified timber property (as defined in § 1.194-3(a)). The election is not available to trusts. Only those reforestation expenditures which result in additions to capital accounts after December 31, 1979 are eligible for this special amortization.

(b) Determination of amortization period. The amortization period must begin on the first day of the first month of the last half of the taxable year during which the taxpayer incurs the reforestation expenditures. For example, the 84-month amortization period begins on July 1 of a taxable year for a calendar year taxpayer, regardless of whether the reforestation expenditures are incurred in January or December of that taxable year. Therefore, a taxpayer will be allowed to claim amortization deductions for only six months of each of the first and eighth taxable years of the period over which the reforestation expenditures will be amortized.

(c) Recapture. If a taxpayer disposes of qualified timber property within ten years of the year in which the amortizable basis was created and the taxpayer has claimed amortization deductions under section 194, part or all of any gain on the disposition may be recaptured as ordinary income. See section 1245.

T.D. 7927, 12/15/83.

§ 1.194-2 Amount of deduction allowable.

Caution: The Treasury has not yet amended Reg § 1.194-2 to reflect changes made by P.L. 109-135, P.L. 108-357.

(a) General rule. The allowable monthly deduction with respect to reforestation expenditures made in a taxable year is determined by dividing the amount of reforestation expenditures made in such taxable year (after applying the limitations of paragraph (b) of this section) by 84. In order to determine the total allowable amortization deduction for a given month, a taxpayer should add the monthly amortization deductions computed under the preceding sentence for qualifying expenditures made by the taxpayer in the taxable year and the preceding seven taxable years.

(b) Dollar limitation. *(1) Maximum amount subject to election.* A taxpayer may elect to amortize up to $10,000 of qualifying reforestation expenditures each year under section 194. However, the maximum amortizable amount is $5,000 in the case of a married individual (as defined in section 143) filing a separate return. No carryover or carryback of expenditures in excess of $10,000 is permitted. The maximum annual amortization deduction for expenditures incurred in any taxable year is $1,428.57 ($10,000/7). The maximum deduction in the first and eighth taxable years of the amortization period is one-half that amount, or $714.29, because of the half-year convention provided in § 1.194-1(b). Total deductions for any one year under this section will reach $10,000 only if a taxpayer incurs and elects to amortize the maximum $10,000 of expenditures each year over an 8-year period.

(2) Allocation of amortizable basis among taxpayer's timber properties. The limit of $10,000 on amortizable reforestation expenditures applies to expenditures paid or incurred during a taxable year on all of the taxpayer's timber properties. A taxpayer who incurs more than $10,000 in qualifying expenditures in connection with more than one qualified timber property during a taxable year may select the properties for which section 194 amortization will be elected as well as the manner in which the $10,000 limitation on amortizable basis is allocated among such properties. For example, A incurred $10,000 of qualifying reforestation expenditures on each of four properties in 1981. A may elect under section 194 to amortize $2,500 of the amount spent on each property, $5,000 of the amount spent on any two properties, the entire $10,000 spent on any one property, or A may allocate the $10,000 maximum amortizable basis among some or all of the properties in any other manner.

(3) Basis. (i) In general. Except as provided in paragraph (b)(3)(ii) of this section, the basis of a taxpayer's interest in qualified timber property for which an election is made under section 194 shall be adjusted to reflect the amount of the section 194 amortization deduction allowable to the taxpayer.

(ii) Special rule for trusts. Although a trust may be a partner of a partnership, income beneficiary of an estate, or (for taxable years beginning after December 31, 1982) shareholder of an S corporation, it may not deduct its allocable share of a section 194 amortization deduction allowable to such a partnership, estate, or S corporation. In addition, the basis of the interest held by the partnership, estate, or S corporation in the qualified timber property shall not be adjusted to reflect the portion of the section 194 amortization deduction that is allocable to the trust.

(4) Allocation of amortizable basis among component members of a controlled group. Component members of a controlled group (as defined in § 1.194-3(d)) on a December 31 shall be treated as one taxpayer in applying the $10,000 limitation of paragraph (b)(1) of this section. The amortizable basis may be allocated to any one such member or allocated (for the taxable year of each such member which includes such December 31) among the several members in any manner, provided that the amount of amortizable basis allocated to any member does not exceed the amount of amortizable basis actually acquired by the member in the taxable year. The allocation is to be made (1) by the common parent corporation if a consolidated return is filed for all component members of the group, or (2) in accordance with an agreement entered into by the members of the group if separate returns are filed. If a consolidated return is filed by some component members of the group and separate returns are filed by other component members, then the common parent of the group filing the consolidated return shall enter into an agreement with those members who do not join in filing the consolidated return allocating the amount between the group filing the return and the other component members of the controlled group who do not join in filing the consolidated return. If a consolidated return is filed, the common parent corporation shall file a separate statement attached to the income tax return on which an election is made to amortize reforestation costs under section 194. See § 1.194-4. If separate returns are filed by some or all component members of the group, each component member to which is allocated any part of the deduction under section 194 shall file a separate statement attached to the income tax return in which an election is made to amortize reforestation expenditures. See § 1.194-4. Such statement shall include the name, address, employer identification number, and the taxable year of each component member of the controlled group, a copy of the allocation agreement signed by persons duly authorized to act on behalf of those members who file separate returns, and a description of the manner in which the deduction under section 194 has been divided among them.

(5) Partnerships. (i) Election to be made by partnership. A partnership makes the election to amortize qualified reforestation expenditures of the partnership. See section 703(b).

(ii) Dollar limitations applicable to partnerships. The dollar limitations of section 194 apply to the partnership as well as to each partner. Thus, a partnership may not elect to amortize more than $10,000 of reforestation expenditures under section 194 in any taxable year.

(iii) Partner's share of amortizable basis. Section 704 and the regulations thereunder shall govern the determination of a partner's share of a partnership's amortizable reforestation expenditures for any taxable year.

(iv) Dollar limitation applicable to partners. A partner shall in no event be entitled in any taxable year to claim a deduction for amortization based on more than $10,000 ($5,000 in the case of a married taxpayer who files a separate return) of amortizable basis acquired in such taxable year regardless of the source of the amortizable basis. In the case of a partner who is a member of two or more partnerships that elect under section 194, the partner's aggregate share of partnership amortizable basis may not exceed $10,000 or $5,000, whichever is applicable. In the case of a member of a partnership that elects under section 194 who also has separately acquired qualified timber property, the aggregate of the member's partnership and nonpartnership amortizable basis may not exceed $10,000 or $5,000 whichever is applicable.

(6) S corporations. For taxable years beginning after December 31, 1982, rules similar to those contained in paragraph (b)(5)(ii) and (iv) of this section shall apply in the case of S corporations (as defined in section 1361(a)) and their shareholders.

(7) Estates. Estates may elect to amortize in each taxable year up to a maximum of $10,000 of qualifying reforestation expenditures under section 194. Any amortizable basis acquired by an estate shall be apportioned between the estate and the income beneficiary on the basis of the income of the estate allocable to each. The amount of amortizable basis apportioned from an estate to a beneficiary shall be taken into account in determining the $10,000 (or $5,000) amount of amortizable basis allowable to such beneficiary under this section.

(c) Life tenant and remainderman. If property is held by one person for life with remainder to another person, the life tenant is entitled to the full benefit of any amortization allowable under section 194 on qualifying expenditures he or she makes. Any remainder interest in the property is ignored for this purpose.

T.D. 7927, 12/15/83.

§ 1.194-3 Definitions.

Caution: The Treasury has not yet amended Reg § 1.194-3 to reflect changes made by P.L. 108-357.

(a) Qualified timber property. The term "qualified timber property" means property located in the United States which will contain trees in significant commercial quantities. The property may be a woodlot or other site but must consist of at least one acre which is planted with tree seedlings in the manner normally used in forestation or reforestation. The property must be held by the taxpayer for the growing and cutting of timber which will either be sold for use in, or used by the taxpayer in, the commercial production of timber products. A taxpayer does not have to own the property in order to be eligible to elect to amortize costs attributable to it under section 194. Thus, a taxpayer may elect to amortize qualifying reforestation expenditures incurred by such taxpayer on leased qualified timber property. Qualified timber property does not include property on which the taxpayer has planted shelter belts (for which current deductions are allowed under section 175) or ornamental trees, such as Christmas trees.

(b) Amortizable basis. The term "amortizable basis" means that portion of the basis of qualified timber property which is attributable to reforestation expenditures.

(c) Reforestation expenditures. *(1) In general.* The term "reforestation expenditures" means direct costs incurred to plant or seed for forestation or reforestation purposes. Qualifying expenditures include amounts spent for site preparation, seed or seedlings, and labor and tool costs, including depreciation on equipment used in planting or seeding. Only those costs which must be capitalized and are included in the adjusted basis of the property qualify as reforestation expenditures. Costs which are currently deductible do not qualify.

(2) Cost-sharing programs. Any expenditures for which the taxpayer has been reimbursed under any governmental reforestation cost-sharing program do not qualify as reforestation expenditures unless the amounts reimbursed have been included in the gross income of the taxpayer.

(d) Definitions of controlled group of corporations and component member of controlled group. For purposes of section 194, the terms "control group of corporations" and "component member" of a controlled group of corporations shall have the same meaning assigned to those terms in section 1583(a) and (b), except that the phrase "more than 50 percent" shall be substituted for the phrase "at least 80 percent" each place it appears in section 1583(a)(1).

T.D. 7927, 12/15/83.

§ 1.194-4 Time and manner of making election.

Caution: The Treasury has not yet amended Reg § 1.194-4 to reflect changes made by P.L. 108-357.

(a) In general. Except as provided in paragraph (b) of this section, an election to amortize reforestation expenditures under section 194 shall be made by entering the amortization deduction claimed at the appropriate place on the taxpayer's income tax return for the year in which the expenditures were incurred, and by attaching a statement to such return. The statement should state the amounts of the expenditures, describe the nature of the expenditures, and give the date on which each was incurred. The statement should also state the type of timber being grown and the purpose for which it is being grown. A separate statement must be included for each property for which reforestation expenditures are being amortized under section 194. The election may only be made on a timely return (taking into account extensions of the time for filing) for the taxable year in which the amortizable expenditures were made.

(b) Special rule. With respect to any return filed before March 15, 1984, on which a taxpayer was eligible to, but did not make an election under section 194, the election to amortize reforestation expenditures under section 194 may be made by a statement on, or attached to, the income tax return (or an amended return) for the taxable year, indicating that an election is being made under section 194 and setting forth the information required under paragraph (a) of this section. An election made under the provisions of this paragraph (b) must be made not later than,

(1) The time prescribed by law (including extensions thereof) for filing the income tax return for the year in which the reforestation expenditures were made, or

(2) March 15, 1984, whichever is later. Nothing in this paragraph shall be construed as extending the time specified in section 6511 within which a claim for credit or refund may be filed.

(c) Revocation. An application for consent to revoke an election under section 194 shall be in writing and shall be addressed to the Commissioner of Internal Revenue, Washington, D.C. 20224. The application shall set forth the name and address of the taxpayer, state the taxable years for which the election was in effect, and state the reason for revoking the election. The application shall be signed by the taxpayer or a duly authorized representative of the taxpayer and shall be filed at least 90 days prior to the time prescribed by law (without regard to extensions thereof) for filing the income tax return for the first taxable year for which the election is to terminate. Ordinarily, the request for consent to revoke the election will not be granted if it appears from all the facts and circumstances that the only reason for the desired change is to obtain a tax advantage.

T.D. 7927, 12/15/83.

§ 1.195-1 Election to amortize start-up expenditures.

[Reserved]. For further guidance, see § 1.195-1T.

T.D. 8797, 12/16/98, amend T.D. 9411, 7/7/2008.

Proposed § 1.195-1 Election to amortize start-up expenditures. [*For Preamble, see ¶ 153,023*]

[The text of this section is the same as the text of § 1.195-1T(a) through (d) published elsewhere in this issue of the Federal Register.] [*See T.D. 9411, 07/08/2008, 73 Fed. Reg. 131.*]

§ 1.195-1T Election to amortize start-up expenditures (temporary).

(a) In general. Under section 195(b), a taxpayer may elect to amortize start-up expenditures as defined in section 195(c)(1). In the taxable year in which a taxpayer begins an active trade or business, an electing taxpayer may deduct an amount equal to the lesser of the amount of the start-up expenditures that relate to the active trade or business, or $5,000 (reduced (but not below zero) by the amount by which the start-up expenditures exceed $50,000). The remainder of the start-up expenditures is deductible ratably over the 180-month period beginning with the month in which the active trade or business begins. All start-up expenditures that relate to the active trade or business are considered in determining whether the start-up expenditures exceed $50,000, including expenditures incurred on or before October 22, 2004.

(b) Time and manner of making election. A taxpayer is deemed to have made an election under section 195(b) to amortize start-up expenditures as defined in section 195(c)(1) for the taxable year in which the active trade or business to which the expenditures relate begins. A taxpayer may choose to forgo the deemed election by clearly electing to capitalize its start-up expenditures on a timely filed Federal income tax return (including extensions) for the taxable year in which the active trade or business to which the expenditures relate begins. The election either to amortize start-up expenditures under section 195(b) or to capitalize start-up expenditures is irrevocable and applies to all start-up expenditures that are related to the active trade or business. A change in the characterization of an item as a start-up expenditure is a change in method of accounting to which sections 446 and 481(a) apply if the taxpayer treated the item consistently for two or more taxable years. A change in the determination of the taxable year in which the active trade or business begins also is treated as a change in method of accounting if the taxpayer amortized start-up expenditures for two or more taxable years.

(c) Examples. The following examples illustrate the application of this section:

Example (1). Expenditures of $5,000 or less. Corporation X, a calendar year taxpayer, incurs $3,000 of start-up expenditures after October 22, 2004, that relate to an active trade or business that begins on July 1, 2009. Under paragraph (b) of this section, Corporation X is deemed to have elected to deduct start-up expenditures under section 195(b) in 2009. Therefore, Corporation X may deduct the entire amount of the start-up expenditures in 2009, the taxable year in which the active trade or business begins.

Example (2). Expenditures of more than $5,000 but less than or equal to $50,000. The facts are the same as in Example 1 except that Corporation X incurs start-up expenditures of $41,000. Under paragraph (b) of this section, Corporation X is deemed to have elected to deduct start-up expenditures under section 195(b) in 2009. Therefore, Corporation X may deduct $5,000 and the portion of the remaining $36,000 that is allocable to July through December of 2009 ($36,000/180 x 6 = $1,200) in 2009, the taxable year in which the active trade or business begins.

Example (3). Subsequent change in the characterization of an item. The facts are the same as in Example 2 except that Corporation X determines in 2011 that Corporation X incurred $10,000 for an additional start-up expenditure erroneously deducted in 2009 under section 162 as a business expense. Under paragraph (b) of this section, Corporation X is deemed to have elected to amortize start-up expenditures under section 195(b) in 2009, including the additional $10,000 of start-up expenditures. Corporation X is using an impermissible method of accounting for the additional $10,000 of start-up expenditures and must change its method under § 1.446-1(e) and the applicable general administrative procedures in effect in 2011.

Example (4). Subsequent redetermination of year in which business begins. The facts are the same as in Example 2 except that, in 2010, Corporation X deducted the start-up expenditures allocable to January through December of 2010 ($36,000/180 x 12 = $2,400). In addition, in 2011 it is determined that Corporation X actually began business in 2010. Under paragraph (b) of this section, Corporation X is deemed to have elected to deduct start-up expenditures under section 195(b) in 2010. Corporation X impermissibly deducted start-up expenditures in 2009, and incorrectly determined the amount of start-up expenditures deducted in 2010. Therefore, Corporation X is using an impermissible method of accounting for the start-up expenditures and must change its method under § 1.446-1(e) and the applicable general administrative procedures in effect in 2011.

Example (5). Expenditures of more than $50,000 but less than or equal to $55,000. The facts are the same as in Example 1 except that Corporation X incurs start-up expenditures of $54,500. Under paragraph (b) of this section, Corporation

X is deemed to have elected to deduct start-up expenditures under section 195(b) in 2009. Therefore, Corporation X may deduct $500 ($5,000-4,500) and the portion of the remaining $54,000 that is allocable to July through December of 2009 ($54,000/180 x 6 = $1,800) in 2009, the taxable year in which the active trade or business begins.

Example (6). Expenditures of more than $55,000. The facts are the same as in Example 1 except that Corporation X incurs start-up expenditures of $450,000. Under paragraph (b) of this section, Corporation X is deemed to have elected to deduct start-up expenditures under section 195(b) in 2009. Therefore, Corporation X may deduct the amounts allocable to July through December of 2009 ($450,000/180 x 6 = $15,000) in 2009, the taxable year in which the active trade or business begins.

(d) Effective/applicability date. This section applies to start-up expenditures paid or incurred after September 8, 2008. However, taxpayers may apply all the provisions of this section to start-up expenditures paid or incurred after October 22, 2004, provided that the period of limitations on assessment of tax for the year the election under paragraph (b) of this section is deemed made has not expired. Otherwise, for start-up expenditures paid or incurred prior to September 8, 2008, see § 1.195-1 in effect prior to that date (§ 1.195-1 as contained in 26 CFR part 1 edition revised as of April 1, 2008).

(e) Expiration date. This section expires on July 7, 2011.

T.D. 9411, 7/7/2008.

Proposed § 1.196-1 Deduction for certain unused investment credits. [*For Preamble, see ¶ 151,105*]

Caution: The Treasury has not yet amended Reg § 1.196-1 to reflect changes made by P.L. 101-508, P.L. 101-239, P.L. 100-647.

(a) In general. Where the amount of the section 38 credit (determined under section 46(a)(2)) for any taxable year exceeds the limitation based on the amount of tax (determined under section 46(a)(3)) for such taxable year and the amount of such excess has not, after the application of 46(b), been allowed to the taxpayer as a credit under section 38 for any taxable year, an amount equal to 50 percent of such excess (to the extent attributable to property the basis of which was reduced under section 48(q)) not so allowed as a credit will be allowed as a deduction in the first taxable year following the last taxable year in which such excess could have been allowed as a credit under section 46(b).

(b) Taxpayers dying or ceasing to exist. *(1) In general.* Except as provided in this paragraph, where the taxpayer dies or ceases to exist prior to the first taxable year following the last taxable year in which the excess credit (described in paragraph (a) of this section) could have been allowed as a credit under section 46(b), then 50 percent of such excess shall be allowed as a deduction to the taxpayer for the taxable year in which such death or cessation occurs.

(2) Special rules. (i) Where the taxpayer dies or ceases to exist prior to the end of the recovery period of section 38 property which was taken into account in computing the section 38 credit with respect to such property, and where the recapture rules of section 47 are applicable, 50 percent of the excess credit described in paragraph (a) of this section that is not required to be recaptured by section 47 shall be allowed as a deduction to the taxpayer for the taxable year in which such death or cessation occurs. The recaptured credit shall be subject to the basis adjustment rules of § 1.48-7(c) or (d). For purposes of this paragraph, a taxpayer (other than an individual) ceases to exist when it no longer continues the active operation of or permanently terminates its trade or business.

(ii) In a case where the taxpayer is a corporation and such corporation ceases to exist, and transfers the assets of its trade or business to a corporation that is entitled to take into account the excess credit of the transferor corporation, the transferor corporation shall not be allowed a deduction for any excess section 38 credit under paragraph (b) of this section.

(c) Qualified rehabilitated buildings. In the case of any credit determined under section 46(a)(2) for any qualified rehabilitation expenditure in connection with a qualified rehabilitated building other than a certified historic structure, the rules of this section shall be applied by inserting the phrase "100 percent of" where the phrase "50 percent of" appears.

(d) Effective date rules. *(1) In general.* This section is effective for taxable years beginning before 1984 for—

(i) Property to which section 46(d) (relating to qualified progress expenditures) does not apply, the construction, reconstruction, or erection of which is completed by the taxpayer on or after January 1, 1983, but only to the extent of the basis thereof attributable to the construction, reconstruction, or erection after 1982,

(ii) Property to which section 46(d) does not apply, acquired by the taxpayer and subsequently placed in service by the taxpayer after 1982, and

(iii) Property to which section 46(d) applies, but only to the extent of the qualified investment (as defined under subsections (c) and (d) of section 46) with respect to qualified progress expenditures made after 1982.

(2) Exception. This section shall not apply to any property which—

(i) Was constructed, reconstructed, erected, or acquired pursuant to a contract which was entered into after August 13, 1981, and was, on July 1, 1982, and at all times thereafter, binding on the taxpayer,

(ii) Was placed in service after December 31, 1982, and before January 1, 1986,

(iii) With respect to which an election under section 168(f)(8)(A) (relating to the safe-harbor leasing provisions) is not in effect at any time, and

(iv) Is not public utility property described in section 167(l)(3)(A).

(3) Special rules. For special rules relating to integrated manufacturing facilities and historic structures, see section 205(c) of Pub. L. 97-248, 96 Stat. 430 (1982).

§ 1.197-0 Table of contents.

This section lists the headings that appear in § 1.197-2.

§ 1.197-2 Amortization of goodwill and certain other intangibles.

(a) Overview.

(1) In general.

(2) Section 167(f) property.

(3) Amounts otherwise deductible.

(b) Section 197 intangibles; in general.

(1) Goodwill.

(2) Going concern value.

(3) Workforce in place.

(4) Information base.

(5) Know-how, etc.

(6) Customer-based intangibles.

(7) Supplier-based intangibles.

(8) Licenses, permits, and other rights granted by governmental units.

(9) Covenants not to compete and other similar arrangements.

(10) Franchises, trademarks, and trade names.

(11) Contracts for the use of, and term interests in, other section 197 intangibles.

(12) Other similar items.

(c) Section 197 intangibles; exceptions.

(1) Interests in a corporation, partnership, trust, or estate.

(2) Interests under certain financial contracts.

(3) Interests in land.

(4) Certain computer software.

(i) Publicly available.

(ii) Not acquired as part of trade or business.

(iii) Other exceptions.

(iv) Computer software defined.

(5) Certain interests in films, sound recordings, video tapes, books, or other similar property.

(6) Certain rights to receive tangible property or services.

(7) Certain interests in patents or copyrights.

(8) Interests under leases of tangible property.

(i) Interest as a lessor.

(ii) Interest as a lessee.

(9) Interests under indebtedness.

(i) In general.

(ii) Exceptions.

(10) Professional sports franchises.

(11) Mortgage servicing rights.

(12) Certain transaction costs.

(13) Rights of fixed duration or amount.

(d) Amortizable section 197 intangibles.

(1) Definition.

(2) Exception for self-created intangibles.

(i) In general.

(ii) Created by the taxpayer.

(A) Defined.

(B) Contracts for the use of intangibles.

(C) Improvements and modifications.

(iii) Exceptions.

(3) Exception for property subject to anti-churning rules.

(e) Purchase of a trade or business.

(1) Goodwill or going concern value.

(2) Franchise, trademark, or trade name.

(i) In general.

(ii) Exceptions.

(3) Acquisitions to be included.

(4) Substantial portion.

(5) Deemed asset purchases under section 338.

(6) Mortgage servicing rights.

(7) Computer software acquired for internal use.

(f) Computation of amortization deduction.

(1) In general.

(2) Treatment of contingent amounts.

(i) Amounts added to basis during 15-year period.

(ii) Amounts becoming fixed after expiration of 15-year period.

(iii) Rules for including amounts in basis.

(3) Basis determinations for certain assets.

(i) Covenants not to compete.

(ii) Contracts for the use of section 197 intangibles; acquired as part of a trade or business.

(A) In general.

(B) Know-how and certain information base.

(iii) Contracts for the use of section 197 intangibles; not acquired as part of a trade or business.

(iv) Applicable rules.

(A) Franchises, trademarks, and trade names.

(B) Certain amounts treated as payable under a debt instrument.

(1) In general.

(2) Rights granted by governmental units.

(3) Treatment of other parties to transaction.

(4) Basis determinations in certain transactions.

(i) Certain renewal transactions.

(ii) Transactions subject to section 338 or 1060.

(iii) Certain reinsurance transactions.

(g) Special rules.

(1) Treatment of certain dispositions.

(i) Loss disallowance rules.

(A) In general.

(B) Abandonment or worthlessness.

(C) Certain nonrecognition transfers.

(ii) Separately acquired property.

(iii) Disposition of a covenant not to compete.

(iv) Taxpayers under common control.

(A) In general.

(B) Treatment of disallowed loss.

(2) Treatment of certain nonrecognition and exchange transactions.

(i) Relationship to anti-churning rules.

(ii) Treatment of nonrecognition and exchange transactions generally.

(A) Transfer disregarded.

(B) Application of general rule.

(C) Transactions covered.

(iii) Certain exchanged-basis property.

(iv) Transfers under section 708(b)(1).

(A) In general.

(B) Termination by sale or exchange of interest.

(C) Other terminations.

(3) Increase in the basis of partnership property under section 732(b), 734(b), 743(b), or 732(d).

(4) Section 704(c) allocations.

(i) Allocations where the intangible is amortizable by the contributor.

(ii) Allocations where the intangible is not amortizable by the contributor.

(5) Treatment of certain insurance contracts acquired in an assumption reinsurance transaction.

(i) In general.

(ii) Determination of adjusted basis of amortizable section 197 intangible resulting from an assumption reinsurance transaction.

(A) In general.

(B) Amount paid or incurred by acquirer (reinsurer) under the assumption reinsurance transaction.

(C) Amount required to be capitalized under section 848 in connection with the transaction.

(1) In general.

(2) Required capitalization amount.

(3) General deductions allocable to the assumption reinsurance transaction.

(4) Treatment of a capitalization shortfall allocable to the reinsurance agreement.

(i) In general.

(ii) Treatment of additional capitalized amounts as the result of an election under § 1.848-2(g)(8).

(5) Cross references and special rules.

(D) Examples.

(E) Effective/applicability date.

(iii) Application of loss disallowance rule upon a disposition of an insurance contract acquired in an assumption reinsurance transaction.

(A) Disposition.

(1) In general.

(2) Treatment of indemnity reinsurance transactions.

(B) Loss.

(C) Examples.

(iv) Effective dates.

(A) In general.

(B) Application to pre-effective date acquisitions and dispositions.

(C) Change in method of accounting.

(1) In general.

(2) Acquisitions and dispositions on or after effective date.

(3) Acquisitions and dispositions before the effective date.

(6) Amounts paid or incurred for a franchise, trademark, or trade name.

(7) Amounts properly taken into account in determining the cost of property that is not a section 197 intangible.

(8) Treatment of amortizable section 197 intangibles as depreciable property.

(h) Anti-churning rules.

(1) Scope and purpose.

(i) Scope.

(ii) Purpose.

(2) Treatment of section 197(f)(9) intangibles.

(3) Amounts deductible under section 1253(d) or § 1.162-11.

(4) Transition period.

(5) Exceptions.

(6) Related person.

(i) In general.

(ii) Time for testing relationships.

(iii) Certain relationships disregarded.

(iv) De minimis rule.

(A) In general.

(B) Determination of beneficial ownership interest.

(7) Special rules for entities that owned or used property at any time during the transition period and that are no longer in existence.

(8) Special rules for section 338 deemed acquisitions.

(9) Gain-recognition exception.

(i) Applicability.

(ii) Effect of exception.

(iii) Time and manner of election.

(iv) Special rules for certain entities.

(v) Effect of nonconforming elections.

(vi) Notification requirements.

(vii) Revocation.

(viii) Election Statement.

(ix) Determination of highest marginal rate of tax and amount of other Federal income tax on gain.

(A) Marginal rate.

(1) Noncorporate taxpayers.

(2) Corporations and tax-exempt entities.

(B) Other Federal income tax on gain.

(x) Coordination with other provisions.

(A) In general.

(B) Section 1374.

(C) Procedural and administrative provisions.

(D) Installment method.

(xi) Special rules for persons not otherwise subject to Federal income tax.

(10) Transactions subject to both anti-churning and nonrecognition rules.

(11) Avoidance purpose.

(12) Additional partnership anti-churning rules

(i) In general.

(ii) Section 732(b) adjustments. [Reserved]

(iii) Section 732(d) adjustments.

(iv) Section 734(b) adjustments. [Reserved]

(v) Section 743(b) adjustments.

(vi) Partner is or becomes a user of partnership intangible.

(A) General rule.

(B) Anti-churning partner.

(C) Effect of retroactive elections.

(vii) Section 704(c) elections.

(A) Allocations where the intangible is amortizable by the contributor.

(B) Allocations where the intangible is not amortizable by the contributor.

(viii) Operating rule for transfers upon death.

(i) Reserved

(j) General anti-abuse rule.

(k) Examples.

(l) Effective dates.

(1) In general.

(2) Application to pre-effective date acquisitions.

(3) Application of regulation project REG-209709-94 to pre-effective date acquisitions.

(4) Change in method of accounting.

(i) In general.

(ii) Application to pre-effective date transactions.

(iii) Automatic change procedures.

T.D. 8865, 1/20/2000, amend T.D. 9257, 4/7/2006, T.D. 9377, 1/22/2008.

Proposed § 1.197-1 Certain elections for intangible property. [*For Preamble, see ¶ 151,563*]

[The text of this proposed section is the same as the text of § 1.197-1T published elsewhere in this issue of the FEDERAL REGISTER]. [*See T.D. 8528, 3/10/94, 59 Fed. Reg. 50.*]

§ 1.197-1T Certain elections for intangible property (temporary).

• ***Caution:*** Under Code Sec. 7805, temporary regulations expire within three years of the date of issuance. This temporary regulation was issued on 3/10/94.

(a) In general. This section provides rules for making the two elections under section 13261 of the Omnibus Budget Reconciliation Act of 1993 (OBRA '93). Paragraph (c) of this section provides rules for making the section 13261(g)(2) election (the retroactive election) to apply the intangibles provisions of OBRA '93 to property acquired after July 25, 1991, and on or before August 10, 1993 (the date of enactment of OBRA '93). Paragraph (d) of this section provides rules for making the section 13261(g)(3) election (binding contract election) to apply prior law to property acquired pursuant to a written binding contract in effect on August 10, 1993, and at all times thereafter before the date of acquisition. The provisions of this section apply only to property for which an election is made under paragraph (c) or (d) of this section.

(b) Definitions and special rules. *(1) Intangibles provisions of OBRA '93.* The intangibles provisions of OBRA '93 are sections 167(f) and 197 of the Internal Revenue Code (Code) and all other pertinent provisions of section 13261 of OBRA '93 (e.g., the amendment of section 1253 in the case of a franchise, trademark, or trade name).

(2) Transition period property. The transition period property of a taxpayer is any property that was acquired by the taxpayer after July 25, 1991, and on or before August 10, 1993.

(3) Eligible section 197 intangibles. The eligible section 197 intangibles of a taxpayer are any section 197 intangibles that—

(i) Are transition period property; and

(ii) Qualify as amortizable section 197 intangibles (within the meaning of section 197(c)) if an election under section 13261(g)(2) of OBRA '93 applies.

(4) Election date. The election date is the date (determined after application of section 7502(a)) on which the taxpayer files the original or amended return to which the election statement described in paragraph (e) of this section is attached.

(5) Election year. The election year is the taxable year of the taxpayer that includes August 10, 1993.

(6) Common control. A taxpayer is under common control with the electing taxpayer if, at any time after August 2, 1993, and on or before the election date (as defined in paragraph (b)(4) of this section), the two taxpayers would be treated as a single taxpayer under section 41(f)(1)(A) or (B).

(7) Applicable convention for sections 197 and 167(f) intangibles. For purposes of computing the depreciation or amortization deduction allowable with respect to transition period property described in section 167(f)(1) or (3) or with respect to eligible section 197 intangibles—

(i) Property acquired at any time during the month is treated as acquired as of the first day of the month and is eligible for depreciation or amortization during the month; and

(ii) Property is not eligible for depreciation or amortization in the month of disposition.

(8) Application to adjustment to basis of partnership property under section 734(b) or 743(b). Any increase in the basis of partnership property under section 734(b) (relating to the optional adjustment to basis of undistributed partnership property) or section 743(b) (relating to the optional adjustment to the basis of partnership property) will be taken into account under this section by a partner as if the increased portion of the basis were attributable to the partner's acquisition of the underlying partnership property on the date the distribution or transfer occurs. For example, if a section 754 election is in effect and, as a result of its acquisition of a partnership interest, a taxpayer obtains an increased basis in an intangible held through the partnership, the increased portion of the basis in the intangible will be treated as an intangible asset newly acquired by that taxpayer on the date of the transaction.

(9) Former member. A former member of a consolidated group is a corporation that was a member of the consolidated group at any time after July 25, 1991, and on or before August 2, 1993, but that is not under common control with the common parent of the group for purposes of paragraph (c)(1)(ii) of this section.

(c) Retroactive election. *(1) Effect of election.* (i) On taxpayer. Except as provided in paragraph (c)(1)(v) of this section, if a taxpayer makes the retroactive election, the intangibles provisions of OBRA '93 will apply to all the taxpayer's transition period property. Thus, for example, section 197 will apply to all the taxpayer's eligible section 197 intangibles.

(ii) On taxpayers under common control. If a taxpayer makes the retroactive election, the election applies to each taxpayer that is under common control with the electing taxpayer. If the retroactive election applies to a taxpayer under common control, the intangibles provisions of OBRA '93 apply to that taxpayer's transition period property in the same manner as if that taxpayer had itself made the retroactive election. However, a retroactive election that applies to a non-electing taxpayer under common control is not treated as an election by that taxpayer for purposes of re-applying the rule of this paragraph (c)(1)(ii) to any other taxpayer.

(iii) On former members of consolidated group. A retroactive election by the common parent of a consolidated group applies to transition period property acquired by a former member while it was a member of the consolidated group and continues to apply to that property in each subsequent consolidated or separate return year of the former member.

(iv) On transferred assets. (A) In general. If property is transferred in a transaction described in paragraph (c)(1)(iv)(C) of this section and the intangibles provisions of OBRA '93 applied to such property in the hands of the transferor, the property remains subject to the intangibles provisions of OBRA '93 with respect to so much of its adjusted basis in the hands of the transferee as does not exceed its adjusted basis in the hands of the transferor. The transferee is not required to apply the intangibles provisions of OBRA '93 to any other transition period property that it owns, however, unless such provisions are otherwise applicable under the rules of this paragraph (c)(1).

(B) Transferee election. If property is transferred in a transaction described in paragraph (c)(1)(iv)(C)(1) of this section and the transferee makes the retroactive election, the transferor is not required to apply the intangibles provisions of OBRA '93 to any of its transition period property (including the property transferred to the transferee in the transaction described in paragraph (c)(1)(iv)(C)(1) of this section), unless such provisions are otherwise applicable under the rules of this paragraph (c)(1).

(C) Transactions covered. This paragraph (c)(1)(iv) applies to—

(1) Any transaction described in section 332, 351, 361, 721, 731, 1031, or 1033; and

(2) Any transaction between corporations that are members of the same consolidated group immediately after the transaction.

(D) Exchanged basis property. In the case of a transaction involving exchanged basis property (e.g., a transaction subject to section 1031 or 1033)—

(1) Paragraph (c)(1)(iv)(A) of this section shall not apply; and

(2) If the intangibles provisions of OBRA '93 applied to the property by reference to which the exchanged basis is determined (the predecessor property), the exchanged basis property becomes subject to the intangibles provisions of OBRA '93 with respect to so much of its basis as does not exceed the predecessor property's basis.

(E) Acquisition date. For purposes of paragraph (b)(2) of this section (definition of transition period property), property (other than exchanged basis property) acquired in a transaction described in paragraph (c)(1)(iv)(C)(1) of this section generally is treated as acquired when the transferor acquired (or was treated as acquiring) the property (or predecessor property). However, if the adjusted basis of the property in the hands of the transferee exceeds the adjusted basis of the property in the hands of the transferor, the property, with respect to that excess basis, is treated as acquired at the time of the transfer. The time at which exchanged basis property is considered acquired is determined by applying similar principles to the transferee's acquisition of predecessor property.

(v) Special rule for property of former member of consolidated group. (A) Intangibles provisions inapplicable for certain periods. If a former member of a consolidated group makes a retroactive election pursuant to paragraph (c)(1)(i) of this section or if an election applies to the former member under the common control rule of paragraph (c)(1)(ii) of this section, the intangibles provisions of OBRA '93 generally apply to all transition period property of the former member. The intangibles provisions of OBRA '93 do not apply, however, to the transition period property of a former member (including a former member that makes or is bound by a retroactive election) during the period beginning immediately after July 25, 1991, and ending immediately before the earlier of—

(1) The first day after July 25, 1991, that the former member was not a member of a consolidated group; or

(2) The first day after July 25, 1991, that the former member was a member of a consolidated group that is otherwise required to apply the intangibles provisions of OBRA '93 to its transition period property (e.g., because the common control election under paragraph (c)(1)(ii) of this section applies to the group).

(B) Subsequent adjustments. See paragraph (c)(5) of this section for adjustments when the intangibles provisions of OBRA '93 first apply to the transition period property of the former member after the property is acquired.

(2) Making the election. (i) Partnerships, S corporations, estates, and trusts. Except as provided in paragraph (c)(2)(ii) of this section, in the case of transition period property of a partnership, S corporation, estate, or trust, only the entity may make the retroactive election for purposes of paragraph (c)(1)(i) of this section.

(ii) Partnerships for which a section 754 election is in effect. In the case of increased basis that is treated as transition period property of a partner under paragraph (b)(8) of this section, only that partner may make the retroactive election for purposes of paragraph (c)(1)(i) of this section.

(iii) Consolidated groups. An election by the common parent of a consolidated group applies to members and former members as described in paragraphs (c)(1)(ii) and (iii) of this section. Further, for purposes of paragraph (c)(1)(ii) of this section, an election by the common parent is not treated as an election by any subsidiary member. A retroactive election cannot be made by a corporation that is a subsidiary member of a consolidated group on August 10, 1993, but an election can be made on behalf of the subsidiary member under paragraph (c)(1)(ii) of this section (e.g., by the common parent of the group). See paragraph (c)(1)(iii) of this section for rules concerning the effect of the common parent's election on transition period property of a former member.

(3) Time and manner of election. (i) Time. In general, the retroactive election must be made by the due date (including extensions of time) of the electing taxpayer's Federal income tax return for the election year. If, however, the taxpayer's original Federal income tax return for the election year is filed before April 14, 1994, the election may be made by amending that return no later than September 12, 1994.

(ii) Manner. The retroactive election is made by attaching the election statement described in paragraph (e) of this section to the taxpayer's original or amended income tax return for the election year. In addition, the taxpayer must—

(A) Amend any previously filed return when required to do so under paragraph (c)(4) of this section; and

(B) Satisfy the notification requirements of paragraph (c)(6) of this section.

(iii) Effect of nonconforming elections. An attempted election that does not satisfy the requirements of this paragraph (c)(3) (including an attempted election made on a return for a taxable year prior to the election year) is not valid.

(4) Amended return requirements. (i) Requirements. A taxpayer subject to this paragraph (c)(4) must amend all previously filed income tax returns as necessary to conform the taxpayer's treatment of transition period property to the

treatment required under the intangibles provisions of OBRA '93. See paragraph (c)(5) of this section for certain adjustments that may be required on the amended returns required under this paragraph (c)(4) in the case of certain consolidated group member dispositions and tax-free transactions.

(ii) Applicability. This paragraph (c)(4) applies to a taxpayer if—

(A) The taxpayer makes the retroactive election; or

(B) Another person's retroactive election applies to the taxpayer or to any property acquired by the taxpayer.

(5) Adjustment required with respect to certain consolidated group member dispositions and tax-free transactions. (i) Application. This paragraph (c)(5) applies to transition period property if the intangibles provisions of OBRA '93 first apply to the property while it is held by the taxpayer but do not apply to the property for some period (the "interim period") after the property is acquired (or considered acquired) by the taxpayer. For example, this paragraph (c)(5) may apply to transition period property held by a former member of a consolidated group if a retroactive election is made by or on behalf of the former member but is not made by the consolidated group. See paragraph (c)(1)(v) of this section.

(ii) Required adjustment to income. If this paragraph (c)(5) applies, an adjustment must be taken into account in computing taxable income of the taxpayer for the taxable year in which the intangibles provisions of OBRA '93 first apply to the property. The amount of the adjustment is equal to the difference for the transition period property between—

(A) The sum of the depreciation, amortization, or other cost recovery deductions that the taxpayer (and its predecessors) would have been permitted if the intangibles provisions of OBRA '93 applied to the property during the interim period; and

(B) The sum of the depreciation, amortization, or other cost recovery deductions that the taxpayer (and its predecessors) claimed during that interim period.

(iii) Required adjustment to basis. The taxpayer also must make a corresponding adjustment to the basis of its transition period property to reflect any adjustment to taxable income with respect to the property under this paragraph (c)(5).

(6) Notification requirements. (i) Notification of commonly controlled taxpayers. A taxpayer that makes the retroactive election must provide written notification of the retroactive election (on or before the election date) to each taxpayer that is under common control with the electing taxpayer.

(ii) Notification of certain former members, former consolidated groups, and transferees. This paragraph (c)(6)(ii) applies to a common parent of a consolidated group that makes or is notified of a retroactive election that applies to transition period property of a former member, a corporation that makes or is notified of a retroactive election that affects any consolidated group of which the corporation is a former member, or a taxpayer that makes or is notified of a retroactive election that applies to transition period property the taxpayer transfers in a transaction described in paragraph (c)(1)(iv)(C) of this section. Such common parent, former member, or transferor must provide written notification of the retroactive election to any affected former member, consolidated group, or transferee. The written notification must be provided on or before the election date in the case of an election by the common parent, former member, or transferor, and within 30 days of the election date in the case of an election by a person other than the common parent, former member, or transferor.

(7) Revocation. Once made, the retroactive election may be revoked only with the consent of the Commissioner.

(8) Examples. The following examples illustrate the application of this paragraph (c).

Example (1). (i) X is a partnership with 5 equal partners, A through E. X acquires in 1989, as its sole asset, intangible asset M. X has a section 754 election in effect for all relevant years. F, an unrelated individual, purchases A's entire interest in the X partnership in January 1993 for $700. At the time of F's purchase, X's inside basis for M is $2,000, and its fair market value is $3,500.

(ii) Under section 743(b), X makes an adjustment to increase F's basis in asset M by $300, the difference between the allocated purchase price and M's inside basis ($700 – $400 = $300). Under paragraphs (b)(8) and (c)(2)(ii) of this section, if F makes the retroactive election, the section 743(b) basis increase of $300 in M is an amortizable section 197 intangible even though asset M is not an amortizable section 197 intangible in the hands of X. F's increase in the basis of asset M is amortizable over 15 years beginning with the month of F's acquisition of the partnership interest. With respect to the remaining $400 of basis, F is treated as stepping into A's shoes and continues A's amortization (if any) in asset M. F's retroactive election applies to all other intangibles acquired by F or a taxpayer under common control with F.

Example (2). A, a calendar year taxpayer, is under common control with B, a June 30 fiscal year taxpayer. A files its original election year Federal income tax return on March 15, 1994, and does not make either the retroactive election or the binding contract election. B files its election year tax return on September 15, 1994, and makes the retroactive election. B is required by paragraph (c)(6)(i) of this section to notify A of its election. Even though A had already filed its election year return, A is bound by B's retroactive election under the common control rules. Additionally, if A had made a binding contract election, it would have been negated by B's retroactive election. Because of B's retroactive election, A must comply with the requirements of this paragraph (c), and file amended returns for the election year and any affected prior years as necessary to conform the treatment of transition period property to the treatment required under the intangibles provisions of OBRA '93.

Example (3). (i) P and Y, calendar year taxpayers, are the common parents of unrelated calendar year consolidated groups. On August 15, 1991, S, a subsidiary member of the P group, acquires a section 197 intangible with an unadjusted basis of $180. Under prior law, no amortization or depreciation was allowed with respect to the acquired intangible. On November 1, 1992, a member of the Y group acquires the S stock in a taxable transaction. On the P group's 1993 consolidated return, P makes the retroactive election. The P group also files amended returns for its affected prior years. Y does not make the retroactive election for the Y group.

(ii) Under paragraph (c)(1)(iii) of this section, a retroactive election by the common parent of a consolidated group applies to all transition period property acquired by a former member while it was a member of the group. The section 197 intangible acquired by S is transition period property that S, a former member of the P group, acquired while a member of the P group. Thus P's election applies to the acquired asset. P must notify S of the election pursuant to paragraph (c)(6)(ii) of this section.

(iii) S amortizes the unadjusted basis of its eligible section 197 intangible ($180) over the 15-year amortization period using the applicable convention beginning as of the first day of the month of acquisition (August 1, 1991). Thus, the P group amends its 1991 consolidated tax return to take into account $5 of amortization ($180/15 years × 5/12 year = $5) for S.

(iv) For 1992, S is entitled to $12 of amortization ($180/15). Assume that under § 1.1502-76, $10 of S's amortization for 1992 is allocated to the P group's consolidated return and $2 is allocated to the Y group's return. The P group amends its 1992 consolidated tax return to reflect the $10 deduction for S. The Y group must amend its 1992 return to reflect the $2 deduction for S.

Example (4). (i) The facts are the same as in Example 3, except that the retroactive election is made for the Y group, not for the P group.

(ii) The Y group amends its 1992 consolidated return to claim a section 197 deduction of $2 ($180/15 years × 2/12 year = $2) for S.

(iii) Under paragraph (c)(1)(ii) of this section, the retroactive election by Y applies to all transition period property acquired by S. However, under paragraph (c)(1)(v)(A) of this section, the intangibles provisions of OBRA '93 do not apply to S's transition period property during the period when it held such property as a member of P group. Instead, these provisions become applicable to S's transition period property beginning on November 1, 1992, when S becomes a member of Y group.

(iv) Because the P group did not make the retroactive election, there is an interim period during which the intangibles provisions of OBRA '93 do not apply to the asset acquired by S. Thus, under paragraph (c)(5) of this section the Y group must take into account in computing taxable income in 1992 an adjustment equal to the difference between the section 197 deduction that would have been permitted if the intangibles provisions of OBRA '93 applied to the property for the interim period (i.e., the period for which S was included in the P group's 1991 and 1992 consolidated returns) and any amortization or depreciation deductions claimed by S for the transferred intangible for that period. The retroactive election does not affect the P group, and the P group is not required to amend its returns.

Example (5). The facts are the same as in Example 3, except that both P and Y make the retroactive election. P must notify S of its election pursuant to paragraph (c)(6)(ii) of this section. Further, both the P and Y groups must file amended returns for affected prior years. Because there is no period of time during which the intangibles provisions of OBRA '93 do not apply to the asset acquired by S, the Y group is permitted no adjustment under paragraph (c)(5) of this section for the asset.

(d) Binding contract election. *(1) General rule.* (i) Effect of election. If a taxpayer acquires property pursuant to a written binding contract in effect on August 10, 1993, and at all times thereafter before the acquisition (an eligible acquisition) and makes the binding contract election with respect to the contract, the law in effect prior to the enactment of OBRA '93 will apply to all property acquired pursuant to the contract. A separate binding contract election must be made with respect to each eligible acquisition to which the law in effect prior to the enactment of OBRA '93 is to apply.

(ii) Taxpayers subject to retroactive election. A taxpayer may not make the binding contract election if the taxpayer or a person under common control with the taxpayer makes the retroactive election under paragraph (c) of this section.

(iii) Revocation. A binding contract election, once made, may be revoked only with the consent of the Commissioner.

(2) Time and manner of election. (i) Time. In general, the binding contract election must be made by the due date (including extensions of time) of the electing taxpayer's Federal income tax return for the election year. If, however, the taxpayer's original Federal income tax return for the election year is filed before April 14, 1994, the election may be made by amending that return no later than September 12, 1994.

(ii) Manner. The binding contract election is made by attaching the election statement described in paragraph (e) of this section to the taxpayer's original or amended income tax return for the election year.

(iii) Effect of nonconforming election. An attempted election that does not satisfy the requirements of this paragraph (d)(2) is not valid.

(e) Election statement. *(1) Filing requirements.* For an election under paragraph (c) or (d) of this section to be valid, the electing taxpayer must:

(i) File (with its Federal income tax return for the election year and with any affected amended returns required under paragraph (c)(4) of this section) a written election statement, as an attachment to Form 4562 (Depreciation and Amortization), that satisfies the requirements of paragraph (e)(2) of this section; and

(ii) Forward a copy of the election statement to the Statistics Branch (QAM:S:6111), IRS Ogden Service Center, ATTN: Chief, Statistics Branch, P.O. Box 9941, Ogden, UT 84409.

(2) Content of the election statement. The written election statement must include the information in paragraphs (e)(2)(i) through (vi) and (ix) of this section in the case of a retroactive election, and the information in paragraphs (e)(2)(i) and (vii) through (ix) of this section in the case of a binding contract election. The required information should be arranged and identified in accordance with the following order and numbering system—

(i) The name, address and taxpayer identification number (TIN) of the electing taxpayer (and the common parent if a consolidated return is filed).

(ii) A statement that the taxpayer is making the retroactive election.

(iii) Identification of the transition period property affected by the retroactive election, the name and TIN of the person from which the property was acquired, the manner and date of acquisition, the basis at which the property was acquired, and the amount of depreciation, amortization, or other cost recovery under section 167 or any other provision of the Code claimed with respect to the property.

(iv) Identification of each taxpayer under common control (as defined in paragraph (b)(6) of this section) with the electing taxpayer by name, TIN, and Internal Revenue Service Center where the taxpayer's income tax return is filed.

(v) If any persons are required to be notified of the retroactive election under paragraph (c)(6) of this section, identification of such persons and certification that written notification of the election has been provided to such persons.

(vi) A statement that the transition period property being amortized under section 197 is not subject to the anti-churning rules of section 197(f)(9).

(vii) A statement that the taxpayer is making the binding contract election.

(viii) Identification of the property affected by the binding contract election, the name and TIN of the person from which the property was acquired, the manner and date of acquisition, the basis at which the property was acquired, and whether any of the property is subject to depreciation under section 167 or to amortization or other cost recovery under any other provision of the Code.

(ix) The signature of the taxpayer or an individual authorized to sign the taxpayer's Federal income tax return.

(f) Effective date. These regulations are effective March 15, 1994.

T.D. 8528, 3/10/94.

---

§ 1.197-2 Amortization of goodwill and certain other intangibles.

Caution: The Treasury has not yet amended Reg § 1.197-2 to reflect changes made by P.L. 108-357.

(a) Overview. *(1) In general.* Section 197 allows an amortization deduction for the capitalized costs of an amortizable section 197 intangible and prohibits any other depreciation or amortization with respect to that property. Paragraphs (b), (c), and (e) of this section provide rules and definitions for determining whether property is a section 197 intangible, and paragraphs (d) and (e) of this section provide rules and definitions for determining whether a section 197 intangible is an amortizable section 197 intangible. The amortization deduction under section 197 is determined by amortizing basis ratably over a 15-year period under the rules of paragraph (f) of this section. Section 197 also includes various special rules pertaining to the disposition of amortizable section 197 intangibles, nonrecognition transactions, anti-churning rules, and anti-abuse rules. Rules relating to these provisions are contained in paragraphs (g), (h), and (j) of this section. Examples demonstrating the application of these provisions are contained in paragraph (k) of this section. The effective date of the rules in this section is contained in paragraph (l) of this section.

(2) Section 167(f) property. Section 167(f) prescribes rules for computing the depreciation deduction for certain property to which section 197 does not apply. See § 1.167(a)-14 for rules under section 167(f) and paragraphs (c)(4), (6), (7), (11), and (13) of this section for a description of the property subject to section 167(f).

(3) Amounts otherwise deductible. Section 197 does not apply to amounts that are not chargeable to capital account under paragraph (f)(3) (relating to basis determinations for covenants not to compete and certain contracts for the use of section 197 intangibles) of this section and are otherwise currently deductible. For this purpose, an amount described in § 1.162-11 is not currently deductible if, without regard to § 1.162-11, such amount is properly chargeable to capital account.

(b) Section 197 intangibles; in general. Except as otherwise provided in paragraph (c) of this section, the term section 197 intangible means any property described in section 197(d)(1). The following rules and definitions provide guidance concerning property that is a section 197 intangible unless an exception applies:

(1) Goodwill. Section 197 intangibles include goodwill. Goodwill is the value of a trade or business attributable to the expectancy of continued customer patronage. This expectancy may be due to the name or reputation of a trade or business or any other factor.

(2) Going concern value. Section 197 intangibles include going concern value. Going concern value is the additional value that attaches to property by reason of its existence as an integral part of an ongoing business activity. Going concern value includes the value attributable to the ability of a trade or business (or a part of a trade or business) to continue functioning or generating income without interruption notwithstanding a change in ownership, but does not include any of the intangibles described in any other provision of this paragraph (b). It also includes the value that is attributable to the immediate use or availability of an acquired trade or business, such as, for example, the use of the revenues or net earnings that otherwise would not be received during any period if the acquired trade or business were not available or operational.

(3) Workforce in place. Section 197 intangibles include workforce in place. Workforce in place (sometimes referred to as agency force or assembled workforce) includes the composition of a workforce (for example, the experience, education, or training of a workforce), the terms and conditions of employment whether contractual or otherwise, and any other value placed on employees or any of their attributes. Thus, the amount paid or incurred for workforce in place includes, for example, any portion of the purchase price of an acquired trade or business attributable to the existence of a highly-skilled workforce, an existing employment contract (or contracts), or a relationship with employees or consultants (including, but not limited to, any key employee contract or relationship). Workforce in place does not include any covenant not to compete or other similar arrangement described in paragraph (b)(9) of this section.

(4) Information base. Section 197 intangibles include any information base, including a customer-related information base. For this purpose, an information base includes business books and records, operating systems, and any other information base (regardless of the method of recording the information) and a customer-related information base is any information base that includes lists or other information with respect to current or prospective customers. Thus, the amount paid or incurred for information base includes, for example, any portion of the purchase price of an acquired trade or business attributable to the intangible value of technical manuals, training manuals or programs, data files, and accounting or inventory control systems. Other examples include the cost of acquiring customer lists, subscription lists, insurance expirations, patient or client files, or lists of newspaper, magazine, radio, or television advertisers.

(5) Know-how, etc. Section 197 intangibles include any patent, copyright, formula, process, design, pattern, knowhow, format, package design, computer software (as defined in paragraph (c)(4)(iv) of this section), or interest in a film, sound recording, video tape, book, or other similar property. (See, however, the exceptions in paragraph (c) of this section.)

(6) Customer-based intangibles. Section 197 intangibles include any customer-based intangible. A customer-based intangible is any composition of market, market share, or other

value resulting from the future provision of goods or services pursuant to contractual or other relationships in the ordinary course of business with customers. Thus, the amount paid or incurred for customer-based intangibles includes, for example, any portion of the purchase price of an acquired trade or business attributable to the existence of a customer base, a circulation base, an undeveloped market or market growth, insurance in force, the existence of a qualification to supply goods or services to a particular customer, a mortgage servicing contract (as defined in paragraph (c)(11) of this section), an investment management contract, or other relationship with customers involving the future provision of goods or services. (See, however, the exceptions in paragraph (c) of this section.) In addition, customer-based intangibles include the deposit base and any similar asset of a financial institution. Thus, the amount paid or incurred for customer-based intangibles also includes any portion of the purchase price of an acquired financial institution attributable to the value represented by existing checking accounts, savings accounts, escrow accounts, and other similar items of the financial institution. However, any portion of the purchase price of an acquired trade or business attributable to accounts receivable or other similar rights to income for goods or services provided to customers prior to the acquisition of a trade or business is not an amount paid or incurred for a customer-based intangible.

(7) Supplier-based intangibles. Section 197 intangibles include any supplier-based intangible. A supplier-based intangible is the value resulting from the future acquisition, pursuant to contractual or other relationships with suppliers in the ordinary course of business, of goods or services that will be sold or used by the taxpayer. Thus, the amount paid or incurred for supplier-based intangibles includes, for example, any portion of the purchase price of an acquired trade or business attributable to the existence of a favorable relationship with persons providing distribution services (such as favorable shelf or display space at a retail outlet), the existence of a favorable credit rating, or the existence of favorable supply contracts. The amount paid or incurred for supplier-based intangibles does not include any amount required to be paid for the goods or services themselves pursuant to the terms of the agreement or other relationship. In addition, see the exceptions in paragraph (c) of this section, including the exception in paragraph (c)(6) of this section for certain rights to receive tangible property or services from another person.

(8) Licenses, permits, and other rights granted by governmental units. Section 197 intangibles include any license, permit, or other right granted by a governmental unit (including, for purposes of section 197, an agency or instrumentality thereof) even if the right is granted for an indefinite period or is reasonably expected to be renewed for an indefinite period. These rights include, for example, a liquor license, a taxi-cab medallion (or license), an airport landing or takeoff right (sometimes referred to as a slot), a regulated airline route, or a television or radio broadcasting license. The issuance or renewal of a license, permit, or other right granted by a governmental unit is considered an acquisition of the license, permit, or other right. (See, however, the exceptions in paragraph (c) of this section, including the exceptions in paragraph (c)(3) of this section for an interest in land, paragraph (c)(6) of this section for certain rights to receive tangible property or services, paragraph (c)(8) of this section for an interest under a lease of tangible property, and paragraph (c)(13) of this section for certain rights granted by a governmental unit. See paragraph (b)(10) of this section for the treatment of franchises.)

(9) Covenants not to compete and other similar arrangements. Section 197 intangibles include any covenant not to compete, or agreement having substantially the same effect, entered into in connection with the direct or indirect acquisition of an interest in a trade or business or a substantial portion thereof. For purposes of this paragraph (b)(9), an acquisition may be made in the form of an asset acquisition (including a qualified stock purchase that is treated as a purchase of assets under section 338), a stock acquisition or redemption, and the acquisition or redemption of a partnership interest. An agreement requiring the performance of services for the acquiring taxpayer or the provision of property or its use to the acquiring taxpayer does not have substantially the same effect as a covenant not to compete to the extent that the amount paid under the agreement represents reasonable compensation for the services actually rendered or for the property or use of the property actually provided.

(10) Franchises, trademarks, and trade names. (i) Section 197 intangibles include any franchise, trademark, or trade name. The term franchise has the meaning given in section 1253(b)(1) and includes any agreement that provides one of the parties to the agreement with the right to distribute, sell, or provide goods, services, or facilities, within a specified area. The term trademark includes any word, name, symbol, or device, or any combination thereof, adopted and used to identify goods or services and distinguish them from those provided by others. The term trade name includes any name used to identify or designate a particular trade or business or the name or title used by a person or organization engaged in a trade or business. A license, permit, or other right granted by a governmental unit is a franchise if it otherwise meets the definition of a franchise. A trademark or trade name includes any trademark or trade name arising under statute or applicable common law, and any similar right granted by contract. The renewal of a franchise, trademark, or trade name is treated as an acquisition of the franchise, trademark, or trade name.

(ii) Notwithstanding the definitions provided in paragraph (b)(10)(i) of this section, any amount that is paid or incurred on account of a transfer, sale, or other disposition of a franchise, trademark, or trade name and that is subject to section 1253(d)(1) is not included in the basis of a section 197 intangible. (See paragraph (g)(6) of this section.)

(11) Contracts for the use of, and term interests in, section 197 intangibles. Section 197 intangibles include any right under a license, contract, or other arrangement providing for the use of property that would be a section 197 intangible under any provision of this paragraph (b) (including this paragraph (b)(11)) after giving effect to all of the exceptions provided in paragraph (c) of this section. Section 197 intangibles also include any term interest (whether outright or in trust) in such property.

(12) Other similar items. Section 197 intangibles include any other intangible property that is similar in all material respects to the property specifically described in section 197(d)(1)(C)(i) through (v) and paragraphs (b)(3) through (7) of this section. (See paragraph (g)(5) of this section for special rules regarding certain reinsurance transactions.)

(c) Section 197 intangibles; exceptions. The term section 197 intangible does not include property described in section 197(e). The following rules and definitions provide guidance concerning property to which the exceptions apply:

(1) Interests in a corporation, partnership, trust, or estate. Section 197 intangibles do not include an interest in a corporation, partnership, trust, or estate. Thus, for example, amortization under section 197 is not available for the cost of acquiring stock, partnership interests, or interests in a trust or estate, whether or not the interests are regularly traded on an established market. (See paragraph (g)(3) of this section for special rules applicable to property of a partnership when a section 754 election is in effect for the partnership.)

(2) Interests under certain financial contracts. Section 197 intangibles do not include an interest under an existing futures contract, foreign currency contract, notional principal contract, interest rate swap, or other similar financial contract, whether or not the interest is regularly traded on an established market. However, this exception does not apply to an interest under a mortgage servicing contract, credit card servicing contract, or other contract to service another person's indebtedness, or an interest under an assumption reinsurance contract. (See paragraph (g)(5) of this section for the treatment of assumption reinsurance contracts. See paragraph (c)(11) of this section and § 1.167(a)-14(d) for the treatment of mortgage servicing rights.)

(3) Interests in land. Section 197 intangibles do not include any interest in land. For this purpose, an interest in land includes a fee interest, life estate, remainder, easement, mineral right, timber right, grazing right, riparian right, air right, zoning variance, and any other similar right, such as a farm allotment, quota for farm commodities, or crop acreage base. An interest in land does not include an airport landing or takeoff right, a regulated airline route, or a franchise to provide cable television service. The cost of acquiring a license, permit, or other land improvement right, such as a building construction or use permit, is taken into account in the same manner as the underlying improvement.

(4) Certain computer software. (i) Publicly available. Section 197 intangibles do not include any interest in computer software that is (or has been) readily available to the general public on similar terms, is subject to a nonexclusive license, and has not been substantially modified. Computer software will be treated as readily available to the general public if the software may be obtained on substantially the same terms by a significant number of persons that would reasonably be expected to use the software. This requirement can be met even though the software is not available through a system of retail distribution. Computer software will not be considered to have been substantially modified if the cost of all modifications to the version of the software that is readily available to the general public does not exceed the greater of 25 percent of the price at which the unmodified version of the software is readily available to the general public or $2,000. For the purpose of determining whether computer software has been substantially modified—

(A) Integrated programs acquired in a package from a single source are treated as a single computer program; and

(B) Any cost incurred to install the computer software on a system is not treated as a cost of the software. However, the costs for customization, such as tailoring to a user's specifications (other than embedded programming options) are costs of modifying the software.

(ii) Not acquired as part of trade or business. Section 197 intangibles do not include an interest in computer software that is not acquired as part of a purchase of a trade or business.

(iii) Other exceptions. For other exceptions applicable to computer software, see paragraph (a)(3) of this section (relating to otherwise deductible amounts) and paragraph (g)(7) of this section (relating to amounts properly taken into account in determining the cost of property that is not a section 197 intangible).

(iv) Computer software defined. For purposes of this section, computer software is any program or routine (that is, any sequence of machine-readable code) that is designed to cause a computer to perform a desired function or set of functions, and the documentation required to describe and maintain that program or routine. It includes all forms and media in which the software is contained, whether written, magnetic, or otherwise. Computer programs of all classes, for example, operating systems, executive systems, monitors, compilers and translators, assembly routines, and utility programs as well as application programs, are included. Computer software also includes any incidental and ancillary rights that are necessary to effect the acquisition of the title to, the ownership of, or the right to use the computer software, and that are used only in connection with that specific computer software. Such incidental and ancillary rights are not included in the definition of trademark or trade name under paragraph (b)(10)(i) of this section. For example, a trademark or trade name that is ancillary to the ownership or use of a specific computer software program in the taxpayer's trade or business and is not acquired for the purpose of marketing the computer software is included in the definition of computer software and is not included in the definition of trademark or trade name. Computer software does not include any data or information base described in paragraph (b)(4) of this section unless the data base or item is in the public domain and is incidental to a computer program. For this purpose, a copyrighted or proprietary data or information base is treated as in the public domain if its availability through the computer program does not contribute significantly to the cost of the program. For example, if a word-processing program includes a dictionary feature used to spell-check a document or any portion thereof, the entire program (including the dictionary feature) is computer software regardless of the form in which the feature is maintained or stored.

(5) Certain interests in films, sound recordings, video tapes, books, or other similar property. Section 197 intangibles do not include any interest (including an interest as a licensee) in a film, sound recording, video tape, book, or other similar property (such as the right to broadcast or transmit a live event) if the interest is not acquired as part of a purchase of a trade or business. A film, sound recording, video tape, book, or other similar property includes any incidental and ancillary rights (such as a trademark or trade name) that are necessary to effect the acquisition of title to, the ownership of, or the right to use the property and are used only in connection with that property. Such incidental and ancillary rights are not included in the definition of trademark or trade name under paragraph (b)(10)(i) of this section. For purposes of this paragraph (c)(5), computer software (as defined in paragraph (c)(4)(iv) of this section) is not treated as other property similar to a film, sound recording, video tape, or book. (See section 167 for amortization of excluded intangible property or interests.)

(6) Certain rights to receive tangible property or services. Section 197 intangibles do not include any right to receive tangible property or services under a contract or from a governmental unit if the right is not acquired as part of a purchase of a trade or business. Any right that is described in the preceding sentence is not treated as a section 197 intangible even though the right is also described in section

197(d)(1)(D) and paragraph (b)(8) of this section (relating to certain governmental licenses, permits, and other rights) and even though the right fails to meet one or more of the requirements of paragraph (c)(13) of this section (relating to certain rights of fixed duration or amount). (See § 1.167(a)-14(c) (1) and (3) for applicable rules.)

(7) Certain interests in patents or copyrights. Section 197 intangibles do not include any interest (including an interest as a licensee) in a patent, patent application, or copyright that is not acquired as part of a purchase of a trade or business. A patent or copyright includes any incidental and ancillary rights (such as a trademark or trade name) that are necessary to effect the acquisition of title to, the ownership of, or the right to use the property and are used only in connection with that property. Such incidental and ancillary rights are not included in the definition of trademark or trade name under paragraph (b)(10)(i) of this section. (See § 1.167(a)-14(c)(4) for applicable rules.)

(8) Interests under leases of tangible property. (i) Interest as a lessor. Section 197 intangibles do not include any interest as a lessor under an existing lease or sublease of tangible real or personal property. In addition, the cost of acquiring an interest as a lessor in connection with the acquisition of tangible property is taken into account as part of the cost of the tangible property. For example, if a taxpayer acquires a shopping center that is leased to tenants operating retail stores, any portion of the purchase price attributable to favorable lease terms is taken into account as part of the basis of the shopping center and in determining the depreciation deduction allowed with respect to the shopping center. (See section 167(c)(2).)

(ii) Interest as a lessee. Section 197 intangibles do not include any interest as a lessee under an existing lease of tangible real or personal property. For this purpose, an airline lease of an airport passenger or cargo gate is a lease of tangible property. The cost of acquiring such an interest is taken into account under section 178 and § 1.162-11(a). If an interest as a lessee under a lease of tangible property is acquired in a transaction with any other intangible property, a portion of the total purchase price may be allocable to the interest as a lessee based on all of the relevant facts and circumstances.

(9) Interests under indebtedness. (i) In general. Section 197 intangibles do not include any interest (whether as a creditor or debtor) under an indebtedness in existence when the interest was acquired. Thus, for example, the value attributable to the assumption of an indebtedness with a below-market interest rate is not amortizable under section 197. In addition, the premium paid for acquiring a debt instrument with an above-market interest rate is not amortizable under section 197. See section 171 for rules concerning the treatment of amortizable bond premium.

(ii) Exceptions. For purposes of this paragraph (c)(9), an interest under an existing indebtedness does not include the deposit base (and other similar items) of a financial institution. An interest under an existing indebtedness includes mortgage servicing rights, however, to the extent the rights are stripped coupons under section 1286.

(10) Professional sports franchises. Section 197 intangibles do not include any franchise to engage in professional baseball, basketball, football, or any other professional sport, and any item (even though otherwise qualifying as a section 197 intangible) acquired in connection with such a franchise.

(11) Mortgage servicing rights. Section 197 intangibles do not include any right described in section 197(e)(7) (concerning rights to service indebtedness secured by residential real property that are not acquired as part of a purchase of a trade or business). (See § 1.167(a)-14(d) for applicable rules.)

(12) Certain transaction costs. Section 197 intangibles do not include any fees for professional services and any transaction costs incurred by parties to a transaction in which all or any portion of the gain or loss is not recognized under part III of subchapter C of the Internal Revenue Code.

(13) Rights of fixed duration or amount. (i) Section 197 intangibles do not include any right under a contract or any license, permit, or other right granted by a governmental unit if the right—

(A) Is acquired in the ordinary course of a trade or business (or an activity described in section 212) and not as part of a purchase of a trade or business;

(B) Is not described in section 197(d)(1)(A), (B), (E), or (F);

(C) Is not a customer-based intangible, a customer-related information base, or any other similar item; and

(D) Either—

(1) Has a fixed duration of less than 15 years; or

(2) Is fixed as to amount and the adjusted basis thereof is properly recoverable (without regard to this section) under a method similar to the unit-of-production method.

(ii) See § 1.167(a)-14(c)(2) and (3) for applicable rules.

(d) Amortizable section 197 intangibles. *(1) Definition.* Except as otherwise provided in this paragraph (d), the term amortizable section 197 intangible means any section 197 intangible acquired after August 10, 1993 (or after July 25, 1991, if a valid retroactive election under § 1.197-1T has been made), and held in connection with the conduct of a trade or business or an activity described in section 212.

(2) Exception for self-created intangibles. (i) In general. Except as provided in paragraph (d)(2)(iii) of this section, amortizable section 197 intangibles do not include any section 197 intangible created by the taxpayer (a self-created intangible).

(ii) Created by the taxpayer. (A) Defined. A section 197 intangible is created by the taxpayer to the extent the taxpayer makes payments or otherwise incurs costs for its creation, production, development, or improvement, whether the actual work is performed by the taxpayer or by another person under a contract with the taxpayer entered into before the contracted creation, production, development, or improvement occurs. For example, a technological process developed specifically for a taxpayer under an arrangement with another person pursuant to which the taxpayer retains all rights to the process is created by the taxpayer.

(B) Contracts for the use of intangibles. A section 197 intangible is not a self-created intangible to the extent that it results from the entry into (or renewal of) a contract for the use of an existing section 197 intangible. Thus, for example, the exception for self-created intangibles does not apply to capitalized costs, such as legal and other professional fees, incurred by a licensee in connection with the entry into (or renewal of) a contract for the use of know-how or similar property.

(C) Improvements and modifications. If an existing section 197 intangible is improved or otherwise modified by the taxpayer or by another person under a contract with the taxpayer, the existing intangible and the capitalized costs (if any) of the improvements or other modifications are each treated as a separate section 197 intangible for purposes of this paragraph (d).

(iii) Exceptions. (A) The exception for self-created intangibles does not apply to any section 197 intangible described in section 197(d)(1)(D) (relating to licenses, permits or other rights granted by a governmental unit), 197(d)(1)(E) (relating to covenants not to compete), or 197(d)(1)(F) (relating to franchises, trademarks, and trade names). Thus, for example, capitalized costs incurred in the development, registration, or defense of a trademark or trade name do not qualify for the exception and are amortized over 15 years under section 197.

(B) The exception for self-created intangibles does not apply to any section 197 intangible created in connection with the purchase of a trade or business (as defined in paragraph (e) of this section).

(C) If a taxpayer disposes of a self-created intangible and subsequently reacquires the intangible in an acquisition described in paragraph (h)(5)(ii) of this section, the exception for self-created intangibles does not apply to the reacquired intangible.

(3) Exception for property subject to anti-churning rules. Amortizable section 197 intangibles do not include any property to which the anti-churning rules of section 197(f)(9) and paragraph (h) of this section apply.

(e) Purchase of a trade or business. Several of the exceptions in section 197 apply only to property that is not acquired in (or created in connection with) a transaction or series of related transactions involving the acquisition of assets constituting a trade or business or a substantial portion thereof. Property acquired in (or created in connection with) such a transaction or series of related transactions is referred to in this section as property acquired as part of (or created in connection with) a purchase of a trade or business. For purposes of section 197 and this section, the applicability of the limitation is determined under the following rules:

(1) Goodwill or going concern value. An asset or group of assets constitutes a trade or business or a substantial portion thereof if their use would constitute a trade or business under section 1060 (that is, if goodwill or going concern value could under any circumstances attach to the assets). See § 1.1060-1(b)(2). For this purpose, all the facts and circumstances, including any employee relationships that continue (or covenants not to compete that are entered into) as part of the transfer of the assets, are taken into account in determining whether goodwill or going concern value could attach to the assets.

(2) Franchise, trademark, or trade name. (i) In general. The acquisition of a franchise, trademark, or trade name constitutes the acquisition of a trade or business or a substantial portion thereof.

(ii) Exceptions. For purposes of this paragraph (e)(2)—

(A) A trademark or trade name is disregarded if it is included in computer software under paragraph (c)(4) of this section or in an interest in a film, sound recording, video tape, book, or other similar property under paragraph (c)(5) of this section;

(B) A franchise, trademark, or trade name is disregarded if its value is nominal or the taxpayer irrevocably disposes of it immediately after its acquisition; and

(C) The acquisition of a right or interest in a trademark or trade name is disregarded if the grant of the right or interest is not, under the principles of section 1253, a transfer of all substantial rights to such property or of an undivided interest in all substantial rights to such property.

(3) Acquisitions to be included. The assets acquired in a transaction (or series of related transactions) include only assets (including a beneficial or other indirect interest in assets where the interest is of a type described in paragraph (c)(1) of this section) acquired by the taxpayer and persons related to the taxpayer from another person and persons related to that other person. For purposes of this paragraph (e)(3), persons are related only if their relationship is described in section 267(b) or 707(b) or they are engaged in trades or businesses under common control within the meaning of section 41(f)(1).

(4) Substantial portion. The determination of whether acquired assets constitute a substantial portion of a trade or business is to be based on all of the facts and circumstances, including the nature and the amount of the assets acquired as well as the nature and amount of the assets retained by the transferor. The value of the assets acquired relative to the value of the assets retained by the transferor is not determinative of whether the acquired assets constitute a substantial portion of a trade or business.

(5) Deemed asset purchases under section 338. A qualified stock purchase that is treated as a purchase of assets under section 338 is treated as a transaction involving the acquisition of assets constituting a trade or business only if the direct acquisition of the assets of the corporation would have been treated as the acquisition of assets constituting a trade or business or a substantial portion thereof.

(6) Mortgage servicing rights. Mortgage servicing rights acquired in a transaction or series of related transactions are disregarded in determining for purposes of paragraph (c)(11) of this section whether the assets acquired in the transaction or transactions constitute a trade or business or substantial portion thereof.

(7) Computer software acquired for internal use. Computer software acquired in a transaction or series of related transactions solely for internal use in an existing trade or business is disregarded in determining for purposes of paragraph (c)(4) of this section whether the assets acquired in the transaction or series of related transactions constitute a trade or business or substantial portion thereof.

(f) Computation of amortization deduction. *(1) In general.* Except as provided in paragraph (f)(2) of this section, the amortization deduction allowable under section 197(a) is computed as follows:

(i) The basis of an amortizable section 197 intangible is amortized ratably over the 15-year period beginning on the later of—

(A) The first day of the month in which the property is acquired; or

(B) In the case of property held in connection with the conduct of a trade or business or in an activity described in section 212, the first day of the month in which the conduct of the trade or business or the activity begins.

(ii) Except as otherwise provided in this section, basis is determined under section 1011 and salvage value is disregarded.

(iii) Property is not eligible for amortization in the month of disposition.

(iv) The amortization deduction for a short taxable year is based on the number of months in the short taxable year.

(2) Treatment of contingent amounts.

(i) Amounts added to basis during 15-year period. Any amount that is properly included in the basis of an amortizable section 197 intangible after the first month of the 15-year period described in paragraph (f)(1)(i) of this section and before the expiration of that period is amortized ratably over the remainder of the 15-year period. For this purpose, the remainder of the 15-year period begins on the first day of the month in which the basis increase occurs.

(ii) Amounts becoming fixed after expiration of 15-year period. Any amount that is not properly included in the basis of an amortizable section 197 intangible until after the expiration of the 15-year period described in paragraph (f)(1)(i) of this section is amortized in full immediately upon the inclusion of the amount in the basis of the intangible.

(iii) Rules for including amounts in basis. See § 1.1275-4(c)(4) and 1.483-4(a) for rules governing the extent to which contingent amounts payable under a debt instrument given in consideration for the sale or exchange of an amortizable section 197 intangible are treated as payments of principal and the time at which the amount treated as principal is included in basis. See § 1.461-1(a)(1) and (2) for rules governing the time at which other contingent amounts are taken into account in determining the basis of an amortizable section 197 intangible.

(3) Basis determinations for certain assets. (i) Covenants not to compete. In the case of a covenant not to compete or other similar arrangement described in paragraph (b)(9) of this section (a covenant), the amount chargeable to capital account includes, except as provided in this paragraph (f)(3), all amounts that are required to be paid pursuant to the covenant, whether or not any such amount would be deductible under section 162 if the covenant were not a section 197 intangible.

(ii) Contracts for the use of section 197 intangibles; acquired as part of a trade or business. (A) In general. Except as provided in this paragraph (f)(3), any amount paid or incurred by the transferee on account of the transfer of a right or term interest described in paragraph (b)(11) of this section (relating to contracts for the use of, and term interests in, section 197 intangibles) by the owner of the property to which such right or interest relates and as part of a purchase of a trade or business is chargeable to capital account, whether or not such amount would be deductible under section 162 if the property were not a section 197 intangible.

(B) Know-how and certain information base. The amount chargeable to capital account with respect to a right or term interest described in paragraph (b)(11) of this section is determined without regard to the rule in paragraph (f)(3)(ii)(A) of this section if the right or interest relates to property (other than a customer-related information base) described in paragraph (b)(4) or (5) of this section and the acquiring taxpayer establishes that—

(1) The transfer of the right or interest is not, under the principles of section 1235, a transfer of all substantial rights to such property or of an undivided interest in all substantial rights to such property; and

(2) The right or interest was transferred for an arm's-length consideration.

(iii) Contracts for the use of section 197 intangibles; not acquired as part of a trade or business. The transfer of a right or term interest described in paragraph (b)(11) of this section by the owner of the property to which such right or interest relates but not as part of a purchase of a trade or business will be closely scrutinized under the principles of section 1235 for purposes of determining whether the transfer is a sale or exchange and, accordingly, whether amounts paid on account of the transfer are chargeable to capital account. If under the principles of section 1235 the transaction is not a sale or exchange, amounts paid on account of the transfer are not chargeable to capital account under this paragraph (f)(3). (iv) Applicable rules.

(A) Franchises, trademarks, and trade names. For purposes of this paragraph (f)(3), section 197 intangibles described in paragraph (b)(11) of this section do not include any property that is also described in paragraph (b)(10) of this section (relating to franchises, trademarks, and trade names).

(B) Certain amounts treated as payable under a debt instrument. (1) In general. For purposes of applying any provision of the Internal Revenue Code to a person making payments of amounts that are otherwise chargeable to capital account under this paragraph (f)(3) and are payable after the acquisition of the section 197 intangible to which they relate, such amounts are treated as payable under a debt instrument given in consideration for the sale or exchange of the section 197 intangible.

(2) Rights granted by governmental units. For purposes of applying any provision of the Internal Revenue Code to any amounts that are otherwise chargeable to capital account with respect to a license, permit, or other right described in paragraph (b)(8) of this section (relating to rights granted by a governmental unit or agency or instrumentality thereof) and are payable after the acquisition of the section 197 intangible to which they relate, such amounts are treated, except as provided in paragraph (f)(4)(i) of this section (relating to renewal transactions), as payable under a debt instrument given in consideration for the sale or exchange of the section 197 intangible.

(3) Treatment of other parties to transaction. No person shall be treated as having sold, exchanged, or otherwise disposed of property in a transaction for purposes of any provision of the Internal Revenue Code solely by reason of the application of this paragraph (f)(3) to any other party to the transaction.

(4) Basis determinations in certain transactions. (i) Certain renewal transactions. The costs paid or incurred for the renewal of a franchise, trademark, or trade name or any license, permit, or other right granted by a governmental unit or an agency or instrumentality thereof are amortized over the 15-year period that begins with the month of renewal. Any costs paid or incurred for the issuance, or earlier renewal, continue to be taken into account over the remaining portion of the amortization period that began at the time of the issuance, or earlier renewal. Any amount paid or incurred for the protection, expansion, or defense of a trademark or trade name and chargeable to capital account is treated as an amount paid or incurred for a renewal.

(ii) Transactions subject to section 338 or 1060. In the case of a section 197 intangible deemed to have been acquired as the result of a qualified stock purchase within the meaning of section 338(d)(3), the basis shall be determined pursuant to section 338(b)(5) and the regulations thereunder. In the case of a section 197 intangible acquired in an applicable asset acquisition within the meaning of section 1060(c), the basis shall be determined pursuant to section 1060(a) and the regulations thereunder.

(iii) Certain reinsurance transactions. See paragraph (g)(5)(ii) of this section for special rules regarding the adjusted basis of an insurance contract acquired through an assumption reinsurance transaction.

(g) Special rules. *(1) Treatment of certain dispositions.* (i) Loss disallowance rules. (A) In general. No loss is recognized on the disposition of an amortizable section 197 intangible if the taxpayer has any retained intangibles. The retained intangibles with respect to the disposition of any amortizable section 197 intangible (the transferred intangible) are all amortizable section 197 intangibles, or rights to use or interests (including beneficial or other indirect interests) in amortizable section 197 intangibles (including the transferred intangible) that were acquired in the same transaction or series of related transactions as the transferred intangible and are retained after its disposition. Except as otherwise provided in paragraph (g)(1)(iv)(B) of this section, the adjusted basis of each of the retained intangibles is increased by the product of—

(1) The loss that is not recognized solely by reason of this rule; and

(2) A fraction, the numerator of which is the adjusted basis of the retained intangible on the date of the disposition and the denominator of which is the total adjusted bases of all the retained intangibles on that date.

(B) Abandonment or worthlessness. The abandonment of an amortizable section 197 intangible, or any other event rendering an amortizable section 197 intangible worthless, is treated as a disposition of the intangible for purposes of this paragraph (g)(1), and the abandoned or worthless intangible is disregarded (that is, it is not treated as a retained intangible) for purposes of applying this paragraph (g)(1) to the subsequent disposition of any other amortizable section 197 intangible.

(C) Certain nonrecognition transfers. The loss disallowance rule in paragraph (g)(1)(i)(A) of this section also applies when a taxpayer transfers an amortizable section 197 intangible from an acquired trade or business in a transaction in which the intangible is transferred basis property and, after the transfer, retains other amortizable section 197 intangibles from the trade or business. Thus, for example, the transfer of an amortizable section 197 intangible to a corporation in exchange for stock in the corporation in a transaction described in section 351, or to a partnership in exchange for an interest in the partnership in a transaction described in section 721, when other amortizable section 197 intangibles acquired in the same transaction are retained, followed by a sale of the stock or partnership interest received, will not avoid the application of the loss disallowance provision to the extent the adjusted basis of the transferred intangible at the time of the sale exceeds its fair market value at that time.

(ii) Separately acquired property. Paragraph (g)(1)(i) of this section does not apply to an amortizable section 197 intangible that is not acquired in a transaction or series of related transactions in which the taxpayer acquires other amortizable section 197 intangibles (a separately acquired intangible). Consequently, a loss may be recognized upon the disposition of a separately acquired amortizable section 197 intangible. However, the termination or worthlessness of only a portion of an amortizable section 197 intangible is not the disposition of a separately acquired intangible. For example, neither the loss of several customers from an acquired customer list nor the worthlessness of only some information from an acquired data base constitutes the disposition of a separately acquired intangible.

(iii) Disposition of a covenant not to compete. If a covenant not to compete or any other arrangement having substantially the same effect is entered into in connection with the direct or indirect acquisition of an interest in one or more trades or businesses, the disposition or worthlessness of the covenant or other arrangement will not be considered to occur until the disposition or worthlessness of all interests in those trades or businesses. For example, a covenant not to compete entered into in connection with the purchase of stock continues to be amortized ratably over the 15-year recovery period (even after the covenant expires or becomes worthless) unless all the trades or businesses in which an interest was acquired through the stock purchase (or all the purchaser's interests in those trades or businesses) also are disposed of or become worthless.

(iv) Taxpayers under common control. (A) In general. Except as provided in paragraph (g)(1)(iv)(B) of this section, all persons that would be treated as a single taxpayer under section 41(f)(1) are treated as a single taxpayer under this paragraph (g)(1). Thus, for example, a loss is not recognized on the disposition of an amortizable section 197 intangible by a member of a controlled group of corporations (as defined in section 41(f)(5)) if, after the disposition, another member retains other amortizable section 197 intangibles acquired in the same transaction as the amortizable section 197 intangible that has been disposed of.

(B) Treatment of disallowed loss. If retained intangibles are held by a person other than the person incurring the disallowed loss, only the adjusted basis of intangibles retained by the person incurring the disallowed loss is increased, and only the adjusted basis of those intangibles is included in the denominator of the fraction described in paragraph (g)(1)(i)(A) of this section. If none of the retained intangibles are held by the person incurring the disallowed loss, the loss is allowed ratably, as a deduction under section 197, over the remainder of the period during which the intangible giving rise to the loss would have been amortizable, except that any remaining disallowed loss is allowed in full on the first date on which all other retained intangibles have been disposed of or become worthless.

(2) Treatment of certain nonrecognition and exchange transactions. (i) Relationship to anti-churning rules. This paragraph (g)(2) provides rules relating to the treatment of section 197 intangibles acquired in certain transactions. If these rules apply to a section 197(f)(9) intangible (within the meaning of paragraph (h)(1)(i) of this section), the intangible is, notwithstanding its treatment under this paragraph (g)(2), treated as an amortizable section 197 intangible only to the extent permitted under paragraph (h) of this section.

(ii) Treatment of nonrecognition and exchange transactions generally. (A) Transfer disregarded. If a section 197 intangible is transferred in a transaction described in paragraph (g)(2)(ii)(C) of this section, the transfer is disregarded in determining—

(1) Whether, with respect to so much of the intangible's basis in the hands of the transferee as does not exceed its basis in the hands of the transferor, the intangible is an amortizable section 197 intangible; and

(2) The amount of the deduction under section 197 with respect to such basis.

(B) Application of general rule. If the intangible described in paragraph (g)(2)(ii)(A) of this section was an amortizable section 197 intangible in the hands of the transferor, the transferee will continue to amortize its adjusted basis, to the extent it does not exceed the transferor's adjusted basis, ratably over the remainder of the transferor's 15-year amortization period. If the intangible was not an amortizable section 197 intangible in the hands of the transferor, the transferee's adjusted basis, to the extent it does not exceed the transferor's adjusted basis, cannot be amortized under section 197. In either event, the intangible is treated, with respect to so much of its adjusted basis in the hands of the transferee as exceeds its adjusted basis in the hands of the transferor, in the same manner for purposes of section 197 as an intangible acquired from the transferor in a transaction that is not described in paragraph (g)(2)(ii)(C) of this section. The rules of this paragraph (g)(2)(ii) also apply to any subsequent transfers of the intangible in a transaction described in paragraph (g)(2)(ii)(C) of this section.

(C) Transactions covered. The transactions described in this paragraph (g)(2)(ii)(C) are—

(1) Any transaction described in section 332, 351, 361, 721, or 731; and

(2) Any transaction between corporations that are members of the same consolidated group immediately after the transaction.

(iii) Certain exchanged-basis property. This paragraph (g)(2)(iii) applies to property that is acquired in a transaction subject to section 1031 or 1033 and is permitted to be acquired without recognition of gain (replacement property). Replacement property is treated as if it were the property by reference to which its basis is determined (the predecessor property) in determining whether, with respect to so much of its basis as does not exceed the basis of the predecessor property, the replacement property is an amortizable section 197 intangible and the amortization period under section 197 with respect to such basis. Thus, if the predecessor property was an amortizable section 197 intangible, the taxpayer will amortize the adjusted basis of the replacement property, to the extent it does not exceed the adjusted basis of the predecessor property, ratably over the remainder of the 15-year amortization period for the predecessor property. If the predecessor property was not an amortizable section 197 intangible, the adjusted basis of the replacement property, to the extent it does not exceed the adjusted basis of the predecessor property, may not be amortized under section 197. In either event, the replacement property is treated, with respect to so much of its adjusted basis as exceeds the adjusted basis of the predecessor property, in the same manner for purposes of section 197 as property acquired from the transferor in a transaction that is not subject to section 1031 or 1033.

(iv) Transfers under section 708(b)(1). (A) In general. Paragraph (g)(2)(ii) of this section applies to transfers of section 197 intangibles that occur or are deemed to occur by reason of the termination of a partnership under section 708(b)(1).

(B) Termination by sale or exchange of interest. In applying paragraph (g)(2)(ii) of this section to a partnership that is terminated pursuant to section 708(b)(1)(B) (relating to deemed terminations from the sale or exchange of an interest), the terminated partnership is treated as the transferor and the new partnership is treated as the transferee with respect to any section 197 intangible held by the terminated partnership immediately preceding the termination. (See paragraph (g)(3) of this section for the treatment of increases in the bases of property of the terminated partnership under section 743(b).)

(C) Other terminations. In applying paragraph (g)(2)(ii) of this section to a partnership that is terminated pursuant to section 708(b)(1)(A) (relating to cessation of activities by a partnership), the terminated partnership is treated as the transferor and the distributee partner is treated as the transferee with respect to any section 197 intangible held by the terminated partnership immediately preceding the termination.

(3) Increase in the basis of partnership property under section 732(b), 734(b), 743(b), or 732(d). Any increase in the adjusted basis of a section 197 intangible under sections 732(b) or 732(d) (relating to a partner's basis in property distributed by a partnership), section 734(b) (relating to the optional adjustment to the basis of undistributed partnership property after a distribution of property to a partner), or section 743(b) (relating to the optional adjustment to the basis of partnership property after transfer of a partnership interest) is treated as a separate section 197 intangible. For purposes of determining the amortization period under section 197 with respect to the basis increase, the intangible is treated as having been acquired at the time of the transaction that causes the basis increase, except as provided in § 1.743-1(j)(4)(i)(B)(2). The provisions of paragraph (f)(2) of this section apply to the extent that the amount of the basis increase is determined by reference to contingent payments. For purposes of the effective date and anti-churning provisions (paragraphs (l)(1) and (h) of this section) for a basis increase under section 732(d), the intangible is treated as having been acquired by the transferee partner at the time of the transfer of the partnership interest described in section 732(d).

(4) Section 704(c) allocations. (i) Allocations where the intangible is amortizable by the contributor. To the extent that the intangible was an amortizable section 197 intangible in the hands of the contributing partner, a partnership may make allocations of amortization deductions with respect to the intangible to all of its partners under any of the permissible methods described in the regulations under section 704(c). See § 1.704-3.

(ii) To the extent that the intangible was not an amortizable section 197 intangible in the hands of the contributing partner, the intangible is not amortizable under section 197 by the partnership. However, if a partner contributes a section 197 intangible to a partnership and the partnership adopts the remedial allocation method for making section 704(c) allocations of amortization deductions, the partnership generally may make remedial allocations of amortization deductions with respect to the contributed section 197 intangible in accordance with § 1.704-3(d). See paragraph (h)(12) of this section to determine the application of the anti-churning rules in the context of remedial allocations.

(5) Treatment of certain insurance contracts acquired in an assumption reinsurance transaction. (i) In general. Section 197 generally applies to insurance and annuity contracts acquired from another person through an assumption reinsurance transaction. See § 1.809-5(a)(7)(ii) for the definition of assumption reinsurance. The transfer of insurance or annuity contracts and the assumption of related liabilities deemed to occur by reason of a section 338 election for a target insurance company is treated as an assumption reinsurance transaction. The transfer of a reinsurance contract by a reinsurer (transferor) to another reinsurer (acquirer) is treated as an assumption reinsurance transaction if the transferor's obligations are extinguished as a result of the transaction.

(ii) Determination of adjusted basis of amortizable section 197 intangible resulting from an assumption reinsurance transaction. (A) In general. Section 197(f)(5) determines the basis of an amortizable section 197 intangible for insurance or annuity contracts acquired in an assumption reinsurance transaction. The basis of such intangible is the excess, if any, of—

(1) The amount paid or incurred by the acquirer (reinsurer) under the assumption reinsurance transaction; over

(2) The amount, if any, required to be capitalized under section 848 in connection with such transaction.

(B) Amount paid or incurred by acquirer (reinsurer) under the assumption reinsurance transaction. The amount paid or incurred by the acquirer (reinsurer) under the assumption reinsurance transaction is—

(1) In a deemed asset sale resulting from an election under section 338, the amount of the adjusted grossed-up basis (AGUB) allocable thereto (see §§ 1.338-6 and 1.338-11(b)(2));

(2) In an applicable asset acquisition within the meaning of section 1060, the amount of the consideration allocable thereto (see §§ 1.338-6, 1.338-11(b)(2), and 1.1060-1(c)(5)); and

(3) In any other transaction, the excess of the increase in the reinsurer's tax reserves resulting from the transaction (computed in accordance with sections 807, 832(b)(4)(B), and 846) over the value of the net assets received from the ceding company in the transaction.

(C) Amount required to be capitalized under section 848 in connection with the transaction. (1) In general. The amount required to be capitalized under section 848 for specified insurance contracts (as defined in section 848(e)) acquired in an assumption reinsurance transaction is the lesser of—

(i) The reinsurer's required capitalization amount for the assumption reinsurance transaction; or

(ii) The reinsurer's general deductions (as defined in section 848(c)(2)) allocable to the transaction.

(2) Required capitalization amount. The reinsurer determines the required capitalization amount for an assumption reinsurance transaction by multiplying the net positive or net negative consideration for the transaction by the applicable percentage set forth in section 848(c)(1) for the category of specified insurance contracts acquired in the transaction. See § 1.848-2(g)(5). If more than one category of specified insurance contracts is acquired in an assumption reinsurance transaction, the required capitalization amount for each category is determined as if the transfer of the contracts in that category were made under a separate assumption reinsurance transaction. See § 1.848-2(f)(7).

(3) General deductions allocable to the assumption reinsurance transaction. The reinsurer determines the general deductions allocable to the assumption reinsurance transaction in accordance with the procedure set forth in § 1.848-2(g)(6). Accordingly, the reinsurer must allocate its general deductions to the amount required under section 848(c)(1) on specified insurance contracts that the reinsurer has issued directly before determining the general deductions allocable to the assumption reinsurance transaction. For purposes of allocating its general deductions under § 1.848-2(g)(6), the reinsurer includes premiums received on the acquired specified insurance contracts after the assumption reinsurance transaction in determining the amount required under section 848(c)(1) on specified insurance contracts that the reinsurer has issued directly. If the reinsurer has entered into multiple reinsurance agreements during the taxable year, the reinsurer determines the general deductions allocable to each reinsurance agreement (including the assumption reinsurance transaction) by allocating the general deductions allocable to reinsurance agreements under § 1.848-2(g)(6) to each reinsurance agreement with a positive required capitalization amount.

(4) Treatment of a capitalization shortfall allocable to the reinsurance agreement. (i) In general. The reinsurer determines any capitalization shortfall allocable to the assumption reinsurance transaction in the manner provided in §§ 1.848-2(g)(4) and 1.848-2(g)(7). If the reinsurer has a capitalization shortfall allocable to the assumption reinsurance transaction, the ceding company must reduce the net negative consideration (as determined under § 1.848-2(f)(2)) for the transaction by the amount described in § 1.848-2(g)(3) unless the parties make the election provided in § 1.848-2(g)(8) to determine the amounts capitalized under section 848 in connection with the transaction without regard to the general deductions limitation of section 848(c)(2).

(ii) Treatment of additional capitalized amounts as the result of an election under § 1.848-2(g)(8). The additional amounts capitalized by the reinsurer as the result of the election under § 1.848-2(g)(8) reduce the adjusted basis of any amortizable section 197 intangible with respect to specified insurance contracts acquired in the assumption reinsurance transaction. If the additional capitalized amounts exceed the adjusted basis of the amortizable section 197 intangible, the reinsurer must reduce its deductions under section 805 or section 832 by the amount of such excess. The additional capitalized amounts are treated as specified policy acquisition expenses attributable to the premiums and other consideration on the assumption reinsurance transaction and are deducted ratably over a 120-month period as provided under section 848(a)(2).

(5) Cross references and special rules. In general, for rules applicable to the determination of specified policy acquisition expenses, net premiums, and net consideration, see section 848(c) and (d), and § 1.848-2(a) and (f). However, the following special rules apply for purposes of this paragraph (g)(5)(ii)(C)—

(i) The amount required to be capitalized under section 848 in connection with the assumption reinsurance transaction cannot be less than zero;

(ii) For purposes of determining the company's general deductions under section 848(c)(2) for the taxable year of the assumption reinsurance transaction, the reinsurer takes into account a tentative amortization deduction under section 197(a) as if the entire amount paid or incurred by the reinsurer for the specified insurance contracts were allocated to an amortizable section 197 intangible with respect to insurance contracts acquired in an assumption reinsurance transaction; and

(iii) Any reduction of specified policy acquisition expenses pursuant to an election under § 1.848-2(i)(4) (relating to an assumption reinsurance transaction with an insolvent insurance company) is disregarded.

(D) Examples. The following examples illustrate the principles of this paragraph (g)(5)(ii):

Example (1). (i) Facts. On January 15, 2006, P acquires all of the stock of T, an insurance company, in a qualified stock purchase and makes a section 338 election for T. T issues individual life insurance contracts which are specified insurance contracts as defined in section 848(e)(1). P and new T are calendar year taxpayers. Under §§ 1.338-6 and 1.338-11(b)(2), the amount of AGUB allocated to old T's individual life insurance contracts is $300,000. On the acquisition date, the tax reserves for old T's individual life insurance contracts are $2,000,000. After the acquisition date, new T receives $1,000,000 of net premiums with respect to new and renewal individual life insurance contracts and incurs $100,000 of general deductions under section 848(c)(2) through December 31, 2006. New T engages in no other reinsurance transactions other than the assumption reinsurance transaction treated as occurring by reason of the section 338 election.

(ii) Analysis. The transfer of insurance contracts and the assumption of related liabilities deemed to occur by reason of the election under section 338 is treated as an assumption reinsurance transaction. New T determines the adjusted basis under section 197(f)(5) for the life insurance contracts acquired in the assumption reinsurance transaction as follows. The amount paid or incurred for the individual life insurance contracts is $300,000. To determine the amount required to be capitalized under section 848 in connection with the assumption reinsurance transaction, new T compares the required capitalization amount for the assumption reinsurance transaction with the general deductions allocable to the transaction. The required capitalization amount for the assumption reinsurance transaction is $130,900, which is determined by multiplying the $1,700,000 net positive consideration for the transaction ($2,000,000 reinsurance premium less $300,000 ceding commission) by the applicable percentage under section 848(c)(1) for the acquired individual life insurance contracts (7.7 percent). To determine its general deductions, new T takes into account a tentative amortization deduction under section 197(a) as if the entire amount paid or incurred for old T's individual life insurance contracts ($300,000) were allocable to an amortizable section 197 intangible with respect to insurance contracts acquired in the assumption reinsurance transaction. Accordingly, for the year of the assumption reinsurance transaction, new T is treated as having general deductions under section 848(c)(2) of $120,000 ($100,000 + $300,000/15). Under § 1.848-2(g)(6), these general deductions are first allocated to the $77,000 capitalization requirement for new T's directly written business ($1,000,000 x .077). Thus, $43,000 ($120,000 – $77,000) of the general deductions are allocable to the assumption reinsurance transaction. Because the general deductions allocable to the assumption reinsurance transaction ($43,000) are less than the required capitalization amount for the transaction ($130,900), new T has a capitalization shortfall of $87,900 ($130,900 – $43,000) with regard to the transaction. Under § 1.848-2(g), this capitalization shortfall would cause old T to reduce the net negative consideration taken into account with respect to the assumption reinsurance transaction by $1,141,558 ($87,900 / .077) unless the parties make the election under § 1.848-2(g)(8) to capitalize specified policy acquisition expenses in connection with the assumption reinsurance transaction without regard to the general deductions limitation. If the parties make the election, the amount capitalized by new T under section 848 in connection with the assumption reinsurance transaction would be $130,900. The $130,900 capitalized by new T under section 848 would reduce new T's adjusted basis of the amortizable section 197 intangible with respect to the specified insurance contracts acquired in the assumption reinsurance transaction. Accordingly, new T would have an adjusted basis under section 197(f)(5) with respect to the individual life insurance contracts acquired from old T of $169,100 ($300,000 – $130,900). New T's actual amortization deduction under section 197(a) with respect to the amortizable section 197 intangible for insurance contracts acquired in the assumption reinsurance transaction would be $11,273 ($169,100 / 15).

Example (2). (i) Facts. The facts are the same as Example 1, except that T only issues accident and health insurance contracts that are qualified long-term care contracts under section 7702B. Under section 7702B(a)(5), T's qualified long-term care insurance contracts are treated as guaranteed renewable accident and health insurance contracts, and, therefore, are considered specified insurance contracts under section 848(e)(1). Under §§ 1.338-6 and 1.338-11(b)(2), the amount of AGUB allocable to T's qualified long-term care insurance contracts is $250,000. The amount of T's tax reserves for the qualified long-term care contracts on the acquisition date is $7,750,000. Following the acquisition, new T receives net premiums of $500,000 with respect to qualified long-term care contracts and incurs general deductions of $75,000 through December 31, 2006.

(ii) Analysis. The transfer of insurance contracts and the assumption of related liabilities deemed to occur by reason of the election under section 338 is treated as an assumption reinsurance transaction. New T determines the adjusted basis under section 197(f)(5) for the insurance contracts acquired in the assumption reinsurance transaction as follows. The amount paid or incurred for the insurance contracts is $250,000. To determine the amount required to be capitalized under section 848 in connection with the assumption reinsurance transaction, new T compares the required capitalization amount for the assumption reinsurance transaction with the general deductions allocable to the transaction. The required capitalization amount for the assumption reinsurance transaction is $577,500, which is determined by multiplying the $7,500,000 net positive consideration for the transaction ($7,750,000 reinsurance premium less $250,000 ceding commission) by the applicable percentage under section 848(c)(1) for the acquired insurance contracts (7.7 percent). To determine its general deductions, new T takes into account a tentative amortization deduction under section 197(a) as if the entire amount paid or incurred for old T's insurance contracts ($250,000) were allocable to an amortizable section 197 intangible with respect to insurance contracts acquired in the assumption reinsurance transaction. Accordingly, for the year of the assumption reinsurance transaction, new T is treated as having general deductions under section 848(c)(2) of $91,667 ($75,000 + $250,000/15). Under § 1.848-2(g)(6), these general deductions are first allocated to the $38,500 capitalization requirement for new T's directly written business ($500,000 x .077). Thus, $53,167 ($91,667 – $38,500) of general deductions are allocable to the assumption reinsurance transaction. Because the general deductions allocable to the assumption reinsurance transaction ($53,167) are less than the required capitalization amount for the transaction ($577,500), new T has a capitalization shortfall of $524,333 ($577,500 – $53,167) with regard to the transaction. Under § 1.848-2(g), this capitalization shortfall would cause old T to reduce the net negative consideration taken into account with respect to the assumption reinsurance transaction by $6,809,519 ($524,333 / .077) unless the parties make the election under § 1.848-2(g)(8) to capitalize specified policy acquisition expenses in connection with the assumption reinsurance transaction without regard to the general deductions limitation. If the parties make the election, the amount capitalized by new T under section 848 in connection with the assumption reinsurance transaction would increase from $53,167 to $577,500. Pursuant to paragraph (g)(5)(ii)(C)(4) of this section, the additional $524,333 ($577,500 – $53,167) capitalized by new T under section 848 would reduce new T's adjusted basis of the amortizable section 197 intangible with respect to the insurance contracts acquired in the assumption reinsurance transaction. Accordingly, new T's adjusted basis of the section 197 intangible with regard to the insurance contracts is reduced from $196,833 ($250,000 – $53,167) to $0. Because the additional $524,333 capitalized pursuant to the § 1.848-2(g)(8) election exceeds the $196,833 adjusted basis of the section 197 intangible before the reduction, new T is required to reduce its deductions under section 805 by the $327,500 ($524,333 – $196,833).

(E) Effective/applicability date. This section applies to acquisitions and dispositions of insurance contracts on or after April 10, 2006.

(iii) Application of loss disallowance rule upon a disposition of an insurance contract acquired in an assumption reinsurance transaction. The following rules apply for purposes of applying the loss disallowance rules of section 197(f)(1)(A) to the disposition of a section 197(f)(5) intangible. For this purpose, a section 197(f)(5) intangible is an amortizable section 197 intangible the basis of which is determined under section 197(f)(5).

(A) Disposition. (1) In general. A disposition of a section 197 intangible is any event as a result of which, absent section 197, recovery of basis is otherwise allowed for Federal income tax purposes.

(2) Treatment of indemnity reinsurance transactions. The transfer through indemnity reinsurance of the right to the future income from the insurance contracts to which a section 197(f)(5) intangible relates does not preclude the recovery of basis by the ceding company, provided that sufficient economic rights relating to the reinsured contracts are transferred to the reinsurer. However, the ceding company is not permitted to recover basis in an indemnity reinsurance transaction if it has a right to experience refunds reflecting a significant portion of the future profits on the reinsured contracts, or if it retains an option to reacquire a significant portion of the future profits on the reinsured contracts through the exercise of a recapture provision. In addition, the ceding company is not permitted to recover basis in an indemnity reinsurance transaction if the reinsurer assumes only a limited portion of the ceding company's risk relating to the reinsured contracts (excess loss reinsurance).

(B) Loss. The loss, if any, recognized by a taxpayer on the disposition of a section 197(f)(5) intangible equals the amount by which the taxpayer's adjusted basis in the section 197(f)(5) intangible immediately before the disposition exceeds the amount, if any, that the taxpayer receives from another person for the future income right from the insurance contracts to which the section 197(f)(5) intangible relates. In determining the amount of the taxpayer's loss on the disposition of a section 197(f)(5) intangible through a reinsurance transaction, any effect of the transaction on the amounts capitalized by the taxpayer as specified policy acquisition expenses under section 848 is disregarded.

(C) Examples. The following examples illustrate the principles of this paragraph (g)(5)(iii):

Example (1). (i) Facts. In a prior taxable year, as a result of a section 338 election with respect to T, new T was treated as purchasing all of old T's insurance contracts that were in force on the acquisition date in an assumption reinsurance transaction. Under §§ 1.338-6 and 1.338-11(b)(2), the amount of AGUB allocable to the future income right from the purchased insurance contracts was $15, net of the amounts required to be capitalized under section 848 as a result of the assumption reinsurance transaction. At the beginning of the current taxable year, as a result of amortization deductions allowed by section 197(a), new T's adjusted basis in the section 197(f)(5) intangible resulting from the assumption reinsurance transaction is $12. During the current taxable year, new T enters into an indemnity reinsurance agreement with R, another insurance company, in which R assumes 100 percent of the risk relating to the insurance contracts to which the section 197(f)(5) intangible relates. In the indemnity reinsurance transaction, R agrees to pay new T a ceding commission of $10 in exchange for the future profits on the underlying reinsured policies. Under the indemnity reinsurance agreement, new T continues to administer the reinsured policies, but transfers investment assets equal to the required reserves for the reinsured policies together with all future premiums to R. The indemnity reinsurance agreement does not contain an experience refund provision or a provision allowing new T to terminate the reinsurance agreement at its sole option. New T retains the insurance licenses and other amortizable section 197 intangibles acquired in the deemed asset sale and continues to underwrite and issue new insurance contracts.

(ii) Analysis. The indemnity reinsurance agreement constitutes a disposition of the section 197(f)(5) intangible because it involves the transfer of sufficient economic rights attributable to the insurance contracts to which the section 197(f)(5) intangible relates such that recovery of basis is allowed. For purposes of applying the loss disallowance rules of section 197(f)(1) and paragraph (g) of this section, new T's loss is $2 (new T's adjusted basis in the section 197(f)(5) intangible immediately before the disposition ($12) less the ceding commission ($10)). Therefore, new T applies $10 of the adjusted basis in the section 197(f)(5) intangible against the amount received from R for the future income right on the reinsured policies and increases its basis in the amortizable section 197 intangibles that it acquired and retained from the deemed asset sale by $2, the amount of the disallowed loss. The amount of new T's disallowed loss under section 197(f)(1)(A) is determined without regard to the effect of the indemnity reinsurance transaction on the amounts capitalized by new T as specified policy acquisition expenses under section 848.

Example (2). (i) Facts. Assume the same facts as in Example 1, except that under the indemnity reinsurance agreement R agrees to pay new T a ceding commission of $5 with respect to the underlying reinsured contracts. In addition, under the indemnity reinsurance agreement, new T is entitled to an experience refund equal to any future profits on the reinsured contracts in excess of the ceding commission plus an annual risk charge. New T also has a right to recapture the business at any time after R has recovered an amount equal to the ceding commission.

(ii) Analysis. The indemnity reinsurance agreement between new T and R does not represent a disposition because it does not involve the transfer of sufficient economic rights with respect to the future income on the reinsured contracts. Therefore, new T may not recover its basis in the section 197(f)(5) intangible to which the contracts relate and must continue to amortize ratably the adjusted basis of the section 197(f)(5) intangible over the remainder of the 15-year recovery period and cannot apply any portion of this adjusted basis to offset the ceding commission received from R in the indemnity reinsurance transaction.

(iv) Effective dates. (A) In general—This paragraph (g)(5) applies to acquisitions and dispositions on or after April 10, 2006. For rules applicable to acquisitions and dispositions before that date, see § 1.197-2 in effect before that date (see 26 CFR part 1, revised April 1, 2001).

(B) Application to pre-effective date acquisitions and dispositions. A taxpayer may choose, on a transaction-by-transaction basis, to apply the provisions of this paragraph (g)(5) to property acquired and disposed of before April 10, 2006.

(C) Change in method of accounting. (1) In general—A change in a taxpayer's treatment of all property acquired and disposed under paragraph (g)(5) is a change in method of accounting to which the provisions of sections 446 and 481 and the regulations thereunder apply.

(2) Acquisitions and dispositions on or after effective date. A Taxpayer is granted the consent of the Commissioner under section 446(e) to change its method of accounting to comply with this paragraph (g)(5) for acquisitions and dispositions on or after April 10, 2006. The change must be made on a cut-off basis with no section 481(a) adjustment. Notwithstanding § 1.446-1(e)(3), a taxpayer should not file a Form 3115, "Application for Change in Accounting Method," to obtain the consent of the Commissioner to change its method of accounting under this paragraph (g)(5)(iv)(C)(2). Instead, a taxpayer must make the change by using the new method on its federal income tax returns.

(3) Acquisitions and dispositions before the effective date. For the first taxable year ending after April 10, 2006, a taxpayer is granted consent of the Commissioner to change its method of accounting for all property acquired in transactions described in paragraph (g)(5)(iv)(B) to comply with this paragraph (g)(5) unless the proper treatment of any such property is an issue under consideration in an examination, before an Appeals office, or before a Federal Court. (For the definition of when an issue is under consideration, see, Rev. Proc. 97-27 (1997-1 C.B. 680); and, § 601.601(d)(2) of this chapter). A taxpayer changing its method of accounting in accordance with this paragraph (g)(5)(iv)(C)(3) must follow the applicable administrative procedures for obtaining the Commissioner's automatic consent to a change in method of accounting (for further guidance, see, for example, Rev. Proc. 2002-9 (2002-1 C.B. 327) as modified and clarified by Announcement 2002-17 (2002-1 C.B. 561), modified and amplified by Rev. Proc. 2002-19 (2002-1 C.B. 696), and amplified, clarified and modified by Rev. Proc. 2002-54 (2002-2 C.B. 432); and, § 601.601(d)(2) of this chapter), except, for purposes of this paragraph (g)(5)(iv)(C)(3), any limitations in such administrative procedures for obtaining the automatic consent of the Commissioner shall not apply. However, if the taxpayer is under examination, before an appeals office, or before a Federal court, the taxpayer must provide a copy of the application to the examining agent(s), appeals officer, or counsel for the government, as appropriate, at the same time that it files the copy of the application with the National Office. The application must contain the name(s) and telephone number(s) of the examining agent(s), appeals officer, or counsel for the government, as appropriate. For purposes of From 3115, "Application for Change in Accounting Method," the designated number for the automatic accounting method change authorized by this paragraph (g)(5)(iv)(C)(3) is "98." A change in method of accounting in accordance with this paragraph (g)(5)(iv)(C)(3) requires an adjustment under section 481(a).

(6) Amounts paid or incurred for a franchise, trademark, or trade name. If an amount to which section 1253(d) (relating to the transfer, sale, or other disposition of a franchise, trademark, or trade name) applies is described in section 1253(d)(1)(B) (relating to contingent serial payments deductible under section 162), the amount is not included in the adjusted basis of the intangible for purposes of section 197. Any other amount, whether fixed or contingent, to which section 1253(d) applies is chargeable to capital account under section 1253(d)(2) and is amortizable only under section 197.

(7) Amounts properly taken into account in determining the cost of property that is not a section 197 intangible. Section 197 does not apply to an amount that is properly taken into account in determining the cost of property that is not a section 197 intangible. The entire cost of acquiring the other property is included in its basis and recovered under other applicable Internal Revenue Code provisions. Thus, for example, section 197 does not apply to the cost of an interest in computer software to the extent such cost is included, without being separately stated, in the cost of the hardware or other tangible property and is consistently treated as part of the cost of the hardware or other tangible property.

(8) Treatment of amortizable section 197 intangibles as depreciable property. An amortizable section 197 intangible is treated as property of a character subject to the allowance for depreciation under section 167. Thus, for example, an amortizable section 197 intangible is not a capital asset for purposes of section 1221, but if used in a trade or business and held for more than one year, gain or loss on its disposition generally qualifies as section 1231 gain or loss. Also, an amortizable section 197 intangible is section 1245 property and section 1239 applies to any gain recognized upon its sale or exchange between related persons (as defined in section 1239(b)).

(h) Anti-churning rules. *(1) Scope and purpose.* (i) Scope. This paragraph (h) applies to section 197(f)(9) intangibles. For this purpose, section 197(f)(9) intangibles are goodwill and going concern value that was held or used at any time during the transition period and any other section 197 intangible that was held or used at any time during the transition period and was not depreciable or amortizable under prior law.

(ii) Purpose. To qualify as an amortizable section 197 intangible, a section 197 intangible must be acquired after the applicable date (July 25, 1991, if the acquiring taxpayer has made a valid retroactive election pursuant to § 1.197-1T; August 10, 1993, in all other cases). The purpose of the anti-churning rules of section 197(f)(9) and this paragraph (h) is to prevent the amortization of section 197(f)(9) intangibles unless they are transferred after the applicable effective date in a transaction giving rise to a significant change in ownership or use. (Special rules apply for purposes of determining whether transactions involving partnerships give rise to a significant change in ownership or use. See paragraph (h)(12) of this section.) The anti-churning rules are to be applied in a manner that carries out their purpose.

(2) Treatment of section 197(f)(9) intangibles. Except as otherwise provided in this paragraph (h), a section 197(f)(9) intangible acquired by a taxpayer after the applicable effective date does not qualify for amortization under section 197 if—

(i) The taxpayer or a related person held or used the intangible or an interest therein at any time during the transition period;

(ii) The taxpayer acquired the intangible from a person that held the intangible at any time during the transition period and, as part of the transaction, the user of the intangible does not change; or

(iii) The taxpayer grants the right to use the intangible to a person that held or used the intangible at any time during the transition period (or to a person related to that person), but only if the transaction in which the taxpayer grants the right and the transaction in which the taxpayer acquired the intangible are part of a series of related transactions.

(3) Amounts deductible under section 1253(d) or § 1.162-11. For purposes of this paragraph (h), deductions allowable under section 1253(d)(2) or pursuant to an election under section 1253(d)(3) (in either case as in effect prior to the enactment of section 197) and deductions allowable under § 1.162-11 are treated as deductions allowable for amortization under prior law.

(4) Transition period. For purposes of this paragraph (h), the transition period is July 25, 1991, if the acquiring taxpayer has made a valid retroactive election pursuant to § 1.197-1T and the period beginning on July 25, 1991, and ending on August 10, 1993, in all other cases.

(5) Exceptions. The anti-churning rules of this paragraph (h) do not apply to—

(i) The acquisition of a section 197(f)(9) intangible if the acquiring taxpayer's basis in the intangible is determined under section 1014(a); or

(ii) The acquisition of a section 197(f)(9) intangible that was an amortizable section 197 intangible in the hands of the seller (or transferor), but only if the acquisition transaction and the transaction in which the seller (or transferor) acquired the intangible or interest therein are not part of a series of related transactions.

(6) Related person. (i) In general. Except as otherwise provided in paragraph (h)(6)(ii) of this section, a person is related to another person for purposes of this paragraph (h) if—

(A) The person bears a relationship to that person that would be specified in section 267(b) (determined without regard to section 267(e)) and, by substitution, section 267(f)(1), if those sections were amended by substituting 20 percent for 50 percent; or

(B) The person bears a relationship to that person that would be specified in section 707(b)(1) if that section were amended by substituting 20 percent for 50 percent; or

(C) The persons are engaged in trades or businesses under common control (within the meaning of section 41(f)(1) (A) and (B)).

(ii) Time for testing relationships. Except as provided in paragraph (h)(6)(iii) of this section, a person is treated as related to another person for purposes of this paragraph (h) if the relationship exists—

(A) In the case of a single transaction, immediately before or immediately after the transaction in which the intangible is acquired; and

(B) In the case of a series of related transactions (or a series of transactions that together comprise a qualified stock purchase within the meaning of section 338(d)(3)), immediately before the earliest such transaction or immediately after the last such transaction.

(iii) Certain relationships disregarded. In applying the rules in paragraph (h)(7) of this section, if a person acquires an intangible in a series of related transactions in which the person acquires stock (meeting the requirements of section 1504(a)(2)) of a corporation in a fully taxable transaction followed by a liquidation of the acquired corporation under section 331, any relationship created as part of such series of transactions is disregarded in determining whether any person is related to such acquired corporation immediately after the last transaction.

(iv) De minimis rule. (A) In general. Two corporations are not treated as related persons for purposes of this paragraph (h) if—

(1) The corporations would (but for the application of this paragraph (h)(6)(iv)) be treated as related persons solely by reason of substituting "more than 20 percent" for "more than 50 percent" in section 267(f)(1)(A); and

(2) The beneficial ownership interest of each corporation in the stock of the other corporation represents less than 10 percent of the total combined voting power of all classes of stock entitled to vote and less than 10 percent of the total value of the shares of all classes of stock outstanding.

(B) Determination of beneficial ownership interest. For purposes of this paragraph (h)(6)(iv), the beneficial ownership interest of one corporation in the stock of another corporation is determined under the principles of section 318(a), except that—

(1) In applying section 318(a)(2)(C), the 50-percent limitation contained therein is not applied; and

(2) Section 318(a)(3)(C) is applied by substituting "20 percent" for "50 percent".

(7) Special rules for entities that owned or used property at any time during the transition period and that are no longer in existence. A corporation, partnership, or trust that owned or used a section 197 intangible at any time during the transition period and that is no longer in existence is deemed, for purposes of determining whether a taxpayer acquiring the intangible is related to such entity, to be in existence at the time of the acquisition.

(8) Special rules for section 338 deemed acquisitions. In the case of a qualified stock purchase that is treated as a deemed sale and purchase of assets pursuant to section 338, the corporation treated as purchasing assets as a result of an election thereunder (new target) is not considered the person that held or used the assets during any period in which the assets were held or used by the corporation treated as selling the assets (old target). Thus, for example, if a corporation (the purchasing corporation) makes a qualified stock purchase of the stock of another corporation after the transition period, new target will not be treated as the owner during the transition period of assets owned by old target during that period even if old target and new target are treated as the same corporation for certain other purposes of the Internal Revenue Code or old target and new target are the same corporation under the laws of the State or other jurisdiction of its organization. However, the anti-churning rules of this paragraph (h) may nevertheless apply to a deemed asset purchase resulting from a section 338 election if new target is related (within the meaning of paragraph (h)(6) of this section) to old target.

(9) Gain-recognition exception. (i) Applicability. A section 197(f)(9) intangible qualifies for the gain-recognition exception if—

(A) The taxpayer acquires the intangible from a person that would not be related to the taxpayer but for the substitution of 20 percent for 50 percent under paragraph (h)(6)(i)(A) of this section; and

(B) That person (whether or not otherwise subject to Federal income tax) elects to recognize gain on the disposition of the intangible and agrees, notwithstanding any other provision of law or treaty, to pay for the taxable year in which the disposition occurs an amount of tax on the gain that, when added to any other Federal income tax on such gain, equals the gain on the disposition multiplied by the highest marginal rate of tax for that taxable year.

(ii) Effect of exception. The anti-churning rules of this paragraph (h) apply to a section 197(f)(9) intangible that qualifies for the gain-recognition exception only to the extent the acquiring taxpayer's basis in the intangible exceeds the gain recognized by the transferor.

(iii) Time and manner of election. The election described in this paragraph (h)(9) must be made by the due date (including extensions of time) of the electing taxpayer's Federal income tax return for the taxable year in which the disposition occurs. The election is made by attaching an election statement satisfying the requirements of paragraph (h)(9)(viii) of this section to the electing taxpayer's original or amended income tax return for that taxable year (or by filing the statement as a return for the taxable year under paragraph (h)(9)(xi) of this section). In addition, the taxpayer must satisfy the notification requirements of paragraph (h)(9)(vi) of this section. The election is binding on the taxpayer and all parties whose Federal tax liability is affected by the election.

(iv) Special rules for certain entities. In the case of a partnership, S corporation, estate or trust, the election under this paragraph (h)(9) is made by the entity rather than by its owners or beneficiaries. If a partnership or S corporation makes an election under this paragraph (h)(9) with respect to the disposition of a section 197(f)(9) intangible, each of its partners or shareholders is required to pay a tax determined in the manner described in paragraph (h)(9)(i)(B) of this section on the amount of gain that is properly allocable to such partner or shareholder with respect to the disposition.

(v) Effect of nonconforming elections. An attempted election that does not substantially comply with each of the requirements of this paragraph (h)(9) is disregarded in determining whether a section 197(f)(9) intangible qualifies for the gain-recognition exception.

(vi) Notification requirements. A taxpayer making an election under this paragraph (h)(9) with respect to the disposition of a section 197(f)(9) intangible must provide written notification of the election on or before the due date of the return on which the election is made to the person acquiring the section 197 intangible. In addition, a partnership or S corporation making an election under this paragraph (h)(9) must attach to the Schedule K-1 furnished to each partner or shareholder a written statement containing all information necessary to determine the recipient's additional tax liability under this paragraph (h)(9).

(vii) Revocation. An election under this paragraph (h)(9) may be revoked only with the consent of the Commissioner.

(viii) Election Statement. An election statement satisfies the requirements of this paragraph (h)(9)(viii) if it is in writing and contains the information listed below. The required information should be arranged and identified in accordance with the following order and numbering system:

(A) The name and address of the electing taxpayer.

(B) Except in the case of a taxpayer that is not otherwise subject to Federal income tax, the taxpayer identification number (TIN) of the electing taxpayer.

(C) A statement that the taxpayer is making the election under section 197(f)(9)(B).

(D) Identification of the transaction and each person that is a party to the transaction or whose tax return is affected by the election (including, except in the case of persons not otherwise subject to Federal income tax, the TIN of each such person).

(E) The calculation of the gain realized, the applicable rate of tax, and the amount of the taxpayer's additional tax liability under this paragraph (h)(9).

(F) The signature of the taxpayer or an individual authorized to sign the taxpayer's Federal income tax return.

(ix) Determination of highest marginal rate of tax and amount of other Federal income tax on gain. (A) Marginal rate. The following rules apply for purposes of determining the highest marginal rate of tax applicable to an electing taxpayer:

(*1*) Noncorporate taxpayers. In the case of an individual, estate, or trust, the highest marginal rate of tax is the highest marginal rate of tax in effect under section 1, determined without regard to section 1(h).

(*2*) Corporations and tax-exempt entities. In the case of a corporation or an entity that is exempt from tax under section 501(a), the highest marginal rate of tax is the highest marginal rate of tax in effect under section 11, determined without regard to any rate that is added to the otherwise applicable rate in order to offset the effect of the graduated rate schedule.

(B) Other Federal income tax on gain. The amount of Federal income tax (other than the tax determined under this paragraph (h)(9)) imposed on any gain is the lesser of—

(*1*) The amount by which the taxpayer's Federal income tax liability (determined without regard to this paragraph (h)(9)) would be reduced if the amount of such gain were not taken into account; or

(*2*) The amount of the gain multiplied by the highest marginal rate of tax for the taxable year.

(x) Coordination with other provisions. (A) In general. The amount of gain subject to the tax determined under this paragraph (h)(9) is not reduced by any net operating loss deduction under section 172(a), any capital loss under section 1212, or any other similar loss or deduction. In addition, the amount of tax determined under this paragraph (h)(9) is not reduced by any credit of the taxpayer. In computing the amount of any net operating loss, capital loss, or other similar loss or deduction, or any credit that may be carried to any taxable year, any gain subject to the tax determined under this paragraph (h)(9) and any tax paid under this paragraph (h)(9) is not taken into account.

(B) Section 1374. No provision of paragraph (h)(9)(iv) of this section precludes the application of section 1374 (relating to a tax on certain built-in gains of S corporations) to any gain with respect to which an election under this paragraph (h)(9) is made. In addition, neither paragraph (h)(9)(iv) nor paragraph (h)(9)(x)(A) of this section precludes a taxpayer from applying the provisions of section 1366(f)(2) (relating to treatment of the tax imposed by section 1374 as a loss sustained by the S corporation) in determining the amount of tax payable under paragraph (h)(9) of this section.

(C) Procedural and administrative provisions. For purposes of subtitle F, the amount determined under this paragraph (h)(9) is treated as a tax imposed by section 1 or 11, as appropriate.

(D) Installment method. The gain subject to the tax determined under paragraph (h)(9)(i) of this section may not be reported under the method described in section 453(a). Any such gain that would, but for the application of this paragraph (h)(9)(x)(D), be taken into account under section

453(a) shall be taken into account in the same manner as if an election under section 453(d) (relating to the election not to apply section 453(a)) had been made.

(xi) Special rules for persons not otherwise subject to Federal income tax. If the person making the election under this paragraph (h)(9) with respect to a disposition is not otherwise subject to Federal income tax, the election statement satisfying the requirements of paragraph (h)(9)(viii) of this section must be filed with the Philadelphia Service Center. For purposes of this paragraph (h)(9) and subtitle F, the statement is treated as an income tax return for the calendar year in which the disposition occurs and as a return due on or before March 15 of the following year.

(10) Transactions subject to both anti-churning and nonrecognition rules. If a person acquires a section 197(f)(9) intangible in a transaction described in paragraph (g)(2) of this section from a person in whose hands the intangible was an amortizable section 197 intangible, and immediately after the transaction (or series of transactions described in paragraph (h)(6)(ii)(B) of this section) in which such intangible is acquired, the person acquiring the section 197(f)(9) intangible is related to any person described in paragraph (h)(2) of this section, the intangible is, notwithstanding its treatment under paragraph (g)(2) of this section, treated as an amortizable section 197 intangible only to the extent permitted under this paragraph (h). (See, for example, paragraph (h)(5)(ii) of this section.)

(11) Avoidance purpose. A section 197(f)(9) intangible acquired by a taxpayer after the applicable effective date does not qualify for amortization under section 197 if one of the principal purposes of the transaction in which it is acquired is to avoid the operation of the anti-churning rules of section 197(f)(9) and this paragraph (h). A transaction will be presumed to have a principal purpose of avoidance if it does not effect a significant change in the ownership or use of the intangible. Thus, for example, if section 197(f)(9) intangibles are acquired in a transaction (or series of related transactions) in which an option to acquire stock is issued to a party to the transaction, but the option is not treated as having been exercised for purposes of paragraph (h)(6) of this section, this paragraph (h)(11) may apply to the transaction.

(12) Additional partnership anti-churning rules. (i) In general. In determining whether the anti-churning rules of this paragraph (h) apply to any increase in the basis of a section 197(f)(9) intangible under section 732(b), 732(d), 734(b), or 743(b), the determinations are made at the partner level and each partner is treated as having owned and used the partner's proportionate share of partnership property. In determining whether the anti-churning rules of this paragraph (h) apply to any transaction under another section of the Internal Revenue Code, the determinations are made at the partnership level, unless under § 1.701-2(e) the Commissioner determines that the partner level is more appropriate.

(ii) Section 732(b) adjustments.

(A) In general. The anti-churning rules of this paragraph (h) apply to any increase in the adjusted basis of a section 197(f)(9) intangible under section 732(b) to the extent that the basis increase exceeds the total unrealized appreciation from the intangible allocable to—

(1) Partners other than the distributee partner or persons related to the distributee partner;

(2) The distributee partner and persons related to the distributee partner if the distributed intangible is a section 197(f)(9) intangible acquired by the partnership on or before August 10, 1993, to the extent that—

(i) The distributee partner and related persons acquired an interest or interests in the partnership after August 10, 1993;

(ii) Such interest or interests were held after August 10, 1993, by a person or persons other than either the distributee partner or persons who were related to the distributee partner; and

(iii) The acquisition of such interest or interests by such person or persons was not part of a transaction or series of related transactions in which the distributee partner (or persons related to the distributee partner) subsequently acquired such interest or interests; and

(3) The distributee partner and persons related to the distributee partner if the distributed intangible is a section 197(f)(9) intangible acquired by the partnership after August 10, 1993, that is not amortizable with respect to the partnership, to the extent that—

(i) The distributee partner and persons related to the distributee partner acquired an interest or interests in the partnership after the partnership acquired the distributed intangible;

(ii) Such interest or interests were held after the partnership acquired the distributed intangible, by a person or persons other than either the distributee partner or persons who were related to the distributee partner; and

(iii) The acquisition of such interest or interests by such person or persons was not part of a transaction or series of related transactions in which the distributee partner (or persons related to the distributee partner) subsequently acquired such interest or interests.

(B) Effect of retroactive elections. For purposes of paragraph (h)(12)(ii)(A) of this section, references to August 10, 1993, are treated as references to July 25, 1991, if the relevant party made a valid retroactive election under § 1.197-1T.

(C) Intangible still subject to anti-churning rules. Notwithstanding paragraph (h)(12)(ii) of this section, in applying the provisions of this paragraph (h) with respect to subsequent transfers, the distributed intangible remains subject to the provisions of this paragraph (h) in proportion to a fraction (determined at the time of the distribution), as follows—

(1) The numerator of which is equal to the sum of—

(i) The amount of the distributed intangible's basis that is nonamortizable under paragraph (g)(2)(ii)(B) of this section; and

(ii) The total unrealized appreciation inherent in the intangible reduced by the amount of the increase in the adjusted basis of the distributed intangible under section 732(b) to which the anti-churning rules do not apply; and

(2) The denominator of which is the fair market value of such intangible.

(D) Partner's allocable share of unrealized appreciation from the intangible. The amount of unrealized appreciation from an intangible that is allocable to a partner is the amount of taxable gain that would have been allocated to that partner if the partnership had sold the intangible immediately before the distribution for its fair market value in a fully taxable transaction.

(E) Acquisition of partnership interest by contribution. Solely for purposes of paragraphs (h)(12)(ii)(A)(2) and (3) of this section, a partner who acquires an interest in a partnership in exchange for a contribution of property to the partnership is deemed to acquire a pro rata portion of that interest in the partnership from each person who is a partner in the partnership at the time of the contribution based on each partner's respective proportionate interest in the partnership.

(iii) Section 732(d) adjustments. The anti-churning rules of this paragraph (h) do not apply to an increase in the basis of a section 197(f)(9) intangible under section 732(d) if, had an election been in effect under section 754 at the time of the transfer of the partnership interest, the distributee partner would have been able to amortize the basis adjustment made pursuant to section 743(b).

(iv) Section 734(b) adjustments—(A) In general. The anti-churning rules of this paragraph (h) do not apply to a continuing partner's share of an increase in the basis of a section 197(f)(9) intangible held by a partnership under section 734(b) to the extent that the continuing partner is an eligible partner.

(B) Eligible partner. For purposes of this paragraph (h)(12)(iv), eligible partner means—

(1) A continuing partner that is not the distributee partner or a person related to the distributee partner;

(2) A continuing partner that is the distributee partner or a person related to the distributee partner, with respect to any section 197(f)(9) intangible acquired by the partnership on or before August 10, 1993, to the extent that—

(i) The distributee partner's interest in the partnership was acquired after August 10, 1993;

(ii) Such interest was held after August 10, 1993 by a person or persons who were not related to the distributee partner; and

(iii) The acquisition of such interest by such person or persons was not part of a transaction or series of related transactions in which the distributee partner or persons related to the distributee partner subsequently acquired such interest; or

(3) A continuing partner that is the distributee partner or a person related to the distributee partner, with respect to any section 197(f)(9) intangible acquired by the partnership after August 10, 1993, that is not amortizable with respect to the partnership, to the extent that—

(i) The distributee partner's interest in the partnership was acquired after the partnership acquired the relevant intangible;

(ii) Such interest was held after the partnership acquired the relevant intangible by a person or persons who were not related to the distributee partner; and

(iii) The acquisition of such interest by such person or persons was not part of a transaction or series of related transactions in which the distributee partner or persons related to the distributee partner subsequently acquired such interest.

(C) Effect of retroactive elections. For purposes of paragraph (h)(12)(iv)(A) of this section, references to August 10, 1993, are treated as references to July 25, 1991, if the distributee partner made a valid retroactive election under § 1.197-1T.

(D) Partner's share of basis increase. (1) In general. Except as provided in paragraph (h)(12)(iv)(D)(2) of this section, for purposes of this paragraph (h)(12)(iv), a continuing partner's share of a basis increase under section 734(b) is equal to—

(i) The total basis increase allocable to the intangible; multiplied by

(ii) A fraction the numerator of which is the amount of the continuing partner's post-distribution capital account (determined immediately after the distribution in accordance with the capital accounting rules of —1.704-1(b)(2)(iv)), and the denominator of which is the total amount of the post-distribution capital accounts (determined immediately after the distribution in accordance with the capital accounting rules of —1.704-1(b)(2)(iv)) of all continuing partners.

(2) Exception where partnership does not maintain capital accounts. If a partnership does not maintain capital accounts in accordance with § 1.704-1(b)(2)(iv), then for purposes of this paragraph (h)(12)(iv), a continuing partner's share of a basis increase is equal to—

(i) The total basis increase allocable to the intangible; multiplied by

(ii) The partner's overall interest in the partnership as determined under § 1.704-1(b)(3) immediately after the distribution.

(E) Interests acquired by contribution. (1) Application of paragraphs (h)(12)(iv)(B) (2) and (3) of this section. Solely for purposes of paragraphs (h)(12)(iv)(B)(2) and (3) of this section, a partner who acquires an interest in a partnership in exchange for a contribution of property to the partnership is deemed to acquire a pro rata portion of that interest in the partnership from each person who is a partner in the partnership at the time of the contribution based on each such partner's proportionate interest in the partnership.

(2) Special rule with respect to paragraph (h)(12)(iv)(B)(1) of this section. Solely for purposes of paragraph (h)(12)(iv)(B)(1) of this section, if a distribution that gives rise to an increase in the basis under section 734(b) of a section 197(f)(9) intangible held by the partnership is undertaken as part of a series of related transactions that include a contribution of the intangible to the partnership by a continuing partner, the continuing partner is treated as related to the distributee partner in analyzing the basis adjustment with respect to the contributed section 197(f)(9) intangible.

(F) Effect of section 734(b) adjustments on partners' capital accounts. If one or more partners are subject to the anti-churning rules under this paragraph (h) with respect to a section 734(b) adjustment allocable to an intangible asset, taxpayers may use any reasonable method to determine amortization of the asset for book purposes, provided that the method used does not contravene the purposes of the anti-churning rules under section 197 and this paragraph (h). A method will be considered to contravene the purposes of the anti-churning rules if the effect of the book adjustments resulting from the method is such that any portion of the tax deduction for amortization attributable to the section 734 adjustment is allocated, directly or indirectly, to a partner who is subject to the anti-churning rules with respect to such adjustment.

(v) Section 743(b) adjustments. (A) General rule. The anti-churning rules of this paragraph (h) do not apply to an increase in the basis of a section 197 intangible under section 743(b) if the person acquiring the partnership interest is not related to the person transferring the partnership interest. In addition, the anti-churning rules of this paragraph (h) do not apply to an increase in the basis of a section 197 intangible under section 743(b) to the extent that—

(1) The partnership interest being transferred was acquired after August 10, 1993, provided—

(i) The section 197(f)(9) intangible was acquired by the partnership on or before August 10, 1993;

(ii) The partnership interest being transferred was held after August 10, 1993, by a person or persons (the post-1993 person or persons) other than the person transferring the partnership interest or persons who were related to the person transferring the partnership interest; and

(iii) The acquisition of such interest by the post-1993 person or persons was not part of a transaction or series of related transactions in which the person transferring the partnership interest or persons related to the person transferring the partnership interest acquired such interest; or

(2) The partnership interest being transferred was acquired after the partnership acquired the section 197(f)(9) intangible, provided—

(i) The section 197(f)(9) intangible was acquired by the partnership after August 10, 1993, and is not amortizable with respect to the partnership;

(ii) The partnership interest being transferred was held after the partnership acquired the section 197(f)(9) intangible by a person or persons (the post-contribution person or persons) other than the person transferring the partnership interest or persons who were related to the person transferring the partnership interest; and

(iii) The acquisition of such interest by the post-contribution person or persons was not part of a transaction or series of related transactions in which the person transferring the partnership interest or persons related to the person transferring the partnership interest acquired such interest.

(B) Acquisition of partnership interest by contribution. Solely for purposes of paragraph (h)(12)(v)(A) (1) and (2) of this section, a partner who acquires an interest in a partnership in exchange for a contribution of property to the partnership is deemed to acquire a pro rata portion of that interest in the partnership from each person who is a partner in the partnership at the time of the contribution based on each such partner's proportionate interest in the partnership.

(C) Effect of retroactive elections. For purposes of paragraph (h)(12)(v)(A) of this section, references to August 10, 1993, are treated as references to July 25, 1991, if the transferee partner made a valid retroactive election under § 1.197-1T.

(vi) Partner is or becomes a user of partnership intangible. (A) General rule. If, as part of a series of related transactions that includes a transaction described in paragraph (h)(12)(ii), (iii), (iv), or (v) of this section, an anti-churning partner or related person (other than the partnership) becomes (or remains) a direct user of an intangible that is treated as transferred in the transaction (as a result of the partners being treated as having owned their proportionate share of partnership assets), the anti-churning rules of this paragraph (h) apply to the proportionate share of such intangible that is treated as transferred by such anti-churning partner, notwithstanding the application of paragraph (h)(12)(ii), (iii), (iv), or (v) of this section.

(B) Anti-churning partner. For purposes of this paragraph (h)(12)(vi), anti-churning partner means—

(1) With respect to all intangibles held by a partnership on or before August 10, 1993, any partner, but only to the extent that

(i) The partner's interest in the partnership was acquired on or before August 10, 1993, or

(ii) The interest was acquired from a person related to the partner on or after August 10, 1993, and such interest was not held by any person other than persons related to such partner at any time after August 10, 1993 (disregarding, for this purpose, a person's holding of an interest if the acquisition of such interest was part of a transaction or series of related transactions in which the partner or persons related to the partner subsequently acquired such interest),

(2) With respect to any section 197(f)(9) intangible acquired by a partnership after August 10, 1993, that is not amortizable with respect to the partnership, any partner, but only to the extent that

(i) The partner's interest in the partnership was acquired on or before the date the partnership acquired the section 197(f)(9) intangible, or

(ii) The interest was acquired from a person related to the partner on or after the date the partnership acquired the section 197(f)(9) intangible, and such interest was not held by any person other than persons related to such partner at any time after the date the partnership acquired the section 197(f)(9) intangible (disregarding, for this purpose, a person's holding of an interest if the acquisition of such interest was part of a transaction or series of related transactions in which the partner or persons related to the partner subsequently acquired such interest).

(C) Effect of retroactive elections. For purposes of paragraph (h)(12)(vi)(B) of this section, references to August 10, 1993, are treated as references to July 25, 1991, if the relevant party made a valid retroactive election under § 1.197-1T.

(vii) Section 704(c) allocations. (A) Allocations where the intangible is amortizable by the contributor. The anti-churning rules of this paragraph (h) do not apply to the curative or remedial allocations of amortization with respect to a section 197(f)(9) intangible if the intangible was an amortizable section 197 intangible in the hands of the contributing partner (unless paragraph (h)(10) of this section applies so as to cause the intangible to cease to be an amortizable section 197 intangible in the hands of the partnership).

(B) Allocations where the intangible is not amortizable by the contributor. If a section 197(f)(9) intangible was not an amortizable section 197 intangible in the hands of the contributing partner, a non-contributing partner generally may receive remedial allocations of amortization under section 704(c) that are deductible for Federal income tax purposes. However, such a partner may not receive remedial allocations of amortization under section 704(c) if that partner is related to the partner that contributed the intangible or if, as part of a series of related transactions that includes the contribution of the section 197(f)(9) intangible to the partnership, the contributing partner or related person (other than the partnership) becomes (or remains) a direct user of the contributed intangible.Notwithstanding paragraph (g)(3)(ii) of this section, where the section 197(f)(9) intangible was not an amortizable section 197 intangible in the hands of the contributing partner, a partner may not receive remedial allocations of amortization under section 704(c) that are deductible for Federal income tax purposes if that partner is related to the partner that contributed the intangible. Taxpayers may use any reasonable method to determine amortization of the asset for book purposes, provided that the method used does not contravene the purposes of the anti-churning rules under section 197 and this paragraph (h). A method will be considered to contravene the purposes of the anti-churning rules if the effect of the book adjustments resulting from the method is such that any portion of the tax deduction for amortization attributable to section 704(c) is allocated, directly or indirectly, to a partner who is subject to the anti-churning rules with respect to such adjustment.

(viii) Operating rule for transfers upon death. For purposes of this paragraph (h)(12), if the basis of a partner's interest in a partnership is determined under section 1014(a), such partner is treated as acquiring such interest from a person who is not related to such partner, and such interest is treated as having previously been held by a person who is not related to such partner.

(i) [Reserved]

(j) General anti-abuse rule. The Commissioner will interpret and apply the rules in this section as necessary and appropriate to prevent avoidance of the purposes of section 197. If one of the principal purposes of a transaction is to achieve a tax result that is inconsistent with the purposes of section 197, the Commissioner will recast the transaction for Federal tax purposes as appropriate to achieve tax results that are consistent with the purposes of section 197, in light of the applicable statutory and regulatory provisions and the pertinent facts and circumstances.

(k) Examples. The following examples illustrate the application of this section:

Example (1). Advertising costs. (i) Q manufactures and sells consumer products through a series of wholesalers and distributors. In order to increase sales of its products by encouraging consumer loyalty to its products and to enhance the value of the goodwill, trademarks, and trade names of the business, Q advertises its products to the consuming public. It regularly incurs costs to develop radio, television, and print advertisements. These costs generally consist of employee costs and amounts paid to independent advertising agencies. Q also incurs costs to run these advertisements in the various media for which they were developed.

(ii) The advertising costs are not chargeable to capital account under paragraph (f)(3) of this section (relating to costs incurred for covenants not to compete, rights granted by governmental units, and contracts for the use of section 197 intangibles) and are currently deductible as ordinary and necessary expenses under section 162. Accordingly, under paragraph (a)(3) of this section, section 197 does not apply to these costs.

Example (2). Computer software. (i) X purchases all of the assets of an existing trade or business from Y. One of the assets acquired is all of Y's rights in certain computer software previously used by Y under the terms of a nonexclusive license from the software developer. The software was developed for use by manufacturers to maintain a comprehensive accounting system, including general and subsidiary ledgers, payroll, accounts receivable and payable, cash receipts and disbursements, fixed asset accounting, and inventory cost accounting and controls. The developer modified the software for use by Y at a cost of $1,000 and Y made additional modifications at a cost of $500. The developer does not maintain wholesale or retail outlets but markets the software directly to ultimate users. Y's license of the software is limited to an entity that is actively engaged in business as a manufacturer.

(ii) Notwithstanding these limitations, the software is considered to be readily available to the general public for purposes of paragraph (c)(4)(i) of this section. In addition, the software is not substantially modified because the cost of the modifications by the developer and Y to the version of the software that is readily available to the general public does not exceed $2,000. Accordingly, the software is not a section 197 intangible.

Example (3). Acquisition of software for internal use. (i) B, the owner and operator of a worldwide package-delivery service, purchases from S all rights to software developed by S. The software will be used by B for the sole purpose of improving its package-tracking operations. B does not purchase any other assets in the transaction or any related transaction.

(ii) Because B acquired the software solely for internal use, it is disregarded in determining for purposes of paragraph (c)(4)(ii) of this section whether the assets acquired in the transaction or series of related transactions constitute a trade or business or substantial portion thereof. Since no other assets were acquired, the software is not acquired as part of a purchase of a trade or business and under paragraph (c)(4)(ii) of this section is not a section 197 intangible.

Example (4). Governmental rights of fixed duration.

(s) City M operates a municipal water system. In order to induce X to locate a new manufacturing business in the city, M grants X the right to purchase water for 16 years at a specified price.

(ii) The right granted by M is a right to receive tangible property or services described in section 197(e)(4)(B) and paragraph (c)(6) of this section and, thus, is not a section 197 intangible. This exclusion applies even though the right does not qualify for exclusion as a right of fixed duration or amount under section 197(e)(4)(D) and paragraph (c)(13) of this section because the duration exceeds 15 years and the right is not fixed as to amount. It is also immaterial that the right would not qualify for exclusion as a self-created intangible under section 197(c)(2) and paragraph (d)(2) of this section because it is granted by a governmental unit.

Example (5). Separate acquisition of franchise. (i) S is a franchiser of retail outlets for specialty coffees. G enters into a franchise agreement (within the meaning of section 1253(b)(1)) with S pursuant to which G is permitted to acquire and operate a store using the S trademark and trade name at the location specified in the agreement. G agrees to pay S $100,000 upon execution of the agreement and also agrees to pay, throughout the term of the franchise, additional amounts that are deductible under section 1253(d)(1). The agreement contains detailed specifications for the construction and operation of the business, but G is not required to purchase from S any of the materials necessary to construct the improvements at the location specified in the franchise agreement.

(ii) The franchise is a section 197 intangible within the meaning of paragraph (b)(10) of this section. The franchise does not qualify for the exclusion relating to self-created intangibles described in section 197(c)(2) and paragraph (d)(2) of this section because the franchise is described in section 197(d)(1)(F). In addition, because the acquisition of the franchise constitutes the acquisition of an interest in a trade or business or a substantial portion thereof, the franchise may not be excluded under section 197(e)(4). Thus, the franchise is an amortizable section 197 intangible, the basis of which must be recovered over a 15-year period. However, the amounts that are deductible under section 1253(d)(1) are not subject to the provisions of section 197 by reason of section 197(f)(4)(C) and paragraph (b)(10)(ii) of this section.

Example (6). Acquisition and amortization of covenant not to compete. (i) As part of the acquisition of a trade or business from C, B and C enter into an agreement containing a covenant not to compete. Under this agreement, C agrees that it will not compete with the business acquired by B within a prescribed geographical territory for a period of three years after the date on which the business is sold to B. In exchange for this agreement, B agrees to pay C $90,000 per year for each year in the term of the agreement. The agreement further provides that, in the event of a breach by

C of his obligations under the agreement, B may terminate the agreement, cease making any of the payments due thereafter, and pursue any other legal or equitable remedies available under applicable law. The amounts payable to C under the agreement are not contingent payments for purposes of § 1.1275-4. The present fair market value of B's rights under the agreement is $225,000. The aggregate consideration paid excluding any amount treated as interest or original issue discount under applicable provisions of the Internal Revenue Code, for all assets acquired in the transaction (including the covenant not to compete) exceeds the sum of the amount of Class I assets and the aggregate fair market value of all Class II, Class III, Class IV, Class V, and Class VI assets by $50,000. See § 1.338-6(b) for rules for determining the assets in each class.

(ii) Because the covenant is acquired in an applicable asset acquisition (within the meaning of section 1060(c)), paragraph (f)(4)(ii) of this section applies and the basis of B in the covenant is determined pursuant to section 1060(a) and the regulations thereunder. Under §§ 1.1060-1(c)(2) and 1.338-6(c)(1), B's basis in the covenant cannot exceed its fair market value. Thus, B's basis in the covenant immediately after the acquisition is $225,000. This basis is amortized ratably over the 15-year period beginning on the first day of the month in which the agreement is entered into. All of the remaining consideration after allocation to the covenant and other Class VI assets, ($50,000) is allocated to Class VII assets (goodwill and going concern value). See §§ 1.1060-1T(c)(2) and 1.338-6T(b).

Example (7). Stand-alone license of technology. (i) X is a manufacturer of consumer goods that does business throughout the world through subsidiary corporations organized under the laws of each country in which business is conducted. X licenses to Y, its subsidiary organized and conducting business in Country K, all of the patents, formulas, designs, and know-how necessary for Y to manufacture the same products that X manufactures in the United States. Assume that the license is not considered a sale or exchange under the principles of section 1235. The license is for a term of 18 years, and there are no facts to indicate that the license does not have a fixed duration. Y agrees to pay X a royalty equal to a specified, fixed percentage of the revenues obtained from selling products manufactured using the licensed technology. Assume that the royalty is reasonable and is not subject to adjustment under section 482. The license is not entered into in connection with any other transaction. Y incurs capitalized costs in connection with entering into the license.

(ii) The license is a contract for the use of a section 197 intangible within the meaning of paragraph (b)(11) of this section. It does not qualify for the exception in section 197(e)(4)(D) and paragraph (c)(13) of this section (relating to rights of fixed duration or amount because it does not have a term of less than 15 years, and the other exceptions in section 197(e) and paragraph (c) of this section are also inapplicable. Accordingly, the license is a section 197 intangible.

(iii) The license is not acquired as part of a purchase of a trade or business. Thus, under paragraph (f)(3)(iii) of this section, the license will be closely scrutinized under the principles of section 1235 for purposes of determining whether the transfer is a sale or exchange and, accordingly, whether the payments under the license are chargeable to capital account. Because the license is not a sale or exchange under the principles of section 1235, the royalty payments are not chargeable to capital account for purposes section 197. The capitalized costs of entering into the license are not within the exception under paragraph (d)(2) of this section for self-created intangibles, and thus are amortized under section 197.

Example (8). License of technology and trademarks.

(s) The facts are the same as in Example 7, except that the license also includes the use of the trademarks and trade names that X uses to manufacture and distribute its products in the United States. Assume that under the principles of section 1253 the transfer is not a sale or exchange of the trademarks and trade names or an undivided interest therein and that the royalty payments are described in section 1253(d)(1)(B).

(ii) As in Example 7, the license is a section 197 intangible. Although the license conveys an interest in X's trademarks and trade names to Y, the transfer of the interest is disregarded for purposes of paragraph (e)(2) of this section unless the transfer is considered a sale or exchange of the trademarks and trade names or an undivided interest therein. Accordingly, the licensing of the technology and the trademarks and trade names is not treated as part of a purchase of a trade or business under paragraph (e)(2) of this section.

(iii) Because the technology license is not part of the purchase of a trade or business, it is treated in the manner described in Example 7. The royalty payments for the use of the trademarks and trade names are deductible under section 1253(d)(1) and, under section 197(f)(4)(C) and paragraph (b)(10)(ii) of this section, are not chargeable to capital account for purposes of section 197. The capitalized costs of entering into the license are treated in the same manner as in example 7.

Example (9). Disguised sale. (i) The facts are the same as in Example 7, except that Y agrees to pay X, in addition to the contingent royalty, a fixed minimum royalty immediately upon entering into the agreement and there are sufficient facts present to characterize the transaction, for federal tax purposes, as a transfer of ownership of the intellectual property from X to Y.

(ii) The purported license of technology is, in fact, an acquisition of an intangible described in section 197(d)(1)(C)(iii) and paragraph (b)(5) of this section (relating to know-how, etc.). As in Example 7, the exceptions in section 197(e) and paragraph (c) of this section do not apply to the transfer. Accordingly, the transferred property is a section 197 intangible. Y's basis in the transferred intangible includes the capitalized costs of entering into the agreement and the fixed minimum royalty payment payable at the time of the transfer. In addition, except to the extent that a portion of any payment will be treated as interest or original issue discount under applicable provisions of the Internal Revenue Code, all of the contingent payments under the purported license are properly chargeable to capital account for purposes of section 197 and this section. The extent to which such payments are treated as payments of principal and the time at which any amount treated as a payment of principal is taken into account in determining basis are determined under the rules of § 1.1275-4(c)(4) or 1.483-4(a), whichever is applicable. Any contingent amount that is included in basis after the month in which the acquisition occurs is amortized under the rules of paragraph (f)(2)(i) or (ii) of this section.

Example (10). License of technology and customer list as part of sale of a trade or business. (i) X is a computer manufacturer that produces, in separate operating divisions, personal computers, servers, and peripheral equipment. In a transaction that is the purchase of a trade or business for purposes of section 197, Y (who is unrelated to X) purchases from X all assets of the operating division producing personal computers, except for certain patents that are also used in the division manufacturing servers and customer lists that are also used in the division manufacturing peripheral equipment. As part of the transaction, X transfers to Y the right to use the retained patents and customer lists solely in connection with the manufacture and sale of personal computers. The transfer agreement requires annual royalty payments contingent on the use of the patents and also requires a payment for each use of the customer list. In addition, Y incurs capitalized costs in connection with entering into the licenses.

(ii) The rights to use the retained patents and customer lists are contracts for the use of section 197 intangibles within the meaning of paragraph (b)(11) of this section. The rights do not qualify for the exception in 197(e)(4)(D) and paragraph (c)(13) of this section (relating to rights of fixed duration or amount) because they are transferred as part of a purchase of a trade or business and the other exceptions in section 197(e) and paragraph (c) of this section are also inapplicable. Accordingly, the licenses are section 197 intangibles.

(iii) Because the right to use the retained patents is described in paragraph (b)(11) of this section and the right is transferred as part of a purchase of a trade or business, the treatment of the royalty payments is determined under paragraph (f)(3)(ii) of this section. In addition, however, the retained patents are described in paragraph (b)(5) of this section. Thus, the annual royalty payments are chargeable to capital account under the general rule of paragraph (f)(3)(ii)(A) of this section unless Y establishes that the license is not a sale or exchange under the principles of section 1235 and the royalty payments are an arm's length consideration for the rights transferred. If these facts are established, the exception in paragraph (f)(3)(ii)(B) of this section applies and the royalty payments are not chargeable to capital account for purposes of section 197. The capitalized costs of entering into the license are treated in the same manner as in Example 7.

(iv) The right to use the retained customer list is also described in paragraph (b)(11) of this section and is transferred as part of a purchase of a trade or business. Thus, the treatment of the payments for use of the customer list is also determined under paragraph (f)(3)(ii) of this section. The customer list, although described in paragraph (b)(6) of this section, is a customer-related information base. Thus, the exception in paragraph (f)(3)(ii)(B) of this section does not apply. Accordingly, payments for use of the list are chargeable to capital account under the general rule of paragraph (f)(3)(ii)(A) of this section and are amortized under section 197. In addition, the capitalized costs of entering into the contract for use of the customer list are treated in the same manner as in Example 7.

Example (11). Loss disallowance rules involving related persons. (i) Assume that X and Y are treated as a single taxpayer for purposes of paragraph (g)(1) of this section. In a single transaction, X and Y acquired from Z all of the assets used by Z in a trade or business. Z had operated this business at two locations, and X and Y each acquired the assets used by Z at one of the locations. Three years after the acquisition, X sold all of the assets it acquired, including amortizable section 197 intangibles, to an unrelated purchaser. The amortizable section intangibles are sold at a loss of $120,000.

(ii) Because X and Y are treated as a single taxpayer for purposes of the loss disallowance rules of section 197(f)(1) and paragraph (g)(1) of this section, X's loss on the sale of the amortizable section 197 intangibles is not recognized. Under paragraph (g)(1)(iv)(B) of this section, X's disallowed loss is allowed ratably, as a deduction under section 197, over the remainder of the 15-year period during which the intangibles would have been amortized, and Y may not increase the basis of the amortizable section 197 intangibles that it acquired from Z by the amount of X's disallowed loss.

Example (12). Disposition of retained intangibles by related person. (i) The facts are the same as in Example 11, except that 10 years after the acquisition of the assets by X and Y and 7 years after the sale of the assets by X, Y sells all of the assets acquired from Z, including amortizable section 197 intangibles, to an unrelated purchaser.

(ii) Under paragraph (g)(1)(iv)(B) of this section, X may recognize, on the date of the sale by Y, any loss that has not been allowed as a deduction under section 197. Accordingly, X recognizes a loss of $50,000, the amount obtained by reducing the loss on the sale of the assets at the end of the third year ($120,000) by the amount allowed as a deduction under paragraph (g)(1)(iv)(B) of this section during the 7 years following the sale by X ($70,000).

Example (13). Acquisition of an interest in partnership with no section 754 election. (i) A, B, and C each contribute $1,500 for equal shares in general partnership P. On January 1, 1998, P acquires as its sole asset an amortizable section 197 intangible for $4,500. P still holds the intangible on January 1, 2003, at which time the intangible has an adjusted basis to P of $3,000, and A, B, and C each have an adjusted basis of $1,000 in their partnership interests. D (who is not related to A) acquires A's interest in P for $1,600. No section 754 election is in effect for 2003.

(ii) Because there is no change in the basis of the intangible under section 743(b), D merely steps into the shoes of A with respect to the intangible. D's proportionate share of P's adjusted basis in the intangible is $1,000, which continues to be amortized over the 10 years remaining in the original 15-year amortization period for the intangible.

Example (14). Acquisition of an interest in partnership with a section 754 election. (i) The facts are the same as in Example 13, except that a section 754 election is in effect for 2003.

(ii) Pursuant to paragraph (g)(3) of this section, for purposes of section 197, D is treated as if P owns two assets. D's proportionate share of P's adjusted basis in one asset is $1,000, which continues to be amortized over the 10 years remaining in the original 15-year amortization period. For the other asset, D's proportionate share of P's adjusted basis is $600 (the amount of the basis increase under section 743 as a result of the section 754 election), which is amortized over a new 15-year period beginning January 2003. With respect to B and C, P's remaining $2,000 adjusted basis in the intangible continues to be amortized over the 10 years remaining in the original 15-year amortization period.

Example (15). Payment to a retiring partner by partnership with a section 754 election. (i) The facts are the same as in Example 13, except that a section 754 election is in effect for 2003 and, instead of D acquiring A's interest in P, A retires from P. A, B, and C are not related to each other within the meaning of paragraph (h)(6) of this section. P borrows $1,600, and A receives a payment under section 736 from P of such amount, all of which is in exchange for A's interest in the intangible asset owned by P. (Assume, for purposes of this example, that the borrowing by P and payment of such funds to A does not give rise to a disguised sale of A's partnership interest under section 707(a)(2)(B).) P makes a positive basis adjustment of $600 with respect to the section 197 intangible under section 734(b).

(ii) Pursuant to paragraph (g)(3) of this section, because of the section 734 adjustment, P is treated as having two amortizable section 197 intangibles, one with a basis of $3,000 and a remaining amortization period of 10 years and the other with a basis of $600 and a new amortization period of 15 years.

Example (16). Termination of partnership under section 708(b)(1)(B). (i) A and B are partners with equal shares in the capital and profits of general partnership P. P's only asset is an amortizable section 197 intangible, which P had acquired on January 1, 1995. On January 1, 2000, the asset had a fair market value of $100 and a basis to P of $50. On that date, A sells his entire partnership interest in P to C, who is unrelated to A, for $50. At the time of the sale, the basis of each of A and B in their respective partnership interests is $25.

(ii) The sale causes a termination of P under section 708(b)(1)(B). Under section 708, the transaction is treated as if P transfers its sole asset to a new partnership in exchange for the assumption of its liabilities and the receipt of all of the interests in the new partnership. Immediately thereafter, P is treated as if it is liquidated, with B and C each receiving their proportionate share of the interests in the new partnership. The contribution by P of its asset to the new partnership is governed by section 721, and the liquidating distributions by P of the interests in the new partnership are governed by section 731. C does not realize a basis adjustment under section 743 with respect to the amortizable section 197 intangible unless P had a section 754 election in effect for its taxable year in which the transfer of the partnership interest to C occurred or the taxable year in which the deemed liquidation of P occurred.

(iii) Under section 197, if P had a section 754 election in effect, C is treated as if the new partnership had acquired two assets from P immediately preceding its termination. Even though the adjusted basis of the new partnership in the two assets is determined solely under section 723, because the transfer of assets is a transaction described in section 721, the application of sections 743(b) and 754 to P immediately before its termination causes P to be treated as if it held two assets for purposes of section 197. See paragraph (g)(3) of this section. B's and C's proportionate share of the new partnership's adjusted basis is $25 each in one asset, which continues to be amortized over the 10 years remaining in the original 15-year amortization period. For the other asset, C's proportionate share of the new partnership's adjusted basis is $25 (the amount of the basis increase resulting from the application of section 743 to the sale or exchange by A of the interest in P), which is amortized over a new 15-year period beginning in January 2000.

(iv) If P did not have a section 754 election in effect for its taxable year in which the sale of the partnership interest by A to C occurred or the taxable year in which the deemed liquidation of P occurred, the adjusted basis of the new partnership in the amortizable section 197 intangible is determined solely under section 723, because the transfer is a transaction described in section 721, and P does not have a basis increase in the intangible. Under section 197(f)(2) and paragraph (g)(2)(ii) of this section, the new partnership continues to amortize the intangible over the 10 years remaining in the original 15-year amortization period. No additional amortization is allowable with respect to this asset.

Example (17). Disguised sale to partnership. (i) E and F are individuals who are unrelated to each other within the meaning of paragraph (h)(6) of this section. E has been engaged in the active conduct of a trade or business as a sole proprietor since 1990. E and F form EF Partnership. E transfers all of the assets of the business, having a fair market value of $100, to EF, and F transfers $40 of cash to EF. E receives a 60 percent interest in EF and the $40 of cash contributed by F, and F receives a 40 percent interest in EF, under circumstances in which the transfer by E is partially treated as a sale of property to EF under § 1.707-3(b).

(ii) Under § 1.707-3(a)(1), the transaction is treated as if E had sold to EF a 40 percent interest in each asset for $40 and contributed the remaining 60 percent interest in each asset to EF in exchange solely for an interest in EF. Because E and EF are related persons within the meaning of paragraph (h)(6) of this section, no portion of any transferred section 197(f)(9) intangible that E held during the transition period (as defined in paragraph (h)(4) of this section) is an amortizable section 197 intangible pursuant to paragraph (h)(2) of this section. Section 197(f)(9)(F) and paragraph (g)(3) of this section do not apply to any portion of the section 197 intangible in the hands of EF because the basis of EF in these assets was not increased under any of sections 732, 734, or 743.

Example (18). Acquisition by related person in nonrecognition transaction. (i) A owns a nonamortizable intangible that A acquired in 1990. In 2000, A sells a one-half interest in the intangible to B for cash. Immediately after the sale, A and B, who are unrelated to each other, form partnership P as equal partners. A and B each contribute their one-half interest in the intangible to P.

(ii) P has a transferred basis in the intangible from A and B under section 723. The nonrecognition transfer rule under paragraph (g)(2)(ii) of this section applies to A's transfer of its one-half interest in the intangible to P, and consequently P steps into A's shoes with respect to A's nonamortizable transferred basis. The anti-churning rules of paragraph (h) of this section apply to B's transfer of its one-half interest in the intangible to P, because A, who is related to P under paragraph (h)(6) of this section immediately after the series of transactions in which the intangible was acquired by P, held B's one-half interest in the intangible during the transition period. Pursuant to paragraph (h)(10) of this section, these rules apply to B's transfer of its one-half interest to P even though the nonrecognition transfer rule under paragraph (g)(2)(ii) of this section would have permitted P to step into B's shoes with respect to B's otherwise amortizable basis. Therefore, P's entire basis in the intangible is nonamortizable. However, if A (not B) elects to recognize gain under paragraph (h)(9) of this section on the transfer of each of the one-half interests in the intangible to B and P, then the intangible would be amortizable by P to the extent provided in section 197(f)(9)(B) and paragraph (h)(9) of this section.

Example (19). Acquisition of partnership interest following formation of partnership. (i) The facts are the same as in Example 18 except that, in 2000, A formed P with an affiliate, S, and contributed the intangible to the partnership and except that in a subsequent year, in a transaction that is properly characterized as a sale of a partnership interest for Federal tax purposes, B purchases a 50 percent interest in P from A. P has a section 754 election in effect and holds no assets other than the intangible and cash.

(ii) For the reasons set forth in Example 16 (iii), B is treated as if P owns two assets. B's proportionate share of P's adjusted basis in one asset is the same as A's proportionate share of P's adjusted basis in that asset, which is not amortizable under section 197. For the other asset, B's proportionate share of the remaining adjusted basis of P is amortized over a new 15-year period.

Example (20). Acquisition by related corporation in nonrecognition transaction. (i) The facts are the same as Example 18, except that A and B form corporation P as equal owners.

(ii) P has a transferred basis in the intangible from A and B under section 362. Pursuant to paragraph (h)(10) of this section, the application of the nonrecognition transfer rule under paragraph (g)(2)(ii) of this section and the anti-churning rules of paragraph (h) of this section to the facts of this Example 18 is the same as in Example 16. Thus, P's entire basis in the intangible is nonamortizable.

Example (21). Acquisition from corporation related to purchaser through remote indirect interest. (i) X, Y, and Z are each corporations that have only one class of issued and outstanding stock. X owns 25 percent of the stock of Y and Y owns 25 percent of the outstanding stock of Z. No other shareholder of any of these corporations is related to any other shareholder or to any of the corporations. On June 30, 2000, X purchases from Z section 197(f)(9) intangibles that Z owned during the transition period (as defined in paragraph (h)(4) of this section).

(ii) Pursuant to paragraph (h)(6)(iv)(B) of this section, the beneficial ownership interest of X in Z is 6.25 percent, determined by treating X as if it owned a proportionate (25 percent) interest in the stock of Z that is actually owned by Y. Thus, even though X is related to Y and Y is related to Z, X and Z are not considered to be related for purposes of the anti-churning rules of section 197.

Example (22). Gain recognition election. (i) B owns 25 percent of the stock of S, a corporation that uses the calendar year as its taxable year. No other shareholder of B or S is related to each other. S is not a member of a controlled group of corporations within the meaning of section 1563(a). S has section 197(f)(9) intangibles that it owned during the transition period. S has a basis of $25,000 in the intangibles. In 2001, S sells these intangibles to B for $75,000. S recognizes a gain of $50,000 on the sale and has no other items of income, deduction, gain, or loss for the year, except that S also has a net operating loss of $20,000 from prior years that it would otherwise be entitled to use in 2001 pursuant to section 172(b). S makes a valid gain recognition election pursuant to section 197(f)(9)(B) and paragraph (h)(9) of this section. In 2001, the highest marginal tax rate applicable to S is 35 percent. But for the election, all of S's taxable income would be taxed at a rate of 15 percent.

(ii) If the gain recognition election had not been made, S would have taxable income of $30,000 for 2001 and a tax liability of $4,500. If the gain were not taken into account, S would have no tax liability for the taxable year. Thus, the amount of tax (other than the tax imposed under paragraph (h)(9) of this section) imposed on the gain is also $4,500. The gain on the disposition multiplied by the highest marginal tax rate is $17,500 ($50,000 × .35). Accordingly, S's tax liability for the year is $4,500 plus an additional tax under paragraph (h)(9) of this section of $13,000 ($17,500—$4,500).

(iii) Pursuant to paragraph (h)(9)(x)(A) of this section, S determines the amount of its net operating loss deduction in subsequent years without regard to the gain recognized on the sale of the section 197 intangible to B. Accordingly, the entire $20,000 net operating loss deduction that would have been available in 2001 but for the gain recognition election may be used in 2002, subject to the limitations of section 172.

(iv) B has a basis of $75,000 in the section 197(f)(9) intangibles acquired from S. As the result of the gain recognition election by S, B may amortize $50,000 of its basis under section 197. Under paragraph (h)(9)(ii) of this section, the remaining basis does not qualify for the gain-recognition exception and may not be amortized by B.

Example (23). Section 338 election. (i) Corporation P makes a qualified stock purchase of the stock of T corporation from two shareholders in July 2000, and a section 338 election is made by P. No shareholder of either T or P owns stock in both of these corporations, and no other shareholder is related to any other shareholder of either corporation.

(ii) Pursuant to paragraph (h)(8) of this section, in the case of a qualified stock purchase that is treated as a deemed sale and purchase of assets pursuant to section 338, the corporation treated as purchasing assets as a result of an election thereunder (new target) is not considered the person that held or used the assets during any period in which the assets were held or used by the corporation treated as selling the assets (old target). Because there are no relationships described in paragraph (h)(6) of this section among the parties to the transaction, any nonamortizable section 197(f)(9) intangible held by old target is an amortizable section 197 intangible in the hands of new target.

(iii) Assume the same facts as set forth in paragraph (i) of this Example 23, except that one of the selling shareholders is an individual who owns 25 percent of the total value of the stock of each of the T and P corporation.

(iv) Old target and new target (as these terms are defined in § 1.338-2(c)(17)) are members of a controlled group of corporations under section 267(b)(3), as modified by section 197(f)(9)(C)(i), and any nonamortizable section 197(f)(9) intangible held by old target is not an amortizable section 197 intangible in the hands of new target. However, a gain recognition election under paragraph (h)(9) of this section may be made with respect to this transaction.

Example (24). Relationship created as part of public offering. (i) On January 1, 2001, Corporation X engages in a series of related transactions to discontinue its involvement in one line of business. X forms a new corporation, Y, with a nominal amount of cash. Shortly thereafter, X transfers all the stock of its subsidiary conducting the unwanted business (Target) to Y in exchange for 100 shares of Y common stock and a Y promissory note. Target owns a nonamortizable section 197(f)(9) intangible. Prior to January 1, 2001, X and an underwriter (U) had entered into a binding agreement pursuant to which U would purchase 85 shares of Y common stock from X and then sell those shares in a public offering. On January 6, 2001, the public offering closes. X and Y make a section 338(h)(10) election for Target.

(ii) Pursuant to paragraph (h)(8) of this section, in the case of a qualified stock purchase that is treated as a deemed sale and purchase of assets pursuant to section 338, the corporation treated as purchasing assets as a result of an election thereunder (new target) is not considered the person that held or used the assets during any period in which the assets were held or used by the corporation treated as selling the assets (old target). Further, for purposes of determining whether the nonamortizable section 197(f)(9) intangible is acquired by new target from a related person, because the transactions are a series of related transactions, the relationship between old target and new target must be tested immediately before the first transaction in the series (the formation of Y) and immediately after the last transaction in the series (the sale to U and the public offering). See paragraph (h)(6)(ii)(B) of this section. Because there was no relationship between old target and new target immediately before the formation of Y (because the section 338 election had not been made) and only a 15% relationship between old target and new target immediately after, old target is not related to new target for purposes of applying the anti-churning rules of paragraph (h) of this section. Accordingly, Target may amortize the section 197 intangible.

Example (25). Other transfers to controlled corporations. (i) In 2001, Corporation A transfers a section 197(f)(9) intangible that it held during the transition period to X, a newly formed corporation, in exchange for 15% of X's stock. As part of the same transaction, B transfers property to X in exchange for the remaining 85% of X stock.

(ii) Because the acquisition of the intangible by X is part of a qualifying section 351 exchange, under section 197(f)(2) and paragraph (g)(2)(ii) of this section, X is treated in the same manner as the transferor of the asset. Accordingly, X may not amortize the intangible. If, however, at the time of the exchange, B has a binding commitment to sell 25 percent of the X stock to C, an unrelated third party, the exchange, including A's transfer of the section 197(f)(9) intangible, would fail to qualify as a section 351 exchange. Because the formation of X, the transfers of property to X, and the sale of X stock by B are part of a series of related transactions, the relationship between A and X must be tested immediately before the first transaction in the series (the transfer of property to X) and immediately after the last transaction in the series (the sale of X stock to C). See paragraph (h)(6)(ii)(B) of this section. Because there was no relationship between A and X immediately before and only a 15% relationship immediately after, A is not related to X for purposes of applying the anti-churning rules of paragraph (h) of this section. Accordingly, X may amortize the section 197 intangible.

Example (26). Relationship created as part of stock acquisition followed by liquidation. (i) In 2001, Partnership P purchases 100 percent of the stock of Corporation X. P and X were not related prior to the acquisition. Immediately after acquiring the X stock, and as part of a series of related transactions, P liquidates X under section 331. In the liquidating distribution, P receives a section 197(f)(9) intangible that was held by X during the transition period.

(ii) Because the relationship between P and X was created pursuant to a series of related transactions where P acquires stock (meeting the requirements of section 1504(a)(2)) in a fully taxable transaction followed by a liquidation under section 331, the relationship immediately after the last transaction in the series (the liquidation) is disregarded. See paragraph (h)(6)(iii) of this section. Accordingly, P is entitled to amortize the section 197(f)(9) intangible.

Example (27). Section 743(b) adjustment with no change in user. (i) On January 1, 2001, A forms a partnership (PRS) with B in which A owns a 40-percent, and B owns a 60-percent, interest in profits and capital. A contributes a nonamortizable section 197(f)(9) intangible with a value of $80 and an adjusted basis of $0 to PRS in exchange for its PRS interest and B contributes $120 cash. At the time of the contribution, PRS licenses the section 197(f)(9) intangible to A. On February 1, 2001, A sells its entire interest in PRS to C, an unrelated person, for $80. PRS has a section 754 election in effect.

(ii) The section 197(f)(9) intangible contributed to PRS by A is not amortizable in the hands of PRS. Pursuant to section (g)(2)(ii) of this section, PRS steps into the shoes of A with respect to A's nonamortizable transferred basis in the intangible.

(iii) When A sells the PRS interest to C, C will have a basis adjustment in the PRS assets under section 743(b) equal to $80. The entire basis adjustment will be allocated to the intangible because the only other asset held by PRS is cash. Ordinarily, under paragraph (h)(12)(v) of this section, the anti-churning rules will not apply to an increase in the basis of partnership property under section 743(b) if the person acquiring the partnership interest is not related to the person transferring the partnership interest. However, A is an anti-churning partner under paragraph (h)(12)(vi)(B)(2)(i) of this section. As a result of the license agreement, A remains a direct user of the section 197(f)(9) intangible after the transfer to C. Accordingly, paragraph (h)(12)(vi)(A) of this section will cause the anti-churning rules to apply to the entire basis adjustment under section 743(b).

Example (28). Example 28. Distribution of section 197(f)(9) intangible to partner who acquired partnership interest prior to the effective date. (i) In 1990, A, B, and C each contribute $150 cash to form general partnership ABC for the purpose of engaging in a consulting business and a software manufacturing business. The partners agree to share partnership profits and losses equally. In 2000, the partnership distributes the consulting business to A in liquidation of A's entire interest in ABC. The only asset of the consulting business is a nonamortizable intangible, which has a fair market value of $180 and a basis of $0. At the time of the distribution, the adjusted basis of A's interest in ABC is $150. A is not related to B or C. ABC does not have a section 754 election in effect.

(ii) Under section 732(b), A's adjusted basis in the intangible distributed by ABC is $150, a $150 increase over the basis of the intangible in ABC's hands. In determining whether the anti-churning rules apply to any portion of the basis increase, A is treated as having owned and used A's proportionate share of partnership property. Thus, A is treated as holding an interest in the intangible during the transition period. Because the intangible was not amortizable prior to the enactment of section 197, the section 732(b) increase in the basis of the intangible may be subject to the anti-churning provisions. Paragraph (h)(12)(ii) of this section provides that the anti-churning provisions apply to the extent that the section 732(b) adjustment exceeds the total unrealized appreciation from the intangible allocable to partners other than A or persons related to A, as well as certain other partners whose purchase of their interests meet certain criteria. Because B and C are not related to A, and A's acquisition of its partnership interest does not satisfy the necessary criteria, the section 732(b) basis increase is subject to the anti-churning provisions to the extent that it exceeds B and C's proportionate share of the unrealized appreciation from the intangible. B and C's proportionate share of the unrealized appreciation from the intangible is $120 (⅔ of $180). This is the amount of gain that would be allocated to B and C if the partnership sold the intangible immediately before the distribution for its fair market value of $180. Therefore, $120 of the section 732(b) basis increase is not subject to the anti-churning rules. The remaining $30 of the section 732(b) basis increase is subject to the anti-churning rules. Accordingly, A is treated as having two intangibles, an amortizable section 197 intangible with an adjusted basis of $120 and a new amortization period of 15 years and a nonamortizable intangible with an adjusted basis of $30.

(iii) In applying the anti-churning rules to future transfers of the distributed intangible, under paragraph (h)(12)(ii)(C) of this section, one-third of the intangible will continue to be subject to the anti-churning rules, determined as follows: The sum of the amount of the distributed intangible's basis that is nonamortizable under paragraph (g)(2)(ii)(B) of this section ($0) and the total unrealized appreciation inherent in the intangible reduced by the amount of the increase in the adjusted basis of the distributed intangible under section 732(b) to which the anti-churning rules do not apply ($180-$120 = $60), over the fair market value of the distributed intangible ($180).

Example (29). Distribution of section 197(f)(9) intangible to partner who acquired partnership interest after the effective date. (i) The facts are the same as in Example 28, except that B and C form ABC in 1990. A does not acquire an interest in ABC until 1995. In 1995, A contributes $150 to ABC in exchange for a one-third interest in ABC. At the time of the distribution, the adjusted basis of A's interest in ABC is $150.

(ii) As in Example 28, the anti-churning rules do not apply to the increase in the basis of the intangible distributed to A under section 732(b) to the extent that it does not exceed the unrealized appreciation from the intangible allocable to B and C. Under paragraph (h)(12)(ii) of this section, the anti-churning provisions also do not apply to the section 732(b) basis increase to the extent of A's allocable share of the unrealized appreciation from the intangible because A acquired the ABC interest from an unrelated person after August 10, 1993, and the intangible was acquired by the partnership before A acquired the ABC interest. Under paragraph (h)(12)(ii)(E) of this section, A is deemed to acquire the ABC partnership interest from an unrelated person because A acquired the ABC partnership interest in exchange for a contribution to the partnership of property other than the distributed intangible and, at the time of the contribution, no partner in the partnership was related to A. Consequently, the increase in the basis of the intangible under section 732(b) is not subject to the anti-churning rules to the extent of the total unrealized appreciation from the intangible allocable to A, B, and C. The total unrealized appreciation from the intangible allocable to A, B, and C is $180 (the gain the partnership would have recognized if it had sold the intangible for its fair market value immediately before the distribution). Because this amount exceeds the section 732(b) basis increase of $150, the entire section 732(b) basis increase is amortizable.

(iii) In applying the anti-churning rules to future transfers of the distributed intangible, under paragraph (h)(12)(ii)(C) of this section, one-sixth of the intangible will continue to be subject to the anti-churning rules, determined as follows: The sum of the amount of the distributed intangible's basis that is nonamortizable under paragraph (g)(2)(ii)(B) of this section ($0) and the total unrealized appreciation inherent in the intangible reduced by the amount of the increase in the adjusted basis of the distributed intangible under section 732(b) to which the anti-churning rules do not apply ($180-$150 = $30), over the fair market value of the distributed intangible ($180).

Example (30). Distribution of section 197(f)(9) intangible contributed to the partnership by a partner. (i) The facts are the same as in Example 29, except that C purchased the intangible used in the consulting business in 1988 for $60 and contributed the intangible to ABC in 1990. At that time, the intangible had a fair market value of $150 and an adjusted tax basis of $60. When ABC distributes the intangible to A in 2000, the intangible has a fair market value of $180 and a basis of $60.

(ii) As in Examples 28 and 29, the adjusted basis of the intangible in A's hands is $150 under section 732(b). However, the increase in the adjusted basis of the intangible under section 732(b) is only $90 ($150 adjusted basis after the distribution compared to $60 basis before the distribution). Pursuant to paragraph (g)(2)(ii)(B) of this section, A steps into the shoes of ABC with respect to the $60 of A's adjusted basis in the intangible that corresponds to ABC's basis in the intangible and this portion of the basis is nonamortizable. B and C are not related to A, A acquired the ABC interest from an unrelated person after August 10, 1993, and the intangible was acquired by ABC before A acquired the ABC interest. Therefore, under paragraph (h)(12)(ii) of this section, the section 732(b) basis increase is amortizable to the extent of A, B, and C's allocable share of the unrealized appreciation from the intangible. The total unrealized appreciation from the intangible that is allocable to A, B, and C is $120. If ABC had sold the intangible immediately before the distribution to A for its fair market value of $180, it would have recognized gain of $120, which would have been allocated $10 to A, $10 to B, and $100 to C under section 704(c). Because A, B, and C's allocable share of the unrealized appreciation from the intangible exceeds the section 732(b) basis increase in the intangible, the entire $90 of basis increase is amortizable by A. Accordingly, after the distribution, A will be treated as having two intangibles, an amortizable section 197 intangible with an adjusted basis of $90 and a new amortization period of 15 years and a nonamortizable intangible with an adjusted basis of $60.

(iii) In applying the anti-churning rules to future transfers of the distributed intangible, under paragraph (h)(12)(ii)(C) of this section, one-half of the intangible will continue to be subject to the anti-churning rules, determined as follows: The sum of the amount of the distributed intangible's basis that is nonamortizable under paragraph (g)(2)(ii)(B) of this section ($60) and the total unrealized appreciation inherent in the intangible reduced by the amount of the increase in the adjusted basis of the distributed intangible under section 732(b) to which the anti-churning rules do not apply ($120-$90 = $30), over the fair market value of the distributed intangible ($180).

Example (31). Partnership distribution causing section 734(b) basis adjustment to section 197(f)(9) intangible. (i) On January 1, 2001, A, B, and C form a partnership (ABC) in which each partner shares equally in capital and income, gain, loss, and deductions. On that date, A contributes a section 197(f)(9) intangible with a zero basis and a value of $150, and B and C each contribute $150 cash. A and B are related, but neither A nor B is related to C. ABC does not adopt the remedial allocation method for making section 704(c) allocations of amortization expenses with respect to the intangible. On December 1, 2004, when the value of the intangible has increased to $600, ABC distributes $300 to B in complete redemption of B's interest in the partnership. ABC has an election under section 754 in effect for the taxable year that includes December 1, 2004. (Assume that, at the time of the distribution, the basis of A's partnership interest remains zero, and the basis of each of B's and C's partnership interest remains $150.)

(ii) Immediately prior to the distribution, the assets of the partnership are revalued pursuant to § 1.704-1(b)(2)(iv)(f), so that the section 197(f)(9) intangible is reflected on the books of the partnership at a value of $600. B recognizes $150 of gain under section 731(a)(1) upon the distribution of $300 in redemption of B's partnership interest. As a result, the adjusted basis of the intangible held by ABC increases by $150 under section 734(b). A does not satisfy any of the tests set forth under paragraph (h)(12)(iv)(B) and thus is not an eligible partner. C is not related to B and thus is an eligible partner under paragraph (h)(12)(iv)(B)(1) of this section. The capital accounts of A and C are equal immediately after the distribution, so, pursuant to paragraph (h)(12)(iv)(D)(1) of this section, each partner's share of the basis increase is equal to $75. Because A is not an eligible partner, the anti-churning rules apply to A's share of the basis increase. The anti-churning rules do not apply to C's share of the basis increase.

(iii) For book purposes, ABC determines the amortization of the asset as follows: First, the intangible that is subject to adjustment under section 734(b) will be divided into three assets: the first, with a basis and value of $75 will be amortizable for both book and tax purposes; the second, with a basis and value of $75 will be amortizable for book, but not tax purposes; and a third asset with a basis of zero and a value of $450 will not be amortizable for book or tax purposes. Any subsequent revaluation of the intangible pursuant to § 1.704-1(b)(2)(iv)(f) will be made solely with respect to the third asset (which is not amortizable for book purposes). The book and tax attributes from the first asset (i.e., book and tax amortization) will be specially allocated to C. The book and tax attributes from the second asset (i.e., book amortization and non-amortizable tax basis) will be specially allocated to A. Upon disposition of the intangible, each partner's share of gain or loss will be determined first by allocating among the partners an amount realized equal to the book value of the intangible attributable to such partner, with any remaining amount realized being allocated in accordance with the partnership agreement. Each partner then will compare its share of the amount realized with its remaining basis in the intangible to arrive at the gain or loss to be allocated to such partner. This is a reasonable method for amortizing the intangible for book purposes, and the results in allocating the income, gain, loss, and deductions attributable to the intangible do not contravene the purposes of the anti-churning rules under section 197 or paragraph (h) of this section.

(l) Effective dates. *(1) In general.* This section applies to property acquired after January 25, 2000, except that paragraph (c)(13) of this section (exception from section 197 for separately acquired rights of fixed duration or amount) applies to property acquired after August 10, 1993 (or July 25, 1991, if a valid retroactive election has been made under § 1.197-1T), and paragraphs (h)(12)(ii), (iii), (iv), (v), (vi)(A), and (vii)(B) of this section (anti-churning rules applicable to partnerships) apply to partnership transactions occurring on or after November 20, 2000.

(2) Application to pre-effective date acquisitions. A taxpayer may choose, on a transaction-by-transaction basis, to apply the provisions of this section and § 1.167(a)-14 to property acquired (or partnership transactions occurring) after August 10, 1993 (or July 25, 1991, if a valid retroactive election has been made under § 1.197-1T) and—

(i) On or before January 25, 2000; or

(ii) With respect to paragraphs (h)(12)(ii), (iii), (iv), (v), (vi)(A), and (vii)(B) of this section, before November 20, 2000.

(3) Application of regulation project REG-209709-94 to pre-effective date acquisitions. A taxpayer may rely on the provisions of regulation project REG-209709-94 (1997-1 C.B. 731) for property acquired after August 10, 1993 (or July 25, 1991, if a valid retroactive election has been made under § 1.197-1T) and on or before January 25, 2000.

(4) Change in method of accounting. (i) In general. For the first taxable year ending after January 25, 2000, a taxpayer that has acquired property to which the exception in § 1.197-2(c)(13) applies is granted consent of the Commissioner to change its method of accounting for such property to comply with the provisions of this section and § 1.167(a)-14 unless the proper treatment of such property is an issue under consideration (within the meaning of Rev. Proc. 97-27 (1997-21 IRB 10)(see § 601.601(d)(2) of this chapter)) in an examination, before an Appeals office, or before a Federal court.

(ii) Application to pre-effective date acquisitions. For the first taxable year ending after January 25, 2000, a taxpayer is granted consent of the Commissioner to change its method of accounting for all property acquired in transactions described in paragraph (l)(2) of this section to comply with the provisions of this section and § 1.167(a)-14 unless the proper treatment of any such property is an issue under consideration (within the meaning of Rev. Proc. 97-27 (1997-21 IRB 10)(see § 601.601(d)(2) of this chapter)) in an examination, before an Appeals office, or before a Federal court.

(iii) Automatic change procedures. A taxpayer changing its method of accounting in accordance with this paragraph (l)(4) must follow the automatic change in accounting method provisions of Rev. Proc. 99-49 (1999-52 IRB 725)(see § 601.601(d)(2) of this chapter) except, for purposes of this paragraph (l)(4), the scope limitations in section 4.02 of Rev. Proc. 99-49 (1999-52 IRB 725) are not applicable. However, if the taxpayer is under examination, before an appeals office, or before a Federal court, the taxpayer must provide a copy of the application to the examining agent(s), appeals officer, or counsel for the government, as appropriate, at the same time that it files the copy of the application with the National Office. The application must contain the name(s) and telephone number(s) of the examining agent(s), appeals officer, or counsel for the government, as appropriate.

T.D. 8865, 1/20/2000, amend T.D. 8907, 11/17/2000, T.D. 8940, 2/12/2001, T.D. 9257, 4/7/2006, T.D. 9377, 1/22/2008.

---

§ 1.199-0 Table of contents.

This section lists the section headings that appear in §§ 1.199-1 through 1.199-9.

§ 1.199-1 Income attributable to domestic production activities.

(a) In general.

(b) Taxable income and adjusted gross income.

(1) In general.

(2) Examples.

(c) Qualified production activities income.

(d) Allocation of gross receipts.

(1) In general.

(2) Reasonable method of allocation.

(3) De minimis rules.
(i) DPGR.
(ii) Non-DPGR.
(4) Example.
(e) Certain multiple-year transactions.
(1) Use of historical data.
(2) Percentage of completion method.
(3) Examples.
§ 1.199-2 Wage limitation.
(a) Rules of application.
(1) In general.
(2) Wages paid by entity other than common law employer.
(3) Requirement that wages must be reported on return filed with the Social Security Administration.
(i) In general.
(ii) Corrected return filed to correct a return that was filed within 60 days of the due date.
(iii) Corrected return filed to correct a return that was filed later than 60 days after the due date.
(4) Joint return.
(b) Application in the case of a taxpayer with a short taxable year.
(c) Acquisition or disposition of a trade or business (or major portion).
(d) Non-duplication rule.
(e) Definition of W-2 wages.
(1) In general.
(2) Limitation on W-2 wages for taxable years beginning after May 17, 2006, the enactment date of the Tax Increase Prevention and Reconciliation Act of 2005.
(i) In general.
(ii) Wage expense safe harbor.
(A) In general.
(B) Wage expense included in cost of goods sold.
(iii) Small business simplified overall method safe harbor.
(iv) Examples.
(3) Methods for calculating W-2 wages.
§ 1.199-3 Domestic production gross receipts.
(a) In general.
(b) Related persons.
(1) In general.
(2) Exceptions.
(c) Definition of gross receipts.
(d) Determining domestic production gross receipts.
(1) In general.
(2) Special rules.
(3) Exception.
(4) Examples.
(e) Definition of manufactured, produced, grown, or extracted.
(1) In general.
(2) Packaging, repackaging, labeling, or minor assembly.
(3) Installing.
(4) Consistency with section 263A.
(5) Examples.
(f) Definition of by the taxpayer.
(1) In general.
(2) Special rule for certain government contracts.
(3) Subcontractor.
(4) Examples.
(g) Definition of in whole or in significant part.
(1) In general.
(2) Substantial in nature.
(3) Safe harbor.
(i) In general.
(ii) Unadjusted depreciable basis.
(iii) Computer software and sound recordings.
(4) Special rules.
(i) Contract with unrelated persons.
(ii) Aggregation.
(5) Examples.
(h) Definition of United States.
(i) Derived from the lease, rental, license, sale, exchange, or other disposition.
(1) In general.
(i) Definition.
(ii) Lease income.
(iii) Income substitutes.
(iv) Exchange of property.
(A) Taxable exchanges.
(B) Safe harbor.
(C) Eligible property.
(2) Examples.
(3) Hedging transactions.
(i) In general.
(ii) Currency fluctuations.
(iii) Effect of identification and nonidentification.
(iv) Other rules.
(4) Allocation of gross receipts.
(i) Embedded services and non-qualified property.
(A) In general.
(B) Exceptions.
(ii) Non-DPGR.
(iii) Examples.
(5) Advertising income.
(i) In general.
(ii) Exceptions.
(A) Tangible personal property.
(B) Computer software.
(C) Qualified film.
(iii) Examples.
(6) Computer software.
(i) In general.
(ii) Gross receipts derived from services.
(iii) Exceptions.
(iv) Definitions and special rules.
(A) Substantially identical software.
(B) Safe harbor for computer software games.
(C) Regular and ongoing basis.

(D) Attribution.
(E) Qualified computer software maintenance agreements.
(F) Advertising income and product-placement income.
(v) Examples.
(7) Qualifying in-kind partnership for taxable years beginning after May 17, 2006, the enactment date of the Tax Increase Prevention and Reconciliation Act of 2005.
(i) In general.
(ii) Definition of qualifying in-kind partnership.
(iii) Other rules.
(iv) Example.
(8) Partnerships owned by members of a single expanded affiliated group for taxable years beginning after May 17, 2006, the enactment date of the Tax Increase Prevention and Reconciliation Act of 2005.
(i) In general.
(ii) Attribution of activities.
(A) In general.
(B) Attribution between EAG partnerships.
(C) Exceptions to attribution.
(iii) Other rules.
(iv) Examples.
(9) Non-operating mineral interests.
(j) Definition of qualifying production property.
(1) In general.
(2) Tangible personal property.
(i) In general.
(ii) Local law.
(iii) Intangible property.
(3) Computer software.
(i) In general.
(ii) Incidental and ancillary rights.
(iii) Exceptions.
(4) Sound recordings.
(i) In general.
(ii) Exception.
(5) Tangible personal property with computer software or sound recordings.
(i) Computer software and sound recordings.
(ii) Tangible personal property.
(k) Definition of qualified film.
(1) In general.
(2) Tangible personal property with a film.
(i) Film not produced by a taxpayer.
(ii) Film produced by a taxpayer.
(A) Qualified film.
(B) Nonqualified film.
(3) Derived from a qualified film.
(i) In general.
(ii) Exceptions.
(4) Compensation for services.
(5) Determination of 50 percent.
(6) Produced by the taxpayer.
(7) Qualified film produced by the taxpayer--safe harbor.
(i) Safe harbor.
(ii) Determination of 50 percent.
(8) Production pursuant to a contract.
(9) Exception.
(10) Examples.
(l) Electricity, natural gas, or potable water.
(1) In general.
(2) Natural gas.
(3) Potable water.
(4) Exceptions.
(i) Electricity.
(ii) Natural gas.
(iii) Potable water.
(iv) De minimis exception.
(A) DPGR.
(B) Non-DPGR.
(5) Example.
(m) Definition of construction performed in the United States.
(1) Construction of real property.
(i) In general.
(ii) Regular and ongoing basis.
(A) In general.
(B) New trade or business.
(iii) De minimis exception.
(A) DPGR.
(B) Non-DPGR.
(2) Activities constituting construction.
(i) In general.
(ii) Tangential services.
(iii) Other construction activities.
(iv) Administrative support services.
(v) Exceptions.
(3) Definition of real property.
(4) Definition of infrastructure.
(5) Definition of substantial renovation.
(6) Derived from construction.
(i) In general.
(ii) Qualified construction warranty.
(iii) Exceptions.
(iv) Land safe harbor.
(A) In general.
(B) Determining gross receipts and costs.
(v) Examples.
(n) Definition of engineering and architectural services.
(1) In general.
(2) Engineering services.
(3) Architectural services.
(4) Administrative support services.
(5) Exceptions.
(6) De minimis exception for performance of services in the United States.
(i) DPGR.
(ii) Non-DPGR.
(7) Example.

(o) Sales of certain food and beverages.

(1) In general.

(2) De minimis exception.

(3) Examples.

(p) Guaranteed payments.

§ 1.199-4 Costs allocable to domestic production gross receipts.

(a) In general.

(b) Cost of goods sold allocable to domestic production gross receipts.

(1) In general.

(2) Allocating cost of goods sold.

(i) In general.

(ii) Gross receipts recognized in an earlier taxable year.

(3) Special rules for imported items or services.

(4) Rules for inventories valued at market or bona fide selling prices.

(5) Rules applicable to inventories accounted for under the last-in, first-out (LIFO) inventory method.

(i) In general.

(ii) LIFO/FIFO ratio method.

(iii) Change in relative base-year cost method.

(6) Taxpayers using the simplified production method or simplified resale method for additional section 263A costs.

(7) Examples.

(c) Other deductions properly allocable to domestic production gross receipts or gross income attributable to domestic production gross receipts.

(1) In general.

(2) Treatment of net operating losses.

(3) W-2 wages.

(d) Section 861 method.

(1) In general.

(2) Deductions for charitable contributions.

(3) Research and experimental expenditures.

(4) Deductions allocated or apportioned to gross receipts treated as domestic production gross receipts.

(5) Treatment of items from a pass-thru entity reporting qualified production activities income.

(6) Examples.

(e) Simplified deduction method.

(1) In general.

(2) Eligible taxpayer.

(3) Total assets.

(i) In general.

(ii) Members of an expanded affiliated group.

(4) Members of an expanded affiliated group.

(i) In general.

(ii) Exception.

(ii) Examples.

(f) Small business simplified overall method.

(1) In general.

(2) Qualifying small taxpayer.

(3) Total costs for the current taxable year.

(i) In general.

(ii) Land safe harbor.

(4) Members of an expanded affiliated group.

(i) In general.

(ii) Exception.

(iii) Examples.

(5) Trusts and estates.

(g) Average annual gross receipts.

(1) In general.

(2) Members of an expanded affiliated group.

§ 1.199-5 Application of section 199 to pass-thru entities for taxable years beginning after May 17, 2006, the enactment date of the Tax Increase Prevention and Reconciliation Act of 2005.

(a) In general.

(b) Partnerships.

(1) In general.

(i) Determination at partner level.

(ii) Determination at entity level.

(2) Disallowed losses or deductions.

(3) Partner's share of paragraph (e)(1) wages.

(4) Transition rule for definition of W-2 wages and for W-2 wage limitation.

(5) Partnerships electing out of subchapter K.

(6) Examples.

(c) S corporations.

(1) In general.

(i) Determination at shareholder level.

(ii) Determination at entity level.

(2) Disallowed losses and deductions.

(3) Shareholder's share of paragraph (e)(1) wages.

(4) Transition rule for definition of W-2 wages and for W-2 wage limitation.

(d) Grantor trusts.

(e) Non-grantor trusts and estates.

(1) Allocation of costs.

(2) Allocation among trust or estate and beneficiaries.

(i) In general.

(ii) Treatment of items from a trust or estate reporting qualified production activities income.

(3) Transition rule for definition of W-2 wages and for W-2 wage limitation.

(4) Example.

(f) Gain or loss from the disposition of an interest in a pass-thru entity.

(g) No attribution of qualified activities.

§ 1.199-6 Agricultural and horticultural cooperatives.

(a) In general.

(b) Cooperative denied section 1382 deduction for portion of qualified payments.

(c) Determining cooperative's qualified production activities income and taxable income.

(d) Special rule for marketing cooperatives.

(e) Qualified payment.

(f) Specified agricultural or horticultural cooperative.

(g) Written notice to patrons.

(h) Additional rules relating to passthrough of section 199 deduction.

(i) W-2 wages.

(j) Recapture of section 199 deduction.

(k) Section is exclusive.

(l) No double counting.

(m) Examples.

§ 1.199-7 Expanded affiliated groups.

(a) In general.

(1) Definition of expanded affiliated group.

(2) Identification of members of an expanded affiliated group.

(i) In general.

(ii) Becoming or ceasing to be a member of an expanded affiliated group.

(3) Attribution of activities.

(i) In general.

(ii) Special rule.

(4) Examples.

(5) Anti-avoidance rule.

(b) Computation of expanded affiliated group's section 199 deduction.

(1) In general.

(2) Example.

(3) Net operating loss carrybacks and carryovers.

(4) Losses used to reduce taxable income of expanded affiliated group.

(i) In general.

(ii) Examples.

(c) Allocation of an expanded affiliated group's section 199 deduction among members of the expanded affiliated group.

(1) In general.

(2) Use of section 199 deduction to create or increase a net operating loss.

(d) Special rules for members of the same consolidated group.

(1) Intercompany transactions.

(2) Attribution of activities in the construction of real property and the performance of engineering and architectural services.

(3) Application of the simplified deduction method and the small business simplified overall method.

(4) Determining the section 199 deduction.

(i) Expanded affiliated group consists of consolidated group and non-consolidated group members.

(ii) Expanded affiliated group consists only of members of a single consolidated group.

(5) Allocation of the section 199 deduction of a consolidated group among its members.

(e) Examples.

(f) Allocation of income and loss by a corporation that is a member of the expanded affiliated group for only a portion of the year.

(1) In general.

(2) Coordination with rules relating to the allocation of income under § 1.1502-76(b).

(g) Total section 199 deduction for a corporation that is a member of an expanded affiliated group for some or all of its taxable year.

(1) Member of the same expanded affiliated group for the entire taxable year.

(2) Member of the expanded affiliated group for a portion of the taxable year.

(3) Example.

(h) Computation of section 199 deduction for members of an expanded affiliated group with different taxable years.

(1) In general.

(2) Example.

§ 1.199-8 Other rules.

(a) In general.

(b) Individuals.

(c) Trade or business requirement.

(1) In general.

(2) Individuals.

(3) Trusts and estates.

(d) Coordination with alternative minimum tax.

(e) Nonrecognition transactions.

(1) In general.

(i) Sections 351, 721, and 731.

(ii) Exceptions.

(A) Section 708(b)(1)(B).

(B) Transfers by reason of death.

(2) Section 1031 exchanges.

(3) Section 381 transactions.

(f) Taxpayers with a 52-53 week taxable year.

(g) Section 481(a) adjustments.

(h) Disallowed losses or deductions.

(i) Effective dates.

(1) In general.

(2) Pass-thru entities.

(3) Non-consolidated EAG members.

(4) Computer software.

(5) Tax Increase Prevention and Reconciliation Act of 2005.

(6) Losses used to reduce taxable income of expanded affiliated group.

(7) Agricultural and horticultural cooperatives.

(8) Qualified film produced by the taxpayer.

(9) Expanded affiliated groups.

§ 1.199-9 Application of section 199 to pass-thru entities for taxable years beginning on or before May 17, 2006, the enactment date of the Tax Increase Prevention and Reconciliation Act of 2005.

(a) In general.

(b) Partnerships.

(1) In general.

(i) Determination at partner level.

(ii) Determination at entity level.

(2) Disallowed losses or deductions.

(3) Partner's share of W-2 wages.

(4) Transition percentage rule for W-2 wages.

(5) Partnerships electing out of subchapter K.

(6) Examples.
(c) S corporations.
(1) In general.
(i) Determination at shareholder level.
(ii) Determination at entity level.
(2) Disallowed losses or deductions.
(3) Shareholder's share of W-2 wages.
(4) Transition percentage rule for W-2 wages.
(d) Grantor trusts.
(e) Non-grantor trusts and estates.
(1) Allocation of costs.
(2) Allocation among trust or estate and beneficiaries.
(i) In general.
(ii) Treatment of items from a trust or estate reporting qualified production activities income.
(3) Beneficiary's share of W-2 wages.
(4) Transition percentage rule for W-2 wages.
(5) Example.
(f) Gain or loss from the disposition of an interest in a pass-thru entity.
(g) Section 199(d)(1)(A)(iii) wage limitation and tiered structures.
(1) In general.
(2) Share of W-2 wages.
(3) Example.
(h) No attribution of qualified activities.
(i) Qualifying in-kind partnership.
(1) In general.
(2) Definition of qualifying in-kind partnership.
(3) Special rules for distributions.
(4) Other rules.
(5) Example.
(j) Partnerships owned by members of a single expanded affiliated group.
(1) In general.
(2) Attribution of activities.
(i) In general.
(ii) Attribution between EAG partnerships.
(iii) Exception to attribution.
(3) Special rules for distributions.
(4) Other rules.
(5) Examples.
(k) Effective dates.

T.D. 9263, 5/24/2006, amend T.D. 9293, 10/18/2006, T.D. 9317, 3/19/2007, T.D. 9381, 2/14/2008, T.D. 9384, 3/6/2008.

Proposed § 1.199-0 Table of contents. [*For Preamble, see ¶ 152,713*]

This section lists the headings that appear in §§ 1.199-1 through 1.199-8.

§ 1.199-1 Income attributable to domestic production activities.
(a) In general.
(b) Taxable income and adjusted gross income.
(1) In general.
(2) Examples.
(c) Qualified production activities income.
(1) In general.
(2) Definition of item.
(i) In general.
(ii) Examples.
(d) Allocation of gross receipts.
(1) In general.
(2) De minimis rule.
(3) Examples.
(e) Timing rules for determining QPAI.
(1) Gross receipts and costs recognized in different taxable years.
(2) Percentage of completion method.
(3) Example.
§ 1.199-2 Wage limitation.
(a) Rules of application.
(1) In general.
(2) Wages paid by entity other than common law employer.
(b) No application in determining whether amounts are wages for employment tax purposes.
(c) Application in case of taxpayer with short taxable year.
(d) Acquisition or disposition of a trade or business (or major portion).
(e) Non-duplication rule.
(f) Definition of W-2 wages.
(1) In general.
(2) Methods for calculating W-2 wages.
(i) Unmodified box method.
(ii) Modified Box 1 method.
(iii) Tracking wages method.
§ 1.199-3 Domestic production gross receipts.
(a) In general.
(b) Related persons.
(1) In general.
(2) Exceptions.
(c) Definition of gross receipts.
(d) Definition of manufactured, produced, grown, or extracted.
(1) In general.
(2) Packaging, repackaging, labeling, or minor assembly.
(3) Installing.
(4) Consistency with section 263A.
(5) Examples.
(e) Definition of by the taxpayer.
(1) In general.
(2) Special rule for certain government contracts.
(3) Examples.
(f) Definition of in whole or in significant part.
(1) In general.
(2) Substantial in nature.
(3) Safe harbor.
(4) Examples.

(g) Definition of United States.

(h) Definition of derived from the lease, rental, license, sale, exchange, or other disposition.

(1) In general.

(2) Examples.

(3) Hedging transactions.

(i) In general.

(ii) Currency fluctuations.

(iii) Other rules.

(4) Allocation of gross receipts — embedded services and non-qualified property.

(i) In general.

(ii) Exceptions.

(iii) Examples.

(5) Advertising income.

(i) Tangible personal property.

(ii) Qualified films.

(iii) Examples.

(6) Computer software.

(i) In general.

(ii) Examples.

(7) Exception for certain oil and gas partnerships.

(i) In general.

(ii) Example.

(8) Partnerships owned by members of a single expanded affiliated group.

(i) In general.

(ii) Special rules for distributions from EAG partnerships.

(iii) Examples.

(9) Non-operating mineral interests.

(i) Definition of qualifying production property.

(1) In general.

(2) Tangible personal property.

(i) In general.

(ii) Local law.

(iii) Machinery.

(iv) Intangible property.

(3) Computer software.

(i) In general.

(ii) Incidental and ancillary rights.

(iii) Exceptions.

(4) Sound recordings.

(i) In general.

(ii) Exception.

(5) Tangible personal property with computer software or sound recordings.

(i) Computer software and sound recordings.

(ii) Tangible personal property.

(j) Definition of qualified film.

(1) In general.

(2) Tangible personal property with a film.

(i) Film licensed by a taxpayer.

(ii) Film produced by a taxpayer.

(A) Qualified films.

(B) Nonqualified films.

(3) Derived from a qualified film.

(4) Examples.

(5) Compensation for services.

(6) Determination of 50 percent.

(7) Exception.

(k) Electricity, natural gas, or potable water.

(1) In general.

(2) Natural gas.

(3) Potable water.

(4) Exceptions.

(i) Electricity.

(ii) Natural gas.

(iii) Potable water.

(iv) De minimis exception.

(5) Example.

(l) Definition of construction performed in the United States.

(1) Construction of real property.

(i) In general.

(ii) De minimis exception.

(2) Activities constituting construction.

(3) Definition of infrastructure.

(4) Definition of substantial renovation.

(5) Derived from construction.

(i) In general.

(ii) Land safe harbor.

(iii) Examples.

(m) Definition of engineering and architectural services.

(1) In general.

(2) Engineering services.

(3) Architectural services.

(4) De minimis exception for performance of services in the United States.

(n) Exception for sales of certain food and beverages.

(1) In general.

(2) Examples.

§ 1.199-4 Costs allocable to domestic production gross receipts.

(a) In general.

(b) Cost of goods sold allocable to domestic production gross receipts.

(1) In general.

(2) Allocating cost of goods sold.

(3) Special rules for imported items or services.

(4) Rules for inventories valued at market or bona fide selling prices.

(5) Rules applicable to inventories accounted for under the last-in, first-out (LIFO) inventory method.

(i) In general.

(ii) LIFO/FIFO ratio method.

(iii) Change in relative base-year cost method.

(6) Taxpayers using the simplified production method or simplified resale method for additional section 263A costs.

(7) Examples.

(c) Other deductions allocable or apportioned to domestic production gross receipts or gross income attributable to domestic production gross receipts.

(1) In general.

(2) Treatment of certain deductions.

(i) In general.

(ii) Net operating losses.

(iii) Deductions not attributable to the conduct of a trade or business.

(d) Section 861 method.

(1) In general.

(2) Deductions for charitable contributions.

(3) Research and experimental expenditures.

(4) Deductions related to gross receipts deemed to be domestic production gross receipts.

(5) Examples.

(e) Simplified deduction method.

(1) In general.

(2) Members of an expanded affiliated group.

(i) In general.

(ii) Exception.

(iii) Examples.

(f) Small business simplified overall method.

(1) In general.

(2) Qualifying small taxpayer.

(3) Members of an expanded affiliated group.

(i) In general.

(ii) Exception.

(iii) Examples.

(4) Ineligible pass-thru entities.

(g) Average annual gross receipts.

(1) In general.

(2) Members of an EAG.

(h) Total assets.

(1) In general.

(2) Members of an EAG.

(i) Total costs for the current taxable year.

(1) In general.

(2) Members of an EAG.

§ 1.199-5 Application of section 199 to pass-thru entities.

(a) Partnerships.

(1) Determination at partner level.

(2) Disallowed deductions.

(3) Partner's share of W-2 wages.

(4) Examples.

(b) S corporations.

(1) Determination at shareholder level.

(2) Disallowed deductions.

(3) Shareholder's share of W-2 wages.

(c) Grantor trusts.

(d) Non-grantor trusts and estates.

(1) Computation of section 199 deduction.

(2) Example.

(e) Gain or loss from the disposition of an interest in a pass-thru entity.

(f) Section 199(d)(1)(B) wage limitation and tiered structures.

(1) In general.

(2) Share of W-2 wages.

(3) Example.

(g) No attribution of qualified activities.

§ 1.199-6 Agricultural and horticultural cooperatives.

(a) In general.

(b) Written notice to patrons.

(c) Determining cooperative's qualified production activities income.

(d) Additional rules relating to pass-through of section 199 deduction.

(e) W-2 wages.

(f) Recapture of section 199 deduction.

(g) Section is exclusive.

(h) No double counting.

(i) Examples.

§ 1.199-7 Expanded affiliated groups.

(a) In general.

(1) Definition of expanded affiliated group.

(2) Identification of members of an expanded affiliated group.

(i) In general.

(ii) Becoming or ceasing to be a member of an expanded affiliated group.

(3) Attribution of activities.

(4) Examples.

(5) Anti-avoidance rule.

(b) Computation of expanded affiliated group's section 199 deduction.

(1) In general.

(2) Net operating loss carryovers.

(c) Allocation of an expanded affiliated group's section 199 deduction among members of the expanded affiliated group.

(1) In general.

(2) Use of section 199 deduction to create or increase a net operating loss.

(d) Special rules for members of the same consolidated group.

(1) Intercompany transactions.

(2) Attribution of activities in the construction of real property and the performance of engineering and architectural services.

(3) Application of the simplified deduction method and the small business simplified overall method.

(4) Determining the section 199 deduction.

(i) Expanded affiliated group consists of consolidated group and non-consolidated group members.

(ii) Expanded affiliated group consists only of members of a single consolidated group.

(5) Allocation of the section 199 deduction of a consolidated group among its members.

(e) Examples.

(f) Allocation of income and loss by a corporation that is a member of the expanded affiliated group for only a portion of the year.

(1) In general.

(i) Pro rata allocation method.

(ii) Section 199 closing of the books method.

(iii) Making the section 199 closing of the books election.

(2) Coordination with rules relating to the allocation of income under § 1.1502-76(b).

(g) Total section 199 deduction for a corporation that is a member of an expanded affiliated group for some or all of its taxable year.

(1) Member of the same expanded affiliated group for the entire taxable year.

(2) Member of the expanded affiliated group for a portion of the taxable year.

(3) Example.

(h) Computation of section 199 deduction for members of an expanded affiliated group with different taxable years.

(1) In general.

(2) Example.

§ 1.199-8 Other rules.

(a) Individuals.

(b) Trade or business requirement.

(c) Coordination with alternative minimum tax.

(d) Nonrecognition transactions.

(1) In general.

(2) Section 1031 exchanges.

(3) Section 381 transactions.

(e) Taxpayers with a 52-53 week taxable year.

(f) Section 481(a) adjustments.

(g) Effective date.

§ 1.199-1 Income attributable to domestic production activities.

(a) In general. A taxpayer may deduct an amount equal to 9 percent (3 percent in the case of taxable years beginning in 2005 or 2006, and 6 percent in the case of taxable years beginning in 2007, 2008, or 2009) of the lesser of the taxpayer's qualified production activities income (QPAI) (as defined in paragraph (c) of this section) for the taxable year, or the taxpayer's taxable income for the taxable year (or, in the case of an individual, adjusted gross income). The amount of the deduction allowable under this paragraph (a) for any taxable year cannot exceed 50 percent of the W-2 wages of the employer for the taxable year (as determined under § 1.199-2). The provisions of this section apply solely for purposes of section 199 of the Internal Revenue Code.

(b) Taxable income and adjusted gross income. *(1) In general.* For purposes of paragraph (a) of this section, the definition of taxable income under section 63 applies, except that taxable income (or alternative minimum taxable income, if applicable) is determined without regard to section 199 and without regard to any amount excluded from gross income pursuant to section 114 or pursuant to section 101(d) of the American Jobs Creation Act of 2004, Public Law 108-357 (118 Stat. 1418) (Act). In the case of individuals, adjusted gross income for the taxable year is determined after applying sections 86, 135, 137, 219, 221, 222, and 469, and without regard to section 199 and without regard to any amount excluded from gross income pursuant to section 114 or pursuant to section 101(d) of the Act. For purposes of determining the tax imposed by section 511, paragraph (a) of this section is applied using unrelated business taxable income. Except as provided in § 1.199-7(c)(2), the deduction under section 199 is not taken into account in computing any net operating loss or the amount of any net operating loss carryback or carryover.

(2) Examples. The following examples illustrate the application of this paragraph (b):

Example (1). X, a corporation that is not part of an expanded affiliated group (EAG) (as defined in § 1.199-7), engages in production activities that generate QPAI and taxable income (without taking into account the deduction under this section and an NOL deduction) of $600 in 2010. During 2010, X incurs W-2 wages as defined in § 1.199-2(e) of $300. X has an NOL carryover to 2010 of $500. X's deduction under this section for 2010 is $9 (.09 x (lesser of QPAI of $600 and taxable income of $100 ($600 taxable income - $500 NOL)). Because the wage limitation is $150 (50% x $300), X's deduction is not limited.

Example (2). (i) Facts. X, a corporation that is not part of an EAG, engages in production activities that generate QPAI and taxable income (without taking into account the deduction under this section and an NOL deduction) of $100 in 2010. X has an NOL carryover to 2010 of $500 that reduces its taxable income for 2010 to $0. X's deduction under this section for 2010 is $0 (.09 x (lesser of QPAI of $100 and taxable income of $0)).

(ii) Carryover to 2011. X's taxable income for purposes of determining its NOL carryover to 2011 is $100. Accordingly, X's NOL carryover to 2011 is $400 ($500 NOL carryover to 2010 - $100 NOL used in 2010).

(c) Qualified production activities income. QPAI for any taxable year is an amount equal to the excess (if any) of the taxpayer's domestic production gross receipts (DPGR) (as defined in § 1.199-3) over the sum of—

(1) The cost of goods sold (CGS) that is allocable to such receipts; and

(2) Other expenses, losses, or deductions (other than the deduction allowed under this section) that are properly allocable to such receipts. See §§ 1.199-3 and 1.199-4.

(d) Allocation of gross receipts. *(1) In general.* A taxpayer must determine the portion of its gross receipts for the taxable year that is DPGR and the portion of its gross receipts that is non-DPGR. Applicable Federal income tax principles apply to determine whether a transaction is, in substance, a lease, rental, license, sale, exchange, or other disposition the gross receipts of which may constitute DPGR (assuming all the other requirements of § 1.199-3 are met), whether it is a service the gross receipts of which may constitute non-DPGR, or some combination thereof. For example, if a taxpayer leases qualifying production property (QPP) (as defined in § 1.199-3(j)(1)) and in connection with that lease, also provides services, the taxpayer must allocate its gross receipts from the transaction using any reasonable method that is satisfactory to the Secretary based on all of the facts and circumstances and that accurately identifies the gross receipts that constitute DPGR and non-DPGR.

(2) Reasonable method of allocation. Factors taken into consideration in determining whether the taxpayer's method of allocating gross receipts between DPGR and non-DPGR is reasonable include whether the taxpayer uses the most accurate information available; the relationship between the gross receipts and the method used; the accuracy of the method chosen as compared with other possible methods; whether the method is used by the taxpayer for internal man-

agement or other business purposes; whether the method is used for other Federal or state income tax purposes; the time, burden, and cost of using alternative methods; and whether the taxpayer applies the method consistently from year to year. Thus, if a taxpayer has the information readily available and can, without undue burden or expense, specifically identify whether the gross receipts derived from an item are DPGR, then the taxpayer must use that specific identification to determine DPGR. If a taxpayer does not have information readily available to specifically identify whether the gross receipts derived from an item are DPGR or cannot, without undue burden or expense, specifically identify whether the gross receipts derived from an item are DPGR, then the taxpayer is not required to use a method that specifically identifies whether the gross receipts derived from an item are DPGR.

(3) De minimis rules. (i) DPGR. All of a taxpayer's gross receipts may be treated as DPGR if less than 5 percent of the taxpayer's total gross receipts are non-DPGR (after application of the exceptions provided in § 1.199-3(i)(4)(i)(B), (l)(4)(iv)(A), (m)(1)(iii)(A), (n)(6)(i), and (o)(2) that may result in gross receipts being treated as DPGR). If the amount of the taxpayer's gross receipts that are non-DPGR equals or exceeds 5 percent of the taxpayer's total gross receipts, then, except as provided in paragraph (d)(3)(ii) of this section, the taxpayer is required to allocate all gross receipts between DPGR and non-DPGR in accordance with paragraph (d)(1) of this section. If a corporation is a member of an EAG, but is not a member of a consolidated group, then the determination of whether less than 5 percent of the taxpayer's total gross receipts are non-DPGR is made at the corporation level. If a corporation is a member of a consolidated group, then the determination of whether less than 5 percent of the taxpayer's total gross receipts are non-DPGR is made at the consolidated group level. In the case of an S corporation, partnership, trust (to the extent not described in § 1.199-5(d) or § 1.199-9(d)) or estate, or other pass-thru entity, the determination of whether less than 5 percent of the pass-thru entity's total gross receipts are non-DPGR is made at the pass-thru entity level. In the case of an owner of a pass-thru entity, the determination of whether less than 5 percent of the owner's total gross receipts are non-DPGR is made at the owner level, taking into account all gross receipts of the owner from its other trade or business activities and the owner's share of the gross receipts of the pass-thru entity.

(ii) Non-DPGR. All of a taxpayer's gross receipts may be treated as non-DPGR if less than 5 percent of the taxpayer's total gross receipts are DPGR (after application of the exceptions provided in § 1.199-3(i)(4)(ii), (l)(4)(iv)(B), (m)(1)(iii)(B), and (n)(6)(ii) that may result in gross receipts being treated as non-DPGR). If a corporation is a member of an EAG, but is not a member of a consolidated group, then the determination of whether less than 5 percent of the taxpayer's total gross receipts are DPGR is made at the corporation level. If a corporation is a member of a consolidated group, then the determination of whether less than 5 percent of the taxpayer's total gross receipts are DPGR is made at the consolidated group level. In the case of an S corporation, partnership, trust (to the extent not described in § 1.199-5(d) or § 1.199-9(d)) or estate, or other pass-thru entity, the determination of whether less than 5 percent of the pass-thru entity's total gross receipts are DPGR is made at the pass-thru entity level. In the case of an owner of a pass-thru entity, the determination of whether less than 5 percent of the owner's total gross receipts are DPGR is made at the owner level, taking into account all gross receipts of the owner from its other trade or business activities and the owner's share of the gross receipts of the pass-thru entity.

(4) Example. The following example illustrates the application of this paragraph (d):

Example. Example. X derives its gross receipts from the sale of gasoline refined by X within the United States and the sale of refined gasoline that X acquired by purchase from an unrelated person. If at least 5% of X's gross receipts are derived from gasoline refined by X within the United States (that qualify as DPGR if all the other requirements of § 1.199-3 are met) and at least 5% of X's gross receipts are derived from the resale of the acquired gasoline (that do not qualify as DPGR), then X does not qualify for the de minimis rules under paragraphs (d)(3)(i) and (ii) of this section, and X must allocate its gross receipts between the gross receipts derived from the sale of gasoline refined by X within the United States and the gross receipts derived from the resale of the acquired gasoline. If less than 5% of X's gross receipts are derived from the resale of the acquired gasoline, then, X may either allocate its gross receipts between the gross receipts derived from the gasoline refined by X within the United States and the gross receipts derived from the resale of the acquired gasoline, or, pursuant to paragraph (d)(3)(i) of this section, X may treat all of its gross receipts derived from the sale of the refined gasoline as DPGR. If X's gross receipts attributable to the gasoline refined by X within the United States constitute less than 5% of X's total gross receipts, then, X may either allocate its gross receipts between the gross receipts derived from the gasoline refined by X within the United States and the gross receipts derived from the resale of the acquired gasoline, or, pursuant to paragraph (d)(3)(ii) of this section, X may treat all of its gross receipts derived from the sale of the refined gasoline as non-DPGR.

(e) Certain multiple-year transactions. *(1) Use of historical data.* If a taxpayer recognizes and reports gross receipts from advance payments or other similar payments on a Federal income tax return for a taxable year, then the taxpayer's use of historical data in making an allocation of gross receipts from the transaction between DPGR and non-DPGR may constitute a reasonable method. If a taxpayer makes allocations using historical data, and subsequently updates the data, then the taxpayer must use the more recent or updated data, starting in the taxable year in which the update is made.

(2) Percentage of completion method. A taxpayer using a percentage of completion method under section 460 must determine the ratio of DPGR and non-DPGR using a reasonable method that is satisfactory to the Secretary based on all of the facts and circumstances that accurately identifies the gross receipts that constitute DPGR. See paragraph (d)(2) of this section for the factors taken into consideration in determining whether the taxpayer's method is reasonable.

(3) Examples. The following examples illustrate the application of this paragraph (e):

Example (1). On December 1, 2007, X, a calendar year accrual method taxpayer, sells for $100 a one-year computer software maintenance agreement that provides for (i) computer software updates that X expects to produce in the United States, and (ii) customer support services. At the end of 2007, X uses a reasonable method that is satisfactory to the Secretary based on all of the facts and circumstances to allocate 60% of the gross receipts ($60) to the computer software updates and 40% ($40) to the customer support services. X treats the $60 as DPGR in 2007. At the expiration of the one-year agreement on November 30, 2008, no computer software updates are provided by X. Pursuant to paragraph (e)(1) of this section, because X used a reasonable method that is satisfactory to the Secretary based on all of the facts and circumstances to identify gross receipts as DPGR, X is not required to make any adjustments to its 2007 Federal income tax return (for example, by amended return) or in 2008 for the $60 that was properly treated as DPGR in 2007, even though no computer software updates were provided under the contract.

Example (2). X manufactures automobiles within the United States and sells 5-year extended warranties to customers. The sales price of the warranty is based on historical data that determines what repairs and services are performed on an automobile during the 5-year period. X sells the 5-year warranty to Y for $1,000 in 2007. Under X's method of accounting, X recognizes warranty revenue when received. Using historical data, X concludes that 60% of the gross receipts attributable to a 5-year warranty will be derived from the sale of parts (QPP) that X manufactures within the United States, and 40% will be derived from the sale of purchased parts X did not manufacture and non-qualifying services. X's method of allocating its gross receipts with respect to the 5-year warranty between DPGR and non-DPGR is a reasonable method that is satisfactory to the Secretary based on all of the facts and circumstances. Therefore, X properly treats $600 as DPGR in 2007.

Example (3). The facts are the same as in Example 2 except that in 2009 X updates its historical data. The updated historical data show that 50% of the gross receipts attributable to a 5-year warranty will be derived from the sale of parts (QPP) that X manufactures within the United States and 50% will be derived from the sale of purchased parts X did not manufacture and non-qualifying services. In 2009, X sells a 5-year warranty for $1,000 to Z. Under all of the facts and circumstances, X's method of allocation is still a reasonable method. Relying on its updated historical data, X properly treats $500 as DPGR in 2009.

Example (4). The facts are the same as in Example 2 except that Y pays for the 5-year warranty over time ($200 a year for 5 years). Under X's method of accounting, X recognizes each $200 payment as it is received. In 2009, X updates its historical data and the updated historical data show that 50% of the gross receipts attributable to a 5-year warranty will be derived from the sale of QPP that X manufactures within the United States and 50% will be derived from the sale of purchased parts X did not manufacture and non-qualifying services. Under all of the facts and circumstances, X's method of allocation is still a reasonable method. When Y makes its $200 payment for 2009, X, relying on its updated historical data, properly treats $100 as DPGR in 2009.

T.D. 9263, 5/24/2006, amend T.D. 9381, 2/14/2008.

Proposed § 1.199-1 Income attributable to domestic production activities. [*For Preamble, see ¶ 152,713*]

(a) In general. A taxpayer may deduct an amount equal to 9 percent (3 percent in the case of taxable years beginning in 2005 or 2006, and 6 percent in the case of taxable years beginning in 2007, 2008, or 2009) of the lesser of the taxpayer's qualified production activities income (QPAI) (as defined in paragraph (c) of this section) for the taxable year, or the taxpayer's taxable income for the taxable year (or, in the case of an individual, adjusted gross income). The amount of the deduction allowable under this paragraph (a) for any taxable year cannot exceed 50 percent of the W-2 wages of the employer for the taxable year (as determined under § 1.199-2).

(b) Taxable income and adjusted gross income. *(1) In general.* For purposes of paragraph (a) of this section, the definition of taxable income under section 63 applies and taxable income is determined without regard to section 199. In the case of individuals, adjusted gross income for the taxable year is determined after applying sections 86, 135, 137, 219, 221, 222, and 469, and without regard to section 199. For purposes of determining the tax imposed by section 511, paragraph (a) of this section is applied using unrelated business taxable income. For purposes of determining the amount of a net operating loss (NOL) carryback or carryover under section 172(b)(2), taxable income is determined without regard to the deduction allowed under section 199.

(2) Examples. The following examples illustrate the application of this paragraph (b):

Example (1). (i) Facts. X, a United States corporation that is not part of an expanded affiliated group (EAG) (as defined in § 1.199-7), engages in production activities that generate QPAI and taxable income (without taking into account the deduction under this section) of $600 in 2010. During 2010, x incurs W-2 wages of $300. x has an NOL carryover to 2010 of $500. X's deduction under this section for 2010 is $9 (.09 x (lesser of QPAI of $600 and taxable income of $100) subject to the wage limitation of $150 (50% x $300)).

Example (2). (i) Facts. X, a United States corporation that is not part of an EAG, engages in production activities that generate QPAI and taxable income (without taking into account the deduction under this section and an NOL deduction) of $100 in 2010. X has an NOL carryover to 2010 of $500. X's deduction under this section for 2010 is $0 (.09 x (lesser of QPAI of $100 and taxable income of $0)).

(ii) Carryover to 2011. X's taxable income for purposes of determining its NOL carryover to 2011 is $100. Accordingly, X's NOL carryover to 2011 is $400 ($500 NOL carryover to 2010–$100 NOL used in 2010).

(c) Qualified production activities income. *(1) In general.* QPAI for any taxable year is an amount equal to the excess (if any) of the taxpayer's domestic production gross receipts (DPGR) over the sum of the cost of goods sold (CGS) that is allocable to such receipts, other deductions, expenses, or losses (collectively, deductions) directly allocable to such receipts, and a ratable portion of deductions that are not directly allocable to such receipts or another class of income. See §§ 1.199-3 and 1.199-4. For purposes of this paragraph (c), QPAI is determined on an item-by-item basis (and not, for example, on a division-by-division, product line-by-product line, or transaction-by-transaction basis) and is the sum of QPAI derived by the taxpayer from each item (as defined in paragraph (c)(2) of this section). For purposes of this determination, QPAI from each item may be positive or negative. DPGR and its related CGS and deductions must be included in the QPAI computation regardless of whether, when viewed in isolation, the DPGR exceeds the CGS and deductions allocated and apportioned thereto. For example, if a taxpayer has $3 of QPAI from the sale of a shirt and derives ($1) of QPAI from the sale of a hat, the taxpayer's QPAI is $2.

(2) Definition of item. (i) In general. Except as otherwise provided in this paragraph, the term item means, for purposes of §§ 1.199-1 through 1.199-8, the property offered for sale to customers that meets all of the requirements under

this section and § 1.199-3. If the property offered for sale does not meet these requirements, a taxpayer must treat as the item any portion of the property offered for sale that meets these requirements. However, in no case shall the portion of the property offered for sale that is treated as the item exclude any other portion that meets these requirements. In no event may an item consist of two or more properties offered for sale that are not packaged and sold together as one item. In addition, in the case of property customarily sold by weight or by volume, the item is determined using the custom of the industry (for example, barrels of oil). In the case of construction (as defined in § 1.199-3(l)(1)) or engineering and architectural services (as defined in § 1.199-3(m)(1)), a taxpayer may use any reasonable method, taking into account all of the facts and circumstances, to determine what construction activities and engineering or architectural services constitute an item.

(ii) Examples. The following examples illustrate the application of paragraph (c)(2)(i) of this section:

Example (1). X manufactures leather and rubber shoe soles in the United States. X imports shoe uppers, which are the parts of the shoe above the sole. X manufactures shoes for sale by sewing or otherwise attaching the soles to the imported uppers. If the shoes do not meet the requirements under this section and § 1.199-3, then under paragraph (c)(2)(i) of this section, X must treat the sole as the item if the sole meets the requirements under this section and § 1.199-3.

Example (2). The facts are the same as in Example 1 except that X also buys some finished shoes from unrelated parties and resells them to retail shoe stores. X sells shoes in individual pairs. X ships the shoes in boxes, each box containing 50 pairs of shoes, some of which X manufactured, and some of which X purchased. X cannot treat a box of 50 pairs of shoes as an item, because the box of shoes is not sold at retail.

Example (3). Y manufactures toy cars in the United States. Y also purchases cars that were manufactured by unrelated parties. In addition to packaging some cars individually, Y also packages some cars in sets of three. Some of the cars in the sets may have been manufactured by Y and some may have been purchased. The three-car packages are sold by toy stores at retail. Y must treat each three-car package as the item. However, if the three-car package does not meet the requirements under this section and § 1.199-3, Y must treat a toy car in the three-car package as the item, provided the toy car meets the requirements under this section and § 1.199-3.

Example (4). The facts are the same as Example 3 except that the toy store follows Y's recommended pricing arrangement for the individual toy cars for sale to customers at three for $10. Frequently, this results in retail customers purchasing three individual cars in one transaction. Y must treat each toy car as an item and cannot treat three individual toy cars as one item, because the individual toy cars are not packaged together for retail sale.

Example (5). Z produces in bulk form in the United States the active ingredient for a pharmaceutical product. Z sells the active ingredient in bulk form to FX, a foreign corporation. This sale qualifies as DPGR assuming all the other requirements of this section and § 1.199-3 are met. FX uses the active ingredient to produce the finished dosage form drug. FX sells the drug in finished dosage to Z, which sells the drug to customers. Under paragraph (c)(2)(i) of this section, if the finished dosage does not meet the requirements under this section and § 1.199-3, Z must treat the active ingredient portion as the item if the ingredient meets the requirements under this section and § 1.199-3.

(d) Allocation of gross receipts. *(1) In general.* A taxpayer must determine the portion of its gross receipts that is DPGR and the portion of its gross receipts that is non-DPGR. Applicable Federal income tax principles apply to determine whether a transaction is, in substance, a lease, rental, license, sale, exchange or other disposition, or whether it is a service (or some combination thereof). For example, if a taxpayer leases, rents, licenses, sells, exchanges, or otherwise disposes of qualifying production property (QPP) (as defined in § 1.199-3(i)(1)), the gross receipts of which constitute DPGR, and engages in transactions with respect to similar property, the gross receipts of which do not constitute DPGR, the taxpayer must allocate its gross receipts from all the transactions based on a reasonable method that is satisfactory to the Secretary based on all of the facts and circumstances and that accurately identifies the gross receipts that constitute DPGR. Factors taken into consideration in determining whether the method is reasonable include whether the taxpayer uses the most accurate information available; the relationship between the gross receipts and the method chosen; the accuracy of the method chosen as compared with other possible methods; whether the method is used by the taxpayer for internal management or other business purposes; whether the method is used for other Federal or state income tax purposes; the time, burden, and cost of using various methods; and whether the taxpayer applies the method consistently from year to year. Thus, if a taxpayer can, without undue burden or expense, specifically identify where an item was manufactured, or if the taxpayer uses a specific identification method for other purposes, then the taxpayer must use that specific identification method to determine DPGR. If a taxpayer does not use a specific identification method for other purposes and cannot, without undue burden or expense, use a specific identification method, then the taxpayer is not required to use a specific identification method to determine DPGR.

(2) De minimis rule. All of a taxpayer's gross receipts may be treated as DPGR if less than 5 percent of the taxpayer's total gross receipts are non-DPGR (after application of exceptions provided in § 1.199-3(h)(4), (k)(4)(iv), (l)(1)(ii), (m)(4), and (n)(1) that result in gross receipts being treated as DPGR). If the amount of the taxpayer's gross receipts that do not qualify as DPGR equals or exceeds 5 percent of the taxpayer's total gross receipts, the taxpayer is required to allocate all gross receipts between DPGR and non-DPGR in accordance with paragraph (d)(1) of this section. If a corporation is a member of an EAG or a consolidated group, the determination of whether less than 5 percent of the taxpayer's total gross receipts are non-DPGR is made at the corporation level rather than at the EAG or consolidated group level, as applicable. In the case of an S corporation, partnership, estate or trust, or other pass-thru entity, the determination of whether less than 5 percent of the pass-thru entity's total gross receipts are non-DPGR is made at the pass-thru entity level. In the case of an owner of a pass-thru entity, the determination of whether less than 5 percent of the owner's total gross receipts are non-DPGR is made at the owner level, taking into account all gross receipts earned by the owner from its activities as well as the owner's share of any pass-thru entity's gross receipts.

(3) Examples. The following examples illustrate the application of this paragraph (d):

Example (1). X derives its gross receipts from the sale of gasoline refined by X within the United States and the sale of refined gasoline that X acquired (either by purchase or in a taxable exchange for gasoline refined by X in the United States) from an unrelated party. X does not commingle the gasoline. X must allocate its gross receipts between the gross receipts attributable to the gasoline refined by X in the United States (that qualify as DPGR if all the other requirements of § 1.199-3 are met) and X's gross receipts derived from the resale of the acquired gasoline (that do not qualify as DPGR) if 5 percent or more of X's total gross receipts are not from the sale of gasoline refined by X within the United States.

Example (2). X manufactures the same type of QPP at facilities within the United States and outside the United States which are sold separately. X must allocate its gross receipts between the receipts from the QPP manufactured within the United States and receipts from the QPP not manufactured within the United States if 5 percent or more of X's total gross receipts are not from the sale of QPP manufactured by X within the United States.

(e) Timing rules for determining QPAI. *(1) Gross receipts and costs recognized in different taxable years.* If a taxpayer recognizes and reports on a Federal income tax return gross receipts that the taxpayer identifies as DPGR, then the taxpayer must treat the CGS and deductions related to such receipts as relating to DPGR, regardless of whether such receipts ultimately qualify as DPGR. Similarly, if a taxpayer pays or incurs and reports on a Federal income tax return CGS or deductions and identifies such CGS or deductions as relating to DPGR, then the taxpayer must treat the gross receipts related to such CGS or deductions as DPGR, regardless of whether such receipts ultimately qualify as DPGR. Similar rules apply if the taxpayer recognizes and reports on a Federal income tax return gross receipts that the taxpayer identifies as non-DPGR, or pays or incurs and reports on a Federal income tax return CGS or deductions that the taxpayer identifies as relating to non-DPGR. The determination of whether gross receipts qualify as DPGR or non-DPGR, and whether CGS or deductions relate to DPGR or non-DPGR, must be made in accordance with the rules provided in §§ 1.199-1 through 1.199-8, as applicable. If the gross receipts are recognized in an intercompany transaction within the meaning of § 1.1502-13, see also § 1.199-7(d). See § 1.199-4 for allocation and apportionment of CGS and deductions.

(2) Percentage of completion method. A taxpayer using the percentage of completion method under section 460 must determine the ratio of DPGR and non-DPGR using a reasonable method that accurately identifies the gross receipts that constitute DPGR. See paragraph (d)(1) of this section for the factors taken into consideration in determining whether the taxpayer's method is reasonable.

(3) Example. The following example illustrates the application of paragraph (e)(1) of this section:

Example. X, a calendar year accrual method taxpayer, enters into a contract with Y, an unrelated person, in 2005 for the sale of QPP. In 2005, X receives an advance payment from Y for the QPP. In 2006, X manufactures the QPP within the United States and delivers the QPP to Y. X's method of accounting requires X to include the entire advance payment in its gross income for Federal income tax purposes in 2005. Assuming X can determine, using any reasonable method, that all the requirements of this section and § 1.199-3 will be met, the advance payment qualifies as DPGR in 2005. The CGS and deductions relating to the QPP under the contract are taken into account under § 1.199-4 in determining X's QPAI in 2006, the taxable year the CGS and deductions are otherwise deductible for Federal income tax purposes and must be treated as relating to DPGR in that taxable year.

§ 1.199-2 Wage limitation.

Caution: The Treasury has not yet amended Reg § 1.199-2 to reflect changes made by P.L. 110-343.

(a) Rules of application. *(1) In general.* The provisions of this section apply solely for purposes of section 199 of the Internal Revenue Code. The amount of the deduction allowable under § 1.199-1(a) (section 199 deduction) to a taxpayer for any taxable year shall not exceed 50 percent of the W-2 wages (as defined in paragraph (e) of this section) of the taxpayer. For this purpose, except as provided in paragraph (a)(3) of this section and paragraph (b) of this section, the Forms W-2, "Wage and Tax Statement," used in determining the amount of W-2 wages are those issued for the calendar year ending during the taxpayer's taxable year for wages paid to employees (or former employees) of the taxpayer for employment by the taxpayer. For purposes of this section, employees of the taxpayer are limited to employees of the taxpayer as defined in section 3121(d)(1) and (2) (that is, officers of a corporate taxpayer and employees of the taxpayer under the common law rules). See paragraph (a)(3) of this section for the requirement that W-2 wages must have been included in a return filed with the Social Security Administration (SSA) within 60 days after the due date (including extensions) of the return.

(2) Wages paid by entity other than common law employer. In determining W-2 wages, a taxpayer may take into account any wages paid by another entity and reported by the other entity on Forms W-2 with the other entity as the employer listed in Box c of the Forms W-2, provided that the wages were paid to employees of the taxpayer for employment by the taxpayer. If the taxpayer is treated as an employer described in section 3401(d)(1) because of control of the payment of wages (that is, the taxpayer is not the common law employer of the payee of the wages), the payment of wages may not be included in determining W-2 wages of the taxpayer. If the taxpayer is paying wages as an agent of another entity to individuals who are not employees of the taxpayer, the wages may not be included in determining the W-2 wages of the taxpayer.

(3) Requirement that wages must be reported on return filed with the Social Security Administration. (i) In general. The term W-2 wages shall not include any amount that is not properly included in a return filed with SSA on or before the 60th day after the due date (including extensions) for such return. Under § 31.6051-2 of this chapter, each Form W-2 and the transmittal Form W-3, "Transmittal of Wage and Tax Statements," together constitute an information return to be filed with SSA. Similarly, each Form W-2c, "Corrected Wage and Tax Statement," and the transmittal Form W-3 or W-3c, "Transmittal of Corrected Wage and Tax Statements," together constitute an information return to be filed with SSA. In determining whether any amount has been properly included in a return filed with SSA on or before the 60th day after the due date (including extensions) for such return, each Form W-2 together with its accompanying Form W-3 shall be considered a separate information return and each Form W-2c together with its accompanying Form W-3 or Form W-3c shall be considered a separate information return. Section 31.6071(a)-1(a)(3) of this chapter provides that each information return in respect of wages as

defined in the Federal Insurance Contributions Act or of income tax withheld from wages which is required to be made under § 31.6051-2 of this chapter shall be filed on or before the last day of February (March 31 if filed electronically) of the year following the calendar year for which it is made, except that if a tax return under § 31.6011(a)-5(a) of this chapter is filed as a final return for a period ending prior to December 31, the information statement shall be filed on or before the last day of the second calendar month following the period for which the tax return is filed. Corrected Forms W-2 are required to be filed with SSA on or before the last day of February (March 31 if filed electronically) of the year following the year in which the correction is made, except that if a tax return under § 31.6011(a)-5(a) is filed as a final return for a period ending prior to December 31 for the period in which the correction is made, the corrected Forms W-2 are required to be filed by the last day of the second calendar month following the period for which the final return is filed.

(ii) Corrected return filed to correct a return that was filed within 60 days of the due date. If a corrected information return (Return B) is filed with SSA on or before the 60th day after the due date (including extensions) of Return B to correct an information return (Return A) that was filed with SSA on or before the 60th day after the due date (including extensions) of the information return (Return A) and paragraph (a)(3)(iii) of this section does not apply, then the wage information on Return B must be included in determining W-2 wages. If a corrected information return (Return D) is filed with SSA later than the 60th day after the due date (including extensions) of Return D to correct an information return (Return C) that was filed with SSA on or before the 60th day after the due date (including extensions) of the information return (Return C), then if Return D reports an increase (or increases) in wages included in determining W-2 wages from the wage amounts reported on Return C, then such increase (or increases) on Return D shall be disregarded in determining W-2 wages (and only the wage amounts on Return C may be included in determining W-2 wages). If Return D reports a decrease (or decreases) in wages included in determining W-2 wages from the amounts reported on Return C, then, in determining W-2 wages, the wages reported on Return C must be reduced by the decrease (or decreases) reflected on Return D.

(iii) Corrected return filed to correct a return that was filed later than 60 days after the due date. If an information return (Return F) is filed to correct an information return (Return E) that was not filed with SSA on or before the 60th day after the due date (including extensions) of Return E, then Return F (and any subsequent information returns filed with respect to Return E) will not be considered filed on or before the 60th day after the due date (including extensions) of Return F (or the subsequent corrected information return). Thus, if a Form W-2c (or corrected Form W-2) is filed to correct a Form W-2 that was not filed with SSA on or before the 60th day after the due date (including extensions) of the information return including the Form W-2 (or to correct a Form W-2c relating to a information return including a Form W-2 that had not been filed with SSA on or before the 60th day after the due date (including extensions) of the information return including the Form W-2), then the information return including this Form W-2c (or corrected Form W-2) shall not be considered to have been filed with SSA on or before the 60th day after the due date (including extensions) for this information return including the Form W-2c (or corrected Form W-2), regardless of when the information return including the Form W-2c (or corrected Form W-2) is filed.

(4) Joint return. An individual and his or her spouse are considered one taxpayer for purposes of determining the amount of W-2 wages for a taxable year, provided that they file a joint return for the taxable year. Thus, an individual filing as part of a joint return may include the wages of employees of his or her spouse in determining W-2 wages, provided the employees are employed in a trade or business of the spouse and the other requirements of this section are met. However, a married taxpayer filing a separate return from his or her spouse for the taxable year may not include the wages of employees of the taxpayer's spouse in determining the taxpayer's W-2 wages for the taxable year.

(b) Application in the case of a taxpayer with a short taxable year. In the case of a taxpayer with a short taxable year, subject to the rules of paragraph (a) of this section, the W-2 wages of the taxpayer for the short taxable year shall include only those wages paid during the short taxable year to employees of the taxpayer, only those elective deferrals (within the meaning of section 402(g)(3)) made during the short taxable year by employees of the taxpayer and only compensation actually deferred under section 457 during the short taxable year with respect to employees of the taxpayer. The Secretary shall have the authority to issue published guidance setting forth the method that is used to calculate W-2 wages in case of a taxpayer with a short taxable year. See paragraph (e)(3) of this section.

(c) Acquisition or disposition of a trade or business (or major portion). If a taxpayer (a successor) acquires a trade or business, the major portion of a trade or business, or the major portion of a separate unit of a trade or business from another taxpayer (a predecessor), then, for purposes of computing the respective section 199 deduction of the successor and of the predecessor, the W-2 wages paid for that calendar year shall be allocated between the successor and the predecessor based on whether the wages are for employment by the successor or for employment by the predecessor. Thus, in this situation, the W-2 wages are allocated based on whether the wages are for employment for a period during which the employee was employed by the predecessor or for employment for a period during which the employee was employed by the successor, regardless of which permissible method for Form W-2 reporting is used.

(d) Non-duplication rule. Amounts that are treated as W-2 wages for a taxable year under any method shall not be treated as W-2 wages of any other taxable year. Also, an amount shall not be treated as W-2 wages by more than one taxpayer.

(e) Definition of W-2 wages. *(1) In general.* Under section 199(b)(2), the term W-2 wages means, with respect to any person for any taxable year of such person, the sum of the amounts described in section 6051(a)(3) and (8) paid by such person with respect to employment of employees by such person during the calendar year ending during such taxable year. Thus, the term W-2 wages includes the total amount of wages as defined in section 3401(a); the total amount of elective deferrals (within the meaning of section 402(g)(3)); the compensation deferred under section 457; and for taxable years beginning after December 31, 2005, the amount of designated Roth contributions (as defined in section 402A).

(2) Limitation on W-2 wages for taxable years beginning after May 17, 2006, the enactment date of the Tax Increase Prevention and Reconciliation Act of 2005 (i) In general.

The term W-2 wages includes only amounts described in paragraph (e)(1) of this section (paragraph (e)(1) wages) that are properly allocable to domestic production gross receipts (DPGR) (as defined in § 1.199-3) for purposes of section 199(c)(1). A taxpayer may determine the amount of paragraph (e)(1) wages that is properly allocable to DPGR using any reasonable method that is satisfactory to the Secretary based on all of the facts and circumstances.

(ii) Wage expense safe harbor. (A) In general. A taxpayer using either the section 861 method of cost allocation under § 1.199-4(d) or the simplified deduction method under § 1.199-4(e) may determine the amount of paragraph (e)(1) wages that is properly allocable to DPGR for a taxable year by multiplying the amount of paragraph (e)(1) wages for the taxable year by the ratio of the taxpayer's wage expense included in calculating qualified production activities income (QPAI) (as defined in § 1.199-1(c)) for the taxable year to the taxpayer's total wage expense used in calculating the taxpayer's taxable income (or adjusted gross income, if applicable) for the taxable year, without regard to any wage expense disallowed by section 465, 469, 704(d), or 1366(d). A taxpayer that uses the section 861 method of cost allocation under § 1.199-4(d) or the simplified deduction method under § 1.199-4(e) to determine QPAI must use the same expense allocation and apportionment methods that it uses to determine QPAI to allocate and apportion wage expense for purposes of this safe harbor. For purposes of this paragraph (e)(2)(ii), the term wage expense means wages (that is, compensation paid by the employer in the active conduct of a trade or business to its employees) that are properly taken into account under the taxpayer's method of accounting.

(B) Wage expense included in cost of goods sold. For purposes of paragraph (e)(2)(ii)(A) of this section, a taxpayer may determine its wage expense included in cost of goods sold (CGS) using any reasonable method that is satisfactory to the Secretary based on all of the facts and circumstances, such as using the amount of direct labor included in CGS or using section 263A labor costs (as defined in § 1.263A-1(h)(4)(ii)) included in CGS.

(iii) Small business simplified overall method safe harbor. A taxpayer that uses the small business simplified overall method under § 1.199-4(f) may use the small business simplified overall method safe harbor for determining the amount of paragraph (e)(1) wages that is properly allocable to DPGR. Under this safe harbor, the amount of paragraph (e)(1) wages that is properly allocable to DPGR is equal to the same proportion of paragraph (e)(1) wages that the amount of DPGR bears to the taxpayer's total gross receipts.

(iv) Examples. The following examples illustrate the application of this paragraph (e)(2). See § 1.199-5(e)(4) for an example of the application of paragraph (e)(2)(ii) of this section to a trust or estate. The examples read as follows:

Example (1). Section 861 method and no EAG. (i) Facts. X, a United States corporation that is not a member of an expanded affiliated group (EAG) (as defined in § 1.199-7) or an affiliated group as defined in the regulations under section 861, engages in activities that generate both DPGR and non-DPGR. X's taxable year ends on April 30, 2011. For X's taxable year ending April 30, 2011, X has $3,000 of paragraph (e)(1) wages reported on 2010 Forms W-2. All of X's production activities that generate DPGR are within Standard Industrial Classification (SIC) Industry Group AAA (SIC AAA). All of X's production activities that generate non-DPGR are within SIC Industry Group BBB (SIC BBB). X is able to specifically identify CGS allocable to DPGR and to non-DPGR. X incurs $900 of research and experimentation expenses (R&E) that are deductible under section 174, $300 of which are performed with respect to SIC AAA and $600 of which are performed with respect to SIC BBB. None of the R&E is legally mandated R&E as described in § 1.861-17(a)(4) and none of the R&E is included in CGS. X incurs section 162 selling expenses that are not includible in CGS and are definitely related to all of X's gross income. For X's taxable year ending April 30, 2011, the adjusted basis of X's assets is $50,000, $40,000 of which generate gross income attributable to DPGR and $10,000 of which generate gross income attributable to non-DPGR. For X's taxable year ending April 30, 2011, the total square footage of X's headquarters is 8,000 square feet, of which 2,000 square feet is set aside for domestic production activities. For its taxable year ending April 30, 2011, X's taxable income is $1,380 based on the following Federal income tax items:

DPGR (all from sales of products within SIC AAA)	$3,000
Non-DPGR (all from sales of products within SIC BBB)	3,000
CGS allocable to DPGR (includes $200 of wage expense)	(600)
CGS allocable to non-DPGR (includes $600 of wage expense)	(1,800)
Section 162 selling expenses (includes $600 of wage expense)	(840)
Section 174 R&E-SIC AAA (includes $100 of wage expense)	(300)
Section 174 R&E-SIC BBB (includes $200 of wage expense)	(600)
Interest expense (not included in CGS)	(300)
Headquarters overhead expense (includes $100 of wage expense)	(180)
X's taxable income	1,380

(ii) X's QPAI. X allocates and apportions its deductions to gross income attributable to DPGR under the section 861 method in § 1.199-4(d). In this case, the section 162 selling expenses and overhead expense are definitely related to all of X's gross income. Based on the facts and circumstances of this specific case, apportionment of the section 162 selling expenses between DPGR and non-DPGR on the basis of X's gross receipts is appropriate. In addition, based on the facts and circumstances of this specific case, apportionment of the headquarters overhead expense between DPGR and non-DPGR on the basis of the square footage of X's headquarters is appropriate. For purposes of apportioning R&E, X elects to use the sales method as described in § 1.861-17(c). X elects to apportion interest expense under the tax book value method of § 1.861-9T(g). X has $2,400 of gross income attributable to DPGR (DPGR of $3,000 - CGS of $600 allocated based on X's books and records). X's QPAI for its taxable year ending April 30, 2011, is $1,395, as shown in the following table:

DPGR (all from sales of products within SIC AAA)	$3,000
CGS allocable to DPGR	(600)
Section 162 selling expenses ($840 x ($3,000 DPGR/$6,000 total gross receipts))	(420)
Section 174 R&E-SIC AAA	(300)
Interest expense (not included in CGS) ($300 x ($40,000 (X's DPGR assets)/$50,000 (X's total assets)))	(240)
Headquarters overhead expense ($180 x (2,000 square feet attributable to DPGR activity/total 8,000 square feet))	(45)

X's QPAI	1,395

(iii) W-2 wages. X chooses to use the wage expense safe harbor under paragraph (e)(2)(ii) of this section to determine its W-2 wages, as shown in the following steps:

(A) Step one. X determines that $625 of wage expense were taken into account in determining its QPAI in paragraph (ii) of this Example 1, as shown in the following table:

CGS wage expense	$200
Section 162 selling expenses wage expense ($600 x ($3,000 DPGR/$6,000 total gross receipts))	300
Section 174 R&E-SIC AAA wage expense	100
Headquarters overhead wage expense ($100 x (2,000 square feet attributable to DPGR activity/ 8,000 total square feet))	25
Total wage expense taken into account	625

(B) Step two. X determines that $1,042 of the $3,000 in paragraph (e)(1) wages are properly allocable to DPGR, and are therefore W-2 wages, as shown in the following calculation:

$$\frac{\text{Step one wage expense}}{\text{X's total wage expense for taxable year ending April 30, 2011}} \times \text{X's paragraph (e)(1) wages}$$

$$\frac{\$625}{\$1,800} \times \$3,000 = \$1,042$$

(iv) Section 199 deduction determination. X's tentative deduction under § 1.199-1(a) (section 199 deduction) is $124 (.09 × (lesser of QPAI of $1,395 or taxable income of $1,380)) subject to the wage limitation under section 199(b)(1) (W-2 wage limitation) of $521 (50% × $1,042). Accordingly, X's section 199 deduction for its taxable year ending April 30, 2011, is $124.

Example (2). Section 861 method and EAG. (i) Facts. The facts are the same as in Example 1 except that X owns stock in Y, a United States corporation, equal to 75% of the total voting power of the stock of Y and 80% of the total value of the stock of Y. X and Y are not members of an affiliated group as defined in section 1504(a). Accordingly, the rules of § 1.861-14T do not apply to X's and Y's selling expenses, R&E, and charitable contributions. X and Y are, however, members of an affiliated group for purposes of allocating and apportioning interest expense (see § 1.861-11T(d)(6)) and are also members of an EAG. Y's taxable year ends April 30, 2011. For Y's taxable year ending April 30, 2011, Y has $2,000 of paragraph (e)(1) wages reported on 2010 Forms W-2. For Y's taxable year ending April 30, 2011, the adjusted basis of Y's assets is $50,000, $20,000 of which generate gross income attributable to DPGR and $30,000 of which generate gross income attributable to non-DPGR. All of Y's activities that generate DPGR are within SIC Industry Group AAA (SIC AAA). All of Y's activities that generate non-DPGR are within SIC Industry Group BBB (SIC BBB). None of X's and Y's sales are to each other. Y is not able to specifically identify CGS allocable to DPGR and non-DPGR. In this case, because CGS is definitely related under the facts and circumstances to all of Y's gross receipts, apportionment of CGS between DPGR and non-DPGR based on gross receipts is appropriate. For Y's taxable year ending April 30, 2011, the total square footage of Y's headquarters is 8,000 square feet, of which 2,000 square feet is set aside for domestic production activities. Y incurs section 162 selling expenses that are not includible in CGS and are definitely related to all of Y's gross income. For Y's taxable year ending April 30, 2011, Y's taxable income is $1,710 based on the following Federal income tax items:

DPGR (all from sales of products within SIC AAA)	$3,000
Non-DPGR (all from sales of products within SIC BBB)	3,000
CGS allocated to DPGR (includes $300 of wage expense)	(1,200)
CGS allocated to non-DPGR (includes $300 of wage expense)	(1,200)
Section 162 selling expenses (includes $300 of wage expense)	(840)
Section 174 R&E-SIC AAA (includes $20 of wage expense)	(100)
Section 174 R&E-SIC BBB (includes $60 of wage expense)	(200)
Interest expense (not included in CGS and not subject to § 1.861-10T)	(500)
Charitable contributions	(50)
Headquarters overhead expense (includes $40 of wage expense)	(200)
Y's taxable income	1,710

(ii) QPAI. (A) X's QPAI. Determination of X's QPAI is the same as in Example 1 except that interest is apportioned to gross income attributable to DPGR based on the combined adjusted bases of X's and Y's assets. See § 1.861-11T(c). Accordingly, X's QPAI for its taxable year ending April 30, 2011, is $1,455, as shown in the following table:

DPGR (all from sales of products within SIC AAA)	$3,000
CGS allocated to DPGR	(600)
Section 162 selling expenses ($840 x ($3,000 DPGR/$6,000 total gross receipts))	(420)
Section 174 R&E-SIC AAA	(300)
Interest expense (not included in CGS and not subject to § 1.861-10T)($300 x ($60,000 (tax book value of X's and Y's DPGR assets)/$100,000 (tax book value of X's and Y's total assets)))	(180)
Headquarters overhead expense ($180 x (2,000 square feet attributable to DPGR activity/total 8,000 square feet))	(45)
X's QPAI	1,455

(B) Y's QPAI. Y makes the same elections under the section 861 method as does X. Y has $1,800 of gross income attributable to DPGR (DPGR of $3,000 - CGS of

$1,200 allocated based on Y's gross receipts). Y's QPAI for its taxable year ending April 30, 2011, is $905, as shown in the following table:

DPGR (all from sales of products within SIC AAA)	$3,000
CGS allocated to DPGR	(1,200)
Section 162 selling expenses ($840 x ($3,000 DPGR/$6,000 total gross receipts))	(420)
Section 174 R&E-SIC AAA	(100)
Interest expense (not included in CGS and not subject to § 1.861-10T) ($500 x ($60,000 (tax book value of X's and Y's DPGR assets)/$100,000 (tax book value of X's and Y's total assets)))	(300)
Charitable contributions (not included in CGS) ($50 x ($1,800 gross income attributable to DPGR/$3,600 total gross income))	(25)
Headquarters overhead expense ($200 x (2,000 square feet attributable to DPGR activity/total 8,000 square feet))	(50)
Y's QPAI	905

(iii) W-2 wages. (A) X's W-2 wages. X's W-2 wages are $1,042, the same as in Example 1.

(B) Y's W-2 wages. Y chooses to use the wage expense safe harbor under paragraph (e)(2)(ii) of this section to determine its W-2 wages, as shown in the following steps: (1) Step one. Y determines that $480 of wage expense were taken into account in determining its QPAI in paragraph (ii)(B) of this Example 2, as shown in the following table:

CGS wage expense	$300
Section 162 selling expenses wage expense ($300 x ($3,000 DPGR/$6,000 total gross receipts))	150
Section 174 R&E-SIC AAA wage expense	20
Headquarters overhead wage expense ($40 x (2,000 square feet attributable to DPGR activity/ 8,000 total square feet))	10
Total wage expense taken into account	480

(2) Step two. Y determines that $941 of the $2,000 paragraph (e)(1) wages are properly allocable to DPGR, and are therefore W-2 wages, as shown in the following calculation:

$$\frac{\text{Step one wage expense}}{\text{Y's total wage expense for taxable year ending April 30, 2011}} \times \text{Y's paragraph (e)(1) wages}$$

$$\frac{\$480}{\$1{,}020} \times \$2{,}000 = \$941$$

(iv) Section 199 deduction determination. The section 199 deduction of the X and Y EAG is determined by aggregating the separately determined taxable income, QPAI, and W-2 wages of X and Y. See § 1.199-7(b). Accordingly, the X and Y EAG's tentative section 199 deduction is $212 (.09 x (lesser of combined QPAI of X and Y of $2,360 (X's QPAI of $1,455 plus Y's QPAI of $905) or combined taxable incomes of X and Y of $3,090 (X's taxable income of $1,380 plus Y's taxable income of $1,710)) subject to the combined W-2 wage limitation of X and Y of $992 (50% x ($1,042 (X's W-2 wages) + $941 (Y's W-2 wages)))). Accordingly, the X and Y EAG's section 199 deduction is $212. The $212 is allocated to X and Y in proportion to their QPAI. See § 1.199-7(c).

Example (3). Simplified deduction method. (i) Facts. Z, a corporation that is not a member of an EAG, engages in activities that generate both DPGR and non-DPGR. Z is able to specifically identify CGS allocable to DPGR and to non-DPGR. Z's taxable year ends on April 30, 2011. For Z's taxable year ending April 30, 2011, Z has $3,000 of paragraph (e)(1) wages reported on 2010 Forms W-2, and Z's taxable income is $1,380 based on the following Federal income tax items:

DPGR	$3,000
Non-DPGR	3,000
CGS allocable to DPGR (includes $200 of wage expense)	(600)
CGS allocable to non-DPGR (includes $600 of wage expense)	(1,800)
Expenses, losses, or deductions (deductions) (includes $1,000 of wage expense)	(2,220)
Z's taxable income	1,380

(ii) Z's QPAI. Z uses the simplified deduction method under § 1.199-4(e) to apportion deductions between DPGR and non-DPGR. Z's QPAI for its taxable year ending April 30, 2011, is $1,290, as shown in the following table:

DPGR	$3,000
CGS allocable to DPGR	(600)
Deductions apportioned to DPGR ($2,220 x ($3,000 DPGR/$6,000 total gross receipts))	(1,110)
Z's QPAI	1,290

(iii) W-2 wages. Z chooses to use the wage expense safe harbor under paragraph (e)(2)(ii) of this section to determine its W-2 wages, as shown in the following steps: (A) Step one. Z determines that $700 of wage expense were taken into account in determining its QPAI in paragraph (ii) of this Example 3, as shown in the following table:

Wage expense included in CGS allocable to DPGR	$200
Wage expense included in deductions ($1,000 in wage expense x ($3,000 DPGR/$6,000 total gross receipts))	500
Wage expense allocable to DPGR	700

(B) Step two. Z determines that $1,167 of the $3,000 paragraph (e)(1) wages are properly allocable to DPGR, and are therefore W-2 wages, as shown in the following calculation:

$$\frac{\text{Step one wage expense}}{\text{Z's total wage expense for taxable year ending April 30, 2011}} \times \text{Z's paragraph (e)(1) wages}$$

$$\frac{\$700}{\$1{,}800} \times \$3{,}000 = \$1{,}167$$

(iv) Section 199 deduction determination. Z's tentative section 199 deduction is $116 (.09 x (lesser of QPAI of $1,290 or taxable income of $1,380)) subject to the W-2 wage limitation of $584 (50% x $1,167). Accordingly, Z's section 199 deduction for its taxable year ending April 30, 2011, is $116.

Example (4). Small business simplified overall method. (i) Facts. Z, a corporation that is not a member of an EAG, engages in activities that generate both DPGR and non-DPGR. Z's taxable year ends on April 30, 2011. For Z's taxable year ending April 30, 2011, Z has $3,000 of paragraph (e)(1) wages reported on 2010 Forms W-2, and Z's taxable income is $1,380 based on the following Federal income tax items:

DPGR	$3,000
Non-DPGR	3,000
CGS and deductions	(4,620)
Z's taxable income	1,380

(ii) Z's QPAI. Z uses the small business simplified overall method under § 1.199-4(f) to apportion CGS and deductions between DPGR and non-DPGR. Z's QPAI for its taxable year ending April 30, 2011, is $690, as shown in the following table:

DPGR	$3,000
CGS and deductions apportioned to DPGR ($4,620 x ($3,000 DPGR/$6,000 total gross receipts))	(2,310)
Z's QPAI	690

(iii) W-2 wages. Z's W-2 wages under paragraph (e)(2)(iii) of this section are $1,500, as shown in the following calculation:

$3,000 in paragraph (e)(1) wages x ($3,000 DPGR/$6,000 total gross receipts)	$1,500

(iv) Section 199 deduction determination. Z's tentative section 199 deduction is $62 (.09 x (lesser of QPAI of $690 or taxable income of $1,380)) subject to the W-2 wage limitation of $750 (50% x $1,500). Accordingly, Z's section 199 deduction for its taxable year ending April 30, 2011, is $62.

Example (5). Corporation uses employees of non-consolidated EAG member. (i) Facts. Corporations S and B are the only members of a single EAG but are not members of a consolidated group. S and B are both calendar year taxpayers. All the activities described in this Example 5 take place during the same taxable year and they are the only activities of S and B. S and B each use the section 861 method described in § 1.199-4(d) for allocating and apportioning their deductions. B is a manufacturer but has only three employees of its own. S employs the remainder of the personnel who perform the manufacturing activities for B. S's only receipts are from supplying employees to B. In 2010, B manufactures qualifying production property (QPP) (as defined in § 1.199-3(j)(1)), using its three employees and S's employees, and sells the QPP for $10,000,000. B's total CGS and other deductions are $6,000,000, including $1,000,000 paid to S for the use of S's employees and $100,000 paid to its own employees. B reports the $100,000 paid to its employees on the 2010 Forms W-2 issued to its employees. S pays its employees $800,000 that is reported on the 2010 Forms W-2 issued to the employees.

(ii) B's W-2 wages. In determining its W-2 wages, B utilizes the wage expense safe harbor described in paragraph (e)(2)(ii) of this section. The entire $100,000 paid by B to its employees is included in B's wage expense included in calculating its QPAI and is the only wage expense used in calculating B's taxable income. Thus, under the wage expense safe harbor described in paragraph (e)(2)(ii) of this section, B's W-2 wages are $100,000 ($100,000 (paragraph (e)(1) wages) x ($100,000 (wage expense used in calculating B's QPAI)/$100,000 (wage expense used in calculating B's taxable income))).

(iii) S's W-2 wages. In determining its W-2 wages, S utilizes the wage expense safe harbor described in paragraph (e)(2)(ii) of this section. Because S's $1,000,000 in receipts from B do not qualify as DPGR and are S's only gross receipts, none of the $800,000 paid by S to its employees is included in S's wage expense included in calculating its QPAI. However, the entire $800,000 is included in calculating S's taxable income. Thus, under the wage expense safe harbor described in paragraph (e)(2)(ii)(A) of this section, S's W-2 wages are $0 ($800,000 (paragraph (e)(1) wages) x ($0 (wage expense used in calculating S's QPAI)/$800,000 (wage expense used in calculating S's taxable income))).

(iv) Determination of EAG's section 199 deduction. The section 199 deduction of the S and B EAG is determined by aggregating the separately determined taxable income or loss, QPAI, and W-2 wages of S and B. See § 1.199-7(b). B's taxable income and QPAI are each $4,000,000 ($10,000,000 DPGR - $6,000,000 CGS and other deductions). S's taxable income is $200,000 ($1,000,000 gross receipts - $800,000 total deductions). S's QPAI is $0 ($0 DPGR - $0 CGS and other deductions). B's W-2 wages (as calculated in paragraph (ii) of this Example 5) are $100,000 and S's W-2 wages (as calculated in paragraph (iii) of this Example 5) are $0. The EAG's tentative section 199 deduction is $360,000 (.09 x (lesser of combined QPAI of $4,000,000 (B's QPAI of $4,000,000 + S's QPAI of $0) or combined taxable income of $4,200,000 (B's taxable income of $4,000,000 + S's taxable income of $200,000))) subject to the W-2 wage limitation of $50,000 (50% x ($100,000 (B's W-2 wages) + $0 (S's W-2 wages))). Accordingly, the S and B EAG's section 199 deduction for 2010 is $50,000. The $50,000 is allocated to S and B in proportion to their QPAI. See § 1.199-7(c). Because S has no QPAI, the entire $50,000 is allocated to B.

Example (6). Corporation using employees of consolidated EAG member. The facts are the same as in Example 5 except that B and S are members of the same consolidated group. Ordinarily, as demonstrated in Example 5, S's $1,000,000 of receipts would not be DPGR and its $800,000 paid to its employees would not be W-2 wages (because the $800,000 would not be properly allocable to DPGR). However, because S and B are members of the same consolidated group, § 1.1502-13(c)(1)(i) provides that the separate entity attributes of S's intercompany items or B's corresponding items, or both, may be redetermined in order to produce the same effect as if S and B were divisions of a single corporation. If S and B were divisions of a single corporation, S and B would have QPAI and taxable income of $4,200,000 ($10,000,000 DPGR received from the sale of the QPP - $5,800,000 CGS and other deductions) and, under the wage expense safe harbor described in paragraph (e)(2)(ii) of this section, would have $900,000 of W-2 wages ($900,000 (combined paragraph (e)(1) wages of S and B) x ($900,000 (wage expense used in calculating QPAI)/$900,000 (wage expense used in calculating taxable income))). The single corporation would have a tentative section 199 deduction equal to 9% of $4,200,000, or $378,000, subject to the W-2 wage limitation of 50% of $900,000, or $450,000. Thus, the single corporation would have a section 199 deduction of $378,000. To obtain this same result for the consolidated group, S's $1,000,000 of receipts from the intercompany transaction are redetermined as DPGR. Thus, S's $800,000 paid to its employees are costs properly allocable to DPGR and S's W-2 wages are $800,000. Accordingly, the consolidated group has QPAI and taxable income of $4,200,000 ($11,000,000 DPGR (from the sale of the QPP and the redetermined intercompany transaction) - $6,800,000 CGS and other deductions) and W-2 wages of $900,000. The consolidated group's section 199 deduction is $378,000, the same as the single corporation. However, for purposes of allocating the section 199 deduction between S and B, the redetermination of S's income as DPGR under § 1.1502-13(c)(1)(i) is not taken into account. See § 1.199-7(d)(5). Accordingly, the consolidated group's entire section 199 deduction of $378,000 is allocated to B.

(3) Methods for calculating W-2 wages. The Secretary may provide by publication in the Internal Revenue Bulletin (see § 601.601(d)(2)(ii)(b) of this chapter) for methods to be used in calculating W-2 wages, including W-2 wages for short taxable years. For example, see Rev. Proc. 2006-22 (2006-23 I.R.B. 1033). (see § 601.601(d)(2) of this chapter).

T.D. 9263, 5/24/2006, amend T.D. 9293, 10/18/2006, T.D. 9381, 2/14/2008.

Proposed § 1.199-2 Wage limitation. [*For Preamble, see ¶ 152,713*]

(a) Rules of application. *(1) In general.* The amount of the deduction allowable under § 1.199-1(a) (section 199 deduction) to a taxpayer for any taxable year shall not exceed 50 percent of the W-2 wages of the taxpayer. For this purpose, except as provided in paragraph (c) of this section, the Forms W-2, "Wage and Tax Statement," used in determining the amount of W-2 wages are those issued for the calendar year ending during the taxpayer's taxable year for wages paid to employees (or former employees) of the taxpayer for employment by the taxpayer. For purposes of this section, employees of the taxpayer are limited to employees of the taxpayer as defined in section 3121(d)(1) and (2) (that is, officers of a corporate taxpayer and employees of the taxpayer under the common law rules). For purposes of section 199(b)(2) and this section, the term taxpayer means employer.

(2) Wages paid by entity other than common law employer. In determining W-2 wages, a taxpayer may take into account any wages paid by another entity and reported by the other entity on Forms W-2 with the other entity as the employer listed in Box c of the Forms W-2, provided that the wages were paid to employees of the taxpayer for employment by the taxpayer. If the taxpayer is treated as an employer described in section 3401(d)(1) because of control of the payment of wages (that is, the taxpayer is not the common law employer of the payee of the wages), the payment of wages may not be included in determining W-2 wages of the taxpayer. If the taxpayer is paying wages as an agent of another entity to individuals who are not employees of the taxpayer, the wages may not be included in determining the W-2 wages of the taxpayer.

(b) No application in determining whether amounts are wages for employment tax purposes. The discussion of wages in this section is for purposes of section 199 only and has no application in determining whether amounts are wages under section 3121(a) for purposes of the Federal Insurance Contributions Act (FICA), under section 3306(b) for purposes of the Federal Unemployment Tax Act (FUTA), under section 3401(a) for purposes of the Collection of Income Tax at Source on Wages (Federal income tax withholding), or any other wage related determination.

(c) Application in case of taxpayer with short taxable year. In the case of a taxpayer with a short taxable year, subject to the rules of paragraph (a) of this section, the W-2 wages of the taxpayer for the short taxable year shall include those wages paid during the short taxable year to employees of the taxpayer as determined under the tracking wages method described in paragraph (f)(2)(iii) of this section. In applying the tracking wages method in the case of a short taxable year, the taxpayer must apply the method as follows—

(1) In paragraph (f)(2)(iii)(A) of this section, the total amount of wages subject to Federal income tax withholding and reported on Form W-2 must include only those wages subject to Federal income tax withholding that are actually paid to employees during the short taxable year and reported on Form W-2 for the calendar year ending within that short taxable year;

(2) In paragraph (f)(2)(iii)(B) of this section, only the supplemental unemployment benefits paid during the short taxable year that were included in the total in paragraph (f)(2)(iii)(A) of this section as modified by paragraph (c)(1) of this section are required to be deducted; and

(3) In paragraph (f)(2)(iii)(C) of this section, only the portion of the amounts reported in Box 12, Codes D, E, F, G, and S, on Forms W-2, that are actually deferred or contributed during the short taxable year may be included in W-2 wages.

(d) Acquisition or disposition of a trade or business (or major portion). If a taxpayer (a successor) acquires a trade or business, the major portion of a trade or business, or the major portion of a separate unit of a trade or business from another taxpayer (a predecessor), then, for purposes of computing the respective section 199 deduction of the successor and of the predecessor, the W-2 wages paid for that calendar year shall be allocated between the successor and the predecessor based on whether the wages are for employment by the successor or for employment by the predecessor. Thus, in this situation, the W-2 wages are allocated based on whether the wages are for employment for a period during which the employee was employed by the predecessor or for employment for a period during which the employee was employed by the successor, regardless of which permissible method for Form W-2 reporting is used.

(e) Non-duplication rule. Amounts that are treated as W-2 wages for a taxable year under any method may not be treated as W-2 wages of any other taxable year. Also, an amount may not be treated as W-2 wages by more than one taxpayer.

(f) Definition of W-2 wages. *(1) In general.* Section 199(b)(2) defines W-2 wages for purposes of section 199(b)(1) as the sum of the amounts required to be included on statements under section 6051(a)(3) and (8) with respect to employment of employees of the taxpayer for the calendar year. Thus, the term W-2 wages includes the total amount of wages as defined in section 3401(a); the total amount of elective deferrals (within the meaning of section 402(g)(3)); the compensation deferred under section 457; and for taxable years beginning after December 31, 2005, the amount of designated Roth contributions (as defined in section 402A). Under the 2004 and 2005 Form W-2, the elective deferrals under section 402(g)(3) and the amounts deferred under section 457 directly correlate to coded items reported in Box 12 on Form W-2. Box 12, Code D, is for elective deferrals to a section 401(k) cash or deferred arrangement; Box 12, Code E, is for elective deferrals under a section 403(b) salary reduction agreement; Box 12, Code F, is for elective deferrals under a section 408(k)(6) salary reduction Simplified Employee Pension (SEP); Box 12, Code G, is for elective deferrals under a section 457(b) plan; and Box 12, Code S, is for employee salary reduction contributions under a section 408(p) SIMPLE (simple retirement account). *(2) Methods for calculating W-2 wages.* For any taxable year, taxpayers may use one of three methods in calculating W-2 wages. These three methods are subject to the non-duplication rule provided in paragraph (e) of this section, and the tracking wages method is subject to the rule provided in paragraph (c) of this section, if applicable.

(i) Unmodified box method. Under the Unmodified box method, W-2 wages are calculated by taking, without modification, the lesser of—

(A) The total entries in Box 1 of all Forms W-2 filed with the Social Security Administration (SSA) by the taxpayer with respect to employees of the taxpayer for employment by the taxpayer; or

(B) The total entries in Box 5 of all Forms W-2 filed with the SSA by the taxpayer with respect to employees of the taxpayer for employment by the taxpayer.

(ii) Modified Box 1 method. Under the Modified Box 1 method, the taxpayer makes modifications to the total entries in Box 1 of Forms W-2 filed with respect to employees of the taxpayer. W-2 wages under this method are calculated as follows—

(A) Total the amounts in Box 1 of all Forms W-2 filed with the SSA by the taxpayer with respect to employees of the taxpayer for employment by the taxpayer;

(B) Subtract from the total in paragraph (f)(2)(ii)(A) of this section amounts included in Box 1 of Forms W-2 that are not wages for Federal income tax withholding purposes and amounts included in Box 1 of Forms W-2 that are treated as wages under section 3402(o) (for example, supplemental unemployment benefits); and

(C) Add to the amount obtained after paragraph (f)(2)(ii)(B) of this section amounts that are reported in Box 12 of Forms W-2 with respect to employees of the taxpayer for employment by the taxpayer and that are properly coded D, E, F, G, or S.

(iii) Tracking wages method. Under the Tracking wages method, the taxpayer actually tracks total wages subject to Federal income tax withholding and makes appropriate modifications. W-2 wages under this method are calculated as follows—

(A) Total the amounts of wages subject to Federal income tax withholding that are paid to employees of the taxpayer for employment by the taxpayer and that are reported on Forms W-2 filed with the SSA by the taxpayer for the calendar year;

(B) Subtract from the total in paragraph (f)(2)(iii)(A) of this section the supplemental unemployment compensation benefits (as defined in section 3402(o)(2)(A)) that were included in the total in paragraph (f)(2)(iii)(A) of this section; and

(C) Add to the amount obtained after paragraph (f)(2)(iii)(B) of this section amounts that are reported in Box 12 of Forms W-2 with respect to employees of the taxpayer for employment by the taxpayer and that are properly coded D, E, F, G, or S.

§ 1.199-3 Domestic production gross receipts.

Caution: The Treasury has not yet amended Reg § 1.199-3 to reflect changes made by P.L. 110-343.

(a) In general. The provisions of this section apply solely for purposes of section 199 of the Internal Revenue Code (Code). Domestic production gross receipts (DPGR) are the gross receipts (as defined in paragraph (c) of this section) of the taxpayer that are—

(1) Derived from any lease, rental, license, sale, exchange, or other disposition (as defined in paragraph (i) of this section) of—

(i) Qualifying production property (QPP) (as defined in paragraph (j)(1) of this section) that is manufactured, produced, grown, or extracted (MPGE) (as defined in paragraph (e) of this section) by the taxpayer (as defined in paragraph (f) of this section) in whole or in significant part (as defined in paragraph (g) of this section) within the United States (as defined in paragraph (h) of this section);

(ii) Any qualified film (as defined in paragraph (k) of this section) produced by the taxpayer; or

(iii) Electricity, natural gas, or potable water (as defined in paragraph (l) of this section) (collectively, utilities) produced by the taxpayer in the United States;

(2) Derived from, in the case of a taxpayer engaged in the active conduct of a construction trade or business, construction of real property (as defined in paragraph (m) of this section) performed in the United States by the taxpayer in the ordinary course of such trade or business; or

(3) Derived from, in the case of a taxpayer engaged in the active conduct of an engineering or architectural services trade or business, engineering or architectural services (as defined in paragraph (n) of this section) performed in the United States by the taxpayer in the ordinary course of such trade or business with respect to the construction of real property in the United States.

(b) Related persons. *(1) In general.* DPGR does not include any gross receipts of the taxpayer derived from property leased, licensed, or rented by the taxpayer for use by any related person. A person is treated as related to another person if both persons are treated as a single employer under either section 52(a) or (b) (without regard to section 1563(b)), or section 414(m) or (o). Any other person is an unrelated person for purposes of §§ 1.199-1 through 1.199-9.

(2) Exceptions. Notwithstanding paragraph (b)(1) of this section, gross receipts derived from any QPP or qualified

film leased or rented by the taxpayer to a related person may qualify as DPGR if the QPP or qualified film is held for sublease or rent, or is subleased or rented, by the related person to an unrelated person for the ultimate use of the unrelated person. Similarly, notwithstanding paragraph (b)(1) of this section, gross receipts derived from the license of QPP or a qualified film to a related person for reproduction and sale, exchange, lease, rental, or sublicense to an unrelated person for the ultimate use of the unrelated person may qualify as DPGR.

(c) Definition of gross receipts. The term gross receipts means the taxpayer's receipts for the taxable year that are recognized under the taxpayer's methods of accounting used for Federal income tax purposes for the taxable year. If the gross receipts are recognized in an intercompany transaction within the meaning of § 1.1502-13, see also § 1.199-7(d). For this purpose, gross receipts include total sales (net of returns and allowances) and all amounts received for services. In addition, gross receipts include any income from investments and from incidental or outside sources. For example, gross receipts include interest (including original issue discount and tax-exempt interest within the meaning of section 103), dividends, rents, royalties, and annuities, regardless of whether the amounts are derived in the ordinary course of the taxpayer's trade of business. Gross receipts are not reduced by cost of goods sold (CGS) or by the cost of property sold if such property is described in section 1221(a)(1), (2), (3), (4), or (5). Gross receipts do not include the amounts received in repayment of a loan or similar instrument (for example, a repayment of the principal amount of a loan held by a commercial lender) and, except to the extent of gain recognized, do not include gross receipts derived from a nonrecognition transaction, such as a section 1031 exchange. Finally, gross receipts do not include amounts received by the taxpayer with respect to sales tax or other similar state and local taxes if, under the applicable state or local law, the tax is legally imposed on the purchaser of the good or service and the taxpayer merely collects and remits the tax to the taxing authority. If, in contrast, the tax is imposed on the taxpayer under the applicable law, then gross receipts include the amounts received that are allocable to the payment of such tax.

(d) Determining domestic production gross receipts. *(1) In general.* For purposes of §§ 1.199-1 through 1.199-9, a taxpayer determines, using any reasonable method that is satisfactory to the Secretary based on all of the facts and circumstances, whether gross receipts qualify as DPGR on an item-by-item basis (and not, for example, on a division-bydivision, product line-by-product line, or transaction-by-transaction basis).

(i) The term item means the property offered by the taxpayer in the normal course of the taxpayer's business for lease, rental, license, sale, exchange, or other disposition (for purposes of this paragraph (d), collectively referred to as disposition) to customers, if the gross receipts from the disposition of such property qualify as DPGR; or

(ii) If paragraph (d)(1)(i) of this section does not apply to the property, then any component of the property described in paragraph (d)(1)(i) of this section is treated as the item, provided that the gross receipts from the disposition of the property described in paragraph (d)(1)(i) of this section that are attributable to such component qualify as DPGR. Each component that meets the requirements under this paragraph (d)(1)(ii) must be treated as a separate item and a component that meets the requirements under this paragraph (d)(1)(ii) may not be combined with a component that does not meet these requirements.

(2) Special rules. The following special rules apply for purposes of paragraph (d)(1) of this section:

(i) For purposes of paragraph (d)(1)(i) of this section, in no event may a single item consist of two or more properties unless those properties are offered for disposition, in the normal course of the taxpayer's business, as a single item (regardless of how the properties are packaged).

(ii) In the case of property customarily sold by weight or by volume, the item is determined using the custom of the industry (for example, barrels of oil).

(iii) In the case of construction activities and services or engineering and architectural services, a taxpayer may use any reasonable method that is satisfactory to the Secretary based on all of the facts and circumstances to determine what construction activities and services or engineering or architectural services constitute an item.

(3) Exception. If a taxpayer MPGE QPP within the United States or produces a qualified film or produces utilities in the United States that it disposes of, and the taxpayer leases, rents, licenses, purchases, or otherwise acquires property that contains or may contain the QPP, qualified film, or the utilities (or a portion thereof), and the taxpayer cannot reasonably determine, without undue burden and expense, whether the acquired property contains any of the original QPP, qualified film, or utilities MPGE or produced by the taxpayer, then the taxpayer is not required to determine whether any portion of the acquired property qualifies as an item for purposes of paragraph (d)(1) of this section. Therefore, the gross receipts derived from the disposition of the acquired property may be treated as non-DPGR. Similarly, the preceding sentences shall apply if the taxpayer can reasonably determine that the acquired property contains QPP, a qualified film, or utilities (or a portion thereof) MPGE or produced by the taxpayer, but cannot reasonably determine, without undue burden or expense, how much, or what type, grade, etc., of the QPP, qualified film, or utilities MPGE or produced by the taxpayer the acquired property contains.

(4) Examples. The following examples illustrate the application of paragraph (d) of this section:

Example (1). Q manufactures leather and rubber shoe soles in the United States. Q imports shoe uppers, which are the parts of the shoe above the sole. Q manufactures shoes for sale by sewing or otherwise attaching the soles to the imported uppers. Q offers the shoes for sale to customers in the normal course of Q's business. If the gross receipts derived from the sale of the shoes do not qualify as DPGR under this section, then under paragraph (d)(1)(ii) of this section, Q must treat the sole as the item if the gross receipts derived from the sale of the sole qualify as DPGR under this section.

Example (2). The facts are the same as in Example 1 except that Q also buys some finished shoes from unrelated persons and resells them to retail shoe stores. Q offers all shoes (manufactured and purchased) for sale to customers, in the normal course of Q's business, in individual pairs, and requires no minimum quantity order. Q ships the shoes in boxes, each box containing as many as 50 pairs of shoes. A full, or partially full, box may contain some shoes that Q manufactured, and some that Q purchased. Under paragraph (d)(2)(i) of this section, Q cannot treat a box of 50 (or fewer) pairs of shoes as an item, because Q offers the shoes for sale in the normal course of Q's business in individual pairs.

Example (3). R manufactures toy cars in the United States. R also purchases cars that were manufactured by unrelated persons. R offers the cars for sale to customers, in the normal course of R's business, in sets of three, and requires no minimum quantity order. R sells the three-car sets to toy stores. A three-car set may contain some cars manufactured by R and some cars purchased by R. If the gross receipts derived from the sale of the three-car sets do not qualify as DPGR under this section, then, under paragraph (d)(1)(ii) of this section, R must treat a toy car in the three-car set as the item, provided the gross receipts derived from the sale of the toy car qualify as DPGR under this section.

Example (4). The facts are the same as Example 3 except that R offers the toy cars for sale individually to customers in the normal course of R's business, rather than in sets of three. R's customers resell the individual toy cars at three for $10. Frequently, this results in retail customers purchasing three individual cars in one transaction. In determining R's DPGR, under paragraph (d)(2)(i) of this section, each toy car is an item and R cannot treat three individual toy cars as one item, because the individual toy cars are not offered for sale in sets of three by R in the normal course of R's business.

Example (5). The facts are the same as in Example 3 except that R offers the toy cars for sale to customers in the normal course of R's business both individually and in sets of three. The results are the same as Example 3 with respect to the three-car sets. The results are the same as in Example 4 with respect to the individual toy cars that are not included in the three-car sets and offered for sale individually. Thus, R has two items, an individual toy car and a set of three toy cars.

Example (6). S produces television sets in the United States. S also produces the same model of television set outside the United States. In both cases, S packages the sets one to a box. S sells the television sets to large retail consumer electronics stores. S requires that its customers purchase a minimum of 100 television sets per order. With respect to a particular order by a customer of 100 television sets, some were manufactured by S in the United States, and some were manufactured by S outside the United States. Under paragraph (d)(2)(i) of this section, a minimum order of 100 television sets is the item provided that the gross receipts derived from the sale of the 100 television sets qualify as DPGR.

Example (7). T produces in bulk form in the United States the active ingredient for a pharmaceutical product. T sells the active ingredient in bulk form to FX, a foreign corporation. This sale qualifies as DPGR assuming all the other requirements of this section are met. FX uses the active ingredient to produce the finished dosage form drug. FX sells the drug in finished dosage to T, which sells the drug to customers. Assume that T knows how much of the active ingredient is in the finished dosage. Under paragraph (d)(1)(ii) of this section, if T's gross receipts derived from the sale of the finished dosage do not qualify as DPGR under this section, then T must treat the active ingredient component as the item because the gross receipts attributable to the active ingredient qualify as DPGR under this section. The exception in paragraph (d)(3) of this section does not apply because T can reasonably determine without undue burden or expense that the finished dosage contains the active ingredient and the quantity of the active ingredient in the finished dosage.

Example (8). U produces steel within the United States and sells its steel to a variety of customers, including V, an unrelated person, who uses the steel for the manufacture of equipment. V also purchases steel from other steel producers. For its steel operations, U purchases equipment from V that may contain steel produced by U. U sells the equipment after 5 years. If U cannot reasonably determine without undue burden and expense whether the equipment contains any steel produced by U, then, under paragraph (d)(3) of this section, U may treat the gross receipts derived from sale of the equipment as non-DPGR.

Example (9). The facts are the same as in Example 8 except that U knows that the equipment purchased from V does contain some amount of steel produced by U. If U cannot reasonably determine without undue burden and expense how much steel produced by U the equipment contains, then, under paragraph (d)(3) of this section, U may treat the gross receipts derived from sale of the equipment as non-DPGR.

Example (10). W manufactures sunroofs, stereos, and tires within the United States. W purchases automobiles from unrelated persons and installs the manufactured components in the automobiles. W, in the normal course of W's business, sells the automobiles with the components to customers. If the gross receipts derived from the sale of the automobiles with the components do not qualify as DPGR under this section, then under paragraph (d)(1)(ii) of this section, W must treat each component (sunroofs, stereos, and tires) that it manufactures as a separate item if the gross receipts derived from the sale of each component qualify as DPGR under this section.

Example (11). X manufacturers leather soles within the United States. X purchases shoe uppers, metal eyelets, and laces. X manufactures shoes by sewing or otherwise attaching the soles to the uppers; attaching the metal eyelets to the shoes; and threading the laces through the eyelets. X, in the normal course of X's business, sells the shoes to customers. If the gross receipts derived from the sale of the shoes do not qualify as DPGR under this section, then under paragraph (d)(1)(ii) of this section, X must treat the sole as the item if the gross receipts derived from the sale of the sole qualify as DPGR under this section. X may not treat the shoe upper, metal eyelets or laces as part of the item because under paragraph (d)(1)(ii) of this section the sole is the component that is treated as the item.

Example (12). Y manufactures glass windshields for automobiles within the United States. Y purchases automobiles from unrelated persons and installs the windshields in the automobiles. Y, in the normal course of Y's business, sells the automobiles with the windshields to customers. If the automobiles with the windshields do not meet the requirements for being an item, then, under paragraph (d)(1)(ii) of this section, Y must treat each windshield that it manufactures as an item if the gross receipts derived from the sale of the windshield qualify as DPGR under this section. Y may not treat any other portion of the automobile as part of the item because under paragraph (d)(1)(ii) of this section the windshield is the component.

(e) Definition of manufactured, produced, grown, or extracted. *(1) In general.* Except as provided in paragraphs (e)(2) and (3) of this section, the term MPGE includes manufacturing, producing, growing, extracting, installing, developing, improving, and creating QPP; making QPP out of scrap, salvage, or junk material as well as from new or raw material by processing, manipulating, refining, or changing the form of an article, or by combining or assembling two or more articles; cultivating soil, raising livestock, fishing, and mining minerals. The term MPGE also includes storage, handling, or other processing activities (other than transportation activities) within the United States related to the sale, exchange, or other disposition of agricultural products, provided the products are consumed in connection with or incorporated into the MPGE of QPP, whether or not by the taxpayer. Pursuant to paragraph (f)(1) of this section, the taxpayer must have the benefits and burdens of ownership of the QPP under Federal income tax principles during the period the MPGE activity occurs in order for gross receipts derived from the MPGE of QPP to qualify as DPGR.

(2) Packaging, repackaging, labeling, or minor assembly. If a taxpayer packages, repackages, labels, or performs minor assembly of QPP and the taxpayer engages in no other MPGE activity with respect to that QPP, the taxpayer's packaging, repackaging, labeling, or minor assembly does not qualify as MPGE with respect to that QPP.

(3) Installing. If a taxpayer installs QPP and engages in no other MPGE activity with respect to the QPP, the taxpayer's installing activity does not qualify as an MPGE activity. Notwithstanding paragraph (i)(4)(i)(B)(4) of this section, if the taxpayer installs QPP MPGE by the taxpayer and, except as provided in paragraph (f)(2) of this section, the taxpayer has the benefits and burdens of ownership of the QPP under Federal income tax principles during the period the installing activity occurs, then the portion of the installing activity that relates to the QPP is an MPGE activity.

(4) Consistency with section 263A. A taxpayer that has MPGE QPP for the taxable year should treat itself as a producer under section 263A with respect to the QPP unless the taxpayer is not subject to section 263A. A taxpayer that currently is not properly accounting for its production activities under section 263A, and wishes to change its method of accounting to comply with the producer requirements of section 263A, must follow the applicable administrative procedures issued under § 1.446-1(e)(3)(ii) for obtaining the Commissioner's consent to a change in accounting method (for further guidance, for example, see Rev. Proc. 97-27 (1997-1 C.B. 680), or Rev. Proc. 2002-9 (2002-1 C.B. 327), whichever applies (see § 601.601(d)(2) of this chapter)).

(5) Examples. The following examples illustrate the application of this paragraph (e):

Example (1). A, B, and C are unrelated persons and are not cooperatives to which Part I of subchapter T of the Code applies. B grows agricultural products in the United States and sells them to A, who owns agricultural storage bins in the United States. A stores the agricultural products and has the benefits and burdens of ownership under Federal income tax principles of the agricultural products while they are being stored. A sells the agricultural products to C, who processes them into refined agricultural products in the United States. The gross receipts from A's, B's, and C's activities are DPGR from the MPGE of QPP.

Example (2). The facts are the same as in Example 1 except that B grows the agricultural products outside the United States and C processes them into refined agricultural products outside the United States. Pursuant to paragraph (e)(1) of this section, the gross receipts derived by A from its sale of the agricultural products to C are DPGR from the MPGE of QPP within the United States. B's and C's respective MPGE activities occur outside the United States and, therefore, their respective gross receipts are non-DPGR.

Example (3). Y is hired to reconstruct and refurbish unrelated customers' tangible personal property. As part of the reconstruction and refurbishment, Y installs purchased replacement parts that constitute QPP in the customers' property. Y's installation of purchased replacement parts does not qualify as MPGE pursuant to paragraph (e)(3) of this section because Y did not MPGE the replacement parts.

Example (4). The facts are the same as in Example 3 except that Y manufactures the replacement parts it uses for the reconstruction and refurbishment of customers' tangible personal property. Y has the benefits and burdens of ownership under Federal income tax principles of the replacement parts during the reconstruction and refurbishment activity and while installing the parts. Y's gross receipts derived from the MPGE of the replacement parts and Y's gross receipts derived from the installation of the replacement parts, which is an MPGE activity pursuant to paragraph (e)(3) of this section, are DPGR (assuming all the other requirements of this section are met).

Example (5). Z MPGE QPP within the United States. The following activities are performed by Z as part of the MPGE of the QPP while Z has the benefits and burdens of ownership under Federal income tax principles: materials analysis and selection, subcontractor inspections and qualifications, testing of component parts, assisting customers in their review and approval of the QPP, routine production inspections, product documentation, diagnosis and correction of system failure, and packaging for shipment to customers. Because Z MPGE the QPP, these activities performed by Z are part of the MPGE of the QPP.

Example (6). X purchases automobiles from unrelated persons and customizes them by adding ground effects, spoilers, custom wheels, specialized paint and decals, sunroofs, roof racks, and similar accessories. X does not manufacture any of the accessories. X's activity is minor assembly under paragraph (e)(2) of this section which is not an MPGE activity.

Example (7). Y manufactures furniture in the United States that it sells to unrelated persons. Y also engraves customers' names on pens and pencils purchased from unrelated persons and sells the pens and pencils to such customers. Although Y's sales of furniture qualify as DPGR if all the other requirements of this section are met, Y must determine whether its gross receipts derived from the sale of the pens and pencils qualify as DPGR. Y's status as a manufacturer of furniture in the United States does not carry over to its other activities.

Example (8). X produces computer software within the United States. In 2007, X enters into an agreement with Y, an unrelated person, under which X will manage Y's networks using computer software that X produced. Pursuant to the terms of the agreement, X also provides to Y for Y's use on Y's own hardware computer software that X produced (additional computer software). Assume that, based on all of the facts and circumstances, the transaction between X and Y relating to the additional computer software is a lease or sale of the additional computer software. Y pays X monthly fees of $100 under the agreement during 2007. No separate charge for the additional computer software is stated in the agreement or in the monthly invoices that X provides to Y. The portion of X's gross receipts that is derived from the lease or sale of the additional computer software is DPGR (assuming all the other requirements of this section are met).

(f) Definition of by the taxpayer. *(1) In general.* With the exception of the rules applicable to an expanded affiliated group (EAG) under § 1.199-7, qualifying in-kind partnerships under paragraph (i)(7) of this section and § 1.199-9(i), EAG partnerships under paragraph (i)(8) of this section and § 1.199-9(j), and government contracts under paragraph (f)(2) of this section, only one taxpayer may claim the deduction under § 1.199-1(a) with respect to any qualifying activity under paragraphs (e)(1), (k)(1), and (l)(1) of this section performed in connection with the same QPP, or the production of a qualified film or utilities. If one taxpayer performs a qualifying activity under paragraph (e)(1), (k)(1), or (l)(1) of this section pursuant to a contract with another party, then only the taxpayer that has the benefit and burdens of ownership of the QPP, qualified film, or utilities under Federal income tax principles during the period in which the qualifying activity occurs is treated as engaged in the qualifying activity.

(2) Special rule for certain government contracts. Gross receipts derived from the MPGE of QPP in whole or in significant part within the United States will be treated as gross receipts derived from the lease, rental, license, sale, exchange, or other disposition of QPP MPGE by the taxpayer in whole or in significant part within the United States notwithstanding the requirements of paragraph (f)(1) of this section if—

(i) The QPP is MPGE by the taxpayer within the United States pursuant to a contract with the Federal government; and

(ii) The Federal Acquisition Regulation (Title 48, Code of Federal Regulations) requires that title or risk of loss with respect to the QPP be transferred to the Federal government before the MPGE of the QPP is completed.

(3) Subcontractor. If a taxpayer (subcontractor) enters into a contract or agreement to MPGE QPP on behalf of a taxpayer to which paragraph (f)(2) of this section applies, and the QPP under the contract or agreement is subject to paragraph (f)(2)(ii) of this section, then, notwithstanding the requirements of paragraph (f)(1) of this section, the subcontractor's gross receipts derived from the MPGE of the QPP in whole or in significant part within the United States will be treated as gross receipts derived from the lease, rental, license, sale, exchange, or other disposition of QPP MPGE by the subcontractor in whole or in significant part within the United States.

(4) Examples. The following examples illustrate the application of this paragraph (f):

Example (1). X designs machines that it uses in its trade or business. X contracts with Y, an unrelated person, for the manufacture of the machines. The contract between X and Y is a fixed-price contract. The contract specifies that the machines will be manufactured in the United States using X's design. X owns the intellectual property attributable to the design and provides it to Y with a restriction that Y may only use it during the manufacturing process and has no right to exploit the intellectual property. The contract specifies that Y controls the details of the manufacturing process while the machines are being produced; Y bears the risk of loss or damage during manufacturing of the machines; and Y has the economic loss or gain upon the sale of the machines based on the difference between Y's costs and the fixed price. Y has legal title during the manufacturing process and legal title to the machines is not transferred to X until final manufacturing of the machines has been completed. Based on all of the facts and circumstances, pursuant to paragraph (f)(1) of this section Y has the benefits and burdens of ownership of the machines under Federal income tax principles during the period the manufacturing occurs and, as a result, Y is treated as the manufacturer of the machines.

Example (2). X designs and engineers machines that it sells to customers. X contracts with Y, an unrelated person, for the manufacture of the machines. The contract between X and Y is a cost-reimbursable type contract. Assume that X has the benefits and burdens of ownership of the machines under Federal income tax principles during the period the manufacturing occurs except that legal title to the machines is not transferred to X until final manufacturing of the machines is completed. Based on all of the facts and circumstances, X is treated as the manufacturer of the machines under paragraph (f)(1) of this section.

Example (3). X manufactures machines within the United States pursuant to a contract with the Federal government and the Federal Acquisition Regulation requires that the title or risk of loss with respect to the machines be transferred to the Federal government before X completes manufacture of the machines. X subcontracts with Y, an unrelated person, for the manufacture of components for the machines that Y manufactures within the United States. Assume that the machines manufactured by X, and the components for the machines manufactured by Y, are QPP. Both the machines and components are subject to the Federal Acquisition Regulation that requires title or risk of loss with respect to the machines and components be transferred to the Federal government before manufacturing of the machines and components are complete. Under paragraph (f)(2) of this section, the gross receipts derived by X from the manufacture within the United States of the machines for the Federal government are treated as having been derived from the lease, rental, license, sale, exchange, or other disposition of the machines manufactured by X in whole or in significant part within the United States. Under paragraph (f)(3) of this section, the gross receipts derived by Y from the manufacture within the United States of the components for X are also treated as having been derived from the lease, rental, license, sale, exchange, or other disposition of the components manufactured by Y in whole or in significant part within the United States.

(g) Definition of in whole or in significant part. *(1) In general.* QPP must be MPGE in whole or in significant part by the taxpayer and in whole or in significant part within the United States to qualify under section 199(c)(4)(A)(i)(I). If a taxpayer enters into a contract with an unrelated person for the unrelated person to MPGE QPP for the taxpayer and the taxpayer has the benefits and burdens of ownership of the QPP under applicable Federal income tax principles during the period the MPGE activity occurs, then, pursuant to paragraph (f)(1) of this section, the taxpayer is considered to MPGE the QPP under this section. The unrelated person must perform the MPGE activity on behalf of the taxpayer in whole or in significant part within the United States in order for the taxpayer to satisfy the requirements of this paragraph (g)(1).

(2) Substantial in nature. QPP will be treated as MPGE in significant part by the taxpayer within the United States for purposes of paragraph (g)(1) of this section if the MPGE of the QPP by the taxpayer within the United States is substantial in nature taking into account all of the facts and circumstances, including the relative value added by, and relative cost of, the taxpayer's MPGE activity within the United States, the nature of the QPP, and the nature of the MPGE activity that the taxpayer performs within the United States. The MPGE of a key component of QPP does not, in itself, meet the substantial-in-nature requirement with respect to the QPP under this paragraph (g)(2). In the case of tangible personal property (as defined in paragraph (j)(2) of this section), research and experimental activities under section 174 and the creation of intangible assets are not taken into account in determining whether the MPGE of QPP is substantial in nature for any QPP other than computer software (as defined in paragraph (j)(3) of this section) and sound recordings (as defined in paragraph (j)(4) of this section). Thus, for

example, a taxpayer may take into account its design and development activities when determining whether its MPGE of computer software is substantial in nature.

(3) Safe harbor. (i) In general. A taxpayer will be treated as having MPGE QPP in whole or in significant part within the United States for purposes of paragraph (g)(1) of this section if, in connection with the QPP, the direct labor and overhead of such taxpayer to MPGE the QPP within the United States account for 20 percent or more of the taxpayer's CGS of the QPP, or in a transaction without CGS (for example, a lease, rental, or license) account for 20 percent or more of the taxpayer's unadjusted depreciable basis (as defined in paragraph (g)(3)(ii) of this section) in the QPP. For taxpayers subject to section 263A, overhead is all costs required to be capitalized under section 263A except direct materials and direct labor. For taxpayers not subject to section 263A, overhead may be computed using any reasonable method that is satisfactory to the Secretary based on all of the facts and circumstances, but may not include any cost, or amount of any cost, that would not be required to be capitalized under section 263A if the taxpayer were subject to section 263A. Research and experimental expenditures under section 174 and the costs of creating intangible assets are not taken into account in determining direct labor or overhead for any tangible personal property. However, for a special rule regarding computer software and sound recordings, see paragraph (g)(3)(iii) of this section. In the case of tangible personal property (as defined in paragraph (j)(2) of this section), research and experimental expenditures under section 174 and any other costs incurred in the creation of intangible assets may be excluded from CGS or unadjusted depreciable basis for purposes of determining whether the taxpayer meets the safe harbor under this paragraph (g)(3).

(ii) Unadjusted depreciable basis. The term unadjusted depreciable basis means the basis of property for purposes of section 1011 without regard to any adjustments described in section 1016(a)(2) and (3). This basis does not reflect the reduction in basis for—

(A) Any portion of the basis the taxpayer properly elects to treat as an expense under section 179 or 179C; or

(B) Any adjustments to basis provided by other provisions of the Code and the regulations under the Code (for example, a reduction in basis by the amount of the disabled access credit pursuant to section 44(d)(7)).

(iii) Computer software and sound recordings. In determining direct labor and overhead under paragraph (g)(3)(i) of this section, the costs of direct labor and overhead for developing computer software as described in Rev. Proc. 2000-50 (2000-1 C.B. 601) (see § 601.601(d)(2) of this chapter), research and experimental expenditures under section 174, and any other costs of creating intangible assets for computer software and sound recordings are treated as direct labor and overhead. These costs must be included in the taxpayer's CGS or unadjusted depreciable basis of computer software and sound recordings for purposes of determining whether the taxpayer meets the safe harbor under paragraph (g)(3)(i) of this section. If the taxpayer expects to lease, rent, license, sell, exchange, or otherwise dispose of computer software or sound recordings over more than one taxable year, the costs of developing computer software as described in Rev. Proc. 2000-50 (2000-1 C.B. 601), research and experimental expenditures under section 174, and any other costs of creating intangible assets for computer software and sound recordings must be allocated over the estimated number of units that the taxpayer expects to lease, rent, license, sell, exchange, or otherwise dispose of.

(4) Special rules. (i) Contract with an unrelated person. If a taxpayer enters into a contract with an unrelated person for the unrelated person to MPGE QPP within the United States for the taxpayer, and the taxpayer is considered to MPGE the QPP pursuant to paragraph (f)(1) of this section, then, for purposes of the substantial-in-nature requirement under paragraph (g)(2) of this section and the safe harbor under paragraph (g)(3)(i) of this section, the taxpayer's MPGE or production activities or direct labor and overhead shall include both the taxpayer's MPGE or production activities or direct labor and overhead to MPGE the QPP within the United States as well as the MPGE or production activities or direct labor and overhead of the unrelated person to MPGE the QPP within the United States under the contract.

(ii) Aggregation. In determining whether the substantial-in-nature requirement under paragraph (g)(2) of this section or the safe harbor under paragraph (g)(3)(i) of this section is met at the time the taxpayer disposes of an item of QPP—

(A) An EAG member must take into account all of the previous MPGE or production activities or direct labor and overhead of the other members of the EAG;

(B) An EAG partnership (as defined in paragraph (i)(8) of this section and § 1.199-9(j)) must take into account all of the previous MPGE or production activities or direct labor and overhead of all members of the EAG in which the partners of the EAG partnership are members (as well as the previous MPGE or production activities of any other EAG partnerships owned by members of the same EAG);

(C) A member of an EAG in which the partners of an EAG partnership are members must take into account all of the previous MPGE or production activities or direct labor and overhead of the EAG partnership (as well as those of any other members of the EAG and any previous MPGE or production activities of any other EAG partnerships owned by members of the same EAG); and

(D) A partner of a qualifying in-kind partnership (as defined in paragraph (i)(7) of this section and § 1.199-9(i)) must take into account all of the previous MPGE or production activities or direct labor and overhead of the qualifying in-kind partnership.

(5) Examples. The following examples illustrate the application of this paragraph (g):

Example (1). X purchases from Y, an unrelated person, unrefined oil extracted outside the United States. X refines the oil in the United States. The refining of the oil by X is an MPGE activity that is substantial in nature.

Example (2). X purchases gemstones and precious metal from outside the United States and then uses these materials to produce jewelry within the United States by cutting and polishing the gemstones, melting and shaping the metal, and combining the finished materials. X's MPGE activities are substantial in nature under paragraph (g)(2) of this section. Therefore, X has MPGE the jewelry in significant part within the United States.

Example (3). (i) Facts. X operates an automobile assembly plant in the United States. In connection with such activity, X purchases assembled engines, transmissions, and certain other components from Y, an unrelated person, and X assembles all of the component parts into an automobile. X also conducts stamping, machining, and subassembly operations, and X uses tools, jigs, welding equipment, and other machinery and equipment in the assembly of automobiles. On a per-unit basis, X 's selling price and costs of such automobiles are as follows:

Selling price:	$2,500
Cost of goods sold:	
Material — Acquired from Y:	$1,475
Direct labor and overhead:	$ 325
Total cost of goods sold:	$1,800
Gross profit:	$ 700
Administrative and selling expenses:	$ 300
Taxable income:	$ 400

(ii) Analysis. Although X's direct labor and overhead are less than 20% of total CGS ($325/$1,800, or 18%) and X is not within the safe harbor under paragraph (g)(3)(i) of this section, the activities conducted by X in connection with the assembly of an automobile are substantial in nature under paragraph (g)(2) of this section taking into account the nature of X's activity and the relative value of X's activity. Therefore, X's automobiles will be treated as MPGE in significant part by X within the United States for purposes of paragraph (g)(1) of this section.

Example (4). X imports into the United States QPP that is partially manufactured. Assume that X completes the manufacture of the QPP within the United States and X's completion of the manufacturing of the QPP within the United States satisfies the in-whole-or-in-significant-part requirement under paragraph (g)(1) of this section. Therefore, X's gross receipts from the lease, rental, license, sale, exchange, or other disposition of the QPP qualify as DPGR if all other applicable requirements under this section are met.

Example (5). X manufactures QPP in significant part within the United States and exports the QPP for further manufacture outside the United States. X retains title to the QPP while the QPP is being further manufactured outside the United States. Assuming X meets all the requirements under this section for the QPP after the further manufacturing, X's gross receipts derived from the lease, rental, license, sale, exchange, or other disposition of the QPP will be considered DPGR, regardless of whether the QPP is imported back into the United States prior to the lease, rental, license, sale, exchange, or other disposition of the QPP.

Example (6). X is a retailer within the United States that sells cigars and pipe tobacco that X purchases from an unrelated person. While being displayed and offered for sale by X, the cigars and pipe tobacco age on X's shelves in a room with controlled temperature and humidity. Although X's cigars and pipe tobacco may become more valuable as they age, the gross receipts derived by X from the sale of the cigars and pipe tobacco are non-DPGR because the aging of the cigars and pipe tobacco while being displayed and offered for sale by X does not qualify as an MPGE activity that is substantial in nature.

Example (7). X incurs $1,000,000 in computer software development costs in direct labor and overhead to develop computer software. X begins producing the computer software and expects to license one million copies of the computer software. In determining its direct labor and overhead for the computer software under paragraph (g)(3)(i) of this section, X must allocate under paragraph (g)(3)(iii) of this section the $1,000,000 to the computer software X expects to produce. Thus, for each copy of the computer software produced by X, $1 ($1,000,000 in computer software development costs/one million estimated number of units to be licensed) in computer software development costs are treated as direct labor and overhead.

Example (8). X creates computer software for microwave ovens. X also manufactures the electric motors used in the ovens. X purchases the other components of the microwave ovens from unrelated persons. X sells each microwave oven individually to customers. Assume that X's assembly of the finished microwave ovens is not minor assembly. To determine whether the manufacture of the microwave ovens satisfies the safe harbor under paragraph (g)(3)(i) of this section, X's direct labor and overhead include X's direct labor and overhead for creating the computer software, manufacturing the electric motors, and assembling the finished microwave ovens that are offered for sale.

Example (9). X designs shirts within the United States, but X cuts and sews the shirts outside of the United States. Because X's design activity is the creation of an intangible, its design activity is not taken into account in determining whether the manufacture of the shirts is substantial in nature under paragraph (g)(2) of this section, and the costs X incurs in creating the design of the shirts are not direct labor or overhead under paragraph (g)(3)(i) of this section. Therefore, X has not MPGE the shirts in significant part within the United States.

Example (10). X manufactures computer chips within the United States. X installs the computer chips that it manufactures in computers that X purchases from unrelated persons and sells the finished computers individually to customers. The computer chips are key components of the computers and the computers will not operate without them. The manufacture of the computer chips is not, in itself, substantial in nature with respect to the finished computers. Therefore, the taxpayer's MPGE activities must meet either the substantial-in-nature requirement under paragraph (g)(2) of this section, or the safe harbor under paragraph (g)(3) of this section, in order to qualify with respect to the finished computers.

(h) Definition of United States. For purposes of this section, the term United States includes the 50 states, the District of Columbia, the territorial waters of the United States, and the seabed and subsoil of those submarine areas that are adjacent to the territorial waters of the United States and over which the United States has exclusive rights, in accordance with international law, with respect to the exploration and exploitation of natural resources. The term United States does not include possessions and territories of the United States or the airspace or space over the United States and these areas.

(i) Derived from the lease, rental, license, sale, exchange, or other disposition. *(1) In general.* (i) Definition. The term derived from the lease, rental, license, sale, exchange, or other disposition is defined as, and limited to, the gross receipts directly derived from the lease, rental, license, sale, exchange, or other disposition of QPP, a qualified film, or utilities, even if the taxpayer has already recognized gross receipts from a previous lease, rental, license, sale, exchange, or other disposition of the same QPP, qualified film, or utilities. Applicable Federal income tax principles apply to determine whether a transaction is, in substance, a lease, rental, license, sale, exchange, or other disposition, whether it is a service, or whether it is some combination thereof.

(ii) Lease income. The financing and interest components of a lease of QPP or a qualified film are considered to be derived from the lease of such QPP or qualified film. However, any portion of the lease income that is attributable to services or non-qualified property as defined in paragraph (i)(4) of this section is not derived from the lease of QPP or a qualified film.

(iii) Income substitutes. The proceeds from business interruption insurance, governmental subsidies, and governmental payments not to produce are treated as gross receipts derived from the lease, rental, license, sale, exchange, or other disposition to the extent that they are substitutes for gross receipts that would qualify as DPGR.

(iv) Exchange of property. (A) Taxable exchanges. Except as provided in paragraph (i)(1)(iv)(B) of this section, the value of property received by a taxpayer in a taxable exchange of QPP MPGE in whole or in significant part by the taxpayer within the United States, a qualified film produced by the taxpayer, or utilities produced by the taxpayer within the United States is DPGR for the taxpayer (assuming all the other requirements of this section are met). However, unless the taxpayer meets all of the requirements under this section with respect to any further MPGE by the taxpayer of the QPP or any further production by the taxpayer of the film or utilities received in the taxable exchange, any gross receipts derived from the sale by the taxpayer of the property received in the taxable exchange are non-DPGR, because the taxpayer did not MPGE or produce such property, even if the property was QPP, a qualified film, or utilities in the hands of the other party to the transaction.

(B) Safe harbor. For purposes of paragraph (i)(1)(iv)(A) of this section, the gross receipts derived by the taxpayer from the sale of eligible property (as defined in paragraph (i)(1)(iv)(C) of this section) received in a taxable exchange, net of any adjustments between the parties involved in the taxable exchange to account for differences in the eligible property exchanged (for example, location differentials and product differentials), may be treated as the value of the eligible property received by the taxpayer in the taxable exchange. For purposes of the preceding sentence, the taxable exchange is deemed to occur on the date of the sale of the eligible property received in the taxable exchange by the taxpayer, to the extent the sale occurs no later than the last day of the month following the month in which the exchanged eligible property is received by the taxpayer. In addition, if the taxpayer engages in any further MPGE or production activity with respect to the eligible property received in the taxable exchange, then, unless the taxpayer meets the in-whole-or-in-significant-part requirement under paragraph (g)(1) of this section with respect to the property sold, for purposes of this paragraph (i)(1)(iv)(B), the taxpayer must also value the property sold without taking into account the gross receipts attributable to the further MPGE or production activity.

(C) Eligible property. For purposes of paragraph (i)(1)(iv)(B) of this section, eligible property is—

(1) Oil, natural gas (as described in paragraph (l)(2) of this section), or petrochemicals, or products derived from oil, natural gas, or petrochemicals; or

(2) Any other property or product designated by publication in the Internal Revenue Bulletin (see § 601.601(d)(2)(ii)(b) of this chapter).

(2) Examples. The following examples illustrate the application of paragraph (i)(1) of this section:

Example (1). X MPGE QPP in whole or in significant part within the United States and uses the QPP in its business. After several years X sells the QPP that it MPGE to Y. The gross receipts derived from the sale of the QPP to Y are DPGR (assuming all the other requirements of this section are met).

Example (2). X MPGE QPP within the United States and sells the QPP to Y, an unrelated person. Y leases the QPP for 3 years to Z, a taxpayer unrelated to both X and Y, and shortly after Y enters into the lease with Z, X repurchases the QPP from Y subject to the lease. At the end of the lease term, Z purchases the QPP from X. X's proceeds derived from the sale of the QPP to Y, from the lease to Z (including any financing and interest components of the lease), and from the sale of the QPP to Z all qualify as DPGR (assuming all the other requirements of this section are met).

Example (3). X MPGE QPP within the United States and sells the QPP to Y, an unrelated person, for $25,000. X finances Y's purchase of the QPP and receives total payments of $35,000, of which $10,000 relates to interest and finance charges. The $25,000 qualifies as DPGR, but the $10,000 in interest and finance charges do not qualify as DPGR because the $10,000 is not derived from the MPGE of QPP within the United States, but rather from X's lending activity.

Example (4). Cable company X charges subscribers $15 a month for its basic cable television. Y, an unrelated person, produces a qualified film within the meaning of paragraph (k)(1) of this section that it licenses to X for $.10 per subscriber per month. The gross receipts derived by Y are derived from the license of a qualified film produced by Y and are DPGR (assuming all the other requirements of this section are met).

Example (5). X manufactures cars within the United States. X also manufactures replacement parts within the United States. The replacement parts are QPP under paragraph (j)(1) of this section. X offers extended warranties to its customers. X sells a car to Y. Y purchases an extended warranty and brings the car to X's service department for maintenance. X repairs the car and replaces damaged parts with replacement parts that X manufactured within the United States. The portion of X's gross receipts derived from the sale of the extended warranty relating to the manufactured parts are DPGR.

(3) Hedging transactions. (i) In general. For purposes of this section, provided that the risk being hedged relates to QPP described in section 1221(a)(1) or relates to property described in section 1221(a)(8) consumed in an activity giving rise to DPGR, and provided that the transaction is a hedging transaction within the meaning of section 1221(b)(2)(A) and § 1.1221-2(b) and is properly identified as a hedging transaction in accordance with § 1.1221-2(f), then—

(A) In the case of a hedge of purchases of property described in section 1221(a)(1), gain or loss on the hedging transaction must be taken into account in determining CGS;

(B) In the case of a hedge of sales of property described in section 1221(a)(1), gain or loss on the hedging transaction must be taken into account in determining DPGR; and

(C) In the case of a hedge of purchases of property described in section 1221(a)(8), gain or loss on the hedging transaction must be taken into account in determining DPGR.

(ii) Currency fluctuations. For purposes of this section, in the case of a transaction that manages the risk of currency fluctuations, the determination of whether the transaction is a hedging transaction within the meaning of § 1.1221-2(b) is made without regard to whether the transaction is a section 988 transaction. See § 1.1221-2(a)(4). The preceding sentence applies only to the extent that § 1.988-5(b) does not apply.

(iii) Effect of identification and nonidentification. If a taxpayer does not make an identification that satisfies all of the requirements of § 1.1221-2(f) but the taxpayer has no reasonable grounds for treating the transaction as other than a hedging transaction, then a loss from the transaction is taken into account under this paragraph (i)(3). If the inadvertent identification rule of § 1.1221-2(g)(1)(ii) or the inadvertent error rule of § 1.1221-2(g)(2)(ii) applies, then the taxpayer is treated as not having identified the transaction as a hedging transaction or as having identified the transaction as a hedging transaction, as the case may be. If a taxpayer identifies a transaction as a hedging transaction in accordance with § 1.1221-2(f)(1), then—

(A) That identification is binding with respect to loss for purposes of this paragraph (i)(3), whether or not all of the requirements of § 1.1221-2(f) are satisfied and whether or not the transaction is in fact a hedging transaction within the meaning of section 1221(b)(2)(A) and § 1.1221-2(b), and

(B) This paragraph (i)(3) does not apply to require gain to be taken into account in determining CGS or DPGR, if the transaction is not in fact a hedging transaction within the meaning of section 1221(b)(2)(A) and § 1.1221-2(b).

(iv) Other rules. See § 1.1221-2(e) for rules applicable to hedging by members of a consolidated group and § 1.446-4 for rules regarding the timing of income, deductions, gains, or losses with respect to hedging transactions.

(4) Allocation of gross receipts. (i) Embedded services and non-qualified property. (A) In general. Except as otherwise provided in paragraph (i)(4)(i)(B), paragraph (m) (relating to construction), and paragraph (n) (relating to engineering and architectural services) of this section, gross receipts derived from the performance of services do not qualify as DPGR. In the case of an embedded service, that is, a service the price of which, in the normal course of the taxpayer's business, is not separately stated from the amount charged for the lease, rental, license, sale, exchange, or other disposition of QPP, a qualified film, or utilities, DPGR include only the gross receipts derived from the lease, rental, license, sale, exchange, or other disposition of QPP, a qualified film, or utilities (assuming all the other requirements of this section are met) and not any receipts attributable to the embedded service. In addition, DPGR does not include the gross receipts derived from the lease, rental, license, sale, exchange, or other disposition of property that does not meet all of the requirements under this section (non-qualified property). The allocation of the gross receipts attributable to the embedded services or non-qualified property will be deemed to be reasonable if the allocation reflects the fair market value of the embedded services or non-qualified property. For example, gross receipts derived from the lease, rental, license, sale, exchange, or other disposition of a replacement part that is non-qualified property does not qualify as DPGR. In addition, see § 1.199-1(e) for other instances when an allocation of gross receipts attributable to embedded services or non-qualified property will be deemed reasonable.

(B) Exceptions. There are six exceptions to the rules under paragraph (i)(4)(i)(A) of this section regarding embedded services and non-qualified property. A taxpayer may include in DPGR, if all the other requirements of this section are met with respect to the underlying item of QPP, qualified films, or utilities to which the embedded services or nonqualified property relate, the gross receipts derived from—

(1) A qualified warranty, that is, a warranty (other than a computer software maintenance agreement described in paragraph (i)(4)(i)(B)(5) of this section) that is provided in connection with the lease, rental, license, sale, exchange, or other disposition of QPP, a qualified film, or utilities if, in the normal course of the taxpayer's business—

(i) The price for the warranty is not separately stated from the amount charged for the lease, rental, license, sale, exchange, or other disposition of the QPP, qualified film, or utilities; and

(ii) The warranty is neither separately offered by the taxpayer nor separately bargained for with customers (that is, a customer cannot purchase the QPP, qualified film, or utilities without the warranty);

(2) A qualified delivery, that is, a delivery or distribution service that is provided in connection with the lease, rental, license, sale, exchange, or other disposition of QPP if, in the normal course of the taxpayer's business—

(i) The price for the delivery or distribution service is not separately stated from the amount charged for the lease, rental, license, sale, exchange, or other disposition of the QPP; and

(ii) The delivery or distribution service is neither separately offered by the taxpayer nor separately bargained for with customers (that is, a customer cannot purchase the QPP without the delivery or distribution service);

(3) A qualified operating manual, that is, a manual of instructions (including electronic instructions) that is provided in connection with the lease, rental, license, sale, exchange, or other disposition of QPP, a qualified film or utilities if, in the normal course of the taxpayer's business—

(i) The price for the manual is not separately stated from the amount charged for the lease, rental, license, sale, exchange, or other disposition of the QPP, qualified film, or utilities;

(ii) The manual is neither separately offered by the taxpayer nor separately bargained for with customers (that is, a customer cannot purchase the QPP, qualified film, or utilities without the manual); and

(iii) The manual is not provided in connection with a training course for customers;

(4) A qualified installation, that is, an installation service (including minor assembly) for tangible personal property that is provided in connection with the lease, rental, license, sale, exchange, or other disposition of the tangible personal property if, in the normal course of the taxpayer's business—

(i) The price for the installation service is not separately stated from the amount charged for the lease, rental, license, sale, exchange, or other disposition of the tangible personal property; and

(ii) The installation is neither separately offered by the taxpayer nor separately bargained for with customers (that is, a customer cannot purchase the tangible personal property without the installation service);

(5) Services performed pursuant to a qualified computer software maintenance agreement. A qualified computer software maintenance agreement is an agreement provided in connection with the lease, rental, license, sale, exchange, or other disposition of the computer software that entitles the customer to receive future updates, cyclical releases, rewrites of the underlying software, or customer support services for the computer software if, in the normal course of the taxpayer's business—

(i) The price for the agreement is not separately stated from the amount charged for the lease, rental, license, sale, exchange, or other disposition of the computer software; and

(ii) The agreement is neither separately offered by the taxpayer nor separately bargained for with customers (that is, a customer cannot purchase the computer software without the agreement); and

(6) A de minimis amount of gross receipts from embedded services and nonqualified property for each item of QPP, qualified films, or utilities. For purposes of the preceding sentence, a de minimis amount of gross receipts from embedded services and non-qualified property is less than 5 percent of the total gross receipts derived from the lease, rental, license, sale, exchange, or other disposition of each item of QPP, qualified films, or utilities. In the case of gross receipts derived from the lease, rental, license, sale, exchange, or other disposition of QPP, a qualified film, or utilities that are received over a period of time (for example, a multi-year lease or installment sale), this de minimis exception is applied by taking into account the total gross receipts for the entire period derived (and to be derived) from the lease, rental, license, sale, exchange, or other disposition of the item of QPP, qualified films, or utilities. For purposes of the preceding sentence, if a taxpayer treats gross receipts as DPGR under this de minimis exception, then the taxpayer must treat the gross receipts recognized in each taxable year consistently as DPGR. The gross receipts that the taxpayer treats as DPGR under paragraphs (i)(4)(i)(B)(1), (2), (3), (4), and (5) and (l)(4)(iv)(A) of this section are treated as DPGR for purposes of applying this de minimis exception. This de minimis exception does not apply if the price of a service or non-qualified property is separately stated by the taxpayer, or if the service or non-qualified property is separately offered or separately bargained for with the customer (that is, the customer can purchase the QPP, qualified film, or utilities without the service or non-qualified property).

(ii) Non-DPGR. All of a taxpayer's gross receipts derived from the lease, rental, license, sale, exchange or other disposition of an item of QPP, qualified films, or utilities may be treated as non-DPGR if less than 5 percent of the taxpayer's total gross receipts derived from the lease, rental, license, sale, exchange or other disposition of that item are DPGR. In the case of gross receipts derived from the lease, rental, license, sale, exchange, or other disposition of QPP, a qualified film, and utilities that are received over a period of time (for example, a multi-year lease or installment sale), this paragraph (i)(4)(ii) is applied by taking into account the total gross receipts for the entire period derived (and to be derived) from the lease, rental, license, sale, exchange, or other disposition of the item of QPP, qualified films, or utilities. For purposes of the preceding sentence, if a taxpayer treats gross receipts as non-DPGR under this de minimis exception, then the taxpayer must treat the gross receipts recognized in each taxable year consistently as non-DPGR.

(iii) Examples. The following examples illustrate the application of this paragraph (i)(4):

Example (1). X MPGE QPP within the United States. As part of the sale of the QPP to Z, X trains Z's employees on how to use and operate the QPP. No other services or property are provided to Z in connection with the sale of the QPP to Z. In the normal course of X's business, the QPP and training services are separately stated in the sales contract. Because, in the normal course of the X's business, the training services are separately stated, the training services are not treated as embedded services under the de minimis exception in paragraph (i)(4)(i)(B)(6) of this section.

Example (2). The facts are the same as in Example 1 except that, in the normal course of X's business, the training services are not separately stated in the sales contract and the customer cannot purchase the QPP without the training services. If the gross receipts for the embedded training services are less than 5% of the gross receipts derived from the sale of X's QPP to Z, after applying the exceptions under paragraphs (i)(4)(i)(B)(1) through (5) of this section, then the gross receipts may be included in DPGR under the de minimis exception in paragraph (i)(4)(i)(B)(6) of this section.

Example (3). X MPGE QPP within the United States. As part of the sale of the QPP to retailers, X charges a fee for delivering the QPP. In the normal course of X's business, the price of the QPP and the delivery fee are separately stated in X's sales contracts. Because, in the normal course of X's business, the delivery fee is separately stated, the delivery fee does not qualify as DPGR under the qualified delivery exception in paragraph (i)(4)(i)(B)(2) of this section or the de minimis exception under paragraph (i)(4)(i)(B)(6) of this section. The result would be the same even if the retailer's customers cannot purchase the QPP without paying the delivery fee.

Example (4). (i) Facts. X manufactures industrial sewing machines within the United States that X offers for sale individually to customers. X enters into a single, lump-sum priced contract with Y, an unrelated person, and the contract has the following terms: X will manufacture industrial sewing machines within the United States for Y; X will deliver the industrial sewing machines to Y; X will provide a one-year warranty on the industrial sewing machines; X will provide operating manuals with the industrial sewing machines; X will provide 100 hours of training and training manuals to Y's employees on the use and maintenance of the industrial sewing machines; X will provide purchased spare parts for the industrial sewing machines; and X will provide a 3-year service agreement for the industrial sewing machines. In the normal course of X's business, none of the services or property described above are separately stated, separately offered or separately bargained for.

(ii) Analysis. The receipts for the manufacture of the industrial sewing machines are DPGR under paragraphs (e)(1) and (g) of this section (assuming all the other requirements of this section are met). X may include in DPGR the gross receipts derived from delivering the industrial sewing machines, which is a qualified delivery under paragraph (i)(4)(i)(B)(2) of this section; the gross receipts derived from the one-year warranty, which is a qualified warranty under paragraph (i)(4)(i)(B)(1) of this section; and the gross receipts derived from the operating manuals, which is a qualified operating manual under paragraph (i)(4)(i)(B)(3) of this section. If the gross receipts allocable to each industrial sewing machine for the embedded services consisting of the employee training and 3-year service agreement, and for the non-qualified property consisting of the purchased spare parts and the employee training manuals, which are not qualified operating manuals, are in total less than 5% of the gross receipts derived from the sale of each industrial sewing machine to Y (after applying the exceptions under paragraphs (i)(4)(i)(B)(1) through (5) of this section), then those gross receipts may be included in DPGR under the de minimis exception in paragraph (i)(4)(i)(B)(6) of this section. If, however, the gross receipts allocable to each industrial sewing machine for the embedded services and non-qualified property consisting of employee training, the 3-year service agreement, purchased spare parts, and employee training manuals equal or exceed, in total, 5% of the gross receipts derived from the sale of each industrial sewing machine to Y (after applying the exceptions under paragraphs (i)(4)(i)(B)(1) through (5) of this section), then those gross receipts do not qualify as DPGR under the de minimis exception in paragraph (i)(4)(i)(B)(6) of this section (and X must allocate gross receipts between DPGR and non-DPGR under § 1.199-1(d)(1)).

(5) Advertising income. (i) In general. Except as provided in paragraph (i)(5)(ii) of this section, gross receipts derived from the lease, rental, license, sale, exchange, or other disposition of QPP, a qualified film, or utilities do not include advertising income and product-placement income.

(ii) Exceptions. (A) Tangible personal property. A taxpayer's gross receipts that are derived from the lease, rental, license, sale, exchange, or other disposition of newspapers, magazines, telephone directories, periodicals, and other similar printed publications that are MPGE in whole or in significant part within the United States include advertising income from advertisements placed in those media, but only if the gross receipts, if any, derived from the lease, rental, license, sale, exchange, or other disposition of the newspapers, magazines, telephone directories, or periodicals are (or would be) DPGR.

(B) Computer software. A taxpayer's gross receipts that are derived from the lease, rental, license, sale, exchange, or other disposition of computer software that is MPGE in whole or in significant part within the United States include advertising income and product-placement income with respect to that computer software, but only if the gross receipts, if any, derived from the lease, rental, license, sale, exchange, or other disposition of computer software are (or would be) DPGR. For this purpose, advertising income and product-placement income mean compensation for placing or integrating advertising or a product into the computer software. This paragraph (i)(5)(ii)(B) does not extend to the exceptions provided in paragraph (i)(6)(iii) of this section. See paragraph (i)(6)(iv)(F) of this section.

(C) Qualified film. A taxpayer's gross receipts that are derived from the lease, rental, license, sale, exchange, or other disposition of a qualified film include advertising income and product-placement income with respect to that qualified film, but only if the gross receipts, if any, derived from the lease, rental, license, sale, exchange, or other disposition of a qualified film are (or would be) DPGR. For this purpose, advertising income and product-placement income mean compensation for placing or integrating advertising or a product into the qualified film.

(iii) Examples. The following examples illustrate the application of this paragraph (i)(5):

Example (1). X MPGE, and sells, newspapers within the United States. X's gross receipts from the newspapers include gross receipts derived from the sale of newspapers to customers and payments from advertisers to publish display advertising or classified advertisements in X's newspapers. X's gross receipts described above are DPGR derived from the sale of X's newspapers.

Example (2). The facts are the same as in Example 1 except that X disposes of the newspapers free of charge to customers, rather than selling them. X's gross receipts from the display advertising or classified advertisements are DPGR.

Example (3). X produces two live television programs that are qualified films. X licenses the first television program to Y's television station and X licenses the second television program to Z's television station. Z broadcasts the second television program on its station. Both television programs contain product placements and advertising for which X received compensation. X and Y are unrelated persons. X and Z are non-consolidated members of an EAG. The gross receipts derived by X from licensing the first television program to Y are DPGR. As a result, pursuant to paragraph (i)(5)(ii)(C) of this section, all of X's product placement and advertising income for the first television program is treated as gross receipts that are derived from the license of the qualified film. The gross receipts derived by X from licensing the second television program to Z are non-DPGR under paragraph (b)(1) of this section. Paragraph (b)(2) of this section does not apply because Z's broadcast of the second television program on Z's television station is not a lease, rental, license, sale, exchange, or other disposition of the second television program. As a result, pursuant to paragraph (i)(5)(ii)(C) of this section, none of X's product placement and advertising income for the second television program is treated as gross receipts derived from the qualified film.

Example (4). The facts are the same as in Example 3 except that Z sublicenses to an unrelated person the television program instead of broadcasting the television program on its station. The gross receipts derived by X from licensing the television program to Z are DPGR under paragraph (b)(2) of this section. As a result, pursuant to paragraph (i)(5)(ii)(C) of this section, X's product placement and advertising income for the television program licensed to Z is treated as gross receipts derived from the qualified film. In addition, Z's receipts from the sublicense of the qualified film are DPGR under § 1.199-7(a)(3)(i).

Example (5). X produces television programs that are qualified films. X licenses the qualified films to Y, an unrelated person, and the license agreement provides that X will receive advertising time slots as part of its payments from Y under the license agreement. X's gross receipts derived from the license of the qualified films to Y include income attributable to the advertising time slots and are DPGR under paragraph (b)(2) of this section.

(6) Computer software. (i) In general. DPGR include the gross receipts of the taxpayer that are derived from the lease, rental, license, sale, exchange, or other disposition of computer software MPGE by the taxpayer in whole or in significant part within the United States. Such gross receipts qualify as DPGR even if the customer provides the computer software to its employees or others over the Internet.

(ii) Gross receipts derived from services. Gross receipts derived from customer and technical support, telephone and other telecommunication services, online services (such as Internet access services, online banking services, providing access to online electronic books, newspapers, and journals), and other similar services do not constitute gross receipts derived from a lease, rental, license, sale, exchange, or other disposition of computer software.

(iii) Exceptions. Notwithstanding paragraph (i)(6)(ii) of this section, if a taxpayer derives gross receipts from providing customers access to computer software MPGE in whole or in significant part by the taxpayer within the United States for the customers' direct use while connected to the Internet or any other public or private communications network (online software), then such gross receipts will be treated as being derived from the lease, rental, license, sale, exchange, or other disposition of computer software only if—

(A) The taxpayer also derives, on a regular and ongoing basis in the taxpayer's business, gross receipts from the lease, rental, license, sale, exchange, or other disposition to customers that are not related persons (as defined in paragraph (b)(1) of this section) of computer software that—

(1) Has only minor or immaterial differences from the online software;

(2) Has been MPGE by the taxpayer in whole or in significant part within the United States; and

(3) Has been provided to such customers either affixed to a tangible medium (for example, a disk or DVD) or by allowing them to download the computer software from the Internet; or

(B) Another person derives, on a regular and ongoing basis in its business, gross receipts from the lease, rental, license, sale, exchange, or other disposition of substantially identical software (as described in paragraph (i)(6)(iv)(A) of this section) (as compared to the taxpayer's online software) to its customers pursuant to an activity described in paragraph (i)(6)(iii)(A)(3) of this section.

(iv) Definitions and special rules. (A) Substantially identical software. For purposes of paragraph (i)(6)(iii)(B) of this section, substantially identical software is computer software that—

(1) From a customer's perspective, has the same functional result as the online software described in paragraph (i)(6)(iii) of this section; and

(2) Has a significant overlap of features or purpose with the online software described in paragraph (i)(6)(iii) of this section.

(B) Safe harbor for computer software games. For purposes of paragraph (i)(6)(iv)(A) of this section, all computer software games are deemed to be substantially identical software. For example, computer software sports games are deemed to be substantially identical to computer software card games.

(C) Regular and ongoing basis. For purposes of paragraph (i)(6)(iii) of this section, in the case of a newly-formed trade or business or a taxpayer in its first taxable year, the taxpayer is considered to be engaged in an activity described in paragraph (i)(6)(iii) of this section on a regular and ongoing basis if the taxpayer reasonably expects that it will engage in the activity on a regular and ongoing basis.

(D) Attribution. For purposes of paragraph (i)(6)(iii)(A) of this section—

(1) All members of an expanded affiliated group (as defined in § 1.199-7(a)(1)) are treated as a single taxpayer; and

(2) In the case of an EAG partnership (as defined in § 1.199-3T(i)(8)), the EAG partnership and all members of the EAG to which the EAG partnership's partners belong are treated as a single taxpayer.

(E) Qualified computer software maintenance agreements. Paragraph (i)(4)(i)(B)(5) of this section does not apply if the computer software is online software under paragraph (i)(6)(iii) of this section.

(F) Advertising income and product-placement income. Paragraph (i)(5)(ii)(B) of this section does not apply if the computer software is online software under paragraph (i)(6)(iii) of this section. If a taxpayer provides a customer with access to online software in conjunction with providing computer software to such customer either affixed to a tangible medium or by download, paragraph (i)(5)(ii)(B) of this section will only apply to compensation for the placement or integration of advertising or a product into the computer software transferred to such customer either affixed to the tangible medium or by download.

(v) Examples. The following examples illustrate the application of this paragraph (i)(6):

Example (1). L is a bank and produces computer software within the United States that enables its customers to receive online banking services for a fee. Under paragraph (i)(6)(ii) of this section, gross receipts derived from online banking services are attributable to a service and do not constitute gross receipts derived from a lease, rental, license, sale, exchange, or other disposition of computer software. Therefore, L's gross receipts derived from the online banking services are non-DPGR.

Example (2). M is an Internet auction company that produces computer software within the United States that enables its customers to participate in Internet auctions for a fee. Under paragraph (i)(6)(ii) of this section, gross receipts derived from online auction services are attributable to a service and do not constitute gross receipts derived from a lease, rental, license, sale, exchange, or other disposition of computer software. M's activities constitute the provision of online services. Therefore, M's gross receipts derived from the Internet auction services are non-DPGR.

Example (3). N provides telephone services, voicemail services, and e-mail services. N produces computer software within the United States that runs all of these services. Under paragraph (i)(6)(ii) of this section, gross receipts derived from telephone and related telecommunication services are attributable to a service and do not constitute gross receipts derived from a lease, rental, license, sale, exchange, or other disposition of computer software. Therefore, N's gross receipts derived from the telephone and other telecommunication services are non-DPGR.

Example (4). O produces tax preparation computer software within the United States. O derives, on a regular and ongoing basis in its business, gross receipts from both the sale to customers that are unrelated persons of O's computer software that has been affixed to a compact disc as well as from the sale to customers of O's computer software that customers have downloaded from the Internet. O also derives gross receipts from providing customers access to the computer software for the customers' direct use while connected to the Internet. The computer software sold on compact disc or by download has only minor or immaterial differences from the online software, and O does not provide any other goods or services in connection with the online software. Under paragraph (i)(6)(iii)(A) of this section, O's gross receipts derived from providing access to the online software will be treated as derived from the lease, rental, license, sale, exchange, or other disposition of computer software and are DPGR (assuming all the other requirements of this section are met).

Example (5). The facts are the same as in Example 4, except that O does not sell the tax preparation computer software to customers affixed to a compact disc or by download. In addition, one of O's competitors, P, derives, on a regular and ongoing basis in its business, gross receipts from the sale to customers of P's substantially identical tax preparation computer software that has been affixed to a compact disc as well as from the sale to customers of P's substantially identical tax preparation computer software that customers have downloaded from the Internet. Under paragraph (i)(6)(iii)(B) of this section, O's gross receipts derived from providing access to its tax preparation online software will be treated as derived from the lease, rental, license, sale, exchange, or other disposition of computer software and are DPGR (assuming all the other requirements of this section are met).

Example (6). Q produces payroll management computer software within the United States. For a fee, Q provides customers access to the payroll management computer software for the customers' direct use while connected to the Internet. This is Q's sole method of providing access to its payroll management computer software to customers. In conjunction with the payroll management computer software, Q provides storage of customers' data and telephone support. One of Q's competitors, R, derives, on a regular and ongoing basis in its business, gross receipts from the sale to customers of R's substantially identical payroll management software that has been affixed to a compact disc as well as from the sale to customers of R's substantially identical payroll management software that customers have downloaded from the Internet. Under paragraph (i)(6)(iii)(B) of this section, Q's gross receipts derived from providing access to its payroll management online software will be treated as derived from the lease, rental, license, sale, exchange, or other disposition of computer software and are DPGR (assuming all the other requirements of this section are met). However, Q's gross receipts derived from the fees that are properly allocable to the storage of customers' data and telephone support are non-DPGR.

Example (7). The facts are the same as in Example 6, except that R produces inventory computer software, not payroll management computer software. R's inventory computer software is not substantially identical software as defined in paragraph (i)(6)(iv)(A) of this section because R's inventory software, from a customer's perspective, does not have the same functional result as Q's payroll management computer software and does not have significant overlap of features or purpose with Q's payroll management computer software. No other person provides substantially identical software to customers affixed to a compact disc or by download. Under paragraph (i)(6)(ii) of this section, gross receipts derived from providing access to Q's payroll online software do not constitute gross receipts derived from a lease, rental, license, sale, exchange or other disposition of payroll computer software. Therefore, Q's gross receipts derived from the payroll management computer software are non-DPGR.

Example (8). S produces computer software games within the United States. S derives, on a regular and ongoing basis in its business, gross receipts from both the sale to customers that are not related to S of S's computer software games that have been affixed to a compact disc as well as from the sale to customers of S's computer software games that customers have downloaded from the Internet. S also derives gross receipts from providing customers access to the computer software games for the customers' direct use while connected to the Internet (online software games). The computer software games sold on compact disc or by download have only minor or immaterial differences from the online software games, and S does not provide any other goods or services in connection with the online software games. Under paragraph (i)(6)(iii)(A) of this section, S's gross receipts derived from providing customers access to its online software games will be treated as derived from the lease, rental, license, sale, exchange, or other disposition of computer software and are DPGR (assuming all the other requirements of this section are met).

Example (9). The facts are the same as in Example 8, except S's gross receipts also include advertising income from integrating advertisers' logos into the computer software games. Under paragraph (i)(5)(ii)(B) of this section, for S's computer software games sold affixed to a compact disc or by download, S's advertising income is treated as gross receipts derived from the sale of the computer software games and, therefore, is DPGR (assuming all the other requirements of this section are met). However, under paragraphs (i)(5)(i) and (i)(6)(iv)(F) of this section, for S's online software games, S's advertising income is not derived from the lease, rental, license, sale, exchange, or other disposition of computer software and, therefore, is non-DPGR.

(7) Qualifying in-kind partnership for taxable years beginning after May 17, 2006, the enactment date of the Tax Increase Prevention and Reconciliation Act of 2005 (i) In general. If a partnership is a qualifying in-kind partnership described in paragraph (i)(7)(ii) of this section, then each partner is treated as having MPGE or produced the property MPGE or produced by the partnership that is distributed to that partner. If a partner of a qualifying in-kind partnership derives gross receipts from the lease, rental, license, sale, exchange, or other disposition of the property that was MPGE or produced by the qualifying in-kind partnership and distributed to that partner, then, provided such partner is a partner of the qualifying in-kind partnership at the time the partner disposes of the property, the partner is treated as conducting the MPGE or production activities previously conducted by the qualifying in-kind partnership with respect to that property. With respect to a lease, rental, or license, the partner is treated as having disposed of the property on the date or dates on which it takes into account its gross receipts derived from the lease, rental, or license under its method of accounting. With respect to a sale, exchange, or other disposition, the partner is treated as having disposed of the property on the date it ceases to own the property for Federal income tax purposes, even if no gain or loss is taken into account.

(ii) Definition of qualifying in-kind partnership. For purposes of this paragraph (i)(7), a qualifying in-kind partnership is a partnership engaged solely in—

(A) The extraction, refining, or processing of oil, natural gas (as described in paragraph (l)(2) of this section), petrochemicals, or products derived from oil, natural gas, or petrochemicals in whole or in significant part within the United States;

(B) The production or generation of electricity in the United States; or

(C) An activity or industry designated by the Secretary by publication in the Internal Revenue Bulletin (see § 601.601(d)(2)(ii)(b) of this chapter).

(iii) Other rules. Except as provided in this paragraph (i)(7), a qualifying in-kind partnership is treated the same as other partnerships for purposes of section 199. Accordingly, a qualifying in-kind partnership is subject to the rules of this section regarding the application of section 199 to pass-thru entities, including application of the section 199(d)(1)(A)(iii) rule for determining a partner's share of the amounts described in § 1.199-2(e)(1) (paragraph (e)(1) wages) from the partnership under § 1.199-5(b)(3). In determining whether a qualifying in-kind partnership or its partners MPGE QPP in whole or in significant part within the United States, see paragraphs (g)(2) and (3) of this section.

(iv) Example. The following example illustrates the application of this paragraph (i)(7). Assume that PRS and X are calendar year taxpayers. The example reads as follows:

Example. X, Y, and Z are partners in PRS, a qualifying in-kind partnership described in paragraph (i)(7)(ii) of this section. X, Y, and Z are corporations. In 2007, PRS distributes oil to X that PRS derived from its oil extraction. PRS incurred $600 of CGS extracting the oil distributed to X, and X's adjusted basis in the distributed oil is $600. X incurs $200 of CGS in refining the oil within the United States. In 2007, X, while it is a partner in PRS, sells the oil to a customer for $1,500. X is treated as having disposed of the property on the date it ceases to own the property for Federal income tax purposes. Under paragraph (i)(7)(i) of this section, X is treated as having extracted the oil. The extraction and refining of the oil each qualify as an MPGE activity under paragraph (e)(1) of this section. Therefore, X's $1,500 of gross receipts qualify as DPGR. X subtracts from the $1,500 of DPGR the $600 of CGS incurred by PRS and the $200 of refining costs it incurred. Thus, X's QPAI is $700 for 2007.

(8) Partnerships owned by members of a single expanded affiliated group for taxable years beginning after May 17, 2006, the enactment date of the Tax Increase Prevention and Reconciliation Act of 2005. (i) In general. For purposes of this section, if all of the interests in the capital and profits of a partnership are owned by members of a single EAG at all times during the taxable year of the partnership (EAG partnership), then the EAG partnership and all members of that EAG are treated as a single taxpayer for purposes of section 199(c)(4) during that taxable year.

(ii) Attribution of activities. (A) In general. If a member of an EAG (disposing member) derives gross receipts from the lease, rental, license, sale, exchange, or other disposition of property that was MPGE or produced by an EAG partnership, all the partners of which are members of the same EAG to which the disposing member belongs at the time that the disposing member disposes of such property, then the disposing member is treated as conducting the MPGE or production activities previously conducted by the EAG partnership with respect to that property. The previous sentence applies only for those taxable years in which the disposing member is a member of the EAG of which all the partners of the EAG partnership are members for the entire taxable year of the EAG partnership. With respect to a lease, rental, or license, the disposing member is treated as having disposed of the property on the date or dates on which it takes into account its gross receipts from the lease, rental, or license under its method of accounting. With respect to a sale, exchange, or other disposition, the disposing member is treated as having disposed of the property on the date it ceases to own the property for Federal income tax purposes, even if no gain or loss is taken into account. Likewise, if an EAG partnership derives gross receipts from the lease, rental, license, sale, exchange, or other disposition of property that was MPGE or produced by a member (or members) of the same EAG (the producing member) to which all the partners of the EAG partnership belong at the time that the EAG partnership disposes of such property, then the EAG partnership is treated as conducting the MPGE or production activities previously conducted by the producing member with respect to that property. The previous sentence applies only for those taxable years in which the producing member is a member of the EAG of which all the partners of the EAG partnership are members for the entire taxable year of the EAG partnership. With respect to a lease, rental, or license, the EAG partnership is treated as having disposed of the property on the date or dates on which it takes into account its gross receipts derived from the lease, rental, or license under its method of accounting. With respect to a sale, exchange, or other disposition, the EAG partnership is treated as having disposed of the property on the date it ceases to own the property for Federal income tax purposes, even if no gain or loss is taken into account. See paragraph (i)(8)(iv) Example 3 of this section.

(B) Attribution between EAG partnerships. If an EAG partnership (disposing partnership) derives gross receipts from the lease, rental, license, sale, exchange, or other disposition of property that was MPGE or produced by another EAG partnership (producing partnership), then the disposing partnership is treated as conducting the MPGE or production activities previously conducted by the producing partnership with respect to that property, provided that each of these partnerships (the producing partnership and the disposing partnership) is owned for its entire taxable year in which the disposing partnership disposes of such property by members of the same EAG. With respect to a lease, rental, or license, the disposing partnership is treated as having disposed of the property on the date or dates on which it takes into account its gross receipts from the lease, rental, or license under its method of accounting. With respect to a sale, exchange, or other disposition, the disposing partnership is treated as having disposed of the property on the date it ceases to own the property for Federal income tax purposes, even if no gain or loss is taken into account.

(C) Exceptions to attribution. Attribution of activities does not apply for purposes of the construction of real property under paragraph (m)(1) of this section and the performance of engineering and architectural services under paragraphs (n)(2) and (3) of this section, respectively.

(iii) Other rules. Except as provided in this paragraph (i)(8), an EAG partnership is treated the same as other partnerships for purposes of section 199. Accordingly, an EAG partnership is subject to the rules of this section regarding the application of section 199 to pass-thru entities, including the section 199(d)(1)(A)(iii) rule under § 1.199-5(b)(3). In determining whether a member of an EAG or an EAG partnership MPGE QPP in whole or in significant part within the United States or produced a qualified film or produced utilities within the United States, see paragraphs (g)(2) and (3) of this section and Example 5 of paragraph (i)(8)(iv) of this section.

(iv) Examples. The following examples illustrate the rules of this paragraph (i)(8). Assume that PRS, X, Y, and Z all are calendar year taxpayers. The examples read as follows:

Example (1). Contribution. X and Y are the only partners in PRS, a partnership, for PRS's entire 2007 taxable year. X and Y are both members of a single EAG for the entire 2007 year. In 2007, X MPGE QPP within the United States and contributes the QPP to PRS. In 2007, PRS sells the QPP for $1,000. Under this paragraph (i)(8), PRS is treated as having MPGE the QPP within the United States, and PRS's $1,000 gross receipts constitute DPGR. PRS, X, and Y must apply the rules of this section regarding the application of section 199 to pass-thru entities with respect to the activity of PRS, including the section 199(d)(1)(A)(iii) rule for determining a partner's share of the paragraph (e)(1) wages from the partnership under § 1.199-5(b)(3).

Example (2). Sale. X, Y, and Z are the only members of a single EAG for the entire 2007 year. X and Y each own 50% of the capital and profits interests in PRS, a partnership, for PRS's entire 2007 taxable year. In 2007, PRS MPGE QPP within the United States and then sells the QPP to X for $6,000, its fair market value at the time of the sale. PRS's gross receipts of $6,000 qualify as DPGR. In 2007, X sells the QPP to customers for $10,000, incurring selling expenses of $2,000. Under paragraph (i)(8)(ii)(A) of this section, X is treated as having MPGE the QPP within the United States, and X's $10,000 of gross receipts qualify as DPGR. PRS, X and Y must apply the rules of this section regarding the application of section 199 to pass-thru entities with respect to the activity of PRS, including application of the section 199(d)(1)(A)(iii) rule for determining a partner's share of the paragraph (e)(1) wages from the partnership under § 1.199-5(b)(3). The results would be the same if PRS sold the QPP to Z rather than to X. However, if PRS did sell the QPP to Z, and Z was not a member of the EAG for

PRS's entire taxable year, the activities previously conducted by PRS with respect to the QPP would not be attributed to Z, and none of Z's $10,000 of gross receipts would qualify as DPGR.

Example (3). Lease. X, Y, and Z are the only members of a single EAG for the entire 2007 year. X and Y each own 50% of the capital and profits interests in PRS, a partnership, for PRS's entire 2007 taxable year. In 2007, PRS MPGE QPP within the United States and then sells the QPP to X for $6,000, its fair market value at the time of the sale. PRS's gross receipts of $6,000 qualify as DPGR. In 2007, X rents the QPP it acquired from PRS to customers unrelated to X. X takes the gross receipts attributable to the rental of the QPP into account under its method of accounting in 2007 and 2008. On July 1, 2008, X ceases to be a member of the same EAG to which Y, the other partner in PRS, belongs. For 2007, X is treated as having MPGE the QPP within the United States under paragraph (i)(8)(ii)(A) of this section, and its gross receipts derived from the rental of the QPP qualify as DPGR. For 2008, however, because X and Y, partners in PRS, are no longer members of the same EAG for the entire year, the gross rental receipts X takes into account in 2008 do not qualify as DPGR.

Example (4). Distribution. X and Y are the only partners in PRS, a partnership, for PRS's entire 2007 taxable year. X and Y are both members of a single EAG for the entire 2007 year. In 2007, PRS MPGE QPP within the United States, incurring $600 of CGS, and then distributes the QPP to X. X's adjusted basis in the QPP is $600. X incurs $200 of CGS to further MPGE the QPP within the United States. In 2007, X sells the QPP for $1,500 to an unrelated customer. X is treated as having disposed of the QPP on the date it ceases to own the QPP for Federal income tax purposes. Under paragraph (i)(8)(ii)(A) of this section, X is treated as having MPGE the QPP within the United States, and X's $1,500 of gross receipts qualify as DPGR.

Example (5). Multiple sales. (i) Facts. X and Y are the only partners in PRS, a partnership, for PRS's entire 2007 taxable year. X and Y are both non-consolidated members of a single EAG for the entire 2007 year. PRS produces in bulk form in the United States the active ingredient for a drug. Assume that PRS's own MPGE activity with respect to the active ingredient is not substantial in nature, taking into account all of the facts and circumstances, and PRS's direct labor and overhead to MPGE the active ingredient within the United States are $15 and account for 15% of PRS's $100 CGS of the active ingredient. In 2007, PRS sells the active ingredient in bulk form to X. X uses the active ingredient to produce the finished dosage form drug. Assume that X's own MPGE activity with respect to the finished dosage form drug is not substantial in nature, taking into account all of the facts and circumstances, and X's direct labor and overhead to MPGE the finished dosage form drug within the United States are $12 and account for 10% of X's $120 CGS of the drug. In 2007, X sells the finished dosage form drug to Y and Y sells the finished dosage form drug to customers. Assume that Y's own MPGE activity with respect to the finished dosage form drug is not substantial in nature, taking into account all of the facts and circumstances, and Y incurs $2 of direct labor and overhead and Y's CGS in selling the finished dosage form drug to customers is $130.

(ii) Analysis. PRS's gross receipts from the sale of the active ingredient to X are non-DPGR because PRS's MPGE activity is not substantial in nature and PRS does not satisfy the safe harbor described in paragraph (g)(3) of this section because PRS's direct labor and overhead account for less than 20% of PRS's CGS of the active ingredient. X's gross receipts from the sale of the finished dosage form drug to Y are DPGR because X is considered to have MPGE the finished dosage form drug in significant part in the United States pursuant to the safe harbor described in paragraph (g)(3) of this section because the $27 ($15 + $12) of direct labor and overhead incurred by PRS and X equals or exceeds 20% of X's total CGS ($120) of the finished dosage form drug at the time X disposes of the finished dosage form drug to Y. Similarly, Y's gross receipts from the sale of the finished dosage form drug to customers are DPGR because Y is considered to have MPGE the finished dosage form drug in significant part in the United States pursuant to the safe harbor described in paragraph (g)(3) of this section because the $29 ($15 + $12 + $2) of direct labor and overhead incurred by PRS, X, and Y equals or exceeds 20% of Y's total CGS ($130) of the finished dosage form drug at the time Y disposes of the finished dosage form drug to Y's customers.

(9) Non-operating mineral interests. DPGR does not include gross receipts derived from non-operating mineral interests (for example, interests other than operating mineral interests within the meaning of § 1.614-2(b)).

(j) Definition of qualifying production property. *(1) In general.* QPP means—

(i) Tangible personal property (as defined in paragraph (j)(2) of this section);

(ii) Computer software (as defined in paragraph (j)(3) of this section); and

(iii) Sound recordings (as defined in paragraph (j)(4) of this section).

(2) Tangible personal property. (i) In general. The term tangible personal property is any tangible property other than land, real property described in paragraph (m)(3) of this section, and any property described in paragraph (j)(3), (j)(4), (k)(1), or (l) of this section. For purposes of the preceding sentence, tangible personal property also includes any gas (other than natural gas described in paragraph (l)(2) of this section), chemical, and similar property, for example, steam, oxygen, hydrogen, and nitrogen. Property such as machinery, printing presses, transportation and office equipment, refrigerators, grocery counters, testing equipment, display racks and shelves, and neon and other signs that are contained in or attached to a building constitutes tangible personal property for purposes of this paragraph (j)(2)(i). Except as provided in paragraphs (j)(5)(ii) and (k)(2)(i) of this section, computer software, sound recordings, and qualified films are not treated as tangible personal property regardless of whether they are affixed to a tangible medium. However, the tangible medium to which such property may be affixed (for example, a videocassette, a computer diskette, or other similar tangible item) is tangible personal property.

(ii) Local law. In determining whether property is tangible personal property, local law is not controlling.

(iii) Intangible property. The term tangible personal property does not include property in a form other than in a tangible medium. For example, mass-produced books are tangible personal property, but neither the rights to the underlying manuscript nor an online version of the book is tangible personal property.

(3) Computer software. (i) In general. The term computer software means any program or routine or any sequence of machine-readable code that is designed to cause a computer to perform a desired function or set of functions, and the documentation required to describe and maintain that pro-

gram or routine. Thus, for example, an electronic book available online or for download is not computer software. For purposes of this paragraph (j)(3), computer software also includes the machine-readable code for video games and similar programs, for equipment that is an integral part of other property, and for typewriters, calculators, adding and accounting machines, copiers, duplicating equipment, and similar equipment, regardless of whether the code is designed to operate on a computer (as defined in section 168(i)(2)(B)). Computer programs of all classes, for example, operating systems, executive systems, monitors, compilers and translators, assembly routines, and utility programs, as well as application programs, are included. Except as provided in paragraph (j)(5) of this section,. if the medium in which the software is contained, whether written, magnetic, or otherwise, is tangible, then such medium is considered tangible personal property for purposes of this section.

(ii) Incidental and ancillary rights. Computer software also includes any incidental and ancillary rights that are necessary to effect the acquisition of the title to, the ownership of, or the right to use the computer software, and that are used only in connection with that specific computer software. Such incidental and ancillary rights are not included in the definition of trademark or trade name under § 1.197-2(b)(10)(i). For example, a trademark or trade name that is ancillary to the ownership or use of a specific computer software program in the taxpayer's trade or business and is not acquired for the purpose of marketing the computer software is included in the definition of computer software and is not included in the definition of trademark or trade name.

(iii) Exceptions. Computer software does not include any data or information base unless the data or information base is in the public domain and is incidental to a computer program. For this purpose, a copyrighted or proprietary data or information base is treated as in the public domain if its availability through the computer program does not contribute significantly to the cost of the program. For example, if a word-processing program includes a dictionary feature that may be used to spell-check a document or any portion thereof, then the entire program (including the dictionary feature) is computer software regardless of the form in which the dictionary feature is maintained or stored.

(4) Sound recordings. (i) In general. The term sound recordings means any works that result from the fixation of a series of musical, spoken, or other sounds under section 168(f)(4). The definition of sound recordings is limited to the master copy of the recordings (or other copy from which the holder is licensed to make and produce copies), and, except as provided in paragraph (j)(5) of this section, if the medium (such as compact discs, tapes, or other phonorecordings) in which the sounds may be embodied is tangible, then the medium is considered tangible personal property for purposes of paragraph (j)(2) of this section.

(ii) Exception. The term sound recordings does not include the creation of copyrighted material in a form other than a sound recording, such as lyrics or music composition.

(5) Tangible personal property with computer software or sound recordings. (i) Computer software and sound recordings. If a taxpayer MPGE in whole or in significant part computer software or sound recordings within the United States that is affixed or added to tangible personal property (for example, a computer diskette, or an appliance), whether or not the taxpayer MPGE such tangible personal property in whole or in significant part within the United States, then for purposes of this section—

(A) The computer software and the tangible personal property may be treated by the taxpayer as computer software. If the taxpayer treats the computer software and the tangible personal property as computer software, activities the cost of which are described in Rev. Proc. 2000-50 (2000-1 C.B. 601), activities giving rise to research and experimental expenditures under section 174, and the creation of intangible assets for computer software are considered in determining whether the taxpayer's MPGE activity is substantial in nature under paragraph (g)(2) of this section. In determining direct labor and overhead under paragraph (g)(3)(i) of this section, the costs of direct labor and overhead for developing the computer software as described in Rev. Proc. 2000-50 (2000-1 C.B. 601), research and experimental expenditures under section 174, and any other costs of creating intangible assets for the computer software are treated as direct labor and overhead. These costs must be included in the taxpayer's CGS of the computer software for purposes of determining whether the taxpayer meets the safe harbor under paragraph (g)(3)(i) of this section. However, any costs under section 174, and the costs to create intangible assets, attributable to the tangible personal property are not considered in determining whether the taxpayer's activity is substantial in nature under paragraph (g)(2) of this section and are not direct labor and overhead under paragraph (g)(3)(i) of this section; and

(B) The sound recordings and the tangible personal property with the sound recordings may be treated by the taxpayer as sound recordings. If the taxpayer treats the sound recordings and the tangible personal property as sound recordings, activities giving rise to research and experimental expenditures under section 174 and the creation of intangible assets for sound recordings are considered in determining whether the taxpayer's MPGE activity is substantial in nature under paragraph (g)(2) of this section. In determining direct labor and overhead under paragraph (g)(3)(i) of this section, research and experimental expenditures under section 174 and any other costs of creating intangible assets for sound recordings are treated as direct labor and overhead. These costs must be included in the taxpayer's CGS of sound recordings for purposes of determining whether the taxpayer meets the safe harbor under paragraph (g)(3)(i) of this section. However, any costs under section 174, and the costs to create intangible assets, attributable to the tangible personal property are not considered in determining whether the taxpayer's activity is substantial in nature under paragraph (g)(2) of this section and are not direct labor and overhead under paragraph (g)(3)(i) of this section.

(ii) Tangible personal property. If a taxpayer MPGE tangible personal property (for example, a computer diskette or an appliance) in whole or in significant part within the United States but not the computer software or sound recordings that is affixed or added to such tangible personal property, then for purposes of this section the tangible personal property with the computer software or sound recordings may be treated by the taxpayer as tangible personal property under paragraph (j)(2) of this section. Any costs under section 174, and the costs to create intangible assets, attributable to the tangible personal property are not considered in determining whether the taxpayer's activity is substantial in nature under paragraph (g)(2) of this section and are not direct labor or overhead under paragraph (g)(3)(i) of this section. For purposes of paragraph (g)(3) of this section, the taxpayer's CGS (or unadjusted depreciable basis, if applicable) for each item of tangible personal property includes the taxpayer's cost of leasing, renting, licensing, buying, or otherwise acquiring the computer software or sound recordings.

(k) Definition of qualified film. *(1) In general.* The term qualified film means any motion picture film or video tape under section 168(f)(3), or live or delayed television programming (film), if not less than 50 percent of the total compensation relating to the production of such film is compensation for services performed in the United States by actors, production personnel, directors, and producers. For purposes of this paragraph (k), the term actors includes players, newscasters, or any other persons who are compensated for their performance or appearance in a film. For purposes of this paragraph (k), the term production personnel includes writers, choreographers and composers who are compensated for providing services during the production of a film, as well as casting agents, camera operators, set designers, lighting technicians, make-up artists, and other persons who are compensated for providing services that are directly related to the production of the film. Except as provided in paragraph (k)(2) of this section, the definition of a qualified film does not include tangible personal property embodying the qualified film, such as DVDs or videocassettes.

(2) Tangible personal property with a film. (i) Film not produced by a taxpayer. If a taxpayer MPGE tangible personal property (for example, a DVD) in whole or in significant part in the United States and a film not produced by a taxpayer is affixed to the tangible personal property, then the taxpayer may treat the tangible personal property with the affixed film as tangible personal property, regardless of whether the film is a qualified film. The determination of whether the gross receipts of such a taxpayer derived from the lease, rental, license, sale, exchange, or other disposition of the tangible personal property with the affixed film are DPGR is made under the rules of this section. For purposes of paragraph (g)(2) of this section, in determining whether the taxpayer's MPGE activity is substantial in nature, the taxpayer must consider the value of the licensed film. For purposes of paragraph (g)(3) of this section, the taxpayer's CGS (or unadjusted depreciable basis, as applicable) for each item of tangible personal property includes the taxpayer's cost of leasing, renting, licensing, buying, or otherwise acquiring the film.

(ii) Film produced by a taxpayer. If a taxpayer produces a film and the film is affixed to tangible personal property (for example, a DVD), then for purposes of this section—

(A) Qualified film. If the film is a qualified film, the taxpayer may treat the tangible personal property, whether or not the taxpayer MPGE such tangible personal property, to which the qualified film is affixed as part of the qualified film; and

(B) Nonqualified film. If the film is not a qualified film (nonqualified film), a taxpayer cannot treat the tangible personal property to which the nonqualified film is affixed as part of the nonqualified film.

(3) Derived from a qualified film. (i) In general. DPGR include the gross receipts of a taxpayer that are derived from any lease, rental, license, sale, exchange, or other disposition of any qualified film produced by such taxpayer.

(ii) Exceptions. The showing of a qualified film (for example, in a movie theater or by broadcast on a television station) by a taxpayer is not a lease, rental, license, sale, exchange, or other disposition of the qualified film by such taxpayer. Ticket sales for viewing a qualified film do not constitute DPGR because the gross receipts are not derived from the lease, rental, license, sale, exchange, or other disposition of a qualified film. Because a taxpayer that merely writes a screenplay or other similar material is not considered to have produced a qualified film under paragraph (k)(1) of this section, the amounts that the taxpayer receives from the sale of the script or screenplay, even if the script is developed into a qualified film, are not gross receipts derived from a qualified film. In addition, revenue from the sale of film-themed merchandise is revenue from the sale of tangible personal property and not gross receipts derived from a qualified film. Gross receipts derived from a license of the right to use or exploit the film characters are not gross receipts derived from a qualified film.

(4) Compensation for services. For purposes of this paragraph (k), the term compensation for services means all payments for services performed by actors, production personnel, directors, and producers relating to the production of the film, including participations and residuals. Payments for services include all elements of compensation as provided for in § 1.263A-1(e)(2)(i)(B) and (3)(ii)(D). Compensation for services is not limited to W-2 wages and includes compensation paid to independent contractors. In the case of a taxpayer that uses the income forecast method of section 167(g) and capitalizes participations and residuals into the adjusted basis of the qualified film, the taxpayer must use the same estimate of participations and residuals in determining compensation for services. In the case of a taxpayer that excludes participations and residuals from the adjusted basis of the qualified film under section 167(g)(7)(D)(i), the taxpayer must use the amount expected to be paid as participations and residuals based on the total forecasted income used in determining income

(5) Determination of 50 percent. The not-less-than-50-percent-of-the-total-compensation requirement under paragraph (k)(1) of this section is calculated using a fraction. The numerator of the fraction is the compensation for services performed in the United States and the denominator is the total compensation for services regardless of where the production activities are performed. A taxpayer may use any reasonable method that is satisfactory to the Secretary based on all of the facts and circumstances, including all historic information available, to determine the compensation for services performed in the United States and the total compensation for services regardless of where the production activities are performed. Among the factors to be considered in determining whether a taxpayer's method of allocating compensation is reasonable is whether the taxpayer uses that method consistently from one taxable year to another.

(6) Produced by the taxpayer. A qualified film will be treated as produced by the taxpayer for purposes of § 199(c)(4)(A)(i)(II) if the production activity performed by the taxpayer is substantial in nature within the meaning of paragraph (g)(2) of this section. The special rules of paragraph (g)(4) of this section regarding a contract with an unrelated person and aggregation apply in determining whether the taxpayer's production activity is substantial in nature. Paragraphs (g)(2) and (4) of this section are applied by substituting the term qualified film for QPP and disregarding the requirement that the production activity must be within the United States. The production activity of the taxpayer must consist of more than the minor or immaterial combination or assembly of two or more components of a film. For purposes of paragraph (g)(2) of this section, the relative value added by affixing trademarks or trade names as defined in § 1.197-2(b)(10)(i) will be treated as zero.

(7) Qualified film produced by the taxpayer--safe harbor. A film will be treated as a qualified film under paragraph

(k)(1) of this section and produced by the taxpayer under paragraph (k)(6) of this section (qualified film produced by the taxpayer) if the taxpayer meets the requirements of paragraphs (k)(7)(i) and (ii) of this section. A taxpayer that chooses to use this safe harbor must apply all the provisions of this paragraph (k)(7).

(i) Safe harbor. A film will be treated as a qualified film produced by the taxpayer if not less than 50 percent of the total compensation for services paid by the taxpayer is compensation for services performed in the United States and the taxpayer satisfies the safe harbor in paragraph (g)(3) of this section. The special rules of paragraph (g)(4) of this section regarding a contract with an unrelated person and aggregation apply in determining whether the taxpayer satisfies paragraph (g)(3) of this section. Paragraphs (g)(3) and (4) of this section are applied by substituting the term qualified film for QPP but not disregarding the requirement that the direct labor and overhead of the taxpayer to produce the qualified film must be within the United States. Paragraph (g)(3)(ii)(A) of this section includes any election under section 181.

(ii) Determination of 50 percent. The not-less-than-50-percent-of-the-total-compensation requirement under paragraph (k)(7)(i) of this section is calculated using a fraction. The numerator of the fraction is the compensation for services paid by the taxpayer for services performed in the United States and the denominator is the total compensation for services paid by the taxpayer regardless of where the production activities are performed. For purposes of this paragraph (k)(7)(ii), the term paid by the taxpayer includes amounts that are treated as paid by the taxpayer under paragraph (g)(4) of this section. A taxpayer may use any reasonable method that is satisfactory to the Secretary based on all of the facts and circumstances, including all historic information available, to determine the compensation for services paid by the taxpayer for services performed in the United States and the total compensation for services paid by the taxpayer regardless of where the production activities are performed. Among the factors to be considered in determining whether a taxpayer's method of allocating compensation is reasonable is whether the taxpayer uses that method consistently from one taxable year to another.

(8) Production pursuant to a contract. With the exception of the rules applicable to an expanded affiliated group (EAG) under § 1.199-7 and EAG partnerships under § 1.199-3(i)(8), only one taxpayer may claim the deduction under § 1.199-1(a) with respect to any activity related to the production of a qualified film performed in connection with the same qualified film. If one taxpayer performs a production activity pursuant to a contract with another party, then only the taxpayer that has the benefits and burdens of ownership of the qualified film under Federal income tax principles during the period in which the production activity occurs is treated as engaging in the production activity.

(9) Exception. A qualified film does not include property with respect to which records are required to be maintained under 18 U.S.C. 2257. Section 2257 of Title 18 requires maintenance of certain records with respect to any book, magazine, periodical, film, videotape, or other matter that—

(i) Contains one or more visual depictions made after November 1, 1990, of actual sexually explicit conduct; and

(ii) Is produced in whole or in part with materials that have been mailed or shipped in interstate or foreign commerce, or is shipped or transported or is intended for shipment or transportation in interstate or foreign commerce.

(10) Examples. The following examples illustrate the application of this paragraph (k):

Example (1). X produces a qualified film and duplicates the film onto purchased DVDs. X sells the DVDs with the qualified film to customers. Under paragraph (k)(2)(ii)(A) of this section, X treats the DVD with the qualified film as a qualified film. Accordingly, X's gross receipts derived from the sale of the qualified film to customers are DPGR (assuming all the other requirements of this section are met).

Example (2). The facts are the same as in Example 1 except that the film is a nonqualified film because the film does not satisfy the not-less-than-50-percent-of-the-total-compensation requirement under (k)(1) of this section and X manufactures the DVDs in the United States. Under paragraph (k)(2)(ii)(B) of this section, X cannot treat the DVD as part of the nonqualified film. X's gross receipts (not including the gross receipts attributable to the nonqualified film) derived from the sale of the tangible personal property are DPGR (assuming all the other requirements of this section are met).

Example (3). X produces live television programs that are qualified films. X shows the programs on its own television station. X sells advertising time slots to advertisers for the television programs. Because showing a qualified film on a television station is not a lease, rental, license, sale, exchange, or other disposition pursuant to paragraph (k)(3)(ii) of this section, the advertising income X receives from advertisers is not derived from the lease, rental, license, sale, exchange, or other disposition of the qualified films and is non-DPGR.

Example (4). The facts are the same as in Example 3 except that X also licenses the qualified films to Y, an unrelated cable company that broadcasts X's qualified films. As part of the license agreement, X can sell advertising time slots. Because X's gross receipts from Y are derived from the licensing of qualified films pursuant to paragraph (k)(3)(i) of this section, X's gross receipts derived from licensing the qualified film are DPGR. In addition, the gross receipts derived from the advertising income X receives that is related to the qualified films licensed to Y is DPGR pursuant to paragraph (i)(5)(ii) of this section. Because showing a qualified film on a television station is not a lease, rental, license, sale, exchange, or other disposition pursuant to paragraph (k)(3)(ii) of this section, the portion of the advertising income X derives from advertisers for the qualified films it broadcasts on its own television station is not derived from the lease, rental, license, sale, exchange, or other disposition of the qualified films and is non-DPGR.

Example (5). X produces a qualified film and contracts with Y, an unrelated person, to duplicate the film onto DVDs. Y manufactures blank DVDs within the United States, duplicates X's film onto the DVDs in the United States, and sells the DVDs with the qualified film to X who then sells them to customers. Y has all of the benefits and burdens of ownership under Federal income tax principles of the DVDs during the MPGE and duplication process. Assume Y's activities relating to manufacture of the blank DVDs and duplicating the film onto the DVDs collectively satisfy the safe harbor under paragraph (g)(3) of this section. Y's gross receipts from manufacturing the DVDs and duplicating the film onto the DVDs are DPGR (assuming all the other requirements of this section are met). X's gross receipts from the sale of the DVDs to customers are DPGR (assuming all the other requirements of this section are met).

Example (6). X creates a television program in the United States that includes scenes from films licensed by X from unrelated persons Y and Z. Assume that Y and Z produced the films licensed by X. The not-less-than-50-percent-of-the-total-compensation requirement under paragraph (k)(1) of this section is determined by reference to all compensation for services paid in the production of the television program, including the films licensed by X from Y and Z, and is calculated using a fraction as described in paragraph (k)(5) of this section. The numerator of the fraction is the compensation for services performed in the United States and the denominator is the total compensation for services regardless of where the production activities are performed. However, for purposes of calculating the denominator, in determining the total compensation paid by Y and Z, X need only include the total compensation paid by Y and Z to actors, production personnel, directors, and producers for the production of the scenes used by X in creating its television program.

(l) Electricity, natural gas, or potable water. *(1) In general.* DPGR include gross receipts derived from any lease, rental, license, sale, exchange, or other disposition of utilities produced by the taxpayer in the United States if all other requirements of this section are met. In the case of an integrated producer that both produces and delivers utilities, see paragraph (l)(4) of this section that describes certain gross receipts that do not qualify as DPGR.

(2) Natural gas. The term natural gas includes only natural gas extracted from a natural deposit and does not include, for example, methane gas extracted from a landfill. In the case of natural gas, production activities include all activities involved in extracting natural gas from the ground and processing the gas into pipeline quality gas.

(3) Potable water. The term potable water means unbottled drinking water. In the case of potable water, production activities include the acquisition, collection, and storage of raw water (untreated water), transportation of raw water to a water treatment facility, and treatment of raw water at such a facility. Gross receipts attributable to any of these activities are included in DPGR if all other requirements of this section are met.

(4) Exceptions. (i) Electricity. Gross receipts attributable to the transmission of electricity from the generating facility to a point of local distribution and gross receipts attributable to the distribution of electricity to customers are non-DPGR.

(ii) Natural gas. Gross receipts attributable to the transmission of pipeline quality gas from a natural gas field (or, if treatment at a natural gas processing plant is necessary to produce pipeline quality gas, from a natural gas processing plant) to a local distribution company's citygate (or to another customer) are non-DPGR. Likewise, gross receipts of a local gas distribution company attributable to distribution from the citygate to the local customers are non-DPGR.

(iii) Potable water. Gross receipts attributable to the storage of potable water after completion of treatment of the potable water, as well as gross receipts attributable to the transmission and distribution of potable water, are non-DPGR.

(iv) De minimis exception. (A) DPGR. Notwithstanding paragraphs (l)(4)(i), (ii), and (iii) of this section, if less than 5 percent of a taxpayer's gross receipts derived from a sale, exchange, or other disposition of utilities are attributable to the transmission or distribution of the utilities and the storage of potable water after completion of treatment of the potable water, then the gross receipts derived from the lease, rental, license, sale, exchange, or other disposition of the utilities that are attributable to the transmission and distribution of the utilities and the storage of potable water after completion of treatment of the potable water may be treated as being DPGR (assuming all other requirements of this section are met). In the case of gross receipts derived from the lease, rental, license, sale, exchange, or other disposition of utilities that are received over a period of time (for example, a multi-year lease or installment sale), this de minimis exception is applied by taking into account the total gross receipts for the entire period derived (and to be derived) from the lease, rental, license, sale, exchange, or other disposition of the utilities. For purposes of the preceding sentence, if a taxpayer treats gross receipts as DPGR under this de minimis exception, then the taxpayer must treat the gross receipts recognized in each taxable year consistently as DPGR.

(B) Non-DPGR. If less than 5 percent of a taxpayer's gross receipts derived from a sale, exchange, or other disposition of utilities are DPGR, then the gross receipts derived from the sale, exchange, or other disposition of the utilities may be treated as non-DPGR. In the case of gross receipts derived from the lease, rental, license, sale, exchange, or other disposition of utilities that are received over a period of time (for example, a multiyear lease or installment sale), this de minimis exception is applied by taking into account the total gross receipts for the entire period derived (and to be derived) from the lease, rental, license, sale, exchange, or other disposition of the utilities. For purposes of the preceding sentence, if a taxpayer treats gross receipts as non-DPGR under this de minimis exception, then the taxpayer must treat the gross receipts recognized in each taxable year consistently as non-DPGR.

(5) Example. The following example illustrates the application of this paragraph (l):

Example. X owns a wind turbine in the United States that generates electricity and Y owns a high voltage transmission line that passes near X's wind turbine and ends near the system of local distribution lines of Z. X sells the electricity produced at the wind turbine to Z and contracts with Y to transmit the electricity produced at the wind turbine to Z who sells the electricity to customers using Z's distribution network. The gross receipts received by X from the sale of electricity produced at the wind turbine are DPGR. The gross receipts of Y derived from transporting X's electricity to Z are non-DPGR under paragraph (l)(4)(i) of this section. Likewise, the gross receipts of Z derived from distributing the electricity are non-DPGR under paragraph (l)(4)(i) of this section. If X made direct sales of electricity to customers in Z's service area and Z receives remuneration for the distribution of electricity, the gross receipts of Z are non-DPGR under paragraph (l)(4)(i) of this section. If X, Y, and Z are related persons (as defined in paragraph (b) of this section), then X, Y, and Z must allocate gross receipts among the production activities (that are DPGR), and the transmission and distribution activities (that are non-DPGR).

(m) Definition of construction performed in the United States. *(1) Construction of real property.* (i) In general. The term construction means activities and services relating to the construction or erection of real property (as defined in paragraph (m)(3) of this section) in the United States by a taxpayer that, at the time the taxpayer constructs the real property, is engaged in a trade or business (but not necessarily its primary, or only, trade or business) that is considered construction for purposes of the North American Industry Classification System (NAICS) on a regular and ongoing basis. A trade or business that is considered construction under the NAICS means a construction activity under the two-digit NAICS code of 23 and any other construction activity in any other NAICS code provided the construction activity relates to the construction of real property such as NAICS code 213111 (drilling oil and gas wells) and 213112 (support activities for oil and gas operations). For purposes of this paragraph (m), the term construction project means the construction activities and services treated as the item under paragraph (d)(2)(iii) of this section. Tangible personal property (for example, appliances, furniture, and fixtures) that is sold as part of a construction project is not considered real property for purposes of this paragraph (m)(1)(i). In determining whether property is real property, the fact that property is real property under local law is not controlling. Conversely, property may be real property for purposes of this paragraph (m)(1)(i) even though under local law the property is considered tangible personal property.

(ii) Regular and ongoing basis. (A) In general. For purposes of paragraph (m)(1)(i) of this section, a taxpayer engaged in a construction trade or business will be considered to be engaged in such trade or business on a regular and ongoing basis if the taxpayer derives gross receipts from an unrelated person by selling or exchanging the constructed real property described in paragraph (m)(3) of this section within 60 months of the date on which construction is complete (for example, on the date a certificate of occupancy is issued for the property).

(B) New trade or business. In the case of a newly-formed trade or business or a taxpayer in its first taxable year, the taxpayer is considered to be engaged in a trade or business on a regular and ongoing basis if the taxpayer reasonably expects that it will engage in a trade or business on a regular and ongoing basis.

(iii) De minimis exception. (A) DPGR. For purposes of paragraph (m)(1)(i) of this section, if less than 5 percent of the total gross receipts derived by a taxpayer from a construction project (as described in paragraph (m)(1)(i) of this section) are derived from activities other than the construction of real property in the United States (for example, from non-construction activities or the sale of tangible personal property or land), then the total gross receipts derived by the taxpayer from the project may be treated as DPGR from construction. If a taxpayer applies the land safe harbor under paragraph (m)(6)(iv) of this section, for a construction project (as described in paragraph (m)(1)(i) of this section), then the gross receipts excluded under the land safe harbor are excluded in determining total gross receipts under this paragraph (m)(1)(iii)(A). If a taxpayer does not apply the land safe harbor and uses any reasonable method (for example, an appraisal of the land) to allocate gross receipts attributable to the land to non-DPGR, then a taxpayer applies this paragraph (m)(1)(iii)(A) by excluding such gross receipts derived from the sale, exchange, or other disposition of the land from total gross receipts. In the case of gross receipts derived from construction that are received over a period of time (for example, an installment sale), this de minimis exception is applied by taking into account the total gross receipts for the entire period derived (and to be derived) from construction. For purposes of the preceding sentence, if a taxpayer treats gross receipts as DPGR under this de minimis exception, then the taxpayer must treat the gross receipts recognized in each taxable year consistently as DPGR.

(B) Non-DPGR. For purposes of paragraph (m)(1)(i) of this section, if less than 5 percent of the total gross receipts derived by a taxpayer from a construction project qualify as DPGR, then the total gross receipts derived by the taxpayer from the construction project may be treated as non-DPGR. In the case of gross receipts derived from construction that are received over a period of time (for example, an installment sale), this de minimis exception is applied by taking into account the total gross receipts for the entire period derived (and to be derived) from construction. For purposes of the preceding sentence, if a taxpayer treats gross receipts as non-DPGR under this de minimis exception, then the taxpayer must treat the gross receipts recognized in each taxable year consistently as non-DPGR.

(2) Activities constituting construction. (i) In general. Activities constituting construction are activities performed in connection with a project to erect or substantially renovate real property, including activities performed by a general contractor or that constitute activities typically performed by a general contractor, for example, activities relating to management and oversight of the construction process such as approvals, periodic inspection of the progress of the construction project, and required job modifications.

(ii) Tangential services. Activities constituting construction do not include tangential services such as hauling trash and debris, and delivering materials, even if the tangential services are essential for construction. However, if the taxpayer performing construction also, in connection with the construction project, provides tangential services such as delivering materials to the construction site and removing its construction debris, then the gross receipts derived from the tangential services are DPGR.

(iii) Other construction activities. Improvements to land that are not capitalizable to the land (for example, landscaping) and painting are activities constituting construction only if these activities are performed in connection with other activities (whether or not by the same taxpayer) that constitute the erection or substantial renovation of real property and provided the taxpayer meets the requirements under paragraph (m)(1) of this section. Services such as grading, demolition (including demolition of structures under section 280B), clearing, excavating, and any other activities that physically transform the land are activities constituting construction only if these services are performed in connection with other activities (whether or not by the same taxpayer) that constitute the erection or substantial renovation of real property and provided the taxpayer meets the requirements under paragraph (m)(1) of this section. A taxpayer engaged in these activities must make a reasonable inquiry or a reasonable determination as to whether the activity relates to the erection or substantial renovation of real property in the United States. Construction activities also include activities relating to drilling an oil or gas well and mining and include any activities the cost of which are intangible drilling and development costs within the meaning of § 1.612-4 or development expenditures for a mine or natural deposit under section 616.

(iv) Administrative support services. If the taxpayer performing construction activities also provides, in connection with the construction project, administrative support services (for example, billing and secretarial services) incidental and necessary to such construction project, then these administrative support services are considered construction activities.

(v) Exceptions. The lease, license, or rental of equipment, for example, bulldozers, generators, or computers, for use in the construction of real property is not a construction activity under this paragraph (m)(2). The term construction does not include any activity that is within the definition of engineering and architectural services under paragraph (n) of this section.

(3) Definition of real property. The term real property means buildings (including items that are structural components of such buildings), inherently permanent structures (as

defined in § 1.263A-8(c)(3)) other than machinery (as defined in § 1.263A-8(c)(4)) (including items that are structural components of such inherently permanent structures), inherently permanent land improvements, oil and gas wells, and infrastructure (as defined in paragraph (m)(4) of this section). For purposes of the preceding sentence, an entire utility plant including both the shell and the interior will be treated as an inherently permanent structure. Property produced by a taxpayer that is not real property in the hands of that taxpayer, but that may be incorporated into real property by another taxpayer, is not treated as real property by the producing taxpayer (for example, bricks, nails, paint, and windowpanes). For purposes of this paragraph (m)(3), structural components of buildings and inherently permanent structures include property such as walls, partitions, doors, wiring, plumbing, central air conditioning and heating systems, pipes and ducts, elevators and escalators, and other similar property.

(4) Definition of infrastructure. The term infrastructure includes roads, power lines, water systems, railroad spurs, communications facilities, sewers, sidewalks, cable, and wiring. The term also includes inherently permanent oil and gas platforms.

(5) Definition of substantial renovation. The term substantial renovation means the renovation of a major component or substantial structural part of real property that materially increases the value of the property, substantially prolongs the useful life of the property, or adapts the property to a new or different use.

(6) Derived from construction. (i) In general. Assuming all the requirements of this section are met, DPGR derived from the construction of real property performed in the United States includes the proceeds from the sale, exchange, or other disposition of real property constructed by the taxpayer in the United States (whether or not the property is sold immediately after construction is completed and whether or not the construction project is completed). DPGR derived from the construction of real property includes compensation for the performance of construction services by the taxpayer in the United States. DPGR derived from the construction of real property includes gross receipts derived from materials and supplies consumed in the construction project or that become part of the constructed real property, assuming all the requirements of this section are met.

(ii) Qualified construction warranty. DPGR derived from the construction of real property includes gross receipts from any qualified construction warranty, that is, a warranty that is provided in connection with the constructed real property if, in the normal course of the taxpayer's business—

(A) The price for the construction warranty is not separately stated from the amount charged for the constructed real property; and

(B) The construction warranty is neither separately offered by the taxpayer nor separately bargained for with customers (that is, the customer cannot purchase the constructed real property without the construction warranty).

(iii) Exceptions. DPGR derived from the construction of real property performed in the United States does not include gross receipts derived from the sale, exchange, or other disposition of real property acquired by the taxpayer even if the taxpayer originally constructed the property. In addition, DPGR derived from the construction of real property does not include gross receipts from the lease or rental of real property constructed by the taxpayer or, except as provided in paragraph (m)(2)(iii) of this section, gross receipts derived from the sale or other disposition of land (including zoning, planning, entitlement costs, and other costs capitalized to the land).

(iv) Land safe harbor. (A) In general. For purposes of paragraph (m)(6)(i) of this section, a taxpayer may allocate gross receipts between the gross receipts derived from the sale, exchange, or other disposition of real property constructed by the taxpayer and the gross receipts derived from the sale, exchange, or other disposition of land by reducing its costs related to DPGR under § 1.199-4 by the costs of the land and any other costs capitalized to the land (collectively, land costs) (including zoning, planning, entitlement costs, and other costs capitalized to the land (except costs for activities listed in paragraph (m)(2)(iii) of this section) and land costs in any common improvements as defined in section 2.01 of Rev. Proc. 92-29 (1992-1 C.B. 748) (see § 601.601(d)(2) of this chapter)) and by reducing its DPGR by those land costs plus a percentage. Generally, the percentage is based on the number of months that elapse between the date the taxpayer acquires the land (not including any options to acquire the land) and ends on the date the taxpayer sells each item of real property on the land. However, a taxpayer will be deemed, for purposes of this paragraph (m)(6)(iv)(A), to acquire the land on the date the taxpayer entered into an option agreement to acquire the land if the taxpayer acquired the land pursuant to such option agreement and the purchase price of the land under the option agreement does not approximate the fair market value of the land. In the case of a sale or disposition of land between related persons (as defined in paragraph (b)(1) of this section) for less than fair market value, for purposes of determining the percentage, the purchaser or transferee of the land must include the months during which the land was held by the seller or transferor. The percentage is 5 percent for land held not more than 60 months, 10 percent for land held more than 60 months but not more than 120 months, and 15 percent for land held more than 120 months but not more than 180 months. Land held by a taxpayer for more than 180 months is not eligible for the safe harbor under this paragraph (m)(6)(iv)(A).

(B) Determining gross receipts and costs. In the case of a taxpayer that uses the small business simplified overall method of cost allocation under § 1.199-4(f), gross receipts derived from the sale, exchange, or other disposition of land, and costs attributable to the land, pursuant to the land safe harbor under paragraph (m)(6)(iv)(A) of this section, are not taken into account for purposes of computing QPAI under §§ 1.199-1 through 1.199-9 except that the gross receipts are taken into account for determining eligibility for that method of cost allocation. All other taxpayers must treat the gross receipts derived from the sale, exchange, or other disposition of land, pursuant to the land safe harbor under paragraph (m)(6)(iv)(A) of this section, as non-DPGR. In the case of a pass-thru entity, if the pass-thru entity would be eligible to use the small business simplified overall method of cost allocation if the method were applied at the pass-thru entity level, then the gross receipts derived from the sale, exchange, or other disposition of land, and costs allocated to the land, pursuant to the land safe harbor under paragraph (m)(6)(iv)(A) of this section, are not taken into account by the pass-thru entity or its owner or owners for purposes of computing QPAI under §§ 1.199-1 through 1.199-9. For purposes of the preceding sentence, in determining whether the pass-thru entity would be eligible for the small business simplified overall method of cost allocation, the gross receipts excluded pursuant to the land safe harbor under paragraph (m)(6)(iv)(A) of this section are taken into account for determining eligibility for that method of cost allocation. All other pass-thru entities (including all trusts and estates described in §§ 1.199-5(e) and 1.199-9(e)) must treat the gross receipts attributable to the sale, exchange, or other disposition of land, pursuant to the land safe harbor under paragraph (m)(6)(iv)(A) of this section, as non-DPGR.

(v) Examples. The following examples illustrate the application of this paragraph (m)(6):

Example (1). A, who is in the trade or business of construction under NAICS code 23 on a regular and ongoing basis, purchases a building in the United States and retains B, an unrelated person, to oversee a substantial renovation of the building (within the meaning of paragraph (m)(5) of this section). Although not licensed as a general contractor, B performs general contractor level work and activities relating to management and oversight of the construction process such as approvals, periodic inspection of the progress of the construction project, and required job modifications. B retains C (a general contractor) to oversee day-to-day operations and hire subcontractors. C hires D (a subcontractor) to install a new electrical system in the building as part of that substantial renovation. The amounts that B receives from A for construction services, the amounts that C receives from B for construction services, and the amounts that D receives from C for construction services qualify as DPGR under paragraph (m)(6)(i) of this section provided B, C, and D meet all of the requirements of paragraph (m)(1) of this section. The gross receipts that A receives from the subsequent sale of the building do not qualify as DPGR because A did not engage in any activity constituting construction under paragraph (m)(2) of this section even though A is in the trade or business of construction. The results would be the same if A, B, C, and D were members of the same EAG under § 1.199-7(a). However, if A, B, C, and D were members of the same consolidated group, see § 1.199-7(d)(2).

Example (2). X is engaged as an electrical contractor under NAICS code 238210 on a regular and ongoing basis. X purchases the wires, conduits, and other electrical materials that it installs in construction projects in the United States. In a particular construction project, all of the wires, conduits, and other electrical materials installed by X for the operation of that building are considered structural components of the building. X's gross receipts derived from installing that property are derived from the construction of real property under paragraph (m)(1) of this section. In addition, pursuant to paragraph (m)(6)(i) of this section, X's gross receipts derived from the purchased materials qualify as DPGR because the wires, conduits, and other electrical materials are consumed during the construction of the building or become structural components of the building.

Example (3). X is engaged in a trade or business on a regular and ongoing basis that is considered construction under the two-digit NAICS code of 23. X buys unimproved land in the United States. X gets the land zoned for residential housing through an entitlement process. X grades the land and sells the land to home builders who construct houses on the land. The gross receipts that X derives from the sale of the land that are attributable to the grading qualify as DPGR under paragraphs (m)(2)(iii) and (6)(i) of this section because those services are undertaken in connection with a construction project in the United States. X's gross receipts derived from the land including capitalized costs of entitlements (including zoning) do not qualify as DPGR under paragraph (m)(6)(i) of this section because the gross receipts are not derived from the construction of real property.

Example (4). The facts are the same as in Example 3 except that X constructs roads, sewers, and sidewalks, and installs power and water lines on the land. X conveys the roads, sewers, sidewalks, and power and water lines to the local government and utilities. The gross receipts that X derives from the sale of lots that are attributable to grading, and the construction of the roads, sewers, sidewalks, and power and water lines (that qualify as infrastructure under paragraph (m)(4) of this section) are DPGR. X's gross receipts derived from the land including capitalized costs of entitlements (including zoning) do not qualify as DPGR under paragraph (m)(6)(i) of this section because the gross receipts are not derived from the construction of real property.

Example (5). (i) Facts. X, who is engaged in the trade or business of construction under NAICS code 23 on a regular and ongoing basis, constructs housing that is real property under paragraph (m)(3) of this section. On June 1, 2007, X pays $50,000,000 and acquires 1,000 acres of land that X will develop as a new housing development. In November 2007, after the expenditure of $10,000,000 for entitlement costs, X receives permits to begin construction. After this expenditure, X's land costs total $60,000,000. The development consists of 1,000 houses to be built on half-acre lots over 5 years. On January 31, 2012, the first house is sold for $300,000. Construction costs for each house are $170,000. Common improvements consisting of streets, sidewalks, sewer lines, playgrounds, clubhouses, tennis courts, and swimming pools that X is contractually obligated or required by law to provide cost $55,000 per lot. The common improvements of $55,000 per lot include $30,000 in land costs underlying the common improvements.

(ii) Land safe harbor. Pursuant to the land safe harbor under paragraph (m)(6)(iv) of this section, X calculates the basis for each house sold as $195,000 (total costs of $255,000 ($170,000 in construction costs plus $55,000 in common improvements (including $30,000 in land costs) plus $30,000 in land costs for the lot), which are reduced by land costs of $60,000). X calculates the DPGR for each house sold by taking the gross receipts of $300,000 and reducing that amount by land costs of $60,000 plus a percentage of $60,000. As X acquired the land on June 1, 2007, for each house sold on the land between January 31, 2012, and June 1, 2012, the percentage reduction for X is 5% because X has held the land for not more than 60 months from the date of acquisition. Thus, X's DPGR for each house is $237,000 ($300,000 - $60,000 - $3,000) with costs for each house of $195,000 ($255,000 - $60,000). For each house sold on the land between June 2, 2012 and June 1, 2017, the percentage reduction for X is 10% because X has held the land for more than 60 months but not more than 120 months from the date of acquisition. Thus, of the $300,000 of gross receipts, X's DPGR for each house is $234,000 ($300,000 - $60,000 - $6,000) with costs for each house of $195,000 ($255,000 - $60,000).

Example (6). The facts are the same as in Example 5 except that on December 31, 2007, after X received the permits to begin construction, X sold the entitled land to Y, an unrelated corporation, for $75,000,000. Y is engaged in a trade or business on a regular and ongoing basis that is considered construction under NAICS code 23. Y subsequently incurred the construction costs and the costs of the common improvements, and Y sold the houses. Because X did not perform any construction activities, none of X's $75,000,000 in gross receipts derived from Y are DPGR and none of X's costs are allocable to DPGR. Pursuant to the land safe harbor under paragraph (m)(6)(iv) of this section, Y calculates the basis for each house sold as $195,000 (total costs of $270,000 ($170,000 in construction costs plus $62,500 in common improvements (including $37,500 in land costs) plus $37,500 in land costs for the lot), which are reduced by land costs of $75,000). Y calculates the DPGR for each house sold by taking the gross receipts of $300,000 and reducing that amount by land costs of $75,000 plus a percentage of $75,000. As Y acquired the land on December 31, 2007, for the houses sold on the land between January 31, 2012, and December 31, 2012, the percentage reduction for Y is 5% because Y held the land for not more than 60 months from the date of acquisition. Thus, of the $300,000 of gross receipts, the DPGR for each house is $221,250 ($300,000 - $75,000 -$3,750) with costs for each house of $195,000. For the houses sold on the land between January 1, 2013, and December 31, 2017, the percentage reduction for Y is 10% because Y held the land for more than 60 months but not more than 120 months from the date of acquisition. Thus, of the $300,000 of gross receipts, the DPGR for each house is $217,500 ($300,000 - $75,000 - $7,500) with costs for each house of $195,000. The results would be the same if X and Y were members of the same EAG, provided X and Y were not members of the same consolidated group.

Example (7). The facts are the same as in Example 6 except that Y is a member of the same consolidated group as X. Pursuant to § 1.1502-13(c)(1)(ii), Y's holding period in the land includes the period of time X held the land. In order to produce the same effect as if X and Y were divisions of a single corporation (see § 1.1502-13(c)(1)(i)), for each house sold between January 31, 2012, and June 1, 2012, Y's DPGR are redetermined to be $237,000, the same as X's DPGR for houses sold between January 31, 2012, and June 1, 2012, in Example 5. Y's costs for each house do not have to be redetermined because Y's costs are $195,000, the same as the costs would be if X and Y were divisions of a single corporation. For each house sold between June 2, 2012, and June 1, 2017, Y's DPGR are redetermined to be $234,000, the same as X's DPGR for each house sold between June 2, 2012, and June 1, 2017, in Example 5. Y's costs for each house do not have to be redetermined because Y's costs are $195,000, the same as the costs would be if X and Y were divisions of a single corporation.

Example (8). X, who is engaged in the trade or business of construction under NAICS code 23 on a regular and ongoing basis, purchases land for development and builds an office building on the land. Y enters into a contract with X to purchase the office building. As part of the contract, X is required to furnish the office space with desks, chairs, and lamps. Upon completion of the sale of the building, X uses the land safe harbor under paragraph (m)(6)(iv) of this section to account for the land. After application of the land safe harbor, X uses the de minimis exception under paragraph (m)(1)(iii)(A) of this section in determining whether the gross receipts derived from the sale of the desks, chairs, and lamps qualify as DPGR. If the gross receipts derived from the sale of the desks, chairs, and lamps are less than 5% of the total gross receipts derived by X from the sale of the furnished office building (excluding any gross receipts taken into account under the land safe harbor pursuant to paragraph (m)(6)(iv)(B) of this section), then all of the gross receipts derived from the sale of the furnished office building, after the reduction under the land safe harbor, may be treated as DPGR.

(n) Definition of engineering and architectural services. *(1) In general.* DPGR include gross receipts derived from engineering or architectural services performed in the United States for a construction project described in paragraph (m)(1)(i) of this section. At the time the taxpayer performs the engineering or architectural services, the taxpayer must be engaged in a trade or business (but not necessarily its primary, or only, trade or business) that is considered engineering or architectural services for purposes of the NAICS, for example NAICS codes 541330 (engineering services) or 541310 (architectural services), on a regular and ongoing basis. In the case of a newly-formed trade or business or a taxpayer in its first taxable year, a taxpayer is considered to be engaged in a trade or business on a regular and ongoing basis if the taxpayer reasonably expects that it will engage in a trade or business on a regular and ongoing basis. DPGR include gross receipts derived from engineering or architectural services, including feasibility studies for a construction project in the United States, even if the planned construction project is not undertaken or is not completed.

(2) Engineering services. Engineering services in connection with any construction project include any professional services requiring engineering education, training, and experience and the application of special knowledge of the mathematical, physical, or engineering sciences to those professional services such as consultation, investigation, evaluation, planning, design, or responsible supervision of construction (for the purpose of assuring compliance with plans, specifications, and design) or erection, in connection with any construction project.

(3) Architectural services. Architectural services in connection with any construction project include the offering or furnishing of any professional services such as consultation, planning, aesthetic and structural design, drawings and specifications, or responsible supervision of construction (for the purpose of assuring compliance with plans, specifications, and design) or erection, in connection with any construction project.

(4) Administrative support services. If the taxpayer performing engineering or architectural services also provides administrative support services (for example, billing and secretarial services) incidental and necessary to such engineering or architectural services, then these administrative support services are considered engineering or architectural services.

(5) Exceptions. Engineering or architectural services do not include postconstruction services such as annual audits and inspections.

(6) De minimis exception for performance of services in the United States.

(i) DPGR. If less than 5 percent of the total gross receipts derived by a taxpayer from engineering or architectural services performed in the United States for a construction project (described in paragraph (m)(1)(i) of this section) are derived from services not relating to a construction project (for example, the services are performed outside the United States or in connection with property other than real property), then the total gross receipts derived by the taxpayer may be treated as DPGR from engineering or architectural services performed in the United States for the construction project. In the case of gross receipts derived from engineering or architectural services that are received over a period of time (for example, an installment sale), this de minimis exception is applied by taking into account the total gross receipts for the entire period derived (and to be derived) from engineering or architectural services. For purposes of the preceding sentence, if a taxpayer treats gross receipts as DPGR under this de minimis exception, then the taxpayer must treat the gross receipts recognized in each taxable year consistently as DPGR.

(ii) Non-DPGR. If less than 5 percent of the total gross receipts derived by a taxpayer from engineering or architectural services performed in the United States for a construction project qualify as DPGR, then the total gross receipts derived by the taxpayer from engineering or architectural services performed in the United States for the construction project may be treated as non-DPGR. In the case of gross receipts derived from engineering or architectural services that are received over a period of time (for example, an installment sale), this de minimis exception is applied by taking into account the total gross receipts for the entire period derived (and to be derived) from engineering or architectural services. For purposes of the preceding sentence, if a taxpayer treats gross receipts as non-DPGR under this de minimis exception, then the taxpayer must treat the gross receipts recognized in each taxable year consistently as non-DPGR.

(7) Example. The following example illustrates the application of this paragraph (n):

Example. X is engaged in the trade or business of providing engineering services under NAICS code 541330 on a regular and ongoing basis. Y buys unimproved land. Y hires X to provide engineering services for roads, sewers, sidewalks, and power and water lines that qualify as infrastructure under paragraph (m)(4) of this section and that will be constructed on Y's land. X's gross receipts from engineering services for the infrastructure are DPGR. X's gross receipts from engineering services relating to land (except as provided in paragraph (m)(2)(iii) of this section) do not qualify as DPGR under paragraph (n)(1) of this section because the gross receipts are not derived from engineering services for a construction project described in paragraph (m)(1)(i) of this section.

(o) Sales of certain food and beverages. *(1) In general.* DPGR does not include gross receipts of the taxpayer that are derived from the sale of food or beverages prepared by the taxpayer at a retail establishment. A retail establishment is defined as tangible property (both real and personal) owned, leased, occupied, or otherwise used by the taxpayer in its trade or business of selling food or beverages to the public at which retail sales are made. In addition, a facility that prepares food and beverages for take out service or delivery is a retail establishment (for example, a caterer). If a taxpayer's facility is a retail establishment, then, for purposes of this section, the taxpayer may allocate its gross receipts between the gross receipts derived from the retail sale of the food and beverages prepared and sold at the retail establishment (that are non-DPGR) and gross receipts derived from the wholesale sale of the food and beverages prepared and sold at the retail establishment (that are DPGR assuming all the other requirements of section 199 are met). Wholesale sales are defined as food and beverages held for resale by the purchaser. The exception for sales of certain food and beverages also applies to food and beverages for non-human consumption. A retail establishment does not include the bonded premises of a distilled spirits plant or wine cellar, or the premises of a brewery (other than a tavern on the brewery premises). See Chapter 51 of Title 26 of the United States Code and the implementing regulations thereunder.

(2) De minimis exception. A taxpayer may treat a facility at which food or beverages are prepared as not being a retail establishment if less than 5 percent of the gross receipts derived from the sale of food or beverages at that facility during the taxable year are attributable to retail sales.

(3) Examples. The following examples illustrate the application of this paragraph (o):

Example (1). X buys coffee beans and roasts those beans at a facility in the United States, the only activity of which is the roasting and packaging of coffee beans. X sells the roasted coffee beans through a variety of unrelated third-party vendors and also sells roasted coffee beans at X's retail establishments. At X's retail establishments, X prepares brewed coffee and other foods. To the extent that the gross receipts of X's retail establishments are derived from the sale of coffee beans roasted at the facility, the receipts are DPGR (assuming all the other requirements of this section are met). To the extent the gross receipts of X's retail establishments are derived from the retail sale of brewed coffee or food prepared at the retail establishments, the receipts are non-DPGR. However, pursuant to § 1.199-1(d)(1)(ii), X must allocate part of the receipts from the retail sale of the brewed coffee as DPGR to the extent of the value of the coffee beans that were roasted at the facility and that were used to brew coffee.

Example (2). Y operates a bonded winery within the United States. Bottles of wine produced by Y at the bonded winery are sold to consumers at the taxpaid premises. Pursuant to paragraph (o)(1) of this section, the bonded premises is not considered a retail establishment and is treated as separate and apart from the taxpaid premises, which is considered a retail establishment for purposes of paragraph (o)(1) of this section. Accordingly, the wine produced by Y in the bonded premises and sold by Y from the taxpaid premises is not considered to have been produced at a retail establishment, and the gross receipts derived from the sales of the wine are DPGR (assuming all the other requirements of this section are met).

(p) Guaranteed payments. DPGR does not include guaranteed payments under section 707(c). Thus, partners, including partners in partnerships described in paragraphs (i)(7) and (8) of this section and § 1.199-9(i) and (j), may not treat guaranteed payments as DPGR. See §§ 1.199-5(b)(6) Example 5 and 1.199-9(b)(6) Example 5.

T.D. 9263, 5/24/2006, amend T.D. 9293, 10/18/2006, T.D. 9317, 3/19/2007, T.D. 9381, 2/14/2008, T.D. 9384, 3/6/2008.

Proposed § 1.199-3 Domestic production gross receipts. *[For Preamble, see ¶ 152,713]*

(a) In general. Domestic production gross receipts (DPGR) are the gross receipts (as defined in paragraph (c) of this section) of the taxpayer that are derived from (as defined in paragraph (h) of this section)—

(1) Any lease, rental, license, sale, exchange, or other disposition of—

(i) Qualifying production property (QPP) (as defined in paragraph (i)(1) of this section) that is manufactured, produced, grown, or extracted (MPGE) (as defined in paragraph (d) of this section) by the taxpayer (as defined in paragraph (e) of this section) in whole or in significant part (as defined in paragraph (f) of this section) within the United States (as defined in paragraph (g) of this section);

(ii) Any qualified film (as defined in paragraph (j) of this section) produced by the taxpayer (in accordance with paragraph (j) of this section); or

(iii) Electricity, natural gas, or potable water (as defined in paragraph (k) of this section) (collectively, utilities) produced by the taxpayer in the United States (in accordance with paragraph (k) of this section);

(2) Construction (as defined in paragraph (l) of this section) performed in the United States (in accordance with paragraph (l) of this section); or

(3) Engineering or architectural services (as defined in paragraph (m) of this section) performed in the United States for construction projects in the United States (in accordance with paragraph (m) of this section).

(b) Related persons. *(1) In general.* DPGR does not include any gross receipts of the taxpayer derived from property leased, licensed, or rented by the taxpayer for use by any related person. A person is treated as related to another person if both persons are treated as a single employer under either section 52(a) or (b) (without regard to section 1563(b)), or section 414(m) or (o).

(2) Exceptions. Paragraph (b)(1) of this section does not apply to any QPP or qualified films leased or rented by the taxpayer to a related person if the QPP or qualified films are held for sublease or rent, or are subleased or rented, by the related person to an unrelated person for the ultimate use of the unrelated person. Similarly, paragraph (b)(1) of this section does not apply to the license of QPP or qualified films to a related person for reproduction and sale, exchange, lease, rental or sublicense to an unrelated person for the ultimate use of the unrelated person.

(c) Definition of gross receipts. The term gross receipts means the taxpayer's receipts for the taxable year that are recognized under the taxpayer's methods of accounting used for Federal income tax purposes for the taxable year. If the gross receipts are recognized in an intercompany transaction within the meaning of § 1.1502-13, see also § 1.199-7(d). For this purpose, gross receipts include total sales (net of returns and allowances) and all amounts received for services. In addition, gross receipts include any income from investments and from incidental or outside sources. For example, gross receipts include interest (including original issue discount and tax-exempt interest within the meaning of section 103), dividends, rents, royalties, and annuities, regardless of whether the amounts are derived in the ordinary course of the taxpayer's trade of business. Gross receipts are not reduced by cost of goods sold (CGS) or by the cost of property sold if such property is described in section 1221(a)(1), (2), (3), (4), or (5). Gross receipts do not include the amounts received in repayment of a loan or similar instrument (for example, a repayment of the principal amount of a loan held by a commercial lender) and, except to the extent of gain recognized, do not include gross receipts derived from a non-recognition transaction, such as a section 1031 exchange. Finally, gross receipts do not include amounts received by the taxpayer with respect to sales tax or other similar state and local taxes if, under the applicable state or local law, the tax is legally imposed on the purchaser of the good or service and the taxpayer merely collects and remits the tax to the taxing authority. If, in contrast, the tax is imposed on the taxpayer under the applicable law, then gross receipts include the amounts received that are allocable to the payment of such tax.

(d) Definition of manufactured, produced, grown, or extracted. *(1) In general.* Except as provided in paragraphs (d)(2) and (3) of this section, the term MPGE includes manufacturing, producing, growing, extracting, installing, developing, improving, and creating QPP; making QPP out of scrap, salvage, or junk material as well as from new or raw material by processing, manipulating, refining, or changing the form of an article, or by combining or assembling two or more articles; cultivating soil, raising livestock, fishing, and mining minerals. The term MPGE also includes storage, handling, or other processing activities (other than transportation activities) within the United States related to the sale, exchange, or other disposition of agricultural products, provided the products are consumed in connection with, or incorporated into, the MPGE of QPP whether or not by the taxpayer. The taxpayer must have the benefits and burdens of ownership of the QPP under Federal income tax principles during the period the MPGE activity occurs, pursuant to paragraph (e)(1) of this section, in order for gross receipts derived from the MPGE of QPP to qualify as DPGR.

(2) Packaging, repackaging, labeling, or minor assembly. If a taxpayer packages, repackages, labels, or performs minor assembly of QPP and the taxpayer engages in no other MPGE activity with respect to that QPP, the taxpayer's packaging, repackaging, labeling, or minor assembly do not qualify as MPGE.

(3) Installing. If a taxpayer installs an item of QPP and engages in no other MPGE with respect to the QPP, the taxpayer's installing activity does not qualify as MPGE. However, if the taxpayer installs an item of QPP MPGE by the taxpayer, and the taxpayer has the benefits and burdens of ownership of the item of QPP under Federal income tax principles during the period the installing activity occurs, the portion of the installing activity that relates to the item of QPP is MPGE.

(4) Consistency with section 263A. A taxpayer that has MPGE QPP for the taxable year should treat itself as a producer under section 263A with respect to the QPP for the taxable year unless the taxpayer is not subject to section 263A. A taxpayer that currently is not properly accounting for its production activities under section 263A, and wishes to change its method of accounting to comply with the producer requirements of section 263A, must follow the applicable administrative procedures issued under § 1.446-1(e)(3)(ii) for obtaining the Commissioner's consent to a change in accounting method (for further guidance, for example, see Rev. Proc. 97-27 (1997-1 C.B. 680), or Rev. Proc. 2002-9 (2002-1 C.B. 327), whichever applies (see § 601.601(d)(2) of this chapter)).

(5) Examples. The following examples illustrate the application of this paragraph (d):

Example (1). A, B, and C are unrelated taxpayers and are not cooperatives to which Part I of subchapter T of the Internal Revenue Code applies. A owns grain storage bins in the United States in which it stores for a fee B's agricultural products that were grown in the United States. B sells its agricultural products to C. C processes B's agricultural products into refined agricultural products in the United States. The gross receipts from A's, B's, and C's activities are DPGR from the MPGE of QPP.

Example (2). The facts are the same as in Example 1 except that B grows the agricultural products outside the United States and C processes B's agricultural products into refined agricultural products outside the United States. Pursuant to paragraph (d)(1) of this section, the gross receipts derived by A are DPGR from the MPGE of QPP within the United States. B's and C's respective activities occur outside the United States and, therefore, their respective gross receipts are non-DPGR.

Example (3). Y is hired to reconstruct and refurbish unrelated customers' tangible personal property. As part of the reconstruction and refurbishment, Y installs purchased replacement parts in the customers' property. Y's installation of purchased replacement parts does not qualify as MPGE pursuant to paragraph (d)(3) of this section because Y did not MPGE the replacement parts.

Example (4). The facts are the same as in Example 3 except that Y manufactures the replacement parts it uses for the reconstruction and refurbishment of customers' tangible personal property. Y has the benefits and burdens of ownership of the replacement parts during the reconstruction and refurbishment activity and while installing the parts. Y's gross receipts from the MPGE of the replacement parts and Y's gross receipts from the installation of the replacement parts, which is an MPGE activity pursuant to paragraph (d)(3) of this section, are DPGR.

Example (5). Z MPGE QPP within the United States. The following activities are performed by Z as part of the MPGE of the QPP while Z has the benefits and burdens of ownership under Federal income tax principles: materials analysis and selection, subcontractor inspections and qualifications, testing of component parts, assisting customers in their review and approval of the QPP, routine production inspections, product documentation, diagnosis and correction of system failure, and packaging for shipment to customers. Because Z MPGE the QPP, these activities performed by Z are part of the MPGE of the QPP.

Example (6). X purchases automobiles from unrelated parties and customizes them by adding ground effects, spoilers, custom wheels, specialized paint and decals, sunroofs, roof racks, and similar accessories. X does not manufacture any of the accessories. X's activity is minor assembly under paragraph (d)(2) of this section which is not an MPGE activity.

Example (7). The facts are the same as in Example 6 except that X manufactures some of the accessories it adds to the automobiles. Pursuant to § 1.199-1(c)(2), if an automobile with accessories does not meet the requirements for being an item, X must treat each accessory that it manufactures as an item for purposes of determining whether X MPGE the item in whole or in significant part within the United States under paragraph (f)(1) of this section and whether the installation of the item is MPGE under paragraph (d)(3) of this section.

Example (8). Y manufactures furniture in the United States that it sells to unrelated persons. Y also engraves customers' names on pens and pencils purchased from unrelated persons and sells the pens and pencils to such customers. Although Y's sales of furniture qualify as DPGR if all the other requirements of this section are met, Y's sales of the engraved pens and pencils do not qualify as DPGR because Y does not MPGE the pens and pencils.

(e) Definition of by the taxpayer. *(1) In general.* With the exception of the rules applicable to an expanded affiliated group (EAG) under § 1.199-7, certain oil and gas partnerships under paragraph (h)(7) of this section, EAG partnerships under paragraph (h)(8) of this section, and government contracts in paragraph (e)(2) of this section, only one taxpayer may claim the deduction under § 1.199-1(a) with respect to any qualifying activity under paragraph (d)(1) of this section performed in connection with the same QPP, or the production of qualified films or utilities. If one taxpayer performs a qualifying activity under paragraph (d)(1), (j)(1), or (k)(1) of this section pursuant to a contract with another party, then only the taxpayer that has the benefits and burdens of ownership of the property under Federal income tax principles during the period the qualifying activity occurs is treated as engaging in the qualifying activity.

(2) Special rule for certain government contracts. QPP, qualified films, or utilities will be treated as MPGE or otherwise produced by the taxpayer notwithstanding the requirements of paragraph (e)(1) of this section if—

(i) The QPP, qualified films, or utilities are MPGE or otherwise produced by the taxpayer pursuant to a contract with the Federal government; and

(ii) The Federal Acquisition Regulation (48 CFR) requires that title or risk of loss with respect to the QPP, qualified films, or utilities be transferred to the Federal government before the MPGE of the QPP, or the production of the qualified films or utilities, is complete.

(3) Examples. The following examples illustrate the application of this paragraph (e):

Example (1). X designs machines that it uses in its trade or business. X contracts with Y, an unrelated taxpayer, for the manufacture of the machines. The contract between X and Y is a fixed-price contract. The contract specifies that the machines will be manufactured in the United States using X's design. X owns the intellectual property attributable to the design and provides it to Y with a restriction that Y may only use it during the manufacturing process and has no right to exploit the intellectual property. The contract specifies that Y controls the details of the manufacturing process while the machines are being produced; Y bears the risk of loss or damage during manufacturing of the machines; and Y has the economic loss or gain upon the sale of the machines based on the difference between Y's costs and the fixed price. Y has legal title during the manufacturing process and legal title to the machines is not transferred to X until final manufacturing of the machines has been completed. Based on all of the facts and circumstances, pursuant to paragraph (e)(1) of this section Y has the benefits and burdens of ownership of the machines under Federal income tax principles during the period the manufacturing occurs and, as a result, Y is treated as the manufacturer of the machines.

Example (2). X designs and engineers machines that it sells to customers. X contracts with Y, an unrelated taxpayer, for the manufacture of the machines. The contract between X and Y is a cost-reimbursable type contract. X has the benefits and burdens of ownership of the machines under Federal income tax principles during the period the manufacturing occurs except that legal title to the machines is not transferred to X until final manufacturing of the machines is completed. Based on all of the facts and circumstances, X is treated as the manufacturer of the machines under paragraph (e)(1) of this section.

(f) Definition of in whole or in significant part. *(1) In general.* QPP must be MPGE in whole or in significant part by the taxpayer and in whole or in significant part within the United States to qualify under section 199(c)(4)(A)(i)(I). If a taxpayer enters into a contract pursuant to paragraph (e)(1) of this section with an unrelated party for the unrelated party to MPGE QPP for the taxpayer and the taxpayer has the benefits and burdens of ownership of the QPP under applicable Federal income tax principles during the period the MPGE activity occurs, then the taxpayer is considered to MPGE the QPP under this section. The unrelated party must perform the MPGE activity on behalf of the taxpayer in whole or in significant part within the United States in order for the taxpayer to satisfy the requirements of this paragraph (f)(1).

(2) Substantial in nature. QPP will be treated as MPGE in significant part by the taxpayer within the United States for purposes of paragraph (f)(1) of this section if the MPGE of

the QPP by the taxpayer within the United States is substantial in nature taking into account all of the facts and circumstances, including the relative value added by, and relative cost of, the taxpayer's MPGE activity within the United States, the nature of the property, and the nature of the MPGE activity that the taxpayer performs within the United States. Research and experimental activities under section 174 and the creation of intangibles do not qualify as substantial in nature for any QPP other than computer software (as defined in paragraph (i)(3) of this section) and sound recordings (as defined in paragraph (i)(4) of this section). In the case of an EAG member, an EAG partnership (as defined in paragraph (h)(8) of this section), or members of an EAG in which the partners of the EAG partnership are members, in determining whether the substantial in nature requirement is met with respect to an item of QPP, all of the previous activities of the members of the EAG, the EAG partnership, and all members of the EAG in which the partners of the EAG partnership are members, as applicable, are taken into account.

(3) Safe harbor. A taxpayer will be treated as having MPGE QPP in whole or in significant part within the United States for purposes of paragraph (f)(1) of this section if, in connection with the QPP, conversion costs (direct labor and related factory burden) of such taxpayer to MPGE the QPP within the United States account for 20 percent or more of the taxpayer's CGS of the QPP. For purposes of the safe harbor under this paragraph (f)(3), research and experimental expenditures under section 174 and the costs of creating intangibles do not qualify as conversion costs for any QPP other than computer software and sound recordings. In the case of tangible personal property (as defined in paragraph (i)(2) of this section), research and experimental expenditures under section 174 and any other costs incurred in the creation of intangibles may be excluded from CGS for purposes of determining whether the taxpayer meets the safe harbor under this paragraph (f)(3). For purposes of this safe harbor, research and experimental expenditures under section 174 and any other costs of creating intangibles for computer software and sound recordings must be allocated to the computer software and sound recordings to which the expenditures and costs relate under § 1.199-4(b). In the case of an EAG member, an EAG partnership, or members of an EAG in which the partners of the EAG partnership are members, in determining whether the requirements of the safe harbor under this paragraph (f)(3) are met with respect to an item of QPP, all of the previous conversion costs of the members of the EAG, the EAG partnership, and all members of the EAG in which the partners of the EAG partnership are members, as applicable, to MPGE the QPP are taken into account. If a taxpayer enters into a contract with an unrelated party for the unrelated party to MPGE QPP for the taxpayer, and the taxpayer is considered pursuant to paragraph (e)(1) of this section to MPGE the QPP, then for purposes of this safe harbor the taxpayer's conversion costs shall include both the taxpayer's conversion costs as well as the conversion costs of the unrelated party to MPGE the QPP under the contract.

(4) Examples. The following examples illustrate the application of this paragraph (f):

Example (1). X purchases from Y unrefined oil extracted outside the United States and X refines the oil in the United States. The refining of the oil by X is an MPGE activity that is substantial in nature.

Example (2). X purchases gemstones and precious metal from outside the United States and then uses these materials to produce jewelry within the United States by cutting and polishing the gemstones, melting and shaping the metal, and combining the finished materials. X's activity is substantial in nature under paragraph (f)(2) of this section. Therefore, X has MPGE the jewelry in significant part within the United States.

Example (3). (i) X operates an automobile assembly plant in the United States. In connection with such activity, X purchases assembled engines, transmissions, and certain other components from Y, an unrelated taxpayer, and X assembles all of the component parts into an automobile. X also conducts stamping, machining, and subassembly operations, and X uses tools, jigs, welding equipment, and other machinery and equipment in the assembly of automobiles. On a per-unit basis, X's selling price and costs of such automobiles are as follows:

Selling price: $2,500

Cost of goods sold:

Material—Acquired from Y: $1,475

Conversion costs (direct labor and factory burden): $325

Total cost of goods sold: $1,800

Gross profit: $700

Administrative and selling expenses: $300

Taxable income: $400

(ii) Although X's conversion costs are less than 20 percent of total CGS ($325/$1,800, or 18 percent), the operations conducted by X in connection with the property purchased and sold are substantial in nature under paragraph (f)(2) of this section because of the nature of X's activity and the relative value of X's activity. Therefore, X's automobiles will be treated as MPGE in significant part by X within the United States for purposes of paragraph (f)(1) of this section.

Example (4). X produces a qualified film (as defined in paragraph (j)(1) of this section) and licenses the film to Y, an unrelated taxpayer, for duplication of the film onto DVDs. Y purchases the DVDs from an unrelated person. Unless Y satisfies the safe harbor under paragraph (f)(3) of this section, Y's income for duplicating X's qualified film onto the DVDs is non-DPGR because the duplication is not substantial in nature relative to the DVD with the film.

Example (5). X imports into the United States QPP that is partially manufactured. X completes the manufacture of the QPP within the United States and X's completion of the manufacturing of the QPP within the United States satisfies the in whole or in significant part requirement under paragraph (f)(1) of this section. Therefore, X's gross receipts from the lease, rental, license, sale, exchange, or other disposition of the QPP qualify as DPGR if all other applicable requirements under this section are met.

Example (6). X manufactures QPP in significant part within the United States and exports the QPP for further manufacture outside the United States. Assuming X meets all the requirements under this section for the QPP after the further manufacturing, X's gross receipts derived from the lease, rental, license, sale, exchange, or other disposition of the QPP will be considered DPGR, regardless of whether the QPP is imported back into the United States prior to the lease, rental, license, sale, exchange, or other disposition of the QPP.

Example (7). X is a retailer that sells cigars and pipe tobacco that X purchases from an unrelated person. While being displayed and offered for sale by X, the cigars and pipe tobacco age on X's shelves in a room with controlled temperature and humidity. Although X's cigars and pipe tobacco may become more valuable as they age, the gross receipts derived by X from the sale of the cigars and pipe tobacco are non-DPGR because the aging of the cigars and pipe tobacco while being displayed and offered for sale by X does not qualify as an MPGE activity that occurs in whole or in significant part within the United States.

(g) Definition of United States. For purposes of this section, the term United States includes the 50 states, the District of Columbia, the territorial waters of the United States, and the seabed and subsoil of those submarine areas that are adjacent to the territorial waters of the United States and over which the United States has exclusive rights, in accordance with international law, with respect to the exploration and exploitation of natural resources. The term United States does not include possessions and territories of the United States or the airspace or space over the United States and these areas.

(h) Definition of derived from the lease, rental, license, sale, exchange, or other disposition. *(1) In general.* The term derived from the lease, rental, license, sale, exchange, or other disposition is defined as, and limited to, the gross receipts directly derived from the lease, rental, license, sale, exchange, or other disposition, even if the taxpayer has already recognized gross receipts from a previous lease, rental, license, sale, exchange, or other disposition of the same property. Applicable Federal income tax principles apply to determine whether a transaction is, in substance, a lease, rental, license, sale, exchange or other disposition, or whether it is a service (or some combination thereof). For example, gross receipts derived from the sale of QPP includes gross receipts derived from the sale of QPP MPGE in whole or in significant part within the United States by a taxpayer for sale, as well as gross receipts derived from the sale of QPP MPGE in whole or in significant part within the United States by a taxpayer and used in the taxpayer's trade or business before being sold. The entire amount of lease income including any interest that is not separately stated is considered derived from the lease of QPP or a qualified film. In addition, the proceeds from business interruption insurance, governmental subsidies, and governmental payments not to produce are treated as gross receipts derived from the lease, rental, license, sale, exchange, or other disposition to the extent that they are substitutes for gross receipts that would qualify as DPGR. The value of property received by a taxpayer in a taxable exchange of QPP MPGE in whole or in significant part within the United States, qualified films, or utilities for an unrelated person's property is DPGR for the taxpayer (assuming all the other requirements of this section are met). However, unless the taxpayer further MPGE the QPP or further produces the qualified films or utilities received in the exchange, any gross receipts from the subsequent sale by the taxpayer of the property received in the exchange are non-DPGR because the taxpayer did not MPGE or otherwise produce such property, even if the property was QPP, qualified films, or utilities in the hands of the other person.

(2) Examples. The following examples illustrate the application of paragraph (h)(1) of this section:

Example (1). X MPGE QPP within the United States and sells the QPP to Y, an unrelated person. Y leases the QPP for 3 years to Z, a taxpayer unrelated to both X and Y, and shortly thereafter, X repurchases the QPP from Y subject to the lease. At the end of the lease term, Z purchases the QPP from X. X's proceeds derived from the sale of the QPP to Y, from the lease to Z, and from the sale of the QPP to Z all qualify as DPGR (assuming all the other requirements of this section are met).

Example (2). X MPGE QPP within the United States and sells the QPP to Y, an unrelated taxpayer, for $25,000. X finances Y's purchase of the QPP and receives total payments of $35,000, of which $10,000 relates to interest and finance charges. The $25,000 qualifies as DPGR but the $10,000 in interest and finance charges do not qualify as DPGR because the $10,000 is not derived from the MPGE of QPP within the United States but rather from X's lending activity.

Example (3). Cable company X charges subscribers $15 a month for its basic cable television. Y, an unrelated taxpayer, produces in the United States all of the programs on its cable channel which it licenses to X for $.10 per subscriber per month. The programs are qualified films within the meaning of paragraph (j)(1) of this section. The gross receipts derived by Y are derived from a license of a qualified film produced by Y and are DPGR (assuming all the other requirements of this section are met).

(3) Hedging transactions. (i) In general. For purposes of this section, provided that the risk being hedged relates to QPP described in section 1221(a)(1) or property described in section 1221(a)(8) consumed in the activity giving rise to DPGR, and provided that the transaction is a hedging transaction within the meaning of section 1221(b)(2) and § 1.1221-2(b), then—

(A) In the case of a hedge of purchases of property described in section 1221(a)(1), gain or loss on the hedging transaction must be taken into account in determining CGS;

(B) In the case of a hedge of sales of property described in section 1221(a)(1), gain or loss on the hedging transaction must be taken into account in determining DPGR; and

(C) In the case of a hedge of purchases of property described in section 1221(a)(8), gain or loss on the hedging transaction must be taken into account in determining DPGR.

(ii) Currency fluctuations. For purposes of this section, in the case of a transaction that manages the risk of currency fluctuations, the determination of whether the transaction is a hedging transaction within the meaning of § 1.1221-2(b) is made without regard to whether the transaction is a section 988 transaction. See § 1.1221-2(a)(4). The preceding sentence applies only to the extent that § 1.988-5(b) does not apply.

(iii) Other rules. See § 1.1221-2(e) for rules applicable to hedging by members of a consolidated group and § 1.446-4 for rules regarding the timing of income, deductions, gain, or loss with respect to hedging transactions.

(4) Allocation of gross receipts—embedded services and non-qualified property. (i) In general. Except as otherwise provided in paragraph (h)(4)(ii), paragraph (l) (relating to construction), and paragraph (m) (relating to architectural and engineering services) of this section, gross receipts derived from the performance of services do not qualify as DPGR. In the case of an embedded service, that is, a service the price of which is not separately stated from the amount charged for the lease, rental, license, sale, exchange, or other disposition of QPP, qualified films, or utilities, DPGR includes only the receipts from the lease, rental, license, sale, exchange, or other disposition of the item (if all the other requirements of this section are met) and not any receipts attributable to the embedded service by the taxpayer. In addition, DPGR does not include the gross receipts derived from the lease, rental, license, sale, exchange, or other disposition of property that does not meet all of the requirements under

this section (non-qualified property). For example, gross receipts derived from the lease, rental, license, sale, exchange, or other disposition of a replacement part that is non-qualified property does not qualify as DPGR.

(ii) Exceptions. There are five exceptions to the rules under paragraph (h)(4)(i) of this section regarding embedded services and non-qualified property. A taxpayer may include in DPGR, if all the other requirements of this section are met with respect to the underlying item of property to which the embedded services or non-qualified property relate, gross receipts derived from—

(A) A qualified warranty, that is, a warranty that is provided in connection with the lease, rental, license, sale, exchange, or other disposition of QPP, qualified films or utilities if—

(1) In the normal course of the taxpayer's business, the price for the warranty is not separately stated from the amount charged for the lease, rental, license, sale, exchange, or other disposition of the property; and

(2) The warranty is neither separately offered by the taxpayer nor separately bargained for with the customer (that is, a customer cannot purchase the property without the warranty);

(B) A qualified delivery, that is, a delivery or distribution service that is provided in connection with the lease, rental, license, sale, exchange, or other disposition of QPP if—

(1) In the normal course of the taxpayer's business, the price for the delivery or distribution service is not separately stated from the amount charged for the lease, rental, license, sale, exchange, or other disposition of the property; and

(2) The delivery or distribution service is neither separately offered by the taxpayer nor separately bargained for with the customer (that is, a customer cannot purchase the property without delivery or distribution service);

(C) A qualified operating manual, that is, a manual of instructions (including electronic instructions) that is provided in connection with the lease, rental, license, sale, exchange, or other disposition of QPP, qualified films or utilities if—

(1) In the normal course of the taxpayer's business, the price for the manual is not separately stated from the amount charged for the lease, rental, license, sale, exchange, or other disposition of the property;

(2) The manual is neither separately offered by the taxpayer nor separately bargained for with the customer (that is, a customer cannot purchase the property without the manual); and

(3) The manual is not provided in connection with a training course for the customer;

(D) A qualified installation, that is, an installation service (including minor assembly) for QPP that is provided in connection with the lease, rental, license, sale, exchange, or other disposition of the QPP if—

(1) In the normal course of the taxpayer's business, the price for the installation service is not separately stated from the amount charged for the lease, rental, license, sale, exchange, or other disposition of the property; and

(2) The installation is neither separately offered by the taxpayer nor separately bargained for with the customer (that is, a customer cannot purchase the property without the installation service); and

(E) A de minimis amount of gross receipts from embedded services and non-qualified property for each item of QPP, qualified films, or utilities. For purposes of the preceding sentence, a de minimis amount of gross receipts from embedded services and non-qualified property is less than 5 percent of the total gross receipts derived from the lease, rental, license, sale, exchange, or other disposition of each item of QPP, qualified films, or utilities (including the gross receipts for the embedded services and property described in paragraphs (h)(4)(ii)(A), (B), (C), (D) and (k)(4)(iv) of this section). The allocation of the gross receipts attributable to the embedded services or non-qualified property will be deemed to be reasonable if the allocation reflects the fair market value of the embedded services or property. In the case of gross receipts derived from the lease, rental, license, sale, exchange, or other disposition of QPP, qualified films, and utilities that are received over a period of time (for example, a multi-year lease or installment sale), this de minimis exception is applied by taking into account the total gross receipts derived from the lease, rental, license, sale, exchange, or other disposition of the item of QPP, qualified films, or utilities. For purposes of applying this de minimis exception, the gross receipts described in paragraphs (h)(4)(ii)(A), (B), (C), (D) and (k)(4)(iv) of this section are treated as DPGR. This de minimis exception does not apply if the prices of the services or non-qualified property are separately stated by the taxpayer, or if the services or non-qualified property are separately offered or separately bargained for with the customer (that is, the customer can purchase the property without the services or non-qualified property).

(iii) Examples. The following examples illustrate the application of this paragraph (h)(4):

Example (1). X MPGE QPP within the United States. As part of the sale of the QPP to Z, X trains Z's employees on how to use and operate the QPP. No other services or property are provided to Z in connection with the sale of the QPP to Z. The QPP and training services are separately stated in the sales contract. Because the training services are separately stated, the training services are not treated as embedded services under the de minimis exception in paragraph (h)(4)(ii)(E) of this section.

Example (2). The facts are the same as in Example 1 except that the training services are not separately stated in the sales contract and the customer cannot purchase the QPP without the training services. If the gross receipts for the embedded training services are less than 5 percent of the gross receipts derived from the sale of X's QPP to Z, including the gross receipts for the training services, then the gross receipts may be included in DPGR under the de minimis exception in paragraph (h)(4)(ii)(E) of this section.

Example (3). X MPGE QPP within the United States. As part of the sale of the QPP to retailers, X charges a fee for delivering the QPP. The price of the QPP and the delivery fee are separately stated in the sales contract. The retailer's customers cannot purchase the QPP without paying for the delivery fee. Because the delivery fee is separately stated, the delivery fee does not qualify as DPGR under the qualified delivery exception in paragraph (h)(4)(ii)(B) of this section or the de minimis exception under paragraph (h)(4)(ii)(E) of this section.

Example (4). X enters into a single, lump-sum priced contract with Y, an unrelated taxpayer, and the contract has the following terms: X will produce QPP within the United States for Y; X will deliver the QPP to Y; X will provide a one-year warranty on the QPP; X will provide operating and maintenance manuals with the QPP; X will provide 100 hours of training and training manuals to Y's employees on the use and maintenance of the QPP; X will provide purchased spare parts for the QPP; and X will provide a 3-year service agreement for the QPP. None of the services or property was separately offered or separately bargained for. The receipts for the production of the QPP are DPGR under paragraphs (d)(1) and (f) of this section (assuming all the other requirements of this section are met). X may include in DPGR the gross receipts for delivering the QPP, which is a qualified delivery under paragraph (h)(4)(ii)(B) of this section; the gross receipts for the one-year warranty, which is a qualified warranty under paragraph (h)(4)(ii)(A) of this section; and the gross receipts for the operating and maintenance manuals, each of which is a qualified operating manual under paragraph (h)(4)(ii)(C) of this section. If the gross receipts for the embedded services consisting of the employee training and 3-year service agreement, and for the non-qualified property consisting of the purchased spare parts and the employee training manuals, which are not qualified operating manuals, are in total less than 5 percent of the gross receipts derived from the sale of X's QPP to Y (including the gross receipts for the embedded services and non-qualified property), those gross receipts may be included in DPGR (assuming there are no other embedded services or non-qualified property under the contract) under the de minimis exception in paragraph (h)(4)(ii)(E) of this section. If, however, the gross receipts for the embedded services and non-qualified property consisting of employee training, the 3-year service agreement, purchased spare parts, and employee training manuals equal or exceed 5 percent of the gross receipts derived from the sale of X's QPP to Y (including the gross receipts for the embedded services and non-qualified property), those gross receipts do not qualify as DPGR under the de minimis exception in paragraph (h)(4)(ii)(E) of this section.

(5) Advertising income. (i) Tangible personal property. A taxpayer's gross receipts that are derived from the lease, rental, license, sale, exchange, or other disposition of newspapers, magazines, telephone directories, or periodicals that are MPGE in whole or in significant part within the United States include advertising income from advertisements placed in those media, but only to the extent the gross receipts, if any, derived from the lease, rental, license, sale, exchange, or other disposition of the newspapers, magazines, telephone directories, or periodicals are DPGR (without regard to this paragraph (h)(5)(i)).

(ii) Qualified films. A taxpayer's gross receipts that are derived from the lease, rental, license, sale, exchange, or other disposition of a qualified film include product-placement income with respect to that qualified film, that is, compensation for placing or integrating a product into the qualified film, but only to the extent the gross receipts derived from the qualified film (if any) are DPGR (without regard to this paragraph (h)(5)(ii)).

(iii) Examples. The following examples illustrate the application of this paragraph (h)(5):

Example (1). X MPGE and sells newspapers within the United States. X's gross receipts from the newspapers include gross receipts derived from the sale of newspapers to customers and payments from advertisers to publish display advertising or classified advertisements in X's newspapers. X's gross receipts described above are DPGR derived from the sale of X's newspapers.

Example (2). The facts are the same as in Example 1 except that X also distributes with its newspapers advertising flyers that are MPGE by the advertiser. The fees X receives for distributing the advertising flyers are not derived from the sale of X's newspapers because X did not MPGE the advertising flyers that it distributes. As a result, the distribution fee is for the provision of a distribution service and is non-DPGR under paragraph (h)(5)(i) of this section.

Example (3). X produces two television programs that are qualified films (as defined in paragraph (j)(1) of this section). X licenses the first television program to Y's television station and X licenses the second television program to Z's television station. Both television programs contain product placements for which X received compensation. Z, but not Y, is a related person to X within the meaning of paragraph (b)(1) of this section. The gross receipts derived by X from licensing the qualified film to Y are DPGR. As a result, pursuant to paragraph (h)(5)(ii) of this section, all of X's product placement income for the first television program is treated as gross receipts that are derived from the license of the qualified film. The gross receipts derived by X from licensing the qualified film to Z are non-DPGR under paragraph (b)(1) of this section. As a result, pursuant to paragraph (h)(5)(ii) of this section, none of X's product placement income for the second television program is treated as gross receipts derived from the qualified film under paragraph (h)(5)(ii) of this section.

(6) Computer software. (i) In general. Gross receipts derived from the lease, rental, license, sale, exchange, or other disposition of computer software (as defined in paragraph (i)(3) of this section) do not include gross receipts derived from Internet access services, online services, customer and technical support, telephone services, online electronic books and journals, games played through a Web site, provider-controlled software online access services, and other similar services that do not constitute the lease, rental, license, sale, exchange, or other disposition of computer software that was developed by the taxpayer.

(ii) Examples. The following examples illustrate the application of this paragraph (h)(6):

Example (1). X produces and prints a newspaper in the United States which it sells to customers. X also has an online version of the newspaper which is available only to subscribers. The gross receipts derived from the sale of the newspaper X produces and prints qualify as DPGR. However, because X's gross receipts from the online newspaper subscription are not derived from the lease, rental, license, sale, exchange, or disposition of computer software under paragraph (h)(6)(i) of this section, the gross receipts attributable to the online newspaper subscription fees are non-DPGR under paragraph (h)(6)(i) of this section.

Example (2). The facts are the same as in Example 1 except that X's gross receipts attributable to the online version of its newspaper are derived from fees from customers to view the newspaper online and payments from advertisers to display advertising online. X's gross receipts derived from allowing customers online access to X's newspaper are non-DPGR because, pursuant to paragraph (h)(6)(i) of this section, the gross receipts relating to online newspapers are not derived from the lease, rental, license, sale, exchange, or other disposition of QPP, but rather is the provision of an online access service. As a result, because X's gross receipts from the online access services are non-DPGR, the related online advertising receipts are similarly non-DPGR under paragraph (h)(5)(i) of this section.

(7) Exception for certain oil and gas partnerships. (i) In general. If a partnership is engaged solely in the extraction, refining, or processing of oil or natural gas, and distributes the oil or natural gas or products derived from the oil or natural gas (products) to one or more partners, then each partner is treated as extracting, refining, or processing any oil or

natural gas or products extracted, refined, or processed by the partnership and distributed to that partner. Thus, to the extent that the extracting, refining, or processing of the distributed oil or natural gas or products occurs in whole or in significant part within the United States, gross receipts derived by each partner from the sale, exchange, or other disposition of the distributed oil or natural gas or products are treated as DPGR (provided all requirements of this section are met). Solely for purposes of section 199(d)(1)(B)(ii), the partnership is treated as having gross receipts in the taxable year of the distribution equal to the fair market value of the distributed oil or natural gas or products at the time of distribution to the partner and the deemed gross receipts are allocated to that partner, provided the partner derives gross receipts from the distributed property during the taxable year of the partner with or within which the partnership's taxable year (in which the distribution occurs) ends. Costs included in the adjusted basis of the distributed oil or natural gas or products and any other relevant deductions are taken into account in computing the partner's QPAI. See § 1.199-5 for the application of section 199 to pass-thru entities.

(ii) Example. The following example illustrates the application of this paragraph (h)(7). Assume that PRS and X are calendar year taxpayers. The example reads as follows:

Example. X is a partner in PRS, a partnership which engages solely in the extraction of oil within the United States. In 2010, PRS distributes oil to X that PRS derived from its oil extraction. PRS incurred $600 of CGS, including $500 of W-2 wages (as defined in § 1.199-2(f)), extracting the oil distributed to X, and X's adjusted basis in the distributed oil is $600. The fair market value of the oil at the time of the distribution to X is $1,000. X incurs $200 of CGS, including $100 of W-2 wages, in refining the oil within the United States. In 2010, X sells the oil for $1,500 to a customer. Under paragraph (h)(7)(i) of this section, X is treated as having extracted the oil. The extraction and refining of the oil qualify as an MPGE activity under paragraph (d)(1) of this section. Therefore, X's $1,500 of gross receipts qualify as DPGR. X subtracts from the $1,500 of DPGR the $600 of CGS incurred by PRS and the $200 of refining costs incurred by X. Thus, X's QPAI is $700 for 2010. In addition, PRS is treated as having $1,000 of DPGR solely for purposes of applying the wage limitation of section 199(d)(1)(B)(ii). Accordingly, X's share of PRS's W-2 wages determined under section 199(d)(1)(B) is $72, the lesser of $500 (X's allocable share of PRS's W-2 wages included in CGS) and $72 (2 x ($400 ($1,000 deemed DPGR less $600 of CGS) x .09)). X adds the $72 of PRS W-2 wages to its $100 of W-2 wages incurred in refining the oil for purposes of section 199(b).

(8) Partnerships owned by members of a single expanded affiliated group. (i) In general. For purposes of this section, if all of the interests in the capital and profits of a partnership are owned by members of a single EAG at all times during the taxable year of the partnership (EAG partnership), then the EAG partnership and all members of that EAG are treated as a single taxpayer for purposes of section 199(c)(4) during that taxable year. Thus, if an EAG partnership MPGE or produces property and distributes, leases, rents, licenses, sells, exchanges, or otherwise disposes of that property to a member of an EAG in which the partners of the EAG partnership are members, then the MPGE or production activity conducted by the EAG partnership will be treated as having been conducted by the members of the EAG. Similarly, if one or more members of an EAG in which the partners of an EAG partnership are members MPGE or produces property and contributes, leases, rents, licenses, sells, exchanges, or otherwise disposes of that property to the EAG partnership, then the MPGE or production activity conducted by the EAG member (or members) will be treated as having been conducted by the EAG partnership. Attribution of activities does not apply for purposes of the construction of real property under § 1.199-3(l)(1) and the performance of engineering and architectural services under § 1.199-3(m)(2) and (3), respectively. An EAG partnership may not use the small business simplified overall method described in § 1.199-4(f). Except as provided in this paragraph (h)(8), an EAG partnership is treated the same as other partnerships for purposes of section 199. Accordingly, an EAG partnership is subject to the rules of § 1.199-5 regarding the application of section 199 to pass-thru entities, including application of the section 199(d)(1)(B) wage limitation under § 1.199-5(a)(3). See paragraphs (f)(2) and (3) of this section for the aggregation of activities and conversion costs among EAG partnerships and all members of the EAG in which the partners of the EAG partnership are members.

(ii) Special rules for distributions from EAG partnerships. If an EAG partnership distributes property to a partner, then, solely for purposes of section 199(d)(1)(B)(ii), the EAG partnership is treated as having gross receipts in the taxable year of the distribution equal to the fair market value of the property at the time of distribution to the partner and the deemed gross receipts are allocated to that partner, provided the partner derives gross receipts from the distributed property during the taxable year of the partner with or within which the partnership's taxable year (in which the distribution occurs) ends. Costs included in the adjusted basis of the distributed property and any other relevant deductions are taken into account in computing the partner's QPAI.

(iii) Examples. The following examples illustrate the rules of this paragraph (h)(8). Assume that PRS, X, Y, and Z all are calendar year taxpayers. The examples read as follows:

Example (1). Contribution. X and Y, both members of a single EAG, are the only partners in PRS, a partnership, for PRS's entire 2010 taxable year. In 2010, X MPGE QPP within the United States and contributes the property to PRS. In 2010, PRS sells the QPP for $1,000. PRS's $1,000 gross receipts constitute DPGR. PRS, X, and Y must apply the rules of § 1.199-5 regarding the application of section 199 to pass-thru entities with respect to the activity of PRS, including application of the section 199(d)(1)(B) wage limitation under § 1.199-5(a)(3).

Example (2). Sale. X, Y, and Z are the only members of a single EAG. X and Y each own 50% of the capital and profits interests in PRS, a partnership, for PRS's entire 2010 taxable year. In 2010, PRS MPGE QPP within the United States and then sells the property to X for $6,000, its fair market value at the time of the sale. PRS's gross receipts of $6,000 qualify as DPGR. In 2010, X sells the QPP to customers for $10,000, incurring selling expenses of $2,000. Under this paragraph (h)(8), X is treated as having MPGE the QPP within the United States, and X's $10,000 of gross receipts qualify as DPGR ($6,000 of CGS and $2,000 of other selling expenses are subtracted from DPGR in determining X's QPAI). The results would be the same if PRS sold the property to Z rather than to X.

Example (3). Distribution. X and Y, both members of a single EAG, are the only partners in PRS, a partnership, for PRS's entire 2010 taxable year. In 2010, PRS MPGE QPP within the United States, incurring $600 of CGS, including $500 of W-2 wages (as defined in § 1.199-2(f)), and then distributes the QPP to X. X's adjusted basis in the QPP is

$600. At the time of the distribution the fair market value of the QPP is $1,000. X incurs $200 of directly allocable costs, including $100 of W-2 wages, to further MPGE the QPP within the United States. In 2010, X sells the QPP for $1,500 to a customer. Under paragraph (h)(8)(i) of this section, X is treated as having MPGE the QPP within the United States, and X's $1,500 of gross receipts qualify as DPGR. X subtracts from the $1,500 of DPGR the $600 of CGS incurred by PRS and the $200 of direct costs incurred by X. Thus, X's QPAI is $700 for 2010. In addition, PRS is treated as having DPGR of $1,000 solely for purposes of applying the wage limitation of section 199(d)(1)(B)(ii). Accordingly, X's share of PRS'S W-2 wages determined under section 199(d)(1)(B) is $72, the lesser of $500 (X's allocable share of PRS'S W-2 wages included in CGS) and $72 (2 x ($400 ($1,000 deemed DPGR less $600 of CGS) x .09)). X adds the $72 of PRS W-2 wages to its $100 of W-2 wages incurred in MPGE the QPP for purposes of section 199(b).

Example (4). Multiple sales. X and Y, both non-consolidated members of a single EAG, are the only partners in PRS, a partnership, for PRS's entire 2010 taxable year. PRS produces in bulk form in the United States the active ingredient for a pharmaceutical product. Assume that PRS's own MPGE activity with respect to the active ingredient is not substantial in nature, taking into account all of the facts and circumstances, and PRS's conversion costs to MPGE the active ingredient within the United States are $15 and account for 15 percent of PRS's $100 CGS of the active ingredient. PRS sells the active ingredient in bulk form to X. X uses the active ingredient to produce the finished dosage form drug. Assume that X's own MPGE activity with respect to the drug is not substantial in nature, taking into account all of the facts and circumstances, and X's conversion costs to MPGE the drug within the United States are $12 and account for 10 percent of X's $120 CGS of the drug. X sells the drug in finished dosage to Y and Y sells the drug to customers. Y incurs $2 of conversion costs and Y's CGS in selling the drug to customers is $130. PRS's gross receipts from the sale of the active ingredient to X are non-DPGR because PRS's MPGE activity is not substantial in nature and PRS does not satisfy the safe harbor described in paragraph (f)(3) of this section because PRS's conversion costs account for less than 20 percent of PRS's CGS of the active ingredient. X's gross receipts from the sale of the drug to Y are DPGR because X is considered to have MPGE the drug in significant part in the United States pursuant to the safe harbor described in paragraph (f)(3) of this section because the $27 ($15 + $12) of conversion costs incurred by PRS and X equals or exceeds 20 percent of X's total CGS ($120) of the drug at the time the drug is sold to Y. Similarly, Y's gross receipts from the sale of the drug to customers are DPGR because Y is considered to have MPGE the drug in significant part in the United States pursuant to the safe harbor described in paragraph (f)(3) of this section because the $29 ($15 + $12 + $2) of conversion costs incurred by PRS, X, and Y equals or exceeds 20 percent of Y's total CGS ($130) of the drug at the time the drug is sold to customers.

(9) Non-operating mineral interests. DPGR does not include gross receipts derived from mineral interests other than operating mineral interests within the meaning of § 1.614-2(b).

(i) Definition of qualifying production property. *(1)* In general. QPP means—

(i) Tangible personal property (as defined in paragraph (i)(2) of this section);

(ii) Computer software (as defined in paragraph (i)(3) of this section); and

(iii) Sound recordings (as defined in paragraph (i)(4) of this section).

(2) Tangible personal property. (i) In general. The term tangible personal property is any tangible property other than land, buildings (including items that are structural components of such buildings), and any property described in paragraph (i)(3), (i)(4), (j)(1), or (k) of this section. Property such as production machinery, printing presses, transportation and office equipment, refrigerators, grocery counters, testing equipment, display racks and shelves, and neon and other signs that are contained in or attached to a building constitutes tangible personal property for purposes of this paragraph (i)(2)(i). Except as provided in paragraphs (i)(5)(ii) and (j)(2)(i) of this section, computer software, sound recordings, and qualified films are not treated as tangible personal property regardless of whether they are fixed on a tangible medium. However, the tangible medium on which such property may be fixed (for example, a videocassette, a computer diskette, or other similar tangible item) is tangible personal property.

(ii) Local law. In determining whether property is tangible personal property, local law is not controlling.

(iii) Machinery. Property that is in the nature of machinery (other than structural components of a building) is tangible personal property even if such property is located outside a building. Thus, for example, a gasoline pump, hydraulic car lift, or automatic vending machine, although annexed to the ground, is considered tangible personal property. A structure that is property in the nature of machinery or is essentially an item of machinery or equipment is not an inherently permanent structure and is tangible personal property. In the case, however, of a building or inherently permanent structure that includes property in the nature of machinery as a structural component, the property in the nature of machinery is real property.

(iv) Intangible property. The term tangible personal property does not include property in a form other than in a tangible medium. For example, mass-produced books are tangible personal property, but neither the rights to the underlying manuscript nor an online version of the book is tangible personal property.

(3) Computer software. (i) In general. The term computer software means any program or routine or any sequence of machine-readable code that is designed to cause a computer to perform a desired function or set of functions, and the documentation required to describe and maintain that program or routine. For purposes of this paragraph (i)(3), computer software also includes the machine-readable code for video games and similar programs, for equipment that is an integral part of other property, and for typewriters, calculators, adding and accounting machines, copiers, duplicating equipment, and similar equipment, regardless of whether the code is designed to operate on a computer (as defined in section 168(i)(2)(B)). Computer programs of all classes, for example, operating systems, executive systems, monitors, compilers and translators, assembly routines, and utility programs, as well as application programs, are included. Except as provided in paragraph (i)(5) of this section, if the medium in which the software is contained, whether written, magnetic, or otherwise, is tangible, then such medium is considered tangible personal property for purposes of this section.

(ii) Incidental and ancillary rights. Computer software also includes any incidental and ancillary rights that are necessary to effect the acquisition of the title to, the ownership of, or the right to use the computer software, and that are used only in connection with that specific computer software. Such incidental and ancillary rights are not included in the definition of trademark or trade name under § 1.197-2(b)(10)(i). For example, a trademark or trade name that is ancillary to the ownership or use of a specific computer software program in the taxpayer's trade or business and is not acquired for the purpose of marketing the computer software is included in the definition of computer software and is not included in the definition of trademark or trade name.

(iii) Exceptions. Computer software does not include any data or information base unless the data or information base is in the public domain and is incidental to a computer program. For this purpose, a copyrighted or proprietary data or information base is treated as in the public domain if its availability through the computer program does not contribute significantly to the cost of the program. For example, if a word-processing program includes a dictionary feature that may be used to spell-check a document or any portion thereof, the entire program (including the dictionary feature) is computer software regardless of the form in which the dictionary feature is maintained or stored.

(4) Sound recordings. (i) In general. The term sound recordings means any works that result from the fixation of a series of musical, spoken, or other sounds under section 168(f)(4). The definition of sound recordings is limited to the master copy of the recordings (or other copy from which the holder is licensed to make and produce copies), and, except as provided in paragraph (i)(5) of this section, if the medium (such as compact discs, tapes, or other phonorecordings) in which the sounds may be embodied is tangible, the medium is considered tangible personal property for purposes of paragraph (i)(2) of this section.

(ii) Exception. The term sound recordings does not include the creation of copyrighted material in a form other than a sound recording, such as lyrics or music composition.

(5) Tangible personal property with computer software or sound recordings. (i) Computer software and sound recordings. If a taxpayer MPGE computer software or sound recordings that is fixed on, or added to, tangible personal property by the taxpayer (for example, a computer diskette, or an appliance), then for purposes of this section—

(A) The computer software and the tangible personal property may be treated by the taxpayer as computer software. If the taxpayer treats the tangible personal property as computer software under this paragraph (i)(5)(i)(A), any costs under section 174 attributable to the tangible personal property are not considered in determining whether the taxpayer's activity is substantial in nature under paragraph (f)(2) of this section and are not conversion costs under paragraph (f)(3) of this section; and

(B) The sound recordings and the tangible personal property with the sound recordings may be treated by the taxpayer as sound recordings. If the taxpayer treats the tangible personal property as sound recordings under this paragraph (i)(5)(i)(B), any costs under section 174 attributable to the tangible personal property are not considered in determining whether the taxpayer's activity is substantial in nature under paragraph (f)(2) of this section and are not conversion costs under paragraph (f)(3) of this section.

(ii) Tangible personal property. If a taxpayer MPGE tangible personal property but not the computer software or sound recordings that the taxpayer fixes on, or adds to, the tangible personal property MPGE by the taxpayer (for example, a computer diskette or an appliance), then for purposes of this section the tangible personal property with the computer software or sound recordings may be treated by the taxpayer as tangible personal property under paragraph (i)(2) of this section. For purposes of paragraph (f)(3) of this section, the taxpayer's CGS for each item includes the taxpayer's cost of licensing the computer software or sound recordings.

(j) Definition of qualified film. *(1) In general.* The term qualified film means any motion picture film or video tape under section 168(f)(3), or live or delayed television programming if not less than 50 percent of the total compensation paid to all actors, production personnel, directors, and producers relating to the production of the motion picture film, video tape, or television programming is compensation for services performed in the United States by those individuals. The term production personnel includes writers, choreographers and composers providing services during the production of a film, casting agents, camera operators, set designers, lighting technicians, make-up artists, and others whose activities are directly related to the production of the film. The term production personnel does not include, however, individuals whose activities are ancillary to the production, such as advertisers and promoters, distributors, studio administrators and managers, studio security personnel, and personal assistants to actors. The term production personnel also does not include individuals whose activities relate to fixing the film on tangible personal property. The definition of qualified film is limited to the master copy of the film (or other copy from which the holder is licensed to make and produce copies), and, except as provided in paragraph (j)(2) of this section, does not include tangible personal property embodying the qualified film, such as DVDs or videocassettes.

(2) Tangible personal property with a film. (i) Film licensed to a taxpayer. If a taxpayer MPGE tangible personal property (such as a DVD) in whole or in significant part in the United States and fixes to the tangible personal property a film that the taxpayer licenses from the producer of the film, then the taxpayer may treat the tangible personal property with the affixed film as QPP, regardless of whether the film is a qualified film. The determination of whether gross receipts of such a taxpayer from the lease, rental, license, sale, exchange, or other disposition of the tangible personal property with the affixed film are DPGR is made under the rules of paragraphs (d), (e), and (f) of this section. For purposes of paragraph (f)(3) of this section, the taxpayer's CGS for each item includes the taxpayer's cost of licensing the film from the producer of the film.

(ii) Film produced by a taxpayer. If a taxpayer produces a film and also fixes the film on tangible personal property (for example, a DVD), then for purposes of this section—

(A) Qualified films. If the film is a qualified film, the taxpayer may treat the tangible personal property on which the qualified film is fixed as part of the qualified film, in which case the gross receipts derived from the lease, rental, license, sale, exchange, or other disposition of the tangible personal property with the affixed qualified film will be DPGR (assuming all the other requirements of this section are met), regardless of whether the taxpayer MPGE the tangible personal property in whole or in significant part within the United States; and

(B) Nonqualified films. If the film is not a qualified film (nonqualified film), any gross receipts derived from the lease, rental, license, sale, exchange, or other disposition of the tangible personal property with the nonqualified film that are allocable to the nonqualified film are non-DPGR. The taxpayer, however, may treat the tangible personal property (without the nonqualified film) as an item of QPP. Thus, the determination of whether gross receipts of such a taxpayer derived from the lease, rental, license, sale, exchange, or other disposition of the tangible personal property with the affixed nonqualified film, that are allocable to the tangible personal property, are DPGR is made under the rules of paragraphs (d), (e), and (f) of this section.

(3) Derived from a qualified film. DPGR includes the gross receipts of the taxpayer which are derived from any lease, rental, license, sale, exchange, or other disposition of any qualified film produced by the taxpayer. Showing a qualified film on a television station is not a lease, rental, license, sale, exchange, or other disposition of the qualified film. Ticket sales for viewing qualified films do not constitute DPGR because the gross receipts are not derived from the lease, rental, license, sale, exchange, or other disposition of a qualified film. Because a taxpayer that merely writes a screenplay or other similar material is not considered to have produced a qualified film under paragraph (j)(1) of this section, the amounts that the taxpayer receives from the sale of the script or screenplay, even if the script is developed into a qualified film, are not gross receipts derived from a qualified film. In addition, revenue from the sale of film-themed merchandise is revenue from the sale of tangible personal property and not gross receipts derived from a qualified film. Gross receipts derived from a license of the right to use the film characters are not gross receipts derived from a qualified film.

(4) Examples. The following examples illustrate the application of paragraphs (j)(2) and (3) of this section:

Example (1). X produces a qualified film in the United States and duplicates the film onto purchased DVDs. X sells the DVDs with the qualified film to customers. Under paragraph (j)(2)(ii)(A) of this section, X may treat the DVD with the qualified film as a qualified film. Accordingly, X's gross receipts derived from the sale of the qualified film to customers are DPGR (assuming all the other requirements of this section are met).

Example (2). The facts are the same as in Example 1 except that the film is a nonqualified film because the film does not satisfy the 50 percent requirement under (j)(1) of this section and X manufactures the DVDs in the United States. Under paragraph (j)(2)(ii)(B) of this section, X may treat the DVD without the nonqualified film as tangible personal property. X's gross receipts (not including the gross receipts attributable to the nonqualified film) derived from the sale of the tangible personal property are DPGR (assuming all the other requirements of this section are met).

Example (3). X produces television programs that are qualified films. X shows the programs on its own television station. X sells advertising time slots to advertisers for the television programs. Because showing qualified films on a television station is not a lease, rental, license, sale, exchange, or other disposition, pursuant to paragraph (j)(3) of this section, the advertising income X receives from advertisers is not derived from the lease, rental, license, sale, exchange, or other disposition of qualified films.

Example (4). X produces a qualified film and contracts with Y, an unrelated taxpayer, to duplicate the film onto DVDs. Y manufactures blank DVDs within the United States, duplicates X's film onto the DVDs in the United States, and sells the DVDs with the qualified film to X who then sells them to customers. Y has all of the benefits and burdens of ownership under Federal income tax principles of the DVDs during the MPGE and duplication process. Assume Y's activities relating to manufacture of the blank DVDs and duplicating the film onto the DVDs collectively satisfy the safe harbor under paragraph (f)(3) of this section. Y's gross receipts from manufacturing the DVDs and duplicating the film onto the DVDs are DPGR. X's gross receipts from the sale of the DVDs to customers are DPGR.

(5) Compensation for services. The term compensation for services means all payments for services performed by actors, production personnel, directors, and producers, including participations and residuals. In the case of a taxpayer that uses the income forecast method of section 167(g) and capitalizes participations and residuals into the adjusted basis of the qualified film, the taxpayer must use the same estimate of participations and residuals for services performed by actors, production personnel, directors, and producers for purposes of this section. In the case of a taxpayer that excludes participations and residuals from the adjusted basis of the qualified film under section 167(g)(7)(D)(i), the taxpayer must determine the compensation expected to be paid for services performed by actors, production personnel, directors, and producers as participations and residuals based on the total forecasted income used in determining income forecast depreciation. Compensation for services includes all direct and indirect compensation costs required to be capitalized under section 263A for film producers under § 1.263A-1(e)(2) and (3). Compensation for services is not limited to W-2 wages and includes compensation paid to independent contractors.

(6) Determination of 50 percent. A taxpayer may use any reasonable method of determining the compensation for services performed in the United States by actors, production personnel, directors, and producers, and the total compensation paid to those individuals for services relating to the production of the property. Among the factors to be considered in determining whether a taxpayer's method of allocating compensation is reasonable is whether the taxpayer uses that method consistently.

(7) Exception. A qualified film does not include property with respect to which records are required to be maintained under 18 U.S.C. 2257. Section 2257 of Title 18 requires maintenance of certain records with respect to any book, magazine, periodical, film, videotape, or other matter that—

(i) Contains one or more visual depictions made after November 1, 1990, of actual sexually explicit conduct; and

(ii) Is produced in whole or in part with materials that have been mailed or shipped in interstate or foreign commerce, or is shipped or transported or is intended for shipment or transportation in interstate or foreign commerce.

(k) Electricity, natural gas, or potable water. *(1) In general.* DPGR includes gross receipts derived from any lease, rental, license, sale, exchange, or other disposition of utilities produced by the taxpayer in the United States if all other requirements of this section are met. In the case of an integrated producer that both produces and delivers utilities, see paragraph (k)(4) of this section that describes certain gross receipts that do not qualify as DPGR, therefore requiring a taxpayer to allocate its gross receipts between DPGR and non-DPGR.

(2) Natural gas. The term natural gas includes only natural gas extracted from a natural deposit and does not include, for example, methane gas extracted from a landfill. In the case of natural gas, production activities include all activities involved in extracting natural gas from the ground and processing the gas into pipeline quality gas.

(3) Potable water. The term potable water means unbottled drinking water. In the case of potable water, production activities include the acquisition, collection, and storage of raw water (untreated water), transportation of raw water to a water treatment facility, and treatment of raw water at such a facility. Gross receipts attributable to any of these activities are included in DPGR if all other requirements of this section are met.

(4) Exceptions. (i) Electricity. Gross receipts attributable to the transmission of electricity from the generating facility to a point of local distribution and gross receipts attributable to the distribution of electricity to final customers are non-DPGR.

(ii) Natural gas. Gross receipts attributable to the transmission of pipeline quality gas from a natural gas field (or, if treatment at a natural gas processing plant is necessary to produce pipeline quality gas, from a natural gas processing plant) to a local distribution company's citygate (or to another customer) are non-DPGR. Likewise, gross receipts of a local gas distribution company attributable to distribution from the citygate to the local customers are non-DPGR.

(iii) Potable water. Gross receipts attributable to the storage of potable water after completion of treatment of the potable water, as well as gross receipts attributable to the transmission and distribution of potable water, are non-DPGR.

(iv) De minimis exception. Notwithstanding paragraphs (k)(4)(i), (ii), and (iii) of this section, if less than 5 percent of a taxpayer's gross receipts derived from a sale, exchange, or other disposition of utilities are attributable to the transmission or distribution of the utilities, then the gross receipts derived from that lease, rental, license, sale, exchange, or other disposition that are attributable to the transmission and distribution of the utilities must be treated for purposes of section 199 as being DPGR if all other requirements of this section are met.

(5) Example. The following example illustrates the application of this paragraph (k):

Example. X owns a wind turbine in the United States that generates electricity and Y owns a high voltage transmission line that passes near X's wind turbine and ends near the system of local distribution lines of Z. X sells the electricity produced at the wind turbine to Z and contracts with Y to transmit the electricity produced at the wind turbine to Z who sells the electricity to customers using Z's distribution network. The gross receipts received by X for the sale of electricity produced at the wind turbine are DPGR. The gross receipts of Y from transporting X's electricity to Z are non-DPGR under paragraph (k)(4)(i) of this section. Likewise, the gross receipts of Z from distributing the electricity are non-DPGR under paragraph (k)(4)(i) of this section. If X made direct sales of electricity to customers in Z's service area and Z receives remuneration for the distribution of electricity, the gross receipts of Z are non-DPGR under paragraph (k)(4)(i) of this section. If X, Y, and Z are related persons (as defined in paragraph (b) of this section), then X, Y, and Z must allocate gross receipts to production activities, transmission activities, and distribution activities.

(l) Definition of construction performed in the United States. *(1) Construction of real property.* (i) In general. The term construction means the construction or erection of real property (that is, residential and commercial buildings (including items that are structural components of such buildings), inherently permanent structures other than tangible personal property in the nature of machinery (see paragraph (i)(2)(iii) of this section), inherently permanent land improvements, oil and gas wells, and infrastructure) in the United States by a taxpayer that, at the time the taxpayer constructs the real property, is engaged in a trade or business (but not necessarily its primary, or only, trade or business) that is considered construction for purposes of the North American Industry Classification System (NAICS) on a regular and ongoing basis. A trade or business that is considered construction under the NAICS means a construction activity under the two-digit NAICS code of 23 and any other construction activity in any other NAICS code provided the construction activity relates to the construction of real property such as NAICS code 213111 (drilling oil and gas wells) and 213112 (support activities for oil and gas operations). Tangible personal property (for example, appliances, furniture, and fixtures) that is sold as part of a construction project is not considered real property for purposes of this paragraph (l)(1)(i). In determining whether property is real property, the fact that property is real property under local law is not controlling. Conversely, property may be real property for purposes of this paragraph (l)(1)(i) even though under local law the property is considered tangible personal property.

(ii) De minimis exception. For purposes of paragraph (l)(1)(i) of this section, if less than 5 percent of the total gross receipts derived by a taxpayer from a construction project (as described in paragraph (l)(1)(i) of this section) are derived from activities other than the construction of real property in the United States (for example, from non-construction activities or the sale of tangible personal property or land) then the total gross receipts derived by the taxpayer from the project are DPGR from construction.

(2) Activities constituting construction. Activities constituting construction include activities performed in connection with a project to erect or substantially renovate real property, but do not include tangential services such as hauling trash and debris, and delivering materials, even if the tangential services are essential for construction. However, if the taxpayer performing construction also, in connection with the construction project, provides tangential services such as delivering materials to the construction site and removing its construction debris, the gross receipts derived from the tangential services are DPGR. Improvements to land that are not capitalizable to the land (for example, landscaping) and painting are activities constituting construction only if these activities are performed in connection with other activities (whether or not by the same taxpayer) that constitute the erection or substantial renovation of real property and provided the taxpayer meets the requirements under paragraph (l)(1) of this section. The taxpayer engaged in these activities must make a reasonable inquiry to determine whether the activity relates to the erection or substantial renovation of real property in the United States. Construction activities also include activities relating to drilling an oil well and mining and include any activities pursuant to which the taxpayer could deduct intangible drilling and development costs under section 263(c) and § 1.612-4 and development expenditures for a mine or natural deposit under section 616. The lease, license, or rental of equipment, for example, bulldozers, generators, or computers, to contractors for use by the contractors in the construction of real property is not a construction activity under this paragraph (l)(2). The term construction does not include any activity that is within the definition of engineering and architectural services under paragraph (m) of this section.

(3) Definition of infrastructure. The term infrastructure includes roads, power lines, water systems, railroad spurs,

communications facilities, sewers, sidewalks, cable, and wiring. The term also includes inherently permanent oil and gas platforms.

(4) Definition of substantial renovation. The term substantial renovation means the renovation of a major component or substantial structural part of real property that materially increases the value of the property, substantially prolongs the useful life of the property, or adapts the property to a new or different use.

(5) Derived from construction. (i) In general. Assuming all the requirements of this section are met, DPGR derived from the construction of real property performed in the United States includes the proceeds from the sale, exchange, or other disposition of real property constructed by the taxpayer in the United States (whether or not the property is sold immediately after construction is completed and whether or not the construction project is complete). DPGR derived from the construction of real property includes compensation for the performance of construction services by the taxpayer in the United States. However, DPGR derived from the construction of real property does not include gross receipts from the lease or rental of real property constructed by the taxpayer or, except as provided in paragraph (l)(5)(ii) of this section, gross receipts attributable to the sale or other disposition of land (including zoning, planning, entitlement costs, and other costs capitalized to the land such as the demolition of structures under section 280B). In addition, DPGR derived from the construction of real property includes gross receipts from any qualified construction warranty, that is, a warranty that is provided in connection with the constructed real property if—

(A) In the normal course of the taxpayer's business, the price for the construction warranty is not separately stated from the amount charged for the constructed real property; and

(B) The construction warranty is neither separately offered by the taxpayer nor separately bargained for with the customer (that is, the customer cannot purchase the constructed real property without the construction warranty).

(ii) Land safe harbor. For purposes of paragraph (l)(5)(i) of this section, a taxpayer may allocate gross receipts between the proceeds from the sale, exchange, or other disposition of real property constructed by the taxpayer and the gross receipts attributable to the sale, exchange, or other disposition of land by reducing its costs related to DPGR under § 1.199-4 by costs of the land and any other costs capitalized to the land (collectively, land costs) (including zoning, planning, entitlement costs, and other costs capitalized to the land such as the demolition of structures under section 280B and land costs in any common improvements as defined in section 2.01 of Rev. Proc. 92-29 (1992-1 C.B. 748) (see § 601.601(d)(2) of this chapter)) and by reducing its DPGR by those land costs plus a percentage. The percentage is based on the number of years that elapse between the date the taxpayer acquires the land, including the date the taxpayer enters into the first option to acquire all or a portion of the land, and ends on the date the taxpayer sells each item of real property on the land. The percentage is 5 percent for years zero through 5; 10 percent for years 6 through 10; and 15 percent for years 11 through 15. Land held by a taxpayer for 16 or more years is not eligible for the safe harbor under this paragraph (l)(5)(ii) and the taxpayer must allocate gross receipts between land and qualifying real property.

(iii) Examples. The following examples illustrate the application of this paragraph (l)(5):

Example (1). X, who is in the trade or business of construction under NAICS code 23 on a regular and ongoing basis, purchases a building in the United States and retains Y, an unrelated taxpayer (a general contractor), to oversee a substantial renovation of the building (within the meaning of paragraph (l)(4) of this section). Y retains Z (a subcontractor) to install a new electrical system in the building as part of that substantial renovation. The amounts that Y receives from X for construction services, and amounts that Z receives from Y for construction services, qualify as DPGR under paragraph (l)(5)(i) of this section provided Y and Z meet all of the requirements of paragraph (l)(1) of this section. The gross receipts that X receives from the subsequent sale of the building do not qualify as DPGR because X did not engage in any activity constituting construction under paragraph (l)(2) of this section even though X is in the trade or business of construction. The results would be the same if X and Y were members of the same EAG under § 1.199-7(a). However, if X and Y were members of the same consolidated group, see § 1.199-7(d)(2).

Example (2). X is engaged as an electrical contractor under NAICS code 238210 on a regular and ongoing basis. X purchases the wires, conduits, and other electrical materials that it installs in construction projects in the United States. In a particular construction project, all of the wires, conduits, and other electrical materials installed by X for the operation of that building are considered structural components of the building. X's gross receipts derived from installing that property are derived from the construction of real property under paragraph (l)(1) of this section. However, X's gross receipts derived from the purchased materials do not qualify as DPGR.

Example (3). X is in a trade or business that is considered construction under the two-digit NAICS code of 23. X buys unimproved land. X gets the land zoned for residential housing through an entitlement process. X grades the land and sells the land to home builders. The gross receipts that X receives from the sale of the land do not qualify as DPGR under paragraph (l)(5)(i) of this section because the gross receipts are not derived from the construction of real property.

Example (4). The facts are the same as in Example 3 except that X builds roads, sewers, sidewalks, and installs power and water lines on the land. The gross receipts that X receives that are attributable to the sale of the roads, sewers, sidewalks, and power and water lines, which qualify as infrastructure under paragraph (l)(3) of this section, are DPGR. X's gross receipts from the land including capitalized costs of entitlements do not qualify as DPGR under paragraph (l)(5)(i) of this section because the gross receipts are not derived from the construction of real property.

Example (5). (i) X is engaged in the business activities of constructing housing within the meaning of paragraph (l)(1) of this section. On June 1, 2005, X pays $50,000,000 for 1,000 acres of land that X will develop as a new housing development. In 2008, after the expenditure of $10,000,000 for entitlement costs, X receives permits to begin construction. After this expenditure, X's land costs total $60,000,000. The development consists of 1,000 houses to be built on half-acre lots over 5 years. On January 31, 2010, the first house is sold for $300,000. Construction costs for each house are $170,000. Common improvements consisting of streets, sidewalks, sewer lines, playgrounds, clubhouses, tennis courts, and swimming pools that X is contractually obligated or required by law to provide cost $55,000 per lot. The common improvements include $30,000 in land costs underlying the common improvements.

(ii) Pursuant to the land safe harbor under paragraph (l)(5)(ii) of this section, X calculates the total costs under § 1.199-4 for each house sold in 2010 as $195,000 (total costs of $255,000 ($170,000 in construction costs plus $55,000 in common improvements (including $30,000 in land costs) plus $30,000 in land costs for the lot), which are reduced by land costs of $60,000). X calculates the DPGR for each house sold by May 31, 2010, by taking the gross receipts of $300,000 and reducing that amount by land costs of $60,000 plus a percentage of $60,000. As X acquired the land on June 1, 2005, and sold the houses on the land between January 31, 2010, and May 31, 2010, the percentage reduction for X is 5 percent because X has held the land for not more than 5 years from the anniversary of the date of acquisition. Thus, the DPGR for each house is $237,000 ($300,000-$60,000-$3,000) with costs for each house of $195,000 for a calculation of QPAI for each house of $42,000.

Example (6). The facts are the same as in Example 5 except some of the houses are sold between June 1, 2010, and December 31, 2010. X calculates the DPGR for each house sold between June 1, 2010, and December 31, 2010, by taking the gross receipts of $300,000 and reducing that amount by land costs of $60,000 plus a percentage of $60,000. As X acquired the land on June 1, 2005, and sold the houses on the land between June 1, 2010, and December 31, 2010, the percentage reduction for X is 10 percent because X has held the land for more than 5 years but not more than 10 years from the anniversary of the date of acquisition. Thus, the DPGR for each house is $234,000 ($300,000-$60,000-$6,000) with costs for each house of $195,000 for a calculation of QPAI for each house of $39,000.

(m) Definition of engineering and architectural services. *(1) In general.* DPGR includes gross receipts derived from engineering or architectural services performed in the United States for a construction project described in paragraph (l) of this section. At the time the taxpayer performs the engineering or architectural services, the taxpayer must be engaged in a trade or business (but not necessarily its primary, or only, trade or business) that is considered engineering or architectural services for purposes of the NAICS, for example NAICS codes 541330 (engineering services) or 541310 (architectural services), on a regular and ongoing basis. DPGR includes gross receipts derived from engineering or architectural services, including feasibility studies for a construction project in the United States, even if the planned construction project is not undertaken or is not completed.

(2) Engineering services. Engineering services in connection with any construction project include any professional services requiring engineering education, training, and experience and the application of special knowledge of the mathematical, physical, or engineering sciences to those professional services such as consultation, investigation, evaluation, planning, design, or responsible supervision of construction for the purpose of assuring compliance with plans, specifications, and design.

(3) Architectural services. Architectural services in connection with any construction project include the offering or furnishing of any professional services such as consultation, planning, aesthetic and structural design, drawings and specifications, or responsible supervision of construction (for the purpose of assuring compliance with plans, specifications, and design) or erection, in connection with any construction project.

(4) De minimis exception for performance of services in the United States. If less than 5 percent of the total gross receipts derived by a taxpayer from engineering or architectural services performed in the United States for a construction project (described in paragraph (l) of this section) are derived from services not relating to a construction project described in paragraph (l) of this section (for example, the services are performed outside the United States or in connection with property other than real property) then the total gross receipts derived by the taxpayer are DPGR from engineering or architectural services performed in the United States for a construction project.

(n) Exception for sales of certain food and beverages. *(1) In general.* DPGR does not include gross receipts of the taxpayer that are derived from the sale of food or beverages prepared by the taxpayer at a retail establishment. A retail establishment is defined as tangible property (both real and personal) leased, occupied, or otherwise used by the taxpayer in its trade or business of selling food or beverages to the public at which retail sales are made. In addition, a facility that prepares food and beverages solely for take out service or delivery is a retail establishment (for example, a caterer). A facility at which food or beverages are prepared will not be treated as a retail establishment if less than 5 percent of the gross receipts from the sale of food or beverages at that facility during the taxable year are attributable to retail sales. If a taxpayer's facility is a retail establishment in the United States, then, for purposes of this section, the taxpayer may allocate its gross receipts between gross receipts derived from the retail sale of the food and beverages prepared and sold at the retail establishment (which are non-DPGR) and gross receipts derived from the wholesale sale of the food and beverages prepared at the retail establishment (which are DPGR). Wholesale sales are sales of food and beverages to be resold by the purchaser. The exception for sales of certain food and beverages also applies to food and beverages for non-human consumption. A retail establishment does not include the bonded premises of a distilled spirits plant or wine cellar, or the premises of a brewery (other than a tavern on the brewery premises). See Chapter 51 of Title 26 of the United States Code and the implementing regulations thereunder.

(2) Examples. The following examples illustrate the application of this paragraph (n):

Example (1). X buys coffee beans and roasts those beans at a facility in the United States, the only activity of which is the roasting and packaging of roasted coffee beans. X sells the roasted coffee beans through a variety of unrelated third-party vendors and also sells roasted coffee beans at X's retail establishments. At X's retail establishments, X prepares brewed coffee and other foods. To the extent that the gross receipts of X's retail establishments represent receipts from the sale of coffee beans roasted at the facility, the receipts are DPGR. To the extent the gross receipts of X's retail establishments represent receipts from the retail sale of brewed coffee or food prepared at the retail establishments, the receipts are non-DPGR. However, pursuant to § 1.199-1(c)(2), X must allocate part of the receipts from the retail sale of the brewed coffee as DPGR to the extent of the value of the coffee beans that were roasted at the facility and that were used to brew coffee.

Example (2). Y operates a bonded winery in California. Bottles of wine produced by Y at the bonded winery are sold to consumers at the taxpaid premises. Pursuant to paragraph (n)(1) of this section, the bonded premises is not considered a retail establishment and is treated as separate and apart from the taxpaid premises, which is considered a retail establishment for purposes of paragraph (n)(1) of this section. Accordingly, the wine produced by Y in the bonded premises and sold by Y from the taxpaid premises is not considered to have been produced at a retail establishment, and the sales of the wine are DPGR (assuming all the other requirements of this section are met).

§ 1.199-4 Costs allocable to domestic production gross receipts.

(a) In general. The provisions of this section apply solely for purposes of section 199 of the Internal Revenue Code (Code). To determine its qualified production activities income (QPAI) (as defined in § 1.199-1(c)) for a taxable year, a taxpayer must subtract from its domestic production gross receipts (DPGR) (as defined in § 1.199-3(a)) the cost of goods sold (CGS) allocable to DPGR and other expenses, losses, or deductions (deductions), other than the deduction allowed under section 199, that are properly allocable to such receipts. Paragraph (b) of this section provides rules for determining CGS allocable to DPGR. Paragraph (c) of this section provides rules for determining the deductions that are properly allocable to DPGR. Paragraph (d) of this section provides that a taxpayer generally must determine deductions allocable to DPGR or to gross income attributable to DPGR using §§ 1.861-8 through 1.861-17 and §§ 1.861-8T through 1.861-14T (the section 861 regulations), subject to the rules in paragraph (d) of this section (the section 861 method). Paragraph (e) of this section provides that certain taxpayers may apportion deductions to DPGR using the simplified deduction method. Paragraph (f) of this section provides a small business simplified overall method that a qualifying small taxpayer may use to apportion CGS and deductions to DPGR.

(b) Cost of goods sold allocable to domestic production gross receipts. *(1) In general.* When determining its QPAI, a taxpayer must subtract from DPGR the CGS allocable to DPGR. A taxpayer determines its CGS allocable to DPGR in accordance with this paragraph (b) or, if applicable, paragraph (f) of this section. In the case of a sale, exchange, or other disposition of inventory, CGS is equal to beginning inventory plus purchases and production costs incurred during the taxable year and included in inventory costs, less ending inventory. CGS is determined under the methods of accounting that the taxpayer uses to compute taxable income. See sections 263A, 471, and 472. If section 263A requires a taxpayer to include additional section 263A costs (as defined in § 1.263A-1(d)(3)) in inventory, additional section 263A costs must be included in determining CGS. CGS allocable to DPGR also includes inventory valuation adjustments such as writedowns under the lower of cost or market method. In the case of a sale, exchange, or other disposition (including, for example, theft, casualty, or abandonment) of non-inventory property, CGS for purposes of this section includes the adjusted basis of the property. CGS allocable to DPGR for a taxable year may include the inventory cost and adjusted basis of qualifying production property (QPP) (as defined in § 1.199-3(j)(1)), a qualified film (as defined in § 1.199-3(k)(1)), or electricity, natural gas, and potable water (as defined in § 1.199-3(l)) (collectively, utilities) that will generate (or have generated) DPGR notwithstanding that the gross receipts attributable to the sale, lease, rental, license, exchange, or other disposition of the QPP, qualified film, or utilities will be, or have been, included in the computation of gross income for a different taxable year. For example, advance payments that are DPGR may be included in gross income under § 1.451-5(b)(1)(i) in a different taxable year than the related CGS allocable to that DPGR. If gross receipts are treated as DPGR pursuant to § 1.199-1(d)(3)(i) or § 1.199-3(i)(4)(i)(B)(6), (l)(4)(iv)(A), (m)(1)(iii)(A), (n)(6)(i), or (o)(2), then CGS must be allocated to such DPGR. Similarly, if gross receipts are treated as non-DPGR pursuant to § 1.199-1(d)(3)(ii) or § 1.199-3(i)(4)(ii), (l)(4)(iv)(B), (m)(1)(iii)(B), or (n)(6)(ii), then CGS must be allocated to such non-DPGR. See § 1.199-3(m)(6)(iv) for rules relating to treatment of certain costs in the case of a taxpayer that uses the land safe harbor under that paragraph.

(2) Allocating cost of goods sold. (i) In general. A taxpayer must use a reasonable method that is satisfactory to the Secretary based on all of the facts and circumstances to allocate CGS between DPGR and non-DPGR. Whether an allocation method is reasonable is based on all of the facts and circumstances including whether the taxpayer uses the most accurate information available; the relationship between CGS and the method used; the accuracy of the method chosen as compared with other possible methods; whether the method is used by the taxpayer for internal management or other business purposes; whether the method is used for other Federal or state income tax purposes; the availability of costing information; the time, burden, and cost of using alternative methods; and whether the taxpayer applies the method consistently from year to year. Depending on the facts and circumstances, reasonable methods may include methods based on gross receipts, number of units sold, number of units produced, or total production costs. Ordinarily, if a taxpayer uses a method to allocate gross receipts between DPGR and non-DPGR, then the use of a different method to allocate CGS that is not demonstrably more accurate than the method used to allocate gross receipts will not be considered reasonable. However, if a taxpayer has information readily available to specifically identify CGS allocable to DPGR and can specifically identify that amount without undue burden or expense, CGS allocable to DPGR is that amount irrespective of whether the taxpayer uses another allocation method to allocate gross receipts between DPGR and non-DPGR. A taxpayer that does not have information readily available to specifically identify CGS allocable to DPGR and that cannot, without undue burden or expense, specifically identify that amount is not required to use a method that specifically identifies CGS allocable to DPGR.

(ii) Gross receipts recognized in an earlier taxable year. If a taxpayer (other than a taxpayer that uses the small business simplified overall method of paragraph (f) of this section) recognizes and reports gross receipts on a Federal income tax return for a taxable year, and incurs CGS related to such gross receipts in a subsequent taxable year, then regardless of whether the gross receipts ultimately qualify as DPGR, the taxpayer must allocate the CGS to—

(A) DPGR if the taxpayer identified the related gross receipts as DPGR in the prior taxable year; or

(B) Non-DPGR if the taxpayer identified the related gross receipts as non-DPGR in the prior taxable year or if the taxpayer recognized under the taxpayer's methods of accounting those gross receipts in a taxable year to which section 199 does not apply.

(3) Special rules for imported items or services. The cost of any item or service brought into the United States (as defined in § 1.199-3(h)) without an arm's length transfer price may not be treated as less than its value immediately after it entered the United States for purposes of determining the CGS to be used in the computation of QPAI. Similarly, the adjusted basis of leased or rented property that gives rise to DPGR that has been brought into the United States (as defined in § 1.199-3(h)) without an arm's length transfer price may not be treated as less than its value immediately after it

entered the United States. When an item or service is imported into the United States that had been exported by the taxpayer for further manufacture, the increase in cost may not exceed the difference between the value of the property when exported and the value of the property when imported back into the United States after further manufacture. For this purpose, the value of property is its customs value as defined in section 1059A(b)(1).

(4) Rules for inventories valued at market or bona fide selling prices. If part of CGS is attributable to inventory valuation adjustments, then CGS allocable to DPGR includes inventory adjustments to QPP that is MPGE in whole or in significant part within the United States, a qualified film produced by the taxpayer, or utilities produced by the taxpayer in the United States. Accordingly, taxpayers that value inventory under § 1.471-4 (inventories at cost or market, whichever is lower) or § 1.471-2(c) (subnormal goods at bona fide selling prices) must allocate a proper share of such adjustments (for example, writedowns) to DPGR based on a reasonable method that is satisfactory to the Secretary based on all of the facts and circumstances. Factors taken into account in determining whether the method is reasonable include whether the taxpayer uses the most accurate information available; the relationship between the adjustment and the allocation base chosen; the accuracy of the method chosen as compared with other possible methods; whether the method is used by the taxpayer for internal management or other business purposes; whether the method is used for other Federal or state income tax purposes; the time, burden, and cost of using alternative methods; and whether the taxpayer applies the method consistently from year to year. If a taxpayer has information readily available to specifically identify the proper amount of inventory valuation adjustments allocable to DPGR, then the taxpayer must allocate that amount to DPGR. A taxpayer that does not have information readily available to specifically identify the proper amount of inventory valuation adjustments allocable to DPGR and that cannot, without undue burden or expense, specifically identify the proper amount of inventory valuation adjustments allocable to DPGR, is not required to use a method that specifically identifies inventory valuations adjustments to DPGR.

(5) Rules applicable to inventories accounted for under the last-in, first-out (LIFO) inventory method. (i) In general. This paragraph applies to inventories accounted for using the specific goods last-in, first-out (LIFO) method or the dollar-value LIFO method. Whenever a specific goods grouping or a dollar-value pool contains QPP, qualified films, or utilities that produces DPGR and goods that do not, the taxpayer must allocate CGS attributable to that grouping or pool between DPGR and non-DPGR using a reasonable method that is satisfactory to the Secretary based on all of the facts and circumstances. Whether a method of allocating CGS between DPGR and non-DPGR is reasonable must be determined in accordance with paragraph (b)(2) of this section. In addition, this paragraph (b)(5) provides methods that a taxpayer may use to allocate CGS for inventories accounted for using the LIFO method. If a taxpayer uses the LIFO/FIFO ratio method provided in paragraph (b)(5)(ii) of this section or the change in relative base-year cost method provided in paragraph (b)(5)(iii) of this section, then the taxpayer must use that method for all inventory accounted for under the LIFO method.

(ii) LIFO/FIFO ratio method. A taxpayer using the specific goods LIFO method or the dollar-value LIFO method may use the LIFO/FIFO ratio method. The LIFO/FIFO ratio method is applied with respect to all LIFO inventory of a taxpayer on a grouping-bygrouping or pool-by-pool basis. Under the LIFO/FIFO ratio method, a taxpayer computes the CGS of a grouping or pool allocable to DPGR by multiplying the CGS of QPP, qualified films, or utilities in the grouping or pool that produced DPGR computed using the first-in, first-out (FIFO) method by the LIFO/FIFO ratio of the grouping or pool. The LIFO/FIFO ratio of a grouping or pool is equal to the total CGS of the grouping or pool computed using the LIFO method over the total CGS of the grouping or pool computed using the FIFO method.

(iii) Change in relative base-year cost method. A taxpayer using the dollar-value LIFO method may use the change in relative base-year cost method. The change in relative base-year cost method is applied with respect to all LIFO inventory of a taxpayer on a pool-by-pool basis. The change in relative base-year cost method determines the CGS allocable to DPGR by increasing or decreasing the total production costs (section 471 costs and additional section 263A costs) of QPP, a qualified film, or utilities that generate DPGR by a portion of any increment or liquidation of the dollar-value pool. The portion of an increment or liquidation allocable to DPGR is determined by multiplying the LIFO value of the increment or liquidation (expressed as a positive number) by the ratio of the change in total base-year cost (expressed as a positive number) of the QPP, qualified film, or utilities that will generate DPGR in ending inventory to the change in total base-year cost (expressed as a positive number) of all goods in the ending inventory. The portion of an increment or liquidation allocable to DPGR may be zero but cannot exceed the amount of the increment or liquidation. Thus, a ratio in excess of 1.0 must be treated as 1.0.

(6) Taxpayers using the simplified production method or simplified resale method for additional section 263A costs. A taxpayer that uses the simplified production method or simplified resale method to allocate additional section 263A costs, as defined in § 1.263A-1(d)(3), to ending inventory must follow the rules in paragraph (b)(2) of this section to determine the amount of additional section 263A costs allocable to DPGR. Allocable additional section 263A costs include additional section 263A costs included in beginning inventory as well as additional section 263A costs incurred during the taxable year. Ordinarily, if a taxpayer uses the simplified production method or the simplified resale method, the additional section 263A costs should be allocated in the same proportion as section 471 costs are allocated.

(7) Examples. The following examples illustrate the application of this paragraph (b) and assume that the taxpayer does not use the small business simplified overall method provided in paragraph (f) of this section:

Example (1). Advance payments. T, a calendar year taxpayer, is a manufacturer of furniture in the United States. Under its method of accounting, T includes advance payments and other gross receipts derived from the sale of furniture in gross income when the payments are received. In December 2007, T receives an advance payment of $5,000 from X with respect to an order of furniture to be manufactured for a total price of $20,000. In 2008, T produces and sells the furniture to X. In 2008, T incurs $14,000 of section 471 and additional section 263A costs to produce the furniture ordered by X. T receives the remaining $15,000 of the contract price from X in 2008. Assuming that in 2007, T can reasonably determine that all the requirements of §§ 1.199-1 and 1.199-3 will be met with respect to the furniture, the advance payment qualifies as DPGR in 2007. Assuming further that all the requirements of §§ 1.199-1 and 1.199-3 are met with respect to the furniture in 2008, the remaining $15,000 of the contract price must be included in income and DPGR when received by T in 2008. T must include the $14,000 it incurred to produce the furniture in CGS and CGS allocable to DPGR in 2008. See § 1.199-4(b)(2)(ii) for rules regarding gross receipts and costs recognized in different taxable years.

Example (2). Use of standard cost method. X, a calendar year taxpayer, manufactures item A in a factory located in the United States and item B in a factory located in Country Y. Item A is produced by X within the United States and the sale of A generates DPGR. X uses the FIFO inventory method to account for its inventory and determines the cost of item A using a standard cost method. At the beginning of its 2007 taxable year, X's inventory contains 2,000 units of item A at a standard cost of $5 per unit. X did not incur significant cost variances in previous taxable years. During the 2007 taxable year, X produces 8,000 units of item A at a standard cost of $6 per unit. X determines that with regard to its production of item A it has incurred a significant cost variance. When X reallocates the cost variance to the units of item A that it has produced, the production cost of item A is $7 per unit. X sells 7,000 units of item A during the taxable year. X can identify from its books and records that CGS related to the sales of item A during the taxable year are $45,000 ((2,000 x $5) + (5,000 x $7)). Accordingly, X has CGS allocable to DPGR of $45,000.

Example (3). Change in relative base-year cost method. (i) Y elects, beginning with the calendar year 2007, to compute its inventories using the dollar-value, LIFO method under section 472. Y establishes a pool for items A and B. Y produces item A within the United States and the sales of item A generate DPGR. Y does not produce item B within the United States and the sale of item B does not generate DPGR. The composition of the inventory for the pool at the base date, January 1, 2007, is as follows:

Item	Unit	Unit cost	Total cost
A	2,000	$5.00	$10,000
B	1,250	4.00	5,000
Total			$15,000

(ii) Y uses a standard cost method to allocate all direct and indirect costs (section 471 and additional section 263A costs) to the units of item A and item B that it produces. During 2007, Y incurs $52,500 of section 471 costs and additional section 263A costs to produce 10,000 units of item A and $114,000 of section 471 costs and additional section 263A costs to produce 20,000 units of item B.

(iii) The closing inventory of the pool at December 31, 2007, contains 3,000 units of item A and 2,500 units of item B. The closing inventory of the pool at December 31, 2007, shown at base-year and current-year cost is as follows:

Item	Quantity	Base-year cost	Amount	Current-year cost	Amount
A	3,000	$5.00	$15,000	$5.25	$15,750
B	2,500	4.00	10,000	5.70	14,250
Totals			$25,000		$30,000

(iv) The base-year cost of the closing LIFO inventory at December 31, 2007, amounts to $25,000, and exceeds the $15,000 base-year cost of the opening inventory for the taxable year by $10,000 (the increment stated at base-year cost). The increment valued at current-year cost is computed by multiplying the increment stated at base-year cost by the ratio of the current-year cost of the pool to total base-year cost of the pool (that is, $30,000/$25,000, or 120%). The increment stated at current-year cost is $12,000 ($10,000 x 120%).

(v) The change in relative base-year cost of item A is $5,000 ($15,000 - $10,000). The change in relative base-year cost (the increment stated at base-year cost) of the total inventory is $10,000 ($25,000 - $15,000). The ratio of the change in base-year cost of item A to the change in base-year cost of the total inventory is 50% ($5,000/$10,000).

(vi) CGS allocable to DPGR is $46,500, computed as follows:

Current-year production costs related to DPGR		$52,500
Less: Increment stated at current-year cost	$12,000	
Ratio	50%	
Total		(6,000)
Total		$46,500

Example (4). Change in relative base-year cost method. (i) The facts are the same as in Example 3 except that, during the calendar year 2008, Y experiences an inventory decrement. During 2008, Y incurs $66,000 of section 471 costs and additional section 263A costs to produce 12,000 units of item A and $150,000 of section 471 costs and additional section 263A costs to produce 25,000 units of item B.

(ii) The closing inventory of the pool at December 31, 2008, contains 2,000 units of item A and 2,500 units of item B. The closing inventory of the pool at December 31, 2008, shown at base-year and current-year cost is as follows:

Item	Quantity	Base-year cost	Amount	Current-year cost	Amount
A	2,000	$5.00	$10,000	$5.50	$11,000
B	2,500	4.00	10,000	6.00	15,000
Totals			$20,000		$26,000

(iii) The base-year cost of the closing LIFO inventory at December 31, 2008, amounts to $20,000, and is less than the $25,000 base-year cost of the opening inventory for that taxable year by $5,000 (the decrement stated at base-year cost). This liquidation is reflected by reducing the most recent layer of increment. The LIFO value of the inventory at December 31, 2008 is:

	Base cost	Index	LIFO value
January 1, 2008, base cost	$15,000	1.00	$15,000
December 31, 2008, increment	5,000	1.20	6,000
Total			$21,000

(iv) The change in relative base-year cost of item A is $5,000 ($15,000 -$10,000). The change in relative base-year cost of the total inventory is $5,000 ($25,000 - $20,000). The ratio of the change in base-year cost of item A to the change in base-year cost of the total inventory is 100% ($5,000/$5,000).

(v) CGS allocable to DPGR is $72,000, computed as follows:

Current-year production costs related to DPGR		$66,000
Plus: LIFO value of decrement	$6,000	
Ratio	100%	
Total		6,000
Total		$72,000

Example (5). LIFO/FIFO ratio method. (i) The facts are the same as in Example 3 except that Y uses the LIFO/FIFO ratio method to determine its CGS allocable to DPGR.

(ii) Y's CGS related to item A on a FIFO basis is $46,750 ((2,000 units at $5) + (7,000 units at $5.25)).

(iii) Y's total CGS computed on a LIFO basis is $154,500 (beginning inventory of $15,000 plus total production costs of $166,500 less ending inventory of $27,000).

(iv) Y's total CGS computed on a FIFO basis is $151,500 (beginning inventory of $15,000 plus total production costs of $166,500 less ending inventory of $30,000).

(v) The ratio of Y's CGS computed using the LIFO method to its CGS computed using the FIFO method is 102% ($154,500/$151,500). Y's CGS related to DPGR computed using the LIFO/FIFO ratio method is $47,685 ($46,750 x 102%).

Example (6). LIFO/FIFO ratio method. (i) The facts are the same as in Example 4 except that Y uses the LIFO/FIFO ratio method to compute CGS allocable to DPGR.

(ii) Y's CGS related to item A on a FIFO basis is $70,750 ((3,000 units at $5.25) + (10,000 units at $5.50)).

(iii) Y's total CGS computed on a LIFO basis is $222,000 (beginning inventory of $27,000 plus total production costs of $216,000 less ending inventory of $21,000).

(iv) Y's total CGS computed on a FIFO basis is $220,000 (beginning inventory of $30,000 plus total production costs of $216,000 less ending inventory of $26,000).

(v) The ratio of Y's CGS computed using the LIFO method to its CGS computed using the FIFO method is 101% ($222,000/$220,000). Y's CGS related to DPGR computed using the LIFO/FIFO ratio method is $71,457 ($70,750 x 101%).

(c) Other deductions properly allocable to domestic production gross receipts or gross income attributable to domestic production gross receipts. *(1) In general.* In determining its QPAI, a taxpayer must subtract from its DPGR, in addition to its CGS allocable to DPGR, the deductions that are properly allocable to DPGR. A taxpayer generally must allocate and apportion these deductions using the rules of the section 861 method. In lieu of the section 861 method, certain taxpayers may apportion these deductions using the simplified deduction method provided in paragraph (e) of this section. Paragraph (f) of this section provides a small business simplified overall method that may be used by a qualifying small taxpayer, as defined in that paragraph. A taxpayer using the simplified deduction method or the small business simplified overall method must use that method for all deductions. A taxpayer eligible to use the small business simplified overall method may choose at any time for any taxable year to use the small business simplified overall method, the simplified deduction method, or the section 861 method for a taxable year. A taxpayer eligible to use the simplified deduction method may choose at any time for any taxable year to use the simplified deduction method or the section 861 method for a taxable year.

(2) Treatment of net operating losses. A deduction under section 172 for a net operating loss is not allocated or apportioned to DPGR or gross income attributable to DPGR.

(3) W-2 wages. Although only W-2 wages as described in § 1.199-2 are taken into account in computing the W-2 wage limitation, all wages paid (or incurred in the case of an accrual method taxpayer) in a taxpayer's trade or business during the taxable year are taken into account in computing QPAI for that taxable year.

(d) Section 861 method. *(1) In general.* Under the section 861 method, a taxpayer must allocate and apportion its deductions using the allocation and apportionment rules provided under the section 861 regulations under which section 199 is treated as an operative section described in § 1.861-8(f). Accordingly, the taxpayer applies the rules of the section 861 regulations to allocate and apportion deductions (including, if applicable, its distributive share of deductions from pass-thru entities) to gross income attributable to DPGR. Gross receipts that are allocable to land under the safe harbor provided in § 1.199-3(m)(6)(iv) are treated as non-DPGR. See § 1.199-3(m)(6)(iv)(B). If the taxpayer applies the allocation and apportionment rules of the section 861 regulations for section 199 and another operative section, then the taxpayer must use the same method of allocation and the same principles of apportionment for purposes of all operative sections (subject to the rules provided in paragraphs (c)(2) and (d)(2) and (3) of this section). See § 1.861-8(f)(2)(i).

(2) Deductions for charitable contributions. Deductions for charitable contributions (as allowed under section 170 and section 873(b)(2) or 882(c)(1)(B)) must be ratably apportioned between gross income attributable to DPGR and gross income attributable to non-DPGR based on the relative amounts of gross income.

(3) Research and experimental expenditures. Research and experimental expenditures must be allocated and apportioned in accordance with § 1.861-17 without taking into account the exclusive apportionment rule of § 1.861-17(b).

(4) Deductions allocated or apportioned to gross receipts treated as domestic production gross receipts. If gross receipts are treated as DPGR pursuant to § 1.199-1(d)(3)(i) or § 1.199-3(i)(4)(i)(B)(6), (l)(4)(iv)(A), (m)(1)(iii)(A), (n)(6)(i), or (o)(2), then deductions must be allocated or apportioned to the gross income attributable to such DPGR. Similarly, if gross receipts are treated as non-DPGR pursuant to § 1.199-1(d)(3)(ii) or § 1.199-3(i)(4)(ii), (l)(4)(iv)(B), (m)(1)(iii)(B), or (n)(6)(ii), then deductions must be allocated or apportioned to the gross income attributable to such non-DPGR.

(5) Treatment of items from a pass-thru entity reporting qualified production activities income. If, pursuant to § 1.199-5(e)(2) or § 1.199-9(e)(2), or to the authority granted in § 1.199-5(b)(1)(ii) or (c)(1)(ii), or § 1.199-9(b)(1)(ii) or (c)(1)(ii), a taxpayer must combine QPAI and W-2 wages from a partnership, S corporation, trust (to the extent not described in § 1.199-5(d) or § 1.199-9(d)) or estate with the taxpayer's total QPAI and W-2 wages from other sources, then for purposes of apportioning the taxpayer's interest expense under this paragraph (d), the taxpayer's interest in such partnership (and, where relevant in apportioning the taxpayer's interest expense, the partnership's assets), the taxpayer's shares in such S corporation, or the taxpayer's interest in such trust shall be disregarded.

(6) Examples. The following examples illustrate the operation of the section 861 method. Assume in the following examples that all corporations are calendar year taxpayers, that

all taxpayers have sufficient W-2 wages as defined in § 1.199-2(e) so that the section 199 deduction is not limited under section 199(b)(1), and that, with respect to the allocation and apportionment of interest expense, § 1.861-10T does not apply.

Example (1). Section 861 method and no EAG. (i) Facts. X, a United States corporation that is not a member of an expanded affiliated group (EAG) (as defined in § 1.199-7), engages in activities that generate both DPGR and non-DPGR. All of X's production activities that generate DPGR are within Standard Industrial Classification (SIC) Industry Group AAA (SIC AAA). All of X's production activities that generate non-DPGR are within SIC Industry Group BBB (SIC BBB). X is able to specifically identify CGS allocable to DPGR and to non-DPGR. X incurs $900 of research and experimentation expenses (R&E) that are deductible under section 174, $300 of which are performed with respect to SIC AAA and $600 of which are performed with respect to SIC BBB. None of the R&E is legally mandated R&E as described in § 1.861-17(a)(4) and none of the R&E is included in CGS. X incurs section 162 selling expenses that are not includible in CGS and are definitely related to all of X's gross income. For 2010, the adjusted basis of X's assets is $5,000, $4,000 of which generates gross income attributable to DPGR and $1,000 of which generates gross income attributable to non-DPGR. For 2010, X's taxable income is $1,380 based on the following Federal income tax items:

DPGR (all from sales of products within SIC AAA)	$3,000
Non-DPGR (all from sales of products within SIC BBB)	$3,000
CGS allocable to DPGR	($ 600)
CGS allocable to non-DPGR	($1,800)
Section 162 selling expenses	($ 840)
Section 174 R&E-SIC AAA	($ 300)
Section 174 R&E-SIC BBB	($ 600)
Interest expense (not included in CGS)	($ 300)
Charitable contributions	($ 180)
X's taxable income	$1,380

(ii) X's QPAI. X allocates and apportions its deductions to gross income attributable to DPGR under the section 861 method of this paragraph (d). In this case, the section 162 selling expenses are definitely related to all of X's gross income. Based on the facts and circumstances of this specific case, apportionment of those expenses between DPGR and non-DPGR on the basis of X's gross receipts is appropriate. For purposes of apportioning R&E, X elects to use the sales method as described in § 1.861-17(c). X elects to apportion interest expense under the tax book value method of § 1.861-9T(g). X has $2,400 of gross income attributable to DPGR (DPGR of $3,000 - CGS of $600 allocated based on X's books and records). X's QPAI for 2010 is $1,320, as shown below:

DPGR (all from sales of products within SIC AAA)	$3,000
CGS allocable to DPGR	($ 600)
Section 162 selling expenses ($840 x ($3,000 DPGR/$6,000 total gross receipts))	($ 420)
Interest expense (not included in CGS) ($300 x ($4,000 (X's DPGR assets)/$5,000 (X's total assets)))	($ 240)
Charitable contributions (not included in CGS) ($180 x ($2,400 gross income attributable to DPGR/$3,600 total gross income))	($ 120)
Section 174 R&E-SIC AAA	($ 300)
X's QPAI	$1,320

(iii) Section 199 deduction determination. X's tentative deduction under § 1.199-1(a) is $119 (.09 x (lesser of QPAI of $1,320 and taxable income of $1,380)). Because the facts of this example assume that X's W-2 wages as defined in § 1.199-2(e) are sufficient to avoid a limitation on the section 199 deduction, X's section 199 deduction for 2010 is $119.

Example (2). Section 861 method and EAG. (i) Facts. The facts are the same as in Example 1 except that X owns stock in Y, a United States corporation, equal to 75% of the total voting power of stock of Y and 80% of the total value of stock in Y. X and Y are not members of an affiliated group as defined in section 1504(a). Accordingly, the rules of § 1.861-14T do not apply to X's and Y's selling expenses, R&E, and charitable contributions. X and Y are, however, members of an affiliated group for purposes of allocating and apportioning interest expense (see § 1.861-11T(d)(6)) and are also members of an EAG. For 2010, the adjusted basis of Y's assets is $45,000, $21,000 of which generates gross income attributable to DPGR and $24,000 of which generates gross income attributable to non-DPGR. All of Y's activities that generate DPGR are within SIC Industry Group AAA (SIC AAA). All of Y's activities that generate non-DPGR are within SIC Industry Group BBB (SIC BBB). None of X's and Y's sales are to each other. Y is not able to specifically identify CGS allocable to DPGR and non-DPGR. In this case, because CGS is definitely related under the facts and circumstances to all of Y's gross receipts, apportionment of CGS between DPGR and non-DPGR based on gross receipts is appropriate. For 2010, Y's taxable income is $1,910 based on the following Federal income tax items:

DPGR (all from sales of products within SIC AAA)	$3,000
Non-DPGR (all from sales of products within SIC BBB)	$3,000
CGS allocated to DPGR	($1,200)
CGS allocated to non-DPGR	($1,200)
Section 162 selling expenses	($ 840)
Section 174 R&E-SIC AAA	($ 100)
Section 174 R&E-SIC BBB	($ 200)
Interest expense (not included in CGS and not subject to § 1.861-10T)	($ 500)
Charitable contributions	($ 50)
Y's taxable income	$1,910

(ii) QPAI. (A) X's QPAI. Determination of X's QPAI is the same as in Example 1 except that interest is apportioned to gross income attributable to DPGR based on the combined adjusted bases of X's and Y's assets. See § 1.861-11T(c). Accordingly, X's QPAI for 2010 is $1,410, as shown below:

DPGR (all from sales of products within SIC AAA)	$3,000
CGS allocated to DPGR	($ 600)
Section 162 selling expenses ($840 x ($3,000 DPGR/$6,000 total gross receipts))	($ 420)
Interest expense (not included in CGS and not subject to § 1861-10T) ($300 x ($25,000 (tax book value of X's and Y's DPGR assets)/$50,000 (tax book value of X's and Y's total assets)))	($ 150)

Charitable contributions (not included in CGS) ($180 x ($2,400 gross income attributable to DPGR/$3,600 total gross income))	($ 120)
Section 174 R&E-SIC AAA	($ 300)
X's QPAI	$1,410

(B) Y's QPAI. Y makes the same elections under the section 861 method as does X. Y has $1,800 of gross income attributable to DPGR (DPGR of $3,000 - CGS of $1,200 allocated based on Y's gross receipts). Y's QPAI for 2010 is $1,005, as shown below:

DPGR (all from sales of products within SIC AAA)	$3,000
CGS allocated to DPGR	($1,200)
Section 162 selling expenses ($840 x ($3,000 DPGR/$6,000 total gross receipts))	($ 420)
Interest expense (not included in CGS and not subject to § 1.861-10T) ($500 x ($25,000 (tax book value of X's and Y's DPGR assets)/$50,000 (tax book value of X's and Y's total assets)))	($ 250)
Charitable contributions (not included in CGS)($50 x ($1,800 gross income attributable to DPGR/$3,600 total gross income))	($ 25)
Section 174 R&E-SIC AAA	($ 100)
Y's QPAI	$1,005

(iii) Section 199 deduction determination. The section 199 deduction of the X and Y EAG is determined by aggregating the separately determined QPAI, taxable income, and W-2 wages of X and Y. See § 1.199-7(b). Accordingly, the X and Y EAG's tentative section 199 deduction is $217 (.09 x (lesser of combined taxable incomes of X and Y of $3,290 (X's taxable income of $1,380 plus Y's taxable income of $1,910) and combined QPAI of $2,415 (X's QPAI of $1,410 plus Y's QPAI of $1,005)). Because the facts of this example assume that the W-2 wages of X and Y are sufficient to avoid a limitation on the section 199 deduction, X and Y EAG's section 199 deduction for 2010 is $217. The $217 is allocated to X and Y in proportion to their QPAI. See § 1.199-7(c).

(e) Simplified deduction method. *(1) In general.* An eligible taxpayer may use the simplified deduction method to apportion deductions between DPGR and non-DPGR. The simplified deduction method does not apply to CGS. Under the simplified deduction method, a taxpayer's deductions (except the net operating loss deduction as provided in paragraph (c)(2) of this section) are ratably apportioned between DPGR and non-DPGR based on relative gross receipts. Accordingly, the amount of deductions for the current taxable year apportioned to DPGR is equal to the same proportion of the total deductions for the current taxable year that the amount of DPGR bears to total gross receipts. Gross receipts that are allocable to land under the safe harbor provided in § 1.199-3(m)(6)(iv) are treated as non-DPGR. See § 1.199-3(m)(6)(iv)(B). Whether a trust (to the extent not described in § 1.199-5(d) or § 1.199-9(d)) or an estate may use the simplified deduction method is determined at the trust or estate level. If a trust or estate qualifies to use the simplified deduction method, the simplified deduction method must be applied at the trust or estate level, taking into account the trust's or estate's DPGR, non-DPGR, and other items from all sources, including its distributive or allocable share of those items of any lower-tier entity, prior to any charitable or distribution deduction. Whether the owner of a pass-thru entity may use the simplified deduction method is determined at the level of the entity's owner. If the owner of a pass-thru entity qualifies and uses the simplified deduction method, then the simplified deduction method is applied at the level of the owner of the pass-thru entity taking into account the owner's DPGR, non-DPGR, and other items from all sources including its distributive or allocable share of those items of the pass-thru entity.

(2) Eligible taxpayer. For purposes of this paragraph (e), an eligible taxpayer is—

(i) A taxpayer that has average annual gross receipts (as defined in paragraph (g) of this section) of $100,000,000 or less; or

(ii) A taxpayer that has total assets (as defined in paragraph (e)(3) of this section) of $10,000,000 or less.

(3) Total assets. (i) In general. For purposes of the simplified deduction method, total assets means the total assets the taxpayer has at the end of the taxable year. In the case of a C corporation, the corporation's total assets at the end of the taxable year is the amount required to be reported on Schedule L of Form 1120, "United States Corporation Income Tax Return,' in accordance with the Form 1120 instructions.

(ii) Members of an expanded affiliated group. To compute the total assets of an EAG, the total assets at the end of the taxable year of each corporation that is a member of the EAG at the end of the taxable year that ends with or within the taxable year of the computing member (as described in § 1.199-7(h)) are aggregated. For purposes of this paragraph, a consolidated group is treated as one member of the EAG.

(4) Members of an expanded affiliated group. (i) In general. Whether the members of an EAG may use the simplified deduction method is determined by reference to all the members of the EAG. If the average annual gross receipts of the EAG are less than or equal to $100,000,000 or the total assets of the EAG are less than or equal to $10,000,000, then each member of the EAG may individually determine whether to use the simplified deduction method, regardless of the cost allocation method used by the other members.

(ii) Exception. Notwithstanding paragraph (e)(4)(i) of this section, all members of the same consolidated group must use the same cost allocation method.

(iii) Examples. The following examples illustrate the application of paragraph (e) of this section:

Example (1). Corporations X, Y, and Z are the only three members of an EAG. Neither X, Y, nor Z is a member of a consolidated group. X, Y, and Z have average annual gross receipts of $20,000,000, $70,000,000, and $5,000,000, respectively. X, Y, and Z each have total assets at the end of the taxable year of $5,000,000. Because the average annual gross receipts of the EAG are less than or equal to $100,000,000, each of X, Y, and Z may use either the simplified deduction method or the section 861 method.

Example (2). The facts are the same as in Example 1 except that X and Y are members of the same consolidated group. X, Y, and Z may use either the simplified deduction method or the section 861 method. However, X and Y must use the same cost allocation method.

Example (3). The facts are the same as in Example 1 except that Z's average annual gross receipts are $15,000,000. Because the average annual gross receipts of the EAG are greater than $100,000,000 and the total assets of the EAG at the end of the taxable year are greater than $10,000,000, X, Y, and Z must each use the section 861 method.

(f) Small business simplified overall method. *(1) In general.* A qualifying small taxpayer may use the small business simplified overall method to apportion CGS and deductions between DPGR and non-DPGR. Under the small business simplified overall method, a taxpayer's total costs for the current taxable year (as defined in paragraph (f)(3) of this section) are apportioned between DPGR and non-DPGR based on relative gross receipts. Accordingly, the amount of total costs for the current taxable year apportioned to DPGR is equal to the same proportion of total costs for the current taxable year that the amount of DPGR bears to total gross receipts. Total gross receipts for this purpose do not include gross receipts that are allocated to land under the land safe harbor provided in § 1.199-3(m)(6)(iv). See § 1.199-3(m)(6)(iv)(B).

(2) Qualifying small taxpayer. Except as provided in paragraph (f)(5), for purposes of this paragraph (f), a qualifying small taxpayer is—

(i) A taxpayer that has average annual gross receipts (as defined in paragraph (g) of this section) of $5,000,000 or less;

(ii) A taxpayer that is engaged in the trade or business of farming that is not required to use the accrual method of accounting under section 447; or

(iii) A taxpayer that is eligible to use the cash method as provided in Rev. Proc. 2002-28 (2002-1 C.B. 815) (that is, certain taxpayers with average annual gross receipts of $10,000,000 or less that are not prohibited from using the cash method under section 448, including partnerships, S corporations, C corporations, or individuals). See § 601.601(d)(2) of this chapter.

(3) Total costs for the current taxable year. (i) In general. For purposes of the small business simplified overall method, total costs for the current taxable year means the total CGS and deductions (excluding the net operating loss deduction as provided in paragraph (c)(2) of this section) for the current taxable year. Total costs for the current taxable year are determined under the methods of accounting that the taxpayer uses to compute taxable income.

(ii) Land safe harbor. A taxpayer that uses the land safe harbor provided in § 1.199-3(m)(6)(iv) must reduce total costs for the current taxable year by the costs of land and any other costs capitalized to the land (except costs for activities listed in § 1.199-3(m)(2)(iii)) prior to applying the small business simplified overall method. See § 1.199-3(m)(6)(iv)(B). For example, if a taxpayer has $1,000 of total costs for the current taxable year and $600 of such costs is attributable to land under the land safe harbor, then only $400 of such costs is apportioned between DPGR and non-DPGR under the small business simplified overall method.

(4) Members of an expanded affiliated group. (i) In general. Whether the members of an EAG may use the small business simplified overall method is determined by reference to all the members of the EAG. If the average annual gross receipts of the EAG are less than or equal to $5,000,000, the EAG (viewed as a single corporation) is engaged in the trade or business of farming that is not required to use the accrual method of accounting under section 447, or the EAG (viewed as a single corporation) is eligible to use the cash method as provided in Rev. Proc. 2002-28, then each member of the EAG may individually determine whether to use the small business simplified overall method, regardless of the cost allocation method used by the other members.

(ii) Exception. Notwithstanding paragraph (f)(4)(i) of this section, all members of the same consolidated group must use the same cost allocation method.

(iii) Examples. The following examples illustrate the application of paragraph (f) of this section:

Example (1). Corporations L, M, and N are the only three members of an EAG. Neither L, M, nor N is a member of a consolidated group. L, M, and N have average annual gross receipts for the current taxable year of $1,000,000, $1,500,000, and $2,000,000, respectively. Because the average annual gross receipts of the EAG are less than or equal to $5,000,000, each of L, M, and N may use the small business simplified overall method, the simplified deduction method, or the section 861 method.

Example (2). The facts are the same as in Example 1 except that M and N are members of the same consolidated group. L, M, and N may use the small business simplified overall method, the simplified deduction method, or the section 861 method. However, M and N must use the same cost allocation method.

Example (3). The facts are the same as in Example 1 except that N has average annual gross receipts of $4,000,000. Unless the EAG, viewed as a single corporation, is engaged in the trade or business of farming that is not required to use the accrual method of accounting under section 447, or the EAG, viewed as a single corporation, is eligible to use the cash method as provided in Rev. Proc. 2002-28, because the average annual gross receipts of the EAG are greater than $5,000,000, L, M, and N are all ineligible to use the small business simplified overall method.

(5) Trusts and estates. Trusts and estates under §§ 1.199-5(e) and 1.199-9(e) may not use the small business simplified overall method.

(g) Average annual gross receipts. *(1) In general.* For purposes of the simplified deduction method and the small business simplified overall method, average annual gross receipts means the average annual gross receipts of the taxpayer (including gross receipts attributable to the sale, exchange, or other disposition of land under the land safe harbor provided in § 1.199-3(m)(6)(iv)) for the 3 taxable years (or, if fewer, the taxable years during which the taxpayer was in existence) preceding the current taxable year, even if one or more of such taxable years began before the effective date of section 199. In the case of any taxable year of less than 12 months (a short taxable year), the gross receipts shall be annualized by multiplying the gross receipts for the short period by 12 and dividing the result by the number of months in the short period.

(2) Members of an expanded affiliated group. To compute the average annual gross receipts of an EAG, the gross receipts, for the entire taxable year, of each corporation that is a member of the EAG at the end of its taxable year that ends with or within the taxable year of the computing member are aggregated. For purposes of this paragraph, a consolidated group is treated as one member of the EAG.

T.D. 9263, 5/24/2006, amend T.D. 9381, 2/14/2008.

Proposed § 1.199-4 Costs allocable to domestic production gross receipts. [*For Preamble, see ¶ 152,713*]

(a) In general. To determine its qualified production activities income (QPAI) (as defined in § 1.199-1(c)) for a taxable year, a taxpayer must subtract from its domestic production gross receipts (DPGR) (as defined in § 1.199-3(a)) the cost of goods sold (CGS) allocable to DPGR, the amount of expenses or losses (deductions) directly allocable to DPGR, and a ratable portion of other deductions not directly allocable to DPGR or to another class of income. Paragraph (b) of this section provides rules for determining CGS allocable to DPGR. Paragraph (c) of this section provides rules for determining the deductions allocated and apportioned to DPGR and a ratable portion of deductions that are not directly allocable to DPGR or to another class of income. Paragraph (d) of this section provides that a taxpayer generally must determine deductions allocated and apportioned to DPGR or to gross income attributable to DPGR using the rules of the regulations at §§ 1.861-8 through 1.861-17 and §§ 1.861-8T through 1.861-14T (the section 861 regulations), subject to the rules in paragraph (d) of this section (the section 861 method). Paragraph (e) of this section provides that certain taxpayers may apportion deductions to DPGR using the simplified deduction method. Paragraph (f) of this section provides a small business simplified overall method that a qualifying small taxpayer may use to apportion CGS and deductions to DPGR.

(b) Cost of goods sold allocable to domestic production gross receipts. *(1) In general.* When determining its QPAI, a taxpayer must reduce DPGR by the CGS allocable to DPGR. A taxpayer determines its CGS allocable to DPGR in accordance with this paragraph (b) or, if applicable, paragraph (f) of this section. In the case of a sale, exchange, or other disposition of inventory, CGS is equal to beginning inventory plus purchases and production costs incurred during the taxable year and included in inventory costs, less ending inventory. CGS is determined under the methods of accounting that the taxpayer uses to compute taxable income. See sections 263A, 471, and 472. Additional section 263A costs, as defined in § 1.263A-1(d)(3), must be included in determining CGS. In the case of a sale, exchange, or other disposition (including, for example, theft, casualty, or abandonment) of non-inventory property, CGS for purposes of this section includes the adjusted basis of the property. CGS allocable to DPGR for a taxable year may include the inventory cost and adjusted basis of qualifying production property (QPP) (as defined in § 1.199-3(i)(1)), a qualified film (as defined in § 1.199-3(j)(1)), or electricity, natural gas, and potable water (as defined in § 1.199-3(k)) (collectively, utilities) that will, or have, generated DPGR notwithstanding that the gross receipts attributable to the sale of the QPP, qualified films, or utilities will, or have been, included in the computation of gross income for a different taxable year. For example, advance payments related to DPGR may be included in gross income under § 1.451-5(b)(1)(i) in a different taxable year than the related CGS allocable to that DPGR. CGS allocable to DPGR includes inventory valuation adjustments such as writedowns under the lower of cost or market method. If non-DPGR is treated as DPGR pursuant to §§ 1.199-1(d)(2) and 1.199-3(h)(4), (k)(4)(iv), (l)(1)(ii), (m)(4), or (n)(1), CGS related to such gross receipts that are treated as DPGR must be allocated or apportioned to DPGR.

(2) Allocating cost of goods sold. A taxpayer must use a reasonable method that is satisfactory to the Secretary to allocate CGS between DPGR and non-DPGR. Whether an allocation method is reasonable is based on all of the facts and circumstances including whether the taxpayer uses the most accurate information available; the relationship between CGS and the method used; the accuracy of the method chosen as compared with other possible methods; whether the method is used by the taxpayer for internal management and other business purposes; whether the method is used for other Federal or state income tax purposes; the availability of costing information; the time, burden, and cost of using various methods; and whether the taxpayer applies the method consistently from year to year. If a taxpayer does, or can, without undue burden or expense, specifically identify from its books and records CGS allocable to DPGR, the CGS allocable to DPGR is that amount irrespective of whether the taxpayer uses another allocation method to allocate gross receipts between DPGR and non-DPGR. A taxpayer that cannot, without undue burden or expense, use a specific identification method to determine CGS allocable to DPGR is not required to use a specific identification method to determine CGS allocable to DPGR. Ordinarily, if a taxpayer uses a method to allocate gross receipts between DPGR and non-DPGR, the use of a different method to allocate CGS that is not demonstrably more accurate than the method used to allocate gross receipts will not be considered reasonable. Depending on the facts and circumstances, reasonable methods may include methods based on gross receipts, number of units sold, number of units produced, or total production costs.

(3) Special rules for imported items or services. The cost of any item or service brought into the United States (as defined in § 1.199-3(g)) without an arm's length transfer price may not be treated as less than its value immediately after it entered the United States for purposes of determining the CGS to be used in the computation of QPAI. When an item or service is imported into the United States that had been exported by the taxpayer for further manufacture, the increase in cost may not exceed the difference between the value of the property when exported and the value of the property when imported back into the United States after further manufacture. For this purpose, the value of property is its customs value as defined in section 1059A(b)(1).

(4) Rules for inventories valued at market or bona fide selling prices. If part of CGS is attributable to inventory valuation adjustments, CGS allocable to DPGR includes inventory adjustments to QPP that is MPGE in whole or in significant part within the United States, qualified films produced in the United States, or utilities produced in the United States. Accordingly, taxpayers that value inventory under § 1.471-4 (inventories at cost or market, whichever is lower) or § 1.471-2(c) (subnormal goods at bona fide selling prices) must allocate a proper share of such adjustments (for example, writedowns) to DPGR based on a reasonable method that is satisfactory to the Secretary based on all of the facts and circumstances. Factors taken into account in determining whether the method is reasonable include whether the taxpayer uses the most accurate information available; the relationship between the adjustment and the allocation base chosen; the accuracy of the method chosen as compared with other possible methods; whether the method is used by the taxpayer for internal management or other business purposes; whether the method is used for other Federal or state income tax purposes; the time, burden, and cost of using various methods; and whether the taxpayer applies the method consistently from year to year. If a taxpayer does, or can, without undue burden or expense, specifically identify from its books and records the proper amount of inventory valuation adjustments allocable to DPGR, then the taxpayer must allocate that amount to DPGR. A taxpayer that cannot, without undue burden or expense, use a specific identification method to determine the proper amount of inventory valuation adjustments allocable to DPGR is not required to use a specific identification method to allocate adjustments to DPGR.

(5) Rules applicable to inventories accounted for under the last-in, first-out (LIFO) inventory method. (i) In general. This paragraph applies to inventories accounted for using the specific goods last-in, first-out (LIFO) method or the dollar-value LIFO method. Whenever a specific goods grouping or a dollar-value pool contains QPP, qualified films, or utilities that produces DPGR and goods that do not, the taxpayer must allocate CGS attributable to that grouping or pool between DPGR and non-DPGR using a reasonable method. Whether a method of allocating CGS between DPGR and non-DPGR is reasonable must be determined in accordance with paragraph (b)(2) of this section. In addition, this paragraph (b)(5) provides methods that a taxpayer may use to allocate CGS for inventories accounted for using the LIFO method. If a taxpayer uses the LIFO/FIFO ratio method provided in paragraph (b)(5)(ii) of this section or the change in relative base-year cost method provided in paragraph (b)(5)(iii) of this section, the taxpayer must use that method for all inventory accounted for under the LIFO method.

(ii) LIFO/FIFO ratio method. A taxpayer using the specific goods LIFO method or the dollar-value LIFO method may use the LIFO/FIFO ratio method. The LIFO/FIFO ratio method is applied with respect to all LIFO inventory of a taxpayer on a grouping-by-grouping or pool-by-pool basis. Under the LIFO/FIFO ratio method, a taxpayer computes the CGS of a grouping or pool allocable to DPGR by multiplying the CGS of QPP, qualified films, or utilities in the grouping or pool that produced DPGR computed using the first-in, first-out (FIFO) method by the LIFO/ FIFO ratio of the grouping or pool. The LIFO/FIFO ratio of a grouping or pool is equal to the total CGS of the grouping or pool computed using the LIFO method over the total CGS of the grouping or pool computed using the FIFO method.

(iii) Change in relative base-year cost method. A taxpayer using the dollar-value LIFO method may use the change in relative base-year cost method. The change in relative base-year cost method is applied with respect to all LIFO inventory of a taxpayer on a pool-by-pool basis. The change in relative base-year cost method determines the CGS allocable to DPGR by increasing or decreasing the total production costs (section 471 costs and additional section 263A costs) of QPP, qualified films, and utilities that generate DPGR by a portion of any increment or liquidation of the dollar-value pool. The portion of an increment or liquidation allocable to DPGR is determined by multiplying the LIFO value of the increment or liquidation (expressed as a positive number) by the ratio of the change in total base-year cost (expressed as a positive number) of the QPP, qualifying films, and utilities that will generate DPGR in ending inventory to the change in total base-year cost (expressed as a positive number) of all goods in the ending inventory. The portion of an increment or liquidation allocable to DPGR may be zero but cannot exceed the amount of the increment or liquidation. Thus, a ratio in excess of 1.0 must be treated as 1.0.

(6) Taxpayers using the simplified production method or simplified resale method for additional section 263A costs. A taxpayer that uses the simplified production method or simplified resale method to allocate additional section 263A costs, as defined in § 1.263A-1(d)(3), to ending inventory must follow the rules in paragraph (b)(2) of this section to determine the amount of additional section 263A costs allocable to DPGR. Allocable additional section 263A costs include additional section 263A costs included in beginning inventory as well as additional section 263A costs incurred during the taxable year. Ordinarily, if a taxpayer uses the simplified production method or the simplified resale method, then additional section 263A costs should be allocated in the same proportion as section 471 costs are allocated.

(7) Examples. The following examples illustrate the application of this paragraph (b):

Example (1). Advance payments.T, a calendar year taxpayer, is a manufacturer of furniture in the United States. Under its method of accounting, T includes advance payments in gross income when the payments are received. In December 2005, T receives an advance payment of $5,000 from X with respect to an order of furniture to be manufactured for a total price of $20,000. In 2006, T produces and ships the furniture to X. In 2006, T incurs $14,000 of section 471 and additional section 263A costs to produce the furniture ordered by X. T receives the remaining $15,000 of the contract price from X in 2006. T must include the $5,000 advance payment in income and DPGR in 2005. The remaining $15,000 of the contract price must be included in income and DPGR when received by T in 2006. T must include the $14,000 it incurred to produce the furniture in CGS and CGS allocable to DPGR in 2006. See § 1.199-1(e)(1) for rules regarding gross receipts and costs recognized in different taxable years.

Example (2). Use of standard cost method. X, a calendar year taxpayer, manufactures item A in a factory located in the United States and item B in a factory located in Country Y. Item A is produced by X in significant part within the United States and the sale of A generates DPGR. X uses the FIFO inventory method to account for its inventory and determines the cost of item A using a standard cost method. At the beginning of its taxable year, X's inventory contains 2,000 units of item A at a standard cost of $5 per unit. X did not incur significant cost variances in previous taxable years. During the 2005 taxable year, X produces 8,000 units of item A at a standard cost of $6 per unit. X determines that with regard to its production of item A it has incurred a significant cost variance. When X reallocates the cost variance to the units of item A that it has produced, the production cost of item A is $7 per unit. X sells 7,000 units of item A during the taxable year. X can identify from its books and records that CGS related to sale of item A is $45,000 ((2,000 x $5) + (5,000 x $7)). Accordingly, X has CGS allocable to DPGR of $45,000.

Example (3). Change in relative base-year cost method. (i) Y elects, beginning with the calendar year 2005, to compute its inventories using the dollar-value, LIFO method under section 472. Y establishes a pool for items A and B. Y produces item A in significant part within the United States and the sales of item A generate DPGR. Y does not produce item B in significant part within the United States and the sale of item B does not generate DPGR. The composition of the inventory for the pool at the base date, January 1, 2005, is as follows:

Item	Unit	Unit cost	Total cost
A	2,000	$5.00	$10,000
B	1,250	4.00	5,000
Total	—	—	15,000

(ii) Y uses a standard cost method to allocate all direct and indirect costs (section 471 and additional section 263A costs) to the units of item A and item B that it produces. During 2005, Y incurs $52,500 of section 471 costs and additional section 263A costs to produce 10,000 units of item A and $114,000 of section 471 costs and additional section 263A costs to produce 20,000 units of item B.

(iii) The closing inventory of the pools at December 31, 2005, contains 3,000 units of item A and 2,500 units of item B. The closing inventory of the pool at December 31, 2005, shown at base-year and current-year cost is as follows:

Item	Quantity	Base-year cost	Amount	Current-year cost	Amount
A	3,000	$5.00	$15,000	$5.25	$15,750
B	2,500	4.00	10,000	5.70	14,250
Totals	—	—	25,000	—	30,000

(iv) The base-year cost of the closing LIFO inventory at December 31, 2005, amounts to $25,000, and exceeds the $15,000 base-year cost of the opening inventory for the taxable year by $10,000 (the increment stated at base-year cost). The increment valued at current-year cost is computed by multiplying the increment stated at base-year cost by the ratio of the current-year cost of the pool to total base-year cost of the pool (that is, $30,000/$25,000, or 120 percent). The increment stated at current-year cost is $12,000 ($10,000 x 120%).

(v) The change in relative base-year cost of item A is $5,000 ($15,000-$10,000). The change in relative base-year cost (the increment stated at base-year cost) of the total inventory is $10,000 ($25,000-$15,000). The ratio of the change in base-year cost of item A to the change in base-year cost of the total inventory is 50% ($5,000/$10,000).

(vi) CGS allocable to DPGR is $46,500, computed as follows:

Current-year production costs related to DPGR	—	$52,500
Less:		
Increment stated at current-year cost	$12,000	—
Ratio	50%	—
Total	—	(6,000)
Total	—	46,500

Example (4). Change in relative base-year cost method. (i) The facts are the same as in Example 3 except that, during the calendar year 2006, Y experiences an inventory decrement. During 2006, Y incurs $66,000 of section 471 costs and additional section 263A costs to produce 12,000 units of item A and $150,000 of section 471 costs and additional section 263A costs to produce 25,000 units of item B.

(ii) The closing inventory of the pool at December 31, 2006, contains 2,000 units of item A and 2,500 units of item B. The closing inventory of the pool at December 31, 2006, shown at base-year and current-year cost is as follows:

Item	Quantity	Base-year cost	Amount	Current-year cost	Amount
A	2,000	$5.00	$10,000	$5.50	$11,000
B	2,500	4.00	10,000	6.00	15,000
Totals	—	—	20,000	—	26,000

(iii) The base-year cost of the closing LIFO inventory at December 31, 2006, amounts to $20,000, and is less than the $25,000 base-year cost of the opening inventory for that year by $5,000 (the decrement stated at base-year cost). This liquidation is reflected by reducing the most recent layer of increment. The LIFO value of the inventory at December 31, 2006 is:

	Base cost	Index	LIFO value
January 1, 2005, base cost	$15,000	1.00	$15,000
December 31, 2005, increment	5,000	1.20	6,000
Total	—	—	21,000

(iv) The change in relative base-year cost of item A is $5,000 ($15,000 - $10,000). The change in relative base-year cost of the total inventory is $5,000 ($25,000 - $20,000). The ratio of the change in base-year cost of item A to the change in base-year cost of the total inventory is 100% ($5,000/$5,000).

(v) CGS allocable to DPGR is $72,000, computed as follows:

Current-year production costs related to DPGR	—	$66,000
Plus:		
LIFO value of decrement	$6,000	—
Ratio	100%	—
Total	—	6,000
Total	—	72,000

Example (5). LIFO/FIFO ratio method. (i) The facts are the same as in Example 3 except that Y uses the LIFO/FIFO ratio method to determine its CGS allocable to DPGR.

(ii) Y's CGS related to item A on a FIFO basis is $46,750 ((2,000 units at $5) + (7,000 units at $5.25)).

(iii) Y's total CGS computed on a LIFO basis is $154,500 (beginning inventory of $15,000 plus total production costs of $166,500 less ending inventory of $27,000).

(iv) Y's total CGS computed on a FIFO basis is $151,500 (beginning inventory of $15,000 plus total production costs of $166,500 less ending inventory of $30,000).

(v) The ratio of Y's CGS computed using the LIFO method to its CGS computed using the FIFO method is 102% ($154,500/$151,500). Y's CGS related to DPGR computed using the LIFO/FIFO ratio method is $47,685 ($46,750 x 102%).

Example (6). LIFO/FIFO ratio method. (i) The facts are the same as in Example 4 except that Y uses the LIFO/FIFO ratio method to compute CGS allocable to DPGR.

(ii) Y's CGS related to item A on a FIFO basis is $70,750 ((3,000 units at $5.25) + (10,000 units at $5.50)).

(iii) Y's total CGS computed on a LIFO basis is $222,000 (beginning inventory of $27,000 plus total production costs of $216,000 less ending inventory of $21,000).

(iv) Y's total CGS computed on a FIFO basis is $220,000 (beginning inventory of $30,000 plus total production costs of $216,000 less ending inventory of $26,000).

(v) The ratio of Y's CGS computed using the LIFO method to its CGS computed using the FIFO method is 101% ($222,000/$220,000). Y's CGS related to DPGR computed using the LIFO/FIFO ratio method is $71,457 ($70,750 x 101%).

(c) Other deductions allocable or apportioned to domestic production gross receipts or gross income attributable to domestic production gross receipts. *(1) In general.* In determining its QPAI, a taxpayer must subtract from its DPGR, in addition to its CGS allocable to DPGR, the deductions that are directly allocable to DPGR, and a ratable portion of deductions that are not directly allocable to DPGR or to another class of income. A taxpayer generally must allocate and apportion these deductions using the rules of the section 861 method. In lieu of the section 861 method, certain taxpayers may apportion these deductions using the simplified deduction method provided in paragraph (e) of this section. Paragraph (f) of this section provides a small business simplified overall method that may be used by a qualified small taxpayer, as defined in that paragraph. A taxpayer using the simplified deduction method or the small business simplified overall method must use that method for all deductions. A taxpayer eligible to use the small business simplified overall method may choose at any time to use the small business simplified overall method, the simplified deduction method, or the section 861 method for a taxable year. A taxpayer eligible to use the simplified deduction method may choose at any time to use the simplified deduction method or the section 861 method for a taxable year.

(2) Treatment of certain deductions. (i) In general. The rules provided in this paragraph (c)(2) apply to net operating losses and certain other deductions for purposes of allocating and apportioning deductions to DPGR or gross income attributable to DPGR for all of the methods provided by this section.

(ii) Net operating losses. A deduction under section 172 for a net operating loss is not allocated or apportioned to DPGR or gross income attributable to DPGR.

(iii) Deductions not attributable to the conduct of a trade or business. Deductions not attributable to the conduct of a trade or business are not allocated or apportioned to DPGR or gross income attributable to DPGR. For example, the standard deduction provided by section 63(c) and the deduction for personal exemptions provided by section 151 are not allocated or apportioned to DPGR or gross income attributable to DPGR.

(d) Section 861 method. *(1) In general.* A taxpayer must allocate and apportion its deductions using the allocation and apportionment rules provided by the section 861 method under which section 199 is treated as an operative section described in § 1.861-8(f). Accordingly, the taxpayer applies the rules of the section 861 regulations to allocate and apportion deductions (including its distributive share of deductions from pass-thru entities) to gross income attributable to DPGR. If the taxpayer applies the allocation and apportionment rules of the section 861 regulations for an operative section other than section 199, the taxpayer must use the same method of allocation and the same principles of apportionment for purposes of all operative sections (subject to the rules provided in paragraphs (c)(2) and (d)(2) and (3) of this section). See § 1.861-8(f)(2)(i).

(2) Deductions for charitable contributions. Deductions for charitable contributions (as allowed under sections 170, 873(b)(2), and 882(c)(1)(B)) must be ratably apportioned be-

tween gross income attributable to DPGR and other gross income based on the relative amounts of gross income. For individuals, this provision applies solely to deductions for charitable contributions that are attributable to the actual conduct of a trade or business.

(3) Research and experimental expenditures. Research and experimental expenditures must be allocated and apportioned in accordance with § 1.861-17 without taking into account the exclusive apportionment rule of § 1.861-17(b).

(4) Deductions related to gross receipts deemed to be domestic production gross receipts. If non-DPGR is treated as DPGR pursuant to §§ 1.199-1(d)(2) and 1.199-3(h)(4), (k)(4)(iv), (l)(1)(ii), (m)(4), or (n)(1), deductions related to such gross receipts that are treated as DPGR must be allocated or apportioned to gross income attributable to DPGR.

(5) Examples. The following examples illustrate the operation of the section 861 method. Assume that with respect to the allocation and apportionment of interest expense, § 1.861-10T does not apply in the following examples. The examples read as follows:

Example (1). General section 861 method. (i) X, a United States corporation that is not a member of an expanded affiliated group (EAG) (as defined in § 1.199-7), engages in activities that generate both DPGR and non-DPGR. All of X's production activities that generate DPGR are within Standard Industrial Classification (SIC) Industry Group AAA (SIC AAA)). All of X's production activities that generate non-DPGR are within SIC Industry Group BBB (SIC BBB). X is able to identify from its books and records CGS allocable to DPGR and to non-DPGR. X incurs $900 of research and experimentation expenses (R&E) that are deductible under section 174, $300 of which are performed with respect to SIC AAA and $600 of which are performed with respect to SIC BBB. None of the R&E is legally mandated R&E as described in § 1.861-17(a)(4) and none of the R&E is included in CGS. X incurs section 162 selling expenses (that include W-2 wages as defined in § 1.199-2(f)) that are not includible in CGS and not directly allocable to any gross income. For 2010, the adjusted basis of X's assets that generate gross income attributable to DPGR and to non-DPGR is, respectively, $4,000 and $1,000. For 2010, X's taxable income is $1,380 based on the following Federal income tax items:

DPGR (all from sales of products within SIC AAA)	$3,000
Non-DPGR (all from sales of products within SIC BBB)	3,000
CGS allocable to DPGR (includes $100 of W-2 wages)	(600)
CGS allocable to non-DPGR (includes $100 of W-2 wages)	(1,800)
Section 162 selling expenses (includes $100 of W-2 wages).	(840)
Section 174 R&E-SIC AAA	(300)
Section 174 R&E-SIC BBB	(600)
Interest expense (not included in CGS)	(300)
Charitable contributions	(180)
X's taxable income	1,380

(ii) X's QPAI. X chooses to allocate and apportion its deductions to gross income attributable to DPGR under the section 861 method of this paragraph (d). In this case, the section 162 selling expenses (including W-2 wages) are definitely related to all of X's gross income. Based on the facts and circumstances of this specific case, apportionment of those expenses between DPGR and non-DPGR on the basis of X's gross receipts is appropriate. For purposes of apportioning R&E, X elects to use the sales method as described in § 1.861-17(c). X elects to apportion interest expense under the tax book value method of § 1.861-9T(g). X has $2,400 of gross income attributable to DPGR (DPGR of $3,000–CGS of $600 (includes $100 of W-2 wages) allocated based on X's books and records). X's QPAI for 2010 is $1,320, as shown below:

DPGR (all from sales of products within SIC AAA)	$3,000
CGS allocable to DPGR (includes $100 of W-2 wages)	(600)
Section 162 selling expenses (includes $100 of W-2 wages) ($840 x ($3,000 DPGR/$6,000 total gross receipts))	(420)
Interest expense (not included in CGS) ($300 x ($4,000 (X's DPGR assets)/$5,000 (X's total assets)))	(240)
Charitable contributions (not included in CGS) ($180 x ($2,400 gross income attributable to DPGR/$3,600 total gross income))	(120)
Section 174 R&E-SIC AAA	(300)
X's QPAI	1,320

(iii) Section 199 deduction determination. X's tentative deduction under § 1.199-1(a) (section 199 deduction) is $119 (.09 x (lesser of QPAI of $1,320 and taxable income of $1,380)) subject to the wage limitation of $150 (50% x $300). Accordingly, X's section 199 deduction for 2010 is $119.

Example (2). Section 861 method and EAG. (i) Facts. The facts are the same as in Example 1 except that X owns stock in Y, a United States corporation, equal to 75 percent of the total voting power of stock of Y and 80 percent of the total value of stock of Y. X and Y are not members of an affiliated group as defined in section 1504(a). Accordingly, the rules of § 1.861-14T do not apply to X's and Y's selling expenses, R&E, and charitable contributions. X and Y are, however, members of an affiliated group for purposes of allocating and apportioning interest expense (see § 1.861-11T(d)(6)) and are also members of an EAG. For 2010, the adjusted basis of Y's assets that generate gross income attributable to DPGR and to non-DPGR is, respectively, $21,000 and $24,000. All of Y's activities that generate DPGR are within SIC Industry Group AAA (SIC AAA). All of Y's activities that generate non-DPGR are within SIC Industry Group BBB (SIC BBB). None of X's and Y's sales are to each other. Y is not able to identify from its books and records CGS allocable to DPGR and non-DPGR. In this case, because CGS is definitely related under the facts and circumstances to all of Y's gross receipts, apportionment of CGS between DPGR and non-DPGR based on gross receipts is appropriate. For 2010, Y's taxable income is $1,910 based on the following tax items:

DPGR (all from sales of products within SIC AAA)	$3,000
Non-DPGR (all from sales of products within SIC BBB)	3,000
CGS allocated to DPGR (includes $300 of W-2 wages)	(1,200)
CGS allocated to non-DPGR (includes $300 of W-2 wages)	(1,200)
Section 162 selling expenses (includes $300 of W-2 wages).	(840)
Section 174 R&E-SIC AAA	(100)
Section 174 R&E-SIC BBB	(200)

Interest expense (not included in CGS and not subject to § 1.861-10T)	(500)
Charitable contributions	(50)
Y's taxable income	1,910

(ii) QPAI. (A) X's QPAI. Determination of X's QPAI is the same as in Example 1 except that interest is apportioned to gross income attributable to DPGR based on the combined adjusted bases of X's and Y's assets. See § 1.861-11T(c). Accordingly, X's QPAI for 2010 is $1,410, as shown below:

DPGR (all from sales of products within SIC AAA)	$3,000
CGS allocated to DPGR (includes $300 of W-2 wages)	(600)
Section 162 selling expenses (includes $100 of W-2 wages) ($840 x ($3,000 DPGR/$6,000 total gross receipts))	(420)
Interest expense (not included in CGS and not subject to § 1.861-10T) ($300 x ($25,000 (tax book value of X's and Y's DPGR assets)/$50,000 (tax book value of X's and Y's total assets)))	(150)
Charitable contributions (not included in CGS) ($180 x ($2,400 gross income attributable to DPGR/$3,600 total gross income))	(120)
Section 174 R&E-SIC AAA	(300)
X's QPAI	1,410

(B) Y's QPAI. Y makes the same elections under the section 861 method as does X. Y has $1,800 of gross income attributable to DPGR (DPGR of $3,000–CGS of $1,200 allocated based on Y's gross receipts). Y's QPAI for 2010 is $1,005, as shown below:

DPGR (all from sales of products within SIC AAA)	$3,000
CGS allocated to DPGR (includes $300 of W-2 wages)	(1,200)
Section 162 selling expenses (includes $300 of W-2 wages) ($840 x ($3,000 DPGR/$6,000 total gross receipts))	(420)
Interest expense (not included in CGS and not subject to § 1.861-10T) ($500 x ($25,000 (tax book value of X's and Y's DPGR assets)/$50,000 (tax book value of X's and Y's total assets)))	(250)
Charitable contributions (not included in CGS) ($50 x ($1,800 gross income attributable to DPGR/$3,600 total gross income))	(25)
Section 174 R&E-SIC AAA	(100)
Y's QPAI	1,005

(iii) Section 199 deduction determination. The section 199 deduction of the X and Y EAG is determined by aggregating the separately determined QPAI, taxable income, and W-2 wages of X and Y. See § 1.199-7(b). Accordingly, the X and Y EAG's tentative section 199 deduction is $217 (.09 x (lesser of combined taxable incomes of X and Y of $3,290 (X's taxable income of $1,380 plus Y's taxable income of $1,910) and combined QPAI of $2,415 (X's QPAI of $1,410 plus Y's QPAI of $1,005)) subject to the wage limitation of $600 (50% x ($300 (X's W-2 wages) + $900 (Y's W-2 wages))). Accordingly, the X and Y EAG's section 199 deduction for 2010 is $217. The $217 is allocated to X and Y in proportion to their QPAI. See § 1.199-7(c).

(e) Simplified deduction method. *(1) In general.* A taxpayer with average annual gross receipts (as defined in paragraph (g) of this section) of $25,000,000 or less, or total assets at the end of the taxable year (as defined in paragraph (h) of this section) of $10,000,000 or less, may use the simplified deduction method to apportion deductions between DPGR and non-DPGR. This paragraph does not apply to CGS. Under the simplified deduction method, a taxpayer's deductions (except the net operating loss deduction as provided in paragraph (c)(2)(ii) of this section and deductions not attributable to the actual conduct of a trade or business as provided in paragraph (c)(2)(iii) of this section) are ratably apportioned between DPGR and non-DPGR based on relative gross receipts. Accordingly, the amount of deductions apportioned to DPGR is equal to the same proportion of the total deductions that the amount of DPGR bears to total gross receipts. Whether an owner of a pass-thru entity may use the simplified deduction method is determined at the level of the owner of the pass-thru entity. Whether a trust or an estate may use the simplified deduction method is determined at the trust or estate level. In the case of a trust or estate, the simplified deduction method is applied at the trust or estate level, taking into account the trust's or estate's DPGR, non-DPGR, and other items from all sources, including its distributive or allocable share of those items of any lower-tier entity, prior to any charitable or distribution deduction. In the case of an owner of any other pass-thru entity, the simplified deduction method is applied at the level of the owner of the pass-thru entity taking into account the owner's DPGR, non-DPGR, and other items from all sources including its distributive or allocable share of those items of the pass-thru entity.

(2) Members of an expanded affiliated group. (i) In general. Whether the members of an EAG may use the simplified deduction method is determined by reference to the average annual gross receipts and total assets of the EAG. If the average annual gross receipts of the EAG are less than or equal to $25,000,000 or the total assets of the EAG at the end of its taxable year are less than or equal to $10,000,000, each member of the EAG may individually determine whether to use the simplified deduction method, regardless of the cost allocation method used by the other members.

(ii) Exception. Notwithstanding paragraph (e)(2)(i) of this section, all members of the same consolidated group must use the same cost allocation method.

(iii) Examples. The following examples illustrate the application of paragraph (e)(2) of this section:

Example (1). Corporations X, Y, and Z are the only three members of an EAG. Neither X, Y, nor Z is a member of a consolidated group. X, Y, and Z have average annual gross receipts of $2,000,000, $7,000,000, and $13,000,000, respectively. X, Y, and Z each have total assets at the end of the taxable year of $5,000,000. Because the average annual gross receipts of the EAG are less than or equal to $25,000,000, each of X, Y, and Z may use either the simplified deduction method or the section 861 method.

Example (2). The facts are the same as in Example 1 except that X and Y are members of the same consolidated group. X, Y, and Z may use either the simplified deduction method or the section 861 method. However, X and Y must use the same cost allocation method.

Example (3). The facts are the same as in Example 1 except that Z's average annual gross receipts are $17,000,000. Because the average annual gross receipts of the EAG are greater than $25,000,000 and the total assets of the EAG at the end of the taxable year are greater than $10,000,000, X, Y, and Z must each use the section 861 method.

(f) Small business simplified overall method. *(1) In general.* A qualifying small taxpayer may use the small business simplified overall method to apportion CGS and deductions between DPGR and non-DPGR. Under the small business simplified overall method, a taxpayer's total costs for the current taxable year (as defined in paragraph (i) of this section) are apportioned between DPGR and other receipts based on relative gross receipts. Accordingly, the amount of total costs for the current taxable year apportioned to DPGR is equal to the same proportion of total costs for the current taxable year that the amount of DPGR bears to total gross receipts. In the case of a pass-thru entity, whether the small business simplified overall method may be used by such entity is determined at the pass-thru entity level and, if such entity is eligible, the small business simplified overall method is applied at the pass-thru entity level.

(2) Qualifying small taxpayer. For purposes of this paragraph (f), a qualifying small taxpayer is—

(i) A taxpayer that has both average annual gross receipts (as defined in paragraph (g) of this section) of $5,000,000 or less and total costs for the current taxable year of $5,000,000 or less;

(ii) A taxpayer that is engaged in the trade or business of farming that is not required to use the accrual method of accounting under section 447; or

(iii) A taxpayer that is eligible to use the cash method as provided in Rev. Proc. 2002-28 (2002-1 C.B. 815) (that is, certain taxpayers with average annual gross receipts of $10,000,000 or less that are not prohibited from using the cash method under section 448, including partnerships, S corporations, C corporations, or individuals). See § 601.601(d)(2) of this chapter.

(3) Members of an expanded affiliated group. (i) In general. Whether the members of an EAG may use the small business simplified overall method is determined by reference to all the members of the EAG. If both the average annual gross receipts and the total costs for the current taxable year of the EAG are less than or equal to $5,000,000; the EAG, viewed as a single corporation, is engaged in the trade or business of farming that is not required to use the accrual method of accounting under section 447; or the EAG, viewed as a single corporation, is eligible to use the cash method as provided in Rev. Proc. 2002-28, then each member of the EAG may individually determine whether to use the small business simplified overall method, regardless of the cost allocation method used by the other members.

(ii) Exception. Notwithstanding paragraph (f)(3)(i) of this section, all members of the same consolidated group must use the same cost allocation method.

(iii) Examples. The following examples illustrate the application of paragraph (f)(3) of this section:

Example (1). Corporations L, M, and N are the only three members of an EAG. Neither L, M, nor N is a member of a consolidated group. L, M, and N have average annual gross receipts and total costs for the current taxable year of $1,000,000, $1,500,000, and $2,000,000, respectively. Because both the average annual gross receipts and total costs for the current taxable year of the EAG are less than or equal to $5,000,000, each of L, M, and N may use the small business simplified overall method, the simplified deduction method, or the section 861 method.

Example (2). The facts are the same as in Example 1 except that M and N are members of the same consolidated group. L, M, and N may use the small business simplified overall method, the simplified deduction method, or the section 861 method. However, M and N must use the same cost allocation method.

Example (3). The facts are the same as in Example 1 except that N has average annual gross receipts of $4,000,000. Unless the EAG, viewed as a single corporation, is engaged in the trade or business of farming that is not required to use the accrual method of accounting under section 447, or the EAG, viewed as a single corporation, is eligible to use the cash method as provided in Rev. Proc. 2002-28, because the average annual gross receipts of the EAG are greater than $5,000,000, L, M, and N are all ineligible to use the small business simplified overall method.

(4) Ineligible pass-thru entities. Qualifying oil and gas partnerships under § 1.199-3(h)(7), EAG partnerships under § 1.199-3(h)(8), and trusts and estates under § 1.199-5(d) may not use the small business simplified overall method.

(g) Average annual gross receipts. *(1) In general.* For purposes of the simplified deduction method and the small business simplified overall method, average annual gross receipts means the average annual gross receipts of the taxpayer for the 3 taxable years (or, if fewer, the taxable years during which the taxpayer was in existence) preceding the current taxable year, even if one or more of such taxable years began before the effective date of section 199. In the case of any taxable year of less than 12 months (a short taxable year), the gross receipts shall be annualized by multiplying the gross receipts for the short period by 12 and dividing the result by the number of months in the short period.

(2) Members of an EAG. To compute the average annual gross receipts of an EAG, the gross receipts, for the entire taxable year, of each corporation that is a member of the EAG at the end of its taxable year that ends with or within the taxable year of the computing member (as described in § 1.199-7(h)) are aggregated.

(h) Total assets. *(1) In general.* For purposes of the simplified deduction method provided by paragraph (e) of this section, total assets means the total assets the taxpayer has at the end of the taxable year that are attributable to the taxpayer's trade or business. In the case of a C corporation, the corporation's total assets at the end of the taxable year is the amount required to be reported on Schedule L of the Form 1120, "United States Corporation Income Tax Return," in accordance with the Form 1120 instructions.

(2) Members of an EAG. To compute the total assets at the end of the taxable year of an EAG, the total assets, at the end of its taxable year, of each corporation that is a member of the EAG at the end of its taxable year that ends with or within the taxable year of the computing member are aggregated.

(i) Total costs for the current taxable year. *(1) In general.* For purposes of the small business simplified overall method, total costs for the current taxable year means the total CGS and deductions (excluding the net operating loss deduction as provided in paragraph (c)(2)(ii) of this section and deductions not attributable to the conduct of a trade or business as provided in paragraph (c)(2)(iii) of this section) for the current taxable year.

(2) Members of an EAG. To compute the total costs for the current taxable year of an EAG, the total costs for the entire taxable year of each corporation that is a member of the EAG at the end of the taxable year that ends with or

within the taxable year of the computing member are aggregated.

§ 1.199-5 Application of section 199 to pass-thru entities for taxable years beginning after May 17, 2006, the enactment date of the Tax Increase Prevention and Reconciliation Act of 2005.

Caution: The Treasury has not yet amended Reg § 1.199-5 to reflect changes made by P.L. 110-343.

(a) In general. The provisions of this section apply solely for purposes of section 199 of the Internal Revenue Code (Code).

(b) Partnerships. *(1) In general.* (i) Determination at partner level. The deduction with respect to the qualified production activities of the partnership allowable under § 1.199-1(a) (section 199 deduction) is determined at the partner level. As a result, each partner must compute its deduction separately. The section 199 deduction has no effect on the adjusted basis of the partner's interest in the partnership. Except as provided by publication pursuant to paragraph (b)(1)(ii) of this section, for purposes of this section, each partner is allocated, in accordance with sections 702 and 704, its share of partnership items (including items of income, gain, loss, and deduction), cost of goods sold (CGS) allocated to such items of income, and gross receipts that are included in such items of income, even if the partner's share of CGS and other deductions and losses exceeds domestic production gross receipts (DPGR) (as defined in § 1.199-3(a)). A partnership may specially allocate items of income, gain, loss, or deduction to its partners, subject to the rules of section 704(b) and the supporting regulations. Guaranteed payments under section 707(c) are not considered allocations of partnership income for purposes of this section. Guaranteed payments under section 707(c) are deductions by the partnership that must be taken into account under the rules of § 1.199-4. See § 1.199-3(p) and paragraph (b)(6) Example 5 of this section. Except as provided in paragraph (b)(1)(ii) of this section, to determine its section 199 deduction for the taxable year, a partner aggregates its distributive share of such items, to the extent they are not otherwise disallowed by the Code, with those items it incurs outside the partnership (whether directly or indirectly) for purposes of allocating and apportioning deductions to DPGR and computing its qualified production activities income (QPAI) (as defined in § 1.199-1(c)).

(ii) Determination at entity level. The Secretary may, by publication in the Internal Revenue Bulletin (see § 601.601(d)(2)(ii)(b) of this chapter), permit a partnership to calculate a partner's share of QPAI and W-2 wages as defined in § 1.199-2(e)(2) (W-2 wages) at the entity level, instead of allocating to the partner, in accordance with sections 702 and 704, the partner's share of partnership items (including items of income, gain, loss, and deduction) and amounts described in § 1.199-2(e)(1) (paragraph (e)(1) wages). If a partnership does calculate QPAI at the entity level—

(A) Each partner is allocated its share of QPAI (subject to the limitations of paragraph (b)(2) of this section) and W-2 wages from the partnership, which are combined with the partner's QPAI and W-2 wages from other sources, if any;

(B) For purposes of computing the partner's QPAI under §§ 1.199-1 through 1.199-8, a partner does not take into account the items from the partnership (for example, a partner does not take into account items from the partnership in determining whether a threshold or de minimis rule applies or in allocating and apportioning deductions) in calculating its QPAI from other sources;

(C) A partner generally does not recompute its share of QPAI from the partnership using another method; however, the partner might have to adjust its share of QPAI from the partnership to take into account certain disallowed losses or deductions, or the allowance of suspended losses or deductions; and

(D) A partner's distributive share of QPAI from a partnership may be less than zero.

(2) Disallowed losses or deductions. Except as provided by publication in the Internal Revenue Bulletin (see § 601.601(d)(2)(ii)(b) of this chapter), losses or deductions of a partnership are taken into account in computing the partner's QPAI for a taxable year only if, and to the extent that, the partner's distributive share of those losses or deductions from all of the partnership's activities is not disallowed by section 465, 469, or 704(d), or any other provision of the Code. If only a portion of the partner's distributive share of the losses or deductions from a partnership is allowed for a taxable year, a proportionate share of those allowed losses or deductions that are allocated to the partnership's qualified production activities, determined in a manner consistent with sections 465, 469, and 704(d), and any other applicable provision of the Code, is taken into account in computing QPAI for that taxable year. To the extent that any of the disallowed losses or deductions are allowed in a later taxable year under section 465, 469, or 704(d), or any other provision of the Code, the partner takes into account a proportionate share of those allowed losses or deductions that are allocated to the partnership's qualified production activities in computing the partner's QPAI for that later taxable year. Losses or deductions of the partnership that are disallowed for taxable years beginning on or before December 31, 2004, however, are not taken into account in a later taxable year for purposes of computing the partner's QPAI for that later taxable year, whether or not the losses or deductions are allowed for other purposes.

(3) Partner's share of paragraph (e)(1) wages. Under section 199(d)(1)(A)(iii), a partner's share of paragraph (e)(1) wages of a partnership for purposes of determining the partner's wage limitation under section 199(b)(1) (W-2 wage limitation) equals the partner's allocable share of those wages. Except as provided by publication in the Internal Revenue Bulletin (see § 601.601(d)(2)(ii)(b) of this chapter), the partnership must allocate the amount of paragraph (e)(1) wages among the partners in the same manner it allocates wage expense among those partners. The partner must add its share of the paragraph (e)(1) wages from the partnership to the partner's paragraph (e)(1) wages from other sources, if any. The partner (other than a partner that itself is a partnership or S corporation) then must calculate its W-2 wages by determining the amount of the partner's total paragraph (e)(1) wages properly allocable to DPGR. If the partner is a partnership or S corporation, the partner must allocate its paragraph (e)(1) wages (including the paragraph (e)(1) wages from a lower-tier partnership) among its partners or shareholders in the same manner it allocates wage expense among those partners or shareholders. See § 1.199-2(e)(2) for the computation of W-2 wages and for the proper allocation of any such wages to DPGR.

(4) Transition rule for definition of W-2 wages and for W-2 wage limitation. If a partnership and any partner in that partnership have different taxable years, only one of which begins after May 17, 2006, the definition of W-2 wages of the partnership and the section 199(d)(1)(A)(iii) rule for de-

termining a partner's share of wages from that partnership is determined under the law applicable to partnerships based on the beginning date of the partnership's taxable year. Thus, for example, for the taxable year of a partnership beginning on or before May 17, 2006, a partner's share of W-2 wages from the partnership is determined under section 199(d)(1)(A)(iii) as in effect for taxable years beginning on or before May 17, 2006, even if the taxable year of that partner in which those wages are taken into account begins after May 17, 2006.

(5) Partnerships electing out of subchapter K. For purposes of §§ 1.199-1 through 1.199-8, the rules of this paragraph (b) apply to all partnerships, including those partnerships electing under section 761(a) to be excluded, in whole or in part, from the application of subchapter K of chapter 1 of the Code.

(6) Examples. The following examples illustrate the application of this paragraph (b). Assume that each partner has sufficient adjusted gross income or taxable income so that the section 199 deduction is not limited under section 199(a)(1)(B). Assume also that the partnership and each of its partners (whether individual or corporate) are calendar year taxpayers. The examples read as follows:

Example (1). Section 861 method with interest expense. (i) Partnership Federal income tax items. X and Y, unrelated United States corporations, are each 50% partners in PRS, a partnership that engages in production activities that generate both DPGR and non-DPGR. X and Y share all items of income, gain, loss, deduction, and credit equally. Both X and Y are engaged in a trade or business. PRS is not able to identify from its books and records CGS allocable to DPGR and non-DPGR. In this case, because CGS is definitely related under the facts and circumstances to all of PRS's gross receipts, apportionment of CGS between DPGR and non-DPGR based on gross receipts is appropriate. For 2010, the adjusted basis of PRS's business assets is $5,000, $4,000 of which generate gross income attributable to DPGR and $1,000 of which generate gross income attributable to non-DPGR. For 2010, PRS has the following Federal income tax items:

DPGR	$3,000
Non-DPGR	3,000
CGS	3,240
Section 162 selling expenses	1,200
Interest expense (not included in CGS)	300

(ii) Allocation of PRS's Federal income tax items. X and Y each receive the following distributive share of PRS's Federal income tax items, as determined under the principles of § 1.704-1(b)(1)(vii):

Gross income attributable to DPGR ($1,500 (DPGR) - $810 (allocable CGS))	$690
Gross income attributable to non-DPGR ($1,500 (non-DPGR) - $810 (allocable CGS))	690
Section 162 selling expenses	600
Interest expense (not included in CGS)	150

(iii) Determination of QPAI. (A) X's QPAI. Because the section 199 deduction is determined at the partner level, X determines its QPAI by aggregating its distributive share of PRS's Federal income tax items with all other such items from all other, non-PRS-related activities. For 2010, X does not have any other such items. For 2010, the adjusted basis of X's non-PRS assets, all of which are investment assets, is $10,000. X's only gross receipts for 2010 are those attributable to the allocation of gross income from PRS. X allocates and apportions its deductible items to gross income attributable to DPGR under the section 861 method of § 1.199-4(d). In this case, the section 162 selling expenses are not included in CGS and are definitely related to all of PRS's gross income. Based on the facts and circumstances of this specific case, apportionment of those expenses between DPGR and non-DPGR on the basis of PRS's gross receipts is appropriate. X elects to apportion its distributive share of interest expense under the tax book value method of § 1.861-9T(g). X's QPAI for 2010 is $366, as shown in the following table:

DPGR	$1,500
CGS allocable to DPGR	(810)
Section 162 selling expenses ($600 x ($1,500 DPGR/$3,000 total gross receipts)	(300)
Interest expense (not included in CGS) ($150 x ($2,000 (X's share of PRS's DPGR assets)/$12,500 (X's non-PRS assets ($10,000) + X's share of PRS assets ($2,500))))	(24)
X's QPAI	366

(B) Y's QPAI. (1) For 2010, in addition to the activities of PRS, Y engages in production activities that generate both DPGR and non-DPGR. Y is able to identify from its books and records CGS allocable to DPGR and to non-DPGR. For 2010, the adjusted basis of Y's non-PRS assets attributable to its production activities that generate DPGR is $8,000 and to other production activities that generate non-DPGR is $2,000. Y has no other assets. Y has the following Federal income tax items relating to its non-PRS activities:

Gross income attributable to DPGR ($1,500 (DPGR) - $900 (allocable CGS))	$ 600
Gross income attributable to non-DPGR ($3,000 (other gross receipts) - $1,620 (allocable CGS))	1,380
Section 162 selling expenses	540
Interest expense (not included in CGS)	90

(2) Y determines its QPAI in the same general manner as X. However, because Y has other trade or business activities outside of PRS, Y must aggregate its distributive share of PRS's Federal income tax items with its own such items. Y allocates and apportions its deductible items to gross income attributable to DPGR under the section 861 method of § 1.199-4(d). In this case, Y's distributive share of PRS's section 162 selling expenses, as well as those selling expenses from Y's non-PRS activities, are definitely related to all of its gross income. Based on the facts and circumstances of this specific case, apportionment of those expenses between DPGR and non-DPGR on the basis of Y's gross receipts (including Y's share of PRS's gross receipts) is appropriate. Y elects to apportion its distributive share of interest expense under the tax book value method of § 1.861-9T(g). Y has $1,290 of gross income attributable to DPGR ($3,000 DPGR ($1,500 from PRS and $1,500 from non-PRS activities)--$1,710 CGS ($810 from PRS and $900 from non-PRS activities)). Y's QPAI for 2010 is $642, as shown in the following table:

DPGR ($1,500 from PRS and $1,500 from non-PRS activities)	$3,000
CGS allocable to DPGR ($810 from PRS and $900 from non-PRS activities)	(1,710)
Section 162 selling expenses ($1,140 ($600 from PRS and $540 from non-PRS activities) x $3,000 ($1,500 PRS DPGR + $1,500 non-PRS DPGR)/ $7,500 ($3,000 PRS total gross receipts + $4,500 non-PRS total gross receipts))	(456)
Interest expense (not included in CGS) ($240 ($150 from PRS and $90 from non-PRS activities) x $10,000 (Y's non-PRS DPGR assets ($8,000) + Y's share of PRS DPGR assets ($2,000))/$12,500 (Y's non-PRS assets ($10,000) + Y's share of PRS assets ($2,500)))	(192)
Y's QPAI	642

(iv) Determination of section 199 deduction. X's tentative section 199 deduction is $33 (.09 x $366, that is, QPAI determined at the partner level) subject to the W-2 wage limitation (50% of W-2 wages). Y's tentative section 199 deduction is $58 (.09 x $642) subject to the W-2 wage limitation.

Example (2). Section 861 method with R&E expense. (i) Partnership Federal income tax items. X and Y, unrelated United States corporations each of which is engaged in a trade or business, are partners in PRS, a partnership that engages in production activities that generate both DPGR and non-DPGR. Neither X nor Y is a member of an affiliated group. X and Y share all items of income, gain, loss, deduction, and credit equally. All of PRS's domestic production activities that generate DPGR are within Standard Industrial Classification (SIC) Industry Group AAA (SIC AAA). All of PRS's production activities that generate non-DPGR are within SIC Industry Group BBB (SIC BBB). PRS is not able to identify from its books and records CGS allocable to DPGR and to non-DPGR. In this case, because CGS is definitely related under the facts and circumstances to all of PRS's gross receipts, apportionment of CGS between DPGR and non-DPGR based on gross receipts is appropriate. PRS incurs $900 of research and experimentation expenses (R&E) that are deductible under section 174, $300 of which are performed with respect to SIC AAA and $600 of which are performed with respect to SIC BBB. None of the R&E is legally mandated R&E as described in § 1.861-17(a)(4) and none is included in CGS. For 2010, PRS has the following Federal income tax items:

DPGR (all from sales of products within SIC AAA)	$3,000
Non-DPGR (all from sales of products within SIC BBB)	3,000
CGS	2,400
Section 162 selling expenses	840
Section 174 R&E-SIC AAA	300
Section 174 R&E-SIC BBB	600

(ii) Allocation of PRS's Federal income tax items. X and Y each receive the following distributive share of PRS's Federal income tax items, as determined under the principles of § 1.704-1(b)(1)(vii):

Gross income attributable to DPGR ($1,500 (DPGR) - $600 (CGS))	$900
Gross income attributable to non-DPGR ($1,500 (other gross receipts) - $600 (CGS))	900
Section 162 selling expenses	420
Section 174 R&E-SIC AAA	150
Section 174 R&E-SIC BBB	300

(iii) Determination of QPAI. (A) X's QPAI. Because the section 199 deduction is determined at the partner level, X determines its QPAI by aggregating its distributive share of PRS's Federal income tax items with all other such items from all other, non-PRS-related activities. For 2010, X does not have any other such tax items. X's only gross receipts for 2010 are those attributable to the allocation of gross income from PRS. As stated, all of PRS's domestic production activities that generate DPGR are within SIC AAA. X allocates and apportions its deductible items to gross income attributable to DPGR under the section 861 method of § 1.199-4(d). In this case, the section 162 selling expenses are definitely related to all of PRS's gross income. Based on the facts and circumstances of this specific case, apportionment of those expenses between DPGR and non-DPGR on the basis of PRS's gross receipts is appropriate. For purposes of apportioning R&E, X elects to use the sales method as described in § 1.861-17(c). Because X has no direct sales of products, and because all of PRS's SIC AAA sales attributable to X's share of PRS's gross income generate DPGR, all of X's share of PRS's section 174 R&E attributable to SIC AAA is taken into account for purposes of determining X's QPAI. Thus, X's total QPAI for 2010 is $540, as shown in the following table:

DPGR (all from sales of products within SIC AAA)	$1,500
CGS	(600)
Section 162 selling expenses ($420 x ($1,500 DPGR/$3,000 total gross receipts))	(210)
Section 174 R&E-SIC AAA	(150)
X's QPAI	540

(B) Y's QPAI. (1) For 2010, in addition to the activities of PRS, Y engages in domestic production activities that generate both DPGR and non-DPGR. With respect to those non-PRS activities, Y is not able to identify from its books and records CGS allocable to DPGR and to non-DPGR. In this case, because non-PRS CGS is definitely related under the facts and circumstances to all of Y's non-PRS gross receipts, apportionment of non-PRS CGS between DPGR and non-DPGR based on Y's non-PRS gross receipts is appropriate. For 2010, Y has the following non-PRS Federal income tax items:

DPGR (from sales of products within SIC AAA)	$1,500
DPGR (from sales of products within SIC BBB)	1,500
Non-DPGR (from sales of products within SIC BBB)	3,000
CGS (allocated to DPGR within SIC AAA)	750
CGS (allocated to DPGR within SIC BBB)	750
CGS (allocated to non-DPGR within SIC BBB)	1,500
Section 162 selling expenses	540
Section 174 R&E-SIC AAA	300
Section 174 R&E-SIC BBB	450

(2) Because Y has DPGR as a result of activities outside PRS, Y must aggregate its distributive share of PRS's Federal income tax items with such items from all its other, non-PRS-related activities. Y allocates and apportions its deductible items to gross income attributable to DPGR under the section 861 method of § 1.199-4(d). In this case, the section 162 selling expenses are definitely related to all of

Y's gross income. Based on the facts and circumstances of the specific case, apportionment of such expenses between DPGR and non-DPGR on the basis of Y's gross receipts (including Y's share of PRS's gross receipts) is appropriate. For purposes of apportioning R&E, Y elects to use the sales method as described in § 1.861-17(c).

(3) With respect to sales that generate DPGR, Y has gross income of $2,400 ($4,500 DPGR ($1,500 from PRS and $3,000 from non-PRS activities) - $2,100 CGS ($600 from sales of products by PRS and $1,500 from non-PRS activities)). Because all of the sales in SIC AAA generate DPGR, all of Y's share of PRS's section 174 R&E attributable to SIC AAA and the section 174 R&E attributable to SIC AAA that Y incurs in its non-PRS activities are taken into account for purposes of determining Y's QPAI. Because only a portion of the sales within SIC BBB generate DPGR, only a portion of the section 174 R&E attributable to SIC BBB is taken into account in determining Y's QPAI. Thus, Y's QPAI for 2010 is $1,282, as shown in the following table:

DPGR ($4,500 DPGR ($1,500 from PRS and $3,000 from non-PRS activities))	$4,500
CGS ($600 from sales of products by PRS and $1,500 from non-PRS activities)	(2,100)
Section 162 selling expenses ($960 ($420 from PRS + $540 from non-PRS activities) x ($4,500 DPGR/$9,000 total gross receipts))	(480)
Section 174 R&E-SIC AAA ($150 from PRS and $300 from non-PRS activities)	(450)
Section 174 R&E-SIC BBB ($750 ($300 from PRS + $450 from non-PRS activities) x ($1,500 DPGR/$6,000 total gross receipts allocated to SIC BBB ($1,500 from PRS + $4,500 from non-PRS activities))..........	(188)
Y's QPAI	1,282

(iv) Determination of section 199 deduction. X's tentative section 199 deduction is $49 (.09 x $540, that is, QPAI determined at the partner level) subject to the W-2 wage limitation (50% of W-2 wages). Y's tentative section 199 deduction is $115 (.09 x $1,282) subject to the W-2 wage limitation.

Example (3). Partnership with special allocations. (i) In general. X and Y are unrelated corporate partners in PRS and each is engaged in a trade or business. PRS is a partnership that engages in a domestic production activity and other activities. In general, X and Y share all partnership items of income, gain, loss, deduction, and credit equally, except that 80% of the wage expense of PRS and 20% of PRS's other expenses are specially allocated to X. Under all the facts and circumstances, these special allocations have substantial economic effect under section 704(b). In the 2010 taxable year, PRS's only wage expense is $2,000 for marketing, which is not included in CGS. PRS has $8,000 of gross receipts ($6,000 of which is DPGR), $4,000 of CGS ($3,500 of which is allocable to DPGR), and $3,000 of deductions (comprised of $2,000 of wage expense for marketing and $1,000 of other expenses). X qualifies for and uses the simplified deduction method under § 1.199-4(e). Y does not qualify to use that method and, therefore, must use the section 861 method under § 1.199-4(d). In the 2010 taxable year, X has gross receipts attributable to non-partnership trade or business activities of $1,000 and wage expense of $200. None of X's non-PRS gross receipts is DPGR. For purposes of this Example 3, with regard to both X and PRS, paragraph (e)(1) wages equal wage expense for the 2010 taxable year.

(ii) Allocation and apportionment of costs. Under the partnership agreement, X's distributive share of the Federal income tax items of PRS is $1,250 of gross income attributable to DPGR ($3,000 DPGR-$1,750 allocable CGS), $750 of gross income attributable to non-DPGR ($1,000 non-DPGR-$250 allocable CGS), and $1,800 of deductions (comprised of X's special allocations of $1,600 of wage expense ($2,000 x 80%) for marketing and $200 of other expenses ($1,000 x 20%)). Under the simplified deduction method, X apportions $1,200 of other deductions to DPGR ($2,000 ($1,800 from the partnership and $200 from non-partnership activities) x ($3,000 DPGR/$5,000 total gross receipts)). Accordingly, X's QPAI is $50 ($3,000 DPGR - $1,750 CGS-$1,200 of deductions). X has $1,800 of paragraph (e)(1) wages ($1,600 (X's 80% share) from PRS + $200 (X's own non-PRS paragraph (e)(1) wages)). To calculate its W-2 wages, X must determine how much of this $1,800 is properly allocable under § 1.199-2(e)(2) to X's total DPGR (including X's share of DPGR from PRS). Thus, X's tentative section 199 deduction for the 2010 taxable year is $5 (.09 x $50), subject to the W-2 wage limitation (50% of X's W-2 wages).

Example (4). Partnership with no paragraph (e)(1) wages. (i) Facts. A and B, both individuals, are partners in PRS. PRS is a partnership that engages in manufacturing activities that generate both DPGR and non-DPGR. A and B share all items of income, gain, loss, deduction, and credit equally. For the 2010 taxable year, PRS has total gross receipts of $2,000 ($1,000 of which is DPGR), CGS of $400 and deductions of $800. PRS has no paragraph (e)(1) wages. Each partner's distributive share of PRS's Federal income tax items is $500 DPGR, $500 non-DPGR, $200 CGS, and $400 of deductions. A has trade or business activities outside of PRS (non-PRS activities). With respect to those activities, A has total gross receipts of $1,000 ($500 of which is DPGR), CGS of $400 (including $50 of paragraph (e)(1) wages), and deductions of $200 for the 2010 taxable year. B has no trade or business activities outside of PRS. A and B each use the small business simplified overall method under § 1.199-4(f).

(ii) A's QPAI. A's total CGS and deductions apportioned to DPGR equal $600 (($1,200 ($200 PRS CGS + $400 non-PRS CGS + $400 PRS deductions + $200 non-PRS trade or business deductions)) x ($1,000 total DPGR ($500 from PRS + $500 from non-PRS activities)/$2,000 total gross receipts ($1,000 from PRS + $1,000 from non-PRS activities))). Accordingly, A's QPAI is $400 ($1,000 DPGR ($500 from PRS + $500 from non-PRS activities) - $600 CGS and deductions).

(iii) A's W-2 wages and section 199 deduction. A has $50 of paragraph (e)(1) wages ($0 from PRS + $50 from A's non-PRS activities). To calculate A's W-2 wages, A determines, under a reasonable method satisfactory to the Secretary, that $40 of this $50 is properly allocable under § 1.199-2(e)(2) to A's DPGR from PRS and non-PRS activities. A's tentative section 199 deduction is $36 (.09 x $400), subject to the W-2 wage limitation of $20 (50% of W-2 wages of $40). Thus, A's section 199 deduction is $20.

(iv) B's QPAI and section 199 deduction. B's CGS and deductions apportioned to DPGR equal $300 (($200 PRS CGS + $400 PRS deductions) x ($500 DPGR from PRS /$1,000 total gross receipts from PRS)). Accordingly, B's QPAI is $200 ($500 DPGR - $300 CGS and deductions). B's tentative section 199 deduction is $18 (.09 x $200), subject to the W-2 wage limitation. In this case, however, the limitation is $0, because B has no paragraph (e)(1) wages. Thus, B's section 199 deduction is $0.

Example (5). Guaranteed payment. (i) Facts. The facts are the same as in Example 4, except that in 2010 PRS also makes a guaranteed payment of $200 to A for services rendered by A (see section 707(c)), and PRS incurs $200 of wage expense for employees' salary, which is included within the $400 of CGS (in this case the wage expense of $200 equals PRS's paragraph (e)(1) wages). The guaranteed payment is taxable to A as ordinary income and is properly deducted by PRS under section 162. Pursuant to § 1.199-3(p), A may not treat any part of this payment as DPGR. Accordingly, PRS has total gross receipts of $2,000 ($1,000 of which is DPGR), CGS of $400 (including $200 of wage expense) and deductions of $1,000 (including the $200 guaranteed payment) for the 2010 taxable year. Each partner's distributive share of the items of the partnership is $500 DPGR, $500 non-DPGR, $200 CGS (including $100 of wage expense), and $500 of deductions.

(ii) A's QPAI and W-2 wages. A's total CGS and deductions apportioned to DPGR equal $591 ($1,300 ($200 PRS CGS + $400 non-PRS CGS + $500 PRS deductions + $200 non-PRS trade or business deductions) x ($1,000 total DPGR ($500 from PRS + $500 from non-PRS activities)/$2,200 total gross receipts ($1,000 from PRS + $200 guaranteed payment + $1,000 from non-PRS activities))). Accordingly, A's QPAI is $409 ($1,000 DPGR-$591 CGS and other deductions). A's total paragraph (e)(1) wages are $150 ($100 from PRS + $50 from non-PRS activities). To calculate its W-2 wages, A must determine how much of this $150 is properly allocable under § 1.199-2(e)(2) to A's total DPGR from PRS and non-PRS activities. A's tentative section 199 deduction is $37 (.09 x $409), subject to the W-2 wage limitation (50% of W-2 wages).

(iii) B's QPAI and W-2 wages. B's QPAI is $150 ($500 DPGR-$350 CGS and other deductions). B has $100 of paragraph (e)(1) wages (all from PRS). To calculate its W-2 wages, B must determine how much of this $100 is properly allocable under § 1.199-2(e)(2) to B's total DPGR. B's tentative section 199 deduction is $14 (.09 x $150), subject to the W-2 wage limitation (50% of B's W-2 wages).

(c) S corporations. *(1) In general.* (i) Determination at shareholder level. The section 199 deduction with respect to the qualified production activities of an S corporation is determined at the shareholder level. As a result, each shareholder must compute its deduction separately. The section 199 deduction has no effect on the adjusted basis of a shareholder's stock in an S corporation. Except as provided by publication pursuant to paragraph (c)(1)(ii) of this section, for purposes of this section, each shareholder is allocated, in accordance with section 1366, its pro rata share of S corporation items (including items of income, gain, loss, and deduction), CGS allocated to such items of income, and gross receipts included in such items of income, even if the shareholder's share of CGS and other deductions and losses exceeds DPGR. Except as provided by publication under paragraph (c)(1)(ii) of this section, to determine its section 199 deduction for the taxable year, the shareholder aggregates its pro rata share of such items, to the extent they are not otherwise disallowed by the Code, with those items it incurs outside the S corporation (whether directly or indirectly) for purposes of allocating and apportioning deductions to DPGR and computing its QPAI.

(ii) Determination at entity level. The Secretary may, by publication in the Internal Revenue Bulletin (see § 601.601(d)(2)(ii)(b) of this chapter), permit an S corporation to calculate a shareholder's share of QPAI and W-2 wages at the entity level, instead of allocating to the shareholder, in accordance with section 1366, the shareholder's pro rata share of S corporation items (including items of income, gain, loss, and deduction) and paragraph (e)(1) wages. If an S corporation does calculate QPAI at the entity level—

(A) Each shareholder is allocated its share of QPAI (subject to the limitations of paragraph (c)(2) of this section) and W-2 wages from the S corporation, which are combined with the shareholder's QPAI and W-2 wages from other sources, if any;

(B) For purposes of computing the shareholder's QPAI under §§ 1.199-1 through 1.199-8, a shareholder does not take into account the items from the S corporation (for example, a shareholder does not take into account items from the S corporation in determining whether a threshold or de minimis rule applies or in allocating and apportioning deductions) in calculating its QPAI from other sources;

(C) A shareholder generally does not recompute its share of QPAI from the S corporation using another method; however, the shareholder might have to adjust its share of QPAI from the S corporation to take into account certain disallowed losses or deductions, or the allowance of suspended losses or deductions; and

(D) A shareholder's share of QPAI from an S corporation may be less than zero.

(2) Disallowed losses or deductions. Except as provided by publication in the Internal Revenue Bulletin (see § 601.601(d)(2)(ii)(b) of this chapter), losses or deductions of the S corporation are taken into account in computing the shareholder's QPAI for a taxable year only if, and to the extent that, the shareholder's pro rata share of the losses or deductions from all of the S corporation's activities is not disallowed by section 465, 469, or 1366(d), or any other provision of the Code. If only a portion of the shareholder's share of the losses or deductions from an S corporation is allowed for a taxable year, a proportionate share of those allowed losses or deductions that are allocated to the S corporation's qualified production activities, determined in a manner consistent with sections 465, 469, and 1366(d), and any other applicable provision of the Code, is taken into account in computing QPAI for that taxable year. To the extent that any of the disallowed losses or deductions are allowed in a later taxable year under section 465, 469, or 1366(d), or any other provision of the Code, the shareholder takes into account a proportionate share of those allowed losses or deductions that are allocated to the S corporation's qualified production activities in computing the shareholder's QPAI for that later taxable year. Losses or deductions of the S corporation that are disallowed for taxable years beginning on or before December 31, 2004, however, are not taken into account in a later taxable year for purposes of computing the shareholder's QPAI for that later taxable year, whether or not the losses or deductions are allowed for other purposes.

(3) Shareholder's share of paragraph (e)(1) wages. Under section 199(d)(1)(A)(iii), an S corporation shareholder's share of the paragraph (e)(1) wages of the S corporation for purposes of determining the shareholder's W-2 wage limitation equals the shareholder's allocable share of those wages. Except as provided by publication in the Internal Revenue Bulletin (see § 601.601(d)(2)(ii)(b) of this chapter), the S corporation must allocate the paragraph (e)(1) wages among the shareholders in the same manner it allocates wage expense among those shareholders. The shareholder then must add its share of the paragraph (e)(1) wages from the S corporation to the shareholder's paragraph (e)(1) wages from other sources, if any, and then must determine the portion of

those total paragraph (e)(1) wages allocable to DPGR to compute the shareholder's W-2 wages. See § 1.199-2(e)(2) for the computation of W-2 wages and for the proper allocation of such wages to DPGR.

(4) Transition rule for definition of W-2 wages and for W-2 wage limitation. If an S corporation and any of its shareholders have different taxable years, only one of which begins after May 17, 2006, the definition of W-2 wages of the S corporation and the section 199(d)(1)(A)(iii) rule for determining a shareholder's share of wages from that S corporation is determined under the law applicable to S corporations based on the beginning date of the S corporation's taxable year. Thus, for example, for the short taxable year of an S corporation beginning after May 17, 2006, and ending in 2006, a shareholder's share of W-2 wages from the S corporation is determined under section 199(d)(1)(A)(iii) for taxable years beginning after May 17, 2006, even if that shareholder's taxable year began on or before May 17, 2006.

(d) Grantor trusts. To the extent that the grantor or another person is treated as owning all or part (the owned portion) of a trust under sections 671 through 679, such person (owner) computes its QPAI with respect to the owned portion of the trust as if that QPAI had been generated by activities performed directly by the owner. Similarly, for purposes of the W-2 wage limitation, the owner of the trust takes into account the owner's share of the paragraph (e)(1) wages of the trust that are attributable to the owned portion of the trust. The provisions of paragraph (e) of this section do not apply to the owned portion of a trust.

(e) Non-grantor trusts and estates. *(1) Allocation of costs.* The trust or estate calculates each beneficiary's share (as well as the trust's or estate's own share, if any) of QPAI and W-2 wages from the trust or estate at the trust or estate level. The beneficiary of a trust or estate may not recompute its share of QPAI or W-2 wages from the trust or estate by using another method to reallocate the trust's or estate's qualified production costs or paragraph (e)(1) wages, or otherwise. Except as provided in paragraph (d) of this section, the QPAI of a trust or estate must be computed by allocating expenses described in section 199(d)(5) in one of two ways, depending on the classification of those expenses under § 1.652(b)-3. Specifically, directly attributable expenses within the meaning of § 1.652(b)-3 are allocated pursuant to § 1.652(b)-3, and expenses not directly attributable within the meaning of § 1.652(b)-3 (other expenses) are allocated under the simplified deduction method of § 1.199-4(e) (unless the trust or estate does not qualify to use the simplified deduction method, in which case it must use the section 861 method of § 1.199-4(d) with respect to such other expenses). For this purpose, depletion and depreciation deductions described in section 642(e) and amortization deductions described in section 642(f) are treated as other expenses described in section 199(d)(5). Also for this purpose, the trust's or estate's share of other expenses from a lower-tier pass-thru entity is not directly attributable to any class of income (whether or not those other expenses are directly attributable to the aggregate pass-thru gross income as a class for purposes other than section 199). A trust or estate may not use the small business simplified overall method for computing its QPAI. See § 1.199-4(f)(5).

(2) Allocation among trust or estate and beneficiaries. (i) In general. The QPAI of a trust or estate (which will be less than zero if the CGS and deductions allocated and apportioned to DPGR exceed the trust's or estate's DPGR) and W-2 wages of a trust or estate are allocated to each beneficiary and to the trust or estate based on the relative proportion of the trust's or estate's distributable net income (DNI), as defined by section 643(a), for the taxable year that is distributed or required to be distributed to the beneficiary or is retained by the trust or estate. For this purpose, the trust or estate's DNI is determined with regard to the separate share rule of section 663(c), but without regard to section 199. To the extent that the trust or estate has no DNI for the taxable year, any QPAI and W-2 wages are allocated entirely to the trust or estate. A trust or estate is allowed the section 199 deduction in computing its taxable income to the extent that QPAI and W-2 wages are allocated to the trust or estate. A beneficiary of a trust or estate is allowed the section 199 deduction in computing its taxable income based on its share of QPAI and W-2 wages from the trust or estate, which are aggregated with the beneficiary's QPAI and W-2 wages from other sources, if any.

(ii) Treatment of items from a trust or estate reporting qualified production activities income. When, pursuant to this paragraph (e), a taxpayer must combine QPAI and W-2 wages from a trust or estate with the taxpayer's total QPAI and W-2 wages from other sources, the taxpayer, when applying §§ 1.199-1 through 1.199-8 to determine the taxpayer's total QPAI and W-2 wages from such other sources, does not take into account the items from such trust or estate. Thus, for example, a beneficiary of an estate that receives QPAI from the estate does not take into account the beneficiary's distributive share of the estate's gross receipts, gross income, or deductions when the beneficiary determines whether a threshold or de minimis rule applies or when the beneficiary allocates and apportions deductions in calculating its QPAI from other sources. Similarly, in determining the portion of the beneficiary's paragraph (e)(1) wages from other sources that is attributable to DPGR (thus, the W-2 wages from other sources), the beneficiary does not take into account DPGR and non-DPGR from the trust or estate.

(3) Transition rule for definition of W-2 wages and for W-2 wage limitation. The definition of W-2 wages of a trust or estate and the section 199(d)(1)(A)(iii) rule for determining the respective shares of wages from that trust or estate, and thus the beneficiary's share of W-2 wages from that trust or estate, is determined under the law applicable to pass-thru entities based on the beginning date of the taxable year of the trust or estate, regardless of the beginning date of the taxable year of the beneficiary.

(4) Example. The following example illustrates the application of this paragraph (e). Assume that the partnership, trust, and trust beneficiary all are calendar year taxpayers. The example reads as follows:

Example. Example. (i) Computation of DNI and inclusion and deduction amounts. (A) Trust's distributive share of partnership items. Trust, a complex trust, is a partner in PRS, a partnership that engages in activities that generate DPGR and non-DPGR. In 2010, PRS distributes $10,000 cash to Trust. PRS properly allocates (in the same manner as wage expense) paragraph (e)(1) wages of $3,000 to Trust. Trust's distributive share of PRS items, which are properly included in Trust's DNI, is as follows:

Gross income attributable to DPGR ($15,000 DPGR - $5,000 CGS (including wage expense of $1,000))	$10,000
Gross income attributable to non-DPGR ($5,000 other gross receipts - $0 CGS)	5,000
Selling expenses attributable to DPGR (includes wage expense of $2,000)	3,000

Other expenses (includes wage expense of $1,000)	2,000

(B) Trust's direct activities. In addition to its cash distribution in 2010 from PRS, Trust directly has the following items which are properly included in Trust's DNI:

Dividends	$10,000
Tax-exempt interest	10,000
Rents from commercial real property operated by Trust as a business	10,000
Real estate taxes	1,000
Trustee commissions	3,000
State income and personal property taxes	5,000
Wage expense for rental business	2,000
Other business expenses	1,000

(C) Allocation of deductions under § 1.652(b)-3. (1) Directly attributable expenses. In computing Trust's DNI for the taxable year, the distributive share of expenses of PRS are directly attributable under § 1.652(b)-3(a) to the distributive share of income of PRS. Accordingly, the $5,000 of CGS, $3,000 of selling expenses, and $2,000 of other expenses are subtracted from the gross receipts from PRS ($20,000), resulting in net income from PRS of $10,000. With respect to the Trust's direct expenses, $1,000 of the trustee commissions, the $1,000 of real estate taxes, and the $2,000 of wage expense are directly attributable under § 1.652(b)-3(a) to the rental income.

(2) Non-directly attributable expenses. Under § 1.652(b)-3(b), the trustee must allocate a portion of the sum of the balance of the trustee commissions ($2,000), state income and personal property taxes ($5,000), and the other business expenses ($1,000) to the $10,000 of tax-exempt interest. The portion to be attributed to tax-exempt interest is $2,222 ($8,000 x ($10,000 tax exempt interest/$36,000 gross receipts net of direct expenses)), resulting in $7,778 ($10,000-$2,222) of net tax-exempt interest. Pursuant to its authority recognized under § 1.652(b)-3(b), the trustee allocates the entire amount of the remaining $5,778 of trustee commissions, state income and personal property taxes, and other business expenses to the $6,000 of net rental income, resulting in $222 ($6,000-$5,778) of net rental income.

(D) Amounts included in taxable income. For 2010, Trust has DNI of $28,000 (net dividend income of $10,000 + net PRS income of $10,000 + net rental income of $222 + net tax-exempt income of $7,778). Pursuant to Trust's governing instrument, Trustee distributes 50%, or $14,000, of that DNI to B, an individual who is a discretionary beneficiary of Trust. Assume that there are no separate shares under Trust, and no distributions are made to any other beneficiary that year. Consequently, with respect to the $14,000 distribution B receives from Trust, B properly includes in B's gross income $5,000 of income from PRS, $111 of rents, and $5,000 of dividends, and properly excludes from B's gross income $3,889 of tax-exempt interest. Trust includes $20,222 in its adjusted total income and deducts $10,111 under section 661(a) in computing its taxable income.

(ii) Section 199 deduction. (A) Simplified deduction method. For purposes of computing the section 199 deduction for the taxable year, assume Trust qualifies for the simplified deduction method under § 1.199-4(e). The determination of Trust's QPAI under the simplified deduction method requires multiple steps to allocate costs. First, the Trust's expenses directly attributable to DPGR under § 1.652(b)-3(a) are subtracted from the Trust's DPGR. In this step, the directly attributable $5,000 of CGS and selling expenses of $3,000 are subtracted from the $15,000 of DPGR from PRS. Second, the Trust's expenses directly attributable under § 1.652(b)-3(a) to non-DPGR from a trade or business are subtracted from the Trust's trade or business non-DPGR. In this step, $4,000 of Trust expenses directly allocable to the real property rental activity ($1,000 of real estate taxes, $1,000 of Trustee commissions, and $2,000 of wages) are subtracted from the $10,000 of rental income. Third, Trust must identify the portion of its other expenses that is attributable to Trust's trade or business activities, if any, because expenses not attributable to trade or business activities are not taken into account in computing QPAI. In this step, in this example, the portion of the trustee commissions not directly attributable to the rental operation ($2,000) is directly attributable to non-trade or business activities. In addition, the state income and personal property taxes are not directly attributable under § 1.652(b)-3(a) to either trade or business or non-trade or business activities, so the portion of those taxes not attributable to either the PRS interests or the rental operation is not a trade or business expense and, thus, is not taken into account in computing QPAI. The portion of the state income and personal property taxes that is treated as an other trade or business expense is $3,000 ($5,000 x $30,000 total trade or business gross receipts/$50,000 total gross receipts). Fourth, Trust then allocates its other trade or business expenses (not directly attributable under § 1.652(b)-3(a)) between DPGR and non-DPGR on the basis of its total gross receipts from the conduct of a trade or business ($20,000 from PRS + $10,000 rental income). Thus, Trust combines its non-directly attributable (other) business expenses ($2,000 from PRS + $4,000 ($1,000 of other business expenses + $3,000 of income and property taxes allocated to a trade or business) from its own activities) and then apportions this total ($6,000) between DPGR and other receipts on the basis of Trust's total trade or business gross receipts ($6,000 of such expenses x $15,000 DPGR/$30,000 total trade or business gross receipts = $3,000). Thus, for purposes of computing Trust's and B's section 199 deduction, Trust's QPAI is $4,000 ($7,000 ($15,000 DPGR-$5,000 CGS-$3,000 selling expenses)-$3,000). Because the distribution of Trust's DNI to B equals one-half of Trust's DNI, Trust and B each has QPAI from PRS for purposes of the section 199 deduction of $2,000. B has $1,000 of QPAI from non-Trust activities that is added to the $2,000 QPAI from Trust for a total of $3,000 of QPAI.

(B) W-2 wages. For the 2010 taxable year, Trust chooses to use the wage expense safe harbor under § 1.199-2(e)(2)(ii) to determine its W-2 wages. For its taxable year ending December 31, 2010, Trust has $5,000 ($3,000 from PRS + $2,000 of Trust) of paragraph (e)(1) wages reported on 2010 Forms W-2. Trust's W-2 wages are $2,917, as shown in the following table:

Wage expense included in CGS directly attributable to DPGR	$1,000
Wage expense included in selling expense directly attributable to DPGR	2,000
Wage expense included in non-directly attributable deductions ($1,000 in wage expense x ($15,000 DPGR/$30,000 total trade or business gross receipts))	500
Wage expense allocable to DPGR	3,500
W-2 wages (($3,500 of wage expense allocable to DPGR/$6,000 of total wage expense) x $5,000 in paragraph (e)(1) wages)	$2,917

(C) Section 199 deduction computation. (1) B's computation. B is eligible to use the small business simplified overall method. Assume that B has sufficient adjusted gross income so that the section 199 deduction is not limited under section 199(a)(1)(B). Because the $14,000 Trust distribution to B equals one-half of Trust's DNI, B has W-2 wages from Trust of $1,459 (50% x $2,917). B has W-2 wages of $100 from trade or business activities outside of Trust and attributable to DPGR (computed without regard to B's interest in Trust pursuant to § 1.199-2(e)) for a total of $1,559 of W-2 wages. B has $1,000 of QPAI from non-Trust activities that is added to the $2,000 QPAI from Trust for a total of $3,000 of QPAI. B's tentative deduction is $270 (.09 x $3,000), limited under the W-2 wage limitation to $780 (50% x $1,559 W-2 wages). Accordingly, B's section 199 deduction for 2010 is $270.

(2) Trust's computation. Trust has sufficient adjusted gross income so that the section 199 deduction is not limited under section 199(a)(1)(B). Because the $14,000 Trust distribution to B equals one-half of Trust's DNI, Trust has W-2 wages of $1,459 (50% x $2,917). Trust's tentative deduction is $180 (.09 x $2,000 QPAI), limited under the W-2 wage limitation to $730 (50% x $1,459 W-2 wages). Accordingly, Trust's section 199 deduction for 2010 is $180.

(f) Gain or loss from the disposition of an interest in a pass-thru entity. DPGR generally does not include gain or loss recognized on the sale, exchange, or other disposition of an interest in a pass-thru entity. However, with respect to a partnership, if section 751(a) or (b) applies, then gain or loss attributable to assets of the partnership giving rise to ordinary income under section 751(a) or (b), the sale, exchange, or other disposition of which would give rise to DPGR, is taken into account in computing the partner's section 199 deduction. Accordingly, to the extent that cash or property received by a partner in a sale or exchange of all or part of its partnership interest is attributable to unrealized receivables or inventory items within the meaning of section 751(c) or (d), respectively, and the sale or exchange of the unrealized receivable or inventory items would give rise to DPGR if sold, exchanged, or otherwise disposed of by the partnership, the cash or property received by the partner is taken into account by the partner in determining its DPGR for the taxable year. Likewise, to the extent that a distribution of property to a partner is treated under section 751(b) as a sale or exchange of property between the partnership and the distributee partner, and any property deemed sold or exchanged would give rise to DPGR if sold, exchanged, or otherwise disposed of by the partnership, the deemed sale or exchange of the property must be taken into account in determining the partnership's and distributee partner's DPGR to the extent not taken into account under the qualifying in-kind partnership rules. See §§ 1.751-1(b) and 1.199-3(i)(7).

(g) No attribution of qualified activities. Except as provided in § 1.199-3(i)(7) regarding qualifying in-kind partnerships and § 1.199-3(i)(8) regarding EAG partnerships, an owner of a pass-thru entity is not treated as conducting the qualified production activities of the pass-thru entity, and vice versa. This rule applies to all partnerships, including partnerships that have elected out of subchapter K under section 761(a). Accordingly, if a partnership manufactures QPP within the United States, or produces a qualified film or produces utilities in the United States, and distributes or leases, rents, licenses, sells, exchanges, or otherwise disposes of such property to a partner who then, without performing its own qualifying activity, leases, rents, licenses, sells, exchanges, or otherwise disposes of such property, then the partner's gross receipts from this latter lease, rental, license, sale, exchange, or other disposition are treated as non-DPGR. In addition, if a partner manufactures QPP within the United States, or produces a qualified film or produces utilities in the United States, and contributes or leases, rents, licenses, sells, exchanges, or otherwise disposes of such property to a partnership which then, without performing its own qualifying activity, leases, rents, licenses, sells, exchanges, or otherwise disposes of such property, then the partnership's gross receipts from this latter disposition are treated as non-DPGR.

T.D. 9263, 5/24/2006, amend T.D. 9293, 10/18/2006, T.D. 9381, 2/14/2008.

Proposed § 1.199-5 Application of section 199 to pass-thru entities. [*For Preamble, see ¶ 152,713*]

(a) Partnerships. *(1) Determination at partner level.* The deduction allowable under § 1.199-1(a) (section 199 deduction) is determined at the partner level. As a result, each partner must compute its deduction separately. For purposes of this section, each partner is allocated, in accordance with sections 702 and 704, its share of partnership items (including items of income, gain, loss, and deduction), cost of goods sold (CGS) allocated to such items of income, and gross receipts that are included in such items of income, even if the partner's share of CGS and other deductions and losses exceeds domestic production gross receipts (DPGR) (as defined in § 1.199-3(a)). A partnership may specially allocate items of income, gain, loss, or deduction to its partners, subject to the rules of section 704(b) and the supporting regulations. To determine its section 199 deduction for the taxable year, a partner generally aggregates its distributive share of such items, to the extent they are not otherwise disallowed by the Internal Revenue Code, with those items it incurs outside the partnership (whether directly or indirectly) for purposes of allocating and apportioning deductions to DPGR and computing its qualified production activities income (QPAI) (as defined in § 1.199-1(c)). However, if a partnership uses the small business simplified overall method described in § 1.199-4(f), then each partner is allocated its share of QPAI and W-2 wages (as defined in § 1.199-2(f)), which (subject to the limitation under section 199(d)(1)(B)) are combined with the partner's QPAI and W-2 wages from other sources. Under this method, a partner's distributive share of QPAI from a partnership may be less than zero.

(2) Disallowed deductions. Deductions of a partnership that otherwise would be taken into account in computing the partner's section 199 deduction are taken into account only if and to the extent the partner's distributive share of those deductions from all of the partnership's activities is not disallowed by section 465, 469, 704(d), or any other provision of the Internal Revenue Code. If only a portion of the partner's distributive share of the losses or deductions is allowed for a taxable year, a proportionate share of those allowable losses or deductions that are allocated to the partnership's qualified production activities, determined in a manner consistent with sections 465, 469, 704(d), and any other applicable provision of the Internal Revenue Code, is taken into account in computing the section 199 deduction for that taxable year. To the extent that any of the disallowed losses or deductions are allowed in a later taxable year, the partner takes into account a proportionate share of those losses or deductions in computing its QPAI for that later taxable year.

(3) Partner's share of W-2 wages. Under section 199(d)(1)(B), a partner's share of W-2 wages of a partner-

ship for purposes of determining the partner's section 199(b) limitation is the lesser of the partner's allocable share of those wages (without regard to section 199(d)(1)(B)), or 2 times 9 percent (3 percent for taxable years beginning in 2005 or 2006, and 6 percent for taxable years beginning in 2007, 2008, or 2009) of the QPAI computed by taking into account only the items of the partnership allocated to the partner for the taxable year of the partnership. In general, this QPAI calculation is performed by the partner using the same cost allocation method that the partner uses in calculating the partner's section 199 deduction. However, if a partnership uses the small business simplified overall method described in § 1.199-4(f), the QPAI used by each partner to determine the wage limitation under section 199(d)(1)(B) is the same as the share of QPAI allocated to the partner. Each partner must compute its share of W-2 wages from the partnership in accordance with section 199(d)(1)(B) (with W-2 wages being allocated to the partner in the same manner as is wage expense), and then add that share to its W-2 wages from other sources, if any. The application of section 199(d)(1)(B) therefore means that if QPAI, computed by taking into account only the items of the partnership allocated to the partner for the taxable year, is not greater than zero, the partner may not take into account any W-2 wages of the partnership in computing the partner's section 199 deduction. See § 1.199-2 for the computation of W-2 wages, and paragraph (f) of this section for rules regarding pass-thru entities in a tiered structure.

(4) Examples. The following examples illustrate the application of this paragraph (a). Assume that each partner has sufficient adjusted gross income or taxable income so that the section 199 deduction is not limited under section 199(a)(1)(B); that the partnership and each of its partners (whether individual or corporate) are calendar year taxpayers; and that the amount of the partnership's W-2 wages equals wage expense for each taxable year. The examples read as follows:

Example (1). Section 861 method with interest expense. (i) Partnership Federal income tax items. X and Y, unrelated United States corporations, are each 50% partners in PRS, a partnership that engages in production activities that generate both DPGR and non-DPGR. X and Y share all items of income, gain, loss, deduction, and credit 50% each. PRS is not able to identify from its books and records CGS allocable to DPGR and non-DPGR. In this case, because CGS is definitely related under the facts and circumstances to all of PRS's gross income, apportionment of CGS between DPGR and non-DPGR based on gross receipts is appropriate. For 2010, the adjusted basis of PRS business assets is $5,000, $4,000 of which generate gross income attributable to DPGR and $1,000 of which generate gross income attributable to non-DPGR. For 2010, PRS has the following Federal income tax items:

DPGR	$3,000
Non-DPGR	3,000
CGS (includes $200 of W-2 wages)	3,240
Section 162 selling expenses (includes $300 of W-2 wages)	1,200
Interest expense (not included in CGS)	300

(ii) Allocation of PRS's items of income, gain, loss, deduction, or credit. X and Y each receive the following distributive share of PRS's items of income, gain, loss, deduction or credit, as determined under the principles of § 1.704-1(b)(1)(vii):

Gross income attributable to DPGR ($1,500 (DPGR) - $810 (allocable CGS, includes $50 of W-2 wages))	$690
Gross income attributable to non-DPGR ($1,500 (non-DPGR) - $810 (allocable CGS, includes $50 of W-2 wages))	690
Section 162 selling expenses (includes $150 of W-2 wages)	600
Interest expense (not included in CGS)	150

(iii) Determination of QPAI. (A) X's QPAI. Because the section 199 deduction is determined at the partner level, X determines its QPAI by aggregating, to the extent necessary, its distributive share of PRS's Federal income tax items with all other such items from all other, non-PRS-related activities. For 2010, X does not have any other such items. For 2010, the adjusted basis of X's non-PRS assets, all of which are investment assets, is $10,000. X's only gross receipts for 2010 are those attributable to the allocation of gross income from PRS. X allocates and apportions its deductible items to gross income attributable to DPGR under the section 861 method of § 1.199-4(d). In this case, the section 162 selling expenses (including W-2 wages) are definitely related to all of PRS's gross receipts. Based on the facts and circumstances of this specific case, apportionment of those expenses between DPGR and non-DPGR on the basis of PRS's gross receipts is appropriate. X elects to apportion its distributive share of interest expense under the tax book value method of § 1.861-9T(g). X's QPAI for 2010 is $366, as shown below:

DPGR	$1,500
CGS allocable to DPGR (includes $50 of W-2 wages)	(810)
Section 162 selling expenses (includes $75 of W-2 wages) ($600 x $1,500/$3,000)	(300)
Interest expense (not included in CGS) ($150 x $2,000 (X's share of PRS's DPGR assets)/ $12,500 (X's non-PRS assets and X's share of PRS assets))	(24)
X's QPAI	366

(B) Y's QPAI. (1) For 2010, in addition to the activities of PRS, Y engages in production activities that generate both DPGR and non-DPGR. Y is able to identify from its books and records CGS allocable to DPGR and to non-DPGR. For 2010, the adjusted basis of Y's non-PRS assets attributable to its production activities that generate DPGR is $8,000 and to other production activities that generate non-DPGR is $2,000. Y has no other assets. Y has the following Federal income tax items relating to its non-PRS activities:

Gross income attributable to DPGR ($1,500 (DPGR)-$900 (allocable CGS, includes $70 of W-2 wages))	$ 600
Gross income attributable to non-DPGR ($3,000 (other gross receipts) - $1,620 (allocable CGS, includes $150 of W-2 wages))	1,380
Section 162 selling expenses (includes $30 of W-2 wages)	540
Interest expense (not included in CGS)	90

(2) Y determines its QPAI in the same general manner as X. However, because Y has activities outside of PRS, Y must aggregate its distributive share of PRS's Federal income tax items with its own such items. Y allocates and apportions its deductible items to gross income attributable to DPGR under the section 861 method of § 1.199-4(d). In this case, Y's distributive share of PRS's section 162 selling ex-

penses (including W-2 wages), as well as those selling expenses from Y's non-PRS activities, are definitely related to all of its gross income. Based on the facts and circumstances of this specific case, apportionment of those expenses between DPGR and non-DPGR on the basis of Y's gross receipts is appropriate. Y elects to apportion its distributive share of interest expense under the tax book value method of § 1.861-9T(g). Y has $1,290 of gross income attributable to DPGR ($3,000 DPGR ($1,500 from PRS and $1,500 from non-PRS activities) -$1,710 CGS ($810 from PRS and $900 from non-PRS activities). Y's QPAI for 2010 is $642, as shown below:

DPGR ($1,500 from PRS and $1,500 from non-PRS activities)	$3,000
CGS allocable to DPGR ($810 from PRS and $900 from non-PRS activities) (includes $120 of W-2 wages)	(1,710)
Section 162 selling expenses (includes $180 of W-2 wages) ($1,140 ($600 from PRS and $540 from non-PRS activities) x ($1,500 PRS DPGR + $1,500 non-PRS DPGR)/($3,000 PRS total gross receipts + $4,500 non-PRS total gross receipts))	(456)
Interest expense (not included in CGS) ($240 ($150 from PRS and $90 from non-PRS activities) x $10,000 (Y's non-PRS DPGR assets and Y's share of PRS DPGR assets)/$12,500 (Y's non-PRS assets and Y's share of PRS assets))	(192)
Y's QPAI	642

(iv) PRS W-2 wages allocated to X and Y under section 199(d)(1)(B). Solely for purposes of calculating the PRS W-2 wages that are allocated to them under section 199(d)(1)(B) for purposes of the wage limitation of section 199(b), X and Y must separately determine QPAI taking into account only the items of PRS allocated to them. X and Y must use the same methods of allocation and apportionment that they use to determine their QPAI in paragraphs (iii)(A) and (B) of this Example 1, respectively. Accordingly, X and Y must apportion deductible section 162 selling expenses which includes W-2 wage expense on the basis of gross receipts, and apportion interest expense according to the tax book value method of § 1.861-9T(g).

(A) QPAI of X and Y, solely for this purpose, is determined by allocating and apportioning each partner's share of PRS expenses to each partner's share of PRS gross income of $690 attributable to DPGR ($1,500 DPGR-$810 CGS, apportioned based on gross receipts). Thus, QPAI of X and Y solely for this purpose is $270, as shown below:

DPGR	$1,500
CGS allocable to DPGR	(810)
Section 162 selling expenses (including W-2 wages) ($600 x ($1,500/$3,000))	(300)
Interest expense (not included in CGS) ($150 x $2,000 (partner's share of adjusted basis of PRS's DPGR assets)/$2,500 (partner's share of adjusted basis of total PRS assets))	(120)
QPAI	270

(B) X's and Y's shares of PRS's W-2 wages determined under section 199(d)(1)(B) for purposes of the wage limitation of section 199(b) are $49, the lesser of $250 (partner's allocable share of PRS's W-2 wages ($100 included in CGS, and $150 included in selling expenses) and $49 (2 x ($270 x .09)).

(v) Section 199 deduction determination. (A) X's tentative section 199 deduction is $33 (.09 x $366 (that is, QPAI determined at partner level)) subject to the wage limitation of $25 (50% x $49). Accordingly, X's section 199 deduction for 2010 is $25.

(B) Y's tentative section 199 deduction is $58 (.09 x $642 (that is, QPAI determined at the partner level) subject to the wage limitation of $150 (50% x ($49 (from PRS)) and $250 (from non-PRS activities)). Accordingly, Y's section 199 deduction for 2010 is $58.

Example (2). Section 861 method with R&E expense. (i) Partnership items of income, gain, loss, deduction or credit. X and Y, unrelated United States corporations, are partners in PRS, a partnership that engages in production activities that generate both DPGR and non-DPGR. Neither X nor Y is a member of an affiliated group. X and Y share all items of income, gain, loss, deduction, and credit 50% each. All of PRS's domestic production activities that generate DPGR are within Standard Industrial Classification (SIC) Industry Group AAA (SIC AAA). All of PRS's production activities that generate non-DPGR are within SIC Industry Group BBB (SIC BBB). PRS is not able to identify from its books and records CGS allocable to DPGR and to non-DPGR and, therefore, apportions CGS to DPGR and non-DPGR based on its gross receipts. PRS incurs $900 of research and experimentation expenses (R&E) that are deductible under section 174, $300 of which are performed with respect to SIC AAA and $600 of which are performed with respect to SIC BBB. None of the R&E is legally mandated R&E as described in § 1.861-17(a)(4) and none is included in CGS. PRS incurs section 162 selling expenses (that include W-2 wage expense) that are not includible in CGS and not directly allocable to any gross income. For 2010, PRS has the following Federal income tax items:

DPGR (all from sales of products within SIC AAA)	$3,000
Non-DPGR (all from sales of products within SIC BBB)	3,000
CGS (includes $200 of W-2 wages)	2,400
Section 162 selling expenses (includes $100 of W-2 wages)	840
Section 174 R&E-SIC AAA	300
Section 174 R&E-SIC BBB	600

(ii) Allocation of PRS's items of income, gain, loss, deduction, or credit. X and Y each receive the following distributive share of PRS's items of income, gain, loss, deduction, or credit, as determined under the principles of § 1.704-1(b)(1)(vii):

Gross income attributable to DPGR ($1,500 (DPGR) -$600 (CGS, includes $50 of W-2 wages))	$900
Gross income attributable to non-DPGR ($1,500 (other gross receipts) - $600 (CGS, includes $50 of W-2 wages))	900
Section 162 selling expenses (includes $50 of W-2 wages)	420
Section 174 R&E-SIC AAA	150
Section 174 R&E-SIC BBB	300

(iii) Determination of QPAI. (A) X's QPAI. Because the section 199 deduction is determined at the partner level, X determines its QPAI by aggregating, to the extent necessary, its distributive shares of PRS's Federal income tax items with all other such items from all other, non-PRS-related activities. For 2010, X does not have any other such tax items.

X's only gross receipts for 2010 are those attributable to the allocation of gross income from PRS. As stated, all of PRS's domestic production activities that generate DPGR are within SIC AAA. X allocates and apportions its deductible items to gross income attributable to DPGR under the section 861 method of § 1.199-4(d). In this case, the section 162 selling expenses (including W-2 wages) are definitely related to all of PRS's gross income. Based on the facts and circumstances of this specific case, apportionment of those expenses between DPGR and non-DPGR on the basis of PRS's gross receipts is appropriate. For purposes of apportioning R&E, X elects to use the sales method as described in § 1.861-17(c). Because X has no direct sales of products, and because all of PRS's SIC AAA sales attributable to X's share of PRS's gross income generate DPGR, all of X's share of PRS's section 174 R&E attributable to SIC AAA is taken into account for purposes of determining X's QPAI. Thus, X's total QPAI for 2010 is $540, as shown below:

DPGR (all from sales of products within SIC AAA)	$1,500
CGS (includes $50 of W-2 wages)	(600)
Section 162 selling expenses (including W-2 wages) ($420 x ($1,500 DPGR/$3,000 total gross receipts))	(210)
Section 174 R&E-SIC AAA	(150)
X's QPAI	540

(B) Y's QPAI. (1) For 2010, in addition to the activities of PRS, Y engages in domestic production activities that generate both DPGR and non-DPGR. With respect to those non-PRS activities, Y is not able to identify from its books and records CGS allocable to DPGR and to non-DPGR. In this case, because CGS is definitely related under the facts and circumstances to all of Y's non-PRS gross receipts, apportionment of CGS between DPGR and non-DPGR based on Y's non-PRS gross receipts is appropriate. For 2010, Y has the following non-PRS Federal income tax items:

DPGR (from sales of products within SIC AAA)	$1,500
DPGR (from sales of products within SIC BBB)	1,500
Non-DPGR (from sales of products within SIC BBB)	3,000
CGS (allocated to DPGR within SIC AAA) (includes $56 of W-2 wages)	750
CGS (allocated to DPGR within SIC BBB) (includes $56 of W-2 wages)	750
CGS (allocated to non-DPGR within SIC BBB) (includes $113 of W-2 wages)	1,500
Section 162 selling expenses (includes $30 of W-2 wages)	540
Section 174 R&E-SIC AAA	300
Section 174 R&E-SIC BBB	450

(2) Because Y has DPGR as a result of activities outside PRS, Y must aggregate its distributive share of PRS's Federal income tax items with such items from all its other, non-PRS-related activities. Y allocates and apportions its deductible items to gross income attributable to DPGR under the section 861 method of § 1.199-4(d). In this case, the section 162 selling expenses (including W-2 wages) are definitely related to all of Y's gross income. Based on the facts and circumstances of the specific case, apportionment of such expenses between DPGR and non-DPGR on the basis of Y's gross receipts is appropriate. For purposes of apportioning R&E, Y elects to use the sales method as described in § 1.861-17(c).

(3) With respect to sales that generate DPGR, Y has gross income of $2,400 ($4,500 DPGR ($1,500 from PRS and $3,000 from non-PRS activities)-$2,100 CGS ($600 from sales of products by PRS and $1,500 from non-PRS activities)). Because all of the sales in SIC AAA generate DPGR, all of Y's share of PRS's section 174 R&E attributable to SIC AAA and the section 174 R&E attributable to SIC AAA that Y incurs in its non-PRS activities are taken into account for purposes of determining Y's QPAI. Because only a portion of the sales within SIC BBB generate DPGR, only a portion of the section 174 R&E attributable to SIC BBB is taken into account in determining Y's QPAI. Thus, Y's QPAI for 2010 is $1,282, as shown below:

DPGR ($4,500 DPGR ($1,500 from PRS and $3,000 from non-PRS activities	$4,500
CGS ($600 from sales of products by PRS and $1,500 from non-PRS activities	(2,100)
Section 162 selling expenses (including W-2 wages) ($420 from PRS + $540 from non-PRS activities) x ($4,500 DPGR/$9,000 total gross receipts))	(480)
Section 174 R&E-SIC AAA ($150 from PRS and $300 from non-PRS activities)	(450)
Section 174 R&E-SIC BBB ($300 from PRS + $450 from non-PRS activities) x ($1,500 DPGR/$6,000 total gross receipts allocated to SIC BBB)	(188)
Y's QPAI	1,282

(iv) PRS W-2 wages allocated to X and Y under section 199(d)(1)(B). Solely for purposes of calculating the PRS W-2 wages that are allocated to X and Y under section 199(d)(1)(B) for purposes of the wage limitation of section 199(b), X and Y must separately determine QPAI taking into account only the items of PRS allocated to them. X and Y must use the same methods of allocation and apportionment that they use to determine their QPAI in paragraphs (iii)(A) and (B) of this Example 2, respectively. Accordingly, X and Y must apportion section 162 selling expense which includes W-2 wage expense on the basis of gross receipts, and apportion section 174 R&E expense under the sales method as described in § 1.861-17(c).

(A) QPAI of X and Y, solely for this purpose, is determined by allocating and apportioning each partner's share of PRS expenses to each partner's share of PRS gross income of $900 attributable to DPGR ($1,500 DPGR-$600 CGS, allocated based on PRS's gross receipts). Because all of PRS's SIC AAA sales generate DPGR, all of X's and Y's shares of PRS's section 174 R&E attributable to SIC AAA is taken into account for purposes of determining X's and Y's QPAI. None of PRS's section 174 R&E attributable to SIC BBB is taken into account because PRS has no DPGR within SIC BBB. Thus, X and Y each has QPAI, solely for this purpose, of $540, as shown below:

DPGR (all from sales of products within SIC AAA)	$1,500
CGS (includes $50 of W-2 wages	(600)
Section 162 selling expenses (including W-2 wages) ($420 x $1,500/$3,000)	(210)
Section 174 R&E-SIC AAA	(150)
QPAI	540

(B) X's and Y's shares of PRS's W-2 wages determined under section 199(d)(1)(B) for purposes of the wage limitation of section 199(b) are $97, the lesser of $150 (partner's allocable share of PRS's W-2 wages ($100 included in CGS, and $50 included in selling expenses)) and $97 (2 x ($540 x .09)).

(v) Section 199 deduction determination. (A) X's tentative section 199 deduction is $49 (.09 x $540 (QPAI determined at partner level)) subject to the wage limitation of $49 (50% x $97). Accordingly, X's section 199 deduction for 2010 is $49.

(B) Y's tentative section 199 deduction is $115 (.09 x $1,282 (QPAI determined at partner level) subject to the wage limitation of $176 (50% x $352 ($97 from PRS + $255 from non-PRS activities)). Accordingly, Y's section 199 deduction for 2010 is $115.

Example (3). Simplified deduction method with special allocations. (i) In general. X and Y are unrelated corporate partners in PRS. PRS engages in a domestic production activity and other activities. In general, X and Y share all partnership items of income, gain, loss, deduction, and credit equally, except that 80% of the wage expense of PRS and 20% of PRS's other expenses are specially allocated to X (substantial economic effect under section 704(b) is presumed). In the 2010 taxable year, PRS's only wage expense is $2,000 for marketing, which is not included in CGS. PRS has $8,000 of gross receipts ($6,000 of which is DPGR), $4,000 of CGS ($3,500 of which is allocable to DPGR), and $3,000 of deductions (comprised of $2,000 of wages for marketing and $1,000 of other expenses). X qualifies for and uses the simplified deduction method under § 1.199-4(e). Y does not qualify to use that method and therefore, must use the section 861 method under § 1.199-4(d). In the 2010 taxable year, X has gross receipts attributable to non-partnership activities of $1,000 and wages of $200. None of X's non-PRS gross receipts is DPGR.

(ii) Allocation and apportionment of costs. Under the partnership agreement, X's distributive share of the items of the partnership is $1,250 of gross income attributable to DPGR ($3,000 DPGR-$1,750 allocable CGS), $750 of gross income attributable to non-DPGR ($1,000 non-DPGR-$250 allocable CGS), and $1,800 of deductions (comprised of X's special allocations of $1,600 of wage expense for marketing and $200 of other expenses). Under the simplified deduction method, X apportions $1,200 of other deductions to DPGR ($2,000 ($1,800 from the partnership and $200 from non-partnership activities) x ($3,000 DPGR/$5,000 total gross receipts)). Accordingly, X's QPAI is $50 ($3,000 DPGR-$1,750 CGS -$1,200 of deductions). However, in determining the section 199(d)(1)(B) wage limitation, QPAI is computed taking into account only the items of the partnership allocated to the partner for the taxable year of the partnership. Thus, X apportions $1,350 of deductions to DPGR ($1,800 x ($3,000 DPGR/ $4,000 total gross receipts from PRS)). Accordingly, X's QPAI for purposes of the section 199(d)(1)(B) wage limitation is $0 ($3,000 DPGR-$1,750 CGS -$1,350 of deductions). X's share of PRS's W-2 wages is $0, the lesser of $1,600 (X's 80% allocable share of $2,000 of wage expense for marketing) or $0 (2 x ($0 QPAI x .09)). X's tentative deduction is $5 ($50 QPAI x .09), subject to the section 199(b)(1) wage limitation of $100 (50% x $200 ($0 of PRS-related W-2 wages + $200 of non-PRS W-2 wages)). Accordingly, X's total section 199 deduction for the 2010 taxable year is $5.

Example (4). Small business simplified overall method. A, an individual, and X, a corporation, are partners in PRS. PRS engages in manufacturing activities that generate both DPGR and non-DPGR. A and X share all items of income, gain, loss, deduction, and credit equally. In the 2010 taxable year, PRS has total gross receipts of $2,000 ($1,000 of which is DPGR), CGS of $800 (including $400 of W-2 wages), and deductions of $800. A and PRS use the small business simplified overall method under § 1.199-4(f). X uses the section 861 method. Under the small business simplified overall method, PRS's CGS and deductions apportioned to DPGR equal $800 (($800 CGS plus $800 of other deductions) x ($1,000 DPGR/$2,000 total gross receipts)). Accordingly, PRS's QPAI is $200 ($1,000 DPGR-$800 CGS and other deductions). Under the partnership agreement, PRS's QPAI is allocated $100 to A and $100 to X. A's share of partnership W-2 wages for purposes of the section 199(d)(1)(B) limitation is $18, the lesser of $200 (A's 50% allocable share of PRS's $400 of W-2 wages) or $18 (2 x ($100 QPAI x .09)). A's tentative deduction is $9 ($100 QPAI x .09), subject to the section 199(b)(1) wage limitation of $9 (50% x $18). Assuming that A engages in no other activities generating DPGR, A's total section 199 deduction for the 2010 taxable year is $9. X must use $100 of QPAI and $18 of W-2 wages to determine its section 199 deduction using the section 861 method.

(b) S corporations. *(1) Determination at shareholder level.* The section 199 deduction is determined at the shareholder level. As a result, each shareholder must compute its deduction separately. For purposes of this section, each shareholder is allocated, in accordance with section 1366, its pro rata share of S corporation items (including items of income, gain, loss, and deduction), CGS allocated to such items of income, and gross receipts included in such items of income, even if the shareholder's share of CGS and other deductions and losses exceeds DPGR. To determine its section 199 deduction for the taxable year, the shareholder generally aggregates its pro rata share of such items, to the extent they are not otherwise disallowed by the Internal Revenue Code, with those items it incurs outside the S corporation (whether directly or indirectly) for purposes of allocating and apportioning deductions to DPGR and computing its QPAI. However, if an S corporation uses the small business simplified overall method described in § 1.199-4(f), then each shareholder is allocated its share of QPAI and W-2 wages, which (subject to the limitation under section 199(d)(1)(B)) are combined with the shareholder's QPAI and W-2 wages from other sources. Under this method, a shareholder's share of QPAI from an S corporation may be less than zero.

(2) Disallowed deductions. Deductions of the S corporation that otherwise would be taken into account in computing the shareholder's section 199 deduction are taken into account only if and to the extent the shareholder's pro rata share of the losses or deductions from all of the S corporation's activities are not disallowed by section 465, 469, 1366(d), or any other provision of the Internal Revenue Code. If only a portion of the shareholder's pro rata share of the losses or deductions is allowed for a taxable year, a proportionate share of the losses or deductions allocated to the S corporation's qualified production activities, determined in a manner consistent with sections 465, 469, 1366(d), and any other applicable provision of the Internal Revenue Code, is taken into account in computing the section 199 deduction for that taxable year. To the extent that any of the disallowed losses or deductions is allowed in a later taxable year, the shareholder takes into account a proportionate share of those losses or deductions in computing its QPAI for that later taxable year.

(3) Shareholder's share of W-2 wages. Under section 199(d)(1)(B), an S corporation shareholder's share of the W-2 wages of the S corporation for purposes of determining the

shareholder's section 199(b) limitation is the lesser of the shareholder's allocable share of those wages (without regard to section 199(d)(1)(B)), or 2 times 9 percent (3 percent for taxable years beginning in 2005 or 2006, and 6 percent for taxable years beginning in 2007, 2008, or 2009) of the QPAI computed by taking into account only the items of the S corporation allocated to the shareholder for the taxable year. In general, this QPAI calculation is performed by the shareholder using the same cost allocation method that the shareholder uses in calculating the shareholder's section 199 deduction. However, if an S corporation uses the small business simplified overall method described in § 1.199-4(f), the QPAI used by each shareholder to determine the wage limitation under section 199(d)(1)(B) is the same as the share of QPAI allocated to the shareholder. Each shareholder must compute its share of W-2 wages from an S corporation in accordance with section 199(d)(1)(B) (with W-2 wages being allocated to the shareholder in the same manner as is wage expense), and then add that share to the shareholder's W-2 wages from other sources, if any. The application of section 199(d)(1)(B) therefore means that if QPAI, computed by taking into account only the items of the S corporation allocated to the shareholder for the taxable year, is not greater than zero, the shareholder may not take into account any W-2 wages of the S corporation in computing the shareholder's section 199 deduction. See § 1.199-2 for the computation of W-2 wages, and paragraph (f) of this section for rules regarding pass-thru entities in a tiered structure.

(c) Grantor trusts. To the extent that the grantor or another person is treated as owning all or part (the owned portion) of a trust under sections 671 through 679, the owner computes its QPAI with respect to the owned portion of the trust as if that QPAI had been generated by activities performed directly by the owner. Similarly, for purposes of the section 199(b) wage limitation, the owner of the trust takes into account the owner's share of the W-2 wages of the trust that are attributable to the owned portion of the trust. The section 199(d)(1)(B) wage limitation is not applicable to the owned portion of the trust.

(d) Non-grantor trusts and estates. *(1) Computation of section 199 deduction.* Except as provided in paragraph (c) of this section, solely for purposes of determining the section 199 deduction for the taxable year, the QPAI of a trust or estate must be computed by allocating expenses described in section 199(d)(5) under § 1.652(b)-3 with respect to directly attributable expenses, and under the simplified deduction method of § 1.199-4(e) with respect to other expenses described in section 199(d)(5) (unless the trust or estate does not qualify to use the simplified deduction method, in which case it must use the section 861 method of § 1.199-4(d) with respect to such other expenses). For this purpose, the trust's or estate's share of other expenses from a lower-tier pass-thru entity is not directly attributable to any class of income (whether or not those other expenses are directly attributable to the aggregate pass-thru gross income as a class for purposes other than section 199). A trust or estate may not use the small business simplified overall method for computing its QPAI. See § 1.199-4(f)(4). The QPAI (which will be less than zero if the CGS and deductions allocated and apportioned to DPGR exceed the trust's or estate's DPGR) and W-2 wages of the trust or estate are allocated to each beneficiary and to the trust or estate based on the relative proportion of the trust's or estate's distributable net income (DNI), as defined by section 643(a), for the taxable year that is distributed or required to be distributed to the beneficiary or is retained by the trust or estate. To the extent that the trust or estate has no DNI for the taxable year, any QPAI and W-2 wages are allocated entirely to the trust or estate. A trust or estate may claim the section 199 deduction in computing its taxable income to the extent that QPAI and W-2 wages are allocated to the trust or estate. A beneficiary of a trust or estate is allowed the section 199 deduction in computing its taxable income based on its share of QPAI and W-2 wages from the trust or estate, which (subject to the wage limitation of section 199(d)(1)(B)) are aggregated with the beneficiary's QPAI and W-2 wages from other sources. Each beneficiary must compute its share of W-2 wages from a trust or estate in accordance with section 199(d)(1)(B). The application of section 199(d)(1)(B) therefore means that if QPAI, computed by taking into account only the items of the trust or estate allocated to the beneficiary for the taxable year, is not greater than zero, the beneficiary may not take into account any W-2 wages of the trust or estate in computing the beneficiary's section 199 deduction. See paragraph (f) of this section for rules applicable to pass-thru entities in a tiered structure.

(2) Example. The following example illustrates the application of this paragraph (d). Assume that the partnership, trust, and trust beneficiary all are calendar year taxpayers. The example is as follows:

Example. (i) Computation of DNI and inclusion and deduction amounts. (A) Trust's distributive share of partnership items. Trust, a complex trust, is a partner in PRS, a partnership that engages in activities that generate DPGR and non-DPGR. In 2010, PRS distributes $10,000 to Trust. Trust's distributive share of PRS items, which are properly included in Trust's DNI, is as follows:

Gross income attributable to DPGR ($15,000 DPGR-$5,000 CGS (including W-2 wages of 1,000))	$10,000
Gross income attributable to other gross receipts ($5,000 other gross receipts-$0 CGS)	5,000
Selling expenses (includes W-2 wages of $2,000)	3,000
Other expenses (includes W-2 wages of $1,000)	2,000

(B) Trust's direct activities. In addition to receiving in 2010 the distribution from PRS, Trust also directly has the following items which are properly included in Trust's DNI:

Dividends	$10,000
Tax-exempt interest	10,000
Rents from commercial real property that is subject to a section 6166 election	10,000
Real estate taxes	1,000
Trustee commissions	3,000
State income and personal property taxes	5,000
W-2 wages	2,000
Other business expenses	1,000

(C) Allocation of deductions under § 1.652(b)-3. (1) Directly attributable expenses. In computing Trust's DNI for the taxable year, the distributive share of expenses of PRS are directly attributable under § 1.652(b)-3(a) to the distributive share of income of PRS. Accordingly, the $20,000 of gross receipts from PRS is reduced by $5,000 of CGS, $3,000 of selling expenses, and $2,000 of other expenses, resulting in net income from PRS of $10,000. With respect to the Trust's direct expenses, $1,000 of the trustee commissions, the $1,000 of real estate taxes, and the $2,000 of W-2 wages are directly attributable under § 1.652(b)-3(a) to the rental income.

(2) Non-directly attributable expenses. Under § 1.652(b)-3(b), the trustee must allocate a portion of the sum of the balance of the trustee commissions ($2,000), state income and personal property taxes ($5,000), and the other business expenses ($1,000) to the $10,000 of tax-exempt interest. The portion to be attributed to tax-exempt interest is $2,222 ($8,000 x ($10,000 tax exempt interest/$36,000 gross receipts net of direct expenses)), resulting in $7,778 ($10,000-$2,222) of net tax-exempt interest. Pursuant to its authority recognized under § 1.652(b)-3(b), the trustee allocates the entire amount of the remaining $5,778 of trustee commissions, state income and personal property taxes, and other business expenses to the $6,000 of net rental income, resulting in $222 ($6,000-$5,778) of net rental income.

(D) Amounts included in taxable income. For 2010, Trust has DNI of $28,000 (net dividend income of $10,000 + net PRS income of $10,000 + net rental income of $222 + net tax-exempt income of $7,778). Pursuant to Trust's governing instrument, Trustee distributes 50%, or $14,000, of that DNI to B, an individual who is a discretionary beneficiary of Trust. Assume that there are no separate shares under Trust, and no distributions are made to any other beneficiary that year. Consequently, with respect to the $14,000 distribution, B properly includes in B's gross income $5,000 of income from PRS, $111 of rents, and $5,000 of dividends, and properly excludes from B's gross income $3,889 of tax-exempt interest. Trust includes $20,222 in its adjusted total income and deducts $10,111 under section 661(a) in computing its taxable income.

(ii) Section 199 deduction. (A) Simplified deduction method. For purposes of computing the section 199 deduction for the taxable year, assume Trust qualifies for the simplified deduction method under § 1.199-4(e). Determining Trust's QPAI under the simplified deduction method requires a multi-step approach to allocating costs. In step 1, the Trust's DPGR is first reduced by the Trust's expenses directly attributable to DPGR under § 1.652(b)-3(a). In this step, the $15,000 of DPGR from PRS is reduced by the directly attributable $5,000 of CGS and selling expenses of $3,000. In step 2, Trust allocates its other business expenses on the basis of its total gross receipts. In this example, the portion of the trustee commissions not directly attributable to the rental operation, as well as the portion of the state income and personal property taxes not directly attributable to either the PRS interests or the rental operation, are not trade or business expenses and, thus, are ignored in computing QPAI. The portion of the state income and personal property taxes that is treated as other trade or business expenses is $3,000 ($5,000 x $30,000 total trade or business gross receipts/$50,000 total gross receipts). Trust then combines its non-directly attributable (other) expenses ($2,000 from PRS + $4,000 ($1,000 + $3,000) from its own activities) and then apportions this total between DPGR and other receipts on the basis of Trust's total gross receipts ($6,000 x $15,000 DPGR/$50,000 total gross receipts = $1,800). Thus, for purposes of computing Trust's and B's section 199 deduction, Trust's QPAI is $5,200 ($7,000 -$1,800). Because the distribution of Trust's DNI to B equals one-half of Trust's DNI, Trust and B each has QPAI from PRS for purposes of the section 199 deduction of $2,600.

(B) Section 199(d)(1)(B) wage limitation. The wage limitation under section 199(d)(1)(B) must be applied both at the Trust level and at B's level. After applying this limitation to the Trust's share of PRS's W-2 wages, Trust is allocated $990 of W-2 wages from PRS (the lesser of Trust's allocable share of PRS's W-2 wages ($4,000) or 2 x 9% of PRS's QPAI ($5,500)). PRS's QPAI for purposes of the section 199(d)(1)(B) limitation is determined by taking into account only the items of PRS allocated to Trust ($15,000 DPGR–($5,000 of CGS + $3,000 selling expenses + $1,500 of other expenses). For this purpose, the $1,500 of other expenses is determined by multiplying $2,000 of other expenses from PRS by $15,000 of DPGR from PRS, divided by $20,000 of total gross receipts from PRS. Trust adds this $990 of W-2 wages to Trust's own $2,000 of W-2 wages (thus, $2,990). Because the $14,000 distribution to B equals one-half of Trust's DNI, Trust and B each has W-2 wages of $1,495. After applying the section 199(d)(1)(B) wage limitation to B's share of the W-2 wages allocated from Trust, B has W-2 wages of $468 from Trust (lesser of $1,495 (allocable share of W-2 wages) or 2 x .09 x $2,600 (Trust's QPAI)). B has W-2 wages of $100 from non-Trust activities for a total of $568 of W-2 wages.

(C) Section 199 deduction computation. (1) B's computation. B is eligible to use the small business simplified overall method. Assume that B has sufficient adjusted gross income so that the section 199 deduction is not limited under section 199(a)(1)(B). B has $1,000 of QPAI from non-Trust activities which is added to the $2,600 QPAI from Trust for a total of $3,600 of QPAI. B's tentative deduction is $324 (.09 x $3,600) which is limited under section 199(b) to $284 (50% x $568 W-2 wages). Accordingly, B's section 199 deduction for 2010 is $284.

(2) Trust's computation. Trust has sufficient taxable income so that the section 199 deduction is not limited under section 199(a)(1)(B). Trust's tentative deduction is $234 (.09 x $2,600 QPAI) which is limited under section 199(b) to $748 (50% x $1,495 W-2 wages). Accordingly, Trust's section 199 deduction for 2010 is $234.

(e) Gain or loss from the disposition of an interest in a pass-thru entity. DPGR generally does not include gain or loss recognized on the sale, exchange, or other disposition of an interest in a pass-thru entity. However, with respect to partnerships, if section 751(a) or (b) applies, gain or loss attributable to assets of the partnership giving rise to ordinary income under section 751(a) or (b), the sale, exchange, or other disposition of which would give rise to DPGR, is taken into account in computing the partner's section 199 deduction. Accordingly, to the extent that money or property received by a partner in a sale or exchange for all or part of its partnership interest is attributable to unrealized receivables or inventory items within the meaning of section 751(c) or (d), respectively, and the sale or exchange of the unrealized receivable or inventory items would give rise to DPGR if sold or exchanged or otherwise disposed of by the partnership, the money or property received is taken into account by the partner in determining its DPGR for the taxable year. Likewise, to the extent that a distribution of property to a partner is treated under section 751(b) as a sale or exchange of property between the partnership and the distributee partner, and any property deemed sold or exchanged would give rise to DPGR if sold or exchanged by the partnership, the deemed sale or exchange of the property must be taken into account in determining the partnership's and distributee partner's DPGR. See § 1.751-1(b).

(f) Section 199(d)(1)(B) wage limitation and tiered structures. *(1) In general.* If a pass-thru entity owns an interest, directly or indirectly, in one or more pass-thru entities, the wage limitation of section 199(d)(1)(B) must be applied at each tier (that is, separately for each entity). Thus, at each tier, the owner of a pass-thru entity calculates the amounts described in sections 199(d)(1)(B)(i) (allocable share) and 199(d)(1)(B)(ii) (twice the applicable percentage of QPAI from that entity) separately with regard to its interest in that pass-thru entity.

(2) Share of W-2 wages. For purposes of section 199(d)(1)(B)(i) and section 199(b), the W-2 wages of the owner of an interest in a pass-thru entity (upper-tier entity) that owns an interest in one or more pass-thru entities (lower-tier entities) are equal to the sum of the owner's allocable share of W-2 wages of the upper-tier entity, as limited in accordance with section 199(d)(1)(B), and the owner's own W-2 wages. The upper-tier entity's W-2 wages are equal to the sum of the upper-tier entity's allocable share of W-2 wages of the next lower-tier entity, as limited in accordance with section 199(d)(1)(B), and the upper-tier entity's own W-2 wages. The W-2 wages of each lower-tier entity in a tiered structure, in turn, is computed as described in the preceding sentence. Although all wages paid during that taxable year are taken into account in computing QPAI, only the W-2 wages as described in § 1.199-2 are taken into account in computing the W-2 wage limitation.

(3) Example. The following example illustrates the application of this paragraph (f). Assume that each partnership and each partner (whether or not an individual) is a calendar year taxpayer. The example is as follows:

Example. (i) In 2010, A, an individual, owns a 50% interest in a partnership, UTP, which in turn owns a 50% interest in another partnership, LTP. All partnership items are allocated in proportion to these ownership percentages. Both partnerships are eligible for and use the small business simplified overall method under § 1.199-4(f). LTP has QPAI of $400 ($900 DPGR–$450 CGS (which includes W-2 wages of $100)–$50 other deductions). Before taking into account its distributive share from LTP, UTP has QPAI of ($500) ($500 DPGR–$500 CGS (which includes W-2 wages of $200)–$500 other deductions). UTP's distributive share of LTP's QPAI is $200.

(ii) UTP's share of LTP's W-2 wages for purposes of the section 199(d)(1)(B) limitation is $36, the lesser of $50 (UTP's allocable share of LTP's W-2 wages paid) or $36 (2 x ($200 QPAI x .09)). After taking into account its distributive share from LTP, UTP has QPAI of ($300) and W-2 wages of $236. A's distributive share of UTP's QPAI is ($150). A's limitation under section 199(d)(1)(B) with respect to A's interest in UTP is $0, the lesser of $118 (A's allocable share of UTP's W-2 wages paid) or $0 (because A's share of QPAI, ($150), is less than zero).

(g) No attribution of qualified activities. Except as provided in § 1.199-3(h)(7) regarding certain qualifying oil and gas partnerships and § 1.199-3(h)(8) regarding EAG partnerships, for purposes of section 199, an owner of a pass-thru entity is not treated as conducting the qualified production activities of the pass-thru entity, and vice versa. This rule applies to all partnerships, including partnerships that have elected out of subchapter K under section 761(a). Accordingly, if a partnership MPGE QPP within the United States, or otherwise produces a qualified film or utilities in the United States, and distributes or leases, rents, licenses, sells, exchanges, or otherwise disposes of the property to a partner who then leases, rents, licenses, sells, exchanges, or otherwise disposes of the property, the partner's gross receipts from this latter lease, rental, license, sale, exchange, or other disposition are not treated as DPGR under § 1.199-3. In addition, if a partner MPGE QPP within the United States, or otherwise produces a qualified film or utilities in the United States, and contributes or leases, rents, licenses, sells, exchanges, or otherwise disposes of the property to a partnership which then leases, rents, licenses, sells, exchanges, or otherwise disposes of the property, the partnership's gross receipts from this latter disposition are not treated as DPGR under § 1.199-3.

§ 1.199-6 Agricultural and horticultural cooperatives.

(a) In general. A patron who receives a qualified payment (as defined in paragraph (e) of this section) from a specified agricultural or horticultural cooperative (cooperative) (as defined in paragraph (f) of this section) is allowed a deduction under § 1.199-1(a) (section 199 deduction) for the taxable year the qualified payment is received for the portion of the cooperative's section 199 deduction passed through to the patron and identified by the cooperative in a written notice mailed to the person during the payment period described in section 1382(d). The provisions of this section apply solely for purposes of section 199 of the Internal Revenue Code (Code).

(b) Cooperative denied section 1382 deduction for portion of qualified payments. A cooperative must reduce its section 1382 deduction by an amount equal to the portion of any qualified payment that is attributable to the cooperative's section 199 deduction passed through to the patron.

(c) Determining cooperative's qualified production activities income and taxable income. For purposes of determining its section 199 deduction, the cooperative's qualified production activities income (QPAI) (as defined in § 1.199-1(c)) and taxable income are computed without taking into account any deduction allowable under section 1382(b) or (c) (relating to patronage dividends, per-unit retain allocations, and nonpatronage distributions).

(d) Special rule for marketing cooperatives. In the case of a cooperative engaged in the marketing of agricultural and/or horticultural products described in paragraph (f) of this section, the cooperative is treated as having manufactured, produced, grown, or extracted (MPGE) (as defined in § 1.199-3(e)) in whole or in significant part (as defined in § 1.199-3(g)) within the United States (as defined in § 1.199-3(h)) any agricultural or horticultural products marketed by the cooperative that its patrons have MPGE.

(e) Qualified payment. The term qualified payment means any amount of a patronage dividend or per-unit retain allocation, as described in section 1385(a)(1) or (3) received by a patron from a cooperative, that is attributable to the portion of the cooperative's QPAI, for which the cooperative is allowed a section 199 deduction. For this purpose, patronage dividends and per-unit retain allocations include any advances on patronage and per-unit retains paid in money during the taxable year.

(f) Specified agricultural or horticultural cooperative. A specified agricultural or horticultural cooperative means a cooperative to which Part I of subchapter T of the Code applies and the cooperative has MPGE in whole or significant part within the United States any agricultural or horticultural product, or has marketed agricultural or horticultural products. For this purpose, agricultural or horticultural products also include fertilizer, diesel fuel, and other supplies used in agricultural or horticultural production.

(g) Written notice to patrons. In order for a patron to qualify for the section 199 deduction, paragraph (a) of this section requires that the cooperative identify in a written notice the patron's portion of the section 199 deduction that is attributable to the portion of the cooperative's QPAI for which the cooperative is allowed a section 199 deduction. This written notice must be mailed by the cooperative to its patrons no later than the 15th day of the ninth month following the close of the taxable year. The cooperative may use the same written notice, if any, that it uses to notify patrons of their respective allocations of patronage dividends, or may use a separate timely written notice(s) to comply with this section. The cooperative must report the amount of the patron's section 199 deduction on Form 1099-PATR, "Taxable Distributions Received From Cooperatives," issued to the patron.

(h) Additional rules relating to passthrough of section 199 deduction. The cooperative may, at its discretion, pass through all, some, or none of the section 199 deduction to its patrons. A cooperative member of a federated cooperative may pass through the section 199 deduction it receives from the federated cooperative to its member patrons. Patrons may claim the section 199 deduction for the taxable year in which they receive the written notice from the cooperative informing them of the section 199 amount without regard to the taxable income limitation under § 1.199-1(a) and (b).

(i) W-2 wages. The W-2 wage limitation described in § 1.199-2 shall be applied at the cooperative level whether or not the cooperative chooses to pass through some or all of the section 199 deduction. Any section 199 deduction that has been passed through by a cooperative to its patrons is not subject to the W-2 wage limitation a second time at the patron level.

(j) Recapture of section 199 deduction. If the amount of the section 199 deduction that was passed through to patrons exceeds the amount allowable as a section 199 deduction as determined on audit or reported on an amended return, then recapture of the excess will occur at the cooperative level in the taxable year the cooperative took the excess section 199 deduction amount into account.

(k) Section is exclusive. This section is the exclusive method for cooperatives and their patrons to compute the amount of the section 199 deduction. Thus, a patron may not deduct any amount with respect to a patronage dividend or a per-unit retain allocation unless the requirements of this section are satisfied.

(l) No double counting. A qualified payment received by a patron of a cooperative is not taken into account by the patron for purposes of section 199.

(m) Examples. The following examples illustrate the application of this section:

Example (1). (i) Cooperative X markets corn grown by its members within the United States for sale to retail grocers. For its calendar year ended December 31, 2007, Cooperative X has gross receipts of $1,500,000, all derived from the sale of corn grown by its members within the United States. Cooperative X pays $370,000 for its members' corn and its W-2 wages (as defined in § 1.199-2(e)) for 2007 total $130,000. Cooperative X has no other costs. Patron A is a member of Cooperative X. Patron A is a cash basis taxpayer and files Federal income tax returns on a calendar year basis. All corn grown by Patron A in 2007 is sold through Cooperative X and Patron A is eligible to share in patronage dividends paid by Cooperative X for that year.

(ii) Cooperative X is a cooperative described in paragraph (f) of this section. Accordingly, this section applies to Cooperative X and its patrons and all of Cooperative X's gross receipts from the sale of its patrons' corn qualify as domestic production gross receipts (as defined § 1.199-3(a)). Cooperative X's QPAI is $1,000,000. Cooperative X's section 199 deduction for its taxable year 2007 is $60,000 (.06 x $1,000,000). Because this amount is less than 50% of Cooperative X's W-2 wages, the entire amount is allowed as a section 199 deduction subject to the rules of section 199(d)(3) and this section.

Example (2). (i) The facts are the same as in Example 1 except that Cooperative X decides to pass its entire section 199 deduction through to its members. Cooperative X declares a patronage dividend for its 2007 taxable year of $1,000,000, which it pays on March 15, 2008. Pursuant to paragraph (g) of this section, Cooperative X notifies members in written notices that accompany the patronage dividend notification that it is allocating to them the section 199 deduction it is entitled to claim in the taxable year 2007. On March 15, 2008, Patron A receives a $10,000 patronage dividend that is a qualified payment under paragraph (e) of this section from Cooperative X. In the notice that accompanies the patronage dividend, Patron A is designated a $600 section 199 deduction. Under paragraph (a) of this section, Patron A must claim a $600 section 199 deduction for the taxable year ending December 31, 2008, without regard to the taxable income limitation under § 1.199-1(a) and (b). Cooperative X must report the amount of Patron A's section 199 deduction on Form 1099-PATR, "Taxable Distributions Received From Cooperatives," issued to Patron A for the calendar year 2008.

(ii) Under paragraph (b) of this section, Cooperative X is required to reduce its patronage dividend deduction of $1,000,000 by the $60,000 section 199 deduction passed through to members (whether or not Cooperative X pays patronage on book or Federal income tax net earnings). As a consequence, Cooperative X is entitled to a patronage dividend deduction for the taxable year ending December 31, 2007, in the amount of $940,000 ($1,000,000 - $60,000) and to a section 199 deduction in the amount of $60,000 ($1,000,000 x .06). Its taxable income for 2007 is $0.

Example (3). (i) The facts are the same as in Example 1 except that Cooperative X paid out $500,000 to its patrons as advances on expected patronage net earnings. In 2007, Cooperative X pays its patrons a $500,000 ($1,000,000 - $500,000 already paid) patronage dividend in cash or a combination of cash and qualified written notices of allocation. Under paragraph (b) of this section and section 1382, Cooperative X is allowed a patronage dividend deduction of $440,000 ($500,000 - $60,000 section 199 deduction), whether patronage net earnings are distributed on book or Federal income tax net earnings.

(ii) The patrons will have received a gross amount of $1,000,000 in qualified payments under paragraph (e) of this section from Cooperative X ($500,000 paid during the taxable year as advances and the additional $500,000 paid as patronage dividends). If Cooperative X passes through its entire section 199 deduction to its members by providing the notice required by paragraph (g) of this section, then the patrons will be allowed a $60,000 section 199 deduction, resulting in a net $940,000 taxable distribution from Cooperative X. Pursuant to paragraph (l) of this section, the $1,000,000 received by the patrons from Cooperative X is not taken into account for purposes of section 199 in the hands of the patrons.

T.D. 9263, 5/24/2006, amend T.D. 9317, 3/19/2007.

Proposed § 1.199-6 Agricultural and horticultural cooperatives. [*For Preamble, see ¶ 152,713*]

(a) In general. This section applies to a cooperative to which Part I of subchapter T of the Internal Revenue Code applies and its patrons if the cooperative has manufactured, produced, grown, or extracted (MPGE) (as defined in § 1.199-3(d)) in whole or significant part (as defined in § 1.199-3(f)) within the United States (as defined in § 1.199-3(g)) any agricultural or horticultural product, or has marketed agricultural or horticultural products. For this purpose, agricultural or horticultural products also include fertilizer, diesel fuel, and other supplies used in agricultural or horticultural production. If any amount of a patronage dividend or per-unit retain allocation received by a patron is allocable to the qualified production activities income (QPAI) (as defined in § 1.199-1(c)) of the cooperative, would be allowable as a deduction under § 1.199-1(a) (section 199 deduction) by the cooperative, and is designated as such in a written notice to the patron during the payment period defined under section 1382(d), then such amount is deductible by the patron as a section 199 deduction. For this purpose, patronage dividends and per-unit retain allocations include any advances on patronage or per-unit retains paid in money during the taxable year.

(b) Written notice to patrons. In order for a patron to qualify for the section 199 deduction, paragraph (a) of this section requires that the cooperative designate in a written notice the amount of the patron's patronage dividend or per-unit retain allocation that is allocable to QPAI and deductible by the cooperative. This written notice designating the patron's portion of the section 199 deduction must be mailed by the cooperative to its patrons no later than the 15th day of the ninth month following the close of the taxable year. The cooperative may use the same written notice, if any, that it uses to notify patrons of their respective allocations of patronage dividends, or may use a separate timely written notice(s) to comply with this section. The cooperative must report the amount of the patron's section 199 deduction on Form 1099-PATR, "Taxable Distributions Received from Cooperative," issued to the patron.

(c) Determining cooperative's qualified production activities income. In determining the portion of the cooperative's QPAI that would be allowable as a section 199 deduction by the cooperative, the cooperative's taxable income is computed without taking into account any deduction allowable under section 1382(b) or (c) (relating to patronage dividends, per-unit retain allocations, and nonpatronage distributions) and, in the case of a cooperative engaged in the marketing of agricultural and/or horticultural products, the cooperative is treated as having MPGE in whole or in significant part within the United States any agricultural or horticultural products marketed by the cooperative that its patrons have MPGE.

(d) Additional rules relating to pass-through of section 199 deduction. The cooperative may, at its discretion, pass through all, some, or none of the section 199 deduction to its patrons. A cooperative member of a federated cooperative may pass through the section 199 deduction it receives from the federated cooperative to its member patrons. Patrons may claim the section 199 deduction for the taxable year in which they receive the written notice from the cooperative informing them of the section 199 amount without regard to the taxable income limitation under § 1.199-1(a) and (b).

(e) W-2 wages. The W-2 wage limitation described in § 1.199-2 shall be applied at the cooperative level whether or not the cooperative chooses to pass through some or all of the section 199 deduction. Any section 199 deduction that has been passed through by a cooperative to its patrons is not subject to the W-2 wage limitation a second time at the patron level.

(f) Recapture of section 199 deduction. If the amount of the section 199 deduction that was passed through to patrons exceeds the amount allowable as a section 199 deduction as determined on audit or reported on the amended return, recapture of the excess will occur at the cooperative level.

(g) Section is exclusive. This section is the exclusive method for cooperatives and their patrons to compute the amount of the section 199 deduction. Thus, a patron may not deduct any amount with respect to a patronage dividend or a per-unit retain allocation unless the requirements of this section are satisfied.

(h) No double counting. A patronage dividend or per-unit retain allocation received by a patron of a cooperative is not QPAI in the hands of the patron.

(i) Examples. The following examples illustrate the application of this section:

Example (1). (i) Cooperative X markets corn grown by its members within the United States for sale to retail grocers. For its calendar year ended December 31, 2005, Cooperative X has gross receipts of $1,500,000, all derived from the sale of corn grown by its members. Cooperative X's W-2 wages for 2005 total $500,000. Cooperative X has no other costs. Patron A is a member of Cooperative X. Patron A is a cash basis taxpayer and files Federal income tax returns on a calendar year basis. All corn grown by Patron A in 2005 is sold through Cooperative X and Patron A is eligible to share in patronage dividends paid by Cooperative X for that year.

(ii) Cooperative X is an agricultural cooperative described in paragraph (a) of this section. Accordingly, this section applies to Cooperative X and its patrons and all of Cooperative X's gross receipts from the sale of its patrons' corn qualify as domestic production gross receipts (as defined § 1.199-3(a)). Cooperative X's QPAI under paragraph (c) of this section is $1,000,000. Cooperative X's section 199 deduction for its taxable year 2005 is $30,000 (.03 x $1,000,000). Since this amount is less than 50% of Cooperative X's W-2 wages, the entire amount is deductible.

Example (2). (i) The facts are the same as in Example 1 except that Cooperative X decides to pass its entire section 199 deduction through to its members. Cooperative X declares a patronage dividend for its 2005 taxable year of $1,000,000, which it pays on March 15, 2006. Pursuant to paragraph (b) of this section, Cooperative X notifies members in written notices which accompany the patronage dividend notification that it is allocating to them the section 199 deduction it is entitled to claim in the taxable year 2005. On March 15, 2006, Patron A receives a $10,000 patronage dividend from Cooperative X. In the notice that accompanies the patronage dividend, Patron A is designated a $300 section 199 deduction. Under paragraph (d) of this section, Patron A may claim a $300 section 199 deduction for the taxable year ending December 31, 2006, without regard to the taxable income limitation under § 1.199-1(a) and (b). Cooperative X must report the amount of Patron A's section 199 deduction on Form 1099-PATR, "Taxable Distributions Received from Cooperative," issued to the Patron A for the calendar year 2006.

(ii) Under section 199(d)(3)(A), Cooperative X is required to reduce its patronage dividend deduction of $1,000,000 by the $30,000 section 199 deduction passed through to members (whether or not Cooperative X pays patronage on book or tax net earnings). As a consequence, Cooperative X is entitled to a patronage dividend deduction for the taxable year ending December 31, 2005, in the amount of $970,000 ($1,000,000-$30,000) and to a section 199 deduction in the amount of $30,000 ($1,000,000 x .03). Its taxable income for 2005 is $0.

Example (3). (i) The facts are the same as in Example 1 except that Cooperative X paid out $500,000 to its patrons as advances on expected patronage net earnings. In 2005, Cooperative X pays its patrons a $500,000 ($1,000,000-$500,000 already paid) patronage dividend in cash or a combination of cash and qualified written notices of allocation. Under sections 199(d)(3)(A) and 1382, Cooperative X is allowed a patronage dividend deduction of $470,000 ($500,000-$30,000 section 199 deduction), whether patronage net earnings are distributed on book or tax net earnings.

(ii) The patrons will have received a gross amount of $1,000,000 from Cooperative X ($500,000 paid during the taxable year as advances and the additional $500,000 paid as qualified patronage dividends). If Cooperative X passes through its entire section 199 deduction to its members by providing the notice required by paragraph (b) of this section, the patrons will be allowed a $30,000 section 199 deduction, resulting in a net $970,000 taxable distribution from Cooperative X. Pursuant to paragraph (h) of this section, the $1,000,000 received by the patrons from Cooperative X is not QPAI in the hands of the patrons.

§ 1.199-7 Expanded affiliated groups.

(a) In general. The provisions of this section apply solely for purposes of section 199 of the Internal Revenue Code (Code). All members of an expanded affiliated group (EAG) are treated as a single corporation for purposes of section 199. Notwithstanding the preceding sentence, except as otherwise provided in the Code and regulations (see, for example, sections 199(c)(7) and 267, § 1.199-3(b), paragraph (a)(3) of this section, and the consolidated return regulations), each member of an EAG is a separate taxpayer that computes its own taxable income or loss, qualified production activities income (QPAI) (as defined in § 1.199-1(c)), and W-2 wages (as defined in § 1.199-2(e)). If members of an EAG are also members of a consolidated group, see paragraph (d) of this section.

(1) Definition of expanded affiliated group. An EAG is an affiliated group as defined in section 1504(a), determined by substituting more than 50 percent for at least 80 percent each place it appears and without regard to section 1504(b)(2) and (4).

(2) Identification of members of an expanded affiliated group. (i) In general. A corporation must determine if it is a member of an EAG on a daily basis.

(ii) Becoming or ceasing to be a member of an expanded affiliated group. If a corporation becomes or ceases to be a member of an EAG, the corporation is treated as becoming or ceasing to be a member of the EAG at the end of the day on which its status as a member changes.

(3) Attribution of activities. (i) In general. If a member of an EAG (the disposing member) derives gross receipts (as defined in § 1.199-3(c)) from the lease, rental, license, sale, exchange, or other disposition (as defined in § 1.199-3(i)) of qualifying production property (QPP) (as defined in § 1.199-3(j)) that was manufactured, produced, grown or extracted (MPGE) (as defined in § 1.199-3(e)), in whole or in significant part (as defined in § 1.199-3(g)) in the United States (as defined in § 1.199-3(h)), a qualified film (as defined in § 1.199-3(k)), or electricity, natural gas, or potable water (as defined in § 1.199-3(l)) (collectively, utilities) that was produced in the United States, such property was MPGE or produced by another corporation (or corporations), and the disposing member is a member of the same EAG as the other corporation (or corporations) at the time that the disposing member disposes of the QPP, qualified film, or utilities, then the disposing member is treated as conducting the previous activities conducted by such other corporation (or corporations) with respect to the QPP, qualified film, or utilities in determining whether its gross receipts are domestic production gross receipts (DPGR) (as defined in § 1.199-3(a)). With respect to a lease, rental, or license, the disposing member is treated as having disposed of the QPP, qualified film, or utilities on the date or dates on which it takes into account the gross receipts derived from the lease, rental, or license under its methods of accounting. With respect to a sale, exchange, or other disposition, the disposing member is treated as having disposed of the QPP, qualified film, or utilities on the date on which it ceases to own the QPP, qualified film, or utilities for Federal income tax purposes, even if no gain or loss is taken into account.

(ii) Special rule. Attribution of activities does not apply for purposes of the construction of real property under § 1.199-3(m) or the performance of engineering and architectural services under § 1.199-3(n). A member of an EAG must engage in a construction activity under § 1.199-3(m)(2), provide engineering services under § 1.199-3(n)(2), or provide architectural services under § 1.199-3(n)(3) in order for the member's gross receipts to be derived from construction, engineering, or architectural services.

(4) Examples. The following examples illustrate the application of paragraph (a)(3) of this section. Assume that all taxpayers are calendar year taxpayers. The examples are as follows:

Example (1). Corporations M and N are members of the same EAG. M is engaged solely in the trade or business of manufacturing furniture in the United States that it sells to unrelated persons. N is engaged solely in the trade or business of engraving companies' names on pens and pencils purchased from unrelated persons and then selling the pens and pencils to such companies. For purposes of this example, assume that if N was not a member of an EAG, its activities would not qualify as MPGE. Accordingly, although M's sales of the furniture qualify as DPGR (assuming all the other requirements of § 1.199-3 are met), N's sales of the engraved pens and pencils do not qualify as DPGR because neither N nor another member of the EAG MPGE the pens and pencils.

Example (2). For the entire 2007 year, Corporations A and B are members of the same EAG. A is engaged solely in the trade or business of MPGE machinery in the United States. A and B each own 45% of partnership C and unrelated persons own the remaining 10%. C is engaged solely in the trade or business of MPGE the same type of machinery in the United States as A. In 2007, B purchases and then resells the machinery MPGE in 2007 by A and C. B also resells machinery it purchases from unrelated persons. If only B's activities were considered, B would not qualify for the deduction under § 1.199-1(a) (section 199 deduction). However, because at the time B disposes of the machinery B is a member of the EAG that includes A, B is treated as conducting A's previous MPGE activities in determining whether B's gross receipts from the sale of the machinery MPGE by A are DPGR. C is not a member of the EAG and thus C's MPGE activities are not attributed to B in determining whether B's gross receipts from the sale of the machinery MPGE by C are DPGR. Accordingly, B's gross receipts attributable to its sale of the machinery it purchases from A are DPGR (assuming all the other requirements of § 1.199-3 are met). B's gross receipts attributable to its sale of the machinery it purchases from C and from the unrelated persons are non-DPGR because no member of the EAG MPGE the machinery and because C does not qualify as an EAG partnership.

Example (3). The facts are the same as in Example 2 except that rather than reselling the machinery, B rents the machinery to unrelated persons and B takes the gross receipts attributable to the rental of the machinery into account under its methods of accounting in 2007, 2008, and 2009. In addition, as of the close of business on December 31, 2008, A and B cease to be members of the same EAG. With respect to the machinery acquired from C and the unrelated persons, B's gross receipts attributable to the rental of the machinery in 2007, 2008, and 2009 are non-DPGR because no member of the EAG MPGE the machinery and because C does not qualify as an EAG partnership. With respect to machinery acquired from A, B's gross receipts in 2007 and 2008 attributable to the rental of the machinery are DPGR because at the time B takes into account the gross receipts derived from the rental of the machinery under its methods of accounting, B is a member of the same EAG as A and B is treated as conducting A's previous MPGE activities. However, with respect to the rental receipts in 2009, because A and B are not members of the same EAG in 2009, B's rental receipts are non-DPGR.

Example (4). For the entire 2007 year, Corporation P owns over 50% of the stock of Corporation S. In 2007, P MPGE QPP in the United States and transfers the QPP to S. On February 28, 2008, P disposes of stock of S, reducing P's ownership of S below 50% and P and S cease to be members of the same EAG. On June 30, 2008, S sells the QPP to an unrelated person. Unless P's transfer of the QPP to S took place in a transaction to which section 381(a) applies (see § 1.199-8(e)(3)), because S is not a member of the same EAG as P on June 30, 2008, S is not treated as conducting the activities conducted by P in determining if S's receipts are DPGR, notwithstanding that P and S were members of the same EAG when P MPGE the QPP and when P transferred the QPP to S.

Example (5). For the entire 2007 year, Corporations X and Y are unrelated corporations. In 2007, X MPGE QPP in the United States and sells the QPP to Y. On August 31, 2008, X acquires over 50% of the stock of Y, thus making X and Y members of the same EAG. On November 30, 2008, Y sells the QPP to an unrelated person. Because X and Y are members of the same EAG on November 30, 2008, Y is treated as conducting the activities conducted by X in 2007 in determining if Y's receipts are DPGR, notwithstanding that X and Y were not members of the same EAG when X MPGE the QPP nor when X sold the QPP to Y.

(5) Anti-avoidance rule. If a transaction between members of an EAG is engaged in or structured with a principal purpose of qualifying for, or increasing the amount of, the section 199 deduction of the EAG or the portion of the section 199 deduction allocated to one or more members of the EAG, adjustments must be made to eliminate the effect of the transaction on the computation of the section 199 deduction.

(b) Computation of expanded affiliated group's section 199 deduction. *(1) In general.* The section 199 deduction for an EAG is determined by the EAG by aggregating each member's taxable income or loss, QPAI, and W-2 wages, if any. For purposes of this determination, a member's QPAI may be positive or negative. A member's taxable income or loss and QPAI shall be determined by reference to the member's methods of accounting.

(2) Example. The following example illustrates the application of paragraph (b)(1) of this section:

Example. Corporations X, Y, and Z, calendar year taxpayers, are the only members of an EAG and are not members of a consolidated group. X has taxable income of $50,000, QPAI of $15,000, and W-2 wages of $1,000. Y has taxable income of ($20,000), QPAI of ($1,000), and W-2 wages of $750. Z has $0 taxable income and $0 QPAI, but has W-2 wages of $2,000. In determining the EAG's section 199 deduction, the EAG aggregates each member's taxable income or loss, QPAI, and W-2 wages. Accordingly, the EAG has taxable income of $30,000 ($50,000 + ($20,000) + $0), QPAI of $14,000 ($15,000 + ($1,000) + $0), and W-2 wages of $3,750 ($1,000 + $750 + $2,000).

(3) Net operating loss carrybacks and carryovers. In determining the taxable income of an EAG, if a member of an EAG has a net operating loss (NOL) carryback or carryover to the taxable year, then the amount of the NOL used to offset taxable income cannot exceed the taxable income of that member.

(4) Losses used to reduce taxable income of expanded affiliated group. (i) In general. The amount of an NOL sustained by any member of an EAG that is used in the year sustained in determining an EAG's taxable income limitation under section 199(a)(1)(B) is not treated as an NOL carryover or NOL carryback to any taxable year in determining the taxable income limitation under section 199(a)(1)(B). For purposes of this paragraph (b)(4), an NOL is considered to be used if it reduces an EAG's aggregate taxable income, regardless of whether the use of the NOL actually reduces the amount of the section 199 deduction that the EAG would otherwise derive. An NOL is not considered to be used to the extent that it reduces an EAG's aggregate taxable income to an amount less than zero. If more than one member of an EAG has an NOL used in the same taxable year to reduce the EAG's taxable income, the members' respective NOLs are deemed used in proportion to the amount of their NOLs.

(ii) Examples. The following examples illustrate the application of this paragraph (b)(4). For purposes of these examples, assume that all relevant parties have sufficient W-2 wages so that the section 199 deduction is not limited under section 199(b)(1). The examples read as follows:

Example (1). (i) Facts. Corporations A and B are the only two members of an EAG. A and B are both calendar year taxpayers, and they do not join in the filing of a consolidated Federal income tax return. Neither A nor B had taxable income or loss prior to 2010. In 2010, A has QPAI and taxable income of $1,000, and B has QPAI of $1,000 and an NOL of $1,500. In 2011, A has QPAI of $2,000 and taxable income of $1,000 and B has QPAI of $2,000 and taxable income prior to the NOL deduction allowed under section 172 of $2,000.

(ii) Section 199 deduction for 2010. In determining the EAG's section 199 deduction for 2010, A's $1,000 of QPAI and B's $1,000 of QPAI are aggregated, as are A's $1,000 of taxable income and B's $1,500 NOL. Thus, for 2010, the EAG has QPAI of $2,000 and taxable income of ($500). The EAG's section 199 deduction for 2010 is 9% of the lesser of its QPAI or its taxable income. Because the EAG has a taxable loss in 2010, the EAG's section 199 deduction is $0.

(iii) Section 199 deduction for 2011. In determining the EAG's section 199 deduction for 2011, A's $2,000 of QPAI and B's $2,000 of QPAI are aggregated, giving the EAG

QPAI of $4,000. Also, $1,000 of B's NOL from 2010 was used in 2010 to reduce the EAG's taxable income to $0. The remaining $500 of B's 2010 NOL is not considered to have been used in 2010 because it reduced the EAG's taxable income below $0. Accordingly, for purposes of determining the EAG's taxable income limitation under section 199(a)(1)(B) in 2011, B is deemed to have only a $500 NOL carryover from 2010 to offset a portion of its 2011 taxable income. Thus, B's taxable income in 2011 is $1,500 which is aggregated with A's $1,000 of taxable income. The EAG's taxable income limitation in 2011 is $2,500. The EAG's section 199 deduction is 9% of the lesser of its QPAI of $4,000 or its taxable income of $2,500. Thus, the EAG's section 199 deduction in 2011 is 9% of $2,500, or $225. The results would be the same if neither A nor B had QPAI in 2010.

Example (2). The facts are the same as in Example 1 except that in 2010 B was not a member of the same EAG as A, but instead was a member of an EAG with Corporation X, which had QPAI and taxable income of $1,000 in 2010, and had neither taxable income nor loss in any other year. There were no other members of the EAG in 2010 besides B and X, and B and X did not file a consolidated Federal income tax return. As $1,000 of B's NOL was used in 2010 to reduce the B and X EAG's taxable income to $0, B is considered to have only a $500 NOL carryover from 2010 to offset a portion of its 2011 taxable income for purposes of the taxable income limitation under section 199(a)(1)(B), just as in Example 1. Accordingly, the results for the A and B EAG in 2011 are the same as in Example 1.

Example (3). The facts are the same as in Example 1 except that B is not a member of any EAG in 2011. Because $1,000 of B's NOL was used in 2010 to reduce the EAG's taxable income to $0, B is considered to have only a $500 NOL carryover from 2010 to offset a portion of its 2011 taxable income for purposes of the taxable income limitation under section 199(a)(1)(B), just as in Example 1. Thus, for purposes of determining B's taxable income limitation in 2011, B is considered to have taxable income of $1,500, and B has a section 199 deduction of 9% of $1,500, or $135.

Example (4). Corporations A, B, and C are the only members of an EAG. A, B, and C are all calendar year taxpayers, and they do not join in the filing of a consolidated Federal income tax return. None of the EAG members (A, B, or C) had taxable income or loss prior to 2010. In 2010, A has QPAI of $2,000 and taxable income of $1,000, B has QPAI of $1,000 and an NOL of $1,000, and C has QPAI of $1,000 and an NOL of $3,000. In 2011, prior to the NOL deduction allowed under section 172, A and B each has taxable income of $200 and C has taxable income of $5,000. In determining the EAG's section 199 deduction for 2010, A's QPAI of $2,000, B's QPAI of $1,000, and C's QPAI of $1,000 are aggregated, as are A's taxable income of $1,000, B's NOL of $1,000, and C's NOL of $3,000. Thus, for 2010, the EAG has QPAI of $4,000 and taxable income of ($3,000). In determining the EAG's taxable income limitation under section 199(a)(1)(B) in 2011, $1,000 of B's and C's aggregate NOLs in 2010 of $4,000 are considered to have been used in 2010 to reduce the EAG's taxable income to $0, in proportion to their NOLs. Thus, $250 of B's NOL from 2010 ($1,000 x $1,000/$4,000) and $750 of C's NOL from 2010 ($1,000 x $3,000/$4,000) are deemed to have been used in 2010. The remaining $750 of B's NOL and the remaining $2,250 of C's NOL are not deemed to have been used because so doing would have reduced the EAG's taxable income in 2010 below $0. Accordingly, for purposes of determining the EAG's taxable income limitation in 2011, B is deemed to have a $750 NOL carryover from 2010 and C is deemed to have a $2,250 NOL carryover from 2010. Thus, for purposes of determining the EAG's taxable income limitation, B's taxable income in 2011 is $0 and C's taxable income in 2011 is $2,750, which are aggregated with A's $200 taxable income. B's unused NOL carryover from 2010 cannot be used to reduce either A's or C's 2011 taxable income. Thus, the EAG's taxable income limitation in 2011 is $2,950, A's taxable income of $200 plus B's taxable income of $0 plus C's taxable income of $2,750.

(c) Allocation of an expanded affiliated group's section 199 deduction among members of the expanded affiliated group. *(1) In general.* An EAG's section 199 deduction as determined in paragraph (b)(1) of this section is allocated among the members of the EAG in proportion to each member's QPAI, regardless of whether the EAG member has taxable income or loss or W-2 wages for the taxable year. For this purpose, if a member has negative QPAI, the QPAI of the member shall be treated as zero.

(2) Use of section 199 deduction to create or increase a net operating loss. Notwithstanding § 1.199-1(b), if a member of an EAG has some or all of the EAG's section 199 deduction allocated to it under paragraph (c)(1) of this section and the amount allocated exceeds the member's taxable income (determined prior to allocation of the section 199 deduction), the section 199 deduction will create an NOL for the member. Similarly, if a member of an EAG, prior to the allocation of some or all of the EAG's section 199 deduction to the member, has an NOL for the taxable year, the portion of the EAG's section 199 deduction allocated to the member will increase the member's NOL.

(d) Special rules for members of the same consolidated group. *(1) Intercompany transactions.* In the case of an intercompany transaction between consolidated group members S and B (as the terms intercompany transaction, S, and B are defined in § 1.1502-13(b)(1)), S takes the intercompany transaction into account in computing the section 199 deduction at the same time and in the same proportion as S takes into account the income, gain, deduction, or loss from the intercompany transaction under § 1.1502-13.

(2) Attribution of activities in the construction of real property and the performance of engineering and architectural services. Notwithstanding paragraph (a)(3)(ii) of this section, a disposing member (as described in paragraph (a)(3)(i) of this section) is treated as conducting the previous activities conducted by each other member of its consolidated group with respect to the construction of real property under § 1.199-3(m) and the performance of engineering and architectural services under § 1.199-3(n), but only with respect to activities performed during the period of consolidation.

(3) Application of the simplified deduction method and the small business simplified overall method. For purposes of applying the simplified deduction method under § 1.199-4(e) and the small business simplified overall method under § 1.199-4(f), a consolidated group determines its QPAI using its members' DPGR, non-DPGR, cost of goods sold (CGS), and all other deductions, expenses, or losses (deductions), determined after application of § 1.1502-13.

(4) Determining the section 199 deduction. (i) Expanded affiliated group consists of consolidated group and non-consolidated group members. In determining the section 199 deduction, if an EAG includes corporations that are members of the same consolidated group and corporations that are not members of the same consolidated group, the consolidated

taxable income or loss, QPAI, and W-2 wages, if any, of the consolidated group (and not the separate taxable income or loss, QPAI, and W-2 wages of the members of the consolidated group), are aggregated with the taxable income or loss, QPAI, and W-2 wages, if any, of the non-consolidated group members. For example, if A, B, C, S1, and S2 are members of the same EAG, and A, S1, and S2 are members of the same consolidated group (the A consolidated group), then the A consolidated group is treated as one member of the EAG. Accordingly, the EAG is considered to have three members, the A consolidated group, B, and C. The consolidated taxable income or loss, QPAI, and W-2 wages, if any, of the A consolidated group are aggregated with the taxable income or loss, QPAI, and W-2 wages, if any, of B and C in determining the EAG's section 199 deduction.

(ii) Expanded affiliated group consists only of members of a single consolidated group. If all the members of an EAG are members of the same consolidated group, the consolidated group's section 199 deduction is determined using the consolidated group's consolidated taxable income or loss, QPAI, and W-2 wages, rather than the separate taxable income or loss, QPAI, and W-2 wages of its members.

(5) Allocation of the section 199 deduction of a consolidated group among its members. The section 199 deduction of a consolidated group (or the section 199 deduction allocated to a consolidated group that is a member of an EAG) is allocated to the members of the consolidated group in proportion to each consolidated group member's QPAI, regardless of whether the consolidated group member has separate taxable income or loss or W-2 wages for the taxable year. In allocating the section 199 deduction of a consolidated group among its members, any redetermination of a corporation's receipts, CGS, or other deductions from an intercompany transaction under § 1.1502-13(c)(1)(i) or (c)(4) for purposes of section 199 is not taken into account. Also, for purposes of this allocation, if a consolidated group member has negative QPAI, the QPAI of the member shall be treated as zero.

(e) Examples. The following examples illustrate the application of paragraphs (a) through (d) of this section:

Example (1). Corporations X and Y are members of the same EAG but are not members of a consolidated group. All the activities described in this example take place during the same taxable year. X and Y each use the section 861 method described in § 1.199-4(d) for allocating and apportioning their deductions. X incurs $5,000 in costs in manufacturing a machine, all of which are capitalized. X is entitled to a $1,000 depreciation deduction for the machine in the current taxable year. X rents the machine to Y for $1,500. Y uses the machine in manufacturing QPP within the United States. Y incurs $1,400 of CGS in manufacturing the QPP. Y sells the QPP to unrelated persons for $7,500. Pursuant to section 199(c)(7) and § 1.199-3(b), X's rental income is non-DPGR (and its related costs are not attributable to DPGR). Accordingly, Y has $4,600 of QPAI (Y's $7,500 DPGR received from unrelated persons - Y's $1,400 CGS allocable to such receipts - Y's $1,500 of rental expense), X has $0 of QPAI, and the EAG has $4,600 of QPAI.

Example (2). The facts are the same as in Example 1 except that X and Y are members of the same consolidated group. Pursuant to section 199(c)(7) and § 1.199-3(b), X's rental income ordinarily would not be DPGR (and its related costs would not be allocable to DPGR). However, because X and Y are members of the same consolidated group, § 1.1502-13(c)(1)(i) provides that the separate entity attributes of X's intercompany items or Y's corresponding items, or both, may be redetermined in order to produce the same effect as if X and Y were divisions of a single corporation. If X and Y were divisions of a single corporation, X and Y would have QPAI of $5,100 ($7,500 DPGR received from unrelated persons - $1,400 CGS allocable to such receipts - $1,000 depreciation deduction). To obtain this same result for the consolidated group, X's rental income is redetermined as DPGR, which results in the consolidated group having $9,000 of DPGR (the sum of Y's DPGR of $7,500 + X's DPGR of $1,500) and $3,900 of costs allocable to DPGR (the sum of Y's $1,400 CGS + Y's $1,500 rental expense + X's $1,000 depreciation expense). For purposes of determining how much of the consolidated group's section 199 deduction is allocated to X and Y, pursuant to paragraph (d)(5) of this section, the redetermination of X's rental income as DPGR under § 1.1502-13(c)(1)(i) is not taken into account (X's costs are considered to be allocable to DPGR because they are allocable to the consolidated group deriving DPGR). Accordingly, for this purpose, X is deemed to have ($1,000) of QPAI (X's $0 DPGR - X's $1,000 depreciation deduction). Because X is deemed to have negative QPAI, also pursuant to paragraph (d)(5) of this section, X's QPAI is treated as zero. Y has $4,600 of QPAI (Y's $7,500 DPGR - Y's $1,400 CGS allocable to such receipts - Y's $1,500 of rental expense). Accordingly, X is allocated $0/($0 + $4,600) of the consolidated group's section 199 deduction and Y is allocated $4,600/($0 + $4,600) of the consolidated group's section 199 deduction.

Example (3). Corporations P and S are members of the same EAG but are not members of a consolidated group. P and S each use the section 861 method for allocating and apportioning their deductions and are both calendar year taxpayers. In 2007, P incurs $1,000 in research and development expenses in creating an intangible asset and deducts these expenses in 2007. P anticipates that it will license the intangible asset to S. On January 1, 2008, P licenses the intangible asset to S for $2,500. S uses the intangible asset in manufacturing QPP within the United States. S incurs $2,000 of additional costs in manufacturing the QPP. On December 31, 2008, S sells the QPP to unrelated persons for $10,000. Because on December 31, 2007, P anticipates that it will license the intangible asset to S, a related person, and also because the intangible asset is not QPP, P's license receipts from S will be non-DPGR. Accordingly, P's research and development expenses in 2007 are not attributable to DPGR. In 2008, S has $5,500 of QPAI (S's $10,000 DPGR received from unrelated persons - S's $2,000 additional costs in manufacturing the QPP - S's $2,500 of license expense), P has $0 of QPAI, and the EAG has $5,500 of QPAI.

Example (4). (i) Determination of consolidated group's QPAI. The facts are the same as in Example 3 except that P and S are members of the same consolidated group. Pursuant to section 199(c)(7) and § 1.199-3(b), and also because the intangible asset is not QPP, P's license income ordinarily would not be DPGR (and its related costs would not be allocable to DPGR). However, because P and S are members of the same consolidated group, § 1.1502-13(c)(1)(i) provides that the separate entity attributes of P's intercompany items or S's corresponding items, or both, may be redetermined in order to produce the same effect as if P and S were divisions of a single corporation. If P and S were divisions of a single corporation, in 2007 the single corporation would have $1,000 of expenses allocable to the anticipated DPGR from the sale of the QPP to unrelated persons, resulting in a negative QPAI (from this individual item) of $1,000. In 2008, the single corporation would have QPAI of $8,000 ($10,000 DPGR received from unrelated persons - $2,000 additional costs in manufacturing the QPP). To obtain this same result for the consolidated group, P's license income from S is redetermined as DPGR. P's research and development expenses are allocable to DPGR. This results in the consolidated group having negative QPAI in 2007 (from the research and development expense) of $1,000. In 2008, the consolidated group has $12,500 of DPGR (the sum of S's DPGR of $10,000 + P's DPGR of $2,500) and $4,500 of costs allocable to DPGR (the sum of S's $2,000 additional costs + S's $2,500 license expense), resulting in $8,000 of QPAI in 2008.

(ii) Allocation of deduction. Since the consolidated group has no QPAI in 2007, there is no section 199 deduction to be allocated between P and S in 2007. In 2008, the consolidated group has $8,000 of QPAI and, assuming that the group has positive taxable income and W-2 wages, the consolidated group will have a section 199 deduction. For purposes of determining how much of the consolidated group's section 199 deduction is allocated to P and S, pursuant to paragraph (d)(5) of this section, the redetermination of P's license income as DPGR under § 1.1502-13(c)(1)(i) is not taken into account.

Accordingly, for purposes of allocating the consolidated group's section 199 deduction between P and S, P is deemed to have $0 DPGR and $0 QPAI in 2008. S has $5,500 of QPAI (S's $10,000 DPGR - S's $2,000 in additional costs allocable to such receipts - S's $2,500 of license expense). Accordingly, P is allocated $0/($0 + $5,500) of the consolidated group's section 199 deduction in 2008 and S is allocated $5,500/($0 + $5,500) of the consolidated group's section 199 deduction.

Example (5). (i) Facts. Corporations A and B are the only two members of an EAG but are not members of a consolidated group. A and B each file Federal income tax returns on a calendar year basis. The average annual gross receipts of the EAG are less than or equal to $100,000,000 and A and B each use the simplified deduction method under § 1.199-4(e). In 2007, A MPGE televisions within the United States. A has $10,000,000 of DPGR from sales of televisions to unrelated persons and $2,000,000 of DPGR from sales of televisions to B. In addition, A has gross receipts from computer consulting services with unrelated persons of $3,000,000. A has CGS of $6,000,000. A is able to determine from its books and records that $4,500,000 of its CGS are attributable to televisions sold to unrelated persons and $1,500,000 are attributable to televisions sold to B (see § 1.199-4(b)(2)). A has other deductions of $4,000,000. A has no other items of income, gain, or deductions. In 2007, B sells the televisions it purchased from A to unrelated persons for $4,100,000. B also pays $100,000 for administrative services performed in 2007. B has no other items of income, gain, or deductions.

(ii) QPAI. (A) A's QPAI. In order to determine A's QPAI, A subtracts its $6,000,000 CGS from its $12,000,000 DPGR. Under the simplified deduction method, A then apportions its remaining $4,000,000 of deductions to DPGR in proportion to the ratio of its DPGR to total gross receipts. Thus, of A's $4,000,000 of deductions, $3,200,000 is apportioned to DPGR ($4,000,000 x $12,000,000/$15,000,000). Accordingly, A's QPAI is $2,800,000 ($12,000,000 DPGR - $6,000,000 CGS - $3,200,000 deductions apportioned to its DPGR).

(B) B's QPAI. Although B did not MPGE the televisions it sold, pursuant to paragraph (a)(3) of this section, B is treated as conducting A's MPGE of the televisions in determining whether B's gross receipts are DPGR. Thus, B has $4,100,000 of DPGR. In order to determine B's QPAI, B subtracts its $2,000,000 CGS from its $4,100,000 DPGR. Under the simplified deduction method, B then apportions its remaining $100,000 of deductions to DPGR in proportion to the ratio of its DPGR to total gross receipts. Thus, because B has no other gross receipts, all of B's $100,000 of deductions is apportioned to DPGR ($100,000 x $4,100,000/$4,100,000). Accordingly, B's QPAI is $2,000,000 ($4,100,000 DPGR - $2,000,000 CGS - $100,000 deductions apportioned to its DPGR).

Example (6). (i) Facts. The facts are the same as in Example 5 except that A and B are members of the same consolidated group, B does not sell the televisions purchased from A until 2008, and B's $100,000 paid for administrative services are paid in 2008 for services performed in 2008. In addition, in 2008, A has $3,000,000 in gross receipts from computer consulting services with unrelated persons and $1,000,000 in related deductions.

(ii) Consolidated group's 2007 QPAI. The consolidated group's DPGR and total gross receipts in 2007 are $10,000,000 and $13,000,000, respectively, because, pursuant to paragraph (d)(1) of this section and § 1.1502-13, the sale of the televisions from A to B is not taken into account in 2007. In order to determine the consolidated group's QPAI, the consolidated group subtracts its $4,500,000 CGS from the televisions sold to unrelated persons from its $10,000,000 DPGR. Under the simplified deduction method, the consolidated group apportions its remaining $4,000,000 of deductions to DPGR in proportion to the ratio of its DPGR to total gross receipts. Thus, $3,076,923 ($4,000,000 x $10,000,000/$13,000,000) is allocated to DPGR. Accordingly, the consolidated group's QPAI for 2007 is $2,423,077 ($10,000,000 DPGR - $4,500,000 CGS - $3,076,923 deductions apportioned to its DPGR).

(iii) Allocation of consolidated group's 2007 section 199 deduction to its members. Because B's only activity during 2007 is the purchase of televisions from A, B has no DPGR or deductions and thus, no QPAI, in 2007. Accordingly, the entire section 199 deduction in 2007 for the consolidated group will be allocated to A.

(iv) Consolidated group's 2008 QPAI. Pursuant to paragraph (d)(1) of this section and § 1.1502-13(c), A's sale of televisions to B in 2007 is taken into account in 2008 when B sells the televisions to unrelated persons. However, because A and B are members of a consolidated group, § 1.1502-13(c)(1)(i) provides that the separate entity attributes of A's intercompany items or B's corresponding items, or both, may be redetermined in order to produce the same effect as if A and B were divisions of a single corporation. Accordingly, A's $2,000,000 of gross receipts are redetermined to be non-DPGR and as not being gross receipts for purposes of allocating costs between DPGR and non-DPGR, and B's $2,000,000 CGS are redetermined to be not allocable to DPGR. Notwithstanding that A's receipts are redetermined to be non-DPGR and as not being gross receipts for purposes of allocating costs between DPGR and non-DPGR, A's CGS are still considered to be allocable to DPGR because they are allocable to the consolidated group deriving DPGR. Accordingly, the consolidated group's DPGR in 2008 is $4,100,000 from B's sales of televisions, and its total receipts are $7,100,000 ($4,100,000 DPGR plus $3,000,000 non-DPGR from A's computer consulting services). To determine the consolidated group's QPAI, the consolidated group subtracts A's $1,500,000 CGS from the televisions sold to B from its $4,100,000 DPGR. Under the simplified deduction method, the consolidated group apportions its remaining $1,100,000 of deductions ($1,000,000 from A and $100,000 from B) to DPGR in proportion to the consolidated group's ratio of its DPGR to total gross receipts. Thus, $635,211 ($1,100,000 x $4,100,000/$7,100,000) is allocated to DPGR. Accordingly, the consolidated group's QPAI for 2008 is $1,964,789 ($4,100,000 DPGR - $1,500,000 CGS - $635,211 deductions apportioned to its DPGR), the same QPAI that would result if A and B were divisions of a single corporation.

(v) Allocation of consolidated group's 2008 section 199 deduction to its members. (A) A's QPAI. For purposes of allocating the consolidated group's section 199 deduction to its members, pursuant to paragraph (d)(5) of this section, the redetermination of A's $2,000,000 in receipts is disregarded. Accordingly, for this purpose, A's DPGR are $2,000,000 (receipts from the sale of televisions to B taken into account in 2008) and its total receipts are $5,000,000 ($2,000,000 DPGR + $3,000,000 non-DPGR from its computer consulting services). In determining A's QPAI, A subtracts its $1,500,000 CGS from the televisions sold to B from its $2,000,000 DPGR. Under the simplified deduction method, A apportions its remaining $1,000,000 of deductions in proportion to the ratio of its DPGR to total receipts. Thus, $400,000 ($1,000,000 x $2,000,000/$5,000,000) is allocated to DPGR. Thus, A's QPAI is $100,000 ($2,000,000 DPGR - $1,500,000 CGS -$400,000 deductions allocated to its DPGR).

(B) B's QPAI. B's DPGR and its total gross receipts are each $4,100,000. For purposes of allocating the consolidated group's section 199 deduction to its members, pursuant to paragraph (d)(5) of this section, the redetermination of B's $2,000,000 CGS as not allocable to DPGR is disregarded. In determining B's QPAI, B subtracts its $2,000,000 CGS from the televisions purchased from A from its $4,100,000 DPGR. Under the simplified deduction method, B apportions its remaining $100,000 deductions in proportion to the ratio of its DPGR to total receipts. Thus, all $100,000 ($100,000 x $4,100,000/$4,100,000) is allocated to DPGR. Thus, B's QPAI is $2,000,000 ($4,100,000 DPGR - $2,000,000 CGS - $100,000 deductions allocated to its DPGR).

(C) Allocation to A and B. Pursuant to paragraph (d)(5) of this section, the consolidated group's section 199 deduction for 2008 is allocated $100,000/($100,000 + $2,000,000) to A and $2,000,000/($100,000 + $2,000,000) to B.

Example (7). Corporations S and B are members of the same consolidated group that files its Federal income tax returns on a calendar year basis. In 2007, S manufactures office furniture for B to use in B's corporate headquarters and S sells the office furniture to B. S and B have no other activities in the taxable year. If S and B were not members of a consolidated group, S's gross receipts from the sale of the office furniture to B would be DPGR (assuming all the other requirements of § 1.199-3 are met) and S's CGS or other deductions, expenses, or losses from the sale to B would be allocable to S's DPGR. However, because S and B are members of a consolidated group, the separate entity attributes of S's intercompany items or B's corresponding items, or both, may be redetermined under § 1.1502-13(c)(1)(i) or (c)(4) in order to produce the same effect as if S and B were divisions of a single corporation. If S and B were divisions of a single corporation, there would be no DPGR with respect to the office furniture because there would be no lease, rental, license, sale, exchange, or other disposition of the furniture by the single corporation (and no CGS or other deductions allocable to DPGR). Thus, in order to produce the same effect as if S and B were divisions of a single corporation, S's gross receipts are redetermined as non-DPGR. Accordingly, the consolidated group has no DPGR (and no CGS or other deductions allocated or apportioned to DPGR) and receives no section 199 deduction in 2007.

Example (8). (i) Facts. A and B are members of the same consolidated group that files its Federal income tax returns on a calendar year basis. On January 1, 2007, A MPGE QPP which is 10-year recovery property for $100 and depreciates it under the straight-line method. On January 1, 2009, A sells the property to B for $130. Under section 168(i)(7), B is treated as A for purposes of section 168 to the extent B's $130 basis does not exceed A's adjusted basis at the time of the sale. B's additional basis is treated as new 10-year recovery property for which B elects the straight-line method of recovery. (To simplify the example, the half-year convention is disregarded.)

(ii) Depreciation; intercompany gain. A claims $10 of depreciation for each taxable year 2007 and 2008 and has an $80 basis at the time of the sale to B. Thus, A has a $50 intercompany gain from its sale to B. For each taxable year 2009 through 2016, B has $10 of depreciation with respect to $80 of its basis (the portion of its $130 basis not exceeding A's adjusted basis) and $5 of depreciation with respect to the $50 of its additional basis that exceeds A's adjusted basis. For each taxable year 2017 and 2018, B has $5 of depreciation with respect to the $50 of its additional basis that exceeds A's adjusted basis.

(iii) Timing. A's $50 gain is taken into account to reflect the difference for each consolidated return year between B's depreciation taken into account with respect to the property and the depreciation that would have been taken into account if A and B were divisions of a single corporation. For each taxable year 2009 through 2016, B takes into account $15 of depreciation rather than the $10 of depreciation that would have been taken into account if A and B were divisions of a single corporation. For each taxable year 2017 and 2018, B takes into account $5 of depreciation rather than the $0 of depreciation that would have been taken into account if A and B were divisions of a single corporation (the QPP would have been fully depreciated after the 2016 taxable year if A and B were divisions of a single corporation). Thus, A takes $5 of gain into account in each of the 2009 through 2018 taxable years (10% of its $50 gain). Pursuant to § 1.199-7(d)(1), A takes its sale to B into account in computing the section 199 deduction at the same time and in the same proportion as A takes into account the income, gain, deduction, or loss from the intercompany transaction under § 1.1502-13. Thus, in each taxable year 2009 through 2018, A takes into account $13 of gross receipts (10% of its $130 gross receipts) from the sale to B. The group's income in each taxable year 2009 through 2016 is a $10 loss ($5 gain - $15 depreciation), the same net amount it would have been if A and B were divisions of a single corporation. The group's income in each taxable year 2017 and 2018 is $0 ($5 gain - $5 depreciation), the same net amount it would have been if A and B were divisions of a single corporation.

(iv) Attributes. If A and B were not members of a consolidated group, A's gross receipts on the sale of the QPP to B would be DPGR (assuming all the other requirements of § 1.199-3 are met). However, because A and B are members of a consolidated group, the separate entity attributes of A's DPGR may be redetermined under § 1.1502-13(c)(1)(i) or (c)(4) in order to produce the same effect as if A and B were divisions of a single corporation. If A and B were divisions of a single corporation, there would be no DPGR with respect to the QPP because there would be no lease, rental, license, sale, exchange, or other disposition of the QPP by the single corporation (and no CGS or other deductions allocable to DPGR). Thus, in order to produce the same effect as if A and B were divisions of a single corporation, A's $13 of gross receipts taken into account in each year is redetermined as non-DPGR. Accordingly, the consolidated group has no DPGR (and no CGS or other deductions allocable or apportioned to DPGR) and receives no section 199 deduction.

Example (9). Corporations X, Y, and Z are members of the same EAG but are not members of a consolidated group. X, Y, and Z each files Federal income tax returns on a calendar year basis. Assume that the EAG has W-2 wages in excess of the section 199(b) wage limitation. Prior to 2007, X had no taxable income or loss. In 2007, X has $0 of taxable income and $2,000 of QPAI, Y has $4,000 of taxable income and $3,000 of QPAI, and Z has $4,000 of taxable income and $5,000 of QPAI. Accordingly, the EAG has taxable income of $8,000, the sum of X's taxable income of $0, Y's taxable income of $4,000, and Z's taxable income of $4,000. The EAG has QPAI of $10,000, the sum of X's QPAI of $2,000, Y's QPAI of $3,000, and Z's QPAI of $5,000. Because X's, Y's, and Z's taxable years all began in 2007, the transition percentage under section 199(a)(2) is 6%. Thus, the EAG's section 199 deduction for 2007 is $480 (6% of the lesser of the EAG's taxable income of $8,000 or the EAG's QPAI of $10,000). Pursuant to paragraph (c)(1) of this section, the $480 section 199 deduction is allocated to X, Y, and Z in proportion to their respective amounts of QPAI, that is $96 to X ($480 x $2,000/$10,000), $144 to Y ($480 x $3,000/$10,000), and $240 to Z ($480 x $5,000/$10,000). Although X's taxable income for 2007 determined prior to allocation of a portion of the EAG's section 199 deduction to it was $0, pursuant to paragraph (c)(2) of this section X will have an NOL for 2007 equal to $96. Because X's NOL for 2007 cannot be carried back to a previous taxable year, X's NOL carryover to 2008 will be $96.

Example (10). (i) Facts. Corporation P owns all of the stock of Corporations S and B. P, S, and B file a consolidated Federal income tax return on a calendar year basis. P, S, and B each uses the section 861 method for allocating and apportioning their deductions. In 2010, S MPGE QPP in the United States at a cost of $1,000. On November 30, 2010, S sells the QPP to B for $2,500. On February 28, 2011, P sells 60% of the stock of B to X, an unrelated person. On June 30, 2011, B sells the QPP to U, another unrelated person, for $3,000.

(ii) Consolidated group's 2010 QPAI. Because S and B are members of a consolidated group in 2010, pursuant to § 1.199-7(d)(1) and § 1.1502-13, neither S's $1,500 of gain on the sale of QPP to B nor S's $2,500 gross receipts from the sale are taken into account in 2010. Accordingly, neither S nor B has QPAI in 2010.

(iii) Consolidated group's 2011 QPAI. B becomes a nonmember of the consolidated group at the end of the day on February 28, 2011, the date on which P sells 60% of the B stock to X. Under § 1.199-7(d)(1) and § 1.1502-13(d), S takes the intercompany transaction into account immediately before B becomes a nonmember of the consolidated group. Pursuant to § 1.1502-13(d)(1)(ii)(A)(1), because the QPP is owned by B, a nonmember of the consolidated group immediately after S's gain is taken into account, B is treated as selling the QPP to a nonmember for $2,500, B's adjusted basis in the property, immediately before B becomes a nonmember of the consolidated group. Accordingly, immediately before B becomes a nonmember of the consolidated group, S takes into account $1,500 of QPAI (S's $2,500 DPGR received from B-S's $1,000 cost of MPGE the QPP).

(iv) B's 2011 QPAI. Pursuant to § 1.1502-13(d)(2)(i)(B), the attributes of B's corresponding item, that is, its sale of the QPP to U, are determined as if the S division (but not the B division) were transferred by the P, S, and B consolidated group (treated as a single corporation) to an unrelated person. Thus, S's activities in MPGE the QPP before the intercompany sale of the QPP to B continue to affect the attributes of B's sale of the QPP. As such, B is treated as having MPGE the QPP. Accordingly, upon its sale of the QPP, B has $500 of QPAI (B's $3,000 DPGR received from U minus B's $2,500 cost of MPGE the QPP).

Example (11). Corporation X is the common parent of a consolidated group, consisting of X and Y, which has filed a consolidated Federal income tax return for many years. Corporation P is the common parent of a consolidated group, consisting of P and S, which has filed a consolidated Federal income tax return for many years. The X and P consolidated groups each file their consolidated Federal income tax returns on a calendar year basis. X, Y, P and S are members of the same EAG in 2008. In 2007, the X consolidated group incurred a consolidated net operating loss (CNOL) of $25,000, none of which was carried back and used to offset taxable income of prior taxable years. Neither P nor S (nor the P consolidated group) has ever incurred an NOL. In 2008, the X consolidated group has (prior to the deduction under section 172) taxable income of $8,000 and the P consolidated group has taxable income of $20,000. The X consolidated group uses $8,000 of its CNOL from 2007 to offset the X consolidated group's taxable income in 2008. None of the X consolidated group's remaining CNOL may be used to offset taxable income of the P consolidated group under paragraph (b)(3) of this section. Accordingly, for purposes of determining the EAG's section 199 deduction, the EAG has taxable income of $20,000 (the X consolidated group's taxable income (after the deduction under section 172) of $0 plus the P consolidated group's taxable income of $20,000).

(f) Allocation of income and loss by a corporation that is a member of the expanded affiliated group for only a portion of the year. *(1) In general.* A corporation that becomes or ceases to be a member of an EAG during its taxable year must allocate its taxable income or loss, QPAI, and W-2 wages between the portion of the taxable year that it is a member of the EAG and the portion of the taxable year that it is not a member of the EAG. This allocation of items is made by using the pro rata allocation method described in this paragraph (f)(1). Under the pro rata allocation method, an equal portion of a corporation's taxable income or loss, QPAI, and W-2 wages for the taxable year is assigned to each day of the corporation's taxable year. Those items assigned to those days that the corporation was a member of the EAG are then aggregated.

(2) Coordination with rules relating to the allocation of income under § 1.1502-76(b). If § 1.1502-76(b) (relating to items included in a consolidated return) applies to a corporation that is a member of an EAG, then any allocation of items required under this paragraph (f) is made only after the allocation of the corporation's items pursuant to § 1.1502-76(b).

(g) Total section 199 deduction for a corporation that is a member of an expanded affiliated group for some or all of its taxable year. *(1) Member of the same expanded affiliated group for the entire taxable year.* If a corporation is a member of the same EAG for its entire taxable year, the corporation's section 199 deduction for the taxable year is the amount of the section 199 deduction allocated to the corporation by the EAG under paragraph (c)(1) of this section.

(2) Member of the expanded affiliated group for a portion of the taxable year. If a corporation is a member of an EAG only for a portion of its taxable year and is either not a member of any EAG or is a member of another EAG, or both, for another portion of the taxable year, the corporation's section 199 deduction for the taxable year is the sum of its section 199 deductions for each portion of the taxable year.

(3) Example. The following example illustrates the application of paragraphs (f) and (g) of this section:

Example. (i) Facts. Corporations X and Y, calendar year corporations, are members of the same EAG for the entire 2010 taxable year. Corporation Z, also a calendar year corporation, is a member of the EAG of which X and Y are members for the first half of 2010 and not a member of any EAG for the second half of 2010. During the 2010 taxable year, neither X, Y, nor Z joins in the filing of a consolidated Federal income tax return. Assume that X, Y, and Z each has W-2 wages in excess of the section 199(b) wage limitation for all relevant periods. In 2010, X has taxable income of $2,000 and QPAI of $600, Y has a taxable loss of $400 and QPAI of ($200), and Z has taxable income of $1,400 and QPAI of $2,400.

(ii) Analysis. Pursuant to the pro rata allocation method, $700 of Z's 2010 taxable income and $1,200 of Z's 2010 QPAI are allocated to the first half of the 2010 taxable year (the period in which Z is a member of the EAG) and $700 of Z's 2010 taxable income and $1,200 of Z's 2010 QPAI are allocated to the second half of the 2010 taxable year (the period in which Z is not a member of any EAG). Accordingly, in 2010, the EAG has taxable income of $2,300 (X's $2,000 + Y's ($400) + Z's $700) and QPAI of $1,600 (X's $600 + Y's ($200) + Z's $1,200). The EAG's section 199 deduction for 2010 is therefore $144 (9% of the lesser of the EAG's $2,300 of taxable income or $1,600 of QPAI). Pursuant to § 1.199-7(c)(1), this $144 deduction is allocated to X, Y, and Z in proportion to their respective QPAI. Accordingly, X is allocated $48 of the EAG's section 199 deduction, Y is allocated $0 of the EAG's section 199 deduction, and Z is allocated $96 of the EAG's section 199 deduction. For the second half of 2010, Z has taxable income of $700 and QPAI of $1,200. Therefore, for the second half of 2010, Z has a section 199 deduction of $63 (9% of the lesser of its $700 taxable income or $1,200 QPAI for the second half of 2010). Accordingly, X's 2010 section 199 deduction is $48, Y's 2010 section 199 deduction is $0, and Z's 2010 section 199 deduction is $159, the sum of the $96 section 199 deduction of the EAG allocated to Z for the first half of 2010 and Z's $63 section 199 deduction for the second half of 2010.

(h) Computation of section 199 deduction for members of an expanded affiliated group with different taxable years. *(1) In general.* If members of an EAG have different taxable years, in determining the section 199 deduction of a member (the computing member), the computing member is required to take into account the taxable income or loss, determined without regard to the section 199 deduction, QPAI, and W-2 wages of each other group member that are both—

(i) Attributable to the period that each other member of the EAG and the computing member are members of the EAG; and

(ii) Taken into account in a taxable year that begins after the effective date of section 199 and such taxable year ends with or within the taxable year of the computing member with respect to which the section 199 deduction is computed.

(2) Example. The following example illustrates the application of this paragraph (h):

Example. (i) Corporations X, Y, and Z are members of the same EAG. Neither X, Y, nor Z is a member of a consolidated group. X and Y are calendar year taxpayers and Z is a June 30 fiscal year taxpayer. Z came into existence on July 1, 2007. Each corporation has taxable income that exceeds its QPAI and has sufficient W-2 wages to avoid the limitation under section 199(b). For the taxable year ending December 31, 2007, X's QPAI is $8,000 and Y's QPAI is ($6,000). For its taxable year ending June 30, 2008, Z's QPAI is $2,000.

(ii) In computing X's and Y's respective section 199 deductions for their taxable years ending December 31, 2007, X's and Y's taxable income, QPAI, and W-2 wages from their respective taxable years ending December 31, 2007, are aggregated. The EAG's QPAI for this purpose is $2,000 (X's QPAI of $8,000 + Y's QPAI of ($6,000)). Because the taxable years of the computing members, X and Y, began in 2007, the transition percentage under section 199(a)(2) is 6%. Accordingly, the EAG's section 199 deduction is $120 ($2,000 x .06). The $120 deduction is allocated to each of X and Y in proportion to their respective QPAI as a percentage of the QPAI of each member of the EAG that was taken into account in computing the EAG's section 199 deduction. Pursuant to paragraph (c)(1) of this section, in allocating the section 199 deduction between X and Y, because Y's QPAI is negative, Y's QPAI is treated as being $0. Accordingly, X's section 199 deduction for its taxable year ending December 31, 2007, is $120 ($120 x $8,000/($8,000 + $0)). Y's section 199 deduction for its taxable year ending December 31, 2007, is $0 ($120 x $0/($8,000 + $0)).

(iii) In computing Z's section 199 deduction for its taxable year ending June 30, 2008, X's and Y's items from their respective taxable years ending December 31, 2007, are taken into account. Therefore, X's and Y's taxable income or loss, determined without regard to the section 199 deduction, QPAI, and W-2 wages from their taxable years ending December 31, 2007, are aggregated with Z's taxable income or loss, QPAI, and W-2 wages from its taxable year ending June 30, 2008. The EAG's QPAI is $4,000 (X's QPAI of $8,000 + Y's QPAI of ($6,000) + Z's QPAI of $2,000). Because the taxable year of the computing member, Z, began in 2007, the transition percentage under section 199(a)(2) is 6%. Accordingly, the EAG's section 199 deduction is $240 ($4,000 x .06). A portion of the $240 deduction is allocated to Z in proportion to its QPAI as a percentage of the QPAI of each member of the EAG that was taken into account in computing the EAG's section 199 deduction. Pursuant to paragraph (c)(1) of this section, in allocating a portion of the $240 deduction to Z, because Y's QPAI is negative, Y's QPAI is treated as being $0. Z's section 199 deduction for its taxable year ending June 30, 2008, is $48 ($240 x $2,000/($8,000 + $0 + $2,000)).

T.D. 9263, 5/24/2006, amend T.D. 9293, 10/18/2006, T.D. 9381, 2/14/2008, T.D. 9384, 3/6/2008.

Proposed § 1.199-7 Expanded affiliated groups. [*For Preamble, see ¶ 152,713*]

(a) In general. All members of an expanded affiliated group (EAG) are treated as a single corporation for purposes of section 199. Notwithstanding the preceding sentence, except as otherwise provided in the Internal Revenue Code and regulations (see, for example, sections 199(c)(7) and 267, § 1.199-3(b), paragraph (a)(3) of this section, and the consolidated return regulations), each member of an EAG is a separate taxpayer that computes its own taxable income or loss, qualified production activites income (QPAI) (as defined in § 1.199-1(c)), and W-2 wages (as defined in § 1.199-2(f)). If members of an EAG are also members of a consolidated group, see paragraph (d) of this section.

(1) Definition of expanded affiliated group. An EAG is an affiliated group as defined in section 1504(a), determined by substituting "more than 50 percent" for "at least 80 percent" each place it appears and without regard to section 1504(b)(2) and (4).

(2) Identification of members of an expanded affiliated group. (i) In general. A corporation must determine if it is a member of an EAG on a daily basis.

(ii) Becoming or ceasing to be a member of an expanded affiliated group. If a corporation becomes or ceases to be a member of an EAG, the corporation is treated as becoming or ceasing to be a member of the EAG at the end of the day on which its status as a member changes.

(3) Attribution of activities. In general, if a member of an EAG (the disposing member) derives gross receipts (as defined in § 1.199-3(c)) from the lease, rental, license, sale, exchange, or other disposition (as defined in § 1.199-3(h)) of qualifying production property (QPP) (as defined in § 1.199-3(i)) that was manufactured, produced, grown or extracted (MPGE) (as defined in § 1.199-3(d)), in whole or in significant part (as defined in § 1.199-3(f)), in the United States (as defined in § 1.199-3(g)), a qualifed film (as defined in § 1.199-3(j)) that was produced in the United States, or electricity, natural gas, or potable water (as defined in § 1.199-3(k)) (collectively, utilities) that was produced in the United States by another member or members of the same EAG, the disposing member is treated as conducting the activities conducted by each other member of the EAG with respect to the QPP, qualified film, or utilities in determining whether its gross receipts are domestic production gross receipts (DPGR) (as defined in § 1.199-3(a)). However, attribution of activities does not apply for purposes of the construction of real property under § 1.199-3(l) or the performance of engineering and architectural services under § 1.199-3(m). A member of an EAG must engage in a construction activity under § 1.199-3(l)(2), provide engineering services under § 1.199-3(m)(2), or provide architectural services under § 1.199-3(m)(3) in order for the member's gross receipts to be derived from construction, engineering, or architectural services.

(4) Examples. The following examples illustrate the application of paragraph (a)(3) of this section:

Example (1). Corporations M and N are members of the same EAG. M is engaged solely in the trade or business of manufacturing furniture in the United States that it sells to unrelated persons. N is engaged solely in the trade or business of engraving companies' names on pens and pencils purchased from unrelated persons and then selling the pens and pencils to such companies. If N was not a member of an EAG, its activities would not qualify as MPGE. Accordingly, although M's sales of the furniture qualify as DPGR (assuming all the other requirements of § 1.199-3 are met), N's sales of the engraved pens and pencils do not qualify as DPGR because neither N nor another member of the EAG MPGE the pens and pencils.

Example (2). For the entire 2006 taxable year, Corporations A and B are members of the same EAG. A is engaged solely in the trade or business of manufacturing QPP in the United States. A and B each own 45 percent of partnership C and unrelated persons own the remaining 10 percent. C is engaged solely in the trade or business of manufacturing the same type of QPP in the United States as A. In 2006, B purchases and then resells the QPP manufactured in 2006 by A and C. B also resells QPP it purchases from unrelated persons. If only B's activities were considered, B would not qualify for the deduction under § 1.199-1(a) (section 199 deduction). However, because B is a member of the EAG that includes A, B is treated as conducting A's manufacturing activities in determining whether B's gross receipts are DPGR. C is not a member of the EAG and thus C's MPGE activities are not attributed to B in determining whether B's gross receipts are DPGR. Accordingly, B's gross receipts attributable to its sale of the QPP it purchases from A are DPGR (assuming all the other requirements of § 1.199-3 are met). B's gross receipts attributable to its sale of the QPP it purchases from C and from the unrelated persons are non-DPGR because no member of the EAG MPGE the QPP. If rather than reselling the QPP, B rented the QPP it acquired from A to unrelated persons, B's gross receipts attributable to the rental of the QPP would also be DPGR (assuming all the other requirements of § 1.199-3 are met).

(5) Anti-avoidance rule. If a transaction between members of an EAG is engaged in or structured with a principal purpose of qualifying for, or increasing the amount of, the section 199 deduction of the EAG or the portion of the section 199 deduction allocated to one or more members of the EAG, adjustments must be made to eliminate the effect of the transaction on the computation of the section 199 deduction.

(b) Computation of expanded affiliated group's section 199 deduction. *(1) In general.* The section 199 deduction for an EAG is determined by aggregating each member's taxable income or loss, QPAI, and W-2 wages. For this purpose, a member's QPAI is determined under § 1.199-1. For purposes of this determination, a member's QPAI may be positive or negative. A member's taxable income or loss and QPAI shall be determined by reference to the member's methods of accounting.

(2) Net operating loss carryovers. In determing the taxable income of an EAG, if a member of an EAG has a net operating loss (NOL) carryback or carryover to the taxable year, then the amount of the NOL used to offset taxable income cannot exceed the taxable income of that member.

(c) Allocation of an expanded affiliated group's section 199 deduction among members of the expanded affiliated group. *(1) In general.* An EAG's section 199 deduction is allocated among the members of the EAG in proportion to each member's QPAI regardless of whether the EAG member has taxable income or loss or W-2 wages for the taxable year. For this purpose, if a member has negative QPAI, the QPAI of the member shall be treated as zero.

(2) Use of section 199 deduction to create or increase a net operating loss. Notwithstanding § 1.199-1(b), which generally prevents the section 199 deduction from creating or increasing an NOL, if a member of an EAG has some or all of the EAG's section 199 deduction allocated to it under paragraph (c)(1) of this section and the amount allocated exceeds the member's taxable income (determined prior to allocation of the section 199 deduction), the section 199 deduction will create an NOL for the member. Similarly, if a member of an EAG, prior to the allocation of some or all of

the EAG's section 199 deduction to the member, has an NOL for the taxable year, the portion of the EAG's section 199 deduction allocated to the member will increase the member's NOL.

(d) Special rules for members of the same consolidated group. *(1) Intercompany transactions.* In the case of an intercompany transaction between consolidated group members S and B (intercompany transaction, S, and B as defined in § 1.1502-13(b)(1)), S takes an intercompany transaction into account in computing the section 199 deduction at the same time and in the same proportion as S takes into account the income, gain, deduction, or loss from the intercompany transaction under § 1.1502-13.

(2) Attribution of activities in the construction of real property and the performance of engineering and architectural services. Notwithstanding paragraph (a)(3) of this section, a disposing member (as described in such paragraph) is treated as conducting the activities conducted by each other member of the consolidated group with respect to the construction of real property under § 1.199-3(l) and the performance of engineering and architectural services under § 1.199-3(m).

(3) Application of the simplified deduction method and the small business simplified overall method. For purposes of applying the simplified deduction method under § 1.199-4(e) and the small business simplified overall method under § 1.199-4(f), a consolidated group determines its QPAI by reference to its members' DPGR, non-DPGR, cost of goods sold (CGS), and all other deductions, expenses, or losses (deductions), determined on a consolidated basis.

(4) Determining the section 199 deduction. (i) Expanded affiliated group consists of consolidated group and non-consolidated group members. If an EAG includes corporations that are members of the same consolidated group and corporations that are not members of the same consolidated group, in computing the taxable income of the EAG, the consolidated taxable income or loss, QPAI, and W-2 wages of the consolidated group, not the separate taxable income or loss, QPAI, and W-2 wages of the members of the consolidated group, are aggregated with the taxable income or loss, QPAI, and W-2 wages of the non-consolidated group members. For example, if A, B, C, S1, and S2 are members of the same EAG, and A, S1, and S2 are members of the same consolidated group (the A consolidated group), the A consolidated group is treated as one member of the EAG. Accordingly, the EAG is considered to have three members, the A consolidated group, B, and C. The consolidated taxable income or loss, QPAI, and W-2 wages of the A consolidated group are aggregated with the taxable income or loss, QPAI, and W-2 wages of B and C in determining the EAG's section 199 deduction.

(ii) Expanded affiliated group consists only of members of a single consolidated group. If all the members of an EAG are members of the same consolidated group, the consolidated group's section 199 deduction is determined by reference to the consolidated group's consolidated taxable income or loss, QPAI, and W-2 wages, not the separate taxable income or loss, QPAI, and W-2 wages of its members.

(5) Allocation of the section 199 deduction of a consolidated group among its members. The section 199 deduction of a consolidated group (or the section 199 deduction allocated to a consolidated group that is a member of an EAG) must be allocated to the members of the consolidated group in proportion to each consolidated group member's QPAI, regardless of whether the consolidated group member has separate taxable income or loss or W-2 wages for the taxable year. For purposes of allocating the section 199 deduction of a consolidated group among its members, any redetermination of a corporation's receipts from an intercompany transaction as DPGR or non-DPGR or as non-receipts, and any redetermination of a corporation's CGS or other deductions from an intercompany transaction as either allocable to or not allocable to DPGR under § 1.1502-13(c)(1)(i) or (c)(4) is not taken into account. Also, for purposes of this allocation, if a consolidated group member has negative QPAI, the QPAI of the member shall be treated as zero.

(e) Examples. The following examples illustrate the application of paragraphs (b), (c), and (d) of this section:

Example (1). Corporations X and Y are members of the same EAG but are not members of a consolidated group. X and Y each use the section 861 method described in § 1.199-4(d) for allocating and apportioning their deductions. X incurs $5,000 in costs in manufacturing a machine, all of which are capitalized. X is entitled to a $1,000 depreciation deduction for the machine in the current taxable year. X rents the machine to Y for $1,500. Y uses the machine in manufacturing QPP within the United States. Y incurs $1,400 of CGS in manufacturing the QPP. Y sells the QPP to unrelated persons for $7,500. Pursuant to section 199(c)(7) and § 1.199-3(b), X's rental income is non-DPGR (and its related costs are not attributable to DPGR). Accordingly, Y has $4,600 of QPAI (Y's $7,500 DPGR received from unrelated persons - Y's $1,400 CGS allocable to such receipts - Y's $1,500 of rental expense), X has $0 of QPAI, and the EAG has $4,600 of QPAI.

Example (2). The facts are the same as in Example 1 except that X and Y are members of the same consolidated group. Pursuant to section 199(c)(7) and § 1.199-3(b), X's rental income ordinarily would not be DPGR (and its related costs would not be allocable to DPGR). However, because X and Y are members of the same consolidated group, § 1.1502-13(c)(1)(i) provides that the separate entity attributes of X's income or Y's expenses, or both X's income and Y's expenses, may be redetermined in order to produce the same effect as if X and Y were divisions of a single corporation. If X and Y were divisions of a single corporation, X and Y would have QPAI of $5,100 ($7,500 DPGR received from unrelated persons - $1,400 CGS allocable to such receipts - $1,000 depreciation deduction). To obtain this same result for the consolidated group, X's rental income is recharacterized as DPGR, which results in the consolidated group having $9,000 of DPGR (the sum of Y's DPGR of $7,500 + X's DPGR of $1,500) and $3,900 of costs allocable to DPGR (the sum of Y's $1,400 CGS + Y's $1,500 rental expense + X's $1,000 depreciation expense). For purposes of determining how much of the consolidated group's section 199 deduction is allocated to X and Y, pursuant to paragraph (d)(5) of this section, the redetermination of X's rental income as DPGR under § 1.1502-13(c)(1)(i) is not taken into account (X's costs are considered to be allocable to DPGR because they are allocable to the consolidated group deriving DPGR). Accordingly, for this purpose, X is deemed to have ($1,000) of QPAI (X's $0 DPGR - X's $1,000 depreciation deduction). Because X is deemed to have negative QPAI, also pursuant to paragraph (d)(5) of this section, X's QPAI is treated as zero. Y has $4,600 of QPAI (Y's $7,500 DPGR - Y's $1,400 CGS allocable to such receipts - Y's $1,500 of rental expense). Accordingly, X is allocated $0/($0 + $4,600) of the consolidated group's section 199 deduction and Y is allocated $4,600/($0 + $4,600) of the consolidated group's section 199 deduction.

Example (3). (i) Facts. Corporations A and B are the only two members of an EAG but are not members of a consolidated group. A and B each file Federal income tax returns on a calendar year basis. The average annual gross receipts of the EAG are less than or equal to $25,000,000 and A and B each use the simplified deduction method under § 1.199-4(e). In 2006, A MPGE televisions within the United States. A has $10,000,000 of DPGR from sales of televisions to unrelated persons and $2,000,000 of DPGR from sales of televisions to B. In addition, A has gross receipts from computer consulting services with unrelated persons of $3,000,000. A has CGS of $6,000,000. A is able to determine from its books and records that $4,500,000 of its CGS are attributable to televisions sold to unrelated persons and $1,500,000 are attributable to televisions sold to B (see § 1.199-4(b)(2)). A has other deductions of $4,000,000. A has no other items of income, gain, or deductions. In 2006, B sells the televisions it purchased from A to unrelated persons for $4,100,000 and pays $100,000 for administrative services performed in 2006. B has no other items of income, gain, or deductions.

(ii) QPAI. (A) A's QPAI. In order to determine A's QPAI, A subtracts its $6,000,000 CGS from its $12,000,000 DPGR. Under the simplified deduction method, A then apportions its remaining $4,000,000 of deductions to DPGR in proportion to the ratio of its DPGR to total gross receipts. Thus, of A's $4,000,000 of deductions, $3,200,000 is apportioned to DPGR ($4,000,000 x $12,000,000/ $15,000,000). Accordingly, A's QPAI is $2,800,000 ($12,000,000 DPGR - $6,000,000 CGS - $3,200,000 deductions apportioned to its DPGR).

(B) B's QPAI. Although B did not MPGE the televisions it sold, pursuant to paragraph (a)(3) of this section, B is treated as conducting A's MPGE of the televisions in determining whether B's gross receipts are DPGR. Thus, B has $4,100,000 of DPGR. In order to determine B's QPAI, B subtracts its $2,000,000 CGS from its $4,100,000 DPGR. Under the simplified deduction method, B then apportions its remaining $100,000 of deductions to DPGR in proportion to the ratio of its DPGR to total gross receipts. Thus, because B has no other gross receipts, all of B's $100,000 of deductions is apportioned to DPGR ($100,000 x $4,100,000/ $4,100,000). Accordingly, B's QPAI is $2,000,000 ($4,100,000 DPGR - $2,000,000 CGS - $100,000 deductions apportioned to its DPGR).

Example (4). (i) Facts. The facts are the same as in Example 3 except that A and B are members of the same consolidated group, B does not sell the televisions purchased from A until 2007, and B's $100,000 paid for administrative services are paid in 2007 for services performed in 2007. In addition, in 2007, A has $3,000,000 in gross receipts from computer consulting services with unrelated persons and $1,000,000 in related deductions.

(ii) Consolidated group's 2006 QPAI. The consolidated group's DPGR and total gross receipts in 2006 are $10,000,000 and $13,000,000, respectively, because, pursuant to paragraph (d)(1) of this section and § 1.1502-13, the sale of the televisions from A to B is not taken into account in 2006. In order to determine the consolidated group's QPAI, the consolidated group subtracts its $4,500,000 CGS from the televisions sold to unrelated persons from its $10,000,000 DPGR. Under the simplified deduction method, the consolidated group apportions its remaining $4,000,000 of deductions to DPGR in proportion to the ratio of its DPGR to total gross receipts. Thus, $3,076,923 ($4,000,000 x $10,000,000/$13,000,000) is allocated to DPGR. Accordingly, the consolidated group's QPAI for 2006 is $2,423,077 ($10,000,000 DPGR - $4,500,000 CGS - $3,076,923 deductions apportioned to its DPGR).

(iii) Allocation of consolidated group's 2006 section 199 deduction to its members. Because B's only activity during 2006 is the purchase of televisions from A, B has no DPGR or deductions and thus, no QPAI, in 2006. Accordingly, the entire section 199 deduction in 2006 for the consolidated group will be allocated to A.

(iv) Consolidated group's 2007 QPAI. Pursuant to paragraph (d)(1) of this section and § 1.1502-13(c), A's sale of televisions to B in 2006 is taken into account in 2007 when B sells the televisions to unrelated persons. However, because A and B are members of a consolidated group, § 1.1502-13(c)(1)(i) provides that the separate entity attributes of A's income or B's expenses, or both A's income and B's expenses, may be redetermined in order to produce the same effect as if A and B were divisions of a single corporation. Accordingly, A's $2,000,000 of gross receipts are redetermined to be non-DPGR and non-receipts and B's $2,000,000 CGS are redetermined to be not allocable to DPGR. Notwithstanding that A's receipts are redetermined to be non-DPGR and non-receipts, A's CGS are still considered to be allocable to DPGR because they are allocable to the consolidated group deriving DPGR. Accordingly, the consolidated group's DPGR in 2007 is $4,100,000 from B's sales of televisions, and its total receipts are $7,100,000 ($4,100,000 DPGR plus $3,000,000 non-DPGR from A's computer consulting services). To determine the consolidated group's QPAI, the consolidated group subtracts A's $1,500,000 CGS from the televisions sold to B from its $4,100,000 DPGR. Under the simplified deduction method, the consolidated group apportions its remaining $1,100,000 of deductions ($1,000,000 from A and $100,000 from B) to DPGR in proportion to the consolidated group's ratio of its DPGR to total gross receipts. Thus, $635,211 ($1,100,000 x $4,100,000/$7,100,000) is allocated to DPGR. Accordingly, the consolidated group's QPAI for 2007 is $1,964,789 ($4,100,000 DPGR - $1,500,000 CGS - $635,211 deductions apportioned to its DPGR), the same QPAI that would result if A and B were divisions of a single corporation.

(v) Allocation of consolidated group's 2007 section 199 deduction to its members. (A) A's QPAI. For purposes of allocating the consolidated group's section 199 deduction to its members, pursuant to paragraph (d)(5) of this section, the redetermination of A's $2,000,000 in receipts as non-DPGR and non-receipts is disregarded. Accordingly, for this purpose, A's DPGR is $2,000,000 (receipts from the sale of televisions to B taken into account in 2007) and its total receipts are $5,000,000 ($2,000,000 DPGR + $3,000,000 non-DPGR from its computer consulting services). In determining A's QPAI, A subtracts its $1,500,000 CGS from the televisions sold to B from its $2,000,000 DPGR. Under the simplified deduction method, A apportions its remaining $1,000,000 of deductions in proportion to the ratio of its DPGR to total receipts. Thus, $400,000 ($1,000,000 x $2,000,000/$5,000,000) is allocated to DPGR. Thus, A's QPAI is $100,000 ($2,000,000 DPGR - $1,500,000 CGS - $400,000 deductions allocated to its DPGR).

(B) B's QPAI. B's DPGR and its total gross receipts are each $4,100,000. For purposes of allocating the consolidated group's section 199 deduction to its members, pursuant to paragraph (d)(5) of this section, the redetermination of B's $2,000,000 CGS as not allocable to DPGR is disregarded. In determining B's QPAI, B subtracts its $2,000,000 CGS from the televisions purchased from A from its $4,100,000 DPGR.

Under the simplified deduction method, B apportions its remaining $100,000 deductions in proportion to the ratio of its DPGR to total receipts. Thus, all $100,000 ($100,000 x $4,100,000/$4,100,000) is allocated to DPGR. Thus, B's QPAI is $2,000,000 ($4,100,000 DPGR - $2,000,000 CGS - $100,000 deductions allocated to its DPGR).

(C) Allocation to A and B. Pursuant to paragraph (d)(5) of this section, the consolidated group's section 199 deduction for 2007 is allocated $100,000/($100,000 + $2,000,000) to A and $2,000,000/ ($100,000 + $2,000,000) to B.

Example (5). Corporations S and B are members of the same consolidated group. In 2006, S manufactures office furniture for B to use in B's corporate headquarters and S sells the office furniture to B. S and B have no other activities in the taxable year. If S and B were not members of a consolidated group, S's gross receipts from the sale of the office furniture to B would be DPGR (assuming all the other requirements of § 1.199-3 are met) and S's CGS or other deductions, expenses, or losses from the sale to B would be allocable to S's DPGR. However, because S and B are members of a consolidated group, the separate entity attributes of S's income or B's expenses, or both S's income and B's expenses, may be redetermined under § 1.1502-13(c)(1)(i) or (c)(4) in order to produce the same effect as if S and B were divisions of a single corporation. If S and B were divisions of a single corporation, there would be no DPGR with respect to the office furniture because there would be no lease, rental, license, sale, exchange, or other disposition of the furniture by the single corporation (and no CGS or other deductions allocable to DPGR). Thus, in order to produce the same effect as if S and B were divisions of a single corporation, S's gross receipts are redetermined as non-DPGR. Accordingly, the consolidated group has no DPGR (and no CGS or other deductions allocated or apportioned to DPGR) and receives no section 199 deduction in 2006.

Example (6). Corporations X, Y, and Z are members of the same EAG but are not members of a consolidated group. X, Y, and Z each files Federal income tax returns on a calendar year basis. Assume that the EAG has W-2 wages in excess of the section 199(b) wage limitation. Prior to 2006, X had no taxable income or loss. In 2006, X has $0 of taxable income and $2,000 of QPAI, Y has $4,000 of taxable income and $3,000 of QPAI, and Z has $4,000 of taxable income and $5,000 of QPAI. Accordingly, the EAG has taxable income of $8,000, the sum of X's taxable income of $0, Y's taxable income of $4,000, and Z's taxable income of $4,000. The EAG has QPAI of $10,000, the sum of X's QPAI of $2,000, Y's QPAI of $3,000, and Z's QPAI of $5,000. Because X's, Y's, and Z's taxable years all began in 2006, the transition percentage under section 199(a)(2) is 3 percent. Thus, the EAG's section 199 deduction for 2006 is $240 (3% of the lesser of the EAG's taxable income of $8,000 or the EAG's QPAI of $10,000). Pursuant to paragraph (c)(1) of this section, the $240 section 199 deduction is allocated to X, Y, and Z in proportion to their respective amounts of QPAI, that is $48 to X ($240 x $2,000/$10,000), $72 to Y ($240 x $3,000/$10,000), and $120 to Z ($240 x $5,000/$10,000). Although X's taxable income for 2006 determined prior to allocation of a portion of the EAG's section 199 deduction to it was $0, pursuant to paragraph (c)(2) of this section X will have an NOL for 2006 equal to $48. Because X's NOL for 2006 cannot be carried back to a previous taxable year, X's NOL carryover to 2007 will be $48.

(f) Allocation of income and loss by a corporation that is a member of the expanded affiliated group for only a portion of the year. *(1) In general.* A corporation that becomes or ceases to be a member of an EAG during its taxable year must allocate its taxable income or loss, QPAI, and W-2 wages between the portion of the taxable year that it is a member of the EAG and the portion of the taxable year that it is not a member of the EAG. In general, this allocation of items must be made by using the pro rata allocation method described in paragraph (f)(1)(i) of this section. However, a corporation may elect to use the section 199 closing of the books method described in paragraph (f)(1)(ii) of this section. Neither the pro rata allocation method nor the section 199 closing of the books method is a method of accounting.

(i) Pro rata allocation method. Under the pro rata allocation method, an equal portion of a corporation's taxable income or loss, QPAI, and W-2 wages for the taxable year is assigned to each day of the corporation's taxable year. Those items assigned to those days that the corporation was a member of the EAG are then aggregated.

(ii) Section 199 closing of the books method. Under the section 199 closing of the books method, a corporation's taxable income or loss, QPAI, and W-2 wages for the period during which the corporation was a member of an EAG are computed by treating the corporation's taxable year as two separate taxable years, the first of which ends at the close of the day on which the corporation's status as a member of the EAG changes and the second of which begins at the beginning of the day after the corporation's status as a member of the EAG changes.

(iii) Making the section 199 closing of the books election. A corporation makes the section 199 closing of the books election by making the following statement: "The section 199 closing of the books election is hereby made with respect to [insert name of corporation and its employer identification number] with respect to the following periods [insert dates of the two periods between which items are allocated pursuant to the closing of the books method]." The statement must be filed with the corporation's timely filed (including extensions) Federal income tax return for the taxable year that includes the periods that are subject to the election. Once made, a section 199 closing of the books election is irrevocable.

(2) Coordination with rules relating to the allocation of income under § 1.1502-76(b). If § 1.1502-76(b) (relating to items included in a consolidated return) applies to a corporation that is a member of an EAG, any allocation of items required under this paragraph (f) is made only after the allocation of the corporation's items pursuant to § 1.1502-76(b).

(g) Total section 199 deduction for a corporation that is a member of an expanded affiliated group for some or all of its taxable year. *(1) Member of the same expanded affiliated group for the entire taxable year.* If a corporation is a member of the same EAG for its entire taxable year, the corporation's section 199 deduction for the taxable year is the amount of the section 199 deduction allocated to the corporation by the EAG under paragraph (c)(1) of this section.

(2) Member of the expanded affiliated group for a portion of the taxable year. If a corporation is a member of an EAG only for a portion of its taxable year and is either not a member of any EAG or is a member of another EAG, or both, for another portion of the taxable year, the corporation's section 199 deduction for the taxable year is the sum of its section 199 deductions for each portion of the taxable year.

(3) Example. The following example illustrates the application of paragraphs (f) and (g) of this section:

Example. Corporations X and Y, calendar year corporations, are members of the same EAG for the entire 2005 taxable year. Corporation Z, also a calendar year corporation, is a member of the EAG of which X and Y are members for the first half of 2005 and not a member of any EAG for the second half of 2005. During the 2005 taxable year, Z does not join in the filing of a consolidated return. Z makes a section 199 closing of the books election. As a result, Z has $80 of taxable income and $100 of QPAI that is allocated to the first half of the taxable year and a $150 taxable loss and ($200) of QPAI that is allocated to the second half of the taxable year. Taking into account Z's taxable income, QPAI, and W-2 wages allocated to the first half of the taxable year pursuant to the section 199 closing of the books election, the EAG has positive taxable income and QPAI for the taxable year and W-2 wages in excess of the section 199(b) wage limitation. Because the EAG has both positive taxable income and QPAI and sufficient W-2 wages, and because Z has positive QPAI for the first half of the year, a portion of the EAG's section 199 deduction is allocated to Z. Because Z has negative QPAI for the second half of the year, Z is allowed no section 199 deduction for the second half of the taxable year. Thus, despite the fact that Z has a $70 taxable loss and ($100) of QPAI for the entire 2005 taxable year, Z is entitled to a section 199 deduction for the taxable year equal to the section 199 deduction allocated to Z as a member of the EAG.

(h) Computation of section 199 deduction for members of an expanded affiliated group with different taxable years. *(1) In general.* If members of an EAG have different taxable years, in determining the section 199 deduction of a member (the computing member), the computing member is required to take into account the taxable income or loss, QPAI, and W-2 wages of each group member that are both—

(i) Attributable to the period that the member of the EAG and the computing member are both members of the EAG; and

(ii) Taken into account in a taxable year that begins after the effective date of section 199 and ends with or within the taxable year of the computing member with respect to which the section 199 deduction is computed.

(2) Example. The following example illustrates the application of this paragraph (h):

Example. (i) Corporations X, Y, and Z are members of the same EAG. Neither X, Y, nor Z is a member of a consolidated group. X and Y are calendar year taxpayers and Z is a June 30 fiscal year taxpayer. Each corporation has taxable income that exceeds its QPAI and has sufficient W-2 wages to avoid the limitation under section 199(b). For its taxable year ending June 30, 2005, Z's QPAI is $4,000. For the taxable year ending December 31, 2005, X's QPAI is $8,000 and Y's QPAI is ($6,000). For its taxable year ending June 30, 2006, Z's QPAI is $2,000.

(ii) Because Z's taxable year ending June 30, 2005, began on July 1, 2004, prior to the effective date of section 199, Z is not allowed a section 199 deduction for its taxable year ending June 30, 2005.

(iii) In computing X's and Y's respective section 199 deductions for their taxable years ending December 31, 2005, Z's items from its taxable year ending June 30, 2005, are not taken into account because Z's taxable year began before the effective date of section 199. Instead, only X's and Y's taxable income, QPAI, and W-2 wages from their respective taxable years ending December 31, 2005, are aggregated. The EAG's QPAI for this purpose is $2,000 (X's QPAI of $8,000 + Y's QPAI of ($6,000)). Because the taxable years of the computing members, X and Y, began in 2005, the transition percentage under section 199(a)(2) is 3 percent. Accordingly, the EAG's section 199 deduction is $60 ($2,000 x .03). The $60 deduction is allocated to each of X and Y in proportion to their respective QPAI as a percentage of the QPAI of each member of the EAG that was taken into account in computing the EAG's section 199 deduction. Pursuant to paragraph (c)(1) of this section, in allocating the section 199 deduction between X and Y, because Y's QPAI is negative, Y's QPAI is treated as being $0. Accordingly, X's section 199 deduction for its taxable year ending December 31, 2005, is $60 ($60 x $8,000/($8,000 + $0)). Y's section 199 deduction for its taxable year ending December 31, 2005, is $0 ($60 x $0/($8,000 + $0)).

(iv) In computing Z's section 199 deduction for its taxable year ending June 30, 2006, X's and Y's items from their respective taxable years ending December 31, 2005, are taken into account. Therefore, X's and Y's taxable income or loss, QPAI, and W-2 wages from their taxable years ending December 31, 2005, are aggregated with Z's taxable income or loss, QPAI, and W-2 wages from its taxable year ending June 30, 2006. The EAG's QPAI is $4,000 (X's QPAI of $8,000 + Y's QPAI of ($6,000) + Z's QPAI of $2,000). Because the taxable year of the computing member, Z, began in 2005, the transition percentage under section 199(a)(2) is 3 percent. Accordingly, the EAG's section 199 deduction is $120 ($4,000 x .03). A portion of the $120 deduction is allocated to Z in proportion to its QPAI as a percentage of the QPAI of each member of the EAG that was taken into account in computing the EAG's section 199 deduction. Pursuant to paragraph (c)(1) of this section, in allocating a portion of the $120 deduction to Z, because Y's QPAI is negative, Y's QPAI is treated as being $0. Z's section 199 deduction for its taxable year ending June 30, 2006, is $24 ($120 x $2,000/($8,000 + $0 + $2,000)).

§ 1.199-8 Other rules.

(a) In general. The provisions of this section apply solely for purposes of section 199 of the Internal Revenue Code (Code). When calculating the deduction under § 1.199-1(a) (section 199 deduction), taxpayers are required to make numerous allocations under § § 1.199-1 through 1.199-9. In making these allocations, taxpayers may use any reasonable method that is satisfactory to the Secretary based on all of the facts and circumstances, unless the regulations under § § 1.199-1 through 1.199-9 specify a method. A change in a taxpayer's method of allocating or apportioning gross receipts, cost of goods sold (CGS), expenses, losses, or deductions (deductions) does not constitute a change in method of accounting to which the provisions of sections 446 and 481 and the regulations thereunder apply. For purposes of §§ 1.199-1 through 1.199-9, use of terms such as payment, paid, incurred, or paid or incurred is not intended to provide any specific rule based upon the use of one term versus another. In general, the use of the term payment, paid, incurred, or paid or incurred is intended to convey the appropriate standard under the taxpayer's method of accounting.

(b) Individuals. In the case of an individual, the section 199 deduction is equal to the applicable percentage of the lesser of the taxpayer's qualified production activities income (QPAI) (as defined in § 1.199-1(c)) for the taxable year, or adjusted gross income (AGI) for the taxable year determined after applying sections 86, 135, 137, 219, 221, 222, and 469, and without regard to section 199.

(c) Trade or business requirement. *(1) In general.* Sections 1.199-1 through 1.199-9 are applied by taking into account only items that are attributable to the actual conduct of a trade or business.

(2) Individuals. An individual engaged in the actual conduct of a trade or business must apply § § 1.199-1 through 1.199-9 by taking into account in computing QPAI only items that are attributable to that trade or business (or trades or businesses) and any items allocated from a pass-thru entity engaged in a trade or business. Compensation received by an individual employee for services performed as an employee is not considered gross receipts for purposes of computing QPAI under § § 1.199-1 through 1.199-9. Similarly, any costs or expenses paid or incurred by an individual employee with respect to those services performed as an employee are not considered CGS or deductions of that employee for purposes of computing QPAI under § § 1.199-1 through 1.199-9.

(3) Trusts and estates. For purposes of this paragraph (c), a trust or estate is treated as an individual.

(d) Coordination with alternative minimum tax. For purposes of determining alternative minimum taxable income (AMTI) under section 55, a taxpayer that is not a corporation must deduct an amount equal to 9 percent (3 percent in the case of taxable years beginning in 2005 or 2006, and 6 percent in the case of taxable years beginning in 2007, 2008, or 2009) of the lesser of the taxpayer's QPAI for the taxable year, or the taxpayer's taxable income for the taxable year, determined without regard to the section 199 deduction (or in the case of an individual, AGI). For purposes of determining AMTI in the case of a corporation (including a corporation subject to tax under section 511(a)), a taxpayer must deduct an amount equal to 9 percent (3 percent in the case of taxable years beginning in 2005 or 2006, and 6 percent in the case of taxable years beginning in 2007, 2008, or 2009) of the lesser of the taxpayer's QPAI for the taxable year, or the taxpayer's AMTI for the taxable year, determined without regard to the section 199 deduction. For purposes of computing AMTI, QPAI is determined without regard to any adjustments under sections 56 through 59. In the case of an individual or a non-grantor trust or estate, AGI and taxable income are also determined without regard to any adjustments under sections 56 through 59. The amount of the deduction allowable under this paragraph (d) for any taxable year cannot exceed 50 percent of the W-2 wages of the employer for the taxable year (as determined under § 1.199-2). The section 199 deduction is not taken into account in determining the amount of the alternative tax net operating loss deduction (ATNOL) allowed under section 56(a)(4). For example, assume that for the calendar year 2007, a corporation has both AMTI (before the NOL deduction and before the section 199 deduction) and QPAI of $1,000,000, and has an ATNOL carryover to 2007 of $5,000,000.

Assume that the taxpayer has W-2 wages in excess of the section 199(b) wage limitation.

Under section 56(d), the ATNOL deduction for 2007 is $900,000 (90 percent of $1,000,000), reducing AMTI to $100,000. The taxpayer must then further reduce the AMTI by the section 199 deduction of $6,000 (six percent of the lesser of $1,000,000 or $100,000) to $94,000. The ATNOL carryover to 2008 is $4,100,000.

(e) Nonrecognition transactions. *(1) In general.* (i) Sections 351, 721, and 731. Except as provided for an EAG partnership (as defined in §§ 1.199-3(i)(8) and 1.199-9(j)) and an expanded affiliated group (EAG) (as defined in § 1.199-7), if property is transferred by the taxpayer to an entity in a transaction to which section 351 or 721 applies, then whether the gross receipts derived by the entity are domestic production gross receipts (DPGR) (as defined in § 1.199-3) shall be determined based solely on the activities performed by the entity without regard to the activities performed by the taxpayer prior to the contribution of the property to the entity. Except as provided for a qualifying in-kind partnership (as defined in §§ 1.199-3(i)(7) and 1.199-9(i)) and an EAG partnership, if property is transferred by a partnership to a partner in a transaction to which section 731 applies, then whether gross receipts derived by the partner are DPGR shall be determined based on the activities performed by the partner without regard to the activities performed by the partnership before the distribution of the property to the partner.

(ii) Exceptions. (A) Section 708(b)(1)(B). If property is deemed to be contributed by a partnership (transferor partnership) to another partnership (transferee partnership) as a result of a termination under section 708(b)(1)(B), then the transferee partnership shall be treated as performing those activities performed by the transferor partnership with respect to the transferred property of the transferor partnership.

(B) Transfers by reason of death. If property is transferred upon or by reason of the death of an individual (decedent), then the decedent's successor(s) in interest shall be treated as having performed those activities performed by or deemed to have been performed (pursuant to § 1.199-3(i)(7) or § 1.199-9(i)) by the decedent with respect to the transferred property. For this purpose, a transfer shall include without limitation the passing of the property by bequest, contractual provision, beneficiary designation, or operation of law, and successor in interest shall include without limitation the decedent's heirs or legatees, the decedent's estate or trust, or the beneficiary or beneficiaries of the decedent's estate or trust.

(2) Section 1031 exchanges. If a taxpayer exchanges property for replacement property in a transaction to which section 1031 applies, then whether the gross receipts derived from the lease, rental, license, sale, exchange, or other disposition of the replacement property are DPGR shall be determined based solely on the activities performed by the taxpayer with respect to the replacement property.

(3) Section 381 transactions. If a corporation (the acquiring corporation) acquires the assets of another corporation (the target corporation) in a transaction to which section 381(a) applies, then the acquiring corporation shall be treated as performing those activities of the target corporation with respect to the acquired assets of the target corporation. Therefore, to the extent that the acquired assets of the target corporation would have given rise to DPGR if leased, rented, licensed, sold, exchanged, or otherwise disposed of by the target corporation, such assets will give rise to DPGR if leased, rented, licensed, sold, exchanged, or otherwise disposed of by the acquiring corporation (assuming all the other requirements of § 1.199-3 are met).

(f) Taxpayers with a 52-53 week taxable year. For purposes of applying § 1.441-2(c)(1) in the case of a taxpayer using a 52-53 week taxable year, any reference in section 199(a)(2) (the phase-in rule), § § 1.199-1 through 1.199-9 to a taxable year beginning after a particular calendar year means a taxable year beginning after December 31st of that year. Similarly, any reference to a taxable year beginning in a particular calendar year means a taxable year beginning after December 31st of the preceding calendar year. For example, a 52-53 week taxable year that begins on December 26, 2006, is deemed to begin on January 1, 2007, and the transition percentage for that taxable year is 6 percent.

(g) Section 481(a) adjustments. For purposes of determining QPAI, a section 481(a) adjustment, whether positive or negative, taken into account by a taxpayer during the taxable year that is solely attributable to either the taxpayer's gross receipts, CGS, or deductions must be allocated or apportioned between DPGR and non-DPGR using the methods used by a taxpayer to allocate or apportion gross receipts, CGS, and deductions between DPGR and non-DPGR for the current taxable year. See § § 1.199-1 and 1.199-4 for rules related to the allocation and apportionment of gross receipts, CGS, and deductions, respectively. For example, if a taxpayer changes its method of accounting for inventories from the last-in, first-out (LIFO) method to the first-in, first-out (FIFO) method and the taxpayer uses the small business simplified overall method to apportion CGS between DPGR and non-DPGR, the taxpayer is required to apportion the resulting section 481(a) adjustment, whether positive or negative, between DPGR and non-DPGR using the small business simplified overall method. If a section 481(a) adjustment is not solely attributable to either gross receipts, CGS, or deductions (for example, the taxpayer changes its overall method of accounting from an accrual method to the cash method) and the section 481(a) adjustment cannot be specifically identified with either gross receipts, CGS, or deductions, then the section 481(a) adjustment, whether positive or negative, must be attributed to, or among, gross receipts, CGS, or deductions using any reasonable method that is satisfactory to the Secretary based on all of the facts and circumstances, and then allocated or apportioned between DPGR and non-DPGR using the same methods the taxpayer uses to allocate or apportion gross receipts, CGS, or deductions between DPGR and non-DPGR for the taxable year or taxable years that the section 481(a) adjustment is taken into account. Factors taken into consideration in determining whether the method is reasonable include whether the taxpayer uses the most accurate information available; the relationship between the section 481(a) adjustment and the apportionment base chosen; the accuracy of the method chosen as compared with other possible methods; and the time, burden, and cost of using alternative methods. If a section 481(a) adjustment is spread over more than one taxable year, then a taxpayer must attribute the section 481(a) adjustment among gross receipts, CGS, or deductions, as applicable, in the same amount for each taxable year within the spread period. For example, if a taxpayer, using a reasonable method that is satisfactory to the Secretary based on all of the facts and circumstances, determines that a section 481(a) adjustment that is required to be spread over four taxable years should be attributed half to gross receipts and half to deductions, then the taxpayer must attribute the section 481(a) adjustment half to gross receipts and half to deductions in each of the four taxable years of the spread period. Further, if such taxpayer uses the simplified deduction method to apportion deductions between DPGR and non-DPGR in the first taxable year of the spread period, then the taxpayer must use the simplified deduction method to apportion half the section 481(a) adjustment for that taxable year between DPGR and non-DPGR for that taxable year. Similarly, if in the second taxable year of the spread period the taxpayer uses the section 861 method to apportion and allocate costs between DPGR and non-DPGR, then the taxpayer must use the section 861 method to allocate and apportion half the section 481(a) adjustment for that taxable year between DPGR and non-DPGR for that taxable year.

(h) Disallowed losses or deductions. Except as provided by publication in the Internal Revenue Bulletin (see § 601.601(d)(2)(ii)(b) of this chapter), losses or deductions of a taxpayer that otherwise would be taken into account in computing the taxpayer's section 199 deduction are taken into account only if and to the extent the deductions are not disallowed by section 465 or 469, or any other provision of the Code. If only a portion of the taxpayer's share of the losses or deductions is allowed for a taxable year, the proportionate share of those allowable losses or deductions that are allocated to the taxpayer's qualified production activities, determined in a manner consistent with sections 465 and 469, and any other applicable provision of the Code, is taken into account in computing QPAI for purposes of the section 199 deduction for that taxable year. To the extent that any of the disallowed losses or deductions are allowed in a later year, the taxpayer takes into account a proportionate share of those losses or deductions in computing it QPAI for that later taxable year. Losses or deductions of the taxpayer that are disallowed for taxable years beginning on or before December 31, 2004, are not taken into account in a later year for purposes of computing the taxpayer's QPAI and the wage limitation of section 199(d)(1)(A)(iii) under § 1.199-9 for that taxable year, regardless of whether the losses or deductions are allowed for other purposes. For taxpayers that are partners in partnerships, see §§ 1.199-5(b)(2) and 1.199-9(b)(2). For taxpayers that are shareholders in S corporations, see §§ 1.199-5(c)(2) and 1.199(c)(2).

(i) Effective dates. *(1) In general.* Section 199 applies to taxable years beginning after December 31, 2004. Sections 1.199-1 through 1.199-8 are applicable for taxable years beginning on or after June 1, 2006. For a taxable year beginning on or before May 17, 2006, the enactment date of the Tax Increase Prevention and Reconciliation Act of 2005 (Public Law 109-222, 120 Stat. 345), a taxpayer may apply § § 1.199-1 through 1.199-9 provided that the taxpayer applies all provisions in § § 1.199-1 through 1.199-9 to the taxable year. For a taxable year beginning after May 17, 2006, and before June 1, 2006, a taxpayer may apply § § 1.199-1 through 1.199-8 provided that the taxpayer applies all provisions in § § 1.199-1 through 1.199-8 to the taxable year. For a taxpayer who chooses not to rely on these final regulations for a taxable year beginning before June 1, 2006, the guidance under section 199 that applies to such taxable year is contained in Notice 2005-14 (2005-1 C.B. 498) (see § 601.601(d)(2) of this chapter). In addition, a taxpayer also may rely on the provisions of REG-105847-05 (2005-47 I.R.B. 987) (see § 601.601(d)(2) of this chapter) for a taxable year beginning before June 1, 2006. If Notice 2005-14 and REG-105847-05 include different rules for the same particular issue, then a taxpayer may rely on either the rule set forth in Notice 2005-14 or the rule set forth in REG-105847-05. However, if REG-105847-05 includes a rule that was not included in Notice 2005-14, then a taxpayer is not permitted to rely on the absence of a rule in Notice 2005-14 to apply a rule contrary to REG-105847-05. For taxable years beginning after May 17, 2006, and before June 1, 2006, a taxpayer may not apply Notice 2005-14, REG-105847-05, or any other guidance under section 199 in a manner inconsistent with amendments made to section 199 by section 514 of the Tax Increase Prevention and Reconciliation Act of 2005.

(2) Pass-thru entities. In determining the deduction under section 199, items arising from a taxable year of a partnership, S corporation, estate, or trust beginning before January 1, 2005, shall not be taken into account for purposes of section 199(d)(1).

(3) Non-consolidated EAG members. A member of an EAG that is not a member of a consolidated group may apply paragraph (i)(1) of this section without regard to how

other members of the EAG apply paragraph (i)(1) of this section.

(4) Computer software. Section 1.199-3(i)(5)(ii)(B) and (i)(6)(ii) through (v) are applicable for taxable years beginning on or after March 20, 2007. A taxpayer may apply § 1.199-3(i)(5)(ii)(B) and (i)(6)(ii) through (v) to taxable years beginning after December 31, 2004, and before March 20, 2007.

(5) Tax Increase Prevention and Reconciliation Act of 2005. Sections 1.199-2(e)(2), 1.199-3(i)(7) and (8), and 1.199-5 are applicable for taxable years beginning on or after October 19, 2006. A taxpayer may apply §§ 1.199-2(e)(2), 1.199-3(i)(7) and (8), and 1.199-5 to taxable years beginning after May 17, 2006, and before October 19, 2006, regardless of whether the taxpayer otherwise relied upon Notice 2005-14 (2005-1 CB 498) (see Sec. 601.601(d)(2)(ii)(b) of this chapter), the provisions of REG-105847-05 (2005-2 CB 987), or §§ 1.199-1 through 1.199-8.

(6) Losses used to reduce taxable income of expanded affiliated group. Section 1.199-7(b)(4) is applicable for taxable years beginning on or after February 15, 2008. For taxable years beginning on or after October 19, 2006, and before February 15, 2008, see § 1.199-7T(b)(4) (see 26 CFR part 1 revised as of April 1, 2007).

(7) Agricultural and horticultural cooperatives. Section 1.199-6(c) is applicable for taxable years beginning on or after March 20, 2007. A taxpayer may apply § 1.199-(6)(c) to taxable years beginning after December 31, 2004, and before March 20, 2007.

(8) Qualified film produced by the taxpayer. Section 1.199-3(k) is applicable to taxable years beginning on or after March 7, 2008. A taxpayer may apply § 1.199-3(k) to taxable years beginning after December 31, 2004, and before March 7, 2008. However, for taxable years beginning before June 1, 2006, a taxpayer may rely on § 1.199-3(k) only if the taxpayer does not apply Notice 2005-14 (2005-1 CB 498) (see § 601.601(d)(2)(ii)(b) of this chapter) or REG-105847-05 (2005-2 CB 987) (see § 601.601(d)(2)(ii)(b) of this chapter) to the taxable year.

(9) Expanded affiliated groups. Section 1.199-7(e), Example 10, (f)(1), and (g)(3) are applicable to taxable years beginning on or after March 7, 2008. A taxpayer may apply § 1.199-7(e), Example 10, to taxable years beginning after December 31, 2004, and before March 7, 2008.

T.D. 9263, 5/24/2006, amend T.D. 9293, 10/18/2006, T.D. 9317, 3/19/2007, T.D. 9381, 2/14/2008, T.D. 9384, 3/6/2008.

Proposed § 1.199-8 Other rules. [*For Preamble, see ¶ 152,713*]

(a) Individuals. In the case of an individual, the deduction under § 1.199-1(a) (section 199 deduction) is equal to the applicable percentage of the lesser of the taxpayer's qualified production activities income (QPAI) (as defined in § 1.199-1(c)) for the taxable year, or adjusted gross income (AGI) for the taxable year determined after applying sections 86, 135, 137, 219, 221, 222, and 469, and without regard to section 199.

(b) Trade or business requirement. Section 1.199-3 is applied by taking into account only items that are attributable to the actual conduct of a trade or business.

(c) Coordination with alternative minimum tax. For purposes of determining alternative minimum taxable income (AMTI) under section 55, a taxpayer that is not a corporation may deduct an amount equal to 9 percent (3 percent in the case of taxable years beginning in 2005 or 2006, and 6 percent in the case of taxable years beginning in 2007, 2008, or 2009) of the lesser of the taxpayer's QPAI for the taxable year, or the taxpayer's taxable income for the taxable year, determined without regard to the section 199 deduction (or in the case of an individual, AGI). For purposes of determining AMTI in the case of a corporation (including a corporation subject to tax under section 511(a)), a taxpayer may deduct an amount equal to 9 percent (3 percent in the case of taxable years beginning in 2005 or 2006, and 6 percent in the case of taxable years beginning in 2007, 2008, or 2009) of the lesser of the taxpayer's QPAI for the taxable year, or the taxpayer's AMTI for the taxable year, determined without regard to the section 199 deduction. For purposes of computing AMTI, QPAI is determined without regard to any adjustments under sections 56 through 59. In the case of an individual or a trust, AGI and taxable income are also determined without regard to any adjustments under sections 56 through 59. The amount of the deduction allowable under this paragraph (c) for any taxable year cannot exceed 50 percent of the W-2 wages of the employer for the taxable year (as determined under § 1.199-2).

(d) Nonrecognition transactions. *(1) In general.* Except as provided for an expanded affiliated group (EAG) (as defined in § 1.199-7) and EAG partnerships (as defined in § 1.199-3(h)(8)), if property is transferred by the taxpayer to an entity in a transaction to which section 351 or 721 applies, then whether the gross receipts derived by the entity are domestic production gross receipts (DPGR) (as defined in § 1.199-3) shall be determined based on the activities performed by the entity without regard to the activities performed by the taxpayer prior to the contribution of the property to the entity. Except as provided in § 1.199-3(h)(7) and (8) (exceptions for certain oil and gas partnerships and EAG partnerships), if property is transferred by a partnership to a partner in a transaction to which section 731 applies, then whether gross receipts derived by the partner are DPGR shall be determined based on the activities performed by the partner without regard to the activities performed by the partnership before the distribution of the property to the partner.

(2) Section 1031 exchanges. If a taxpayer exchanges property for replacement property in a transaction to which section 1031 applies, then whether the gross receipts derived from the lease, rental, license, sale, exchange, or other disposition of the replacement property are DPGR shall be determined based solely on the activities performed by the taxpayer with respect to the replacement property.

(3) Section 381 transactions. If a corporation (the acquiring corporation) acquires the assets of another corporation (the target corporation) in a transaction to which section 381(a) applies, the acquiring corporation shall be treated as performing those activities of the target corporation with respect to the acquired assets of the target corporation. Therefore, to the extent that the acquired assets of the target corporation would have given rise to DPGR if leased, rented, licensed, sold, exchanged, or otherwise disposed of by the target corporation, then the assets will give rise to DPGR if leased, rented, licensed, sold, exchanged, or otherwise disposed of by the acquiring corporation.

(e) Taxpayers with a 52-53 week taxable year. For purposes of applying § 1.441-2(c)(1) in the case of a taxpayer using a 52-53 week taxable year, any reference in section 199(a)(2) (the phase-in rule), §§ 1.199-1 through 1.199-7, and this section to a taxable year beginning after a particular calendar year means a taxable year beginning after December 31st of that year. Similarly, any reference to a taxable year beginning in a particular calendar year means a taxable year beginning after December 31st of the preceding calendar year. For example, a 52-53 week taxable year that begins on December 26, 2004, is deemed to begin on January 1, 2005, and the transition percentage for that taxable year is 3 percent.

(f) Section 481(a) adjustments. For purposes of determining QPAI, a section 481(a) adjustment, whether positive or negative, taken into account during the taxable year that is solely attributable to either gross receipts, cost of goods sold (CGS), or deductions, expenses, or losses (deductions) must be allocated or apportioned in the same manner as the gross receipts, CGS, or deductions to which it is attributable. See §§ 1.199-1(d), 1.199-4(b), and 1.199-4(c) for rules related to the allocation and apportionment of gross receipts, CGS, and deductions. For example, if a taxpayer changes its method of accounting for inventories from the last-in, first-out (LIFO) method to the first-in, first-out (FIFO) method, the taxpayer is required to allocate the resulting section 481(a) adjustment, whether positive or negative, in the same manner as the CGS computed for the taxable year with respect to those inventories. If a section 481(a) adjustment is not solely attributable to either gross receipts, CGS, or deductions (for example, the taxpayer changes its overall method of accounting from an accrual method to the cash method and the section 481(a) adjustment cannot be specifically identified with either gross receipts, CGS, or deductions), the section 481(a) adjustment, whether positive or negative, must be attributed to, or among, gross receipts, CGS, or deductions using any reasonable method that is satisfactory to the Secretary and allocated or apportioned in the same manner as the gross receipts, CGS, or deductions to which it is attributable. Factors taken into consideration in determining whether the method is reasonable include whether the taxpayer uses the most accurate information available; the relationship between the section 481(a) adjustment and the apportionment base chosen; the accuracy of the method chosen as compared with other possible methods; and the time, burden, and cost of using various methods. If a section 481(a) adjustment is spread over more than one taxable year, a taxpayer must attribute the section 481(a) adjustment among gross receipts, CGS, or deductions, as applicable, in the same manner for each taxable year within the spread period. For example, if a taxpayer, using a reasonable method, determines that a section 481(a) adjustment that is required to be spread over four taxable years should be attributed entirely to gross receipts, then the taxpayer must attribute the section 481(a) adjustment entirely to gross receipts in each of the four taxable years of the spread period.

(g) Effective date. The final regulations will be applicable to taxable years beginning after December 31, 2004. In the case of pass-thru entities described in § 1.199-5, the final regulations will be applicable to taxable years of pass-thru entities beginning after December 31, 2004. Until the date final regulations are published in the Federal Register, taxpayers may rely on the interim guidance on section 199 as set forth in Notice 2005-14 (2005-7 I.R.B. 498) (see § 601.601(d)(2) of this chapter), as well as the proposed regulations under §§ 1.199-1 through 1.199-7, and this section. For this purpose, if the proposed regulations and Notice 2005-14 include different rules for the same particular issue, then the taxpayer may rely on either the rule set forth in the proposed regulations or the rule set forth in Notice 2005-14. However, if the proposed regulations include a rule that was not included in Notice 2005-14, taxpayers are not permitted to rely on the absence of a rule to apply a rule contrary to the proposed regulations.

§ 1.199-9 Application of section 199 to pass-thru entities for taxable years beginning on or before May 17, 2006, the enactment date of the Tax Increase Prevention and Reconciliation Act of 2005.

(a) In general. The provisions of this section apply solely for purposes of section 199 of the Internal Revenue Code (Code).

(b) Partnerships. *(1) In general.* (i) Determination at partner level. The deduction with respect to the qualified production activities of the partnership allowable under § 1.199-1(a) (section 199 deduction) is determined at the partner level. As a result, each partner must compute its deduction separately. The section 199 deduction has no effect on the adjusted basis of the partner's interest in the partnership. Except as provided by publication pursuant to paragraph (b)(1)(ii) of this section, for purposes of this section, each partner is allocated, in accordance with sections 702 and 704, its share of partnership items (including items of income, gain, loss, and deduction), cost of goods sold (CGS) allocated to such items of income, and gross receipts that are included in such items of income, even if the partner's share of CGS and other deductions and losses exceeds domestic production gross receipts (DPGR) (as defined in § 1.199-3(a)) and regardless of the amount of the partner's share of W-2 wages (as defined in § 1.199-2(e)) of the partnership for the taxable year. A partnership may specially allocate items of income, gain, loss, or deduction to its partners, subject to the rules of section 704(b) and the supporting regulations. Guaranteed payments under section 707(c) are not considered allocations of partnership income for purposes of this section. Guaranteed payments under section 707(c) are deductions by the partnership that must be taken into account under the rules of § 1.199-4. See § 1.199-3(p) and paragraph (b)(6) Example 5 of this section. Except as provided in paragraph (b)(1)(ii) of this section, to determine its section 199 deduction for the taxable year, a partner aggregates its distributive share of such items, to the extent they are not otherwise disallowed by the Code, with those items it incurs outside the partnership (whether directly or indirectly) for purposes of allocating and apportioning deductions to DPGR and computing its qualified production activities income (QPAI) (as defined in § 1.199-1(c)).

(ii) Determination at entity level. The Secretary may, by publication in the Internal Revenue Bulletin (see § 601.601(d)(2)(ii)(b) of this chapter), permit a partnership to calculate a partner's share of QPAI at the entity level, instead of allocating, in accordance with sections 702 and 704, the partner's share of partnership items (including items of income, gain, loss, and deduction). If a partnership does calculate QPAI at the entity level—

(A) The partner is allocated its share of QPAI and W-2 wages (as defined in § 1.199-2(e)), which (subject to the limitations of paragraph (b)(2) of this section and section 199(d)(1)(A)(iii), respectively) are combined with the partner's QPAI and W-2 wages from other sources;

(B) For purposes of computing the partner's QPAI under §§ 1.199-1 through 1.199-9, a partner does not take into account the items from the partnership (for example, a partner does not take into account items from the partnership in determining whether a threshold or de minimis rule applies or in allocating and apportioning deductions) in calculating its QPAI from other sources;

(C) A partner generally does not recompute its share of QPAI from the partnership using another method; however, the partner might have to adjust its share of QPAI from the partnership to take into account certain disallowed losses or deductions, or the allowance of suspended losses or deductions; and

(D) A partner's distributive share of QPAI from a partnership may be less than zero.

(2) Disallowed losses or deductions. Except as provided by publication in the Internal Revenue Bulletin (see § 601.601(d)(2)(ii)(b) of this chapter), losses or deductions of a partnership that otherwise would be taken into account in computing the partner's section 199 deduction for a taxable year are taken into account in that year only if and to the extent the partner's distributive share of those losses or deductions from all of the partnership's activities is not disallowed by section 465, 469, or 704(d), or any other provision of the Code. If only a portion of the partner's distributive share of the losses or deductions is allowed for a taxable year, a proportionate share of those allowable losses or deductions that are allocated to the partnership's qualified production activities, determined in a manner consistent with sections 465, 469, and 704(d), and any other applicable provision of the Code, is taken into account in computing QPAI and the wage limitation of section 199(d)(1)(A)(iii) for that taxable year. To the extent that any of the disallowed losses or deductions are allowed in a later taxable year, the partner takes into account a proportionate share of those losses or deductions in computing its QPAI for that later taxable year. Losses or deductions of the partnership that are disallowed for taxable years beginning on or before December 31, 2004, are not taken into account in a later taxable year for purposes of computing the partner's QPAI or the wage limitation of section 199(d)(1)(A)(iii) for that taxable year, regardless of whether the losses or deductions are allowed for other purposes.

(3) Partner's share of W-2 wages. Under section 199(d)(1)(A)(iii), a partner's share of W-2 wages of a partnership for purposes of determining the partner's section 199(b) wage limitation is the lesser of the partner's allocable share of those wages (without regard to section 199(d)(1)(A)(iii)), or 2 times 3 percent of the QPAI computed by taking into account only the items of the partnership allocated to the partner for the taxable year of the partnership. Except as provided by publication in the Internal Revenue Bulletin (see § 601.601(d)(2)(ii)(b) of this chapter), this QPAI calculation is performed by the partner using the same cost allocation method that the partner uses in calculating the partner's section 199 deduction. The partnership must allocate W-2 wages (prior to the application of the wage limitation) among the partners in the same manner as wage expense. The partner must add the partner's share of the W-2 wages from the partnership, as limited by section 199(d)(1)(A)(iii), to the partner's W-2 wages from other sources, if any. If QPAI, computed by taking into account only the items of the partnership allocated to the partner for the taxable year (as required by the wage limitation of section 199(d)(1)(A)(iii)) is not greater than zero, then the partner may not take into account any W-2 wages of the partnership in applying the wage limitation of § 1.199-2 (but the partner will, nevertheless, aggregate its distributive share of partnership items including wage expense with those items not from the partnership in computing its QPAI when determining its section 199 deduction). See § 1.199-2 for the computation of W-2 wages, and paragraph (g) of this section for rules regarding pass-thru entities in a tiered structure.

(4) Transition percentage rule for W-2 wages. With regard to partnerships, for purposes of section 199(d)(1)(A)(iii)(II) the transition percentages determined under section 199(a)(2) shall be determined by reference to the partnership's taxable year. Thus, if a partner uses a calendar year taxable year, and owns an interest in a partnership that has a taxable year ending on April 30, the partner's section 199(d)(1)(A)(iii) wage limitation for the partnership's taxable year beginning on May 1, 2006, would be calculated using 3 percent, even though the partner includes the partner's distributive share of partnership items from that taxable year on the partner's 2007 Federal income tax return.

(5) Partnerships electing out of subchapter K. For purposes of § § 1.199-1 through 1.199-9, the rules of this paragraph (b) apply to all partnerships, including those partnerships electing under section 761(a) to be excluded, in whole or in part, from the application of subchapter K of chapter 1 of the Code.

(6) Examples. The following examples illustrate the application of this paragraph (b). Assume that each partner has sufficient adjusted gross income or taxable income so that the section 199 deduction is not limited under section 199(a)(1)(B); that the partnership and each of its partners (whether individual or corporate) are calendar year taxpayers; and that the amount of the partnership's W-2 wages equals wage expense for each taxable year. The examples are as follows:

Example (1). Section 861 method with interest expense. (i) Partnership Federal income tax items. X and Y, unrelated United States corporations, are each 50% partners in PRS, a partnership that engages in production activities that generate both DPGR and non-DPGR. X and Y share all items of income, gain, loss, deduction, and credit 50% each. Both X and Y are engaged in a trade or business. PRS is not able to specifically identify CGS allocable to DPGR and non-DPGR. In this case, because CGS is definitely related under the facts and circumstances to all of PRS's gross income, apportionment of CGS between DPGR and non-DPGR based on gross receipts is appropriate. For 2006, the adjusted basis of PRS's business assets is $5,000, $4,000 of which generate gross income attributable to DPGR and $1,000 of which generate gross income attributable to non-DPGR. For 2006, PRS has the following Federal income items:

DPGR	$3,000
Non-DPGR	$3,000
CGS (includes $200 of W-2 wages)	$3,240
Section 162 selling expenses (includes $300 of W-2 wages)	$1,200
Interest expense (not included in CGS)	$ 300

(ii) Allocation of PRS's items of income, gain, loss, deduction, or credit. X and Y each receive the following distributive share of PRS's items of income, gain, loss, deduction or credit, as determined under the principles of § 1.704-1(b)(1)(vii):

Gross income attributable to DPGR ($1,500 (DPGR) - $810 (allocable CGS, includes $50 of W-2 wages))	$690
Gross income attributable to non-DPGR ($1,500 (non-DPGR) - $810 (allocable CGS, includes $50 of W-2 wages))	$690
Section 162 selling expenses (includes $150 of W-2 wages)	$600
Interest expense (not included in CGS)	$150

(iii) Determination of QPAI. (A) X's QPAI. Because the section 199 deduction is determined at the partner level, X determines its QPAI by aggregating, to the extent necessary, its distributive share of PRS's Federal income tax items with all other such items from all other, non-PRS-related activities. For 2006, X does not have any other such items. For 2006, the adjusted basis of X's non-PRS assets, all of which are investment assets, is $10,000. X's only gross receipts for 2006 are those attributable to the allocation of gross income from PRS. X allocates and apportions its deductible items to gross income attributable to DPGR under the section 861 method of § 1.199-4(d). In this case, the section 162 selling expenses (including W-2 wages) are definitely related to all of PRS's gross receipts. Based on the facts and circumstances of this specific case, apportionment of those expenses between DPGR and non-DPGR on the basis of PRS's gross receipts is appropriate. X elects to apportion its distributive share of interest expense under the tax book value method of § 1.861-9T(g). X's QPAI for 2006 is $366, as shown below:

DPGR	$1,500
CGS allocable to DPGR (includes $50 of W-2 wages)	($ 810)
Section 162 selling expenses (includes $75 of W-2 wages) ($600 x $1,500/$3,000)	($ 300)
Interest expense (not included in CGS) ($150 x $2,000 (X's share of PRS's DPGR assets)/$12,500 (X's non-PRS assets ($10,000) and X's share of PRS assets ($2,500)))	($ 24)
X's QPAI	$ 366

(B) Y's QPAI. (1) For 2006, in addition to the activities of PRS, Y engages in production activities that generate both DPGR and non-DPGR. Y is able to specifically identify CGS allocable to DPGR and to non-DPGR. For 2006, the adjusted basis of Y's non-PRS assets attributable to its production activities that generate DPGR is $8,000 and to other production activities that generate non-DPGR is $2,000. Y has no other assets. Y has the following Federal income tax items relating to its non-PRS activities:

Gross income attributable to DPGR ($1,500 (DPGR) - $900 (allocable CGS, includes $70 of W-2 wages))	$ 600
Gross income attributable to non-DPGR ($3,000 (other gross receipts) - $1,620 (allocable CGS, includes $150 of W-2 wages))	$1,380
Section 162 selling expenses (includes $30 of W-2 wages)	$ 540
Interest expense (not included in CGS)	$ 90

(2) Y determines its QPAI in the same general manner as X. However, because Y has other trade or business activities outside of PRS, Y must aggregate its distributive share of PRS's Federal income tax items with its own such items. Y allocates and apportions its deductible items to gross income attributable to DPGR under the section 861 method of § 1.199-4(d). In this case, Y's distributive share of PRS's section 162 selling expenses (including W-2 wages), as well as those selling expenses from Y's non-PRS activities, are definitely related to all of its gross income. Based on the facts and circumstances of this specific case, apportionment of those expenses between DPGR and non-DPGR on the basis of Y's gross receipts is appropriate. Y elects to apportion its distributive share of interest expense under the tax book value method of § 1.861-9T(g). Y has $1,290 of gross income attributable to DPGR ($3,000 DPGR ($1,500 from PRS and $1,500 from non-PRS activities)— $1,710 CGS ($810 from PRS and $900 from non-PRS activities)). Y's QPAI for 2006 is $642, as shown below:

DPGR ($1,500 from PRS and $1,500 from non-PRS activities)	$3,000
CGS allocable to DPGR ($810 from PRS and $900 from non-PRS activities) (includes $120 of W-2 wages)	($1,710)
Section 162 selling expenses (includes $180 of W-2 wages) ($1,140 ($600 from PRS and $540 from non-PRS activities) x ($1,500 PRS DPGR + $1,500 non-PRS DPGR)/($3,000 PRS total gross receipts + $4,500 non-PRS total gross receipts))	($ 456)
Interest expense (not included in CGS) ($240 ($150 from PRS and $90 from non-PRS activities) x $10,000 (Y's non-PRS DPGR assets ($8,000) and Y's share of PRS DPGR assets ($2,000))/$12,500 (Y's non-PRS assets ($10,000) and Y's share of PRS assets ($2,500)))	($ 192)
Y's QPAI	$ 642

(iv) PRS W-2 wages allocated to X and Y under section 199(d)(1)(A)(iii). Solely for purposes of calculating the PRS W-2 wages that are allocated to them under section 199(d)(1)(A)(iii) for purposes of the wage limitation of section 199(b), X and Y must separately determine QPAI taking into account only the items of PRS allocated to them. X and Y must use the same methods of allocation and apportionment that they use to determine their QPAI in paragraphs (iii)(A) and (B) of this Example 1, respectively. Accordingly, X and Y must apportion deductible section 162 selling expenses that include W-2 wage expense on the basis of gross receipts, and must apportion interest expense according to the tax book value method of § 1.861-9T(g).

(A) QPAI of X and Y, solely for this purpose, is determined by allocating and apportioning each partner's share of PRS expenses to each partner's share of PRS gross income of $690 attributable to DPGR ($1,500 DPGR - $810 CGS, apportioned based on gross receipts). Thus, QPAI of X and Y solely for this purpose is $270, as shown below:

DPGR	$1,500
CGS allocable to DPGR	($ 810)
Section 162 selling expenses (including W-2 wages) ($600 x ($1,500/$3,000))	($ 300)
Interest expense (not included in CGS) ($150 x $2,000 (partner's share of adjusted basis of PRS's DPGR assets)/ $2,500 (partner's share of adjusted basis of total PRS assets))	($ 120)
QPAI	$ 270

(B) X's and Y's shares of PRS's W-2 wages determined under section 199(d)(1)(A)(iii) for purposes of the wage limitation of section 199(b) are $16, the lesser of $250 (partner's allocable share of PRS's W-2 wages ($100 included in total CGS, and $150 included in selling expenses) and $16 (2 x ($270 x .03)).

(v) Section 199 deduction determination. (A) X's tentative section 199 deduction is $11 (.03 x $366 (that is, QPAI determined at partner level)) subject to the wage limitation of $8 (50% x $16). Accordingly, X's section 199 deduction for 2006 is $8.

(B) Y's tentative section 199 deduction is $19 (.03 x $642 (that is, QPAI determined at the partner level) subject to the wage limitation of $133 (50% x ($16 from PRS and $250 from non-PRS activities)). Accordingly, Y's section 199 deduction for 2006 is $19.

Example (2). Section 861 method with R&E expense. (i) Partnership items of income, gain, loss, deduction or credit. X and Y, unrelated United States corporations each of which is engaged in a trade or business, are partners in PRS, a partnership that engages in production activities that generate both DPGR and non-DPGR. Neither X nor Y is a member of an affiliated group. X and Y share all items of income, gain, loss, deduction, and credit 50% each. All of PRS's domestic production activities that generate DPGR are within Standard Industrial Classification (SIC) Industry Group AAA (SIC AAA). All of PRS's production activities that generate non-DPGR are within SIC Industry Group BBB (SIC BBB). PRS is not able to specifically identify CGS allocable to DPGR and to non-DPGR and, therefore, apportions CGS to DPGR and non-DPGR based on its gross receipts. PRS incurs $900 of research and experimentation expenses (R&E) that are deductible under section 174, $300 of which are performed with respect to SIC AAA and $600 of which are performed with respect to SIC BBB. None of the R&E is legally mandated R&E as described in § 1.861-17(a)(4) and none is included in CGS. PRS incurs section 162 selling expenses (that include W-2 wage expense) that are not includible in CGS and are definitely related to all of PRS's gross income. For 2006, PRS has the following Federal income tax items:

DPGR (all from sales of products within SIC AAA)	$3,000
Non-DPGR (all from sales of products within SIC BBB)	$3,000
CGS (includes $200 of W-2 wages)	$2,400
Section 162 selling expenses (includes $100 of W-2 wages)	$ 840
Section 174 R&E-SIC AAA	$ 300
Section 174 R&E-SIC BBB	$ 600

(ii) Allocation of PRS's items of income, gain, loss, deduction, or credit. X and Y each receive the following distributive share of PRS's items of income, gain, loss, deduction, or credit, as determined under the principles of § 1.704-1(b)(1)(vii):

Gross income attributable to DPGR ($1,500 DPGR) - $600 (CGS, includes $50 of W-2 wages))	$900
Gross income attributable to non-DPGR ($1,500 (other gross receipts) - $600 (CGS, includes $50 of W-2 wages))	$900
Section 162 selling expenses (includes $50 of W-2 wages)	$420
Section 174 R&E-SIC AAA	$150
Section 174 R&E-SIC BBB	$300

(iii) Determination of QPAI. (A) X's QPAI. Because the section 199 deduction is determined at the partner level, X determines its QPAI by aggregating, to the extent necessary, its distributive shares of PRS's Federal income tax items with all other such items from all other, non-PRS-related activities. For 2006, X does not have any other such tax items. X's only gross receipts for 2006 are those attributable to the allocation of gross income from PRS. As stated, all of PRS's domestic production activities that generate DPGR are within SIC AAA. X allocates and apportions its deductible items to gross income attributable to DPGR under the section 861 method of § 1.199-4(d). In this case, the section 162 selling expenses (including W-2 wages) are definitely related to all of PRS's gross income. Based on the facts and circumstances of this specific case, apportionment of those expenses between DPGR and non-DPGR on the basis of PRS's gross receipts is appropriate. For purposes of apportioning R&E, X elects to use the sales method as described in § 1.861-17(c). Because X has no direct sales of products, and because all of PRS's SIC AAA sales attributable to X's share of PRS's gross income generate DPGR, all of X's share of PRS's section 174 R&E attributable to SIC AAA is taken into account for purposes of determining X's QPAI. Thus, X's total QPAI for 2006 is $540, as shown below:

DPGR (all from sales of products within SIC AAA)	$1,500
CGS (includes $50 of W-2 wages)	($ 600)
Section 162 selling expenses (including W-2 wages) ($420 x ($1,500 DPGR/ $3,000 total gross receipts))	($ 210)
Section 174 R&E-SIC AAA	($ 150)
X's QPAI	$ 540

(B) Y's QPAI. (1) For 2006, in addition to the activities of PRS, Y engages in domestic production activities that generate both DPGR and non-DPGR. With respect to those non-PRS activities, Y is not able to specifically identify CGS allocable to DPGR and to non-DPGR. In this case, because CGS is definitely related under the facts and circumstances to all of Y's non-PRS gross receipts, apportionment of CGS between DPGR and non-DPGR based on Y's non-PRS gross receipts is appropriate. For 2006, Y has the following non-PRS Federal income tax items:

DPGR (from sales of products within SIC AAA)	$1,500
DPGR (from sales of products within SIC BBB)	$1,500
Non-DPGR (from sales of products within SIC BBB)	$3,000
CGS (allocated to DPGR within SIC AAA) (includes $56 of W-2 wages)	$ 750
CGS (allocated to DPGR within SIC BBB) (includes $56 of W-2 wages)	$ 750
CGS (allocated to non-DPGR within SIC BBB) (includes $113 of W-2 wages)	$1,500
Section 162 selling expenses (includes $30 of W-2 wages)	$ 540
Section 174 R&E-SIC AAA	$ 300
Section 174 R&E-SIC BBB	$ 450

(2) Because Y has DPGR as a result of activities outside PRS, Y must aggregate its distributive share of PRS's Federal income tax items with such items from all its other, non-PRS-related activities. Y allocates and apportions its deductible items to gross income attributable to DPGR under the section 861 method of § 1.199-4(d). In this case, the section 162 selling expenses (including W-2 wages) are definitely related to all of Y's gross income. Based on the facts and circumstances of the specific case, apportionment of such expenses between DPGR and non-DPGR on the basis of Y's gross receipts is appropriate. For purposes of apportioning R&E, Y elects to use the sales method as described in § 1.861-17(c).

(3) With respect to sales that generate DPGR, Y has gross income of $2,400 ($4,500 DPGR ($1,500 from PRS and $3,000 from non-PRS activities) - $2,100 CGS ($600 from sales of products by PRS and $1,500 from non-PRS activities)). Because all of the sales in SIC AAA generate DPGR, all of Y's share of PRS's section 174 R&E attributable to SIC AAA and the section 174 R&E attributable to SIC AAA that Y incurs in its non-PRS activities are taken into account for purposes of determining Y's QPAI. Because only a portion of the sales within SIC BBB generate DPGR, only a portion of the section 174 R&E attributable to SIC BBB is taken into account in determining Y's QPAI. Thus, Y's QPAI for 2006 is $1,282, as shown below:

DPGR ($4,500 DPGR ($1,500 from PRS and $3,000 from non-PRS activities)	$4,500
CGS ($600 from sales of products by PRS and $1,500 from non-PRS activities)	(2,100)
Section 162 selling expenses (including W-2 wages) ($420 from PRS + $540 from non-PRS activities) x ($4,500 DPGR/ $9,000 total gross receipts)	(480)
Section 174 R&E-SIC AAA ($150 from PRS and $300 from non-PRS activities)......	(450)
Section 174 R&E-SIC BBB ($300 from PRS + $450 from non-PRS activities) x ($1,500 DPGR/$6,000 total gross receipts allocated to SIC BBB ($1,500 from PRS and $4,500 from non-PRS activities))........	(188)
Y's QPAI................................	1,282

(iv) PRS W-2 wages allocated to X and Y under section 199(d)(1)(A)(iii). Solely for purposes of calculating the PRS W-2 wages that are allocated to X and Y under section 199(d)(1)(A)(iii) for purposes of the wage limitation of section 199(b), X and Y must separately determine QPAI taking into account only the items of PRS allocated to them. X and Y must use the same methods of allocation and apportionment that they use to determine their QPAI in paragraphs (iii)(A) and (B) of this Example 2, respectively. Accordingly, X and Y must apportion section 162 selling expenses that include W-2 wage expense on the basis of gross receipts, and apportion section 174 R&E expense under the sales method as described in § 1.861-17(c).

(A) QPAI of X and Y, solely for this purpose, is determined by allocating and apportioning each partner's share of PRS expenses to each partner's share of PRS gross income of $900 attributable to DPGR ($1,500 DPGR - $600 CGS, allocated based on PRS's gross receipts). Because all of PRS's SIC AAA sales generate DPGR, all of X's and Y's shares of PRS's section 174 R&E attributable to SIC AAA is taken into account for purposes of determining X's and Y's QPAI. None of PRS's section 174 R&E attributable to SIC BBB is taken into account because PRS has no DPGR within SIC BBB. Thus, X and Y each has QPAI, solely for this purpose, of $540, as shown below:

DPGR (all from sales of products within SIC AAA)	$1,500
CGS (includes $50 of W-2 wages)	($ 600)
Section 162 selling expenses (including W-2 wages) ($420 x $1,500/$3,000)	($ 210)
Section 174 R&E-SIC AAA	($ 150)
QPAI	$ 540

(B) X's and Y's shares of PRS's W-2 wages determined under section 199(d)(1)(A)(iii) for purposes of the wage limitation of section 199(b) are $32, the lesser of $150 (partner's allocable share of PRS's W-2 wages ($100 included in CGS, and $50 included in selling expenses)) and $32 (2 x ($540 x .03)).

(v) Section 199 deduction determination. (A) X's tentative section 199 deduction is $16 (.03 x $540 (QPAI determined at partner level)) subject to the wage limitation of $16 (50% x $32). Accordingly, X's section 199 deduction for 2006 is $16.

(B) Y's tentative section 199 deduction is $38 (.03 x $1,282 (QPAI determined at partner level) subject to the wage limitation of $144 (50% x $287 ($32 from PRS + $255 from non-PRS activities)). Accordingly, Y's section 199 deduction for 2006 is $38.

Example (3). Partnership with special allocations. (i) In general. X and Y are unrelated corporate partners in PRS and each is engaged in a trade or business. PRS is a partnership that engages in a domestic production activity and other activities. In general, X and Y share all partnership items of income, gain, loss, deduction, and credit equally, except that 80% of the wage expense of PRS and 20% of PRS's other expenses are specially allocated to X (substantial economic effect under section 704(b) is presumed). In the 2006 taxable year, PRS's only wage expense is $2,000 for marketing, which is not included in CGS. PRS has $8,000 of gross receipts ($6,000 of which is DPGR), $4,000 of CGS ($3,500 of which is allocable to DPGR), and $3,000 of deductions (comprised of $2,000 of wages for marketing and $1,000 of other expenses). X qualifies for and uses the simplified deduction method under § 1.199-4(e). Y does not qualify to use that method and, therefore, must use the section 861 method under § 1.199-4(d). In the 2006 taxable year, X has gross receipts attributable to non-partnership trade or business activities of $1,000 and wages of $200. None of X's non-PRS gross receipts is DPGR.

(ii) Allocation and apportionment of costs. Under the partnership agreement, X's distributive share of the items of PRS is $1,250 of gross income attributable to DPGR ($3,000 DPGR - $1,750 allocable CGS), $750 of gross income attributable to non-DPGR ($1,000 non-DPGR - $250 allocable CGS), and $1,800 of deductions (comprised of X's special allocations of $1,600 of wage expense ($2,000 x 80%) for marketing and $200 of other expenses ($1,000 x 20%)). Under the simplified deduction method, X apportions $1,200 of other deductions to DPGR ($2,000 ($1,800 from the partnership and $200 from non-partnership activities) x ($3,000 DPGR/$5,000 total gross receipts)). Accordingly, X's QPAI is $50 ($3,000 DPGR - $1,750 CGS - $1,200 of deductions). However, in determining the section 199(d)(1)(A)(iii) wage limitation, QPAI is computed taking into account only the items of PRS allocated to X for the taxable year of PRS. Thus, X apportions $1,350 of deductions to DPGR ($1,800 x ($3,000 DPGR/$4,000 total gross receipts from PRS)). Accordingly, X's QPAI for purposes of the section 199(d)(1)(A)(iii) wage limitation is $0 ($3,000 DPGR - $1,750 CGS - $1,350 of deductions). X's share of PRS's W-2 wages is $0, the lesser of $1,600 (X's 80% allocable share of $2,000 of wage expense for marketing) and $0 (2 x ($0 QPAI x .03)). X's tentative deduction is $2 ($50 QPAI x .03), subject to the section 199(b)(1) wage limitation of $100 (50% x $200 ($0 of PRS-related W-2 wages + $200 of non-PRS W-2 wages)). Accordingly, X's section 199 deduction for the 2006 taxable year is $2.

Example (4). Partnership with no W-2 wages. (i) Facts. A, an individual, and B, an individual, are partners in PRS. PRS is a partnership that engages in manufacturing activities that generate both DPGR and non-DPGR. A and B share all items of income, gain, loss, deduction, and credit equally. In the 2006 taxable year, PRS has total gross receipts of $2,000 ($1,000 of which is DPGR), CGS of $400 and deductions of $800. PRS has no W-2 wages. A and B each use the small business simplified overall method under § 1.199-4(f). A has trade or business activities outside of PRS. With respect to those activities, A has total gross receipts of $1,000 ($500 of which is DPGR), CGS of $400 (including $50 of W-2 wages) and deductions of $200 for the 2006 taxable year. B has no trade or business activities outside of PRS and pays $0 of W-2 wages directly for the 2006 taxable year. A's distributive share of the items of the partnership is $500 DPGR, $500 non-DPGR, $200 CGS, and $400 of deductions.

(ii) Section 199(d)(1)(A)(iii) wage limitation. A's CGS and deductions apportioned to DPGR from PRS equal $300 (($200 CGS + $400 of other deductions) x ($500 DPGR/$1,000 total gross receipts)). Accordingly, for purposes of the wage limitation of section 199(d)(1)(A)(iii), A's QPAI is $200 ($500 DPGR - $300 CGS and other deductions). A's share of partnership W-2 wages after application of the section 199(d)(1)(A)(iii) limitation is $0, the lesser of $0 (A's 50% allocable share of PRS's $0 of W-2 wages) or $12 (2 x ($200 QPAI x .03)). B's share of PRS's W-2 wages also is $0.

(iii) Section 199 deduction computation. A's total CGS and deductions apportioned to DPGR equal $600 (($200 PRS CGS + $400 outside trade or business CGS + $400 PRS deductions + $200 outside trade or business deductions) x ($1,000 total DPGR ($500 from PRS + $500 from outside trade or business)/$2,000 total gross receipts ($1,000 from PRS + $1,000 from outside trade or business)). Accordingly, A's QPAI is $400 ($1,000 DPGR - $600 CGS and deductions). A's tentative deduction is $12 ($400 QPAI x .03), subject to the section 199(b)(1) wage limitation of $25 (50% x $50 total W-2 wages). A's section 199 deduction for the 2006 taxable year is $12. B's total section 199 deduction for the 2006 taxable year is $0 because B has no W-2 wages for the 2006 taxable year.

Example (5). Guaranteed payment. (i) Facts. The facts are the same as Example 4 except that in 2006 PRS also makes a guaranteed payment of $200 to A for services, and PRS pays $200 of W-2 wages to PRS employees, which is included within the $400 of CGS. See section 707(c). This guaranteed payment is taxable to A as ordinary income and is properly deducted by PRS under section 162. Pursuant to § 1.199-3(p), A may not treat any part of this payment as DPGR. Accordingly, PRS has total gross receipts of $2,000 ($1,000 of which is DPGR), CGS of $400 (including $200 of W-2 wages) and deductions of $1,000 (including the $200 guaranteed payment) for the 2006 taxable year. A's distributive share of the items of the partnership is $500 DPGR, $500 non-DPGR, $200 CGS, and $500 of deductions.

(ii) Section 199(d)(1)(A)(iii) wage limitation. A's CGS and deductions apportioned to DPGR from PRS equal $350 (($200 CGS + $500 of other deductions) x ($500 DPGR/$1,000 total gross receipts)). Accordingly, for purposes of the wage limitation of section 199(d)(1)(A)(iii), A's QPAI is $150 ($500 DPGR - $350 CGS and other deductions). A's share of partnership W-2 wages after application of the section 199(d)(1)(A)(iii) limitation is $9, the lesser of $100 (A's 50% allocable share of PRS's $200 of W-2 wages) or $9 (2 x ($150 QPAI x .03)). B's share of PRS's W-2 wages after application of section 199(d)(1)(A)(iii) also is $9.

(iii) A's section 199 deduction computation. A's total CGS and deductions apportioned to DPGR equal $591 (($200 PRS CGS + $400 outside trade or business CGS + $500 PRS deductions + $200 outside trade or business deductions) x ($1,000 total DPGR ($500 from PRS + $500 from outside trade or business)/$2,200 total gross receipts ($1,000 from PRS + $200 guaranteed payment + $1,000 from outside trade or business)). Accordingly, A's QPAI is $409 ($1,000 DPGR - $591 CGS and other deductions). A's tentative deduction is $12 ($409 QPAI x .03), subject to the section 199(b)(1) wage limitation of $30 (50% x $59 ($9 PRS W-2 wages + $50 W-2 wages from A's trade or business activities outside of PRS)). A's section 199 deduction for the 2006 taxable year is $12.

(iv) B's section 199 deduction computation. B's QPAI is $150 ($500 DPGR - $350 CGS and other deductions). B's tentative deduction is $5 ($150 QPAI x .03), subject to the section 199(b)(1) wage limitation of $5 (50% x $9). Assuming that B engages in no other activities generating DPGR, B's section 199 deduction for the 2006 taxable year is $5.

(c) S corporations. *(1) In general.* (i) Determination at shareholder level. The section 199 deduction with respect to the qualified production activities of an S corporation is determined at the shareholder level. As a result, each shareholder must compute its deduction separately. The section 199 deduction will have no effect on the basis of a shareholder's stock in an S corporation. Except as provided by publication pursuant to paragraph (c)(1)(ii) of this section, for purposes of this section, each shareholder is allocated, in accordance with section 1366, its pro rata share of S corporation items (including items of income, gain, loss, and deduction), CGS allocated to such items of income, and gross receipts included in such items of income, even if the shareholder's share of CGS and other deductions and losses exceeds DPGR, and regardless of the amount of the shareholder's share of the W-2 wages of the S corporation for the taxable year. Except as provided by publication under paragraph (c)(1)(ii) of this section, to determine its section 199 deduction for the taxable year, the shareholder aggregates its pro rata share of such items, to the extent they are not otherwise disallowed by the Code, with those items it incurs outside the S corporation (whether directly or indirectly) for purposes of allocating and apportioning deductions to DPGR and computing its QPAI.

(ii) Determination at entity level. The Secretary may, by publication in the Internal Revenue Bulletin (see § 601.601(d)(2)(ii)(b) of this chapter), permit an S corporation to calculate a shareholder's share of QPAI at the entity level, instead of allocating, in accordance with section 1366, the shareholder's pro rata share of S corporation items (including items of income, gain, loss, and deduction). If an S corporation does calculate QPAI at the entity level—

(A) Each shareholder is allocated its share of QPAI and W-2 wages, which (subject to the limitations under paragraph (c)(2) of this section and section 199(d)(1)(A)(iii), respectively) are combined with the shareholder's QPAI and W-2 wages from other sources;

(B) For purposes of computing the shareholder's QPAI under §§ 1.199-1 through 1.199-9, a shareholder does not take into account the items from the S corporation (for example, a shareholder does not take into account items from the S corporation in determining whether a threshold or de minimis rule applies or in allocating and apportioning deductions) in calculating its QPAI from other sources;

(C) A shareholder generally does not recompute its share of QPAI from the S corporation using another method; however, the shareholder might have to adjust its share of QPAI from the S corporation to take into account certain disallowed losses or deductions, or the allowance of suspended losses or deductions; and

(D) A shareholder's share of QPAI from an S corporation may be less than zero.

(2) Disallowed losses or deductions. Except as provided by publication in the Internal Revenue Bulletin (see § 601.601(d)(2)(ii)(b) of this chapter), losses or deductions of the S corporation that otherwise would be taken into account in computing the shareholder's section 199 deduction for a taxable year are taken into account in that year only if and to the extent the shareholder's pro rata share of the losses or deductions from all of the S corporation's activities is not disallowed by section 465, 469, or 1366(d), or any other provision of the Code. If only a portion of the shareholder's share of the losses or deductions is allowed for a taxable year, a proportionate share of those allowable losses or deductions that are allocated to the S corporation's qualified production activities, determined in a manner consistent with sections 465, 469, and 1366(d), and any other applicable provision of the Code, is taken into account in computing the QPAI and the wage limitation of section 199(d)(1)(A)(iii) for that taxable year. To the extent that any of the disallowed losses or deductions are allowed in a later taxable year, the shareholder takes into account a proportionate share of those losses or deductions in computing its QPAI for that later taxable year. Losses or deductions of the S corporation that are disallowed for taxable years beginning on or before December 31, 2004, are not taken into account in a later taxable year for purposes of computing the shareholder's QPAI or the wage limitation of section 199(d)(1)(A)(iii) for that taxable year, regardless of whether the losses or deductions are allowed for other purposes.

(3) Shareholder's share of W-2 wages. Under section 199(d)(1)(A)(iii), an S corporation shareholder's share of the W-2 wages of the S corporation for purposes of determining the shareholder's section 199(b) limitation is the lesser of the shareholder's allocable share of those wages (without regard to section 199(d)(1)(A)(iii)), or 2 times 3 percent of the QPAI computed by taking into account only the items of the S corporation allocated to the shareholder for the taxable year of the S corporation. Except as provided by publication in the Internal Revenue Bulletin (see § 601.601(d)(2)(ii)(b) of this chapter), this QPAI calculation is performed by the shareholder using the same cost allocation method that the shareholder uses in calculating the shareholder's section 199 deduction. The S corporation must allocate W-2 wages (prior to the application of the wage limitation) among the shareholders in the same manner as wage expense. The shareholder must add the shareholder's share of W-2 wages from the S corporation, as limited by section 199(d)(1)(A)(iii), to the shareholder's W-2 wages from other sources, if any. If QPAI, computed by taking into account only the items of the S corporation allocated to the shareholder for the taxable year (as required by the wage limitation of section 199(d)(1)(A)(iii)), is not greater than zero, then the shareholder may not take into account any W-2 wages of the S corporation in applying the wage limitation of § 1.199-2 (but the shareholder will, nevertheless, aggregate its distributive share of S corporation items including wage expense with those items not from the S corporation in computing its QPAI when determining its section 199 deduction). See § 1.199-2 for the computation of W-2 wages, and paragraph (g) of this section for rules regarding pass-thru entities in a tiered structure.

(4) Transition percentage rule for W-2 wages. With regard to S corporations, for purposes of section 199(d)(1)(A)(iii)(II) the transition percentages determined under section 199(a)(2) shall be determined by reference to the S corporation's taxable year. Thus, if an S corporation shareholder uses a calendar year taxable year, and owns stock in an S corporation that has a taxable year ending on April 30, the shareholder's section 199(d)(1)(A)(iii) wage limitation for the S corporation's taxable year beginning on May 1, 2006, would be calculated using 3 percent, even though the shareholder includes the shareholder's pro rata share of S corporation items from that taxable year on the shareholder's 2007 Federal income tax return.

(d) Grantor trusts. To the extent that the grantor or another person is treated as owning all or part (the owned portion) of a trust under sections 671 through 679, such person (owner) computes its QPAI with respect to the owned portion of the trust as if that QPAI had been generated by activities performed directly by the owner. Similarly, for purposes of the section 199(b) wage limitation, the owner of the trust takes into account the owner's share of the W-2 wages of the trust that are attributable to the owned portion of the trust. The section 199(d)(1)(A)(iii) wage limitation is not applicable to the owned portion of the trust. The provisions of paragraph (e) of this section do not apply to the owned portion of a trust.

(e) Non-grantor trusts and estates. *(1) Allocation of costs.* The trust or estate calculates each beneficiary's share (as well as the trust's or estate's own share, if any) of QPAI and W-2 wages from the trust or estate at the trust or estate level. The beneficiary of a trust or estate is not permitted to use another cost allocation method to recompute its share of QPAI from the trust or estate or to reallocate the costs of the trust or estate. Except as provided in paragraph (d) of this section, the QPAI of a trust or estate must be computed by allocating expenses described in section 199(d)(5) in one of two ways, depending on the classification of those expenses under § 1.652(b) 3. Specifically, directly attributable expenses within the meaning of § 1.652(b)-3 are allocated pursuant to § 1.652(b)-3, and expenses not directly attributable within the meaning of § 1.652(b)-3 (other expenses) are allocated under the simplified deduction method of § 1.199-4(e) (unless the trust or estate does not qualify to use the simplified deduction method, in which case it must use the section 861 method of § 1.199-4(d) with respect to such other expenses). For this purpose, depletion and depreciation deductions described in section 642(e) and amortization deductions described in section 642(f) are treated as other expenses described in section 199(d)(5). Also for this purpose, the trust's or estate's share of other expenses from a lower-tier pass-thru entity is not directly attributable to any class of income (whether or not those other expenses are directly attributable to the aggregate pass-thru gross income as a class for purposes other than section 199). A trust or estate may not use the small business simplified overall method for computing its QPAI. See § 1.199-4(f)(5).

(2) Allocation among trust or estate and beneficiaries. (i) In general. The QPAI of a trust or estate (which will be less than zero if the CGS and deductions allocated and apportioned to DPGR exceed the trust's or estate's DPGR) and W-2 wages of a trust or estate are allocated to each beneficiary and to the trust or estate based on the relative proportion of the trust's or estate's distributable net income (DNI), as defined by section 643(a), for the taxable year that is distrib-

uted or required to be distributed to the beneficiary or is retained by the trust or estate. For this purpose, the trust or estate's DNI is determined with regard to the separate share rule of section 663(c), but without regard to section 199. To the extent that the trust or estate has no DNI for the taxable year, any QPAI and W-2 wages are allocated entirely to the trust or estate. A trust or estate is allowed the section 199 deduction in computing its taxable income to the extent that QPAI and W-2 wages are allocated to the trust or estate. A beneficiary of a trust or estate is allowed the section 199 deduction in computing its taxable income based on its share of QPAI and W-2 wages from the trust or estate, which (subject to the wage limitation as described in paragraph (e)(3) of this section) are aggregated with the beneficiary's QPAI and W-2 wages from other sources, if any.

(ii) Treatment of items from a trust or estate reporting qualified production activities income. When, pursuant to this paragraph (e), a taxpayer must combine QPAI and W-2 wages from a trust or estate with the taxpayer's total QPAI and W-2 wages from other sources, the taxpayer, when applying §§ 1.199-1 through 1.199-9 to determine the taxpayer's total QPAI and W-2 wages from such other sources, does not take into account the items from such trust or estate. Thus, for example, a beneficiary of an estate that receives QPAI from the estate does not take into account the beneficiary's distributive share of the estate's gross receipts, gross income, or deductions when the beneficiary determines whether a threshold or de minimis rule applies or when the beneficiary allocates and apportions deductions in calculating its QPAI from other sources.

(3) Beneficiary's share of W-2 wages. The trust or estate must compute each beneficiary's share of W-2 wages from the trust or estate in accordance with section 199(d)(1)(A)(iii), as if the beneficiary were a partner in a partnership. The application of section 199(d)(1)(A)(iii) to each trust and estate therefore means that if QPAI, computed by taking into account only the items of the trust or estate allocated to the beneficiary for the taxable year, is not greater than zero, then the beneficiary may not take into account any W-2 wages of the trust or estate in applying the wage limitation of § 1.199-2 (but the beneficiary will, nevertheless, aggregate its QPAI from the trust or estate with its QPAI from other sources when determining the beneficiary's section 199 deduction). See paragraph (g) of this section for rules applicable to pass-thru entities in a tiered structure.

(4) Transition percentage rule for W-2 wages. With regard to trusts and estates, for purposes of section 199(d)(1)(A)(iii)(II), the transition percentages determined under section 199(a)(2) shall be determined by reference to the taxable year of the trust or estate.

(5) Example. The following example illustrates the application of this paragraph (e) and paragraph (g) of this section. Assume that the partnership, trust, and trust beneficiary all are calendar year taxpayers.

Example. (i) Computation of DNI and inclusion and deduction amounts. (A) Trust's distributive share of partnership items. Trust, a complex trust, is a partner in PRS, a partnership that engages in activities that generate DPGR and non-DPGR. In 2006, PRS distributes $10,000 cash to Trust. Trust's distributive share of PRS items, which are properly included in Trust's DNI, is as follows:

Gross income attributable to DPGR ($15,000 DPGR - $5,000 CGS (including W-2 wages of $1,000))	$10,000
Gross income attributable to non-DPGR ($5,000 other gross receipts - $0 CGS)	$ 5,000
Selling expenses (includes W-2 wages of $2,000)	$ 3,000
Other expenses (includes W-2 wages of $1,000)	$ 2,000

(B) Trust's direct activities. In addition to its cash distribution in 2006 from PRS, Trust also directly has the following items which are properly included in Trust's DNI:

Dividends	$10,000
Tax-exempt interest	$10,000
Rents from commercial real property operated by Trust as a business	$10,000
Real estate taxes	$ 1,000
Trustee commissions	$ 3,000
State income and personal property taxes	$ 5,000
W-2 wages for rental business	$ 2,000
Other business expenses	$ 1,000

(C) Allocation of deductions under § 1.652(b)-3. (1) Directly attributable expenses. In computing Trust's DNI for the taxable year, the distributive share of expenses of PRS are directly attributable under § 1.652(b)-3(a) to the distributive share of income of PRS. Accordingly, the $5,000 of CGS, $3,000 of selling expenses, and $2,000 of other expenses are subtracted from the gross receipts from PRS ($20,000), resulting in net income from PRS of $10,000. With respect to the Trust's direct expenses, $1,000 of the trustee commissions, the $1,000 of real estate taxes, and the $2,000 of W-2 wages are directly attributable under § 1.652(b)-3(a) to the rental income.

(2) Non-directly attributable expenses. Under § 1.652(b)-3(b), the trustee must allocate a portion of the sum of the balance of the trustee commissions ($2,000), state income and personal property taxes ($5,000), and the other business expenses ($1,000) to the $10,000 of tax-exempt interest. The portion to be attributed to tax-exempt interest is $2,222 ($8,000 x ($10,000 tax exempt interest/$36,000 gross receipts net of direct expenses)), resulting in $7,778 ($10,000 - $2,222) of net tax-exempt interest. Pursuant to its authority recognized under § 1.652(b)-3(b), the trustee allocates the entire amount of the remaining $5,778 of trustee commissions, state income and personal property taxes, and other business expenses to the $6,000 of net rental income, resulting in $222 ($6,000 - $5,778) of net rental income.

(D) Amounts included in taxable income. For 2006, Trust has DNI of $28,000 (net dividend income of $10,000 + net PRS income of $10,000 + net rental income of $222 + net tax-exempt income of $7,778). Pursuant to Trust's governing instrument, Trustee distributes 50%, or $14,000, of that DNI to B, an individual who is a discretionary beneficiary of Trust. Assume that there are no separate shares under Trust, and no distributions are made to any other beneficiary that year. Consequently, with respect to the $14,000 distribution B receives from Trust, B properly includes in B's gross income $5,000 of income from PRS, $111 of rents, and $5,000 of dividends, and properly excludes from B's gross income $3,889 of tax-exempt interest. Trust includes $20,222 in its adjusted total income and deducts $10,111 under section 661(a) in computing its taxable income.

(ii) Section 199 deduction. (A) Simplified deduction method. For purposes of computing the section 199 deduction for the taxable year, assume Trust qualifies for the simplified deduction method under § 1.199-4(e). The determination of Trust's QPAI under the simplified deduction method requires multiple steps to allocate costs. First, the

Trust's expenses directly attributable to DPGR under § 1.652(b)-3(a) are subtracted from the Trust's DPGR. In this step, the directly attributable $5,000 of CGS and selling expenses of $3,000 are subtracted from the $15,000 of DPGR from PRS. Next, Trust must identify its other trade or business expenses directly related to non-DPGR trade or business income. In this example, the portion of the trustee commissions not directly attributable to the rental operation ($2,000), as well as the portion of the state income and personal property taxes not directly attributable to either the PRS interests or the rental operation, are not trade or business expenses and, thus, are ignored in computing QPAI. The portion of the state income and personal property taxes that is treated as other trade or business expenses is $3,000 ($5,000 x $30,000 total trade or business gross receipts/$50,000 total gross receipts). Trust then allocates its other trade or business expenses on the basis of its total gross receipts from the conduct of a trade or business ($20,000 from PRS + $10,000 rental income). Trust then combines its non-directly attributable (other) business expenses ($2,000 from PRS + $4,000 ($1,000 of other expenses + $3,000 of income and property taxes) from its own activities) and then apportions this total between DPGR and other receipts on the basis of Trust's total trade or business gross receipts ($6,000 x $15,000 DPGR/$30,000 total trade or business gross receipts = $3,000). Thus, for purposes of computing Trust's and B's section 199 deduction, Trust's QPAI is $4,000 ($7,000 - $3,000). Because the distribution of Trust's DNI to B equals one-half of Trust's DNI, Trust and B each has QPAI from PRS for purposes of the section 199 deduction of $2,000.

(B) Section 199(d)(1)(A)(iii) wage limitation. The wage limitation under section 199(d)(1)(A)(iii) must be applied both at the Trust level and at B's level. After applying this limitation to the Trust's share of PRS's W-2 wages, Trust is allocated $330 of W-2 wages from PRS (the lesser of Trust's allocable share of PRS's W-2 wages ($4,000) or 2 x 3% of Trust's QPAI from PRS ($5,500)). Trust's QPAI from PRS for purposes of the section 199(d)(1)(A)(iii) limitation is determined by taking into account only the items of PRS allocated to Trust ($15,000 DPGR - ($5,000 of CGS + $3,000 selling expenses + $1,500 of other expenses)). For this purpose, the $1,500 of other expenses is determined by multiplying $2,000 of other expenses from PRS by $15,000 of DPGR from PRS, divided by $20,000 of total gross receipts from PRS. Trust adds this $330 of W-2 wages to Trust's own $2,000 of W-2 wages (thus, $2,330). Because the $14,000 Trust distribution to B equals one-half of Trust's DNI, Trust and B each has W-2 wages of $1,165. After applying the section 199(d)(1)(A)(iii) wage limitation to B's share of the W-2 wages allocated from Trust, B has W-2 wages of $120 from Trust (lesser of $1,165 (allocable share of W-2 wages) or 2 x .03 x $2,000 (B's share of Trust's QPAI)). B has W-2 wages of $100 from non-Trust activities for a total of $220 of W-2 wages.

(C) Section 199 deduction computation. (1) B's computation. B is eligible to use the small business simplified overall method. Assume that B has sufficient adjusted gross income so that the section 199 deduction is not limited under section 199(a)(1)(B). B has $1,000 of QPAI from non-Trust activities that is added to the $2,000 QPAI from Trust for a total of $3,000 of QPAI. B's tentative deduction is $90 (.03 x $3,000), but it is limited under section 199(b) to $110 (50% x $220 W-2 wages). Accordingly, B's section 199 deduction for 2006 is $90.

(2) Trust's computation. Trust has sufficient adjusted gross income so that the section 199 deduction is not limited under section 199(a)(1)(B). Trust's tentative deduction is $60 (.03 x $2,000 QPAI), but it is limited under section 199(b) to $583 (50% x $1,165 W-2 wages). Accordingly, Trust's section 199 deduction for 2006 is $60.

(f) Gain or loss from the disposition of an interest in a pass-thru entity. DPGR generally does not include gain or loss recognized on the sale, exchange, or other disposition of an interest in a pass-thru entity. However, with respect to a partnership, if section 751(a) or (b) applies, then gain or loss attributable to assets of the partnership giving rise to ordinary income under section 751(a) or (b), the sale, exchange, or other disposition of which would give rise to DPGR, is taken into account in computing the partner's section 199 deduction. Accordingly, to the extent that cash or property received by a partner in a sale or exchange for all or part of its partnership interest is attributable to unrealized receivables or inventory items within the meaning of section 751(c) or (d), respectively, and the sale or exchange of the unrealized receivable or inventory items would give rise to DPGR if sold, exchanged, or otherwise disposed of by the partnership, the cash or property received by the partner is taken into account by the partner in determining its DPGR for the taxable year. Likewise, to the extent that a distribution of property to a partner is treated under section 751(b) as a sale or exchange of property between the partnership and the distributee partner, and any property deemed sold or exchanged would give rise to DPGR if sold, exchanged, or otherwise disposed of by the partnership, the deemed sale or exchange of the property must be taken into account in determining the partnership's and distributee partner's DPGR to the extent not taken into account under the qualifying in-kind partnership rules. See § 1.751-1(b) and paragraph (i) of this section.

(g) Section 199(d)(1)(A)(iii) wage limitation and tiered structures. *(1) In general.* If a pass-thru entity owns an interest, directly or indirectly, in one or more pass-thru entities, then the wage limitation of section 199(d)(1)(A)(iii) must be applied at each tier (that is, separately for each entity). For purposes of this wage limitation, references to pass-thru entities includes partnerships, S corporations, trusts (to the extent not described in paragraph (d) of this section) and estates. Thus, at each tier, the owner of a pass-thru entity (or the entity on behalf of the owner) calculates the amounts described in sections 199(d)(1)(A)(iii)(I) (owner's allocable share) and 199(d)(1)(A)(iii)(II) (twice the applicable percentage of the owner's QPAI from that entity) separately with regard to its interest in that pass-thru entity.

(2) Share of W-2 wages. For purposes of section 199(d)(1)(A)(iii) and section 199(b), the W-2 wages of the owner of an interest in a pass-thru entity (upper-tier entity) that owns an interest in one or more pass-thru entities (lower-tier entities) are equal to the sum of the owner's allocable share of W-2 wages of the upper-tier entity, as limited in accordance with section 199(d)(1)(A)(iii), and the owner's own W-2 wages. The upper-tier entity's W-2 wages are equal to the sum of the upper-tier entity's allocable share of W-2 wages of the next lower-tier entity, as limited in accordance with section 199(d)(1)(A)(iii), and the upper-tier entity's own W-2 wages. The W-2 wages of each lower-tier entity in a tiered structure, in turn, is computed as described in the preceding sentence. Except as provided by publication in the Internal Revenue Bulletin (see § 601.601(d)(2)(ii)(b) of this chapter)—

(i) An upper-tier entity may compute its share of QPAI attributable to items from a lower-tier entity solely for purposes of section 199(d)(1)(A)(iii)(II) by applying either the section 861 method described in § 1.199-4(d) or the simplified deduction method described in § 1.199-4(e), provided the upper tier entity would otherwise qualify to use such method.

(ii) Alternatively, the upper-tier entity (other than a trust or estate described in paragraph (e) of this section) may compute its share of QPAI attributable to items from a lower-tier entity solely for purposes of section 199(d)(1)(A)(iii)(II) by applying the small business simplified overall method described in § 1.199-4(f), regardless of whether such upper-tier entity would otherwise qualify to use the small business simplified overall method.

(3) Example. The following example illustrates the application of this paragraph (g). Assume that each partnership and each partner (whether or not an individual) is a calendar year taxpayer.

Example. (i) In 2006, A, an individual, owns a 50% interest in a partnership, UTP, which in turn owns a 50% interest in another partnership, LTP. All partnership items are allocated in proportion to these ownership percentages. LTP has $900 DPGR, $450 CGS (which includes W-2 wages of $100), and $50 other deductions. Before taking into account its share of items from LTP, UTP has $500 DPGR, $500 CGS (which includes W-2 wages of $200), and $500 other deductions. UTP chooses to compute its share of QPAI attributable to items from LTP for purposes of section 199(d)(1)(A)(iii)(II) by applying the small business simplified overall method described in § 1.199-4(f). For purposes of the wage limitation of section 199(d)(1)(A)(iii), UTP's distributive share of LTP's QPAI is $200 ($450 DPGR - $250 CGS and other deductions).

(ii) UTP's share of LTP's W-2 wages for purposes of the section 199(d)(1)(A)(iii) limitation is $12, the lesser of $50 (UTP's 50% allocable share of LTP's $100 of W-2 wages) or $12 (2 x ($200 QPAI x .03)). After taking into account its share of items from LTP, UTP has $950 DPGR, $725 CGS, and $525 other deductions. A is eligible for and uses the simplified deduction method described in § 1.199-4(e). For purposes of the wage limitation of section 199(d)(1)(A)(iii), A's distributive share of UTP's QPAI is ($151) ($475 DPGR - $363 CGS - $263 other deductions). A's wage limitation under section 199(d)(1)(A)(iii) with respect to A's interest in UTP is $0, the lesser of $106 (A's 50% allocable share of UTP's $212 of W-2 wages) or $0 (because A's share of UTP's QPAI ($151), is less than zero).

(h) No attribution of qualified activities. Except as provided in paragraph (i) of this section regarding qualifying in-kind partnerships and paragraph (j) of this section regarding EAG partnerships, an owner of a pass-thru entity is not treated as conducting the qualified production activities of the pass-thru entity, and vice versa. This rule applies to all partnerships, including partnerships that have elected out of subchapter K under section 761(a). Accordingly, if a partnership MPGE QPP within the United States, or produces a qualified film or produces utilities in the United States, and distributes or leases, rents, licenses, sells, exchanges, or otherwise disposes of such property to a partner who then, without performing its own qualifying MPGE or other production, leases, rents, licenses, sells, exchanges, or otherwise disposes of such property, then the partner's gross receipts from this latter lease, rental, license, sale, exchange, or other disposition are treated as non-DPGR. In addition, if a partner MPGE QPP within the United States, or produces a qualified film or produces utilities in the United States, and contributes or leases, rents, licenses, sells, exchanges, or otherwise disposes of such property to a partnership which then, without performing its own qualifying MPGE or other production, leases, rents, licenses, sells, exchanges, or otherwise disposes of such property, then the partnership's gross receipts from this latter disposition are treated as non-DPGR.

(i) Qualifying in-kind partnership. *(1) In general.* If a partnership is a qualifying in-kind partnership described in paragraph (i)(2) of this section, then each partner is treated as MPGE or producing the property MPGE or produced by the partnership that is distributed to that partner. If a partner of a qualifying in-kind partnership derives gross receipts from the lease, rental, license, sale, exchange, or other disposition of the property that was MPGE or produced by the qualifying in-kind partnership, then, provided such partner is a partner of the qualifying in-kind partnership at the time the partner disposes of the property, the partner is treated as conducting the MPGE or production activities previously conducted by the qualifying in-kind partnership with respect to that property. With respect to a lease, rental, or license, the partner is treated as having disposed of the property on the date or dates on which it takes into account its gross receipts derived from the lease, rental, or license under its methods of accounting. With respect to a sale, exchange, or other disposition, the partner is treated as having disposed of the property on the date on which it ceases to own the property for Federal income tax purposes, even if no gain or loss is taken into account.

(2) Definition of qualifying in-kind partnership. For purposes of this paragraph (i), a qualifying in-kind partnership is a partnership engaged solely in—

(i) The extraction, refining, or processing of oil, natural gas (as described in § 1.199-3(l)(2)), petrochemicals, or products derived from oil, natural gas, or petrochemicals in whole or in significant part within the United States;

(ii) The production or generation of electricity in the United States; or

(iii) An activity or industry designated by the Secretary by publication in the Internal Revenue Bulletin (see § 601.601(d)(2)(ii)(b) of this chapter).

(3) Special rules for distributions. If a qualifying in-kind partnership distributes property to a partner, then, solely for purposes of section 199(d)(1)(A)(iii)(II), the partnership is treated as having gross receipts in the taxable year of the distribution equal to the fair market value of the distributed property at the time of distribution to the partner and the deemed gross receipts are allocated to that partner, provided that the partner derives gross receipts from the distributed property (and takes into account such receipts under its method of accounting) during the taxable year of the partner with or within which the partnership's taxable year (in which the distribution occurs) ends. For rules for taking costs into account (such as costs included in the adjusted basis of the distributed property), see § 1.199-4.

(4) Other rules. Except as provided in this paragraph (i), a qualifying in-kind partnership is treated the same as other partnerships for purposes of section 199. Accordingly, a qualifying in-kind partnership is subject to the rules of this section regarding the application of section 199 to pass-thru entities, including application of the section 199(d)(1)(A)(iii) wage limitation under paragraph (b)(3) of this section. In determining whether a qualifying in-kind partnership or its

partners MPGE QPP in whole or in significant part within the United States, see § 1.199-3(g)(2) and (3).

(5) Example. The following example illustrates the application of this paragraph (i). Assume that PRS and X are calendar year taxpayers.

Example. X, Y and Z are partners in PRS, a qualifying in-kind partnership described in paragraph (i)(2) of this section. X, Y, and Z are corporations. In 2006, PRS distributes oil to X that PRS derived from its oil extraction. PRS incurred $600 of CGS, including $500 of W-2 wages (as defined in § 1.199-2(e)), extracting the oil distributed to X, and X's adjusted basis in the distributed oil is $600. The fair market value of the oil at the time of the distribution to X is $1,000. X incurs $200 of CGS, including $100 of W-2 wages, in refining the oil within the United States. In 2006, X, while it is a partner in PRS, sells the oil to a customer for $1,500, taking the gross receipts into account under its method of accounting in the same taxable year. Under paragraph (i)(1) of this section, X is treated as having extracted the oil. The extraction and refining of the oil qualify as an MPGE activity under § 1.199-3(e)(1). Therefore, X's $1,500 of gross receipts qualify as DPGR. X subtracts from the $1,500 of DPGR the $600 of CGS incurred by PRS and the $200 of refining costs incurred by X. Thus, X's QPAI is $700 for 2006. In addition, PRS is treated as having $1,000 of DPGR solely for purposes of applying the wage limitation in section 199(d)(1)(A)(iii) based on the applicable percentage of QPAI. Accordingly, X's share of PRS's W-2 wages determined under section 199(d)(1)(A)(iii) is $24, the lesser of $500 (X's allocable share of PRS's W-2 wages included in CGS) and $24 (2 x ($400 ($1,000 deemed DPGR less $600 of CGS) x .03)). X adds the $24 of PRS W-2 wages to its $100 of W-2 wages incurred in refining the oil for purposes of section 199(b).

(j) Partnerships owned by members of a single expanded affiliated group. *(1) In general.* For purposes of this section, if all of the interests in the capital and profits of a partnership are owned by members of a single EAG at all times during the taxable year of the partnership (EAG partnership), then the EAG partnership and all members of that EAG are treated as a single taxpayer for purposes of section 199(c)(4) during that taxable year.

(2) Attribution of activities. (i) In general. If a member of an EAG (disposing member) derives gross receipts from the lease, rental, license, sale, exchange, or other disposition of property that was MPGE or produced by an EAG partnership, all the partners of which are members of the same EAG to which the disposing member belongs at the time that the disposing member disposes of such property, then the disposing member is treated as conducting the MPGE or production activities previously conducted by the EAG partnership with respect to that property. The previous sentence applies only for those taxable years in which the disposing member is a member of the EAG of which all the partners of the EAG partnership are members for the entire taxable year of the EAG partnership. With respect to a lease, rental, or license, the disposing member is treated as having disposed of the property on the date or dates on which it takes into account its gross receipts from the lease, rental, or license under its methods of accounting. With respect to a sale, exchange, or other disposition, the disposing member is treated as having disposed of the property on the date on which it ceases to own the property for Federal income tax purposes, even if no gain or loss is taken into account. Likewise, if an EAG partnership derives gross receipts from the lease, rental, license, sale, exchange, or other disposition of property that was MPGE or produced by a member (or members) of the same EAG (the producing member) to which all the partners of the EAG partnership belong at the time that the EAG partnership disposes of such property, then the EAG partnership is treated as conducting the MPGE or production activities previously conducted by the producing member with respect to that property. The previous sentence applies only for those taxable years in which the producing member is a member of the EAG of which all the partners of the EAG partnership are members for the entire taxable year of the EAG partnership. With respect to a lease, rental, or license, the EAG partnership is treated as having disposed of the property on the date or dates on which it takes into account its gross receipts derived from the lease, rental, or license under its methods of accounting. With respect to a sale, exchange, or other disposition, the EAG partnership is treated as having disposed of the property on the date on which it ceases to own the property for Federal income tax purposes, even if no gain or loss is taken into account. See paragraph (j)(5) Example 3 of this section.

(ii) Attribution between EAG partnerships. If an EAG partnership (disposing partnership) derives gross receipts from the lease, rental, license, sale, exchange, or other disposition of property that was MPGE or produced by another EAG partnership (producing partnership), then the disposing partnership is treated as conducting the MPGE or production activities previously conducted by the producing partnership with respect to that property, provided that the producing partnership and the disposing partnership are owned by members of the same EAG for the entire taxable year of the respective partnership in which the disposing partnership disposes of such property. With respect to a lease, rental, or license, the disposing partnership is treated as having disposed of the property on the date or dates on which it takes into account its gross receipts from the lease, rental, or license under its methods of accounting. With respect to a sale, exchange, or other disposition, the disposing partnership is treated as having disposed of the property on the date on which it ceases to own the property for Federal income tax purposes, even if no gain or loss is taken into account.

(iii) Exceptions to attribution. Attribution of activities does not apply for purposes of the construction of real property under § 1.199-3(m)(1) and the performance of engineering and architectural services under § 1.199-3(n)(2) and (3), respectively.

(3) Special rules for distributions. If an EAG partnership distributes property to a partner, then, solely for purposes of section 199(d)(1)(A)(iii)(II), the EAG partnership is treated as having gross receipts in the taxable year of the distribution equal to the fair market value of the property at the time of distribution to the partner and the deemed gross receipts are allocated to that partner, provided that the partner derives gross receipts from the distributed property (and takes such receipts into account under its methods of accounting) during the taxable year of the partner with or within which the partnership's taxable year (in which the distribution occurs) ends. For rules for taking costs into account (such as costs included in the adjusted basis of the distributed property), see § 1.199-4.

(4) Other rules. Except as provided in this paragraph (j), an EAG partnership is treated the same as other partnerships for purposes of section 199. Accordingly, an EAG partnership is subject to the rules of this section regarding the application of section 199 to pass-thru entities, including application of the section 199(d)(1)(A)(iii) wage limitation under paragraph (b)(3) of this section. In determining whether a

member of an EAG or an EAG partnership MPGE QPP in whole or in significant part within the United States or produced a qualified film or produced utilities within the United States, see § 1.199-3(g)(2) and (3) and Example 5 of paragraph (j)(5) of this section.

(5) Examples. The following examples illustrate the rules of this paragraph (j). Assume that PRS, X, Y, and Z all are calendar year taxpayers.

Example (1). Contribution. X and Y are the only partners in PRS, a partnership, for PRS's entire 2006 taxable year. X and Y are both members of a single EAG for the entire 2006 year. In 2006, X MPGE QPP within the United States and contributes the property to PRS. In 2006, PRS sells the QPP for $1,000. Under this paragraph (j), PRS is treated as having MPGE the QPP within the United States, and PRS's $1,000 gross receipts constitute DPGR. PRS, X, and Y must apply the rules of this section regarding the application of section 199 to pass-thru entities with respect to the activity of PRS, including application of the section 199(d)(1)(A)(iii) wage limitation under paragraph (b)(3) of this section.

Example (2). Sale. X, Y, and Z are the only members of a single EAG for the entire 2006 year. X and Y each own 50% of the capital and profits interests in PRS, a partnership, for PRS's entire 2006 taxable year. In 2006, PRS MPGE QPP within the United States and then sells the property to X for $6,000, its fair market value at the time of the sale. PRS's gross receipts of $6,000 qualify as DPGR. In 2006, X sells the QPP to customers for $10,000, incurring selling expenses of $2,000. Under this paragraph (j), X is treated as having MPGE the QPP within the United States, and X's $10,000 of gross receipts qualify as DPGR. PRS, X and Y must apply the rules of this section regarding the application of section 199 to pass-thru entities with respect to the activity of PRS, including application of the section 199(d)(1)(A)(iii) wage limitation under paragraph (b)(3) of this section. The results would be the same if PRS sold the property to Z rather than to X.

Example (3). Lease. X, Y, and Z are the only members of a single EAG for the entire 2005 year. X and Y each own 50% of the capital and profits interests in PRS, a partnership, for PRS's entire 2005 taxable year. In 2005, PRS MPGE QPP within the United States and then sells the property to X for $6,000, its fair market value at the time of the sale. PRS's gross receipts of $6,000 qualify as DPGR. In 2005, X rents the QPP it acquired from PRS to customers unrelated to X. X takes the gross receipts attributable to the rental of the QPP into account under its methods of accounting in 2005 and 2006. On July 1, 2006, X ceases to be a member of the same EAG to which Y, the other partner in PRS, belongs. For 2005, X is treated as having MPGE the QPP in the United States, and its gross receipts derived from the rental of the QPP qualify as DPGR. For 2006, however, because X and Y, partners in PRS, are no longer members of the same EAG for the entire year, the gross rental receipts X takes into account in 2006 do not qualify as DPGR.

Example (4). Distribution. X and Y are the only partners in PRS, a partnership, for PRS's entire 2006 taxable year. X and Y are both members of a single EAG for the entire 2006 year. In 2006, PRS MPGE QPP within the United States, incurring $600 of CGS, including $500 of W-2 wages (as defined in § 1.199-2(e)), and then distributes the QPP to X. X's adjusted basis in the QPP is $600. At the time of the distribution, the fair market value of the QPP is $1,000. X incurs $200 of CGS, including $100 of W-2 wages, to further MPGE the QPP within the United States. In 2006, X sells the QPP for $1,500 to an unrelated customer and takes the gross receipts into account under its method of accounting in the same taxable year. Under paragraph (j)(1) of this section, X is treated as having MPGE the QPP within the United States, and X's $1,500 of gross receipts qualify as DPGR. In addition, PRS is treated as having DPGR of $1,000 solely for purposes of applying the wage limitation in section 199(d)(1)(A)(iii) based on the applicable percentage of QPAI.

Example (5). Multiple sales. (i) Facts. X and Y are the only partners in PRS, a partnership, for PRS's entire 2006 taxable year. X and Y are both non-consolidated members of a single EAG for the entire 2006 year. PRS produces in bulk form in the United States the active ingredient for a pharmaceutical product. Assume that PRS's own MPGE activity with respect to the active ingredient is not substantial in nature, taking into account all of the facts and circumstances, and PRS's direct labor and overhead to MPGE the active ingredient within the United States are $15 and account for 15% of PRS's $100 CGS of the active ingredient. In 2006, PRS sells the active ingredient in bulk form to X. X uses the active ingredient to produce the finished dosage form finished dosage form drug. Assume that X's own MPGE activity with respect to the finished dosage form drug is not substantial in nature, taking into account all of the facts and circumstances, and X's direct labor and overhead to MPGE the finished dosage form drug within the United States are $12 and account for 10% of X's $120 CGS of the finished dosage form drug. In 2006, X sells the finished dosage form drug in finished dosage to Y and Y sells the finished dosage form drug to customers. Assume that Y's own MPGE activity with respect to the finished dosage form drug is not substantial in nature, taking into account all of the facts and circumstances, and Y incurs $2 of direct labor and overhead and Y's CGS in selling the finished dosage form drug to customers is $130.

(ii) Analysis. PRS's gross receipts from the sale of the active ingredient to X are non-DPGR because PRS's MPGE activity is not substantial in nature and PRS does not satisfy the safe harbor described in § 1.199-3(g)(3) because PRS's direct labor and overhead account for less than 20% of PRS's CGS of the active ingredient. X's gross receipts from the sale of the finished dosage form drug to Y are DPGR because X is considered to have MPGE the finished dosage form drug in significant part in the United States pursuant to the safe harbor described in § 1.199-3(g)(3) because the $27 ($15 + $12) of direct labor and overhead incurred by PRS and X equals or exceeds 20% of X's total CGS ($120) of the finished dosage form drug at the time X disposes of the finished dosage form drug to Y. Similarly, Y's gross receipts from the sale of the finished dosage form drug to customers are DPGR because Y is considered to have MPGE the finished dosage form drug in significant part in the United States pursuant to the safe harbor described in § 1.199-3(g)(3) because the $29 ($15 + $12 + $2) of direct labor and overhead incurred by PRS, X, and Y equals or exceeds 20% of Y's total CGS ($130) of the finished dosage form drug at the time Y disposes of the finished dosage form drug to Y's customers.

(k) Effective dates. Section 199 applies to taxable years beginning after December 31, 2004. In determining the deduction under section 199, items arising from a taxable year of a partnership, S corporation, estate, or trust beginning before January 1, 2005, shall not be taken into account for purposes of section 199(d)(1). Section 1.199-9 does not apply to taxable years beginning after May 17, 2006, the enactment date of the Tax Increase Prevention and Reconciliation Act of 2005 (Public Law 109-222, 120 Stat. 345). For taxable years beginning on or before May 17, 2006, a taxpayer must apply § 1.199-9 if the taxpayer applies §§ 1.199-1 through 1.199-8 to that taxable year. Notwithstanding the preceding sentence, a partnership or S corporation that is a qualifying small taxpayer under § 1.199-4(f) of REG-105847-05 (2005-47 I.R.B. 987) (see § 601.601(d)(2) of this chapter) may use the small business simplified overall method to apportion CGS and deductions between DPGR and non-DPGR at the entity level under § 1.199-4(f) of REG-105847-05 for taxable years beginning on or before May 17, 2006. If a taxpayer chooses not to rely on §§ 1.199-1 through 1.199-9 (as provided in § 1.199-8(i)) for a taxable year beginning before June 1, 2006, the guidance under section 199 that applies to taxable years beginning before June 1, 2006, is contained in Notice 2005-14 (2005-1 C.B. 498) (see § 601.601(d)(2) of this chapter). In addition, a taxpayer also may rely on the provisions of REG-105847-05 for taxable years beginning before June 1, 2006. If Notice 2005-14 and REG-105847-05 include different rules for the same particular issue, then a taxpayer may rely on either the rule set forth in Notice 2005-14 or the rule set forth in REG-105847-05. However, if REG-105847-05 includes a rule that was not included in Notice 2005-14, then a taxpayer is not permitted to rely on the absence of a rule in Notice 2005-14 to apply a rule contrary to REG-105847-05. For taxable years beginning after May 17, 2006, and before June 1, 2006, a taxpayer may not apply Notice 2005-14, REG-105847-05, or any other guidance under section 199 in a manner inconsistent with amendments made to section 199 by section 514 of the Tax Increase Prevention and Reconciliation Act of 2005.

T.D. 9263, 5/24/2006, amend T.D. 9381, 2/14/2008.

§ 1.211-1 Allowance of deductions.

In computing taxable income under section 63(a), the deductions provided by sections 212, 213, 214, 215, 216, and 217 shall be allowed subject to the exceptions provided in part IX, subchapter B, chapter 1 of the Code (section 261 and following, relating to items not deductible).

T.D. 6279, 12/13/57, amend T.D. 6796, 1/29/65.

§ 1.212-1 Nontrade or nonbusiness expenses.

(a) An expense may be deducted under section 212 only if—

(1) It has been paid or incurred by the taxpayer during the taxable year (i) for the production or collection of income which, if and when realized, will be required to be included in income for Federal income tax purposes, or (ii) for the management, conservation, or maintenance of property held for the production of such income, or (iii) in connection with the determination, collection, or refund of any tax; and

(2) It is an ordinary and necessary expense for any of the purposes stated in subparagraph (1) of this paragraph.

(b) The term "income" for the purpose of section 212 includes not merely income of the taxable year but also income which the taxpayer has realized in a prior taxable year or may realize in subsequent taxable years; and is not confined to recurring income but applies as well to gains from the disposition of property. For example, if defaulted bonds, the interest from which if received would be includible in income, are purchased with the expectation of realizing capital gain on their resale, even though no current yield thereon is anticipated, ordinary and necessary expenses thereafter paid or incurred in connection with such bonds are deductible. Similarly, ordinary and necessary expenses paid or incurred in the management, conservation, or maintenance of a building devoted to rental purposes are deductible notwithstanding that there is actually no income therefrom in the taxable year, and regardless of the manner in which or the purpose for which the property in question was acquired. Expenses paid or incurred in managing, conserving, or maintaining property held for investment may be deductible under section 212 even though the property is not currently productive and there is no likelihood that the property will be sold at a profit or will otherwise be productive of income and even though the property is held merely to minimize a loss with respect thereto.

(c) In the case of taxable years beginning before January 1, 1970, expenses of carrying on transactions which do not constitute a trade or business of the taxpayer and are not carried on for the production or collection of income or for the management, conservation, or maintenance of property held for the production of income, but which are carried on primarily as a sport, hobby, or recreation are not allowable as nontrade or nonbusiness expenses. The question whether or not a transaction is carried on primarily for the production of income or for the management, conservation, or maintenance of property held for the production or collection of income, rather than primarily as a sport, hobby, or recreation, is not to be determined solely from the intention of the taxpayer but rather from all the circumstances of the case. For example, consideration will be given to the record of prior gain or loss of the taxpayer in the activity, the relation between the type of activity and the principal occupation of the taxpayer, and the uses to which the property or what it produces is put by the taxpayer. For provisions relating to activities not engaged in for profit applicable to taxable years beginning after December 31, 1969, see section 183 and the regulations thereunder.

(d) Expenses, to be deductible under section 212, must be "ordinary and necessary". Thus, such expenses must be reasonable in amount and must bear a reasonable and proximate relation to the production or collection of taxable income or to the management, conservation, or maintenance of property held for the production of income.

(e) A deduction under section 212 is subject to the restrictions and limitations in part IX (section 261 and following), subchapter B, chapter 1 of the Code, relating to items not deductible. Thus, no deduction is allowable under section 212 for any amount allocable to the production or collection of one or more classes of income which are not includible in gross income, or for any amount allocable to the management, conservation, or maintenance of property held for the production of income which is not included in gross income. See section 265. Nor does section 212 allow the deduction of any expenses which are disallowed by any of the provisions of subtitle A of the Code, even though such expenses may be paid or incurred for one of the purposes specified in section 212.

(f) Among expenditures not allowable as deductions under section 212 are the following: Commuter's expenses; expenses of taking special courses or training; expenses for improving personal appearance; the cost of rental of a safe-deposit box for storing jewelry and other personal effects; expenses such as those paid or incurred in seeking employment or in placing oneself in a position to begin rendering personal services for compensation, campaign expenses of a candidate for public office, bar examination fees and other expenses paid or incurred in securing admission to the bar, and corresponding fees and expenses paid or incurred by physicians, dentists, accountants, and other taxpayers for securing the right to practice their respective professions. See, however, section 162 and the regulations thereunder.

(g) Fees for services of investment counsel, custodial fees, clerical help, office rent, and similar expenses paid or incurred by a taxpayer in connection with investments held by him are deductible under section 212 only if (1) they are paid or incurred by the taxpayer for the production or collection of income or for the management, conservation, or maintenance of investments held by him for the production of income; and (2) they are ordinary and necessary under all the circumstances, having regard of the type of investment and to the relation of the taxpayer to such investment.

(h) Ordinary and necessary expenses paid or incurred in connection with the management, conservation, or maintenance of property held for use as a residence by the taxpayer are not deductible. However, ordinary and necessary expenses paid or incurred in connection with the management, conservation, or maintenance of property held by the taxpayer as rental property are deductible even though such property was formerly held by the taxpayer for use as a home.

(i) Reasonable amounts paid or incurred by the fiduciary of an estate or trust on account of administration expenses, including fiduciaries' fees and expenses of litigation, which are ordinary and necessary in connection with the performance of the duties of administration are deductible under section 212, notwithstanding that the estate or trust is not engaged in a trade or business, except to the extent that such expenses are allocable to the production or collection of tax-exempt income. But see section 642(g) and the regulations thereunder for disallowance of such deductions to an estate where such items are allowed as a deduction under section 2053 or 2054 in computing the net estate subject to the estate tax.

(j) Reasonable amounts paid or incurred for the services of a guardian or committee for a ward or minor, and other expenses of guardians and committees which are ordinary and necessary, in connection with the production or collection of income inuring to the ward or minor, or in connection with the management, conservation, or maintenance of property, held for the production of income, belonging to the ward or minor, are deductible.

(k) Expenses paid or incurred in defending or perfecting title to property, in recovering property (other than investment property and amounts of income which, if and when recovered, must be included in gross income), or in developing or improving property, constitute a part of the cost of the property and are not deductible expenses. Attorneys' fees paid in a suit to quiet title to lands are not deductible; but if the suit is also to collect accrued rents thereon, that portion of such fees is deductible which is properly allocable to the services rendered in collecting such rents. Expenses paid or incurred in protecting or asserting one's right to property of a decedent as heir or legatee, or as beneficiary under a testamentary trust, are not deductible.

(l) Expenses paid or incurred by an individual in connection with the determination, collection, or refund of any tax, whether the taxing authority be Federal, State, or municipal, and whether the tax be income, estate, gift, property, or any other tax, are deductible. Thus, expenses paid or incurred by a taxpayer for tax counsel or expenses paid or incurred in connection with the preparation of his tax returns or in connection with any proceedings involved in determining the extent of his tax liability or in contesting his tax liability are deductible.

(m) An expense (not otherwise deductible) paid or incurred by an individual in determining or contesting a liability asserted against him does not become deductible by reason of the fact that property held by him for the production of income may be required to be used or sold for the purpose of satisfying such liability.

(n) Capital expenditures are not allowable as nontrade or nonbusiness expenses. The deduction of an item otherwise allowable under section 212 will not be disallowed simply because the taxpayer was entitled under subtitle A of the Code to treat such item as a capital expenditure, rather than to deduct it as an expense. For example, see section 266. Where, however, the item may properly be treated only as a capital expenditure or where it was properly so treated under an option granted in subtitle A of the Code, no deduction is allowable under section 212; and this is true regardless of whether any basis adjustment is allowed under any other provision of the Code.

(o) The provisions of section 212 are not intended in any way to disallow expenses which would otherwise be allowable under section 162 and the regulations thereunder. Double deductions are not permitted. Amounts deducted under one provision of the Internal Revenue Code of 1954 cannot again be deducted under any other provision thereof.

(p) Frustration of public policy. The deduction of a payment will be disallowed under section 212 if the payment is of a type for which a deduction would be disallowed under section 162(c), (f), or (g) and the regulations thereunder in the case of a business expense.

T.D. 6279, 12/13/57, amend T.D. 7198, 7/12/72, T.D. 7345, 2/19/75.

PAR. 3. In § 1.212-1, paragraph (q) is added to read as follows:

Proposed § 1.212-1 Nontrade or nonbusiness expenses. [*For Preamble, see ¶ 152,497*]

* * * * *

(q) Notional principal contract payments. *(1)* Amounts taken into account by an individual pursuant to § 1.446-3(d)(1) (including mark-to-market deductions) with respect to a notional principal contract as defined in § 1.446-3(c)(1)(i), are ordinary and necessary, and are deductible to the extent these amounts are paid or incurred in connection with the production or collection of income. However, this section will not apply to any amount representing interest expense on the deemed loan component of a significant nonperiodic payment as described in § 1.446-3(g)(4). For any loss arising from a termination payment as defined in § 1.446-3(h)(1), see section 1234A and the regulations thereunder. For the timing of deductions with respect to notional principal contracts, see § 1.446-3.

(2) Effective date. Paragraph (q) of this section is applicable to notional principal contracts entered into on or after 30 days after the date a Treasury decision based on these proposed regulations is published in the Federal Register.

PAR. 2. Paragraph (h) of § 1.212-1 is amended by adding at the end thereof a new sentence to read as follows:

Proposed § 1.212-1 Nontrade or nonbusiness expenses. [*For Preamble, see ¶ 150,615*]

* * * * *

(h) * * * But see section 280A and the regulations thereunder.

* * * * *

§ 1.213-1 Medical, dental, etc., expenses.

Caution: The Treasury has not yet amended Reg § 1.213-1 to reflect changes made by P.L. 104-191, P.L. 103-66, P.L. 101-508, P.L. 99-514, P.L. 98-369, P.L. 97-248.

(a) Allowance of deduction. *(1)* Section 213 permits a deduction of payments for certain medical expenses (including expenses for medicine and drugs). Except as provided in paragraph (d) of this section (relating to special rule for decedents) a deduction is allowable only to individuals and only with respect to medical expenses actually paid during the taxable year, regardless of when the incident or event which occasioned the expenses occurred and regardless of the method of accounting employed by the taxpayer in making his income tax return. Thus, if the medical expenses are incurred but not paid during the taxable year, no deduction for such expenses shall be allowed for such year.

(2) Except as provided in subparagraph (4)(i) and (5)(i) of this paragraph, only such medical expenses (including the allowable expenses for medicine and drugs) are deductible as exceed 3 percent of the adjusted gross income for the taxable year. For taxable years beginning after December 31, 1966, the amounts paid during the taxable year for insurance that constitute expenses paid for medical care shall, for purposes of computing total medical expenses, be reduced by the amount determined under subparagraph (5)(i) of this paragraph. For the amounts paid during the taxable year for medicine and drugs which may be taken into account in computing total medical expenses, see paragraph (b) of this section. For the maximum deduction allowable under section 213 in the case of certain taxable years, see paragraph (c) of this section. As to what constitutes "adjusted gross income", see section 62 and the regulations thereunder.

(3) (i) For medical expenses paid (including expenses paid for medicine and drugs) to be deductible, they must be for medical care of the taxpayer, his spouse, or a dependent of the taxpayer and not be compensated for by insurance or otherwise. Expenses paid for the medical care of a dependent, as defined in section 152 and the regulations thereunder, are deductible under this section even though the dependent has gross income equal to or in excess of the amount determined pursuant to § 1.151-2 applicable to the calendar year in which the taxable year of the taxpayer begins. Where such expenses are paid by two or more persons and the conditions of section 152 (c) and the regulations thereunder are met, the medical expenses are deductible only by the person designated in the multiple support agreement filed by such persons and such deduction is limited to the amount of medical expenses paid by such person.

(ii) An amount excluded from gross income under section 105(c) or (d) (relating to amounts received under accident and health plans) and the regulations thereunder shall not constitute compensation for expenses paid for medical care. Exclusion of such amounts from gross income will not affect the treatment of expenses paid for medical care.

(iii) The application of the rule allowing a deduction for medical expenses to the extent not compensated for by insurance or otherwise may be illustrated by the following example in which it is assumed that neither the taxpayer nor his wife has attained the age of 65:

Example. Taxpayer H, married to W and having one dependent child, had adjusted gross income for 1956 of $3,000. During 1956 he paid $300 for medical care, of which $100 was for treatment of his dependent child and $200 for an operation on W which was performed in September 1955. In 1956 he received a payment of $50 for health insurance to cover the portion of the cost of W's operation performed during 1955. The deduction allowable under section 213 for the calendar year 1956, provided the taxpayer itemizes his deductions and does not compute his tax under section 3 by use of the tax table, is $160, computed as follows:

Payments in 1956 for medical care	$300
Less: Amount of insurance received in 1956	50
Payments in 1956 for medical care not compensated for during 1956	250
Less: 3 percent of $3,000 (adjusted gross income)	90
Excess allowable as a deduction for 1956	160

(4) (i) For taxable years beginning before January 1, 1967, where either the taxpayer or his spouse has attained the age of 65 before the close of the taxable year, the 3-percent limitation on the deduction for medical expenses for medical care of the taxpayer or his spouse. Moreover, for taxpayer years beginning after December 31, 1959, and before January 1, 1967, the 3-percent limitation on the deduction for medical expenses does not apply to amounts paid for the medical care of a dependent (as defined in section 152) who is the mother or father of the taxpayer or of his spouse and who has attained the age of 65 before the close of the taxpayer's taxable year. For taxable years beginning before January 1, 1964, and for taxable years beginning after December 31, 1966, all amounts paid by the taxpayer for medicine and drugs are subject to the 1-percent limitation provided by section 213(b). For taxable years beginning after December 31, 1963, and before January 1, 1967, the 1-percent limitation provided by section 213(b) does not apply, under certain circumstances, to amounts paid by the taxpayer for medicine and drugs for the taxpayer and his spouse or for a dependent (as defined in sec. 152) who is the mother or father of the taxpayer or of his spouse. (For additional provisions relating to the 1-percent limitation with respect to medicine and drugs, see paragraph (b) of this section.) For taxable years beginning before January 1, 1967, whether or not the 3-percent or 1-percent limitation applies, the total medical expenses deductible under section 213 are subject to the limitations described in section 213(c) and paragraph (c) of this section and, where applicable, to the limitations described in section 213(g) and § 1.213-2.

(ii) The age of a taxpayer shall be determined as of the last day of his taxable year. In the event of the taxpayer's death, his taxable year shall end as of the date of his death. The age of a taxpayer's spouse shall be determined as of the last day of the taxpayer's taxable year, except that, if the spouse dies within such taxable year, her age shall be determined as of the date of her death. Likewise, the age of the taxpayer's dependent who is the mother or father of the taxpayer or of his spouse shall be determined as of the last day of the taxpayer's taxable year but not later than the date of death of such dependent.

(iii) The application of subdivision (i) of this subparagraph may be illustrated by the following examples:

Example (1). Taxpayer A, who attained the age of 65 on February 22, 1956, makes his return on the basis of the calendar year. During the year 1956, A had adjusted gross income of $8,000, and paid the following medical bills: (a) $560 (7 percent of adjusted gross income) for the medical care of himself and his spouse, and (b) $160 (2 percent of adjusted gross income) for the medical care of his dependent son. No part of these payments was for medicine and drugs nor compensated for by insurance or otherwise. The allowable deduction under section 213 for 1956 is $560, the full amount of the medical expenses for the taxpayer and his spouse. No deduction is allowable for the amount of $160 paid for medical care of the dependent son since the amount of such payment (determined without regard to the payments for the care of the taxpayer and his spouse) does not exceed 3 percent of adjusted gross income.

Example (2). H and W, who have a dependent child, made a joint return for the calendar year 1956. H became 65 years of age on August 15, 1956. The adjusted gross income of H and W in 1956 was $40,000 and they paid in such year the following amounts for medical care: (a) $3,000 for the medical care of H; (b) $2,000 for the medical care of W; and (c) $3,000 for the medical care of the dependent child. No part of these payments was for medicine and drugs nor compensated for by insurance or otherwise. The allowable deduction under section 213 for medical expenses paid in 1956 is $6,800 computed as follows:

Payments for medical care of H and W in 1956 ...		$5,000
Payments for medical care of the dependent in 1956	$3,000	
Less: 3 percent of $40,000 (adjusted gross income)	1,200	
		1,800
Allowable deduction for 1956		6,800

Example (3). D and his wife, E, made a joint income tax return for the calendar year 1962, and reported adjusted gross income of $30,000. On December 13, 1962, D attained the age of 65. During the year 1962, D's father, F, who was 87 years of age, received over half of his support from, and was a dependent (as defined in section 152) of, D. However, D could not claim an exemption under section 151 for F because F had gross income from rents in 1962 of $800. D paid the following medical expenses in 1962, none of which were compensated for by insurance or otherwise: hospital and doctor bills for D and E, $6,500; hospital and doctor bills for F, $4,850; medicine and drugs for D and E, $225, and for F, $225. Since none of the medical expenses are subject to the 3-percent limitation, the amount of medical expenses to be taken into account (before computing the maximum deduction) is $11,500, computed as follows:

Hospital and doctor bills—for D and E		$6,500
Hospital and doctor bills—for F		4,850
Medicine and drugs—for D and E	$225	
Medicine and drugs—for F	225	
Total medicine and drugs	450	
Less: 1 percent of adjusted gross income ($30,000)	300	
Allowable expenses for medicine and drugs.		150
Total medical expenses taken into account		11,500

Since an exemption cannot be claimed for F on the 1962 return of D and E, their deduction for medical expenses (assuming that section 213(g) does not apply) is limited to $10,000 for that year ($5,000 multiplied by the two exemptions allowed for D and E under section 151(b)). If these identical facts had occurred in a taxable year beginning before January 1, 1962, the medical expense deduction for D and E would, for such taxable year, be limited to $5,000 ($2,500 multiplied by the two exemptions allowed for D and E under section 151(b)). See paragraph (c) of this section.

Example (4). Assume the same facts as in Example (3), except that D furnished the entire support of his father's twin sister, G, who had no gross income during 1962 and for whom D was entitled to a dependency exemption. In addition, D paid $4,800 to doctors and hospitals during 1962 for the medical care of G. No part of the $4,800 was for medicine and drugs, and no amount was compensated for by insurance or otherwise. For purposes of the maximum limitation under section 213(c), the maximum deduction for medical expenses on the 1962 return of D and E is limited to $15,000 ($5,000 multiplied by 3, the number of exemptions allowed under section 151, exclusive of the exemptions for old age or blindness). If these identical facts had occurred in a taxable year beginning before January 1, 1962, the medical expense deduction for D and E would, for such taxable year, be limited to $7,500 ($2,500 multiplied by the three exemptions allowed under section 151, exclusive of the exemptions for old age or blindness). The medical expenses to be taken into account by D and E for 1962 and the maximum deductions allowable for such expenses are $15,400 and $15,000, respectively, computed as follows:

Medical expenses per example (3)		$11,500
Add: Expenses paid for G	$4,800	
Less: 3 percent of adjusted gross income ($30,000)	900	
		3,900
Total medical expenses taken into account		15,400
Maximum deduction for 1962 ($5,000 multiplied by 3 exemptions)		15,000
Medical expenses not deductible................		400

Example (5). Assume that the facts set forth in Example (3) had occurred in respect of the calendar year 1964 rather than the calendar year 1962. Since both D and his father, F, had attained the age of 65 before the close of the taxable year, the 1-percent limitation does not apply to the amounts, paid for medicine and drugs for D, E, and F. Accordingly, the total medical expenses taken into account by D and E for 1964 would be $11,800 (rather than $11,500 as in Example (3)) computed as follows:

Hospital and doctor bills—for D and E	$6,500
Hospital and doctor bills—for F................	4,850
Medicine and drugs—for D and E	225
Medicine and drugs—for F	225
Total medical expenses taken into account.....	11,800

(5) (i) For taxable years beginning after December 31, 1966, there may be deducted without regard to the 3-percent limitation the lesser of—(a) One-half of the amounts paid during the taxable year for insurance which constitute expenses for medical care for the taxpayer, his spouse, and dependents; or (b) $150.

(ii) The application of subdivision (i) of this subparagraph may be illustrated by the following example:

Example. H and W made a joint return for the calendar year 1967. The adjusted gross income of H and W for 1967 was $10,000 and they paid in such year $370 for medical care of which amount $350 was paid for insurance which constitutes medical care for H and W. No part of the payment was for medicine and drugs or was compensated for by insurance or otherwise. The allowable deduction under section 213 for medical expenses paid in 1967 is $150, computed as follows:

(1) Lesser of $175 (one-half of amounts paid for insurance) or $150		$150
(2) Payments for medical care	$370	
(3) Less line 1	150	
(4) Medical expenses to be taken into account under 3-percent limitation (line 2 minus line 3)		$220
(5) Less: 3 percent of $10,000 (adjusted gross income)	300	
(6) Excess allowable as a deduction for 1967 (excess of line 4 over line 5)		0
(7) Allowable medical expense deduction for 1967 (line 1 plus line 6)		$150

(b) Limitation with respect to medicine and drugs. *(1) Taxable years beginning before January 1, 1964.* (i) Amounts paid during taxable years beginning before January 1, 1964, for medicine and drugs are to be taken into account in computing the allowable deduction for medical expenses paid during the taxable year only to the extent that the aggregate of such amounts exceeds 1 percent of the adjusted gross income for the taxable year. Thus, if the aggregate of the amounts paid for medicine and drugs exceeds 1 percent of adjusted gross income, the excess is added to other medical expenses for the purpose of computing the medical expense deduction. The application of this subdivision may be illustrated by the following example:

Example. The taxpayer, a single individual with no dependents, had an adjusted gross income of $6,000 for the calendar year 1956. During 1956, he paid a doctor $300 for medical services, a hospital $100 for hospital care, and also spent $100 for medicine and drugs. These payments were not compensated for by insurance or otherwise. The deduction allowable under section 213 for the calendar year 1956 is $260, computed as follows:

Payments for medical care in 1956:

Doctor		$300
Hospital		100
Medicine and drugs	$100	
Less: 1 percent of $6,000 (adjusted gross income)	60	40
Total medical expenses taken into account		440
Less: 3 percent of $6,000 (adjusted gross income)		180
Allowable deduction for 1956		260

(ii) For taxable years beginning before January 1, 1964, the 1-percent limitation is applicable to all amounts paid by a taxpayer during the taxable year for medicine and drugs. Moreover, this limitation applies regardless of the fact that the amounts paid are for medicine and drugs for the taxpayer, his spouse, or dependent parent (the mother or father of the taxpayer or of his spouse) who has attained the age of 65 before the close of the taxable year. In a case where either a taxpayer or his spouse has attained the age of 65 and the taxpayer pays an amount in excess of 1 percent of adjusted gross income for medicine and drugs for himself, his spouse, and his dependents, it is necessary to apportion the 1 percent of adjusted gross income (the portion which is not taken into account as expenses paid for medical care) between the taxpayer and his spouse on the one hand and his dependents on the other. The part of the 1 percent allocable to the taxpayer and his spouse is an amount which bears the same ratio to 1 percent of his adjusted gross income which the amount paid for medicine and drugs for the taxpayer and his spouse bears to the total amount paid for medicine and drugs for the taxpayer, his spouse, and his dependents. The balance of the 1 percent shall be allocated to his dependents. The amount paid for medicine and drugs in excess of the allocated part of the 1 percent shall be taken into account as payments for medical care for the taxpayer and his spouse on the one hand and his dependents on the other, respectively. A similar apportionment must be made in the case of a dependent parent (65 years of age or over) of the taxpayer or his spouse. The application of this subdivision (ii) may be illustrated by the following example:

Example. H and W, who have a dependent child, made a joint return for the calendar year 1956. H became 65 years of age on September 15, 1956. The adjusted gross income of H and W for 1956 is $10,000. During the year, H and W paid the following amounts for medical care: (i) $1,000 for doctors and hospital expenses and $180 for medicine and drugs for themselves; and (ii) $500 for doctors and hospital expenses and $140 for medicine and drugs for the dependent child. These payments were not compensated for by insurance or otherwise. The deduction allowable under section 213(a)(2) for medical expenses paid in 1956 is $1,420, computed as follows:

H and W:			
Payments for doctors and hospital			$1,000.00
Payments for medicine and drugs		$180.00	
Less: Limitation for medicine and drugs (see computation below)		56.25	
			123.75
Medical expenses for H and W to be taken into account			1,123.75
Dependent:			
Payments for doctors and hospital		500.00	
Payments for medicine and drugs	$140.00		
Less: Limitation for medicine and drugs (see computation below)	43.75		
		96.25	
Total medical expenses		596.25	
Less: 3 percent of $10,000 (adjusted gross income)		300.00	
Medical expenses for the dependent to be taken into account			296.25
Allowable deductions for 1956			1,420.00
Payments for medicine and drugs:			
H and W			180.00
Dependent			140.00

Total payments	320.00
Less: 1 percent of $10,000 (adjusted gross income)	100.00
Payments to be taken into account	220.00
Allocation of 1-percent exclusion:	
H and W $\frac{180}{320} \times \$100$	56.25
Dependent $\frac{140}{320} \times \$100$	43.75
Total	100.00

(2) *Taxable years beginning after December 31, 1963.* (i) Except as otherwise provided in subdivision (ii) of this subparagraph, amounts paid during taxable years beginning after December 31, 1963, for medicine and drugs are to be taken into account in computing the allowable deduction for medical expenses paid during the taxable year only to the extent that the aggregate of such amounts exceeds 1 percent of the adjusted gross income for the taxable year. Thus, if the aggregate of the amounts paid for medicine and drugs which are subject to the 1-percent limitation exceeds 1 percent of adjusted gross income, the excess is added to other medical expenses for the purpose of computing the medical expense deduction.

(ii) The 1-percent limitation provided by section 213 does not apply to amounts paid by a taxpayer during a taxable year beginning after December 31, 1963, and before January 1, 1967, for medicine and drugs for the medical care of the taxpayer and his spouse if either has attained the age of 65 before the close of the taxable year. Moreover, for taxable years beginning after December 31, 1963, and before January 1, 1967, the 1-percent limitation with respect to medicine and drugs does not apply to amounts paid for the medical care of a dependent (as defined in sec. 152) who is the mother or father of the taxpayer or of his spouse and who has attained the age of 65 before the close of the taxpayer's taxable year. Amounts paid for medicine and drugs which are not subject to the limitation on medicine and drugs are added to other medical expenses of a taxpayer and his spouse or the dependent (as the case may be) for the purpose of computing the medical expense deduction.

(iii) The application of this subparagraph may be illustrated by the following examples:

Example (1). H and W, who have a dependent child, C, were both under 65 years of age at the close of the calendar year 1964 and made a joint return for that calendar year. During the year 1964, H's mother, M, attained the age of 65, and was a dependent (as defined in section 152) of H. The adjusted gross income of H and W in 1964 was $12,000. During 1964 H and W paid the following amounts for medical care: (i) $600 for doctors and hospital expenses and $120 for medicine and drugs for themselves; (ii) $350 for doctors and hospital expenses and $60 for medicine and drugs for C; and (iii) $400 for doctors and hospital expenses and $100 for medicine and drugs for M. These payments were not compensated for by insurance or otherwise. The deduction allowable under section 213(a)(1) for medical expenses paid in 1964 is $1,150, computed as follows:

H, W, and C:			
Payments for doctors and hospital		$950	
Payments for medicine and drugs	$180		
Less: 1 percent of $12,000 (adjusted gross income)	120	60	
Total medical expenses		1,010	
Less: 3 percent of $12,000 (adjusted gross income)		360	
Medical expenses of H, W, and C to be taken into account			$650
M:			
Payments for doctors and hospitals		400	
Payments for medicine and drugs		100	
Medical expenses of M to be taken into account			500
Allowable deduction for 1964			1,150

Example (2). H and W, who have a dependent child, C, made a joint return for the calendar year 1964, and reported adjusted gross income of $12,000. H became 65 years of age on January 23, 1964. F, the 87 year old father of W, was a dependent of H. During 1964, H and W paid the following amounts for medical care: (i) $400 for doctors and hospital expenses and $75 for medicine and drugs for H; (ii) $200 for doctors and hospital expenses and $100 for medicine and drugs for W; (iii) $200 for doctors and hospital expenses and $175 for medicine and drugs for C; and (iv) $700 for doctors and hospital expenses and $150 for medicine and drugs for F. These payments were not compensated for by insurance or otherwise. The deduction allowable under section 213(a)(2) for medical expenses paid in 1964 is $1,625, computed as follows:

H and W:			
Payments for doctors and hospital		$600	
Payments for medicine and drugs		175	
Medical expenses for H and W to be taken into account			$ 775
F:			
Payments for doctors and hospital		700	
Payments for medicine and drugs		150	
Medical expenses for F to be taken into account			850
C:			
Payments for doctors and hospital		200	
Payments for medicine and drugs	$175		
Less: 1 percent of $12,000 (adjusted gross income)	120	55	
Total medical expenses		255	
Less: 3 percent of $12,000 (adjusted gross income)		360	
Medical expenses for C to be taken into account			0

Allowable deduction for 1964 ..		1,625

Example (3). Assume the same facts as example (2) except that the calendar year of the return is 1967 and the amounts paid for medical care were paid during 1967. The deduction allowable under section 213(a) for medical expenses paid in 1967 is $1,520, computed as follows:

Payments for doctors and hospitals:			
H			$ 400
W			200
C			200
F			700
			$1,500
Payments for medicine and drugs:			
H	75		
W	100		
C	175		
F	150		
	$500		
Less: 1 percent of $12,000 (adjusted gross income)	120	380	
Medical expenses to be taken into account			$1,880
Less: 3 percent of $12,000 (adjusted gross income)			360
Allowable medical expense deduction for 1967			1,520

(3) Definition of medicine and drugs. For definition of medicine and drugs, see paragraph (e)(2) of this section.

(c) Maximum limitations. *(1)* For taxable years beginning after December 31, 1966, there shall be no maximum limitation on the amount of the deduction allowable for payment of medical expenses.

(2) Except as provided in section 213(g) and § 1.213-2 (relating to maximum limitations with respect to certain aged and disabled individuals for taxable years beginning before January 1, 1967), for taxable years beginning after December 31, 1961, and before January 1, 1967, the maximum deduction allowable for medical expenses paid in any one taxable year is the lesser of:

(i) $5,000 multiplied by the number of exemptions allowed under section 151 (exclusive of exemptions allowed under section 151(c) for a taxpayer or spouse attaining the age of 65, or section 151(d) for a taxpayer who is blind or a spouse who is blind);

(ii) $10,000, if the taxpayer is single, not the head of a household (as defined in section 1(b)(2)) and not a surviving spouse (as defined in section 2(b)), or is married and files a separate return; or

(iii) $20,000 if the taxpayer is married and files a joint return with his spouse under section 6013, or is the head of a household (as defined in section 1(b)(2)), or a surviving spouse (as defined in section 2(b)).

(3) The application of subparagraph (2) of this paragraph may be illustrated by the following example:

Example. H and W made a joint return for the calendar year 1962 and were allowed five exemptions (exclusive of exemptions under sec. 151 (c) and (d)), one for each taxpayer and three for their dependents. The adjusted gross income of H and W in 1962 was $80,000. They paid during such year $26,000 for medical care, no part of which is compensated for by insurance or otherwise. The deduction allowable under section 213 for the calendar year 1962 is $20,000, computed as follows:

Payments for medical care in 1962	$26,000
Less: 3 percent of $80,000 (adjusted gross income)	2,400
Excess of medical expenses in 1962 over 3 percent of adjusted gross income	23,600
Allowable deduction for 1962 ($5,000 multiplied by five exemptions allowed under sec. 151(b) and (e) but not in excess of $20,000)	20,000

(4) Except as provided in section 213(g) and § 1.213-2 (relating to certain aged and disabled individuals), for taxable years beginning before January 1, 1962, the maximum deduction allowable for medical expenses paid in any 1 taxable year is the lesser of:

(i) $2,500 multiplied by the number of exemptions allowed under section 151 (exclusive of exemptions allowed under section 151(c) for a taxpayer or spouse attaining the age of 65, or section 151(d) for a taxpayer who is blind or a spouse who is blind);

(ii) $5,000, if the taxpayer is single, not the head of a household (as defined in section 1(b)(2)) and not a surviving spouse (as defined in section 2(b)) or is married and files a separate return; or

(iii) $10,000, if the taxpayer is married and files a joint return with his spouse under section 6013, or is head of a household (as defined in section 1(b)(2)), or a surviving spouse (as defined in section 2(b)).

(5) For the maximum deduction allowable for taxable years beginning before January 1, 1967, if the taxpayer or his spouse is age 65 or over and is disabled, see § 1.213-2.

(d) Special rule for decedents. *(1)* For the purpose of section 213(a), expenses for medical care of the taxpayer which are paid out of his estate during the 1-year period beginning with the day after the date of his death shall be treated as paid by the taxpayer at the time the medical services were rendered. However, no credit or refund of tax shall be allowed for any taxable year for which the statutory period for filing a claim has expired. See section 6511 and the regulations thereunder.

(2) The rule prescribed in subparagraph (1) of this paragraph shall not apply where the amount so paid is allowable under section 2053 as a deduction in computing the taxable estate of the decedent unless there is filed in duplicate (i) a statement that such amount has not been allowed as a deduction under section 2053 in computing the taxable estate of the decedent and (ii) a waiver of the right to have such amount allowed at any time as a deduction under section 2053. The statement and waiver shall be filed with or for association with the return, amended return, or claim for credit or refund for the decedent for any taxable year for which such an amount is claimed as a deduction.

(e) Definitions. *(1) General.* (i) The term "medical care" includes the diagnosis, cure, mitigation, treatment, or prevention of disease. Expenses paid for "medical care" shall include those paid for the purpose of affecting any structure or function of the body or for transportation primarily for and essential to medical care. See subparagraph (4) of this paragraph for provisions relating to medical insurance.

(ii) Amounts paid for operations or treatments affecting any portion of the body, including obstetrical expenses and expenses of therapy or X-ray treatments, are deemed to be for the purpose of affecting any structure or function of the body and are therefore paid for medical care. Amounts expended for illegal operations or treatments are not deductible. Deductions for expenditures for medical care allowable under section 213 will be confined strictly to expenses incurred primarily for the prevention or alleviation of a physical or mental defect or illness. Thus, payments for the following are payments for medical care: hospital services, nursing services (including nurse's board where paid by the taxpayer), medical, laboratory, surgical, dental and other diagnostic and healing services, X-rays, medicine and drugs (as defined in subparagraph (2) of this paragraph, subject to the 1-percent limitation in paragraph (b) of this section), artificial teeth or limbs, and ambulance hire. However, an expenditure which is merely beneficial to the general health of an individual, such as an expenditure for a vacation, is not an expenditure for medical care.

(iii) Capital expenditures are generally not deductible for Federal income tax purposes. See section 263 and the regulations thereunder. However, an expenditure which otherwise qualifies as a medical expense under section 213 shall not be disqualified merely because it is a capital expenditure. For purposes of section 213 and this paragraph, a capital expenditure made by the taxpayer may qualify as a medical expense, if it has as its primary purpose the medical care (as defined in subdivisions (i) and (ii) of this subparagraph) of the taxpayer, his spouse, or his dependent. Thus, a capital expenditure which is related only to the sick person and is not related to permanent improvement or betterment of property, if it otherwise qualifies as an expenditure for medical care, shall be deductible; for example, an expenditure for eye glasses, a seeing eye dog, artificial teeth and limbs, a wheel chair, crutches, an inclinator or an air conditioner which is detachable from the property and purchased only for the use of a sick person, etc. Moreover, a capital expenditure for permanent improvement or betterment of property which would not ordinarily be for the purpose of medical care (within the meaning of this paragraph) may, nevertheless, qualify as a medical expense to the extent that the expenditure exceeds the increase in the value of the related property, if the particular expenditure is related directly to medical care. Such a situation could arise, for example, where a taxpayer is advised by a physician to install an elevator in his residence so that the taxpayer's wife who is afflicted with heart disease will not be required to climb stairs. If the cost of installing the elevator is $1,000 and the increase in the value of the residence is determined to be only $700, the difference of $300, which is the amount in excess of the value enhancement, is deductible as a medical expense. If, however, by reason of this expenditure, it is determined that the value of the residence has not been increased, the entire cost of installing the elevator would qualify as a medical expense. Expenditures made for the operation or maintenance of a capital asset are likewise deductible medical expenses if they have as their primary purpose the medical care (as defined in subdivisions (i) and (ii) of this subparagraph) of the taxpayer, his spouse, or his dependent. Normally, if a capital expenditure qualifies as a medical expense, expenditures for the operation or maintenance of the capital asset would also qualify provided that the medical reason for the capital expenditure still exists. The entire amount of such operation and maintenance expenditures qualifies, even if none or only a portion of the original cost of the capital asset itself qualified.

(iv) Expenses paid for transportation primarily for and essential to the rendition of the medical care are expenses paid for medical care. However, an amount allowable as a deduction for "transportation primarily for and essential to medical care" shall not include the cost of any meals and lodging while away from home receiving medical treatment. For example, if a doctor prescribes that a taxpayer go to a warm climate in order to alleviate a specific chronic ailment, the cost of meals and lodging while there would not be deductible. On the other hand, if the travel is undertaken merely for the general improvement of a taxpayer's health, neither the cost of transportation nor the cost of meals and lodging would be deductible. If a doctor prescribes an operation or other medical care, and the taxpayer chooses for purely personal considerations to travel to another locality (such as a resort area) for the operation or the other medical care, neither the cost of transportation nor the cost of meals and lodging (except where paid as part of a hospital bill) is deductible.

(v) The cost of in-patient hospital care (including the cost of meals and lodging therein) is an expenditure for medical care. The extent to which expenses for care in an institution other than a hospital shall constitute medical care is primarily a question of fact which depends upon the condition of the individual and the nature of the services he receives (rather than the nature of the institution). A private establishment which is regularly engaged in providing the types of care or services outlined in this subdivision shall be considered an institution for purposes of the rules provided herein. In general, the following rules will be applied:

(a) Where an individual is in an institution because his condition is such that the availability of medical care (as defined in subdivisions (i) and (ii) of this subparagraph) in such institution is a principal reason for his presence there, and meals and lodging are furnished as a necessary incident to such care, the entire cost of medical care and meals and lodging at the institution, which are furnished while the individual requires continual medical care, shall constitute an expense for medical care. For example, medical care includes the entire cost of institutional care for a person who is mentally ill and unsafe when left alone. While ordinary education is not medical care, the cost of medical care includes the cost of attending a special school for a mentally or physically handicapped individual, if his condition is such that the resources of the institution for alleviating such mental or physical handicap are a principal reason for his presence there. In such a case, the cost of attending such a special school will include the cost of meals and lodging, if supplied, and the cost of ordinary education furnished which is incidental to the special services furnished by the school. Thus, the cost of medical care includes the cost of attending a special school designed to compensate for or overcome a physical handicap, in order to qualify the individual for future normal education or for normal living, such as a school for the teaching of braille or lip reading. Similarly, the cost of care and supervision, or of treatment and training, of a mentally retarded or physically handicapped individual at an institution is within the meaning of the term "medical care".

(b) Where an individual is in an institution, and his condition is such that the availability of medical care in such institution is not a principal reason for his presence there, only that part of the cost of care in the institution as is attributable to medical care (as defined in subdivisions (i) and (ii) of this subparagraph) shall be considered as a cost of medical care; meals and lodging at the institution in such a case are not considered a cost of medical care for purposes of this section. For example, an individual is in a home for the aged for personal or family considerations and not because he requires medical or nursing attention. In such case, medical care consists only of that part of the cost for care in the home which is attributable to medical care or nursing attention furnished to him; his meals and lodging at the home are not considered a cost of medical care.

(c) It is immaterial for purposes of this subdivision whether the medical care is furnished in a Federal or State institution or in a private institution.

(vi) See section 262 and the regulations thereunder for disallowance of deduction for personal, living, and family expenses not falling within the definition of medical care.

(2) Medicine and drugs. The term "medicine and drugs" shall include only items which are legally procured and which are generally accepted as falling within the category of medicine and drugs (whether or not requiring a prescription). Such term shall not include toiletries or similar preparations (such as toothpaste, shaving lotion, shaving cream, etc.) nor shall it include cosmetics (such as face creams, deodorants, hand lotions, etc., or any similar preparation used for ordinary cosmetic purposes) or sundry items. Amounts expended for items which, under this subparagraph, are excluded from the term "medicine and drugs" shall not constitute amounts expended for "medical care".

(3) Status as spouse or dependent. In the case of medical expenses for the care of a person who is the taxpayer's spouse or dependent, the deduction under section 213 is allowable if the status of such person as "spouse" or "dependent" of the taxpayer exists either at the time the medical services were rendered or at the time the expenses were paid. In determining whether such status as "spouse" exists, a taxpayer who is legally separated from his spouse under a decree of separate maintenance is not considered as married. Thus, payments made in June 1956 by A, for medical services rendered in 1955 to B, his wife, may be deducted by A for 1956 even though, before the payments were made, B may have died or in 1956 secured a divorce. Payments made in July 1956 by C, for medical services rendered to D in 1955 may be deducted by C for 1956 even though C and D were not married until June 1956.

(4) Medical insurance. (i) (a) For taxable years beginning after December 31, 1966, expenditures for insurance shall constitute expenses paid for medical care only to the extent that such amounts are paid for insurance covering expenses of medical care referred to in subparagraph (1) of this paragraph. In the case of an insurance contract under which amounts are payable for other than medical care (as, for example, a policy providing an indemnity for loss of income or for loss of life, limb, or sight)—

(1) No amount shall be treated as paid for insurance covering expenses of medical care referred to in subparagraph (1) of this paragraph unless the charge for such insurance is either separately stated in the contract or furnished to the policyholder by the insurer in a separate statement,

(2) The amount taken into account as the amount paid for such medical insurance shall not exceed such charge, and

(3) No amount shall be treated as paid for such medical insurance if the amount specified in the contract (or furnished to the policyholder by the insurer in a separate statement) as the charge for such insurance is unreasonably large in relation to the total charges under the contract.

For purposes of the preceding sentence, amounts will be considered payable for other than medical care under the contract if the contract provides for the waiver of premiums upon the occurrence of an event. In determining whether a separately stated charge for insurance covering expenses of medical care is unreasonably large in relation to the total premium, the relationship of the coverages under the contract together with all of the facts and circumstances shall be considered. In determining whether a contract constitutes an "insurance" contract it is irrelevant whether the benefits are payable in cash or in services. For example, amounts paid for hospitalization insurance, for membership in an association furnishing cooperative or so-called free-choice medical service, or for group hospitalization and clinical care are expenses paid for medical care. Premiums paid under Part B, Title XVIII of the Social Security Act (42 U.S.C. 1395j-1395w), relating to supplementary medical insurance benefits for the aged, are amounts paid for insurance covering expenses of medical care. Taxes imposed by any governmental unit do not, however, constitute amounts paid for such medical insurance.

(b) For taxable years beginning after December 31, 1966, subject to the rules of (a) of this subdivision, premiums paid during a taxable year by a taxpayer under the age of 65 for insurance covering expenses of medical care for the taxpayer, his spouse, or a dependent after the taxpayer attains the age of 65 are to be treated as expenses paid during the taxable year for insurance covering expenses of medical care if the premiums for such insurance are payable (on a level payment basis) under the contract—

(1) For a period of 10 years or more, or

(2) Until the year in which the taxpayer attains the age of 65 (but in no case for a period of less than 5 years).

For purposes of this subdivision (b), premiums will be considered payable on a level payment basis if the total premium under the contract is payable in equal annual or more frequent installments. Thus, a total premium of $10,000 payable over a period of 10 years at $1,000 a year shall be considered payable on a level payment basis.

(ii) For taxable years beginning before January 1, 1967, expenses paid for medical care shall include amounts paid for accident or health insurance. In determining whether a contract constitutes an "insurance" contract it is irrelevant whether the benefits are payable in cash or in services. For example, amounts paid for hospitalization insurance, for membership in an association furnishing co-operative or so-called free-choice medical service, or for group hospitalization and clinical care are expenses paid for medical care.

(f) Exclusion of amounts allowed for care of certain dependents. Amounts taken into account under section 44A in computing a credit for the care of certain dependents shall not be treated as expenses paid for medical care.

(g) Reimbursement for expenses paid in prior years. *(1)* Where reimbursement, from insurance or otherwise, for medical expenses is received in a taxable year subsequent to a year in which a deduction was claimed on account of such expenses, the reimbursement must be included in gross income in such subsequent year to the extent attributable to (and not in excess of) deductions allowed under section 213 for any prior taxable year. See section 104, relating to compensation for injuries or sickness, and section 105(b), relating to amounts expended for medical care, and the regulations thereunder, with regard to amounts in excess of or not attributable to deductions allowed.

(2) If no medical expense deduction was taken in an earlier year, for example, if the standard deduction under section 141 was taken for the earlier year, the reimbursement received in the taxable year for the medical expense of the earlier year is not includible in gross income.

(3) In order to allow the same aggregate medical expense deductions as if the reimbursement received in a subsequent year or years had been received in the year in which the

payments for medical care were made, the following rules shall be followed:

(i) If the amount of the reimbursement is equal to or less than the amount which was deducted in a prior year, the entire amount of the reimbursement shall be considered attributable to the deduction taken in such prior year (and hence includible in gross income); or

(ii) If the amount of the reimbursement received in such subsequent year or years is greater than the amount which was deducted for the prior year, that portion of the reimbursement received which is equal in amount to the deduction taken in the prior year shall be considered as attributable to such deduction (and hence includible in gross income); but

(iii) If the deduction for the prior year would have been greater but for the limitations on the maximum amount of such deduction provided by section 213(c), then the amount of the reimbursement attributable to such deduction (and hence includible in gross income) shall be the amount of the reimbursement received in a subsequent year or years reduced by the amount disallowed as a deduction because of the maximum limitation, but not in excess of the deduction allowed for the previous year.

(4) The application of subparagraphs (1), (2), and (3) of this paragraph may be illustrated by the following examples: Examples (1) and (2) reflect the maximum limitation on the medical expense deduction applicable to taxable years beginning after December 31, 1961. Examples (3) and (4) reflect the maximum limitation on the medical expense deduction applicable to taxable years beginning prior to January 1, 1962. For explanation of such maximum medical expense limitations, see paragraph (c) of this section.

Example (1). Taxpayer A, a single individual (not the head of a household and not a surviving spouse) with one dependent, is entitled to two exemptions under the provisions of section 151. He had an adjusted gross income of $35,000 for the calendar year 1962. During 1962 he paid $16,000 for medical care. A received no reimbursement for such medical expenses in 1962, but in 1963 he received $6,000 upon an insurance policy covering the medical expenses which he paid in 1962. A was allowed a deduction of $10,000 (the maximum) from his adjusted gross income for 1962. The amount which A must include in his gross income for 1963 is $1,050, and the amount to be excluded from gross income for 1963 is $4,950, computed as follows:

Payments for medical care in 1962 (not reimbursed in 1962)	$16,000
Less: 3 percent of $35,000 (adjusted gross income)	1,050
Excess of medical expenses not reimbursed in 1962 over 3 percent of adjusted gross income	14,950
Allowable deduction for 1962	10,000
Amount by which the medical deductions for 1962 would have been greater than $10,000 but for the limitations on the maximum amount provided by section 213	4,950
Reimbursement received in 1963	$ 6,000
Less: Amount by which the medical deduction for 1962 would have been greater than $10,000 but for the limitations on the maximum amount provided by section 213	4,950
Reimbursement received in 1963 reduced by the amount by which the medical deduction for 1962 would have been greater than $10,000 but for the limitations on the maximum amount provided by section 213	1,050
Amount attributed to medical deduction taken for 1962	1,050
Amount to be included in gross income for 1963	1,050
Amount to be excluded from gross income for 1963 ($6,000 less $1,050)	4,950

Example (2). Assuming that A, in example (1), received $15,000 in 1963 as reimbursement for the medical expenses which he paid in 1962, the amount which A must include in his gross income for 1963 is $10,000, and the amount to be excluded from gross income for 1963 is $5,000, computed as follows:

Reimbursement received in 1963	$15,000
Less: Amount by which the medical deduction for 1962 would have been greater than $10,000 but for the limitations on the maximum amount provided by section 213	4,950
Reimbursement received in 1963 reduced by the amount by which the medical deduction for 1962 would have been greater than $10,000 but for the limitations on the maximum amount provided by section 213	10,050
Deduction allowable for 1962	10,000
Amount of reimbursement received in 1963 to be included in gross income for 1963 as attributable to deduction allowable for 1962	10,000
Amount to be excluded from gross income for 1963 ($15,000 less $10,000)	5,000

Example (3). Taxpayer A, a single individual (not the head of a household and not a surviving spouse) with one dependent, is entitled to two exemptions under the provisions of section 151. He had an adjusted gross income of $35,000 for the calendar year 1956. During 1956 he paid $9,000 for medical care. A received no reimbursement for such medical expenses in 1956, but in 1957 he received $6,000 upon an insurance policy covering the medical expenses which he paid in 1956. A was allowed a deduction of $5,000 (the maximum) from his adjusted gross income for 1956. The amount which A must include in his gross income for 1957 is $3,050 and the amount to be excluded from gross income for 1957 is $2,950, computed as follows:

Payments for medical care in 1956 (not reimbursed in 1956)	$9,000
Less: 3 percent of $35,000 (adjusted gross income)	1,050
Excess of medical expenses not reimbursed in 1956 over 3 percent of adjusted gross income	7,950
Allowable deduction for 1956	5,000
Amount by which the medical deductions for 1956 would have been greater than $5,000 but for the limitations on the maximum amount provided by section 213	2,950
Reimbursement received in 1957	6,000
Less: Amount by which the medical deduction for 1956 would have been greater than $5,000 but for the limitations on the maximum amount provided by section 213	2,950

Reimbursement received in 1957 reduced by the amount by which the medical deduction for 1956 would have been greater than $5,000 but for the limitations on the maximum amount provided by section 213	3,050
Amount attributed to medical deduction taken for 1956	3,050
Amount to be included in gross income for 1957	3,050
Amount to be excluded from gross income for 1957 ($6,000 less $3,050)	2,950

Example (4). Assuming that A, in example (3), received $8,000 in 1957 as reimbursement for the medical expenses which he paid in 1956, the amount which A must include in his gross income for 1957 is $5,000 and the amount to be excluded from gross income for 1957 is $3,000 computed as follows:

Reimbursement received in 1957	$8,000
Less: Amount by which the medical deduction for 1956 would have been greater than $5,000 but for the limitations on the maximum amount provided by section 213	2,950
Reimbursement received in 1957 reduced by the amount by which the medical deduction for 1956 would have been greater than $5,000 but for the limitations on the maximum amount provided by section 213	5,050
Deduction allowable for 1956	$5,000
Amount of reimbursement received in 1957 to be included in gross income for 1957 as attributable to deduction allowable for 1956	5,000
Amount to be excluded from gross income for 1957 ($8,000 less $5,000)	3,000

(h) Substantiation of deductions. In connection with claims for deductions under section 213, the taxpayer shall furnish the name and address of each person to whom payment for medical expenses was made and the amount and date of the payment thereof in each case. If payment was made in kind, such fact shall be so reflected. Claims for deductions must be substantiated, when requested by the district director, by a statement or itemized invoice from the individual or entity to which payment for medical expenses was made showing the nature of the service rendered, and to or for whom rendered; the nature of any other item of expense and for whom incurred and for what specific purpose, the amount paid therefor and the date of the payment thereof; and by such other information as the district director may deem necessary.

T.D. 6279, 12/13/57, amend T.D. 6451, 2/3/60, T.D. 6604, 7/23/62, T.D. 6661, 6/26/63, T.D. 6761, 9/28/64, T.D. 6946, 2/12/68, T.D. 6985, 12/26/68, T.D. 7114, 5/17/71, T.D. 7317, 6/27/74, T.D. 7643, 8/27/79.

§ 1.215-1 Periodic alimony, etc., payments.

(a) A deduction is allowable under section 215 with respect to periodic payments in the nature of, or in lieu of, alimony or an allowance for support actually paid by the taxpayer during his taxable year and required to be included in the income of the payee wife or former wife, as the case may be, under section 71. As to the amounts required to be included in the income of such wife or former wife, see section 71 and the regulations thereunder. For definition of "husband" and "wife" see section 7701(a)(17).

(b) The deduction under section 215 is allowed only to the obligor spouse. It is not allowed to an estate, trust, corporation, or any other person who may pay the alimony obligation of such obligor spouse. The obligor spouse, however, is not allowed a deduction for any periodic payment includible under section 71 in the income of the wife or former wife, which payment is attributable to property transferred in discharge of his obligation and which, under section 71(d) or section 682, is not includible in his gross income.

(c) The following examples, in which both H and W file their income tax returns on the basis of a calendar year, illustrate cases in which a deduction is or is not allowed under section 215:

Example (1). Pursuant to the terms of a decree of divorce, H, in 1956, transferred securities valued at $100,000 in trust for the benefit of W, which fully discharged all his obligations to W. The periodic payments made by the trust to W are required to be included in W's income under section 71. Such payments are stated in section 71(d) not to be includible in H's income and, therefore, under section 215 are not deductible from his income.

Example (2). A decree of divorce obtained by W from H incorporated a previous agreement of H to establish a trust, the trustees of which were instructed to pay W $5,000 a year for the remainder of her life. The court retained jurisdiction to order H to provide further payments if necessary for the support of W. In 1956 the trustee paid to W $4,000 from the income of the trust and $1,000 from the corpus of the trust. Under the provisions of sections 71 and 682(b), W would include $5,000 in her income for 1956. H would not include any part of the $5,000 in his income nor take a deduction therefor. If H had paid the $1,000 to W pursuant to court order rather than allowing the trustees to pay it out of corpus, he would have been entitled to a deduction of $1,000 under the provisions of section 215.

(d) For other examples, see sections 71 and 682 and the regulations thereunder.

T.D. 6279, 12/13/57.

§ 1.215-1T Alimony, etc., payments (temporary).

Q-1. What information is required by the Internal Revenue Service when an alimony or separate maintenance payment is claimed as a deduction by a payor?

A-1. The payor spouse must include on his/her first filed return of tax (Form 1040) for the taxable year in which the payment is made the payee's social security number, which the payee is required to furnish to the payor. For penalties applicable to a payor spouse who fails to include such information on his/her return of tax or to a payee spouse who fails to furnish his/her social security number to the payor spouse, see section 6676.

T.D. 7973, 8/30/84.

§ 1.216-1 Amounts representing taxes and interest paid to cooperative housing corporation.

Caution: The Treasury has not yet amended Reg § 1.216-1 to reflect changes made by P.L. 110-142.

(a) General rule. A tenant-stockholder of a cooperative housing corporation may deduct from his gross income amounts paid or accrued within his taxable year to a cooperative housing corporation representing his proportionate share of:

(1) The real estate taxes allowable as a deduction to the corporation under section 164 which are paid or incurred by

the corporation before the close of the taxable year of the tenant-stockholder on the houses (or apartment building) and the land on which the houses (or apartment building) are situated, or

(2) The interest allowable as a deduction to the corporation under section 163 which is paid or incurred by the corporation before the close of the taxable year of the tenant-stockholder on its indebtedness contracted in the acquisition, construction, alteration, rehabilitation, or maintenance of the houses (or apartment building), or in the acquisition of the land on which the houses (or apartment building) are situated.

(b) Limitation. The deduction allowable under section 216 shall not exceed the amount of the tenant-stockholder's proportionate share of the taxes and interest described therein. If a tenant-stockholder pays or incurs only a part of his proportionate share of such taxes and interest to the corporation, only the amount so paid or incurred which represents taxes and interest is allowable as a deduction under section 216. If a tenant-stockholder pays an amount, or incurs an obligation for an amount, to the corporation on account of such taxes and interest and other items, such as maintenance, overhead expenses, and reduction of mortgage indebtedness, the amount representing such taxes and interest is an amount which bears the same ratio to the total amount of the tenant-stockholder's payment or liability, as the case may be, as the total amount of the tenant-stockholder's proportionate share of such taxes and interest bears to the total amount of the tenant-stockholder's proportionate share of the taxes, interest, and other items on account of which such payment is made or liability incurred. No deduction is allowable under section 216 for that part of amounts representing the taxes or interest described in that section which are deductible by a tenant-stockholder under any other provision of the Code.

(c) Disallowance of deduction for certain payments to the corporation. For taxable years beginning after December 31, 1986, no deduction shall be allowed to a stockholder during any taxable year for any amount paid or accrued to a cooperative housing corporation (in excess of the stockholder's proportionate share of the items described in paragraphs (a)(1) and (2) of this section) which is allocable to amounts that are paid or incurred at any time by the cooperative housing corporation and which is chargeable to the corporation's capital account. Examples of expenditures chargeable to the corporation's capital account include the cost of paving a community parking lot, the purchase of a new boiler or roof, and the payment of the principal of the corporation's building mortgage. The adjusted basis of the stockholder's stock in such corporation shall be increased by the amount of such disallowance. This paragraph may be illustrated by the following example:

Example. The X corporation is a cooperative housing corporation within the meaning of section 216. In 1988 X uses $275,000 that it received from its shareholders in such year to purchase and place in service a new boiler. The $275,000 will be chargeable to the corporation's capital account. A owns 10% of the shares of X and uses in a trade or business the dwelling unit appurtenant to A's shares and was responsible for paying 10% of the cost of the boiler. A is thus responsible for $27,500 of the cost of the boiler, which amount A will not be able to deduct currently. A will, however, add the $27,500 to A's basis for A's shares in X.

(d) Tenant-stockholder's proportionate share. *(1) General rule.* The tenant-stockholder's proportionate share is that proportion which the stock of the cooperative housing corporation owned by the tenant-stockholder is of the total outstanding stock of the corporation, including any stock held by the corporation. For taxable years beginning after December 31, 1969, if the cooperative housing corporation had issued stock to a governmental unit, as defined in paragraph (g) of this section, then in determining the total outstanding stock of the corporation, the governmental unit shall be deemed to hold the number of shares that it would have held, with respect to the apartments or houses it is entitled to occupy, if it has been a tenant-stockholder. That is, the number of shares the governmental unit is deemed to hold is determined in the same manner as if stock had been issued to it as a tenant-stockholder. For example, if a cooperative housing corporation requires each tenant-stockholder to buy one share of stock for each one thousand dollars of value of the apartment he is entitled to occupy, a governmental unit shall be deemed to hold one share of stock for each one thousand dollars of value of the apartments it is entitled to occupy, regardless of the number of shares formally issued to it.

(2) Special rule. (i) In general. For taxable years beginning after December 31, 1986, if a cooperative housing corporation allocates to each tenant-stockholder a portion of the real estate taxes or interest (or both) that reasonably reflects the cost to the corporation of the taxes or interest attributable to each tenant-stockholder's dwelling unit (and the unit's share of the common areas), the cooperative housing corporation may elect to treat the amounts so allocated as the tenant-stockholders' proportionate shares.

(ii) Time and manner of making election. The election referred to in paragraph (d)(2)(i) of this section is effective only if, by January 31 of the year following the first calendar year that includes any period to which the election applies, the cooperative housing corporation furnishes to each person that is a tenant-stockholder during that period a written statement showing the amount of real estate taxes or interest (or both) allocated to the tenant-stockholder with respect to the tenant-stockholder's dwelling unit or units and share of common areas for that period. The election must be made by attaching a statement to the corporation's timely filed tax return (taking extensions into account) for the first taxable year for which the election is to be effective. The statement must contain the name, address, and taxpayer identification number of the cooperative housing corporation, identify the election as an election under section 216(b)(3)(B)(ii) of the Code, indicate whether the election is being made with respect to the allocation of real estate taxes or interest (or both), and include a description of the method of allocation being elected. The election applies for the taxable year and succeeding taxable years. It is revocable only with the consent of the Commissioner and will be binding on all tenant-stockholders.

(iii) Reasonable allocation. It is reasonable to allocate to each tenant-stockholder a portion of the real estate taxes or interest (or both) that bears the same ratio to the cooperative housing corporation's total interest or real estate taxes as the fair market value of each dwelling unit (including the unit's share of the common areas) bears to the fair market value of all the dwelling units with respect to which stock is outstanding (including stock held by the corporation) at the time of allocation. If real estate taxes are separately assessed on each dwelling unit by the relevant taxing authority, an allocation of real estates taxes to tenant-stockholders based on separate assessments is a reasonable allocation. If one or more of the tenant-stockholders prepays any portion of the principal of the indebtedness and gives rise to interest, and allocation of interest to those tenant-stockholders will be a reasonable allocation of interest if the allocation is reduced to reflect the reduction in the debt service attributable to the prepayment. In addition, similar kinds of allocations may also be reasonable, depending on the facts and circumstances.

(3) Examples. The provisions of this paragraph may be illustrated by the following examples:

Example (1). The X Corporation is a cooperative housing corporation within the meaning of section 216. In 1970, it acquires a building containing 40 category A apartments and 25 category B apartments, for $750,000. The value of each category A apartment is $12,500, and of each category B apartment is $10,000. X values each share of stock issued with respect to the category A apartments at $125, and sells 4,000 shares of its stock, along with the right to occupy the 40 category A apartments, to 40 tenant-stockholders for $500,000. X also sells 1,000 shares of nonvoting stock to G, a State housing authority qualifying as a governmental unit under paragraph (f) of this section for $250,000. The purchase of this stock gives G the right to occupy all the category B apartments. G is deemed to hold the number of shares that it would have held if it had been a tenant-stockholder. G is therefore deemed to own 2,000 shares of stock of X. All stockholders are required to pay a specified part of the corporation's expenses. F, one of the tenant-stockholders, purchased 100 shares of the category A stock for $12,500 in order to obtain a right to occupy a category A apartment. Since there are 6,000 total shares deemed outstanding, F's proportionate share is 1/60 (100/6,000).

Example (2). The X Corporation is a cooperative housing corporation within the meaning of section 216. In 1960 it required a housing development containing 100 detached houses, each house having the same value. X issued one share of stock to each of 100 tenant-stockholders, each share carrying the right to occupy one of the houses. In 1971 X redeemed 40 of its 100 shares. It then sold to G, a municipal housing authority qualifying as a governmental unit under paragraph (f) of this section, 1,000 shares of preferred stock and the right to occupy the 40 houses with respect to which the stock had been redeemed. X sold the preferred stock to G for an amount equal to the cost of redeeming the 40 shares. G also agreed to pay 40 percent of X's expenses. For purposes of determining the total stock which X has outstanding, G is deemed to hold 40 shares of X.

Example (3). The X Corporation is a cooperative housing corporation within the meaning of section 216. In 1987, it acquires for $1,000,000 a building containing 10 category A apartments, 10 category B apartments, and 10 category C apartments. The value of each category A apartment is $20,000, of each category B apartment is $30,000 and of each category C apartment is $50,000. X issues 1 share of stock to each of the 30 tenant-stockholders, each share carrying the right to occupy one of the apartments. X allocates the real estate taxes and interest to the tenant-stockholders on the basis of the fair market value of their respective apartments. Since the total fair market value of all of the apartments is $1,000,000, the allocation of taxes and interest to each tenant-stockholder that has the right to occupy a category A apartment is 2/100 ($20,000/$1,000,000). Similarly, the allocation of taxes and interest to each tenant-stockholder who has a right to occupy a category B apartment is 3/100 ($30,000/$1,000,000) and of a category C apartment is 5/100 ($50,000/$1,000,000). X may elect in accordance with the rules described in paragraph (d)(2) of this section to treat the amounts so allocated as each tenant-stockholder's proportionate share of real estate taxes and interest.

Example (4). The Y Corporation is a cooperative housing corporation within the meaning of section 216. In 1987, it acquires a housing development containing 5 detached houses for $1,500,000, incurring an indebtedness of $1,000,000 for the purchase of the property. Each house is valued at $300,000, although the shares appurtenant to those houses have been sold to tenant-stockholders for $100,000. Y issues one share of stock to each of the five tenant-stockholders, each share carrying the right to occupy one of the houses. A, a tenant-stockholder, prepays all of the corporation's indebtedness allocable to A's house. The periodic charges payable to Y by A are reduced commensurately with the reduction in Y's debt service. Because no part of the indebtedness remains outstanding with respect to A's house, A's share of the interest expense is $0. The other four tenant-stockholders do not prepay their share of the indebtedness. Accordingly, ¼ of the interest is allocated to each of the tenant-stockholders other than A. Y may elect in accordance with the rules described in paragraph (d)(2) of this section to treat the amounts so allocated as each tenant-stockholder's proportionate share of interest.

Example (5). The Z Corporation is a cooperative housing corporation within the meaning of section 216. In 1987, it acquires a building containing 10 apartments. One of the apartments is occupied by a senior citizen. Under local law, a senior citizen who owns and occupies a residential apartment is entitled to a $500 reduction in local property taxes assessed upon the apartment. As a result, Z Corporation is eligible under local law for a reduction in local property taxes assessed upon the building. Z's real estate tax assessment for the year would have been $10,000 however, with the senior citizen reduction, the assessment is $9,500. The proprietary lease provides for a reduced maintenance fee to the senior citizen tenant-stockholder in accordance with the real estate tax reduction. Accordingly, each apartment owner is assessed $1,000 for local real estate taxes, except the senior citizen tenant-shareholder, who is assessed $500. Z may elect in accordance with the rules described in paragraph (d)(2) of this section to treat the amounts so allocated as each tenant-stockholder's proportionate share of taxes.

(e) Cooperative housing corporation. In order to qualify as a "cooperative housing corporation" under section 216, the requirements of subparagraphs (1) through (4) of this paragraph must be met.

(1) One class of stock. The corporation shall have one and only one class of stock outstanding. However, a special classification of preferred stock, in a nominal amount not exceeding $100, issued to a Federal housing agency or other governmental agency solely for the purpose of creating a security device on the mortgage indebtedness of the corporation, shall be disregarded for purposes of determining whether the corporation has one class of stock outstanding and such agency will not be considered a stockholder for purposes of section 216 and this section. Furthermore, for taxable years beginning after December 31, 1969, a special class of stock issued to a governmental unit, as defined in paragraph (g) of this section, shall also be disregarded for purposes of this paragraph in determining whether the corporation has one class of stock outstanding.

(2) Right of occupancy. Each stockholder of the corporation, whether or not the stockholder qualifies as a tenant-stockholder under section 216(b)(2) and paragraph (f) of this section, must be entitled to occupy for dwelling purposes an apartment in a building or a unit in a housing development

owned or leased by such corporation. The stockholder is not required to occupy the premises. The right as against the corporation to occupy the premises is sufficient. Such right must be conferred on each stockholder solely by reasons of his or her ownership of stock in the corporation. That is, the stock must entitle the owner thereof either to occupy the premises or to a lease of the premises. The fact that the right to continue to occupy the premises is dependent upon the payment of charges to the corporation in the nature of rentals or assessments is immaterial. For taxable years beginning after December 31, 1986, the fact that, by agreement with the cooperative housing corporation, a person or his nominee may not occupy the house or apartment without the prior approval of such corporation will not be taken into account for purposes of this paragraph in the following cases.

(i) In any case where a person acquires stock of the cooperative housing corporation by operation of law, by inheritance, or by foreclosure (or by instrument in lieu of foreclosure),

(ii) In any case where a person other than an individual acquires stock in the cooperative housing corporation, and

(iii) In any case where the person from whom the corporation has acquired the apartments or houses (or leaseholds therein) acquires any stock of the cooperative housing corporation from the corporation not later than one year after the date on which the apartments or houses (or leaseholds therein) are transferred to the corporation by such person. For purposes of the preceding sentence, paragraphs (e)(2)(i) and (ii) of this section will not apply to acquisitions of stock by foreclosure by the person from whom the corporation has acquired the apartments or houses (or leaseholds therein).

(3) Distributions. None of the stockholders of the corporation may be entitled, either conditionally or unconditionally, except upon a complete or partial liquidation of the corporation, to receive any distribution other than out of earnings or profits of the corporation.

(4) Gross income. Eighty percent or more of the gross income of the corporation for the taxable year of the corporation in which the taxes and interest are paid or incurred must be derived from the tenant-stockholders. For purposes of the 80-percent test, in taxable years beginning after December 31, 1969, gross income attributable to any house or apartment which a governmental unit is entitled to occupy, pursuant to a lease or stock ownership, shall be disregarded.

(f) Tenant-stockholder. The term "tenant-stockholder" means a person that is a stockholder in a cooperative housing corporation, as defined in section 216(b)(1) and paragraph (e) of this section, and whose stock is fully paid up in an amount at least equal to an amount shown to the satisfaction of the district director as bearing a reasonable relationship to the portion of the fair market value, as of the date of the original issuance of the stock, of the corporation's equity in the building and the land on which it is situated that is attributable to the apartment or housing unit which such person is entitled to occupy (within the meaning of paragraphs (e)(2) of this section). Notwithstanding the preceding sentence, for taxable years beginning before January 1, 1987, tenant-stockholders include only individuals, certain lending institutions, and certain persons from whom the cooperative housing corporation has acquired the apartments or houses (or leaseholds thereon).

(g) Governmental unit. For purposes of section 216(b) and this section, the term "governmental unit" means the United States or any of its possessions, a State or any political subdivision thereof, or any agency or instrumentality of the foregoing empowered to acquire shares in a cooperative housing corporation for the purpose of providing housing facilities.

(h) Examples. The application of section 216(a) and (b) and this section may be illustrated by the following examples, which refer to apartments but which are equally applicable to housing units:

Example (1). The X Corporation is a cooperative housing corporation within the meaning of section 216. In 1970, at a total cost of $200,000, it purchased a site and constructed thereon a building with 15 apartments. The fair market value of the land and building was $200,000 at the time of completion of the building. The building contains five category A apartment units, each of equal value, and 10 category B apartment units. The total value of all of the category A apartment units is $100,000. The total value of all of the category B apartments is also $100,000. Upon completion of the building, the X Corporation mortgaged the land and building for $100,000, and sold its total authorized capital stock for $100,000. The stock attributable to the category A apartments was purchased by five individuals, each of whom paid $10,000 for 100 shares, or $100 a share. Each certificate for 100 shares of such stock provides that the holder thereof is entitled to a lease of a particular apartment in the building for a specified term of years. The stock attributable to the category B apartments was purchased by a governmental unit for $50,000. Since the shares sold to the tenant-stockholders are valued at $100 per share, the governmental unit is deemed to hold a total of 500 shares. The certificate of such stock provides that the governmental unit is entitled to a lease of all of the category B apartments. All leases provide that the lessee shall pay his proportionate part of the corporation's expenses. In 1970 the original owner of 100 shares of stock attributable to the category A apartments and to the lease to apartment No. 1 made a gift of the stock and lease to A, an individual. The taxable year of A and of the X Corporation is the calendar year. The corporation computes its taxable income on an accrual method, while A computes his taxable income on the cash receipts and disbursements method. In 1971, the X Corporation incurred expenses aggregating $13,800, including $4,000 for the real estate taxes on the land and building, and $5,000 for the interest on the mortgage. In 1972, A pays the X Corporation $1,380, representing his proportionate part of the expenses incurred by the corporation. The entire gross income of the X Corporation for 1971 was derived from the five tenant-stockholders and from the governmental unit. A is entitled under section 216 to a deduction of $900 in computing his taxable income for 1972. The deduction is computed as follows:

Shares of X Corporation owned by A		100
Shares of X Corporation owned by four other tenant-stockholders		400
Shares of stock of X Corporation deemed owned by governmental unit		500
Total shares of stock of X Corporation outstanding		1,000
A's proportionate share of the stock of X Corporation (100/1,000)		1/10
Expenses incurred by X Corporation:		
Real estate taxes	$4,000	
Interest	5,000	
Other	4,800	
Total		$13,800

Amount paid by A	$ 1,380
A's proportionate share of real estate and interest based on his stock ownership (1/10 of $9,000)	$ 900
A's proportionate share of total corporate expenses based on his stock ownership (1/10 of $13,800)	$ 1,380
Amount of A's payment representing real estate taxes and interest (900/1,380 of $1,380)	$ 900
A's allowable deduction	$ 900

Since the stock which A acquired by gift was fully paid up by his donor in an amount equal to the portion of the fair market value, as of the date of the original issuance of the stock, of the corporation's equity in the land and building which is attributable to apartment No. 1, the requirement of section 216 in this regard is satisfied. The fair market value at the time of the gift of the corporation's equity attributable to the apartment is immaterial.

Example (2). The facts are the same as in example (1) except that the building constructed by the X Corporation contained, in addition to the 15 apartments, business space on the ground floor, which the corporation rented at $2,400 for the calendar year 1971. The corporation deducted the $2,400 from its expenses in determining the amount of the expenses to be prorated among its tenant-stockholders. The amount paid by A to the corporation in 1972 is $1,140 instead of $1,380. More than 80 percent of the gross income of the corporation for 1971 was derived from tenant-stockholders. A is entitled under section 216 to a deduction of $743.48 in computing his taxable income for 1972. The deduction is computed as follows:

Expenses incurred by X Corporation	$13,800.00	
Less: Rent from business space	2,400.00	
Expenses to be prorated among tenant-stockholders		$11,400.00
Amount paid by A		1,140.00
A's proportionate share of real estate taxes and interest based on his stock ownership (1/10 of $9,000)		900.00
A's proportionate share of total corporate expenses based on his stock ownership (1/10 of $13,800)		1,380.00
Amount of A's payment representing real estate taxes and interest (900/1380 of $1,140)		743.48
A's allowable deduction		743.48

Since the portion of A's payment allocable to real estate taxes and interest is only $743.48, that amount instead of $900 is allowable as a deduction in computing A's taxable income for 1972.

Example (3). The facts are the same as in example (1) except that the amount paid by A to the X corporation in 1972 is $1,000 instead of $1,380. A is entitled under section 216 to a deduction of 652.17 in computing his taxable income for 1972. The deduction is computed as follows:

Amount paid by A	$1,000.00
A's proportionate share of real estate taxes and interest based on his stock ownership (1/10 of $9,000)	900.00
A's proportionate share of total corporate expenses based on his stock ownership (1/10 of $13,800)	1,380.00
Amount of A's payment representing real estate taxes and interest (900/1380 of $1,000)	652.17
A's allowable deduction	652.17

Since the portion of A's payment allocable to real estate taxes and interest is only $652.17, that amount instead of $900 is allowable as a deduction in computing A's taxable income for 1972.

Example (4). The facts are the same as in example (1) except that X Corporation leases recreational facilities from Y Corporation for use by the tenant-stockholders of X. Under the terms of the lease, X is obligated to pay an annual rate of $5,000 plus all real estate taxes assessed against the facilities. In 1971 X paid, in addition to the $13,800 of expenses enumerated in example (1), $5,000 rent and $1,000 real estate taxes. In 1972 A pays the X Corporation $2,000, no part of which is refunded to him in 1972. A is entitled under section 216 to a deduction of $900 in computing his taxable income for 1972. The deduction is computed as follows:

Expenses to be prorated among tenant-stockholders	$ 19,800.00
Amount paid by A	2,000.00
A's proportionate share of real estate taxes and interest based on his stock ownership (1/10 of $9,000)	900.00
A's proportionate share of total corporate expenses based on his stock ownership (1/10 of $19,800)	1,980.00
Amount of A's payment representing real estate taxes and interest (900/1,980 of $1,980)	900.00
A's allowable deduction	900.00

The $1,000 of real estate taxes assessed against the recreational facilities constitutes additional rent and hence is not deductible by A as taxes under section 216. A's allowable deduction is limited to his proportionate share of real estate taxes and interest based on stock ownership and cannot be increased by the payment of an amount in excess of his proportionate share.

T.D. 6277, 12/9/57, amend T.D. 7092, 3/9/71, T.D. 8316, 10/16/90.

§ 1.216-2 Treatment as property subject to depreciation.

(a) General rule. For taxable years beginning after December 31, 1961, stock in a cooperative housing corporation (as defined by section 216(b)(1) and paragraph (c) of § 1.216-1) owned by a tenant-stockholder (as defined by section 216(b)(2) and paragraph (d) of § 1.216-1) who uses the proprietary lease or right of tenancy, which was conferred on him solely by reason of his ownership of such stock, in a trade or business or for the production of income shall be treated as property subject to the allowance for depreciation under section 167(a) in the manner and to the extent prescribed in this section.

(b) Determination of allowance for depreciation. *(1) In general.* Subject to the special rules provided in subparagraphs (2) and (3) of this paragraph and the limitation provided in paragraph (c) of this section, the allowance for depreciation for the taxable year with respect to stock of a tenant-stockholder, subject to the extent provided in this section to an allowance for depreciation, shall be determined—

(i) By computing the amount of depreciation (amortization in the case of a leasehold) which would be allowable under one of the methods of depreciation prescribed in section 167(b) and the regulations thereunder (in paragraph (a) of § 1.162-11 and § 1.167(a)-4 in the case of a leasehold) in respect of the depreciable (amortizable) real property owned by the cooperative housing corporation in which such tenant-stockholder has a proprietary lease or right of tenancy,

(ii) By reducing the amount of depreciation (amortization) so computed in the same ratio as the rentable space in such property which is not subject to a proprietary lease or right of tenancy by reason of stock ownership but which is held for rental purposes bears to the total rentable space in such property, and

(iii) By computing such tenant-stockholder's proportionate share of such annual depreciation (amortization), so reduced.

As used in this section, the terms "depreciation" and "depreciable real property" include amortization and amortizable leasehold of real property. As used in this section, the tenant-stockholder's proportionate share is that proportion which stock of the cooperative housing corporation owned by the tenant-stockholder is of the total outstanding stock of the corporation, including any stock held by the corporation. In order to determine whether a tenant-stockholder may use one of the methods of depreciation prescribed in section 167(b)(2), (3), or (4) for purposes of subdivision (i) of this subparagraph, the limitations provided in section 167(c) on the use of such methods of depreciation shall be applied with respect to the depreciable real property owned by the cooperative housing corporation in which the tenant-stockholder has a proprietary lease or right of tenancy, rather than with respect to the stock in the cooperative housing corporation owned by the tenant-stockholder or with respect to the proprietary lease or right of tenancy conferred on the tenant-stockholder by reason of his ownership of such stock. The allowance for depreciation determined under this subparagraph shall be properly adjusted where only a portion of the property occupied under a proprietary lease or right of tenancy is used in a trade or business or for the production of income.

(2) Stock acquired subsequent to first offering. Except as provided in subparagraph (3), in the case of a tenant-stockholder who purchases stock other than as part of the first offering of stock by the corporation, the basis of the depreciable real property for purposes of the computation required by subparagraph (1)(i) of this paragraph shall be the amount obtained by—

(i) Multiplying the taxpayer's cost per share by the total number of outstanding shares of stock of the corporation, including any shares held by the corporation,

(ii) Adding thereto the mortgage indebtedness to which such depreciable real property is subject on the date of purchase of such stock, and

(iii) Subtracting from the sum so obtained the portion thereof not properly allocable as of the date such stock was purchased to the depreciable real property owned by the cooperative housing corporation in which such tenant-stockholder has a proprietary lease or right of tenancy.

In order to prevent an overstatement or understatement of the basis of the depreciable real property for purposes of the computation required by subparagraph (1)(i) of this paragraph, appropriate adjustment for purposes of the computations described in subdivisions (i) and (ii) of this subparagraph shall be made in respect of prepayments and delinquencies on account of the corporation's mortgage indebtedness. Thus, for purposes of subdivision (i) of this subparagraph, the taxpayer's cost per share shall be reduced by an amount determined by dividing the total mortgage indebtedness prepayments in respect of the shares purchased by the taxpayer by the number of such shares. For purposes of subdivision (ii) of this subparagraph, the mortgage indebtedness shall be increased by the sum of all prepayments applied in reduction of the mortgage indebtedness and shall be decreased by any amount due under the terms of the mortgage and unpaid.

(3) Conversion subsequent to date of acquisition. In the case of a tenant-stockholder whose proprietary lease or right of tenancy is converted, in whole or in part, to use in a trade or business or for the production of income on a date subsequent to the date on which he acquired the stock conferring on him such lease or right of tenancy, the basis of the depreciable real property for purposes of the computation required by subparagraph (1)(i) of this paragraph shall be the fair market value of such depreciable real property on the date of the conversion if the fair market value is less than the adjusted basis of such property in the hands of the cooperative housing corporation provided in section 1011 without taking into account any adjustment for depreciation required by section 1016(a)(2). Such fair market value shall be deemed to be equal to the adjusted basis of such property, taking into account adjustments required by section 1016(a)(2) computed as if the corporation had used the straight line method of depreciation, in the absence of evidence establishing that the fair market value so attributed to the property is unrealistic. In the case of a tenant-stockholder who purchases stock other than as part of the first offering of stock of the corporation, and at a later date converts his proprietary lease to use for business or production of income—

(i) The adjusted basis of the cooperative housing corporation's depreciable real property without taking into account any adjustment for depreciation shall be the amount determined in accordance with subdivisions (i), (ii), and (iii) of subparagraph (2) of this paragraph, and

(ii) The fair market value shall be deemed to be equal to such adjusted basis reduced by the amount of depreciation, computed under the straight line method, which would have been allowable in respect of depreciable real property having a cost or other basis equal to the amount representing such adjusted basis in the absence of evidence establishing that the fair market value so attributed to the property is unrealistic.

(c) Limitation. If the allowance for depreciation for the taxable year determined in accordance with the provisions of paragraph (b) of this section exceeds the adjusted basis (provided in section 1011) of the stock described in paragraph (a) of this section allocable to the tenant-stockholder's proprietary lease or right of tenancy used in a trade or business or for the production of income, such excess is not allowable as a deduction. For taxable years beginning after December 31, 1986, such excess, subject to the provisions of this paragraph (c), is allowable as a deduction for depreciation in the succeeding taxable year. To determine the portion of the adjusted basis of such stock which is allocable to such proprietary lease or right of tenancy, the adjusted basis is reduced by taking into account the same factors as are taken into account under paragraph (b)(1) of this section in determining the allowance for depreciation.

(d) Examples. The provisions of section 216(c) and this section may be illustrated by the following examples:

Example (1). The Y corporation, a cooperative housing corporation within the meaning of section 216, in 1961 purchased a site and constructed thereon a building with 10 apartments at a total cost of $250,000 ($200,000 being allocable to the building and $50,000 being allocable to the land). Such building was completed on January 1, 1962, and at that time had an estimated useful life of 50 years, with an estimated salvage value of $20,000. Each apartment is of equal value. Upon completion of the building, Y corporation mortgaged the land and building for $150,000 and sold its total authorized capital stock, consisting of 1000 shares of common stock, for $100,000. The stock was purchased by 10 individuals each of whom paid $10,000 for 100 shares. Each certificate for 100 shares provides that the holder thereof is entitled to a proprietary lease of a particular apartment in the building. Each lease provides that the lessee shall pay his proportionate share of the corporation's expenses including an amount on account of the curtailment of Y's mortgage indebtedness. B, a calendar year taxpayer, is the original owner of 100 shares of stock in Y corporation. On January 1, 1962, B subleases his apartment for a term of 5 years. B's stock in Y corporation is treated as property subject to the allowance for depreciation under section 167(a), and B, who uses the straight line method of depreciation for purposes of the computation prescribed by paragraph (b)(1)(i) of this section, computes the allowance for depreciation for the taxable year 1962 with respect to such stock as follows:

Y's basis in the building	$200,000
Less: Estimated salvage value	20,000
Y's basis for depreciation	180,000
Annual straight line depreciation on Y's building (1/50 of $180,000)	3,600
Proportion of outstanding shares of stock of Y corporation (1,000) owned by B (100)	1/10
B's proportionate share of annual depreciation (1/10 of $3,600)	360
Depreciation allowance for 1962 with respect to B's stock (if the limitation in paragraph (c) of this section is not applicable)	360

Example (2). The facts are the same as in example (1) except that the building constructed by Y corporation contained, in addition to the 10 apartments, space on the ground floor for 2 stores which were rented to persons who do not have a proprietary lease of such space by reason of stock ownership. Y corporation's building has a total area of 16,000 square feet, the 10 apartments in such building have an area of 10,000 square feet, and the 2 stores on the ground floor have an area of 2,000 square feet. Thus, the total rentable space in Y corporation's building is 12,000 square feet. B, who uses the straight line method of depreciation for purposes of the computation prescribed by paragraph (b)(1)(i) of this section, computes the allowance for depreciation for the taxable year 1962 with respect to his stock in Y corporation as follows:

Y's basis in the building	$200,000
Less: Estimated salvage value	20,000
Y's basis for depreciation	180,000
Annual straight line depreciation on Y's building (1/50 of $180,000)	3,600
Less: Amount representing rentable space not subject to proprietary lease but held for rental purposes over total rentable space	
$\left(\frac{2,000}{12,000} \text{ of } \$3,600\right)$	600
Annual depreciation as reduced	3,000
B's proportionate share of annual depreciation (1/10 of $3,000)	300
Depreciation allowance for 1962 with respect to B's stock (if the limitation in paragraph (c) of this section is not applicable)	300

Example (3). The facts are the same as in example (1) except that B occupies his apartment from January 1, 1962, until December 31, 1966, and that on January 1, 1967, B sells his stock to C, an individual, for $15,000. C thereby obtains a proprietary lease from Y corporation with the same rights and obligations as B's lease provided. Y corporation's records disclose that its outstanding mortgage indebtedness is $135,000 on January 1, 1967. C, a physician, uses the entire apartment solely as an office. C's stock in Y corporation is treated as property subject to the allowance for depreciation under section 167(a), and C, who uses the straight line method of depreciation for purposes of the computation prescribed by paragraph (b)(1)(i) of this section, computes the allowance for depreciation for the taxable year 1967 with respect to such stock as follows:

Price paid for each share of stock in Y corporation purchaser by C on 1-1-67 ($15,000 ÷ 100)	$ 150
Per share price paid by C multiplied by total shares of stock in Y corporation outstanding on 1-1-67 ($150 × 1,000)	150,000
Y's mortgage indebtedness outstanding on 1-1-67	$135,000
	228,000
Less: Amount attributable to land (assumed to be 1/5 of $285,000)	57,000
	228,000
Less: Estimated salvage value	20,000
Basis of Y's building for purposes of computing C's depreciation	208,000
Annual straight line depreciation (1/45 of $208,000	4,622.22
C's proportionate share of annual depreciation (1/10 of $4,622.22)	462.22
Depreciation allowance for 1967 with respect to C's stock (if the limitation in paragraph (c) of this section is not applicable)	462.22

T.D. 6725, 4/28/64, amend T.D. 8316, 10/16/90.

§ 1.217-1 Deduction for moving expenses paid or incurred in taxable years beginning before January 1, 1970.

(a) Allowance of deduction. *(1) In general.* Section 217(a) allows a deduction from gross income for moving expenses paid or incurred by the taxpayer during the taxable year in connection with the commencement of work as an employee at a new principal place of work. Except as provided in section 217, no deduction is allowable for any expenses incurred by the taxpayer in connection with moving himself, the members of his family or household, or household goods and personal effects. The deduction is allowable only for expenses incurred after December 31, 1963, in taxable years ending after such date and beginning before January 1, 1970, except in cases where a taxpayer makes an election under paragraph (g) of § 1.217-2 with respect to moving expenses paid or incurred before January 1, 1971, in connection with the commencement of work by such taxpayer as an employee at a new principal place of work of which such taxpayer has been notified by his employer on or before December 19, 1969. To qualify for the deduction the expenses must meet the definition of the term "moving expenses" provided in section 217(b); the taxpayer must meet the conditions set forth in section 217(c); and, if the taxpayer receives a reimbursement or other expense allowance for an item of expense, the deduction for the portion of the expense reimbursed is allowable only to the extent that such reimbursement or other expense allowance is included in his gross income as provided in section 217(e). The deduction is allowable only to a taxpayer who pays or incurs moving expenses in connection with his commencement of work as an employee and is not allowable to a taxpayer who pays or incurs such expenses in connection with his commencement of work as a self-employed individual. The term "employee" as used in this section has the same meaning as in § 31.3401(c)-1 of this chapter (Employment Tax Regulations). All references to section 217 in this section are to section 217 prior to the effective date of section 231 of the Tax Reform Act of 1969 (83 Stat. 577).

(2) Commencement of work. To be deductible, the moving expenses must be paid or incurred by the taxpayer in connection with the commencement of work by him at a new principal place of work (see paragraph (c)(3) of this section for a discussion of the term "principal place of work"). While it is not necessary that the taxpayer have a contract or commitment of employment prior to his moving to a new location, the deduction is not allowable unless employment actually does occur. The term "commencement" includes (i) the beginning of work by a taxpayer for the first time or after a substantial period of unemployment or part-time employment, (ii) the beginning of work by a taxpayer for a different employer, or (iii) the beginning of work by a taxpayer for the same employer at a new location. To qualify as being in connection with the commencement of work, the move for which moving expenses are incurred must bear a reasonable proximity both in time and place to such commencement. In general, moving expenses incurred within one year of the date of the commencement of work are considered to be reasonably proximate to such commencement. Moving expenses incurred in relocating the taxpayer's residence to a location which is farther from his new principal place of work than was his former residence are not generally to be considered as incurred in connection with such commencement of work. For example, if A is transferred by his employer from place X to place Y and A's old residence while he worked at place X is 25 miles from Y, A will not generally be entitled to deduct moving expenses in moving to a new residence 40 miles from Y even though the minimum distance limitation contained in section 217(c)(1) is met. If, however, A is required, as a condition of his employment, to reside at a particular place, or if such residency will result in an actual decrease in his commuting time or expense, the expenses of the move may be considered as incurred in connection with his commencement of work at place Y.

(b) Definition of moving expenses. *(1) In general.* Section 217(b) defines the term "moving expenses" to mean only the reasonable expenses (i) of moving household goods and personal effects from the taxpayer's former residence to his new residence, and (ii) of traveling (including meals and lodging) from the taxpayer's former residence to his new place of residence. The test of deductibility thus is whether the expenses are reasonable and are incurred for the items set forth in (i) and (ii) above.

(2) Reasonable expenses. (i) The term "moving expenses" includes only those expenses which are reasonable under the circumstances of the particular move. Generally, expenses are reasonable only if they are paid or incurred for movement by the shortest and most direct route available from the taxpayer's former residence to his new residence by the conventional mode or modes of transportation actually used and in the shortest period of time commonly required to travel the distance involved by such mode. Expenses paid or incurred in excess of a reasonable amount are not deductible. Thus, if moving or travel arrangements are made to provide a circuitous route for scenic, stopover, or other similar reasons, the additional expenses resulting therefrom are not deductible since they do not meet the test of reasonableness.

(ii) The application of this subparagraph may be illustrated by the following example:

Example. A, an employee of the M Company works and maintains his principal residence in Boston, Massachusetts. Upon receiving orders from his employer that he is to be transferred to M's Los Angeles, California office, A motors to Los Angeles with his family with stopovers at various cities between Boston and Los Angeles to visit friends and relatives. In addition, A detours into Mexico for sight-seeing. Because of the stopovers and tour into Mexico, A's travel time and distance are increased over what they would have been had he proceeded directly to Los Angeles. To the extent that A's route of travel between Boston and Los Angeles is in a general southwesterly direction it may be said that he is traveling by the shortest and most direct route available by motor vehicle. Since A's excursion into Mexico is away from the usual Boston-Los Angeles route, the portion of the expenses paid or incurred attributable to such excursion is not deductible. Likewise, that portion of the expenses attributable to A's delays en route not necessitated by reasons or rest of repair of his vehicle are not deductible.

(3) Expenses of moving household goods and personal effects. Expenses of moving household goods and personal effects include expenses of transporting such goods and effects owned by the taxpayer or a member of his household from the taxpayer's former residence to his new residence, and expenses of packing, crating and in-transit storage and insurance for such goods and effects. Expenses paid or incurred in moving household goods and personal effects to a taxpayer's new residence from a place other than his former residence are allowable, but only to the extent that such expenses do not exceed the amount which would be allowable had such goods and effects been moved from the taxpayer's former residence. Examples of items not deductible as moving expenses include, but are not limited to, storage charges (other than in-transit), costs incurred in the acquisition of property, costs incurred and losses sustained in the disposition of property, penalties for breaking leases, mortgage penalties, expenses of refitting rugs or draperies, expenses of connecting or disconnecting utilities, losses sustained on the disposal of memberships in clubs, tuition fees, and similar items.

(4) Expenses of traveling. Expenses of traveling include the cost of transportation and of meals and lodging en route (including the date of arrival) of both the taxpayer and members of his household, who have both the taxpayer's former residence and the taxpayer's new residence as their principal place of abode, from the taxpayer's former residence to his new place of residence. Expenses of traveling do not include, for example: living or other expenses of the taxpayer and members of his household following their date of arrival at the new place of residence and while they are waiting to enter the new residence or waiting for their household goods to arrive; expenses in connection with house or apartment hunting; living expenses preceding the date of departure for the new place of residence; expenses of trips for purposes of selling property; expenses of trips to the former residence by the taxpayer pending the move by his family to the new

place of residence; or any allowance for depreciation. The deduction for traveling expenses is allowable for only one trip made by the taxpayer and members of his household; however, it is not necessary that the taxpayer and all members of his household travel together or at the same time.

(5) Residence. The term "former residence" refers to the taxpayer's principal residence before his departure for his new principal place of work. The term "new residence" refers to the taxpayer's principal residence within the general location of his new principal place of work. Thus, neither term includes other residences owned or maintained by the taxpayer or members of his family or seasonal residences such as a summer beach cottage. Whether or not property is used by the taxpayer as his residence, and whether or not property is used by the taxpayer as his principal residence (in the case of a taxpayer using more than one property as a residence), depends upon all the facts and circumstances in each case. Property used by the taxpayer as his principal residence may include a houseboat, a house trailer, or similar dwelling. The term "new place of residence" generally includes the area within which the taxpayer might reasonably be expected to commute to his new principal place of work. The application of the terms "former residence", "new residence" and "new place of residence" as defined in this paragraph and as used in section 217(b)(1) may be illustrated in the following manner: Expenses of moving household goods and personal effects are moving expenses when paid or incurred for transporting such items from the taxpayer's former residence to the taxpayer's new residence (such as from one street address to another). Expenses of traveling, on the other hand, are limited to those incurred between the taxpayer's former residence (a geographic point) and his new place of residence (a commuting area) up to and including the date of arrival. The date of arrival is the day the taxpayer secures lodging within that commuting area, even if on a temporary basis.

(6) Individuals other than taxpayer. In addition to the expenses set forth in section 217(b)(1) which are attributable to the taxpayer alone, the same type of expenses attributable to certain individuals other than the taxpayer, if paid or incurred by the taxpayer, are deductible. Those other individuals must (i) be members of the taxpayer's household, and (ii) have both the taxpayer's former residence and his new residence as their principal place of abode. A member of the taxpayer's household may not be, for example, a tenant residing in the taxpayer's residence, nor an individual such as a servant, governess, chauffeur, nurse, valet, or personal attendant.

(c) Conditions for allowance. *(1) In general.* Section 217(c) provides two conditions which must be satisfied in order for a deduction of moving expenses to be allowed under section 217(a). The first is a minimum distance requirement prescribed by section 217(c)(1), and the second is a minimum period of employment requirement prescribed by section 217(c)(2).

(2) Minimum distance. For purposes of applying the minimum distance requirement of section 217(c)(1) all taxpayers are divided into one or the other of the following categories: taxpayers having a former principal place of work, and taxpayers not having a former principal place of work. In this latter category are individuals who are seeking full-time employment for the first time (for example, recent high school or college graduates), or individuals who are re-entering the labor force after a substantial period of unemployment or part-time employment.

(i) In the case of a taxpayer having a former principal place of work, section 217(c)(1)(A) provides that no deduction is allowable unless the distance between his new principal place of work and his former residence exceeds by at least 20 miles the distance between his former principal place of work and such former residence.

(ii) In the case of a taxpayer not having a former principal place of work, section 217(c)(1)(B) provides that no deduction is allowable unless the distance between his new principal place of work and his former residence is at least 20 miles.

(iii) For purposes of measuring distances under section 217(c)(1) all computations are to be made on the basis of a straight-line measurement.

(3) Principal place of work. (i) A taxpayer's "principal place of work" usually is the place at which he spends most of his working time. Generally, where a taxpayer performs services as an employee, his principal place of work is his employer's plant, office, shop, store or other property. However, a taxpayer may have a principal place of work even if there is no one place at which he spends a substantial portion of his working time. In such case, the taxpayer's principal place of work is the place at which his business activities are centered—for example, because he reports there for work, or is otherwise required either by his employer or the nature of his employment to "base" his employment there. Thus, while a member of a railroad crew, for example, may spend most of his working time aboard a train, his principal place of work is his home terminal, station, or other such central point where he reports in, checks out, or receives instructions. In those cases where the taxpayer is employed by a number of employers on a relatively short-term basis, and secures employment by means of a union hall system (such as a construction or building trades worker), the taxpayer's principal place of work would be the union hall.

(ii) In cases where a taxpayer has more than one employment (i.e., more than one employer at any particular time) his principal place of work is usually determined with reference to his principal employment. The location of a taxpayer's principal place of work is necessarily a question of fact which must be determined on the basis of the particular circumstances in each case. The more important factors to be considered in making a factual determination regarding the location of a taxpayer's principal place of work are (a) the total time ordinarily spent by the taxpayer at each place, (b) the degree of the taxpayer's business activity at each place, and (c) the relative significance of the financial return to the taxpayer from each place.

(iii) In general, a place of work is not considered to be the taxpayer's principal place of work for purposes of this section if the taxpayer maintains an inconsistent position, for example, by claiming an allowable deduction under section 162 (relating to trade or business expenses) for traveling expenses "while away from home" with respect to expenses incurred while he is not away from such place of work and after he has incurred moving expenses for which a deduction is claimed under this section.

(4) Minimum period of employment. Under section 217(c)(2), no deduction is allowed unless, during the 12-month period immediately following the taxpayer's arrival in the general location of his new principal place of work, he is a full-time employee, in such general location, during at least 39 weeks.

(i) The 12-month period and the 39-week period set forth in section 217(c)(2) are measured from the date of the taxpayer's arrival in the general location of his new principal place of work. Generally, the taxpayer's date of arrival is the date of the termination of the last trip preceding the taxpayer's commencement of work on a regular basis, regardless of the date on which the taxpayer's family or household goods and effects arrive.

(ii) It is not necessary that the taxpayer remain in the employ of the same employer for 39 weeks, but only that he be employed in the same general location of his new principal place of work during such period. The "general location" of the new principal place of work refers to the area within which an individual might reasonably be expected to commute to such place of work, and will usually be the same area as is known as the "new place of residence"; see paragraph (b)(5) of this section.

(iii) Only a week during which the taxpayer is a full-time employee qualifies as a week of work for purposes of the 39-week requirement of section 217(c)(2). Whether an employee is a full-time employee during any particular week depends upon the customary practices of the occupation in the geographic area in which the taxpayer works. In the case of occupations where employment is on a seasonal basis, weeks occurring in the off-season when no work is required or available (as the case may be) may be counted as weeks of full-time employment only if the employee's contract or agreement of employment covers the off-season period and the off-season period is less than 6 months. Thus, a schoolteacher whose employment contract covers a 12-month period and who teaches on a full-time basis for more than 6 months in fulfillment of such contract is considered a full-time employee during the entire 12-month period. A taxpayer will not be deemed as other than a full-time employee during any week merely because of periods of involuntary temporary absence from work, such as those due to illness, strikes, shutouts, layoffs, natural disasters, etc.

(iv) In the case of taxpayers filing a joint return, either spouse may satisfy this 39-week requirement. However, weeks worked by one spouse may not be added to weeks worked by the other spouse in order to satisfy such requirement.

(v) The application of this subparagraph may be illustrated by the following examples:

Example (1). A is an electrician residing in New York City. Having heard of the possibility of better employment prospects in Denver, Colorado, he moves himself, his family and his household goods and personal effects, at his own expense, to Denver where he secures employment with the M Aircraft Corporation. After working full time for 30 weeks his job is terminated, and he subsequently moves to and secures employment in Los Angeles, California, which employment lasts for more than 39 weeks. Since A was not employed in the general location of his new principal place of employment while in Denver for at least 39 weeks, no deduction is allowable for moving expenses paid or incurred between New York City and Denver. A will be allowed to deduct only those moving expenses attributable to his move from Denver to Los Angeles, assuming all other conditions of section 217 are met.

Example (2). Assume the same facts as in example (1), except that B, A's wife, secures employment in Denver at the same time as A, and that she continues to work in Denver for at least 9 weeks after A's departure for Los Angeles. Since she has met the 39-week requirement in Denver, and assuming all other requirements of section 217 are met, the moving expenses paid by A attributable to the move from New York City to Denver will be allowed as a deduction, provided A and B file a joint return.

Example (3). Assume the same facts as in example (1), except that B, A's wife, secures employment in Denver on the same day that A departs for Los Angeles, and continues to work in Denver for 9 weeks thereafter. Since neither A (who has worked 30 weeks) nor B (who has worked 9 weeks) has independently satisfied the 39-week requirement, no deduction for moving expenses attributable to the move from New York City to Denver is allowable.

(d) Rules for application of section 217(c)(2). *(1) Inapplicability of 39-week test to reimbursed expenses.* (i) Paragraph (1) of section 217(d) provides that the 39-week employment condition of section 217(c)(2) does not apply to any moving expense item to the extent that the taxpayer receives reimbursement or other allowance from his employer for such item. A reimbursement or other allowance to an employee for expenses of moving, in the absence of a specific allocation by the employer, is allocated first to items deductible under section 217(a) and then, if a balance remains, to items not so deductible.

(ii) The application of this subparagraph may be illustrated by the following examples:

Example (1). A, a recent college graduate, with his residence in Washington, D.C., is hired by the M Corporation in San Francisco, California. Under the terms of the employment contract, M agrees to reimburse A for three-fifths of his moving expenses from Washington to San Francisco. A moves to San Francisco, and pays $1,000 for expenses incurred, for which he is reimbursed $600 by M. After working for M for a period of 3 months, A becomes dissatisfied with the job, and returns to Washington to continue his education. Since he has failed to satisfy the 39-week requirement of section 217(c)(2) the expenses totaling $400 for which A has received no reimbursement are not deductible. Under the special rule of section 217(d)(1), however, the deduction for the $600 reimbursed moving expenses is not disallowed by reason of section 217(c)(2).

Example (2). B, a self-employed accountant, who works and resides in Columbus, Ohio, is hired by the N Company in St. Petersburg, Florida. Pursuant to its policy with respect to newly hired employees, N agrees to reimburse B to the extent of $1,000 of the expenses incurred by him in connection with his move to St. Petersburg, allocating $700 for the items specified in section 217(b)(1), and $300 for "temporary living expenses." B moves to St. Petersburg, and incurs $800 of "moving expenses" and $300 of "temporary living expenses" in St. Petersburg. B receives reimbursement of $1,000 from N, which amount is included in his gross income. Assuming B fails to satisfy the 39-week test of section 217(c)(2), he will nevertheless be allowed to deduct $700 as a moving expense. On the other hand, had N made no allocation between deductible and non-deductible items, B would have been allowed to deduct $800 since, in the absence of a specific allocation of the reimbursement by N, it is presumed that the reimbursement was for items specified in section 217(b)(1) to the extent thereof.

(2) Election of deduction before 39-week test is satisfied. (i) Paragraph (2) of section 217(d) provides a special rule which applies in those cases where a taxpayer paid or incurred, in a particular taxable year, moving expenses which would be deductible in that taxable year except for the fact that the 39-week employment condition of section 217(c)(2) has not been satisfied before the time prescribed by law (including extensions thereof) for filing the return for such taxable year. The rule provides that where a taxpayer has paid

or incurred moving expenses and as of the date prescribed by section 6072 for filing his return for such taxable year, including extensions thereof as may be allowed under section 6081, there remains unexpired a sufficient portion of the 12-month period so that it is still possible for the taxpayer to satisfy the 39-week requirement, then the taxpayer may elect to claim a deduction for such moving expenses on the return for such taxable year. The election shall be exercised by taking the deduction on the return filed within the time prescribed by section 6072 (including extensions as may be allowed under section 6081). It is not necessary that the taxpayer wait until the date prescribed by law for filing his return in order to make the election. He may make the election on an early return based upon the facts known on the date such return is filed. However, an election made on an early return will become invalid if, as of the date prescribed by law for filing the return, it is not possible for the taxpayer to satisfy the 39-week requirement.

(ii) In the event that a taxpayer does not elect to claim a deduction for moving expenses on the return for the taxable year in which such expenses were paid or incurred in accordance with (i) of this subparagraph, and the 39-week employment condition of section 217(c)(2) (as well as all other requirements of section 217) is subsequently satisfied, then the taxpayer may file an amended return for the taxable year in which such moving expenses were paid or incurred on which he may claim a deduction under section 217. The taxpayer may, in lieu of filing an amended return, file a claim for refund based upon the deduction allowable under section 217.

(iii) The application of this subparagraph may be illustrated by the following examples:

Example (1). A is transferred by his employer, M, from Boston, Massachusetts, to Cleveland, Ohio, and begins working there on November 1, 1964, followed by his family and household goods and personal effects on November 15, 1964. Moving expenses are paid or incurred by A in 1964 in connection with this move. On April 15, 1965, when A files his income tax return for the year 1964, A has been a full-time employee in Cleveland for approximately 24 weeks. Notwithstanding the fact that as of April 15, 1965, A has not satisfied the 39-week employment condition of section 217(c)(2) he may nevertheless elect to claim his 1964 moving expenses on his 1964 income tax return since there is still sufficient time remaining before November 1, 1965, within which to satisfy the 39-week requirement.

Example (2). Assume the facts are the same as in example (1), except that as of April 15, 1965, A has left the employ of M, and is in the process of seeking further employment in Cleveland. Since under these conditions, A may be unsure whether or not he will be able to satisfy the 39-week requirement by November 1, 1965, he may not wish to avail himself of the election provided by section 217(d)(2). In such event, A may wait until he has actually satisfied the 39-week requirement, at which time he may file an amended return claiming as a deduction the moving expenses paid or incurred in 1964. A may, in lieu of filing an amended return, file a claim for refund based upon a deduction for such expenses. Should A fail to satisfy the 39-week requirement on or before November 1, 1965, no deduction is allowable for moving expenses incurred in 1964.

(3) Recapture of deduction where 39-week test is not met. Paragraph (3) of section 217(d) provides a special rule which applies in cases where a taxpayer has deducted moving expenses under the election provided in section 217(d)(2) prior to his satisfying the 39-week employment condition of section 217(c)(2), and the 39-week test is not satisfied during the taxable year immediately following the taxable year in which the expenses were deducted. In such cases an amount equal to the expenses which were deducted must be included in the taxpayer's gross income for the taxable year immediately following the taxable year in which the expenses were deducted. In the event the taxpayer has deducted moving expenses under the election provided in section 217(d)(2) for the taxable year, and subsequently files an amended return for such year on which he eliminates such deduction, such expenses will not be deemed to have been deducted for purposes of the recapture rule of the preceding sentence.

(e) Disallowance of deduction with respect to reimbursements not included in gross income. Section 217(e) provides that no deduction shall be allowed under section 217 for any item to the extent that the taxpayer receives reimbursement or other expense allowance for such item unless the amount of such reimbursement or other expense allowance is included in his gross income. A reimbursement or other allowance to an employee for expenses of moving, in the absence of a specific allocation by the employer, is allocated first to items deductible under section 217(a) and then, if a balance remains, to items not so deductible. For purposes of this section, moving services furnished in-kind, directly or indirectly, by a taxpayer's employer to the taxpayer or members of his household are considered as being a reimbursement or other allowance received by the taxpayer for moving expenses. If a taxpayer pays or incurs moving expenses and either prior or subsequent thereto receives reimbursement or other expense allowance for such item, no deduction is allowed for such moving expenses unless the amount of the reimbursement or other expense allowance is included in his gross income in the year in which such reimbursement or other expense allowance is received. In those cases where the reimbursement or other expense allowance is received by a taxpayer for an item of moving expense subsequent to his having claimed a deduction for such item, and such reimbursement or other expense allowance is properly excluded from gross income in the year in which received, the taxpayer must file an amended return for the taxable year in which the moving expenses were deducted and decrease such deduction by the amount of the reimbursement or other expense allowance not included in gross income. This does not mean, however, that a taxpayer has an option to include or not include in his gross income an amount received as reimbursement or other expense allowance in connection with his move as an employee. This question remains one which must be resolved under section 61(a) (relating to the definition of gross income).

T.D. 6796, 1/29/65, amend T.D. 7195, 7/10/72.

§ 1.217-2 Deduction for moving expenses paid or incurred in taxable years beginning after December 31, 1969.

Caution: The Treasury has not yet amended Reg § 1.217-2 to reflect changes made by P.L. 103-66.

(a) Allowance of deduction. *(1) In general.* Section 217(a) allows a deduction from gross income for moving expenses paid or incurred by the taxpayer during the taxable year in connection with his commencement of work as an employee or as a self-employed individual at a new principal place of work. For purposes of this section, amounts are considered as being paid or incurred by an individual whether goods or services are furnished to the taxpayer directly (by an employer, a client, a customer, or similar person) or indirectly (paid to a third party on behalf of the taxpayer by an employer, a client, a customer, or similar person). A cash basis taxpayer will treat moving expenses as being paid for purposes of section 217 and this section in the year in which the taxpayer is considered to have received such payment under section 82 and § 1.82-1. No deduction is allowable under section 162 for any expenses incurred by the taxpayer in connection with moving from one residence to another residence unless such expenses are deductible under section 162 without regard to such change in residence. To qualify for the deduction under section 217 the expenses must meet the definition of the term "moving expenses" provided in section 217(b) and the taxpayer must meet the conditions set forth in section 217(c). The term "employee" as used in this section has the same meaning as in § 31.3401(c)-1 of this chapter (Employment Tax Regulations). The term "self-employed individual" as used in this section is defined in paragraph (f)(1) of this section.

(2) Expenses paid in a taxable year other than the taxable year in which reimbursement representing such expenses is received. In general, moving expenses are deductible in the year paid or incurred. If a taxpayer who uses the cash receipts and disbursements method of accounting receives reimbursement for a moving expense in a taxable year other than the taxable year the taxpayer pays such expense, he may elect to deduct such expense in the taxable year that he receives such reimbursement, rather than the taxable year when he paid such expense in any case where—

(i) The expense is paid in a taxable year prior to the taxable year in which the reimbursement is received, or

(ii) The expense is paid in the taxable year immediately following the taxable year in which the reimbursement is received, provided that such expense is paid on or before the due date prescribed for filing the return (determined with regard to any extension of time for such filing) for the taxable year in which the reimbursement is received. An election to deduct moving expenses in the taxable year that the reimbursement is received shall be made by claiming the deduction on the return, amended return, or claim for refund for the taxable year in which the reimbursement is received.

(3) Commencement of work. (i) To be deductible the moving expenses must be paid or incurred by the taxpayer in connection with his commencement of work at a new principal place of work (see paragraph (c)(3) of this section for a discussion of the term "principal place of work"). Except for those expenses described in section 217(b)(1)(C) and (D) it is not necessary for the taxpayer to have made arrangements to work prior to his moving to a new location; however, a deduction is not allowable unless employment or self-employment actually does occur. The term "commencement" includes (a) the beginning of work by a taxpayer as an employee or as a self-employed individual for the first time or after a substantial period of unemployment or part-time employment, (b) the beginning of work by a taxpayer for a different employer or in the case of a self-employed individual in a new trade or business, or (c) the beginning of work by a taxpayer for the same employer or in the case of a self-employed individual in the same trade or business at a new location. To qualify as being in connection with the commencement of work, the move must bear a reasonable proximity both in time and place to such commencement at the new principal place of work. In general, moving expenses incurred within 1 year of the date of the commencement of work are considered to be reasonably proximate in time to such commencement. Moving expenses incurred after the 1-year period may be considered reasonably proximate in time if it can be shown that circumstances existed which prevented the taxpayer from incurring the expenses of moving within the 1-year period allowed. Whether circumstances existed which prevented the taxpayer from incurring the expenses of moving within the period allowed is dependent upon the facts and circumstances of each case. The length of the delay and the fact that the taxpayer may have incurred part of the expenses of the move within the 1-year period allowed shall be taken into account in determining whether expenses incurred after such period are allowable. In general, a move is not considered to be reasonably proximate in place to the commencement of work at the new principal place of work where the distance between the taxpayer's new residence and his new principal place of work exceeds the distance between his former residence and his new principal place of work. A move to a new residence which does not satisfy this test may, however, be considered reasonably proximate in place to the commencement of work if the taxpayer can demonstrate, for example, that he is required to live at such residence as a condition of employment or that living at such residence will result in an actual decrease in commuting time or expense. For example, assume that in 1977 A is transferred by his employer to a new principal place of work and the distance between his former residence and his new principal place of work is 35 miles greater than was the distance between his former residence and his former principal place of work. However, the distance between his new residence and his new principal place of work is 10 miles greater than was the distance between his former residence and his new principal place of work. Although the minimum distance requirement of section 217(c)(1) is met the expenses of moving to the new residence are not considered as incurred in connection with A's commencement of work at his new principal place of work since the new residence is not proximate in place to the new place of work. If, however, A can demonstrate, for example, that he is required to live at such new residence as a condition of employment or if living at such new residence will result in an actual decrease in commuting time or expense, the expenses of the move may be considered as incurred in connection with A's commencement of work at his new principal place of work.

(ii) The provisions of subdivision (i) of this subparagraph may be illustrated by the following examples:

Example (1). Assume that A is transferred by his employer from Boston, Mass., to Washington, D.C. A moves to a new residence in Washington, D.C., and commences work on February 1, 1971. A's wife and his two children remain in Boston until June 1972 in order to allow A's children to complete their grade school education in Boston. On June 1, 1972, A sells his home in Boston and his wife and children move to the new residence in Washington, D.C. The expenses incurred on June 1, 1972, in selling the old residence and in moving A's family, their household goods, and personal effects to the new residence in Washington are allowable as a deduction although they were incurred 16 months after the date of the commencement of work by A since A has moved to and established a new residence in Washington, D.C., and thus incurred part of the total expenses of the move prior to the expiration of the 1-year period.

Example (2). Assume that A is transferred by his employer from Washington, D.C., to Baltimore, Md. A commences work on January 1, 1971, in Baltimore. A commutes from his residence in Washington to his new principal place of work in Baltimore for a period of 18 months. On July 1, 1972, A decides to move to and establish a new residence in

Baltimore. None of the moving expenses otherwise allowable under section 217 may be deducted since A neither incurred the expenses within 1 year nor has shown circumstances under which he was prevented from moving within such period.

(b) Definition of moving expenses. *(1) In general.* Section 217(b) defines the term "moving expenses" to mean only the reasonable expenses (i) of moving household goods and personal effects from the taxpayer's former residence to his new residence, (ii) of traveling (including meals and lodging) from the taxpayer's former residence to his new place of residence, (iii) of traveling including meals and lodging), after obtaining employment, from the taxpayer's former residence to the general location of his new principal place of work and return, for the principal purpose of searching for a new residence, (iv) of meals and lodging while occupying temporary quarters in the general location of the new principal place of work during any period of 30 consecutive days after obtaining employment, or (v) of a nature constituting qualified residence sale, purchase, or lease expenses. Thus, the test of deductibility is whether the expenses are reasonable and are incurred for the items set forth in subdivisions (i) through (v) of this subparagraph.

(2) Reasonable expenses. (i) The term "moving expenses" includes only those expenses which are reasonable under the circumstances of the particular move. Expenses paid or incurred in excess of a reasonable amount are not deductible. Generally, expenses paid or incurred for movement of household goods and personal effects or for travel (including meals and lodging) are reasonable only to the extent that they are paid or incurred for such movement or travel by the shortest and most direct route available from the former residence to the new residence by the conventional mode or modes of transportation actually used and in the shortest period of time commonly required to travel the distance involved by such mode. Thus, if moving or travel arrangements are made to provide a circuitous route for scenic, stopover, or other similar reasons, additional expenses resulting therefrom are not deductible since they are not reasonable nor related to the commencement of work at the new principal place of work. In addition, expenses paid or incurred for meals and lodging while traveling from the former residence to the new place of residence or to the general location of the new principal place of work and return or occupying temporary quarters in the general location of the new principal place of work are reasonable only if under the facts and circumstances involved such expenses are not lavish or extravagant.

(ii) The application of this subparagraph may be illustrated by the following example:

Example. A, an employee of the M Company works and maintains his residence in Boston, Mass. Upon receiving orders from his employer that he is to be transferred to M's Los Angeles, Calif., office, A motors to Los Angeles with his family with stopovers at various cities between Boston and Los Angeles to visit friends and relatives. In addition, A detours into Mexico for sight-seeing. Because of the stopovers and tour into Mexico, A's travel time and distance are increased over what they would have been had he proceeded directly to Los Angeles. To the extent that A's route of travel between Boston and Los Angeles is in a generally southwesterly direction it may be said that he is traveling by the shortest and most direct route available by motor vehicle. Since A's excursion into Mexico is away from the usual Boston-Los Angeles route, the portion of the expenses paid or incurred attributable to such excursion is not deductible. Likewise, that portion of the expenses attributable to A's delay en route in visiting personal friends and sight-seeing are not deductible.

(3) Expense of moving household goods and personal effects. Expenses of moving household goods and personal effects include expenses of transporting such goods and effects from the taxpayer's former residence to his new residence, and expenses of packing, crating, and in-transit storage and insurance for such goods and effects. Such expenses also include any costs of connecting or disconnecting utilities required because of the moving of household goods, appliances, or personal effects. Expenses of storing and insuring household goods and personal effects constitute in transit expenses if incurred within any consecutive 30-day period after the day such goods and effects are moved from the taxpayer's former residence and prior to delivery at the taxpayer's new residence. Expenses paid or incurred in moving household goods and personal effects to the taxpayer's new residence from a place other than his former residence are allowable, but only to the extent that such expenses do not exceed the amount which would be allowable had such goods and effects been moved from the taxpayer's former residence. Expenses of moving household goods and personal effects do not include, for example, storage charges (other than in-transit), costs incurred in the acquisition of property, costs incurred and losses sustained in the disposition of property, penalties for breaking leases, mortgage penalties, expenses of refitting rugs or draperies, losses sustained on the disposal of memberships in clubs, tuition fees, and similar items. The above expenses may, however, be described in other provisions of section 217(b) and if so a deduction may be allowed for them subject to the allowable dollar limitations.

(4) Expenses of traveling from the former residence to the new place of residence. Expenses of traveling from the former residence to the new place of residence include the cost of transportation and of meals and lodging en route (including the date of arrival) from the taxpayer's former residence to his new place of residence. Expenses of meals and lodging incurred in the general location of the former residence within 1 day after the former residence is no longer suitable for occupancy because of the removal of household goods and personal effects shall be considered as expenses of traveling for purposes of this subparagraph. The date of arrival is the day the taxpayer secures lodging at the new place of residence, even if on a temporary basis. Expenses of traveling from the taxpayer's former residence to his new place of residence do not include, for example, living or other expenses following the date of arrival at the new place of residence and while waiting to enter the new residence or waiting for household goods to arrive, expenses in connection with house or apartment hunting, living expenses preceding date of departure for the new place of residence (other than expenses of meals and lodging incurred within 1 day after the former residence is no longer suitable for occupancy), expenses of trips for purposes of selling property, expenses of trips to the former residence by the taxpayer pending the move by his family to the new place of residence, or any allowance for depreciation. The above expenses may, however, be described in other provisions of section 217(b) and if so a deduction may be allowed for them subject to the allowable dollar limitations. The deduction for traveling expenses from the former residence to the new place of residence is allowable for only one trip made by the taxpayer and members of his household; however, it is not necessary

that the taxpayer and all members of his household travel together or at the same time.

(5) Expenses of traveling for the principal purpose of looking for a new residence. Expenses of traveling, after obtaining employment, from the former residence to the general location of the new principal place of work and return, for the principal purpose of searching for a new residence include the cost of transportation and meals and lodging during such travel and while at the general location of the new place of work for the principal purpose of searching for a new residence. However, such expenses do not include, for example, expenses of meals and lodging of the taxpayer and members of his household before departing for the new principal place of work, expenses for trips for purposes of selling property, expenses of trips to the former residence by the taxpayer pending the move by his family to the place of residence, or any allowance for depreciation. The above expenses may, however, be described in other provisions of section 217(b) and if so a deduction may be allowed for them. The deduction for expenses of traveling for the principal purpose of looking for a new residence is not limited to any number of trips by the taxpayer and by members of his household. In addition, the taxpayer and all members of his household need not travel together or at the same time. Moreover, a trip need not result in acquisition of a lease of property or purchase of property. An employee is considered to have obtained employment in the general location of the new principal place of work after he has obtained a contract or agreement of employment. A self-employed individual is considered to have obtained employment when he has made substantial arrangements to commence work at the new principal place of work (see paragraph (f)(2) of this section for a discussion of the term "made substantial arrangements to commence to work").

(6) Expenses of occupying temporary quarters. Expenses of occupying temporary quarters include only the cost of meals and lodging while occupying temporary quarters in the general location of the new principal place of work during any period of 30 consecutive days after the taxpayer has obtained employment in such general location. Thus, expenses of occupying temporary quarters do not include, for example, the cost of entertainment, laundry, transportation, or other personal, living family expenses, or expenses of occupying temporary quarters in the general location of the former place of work. The 30 consecutive day period is any one period of 30 consecutive days which can begin, at the option of the taxpayer, on any day after the day the taxpayer obtains employment in the general location of the new principal place of work.

(7) Qualified residence sale, purchase, or lease expenses. Qualified residence sale, purchase, or lease expenses (hereinafter "qualified real estate expenses") are only reasonable amounts paid or incurred for any of the following purposes:

(i) Expenses incident to the sale or exchange by the taxpayer or his spouse of the taxpayer's former residence which, but for section 217(b) and (e), would be taken into account in determining the amount realized on the sale or exchange of the residence. These expenses include real estate commissions, attorneys' fees, title fees, escrow fees, so called "points" or loan placement charges which the seller is required to pay, State transfer taxes and similar expenses paid or incurred in connection with the sale or exchange. No deduction, however, is permitted under section 217 and this section for the cost of physical improvements intended to enhance salability by improving the condition or appearance of the residence.

(ii) Expenses incident to the purchase by the taxpayer or his spouse of a new residence in the general location of the new principal place of work which, but for section 217(b) and (e), would be taken into account in determining either the adjusted basis of the new residence or the cost of a loan. These expenses include attorneys' fees, escrow fees, appraisal fees, title costs, so-called "points" or loan placement charges not representing payments or prepayments of interest, and similar expenses paid or incurred in connection with the purchase of the new residence. No deduction, however, is permitted under section 217 and this section for any portion of real estate taxes or insurance, so-called "points" or loan placement charges which are, in essence, prepayments of interest, or the purchase price of the residence.

(iii) Expenses incident to the settlement of an unexpired lease held by the taxpayer or his spouse on property used by the taxpayer as his former residence. These expenses include consideration paid to a lessor to obtain a release from a lease, attorneys' fees, real estate commissions, or similar expenses incident to obtaining a release from a lease or to obtaining an assignee or a sublessee such as the difference between rent paid under a primary lease and rent received under a sublease. No deduction, however, is permitted under section 217 and this section for the cost of physical improvement intended to enhance marketability of the leasehold by improving the condition or appearance of the residence.

(iv) Expenses incident to the acquisition of a lease by the taxpayer or his spouse. These expenses include the cost of fees or commissions for obtaining a lease, a sublease, or an assignment of an interest in property used by the taxpayer as his new residence in the general location of the new principal place of work. No deduction, however, is permitted under section 217 and this section for payments or prepayments of rent or payments representing the cost of a security or other similar deposit.

Qualified real estate expenses do not include losses sustained on the disposition of property or mortgage penalties, to the extent that such penalties are otherwise deductible as interest.

(8) Residence. The term "former residence" refers to the taxpayer's principal residence before his departure for his new principal place of work. The term "new residence" refers to the taxpayer's principal residence within the general location of his new principal place of work. Thus, neither term includes other residences owned or maintained by the taxpayer or members of his family or seasonal residences such as a summer beach cottage. Whether or not property is used by the taxpayer as his principal residence depends upon all the facts and circumstances in each case. Property used by the taxpayer as his principal residence may include a houseboat, a housetrailer, or similar dwelling. The term "new place of residence" generally includes the area within which the taxpayer might reasonably be expected to commute to his new principal place of work.

(9) Dollar limitations. (i) Expenses described in subparagraphs (A) and (B) of section 217(b)(1) are not subject to an overall dollar limitation. Thus, assuming all other requirements of section 217 are satisfied, a taxpayer who, in connection with his commencement of work at a new principal place of work, pays or incurs reasonable expenses of moving household goods and personal effects from his former residence to his new place of residence and reasonable expenses of traveling, including meals and lodging, from his former residence to his new place of residence is permitted to deduct the entire amount of these expenses.

each place, and (c) the relative significance of the financial return to the taxpayer from each place.

(iii) Where a taxpayer maintains inconsistent positions by claiming a deduction for expenses of meals and lodging while away from home (incurred in the general location of the new principal place of work) under section 162 (relating to trade or business expenses) and by claiming a deduction under this section for moving expenses incurred in connection with the commencement of work at such place of work, it will be a question of facts and circumstances as to whether such new place of work will be considered a principal place of work, and accordingly, which category of deductions he will be allowed.

(4) Minimum period of employment. (i) Under section 217(c)(2) no deduction is allowed unless—

(a) Where a taxpayer is an employee, during the 12-month period immediately following his arrival in the general location of the new principal place of work, he is a full-time employee, in such general location, during at least 39 weeks, or

(b) Where a taxpayer is a self-employed individual (including a taxpayer who is also an employee, but is unable to satisfy the requirements of the 39-week test of (a) of this subdivision (i)), during the 24-month period immediately following his arrival in the general location of the new principal place of work, he is a full-time employee or performs services as a self-employed individual on a full-time basis, in such general location, during at least 78 weeks, of which not less than 39 weeks are during the 12-month period referred to above.

Where a taxpayer works as an employee and at the same time performs services as a self-employed individual his principal employment (determined according to subdivision (i) of subparagraph (3) of this paragraph) governs whether the 39-week or 78-week test is applicable.

(ii) The 12-month period and the 39-week period set forth in subparagraph (A) of section 217(c)(2) and the 12- and 24-month periods as well as 39- and 78-week periods set forth in subparagraph (B) of such section are measured from the date of the taxpayer's arrival in the general location of the new principal place of work. Generally, date of arrival is the date of the termination of the last trip preceding the taxpayer's commencement of work on a regular basis and is not the date the taxpayer's family or household goods and effects arrive.

(iii) The taxpayer need not remain in the employ of the same employer or remain self-employed in the same trade or business for the required number of weeks. However, he must be employed in the same general location of the new principal place of work during such period. The "general location" of the new principal place of work refers to a general commutation area and is usually the same area as the "new place of residence"; see paragraph (b)(8) of this section.

(iv) Only those weeks during which the taxpayer is a full-time employee or during which he performs services as a self-employed individual on a full-time basis qualify as a week of work for purposes of the minimum period of employment condition of section 217(c)(2).

(a) Whether an employee is a full-time employee during any particular week depends upon the customary practices of the occupation in the geographic area in which the taxpayer works. Where employment is on a seasonal basis, weeks occurring in the off-season when no work is required or available may be counted as weeks of full-time employment only if the employee's contract or agreement of employment covers the off-season period and such period is less than 6 months. Thus, for example, a schoolteacher whose employment contract covers a 12-month period and who teaches on a full-time basis for more than 6 months is considered a full-time employee during the entire 12-month period. A taxpayer will be treated as a full-time employee during any week of involuntary temporary absence from work because of illness, strikes, shutouts, layoffs, natural disasters, etc. A taxpayer will, also, be treated as a full-time employee during any week in which he voluntarily absents himself from work for leave or vacation provided for in his contract or agreement of employment.

(b) Whether a taxpayer performs services as a self-employed individual on a full-time basis during any particular week depends on the practices of the trade or business in the geographic area in which the taxpayer works. For example, a self-employed dentist maintaining office hours 4 days a week is considered to perform services as a self-employed individual on a full-time basis providing it is not unusual for other self-employed dentists in the geographic area in which the taxpayer works to maintain office hours only 4 days a week. Where a trade or business is seasonal, weeks occurring during the off-season when no work is required or available may be counted as weeks of performance of services on a full-time basis only if the off-season is less than 6 months and the taxpayer performs services on a full-time basis both before and after the off-season. For example, a taxpayer who owns and operates a motel at a beach resort is considered to perform services as a self-employed individual on a full-time basis if the motel is closed for a period not exceeding 6 months during the off-season and if he performs services on a full-time basis as the operator of a motel both before and after the off-season. A taxpayer will be treated as performing services as a self-employed individual on a full-time basis during any week of involuntary temporary absence from work because of illness, strikes, natural disasters, etc.

(v) Where taxpayers file a joint return, either spouse may satisfy the minimum period of employment condition. However, weeks worked by one spouse may not be added to weeks worked by the other spouse in order to satisfy such condition. The taxpayer seeking to satisfy the minimum period of employment condition must satisfy the condition applicable to him. Thus, if a taxpayer is subject to the 39-week condition and his spouse is subject to the 78-week condition and the taxpayer satisfies the 39-week condition, his spouse need not satisfy the 78-week condition. On the other hand, if the taxpayer does not satisfy the 39-week condition, his spouse in such case must satisfy the 78-week condition.

(vi) The application of this subparagraph may be illustrated by the following examples:

Example (1). A is an electrician residing in New York City. He moves himself, his family, and his household goods and personal effects, at his own expense, to Denver where he commences employment with the M Aircraft Corporation. After working full-time for 30 weeks he voluntarily leaves his job, and he subsequently moves to and commences employment in Los Angeles, Calif., which employment lasts for more than 39 weeks. Since A was not employed in the general location of his new principal place of employment in Denver for at least 39 weeks, no deduction is allowable for moving expenses paid or incurred between New York City and Denver. A will be allowed to deduct only those moving expenses attributable to his move from Denver to Los Angeles, assuming all other conditions of section 217 are met.

Example (2). Assume the same facts as in example (1), except that A's wife commences employment in Denver at the same time as A, and that she continues to work in Denver for at least 9 weeks after A's departure for Los Angeles. Since she has met the 39-week requirement in Denver, and assuming all other requirements of section 217 are met, the moving expenses paid by A attributable to the move from New York City to Denver will be allowed as a deduction, provided A and his wife file a joint return. If A and his wife file separate returns moving expenses paid by A's wife attributable to the move from New York City to Denver will be allowed as a deduction on A's wife's return.

Example (3). Assume the same facts as in example (1), except that A's wife commences employment in Denver on the same day that A departs for Los Angeles, and continues to work in Denver for 9 weeks thereafter. Since neither A (who has worked 30 weeks) nor his wife (who has worked 9 weeks) has independently satisfied the 39-week requirement, no deduction for moving expenses attributable to the move from New York City to Denver is allowable.

(d) Rules for application of section 217(c)(2). *(1) Inapplicability of minimum period of employment condition in certain cases.* Section 217(d)(1) provides that the minimum period of employment condition of section 217(c)(2) does not apply in the case of a taxpayer who is unable to meet such condition by reason of—

(i) Death or disability, or

(ii) Involuntary separation (other than for willful misconduct) from the service of an employer or separation by reason of transfer for the benefit of an employer after obtaining full-time employment in which the taxpayer could reasonably have been expected to satisfy such condition.

For purposes of subdivision (i) of this paragraph disability shall be determined according to the rules in section 72(m)(7) and § 172.-17(f). Subdivision (ii) of this subparagraph applies only where the taxpayer has obtained full-time employment in which he could reasonably have been expected to satisfy the minimum period of employment condition. A taxpayer could reasonably have been expected to satisfy the minimum period of employment condition if at the time he commences work at the new principal place of work he could have been expected, based upon the facts known to him at such time, to satisfy such condition. Thus, for example, if the taxpayer at the time of transfer was not advised by his employer that he planned to transfer him within 6 months to another principal place of work, the taxpayer could, in the absence of other factors, reasonably have been expected to satisfy the minimum employment period condition at the time of the first transfer. On the other hand, a taxpayer could not reasonably have been expected to satisfy the minimum employment condition if at the time of the commencement of the move he knew that his employer's retirement age policy would prevent his satisfying the minimum employment period condition.

(2) Election of deduction before minimum period of employment condition is satisfied. (i) Paragraph (2) of section 217(d) provides a rule which applies where a taxpayer paid or incurred, in a taxable year, moving expenses which would be deductible in that taxable year except that the minimum period of employment condition of section 217(c)(2) has not been satisfied before the time prescribed by law for filing the return for such taxable year. The rule provides that where a taxpayer has paid or incurred moving expenses and as of the date prescribed by section 6072 for filing his return for such taxable year (determined with regard to extensions of time for filing) there remains unexpired a sufficient portion of the 12-month or the 24-month period so that it is still possible for the taxpayer to satisfy the applicable period of employment condition, the taxpayer may elect to claim a deduction for such moving expenses on the return for such taxable year. The election is exercised by taking the deduction on the return.

(ii) Where a taxpayer does not elect to claim a deduction for moving expenses on the return for the taxable year in which such expenses were paid or incurred in accordance with subdivision (i) of this subparagraph and the applicable minimum period of employment condition of section 217(c)(2) (as well as all other requirements of section 217) is subsequently satisfied, the taxpayer may file an amended return or a claim for refund for the taxable year such moving expenses were paid or incurred on which he may claim a deduction under section 217.

(iii) The application of this subparagraph may be illustrated by the following examples:

Example (1). A is transferred by his employer from Boston, Massachusetts, to Cleveland, Ohio. He begins working there on November 1, 1970. Moving expenses are paid by A in 1970 in connection with this move. On April 15, 1971, when he files his income tax return for the year 1970, A has been a full-time employee in Cleveland for approximately 24 weeks. Although he has not satisfied the 39-week employment condition at this time, A may elect to claim his 1970 moving expenses on his 1970 income tax return as there is still sufficient time remaining before November 1, 1971, to satisfy such condition.

Example (2). Assume the same facts as in example (1), except that on April 15, 1971, A has voluntarily left his employer and is looking for other employment in Cleveland. A may not be sure he will be able to meet the 39-week employment condition by November 1, 1971. Thus, he may if he wishes wait until such condition is met and file an amended return claiming as a deduction the expenses paid in 1970. Instead of filing an amended return A may file a claim for refund based on a deduction for such expenses. If A fails to meet the 39-week employment condition on or before November 1, 1971, no deduction is allowable for such expenses.

Example (3). B is a self-employed accountant. He moves from Rochester, N.Y., to New York, N.Y., and begins to work there on December 1, 1970. Moving expenses are paid by B in 1970 and 1971 in connection with this move. On April 15, 1971, when he files his income tax return for the year 1970, B has been performing services as a self-employed individual on a full-time basis in New York City for approximately 20 weeks. Although he has not satisfied the 78-week employment condition at this time, A may elect to claim his 1970 moving expenses on his 1970 income tax return as there is still sufficient time remaining before December 1, 1972, to satisfy such condition. On April 15, 1972, when he files his income tax return for the year 1971, B has been performing services as a self-employed individual on a full-time basis in New York City for approximately 72 weeks. Although he has not met the 78-week employment condition at this time, B may elect to claim his 1971 moving expenses on his 1971 income tax return as there is still sufficient time remaining before December 1, 1972, to satisfy such requirement.

(3) Recapture of deduction. Paragraph (3) of section 217(d) provides a rule which applies where a taxpayer has deducted moving expenses under the election provided in section 217(d)(2) prior to satisfying the applicable minimum period of employment condition and such condition cannot

be satisfied at the close of a subsequent taxable year. In such cases an amount equal to the expenses deducted must be included in the taxpayer's gross income for the taxable year in which the taxpayer is no longer able to satisfy such minimum period of employment condition. Where the taxpayer has deducted moving expenses under the election provided in section 217(d)(2) for the taxable year and subsequently files an amended return for such year on which he does not claim the deduction, such expenses are not treated as having been deducted for purposes of the recapture rule of the preceding sentence.

(e) Denial of double benefit. *(1) In general.* Section 217(e) provides a rule for computing the amount realized and the basis where qualified real estate expenses are allowed as a deduction under section 217(a).

(2) Sale or exchange of residence. Section 217(e) provides that the amount realized on the sale or exchange of a residence owned by the taxpayer, by the taxpayer's spouse, or by the taxpayer and his spouse and used by the taxpayer as his principal place of residence is not decreased by the amount of any expenses described in subparagraph (A) of section 217(b)(2) and deducted under section 217(a). For the purposes of section 217(e) and of this paragraph the term "amount realized" has the same meaning as under section 1001(b) and the regulations thereunder. Thus, for example, if the taxpayer sells a residence used as his principal place of residence and real estate commissions or similar expenses described in subparagraph (A) of section 217(b)(2) are deducted by him pursuant to section 217(a), the amount realized on the sale of the residence is not reduced by the amount of such real estate commissions or such similar expenses described in subparagraph (A) of section 217(b)(2).

(3) Purchase of a residence. Section 217(e) provides that the basis of a residence purchased or received in exchange for other property by the taxpayer, by the taxpayer's spouse, or by the taxpayer and his spouse and used by the taxpayer as his principal place of residence is not increased by the amount of any expenses described in subparagraph (B) of section 217(b)(2) and deducted under section 217(a). For the purposes of section 217(e) and of this paragraph the term "basis" has the same meaning as under section 1011 and the regulations thereunder. Thus, for example, if a taxpayer purchases a residence to be used as his principal place of residence and attorneys' fees or similar expenses described in subparagraph (B) of section 217(b)(2) are deducted pursuant to section 217(a), the basis of such residence is not increased by the amount of such attorneys' fees or such similar expenses described in subparagraph (B) of section 217(b)(2).

(4) Inapplicability of section 217(e). (i) Section 217(e) and subparagraphs (1) through (3) of this paragraph do not apply to any expenses with respect to which an amount is included in gross income under section 217(d)(3). Thus, the amount of any expenses described in subparagraph (A) of section 217(b)(2) deducted in the year paid or incurred pursuant to the election under section 217(d)(2) and subsequently recaptured pursuant to section 217(d)(3) may be taken into account in computing the amount realized on the sale or exchange of the residence described in such subparagraph. Also, the amount of expenses described in subparagraph (B) of section 217(b)(2) deducted in the year paid or incurred pursuant to such election under section 217(d)(2) and subsequently recaptured pursuant to section 217(d)(3) may be taken into account as an adjustment to the basis of the residence described in such subparagraph.

(ii) The application of subdivision (i) of this subparagraph may be illustrated by the following examples:

Example (1). A was notified of his transfer effective December 15, 1972, from Seattle, Wash., to Philadelphia, Pa. In connection with the transfer A sold his house in Seattle on November 10, 1972. Expenses incident to the sale of the house of $2,500 were paid by A prior to or at the time of the closing of the contract of sale on December 10, 1972. The amount realized on the sale of the house was $47,500 and the adjusted basis of the house was $30,000. Pursuant to the election provided in section 217(d)(2), A deducted the expenses of moving from Seattle to Philadelphia including the expenses incident to the sale of his former residence in taxable year 1972. Dissatisfied with his position with his employer in Philadelphia, A took a position with an employer in Chicago, Ill., on July 15, 1973. Since A was no longer able to satisfy the minimum period employment condition at the close of taxable year 1973 he included an amount equal to the amount deducted as moving expenses including the expenses incident to the sale of his former residence in gross income for taxable year 1973. A is permitted to decrease the amount realized on the sale of the house by the amount of the expenses incident to the sale of the house deducted from gross income and subsequently included in gross income. Thus, the amount realized on the sale of the house is decreased from $47,500 to $45,000 and thus, the gain on the sale of the house is reduced from $17,500 to $15,000. A is allowed to file an amended return or a claim for refund in order to reflect the recomputation of the amount realized.

Example (2). B, who is self-employed decided to move from Washington, D.C., to Los Angeles, Calif. In connection with the commencement of work in Los Angeles on March 1, 1973, B purchased a house in a suburb of Los Angeles for $65,000. Expenses incident to the purchase of the house in the amount of $1,500 were paid by B prior to or at the time of the closing of the contract of sale on September 15, 1973. Pursuant to the election provided in section 217(d)(2), B deducted the expenses of moving from Washington to Los Angeles including the expenses incident to the purchase of his new residence in taxable year 1973. Dissatisfied with his prospects in Los Angeles, B moved back to Washington on July 1, 1974. Since B was no longer able to satisfy the minimum period of employment condition at the close of taxable year 1974 he included an amount equal to the amount deducted as moving expenses incident to the purchase of the former residence in gross income for taxable year 1974. B is permitted to increase the basis of the house by the amount of the expenses incident to the purchase of the house deducted from gross income and subsequently included in gross income. Thus, the basis of the house is increased to $66,500.

(f) Rules for self-employed individuals. *(1) Definition.* Section 217(f)(1) defines the term "self-employed individual" for purposes of section 217 to mean an individual who performs personal services either as the owner of the entire interest in an unincorporated trade or business or as a partner in a partnership carrying on a trade or business. The term "self-employed individual" does not include the semiretired, part-time students, or other similarly situated taxpayers who work only a few hours each week. The application of this subparagraph may be illustrated by the following example:

Example. A is the owner of the entire interest in an unincorporated construction business. A hires a manager who performs all of the daily functions of the business including the negotiation of contracts with customers, the hiring and firing of employees, the purchasing of materials used on the projects, and other similar services. A and his manager discuss the operations of the business about once a week over the telephone. Otherwise A does not perform any managerial services for the business. For the purposes of section 217, A is not considered to be a self-employed individual.

(2) Rule for application of subsection (b)(1) (C) and (D). Section 217(f)(2) provides that for purposes of subparagraphs (C) and (D) of section 217(b)(1) an individual who commences work at a new principal place of work as a self-employed individual is treated as having obtained employment when he has made substantial arrangements to commence such work. Whether the taxpayer has made substantial arrangements to commence work at a new principal place of work is determined on the basis of all the facts and circumstances in each case. The factors to be considered in this determination depend upon the nature of the taxpayer's trade or business and include such considerations as whether the taxpayer has: (i) Leased or purchased a plant, office, shop, store, equipment, or other property to be used in the trade or business, (ii) made arrangements to purchase inventory or supplies to be used in connection with the operation of the trade or business, (iii) entered into commitments with individuals to be employed in the trade or business, and (iv) made arrangements to contact customers or clients in order to advertise the business in the general location of the new principal place of work. The application of this subparagraph may be illustrated by the following examples:

Example (1). A, a partner in a growing chain of drug stores decided to move from Houston, Tex., to Dallas, Tex., in order to open a drug store in Dallas. A made several trips to Dallas for the purpose of looking for a site for the drug store. After the signing of a lease on a building in a shopping plaza, suppliers were contacted, equipment was purchased, and employees were hired. Shortly before the opening of the store A and his wife moved from Houston to Dallas and took up temporary quarters in a motel until the time their apartment was available. By the time he and his wife took up temporary quarters in the motel A was considered to have made substantial arrangements to commence work at the new principal place of work.

Example (2). B, who is a partner in a securities brokerage firm in New York, N.Y., decided to move to Rochester, N.Y., to become the resident partner in the firm's new Rochester office. After a lease was signed on an office in downtown Rochester B moved to Rochester and took up temporary quarters in a motel until his apartment became available. Before the opening of the office B supervised the decoration of the office, the purchase of equipment and supplies necessary for the operation of the office, the hiring of personnel for the office, as well as other similar activities. By the time B took up temporary quarters in the motel he was considered to have made substantial arrangements to commence to work at the new principal place of work.

Example (3). C, who is about to complete his residency in ophthalmology at a hospital in Pittsburgh, Pa., decided to fly to Philadelphia, Pa., for the purpose of looking into opportunities for practicing in that city. Following his arrival in Philadelphia C decided to establish his practice in that city. He leased an office and an apartment. At the time he departed Pittsburgh for Philadelphia C was not considered to have made substantial arrangements to commence work at the new principal place of work, and, therefore, is not allowed to deduct expenses described in subparagraph (C) of section 217(b)(1) (relating to expenses of traveling (including meals and lodging), after obtaining employment, from the former residence to the general location of the new principal place of work and return, for the principal purpose of searching for a new residence).

(g) Rules for members of the Armed Forces of the United States. *(1) In general.* The rules in paragraphs (a)(1) and (2), (b), and (e) of this section apply to moving expenses paid or incurred by members of the Armed Forces of the United States on active duty who move pursuant to a military order and incident to a permanent change of station, except as provided in this paragraph (g). However, if the moving expenses are not paid or incurred incident to a permanent change of station, this paragraph (g) does not apply, but all other paragraphs of this section do apply. The provisions of this paragraph apply to taxable years beginning after December 31, 1975.

(2) Treatment of services or reimbursement provided by Government. (i) Services in kind. The value of any moving or storage services furnished by the United States Government to members of the Armed Forces, their spouses, or their dependents in connection with a permanent change of station is not includible in gross income. The Secretary of Defense and (in cases involving members of the peacetime Coast Guard) the Secretary of Transportation are not required to report or withhold taxes with respect to those services. Services furnished by the Government include services rendered directly by the Government or rendered by a third party who is compensated directly by the Government for the services.

(ii) Reimbursements. The following rules apply to reimbursements or allowances by the Government to members of the Armed Forces, their spouses, or their dependents for moving or storage expenses paid or incurred by them in connection with a permanent change of station. If the reimbursement or allowance exceeds the actual expenses paid or incurred, the excess is includible in the gross income of the member, and the Secretary of Defense or Secretary of Transportation must report the excess as payment of wages and withhold income taxes under section 3402 and the employee taxes under section 3102 with respect to that excess. If the reimbursement or allowance does not exceed the actual expenses, the reimbursement or allowance is not includible in gross income, and no reporting or withholding by the Secretary of Defense or Secretary of Transportation is required. If the actual expenses, as limited by paragraph (b)(9) of this section, exceed the reimbursement or allowance, the member may deduct the excess if the other requirements of this section, as modified by this paragraph, are met. The determination of the limitation on actual expenses under paragraph (b)(9) of this section is made without regard to any services in kind furnished by the Government.

(3) Permanent change of station. For purposes of this section, the term "permanent change of station" includes the following situations:

(i) A move from home to the first post of duty when appointed, reappointed, reinstated, called to active duty, enlisted, or inducted.

(ii) A move from the last post of duty to home or a nearer point in the United States in connection with retirement, discharge, resignation, separation under honorable conditions, transfer, relief from active duty, temporary disability retirement, or transfer to a Fleet Reserve, if such move occurs within 1 year of such termination of active duty or within the period prescribed by the Joint Travel Regulations promulgated under the authority contained in sections 404 through 411 of title 37 of the United States Code.

(iii) A move from one permanent post of duty to another permanent post of duty at a different duty station, even if the member separates from the Armed Forces immediately or shortly after the move.

The terms "permanent," "post of duty," "duty station," and "honorable" have the meanings given them in appropriate Department of Defense or Department of Transportation rules and regulations.

(4) Storage expenses. This paragraph applies to storage expenses as well as to moving expenses described in paragraph (b)(1) of this section. The term "storage expenses" means the cost of storing personal effects of members of the Armed Forces, their spouses, and their dependents.

(5) Moves of spouses and dependents. (i) The following special rule applies for purposes of paragraphs (b)(9) and (10) of this section, if the spouse or dependents of a member of the Armed Forces move to or from a different location than does the member. In this case, the spouse is considered to have commenced work as an employee at a new principal place of work that is within the same general location as the location to which the member moves.

(ii) The following special rule applies for purposes of this paragraph to moves by spouses or dependents of members of the Armed Forces who die, are imprisoned, or desert while on active duty. In these cases, a move to a member's place of enlistment or induction or the member's, spouse's, or dependent's home of record or nearer point in the United States is considered incident to a permanent change of station.

(6) Disallowance of deduction. No deduction is allowed under this section for any moving or storage expense reimbursed by an allowance that is excluded from gross income.

(h) Special rules for foreign moves. *(1) Increase in limitations.* In the case of a foreign move (as defined in paragraph (h)(3) of this section), paragraph (b)(6) of this section shall be applied by substituting "90 consecutive" for "30 consecutive" each time it appears. Paragraph (b)(9)(ii), (iii) and (v) of this section shall be applied by substituting "$6,000" for "$3,000" each time it appears and by substituting "$4,500" for "$1,500" each time it appears. Paragraph (b)(9)(ii) of this section shall be applied by substituting "$5,000" for "$2,000" each time it appears and by substituting "1979" for "1977" and "1980" for "1978" each time they appear in the last sentence. Paragraph (b)(9)(v) of this section shall be applied by substituting "$2,250" for "$750" each time it appears. Paragraph (b)(9)(vi) of this section does not apply.

(2) Allowance of certain storage fees. In the case of a foreign move, for purposes of this section, the moving expenses described in paragraph (b)(3) of this section shall include the reasonable expenses of moving household goods and personal effects to and from storage, and of storing such goods and effects for part or all of the period during which the new place of work continues to be the taxpayer's principal place of work.

(3) Foreign move. For purposes of this paragraph, the term "foreign move" means a move in connection with the commencement of work by the taxpayer at a new principal place of work located outside the United States. Thus, a move from the United States to a foreign country or from one foreign country to another foreign country qualifies as a foreign move. A move within a foreign country also qualifies as a foreign move. A move from a foreign country to the United States does not qualify as a foreign move.

(4) United States. For purposes of this paragraph, the term "United States" includes the possessions of the United States.

(5) Effective date. The provisions of this paragraph apply to expenses paid or incurred in taxable years beginning after December 31, 1978. The paragraph also applies to the expenses paid or incurred in the taxable year beginning during 1978 of taxpayers who do not make an election pursuant to section 209(c) of the Foreign Earned Income Act of 1978 (Pub. L. 95-615, 92 Stat. 3109) to have section 911 under prior law apply to that taxable year.

(i) Allowance of deductions in case of retirees or decedents who were working abroad. *(1) In general.* In the case of any qualified retiree moving expenses or qualified survivor moving expenses, this section (other than paragraph (h)) shall be applied to such expenses as if they were incurred in connection with the commencement of work by the taxpayer as an employee at a new principal place of work located within the United States and the limitations of paragraph (c)(4) of this section (relating to the minimum period of employment) shall not apply.

(2) Qualified retiree moving expenses. For purposes of this paragraph, the term "qualified retiree moving expenses" means any moving expenses which are incurred by an individual whose former principal place of work and former residence were outside the United States and which are incurred for a move to a new residence in the United States in connection with the bona fide retirement of the individual. "Bona fide retirement" means the permanent withdrawal from gainful full-time employment and self-employment. An individual who at the time of withdrawal from gainful full-time employment or self-employment, intends the withdrawal to be permanent shall be considered to be a "bona fide retiree" even though the individual ultimately resumes gainful full-time employment or self-employment. An individual's intention may be evidenced by relevant facts and circumstances which include the age and health of the individual, the customary retirement age of employees engaged in similar work, whether the individual is receiving a retirement allowance under a pension annuity, retirement or similar fund or system, and the length of time before resuming full-time employment or self-employment.

(3) Qualified survivor moving expenses. (i) For purposes of this paragraph, the term "qualified survivor moving expenses" means any moving expenses—

(A) Which are paid or incurred by the spouse or any dependent (as defined in section 152) of any decedent who (as of the time of his death) had a principal place of work outside the United States, and

(B) Which are incurred for a move which begins within 6 months after the death of the decedent and which is to a residence in the United States from a former residence outside the United States which (as of the time of the decedent's death) was the residence of such decedent and the individual paying or incurring the expense.

(ii) For purposes of paragraph (i)(3)(i)(B) of this section, a move begins when—

(A) The taxpayer contracts for the moving of his or her household goods and personal effects to a residence in the United States but only if the move is completed within a reasonable time thereafter;

(B) The taxpayer's household goods and personal effects are packed and in transit to a residence in the United States; or

(C) The taxpayer leaves the former residence to travel to a new place of residence in the United States.

(4) United States. For purposes of this paragraph, the term "United States" includes the possessions of the United States.

(5) Effective date. The provisions of this paragraph apply to expenses paid or incurred in taxable years beginning after December 31, 1978. The paragraph also applies to the expenses paid or incurred in the taxable year beginning during 1978 of taxpayers who do not make an election pursuant to section 209(c) of the Foreign Earned Income Act of 1978 (Pub. L. 95-615, 92 Stat. 3109) to have section 911 under prior law apply to that taxable year.

(j) Effective date. *(1) In general.* This section, except as provided in subparagraphs (2) and (3) of this paragraph, is applicable to items paid or incurred in taxable years beginning after December 31, 1969.

(2) Reimbursement not included in gross income. This section does not apply to items to the extent that the taxpayer received or accrued in a taxable year beginning before January 1, 1970, a reimbursement or other expense allowance for such items which was not included in his gross income.

(3) Election in cases of expenses paid or incurred before January 1, 1971, in connection with certain moves. (i) In general. A taxpayer who was notified by his employer on or before December 19, 1969, of a transfer to a new principal place of work and who pays or incurs moving expenses after December 31, 1969, but before January 1, 1971, in connection with such transfer may elect to have the rules governing moving expenses in effect prior to the effective date of section 231 of the Tax Reform Act of 1969 (83 Stat. 577) govern such expenses. If such election is made, this section and section 82 and the regulations thereunder do not apply to such expenses. A taxpayer is considered to have been notified on or before December 19, 1969, by his employer of a transfer, for example, if before such date the employer has sent a notice to all employees or a reasonably defined group of employees, which includes such taxpayer, of a relocation of the operations of such employer from one plant or facility to another plant or facility. An employee who is transferred to a new principal place of work for the benefit of his employer and who makes an election under this paragraph is permitted to exclude amounts received or accrued, directly or indirectly, as payment for or reimbursement of expenses of moving household goods and personal effects from the former residence to the new residence and of traveling (including meals and lodging) from the former residence to the new place of residence. Such exclusion is limited to amounts received or accrued, directly or indirectly, as a payment for or reimbursement of the expenses described above. Amounts in excess of actual expenses paid or incurred must be included in gross income. No deduction is allowable under section 217 for expenses representing amounts excluded from gross income. Also, an employee who is transferred to a new principal place of work which is less than 50 miles but at least 20 miles farther from his former residence than was his former principal place of work and who is not reimbursed, either directly or indirectly, for the expenses described above is permitted to deduct such expenses providing all of the requirements of section 217 and the regulations thereunder prior to the effective date of section 231 of the Tax Reform Act of 1969 (83 Stat. 577) are satisfied.

(ii) Election made before the date of publication of this notice as a Treasury decision. An election under this subparagraph made before the date of publication of this notice as a Treasury decision shall be made pursuant to the procedure prescribed in temporary income tax regulations relating to treatment of payments of expenses of moving from one residence to another residence (Part 13 of this chapter) T.D. 7032 (35 F.R. 4330), approved March 11, 1970.

(iii) Election made on or after the date of publication of this notice as a Treasury decision. An election made under this subparagraph on or after the date of publication of this notice as a Treasury decision shall be made not later than the time, including extensions thereof, prescribed by law for filing the income tax return for the year in which the expenses were paid or 30 days after the date of publication of this notice as a Treasury decision, whichever occurs last. The election shall be made by a statement attached to the return (or the amended return) for the taxable year, setting forth the following information:

(a) The items to which the election relates;

(b) The amount of each item;

(c) The date each item was paid or incurred; and

(d) The date the taxpayer was informed by his employer of his transfer to the new principal place of work.

(iv) Revocation of election. An election made in accordance with this subparagraph is revocable upon the filing by the taxpayer of an amended return or a claim for refund with the district director, or the director of the Internal Revenue service center with whom the election was filed not later than the time prescribed by law, including extensions thereof, for the filing of a claim for refund with respect to the items to which the election relates.

T.D. 7195, 7/10/72, amend T.D. 7578, 12/19/78, T.D. 7608, 3/29/79, T.D. 7689, 3/28/80, T.D. 7810, 2/5/82, T.D. 8607, 8/4/95.

§ 1.219-1 Deduction for retirement savings.

Caution: The Treasury has not yet amended Reg § 1.219-1 to reflect changes made by P.L. 108-357, P.L. 105-34, P.L. 104-188, P.L. 101-239, P.L. 100-647, P.L. 100-203, P.L. 99-514, P.L. 98-369, P.L. 97-248, P.L. 97-34.

(a) In general. Subject to the limitations and restrictions of paragraph (b) and the special rules of paragraph (c)(3) of this section, there shall be allowed a deduction under section 62 from gross income of amounts paid for the taxable year of an individual on behalf of such individual to an individual retirement account described in section 408(a), for an individual retirement annuity described in section 408(b), or for a retirement bond described in section 409. The deduction described in the preceding sentence shall be allowed only to the individual on whose behalf such individual retirement account, individual retirement annuity, or retirement bond is maintained. The first sentence of this paragraph shall apply only in the case of a contribution of cash. A contribution of property other than cash is not allowable as a deduction under this section. In the case of a retirement bond, a deduction will not be allowed if the bond is redeemed within 12 months of its issue date.

(b) Limitations and restrictions. *(1) Maximum deduction.* The amount allowable as a deduction under section 219(a) to an individual for any taxable year cannot exceed an amount equal to 15 percent of the compensation includible in the gross income of the individual for such taxable year, or $1,500, whichever is less.

(2) Restrictions. (i) Individuals covered by certain other plans. No deduction is allowable under section 219(a) to an individual for the taxable year if for any part of such year—

(A) He was an active participant in—

(1) A plan described in section 401(a) which includes a trust exempt from tax under section 501(a).

(2) An annuity plan described in section 403(a),

(3) A qualified bond purchase plan described in section 405(a), or

(4) A retirement plan established for its employees by the United States, by a State or political subdivision thereof, or by an agency or instrumentality of any of the foregoing, or

(B) Amounts were contributed by his employer for an annuity contract described in section 403(b) (whether or not the individual's rights in such contract are nonforfeitable).

(ii) Contributions after age 70½. No deduction is allowable under section 219 (a) to an individual for the taxable year of the individual, if he has attained the age of 70½ before the close of such taxable year.

(iii) Rollover contributions. No deduction is allowable under section 219 for any taxable year of an individual with respect to a rollover contribution described in section 402(a)(5), 402(a)(7), 403(a)(4), 403(b)(8), 408(d)(3), or 409(b)(3)(C).

(3) Amounts contributed under endowment contracts. (i) For any taxable year, no deduction is allowable under section 219(a) for amounts paid under an endowment contract described in § 1.408-3(e) which is allocable under subdivision (ii) of this subparagraph to the cost of life insurance.

(ii) For any taxable year, the cost of current life insurance protection under an endowment contract described in paragraph (b)(3)(i) of this section is the product of the net premium cost, as determined by the Commissioner, and the excess, if any, of the death benefit payable under the contract during the policy year beginning in the taxable year over the cash value of the contract at the end of such policy year.

(iii) The provisions of this subparagraph may be illustrated by the following examples:

Example (1). A, an individual who is otherwise entitled to the maximum deduction allowed under section 219, purchases, at age 20, an endowment contract described in § 1.408-3(e) which provides for the payment of an annuity of $100 per month, at age 65, with a minimum death benefit of $10,000 and an annual premium of $220. The cash value at the end of the first policy year is 0. The net premium cost, as determined by the Commissioner, for A's age is $1.61 per thousand dollars of life insurance protection. The cost of current life insurance protection is $16.10 ($1.61 × 10). A's maximum deduction under section 219 with respect to amounts paid under the endowment contract for the taxable year in which the first policy year begins is $203.90 ($220 – $16.10).

Example (2). Assume the same facts as in example (1), except that the cash value at the end of the second policy year is $200 and the net premium cost is $1.67 per thousand for A's age. The cost of current life insurance protection is $16.37 ($1.67 × 9.8). A's maximum deduction under section 219 with respect to amounts paid under the endowment contract for the taxable year in which the second policy year begins is $203.63 ($220 – $16.37).

(c) Definitions and special rules. *(1) Compensation.* For purposes of this section, the term "compensation" means wages, salaries, professional fees, or other amounts derived from or received for personal service actually rendered (including, but not limited to, commissions paid salesmen, compensation for services on the basis of a percentage of profits, commissions on insurance premiums, tips, and bonuses) and includes earned income, as defined in section 401(c)(2), but does not include amounts derived from or received as earnings or profits from property (including, but not limited to, interest and dividends) or amounts not includible in gross income.

(2) Active participant. For the definition of active participant, see § 1.219-2.

(3) Special rules. (i) The maximum deduction allowable under section 219(b)(1) is computed separately for each individual. Thus, if a husband and wife each has compensation of $10,000 for the taxable year and they are each otherwise eligible to contribute to an individual retirement account and they file a joint return, then the maximum amount allowable as a deduction under section 219 is $3,000, the sum of the individual maximums of $1,500. However, if, for example, the husband has compensation of $20,000, the wife has no compensation, each is otherwise eligible to contribute to an individual retirement account for the taxable year, and they file a joint return, the maximum amount allowable as a deduction under section 219 is $1,500.

(ii) Section 219 is to be applied without regard to any community property laws. Thus, if, for example, a husband and wife, who are otherwise eligible to contribute to an individual retirement account, live in a community property jurisdiction and the husband alone has compensation of $20,000 for the taxable year, then the maximum amount allowable as a deduction under section 219 is $1,500.

(4) Employer contributions. For purposes of this chapter, any amount paid by an employer to an individual retirement annuity or retirement bond constitutes the payment of compensation to the employee (other than a self-employed individual who is an employee within the meaning of section 401(c)(1)) includible in his gross income, whether or not a deduction for such payment is allowable under section 219 to such employee after the application of section 219(b). Thus, an employer will be entitled to a deduction for compensation paid to an employee for amounts the employer contributes on the employee's behalf to an individual retirement account, for an individual retirement annuity, or for a retirement bond if such deduction is otherwise allowable under section 162.

T.D. 7714, 8/7/80.

PAR. 2. Section 1.219-1 is revised by adding: (1) a new subdivision (iv) to paragraph (b)(2), and (2) new paragraphs (d) and (e) to read as follows:

Proposed § 1.219-1 Deduction for retirement savings.

[*For Preamble, see ¶ 150,703*]

* * * * *

(b) Limitations and restrictions. * * *

(2) Restrictions. * * *

(iv) Alternative deduction. No deduction is allowed under subsection (a) for the taxable year if the individual claims the deduction allowed by section 220 (relating to retirement savings for certain married individuals) for the taxable year.

* * * * *

(d) Time when contributions deemed made. *(1) Taxable years beginning before January 1, 1978.* For taxable years beginning before January 1, 1977, a taxpayer must make a contribution to an individual retirement plan during a taxable year in order to receive a deduction for such taxable year. For taxable years beginning after December 31, 1976, and before January 1, 1978, a taxpayer shall be deemed to have made a contribution on the last day of the preceding taxable year if the contribution is made on account of such taxable year and is made not later than 45 days after the end of such taxable year. A contribution made not later than 45 days after the end of a taxable year shall be treated as made on account of such taxable year if the individual specifies in writing to the trustee, insurance company, or custodian that the amounts contributed are for such taxable year.

(2) Taxable years beginning after December 31, 1977. For taxable years beginning after December 31, 1977, a taxpayer shall be deemed to have made a contribution on the last day of the preceding taxable year if the contribution is made on account of such taxable year and is made not later than the time prescribed by law for filing the return for such taxable year (including extensions thereof). A contribution made not later than the time prescribed by law for filing the return for a taxable year (including extensions thereof) shall be treated as made on account of such taxable year if it is irrevocably specified in writing to the trustee, insurance company, or custodian that the amounts contributed are for such taxable year.

(3) Time when individual retirement plan must be established. For purposes of this paragraph, an individual retirement plan need not be established until the contribution is made.

(4) Year of inclusion in income. Any amount paid by an employer to an individual retirement account, for an individual retirement annuity or for an individual retirement bond (including an individual retirement account or individual retirement annuity maintained as part of a simplified employee pension plan) shall be included in the gross income of the employee for the taxable year for which the contribution is made.

(e) Excess contributions treated as contribution made during subsequent year for which there is an unused limitation. *(1) In general.* If for the taxable year the maximum amount allowable as a deduction under this section exceeds the amount contributed, then the taxpayer, whether or not a deduction is actually claimed, shall be treated as having made an additional contribution for the taxable year in an amount equal to the lesser of—

(i) The amount of such excess, or

(ii) The amount of the excess contributions for such taxable year (determined under section 4973(b)(2) without regard to subparagraph (C) thereof).

(2) Amount contributed. For purposes of this paragraph, the amount contributed—

(i) Shall be determined without regard to this paragraph, and

(ii) Shall not include any rollover contribution.

(3) Special rule where excess deduction was allowed for closed year. Proper reduction shall be made in the amount allowable as a deduction by reason of this paragraph for any amount allowed as a deduction under this section or section 220 for a prior taxable year for which the period for assessing a deficiency has expired if the amount so allowed exceeds the amount which should have been allowed for such prior taxable year.

(4) Effective date. (i) This paragraph shall apply to the determination of deductions for taxable years beginning after December 31, 1975.

(ii) If, but for this subdivision, an amount would be allowable as a deduction by reason of section 219(c)(5) for a taxable year beginning before January 1, 1978, such amount shall be allowable only for the taxpayer's first taxable year beginning in 1978.

(5) Examples. The provisions of this paragraph may be illustrated by the following examples. (Assume in each example, unless otherwise stated, that B is less than age 70½ and is not covered by a simplified employee pension or a plan described in section 219(b)(2).)

Example (1). (i) B, a calendar-year taxpayer, earns $8,000 in compensation includible in gross income for 1979. On December 1, 1979, B establishes an individual retirement account (IRA) and contributes $1,500 to the account. B does not withdraw any money from the IRA after the initial contribution. Under section 219(b)(1), the maximum amount that B can deduct for 1979 is 15% of $8,000 or $1,200. B has an excess contribution for 1979 of $300.

(ii) For 1980, B has compensation includible in gross income of $12,000. B makes a $1,000 contribution to his IRA for 1980.

(iii) Although B made only a $1,000 contribution to his IRA for 1980, under the rules contained in this paragraph, B is treated as having made an additional contribution of $300 for 1980 and will be allowed to deduct $1,300 as his 1980 IRA contribution.

Example (2). (i) For 1979, the facts are the same as in Example (1).

(ii) For 1980, B has compensation includible in gross income of $12,000. B makes a $1,500 contribution to his IRA for 1980.

(iii) B will be allowed a $1,500 deduction for 1980 (the amount of his contribution). B will not be allowed a deduction for the $300 excess contribution made in 1979 because the maximum amount allowable for 1980 does not exceed the amount contributed.

Example (3). (i) For 1979, the facts are the same as in Example (1).

(ii) For 1980, B has compensation includible in gross income of $12,000. B makes a $1,400 contribution to his IRA for 1980.

(iii) For 1980, B will be allowed to deduct his contribution of $1,400 and $100 of the excess contribution made for 1979. He will not be allowed to deduct the remaining $200 of the excess contribution made for 1979 because that would make his deduction for 1980 more than $1,500, his allowable deduction for 1980.

(iv) For 1981, B has compensation includible in gross income of $15,000. B makes a $1,300 contribution to his IRA for 1981.

(v) B will be allowed to deduct the remaining $200 and his $1,300 contribution for 1981.

Example (4). (i) For 1979, the facts are the same as in *Example (1).*

(ii) For 1980, B has compensation includible in gross income of $12,000. B makes a $1,000 contribution to his IRA for 1980. B is allowed to deduct the $300 excess contribution for 1980 but fails to do so on his return. Consequently, B deducts only $1,000 for 1980.

(iii) Under no circumstances will B be allowed to deduct the $300 excess contribution made for 1979 for any taxable year after 1980 because B is treated as having made the contribution for 1980.

Example (5). (i) For 1979, the facts are the same as in *Example (1).*

(ii) For 1980, B has compensation includible in gross income of $15,000 and is an active participant in a plan described in section 219(b)(2)(A).

(iii) B will not be allowed to deduct for 1980 the $300 excess contribution for 1979 because the maximum amount allowable as a deduction under sections 219(b)(1) and 219(b)(2) is $0.

§ 1.219-2 Definition of active participant.

Caution: The Treasury has not yet amended Reg § 1.219-2 to reflect changes made by P.L. 105-34, P.L. 101-239, P.L. 100-647, P.L. 100-203, P.L. 99-514, P.L. 98-369, P.L. 97-34.

(a) In general. This section defines the term "active participant" for individuals who participate in retirement plans described in section 219(b)(2). Any individual who is an active participant in such a plan is not allowed a deduction under section 219(a) for contributions to an individual retirement account.

(b) Defined benefit plans. *(1) In general.* Except as provided in subparagraphs (2), (3) and (4) of this paragraph, an individual is an active participant in a defined benefit plan if for any portion of the plan year ending with or within such individual's taxable year he is not excluded under the eligibility provisions of the plan. An individual is not an active participant in a particular taxable year merely because the individual meets the plan's eligibility requirements during a plan year beginning in that particular taxable year but ending in a later taxable year of the individual. However, for purposes of this section, an individual is deemed not to satisfy the eligibility provisions for a particular plan year if his compensation is less than the minimum amount of compensation needed under the plan to accrue a benefit. For example, assume a plan is integrated with Social Security and only those individuals whose compensation exceeds a certain amount accrue benefits under the plan. An individual whose compensation for the plan year ending with or within his taxable year is less than the amount necessary under the plan to accrue a benefit is not an active participant in such plan.

(2) Rules for plans maintained by more than one employer. In the case of a defined benefit plan described in section 413(a) and funded at least in part by service-related contributions, e.g., so many cents-per-hour, an individual is an active participant if an employer is contributing or is required to contribute to the plan an amount based on that individual's service taken into account for the plan year ending with or within the individual's taxable year. The general rule in paragraph (b)(1) of this section applies in the case of plans described in section 413(a) and funded only on some non-service-related unit. e.g., so many cents-per-ton of coal.

(3) Plans in which accruals for all participants have ceased. In the case of a defined benefit plan in which accruals for all participants have ceased, an individual in such a plan is not an active participant. However, any benefit that may vary with future compensation of an individual provides additional accruals. For example, a plan in which future benefit accruals have ceased, but the actual benefit depends upon final average compensation will not be considered as one in which accruals have ceased.

(4) No accruals after specified age. An individual in a defined benefit plan who accrues no additional benefits in a plan year ending with or within such individual's taxable year by reason of attaining a specified age is not an active participant by reason of his participation in that plan.

(c) Money purchase plan. An individual is an active participant in a money purchase plan if under the terms of the plan employer contributions must be allocated to the individual's account with respect to the plan year ending with or within the individual's taxable year. This rule applies even if an individual is not employed at any time during the individual's taxable year.

(d) Profit-sharing and stock-bonus plans. *(1) In general.* This paragraph applies to profit-sharing and stock bonus plans. An individual is an active participant in such plans in a taxable year if a forfeiture is allocated to his account as of a date in such taxable year. An individual is also an active participant in a taxable year in such plans if an employer contribution is added to the participant's account in such taxable year. A contribution is added to a participant's account as of the later of the following two dates: the date the contribution is made or the date as of which it is allocated. Thus, if a contribution is made in an individual's taxable year 2 and allocated as of a date in individual's taxable year 1, the later of the relevant dates is the date the contribution is made. Consequently, the individual is an active participant in year 2 but not in year 1 as a result of that contribution.

(2) Special rule. An individual is not an active participant for a particular taxable year by reason of a contribution made in such year allocated to a previous year if such individual was an active participant in such previous year by reason of a prior contribution that was allocated as of a date in such previous year.

(e) Employee contributions. If an employee makes a voluntary or mandatory contribution to a plan described in paragraphs (b), (c), or (d) of this section, such employee is an active participant in the plan for the taxable year in which such contribution is made.

(f) Certain individuals not active participants. For purposes of this section, an individual is not an active participant under a plan for any taxable year of such individual for which such individual elects, pursuant to the plan, not to participate in such plan.

(g) Retirement savings for married individuals. The provisions of this section apply in determining whether an individual or his spouse is an active participant in a plan for purposes of section 220 (relating to retirement savings for certain married individuals).

(h) Examples. The provisions of this section may be illustrated by the following examples:

Example (1). The X Corporation maintains a defined benefit plan which has the following rules on participation and accrual of benefits. Each employee who has attained the age of 25 or has completed one year of service is a participant in the plan. The plan further provides that each participant shall receive upon retirement $12 per month for each year of service in which the employee completes 1,000 hours of service. The plan year is the calendar year. B, a calendar-year taxpayer, enters the plan on January 2, 1980, when he is 27 years of age. Since B has attained the age of 25, he is a participant in the plan. However, B completes less than 1,000 hours of service in 1980 and 1981. Although B is not accruing any benefits under the plan in 1980 and 1981, he is an active participant under section 219(b)(2) because he is a participant in the plan. Thus, B cannot make deductible contributions to an individual retirement arrangement for his taxable years of 1980 and 1981.

Example (2). The Y Corporation maintains a profit-sharing plan for its employees. The plan year of the plan is the calendar year. C is a calendar-year taxpayer and a participant in the plan. On June 30, 1980, the employer makes a contribution for 1980 which as allocated on July 31, 1980. In

1981 the employer makes a second contribution for 1980, allocated as of December 31, 1980. Under the general rule stated in § 1.219-2(d)(1), C is an active participant in 1980. Under the special rule stated in § 1.219-2(d)(2), however, C is not an active participant in 1981 by reason of that contribution made in 1981.

(i) Effective date. The provisions set forth in this section are effective for taxable years beginning after December 31, 1978.

T.D. 7714, 8/7/80.

PAR. 3. Section 1.219-2 is amended by: (1) revising the first sentence of paragraph (b)(1); (2) renumbering paragraph (b)(2), (3), and (4) as paragraph (b)(3), (4) and (5), respectively, and adding a new paragraph (b)(2) before the renumbered paragraph (b)(3), (4) and (5); (3) revising paragraph (f) and (4) adding new examples (3), (4) and (5) after *Example (2)* in paragraph (h). These revised and added provisions read as follows:

Proposed § 1.219-2 Definition of active participant. [*For Preamble, see ¶ 150,703*]

* * * * *

(b) Defined benefit plans. *(1) In general.* Except as provided in subparagraphs (2), (3), (4) and (5) of this paragraph, an individual is an active participant in a defined benefit plan if for any portion of the plan year ending with or within such individual's taxable year he is not excluded under the eligibility provisions of the plan. * * *

(2) Special rule for offset plans. For taxable years beginning after December 31, 1980, an individual who satisfies the eligibility requirements of a plan under which benefits are offset by Social Security or Railroad Retirement benefits is not considered an active participant by virtue of participation in such plan for a particular plan year if such individual's compensation for the calendar year during which such plan year ends does not exceed the offset plan's breakpoint compensation amount for such plan year. Breakpoint compensation is the maximum compensation determined for the plan for a plan year tht any participant could earn and have a projected benefit from the offset plan of $0. For purposes of determining the projected plan benefit, the following assumptions are made: plan participation begins at age 25 and maximum credited service is earned for participation from age 25 to age 65 regardless of the participant's actual participation; plan benefits, including the offset, are based on W-2 earnings from the employer for such calendar year regardless of the definition of compensation on which plan benefits are based; and the projected Social Security Primary Insurance Amount (PIA) is computed under a formula that the Commissioner may, from time to time, prescribe for this purpose.

* * * * *

(f) Certain individuals not active participants. *(1) Election out of plan.* For purposes of this section, an individual who elects pursuant to the plan not to participate in the plan will be considered to be ineligible for participation for the period to which the election applies. In the case of a defined benefit plan, such an election shall be effective no earlier than the first plan year commencing after the date of the election.

(2) Members of reserve components. A member of a reserve component of the armed forces (as defined in section 261(a) of Title 10 of the United States Code) is not considered to be an active participant in a plan described in section 219(b)(2)(A)(iv) for a taxable year solely because he is a member of a reserve component unless he has served in excess of 90 days on active duty (other than military duty for training) during the year.

(3) Volunteer firefighters. An individual whose participation in a plan described in section 219(b)(2)(A)(iv) is based solely upon his activity as a volunteer firefighter and whose accrued benefit as of the beginning of the taxable year is not more than an annual benefit of $1,800 (when expressed as a single life annuity commencing at age 65) is not considered to be an active participant in such a plan for the taxable year.

* * * * *

(h) Examples. * * *

Example (3). (i) For plan year X the annual projected Social Security PIA is determined as follows:

Compensation range[1]	PIA formula[1]
$0 to $1,626	PIA = $1,464.
$1,627 to $2,160	PIA = .90 (compensation).
$2,161 to $13,020 ...	PIA = .32 (compensation) + $1,253.
$13,021 to $22,900 ..	PIA = .15 (compensation) + $3,466.
$22,901 and over ...	PIA = $6,901.

[1] These numbers are for illustrative purposes only.

(ii) V is a defined benefit plan which provides a normal retirement benefit of 1.5% of high five-year average earnings excluding overtime pay, minus 2% of Social Security PIA, the difference multiplied by years of plan participation up to a maximum of 30 years, V provides that individuals commence plan participation on their date of employment. Normal retirement age is 62. V's breakpoint compensation for the plan year ending in year X can be determined as follows:

I. Determine V's projected benefits:

An individual credited with 40 years of service (from age 25 to 65) would have a projected benefit of:

(30) (1.5% (compensation) − 2% (PIA))

or

45% (compensation) − 60% (PIA).

Note that in the determination of the projected benefit, the normal retirement age is assumed to be age 65 rather than the actual normal retirement age of 62, the participant is assumed to have 40 years of credited service, and the plan definition of compensation is assumed to be the same as is used to compute the Social Security benefit.

II. Determine V's formula compensation changepoints. The formula compensation changepoints are amounts where the projected benefit formula, expressed in terms of compensation, changes:

Since V's benefit formula applies uniformly to all compensation, the compensation changepoints are determined by the PIA portion only, and are

a. $1,626. b. 2,160. c. 13,020. d. 22,900.

III. Determine which of the formula compensation changepoints first produces a projected benefit greater than 0. This can be done by testing the projected benefit for compensation amounts equal to V's compensation changepoints:

a. Formula compensation changepoint equal to $1,626.

i. Projected benefit = 45% × 1,626 − 60% × 1,464 = 0.

V's compensation breakpoint, therefore, exceeds $1,626.

b. Formula compensation changepoint equal to $2,160.

i. Projected benefit = 45% × 2,160 − 60% × (90 × 2,160) = 0.

V's compensation breakpoint, therefore, exceeds $2,160.

c. Formula compensation changepoint equal to $13,020.

i. Projected benefit = 45% × 13,020 − 60% × (.32 × 13,020 + 1,253) = 2,607.

V's compensation breakpoint is, therefore, in the compensation range $2,161 to $13,020.

IV. Determine V's compensation breakpoint within the $2,161 to $13,020 compensation range.

V's compensation breakpoint can be determined by finding the greatest compensation that will result in a projected benefit of 0 for this compensation range:

a. 45% × compensation − 60% × (.32 × compensation + 1,253) = 0.

b. Eliminate the parentheses in equation a by multiplying each of the terms within the parentheses by − 60%. 45% × compensation − 19.2% × compensation − 751.80 = 0.

c. Add 751.80 to both sides of equation in b and combine the first two terms. 25.8% × compensation = 751.80.

d. Dividing both sides of the equation in c by 25.8%, V's breakpoint compensation for 1979 = $2,914.

V. Therefore, individuals whose W-2 earnings from the employer do not exceed $2,914 in year X are not considered active participants by virtue of participating in Plan V.

Example (4). For year X the annual projected Social Security PIA is determined as in *Example (3).*

T is a defined benefit plan which provides a normal retirement benefit equal to 20% of final average earnings plus 10% of such earnings in excess of $2,000 minus 45% of PIA, the net result reduced pro-rata for participation less than 15 years. Participation commerces upon attainment of age 20. Normal retirement age is 65.

I. Determine T's projected benefit for year X.

An individual credited with 40 years of service (from age 25 to 65) would have projected benefit of:

20% of compensation plus 10% of

compensation in excess of $2,000, if any

minus

45% of PIA

II. Determine T's formula compensation changepoints.

$2,000 is a formula compensation changepoint, in addition to the four PIA changepoints, since T's benefit formula changes at this compensation amount. The five formula compensation changepoints are:

a. $1,626. b. 2,000. c. 2,160. d. 13,020. e. 22,900.

III. Determine which of T's formula compensation changepoints first produces a projected benefit greater than 0.

a. Compensation changepoint equal to $1,626.

i. Projected benefit = 20% × 1,626 + 10% × 0 − 45% × 1,424 = 0.

T's compensation breakpoint, therefore, exceeds $1,626.

b. Compensation changepoint equal to $2,000

i. Projected benefit = 20% × 2,000 + 10% × 0 − 45% × (.90 × 2,000) = 0.

T's compensation breakpoint, therefore, exceeds $2,000.

c. Compensation changepoint equal to $2,160.

i. Projected benefit = 20% × 2,160 + 10% × (2,160 − 2,000) − 45% × (.90 × 2,160) = 0.

T's compensation breakpoint, therefore, exceeds $2,160.

d. Compensation changepoint equal to $13,020.

i. Projected benefit = 20% × 13,020 + 10% (13,020 − 2,000) − 45% × (.32 × 13,020 + 1,253) = 1,267.

T's compensation breakpoint, therefore, in the compensation range $2,160 to $13,020.

IV. Determine T's breakpoint compensation within the $2,160 to $13,020 range.

T's compensation breakpoint can be determined by finding the greatest compensation that will result in a projected benefit of 0 for this range:

a. 20% × comp. + 10% × (comp. − 2,000) − 45% × (.32 × comp. + 1,253) = 0.

b. Eliminating both parenthesis in equation a. by multiplying each of the terms within by the appropriate percentage.

20% × comp. + 10% × comp. − 200 − 14.4% × comp. − 563.85 = 0.

c. Add 763.85 to both sides of equation and combine remaining terms in equation b.

15.6% × comp. = 763.85.

d. Dividing each side of equation c. by 15.6%, T's breakpoint compensation for year X = $4,896.

V. Therefore, individuals whose W-2 earnings do not exceed $4,896 in year X are not considered active participants by virtue of participating in Plan T.

Example (5). Assume the same facts as *Example (4)*, except that T also provides a minimum monthly benefit of $100 for participants with 15 or more years of plan participation. There is no compensation amount which will produce a projected benefit of $0. Therefore, all individuals who satisfy T's eligibility requirements are considered active participants.

Proposed § 1.219-3 Limitation on simplified employee pension deductions. [*For Preamble, see ¶ 150,703*]

Caution: The Treasury has not yet amended Reg § 1.219-3 to reflect changes made by P.L. 99-514, P.L. 98-369, P.L. 97-34.

(a) General rule. *(1) In general.* Under section 219(b)(7), if an employer contribution is made on behalf of an employee to a simplified employee pension described in section 408(k), the limitations of this action, and not section 219(b)(1) and § 1.219-1(b)(1), shall apply for purposes of computing the maximum allowable deduction for that individual employee. The other rules of section 219 and §§ 1.219-1 and 1.219-2 apply for purposes of computing an individual's deduction except as modified by this section.

(2) Employer limitation. The maximum deduction limitation under section 219(a) for an employee with respect to an employer contribution to the employee's simplified employee pension under that employer's arrangement cannot exceed an amount equal to the lesser of—

(i) 15 percent of the employee's compensation from that employer (determined without regard to the employer contribution to the simplified employee pension) includible in the employee's gross income for the taxable year, or

(ii) The amount contributed by that employer to the employee's simplified employee pension and included in gross income (but not in excess of $7,500).

(3) Special rules. (i) Compensation. Compensation referred to in paragraph (a)(2)(i) has the same meaning as under § 1.219-1(c)(1) except that it includes only the compensation from the employer making the contribution to the simplified employee pension. Thus, if an individual earns $50,000 from employer A and $20,000 from employer B and employer B contributes $4,000 to a simplified employee pension on behalf of the individual, the maximum amount the individual will be able to deduct under section 219(b)(7) is 15 percent of $20,000, or $3,000.

(ii) Special rule for officers, shareholders, and owner-employees. In the case of an employee who is an officer, shareholder, or owner-employee described in section 408(k)(3) with respect to a particular employer, the $7,500 amount referred to in paragraph (a)(2)(ii) shall be reduced by the amount of tax taken into account with respect to such individual under section 408(k)(3)(D).

(iii) More than one employer arrangement. Except as provided in paragraph (c), below, the maximum deduction under paragraph (a)(2) for an individual who receives simplified employee pension contributions under two or more employers' simplified employee pension arrangements cannot exceed the sum of the maximum deduction limitations computed separately for that individual under each such employer's arrangement.

(iv) Section 408 rules. Under section 408(j), for purposes of applying the $7,500 limitations under section 408(a)(1), (b)(1), (b)(2)(B) and (d)(5) (§ 1.408-2(b)(1), § 1.408-3(b)(2) and § 1.408-4(h)(3)(i), respectively), the $7,500 limitations shall be applied separately with respect to each employer's contributions to a individual's simplified employee pension.

(b) Limitations not applicable to SEP contributions. *(1) Active participant.* The limitations on coverage by certain other plans in section 219(b)(2) and § 1.219-1(b)(2)(i) shall not apply with respect to the employer contribution to a simplified employee pension. Thus, an employee is allowed a deduction for an employer's contribution to a simplified employee pension even though he is an active participant in an employer's qualified plan.

(2) Contributions to simplified employee pensions after age 70½. The denial of deductions for contributions after age 70½ contained in section 219(b)(3) and § 1.219-1(b)(2)(ii) shall not apply with respect to the employer contribution to a simplified employee pension.

(c) Multiple employer, etc. limitations. *(1) Section 414(b) and (c) employers.* In the case of a controlled group of employers within the meaning of section 414(b) or (c), the maximum deduction limitation for an employee under paragraph (a)(2) shall be computed by treating such employers as one employer maintaining a single simplified pension arrangement and by treating the compensation of that employee from such employers as if from one employer. Thus, for example, for a particular employee the 15 percent limitation on compensation would be determined with regard to the compensation from all employers within such group. Further, the maximum deduction with respect to such group could not exceed $7,500.

(2) Self-employed individuals. In the case of an employee who is a self-employed individual within the meaning of section 401(c)(1) with respect to more than one trade or business, the maximum deduction limitation for such an employee under paragraph (a)(2) shall not exceed the lesser of the sum of such limitation applied separately with respect to the simplified employee pension arrangement of each trade or business or such limitation determined by treating such trades or businesses as if they constituted a single employer.

(d) Additional deduction for employee contributions. If the maximum allowable deduction for an individual employee determined under paragraph (a) for employer contributions to that individual's simplified employee pensions is less than $1,500, the individual shall be entitled to an additional deduction for contributions to individual retirement programs maintained on his behalf. The additional deduction shall equal the excess, if any, of the section 219(b)(1) and § 1.219-1(b)(1) maximum deduction limitation over the maximum deduction limitation determined under paragraph (a). For purpose of determining the compensation limit of section 219(b)(1), employer simplified employee pension contributions shall not be taken into account. Thus, for example, if $1,000 is deductible by individual A for employer contributions under a simplified employee pension arrangement and A's compensation, not including the $1,000 SEP contribution, is $10,000, than A would be entitled to an additional deduction of $500.

(e) Examples. The provisions of this section may be illustrated by the following examples:

Example (1). Corporation X is a calendar-year, cash basis taxpayer. It adopts a simplified employee pension agreement in 1980 and wishes to contribute the maximum amount on behalf of each employee for 1980. Individual E is a calendar-year taxpayer who is employed solely by Corporation X in 1980. Beginning in June 1980, Corporation X pays $100 each month into a simplified employee pension maintained on behalf of E. X makes a total payment to E's simplified employee pension during the year of $700. E's other compensation from X for the year totals $15,000. The maximum amount which E will be allowed to deduct as a simplified employee pension contribution is 15% of $15,000, or $2,250. Therefore, X may make an additional contribution for 1980 to E's simplified employee pension of $1,550. X makes this additional contribution to E's simplified employee pension in February of 1981. E's total compensation for 1980 includible in gross income is $15,000 + $2,250 or $17,250.

Example (2). (i) Corporation G is a calendar-year taxpayer which does not maintain an integrated plan is defined in section 408(k)(3)(E). It adopts a simplified employee pension agreement for 1980. It wishes to contribute 15% of compensation on behalf of each employee reduced by its tax under section 3111(a). The corporation has 4 employees, A, B, C, and D. D is a shareholder. The compensation for these employees for 1980 is as follows:

A = $10,000

B = 20,000

C = 30,000

D = 60,000

(ii) The amount of money which the corporation will be allowed to contributed on behalf of each employee under this allocation formula and the amount of the employer contribution each employee will be allowed to deduct is set forth in the following table:

Employee	Compensation	Lesser of $7,500 or 15% Comp.	3111(a)[1] Tax	SEP[2] Contribution	219(b)(7) deduction
A	$10,000	$1,500	$ 508.00	$ 992.00	$ 992.00

B	20,000	3,000	1,016.00	1,984.00	1,984.00
C	30,000	4,500	1,315.72	3,184.28	3,184.28
D	60,000	7,500	1,315.72	6,184.28	6,184.28

[1] The section 3111(a) tax is computed by multiplying compensation up to the taxable wage base ($25,900 for 1980) by the tax rate (5.08% for 1980).

[2] Simplified Employee Pension.

Example (3). Corporations A and B are calendar year taxpayers. Corporations A and B are not members of a controlled group of employers within the meaning of section 414(b) or (c). Individual M is employed full-time by Corporation A and part-time by Corporation B. Corporation A adopts a simplified employee pension agreement for calendar year 1980 and agrees to contribute 15% of compensation for each participant. M is a participant under Corporation A's simplified employee pension agreement and earns $15,000 for 1980 from Corporation A before A's contribution to his simplified employee pension. M also earns $5,000 as a part-time employee of Corporation B for 1980. Corporation A contributes $2,500 to M's simplified employee pension. The maximum amount that M will be allowed to deduct under section 219(b)(7) for 1980 is 15% of $15,000 or $2,250. The remaining $250 is an excess contribution because M cannot consider the compensation earned from Corporation B under § 1.219-3(a)(3)(i).

Example (4). Individual P is employed by Corporation H and Corporation O. Corporation H and O are not members of a controlled group of employers within the meaning of section 414(b) or (c). Both Corporation H and Corporation O maintain a simplified employee pension arrangement and contribute 15 percent of compensation on behalf of each employee. P earns $50,000 from Corporation H and $60,000 from Corporation O. Corporation H and O each contributes $7,500 under its simplified employee pension arrangement to an individual retirement account maintained on behalf of P. P will be allowed to deduct $15,000 for employer contributions to simplified employee pensions because each employer has a simplified employee pension arrangement and the SEP contributions by Corporation H and O do not exceed the applicable $7,500 – 15 percent limitation.

Proposed § 1.219(a)-1 Deduction for contributions to individual retirement plans and employer plans under the Economic Recovery Tax Act of 1981. [*For Preamble, see ¶ 150,933*]

Caution: The Treasury has not yet amended Reg § 1.219(a)-1 to reflect changes made by P.L. 100-647, P.L. 100-318, P.L. 99-514.

(a) In general. Under section 219, as amended by the Economic Recovery Tax Act of 1981, an individual is allowed a deduction from gross income for amounts paid on his behalf to an individual retirement plan or to certain employer retirement plans. The following table indicates the location of the rules for deductions on behalf of individuals to individual retirement plans or employer plans.

§ 1.219(a)-2. Individual retirement plans.

§ 1.219(a)-3. Spousal individual retirement accounts.

§ 1.219(a)-4. Simplified employee pensions.

§ 1.219(a)-5. Employer plans.

§ 1.219(a)-6. Divorced individuals.

(b) Definitions. The following is a list of terms and their definitions to be used for purposes of this section and §§ 1.219(a)-2 through 1.219(a)-6:

(1) Individual retirement plan. The term "individual retirement plan" means an individual retirement account described in section 408(a), an individual retirement annuity described in section 408(b), and a retirement bond described in section 409.

(2) Simplified employee pension. The term "simplified employee pension" has the meaning set forth in § 1.408-7(a).

(3) Compensation. The term "compensation" means wages, salaries, professional fees, or other amounts derived from or received for personal service actually rendered (including, but not limited to, commissions paid salesmen, compensation for services on the basis of a percentage of profits, commissions on insurance premiums, tips, and bonuses), but does not include amounts derived from or received as earnings or profits from property (including, but not limited to, interest and dividends) or amounts not includible in gross income such as amounts excluded under section 911. Compensation includes earned income, as defined in section 401(c)(2), reduced by amounts deductible under sections 404 and 405. Compensation does not include amounts received as deferred compensation, including any pension or annuity payment. Compensation does not include unemployment compensation within the meaning of section 85(c).

(4) Qualified voluntary employee contribution. The term "qualified voluntary employee contribution" means any employee contribution which is not a mandatory contribution within the meaning of section 411(c)(2)(C) made by an individual as an employee under a qualified employer plan or government plan, which plan allows an employee to make such contributions, and which the individual has not designated as a contribution other than a qualified voluntary employee contribution. Thus, if employee contributions are required as a condition of plan participation, they are mandatory contributions within the meaning of section 411(c)(2)(C) and cannot be treated as qualified voluntary employee contributions.

(5) Qualified retirement contribution. The term "qualified retirement contribution" means any amount paid in cash for the taxable year by or on behalf of an individual for his benefit to an individual retirement plan and any qualified voluntary employee contribution paid in cash by the individual for the taxable year.

(6) Deductible employee contribution. The term "deductible employee contribution" means any qualified voluntary employee contribution made after December 31, 1981, in a taxable year beginning after such date and allowable as a deduction under section 219(a) for such taxable year.

(7) Qualified employer plan. The term "qualified employer plan" means—

(i) A plan described in section 401(a) which includes a trust exempt from tax under section 501(a),

(ii) An annuity plan described in section 403(a),

(iii) A qualified bond purchase plan described in section 405(a), and

(iv) A plan under which amounts are contributed by an individual's employer for an annuity contract described in section 403(b).

(8) Government plan. The term "government plan" means any retirement plan, whether or not qualified, established and maintained for its employees by the United States, by a State or political subdivision thereof, or by an agency or instrumentality of any of the foregoing.

(c) Effective date. This section and §§ 1.219(a)-2 through 1.219(a)-6 are effective for taxable years of individuals beginning after December 31, 1981.

Proposed § 1.219(a)-2 Deduction for contributions to individuals retirement plans under the Economic Recovery Tax Act of 1981. [*For Preamble, see ¶ 150,933*]

Caution: The Treasury has not yet amended Reg § 1.219(a)-2 to reflect changes made by P.L. 100-647, P.L. 99-514.

(a) In general. Subject to the limitations and restrictions of paragraph (b) and the special rules of paragraph (c)(3) of this section, there shall be allowed a deduction under section 62 from gross income of amounts paid for the taxable year of an individual by or on behalf of such individual to an individual retirement plan. The deduction described in the preceding sentence shall be allowed only to the individual on whose behalf such individual retirement plan is maintained and only in the case of a contribution of cash. No deduction is allowable under this section for a contribution of property other than cash. In the case of a retirement bond, no deduction is allowed if the bond is redeemed within 12 months of its issue date.

(b) Limitations and restrictions. *(1) Maximum deduction.* The amount allowable as a deduction for contributions to an individual retirement plan to an individual for any taxable year cannot exceed the lesser of—

(i) $2,000, or

(ii) An amount equal to the compensation includible in the individual's gross income for the taxable year,

reduced by the amount of the individual's qualified voluntary employee contributions for the taxable year.

(2) Contributions after age 70½. No deduction is allowable for contributions to an individual retirement plan to an individual for the taxable year of the individual if he has attained the age of 70½ before the close of such taxable year.

(3) Rollover contributions. No deduction is allowable under § 1.219(a)-2(a) for any taxable year of an individual with respect to a rollover contribution described in section 402(a)(5), 402(a)(7), 403(a)(4), 403(b)(8), 405(d)(3), 408(d)(3), or 409(b)(3)(C).

(4) Amounts contributed under endowment contracts. (i) For any taxable year, no deduction is allowable under § 1.219(a)-2(a) for amounts paid under an endowment contract described in § 1.408-3(e) which is allocable under subdivision (ii) of this subparagraph to the cost of life insurance.

(ii) For any taxable year, the cost of current life insurance protection under an endowment contract described in paragraph (b)(4)(i) of this section is the product of the net premium cost, as determined by the Commissioner, and the excess, if any, of the death benefit payable under the contract during the policy year beginning in the taxable year over the cash value of the contract at the end of such policy year.

(c) Special rules. *(1) Separate deduction for each individual.* The maximum deduction allowable for contributions to an individual retirement plan is computed separately for each individual. Thus, if a husband and wife each has compensation of $15,000 for the taxable year, the maximum amount allowable as a deduction on their joint return is $4,000. See § 1.219(a)-3 for the maximum deduction for a spousal individual retirement plan when one spouse has no compensation.

(2) Community property. Section 219 is to be applied without regard to any community property laws. Thus, if, for example, a husband and wife, live in a community property jurisdiction, the husband has compensation of $30,000 for the taxable year, and the wife has no compensation for the taxable year, then the maximum amount allowable as a deduction for contributions to an individual retirement plan, other than a spousal individual retirement plan, is $2,000.

(3) Employer contributions. For purposes of this chapter, any amount paid by an employer to an individual retirement plan of an employee (other than a self-employed individual who is an employee within the meaning of section 401(c)(1)) constitutes the payment of compensation to the employee. The payment is includible in the employee's gross income, whether or not a deduction for such payment is allowable under section 219 to this employee. An employer will be entitled to a deduction for compensation paid to an employee for amounts the employer contributes on the employee's behalf to an individual retirement plan if such deduction is otherwise allowable under section 162. See § 1.404(h)-1 for certain limitations on this deduction in the case of employer contributions to a simplified employee pension.

(4) Year of inclusion in income. Any amount paid by an employer to an individual retirement plan (including an individual retirement account or individual retirement annuity maintained as part of a simplified employee pension arrangement) shall be included in the gross income of the employee for the taxable year for which the contribution was made.

(5) Time when contributions deemed made. A taxpayer shall be deemed to have made a contribution on the last day of the preceding taxable year if the contribution is made on account of the taxable year which includes such last day and is made not later than the time prescribed by law for filing the return for such taxable year (including extensions thereof). A contribution made not later than the time prescribed by law for filing the return for a taxable year (including extensions thereof) shall be treated as made on account of such taxable year if it is irrevocably specified in writing to the trustee, insurance company, or custodian that the amounts contributed are for such taxable year.

(d) Excess contributions treated as contribution made during subsequent year for which there is an unused limitation. *(1) In general.* This paragraph sets forth rules for the possible deduction of excess contributions made to an individual retirement plan for the taxable years following the taxable year of the excess contributions. If for a taxable year subsequent to the taxable year for which the excess contribution was made, the maximum amount allowable as a deduction for contributions to an individual retirement plan exceeds the amount contributed, then the taxpayer, whether or not a deduction is actually claimed, shall be treated as having made an additional contribution for the taxable year in an amount equal to the lesser of—

(i) The amount of such excess, or

(ii) The amount of the excess contributions for such taxable year (determined under section 4973(b)(2) without regard to subparagraph (C) thereof).

(2) Amount contributed. For purposes of this paragraph, the amount contributed—

(i) Shall be determined without regard to this paragraph, and

(ii) Shall not include any rollover contribution.

(3) Special rule where excess deduction was allowed for closed year. Proper reduction shall be made in the amount allowable as a deduction by reason of this paragraph for any amount allowed as a deduction for contributions to an individual retirement plan for a prior taxable year for which the period for assessing a deficiency has expired if the amount

so allowed exceeds the amount which should have been allowed for such prior taxable year.

(4) Excise tax consequences. See section 4973 and the regulations thereunder for the excise tax applicable to excess contributions made to individual retirement plans.

(5) Examples. The provisions of this paragraph may be illustrated by the following examples. (Assume in each example, unless otherwise stated, that T is less than age 70½ and is not married.)

Example (1). (i) T, a calendar-year taxpayer, earns $1,500 in compensation includible in gross income for 1982. On December 1, 1982, T establishes an individual retirement account (IRA) and contributes $2,000 to the account T does not withdraw any money from the IRA after the initial contribution. Under section 219(b)(1), the maximum amount that T can deduct for 1982 is $1,500. T has an excess contribution for 1982 of $500.

(ii) For 1983, T has compensation includible in gross income of $12,000. T makes a $1,000 contribution to his IRA for 1983.

(iii) Although T made only a $1,000 contribution to his IRA for 1983, under the rules contained in this paragraph, T is treated as having made an additional contribution of $500 for 1983 and will be allowed to deduct $1,500 as his 1983 IRA contribution.

Example (2). (i) For 1982, the facts are the same as in Example (1).

(ii) For 1983, T has compensation includible in gross income of $12,000. T makes a $2,000 contribution to his IRA for 1983.

(iii) T will be allowed a $2,000 deduction for 1983 (the amount of his contribution). T will not be allowed a deduction for the $500 excess contribution made in 1982 because the maximum amount allowable for 1983 does not exceed the amount contributed.

Example (3). (i) For 1982, the facts are the same as in Example (1).

(ii) For 1983, T has compensation includible in gross income of $12,000. T makes a $1,800 contribution to his IRA for 1983.

(iii) For 1983, T will be allowed to deduct his contribution of $1,800 and $200 of the excess contribution made for 1982. He will not be allowed to deduct the remaining $300 of the excess contribution made for 1982 because his deduction for 1983 would then exceed $2,000, his allowable deduction for 1983.

(iv) For 1984, T has compensation includible in gross income of $15,000. T makes a $1,300 contribution to his IRA for 1984.

(v) T will be allowed to deduct both his $1,300 contribution for 1984 and the remaining $300 contribution made for 1982.

Example (4). (i) For 1982, the facts are the same as in Example (1).

(ii) For 1983, T has compensation includible in gross income of $12,000. T makes a $1,000 contribution to his IRA for 1983. T is allowed to deduct the $500 excess contribution for 1983 but fails to do so on his return. Consequently, T deducts only $1,000 for 1983.

(iii) Under no circumstances will T be allowed to deduct the $500 excess contribution made for 1982 for any taxable year after 1983 because T is treated as having made the contribution for 1983.

Example (5). (i) For 1982, the facts are the same as in Example (1).

(ii) For 1983, T has no compensation includible in gross income.

(iii) T will not be allowed to deduct for 1983 the $500 excess contribution for 1982 because the maximum amount allowable as a deduction under section 219(b)(1) is $0.

Proposed § 1.219(a)-3 Deduction for retirement savings for certain married individuals. [*For Preamble, see ¶ 150,933*]

Caution: The Treasury has not yet amended Reg § 1.219(a)-3 to reflect changes made by P.L. 100-647, P.L. 99-514.

(a) In general. Subject to the limitations and restrictions of paragraphs (c) and (d) and the special rules of paragraph (e) of this section, there shall be allowed a deduction under section 62 from gross income of amounts paid for the taxable year of an individual by or on behalf of such individual for the benefit of his spouse to an individual retirement plan. The amounts contributed to an individual retirement plan by or on behalf of an individual for the benefit of his spouse shall be deductible only by such individual and only in the case of a contribution of cash. No deduction is allowable under this section for a contribution of property other than cash. In the case of an individual retirement bond, no deduction is allowed if the bond is redeemed within 12 months of its issue date.

(b) Definition of compensation. For purposes of this section, the term " compensation" has the meaning set forth in § 1.219(a)-1(b)(3).

(c) Maximum deduction. The amount allowable as a deduction under this section to an individual for any taxable year may not exceed the smallest of—

(1) $2,000,

(2) An amount equal to the compensation includible in the individual's gross income for the taxable year less the amount allowed as a deduction under section 219(a) (determined without regard to contributions to a simplified employee pension allowed under section 219(b)(2)), § 1.219(a)-2 and § 1.219(a)-5 for the taxable year, or

(3) $2,250 less the amount allowed as a deduction under section 219(a) (determined without regard to contributions to a simplified employee pension allowed under section 219(b)(2)), § 1.219(a)-2 and § 1.219(a)-5 for the taxable year.

(d) Limitations and restrictions. *(1) Requirement to file joint return.* No deduction is allowable under this section for a taxable year unless the individual and his spouse file a joint return under section 6013 for the taxable year.

(2) Employed spouses. No deduction is allowable under this section if the spouse of the individual has any compensation for the taxable year of such spouse ending with or within the taxable year of the individual. For purposes of this subparagraph, compensation has the meaning set forth in § 1.219(a)-1(b)(3), except that compensation shall include amounts excluded under section 911.

(3) Contributions after age 70½. No deduction is allowable under this section with respect to any payment which is made for a taxable year of an individual if the individual for whose benefit the individual retirement plan is maintained has attained age 70½ before the close of such taxable year.

(4) Recontributed amounts. No deduction is allowable under this section for any taxable year of an individual with

respect to a rollover contribution described in section 402(a)(5), 402(a)(7), 403(a)(4), 403(b)(8), 405(d)(3), 408(d)(3), or 409(b)(3)(C).

(5) Amounts contributed under endowment contracts. The rules for endowment contracts under this section are the same as the provisions for such contracts under § 1.219(a)-2(b)(4).

(e) Special rules. *(1) Community property.* This section is to be applied without regard to any community property laws.

(2) Time when contributions deemed made. The time when contributions are deemed made is determined under section 219(f)(3). See § 1.219(a)-2(c)(5).

Proposed § 1.219(a)-4 Deduction for contributions to simplified employee pensions. [*For Preamble, see ¶ 150,933*]

Caution: The Treasury has not yet amended Reg § 1.219(a)-4 to reflect changes made by P.L. 100-647, P.L. 99-514.

(a) General rule. *(1) In general.* Under section 219(b)(2), if an employer contribution is made on behalf of an employee to a simplified employee pension described in section 408(k), the limitations of this section, and not section 219(b)(1) and § 1.219(a)-2, shall apply for purposes of computing the maximum allowable deduction with respect to that contribution for that individual employee.

(2) Employer limitation. The maximum deduction under section 219(b)(2) for an employee with respect to an employer contribution to the employee's simplified employee pension under that employer's arrangement cannot exceed an amount equal to the lesser of—

(i) 15 percent of the employee's compensation from that employer (determined without regard to the employer contribution to the simplified employee pension) includible in the employee's gross income for the taxable year, or

(ii) The amount contributed by that employer to the employee's simplified employee pension and included in gross income (but not in excess of $15,000).

(3) Special rules. (i) Compensation. Compensation referred to in paragraph (a)(2)(i) has the same meaning as under § 1.219(a)-1(b)(3) except that it includes only the compensation from the employer making the contribution to the simplified employee pension. Thus, if an individual earns $50,000 from employer A and $20,000 from employer B and employer B contributes $4,000 to a simplified employee pension on behalf of the individual, the maximum amount the individual will be able to deduct under section 219(b)(2) is 15 percent of $20,000, or $3,000.

(ii) Special rule for officers, shareholders, and owner-employees. In the case of an employee who is an officer, shareholder, or owner-employee described in section 408(k)(3) with respect to a particular employer, the $15,000 amount referred to in paragraph (a)(2)(ii) shall be reduced by the amount of tax taken into account with respect to such individual under section 408(k)(3)(D).

(iii) More than one employer arrangement. Except as provided in paragraph (c), below, the maximum deduction under paragraph (a)(2) for an individual who receives simplified employee pension contributions under two or more employers' simplified employee pension arrangements cannot exceed the sum of the maximum deduction limitations computed separately for that individual under each such employer's arrangement.

(iv) Section 408 rules. Under section 408(j), the limitations under section 408(a)(1) and (b)(2)(B) (§ 1.408-2(b)(1) and § 1.408-3(b)(2)), shall be applied separately with respect to each employer's contributions to an individual's simplified employee pension.

(4) Additional deduction for individual retirement plan and qualified voluntary employee contribution. The deduction under this paragraph is in addition to any deduction allowed under section 219(a) to the individual for qualified retirement contributions.

(b) Contributions to simplified employee pensions after age 70½. The denial of deductions for contributions after age 70½ contained in section 219(d)(1) and § 1.219(a)-2(b)(2) shall not apply with respect to employer contributions to a simplified employee pension.

(c) Multiple employer, etc. limitations. *(1) Section 414(b), (c) and (m) employers.* In the case of a controlled group of employers within the meaning of section 414(b) or (c) or employers aggregated under section 414(m), the maximum deduction limitation for an employee under paragraph (a)(2) shall be computed by treating such employers as one employer maintaining a single simplified employee pension arrangement and by treating the compensation of that employee from such employers as if from one employer. Thus, for example, for a particular employee the 15 percent limitation on compensation would be determined with regard to the compensation from all employers within such group. Further, the maximum deduction with respect to contributions made by employers included within such group could not exceed $15,000.

(2) Self-employed individuals. In the case of an employee who is a self-employed individual within the meaning of section 401(c)(1) with respect to more than one trade or business, the maximum deduction limitation for such an employee under paragraph (a)(2) shall not exceed the lesser of the sum of such limitation applied separately with respect to the simplified employee pension arrangement of each trade or business or such limitation determined by treating such trades or businesses as if they constituted a single employer.

(d) Examples. The provisions of this section may be illustrated by the following examples:

Example (1). Corporation X is a calendar-year, cash basis taxpayer. It adopts a simplified employee pension agreement in 1982 and wishes to contribute the maximum amount on behalf of each employee for 1982. Individual E is a calendar-year taxpayer who is employed solely by Corporation X in 1982. Beginning in June, 1982, Corporation X pays $100 each month into a simplified employee pension maintained on behalf of E. X makes a total payment to E's simplified employee pension during the year of $700. E's other compensation from X for the year totals $15,000. The maximum amount which E will be allowed to deduct as a simplified employee pension contribution is 15% of $15,000, or $2,250. Therefore, X may make an additional contribution for 1982 to E's simplified employee pension of $1,550. X makes this additional contribution to E's simplified employee pension in February of 1983. E's total compensation includible in gross income for 1982 is $15,000 + $2,250 or $17,250.

Example (2). (i) Corporation G is a calendar-year taxpayer which adopts a simplified employee pension agreement for 1982. It does not maintain an integrated plan as defined in section 408(k)(3)(E). It wishes to contribute 15% of compensation on behalf of each employee reduced by its tax under section 3111(a). The corporation has 4 employees, A, B, C, and D. D is a shareholder. The compensation for these employees for 1982 is as follows: A = $10,000

B = $20,000

C = $30,000

D = $120,000

(ii) The amount of money which the corporation will be allowed to contribute on behalf of each employee under this allocation formula and the amount of the employer contribution each employee will be allowed to deduct is set forth in the following table:

Employee	Compen-sation	Lesser of $15,000 or 15% of Comp.	3111(a)[1] Tax	SEP[2] Con-tribution	Sec. 219(b)(2) deduction
A	$ 10,000	$ 1,500	$ 540.00	$ 960.00	$ 960.00
B	20,000	3,000	1,080.00	1,920.00	1,920.00
C	30,000	4,500	1,620.00	2,880.00	2,880.00
D	120,000	15,000	1,749.60	13,250.40	13,250.40

[1] The section 3111(a) tax is computed by multiplying compensation up to the taxable wage base (32,400 for 1982) by the tax rate (5.40% for 1982).

[2] Simplified Employee Pension.

Example (3). Corporations A and B are calendar year taxpayers. Corporations A and B are not aggregated employers under section 414(b), (c) or (m). Individual M is employed full-time by Corporation A and part-time by Corporation B. Corporation A adopts a simplified employee pension agreement for calendar year 1982 and agrees to contribute 15% of compensation for each participant. M is a participant under Corporation A's simplified employee pension agreement and earns $15,000 for 1982 from Corporation A before A's contribution to his simplified employee pension. M also earns $5,000 as a part-time employee of Corporation B for 1982 Corporation A contributes $2,500 to M's simplified employee pension. The maximum amount that M will be allowed to deduct under section 219(b)(2) for 1982 is 15% of $15,000 or $2,250. In addition, M would be allowed to deduct the remaining $250 under section 219(a) for qualified retirement contributions.

Example (4). Individual P is employed by Corporation H and Corporation O. Corporations H and O are not aggregated employers under section 414(b), (c) or (m). Both Corporation H and Corporation O maintain a simplified employee pension arrangement and contribute 15 percent of compensation on behalf of each employee, up to a maximum of $15,000. P earns $100,000 from Corporation H and $120,000 from Corporation O. Corporation H and O each contribute $15,000 under its simplified employee pension arrangement to an individual retirement account maintained on behalf of P. P will be allowed to deduct $30,000 for employer contributions to simplified employee pensions because each employer has a simplified employee pension arrangement and the SEP contributions by Corporation H and O do not exceed the applicable $15,000—15 percent limitation with respect to compensation received from each employer. In addition, P would be allowed to deduct $2,000 under section 219(a) for qualified retirement contributions.

Proposed § 1.219(a)-5 Deduction for employee contributions to employer plans. [*For Preamble, see ¶ 150,933*]

Caution: The Treasury has not yet amended Reg § 1.219(a)-5 to reflect changes made by P.L. 99-514.

(a) Deduction allowed. In the case of an individual, there is allowed as a deduction amounts contributed in cash to a qualified employer plan or government plan (as defined, respectively, in paragraphs (b)(7) and (b)(8) of § 1.219(a)-1) and designated as qualified voluntary employee contributions. If an employee transfers an amount of cash from one account in a plan to the qualified voluntary employee contribution account, such transfer is a distribution for purposes of sections 72, 402 and 403, and the amounts are considered recontributed as qualified voluntary employee contributions. No deduction will be allowed for a contribution of property other than cash.

(b) Limitations. *(1) Maximum amount of deduction.* The amount allowable as a deduction under paragraph (a) to any individual for any taxable year shall not exceed the lesser of $2,000 or an amount equal to the compensation (from the employer who maintains the plan) includible in the individual's gross income for such taxable year.

(2) Contributions after age 70½. No deduction is allowable for contributions under paragraph (a) to an individual for the taxable year of the individual if he has attained the age of 70½ before the close of such taxable year.

(3) Rollover contributions. No deduction is allowable under paragraph (a) for any taxable year of an individual with respect to a rollover contribution described in section 402(a)(5), 402(a)(7), 403(a)(4), 403(b)(8), 405(d)(3), 408(d)(3), or 409(b)(3)(C).

(c) Rules for plans accepting qualified voluntary employee contributions. *(1) Plan provision, etc.* (i) No plan may receive qualified voluntary employee contributions unless the plan document provides for acceptance of voluntary contributions. No plan may receive qualified voluntary employee contributions unless either the plan document provides for acceptance of qualified voluntary employee contributions or the employer or the plan administrator manifests an intent to accept such contributions. Such intention must be communicated to the employees. Any manner of communication that satisfies § 1.7476-2(c)(1) shall satisfy the requirements of this subparagraph.

(ii) If the plan document provides for the acceptance of voluntary contributions, but does not specifically provide for acceptance of qualified voluntary employee contributions, the plan qualification limitation on voluntary contributions (the limit of 10 percent of the employee's cumulative compensation less prior voluntary contributions) would apply to both qualified voluntary employee contributions and other voluntary contributions. On the other hand, if the plan document provides for acceptance of both qualified voluntary employee contributions and other voluntary contributions, the plan qualification limitation on voluntary contributions would apply only to the contributions other than the qualified voluntary employee contributions.

(2) Plans accepting only qualified voluntary employee contributions. A qualified pension plan or stock bonus plan may be established that provides only for qualified voluntary employee contributions. Similarly, a government plan may be established that provides only for qualified voluntary employee contributions. A plan that provides only for qualified voluntary employee contributions would not satisfy the qualification requirements for a profit-sharing plan.

(3) Recordkeeping provisions. Separate accounting for qualified voluntary employee contributions that are deductible under this section is not required as a condition for receiving qualified voluntary employee contributions. However, failure to properly account for such contributions may result in adverse tax consequences to employees upon subsequent plan distributions and reporting and recordkeeping

penalties for employers. See section 72(o) for rules for accounting for such contributions.

(4) Status as employee. An amount will not be considered as a qualified voluntary employee contribution on behalf of an individual unless the individual is an employee of the employer at some time during the calendar year for which the voluntary contribution is made. See section 415(c) concerning the effect of a nondeductible voluntary employee contribution on plan qualification.

(5) Contribution before receipt of compensation. A plan may allow an individual to make a qualified voluntary employee contribution greater than the amount he has received in compensation from the employer at the time the contribution is made. However, see paragraph (f) of this section.

(d) Designations, procedures, etc. *(1) Plan procedures.* (i) A plan which accepts qualified voluntary employee contributions may adopt procedures by which an employee can designate the character of the employee's voluntary contributions as either qualified voluntary employee contributions or other employee contributions. Such procedures may, but need not, be in the plan document.

(ii) In the absence of such plan procedures, all voluntary employee contributions shall be deemed to be qualified voluntary employee contributions unless the employee notifies the employer that the contributions are not qualified voluntary employee contributions. Such notification must be received by April 15 following the calendar year for which such contributions were made. If such notification is not received, contributions are deemed to be qualified voluntary employee contributions for the prior year.

(2) Characterization procedures, etc. (i) The plan procedures may allow an employee to elect whether or not an employee contribution is to be treated as a qualified voluntary employee contribution or as other voluntary contributions. This election can be required either prior to or after the contribution is made. If a contribution may be treated under such procedures as a qualified voluntary employee contribution or other voluntary contribution for a calendar year and the employee has not by April 15 of the subsequent calendar year designated the character of the contribution, the contribution must be treated as a qualified voluntary employee contribution for the calendar year. An employer may allow the election to be irrevocable or revocable. A procedure allowing revocable elections may limit the time within which an election may be revoked. The revocation of an election after April 15 following the calendar year for which the contribution was made is deemed to be ineffective in changing the character of employee contributions.

(ii) For purposes of this section, if the plan procedures allow employees to make contributions on account of the immediately preceding calendar year, a taxpayer shall be deemed to have made a qualified voluntary employee contribution to such plan on the last day of the preceding calendar year if the contribution is on account of such year and is made by April 15 of the calendar year or such earlier time as provided by the plan procedure.

(e) Nondiscrimination requirements. *(1) General rule.* Plans subject to the nondiscrimination requirements of section 401(a)(4) which accept qualified voluntary employee contributions must permit such contributions in a nondiscriminatory manner in order to satisfy section 401(a)(4). If a plan permits participants to make qualified voluntary employee contributions, the opportunity to make such contributions must be reasonably available to a nondiscriminatory group of employees. The availability standard will be satisfied if a nondiscriminatory group of employees is eligible to make qualified voluntary employee contributions under the terms of the plan and if a nondiscriminatory group of employees actually has the opportunity to make qualified voluntary employee contributions when plan restrictions are taken into account.

(2) Eligible employees. A nondiscriminatory group of employees is eligible to make qualified voluntary employee contribution under the terms of the plan if the group either meets the percentage requirements of section 410(b)(1)(A) or comprises a classification of employees that does not discriminate in favor of employees who are officers, shareholders, or highly compensated, as provided in section 410(b)(1)(B).

(3) Plan restrictions. In some cases, an employee may not be permitted to make qualified voluntary employee contributions until a plan restriction (such as making a certain level of mandatory employee contributions) is satisfied. In this case, it is necessary to determine whether a nondiscriminatory group of employees actually has the opportunity to make qualified voluntary employee contributions. For this purpose, only employees who have satisfied the plan restriction will be considered to have the opportunity to make deductible contributions. Thus, for example, if a plan requires an employee to make mandatory contributions of 6 percent of compensation in order to make qualified voluntary employee contributions and if only a small percentage of employees make the 6 percent mandatory contributions, then the group of employees who have the opportunity to make qualified voluntary employee contributions may not satisfy either test under section 410(b). A similar rule is applicable to integrated plans: Employees who are not permitted to make qualified voluntary employee contributions to such a plan because they earn less than the integration level amount will be considered as employees who do not have the opportunity to make qualified voluntary employee contributions.

(4) Permissible contributions. If the availability standards are met, and if the qualified voluntary employee contributions permitted are not higher, as a percentage of compensation, for officers, shareholders or highly compensated employees than for other participants, the qualified voluntary employee contribution feature will meet the requirement that contributions or benefits not discriminate in favor of employees who are officers, shareholders, or highly compensated. This is so because the contributions are made by the employee, not the employer.

(5) Acceptable contributions. A plan may accept qualified voluntary employee contributions in an amount less than the maximum deduction allowable to an individual.

(f) Excess qualified voluntary employee contributions. Voluntary employee contributions which exceed the amount allowable as a deduction under paragraph (b) of this section will be treated as nondeductible voluntary employee contributions to the plan. See § 1.415-6(b)(8).

(g) Reports. *(1) Requirements.* Each employer who maintains a plan which accepts qualified voluntary employee contributions must furnish to each employee—

(i) A report showing the amount of qualified voluntary employee contributions the employee made for the calendar year, and

(ii) A report showing the amount of withdrawals made by the employee of qualified voluntary employee contributions during the calendar year.

(2) Times. (i) The report required by paragraph (g)(1)(i) of this section must be furnished by the later of January 31

following the year for which the contributions was made or the time the contribution is made.

(ii) The report required by paragraph (g)(1)(ii) of this section must be furnished by January 31 following the year of withdrawal.

(3) Authority for additional reports. The Commissioner may require additional reports to be given to individuals or to be filed with the Service. Such reports shall be furnished at the time and in the manner that the Commissioner specifies.

(4) Authority to modify reporting requirements. The Commissioner may, in his discretion, modify the reporting requirements of this paragraph. Such modification may include: the matters to be reported, the forms to be used for the reports, the time when the reports must be filed or furnished, who must receive the reports, the substitution of the plan administrator for the employer as the person required to file or furnish the reports, and the deletion of some or all of the reporting requirements. The Commissioner may, in his discretion, relieve employers from making the reports required by section 219(f)(4) and this paragraph (g). This discretion includes the ability to relieve categories of employers (but not individual employers) from furnishing or filing any report required by section 219(f)(4) and this paragraph (g).

(5) Effective date. This paragraph shall apply to reports for calendar years after 1982.

Proposed § 1.219(a)-6 Alternative deduction for divorced individuals. [*For Preamble, see ¶ 150,933*]

Caution: The Treasury has not yet amended Reg § 1.219(a)-6 to reflect changes made by P.L. 100-647, P.L. 99-514.

(a) In general. A divorced individual may use the provisions of this section rather than § 1.219(a)-2 in computing the maximum amount he may deduct as a contribution to an individual retirement plan. A divorced individual is not required to use the provisions of this section; he may use the provisions of § 1.219(a)-2 in computing the maximum amount he may deduct as a contribution to an individual retirement plan.

(b) Individuals who may use this section. An individual may compute the deduction for a contribution to an individual retirement plan under this section if—

(1) An individual retirement plan was established for the benefit of the individual at least five years before the beginning of the calendar year in which the decree of divorce or separate maintenance was issued, and

(2) For at least three of the former spouse's most recent five taxable years ending before the taxable year in which the decree was issued, such former spouse was allowed a deduction under section 219(c) (or the corresponding provisions of prior law) for contributions to such individual retirement plan.

(c) Limitations. *(1) Amount of deduction.* An individual who computes his deduction for contributions to an individual retirement plan under this section may deduct the smallest of—

(i) The amount contributed to the individual retirement plan for the taxable year,

(ii) $1,125, or

(iii) The sum of the amount of compensation includible in the individual's gross income for the taxable year and any qualifying alimony received by the individual during the taxable year.

(2) Contributions after age 70½. No deduction is allowable for contributions to an individual retirement plan to an individual for the taxable year of the individual if he has attained the age of 70½ before the close of such taxable year.

(3) Rollover contributions. No deduction is allowable under this section for any taxable year of an individual with respect to a rollover contribution described in section 402(a)(5), 402(a)(7), 403(a)(4), 403(b)(8), 405(d)(3), 408(d)(3), or 409(b)(3)(C).

(d) Qualifying alimony. For purposes of this section, the term " qualifying alimony" means amounts includible in the individual's gross income under section 71(a)(1) (relating to a decree of divorce or separate maintenance).

Proposed § 1.220-1 Deduction for retirement savings for certain married individuals. [*For Preamble, see ¶ 150,703*]

(a) In general. Subject to the limitations and restrictions of paragraphs (c), (d) and (e) and the special rules of paragraph (f) of this section, there shall be allowed a deduction under section 62 from gross income of amounts paid for the taxable year of an individual by or on behalf of such individual for the benefit of himself and his spouse to an individual retirement account described in section 408(a), for an individual retirement annuity described in section 408(b), or for an individual retirement bond described in section 409. The amounts contributed to an individual retirement account, for an individual retirement annuity, or for an individual retirement bond by or on behalf of an individual for the benefit of himself and his spouse shall be deductible only by such individual. The first sentence of this paragraph shall apply only in the case of a contribution of cash; a contribution of property other than cash is not allowable as a deduction. In the case of an individual retirement bond, a deduction will not be allowed if the bond is redeemed within 12 months of its issue date.

(b) Definitions. *(1) Compensation.* For purposes of this section, the term "compensation" has the meaning set forth in § 1.219-1(c)(1).

(2) Active participant. For purposes of this section, the term "active participant" has the meaning set forth in § 1.219-2.

(3) Individual retirement subaccount. For purposes of this section, the term individual retirement subaccount is that part of an individual retirement account maintained for the exclusive benefit of the individual or the individual's spouse and which meets the following requirements:

(i) The individual or spouse for whom the subaccount is maintained has exclusive control over the subaccount after deposits have been made,

(ii) The subaccount, by itself, meets the requirements of section 408(a), except that it is not a separate trust,

(iii) The trustee or custodian maintains records indicating the ownership of the funds, and

(iv) The individual and spouse do not jointly own the individual retirement account of which the subaccount is a part.

(c) Types of funding arrangements permitted. The deduction under paragraph (a) of this section shall be allowed only if one of the following types of funding arrangements is used:

(1) A separate individual retirement account, individual retirement annuity, or individual retirement bond is established or purchased for the benefit of the individual and a separate

individual retirement account, individual retirement annuity or individual retirement bond is established or purchased for the individual's spouse.

(2) A single individual retirement account described in section 408(a) is established or purchased and such account has an individual retirement subaccount for the benefit of the individual and an individual retirement subaccount for the benefit of the spouse. The single individual retirement account cannot be owned jointly by the husband and wife.

(3) An individual retirement account described in section 408(c) is maintained by an employer or employee association and such account has arrangements described in subparagraphs (1) or (2).

(d) Maximum deduction. The amount allowable as a deduction under section 220(a) to an individual for any taxable year may not exceed—

(1) Twice the amount paid (including prior excess contributions) to the account, subaccount, annuity, or for the bond, established for the individual or for the spouse to or for which the lesser amount was paid for the taxable year,

(2) An amount equal to 15 percent of the compensation includible in the individual's gross income for the taxable year, or

(3) $1,750 whichever is the smallest amount.

(e) Limitations and restrictions. *(1) Alternative deduction.* No deduction is allowable under section 220(a) for the taxable year if the individual claims the deduction allowed by section 219(a) for the taxable year.

(2) Individual or spouse covered by certain other plans. No deduction is allowable under section 220(a) to an individual for the taxable year if for any part of such year—

(i) He or his spouse was an active participant (as defined in § 1.219-2), or

(ii) Amounts were contributed by his employer, or his spouse's employer, on the individual's or spouse's behalf for an annuity contract described in section 403(b) (whether or not his, or his spouse's, rights in such contract are nonforfeitable).

(3) Contributions after age 70½. No deduction is allowable under section 220(a) with respect to any payment which is made for a taxable year of an individual if either the individual or his spouse has attained age 70½ before the close of such taxable year.

(4) Recontributed amounts. No deduction is allowable under section 220(a) for any taxable year of an individual with respect to a rollover contribution described in section 402(a)(5), 402(a)(7), 403(a)(4), 403(b)(8), 408(d)(3), or 409(b)(3)(C).

(5) Amounts contributed under endowment contracts. The rules for endowment contracts under section 220 are the same as the provisions for such contracts under § 1.219-1(b)(3).

(6) Employed spouses. No deduction is allowable under section 220(a) if the spouse of the individual has any compensation (as defined in § 1.219-1(c)(1) determined without regard to section 911) for the taxable year of such spouse ending with or within the taxable year of the individual.

(f) Special rules. *(1) Community property.* Section 220 is to be applied without regard to any community property laws.

(2) Time when contributions deemed made. The time when contributions are deemed made is determined in the same manner as under section 219(c)(3). See § 1.219-1(d).

(g) Excess contributions treated as contribution made during subsequent year for which there is an unused limitation. *(1) In general.* If for the taxable year the maximum amount allowable as a deduction under this section exceeds the amount contributed, then the taxpayer, whether or not a deduction is actually claimed, shall be treated as having made an additional contribution for the taxable year in an amount equal to the lesser of—

(i) The amount of such excess, or

(ii) The amount of the excess contributions for such taxable year (determined under section 4973(b)(2) without regard to subparagraph (C) thereof).

For purposes of computing the maximum deduction under section 220(b)(1), the excess contribution for a previous year shall be treated as made for the current year.

(2) Amount contributed. For purposes of this paragraph, the amount contributed—

(i) Shall be determined without regard to this paragraph, and

(ii) Shall not include any rollover contribution.

(3) Special rule where excess contribution was allowed for closed year. Proper reduction shall be made in the amount allowable as a deduction by reason of this paragraph for any amount allowed as a deduction under this section or section 219 for a prior taxable year for which the period for assessing a deficiency has expired if the amount so allowed exceeds the amount which should have been allowed for such prior taxable year.

(4) Examples. The provisions of this paragraph may be illustrated by the following examples:

Example (1). (i) H, a calendar-year taxpayer, earns $10,000 in compensation includible in gross income for 1979. H is married to W, also a calendar-year taxpayer, who has no compensation for 1979. For 1979, neither H nor W is covered by certain other plans within the meaning of section 220(b)(3). On November 24, 1979, H establishes an individual retirement account (IRA) for himself and an individual retirement account for W. H contributes $850 to each account. Neither H nor W withdraws any money from either account after the initial contribution. Under section 220(b)(1) the maximum amount that H can deduct for 1979 is 15 percent of the compensation includible in his gross income or $1,500. H has made an excess contribution of $200 for 1979.

(ii) for 1980, H has compensation includible in gross income of $12,000. W has no compensation for 1980. For 1980, neither H nor W is covered by certain other plans, within the meaning of section 220(b)(3). No contributions are made to the IRA of H or W for 1980.

(iii) Although H made no contributions to either his or W's IRA for 1980, under the rules contained in this paragraph, H is treated as having made an additional contribution of $100 to his IRA and $100 to W's IRA for 1980 and will be allowed to deduct $200 as his 1980 IRA contribution.

Example (2). (i) For 1979, the facts are the same as in *Example (1).*

(ii) For 1980, H has compensation of $15,000 includible in gross income and is not covered by any other plans within the meaning of section 219(b)(2). W also goes to work in 1980 and has compensation of $6,000, but is not covered by certain other plans within the meaning of section 219(b)(2). H will not be treated as having made a deductible contribution of a previous year's excess contribution within the meaning of section 220(c)(6) because W has compensation for 1980. However, both H and W now meet the deduction standards of section 219 and each will be treated as having made a deductible contribution of $100 to their separate IRA's for 1980 under section 219(c)(5).

Example (3). (i) For 1979, the facts are the same as in *Example (1).*

(ii) For 1980, H has compensation of $15,000 includible in gross income and is covered by certain other plans within the meaning of section 220(b)(3). W has no compensation for 1980 and is not covered by certain other plans within the meaning of section 220(b)(3). H will not be treated as having made a deductible contribution of a previous year's excess contribution within the meaning of section 219(c)(5) or 220(c)(6) because H is covered by other plans for 1980 and has no allowable deduction under section 219 or 220.

(iii) W will not be treated as having made a deductible contribution of a previous year's excess contribution within the meaning of section 219(c)(5) because W has no compensation for 1980 and thus no allowable deduction under section 219.

(h) Effective date. (1) This section is effective for taxable years beginning after December 31, 1976.

(2) If, but for this subparagraph, an amount would be allowable as a deduction by reason of section 220(c)(6) and paragraph (g) for a taxable year beginning before January 1, 1978, such amount shall be allowable only for the taxpayer's first taxable year beginning in 1978.

§ 1.221-1 Deduction for interest paid on qualified education loans after December 31, 2001.

Caution: The Treasury has not yet amended Reg § 1.221-1 to reflect changes made by P.L. 108-357.

(a) In general. *(1) Applicability.* Under section 221, an individual taxpayer may deduct from gross income certain interest paid by the taxpayer during the taxable year on a qualified education loan. See paragraph (b)(4) of this section for rules on payments of interest by third parties. The rules of this section are applicable to periods governed by section 221 as amended in 2001, which relates to deductions for interest paid on qualified education loans after December 31, 2001, in taxable years ending after December 31, 2001, and on or before December 31, 2010. For rules applicable to interest due and paid on qualified education loans after January 21, 1999, if paid before January 1, 2002, see § 1.221-2. Taxpayers also may apply § 1.221-2 to interest due and paid on qualified education loans after December 31, 1997, but before January 21, 1999. To the extent that the effective date limitation (sunset) of the 2001 amendment remains in force unchanged, section 221 before amendment in 2001, to which § 1.221-2 relates, also applies to interest due and paid on qualified education loans in taxable years beginning after December 31, 2010.

(2) Example. The following example illustrates the rules of this paragraph (a). In the example, assume that the institution the student attends is an eligible educational institution, the loan is a qualified education loan, the student is legally obligated to make interest payments under the terms of the loan, and any other applicable requirements, if not otherwise specified, are fulfilled. The example is as follows:

Example. Effective dates. Student A begins to make monthly interest payments on her loan beginning January 1, 1997. Student A continues to make interest payments in a timely fashion. However, under the effective date provisions of section 221, no deduction is allowed for interest Student A pays prior to January 1, 1998. Student A may deduct interest due and paid on the loan after December 31, 1997. Student A may apply the rules of § 1.221-2 to interest due and paid during the period beginning January 1, 1998, and ending January 20, 1999. Interest due and paid during the period January 21, 1999, and ending December 31, 2001, is deductible under the rules of § 1.221-2, and interest paid after December 31, 2001, is deductible under the rules of this section.

(b) Eligibility. *(1) Taxpayer must have a legal obligation to make interest payments.* A taxpayer is entitled to a deduction under section 221 only if the taxpayer has a legal obligation to make interest payments under the terms of the qualified education loan.

(2) Claimed dependents not eligible. (i) In general. An individual is not entitled to a deduction under section 221 for a taxable year if the individual is a dependent (as defined in section 152) for whom another taxpayer is allowed a deduction under section 151 on a Federal income tax return for the same taxable year (or, in the case of a fiscal year taxpayer, the taxable year beginning in the same calendar year as the individual's taxable year).

(ii) Examples. The following examples illustrate the rules of this paragraph (b)(2):

Example (1). Student not claimed as dependent. Student B pays $750 of interest on qualified education loans during 2003. Student B's parents are not allowed a deduction for her as a dependent for 2003. Assuming fulfillment of all other relevant requirements, Student B may deduct under section 221 the $750 of interest paid in 2003.

Example (2). Student claimed as dependent. Student C pays $750 of interest on qualified education loans during 2003. Only Student C has the legal obligation to make the payments. Student C's parent claims him as a dependent and is allowed a deduction under section 151 with respect to Student C in computing the parent's 2003 Federal income tax. Student C is not entitled to a deduction under section 221 for the $750 of interest paid in 2003. Because Student C's parent was not legally obligated to make the payments, Student C's parent also is not entitled to a deduction for the interest.

(3) Married taxpayers. If a taxpayer is married as of the close of a taxable year, he or she is entitled to a deduction under this section only if the taxpayer and the taxpayer's spouse file a joint return for that taxable year.

(4) Payments of interest by a third party. (i) In general. If a third party who is not legally obligated to make a payment of interest on a qualified education loan makes a payment of interest on behalf of a taxpayer who is legally obligated to make the payment, then the taxpayer is treated as receiving the payment from the third party and, in turn, paying the interest.

(ii) Examples. The following examples illustrate the rules of this paragraph (b)(4):

Example (1). Payment by employer. Student D obtains a qualified education loan to attend college. Upon Student D's graduation from college, Student D works as an intern for a non-profit organization during which time Student D's loan is in deferment and Student D makes no interest payments. As part of the internship program, the non-profit organization makes an interest payment on behalf of Student D after the deferment period. This payment is not excluded from Student D's income under section 108(f) and is treated as additional compensation includible in Student D's gross income. Assuming fulfillment of all other requirements of section 221, Student D may deduct this payment of interest for Federal income tax purposes.

Example (2). Payment by parent. Student E obtains a qualified education loan to attend college. Upon graduation from college, Student E makes legally required monthly payments of principal and interest. Student E's mother makes a required monthly payment of interest as a gift to Student E. A deduction for Student E as a dependent is not allowed on another taxpayer's tax return for that taxable year. Assuming fulfillment of all other requirements of section 221, Student E may deduct this payment of interest for Federal income tax purposes.

(c) Maximum deduction. The amount allowed as a deduction under section 221 for any taxable year may not exceed $2,500.

(d) Limitation based on modified adjusted gross income. *(1) In general.* The deduction allowed under section 221 is phased out ratably for taxpayers with modified adjusted gross income between $50,000 and $65,000 ($100,000 and $130,000 for married individuals who file a joint return). Section 221 does not allow a deduction for taxpayers with modified adjusted gross income of $65,000 or above ($130,000 or above for married individuals who file a joint return). See paragraph (d)(3) of this section for inflation adjustment of amounts in this paragraph (d)(1).

(2) Modified adjusted gross income defined. The term modified adjusted gross income means the adjusted gross income (as defined in section 62) of the taxpayer for the taxable year increased by any amount excluded from gross income under section 911, 931, or 933 (relating to income earned abroad or from certain United States possessions or Puerto Rico). Modified adjusted gross income must be determined under this section after taking into account the inclusions, exclusions, deductions, and limitations provided by sections 86 (social security and tier 1 railroad retirement benefits), 135 (redemption of qualified United States savings bonds), 137 (adoption assistance programs), 219 (deductible qualified retirement contributions), and 469 (limitation on passive activity losses and credits), but before taking into account the deductions provided by sections 221 and 222 (qualified tuition and related expenses).

(3) Inflation adjustment. For taxable years beginning after 2002, the amounts in paragraph (d)(1) of this section will be increased for inflation occurring after 2001 in accordance with section 221(f)(1). If any amount adjusted under section 221(f)(1) is not a multiple of $5,000, the amount will be rounded to the next lowest multiple of $5,000.

(e) Definitions. *(1) Eligible educational institution.* In general, an eligible educational institution means any college, university, vocational school, or other postsecondary educational institution described in section 481 of the Higher Education Act of 1965 (20 U.S.C. 1088), as in effect on August 5, 1997, and certified by the U.S. Department of Education as eligible to participate in student aid programs administered by the Department, as described in section 25A(f)(2) and § 1.25A-2(b). For purposes of this section, an eligible educational institution also includes an institution that conducts an internship or residency program leading to a degree or certificate awarded by an institution, a hospital, or a health care facility that offers postgraduate training.

(2) Qualified higher education expenses. (i) In general. Qualified higher education expenses means the cost of attendance (as defined in section 472 of the Higher Education Act of 1965, 20 U.S.C. 1087ll, as in effect on August 4, 1997), at an eligible educational institution, reduced by the amounts described in paragraph (e)(2)(ii) of this section. Consistent with section 472 of the Higher Education Act of 1965, a student's cost of attendance is determined by the eligible educational institution and includes tuition and fees normally assessed a student carrying the same academic workload as the student, an allowance for room and board, and an allowance for books, supplies, transportation, and miscellaneous expenses of the student.

(ii) Reductions. Qualified higher education expenses are reduced by any amount that is paid to or on behalf of a student with respect to such expenses and that is—

(A) A qualified scholarship that is excludable from income under section 117;

(B) An educational assistance allowance for a veteran or member of the armed forces under chapter 30, 31, 32, 34 or 35 of title 38, United States Code, or under chapter 1606 of title 10, United States Code;

(C) Employer-provided educational assistance that is excludable from income under section 127;

(D) Any other amount that is described in section 25A(g)(2)(C) (relating to amounts excludable from gross income as educational assistance);

(E) Any otherwise includible amount excluded from gross income under section 135 (relating to the redemption of United States savings bonds);

(F) Any otherwise includible amount distributed from a Coverdell education savings account and excluded from gross income under section 530(d)(2); or

(G) Any otherwise includible amount distributed from a qualified tuition program and excluded from gross income under section 529(c)(3)(B).

(3) Qualified education loan. (i) In general. A qualified education loan means indebtedness incurred by a taxpayer solely to pay qualified higher education expenses that are—

(A) Incurred on behalf of a student who is the taxpayer, the taxpayer's spouse, or a dependent (as defined in section 152) of the taxpayer at the time the taxpayer incurs the indebtedness;

(B) Attributable to education provided during an academic period, as described in section 25A and the regulations thereunder, when the student is an eligible student as defined in section 25A(b)(3) (requiring that the student be a degree candidate carrying at least half the normal full-time workload); and

(C) Paid or incurred within a reasonable period of time before or after the taxpayer incurs the indebtedness.

(ii) Reasonable period. Except as otherwise provided in this paragraph (e)(3)(ii), what constitutes a reasonable period of time for purposes of paragraph (e)(3)(i)(C) of this section generally is determined based on all the relevant facts and circumstances. However, qualified higher education expenses are treated as paid or incurred within a reasonable period of time before or after the taxpayer incurs the indebtedness if—

(A) The expenses are paid with the proceeds of education loans that are part of a Federal postsecondary education loan program; or

(B) The expenses relate to a particular academic period and the loan proceeds used to pay the expenses are disbursed within a period that begins 90 days prior to the start of that academic period and ends 90 days after the end of that academic period.

(iii) Related party. A qualified education loan does not include any indebtedness owed to a person who is related to the taxpayer, within the meaning of section 267(b) or 707(b)(1). For example, a parent or grandparent of the taxpayer is a related person. In addition, a qualified education loan does not include a loan made under any qualified employer plan as defined in section 72(p)(4) or under any contract referred to in section 72(p)(5).

(iv) Federal issuance or guarantee not required. A loan does not have to be issued or guaranteed under a Federal postsecondary education loan program to be a qualified education loan.

(v) Refinanced and consolidated indebtedness. (A) In general. A qualified education loan includes indebtedness incurred solely to refinance a qualified education loan. A qualified education loan includes a single, consolidated indebtedness incurred solely to refinance two or more qualified education loans of a borrower.

(B) Treatment of refinanced and consolidated indebtedness. [Reserved.]

(4) Examples. The following examples illustrate the rules of this paragraph (e):

Example (1). Eligible educational institution. University F is a postsecondary educational institution described in section 481 of the Higher Education Act of 1965. The U.S. Department of Education has certified that University F is eligible to participate in federal financial aid programs administered by that Department, although University F chooses not to participate. University F is an eligible educational institution.

Example (2). Qualified higher education expenses. Student G receives a $3,000 qualified scholarship for the 2003 fall semester that is excludable from Student G's gross income under section 117. Student G receives no other forms of financial assistance with respect to the 2003 fall semester. Student G's cost of attendance for the 2003 fall semester, as determined by Student G's eligible educational institution for purposes of calculating a student's financial need in accordance with section 472 of the Higher Education Act, is $16,000. For the 2003 fall semester, Student G has qualified higher education expenses of $13,000 (the cost of attendance as determined by the institution ($16,000) reduced by the qualified scholarship proceeds excludable from gross income ($3,000)).

Example (3). Qualified education loan. Student H borrows money from a commercial bank to pay qualified higher education expenses related to his enrollment on a half-time basis in a graduate program at an eligible educational institution. Student H uses all the loan proceeds to pay qualified higher education expenses incurred within a reasonable period of time after incurring the indebtedness. The loan is not federally guaranteed. The commercial bank is not related to Student H within the meaning of section 267(b) or 707(b)(1). Student H's loan is a qualified education loan within the meaning of section 221.

Example (4). Qualified education loan. Student I signs a promissory note for a loan on August 15, 2003, to pay for qualified higher education expenses for the 2003 fall and 2004 spring semesters. On August 20, 2003, the lender disburses loan proceeds to Student I's college. The college credits them to Student I's account to pay qualified higher education expenses for the 2003 fall semester, which begins on August 25, 2003. On January 26, 2004, the lender disburses additional loan proceeds to Student I's college. The college credits them to Student I's account to pay qualified higher education expenses for the 2004 spring semester, which began on January 12, 2004. Student I's qualified higher education expenses for the two semesters are paid within a reasonable period of time, as the first loan disbursement occurred within the 90 days prior to the start of the fall 2003 semester and the second loan disbursement occurred during the spring 2004 semester.

Example (5). Qualified education loan. The facts are the same as in Example 4 except that in 2005 the college is not an eligible educational institution because it loses its eligibility to participate in certain federal financial aid programs administered by the U.S. Department of Education. The qualification of Student I's loan, which was used to pay for qualified higher education expenses for the 2003 fall and 2004 spring semesters, as a qualified education loan is not affected by the college's subsequent loss of eligibility.

Example (6). Mixed-use loans. Student J signs a promissory note for a loan secured by Student J's personal residence. Student J will use part of the loan proceeds to pay for certain improvements to Student J's residence and part of the loan proceeds to pay qualified higher education expenses of Student J's spouse. Because Student J obtains the loan not solely to pay qualified higher education expenses, the loan is not a qualified education loan.

(f) Interest. *(1) In general.* Amounts paid on a qualified education loan are deductible under section 221 if the amounts are interest for Federal income tax purposes. For example, interest includes—

(i) Qualified stated interest (as defined in § 1.1273-1(c)); and

(ii) Original issue discount, which generally includes capitalized interest. For purposes of section 221, capitalized interest means any accrued and unpaid interest on a qualified education loan that, in accordance with the terms of the loan, is added by the lender to the outstanding principal balance of the loan.

(2) Operative rules for original issue discount. (i) In general. The rules to determine the amount of original issue discount on a loan and the accruals of the discount are in sections 163(e), 1271 through 1275, and the regulations thereunder. In general, original issue discount is the excess of a loan's stated redemption price at maturity (all payments due under the loan other than qualified stated interest payments) over its issue price (the amount loaned). Although original issue discount generally is deductible as it accrues under section 163(e) and § 1.163-7, original issue discount on a qualified education loan is not deductible until paid. See paragraph (f)(3) of this section to determine when original issue discount is paid.

(ii) Treatment of loan origination fees by the borrower. If a loan origination fee is paid by the borrower other than for property or services provided by the lender, the fee reduces the issue price of the loan, which creates original issue discount (or additional original issue discount) on the loan in an amount equal to the fee. See § 1.1273-2(g). For an example of how a loan origination fee is taken into account, see Example 2 of paragraph (f)(4) of this section.

(3) Allocation of payments. See §§ 1.446-2(e) and 1.1275-2(a) for rules on allocating payments between interest and principal. In general, these rules treat a payment first as a payment of interest to the extent of the interest that has accrued and remains unpaid as of the date the payment is due, and second as a payment of principal. The characterization of a payment as either interest or principal under these rules applies regardless of how the parties label the payment (ei-

ther as interest or principal). Accordingly, the taxpayer may deduct the portion of a payment labeled as principal that these rules treat as a payment of interest on the loan, including any portion attributable to capitalized interest or loan origination fees.

(4) Examples. The following examples illustrate the rules of this paragraph (f). In the examples, assume that the institution the student attends is an eligible educational institution, the loan is a qualified education loan, the student is legally obligated to make interest payments under the terms of the loan, and any other applicable requirements, if not otherwise specified, are fulfilled. The examples are as follows:

Example (1). Capitalized interest. Interest on Student K's loan accrues while Student K is in school, but Student K is not required to make any payments on the loan until six months after he graduates or otherwise leaves school. At that time, the lender capitalizes all accrued but unpaid interest and adds it to the outstanding principal amount of the loan. Thereafter, Student K is required to make monthly payments of interest and principal on the loan. The interest payable on the loan, including the capitalized interest, is original issue discount. See section 1273 and the regulations thereunder. Therefore, in determining the total amount of interest paid on the loan each taxable year, Student K may deduct any payments that § 1.1275-2(a) treats as payments of interest, including any principal payments that are treated as payments of capitalized interest. See paragraph (f)(3) of this section.

Example (2). Allocation of payments. The facts are the same as in Example 1, except that, in addition, the lender charges Student K a loan origination fee, which is not for any property or services provided by the lender. Under § 1.1273-2(g), the loan origination fee reduces the issue price of the loan, which reduction increases the amount of original issue discount on the loan by the amount of the fee. The amount of original issue discount (which includes the capitalized interest and loan origination fee) that accrues each year is determined under section 1272 and § 1.1272-1. In effect, the loan origination fee accrues over the entire term of the loan. Because the loan has original issue discount, the payment ordering rules in § 1.1275-2(a) must be used to determine how much of each payment is interest for federal tax purposes. See paragraph (f)(3) of this section. Under § 1.1275-2(a), each payment (regardless of its designation by the parties as either interest or principal) generally is treated first as a payment of original issue discount, to the extent of the original issue discount that has accrued as of the date the payment is due and has not been allocated to prior payments, and second as a payment of principal. Therefore, in determining the total amount of interest paid on the qualified education loan for a taxable year, Student K may deduct any payments that the parties label as principal but that are treated as payments of original issue discount under § 1.1275-2(a).

(g) Additional rules. *(1) Payment of interest made during period when interest payment not required.* Payments of interest on a qualified education loan to which this section is applicable are deductible even if the payments are made during a period when interest payments are not required because, for example, the loan has not yet entered repayment status or is in a period of deferment or forbearance.

(2) Denial of double benefit. No deduction is allowed under this section for any amount for which a deduction is allowable under another provision of Chapter 1 of the Internal Revenue Code. No deduction is allowed under this section for any amount for which an exclusion is allowable under section 108(f) (relating to cancellation of indebtedness).

(3) Examples. The following examples illustrate the rules of this paragraph (g). In the examples, assume that the institution the student attends is an eligible educational institution, the loan is a qualified education loan, and the student is legally obligated to make interest payments under the terms of the loan:

Example (1). Voluntary payment of interest before loan has entered repayment status. Student L obtains a loan to attend college. The terms of the loan provide that interest accrues on the loan while Student L earns his undergraduate degree but that Student L is not required to begin making payments of interest until six full calendar months after he graduates or otherwise leaves school. Nevertheless, Student L voluntarily pays interest on the loan during 2003, while enrolled in college. Assuming all other relevant requirements are met, Student L is allowed a deduction for interest paid while attending college even though the payments were made before interest payments were required.

Example (2). Voluntary payment during period of deferment or forbearance. The facts are the same as in Example 2, except that Student L makes no payments on the loan while enrolled in college. Student L graduates in June 2003 and begins making monthly payments of principal and interest on the loan in January 2004, as required by the terms of the loan. In August 2004, Student L enrolls in graduate school on a full-time basis. Under the terms of the loan, Student L may apply for deferment of the loan payments while Student L is enrolled in graduate school. Student L applies for and receives a deferment on the outstanding loan. However, Student L continues to make some monthly payments of interest during graduate school. Student L may deduct interest paid on the loan during the period beginning in January 2004, including interest paid while Student L is enrolled in graduate school.

(h) Effective date. This section is applicable to periods governed by section 221 as amended in 2001, which relates to interest paid on a qualified education loan after December 31, 2001, in taxable years ending after December 31, 2001, and on or before December 31, 2010.

T.D. 9125, 5/6/2004.

§ 1.221-2 Deduction for interest due and paid on qualified education loans before January 1, 2002.

(a) In general. Under section 221, an individual taxpayer may deduct from gross income certain interest due and paid by the taxpayer during the taxable year on a qualified education loan. The deduction is allowed only with respect to interest due and paid on a qualified education loan during the first 60 months that interest payments are required under the terms of the loan. See paragraph (e) of this section for rules relating to the 60-month rule. See paragraph (b)(4) of this section for rules on payments of interest by third parties. The rules of this section are applicable to interest due and paid on qualified education loans after January 21, 1999, if paid before January 1, 2002. Taxpayers also may apply the rules of this section to interest due and paid on qualified education loans after December 31, 1997, but before January 21, 1999. To the extent that the effective date limitation ("sunset") of the 2001 amendment remains in force unchanged, section 221 before amendment in 2001, to which this section relates, also applies to interest due and paid on qualified education loans in taxable years beginning after December 31, 2010. For rules applicable to periods governed by section 221 as amended in 2001, which relates to deductions for interest paid on qualified education loans after December 31, 2001, in taxable years ending after December 31, 2001, and before January 1, 2011, see § 1.221-1.

(b) Eligibility. *(1) Taxpayer must have a legal obligation to make interest payments.* A taxpayer is entitled to a deduction under section 221 only if the taxpayer has a legal obligation to make interest payments under the terms of the qualified education loan.

(2) Claimed dependents not eligible. (i) In general. An individual is not entitled to a deduction under section 221 for a taxable year if the individual is a dependent (as defined in section 152) for whom another taxpayer is allowed a deduction under section 151 on a Federal income tax return for the same taxable year (or, in the case of a fiscal year taxpayer, the taxable year beginning in the same calendar year as the individual's taxable year).

(ii) Examples. The following examples illustrate the rules of this paragraph (b)(2):

Example (1). Student not claimed as dependent. Student A pays $750 of interest on qualified education loans during 1998. Student A's parents are not allowed a deduction for her as a dependent for 1998. Assuming fulfillment of all other relevant requirements, Student A may deduct the $750 of interest paid in 1998 under section 221.

Example (2). Student claimed as dependent. Student B pays $750 of interest on qualified education loans during 1998. Only Student B has the legal obligation to make the payments. Student B's parent claims him as a dependent and is allowed a deduction under section 151 with respect to Student B in computing the parent's 1998 Federal income tax. Student B may not deduct the $750 of interest paid in 1998 under section 221. Because Student B's parent was not legally obligated to make the payments, Student B's parent also may not deduct the interest.

(3) Married taxpayers. If a taxpayer is married as of the close of a taxable year, he or she is entitled to a deduction under this section only if the taxpayer and the taxpayer's spouse file a joint return for that taxable year.

(4) Payments of interest by a third party. (i) In general. If a third party who is not legally obligated to make a payment of interest on a qualified education loan makes a payment of interest on behalf of a taxpayer who is legally obligated to make the payment, then the taxpayer is treated as receiving the payment from the third party and, in turn, paying the interest.

(ii) Examples. The following examples illustrate the rules of this paragraph (b)(4):

Example (1). Payment by employer. Student C obtains a qualified education loan to attend college. Upon Student C's graduation from college, Student C works as an intern for a non-profit organization during which time Student C's loan is in deferment and Student C makes no interest payments. As part of the internship program, the non-profit organization makes an interest payment on behalf of Student C after the deferment period. This payment is not excluded from Student C's income under section 108(f) and is treated as additional compensation includible in Student C's gross income. Assuming fulfillment of all other requirements of section 221, Student C may deduct this payment of interest for Federal income tax purposes.

Example (2). Payment by parent. Student D obtains a qualified education loan to attend college. Upon graduation from college, Student D makes legally required monthly payments of principal and interest. Student D's mother makes a required monthly payment of interest as a gift to Student D. A deduction for Student D as a dependent is not allowed on another taxpayer's tax return for that taxable year. Assuming fulfillment of all other requirements of section 221, Student D may deduct this payment of interest for Federal income tax purposes.

(c) Maximum deduction. In any taxable year beginning before January 1, 2002, the amount allowed as a deduction under section 221 may not exceed the amount determined in accordance with the following table:

Taxable year beginning in:	Maximum deduction
1998	$1,000
1999	1,500
2000	2,000
2001	2,500

(d) Limitation based on modified adjusted gross income. *(1) In general.* The deduction allowed under section 221 is phased out ratably for taxpayers with modified adjusted gross income between $40,000 and $55,000 ($60,000 and $75,000 for married individuals who file a joint return). Section 221 does not allow a deduction for taxpayers with modified adjusted gross income of $55,000 or above ($75,000 or above for married individuals who file a joint return).

(2) Modified adjusted gross income defined. The term modified adjusted gross income means the adjusted gross income (as defined in section 62) of the taxpayer for the taxable year increased by any amount excluded from gross income under section 911, 931, or 933 (relating to income earned abroad or from certain United States possessions or Puerto Rico). Modified adjusted gross income must be determined under this section after taking into account the inclusions, exclusions, deductions, and limitations provided by sections 86 (social security and tier 1 railroad retirement benefits), 135 (redemption of qualified United States savings bonds), 137 (adoption assistance programs), 219 (deductible qualified retirement contributions), and 469 (limitation on passive activity losses and credits), but before taking into account the deduction provided by section 221.

(e) 60-month rule. *(1) In general.* A deduction for interest paid on a qualified education loan is allowed only for payments made during the first 60 months that interest payments are required on the loan. The 60-month period begins on the first day of the month that includes the date on which interest payments are first required and ends 60 months later, unless the 60-month period is suspended for periods of deferment or forbearance within the meaning of paragraph (e)(3) of this section. The 60-month period continues to run regardless of whether the required interest payments are actually made. The date on which the first interest payment is required is determined under the terms of the loan agreement or, in the case of a loan issued or guaranteed under a federal postsecondary education loan program (such as loan programs under Title IV of the Higher Education Act of 1965 (20 U.S.C. 1070) and Titles VII and VIII of the Public Health Service Act (42 U.S.C. 292., and 42 U.S.C. 296)) under applicable Federal regulations. For a discussion of interest, see paragraph (h) of this section. For special rules relating to loan refinancings, consolidated loans, and collapsed loans, see paragraph (i) of this section.

(2) Loans that entered repayment status prior to January 1, 1998. In the case of any qualified education loan that entered repayment status prior to January 1, 1998, section 221 allows no deduction for interest paid during the portion of the 60-month period described in paragraph (e)(1) of this section that occurred prior to January 1, 1998. Section 221 allows a deduction only for interest due and paid during that portion, if any, of the 60-month period remaining after December 31, 1997.

(3) Periods of deferment or forbearance. The 60-month period described in paragraph (e)(1) of this section generally is suspended for any period when interest payments are not required on a qualified education loan because the lender has granted the taxpayer a period of deferment or forbearance (including postponement in anticipation of cancellation). However, in the case of a qualified education loan that is not issued or guaranteed under a Federal postsecondary education loan program, the 60-month period will be suspended under this paragraph (e)(3) only if the promissory note contains conditions substantially similar to the conditions for deferment or forbearance established by the U.S. Department of Education for Federal student loan programs under Title IV of the Higher Education Act of 1965, such as half-time study at a postsecondary educational institution, study in an approved graduate fellowship program or in an approved rehabilitation program for the disabled, inability to find full-time employment, economic hardship, or the performance of services in certain occupations or federal programs, and the borrower satisfies one of those conditions. For any qualified education loan, the 60-month period is not suspended if under the terms of the loan interest continues to accrue while the loan is in deferment or forbearance and either—

(i) In the case of deferment, the taxpayer agrees to pay interest currently during the deferment period; or

(ii) In the case of forbearance, the taxpayer agrees to make reduced payments, or payments of interest only, during the forbearance period.

(4) Late payments. A deduction is allowed for a payment of interest required in one month but actually made in a subsequent month prior to the expiration of the 60-month period. A deduction is not allowed for a payment of interest required in one month but actually made in a subsequent month after the expiration of the 60-month period. A late payment made during a period of deferment or forbearance is treated, solely for purposes of determining whether it is made during the 60-month period, as made on the date it is due.

(5) Examples. The following examples illustrate the rules of this paragraph (e). In the examples, assume that the institution the student attends is an eligible educational institution, the loan is a qualified education loan and is issued or guaranteed under a federal postsecondary education loan program, the student is legally obligated to make interest payments under the terms of the loan, the interest payments occur after December 31, 1997, but before January 1, 2002, and with respect to any period after December 31, 1997, but before January 21, 1999, the taxpayer elects to apply the rules of this section. The examples are as follows:

Example (1). Payment prior to 60-month period. Student E obtains a loan to attend college. The terms of the loan provide that interest accrues on the loan while Student E earns his undergraduate degree but that Student E is not required to begin making payments of interest until six full calendar months after he graduates. Nevertheless, Student E voluntarily pays interest on the loan while attending college. Student E is not allowed a deduction for interest paid during that period, because those payments were made prior to the start of the 60-month period. Similarly, Student E would not be allowed a deduction for any interest paid during the six month grace period after graduation when interest payments are not required.

Example (2). Deferment option not exercised. The facts are the same as in Example 1 except that Student E makes no payments on the loan while enrolled in college. Student E graduates in June 1999, and is required to begin making monthly payments of principal and interest on the loan in January 2000. The 60-month period described in paragraph (e)(1) of this section begins in January 2000. In August 2000, Student E enrolls in graduate school on a full-time basis. Under the terms of the loan, Student E may apply for deferment of the loan payments while enrolled in graduate school. However, Student E elects not to apply for deferment and continues to make required monthly payments on the loan during graduate school. Assuming fulfillment of all other relevant requirements, Student E may deduct interest paid on the loan during the 60-month period beginning in January 2000, including interest paid while enrolled in graduate school.

Example (3). Late payment, within 60-month period. The facts are the same as in Example 2 except that, after the loan enters repayment status in January 2000, Student E makes no interest payments until March 2000. In March 2000, Student E pays interest required for the months of January, February, and March 2000. Assuming fulfillment of all other relevant requirements, Student E may deduct the interest paid in March for the months of January, February, and March because the interest payments are required under the terms of the loan and are paid within the 60-month period, even though the January and February interest payments may be late.

Example (4). Late payment during deferment but within 60-month period. The terms of Student F's loan require her to begin making monthly payments of interest on the loan in January 2000. The 60-month period described in paragraph (e)(1) of this section begins in January 2000. Student F fails to make the required interest payments for the months of November and December 2000. In January 2001, Student F enrolls in graduate school on a half-time basis. Under the terms of the loan, Student F obtains a deferment of the loan payments due while enrolled in graduate school. The deferment becomes effective January 1, 2001. In March 2001, while the loan is in deferment, Student F pays the interest due for the months of November and December 2000. Assuming fulfillment of all other relevant requirements, Student F may deduct interest paid in March 2001, for the months of November and December 2000, because the late interest payments are treated, solely for purposes of determining whether they were made during the 60-month period, as made in November and December 2000.

Example (5). 60-month period. The terms of Student G's loan require him to begin making monthly payments of interest on the loan in November 1999. The 60-month period described in paragraph (e)(1) of this section begins in November 1999. In January 2000, Student G enrolls in graduate school on a half-time basis. As permitted under the terms of the loan, Student G applies for deferment of the loan payments due while enrolled in graduate school. While awaiting formal approval from the lender of his request for deferment, Student G pays interest due for the month of January 2000. In February 2000, the lender approves Student G's request for deferment, effective as of January 1, 2000. Assuming fulfillment of all other relevant requirements, Student G may deduct interest paid in January 2000, prior to his receipt of the lender's approval, even though the deferment was retroactive to January 1, 2000. As of February 2000, there are 57 months remaining in the 60-month period for that loan. Because Student G is not required to make interest payments during the period of deferment, the 60-month period is suspended. After January 2000, Student G may not deduct any voluntary payments of interest made during the period of deferment.

Example (6). 60-month period. The terms of Student H's loan require her to begin making monthly payments of interest on the loan in November 1999. The 60-month period described in paragraph (e)(1) of this section begins in November 1999. In January 2000, Student H enrolls in graduate school on a half-time basis. As permitted under the terms of the loan, Student H applies to make reduced payments of principal and interest while enrolled in graduate school. After the lender approves her application, Student H pays principal and interest due for the month of January 2000 at the reduced rate. Assuming fulfillment of all other relevant requirements, Student H may deduct interest paid in January 2000. As of February 2000, there are 57 months remaining in the 60-month period for that loan.

Example (7). Reduction of 60-month period for months prior to January 1, 1998. The first payment of interest on a loan is due in January 1997. Thereafter, interest payments are required on a monthly basis. The 60-month period described in paragraph (e)(1) of this section for this loan begins on January 1, 1997, the first day of the month that includes the date on which the first interest payment is required. However, the borrower may not deduct interest paid prior to January 1, 1998, under the effective date provisions of section 221. Assuming fulfillment of all other relevant requirements, the borrower may deduct interest due and paid on the loan during the 48 months beginning on January 1, 1998 (unless such period is extended for periods of deferment or forbearance under paragraph (e)(3) of this section).

(f) Definitions. *(1) Eligible educational institution.* In general, an eligible educational institution means any college, university, vocational school, or other post-secondary educational institution described in section 481 of the Higher Education Act of 1965, 20 U.S.C. 1088, as in effect on August 5, 1997, and certified by the U.S. Department of Education as eligible to participate in student aid programs administered by the Department, as described in section 25A(f)(2) and § 1.25A-2(b). For purposes of this section, an eligible educational institution also includes an institution that conducts an internship or residency program leading to a degree or certificate awarded by an institution, a hospital, or a health care facility that offers postgraduate training.

(2) Qualified higher education expenses. (i) In general. Qualified higher education expenses means the cost of attendance (as defined in section 472 of the Higher Education Act of 1965, 20 U.S.C. 1087ll, as in effect on August 4, 1997), at an eligible educational institution, reduced by the amounts described in paragraph (f)(2)(ii) of this section. Consistent with section 472 of the Higher Education Act of 1965, a student's cost of attendance is determined by the eligible educational institution and includes tuition and fees normally assessed a student carrying the same academic workload as the student, an allowance for room and board, and an allowance for books, supplies, transportation, and miscellaneous expenses of the student.

(ii) Reductions. Qualified higher education expenses are reduced by any amount that is paid to or on behalf of a student with respect to such expenses and that is—

(A) A qualified scholarship that is excludable from income under section 117;

(B) An educational assistance allowance for a veteran or member of the armed forces under chapter 30, 31, 32, 34 or 35 of title 38, United States Code, or under chapter 1606 of title 10, United States Code;

(C) Employer-provided educational assistance that is excludable from income under section 127;

(D) Any other amount that is described in section 25A(g)(2)(C) (relating to amounts excludable from gross income as educational assistance);

(E) Any otherwise includible amount excluded from gross income under section 135 (relating to the redemption of United States savings bonds); or

(F) Any otherwise includible amount distributed from a Coverdell education savings account and excluded from gross income under section 530(d)(2).

(3) Qualified education loan. (i) In general. A qualified education loan means indebtedness incurred by a taxpayer solely to pay qualified higher education expenses that are—

(A) Incurred on behalf of a student who is the taxpayer, the taxpayer's spouse, or a dependent (as defined in section 152) of the taxpayer at the time the taxpayer incurs the indebtedness;

(B) Attributable to education provided during an academic period, as described in section 25A and the regulations thereunder, when the student is an eligible student as defined in section 25A(b)(3) (requiring that the student be a degree candidate carrying at least half the normal full-time workload); and

(C) Paid or incurred within a reasonable period of time before or after the taxpayer incurs the indebtedness.

(ii) Reasonable period. Except as otherwise provided in this paragraph (f)(3)(ii), what constitutes a reasonable period of time for purposes of paragraph (f)(3)(i)(C) of this section generally is determined based on all the relevant facts and circumstances. However, qualified higher education expenses are treated as paid or incurred within a reasonable period of time before or after the taxpayer incurs the indebtedness if—

(A) The expenses are paid with the proceeds of education loans that are part of a federal postsecondary education loan program; or

(B) The expenses relate to a particular academic period and the loan proceeds used to pay the expenses are disbursed within a period that begins 90 days prior to the start of that academic period and ends 90 days after the end of that academic period.

(iii) Related party. A qualified education loan does not include any indebtedness owed to a person who is related to the taxpayer, within the meaning of section 267(b) or 707(b)(1). For example, a parent or grandparent of the taxpayer is a related person. In addition, a qualified education loan does not include a loan made under any qualified employer plan as defined in section 72(p)(4) or under any contract referred to in section 72(p)(5).

(iv) Federal issuance or guarantee not required. A loan does not have to be issued or guaranteed under a federal postsecondary education loan program to be a qualified education loan.

(v) Refinanced and consolidated indebtedness. (A) In general. A qualified education loan includes indebtedness incurred solely to refinance a qualified education loan. A qualified education loan includes a single, consolidated indebtedness incurred solely to refinance two or more qualified education loans of a borrower.

(B) Treatment of refinanced and consolidated indebtedness. [Reserved.]

(4) Examples. The following examples illustrate the rules of this paragraph (f):

Example (1). Eligible educational institution. University J is a postsecondary educational institution described in section 481 of the Higher Education Act of 1965. The U.S. Department of Education has certified that University J is eligible to participate in federal financial aid programs administered by that Department, although University J chooses not to participate. University J is an eligible educational institution.

Example (2). Qualified higher education expenses. Student K receives a $3,000 qualified scholarship for the 1999 fall semester that is excludable from Student K's gross income under section 117. Student K receives no other forms of financial assistance with respect to the 1999 fall semester. Student K's cost of attendance for the 1999 fall semester, as determined by Student K's eligible educational institution for purposes of calculating a student's financial need in accordance with section 472 of the Higher Education Act, is $16,000. For the 1999 fall semester, Student K has qualified higher education expenses of $13,000 (the cost of attendance as determined by the institution ($16,000) reduced by the qualified scholarship proceeds excludable from gross income ($3,000)).

Example (3). Qualified education loan. Student L borrows money from a commercial bank to pay qualified higher education expenses related to his enrollment on a half-time basis in a graduate program at an eligible educational institution. Student L uses all the loan proceeds to pay qualified higher education expenses incurred within a reasonable period of time after incurring the indebtedness. The loan is not federally guaranteed. The commercial bank is not related to Student L within the meaning of section 267(b) or 707(b)(1). Student L's loan is a qualified education loan within the meaning of section 221.

Example (4). Qualified education loan. Student M signs a promissory note for a loan on August 15, 1999, to pay for qualified higher education expenses for the 1999 fall and 2000 spring semesters. On August 20, 1999, the lender disburses loan proceeds to Student M's college. The college credits them to Student M's account to pay qualified higher education expenses for the 1999 fall semester, which begins on August 23, 1999. On January 25, 2000, the lender disburses additional loan proceeds to Student M's college. The college credits them to Student M's account to pay qualified higher education expenses for the 2000 spring semester, which began on January 10, 2000. Student M's qualified higher education expenses for the two semesters are paid within a reasonable period of time, as the first loan disbursement occurred within the 90 days prior to the start of the fall 1999 semester, and the second loan disbursement occurred during the spring 2000 semester.

Example (5). Qualified education loan. The facts are the same as in Example 4, except that in 2001 the college is not an eligible educational institution because it loses its eligibility to participate in certain federal financial aid programs administered by the U.S. Department of Education. The qualification of Student M's loan, which was used to pay for qualified higher education expenses for the 1999 fall and 2000 spring semesters, as a qualified education loan is not affected by the college's subsequent loss of eligibility.

Example (6). Mixed-use loans. Student N signs a promissory note for a loan that is secured by Student N's personal residence. Student N will use part of the loan proceeds to pay for certain improvements to Student N's residence and part of the loan proceeds to pay qualified higher education expenses of Student N's spouse. Because Student N obtains the loan not solely to pay qualified higher education expenses, the loan is not a qualified education loan.

(g) Denial of double benefit. No deduction is allowed under this section for any amount for which a deduction is allowable under another provision of Chapter 1 of the Internal Revenue Code. No deduction is allowed under this section for any amount for which an exclusion is allowable under section 108(f) (relating to cancellation of indebtedness).

(h) Interest. *(1) In general.* Amounts paid on a qualified education loan are deductible under section 221 if the amounts are interest for Federal income tax purposes. For example, interest includes—

(i) Qualified stated interest (as defined in § 1.1273-1(c)); and

(ii) Original issue discount, which generally includes capitalized interest. For purposes of section 221, capitalized interest means any accrued and unpaid interest on a qualified education loan that, in accordance with the terms of the loan, is added by the lender to the outstanding principal balance of the loan.

(2) Operative rules for original issue discount. (i) In general. The rules to determine the amount of original issue discount on a loan and the accruals of the discount are in sections 163(e), 1271 through 1275, and the regulations thereunder. In general, original issue discount is the excess of a loan's stated redemption price at maturity (all payments due under the loan other than qualified stated interest payments) over its issue price (the amount loaned). Although original issue discount generally is deductible as it accrues under section 163(e) and § 1.163-7, original issue discount on a qualified education loan is not deductible until paid. See paragraph (h)(3) of this section to determine when original issue discount is paid.

(ii) Treatment of loan origination fees by the borrower. If a loan origination fee is paid by the borrower other than for property or services provided by the lender, the fee reduces the issue price of the loan, which creates original issue discount (or additional original issue discount) on the loan in an amount equal to the fee. See § 1.1273-2(g). For an example of how a loan origination fee is taken into account, see Example 2 of paragraph (h)(4) of this section.

(3) Allocation of payments. See §§ 1.446-2(e) and 1.1275-2(a) for rules on allocating payments between interest and principal. In general, these rules treat a payment first as a

payment of interest to the extent of the interest that has accrued and remains unpaid as of the date the payment is due, and second as a payment of principal. The characterization of a payment as either interest or principal under these rules applies regardless of how the parties label the payment (either as interest or principal). Accordingly, the taxpayer may deduct the portion of a payment labeled as principal that these rules treat as a payment of interest on the loan, including any portion attributable to capitalized interest or loan origination fees.

(4) Examples. The following examples illustrate the rules of this paragraph (h). In the examples, assume that the institution the student attends is an eligible educational institution, the loan is a qualified education loan, the student is legally obligated to make interest payments under the terms of the loan, and any other applicable requirements, if not otherwise specified, are fulfilled. The examples are as follows:

Example (1). Capitalized interest. Interest on Student O's qualified education loan accrues while Student O is in school, but Student O is not required to make any payments on the loan until six months after he graduates or otherwise leaves school. At that time, the lender capitalizes all accrued but unpaid interest and adds it to the outstanding principal amount of the loan. Thereafter, Student O is required to make monthly payments of interest and principal on the loan. The interest payable on the loan, including the capitalized interest, is original issue discount. Therefore, in determining the total amount of interest paid on the qualified education loan during the 60-month period described in paragraph (e)(1) of this section, Student O may deduct any payments that § 1.1275-2(a) treats as payments of interest, including any principal payments that are treated as payments of capitalized interest. See paragraph (h)(3) of this section.

Example (2). Allocation of payments. The facts are the same as in Example 1 of this paragraph (h)(4), except that, in addition, the lender charges Student O a loan origination fee, which is not for any property or services provided by the lender. Under § 1.1273-2(g), the loan origination fee reduces the issue price of the loan, which reduction increases the amount of original issue discount on the loan by the amount of the fee. The amount of original issue discount (which includes the capitalized interest and loan origination fee) that accrues each year is determined under section § 1272 and § 1.1272-1. In effect, the loan origination fee accrues over the entire term of the loan. Because the loan has original issue discount, the payment ordering rules in § 1.1275-2(a) must be used to determine how much of each payment is interest for federal tax purposes. See paragraph (h)(3) of this section. Under § 1.1275-2(a), each payment (regardless of its designation by the parties as either interest or principal) generally is treated first as a payment of original issue discount, to the extent of the original issue discount that has accrued as of the date the payment is due and has not been allocated to prior payments, and second as a payment of principal. Therefore, in determining the total amount of interest paid on the qualified education loan during the 60-month period described in paragraph (e)(1) of this section, Student O may deduct any payments that the parties label as principal but that are treated as payments of original issue discount under § 1.1275-2(a). The 60-month period does not begin in the month in which the lender charges Student O the loan origination fee.

(i) Special rules regarding 60-month limitation. *(1) Refinancing.* A qualified education loan and all indebtedness incurred solely to refinance that loan constitute a single loan for purposes of calculating the 60-month period described in paragraph (e)(1) of this section.

(2) Consolidated loans. A consolidated loan is a single loan that refinances more than one qualified education loan of a borrower. For consolidated loans, the 60-month period described in paragraph (e)(1) of this section begins on the latest date on which any of the underlying loans entered repayment status and includes any subsequent month in which the consolidated loan is in repayment status.

(3) Collapsed loans. A collapsed loan is two or more qualified education loans of a single taxpayer that constitute a single qualified education loan for loan servicing purposes and for which the lender or servicer does not separately account. For a collapsed loan, the 60-month period described in paragraph (e)(1) of this section begins on the latest date on which any of the underlying loans entered repayment status and includes any subsequent month in which any of the underlying loans is in repayment status.

(4) Examples. The following examples illustrate the rules of this paragraph (i):

Example (1). Refinancing. Student P obtains a qualified education loan to pay for an undergraduate degree at an eligible educational institution. After graduation, Student P is required to make monthly interest payments on the loan beginning in January 2000. Student P makes the required interest payments for 15 months. In April 2001, Student P borrows money from another lender exclusively to repay the first qualified education loan. The new loan requires interest payments to start immediately. At the time Student P must begin interest payments on the new loan, which is a qualified education loan, there are 45 months remaining of the original 60-month period referred to in paragraph (e)(1) of this section.

Example (2). Collapsed loans. To finance his education, Student Q obtains four separate qualified education loans from Lender R. The loans enter repayment status, and their respective 60-month periods described in paragraph (e)(1) of this section begin, in July, August, September, and December of 1999. After all of Student Q's loans have entered repayment status, Lender R informs Student Q that Lender R will transfer all four loans to Lender S. Following the transfer, Lender S treats the loans as a single loan for loan servicing purposes. Lender S sends Student Q a single statement that shows the total principal and interest, and does not keep separate records with respect to each loan. With respect to the single collapsed loan, the 60-month period described in paragraph (e)(1) of this section begins in December 1999.

(j) Effective date. This section is applicable to interest due and paid on qualified education loans after January 21, 1999, if paid before January 1, 2002. Taxpayers also may apply this section to interest due and paid on qualified education loans after December 31, 1997, but before January 21, 1999. This section also applies to interest due and paid on qualified education loans in a taxable year beginning after December 31, 2010.

T.D. 9125, 5/6/2004.

§ 1.241-1 Allowance of special deductions.

A corporation, in computing its taxable income, is allowed as deductions the items specified in part VIII (section 242 and following), subchapter B, chapter 1 of the Code, in addition to the deductions provided in part VI (section 161 and following) subchapter B, chapter 1 of the Code.

T.D. 6183, 6/13/56.

§ 1.242-1 Deduction for partially tax-exempt interest.

A corporation is allowed a deduction under section 242(a) in an amount equal to certain interest received on obligations of the United States, or an obligation of corporations organized under Acts of Congress which are instrumentalities of the United States. The interest for which a deduction shall be allowed is interest which is included in gross income and which is exempt from normal tax under the act, as amended and supplemented, which authorized the issuance of the obligations. The deduction allowed by section 242(a) is allowed only for the purpose of computing normal tax, and therefore, no deduction is allowed for such interest in the computation of any surtax imposed by Subtitle A of the Internal Revenue Code of 1954.

T.D. 7100, 5/20/71.

§ 1.243-1 Deduction for dividends received by corporations.

Caution: The Treasury has not yet amended Reg § 1.243-1 to reflect changes made by P.L. 100-203, P.L. 99-514.

(a) *(1)* A corporation is allowed a deduction under section 243 for dividends received from a domestic corporation which is subject to taxation under chapter 1 of the Internal Revenue Code of 1954.

(2) Except as provided in section 243(c) and in section 246, the deduction is:

(i) For the taxable year, an amount equal to 85 percent of the dividends received from such domestic corporations during the taxable year (other than dividends to which subdivision (ii) or (iii) of this subparagraph applies).

(ii) For a taxable year beginning after September 2, 1958, an amount equal to 100 percent of the dividends received from such domestic corporations if at the time of receipt of such dividends the recipient corporation is a Federal licensee under the Small Business Investment Act of 1958 (15 U.S.C. ch. 14B). However, to claim the deduction provided by section 243(a)(2) the company must file with its return a statement that it was a Federal licensee under the Small Business Investment Act of 1958 at the time of the receipt of the dividends.

(iii) For a taxable year ending after December 31, 1963, an amount equal to 100 percent of the dividends received which are "qualifying dividends," as defined in section 243(b) and § 1.243-4.

(3) To determine the amount of the distribution to a recipient corporation and the amount of the dividend, see §§ 1.301-1 and 1.316-1.

(b) The deductions allowed by section 243(a) and (b) shall be determined without regard to any dividends described in paragraph (1) of section 244 (relating to dividends on the preferred stock of a public utility). That is, such deductions shall be determined without regard to any dividends received on the preferred stock of a public utility which is subject to taxation under chapter 1 of the Code and with respect to which a deduction is allowed by section 247 (relating to dividends paid on certain preferred stock of public utilities). For a deduction with respect to such dividends received on the preferred stock of a public utility, see section 244. If a deduction for dividends paid is not allowable to the distributing corporation under section 247 with respect to the dividends on its preferred stock, such dividends received from a domestic public utility corporation subject to taxation under chapter 1 of the Code are includible in determining the deduction allowed by section 243(a) or (b).

(c) For limitation of dividends received deduction, see section 246 and the regulations thereunder.

T.D. 6183, 6/13/56, amend T.D. 6449, 1/27/60, T.D. 6992, 1/17/69.

§ 1.243-2 Special rules for certain distributions.

(a) Dividends paid by mutual savings banks, etc. In determining the deduction provided in section 243(a), any amount allowed as a deduction under section 591 (relating to deduction for dividends paid by mutual savings banks, cooperative banks, and domestic building and loan associations) shall not be considered as a dividend.

(b) Dividends received from regulated investment companies. In determining the deduction provided in section 243(a), dividends received from a regulated investment company shall be subject to the limitations provided in section 854.

(c) Dividends received from real estate investment trusts. See section 857(c) and paragraph (d) of § 1.857-6 for special rules which deny a deduction under section 243 in the case of dividends received from a real estate investment trust with respect to a taxable year for which such trust is taxable under part II, subchapter M, chapter 1 of the Code.

(d) Dividends received on preferred stock of a public utility. The deduction allowed by section 243(a) shall be determined without regard to any dividends described in section 244 (relating to dividends on the preferred stock of a public utility). That is, such deduction shall be determined without regard to any dividends received on the preferred stock of a public utility which is subject to taxation under chapter 1 of the Code and with respect to which a deduction is allowed by section 247 (relating to dividends paid on certain preferred stock of public utilities). For a deduction with respect to such dividends received on the preferred stock of a public utility, see section 244. If a deduction for dividends paid is not allowable to the distributing corporation under section 247 with respect to the dividends on its preferred stock, such dividends received from a domestic public utility corporation subject to taxation under chapter 1 of the Code are includible in determining the deduction allowed by section 243(a).

T.D. 6183, 6/13/56, amend T.D. 6449, 1/27/60, T.D. 6598, 4/25/62, T.D. 6992, 1/17/69, T.D. 7767, 2/3/81.

§ 1.243-3 Certain dividends from foreign corporations.

Caution: The Treasury has not yet amended Reg § 1.243-3 to reflect changes made by P.L. 100-203.

(a) In general. *(1)* In determining the deduction provided in section 243(a), section 243(d) provides that a dividend received from a foreign corporation after December 31, 1959, shall be treated as a dividend from a domestic corporation which is subject to taxation under chapter 1 of the Code, but only to the extent that such dividend is out of earnings and profits accumulated by a domestic corporation during a period with respect to which such domestic corporation was subject to taxation under chapter 1 of the Code (or corresponding provisions of prior law). Thus, for example, if a domestic corporation accumulates earnings and profits during a period or periods with respect to which it is subject to taxation under chapter 1 of the Code (or corresponding provisions of prior law) and subsequently such domestic corporation reincorporates in a foreign country, any dividends paid out of such earnings and profits after such reincorporation are eligible for the deduction provided in section 243(a)(1) and (2).

(2) Section 253(d) and this section do not apply to dividends paid out of earnings and profits accumulated (i) by a corporation organized under the China Trade Act, 1922, (ii) by a domestic corporation during any period with respect to which such corporation was exempt from taxation under section 501 (relating to certain charitable, etc. organizations) or 521 (relating to farmers' cooperative associations), or (iii) by a domestic corporation during any period to which section 931 (relating to income from sources within possessions of the UnitedStates), as in effect for taxable years beginning before January 1, 1976, applied.

(b) Establishing separate earnings and profits accounts. A foreign corporation shall, for purposes of section 243(d), maintain a separate account for earnings and profits to which it succeeds which were accumulated by a domestic corporation, and such foreign corporation shall treat such earnings and profits as having been accumulated during the accounting periods in which earned by such domestic corporation. Such foreign corporation shall maintain such a separate account for the earnings and profits, or deficit in earnings and profits, accumulated by it or accumulated by any other corporations to the earnings and profits of which it succeeds.

(c) Effect of dividends on earnings and profits accounts. Dividends paid out of the accumulated earnings and profits (see section 361(a)(1)) of such foreign corporation shall be treated as having been paid out of the most recently accumulated earnings and profits of such corporation. A deficit in an earnings and profits account for any accounting period shall reduce the most recently accumulated earnings and profits for a prior accounting period in such account. If there are no accumulated earnings and profits in an earnings and profits account because of a deficit incurred in a prior accounting period, such deficit must be restored before earnings and profits can be accumulated in a subsequent accounting period. If a dividend is paid out of earnings and profits of a foreign corporation which maintains two or more accounts (established under the provisions of paragraph (b) of this section) with respect to two or more accounting periods ending on the same day, then the portion of such dividend considered as paid out of each account shall be the same proportion of the total dividend as the amount of earnings and profits in that account bears to the sum of the earnings and profits in all such accounts.

(d) Illustration. The application of the principles of this section in the determination of the amount of the dividends received deduction may be illustrated by the following example:

Example. On December 31, 1960, corporation X, a calendar-year corporation organized in the United States on January 1, 1958, consolidated with corporation Y, a foreign corporation organized on January 1, 1958, which used an annual accounting period based on the calendar year, to from corporation Z, a foreign corporation not engaged in trade or business within the United States. Corporation Z is a wholly-owned subsidiary of corporation M, a domestic corporation. On January 1, 1961, corporation Z's accumulated earnings and profits of $31,000 are, under the provisions of paragraph (b) of this section, maintained in separate earnings and profits accounts containing the following amounts:

Earnings and profits accumulated for—	Domestic corporation X	Foreign corporation Y
1958	($ 1,000)	$11,000
1959	10,000	9,000
1960	5,000	(3,000)

Corporation Z had earnings and profits of $10,000 in each of the years 1961, 1962, and 1963 and makes distributions with respect to its stock to corporation M for such years in the following amounts:

1961	$14,000
1962	23,000
1963	16,000

(1) For 1961, a deduction of $3,400 is allowable to M with respect to the $14,000 distribution from Z, computed as follows:

(i) Dividend from current year earnings and profits (1961)		$10,000
(ii) Dividend from earnings and profits of corporation X accumulated for 1960		4,000
(iii) Deduction: 85 percent of $4,000 (the amount distributed from the accumulated earnings and profits of corporation X)		3,400

(2) For 1962, a deduction of $6,970 is allowable to corporation M with respect to the $23,000 distribution from corporation Z, computed as follows:

(i) Dividend from current year earnings and profits (1962)		$10,000
(ii) Dividend from earnings and profits of corporation X accumulated for:		
1960	$1,000	
1959: $9,000 (i.e., $10,000 − $1,000) divided by $15,000 (i.e., $9,000 + $9,000 − $3,000) multiplied by $12,000 (i.e., $23,000 − $11,000)	7,200	
Total		8,200
(iii) Dividend from earnings and profits of corporation Y accumulated for: 1959: $6,000/$15,000 × $12,000		4,800
(iv) Deduction: 85 percent of $8,200 (the amount distributed from the accumulated earnings and profits of corporation X)		6,970

(3) For 1963, a deduction of $1,530 is allowable to M with respect to the $16,000 distribution from Z, computed as follows:

(i) Dividend from current year earnings and profits (1963)	$10,000
(ii) Dividend from earnings and profits of corporation X accumulated for 1959: Earnings and profits remaining after 1962 distribution (i.e., $9,000 − $7,200)	1,800
(iii) Dividend from earnings and profits of corporation Y accumulated for 1959: Earnings and profits remaining after 1962 distribution (i.e., $6,000 − $4,800)	1,200
1958	3,000
(iv) Deduction: 85 percent of $1,800 (the amount distributed from the accumulated earnings and profits of corporation X)	1,530

T.D. 6830, 6/22/65, amend T.D. 9194, 4/6/2005.

§ 1.243-4 Qualifying dividends.

Caution: The Treasury has not yet amended Reg § 1.243-4 to reflect changes made by P.L. 101-508.

(a) Definition of qualifying dividends. *(1) General.* For purposes of section 243(a)(3), the term "qualifying dividends" means dividends received by a corporation if—

(i) At the close of the day the dividends are received, such corporation is a member of the same affiliated group of corporations (as defined in paragraph (b) of this section) as the corporation distributing the dividends,

(ii) An election by such affiliated group under section 243(b)(2) and paragraph (c) of this section is effective for the taxable years of its members which include such day, and

(iii) The dividends are distributed out of earnings and profits specified in subparagraph (2) of this paragraph.

(2) Earnings and profits. The earnings and profits specified in this subparagraph are earnings and profits of a taxable year of the distributing corporation (or a predecessor corporation) which satisfies each of the following conditions:

(i) Such year must end after December 31, 1963;

(ii) On each day of such year the distributing corporation (or the predecessor corporation) and the corporation receiving the dividends must have been members of the affiliated group of which the distributing corporation and the corporation receiving the dividends are members on the day the dividends are received; and

(iii) An election under section 1562 (relating to the election of multiple surtax exemptions) was never effective (or is no longer effective pursuant to section 1562(c)) for such year.

(3) Special rule for insurance companies. Notwithstanding the provisions of subparagraph (2) of this paragraph, if an insurance company subject to taxation under section 802 or 821 distributes a dividend out of earnings and profits of a taxable year with respect to which the company would have been a component member of a controlled group of corporations within the meaning of section 1563 were it not for the application of section 1563(b)(2)(D), such dividend shall not be treated as a qualifying dividend unless an election under section 243(b)(2) is effective for such taxable year.

(4) Predecessor corporations. For purposes of this paragraph, a corporation shall be considered to be a predecessor corporation with respect to a distributing corporation if the distributing corporation succeeds to the earnings and profits of such corporation, for example, as the result of a transaction to which section 381(a) applies. A distributing corporation shall, for purposes of this section, maintain, in respect of each predecessor corporation, a separate account for earnings and profits to which it succeeds, and such earnings and profits shall be considered to be earnings and profits of the predecessor's taxable year in which the earnings and profits were accumulated.

(5) Mere change in form. (i) For purposes of subparagraph (2)(ii) of this paragraph, the affiliated group in existence during the taxable year out of the earnings and profits of which the dividend is distributed shall not be considered as a different group from that in existence on the day on which the dividend is received merely because—

(a) The common parent corporation has undergone a mere change in identity, form, or place of organization (within the meaning of section 368(a)(1)(F)), or

(b) A newly organized corporation (the "acquiring corporation") has acquired substantially all of the outstanding stock of the common parent corporation (the "acquired corporation") solely in exchange for stock of such acquiring corporation, and the stockholders (immediately before the acquisition) of the acquired corporation, as a result of owning stock of the acquired corporation, own (immediately after the acquisition) all of the outstanding stock of the acquiring corporation.

If a transaction described in the preceding sentence has occurred, the acquiring corporation shall be treated as having been a member of the affiliated group for the entire period during which the acquired corporation was a member of such group.

(ii) For purposes of subdivision (i)(b) of this subparagraph, if immediately before the acquisition—

(a) The stockholders of the acquired corporation also owned all of the outstanding stock of another corporation (the "second corporation"), and

(b) Stock of the acquired corporation and of the second corporation could be acquired or transferred only as a unit (hereinafter referred to as the "limitation on transferability"),

then the second corporation shall be treated as an acquired corporation and such second corporation shall be treated as having been a member of the affiliated group for the entire period (while such group was in existence) during which the limitation on transferability was in existence, and if the second corporation is itself the common parent corporation of an affiliated group (the "second group") any other member of the second group shall be treated as having been a member of the affiliated group for the entire period during which it was a member of the second group while the limitation on transferability existed. For purposes of (a) of this subdivision and subdivision (i)(b) of this subparagraph, if the limitation on transferability of stock of the acquired corporation and the second corporation is achieved by using a voting trust, then the stock owned by the trust shall be considered as owned by the holders of the beneficial interests in the trust.

(6) Source of distributions. In determining from what year's earnings and profits a dividend is treated as having been distributed for purposes of this section, the principles of paragraph (a) of § 1.316-2 shall apply. A dividend shall be considered to be distributed, first, out of the earnings and profits of the taxable year which includes the date the dividend is distributed, second, out of the earnings and profits accumulated for the immediately preceding taxable year, third, out of the earnings and profits accumulated for the second preceding taxable year, etc. A deficit in an earnings and profits account for any taxable year shall reduce the most recently accumulated earnings and profits for a prior year in such account. If there are no accumulated earnings and profits in an earnings and profits account because of a deficit incurred in a prior year, such deficit must be restored before earnings and profits can be accumulated in a subsequent year. If a dividend is distributed out of separate earnings and profits accounts (established under the provisions of subparagraph (4) of this paragraph) for two or more taxable years ending on the same day, then the portion of such dividend considered as distributed out of each account shall be the same proportion of the total dividend as the amount of earnings and profits in that account bears to the sum of the earnings and profits in all such accounts.

(7) Examples. The provisions of this paragraph may be illustrated by the following examples:

Example (1). On March 1, 1965, corporation P, a publicly owned corporation, acquires all of the stock of corporation S and continues to hold the stock throughout the remainder of 1965 and all of 1966. P and S are domestic corporations which file separate returns on the basis of a calendar year. The affiliated group consisting of P and S makes an election under section 243(b)(2) which is effective for the 1966 taxable years of P and S. A multiple surtax exemption election under section 1562 is not effective for their 1965 taxable years. On February 1, 1966, S distributes $50,000 with respect to its stock which is received by P on the same date. S had earnings and profits of $40,000 for 1966 (computed without regard to distributions during 1966). S also had earnings and profits accumulated for 1965 of $70,000. Since $40,000 was distributed out of earnings and profits for 1966 and since each of the conditions prescribed in subparagraphs (1) and (2) of this paragraph is satisfied, P is entitled to a 100-percent dividends received deduction with respect to $40,000 of the $50,000 distribution. However, since $10,000 was distributed out of earnings and profits accumulated for 1965, and since on each day of 1965 S and P were not members of the affiliated group of which S and P were members on February 1, 1966, $10,000 of the $50,000 distribution does not satisfy the condition specified in subparagraph (2)(ii) of this paragraph and thus does not qualify for the 100-percent dividends received deduction.

Example (2). Assume the same facts as in example (1), except that corporation P acquires all the stock of corporation S on January 1, 1965, and sells such stock on November 1, 1966. Since $10,000 is distributed out of earnings and profits for 1965, and since each of the conditions prescribed in subparagraphs (1) and (2) of this paragraph is satisfied, P is entitled to a 100-percent dividends received deduction with respect to $10,000 of the $50,000 distribution. However, since $40,000 of the $50,000 distribution was made out of earnings and profits of S for its 1966 taxable year, and on each day of such year S and P were not members of the affiliated group of which S and P were members on February 1, 1966, $40,000 of the distribution does not satisfy the condition specified in subparagraph (2)(ii) of this paragraph and thus does not qualify for the 100-percent dividends received deduction.

Example (3). Assume the same facts as in example (1), except that corporation P acquires all the stock of corporation S on January 1, 1965, and that a multiple surtax exemption election under section 1562 is effective for P's and S's 1965 taxable years. Further assume that the section 1562 election is terminated effective with respect to their 1966 taxable years, and that an election under section 243(b)(2) is effective for such taxable years. Since $10,000 of the February 1, 1966, distribution was made out of earnings and profits of S for its 1965 taxable year and since a multiple surtax exemption election is effective for such year, $10,000 of the distribution does not satisfy the condition specified in subparagraph (2)(iii) of this paragraph and thus does not qualify for the 100-percent dividends received deduction. However, the portion of the distribution which was distributed out of earnings and profits of S's 1966 year ($40,000) qualifies for the 100-percent dividends received deduction.

Example (4). Assume the same facts as in example (1), except that corporation P acquires all the stock of corporation S on January 1, 1965, and that S is a life insurance company subject to taxation under section 802. Accordingly, S would have been a member of a controlled group of corporations except for the application of section 1563(b)(2)(D). Since $10,000 of the distribution was made out of earnings and profits of S for its 1965 taxable year, and since with respect to such year an election under section 243(b)(2) was not effective, $10,000 of the distribution is not a qualifying dividend by reason of subparagraph (3) of this paragraph. On the other hand, the portion of the distribution which was distributed out of earnings and profits for S's 1966 year ($40,000) does qualify for the 100-percent dividends received deduction because the distribution was out of earnings and profits of a year for which an election under section 243(b)(2) is effective, and because the other conditions specified in subparagraphs (1) and (2) of this paragraph are satisfied. However, if P were also a life insurance company subject to taxation under section 802, then subparagraph (3) of this paragraph would not result in the disqualification of the portion of the distribution made out of S's 1965 earnings and profits because S would be a component member of an insurance group of corporations (as defined in section 1563(a)(4)), consisting of P and S, with respect to its 1965 year.

Example (5). Corporation X owns all the stock of corporation Y from January 1, 1965, through December 31, 1969. X and Y are domestic corporations which file separate returns on the basis of a calendar year. On June 30, 1965, Y acquired all the stock of domestic corporation Z, a calendar year taxpayer, and on December 31, 1967, Y acquired the assets of Z in a transaction to which section 381(a) applied. A multiple surtax exemption election under section 1562 was not effective for any taxable year of X, Y, or Z, and an election under section 243(b)(2) is effective for the 1968 and 1969 taxable years of X and Y. On January 1, 1968, Y's accumulated earnings and profits are, under the provisions of subparagraph (4) of this paragraph, maintained in separate earnings and profits accounts containing the following amounts:

Earnings and profits accumulated for—	Corporation Y	Corporation Z
1964	$60,000	$40,000
1965	30,000	15,000
1966	(5,000)	2,000
1967	12,000	6,000

Corporation Y had earnings and profits of $10,000 in each of the years 1968 and 1969, and made distributions during such years in the following amounts:

1968	$29,000
1969	31,000

(i) The source of the 1968 distribution, determined in accordance with the rules of subparagraph (6) of this paragraph, is as follows:

(a) Dividend from Y's current year's earnings and profits (1968)	$10,000
(b) Dividend from earnings and profits of Y accumulated for 1967	12,000
(c) Dividend from earnings and profits of Z accumulated for:	
1967	6,000
1966	1,000
	29,000

Since the 1968 dividend is considered paid out of earnings and profits of Y's 1968 and 1967 years, and Z's 1967 and 1966 years, and since each of these years satisfies each of the conditions specified in subparagraph (2) of this paragraph, X is entitled to a 100-percent dividends received deduction with respect to the entire 1968 distribution of $29,000 from Y.

(ii) The source of the 1969 distribution of $31,000, determined in accordance with the rules of subparagraph (6) of this paragraph, is as follows:

(a) Dividend from Y's current year's earnings and profits (1969)	$10,000
(b) Dividend from earnings and profits of Z accumulated for 1966 (1966 earnings and profits remaining after 1968 distribution, i.e., $2,000 – $1,000)	1,000
(c) Dividend from earnings and profits of Y and Z accumulated for 1965:	
Corporation Y: $25,000 (i.e., $30,000 – $5,000 deficit) divided by $40,000 (i.e., the sum of the 1965 earnings and profits of Y and Z) multiplied by $20,000 (the portion of the distribution from the 1965 earnings and profits of Y and Z)	12,500
Corporation Z: $15,000 divided by $40,000 multiplied by $20,000	7,500
	31,000

The sum of the dividends from Y's 1969 year ($10,000), Z's 1966 year ($1,000), and Y's 1965 year ($12,000), or $23,500, qualifies for the 100-percent dividends received deduction. However, the dividends paid out of Z's 1965 year ($7,500) do not qualify because on each day of 1965 Z and X were not members of the affiliated group of which Y (the distributing corporation) and X (the corporation receiving the dividends) were members on the day in 1969 when the dividends were received by X.

(b) Definition of affiliated group. For purposes of this section and § 1.243-5, the term "affiliated group" shall have the meaning assigned to it by section 1504(a), except that insurance companies subject to taxation under section 802 or 821 shall be treated as includible corporations (notwithstanding section 1504(b)(2)), and the provisions of section 1504(c) shall not apply.

(c) Election. *(1) Manner and time of making election.* (i) General. The election provided by section 243(b)(2) shall be made for an affiliated group by the common parent corporation and shall be made for a particular taxable year of the common parent corporation. Such election may not be made for any taxable year of the common parent corporation for which a multiple surtax exemption election under section 1562 is effective. The election shall be made by means of a statement, signed by any person who is duly authorized to act on behalf of the common parent corporation, stating that the affiliated group elects under section 243(b)(2) for such taxable year. The statement shall be filed with the district director for the internal revenue district in which is located the principal place of business or principal office or agency of the common parent. The statement shall set forth the name, address, taxpayer account number, and taxable year of each corporation (including wholly-owned subsidiaries) that is a member of the affiliated group at the time the election is filed. The statement may be filed at any time, provided that, with respect to each corporation the tax liability of which for its matching taxable year of election (or for any subsequent taxable year) would be increased because of the election, at the time of filing there is at least 1 year remaining in the statutory period (including any extensions thereof) for the assessment of a deficiency against such corporation for such year. (If there is less than 1 year remaining with respect to any taxable year, the district director for the internal revenue district in which is located the principal place of business or principal office or agency of the corporation will ordinarily, upon request, enter into an agreement to extend such statutory period for assessment and collection of deficiencies.)

(ii) Information statement by common parent. If a corporation becomes a member of the affiliated group after the date on which the election is filed and during its matching taxable year of election, then the common parent shall file, within 60 days after such corporation becomes a member of the affiliated group, an additional statement containing the name, address, taxpayer account number, and taxable year of such corporation. Such additional statement shall be filed with the internal revenue officer with whom the election was filed.

(iii) Definition of matching taxable year of election. For purposes of this paragraph and paragraphs (d) and (e) of this section, the term "matching taxable year of election" shall mean the taxable year of each member (including the common parent corporation) of the electing affiliated group which includes the last day of the taxable year of the common parent corporation for which an election by the affiliated group is made under section 243(b)(2).

(2) Consents by subsidiary corporations. (i) General. Each corporation (other than the common parent corporation) which is a member of the electing affiliated group (including any member which joins in the filing of a consolidated return) at any time during its matching taxable year of election must consent to such election in the manner and time provided in subsection (ii) or (iii) of this subparagraph whichever is applicable.

(ii) Wholly owned subsidiary. If all of the stock of a corporation is owned by a member of the affiliated group on each day of such corporation's matching taxable year of election, then such corporation (referred to in this paragraph as a "wholly owned subsidiary") shall be deemed to consent to such election.

(iii) Other members. The consent of each member of the affiliated group (other than a wholly owned subsidiary) shall be made by means of a statement, signed by any person who is duly authorized to act on behalf of the consenting member, stating that such member consents to the election under section 243(b)(2). The statement shall set forth the name, address, taxpayer account number, and taxable year of the consenting member and of the common parent corporation, and in the case of a statement filed after December 31, 1968 the identity of the internal revenue district in which is located the principal place of business or principal office or agency of the common parent corporation. The consent of more than one such member may be incorporated in a single statement. The statement (or statements) shall be attached to the election filed by the common parent corporation. The consent of a corporation that, after the date the election was filed and during its matching taxable year of election, either (a) becomes a member, or (b) ceases to be a wholly owned subsidiary but continues to be a member, shall be filed with the internal revenue officer with whom the election was filed and shall be filed on or before the date prescribed by law (including extensions of time) for the filing of the consenting member's income tax return for such taxable year, or on or before June 10, 1964, whichever is later.

(iv) Statement attached to return. Each corporation that consents to an election by means of a statement described in subdivision (iii) of this subparagraph should attach a copy of the statement to its income tax return for its matching taxable year of election, or, if such return has already been filed, to its first income tax return filed on or after the date on which the statement is filed. However, if such return is filed on or before June 10, 1964, a copy of such statement should be filed on or before June 10, 1964, with the district director with whom such return is filed. Each wholly owned subsidiary should attach a statement to its income tax return for its matching taxable year of election, or, if such return has already been filed, to its first income tax return filed on or after the date on which the statement is filed stating that it is subject to an election under section 243(b)(2) and the taxable year to which the election applies, and setting forth the name, address, taxpayer account number, and taxable year of the common parent corporation, and in the case of a statement filed after December 31, 1968, the identity of the internal revenue district in which is located the principal place of business or principal office or agency of the common parent corporation. However, if the due date for such return (including extensions of time) is before June 10, 1964, such statement should be filed on or before June 10, 1964, with the district director with whom such return is filed.

(3) Information statement by member. If a corporation becomes a member of the affiliated group during a taxable year that begins after the last day of the common parent corporation's matching taxable year of election, then (unless such election has been terminated) such corporation should attach a statement to its income tax return for such taxable year stating that it is subject to an election under section 243(b)(2) for such taxable year and setting forth the name, address, taxpayer account number, and taxable year of the common parent corporation, and the identity of the internal revenue district in which is located the principal place of business or principal office or agency of the common parent corporation. In the case of an affiliated group that made an election under the rules provided in Treasury Decision 6721 approved April 8, 1964 (29 F.R. 4997, C.B. 1964-1 (Part 1), 625), such statement shall be filed, on or before March 15, 1969, with the district director for the internal revenue district in which is located such member's principal place of business or principal office or agency.

(4) Years for which election effective. (i) General rule. An election under section 243(b)(2) by an affiliated group shall be effective—

(a) In the case of each corporation which is a member of such group at any time during its matching taxable year of election for such taxable year, and

(b) In the case of each corporation which is a member of such group at any time during a taxable year ending after the last day of the common parent's taxable year of election but which does not include such last day, for such taxable year, unless the election is terminated under section 243(b)(4) and paragraph (e) of this section. Thus, the election has a continuing effect and need not be renewed annually.

(ii) Special rule for certain taxable years ending in 1964. In the case of a taxable year of a member (other than the common parent corporation) of the affiliated group (a) which begins in 1963 and ends in 1964, and (b) for which an election is not effective under subdivision (i)(a) of this subparagraph, if an election under section 243(b)(2) is effective for the taxable year of the common parent corporation which includes the last day of such taxable year of such member, then such election shall be effective for such taxable year of such member if such member files a separate consent with respect to such taxable year. However, in order for a dividend distributed by such member during such taxable year to meet the requirements of section 243(b)(1), an election under section 243(b)(2) must be effective for the taxable year of each member of the affiliated group which includes the date such dividend is received. See section 243(b)(1)(A) and paragraph (a)(1) of this section. Accordingly, if the dividend is to qualify for the 100-percent dividends received deduction under section 243(a)(3), a consent must be filed under this subdivision by each member of the affiliated group with respect to its taxable year which includes the day the dividend is received (unless an election is effective for such taxable year under subdivision (i)(a) of this subparagraph). For purposes of this subdivision, a consent shall be made by means of a statement meeting the requirements of subparagraph (2)(iii) of this paragraph, and shall be attached to the election made by the common parent corporation for its taxable year which includes the last day of the taxable year of the member with respect to which the consent is made. A copy of the statement should be filed, within 60 days after such election is filed by the common parent corporation, with the district director with whom the consenting member filed its income tax return for such taxable year.

(iii) Examples. The provisions of subdivision (ii) of this subparagraph, relating to the special rule for certain taxable years ending in 1964, may be illustrated by the following examples:

Example (1). P Corporation owns all the stock of S-1 Corporation on each day of 1963, 1964, and 1965. P uses the calendar year as its taxable year and S-1 uses a fiscal year ending June 30 as its taxable year. P makes an election under section 243(b)(2) for 1964. Since S-1 is a wholly owned subsidiary for its taxable year ending June 30, 1965, it is deemed to consent to the election. However, in order for the election to be effective with respect to S-1's taxable year ending June 30, 1964, a statement specifying that S-1 consents to the election with respect to such taxable year and containing the information required in a statement of consent under subparagraph (2)(iii) of this paragraph must be attached to the election.

Example (2). Assume the same facts as in example (1), except that P also owns all the stock of S-2 Corporation on each day of 1963, 1964, and 1965. S-2 uses a fiscal year ending May 31 as its taxable year. If S-1 distributes a dividend to P on January 15, 1964, the dividend may qualify under section 243(a)(3) only if S-1 and S-2 both consent to the election made by P for 1964 with respect to their taxable years ending in 1964.

Example (3). Assume the same facts as in example (1), except that P uses a fiscal year ending on January 31 as its taxable year and makes an election under subparagraph (1) of this paragraph for its taxable year ending January 31, 1964. Since S-1's taxable year beginning in 1963 and ending in 1964 includes January 31, 1964, the last day of P's taxable year for which the election was made, the election is effective under subdivision (i) *(a)* of this subparagraph, for S-1's taxable year ending June 30, 1964. Accordingly, the special rule of subdivision (ii) of this subparagraph has no application.

(d) Effect of election. For restrictions and limitations applicable to corporations which are members of an electing affiliated group on each day of their taxable years, see § 1.243-5.

(e) Termination of election. *(1) In general.* An election under section 243(b)(2) by an affiliated group may be terminated with respect to any taxable year of the common parent corporation after the matching taxable year of election of the common parent corporation. The election is terminated as a result of one of the occurrences described in subparagraph (2) or (3) of this paragraph. For years affected by termination, see subparagraph (4) of this paragraph.

(2) Consent of members. (i) General. An election may be terminated for an affiliated group by its common parent corporation with respect to a taxable year of the common parent corporation provided each corporation (other than the common parent) that was a member of the affiliated group at any time during its taxable year that includes the last day of such year of the common parent (the "matching taxable year of termination") consents to such termination. The statement of termination may be filed by the common parent corporation at any time, provided that, with respect to each corporation the tax liability of which for its matching taxable year of termination (or for any subsequent taxable year) would be increased because of the termination, at the time of filing there is at least 1 year remaining in the statutory period (including any extensions thereof) for the assessment of a deficiency against such corporation for such year. (If there is less than 1 year remaining with respect to any taxable year, the district director for the internal revenue district in which is located the principal place of business or principal office or agency of the corporation will ordinarily, upon request, enter into an agreement to extend such statutory period for assessment and collection of deficiencies.)

(ii) Statements filed after December 31, 1968. With respect to statements of termination filed after December 31, 1968—

(a) The statement shall be filed with the district director for the internal revenue district in which is located the principal place of business or principal office or agency of the common parent corporation:

(b) The statement shall be signed by any person who is duly authorized to act on behalf of the common parent corporation and shall state that the affiliated group terminates the election under section 243(b)(2) for such taxable year;

(c) The statement shall set forth the name, address, taxpayer account number, and taxable year of each corporation (including wholly owned subsidiaries) which is a member of the affiliated group at the time the termination is filed; and

(d) The consents to the termination shall be given in accordance with the rules prescribed in paragraph (c)(2) of this section, relating to manner and time for giving consents to an election under section 243(b)(2).

(3) Refusal by new member to consent. (i) Manner of giving refusal. If any corporation which is a new member of an affiliated group with respect to a taxable year of the common parent corporation (other than the matching taxable year of election of the common parent corporation) files a statement that it does not consent to an election under section 243(b)(2) with respect to such taxable year, then such election shall terminate with respect to such taxable year. Such statement shall be signed by any person who is duly authorized to act on behalf of the new member, and shall be filed with the timely filed income tax return of such new member for its taxable year within which falls the last day of such taxable year of the common parent corporation. In the event of a termination under this subparagraph, each corporation (other than such new member) that is a member of the affiliated group at any time during its taxable year which includes such last day should, within 30 days after such new member files the statement of refusal to consent, notify the district director of such termination. Such notification should be filed with the district director for the internal revenue district in which is located the principal place of business or principal office or agency of the corporation.

(ii) Corporation considered as new member. For purposes of subdivision (i) of this subparagraph, a corporation shall be considered to be a new member of an affiliated group of corporations with respect to a taxable year of the common parent corporation if such corporation—

(a) Is a member of the affiliated group at any time during such taxable year of the common parent corporation, and

(b) Was not a member of the affiliated group at any time during the common parent corporation's immediately preceding taxable year.

(4) Effect of termination. A termination under subparagraph (2) or (3) of this paragraph is effective with respect to (i) the common parent corporation's taxable year referred to in the particular subparagraph under which the termination occurs, and (ii) the taxable years of the other members of the affiliated group which include the last day of such taxable year of the common parent. An election, once terminated, is no longer effective. Accordingly, the termination is also effective with respect to the succeeding taxable years of the members of the group. However, the affiliated group may make a new election in accordance with the provisions of section 243(b)(2) and paragraph (c) of this section.

T.D. 6992, 1/17/69.

§ 1.243-5 Effect of election.

Caution: The Treasury has not yet amended Reg § 1.243-5 to reflect changes made by P.L. 101-508, P.L. 99-514, P.L. 98-369, P.L. 94-455.

(a) General. *(1) Corporations subject to restrictions and limitations.* If an election by an affiliated group under section 243(b)(2) is effective with respect to a taxable year of the common parent corporation, then each corporation (including the common parent corporation) which is a member of such group on each day of its matching taxable year shall be subject to the restrictions and limitations prescribed by paragraphs (b), (c), and (d) of this section for such taxable year. For purposes of this section, the term "matching taxable year" shall mean the taxable year of each member (including the common parent corporation) of an affiliated group which includes the last day of a particular taxable year of the common parent corporation for which an election by the affiliated group under section 243(b)(2) is effective. If a corporation is a member of an affiliated group on each day of a short taxable year which does not include the last day of a taxable year of the common parent corporation, and if an election under section 243(b)(2) is effective for such short year, see paragraph (g) of this section. In the case of taxable years beginning in 1963 and ending in 1964 for which an election under section 243(b)(2) is effective under paragraph (c)(4)(ii) of § 1.243-4, see paragraph (f)(9) of this section.

(2) Members filing consolidated returns. The restrictions and limitations prescribed by this section shall apply notwithstanding the fact that some of the corporations which are members of the electing affiliated group (within the meaning of section 243(b)(5)) join in the filing of a consolidated return. Thus, for example, if an electing affiliated group includes one or more corporations taxable under section 11 of the Code and two or more insurance companies taxable under section 802 of the Code, and if the insurance companies join in the filing of a consolidated return, the amount of such companies' exemptions from estimated tax (for purposes of sections 6016 and 6655) shall be the amounts determined under paragraph (d)(5) of this section and not the amounts determined pursuant to the regulations under section 1502.

(b) Multiple surtax exemption election. *(1) General rule.* If an election by an affiliated group under section 243(b)(2) is effective with respect to a taxable year of the common parent corporation, then no corporation which is a member of such affiliated group on each day of its matching taxable year may consent (or shall be deemed to consent) to an election under section 1562(a)(1), relating to election of multiple surtax exemptions, which would be effective for such matching taxable year. Thus, each corporation which is a component member of the controlled group of corporations with respect to its matching taxable year (determined by applying section 1563(b) without regard to paragraph (2)(D) thereof) shall determine its surtax exemption for such taxable year in accordance with section 1561 and the regulations thereunder.

(2) Special rule for certain insurance companies. Under section 243(b)(6)(A), if the provisions of subparagraph (1) of this paragraph apply with respect to the taxable year of an insurance company subject to taxation under section 802 or 821, then the surtax exemption of such insurance company for such taxable year shall be determined by applying part II (section 1561 and following), subchapter B, chapter 6 of the Code, with respect to such insurance company and the other corporations which are component members of the controlled group of corporations (as determined under section 1563 without regard to subsections (a)(4) and (b)(2)(D) thereof) of which such insurance company is a member, without regard to section 1563(a)(4) (relating to certain insurance companies treated as a separate controlled group) and section 1563(b)(2)(D) (relating to certain insurance companies treated as excluded members).

(3) Example. The provisions of this paragraph may be illustrated by the following example:

Example. Throughout 1965 corporation M owns all the stock of corporations L-1, L-2, S-1, and S-2. M is a domestic mutual insurance company subject to tax under section 821 of the Code, L-1 and L-2 are domestic life insurance companies subject to tax under section 802 of the Code, and S-1 and S-2 are domestic corporations subject to tax under section 11 of the Code. Each corporation uses the calendar year as its taxable year. M makes a valid election under section 243(b)(2) for the affiliated group consisting of M, L-1, L-2, S-1, and S-2. If part II, subchapter B, chapter 6 of the Code were applied with respect to the 1965 taxable years of the corporations without regard to section 243(b)(6)(A), the following would result: S-1 and S-2 would be treated as component members of a controlled group of corporations on such date; L-1 and L-2 would be treated as component members of a separate controlled group on such date; and M would be treated as an excluded member. However, since section 243(b)(6)(A) requires that part II of subchapter B be applied without regard to section 1563(a)(4) and (b)(2)(D), for purposes of determining the surtax exemptions of M, L-1, L-2, S-1, and S-2 for their 1965 taxable years, such corporations are treated for purposes of such part II as component members of a single controlled group of corporations on December 31, 1965. Moreover, by reason of having made the election under section 243(b)(2), M, L-1, L-2, S-1, and S-2 cannot consent to multiple surtax exemption elections under section 1562 which would be effective for their 1965 taxable years. Thus, such corporations are limited to a single $25,000 surtax exemption for such taxable years (to be apportioned among such corporations in accordance with section 1561 and the regulations thereunder).

(c) Foreign tax credit. *(1) General.* If an election by an affiliated group under section 243(b)(2) is effective with respect to a taxable year of the common parent corporation, then—

(i) The credit under section 901 for taxes paid or accrued to any foreign country or possession of the United States shall be allowed to a corporation which is a member of such affiliated group for each day of its matching taxable year only if each other corporation which pays or accrues such foreign taxes to any foreign country or possession, and which is a member of such group on each day of its matching taxable year, does not deduct such taxes in computing its tax liability for its matching taxable year, and

(ii) A corporation which is a member of such affiliated group on each day of its matching taxable year may use the overall limitation provided in section 904(a)(2) for such matching taxable year only if each other corporation which pays or accrues foreign taxes to any foreign country or possession, and which is a member of such group on each day of its matching taxable year, uses such limitation for its matching taxable year.

(2) Consent of the Commissioner. In the absence of unusual circumstances, a request by a corporation for the consent of the Commissioner to the revocation of an election of the overall limitation, or to a new election of the overall limitation, for the purpose of satisfying the requirements of subparagraph (1)(i) of this paragraph will be given favorable consideration, notwithstanding the fact that there has been no change in the basic nature of the corporation's business or changes in conditions in a foreign country which substantially affect the corporation's business. See paragraph (d)(3) of § 1.904-1.

(d) Other restrictions and limitations. *(1) General rule.* If an election by an affiliated group under section 243(b)(2) is effective with respect to a taxable year of the common parent corporation, then, except to the extent that an apportionment plan adopted under paragraph (f) of this section for such taxable year provides otherwise with respect to a restriction or limitation described in this paragraph, the rules provided in subparagraphs (2), (3), (4), and (5) of this paragraph shall apply to each corporation which is a member of such affiliated group on each day of its matching taxable year for the purpose of computing the amount of such restriction or limitation for its matching taxable year. For purposes of this paragraph, each corporation which is a member of an electing affiliated group (including any member which joins in filing a consolidated return) shall be treated as a separate corporation for purposes of determining the amount of such restrictions and limitations.

(2) Accumulated earnings credit. (i) General. Except as provided in subdivision (ii) of this subparagraph, in determining the minimum accumulated earnings credit under section 535(c)(2) (or the accumulated earnings credit of a mere holding or investment company under section 535(c)(3)) for each corporation which is a member of the affiliated group on each day of its matching taxable year, in lieu of the $150,000 amount ($100,000 amount in the case of taxable years beginning before January 1, 1975) mentioned in such sections there shall be substituted an amount equal to (a) $150,000 ($100,000 in the case of taxable years beginning before January 1, 1975), divided by *(b)* the number of such members.

(ii) Allocation of excess. If, with respect to one or more members, the amount determined under subdivision (i) of this subparagraph exceeds the sum of (a) such member's accumulated earnings and profits as of the close of the preceding taxable year, plus (b) such member's earnings and profits for the taxable year which are retained (within the meaning of section 535(c)(1)), then any such excess shall be subtracted from the amount determined under subdivision (i) of this subparagraph and shall be divided equally among those remaining members of the affiliated group that do not have such an excess (until no such excess remains to be divided among those remaining members that have not had such an excess). The excess so divided among such remaining members shall be added to the amount determined under subdivision (i) with respect to such members.

(iii) Apportionment plan not allowed. An affiliated group may not adopt an apportionment plan, as provided in paragraph (f) of this section, with respect to the amounts computed under the provisions of this subparagraph.

(iv) Example. The provisions of this subparagraph may be illustrated by the following example:

Example. An affiliated group is composed of four member corporations, W, X, Y, and Z. The sum of the accumulated earnings and profits (as of the close of the preceding taxable year ending December 31, 1975) plus the earnings and profits for the taxable year ending December 31, 1976 which are retained is $15,000, $75,000, $37,500, and $300,000 in the case of W, X, Y, and Z, respectively. The amounts determined under this subparagraph for W, X, Y, and Z are $15,000, $48,750, $37,500 and $48,750, respectively, computed as follows:

	Component Member			
	W	X	Y	Z
Earnings and profits	$15,000	$75,000	$37,000	$300,000
Amount computed under subpar. (1)	37,500	37,500	37,500	37,500
Excess	22,500	0	0	0
Allocation of excess		7,500	7,500	7,500
New excess			7,500	
Reallocation of new excess		3,750		3,750
Amount to be used for purposes of section 535(c)(2) and (3)	15,000	48,750	37,500	48,750

(3) Mine exploration expenditures. (i) Limitation under section 615(a). If the aggregate of the expenditures to which section 615(a) applies, which are paid or incurred by corporations which are members of the affiliated group on each day of their matching taxable years (during such taxable years) exceeds $100,000, then the deduction (or amount deferrable) under section 615 for any such member for its matching taxable year shall be limited to an amount equal to the amount which bears the same ratio to $100,000 as the amount deductible or deferrable by such member under section 615 (computed without regard to this subdivision) bears to the aggregate of the amounts deductible or deferrable under section 615 (as so computed) by all such members.

(ii) Limitation under section 615(c). If the aggregate of the expenditures to which section 615(a) applies which are paid or incurred by the corporations which are members of such affiliated group on each day of their matching taxable years (during such taxable years) would, when added to the aggregate of the amounts deducted or deferred in prior taxable years which are taken into account by such corporations in applying the limitation of section 615(c), exceed $400,000, then section 615 shall not apply to any such expenditure so paid or incurred by any such member to the extent such expenditure would exceed the amount which bears the same ratio to (a) the amount, if any, by which $400,000 exceeds the amounts so deducted or deferred in prior years, as (b) such member's deduction (or amount deferrable) under section 615 (computed without regard to this subdivision) for such expenditures paid or incurred by such member during its matching taxable year, bears to (c) the aggregate of the amounts deductible or deferrable under section 615 (as so computed) by all such members during their matching taxable years.

(iii) Treatment of corporations filing consolidated returns. For purposes of making the computations under subdivisions (i) and (ii) of this subparagraph, a corporation which joins in the filing of a consolidated return shall be treated as if it filed a separate return.

(iv) Estimate of exploration expenditures. If, on the date a corporation (which is a member of an affiliated group on each day of its matching taxable year) files its income tax return for such taxable year, it cannot be determined whether or not the $100,000 limitation prescribed by subdivision (i) of this subparagraph, or the $400,000 limitation prescribed by subdivision (ii) of this subparagraph, will apply with respect to such taxable year, then such member shall, for purposes of such return, apply the provisions of such subdivisions (i) and (ii) with respect to such taxable year on the basis of an estimate of the aggregate of the exploration expenditures by all such members of the affiliated group for their matching taxable years. Such estimate shall be made on the basis of the facts and circumstances known at the time of such estimate. If an estimate is used by any such member of the affiliated group pursuant to this subdivision, and if the actual expenditures by all such members differ from the estimate, then each such member shall file as soon as possible an original or amended return reflecting an amended apportionment (either pursuant to an apportionment plan adopted under paragraph (f) of this section or pursuant to the application of the rule provided by subdivision (i) or (ii) of this subparagraph) based upon such actual expenditures.

(v) Amount apportioned under apportionment plan. If an electing affiliated group adopts an apportionment plan as provided in paragraph (f) of this section with respect to the limitation under section 615(a) or 615(c), then the amount apportioned under such plan to any corporation which is a member of such group may not exceed the amount which such member could have deducted (or deferred) under section 615 had such affiliated group not filed an election under section 243(b)(2).

(4) Small business deductions of life insurance companies. In the case of a life insurance company taxable under section 802 which is a member of such affiliated group on each day of its matching taxable year, the small business deduction under section 804(a)(4) and 809(d)(10) shall not exceed an amount equal to $25,000 divided by the number of life insurance companies taxable under section 802 which are members of such group on each day of their matching taxable years.

(5) Estimated tax. (i) Exemption from estimated tax. Except as otherwise provided in subdivision (ii) of this subparagraph, the exemption from estimated tax (for purposes of estimated tax filing requirements under section 6016 and the addition to tax under section 6655 for failure to pay estimated tax) of each corporation which is a member of such affiliated group on each day of its matching taxable year shall be (in lieu of the $100,000 amount specified in section 6016(a) and (b)(2)(A) and in section 6655(d)(1) and (e)(2)(A)) an amount equal to $100,000 divided by the number of such members.

(ii) Nonapplication to certain taxable years beginning in 1963 and ending in 1964. For purposes of this section, if a corporation has a taxable year beginning in 1963 and ending in 1964 the last day of the eighth month of which falls on or before April 10, 1964, then (notwithstanding the fact that an election under section 243(b)(2) is effective for such taxable year) subdivision (i) of this subparagraph shall not apply to such corporation for such taxable year. Thus, such corporation shall be entitled to a $100,000 exemption from estimated tax for such taxable year. Also, with respect to a taxable year described in the first sentence of this subdivision, any such corporation shall not be considered to be a member of the affiliated group for purposes of determining the number of members referred to in subdivision (i) of this subparagraph.

(iii) Examples. The provisions of subdivision (i) of this subparagraph may be illustrated by the following examples:

Example (1). Corporation P owns all the stock of corporation S-1 on each day of 1965. On March 1, 1965, P acquires all the stock of corporation S-2. Corporations P, S-1, and S-2 file separate returns on a calendar year basis. On March 31, 1965, the affiliated group consisting of P, S-1, and S-2 anticipates making an election under section 243(b)(2) for P's 1965 taxable year. If the affiliated group does make a valid election under section 243(b)(2) for P's 1965 year, under subdivision (i) of this subparagraph the exemption from estimated tax of P for 1965, and the exemption from estimated tax of S-1 for 1965, will be (assuming an apportionment plan is not filed pursuant to paragraph (f) of this section) an amount equal to $50,000 ($100,000 ÷ 2). (Since S-2 is not a member of the affiliated group on each day of 1965, S-2's exemption from estimated tax will be determined for the year 1965 without regard to subdivision (i) of this subparagraph, whether or not the affiliated group makes the election under section 243(b)(2).) P and S-1 file declarations of estimated tax on April 15, 1965, on such basis and make payments with respect to such declarations on such basis. Thus, if the affiliated group does make a valid election under section 243(b)(2) for P's 1965 year, P and S-1 will not incur (as a result of the application of subdivision (i) of this subparagraph to their 1965 years) additions to tax under section 6655 for failure to pay estimated tax.

Example (2). Assume the same facts as in example (1), except that, on March 31, 1965, S-1 anticipates that it will incur a loss for its 1965 year. Accordingly, in anticipation of making an election under section 243(b)(2) for P's 1965 year and adopting an apportionment plan under paragraph (f) of this section, P computes its estimated tax liability for 1965 on the basis of a $100,000 exemption, and S-1 computes its estimated tax liability for 1965 on the basis of a zero exemption. Assume S-1 incurs a loss for 1965 as anticipated. Thus, if P does make the election for 1965, and an apportionment plan is adopted apportioning $100,000 to P and zero to S-1 (for their 1965 years), P and S-1 will not incur (as a result of the application of subdivision (i) of this subparagraph to their 1965 years) additions to tax under section 6655 for failure to pay estimated tax.

Example (3). Assume the same facts as in example (1), except that P and S-1 file declarations of estimated tax on April 15, 1965, on the basis of separate $100,000 exemptions from estimated tax for their 1965 years, and make payments with respect to such declarations on such basis. Assume that the affiliated group makes an election under section 243(b)(2) for P's 1965 year. Under subdivision (i) of this subparagraph, P and S-1 are limited in the aggregate to a single $100,000 exemption from estimated tax for their 1965 years. The provisions of section 6655 will be applied to the 1965 year of P and the 1965 year of S-1 on the basis of a $50,000 exemption from estimated tax for each corporation, unless a different apportionment of the $100,000 amount is adopted under paragraph (f) of this section. Since the election was made under section 243(b)(2), regardless of whether or not the affiliated group anticipated making the election, P or S-1 (or both) may incur additions to tax under section 6655 for failure to pay estimated tax.

(e) Effect of election for certain taxable years beginning in 1963 and ending in 1964. If an election under section 243(b)(2) by an affiliated group is effective for a taxable year of a corporation under paragraph (c)(4)(ii) of § 1.243-4 relating to election for certain taxable years beginning in 1963 and ending in 1964, and if such corporation is a member of such group on each day of such taxable year, then the restrictions and limitations prescribed by paragraphs (b), (c), and (d) of this section shall apply to all such members having such taxable years (for such taxable years). For purposes of this paragraph, such paragraphs shall be applied with respect to such taxable years as if such taxable years included the last day of a taxable year of the common parent corporation for which an election was effective under section 243(b)(2), *i.e.,* as if such taxable years were matching taxable years. For apportionment plans with respect to such taxable years, see paragraph (f)(9) of this section.

(f) Apportionment plans. *(1) In general.* In the case of corporations which are members of an affiliated group of corporations on each day of their matching taxable years—

(i) The $100,000 amount referred to in paragraph (d)(3)(i) of this section (relating to limitation under section 615(a)),

(ii) The amount determined under paragraph (d)(3)(ii)(a) of this section (relating to limitation under section 615(c)),

(iii) The $25,000 amount referred to in paragraph (d)(4) of this section (relating to small business deduction of life insurance companies), and

(iv) The $100,000 amount referred to in paragraph (d)(5)(i) of this section (relating to exemption from estimated tax),

may be apportioned among such members (for such taxable years) if the common parent corporation files an apportionment plan with respect to such taxable years in the manner provided in subparagraph (4) of this paragraph, and if all other members consent to the plan, in the manner provided in subparagraph (5) or (6) of this paragraph (whichever is applicable). The plan may provide for the apportionment to one or more of such members, in fixed dollar amounts, of one or more of the amounts referred to in subdivisions (i), (ii), (iii), and (iv) of this subparagraph, but in no event shall the sum of the amounts so apportioned in respect to any such subdivision exceed the amount referred to in such subdivision. See also paragraph (d)(3)(v) of this section, relating to the maximum amount that may be apportioned to a corporation under this subparagraph with respect to exploration expenditures to which section 615 applies.

(2) Time for adopting plan. An affiliated group may adopt an apportionment plan with respect to the matching taxable years of its members only if, at the time such plan is sought to be adopted, there is at least 1 year remaining in the statutory period (including any extensions thereof) for the assessment of a deficiency against any corporation the tax liability of which for any taxable year would be increased by the adoption of such plan. (If there is less than 1 year remaining with respect to any taxable year, the district director for the internal revenue district in which is located the principal place of business or principal office or agency of the corporation will ordinarily, upon request, enter into an agreement to extend such statutory period for assessment and collection of deficiencies.)

(3) Years for which effective. A valid apportionment plan with respect to matching taxable years of members of an affiliated group shall be effective for such matching taxable years, and for all succeeding matching taxable years of such members, unless the plan is amended in accordance with subparagraph (8) of this paragraph or is terminated. Thus, the apportionment plan (including any amendments thereof) has a continuing effect and need not be renewed annually. An apportionment plan with respect to a particular taxable year of the common parent shall terminate with respect to the taxable years of the members of the affiliated group which include the last day of a succeeding taxable year of the common parent if—

(i) Any corporation which was a member of the affiliated group on each day of its matching taxable year which included the last day of the particular taxable year of the common parent is not a member of such group on each day of its taxable year which includes the last day of each succeeding taxable year of the common parent, or

(ii) Any corporation which was not a member of such group on each day of its taxable year which included the last day of the particular taxable year of the common parent is a member of such group on each day of its taxable year which includes the last day of such succeeding taxable year of the common parent.

An apportionment plan, once terminated, is no longer effective. Accordingly, unless a new apportionment plan is filed and consented to (or the section 243(b)(2) election is terminated) the amounts referred to in subparagraph (1) of this paragraph will be apportioned among the corporations which are members of the affiliated group on each day of their matching taxable years in accordance with the rules provided in paragraphs (d)(3)(i), (d)(3)(ii), (d)(4), and (d)(5)(i) of this section.

(4) Filing of plan. The apportionment plan shall be in the form of a statement filed by the common parent corporation with the district director for the internal revenue district in which is located the principal place of business or principal office or agency of such common parent. The statement shall be signed by any person who is duly authorized to act on behalf of the common parent corporation and shall set forth the name, address, internal revenue district, taxpayer account number, and taxable year of each member to whom the common parent could apportion an amount under subparagraph (1) of this paragraph (or, in the case of an apportionment plan referred to in subparagraph (9) of this paragraph, each member to whom the common parent could apportion an amount under such subparagraph) and the amount (or amounts) apportioned to each such member of the plan.

(5) Consent of wholly owned subsidiaries. If all the stock of a corporation which is a member of the affiliated group on each day of its matching taxable year is owned on each such day by another corporation (or corporations) which is a member of such group on each day of its matching taxable year, such corporation (hereinafter in this paragraph referred to as a "wholly owned subsidiary") shall be deemed to consent to the apportionment plan. Each wholly owned subsidiary should attach a copy of the plan filed by the common parent corporation to an income tax return, amended return, or claim for refund for its matching taxable year.

(6) Consent of other members. The consent of each member (other than the common parent corporation and wholly owned subsidiaries) to an appointment plan shall be in the form of a statement signed by any person who is duly authorized to act on behalf of the member consenting to the plan, stating that such member consents to the plan. The consent of more than one such member may be incorporated in a single statement. The statement (or statements) shall be attached to the apportionment plan filed by the common parent corporation. The consent of any such member which, after the date of apportionment plan was filed and during its matching taxable year referred to in subparagraph (1) of this paragraph, ceases to be a wholly owned subsidiary but continues to be a member, shall be filed with the district director with whom the apportionment plan is filed (as soon as possible after it ceases to be a wholly owned subsidiary). Each consenting member should attach a copy of the apportionment plan filed by the common parent to an income tax return, amended return, or claim for refund for its matching taxable year which includes the last day of the taxable year of the common parent corporation for which the apportionment plan was filed.

(7) Members of group filing consolidated return. (i) General rule. Except as provided in subdivision (ii) of this subparagraph, if the members of an affiliated group of corporations include one or more corporations taxable under section 11 of the Code and one or more insurance companies taxable under section 802 or 821 of the Code and if the affiliated group includes corporations which join in the filing of a consolidated return, then, for purposes of determining the amount to be apportioned to a corporation under an apportionment plan adopted under this paragraph, the corporations filing the consolidated return shall be treated as a single member.

(ii) Consenting to an apportionment plan. For purposes of consenting to an apportionment plan under subparagraph (5) and (6) of this paragraph, if the members of an affiliated group of corporations include corporations which join in the filing of a consolidated return, each corporation which joins in filing the consolidated return shall be treated as a separate member.

(8) Amendment of plan. An apportionment plan, which is effective for the matching taxable years of members of an affiliated group, may be amended if an amended plan is filed (and consented to) within the time and in accordance with the rules prescribed in this paragraph for the adoption of an original plan with respect to such taxable years.

(9) Certain taxable years beginning in 1963 and ending in 1964. In the case of corporations which are members of an affiliated group of corporations on each day of their taxable years referred to in paragraph (e) of this section—

(i) The $100,000 amount referred to in paragraph (d)(3)(i) of this section (relating to limitation under section 615(a)),

(ii) The amount determined under paragraph (d)(3)(ii)(a) of this section (relating to limitation under section 615(c)),

(iii) The $25,000 amount referred to in paragraph (d)(4) of this section (relating to small business deduction of life insurance companies), and

(iv) The $100,000 amount referred to in paragraph (d)(5)(i) of this section (relating to exemption from estimated tax),

may be apportioned among such members (for such taxable years) if an apportionment plan is filed (and consented to) with respect to such taxable years in accordance with the rules provided in subparagraph (2), (4), (5), (6), (7), and (8) of this paragraph. For purposes of this subparagraph, such subparagraphs shall be applied as if such taxable years included the last day of a taxable year of the common parent corporation, i.e., as if such taxable years were matching taxable years. An apportionment plan adopted under this subparagraph shall be effective only with respect to taxable years referred to in paragraph (e) of this section. The plan may provide for the apportionment of one or more of such members, in fixed dollar amounts, of one or more of the amounts referred to in subdivisions (i), (ii), (iii), and (iv) of this subparagraph, but in no event shall the sum of the amounts so apportioned in respect of any such subdivision exceed the amount referred to in such subdivision. See also paragraph (d)(3)(v) of this section, relating to the maximum amount that may be apportioned to a corporation under an apportionment plan described in this subparagraph with respect to exploration expenditures to which section 615 applies.

(g) Short taxable years. *(1) General.* If—

(i) The return of a corporation is for a short period (ending after December 31, 1963) on each day of which such corporation is a member of an affiliated group,

(ii) The last day of the common parent's taxable year does not end with or within such short period, and

(iii) An election under section 243(b)(2) by such group is effective under paragraph (c)(4)(i) of § 1.243-4 for the taxable year of the common parent within which falls such short period,

then the restrictions and limitations prescribed by section 243(b)(3) shall be applied in the manner provided in subparagraph (2) of this paragraph.

(2) Manner of applying restrictions. In the case of a corporation described in subparagraph (1) of this paragraph having a short period described in such subparagraph—

(i) Such corporation may not consent to an election under section 1562, relating to election of multiple surtax exemptions, which would be effective for such short period;

(ii) The credit under section 901 shall be allowed to such corporation for such short period if, and only if, each corporation, which pays or accrues foreign taxes and which is a member of the affiliated group on each day of its taxable year which includes the last day of the common parent's taxable year within which falls such short period, does not deduct such taxes in computing its tax liability for its taxable year which includes such last day;

(iii) The overall limitation provided in section 904(a)(2) shall be allowed to such corporation for such short period if, and only if, each corporation, which pays or accrues foreign taxes and which includes the last day of the common parent's taxable year within which falls such short period, uses such limitation for its taxable year which includes such last day;

(iv) The minimum accumulated earnings credit provided by section 535(c)(2) (or in the case of a mere holding or investment company, the accumulated earnings credit provided by section 535(c)(3)) allowable for such short period shall be the amount computed by dividing (a) the amount (if any) by which $100,000 exceeds the aggregate of the accumulated earnings and profits of the corporations, which are members of the affiliated group on the last day of such short period, as of the close of their taxable years preceding the taxable year which includes the last day of such short period, by (b) the number of such members on the last day of such short period;

(v) The deduction allowable under section 615(a) for such short period shall be limited to an amount equal to $100,000 divided by the number of corporations which are members of the affiliated group on the last day of such short period;

(vi) If the expenditures to which section 615(a) applies which are paid or incurred by such corporation during such short period would, when added to the aggregate of the amounts deducted or deferred (in taxable years ending before the last day of such short period) which are taken into account in applying the limitation of section 615(c) by corporations which are members of the affiliated group on the last day of such short period exceed $400,000, then section 615 shall not apply to any such expenditure so paid or incurred by such corporation to the extent such expenditure would exceed an amount equal to (a) the amount (if any) by which $400,000 exceeds the aggregate of the amounts so deducted or deferred in such taxable years (computed as if each member filed a separate return), divided by (b) the number of corporations in the group which have taxable years ending on such last day;

(vii) If such corporation is a life insurance company taxable under section 802, the small business deduction under sections 804(a)(4) and 809(d)(10) shall not exceed an amount equal to (a) $25,000, divided by (b) the number of life insurance companies taxable under section 802 which are members of the affiliated group on the last day of such short period; and

(viii) The exemption from estimated tax (for purposes of estimated tax filing requirements under section 6016 and the addition to tax under section 6655 for failure to pay estimated tax) for such short period shall be an amount equal to $100,000 divided by the number of corporations which are members of the affiliated group on the last day of such short period.

T.D. 6992, 1/17/69, amend T.D. 7376, 9/15/75.

§ 1.244-1 Deduction for dividends received on certain preferred stock.

A corporation is allowed a deduction under section 244 for dividends received on certain preferred stock of certain public utility corporations subject to taxation under chapter 1 of the Code. The deduction is allowable only for dividends received on the preferred stock of a public utility with respect to which the deduction for dividends paid provided in section 247 (relating to dividends paid on certain preferred stock of public utilities) is allowable to the distributing corporation.

T.D. 6183, 6/13/56.

§ 1.244-2 Computation of deduction.

Caution: The Treasury has not yet amended Reg § 1.244-2 to reflect changes made by P.L. 100-203, P.L. 99-514, P.L. 95-600.

(a) General rule. Section 244(a) provides a formula for the computation of the deduction for dividends received on the preferred stock of a public utility. For purposes of this computation, the normal tax rate referred to in section 244(a)(2)(B) shall be determined without regard to any additional tax imposed by section 1562(b). See section 1562(b)(4). The deduction computed under section 244(a) is subject to the limitation provided in section 246.

(b) Qualifying dividends. Section 244(b) provides that in the case of dividends received on the preferred stock of a public utility in taxable years ending after December 31, 1963, which are "qualifying dividends" (as defined in section 243(b)(1), but determined without regard to section 243(c)(4)), the computation of the deduction for dividends received shall be made by applying the formula provided by section 244(a) separately to such qualifying dividends. For such purposes, 100 percent shall be used in lieu of the 85 percent specified in section 244(a)(3).

(c) Examples. The computation of the deduction provided in section 244 may be illustrated by the following examples:

Example (1). Corporation X, which files its income tax returns on the calendar year basis, received in 1965 $100,000 as dividends on the preferred stock of corporation Y, a public utility corporation which is subject to taxation under chapter 1 of the Code. The deduction provided in section 247 is allowable to Y, the distributing corporation, with respect to these dividends and they are not "qualifying dividends" (as defined in section 243(b)(1) but determined without regard to section 243(c)(4)). The corporation normal tax rate and the surtax rate for the calendar year 1965 are 22 percent and 26 percent, respectively. The deduction allowable to X under section 244(a) for the year 1965 with respect to these dividends is $60,208.33, computed as follows:

Dividends received on preferred stock of corporation Y	$100,000.00
Less: The fraction specified in section 244(a)(2): 14/48 × $100,000	29,166.67
Amount subject to 85-percent deduction	70,833.33
Deduction—85 percent of $70,833.33	60,208.33

The result would be the same if X or Y (or both) were subject to the 6-percent additional tax imposed by section 1562(b) for 1965.

Example (2). Assume the same facts as in example (1) and also assume that in 1965 corporation X received $200,000 as dividends on the preferred stock of Corporation Z, a public utility corporation which is subject to taxation under chapter 1 of the Code. Assume further that such dividends are "qualifying dividends" (as defined in section 243(b)(1) but determined without regard to section 243(c)(4)). The deduction provided in section 247 is allowable to Z, the distributing corporation, with respect to these dividends. The deduction allowable to X under section 244 for the year 1965 is $201,875, computed as follows:

Deduction allowable under section 244(a) with respect to the dividend received from Y (see example (1))	$ 60,208.33
Deduction allowable under section 244(b) with respect to the dividend received from Z:	
Qualifying dividends received on preferred stock of corporation Z	200,000.00
Less: The fraction specified in section 244(a)(2): 14/48 × $200,000	58,333.33
Deduction	141,666.67
Deduction allowable under section 244 for 1965	201,875.00

T.D. 6183, 6/13/56, amend T.D. 6992, 1/17/69.

§ 1.245-1 Dividends received from certain foreign corporations.

Caution: The Treasury has not yet amended Reg § 1.245-1 to reflect changes made by P.L. 100-647, P.L. 99-514.

(a) General rule. *(1)* A corporation is allowed a deduction under section 245(a) for dividends received from a foreign corporation (other than a foreign personal holding company as defined in section 552) which is subject to taxation under chapter 1 of the Code if, for an uninterrupted period of not less than 36 months ending with the close of the foreign corporation's taxable year in which the dividends are paid, (i) the foreign corporation is engaged in trade or business in the United States, and (ii) 50 percent or more of the foreign corporation's entire gross income is effectively connected with the conduct of a trade or business in the United States by that corporation. If the foreign corporation has been in existence less than 36 months as of the close of the taxable year in which the dividends are paid, then the applicable uninterrupted period to be taken into consideration in lieu of the uninterrupted period of 36 or more months is the entire period such corporation has been in existence as of the close of such taxable year. An uninterrupted period which satisfied the twofold requirement with respect to business activity and gross income may start at a date later than the date on which the foreign which satisfied the twofold requirement with respect to business activity and gross income may start a date later than the date on which the foreign corporation first commenced an uninterrupted period of engaging in trade or business within the United States, but the applicable uninterrupted period is in any event the longest uninterrupted period which satisfies such twofold requirement. The deduction under section 245(a) is allowable to any corporation, whether foreign or domestic, receiving dividends from a distributing corporation which meets the requirements of that section.

(2) Any taxable year of a foreign corporation which falls within the uninterrupted period described in section 245(a)(2) shall not be taken into account in applying section 245(a)(2) and this paragraph if the 100 percent dividends received deduction would be allowable under paragraph (b) of this section, whether or not in fact allowed, with respect to any dividends payable, whether or not in fact paid, out of the earnings and profits of such foreign corporation or that taxable year. Thus, in such case the foreign corporation shall be treated as having no earnings and profits for that taxable year or purposes of determining the dividends received deduction allowable under section 245(a) and this paragraph. However, that taxable year may be taken into account for purposes of determining whether the foreign corporation meets the requirements of section 245(a) that, for the uninterrupted period specified therein, the foreign corporation is

engaged in trade or business in the United States and meets the 50 percent gross income requirement.

(b) Dividends from wholly owned foreign subsidiaries. *(1)* A domestic corporation is allowed a deduction under section 245(b) for any taxable year beginning after December 31, 1966, for dividends received from a foreign corporation (other than a foreign personal holding company as defined in section 552) which is subject to taxation under chapter 1 of the Code if—

(i) The domestic corporation owns either directly or indirectly all of the outstanding stock of the foreign corporation during the entire taxable year of the domestic corporation in which the dividends are received, and

(ii) The dividends are paid out of earnings and profits of a taxable year of the foreign corporation during which (a) the domestic corporation receiving the dividends owns directly or indirectly throughout such year all of the outstanding stock of the foreign corporation, and (b) all of the gross income of the foreign corporation from all sources is effectively connected for that year with the conduct of a trade or business in the United States by that corporation.

(2) The deduction allowed by section 245(b) does not apply if an election under section 1562, relating to the privilege of a controlled group of corporations to elect multiple surtax exemptions, is effective for either the taxable year of the domestic corporation in which the dividends are received or the taxable year of the foreign corporation out of the earnings and profits of which the dividends are paid.

(c) Rules of application. *(1)* Except as provided in section 246, the deduction provided by section 245 for any taxable year is the sum of the amounts computed under paragraphs (1) and (2) of section 245(a) plus, in the case of a domestic corporation for any taxable year beginning after December 31, 1966, the sum of the amounts computed under section 245(b)(2).

(2) To the extent that a dividend received from a foreign corporation is treated as a dividend from a domestic corporation in accordance with section 243(d) and § 1.243-3, it shall not be treated as a dividend received from a foreign corporation for purposes of this section.

(3) For purposes of section 245(a) and (b), the amount of a distribution shall be determined under subparagraph (B) (without reference to subparagraph (C)) of section 301(b)(1).

(4) In determining from what year's earnings and profits a dividend is treated as having been distributed for purposes of this section, the principles of paragraph (a) of § 1.316-2 shall apply. A dividend shall be considered to be distributed, first, out of the earnings and profits of the taxable year which includes the date the dividend is distributed, second, out of the earnings and profits accumulated for the immediately preceding taxable year, third, out of the earnings and profits accumulated for the second preceding taxable year, etc. A deficit in an earnings and profits account for any taxable year shall reduce the most recently accumulated earnings and profits for a prior year in such account. If there are no accumulated earnings and profits in an earnings and profits account because of a deficit incurred in a prior year, such deficit must be restored before earnings and profits can be accumulated in a subsequent accounting year. See also paragraph (c) of § 1.243-3 and paragraph (a)(6) of § 1.243-4.

(5) For purposes of this section the gross income of a foreign corporation for any period before its first taxable year beginning after December 31, 1966, which is from sources within the United States shall be treated as gross income which is effectively connected for that period with the conduct of a trade or business in the United States by that corporation.

(6) For the determination of the source of income and the income which is effectively connected with the conduct of a trade or business in the United States, see sections 861 through 864, and the regulations thereunder.

(d) Illustrations. The application of this section may be illustrated by the following examples:

Example (1). Corporation A (a foreign corporation filing its income tax returns on a calendar year basis) whose stock is 100 percent owned by Corporation B (a domestic corporation filing its income tax returns on a calendar year basis) for the first time engaged in trade or business within the United States on January 1, 1943, and qualifies under section 245 for the entire period beginning on that date and ending on December 31, 1954. Corporation A had accumulated earnings and profits of $50,000 immediately prior to January 1, 1943, and had earnings and profits of $10,000 for each taxable year during the uninterrupted period from January 1, 1943, through December 31, 1954. It derived for the period from January 1, 1943, through December 31, 1953, 90 percent of its gross income from sources within the United States and in 1954 derived 95 percent of its gross income from sources within the United States. During the calendar years 1943, 1944, 1945, 1946, and 1947 Corporation A distributed in each year $15,000; during the calendar years 1948, 1949, 1950, 1951, 1952, and 1953 it distributed in each year $5,000; and during the year 1954, $50,000. An analysis of the accumulated earnings and profits under the above statement of facts discloses that at December 31, 1953, the accumulation amounted to $55,000, of which $25,000 was accumulated prior to the "uninterrupted period" and $30,000 was accumulated during the uninterrupted period. (See section 316(a) and paragraph(c) of this section.) For 1954 a deduction under section 245 of $31,025 ($8,075 on 1954 earnings of the foreign corporation, plus $22,950 from the $30,000 accumulation at December 31, 1953) for dividends received from a foreign corporation is allowable to Corporation B with respect to the $50,000 received from Corporation A, computed as follows:

(i) $8,075, which is $8,500 (85 percent—the percent specified in section 243 for the calendar year 1954—of the $10,000 of earnings and profits of the taxable year) multiplied by 95 percent (the portion of the gross income of Corporation A derived during the taxable year 1954 from sources within the United States), plus

(ii) $22,950, which is $25,500 (85 percent—the percent specified in section 243 for the calendar year 1954—of $30,000, the part of the earnings and profits accumulated after the beginning of the uninterrupted period) multiplied by 90 percent (the portion of the gross income of Corporation A derived from sources within the United States during that portion of the uninterrupted period ending at the beginning of the taxable year 1954).

Example (2). If in example (1), Corporation A for the taxable year 1954 had incurred a deficit of $10,000 (shown to have been incurred before December 31) the amount of the earnings and profits accumulated after the beginning of the uninterrupted period would be $20,000. If Corporation A had distributed $50,000 on December 31, 1954, the deduction under section 245 for dividends received from a foreign corporation allowable to Corporation B for 1954 would be $15,300, computed by multiplying $17,000 (85 percent—the percent specified in section 243 for the calendar year 1954—of $20,000 earnings and profits accumulated after the beginning of the uninterrupted period) by 90 percent (the portion of the gross income of Corporation A derived from United States sources during that portion of the uninterrupted period ending at the beginning of the taxable year 1954).

Example (3). Corporation A (a foreign corporation filing its income tax returns on a calendar year basis) whose stock is 100 percent owned by corporation B (a domestic corporation filing its income tax returns on a calendar year basis) for the first time engaged in trade or business within the United States on January 1, 1960, and qualifies under section 245 for the entire period beginning on that date and ending on December 31, 1963. In 1963, A derived 75 percent of its gross income from sources within the United States. A's earnings and profits for 1963 (computed as of the close of the taxable year without diminution by reason of any distributions made during the taxable year) are $200,000. On December 31, 1963, corporation A distributes to corporation B 100 shares of corporation C stock which have an adjusted basis in A's hands of $40,000 and a fair market value of $100,000. For purposes of computing the deduction under section 245 for dividends received from a foreign corporation, the amount of the distribution is $40,000. B is allowed a deduction under section 245 of $25,500, i.e., $34,000 ($40,000 multiplied by 85 percent, the percent specified in section 243 for 1963), multiplied by 75 percent (the portion of the gross income of corporation A derived during 1963 from sources within the United States).

T.D. 6183, 6/13/56, amend T.D. 6752, 9/8/64, T.D. 6830, 6/22/65, T.D. 7293, 11/27/73.

§ 1.246-1 Deductions not allowed for dividends from certain corporations.

Caution: The Treasury has not yet amended Reg § 1.246-1 to reflect changes made by P.L. 99-514, P.L. 98-369.

The deductions provided in sections 243 (relating to dividends received by corporations), 244 (relating to dividends received on certain preferred stock), and 245 (relating to dividends received from certain foreign corporations), are not allowable with respect to any dividend received from:

(a) A corporation organized under the China Trade Act, 1922 (15 U.S.C. ch. 4) (see section 941); or

(b) A corporation which is exempt from tax under section 501 (relating to certain charitable, etc., organizations) or section 521 (relating to farmers' cooperative associations) for the taxable year of the corporation in which the distribution is made or for its next preceding taxable year; or

(c) A corporation to which section 931 (relating to income from sources within possessions of the United States) applies for the taxable year of the corporation in which the distribution is made or for its next preceding taxable year; or

(d) A real estate investment trust which, for its taxable year in which the distribution is made, is taxable under part II, subchapter M, chapter 1 of the Code. See section 243(c)(3), paragraph (c) of § 1.243-2, section 857(c), and paragraph (d) of § 1.857-6.

T.D. 6183, 6/13/56, amend T.D. 6598, 4/25/62, T.D. 7767, 2/3/81.

§ 1.246-2 Limitation on aggregate amount of deductions.

Caution: The Treasury has not yet amended Reg § 1.246-2 to reflect changes made by P.L. 108-357, P.L. 99-514, P.L. 98-369.

(a) General rule. The sum of the deductions allowed by sections 243(a)(1) (relating to dividends received by corporations). 244(a) (relating to dividends received on certain preferred stock), and 245 (relating to dividends received from certain foreign corporations), except as provided in section 246(b)(2) and in paragraph (b) of this section, is limited to 85 percent of the taxable income of the corporation. The taxable income of the corporation for this purpose is computed without regard to the net operating loss deduction allowed by section 172, the deduction for dividends paid on certain preferred stock of public utilities allowed by section 247, any capital loss carryback under section 1212(a)(1), and the deductions provided in sections 243(a)(1), 244(a) and 245. For definition of the term "taxable income", see section 63.

(b) Effect of net operating loss. If the shareholder corporation has a net operating loss (as determined under sec. 172) for a taxable year, the limitation provided in section 246(b)(1) and in paragraph (a) of this section is not applicable for such taxable year. In that event, the deductions provided in sections 243(a)(1), 244(a), and 245 shall be allowable for all tax purposes to the shareholder corporation for such taxable year without regard to such limitation. If the shareholder corporation does not have a net operating loss for the taxable year, however, the limitation will be applicable for all tax purposes for such taxable year. In determining whether the shareholder corporation has a net operating loss for a taxable year under section 172, the deductions allowed by sections 243(a)(1), 244(a), and 245 are to be computed without regard to the limitation provided in section 246(b)(1) and in paragraph (a) of this section.

T.D. 6183, 6/13/56, amend T.D. 6449, 1/27/60, T.D. 6992, 1/17/69, T.D. 7301, 1/3/74.

§ 1.246-3 Exclusion of certain dividends.

Caution: The Treasury has not yet amended Reg § 1.246-3 to reflect changes made by P.L. 105-34, P.L. 99-514, P.L. 98-369.

(a) In general. Corporate taxpayers are denied, in certain cases, the dividends-received deduction provided by section 243 (dividends received by corporations), section 244 (dividends received on certain preferred stock), and section 245 (dividends received from certain foreign corporations). The above-mentioned dividends-received deductions are denied, under section 246(c)(1), to corporate shareholders:

(1) If the dividend is in respect of any share of stock which is sold or otherwise disposed of in any case where the taxpayer has held such share for 15 days or less; or

(2) If and to the extent that the taxpayer is under an obligation to make corresponding payments with respect to substantially identical stock or securities. It is immaterial whether the obligation has arisen pursuant to a short sale or otherwise.

(b) Ninety-day rule for certain preference dividends. In the case of any stock having a preference in dividends, a special rule is provided by section 246(c)(2) in lieu of the 15-day rule described in section 246(c)(1) and paragraph (a)(1) of this section. If the taxpayer receives dividends on such stock which are attributable to a period or periods aggregating in excess of 366 days, the holding period specified in section 246(c)(1)(A) shall be 90 days (in lieu of 15 days).

(c) Definitions. *(1) "Otherwise disposed of".* As used in this section the term "otherwise disposed of" includes disposal by gift.

(2) "Substantially identical stock or securities". The term "substantially identical stock or securities" is to be applied according to the facts and circumstances in each case. In general, the term has the same meaning as the corresponding terms in sections 1091 and 1233 and the regulations thereunder. See paragraph (d)(1) of § 1.1233-1.

(3) Obligation to make corresponding payments. (i) Section 246(c)(1)(B) of the Code denies the dividends-received deduction to a corporate taxpayer to the extent that such taxpayer is under an obligation, with respect to substantially identical stock or securities, to make payments corresponding to the dividend received. Thus, for example, where a corporate taxpayer is in both a "long" and "short" position with respect to the same stock on the date that such stock goes ex-dividend, the dividend received on the stock owned by the taxpayer will not be eligible for the dividends-received deduction to the extent that the taxpayer is obligated to make payments to cover the dividends with respect to its offsetting short position in the same stock. The dividends-received deduction is denied in such a case without regard to the length of time the taxpayer had held the stock on which such dividends are received.

(ii) The provisions of subdivision (i) of this subparagraph may be illustrated by the following example:

Example. Y Corporation owns 100 shares of the Z Corporation's common stock on January 1, 1959. Z Corporation on January 15, 1959, declares a dividend of $1.00 per share payable to shareholders of record on January 30, 1959. On January 21, 1959, Y Corporation sells short 25 shares of the Z Corporation's common stock and remains in the short position on January 31, 1959, the day that Z Corporation's common stock goes ex-dividend. Y Corporation is therefore obligated to make a payment to the lender of the 25 shares of Z Corporation's common stock which were sold short, corresponding to the $1.00 a share dividend that the lender would have received on those 25 shares, or $25.00. Therefore, $25.00 of the $100.00 that the Y Corporation receives as dividends from the Z Corporation with respect to the 100 shares of common stock in which it has a long position is not eligible for the dividends-received deduction.

(d) Determination of holding period. *(1) In general.* Special rules are provided by paragraph (3) of section 246(c) for determining the period for which the taxpayer has held any share of stock for purposes of the restriction provided by each section. In computing the holding period the day of disposition but not the day of acquisition shall be taken into account. Also, there shall not be taken into account any day which is more than 15 days after the date on which the share of stock becomes ex-dividend. Thus, the holding period is automatically terminated at the end of such 15-day period without regard to how long the stock may be held after that date. In the case of stock qualifying under paragraph (2) of section 246(c) (as having preference in dividends) a 90-day period is substituted for the 15-day period prescribed in this subparagraph. Finally, section 1223(4), relating to holding periods in the case of wash sales, shall not apply. Therefore, tacking of the holding period of the stock disposed of to the holding period of the stock acquired where a wash sale occurs is not permitted for purposes of determining the holding period described in section 246(c).

(2) Special rules. Section 246(c) requires that the holding periods determined thereunder shall be appropriately reduced for any period that the taxpayer's stock holding is offset by a corresponding short position resulting from an option to sell, a contractual obligation to sell, or a short sale of, substantially identical stock or securities. The holding periods of stock held for a period of 15 days or less on the date such short position is created shall accordingly be reduced to the extent of such short position. Where the amount of stock acquired within such period exceeds the amount as to which the taxpayer establishes a short position, the stock the holding period of which must be reduced because of such short position shall be that most recently acquired within such period. If, on the date the short position is created, the amount of stock subject to the short position exceeds the amount, if any, of stock held by the taxpayer for 15 days or less, the excess shares of stock sold short shall, to the extent thereof, postpone until the termination of the short position the commencement of the holding periods of subsequently acquired stock. Stock having a preference in dividends is also subject to the rules prescribed in this subparagraph, except that the 90-day period provided by paragraph (b) of this section shall apply in lieu of the 15-day period otherwise applicable. The rules prescribed in this subparagraph may be illustrated by the following examples:

Example (1). L Company purchased 100 shares of Z Corporation's common stock during January 1959. On November 26, 1959, L Company purchased an additional 100 shares of the same stock. On December 1, 1959, Z Corporation declared a dividend payable on its common stock to shareholders of record on December 20, 1959. Also on December 1, L Company sold short 150 shares of Z Corporation's common stock. On December 16, 1959 (before the stock went ex-dividend), L Company closed its short sale with 150 shares purchased on that date. In determining, for purposes of section 246(c), whether L Company has held the 100 shares of stock acquired on November 26 for a period in excess of 15 days, the period of the short position (from December 2 through December 16) shall be excluded. Thus, if on or before December 26, 1959, L Company sold the 100 shares of Z Corporation stock which it purchased on November 26, 1959, it would not be entitled to a dividends-received deduction for the dividends received on such shares because it would have held such shares for 15 days or less on the date of the sale. Since L Company had held the 100 shares acquired during January 1959 for for more than 15 days on December 2, 1959, and since it was under no obligation to make payments corresponding to the dividends received thereon, section 246(c) is inapplicable to the dividends received with respect to those shares.

Example (2). Assume the same facts as in example (1) above except that the additional 100 shares of Z Corporation common stock were purchased by L Company on December 10, 1959, rather than November 26, 1959. In determining, for purposes of section 246(c), whether L Company has held such shares for a period in excess of 15 days, the period from December 11, 1959, until December 16, 1959 (the date the short sale made on December 1 was closed), shall be excluded.

(e) Effective date. The provisions of this section shall apply to stock acquired after December 31, 1957, or with respect to stock acquired before that date where the taxpayer has made a short sale of substantially identical stock or securities after that date.

T.D. 6440, 1/4/60.

§ 1.246-4 Dividends from a DISC or former DISC.

The deduction provided in section 243 (relating to dividends received by corporations) is not allowable with respect to any dividend (whether in the form of a deemed or actual distribution or an amount treated as a dividend pursuant to section 995(c)) from a corporation which is a DISC or former DISC (as defined in section 992(a)(1) or (3) as the case may be) to the extent such dividend is from the corporation's accumulated DISC income (as defined in section 996(f)(1)) or previously taxed income (as defined in section 996(f)(2)) or is a deemed distribution pursuant to section 995(b)(1) in a taxable year for which the corporation qualifies (or is treated) as a DISC. To the extent that a dividend is paid out of earnings and profits which are not made up of accumulated DISC income or previously taxed income, the corporate recipient is entitled to the deduction provided in section 243 in the same manner and to the same extent as a dividend from a domestic corporation which is not a DISC or former DISC.

T.D. 7283, 8/2/73.

§ 1.246-5 Reduction of holding periods in certain situations.

(a) In general. Under section 246 (c)(4)(C), the holding period of stock for purposes of the dividends received deduction is appropriately reduced for any period in which a taxpayer has diminished its risk of loss by holding one or more other positions with respect to substantially similar or related property. This section provides rules for applying section 246(c)(4)(C).

(b) Definitions. *(1) Substantially similar or related property.* The term substantially similar or related property is applied according to the facts and circumstances in each case. In general, property is substantially similar or related to stock when—

(i) The fair market values of the stock and the property primarily reflect the performance of—

(A) A single firm or enterprise;

(B) The same industry or industries; or

(C) The same economic factor or factors such as (but not limited to) interest rates, commodity prices, or foreign-currency exchange rates; and

(ii) Changes in the fair market value of the stock are reasonably expected to approximate, directly or inversely, changes in the fair market value of the property, a fraction of the fair market value of the property, or a multiple of the fair market value of the property.

(2) Diminished risk of loss. A taxpayer has diminished its risk of loss on its stock by holding positions with respect to substantially similar or related property if changes in the fair market values of the stock and the positions are reasonably expected to vary inversely.

(3) Position. For purposes of this section, a position with respect to property is an interest (including a futures or forward contract or an option) in property or any contractual right to a payment, whether or not severable from stock or other property. A position does not include traditional equity rights to demand payment from the issuer, such as the rights traditionally provided by mandatorily redeemable preferred stock.

(4) Reasonable expectations. For purposes of paragraphs (b)(1)(i), (b)(2), or (c)(1)(vi) of this section, reasonable expectations are the expectations of a reasonable person, based on all the facts and circumstances at the later of the time the stock is acquired or the positions are entered into. Reasonable expectations include all explicit or implicit representations made with respect to the marketing or sale of the position.

(c) Special rules. *(1) Positions in more than one stock.* (i) In general. This paragraph (c)(1) provides rules for the treatment of positions that reflect the value of more than one stock. In general, positions that reflect the value of a portfolio of stocks are treated under the rules of paragraphs (c)(1)(ii) through (iv) of this section, and positions that reflect the value of more than one stock but less than a portfolio are treated under the rules of paragraph (c)(1)(v) of this section. A portfolio for this purpose is any group of stocks of 20 or more unrelated issuers. Paragraph (c)(1)(vi) of this section provides an anti-abuse rule.

(ii) Portfolios. Notwithstanding paragraph (b)(1) of this section, a position reflecting the value of a portfolio of stocks is substantially similar or related to the stocks held by the taxpayer only if the position and the taxpayer's holdings substantially overlap as of the most recent testing date. A position may be substantially similar or related to a taxpayer's entire stock holdings or a portion of a taxpayer's stock holdings.

(iii) Determining substantial overlap. This paragraph (c)(1)(iii) provides rules for determining whether a position and a taxpayer's stock holdings or a portion of a taxpayer's stock holdings substantially overlap. Paragraphs (c)(1)(iii)(A) through (C) of this section determine whether there is substantial overlap as of any testing date.

(A) Step One. Construct a subportfolio (the Subportfolio) that consists of stock in an amount equal to the lesser of the fair market value of each stock represented in the position and the fair market value of the stock in the taxpayer's stock holdings. (The Subportfolio may contain fewer than 20 stocks.)

(B) Step Two. If the fair market value of the Subportfolio is equal to or greater than 70 percent of the fair market value of the stocks represented in the position, the position and the Subportfolio substantially overlap.

(C) Step Three. If the position does not substantially overlap with the Subportfolio, repeat Steps One and Two (paragraphs (c)(1)(iii)(A) and (B) of this section) reducing the size of the position. The largest percentage of the position that results in a substantial overlap is substantially similar or related to the Subportfolio determined with respect to that percentage of the position.

(iv) Testing date. A testing date is any day on which the taxpayer purchases or sells any stock if the fair market value of the stock or the fair market value of substantially similar or related property is reflected in the position, any day on which the taxpayer changes the position, or any day on which the composition of the position changes.

(v) Nonportfolio positions. A position that reflects the fair market value of more than one stock but not of a portfolio of stocks is treated as a separate position with respect to each of the stocks the value of which the position reflects.

(vi) Anti-abuse rule. Notwithstanding paragraphs (c)(1)(i) through (v) of this section, a position that reflects the value of more than one stock is a position in substantially similar or related property to the appropriate portion of the taxpayer's stock holdings if—

(A) Changes in the value of the position or the stocks reflected in the position are reasonably expected to virtually track (directly or inversely) changes in the value of the taxpayer's stock holdings, or any portion of the taxpayer's stock holdings and other positions of the taxpayer; and

(B) The position is acquired or held as part of a plan a principal purpose of which is to obtain tax savings (including by deferring tax) the value of which is significantly in excess of the expected pre-tax economic profits from the plan.

(2) Options. (i) Options that are significantly out of the money. For purposes of paragraph (b)(2) of this section, an option to sell that is significantly out of the money does not diminish the taxpayer's risk of loss on its stock unless the option is held as part of a strategy to substantially offset changes in the fair market value of the stock.

(ii) Conversion rights. Notwithstanding paragraphs (b)(1) and (2) of this section, a taxpayer is treated as diminishing its risk of loss by holding substantially similar or related property if it engages in the following transactions or their substantial equivalents—

(A) A short sale of common stock while holding convertible preferred stock of the same issuer and the price changes of the convertible preferred stock and the common stock are related;

(B) A short sale of a convertible debenture while holding convertible preferred stock into which the debenture is convertible or common stock; or

(C) A short sale of convertible preferred stock while holding common stock.

(3) Stacking rule. If a taxpayer diminishes its risk of loss by holding a position in substantially similar or related property with respect to only a portion of the shares that the taxpayer holds in a particular stock, the holding period of those shares having the shortest holding period is reduced.

(4) Guarantees, surety agreements, or similar arrangements. A taxpayer has diminished its risk of loss on stock by holding a position in substantially similar or related property if the taxpayer is the beneficiary of a guarantee, surety agreement, or similar arrangement and the guarantee, surety agreement, or similar arrangement provides for payments that will substantially offset decreases in the fair market value of the stock.

(5) Hedges counted only once. A position established as a hedge of one outstanding position, transaction, or obligation of the taxpayer (other than stock) is not treated as diminishing the risk of loss with respect to any other position held by the taxpayer. In determining whether a position is established to hedge an outstanding position, transaction, or obligation of the taxpayer, substantial deference will be given to the relationships that are established in its books and records at the time the position is entered into.

(6) Use of related persons or pass-through entities. Positions held by a party related to the taxpayer within the meaning of sections 267(b) or 707(b)(1) are treated as positions held by the taxpayer if the positions are held with a view to avoiding the application of this section or § 1.1092(d)-2. In addition, a taxpayer is treated as diminishing its risk of loss by holding substantially similar or related property if the taxpayer holds an interest in, or is the beneficiary of, a pass-through entity, intermediary, or other arrangement with a view to avoiding the application of this section or § 1.1092(d)-2.

(7) Notional principal contracts. For purposes of this section, rights and obligations under notional principal contracts are considered separately even though payments with regard to those rights and obligations are generally netted for other purposes. Therefore, if a taxpayer is treated under the preceding sentence as receiving payments under a notional principal contract when the fair market value of the taxpayer's stock declines, the taxpayer has diminished its risk of loss by holding a position in substantially similar or related property regardless of the netting of the payments under the contract for any other purposes.

(d) Examples. The following examples illustrate the provisions of this section:

Example (1). General application to common stock. Corporation A and Corporation B are both automobile manufacturers. The fair market values of Corporation A and Corporation B common stock primarily reflect the value of the same industry. Because Corporation A and Corporation B common stock are affected not only by the general level of growth in the industry but also by individual corporate management decisions and corporate capital structures, changes in the fair market value of Corporation A common stock are not reasonably expected to approximate changes in the fair market value of the Corporation B common stock. Under paragraph (b)(1) of this section, Corporation A common stock is not substantially similar or related to Corporation B common stock.

Example (2). Common stock value primarily reflects commodity price. Corporation C and Corporation D both hold gold as their primary asset, and historically changes in the fair market value of Corporation C common stock approximated changes in the fair market value of Corporation D common stock. Corporation M purchased Corporation C common stock and sold short Corporation D common stock. Corporation C common stock is substantially similar or related to Corporation D common stock because their fair market values primarily reflect the performance of the same economic factor, the price of gold, and changes in the fair market value of Corporation C common stock are reasonably expected to approximate changes in the fair market value of Corporation D common stock. It was reasonably expected that changes in the fair market values of the Corporation C common stock and the short position in Corporation D common stock would vary inversely. Thus, Corporation M has diminished its risk of loss on its Corporation C common stock for purposes of section 246(c)(4)(C) and this section by holding a position in substantially similar or related property.

Example (3). Portfolios of stocks.

(i) Corporation Z holds a portfolio of stocks and acquires a short position on a publicly traded index through a regulated futures contract (RFC) that reflects the value of a portfolio of stocks as defined in paragraph (c)(1)(i) of this section. The index reflects the fair market value of stocks A through T. The values of stocks reflected in the index and the values of the same stocks in Corporation Z's holdings are as follows:

Stock	Z's Holdings	RFC	Subportfolio
A	$ 300	$ 300	$ 300
B	300	300	300
C	-0-	300	-0-
D	400	500	400
E	300	500	300
F	300	500	300
G	500	600	500
H	300	300	300
I	-0-	300	-0-
J	400	450	400
K	200	500	200
L	200	400	200
M	200	500	200
N	100	200	100
O	-0-	200	-0-

P	200	200	200
Q	100	300	100
R	200	100	100
S	100	100	100
T	100	200	100
Totals	$4,200	$6,750	$4,100

(ii) The position is substantially similar or related to Z's stock holdings only if they substantially overlap. To determine whether they substantially overlap, Corporation Z must construct a Subportfolio of stocks with the lesser of the value of the stock as reflected in the RFC and its holdings. The Subportfolio is given in the rightmost column above. The value of the Subportfolio is 60.74 percent of the value of the stocks represented in the position ($4100 section $6750), so the position and the Subportfolio do not substantially overlap.

(iii) To determine whether any portion of the position substantially overlaps with any portion of the Z's stock holdings, the values of the stocks in the RFC are reduced for purposes of the above steps. Eighty percent of the position and the corresponding subportfolio (consisting of stocks with a value of the lesser of the stocks represented in Z's holdings and in 80 percent of the RFC) substantially overlap, computed as follows:

Stock	Z's Holdings	80% of RFC	Subportfolio
A	$ 300	$ 240	$ 240
B	300	240	240
C	-0-	240	-0-
D	400	400	400
E	300	400	300
F	300	400	300
G	500	480	480
H	300	240	240
I	-0-	240	-0-
J	400	360	360
K	200	400	200
L	200	320	200
M	200	400	200
N	100	160	100
O	-0-	160	-0-
P	200	160	160
Q	100	240	100
R	200	80	80
S	100	80	80
T	100	160	100
Totals	$4,200	$5,400	$3,780

(iv) Because $3,780 is 70 percent of $5,400, the Subportfolio substantially overlaps with 80 percent of the position. Under paragraph (c)(3) of this section, Z's stocks having the shortest holding period are treated as included in the Subportfolio. A larger portion of Z's stocks may be treated as substantially similar or related property under the anti-abuse rule of paragraph (c)(1)(vi) of this section.

Example (4). Hedges counted only once. On January 1, 1996, Corporation X owns a $100 million portfolio of stocks all of which would substantially overlap with a $100 million regulated futures contract (RFC) on a commonly used index (the Index). On January 15, Corporation X enters into a $100 million short position in an RFC on the Index with a March delivery date and enters into a $75 million long position in an RFC on the Index for June delivery. Also on January 15, 1996, Corporation X indicates in its books and records that the long and short RFC positions are intended to offset one another. Under paragraph (c)(5) of this section, $75 million of the short position in the RFC is not treated as diminishing the risk of loss on the stock portfolio and instead is treated as a straddle or a hedging transaction, as appropriate, with respect to the $75 million long position in the RFC, under section 1092. The remaining $25 million short position is treated as diminishing the risk of loss on the portfolio by holding a position in substantially similar or related property. The rules of paragraph (c)(1) determine how much of the portfolio is subject to this rule and the rules of paragraph (c)(3) determine which shares have their holding periods tolled.

(e) Effective date. *(1) In general.* The provisions of this section apply to dividends received on or after March 17, 1995, on stock acquired after July 18, 1984.

(2) Special rule for dividends received on certain stock. Notwithstanding paragraph (e)(1) of this section, this section applies to any dividends received by a taxpayer on stock acquired after July 18, 1984, if the taxpayer has diminished its risk of loss by holding substantially similar or related property involving the following types of transactions—

(i) The short sale of common stock when holding convertible preferred stock of the same issuer and the price changes of the two stocks are related, or the short sale of a convertible debenture while holding convertible preferred stock into which the debenture is convertible (or common stock), or a short sale of convertible preferred stock while holding common stock; or

(ii) The acquisition of a short position in a regulated futures contract on a stock index, or the acquisition of an option to sell the regulated futures contract or the stock index itself, or the grant of a deep-in-the-money option to buy the regulated futures contract or the stock index while holding the stock of an investment company whose principal holdings mimic the performance of the stocks included in the stock index; or alternatively, while holding a portfolio composed of stocks that mimic the performance of the stocks included in the stock index.

T.D. 8590, 3/17/95.

§ 1.247-1 Deduction for dividends paid on preferred stock of public utilities.

Caution: The Treasury has not yet amended Reg § 1.247-1 to reflect changes made by P.L. 95-600, P.L. 94-455.

(a) Amount of deduction. *(1)* A deduction is provided in section 247 for dividends paid during the taxable year by certain public utility corporations (see paragraph (b) of this section) on certain preferred stock (see paragraph (c) of this section). This deduction is an amount equal to the product of a specified fraction times the lesser of (i) the amount of the dividends paid during the taxable year by a public utility on its preferred stock (as defined in paragraph (c) of this section), or (ii) the taxable income of the public utility for such taxable year (computed without regard to the deduction allowed by section 247). The specified fraction for any taxable year is the fraction the numerator of which is 14 and the denominator of which is the sum of the corporation normal tax rate and the surtax rate for such taxable year specified in section 11. Since section 11 provides that for the calendar year 1954 the corporation normal tax rate is 30 percent and the surtax rate is 22 percent, the sum of the two tax rates is 52 percent and the specified fraction for the calendar year 1954 is 14/52. If, for example, section 11 should specify that the corporation's normal tax rate is 25 percent and the surtax rate is 22 percent for the calendar year, the sum of the two tax rates will be 47 percent and the specified fraction for the calendar year will be $^{14}/_{47}$. If Corporation A, a public utility which files its income tax return on the calendar year basis, pays $100,000 dividends on its preferred stock in the calendar year 1954 and if its taxable income for such year is greater than $100,000 the deduction allowable to Corporation A under section 247 for 1954 is $100,000 times $^{14}/_{52}$, or $26,923.08. If in 1954 Corporation A's taxable income, computed without regard to the deduction provided in section 247, had been $90,000 (that is, less than the amount of the dividends which it paid on its preferred stock in that year), the deduction allowable under section 247 for 1954 would have been $90,000 times $^{14}/_{52}$, or $24,230.77.

(2) For the purpose of determining the amount of the deduction provided in section 247(a) and in subparagraph (1) of this paragraph, the amount of dividends paid in a given taxable year shall not include any amount distributed in such year with respect to dividends unpaid and accumulated in any taxable year ending before October 1, 1942. If any distribution is made in the current taxable year with respect to dividends unpaid and accumulated for a prior taxable year, such distribution will be deemed to have been made with respect to the earliest year or years for which there are dividends unpaid and accumulated. Thus, if a public utility makes a distribution with respect to a prior taxable year, it shall be considered that such distribution was made with respect to the earliest year or years for which there are dividends unpaid and accumulated, whether or not the public utility states that the distribution was made with respect to such year or years and even though the public utility states that the distribution was made with respect to a later year. Even though it has dividends unpaid and accumulated with respect to a taxable year ending before October 1, 1942, a public utility may, however, include the dividends paid with respect to the current taxable year in computing the deduction under section 247. If there are no dividends unpaid and accumulated with respect to a taxable year ending before October 1, 1942, a public utility may include the dividends paid with respect to a prior taxable year which ended after October 1, 1942, in computing the deduction under section 247: such public utility in addition may include the dividends paid with respect to the current taxable year in computing the deduction under section 247. However, if local law or its own charter requires a public utility to pay all unpaid and accumulated dividends before any dividends can be paid with respect to the current taxable year, such public utility may not include any distribution in the current year in computing the deduction under section 247 to the extent that there are dividends unpaid and accumulated with respect to taxable years ending before October 1, 1942.

(3) If a corporation which is engaged in one or more of the four types of business activities (called utility activities in this section) enumerated in section 247(b)(1) (the furnishing of telephone service or the sale of electrical energy, gas, or water) is also engaged in some other business that does not fall within any of the enumerated categories, the deduction under section 247 is allowable only for such portion of the amount computed under section 247(a) as is allocable to the income from utility activities. For this purpose, the allocation may be made on the basis of the ratio which the total income from the utility activities bears to total income from all sources (total income being considered either gross income or gross receipts, whichever method results in the higher deduction). However, if such an allocation reaches an inequitable result and the books of the corporation are so kept that the taxable income attributable to the utility activities can be readily determined, particularly where the books of the corporation are required by governmental bodies to be so kept for rate making or other purposes, the allocation may be made upon the basis of taxable income. No such apportionment will be required if the income from sources other than utility activities is less than 20 percent of the total income of the corporation, irrespective of the method used in determining such total income.

(b) Public utility. As used in section 247 and this section, public utility means a corporation engaged in the furnishing of telephone service, or in the sale of electric energy, gas, or water if the rates charged by such corporation for such furnishing or sale, as the case may be, have been established or approved by a State or political subdivision thereof or by an agency or instrumentality of the United States or by a public utility or public service commission or other similar body of the District of Columbia or of any State or political subdivision thereof. If a schedule of rates has been filed with any of the above bodies having the power to disapprove such rates, then such rates shall be considered as established or approved rates even though such body has taken no action on the filed schedule. Rates fixed by contract between the corporation and the purchaser, except where the purchaser is the United States, a State, the District of Columbia, or an agency or political subdivision of the United States, a State, or the District of Columbia, shall not be considered as established or approved rates in those cases where they are not subject to direct control, or where no maximum rate for such contract rates has been established by the United States, a State, the District of Columbia, or by an agency or political subdivision thereof. The deduction provided in section 247 will not be denied solely because part of the gross income of the corporation consists of revenue derived from such furnishing or sale at rates which are not so regulated, provided the corporation establishes to the satisfaction of the Commissioner (1) that the revenue from regulated rates and the revenue from unregulated rates are derived from the operation of a single interconnected and coordinated system within a single area or region in one or more States, or from the operation of more than one such system and (2) that the regulation to which it is subject in part of its operating territory in one such system is effective to control rates within the unregulated territory of the same system so that the rates within the unregulated territory have been and are substantially as favorable to users and consumers as are the rates within the regulated territory.

(c) Preferred stock. *(1)* For the purposes of section 247 and this section, preferred stock means stock (i) which was issued before October 1, 1942, (ii) the dividends in respect of which (during the whole of the taxable year, or the part of the taxable year after the actual date of the issue of such stock) were cumulative, nonparticipating as to current distributions, and payable in preference to the payment of dividends on other stock, and (iii) the rate of return on which is fixed and cannot be changed by a vote of the board of directors or by some similar method. However, if there are several classes of preferred stock, all of which meet the above requirements, the deduction provided in section 247 shall not be denied in the case of a given class of preferred stock merely because there is another class of preferred stock whose dividends are to be paid before those of the given class of stock. Likewise, it is immaterial for the purposes of section 247 and this section whether the stock be voting or nonvoting stock.

(2) Preferred stock issued on or after October 1, 1942, under certain circumstances will be considered as having been issued before October 1, 1942, for purposes of the deduction provided in section 247. If the new stock is issued on or after October 1, 1942, to refund or replace bonds or debentures which were issued before October 1, 1942, or to refund or replace other stock which was preferred stock within the meaning of section 247(b)(2) (or the corresponding provision of the Internal Revenue Code of 1939), such new stock shall be considered as having been issued before October 1, 1942. If preferred stock is issued to refund or replace stock which was preferred stock within the meaning of section 247(b)(2) (or the corresponding provision of the Internal Revenue Code of 1939), it shall be immaterial whether the preferred stock so refunded or replaced was issued before, on, or after October 1, 1942. If stock issued on or after October 1, 1942, to refund or replace stock which was issued before October 1, 1942, and which was preferred stock within the meaning of section 247(b)(2) (or the corresponding provision of the Internal Revenue Code of 1939), is not itself preferred stock within the meaning of section 247(b)(2) (or the corresponding provision of the Internal Revenue Code of 1939), no stock issued to refund or replace such stock can be considered preferred stock for purposes of the deduction provided in section 247.

(3) In the case of any preferred stock issued on or after October 1, 1942, to refund or replace bonds or debentures issued before October 1, 1942, or to refund or replace other stock which was preferred stock within the meaning of section 247(b)(2) (or the corresponding provision of the Internal Revenue Code of 1939), only that portion of the stock issued on or after October 1, 1942, will be considered as having been issued before October 1, 1942, the par or stated value of which does not exceed the par, stated, or face value of such bonds, debentures, or other preferred stock which the new stock was issued to refund or replace. In such case no shares of the new stock issued on or after October 1, 1942, shall be earmarked in determining the deduction allowable under section 247, but the appropriate allocable portion of the total amount of dividends paid on such stock will be considered as having been paid on stock which was issued before October 1, 1942.

(4) The provisions of section 247(b)(2) may be illustrated by the following example:

Example. A public utility has outstanding 1,000 bonds which were issued before October 1, 1942, and each of which has a face value of $100. On or after October 1, 1942, each of such bonds is retired in exchange for 1$\frac{1}{10}$ shares of preferred stock issued on or after October 1, 1942, and having a par value of $100 per share. Only $\frac{10}{11}$ of the dividends paid on the preferred stock thus issued in exchange for the bonds will be considered as having been paid on stock which was issued before October 1, 1942. Likewise, if preferred stock which is issued on or after October 1, 1942, has no par value but a stated value of $50 per share and such stock is issued in a ratio of three shares to one share to refund or replace preferred stock having a par value of $100 per share, only two-thirds of the dividends paid on the new shares of stock will be considered as having been paid on stock which was issued before October 1, 1942.

(5) Whether or not preferred stock issued on or after October 1, 1942, was issued to refund or replace bonds or debentures issued before October 1, 1942, or to refund or replace other preferred stock, is in each case a question of fact. Among the factors to be considered is whether such stock is new in an economic sense to the corporation or whether it was issued merely to take the place, directly or indirectly, of bonds, debentures, or other preferred stock of such corporation. It is not necessary that the new preferred stock be issued in exchange for such bonds, debentures, or other preferred stock. The mere fact that the bonds, debentures, or other preferred stock remain in existence for a short period of time after the issuance of the new stock (or were retired before the issuance of the new stock) does not necessarily mean that such new stock was not issued to refund or replace such bonds, debentures, or other preferred stock. It is necessary to consider the entire transaction, including the issuance of the new preferred stock, the date of such issuance, the retirement of the old bonds, debentures, or preferred stock, and the date of such retirement, in order to determine whether such new stock really was issued to take the place of bonds, debentures, or other preferred stock of the corporation or whether it represents something essentially new in an economic sense in the corporation's financial structure. If, for example, a public utility, which has outstanding bonds issued before October 1, 1942, issues new preferred stock on October 1, 1954, in order to secure funds with which to retire such bonds and with the money paid in for such stock retires the bonds on November 1, 1954, such stock may be considered as having been issued to refund or replace bonds issued before October 1, 1942. Whether the money used to retire the bonds can be traced back and identified as the money paid in for the stock will have evidentiary value, but will not be conclusive, in determining whether the stock was issued to refund or replace the bonds. Similarly, whether the amount of money used to retire the bonds was smaller than, equal to, or greater than that paid in for the stock, or whether the entire issue of bonds is retired, will be important, but not decisive, in making such determination.

(6) Preferred stock issued on or after October 1, 1942, by a corporation to refund or replace bonds or debentures of a second corporation which were issued before October 1, 1942, or to refund or replace other preferred stock of such second corporation, may be considered as having been issued before October 1, 1942, if such new stock was issued (i) in a transaction which is a reorganization within the meaning of section 368(a) or the corresponding provisions of the Internal Revenue Code of 1939; or (ii) in a transaction to which section 371 (relating to insolvency reorganizations), or the corresponding provisions of the Internal Revenue Code of 1939, is applicable; or (iii) in a transaction which is subject to the provisions of part VI, subchapter O, chapter 1 of the Code (relating to exchanges and distributions in obedience to orders of the Securities and Exchange Commission) or to the corresponding provisions of the Internal Revenue Code of 1939. Whether the stock actually was issued to refund or replace bonds or debentures of the second corporation issued before October 1, 1942, or to refund or replace preferred stock of such second corporation, shall be determined under the same principles as if only one corporation were involved. A corporation may issue stock to refund or replace its own bonds, debentures, or other preferred stock in a transaction which is a reorganization within the meaning of section 368(a) or the corresponding provisions of the Internal Revenue Code of 1939, in a transaction to which section 371 or the corresponding provisions of the Internal Revenue Code of 1939 is applicable, or in a transaction which is subject to the provisions of part VI, subchapter O, chapter 1 of the Code, or to the corresponding provisions of the Internal Revenue Code of 1939. The provisions of this paragraph, in addition, are applicable in case a corporation issues stock on or after October 1, 1942, to refund or replace its own bonds,

debentures, or other preferred stock even though the issuance of such stock may not fall within one of the categories enumerated above.

(7) Even though stock issued on or after October 1, 1942, is considered as having been issued before October 1, 1942, by reason of having been issued to refund or replace bonds or debentures issued before October 1, 1942, or to refund or replace other preferred stock, such stock will not be deemed to be preferred stock within the meaning of section 247(b)(2), and no deduction will be allowable in respect of dividends paid on such stock, unless the stock fulfills all the other requirements of a preferred stock set forth in section 247(b)(2) and in this paragraph.

T.D. 6183, 6/13/56.

---

§ 1.248-1 Election to amortize organizational expenditures.

(a) [Reserved]. For further guidance, see § 1.248-1T(a).

(b) Organizational expenditures defined. *(1)* Section 248(b) defines the term "organizational expenditures." Such expenditures, for purposes of section 248 and this section, are those expenditures which are directly incident to the creation of the corporation. An expenditure, in order to qualify as an organizational expenditure, must be (i) incident to the creation of the corporation, (ii) chargeable to the capital account of the corporation, and (iii) of a character which, if expended incident to the creation of a corporation having a limited life, would be amortizable over such life. An expenditure which fails to meet each of these three tests may not be considered an organizational expenditure for purposes of section 248 and this section.

(2) The following are examples of organizational expenditures within the meaning of section 248 and this section: legal services incident to the organization of the corporation, such as drafting the corporate charter, by-laws, minutes of organizational meetings, terms of original stock certificates, and the like; necessary accounting services; expenses of temporary directors and of organizational meetings of directors or stockholders; and fees paid to the State of incorporation.

(3) The following expenditures are not organizational expenditures within the meaning of section 248 and this section:

(i) Expenditures connected with issuing or selling shares of stock or other securities, such as commissions, professional fees, and printing costs. This is so even where the particular issue of stock to which the expenditures relate is for a fixed term of years;

(ii) Expenditures connected with the transfer of assets to a corporation.

(4) Expenditures connected with the reorganization of a corporation, unless directly incident to the creation of a corporation, are not organizational expenditures within the meaning of section 248 and this section.

(c) Time and manner of making election. The election provided by section 248(a) and paragraph (a) of this section shall be made in a statement attached to the taxpayer's return for the taxable year in which it begins business. Such taxable year must be one which begins after December 31, 1953. The return and statement must be filed not later than the date prescribed by law for filing the return (including any extensions of time) for the taxable year in which the taxpayer begins business. The statement shall set forth the description and amount of the expenditures involved, the date such expenditures were incurred, the month in which the corporation began business, and the number of months (not less than 60 and beginning with the month in which the taxpayer began business) over which such expenditures are to be deducted ratably.

(c) through (g) [Reserved]. For further guidance, see § 1.248-1T(c) through (g).

T.D. 6183, 6/13/56, amend T.D. 7605, 3/29/79, T.D. 9411, 7/7/2008.

PAR. 3. Section 1.248-1 is amended by revising paragraphs (a) and (c), and adding paragraphs (d) through (f), to read as follows:

Proposed § 1.248-1 Election to amortize organizational expenditures. [*For Preamble, see ¶ 153,023*]

(a) [The text of this proposed amendment to § 1.248-1(a) is the same as the text of § 1.248-1T(a) published elsewhere in this issue of the Federal Register.] [*See T.D. 9411, 07/08/2008, 73 Fed. Reg. 131.*]

* * * * *

(c) through (f) [The text of these proposed amendments to § 1.248-1(c) through (f) are the same as the text of § 1.248-1T(c) through (f) published elsewhere in this issue of the Federal Register.] [*See T.D. 9411, 07/08/2008, 73 Fed. Reg. 131.*]

§ 1.248-1T Election to amortize organizational expenditures (temporary).

(a) In general. Under section 248(a), a corporation may elect to amortize organizational expenditures as defined in section 248(b) and § 1.248-1(b). In the taxable year in which a corporation begins business, an electing corporation may deduct an amount equal to the lesser of the amount of the organizational expenditures of the corporation, or $5,000 (reduced (but not below zero) by the amount by which the organizational expenditures exceed $50,000). The remainder of the organizational expenditures is deducted ratably over the 180-month period beginning with the month in which the corporation begins business. All organizational expenditures of the corporation are considered in determining whether the organizational expenditures exceed $50,000, including expenditures incurred on or before October 22, 2004.

(b) [Reserved]. For further guidance, see § 1.248-1(b).

(c) Time and manner of making election. A corporation is deemed to have made an election under section 248(a) to amortize organizational expenditures as defined in section 248(b) and § 1.248-1(b) for the taxable year in which the corporation begins business. A corporation may choose to forgo the deemed election by clearly electing to capitalize its organizational expenditures on a timely filed Federal income tax return (including extensions) for the taxable year in which the corporation begins business. The election either to amortize organizational expenditures under section 248(a) or to capitalize organizational expenditures is irrevocable and applies to all organizational expenditures of the corporation. A change in the characterization of an item as an organizational expenditure is a change in method of accounting to which sections 446 and 481(a) apply if the corporation treated the item consistently for two or more taxable years. A change in the determination of the taxable year in which the corporation begins business also is treated as a change in method of accounting if the corporation amortized organizational expenditures for two or more taxable years.

(d) Determination of when corporation begins business. The deduction allowed under section 248 must be spread over a period beginning with the month in which the corporation begins business. The determination of the date the corporation begins business presents a question of fact which must be determined in each case in light of all the circumstances of the particular case. The words "begins business," however, do not have the same meaning as "in existence." Ordinarily, a corporation begins business when it starts the business operations for which it was organized; a corporation comes into existence on the date of its incorporation. Mere organizational activities, such as the obtaining of the corporate charter, are not alone sufficient to show the beginning of business. If the activities of the corporation have advanced to the extent necessary to establish the nature of its business operations, however, it will be deemed to have begun business. For example, the acquisition of operating assets which are necessary to the type of business contemplated may constitute the beginning of business.

(e) Examples. The following examples illustrate the application of this section:

Example (1). Expenditures of $5,000 or less. Corporation X, a calendar year taxpayer, incurs $3,000 of organizational expenditures after October 22, 2004, and begins business on July 1, 2009. Under paragraph (c) of this section, Corporation X is deemed to have elected to deduct organizational expenditures under section 248(a) in 2009. Therefore, Corporation X may deduct the entire amount of the organizational expenditures in 2009, the taxable year in which Corporation X begins business.

Example (2). Expenditures of more than $5,000 but less than or equal to $50,000. The facts are the same as in Example 1 except that Corporation X incurs organizational expenditures of $41,000. Under paragraph (c) of this section, Corporation X is deemed to have elected to deduct organizational expenditures under section 248(a) in 2009. Therefore, Corporation X may deduct $5,000 and the portion of the remaining $36,000 that is allocable to July through December of 2009 ($36,000/180 x 6 = $1,200) in 2009, the taxable year in which Corporation X begins business.

Example (3). Subsequent change in the characterization of an item. The facts are the same as in Example 2 except that Corporation X determines in 2011 that Corporation X incurred $10,000 for an additional organizational expenditure erroneously deducted in 2009 under section 162 as a business expense. Under paragraph (c) of this section, Corporation X is deemed to have elected to amortize organizational expenditures under section 248(a) in 2009, including the additional $10,000 of organizational expenditures. Corporation X is using an impermissible method of accounting for the additional $10,000 of organizational expenditures and must change its method under § 1.446-1(e) and the applicable general administrative procedures in effect in 2011.

Example (4). Subsequent redetermination of year in which business begins. The facts are the same as in Example 2 except that, in 2010, Corporation X deducted the organizational expenditures allocable to January through December of 2010 ($36,000/180 x 12 = $2,400). In addition, in 2011 it is determined that Corporation X actually began business in 2010. Under paragraph (c) of this section, Corporation X is deemed to have elected to deduct organizational expenditures under section 248(a) in 2010. Corporation X impermissibly deducted organizational expenditures in 2009, and incorrectly determined the amount of organizational expenditures deducted in 2010. Therefore, Corporation X is using an impermissible method of accounting for the organizational expenditures and must change its method under § 1.446-1(e) and the applicable general administrative procedures in effect in 2011.

Example (5). Expenditures of more than $50,000 but less than or equal to $55,000. The facts are the same as in Example 1 except that Corporation X incurs organizational expenditures of $54,500. Under paragraph (c) of this section, Corporation X is deemed to have elected to deduct organizational expenditures under section 248(a) in 2009. Therefore, Corporation X may deduct $500 ($5,000-4,500) and the portion of the remaining $54,000 that is allocable to July through December of 2009 ($54,000/180 x 6 = $1,800) in 2009, the taxable year in which Corporation X begins business.

Example (6). Expenditures of more than $55,000. The facts are the same as in Example 1 except that Corporation X incurs organizational expenditures of $450,000. Under paragraph (c) of this section, Corporation X is deemed to have elected to deduct organizational expenditures under section 248(a) in 2009. Therefore, Corporation X may deduct the amounts allocable to July through December of 2009 ($450,000/180 x 6 = $15,000) in 2009, the taxable year in which Corporation X begins business.

(f) Effective/applicability date. This section applies to organizational expenditures paid or incurred after September 8, 2008. However, taxpayers may apply all the provisions of this section to organizational expenditures paid or incurred after October 22, 2004, provided that the period of limitations on assessment of tax for the year the election under paragraph (c) of this section is deemed made has not expired. Otherwise, for organizational expenditures paid or incurred prior to September 8, 2008, see § 1.248-1 in effect prior to that date (§ 1.248-1 as contained in 26 CFR part 1 edition revised as of April 1, 2008).

(g) Expiration date. This section expires on July 7, 2011.

T.D. 9411, 7/7/2008.

§ 1.249-1 Limitation on deduction of bond premium on repurchase.

Caution: The Treasury has not yet amended Reg § 1.249-1 to reflect changes made by P.L. 98-369.

(a) Limitation. *(1) General rule.* No deduction is allowed to the issuing corporation for any "repurchase premium" paid or incurred to repurchase a convertible obligation to the extent the repurchase premium exceeds a "normal call premium."

(2) Exception. Under paragraph (e) of this section, the preceding sentence shall not apply to the extent the corporation demonstrates that such excess is attributable to the cost of borrowing and not to the conversion feature.

(b) Obligations. *(1) Definition.* For purposes of this section, the term "obligation" means any bond, debenture, note, or certificate or other evidence of indebtedness.

(2) Convertible obligation. Section 249 applies to an obligation which is convertible into the stock of the issuing corporation or a corporation which, at the time the obligation is issued or repurchased, is in control of or controlled by the issuing corporation. For purposes of this subparagraph, the term "control" has the meaning assigned to such term by section 368(c).

(3) Comparable nonconvertible obligation. A nonconvertible obligation is comparable to a convertible obligation if both obligations are of the same grade and classification,

with the same issue and maturity dates, and bearing the same rate of interest. The term "comparable nonconvertible obligation" does not include any obligation which is convertible into property.

(c) Repurchase premium. For purposes of this section, the term *repurchase premium* means the excess of the repurchase price paid or incurred to repurchase the obligation over its adjusted issue price (within the meaning of § 1.1275-1(b)) as of the repurchase date. For the general rules applicable to the deductibility of repurchase premium, see § 1.163-7(c). This paragraph (c) applies to convertible obligations repurchased on or after March 2, 1998.

(d) Normal call premium. *(1) In general.* Except as provided in subparagraph (2) of this paragraph, for purposes of this section, a "normal call premium" on a convertible obligation is an amount equal to a normal call premium on a nonconvertible obligation which is comparable to the convertible obligation. A normal call premium on a comparable nonconvertible obligation is a call premium specified in dollars under the terms of such obligation. Thus, if such a specified call premium is constant over the entire term of the obligation, the normal call premium is the amount specified. If, however, the specified call premium varies during the period the comparable nonconvertible obligation is callable or if such obligation is not callable over its entire term, the normal call premium is the amount specified for the period during the term of such comparable nonconvertible obligation which corresponds to the period during which the convertible obligation was repurchased.

(2) One-year's interest rule. For a convertible obligation repurchased on or after March 2, 1998, a call premium specified in dollars under the terms of the obligation is considered to be a normal call premium on a nonconvertible obligation if the call premium applicable when the obligation is repurchased does not exceed an amount equal to the interest (including original issue discount) that otherwise would be deductible for the taxable year of repurchase (determined as if the obligation were not repurchased). The provisions of this subparagraph shall not apply if the amount of interest payable for the corporation's taxable year is subject under the terms of the obligation to any contingency other than repurchase prior to the close of such taxable year.

(e) Exception. *(1) In general.* If a repurchase premium exceeds a normal call premium, the general rule of paragraph (a)(1) of this section does not apply to the extent that the corporation demonstrates to the satisfaction of the Commissioner or his delegate that such repurchase premium is attributable to the cost of borrowing and is not attributable to the conversion feature. For purposes of this paragraph, if a normal call premium cannot be established under paragraph (d) of this section, the amount thereof shall be considered to be zero.

(2) Determination of the portion of a repurchase premium attributable to the cost of borrowing and not attributable to the conversion feature. (i) For purposes of subparagraph (1) of this paragraph, the portion of a repurchase premium which is attributable to the cost of borrowing and which is not attributable to the conversion feature is the amount by which the selling price of the convertible obligation increased between the dates it was issued and repurchased by reason of a decline in yields on comparable nonconvertible obligations traded on an established securities market or, if such comparable traded obligations do not exist, by reason of a decline in yields generally on nonconvertible obligations which are as nearly comparable as possible.

(ii) In determining the amount under subdivision (i) of this subparagraph, appropriate consideration shall be given to all factors affecting the selling price or yields of comparable nonconvertible obligations. Such factors include general changes in prevailing yields of comparable obligations between the dates the convertible obligation was issued and repurchased and the amount (if any) by which the selling price of the nonconvertible obligation was affected by reason of any change in the issuing corporation's credit rating or the credit rating of the obligation during such period (determined on the basis of widely published ratings of recognized credit rating services or on the basis of other relevant facts and circumstances which reflect the relative credit ratings of the corporation or the comparable obligation).

(iii) The relationship between selling price and yields in subdivision (i) of this subparagraph shall ordinarily be determined by means of standard bond tables.

(f) Effective date. *(1) In general.* Under section 414(c) of the Tax Reform Act of 1969, the provisions of section 249 and this section shall apply to any repurchase of a convertible obligation occurring after April 22, 1969, other than a convertible obligation repurchased pursuant to a binding obligation incurred on or before April 22, 1969, to repurchase such convertible obligation at a specified call premium. A binding obligation on or before such date may arise if, for example, the issuer irrevocably obligates itself, on or before such date, to repurchase the convertible obligation at a specified price after such date, or if, for example, the issuer, without regard to the terms of the convertible obligation, negotiates a contract which, on or before such date, irrevocably obligates the issuer to repurchase the convertible obligation at a specified price after such date. A binding obligation on or before such date does not include a privilege in the convertible obligation permitting the issuer to call such convertible obligation after such date, which privilege was not exercised on or before such date.

(2) Effect on transactions not subject to this section. No inferences shall be drawn from the provisions of section 249 and this section as to the proper treatment of transactions not subject to such provisions because of the effective date limitations thereof. For provisions relating to repurchases of convertible bonds or other evidences of indebtedness to which section 249 and this section do not apply, see §§ 1.163-3(c) and 1.163-4(c).

(g) Example. The provisions of this section may be illustrated by the following example:

Example. On May 15, 1968, corporation A issues a callable 20-year convertible bond at face for $1,000 bearing interest at 10 percent per annum. The bond is convertible at any time into 2 shares of the common stock of corporation A. Under the terms of the bond, the applicable call price prior to May 15, 1975, is $1,100. On June 1, 1974, corporation A calls the bond for $1,100. Since the repurchase premium, $100 (i.e., $1,100 minus $1,000), was specified in dollars in the obligation and does not exceed 1 year's interest at the rate fixed in the obligation, the $100 is considered under paragraph (d)(2) of this section to be a normal call premium on a comparable nonconvertible obligation. Accordingly, A may deduct the $100 under § 1.163-3(c).

T.D. 7259, 2/9/73, amend T.D. 8746, 12/30/97.

PAR. 6. Section 1.249-1 is amended as follows:

1. In paragraph (c)(2) by removing the phrase "section 1232(b)" and adding in its place the phrase "sections

1273(b) and 1274", and by removing the phrase "§§ 1.163-3 and 1.163-4." and adding in its place the phrase "§§ 1.163-3, 1.163-4, and 1.163-7.".

2. In paragraph (d)(2), the first sentence, by removing the phrase "§§ 1.163-3, 1.163-4." and adding in its place the phrase "§§ 1.163-3 and 1.163-4, and 1.163-7.".

3. In paragraph (f)(2), the second sentence, by removing the phrase "§§ 1.163-3(c) and 1.163-4(c)." and adding in its place the phrase "§§ 1.163-3(c), 1.163-4(c), and 1.163-7(f).".

Proposed § 1.249-1 [Amended] [*For Preamble, see ¶ 151,065*]

• ***Caution:*** Prop reg § 1.482-2 was finalized by T.D. 8204, 5/20/88. Prop regs §§ 1.163-7, 1.446-2, 1.483-1 through -5, 1.1001-1, 1.1012-1, 1.1271 through -3, 1.1272-1, 1.1273-1, 1.1273-2, 1.1274-1 throught -7, 1.1274A-1, 1.1275-1 through -3, and 1.1275-5 were withdrawn by the Treasury on 12/22/92, 57 Fed. Reg. 67050. Prop reg § 1.1275-4 was superseded by the Treasury on 12/16/94, Fed. Reg. 59, 64884, which was finalized by T.D. 8674, 6/11/96.

§ 1.261-1 General rule for disallowance of deductions.

In computing taxable income, no deduction shall be allowed, except as otherwise expressly provided in chapter 1 of the Code, in respect of any of the items specified in part IX (section 262 and following), subchapter B, chapter 1 of the Code, and the regulations thereunder.

T.D. 6313, 9/16/58.

§ 1.262-1 Personal, living, and family expenses.

(a) In general. In computing taxable income, no deduction shall be allowed, except as otherwise expressly provided in chapter 1 of the Code, for personal, living, and family expenses.

(b) Examples of personal, living, and family expenses. Personal, living, and family expenses are illustrated in the following examples:

(1) Premiums paid for life insurance by the insured are not deductible. See also section 264 and the regulations thereunder.

(2) The cost of insuring a dwelling owned and occupied by the taxpayer as a personal residence is not deductible.

(3) Expenses of maintaining a household, including amounts paid for rent, water, utilities, domestic service, and the like, are not deductible. A taxpayer who rents a property for residential purposes, but incidentally conducts business there (his place of business being elsewhere) shall not deduct any part of the rent. If, however, he uses part of the house as his place of business, such portion of the rent and other similar expenses as is properly attributable to such place of business is deductible as a business expense.

(4) Losses sustained by the taxpayer upon the sale or other disposition of property held for personal, living, and family purposes are not deductible. But see section 165 and the regulations thereunder for deduction of losses sustained to such property by reason of casualty, etc.

(5) Expenses incurred in traveling away from home (which include transportation expenses, meals, and lodging) and any other transportation expenses are not deductible unless they qualify as expenses deductible under section 162, § 1.162-2, and paragraph (d) of § 1.162-5 (relating to trade or business expenses), section 170 and paragraph (a)(2) of § 1.170-2 (relating to charitable contributions), section 212 and § 1.212-1 (relating to expenses for production of income), section 213(e) and paragraph (e) of § 1.213-1 (relating to medical expenses) or section 217(a) and paragraph (a) of § 1.217-1 (relating to moving expenses). The taxpayer's costs of commuting to his place of business or employment are personal expenses and do not qualify as deductible expenses. The costs of the taxpayer's lodging not incurred in traveling away from home are personal expenses and are not deductible unless they qualify as deductible expenses under section 217. Except as permitted under section 162, 212, or 217, the costs of the taxpayer's meals not incurred in traveling away from home are personal expenses.

(6) Amounts paid as damages for breach of promise to marry, and attorney's fees and other costs of suit to recover such damages, are not deductible.

(7) Generally, attorney's fees and other costs paid in connection with a divorce, separation, or decree for support are not deductible by either the husband or the wife. However, the part of an attorney's fee and the part of the other costs paid in connection with a divorce, legal separation, written separation agreement, or a decree for support, which are properly attributable to the production or collection of amounts includible in gross income under section 71 are deductible by the wife under section 212.

(8) The cost of equipment of a member of the armed services is deductible only to the extent that it exceeds nontaxable allowances received for such equipment and to the extent that such equipment is especially required by his profession and does not merely take the place of articles required in civilian life. For example, the cost of a sword is an allowable deduction in computing taxable income, but the cost of a uniform is not. However, amounts expended by a reservist for the purchase and maintenance of uniforms which may be worn only when on active duty for training for temporary periods, when attending service school courses, or when attending training assemblies are deductible except to the extent that nontaxable allowances are received for such amounts.

(9) Expenditures made by a taxpayer in obtaining an education or in furthering his education are not deductible unless they qualify under section 162 and § 1.162-5 (relating to trade or business expenses).

(c) Cross references. Certain items of a personal, living, or family nature are deductible to the extent expressly provided under the following sections, and the regulations under those sections:

(1) Section 163 (interest).

(2) Section 164 (taxes).

(3) Section 165 (losses).

(4) Section 166 (bad debts).

(5) Section 170 (charitable, etc., contributions and gifts).

(6) Section 213 (medical, dental, etc., expenses).

(7) Section 214 (expenses for care of certain dependents).

(8) Section 215 (alimony, etc., payments).

(9) Section 216 (amounts representing taxes and interest paid to cooperative housing corporation).

(10) Section 217 (moving expenses).

T.D. 6313, 9/16/58, amend T.D. 6796, 1/29/65, T.D. 6918, 5/1/67, T.D. 7207, 10/3/72.

PAR. 3. Paragraph (b)(3) of § 1.262-1 is amended to read as follows:

Proposed § 1.262-1 Personal, living and family expenses.
[*For Preamble, see ¶ 150,615*]

* * * * *

(b) Examples of personal, living, and family expenses. * * *

(3) Expenses of maintaining a household, including amounts paid for rent, water, utilities, domestic service, and the like are not deductible. For rules relating to expenses incurred in connection with dwelling units used for both business purposes and personal purposes, see section 280A and the regulations thereunder.

* * * * *

§ 1.263(a)-0 Table of contents.

This section lists major captions contained in §§ 1.263(a)-1 through 1.263(a)-5.

§ 1.263(a)-1 Capital expenditures; in general.

§ 1.263(a)-2 Examples of capital expenditures.

§ 1.263(a)-3 Election to deduct or capitalize certain expenditures.

§ 1.263(a)-4 Amounts paid to acquire or create intangibles.

(a) Overview.

(b) Capitalization with respect to intangibles.

(1) In general.

(2) Published guidance.

(3) Separate and distinct intangible asset.

(i) Definition.

(ii) Creation or termination of contract rights.

(iii) Amounts paid in performing services.

(iv) Creation of computer software.

(v) Creation of package design.

(4) Coordination with other provisions of the Internal Revenue Code.

(i) In general.

(ii) Example.

(c) Acquired intangibles.

(1) In general.

(2) Readily available software.

(3) Intangibles acquired from an employee.

(4) Examples.

(d) Created intangibles.

(1) In general.

(2) Financial interests.

(i) In general.

(ii) Amounts paid to create, originate, enter into, renew or renegotiate.

(iii) Renegotiate.

(iv) Coordination with other provisions of this paragraph (d).

(v) Coordination with § 1.263(a)-5.

(vi) Examples.

(3) Prepaid expenses.

(i) In general.

(ii) Examples.

(4) Certain memberships and privileges.

(i) In general.

(ii) Examples.

(5) Certain rights obtained from a government agency.

(i) In general.

(ii) Examples.

(6) Certain contract rights.

(i) In general.

(ii) Amounts paid to create, originate, enter into, renew or renegotiate.

(iii) Renegotiate.

(iv) Right.

(v) De minimis amounts.

(vi) Exception for lessee construction allowances.

(vii) Examples.

(7) Certain contract terminations.

(i) In general.

(ii) Certain break-up fees.

(iii) Examples.

(8) Certain benefits arising from the provision, production, or improvement of real property.

(i) In general.

(ii) Exclusions.

(iii) Real property.

(iv) Impact fees and dedicated improvements.

(v) Examples.

(9) Defense or perfection of title to intangible property.

(i) In general.

(ii) Certain break-up fees.

(iii) Example.

(e) Transaction costs.

(1) Scope of facilitate.

(i) In general.

(ii) Treatment of termination payments.

(iii) Special rule for contracts.

(iv) Borrowing costs.

(v) Special rule for stock redemption costs of open-end regulated investment companies.

(2) Coordination with paragraph (d) of this section.

(3) Transaction.

(4) Simplifying conventions.

(i) In general.

(ii) Employee compensation.

(iii) De minimis costs.

(iv) Election to capitalize.

(5) Examples.

(f) 12-month rule.

(1) In general.

(2) Duration of benefit for contract terminations.

(3) Inapplicability to created financial interests and self-created amortizable section 197 intangibles.

(4) Inapplicability to rights of indefinite duration.

(5) Rights subject to renewal.

(i) In general.
(ii) Reasonable expectancy of renewal.
(iii) Safe harbor pooling method.
(6) Coordination with section 461.
(7) Election to capitalize.
(8) Examples.
(g) Treatment of capitalized costs.
(1) In general.
(2) Financial instruments.
(h) Special rules applicable to pooling.
(1) In general.
(2) Method of accounting.
(3) Adopting or changing to a pooling method.
(4) Definition of pool.
(5) Consistency requirement.
(6) Additional guidance pertaining to pooling.
(7) Example.
(i) [Reserved].
(j) Application to accrual method taxpayers.
(k) Treatment of related parties and indirect payments.
(l) Examples.
(m) Amortization.
(n) Intangible interests in land [Reserved].
(o) Effective date.
(p) Accounting method changes.
(1) In general.
(2) Scope limitations.
(3) Section 481(a) adjustment.

§ 1.263(a)-5 Amounts paid or incurred to facilitate an acquisition of a trade or business, a change in the capital structure of a business entity, and certain other transactions.

(a) General rule.
(b) Scope of facilitate.
(1) In general.
(2) Ordering rules.
(c) Special rules for certain costs.
(1) Borrowing costs.
(2) Costs of asset sales.
(3) Mandatory stock distributions.
(4) Bankruptcy reorganization costs.
(5) Stock issuance costs of open-end regulated investment companies.
(6) Integration costs.
(7) Registrar and transfer agent fees for the maintenance of capital stock records.
(8) Termination payments and amounts paid to facilitate mutually exclusive transactions.
(d) Simplifying conventions.
(1) In general.
(2) Employee compensation.
(i) In general.
(ii) Certain amounts treated as employee compensation.
(3) De minimis costs.
(i) In general.
(ii) Treatment of commissions.
(4) Election to capitalize.
(e) Certain acquisitive transactions.
(1) In general.
(2) Exception for inherently facilitative amounts.
(3) Covered transactions.
(f) Documentation of success-based fees.
(g) Treatment of capitalized costs.
(1) Tax-free acquisitive transactions [Reserved].
(2) Taxable acquisitive transactions.
(i) Acquirer.
(ii) Target.
(3) Stock issuance transactions [Reserved].
(4) Borrowings.
(5) Treatment of capitalized amounts by option writer.
(h) Application to accrual method taxpayers.
(i) [Reserved].
(j) Coordination with other provisions of the Internal Revenue Code.
(k) Treatment of indirect payments.
(l) Examples.
(m) Effective date.
(n) Accounting method changes.
(1) In general.
(2) Scope limitations.
(3) Section 481(a) adjustment.

T.D. 6313, 9/16/58, amend T.D. 6548, 2/21/61, T.D. 6794, 1/25/65, T.D. 8121, 1/5/87, T.D. 8131, 3/24/87, T.D. 8408, 4/9/92, T.D. 8482, 8/6/93, T.D. 9107, 12/31/2003.

PAR. 5. Section 1.263(a)-0 is amended by revising the entries for §§ 1.263(a)-1, 1.263(a)-2 and 1.263(a)-3 to read as follows:

Proposed § 1.263(a)-0 Table of contents. [*For Preamble, see ¶ 152,973*]

* * * * *

§ 1.263(a)-1 Capital expenditures; in general.

(a) General rule for capital expenditures.
(b) Coordination with section 263A.
(c) Examples of capital expenditures.
(d) Amounts paid to sell property.
(1) In general.
(2) Treatment of capitalized amount.
(3) Examples.
(e) Amount paid.
(f) [Reserved]
(g) Effective/applicability date.

§ 1.263(a)-2 Amounts paid to acquire or produce tangible property.

(a) Overview.
(b) Definitions.
(1) Amount paid.
(2) Personal property.
(3) Real property.
(4) Produce.

(c) Coordination with other provisions of the Internal Revenue Code.
(1) In general.
(2) Materials and supplies.
(d) Acquired or produced tangible property.
(1) In general.
(i) Requirement of capitalization.
(ii) Examples.
(2) Defense or perfection of title to property.
(i) In general.
(ii) Examples.
(3) Transaction costs.
(i) In general.
(ii) Scope of facilitate.
(A) In general.
(B) Inherently facilitative amounts.
(C) Special rule for acquisitions of real property.
(D) Employee compensation and overhead costs.
(1) In general.
(2) Election to capitalize.
(iii) Treatment of transaction costs.
(iv) Examples.
(4) De minimis rule.
(i) In general.
(ii) Exceptions to de minimis rule.
(iii) Safe harbor.
(iv) Additional rules.
(v) Election to capitalize.
(vi) Definition of applicable financial statement.
(vii) Examples.
(e) Treatment of capital expenditures.
(f) Recovery of capitalized amounts.
(1) In general.
(2) Examples.
(g) [Reserved]
(h) Effective/applicability date.
§ 1.263(a)-3 Amounts paid to improve tangible property.
(a) Overview.
(b) Definitions.
(1) Amount paid.
(2) Personal property.
(3) Real property.
(4) Applicable financial statement.
(c) Coordination with other provisions of the Internal Revenue Code.
(1) In general.
(2) Example.
(d) Improved property.
(1) Capitalization rule.
(2) Determining the unit of property.
(i) In general.
(ii) Building and structural components.
(iii) Property other than buildings.
(A) In general.
(B) Plant property.
(1) Definition.
(2) Unit of property for plant property.
(C) Network assets.
(1) Definition.
(2) [Reserved]
(D) Additional rules.
(iv) Examples.
(3) Compliance with regulatory requirements.
(4) Repairs and maintenance performed during an improvement.
(i) In general.
(ii) Exception for individuals.
(5) Aggregate of related amounts.
(e) Safe harbor for routine maintenance.
(1) In general.
(2) Exceptions.
(3) Rotable or temporary spare parts.
(4) Class life.
(5) Examples.
(f) Capitalization of betterments.
(1) In general.
(2) Application of general rule.
(i) Facts and circumstances.
(ii) Unavailability of replacement parts.
(iii) Appropriate comparison.
(A) In general.
(B) Normal wear and tear.
(C) Particular event.
(3) Examples.
(g) Capitalization of restorations.
(1) In general.
(2) Rebuild to like-new condition.
(i) In general.
(A) Like-new condition.
(B) Economic useful life.
(ii) Exception.
(3) Replacement of a major component or substantial structural part.
(i) In general.
(ii) Exception.
(4) Examples.
(h) Capitalization of amounts to adapt property to a new or different use.
(1) In general.
(2) Examples.
(i) Optional regulatory accounting method.
(1) In general.
(2) Eligibility for regulatory accounting method.
(3) Description of regulatory accounting method.
(4) [Reserved]
(5) Examples.
(j) Repair allowance.
(k) Treatment of capital expenditures.

(l) Recovery of capitalized amounts.

(m) [Reserved]

(n) Effective/applicability date.

§ 1.263(a)-1 Capital expenditures; in general.

Caution: The Treasury has not yet amended Reg § 1.263(a)-1 to reflect changes made by P.L. 110-246, P.L. 109-58, P.L. 108-357.

(a) Except as otherwise provided in chapter 1 of the Code, no deduction shall be allowed for—

(1) Any amount paid out for new buildings or for permanent improvements or betterments made to increase the value of any property or estate, or

(2) Any amount expended in restoring property or in making good the exhaustion thereof for which an allowance is or has been made in the form of a deduction for depreciation, amortization, or depletion.

(b) In general, the amounts referred to in paragraph (a) of this section include amounts paid or incurred (1) to add to the value, or substantially prolong the useful life, of property owned by the taxpayer, such as plant or equipment, or (2) to adapt property to a new or different use. Amounts paid or incurred for incidental repairs and maintenance of property are not capital expenditures within the meaning of subparagraphs (1) and (2) of this paragraph. See section 162 and § 1.162-4. See section 263A and the regulations thereunder for cost capitalization rules which apply to amounts referred to in paragraph (a) of this section with respect to the production of real and tangible personal property (as defined in § 1.263A-2(a)(2)), including films, sound recordings, video tapes, books, or similar properties. An amount referred to in paragraph (a) of this section is a capital expenditure that is taken into account through inclusion in inventory costs or a charge to capital accounts or basis no earlier than the taxable year during which the amount is incurred within the meaning of § 1.446-1(c)(1)(ii). Capital expenditures are subsequently recovered through depreciation, amortization, cost of goods sold, as an adjustment to basis, or otherwise, at such time as the property to which the amount relates is used, sold or otherwise disposed of by the taxpayer, in accordance with applicable Code sections and guidance published by the Secretary.

(c) The provisions of paragraph (a)(1) of this section shall not apply to expenditures deductible under—

(1) Section 616 and §§ 1.616-1 through 1.616-3, relating to the development of mines or deposits,

(2) Section 174 and §§ 1.174-1 through 1.174-4, relating to research and experimentation,

(3) Section 175 and §§ 1.175-1 through 1.175-6, relating to soil and water conservation,

(4) Section 179 and §§ 1.179-1 through 1.179-5, relating to election to expense certain depreciable business assets.

(5) Section 180 and §§ 1.180-1 and 1.180-2, relating to expenditures by farmers for fertilizer, lime, etc., and

(6) Section 182 and §§ 1.182-1 through 1.182-6, relating to expenditures by farmers for clearing land.

T.D. 6313, 9/16/58, amend T.D. 6548, 2/21/61, T.D. 6794, 1/25/65, T.D. 8121, 1/5/87, T.D. 8131, 3/24/87, T.D. 8408, 4/9/92, T.D. 8482, 8/6/93.

PAR. 6. Section 1.263(a)-1 is revised to read as follows:

Proposed § 1.263(a)-1 Capital expenditures; in general.
[*For Preamble, see ¶ 152,973*]

(a) General rule for capital expenditures. Except as provided in chapter 1 of the Internal Revenue Code (Code), no deduction is allowed for—

(1) Any amount paid for new buildings or for permanent improvements or betterments made to increase the value of any property or estate, or

(2) Any amount paid in restoring property or in making good the exhaustion thereof for which an allowance is or has been made.

(b) Coordination with section 263A. Section 263(a) generally requires taxpayers to capitalize an amount paid to acquire, produce, or improve real or personal tangible property. Section 263A generally prescribes the direct and indirect costs that must be capitalized to property produced or improved by the taxpayer and property acquired for resale.

(c) Examples of capital expenditures. The following amounts paid are examples of capital expenditures:

(1) An amount paid to acquire or produce real or personal tangible property. See § 1.263(a)-2.

(2) An amount paid to improve real or personal tangible property. See § 1.263(a)-3.

(3) An amount paid to acquire or create intangibles. See § 1.263(a)-4.

(4) An amount paid or incurred to facilitate an acquisition of a trade or business, a change in capital structure of a business entity, and certain other transactions. See § 1.263(a)-5.

(5) An amount paid to acquire or create interests in land, such as easements, life estates, mineral interests, timber rights, zoning variances, or other interests in land.

(6) An amount assessed and paid under an agreement between bondholders or shareholders of a corporation to be used in a reorganization of the corporation or voluntary contributions by shareholders to the capital of the corporation for any corporate purpose. See section 118 and § 1.118-1.

(7) An amount paid by a holding company to carry out a guaranty of dividends at a specified rate on the stock of a subsidiary corporation for the purpose of securing new capital for the subsidiary and increasing the value of its stockholdings in the subsidiary. This amount must be added to the cost of the stock in the subsidiary.

(d) Amounts paid to sell property. *(1) In general.* Except in the case of dealers in property, commissions and other transaction costs paid to facilitate the sale of property generally must be capitalized. However, in the case of dealers in property, amounts paid to facilitate the sale of property are treated as ordinary and necessary business expenses. See § 1.263(a)-5(g) for the treatment of amounts paid to facilitate the disposition of assets that constitute a trade or business.

(2) Treatment of capitalized amount. Amounts capitalized under paragraph (d)(1) of this section are treated as a reduction in the amount realized and generally are taken into account either in the taxable year in which the sale occurs or in the taxable year in which the sale is abandoned if a loss deduction is permissible. The capitalized amount is not added to the basis of the property and is not treated as an intangible under § 1.263(a)-4.

(3) Examples. The following examples, which assume the sale is not an installment sale under section 453, illustrate the rules of this paragraph (d):

Example (1). Sales costs of real property. X owns a parcel of real estate. X sells the real estate and pays legal fees, recording fees, and sales commissions to facilitate the sale. X must capitalize the fees and commissions and, in the taxable year of the sale, offset the fees and commissions against the amount realized from the sale of the real estate.

Example (2). Sales costs of dealers. Assume the same facts as in Example 1, except that X is a dealer in real estate. The commissions and fees paid to facilitate the sale of the real estate are treated as ordinary and necessary business expenses under section 162.

Example (3). Sales costs of personal property used in a trade or business. X owns a truck for use in X's trade or business. X decides to sell the truck and on November 15, 2008, X pays for an appraisal to determine a reasonable asking price. On February 15, 2009, X sells the truck to Y. X is required to capitalize in 2008 the amount paid to appraise the truck and, in 2009, is required to offset the amount paid against the amount realized from the sale of the truck.

Example (4). Costs of abandoned sale of personal property used in a trade or business. Assume the same facts as in Example 3, except that, instead of selling the truck on February 15, 2009, X decides on that date not to sell the truck and takes the truck off the market. X is required to capitalize in 2008 the amount paid to appraise the truck. However, X may treat the amount paid to appraise the truck as a loss under section 165 in 2009 when the sale is abandoned.

Example (5). Sales costs of personal property not used in a trade or business. Assume the same facts as in Example 3, except that X does not use the truck in X's trade or business, but instead uses it for personal purposes. X decides to sell the truck and on November 15, 2008, X pays for an appraisal to determine a reasonable asking price. On February 15, 2009, X sells the truck to Y. X is required to capitalize in 2008 the amount paid to appraise the truck and, in 2009, is required to offset the amount paid against the amount realized from the sale of the truck.

Example (6). Costs of abandoned sale of personal property not used in a trade or business. Assume the same facts as in Example 5, except that, instead of selling the truck on February 15, 2009, X decides on that date not to sell the truck and takes the truck off the market. X is required to capitalize in 2008 the amount paid to appraise the truck. Although the sale is abandoned in 2009, X may not treat the amount paid to appraise the truck as a loss under section 165 because the truck was not used in X's trade or business or in a transaction entered into for profit.

(e) Amount paid. In the case of a taxpayer using an accrual method of accounting, the terms amount paid and payment mean a liability incurred (within the meaning of § 1.446-1(c)(1)(ii)). A liability may not be taken into account under this section prior to the taxable year during which the liability is incurred.

(f) [Reserved]

(g) Effective/applicability date. The rules in this section apply to taxable years beginning on or after the date of publication of the Treasury decision adopting these rules as final regulations in the Federal Register.

§ 1.263(a)-2 Examples of capital expenditures.

The following paragraphs of this section include examples of capital expenditures:

(a) The cost of acquisition, construction, or erection of buildings, machinery and equipment, furniture and fixtures, and similar property having a useful life substantially beyond the taxable year.

(b) Amounts expended for securing a copyright and plates, which remain the property of the person making the payments. See section 263A and the regulations thereunder for capitalization rules which apply to amounts expended in securing and producing a copyright and plates in connection with the production of property, including films, sound recordings, video tapes, books, or similar properties.

(c) The cost of defending or perfecting title to property.

(d) The amount expended for architect's services.

(e) Commissions paid in purchasing securities. Commissions paid in selling securities are an offset against the selling price, except that in the case of dealers in securities such commissions may be treated as an ordinary and necessary business expense.

(f) Amounts assessed and paid under an agreement between bondholders or shareholders of a corporation to be used in a reorganization of the corporation or voluntary contributions by shareholders to the capital of the corporation for any corporate purpose. Such amounts are capital investments and are not deductible. See section 118 and § 1.118-1.

(g) A holding company which guarantees dividends at a specified rate on the stock of a subsidiary corporation for the purpose of securing new capital for the subsidiary and increasing the value of its stockholdings in the subsidiary shall not deduct amounts paid in carrying out this guaranty in computing its taxable income, but such payments are capital expenditures to be added to the cost of its stock in the subsidiary.

(h) The cost of good will in connection with the acquisition of the assets of a going concern is a capital expenditure.

T.D. 6313, 9/16/58, amend T.D. 8131, 3/24/87.

PAR. 7. Section 1.263(a)-2 is revised to read as follows:

Proposed § 1.263(a)-2 Amounts paid to acquire or produce tangible property. [*For Preamble, see ¶ 152,973*]

(a) Overview. This section provides rules for applying section 263(a) to amounts paid to acquire or produce a unit of real or personal property. Paragraph (b) of this section contains definitions. Paragraph (c) of this section contains the rules for coordinating this section with other provisions of the Internal Revenue Code (Code). Paragraph (d) of this section provides the rules for determining the treatment of amounts paid to acquire or produce a unit of real or personal property, including amounts paid to defend or perfect title to real or personal property and amounts paid to facilitate the acquisition of property. Paragraph (d) also provides a de minimis rule.

(b) Definitions. For purposes of this section, the following definitions apply:

(1) Amount paid. In the case of a taxpayer using an accrual method of accounting, the terms amount paid and payment mean a liability incurred (within the meaning of § 1.446-1(c)(1)(ii)). A liability may not be taken into account under this section prior to the taxable year during which the liability is incurred.

(2) Personal property means tangible personal property as defined in § 1.48-1(c).

(3) Real property means land and improvements thereto, such as buildings or other inherently permanent structures (including items that are structural components of the buildings or structures) that are not personal property as defined in paragraph (b)(2) of this section. Any property that constitutes other tangible property under § 1.48-1(d) is treated as real property for purposes of this section. Local law is not

controlling in determining whether property is real property for purposes of this section.

(4) Produce means construct, build, install, manufacture, develop, create, raise, or grow. This definition is intended to have the same meaning as the definition used for purposes of section 263A(g)(1) and § 1.263A-2(a)(1)(i), except that improvements are excluded from the definition in this paragraph (b)(4) and are separately defined and addressed in § 1.263(a)-3.

(c) Coordination with other provisions of the Internal Revenue Code. *(1) In general.* Nothing in this section changes the treatment of any amount that is specifically provided for under any provision of the Code or regulations other than section 162(a) or section 212 and the regulations under those sections. For example, see section 263A requiring taxpayers to capitalize the direct and certain indirect costs of producing property or acquiring property for resale.

(2) Materials and supplies. Nothing in this section changes the treatment of amounts paid to acquire or produce property that is properly treated as materials and supplies under § 1.162-3.

(d) Acquired or produced tangible property. *(1) In general.* (i) Requirement of capitalization. Except as provided in paragraph (d)(4) of this section (relating to the de minimis rule) and in § 1.162-3(d)(1)(ii), (iii), and (iv) (relating to certain materials and supplies), a taxpayer must capitalize amounts paid to acquire or produce a unit of real or personal property (as determined under § 1.263(a)-3(d)(2)), including leasehold improvement property, land and land improvements, buildings, machinery and equipment, and furniture and fixtures. Amounts paid to acquire or produce a unit of real or personal property include the invoice price, transaction costs as determined under paragraph (d)(3) of this section, and costs for work performed prior to the date that the unit of property is placed in service by the taxpayer (without regard to any applicable convention under section 168(d)). A taxpayer also must capitalize amounts paid to acquire real or personal property for resale and to produce real or personal property. See section 263A for the costs required to be capitalized to property produced by the taxpayer or to property acquired for resale.

(ii) Examples. The rules of this section are illustrated by the following examples, in which it is assumed that the taxpayer does not apply the de minimis rule under paragraph (d)(4) of this section:

Example (1). Acquisition of personal property. In 2008, X purchases new cash registers for use in its retail store located in leased space in a shopping mall. Assume each cash register is a unit of property as determined under § 1.263(a)-3(d)(2), and is not a material or supply under § 1.162-3. X must capitalize under this paragraph (d)(1) the amount paid to purchase each cash register.

Example (2). Relocation of personal property. Assume the same facts as in Example 1, except that X's lease expires in 2009 and X decides to relocate its retail store to a different building. In addition to various other costs, X pays $5,000 to move the cash registers. X is not required to capitalize under this paragraph (d)(1) the $5,000 amount paid for moving the cash registers.

Example (3). Acquisition of personal property that is not a unit of property; coordination with § 1.162-3. X operates a fleet of aircraft. In 2008, X purchases a stock of spare parts, which it uses to maintain and repair its aircraft. Assume that the spare parts are not units of property as determined under § 1.263(a)-3(d)(2). X does not make elections under § 1.162-3(e) to treat the materials and supplies as capital expenditures. In 2009, X uses the spare parts in a repair and maintenance activity that does not improve the property under § 1.263(a)-3. Because the parts are not units of property, X is not required to capitalize the amounts paid for the parts under this paragraph (d)(1). Rather, X must apply the rules in § 1.162-3, governing the treatment of materials and supplies, to determine the treatment of these amounts.

Example (4). Acquisition of unit of personal property; coordination with § 1.162-3. X operates a rental business that rents out a variety of small individual items to customers (rental items). X maintains a supply of rental items on hand to replace worn or damaged items. In 2008, X purchases a large quantity of rental items to be used in its business. Assume that each of these items is a unit of property under § 1.263(a)-3(d)(2) and that several of these rental items are materials and supplies under the definition provided in § 1.162-3(d). Therefore, X must apply the rules in § 1.162-3 to determine the treatment of the amounts paid to acquire rental items that are materials and supplies. Under this paragraph (d)(1), X must capitalize the amounts paid for the rental items that are units of property and do not otherwise qualify as materials and supplies under § 1.162-3(d).

Example (5). Acquisition or production cost. X purchases or produces jigs, dies, molds, and patterns for use in the manufacture of X's products. Assume that each of these items is a unit of property as determined under § 1.263(a)-3(d)(2), and is not a material and supply under § 1.162-3(d). X is required to capitalize under this paragraph (d)(1) the amounts paid to produce or purchase the jigs, dies, molds, and patterns. See section 263A for the costs to be capitalized to property produced by X.

Example (6). Acquisition of land. X purchases a parcel of undeveloped real estate. X must capitalize under this paragraph (d)(1) the amount paid to acquire the real estate. See § 1.263(a)-2(d)(3) for the treatment of amounts paid to facilitate the acquisition of real property.

Example (7). Acquisition of building. X purchases a building. X must capitalize under this paragraph (d)(1) the amount paid to acquire the building. See § 1.263(a)-2(d)(3) for the treatment of amounts paid to facilitate the acquisition of real property.

Example (8). Acquisition of property for resale. X purchases goods for resale. X must capitalize under this paragraph (d)(1) the amounts paid to acquire the goods. See section 263A for the costs to be capitalized to property acquired for resale.

Example (9). Production of property for sale. X produces goods for sale. X must capitalize under this paragraph (d)(1) the amount paid to produce the goods. See section 263A for the costs to be capitalized to property produced by X.

Example (10). Production of building. X constructs a building. X must capitalize under this paragraph (d)(1) the amount paid to construct the building. See section 263A for the costs to be capitalized to real property produced by X.

Example (11). Acquisition of assets constituting a trade or business. Y owns tangible and intangible assets that constitute a trade or business. X purchases all the assets of Y in a taxable transaction. X must capitalize under this paragraph (d)(1) the amount paid for the tangible assets of Y. See § 1.263(a)-4 for the treatment of amounts paid to acquire intangibles and § 1.263(a)-5 for the treatment of amounts paid to facilitate the acquisition of assets that constitute a trade or business. See section 1060 for special allocation rules for certain asset acquisitions.

Example (12). Work performed prior to placing the property in service. In 2008, X purchases a building for use as a business office. The building is in a state of disrepair. Prior to placing the building in service, X incurs costs to repair cement steps, shore up parts of the first and second floors, replace electrical wiring, remove and replace old plumbing, and paint the outside and inside of the building. All the work was performed on the building or its structural components. In 2010, X places the building in service and begins using the building as its business office. Assume the building and its structural components is the unit of property. The amounts paid must be capitalized as costs of acquiring the building because they were for work performed prior to X's placing the building in service.

Example (13). Work performed prior to placing the property in service. In January 2008, X purchases a new machine for use in an existing production line of its manufacturing business. Assume that the machine is a unit of property under § 1.263(a)-3(d)(2). After the machine is installed, X performs critical testing on the machine to ensure that it is operational. On November 1, 2008, the critical testing is complete and X places the machine in service on the production line. X continues to perform testing for quality control. The amounts paid for the installation and critical testing must be capitalized as costs of acquiring the machine because they were for work performed prior to X's placing the machine in service. However, amounts paid for quality control testing after the machine is placed in service by X are not required to be capitalized as a cost of acquiring the machine.

(2) Defense or perfection of title to property. (i) In general. Amounts paid to defend or perfect title to real or personal property are amounts paid to acquire or produce property within the meaning of this section and must be capitalized. See section 263A for the costs required to be capitalized to property produced by the taxpayer or to property acquired for resale.

(ii) Examples. The following examples illustrate the rule of this paragraph (d)(2):

Example (1). Amounts paid to contest condemnation. X owns real property located in County. County files an eminent domain complaint condemning a portion of X's property to use as a roadway. X hires an attorney to contest the condemnation. Amounts paid by X to the attorney must be capitalized because they were to defend X's title to the property.

Example (2). Amounts paid to invalidate ordinance. X is in the business of quarrying and supplying for sale sand and stone in a certain municipality. Several years after X establishes its business, the municipality in which it is located passes an ordinance that prohibits the operation of X's business. X incurs attorney's fees in a successful prosecution of a suit to invalidate the municipal ordinance. X prosecutes the suit to preserve its business activities and not to defend X's title in the property. Therefore, attorney's fees paid by X are not required to be capitalized under this paragraph (d)(2). However, under section 263A, all indirect costs, including otherwise deductible costs, that directly benefit or are incurred by reason of the taxpayer's production activities must be capitalized to the property produced for sale. See § 1.263A-1(e)(3)(i). Therefore, because the amounts paid to invalidate the ordinance are incurred by reason of X's production activities, the amounts paid must be capitalized under section 263A to the property produced for sale by X.

Example (3). Amounts paid to challenge building line. The board of public works of a municipality establishes a building line across X's business property, adversely affecting the value of the property. X incurs legal fees in unsuccessfully litigating the establishment of the building line. Amounts paid by X to the attorney must be capitalized because they were to defend X's title to the property.

(3) Transaction costs. (i) In general. A taxpayer must capitalize amounts paid to facilitate the acquisition or production of real or personal property. See section 263A for the costs required to be capitalized to property produced by the taxpayer or to property acquired for resale. See § 1.263(a)-5 for the treatment of amounts paid to facilitate the acquisition of assets that constitute a trade or business.

(ii) Scope of facilitate. (A) In general. Except as otherwise provided in this section, an amount is paid to facilitate the acquisition of real or personal property if the amount is paid in the process of investigating or otherwise pursuing the acquisition. Whether an amount is paid in the process of investigating or otherwise pursuing the acquisition is determined based on all of the facts and circumstances. In determining whether an amount is paid to facilitate an acquisition, the fact that the amount would (or would not) have been paid but for the acquisition is relevant, but is not determinative. These amounts include, but are not limited to, inherently facilitative amounts specified in paragraph (d)(3)(ii)(B) of this section.

(B) Inherently facilitative amounts. An amount paid in the process of investigating or otherwise pursuing the acquisition of real or personal property facilitates the acquisition if the amount is inherently facilitative. An amount is inherently facilitative if the amount is paid for—

(1) Transporting the property (for example, shipping fees and moving costs);

(2) Securing an appraisal or determining the value or price of property;

(3) Negotiating the terms or structure of the acquisition and obtaining tax advice on the acquisition;

(4) Application fees, bidding costs, or similar expenses;

(5) Preparing and reviewing the documents that effectuate the acquisition of the property (for example, preparing the bid, offer, sales contract, or purchase agreement);

(6) Examining and evaluating the title of property;

(7) Obtaining regulatory approval of the acquisition or securing permits related to the acquisition, including application fees;

(8) Conveying property between the parties, including sales and transfer taxes, and title registration costs;

(9) Finders' fees or brokers' commissions, including amounts paid that are contingent on the successful closing of the acquisition;

(10) Architectural, geological, engineering, environmental or inspection services pertaining to particular properties; and

(11) Services provided by a qualified intermediary or other facilitator of an exchange under section 1031.

(C) Special rule for acquisitions of real property. Except as provided in paragraph (d)(3)(ii)(B) of this section (relating to inherently facilitative amounts), an amount paid by the taxpayer in the process of investigating or otherwise pursuing the acquisition of real property does not facilitate the acquisition if it relates to activities performed in the process of determining whether to acquire real property and which real property to acquire.

(D) Employee compensation and overhead costs. (1) In general. For purposes of this paragraph (d)(3), amounts paid for employee compensation (within the meaning of § 1.263(a)-4(e)(4)(ii)) and overhead are treated as amounts that do not facilitate the acquisition of real or personal property. See section 263A for the treatment of employee compensation and overhead costs required to be capitalized to property produced by the taxpayer or to property acquired for resale.

(2) Election to capitalize. A taxpayer may elect to treat amounts paid for employee compensation or overhead as amounts that facilitate the acquisition of property. The election is made separately for each acquisition and applies to employee compensation or overhead, or both. For example, a taxpayer may elect to treat overhead, but not employee compensation, as amounts that facilitate the acquisition of property. A taxpayer makes the election by treating the amounts to which the election applies as amounts that facilitate the acquisition in the taxpayer's timely filed original Federal income tax return (including extensions) for the taxable year during which the amounts are paid. In the case of an S corporation or partnership, the election is made by the S corporation or by the partnership, and not by the shareholders or partners. A taxpayer may revoke an election made under this paragraph (d)(3)(ii)(D)(2) with respect to each acquisition only by filing a request for a private letter ruling and obtaining the Commissioner's consent to revoke the election. An election may not be made or revoked through the filing of an application for change in accounting method or by an amended Federal income tax return.

(iii) Treatment of transaction costs. All amounts paid to facilitate the acquisition or production of real or personal property are capital expenditures. Inherently facilitative amounts allocable to real or personal property are capital expenditures related to such property even if the property is not eventually acquired or produced. Facilitative amounts allocable to real or personal property actually acquired or produced must be included in the basis of the property acquired or produced. See paragraph (f) of this section for the recovery of capitalized amounts.

(iv) Examples. The following examples illustrate the rules of this paragraph (d)(3):

Example (1). Broker's fees to facilitate an acquisition. X decides to purchase a building in which to relocate its offices and hires a real estate broker to find a suitable building. X pays fees to the broker to find property for X to acquire. Under paragraph (d)(3)(i) of this section, X must capitalize the amounts paid to the broker because these costs are inherently facilitative of the acquisition of real property.

Example (2). Inspection and survey costs to facilitate an acquisition. X decides to purchase building A and pays amounts to third-party contractors for a termite inspection and an environmental survey of building A. Under paragraph (d)(3)(i) of this section, X must capitalize the amounts paid for the inspection and the survey of the building because these costs are inherently facilitative of the acquisition of real property.

Example (3). Moving costs to facilitate an acquisition. X purchases all the assets of Y and, in connection with the purchase, hires a transportation company to move storage tanks from Y's plant to X's plant. Under paragraph (d)(3)(i) of this section, X must capitalize the amount paid to move the storage tanks from Y's plant to X's plant because this cost is inherently facilitative to the acquisition of personal property.

Example (4). Scope of facilitate. X is in the business of providing legal services to clients. X is interested in acquiring a new conference table for its office. X hires and incurs fees for an interior designer to shop for, evaluate, and make recommendations to X regarding which new table to acquire. Under paragraph (d)(3)(i) of this section, X must capitalize the amounts paid to the interior designer to provide these services because they are paid in the process of investigating or otherwise pursuing the acquisition of personal property.

Example (5). Transaction costs allocable to other property. X, a retailer, wants to acquire land for the purpose of building a new distribution facility for its products. X considers various properties on highway A in state B. In evaluating the feasibility of several sites, X incurs fees for the services of an architect to advise and prepare preliminary plans for a facility that X is reasonably likely to construct at one of the sites. The architect's fees are not inherently facilitative to the acquisition of land, but are inherently facilitative to the acquisition of a building under paragraph (d)(3)(ii)(B)(10) of this section. In addition, these costs are allocable as construction costs of the building under section 263A. Therefore, X does not capitalize these fees as amounts to acquire the building under paragraph (d)(3)(ii)(B) of this section, but instead must capitalize these costs as indirect costs allocable to the production of property under section 263A.

Example (6). Special rule for acquisitions of real property. X owns several retail stores. X decides to examine the feasibility of opening a new store in City A. In October 2008, X hires and incurs costs for a development consulting firm to study City A and perform market surveys, evaluate zoning and environmental requirements, and make preliminary reports and recommendations as to areas that X should consider for purposes of locating a new store. In December 2008, X continues to consider whether to purchase real property in City A and which property to acquire. X hires, and incurs fees for, an appraiser to perform appraisals on two different sites to determine a fair offering price for each site. In March 2009, X decides to acquire one of these two sites for the location of its new store. At the same time, X determines not to acquire the other site. Under paragraph (d)(3)(ii)(C) of this section, X is not required to capitalize amounts paid to the development consultant in 2008 because the amounts relate to activities performed in the process of determining whether to acquire real property and which real property to acquire and the amounts are not inherently facilitative costs under paragraph (d)(3)(ii)(B) of this section. However, X must capitalize amounts paid to the appraiser in 2008 because the appraisal costs are inherently facilitative costs under paragraph (d)(3)(ii)(B)(2) of this section. In 2009, X must include the appraisal costs allocable to property acquired in the basis of the property acquired and may recover the appraisal costs allocable to the property not acquired in accordance with paragraph (f) of this section.

Example (7). Employee compensation and overhead. X, a freight carrier, maintains an acquisition department whose sole function is to arrange for the purchase of vehicles and aircraft from manufacturers or other parties to be used in its freight carrying business. As provided in paragraph (d)(3)(ii)(D)(1) of this section, X is not required to capitalize any portion of the compensation paid to employees in its acquisition department or any portion of its overhead allocable to its acquisition department. However, under paragraph (d)(3)(ii)(D)(2) of this section, X may elect to capitalize the compensation and overhead costs allocable to the acquisition of a vehicle or aircraft by treating these amounts as costs that facilitate the acquisition of that property in its timely filed original Federal income tax return for the year the amounts are paid.

(4) De minimis rule. (i) In general. Except as otherwise provided in this paragraph (d)(4), a taxpayer is not required to capitalize under paragraph (d) of this section amounts paid for the acquisition or production (including any amounts paid to facilitate the acquisition or production) of a unit of property (as determined under § 1.263(a)-3(d)(2)) if—

(A) The taxpayer has an applicable financial statement (as defined in § 1.263(a)-2(d)(4)(vi));

(B) The taxpayer has at the beginning of the taxable year, written accounting procedures treating as an expense for non-tax purposes the amounts paid for property costing less than a certain dollar amount;

(C) The taxpayer treats the amounts paid during the taxable year as an expense on its applicable financial statement in accordance with its written accounting procedures; and

(D) The total aggregate of amounts paid and not capitalized under paragraphs (d)(4)(i)(A), (B), and (C) of this section for the taxable year do not distort the taxpayer's income for the taxable year.

(ii) Exceptions to de minimis rule. The de minimis rule in paragraph (d)(4)(i) of this section does not apply to the following:

(A) Amounts paid to improve property under § 1.263(a)-3.

(B) Amounts paid for property that is or is intended to be included in property produced or acquired for resale.

(C) Amounts paid for land.

(iii) Safe harbor. The total aggregate amount that is not required to be capitalized under the de minimis rule of paragraphs (d)(4)(i)(A), (B) and (C) of this section for the taxable year is deemed to not distort the taxpayer's income under paragraph (d)(4)(i)(D) of this section if this amount, added to the amount the taxpayer deducts in the taxable year as materials and supplies under the definition provided under § 1.162-3(d)(1)(iii) (relating to certain property costing $100 or less), is less than or equal to the lesser of—

(A) 0.1 percent of the taxpayer's gross receipts for the taxable year; or

(B) 2 percent of the taxpayer's total depreciation and amortization expense for the taxable year as determined in its applicable financial statement.

(iv) Additional rules. Property to which a taxpayer applies the de minimis rule contained in paragraph (d)(4) of this section is not treated upon sale or disposition as a capital asset under section 1221 or as property used in the trade or business under section 1231. Property to which a taxpayer applies the de minimis rule contained in paragraph (d)(4) of this section is not a material or supply under § 1.162-3. The cost of property to which a taxpayer properly applies the de minimis rule contained in paragraph (d)(4) of this section is not required to be capitalized under section 263A to a separate unit of property, but may be required to be capitalized as a cost of other property if incurred by reason of the production of the other property. See, for example, § 1.263A-1(e)(3)(ii)(O) requiring taxpayers to capitalize repair and maintenance costs allocable to property produced or acquired for resale.

(v) Election to capitalize. A taxpayer may elect not to apply the de minimis rule contained in paragraph (d)(4)(i) of this section. An election made under this paragraph (d)(4)(v) applies to any unit of property during the taxable year to which paragraphs (d)(4)(i)(A), (B), and (C) of this section would apply (but for the election under this paragraph (d)(4)(v)). A taxpayer makes the election by treating the amount paid as a capital expenditure in its timely filed original Federal income tax return (including extensions) for the taxable year in which the amount is paid. In the case of an S corporation or partnership, the election is made by the S corporation or by the partnership, and not by the shareholders or partners. A taxpayer may revoke an election made under this paragraph (d)(4)(v) with respect to a unit of property only by filing a request for a private letter ruling and obtaining the Commissioner's consent to revoke the election. An election may not be made or revoked through the filing of an application for change in accounting method or by an amended Federal income tax return.

(vi) Definition of applicable financial statement. For purposes of this paragraph (d)(4), the taxpayer's applicable financial statement is the taxpayer's financial statement listed in paragraphs (d)(4)(vi)(A) through (C) of this section that has the highest priority (including within paragraph (d)(4)(vi)(B) of this section). The financial statements are, in descending priority—

(A) A financial statement required to be filed with the Securities and Exchange Commission (SEC) (the 10-K or the Annual Statement to Shareholders);

(B) A certified audited financial statement that is accompanied by the report of an independent CPA (or in the case of a foreign entity, by the report of a similarly qualified independent professional), that is used for—

(1) Credit purposes;

(2) Reporting to shareholders, partners, or similar persons; or

(3) Any other substantial non-tax purpose; or

(C) A financial statement (other than a tax return) required to be provided to the Federal or a state government or any Federal or state agencies (other than the SEC or the Internal Revenue Service).

(vii) Examples. The following examples illustrate the rule of this paragraph (d)(4):

Example (1). De minimis rule. X purchases 10 printers at $200 each for a total cost of $2000. Assume that each printer is a unit of property under § 1.263(a)-3(d)(2). X has an applicable financial statement. X has a written policy at the beginning of the taxable year to expense amounts paid for property costing less than $500. X treats the amounts paid for the printers as an expense on its applicable financial statement. Assuming the total aggregate amounts not capitalized under the de minimis rule for the taxable year do not distort the taxpayer's income, X is not required to capitalize the amounts paid for the printers.

Example (2). De minimis rule safe harbor not met. X is a member of an affiliated group that files a consolidated return. In 2008, X purchases 300 computers at $400 each for a total cost of $120,000. Assume that each computer is a unit of property under § 1.263(a)-3(d)(2). X has a written policy at the beginning of the taxable year to expense amounts paid for property costing less than $500. X treats the amounts paid for the computers as an expense on its applicable financial statement. In addition, in 2008 X purchases 300 desk chairs for $50 each for a total cost of $15,000. X intends to deduct the amounts paid for the desk chairs when used or consumed as non-incidental materials and supplies under § 1.162-3(a)(1) and § 1.162-3(d)(1)(iii) because they are units of property costing less than $100. For its 2008 taxable year, X has gross receipts of $125,000,000 and reports $7,000,000 of depreciation and amortization on its applicable financial statement. Thus, in order to meet the de minimis rule safe harbor for 2008, the sum of the amounts not required to be capitalized under the de minimis rule for 2008 ($120,000) plus the amounts X intends to deduct as materials and supplies under § 1.162-3(a)(1) and § 1.162-3(d)(1)(iii) for 2008 ($15,000), must be less than or equal to $125,000 (0.1% of X's total gross receipts of $125,000,000), which is less than $140,000 (2% of X's total depreciation and amortization of $7,000,000). Because $135,000 ($120,000 + $15,000) exceeds $125,000, X will not meet the de minimis rule safe harbor for its 2008 taxable year. As a result, to apply the de minimis rule to the $120,000 paid to acquire the computers, X will have to otherwise establish that this amount does not distort the taxpayer's income in 2008.

Example (3). De minimis rule safe harbor met. Assume the same facts as in Example 2, except X makes an election under paragraph (d)(4)(v) of this section to capitalize the $10,000 paid to acquire 25 of the 300 computers at $400 each. In this case, X is not required to capitalize the $110,000 paid to acquire the remaining 275 computers under paragraph (d)(4)(i) because this amount, when added to the $15,000 that X intends to deduct in 2008 as materials and supplies under § 1.162-3(a)(1) and § 1.162-3(d)(1)(iii), does not exceed the de minimis rule safe harbor of $125,000 for 2008.

Example (4). De minimis rule safe harbor; election to capitalize. Assume the same facts as in Example 2, except X does not otherwise establish that the deduction of amounts in excess of the $125,000 safe harbor do not distort X's income in 2008. Rather, X makes an election under § 1.162-3(e) to capitalize $10,000 paid to acquire 200 of the 300 desk chairs at $50 each. In this case, X is not required to capitalize the $120,000 paid to acquire the 300 computers under paragraph (d)(4)(i) of this section because this amount, when added to the $5000 (the remaining 100 desk chairs at $50 each) that X intends to deduct in 2008 as materials and supplies under § 1.162-3(a)(1) and § 1.162-3(d)(1)(iii), does not exceed the de minimis rule safe harbor of $125,000 for 2008.

(e) Treatment of capital expenditures. Amounts required to be capitalized under this section are capital expenditures and must be taken into account through a charge to capital account or basis, or in the case of property that is inventory in the hands of a taxpayer, through inclusion in inventory costs. See section 263A for the treatment of amounts referred to in this section as well as other amounts paid in connection with the production of real property and personal property, including films, sound recordings, video tapes, books, or similar properties.

(f) Recovery of capitalized amounts. *(1) In general.* Amounts that are capitalized under this section are recovered through depreciation, cost of goods sold, or by an adjustment to basis at the time the property is placed in service, sold, used, or otherwise disposed of by the taxpayer. Cost recovery is determined by the applicable Code and regulation provisions relating to the use, sale, or disposition of property.

(2) Examples. The following examples illustrate the rule of this paragraph (f)(1). Assume that X does not apply the de minimis rule under paragraph (d)(4) of this section.

Example (1). Recovery when property placed in service. X owns a 10-unit apartment building. The refrigerator in one of the apartments stops functioning and X purchases a new refrigerator to replace the old one. X pays for the acquisition, delivery, and installation of the new refrigerator to replace the old refrigerator. Assume that the refrigerator is the unit of property, as determined under § 1.263(a)-3(d)(2), and is not a material or supply under § 1.162-3. Under paragraph (d) of this section, X is required to capitalize the amounts paid for the acquisition, delivery, and installation of the refrigerator. Under this paragraph (f), the capitalized amounts are recovered through depreciation when the refrigerator is placed in service by X.

Example (2). Recovery when property used in the production of property. X operates a plant where it manufactures widgets. X purchases a tractor/loader to move raw materials into and around the plant for use in the manufacturing process. Assume that the tractor/ loader is a unit of property, as determined under § 1.263(a)-3(d)(2), and is not a material or supply under § 1.162-3. Under paragraph (d) of this section, X is required to capitalize the amounts paid to acquire the tractor/loader. Under this paragraph (f), the capitalized amounts are recovered through depreciation when the tractor/loader is placed in service by X. However, because the tractor/loader is used in the production of property, under section 263A the cost recovery (that is, the depreciation) on the capitalized amounts must be capitalized to X's property produced, and consequently, recovered through cost of goods sold. See § 1.263A-1(e)(3)(ii)(I).

(g) [Reserved]

(h) Effective/applicability date. The rules in this section apply to taxable years beginning on or after the date of publication of the Treasury decision adopting these rules as final regulations in the Federal Register.

§ 1.263(a)-3 Election to deduct or capitalize certain expenditures.

Caution: The Treasury has not yet amended Reg § 1.263(a)-3 to reflect changes made by P.L. 110-246, P.L. 99-514.

(a) Under certain provisions of the Code, taxpayers may elect to treat capital expenditures as deductible expenses or as deferred expenses, or to treat deductible expenses as capital expenditures.

(b) The sections referred to in paragraph (a) of this section include:

(1) Section 173 (circulation expenditures).

(2) Section 174 (research and experimental expenditures).

(3) Section 175 (soil and water conservation expenditures).

(4) Section 177 (trademark and trade name expenditures).

(5) Section 179 (election to expense certain depreciable business assets).

(6) Section 180 (expenditures by farmers for fertilizer, lime, etc.).

(7) Section 182 (expenditures by farmers for clearing land).

(8) Section 248 (organizational expenditures of a corporation).

(9) Section 266 (carrying charges).

(10) Section 615 (exploration expenditures).

(11) Section 616 (development expenditures).

T.D. 6313, 9/16/58, amend T.D. 6548, 2/21/61, T.D. 6794, 1/25/65, T.D. 8121, 1/5/87.

PAR. 8. Section 1.263(a)-3 is revised to read as follows:

Proposed § 1.263(a)-3 Amounts paid to improve tangible property. [*For Preamble, see ¶ 152,973*]

(a) Overview. This section provides rules for applying section 263(a) to amounts paid to improve tangible property. Paragraph (b) of this section provides definitions. Paragraph (c) of this section provides rules for coordinating this section with other provisions of the Internal Revenue Code (Code). Paragraph (d) of this section provides rules for determining the treatment of amounts paid to improve tangible property, including rules for determining the appropriate unit of property. Paragraph (e) of this section provides a safe harbor for routine maintenance costs. Paragraph (f) of this section provides rules for determining whether amounts paid result in betterments to the unit of property. Paragraph (g) of this section provides rules for determining whether amounts paid restore the unit of property. Paragraph (h) of this section provides rules for amounts paid to adapt the unit of property to a new or different use. Paragraph (i) of this section provides an optional regulatory accounting method safe harbor. Paragraph (j) of this section provides an optional repair allowance. Paragraphs (k) through (m) of this section provide additional rules related to these provisions. Paragraph (n) of this section provides the applicability date of the rules in this section.

(b) Definitions. For purposes of this section, the following definitions apply:

(1) Amount paid. In the case of a taxpayer using an accrual method of accounting, the terms amounts paid and payment mean a liability incurred (within the meaning of § 1.446-1(c)(1)(ii)). A liability may not be taken into account under this section prior to the taxable year during which the liability is incurred.

(2) Personal property means tangible personal property as defined in § 1.48-1(c).

(3) Real property means land and improvements thereto, such as buildings or other inherently permanent structures (including items that are structural components of the buildings or structures) that are not personal property as defined in paragraph (b)(2) of this section. Any property that constitutes other tangible property under § 1.48-1(d) is also treated as real property for purposes of this section. Local law is not controlling in determining whether property is real property for purposes of this section.

(4) Applicable financial statement. The applicable financial statement is the taxpayer's financial statement listed in paragraphs (b)(4)(i) through (iii) of this section that has the highest priority (including within paragraph (b)(4)(ii) of this section). The financial statements are, in descending priority—

(i) A financial statement required to be filed with the Securities and Exchange Commission (SEC) (the 10-K or the Annual Statement to Shareholders);

(ii) A certified audited financial statement that is accompanied by the report of an independent CPA (or in the case of a foreign entity, by the report of a similarly qualified independent professional), that is used for—

(A) Credit purposes,

(B) Reporting to shareholders, partners, or similar persons; or

(C) Any other substantial non-tax purpose; or

(iii) A financial statement (other than a tax return) required to be provided to the Federal or a state government or any Federal or state agencies (other than the SEC or the Internal Revenue Service).

(c) Coordination with other provisions of the Internal Revenue Code. *(1) In general.* Nothing in this section changes the treatment of any amount that is specifically provided for under any provision of the Code or regulations (other than section 162(a) or section 212 and the regulations under those sections). See, for example, § 1.263A-1(e)(3), requiring taxpayers to capitalize costs that directly benefit or are incurred by reason of the performance of production or resale activities, including repair and maintenance costs allocable to property produced or acquired for resale.

(2) Example. The following example illustrates the rules of this paragraph (c):

Example. Railroad rolling stock. X is a railroad that properly treats amounts paid for the rehabilitation of railroad rolling stock as deductible expenses under section 263(d). X is not required to capitalize the amounts paid because nothing in this section changes the treatment of amounts specifically provided for under section 263(d).

(d) Improved property. *(1) Capitalization rule.* Except as provided in the optional regulatory accounting method in paragraph (i) of this section or under any repair allowance method published in accordance with paragraph (j) of this section, a taxpayer must capitalize the aggregate of related amounts paid to improve a unit of property, whether the improvements are made by the taxpayer or by a third party, and whether the taxpayer is an owner or lessee of the property. For purposes of this section, a unit of property includes units of property for which the acquisition or production costs were deducted as materials and supplies under § 1.162-3(a)(1) or under the de minimis rule in § 1.263(a)-2(d)(4). See section 263A for the costs required to be capitalized to property produced by the taxpayer or to property acquired for resale; section 1016 for adding capitalized amounts to the basis of the unit of property; and section 168 for the treatment of additions or improvements for depreciation purposes. For purposes of this section, a unit of property is improved if the amounts paid for activities performed after the property is placed in service by the taxpayer—

(i) Result in a betterment to the unit of property (see paragraph (f) of this section); or

(ii) Restore the unit of property (see paragraph (g) of this section); or

(iii) Adapt the unit of property to a new or different use (see paragraph (h) of this section).

(2) Determining the appropriate unit of property. (i) In general. The unit of property rules in this paragraph (d)(2) apply only for purposes of section 263(a) and §§ 1.263(a)-1, 1.263(a)-2, 1.263(a)-3, and 1.162-3(d). In general, the unit of property determination is based upon the functional interdependence standard provided in paragraph (d)(2)(iii)(A) of this section. However, special rules are provided for buildings (see paragraph (d)(2)(ii) of this section), plant property (see paragraph (d)(2)(iii)(B) of this section), and network assets (see paragraph (d)(2)(iii)(C) of this section). Additional rules are provided if a taxpayer has assigned different financial statement economic useful lives or MACRS classes or depreciation methods to components of property (see paragraph (d)(2)(iii)(D) of this section). Property that is aggregated and subject to a general asset account election or accounted for in a multiple asset account (that is, pooled) may not be treated as a single unit of property. In addition, an improvement to a unit of property as determined under this section, other than a leasehold improvement, is not a unit of property separate from the unit of property improved.

(ii) Buildings and structural components. In the case of a building (as defined in § 1.48-1(e)(1)), the building and its structural components (as defined in § 1.48-1(e)(2)) are a single unit of property. In the case of a leasehold improvement made by a lessee and that is section 1250 property, the leasehold improvement is a separate unit of property. In the case of a taxpayer that owns or occupies an individual unit in a building with multiple units (such as a condominium or cooperative), the unit of property is the individual unit owned and/or occupied by the taxpayer.

(iii) Property other than buildings. (A) In general. Except as provided in paragraph (d)(2)(iii)(B), (C) and (D) of this section, in the case of real or personal property other than property described in paragraph (d)(2)(ii) of this section, all the components that are functionally interdependent comprise a single unit of property. Components of property are functionally interdependent if the placing in service of one component by the taxpayer is dependent on the placing in service of the other component by the taxpayer.

(B) Plant property. (1) Definition. For purposes of this paragraph (d)(2) of this section, the term plant property means functionally interdependent machinery or equipment, other than network assets, used to perform an industrial process, such as manufacturing, generation, warehousing, distribution, automated materials handling in service industries, or other similar activities.

(2) Unit of property for plant property. In the case of plant property, a unit of property is comprised of each component (or group of components) within the unit of property determined under the general rule of paragraph (d)(2)(iii)(A) of this section that performs a discrete and major function or operation within the functionally interdependent machinery or equipment.

(C) Network assets. (1) Definition. For purposes of this paragraph (d)(2), the term network assets means railroad track, oil and gas pipelines, water and sewage pipelines, power transmission and distribution lines, and telephone and cable lines that are owned or leased by taxpayers in each of those respective industries. The term includes, for example, trunk and feeder lines, pole lines, and buried conduit. It does not include property that would be included as a structural component of a building under paragraph (d)(2)(ii) of this section, nor does it include separate property that is adjacent to, but not part of a network asset, such as bridges, culverts, or tunnels.

(2) [Reserved]

(D) Additional rules. Notwithstanding the unit of property determination under paragraphs (d)(2)(iii)(A), (B), and (C) of this section, a component (or a group of components) of a unit property must be treated as a separate unit of property if— (1) At the time the unit of property (as determined under paragraph (d)(2)(iii)(A), (B), and (C) of this section) is placed in service by the taxpayer (without regard to subsequent improvements), the taxpayer has recorded on its books and records for financial or regulatory accounting purposes an economic useful life for the component that is different from the economic useful life of the unit of property of which the component is a part; or

(2) The taxpayer has properly treated the component as being within a different class of property under section 168(e) (MACRS classes) than the class of the unit of property of which the component is a part or, the taxpayer, at the time the component was placed in service by the taxpayer, has properly depreciated the component using a different depreciation method under section 167 or section 168 than the depreciation method of the unit of property of which the component is a part.

(iv) Examples. The rules of this paragraph (d)(2) are illustrated by the following examples, in which it is assumed that the taxpayer has not made a general asset account election with regard to property or accounted for property in a multiple asset account.

Example (1). Buildings and structural components; plant property. X owns a building containing various types of manufacturing equipment that are not structural components of the building. Because the property is a building, as defined in § 1.48-1(e)(1), the unit of property for the building must be determined under paragraph (d)(2)(ii) of this section. Under the rules of that paragraph, X must treat the building and all its structural components as a single unit of property. In addition, because the manufacturing equipment contained within the building constitutes property other than a building, the units of property for the manufacturing equipment are initially determined under the general rule in paragraph (d)(2)(iii)(A) of this section and are therefore comprised of all the components that are functionally interdependent. Moreover, because the manufacturing equipment is plant property, under paragraph (d)(2)(iii)(B) of this section, the units of property under the general rule are further divided into smaller units of property by determining the components (or groups of components) that perform discrete and major functions within the plant. Finally, X must apply the additional rules in paragraph (d)(2)(iii)(D) of this section to determine whether any of the units of property determined under paragraphs (d)(2)(iii)(A) and (B) of this section contain components that must be treated as separate units of property.

Example (2). Buildings and structural components; property other than plants. X, a manufacturer, owns a building adjacent to its manufacturing facility that contains office space and related facilities for X's employees that manage and administer X's manufacturing operations. The office building contains equipment, such as desks, chairs, computers, telephones, and bookshelves, that are not structural components of the building. Because the office building is a building, as defined in § 1.48-1(e)(1), the unit of property for the building must be determined under paragraph (d)(2)(ii) of this section. Under the rules of that paragraph, X must treat the office building and all its structural components as a single unit of property. In addition, because the equipment contained within the office building constitutes property other than a building, the units of property for the office equipment are initially determined under the general rule in paragraph (d)(2)(iii)(A) of this section and are comprised of the groups of components that are functionally interdependent. X then must apply the additional rules in paragraph (d)(2)(iii)(D) of this section to determine whether any of the units of property determined under paragraph (d)(2)(iii)(A) of this section contain components that must be treated as separate units of property.

Example (3). Plant property; discrete and major function. X is an electric utility company that operates a power plant to generate electricity. The power plant includes a structure that is not a building under § 1.48-1(e)(1), four pulverizers that grind coal, one boiler that produces steam, one turbine that converts the steam into mechanical energy, and one generator that converts mechanical energy into electrical energy. In addition, the turbine contains a series of blades that cause the turbine to rotate when affected by the steam. When X placed the plant into service, X recorded all the components of the plant as having the same economic useful life on its books and records for financial and regulatory accounting purposes. X also treated all the components of the plant as being within the same class of property under section 168(e) and has depreciated all the components using the same depreciation methods. Because the plant is composed of real and personal tangible property other than a building, the unit of property for the generating equipment is initially determined under the general rule in paragraph (d)(2)(iii)(A) of this section and is comprised of all the components that are functionally interdependent. Under this rule, the initial unit of property is the entire plant because the components of the plant are functionally interdependent. However, because the power plant is plant property under paragraph (d)(2)(iii)(B) of this section, the initial unit of property is further divided into smaller units of property by determining the components (or groups of components) that perform discrete and major functions within the plant. Under this paragraph, X must treat the structure, the boiler, the turbine, and the generator each as a separate unit of property, and each of the four pulverizers as a separate unit of property because each of these components performs a discrete and major function within the power plant. X is not required to treat components, such as the turbine blades, as separate units of property because each of these components does not perform a discrete and major function within the plant.

Example (4). Plant property; discrete and major function. X is engaged in a uniform and linen rental business that operates a plant to treat and launder items used in its business. Within the plant, X utilizes an assembly line-like process that incorporates many different machines and equipment to launder and prepare the items to be returned to customers. X utilizes two laundering lines in its plant, each of which can operate independently. One line is used for uniforms and another line is used for linens. Both lines incorporate several sorters, boilers, washers, dryers, ironers, folders, and waste water treatment systems. Because the laundering equipment contained within the plant is personal property, the unit of property for the laundering equipment is initially determined under the general rule in paragraph (d)(2)(iii)(A) of this section and is comprised of all the components that are functionally interdependent. Under this rule, the initial units of property are each laundering line because each line is functionally independent and is comprised of components that are functionally interdependent. However, because each line is comprised of plant property under paragraph (d)(2)(iii)(B) of this section, the initial units of property are further divided into smaller units of property by determining the components (or groups of components) that perform discrete and major functions within the line. Under paragraph (d)(2)(iii)(B) of this section, X must treat each sorter, boiler, washer, dryer, ironer, folder, and waste water treatment system in each line as a separate unit of property because each of these components performs a discrete and major function within the line. Finally, X must apply the additional rules in paragraph (d)(2)(iii)(D) of this section to determine whether any of the units of property determined under paragraph (d)(2)(iii)(B) of this section contain components that must be treated as separate units of property.

Example (5). Plant property; industrial process. X operates a restaurant that prepares and serves food to retail customers. Within its restaurant, X has a large piece of equipment that uses an assembly line-like process to prepare and cook tortillas that X serves to its customers. Because the tortilla-making equipment is personal property, the unit of property for the equipment is initially determined under the general rule in paragraph (d)(2)(iii)(A) of this section and is comprised of all the components that are functionally interdependent. Under this rule, the initial unit of property is the entire tortilla-making equipment because the various components of the equipment are functionally interdependent. Although the equipment is used to perform a manufacturing process, the equipment is not being used in an industrial process, as it performs a small-scale function as part of X's retail restaurant operations. Therefore, the equipment is not plant property under paragraph (d)(2)(iii)(B) of this section. Finally, X must apply the additional rules in paragraph (d)(2)(iii)(D) of this section to determine whether the equipment contains components that must be treated as separate units of property.

Example (6). Personal property. X owns locomotives that it uses in its railroad business. Each locomotive consists of various components, such as an engine, generators, batteries and trucks. X acquired a locomotive with all its components and recorded all the components as having the same economic useful life on its books and records for financial and regulatory accounting. X also treated all the components of the locomotive as being within the same class of property under section 168(e) and has depreciated all the components using the same depreciation methods. Because X's locomotive is property other than a building, the initial unit of property is determined under paragraph (d)(2)(iii)(A) of this section. Under this paragraph, the locomotive is a single unit of property because it consists entirely of components that are functionally interdependent. Because the additional rules under paragraph (d)(2)(iii)(D) of this section do not apply under these facts, the locomotive is a single unit of property.

Example (7). Personal property. X is engaged in the business of transporting freight throughout the United States. To conduct its business, X owns a fleet of tractors and trailers. Each tractor and trailer is comprised of various components, including tires. X purchases a truck trailer with all of its components, including 16 tires. At the time the trailer was placed in service by X, X treated the trailer and the tires as being within the same class of property under section 168(e) and has depreciated all the components using the same depreciation methods. However, on its books and records for financial accounting purposes, X recorded economic useful lives for the tires that were different from the economic useful life that it recorded for the trailer. Because X's trailer is property other than a building, the initial units of property for the trailer are determined under the general rule in paragraph (d)(2)(iii)(A) of this section and are comprised of all the components that are functionally interdependent. Under this rule, the truck trailer, including its 16 tires, is a single unit of property because the trailer and the tires are functionally interdependent (that is, the placing in service of the tires is dependent upon the placing in service of the trailer). X then must apply the additional rules in paragraph (d)(2)(iii)(D) of this section to determine whether the initial unit of property determined under paragraph (d)(2)(iii)(A) of this section contains components that must be treated as separate units of property. Under paragraph (d)(2)(iii)(D)(1) of this section, because X recorded on its books and records economic useful lives for the tires that are different from the economic useful lives that it recorded for the trailer, the tires must be treated as separate units of property.

Example (8). Personal property. X provides legal services to customers. X purchased a laptop computer and a printer to be used by its employees in providing services. When X placed the computer and printer into service, X recorded both items and all their components as having the same economic useful life on its books and records for financial accounting purposes. X also treated the computer and printer and all their components as being within the same class of property under section 168(e) and has depreciated all the components using the same depreciation methods. Because the computer and printer are property other than a building, the initial units of property are determined under the general rule in paragraph (d)(2)(iii)(A) of this section and are comprised of the components that are functionally interdependent. Under this paragraph (d)(2)(iii)(A), the computer and the printer are separate units of property because the computer and the printer are not components that are functionally interdependent (that is, the placing in service of the computer is not dependent on the placing in service of the printer). The additional rules in paragraph (d)(2)(iii)(D) of this section do not apply under these facts. Accordingly, the computer and the printer each constitute separate units of property.

(3) Compliance with regulatory requirements. For purposes of this section, a Federal, state, or local regulator's requirement that a taxpayer perform certain repairs or maintenance on a unit of property to continue operating the property is not relevant in determining whether the amount paid improves the unit of property.

(4) Repairs and maintenance performed during an improvement. (i) In general. A taxpayer must capitalize all the direct costs of an improvement and all the indirect costs (including otherwise deductible repair costs) that directly benefit or are incurred by reason of an improvement in accordance with the rules under section 263A. Repairs and maintenance that do not directly benefit or are not incurred by reason of an improvement are not required to be capitalized under section 263(a), regardless of whether they are made at the same time as an improvement.

(ii) Exception for individuals' residences. A taxpayer who is an individual may capitalize amounts paid for repairs and maintenance that are made at the same time as substantial capital improvements to property not used in the taxpayer's trade or business or for the production of income if the repairs are done as part of a remodeling of the taxpayer's residence.

(5) Aggregate of related amounts. For purposes of paragraph (d)(1) of this section, the aggregate of related amounts paid to improve a unit of property may be incurred over a period of more than one taxable year. Whether amounts are related to the same improvement depends on the facts and circumstances of the activities being performed and whether the costs are incurred by reason of a single improvement or directly benefit a single improvement.

(e) Safe harbor for routine maintenance. *(1) In general.* An amount paid for routine maintenance performed on a unit of property is deemed to not improve that unit of property. Routine maintenance is the recurring activities that a taxpayer expects to perform as a result of the taxpayer's use of the unit of property to keep the unit of property in its ordinarily efficient operating condition. Routine maintenance activities include, for example, the inspection, cleaning, and testing of the unit of property, and the replacement of parts of the unit of property with comparable and commercially available and reasonable replacement parts. The activities are routine only if, at the time the unit of property is placed in service by the taxpayer, the taxpayer reasonably expects to perform the activities more than once during the class life (as defined in paragraph (e)(4) of this section) of the unit of property. Among the factors to be considered in determining whether a taxpayer is performing routine maintenance are the recurring nature of the activity, industry practice, manufacturers' recommendations, the taxpayer's experience, and the taxpayer's treatment of the activity on its applicable financial statement (as defined in paragraph (b)(4) of this section). With respect to a taxpayer that is a lessor of a unit of property, the taxpayer's use of the unit of property includes the lessee's use of the unit of property.

(2) Exceptions. Routine maintenance does not include the following—

(i) Amounts paid for the replacement of a component of a unit of property if the taxpayer has properly deducted a loss for that component (other than a casualty loss under § 1.165-7);

(ii) Amounts paid for the replacement of a component of a unit of property if the taxpayer has properly taken into account the adjusted basis of the component in realizing gain or loss resulting from the sale or exchange of the component;

(iii) Amounts paid for the repair of damage to a unit of property for which the taxpayer has taken a basis adjustment as a result of a casualty loss under section 165 or relating to a casualty event described in section 165; and

(iv) Amounts paid to return a unit of property to its former ordinarily efficient operating condition, if the property has deteriorated to a state of disrepair and is no longer functional for its intended use.

(3) Rotable or temporary spare parts. For purposes of paragraph (e)(1) of this section, amounts paid for routine maintenance include routine maintenance performed on (and with regard to) rotable and temporary spare parts. But see § 1.162-3(b), which provides that rotable and temporary spare parts are used or consumed by the taxpayer in the taxable year in which the taxpayer disposes of the part.

(4) Class life. The class life of a unit of property is the recovery period prescribed for the property under section 168(g)(2) and (3) for purposes of the alternative depreciation system, regardless of whether the property is depreciated under section 168(g). For purposes of determining class life under this paragraph (e), section 168(g)(3)(A) (relating to tax-exempt use property subject to lease) does not apply.

(5) Examples. The following examples illustrate the rules of this paragraph (e).

Example (1). Routine maintenance on rotable component. (i) X is a commercial airline engaged in the business of transporting passengers and freight throughout the United States and abroad. To conduct its business, X owns or leases various types of aircraft. As a condition of maintaining its airworthiness certification for these aircraft, X is required by the Federal Aviation Administration (FAA) to establish and adhere to a continuous maintenance program for each aircraft within its fleet. These programs, which are designed by X and the aircraft's manufacturer and approved by the FAA, are incorporated into each aircraft's maintenance manual. The maintenance manuals require a variety of periodic maintenance visits at various intervals. One type of maintenance visit is an engine shop visit (ESV), which X expects to perform on its aircraft engines approximately every 4 years in order to keep its aircraft in its ordinarily efficient operating condition. In 2004, X purchased a new aircraft and four new engines to use in that aircraft and later, in other aircraft in its fleet. The aircraft engines are rotable spare parts because they are removable from the aircraft, and repaired and reinstalled on other aircraft or stored for later installation on other aircraft. See § 1.162-3(b) (treatment of materials and supplies). In 2008, X performs its first ESV on the aircraft engines. The ESV includes disassembly, cleaning, inspection, repair, replacement, reassembly, and testing of the engine and its component parts. During the ESV, the engine is removed from the aircraft and shipped to an outside vendor who performs the ESV. If inspection or testing discloses a discrepancy in a part's conformity to the specifications in X's maintenance program, the part is repaired, or if necessary, replaced with a comparable and commercially available and reasonable replacement part. After the ESVs, the engines are returned to X to be reinstalled on another aircraft or stored for later installation. Assume the unit of property for X's aircraft is the entire aircraft, including the aircraft engines, and that the class life for X's aircraft is 12 years. Assume that none of the exceptions set out in paragraph (e)(2) of this section applies to the costs of performing the ESVs.

(ii) Because the ESVs involve the recurring activities that X expects to perform as a result of its use of the aircraft to keep the aircraft in ordinarily efficient operating condition, and consist of maintenance activities that X expects to perform more than once during the 12 year class life of the aircraft, X's ESVs are within the routine maintenance safe harbor under paragraph (e) of this section. Accordingly, the amounts paid by X for the ESVs are deemed not to improve the aircraft and are not required to be capitalized under paragraph (d)(1) of this section. For the treatment of costs to acquire the engines, see § 1.162-3.

Example (2). Routine maintenance after economic useful life. Assume the same facts as in Example 1, except that X incurs costs to perform an ESV on one of its aircraft engines in 2024, after the end of the economic useful life that X anticipated for the aircraft. Because this ESV involves the same routine maintenance activities that were performed on aircraft engines in Example 1, this ESV also is within the routine maintenance safe harbor under paragraph (e) of this section. Accordingly, the amounts paid by X for this ESV, even though performed after the economic useful life of the aircraft, are deemed not to improve the aircraft and are not required to be capitalized under paragraph (d)(1) of this section.

Example (3). Routine maintenance resulting from prior owner's use. (i) In January 2008, X purchases a used machine for use its manufacturing operations. Assume that the machine is the unit of property and has a class life of 10 years. The machine is fully operational at the time it is purchased by X and is immediately placed in service in X's business. At the time it is placed in service by X, X expects to perform manufacturer recommended scheduled maintenance on the machine approximately every three years. The scheduled maintenance includes the cleaning and oiling of the machine, the inspection of parts for defects, and the replacement of minor items such as springs, bearings, and seals with comparable and commercially available and reasonable replacement parts. At the time the machine is purchased, it is approaching the end of a three-year scheduled maintenance period. As a result, in February 2008, X incurs costs to perform the manufacturer recommended scheduled maintenance. Assume that none of the exceptions set out in paragraph (e)(2) of this section apply to the amounts paid for the scheduled maintenance.

(ii) The majority of the costs incurred by X do not qualify under the routine maintenance safe harbor in paragraph (e) of this section because the costs were primarily incurred as a result of the prior owner's use of the property and not X's use. The condition of the machine at the time that it was placed in service by X was that of a machine nearing the end of a scheduled maintenance period. Accordingly, the amounts paid by X for the scheduled maintenance resulting from the prior owner's use of the property must be capitalized if those amounts result in a betterment under paragraph (f) of this section, including the amelioration of a material condition or defect, or otherwise result in an improvement under paragraph (d)(1) of this section. See also section 263A requiring taxpayers to capitalize the direct and allocable share of indirect costs of property produced or acquired for resale.

Example (4). Routine maintenance resulting from new owner's use. Assume the same facts as in Example 3, except that after X incurs costs for the maintenance in 2008, X continues to operate the machine in its manufacturing business. In 2011, X incurs costs to perform the next scheduled manufacturer recommended maintenance on the machine. Assume that the scheduled maintenance activities performed are the same as those performed in Example 3 and that none of the exceptions set out in paragraph (e)(2) of this section apply to the amounts paid for the scheduled maintenance. Because the scheduled maintenance performed in 2011 involves the recurring activities that X performs as a result of its use of the machine, keeps the machine in an ordinarily efficient operating condition, and consists of maintenance activities that X expects to perform more than once during the 10 year class life of the machine, X's scheduled maintenance costs are within the routine maintenance safe harbor under paragraph (e) of this section. Accordingly, the amounts paid by X for the scheduled maintenance in 2011 are deemed not to improve the machine and are not required to be capitalized under paragraph (d)(1) of this section. However, because the amounts paid for the scheduled maintenance are incurred by reason of X's manufacturing operations, X is required to capitalize the amounts paid for the maintenance to products produced by X. See § 1.263A-1(e)(3)(ii).

Example (5). Routine maintenance; replacement of substantial structural part. X is in the business of producing commercial products for sale. As part of the production process, X places raw materials into lined containers in which a chemical reaction is used to convert raw materials into the finished product. The lining is a substantial structural part of the container, and comprises 60% of the total physical structure of the container. Assume that each container, including its lining, is the unit of property and that a container has a class life of 12 years. At the time that X placed the container into service, X was aware that approximately every three years, X would be required to replace the lining in the container with comparable and commercially available and reasonable replacement materials. At the end of that period, the container will continue to function, but will become less efficient and the replacement of the lining will be necessary to keep the container in an ordinarily efficient operating condition. In 2003, X acquired 10 new containers and placed them into service. In 2006, 2009, 2011, and 2014, X pays amounts to replace the containers' linings with comparable and commercially available and reasonable replacement parts. Assume that none of the exceptions set out in paragraph (e)(2) of this section apply to the amounts paid for the replacement linings. Because the replacement of the linings involves recurring activities that X expects to perform as a result of its use of the containers to keep the containers in their ordinarily efficient operating condition, and consists of maintenance activities that X expects to perform more than once during the 12 year class lives of the containers, X's lining replacement costs are within the routine maintenance safe harbor under paragraph (e) of this section. Accordingly, the amounts paid by X for the replacement of the container linings are deemed not to improve the containers and are not required to be capitalized under paragraph (d)(1) of this section. However, because the amounts paid to replace the container linings are incurred by reason of X's manufacturing operations, X is required to capitalize the amounts paid for the replacements to products produced by X. See § 1.263A-1(e)(3)(ii).

Example (6). Routine maintenance once during class life. X is a Class I railroad that owns a fleet of freight cars. Assume that a freight car, including all its components, is a unit of property and has a class life of 14 years. At the time that X places a freight car into service, X expects to perform cyclical reconditioning to the car every 8 to 10 years in order to keep the freight car in ordinarily efficient operating condition. During this reconditioning, X incurs costs to disassemble, inspect, and recondition and/or replace components of the freight car with comparable and commercially available and reasonable replacement parts. Ten years after the freight car is placed in service by X, X incurs costs to perform a cyclical reconditioning on the car. Because X expects to perform the reconditioning only once during the 14 year class life of the freight car, the costs incurred for reconditioning do not qualify for the routine maintenance safe harbor under paragraph (e) of this section. Accordingly, X must capitalize the amounts paid for the reconditioning of the freight car if these amounts result in an improvement under paragraph (d)(1) of this section.

Example (7). Routine maintenance on non-rotable part. X is, a towboat operator that owns and leases a fleet of towboats. Each towboat is equipped with two diesel-powered engines. Assume that each towboat, including its engines, is the unit of property and that a towboat has a class life of 18 years. At the time that X places its towboats into service, X is aware that approximately every three to four years, X will need to perform scheduled maintenance on the two towboat engines to keep the engines in their ordinarily efficient operating condition. This maintenance is completed while the engines are attached to the towboat and involves the cleaning and inspecting of the engines to determine which parts are within acceptable operating tolerances and can continue to be used, which parts must be reconditioned to be brought back to acceptable tolerances, and which parts must be replaced. Engine parts replaced during these procedures are replaced with comparable and commercially available and reasonable replacement parts. Assume the towboat engines are not rotable spare parts under § 1.162-3(b). In 2005, X acquired a new towboat, including its two engines, and placed the towboat into service. In 2009, X incurs amounts to perform scheduled maintenance on both engines in the towboat. Assume that none of the exceptions set out in paragraph (e)(2) of this section apply to the scheduled maintenance costs. The scheduled maintenance involves recurring activities that X expects to perform more than once during the 18 year class life of the towboat. Because this maintenance results from X's use of the towboat, and is performed to keep the towboat in an ordinarily efficient operating condition, the scheduled maintenance on X's towboat is within the routine maintenance safe harbor under paragraph (e) of this section. Accordingly, the amounts paid by X for the scheduled maintenance to its towboat engines in 2009 are deemed not to improve the towboat and are not required to be capitalized under paragraph (d)(1) of this section.

Example (8). Routine maintenance with betterments. Assume the same facts as Example 7, except that in 2013, X's towboat engines are due for another scheduled maintenance visit. At this time X decides to upgrade the engines to increase their horsepower and propulsion, which would permit the towboats to tow heavier loads. Accordingly, in 2013 X incurs costs to perform many of the same activities that it would perform during the typical scheduled maintenance activities such as cleaning, inspecting, reconditioning, and replacing minor parts, but at the same time, X incurs costs to upgrade certain engine parts to increase the towing capacity of the boats in excess of the capacity when the boats were placed in service by X. Both the scheduled maintenance procedures and the replacement of parts with new and upgraded parts are necessary to increase the horsepower of the engines and the towing capacity of the boat. Thus, the work done on the engines encompasses more than the recurring activities that X expected to perform as a result of its use of the towboats and did more than keep the towboat in its ordinarily efficient operating condition. In addition, the scheduled maintenance procedures directly benefit and are incurred by reason of the upgrades. Therefore, the amounts paid by X in 2013 for the maintenance and upgrade of the engines do not qualify for the routine maintenance safe harbor described under paragraph (e) of this section. These amounts must be capitalized if they result in a betterment under paragraph (f) of this section, including a material increase in the capacity of the towboat, or otherwise result in an improvement under paragraph (d)(1) of this section. See also section 263A requiring taxpayers to capitalize all the direct costs of an improvement to property and all the indirect costs that directly benefit or are incurred by reason of an improvement to property.

Example (9). Exceptions to routine maintenance. X owns and operates a farming and cattle ranch with an irrigation system that provides water for crops. Assume that each canal in the irrigation system is a single unit of property and has a class life of 20 years. When X placed the canals into service, X expected to have to perform major maintenance on the canals every 3 years to keep the canals in their ordinarily efficient operating condition. This maintenance included draining the canals, and then cleaning, inspecting, repairing, reconditioning or replacing parts of the canal with comparable and commercially available and reasonable replacement parts. X placed the canals into service in 2005 and did not perform any maintenance on the canals until 2010. At that time, the canals had fallen into a state of disrepair and no longer functioned for irrigation. In 2010, X paid amounts to drain the canals, and do extensive cleaning, repairing, reconditioning and replacing parts of the canals with comparable and commercially available and reasonable replacement parts. Although the work performed on X's canals was similar to the activities that X expected to perform, but did not perform, every three years, the costs of these activities do not fall within the routine maintenance safe harbor. Specifically, under paragraph (e)(2)(iv) of this section, routine maintenance does not include amounts paid to return a unit of property to its former ordinarily efficient operating condition if the property has deteriorated to a state of disrepair and is no longer functional for its intended use. Accordingly, amounts paid by X for work performed on the canals in 2010 must be capitalized if they result in improvements under paragraph (d)(1) of this section (for example, restorations under paragraph (g) of this section).

(f) Capitalization of betterments. *(1) In general.* A taxpayer must capitalize amounts paid that result in the betterment of a unit of property. An amount paid results in the betterment of a unit of property only if it-

(i) Ameliorates a material condition or defect that either existed prior to the taxpayer's acquisition of the unit of property or arose during the production of the unit of property, whether or not the taxpayer was aware of the condition or defect at the time of acquisition or production;

(ii) Results in a material addition (including a physical enlargement, expansion, or extension) to the unit of property; or

(iii) Results in a material increase in capacity (including additional cubic or square space), productivity, efficiency, strength, or quality of the unit of property or the output of the unit of property.

(2) Application of general rule. (i) Facts and circumstances. To determine whether an amount paid results in a betterment described in paragraph (f)(1) of this section, it is appropriate to consider all the facts and circumstances including, but not limited to, the purpose of the expenditure, the physical nature of the work performed, the effect of the expenditure on the unit of property, and the taxpayer's treatment of the expenditure on its applicable financial statement (as defined in paragraph (b)(4) of this section).

(ii) Unavailability of replacement parts. If a taxpayer needs to replace part of a unit of property that cannot practicably be replaced with the same type of part (for example, because of technological advancements or product enhancements), the replacement of the part with an improved but comparable part does not, by itself, result in a betterment to the unit of property.

(iii) Appropriate comparison. (A) In general. In cases in which a particular event necessitates an expenditure, the determination of whether an expenditure results in a betterment of the unit of property is made by comparing the condition of the property immediately after the expenditure with the condition of the property immediately prior to the circumstances necessitating the expenditure.

(B) Normal wear and tear. If the expenditure is made to correct the effects of normal wear and tear to the unit of property (including the amelioration of a condition or defect that existed prior to the taxpayer's acquisition of the unit of property resulting from normal wear and tear), the condition of the property immediately prior to the circumstances necessitating the expenditure is the condition of the property after the last time the taxpayer corrected the effects of normal wear and tear (whether the amounts paid were for maintenance or improvements) or, if the taxpayer has not previously corrected the effects of normal wear and tear, the condition of the property when placed in service by the taxpayer.

(C) Particular event. If the expenditure is made as a result of a particular event, the condition of the property immediately prior to the circumstances necessitating the expenditure is the condition of the property immediately prior to the particular event.

(3) Examples. The following examples illustrate solely the rules of this paragraph (f). Even if capitalization is not required in an example under this paragraph (f), the amounts paid in the example may be subject to capitalization under a different provision of this section.

Example (1). Amelioration of pre-existing material condition or defect. In 2008, X purchases a store located on a parcel of land that contained underground gasoline storage tanks left by prior occupants. Assume that the parcel of land is the unit of property. The tanks had leaked, causing soil contamination. X is not aware of the contamination at the time of purchase. In 2009, X discovers the contamination and incurs costs to remediate the soil. The remediation costs incurred by X result in a betterment to the land under paragraph (f)(1)(i) of this section because the costs were incurred to ameliorate a material condition or defect that existed prior to the taxpayer's acquisition of the land.

Example (2). Not amelioration of pre-existing condition or defect. X owned a building that was constructed with insulation that contained asbestos. The health dangers of asbestos were not widely known when the building was constructed. In 2008, X determined that certain areas of asbestos-containing insulation had begun to deteriorate and could eventually pose a health risk to employees. Therefore, X decided to remove the asbestos-containing insulation from the building and replace it with new insulation that was safer to employees, but no more efficient or effective than the asbestos insulation. Assume the building and its structural components (including the asbestos insulation) is the unit of property. The amounts paid to remove and replace the asbestos insulation are not required to be capitalized as a betterment under paragraphs (f)(1)(i) and (f)(2)(i) of this section because the asbestos, although later determined to be unsafe under certain circumstances, was not an inherent and material defect to the property. In addition, the removal and replacement of the asbestos did not result in any material additions to the building or material increases in capacity, productivity, efficiency, strength or quality of the building or the output of the building under paragraphs (f)(1)(ii) and (f)(1)(iii) of this section.

Example (3). Not amelioration of pre-existing material condition or defect. (i) In January 2008, X purchases a used machine for use in its manufacturing operations. Assume that the machine is a unit of property and it has a class life of 10 years. The machine is fully operational at the time it is purchased by X and is immediately placed in service in X's business. At the time it is placed in service by X, X expects to perform manufacturer recommended scheduled maintenance on the machine every three years. The scheduled maintenance includes the cleaning and oiling of the machine, the inspection of parts for defects, and the replacement of minor items such as springs, bearings, and seals with comparable and commercially available and reasonable replacement parts. The scheduled maintenance does not result in any material additions or material increases in capacity, productivity, efficiency, strength or quality of the machine or the output of the machine. At the time the machine is purchased, it is approaching the end of a three-year scheduled maintenance period. As a result, in February 2008, X incurs costs to perform the manufacturer recommended scheduled maintenance to keep the machine in its ordinarily efficient operating condition.

(ii) The majority of the costs incurred by X do not qualify under the routine maintenance safe harbor in paragraph (e) of this section because the costs were primarily incurred as a result of the prior owner's use of the property and not the taxpayer's use. The condition of the machine at the time that it was placed in service by X was that of a machine nearing the end of a scheduled maintenance period. Accordingly, the amounts paid by X for the scheduled maintenance resulting from the prior owner's use of the property ameliorate conditions or defects that existed prior to X's ownership of the machine. Nevertheless, considering the facts and circumstances under paragraph (f)(2)(i) of this section, including the purpose and minor nature of the work performed, those amounts do not ameliorate a material condition or defect under paragraph (f)(1)(i) of this section and accordingly do not result in a betterment that must be capitalized under this paragraph (f).

Example (4). Not amelioration of pre-existing material condition or defect. In 2008, X purchases a used ice resurfacing machine for use in the operation of its ice skating rink. To comply with local regulations, X is required to routinely monitor the air quality in the ice skating rink. One week after X places the machine into service, during a routine air quality check, X discovers that the operation of the machine is adversely affecting the air quality in the skating rink. As a result, X incurs costs to inspect and retune the machine, which includes replacing minor components of the engine, which had worn out prior to X's acquisition of the machine. Assume the resurfacing machine, including the engine, is the unit of property. The routine maintenance safe harbor in paragraph (e) of this section does not apply to the amounts paid because the activities performed do more than return the machine to the condition that existed at the time it was placed in service by X. The amounts paid by X to inspect, retune, and replace minor components of the ice resurfacing machine ameliorated a condition or defect that existed prior to X's acquisition of the equipment. Nevertheless, considering the facts and circumstances under paragraph (f)(2)(i) of this section, including the purpose and minor nature of the work performed, these amounts do not ameliorate a material condition or defect under paragraph (f)(1)(i) of this section, result in a material addition to the machine under paragraph (f)(1)(ii) of this section, or result in a material increase in the capacity, productivity, efficiency, strength or quality of the machine or the output of the machine. Accordingly, the amounts paid by X to inspect, retune, and replace minor components of the machine do not result in a betterment that must be capitalized under this paragraph (f).

Example (5). Amelioration of material condition or defect; increase in quality. (i) In January 2009, X acquires a building for use in its business of providing assisted living services. Before and after the purchase, the building functions as an assisted living facility. However, at the time of the purchase, X is aware that the building is in a condition that is below the standards that X requires for facilities used in its business. Beginning in 2009 and over the next two years, while X continues to use the building as an assisted living facility, X incurs costs for repairs, maintenance, and the acquisition of new property to bring the facility into the high-quality condition for which X's facilities are known. The work includes repainting; replacing flooring materials, windows, and tiling and fixtures in bathrooms; replacing window treatments, furniture, and cabinets; and repairing or replacing roofing materials, heating and cooling systems. On its applicable financial statements, X capitalizes the costs of the repairs, maintenance, and acquisitions over the remaining economic useful life recorded for the building. Assume that the building, including its structural components, is a single unit of property and that each section 1245 property is a separate unit of property.

(ii) Considering the facts and circumstances under paragraph (f)(2)(i) of this section, including the purpose of the expenditures, the effect of the expenditures on the building, and the treatment of the expenditures in X's applicable financial statements, the amounts paid by X for repairs and maintenance to the building and its structural components ameliorated material conditions and defects that existed prior to X's acquisition of the building. In addition, these amounts materially increased the quality of the building as compared to the condition of the building when it was placed in service by X. Accordingly, the amounts paid by X for repairs and maintenance to the building and its structural components (that is, repainting, replacing windows, replacing bathroom fixtures, repairing and replacing roofing materials and heating and cooling systems) result in betterments that must be capitalized under this paragraph (f). Moreover, X is required to capitalize the amounts paid to acquire and install each section 1245 property, including the flooring materials, tiling, each window treatment, each item of furniture, and each cabinet, in accordance with § 1.263(a)-2(d).

Example (6). Not a betterment. (i) X owns a nationwide chain of retail stores that sell a wide variety of items. To remain competitive in the industry, X periodically changes the layout and appearance of its stores. These changes include the reconfiguration of the stores to provide better exposure of the merchandise and cosmetic alterations to keep the store modern and attractive to customers. The work is not undertaken for the purpose of repairing damaged property but rather to renew the appearance of the property. X incurs costs to update 50 stores during the taxable year. In its applicable financial statement, X capitalizes all the costs of the updates over a 5-year period until which X anticipates it would have to update again. Assume that each store building, including its structural components, is a unit of property and that each section 1245 property within the store is a separate unit of property. Also assume that the work performed did not ameliorate any material conditions or defects that existed when X acquired the store buildings or result in any material additions to the store buildings.

(ii) Considering the facts and circumstances under paragraph (f)(2)(i) of this section, including the purpose of the expenditure, the nature of the work performed, and the treatment of the work on X's applicable financial statements, the amounts paid by X for updates to its store buildings (including their structural components) do not result in material increases in capacity, productivity, efficiency, strength or quality of the store buildings. Accordingly, the amounts paid by X for the updates on the store buildings (including their structural components) do not result in betterments that must be capitalized under this paragraph (f). However, X is required to capitalize the amounts paid to acquire and install each section 1245 property in accordance with § 1.263(a)-2(d).

Example (7). Betterment; regulatory requirement. X owns a hotel in City that includes five foot high unreinforced terra cotta and concrete parapets with overhanging cornices around the entire roof perimeter. The parapets and cornices are in good condition. In 2008, City passes an ordinance setting higher safety standards for parapets and cornices because of the hazardous conditions caused by earthquakes. To comply with the ordinance, X replaces the old parapets and cornices with new ones made of glass fiber reinforced concrete, which makes them lighter and stronger than the original ones. They are attached to the hotel using welded connections instead of wire supports, making them more resistant to damage from lateral movement. Assume the hotel building and its structural components are the unit of property. The event necessitating the expenditure was the 2008 City ordinance. Prior to the ordinance, the old parapets and cornices were in good condition, but were determined by City to create a potential hazard. After the expenditure, the new parapets and cornices materially increased the structural soundness (that is, the strength) of the hotel building. Therefore, the amounts paid by X to replace the parapets and cornices must be capitalized because they resulted in a betterment to the hotel. City's requirement that X correct the potential hazard to continue operating the hotel is not relevant in determining whether the amount paid improved the hotel. See paragraph (d)(3) of this section.

Example (8). Not a betterment; regulatory requirement. X owns a meat processing plant. In 2008, X discovers that oil was seeping through the concrete walls of the plant, creating a fire hazard. Federal meat inspectors advise X that it must correct the seepage problem or shut down its plant. To correct the problem, X incurs costs to add a concrete lining to the walls from the floor to a height of about four feet and also to add concrete to the floor of the plant. Assume the plant building and its structural components are the unit of property. The event necessitating the expenditure was the seepage of the oil. Prior to the seepage, the plant did not leak and was functioning for its intended use. The expenditure did not result in a material addition or material increase in capacity, productivity, efficiency, strength or quality of the plant or its output compared to the condition of the plant prior to the seepage of the oil. Therefore, the amounts paid by X to correct the seepage do not result in a betterment to the plant. X is not required to capitalize as an improvement under this paragraph (f) amounts paid to correct the seepage problem. The Federal meat inspectors' requirement that X correct the seepage to continue operating the plant is not relevant in determining whether the amount paid improved the plant. See paragraph (d)(3) of this section.

Example (9). Not a betterment; replacement with same part. X owns a small retail shop. In 2008, a storm damages the roof of X's shop by displacing numerous wooden shingles. X decides to replace all the wooden shingles on the roof and hires a contractor to replace all the shingles on the roof with new wooden shingles. Assume the shop building and its structural components are the unit of property. The event necessitating the expenditure was the storm. Prior to the storm, the retail shop was functioning for its intended use. The expenditure did not result in a material addition, or material increase in the capacity, productivity, efficiency, strength or quality of the shop or the output of the shop compared to the condition of the shop prior to the storm. Therefore, the amounts paid by X to reshingle the roof with wooden shingles do not result in betterment to the shop building. X is not required to capitalize as an improvement under this paragraph (f) amounts paid to replace the shingles.

Example (10). Not a betterment; replacement with comparable part. Assume the same facts as in Example 9, except that wooden shingles are not available on the market. X decides to replace all the wooden shingles with comparable asphalt shingles. The amounts paid by X to reshingle the roof with asphalt shingles do not result in a betterment to the shop, even though the asphalt shingles may be stronger than the wooden shingles. Because the wooden shingles could not practicably be replaced with new wooden shingles, the replacement of the old shingles with comparable asphalt shingles does not, by itself, result in an improvement to the shop. X is not required to capitalize as an improvement under this paragraph (f) amounts paid to replace the shingles.

Example (11). Betterment; replacement with improved parts. Assume the same facts as in Example 9, except that, instead of replacing the wooden shingles with asphalt shingles, X decides to replace all the wooden shingles with shingles made of lightweight composite materials that are maintenance-free and do not absorb moisture. The new shingles have a 50-year warranty and a Class A fire rating. The expenditure for these shingles resulted in a material increase in the quality of the shop building as compared to the condition of the shop building prior to the storm. X must capitalize amounts paid to reshingle the roof as an improvement under this paragraph (f) because they result in a betterment to the shop.

Example (12). Material increase in capacity. X owns a factory building with a storage area on the second floor. In 2008, X replaces the columns and girders supporting the second floor to permit storage of supplies with a gross weight 50 percent greater than the previous load-carrying capacity of the storage area. Assume the factory building and its structural components are the unit of property. X must capitalize as an improvement amounts paid for the columns and girders because they result in a material increase in the load-carrying capacity of the building. The comparison rule in paragraph (f)(2)(iii) of this section does not apply to these amounts paid because the expenditure was not necessitated by a particular event.

Example (13). Material increase in capacity. In 2008, X purchases harbor facilities consisting of a slip for the loading and unloading of barges and a channel leading from the slip to the river. At the time of purchase, the channel is 150 feet wide, 1,000 feet long, and 10 feet deep. To allow for ingress and egress and for the unloading of its barges, X needs to deepen the channel to a depth of 20 feet. X hires a contractor to dredge the channel to the required depth. Assume the channel is the unit of property. X must capitalize as an improvement amounts paid for the dredging because it resulted in a material increase in the capacity of the channel. The comparison rule in paragraph (f)(2)(iii) of this section does not apply to these amounts paid because the expenditure was not necessitated by a particular event.

Example (14). Not a material increase in capacity. Assume the same facts as in Example 13, except that the channel was susceptible to siltation and, by 2009, the channel depth had been reduced to 18 feet. X hired a contractor to redredge the channel to a depth of 20 feet. The event necessitating the expenditure was the siltation of the channel. Both prior to the siltation and after the redredging, the depth of the channel was 20 feet. Therefore, the amounts paid by X for redredging the channel did not result in a material addition to the unit of property or a material increase in the capacity, productivity, efficiency, strength or quality of the unit of property or the output of the unit of property. X is not required to capitalize as a betterment under paragraph (f) of this section amounts paid to redredge the channel.

Example (15). Not a material increase in capacity. X owns a building used in its trade or business. The first floor has a drop-ceiling. X decides to remove the drop-ceiling and repaint the original ceiling. Assume the building and its structural components are the unit of property. The removal of the drop-ceiling does not create additional capacity in the building that was not there prior to the removal. Therefore, the amounts paid by X to remove the drop-ceiling and repaint the original ceiling did not result in a material addition or a material increase to the capacity, productivity, efficiency, strength or quality of the unit of property or output of the unit of property. X is not required to capitalize as a betterment under this paragraph (f) amounts paid related to removing the drop-ceiling. The comparison rule in paragraph (f)(2)(iii) of this section does not apply to these amounts paid because the expenditure was not necessitated by a particular event.

(g) Capitalization of restorations. *(1) In general.* A taxpayer must capitalize amounts paid to restore a unit of property, including amounts paid in making good the exhaustion for which an allowance is or has been made. An amount is paid to restore a unit of property if it—

(i) Is for the replacement of a component of a unit of property and the taxpayer has properly deducted a loss for that component (other than a casualty loss under § 1.165-7);

(ii) Is for the replacement of a component of a unit of property and the taxpayer has properly taken into account the adjusted basis of the component in realizing gain or loss resulting from the sale or exchange of the component;

(iii) Is for the repair of damage to a unit of property for which the taxpayer has properly taken a basis adjustment as a result of a casualty loss under section 165, or relating to a casualty event described in section 165;

(iv) Returns the unit of property to its ordinarily efficient operating condition if the property has deteriorated to a state of disrepair and is no longer functional for its intended use;

(v) Results in the rebuilding of the unit of property to a like-new condition after the end of its economic useful life (see paragraph (g)(2) of this section); or

(vi) Is for the replacement of a major component or a substantial structural part of the unit of property (see paragraph (g)(3) of this section).

(2) Rebuild to like-new condition. (i) In general. For purposes of paragraph (g)(1)(v) of this section, the following definitions apply:

(A) Like-new condition. A unit of property is rebuilt to a like-new condition if it is brought to the status of new, rebuilt, remanufactured, or similar status under the terms of any Federal regulatory guideline or the manufacturer's original specifications.

(B) Economic useful life. The economic useful life of a unit of property is not necessarily the useful life inherent in the property but is the period over which the property may reasonably be expected to be useful to the taxpayer or, if the taxpayer is engaged in a trade or business or an activity for the production of income, the period over which the property may reasonably be expected to be useful to the taxpayer in its trade or business or for the production of income, as applicable. See § 1.167(a)-1(b) for the factors to be considered in determining this period.

(ii) Exception. An amount paid is not required to be capitalized under paragraph (g)(1)(v) of this section if it is paid during the recovery period prescribed in section 168(c) (taking into account the applicable convention) for the property, regardless of whether the property is depreciated under section 168(a).

(3) Replacement of a major component or a substantial structural part. (i) In general. For purposes of paragraph (g)(1)(vi) of this section, the replacement of a major component or a substantial structural part means the replacement of—

(A) A part or a combination of parts of the unit of property, the cost of which comprises 50 percent or more of the replacement cost of the unit of property; or

(B) A part or a combination of parts of the unit of property that comprise 50 percent or more of the physical structure of the unit of property.

(ii) Exception. An amount paid is not required to be capitalized under paragraph (g)(1)(vi) of this section if it is paid during the recovery period prescribed in section 168(c) (taking into account the applicable convention) for the property, regardless of whether the property is depreciated under section 168(a).

(4) Examples. The following examples illustrate solely the rules of this paragraph (g). Even if capitalization is not required in an example under the cited subparagraph under this paragraph (g), the amounts paid in the example may be subject to capitalization under a different provision of this section, or under a different subparagraph in this paragraph (g).

Example (1). Replacement of loss component. X owns a manufacturing building containing various types of manufacturing equipment. X does a cost segregation study of the manufacturing building and properly determines that a walk-in freezer in the manufacturing equipment is section 1245 property as defined in section 1245(a)(3). The freezer is not part of the HVAC system that relates to the general operation or maintenance of the building. The components of the walk-in freezer cease to function and X decides to replace them. X abandons the freezer components and properly recognizes a loss from the abandonment of the components. X replaces the abandoned freezer components with new components and incurs costs to acquire and install the new components. Under paragraph (g)(1)(i) of this section, X must capitalize the amounts paid to acquire and install the new freezer components because X replaced components for which it had properly deducted a loss.

Example (2). Replacement of sold component. Assume the same facts as in Example 1 except that X did not abandon the components, but instead sold them to another party and properly recognized a loss on the sale. Under paragraph (g)(1)(ii) of this section, X must capitalize the amounts paid to acquire and install the new freezer components because X replaced components for which it had properly taken into account the adjusted basis of the components in realizing a loss from the sale of the components.

Example (3). Restoration after casualty loss. X owns an office building that it uses in its trade or business. A storm damages the office building at a time when the building has an adjusted basis of $500,000. X deducts under section 165 a casualty loss in the amount of $50,000 and properly reduces its basis in the office building to $450,000. X hires a contractor to repair the damage to the building and pays the contractor $50,000 for the work. Under paragraph (g)(1)(iii) of this section, X must capitalize the $50,000 amount paid to the contractor because X properly adjusted its basis as a result of a casualty loss under section 165.

Example (4). Restoration after casualty event. Assume the same facts as in Example 3, except that X receives insurance proceeds of $50,000 after the casualty to compensate for its loss. X cannot deduct a casualty loss under section 165 because its loss was compensated by insurance. However, X properly reduces its basis in the property by the amount of the insurance proceeds. Under paragraph (g)(1)(iii) of this section, X must capitalize the $50,000 amount paid to the contractor because X has properly taken a basis adjustment relating to a casualty event described in section 165.

Example (5). Restoration of property in a state of disrepair. X owns and operates a farm with several barns and outbuildings. One of the outbuildings is not used or maintained by X on a regular basis and falls into a state of disrepair. The outbuilding previously was used for storage but can no longer be used for that purpose because the building is not structurally sound. X decides to restore the outbuilding and incurs costs to shore up the walls and replace the siding. Under paragraph (g)(1)(iv) of this section, X must capitalize the amounts paid to restore the outbuilding because they return the outbuilding to its ordinarily efficient operating condition after it had deteriorated to a state of disrepair and was no longer functional for its intended use.

Example (6). Rebuild of property to like-new condition before end of economic useful life. X is a Class I railroad that owns a fleet of freight cars. Freight cars have a recovery period of 7 years under section 168(c) and an economic useful life of 30 years. Every 8 to 10 years, X rebuilds its freight cars. Ten years after the freight car is placed in service by X, X performs a rebuild, which includes a complete disassembly, inspection, and reconditioning and/ or replacement of components of the suspension and draft systems, trailer hitches, and other special equipment. X modifies the car to upgrade various components to the latest engineering standards. The freight car essentially is stripped to the frame, with all of its substantial components either reconditioned or replaced. The frame itself is the longest-lasting part of the car and is reconditioned. The walls of the freight car are replaced or are sandblasted and repainted. New wheels are installed on the car. All the remaining components of the car are restored before they are reassembled. At the end of the rebuild, the freight car has been restored to a rebuilt condition under the manufacturer's specifications. Assume the freight car is the unit of property. X is not required to capitalize under paragraph (g)(1)(v) of this section the amounts paid to rebuild the freight car because, although the amounts paid restore the freight car to a like-new condition, the amounts were not paid after the end of the economic useful life of the freight car.

Example (7). Rebuild of property to like-new condition after end of economic useful life. Assume the same facts as in Example 6, except that X rebuilds the freight car 40 years after it is placed in service by X. Under paragraph (g)(1)(v) of this section, X must capitalize the amounts paid to rebuild the freight car because the amounts paid restore the freight car to a like-new condition after the end of the economic useful life of the freight car.

Example (8). Replacement of major component. X is a common carrier that owns a fleet of petroleum hauling trucks. X replaces the existing engine, cab, and petroleum tank with a new engine, cab, and tank. The new engine and cab cost $25,000; the new tank costs $10,000. The cost of a new tractor is $50,000 and the cost of a new trailer is $30,000. Assume the tractor of the truck (which includes the cab and the engine) is a separate unit of property from the rest of the truck, and that the trailer (which contains the petroleum tank) is a separate unit of property from the rest of the truck. Also assume that X replaced the components after the end of the recovery periods under section 168(c) for the tractor and the trailer. The amounts paid for the new engine and cab comprise 50% of the cost of a new tractor and must be capitalized under paragraph (g)(1)(vi) of this section. The amounts paid for the new petroleum tank do not comprise 50% or more of the cost of a new trailer; however, the tank comprises more than 50% of the physical structure of the trailer. Therefore, the amounts paid for the new tank also must be capitalized under paragraph (g)(1)(vi) of this section.

Example (9). Repair performed during a restoration. Assume the same facts as in Example 8, except that, at the same time the engine and cab of the tractor are replaced, X paints the cab of the tractor with its company logo and fixes a broken taillight on the tractor. The repair of the broken taillight and the painting of the cab generally are deductible expenses under § 1.162-4. However, under paragraph (d)(4)(i) of this section, a taxpayer must capitalize all the direct costs of an improvement and all the indirect costs that directly benefit or are incurred by reason of an improvement in accordance with the rules under section 263A. Repairs and maintenance that do not directly benefit or are not incurred by reason of an improvement are not required to be capitalized under section 263(a), regardless of whether they are made at the same time as an improvement. Therefore, all amounts paid that directly benefit or are incurred by reason of the tractor restoration must be capitalized, including amounts paid for activities that usually would be deductible maintenance expenses, such as the painting of the cab. Amounts paid to repair the broken taillight, however, are not incurred by reason of the restoration of the tractor, nor do the amounts paid directly benefit the tractor restoration, despite that the repair was performed at the same time as the restoration. Thus, X must capitalize to the restoration of the tractor the amounts paid to paint the cab, but X is not required to capitalize to the restoration of the tractor the amounts paid to repair the broken taillight.

Example (10). Not a replacement of substantial structural part. X owns a large retail store. X discovers a leak in the roof of the store and hires a contractor to inspect and fix the roof. The contractor discovers that a major portion of the sheathing and rafters has rotted, and recommends the replacement of the entire roof. X pays the contractor to replace the roof. Assume the store and its structural components are the unit of property and that the roof does not comprise 50% or more of the physical structure of the store. Also assume the cost of the roof does not comprise 50% or more of the cost to acquire a new store. Consequently, the new roof is not a major component or substantial structural part of the store. Therefore, X is not required to capitalize under paragraph (g)(1)(vi) of this section the amounts paid to replace the roof.

Example (11). Related amounts to replace major component. (i) X owns a retail gasoline station, consisting of a paved area used for automobile access to the pumps and parking areas, a building used to market gasoline, and a canopy covering the gasoline pumps. The premises also consist of underground storage tanks (USTs) that are connected by piping to the pumps and are part of the machinery used in the immediate retail sale of gas. To comply with regulations issued by the Environmental Protection Agency, X is required to remove and replace leaking USTs. In 2008, X hires a contractor to perform the removal and replacement, which consists of removing the old tanks and installing new tanks with leak detection systems. The removal of the old tanks includes removing the paving material covering the tanks, excavating a hole large enough to gain access to the old tanks, disconnecting any strapping and pipe connections to the old tanks, and lifting the old tanks out of the hole. Installation of the new tanks includes placement of a liner in the excavated hole, placement of the new tanks, installation of a leak detection system, installation of an overfill system, connection of the tanks to the pipes leading to the pumps, backfilling of the hole, and replacement of the paving. Assume the new tanks comprise 50% or more of the physical structure of the gasoline distribution system. X also is required to pay a permit fee to the county to undertake the installation of the new tanks.

(ii) X pays the permit fee to the county on October 15, 2008. The contractor performs all of the required work and, on November 1, 2008, bills X for the costs of removing the old USTs. On November 15, 2008, the contractor bills X for the remainder of the work. Assume the gasoline distribution system is the unit of property. The USTs are major components of the gasoline distribution system. Therefore, under paragraphs (d)(5) and (g)(1)(vi) of this section, X must capitalize as an improvement to the distribution system the aggregate of related amounts paid to replace the USTs, which related amounts include the amount paid to the county, the amount paid to remove the old USTs, and the amount paid to install the new USTs (regardless that the amounts were separately invoiced and paid to two different parties).

Example (12). Minor part replacement; coordination with section 263A. X is in the business of smelting aluminum. X's aluminum smelting facility includes a plant where molten aluminum is poured into molds and allowed to solidify. Because of the potential of fire from a molten metal explosion, the plant's roof must be made of fire-resistant material. The roof must also be without leaks because rain water hitting the molten aluminum could cause an explosion. During 2008, X removed and replaced a major portion of the plant's roof decking and roofing material. Assume the plant building and its structural components are the unit of property and that the portion of the roof that is replaced is not a major component or substantial structural part of the building. X is not required to capitalize under paragraph (g)(1)(vi) of this section the amounts paid to remove and replace the roof decking and materials. However, under section 263A, all direct and indirect costs, including otherwise deductible costs, that directly benefit or are incurred by reason of X's manufacturing activities must be capitalized to the property produced by X. Therefore, because the amounts paid for the roof decking and materials are incurred by reason of X's manufacturing operations, the amounts paid must be capitalized under section 263A to the property produced by X.

(h) Capitalization of amounts to adapt property to a new or different use. *(1) In general.* Taxpayers must capitalize amounts paid to adapt a unit of property to a new or different use. In general, an amount is paid to adapt a unit of property to a new or different use if the adaptation is not consistent with the taxpayer's intended ordinary use of the unit of property at the time originally placed in service by the taxpayer.

(2) Examples. The following examples illustrate solely the rules of this paragraph (h). Even if capitalization is not required in an example under this paragraph (h), the amounts paid in the example may be subject to capitalization under a different provision of this section.

Example (1). New or different use. X is a manufacturer and owns a manufacturing facility that it has used for manufacturing since 1970, when it was placed in service by X. Assume the manufacturing facility is a unit of property. In 2008, X incurred costs to convert its manufacturing facility into a showroom for its business. To convert the facility, X replaces various structural components to provide a better layout for the showroom and its offices. X also rewires and repaints the building as part of the conversion. None of the materials used, such as the wiring, are better than existing materials in the building. Under this paragraph (h), the amounts paid by X to convert the manufacturing facility into a showroom are paid to adapt the building to a new or different use because the conversion is not consistent with X's intended ordinary use of the property at the time it was placed in service. Therefore, X is required to capitalize these amounts under paragraph (h)(1) of this section.

Example (2). Not a new or different use. X owns a building, which is a unit of property, consisting of twenty retail spaces. The space was designed to be reconfigured; that is, adjoining spaces could be combined into one space. In 2008, one of the tenants expanded its occupancy to include two adjoining retail spaces. To facilitate the new lease, X incurred costs to remove the walls between the three retail spaces. Under this paragraph (h), the amounts paid by X to convert three retail spaces into one larger space for an existing tenant do not adapt X's building to a new or different use because the combination of retail spaces is consistent with X's intended, ordinary use of the building. Therefore, the costs are not required by this paragraph (h) to be capitalized.

Example (3). Not a new or different use. X owns a building, which is a unit of property, consisting of twenty retail spaces. X decides to sell the building. In anticipation of selling the building, X repaints the interior walls and refinishes the hardwood floors. Preparing the building for sale does not constitute a new or different use for the building. Therefore, amounts paid in preparing the building for sale are not required by this paragraph (h) to be capitalized.

Example (4). New or different use. Since 1930, X has owned a parcel of land on which it previously operated a manufacturing facility. Assume that the land is the unit of property. During the course of X's operation of the manufacturing facility, the land became contaminated with wastes from its manufacturing processes. In 1995, X discontinued manufacturing operations at the site. In 2008, X decides to sell the property to a developer that intends to use the property for residential housing. In anticipation of selling the land, X pays amounts to cleanup the land to a standard that is required for the land to be used for residential purposes. In addition, X pays amounts to regrade the land so that it can be used for residential purposes. Amounts paid by X to cleanup wastes that were discharged in the course of X's manufacturing operations do not adapt the land to a new or different use, regardless of the extent to which the land was cleaned. However, amounts to regrade the land so that it can be used for residential purposes adapts the land to a new or different use that is inconsistent with X's intended ordinary use of the property at the time it was placed in service. Accordingly, the amounts paid by X to regrade the land must be capitalized under paragraph (h)(1) of this section.

(i) Optional regulatory accounting method. *(1) In general.* This paragraph (i) provides an optional simplified method (the regulatory accounting method) for regulated taxpayers to determine whether amounts paid to repair, maintain, or improve tangible property are to be treated as deductible expenses or capital expenditures. A taxpayer that elects to use the regulatory accounting method described in paragraph (i)(3) of this section must use that method for property subject to regulatory accounting instead of determining whether amounts paid to repair, maintain, or improve property are capital expenditures or deductible expenses under the general principles of sections 162(a), 212, and 263(a). Thus, the capitalization rules in § 1.263(a)-3(d) (and the routine maintenance safe harbor described in paragraph (e) of this section) do not apply to amounts paid to repair, maintain, or improve property subject to regulatory accounting by taxpayers that elect to use the regulatory accounting method under this paragraph (i). However, section 263A continues to apply to costs required to be capitalized to property produced by the taxpayer or to property acquired for resale.

(2) Eligibility for regulatory accounting method. A taxpayer that is engaged in a trade or business in a regulated industry may use the regulatory accounting method under this paragraph (i). For purposes of this paragraph (i), a taxpayer in a regulated industry is a taxpayer that is subject to the regulatory accounting rules of the Federal Energy Regulatory Commission (FERC), the Federal Communications Commission (FCC), or the Surface Transportation Board (STB).

(3) Description of regulatory accounting method. Under the regulatory accounting method, a taxpayer must follow its

method of accounting for regulatory accounting purposes in determining whether an amount paid improves property under this section. Therefore, a taxpayer must capitalize for Federal income tax purposes an amount paid that is capitalized as an improvement for regulatory accounting purposes. A taxpayer must not capitalize for Federal income tax purposes under this section an amount paid that is not capitalized as an improvement for regulatory accounting purposes. A taxpayer that uses the regulatory accounting method must use that method for all of its tangible property that is subject to regulatory accounting rules. The method does not apply to tangible property that is not subject to regulatory accounting rules.

(4) [Reserved]

(5) Examples. The rules of this paragraph (i) are illustrated by the following examples.

Example (1). Taxpayer subject to regulatory accounting rules of FERC. X is an electric utility company that operates a power plant to generate electricity. X is subject to the regulatory accounting rules of FERC and X chooses to use the regulatory accounting method under this paragraph (i). X does not capitalize on its books and records for regulatory accounting purposes the cost of repairs made to its turbines. Under the regulatory accounting method, X must not capitalize for Federal income tax purposes amounts paid for repairs made to its turbines.

Example (2). Taxpayer not subject to regulatory accounting rules of FERC. X is an electric utility company that operates a power plant to generate electricity. X previously was subject to the regulatory accounting rules of FERC but, for various reasons, X is no longer required to use FERC's regulatory accounting rules. X cannot use the regulatory accounting method provided in this paragraph (i).

Example (3). Taxpayer subject to regulatory accounting rules of FCC. X is a telecommunications company that is subject to the regulatory accounting rules of the FCC. X chooses to use the regulatory accounting method under this paragraph (i). The assets of X include a telephone central office switching center, which contains numerous switches and various switching equipment. X capitalizes on its books and records for regulatory accounting purposes the cost of replacing each switch. Under the regulatory accounting method, X is required to capitalize for Federal income tax purposes amounts paid to replace each switch.

Example (4). Taxpayer subject to regulatory accounting rules of STB. X is a Class I railroad that is subject to the regulatory accounting rules of the STB. X chooses to use the regulatory accounting method under this paragraph (i). X capitalizes on its books and records for regulatory accounting purposes the cost of locomotive rebuilds. Under the regulatory accounting method, X is required to capitalize for Federal income tax purposes amounts paid to rebuild its locomotives.

(j) Repair allowance. A taxpayer may use a repair allowance method of accounting that is identified in published guidance in the Federal Register or in the Internal Revenue Bulletin (see § 601.601(d)(2)(ii)(b) of this chapter).

(k) Treatment of capital expenditures. Amounts required to be capitalized under this section are capital expenditures and must be taken into account through a charge to capital account or basis, or in the case of property that is inventory in the hands of a taxpayer, through inclusion in inventory costs. See section 263A for the treatment of amounts referred to in this section as well as other amounts paid in connection with the production of real property and personal property, including films, sound recordings, video tapes, books, or similar properties.

(l) Recovery of capitalized amounts. Amounts that are capitalized under this section are recovered through depreciation, cost of goods sold, or by an adjustment to basis at the time the property is placed in service, sold, used, or otherwise disposed of by the taxpayer. Cost recovery is determined by the applicable Code and regulation provisions relating to the use, sale, or disposition of property.

(m) [Reserved]

(n) Effective/applicability date. The rules in this section apply to taxable years beginning on or after the date of publication of the Treasury decision adopting these rules as final regulations in the Federal Register.

§ 1.263(a)-4 Amounts paid to acquire or create intangibles.

(a) Overview. This section provides rules for applying section 263(a) to amounts paid to acquire or create intangibles. Except to the extent provided in paragraph (d)(8) of this section, the rules provided by this section do not apply to amounts paid to acquire or create tangible assets. Paragraph (b) of this section provides a general principle of capitalization. Paragraphs (c) and (d) of this section identify intangibles for which capitalization is specifically required under the general principle. Paragraph (e) of this section provides rules for determining the extent to which taxpayers must capitalize transaction costs. Paragraph (f) of this section provides a 12-month rule intended to simplify the application of the general principle to certain payments that create benefits of a brief duration. Additional rules and examples relating to these provisions are provided in paragraphs (g) through (n) of this section. The applicability date of the rules in this section is provided in paragraph (o) of this section. Paragraph (p) of this section provides rules applicable to changes in methods of accounting made to comply with this section.

(b) Capitalization with respect to intangibles. *(1) In general.* Except as otherwise provided in this section, a taxpayer must capitalize—

(i) An amount paid to acquire an intangible (see paragraph (c) of this section);

(ii) An amount paid to create an intangible described in paragraph (d) of this section;

(iii) An amount paid to create or enhance a separate and distinct intangible asset within the meaning of paragraph (b)(3) of this section;

(iv) An amount paid to create or enhance a future benefit identified in published guidance in the Federal Register or in the Internal Revenue Bulletin (see § 601.601(d)(2)(ii) of this chapter) as an intangible for which capitalization is required under this section; and

(v) An amount paid to facilitate (within the meaning of paragraph (e)(1) of this section) an acquisition or creation of an intangible described in paragraph (b)(1)(i), (ii), (iii) or (iv) of this section.

(2) Published guidance. Any published guidance identifying a future benefit as an intangible for which capitalization is required under paragraph (b)(1)(iv) of this section applies only to amounts paid on or after the date of publication of the guidance.

(3) Separate and distinct intangible asset. (i) Definition. The term separate and distinct intangible asset means a property interest of ascertainable and measurable value in money's worth that is subject to protection under applicable

State, Federal or foreign law and the possession and control of which is intrinsically capable of being sold, transferred or pledged (ignoring any restrictions imposed on assignability) separate and apart from a trade or business. In addition, for purposes of this section, a fund (or similar account) is treated as a separate and distinct intangible asset of the taxpayer if amounts in the fund (or account) may revert to the taxpayer. The determination of whether a payment creates a separate and distinct intangible asset is made based on all of the facts and circumstances existing during the taxable year in which the payment is made.

(ii) Creation or termination of contract rights. Amounts paid to another party to create, originate, enter into, renew or renegotiate an agreement with that party that produces rights or benefits for the taxpayer (and amounts paid to facilitate the creation, origination, enhancement, renewal or renegotiation of such an agreement) are treated as amounts that do not create (or facilitate the creation of) a separate and distinct intangible asset within the meaning of this paragraph (b)(3). Further, amounts paid to another party to terminate (or facilitate the termination of) an agreement with that party are treated as amounts that do not create a separate and distinct intangible asset within the meaning of this paragraph (b)(3). See paragraphs (d)(2), (d)(6), and (d)(7) of this section for rules that specifically require capitalization of amounts paid to create or terminate certain agreements.

(iii) Amounts paid in performing services. Amounts paid in performing services under an agreement are treated as amounts that do not create a separate and distinct intangible asset within the meaning of this paragraph (b)(3), regardless of whether the amounts result in the creation of an income stream under the agreement.

(iv) Creation of computer software. Except as otherwise provided in the Internal Revenue Code, the regulations thereunder, or other published guidance in the Federal Register or in the Internal Revenue Bulletin (see § 601.601(d)(2)(ii) of this chapter), amounts paid to develop computer software are treated as amounts that do not create a separate and distinct intangible asset within the meaning of this paragraph (b)(3).

(v) Creation of package design. Amounts paid to develop a package design are treated as amounts that do not create a separate and distinct intangible asset within the meaning of this paragraph (b)(3). For purposes of this section, the term package design means the specific graphic arrangement or design of shapes, colors, words, pictures, lettering, and other elements on a given product package, or the design of a container with respect to its shape or function.

(4) Coordination with other provisions of the Internal Revenue Code. (i) In general. Nothing in this section changes the treatment of an amount that is specifically provided for under any other provision of the Internal Revenue Code (other than section 162(a) or 212) or the regulations thereunder.

(ii) Example. The following example illustrates the rule of this paragraph (b)(4):

Example. On January 1, 2004, G enters into an interest rate swap agreement with unrelated counterparty H under which, for a term of five years, G is obligated to make annual payments at 11% and H is obligated to make annual payments at LIBOR on a notional principal amount of $100 million. At the time G and H enter into this swap agreement, the rate for similar on-market swaps is LIBOR to 10%. To compensate for this difference, on January 1, 2004, H pays G a yield adjustment fee of $3,790,786. This yield adjustment fee constitutes an amount paid to create an intangible and would be capitalized under paragraph (d)(2) of this section. However, because the yield adjustment fee is a nonperiodic payment on a notional principal contract as defined in § 1.446-3(c), the treatment of this fee is governed by § 1.446-3 and not this section.

(c) Acquired intangibles. *(1) In general.* A taxpayer must capitalize amounts paid to another party to acquire any intangible from that party in a purchase or similar transaction. Examples of intangibles within the scope of this paragraph (c) include, but are not limited to, the following (if acquired from another party in a purchase or similar transaction):

(i) An ownership interest in a corporation, partnership, trust, estate, limited liability company, or other entity.

(ii) A debt instrument, deposit, stripped bond, stripped coupon (including a servicing right treated for federal income tax purposes as a stripped coupon), regular interest in a REMIC or FASIT, or any other intangible treated as debt for federal income tax purposes.

(iii) A financial instrument, such as—

(A) A notional principal contract;

(B) A foreign currency contract;

(C) A futures contract;

(D) A forward contract (including an agreement under which the taxpayer has the right and obligation to provide or to acquire property (or to be compensated for such property, regardless of whether the taxpayer provides or acquires the property));

(E) An option (including an agreement under which the taxpayer has the right to provide or to acquire property (or to be compensated for such property, regardless of whether the taxpayer provides or acquires the property)); and

(F) Any other financial derivative.

(iv) An endowment contract, annuity contract, or insurance contract.

(v) Non-functional currency.

(vi) A lease.

(vii) A patent or copyright.

(viii) A franchise, trademark or tradename (as defined in § 1.197-2(b)(10)).

(ix) An assembled workforce (as defined in § 1.197-2(b)(3)).

(x) Goodwill (as defined in § 1.197-2(b)(1)) or going concern value (as defined in § 1.197-2(b)(2)).

(xi) A customer list.

(xii) A servicing right (for example, a mortgage servicing right that is not treated for Federal income tax purposes as a stripped coupon).

(xiii) A customer-based intangible (as defined in § 1.197-2(b)(6)) or supplier-based intangible (as defined in § 1.197-2(b)(7)).

(xiv) Computer software.

(xv) An agreement providing either party the right to use, possess or sell an intangible described in paragraphs (c)(1)(i) through (v) of this section.

(2) Readily available software. An amount paid to obtain a nonexclusive license for software that is (or has been) readily available to the general public on similar terms and has not been substantially modified (within the meaning of § 1.197-2(c)(4)) is treated for purposes of this paragraph (c) as an amount paid to another party to acquire an intangible from that party in a purchase or similar transaction.

(3) Intangibles acquired from an employee. Amounts paid to an employee to acquire an intangible from that employee are not required to be capitalized under this section if the amounts are includible in the employee's income in connection with the performance of services under section 61 or 83. For purposes of this section, whether an individual is an employee is determined in accordance with the rules contained in section 3401(c) and the regulations thereunder.

(4) Examples. The following examples illustrate the rules of this paragraph (c):

Example (1). Debt instrument. X corporation, a commercial bank, purchases a portfolio of existing loans from Y corporation, another financial institution. X pays Y $2,000,000 in exchange for the portfolio. The $2,000,000 paid to Y constitutes an amount paid to acquire an intangible from Y and must be capitalized.

Example (2). Option. W corporation owns all of the outstanding stock of X corporation. Y corporation holds a call option entitling it to purchase from W all of the outstanding stock of X at a certain price per share. Z corporation acquires the call option from Y in exchange for $5,000,000. The $5,000,000 paid to Y constitutes an amount paid to acquire an intangible from Y and must be capitalized.

Example (3). Ownership interest in a corporation. Same as Example 2, but assume Z exercises its option and purchases from W all of the outstanding stock of X in exchange for $100,000,000. The $100,000,000 paid to W constitutes an amount paid to acquire an intangible from W and must be capitalized.

Example (4). Customer list. N corporation, a retailer, sells its products through its catalog and mail order system. N purchases a customer list from R corporation. N pays R $100,000 in exchange for the customer list. The $100,000 paid to R constitutes an amount paid to acquire an intangible from R and must be capitalized.

Example (5). Goodwill. Z corporation pays W corporation $10,000,000 to purchase all of the assets of W in a transaction that constitutes an applicable asset acquisition under section 1060(c). Of the $10,000,000 consideration paid in the transaction, $9,000,000 is allocable to tangible assets purchased from W and $1,000,000 is allocable to goodwill. The $1,000,000 allocable to goodwill constitutes an amount paid to W to acquire an intangible from W and must be capitalized.

(d) Created intangibles. *(1) In general.* Except as provided in paragraph (f) of this section (relating to the 12-month rule), a taxpayer must capitalize amounts paid to create an intangible described in this paragraph (d). The determination of whether an amount is paid to create an intangible described in this paragraph (d) is to be made based on all of the facts and circumstances, disregarding distinctions between the labels used in this paragraph (d) to describe the intangible and the labels used by the taxpayer and other parties to the transaction.

(2) Financial interests. (i) In general. A taxpayer must capitalize amounts paid to another party to create, originate, enter into, renew or renegotiate with that party any of the following financial interests, whether or not the interest is regularly traded on an established market:

(A) An ownership interest in a corporation, partnership, trust, estate, limited liability company, or other entity.

(B) A debt instrument, deposit, stripped bond, stripped coupon (including a servicing right treated for federal income tax purposes as a stripped coupon), regular interest in a REMIC or FASIT, or any other intangible treated as debt for Federal income tax purposes.

(C) A financial instrument, such as—

(1) A letter of credit;

(2) A credit card agreement;

(3) A notional principal contract;

(4) A foreign currency contract;

(5) A futures contract;

(6) A forward contract (including an agreement under which the taxpayer has the right and obligation to provide or to acquire property (or to be compensated for such property, regardless of whether the taxpayer provides or acquires the property));

(7) An option (including an agreement under which the taxpayer has the right to provide or to acquire property (or to be compensated for such property, regardless of whether the taxpayer provides or acquires the property)); and

(8) Any other financial derivative.

(D) An endowment contract, annuity contract, or insurance contract that has or may have cash value.

(E) Non-functional currency.

(F) An agreement providing either party the right to use, possess or sell a financial interest described in this paragraph (d)(2).

(ii) Amounts paid to create, originate, enter into, renew or renegotiate. An amount paid to another party is not paid to create, originate, enter into, renew or renegotiate a financial interest with that party if the payment is made with the mere hope or expectation of developing or maintaining a business relationship with that party and is not contingent on the origination, renewal or renegotiation of a financial interest with that party.

(iii) Renegotiate. A taxpayer is treated as renegotiating a financial interest if the terms of the financial interest are modified. A taxpayer also is treated as renegotiating a financial interest if the taxpayer enters into a new financial interest with the same party (or substantially the same parties) to a terminated financial interest, the taxpayer could not cancel the terminated financial interest without the consent of the other party (or parties), and the other party (or parties) would not have consented to the cancellation unless the taxpayer entered into the new financial interest. A taxpayer is treated as unable to cancel a financial interest without the consent of the other party (or parties) if, under the terms of the financial interest, the taxpayer is subject to a termination penalty and the other party (or parties) to the financial interest modifies the terms of the penalty.

(iv) Coordination with other provisions of this paragraph (d). An amount described in this paragraph (d)(2) that is also described elsewhere in paragraph (d) of this section is treated as described only in this paragraph (d)(2).

(v) Coordination with § 1.263(a)-5. See § 1.263(a)-5 for the treatment of borrowing costs and the treatment of amounts paid by an option writer.

(vi) Examples. The following examples illustrate the rules of this paragraph (d)(2):

Example (1). Loan. X corporation, a commercial bank, makes a loan to A in the principal amount of $250,000. The $250,000 principal amount of the loan paid to A constitutes an amount paid to another party to create a debt instrument with that party under paragraph (d)(2)(i)(B) of this section and must be capitalized.

Example (2). Option. W corporation owns all of the outstanding stock of X corporation. Y corporation pays W $1,000,000 in exchange for W's grant of a 3-year call option to Y permitting Y to purchase all of the outstanding stock of X at a certain price per share. Y's payment of $1,000,000 to W constitutes an amount paid to another party to create an option with that party under paragraph (d)(2)(i)(C)(7) of this section and must be capitalized.

Example (3). Partnership interest. Z corporation pays $10,000 to P, a partnership, in exchange for an ownership interest in P. Z's payment of $10,000 to P constitutes an amount paid to another party to create an ownership interest in a partnership with that party under paragraph (d)(2)(i)(A) of this section and must be capitalized.

Example (4). Take or pay contract. Q corporation, a producer of natural gas, pays $1,000,000 to R during 2005 to induce R corporation to enter into a 5-year "take or pay" gas purchase contract. Under the contract, R is liable to pay for a specified minimum amount of gas, whether or not R takes such gas. Q's payment of $1,000,000 is an amount paid to another party to induce that party to enter into an agreement providing Q the right and obligation to provide property or be compensated for such property (regardless of whether the property is provided) under paragraph (d)(2)(i)(C)(6) of this section and must be capitalized.

Example (5). Agreement to provide property. P corporation pays R corporation $1,000,000 in exchange for R's agreement to purchase 1,000 units of P's product at any time within the three succeeding calendar years. The agreement describes P's $1,000,000 as a sales discount. P's $1,000,000 payment is an amount paid to induce R to enter into an agreement providing P the right and obligation to provide property under paragraph (d)(2)(i)(C)(6) of this section and must be capitalized.

Example (6). Customer incentive payment. S corporation, a computer manufacturer, seeks to develop a business relationship with V corporation, a computer retailer. As an incentive to encourage V to purchase computers from S, S enters into an agreement with V under which S agrees that, if V purchases $20,000,000 of computers from S within 3 years from the date of the agreement, S will pay V $2,000,000 on the date that V reaches the $20,000,000 threshold. V reaches the $20,000,000 threshold during the third year of the agreement, and S pays V $2,000,000. S is not required to capitalize its payment to V under this paragraph (d)(2) because the payment does not provide S the right or obligation to provide property and does not create a separate and distinct intangible asset for S within the meaning of paragraph (b)(3)(i) of this section.

(3) Prepaid expenses. (i) In general. A taxpayer must capitalize prepaid expenses.

(ii) Examples. The following examples illustrate the rules of this paragraph (d)(3):

Example (1). Prepaid insurance. N corporation, an accrual method taxpayer, pays $10,000 to an insurer to obtain three years of coverage under a property and casualty insurance policy. The $10,000 is a prepaid expense and must be capitalized under this paragraph (d)(3). Paragraph (d)(2) of this section does not apply to the payment because the policy has no cash value.

Example (2). Prepaid rent. X corporation, a cash method taxpayer, enters into a 24-month lease of office space. At the time of the lease signing, X prepays $240,000. No other amounts are due under the lease. The $240,000 is a prepaid expense and must be capitalized under this paragraph (d)(3).

(4) Certain memberships and privileges. (i) In general. A taxpayer must capitalize amounts paid to an organization to obtain, renew, renegotiate, or upgrade a membership or privilege from that organization. A taxpayer is not required to capitalize under this paragraph (d)(4) an amount paid to obtain, renew, renegotiate or upgrade certification of the taxpayer's products, services, or business processes.

(ii) Examples. The following examples illustrate the rules of this paragraph (d)(4):

Example (1). Hospital privilege. B, a physician, pays $10,000 to Y corporation to obtain lifetime staff privileges at a hospital operated by Y. B must capitalize the $10,000 payment under this paragraph (d)(4).

Example (2). Initiation fee. X corporation pays a $50,000 initiation fee to obtain membership in a trade association. X must capitalize the $50,000 payment under this paragraph (d)(4).

Example (3). Product rating. V corporation, an automobile manufacturer, pays W corporation, a national quality ratings association, $100,000 to conduct a study and provide a rating of the quality and safety of a line of V's automobiles. V's payment is an amount paid to obtain a certification of V's product and is not required to be capitalized under this paragraph (d)(4).

Example (4). Business process certification. Z corporation, a manufacturer, seeks to obtain a certification that its quality control standards meet a series of international standards known as ISO 9000. Z pays $50,000 to an independent registrar to obtain a certification from the registrar that Z's quality management system conforms to the ISO 9000 standard. Z's payment is an amount paid to obtain a certification of Z's business processes and is not required to be capitalized under this paragraph (d)(4).

(5) Certain rights obtained from a governmental agency. (i) In general. A taxpayer must capitalize amounts paid to a governmental agency to obtain, renew, renegotiate, or upgrade its rights under a trademark, trade name, copyright, license, permit, franchise, or other similar right granted by that governmental agency.

(ii) Examples. The following examples illustrate the rules of this paragraph (d)(5):

Example (1). Business license. X corporation pays $15,000 to state Y to obtain a business license that is valid indefinitely. Under this paragraph (d)(5), the amount paid to state Y is an amount paid to a government agency for a right granted by that agency. Accordingly, X must capitalize the $15,000 payment.

Example (2). Bar admission. A, an individual, pays $1,000 to an agency of state Z to obtain a license to practice law in state Z that is valid indefinitely, provided A adheres to the requirements governing the practice of law in state Z. Under this paragraph (d)(5), the amount paid to state Z is an amount paid to a government agency for a right granted by that agency. Accordingly, A must capitalize the $1,000 payment.

(6) Certain contract rights. (i) In general. Except as otherwise provided in this paragraph (d)(6), a taxpayer must capitalize amounts paid to another party to create, originate, enter into, renew or renegotiate with that party—

(A) An agreement providing the taxpayer the right to use tangible or intangible property or the right to be compensated for the use of tangible or intangible property;

(B) An agreement providing the taxpayer the right to provide or to receive services (or the right to be compensated for services regardless of whether the taxpayer provides such services);

(C) A covenant not to compete or an agreement having substantially the same effect as a covenant not to compete (except, in the case of an agreement that requires the performance of services, to the extent that the amount represents reasonable compensation for services actually rendered);

(D) An agreement not to acquire additional ownership interests in the taxpayer; or

(E) An agreement providing the taxpayer (as the covered party) with an annuity, an endowment, or insurance coverage.

(ii) Amounts paid to create, originate, enter into, renew or renegotiate. An amount paid to another party is not paid to create, originate, enter into, renew or renegotiate an agreement with that party if the payment is made with the mere hope or expectation of developing or maintaining a business relationship with that party and is not contingent on the origination, renewal or renegotiation of an agreement with that party.

(iii) Renegotiate. A taxpayer is treated as renegotiating an agreement if the terms of the agreement are modified. A taxpayer also is treated as renegotiating an agreement if the taxpayer enters into a new agreement with the same party (or substantially the same parties) to a terminated agreement, the taxpayer could not cancel the terminated agreement without the consent of the other party (or parties), and the other party (or parties) would not have consented to the cancellation unless the taxpayer entered into the new agreement. A taxpayer is treated as unable to cancel an agreement without the consent of the other party (or parties) if, under the terms of the agreement, the taxpayer is subject to a termination penalty and the other party (or parties) to the agreement modifies the terms of the penalty.

(iv) Right. An agreement does not provide the taxpayer a right to use property or to provide or receive services if the agreement may be terminated at will by the other party (or parties) to the agreement before the end of the period prescribed by paragraph (f)(1) of this section. An agreement is not terminable at will if the other party (or parties) to the agreement is economically compelled not to terminate the agreement until the end of the period prescribed by paragraph (f)(1) of this section. All of the facts and circumstances will be considered in determining whether the other party (or parties) to an agreement is economically compelled not to terminate the agreement. An agreement also does not provide the taxpayer the right to provide services if the agreement merely provides that the taxpayer will stand ready to provide services if requested, but places no obligation on another person to request or pay for the taxpayer's services.

(v) De minimis amounts. A taxpayer is not required to capitalize amounts paid to another party (or parties) to create, originate, enter into, renew or renegotiate with that party (or those parties) an agreement described in paragraph (d)(6)(i) of this section if the aggregate of all amounts paid to that party (or those parties) with respect to the agreement does not exceed $5,000. If the aggregate of all amounts paid to the other party (or parties) with respect to that agreement exceeds $5,000, then all amounts must be capitalized. For purposes of this paragraph (d)(6), an amount paid in the form of property is valued at its fair market value at the time of the payment. In general, a taxpayer must determine whether the rules of this paragraph (d)(6)(v) apply by accounting for the specific amounts paid with respect to each agreement. However, a taxpayer that reasonably expects to create, originate, enter into, renew or renegotiate at least 25 similar agreements during the taxable year may establish a pool of agreements for purposes of determining the amounts paid with respect to the agreements in the pool. Under this pooling method, the amount paid with respect to each agreement included in the pool is equal to the average amount paid with respect to all agreements included in the pool. A taxpayer computes the average amount paid with respect to all agreements included in the pool by dividing the sum of all amounts paid with respect to all agreements included in the pool by the number of agreements included in the pool. See paragraph (h) of this section for additional rules relating to pooling.

(vi) Exception for lessee construction allowances. Paragraph (d)(6)(i) of this section does not apply to amounts paid by a lessor to a lessee as a construction allowance to the extent the lessee expends the amount for the tangible property that is owned by the lessor for Federal income tax purposes (see, for example, section 110).

(vii) Examples. The following examples illustrate the rules of this paragraph (d)(6):

Example (1). New lease agreement. V seeks to lease commercial property in a prominent downtown location of city R. V pays Z, the owner of the commercial property, $50,000 in exchange for Z entering into a 10-year lease with V. V's payment is an amount paid to another party to enter into an agreement providing V the right to use tangible property. Because the $50,000 payment exceeds $5,000, no portion of the amount paid to Z is de minimis for purposes of paragraph (d)(6)(v) of this section. Under paragraph (d)(6)(i)(A) of this section, V must capitalize the entire $50,000 payment.

Example (2). Modification of lease agreement. Partnership Y leases a piece of equipment for use in its business from Z corporation. When the lease has a remaining term of 3 years, Y requests that Z modify the existing lease by extending the remaining term by 5 years. Y pays $50,000 to Z in exchange for Z's agreement to modify the existing lease. Y's payment of $50,000 is an amount paid to another party to renegotiate an agreement providing Y the right to use property. Because the $50,000 payment exceeds $5,000, no portion of the amount paid to Z is de minimis for purposes of paragraph (d)(6)(v) of this section. Under paragraph (d)(6)(i)(A) of this section, Y must capitalize the entire $50,000 payment.

Example (3). Modification of lease agreement. In 2004, R enters into a 5-year, non-cancelable lease of a mainframe computer for use in its business. R subsequently determines that the mainframe computer that R is leasing is no longer adequate for its needs. In 2006, R and P corporation (the lessor) agree to terminate the 2004 lease and to enter into a new 5-year lease for a different and more powerful mainframe computer. R pays P a $75,000 early termination fee. P would not have agreed to terminate the 2004 lease unless R agreed to enter into the 2006 lease. R's payment of $75,000 is an amount paid to another party to renegotiate an agreement providing R the right to use property. Because the $75,000 payment exceeds $5,000, no portion of the amount paid to P is de minimis for purposes of paragraph (d)(6)(v) of this section. Under paragraph (d)(6)(i)(A) of this section, R must capitalize the entire $75,000 payment.

Example (4). Modification of lease agreement. Same as Example 3, except the 2004 lease agreement allows R to terminate the lease at any time subject to a $75,000 early termination fee. Because R can terminate the lease without P's approval, R's payment of $75,000 is not an amount paid to another party to renegotiate an agreement. Accordingly, R is not required to capitalize the $75,000 payment under this paragraph (d)(6).

Example (5). Modification of lease agreement. Same as Example 4, except P agreed to reduce the early termination fee to $60,000. Because R did not pay an amount to renegotiate the early termination fee, R's payment of $60,000 is not an amount paid to another party to renegotiate an agreement. Accordingly, R is not required to capitalize the $60,000 payment under this paragraph (d)(6).

Example (6). Covenant not to compete. R corporation enters into an agreement with A, an individual, that prohibits A from competing with R for a period of three years. To encourage A to enter into the agreement, R agrees to pay A $100,000 upon the signing of the agreement. R's payment is an amount paid to another party to enter into a covenant not to compete. Because the $100,000 payment exceeds $5,000, no portion of the amount paid to A is de minimis for purposes of paragraph (d)(6)(v) of this section. Under paragraph (d)(6)(i)(C) of this section, R must capitalize the entire $100,000 payment.

Example (7). Standstill agreement. During 2004 through 2005, X corporation acquires a large minority interest in the stock of Z corporation. To ensure that X does not take control of Z, Z pays X $5,000,000 for a standstill agreement under which X agrees not to acquire any more stock in Z for a period of 10 years. Z's payment is an amount paid to another party to enter into an agreement not to acquire additional ownership interests in Z. Because the $5,000,000 payment exceeds $5,000, no portion of the amount paid to X is de minimis for purposes of paragraph (d)(6)(v) of this section. Under paragraph (d)(6)(i)(D) of this section, Z must capitalize the entire $5,000,000 payment.

Example (8). Signing bonus. Employer B pays a $25,000 signing bonus to employee C to induce C to come to work for B. C can leave B's employment at any time to work for a competitor of B and is not required to repay the $25,000 bonus to B. Because C is not economically compelled to continue his employment with B, B's payment does not provide B the right to receive services from C. Accordingly, B is not required to capitalize the $25,000 payment.

Example (9). Renewal. In 2000, M corporation and N corporation enter into a 5-year agreement that gives M the right to manage N's investment portfolio. In 2005, N has the option of renewing the agreement for another three years. During 2004, M pays $10,000 to send several employees of N to an investment seminar. M pays the $10,000 to help develop and maintain its business relationship with N with the expectation that N will renew its agreement with M in 2005. Because M's payment is not contingent on N agreeing to renew the agreement, M's payment is not an amount paid to renew an agreement under paragraph (d)(6)(ii) of this section and is not required to be capitalized.

Example (10). De minimis payments. X corporation is engaged in the business of providing wireless telecommunications services to customers. To induce customer B to enter into a 3-year non-cancelable telecommunications contract, X provides B with a free wireless telephone. The fair market value of the wireless telephone is $300 at the time it is provided to B. X's provision of a wireless telephone to B is an amount paid to B to induce B to enter into an agreement providing X the right to provide services, as described in paragraph (d)(6)(i)(B) of this section. Because the amount of the inducement is $300, the amount of the inducement is de minimis under paragraph (d)(6)(v) of this section. Accordingly, X is not required to capitalize the amount of the inducement provided to B.

(7) Certain contract terminations. (i) In general. A taxpayer must capitalize amounts paid to another party to terminate—

(A) A lease of real or tangible personal property between the taxpayer (as lessor) and that party (as lessee);

(B) An agreement that grants that party the exclusive right to acquire or use the taxpayer's property or services or to conduct the taxpayer's business (other than an intangible described in paragraph (c)(1)(i) through (iv) of this section or a financial interest described in paragraph (d)(2) of this section); or

(C) An agreement that prohibits the taxpayer from competing with that party or from acquiring property or services from a competitor of that party.

(ii) Certain break-up fees. Paragraph (d)(7)(i) of this section does not apply to the termination of a transaction described in § 1.263(a)-5(a) (relating to an acquisition of a trade or business, a change in the capital structure of a business entity, and certain other transactions). See § 1.263(a)-5(c)(8) for rules governing the treatment of amounts paid to terminate a transaction to which that section applies.

(iii) Examples. The following examples illustrate the rules of this paragraph (d)(7):

Example (1). Termination of exclusive license agreement. On July 1, 2005, N enters into a license agreement with R corporation under which N grants R the exclusive right to manufacture and distribute goods using N's design and trademarks for a period of 10 years. On June 30, 2007, N pays R $5,000,000 in exchange for R's agreement to terminate the exclusive license agreement. N's payment to terminate its license agreement with R constitutes a payment to terminate an exclusive license to use the taxpayer's property, as described in paragraph (d)(7)(i)(B) of this section. Accordingly, N must capitalize its $5,000,000 payment to R.

Example (2). Termination of exclusive distribution agreement. On March 1, 2005, L, a manufacturer, enters into an agreement with M granting M the right to be the sole distributor of L's products in state X for 10 years. On July 1, 2008, L pays M $50,000 in exchange for M's agreement to terminate the distribution agreement. L's payment to terminate its agreement with M constitutes a payment to terminate an exclusive right to acquire L's property, as described in paragraph (d)(7)(i)(B) of this section. Accordingly, L must capitalize its $50,000 payment to M.

Example (3). Termination of covenant not to compete. On February 1, 2005, Y corporation enters into a covenant not to compete with Z corporation that prohibits Y from competing with Z in city V for a period of 5 years. On January 31, 2007, Y pays Z $1,000,000 in exchange for Z's agreement to terminate the covenant not to compete. Y's payment to terminate the covenant not to compete with Z constitutes a payment to terminate an agreement that prohibits Y from competing with Z, as described in paragraph (d)(7)(i)(C) of this section. Accordingly, Y must capitalize its $1,000,000 payment to Z.

Example (4). Termination of merger agreement. N corporation and U corporation enter into an agreement under which N agrees to merge into U. Subsequently, N pays U $10,000,000 to terminate the merger agreement. As provided in paragraph (d)(7)(ii) of this section, N's $10,000,000 payment to terminate the merger agreement with U is not required to be capitalized under this paragraph (d)(7). In addition, N's $10,000,000 does not create a separate and distinct intangible asset for N within the meaning of paragraph (b)(3)(i) of this section. (See § 1.263(a)-5 for additional rules regarding termination of merger agreements).

(8) Certain benefits arising from the provision, production, or improvement of real property. (i) In general. A taxpayer must capitalize amounts paid for real property if the taxpayer transfers ownership of the real property to another person (except to the extent the real property is sold for fair market value) and if the real property can reasonably be expected to produce significant economic benefits to the taxpayer after the transfer. A taxpayer also must capitalize amounts paid to produce or improve real property owned by another (except to the extent the taxpayer is selling services at fair market value to produce or improve the real property) if the real property can reasonably be expected to produce significant economic benefits for the taxpayer.

(ii) Exclusions. A taxpayer is not required to capitalize an amount under paragraph (d)(8)(i) of this section if the taxpayer transfers real property or pays an amount to produce or improve real property owned by another in exchange for services, the purchase or use of property, or the creation of an intangible described in paragraph (d) of this section (other than in this paragraph (d)(8)). The preceding sentence does not apply to the extent the taxpayer does not receive fair market value consideration for the real property that is relinquished or for the amounts that are paid by the taxpayer to produce or improve real property owned by another.

(iii) Real property. For purposes of this paragraph (d)(8), real property includes property that is affixed to real property and that will ordinarily remain affixed for an indefinite period of time, such as roads, bridges, tunnels, pavements, wharves and docks, breakwaters and sea walls, elevators, power generation and transmission facilities, and pollution control facilities.

(iv) Impact fees and dedicated improvements. Paragraph (d)(8)(i) of this section does not apply to amounts paid to satisfy one-time charges imposed by a State or local government against new development (or expansion of existing development) to finance specific offsite capital improvements for general public use that are necessitated by the new or expanded development. In addition, paragraph (d)(8)(i) of this section does not apply to amounts paid for real property or improvements to real property constructed by the taxpayer where the real property or improvements benefit new development or expansion of existing development, are immediately transferred to a State or local government for dedication to the general public use, and are maintained by the State or local government. See section 263A and the regulations thereunder for capitalization rules that apply to amounts referred to in this paragraph (d)(8)(iv).

(v) Examples. The following examples illustrate the rules of this paragraph (d)(8):

Example (1). Amount paid to produce real property owned by another. W corporation operates a quarry on the east side of a river in city Z and a crusher on the west side of the river. City Z's existing bridges are of insufficient capacity to be traveled by trucks in transferring stone from W's quarry to its crusher. As a result, the efficiency of W's operations is greatly reduced. W contributes $1,000,000 to city Z to defray in part the cost of constructing a publicly owned bridge capable of accommodating W's trucks. W's payment to city Z is an amount paid to produce or improve real property (within the meaning of paragraph (d)(8)(iii) of this section) that can reasonably be expected to produce significant economic benefits for W. Under paragraph (d)(8)(i) of this section, W must capitalize the $1,000,000 paid to city Z.

Example (2). Transfer of real property to another. K corporation, a shipping company, uses smaller vessels to unload its ocean-going vessels at port X. There is no natural harbor at port X, and during stormy weather the transfer of freight between K's ocean vessels and port X is extremely difficult and sometimes impossible, which can be very costly to K. Consequently, K constructs a short breakwater at a cost of $50,000. The short breakwater, however, is inadequate, so K persuades the port authority to build a larger breakwater that will allow K to unload its vessels at any time of the year and during all kinds of weather. K contributes the short breakwater and pays $200,000 to the port authority for use in building the larger breakwater. Because the transfer of the small breakwater and $200,000 is reasonably expected to produce significant economic benefits for K, K must capitalize both the adjusted basis of the small breakwater (determined at the time the small breakwater is contributed) and the $200,000 payment under this paragraph (d)(8).

Example (3). Dedicated improvements. X corporation is engaged in the development and sale of residential real estate. In connection with a residential real estate project under construction by X in city Z, X is required by city Z to construct ingress and egress roads to and from its project and immediately transfer the roads to city Z for dedication to general public use. The roads will be maintained by city Z. X pays its subcontractor $100,000 to construct the ingress and egress roads. X's payment is a dedicated improvement within the meaning of paragraph (d)(8)(iv) of this section. Accordingly, X is not required to capitalize the $100,000 payment under this paragraph (d)(8). See section 263A and the regulations thereunder for capitalization rules that apply to amounts referred to in paragraph (d)(8)(iv) of this section.

(9) Defense or perfection of title to intangible property. (i) In general. A taxpayer must capitalize amounts paid to another party to defend or perfect title to intangible property if that other party challenges the taxpayer's title to the intangible property.

(ii) Certain break-up fees. Paragraph (d)(9)(i) of this section does not apply to the termination of a transaction described in § 1.263(a)-5(a) (relating to an acquisition of a trade or business, a change in the capital structure of a business entity, and certain other transactions). See § 1.263(a)-5 for rules governing the treatment of amounts paid to terminate a transaction to which that section applies. Paragraph (d)(9)(i) of this section also does not apply to an amount paid to another party to terminate an agreement that grants that party the right to purchase the taxpayer's intangible property.

(iii) Example. The following example illustrates the rules of this paragraph (d)(9):

Example. Defense of title. R corporation claims to own an exclusive patent on a particular technology. U corporation brings a lawsuit against R, claiming that U is the true owner of the patent and that R stole the technology from U. The sole issue in the suit involves the validity of R's patent. R chooses to settle the suit by paying U $100,000 in exchange for U's release of all future claim to the patent. R's payment to U is an amount paid to defend or perfect title to intangible property under paragraph (d)(9) of this section and must be capitalized.

(e) Transaction costs. *(1) Scope of facilitate.* (i) In general. Except as otherwise provided in this section, an amount is paid to facilitate the acquisition or creation of an intangible (the transaction) if the amount is paid in the process of investigating or otherwise pursuing the transaction. Whether an amount is paid in the process of investigating or otherwise pursuing the transaction is determined based on all of the facts and circumstances. In determining whether an amount is paid to facilitate a transaction, the fact that the amount would (or would not) have been paid but for the transaction is relevant, but is not determinative. An amount paid to determine the value or price of an intangible is an amount paid in the process of investigating or otherwise pursuing the transaction.

(ii) Treatment of termination payments. An amount paid to terminate (or acilitate the termination of) an existing agreement does not facilitate the acquisition or creation of another agreement under this section. See paragraph (d)(6)(iii) of this section for the treatment of termination fees paid to the other party (or parties) of a renegotiated agreement.

(iii) Special rule for contracts. An amount is treated as not paid in the process of investigating or otherwise pursuing the creation of an agreement described in paragraph (d)(2) or (d)(6) of this section if the amount relates to activities performed before the earlier of the date the taxpayer begins preparing its bid for the agreement or the date the taxpayer begins discussing or negotiating the agreement with another party to the agreement.

(iv) Borrowing costs. An amount paid to facilitate a borrowing does not facilitate an acquisition or creation of an intangible described in paragraphs (b)(1)(i) through (iv) of this section. See §§ 1.263(a)-5 and 1.446-5 for the treatment of an amount paid to facilitate a borrowing.

(v) Special rule for stock redemption costs of open-end regulated investment companies. An amount paid by an open-end regulated investment company (within the meaning of section 851) to facilitate a redemption of its stock is treated as an amount that does not facilitate the acquisition of an intangible under this section.

(2) Coordination with paragraph (d) of this section. In the case of an amount paid to facilitate the creation of an intangible described in paragraph (d) of this section, the provisions of this paragraph (e) apply regardless of whether a payment described in paragraph (d) is made.

(3) Transaction. For purposes of this section, the term transaction means all of the factual elements comprising an acquisition or creation of an intangible and includes a series of steps carried out as part of a single plan. Thus, a transaction can involve more than one invoice and more than one intangible. For example, a purchase of intangibles under one purchase agreement constitutes a single transaction, notwithstanding the fact that the acquisition involves multiple intangibles and the amounts paid to facilitate the acquisition are capable of being allocated among the various intangibles acquired.

(4) Simplifying conventions. (i) In general. For purposes of this section, employee compensation (within the meaning of paragraph (e)(4)(ii) of this section), overhead, and de minimis costs (within the meaning of paragraph (e)(4)(iii) of this section) are treated as amounts that do not facilitate the acquisition or creation of an intangible.

(ii) Employee compensation. (A) In general. The term employee compensation means compensation (including salary, bonuses and commissions) paid to an employee of the taxpayer. For purposes of this section, whether an individual is an employee is determined in accordance with the rules contained in section 3401(c) and the regulations thereunder.

(B) Certain amounts treated as employee compensation. For purposes of this section, a guaranteed payment to a partner in a partnership is treated as employee compensation. For purposes of this section, annual compensation paid to a director of a corporation is treated as employee compensation. For example, an amount paid to a director of a corporation for attendance at a regular meeting of the board of directors (or committee thereof) is treated as employee compensation for purposes of this section. However, an amount paid to a director for attendance at a special meeting of the board of directors (or committee thereof) is not treated as employee compensation. An amount paid to a person that is not an employee of the taxpayer (including the employer of the individual who performs the services) is treated as employee compensation for purposes of this section only if the amount is paid for secretarial, clerical, or similar administrative support services. In the case of an affiliated group of corporations filing a consolidated Federal income tax return, a payment by one member of the group to a second member of the group for services performed by an employee of the second member is treated as employee compensation if the services provided by the employee are provided at a time during which both members are affiliated.

(iii) De minimis costs. (A) In general. Except as provided in paragraph (e)(4)(iii)(B) of this section, the term de minimis costs means amounts (other than employee compensation and overhead) paid in the process of investigating or otherwise pursuing a transaction if, in the aggregate, the amounts do not exceed $5,000 (or such greater amount as may be set forth in published guidance). If the amounts exceed $5,000 (or such greater amount as may be set forth in published guidance), none of the amounts are de minimis costs within the meaning of this paragraph (e)(4)(iii)(A). For purposes of this paragraph (e)(4)(iii), an amount paid in the form of property is valued at its fair market value at the time of the payment. In determining the amount of transaction costs paid in the process of investigating or otherwise pursuing a transaction, a taxpayer generally must account for the specific costs paid with respect to each transaction. However, a taxpayer that reasonably expects to enter into at least 25 similar transactions during the taxable year may establish a pool of similar transactions for purposes of determining the amount of transaction costs paid in the process of investigating or otherwise pursuing the transactions in the pool. Under this pooling method, the amount of transaction costs paid in the process of investigating or otherwise pursuing each transaction included in the pool is equal to the average transaction costs paid in the process of investigating or otherwise pursuing all transactions included in the pool. A taxpayer computes the average transaction costs paid in the process of investigating or otherwise pursuing all transactions included in the pool by dividing the sum of all transaction costs paid in the process of investigating or otherwise pursuing all transactions included in the pool by the number of transactions included in the pool. See paragraph (h) of this section for additional rules relating to pooling.

(B) Treatment of commissions. The term de minimis costs does not include commissions paid to facilitate the acquisition of an intangible described in paragraphs (c)(1)(i) through (v) of this section or to facilitate the creation, origination, entrance into, renewal or renegotiation of an intangible described in paragraph (d)(2)(i) of this section.

(iv) Election to capitalize. A taxpayer may elect to treat employee compensation, overhead, or de minimis costs paid in the process of investigating or otherwise pursuing a transaction as amounts that facilitate the transaction. The election is made separately for each transaction and applies to employee compensation, overhead, or de minimis costs, or to any combination thereof. For example, a taxpayer may elect to treat overhead and de minimis costs, but not employee compensation, as amounts that facilitate the transaction. A taxpayer makes the election by treating the amounts to which the election applies as amounts that facilitate the transaction in the taxpayer's timely filed original Federal income tax return (including extensions) for the taxable year during which the amounts are paid. In the case of an affiliated group of corporations filing a consolidated return, the election is made separately with respect to each member of the group, and not with respect to the group as a whole. In the case of an S corporation or partnership, the election is made by the S corporation or by the partnership, and not by the shareholders or partners. An election made under this paragraph (e)(4)(iv) is revocable with respect to each taxable year for which made only with the consent of the Commissioner.

(5) Examples. The following examples illustrate the rules of this paragraph (e):

Example (1). Costs to facilitate. In December 2005, R corporation, a calendar year taxpayer, enters into negotiations with X corporation to lease commercial property from X for a period of 25 years. R pays A, its outside legal counsel, $4,000 in December 2005 for services rendered by A during December in assisting with negotiations with X. In January 2006, R and X finalize the terms of the lease and execute the lease agreement. R pays B, another of its outside legal counsel, $2,000 in January 2006 for services rendered by B during January in drafting the lease agreement. The agreement between R and X is an agreement providing R the right to use property, as described in paragraph (d)(6)(i)(A) of this section. R's payments to its outside counsel are amounts paid to facilitate the creation of the agreement. As provided in paragraph (e)(4)(iii)(A) of this section, R must aggregate its transaction costs for purposes of determining whether the transaction costs are de minimis. Because R's aggregate transaction costs exceed $5,000, R's transaction costs are not de minimis costs within the meaning of paragraph (e)(4)(iii)(A) of this section. Accordingly, R must capitalize the $4,000 paid to A and the $2,000 paid to B under paragraph (b)(1)(v) of this section.

Example (2). Costs to facilitate. Partnership X leases its manufacturing equipment from Y corporation under a 10-year lease. During 2005, when the lease has a remaining term of 4 years, X enters into a written agreement with Z corporation, a competitor of Y, under which X agrees to lease its manufacturing equipment from Z, subject to the condition that X first successfully terminates its lease with Y. X pays Y $50,000 in exchange for Y's agreement to terminate the equipment lease. Under paragraph (e)(1)(ii), X's $50,000 payment does not facilitate the creation of the new lease with Z. In addition, X's $50,000 payment does not terminate an agreement described in paragraph (d)(7) of this section. Accordingly, X is not required to capitalize the $50,000 termination payment under this section.

Example (3). Costs to facilitate. W corporation enters into a lease agreement with X corporation under which W agrees to lease property to X for a period of 5 years. W pays its outside counsel $7,000 for legal services rendered in drafting the lease agreement and negotiating with X. The agreement between W and X is an agreement providing W the right to be compensated for the use of property, as described in paragraph (d)(6)(i)(A) of this section. Under paragraph (e)(1)(i) of this section, W's payment to its outside counsel is an amount paid to facilitate the creation of that agreement. As provided by paragraph (e)(2) of this section, W must capitalize its $7,000 payment to outside counsel notwithstanding the fact that W made no payment described in paragraph (d)(6)(i) of this section.

Example (4). Costs to facilitate. U corporation, which owns a majority of the common stock of T corporation, votes its controlling interest in favor of a perpetual extension of T's charter. M, a minority shareholder in T, votes against the extension. Under applicable state law, U is required to purchase the stock of T held by M. When U and M are unable to agree on the value of M's shares, U brings an action in state court to appraise the value of M's stock interest. U pays attorney, accountant and appraisal fees of $25,000 for services rendered in connection with the negotiation and litigation with M. Because U's attorney, accountant and appraisal costs help establish the purchase price of M's stock, U's $25,000 payment facilitates the acquisition of stock. Accordingly, U must capitalize the $25,000 payment under paragraph (b)(1)(v) of this section.

Example (5). Costs to facilitate. For several years, H corporation has provided services to J corporation whenever requested by J. H wants to enter into a multiple-year contract with J that would give H the right to provide services to J. On June 10, 2004, H starts to prepare a bid to provide services to J and pays a consultant $15,000 to research potential competitors. On August 10, 2004, H raises the possibility of a multi-year contract with J. On October 10, 2004, H and J enter into a contract giving H the right to provide services to J for five years. During 2004, H pays $7,000 to travel to the city in which J's offices are located to continue providing services to J under their prior arrangement and pays $6,000 for travel to the city in which J's offices are located to further develop H's business relationship with J (for example, to introduce new employees, update J on current developments and take J's executives to dinner). H also pays $8,000 for travel costs to meet with J to discuss and negotiate the contract. Because the contract gives H the right to provide services to J, H must capitalize amounts paid to facilitate the creation of the contract. The $7,000 of travel expenses paid to provide services to J under their prior arrangement does not facilitate the creation of the contract and is not required to be capitalized, regardless of when the travel occurs. The $6,000 of travel expenses paid to further develop H's business relationship with J is paid in the process of pursuing the contract (and therefore must be capitalized) only to the extent the expenses relate to travel on or after June 10, 2004 (the date H begins to prepare a bid) and before October 11, 2004 (the date after H and J enter into the contract). The $8,000 of travel expenses paid to meet with J to discuss and negotiate the contract is paid in the process of pursuing the contact and must be capitalized. The $15,000 of consultant fees is paid to investigate the contract and also must be capitalized.

Example (6). Costs that do not facilitate. X corporation brings a legal action against Y corporation to recover lost profits resulting from Y's alleged infringement of X's copyright. Y does not challenge X's copyright, but argues that it did not infringe upon X's copyright. X pays its outside counsel $25,000 for legal services rendered in pursuing the suit against Y. Because X's title to its copyright is not in question, X's action against Y does not involve X's defense or perfection of title to intangible property. Thus, the amount paid to outside counsel does not facilitate the creation of an intangible described in paragraph (d)(9) of this section. Accordingly, X is not required to capitalize its $25,000 payment under this section.

Example (7). De minimis rule. W corporation, a commercial bank, acquires a portfolio containing 100 loans from Y corporation. As part of the acquisition, W pays an independent appraiser a fee of $10,000 to appraise the portfolio. The fee is an amount paid to facilitate W's acquisition of an intangible. The acquisition of the loan portfolio is a single transaction within the meaning of paragraph (e)(3) of this section. Because the amount paid to facilitate the transaction exceeds $5,000, the amount is not de minimis as defined in paragraph (e)(4)(iii)(A) of this section. Accordingly, W must capitalize the $10,000 fee under paragraph (b)(1)(v) of this section.

Example (8). Compensation and overhead. P corporation, a commercial bank, maintains a loan acquisition department whose sole function is to acquire loans from other financial institutions. As provided in paragraph (e)(4)(i) of this section, P is not required to capitalize any portion of the compensation paid to the employees in its loan acquisition department or any portion of its overhead allocable to the loan acquisition department.

(f) 12-month rule. *(1) In general.* Except as otherwise provided in this paragraph (f), a taxpayer is not required to capitalize under this section amounts paid to create (or to facilitate the creation of) any right or benefit for the taxpayer that does not extend beyond the earlier of—

(i) 12 months after the first date on which the taxpayer realizes the right or benefit; or

(ii) The end of the taxable year following the taxable year in which the payment is made.

(2) Duration of benefit for contract terminations. For purposes of this paragraph (f), amounts paid to terminate a contract or other agreement described in paragraph (d)(7)(i) of this section prior to its expiration date (or amounts paid to facilitate such termination) create a benefit for the taxpayer that lasts for the unexpired term of the agreement immediately before the date of the termination. If the terms of a contract or other agreement described in paragraph (d)(7)(i) of this section permit the taxpayer to terminate the contract or agreement after a notice period, amounts paid by the taxpayer to terminate the contract or agreement before the end of the notice period create a benefit for the taxpayer that lasts for the amount of time by which the notice period is shortened.

(3) Inapplicability to created financial interests and self-created amortizable section 197 intangibles. Paragraph (f)(1) of this section does not apply to amounts paid to create (or facilitate the creation of) an intangible described in paragraph (d)(2) of this section (relating to amounts paid to create financial interests) or to amounts paid to create (or facilitate the creation of) an intangible that constitutes an amortizable section 197 intangible within the meaning of section 197(c).

(4) Inapplicability to rights of indefinite duration. Paragraph (f)(1) of this section does not apply to amounts paid to create (or facilitate the creation of) an intangible of indefinite duration. A right has an indefinite duration if it has no period of duration fixed by agreement or by law, or if it is not based on a period of time, such as a right attributable to an agreement to provide or receive a fixed amount of goods or services. For example, a license granted by a governmental agency that permits the taxpayer to operate a business conveys a right of indefinite duration if the license may be revoked only upon the taxpayer's violation of the terms of the license.

(5) Rights subject to renewal. (i) In general. For purposes of paragraph (f)(1) of this section, the duration of a right includes any renewal period if all of the facts and circumstances in existence during the taxable year in which the right is created indicate a reasonable expectancy of renewal.

(ii) Reasonable expectancy of renewal. The following factors are significant in determining whether there exists a reasonable expectancy of renewal:

(A) Renewal history. The fact that similar rights are historically renewed is evidence of a reasonable expectancy of renewal. On the other hand, the fact that similar rights are rarely renewed is evidence of a lack of a reasonable expectancy of renewal. Where the taxpayer has no experience with similar rights, or where the taxpayer holds similar rights only occasionally, this factor is less indicative of a reasonable expectancy of renewal.

(B) Economics of the transaction. The fact that renewal is necessary for the taxpayer to earn back its investment in the right is evidence of a reasonable expectancy of renewal. For example, if a taxpayer pays $14,000 to enter into a renewable contract with an initial 9-month term that is expected to generate income to the taxpayer of $1,000 per month, the fact that renewal is necessary for the taxpayer to earn back its $14,000 payment is evidence of a reasonable expectancy of renewal.

(C) Likelihood of renewal by other party. Evidence that indicates a likelihood of renewal by the other party to a right, such as a bargain renewal option or similar arrangement, is evidence of a reasonable expectancy of renewal. However, the mere fact that the other party will have the opportunity to renew on the same terms as are available to others is not evidence of a reasonable expectancy of renewal.

(D) Terms of renewal. The fact that material terms of the right are subject to renegotiation at the end of the initial term is evidence of a lack of a reasonable expectancy of renewal. For example, if the parties to an agreement must renegotiate price or amount, the renegotiation requirement is evidence of a lack of a reasonable expectancy of renewal.

(E) Terminations. The fact that similar rights are typically terminated prior to renewal is evidence of a lack of a reasonably expectancy of renewal.

(iii) Safe harbor pooling method. In lieu of applying the reasonable expectancy of renewal test described in paragraph (f)(5)(ii) of this section to each separate right created during a taxable year, a taxpayer that reasonably expects to enter into at least 25 similar rights during the taxable year may establish a pool of similar rights for which the initial term does not extend beyond the period prescribed in paragraph (f)(1) of this section and may elect to apply the reasonable expectancy of renewal test to that pool. See paragraph (h) of this section for additional rules relating to pooling. The application of paragraph (f)(1) of this section to each pool is determined in the following manner:

(A) All amounts (except de minimis costs described in paragraph (d)(6)(v) of this section) paid to create the rights included in the pool and all amounts paid to facilitate the creation of the rights included in the pool are aggregated.

(B) If less than 20 percent of the rights in the pool are reasonably expected to be renewed beyond the period prescribed in paragraph (f)(1) of this section, all rights in the pool are treated as having a duration that does not extend beyond the period prescribed in paragraph (f)(1) of this section, and the taxpayer is not required to capitalize under this section any portion of the aggregate amount described in paragraph (f)(5)(iii)(A) of this section.

(C) If more than 80 percent of the rights in the pool are reasonably expected to be renewed beyond the period prescribed in paragraph (f)(1) of this section, all rights in the pool are treated as having a duration that extends beyond the period prescribed in paragraph (f)(1) of this section, and the taxpayer is required to capitalize under this section the aggregate amount described in paragraph (f)(5)(iii)(A) of this section.

(D) If 20 percent or more, but 80 percent or less, of the rights in the pool are reasonably expected to be renewed beyond the period prescribed in paragraph (f)(1) of this section, the aggregate amount described in paragraph (f)(5)(iii)(A) of this section is multiplied by the percentage of the rights in the pool that are reasonably expected to be renewed beyond the period prescribed in paragraph (f)(1) of this section and the taxpayer must capitalize the resulting amount under this section by treating such amount as creating a separate intangible. The amount determined by multiplying the aggregate amount described in paragraph (f)(5)(iii)(A) of this section by the percentage of rights in the pool that are not reasonably expected to be renewed beyond the period prescribed in paragraph (f)(1) of this section is not required to be capitalized under this section.

(6) Coordination with section 461. In the case of a taxpayer using an accrual method of accounting, the rules of this paragraph (f) do not affect the determination of whether a liability is incurred during the taxable year, including the determination of whether economic performance has occurred with respect to the liability. See § 1.461-4 for rules relating to economic performance.

(7) Election to capitalize. A taxpayer may elect not to apply the rule contained in paragraph (f)(1) of this section. An election made under this paragraph (f)(7) applies to all similar transactions during the taxable year to which paragraph (f)(1) of this section would apply (but for the election under this paragraph (f)(7)). For example, a taxpayer may elect under this paragraph (f)(7) to capitalize its costs of prepaying insurance contracts for 12 months, but may continue to apply the rule in paragraph (f)(1) to its costs of entering into non-renewable, 12-month service contracts. A taxpayer makes the election by treating the amounts as capital expenditures in its timely filed original federal income tax return (including extensions) for the taxable year during which the amounts are paid. In the case of an affiliated group of corporations filing a consolidated return, the election is made separately with respect to each member of the group, and not with respect to the group as a whole. In the case of an S corporation or partnership, the election is made by the S corporation or by the partnership, and not by the shareholders or partners. An election made under this paragraph (f)(7) is revocable with respect to each taxable year for which made only with the consent of the Commissioner.

(8) Examples. The rules of this paragraph (f) are illustrated by the following examples, in which it is assumed (unless otherwise stated) that the taxpayer is a calendar year, accrual method taxpayer that does not have a short taxable year in any taxable year and has not made an election under paragraph (f)(7) of this section:

Example (1). Prepaid expenses. On December 1, 2005, N corporation pays a $10,000 insurance premium to obtain a property insurance policy (with no cash value) with a 1-year term that begins on February 1, 2006. The amount paid by N is a prepaid expense described in paragraph (d)(3) of this section and not paragraph (d)(2) of this section. Because the right or benefit attributable to the $10,000 payment extends beyond the end of the taxable year following the taxable year in which the payment is made, the 12-month rule provided by this paragraph (f) does not apply. N must capitalize the $10,000 payment.

Example (2). Prepaid expenses. (i) Assume the same facts as in Example 1, except that the policy has a term beginning on December 15, 2005. The 12-month rule of this paragraph (f) applies to the $10,000 payment because the right or benefit attributable to the payment neither extends more than 12 months beyond December 15, 2005 (the first date the benefit is realized by the taxpayer) nor beyond the end of the taxable year following the taxable year in which the payment is made. Accordingly, N is not required to capitalize the $10,000 payment.

(ii) Alternatively, assume N capitalizes prepaid expenses for financial accounting and reporting purposes and elects under paragraph (f)(7) of this section not to apply the 12-month rule contained in paragraph (f)(1) of this section. N must capitalize the $10,000 payment for Federal income tax purposes.

Example (3). Financial interests. On October 1, 2005, X corporation makes a 9-month loan to B in the principal amount of $250,000. The principal amount of the loan to B constitutes an amount paid to create or originate a financial interest under paragraph (d)(2)(i)(B) of this section. The 9-month term of the loan does not extend beyond the period prescribed by paragraph (f)(1) of this section. However, as provided by paragraph (f)(3) of this section, the rules of this paragraph (f) do not apply to intangibles described in paragraph (d)(2) of this section. Accordingly, X must capitalize the $250,000 loan amount.

Example (4). Financial interests. X corporation owns all of the outstanding stock of Z corporation. On December 1, 2005, Y corporation pays X $1,000,000 in exchange for X's grant of a 9-month call option to Y permitting Y to purchase all of the outstanding stock of Z. Y's payment to X constitutes an amount paid to create or originate an option with X under paragraph (d)(2)(i)(C)(7) of this section. The 9-month term of the option does not extend beyond the period prescribed by paragraph (f)(1) of this section. However, as provided by paragraph (f)(3) of this section, the rules of this paragraph (f) do not apply to intangibles described in paragraph (d)(2) of this section. Accordingly, Y must capitalize the $1,000,000 payment.

Example (5). License. (i) On July 1, 2005, R corporation pays $10,000 to state X to obtain a license to operate a business in state X for a period of 5 years. The terms of the license require R to pay state X an annual fee of $500 due on July 1, 2005, and each of the succeeding four years. R pays the $500 fee on July 1 as required by the license.

(ii) R's payment of $10,000 is an amount paid to a governmental agency for a license granted by that agency to which paragraph (d)(5) of this section applies. Because R's payment creates rights or benefits for R that extend beyond 12 months after the first date on which R realizes the rights or benefits attributable to the payment and beyond the end of 2006 (the taxable year following the taxable year in which the payment is made), the rules of this paragraph (f) do not apply to R's payment. Accordingly, R must capitalize the $10,000 payment.

(iii) R's payment of each $500 annual fee is a prepaid expense described in paragraph (d)(3) of this section. R is not required to capitalize the $500 fee in each taxable year. The rules of this paragraph (f) apply to each such payment because each payment provides a right or benefit to R that does not extend beyond 12 months after the first date on which R realizes the rights or benefits attributable to the payment and does not extend beyond the end of the taxable year following the taxable year in which the payment is made.

Example (6). Lease. On December 1, 2005, W corporation enters into a lease agreement with X corporation under which W agrees to lease property to X for a period of 9 months, beginning on December 1, 2005. W pays its outside counsel $7,000 for legal services rendered in drafting the lease agreement and negotiating with X. The agreement between W and X is an agreement providing W the right to be compensated for the use of property, as described in paragraph (d)(6)(i)(A) of this section. W's $7,000 payment to its outside counsel is an amount paid to facilitate W's creation of the lease as described in paragraph (e)(1)(i) of this section. The 12-month rule of this paragraph (f) applies to the $7,000 payment because the right or benefit that the $7,000 payment facilitates the creation of neither extends more than 12 months beyond December 1, 2005 (the first date the benefit is realized by the taxpayer) nor beyond the end of the taxable year following the taxable year in which the payment is made. Accordingly, W is not required to capitalize its payment to its outside counsel.

Example (7). Certain contract terminations. V corporation owns real property that it has leased to A for a period of 15 years. When the lease has a remaining unexpired term of 5 years, V and A agree to terminate the lease, enabling V to use the property in its trade or business. V pays A $100,000 in exchange for A's agreement to terminate the lease. V's payment to A to terminate the lease is described in paragraph (d)(7)(i)(A) of this section. Under paragraph (f)(2) of this section, V's payment creates a benefit for V with a duration of 5 years, the remaining unexpired term of the lease as of the date of the termination. Because the benefit attributable to the expenditure extends beyond 12 months after the first date on which V realizes the rights or benefits attributable to the payment and beyond the end of the taxable year following the taxable year in which the payment is made, the rules of this paragraph (f) do not apply to the payment. V must capitalize the $100,000 payment.

Example (8). Certain contract terminations. Assume the same facts as in Example 7, except that the lease is terminated when it has a remaining unexpired term of 10 months. Under paragraph (f)(2) of this section, V's payment creates a benefit for V with a duration of 10 months. The 12-month rule of this paragraph (f) applies to the payment because the benefit attributable to the payment neither extends more than 12 months beyond the date of termination (the first date the benefit is realized by V) nor beyond the end of the taxable year following the taxable year in which the payment is made. Accordingly, V is not required to capitalize the $100,000 payment.

Example (9). Certain contract terminations. Assume the same facts as in Example 7, except that either party can terminate the lease upon 12 months notice. When the lease has a remaining unexpired term of 5 years, V wants to terminate the lease, however, V does not want to wait another 12 months. V pays A $50,000 for the ability to terminate the lease with one month's notice. V's payment to A to terminate the lease is described in paragraph (d)(7)(i)(A) of this section. Under paragraph (f)(2) of this section, V's payment creates a benefit for V with a duration of 11 months, the time by which the notice period is shortened. The 12-month rule of this paragraph (f) applies to V's $50,000 payment because the benefit attributable to the payment neither extends more than 12 months beyond the date of termination (the first date the benefit is realized by V) nor beyond the end of the taxable year following the taxable year in which the payment is made. Accordingly, V is not required to capitalize the $50,000 payment.

Example (10). Coordination with section 461. (i) U corporation leases office space from W corporation at a monthly rental rate of $2,000. On August 1, 2005, U prepays its office rent expense for the first six months of 2006 in the amount of $12,000. For purposes of this example, it is assumed that the recurring item exception provided by § 1.461-5 does not apply and that the lease between W and U is not a section 467 rental agreement as defined in section 467(d).

(ii) Under § 1.461-4(d)(3), U's prepayment of rent is a payment for the use of property by U for which economic performance occurs ratably over the period of time U is entitled to use the property. Accordingly, because economic performance with respect to U's prepayment of rent does not occur until 2006, U's prepaid rent is not incurred in 2005 and therefore is not properly taken into account through capitalization, deduction, or otherwise in 2005. Thus, the rules of this paragraph (f) do not apply to U's prepayment of its rent.

(iii) Alternatively, assume that U uses the cash method of accounting and the economic performance rules in § 1.461-4 therefore do not apply to U. The 12-month rule of this paragraph (f) applies to the $12,000 payment because the rights or benefits attributable to U's prepayment of its rent do not extend beyond December 31, 2006. Accordingly, U is not required to capitalize its prepaid rent.

Example (11). Coordination with section 461. N corporation pays R corporation, an advertising and marketing firm, $40,000 on August 1, 2005, for advertising and marketing services to be provided to N throughout calendar year 2006. For purposes of this example, it is assumed that the recurring item exception provided by § 1.461-5 does not apply. Under § 1.461-4(d)(2), N's payment arises out of the provision of services to N by R for which economic performance occurs as the services are provided. Accordingly, because economic performance with respect to N's prepaid advertising expense does not occur until 2006, N's prepaid advertising expense is not incurred in 2005 and therefore is not properly taken into account through capitalization, deduction, or otherwise in 2005. Thus, the rules of this paragraph (f) do not apply to N's payment.

(g) Treatment of capitalized costs. *(1) In general.* An amount required to be capitalized by this section is not currently deductible under section 162. Instead, the amount generally is added to the basis of the intangible acquired or created. See section 1012.

(2) Financial instruments. In the case of a financial instrument described in paragraph (c)(1)(iii) or (d)(2)(i)(C) of this section, notwithstanding paragraph (g)(1) of this section, if under other provisions of law the amount required to be capitalized is not required to be added to the basis of the intangible acquired or created, then the other provisions of law will govern the tax treatment of the amount.

(h) Special rules applicable to pooling. *(1) In general.* Except as otherwise provided, the rules of this paragraph (h) apply to the pooling methods described in paragraph (d)(6)(v) of this section (relating to de minimis rules applicable to certain contract rights), paragraph (e)(4)(iii)(A) of this section (relating to de minimis rules applicable to transaction costs), and paragraph (f)(5)(iii) of this section (relating to the application of the 12-month rule to renewable rights).

(2) Method of accounting. A pooling method authorized by this section constitutes a method of accounting for purposes of section 446. A taxpayer that adopts or changes to a pooling method authorized by this section must use the method for the year of adoption and for all subsequent taxable years during which the taxpayer qualifies to use the pooling method unless a change to another method is required by the Commissioner in order to clearly reflect income, or unless permission to change to another method is granted by the Commissioner as provided in § 1.446-1(e).

(3) Adopting or changing to a pooling method. A taxpayer adopts (or changes to) a pooling method authorized by this section for any taxable year by establishing one or more pools for the taxable year in accordance with the rules governing the particular pooling method and the rules prescribed by this paragraph (h), and by using the pooling method to compute its taxable income for the year of adoption (or change).

(4) Definition of pool. A taxpayer may use any reasonable method of defining a pool of similar transactions, agreements or rights, including a method based on the type of customer or the type of product or service provided under a contract. However, a taxpayer that pools similar transactions, agreements or rights must include in the pool all similar transactions, agreements or rights created during the taxable year. For purposes of the pooling methods described in paragraph (d)(6)(v) of this section (relating to de minimis rules applicable to certain contract rights) and paragraph (e)(4)(iii)(A) of this section (relating to de minimis rules applicable to transaction costs), an agreement (or a transaction) is treated as not similar to other agreements (or transactions) included in the pool if the amount at issue with respect to that agreement (or transaction) is reasonably expected to differ significantly from the average amount at issue with respect to the other agreements (or transactions) properly included in the pool.

(5) Consistency requirement. A taxpayer that uses the pooling method described in paragraph (f)(5)(iii) of this section for purposes of applying the 12-month rule to a right or benefit—

(i) Must use the pooling methods described in paragraph (d)(6)(v) of this section (relating to de minimis rules applicable to certain contract rights) and paragraph (e)(4)(iii)(A) of this section (relating to de minimis rules applicable to transaction costs) for purposes of determining the amount paid to create, or facilitate the creation of, the right or benefit; and

(ii) Must use the same pool for purposes of paragraph (d)(6)(v) of this section and paragraph (e)(4)(iii)(A) of this section as is used for purposes of paragraph (f)(5)(iii) of this section.

(6) Additional guidance pertaining to pooling. The Internal Revenue Service may publish guidance in the Internal Revenue Bulletin (see § 601.601(d)(2) of this chapter) prescribing additional rules for applying the pooling methods authorized by this section to specific industries or to specific types of transactions.

(7) Example. The following example illustrates the rules of this paragraph (h):

Example. Pooling. (i) In the course of its business, W corporation enters into 3-year non-cancelable contracts that provide W the right to provide services to its customers. W generally pays certain amounts in the process of pursuing an agreement with a customer, including amounts paid to credit reporting agencies to verify the credit history of the potential customer and commissions paid to the independent sales agent who secures the agreement with the customer. In the case of agreements that W enters into with customers who are individuals, the agreements contain substantially similar terms and conditions and W typically pays between $100 and $200 in the process of pursuing each transaction. During 2005, W enters into agreements with 300 individuals. Also during 2005, W enters into an agreement with X corporation containing terms and conditions that are substantially similar to those contained in the agreements W enters into with its customers who are individuals. W pays certain amounts in the process of pursuing the agreement with X that W would not typically incur in the process of pursuing an agreement with its customers who are individuals. For example, W pays amounts to prepare and submit a bid for the agreement with X and amounts to travel to X's headquarters to make a sales presentation to X's management. In the aggregate, W pays $11,000 in the process of obtaining the agreement with X.

(ii) The agreements between W and its customers are agreements providing W the right to provide services, as described in paragraph (d)(6)(i)(B) of this section. Under paragraph (b)(1)(v) of this section, W must capitalize transaction costs paid to facilitate the creation of these agreements. Because W enters into at least 25 similar transactions during 2005, W may pool its transactions for purposes of determining whether its transaction costs are de minimis within the meaning of paragraph (e)(4)(iii)(A) of this section. W adopts a pooling method by establishing one or more pools of similar transactions and by using the pooling method to compute its taxable income beginning in its 2005 taxable year. If W adopts a pooling method, W must include all similar transactions in the pool. Under paragraph (h)(4) of this section, the transaction with X is not similar to the transactions W enters into with its customers who are individuals. While the agreement with X contains terms and conditions that are substantially similar to those contained in the agreements W enters into with its customers who are individuals, the transaction costs paid in the process of pursuing the agreement with X are reasonably expected to differ significantly from the average transaction costs attributable to transactions with its customers who are individuals. Accordingly, W may not include the transaction with X in the pool of transactions with customers who are individuals.

(i) [Reserved]

(j) Application to accrual method taxpayers. For purposes of this section, the terms amount paid and payment mean, in the case of a taxpayer using an accrual method of accounting, a liability incurred (within the meaning of § 1.446-1(c)(1)(ii)). A liability may not be taken into account under this section prior to the taxable year during which the liability is incurred.

(k) Treatment of related parties and indirect payments. For purposes of this section, references to a party other than the taxpayer include persons related to that party and persons acting for or on behalf of that party (including persons to whom the taxpayer becomes obligated as a result of assuming a liability of that party). For this purpose, persons are related only if their relationship is described in section 267(b) or 707(b) or they are engaged in trades or businesses under common control within the meaning of section 41(f)(1). References to an amount paid to or by a party include an amount paid on behalf of that party.

(l) Examples. The rules of this section are illustrated by the following examples in which it is assumed that the Internal Revenue Service has not published guidance that requires capitalization under paragraph (b)(1)(iv) of this section (relating to amounts paid to create or enhance a future benefit that is identified in published guidance as an intangible for which capitalization is required):

Example (1). License granted by a governmental unit. (i) X corporation pays $25,000 to state R to obtain a license to sell alcoholic beverages in its restaurant. The license is valid indefinitely, provided X complies with all applicable laws regarding the sale of alcoholic beverages in state R. X pays its outside counsel $4,000 for legal services rendered in preparing the license application and otherwise representing X during the licensing process. In addition, X determines that $2,000 of salaries paid to its employees is allocable to services rendered by the employees in obtaining the license.

(ii) X's payment of $25,000 is an amount paid to a governmental unit to obtain a license granted by that agency, as described in paragraph (d)(5)(i) of this section. The right has an indefinite duration and constitutes an amortizable section 197 intangible. Accordingly, as provided in paragraph (f)(3) of this section, the provisions of paragraph (f) of this section (relating to the 12-month rule) do not apply to X's payment. X must capitalize its $25,000 payment to obtain the license from state R.

(iii) As provided in paragraph (e)(4) of this section, X is not required to capitalize employee compensation because such amounts are treated as amounts that do not facilitate the acquisition or creation of an intangible. Thus, X is not required to capitalize the $2,000 of employee compensation allocable to the transaction.

(iv) X's payment of $4,000 to its outside counsel is an amount paid to facilitate the creation of an intangible, as described in paragraph (e)(1)(i) of this section. Because X's transaction costs do not exceed $5,000, X's transaction costs are de minimis within the meaning of paragraph (e)(4)(iii)(A) of this section. Accordingly, X is not required to capitalize the $4,000 payment to its outside counsel under this section.

Example (2). Franchise agreement. (i) R corporation is a franchisor of income tax return preparation outlets. V corporation negotiates with R to obtain the right to operate an income tax return preparation outlet under a franchise from R. V pays an initial $100,000 franchise fee to R in exchange for the franchise agreement. In addition, V pays its outside counsel $4,000 to represent V during the negotiations with R. V also pays $2,000 to an industry consultant to advise V during the negotiations with R.

(ii) Under paragraph (d)(6)(i)(A) of this section, V's payment of $100,000 is an amount paid to another party to enter into an agreement with that party providing V the right to use tangible or intangible property. Accordingly, V must capitalize its $100,000 payment to R. The franchise agreement is a self-created amortizable section 197 intangible within the meaning of section 197(c). Accordingly, as provided in paragraph (f)(3) of this section, the 12-month rule contained in paragraph (f)(1) of this section does not apply.

(iii) V's payment of $4,000 to its outside counsel and $2,000 to the industry consultant are amounts paid to facilitate the creation of an intangible, as described in paragraph (e)(1)(i) of this section. Because V's aggregate transaction costs exceed $5,000, V's transaction costs are not de minimis within the meaning of paragraph (e)(4)(iii)(A) of this section. Accordingly, V must capitalize the $4,000 payment to its outside counsel and the $2,000 payment to the industry consultant under this section into the basis of the franchise, as provided in paragraph (g) of this section.

Example (3). Covenant not to compete. (i) On December 1, 2005, N corporation, a calendar year taxpayer, enters into a covenant not to compete with B, a key employee that is leaving the employ of N. The covenant not to compete is not entered into in connection with the acquisition of an interest in a trade or business. The covenant not to compete prohibits B from competing with N for a period of 9 months, beginning December 1, 2005. N pays B $25,000 in full consideration for B's agreement not to compete. In addition, N pays its outside counsel $6,000 to facilitate the creation of the covenant not to compete with B. N does not have a short taxable year in 2005 or 2006.

(ii) Under paragraph (d)(6)(i)(C) of this section, N's payment of $25,000 is an amount paid to another party to induce that party to enter into a covenant not to compete with N. However, because the covenant not to compete has a duration that does not extend beyond 12 months after the first date on which N realizes the rights attributable to its payment (i.e., December 1, 2005) or beyond the end of the taxable year following the taxable year in which payment is made, the 12-month rule contained in paragraph (f)(1) of this section applies. Accordingly, N is not required to capitalize its $25,000 payment to B or its $6,000 payment to facilitate the creation of the covenant not to compete.

Example (4). Demand-side management. (i) X corporation, a public utility engaged in generating and distributing electrical energy, provides programs to its customers to promote energy conservation and energy efficiency. These programs are aimed at reducing electrical costs to X's customers, building goodwill with X's customers, and reducing X's future operating and capital costs. X provides these programs without obligating any of its customers participating in the programs to purchase power from X in the future. Under these programs, X pays a consultant to help industrial customers design energy-efficient manufacturing processes, to conduct "energy efficiency audits" that serve to identify for customers inefficiencies in their energy usage patterns, and to provide cash allowances to encourage residential customers to replace existing appliances with more energy efficient appliances.

(ii) The amounts paid by X to the consultant are not amounts to acquire or create an intangible under paragraph (c) or (d) of this section or to facilitate such an acquisition or creation. In addition, the amounts do not create a separate and distinct intangible asset within the meaning of paragraph (b)(3) of this section. Accordingly, the amounts paid to the consultant are not required to be capitalized under this section. While the amounts may serve to reduce future operating and capital costs and create goodwill with customers, these benefits, without more, are not intangibles for which capitalization is required under this section.

Example (5). Business process re-engineering. (i) V corporation manufactures its products using a batch production system. Under this system, V continuously produces component parts of its various products and stockpiles these parts until they are needed in V's final assembly line. Finished goods are stockpiled awaiting orders from customers. V discovers that this process ties up significant amounts of V's capital in work-in-process and finished goods inventories. V hires B, a consultant, to advise V on improving the efficiency of its manufacturing operations. B recommends a complete re-engineering of V's manufacturing process to a process known as just-in-time manufacturing. Just-in-time manufacturing involves reconfiguring a manufacturing plant to a configuration of "cells" where each team in a cell performs the entire manufacturing process for a particular customer order, thus reducing inventory stockpiles.

(ii) V incurred three categories of costs to convert its manufacturing process to a just-in-time system. First, V paid B, a consultant, $250,000 in professional fees to implement the conversion of V's plant to a just-in-time system. Second, V paid C, a contractor, $100,000 to relocate and reconfigure V's manufacturing equipment from an assembly line layout to a configuration of cells. Third, V paid D, a consultant, $50,000 to train V's employees in the just-in-time manufacturing process.

(iii) The amounts paid by V to B, C, and D are not amounts to acquire or create an intangible under paragraph (c) or (d) of this section or to facilitate such an acquisition or creation. In addition, the amounts do not create a separate and distinct intangible asset within the meaning of paragraph (b)(3) of this section. Accordingly, the amounts paid to B, C, and D are not required to be capitalized under this section. While the amounts produce long term benefits to V in the form of reduced inventory stockpiles, improved product quality, and increased efficiency, these benefits, without more, are not intangibles for which capitalization is required under this section.

Example (6). Defense of business reputation. (i) X, an investment adviser, serves as the fund manager of a money market investment fund. X, like its competitors in the industry, strives to maintain a constant net asset value for its money market fund of $1.00 per share. During 2005, in the course of managing the fund assets, X incorrectly predicts the direction of market interest rates, resulting in significant investment losses to the fund. Due to these significant losses, X is faced with the prospect of reporting a net asset value that is less than $1.00 per share. X is not aware of any investment adviser in its industry that has ever reported a net asset value for its money market fund of less than $1.00 per share. X is concerned that reporting a net asset value of less than $1.00 per share will significantly harm its reputation as an investment adviser, and could lead to litigation by shareholders. X decides to contribute $2,000,000 to the fund in order to raise the net asset value of the fund to $1.00 per share. This contribution is not a loan to the fund and does not give X any ownership interest in the fund.

(ii) The $2,000,000 contribution is not an amount paid to acquire or create an intangible under paragraph (c) or (d) of this section or to facilitate such an acquisition or creation. In addition, the amount does not create a separate and distinct intangible asset within the meaning of paragraph (b)(3) of this section. Accordingly, the amount contributed to the fund is not required to be capitalized under this section. While the amount serves to protect the business reputation of the taxpayer and may protect the taxpayer from litigation by shareholders, these benefits, without more, are not intangibles for which capitalization is required under this section.

Example (7). Product launch costs. (i) R corporation, a manufacturer of pharmaceutical products, is required by law to obtain regulatory approval before selling its products. While awaiting regulatory approval on Product A, R pays to develop and implement a marketing strategy and an advertising campaign to raise consumer awareness of the purported need for Product A. R also pays to train health care professionals and other distributors in the proper use of Product A.

(ii) The amounts paid by R are not amounts paid to acquire or create an intangible under paragraph (c) or (d) of this section or to facilitate such an acquisition or creation. In addition, the amounts do not create a separate and distinct intangible asset within the meaning of paragraph (b)(3) of this section. Accordingly, R is not required to capitalize these amounts under this section. While the amounts may benefit R by creating consumer demand for Product A and increasing awareness of Product A among distributors, these benefits, without more, are not intangibles for which capitalization is required under this section.

Example (8). Stocklifting costs. (i) N corporation is a wholesale distributor of Brand A aftermarket automobile replacement parts. In an effort to induce a retail automobile parts supply store to stock only Brand A parts, N offers to replace all of the store's inventory of other branded parts with Brand A parts, and to credit the store for its cost of other branded parts. The store is under no obligation to continue stocking Brand A parts or to purchase a minimum volume of Brand A parts from N in the future.

(ii) The amount paid by N as a credit to the store for the cost of other branded parts is not an amount paid to acquire or create an intangible under paragraph (c) or (d) of this section or to facilitate such an acquisition or creation. In addition, the amount does not create a separate and distinct intangible asset within the meaning of paragraph (b)(3) of this section. Accordingly, N is not required to capitalize the amount under this section. While the amount may create a hope or expectation by N that the store will continue to stock Brand A parts, this benefit, without more, is not an intangible for which capitalization is required under this section.

(iii) Alternatively, assume that N agrees to credit the store for its cost of other branded parts in exchange for the store's agreement to purchase all of its inventory requirements for such parts from N for a period of at least 3 years. The amount paid by N as a credit to the store for the cost of other branded parts is an amount paid to induce the store to enter into an agreement providing R the right to provide property. Accordingly, R must capitalize its payment.

Example (9). Package design costs. (i) Z corporation manufactures and markets personal care products. Z pays $100,000 to a consultant to develop a package design for Z's newest product, Product A. Z also pays a fee to a government agency to obtain trademark and copyright protection on certain elements of the package design. Z pays its outside legal counsel $10,000 for services rendered in preparing and filing the trademark and copyright applications and for other services rendered in securing the trademark and copyright protection.

(ii) The $100,000 paid by Z to the consultant for development of the package design is not an amount paid to acquire or create an intangible under paragraph (c) or (d) of this section or to facilitate such an acquisition or creation. In addition, as provided in paragraph (b)(3)(v) of this section, amounts paid to develop a package design are treated as amounts that do not create a separate and distinct intangible asset. Accordingly, Z is not required to capitalize the $100,000 payment under this section.

(iii) The amounts paid by Z to the government agency to obtain trademark and copyright protection are amounts paid to a government agency for a right granted by that agency. Accordingly, Z must capitalize the payment. In addition, the $10,000 paid by Z to its outside counsel is an amount paid to facilitate the creation of the trademark and copyright. Because the aggregate amounts paid to facilitate the transaction exceed $5,000, the amounts are not de minimis as defined in paragraph (e)(4)(iii)(A) of this section. Accordingly, Z must capitalize the $10,000 payment to its outside counsel under paragraph (b)(1)(v) of this section.

(iv) Alternatively, assume that Z acquires an existing package design for Product A as part of an acquisition of a trade or business that constitutes an applicable asset acquisition within the meaning of section 1060(c). Assume further that $100,000 of the consideration paid by N in the acquisition is properly allocable to the package design for Product A. Under paragraph (c)(1) of this section, Z must capitalize the $100,000 payment.

Example (10). Contract to provide services. (i) Q corporation, a financial planning firm, provides financial advisory services on a fee-only basis. During 2005, Q and several other financial planning firms submit separate bids to R corporation for a contract to become one of three providers of financial advisory services to R's employees. Q pays $2,000 to a printing company to develop and produce materials for its sales presentation to R's management. Q also pays $6,000 to travel to R's corporate headquarters to make the sales presentation, and $20,000 of salaries to its employees for services performed in preparing the bid and making the presentation to R's management. Q's bid is successful and Q enters into an agreement with R in 2005 under which Q agrees to provide financial advisory services to R's employees, and R agrees to pay Q's fee on behalf of each employee who chooses to utilize such services. R enters into similar agreements with two other financial planning firms, and R's employees may choose to use the services of any one of the three firms. Based on its past experience, Q reasonably expects to provide services to at least 5 percent of R's employees.

(ii) Q's agreement with R is not an agreement providing Q the right to provide services, as described in paragraph (d)(6)(i)(B) of this section. Under paragraph (d)(6)(iv) the agreement places no obligation on another person to request or pay for Q's services. Accordingly, Q is not required to capitalize any of the amounts paid in the process of pursuing the agreement with R.

Example (11). Mutual fund distributor. (i) D incurs costs to enter into a distribution agreement with M, a mutual fund. The initial term of the distribution agreement is two years, and afterwards must be approved annually by M. The distribution agreement can be terminated by either party on 60 days notice. Although distribution agreements are rarely terminated in the mutual fund industry, M is not economically compelled to continue D's distribution agreement. Under the distribution agreement, D has the exclusive right to sell shares of M and agrees to use its best efforts to solicit orders for the sale of shares of M. D sells shares in M directly to the general public as well as through brokers. When an investor places an order for M shares with a broker, D pays the broker a commission for selling the shares to the investor. Under the distribution agreement, D receives compensation from M in the form of 12b-1 fees (which equal a percentage of M's net asset value attributable to investors that have held their shares for up to 6 years) and contingent deferred sales charges (which are paid if the investor redeems the purchased shares within 6 years).

(ii) The distribution agreement is not an agreement providing D with the right to provide services, as described in paragraph (d)(6)(i)(B) of this section, because the distribution agreement can be terminated by M at will upon 60 days notice and M is not economically compelled to continue the distribution agreement. Accordingly, D is not required to capitalize the costs of creating (or facilitating the creation of) the distribution agreement under paragraphs (b)(1)(ii) or (v) of this section. In addition, as provided in paragraph (b)(3)(ii) of this section, amounts paid to create an agreement are treated as amounts that do not create a separate and distinct intangible asset. Accordingly, D also is not required to capitalize the costs of creating (or facilitating the creation of) the distribution agreement under paragraph (b)(1)(iii) or (v) of this section.

(iii) Under paragraph (b)(3)(iii), the broker commissions paid by D in performing services under the distribution agreement do not create (or facilitate the creation of) a separate and distinct intangible asset. In addition, the broker commissions do not create an intangible described in paragraph (d) of this section. Accordingly, D is not required to capitalize the broker commissions under this section.

(m) Amortization. For rules relating to amortization of certain intangibles, see § 1.167(a)-3.

(n) Intangible interests in land. [Reserved].

(o) Effective date. This section applies to amounts paid or incurred on or after December 31, 2003.

(p) Accounting method changes. *(1) In general.* A taxpayer seeking to change a method of accounting to comply with this section must secure the consent of the Commissioner in accordance with the requirements of § 1.446-1(e). For the taxpayer's first taxable year ending on or after December 31, 2003, the taxpayer is granted the consent of the Commissioner to change its method of accounting to comply with this section, provided the taxpayer follows the administrative procedures issued under § 1.446-1(e)(3)(ii) for obtaining the Commissioner's automatic consent to a change in accounting method (for further guidance, for example, see Rev. Proc. 2002-9 (2002-1 C.B. 327) and § 601.601(d)(2)(ii)(b) of this chapter).

(2) Scope limitations. Any limitations on obtaining the automatic consent of the Commissioner do not apply to a taxpayer seeking to change to a method of accounting to comply with this section for its first taxable year ending on or after December 31, 2003.

(3) Section 481(a) adjustment. With the exception of a change to a pooling method authorized by this section, the section 481(a) adjustment for a change in method of accounting to comply with this section for a taxpayer's first taxable year ending on or after December 31, 2003 is determined by taking into account only amounts paid or incurred in taxable years ending on or after January 24, 2002. A taxpayer seeking to change to a pooling method authorized by this section on or after the effective date of these regulations must change to the method using a cut-off method.

T.D. 9107, 12/31/2003.

§ 1.263(a)-5 Amounts paid or incurred to facilitate an acquisition of a trade or business, a change in the capital structure of a business entity, and certain other transactions.

(a) General rule. A taxpayer must capitalize an amount paid to facilitate (within the meaning of paragraph (b) of this section) each of the following transactions, without regard to whether the transaction is comprised of a single step or a series of steps carried out as part of a single plan and without regard to whether gain or loss is recognized in the transaction:

(1) An acquisition of assets that constitute a trade or business (whether the taxpayer is the acquirer in the acquisition or the target of the acquisition).

(2) An acquisition by the taxpayer of an ownership interest in a business entity if, immediately after the acquisition, the taxpayer and the business entity are related within the meaning of section 267(b) or 707(b) (see § 1.263(a)-4 for rules requiring capitalization of amounts paid by the taxpayer to acquire an ownership interest in a business entity, or to facilitate the acquisition of an ownership interest in a business entity, where the taxpayer and the business entity are not related within the meaning of section 267(b) or 707(b) immediately after the acquisition).

(3) An acquisition of an ownership interest in the taxpayer (other than an acquisition by the taxpayer of an ownership interest in the taxpayer, whether by redemption or otherwise).

(4) A restructuring, recapitalization, or reorganization of the capital structure of a business entity (including reorganizations described in section 368 and distributions of stock by the taxpayer as described in section 355).

(5) A transfer described in section 351 or section 721 (whether the taxpayer is the transferor or transferee).

(6) A formation or organization of a disregarded entity.

(7) An acquisition of capital.

(8) A stock issuance.

(9) A borrowing.

For purposes of this section, a borrowing means any issuance of debt, including an issuance of debt in an acquisition of capital or in a recapitalization. A borrowing also includes debt issued in a debt for debt exchange under § 1.1001-3.

(10) Writing an option.

(b) Scope of facilitate. *(1) In general.* Except as otherwise provided in this section, an amount is paid to facilitate a transaction described in paragraph (a) of this section if the amount is paid in the process of investigating or otherwise pursuing the transaction. Whether an amount is paid in the process of investigating or otherwise pursuing the transaction is determined based on all of the facts and circumstances. In determining whether an amount is paid to facilitate a transaction, the fact that the amount would (or would not) have been paid but for the transaction is relevant, but is not determinative. An amount paid to determine the value or price of a transaction is an amount paid in the process of investigating or otherwise pursuing the transaction. An amount paid to another party in exchange for tangible or intangible property is not an amount paid to facilitate the exchange. For example, the purchase price paid to the targetof an asset acquisition in exchange for its assets is not an amount paid to facilitate the acquisition. Similarly, the purchase price paid by an acquirer to the target's shareholders in exchange for their stock in a stock acquisition is not an amount paid to facilitate the acquisition of the stock. See § 1.263(a)-1, § 1.263(a)-2, and § 1.263(a)-4 for rules requiring capitalization of the purchase price paid to acquire property.

(2) Ordering rules. An amount paid in the process of investigating or otherwise pursuing both a transaction described in paragraph (a) of this section and an acquisition or creation of an intangible described in § 1.263(a)-4 is subject to the rules contained in this section, and not to the rules contained in § 1.263(a)-4. In addition, an amount required to be capitalized by § 1.263(a)-1, § 1.263(a)-2, or § 1.263(a)-4 does not facilitate a transaction described in paragraph (a) of this section.

(c) Special rules for certain costs. *(1) Borrowing costs.* An amount paid to facilitate a borrowing does not facilitate another transaction (other than the borrowing) described in paragraph (a) of this section.

(2) Costs of asset sales. An amount paid by a taxpayer to facilitate a sale of its assets does not facilitate another transaction (other than the sale) described in paragraph (a) of this section. For example, where a target corporation, in preparation for a merger with an acquiring corporation, sells assets that are not desired by the acquiring corporation, amounts paid to facilitate the sale of the unwanted assets are not required to be capitalized as amounts paid to facilitate the merger.

(3) Mandatory stock distributions. An amount paid in the process of investigating or otherwise pursuing a distribution of stock by a taxpayer to its shareholders does not facilitate a transaction described in paragraph (a) of this section if the divestiture of the stock (or of properties transferred to an entity whose stock is distributed) is required by law, regulatory mandate, or court order. A taxpayer is not required to capitalize (under this section or § 1.263(a)-4) an amount paid to organize (or facilitate the organization of) an entity if the entity is organized solely to receive properties that the taxpayer is required to divest by law, regulatory mandate, or court order and if the taxpayer distributes the stock of the entity to its shareholders. A taxpayer also is not required to capitalize (under this section or § 1.263(a)-4) an amount paid to transfer property to an entity if the taxpayer is required to divest itself of that property by law, regulatory mandate, or court order and if the stock of the recipient entity is distributed to the taxpayer's shareholders.

(4) Bankruptcy reorganization costs. An amount paid to institute or administer a proceeding under Chapter 11 of the Bankruptcy Code by a taxpayer that is the debtor under the proceeding constitutes an amount paid to facilitate a reorganization within the meaning of paragraph (a)(4) of this section, regardless of the purpose for which the proceeding is instituted. For example, an amount paid to prepare and file a petition under Chapter 11, to obtain an extension of the exclusivity period under Chapter 11, to formulate plans of reorganization under Chapter 11, to analyze plans of reorganization formulated by another party in interest, or to contest or obtain approval of a plan of reorganization under Chapter 11 facilitates a reorganization within the meaning of this section. However, amounts specifically paid to formulate, analyze, contest or obtain approval of the portion of a plan of reorganization under Chapter 11 that resolves tort liabilities of the taxpayer do not facilitate a reorganization within the meaning of paragraph (a)(4) of this section if the amounts would have been treated as ordinary and necessary business expenses under section 162 had the bankruptcy proceeding not been instituted. In addition, an amount paid by the taxpayer to defend against the commencement of an involuntary bankruptcy proceeding against the taxpayer does not facilitate a reorganization within the meaning of paragraph (a)(4) of this section. An amount paid by the debtor to operate its business during a Chapter 11 bankruptcy proceeding is not an amount paid to institute or administer the bankruptcy proceeding and does not facilitate a reorganization. Such amount is treated in the same manner as it would have been treated had the bankruptcy proceeding not been instituted.

(5) Stock issuance costs of open-end regulated investment companies. Amounts paid by an open-end regulated investment company (within the meaning of section 851) to facilitate an issuance of its stock are treated as amounts that do not facilitate a transaction described in paragraph (a) of this

section unless the amounts are paid during the initial stock offering period.

(6) Integration costs. An amount paid to integrate the business operations of the taxpayer with the business operations of another does not facilitate a transaction described in paragraph (a) of this section, regardless of when the integration activities occur.

(7) Registrar and transfer agent fees for the maintenance of capital stock records. An amount paid by a taxpayer to a registrar or transfer agent in connection with the transfer of the taxpayer's capital stock does not facilitate a transaction described in paragraph (a) of this section unless the amount is paid with respect to a specific transaction described in paragraph (a). For example, a taxpayer is not required to capitalize periodic payments to a transfer agent for maintaining records of the names and addresses of shareholders who trade the taxpayer's shares on a national exchange. By comparison, a taxpayer is required to capitalize an amount paid to the transfer agent for distributing proxy statements requesting shareholder approval of a transaction described in paragraph (a) of this section.

(8) Termination payments and amounts paid to facilitate mutually exclusive transactions. An amount paid to terminate (or facilitate the termination of) an agreement to enter into a transaction described in paragraph (a) of this section constitutes an amount paid to facilitate a second transaction described in paragraph (a) of this section only if the transactions are mutually exclusive. An amount paid to facilitate a transaction described in paragraph (a) of this section is treated as an amount paid to facilitate a second transaction described in paragraph (a) of this section only if the transactions are mutually exclusive.

(d) Simplifying conventions. *(1) In general.* For purposes of this section, employee compensation (within the meaning of paragraph (d)(2) of this section), overhead, and de minimis costs (within the meaning of paragraph (d)(3) of this section) are treated as amounts that do not facilitate a transaction described in paragraph (a) of this section.

(2) Employee compensation. (i) In general. The term employee compensation means compensation (including salary, bonuses and commissions) paid to an employee of the taxpayer. For purposes of this section, whether an individual is an employee is determined in accordance with the rules contained in section 3401(c) and the regulations thereunder.

(ii) Certain amounts treated as employee compensation. For purposes of this section, a guaranteed payment to a partner in a partnership is treated as employee compensation. For purposes of this section, annual compensation paid to a director of a corporation is treated as employee compensation. For example, an amount paid to a director of a corporation for attendance at a regular meeting of the board of directors (or committee thereof) is treated as employee compensation for purposes of this section. However, an amount paid to the director for attendance at a special meeting of the board of directors (or committee thereof) is not treated as employee compensation. An amount paid to a person that is not an employee of the taxpayer (including the employer of the individual who performs the services) is treated as employee compensation for purposes of this section only if the amount is paid for secretarial, clerical, or similar administrative support services (other than services involving the preparation and distribution of proxy solicitations and other documents seeking shareholder approval of a transaction described in paragraph (a) of this section). In the case of an affiliated group of corporations filing a consolidated federal income tax return, a payment by one member of the group to a second member of the group for services performed by an employee of the second member is treated as employee compensation if the services provided by the employee are provided at a time during which both members are affiliated.

(3) De minimis costs. (i) In general. The term de minimis costs means amounts (other than employee compensation and overhead) paid in the process of investigating or otherwise pursuing a transaction described in paragraph (a) of this section if, in the aggregate, the amounts do not exceed $5,000 (or such greater amount as may be set forth in published guidance). If the amounts exceed $5,000 (or such greater amount as may be set forth in published guidance), none of the amounts are de minimis costs within the meaning of this paragraph (d)(3). For purposes of this paragraph (d)(3), an amount paid in the form of property is valued at its fair market value at the time of the payment.

(ii) Treatment of commissions. The term de minimis costs does not include commissions paid to facilitate a transaction described in paragraph (a) of this section.

(4) Election to capitalize. A taxpayer may elect to treat employee compensation, overhead, or de minimis costs paid in the process of investigating or otherwise pursuing a transaction described in paragraph (a) of this section as amounts that facilitate the transaction. The election is made separately for each transaction and applies to employee compensation, overhead, or de minimis costs, or to any combination thereof. For example, a taxpayer may elect to treat overhead and de minimis costs, but not employee compensation, as amounts that facilitate the transaction. A taxpayer makes the election by treating the amounts to which the election applies as amounts that facilitate the transaction in the taxpayer's timely filed original federal income tax return (including extensions) for the taxable year during which the amounts are paid. In the case of an affiliated group of corporations filing a consolidated return, the election is made separately with respect to each member of the group, and not with respect to the group as a whole. In the case of an S corporation or partnership, the election is made by the S corporation or by the partnership, and not by the shareholders or partners. An election made under this paragraph (d)(4) is revocable with respect to each taxable year for which made only with the consent of the Commissioner.

(e) Certain acquisitive transactions. *(1) In general.* Except as provided in paragraph (e)(2) of this section (relating to inherently facilitative amounts), an amount paid by the taxpayer in the process of investigating or otherwise pursuing a covered transaction (as described in paragraph (e)(3) of this section) facilitates the transaction within the meaning of this section only if the amount relates to activities performed on or after the earlier of—

(i) The date on which a letter of intent, exclusivity agreement, or similar written communication (other than a confidentiality agreement) is executed by representatives of the acquirer and the target; or

(ii) The date on which the material terms of the transaction (as tentatively agreed to by representatives of the acquirer and the target) are authorized or approved by the taxpayer's board of directors (or committee of the board of directors) or, in the case of a taxpayer that is not a corporation, the date on which the material terms of the transaction (as tentatively agreed to by representatives of the acquirer and the target) are authorized or approved by the appropriate governing officials of the taxpayer. In the case of a transaction that does not require authorization or approval of the taxpayer's board of directors (or appropriate governing officials in the case of a taxpayer that is not a corporation) the date determined under this paragraph (e)(1)(ii) is the date on which the acquirer and the target execute a binding written contract reflecting the terms of the transaction.

(2) Exception for inherently facilitative amounts. An amount paid in the process of investigating or otherwise pursuing a covered transaction facilitates that transaction if the amount is inherently facilitative, regardless of whether the amount is paid for activities performed prior to the date determined under paragraph (e)(1) of this section. An amount is inherently facilitative if the amount is paid for—

(i) Securing an appraisal, formal written evaluation, or fairness opinion related to the transaction;

(ii) Structuring the transaction, including negotiating the structure of the transaction and obtaining tax advice on the structure of the transaction (for example, obtaining tax advice on the application of section 368);

(iii) Preparing and reviewing the documents that effectuate the transaction (for example, a merger agreement or purchase agreement);

(iv) Obtaining regulatory approval of the transaction, including preparing and reviewing regulatory filings;

(v) Obtaining shareholder approval of the transaction (for example, proxy costs, solicitation costs, and costs to promote the transaction to shareholders); or

(vi) Conveying property between the parties to the transaction (for example, transfer taxes and title registration costs).

(3) Covered transactions. For purposes of this paragraph (e), the term covered transaction means the following transactions:

(i) A taxable acquisition by the taxpayer of assets that constitute a trade or business.

(ii) A taxable acquisition of an ownership interest in a business entity (whether the taxpayer is the acquirer in the acquisition or the target of the acquisition) if, immediately after the acquisition, the acquirer and the target are related within the meaning of section 267(b) or 707(b).

(iii) A reorganization described in section 368(a)(1)(A), (B), or (C) or a reorganization described in section 368(a)(1)(D) in which stock or securities of the corporation to which the assets are transferred are distributed in a transaction which qualifies under section 354 or 356 (whether the taxpayer is the acquirer or the target in the reorganization).

(f) Documentation of success-based fees. An amount paid that is contingent on the successful closing of a transaction described in paragraph (a) of this section is an amount paid to facilitate the transaction except to the extent the taxpayer maintains sufficient documentation to establish that a portion of the fee is allocable to activities that do not facilitate the transaction. This documentation must be completed on or before the due date of the taxpayer's timely filed original federal income tax return (including extensions) for the taxable year during which the transaction closes. For purposes of this paragraph (f), documentation must consist of more than merely an allocation between activities that facilitate the transaction and activities that do not facilitate the transaction, and must consist of supporting records (for example, time records, itemized invoices, or other records) that identify—

(1) The various activities performed by the service provider;

(2) The amount of the fee (or percentage of time) that is allocable to each of the various activities performed;

(3) Where the date the activity was performed is relevant to understanding whether the activity facilitated the transaction, the amount of the fee (or percentage of time) that is allocable to the performance of that activity before and after the relevant date; and

(4) The name, business address, and business telephone number of the service provider.

(g) Treatment of capitalized costs. *(1) Tax-free acquisitive transactions.* [Reserved]

(2) Taxable acquisitive transactions. (i) Acquirer. In the case of an acquisition, merger, or consolidation that is not described in section 368, an amount required to be capitalized under this section by the acquirer is added to the basis of the acquired assets (in the case of a transaction that is treated as an acquisition of the assets of the target for federal income tax purposes) or the acquired stock (in the case of a transaction that is treated as an acquisition of the stock of the target for federal income tax purposes).

(ii) Target. (A) Asset acquisition. In the case of an acquisition, merger, or consolidation that is not described in section 368 and that is treated as an acquisition of the assets of the target for federal income tax purposes, an amount required to be capitalized under this section by the target is treated as a reduction of the target's amount realized on the disposition of its assets.

(B) Stock acquisition. [Reserved]

(3) Stock issuance transactions. [Reserved]

(4) Borrowings. For the treatment of amounts required to be capitalized under this section with respect to a borrowing, see § 1.446-5.

(5) Treatment of capitalized amounts by option writer. An amount required to be capitalized by an option writer under paragraph (a)(10) of this section is not currently deductible under section 162 or 212. Instead, the amount required to be capitalized generally reduces the total premium received by the option writer. However, other provisions of law may limit the reduction of the premium by the capitalized amount (for example, if the capitalized amount is never deductible by the option writer).

(h) Application to accrual method taxpayers. For purposes of this section, the terms amount paid and payment mean, in the case of a taxpayer using an accrual method of accounting, a liability incurred (within the meaning of § 1.446-1(c)(1)(ii)). A liability may not be taken into account under this section prior to the taxable year during which the liability is incurred.

(i) [Reserved]

(j) Coordination with other provisions of the Internal Revenue Code. Nothing in this section changes the treatment of an amount that is specifically provided for under any other provision of the Internal Revenue Code (other than section 162(a) or 212) or regulations thereunder.

(k) Treatment of indirect payments. For purposes of this section, references to an amount paid to or by a party include an amount paid on behalf of that party.

(l) Examples. The following examples illustrate the rules of this section:

Example (1). Costs to facilitate. Q corporation pays its outside counsel $20,000 to assist Q in registering its stock with the Securities and Exchange Commission. Q is not a regulated investment company within the meaning of section

851. Q's payments to its outside counsel are amounts paid to facilitate the issuance of stock. Accordingly, Q must capitalize its $20,000 payment under paragraph (a)(8) of this section (whether incurred before or after the issuance of the stock and whether or not the registration is productive of equity capital).

Example (2). Costs to facilitate. Q corporation seeks to acquire all of the outstanding stock of Y corporation. To finance the acquisition, Q must issue new debt. Q pays an investment banker $25,000 to market the debt to the public and pays its outside counsel $10,000 to prepare the offering documents for the debt. Q's payment of $35,000 facilitates a borrowing and must be capitalized under paragraph (a)(9) of this section. As provided in paragraph (c)(1) of this section, Q's payment does not facilitate the acquisition of Y, notwithstanding the fact that Q incurred the new debt to finance its acquisition of Y. See § 1.446-5 for the treatment of Q's capitalized payment.

Example (3). Costs to facilitate. (i) Z agrees to pay investment banker B $1,000,000 for B's services in evaluating four alternative transactions ($250,000 for each alternative): An initial public offering; a borrowing of funds; an acquisition by Z of a competitor; and an acquisition of Z by a competitor. Z eventually decides to pursue a borrowing and abandons the other options. The $250,000 payment to evaluate the possibility of a borrowing is an amount paid in the process of investigating or otherwise pursuing a transaction described in paragraph (a)(9) of this section. Accordingly Z must capitalize that $250,000 payment to B. See § 1.446-5 for the treatment of Z's capitalized payment.

(iii) The $250,000 payment to evaluate the possibility of an initial public offering is an amount paid in the process of investigating or otherwise pursuing a transaction described in paragraph (a)(8) of this section. Accordingly, Z must capitalize that $250,000 payment to B under this section. Because the borrowing and the initial public offering are not mutually exclusive transactions, the $250,000 is not treated as an amount paid to facilitate the borrowing. When Z abandons the initial public offering, Z may recover under section 165 the $250,000 paid to facilitate the initial public offering.

(iv) The $500,000 paid by Z to evaluate the possibilities of an acquisition of Z by a competitor and an acquisition of a competitor by Z are amounts paid in the process of investigating or otherwise pursuing transactions described in paragraphs (a) and (e)(3) of this section. Accordingly, Z is only required to capitalize under this section the portion of the $500,000 payment that relates to inherently facilitative activities under paragraph (e)(2) of this section or to activities performed on or after the date determined under paragraph (e)(1) of this section. Because the borrowing and the possible acquisitions are not mutually exclusive transactions, no portion of the $500,000 is treated as an amount paid to facilitate the borrowing. When Z abandons the acquisition transactions, Z may recover under section 165 any portion of the $500,000 that was paid to facilitate the acquisitions.

Example (4). Corporate acquisition. (i) On February 1, 2005, R corporation decides to investigate the acquisition of three potential targets: T corporation, U corporation, and V corporation. R's consideration of T, U, and V represents the consideration of three distinct transactions, any or all of which R might consummate and has the financial ability to consummate. On March 1, 2005, R enters into an exclusivity agreement with T and stops pursuing U and V. On July 1, 2005, R acquires all of the stock of T in a transaction described in section 368. R pays $1,000,000 to an investment banker and $50,000 to its outside counsel to conduct due diligence on T, U, and V; determine the value of T, U, and V; negotiate and structure the transaction with T; draft the merger agreement; secure shareholder approval; prepare SEC filings; and obtain the necessary regulatory approvals.

(ii) Under paragraph (e)(1) of this section, the amounts paid to conduct due diligence on T, U and V prior to March 1, 2005 (the date of the exclusivity agreement) are not amounts paid to facilitate the acquisition of the stock of T, U or V and are not required to be capitalized under this section. However, the amounts paid to conduct due diligence on T on and after March 1, 2005, are amounts paid to facilitate the acquisition of the stock of T and must be capitalized under paragraph (a)(2) of this section.

(iii) Under paragraph (e)(2) of this section, the amounts paid to determine the value of T, negotiate and structure the transaction with T, draft the merger agreement, secure shareholder approval, prepare SEC filings, and obtain necessary regulatory approvals are inherently facilitative amounts paid to facilitate the acquisition of the stock of T and must be capitalized, regardless of whether those activities occur prior to, on, or after March 1, 2005.

(iv) Under paragraph (e)(2) of this section, the amounts paid to determine the value of U and V are inherently facilitative amounts paid to facilitate the acquisition of U or V and must be capitalized. Because the acquisition of U, V, and T are not mutually exclusive transactions, the costs that facilitate the acquisition of U and V do not facilitate the acquisition of T. Accordingly, the amounts paid to determine the value of U and V may be recovered under section 165 in the taxable year that R abandons the planned mergers with U and V.

Example (5). Corporate acquisition; employee bonus. Assume the same facts as in Example 4, except R pays a bonus of $10,000 to one of its corporate officers who negotiated the acquisition of T. As provided by paragraph (d)(1) of this section, Y is not required to capitalize any portion of the bonus paid to the corporate officer.

Example (6). Corporate acquisition; integration costs. Assume the same facts as in Example 4, except that, before and after the acquisition is consummated, R incurs costs to relocate personnel and equipment, provide severance benefits to terminated employees, integrate records and information systems, prepare new financial statements for the combined entity, and reduce redundancies in the combined business operations. Under paragraph (c)(6) of this section, these costs do not facilitate the acquisition of T. Accordingly, R is not required to capitalize any of these costs under this section.

Example (7). Corporate acquisition; compensation to target's employees. Assume the same facts as in Example 4, except that, prior to the acquisition, certain employees of T held unexercised options issued pursuant to T's stock option plan. These options granted the employees the right to purchase T stock at a fixed option price. The options did not have a readily ascertainable value (within the meaning of § 1.83-7(b)), and thus no amount was included in the employees' income when the options were granted. As a condition of the acquisition, T is required to terminate its stock option plan. T therefore agrees to pay its employees who hold unexercised stock options the difference between the option price and the current value of T's stock in consideration of their agreement to cancel their unexercised options. Under paragraph (d)(1) of this section, T is not required to capitalize the amounts paid to its employees. See section 83 for the treatment of amounts received in cancellation of stock options.

Example (8). Asset acquisition; employee compensation. N corporation owns tangible and intangible assets that constitute a trade or business. M corporation purchases all the assets of N in a taxable transaction. Under paragraph (a)(1) of this section, M must capitalize amounts paid to facilitate the acquisition of the assets of N. Under paragraph (d)(1) of this section, no portion of the salaries of M's employees who work on the acquisition are treated as facilitating the transaction.

Example (9). Corporate acquisition; retainer. Y corporation's outside counsel charges Y $60,000 for services rendered in facilitating the friendly acquisition of the stock of Y corporation by X corporation. Y has an agreement with its outside counsel under which Y pays an annual retainer of $50,000. Y's outside counsel has the right to offset amounts billed for any legal services rendered against the annual retainer. Pursuant to this agreement, Y's outside counsel offsets $50,000 of the legal fees from the acquisition against the retainer and bills Y for the balance of $10,000. The $60,000 legal fee is an amount paid to facilitate the acquisition of an ownership interest in Y as described in paragraph (a)(3) of this section. Y must capitalize the full amount of the $60,000 legal fee.

Example (10). Corporate acquisition; antitrust defense costs. On March 1, 2005, V corporation enters into an agreement with X corporation to acquire all of the outstanding stock of X. On April 1, 2005, federal and state regulators file suit against V to prevent the acquisition of X on the ground that the acquisition violates antitrust laws. V enters into a consent agreement with regulators on May 1, 2005, that allows the acquisition to proceed, but requires V to hold separate the business operations of X pending the outcome of the antitrust suit and subjects V to possible divestiture. V acquires title to all of the outstanding stock of X on June 1, 2005. After June 1, 2005, the regulators pursue antitrust litigation against V seeking rescission of the acquisition. V pays $50,000 to its outside counsel for services rendered after June 1, 2005, to defend against the antitrust litigation. V ultimately prevails in the antitrust litigation. V's costs to defend the antitrust litigation are costs to facilitate its acquisition of the stock of X under paragraph (a)(2) of this section and must be capitalized. Although title to the shares of X passed to V prior to the date V incurred costs to defend the antitrust litigation, the amounts paid by V are paid in the process of pursuing the acquisition of the stock of X because the acquisition was not complete until the antitrust litigation was ultimately resolved. V must capitalize the $50,000 in legal fees.

Example (11). Corporate acquisition; defensive measures. (i) On January 15, 2005, Y corporation, a publicly traded corporation, becomes the target of a hostile takeover attempt by Z corporation. In an effort to defend against the takeover, Y pays legal fees to seek an injunction against the takeover and investment banking fees to locate a potential "white knight" acquirer. Y also pays amounts to complete a defensive recapitalization, and pays $50,000 to an investment banker for a fairness opinion regarding Z's initial offer. Y's efforts to enjoin the takeover and locate a white knight acquirer are unsuccessful, and on March 15, 2005, Y's board of directors decides to abandon its defense against the takeover and negotiate with Z in an effort to obtain the highest possible price for its shareholders. After Y abandons its defense against the takeover, Y pays an investment banker $1,000,000 for a second fairness opinion and for services rendered in negotiating with Z.

(ii) The legal fees paid by Y to seek an injunction against the takeover are not amounts paid in the process of investigating or otherwise pursuing the transaction with Z. Accordingly, these legal fees are not required to be capitalized under this section.

(iii) The investment banking fees paid to search for a white knight acquirer do not facilitate an acquisition of Y by a white knight because none of Y's costs with respect to a white knight were inherently facilitative amounts and because Y did not reach the date described in paragraph (e)(1) of this section with respect to a white knight. Accordingly, these amounts are not required to be capitalized under this section.

(iv) The amounts paid by Y to investigate and complete the recapitalization must be capitalized under paragraph (a)(4) of this section.

(v) The $50,000 paid to the investment bankers for a fairness opinion during Y's defense against the takeover and the $1,000,000 paid to the investment bankers after Y abandons its defense against the takeover are inherently facilitative amounts with respect to the transaction with Z and must be capitalized under paragraph (a)(3) of this section.

Example (12). Corporate acquisition; acquisition by white knight. (i) Assume the same facts as in Example 11, except that Y's investment bankers identify three potential white knight acquirers: U corporation, V corporation, and W corporation. Y pays its investment bankers to conduct due diligence on the three potential white knight acquirers. On March 15, 2005, Y's board of directors approves a tentative acquisition agreement under which W agrees to acquire all of the stock of Y, and the investment bankers stop due diligence on U and V. On June 15, 2005, W acquires all of the stock of Y.

(ii) Under paragraph (e)(1) of this section, the amounts paid to conduct due diligence on U, V, and W prior to March 15, 2005 (the date of board of directors' approval) are not amounts paid to facilitate the acquisition of the stock of Y and are not required to be capitalized under this section. However, the amounts paid to conduct due diligence on W on and after March 15, 2005, facilitate the acquisition of the stock of Y and are required to be capitalized.

Example (13). Corporate acquisition; mutually exclusive costs. (i) Assume the same facts as in Example 11, except that Y's investment banker finds W, a white knight. Y and W execute a letter of intent on March 10, 2005. Under the terms of the letter of intent, Y must pay W a $10,000,000 break-up fee if the merger with W does not occur. On April 1, 2005, Z significantly increases the amount of its offer, and Y decides to accept Z's offer instead of merging with W. Y pays its investment banker $500,000 for inherently facilitative costs with respect to the potential merger with W. Y also pays its investment banker $2,000,000 for due diligence costs with respect to the potential merger with W, $1,000,000 of which relates to services performed on or after March 10, 2005.

(ii) Y's $500,000 payment for inherently facilitative costs and Y's $1,000,000 payment for due diligence activities performed on or after March 10, 2005 (the date the letter of intent with W is entered into) facilitate the potential merger with W. Because Y could not merge with both W and Z, under paragraph (c)(8) of this section the $500,000 and $1,000,000 payments also facilitate the transaction between Y and Z. Accordingly, Y must capitalize the $500,000 and $1,000,000 payments as amounts that facilitate the transaction with Z.

(iii) Similarly, because Y could not merge with both W and Z, under paragraph (c)(8) of this section the $10,000,000 termination payment facilitates the transaction between Y and Z. Accordingly, Y must capitalize the $10,000,000 termination payment as an amount that facilitates the transaction with Z.

Example (14). Break-up fee; transactions not mutually exclusive. N corporation and U corporation enter into an agreement under which U would acquire all the stock or all the assets of N in exchange for U stock. Under the terms of the agreement, if either party terminates the agreement, the terminating party must pay the other party $10,000,000. U decides to terminate the agreement and pays N $10,000,000. Shortly thereafter, U acquires all the stock of V corporation, a competitor of N. U had the financial resources to have acquired both N and V. U's $10,000,000 payment does not facilitate U's acquisition of V. Accordingly, U is not required to capitalize the $10,000,000 payment under this section.

Example (15). Corporate reorganization; initial public offering. Y corporation is a closely held corporation. Y's board of directors authorizes an initial public offering of Y's stock to fund future growth. Y pays $5,000,000 in professional fees for investment banking services related to the determination of the offering price and legal services related to the development of the offering prospectus and the registration and issuance of stock. The investment banking and legal services are performed both before and after board authorization. Under paragraph (a)(8) of this section, the $5,000,000 is an amount paid to facilitate a stock issuance.

Example (16). Auction. (i) N corporation seeks to dispose of all of the stock of its wholly owned subsidiary, P corporation, through an auction process and requests that each bidder submit a non-binding purchase offer in the form of a draft agreement. Q corporation hires an investment banker to assist in the preparation of Q's bid to acquire P and to conduct a due diligence investigation of P. On July 1, 2005, Q submits its draft agreement. On August 1, 2005, N informs Q that it has accepted Q's offer, and presents Q with a signed letter of intent to sell all of the stock of P to Q. On August 5, 2005, Q's board of directors approves the terms of the transaction and authorizes Q to execute the letter of intent. Q executes a binding letter of intent with N on August 6, 2005.

(ii) Under paragraph (e)(1) of this section, the amounts paid by Q to its investment banker that are not inherently facilitative and that are paid for activities performed prior to August 5, 2005 (the date Q's board of directors approves the transaction) are not amounts paid to facilitate the acquisition of P. Amounts paid by Q to its investment banker for activities performed on or after August 5, 2005, and amounts paid by Q to its investment banker that are inherently facilitative amounts within the meaning of paragraph (e)(2) of this section are required to be capitalized under this section.

Example (17). Stock distribution. Z corporation distributes natural gas throughout state Y. The federal government brings an antitrust action against Z seeking divestiture of certain of Z's natural gas distribution assets. As a result of a court ordered divestiture, Z and the federal government agree to a plan of divestiture that requires Z to organize a subsidiary to receive the divested assets and to distribute the stock of the subsidiary to its shareholders. During 2005, Z pays $300,000 to various independent contractors for the following services: studying customer demand in the area to be served by the divested assets, identifying assets to be transferred to the subsidiary, organizing the subsidiary, structuring the transfer of assets to the subsidiary to qualify as a tax-free transaction to Z, and distributing the stock of the subsidiary to the stockholders. Under paragraph (c)(3) of this section, Z is not required to capitalize any portion of the $300,000 payments.

Example (18). Bankruptcy reorganization. (i) X corporation is the defendant in numerous lawsuits alleging tort liability based on X's role in manufacturing certain defective products. X files a petition for reorganization under Chapter 11 of the Bankruptcy Code in an effort to manage all of the lawsuits in a single proceeding. X pays its outside counsel to prepare the petition and plan of reorganization, to analyze adequate protection under the plan, to attend hearings before the Bankruptcy Court concerning the plan, and to defend against motions by creditors and tort claimants to strike the taxpayer's plan.

(ii) X's reorganization under Chapter 11 of the Bankruptcy Code is a reorganization within the meaning of paragraph (a)(4) of this section. Under paragraph (c)(4) of this section, amounts paid by X to its outside counsel to prepare, analyze or obtain approval of the portion of X's plan of reorganization that resolves X's tort liability do not facilitate the reorganization and are not required to be capitalized, provided that such amounts would have been treated as ordinary and necessary business expenses under section 162 had the bankruptcy proceeding not been instituted. All other amounts paid by X to its outside counsel for the services described above (including all amounts paid to prepare the bankruptcy petition) facilitate the reorganization and must be capitalized.

(m) Effective date. This section applies to amounts paid or incurred on or after December 31, 2003.

(n) Accounting method changes. *(1) In general.* A taxpayer seeking to change a method of accounting to comply with this section must secure the consent of the Commissioner in accordance with the requirements of § 1.446-1(e). For the taxpayer's first taxable year ending on or after December 31, 2003, the taxpayer is granted the consent of the Commissioner to change its method of accounting to comply with this section, provided the taxpayer follows the administrative procedures issued under § 1.446-1(e)(3)(ii) for obtaining the Commissioner's automatic consent to a change in accounting method (for further guidance, for example, see Rev. Proc. 2002-9 (2002-1 C.B. 327) and § 601.601(d)(2)(ii)(b) of this chapter).

(2) Scope limitations. Any limitations on obtaining the automatic consent of the Commissioner do not apply to a taxpayer seeking to change to a method of accounting to comply with this section for its first taxable year ending on or after December 31, 2003.

(3) Section 481(a) adjustment. The section 481(a) adjustment for a change in method of accounting to comply with this section for a taxpayer's first taxable year ending on or after December 31, 2003 is determined by taking into account only amounts paid or incurred in taxable years ending on or after January 24, 2002.

T.D. 9107, 12/31/2003.

§ 1.263(b)-1 Expenditures for advertising or promotion of good will.

Caution: The Treasury has not yet amended Reg § 1.263(b)-1 to reflect changes made by P.L. 101-508.

See § 1.162-14 for the rules applicable to a corporation which has elected to capitalize expenditures for advertising or the promotion of good will under the provisions of section 733 or section 451 of the Internal Revenue Code of 1939, in computing its excess profits tax credit under subchapter E, chapter 2, or subchapter D, chapter 1, of the Internal Revenue Code of 1939.

T.D. 6313, 9/16/58.

§ 1.263(c)-1 Intangible drilling and development costs in the case of oil and gas wells.

For rules relating to the option to deduct as expenses intangible drilling and development costs in the case of oil and gas wells, see § 1.612-4.

T.D. 6313, 9/16/58.

§ 1.263(e)-1 Expenditures in connection with certain railroad rolling stock.

Caution: The Treasury has not yet amended Reg § 1.263(e)-1 to reflect changes made by P.L. 94-455.

(a) Allowance of deduction. *(1) Election.* Under section 263(e), for any taxable year beginning after December 31, 1969, a taxpayer may elect to treat certain expenditures paid or incurred during such taxable year as deductible repairs under section 162 or 212. This election applies only to expenditures described in paragraph (c) of this section in connection with the rehabilitation of a unit of railroad rolling stock (as defined in paragraph (b)(2) of this section) used by a domestic common carrier by railroad (as defined in paragraphs (b)(3) and (4) of this section). However, an election under section 263(e) may not be made with respect to expenditures in connection with any unit of railroad rolling stock for which an election under section 263(f) and the regulations thereunder is in effect. An election made under section 263(e) is an annual election which may be made with respect to one or more of the units of railroad rolling stock owned by the taxpayer.

(2) Special 20 percent rule. Section 263(e) shall not apply if, under paragraph (d) of this section, expenditures paid or incurred during any period of 12 calendar months in connection with the rehabilitation of a unit exceed 20 percent of the basis (as defined in paragraph (b)(1) of this section) of such unit in the hands of the taxpayer. However, section 263(e) does not constitute a limit on the deduction of expenditures for repairs which are deductible without regard to such section. Accordingly, amounts otherwise deductible as repairs will continue to be deductible even though such amounts exceed 20 percent of the basis of the unit of railroad rolling stock in the hands of the taxpayer.

(3) Time and manner of making election. (i) An election by a taxpayer under section 263(e) shall be made by a statement to that effect attached to its income tax return or amended income tax return for the taxable year for which the election is made if such return or amended return is filed no later than the time prescribed by law (including extensions thereof) for filing the return for the taxable year of election. An election under section 263(e) may be made with respect to one or more of the units of railroad rolling stock owned by the taxpayer. If an election is not made within the time and in the manner prescribed in this subparagraph, no election may be made (by the filing of an amended return or in any other manner) with respect to the taxable year.

(ii) If the taxpayer has filed a return on or before [the 30th day after the date of publication in the FEDERAL REGISTER of final regulations under section 263(e)] and has claimed a deduction under section 162 or 212 by reason of section 263(e), and if the taxpayer does not desire to make an election under section 263(e) for the taxable year with respect to which such return was filed, the taxpayer shall file an amended return for such taxable year on or before [the 90th day after such date of publication], and shall pay any additional tax due for such year. The taxpayer shall also file an amended return for each taxable year which is affected by the filing of an amended return under the preceding sentence and shall pay any additional tax due for such year. Nothing in this subdivision shall be construed as extending the time specified in section 6511 within which a claim for credit or refund may be filed.

(iii) If an election under section 263(e) was not made at the time the return for a taxable year was filed, and it is subsequently determined that an expenditure was erroneously treated as an expenditure which was not in connection with rehabilitation (as determined under paragraph (c) of this section), an election under section 263(e) may be made with respect to the unit of railroad rolling stock for which such expenditure was made for such taxable year, notwithstanding any provision in this subparagraph (3) to the contrary. Nothing in this subdivision shall be construed as extending the time specified in section 6511 within which a claim for credit or refund may be filed.

(iv) The statement required by subdivision (i) of this subparagraph shall include the following information:

(a) The total number of units of railroad rolling stock with respect to which an election is being made under section 263(e).

(b) The aggregate basis (as defined in paragraph (b)(1) of this section) of the units described in (a) of this subdivision (iv), and

(c) The total deduction being claimed under section 263(e) for the taxable year.

(b) Definitions. *(1) Basis.* (i) In general, for purposes of section 263(e) the basis of a unit of rolling stock shall be the adjusted basis of such unit determined without regard to the adjustments provided in paragraphs (1), (2), and (3) of section 1016(a) and section 1017. Thus, the basis of property would generally be its cost without regard to adjustments to basis such as for depreciation or for capital improvements. If the basis of a unit in the hands of a transferee is determined in whole or in part by reference to its basis in the hands of the transferor, for example, by reason of the application of section 362 (relating to basis to corporations), 374 (relating to gain or loss not recognized in certain railroad reorganizations) or 723 (relating to the basis of property contributed to a partnership), then the basis of such unit in the hands of the transferor for purposes of section 263(e) shall be its basis for purposes of section 263(e) in the hands of the transferee. Similarly, when the basis of a unit of railroad rolling stock in the hands of the taxpayer is determined in whole or in part by reference to the basis of another unit, for example, by reason of the application of the first sentence of section 1033(c) (relating to involuntary conversions), then the basis of the latter unit for purposes of section 263(e) shall be the basis for purposes of section 263(e) of the former unit. The question whether a capital expenditure in connection with a unit of railroad rolling stock results in the retirement of such unit and the creation of another unit of railroad rolling stock shall be determined without regard to rules under the uniform system of accounts prescribed by the Interstate Commerce Commission.

(ii) For example, if a unit of railroad rolling stock has a cost to M of $10,000 and because of depreciation adjustments of $4,000 and capital expenditures of $3,000, such unit has an adjusted basis in the hands of M of $9,000, the basis for purposes of section 263(e) of such unit in the hands of M is $10,000. Further, if M transfers such unit to N in a transaction in which no gain or loss is recognized such as, for example, a transaction to which section 351(a) (relating to a transfer to a corporation controlled by the transferor) applies, the basis of such unit for purposes of section 263(e) is $10,000 in the hands of N.

(2) Railroad rolling stock. For purposes of this section, the term "unit" or "unit of railroad rolling stock" means a unit of transportation equipment the expenditures for which are of a type chargeable (or in the case of property leased to a domestic common carrier by railroad, would be chargeable) to the equipment investment accounts in the uniform system of accounts for railroad companies prescribed by the Interstate Commerce Commission (49 CFR Part 1201), but only if (i) such unit exclusively moves on, moves under, or is guided by rail, and (ii) such unit is not a locomotive. Thus, for example, a unit of railroad rolling stock includes a box car, a gondola car, a passenger car, a car designed to carry truck trailers and containerized freight, a wreck crane, and a bunk car. However, such term does not include equipment which does not exclusively move on, move under, or is not exclusively guided by rail such as, for example, a barge, a tugboat, a container which is used on cars designed to carry containerized freight, a truck trailer, or an automobile. A locomotive is self-propelled equipment, the sole function of which is to push or pull railroad rolling stock. Thus, a self-propelled passenger or freight car is not a locomotive.

(3) Domestic common carrier by railroad. The term "domestic common carrier by railroad" means a railroad subject to regulation under Part I of the Interstate Commerce Act (49 U.S.C. 1 *et seq.*) or a railroad which would be subject to regulation under Part I of the Interstate Commerce Act if it were engaged in interstate commerce.

(4) Use. For purposes of this section, a unit of railroad rolling stock is not used by a domestic common carrier by railroad if it is owned by a person other than a domestic common carrier by railroad and (i) is exclusively used for transportation by the owner or (ii) is exclusively used for transportation by another person which is not a domestic common carrier by railroad. Thus, for example, a unit of railroad rolling stock which is owned by a person which is not a domestic common carrier by railroad and is leased to a manufacturing company by the owner is not a unit of railroad rolling stock used by a domestic common carrier by railroad.

(c) Expenditures considered in connection with rehabilitation. For purposes of section 263(e) and this section all expenditures which would be properly chargeable to capital account but for the application of section 263(e) or (f) shall be considered to be expenditures in connection with the rehabilitation of a unit of railroad rolling stock. Expenditures which are paid or incurred in connection with incidental repairs or maintenance of a unit of railroad rolling stock and which are deductible without regard to section 263(e) or (f) shall not be included in any determination or computation under section 263(e) and shall not be treated as paid or incurred in connection with the rehabilitation of a unit of railroad rolling stock for purposes of section 263(e). The determination of whether an item would be, but for section 263(e) or (f), properly chargeable to capital account shall be made in a manner consistent with the principles for classification of expenditures as between capital and expenses under the Internal Revenue Code. See, for example, §§ 1.162-4, 1.263(a)-1, 1.263(a)-2, and paragraph (a)(4)(ii) and (iii) of § 1.446-1. An expenditure shall be classified as capital or as expense without regard to its classification under the uniform system of accounts prescribed by the Interstate Commerce Commission.

(d) 20-percent limitation. *(1) In general.* No expenditures in connection with the rehabilitation of a unit of railroad rolling stock shall be treated as a deductible repair by reason of an election under section 263(e) if, during any period of 12 calendar months in which the month the expenditure is included falls, all such expenditures exceed an amount equal to 20 percent of the basis (as defined in paragraph (b)(1) of this section) of such unit in the hands of the taxpayer. All such expenditures shall be included in the computation of the 20-percent limitation even if such expenditures were deducted under section 263(f) in either the preceding or succeeding taxable year. Solely for purposes of the 20-percent limitation in this paragraph, such expenditures shall be deemed to be included in the month in which a rehabilitation of the unit of railroad rolling stock is completed. For the requirement that expenditures treated as repairs solely by reason of an election under section 263(e) be deducted in the taxable year paid or incurred, see paragraph (a) of this section.

(2) 12-month period. For purposes of this section, any period of 12 calendar months shall consist of any 12 consecutive calendar months except that calendar months prior to the calendar month of January 1970 shall not be included in determining such period.

(3) Period for certain corporate acquisitions. If a unit of railroad rolling stock to which section 263(e) applies is sold, exchanged, or otherwise disposed of in a transaction in which its basis in the hands of the transferee is determined in whole or in part by reference to its basis in the hands of the transferor (see paragraph (b)(1) of this section), calendar months during which such unit is in the hands of the transferor and in the hands of such transferee shall both be included in the calendar months used by the transferor and the transferee to determine any period of 12 calendar months for purposes of section 263(e).

(4) Deduction allowed in year paid or incurred. If, based on the information available when the income tax return for the taxable year is filed, an expenditure paid or incurred in such taxable year would be deductible by reason of the application of section 263(e) but for the fact that it cannot be established whether the 20-percent limitation in subparagraph (1) of this paragraph will be exceeded, the expenditure shall be deducted for such taxable year. If by reason of the application of such 20-percent limitation it is subsequently determined that such expenditure is not deductible as a repair, an amended return shall be filed for the year in which such deduction was treated as a deductible repair and additional tax, if any, for such year shall be paid. Appropriate adjustment with respect to the taxpayer's tax liability for any other affected year shall be made. Nothing in this subparagraph shall be construed as extending the time specified in section 6511 within which a claim for credit or refund may be filed.

(e) Recordkeeping requirements. *(1) In general.* Such records as will enable the accurate determination of the expenditures which may be subject to the treatment provided in section 263(e) shall be maintained. No deduction shall be allowed under section 162 or 212 by reason of section 263(e) with respect to a unit unless the taxpayer substantiates by adequate records that expenditures in connection with such unit of railroad rolling stock meet the requirements and limitations of this section.

(2) Separate records. A separate section 263(e) record shall be maintained for each unit with respect to which an election under section 263(e) is made. Such record shall—

(i) Identify the unit,

(ii) State the basis (as defined in paragraph (b)(1) of this section) and the date of acquisition of the unit,

(iii) Enumerate for each unit the amount of all expenditures incurred in connection with rehabilitation of such unit which would, but for section 263(e) or (f), be properly chargeable to capital account (including expenditures incurred by the taxpayer in connection with rehabilitation of such unit undertaken by a person other than the taxpayer) regardless of whether such expenditures during any 12-month period exceed 20 percent of the basis of such unit.

(iv) Describe the nature of the work in connection with each expenditure, and

(v) Specify the calendar month in which the rehabilitation is completed and the taxable year in which each expenditure is paid or incurred. A section 263(e) record need only be prepared for a unit of railroad rolling stock for the period beginning on the first day of the eleventh calendar month immediately preceding the month in which the rehabilitation of such unit is completed and ending on the last day of the eleventh calendar month immediately succeeding such month. No section 263(e) record need be prepared for calendar months before January 1970.

(3) Records for certain expenditures. Expenditures determined to be incidental repairs and maintenance (referred to in paragraph (c) of this section) shall not be entered in the section 263(e) record. However, each taxpayer shall maintain records to reflect that such expenditures are properly deductible.

(4) Convenience rule. In general, expenditures and information maintained in compliance with subparagraphs (1) and (2) of this paragraph shall be recorded in the section 263(e) record of the specific unit with respect to which such expenditures are incurred. However, when a group of units of the same type are rehabilitated in a single project and the expenditure for each unit in the project will approximate the average expenditure per unit for the project, expenditures for the project may be aggregated without regard to the unit in the project with respect to which each expenditure is connected, and an amount equal to the aggregate expenditures for the project divided by the number of units in the project may be entered in the section 263(e) account of each unit in the project.

(f) Examples. The provisions of this section may be illustrated by the following examples:

Example (1). M Corporation, a domestic common carrier by railroad, uses the calendar year as its taxable year. M owns and uses several gondola cars to which an election under section 263(e) applies for its taxable years 1970-1972. Gondola car #1 has a basis (defined in paragraph (b)(1) of this section) of $10,000. No expenditures properly chargeable to the section 263(e) record are made on gondola car #1 in 1970 and 1971, except in January 1971. In January 1971, M at a cost of $1,500 performed rehabilitation work on gondola car #1. Such amount was properly entered in the section 263(e) record for gondola car #1. Since the expenditures in such record do not exceed an amount equal to 20 percent of the basis of gondola car #1 ($2,000) during any period of 12 calendar months in which January 1971 falls, the expenditures during January 1971 shall be treated as a deductible expense regardless of what the treatment would have been if section 263(e) had not been enacted.

Example (2). Assume the same facts as in example (1). Assume further that for 1970, 1971, and 1972, only the following expenditures in connection with rehabilitation which would, but for section 263(e), be properly chargeable to capital account were deemed included for gondola car #2:

(a) December 1970	$1,500
(b) November 1971	600
(c) December 1971	400
(d) January 1972	1,050

Assume further that gondola car #2 has a basis (as defined in paragraph (b)(1) of this section) equal to $10,000, that M files its tax return by September 15 following each taxable year, and that each rehabilitation was completed in the month in which expenditures in connection with it were incurred. Any expenditures in connection with each gondola car (#1 or #2) have no effect on the treatment of expenditures in connection with the other gondola car. With respect to gondola car #2, the expenditures of December 1970 are treated as deductible repairs at the time M's income tax return for 1970 is filed because, based on the information available when the income tax return for 1970 is filed, such expenditure would be deductible by reason of application of section 263(e) but for the fact that it cannot be established whether the 20-percent limitation in paragraph (d)(1) of this section will be exceeded. Nevertheless, because such expenditures during the period of 12 calendar months including calendar months December 1970 and November 1971 exceed $2,000, the December 1970 rehabilitation expenditures are not subject to the provisions of section 263(e). Because such rehabilitation expenditures during the period of 12 calendar months including calendar months February 1971 and January 1972 exceed $2,000, rehabilitation expenditures in 1971 are not subject to the provisions of section 263(e). Similarly, the 1972 rehabilitation expenditures are not subject to the provisions of section 263(e).

T.D. 7257, 2/9/73.

§ 1.263(f)-1 Reasonable repair allowance.

Caution: The Treasury has not yet amended Reg § 1.263(f)-1 to reflect changes made by P.L. 97-34.

(a) For rules regarding the election of the repair allowance authorized by section 263(f), the definition of repair allowance property, and the conditions under which an election may be made, see paragraphs (d)(2) and (f) of § 1.167(a)-11. An election may be made under this section for a taxable year only if the taxpayer makes an election under § 1.167(a)-11 for such taxable year.

T.D. 7272, 4/20/73, amend T.D. 7593, 1/25/79.

Proposed § 1.263(g)-1 Treatment of interest and carrying charges in the case of straddles; in general. [*For Preamble, see ¶ 152,157*]

(a) Under section 263(g), no deduction is allowed for interest and carrying charges allocable to personal property that is part of astraddle (as defined in section 1092(c)). The purpose of section 263(g) is to coordinate the character and the timing of items of income and loss attributable to a taxpayer's positions that are part of a straddle. In order to prevent payments or accruals related to a straddle transaction from giving rise to recognition of deductions or losses before related income is recognized and to prevent the items of loss and income from having different character, no deduction is allowed for interest and carrying charges properly allocable to personal property that is part of a straddle. Rather, such amounts are chargeable to the capital account of the personal property to which the interest and carrying charges are properly allocable.

(b) Section 263(g) does not apply if none of the taxpayer's positions that are part of the straddle are personal property. Section 263(g) also does not apply to hedging transactions as defined in section 1256(e) (see section 263(g)(3)) or to securities to which the mark-to-market accounting method provided by section 475 applies (see section 475(d)(1)).

(c) Section 1.263(g)-2 provides a definition of personal property for purposes of section 263(g) and §§ 1.263(g)-1 through 1.263(g)-5. Section 1.263(g)-3 provides a definition of interest and carrying charges for purposes of section 263(g), section 1092, §§ 1.263(g)-1 through 1.263(g)-5, and § 1.1092(b)-4T. Section 1.263(g)-4 provides a set of allocation rules governing the capitalization of amounts to which section 263(g) applies.

Proposed § 1.263(g)-2 Personal property to which interest and carrying charges may properly be allocable. [*For Preamble, see ¶ 152,157*]

(a) Definition of personal property. For purposes of section 263(g) and of §§ 1.263(g)-1 through 1.263(g)-5, personal property means property, whether or not actively traded, that is not real property. For purposes of the preceding sentence, a position in personal property may itself be property. In general, however, a position in personal property is not property of a taxpayer unless the position confers or may confer substantial rights on the taxpayer.

(1) Application to certain financial instruments. Personal property includes a stockholder's ownership of common stock, a holder's ownership of a debt instrument, and either party's position in a forward contract or in a conventional swap agreement. Personal property does not include a position that imposes obligations but does not confer substantial rights on the taxpayer. Therefore, the obligor's position in a debt instrument generally is not personal property, even though the obligor may have typical rights of a debtor, such as the right to prepay the debt. However, the obligor on a debt instrument has a position in any personal property underlying the debt instrument. See § 1.1092(d)-1(d).

(2) Options. For the purposes of applying this section, a put option or call option imposes obligations but does not confer substantial rights on the grantor, whether or not the option is cash-settled.

(b) Example. The following example illustrates the rules stated in paragraph (a) of this section:

Example. (i) Facts. A purchases 100 ounces of gold at a cost of $x. A transfers the 100 ounces of gold to a trust that issues multiple classes of trust certificates and is treated as a partnership for tax purposes. In return, A receives two trust certificates that are not personal property of a type that is actively traded within the meaning of section 1092(d)(1). One certificate entitles A to a payment on termination of the trust at the end of four years equal to the value of the 100 ounces of gold up to a maximum value of $(x + y). The other certificate entitles A to a payment equal to the amount by which the value of 100 ounces of gold exceeds $(x + y) on termination of the trust. A sells the second certificate and keeps the first certificate.

(ii) Analysis. The trust certificate retained by A is property that is not real property. In addition, ownership of the trust certificate confers certain substantial rights on A. Therefore, although the trust certificate is not personal property of a type that is actively traded, A's interest in the trust certificate is personal property for purposes of section 263(g).

Proposed § 1.263(g)-3 Interest and carrying charges properly allocable to personal property that is part of a straddle. [*For Preamble, see ¶ 152,157*]

(a) In general. For purposes of section 263(g), section 1092, §§ 1.263(g)-1 through 1.263(g)-5, and § 1.1092(b)-4T, interest and carrying charges properly allocable to personal property that is part of a straddle means the excess of interest and carrying charges (as defined in paragraph (b) of this section) over the allowable income offsets (as defined in paragraph (e) of this section).

(b) Interest and carrying charges. Interest and carrying charges are otherwise deductible amounts paid or accrued with respect to indebtedness or other financing incurred or continued to purchase or carry personal property that is part of a straddle and otherwise deductible amounts paid or incurred to carry personal property that is part of a straddle. As provided in section 263(g)(2), interest includes any amount paid or incurred in connection with personal property used in a short sale. Interest and carrying charges include—

(1) Otherwise deductible payments or accruals (including interest and original issue discount) on indebtedness or other financing issued or continued to purchase or carry personal property that is part of a straddle;

(2) Otherwise deductible fees or expenses paid or incurred in connection with acquiring or holding personal property that is part of a straddle including, but not limited to, fees or expenses incurred to purchase, insure, store, maintain or transport the personal property; and

(3) Other otherwise deductible payments or accruals on financial instruments that are part of a straddle or that carry part of a straddle.

(c) Indebtedness or other financing incurred or continued to purchase or carry personal property that is part of a straddle. For purposes of paragraph (b)(1) of this section, indebtedness or other financing that is incurred or continued to purchase or carry personal property that is part of a straddle includes—

(1) Indebtedness or other financing the proceeds of which are used directly or indirectly to purchase or carry personal property that is part of the straddle;

(2) Indebtedness or other financing that is secured directly or indirectly by personal property that is part of the straddle; and

(3) Indebtedness or other financing the payments on which are determined by reference to payments with respect to the personal property or the value of, or change in value of, the personal property.

(d) Financial instruments that are part of a straddle or that carry part of a straddle. For purposes of paragraph (b)(3), financial instruments that are part of a straddle or that carry part of a straddle include—

(1) A financial instrument that is part of the straddle;

(2) A financial instrument that is issued in connection with the creation or acquisition of a position in personal property if that position is part of the straddle;

(3) A financial instrument that is sold or marketed as part of an arrangement that involves a taxpayer's position in personal property that is part of the straddle and that is purported to result in either economic realization of all or part of the appreciation in an asset without simultaneous recognition of taxable income or a current tax deduction (for interest, carrying charges, payments on a notional principal contract, or otherwise) reflecting a payment or expense that is economically offset by an increase in value that is not concurrently recognized for tax purposes or has a different tax character (for example, an interest payment that is economically offset by an increase in value that may result in a capital gain in a later tax period); and

(4) Any other financial instrument if the totality of the facts and circumstances support a reasonable inference that the issuance, purchase, or continuation of the financial instrument by the taxpayer was intended to purchase or carry personal property that is part of the straddle.

(e) Allowable income offsets. The allowable income offsets are:

(1) The amount of interest (including original issue discount) includible in gross income for the taxable year with respect to such personal property;

(2) Any amount treated as ordinary income under section 1271(a)(3)(A), 1278, or 1281(a) with respect to such personal property for the taxable year;

(3) The excess of any dividends includible in gross income with respect to such property for the taxable year over the amount of any deductions allowable with respect to such dividends under section 243, 244, or 245;

(4) Any amount that is a payment with respect to a security loan (within the meaning of section 512(a)(5)) includible in income with respect to the personal property for the taxable year; and

(5) Any amount that is a receipt or accrual includible in income for the taxable year with respect to a financial instrument described in § 1.263(g)-3(d) to the extent the financial instrument is entered into to purchase or carry the personal property.

Proposed § 1.263(g)-4 Rules for allocating amounts to personal property that is part of a straddle. [*For Preamble, see ¶ 152,157*]

(a) Allocation rules. *(1)* Interest and carrying charges paid or accrued on indebtedness or other financing issued or continued to purchase or carry personal property that is part of a straddle are allocated, in the order listed—

(i) To personal property that is part of the straddle purchased, directly or indirectly, with the proceeds of the indebtedness or other financing;

(ii) To personal property that is part of the straddle and directly or indirectly secures the indebtedness or other financing; or

(iii) If all or a portion of such interest and carrying charges are determined by reference to the value or change in value of personal property, to such personal property.

(2) Fees and expenses described in § 1.263(g)-3(b)(2) are allocated to the personal property, the acquisition or holding of which resulted in the fees and expenses being paid or incurred.

(3) In all other cases, interest and carrying charges are allocated to personal property that is part of a straddle in the manner that under all the facts and circumstances is most appropriate.

(b) Coordination with other provisions. In the case of a short sale, section 263(g) applies after section 263(h). See sections 263(g)(4)(A) and (h)(6). In case of an obligation to which section 1277 (dealing with deferral of interest deduction allocable to accrued market discount) or 1282 (dealing with deferral of interest deduction allocable to certain accruals on short-term indebtedness) applies, section 263(g) applies after section 1277 and section 1282. See section 263(g)(4)(B). Capitalization under section 263(g) applies before loss deferral under section 1092.

(c) Examples. The following examples illustrate the rules stated in §§ 1.263(g)-2, 1.263(g)-3, and 1.263(g)-4.

Example (1). Cash and Carry Silver. (i) Facts. On January 1, 2002, A borrows $x at 6% interest and uses the proceeds to purchase y ounces of silver from B. At approximately the same time, A enters into a forward contract with C to deliver y ounces of silver to C in one year.

(ii) Analysis. The y ounces of silver and the forward contract to deliver y ounces of silver in one year are offsetting positions with respect to the same personal property and therefore constitute a straddle. See sections 1092(c)(1), (c)(3)(A)(i). The proceeds of the debt instrument were used to purchase personal property that is part of the straddle. Consequently, A's interest payments are interest and carrying charges properly allocable to personal property that is part of a straddle. See § 1.263(g)-3(b)(1) and (c)(1). Under § 1.263(g)-4(a)(1)(i), the interest payments must be charged to the capital account for the y ounces of silver purchased by A with the proceeds of the borrowing.

Example (2). Additional indebtedness issued to carry personal property. (i) Facts. The facts are the same as for Example 1 except that during the year 2002, the market price of silver increases and A is required to post variation margin as security for its obligation to deliver y ounces of silver to C. A incurs additional indebtedness to obtain funds necessary to meet A's variation margin requirement.

(ii) Analysis. The additional indebtedness is incurred to continue to carry A's holding of z ounces of silver. Consequently, A's interest payments on the additional indebtedness are interest and carrying charges properly allocable to personal property that is part of a straddle and must be charged to the capital account for the y ounces of silver.

Example (3). Contingent payment debt instrument. (i) Facts. On January 1, 2002, D enters into a contract to deliver x barrels of fuel oil to E on July 1, 2004, at an aggregate price equal to $y. Soon afterward, D issues a contingent payment debt instrument to F with a principal amount of $z and a 2-year term that pays interest quarterly at a rate determined at the beginning of each quarter equal to the greater of zero and the London Interbank Offered Rate (LIBOR) adjusted by an index that varies inversely with changes in the price of fuel oil (so that the interest rate increases as the price of fuel oil decreases and vice versa). The change in the aggregate amount of interest paid on the $z of debt due to the functioning of the index approximates the concurrent aggregate change in value of x barrels of fuel oil and, thus, the value of D's interest in the forward contract.

(ii) Analysis. The debt instrument and the forward contract are offsetting positions with respect to the same personal property and constitute a straddle. See section 1092(c)(1), (c)(3)(A)(i). When issued, the debt instrument is a position in personal property that is part of a straddle. See § 1.1092(d)-1(d). Consequently, D's interest payments are interest and carrying charges properly allocable to personal property that is part of a straddle and must be allocated to the capital account for the forward contract for the delivery of x barrels of fuel oil to E. See §§ 1.263(g)-3(b)(1), (b)(3), (c)(3), and (d)(1) and -4(a)(1)(iii).

Example (4). Financial instrument issued to carry personalproperty that is part of a straddle. (i) Facts. The facts are the same as for Example 3 except that D also enters into a two-year interest rate swap under which D receives LIBOR times a notional principal amount equal to $z and pays 7% times $z.

(ii) Analysis. Because of the relationship between the two-year debt instrument issued by D and the interest rate swap, the interest rate swap is a financial instrument that carries personal property that is part of a straddle. See § 1.263(g)-3(d)(4). Net payments made by D under the interest rate swap are chargeable to the capital account for the forward contract for the delivery of x barrels of fuel oil to E. Similarly, net payments received by D under the interest rate swap are allowable offsets. See § 1.263(g)-3(e)(5).

Example (5). Contingent payment debt instrument with embedded short position. (i) Facts. On January 1, 1998, G purchases 100,000 shares of the common stock of XYZ corporation (which is publicly traded). On January 1, 2002, the 100,000 shares of XYZ corporation common stock were worth $x per share. On that date, G issued a contingent payment debt instrument for $100,000x. The terms of the debt instrument provided that the holder would receive an annual payment of $2,000x on December 31 of each year up to and including the maturity date of December 31, 2007. On the maturity date, the holders would also receive a payment of $100,000x plus an additional amount, if the price of an XYZ share exceeded $1.2x on such date, equal to 100,000 times three-quarters of the amount of such excess per share. Thus, G's aggregate payments on the debt instrument varied directly with the increase in value in the XYZ shares.

(ii) Analysis. The debt instrument is a position in XYZ stock. See § 1.1092(d)-1(d). The XYZ stock is personal property within the meaning of section 1092(d)(3)(B) because the debt instrument is a position with respect to substantially similar or related property (other than stock) within the meaning of section 1092(d)(3)(B)(i)(II). See § 1.1092(d)-2(c). The debt instrument and the XYZ shares are offsetting positions with respect to the same personal property and constitute a straddle. See sections 1092(c)(1), (c)(3)(A)(i). Consequently, G's interest payments are interest and carrying charges properly allocable to personal property that is part of a straddle, see §§ 1.263(g)-3(b)(1), (b)(3), (c)(3), and (d)(1), and must be allocated to the capital account for the XYZ common stock, see § 1.263(g)-4(a)(1)(iii) and (a)(3).

Example (6). Straddle including partnership interest. (i) Facts. H borrows money from I to purchase 100 ounces of gold at a cost of $u. H transfers the 100 ounces of gold and $v to a newly created trust that issues multiple classes of trust certificates and is treated as a partnership for tax purposes. In return, H receives two trust certificates. One certificate entitles the holder to a payment on termination of the trust at the end of four years equal to the value of the 100 ounces of gold up to a maximum value of $(u + w). The other certificate entitles the holder to a payment equal to the amount by which the value of 100 ounces of gold exceeds $(u + w) on termination of the trust. H sells the second certificate and keeps the first certificate. H also enters into a forward contract to sell 100 ounces of gold for $1.12u per ounce on a date two years after creation of the trust. The trust uses part of the $v and similar cash contributions from other investors to pay costs of storing the gold held by the trust and allocates H's share of the expenses to H.

(ii) Analysis. The trust certificate retained by H and the forward contract entered into by H are personal property for the purposes of section 263(g). See § 1.263(g)-2(a). They are also offsetting positions and constitute a straddle. Section 1092(c)(1). The borrowing from I is an indebtedness incurred to purchase personal property that is part of a straddle. See §§ 1.263(g)-3(b)(1) and (c)(1). Similarly, the gold storage expenses are expenses incurred due to the taxpayer's holding personal property that is part of a straddle. See § 1.263(g)-3(b)(2). Therefore both the interest on the borrowing and the gold storage expenses must be allocated to the capital account for the partnership interest represented by the retained trust certificate. See § 1.263(g)-4(a)(1)(i) and (a)(2).

Example (7). Equity Swap. (i) Facts. On January 1, 1998, J purchases 100,000 shares of the common stock of XYZ corporation (which is publicly traded). On December 31, 2001, the 100,000 shares of XYZ corporation common stock were worth $x per share. On that date, J entered into a NPC with K. The terms of the NPC provided that K would receive an annual payment on December 31 of each year equal to 100,000 times any appreciation in the value of a share of XYZ corporation stock above its price at the end of trading on December 31 of the preceding year and 100,000 times the dividends paid during the year on each share of XYZ corporation stock. In return, on December 31 of each year, J would receive an amount equal to LIBOR times the value of 100,000 XYZ shares at the end of trading on December 31 of the preceding year plus 100,000 times the amount of any decrease in the value of a share of XYZ corporation stock below its price at the end of trading on December 31 of the preceding year. Payments between J and K would be netted and continue up to and including the maturity date of the NPC on December 31, 2008. Thus, J's aggregate payments on the NPC varied directly with the increase in value in the XYZ shares.

(ii) Analysis. The NPC is a position in XYZ stock. See § 1.1092(d)-2(c). The XYZ stock is personal property within the meaning of section 1092(d)(3)(B) because the NPC is a position with respect to substantially similar or related property (other than stock) within the meaning of section 1092(b)(3)(B)(i)(II). See § 1.1092(d)-2(a)(1)(ii). The NPC and the XYZ shares are offsetting positions with respect to the same personal property and constitute a straddle. See sections 1092(c)(1), (c)(3)(A)(i). Consequently, J's payments are interest and carrying charges properly allocable to personal property that is part of a straddle. See §§ 1.263(g)-3(b)(3) and (d)(1). Therefore, they should be allocated to the personal property that is part of the straddle in the manner that is most appropriate under all the facts and circumstances. In this case, because these payments are incurred to carry the XYZ shares, they should be allocated to the capital account for the XYZ common stock. See § 1.263(g)-4(a)(3).

Proposed § 1.263(g)-5 Effective dates. [*For Preamble, see ¶ 152,157*]

Sections 1.263(g)-1, 1.263(g)-2, 1.263(g)-3, and 1.263(g)-4 apply to interest and carrying charges properly allocable to personal property that are paid, incurred, or accrued after the date these regulations are adopted as final regulations by publication in the Federal Register for a straddle established on or after January 17, 2001.

§ 1.263A-0 Outline of regulations under section 263A.

This section lists the paragraphs in §§ 1.263A-1 through 1.263A-4 and §§ 1.263A-7 through 1.263A-15 as follows:

§ 1.263A-1 Uniform capitalization of costs.

(a) Introduction.

(1) In general.

(2) Effective dates.

(3) General scope.

(i) Property to which section 263A applies.

(ii) Property produced.

(iii) Property acquired for resale.

(iv) Inventories valued at market.

(v) Property produced in a farming business.

(vi) Creative property.

(vii) Property produced or property acquired for resale by foreign persons.

(b) Exceptions.

(1) Small resellers.

(2) Long-term contracts.

(3) Costs incurred in certain farming businesses.

(4) Costs incurred in raising, harvesting, or growing timber.

(5) Qualified creative expenses.

(6) Certain not-for-profit activities.

(7) Intangible drilling and development costs.

(8) Natural gas acquired for resale.

(i) Cushion gas.

(ii) Emergency gas.

(9) Research and experimental expenditures.

(10) Certain property that is substantially constructed.

(11) Certain property provided incident to services.

(i) In general.

(ii) Definition of services.

(iii) De minimis property provided incident to services.

(12) De minimis rule for certain producers with total indirect costs of $ 200,000 or less.

(13) Exception for the origination of loans.

(c) General operation of section 263A.

(1) Allocations.

(2) Otherwise deductible.

(3) Capitalize.

(4) Recovery of capitalized costs.

(d) Definitions.

(1) Self-constructed assets.

(2) Section 471 costs.

(i) In general.

(ii) New taxpayers.

(iii) Method changes.

(3) Additional section 263A costs.

(4) Section 263A costs.

(e) Types of costs subject to capitalization.

(1) In general.

(2) Direct costs.

(i) Producers.

(A) Direct material costs.

(B) Direct labor costs.

(ii) Resellers.

(3) Indirect costs.

(i) In general.

(ii) Examples of indirect costs required to be capitalized.

(A) Indirect labor costs.

(B) Officers' compensation.

(C) Pension and other related costs.

(D) Employee benefit expenses.

(E) Indirect material costs.

(F) Purchasing costs.

(G) Handling costs.

(H) Storage costs.

(I) Cost recovery.

(J) Depletion.

(K) Rent.

(L) Taxes.

(M) Insurance.

(N) Utilities.

(O) Repairs and maintenance.

(P) Engineering and design costs.

(Q) Spoilage.

(R) Tools and equipment.

(S) Quality control.

(T) Bidding costs.

(U) Licensing and franchise costs.

(V) Interest.

(W) Capitalizable service costs.

(iii) Indirect costs not capitalized.

(A) Selling and distribution costs.

(B) Research and experimental expenditures.

(C) Section 179 costs.

(D) Section 165 losses.

(E) Cost recovery allowances on temporarily idle equipment and facilities.

(1) In general.

(2) Examples.

(F) Taxes assessed on the basis of income.

(G) Strike expenses.

(H) Warranty and product liability costs.

(I) On-site storage costs.

(J) Unsuccessful bidding expenses.

(K) Deductible service costs.

(4) Service costs.

(i) Introduction.

(A) Definition of service costs.

(B) Definition of service departments.

(ii) Various service cost categories.

(A) Capitalizable service costs.

(B) Deductible service costs.

(C) Mixed service costs.

(iii) Examples of capitalizable service costs.

(iv) Examples of deductible service costs.

(f) Cost allocation methods.

(1) Introduction.
(2) Specific identification method.
(3) Burden rate and standard cost methods.
(i) Burden rate method.
(A) In general.
(B) Development of burden rates.
(C) Operation of the burden rate method.
(ii) Standard cost method.
(A) In general.
(B) Treatment of variances.
(4) Reasonable allocation methods.
(g) Allocating categories of costs.
(1) Direct materials.
(2) Direct labor.
(3) Indirect costs.
(4) Service costs.
(i) In general.
(ii) De minimis rule.
(iii) Methods for allocating mixed service costs.
(A) Direct reallocation method.
(B) Step-allocation method.
(C) Examples.
(iv) Illustrations of mixed service cost allocations using reasonable factors or relationships.
(A) Security services.
(B) Legal services.
(C) Centralized payroll services.
(D) Centralized data processing services.
(E) Engineering and design services.
(F) Safety engineering services.
(v) Accounting method change.
(h) Simplified service cost method.
(1) Introduction.
(2) Eligible property.
(i) In general.
(A) Inventory property.
(B) Non-inventory property held for sale.
(C) Certain self-constructed assets.
(D) Self-constructed assets produced on a repetitive basis.
(ii) Election to exclude self-constructed assets.
(3) General allocation formula.
(4) Labor-based allocation ratio.
(5) Production cost allocation ratio.
(6) Definition of total mixed service costs.
(7) Costs allocable to more than one business.
(8) De minimis rule.
(9) Separate election.
(i) [Reserved]
(j) Special rules.
(1) Costs provided by a related person.
(i) In general.
(ii) Exceptions.
(2) Optional capitalization of period costs.
(i) In general.
(ii) Period costs eligible for capitalization.
(3) Trade or business application.
(4) Transfers with a principal purpose of tax avoidance. [Reserved]

§ 1.263A-2 Rules relating to property produced by the taxpayer.

(a) In general.
(1) Produce.
(i) In general.
(ii) Ownership.
(A) General rule.
(B) Property produced for the taxpayer under a contract.
(1) In general.
(2) Definition of contract.
(C) Home construction contracts.
(2) Tangible personal property.
(i) General rule.
(ii) Intellectual or creative property.
(A) Intellectual or creative property that is tangible personal property.
(1) Books.
(2) Sound recordings.
(B) Intellectual or creative property that is not tangible personal property.
(1) Evidences of value.
(2) Property provided incident to services.
(3) Costs required to be capitalized by producers.
(i) In general.
(ii) Pre-production costs.
(iii) Post-production costs.
(4) Practical capacity concept.
(5) Taxpayers required to capitalize costs under this section.
(b) Simplified production method.
(1) Introduction.
(2) Eligible property.
(i) In general.
(A) Inventory property.
(B) Non-inventory property held for sale.
(C) Certain self-constructed assets.
(D) Self-constructed assets produced on a repetitive basis.
(ii) Election to exclude self-constructed assets.
(3) Simplified production method without historic absorption ratio election.
(i) General allocation formula.
(ii) Definitions.
(A) Absorption ratio.
(1) Additional section 263A costs incurred during the taxable year.
(2) Section 471 costs incurred during the taxable year.
(B) Section 471 costs remaining on hand at year end.
(iii) LIFO taxpayers electing the simplified production method.
(A) In general.
(B) LIFO increment.
(C) LIFO decrement.

(iv) De minimis rule for producers with total indirect costs of $ 200,000 or less.

(A) In general.

(B) Related party and aggregation rules.

(v) Examples.

(4) Simplified production method with historic absorption ratio election.

(i) In general.

(ii) Operating rules and definitions.

(A) Historic absorption ratio.

(B) Test period.

(1) In general.

(2) Updated test period.

(C) Qualifying period.

(1) In general.

(2) Extension of qualifying period.

(iii) Method of accounting.

(A) Adoption and use.

(B) Revocation of election.

(iv) Reporting and recordkeeping requirements.

(A) Reporting.

(B) Recordkeeping.

(v) Transition rules.

(vi) Example.

(c) Additional simplified methods for producers.

(d) Cross reference.

§ 1.263A-3 Rules relating to property acquired for resale.

(a) Capitalization rules for property acquired for resale.

(1) In general.

(2) Resellers with production activities.

(i) In general.

(ii) Exception for small resellers.

(iii) De minimis production activities.

(A) In general.

(B) Example.

(3) Resellers with property produced under a contract.

(4) Use of the simplified resale method.

(i) In general.

(ii) Resellers with de minimis production activities.

(iii) Resellers with property produced under a contract.

(iv) Application of simplified resale method.

(b) Gross receipts exception for small resellers.

(1) In general.

(i) Test period for new taxpayers.

(ii) Treatment of short taxable year.

(2) Definition of gross receipts.

(i) In general.

(ii) Amounts excluded.

(3) Aggregation of gross receipts.

(i) In general.

(ii) Single employer defined.

(iii) Gross receipts of a single employer.

(iv) Examples.

(c) Purchasing, handling, and storage costs.

(1) In general.

(2) Costs attributable to purchasing, handling, and storage.

(3) Purchasing costs.

(i) In general.

(ii) Determination of whether personnel are engaged in purchasing activities.

(A) 1/3-2/3 rule for allocating labor costs.

(B) Example.

(4) Handling costs.

(i) In general.

(ii) Processing costs.

(iii) Assembling costs.

(iv) Repackaging costs.

(v) Transportation costs.

(vi) Costs not considered handling costs.

(A) Distribution costs.

(B) Delivery of custom-ordered items.

(C) Repackaging after sale occurs.

(5) Storage costs.

(i) In general.

(ii) Definitions.

(A) On-site storage facility.

(B) Retail sales facility.

(C) An integral part of a retail sales facility.

(D) On-site sales.

(E) Retail customer.

(1) In general.

(2) Certain non-retail customers treated as retail customers.

(F) Off-site storage facility.

(G) Dual-function storage facility.

(iii) Treatment of storage costs incurred at a dual-function storage facility.

(A) In general.

(B) Dual-function storage facility allocation ratio.

(1) In general.

(2) Illustration of ratio allocation.

(3) Appropriate adjustments for other uses of a dual-function storage facility.

(C) De minimis 90-10 rule for dual-function storage facilities.

(iv) Costs not attributable to an off-site storage facility.

(v) Examples.

(d) Simplified resale method.

(1) Introduction.

(2) Eligible property.

(3) Simplified resale method without historic absorption ratio election.

(i) General allocation formula.

(A) In general.

(B) Effect of allocation.

(C) Definitions.

(1) Combined absorption ratio.

(2) Section 471 costs remaining on hand at year end.

(D) Storage and handling costs absorption ratio.

(E) Purchasing costs absorption ratio.
(F) Allocable mixed service costs.
(ii) LIFO taxpayers electing simplified resale method.
(A) In general.
(B) LIFO increment.
(C) LIFO decrement.
(iii) Permissible variations of the simplified resale method.
(iv) Examples.
(4) Simplified resale method with historic absorption ratio election.
(i) In general.
(ii) Operating rules and definitions.
(A) Historic absorption ratio.
(B) Test period.
(1) In general.
(2) Updated test period.
(C) Qualifying period.
(1) In general.
(2) Extension of qualifying period.
(iii) Method of accounting.
(A) Adoption and use.
(B) Revocation of election.
(iv) Reporting and recordkeeping requirements.
(A) Reporting.
(B) Recordkeeping.
(v) Transition rules.
(vi) Example.
(5) Additional simplified methods for resellers.
(e) Cross reference.

§ 1.263A-4 Rules for property produced in a farming business.

(a) Introduction.
(1) In general.
(2) Exception.
(i) In general.
(ii) Tax shelter.
(A) In general.
(B) Presumption.
(iii) Examples.
(3) Costs required to be capitalized or inventoried under another provision.
(4) Farming business.
(i) In general.
(A) Plant.
(B) Animal.
(ii) Incidental activities.
(A) In general.
(B) Activities that are not incidental.
(iii) Examples.
(b) Application of section 263A to property produced in a farming business.
(1) In general.
(i) Plants.
(ii) Animals.
(2) Preproductive period.
(i) Plant.
(A) In general.
(B) Applicability of section 263A.
(C) Actual preproductive period.
(1) Beginning of the preproductive period.
(2) End of the preproductive period.
(i) In general.
(ii) Marketable quantities.
(D) Examples.
(ii) Animal.
(A) Beginning of the preproductive period.
(B) End of the preproductive period.
(C) Allocation of costs between animal and first yield.
(c) Inventory methods.
(1) In general.
(2) Available for property used in a trade or business.
(3) Exclusion of property to which section 263A does not apply.
(d) Election not to have section 263A apply.
(1) Introduction.
(2) Availability of the election.
(3) Time and manner of making the election.
(i) Automatic election.
(ii) Nonautomatic election.
(4) Special rules.
(i) Section 1245 treatment.
(ii) Required use of alternative depreciation system.
(iii) Related person.
(A) In general.
(B) Members of family.
(5) Examples.
(e) Exception for certain costs resulting from casualty losses.
(1) In general.
(2) Ownership.
(3) Examples.
(4) Special rule for citrus and almond groves.
(i) In general.
(ii) Example.
(f) Effective date and change in method of accounting.
(1) Effective date.
(2) Change in method of accounting.

§ 1.263A-7 Changing a method of accounting under section 263A.

(a) Introduction.
(1) Purpose.
(2) Taxpayers that adopt a method of accounting under section 263A.
(3) Taxpayers that change a method of accounting under section 263A.
(4) Effective date.
(5) Definition of change in method of accounting.
(b) Rules applicable to a change in method of accounting.
(1) General rules.
(2) Special rules.

(i) Ordering rules when multiple changes in method of accounting occur in the year of change.

(A) In general.

(B) Exceptions to the general ordering rule.

(1) Change from the LIFO inventory method.

(2) Change from the specific goods LIFO inventory method.

(3) Change in overall method of accounting.

(4) Change in method of accounting for depreciation.

(ii) Adjustment required by section 481(a).

(iii) Base year.

(A) Need for a new base year.

(1) Facts and circumstances revaluation method used.

(2) 3-year average method used.

(i) Simplified method not used.

(ii) Simplified method used.

(B) Computing a new base year.

(c) Inventory.

(1) Need for adjustments.

(2) Revaluing beginning inventory.

(i) In general.

(ii) Methods to revalue inventory.

(iii) Facts and circumstances revaluation method.

(A) In general.

(B) Exception.

(C) Estimates and procedures allowed.

(D) Use by dollar-value LIFO taxpayers.

(E) Examples.

(iv) Weighted average method.

(A) In general.

(B) Weighted average method for FIFO taxpayers.

(1) In general.

(2) Example.

(C) Weighted average method for specific goods LIFO taxpayers.

(1) In general.

(2) Example.

(D) Adjustments to inventory costs from prior years.

(v) 3-year average method.

(A) In general.

(B) Consecutive year requirement.

(C) Example.

(D) Short taxable years.

(E) Adjustments to inventory costs from prior years.

(1) General rule.

(2) Examples of costs eligible for restatement adjustment procedure.

(F) Restatement adjustment procedure.

(1) In general.

(2) Examples of restatement adjustment procedure.

(3) Intercompany items.

(i) Revaluing intercompany transactions.

(ii) Example.

(iii) Availability of revaluation methods.

(4) Anti-abuse rule.

(i) In general.

(ii) Deemed avoidance of this section.

(A) Scope.

(B) General rule.

(iii) Election to use transferor's LIFO layers.

(iv) Tax avoidance intent not required.

(v) Related corporation.

(d) Non-inventory property.

(1) Need for adjustments.

(2) Revaluing property.

§ 1.263A-8 Requirement to capitalize interest.

(a) In general.

(1) General rule.

(2) Treatment of interest required to be capitalized.

(3) Methods of accounting under section 263A(f).

(4) Special definitions.

(i) Related person.

(ii) Placed in service.

(b) Designated property.

(1) In general.

(2) Special rules.

(i) Application of thresholds.

(ii) Relevant activities and costs.

(iii) Production period and cost of production.

(3) Excluded property.

(4) De minimis rule.

(i) In general.

(ii) Determination of total production expenditures.

(c) Definition of real property.

(1) In general.

(2) Unsevered natural products of land.

(3) Inherently permanent structures.

(4) Machinery.

(i) Treatment.

(ii) Certain factors not determinative.

(d) Production.

(1) Definition of produce.

(2) Property produced under a contract.

(i) Customer.

(ii) Contractor.

(iii) Definition of a contract.

(iv) Determination of whether thresholds are satisfied.

(A) Customer.

(B) Contractor.

(v) Exclusion for property subject to long-term contract rules.

(3) Improvements to existing property.

(i) In general.

(ii) Real property.

(iii) Tangible personal property.

§ 1.263A-9 The avoided cost method.

(a) In general.

(1) Description.

(2) Overview.

(i) In general.
(ii) Rules that apply in determining amounts.
(3) Definitions of interest and incurred.
(4) Definition of eligible debt.
(b) Traced debt amount.
(1) General rule.
(2) Identification and definition of traced debt.
(3) Example.
(c) Excess expenditure amount.
(1) General rule.
(2) Interest required to be capitalized.
(3) Example.
(4) Treatment of interest subject to a deferral provision.
(5) Definitions.
(i) Nontraced debt.
(A) Defined.
(B) Example.
(ii) Average excess expenditures.
(A) General rule.
(B) Example.
(iii) Weighted average interest rate.
(A) Determination of rate.
(B) Interest incurred on nontraced debt.
(C) Average nontraced debt.
(D) Special rules if taxpayer has no nontraced debt or rate is contingent.
(6) Examples.
(7) Special rules where the excess expenditure amount exceeds incurred interest.
(i) Allocation of total incurred interest to units.
(ii) Application of related person rules to average excess expenditures.
(iii) Special rule for corporations.
(d) Election not to trace debt.
(1) General rule.
(2) Example.
(e) Election to use external rate.
(1) In general.
(2) Eligible taxpayer.
(f) Selection of computation period and measurement dates and application of averaging conventions.
(1) Computation period.
(i) In general.
(ii) Method of accounting.
(iii) Production period beginning or ending during the computation period.
(2) Measurement dates.
(i) In general.
(ii) Measurement period.
(iii) Measurement dates on which accumulated production expenditures must be taken into account.
(iv) More frequent measurement dates.
(3) Examples.
(g) Special rules.
(1) Ordering rules.
(i) Provisions preempted by section 263A(f).
(ii) Deferral provisions applied before this section.
(2) Application of section 263A(f) to deferred interest.
(i) In general.
(ii) Capitalization of deferral amount.
(iii) Deferred capitalization.
(iv) Substitute capitalization.
(A) General rule.
(B) Capitalization of amount carried forward.
(C) Method of accounting.
(v) Examples.
(3) Simplified inventory method.
(i) In general.
(ii) Segmentation of inventory.
(A) General rule.
(B) Example.
(iii) Aggregate interest capitalization amount.
(A) Computation period and weighted average interest rate.
(B) Computation of the tentative aggregate interest capitalization amount.
(C) Coordination with other interest capitalization computations.
(1) In general.
(2) Deferred interest.
(3) Other coordinating provisions.
(D) Treatment of increases or decreases in the aggregate interest capitalization amount.
(E) Example.
(iv) Method of accounting.
(4) Financial accounting method disregarded.
(5) Treatment of intercompany transactions.
(i) General rule.
(ii) Special rule for consolidated group with limited outside borrowing.
(iii) Example.
(6) Notional principal contracts and other derivatives. [Reserved]
(7) 15-day repayment rule.

§ 1.263A-10 Unit of property.

(a) In general.
(b) Units of real property.
(1) In general.
(2) Functional interdependence.
(3) Common features.
(4) Allocation of costs to unit.
(5) Treatment of costs when a common feature is included in a unit of real property.
(i) General rule.
(ii) Production activity not undertaken on benefitted property.
(A) Direct production activity not undertaken.
(1) In general.
(2) Land attributable to a benefitted property.
(B) Suspension of direct production activity after clearing and grading undertaken.

(1) General rule.

(2) Accumulated production expenditures.

(iii) Common feature placed in service before the end of production of a benefitted property.

(iv) Benefitted property sold before production completed on common feature.

(v) Benefitted property placed in service before production completed on common feature.

(6) Examples.

(c) Units of tangible personal property.

(d) Treatment of installations.

§ 1.263A-11 Accumulated production expenditures.

(a) General rule.

(b) When costs are first taken into account.

(1) In general.

(2) Dedication rule for materials and supplies.

(c) Property produced under a contract.

(1) Customer.

(2) Contractor.

(d) Property used to produce designated property.

(1) In general.

(2) Example.

(3) Excluded equipment and facilities.

(e) Improvements.

(1) General rule.

(2) De minimis rule.

(f) Mid-production purchases.

(g) Related person costs.

(h) Installation.

§ 1.263A-12 Production period.

(a) In general.

(b) Related person activities.

(c) Beginning of production period.

(1) In general.

(2) Real property.

(3) Tangible personal property.

(d) End of production period.

(1) In general.

(2) Special rules.

(3) Sequential production or delivery.

(4) Examples.

(e) Physical production activities.

(1) In general.

(2) Illustrations.

(f) Activities not considered physical production.

(1) Planning and design.

(2) Incidental repairs.

(g) Suspension of production period.

(1) In general.

(2) Special rule.

(3) Method of accounting.

(4) Example.

§ 1.263A-13 Oil and gas activities.

(a) In general.

(b) Generally applicable rules.

(1) Beginning of production period.

(i) Onshore activities.

(ii) Offshore activities.

(2) End of production period.

(3) Accumulated production expenditures.

(i) Costs included.

(ii) Improvement unit.

(c) Special rules when definite plan not established.

(1) In general.

(2) Oil and gas units.

(i) First productive well unit.

(ii) Subsequent units.

(3) Beginning of production period.

(i) First productive well unit.

(ii) Subsequent wells.

(4) End of production period.

(5) Accumulated production expenditures.

(i) First productive well unit.

(ii) Subsequent well unit.

(6) Allocation of interest capitalized with respect to first productive well unit.

(7) Examples.

§ 1.263A-14 Rules for related persons.

§ 1.263A-15 Effective dates, transitional rules, and anti-abuse rule.

(a) Effective dates.

(b) Transitional rule for accumulated production expenditures.

(1) In general.

(2) Property used to produce designated property.

(c) Anti-abuse rule.

T.D. 8482, 8/6/93, amend T.D. 8584, 12/28/94, T.D. 8728, 8/4/97, T.D. 8897, 8/18/2000.

---

§ 1.263A-1 Uniform capitalization of costs.

Caution: The Treasury has not yet amended Reg § 1.263A-1 to reflect changes made by P.L. 108-357.

(a) Introduction. *(1) In general.* The regulations under §§ 1.263A-1 through 1.263A-6 provide guidance to taxpayers that are required to capitalize certain costs under section 263A. These regulations generally apply to all costs required to be capitalized under section 263A except for interest that must be capitalized under section 263A(f) and the regulations thereunder. Statutory or regulatory exceptions may provide that section 263A does not apply to certain activities or costs; however, those activities or costs may nevertheless be subject to capitalization requirements under other provisions of the Internal Revenue Code and regulations.

(2) Effective dates. (i) In general, this section and §§ 1.263A-2 and 1.263A-3 apply to costs incurred in taxable years beginning after December 31, 1993. In the case of property that is inventory in the hands of the taxpayer, however, these sections are effective for taxable years beginning after December 31, 1993. Changes in methods of accounting necessary as a result of the rules in this section and §§ 1.263A-2 and 1.263A-3 must be made under terms and conditions prescribed by the Commissioner. Under these

terms and conditions, the principles of § 1.263A-7 generally must be applied in revaluing inventory property.

(ii) For taxable years beginning before January 1, 1994, taxpayers must take reasonable positions on their federal income tax returns when applying section 263A. For purposes of this paragraph (a)(2)(iii), a reasonable position is a position consistent with the temporary regulations, revenue rulings, revenue procedures, notices, and announcements concerning section 263A applicable in taxable years beginning before January 1, 1994. See § 601.601(d)(2)(ii)(b) of this chapter.

(3) General scope. (i) Property to which section 263A applies. Taxpayers subject to section 263A must capitalize all direct costs and certain indirect costs properly allocable to—

(A) Real property and tangible personal property produced by the taxpayer; and

(B) Real property and personal property described in section 1221(1), which is acquired by the taxpayer for resale.

(ii) Property produced. Taxpayers that produce real property and tangible personal property (producers) must capitalize all the direct costs of producing the property and the property's properly allocable share of indirect costs (described in paragraphs (e)(2)(i) and (3) of this section), regardless of whether the property is sold or used in the taxpayer's trade or business. See § 1.263A-2 for rules relating to producers.

(iii) Property acquired for resale. Retailers, wholesalers, and other taxpayers that acquire property described in section 1221(1) for resale (resellers) must capitalize the direct costs of acquiring the property and the property's properly allocable share of indirect costs (described in paragraphs (e)(2)(ii) and (3) of this section). See § 1.263A-3 for rules relating to resellers. See also section 263A(b)(2)(B), which excepts from section 263A personal property acquired for resale by a small reseller.

(iv) Inventories valued at market. Section 263A does not apply to inventories valued at market under either the market method or the lower of cost or market method if the market valuation used by the taxpayer generally equals the property's fair market value. For purposes of this paragraph (a)(3)(iv), the term fair market value means the price at which the taxpayer sells its inventory to its customers (e.g., as in the market value definition provided in § 1.471-4(b)) less, if applicable, the direct cost of disposing of the inventory. However, section 263A does apply in determining the market value of any inventory for which market is determined with reference to replacement cost or reproduction cost. See §§ 1.471-4 and 1.471-5.

(v) Property produced in a farming business. Section 263A generally requires taxpayers engaged in a farming business to capitalize certain costs. See section 263A(d) and § 1.263A-4 for rules relating to taxpayers engaged in a farming business.

(vi) Creative property. Section 263A generally requires taxpayers engaged in the production and resale of creative property to capitalize certain costs.

(vii) Property produced or property acquired for resale by foreign persons. Section 263A generally applies to foreign persons.

(b) Exceptions. *(1) Small resellers.* See section 263A(b)(2)(B) for the $10,000,000 gross receipts exception for small resellers of personal property. See § 1.263A-3(b) for rules relating to this exception. See also the exception for small resellers with de minimis production activities in § 1.263A-3(a)(2)(ii) and the exception for small resellers that have property produced under contract in § 1.263A-3(a)(3).

(2) Long-term contracts. Except for certain home construction contracts described in section 460(e)(1), section 263A does not apply to any property produced by the taxpayer pursuant to a long-term contract as defined in section 460(f), regardless of whether the taxpayer uses an inventory method to account for such production.

(3) Costs incurred in certain farming businesses. See section 263A(d) for an exception for costs paid or incurred in certain farming businesses. See § 1.263A-4 for specific rules relating to taxpayers engaged in the trade or business of farming.

(4) Costs incurred in raising, harvesting, or growing timber. See section 263A(c)(5) for an exception for costs paid or incurred in raising, harvesting, or growing timber and certain ornamental trees. See § 1.263A-4, however, for rules relating to taxpayers producing certain trees to which section 263A applies.

(5) Qualified creative expenses. See section 263A(h) for an exception for qualified creative expenses paid or incurred by certain free-lance authors, photographers, and artists.

(6) Certain not-for-profit activities. See section 263A(c)(1) for an exception for property produced by a taxpayer for use by the taxpayer other than in a trade or business or an activity conducted for profit. This exception does not apply, however, to property produced by an exempt organization in connection with its unrelated trade or business activities.

(7) Intangible drilling and development costs. See section 263A(c)(3) for an exception for intangible drilling and development costs. Additionally, section 263A does not apply to any amount allowable as a deduction under section 59(e) with respect to qualified expenditures under sections 263(c), 616(a), or 617(a).

(8) Natural gas acquired for resale. Under this paragraph (b)(8), section 263A does not apply to any costs incurred by a taxpayer relating to natural gas acquired for resale to the extent such costs would otherwise be allocable to cushion gas.

(i) Cushion gas. Cushion gas is the portion of gas stored in an underground storage facility or reservoir that is required to maintain the level of pressure necessary for operation of the facility. However, section 263A applies to costs incurred by a taxpayer relating to natural gas acquired for resale to the extent such costs are properly allocable to emergency gas.

(ii) Emergency gas. Emergency gas is natural gas stored in an underground storage facility or reservoir for use during periods of unusually heavy customer demand.

(9) Research and experimental expenditures. See section 263A(c)(2) for an exception for any research and experimental expenditure allowable as a deduction under section 174 or the regulations thereunder. Additionally, section 263A does not apply to any amount allowable as a deduction under section 59(e) with respect to qualified expenditures under section 174.

(10) Certain property that is substantially constructed. Section 263A does not apply to any property produced by a taxpayer for use in its trade or business if substantial construction occurred before March 1, 1986.

(i) For purposes of this section, substantial construction is deemed to have occurred if the lesser of—

(A) 10 percent of the total estimated costs of construction; or

(B) The greater of $10 million or 2 percent of the total estimated costs of construction, was incurred before March 1, 1986.

(ii) For purposes of this provision, the total estimated costs of construction shall be determined by reference to a reasonable estimate, on or before March 1, 1986, of such amount. Assume, for example, that on March 1, 1986, the estimated costs of constructing a facility were $150 million. Assume that before March 1, 1986, $12 million of construction costs had been incurred. Based on the above facts, substantial construction would be deemed to have occurred before March 1, 1986, because $12 million (the costs of construction incurred before such date) is greater than $10 million (the lesser of $15 million; or the greater of $10 million or $3 million). For purposes of this provision, construction costs are defined as those costs incurred after construction has commenced at the site of the property being constructed (unless the property will not be located on land and, therefore, the initial construction of the property must begin at a location other than the intended site). For example, in the case of a building, construction commences when work begins on the building, such as the excavation of the site, the pouring of pads for the building, or the driving of foundation pilings into the ground. Preliminary activities such as project engineering and architectural design do not constitute the commencement of construction, nor are such costs considered construction costs, for purposes of this paragraph (b)(10).

(11) Certain property provided incident to services. (i) In general. Under this paragraph (b)(11), section 263A does not apply to property that is provided to a client (or customer) incident to the provision of services by the taxpayer if the property provided to the client is—

(A) De minimis in amount; and

(B) Not inventory in the hands of the service provider.

(ii) Definition of services. For purposes of this paragraph (b)(11), services is defined with reference to its ordinary and accepted meaning under federal income tax principles. In determining whether a taxpayer is a bona-fide service provider under this paragraph (b)(11), the nature of the taxpayer's trade or business and the facts and circumstances surrounding the taxpayer's trade or business activities must be considered. Examples of taxpayers qualifying as service providers under this paragraph include taxpayers performing services in the fields of health, law, engineering, architecture, accounting, actuarial science, performing arts, or consulting.

(iii) De minimis property provided incident to services. In determining whether property provided to a client by a service provider is de minimis in amount, all facts and circumstances, such as the nature of the taxpayer's trade or business and the volume of its service activities in the trade or business, must be considered. A significant factor in making this determination is the relationship between the acquisition or direct materials costs of the property that is provided to clients and the price that the taxpayer charges its clients for its services and the property. For purposes of this paragraph (b)(11), if the acquisition or direct materials cost of the property provided to a client incident to the services is less than or equal to five percent of the price charged to the client for the services and property, the property is de minimis. If the acquisition or direct materials cost of the property exceeds five percent of the price charged for the services and property, the property may be de minimis if additional facts and circumstances so indicate.

(12) De minimis rule for certain producers with total indirect costs of $200,000 or less. See § 1.263A-2(b)(3)(iv) for a de minimis rule that treats producers with total indirect costs of $200,000 or less as having no additional section 263A costs (as defined in paragraph (d)(3) of this section) for purposes of the simplified production method.

(13) Exception for the origination of loans. For purposes of section 263A(b)(2)(A), the origination of loans is not considered the acquisition of intangible property for resale. (But section 263A(b)(2)(A) does include the acquisition by a taxpayer of pre-existing loans from other persons for resale.)

(c) General operation of section 263A. *(1) Allocations.* Under section 263A, taxpayers must capitalize their direct costs and a properly allocable share of their indirect costs to property produced or property acquired for resale. In order to determine these capitalizable costs, taxpayers must allocate or apportion costs to various activities, including production or resale activities. After section 263A costs are allocated to the appropriate production or resale activities, these costs are generally allocated to the items of property produced or property acquired for resale during the taxable year and capitalized to the items that remain on hand at the end of the taxable year. See however, the simplified production method and the simplified resale method in §§ 1.263A-2(b) and 1.263A-3(d).

(2) Otherwise deductible. (i) Any cost which (but for section 263A and the regulations thereunder) may not be taken into account in computing taxable income for any taxable year is not treated as a cost properly allocable to property produced or acquired for resale under section 263A and the regulations thereunder. Thus, for example, if a business meal deduction is limited by section 274(n) to 80 percent of the cost of the meal, the amount properly allocable to property produced or acquired for resale under section 263A is also limited to 80 percent of the cost of the meal.

(ii) The amount of any cost required to be capitalized under section 263A may not be included in inventory or charged to capital accounts or basis any earlier than the taxable year during which the amount is incurred within the meaning of § 1.446-1(c)(1)(ii).

(3) Capitalize. Capitalize means, in the case of property that is inventory in the hands of a taxpayer, to include in inventory costs and, in the case of other property, to charge to a capital account or basis.

(4) Recovery of capitalized costs. Costs that are capitalized under section 263A are recovered through depreciation, amortization, cost of goods sold, or by an adjustment to basis at the time the property is used, sold, placed in service, or otherwise disposed of by the taxpayer. Cost recovery is determined by the applicable Internal Revenue Code and regulation provisions relating to the use, sale, or disposition of property.

(d) Definitions. *(1) Self-constructed assets.* Self-constructed assets are assets produced by a taxpayer for use by the taxpayer in its trade or business. Self-constructed assets are subject to section 263A.

(2) Section 471 costs. (i) In general. Except as otherwise provided in paragraphs (d)(2)(ii) and (iii) of this section, for purposes of the regulations under section 263A, a taxpayer's section 471 costs are the costs, other than interest, capitalized under its method of accounting immediately prior to the effective date of section 263A. Thus, although section 471 applies only to inventories, section 471 costs include any non-inventory costs, other than interest, capitalized or included in acquisition or production costs under the tax-

payer's method of accounting immediately prior to the effective date of section 263A.

(ii) New taxpayers. In the case of a new taxpayer, section 471 costs are those acquisition or production costs, other than interest, that would have been required to be capitalized by the taxpayer if the taxpayer had been in existence immediately prior to the effective date of section 263A.

(iii) Method changes. If a taxpayer included a cost described in § 1.471-11(c)(2)(iii) in its inventoriable costs immediately prior to the effective date of section 263A, that cost is included in the taxpayer's section 471 costs under paragraph (d)(2)(i) of this section. Except as provided in the following sentence, a change in the financial reporting practices of a taxpayer for costs described in § 1.471-11(c)(2)(iii) subsequent to the effective date of section 263A does not affect the classification of these costs as section 471 costs. A taxpayer may change its established methods of accounting used in determining section 471 costs only with the consent of the Commissioner as required under section 446(e) and the regulations thereunder.

(3) Additional section 263A costs. Additional section 263A costs are defined as the costs, other than interest, that were not capitalized under the taxpayer's method of accounting immediately prior to the effective date of section 263A (adjusted as appropriate for any changes in methods of accounting for section 471 costs under paragraph (d)(2)(iii) of this section), but that are required to be capitalized under section 263A. For new taxpayers, additional section 263A costs are defined as the costs, other than interest, that the taxpayer must capitalize under section 263A, but which the taxpayer would not have been required to capitalize if the taxpayer had been in existence prior to the effective date of section 263A.

(4) Section 263A costs. Section 263A costs are defined as the costs that a taxpayer must capitalize under section 263A. Thus, section 263A costs are the sum of a taxpayer's section 471 costs, its additional section 263A costs, and interest capitalizable under section 263A(f).

(e) Types of costs subject to capitalization. *(1) In general.* Taxpayers subject to section 263A must capitalize all direct costs and certain indirect costs properly allocable to property produced or property acquired for resale. This paragraph (e) describes the types of costs subject to section 263A.

(2) Direct costs. (i) Producers. Producers must capitalize direct material costs and direct labor costs.

(A) Direct material costs include the costs of those materials that become an integral part of specific property produced and those materials that are consumed in the ordinary course of production and that can be identified or associated with particular units or groups of units of property produced.

(B) Direct labor costs include the costs of labor that can be identified or associated with particular units or groups of units of specific property produced. For this purpose, labor encompasses full-time and part-time employees, as well as contract employees and independent contractors. Direct labor costs include all elements of compensation other than employee benefit costs described in paragraph (e)(3)(ii)(D) of this section. Elements of direct labor costs include basic compensation, overtime pay, vacation pay, holiday pay, sick leave pay (other than payments pursuant to a wage continuation plan under section 105(d) as it existed prior to its repeal in 1983), shift differential, payroll taxes, and payments to a supplemental unemployment benefit plan.

(ii) Resellers. Resellers must capitalize the acquisition costs of property acquired for resale. In the case of inventory, the acquisition cost is the cost described in § 1.471-3(b).

(3) Indirect costs. (i) In general. Indirect costs are defined as all costs other than direct material costs and direct labor costs (in the case of property produced) or acquisition costs (in the case of property acquired for resale). Taxpayers subject to section 263A must capitalize all indirect costs properly allocable to property produced or property acquired for resale. Indirect costs are properly allocable to property produced or property acquired for resale when the costs directly benefit or are incurred by reason of the performance of production or resale activities. Indirect costs may be allocable to both production and resale activities, as well as to other activities that are not subject to section 263A. Taxpayers subject to section 263A must make a reasonable allocation of indirect costs between production, resale, and other activities.

(ii) Examples of indirect costs required to be capitalized. The following are examples of indirect costs that must be capitalized to the extent they are properly allocable to property produced or property acquired for resale:

(A) Indirect labor costs. Indirect labor costs include all labor costs (including the elements of labor costs set forth in paragraph (e)(2)(i) of this section) that cannot be directly identified or associated with particular units or groups of units of specific property produced or property acquired for resale (e.g., factory labor that is not direct labor). As in the case of direct labor, indirect labor encompasses full-time and part-time employees, as well as contract employees and independent contractors.

(B) Officers' compensation. Officers' compensation includes compensation paid to officers of the taxpayer.

(C) Pension and other related costs. Pension and other related costs include contributions paid to or made under any stock bonus, pension, profit-sharing or annuity plan, or other plan deferring the receipt of compensation, whether or not the plan qualifies under section 401(a). Contributions to employee plans representing past services must be capitalized in the same manner (and in the same proportion to property currently being acquired or produced) as amounts contributed for current service.

(D) Employee benefit expenses. Employee benefit expenses include all other employee benefit expenses (not described in paragraph (e)(3)(ii)(C) of this section) to the extent such expenses are otherwise allowable as deductions under chapter 1 of the Internal Revenue Code. These other employee benefit expenses include: worker's compensation; amounts otherwise deductible or allowable in reducing earnings and profits under section 404A; payments pursuant to a wage continuation plan under section 105(d) as it existed prior to its repeal in 1983; amounts includible in the gross income of employees under a method or arrangement of employer contributions or compensation that has the effect of a stock bonus, pension, profit-sharing or annuity plan, or other plan deferring receipt of compensation or providing deferred benefits; premiums on life and health insurance; and miscellaneous benefits provided for employees such as safety, medical treatment, recreational and eating facilities, membership dues, etc. Employee benefit expenses do not, however, include direct labor costs described in paragraph (e)(2)(i) of this section.

(E) Indirect material costs. Indirect material costs include the cost of materials that are not an integral part of specific property produced and the cost of materials that are consumed in the ordinary course of performing production or resale activities that cannot be identified or associated with particular units or groups of units of property. Thus, for example, a cost described in § 1.162-3, relating to the cost of a material or supply, is an indirect material cost.

(F) Purchasing costs. Purchasing costs include costs attributable to purchasing activities. See § 1.263A-3(c)(3) for a further discussion of purchasing costs.

(G) Handling costs. Handling costs include costs attributable to processing, assembling, repackaging and transporting goods, and other similar activities. See § 1.263A-3(c)(4) for a further discussion of handling costs.

(H) Storage costs. Storage costs include the costs of carrying, storing, or warehousing property. See § 1.263A-3(c)(5) for a further discussion of storage costs.

(I) Cost recovery. Cost recovery includes depreciation, amortization, and cost recovery allowances on equipment and facilities (including depreciation or amortization of self-constructed assets or other previously produced or acquired property to which section 263A or section 263 applies).

(J) Depletion. Depletion includes allowances for depletion, whether or not in excess of cost. Depletion is, however, only properly allocable to property that has been sold (i.e., for purposes of determining gain or loss on the sale of the property).

(K) Rent. Rent includes the cost of renting or leasing equipment, facilities, or land.

(L) Taxes. Taxes include those taxes (other than taxes described in paragraph (e)(3)(iii)(F) of this section) that are otherwise allowable as a deduction to the extent such taxes are attributable to labor, materials, supplies, equipment, land, or facilities used in production or resale activities.

(M) Insurance. Insurance includes the cost of insurance on plant or facility, machinery, equipment, materials, property produced, or property acquired for resale.

(N) Utilities. Utilities include the cost of electricity, gas, and water.

(O) Repairs and maintenance. Repairs and maintenance include the cost of repairing and maintaining equipment or facilities.

(P) Engineering and design costs. Engineering and design costs include pre-production costs, such as costs attributable to research, experimental, engineering, and design activities (to the extent that such amounts are not research and experimental expenditures as described in section 174 and the regulations thereunder).

(Q) Spoilage. Spoilage includes the costs of rework labor, scrap, and spoilage.

(R) Tools and equipment. Tools and equipment include the costs of tools and equipment which are not otherwise capitalized.

(S) Quality control. Quality control includes the costs of quality control and inspection.

(T) Bidding costs. Bidding costs are costs incurred in the solicitation of contracts (including contracts pertaining to property acquired for resale) ultimately awarded to the taxpayer. The taxpayer must defer all bidding costs paid or incurred in the solicitation of a particular contract until the contract is awarded. If the contract is awarded to the taxpayer, the bidding costs become part of the indirect costs allocated to the subject matter of the contract. If the contract is not awarded to the taxpayer, bidding costs are deductible in the taxable year that the contract is awarded to another party, or in the taxable year that the taxpayer is notified in writing that no contract will be awarded and that the contract (or a similar or related contract) will not be rebid, or in the taxable year that the taxpayer abandons its bid or proposal, whichever occurs first. Abandoning a bid does not include modifying, supplementing, or changing the original bid or proposal. If the taxpayer is awarded only part of the bid (for example, the taxpayer submitted one bid to build each of two different types of products, and the taxpayer was awarded a contract to build only one of the two types of products), the taxpayer shall deduct the portion of the bidding costs related to the portion of the bid not awarded to the taxpayer. In the case of a bid or proposal for a multi-unit contract, all bidding costs must be included in the costs allocated to the subject matter of the contract awarded to the taxpayer to produce or acquire for resale any of such units. For example, where the taxpayer submits one bid to produce three similar turbines and the taxpayer is awarded a contract to produce only two of the three turbines, all bidding costs must be included in the cost of the two turbines. For purposes of this paragraph (e)(3)(ii)(T), a contract means—

(1) In the case of a specific unit of property, any agreement under which the taxpayer would produce or sell property to another party if the agreement is entered into before the taxpayer produces or acquires the specific unit of property to be delivered to the party under the agreement; and

(2) In the case of fungible property, any agreement to the extent that, at the time the agreement is entered into, the taxpayer has on hand an insufficient quantity of completed fungible items of such property that may be used to satisfy the agreement (plus any other production or sales agreements of the taxpayer).

(U) Licensing and franchise costs. Licensing and franchise costs include fees incurred in securing the contractual right to use a trademark, corporate plan, manufacturing procedure, special recipe, or other similar right associated with property produced or property acquired for resale. These costs include the otherwise deductible portion (e.g., amortization) of the initial fees incurred to obtain the license or franchise and any minimum annual payments and royalties that are incurred by a licensee or a franchisee.

(V) Interest. Interest includes interest on debt incurred or continued during the production period to finance the production of real property or tangible personal property to which section 263A(f) applies.

(W) Capitalizable service costs. Service costs that are required to be capitalized include capitalizable service costs and capitalizable mixed service costs as defined in paragraph (e)(4) of this section.

(iii) Indirect costs not capitalized. The following indirect costs are not required to be capitalized under section 263A:

(A) Selling and distribution costs. These costs are marketing, selling, advertising, and distribution costs.

(B) Research and experimental expenditures. Research and experimental expenditures are expenditures described in section 174 and the regulations thereunder.

(C) Section 179 costs. Section 179 costs are expenses for certain depreciable assets deductible at the election of the taxpayer under section 179 and the regulations thereunder.

(D) Section 165 losses. Section 165 losses are losses under section 165 and the regulations thereunder.

(E) Cost recovery allowances on temporarily idle equipment and facilities. (1) In general. Cost recovery allowances on temporarily idle equipment and facilities include only depreciation, amortization, and cost recovery allowances on equipment and facilities that have been placed in service but are temporarily idle. Equipment and facilities are temporarily idle when a taxpayer takes them out of service for a finite period. However, equipment and facilities are not considered temporarily idle—

(i) During worker breaks, non-working hours, or on regularly scheduled non-working days (such as holidays or weekends);

(ii) During normal interruptions in the operation of the equipment or facilities;

(iii) When equipment is enroute to or located at a job site; or

(iv) When under normal operating conditions, the equipment is used or operated only during certain shifts.

(2) Examples. The provisions of this paragraph (e)(3)(iii)(E) are illustrated by the following examples:

Example (1). Equipment operated only during certain shifts. Taxpayer A manufactures widgets. Although A's manufacturing facility operates 24 hours each day in three shifts, A only operates its stamping machine during one shift each day. Because A only operates its stamping machine during certain shifts, A's stamping machine is not considered temporarily idle during the two shifts that it is not operated.

Example (2). Facility shut down for retooling. Taxpayer B owns and operates a manufacturing facility. B closes its manufacturing facility for two weeks to retool its assembly line. B's manufacturing facility is considered temporarily idle during this two-week period.

(F) Taxes assessed on the basis of income. Taxes assessed on the basis of income include only state, local, and foreign income taxes, and franchise taxes that are assessed on the taxpayer based on income.

(G) Strike expenses. Strike expenses include only costs associated with hiring employees to replace striking personnel (but not wages of replacement personnel), costs of security, and legal fees associated with settling strikes.

(H) Warranty and product liability costs. Warranty costs and product liability costs are costs incurred in fulfilling product warranty obligations for products that have been sold and costs incurred for product liability insurance.

(I) On-site storage costs. On-site storage costs are storage and warehousing costs incurred by a taxpayer at an on-site storage facility, as defined in § 1.263A-3(c)(5)(ii)(A), with respect to property produced or property acquired for resale.

(J) Unsuccessful bidding expenses. Unsuccessful bidding costs are bidding expenses incurred in the solicitation of contracts not awarded to the taxpayer.

(K) Deductible service costs. Service costs that are not required to be capitalized include deductible service costs and deductible mixed service costs as defined in paragraph (e)(4) of this section.

(4) Service costs. (i) Introduction. This paragraph (e)(4) provides definitions and categories of service costs. Paragraph (g)(4) of this section provides specific rules for determining the amount of service costs allocable to property produced or property acquired for resale. In addition, paragraph (h) of this section provides a simplified method for determining the amount of service costs that must be capitalized.

(A) Definition of service costs. Service costs are defined as a type of indirect costs (e.g., general and administrative costs) that can be identified specifically with a service department or function or that directly benefit or are incurred by reason of a service department or function.

(B) Definition of service departments. Service departments are defined as administrative, service, or support departments that incur service costs. The facts and circumstances of the taxpayer's activities and business organization control whether a department is a service department. For example, service departments include personnel, accounting, data processing, security, legal, and other similar departments.

(ii) Various service cost categories. (A) Capitalizable service costs. Capitalizable service costs are defined as service costs that directly benefit or are incurred by reason of the performance of the production or resale activities of the taxpayer. Therefore, these service costs are required to be capitalized under section 263A. Examples of service departments or functions that incur capitalizable service costs are provided in paragraph (e)(4)(iii) of this section.

(B) Deductible service costs. Deductible service costs are defined as service costs that do not directly benefit or are not incurred by reason of the performance of the production or resale activities of the taxpayer, and therefore, are not required to be capitalized under section 263A. Deductible service costs generally include costs incurred by reason of the taxpayer's overall management or policy guidance functions. In addition, deductible service costs include costs incurred by reason of the marketing, selling, advertising, and distribution activities of the taxpayer. Examples of service departments or functions that incur deductible service costs are provided in paragraph (e)(4)(iv) of this section.

(C) Mixed service costs. Mixed service costs are defined as service costs that are partially allocable to production or resale activities (capitalizable mixed service costs) and partially allocable to non-production or non-resale activities (deductible mixed service costs). For example, a personnel department may incur costs to recruit factory workers, the costs of which are allocable to production activities, and it may incur costs to develop wage, salary, and benefit policies, the costs of which are allocable to non-production activities.

(iii) Examples of capitalizable service costs. Costs incurred in the following departments or functions are generally allocated among production or resale activities:

(A) The administration and coordination of production or resale activities (wherever performed in the business organization of the taxpayer).

(B) Personnel operations, including the cost of recruiting, hiring, relocating, assigning, and maintaining personnel records or employees.

(C) Purchasing operations, including purchasing materials and equipment, scheduling and coordinating delivery of materials and equipment to or from factories or job sites, and expediting and follow-up.

(D) Materials handling and warehousing and storage operations.

(E) Accounting and data services operations, including, for example, cost accounting, accounts payable, disbursements, and payroll functions (but excluding accounts receivable and customer billing functions).

(F) Data processing.

(G) Security services.

(H) Legal services.

(iv) Examples of deductible service costs. Costs incurred in the following departments or functions are not generally allocated to production or resale activities:

(A) Departments or functions responsible for overall management of the taxpayer or for setting overall policy for all of the taxpayer's activities or trades or businesses, such as the board of directors (including their immediate staff), and the chief executive, financial, accounting, and legal officers (including their immediate staff) of the taxpayer, provided that no substantial part of the cost of such departments or functions benefits a particular production or resale activity.

(B) Strategic business planning.

(C) General financial accounting.

(D) General financial planning (including general budgeting) and financial management (including bank relations and cash management).

(E) Personnel policy (such as establishing and managing personnel policy in general; developing wage, salary, and benefit policies; developing employee training programs unrelated to particular production or resale activities; negotiating with labor unions; and maintaining relations with retired workers).

(F) Quality control policy.

(G) Safety engineering policy.

(H) Insurance or risk management policy (but not including bid or performance bonds or insurance related to activities associated with property produced or property acquired for resale).

(I) Environmental management policy (except to the extent that the costs of any system or procedure benefits a particular production or resale activity).

(J) General economic analysis and forecasting.

(K) Internal audit.

(L) Shareholder, public, and industrial relations.

(M) Tax services.

(N) Marketing, selling, or advertising.

(f) Cost allocation methods. *(1) Introduction.* This paragraph (f) sets forth various detailed or specific (facts-and-circumstances) cost allocation methods that taxpayers may use to allocate direct and indirect costs to property produced and property acquired for resale. Paragraph (g) of this section provides general rules for applying these allocation methods to various categories of costs (i.e., direct materials, direct labor, and indirect costs, including service costs). In addition, in lieu of a facts-and-circumstances allocation method, taxpayers may use the simplified methods provided in §§ 1.263A-2(b) and 1.263A-3(d) to allocate direct and indirect costs to eligible property produced or eligible property acquired for resale; see those sections for definitions of eligible property. Paragraph (h) of this section provides a simplified method for determining the amount of mixed service costs required to be capitalized to eligible property. The methodology set forth in paragraph (h) of this section for mixed service costs may be used in conjunction with either a facts-and-circumstances or a simplified method of allocating costs to eligible property produced or eligible property acquired for resale.

(2) Specific identification method. A specific identification method traces costs to a cost objective, such as a function, department, activity, or product, on the basis of a cause and effect or other reasonable relationship between the costs and the cost objective.

(3) Burden rate and standard cost methods. (i) Burden rate method. (A) In general. A burden rate method allocates an appropriate amount of indirect costs to property produced or property acquired for resale during a taxable year using predetermined rates that approximate the actual amount of indirect costs incurred by the taxpayer during the taxable year. Burden rates (such as ratios based on direct costs, hours, or similar items) may be developed by the taxpayer in accordance with acceptable accounting principles and applied in a reasonable manner. A taxpayer may allocate different indirect costs on the basis of different burden rates. Thus, for example, the taxpayer may use one burden rate for allocating the cost of rent and another burden rate for allocating the cost of utilities. Any periodic adjustment to a burden rate that merely reflects current operating conditions, such as increases in automation or changes in operation or prices, is not a change in method of accounting under section 446(e). A change, however, in the concept or base upon which such rates are developed, such as a change from basing the rates on direct labor hours to basing them on direct machine hours, is a change in method of accounting to which section 446(e) applies.

(B) Development of burden rates. The following factors, among others, may be used in developing burden rates:

(1) The selection of an appropriate level of activity and a period of time upon which to base the calculation of rates reflecting operating conditions for purposes of the unit costs being determined.

(2) The selection of an appropriate statistical base, such as direct labor hours, direct labor dollars, machine hours, or a combination thereof, upon which to apply the overhead rate.

(3) The appropriate budgeting, classification and analysis of expenses (for example, the analysis of fixed versus variable costs).

(C) Operation of the burden rate method. The purpose of the burden rate method is to allocate an appropriate amount of indirect costs to production or resale activities through the use of predetermined rates intended to approximate the actual amount of indirect costs incurred. Accordingly, the proper use of the burden rate method under this section requires that any net negative or net positive difference between the total predetermined amount of costs allocated to property and the total amount of indirect costs actually incurred and required to be allocated to such property (i.e., the under or over-applied burden) must be treated as an adjustment to the taxpayer's ending inventory or capital account (as the case may be) in the taxable year in which such difference arises. However, if such adjustment is not significant in amount in relation to the taxpayer's total indirect costs incurred with respect to production or resale activities for the year, such adjustment need not be allocated to the property produced or property acquired for resale unless such allocation is made in the taxpayer's financial reports. The taxpayer must treat both positive and negative adjustments consistently.

(ii) Standard cost method. (A) In general. A standard cost method allocates an appropriate amount of direct and indirect costs to property produced by the taxpayer through the use of preestablished standard allowances, without reference to costs actually incurred during the taxable year. A taxpayer may use a standard cost method to allocate costs, provided variances are treated in accordance with the procedures prescribed in paragraph (f)(3)(ii)(B) of this section. Any periodic adjustment to standard costs that merely reflects current operating conditions, such as increases in automation or changes in operation or prices, is not a change in method of accounting under section 446(e). A change, however, in the concept or base upon which standard costs are developed is a change in method of accounting to which section 446(e) applies.

(B) Treatment of variances. For purposes of this section, net positive overhead variance means the excess of total standard indirect costs over total actual indirect costs and net negative overhead variance means the excess of total actual indirect costs over total standard indirect costs. The proper use of a standard cost method requires that a taxpayer must reallocate to property a pro rata portion of any net negative or net positive overhead variances and any net negative or net positive direct cost variances. The taxpayer must apportion such variances to or among the property to which the costs are allocable. However, if such variances are not significant in amount relative to the taxpayer's total indirect costs incurred with respect to production and resale activities for the year, such variances need not be allocated to property produced or property acquired for resale unless such allocation is made in the taxpayer's financial reports. A taxpayer must treat both positive and negative variances consistently.

(4) Reasonable allocation methods. A taxpayer may use the methods described in paragraph (f)(2) or (3) of this section if they are reasonable allocation methods within the meaning of this paragraph (f)(4). In addition, a taxpayer may use any other reasonable method to properly allocate direct and indirect costs among units of property produced or property acquired for resale during the taxable year. An allocation method is reasonable if, with respect to the taxpayer's production or resale activities taken as a whole—

(i) The total costs actually capitalized during the taxable year do not differ significantly from the aggregate costs that would be properly capitalized using another permissible method described in this section or in §§ 1.263A-2 and 1.263A-3, with appropriate consideration given to the volume and value of the taxpayer's production or resale activities, the availability of costing information, the time and cost of using various allocation methods, and the accuracy of the allocation method chosen as compared with other allocation methods;

(ii) The allocation method is applied consistently by the taxpayer; and

(iii) The allocation method is not used to circumvent the requirements of the simplified methods in this section or in § 1.263A-2, § 1.263A-3, or the principles of section 263A.

(g) Allocating categories of costs. *(1) Direct materials.* Direct material costs (as defined in paragraph (e)(2) of this section) incurred during the taxable year must be allocated to the property produced or property acquired for resale by the taxpayer using the taxpayer's method of accounting for materials (e.g., specific identification; first-in, first-out (FIFO); or last-in, first-out (LIFO)), or any other reasonable allocation method (as defined under the principles of paragraph (f)(4) of this section).

(2) Direct labor. Direct labor costs (as defined in paragraph (e)(2) of this section) incurred during the taxable year are generally allocated to property produced or property acquired for resale using a specific identification method, standard cost method, or any other reasonable allocation method (as defined under the principles of paragraph (f)(4) of this section). All elements of compensation, other than basic compensation, may be grouped together and then allocated in proportion to the charge for basic compensation. Further, a taxpayer is not treated as using an erroneous method of accounting if direct labor costs are treated as indirect costs under the taxpayer's allocation method, provided such costs are capitalized to the extent required by paragraph (g)(3) of this section.

(3) Indirect costs. Indirect costs (as defined in paragraph (e)(3) of this section) are generally allocated to intermediate cost objectives such as departments or activities prior to the allocation of such costs to property produced or property acquired for resale. Indirect costs are allocated using either a specific identification method, a standard cost method, a burden rate method, or any other reasonable allocation method (as defined under the principles of paragraph (f)(4) of this section).

(4) Service costs. (i) In general. Service costs are a type of indirect costs that may be allocated using the same allocation methods available for allocating other indirect costs described in paragraph (g)(3) of this section. Generally, taxpayers that use a specific identification method or another reasonable allocation method must allocate service costs to particular departments or activities based on a factor or relationship that reasonably relates the service costs to the benefits received from the service departments or activities. For example, a reasonable factor for allocating legal services to particular departments or activities is the number of hours of legal services attributable to each department or activity. See paragraph (g)(4)(iv) of this section for other illustrations. Using reasonable factors or relationships, a taxpayer must allocate mixed service costs under a direct reallocation method described in paragraph (g)(4)(iii)(A) of this section, a step-allocation method described in paragraph (g)(4)(iii)(B) of this section, or any other reasonable allocation method (as defined under the principles of paragraph (f)(4) of this section).

(ii) De minimis rule. For purposes of administrative convenience, if 90 percent or more of a mixed service department's costs are deductible service costs, a taxpayer may elect not to allocate any portion of the service department's costs to property produced or property acquired for resale. For example, if 90 percent of the costs of an electing taxpayer's industrial relations department benefit the taxpayer's overall policy-making activities, the taxpayer is not required to allocate any portion of these costs to a production activity. Under this election, however, if 90 percent or more of a mixed service department's costs are capitalizable service costs, a taxpayer must allocate 100 percent of the department's costs to the production or resale activity benefitted. For example, if 90 percent of the costs of an electing taxpayer's accounting department benefit the taxpayer's manufacturing activity, the taxpayer must allocate 100 percent of the costs of the accounting department to the manufacturing activity. An election under this paragraph (g)(4)(ii) applies to all of a taxpayer's mixed service departments and constitutes the adoption of a (or a change in) method of accounting under section 446 of the Internal Revenue Code.

(iii) Methods for allocating mixed service costs. (A) Direct reallocation method. Under the direct reallocation method, the total costs (direct and indirect) of all mixed service departments are allocated only to departments or cost centers engaged in production or resale activities and then from those departments to particular activities. This direct reallocation method ignores benefits provided by one mixed service department to other mixed service departments, and also excludes other mixed service departments from the base used to make the allocation.

(B) Step-allocation method. (1) Under a step-allocation method, a sequence of allocations is made by the taxpayer. First, the total costs of the mixed service departments that benefit the greatest number of other departments are allocated to—

(i) Other mixed service departments;

(ii) Departments that incur only deductible service costs; and

(iii) Departments that exclusively engage in production or resale activities.

(2) A taxpayer continues allocating mixed service costs in the manner described in paragraph (g)(4)(iii)(B)(1) of this section (i.e., from the service departments benefitting the greatest number of departments to the service departments benefitting the least number of departments) until all mixed service costs are allocated to the types of departments listed in this paragraph (g)(4)(iii). Thus, a step-allocation method recognizes the benefits provided by one mixed service department to another mixed service department and also includes mixed service departments that have not yet been allocated in the base used to make the allocation.

(C) Examples. The provisions of this paragraph (g)(4)(iii) are illustrated by the following examples:

Example (1). Direct reallocation method. (i) Taxpayer E has the following five departments: the Assembling Department, the Painting Department, and the Finishing Department (production departments), and the Personnel Department and the Data Processing Department (mixed service departments). E allocates the Personnel Department's costs on the basis of total payroll costs and the Data Processing Department's costs on the basis of data processing hours.

(ii) Under a direct reallocation method, E allocates the Personnel Department's costs directly to its Assembling, Painting, and Finishing Department, and not to its Data Processing department.

Department	Total dept. costs	Amount of payroll costs	Allocation ratio	Amount allocated
Personnel	$ 500,000	$ 50,000	—	<$500,000>
Data Proc'g	250,000	15,000	—	—
Assembling	250,000	15,000	15,000/285,000	26,315
Painting	1,000,000	90,000	90,000/285,000	157,895
Finishing	2,000,000	180,000	180,000/285,000	315,790
Total	$4,000,000	$350,000	—	—

(iii) After E allocates the Personnel Department's costs, E then allocates the costs of its Data Processing Department in the same manner.

Department	Total dept. cost after initial allocation	Total data proc. hours	Allocation ratio	Amount allocated	Total dept. cost after final allocation
Personnel	$ 0	2,000	—		0
Data Proc'g	250,000	—	—	<$250,000>	—
Assembling	276,315	2,000	2,000/10,000	50,000	$ 326,315
Painting	1,157,895	0	0/10,000	0	1,157,895
Finishing	2,315,790	8,000	8,000/10,000	200,000	2,515,790
Total	$4,000,000	12,000			$4,000,000

Example (2). Step-allocation method. (i) Taxpayer F has the following five departments: the Manufacturing Department (a production department), the Marketing Department and the Finance Department (departments that incur only deductible service costs), the Personnel Department and the Data Processing Department (mixed service departments). F uses a step-allocation method and allocates the Personnel Department's costs on the basis of total payroll costs and the Data Processing Department's costs on the basis of data processing hours. F's Personnel Department benefits all four of F's other departments, while its Data Processing Department benefits only three departments. Because F's Personnel Department benefits the greatest number of other departments, F first allocates its Personnel Department's costs to its Manufacturing, Marketing, Finance and Data processing departments, as follows:

Department	Total cost of dept.	Total payroll costs	Allocation ratio	Amount allocated
Personnel	$ 500,000	$ 50,000	—	<$500,000>
Data Proc'g	250,000	15,000	15,000/300,000	25,000
Finance	250,000	15,000	15,000/300,000	25,000
Marketing	1,000,000	90,000	90,000/300,000	150,000
Manufac'g	2,000,000	180,000	180,000/300,000	300,000
	4,000,000	350,000	—	—

(ii) Under a step-allocation method, the denominator of F's allocation ratio includes the payroll costs of its Manufacturing, Marketing, Finance, and Data Processing departments.

(iii) Next, F allocates the costs of its Data Processing Department on the basis of data processing hours. Because the costs incurred by F's Personnel Department have already been allocated, no allocation is made to the Personnel Department.

Department	Total dept. cost after initial allocation	Total data proc. hours	Allocation ratio	Amount allocated	Total dept. cost after final allocation
Personnel	$ 0	2,000	—	—	$ 0
Data Proc'g	275,000	—	—	<$275,000>	0
Finance	275,000	2,000	2,000/10,000	55,000	330,000
Marketing	1,150,000	0	0/10,000	0	1,150,000
Manufac'g	2,300,000	8,000	8,000/10,000	220,000	2,520,000
	4,000,000	12,000	—	—	4,000,000

(iv) Under the second step of F's step-allocation method, the denominator of F's allocation ratio includes the data processing hours of its Manufacturing, Marketing, and Finance Departments, but does not include the data processing hours of its Personnel Department (the other mixed service department) because the costs of that department have previously been allocated.

(iv) Illustrations of mixed service cost allocations using reasonable factors or relationships. This paragraph (g)(4)(iv) illustrates various reasonable factors and relationships that may be used in allocating different types of mixed service costs. Taxpayers, however, are permitted to use other reasonable factors and relationships to allocate mixed service costs. In addition, the factors or relationships illustrated in this paragraph (g)(4)(iv) may be used to allocate other types of service costs not illustrated in this paragraph (g)(4)(iv).

(A) Security services. The costs of security or protection services must be allocated to each physical area that receives the services using any reasonable method applied consistently (e.g., the size of the physical area, the number of employees in the area, or the relative fair market value of assets located in the area).

(B) Legal services. The costs of legal services are generally allocable to a particular production or resale activity on the basis of the approximate number of hours of legal service performed in connection with the activity, including research, bidding, negotiating, drafting, reviewing a contract, obtaining necessary licenses and permits, and resolving disputes. Different hourly rates may be appropriate for different services. In determining the number of hours allocable to any activity, estimates are appropriate, detailed time records are not required to be kept, and insubstantial amounts of services provided to an activity by senior legal staff (such as administrators or reviewers) may be ignored. Legal costs may also be allocated to a particular production or resale activity based on the ratio of the total direct costs incurred for the activity to the total direct costs incurred with respect to all production or resale activities. The taxpayer must also allocate directly to an activity the cost incurred for any outside legal services. Legal costs relating to general corporate functions are not required to be allocated to a particular production or resale activity.

(C) Centralized payroll services. The costs of a centralized payroll department or activity are generally allocated to the departments or activities benefitted on the basis of the gross dollar amount of payroll processed.

(D) Centralized data processing services. The costs of a centralized data processing department are generally allocated to all departments or activities benefitted using any reasonable basis, such as total direct data processing costs or the number of data processing hours supplied. The costs of data processing systems or applications developed for a particular activity are directly allocated to that activity.

(E) Engineering and design services. The costs of an engineering or a design department are generally directly allocable to the departments or activities benefitted based on the ratio of the approximate number of hours of work performed with respect to the particular activity to the total number of hours of engineering or design work performed for all activities. Different services may be allocated at different hourly rates.

(F) Safety engineering services. The costs of a safety engineering departments or activities generally benefit all of the taxpayer's activities and, thus, should be allocated using a reasonable basis, such as: the approximate number of safety inspections made in connection with a particular activity as a fraction of total inspections, the number of employees assigned to an activity as a fraction of total employees, or the total labor hours worked in connection with an activity as a fraction of total hours. However, in determining the allocable costs of a safety engineering department, costs attributable to providing a safety program relating only to a particular activity must be directly assigned to such activity. Additionally, the cost of a safety engineering department only responsible for setting safety policy and establishing safety procedures to be used in all of the taxpayer's activities is not required to be allocated.

(v) Accounting method change. A change in the method or base used to allocate service costs (such as changing from an allocation base using direct labor costs to a base using direct labor hours), or a change in the taxpayer's determination of what functions or departments of the taxpayer are to be allocated, is a change in method of accounting to which section 446(e) and the regulations thereunder apply.

(h) Simplified service cost method. *(1) Introduction.* This paragraph (h) provides a simplified method for determining capitalizable mixed service costs incurred during the taxable year with respect to eligible property (i.e., the aggregate portion of mixed service costs that are properly allocable to the taxpayer's production or resale activities).

(2) Eligible property. (i) In general. Except as otherwise provided in paragraph (h)(2)(ii) of this section, the simplified service cost method, if elected for any trade or business of the taxpayer, must be used for all production and resale activities of the trade or business associated with any of the following categories of property that are subject to section 263A:

(A) Inventory property. Stock in trade or other property properly includible in the inventory of the taxpayer.

(B) Non-inventory property held for sale. Non-inventory property held by a taxpayer primarily for sale to customers in the ordinary course of the taxpayer's trade or business.

(C) Certain self-constructed assets. Self-constructed assets substantially identical in nature to, and produced in the same manner as, inventory property produced by the taxpayer or other property produced by the taxpayer and held primarily for sale to customers in the ordinary course of the taxpayer's trade or business.

(D) Self-constructed tangible personal property produced on a routine and repetitive basis. (1) In general. Self-constructed tangible personal property produced by the taxpayer on a routine and repetitive basis in the ordinary course of the taxpayer's trade or business. Self-constructed tangible personal property is produced by the taxpayer on a routine and repetitive basis in the ordinary course of the taxpayer's trade or business when units of tangible personal property (as defined in § 1.263A-10(c)) are mass-produced, that is, numerous substantially identical assets are manufactured within a taxable year using standardized designs and assembly line techniques, and either the applicable recovery period of the property determined under section 168(c) is not longer than 3 years or the property is a material or supply that will be used and consumed within 3 years of being produced. For purposes of this paragraph (h)(2)(i)(D), the applicable recovery period of the assets will be determined at the end of the taxable year in which the assets are placed in service for purposes of § 1.46-3(d). Subsequent changes to the applicable recovery period after the assets are placed in service will not affect the determination of whether the assets are produced on a routine and repetitive basis for purposes of this paragraph (h)(2)(i)(D).

(2) Examples. The following examples illustrate this paragraph (h)(2)(i)(D):

Example (1). Y is a manufacturer of automobiles. During the taxable year Y produces numerous substantially identical dies and molds using standardized designs and assembly line techniques. The dies and molds have a 3-year applicable recovery period for purposes of section 168(c). Y uses the dies and molds to produce or process particular automobile components and does not hold them for sale. The dies and molds are produced on a routine and repetitive basis in the ordinary course of Y's business for purposes of this paragraph because the dies and molds are both mass-produced and have a recovery period of not longer than 3 years.

Example (2). Z is an electric utility that regularly manufactures and installs identical poles that are used in transmitting and distributing electricity. The poles have a 20-year applicable recovery period for purposes of section 168(c). The poles are not produced on a routine and repetitive basis in the ordinary course of Z's business for purposes of this paragraph because the poles have an applicable recovery period that is longer than 3 years.

(ii) Election to exclude self-constructed assets. At the taxpayer's election, the simplified service cost method may be applied within a trade or business to only the categories of inventory property and non-inventory property held for sale described in paragraphs (h)(2)(i)(A) and (B) of this section. Taxpayers electing to exclude the self-constructed assets described in paragraphs (h)(2)(i)(C) and (D) of this section from application of the simplified service cost method must, however, allocate service costs to such property in accordance with paragraph (g)(4) of this section.

(3) General allocation formula. (i) Under the simplified service cost method, a taxpayer computes its capitalizable mixed service costs using the following formula:

Allocation ratio × Total mixed service costs.

(ii) A producer may elect one of two allocation ratios, the labor-based allocation ratio or the production cost allocation ratio. A reseller that satisfies the requirements for using the simplified resale method of § 1.263A-3(d) (whether or not that method is elected) may elect the simplified service cost method, but must use a labor-based allocation ratio. (See § 1.263A-3(d) for labor-based allocation ratios to be used in conjunction with the simplified resale method.) The allocation ratio used by a trade or business of a taxpayer is a method of accounting which must be applied consistently within the trade or business.

(4) Labor-based allocation ratio. (i) The labor-based allocation ratio is computed as follows:

$$\frac{\text{Section 263A labor costs}}{\text{Total labor costs}}$$

(ii) Section 263A labor costs are defined as the total labor costs (excluding labor costs included in mixed service costs) allocable to property produced and property acquired for resale under section 263A that are incurred in the taxpayer's trade or business during the taxable year. Total labor costs are defined as the total labor costs (excluding labor costs included in mixed service costs) incurred in the taxpayer's trade or business during the taxable year. Total labor costs include labor costs incurred in all parts of the trade or business (i.e., if the taxpayer has both property produced and property acquired for resale, the taxpayer must include labor costs from resale activities as well as production activities). For example, taxpayer G incurs $ 1,000 of total mixed service costs during the taxable year. G's section 263A labor costs are $ 5,000 and its total labor costs are $ 10,000. Under the labor-based allocation ratio, G's capitalizable mixed service costs are $ 500 (i.e., $ 1,000 × ($ 5,000 divided by $ 10,000)).

(5) Production cost allocation ratio. (i) Producers may use the production cost allocation ratio, computed as follows:

$$\frac{\text{Section 263A production costs}}{\text{Total costs}}$$

(ii) Section 263A production costs are defined as the total costs (excluding mixed service costs and interest) allocable to property produced (and property acquired for resale if the producer is also engaged in resale activities) under section 263A that are incurred in the taxpayer's trade or business during the taxable year. Total costs are defined as all costs (excluding mixed service costs and interest) incurred in the taxpayer's trade or business during the taxable year. Total costs include all direct and indirect costs allocable to property produced (and property acquired for resale if the producer is also engaged in resale activities) as well as all other costs of the taxpayer's trade or business, including, but not limited to: salaries and other labor costs of all personnel; all depreciation taken for federal income tax purposes; research and experimental expenditures; and selling, marketing, and distribution costs. Such costs do not include, however, taxes described in paragraph (e)(3)(iii)(F) of this section. For example, taxpayer H, a producer, incurs $ 1,000 of total mixed service costs in the taxable year. H's section 263A production costs are $ 10,000 and its total costs are $ 20,000. Under the production cost allocation ratio, H's capitalizable mixed service costs are $ 500 (i.e., $ 1,000 X ($ 10,000 divided by $ 20,000)).

(6) Definition of total mixed service costs. Total mixed service costs are defined as the total costs incurred during the taxable year in all departments or functions of the tax-

payer's trade or business that perform mixed service activities. See paragraph (e)(4)(ii)(C) of this section which defines mixed service costs. In determining the total mixed service costs of a trade or business, the taxpayer must include all costs incurred in its mixed service departments and cannot exclude any otherwise deductible service costs. For example, if the accounting department within a trade or business is a mixed service department, then in determining the total mixed service costs of the trade or business, the taxpayer cannot exclude the costs of personnel in the accounting department that perform services relating to non-production activities (e.g., accounts receivable or customer billing activities). Instead, the entire cost of the accounting department must be included in the total mixed service costs.

(7) Costs allocable to more than one business. To the extent mixed service costs, labor costs, or other costs are incurred in more than one trade or business, the taxpayer must determine the amounts allocable to the particular trade or business for which the simplified service cost method is being applied by using any reasonable allocation method consistent with the principles of paragraph (f)(4) of this section.

(8) De minimis rule. If the taxpayer elects to apply the de minimis rule of paragraph (g)(4)(ii) of this section to any mixed service department, the department is not considered a mixed service department for purposes of the simplified service cost method. Instead, the costs of such department are allocated exclusively to the particular activity satisfying the 90-percent test.

(9) Separate election. A taxpayer may elect the simplified service cost method in conjunction with any other allocation method used at the trade or business level, including the simplified methods described in §§ 1.263A-2(b) and 1.263A-3(d). However, the election of the simplified service cost method must be made independently of the election to use those other simplified methods.

(i) [Reserved]

(j) Special rules. *(1) Costs provided by a related person.* (i) In general. A taxpayer subject to section 263A must capitalize an arm's-length charge for any section 263A costs (e.g., costs of materials, labor, or services) incurred by a related person that are properly allocable to the property produced or property acquired for resale by the taxpayer. Both the taxpayer and the related person must account for the transaction as if an arm's-length charge had been incurred by the taxpayer with respect to its property produced or property acquired for resale. For purposes of this paragraph (j)(1)(i), a taxpayer is considered related to another person if the taxpayer and such person are described in section 482. Further, for purposes of this paragraph (j)(1)(i), arm's-length charge means the arm's-length charge (or other appropriate charge where permitted and applicable) under the principles of section 482. Any correlative adjustments necessary because of the arm's-length charge requirement of this paragraph (j)(1)(i) shall be determined under the principles of section 482.

(ii) Exceptions. The provisions of paragraph (j)(1)(i) of this section do not apply if, and to the extent that—

(A) It would be inappropriate under the principles of section 482 for the Commissioner to adjust the income of the taxpayer or the related person with respect to the transaction at issue; or

(B) A transaction is accounted for under an alternative Internal Revenue Code section resulting in the capitalization (or deferral of the deduction) of the costs of the items provided by the related party and the related party does not deduct such costs earlier than the costs would have been deducted by the taxpayer if the costs were capitalized under section 263A. See § 1.1502-13.

(2) Optional capitalization of period costs. (i) In general. Taxpayers are not required to capitalize indirect costs that do not directly benefit or are not incurred by reason of the production of property or acquisition of property for resale (i.e., period costs). A taxpayer may, however, elect to capitalize certain period costs if: The method is consistently applied; is used in computing beginning inventories, ending inventories, and cost of goods sold; and does not result in a material distortion of the taxpayer's income. A material distortion relates to the source, character, amount, or timing of the cost capitalized or any other item affected by the capitalization of the cost. Thus, for example, a taxpayer may not capitalize a period cost under section 263A if capitalization would result in a material change in the computation of the foreign tax credit limitation under section 904. An election to capitalize a period cost is the adoption of (or a change in) a method of accounting under section 446 of the Internal Revenue Code.

(ii) Period costs eligible for capitalization. The types of period costs eligible for capitalization under this paragraph (j)(2) include only the types of period costs (e.g., under paragraph (e)(3)(iii) of this section) for which some portion of the costs incurred is properly allocable to property produced or property acquired for resale in the year of the election. Thus, for example, marketing or advertising costs, no portion of which are properly allocable to property produced or property acquired for resale, do not qualify for elective capitalization under this paragraph (j)(2).

(3) Trade or business application. Notwithstanding the references generally to taxpayer throughout this section and §§ 1.263A-2 and 1.263A-3, the methods of accounting provided under section 263A are to be elected and applied independently for each separate and distinct trade or business of the taxpayer in accordance with the provisions of section 446(d) and the regulations thereunder.

(4) Transfers with a principal purpose of tax avoidance. The District Director may require appropriate adjustments to valuations of inventory and other property subject to section 263A if a transfer of property is made to another person for a principal purpose of avoiding the application of section 263A. Thus, for example, the District Director may require a taxpayer using the simplified production method of § 1.263A-2(b) to apply that method to transferred inventories immediately prior to a transfer under section 351 if a principal purpose of the transfer is to avoid the application of section 263A.

(k) Change in method of accounting. *(1) In general.* A change in a taxpayer's treatment of mixed service costs to comply with paragraph (h)(2)(i)(D) of this section is a change in method of accounting to which the provisions of sections 446 and 481 and the regulations under those sections apply. See § 1.263A-7. For a taxpayer's first taxable year ending on or after August 2, 2005, the taxpayer is granted the consent of the Commissioner to change its method of accounting to comply with paragraph (h)(2)(i)(D) of this section, provided the taxpayer follows the administrative procedures, as modified by paragraphs (k)(2) through (4) of this section, issued under § 1.446-1(e)(3)(ii) for obtaining the Commissioner's automatic consent to a change in accounting method (for further guidance, for example, see Rev. Proc. 2002-9 (2002-1 CB 327), as modified and clarified by Announcement 2002-17 (2002-1 CB 561), modified and amplified by Rev. Proc. 2002-19 (2002-1 CB 696), and amplified, clarified, and modified by Rev. Proc. 2002-54

(2002-2 CB 432), and § 601.601(d)(2)(ii)(b) of this chapter). For purposes of Form 3115, "Application for Change in Accounting Method," the designated number for the automatic accounting method change authorized by this paragraph (k) is "95." If Form 3115 is revised or renumbered, any reference in this section to that form is treated as a reference to the revised or renumbered form. Alternatively, notwithstanding the provisions of any administrative procedures that preclude a taxpayer from requesting the advance consent of the Commissioner to change a method of accounting that is required to be made pursuant to a published automatic change procedure, for its first taxable year ending on or after August 2, 2005, a taxpayer may request the advance consent of the Commissioner to change its method of accounting to comply with paragraph (h)(2)(i)(D) of this section, provided the taxpayer follows the administrative procedures, as modified by paragraphs (k)(2) through (5) of this section, for obtaining the advance consent of the Commissioner (for further guidance, for example, see Rev. Proc. 97-27 (1997-1 CB 680), as modified and amplified by Rev. Proc. 2002-19 (2002-1 CB 696), as amplified and clarified by Rev. Proc. 2002-54 (2002-2 CB 432), and § 601.601(d)(2)(ii)(b) of this chapter). For the taxpayer's second and subsequent taxable years ending on or after August 2, 2005, requests to secure the consent of the Commissioner must be made under the administrative procedures, as modified by paragraphs (k)(3) and (4) of this section, for obtaining the Commissioner's advance consent to a change in accounting method.

(2) Scope limitations. Any limitations on obtaining the automatic consent or advance consent of the Commissioner do not apply to a taxpayer seeking to change its method of accounting to comply with paragraph (h)(2)(i)(D) of this section for its first taxable year ending on or after August 2, 2005.

(3) Audit protection. A taxpayer that changes its method of accounting in accordance with this paragraph (k) to comply with paragraph (h)(2)(i)(D) of this section does not receive audit protection if its method of accounting for mixed service costs is an issue under consideration at the time the application is filed with the national office.

(4) Section 481(a) adjustment. A change in method of accounting to conform to paragraph (h)(2)(i)(D) of this section requires a section 481(a) adjustment. The section 481(a) adjustment period is two taxable years for a net positive adjustment for an accounting method change that is made to conform to paragraph (h)(2)(i)(D) of this section.

(5) Time for requesting change. Notwithstanding the provisions of § 1.446-1(e)(3)(i) and any contrary administrative procedure, a taxpayer may submit a request for advance consent to change its method of accounting to comply with paragraph (h)(2)(i)(D) of this section for its first taxable year ending on or after August 2, 2005, on or before the date that is 30 days after the end of the taxable year for which the change is requested.

(l) Effective date. Paragraphs (h)(2)(i)(D), (k), and (l) of this section apply for taxable years ending on or after August 2, 2005.

T.D. 8482, 8/6/93, amend T.D. 8559, 8/2/94, T.D. 8584, 12/28/94, T.D. 8597, 7/12/95, T.D. 8728, 8/4/97, T.D. 8729, 8/21/97, T.D. 8897, 8/18/2000, T.D. 9217, 8/2/2005, T.D. 9318, 3/28/2007.

PAR. 9. Section 1.263A-1 is amended by adding paragraph (b)(14) as follows:

Proposed § 1.263A-1 Uniform capitalization of costs.

[*For Preamble, see ¶ 152,973*]

* * * * *

(b) * * *

(14) Property subject to de minimis rule. Section 263A does not apply to the costs of property produced by a taxpayer to which the taxpayer properly applies the de minimis rule under § 1.263(a)-2(d)(4). However, the cost of property to which a taxpayer properly applies the de minimis rule under § 1.263(a)-2(d)(4) may be required to be capitalized to other property as a cost incurred by reason of the production of the other property that is subject to section 263A.

* * * * *

§ 1.263A-2 Rules relating to property produced by the taxpayer.

(a) In general. Section 263A applies to real property and tangible personal property produced by a taxpayer for use in its trade or business or for sale to its customers. In addition, section 263A applies to property produced for a taxpayer under a contract with another party. The principal terms related to the scope of section 263A with respect to producers are provided in this paragraph (a). See § 1.263A-1(b)(11) for an exception in the case of certain de minimis property provided to customers incident to the provision of services.

(1) Produce. (i) In general. For purposes of section 263A, produce includes the following: construct, build, install, manufacture, develop, improve, create, raise, or grow.

(ii) Ownership. (A) General rule. Except as provided in paragraphs (a)(1)(ii)(B) and (C) of this section, a taxpayer is not considered to be producing property unless the taxpayer is considered an owner of the property produced under federal income tax principles. The determination as to whether a taxpayer is an owner is based on all of the facts and circumstances, including the various benefits and burdens of ownership vested with the taxpayer. A taxpayer may be considered an owner of property produced, even though the taxpayer does not have legal title to the property.

(B) Property produced for the taxpayer under a contract. (1) In general. Property produced for the taxpayer under a contract with another party is treated as property produced by the taxpayer to the extent the taxpayer makes payments or otherwise incurs costs with respect to the property. A taxpayer has made payment under this section if the transaction would be considered payment by a taxpayer using the cash receipts and disbursements method of accounting.

(2) Definition of a contract. (i) General rule. Except as provided under paragraph (a)(1)(ii)(B)(2)(ii) of this section, a contract is any agreement providing for the production of property if the agreement is entered into before the production of the property to be delivered under the contract is completed. Whether an agreement exists depends on all the facts and circumstances. Facts and circumstances indicating an agreement include, for example, the making of a prepayment, or an arrangement to make a prepayment, for property prior to the date of the completion of production of the property, or the incurring of significant expenditures for property of specialized design or specialized application that is not intended for self-use.

(ii) Routine purchase order exception. A routine purchase order for fungible property is not treated as a contract for purposes of this section. An agreement will not be treated as a routine purchase order for fungible property, however, if the contractor is required to make more than de minimis modifications to the property to tailor it to the customer's specific needs, or if at the time the agreement is entered into, the customer knows or has reason to know that the contractor cannot satisfy the agreement within 30 days out of existing stocks and normal production of finished goods.

(C) Home construction contracts. Section 460(e)(1) provides that section 263A applies to a home construction contract unless that contract will be completed within two years of the contract commencement date and the taxpayer's average annual gross receipts for the three preceding taxable years do not exceed $10,000,000. Section 263A applies to such a contract even if the contractor is not considered the owner of the property produced under the contract under federal income tax principles.

(2) Tangible personal property. (i) General rule. In general, section 263A applies to the costs of producing tangible personal property, and not to the costs of producing intangible property. For example, section 263A applies to the costs manufacturers incur to produce goods, but does not apply to the costs financial institutions incur to originate loans.

(ii) Intellectual or creative property. For purposes of determining whether a taxpayer producing intellectual or creative property is producing tangible personal property or intangible property, the term tangible personal property includes films, sound recordings, video tapes, books, and other similar property embodying words, ideas, concepts, images, or sounds by the creator thereof. Other similar property for this purpose generally means intellectual or creative property for which, as costs are incurred in producing the property, it is intended (or is reasonably likely) that any tangible medium in which the property is embodied will be mass distributed by the creator or any one or more third parties in a form that is not substantially altered. However, any intellectual or creative property that is embodied in a tangible medium that is mass distributed merely incident to the distribution of a principal product or good of the creator is not other similar property for these purposes.

(A) Intellectual or creative property that is tangible personal property. Section 263A applies to tangible personal property defined in this paragraph (a)(2) without regard to whether such property is treated as tangible or intangible property under other sections of the Internal Revenue Code. Thus, for example, section 263A applies to the costs of producing a motion picture or researching and writing a book even though these assets may be considered intangible for other purposes of the Internal Revenue Code. Tangible personal property includes, for example, the following:

(1) Books. The costs of producing and developing books (including teaching aids and other literary works) required to be capitalized under this section include costs incurred by an author in researching, preparing, and writing the book. (However, see section 263A(h), which provides an exemption from the capitalization requirements of section 263A in the case of certain free-lance authors.) In addition, the costs of producing and developing books include prepublication expenditures incurred by publishers, including payments made to authors (other than commissions for sales of books that have already taken place), as well as costs incurred by publishers in writing, editing, compiling, illustrating, designing, and developing the books. The costs of producing a book also include the costs of producing the underlying manuscript, copyright, or license. (These costs are distinguished from the separately capitalizable costs of printing and binding the tangible medium embodying the book (e.g., paper and ink).) See § 1.174-2(a)(1), which provides that the term research or experimental expenditures does not include expenditures incurred for research in connection with literary, historical, or similar projects.

(2) Sound recordings. A sound recording is a work that results from the fixation of a series of musical, spoken, or other sounds, regardless of the nature of the material objects, such as discs, tapes, or other phonorecordings, in which such sounds are embodied.

(B) Intellectual or creative property that is not tangible personal property. Items that are not considered tangible personal property within the meaning of section 263A(b) and paragraph (a)(2)(ii) of this section include:

(1) Evidences of value. Tangible personal property does not include property that is representative or evidence of value, such as stock, securities, debt instruments, mortgages, or loans.

(2) Property provided incident to services. Tangible personal property does not include de minimis property provided to a client or customer incident to the provision of services, such as wills prepared by attorneys, or blueprints prepared by architects. See § 1.263A-1(b)(11).

(3) Costs required to be capitalized by producers. (i) In general. Except as specifically provided in section 263A(f) with respect to interest costs, producers must capitalize direct and indirect costs properly allocable to property produced under section 263A, without regard to whether those costs are incurred before, during, or after the production period (as defined in section 263A(f)(4)(B)).

(ii) Pre-production costs. If property is held for future production, taxpayers must capitalize direct and indirect costs allocable to such property (e.g., purchasing, storage, handling, and other costs), even though production has not begun. If property is not held for production, indirect costs incurred prior to the beginning of the production period must be allocated to the property and capitalized if, at the time the costs are incurred, it is reasonably likely that production will occur at some future date. Thus, for example, a manufacturer must capitalize the costs of storing and handling raw materials before the raw materials are committed to production. In addition, a real estate developer must capitalize property taxes incurred with respect to property if, at the time the taxes are incurred, it is reasonably likely that the property will be subsequently developed.

(iii) Post-production costs. Generally, producers must capitalize all indirect costs incurred subsequent to completion of production that are properly allocable to the property produced. Thus, for example, storage and handling costs incurred while holding the property produced for sale after production must be capitalized to the property to the extent properly allocable to the property. However, see § 1.263A-3(c) for exceptions.

(4) Practical capacity concept. Notwithstanding any provision to the contrary, the use, directly or indirectly, of the practical capacity concept is not permitted under section 263A. For purposes of section 263A, the term practical capacity concept means any concept, method, procedure, or formula (such as the practical capacity concept described in § 1.471-11(d)(4)) whereunder fixed costs are not capitalized because of the relationship between the actual production at the taxpayer's production facility and the practical capacity of the facility. For purposes of this section, the practical capacity of a facility includes either the practical capacity or theoretical capacity of the facility, as defined in § 1.471-11(d)(4), or any similar determination of productive or operating capacity. The practical capacity concept may not be used with respect to any activity to which section 263A applies (i.e., production or resale activities). A taxpayer shall not be considered to be using the practical capacity concept

solely because the taxpayer properly does not capitalize costs described in § 1.263A-1(e)(3)(iii)(E), relating to certain costs attributable to temporarily idle equipment.

(5) Taxpayers required to capitalize costs under this section. This section generally applies to taxpayers that produce property. If a taxpayer is engaged in both production activities and resale activities, the taxpayer applies the principles of this section as if it read production or resale activities, and by applying appropriate principles from § 1.263A-3. If a taxpayer is engaged in both production and resale activities, the taxpayer may elect the simplified production method provided in this section, but generally may not elect the simplified resale method discussed in § 1.263A-3(d). If elected, the simplified production method must be applied to all eligible property produced and all eligible property acquired for resale by the taxpayer.

(b) Simplified production method. *(1) Introduction.* This paragraph (b) provides a simplified method for determining the additional section 263A costs properly allocable to ending inventories of property produced and other eligible property on hand at the end of the taxable year.

(2) Eligible property. (i) In general. Except as otherwise provided in paragraph (b)(2)(ii) of this section, the simplified production method, if elected for any trade or business of a producer, must be used for all production and resale activities associated with any of the following categories of property to which section 263A applies:

(A) Inventory property. Stock in trade or other property properly includible in the inventory of the taxpayer.

(B) Non-inventory property held for sale. Non-inventory property held by a taxpayer primarily for sale to customers in the ordinary course of the taxpayer's trade or business.

(C) Certain self-constructed assets. Self-constructed assets substantially identical in nature to, and produced in the same manner as, inventory property produced by the taxpayer or other property produced by the taxpayer and held primarily for sale to customers in the ordinary course of the taxpayer's trade or business.

(D) Self-constructed tangible personal property produced on a routine and repetitive basis. (1) In general. Self-constructed tangible personal property produced by the taxpayer on a routine and repetitive basis in the ordinary course of the taxpayer's trade or business. Self-constructed tangible personal property is produced by the taxpayer on a routine and repetitive basis in the ordinary course of the taxpayer's trade or business when units of tangible personal property (as defined in § 1.263A-10(c)) are mass-produced, that is, numerous substantially identical assets are manufactured within a taxable year using standardized designs and assembly line techniques, and either the applicable recovery period of the property determined under section 168(c) is not longer than 3 years or the property is a material or supply that will be used and consumed within 3 years of being produced. For purposes of this paragraph (b)(2)(i)(D), the applicable recovery period of the assets will be determined at the end of the taxable year in which the assets are placed in service for purposes of § 1.46-3(d). Subsequent changes to the applicable recovery period after the assets are placed in service will not affect the determination of whether the assets are produced on a routine and repetitive basis for purposes of this paragraph (b)(2)(i)(D).

(2) Examples. The following examples illustrate this paragraph (b)(2)(i)(D):

Example (1). Y is a manufacturer of automobiles. During the taxable year Y produces numerous substantially identical dies and molds using standardized designs and assembly line techniques. The dies and molds have a 3-year applicable recovery period for purposes of section 168(c). Y uses the dies and molds to produce or process particular automobile components and does not hold them for sale. The dies and molds are produced on a routine and repetitive basis in the ordinary course of Y's business for purposes of this paragraph because the dies and molds are both mass-produced and have a recovery period of not longer than 3 years.

Example (2). Z is an electric utility that regularly manufactures and installs identical poles that are used in transmitting and distributing electricity. The poles have a 20-year applicable recovery period for purposes of section 168(c). The poles are not produced on a routine and repetitive basis in the ordinary course of Z's business for purposes of this paragraph because the poles have an applicable recovery period that is longer than 3 years.

(ii) Election to exclude self-constructed assets. At the taxpayer's election, the simplified production method may be applied within a trade or business to only the categories of inventory property and non-inventory property held for sale described in paragraphs (b)(2)(i)(A) and (B) of this section. Taxpayers electing to exclude the self-constructed assets, defined in paragraphs (b)(2)(i)(C) and (D) of this section, from application of the simplified production method must, however, allocate additional section 263A costs to such property in accordance with § 1.263A-1(f).

(3) Simplified production method without historic absorption ratio election. (i) General allocation formula. (A) In general. Except as otherwise provided in paragraph (b)(3)(iv) of this section, the additional section 263A costs allocable to eligible property remaining on hand at the close of the taxable year under the simplified production method are computed as follows:

$$\text{Absorption ratio} \times \text{Section 471 costs remaining on hand at year end}$$

(B) Effect of allocation. The absorption ratio generally is multiplied by the section 471 costs remaining in ending inventory or otherwise on hand at the end of each taxable year in which the simplified production method is applied. The resulting product is the additional section 263A costs that are added to the taxpayer's ending section 471 costs to determine the section 263A costs that are capitalized. See, however, paragraph (b)(3)(iii) of this section for special rules applicable to LIFO taxpayers. Except as otherwise provided in this section or in § 1.263A-1 or 1.263A-3, additional section 263A costs that are allocated to inventories on hand at the close of the taxable year under the simplified production method of this paragraph (b) are treated as inventory costs for all purposes of the Internal Revenue Code.

(ii) Definitions. (A) Absorption ratio. Under the simplified production method, the absorption ratio is determined as follows:

$$\frac{\text{Additional section 263A costs incurred during the taxable year}}{\text{Section 471 costs incurred during the taxable year}}$$

(1) Additional section 263A costs incurred during the taxable year. Additional section 263A costs incurred during the taxable year are defined as the additional section 263A costs described in § 1.263A-1(d)(3) that a taxpayer incurs during its current taxable year.

(2) Section 471 costs incurred during the taxable year. Section 471 costs incurred during the taxable year are defined as the section 471 costs described in § 1.263A-1(d)(2) that a taxpayer incurs during its current taxable year.

(B) Section 471 costs remaining on hand at year end. Section 471 costs remaining on hand at year end means the section 471 costs, as defined in § 1.263A-1(d)(2), that a taxpayer incurs during its current taxable year which remain in its ending inventory or are otherwise on hand at year end. For LIFO inventories of a taxpayer, the section 471 costs remaining on hand at year end means the increment, if any, for the current year stated in terms of section 471 costs. See paragraph (b)(3)(iii) of this section.

(iii) LIFO taxpayers electing the simplified production method. (A) In general. Under the simplified production method, a taxpayer using a LIFO method must calculate a particular year's index (e.g., under § 1.472-8(e)) without regard to its additional section 263A costs. Similarly, a taxpayer that adjusts current-year costs by applicable indexes to determine whether there has been an inventory increment or decrement in the current year for a particular LIFO pool must disregard the additional section 263A costs in making that determination.

(B) LIFO increment. If the taxpayer determines there has been an inventory increment, the taxpayer must state the amount of the increment in current-year dollars (stated in terms of section 471 costs). The taxpayer then multiplies this amount by the absorption ratio. The resulting product is the additional section 263A costs that must be added to the taxpayer's increment for the year stated in terms of section 471 costs.

(C) LIFO decrement. If the taxpayer determines there has been an inventory decrement, the taxpayer must state the amount of the decrement in dollars applicable to the particular year for which the LIFO layer has been invaded. The additional section 263A costs incurred in prior years that are applicable to the decrement are charged to cost of goods sold. The additional section 263A costs that are applicable to the decrement are determined by multiplying the additional section 263A costs allocated to the layer of the pool in which the decrement occurred by the ratio of the decrement (excluding additional section 263A costs) to the section 471 costs in the layer of that pool.

(iv) De minimis rule for producers with total indirect costs of $200,000 or less. (A) In general. If a producer using the simplified production method incurs $200,000 or less of total indirect costs in a taxable year, the additional section 263A costs allocable to eligible property remaining on hand at the close of the taxable year are deemed to be zero. Solely for purposes of this paragraph (b)(3)(iv), taxpayers are permitted to exclude any category of indirect costs (listed in § 1.263A-1(e)(3)(iii)) that is not required to be capitalized (e.g., selling and distribution costs) in determining total indirect costs.

(B) Related party and aggregation rules. In determining whether the producer incurs $200,000 or less of total indirect costs in a taxable year, the related party and aggregation rules of § 1.263A-3(b)(3) are applied by substituting total indirect costs for gross receipts wherever gross receipts appears.

(v) Examples. The provisions of this paragraph (b) are illustrated by the following examples.

Example (1). FIFO inventory method. (i) Taxpayer J uses the FIFO method of accounting for inventories. J's beginning inventory for 1994 (all of which is sold during 1994) is $2,500,000 (consisting of $2,000,000 of section 471 costs and $500,000 of additional section 263A costs). During 1994, J incurs $10,000,000 of section 471 costs and $1,000,000 of additional section 263A costs. J's additional section 263A costs include capitalizable mixed service costs computed under the simplified service cost method as well as other allocable costs. J's section 471 costs remaining in ending inventory at the end of 1994 are $3,000,000. J computes its absorption ratio for 1994, as follows:

$$\frac{\text{Additional § 263A costs incurred during 1994}}{\text{Section 471 costs incurred during 1994}} = \frac{\$1{,}000{,}000}{\$10{,}000{,}000} = 10\%$$

(ii) Under the simplified production method, J determines the additional section 263A costs allocable to its ending inventory by multiplying the absorption ratio by the section 471 costs remaining in its ending inventory:

Additional § 263A costs = 10% × $3,000,000 = $300,000

(iii) J adds this $300,000 to the $3,000,000 of section 471 costs remaining in its ending inventory to calculate its total ending inventory of $3,300,000. The balance of J's additional section 263A costs incurred during 1994, $700,000, ($1,000,000 less $300,000) is taken into account in 1994 as part of J's cost of goods sold.

Example (2). LIFO inventory method. (i) Taxpayer K uses a dollar-value LIFO inventory method. K's beginning inventory for 1994 is $2,500,000 (consisting of $2,000,000 of section 471 costs and $500,000 of additional section 263A costs). During 1994, K incurs $10,000,000 of section 471 costs and $1,000,000 of additional section 263A costs. K's 1994 LIFO increment is $1,000,000 ($3,000,000 of section 471 costs in ending inventory less $2,000,000 of section 471 costs in beginning inventory).

(ii) To determine the additional section 263A costs allocable to its ending inventory, K multiplies the 10% absorption ratio ($1,000,000 of additional section 263A costs divided by $10,000,000 of section 471 costs) by the $1,000,000 LIFO increment. Thus, K's additional section 263A costs allocable to its ending inventory are $100,000 ($1,000,000 multiplied by 10%). This $100,000 is added to the $1,000,000 to determine a total 1994 LIFO increment of $1,100,000. K's ending inventory is $3,600,000 (its beginning inventory of $2,500,000 plus the $1,100,000 increment). The balance of K's additional section 263A costs incurred during 1994, $900,000 ($1,000,000 less $100,000), is taken into account in 1994 as part of K's cost of goods sold.

(iii) In 1995, K sells one-half of the inventory in its 1994 LIFO increment. K must include in its cost of goods sold for 1995 the amount of additional section 263A costs relating to this inventory, $50,000 (one-half of the additional section 263A costs capitalized in 1994 ending inventory, or $100,000).

Example (3). LIFO pools. (i) Taxpayer L begins its business in 1994 and adopts the LIFO inventory method. During 1994, L incurs $10,000 of section 471 costs and $1,000 of additional section 263A costs. At the end of 1994, L's ending inventory includes $3,000 of section 471 costs contained in three LIFO pools (X, Y, and Z) as shown below. Under the simplified production method, L computes its absorption ratio and inventory for 1994 as follows:

$$\frac{\text{Additional § 263A costs incurred during 1994}}{\text{Section 471 costs incurred during 1994}} = \frac{\$1{,}000}{\$10{,}000} = 10\%$$

	Total	X	Y	Z
1994:				
Ending section 471 costs	$3,000	$1,600	$600	$800
Additional section 263A costs (10%)	300	160	60	80
1994 ending inventory	$3,300	$1,760	$660	$880

(ii) During 1995, L incurs $2,000 of section 471 costs as shown below and $400 of additional section 263A costs. Moreover, L sells goods from pools X, Y, and Z having a total cost of $1,000. L computes its absorption ratio and inventory for 1995:

$$\frac{\text{Additional § 263A costs incurred during 1995}}{\text{Section 471 costs incurred during 1995}} = \frac{\$400}{\$2{,}000} = 20\%$$

	Total	X	Y	Z
1995:				
Beginning section 471 costs	$3,000	$1,600	$600	$800
1995 section 471 costs	2,000	1,500	300	200
Section 471 cost of goods sold	(1,000)	(300)	(300)	(400)
1995 ending section 471 costs	$4,000	$2,800	$600	$600
Consisting of:				
1994 layer	$2,800	$1,600	$600	$600
1995 layer	1,200	1,200		
	$4,000	$2,800	$600	$600
Additional section 263A costs:				
1994 (10%)	$ 280	$ 160	$ 60	$ 60
1995 (20%)	240	240		
	$ 520	$ 400	$ 60	$ 60
1995 ending inventory	$4,520	$3,200	$660	$660

(iii) In 1995, L experiences a $200 decrement in pool Z. Thus, L must charge the additional section 263A costs incurred in prior years applicable to the decrement to 1995's cost of goods sold. To do so, L determines a ratio by dividing the decrement by the section 471 costs in the 1994 layer ($200 divided by $800, or 25%). L then multiplies this ratio (25%) by the additional section 263A costs in the 1994 layer ($80) to determine the additional section 263A costs applicable to the decrement ($20). Therefore, $20 is taken into account by L in 1995 as part of its cost of goods sold ($80 multiplied by 25%).

(4) Simplified production method with historic absorption ratio election. (i) In general. This paragraph (b)(4) generally permits producers using the simplified production method to elect a historic absorption ratio in determining additional section 263A costs allocable to eligible property remaining on hand at the close of their taxable years. Except as provided in paragraph (b)(4)(v) of this section, a taxpayer may only make a historic absorption ratio election if it has used the simplified production method for three or more consecutive taxable years immediately prior to the year of election and has capitalized additional section 263A costs using an actual absorption ratio (as defined under paragraph (b)(3)(ii) of this section) for its three most recent consecutive taxable years. This method is not available to a taxpayer that is deemed to have zero additional section 263A costs under paragraph (b)(3)(iv) of this section. The historic absorption ratio is used in lieu of an actual absorption ratio computed under paragraph (b)(3)(ii) of this section and is based on costs capitalized by a taxpayer during its test period. If elected, the historic absorption ratio must be used for each taxable year within the qualifying period described in paragraph (b)(4)(ii)(C) of this section.

(ii) Operating rules and definitions. (A) Historic absorption ratio. (1) The historic absorption ratio is equal to the following ratio:

$$\frac{\text{Additional section 263A costs incurred during the test period}}{\text{Section 471 costs incurred during the test period}}$$

(2) Additional section 263A costs incurred during the test period are defined as the additional section 263A costs described in § 1.263A-1(d)(3) that the taxpayer incurs during the test period described in paragraph (b)(4)(ii)(B) of this section.

(3) Section 471 costs incurred during the test period mean the section 471 costs described in § 1.263A-1(d)(2) that the taxpayer incurs during the test period described in paragraph (b)(4)(ii)(B) of this section.

(B) Test period. (1) In general. The test period is generally the three taxable-year period immediately prior to the taxable year that the historic absorption ratio is elected.

(2) Updated test period. The test period begins again with the beginning of the first taxable year after the close of a qualifying period. This new test period, the updated test period, is the three taxable-year period beginning with the first taxable year after the close of the qualifying period as defined in paragraph (b)(4)(ii)(C) of this section.

(C) Qualifying period. (1) In general. A qualifying period includes each of the first five taxable years beginning with the first taxable year after a test period (or an updated test period).

(2) Extension of qualifying period. In the first taxable year following the close of each qualifying period, (e.g., the sixth taxable year following the test period), the taxpayer must compute the actual absorption ratio under the simplified production method. If the actual absorption ratio computed for this taxable year (the recomputation year) is within one-half of one percentage point (plus or minus) of the historic absorption ratio used in determining capitalizable costs for the qualifying period (i.e., the previous five taxable years), the qualifying period is extended to include the recomputation year and the following five taxable years, and the taxpayer must continue to use the historic absorption ratio throughout the extended qualifying period. If, however, the actual absorption ratio computed for the recomputation year is not within one-half of one percentage point (plus or minus) of the historic absorption ratio, the taxpayer must use actual absorption ratios beginning with the recomputation year under the simplified production method and throughout the updated test period. The taxpayer must resume using the historic absorption ratio (determined with reference to the updated test period) in the third taxable year following the recomputation year.

(iii) Method of accounting. (A) Adoption and use. The election to use the historic absorption ratio is a method of accounting. A taxpayer using the simplified production method may elect the historic absorption ratio in any taxable year if permitted under this paragraph (b)(4), provided the taxpayer has not obtained the Commissioner's consent to revoke the historic absorption ratio election within its prior six taxable years. The election is to be effected on a cut-off basis, and thus, no adjustment under section 481(a) is required or permitted. The use of a historic absorption ratio has no effect on other methods of accounting adopted by the taxpayer and used in conjunction with the simplified production method in determining its section 263A costs. Accordingly, in computing its actual absorption ratios, the taxpayer must use the same methods of accounting used in computing its historic absorption ratio during its most recent test period unless the taxpayer obtains the consent of the Commissioner. Finally, for purposes of this paragraph (b)(4)(iii), the recomputation of the historic absorption ratio during an updated test period and the change from a historic absorption ratio to an actual absorption ratio by reason of the requirements of this paragraph (b)(4) are not considered changes in methods of accounting under section 446(e) and, thus, do not require the consent of the Commissioner or any adjustments under section 481(a).

(B) Revocation of election. A taxpayer may only revoke its election to use the historic absorption ratio with the consent of the Commissioner in a manner prescribed under section 446(e) and the regulations thereunder. Consent to the change for any taxable year that is included in the qualifying period (or an extended qualifying period) will be granted only upon a showing of unusual circumstances.

(iv) Reporting and recordkeeping requirements. (A) Reporting. A taxpayer making an election under this paragraph (b)(4) must attach a statement to its federal income tax return for the taxable year in which the election is made showing the actual absorption ratios determined under the simplified production method during its first test period. This statement must disclose the historic absorption ratio to be used by the taxpayer during its qualifying period. A similar statement must be attached to the federal income tax return for the first taxable year within any subsequent qualifying period (i.e., after an updated test period).

(B) Recordkeeping. A taxpayer must maintain all appropriate records and details supporting the historic absorption ratio until the expiration of the statute of limitations for the last year for which the taxpayer applied the particular historic absorption ratio in determining additional section 263A costs capitalized to eligible property.

(v) Transition rules. Taxpayers will be permitted to elect a historic absorption ratio in their first, second, or third taxable year beginning after December 31, 1993, under such terms and conditions as may be prescribed by the Commissioner. Taxpayers are eligible to make an election under these transition rules whether or not they previously used the simplified production method. A taxpayer making such an election must recompute (or compute) its additional section 263A costs, and thus, its historic absorption ratio for its first test period as if the rules prescribed in this section and §§ 1.263A-1 and 1.263A-3 had applied throughout the test period.

(vi) Example. The provisions of this paragraph (b)(4) are illustrated by the following example:

Example. (i) Taxpayer M uses the FIFO method of accounting for inventories and for 1994 elects to use the historic absorption ratio with the simplified production method. After recomputing its additional section 263A costs in accordance with the transition rules of paragraph (b)(4)(v) of this section, M identifies the following costs incurred during the test period:

1991:

Add'l section 263A costs—$100 Section 471 costs—$3,000

1992:

Add'l section 263A costs—200 Section 471 costs—4,000

1993:

Add'l section 263A costs—300 Section 471 costs—5,000

(ii) Therefore, M computes a 5% historic absorption ratio determined as follows:

$$\text{Historic absorption ratio} = \frac{\$100 + 200 + 300}{\$3,000 + 4,000 + 5,000} = \frac{\$600}{\$12,000} = 5\%$$

(iii) In 1994, M incurs $10,000 of section 471 costs of which $3,000 remain in inventory at the end of the year. Under the simplified production method using a historic absorption ratio, M determines the additional section 263A costs allocable to its ending inventory by multiplying its historic absorption ratio (5%) by the section 471 costs remaining in its ending inventory as follows:

$$\text{Additional section 263A costs} = 5\% \times \$3,000 = \$150$$

(iv) To determine its ending inventory under section 263A, M adds the additional section 263A costs allocable to ending inventory to its section 471 costs remaining in ending inventory ($3,150 = $150 + $3,000). The balance of M's additional section 263A costs incurred during 1994 is taken into account in 1994 as part of M's cost of goods sold.

(v) M's qualifying period ends with the close of its 1998 taxable year. Therefore, 1999 is a recomputation year in which M must compute its actual absorption ratio. M determines its actual absorption ratio for 1999 to be 5.25% and compares that ratio to its historic absorption ratio (5.0%). Therefore, M must continue to use its historic absorption ratio of 5.0% throughout an extended qualifying period, 1999 through 2004 (the recomputation year and the following five taxable years).

(vi) If, instead, M's actual absorption ratio for 1999 were not between 4.5% and 5.5%, M's qualifying period would end and M would be required to compute a new historic absorption ratio with reference to an updated test period of 1999, 2000, and 2001. Once M's historic absorption ratio is determined for the updated test period, it would be used for a new qualifying period beginning in 2002.

(c) Additional simplified methods for producers. The Commissioner may prescribe additional elective simplified methods by revenue ruling or revenue procedure.

(d) Cross reference. See § 1.6001-1(a) regarding the duty of taxpayers to keep such records as are sufficient to establish the amount of gross income, deductions, etc.

(e) Change in method of accounting. *(1) In general.* A change in a taxpayer's treatment of additional section 263A costs to comply with paragraph (b)(2)(i)(D) of this section is a change in method of accounting to which the provisions of sections 446 and 481 and the regulations under those sections apply. See § 1.263A-7. For a taxpayer's first taxable year ending on or after August 2, 2005, the taxpayer is granted the consent of the Commissioner to change its method of accounting to comply with paragraph (b)(2)(i)(D) of this section, provided the taxpayer follows the administrative procedures, as modified by paragraphs (e)(2) through (4) of this section, issued under § 1.446-1(e)(3)(ii) for obtaining the Commissioner's automatic consent to a change in accounting method (for further guidance, for example, see Rev. Proc. 2002-9 (2002-1 CB 327), as modified and clarified by Announcement 2002-17 (2002-1 CB 561), modified and amplified by Rev. Proc. 2002-19 (2002-1 CB 696), and amplified, clarified, and modified by Rev. Proc. 2002-54 (2002-2 CB 432), and § 601.601(d)(2)(ii)(b) of this chapter). For purposes of Form 3115, "Application for Change in Accounting Method," the designated number for the automatic accounting method change authorized by this paragraph (e) is "95." If Form 3115 is revised or renumbered, any reference in this section to that form is treated as a reference to the revised or renumbered form. Alternatively, notwithstanding the provisions of any administrative procedures that preclude a taxpayer from requesting the advance consent of the Commissioner to change a method of accounting that is required to be made pursuant to a published automatic change procedure, for its first taxable year ending on or after August 2, 2005, a taxpayer may request the advance consent of the Commissioner to change its method of accounting to comply with paragraph (b)(2)(i)(D) of this section, provided the taxpayer follows the administrative procedures, as modified by paragraphs (e)(2) through (5) of this section, for obtaining the advance consent of the Commissioner (for further guidance, for example, see Rev. Proc. 97-27 (1997-1 CB 680), as modified and amplified by Rev. Proc. 2002-19 (2002-1 CB 696), as amplified and clarified by Rev. Proc. 2002-54 (2002-2 CB 432), and § 601.601(d)(2)(ii)(b) of this chapter). For the taxpayer's second and subsequent taxable years ending on or after August 2, 2005, requests to secure the consent of the Commissioner must be made under the administrative procedures, as modified by paragraphs (e)(3) and (4) of this section, for obtaining the Commissioner's advance consent to a change in accounting method.

(2) Scope limitations. Any limitations on obtaining the automatic consent or advance consent of the Commissioner do not apply to a taxpayer seeking to change its method of accounting to comply with paragraph (b)(2)(i)(D) of this section for its first taxable year ending on or after August 2, 2005.

(3) Audit protection. A taxpayer that changes its method of accounting in accordance with this paragraph (e) to comply with paragraph (b)(2)(i)(D) of this section does not receive audit protection if its method of accounting for additional section 263A costs is an issue under consideration at the time the application is filed with the national office.

(4) Section 481(a) adjustment. A change in method of accounting to conform to paragraph (b)(2)(i)(D) of this section requires a section 481(a) adjustment. The section 481(a) adjustment period is two taxable years for a net positive adjustment for an accounting method change that is made to conform to paragraph (b)(2)(i)(D) of this section.

(5) Time for requesting change. Notwithstanding the provisions of § 1.446-1(e)(3)(i) and any contrary administrative procedure, a taxpayer may submit a request for advance consent to change its method of accounting to comply with paragraph (b)(2)(i)D) of this section for its first taxable year ending on or after August 2, 2005, on or before the date that is 30 days after the end of the taxable year for which the change is requested.

(f) Effective date. Paragraphs (b)(2)(i)(D), (e), and (f) of this section apply for taxable years ending on or after August 2, 2005.

T.D. 8482, 8/6/93, amend T.D. 8584, 12/28/94, T.D. 9217, 8/2/2005, T.D. 9318, 3/28/2007.

§ 1.263A-3 Rules relating to property acquired for resale.

(a) Capitalization rules for property acquired for resale. *(1) In general.* Section 263A applies to real property and personal property described in section 1221(1) acquired for resale by a retailer, wholesaler, or other taxpayer (reseller). However, section 263A does not apply to personal property described in section 1221(1) acquired for resale by a reseller whose average annual gross receipts for the three previous taxable years do not exceed $10,000,000 (small reseller). For this purpose, personal property includes both tangible and intangible property. Property acquired for resale includes stock in trade of the taxpayer or other property which is includible in the taxpayer's inventory if on hand at the close of the taxable year, and property held by the taxpayer primarily for sale to customers in the ordinary course of the taxpayer's trade or business. See, however, § 1.263A-1(b)(11) for an exception for certain de minimis property provided to customers incident to the provision of services.

(2) Resellers with production activities. (i) In general. Generally, a taxpayer must capitalize all direct costs and certain indirect costs associated with real property and tangible personal property it produces. See § 1.263A-2(a). Thus, except as provided in paragraphs (a)(2)(ii) and (3) of this section, a reseller, including a small reseller, that also produces property must capitalize the additional section 263A costs associated with any property it produces.

(ii) Exception for small resellers. Under this paragraph (a)(2)(ii), a small reseller is not required to capitalize additional section 263A costs associated with any personal property that is produced incident to its resale activities, provided the production activities are de minimis (within the meaning of paragraph (a)(2)(iii) of this section).

(iii) De minimis production activities. (A) In general. (1) In determining whether a taxpayer's production activities are de minimis, all facts and circumstances must be considered. For example, the taxpayer must consider the volume of the production activities in its trade or business. Production activities are presumed de minimis if—

(i) The gross receipts from the sale of the property produced by the reseller are less than 10 percent of the total gross receipts of the trade or business; and

(ii) The labor costs allocable to the trade or business' production activities are less than 10 percent of the reseller's total labor costs allocable to its trade or business.

(2) For purposes of this de minimis presumption, gross receipts has the same definition as provided in paragraph (b) of this section except that gross receipts are measured at the trade-or-business level rather than at the single-employer level.

(B) Example. The application of this paragraph (a)(2) may be illustrated by the following example:

Example. Small reseller with de minimis production activities. Taxpayer N is a small reseller in the retail grocery business whose average annual gross receipts for the three previous taxable years are less than $10,000,000. N's grocery stores typically contain bakeries where customers may purchase baked goods produced by N. N's gross receipts from its bakeries are 5% of the entire grocery business. N's labor costs from its bakeries are 3% of its total labor costs allocable to the entire grocery business. Because both ratios are less than 10%, N's production activities are de minimis. Further, because N's production activities are incident to its resale activities, N is not required to capitalize any additional section 263A costs associated with its produced property.

(3) Resellers with property produced under contract. Generally, property produced for a taxpayer under a contract (within the meaning of § 1.263A-2(a)(1)(ii)(B)(2)) is treated as property produced by the taxpayer. See § 1.263A-2(a)(1)(ii)(B). However, a small reseller is not required to capitalize additional section 263A costs to personal property produced for it under contract with an unrelated person if the contract is entered into incident to the resale activities of the small reseller and the property is sold to its customers. For purposes of this paragraph, persons are related if they are described in section 267(b) or 707(b).

(4) Use of the simplified resale method. (i) In general. Except as provided in paragraphs (a)(4)(ii) and (iii) of this section, a taxpayer may elect the simplified production method (as described in § 1.263A-2(b)) but may not elect the simplified resale method (as described in paragraph (d) of this section) if the taxpayer is engaged in both production and resale activities with respect to the items of eligible property listed in § 1.263A-2(b)(2).

(ii) Resellers with de minimis production activities. A reseller otherwise permitted to use the simplified resale method in paragraph (d) of this section may use the simplified resale method if its production activities with respect to the items of eligible property listed in § 1.263A-2(b)(2) are de minimis (within the meaning of paragraph (a)(2)(iii) of this section) and incident to its resale of personal property described in section 1221(1).

(iii) Resellers with property produced under a contract. A reseller otherwise permitted to use the simplified resale method in paragraph (d) of this section may use the simplified resale method even though it has personal property produced for it (e.g., private label goods) under a contract with an unrelated person if the contract is entered into incident to its resale activities and the property is sold to its customers. For purposes of this paragraph (a)(4)(iii), persons are related if they are described in section 267(b) or 707(b).

(iv) Application of simplified resale method. A taxpayer that uses the simplified resale method and has de minimis production activities incident to its resale activities or property produced under contract must capitalize all costs allocable to eligible property produced using the simplified resale method.

(b) Gross receipts exception for small resellers. *(1) In general.* Section 263A does not apply to any personal property acquired for resale during any taxable year if the taxpayer's (or its predecessors') average annual gross receipts for the three previous taxable years (test period) do not exceed $10,000,000. However, taxpayers that acquire real property for resale are subject to section 263A with respect to real property regardless of their gross receipts. See section 263A(b)(2)(B).

(i) Test period for new taxpayers. For purposes of applying this exception, if a taxpayer has been in existence for less than three taxable years, the taxpayer determines its average annual gross receipts for the number of taxable years (including short taxable years) that the taxpayer (or its predecessor) has been in existence.

(ii) Treatment of short taxable year. In the case of a short taxable year, the taxpayer's gross receipts are annualized by—

(A) Multiplying the gross receipts of the short taxable year by 12; and

(B) Dividing the product determined in paragraph (b)(1)(ii)(A) of this section by the number of months in the short taxable year.

(2) Definition of gross receipts. (i) In general. Gross receipts are the total amount, as determined under the taxpayer's method of accounting, derived from all of the taxpayer's trades or businesses (e.g., revenues derived from the sale of inventory before reduction for cost of goods sold).

(ii) Amounts excluded. For purposes of this paragraph (b), gross receipts do not include amounts representing—

(A) Returns or allowances;

(B) Interest, dividends, rents, royalties, or annuities, not derived in the ordinary course of a trade or business;

(C) Receipts from the sale or exchange of capital assets, as defined in section 1221;

(D) Repayments of loans or similar instruments (e.g., a repayment of the principal amount of a loan held by a commercial lender);

(E) Receipts from a sale or exchange not in the ordinary course of business, such as the sale of an entire trade or business or the sale of property used in a trade or business as defined under section 1221(2); and

(F) Receipts from any activity other than a trade or business or an activity engaged in for profit.

(3) Aggregation of gross receipts. (i) In general. In determining gross receipts, all persons treated as a single employer under section 52(a) or (b), section 414(m), or any regulation prescribed under section 414 (or persons that would be treated as a single employer under any of these provisions if they had employees) shall be treated as one taxpayer. The gross receipts of a single employer (or the group) are determined by aggregating the gross receipts of all persons (or the members) of the group, excluding any gross receipts attributable to transactions occurring between group members.

(ii) Single employer defined. A controlled group, which is treated as a single employer under section 52(a), includes members of a controlled group within the meaning of section 1563(a), regardless of whether such members would be treated as component members of such group under section 1563(b). (See § 1.52-1(c).) Thus, for example, the gross receipts of a franchised corporation that is treated as an excluded member for purposes of section 1563(b) are included in the single employer's gross receipts under this aggregation rule, if such corporation and the taxpayer were members of the same controlled group under section 1563(a).

(iii) Gross receipts of a single employer. The gross receipts of a single employer for the test period include the gross receipts of all group members (or their predecessors) that are members of the group as of the first day of the taxable year in issue, regardless of whether such persons were members of the group for any of the three preceding taxable years. The gross receipts of the single employer for the test period do not, however, include the gross receipts of any member that was a group member (including any predecessor) for any or all of the three preceding taxable years, and is no longer a group member as of the first day of the taxable year in issue. Any group member that has a taxable year of less than 12 months must annualize its gross receipts in accordance with paragraph (b)(1)(ii) of this section.

(iv) Examples. The provisions of this paragraph (b)(3) are illustrated by the following examples:

Example (1). Subsidiary acquired during the taxable year. A parent corporation, (P), has owned 100% of the stock of another corporation, (S1), continually since 1989. P and S1 are calendar year taxpayers. S1 acquires property for resale. On January 1, 1994, P acquires 100% of the stock of another calendar year corporation (S2). In determining whether S1's resale activities are subject to the provisions of section 263A for 1994, the gross receipts of P, S1, and S2 for 1991, 1992, and 1993 are aggregated, excluding the gross receipts, if any, attributable to transactions occurring between the three corporations.

Example (2). Subsidiary sold during the taxable year. Since 1989, a parent corporation, (P), has continually owned 100% of the stock of two other corporations, (S1) and (S2). The three corporations are calendar year taxpayers. S1 acquires property for resale. On December 31, 1993, P sells all of its stock in S2. In determining whether S1's resale activities are subject to the provisions of section 263A for 1994, only the gross receipts of P and S1 for 1991, 1992, and 1993 must be aggregated, excluding the gross receipts, if any, attributable to transactions occurring between the two corporations.

(c) Purchasing, handling, and storage costs. *(1) In general.* Generally, § 1.263A-1(e) describes the types of costs that must be capitalized by taxpayers. Resellers must capitalize the acquisition cost of property acquired for resale, as well as indirect costs described in § 1.263A-1(e)(3), which are properly allocable to property acquired for resale. The indirect costs most often incurred by resellers are purchasing, handling, and storage costs. This paragraph (c) provides additional guidance regarding each of these categories of costs. As provided in § 1.263A-1(e), this paragraph (c) also applies to producers incurring purchasing, handling, and storage costs.

(2) Costs attributable to purchasing, handling, and storage. The costs attributable to purchasing, handling, and storage activities generally consist of direct and indirect labor costs (including the costs of pension plans and other fringe benefits); occupancy expenses including rent, depreciation, insurance, security, taxes, utilities and maintenance; materials and supplies; rent, maintenance, depreciation, and insurance of vehicles and equipment; tools; telephone; travel; and the general and administrative costs that directly benefit or are incurred by reason of the taxpayer's activities.

(3) Purchasing costs. (i) In general. Purchasing costs are costs associated with operating a purchasing department or office within a trade or business, including personnel costs (e.g., of buyers, assistant buyers, and clerical workers), relating to—

(A) The selection of merchandise;

(B) The maintenance of stock assortment and volume;

(C) The placement of purchase orders;

(D) The establishment and maintenance of vendor contacts; and

(E) The comparison and testing of merchandise.

(ii) Determination of whether personnel are engaged in purchasing activities. The determination of whether a person is engaged in purchasing activities is based upon the activities performed by that person and not upon the person's title or job classification. Thus, for example, although an employee's job function may be described in such a way as to indicate activities outside the area of purchasing (e.g., a marketing representative), such activities must be analyzed on the basis of the activities performed by that employee. If a person performs both purchasing and non-purchasing activities, the taxpayer must reasonably allocate the person's labor costs between these activities. For example, a reasonable allocation is one based on the amount of time the person spends on each activity.

(A) 1/3-2/3 rule for allocating labor costs. A taxpayer may elect the 1/3-2/3 rule for allocating labor costs of persons performing both purchasing and non-purchasing activities. If elected, the taxpayer must allocate the labor costs of all such persons using the 1/3-2/3 rule. Under this rule—

(1) If less than one-third of a person's activities are related to purchasing, none of that person's labor costs are allocated to purchasing;

(2) If more than two-thirds of a person's activities are related to purchasing, all of that person's labor costs are allocated to purchasing; and

(3) In all other cases, the taxpayer must reasonably allocate labor costs between purchasing and non-purchasing activities.

(B) Example. The application of paragraph (c)(3)(ii)(A) of this section may be illustrated by the following example:

Example. Taxpayer O is a reseller that employs three persons, A, B, and C, who perform both purchasing and non-purchasing activities. These persons spend the following time performing purchasing activities: A-25%; B-70%; and C-50%. Under the 1/3-2/3 rule, Taxpayer O treats none of A's labor costs as purchasing costs, all of B's labor costs as purchasing costs, and Taxpayer O allocates 50% of C's labor costs as purchasing costs.

(4) Handling costs. (i) In general. Handling costs include costs attributable to processing, assembling, repackaging, transporting, and other similar activities with respect to property acquired for resale, provided the activities do not come within the meaning of the term produce as defined in § 1.263A-2(a)(1). Handling costs are generally required to be capitalized under section 263A. Under this paragraph (c)(4)(i), however, handling costs incurred at a retail sales facility (as defined in paragraph (c)(5)(ii)(B) of this section) with respect to property sold to retail customers at the facility are not required to be capitalized. Thus, for example, handling costs incurred at a retail sales facility to unload, unpack, mark, and tag goods sold to retail customers at the facility are not required to be capitalized. In addition, handling costs incurred at a dual-function storage facility (as defined in paragraph (c)(5)(ii)(G) of this section) with respect to property sold to customers from the facility are not required to be capitalized to the extent that the costs are incurred with respect to property sold in on-site sales. Handling costs attributable to property sold to customers from a dual-function storage facility in on-site sales are determined by applying the ratio in paragraph (c)(5)(iii)(B) of this section.

(ii) Processing costs. Processing costs are the costs a reseller incurs in making minor changes or alterations to the nature or form of a product acquired for resale. Minor changes to a product include, for example, monogramming a sweater, altering a pair of pants, and other similar activities.

(iii) Assembling costs. Generally, assembling costs are costs associated with incidental activities that are necessary in readying property for resale (e.g., attaching wheels and handlebars to a bicycle acquired for resale).

(iv) Repackaging costs. Repackaging costs are the costs a taxpayer incurs to package property for sale to its customers.

(v) Transportation costs. Generally, transportation costs are the costs a taxpayer incurs moving or shipping property acquired for resale. These costs include the cost of dispatching trucks; loading and unloading shipments; and sorting, tagging, and marking property. Transportation costs may consist of depreciation on trucks and equipment and the costs of fuel, insurance, labor, and similar costs. Generally, transportation costs required to be capitalized include costs incurred in transporting property—

(A) From the vendor to the taxpayer;

(B) From one of the taxpayer's storage facilities to another of its storage facilities;

(C) From the taxpayer's storage facility to its retail sales facility;

(D) From the taxpayer's retail sales facility to its storage facility; and

(E) From one of the taxpayer's retail sales facilities to another of its retail sales facilities.

(vi) Costs not required to be capitalized as handling costs. (A) Distribution costs. (1) In general. Distribution costs are not required to be capitalized. Distribution costs are any transportation costs incurred outside a storage facility in delivering goods to a customer. For this purpose, any costs incurred on a loading dock are treated as incurred outside a storage facility.

(2) Costs incurred in transporting goods to a related person. Distribution costs do not include costs incurred by a taxpayer in delivering goods to a related person. Thus, for example, when a taxpayer sells goods to a related person, the costs of transporting the goods are included in determining the basis of the goods that are sold, and hence in determining the resulting gain or loss from the sale, for all purposes of the Internal Revenue Code and the regulations thereunder. See, e.g., sections 267, 707, and 1502. For purposes of this provision, persons are related if they are described in section 267(b) or section 707(b).

(B) Delivery of custom-ordered items. Generally, costs incurred in transporting goods from a taxpayer's storage facility to its retail sales facility must be capitalized. However, costs incurred outside a storage facility in delivering custom-ordered items to a retail sales facility are not required to be capitalized. For this purpose, any costs incurred on a loading dock are treated as incurred outside a storage facility. Delivery of custom-ordered items occurs when a taxpayer can demonstrate that a delivery to the taxpayer's retail sales facility is made to fill an identifiable order of a particular customer (placed by the customer before the delivery of the goods occurs) for the particular goods in question. Factors that may demonstrate the existence of a specific, identifiable delivery include the following—

(1) The customer has paid for the item in advance of the delivery;

(2) The customer has submitted a written order for the item;

(3) The item is not normally available at the retail sales facility for on-site customer purchases; and

(4) The item will be returned to the storage facility (and not held for sale at the retail sales facility) if the customer cancels an order.

(C) Pick and pack costs. (1) In general. Generally, handling costs incurred inside a storage or warehousing facility must be capitalized. However, costs attributable to pick and pack activities inside a storage or warehousing facility are not required to be capitalized. Pick and pack activities are activities undertaken in preparation for imminent shipment to a particular customer after the customer has ordered the specific goods in question. Examples of pick and pack activities include:

(i) Moving specific goods from a storage location in preparation for shipment to the customer;

(ii) Packing or repacking those goods for shipment to the customer; and

(iii) Staging those goods for shipment to the customer.

(2) Activities that are not pick and pack activities. Pick and pack activities do not include:

(i) Unloading goods that are received for storage;

(ii) Checking the quantity and quality of goods received;

(iii) Comparing the quantity of goods received to the amounts ordered and preparing the receiving documents;

(iv) Moving the goods to their storage location, e.g., bins, racks, containers, etc.; and

(v) Storing the goods.

(3) Costs not attributable to pick and pack activities. Occupancy costs, such as rent, depreciation, insurance, security, taxes, utilities, and maintenance costs properly allocable to the storage or warehousing facility, are not costs attributable to pick and pack activities.

(5) Storage costs. (i) In general. Generally, storage costs are capitalized under section 263A to the extent they are attributable to the operation of an off-site storage or warehousing facility (an off-site storage facility). However, storage costs attributable to the operation of an on-site storage facility (as defined in paragraph (c)(5)(ii)(A) of this section) are not required to be capitalized under section 263A. Storage costs attributable to a dual-function storage facility (as defined in paragraph (c)(5)(ii)(G) of this section) must be capitalized to the extent that the facility's costs are allocable to off-site storage.

(ii) Definitions. (A) On-site storage facility. An on-site storage facility is defined as a storage or warehousing facility that is physically attached to, and an integral part of, a retail sales facility.

(B) Retail sales facility. (1) A retail sales facility is defined as a facility where a taxpayer sells merchandise exclusively to retail customers in on-site sales. For this purpose, a retail sales facility includes those portions of any specific retail site—

(i) Which are customarily associated with and are an integral part of the operations of that retail site;

(ii) Which are generally open each business day exclusively to retail customers;

(iii) On or in which retail customers normally and routinely shop to select specific items of merchandise; and

(iv) which are adjacent to or in immediate proximity to other portions of the specific retail site.

(2) Thus, for example, two lots of an automobile dealership physically separated by an alley or an access road would generally be considered one retail sales facility, provided customers routinely shop on both of the lots to select the specific automobiles that they wish to acquire.

(C) An internal part of a retail sales facility. A storage facility is considered an integral part of a retail sales facility when the storage facility is an essential and indispensable part of the retail sales facility. For example, if the storage facility is used exclusively for filling orders or completing sales at the retail sales facility, the storage facility is an integral part of the retail sales facility.

(D) On-site sales. On-site sales are defined as sales made to retail customers physically present at a facility. For example, mail order and catalog sales are made to customers not physically present at the facility, and thus, are not on-site sales.

(E) Retail customer. (1) In general. A retail customer is defined as the final purchaser of the merchandise. A retail customer does not include a person who resells the merchandise to others, such as a contractor or manufacturer that incorporates the merchandise into another product for sale to customers.

(2) Certain non-retail customers treated as retail customers. For purposes of this section, a non-retail customer is treated as a retail customer with respect to a particular facility if the following requirements are satisfied—

(i) The non-retail customer purchases goods under the same terms and conditions as are available to retail customers (e.g., no special discounts);

(ii) The non-retail customer purchases goods in the same manner as a retail customer (e.g., the non-retail customer may not place orders in advance and must come to the facility to examine and select goods);

(iii) Retail customers shop at the facility on a routine basis (i.e., on most business days), and no special days or hours are reserved for non-retail customers; and

(iv) More than 50 percent of the gross sales of the facility are made to retail customers.

(F) Off-site storage facility. An off-site storage facility is defined as a storage facility that is not an on-site storage facility.

(G) Dual-function storage facility. A dual-function storage facility is defined as a storage facility that serves as both an off-site storage facility and an on-site storage facility. For example, a dual-function storage facility would include a regional warehouse that serves the taxpayer's separate retail sales outlets and also contains a sales outlet therein. A dual-function storage facility also includes any facility where sales are made to retail customers in on-site sales and to—

(1) Retail customers in sales that are not on-site sales; or

(2) Other customers.

(iii) Treatment of storage costs incurred at a dual-function storage facility. (A) In general. Storage costs associated with a dual-function storage facility must be allocated between the off-site storage function and the on-site storage function. To the extent that the dual-function storage facility's storage costs are allocable to the off-site storage function, they must be capitalized. To the extent that the dual-function storage facility's storage costs are allocable to the on-site storage function, they are not required to be capitalized.

(B) Dual-function storage facility allocation ratio. (1) In general. Storage costs associated with a dual-function storage facility must be allocated between the off-site storage function and the on-site storage function using the ratio of—

(i) Gross on-site sales of the facility (i.e., gross sales of the facility made to retail customers visiting the premises in person and purchasing merchandise stored therein); to

(ii) Total gross sales of the facility. For this purpose, the total gross sales of the facility include the value of items shipped to other facilities of the taxpayer.

(2) Illustration of ratio allocation. For example, if a dual-function storage facility's on-site sales are 40 percent of the total gross sales of the facility, then 40 percent of the facility's storage costs are allocable to the on-site storage function and are not required to be capitalized under section 263A.

(3) Appropriate adjustments for other uses of a dual-function storage facility. Prior to computing the allocation ratio in paragraph (c)(5)(iii)(B) of this section, a taxpayer must apply the principles of paragraph (c)(5)(iv) of this section in determining the portion of the facility that is a dual-function storage facility (and the costs attributable to such portion).

(C) De minimis 90-10 rule for dual-function storage facilities. If 90 percent or more of the costs of a facility are attributable to the on-site storage function, the entire storage facility is deemed to be an on-site storage facility. In contrast, if 10 percent or less of the costs of a storage facility are attributable to the on-site storage function, the entire storage facility is deemed to be an off-site storage facility.

(iv) Costs not attributable to an off-site storage facility. To the extent that costs incurred at an off-site storage facility are not properly allocable to the taxpayer's storage function, the costs are not accounted for as off-site storage costs. For example, if a taxpayer has an office attached to its off-site storage facility where work unrelated to the storage function is performed, such as a sales office, costs associated with this office are not off-site storage costs. However, if a taxpayer uses a portion of an off-site storage facility in a manner related to the storage function, for example, to store equipment or supplies that are not offered for sale to customers, costs associated with this portion of the facility are off-site storage costs.

(v) Examples. The provisions of this paragraph (c)(5) are illustrated by the following examples:

Example (1). Catalog or mail order center. Taxpayer P operates a mail order catalog business. As part of its business, P stores merchandise for shipment to customers who purchase the merchandise through orders placed by telephone or mail. P's storage facility is not an on-site storage facility because no on-site sales are made at the facility.

Example (2). Pooled-stock facility. Taxpayer Q maintains a pooled-stock facility, which functions as a back-up regional storage facility for Q's retail sales outlets in the nearby area. Q's pooled stock facility is an off-site storage facility because it is neither physically attached to nor an integral part of a retail sales facility.

Example (3). Wholesale warehouse. Taxpayer R operates a wholesale warehouse where wholesale sales are made to customers physically present at the facility. R's customers resell the goods they purchase from R to final retail customers. Because no retail sales are conducted at the facility, all storage costs attributable to R's wholesale warehouse must be capitalized.

(d) Simplified resale method. *(1) Introduction.* This paragraph (d) provides a simplified method for determining the additional section 263A costs properly allocable to property acquired for resale and other eligible property on hand at the end of the taxable year.

(2) Eligible property. Generally, the simplified resale method is only available to a trade or business exclusively engaged in resale activities. However, certain resellers with property produced as a result of de minimis production activities or property produced under contract may elect the simplified resale method, as described in paragraph (a)(4) of this section. Eligible property for purposes of the simplified resale method, therefore, includes any real or personal property described in section 1221(1) that is acquired for resale and any eligible property (within the meaning of § 1.263A-2(b)(2)) that is described in paragraph (a)(4) of this section.

(3) Simplified resale method without historic absorption ratio election. (i) General allocation formula. (A) In general. Under the simplified resale method, the additional section 263A costs allocable to eligible property remaining on hand at the close of the taxable year are computed as follows:

$$\text{Combined absorption ratio} \times \text{Section 471 costs remaining on hand at year end}$$

(B) Effect of allocation. The resulting product under the general allocation formula is the additional section 263A costs that are added to the taxpayer's ending section 471 costs to determine the section 263A costs that are capitalized.

(C) Definitions. (1) Combined absorption ratio. The combined absorption ratio is defined as the sum of the storage and handling costs absorption ratio as defined in paragraph (d)(3)(i)(D) of this section and the purchasing costs absorption ratio as defined in paragraph (d)(3)(i)(E) of this section.

(2) Section 471 costs remaining on hand at year end. Section 471 costs remaining on hand at year end mean the section 471 costs, as defined in § 1.263A-1(d)(2), that the taxpayer incurs during its current taxable year, which remain in its ending inventory or are otherwise on hand at year end. For LIFO inventories of a taxpayer, the section 471 costs remaining on hand at year end means the increment, if any, for the current year stated in terms of section 471 costs. See paragraph (d)(3)(ii) of this section for special rules applicable to LIFO taxpayers. Except as otherwise provided in this section or in § 1.263A-1 or 1.263A-2, additional section 263A costs that are allocated to inventories on hand at the close of the taxable year under the simplified resale method of this paragraph (d) are treated as inventory costs for all purposes of the Internal Revenue Code.

(D) Storage and handling costs absorption ratio.

(1) Under the simplified resale method, the storage and handling costs absorption ratio is determined as follows:

$$\frac{\text{Current year's storage and handling costs}}{\text{Beginning inventory plus current year's purchases}}$$

(2) Current year's storage and handling costs are defined as the total storage costs plus the total handling costs incurred during the taxable year that relate to the taxpayer's property acquired for resale and other eligible property. See paragraph (c) of this section, which discusses storage and handling costs. Storage and handling costs must include the amount of allocable mixed service costs as described in paragraph (d)(3)(i)(F) of this section. Beginning inventory in the denominator of the storage and handling costs absorption ratio refers to the section 471 costs of any property acquired for resale or other eligible property held by the taxpayer as of the beginning of the taxable year. Current year's purchases generally mean the taxpayer's section 471 costs incurred with respect to purchases of property acquired for resale during the current taxable year. In computing the denominator of the storage and handling costs absorption ratio,

a taxpayer using a dollar-value LIFO method of accounting, must state beginning inventory amounts using the LIFO carrying value of the inventory and not current-year dollars.

(E) Purchasing costs absorption ratio. (1) Under the simplified resale method, the purchasing costs absorption ratio is determined as follows:

$$\frac{\text{Current year's purchasing costs}}{\text{Current year's purchases}}$$

(2) Current year's purchasing costs are defined as the total purchasing costs incurred during the taxable year that relate to the taxpayer's property acquired for resale and eligible property. See paragraph (c)(3) of this section, which discusses purchasing costs. Purchasing costs must include the amount of allocable mixed service costs determined in paragraph (d)(3)(i)(F) of this section. Current year's purchases generally mean the taxpayer's section 471 costs incurred with respect to purchases of property acquired for resale during the current taxable year.

(F) Allocable mixed service costs. (1) If a taxpayer allocates its mixed service costs to purchasing costs, storage costs, and handling costs using a method described in § 1.263A-1(g)(4), the taxpayer is not required to determine its allocable mixed service costs under this paragraph (d)(3)(i)(F). However, if the taxpayer uses the simplified service cost method, the amount of mixed service costs allocated to and included in purchasing costs, storage costs, and handling costs in the absorption ratios in paragraphs (d)(3)(i)(D) and (E) of this section is determined as follows:

$$\frac{\text{Labor costs allocable to activity}}{\text{Total labor costs}} \times \text{Total mixed service costs}$$

(2) Labor costs allocable to activity are defined as the total labor costs allocable to each particular activity (i.e., purchasing, handling, and storage), excluding labor costs included in mixed service costs. Total labor costs are defined as the total labor costs (excluding labor costs included in mixed service costs) that are incurred in the taxpayer's trade or business during the taxable year. See § 1.263A-1(h)(6) for the definition of total mixed service costs.

(ii) LIFO taxpayers electing simplified resale method. (A) In general. Under the simplified resale method, a taxpayer using a LIFO method must calculate a particular year's index (e.g., under § 1.472-8(e)) without regard its additional section 263A costs. Similarly, a taxpayer that adjusts current-year costs by applicable indexes to determine whether there has been an inventory increment or decrement in the current year for a particular LIFO pool must disregard the additional section 263A costs in making that determination.

(B) LIFO increment. If the taxpayer determines there has been an inventory increment, the taxpayer must state the amount of the increment in current-year dollars (stated in terms of section 471 costs). The taxpayer then multiplies this amount by the combined absorption ratio. The resulting product is the additional section 263A costs that must be added to the taxpayer's increment for the year stated in terms of section 471 costs.

(C) LIFO decrement. If the taxpayer determines there has been an inventory decrement, the taxpayer must state the amount of the decrement in dollars applicable to the particular year for which the LIFO layer has been invaded. The additional section 263A costs incurred in prior years that are applicable to the decrement are charged to cost of goods sold. The additional section 263A costs that are applicable to the decrement are determined by multiplying the additional section 263A costs allocated to the layer of the pool in which the decrement occurred by the ratio of the decrement (excluding additional section 263A costs) to the section 471 costs in the layer of that pool.

(iii) Permissible variations of the simplified resale method. The following variations of the simplified resale method are permitted:

(A) The exclusion of beginning inventories from the denominator in the storage and handling costs absorption ratio formula in paragraph (d)(3)(i)(D) of this section; or

(B) Multiplication of the storage and handling costs absorption ratio in paragraph (d)(3)(i)(D) of this section by the total of section 471 costs included in a LIFO taxpayer's ending inventory (rather than just the increment, if any, experienced by the LIFO taxpayer during the taxable year) for purposes of determining capitalizable storage and handling costs.

(iv) Examples. The provisions of this paragraph (d)(3) are illustrated by the following examples:

Example (1). FIFO inventory method. (i) Taxpayer S uses the FIFO method of accounting for inventories. S's beginning inventory for 1994 (all of which was sold during 1994) was \$2,100,000 (consisting of \$2,000,000 of section 471 costs and \$100,000 of additional section 263A costs). During 1994, S makes purchases of \$10,000,000. In addition, S incurs purchasing costs of \$460,000, storage costs of \$110,000, and handling costs of \$90,000. S's purchases (section 471 costs) remaining in ending inventory at the end of 1994 are \$ 3,000,000.

(ii) In 1994, S incurs \$400,000 of total mixed service costs and \$1,000,000 of total labor costs (excluding labor costs included in mixed service costs). In addition, S incurs the following labor costs (excluding labor costs included in mixed service costs): purchasing—\$100,000, storage—\$200,000, and handling—\$ 200,000. Accordingly, the following mixed service costs must be included in purchasing costs, storage costs, and handling costs as capitalizable mixed service costs: purchasing—\$40,000 ([\$100,000 divided by \$1,000,000] multiplied by \$400,000); storage—\$80,000 ([\$200,000 divided by \$1,000,000] multiplied by \$400,000); and handling—\$80,000 ([\$200,000 divided by \$1,000,000] multiplied by \$400,000).

(iii) S computes its purchasing costs absorption ratio for 1994 as follows:

$$\frac{\text{1994 purchasing costs}}{\text{1994 purchases}} = \frac{\$460{,}000 + \$40{,}000}{\$10{,}000{,}000} = \frac{\$500{,}000}{\$10{,}000{,}000} = 5.0\%$$

(iv) S computes its storage and handling costs absorption ratio for 1994 as follows:

$$\frac{\text{Storage and handling costs}}{\text{Beginning inventory plus 1994 purchases}} = \frac{(\$110{,}000 + \$80{,}000) + (\$90{,}000 + \$80{,}000)}{\$2{,}000{,}000 + \$10{,}000{,}000} = \frac{\$190{,}000 + \$170{,}000}{\$12{,}000{,}000} = \frac{\$360{,}000}{\$12{,}000{,}000} = 3.0\%$$

(v) S's combined absorption ratio is 8.0%, or the sum of the purchasing costs absorption ratio (5.0%) and the storage and handling costs absorption ratio (3.0%). Under the simplified resale method, S determines the additional section 263A costs allocable to its ending inventory by multiplying the combined absorption ratio by its section 471 costs with respect to current year's purchases remaining in ending inventory:

Additional § 263A costs = 8.0% × $3,000,000 = $240,000

(vi) S adds this $240,000 to the $3,000,000 of purchases remaining in its ending inventory to determine its total ending FIFO inventory of $3,240,000.

Example (2). LIFO inventory method. (i) Taxpayer T uses a dollar-value LIFO inventory method. T's beginning inventory for 1994 is $2,100,000 (consisting of $2,000,000 of section 471 costs and $100,000 of additional section 263A costs). During 1994, T makes purchases of $10,000,000. In addition, T incurs purchasing costs of $460,000, storage costs of $110,000, and handling costs of $90,000. T's 1994 LIFO increment is $1,000,000 ($3,000,000 of section 471 costs in ending inventory less $2,000,000 of section 471 costs in beginning inventory).

(ii) In 1994, T incurs $400,000 of total mixed service costs and $1,000,000 of total labor costs (excluding labor costs included in mixed service costs). In addition, T incurs the following labor costs (excluding labor costs included in mixed service costs): purchasing—$100,000, storage—$200,000, and handling—$200,000. Accordingly, the following mixed service costs must be included in purchasing costs, storage costs, and handling costs as capitalizable mixed service costs: purchasing—$40,000 ([$100,000 divided by $1,000,000] multiplied by $400,000); storage—$80,000 ([$200,000 divided by $1,000,000] multiplied by $400,000); and handling— $80,000 ([$200,000 divided by $1,000,000] multiplied by $400,000).

(iii) Based on these facts, T determines that it has a combined absorption ratio of 8.0%. To determine the additional section 263A costs allocable to its ending inventory, T multiplies its combined absorption ratio (8.0%) by the $1,000,000 LIFO increment. Thus, T's additional section 263A costs allocable to its ending inventory are $80,000 ($1,000,000 multiplied by 8.0%). This $80,000 is added to the $1,000,000 to determine a total 1994 LIFO increment of $1,080,000. T's ending inventory is $3,180,000 (its beginning inventory of $2,100,000 plus the $1,080,000 increment).

(iv) In 1995, T sells one-half of the inventory in its 1994 LIFO increment. T must include in its cost of goods sold for 1995 the amount of additional section 263A costs relating to this inventory, i.e., one-half of the $80,000 additional section 263A costs capitalized in 1994 ending inventory, or $40,000.

Example (3). LIFO pools. (i) Taxpayer U begins its business in 1994, and adopts the LIFO inventory method. During 1994, U makes purchases of $10,000, and incurs $400 of purchasing costs, $350 of storage costs and $250 of handling costs. U's purchasing costs, storage costs, and handling costs include their proper allocable share of mixed service costs.

(ii) U computes its purchasing costs absorption ratio for 1994, as follows:

$$\frac{\text{1994 purchasing costs}}{\text{1994 purchases}} = \frac{\$400}{\$10{,}000} = 4.0\%$$

(iii) U computes its storage and handling costs absorption ratio 1994, as follows:

$$\frac{\text{1994 storage and handling costs}}{\text{Beginning inventory plus 1994 purchases}} = \frac{\$350 + \$250}{\$0 + \$10{,}000} = \frac{\$600}{\$10{,}000} = 6.0\%$$

(iv) U's combined absorption ratio is 10%, or the sum of the purchasing costs absorption ratio (4.0%) and the storage and handling costs absorption ratio (6.0%). At the end of 1994, U's ending inventory included $3,000 of current year purchases, contained in three LIFO pools (X, Y, and Z) as shown below. Under the simplified resale method, U computes its ending inventory for 1994 as follows:

1994	Total	X	Y	Z
Ending section 471 costs	$3,000	$1,600	$600	$800
Additional section 263A costs (10%)	300	160	60	80
1994 Ending inventory	$3,300	$1,760	$660	$880

(v) During 1995, U makes purchases of $2,000 as shown below, and incurs $200 of purchasing costs, $325 of storage costs and $ 175 of handling costs. U's purchasing costs, storage costs, and handling costs include their proper share of mixed service costs. Moreover, U sold goods from pools X, Y, and Z having a total cost of $1,000. U computes its ending inventory for 1995 as follows.

(vi) U computes its purchasing costs absorption ratio for 1995:

$$\frac{\text{1995 purchasing costs}}{\text{1995 purchases}} = \frac{\$200}{\$2{,}000} = 10.0\%$$

(vii) U computes its storage and handling costs absorption ratio for 1995:

$$\frac{\text{1995 storage and handling costs}}{\text{Beginning inventory plus 1995 purchases}} = \frac{\$325 + \$175}{\$3{,}000 + \$2{,}000} = \frac{\$500}{\$5{,}000} = 10.0\%$$

(viii) U's combined absorption ratio is 20.0% or the sum of the purchasing costs absorption ratio (10.0%) and the storage and handling costs absorption ratio (10.0%).

1995	Total	X	Y	Z
Beginning section 471 costs	$3,000	$1,600	$600	$800
1995 section 471 costs	2,000	1,500	300	200
Section 471 cost of goods sold	(1,000)	(300)	(300)	(400)
1995 Ending section 471 costs	$4,000	$2,800	$600	$600
Consisting of:				
1994 layer	$2,800	$1,600	$600	$600
1995 layer	1,200	1,200	—	—
	$4,000	$2,800	$600	$600
Additional section 263A costs:				
1994 (10%)	$ 280	$ 160	$ 60	$ 60
1995 (20%)	240	240	—	—
	$ 520	$ 400	$ 60	$ 60
1995 ending inventory	$4,520	$3,200	$660	$660

(ix) In 1995, U experiences a $200 decrement in Pool Z. Thus, U must charge the additional section 263A costs incurred in prior years applicable to the decrement to 1995's cost of goods sold. To do so, U determines a ratio by dividing the decrement by the section 471 costs in the 1994 layer ($200 divided by $800, or 25%). U then multiplies this ratio (25%) by the additional section 263A costs in the 1994 layer ($80) to determine the additional section 263A costs applicable to the decrement ($20). Therefore, $20 is taken into account by U in 1995 as part of its cost of goods sold ($80 multiplied by 25%).

(4) Simplified resale method with historic absorption ratio election. (i) In general. This paragraph (d)(4) permits resellers using the simplified resale method to elect a historic ab-

sorption ratio in determining additional section 263A costs allocable to eligible property remaining on hand at the close of their taxable years. Except as provided in paragraph (d)(4)(v) of this section, a taxpayer may only make a historic absorption ratio election if it has used the simplified resale method for three or more consecutive taxable years immediately prior to the year of election. The historic absorption ratio is used in lieu of an actual combined absorption ratio computed under paragraph (d)(3)(i)(C)(1) of this section and is based on costs capitalized by a taxpayer during its test period. If elected, the historic absorption ratio must be used for the qualifying period described in paragraph (d)(4)(ii)(C) of this section.

(ii) Operating rules and definitions. (A) Historic absorption ratio. (1) The historic absorption ratio is equal to the following ratio:

$$\frac{\text{Additional section 263A costs incurred during the test period}}{\text{Section 471 costs incurred during the test period}}$$

(2) Additional section 263A costs incurred during the test period are defined as the sum of the products of the combined absorption ratios (defined in paragraph (d)(3)(i)(C)(1) of this section) multiplied by a taxpayer's section 471 costs incurred with respect to purchases, for each taxable year of the test period.

(3) Section 471 costs incurred during the test period mean the section 471 costs described in § 1.263A-1(d)(2) that a taxpayer incurs generally with respect to its purchases during the test period described in paragraph (d)(4)(ii)(B) of this section.

(B) Test period. (1) In general. The test period is generally the three taxable-year period immediately prior to the taxable year that the historic absorption ratio is elected.

(2) Updated test period. The test period begins again with the beginning of the first taxable year after the close of a qualifying period (as defined in paragraph (d)(4)(ii)(C) of this section). This new test period, the updated test period, is the three taxable-year period beginning with the first taxable year after the close of the qualifying period.

(C) Qualifying period. (1) In general. A qualifying period includes each of the first five taxable years beginning with the first taxable year after a test period (or updated test period).

(2) Extension of qualifying period. In the first taxable year following the close of each qualifying period (e.g., the sixth taxable year following the test period), the taxpayer must compute the actual combined absorption ratio under the simplified resale method. If the actual combined absorption ratio computed for this taxable year (the recomputation year) is within one-half of one percentage point (plus or minus) of the historic absorption ratio used in determining capitalizable costs for the qualifying period (i.e., the previous five taxable years), the qualifying period must be extended to include the recomputation year and the following five taxable years, and the taxpayer must continue to use the historic absorption ratio throughout the extended qualifying period. If, however, the actual combined absorption ratio computed for the recomputation year is not within one-half of one percentage point (plus or minus) of the historic absorption ratio, the taxpayer must use actual combined absorption ratios beginning with the recomputation year under the simplified resale method and throughout the updated test period. The taxpayer must resume using the historic absorption ratio (determined with reference to the updated test period) in the third taxable year following the recomputation year.

(iii) Method of accounting. (A) Adoption and use. The election to use the historic absorption ratio is a method of accounting. A taxpayer using the simplified resale method may elect the historic absorption ratio in any taxable year if permitted under this paragraph (d)(4), provided the taxpayer has not obtained the Commissioner's consent to revoke the historic absorption ratio election within its prior six taxable years. The election is to be effected on a cut-off basis, and thus, no adjustment under section 481(a) is required or permitted. The use of a historic absorption ratio has no effect on other methods of accounting adopted by the taxpayer and used in conjunction with the simplified resale method in determining its section 263A costs. Accordingly, in computing its actual combined absorption ratios, the taxpayer must use the same methods of accounting used in computing its historic absorption ratio during its most recent test period unless the taxpayer obtains the consent of the Commissioner. Finally, for purposes of this paragraph (d)(4)(iii)(A), the recomputation of the historic absorption ratio during an updated test period and the change from a historic absorption ratio to an actual combined absorption ratio during an updated test period by reason of the requirements of this paragraph (d)(4) are not considered changes in methods of accounting under section 446(e) and, thus, do not require the consent of the Commissioner or any adjustments under section 481(a).

(B) Revocation of election. A taxpayer may only revoke its election to use the historic absorption ratio with the consent of the Commissioner in a manner prescribed under section 446(e) and the regulations thereunder. Consent to the change for any taxable year that is included in the qualifying period (or an extended qualifying period) will be granted only upon a showing of unusual circumstances.

(iv) Reporting and recordkeeping requirements. (A) Reporting. A taxpayer making an election under this paragraph (d)(4) must attach a statement to its federal income tax return for the taxable year in which the election is made showing the actual combined absorption ratios determined under the simplified resale method during its first test period. This statement must disclose the historic absorption ratio to be used by the taxpayer during its qualifying period. A similar statement must be attached to the federal income tax return for the first taxable year within any subsequent qualifying period (i.e., after an updated test period).

(B) Recordkeeping. A taxpayer must maintain all appropriate records and details supporting the historic absorption ratio until the expiration of the statute of limitations for the last year for which the taxpayer applied the particular historic absorption ratio in determining additional section 263A costs capitalized to eligible property.

(v) Transition rules. Taxpayers will be permitted to elect a historic absorption ratio in their first, second, or third taxable year beginning after December 31, 1993, under such terms and conditions as may be prescribed by the Commissioner. Taxpayers are eligible to make an election under these transition rules whether or not they previously used the simplified resale method. A taxpayer making such an election must recompute (or compute) its additional section 263A costs, and thus, its historic absorption ratio for its first test period as if the rules prescribed in this section and §§ 1.263A-1 and 1.263A-2 had applied throughout the test period.

(vi) Example. The provisions of this paragraph (d)(4) are illustrated by the following example:

Example. (i) Taxpayer V uses the FIFO method of accounting for inventories and in 1994 elects to use the historic absorption ratio with the simplified resale method. After recomputing its additional section 263A costs in accordance with the transition rules of paragraph (d)(4)(v) of this section, V identifies the following costs incurred during the test period:

1991:
Add'l section 263A costs—$100 Section 471 costs—$3,000
1992:
Add'l section 263A costs—200 Section 471 costs—4,000
1993:
Add'l section 263A costs—300 Section 471 costs—5,000

(ii) Therefore, V computes a 5% historic absorption ratio determined as follows:

$$\text{Historic absorption ratio} = \frac{\$100 + 200 + 300}{\$3{,}000 + 4{,}000 + 5{,}000} = \frac{\$600}{\$12{,}000} = 5\%$$

(iii) In 1994, V incurs $10,000 of section 471 costs of which $3,000 remain in inventory at the end of the year. Under the simplified resale method using a historic absorption ratio, V determines the additional section 263A costs allocable to its ending inventory by multiplying its historic ratio (5%) by the section 471 costs remaining in its ending inventory:

$$\text{Additional section 263A costs} = 5\% \times \$3{,}000 = \$150$$

(iv) To determine its ending inventory under section 263A, V adds the additional section 263A costs allocable to ending inventory to its section 471 costs remaining in ending inventory ($3,150 = $150 + $3,000). The balance of V's additional section 263A costs incurred during 1994 is taken into account in 1994 as part of V's cost of goods sold.

(v) V's qualifying period ends as of the close of its 1998 taxable year. Therefore, 1999 is a recomputation year in which V must compute its actual combined absorption ratio. V determines its actual absorption ratio for 1999 to be 5.25% and compares that ratio to its historic absorption ratio (5.0%). Therefore, V must continue to use its historic absorption ratio of 5.0% throughout an extended qualifying period, 1999 through 2004 (the recomputation year and the following five taxable years).

(vi) If, instead, V's actual combined absorption ratio for 1999 were not between 4.5 % and 5.5 %, V's qualifying period would end and V would be required to compute a new historic absorption ratio with reference to an updated test period of 1999, 2000, and 2001. Once V's historic absorption ratio is determined for the updated test period, it would be used for a new qualifying period beginning in 2002.

(5) Additional simplified methods for resellers. The Commissioner may prescribe additional elective simplified methods by revenue ruling or revenue procedure.

(e) Cross reference. See § 1.6001-1(a) regarding the duty of taxpayers to keep such records as are sufficient to establish the amount of gross income, deductions, etc.

T.D. 8482, 8/6/93, amend T.D. 8559, 8/2/94.

§ 1.263A-4 Rules for property produced in a farming business.

Caution: The Treasury has not yet amended Reg § 1.263A-4 to reflect changes made by P.L. 110-246.

(a) Introduction *(1) In general.* This section provides guidance with respect to the application of section 263A to property produced in a farming business as defined in paragraph (a)(4) of this section. Except as otherwise provided by the rules of this section, the general rules of §§ 1.263A-1 through 1.263A-3 and §§ 1.263A-7 through 1.263A-15 apply to property produced in a farming business. A taxpayer that engages in the raising or growing of any agricultural or horticultural commodity, including both plants and animals, is engaged in the production of property. Section 263A generally requires the capitalization of the direct costs and an allocable portion of the indirect costs that directly benefit or are incurred by reason of the production of this property. The direct and indirect costs of producing plants or animals generally include preparatory costs allocable to the plant or animal and preproductive period costs of the plant or animal. Except as provided in paragraphs (a)(2) and (e) of this section, taxpayers must capitalize the costs of producing all plants and animals unless the election described in paragraph (d) of this section is made.

(2) Exception. (i) In general. Section 263A does not apply to the costs of producing plants with a preproductive period of 2 years or less or the costs of producing animals in a farming business, if the taxpayer is not—

(A) A corporation or partnership required to use an accrual method of accounting (accrual method) under section 447 in computing its taxable income from farming; or

(B) A tax shelter prohibited from using the cash receipts and disbursements method of accounting (cash method) under section 448(a)(3).

(ii) Tax shelter.

(A) In general. A farming business is considered a tax shelter, and thus a taxpayer prohibited from using the cash method under section 448(a)(3), if the farming business is—

(1) A farming syndicate as defined in section 464(c); or

(2) A tax shelter, within the meaning of section 6662(d)(2)(C)(iii).

(B) Presumption. Marketed arrangements in which persons carry on farming activities using the services of a common managerial or administrative service will be presumed to have the principal purpose of tax avoidance, within the meaning of section 6662(d)(2)(C)(iii), if such persons prepay a substantial portion of their farming expenses with borrowed funds.

(iii) Examples. The following examples illustrate the provisions of this paragraph (a)(2):

Example (1). Farmer A grows trees that have a preproductive period in excess of 2 years, and that produce an annual crop. Farmer A is not required by section 447 to use an accrual method or prohibited by section 448(a)(3) from using the cash method. Accordingly, Farmer A qualifies for the exception described in this paragraph (a)(2). Since the trees have a preproductive period in excess of 2 years, Farmer A must capitalize the direct costs and an allocable portion of the indirect costs that directly benefit or are incurred by reason of the production of the trees. Since the annual crop has a preproductive period of 2 years or less, Farmer A is not required to capitalize the costs of producing the crops.

Example (2). Assume the same facts as Example 1, except that Farmer A is required by section 447 to use an accrual method or prohibited by 448(a)(3) from using the cash method. Farmer A does not qualify for the exception described in this paragraph (a)(2). Farmer A is required to capitalize the direct costs and an allocable portion of the indirect costs that directly benefit or are incurred by reason of the production of the trees and crops.

(3) Costs required to be capitalized or inventoried under another provision. The exceptions from capitalization provided in paragraphs (a)(2), (d) and (e) of this section do not apply to any cost that is required to be capitalized or inventoried under another Internal Revenue Code or regulatory provision, such as section 263 or 471.

(4) Farming business. (i) In general. A farming business means a trade or business involving the cultivation of land or the raising or harvesting of any agricultural or horticultural commodity. Examples include the trade or business of operating a nursery or sod farm; the raising or harvesting of trees bearing fruit, nuts, or other crops; the raising of ornamental trees (other than evergreen trees that are more than 6 years old at the time they are severed from their roots); and the raising, shearing, feeding, caring for, training, and management of animals. For purposes of this section, the term harvesting does not include contract harvesting of an agricultural or horticultural commodity grown or raised by another. Similarly, merely buying and reselling plants or animals grown or raised entirely by another is not raising an agricultural or horticultural commodity. A taxpayer is engaged in raising a plant or animal, rather than the mere resale of a plant or animal, if the plant or animal is held for further cultivation and development prior to sale. In determining whether a plant or animal is held for further cultivation and development prior to sale, consideration will be given to all of the facts and circumstances, including: the value added by the taxpayer to the plant or animal through agricultural or horticultural processes; the length of time between the taxpayer's acquisition of the plant or animal and the time that the taxpayer makes the plant or animal available for sale; and in the case of a plant, whether the plant is kept in the container in which purchased, replanted in the ground, or replanted in a series of larger containers as it is grown to a larger size.

(A) Plant. A plant produced in a farming business includes, but is not limited to, a fruit, nut, or other crop bearing tree, an ornamental tree, a vine, a bush, sod, and the crop or yield of a plant that will have more than one crop or yield raised by the taxpayer. Sea plants are produced in a farming business if they are tended and cultivated as opposed to merely harvested.

(B) Animal. An animal produced in a farming business includes, but is not limited to, any stock, poultry or other bird, and fish or other sea life raised by the taxpayer. Thus, for example, the term animal may include a cow, chicken, emu, or salmon raised by the taxpayer. Fish and other sea life are produced in a farming business if they are raised on a fish farm. A fish farm is an area where fish or other sea life are grown or raised as opposed to merely caught or harvested.

(ii) Incidental activities. (A) In general. A farming business includes processing activities that are normally incident to the growing, raising, or harvesting of agricultural or horticultural products. For example, a taxpayer in the trade or business of growing fruits and vegetables may harvest, wash, inspect, and package the fruits and vegetables for sale. Such activities are normally incident to the raising of these crops by farmers. The taxpayer will be considered to be in the trade or business of farming with respect to the growing of fruits and vegetables and the processing activities incident to their harvest.

(B) Activities that are not incidental. Farming business does not include the processing of commodities or products beyond those activities that are normally incident to the growing, raising, or harvesting of such products.

(iii) Examples. The following examples illustrate the provisions of this paragraph (a)(4):

Example (1). Individual A operates a retail nursery. Individual A has three categories of plants. The first category is comprised of plants that Individual A grows from seeds or cuttings. The second category is comprised of plants that Individual A purchases in containers and grows for a period of from several months to several years. Individual A replants some of these plants in the ground. The others are replanted in a series of larger containers as they grow. The third category is comprised of plants that are purchased by Individual A in containers. Individual A does not grow these plants to a larger size before making them available for resale. Instead, Individual A makes these plants available for resale, in the container in which purchased, shortly after receiving them. Thus, no value is added to these plants by Individual A through horticultural processes. Individual A also sells soil, mulch, chemicals, and yard tools. Individual A is producing property in the farming business with respect to the first two categories of plants because these plants are held for further cultivation and development prior to sale. The plants in the third category are not held for further cultivation and development prior to sale and, therefore, are not regarded as property produced in a farming business for purposes of section 263A. Accordingly, Individual A must account for the third category of plants, along with the soil, mulch, chemicals, and yard tools, as property acquired for resale. If Individual A's average annual gross receipts are less than $10 million, Individual A will not be required to capitalize costs with respect to its resale activities under section 263A.

Example (2). Individual B is in the business of growing and harvesting wheat and other grains. Individual B also processes grain that Individual B has harvested in order to produce breads, cereals, and other similar food products, which Individual B then sells to customers in the course of its business. Although Individual B is in the farming business with respect to the growing and harvesting of grain, Individual B is not in the farming business with respect to the processing of such grain to produce the food products.

Example (3). Individual C is in the business of raising poultry and other livestock. Individual C also operates a meat processing operation in which the poultry and other livestock are slaughtered, processed, and packaged or canned. The packaged or canned meat is sold to Individual C's customers. Although Individual C is in the farming business with respect to the raising of poultry and other livestock, Individual C is not in the farming business with respect to the slaughtering, processing, packaging, and canning of such animals to produce the food products.

(b) Application of section 263A to property produced in a farming business. *(1) In general.* Unless otherwise provided in this section, section 263A requires the capitalization of the direct costs and an allocable portion of the indirect costs that directly benefit or are incurred by reason of the production of any property in a farming business (including animals and plants without regard to the length of their preproductive period). Section 1.263A-1(e) describes the types of direct and indirect costs that generally must be capitalized by taxpayers under section 263A and paragraphs (b)(1)(i) and (ii) of this section provide specific examples of the types of costs typically incurred in the trade or business of farming. For purposes of this section, soil and water conservation expenditures that a taxpayer has elected to deduct under section 175 and fertilizer that a taxpayer has elected to deduct under section 180 are not subject to capitalization under section 263A, except to the extent these costs are required to be capitalized as a preproductive period cost of a plant or animal.

(i) Plants. The costs of producing a plant typically required to be capitalized under section 263A include the costs incurred so that the plant's growing process may begin (preparatory costs), such as the acquisition costs of the seed, seedling, or plant, and the costs of planting, cultivating, maintaining, or developing the plant during the preproductive period (preproductive period costs). Preproductive period costs include, but are not limited to, management, irrigation, pruning, soil and water conservation (including costs that the taxpayer has elected to deduct under section 175), fertilizing (including costs that the taxpayer has elected to deduct under section 180), frost protection, spraying, harvesting, storage and handling, upkeep, electricity, tax depreciation and repairs on buildings and equipment used in raising the plants, farm overhead, taxes (except state and Federal income taxes), and interest required to be capitalized under section 263A(f).

(ii) Animals. The costs of producing an animal typically required to be capitalized under section 263A include the costs incurred so that the animal's raising process may begin (preparatory costs), such as the acquisition costs of the animal, and the costs of raising or caring for such animal during the preproductive period (preproductive period costs). Preproductive period costs include, but are not limited to, management, feed (such as grain, silage, concentrates, supplements, haylage, hay, pasture and other forages), maintaining pasture or pen areas (including costs that the taxpayer has elected to deduct under sections 175 or 180), breeding, artificial insemination, veterinary services and medicine, livestock hauling, bedding, fuel, electricity, hired labor, tax depreciation and repairs on buildings and equipment used in raising the animals (for example, barns, trucks, and trailers), farm overhead, taxes (except state and Federal income taxes), and interest required to be capitalized under section 263A(f).

(2) Preproductive period. (i) Plant. (A) In general. The preproductive period of property produced in a farming business means—

(1) In the case of a plant that will have more than one crop or yield (for example, an orange tree), the period before the first marketable crop or yield from such plant;

(2) In the case of the crop or yield of a plant that will have more than one crop or yield (for example, the orange), the period before such crop or yield is disposed of; or

(3) In the case of any other plant, the period before such plant is disposed of.

(B) Applicability of section 263A. For purposes of determining whether a plant has a preproductive period in excess of 2 years, the preproductive period of plants grown in commercial quantities in the United States is based on the nationwide weighted average preproductive period for such plant. The Commissioner will publish a noninclusive list of plants with a nationwide weighted average preproductive period in excess of 2 years. In the case of other plants grown in commercial quantities in the United States, the nationwide weighted average preproductive period must be determined based on available statistical data. For all other plants, the taxpayer is required, at or before the time the seed or plant is acquired or planted, to reasonably estimate the preproductive period of the plant. If the taxpayer estimates a preproductive period in excess of 2 years, the taxpayer must capitalize the costs of producing the plant. If the estimate is reasonable, based on the facts in existence at the time it is made, the determination of whether section 263A applies is not modified at a later time even if the actual length of the preproductive period differs from the estimate. The actual length of the preproductive period will, however, be considered in evaluating the reasonableness of the taxpayer's future estimates. The nationwide weighted average preproductive period or the estimated preproductive period is only used for purposes of determining whether the preproductive period of a plant is greater than 2 years.

(C) Actual preproductive period. The plant's actual preproductive period is used for purposes of determining the period during which a taxpayer must capitalize preproductive period costs with respect to a particular plant.

(1) Beginning of the preproductive period. The actual preproductive period of a plant begins when the taxpayer first incurs costs that directly benefit or are incurred by reason of the plant. Generally, this occurs when the taxpayer plants the seed or plant. In the case of a taxpayer that acquires plants that have already been permanently planted, or plants that are tended by the taxpayer or another prior to permanent planting, the actual preproductive period of the plant begins upon acquisition of the plant by the taxpayer. In the case of the crop or yield of a plant that will have more than one crop or yield, the actual preproductive period begins when the plant has become productive in marketable quantities and the crop or yield first appears, for example, in the form of a sprout, bloom, blossom, or bud.

(2) End of the preproductive period.

(i) In general. In the case of a plant that will have more than one crop or yield, the actual preproductive period ends when the plant first becomes productive in marketable quantities. In the case of any other plant (including the crop or yield of a plant that will have more than one crop or yield), the actual preproductive period ends when the plant, crop, or yield is sold or otherwise disposed of. Field costs, such as irrigating, fertilizing, spraying and pruning, that are incurred after the harvest of a crop or yield but before the crop or yield is sold or otherwise disposed of are not required to be included in the preproductive period costs of the harvested crop or yield because they do not benefit and are unrelated to the harvested crop or yield.

(ii) Marketable quantities. A plant that will have more than one crop or yield becomes productive in marketable quantities once a crop or yield is produced in sufficient quantities to be harvested and marketed in the ordinary course of the taxpayer's business. Factors that are relevant to determining whether a crop or yield is produced in sufficient quantities to be harvested and marketed in the ordinary course include: whether the crop or yield is harvested that is more than de minimis, although it may be less than expected at the maximum bearing stage, based on a comparison of the quantities per acre harvested in the year in question to the quantities per acre expected to be harvested when the plant reaches full maturity; and whether the sales proceeds exceed the costs of harvest and make a reasonable contribution to an allocable share of farm expenses.

(D) Examples. The following examples illustrate the provisions of this paragraph (b)(2):

Example (1). (i) Farmer A, a taxpayer that qualifies for the exception in paragraph (a)(2) of this section, grows plants that will have more than one crop or yield. The plants are grown in commercial quantities in the United States. Farmer A acquires 1 year-old plants by purchasing them from an unrelated party, Corporation B, and plants them immediately. The nationwide weighted average preproductive period of the plant is 4 years. The particular plants grown by Farmer A do not begin to produce in marketable quantities until 3 years and 6 months after they are planted by Farmer A.

(ii) Since the plants are deemed to have a preproductive period in excess of 2 years, Farmer A is required to capitalize the costs of producing the plants. See paragraphs (a)(2) and (b)(2)(i)(B) of this section. In accordance with paragraph (b)(2)(i)(C)(1) of this section, Farmer A must begin to capitalize the preproductive period costs when the plants are planted. In accordance with paragraph (b)(2)(i)(C)(2) of this section, Farmer A must continue to capitalize preproductive period costs to the plants until the plants begin to produce in marketable quantities. Thus, Farmer A must capitalize the preproductive period costs for a period of 3 years and 6 months (that is, until the plants are 4 years and 6 months old), notwithstanding the fact that the plants, in general, have a nationwide weighted average preproductive period of 4 years.

Example (2). (i) Farmer B, a taxpayer that qualifies for the exception in paragraph (a)(2) of this section, grows plants that will have more than one crop or yield. The plants are grown in commercial quantities in the United States. The nationwide weighted average preproductive period of the plant is 2 years and 5 months. Farmer B acquires 1 month-old plants by purchasing them from an unrelated party, Corporation B. Farmer B enters into a contract with Corporation B under which Corporation B will retain and tend the plants for 7 months following the sale. At the end of 7 months, Farmer B takes possession of the plants and plants them in the permanent orchard. The plants become productive in marketable quantities 1 year and 11 months after they are planted by Farmer B.

(ii) Since the plants are deemed to have a preproductive period in excess of 2 years, Farmer B is required to capitalize the costs of producing the plants. See paragraphs (a)(2) and (b)(2)(i)(B) of this section. In accordance with paragraph (b)(2)(i)(C)(1) of this section, Farmer B must begin to capitalize the preproductive period costs when the purchase occurs. In accordance with paragraph (b)(2)(i)(C)(2) of this section, Farmer B must continue to capitalize the preproductive period costs to the plants until the plants begin to produce in marketable quantities. Thus, Farmer B must capitalize the preproductive period costs of the plants for a period of 2 years and 6 months (the 7 months the plants are tended by Corporation B and the 1 year and 11 months after the plants are planted by Farmer B), that is, until the plants are 2 years and 7 months old, notwithstanding the fact that the plants, in general, have a nationwide weighted average preproductive period of 2 years and 5 months.

Example (3). (i) Assume the same facts as in Example 2, except that Farmer B acquires the plants by purchasing them from Corporation B when the plants are 8 months old and that the plants are planted by Farmer B upon acquisition.

(ii) Since the plants are deemed to have a preproductive period in excess of 2 years, Farmer B is required to capitalize the costs of producing the plants. See paragraphs (a)(2) and (b)(2)(i)(B) of this section. In accordance with paragraph (b)(2)(i)(C)(1) of this section, Farmer B must begin to capitalize the preproductive period costs when the plants are planted. In accordance with paragraph (b)(2)(i)(C)(2) of this section, Farmer B must continue to capitalize the preproductive period costs to the plants until the plants begin to produce in marketable quantities. Thus, Farmer B must capitalize the preproductive period costs of the plants for a period of 1 year and 11 months.

Example (4). (i) Farmer C, a taxpayer that qualifies for the exception in paragraph (a)(2) of this section, grows plants that will have more than one crop or yield. The plants are grown in commercial quantities in the United States. Farmer C acquires 1 month-old plants from an unrelated party and plants them immediately. The nationwide weighted average preproductive period of the plant is 2 years and 3 months. The particular plants grown by Farmer C begin to produce in marketable quantities 1 year and 10 months after they are planted by Farmer C.

(ii) Since the plants are deemed to have a nationwide weighted average preproductive period in excess of 2 years, Farmer C is required to capitalize the costs of producing the plants, notwithstanding the fact that the particular plants grown by Farmer C become productive in less than 2 years. See paragraph (b)(2)(i)(B) of this section. In accordance with paragraph (b)(2)(i)(C)(1) of this section, Farmer C must begin to capitalize the preproductive period costs when it plants the plants. In accordance with paragraph (b)(2)(i)(C)(2) of this section, Farmer C properly ceases capitalization of preproductive period costs when the plants become productive in marketable quantities (that is, 1 year and 10 months after they are planted, which is when they are 1 year and 11 months old).

Example (5). (i) Farmer D, a taxpayer that qualifies for the exception in paragraph (a)(2) of this section, grows plants that will have more than one crop or yield. The plants are not grown in commercial quantities in the United States. Farmer D acquires and plants the plants when they are 1 year old and estimates that they will become productive in marketable quantities 3 years after planting. Thus, at the time the plants are acquired and planted Farmer D reasonably estimates that the plants will have a preproductive period of 4 years. The actual plants grown by Farmer D do not begin to produce in marketable quantities until 3 years and 6 months after they are planted by Farmer D.

(ii) Since the plants have an estimated preproductive period in excess of 2 years, Farmer D is required to capitalize the costs of producing the plants. See paragraph (b)(2)(i)(B) of this section. In accordance with paragraph (b)(2)(i)(C)(1) of this section, Farmer D must begin to capitalize the preproductive period costs when it acquires and plants the plants. In accordance with paragraph (b)(2)(i)(C)(2) of this section, Farmer D must continue to capitalize the preproductive period costs until the plants begin to produce in marketable quantities. Thus, Farmer D must capitalize the preproductive period costs of the plants for a period of 3 years and 6 months (that is, until the plants are 4 years and 6 months old), notwithstanding the fact that Farmer D estimated that the plants would become productive after 4 years.

Example (6). (i) Farmer E, a taxpayer that qualifies for the exception in paragraph (a)(2) of this section grows plants from seed. The plants are not grown in commercial quantities in the United States. The plants do not have more than 1 crop or yield. At the time the seeds are planted Farmer E reasonably estimates that the plants will have a preproductive period of 1 year and 10 months. The actual plants grown by Farmer E are not ready for harvesting and disposal until 2 years and 2 months after the seeds are planted by Farmer E.

(ii) Because Farmer E's estimate of the preproductive period (which was 2 years or less) was reasonable at the time made based on the facts, Farmer E will not be required to capitalize the costs of producing the plants under section 263A, notwithstanding the fact that the actual preproductive period of the plants exceeded 2 years. See paragraph (b)(2)(i)(B) of this section. However, Farmer E must take the actual preproductive period of the plants into consideration when making future estimates of the preproductive period of such plants.

Example (7). (i) Farmer F, a calendar year taxpayer that does not qualify for the exception in paragraph (a)(2) of this section, grows trees that will have more than one crop. Farmer F acquires and plants the trees in April, Year 1. On October 1, Year 6, the trees become productive in marketable quantities.

(ii) The costs of producing the plant, including the preproductive period costs incurred by Farmer F on or before October 1, Year 6, are capitalized to the trees. Preproductive period costs incurred after October 1, Year 6, are capitalized to a crop when incurred during the preproductive period of the crop and deducted as a cost of maintaining the tree when incurred between the disposal of one crop and the appearance of the next crop. See paragraphs (b)(2)(i)(A), (b)(2)(i)(C)(1) and (b)(2)(i)(C)(2) of this section.

Example (8). (i) Farmer G, a taxpayer that qualifies for the exception in paragraph (a)(2) of this section, produces fig trees on 10 acres of land. The fig trees are grown in commercial quantities in the United States and have a nationwide weighted average preproductive period in excess of 2 years. Farmer G acquires and plants the fig trees in their permanent grove during Year 1. When the fig trees are mature, Farmer G expects to harvest 10x tons of figs per acre. At the end of Year 4, Farmer G harvests .5x tons of figs per acre that it sells for $100x. During Year 4, Farmer G incurs expenses related to the fig operation of: $50x to harvest the figs and transport them to market and other direct and indirect costs related to the fig operation in the amount of $1000x.

(ii) Since the fig trees have a preproductive period in excess of 2 years, Farmer G is required to capitalize the costs of producing the fig trees. See paragraphs (a)(2) and (b)(2)(i)(B) of this section. In accordance with paragraph (b)(2)(i)(C)(2) of this section, Farmer G must continue to capitalize preproductive period costs to the trees until they become productive in marketable quantities. The following factors weigh in favor of a determination that the fig trees did not become productive in Year 4: the quantity of harvested figs is de minimis based on the fact that the yield is only 5 percent of the expected yield at maturity and the proceeds from the sale of the figs are sufficient, after covering the costs of harvesting and transporting the figs, to cover only a negligible portion of the allocable farm expenses. Based on these facts and circumstances, the fig trees did not become productive in marketable quantities in Year 4.

(ii) Animal. An animal's actual preproductive period is used to determine the period that the taxpayer must capitalize preproductive period costs with respect to a particular animal.

(A) Beginning of the preproductive period. The preproductive period of an animal begins at the time of acquisition, breeding, or embryo implantation.

(B) End of the preproductive period. In the case of an animal that will be used in the trade or business of farming (for example, a dairy cow), the preproductive period generally ends when the animal is (or would be considered) placed in service for purposes of section 168 (without regard to the applicable convention). However, in the case of an animal that will have more than one yield (for example, a breeding cow), the preproductive period ends when the animal produces (for example, gives birth to) its first yield. In the case of any other animal, the preproductive period ends when the animal is sold or otherwise disposed of.

(C) Allocation of costs between animal and yields. In the case of an animal that will have more than one yield, the costs incurred after the beginning of the preproductive period of the first yield but before the end of the preproductive period of the animal must be allocated between the animal and the yield using any reasonable method. Any depreciation allowance on the animal may be allocated entirely to the yield. Costs incurred after the beginning of the preproductive period of the second yield, but before the first yield is weaned from the animal must be allocated between the first and second yield using any reasonable method. However, a taxpayer may elect to allocate these costs entirely to the second yield. An allocation method used by a taxpayer is a method of accounting that must be used consistently and is subject to the rules of section 446 and the regulations thereunder.

(c) Inventory methods. *(1) In general.* Except as otherwise provided, the costs required to be allocated to any plant or animal under this section may be determined using reasonable inventory valuation methods such as the farm-price method or the unit-livestock-price method. See § 1.471-6. Under the unit-livestock-price method, unit prices must include all costs required to be capitalized under section 263A. A taxpayer using the unit-livestock-price method may elect to use the cost allocation methods in § 1.263A-1(f) or 1.263A-2(b) to allocate its direct and indirect costs to the property produced in the business of farming. In such a situation, section 471 costs are the costs taken into account by the taxpayer under the unit-livestock-price method using the taxpayer's standard unit price as modified by this paragraph (c)(1). Tax shelters, as defined in paragraph (a)(2)(ii) of this section, that use the unit-livestock-price method for inventories must include in inventory the annual standard unit price for all animals that are acquired during the taxable year, regardless of whether the purchases are made during the last 6 months of the taxable year. Taxpayers required by section 447 to use an accrual method or prohibited by section 448(a)(3) from using the cash method that use the unit-livestock-price method must modify the annual standard price in order to reasonably reflect the particular period in the taxable year in which purchases of livestock are made, if such modification is necessary in order to avoid significant distortions in income that would otherwise occur through operation of the unit-livestock-price method.

(2) Available for property used in a trade or business. The farm-price method or the unit-livestock-price method may be used by any taxpayer to allocate costs to any plant or animal under this section, regardless of whether the plant or animal is held or treated as inventory property by the taxpayer. Thus, for example, a taxpayer may use the unit-livestock-price method to account for the costs of raising livestock that will be used in the trade or business of farming (for example, a breeding animal or a dairy cow) even though the property in question is not inventory property.

(3) Exclusion of property to which section 263A does not apply. Notwithstanding a taxpayer's use of the farm-price method with respect to farm property to which the provisions of section 263A apply, that taxpayer is not required, solely by such use, to use the farm-price method with respect to farm property to which the provisions of section 263A do not apply. Thus, for example, assume Farmer A raises fruit trees that have a preproductive period in excess of 2 years and to which the provisions of section 263A, therefore, apply. Assume also that Farmer A raises cattle and is not required to use an accrual method by section 447 or prohibited from using the cash method by section 448(a)(3). Because Farmer A qualifies for the exception in paragraph (a)(2) of this section, Farmer A is not required to capitalize the costs of raising the cattle. Although Farmer A may use the farm-price method with respect to the fruit trees, Farmer A is not required to use the farm-price method with respect to the cattle. Instead, Farmer A's accounting for the cattle is determined under other provisions of the Code and regulations.

(d) Election not to have section 263A apply. *(1) Introduction.* This paragraph (d) permits certain taxpayers to make an election not to have the rules of this section apply to any plant produced in a farming business conducted by the electing taxpayer. The election is a method of accounting under section 446, and once an election is made, it is revocable only with the consent of the Commissioner.

(2) Availability of the election. The election described in this paragraph (d) is available to any taxpayer that produces plants in a farming business, except that no election may be made by a corporation, partnership, or tax shelter required to use an accrual method under section 447 or prohibited from using the cash method by section 448(a)(3). Moreover, the election does not apply to the costs of planting, cultivation, maintenance, or development of a citrus or almond grove (or any part thereof) incurred prior to the close of the fourth taxable year beginning with the taxable year in which the trees were planted in the permanent grove (including costs incurred prior to the permanent planting). If a citrus or almond grove is planted in more than one taxable year, the portion of the grove planted in any one taxable year is treated as a separate grove for purposes of determining the year of planting.

(3) Time and manner of making the election. (i) Automatic election. A taxpayer makes the election under this paragraph (d) by not applying the rules of section 263A to determine the capitalized costs of plants produced in a farming business and by applying the special rules in paragraph (d)(4) of this section on its original return for the first taxable year in which the taxpayer is otherwise required to capitalize section 263A costs. Thus, in order to be treated as having made the election under this paragraph (d), it is necessary to report both income and expenses in accordance with the rules of this paragraph (d) (for example, it is necessary to use the alternative depreciation system as provided in paragraph (d)(4)(ii) of this section). For example, a farmer who deducts costs that are otherwise required to be capitalized under section 263A but fails to use the alternative depreciation system under section 168(g)(2) for applicable property placed in service has not made an election under this paragraph (d) and is not in compliance with the provisions of section 263A. In the case of a partnership or S corporation, the election must be made by the partner, shareholder, or member.

(ii) Nonautomatic election. A taxpayer that does not make the election under this paragraph (d) as provided in paragraph (d)(3)(i) must obtain the consent of the Commissioner to make the election by filing a Form 3115, Application for Change in Method of Accounting, in accordance with § 1.446-1(e)(3).

(4) Special rules. If the election under this paragraph (d) is made, the taxpayer is subject to the special rules in this paragraph (d)(4).

(i) Section 1245 treatment. The plant produced by the taxpayer is treated as section 1245 property and any gain resulting from any disposition of the plant is recaptured (that is, treated as ordinary income) to the extent of the total amount of the deductions that, but for the election, would have been required to be capitalized with respect to the plant. In calculating the amount of gain that is recaptured under this paragraph (d)(4)(i), a taxpayer may use the farm-price method or another simplified method permitted under these regulations in determining the deductions that otherwise would have been capitalized with respect to the plant.

(ii) Required use of alternative depreciation system. If the taxpayer or a related person makes an election under this paragraph (d), the alternative depreciation system (as defined in section 168(g)(2)) must be applied to all property used predominantly in any farming business of the taxpayer or related person and placed in service in any taxable year during which the election is in effect. The requirement to use the alternative depreciation system by reason of an election under this paragraph (d) will not prevent a taxpayer from making an election under section 179 to deduct certain depreciable business assets.

(iii) Related person. (A) In general. For purposes of this paragraph (d)(4), related person means—

(1) The taxpayer and members of the taxpayer's family;

(2) Any corporation (including an S corporation) if 50 percent or more of the stock (in value) is owned directly or indirectly (through the application of section 318) by the taxpayer or members of the taxpayer's family;

(3) A corporation and any other corporation that is a member of the same controlled group (within the meaning of section 1563(a)(1)); and

(4) Any partnership if 50 percent or more (in value) of the interests in such partnership is owned directly or indirectly by the taxpayer or members of the taxpayer's family.

(B) Members of family. For purposes of this paragraph (d)(4)(iii), the terms "members of the taxpayer's family", and "members of family" (for purposes of applying section 318(a)(1)), means the spouse of the taxpayer (other than a spouse who is legally separated from the individual under a decree of divorce or separate maintenance) and any of the taxpayer's children (including legally adopted children) who have not reached the age of 18 as of the last day of the taxable year in question.

(5) Examples. The following examples illustrate the provisions of this paragraph (d):

Example (1). (i) Farmer A, an individual, is engaged in the trade or business of farming. Farmer A grows apple trees that have a preproductive period greater than 2 years. In addition, Farmer A grows and harvests wheat and other grains. Farmer A elects under this paragraph (d) not to have the rules of section 263A apply to the costs of growing the apple trees.

(ii) In accordance with paragraph (d)(4) of this section, Farmer A is required to use the alternative depreciation system described in section 168(g)(2) with respect to all property used predominantly in any farming business in which Farmer A engages (including the growing and harvesting of wheat) if such property is placed in service during a year for which the election is in effect. Thus, for example, all assets and equipment (including trees and any equipment used to grow and harvest wheat) placed in service during a year for which the election is in effect must be depreciated as provided in section 168(g)(2).

Example (2). Assume the same facts as in Example 1, except that Farmer A and members of Farmer A's family (as defined in paragraph (d)(4)(iii)(B) of this section) also own 51 percent (in value) of the interests in Partnership P, which is engaged in the trade or business of growing and harvesting corn. Partnership P is a related person to Farmer A under the provisions of paragraph (d)(4)(iii) of this section. Thus, the requirements to use the alternative depreciation system under section 168(g)(2) also apply to any property used predominantly in a trade or business of farming which Partnership P places in service during a year for which an election made by Farmer A is in effect.

(e) Exception for certain costs resulting from casualty losses. *(1) In general.* Section 263A does not require the capitalization of costs that are attributable to the replanting, cultivating, maintaining, and developing of any plants bearing an edible crop for human consumption (including, but not limited to, plants that constitute a grove, orchard, or vineyard) that were lost or damaged while owned by the taxpayer by reason of freezing temperatures, disease, drought, pests, or other casualty (replanting costs). Such replanting costs may be incurred with respect to property other than the property on which the damage or loss occurred to the extent the acreage of the property with respect to which the replanting costs are incurred is not in excess of the acreage of the property on which the damage or loss occurred. This paragraph (e) applies only to the replanting of plants of the same type as those lost or damaged. This paragraph (e) applies to plants replanted on the property on which the damage or loss occurred or property of the same or lesser acreage in the United States irrespective of differences in density between the lost or damaged and replanted plants. Plants bearing crops for human consumption are those crops normally eaten or drunk by humans. Thus, for example, costs incurred with respect to replanting plants bearing jojoba beans do not qualify for the exception provided in this paragraph (e) because that crop is not normally eaten or drunk by humans.

(2) Ownership. Replanting costs described in paragraph (e)(1) of this section generally must be incurred by the taxpayer that owned the property at the time the plants were lost or damaged. Paragraph (e)(1) of this section will apply, however, to costs incurred by a person other than the taxpayer that owned the plants at the time of damage or loss if—

(i) The taxpayer that owned the plants at the time the damage or loss occurred owns an equity interest of more than 50 percent in such plants at all times during the taxable year in which the replanting costs are paid or incurred; and

(ii) Such other person owns any portion of the remaining equity interest and materially participates in the replanting, cultivating, maintaining, or developing of such plants during the taxable year in which the replanting costs are paid or incurred. A person will be treated as materially participating for purposes of this provision if such person would otherwise meet the requirements with respect to material participation within the meaning of section 2032A(e)(6).

(3) Examples. The following examples illustrate the provisions of this paragraph (e):

Example (1). (i) Farmer A grows cherry trees that have a preproductive period in excess of 2 years and produce an annual crop. These cherries are normally eaten by humans. Farmer A grows the trees on a 100 acre parcel of land (parcel 1) and the groves of trees cover the entire acreage of parcel 1. Farmer A also owns a 150 acre parcel of land (parcel 2) that Farmer A holds for future use. Both parcels are in the United States. In 2000, the trees and the irrigation and drainage systems that service the trees are destroyed in a casualty (within the meaning of paragraph (e)(1) of this section). Farmer A installs new irrigation and drainage systems on parcel 1, purchases young trees (seedlings), and plants the seedlings on parcel 1.

(ii) The costs of the irrigation and drainage systems and the seedlings must be capitalized. In accordance with paragraph (e)(1) of this section, the costs of planting, cultivating, developing, and maintaining the seedlings during their preproductive period are not required to be capitalized by section 263A.

Example (2). (i) Assume the same facts as in Example 1 except that Farmer A decides to replant the seedlings on parcel 2 rather than on parcel 1. Accordingly, Farmer A installs the new irrigation and drainage systems on 100 acres of parcel 2 and plants seedlings on those 100 acres.

(ii) The costs of the irrigation and drainage systems and the seedlings must be capitalized. Because the acreage of the related portion of parcel 2 does not exceed the acreage of the destroyed orchard on parcel 1, the costs of planting, cultivating, developing, and maintaining the seedlings during their preproductive period are not required to be capitalized by section 263A. See paragraph (e)(1) of this section.

Example (3). (i) Assume the same facts as in Example 1 except that Farmer A replants the seedlings on parcel 2 rather than on parcel 1, and Farmer A additionally decides to expand its operations by growing 125 rather than 100 acres of trees. Accordingly, Farmer A installs new irrigation and drainage systems on 125 acres of parcel 2 and plants seedlings on those 125 acres.

(ii) The costs of the irrigation and drainage systems and the seedlings must be capitalized. The costs of planting, cultivating, developing, and maintaining 100 acres of the trees during their preproductive period are not required to be capitalized by section 263A. The costs of planting, cultivating, maintaining, and developing the additional 25 acres are, however, subject to capitalization under section 263A. See paragraph (e)(1) of this section.

(4) Special rule for citrus and almond groves. (i) In general. The exception in this paragraph (e) is available with respect to replanting costs of a citrus or almond grove incurred prior to the close of the fourth taxable year after replanting, notwithstanding the taxpayer's election to have section 263A not apply (described in paragraph (d) of this section).

(ii) Example. The following example illustrates the provisions of this paragraph (e)(4):

Example. (i) Farmer A, an individual, is engaged in the trade or business of farming. Farmer A grows citrus trees that have a preproductive period of 5 years. Farmer A elects, under paragraph (d) of this section, not to have section 263A apply. This election, however, is unavailable with respect to the costs of producing a citrus grove incurred within the first 4 years beginning with the year the trees were planted. See paragraph (d)(2) of this section. In year 10, after the citrus grove has become productive in marketable quantities, the citrus grove is destroyed by a casualty within the meaning of paragraph (e)(1) of this section. In year 10, Farmer A acquires and plants young citrus trees in the same grove to replace those destroyed by the casualty.

(ii) Farmer A must capitalize the costs of producing the citrus grove incurred before the close of the fourth taxable year beginning with the year in which the trees were permanently planted. As a result of the election not to have section 263A apply, Farmer A may deduct the preproductive period costs incurred in the fifth year. In year 10, Farmer A must capitalize the acquisition cost of the young trees. However, the costs of planting, cultivating, developing, and maintaining the young trees that replace those destroyed by the casualty are exempted from capitalization under this paragraph (e).

(f) Effective date and change in method of accounting. *(1) Effective date.* In the case of property that is not inventory in the hands of the taxpayer, this section is applicable to costs incurred after August 21, 2000 in taxable years ending after August 21, 2000. In the case of inventory property, this section is applicable to taxable years beginning after August 21, 2000.

(2) Change in method of accounting. Any change in a taxpayer's method of accounting necessary to comply with this section is a change in method of accounting to which the provisions of sections 446 and 481 and the regulations thereunder apply. For property that is not inventory in the hands of the taxpayer, a taxpayer is granted the consent of the Commissioner to change its method of accounting to comply with the provisions of this section for costs incurred after August 21, 2000, provided the change is made for the first taxable year ending after August 21, 2000. For inventory property, a taxpayer is granted the consent of the Commissioner to change its method of accounting to comply with the provisions of this section for the first taxable year beginning after August 21, 2000. A taxpayer changing its method of accounting under this paragraph (f)(2) must file a Form 3115, "Application for Change in Accounting Method," in accordance with the automatic consent procedures in Rev. Proc. 99-49 (1999-2 I.R.B. 725) (see § 601.601(d)(2) of this chapter). However, the scope limitations in section 4.02 of Rev. Proc. 99-49 do not apply, provided the taxpayer's method of accounting for property produced in a farming business is not an issue under consideration within the meaning of section 3.09 of Rev. Proc. 99-49. If the taxpayer is under examination, before an appeals office, or before a federal court at the time that a copy of the Form 3115 is filed with the national office, the taxpayer must provide a duplicate copy of the Form 3115 to the examining agent, appeals officer, or counsel for the government, as appropriate, at the time the copy of the Form 3115 is filed. The form 3115 must contain the name(s) and telephone number(s) of the examining agent, appeals officer, or counsel for the government, as appropriate. Further, in the case of property that is not inventory in the hands of the taxpayer, a change under this paragraph (f)(2) is made on a cutoff basis as described in section 2.06 of Rev. Proc. 99-49 and without the audit protection provided in section 7 of Rev. Proc. 99-49. However, a taxpayer may receive such audit protection for non-inventory property by taking into account any section 481(a) adjustment that results from the change in method of accounting to comply with this section. A taxpayer that opts to determine a section 481(a) adjustment (and, thus, obtain audit protection) for non-inventory property must take into account only additional section 263A costs incurred after December 31, 1986, in taxable years ending after December 31, 1986. Any change in method of accounting that is not made for the taxpayer's first taxable year ending or beginning after August 21, 2000, whichever is applicable, must be made in accord with the procedures in Rev. Proc. 97-27 (1997-1 C.B. 680) (see § 601.601(d)(2) of this chapter).

T.D. 8897, 8/18/2000.

§ 1.263A-5 Exception for qualified creative expenses incurred by certain free-lance authors, photographers, and artists. [Reserved]

§ 1.263A-6 Rules for foreign persons. [Reserved]

§ 1.263A-7 Changing a method of accounting under section 263A.

(a) Introduction. *(1) Purpose.* These regulations provide guidance to taxpayers changing their methods of accounting for costs subject to section 263A. The principal purpose of these regulations is to provide guidance regarding how taxpayers are to revalue property on hand at the beginning of the taxable year in which they change their method of accounting for costs subject to section 263A. Paragraph (c) of this section provides guidance regarding how items or costs included in beginning inventory in the year of change must be revalued. Paragraph (d) of this section provides guidance regarding how non-inventory property should be revalued in the year of change.

(2) Taxpayers that adopt a method of accounting under section 263A. Taxpayers may adopt a method of accounting for costs subject to section 263A in the first taxable year in which they engage in resale or production activities. For purposes of this section, the adoption of a method of accounting has the same meaning as provided in § 1.446-1(e)(1). Taxpayers are not subject to the provisions of these regulations to the extent they adopt, as opposed to change, a method of accounting.

(3) Taxpayers that change a method of accounting under section 263A. Taxpayers changing their method of accounting for costs subject to section 263A are subject to the revaluation and other provisions of this section. Taxpayers subject to these regulations include, but are not limited to —

(i) Resellers of personal property whose average annual gross receipts for the immediately preceding 3-year period (or lesser period if the taxpayer was not in existence for the three preceding taxable years) exceed $10,000,000 where the taxpayer was not subject to section 263A in the prior taxable year;

(ii) Resellers of real or personal property that are using a method that fails to comply with section 263A and desire to change to a method of accounting that complies with section 263A;

(iii) Producers of real or tangible personal property that are using a method that fails to comply with section 263A and desire to change to a method of accounting that complies with section 263A; and

(iv) Resellers and producers that desire to change from one permissible method of accounting for costs subject to section 263A to another permissible method.

(4) Effective date. The provisions of this section are effective for taxable years beginning on or after August 5, 1997. For taxable years beginning before August 5, 1997, the rules of § 1.263A-7T contained in the 26 CFR part 1 edition revised as of April 1, 1997, as modified by other administrative guidance, will apply.

(5) Definition of change in method of accounting. For purposes of this section, a change in method of accounting has the same meaning as provided in § 1.446-1(e)(2)(ii). Changes in method of accounting for costs subject to section 263A include changes to methods required or permitted by section 263A and the regulations thereunder. Changes in method of accounting may be described in the preceding sentence irrespective of whether the taxpayer's previous method of accounting resulted in the capitalization of more (or fewer) costs than the costs required to be capitalized under section 263A and the regulations thereunder, and irrespective of whether the taxpayer's previous method of accounting was a permissible method under the law in effect when the method was being used. However, changes in method of accounting for costs subject to section 263A do not include changes relating to factors other than those described therein. For example, a change in method of accounting for costs subject to section 263A does not include a change from one inventory identification method to another inventory identification method, such as a change from the last-in, first-out (LIFO) method to the first-in, first-out (FIFO) method, or vice versa, or a change from one inventory valuation method to another inventory valuation method under section 471, such as a change from valuing inventory at cost to valuing the inventory at cost or market, whichever is lower, or vice versa. In addition, a change in method of accounting for costs subject to section 263A does not include a change within the LIFO inventory method, such as a change from the double extension method to the link- chain method, or a change in the method used for determining the number of pools. Further, a change from the modified resale method set forth in Notice 89-67 (1989-1 C.B. 723), see § 601.601(d)(2) of this chapter, to the simplified resale method set forth in § 1.263A-3(d) is not a change in method of accounting within the meaning of § 1.446-1(e)(2)(ii) and is therefore not subject to the provisions of this section. However, a change from the simplified resale method set forth in former § 1.263A-1T(d)(4) to the simplified resale method set forth in § 1.263A-3(d) is a change in method of accounting within the meaning of § 1.446-1(e)(2)(ii) and is subject to the provisions of this section.

(b) Rules applicable to a change in method of accounting. *(1) General rules.* All changes in method of accounting for costs subject to section 263A are subject to the rules and procedures provided by the Code, regulations, and administrative procedures applicable to such changes. The Internal Revenue Service has issued specific revenue procedures that govern certain accounting method changes for costs subject to section 263A. Where a specific revenue procedure is not applicable, changes in method of accounting for costs subject to section 263A are subject to the same rules and procedures that govern other accounting method changes. See Rev. Proc. 97-27 (1997-21 I.R.B. 10) and § 601.601(d)(2) of this chapter.

(2) Special rules. (i) Ordering rules when multiple changes in method of accounting occur in the year of change. (A) In general. A change in method of accounting for costs subject to section 263A is generally deemed to occur (including the computation of the adjustment under section 481(a)) before any other change in method of accounting is deemed to occur for that same taxable year.

(B) Exceptions to the general ordering rule. (1) Change from the LIFO inventory method. In the case of a taxpayer that is discontinuing its use of the LIFO inventory method in the same taxable year it is changing its method of accounting for costs subject to section 263A, the change from the LIFO method may be made before the change in method of accounting (and the computation of the corresponding adjustment under section 481 (a)) under section 263A is made.

(2) Change from the specific goods LIFO inventory method. In the case of a taxpayer that is changing from the specific goods LIFO inventory method to the dollar-value LIFO inventory method in the same taxable year it is changing its method of accounting for costs subject to section 263A, the change from the specific goods LIFO inventory method may be made before the change in method of accounting under section 263A is made.

(3) Change in overall method of accounting. In the case of a taxpayer that is changing its overall method of accounting from the cash receipts and disbursements method to an accrual method in the same taxable year it is changing its method of accounting for costs subject to section 263A, the taxpayer must change to an accrual method for capitalizable costs (see § 1.263A-1(c)(2)(ii)) before the change in method of accounting (and the computation of the corresponding adjustment under section 481(a)) under section 263A is made.

(4) Change in method of accounting for depreciation. In the case of a taxpayer that is changing its method of accounting for depreciation in the same taxable year it is changing its method of accounting for costs subject to section 263A and any portion of the depreciation is subject to section 263A, the change in method of accounting for depreciation must be made before the change in method of accounting (and the computation of the corresponding adjustment under section 481(a)) under section 263A is made.

(ii) Adjustment required by section 481(a). In the case of any taxpayer required or permitted to change its method of accounting for any taxable year under section 263A and the regulations thereunder, the change will be treated as initiated by the taxpayer for purposes of the adjustment required by section 481(a). The taxpayer must take the net section 481(a) adjustment into account over the section 481(a) adjustment period as determined under the applicable administrative procedures issued under § 1.446-1(e)(3)(ii) for obtaining the Commissioner's consent to a change in accounting method (for example, see Rev. Proc. 2002-9 (2002-1 C.B. 327) and Rev. Proc. 97-27 (1997-1 C.B. 680) (also see § 601.601(d)(2) of this chapter)). This paragraph applies to taxable years ending on or after June 16, 2004.

(iii) Base year. (A) Need for a new base year. Certain dollar-value LIFO taxpayers (whether using double extension or link-chain) must establish a new base year when they revalue their inventories under section 263A.

(1) Facts and circumstances revaluation method used. A dollar-value LIFO taxpayer that uses the facts and circumstances revaluation method is permitted, but not required, to establish a new base year.

(2) 3-year average method used. (i) Simplified method not used. A dollar-value LIFO taxpayer using the 3-year average method but not the simplified production method or the simplified resale method to revalue its inventory is required to establish a new base year.

(ii) Simplified method used. A dollar-value LIFO taxpayer using the 3-year average method and either the simplified production method or the simplified resale method to revalue its inventory is permitted, but not required, to establish a new base year.

(B) Computing a new base year. For purposes of determining future indexes, the year of change becomes the new base year (that is, the index at the beginning of the year of change generally must be 1.00) and all costs are restated in new base year costs for purposes of extending such costs in future years. However, when a new base year is established, costs associated with old layers retain their separate identity within the base year, with such layers being restated in terms of the new base year index. For example, for purposes of determining whether a particular layer has been invaded, each layer must retain its separate identity. Thus, if a decrement in an inventory pool occurs, layers accumulated in more recent years must be viewed as invaded first, in order of priority.

(c) Inventory. *(1) Need for adjustments.* When a taxpayer changes its method of accounting for costs subject to section 263A, the taxpayer generally must, in computing its taxable income for the year of change, take into account the adjustments required by section 481(a). The adjustments required by section 481(a) relate to revaluations of inventory property, whether the taxpayer produces the inventory or acquires it for resale. See paragraph (d) of this section in regard to the adjustments required by section 481(a) that relate to non-inventory property.

(2) Revaluing beginning inventory. (i) In general. If a taxpayer changes its method of accounting for costs subject to section 263A, the taxpayer must revalue the items or costs included in its beginning inventory in the year of change as if the new method (that is, the method to which the taxpayer is changing) had been in effect during all prior years. In revaluing inventory costs under this procedure, all of the capitalization provisions of section 263A and the regulations thereunder apply to all inventory costs accumulated in prior years. The necessity to revalue beginning inventory as if these capitalization rules had been in effect for all prior years includes, for example, the revaluation of costs or layers incurred in taxable years preceding the transition period to the full absorption method of inventory costing as described in § 1.471-11(e), regardless of whether a taxpayer employed a cut-off method under those regulations. The difference between the inventory as originally valued using the former method (that is, the method from which the taxpayer is changing) and the inventory as revalued using the new method is equal to the amount of the adjustment required under section 481(a).

(ii) Methods to revalue inventory. There are three methods available to revalue inventory. The first method, the facts and circumstances revaluation method, may be used by all taxpayers. Under this method, a taxpayer determines the direct and indirect costs that must be assigned to each item of inventory based on all the facts and circumstances. This method is described in paragraph (c)(2)(iii) of this section. The second method, the weighted average method, is available only in certain situations to taxpayers using the FIFO inventory method or the specific goods LIFO inventory method. This method is described in paragraph (c)(2)(iv) of this section. The third method, the 3-year average method, is available to all taxpayers using the dollar-value LIFO inventory method of accounting. This method is described in paragraph (c)(2)(v) of this section. The weighted average method and the 3-year average method revalue inventory through processes of estimation and extrapolation, rather than based on the facts and circumstances of a particular year's data. All three methods are available regardless of whether the taxpayer elects to use a simplified method to capitalize costs under section 263A.

(iii) Facts and circumstances revaluation method. (A) In general. Under the facts and circumstances revaluation method, a taxpayer generally is required to revalue inventories by applying the capitalization rules of section 263A and the regulations thereunder to the production and resale activities of the taxpayer, with the same degree of specificity as required of inventory manufacturers under the law immediately prior to the effective date of the Tax Reform Act of 1986 (Public Law 99-514, 100 Stat. 2085, 1986-3 C.B. (Vol. 1)). Thus, for example, with respect to any prior year that is relevant in determining the total amount of the revalued balance as of the beginning of the year of change, the taxpayer must analyze the production and resale data for that particular year and apply the rules and principles of section 263A and the regulations thereunder to determine the appropriate revalued inventory costs. However, under the facts and circumstances revaluation method, a taxpayer may utilize reasonable estimates and procedures in valuing inventory costs if—

(1) The taxpayer lacks, and is not able to reconstruct from its books and records, actual financial and accounting data which is required to apply the capitalization rules of section 263A and the regulations thereunder to the relevant facts and circumstances surrounding a particular item of inventory or cost; and

(2) The total amounts of costs for which reasonable estimates and procedures are employed are not significant in comparison to the total restated value (including costs previously capitalized under the taxpayer's former method) of the items or costs for the period in question.

(B) Exception. A taxpayer that is not able to comply with the requirement of paragraph (c)(2)(iii)(A)(2) of this section because of the existence of a significant amount of costs that would require the use of estimates and procedures must revalue its inventories under the procedures provided in paragraph (c)(2)(iv) or (v) of this section.

(C) Estimates and procedures allowed. The estimates and procedures of this paragraph (c)(2)(iii) include—

(1) The use of available information from more recent years to estimate the amount and nature of inventory costs applicable to earlier years; and

(2) The use of available information with respect to comparable items of inventory produced or acquired during the same year in order to estimate the costs associated with other items of inventory.

(D) Use by dollar-value LIFO taxpayers. Generally, a dollar-value LIFO taxpayer must recompute its LIFO inventory for each taxable year that the LIFO inventory method was used.

(E) Examples. The provisions of this paragraph (c)(2)(iii) are illustrated by the following three examples. The principles set forth in these examples are applicable both to production and resale activities and the year of change in all three examples is 1997. The examples read as follows:

Example (1). Taxpayer X lacks information for the years 1993 and earlier, regarding the amount of costs incurred in transporting finished goods from X's factory to X's warehouse and in storing those goods at the warehouse until their sale to customers. X determines that, for 1994 and subsequent years, these transportation and storage costs constitute

4 percent of the total costs of comparable goods under X's method of accounting for such years. Under this paragraph (c)(2)(iii), X may assume that transportation and storage costs for the years 1993 and earlier constitute 4 percent of the total costs of such goods.

Example (2). Assume the same facts as in Example 1, except that for the year 1993 and earlier, X used a different method of accounting for inventory costs whereunder significantly fewer costs were capitalized than amounts capitalized in later years. Thus, the application of transportation and storage based on a percentage of costs for 1994 and later years would not constitute a reasonable estimate for use in earlier years. X may use the information from 1994 and later years, if appropriate adjustments are made to reflect the differences in inventory costs for the applicable years, including, for example—

(i) Increasing the percentage of costs that are intended to represent transportation and storage costs to reflect the aggregate differences in capitalized amounts under the two methods of accounting; or

(ii) Taking the absolute dollar amount of transportation and storage costs for comparable goods in inventory and applying that amount (adjusted for changes in general price levels, where appropriate) to goods associated with 1993 and prior periods.

Example (3). Taxpayer Z lacks information for certain years with respect to factory administrative costs, subject to capitalization under section 263A and the regulations thereunder, incurred in the production of inventory in factory A. Z does have sufficient information to determine factory administrative costs with respect to production of inventory in factory B, wherein inventory items were produced during the same years as Factory A. Z may use the information from factory B to determine the appropriate amount of factory administrative costs to capitalize as inventory costs for comparable items produced in factory A during the same years.

(iv) Weighted average method. (A) In general. A taxpayer using the FIFO method or the specific goods LIFO method of accounting for inventories may use the weighted average method as provided in this paragraph (c)(2)(iv) to estimate the change in the amount of costs that must be allocated to inventories for prior years. The weighted average method under this paragraph (c)(2)(iv) is only available to a taxpayer that lacks sufficient data to revalue its inventory costs under the facts and circumstances revaluation method provided for in paragraph (c)(2)(iii) of this section. Moreover, a taxpayer that qualifies for the use of the weighted average method under this paragraph (c)(2)(iv) must utilize such method only with respect to items or costs for which it lacks sufficient information to revalue under the facts and circumstances revaluation method. Particular items or costs must be revalued under the facts and circumstances revaluation method if sufficient information exists to make such a revaluation. If a taxpayer lacks sufficient information to otherwise apply the weighted average method under this paragraph (c)(2)(iv) (for example, the taxpayer is unable to revalue the costs of any of its items in inventory due to a lack of information), then the taxpayer must use reasonable estimates and procedures, as described in the facts and circumstances revaluation method, to whatever extent is necessary to allow the taxpayer to apply the weighted average method.

(B) Weighted average method for FIFO taxpayers. (1) In general. This paragraph (c)(2)(iv)(B) sets forth the mechanics of the weighted average method as applicable to FIFO taxpayers. Under the weighted average method, an item in ending inventory for which sufficient data is not available for revaluation under section 263A and the regulations thereunder must be revalued by using the weighted average percentage increase or decrease with respect to such item for the earliest subsequent taxable year for which sufficient data is available. With respect to an item for which no subsequent data exists, such item must be revalued by using the weighted average percentage increase or decrease with respect to all reasonably comparable items in the taxpayer's inventory for the same year or the earliest subsequent taxable year for which sufficient data is available.

(2) Example. The provisions of this paragraph (c)(2)(iv)(B) are illustrated by the following example. The principles set forth in this example are applicable both to production and resale activities and the year of change in the example is 1997. The example reads as follows:

Example. Taxpayer A manufactures bolts and uses the FIFO method to identify inventories. Under A's former method, A did not capitalize all of the costs required to be capitalized under section 263A. A maintains inventories of bolts, two types of which it no longer produces. Bolt A was last produced in 1994. The revaluation of the costs of Bolt A under this section for bolts produced in 1994 results in a 20 percent increase of the costs of Bolt A. A portion of the inventory of Bolt A, however, is attributable to 1993. A does not have sufficient data for revaluation of the increase determined for 1994 to the 1993 production as an acceptable estimate. Bolt B was last produced in 1992 and no data exists that would allow revaluation of the inventory cost of Bolt B. The inventories of all other bolts for which information is available are attributable to 1994 and 1995. Revaluation of the costs of these other bolts using available data results in an average increase in inventory costs of 15 percent for 1994 production. With respect to Bolt B, the overall 15 percent increase for A's inventory for 1994 may be used in revaluing the cost of Bolt B.

(C) Weighted average method for specific goods LIFO taxpayers. (1) In general. This paragraph (c)(2)(iv)(C) sets forth the mechanics of the weighted average method as applicable to LIFO taxpayers using the specific goods method of valuing inventories. Under the weighted average method, the inventory layers with respect to an item for which data is available are revalued under this section and the increase or decrease in amount for each layer is expressed as a percentage of change from the cost in the layer as originally valued. A weighted average of the percentage of change for all layers for each type of good is computed and applied to all earlier layers for each type of good that lack sufficient data to allow for revaluation. In the case of earlier layers for which sufficient data exists, such layers are to be revalued using actual data. In cases where sufficient data is not available to make a weighted average estimate with respect to a particular item of inventory, a weighted average increase or decrease is to be determined using all other inventory items revalued by the taxpayer in the same specific goods grouping. This percentage increase or decrease is then used to revalue the cost of the item for which data is lacking. If the taxpayer lacks sufficient data to revalue any of the inventory items contained in a specific goods grouping, then the weighted average increase or decrease of substantially similar items (as determined by principles similar to the rules applicable to dollar-value LIFO taxpayers in § 1.472-8(b)(3)) must be applied in the revaluation of the items in such grouping. If insufficient data exists with respect to all the items in a specific goods grouping and to all items that are substantially similar (or such items do not exist), then the weighted average for all revalued items in the taxpayer's inventory must be applied in revaluing items for which data is lacking.

(2) Example. The provisions of this paragraph (c)(2)(iv)(C) are illustrated by the following example. The principles set forth in this example are applicable both to production and resale activities and the year of change in the example is 1997. The example reads as follows:

Example. (i) Taxpayer M is a manufacturer that produces two different parts. Under M's former method, M did not capitalize all of the costs required to be capitalized under section 263A. Work-in-process inventory is recorded in terms of equivalent units of finished goods. M's records show the following at the end of 1996 under the specific goods LIFO inventory method:

LIFO Product and layer	Number	Cost	Carrying values
Product #1:			
1993	150	$5.00	$ 750
1994	100	6.00	600
1995	100	6.50	650
1996	50	7.00	350
			$2,350
Product #2:			
1993	200	$4.00	$ 800
1994	200	4.50	900
1995	100	5.00	500
1996	100	6.00	600
			$2,800

Total carrying value of Product #1 and #2 under M's former method—$5,150

(ii) M has sufficient data to revalue the unit costs of Product #1 using its new method for 1994, 1995 and 1996. These costs are: $7.00 in 1994, $7.75 in 1995, and $9.00 in 1996. This data for Product #1 results in a weighted average percentage change of 20.31 percent [(100 × ($7.00 − $6.00)) + (100 × ($7.75 − $6.50)) + (50 × ($9.00 − $7.00)) divided by (100 × $6.00) + (100 × $6.50) + (50 × $7.00)]. M has sufficient data to revalue the unit costs of Product #2 only in 1995 and 1996. These costs are: $6.00 in 1995 and $7.00 in 1996. This data for Product #2 results in a weighted average percentage change of 18.18 percent [(100 + ($6.00 − $5.00)) + (100 × ($7.00 − $6.00)) divided by (100 × $5.00) + (100 × $6.00)].

(iii) M can estimate its revalued costs for Product #1 for 1993 by applying the weighted average increase computed for Product #1 (20.31 percent) to the unit costs originally carried on M's records for 1993 under M's former method. The estimated revalued unit cost of Product #1 would be $6.02 ($5.00 + 1.2031). M estimates its revalued costs for Product #2 for 1993 and 1994 in a similar fashion. M applies the weighted average increase determined for Product #2 (18.18 percent) to the unit costs of $4.00 and $4.50 for 1993 and 1994 respectively. The revalued unit costs of Product #2 are $4.73 for 1993 ($4.00 × 1.1818) and $5.32 for 1994 ($4.50 × 1.1818).

(iv) M's inventory would be revalued as follows:

LIFO Product and layer	Number	Cost	Carrying values
Product #1:			
1993	150	$6.02	$ 903
1994	100	7.00	700
1995	100	7.75	775
1996	50	9.00	450
			$2,828
Product #2:			
1993	200	$4.73	$ 946
1994	200	5.32	1,064
1995	100	6.00	600
1996	100	7.00	700
			$3,310

Total value of Products #1 and #2 as revalued under M's new method—$6,138

Total amount of adjustment required under section 481(a) [$6,138 − $5,150]—$988

(D) Adjustments to inventory costs from prior years. For special rules applicable when a revaluation using the weighted average method includes costs not incurred in prior years, see paragraph (c)(2)(v)(E) of this section.

(v) 3-year average method. (A) In general. A taxpayer using the dollar-value LIFO method of accounting for inventories may revalue all existing LIFO layers of a trade or business based on the 3-year average method as provided in this paragraph (c)(2)(v). The 3-year average method is based on the average percentage change (the 3-year revaluation factor) in the current costs of inventory for each LIFO pool based on the three most recent taxable years for which the taxpayer has sufficient information (typically, the three most recent taxable years of such trade or business). The 3-year revaluation factor is applied to all layers for each pool in beginning inventory in the year of change. The 3-year average method is available to any dollar-value taxpayer that complies with the requirements of this paragraph (c)(2)(v) regardless of whether such taxpayer lacks sufficient data to revalue its inventory costs under the facts and circumstances revaluation method prescribed in paragraph (c)(2)(iii) of this section. The 3-year average method must be applied with respect to all inventory in a taxpayer's trade or business. A taxpayer is not permitted to apply the method for the revaluation of some, but not all, inventory costs on the basis of pools, business units, or other measures of inventory amounts that do not constitute a separate trade or business. Generally, a taxpayer revaluing its inventory using the 3-year average method must establish a new base year. See, paragraph (b)(2)(iii)(A)(2)(i) of this section. However, a dollar-value LIFO taxpayer using the 3-year average method and either the simplified production method or the simplified resale method to revalue its inventory is permitted, but not required, to establish a new base year. See, paragraph (b)(2)(iii)(A)(2)(ii) of this section. If a taxpayer lacks sufficient information to otherwise apply the 3-year average method under this paragraph (c)(2)(v) (for example, the taxpayer is unable to revalue the costs of any of its LIFO pools for three years due to a lack of information), then the taxpayer must use reasonable estimates and procedures, as described in the facts and circumstances revaluation method under paragraph (c)(2)(iii) of this section, to whatever extent is necessary to allow the taxpayer to apply the 3-year average method.

(B) Consecutive year requirement. Under the 3-year average method, if sufficient data is available to calculate the revaluation factor for more than three years, the taxpayer may use data from such additional years in determining the average percentage increase or decrease only if the additional years are consecutive to and prior to the year of change. The requirement under the preceding sentence to use consecutive years is applicable under this method regardless of whether any inventory costs in beginning inventory as of the year of change are viewed as incurred in, or attributable to, those consecutive years under the LIFO inventory method. Thus, the requirement to use data from consecutive years may result in using information from a year in which no LIFO increment occurred. For example, if a taxpayer is changing its method of accounting in 1997 and has sufficient data to revalue its inventory for the years 1991 through 1996, the taxpayer may calculate the revaluation factor using all six years. If, however, the taxpayer has sufficient data to revalue its inventory for the years 1990 through 1992, and 1994 through 1996, only the three years consecutive to the year of change, that is, 1994 through 1996, may be used in determining the revaluation factor. Similarly, for example, a taxpayer with LIFO increments in 1995, 1993, and 1992 may not calculate the revaluation factor based on the data from those years alone, but instead must use the data from consecutive years for which the taxpayer has information.

(C) Example. The provisions of this paragraph (c)(2)(v) are illustrated by the following example. The principles set forth in this example are applicable both to production and resale activities and the year of change in the example is 1997. The example reads as follows:

Example. (i) Taxpayer G, a calendar year taxpayer, is a reseller that is required to change its method of accounting under section 263A. G will not use either the simplified production method or the simplified resale method. G adopted the dollar-value LIFO inventory method in 1991, using a single pool and the double extension method. G's beginning LIFO inventory as of January 1, 1997, computed using its former method, for the year of change is as follows:

	Base year costs	Index	LIFO carrying value
Base layer	$14,000	1.00	$14,000
1991 layer	4,000	1.20	4,800
1992 layer	5,000	1.30	6,500
1993 layer	2,000	1.35	2,700
1994 layer	0	1.40	0
1995 layer	4,000	1.50	6,000
1996 layer	5,000	1.60	8,000
Total	$34,000		$42,000

(ii) G is able to recompute total inventoriable costs incurred under its new method for the three preceding taxable years as follows:

	Current cost as recorded (former) method	Current cost as adjusted (new method)	Weighted Percentage change
1994r	$ 35,000	$ 45,150	.29
1995	43,500	54,375	.25
1996	54,400	70,720	.30
Total	$132,900	$170,245	.28

(iii) Applying the average revaluation factor of .28 to each layer, G's inventory is restated as follows:

	Restated base year costs	Index	Restated LIFO carrying value
Base layer	$17,920	1.00	$17,920
1991 layer	5,120	1.20	6,144
1992 layer	6,400	1.30	8,320
1993 layer	2,560	1.35	3,456
1994 layer	0	1.40	0
1995 layer	5,120	1.50	7,680
1996 layer	6,400	1.60	10,240
Total	$43,520		$53,760

(iv) The adjustment required by section 481(a) is $11,760. This amount may be computed by multiplying the average percentage of .28 by the LIFO carrying value of G's inventory valued using its former method ($42,000). Alternatively, the adjustment required by section 481(a) may be computed by the difference between—

(A) The revalued costs of the taxpayer's inventory under its new method ($53,760), and

(B) The costs of the taxpayer's inventory using its former method ($42,000).

(v) In addition, the inventory as of the first day of the year of change (January 1, 1997) becomes the new base year cost for purposes of determining the LIFO index in future years. See, paragraphs (b)(2)(iii)(A)(2)(i) and (b)(2)(iii)(B) of this section. This requires that layers in years prior to the base year be restated in terms of the new base year index. The current year cost of G's inventory, as adjusted, is $70,720. Such cost must be apportioned to each layer in proportion to the restated base year cost of that layer to total restated base year costs ($43,520), as follows:

	Restated base year costs	Index	Restated LIFO carrying value
Old base layer	$29,120	.615	$17,920
1991 layer	8,320	.738	6,144
1992 layer	10,400	.80	8,320
1993 layer	4,160	.80	3,456
1994 layer	0		0
1995 layer	8,320	.923	7,680
1996 layer	10,400	.985	10,240
Total	$70,720		$53,760

(D) Short taxable years. A short taxable year is treated as a full 12 months.

(E) Adjustments to inventory costs from prior years. (1) General rule. (i) The use of the revaluation factor, based on current costs, to estimate the revaluation of prior inventory layers under the 3-year average method, as described in paragraph (c)(2)(v) of this section, may result in an allocation of costs that include amounts attributable to costs not incurred during the year in which the layer arose. To the extent a taxpayer can demonstrate that costs that contributed to the determination of the revaluation factor could not have affected a prior year, the revaluation factor as applied to that year may be adjusted under the restatement adjustment procedure, as described in paragraph (c)(2)(v)(F) of this section. The determination that a cost could not have affected a prior year must be made by a taxpayer only upon showing that the type of cost incurred during the years used to calculate the revaluation factor (revaluation years) was not present during such prior year. An item of cost will not be eligible for the restatement adjustment procedure simply because the cost varies in amount from year to year or the same type of cost is described or referred to by a different name from year to year. Thus, the restatement adjustment procedure allowed under paragraph (c)(2)(v)(F) of this section is not available in a prior year with respect to a particular cost if the same type of cost was incurred both in the revaluation years and in such prior year, although the amount of such cost and the name or description thereof may vary.

(ii) The provisions of this paragraph (c)(2)(v)(E) are also applicable to taxpayers using the weighted average method in revaluing inventories under paragraph (c)(2)(iv) of this section. Thus, to the extent a taxpayer can demonstrate that costs that contributed to the determination of the restatement of a particular year or item could not have affected a prior year or item, the taxpayer may adjust the revaluation of that prior year or item accordingly under the weighted average method. All the requirements and definitions, however, applicable to the restatement adjustment procedure under this paragraph (c)(2)(v)(E) fully apply to a taxpayer using the weighted average method to revalue inventories.

(2) Examples of costs eligible for restatement adjustment procedure. The provisions of this paragraph (c)(2)(v)(E) are illustrated by the following four examples. The principles set forth in these examples are applicable both to production and resale activities and the year of change in the four examples is 1997. The examples read as follows:

Example (1). Taxpayer A is a reseller that introduced a defined benefit pension plan in 1994, and made the plan available to personnel whose labor costs were (directly or indirectly) properly allocable to resale activities. A determines the revaluation factor based on data available for the years 1994 through 1996, for which the pension plan was in existence. Based on these facts, the costs of the pension plan in the revaluation years are eligible for the restatement adjustment procedure for years prior to 1994.

Example (2). Assume the same facts as in Example 1, except that a defined contribution plan was available, during prior years, to personnel whose labor costs were properly allocable to resale activities. The defined contribution plan was terminated before the introduction of the defined benefit plan in 1994. Based on these facts, the costs of the defined benefit pension plan in the revaluation years are not eligible for the restatement adjustment procedure with respect to years for which the defined contribution plan existed.

Example (3). Taxpayer C is a manufacture that established a security department in 1995 to patrol and safeguard its production and warehouse areas used in C's trade or business. Prior to 1995, C had not been required to utilize security personnel in its trade or business; C established the security department in 1995 in response to increasing vandalism and theft at its plant locations. Based on these facts, the costs of the security department are eligible for restatement adjustment procedure for years prior to 1995.

Example (4). Taxpayer D is a reseller that established a payroll department in 1995 to process the company's weekly payroll. In the years 1991 through 1994, D engaged the services of an outside vendor to process the company's payroll. Prior to 1991, D's payroll processing was done by D's accounting department, which was responsible for payroll processing as well as for other accounting functions. Based on these facts, the costs of the payroll department are not eligible for the restatement adjustment procedure. D was incurring the same type of costs in earlier years as D was incurring in the payroll department in 1995 and subsequent years, although these costs were designated by a different name or description.

(F) Restatement adjustment procedure. (1) In general. (i) This paragraph (c)(2)(v)(F) provides a restatement adjustment procedure whereunder a taxpayer may adjust the restatement of inventory costs in prior taxable years in order to produce a different restated value than the value that would otherwise occur through application of the revaluation factor to such prior taxable years.

(ii) Under the restatement adjustment procedure as applied to a particular prior year, a taxpayer must determine the particular items of cost that are eligible for the restatement adjustment with respect to such prior year. The taxpayer must then recompute, using reasonable estimates and procedures, the total inventoriable costs that would have been incurred for each revaluation year under the taxpayer's former method and the taxpayer's new method by making appropriate adjustments in the data for such revaluation year to reflect the particular costs eligible for adjustment.

(iii) The taxpayer must then compute the total percentage change with respect to each revaluation year, using the revised estimates of total inventoriable costs for such year as described in paragraph (c)(2)(v)(F)(1)(ii) of this section. The percentage change must be determined by calculating the ratio of the revised total of the inventoriable costs for such revaluation year under the taxpayer's new method to the revised total of the inventoriable costs for such revaluation year under the taxpayer's former method.

(iv) An average of the resulting percentage change for all revaluation years is then calculated, and the resulting average is applied to the prior year in issue.

(2) Examples of restatement adjustment procedure. The provisions of this paragraph (c)(2)(v)(F) are illustrated by the following two examples. The principles set forth in these examples are applicable both to production and resale activities and the year of change in the two examples is 1997. The examples read as follows:

Example (1). Taxpayer A is a reseller that is eligible to make a restatement adjustment by reason of the costs of a defined benefit pension plan that was introduced in 1994, during the revaluation period. The revaluation factor, before adjustment of data to reflect the pension costs, is as provided in the example in paragraph (c)(2)(v)(C) of this section. Thus, for example, with respect to the year 1994, the total inventoriable costs under A's former method is $35,000, the total inventoriable costs under A's new method is $45,150, and the percentage change is .29. Under the method of accounting used by A during 1994 (the former method), none of the pension costs were included as inventoriable costs. Thus, under the restatement adjustment procedure, the total inventoriable cost under A's former method would remain at $35,000 if the pension plan had not been in existence. Similarly, A determines that the total inventoriable costs for 1994 under A's new method, if the pension plan had not been in existence, would have been $42,000. The restatement adjustment for 1994 determined under this paragraph (c)(2)(v)(F) would then be equal to .20 ([$42,000 − $35,000]/$35,000). A would make similar calculations with respect to 1995 and 1996. The average of such amounts for each of the three years in the revaluation period would then be determined as in the example in paragraph (c)(2)(v)(C) of this section. Such average would be used to revalue cost layers for years for which the pension plan was not in existence. Such revalued layers would then be viewed as restated in compliance with the requirements of this paragraph. With respect to cost layers incurred during years for which the pension plan was in existence, no adjustment of the revaluation factor would occur.

Example (2). Assume the same facts as in Example 1, except that a portion of the pension costs were included as inventoriable costs under the method used by A during 1994 (the former method). Under the restatement adjustment procedure, A determines that the total inventoriable costs for 1994 under the former method, if the pension plan had not been in existence, would have been $34,000. Similarly, A determines that the total inventoriable costs for 1994 under A's new method, if the pension plan had not been in existence, would have been $42,000. The restatement adjustment for 1994 determined under this paragraph (c)(2)(v)(F) would then be equal to .24 ([$42,000 − $34,000]/$34,000). A would make similar calculations with respect to 1995 and 1996. The average of such amounts for each of the three years in the revaluation period would then be determined as in the example in paragraph (c)(2)(v)(C) of this section. Such average would be used to revalue cost layers for years for which the pension plan was not in existence.

(3) Intercompany items. (i) Revaluing intercompany transactions. Pursuant to any change in method of accounting for costs subject to section 263A, taxpayers are required to revalue the amount of any intercompany item resulting from the sale or exchange of inventory property in an intercompany transaction to an amount equal to the intercompany item that would have resulted had the cost of goods sold for that inventory property been determined under the taxpayer's new method. The requirement of the preceding sentence applies with respect to both inventory produced by a taxpayer and inventory acquired by the taxpayer for resale. In addition, the requirements of this paragraph (c)(3) apply only to any intercompany item of the taxpayer as of the beginning of the year of change in method of accounting. See § 1.1502-13(b)(2)(ii). A taxpayer must revalue the amount of any intercompany item only if the inventory property sold in the intercompany transaction is held as inventory by a buying member as of the date the taxpayer changes its method of accounting under section 263A. Corresponding changes to the adjustment required under section 481(a) must be made with respect to any adjustment of the intercompany item required under this paragraph (c)(3). Moreover, the requirements of this paragraph (c)(3) apply regardless of whether the taxpayer has any items in beginning inventory as of the year of change in method of accounting. See § 1.1502-13 for the definition of intercompany transaction.

(ii) Example.The provisions of this paragraph (c)(3) are illustrated by the following example. The principles set forth in this example are applicable both to production and resale activities and the year of change in the example is 1997. The example reads as follows:

(iii) Availability of revaluation methods. In revaluing the amount of any intercompany item resulting from the sale or exchange of inventory property in an intercompany transaction to an amount equal to the intercompany item that would have resulted had the cost of goods sold for that inventory property been determined under the taxpayer's new method, a taxpayer may use the other methods and procedures otherwise properly available to that particular taxpayer in revaluing inventory under section 263A and the regulations thereunder, including, if appropriate, the various simplified methods provided in section 263A and the regulations thereunder and the various procedures described in this paragraph (c).

(4) Anti-abuse rule. (i) In general. Section 263A(i)(1) provides that the Secretary shall prescribe such regulations as may be necessary or appropriate to carry out the purposes of section 263A, including regulations to prevent the use of related parties, pass-thru entities, or intermediaries to avoid the application of section 263A and the regulations thereunder. One way in which the application of section 263A and the regulations thereunder would be otherwise avoided is through the use of entities described in the preceding sentence in such a manner as to effectively avoid the necessity to restate beginning inventory balances under the change in method of accounting required or permitted under section 263A and the regulations thereunder.

(ii) Deemed avoidance of this section. (A) Scope. For purposes of this paragraph (c), the avoidance of the application of section 263A and the regulations thereunder will be deemed to occur if a taxpayer using the LIFO method of accounting for inventories, transfers inventory property to a related corporation in a transaction described in section 351, and such transfer occurs:

(1) On or before the beginning of the transferor's taxable year beginning in 1987; and

(2) After September 18, 1986.

(B) General rule. Any transaction described in paragraph (c)(4)(ii)(A) of this section will be treated in the following manner:

(1) Notwithstanding any provision to the contrary (for example, section 381), the transferee corporation is required to revalue the inventories acquired from the transferor under the provisions of this paragraph (c) relating to the change in method of accounting and the adjustment required by section 481(a), as if the inventories had never been transferred and were still in the hands of the transferor; and

(2) Absent an election as described in paragraph (c)(4)(iii) of this section, the transferee must account for the inventories acquired from the transferor by treating such inventories as if they were contained in the transferee's LIFO layer(s).

(iii) Election to use transferor's LIFO layers. If a transferee described in paragraph (c)(4)(ii) of this section so elects, the transferee may account for the inventories acquired from the transferor by allocating such inventories to LIFO layers corresponding to the layers to which such properties were properly allocated by the transferor, prior to their transfer. The transferee must account for such inventories for all subsequent periods with reference to such layers to which the LIFO costs were allocated. Any such election is to be made on a statement attached to the timely filed federal income tax return of the transferee for the first taxable year for which section 263A and the regulations thereunder applies to the transferee.

(iv) Tax avoidance intent not required. The provisions of paragraph (c)(4)(ii) of this section will apply to any transaction described therein, without regard to whether such transaction was consummated with an intention to avoid federal income taxes.

(v) Related corporation. For purposes of this paragraph (c)(4), a taxpayer is related to a corporation if—

(A) the relationship between such persons is described in section 267(b)(1), or

(B) such persons are engaged in trades or businesses under common control (within the meaning of paragraphs (a) and (b) of section 52).

(d) Non-inventory property. *(1) Need for adjustments.* A taxpayer that changes its method of accounting for costs subject to section 263A with respect to non-inventory property must revalue the non-inventory property on hand at the beginning of the year of change as set forth in paragraph (d)(2) of this section, and compute an adjustment under section 481(a). The adjustment under section 481(a) will equal the difference between the adjusted basis of the property as revalued using the taxpayer's new method and the adjusted basis of the property as originally valued using the taxpayer's former method.

(2) Revaluing property. A taxpayer must revalue its non-inventory property as of the beginning of the year of change in method of accounting. The facts and circumstances revaluation method of paragraph (c)(2)(iii) of this section must be used to revalue this property. In revaluing non-inventory property, however, the only additional section 263A costs that must be taken into account are those additional section 263A costs incurred after the later of December 31, 1986, or the date the taxpayer first becomes subject to section 263A, in taxable years ending after that date. See § 1.263A-1(d)(3) for the definition of additional section 263A costs.

T.D. 8728, 8/4/97, amend T.D. 9131, 6/15/2004.

§ 1.263A-8 Requirement to capitalize interest.

(a) In general. *(1) General rule.* Capitalization of interest under the avoided cost method described in § 1.263A-9 is required with respect to the production of designated property described in paragraph (b) of this section.

(2) Treatment of interest required to be capitalized. In general, interest that is capitalized under this section is treated as a cost of the designated property and is recovered in accordance with § 1.263A-1(c)(4). Interest capitalized by reason of assets used to produce designated property (within the meaning of § 1.263A-11(d)) is added to the basis of the designated property rather than the bases of the assets used to produce the designated property. Interest capitalized with respect to designated property that includes both components subject to an allowance for depreciation or depletion and components not subject to an allowance for depreciation or depletion is ratably allocated among, and is treated as a cost of, components that are subject to an allowance for depreciation or depletion.

(3) Methods of accounting under section 263A(f). Except as otherwise provided, methods of accounting and other computations under §§ 1.263A-8 through 1.263A-15 are applied on a taxpayer, as opposed to a separate and distinct trade or business, basis.

(4) Special definitions. (i) Related person. Except as otherwise provided, for purposes of §§ 1.263A-8 through 1.263A-15, a person is related to a taxpayer if their relationship is described in section 267(b) or 707(b).

(ii) Placed in service. For purposes of §§ 1.263A-8 through 1.263A-15, placed in service has the same meaning as set forth in § 1.46-3(d).

(b) Designated property. *(1) In general.* Except as provided in paragraphs (b)(3) and (b)(4) of this section, designated property means any property that is produced and that is either:

(i) Real property; or

(ii) Tangible personal property (as defined in § 1.263A-2(a)(2)) which meets any of the following criteria:

(A) Property with a class life of 20 years or more under section 168 (long-lived property), but only if the property is not property described in section 1221(1) in the hands of the taxpayer or a related person,

(B) Property with an estimated production period (as defined in § 1.263A-12) exceeding 2 years (2-year property), or

(C) Property with an estimated production period exceeding 1 year and an estimated cost of production exceeding $1,000,000 (1-year property).

(2) Special rules. (i) Application of thresholds. The thresholds described in paragraphs (b)(1)(ii)(A), (B), and (C) of this section are applied separately for each unit of property (as defined in § 1.263A-10).

(ii) Relevant activities and costs. For purposes of determining whether property is designated property, all activities and costs are taken into account if they are performed or incurred by, or for, the taxpayer or any related person and they directly benefit or are incurred by reason of the production of the property.

(iii) Production period and cost of production. For purposes of applying the classification thresholds under paragraphs (b)(1)(ii)(B) and (C) of this section to a unit of property, the taxpayer is required, at the beginning of the production period, to reasonably estimate the production period and the total cost of production for the unit of property. The taxpayer must maintain contemporaneous written records supporting the estimates and classification. If the estimates are reasonable based on the facts in existence at the beginning of the production period, the taxpayer's classification of the property is not modified in subsequent periods, even if the actual length of the production period or the actual cost of production differs from the estimates. To be considered reasonable, estimates of the production period and the total cost of production must include anticipated expense and time for delay, rework, change orders, and technological, design or other problems. To the extent that several distinct activities related to the production of the property are expected to occur simultaneously, the period during which these distinct activities occur is not counted more than once. The bases of assets used to produce a unit of property (within the meaning of § 1.263A-11(d)) and any interest that would be required to be capitalized if a unit of property were designated property are disregarded in making estimates of the total cost of production for purposes of this paragraph (b)(2)(iii).

(3) Excluded property. Designated property does not include:

(i) Timber and evergreen trees that are more than 6 years old when severed from the roots, or

(ii) Property produced by the taxpayer for use by the taxpayer other than in a trade or business or an activity conducted for profit.

(4) De minimis rule. (i) In general. Designated property does not include property for which—

(A) The production period does not exceed 90 days; and

(B) The total production expenditures do not exceed $1,000,000 divided by the number of days in the production period.

(ii) Determination of total production expenditures. For purposes of determining whether the condition of paragraph (b)(4)(i)(B) of this section is met with respect to property, the cost of land, the adjusted basis of property used to produce property, and interest that would be capitalized with respect to property if it were designated property are excluded from total production expenditures.

(c) Definition of real property. *(1) In general.* Real property includes land, unsevered natural products of land, buildings, and inherently permanent structures. Any interest in real property of a type described in this paragraph (c), including fee ownership, co-ownership, a leasehold, an option, or a similar interest is real property under this section. Real property includes the structural components of both buildings and inherently permanent structures, such as walls, partitions, doors, wiring, plumbing, central air conditioning and heating systems, pipes and ducts, elevators and escalators, and other similar property. Tenant improvements to a building that are inherently permanent or otherwise classified as real property within the meaning of this paragraph (c)(1) are real property under this section. However, property produced for sale that is not real property in the hands of the taxpayer or a related person, but that may be incorporated into real property by an unrelated buyer, is not treated as real property by the producing taxpayer (e.g., bricks, nails, paint, and windowpanes).

(2) Unsevered natural products of land. Unsevered natural products of land include growing crops and plants, mines, wells, and other natural deposits. Growing crops and plants, however, are real property only if the preproductive period of the crop or plant exceeds 2 years.

(3) Inherently permanent structures. Inherently permanent structures include property that is affixed to real property and that will ordinarily remain affixed for an indefinite period of time, such as swimming pools, roads, bridges, tunnels, paved parking areas and other pavements, special foundations, wharves and docks, fences, inherently permanent advertising displays, inherently permanent outdoor lighting facilities, railroad tracks and signals, telephone poles, power generation and transmission facilities, permanently installed telecommunications cables, broadcasting towers, oil and gas pipelines, derricks and storage equipment, grain storage bins and silos. For purposes of this section, affixation to real property may be accomplished by weight alone. Property may constitute an inherently permanent structure even though it is not classified as a building for purposes of former section 48(a)(1)(B) and § 1.48-1. Any property not otherwise described in this paragraph (c)(3) that constitutes other tangible property under the principles of former section 48(a)(1)(B) and § 1.48-1(d) is treated for the purposes of this section as an inherently permanent structure.

(4) Machinery. (i) Treatment. A structure that is property in the nature of machinery or is essentially an item of machinery or equipment is not an inherently permanent structure and is not real property. In the case, however, of a building or inherently permanent structure that includes property in the nature of machinery as a structural component, the property in the nature of machinery is real property.

(ii) Certain factors not determinative. A structure may be an inherently permanent structure, and not property in the nature of machinery or essentially an item of machinery, even if the structure is necessary to operate or use, supports, or is otherwise associated with, machinery.

(d) Production. *(1) Definition of produce.* Produce is defined as provided in section 263A(g) and § 1.263A-2(a)(1)(i).

(2) Property produced under a contract. (i) Customer. A taxpayer is treated as producing any property that is produced for the taxpayer (the customer) by another party (the contractor) under a contract with the taxpayer or an intermediary. Property produced under a contract is designated property to the customer if it is real property or tangible personal property that satisfies the classification thresholds described in paragraph (b)(1)(ii) of this section. If property produced under a contract will become part of a unit of designated property produced by the customer in the customer's hands, the property produced under the contract is designated property to the customer.

(ii) Contractor. Property produced under a contract is designated property to the contractor if it is real property, 2-year property, or 1-year property and the property produced under the contract is not excluded by reason of paragraph (d)(2)(v) of this section.

(iii) Definition of a contract. For purposes of this paragraph (d)(2), contract has the same meaning as under § 1.263A-2(a)(1)(ii)(B)(2).

(iv) Determination of whether thresholds are satisfied. In the case of tangible personal property produced under a contract, the customer and the contractor each determine under this paragraph (d)(2), whether the property satisfies the classification thresholds described in paragraph (b)(1)(ii) of this section. Thus, tangible personal property may be designated property with respect to either, or both, the customer and the contractor. The provisions of paragraph (b)(2)(iii) of this section are modified as set forth in this paragraph (d)(2)(iv) for purposes of determining whether tangible personal property produced under a contract is 2-year property or 1-year property.

(A) Customer. In determining a customer's estimated cost of production, the customer takes into account costs and payments that are reasonably expected to be incurred by the customer, but does not take into account costs incurred (or to be incurred) by an unrelated contractor. In determining the customer's estimated length of the production period, the production period is treated as beginning on the earlier of the date the contract is executed or the date that the customer's accumulated production expenditures for the unit are at least 5 percent of the customer's total estimated production expenditures for the unit. The customer, however, may elect to treat the production period as beginning on the date the sum of the accumulated production expenditures of the contractor (or contractors if more than one contractor is producing components for the unit of property) and of the customer are at least 5 percent of the customer's estimated production expenditures for the unit.

(B) Contractor. In determining a contractor's estimated cost of production, the contractor takes into account only the costs that are reasonably expected to be incurred by the contractor, without any reduction for payments from the customer. In determining the contractor's estimated length of the production period, the production period is treated as beginning on the date the contractor's accumulated production expenditures (without any reduction for payments from the customer) are at least 5 percent of the contractor's total estimated accumulated production expenditures.

(v) Exclusion for property subject to long-term contract rules. Property described in paragraph (b) of this section is designated property with respect to a contractor only if—

(A) The contract is not a long-term contract (within the meaning of section 460(f)); or

(B) The contract is a home construction contract (within the meaning of section 460(e)(6)(A)) with respect to which the requirements of section 460(e)(1)(B)(i) and (ii) are not met.

(3) Improvements to existing property. (i) In general. Any improvement to property described in § 1.263(a)-1(b) consti-

tutes the production of property. Generally, any improvement to designated property constitutes the production of designated property. An improvement is not treated as the production of designated property, however, if the de minimis exception described in paragraph (b)(4) of this section applies to the improvement. In addition, paragraph (d)(3)(iii) of this section provides an exception for certain improvements to tangible personal property. Incidental maintenance and repairs are not treated as improvements under this paragraph (d)(3). See § 1.162-4.

(ii) Real property. The rehabilitation or preservation of a standing building, the clearing of raw land prior to sale, and the drilling of an oil well are activities constituting improvements to real property and, therefore, the production of designated property. Similarly, the demolition of a standing building generally constitutes an activity that is an improvement to real property and, therefore, the production of designated property. See the exceptions, however, in paragraphs (b)(3) and (b)(4) of this section.

(iii) Tangible personal property. If the taxpayer has treated a unit of tangible personal property as designated property under this section, an improvement to such property constitutes the production of designated property regardless of the remaining useful life of the improved property (or the improvement) and, except as provided in paragraph (b)(4) of this section, regardless of the estimated length of the production period or the estimated cost of the improvement. If the taxpayer has not treated a unit of tangible personal property as designated property under this section, an improvement to such property constitutes the production of designated property only if the improvement independently meets the classification thresholds described in paragraph (b)(1)(ii) of this section.

T.D. 8584, 12/28/94.

§ 1.263A-9 The avoided cost method.

(a) In general. *(1) Description.* The avoided cost method described in this section must be used to calculate the amount of interest required to be capitalized under section 263A(f). Generally, any interest that the taxpayer theoretically would have avoided if accumulated production expenditures (as defined in § 1.263A-11) had been used to repay or reduce the taxpayer's outstanding debt must be capitalized under the avoided cost method. The application of the avoided cost method does not depend on whether the taxpayer actually would have used the amounts expended for production to repay or reduce debt. Instead, the avoided cost method is based on the assumption that debt of the taxpayer would have been repaid or reduced without regard to the taxpayer's subjective intentions or to restrictions (including legal, regulatory, contractual, or other restrictions) against repayment or use of the debt proceeds.

(2) Overview. (i) In general. For each unit of designated property (within the meaning of § 1.263A-8(b)), the avoided cost method requires the capitalization of—

(A) The traced debt amount under paragraph (b) of this section, and

(B) The excess expenditure amount under paragraph (c) of this section.

(ii) Rules that apply in determining amounts. The traced debt and excess expenditure amounts are determined for each taxable year or shorter computation period that includes the production period (as defined in § 1.263A-12) of a unit of designated property. Paragraph (d) of this section provides an election not to trace debt to specific units of designated property. Paragraph (f) of this section provides rules for selecting the computation period, for calculating averages, and for determining measurement dates within the computation period. Special rules are in paragraph (g) of this section.

(3) Definitions of interest and incurred. Except as provided in the case of certain expenses that are treated as a substitute for interest under paragraphs (c)(2)(iii) and (g)(2)(iv) of this section, interest refers to all amounts that are characterized as interest expense under any provision of the Code, including, for example, sections 482, 483, 1272, 1274, and 7872. Incurred refers to the amount of interest that is properly accruable during the period of time in question determined by taking into account the loan agreement and any applicable provisions of the Internal Revenue laws and regulations such as section 163, § 1.446-2, and sections 1271 through 1275.

(4) Definition of eligible debt. Except as provided in this paragraph (a)(4), eligible debt includes all outstanding debt (as evidenced by a contract, bond, debenture, note, certificate, or other evidence of indebtedness). Eligible debt does not include—

(i) Debt (or the portion thereof) bearing interest that is disallowed under a provision described in § 1.163-8T(m)(7)(ii);

(ii) Debt, such as accounts payable and other accrued items, that bears no interest, except to the extent that such debt is traced debt (as defined in paragraph (b)(2) of this section);

(iii) Debt that is borrowed directly or indirectly from a person related to the taxpayer and that bears a rate of interest that is less than the applicable Federal rate in effect under section 1274(d) on the date of issuance;

(iv) Debt (or the portion thereof) bearing personal interest within the meaning of section 163(h)(2);

(v) Debt (or the portion thereof) bearing qualified residence interest within the meaning of section 163(h)(3);

(vi) Debt incurred by an organization that is exempt from Federal income tax under section 501(a), except to the extent interest on such debt is directly attributable to an unrelated trade or business of the organization within the meaning of section 512;

(vii) Reserves, deferred tax liabilities, and similar items that are not treated as debt for Federal income tax purposes, regardless of the extent to which the taxpayer's applicable financial accounting or other regulatory reporting principles require or support treating these items as debt;

(viii) Federal, State, and local income tax liabilities, deferred tax liabilities under section 453A, and hypothetical tax liabilities under the look-back method of section 460(b) or similar provisions; and

(ix) A purchase money obligation given by the lessor to the lessee (or a party that is related to the lessee) in a sale and leaseback transaction involving an agreement qualifying as a lease under § 5c.168(f)(8)-1 through § 5c.168(f)(8)-11 of this chapter. See § 5c.168(f)(8)-1(e) Example (2) of this chapter.

(b) Traced debt amount. *(1) General rule.* Interest must be capitalized with respect to a unit of designated property in an amount (the traced debt amount) equal to the total interest incurred on the traced debt during each measurement period (as defined in paragraph (f)(2)(ii) of this section) that ends on a measurement date described in paragraph (f)(2)(iii) of this section. See the example in paragraph (b)(3) of this section. If any interest incurred on the traced debt is not taken into account for the taxable year that includes the measurement period because of a deferral provision, see paragraph (g)(2) of this section for the time and manner for capitalizing and recovering that amount. This paragraph (b)(1) does not apply if the taxpayer elects under paragraph (d) of this section not to trace debt.

(2) Identification and definition of traced debt. On each measurement date described in paragraph (f)(2)(iii) of this section, the taxpayer must identify debt that is traced debt with respect to a unit of designated property. On each such date, traced debt with respect to a unit of designated property is the outstanding eligible debt (as defined in paragraph (a)(4) of this section) that is allocated, on that date, to accumulated production expenditures with respect to the unit of designated property under the rules of § 1.163-8T. Traced debt also includes unpaid interest that has been capitalized with respect to such unit under paragraph (b)(1) of this section and that is included in accumulated production expenditures on the measurement date.

(3) Example. The provisions of paragraphs (b)(1) and (b)(2) of this section are illustrated by the following example.

Example. Corporation X, a calendar year taxpayer, is engaged in the production of a single unit of designated property during 1995 (unit A). Corporation X adopts a taxable year computation period and quarterly measurement dates. Production of unit A starts on January 14, 1995, and ends on June 16, 1995. On March 31, 1995 and on June 30, 1995, Corporation X has outstanding a $1,000,000 loan that is allocated under the rules of § 1.163-8T to production expenditures with respect to unit A. During the period January 1, 1995, through June 30, 1995, Corporation X incurs $50,000 of interest related to the loan. Under paragraph (b)(1) of this section, the $50,000 of interest Corporation X incurs on the loan during the period January 1, 1995, through June 30, 1995, must be capitalized with respect to unit A.

(c) Excess expenditure amount. *(1) General rule.* If there are accumulated production expenditures in excess of traced debt with respect to a unit of designated property on any measurement date described in paragraph (f)(2)(iii) of this section, the taxpayer must, for the computation period that includes the measurement date, capitalize with respect to the unit the excess expenditure amount calculated under this paragraph (c)(1). However, if the sum of the excess expenditure amounts for all units of designated property of a taxpayer exceeds the total interest described in paragraph (c)(2) of this section, only a prorata amount (as determined under paragraph (c)(7) of this section) of such interest must be capitalized with respect to each unit. For each unit of designated property, the excess expenditure amount for a computation period equals the product of—

(i) The average excess expenditures (as determined under paragraph (c)(5)(ii) of this section) for the unit of designated property for that period, and

(ii) The weighted average interest rate (as determined under paragraph (c)(5)(iii) of this section) for that period.

(2) Interest required to be capitalized. With respect to an excess expenditure amount, interest incurred during the computation period is capitalized from the following sources and in the following sequence but not in excess of the excess expenditure amount for all units of designated property:

(i) Interest incurred on nontraced debt (as defined in paragraph (c)(5)(i) of this section);

(ii) Interest incurred on borrowings described in paragraph (a)(4)(iii) of this section (relating to certain borrowings from related persons); and

(iii) In the case of a partnership, guaranteed payments for the use of capital (within the meaning of section 707(c)) that would be deductible by the partnership if section 263A(f) did not apply.

(3) Example. The provisions of paragraph (c)(1) and (2) of this section are illustrated by the following example.

Example. (i) P, a partnership owned equally by Corporation A and Individual B, is engaged in the construction of an office building during 1995. Average excess expenditures for the office building for 1995 are $2,000,000. When P was formed, A and B agreed that A would be entitled to an annual guaranteed payment of $70,000 in exchange for A's capital contribution. The only borrowing of P, A, and B for 1995 is a loan to P from an unrelated lender of $1,000,000 (loan #1). The loan is nontraced debt and bears interest at an annual rate of 10 percent. Thus, P's weighted average interest rate (determined under paragraph (c)(5)(iii) of this section) is 10 percent and interest incurred during 1995 is $100,000.

(ii) In accordance with paragraph (c)(1) of this section, the excess expenditure amount is $200,000 ($2,000,000 × 10%). The interest capitalized under paragraph (c)(2) of this section is $170,000 ($100,000 of interest plus $70,000 of guaranteed payments).

(4) Treatment of interest subject to a deferral provision. If any interest described in paragraph (c)(2) of this section is not taken into account for the taxable year that includes the computation period because of a deferral provision described in paragraph (g)(1)(ii) of this section, paragraph (c)(2) of this section is first applied without regard to the amount of the deferred interest. After applying paragraph (c)(2) without regard to the deferred interest, if the amount of interest capitalized with respect to all units of designated property for the computation period is less than the amount that would have been capitalized if a deferral provision did not apply, see paragraph (g)(2) of this section for the time and manner for capitalizing and recovering the difference (the shortfall amount).

(5) Definitions. (i) Nontraced debt. (A) Defined. Nontraced debt means all eligible debt on a measurement date other than any debt that is treated as traced debt with respect to any unit of designated property on that measurement date. For example, nontraced debt includes eligible debt that is allocated to expenditures that are not capitalized under section 263A(a) (e.g., expenditures deductible under section 174(a) or 263(c)). Similarly, even if eligible debt is allocated to a production expenditure for a unit of designated property, the debt is included in nontraced debt on measurement dates before the first or after the last measurement date for that unit of designated property. Thus, nontraced debt may include debt that was previously treated as traced debt or that will be treated as traced debt on a future measurement date.

(B) Example. The provisions of paragraph (c)(5)(i)(A) of this section are illustrated by the following example.

Example. In 1995, Corporation X begins, but does not complete, the construction of two office buildings that are separate units of designated property as defined in § 1.263A-10 (Property D and Property E). At the beginning of 1995, X borrows $2,500,000 (the $2,500,000 loan), which will be used exclusively to finance production expenditures for Property D. Although interest is paid currently, the entire principal amount of the loan remains outstanding at the end of 1995. Corporation X also has outstanding during all of 1995 a long-term loan with a principal amount of $2,000,000 (the $2,000,000 loan). The proceeds of the $2,000,000 loan were used exclusively to finance the production of Property C, a unit of designated property that was completed in 1994. Under the rules of paragraph (b)(2) of this section, the portion of the $2,500,000 loan allocated to accumulated production expenditures for property D at each measurement date during 1995 is treated as traced debt for that measurement date. The excess, if any, of $2,500,000 over the amount treated as traced debt at each measurement date during 1995 is treated as nontraced debt for that measurement date, even though it is expected that the entire $2,500,000 will be treated as traced debt with respect to Property D on subsequent measurement dates as more of the proceeds of the loan are used to finance additional production expenditures. In addition, the entire principal amount of the $2,000,000 loan is treated as nontraced debt for 1995, even though it was treated as traced debt with respect to Property C in a previous period.

(ii) Average excess expenditures. (A) General rule. The average excess expenditures for a unit of designated property for a computation period are computed by—

(1) Determining the amount (if any) by which accumulated production expenditures exceed traced debt at each measurement date during the computation period; and

(2) Dividing the sum of these amounts by the number of measurement dates during the computation period.

(B) Example. The provisions of paragraph (c)(5)(ii)(A) of this section are illustrated by the following example.

Example. Corporation X, a calendar year taxpayer, is engaged in the production of a single unit of designated property during 1995 (unit A). Corporation X adopts the taxable year as the computation period and quarterly measurement dates. The production period for unit A begins on January 14, 1995, and ends on June 16, 1995. On March 31, 1995, and on June 30, 1995, Corporation X has outstanding $1,000,000 of traced debt with respect to unit A. Accumulated production expenditures for unit A on March 31, 1995, are $1,400,000 and on June 30, 1995, are $1,600,000. Accumulated production expenditures in excess of traced debt for unit A on March 31, 1995, are $400,000 and on June 30, 1995, are $600,000. Average excess expenditures for unit A during 1995 are therefore $250,000 ([$400,000 + $600,000 + $0 + $0] section 4).

(iii) Weighted average interest rate. (A) Determination of rate. The weighted average interest rate for a computation period is determined by dividing interest incurred on nontraced debt during the period by average nontraced debt for the period.

(B) Interest incurred on nontraced debt. Interest incurred on nontraced debt during the computation period is equal to the total amount of interest incurred during the computation period on all eligible debt minus the amount of interest incurred during the computation period on traced debt. Thus, all interest incurred on nontraced debt during the computation period is included in the numerator of the weighted average interest rate, even if the underlying nontraced debt is repaid before the end of a measurement period and excluded from nontraced debt outstanding for measurement dates after repayment, in determining the denominator of the weighted average interest rate. However, see paragraph (g)(7) of this section for an election to treat eligible debt that is repaid within the 15-day period immediately preceding a quarterly measurement date as outstanding on that measurement date. See paragraph (a)(3) of this section for the definitions of interest and incurred.

(C) Average nontraced debt. The average nontraced debt for a computation period is computed by—

(1) Determining the amount of nontraced debt outstanding on each measurement date during the computation period; and

(2) Dividing the sum of these amounts by the number of measurement dates during the computation period.

(D) Special rules if taxpayer has no nontraced debt or rate is contingent. If the taxpayer does not have nontraced debt outstanding during the computation period, the weighted average interest rate for purposes of applying paragraphs (c)(1) and (c)(2) of this section is the highest applicable Federal rate in effect under section 1274(d) during the computation period. If interest is incurred at a rate that is contingent at the time the return for the year that includes the computation period is filed, the amount of interest is determined using the higher of the fixed rate of interest (if any) on the underlying debt or the applicable Federal rate in effect under section 1274(d) on the date of issuance.

(6) Examples. The following examples illustrate the principles of this paragraph (c):

Example (1). (i) W, a calendar year taxpayer, is engaged in the production of a unit of designated property during 1995. For purposes of applying the avoided cost method of this section, W uses the taxable year as the computation period. During 1995, W's only debt is a $1,000,000 loan bearing interest at a rate of 7 percent from Y, a person that is related to W. Assuming the applicable Federal rate in effect under section 1274(d) on the date of issuance of the loan is 10 percent, the loan is not eligible debt under paragraph (a)(4) of this section. However, even though W has no eligible debt, W incurs $70,000 ($1,000,000 × 7%) of interest during the computation period. This interest is described in paragraph (c)(2) of this section and must be capitalized under paragraph (c)(1) of this section to the extent it does not exceed W's excess expenditure amount for the unit of property.

(ii) W determines, under paragraph (c)(5)(ii) of this section, that average excess expenditures for the unit of property are $600,000. Assuming the highest applicable Federal rate in effect under section 1274(d) during the computation period is 10 percent, W uses 10 percent as the weighted average interest rate for purposes of determining the excess expenditure amount. See paragraph (c)(5)(iii)(D) of this section. In accordance with paragraph (c)(1) of this section, the excess expenditure amount is therefore $60,000. Because this amount does not exceed the total amount of interest described in paragraph (c)(2) of this section ($70,000), W is required to capitalize $60,000 of interest with respect to the unit of designated property for the 1995 computation period.

Example (2). (i) Corporation X, a calendar year taxpayer, is engaged in the production of a single unit of designated property during 1995 (unit A). Corporation X adopts the taxable year as the computation period and quarterly measurement dates. Production of unit A begins in 1994 and ends on June 30, 1995. On March 31, 1995, and on June 30, 1995, Corporation X has outstanding $1,000,000 of eligible debt (loan #1) that is allocated under the rules of § 1.163-8T to production expenditures for unit A. During each of the first two quarters of 1995, $30,000 of interest is incurred on loan #1. The loan is repaid on July 1, 1995. Throughout 1995, Corporation X also has outstanding $2,000,000 of eligible debt (loan #2) which is not allocated under the rules of

§ 1.163-8T to the production of unit A. During 1995, $200,000 of interest is incurred on this nontraced debt. Accumulated production expenditures on March 31, 1995, are $1,400,000 and on June 30, 1995, are $1,600,000. Accumulated production expenditures in excess of traced debt on March 31, 1995, are $400,000 and on June 30, 1995, are $600,000.

(ii) Under paragraph (b)(1) of this section, the amount of interest capitalized with respect to traced debt is $60,000 ($30,000 for the measurement period ending March 31, 1995, and $30,000 for the measurement period ending June 30, 1995). Under paragraph (c)(5)(ii) of this section, average excess expenditures for unit A are $250,000 ([($1,400,000 − $1,000,000) + ($1,600,000 − $1,000,000) + $0 + $0] section 4). Under paragraph (c)(5)(iii)(C) of this section, average nontraced debt is $2,000,000 ([2,000,000 + $2,000,000 + $2,000,000 + $2,000,000] ÷ 4). Under paragraph (c)(5)(iii)(B) of this section, interest incurred on nontraced debt is $200,000 ($260,000 of interest incurred on all eligible debt less $60,000 of interest incurred on traced debt). Under paragraph (c)(5)(iii)(A) of this section, the weighted average interest rate is 10 percent ($200,000 ÷ $2,000,000). Under paragraph (c)(1) of this section, Corporation X capitalizes the excess expenditure amount of $25,000 ($250,000 × 10%), because it does not exceed the total amount of interest subject to capitalization under paragraph (c)(2) of this section ($200,000). Thus, the total interest capitalized with respect to unit A during 1995 is $85,000 ($60,000 + $25,000).

(7) Special rules where the excess expenditure amount exceeds incurred interest. (i) Allocation of total incurred interest to units. For a computation period in which the sum of the excess expenditure amounts under paragraph (c)(1) of this section for all units of designated property exceeds the total amount of interest (including deferred interest) available for capitalization, as determined under paragraph (c)(2) of this section, the amount of interest that is allocated to a unit of designated property is equal to the product of—

(A) The total amount of interest (including deferred interest) available for capitalization, as determined under paragraph (c)(2) of this section; and

(B) A fraction, the numerator of which is the average excess expenditures for the unit of designated property and the denominator of which is the sum of the average excess expenditures for all units of designated property.

(ii) Application of related person rules to average excess expenditures. Certain excess expenditures must be taken into account by the persons (if any) required to capitalize interest with respect to production expenditures of the taxpayer under applicable related person rules. For each computation period, the amount of average excess expenditures that must be taken into account by such persons for each unit of the taxpayer's property is computed by—

(A) Determining, for the computation period, the amount (if any) by which the excess expenditure amount for the unit exceeds the amount of interest allocated to the unit under paragraph (c)(7)(i) of this section; and

(B) Dividing the excess by the weighted average interest rate for the period.

(iii) Special rule for corporations. If a corporation is related to another person for the purposes of the applicable related party rules, the District Director upon examination may require that the corporation apply this paragraph (c)(7) and other provisions of the regulations by excluding deferred interest from the total interest available for capitalization.

(d) Election not to trace debt. *(1) General rule.* Taxpayers may elect not to trace debt. If the election is made, the average excess expenditures and weighted average interest rate under paragraph (c)(5) of this section are determined by treating all eligible debt as nontraced debt. For this purpose, debt specified in paragraph (a)(4)(ii) of this section (e.g., accounts payable) may be included in eligible debt, provided it would be treated as traced debt but for an election under this paragraph (d). The election not to trace debt is a method of accounting that applies to the determination of capitalized interest for all designated property of the taxpayer. The making or revocation of the election is a change in method of accounting requiring the consent of the Commissioner under section 446(e) and § 1.446-1(e).

(2) Example. The provisions of paragraph (d)(1) of this section are illustrated by the following example.

Example. (i) Corporation X, a calendar year taxpayer, is engaged in the production of a single unit of designated property during 1995 (unit A). Corporation X adopts the taxable year as the computation period and quarterly measurement dates. At each measurement date (March 31, June 30, September 30, and December 31) Corporation X has the following outstanding indebtedness:

Noninterest-bearing accounts payable traced to unit A	$100,000
Noninterest-bearing accounts payable that are not traced to unit A	$300,000
Interest-bearing loans that are eligible debt within the meaning of paragraph (a)(4) of this section	$900,000

(ii) Corporation X elects under this paragraph (d) not to trace debt. Eligible debt at each measurement date for purposes of calculating the weighted average interest rate under paragraph (c)(5)(iii) of this section is $1,000,000 ($100,000 + $900,000).

(e) Election to use external rate. *(1) In general.* An eligible taxpayer may elect to use the highest applicable Federal rate (AFR) under section 1274(d) in effect during the computation period plus 3 percentage points (AFR plus 3) as a substitute for the weighted average interest rate determined under paragraph (c)(5)(iii) of this section. A taxpayer that makes this election may not trace debt. The use of the AFR plus 3 as provided under this paragraph (e)(1) constitutes a method of accounting. A taxpayer makes the election to use the AFR plus 3 method by using the AFR plus 3 as the taxpayer's weighted average interest rate, and any change to the AFR plus 3 method by a taxpayer that has never previously used the method does not require the consent of the Commissioner. Any other change to or from the use of the AFR plus 3 method under this paragraph (e)(1) (other than by reason of a taxpayer ceasing to be an eligible taxpayer) is a change in method of accounting requiring the consent of the Commissioner under section 446(e) and § 1.446-1(e). All changes to or from the AFR plus 3 method are effected on a cut-off basis.

(2) Eligible taxpayer. A taxpayer is an eligible taxpayer for a taxable year for purposes of this paragraph (e) if the average annual gross receipts of the taxpayer for the three previous taxable years do not exceed $10,000,000 (the $10,000,000 gross receipts test) and the taxpayer has met the $10,000,000 gross receipts test for all prior taxable years beginning after December 31, 1994. For purposes of this paragraph (e)(2), the principles of section 263A(b)(2)(B) and (C) and § 1.263A-3(b) apply in determining whether a taxpayer is an eligible taxpayer for a taxable year.

(f) Selection of computation period and measurement dates and application of averaging conventions. *(1) Computation period.* (i) In general. A taxpayer may (but is not required to) make the avoided cost calculation on the basis of a full taxable year. If the taxpayer uses the taxable year as the computation period, a single avoided cost calculation is made for each unit of designated property for the entire taxable year. If the taxpayer uses a computation period that is shorter than the full taxable year, an avoided cost calculation is made for each unit of designated property for each shorter computation period within the taxable year. If the taxpayer uses a shorter computation period, the computation period may not include portions of more than one taxable year and, except as provided in the case of short taxable years, each computation period within a taxable year must be the same length. In the case of a short taxable year, a taxpayer may treat a period shorter than the taxpayer's regular computation period as the first or last computation period, or as the only computation period for the year if the year is shorter than the taxpayer's regular computation period. A taxpayer must use the same computation periods for all designated property produced during a single taxable year.

(ii) Method of accounting. The choice of a computation period is a method of accounting. Any change in the computation period is a change in method of accounting requiring the consent of the Commissioner under section 446(e) and § 1.446-1(e).

(iii) Production period beginning or ending during the computation period. The avoided cost method applies to the production of a unit of designated property on the basis of a full computation period, regardless of whether the production period for the unit of designated property begins or ends during the computation period.

(2) Measurement dates. (i) In general. If a taxpayer uses the taxable year as the computation period, measurement dates must occur at quarterly or more frequent regular intervals. If the taxpayer uses computation periods that are shorter than the taxable year, measurement dates must occur at least twice during each computation period and at least four times during the taxable year (or consecutive 12-month period in the case of a short taxable year). The taxpayer must use the same measurement dates for all designated property produced during a computation period. Except in the case of a computation period that differs from the taxpayer's regular computation period by reason of a short taxable year (see paragraph (f)(1)(i) of this section), measurement dates must occur at equal intervals during each computation period that falls within a single taxable year. For any computation period that differs from the taxpayer's regular computation period by reason of a short taxable year, the measurement dates used by the taxpayer during that period must be consistent with the principles and purposes of section 263A(f). A taxpayer is permitted to modify the frequency of measurement dates from year to year.

(ii) Measurement period. For purposes of this section, measurement period means the period that begins on the first day following the preceding measurement date and that ends on the measurement date.

(iii) Measurement dates on which accumulated production expenditures must be taken into account. The first measurement date on which accumulated production expenditures must be taken into account with respect to a unit of designated property is the first measurement date following the beginning of the production period for the unit of designated property. The final measurement date on which accumulated production expenditures with respect to a unit of designated property must be taken into account is the first measurement date following the end of the production period for the unit of designated property. Accumulated production expenditures with respect to a unit of designated property must also be taken into account on all intervening measurement dates. See § 1.263A-12 to determine when the production period begins and ends.

(iv) More frequent measurement dates. When in the opinion of the District Director more frequent measurement dates are necessary to determine capitalized interest consistent with the principles and purposes of section 263A(f) for a particular computation period, the District Director may require the use of more frequent measurement dates. If a significant segment of the taxpayer's production activities (the first segment) requires more frequent measurement dates than another significant segment of the taxpayer's production activities, the taxpayer may request a ruling from the Internal Revenue Service permitting, for a taxable year and all subsequent taxable years, a segregation of the two segments and, notwithstanding paragraph (f)(2)(i) of this section, the use of the more frequent measurement dates for only the first segment. The request for a ruling must be made in accordance with any applicable rules relating to submissions of ruling requests. The request must be filed on or before the due date (including extensions) of the original Federal income tax return for the first taxable year to which it will apply.

(3) Examples. The following examples illustrate the principles of this paragraph (f):

Example (1). Corporation X, a calendar year taxpayer, is engaged in the production of designated property during 1995. Corporation X adopts the taxable year as the computation period and quarterly measurement dates. Corporation X must identify traced debt, accumulated production expenditures, and nontraced debt at each quarterly measurement date (March 31, June 30, September 30, and December 31). Under paragraph (c)(5)(ii) of this section, Corporation X must calculate average excess expenditures for each unit of designated property by determining the amount by which accumulated production expenditures exceed traced debt for each unit at the end of each quarter and dividing the sum of these amounts by four. Under paragraph (c)(5)(iii)(C) of this section, Corporation X must calculate average nontraced debt by determining the amount of nontraced debt outstanding at the end of each quarter and dividing the sum of these amounts by four.

Example (2). Corporation X, a calendar year taxpayer, is engaged in the production of designated property during 1995. Corporation X adopts a 6-month computation period with two measurement dates within each computation period. Corporation X must identify traced debt, accumulated production expenditures, and nontraced debt at each measurement date (March 31 and June 30 for the first computation period and September 30 and December 31 for the second computation period). Under paragraph (c)(5)(ii) of this section, Corporation X must, for each computation period, calculate average excess expenditures for each unit of designated property by determining the amount by which accumulated production expenditures exceed traced debt for each unit at each measurement date during the period and dividing the sum of these amounts by two. Under paragraph (c)(5)(iii)(C) of this section, Corporation X must calculate average nontraced debt for each computation period by determining the amount of nontraced debt outstanding at each measurement date during the period and dividing the sum of these amounts by two.

Example (3). (i) Corporation X, a calendar year taxpayer, is engaged in the production of two units of designated property during 1995. Production of Unit A starts in 1994 and ends on June 20, 1995. Production of Unit B starts on April 15, 1995, but does not end until 1996. Corporation X adopts the taxable year as its computation period and does not elect under paragraph (d) of this section not to trace debt. Corporation X uses quarterly measurement dates and pays all interest on eligible debt in the quarter in which the interest is incurred. During 1995, Corporation X has two items of eligible debt. The debt and the manner in which it is used are as follows:

#	Principal	Annual rate	Period Outstanding	Use of proceeds
1	$1,000,000	9%	1/01-9/01	Unit A
2	2,000,000	11%	6/01-12/31	Nontraced

(ii) Based on the annual 9 percent rate of interest, Corporation X incurs $7,500 of interest during each month that Loan #1 is outstanding.

(iii) Accumulated production expenditures at the end of each quarter during 1995 are as follows:

Measurement Date	Unit A	Unit B
March 31	$1,200,000	$ -0-
June 30	$1,800,000	$ 500,000
Sept. 30	-0-	$1,000,000
Dec. 31	-0-	$1,600,000

(iv) Corporation X must first determine the amount of interest incurred on traced debt and capitalize the interest incurred on this debt (the traced debt amount). Loan #1 is allocated to Unit A on the March 31 and June 30 measurement dates. Accordingly, Loan #1 is treated as traced debt with respect to unit A for the measurement periods beginning January 1 and ending June 30. The interest incurred on Loan #1 during the period that Loan #1 is treated as traced debt must be capitalized with respect to Unit A. Thus, $45,000 ($7,500 per month for 6 months) is capitalized with respect to Unit A.

(v) Second, Corporation X must determine average excess expenditures for Unit A and Unit B. For Unit A, this amount is $250,000 ([$200,000 + $800,000 + $0 + $0] ÷ 4). For Unit B, this amount is $775,000 ([$0 + $500,000 + $1,000,000 + $1,600,000] ÷ 4).

(vi) Third, Corporation X must determine the weighted average interest rate and apply that rate to the average excess expenditures for Units A and B. The rate is equal to the total amount of interest incurred on nontraced debt (i.e., interest incurred on all eligible debt reduced by interest incurred on traced debt) divided by the average nontraced debt. The interest incurred on nontraced debt equals $143,333 ([$1,000,000 × 9% × 8/12] + [$2,000,000 × 11% × 7/12] − $45,000). The average nontraced debt equals $1,500,000 ([$0 + $2,000,000 + $2,000,000 + $2,000,000] ÷ 4). The weighted average interest rate of 9.56 percent ($143,333 ÷ $1,500,000), is then applied to average excess expenditures for Units A and B. Accordingly, Corporation X capitalizes an additional $23,900 ($250,000 × 9.56%) with respect to Unit A and $74,090 ($775,000 × 9.56%) with respect to Unit B (the excess expenditure amounts).

(g) Special rules. *(1) Ordering rules.* (i) Provisions preempted by section 263A(f). Interest must be capitalized under section 263A(f) before the application of section 163(d) (regarding the investment interest limitation), section 163(j) (regarding the limitation on interest paid to a tax-exempt related person), section 266 (regarding the election to capitalize carrying charges), section 469 (regarding the limitation on passive losses), and section 861 (regarding the allocation of interest to United States sources). Any interest that is capitalized under section 263A(f) is not taken into account as interest under those sections. However, in applying section 263A(f) with respect to the excess expenditure amount, the taxpayer must capitalize all interest that is neither investment interest under section 163(d), exempt related person interest under section 163(j), nor passive interest under section 469 before capitalizing any interest that is either investment interest, exempt related person interest, or passive interest. Any interest that is not required to be capitalized after the application of section 263A(f) is then taken into account as interest subject to sections 163(d), 163(j), 266, 469, and 861. If, after the application of section 263A(f), interest is deferred under sections 163(d), 163(j), 266, or 469, that interest is not subject to capitalization under section 263A(f) in any subsequent taxable year.

(ii) Deferral provisions applied before this section. Interest (including contingent interest) that is subject to a deferral provision described in this paragraph (g)(1)(ii) is subject to capitalization under section 263A(f) only in the taxable year in which it would be deducted if section 263A(f) did not apply. Deferral provisions include sections 163(e)(3), 267, 446, and 461, and all other deferral or limitation provisions that are not described in paragraph (g)(1)(i) of this section. In contrast to the provisions of paragraph (g)(1)(i) of this section, deferral provisions are applied before the application of section 263A(f).

(2) Application of section 263A(F) to deferred interest. (i) In general. This paragraph (g)(2) describes the time and manner of capitalizing and recovering the deferral amount. The deferral amount for any computation period equals the sum of—

(A) The amount of interest that is incurred on traced debt that is deferred during the computation period and is not deductible for the taxable year that includes the computation period because of a deferral provision described in paragraph (g)(1)(ii) of this section, and

(B) The shortfall amount described in paragraph (c)(4) of this section.

(ii) Capitalization of deferral amount. The rules described in paragraph (g)(2)(iii) of this section apply to the deferral amount unless the taxpayer elects under paragraph (g)(2)(iv) of this section to capitalize substitute costs.

(iii) Deferred capitalization. If the taxpayer does not elect under paragraph (g)(2)(iv) of this section to capitalize substitute costs, deferred interest to which the deferral amount is attributable (determined under any reasonable method) is capitalized in the year or years in which the deferred interest would have been deductible but for the application of section 263A(f) (the capitalization year). For this purpose, any interest that is deferred from a prior computation period is taken into account in subsequent capitalization years in the same order in which the interest was deferred. If a unit of designated property to which previously deferred interest relates is sold before the capitalization year, the deferred interest applicable to that unit of property is taken into account in the capitalization year and treated as if recovered from the sale of the property. If the taxpayer continues to hold, throughout the capitalization year, a unit of depreciable property to which previously deferred interest relates, the adjusted basis and applicable recovery percentages for the unit of property are redetermined for the capitalization year and subsequent years so that the increase in basis is accounted for over the remaining recovery periods beginning with the capitalization year. See Example 2 of paragraph (g)(2)(v) of this section.

(iv) Substitute capitalization. (A) General rule. In lieu of deferred capitalization under paragraph (g)(2)(iii) of this section, the taxpayer may elect the substitute capitalization method described in this paragraph (g)(2)(iv). Under this method, the taxpayer capitalizes for the computation period in which interest is incurred and deferred (the deferral period) costs that would be deducted but for this paragraph (g)(2)(iv) (substitute costs). The taxpayer must capitalize an amount of substitute costs equal to the deferral amount for each unit of designated property, or if less, a prorata amount (determined in accordance with the principles of paragraph (c)(7)(i) of this section) of the total substitute costs that would be deducted but for this paragraph (g)(2)(iv) during the deferral period. If the entire deferral amount is capitalized pursuant to this paragraph (g)(2)(iv) in the deferral period, any interest incurred and deferred in the deferral period is neither capitalized nor deducted during the deferral period and, unless subsequently capitalized as a substitute cost under this paragraph (g)(2)(iv), is deductible in the appropriate subsequent period without regard to section 263A(f).

(B) Capitalization of amount carried forward. If the taxpayer has an insufficient amount of substitute costs in the deferral period, the amount by which substitute costs are insufficient with respect to each unit of designated property is a deferral amount carryforward to succeeding computation periods beginning with the next computation period. In any carryforward year, the taxpayer must capitalize an amount of substitute costs equal to the deferral amount carryforward or, if less, a prorata amount (determined in accordance with the principles of paragraph (c)(7)(i) of this section) of the total substitute costs that would be deducted during the carryforward year or years (the carryforward capitalization year) but for this paragraph (g)(2)(iv) (after applying the substitute cost method of this paragraph (g)(2)(iv) to the production of designated property in the carryforward period). If a unit of designated property to which the deferral amount carryforward relates is sold prior to the carryforward capitalization year, substitute costs applicable to that unit of property are taken into account in the carryforward capitalization year and treated as if recovered from the sale of the property. If the taxpayer continues to hold, throughout the capitalization year, a unit of depreciable property to which a deferral amount carryforward relates, the adjusted basis and applicable recovery percentages for the unit of property are redetermined for the carryforward capitalization year and subsequent years so that the increase in basis is accounted for over the remaining recovery periods beginning with the carryforward capitalization year. See Example 2 of paragraph (g)(2)(v) of this section.

(C) Method of accounting. The substitute capitalization method under this paragraph (g)(2)(iv) is a method of accounting that applies to all designated property of the taxpayer. A change to or from the substitute capitalization method is a change in method of accounting requiring the consent of the Commissioner under section 446(e) and § 1.446-1(e).

(v) Examples. The following examples illustrate the application of the avoided cost method when interest is subject to a deferral provision:

Example (1). (i) Corporation X is a calendar year taxpayer and uses the taxable year as its computation period. During 1995, X is engaged in the construction of a warehouse which X will use in its storage business. The warehouse is completed and placed in service in December 1995. X's average excess expenditures for 1995 equal $1,000,000. Throughout 1995, X's only outstanding debt is nontraced debt of $900,000 and $1,200,000, bearing interest at 15 percent and 9 percent, respectively, per year. Of the $243,000 interest incurred during the year ([$900,000 × 15%] + [$1,200,000 × 9%] = [$135,000 + $108,000]), $75,000 is deferred under section 267(a)(2).

(ii) X must first determine the amount of interest required to be capitalized under paragraph (c)(1) of this section for 1995 (the deferral period) without applying section 267(a)(2). The weighted average interest rate is 11.6 percent ([$135,000 + $108,000] ÷ $2,100,000), and the excess expenditure amount under paragraph (c)(1) of this section is $116,000 ($1,000,000 × 11.6%). Under paragraph (c)(4) of this section, X must then determine the amount of interest that would be capitalized by applying paragraph (c)(2) of this section without regard to the amount of deferred interest. Disregarding deferred interest, the amount of interest available for capitalization is $168,000 ([$900,000 × 15%] + [$1,200,000 × 9%] − $75,000). Thus, the full excess expenditure amount ($116,000) is capitalized from interest that is not deferred under section 267(a)(2) and there is no shortfall amount.

Example (2). (i) The facts are the same as in Example 1, except that $140,000 of interest is deferred under section 267 (a)(2) in 1995. The taxpayer does not elect to use the substitute capitalization method. This interest is also deferred in 1996 but would be deducted in 1997 if section 263A(f) did not apply. As in Example 1, the excess expenditure amount is $116,000. However, the amount of interest available for capitalization after excluding the amount of deferred interest is $103,000 ([$900,000 × 15%] + [$1,200,000 × 9%] − $140,000). Thus, only $103,000 of interest is capitalized with respect to the warehouse in 1995. Since $116,000 of interest would be capitalized if section 267(a)(2) did not apply, the deferral amount determined under paragraphs (c)(2) and (g)(2)(i) of this section is $13,000 ($116,000 − $103,000), and $13,000 of deferred interest must be capitalized in the year in which it would be deducted if section 263A(f) did not apply.

(ii) The $140,000 of interest deferred under section 267(a)(2) in 1995 would be deducted in 1997 if section 263A(f) did not apply. X is therefore required to capitalize an additional $13,000 of interest with respect to the warehouse in 1997 and must redetermine its basis and recovery percentage.

(3) Simplified inventory method. (i) In general. This paragraph (g)(3) provides a simplified method of capitalizing interest expense with respect to designated property that is inventory. Under this method, the taxpayer determines beginning and ending inventory and cost of goods sold applying all other capitalization provisions, including, for example, the simplified production method of § 1.263A-2(b), but without regard to the capitalization of interest with respect to inventory. The taxpayer must establish a separate capital asset, however, in an amount equal to the aggregate

interest capitalization amount (as defined in paragraph (g)(3)(iii)(C) of this section). Under the simplified inventory method, increases in the aggregate interest capitalization amount from one year to the next generally are treated as reductions in interest expense, and decreases in the aggregate interest capitalization amount from one year to the next are treated as increases to cost of goods sold.

(ii) Segmentation of inventory. (A) General rule. Under the simplified inventory method, the taxpayer first separates its total ending inventory value into segments that are equal to the total ending inventory value divided by the inverse inventory turnover rate. Each inventory segment is then assigned an age starting with one year and increasing by one year for each additional segment. The inverse inventory turnover rate is determined by finding the average of beginning and ending inventory, dividing the average by the cost of goods sold for the year, and rounding the result to the nearest whole number. Beginning and ending inventory amounts are determined using total current cost of inventory for the year (rather than carrying value). Cost of goods sold, however, may be determined using either total current cost or the taxpayer's inventory method. In addition, for purposes of this paragraph (g)(3)(ii), current costs for a year (and, if applicable, the cost of goods sold for the year under the taxpayer's inventory method) are determined without regard to the capitalization of interest with respect to inventory.

(B) Example. The provisions of paragraph (g)(3)(ii)(A) of this section are illustrated by the following example.

Example. X, a taxpayer using the FIFO inventory method, determines that total cost of goods sold for 1995 equals $900, and the cost of both beginning and ending inventory equals $3,000. Thus, X's inverse inventory turnover rate equals 3 (3.33 rounded to the nearest whole number). Total ending inventory of $3,000 is divided into three segments of $1,000 each. One segment is treated as 3-year-old inventory, one segment is treated as 2-year-old inventory, and one segment is treated as 1-year-old inventory.

(iii) Aggregate interest capitalization amount. (A) Computation period and weighed average interest rate. If a taxpayer elects the simplified inventory method, the taxpayer must use the taxable year as its computation period and use the weighted average interest rate determined under this paragraph (g)(3)(iii)(A) in determining the aggregate interest capitalization amount defined in paragraph (g)(3)(iii)(C) of this section and in determining the amount of interest capitalized with respect to any designated property that is not inventory. Under the simplified inventory method, the taxpayer determines the weighted average interest rate in accordance with paragraph (c)(5)(iii) of this section, treating all eligible debt (other than debt traced to noninventory property in the case of a taxpayer tracing debt) as nontraced debt (i.e., without tracing debt to inventory). A taxpayer that has elected under paragraph (e) of this section to use an external rate as a substitute for the weighted average interest rate determined under paragraph (c)(5)(iii) of this section uses the rate described in paragraph (e)(1) as the weighted average interest rate.

(B) Computation of the tentative aggregate interest capitalization amount. The weighted average interest rate is compounded annually by the number of years assigned to a particular inventory segment to produce an interest factor (applicable interest factor) for that segment. The amounts determined by multiplying the value of each inventory segment by its applicable interest factor are then combined to produce a tentative aggregate interest capitalization amount.

(C) Coordination with other interest capitalization computations. (1) In general. If the tentative aggregate interest capitalization amount for a year exceeds the aggregate interest capitalization amount (defined in paragraph (g)(3)(iii)(D) of this section) as of the close of the preceding year, then, for purposes of applying the rules of paragraph (c)(7) of this section, the excess is treated as an excess expenditure amount and the inventory to which the simplified inventory method of this paragraph (g)(3) applies is treated as a single unit of designated property. If, after these modifications, no paragraph (c)(7) interest allocation is necessary (i.e., the excess expenditure amounts for all units of designated property do not exceed the total amount of interest (including deferred interest) available for capitalization), the aggregate interest capitalization amount generally equals the tentative aggregate interest capitalization amount. If, on the other hand, a paragraph (c)(7) allocation is necessary, the tentative aggregate interest capitalization amount is generally adjusted to reflect the results of that allocation (i.e., the increase in the aggregate interest capitalization amount is limited to the amount of interest allocated to inventory, reduced, however, by any substitute costs that are capitalized with respect to inventory under applicable related party rules).

(2) Deferred interest. In determining the aggregate interest capitalization amount, the tentative aggregate interest capitalization amount is adjusted (after the application of paragraph (c)(7) of this section) as appropriate to reflect the deferred interest rules of paragraph (g)(2) of this section. The tentative aggregate interest capitalization amount would be reduced, for example, by the amount of a taxpayer's deferred interest for a taxable year unless the taxpayer has elected the substitute capitalization method under paragraph (g)(2)(iv).

(3) Other coordinating provisions. The Commissioner may prescribe, by revenue ruling or revenue procedure, additional provisions to coordinate the election and use of the simplified inventory method with other interest capitalization requirements and methods. See § 601.601(d)(2)(ii)(b) of this chapter.

(D) Treatment of increases or decreases in the aggregate interest capitalization amount. Except as otherwise provided in this paragraph (g)(3)(iii)(D), increases in the aggregate interest capitalization amount from one year to the next are treated as reductions in interest expense, and decreases in the aggregate interest capitalization amount from one year to the next are treated as increases to cost of goods sold. To the extent a taxpayer capitalizes substitute costs under either applicable related party rules or the deferred interest rules in paragraph (g)(2) of this section, increases in the aggregate interest capitalization amount are treated as reductions in applicable substitute costs, rather than interest expense.

(E) Example. The provisions of this paragraph (g)(3)(iii) are illustrated by the following example.

Example. The facts are the same as in the example in paragraph (g)(3)(ii)(B) of this section, and, in addition X determines that its weighted average interest rate for 1995 is 10 percent. Additionally, assume that X has no deferred interest in 1995 or 1996 and no deferral amount carryforward to either 1995 or 1996. (See paragraph (g)(2) of this section.) Also assume that no allocation is necessary under paragraph (c)(7) of this section in either 1995 or 1996. Under the rules of paragraph (g)(3)(ii) of this section, X divides ending inventory into segments of $1,000 each. One segment is 1-year old inventory, one segment is 2-year old inventory, and one segment is 3-year old inventory. Under paragraph (g)(3)(iii)(B) of this section, X must compute the applicable interest factor for each segment. The applicable interest factor for the 1-year old inventory is not compounded. The applicable interest factor for the 2-year old inventory is compounded for 1 year. The applicable interest factor for the 3-year old inventory is compounded for 2 years. The interest factor applied to the 1- year old inventory segment is .1. The interest factor applied to the 2-year old inventory segment is .21 [(1.1 × 1.1) − 1]. The interest factor applied to the 3-year old inventory is .331 [(1.1 × 1.1 × 1.1) − 1]. Thus, the tentative aggregate interest capitalization amount for 1995 is $641 (1,000 × [.1 + .21 + .331]). Because X has no deferred interest in 1995, no deferral amount carryforward to 1995, and no required allocation under paragraph (c)(7) of this section in 1995, X's aggregate interest capitalization amount equals its $641 tentative aggregate interest capitalization amount. If, in 1996, X computes an aggregate interest capitalization amount of $750, the $109 increase in the amount from 1995 to 1996 would be treated as a reduction in interest expense for 1996.

(iv) Method of accounting. The simplified inventory method is a method of accounting that must be elected for and applied to all inventory within a single trade or business of the taxpayer (within the meaning of section 446 (d) and § 1.446-1(d)). This method may be elected only if the inventory in that trade or business consists only of designated property and only if the taxpayer's inverse inventory turnover rate for that trade or business (as defined in paragraph (g)(3)(ii)(A) of this section) is greater than or equal to one. A change from or to the simplified inventory method is a change in method of accounting requiring the consent of the Commissioner under section 446(e) and § 1.446-(1)(e).

(4) Financial accounting method disregarded. The avoided cost method is applied under this section without regard to any financial or regulatory accounting principles for the capitalization of interest. For example, this section determines the amount of interest that must be capitalized without regard to Financial Accounting Standards Board (FASB) Statement Nos. 34, 71, and 90, issued by the Financial Accounting Standards Board, Norwalk, CT 06856-5116. Similarly, taxpayers are not permitted to net interest income and interest expense in determining the amount of interest that must be capitalized under this section with respect to certain restricted tax-exempt borrowings even though netting is permitted under FASB Statement No. 62.

(5) Treatment of intercompany transactions. (i) General rule. If interest capitalized under section 263A(f) by a member of a consolidated group (within the meaning of § 1.1502-1(h)) with respect to a unit of designated property is attributable to a loan from another member of the group (the lending member), the intercompany transaction provisions of the consolidated return regulations do not apply to the lending member's interest income with respect to that loan, except as provided in paragraph (g)(5)(ii) of this section. For this purpose, the capitalized interest expense that is attributable to a loan from another member is determined under any method that reasonably reflects the principles of the avoided cost method, including the traced and nontraced concepts. For purposes of this paragraph (g)(5)(i) and paragraph (g)(5)(ii) of this section, in order for a method to be considered reasonable it must be consistently applied.

(ii) Special rule for consolidated group with limited outside borrowing. If, for any year, the aggregate amount of interest income described in paragraph (g)(5)(i) of this section for all members of the group with respect to all units of designated property exceeds the total amount of interest that is deductible for that year by all members of the group with respect to debt of a member owed to nonmembers (group deductible interest) after applying section 263A(f), the intercompany transaction provisions of the consolidated return regulations are applied to the excess, and the amount of interest income that must be taken into account by the group under paragraph (g)(5)(i) of this section is limited to the amount of the group deductible interest. The amount to which the intercompany transaction provisions of the consolidated return regulations apply by reason of this paragraph (g)(5)(ii) is allocated among the lending members under any method that reasonably reflects each member's share of interest income described in paragraph (g)(5)(i) of this section. If a lending member has interest income that is attributable to more than one unit of designated property, the amount to which the intercompany transaction provisions of the consolidated return regulations apply by reason of this paragraph (g)(5)(ii) with respect to the member is allocated among the units in accordance with the principles of paragraph (c)(7)(i) of this section.

(iii) Example. The provisions of paragraph (g)(5)(ii) of this section are illustrated by the following example.

Example. (i) P and S1 are the members of a consolidated group. In 1995, S1 begins and completes the construction of a shopping center and is required to capitalize interest with respect to the construction. S1's average excess expenditures for 1995 are $5,000,000. Throughout 1995, S1's only borrowings include a $6,000,000 loan from P bearing interest at an annual rate of 10 percent ($600,000 per year). Under the avoided cost method, S1 is required to capitalize interest in the amount of $500,000 ([$600,000 ÷ $6,000,000] × $5,000,000).

(ii) P's only borrowing from unrelated lenders is a $2,000,000 loan bearing interest at an annual rate of 10 percent ($200,000 per year). Under the principles of paragraph (g)(5)(ii) of this section, because the aggregate amount of interest described in paragraph (g)(5)(i) of this section ($500,000) exceeds the aggregate amount of currently deductible interest of the group ($200,000), the intercompany transaction provisions of the consolidated return regulations apply to the excess of $300,000 and the amount of P's interest income that is subject to current inclusion by reason of paragraph (g)(5)(i) of this section is limited to $200,000.

(6) Notional principal contracts and other derivatives. [Reserved]

(7) 15-Day repayment rule. A taxpayer may elect to treat an eligible debt that is repaid within the 15-day period immediately preceding a quarterly measurement date as outstanding as of that measurement date for purposes of determining traced debt, average nontraced debt, and the weighted average interest rate. This election may be made or discontinued for any computation period and is not a method of accounting.

T.D. 8584, 12/28/94, amend T.D. 9129, 5/20/2004, T.D. 9179, 2/22/2005.

§ 1.263A-10 Unit of property.

(a) In general. The unit of property as defined in this section is used as the basis to determine accumulated production expenditures under § 1.263A-11 and the beginning and end of the production period under § 1.263A-12. Whether property is 1-year or 2-year property under § 1.263A-8(b)(1)(ii) is also determined separately with respect to each unit of property as defined in this section.

(b) Units of real property. *(1) In general.* A unit of real property includes any components of real property owned by the taxpayer or a related person that are functionally interdependent and an allocable share of any common feature owned by the taxpayer or a related person that is real property even though the common feature does not meet the functional interdependence test. When the production period begins with respect to any functionally interdependent component or any common feature of the unit of real property, the production period has begun for the entire unit of real property. See, however, paragraph (b)(5) of this section for rules under which the costs of a common feature or benefitted property are excluded from accumulated production expenditures for one or more measurement dates. The portion of land included in a unit of real property includes land on which real property (including a common feature) included in the unit is situated, land subject to setback restrictions with respect to such property, and any other contiguous portion of the tract of land other than land that the taxpayer holds for a purpose unrelated to the unit being produced (e.g., investment purposes, personal use purposes, or specified future development as a separate unit of real property).

(2) Functional interdependence. Components of real property produced by, or for, the taxpayer, for use by the taxpayer or a related person are functionally interdependent if the placing in service of one component is dependent on the placing in service of the other component by the taxpayer or a related person. In the case of property produced for sale, components of real property are functionally interdependent if they are customarily sold as a single unit. For example, the real property components of a single-family house (e.g., the land, foundation, and walls) are functionally interdependent. In contrast, components of real property that are expected to be separately placed in service or held for resale are not functionally interdependent. Thus, dwelling units within a multi-unit building that are separately placed in service or sold (within the meaning of § 1.263A-12(d)(1)) are treated as functionally independent of any other units, even though the units are located in the same building.

(3) Common features. For purposes of this section, a common feature generally includes any real property (as defined in § 1.263A-8(c)) that benefits real property produced by, or for, the taxpayer or a related person, and that is not separately held for the production of income. A common feature need not be physically contiguous to the real property that it benefits. Examples of common features include streets, sidewalks, playgrounds, clubhouses, tennis courts, sewer lines, and cables that are not held for the production of income separately from the units of real property that they benefit.

(4) Allocation of costs to unit. Except as provided in paragraph (b)(5) of this section, the accumulated production expenditures for a unit of real property include, in all cases, the costs that directly benefit, or are incurred by reason of the production of, the unit of real property. Accumulated production expenditures also include the adjusted basis of property used to produce the unit of real property. The accumulated costs of a common feature or land that benefits more than one unit of real property, or that benefits designated property and property other than designated property, is apportioned among the units of designated property, or among the designated property and property other than designated property, in determining accumulated production expenditures. The apportionment of the accumulated costs of the common feature (allocable share) or land (attributable land costs) generally may be made using any method that is applied on a consistent basis and that reasonably reflects the benefits provided. For example, an apportionment based on relative costs to be incurred, relative space to be occupied, or relative fair market values may be reasonable.

(5) Treatment of costs when a common feature is included in a unit of real property. (i) General rule. Except as provided in this paragraph (b)(5), the accumulated production expenditures of a unit of real property include the costs of functionally interdependent components (benefitted property) and an allocable share of the cost of common features throughout the entire production period of the unit. See § 1.263A-12, relating to the production period of a unit of property.

(ii) Production activity not undertaken on benefitted property. (A) Direct production activity not undertaken. (1) In general. The costs of land attributable to a benefitted property may be treated as not included in accumulated production expenditures for a unit of real property for measurement dates prior to the first date a production activity (direct production activity), including the clearing and grading of land, has been undertaken with respect to the land attributable to the benefitted property. Thus, the costs of land attributable to a benefitted property (as opposed to land attributable to the common features) with respect to which no direct production activities have been undertaken may be treated as not included in the accumulated production expenditures of a unit of real property even though a production activity has begun on a common feature allocable to the unit.

(2) Land attributable to a benefitted property. For purposes of this paragraph (b)(5)(ii), land attributable to a benefitted property includes all land in the unit of real property that includes the benefitted property other than land for a common feature. (Thus, land attributable to a benefitted property does not include land attributable to a common feature.)

(B) Suspension of direct production activity after clearing and grading undertaken. (1) General rule. This paragraph (b)(5)(ii)(B) may be used to determine the accumulated production expenditures for a unit of real property, if the only production activity with respect to a benefitted property has been clearing and grading and no further direct production activity is undertaken with respect to the benefitted property for at least 120 consecutive days (i.e., direct production activity has ceased). Under this paragraph (b)(5)(ii)(B), the accumulated production expenditures attributable to a benefitted property qualifying under this paragraph (b)(5)(ii)(B) may be excluded from the accumulated production expenditures of the unit of real property even though production continues on a common feature allocable to the unit. For purposes of this paragraph (b)(5)(ii)(B), production activity is considered to occur during any time which would not qualify as a cessation of production activities under the suspension period rules of § 1.263A-12(g).

(2) Accumulated production expenditures. If this paragraph (b)(5)(ii)(B) applies, accumulated production expenditures attributable to the benefitted property of the unit of real property may be treated as not included in the accumulated production expenditures for the unit starting with the first measurement period beginning after the first day of the 120 consecutive day period, but must be included in the accumulated production expenditures for the unit beginning in the measurement period in which direct production activity has resumed on the benefitted property. Accumulated production expenditures with respect to common features allocable to the unit of real property may not be excluded under this paragraph (b)(5)(ii)(B).

(iii) Common feature placed in service before the end of production of a benefitted property. To the extent that a common feature with respect to which all production activities to be undertaken by, or for, a taxpayer or a related person are completed is placed in service before the end of the production period of a unit that includes an allocable share of the costs of the common feature, the costs of the common feature are not treated as included in accumulated production expenditures of the unit for measurement periods beginning after the date the common feature is placed in service.

(iv) Benefitted property sold before production completed on common feature. If a unit of real property is sold before common features included in the unit are completed, the production period of the unit ends on the date of sale. Thus, common feature costs actually incurred and properly allocable to the unit as of the date of sale are excluded from accumulated production expenditures for measurement periods beginning after the date of sale. Common feature costs properly allocable to the unit and actually incurred after the sale are not taken into account in determining accumulated production expenditures.

(v) Benefitted property placed in service before production completed on common feature. Where production activities remain to be undertaken on a common feature allocable to a unit of real property that includes benefitted property, the costs of the benefitted property are not treated as included in the accumulated production expenditures for the unit for measurement periods beginning after the date the benefitted property is placed in service and all production activities reasonably expected to be undertaken by, or for, the taxpayer or a related person with respect to the benefitted property are completed.

(6) Examples. The principles of paragraph (b) of this section are illustrated by the following examples:

Example (1). B, an individual, is in the trade or business of constructing custom-built houses for sale. B owns a 10-acre tract upon which B intends to build four houses on 2-acre lots. In addition, on the remaining 2 acres B plans to construct a perimeter road that benefits the four houses and is not held for the production of income separately from the sale of the houses. In 1995, B begins constructing the perimeter road and clears the land for one house. Under the principles of paragraph (b)(1) of this section, each planned house (including attributable land) is part of a separate unit of real property (house unit). Under the principles of paragraph (b)(3) of this section, the perimeter road (including attributable land) constitutes a common feature with respect to each planned house (i.e., benefitted property). In accordance with paragraph (b)(1), the production period for all four house units begins when production commences on the perimeter road in 1995. In addition, under the principles of paragraph (b)(4) of this section, the accumulated production expenditures for the four house units include the allocable costs of the road. In addition, for the house with respect to which B has cleared the land, the accumulated production expenditures for the house unit include the land costs attributable to the house. See paragraph (b)(5)(i) of this section. However, the accumulated production expenditures for each of the three house units that include a house for which B has not yet undertaken a direct production activity do not include the land costs attributable to the house. See paragraph (b)(5)(ii) of this section.

Example (2). Assume the same facts as Example 1, except that B undertakes no further direct production activity with respect to the house for which the land was cleared for a period of at least 120 days but continues constructing the perimeter road during this period. In accordance with paragraph (b)(5)(ii)(B) of this section, B may exclude the accumulated production expenditures attributable to the benefitted property from the accumulated production expenditures of the house unit starting with the first measurement period that begins after the first day of the 120 consecutive day period. B must include the accumulated production expenditures attributable to the benefitted property in the accumulated production expenditures for the house unit beginning with the measurement period in which direct production resumes on the benefitted property. The house unit will continue to include the accumulated production expenditures attributable to the perimeter road during the period in which direct production activity was suspended on the benefitted property.

Example (3). (i) D, a corporation, is in the trade or business of developing commercial real property. D owns a 20-acre tract upon which D intends to build a shopping center with 150 stores. D intends to lease the stores. D will also provide on the 20 acres a 1500-car parking lot, which is not held by D for the production of income separately from the stores in the shopping center. Additionally, D will not produce any other common features as part of the project. D intends to complete the shopping center in phases and expects that each store will be placed in service independently of any other store.

(ii) Under paragraphs (b)(1) and (b)(2) of this section, each store (including attributable land) is part of a separate unit of real property (store unit). The 1500-car parking lot is a common feature benefitting each store, and D must include an allocable share of the parking lot in each store unit. See paragraphs (b)(1) and (b)(3). In accordance with paragraph (b)(5)(i), D includes in the accumulated production expenditures for each store unit during each store unit's production period: the costs capitalized with respect to the store (including attributable land costs in accordance with paragraph (b)(5) of this section) and an allocable share of the parking lot costs (including attributable land costs in accordance with paragraph (b)(5) of this section). Under paragraph (b)(4), the portion of the parking lot costs that is included in the accumulated production expenditures of a store unit is determined using a reasonable method of allocation.

Example (4). X, a real estate developer, begins a project to construct a condominium building and a convenience store for the benefit of the condominium. X intends to separately lease the convenience store. Because the convenience store is held for the production of income separately from the condominium units that it benefits, the convenience store is not a common feature with respect to the condominium building. Instead, the convenience store is a separate unit of property with a separate production period and for which a separate determination of accumulated production expenditures must be made.

Example (5). (i) In 1995, X, a real estate developer, begins a project consisting of a condominium building and a common swimming pool that is not held for the production of income separately from the condominium sales. The condominium building consists of 10 stories, and each story is occupied by a single condominium. Production of the swimming pool begins in January. No direct production activity is undertaken on any condominium until September, when direct production activity commences on each condominium. On December 31, 1995, 1 condominium that was completed in December has been sold, 3 condominiums that were completed in December have not been sold, and 6 condominiums are only partially complete; additionally, the swimming pool is completed. X is a calendar year taxpayer that uses a full taxable year as the computation period, and quarterly measurement dates.

(ii) Under paragraphs (b)(1) and (b)(2) of this section, each condominium (including attributable land) is part of a separate unit of real property. Under the principles of paragraph (b)(3) of this section, the swimming pool is a common feature with respect to each condominium and under paragraph (b)(4) of this section the cost of the swimming pool is allocated equally among the condominiums.

(iii) Under paragraph (b)(1) of this section, the production period of each of the 10 condominium units begins in January when production of the swimming pool begins. On X's March 31, 1995, and June 30, 1995, measurement dates, the accumulated production expenditures for each condominium unit include the allocable costs of the swimming pool, but not the land costs attributable to the condominium because no direct production activity has been undertaken on the condominium. See paragraph (b)(5)(ii)(A) of this section. On X's September 30, 1995, and December 31, 1995, measurement dates, the accumulated production expenditures for each unit include the allocable costs of the swimming pool, and the costs of the condominium (including attributable land costs) because a direct production activity has commenced on the condominium. See paragraph (b)(5)(i) of this section.

(iv) The production period for the condominium unit that includes the condominium that is sold as of the end of 1995 ends on the date the condominium is sold. See paragraph (b)(5)(iv) of this section. The production period of each unit that is ready to be held for sale ends when all production activities have been completed on the unit, in this case on December 31, 1995, the date that the swimming pool included in the unit is completed. See § 1.263A-12(d). Accordingly, interest capitalization ceases for each such unit that is sold or ready to be held for sale as of the end of 1995 (including each unit's allocable share of the completed swimming pool).

(v) The production periods for the condominium units that include the condominiums that are only partially complete at the end of 1995 continue after 1995. The accumulated production expenditures for each partially completed condominium unit continue to include the costs of the condominium (including attributable land costs) in addition to the costs of an allocable share of the completed swimming pool (including attributable land costs).

Example (6). Assume the same facts as in Example 5, except that the swimming pool is only partially complete as of the end of 1995. Under these facts, X capitalizes no interest during 1996 for the 1 unit that includes the condominium sold during 1995 (including the costs of the allocable share of the swimming pool). See paragraph (b)(5)(iv) of this section. However, with respect to the 6 condominiums that are partially complete and the 3 condominiums that are completed but unsold, interest capitalization continues after the end of 1995. The accumulated production expenditures for each of these 9 units include the costs of an allocable share of the swimming pool. See paragraph (b)(5)(i) of this section. In determining the costs of an allocable share of the swimming pool included in the accumulated production expenditures for each of the 9 units, X includes all costs of the swimming pool properly allocable to each unit, including those costs incurred as of the date of the sale of unit 1 that may have been used under applicable administrative procedures (e.g., Rev. Proc. 92-29, 1992-1 C.B. 748) in determining the basis of unit 1 solely for purposes of computing gain or loss on the sale of unit 1. See § 601.601(d)(2)(ii)(b) of this chapter.

Example (7). (i) Assume the same facts as in Example 5, except that X intends to lease rather than sell the condominiums and the completed swimming pool is placed in service for depreciation purposes on December 31, 1995. Additionally, assume that all 10 condominiums are partially completed at the end of 1995.

(ii) Under these facts, because the swimming pool is a common feature that is placed in service separately from the condominiums that it benefits, under paragraph (b)(5)(iii) of this section, the accumulated production expenditures of each of the condominium units do not include the costs of the allocable share of the swimming pool after 1995.

(c) Units of tangible personal property. Components of tangible personal property are a single unit of property if the components are functionally interdependent. Components of tangible personal property that are produced by, or for, the taxpayer, for use by the taxpayer or a related person, are functionally interdependent if the placing in service of one component is dependent on the placing in service of the other component by the taxpayer or a related person. In the case of tangible personal property produced for sale, components of tangible personal property are functionally interdependent if they are customarily sold as a single unit. For example, if an aircraft manufacturer customarily sells completely assembled aircraft, the unit of property includes all components of a completely assembled aircraft. If the manufacturer also customarily sells aircraft engines separately, any engines that are reasonably expected to be sold separately are treated as single units of property.

(d) Treatment of installations. If the taxpayer produces or is treated as producing any property that is installed on or in other property, the production activity and installation activity relating to each unit of property generally are not aggregated for purposes of this section. However, if the taxpayer is treated as producing and installing any property for use by the taxpayer or a related person or if the taxpayer enters into a contract requiring the taxpayer to install property for use by a customer, the production activity and installation activity are aggregated for purposes of this section.

T.D. 8584, 12/28/94.

§ 1.263A-11 Accumulated production expenditures.

(a) General rule. Accumulated production expenditures generally means the cumulative amount of direct and indirect costs described in section 263A(a) that are required to be capitalized with respect to the unit of property (as defined in § 1.263A-10), including interest capitalized in prior computation periods, plus the adjusted bases of any assets described in paragraph (d) of this section that are used to produce the unit of property during the period of their use. Accumulated production expenditures may also include the basis of any property received by the taxpayer in a nontaxable transaction.

(b) When costs are first taken into account. *(1) In general.* Except as provided in paragraph (c)(1) of this section, costs are taken into account in the computation of accumulated production expenditures at the time and to the extent they would otherwise be taken into account under the taxpayer's method of accounting (e.g., after applying the requirements of section 461, including the economic performance requirement of section 461(h)). Costs that have been incurred and capitalized with respect to a unit of property prior to the beginning of the production period are taken into account as accumulated production expenditures beginning on the date on which the production period of the property begins (as defined in § 1.263A-12(c)). Thus, for example, the cost of raw land acquired for development, the cost of a leasehold in mineral properties acquired for development, and the capitalized cost of planning and design activities are taken into account as accumulated production expenditures beginning on the first day of the production period. For purposes of determining accumulated production expenditures on any measurement date during a computation period, the interest required to be capitalized for the computation period is deemed to be capitalized on the day immediately following the end of the computation period. For any subsequent measurement dates and computation periods, that interest is included in accumulated production expenditures. If the cost of land or common features is allocated among planned units of property that are completed in phases, any portion of the cost properly allocated to completed units is not reallocated to any incomplete units of property.

(2) Dedication rule for materials and supplies. The costs of raw materials, supplies, or similar items are taken into account as accumulated production expenditures when they are incurred and dedicated to production of a unit of property. Dedicated means the first date on which the raw materials, supplies, or similar items are specifically associated with the production of any unit of property, including by record, assignment to the specific job site, or physical incorporation. In contrast, in the case of a component or subassembly that is reasonably expected to be become a part of (e.g., be incorporated into) any unit of property, costs incurred (including dedicated raw materials) for the component or subassembly are taken into account as accumulated production expenditures during the production of any portion of the component or subassembly and prior to its connection with (e.g., incorporation into) any specific unit of property. For purposes of the preceding sentence, components and subassemblies must be aggregated at each measurement date in a reasonable manner that is consistent with the purposes of section 263A(f).

(c) Property produced under a contract. *(1) Customer.* If a unit of property produced under a contract is designated property under § 1.263A-8(d)(2)(i) with respect to the customer, the customer's accumulated production expenditures include any payments under the contract that represent part of the purchase price of the unit of designated property or, to the extent costs are incurred earlier than payments are made (determined on a cumulative basis for each unit of designated property), any part of such price for which the requirements of section 461 have been satisfied. The customer has made a payment under this section if the transaction would be considered a payment by a taxpayer using the cash receipts and disbursements method of accounting. The customer's accumulated production expenditures also include any other costs incurred by the customer, such as interest, or any other direct or indirect costs that are required to be capitalized under section 263A(a) and the regulations thereunder with respect to the production of the unit of designated property.

(2) Contractor. If a unit of property produced under a contract is designated property under § 1.263A-8(d)(2)(ii) with respect to the contractor, the contractor must treat the cumulative amount of payments made by the customer under the contract attributable to the unit of property as a reduction in the contractor's accumulated production expenditures. The customer has made a payment under this section if the transaction would be considered a payment by a taxpayer using the cash receipts and disbursements method of accounting.

(d) Property used to produce designated property. *(1) In general.* Accumulated production expenditures include the adjusted bases (or portion thereof) of any equipment, facilities, or other similar assets, used in a reasonably proximate manner for the production of a unit of designated property during any measurement period in which the asset is so used. Examples of assets used in a reasonably proximate manner include machinery and equipment used directly or indirectly in the production process, such as assembly-line structures, cranes, bulldozers, and buildings. A taxpayer apportions the adjusted basis of an asset used in the production of more than one unit of designated property in a measurement period among such units of designated property using reasonable criteria corresponding to the use of the asset, such as machine hours, mileage, or units of production. If an asset used in a reasonably proximate manner for the production of a unit of designated property is temporarily idle (within the meaning of § 1.263A-1(e)(3)(iii)(E)) for an entire measurement period, the adjusted basis of the asset is excluded from the accumulated production expenditures for the unit during that measurement period. Notwithstanding this paragraph (d)(1), the portion of the depreciation allowance for equipment, facilities, or any other asset that is capitalized with respect to a unit of designated property in accordance with § 1.263A-1(e)(3)(ii)(I) is included in accumulated production expenditures without regard to the extent of use under this paragraph (d)(1) (i.e., without regard to whether the asset is used in a reasonably proximate manner for the production of the unit of designated property).

(2) Example. The following example illustrates how the basis of an asset is allocated on the basis of time:

Example. In 1995, X uses a bulldozer exclusively to clear the land on several adjacent real estate development projects, A, B, and C. A, B, and C are treated as separate units of property under the principles of § 1.263A-10. X decides to allocate the basis of the bulldozer among the three projects on the basis of time. At the end of the first quarter of 1995, the production period has commenced for all three projects. The bulldozer was operated for 30 hours on project A, 80 hours on project B, and 10 hours on project C, for a total of 120 hours for the entire period. For purposes of determining accumulated production expenditures as of the end of the first quarter, 1/4 of the adjusted basis of the bulldozer is allocated to project A, 2/3 to project B, and 1/12 to project C. Nonworking hours, regularly scheduled nonworking days, or other periods in which the bulldozer is temporarily idle (within the meaning of § 1.263A-1(e)(3)(iii)(E)) during the measurement period are not taken into account in allocating the basis of the bulldozer.

(3) Excluded equipment and facilities. The adjusted bases of equipment, facilities, or other assets that are not used in a reasonably proximate manner to produce a unit of property are not included in the computation of accumulated production expenditures. For example, the adjusted bases of equipment and facilities, including buildings and other structures, used in service departments performing administrative, purchasing, personnel, legal, accounting, or similar functions, are excluded from the computation of accumulated production expenditures under this paragraph (d)(3).

(e) Improvements. *(1) General rule.* If an improvement constitutes the production of designated property under § 1.263A-8(d)(3), accumulated production expenditures with respect to the improvement consist of —

(i) All direct and indirect costs required to be capitalized with respect to the improvement,

(ii) In the case of an improvement to a unit of real property—

(A) An allocable portion of the cost of land, and

(B) For any measurement period, the adjusted basis of any existing structure, common feature, or other property that is not placed in service or must be temporarily withdrawn from service to complete the improvement (associated property) during any part of the measurement period if the associated property directly benefits the property being improved, the associated property directly benefits from the improvement, or the improvement was incurred by reason of the associated property. See, however, the de minimis rule under paragraph (e)(2) of this section that applies in the case of associated property.

(iii) In the case of an improvement to a unit of tangible personal property, the adjusted basis of the asset being improved if that asset either is not placed in service or must be temporarily withdrawn from service to complete the improvement.

(2) De minimis rule. For purposes of paragraph (e)(1)(ii) of this section, the total costs of all associated property for an improvement unit (associated property costs) are excluded from the accumulated production expenditures for the improvement unit during its production period if, on the date the production period of the unit begins, the taxpayer reasonably expects that at no time during the production period of the unit will the accumulated production expenditures for the unit, determined without regard to the associated property costs, exceed 5 percent of the associated property costs.

(f) Mid-production purchases. If a taxpayer purchases a unit of property for further production, the taxpayer's accumulated production expenditures include the full purchase price of the property plus, in accordance with the principles of paragraph (e) of this section, additional direct and indirect costs incurred by the taxpayer.

(g) Related person costs. The activities of a related person are taken into account in applying the classification thresholds under § 1.263A-8(b)(1)(ii)(B) and (C), and in determining the production period of a unit of designated property under § 1.263A-12. However, only those costs incurred by the taxpayer are taken into account in the taxpayer's accumulated production expenditures under this section because the related person includes its own capitalized costs in the related person's accumulated production expenditures with respect to any unit of designated property upon which the parties engage in mutual production activities. For purposes of the preceding sentence, the accumulated production expenditures of any property transferred to a taxpayer in a nontaxable transaction are treated as accumulated production expenditures incurred by the taxpayer.

(h) Installation. If the taxpayer installs property that is purchased by the taxpayer, accumulated production expenditures include the cost of the property that is installed in addition to the direct and indirect costs of installation.

T.D. 8584, 12/28/94.

§ 1.263A-12 Production period.

(a) In general. Capitalization of interest is required under § 1.263A-9 for computation periods (within the meaning of § 1.263A-9(f)(1)) that include the production period of a unit of designated property. In contrast, section 263A(a) requires the capitalization of all other direct or indirect costs, such as insurance, taxes, and storage, that directly benefit or are incurred by reason of the production of property without regard to whether they are incurred during a period in which production activity occurs.

(b) Related person activities. Activities performed and costs incurred by a person related to the taxpayer that directly benefit or are incurred by reason of the taxpayer's production of designated property are taken into account in determining the taxpayer's production period (regardless of whether the related person is performing only a service or is producing a subassembly or component that the related person is required to treat as an item of designated property). These activities and the related person's costs are also taken into account in determining whether tangible personal property produced by the taxpayer is 1-year or 2-year property under § 1.263A-8(b)(1)(ii)(B) and (C).

(c) Beginning of production period. *(1) In general.* A separate production period is determined for each unit of property defined in § 1.263A-10. The production period begins on the date that production of the unit of property begins.

(2) Real property. The production period of a unit of real property begins on the first date that any physical production activity (as defined in paragraph (e) of this section) is performed with respect to a unit of real property. See § 1.263A-10(b)(1). The production period of a unit of real property produced under a contract begins for the contractor on the date the contractor begins physical production activity on the property. The production period of a unit of real property produced under a contract begins for the customer on the date either the customer or the contractor begins physical production activity on the property.

(3) Tangible personal property. The production period of a unit of tangible personal property begins on the first date by which the taxpayer's accumulated production expenditures, including planning and design expenditures, are at least 5 percent of the taxpayer's total estimated accumulated production expenditures for the property unit. Thus, the beginning of the production period is determined without regard to whether physical production activity has commenced. The production period of a unit of tangible personal property produced under a contract begins for the contractor when the contractor's accumulated production expenditures, without any reduction for payments from the customer, are at least 5 percent of the contractor's total estimated accumulated production expenditures. The production period for a unit of tangible personal property produced under a contract begins for the customer when the customer's accumulated production expenditures are at least 5 percent of the customer's total estimated accumulated production expenditures.

(d) End of production period. *(1) In general.* The production period for a unit of property produced for self use ends on the date that the unit is placed in service and all production activities reasonably expected to be undertaken by, or for, the taxpayer or a related person are completed. The production period for a unit of property produced for sale ends on the date that the unit is ready to be held for sale and all production activities reasonably expected to be undertaken by, or for, the taxpayer or a related person are completed. See, however, § 1.263A-10(b)(5)(iv) providing an exception for common features in the case of a benefitted property that is sold. In the case of a unit of property produced under a contract, the production period for the customer ends when the property is placed in service by the customer and all production activities reasonably expected to be undertaken are complete (i.e., generally, no earlier than when the customer takes delivery). In the case of property that is customarily aged (such as tobacco, wine, or whiskey) before it is sold, the production period includes the aging period.

(2) Special rules. The production period does not end for a unit of property prior to the completion of physical production activities by the taxpayer even though the property is held for sale or lease, since all production activities reasonably expected to be undertaken by the taxpayer with respect to such property have not in fact been completed. See, however, § 1.263A-10(b)(5) regarding separation of certain common features.

(3) Sequential production or delivery. The production period ends with respect to each unit of property (as defined in § 1.263A-10) and its associated accumulated production expenditures as the unit of property is completed within the meaning of paragraph (d)(1) of this section, without regard to the production activities or costs of any other units of property. Thus, for example, in the case of separate apartments in a multi-unit building, each of which is a separate unit of property within the meaning of § 1.263A-10, the production period ends for each separate apartment when it is ready to be held for sale or placed in service within the meaning of paragraph (d)(1) of this section. In the case of a single unit of property that merely undergoes separate and distinct stages of production, the production period ends at the same time (i.e., when all separate stages of production are completed with respect to the entire amount of accumulated production expenditures for the property).

(4) Examples. The provisions of paragraph (d) of this section are illustrated by the following examples:

Example (1). E is engaged in the original construction of a high-rise office building with two wings. At the end of 1995, Wing #1, but not Wing #2, is placed in service. Moreover, at the end of 1995, all production activities reasonably expected to be undertaken on Wing #1 are completed. In accordance with § 1.263A-10(b)(1), Wing #1 and Wing #2 are separate units of designated property. E may stop capitalizing interest on Wing #1 but not on Wing #2.

Example (2). F is in the business of constructing finished houses. F generally paints and finishes the interior of the house, although this does not occur until a potential buyer is located. Because F reasonably expects to undertake production activity (painting and finishing), the production period of each house does not end until these activities are completed.

(e) Physical production activities. *(1) In general.* The term physical production activities includes any physical activity that constitutes production within the meaning of § 1.263A-8(d)(1). The production period begins and interest must be capitalized with respect to real property if any physical production activities are undertaken, whether alone or in preparation for the construction of buildings or other structures, or with respect to the improvement of existing structures. For example, the clearing of raw land constitutes the production of designated property, even if only cleared prior to resale.

(2) Illustrations. The following is a partial list of activities any one of which constitutes a physical production activity with respect to the production of real property:

(i) Clearing, grading, or excavating of raw land;

(ii) Demolishing a building or gutting a standing building;

(iii) Engaging in the construction of infrastructure, such as roads, sewers, sidewalks, cables, and wiring;

(iv) Undertaking structural, mechanical, or electrical activities with respect to a building or other structure; or

(v) Engaging in landscaping activities.

(f) Activities not considered physical production. The activities described in paragraphs (f)(1) and (f)(2) of this section are not considered physical production activities:

(1) Planning and design. Soil testing, preparing architectural blueprints or models, or obtaining building permits.

(2) Incidental repairs. Physical activities of an incidental nature that may be treated as repairs under § 1.162-4.

(g) Suspension of production period. *(1) In general.* If production activities related to the production of a unit of designated property cease for at least 120 consecutive days (cessation period), a taxpayer may suspend the capitalization of interest with respect to the unit of designated property starting with the first measurement period that begins after the first day in which production ceases. The taxpayer must resume the capitalization of interest with respect to a unit beginning with the measurement period during which production activities resume. In addition, production activities are not considered to have ceased if they cease because of circumstances inherent in the production process, such as normal adverse weather conditions, scheduled plant shutdowns, or delays due to design or construction flaws, the obtaining of a permit or license, or the settlement of groundfill to construct property. Interest incurred on debt that is traced debt with respect to a unit of designated property during the suspension period is subject to capitalization with respect to the production of other units of designated property as interest on nontraced debt. See § 1.263A-9(c)(5)(i) of this section. For applications of the avoided cost method after the end of the suspension period, the accumulated production expenditures for the unit include the balance of accumulated production expenditures as of the beginning of the suspension period, plus any additional capitalized costs incurred during the suspension period. No further suspension of interest capitalization may occur unless the requirements for a new suspension period are satisfied.

(2) Special rule. If a cessation period spans more than one taxable year, the taxpayer may suspend the capitalization of interest with respect to a unit beginning with the first measurement period of the taxable year in which the 120-day period is satisfied.

(3) Method of accounting. An election to suspend interest capitalization under paragraph (g)(1) of this section is a method of accounting that must be consistently applied to all units that satisfy the requirements of paragraph (g)(1) of this section. However, the special rule in paragraph (g)(2) of this section is applied on an annual basis to all units of an electing taxpayer that satisfy the requirements of paragraph (g)(2) of this section.

(4) Example. The provisions of paragraph (g)(1) of this section are illustrated by the following example.

Example. (i) D, a calendar-year taxpayer, began production of a residential housing development on January 1, 1995. D, in applying the avoided cost method, chose a taxable year computation period and quarterly measurement dates. On April 10, 1995, all production activities ceased with respect to the units in the development until December 1, 1996. The cessation, which occurred for a period of at least 120 consecutive days, was not attributable to circumstances inherent in the production process. With respect to the units in the development, D incurred production expenditures of $2,000,000 from January 1, 1995 through April 10, 1995. D incurred interest of $100,000 on traced debt with respect to the units for the period beginning January 1, 1995, and ending June 30, 1995. D did not incur any production expenditures for the more than 20-month cessation beginning April 10, 1995, and ending December 1, 1996, but incurred $200,000 of production expenditures from December 1, 1996, through December 31, 1996.

(ii) D is required to capitalize the $100,000 interest on traced debt incurred during the two measurement periods beginning January 1, 1995, and ending June 30, 1995. Because D satisfied the 120-day rule under this paragraph (g), D is not required to capitalize interest with respect to the accumulated production expenditures for the units for the measurement period beginning July 1, 1995, and ending September 30, 1995, which is the first measurement period that begins after the date production activities ceased. D is required to resume interest capitalization with respect to the $ 2,300,000 (2,000,000 + 100,000 + 200,000) of accumulated production expenditures for the units for the measurement period beginning October 1, 1996, and ending December 31, 1996 (the measurement period during which production activities resume). Accordingly, D may suspend the capitalization of interest with respect to the units from July 1, 1995, through September 30, 1996.

T.D. 8584, 12/28/94.

§ 1.263A-13 Oil and gas activities.

(a) In general. This section provides rules that are to be applied in tandem with § 1.263A-8 through 1.263A-12, 1.263A-14, and 1.263A-15 in capitalizing interest with respect to the development (within the meaning of section 263A(g)) of oil or gas property. For this purpose, oil or gas property consists of each separate operating mineral interest in oil or gas as defined in section 614(a), or, if a taxpayer makes an election under section 614(b), the aggregate of two or more separate operating mineral interests in oil or gas as described in section 614(b) (section 614 property). Thus, an oil or gas property is designated property unless the de minimis rule applies. A taxpayer must apply the rules in paragraph (c) of this section if the taxpayer cannot establish, at the beginning of the production period of the first well drilled on the property, a definite plan that identifies the number and location of other wells planned with respect to the property. If a taxpayer can establish such a plan at the beginning of the production period of the first well drilled on the property, the taxpayer may either apply the rules of paragraph (c) of this section or treat each of the planned wells as a separate unit and partition the leasehold acquisition costs and costs of common features based on the number of planned well units.

(b) Generally applicable rules. *(1) Beginning of production period.* (i) Onshore activities. In the case of onshore oil or gas development activities, the production period for a unit begins on the first date physical site preparation activities (such as building an access road, leveling a site for a drilling rig, or excavating a mud pit) are undertaken with respect to the unit.

(ii) Offshore activities. In the case of offshore development activities, the production period for a unit begins on the first date physical site preparation activities, other than activities undertaken with respect to expendable wells, are undertaken with respect to the unit. For purposes of the preceding sentence, the first physical site preparation activity undertaken with respect to a section 614 property is generally the first activity undertaken with respect to the anchoring of a platform (e.g., drilling to drive the piles). For purposes of this section, an expendable well is a well drilled solely to determine the location and delineation of offshore hydrocarbon deposits.

(2) End of production period. The production period ends for a productive well unit on the date the well is placed in service and all production activities reasonably expected to be undertaken by, or for, the taxpayer or a related person are completed. See § 1.263A-12(d).

(3) Accumulated production expenditures. (i) Costs included. Accumulated production expenditures for a well unit include the following costs (to the extent they are not intangible drilling and development costs allowable as a deduction under section 263(c), 263(i), or 291(b)(2)): the costs of acquiring the section 614 leasehold and the costs of taxes and similar items that are required to be capitalized under section 263A(a) with respect to the section 614 leasehold; the costs of real property associated with developing the section 614 property (e.g., casing); the basis of real property that constitutes a common feature within the meaning of § 1.263A-10(b)(3); and the adjusted basis of property used to produce property (such as a mobile rig, drilling ship, or an offshore drilling platform).

(ii) Improvement unit. To the extent section 614 costs are allocated to a well unit, the undepleted portion of those section 614 costs must also be included in the accumulated production expenditures for any improvement unit (within the meaning of § 1.263A-8(d)(3)) with respect to that well unit.

(c) Special rules when definite plan not established. *(1) In general.* The special rules of this paragraph (c) must be applied by a taxpayer that cannot establish, at the beginning of the production period of the first well drilled on the property, a definite plan that identifies the number and location of the wells planned with respect to the property. A taxpayer that can establish such a plan is permitted, but not required, to apply the rules of this paragraph (c), provided the rules of this paragraph (c) are consistently applied for all the taxpayer's oil or gas properties for which a definite plan can be established.

(2) Oil and gas units. (i) First productive well unit. Until the first productive well is placed in service and all production activities reasonably expected to be undertaken by, or for, the taxpayer or a related person are completed, a first productive well unit includes the section 614 property and all real property associated with the development of the section 614 property. Thus, for example, a first productive well unit includes the section 614 property and real property associated with any nonproductive well drilled on the section 614 property on or before the date the first productive well is placed in service and all production activities reasonably expected to be undertaken by, or for, the taxpayer or a related person are completed. For purposes of this section, a productive well is a well that produces in commercial quantities. See paragraph (c)(5) of this section, which provides a special rule whereby the costs of a section 614 property and common feature costs for a section 614 property generally are included only in the accumulated production expenditures for the first productive well unit.

(ii) Subsequent units. Generally, real property associated with each productive or nonproductive well with respect to which production activities begin after the date the first productive well is placed in service and all production activities reasonably expected to be undertaken by, or for, the taxpayer or a related person are completed, constitutes a unit of real property. Additionally, a productive or nonproductive well that is included in a first productive well unit and for which development continues after the date the first productive well is placed in service and all production activities reasonably expected to be undertaken by, or for, the taxpayer or a related person are completed, generally is treated as a separate unit of property after that date. See, however, paragraph (c)(5) of this section, which provides rules for the treatment of costs included in the accumulated production expenditures of a first productive well unit.

(3) Beginning of production period. (i) First productive well unit. The beginning of the production period of the first productive well unit is determined as provided in paragraph (b) of this section.

(ii) Subsequent wells. In applying paragraph (b) of this section to subsequent well units (as described in paragraph (c)(2)(ii) of this section), any activities occurring prior to the date the production period ends for the first productive well unit are not taken into account in determining the beginning of the production period for the subsequent well units.

(4) End of production period. The end of the production period for both the first productive well unit and subsequent productive well units is determined as provided in paragraph (b)(2) of this section. See § 1.263A-12(d). Nonproductive wells included in the first productive well unit need not be plugged and abandoned for the production period to end for a first productive well unit.

(5) Accumulated production expenditures. (i) First productive well unit. The accumulated production expenditures for a first productive well unit include all costs incurred with respect to the section 614 property and associated real property at any time through the end of the production period for the first productive well unit. Thus, the costs of acquiring the section 614 property, the costs of taxes and similar items that are required to be capitalized under section 263A(a) with respect to the section 614 property, and the costs of common features, that are incurred at any time through the end of the production period of the first productive well unit (section 614 costs) are included in the accumulated production expenditures for the first productive well unit.

(ii) Subsequent well unit. The accumulated production expenditures for a subsequent well do not include any costs included in the accumulated production expenditures for a first productive well unit. In the event that section 614 costs or common feature costs with respect to a section 614 property are incurred subsequent to the end of the production period of the first productive well unit, those common feature costs and undepleted section 614 costs are allocated among the accumulated production expenditures of wells being drilled as of the date such costs are incurred.

(6) Allocation of interest capitalized with respect to first productive well unit. Interest attributable to any productive or nonproductive well included in the first productive well unit (within the meaning of paragraph (c)(2)(ii) of this section) is allocated among and capitalized to the basis of the property associated with the first productive well unit. See § 1.263A-8(a)(2).

(7) Example. The provisions of this paragraph (c) are illustrated by the following example.

Example. (i) Corporation Z, an oil company, acquired a section 614 property in an onshore tract, Tract B, for development. In 1995, Corporation Z began site preparation activities on Tract B and also commenced drilling Well 1 on Tract B. Corporation Z was unable to establish, as provided in paragraph (a) of this section, a definite plan identifying the number and location of other wells planned on Tract B. In 1996, Corporation Z began drilling Well 2. On May 1, 1997, Well 2, a productive well, was placed in service and all production activities reasonably expected to be undertaken with respect to Well 2 were completed. By that date, also, Well 1 was abandoned.

(ii) Well 2 is a first productive well (within the meaning of paragraph (c)(2)(i) of this section). Well 1 is a nonproductive well drilled prior to a first productive well. Under paragraph (c) of this section, Corporation Z must treat both Well 1 and Well 2 as part of the first productive well unit on the section 614 property. In accordance with paragraphs (c)(3) and (c)(4) of this section, the production period of the first productive well unit begins on the date physical site preparation activities are undertaken with respect to Well 1 in 1995 and ends on May 1, 1997, the date that Well 2 is placed in service and all production activities reasonably expected to be undertaken are completed. In accordance with paragraph (c)(5) of this section, the accumulated production expenditures for the first productive well unit include, among other capitalized costs, the entire section 614 property costs capitalized with respect to Tract B and all common feature costs incurred with respect to the section 614 property through May 1, 1997.

(iii) Any well that Corporation Z begins after May 1, 1997, is a separate unit of property. See paragraph (c)(2)(ii) of this section. Under paragraph (c)(3)(ii) of this section, the production period for any such well unit begins on the first day after May 1, 1997, on which Corporation Z undertakes physical site preparation activities with respect to the well unit. Moreover, Corporation Z does not include any of the section 614 property costs in the accumulated production expenditures for any well unit begun after May 1, 1997.

T.D. 8584, 12/28/94.

§ 1.263A-14 Rules for related persons.

Taxpayers must account for average excess expenditures allocated to related persons under applicable administrative pronouncements interpreting section 263A(f). See § 601.601(d)(2)(ii)(b) of this chapter.

T.D. 8584, 12/28/94.

§ 1.263A-15 Effective dates, transitional rules, and anti-abuse rule.

(a) Effective dates. *(1)* Sections 1.263A-8 through 1.263A-15 generally apply to interest incurred in taxable years beginning on or after January 1, 1995. In the case of property that is inventory in the hands of the taxpayer, however, these sections are effective for taxable years beginning on or after January 1, 1995. Changes in methods of accounting necessary as a result of the rules in § 1.263A-8 through 1.263A-15 must be made under the terms and conditions prescribed by the Commissioner. Under these terms and conditions, the principles of § 1.263A-7 must be applied in revaluing inventory property.

(2) For taxable years beginning before January 1, 1995, taxpayers must take reasonable positions on their federal income tax returns when applying section 263A(f). For purposes of this paragraph (a)(2), a reasonable position is a position consistent with the temporary regulations, revenue rulings, revenue procedures, notices, and announcements concerning section 263A applicable in taxable years beginning before January 1, 1995. See § 601.601(d)(2)(ii)(b) of this chapter. For this purpose, Notice 88-99, 1988-2 C.B. 422, applies to taxable years beginning after August 17, 1988, in the case of inventory, and to interest incurred in taxable years beginning after August 17, 1988, in all other cases. Finally, under administrative procedures issued by the

Commissioner, taxpayers may elect early application of §§ 1.263A-8 through 1.263A-15 to taxable years beginning on or after January 1, 1994, in the case of inventory property, and to interest incurred in taxable years beginning on or after January 1, 1994, in the case of property that is not inventory in the hands of the taxpayer.

(3) Section 1.263A-9(a)(4)(ix) generally applies to interest incurred in taxable years beginning on or after May 20, 2004. In the case of property that is inventory in the hands of the taxpayer, § 1.263A-9(a)(4)(ix) applies to taxable years beginning on or after May 20, 2004. Taxpayers may elect to apply § 1.263A-9(a)(4)(ix) to interest incurred in taxable years beginning on or after January 1, 1995, or, in the case of property that is inventory in the hands of the taxpayer, to taxable years beginning on or after January 1, 1995. A change in a taxpayer's treatment of interest to a method consistent with § 1.263A-9(a)(4)(ix) is a change in method of accounting to which sections 446 and 481 apply.

(b) Transitional rule for accumulated production expenditures. *(1) In general.* Except as provided in paragraph (b)(2) of this section, costs incurred before the effective date of section 263A are included in accumulated production expenditures (within the meaning of § 1.263A-11) with respect to noninventory property only to the extent those costs were required to be capitalized under section 263 when incurred and would have been taken into account in determining the amount of interest required to be capitalized under former section 189 (relating to the capitalization of real property interest and taxes) or pursuant to an election that was in effect under section 266 (relating to the election to capitalize certain carrying charges).

(2) Property used to produce designated property. The basis of property acquired prior to 1987 and used to produce designated noninventory property after December 31, 1986, is included in accumulated production expenditures in accordance with § 1.263A-11(d) without regard to whether the basis would have been taken into account under former section 189 or section 266.

(c) Anti-abuse rule. The interest capitalization rules contained in § 1.263A-8 through 1.263A-15 must be applied by the taxpayer in a manner that is consistent with and reasonably carries out the purposes of section 263A(f). For example, in applying § 1.263A-10, regarding the definition of a unit of property, taxpayers may not divide a single unit of property to avoid properly classifying the property as designated property. Similarly, taxpayers may not use loans in lieu of advance payments, tax-exempt parties, loan restructurings at measurement dates, or obligations bearing an unreasonably low rate of interest (even if such rate equals or exceeds the applicable Federal rate under section 1274(d)) to avoid the purposes of section 263A(f). For purposes of this paragraph (c), the presence of back-to-back loans with different rates of interest, and other uses of related parties to facilitate an avoidance of interest capitalization, evidences abuse. In such cases, the District Director may, based upon all the facts and circumstances, determine the amount of interest that must be capitalized in a manner that is consistent with and reasonably carries out the purposes of section 263A(f).

T.D. 8584, 12/28/94, amend T.D. 8728, 8/4/97, T.D. 9179, 2/22/2005.

§ 1.264-1 Premiums on life insurance taken out in a trade or business.

Caution: The Treasury has not yet amended Reg § 1.264-1 to reflect changes made by P.L. 105-34, P.L. 104-191, P.L. 99-514, P.L. 88-272.

(a) When premiums are not deductible. Premiums paid by a taxpayer on a life insurance policy are not deductible from the taxpayer's gross income, even though they would otherwise be deductible as trade or business expenses, if they are paid on a life insurance policy covering the life of any officer or employee of the taxpayer, or any person (including the taxpayer) who is financially interested in any trade or business carried on by the taxpayer, when the taxpayer is directly or indirectly a beneficiary of the policy. For additional provisions relating to the nondeductibility of premiums paid on life insurance policies (whether under section 162 or any other section of the Code), see section 262, relating to personal, living, and family expenses, and section 265, relating to expenses allocable to tax-exempt income.

(b) When taxpayer is a beneficiary. If a taxpayer takes out a policy for the purpose of protecting himself from loss in the event of the death of the insured, the taxpayer is considered a beneficiary directly or indirectly under the policy. However, if the taxpayer is not a beneficiary under the policy, the premiums so paid will not be disallowed as deductions merely because the taxpayer may derive a benefit from the increased efficiency of the officer or employee insured. See section 162 and the regulations thereunder. A taxpayer is considered a beneficiary under a policy where, for example, he, as a principal member of a partnership, takes out an insurance policy on his own life irrevocably designating his partner as the sole beneficiary in order to induce his partner to retain his investment in the partnership. Whether or not the taxpayer is a beneficiary under a policy, the proceeds of the policy paid by reason of the death of the insured may be excluded from gross income whether the beneficiary is an individual or a corporation, except in the case of (1) certain transferees, as provided in section 101(a)(2); (2) portions of amounts of life insurance proceeds received at a date later than death under the provisions of section 101(d); and (3) life insurance policy proceeds which are includible in the gross income of a husband or wife under section 71 (relating to alimony) or section 682 (relating to income of an estate or trust in case of divorce, etc.). (See section 101(e).) For further reference, see, generally, section 101 and the regulations thereunder.

T.D. 6228, 4/17/57.

§ 1.264-2 Single premium life insurance, endowment, or annuity contracts.

Caution: The Treasury has not yet amended Reg § 1.264-2 to reflect changes made by P.L. 104-191, P.L. 99-514, P.L. 88-272.

Amounts paid or accrued on indebtedness incurred or continued, directly or indirectly, to purchase or to continue in effect a single premium life insurance or endowment contract, or to purchase or to continue in effect a single premium annuity contract purchased (whether from the insurer, annuitant, or any other person) after March 1, 1954, are not deductible under section 163 or any other provision of chapter 1 of the Code. This prohibition applies even though the insurance is not on the life of the taxpayer and regardless of whether or not the taxpayer is the annuitant or payee of such annuity contract. A contract is considered a single premium life insurance, endowment, or annuity contract, for the purposes of this section, if substantially all the premiums on the contract are paid within four years from the date on which the contract was purchased, or if an amount is deposited after March 1, 1954, with the insurer for payment of a substantial number of future premiums on the contract.

T.D. 6228, 4/17/57.

§ 1.264-3 Effective date; taxable years ending after March 1, 1954, subject to the Internal Revenue Code of 1939.

Caution: The Treasury has not yet amended Reg § 1.264-3 to reflect changes made by P.L. 104-191, P.L. 99-514, P.L. 88-272.

Pursuant to section 7851(a)(1)(C), the regulations prescribed in § 1.264-2, to the extent that they relate to amounts paid or accrued on indebtedness incurred or continued to purchase or carry a single premium annuity contract purchased after March 1, 1954, and to the extent they consider a contract a single premium life insurance, endowment, or annuity contract if an amount is deposited after March 1, 1954, with the insurer for payment of a substantial number of future premiums on the contract, shall also apply to taxable years beginning before January 1, 1954, and ending after March 1, 1954, and to taxable years beginning after December 31, 1953, and ending after March 1, 1954, but before August 17, 1954, although such years are subject to the Internal Revenue Code of 1939.

T.D. 6228, 4/17/57.

§ 1.264-4 Other life insurance, endowment, or annuity contracts.

Caution: The Treasury has not yet amended Reg § 1.264-4 to reflect changes made by P.L. 104-191, P.L. 99-514.

(a) General rule. Except as otherwise provided in paragraphs (d) and (e) of this section, no deduction shall be allowed under section 163 or any other provision of chapter 1 of the Code for any amount (determined under paragraph (b) of this section) paid or accrued during the taxable year on indebtedness incurred or continued to purchase or continue in effect a life insurance, endowment, or annuity contract (other than a single premium contract or a contract treated as a single premium contract) if such indebtedness is incurred pursuant to a plan of purchase which contemplates the systematic direct or indirect borrowing of part or all of the increases in the cash value of such contract (either from the insurer or otherwise). For the purposes of the preceding sentence, the term "of purchase" includes the payment of part or all of the premiums on a contract, and not merely payment of the premium due upon initial issuance of the contract. The rule of this paragraph applies whether or not the taxpayer is the insured, payee, or annuitant under the contract. The rule of this paragraph does not apply to contracts purchased by the taxpayer on or before August 6, 1963, even though there is a substantial increase in premiums after such date. The rule of this paragraph does not apply to any amount paid or accrued on indebtedness incurred or continued to purchase or carry a single premium life insurance, endowment, or annuity contract (including a contract treated as a single premium contract); the treatment of such amounts is governed by § 1.264-2.

(b) Determination of amount not allowed. The amount not allowed as a deduction under paragraph (a) of this section is determined with reference to the entire amount of borrowing to purchase or carry the contract, and is not limited with reference to the amount of borrowing of increases in the cash value. The rule of this paragraph may be illustrated by the following example:

Example. A, a calendar year taxpayer using the cash receipts and disbursements method of accounting, on January 1, 1964, purchases from a life insurance company a policy in the amount of $100,000 with an annual gross premium of $2,200. For the first policy year, A pays the annual premium by means other than by borrowing. For the second, third, fourth, and fifth policy years, A continues the policy in effect by incurring indebtedness pursuant to a plan referred to in paragraph (a) of this section. The years and amounts applicable to the policy are as follows:

Years	Cumulative cash value of contract	Total loan outstanding	Interest paid at 4.8 percent
1964	$ 370	0	0
1965	2,175	$2,200	$105.60
1966	4,000	4,400	211.20
1967	5,865	6,600	316.80
1968	7,745	8,800	422.40

On these facts (assuming that none of the exceptions contained in paragraph (d) of this section are applicable), no deduction is allowed for the interest paid during the year 1968. Moreover, the interest deduction will be disallowed for the taxable years 1965 through 1967 if such taxable years are not closed by reason of the statute of limitations or other rule of law.

(c) Special rules. For purposes of this section—

(1) Determination of existence of a plan which contemplates systematic borrowing. (i) In general. The determination of whether indebtedness is incurred or continued pursuant to a plan referred to in paragraph (a) of this section shall be made on the basis of all the facts and circumstances in each case. Unless the taxpayer shows otherwise, in the case of borrowing in connection with premiums for more than three years, the existence of a plan referred to in paragraph (a) of this section will be presumed. The mere fact that a taxpayer does not borrow to pay a premium in a particular year does not in and of itself preclude the existence of a plan referred to in paragraph (a) of this section. A plan referred to in paragraph (a) of this section need not exist at the time the contract is entered into, but may come into existence at any time during the 7-year period following the taxpayer's purchase of the contract or following a substantial increase (referred to in paragraph (d)(1) of this section) in premiums on the contract.

(ii) Premium attributable to more than one year. For purposes of subdivision (i) of this subparagraph, if the stated annual premiums due on a contract vary in amount, borrowing in connection with any premium, the amount of which exceeds the amount of any other premium, on such contract may be considered borrowing to pay premiums for more than one year. The preceding sentence shall not apply where the borrowing is in connection with a substantially increased premium within the meaning of paragraph (d)(1) of this section.

(2) Direct or indirect. A plan referred to in paragraph (a) of this section may contemplate direct or indirect borrowing of increases in cash value of the contract directly or indirectly to pay premiums and may contemplate borrowing either from an insurance carrier, from a bank, or from any other person. Thus, for example, if a taxpayer borrows

$100,000 from a bank and uses the funds to purchase securities, later borrows $100,000 from a second bank and uses the funds to repay the first bank, later sells the securities and uses the funds as a part of a plan referred to in paragraph (a) of this section to pay premiums on a contract of cash value life insurance, the deduction for interest paid in continuing the loan from the second bank shall not be allowed (assuming that none of the exceptions contained in paragraph (d) of this section are applicable). Moreover, a plan referred to in paragraph (a) of this section need not involve a pledge of the contract, but may contemplate unsecured borrowing or the use of other property.

(d) Exceptions. No deduction shall be denied under paragraph (a) of this section with respect to any amount paid or accrued during a taxable year on indebtedness incurred or continued as part of a plan referred to in paragraph (a) of this section if any of the following exceptions apply.

(1) The 7-year exception. (i) In general. No part of 4 of the annual premiums due during the 7-year period (beginning with the date the first premium on the contract to which such plan relates was paid) is paid under such plan by means of indebtedness. For purposes of this exception, in the event of a substantial increase in any annual premium on a contract, a new 7-year period begins on the date such increased premium is paid. If premiums on a contract are payable other than on an annual basis (for example, monthly), the annual premium is the aggregate of premiums due for the year. See paragraph (c)(1)(ii) of this section for cases where one premium on a contract paid by means of indebtedness may be considered as more than one annual premium.

(ii) Application of borrowings. For purposes of subdivision (i) of this subparagraph, if during a 7-year period referred to in such subdivision the taxpayer, directly or indirectly, borrows with respect to more than one annual premium on a contract, such borrowing shall be considered first attributable to the premium for the current policy year (within the meaning of subdivision (iii) of this subparagraph) and then attributable to premiums for prior policy years beginning with the most recent prior policy year (but not including any prior policy year to the extent that such taxpayer has indebtedness outstanding with respect to the premium for such prior policy year). If such borrowing exceeds the premiums paid for the current policy year and for prior policy years and the taxpayer has, with respect to the current policy year, deposited premiums in advance of the due date of such premiums, such excess borrowing shall be considered indebtedness incurred to carry the contract which is attributable to the premiums deposited for succeeding policy years beginning with the premium for the next succeeding policy year. The preceding sentence shall not apply to a single premium contract referred to in § 1.264-2.

(iii) Current policy year. For purposes of subdivision (ii) of this subparagraph, the term "current policy year" refers to the policy year which begins with or within the taxable year of the taxpayer.

(iv) Illustrations. The provisions of subdivision (ii) of this subparagraph may be illustrated by the following examples:

Example (1). A, a calendar year taxpayer using the cash receipts and disbursements method of accounting, on January 1, 1964, purchases from a life insurance company a policy in the amount of $100,000 with an annual gross premium of $2,200. For the first four policy years, A initially pays the annual premium by means other than borrowing. On January 1, 1968, pursuant to a plan referred to in paragraph (a) of this section, A borrows $10,000 with respect to the policy. Such borrowing is considered first attributable to paying the premium for the year 1968 and then attributable to paying the premiums for the years 1967, 1966, 1965, and 1964 (in part). No deduction is allowed for the interest paid by A on the $10,000 indebtedness during the year 1968.

Example (2). The facts are the same as in example (1), except that on January 1, 1964, A pays the first annual premium and deposits an amount equal to the second and third annual premiums, all such amounts initially being paid or deposited by means other than borrowing. On January 1, 1965, A deposits an amount equal to the fourth, fifth, and sixth annual premiums, and borrows $4,400 pursuant to a plan referred to in paragraph (a) of this section. Such borrowing is considered attributable to the premiums paid for the policy years 1965 and 1964. On January 1, 1966, A deposits an amount equal to the seventh, eighth, and ninth annual premiums, and borrows $6,600 pursuant to such plan. Such borrowing is considered attributable to the premium paid for the policy year 1966 and deposited for the policy years 1967 and 1968. No deduction is allowed for interest paid by A on the $11,000 indebtedness during 1966. Moreover, the interest deduction will be disallowed for the taxable year 1965. However, if this contract is treated as a single premium contract under § 1.264-2 (by reason of deposit with the insurer of an amount for payment of a substantial number of future premiums), the deduction for interest on indebtedness incurred or continued to purchase or carry the contract would be denied without reference to this section.

(2) The $100 exception. The total amount paid or accrued during the taxable year by the taxpayer who has entered one or more plans referred to in paragraph (a) of this section for which (without regard to this subparagraph) no deduction would be allowable under paragraph (a) of this section does not exceed $100. Where the amount so paid or accrued during the taxable year exceeds $100, the entire amount shall be subject to the general rule of paragraph (a) of this section.

(3) The unforeseen events exception. The amount is paid or accrued by the taxpayer on indebtedness incurred because of an unforeseen substantial loss of such taxpayer's income or an unforeseen substantial increase in such taxpayer's financial obligations. A loss of income or increase in financial obligations is not unforeseen, within the meaning of this subparagraph, if at the time of the purchase of the contract such event was or could have been foreseen. College education expenses are foreseeable; however, if college expenses substantially increase, then to the extent that such increases are unforeseen, this exception will apply. This exception applies only if the plan referred to in paragraph (a) of this section arises because of the unforeseen event. Thus, for example, if a taxpayer or his family incur substantial unexpected medical expenses or the taxpayer is laid off from his job, and for that reason systematically borrows against the cash value of a previously purchased contract, the deduction for the interest paid on the loan will not be denied, whether or not the loan is used to pay a premium on the contract.

(4) The trade or business exception. The indebtedness is incurred by the taxpayer in connection with his trade or business. To be within this exception, the indebtedness must be incurred to finance business obligations rather than to finance cash value life insurance. Thus, if a taxpayer pledges a life insurance, endowment, or annuity contract as part of the collateral for a loan to finance the expansion of inventory or capital improvements for his business, no part of the deduction for interest on such loan will be denied under paragraph (a) of this section. Borrowing by a business taxpayer to finance business life insurance such as under so-called

keyman, split dollar, or stock retirement plans is not considered to be incurred in connection with the taxpayer's trade or business within the meaning of this subparagraph. The determination of whether the indebtedness is incurred in connection with the taxpayer's trade or business, within the meaning of this exception, rather than to finance cash value life insurance shall be made on the basis of all the facts and circumstances. The provisions of this subparagraph may be illustrated by the following examples:

Example (1). Corporation M each year borrows substantial sums to carry on its business. Corporation M agrees to provide a retirement plan for its employees and purchases level premium life insurance to fund its obligation under the plan. The mere fact that M Corporation purchases a cash value life insurance policy will not cause its deduction for interest paid on its normal indebtedness to be denied even though the policy is later used as part of the collateral for its normal indebtedness.

Example (2). Corporation R has $200,000 of bonds outstanding and purchases cash value life insurance policies on several of its key employees. Such purchase by R Corporation will not, of itself, cause its deduction for interest on its bonded indebtedness to be denied. If, however, the premiums on the life insurance policies are $10,000 each year, the cash value increases by $8,000 each year, and R Corporation increases its indebtedness by $10,000 each year, its deduction for interest on such indebtedness will not be allowed under the rule of paragraph (a) of this section. On the other hand, the absence of such a directly parallel increase will not of itself establish that the deduction for interest is allowable.

(e) Applicability of section. The rules of this section apply with respect to taxable years beginning after December 31, 1963, but only with respect to contracts purchased after August 6, 1963. With respect to contracts entered into on or before August 6, 1963, but purchased or acquired whether from the insurer, insured, or any other person (other than by gift, bequest, or inheritance, or in a transaction to which section 381(a) of the Code applies) after such date, the rules of this section apply after such purchase or acquisition.

T.D. 6773, 11/23/64.

§ 1.265-1 Expenses relating to tax-exempt income.

Caution: The Treasury has not yet amended Reg § 1.265-1 to reflect changes made by P.L. 99-514.

(a) Nondeductibility of expenses allocable to exempt income. *(1)* No amount shall be allowed as a deduction under any provision of the Code for any expense or amount which is otherwise allowable as a deduction and which is allocable to a class or classes of exempt income other than a class or classes of exempt interest income.

(2) No amount shall be allowed as a deduction under section 212 (relating to expenses for production of income) for any expense or amount which is otherwise allowable as a deduction and which is allocable to a class or classes of exempt interest income.

(b) Exempt income and nonexempt income. *(1)* As used in this section, the term "class of exempt income" means any class of income (whether or not any amount of income of such class is received or accrued) wholly exempt from the taxes imposed by subtitle A of the Code. For purposes of this section, a class of income which is considered as wholly exempt from the taxes imposed by subtitle A includes any class of income which is—

(i) Wholly excluded from gross income under any provision of subtitle A, or

(ii) Wholly exempt from the taxes imposed by subtitle A under the provisions of any other law.

(2) As used in this section the term "nonexempt income" means any income which is required to be included in gross income.

(c) Allocation of expenses to a class or classes of exempt income. Expenses and amounts otherwise allowable which are directly allocable to any class or classes of exempt income shall be allocated thereto; and expenses and amounts directly allocable to any class or classes of nonexempt income shall be allocated thereto. If an expense or amount otherwise allowable is indirectly allocable to both a class of nonexempt income and a class of exempt income, a reasonable proportion thereof determined in the light of all the facts and circumstances in each case shall be allocated to each.

(d) Statement of classes of exempt income; records. *(1)* A taxpayer receiving any class of exempt income or holding any property or engaging in any activity the income from which is exempt shall submit with his return as a part thereof an itemized statement, in detail, showing (i) the amount of each class of exempt income, and (ii) the amount of expenses and amounts otherwise allowable allocated to each such class (the amount allocated by apportionment being shown separately) as required by paragraph (c) of this section. If an item is apportioned between a class of exempt income and a class of nonexempt income, the statement shall show the basis of the apportionment. Such statement shall also recite that each deduction claimed in the return is not in any way attributable to a class of exempt income.

(2) The taxpayer shall keep such records as will enable him to make the allocations required by this section. See section 6001 and the regulations thereunder.

T.D. 6313, 9/16/58.

§ 1.265-2 Interest relating to tax-exempt income.

Caution: The Treasury has not yet amended Reg § 1.265-2 to reflect changes made by P.L. 105-34, P.L. 99-514, P.L. 98-369, P.L. 97-34, P.L. 96-223, P.L. 94-455.

(a) In general. No amount shall be allowed as a deduction for interest on any indebtedness incurred or continued to purchase or carry obligations, the interest on which is wholly exempt from tax under subtitle A of the Code, such as municipal bonds, Panama Canal loan 3-percent bonds, or obligations of the United States, the interest on which is wholly exempt from tax under subtitle A, and which were issued after September 24, 1917, and not originally subscribed for by the taxpayer. Interest paid or accrued within the taxable year on indebtedness incurred or continued to purchase or carry (a) obligations of the United States issued after September 24, 1917, the interest on which is not wholly exempt from the taxes imposed under subtitle A of the Code, or (b) obligations of the United States issued after September 24, 1917, and originally subscribed for by the taxpayer, the interest on which is wholly exempt from the taxes imposed by subtitle A of the Code, is deductible. For rules as to the inclusion in gross income of interest on certain governmental obligations, see section 103 and the regulations thereunder.

(b) Special rule for certain financial institutions. *(1)* No deduction shall be disallowed, for taxable years ending after February 26, 1964, under section 265 (2) for interest paid or accrued by a financial institution which is a face-amount certificate company registered under the Investment Company Act of 1940 (15 U.S.C. 80a-1 and following) and which is subject to the banking laws of the State in which it is incorporated, on face-amount certificates (as defined in section 2(a)(15) of the Investment Company Act of 1940) issued by such institution and on amounts received for the purchase of such certificates to be issued by the institution, if the average amount of obligations, the interest on which is wholly exempt from the taxes imposed by subtitle A of the Code, held by such institution during the taxable year, does not exceed 15 percent of the average amount of the total assets of such institution during such year. See subparagraph (3) of this paragraph for treatment of interest paid or accrued on face-amount certificates where the figure is in excess of 15 percent. Interest expense other than that paid or accrued on face-amount certificates or on amounts received for the purchase of such certificates does not come within the rules of this paragraph.

(2) This subparagraph is prescribed under the authority granted the Secretary or his delegate under section 265(2) to prescribe regulations governing the determination of the average amount of tax-exempt obligations and of the total assets held during an institution's taxable year. The average amount of tax-exempt obligations held during an institution's taxable year shall be the average of the amounts of tax-exempt obligations held at the end of each month ending within such taxable year. The average amount of total assets for a taxable year shall be the average of the total assets determined at the beginning and end of the institution's taxable year. If the Commissioner, however, determines that any such amount is not fairly representative of the average amount of tax-exempt obligations or total assets, as the case may be, held by such institution during such taxable year, the Commissioner shall determine the amount which is fairly representative of the average amount of tax-exempt obligations or total assets, as the case may be. The percentage which the average amount of tax-exempt obligations is of the average amount of total assets is determined by dividing the average amount of tax-exempt obligations by the average amount of total assets, and multiplying by 100. The amount of tax-exempt obligations means that portion of the total assets of the institution which consists of obligations the interest on which is wholly exempt from tax under subtitle A of the Code, and valued at their adjusted basis, appropriately adjusted for amortization of premium or discount. Total assets means the sum of the money, plus the aggregate of the adjusted basis of the property other than money held by the taxpayer in good faith for the purpose of the business. Such adjusted basis for any asset is its adjusted basis for determining gain upon sale or exchange for Federal income tax purposes.

(3) If the percentage computation required by subparagraph (2) of this paragraph results in a figure in excess of 15 percent for the taxable year, there is interest that does not come within the special rule for certain financial institutions contained in section 265(2). The amount of such interest is obtained by multiplying the total interest paid or accrued for the taxable year on face-amount certificates and on amounts received for the purchase of such certificates by the percentage figure equal to the excess of the percentage figure computed under subparagraph (2) of this paragraph over 15 percent. See paragraph (a) for the disallowance of interest on indebtedness incurred or continued to purchase or carry obligations the interest on which is wholly exempt from tax under subtitle A of the Code.

(4) Every financial institution claiming the benefits of the special rule for certain financial institutions contained in section 265(2) shall file with its return for the taxable year:

(i) A statement showing that it is a face-amount certificate company registered under the Investment Company Act of 1940 (15 U.S.C. 80a-1 and following) and that it is subject to the banking laws of the State in which it is incorporated.

(ii) A detailed schedule showing the computation of the average amount of tax-exempt obligations, the average amount of total assets of such institution, and the total amount of interest paid or accrued on face-amount certificates and on amounts received for the purchase of such certificates for the taxable year.

T.D. 6313, 9/16/58, amend T.D. 6927, 9/18/67.

PAR. 2. In § 1.265-2, paragraph (c) is added to read as follows:

Proposed § 1.265-2 Interest relating to tax-exempt income. [*For Preamble, see ¶ 152,525*]

* * * * *

(c) Special rule for consolidated groups. *(1) Treatment of intercompany obligations.* (i) Direct tracing to nonmember indebtedness. If a member of a consolidated group incurs or continues indebtedness to a nonmember, that indebtedness is directly traceable to all or a portion of an intercompany obligation (as defined in § 1.1502-13(g)(2)(ii)) extended to a member of the group (B) by another member of the group (S), and section 265(a)(2) applies to disallow a deduction for all or a portion of B's interest expense incurred with respect to the intercompany obligation, then § 1.1502-13(c)(6)(i) will not apply to exclude an amount of S's interest income with respect to the intercompany obligation that equals the amount of B's disallowed interest deduction.

(ii) Limitation. The amount of interest income to which § 1.1502-13(c)(6)(i) will not apply as a result of the application of paragraph (c)(1)(i) of this section cannot exceed the interest expense on the portion of the indebtedness to the nonmember that is directly traceable to the intercompany obligation.

(2) Examples. The rules of this paragraph (c) are illustrated by the following examples. For purposes of these examples, unless otherwise stated, P and S are members of a consolidated group of which P is the common parent. P owns all of the outstanding stock of S. The taxable year of the P group is the calendar year and all members of the P group use the accrual method of accounting. L is a bank unrelated to any member of the consolidated group. All obligations are on the same terms and conditions, remain outstanding at the end of the applicable year, and provide for payments of interest on December 31 of each year that are greater than the appropriate applicable Federal rate (AFR). The examples are as follows:

Example (1). (i) Facts. On January 1, 2005, P borrows $100x from L and lends the entire $100x of borrowed proceeds to S. S uses the $100x of borrowed proceeds to purchase tax-exempt securities. P's indebtedness to L is directly traceable to the intercompany obligation between P and S. In addition, there is direct evidence that the proceeds of S's intercompany obligation to P were used to fund S's purchase or carrying of tax-exempt obligations. During the 2005 taxable year, P incurs $10x of interest expense on its loan from L, and S incurs $10x of interest expense on its loan from P. Under section 265(a)(2), the entire $10x of S's interest expense on the intercompany obligation to P is disallowed as a deduction.

(ii) Analysis. Because section 265(a)(2) permanently and explicitly disallows $10x of S's interest expense, ordinarily $10x of P's interest income on the intercompany obligation would be redetermined to be excluded from P's gross income under § 1.1502-13(c)(6)(i). However, under this paragraph (c), § 1.1502-13(c)(6)(i) will not apply to exclude P's interest income with respect to the intercompany obligation in an amount that equals S's disallowed interest deduction with respect to the intercompany obligation. Accordingly, § 1.1502-13(c)(6)(i) will not apply to exclude P's $10x of interest income on the intercompany obligation and P must include in income $10x of interest income from the intercompany obligation.

Example (2). (i) Facts. The facts are the same as in Example 1, except that P incurs only $8x of interest expense on its loan from L.

(ii) Analysis. Section 1.1502-13(c)(6)(i) will apply to exclude only a portion of P's $10x of interest income on the intercompany obligation. Under paragraph (c)(1)(ii) of this section, the amount of P's interest income that § 1.1502-13(c)(6)(i) will not apply to exclude is $8x, the total interest expense incurred by P on its indebtedness to L. Consequently, P must include in income $8x of interest income from the intercompany obligation and § 1.1502-13(c)(6)(i) will apply to exclude $2x of interest income from the intercompany obligation.

(3) Effective date. The provisions of this section shall apply to taxable years beginning on or after the date these regulations are published as final regulations in the Federal Register.

§ 1.265-3 Nondeductibility of interest relating to exempt-interest dividends

(a) In general. No deduction is allowed to a shareholder of a regulated investment company for interest on indebtedness that relates to exempt-interest dividends distributed by the company to the shareholder during the shareholder's taxable year.

(b) Interest relating to exempt-interest dividends. *(1)* All or a portion of the interest on an indebtedness relates to exempt-interest dividends if the indebtedness is either incurred or continued to purchase or carry shares of stock of a regulated investment company that distributes exempt-interest dividends (as defined in section 852(b)(5) of the Code) to the holder of the shares during the shareholder's taxable year.

(2) To determine the amount of interest that relates to the exempt-interest dividends the total amount of interest paid or accrued on the indebtedness is multiplied by a fraction. The numerator of the fraction is the amount of exempt-interest dividends received by the shareholder. The denominator of the fraction is the sum of the exempt-interest dividends and taxable dividends received by the shareholder (excluding capital gain dividends received by the shareholder and capital gains required to be included in the shareholder's computation of long-term capital gains under section 852(b)(3)(D)).

T.D. 7601, 3/15/79.

§ 1.266-1 Taxes and carrying charges chargeable to capital account and treated as capital items.

(a) *(1) In general.* In accordance with section 266, items enumerated in paragraph (b)(1) of this section may be capitalized at the election of the taxpayer. Thus, taxes and carrying charges with respect to property of the type described in this section are chargeable to capital account at the election of the taxpayer, notwithstanding that they are otherwise expressly deductible under provisions of subtitle A of the Code. No deduction is allowable for any items so treated.

(2) See §§ 1.263A-8 through 1.263A-15 for rules regarding the requirement to capitalize interest, that apply prior to the application of this section. After applying §§ 1.263A-8 through 1.263A-15, a taxpayer may elect to capitalize interest under section 266 with respect to designated property within the meaning of § 1.263A-8(b), provided a computation under any provision of the Internal Revenue Code is not thereby materially distorted, including computations relating to the source of deductions.

(b) Taxes and carrying charges. *(1)* The taxpayer may elect, as provided in paragraph (c) of this section, to treat the items enumerated in this subparagraph which are otherwise expressly deductible under the provisions of subtitle A of the Code as chargeable to capital account either as a component of original cost or other basis, for the purposes of section 1012, or as an adjustment to basis, for the purposes of section 1016(a)(1). The items thus chargeable to capital account are—

(i) In the case of unimproved and unproductive real property: Annual taxes, interest on a mortgage, and other carrying charges.

(ii) In the case of real property, whether improved or unimproved and whether productive or unproductive:

(a) Interest on a loan (but not theoretical interest of a taxpayer using his own funds),

(b) Taxes of the owner of such real property measured by compensation paid to his employees,

(c) Taxes of such owner imposed on the purchase of materials, or on the storage, use, or other consumption of materials, and

(d) Other necessary expenditures, paid or incurred for the development of the real property or for the construction of an improvement or additional improvement to such real property, up to the time the development or construction work has been completed. The development or construction work with respect to which such items are incurred may relate to unimproved and unproductive real estate whether the construction work will make the property productive of income subject to tax (as is the case of a factory) or not (as in the case of a personal residence), or may relate to property already improved or productive (as in the case of a plant addition or improvement, such as the construction of another floor on a factory or the installation of insulation therein).

(iii) In the case of personal property:

(a) Taxes of an employer measured by compensation for services rendered in transporting machinery or other fixed assets to the plant or installing them therein,

(b) Interest on a loan to purchase such property or to pay for transporting or installing the same, and

(c) Taxes of the owner thereof imposed on the purchase of such property or on the storage, use, or other consumption of such property,

paid or incurred up to the date of installation or the date when such property is first put into use by the taxpayer, whichever date is later.

(iv) Any other taxes and carrying charges with respect to property, otherwise deductible, which in the opinion of the

Commissioner are, under sound accounting principles, chargeable to capital account.

(2) The sole effect of section 266 is to permit the items enumerated in subparagraph (1) of this paragraph to be chargeable to capital account notwithstanding that such items are otherwise expressly deductible under the provisions of subtitle A of the Code. An item not otherwise deductible may not be capitalized under 266.

(3) In the absence of a provision in this section for treating a given item as a capital item, this section has no effect on the treatment otherwise accorded such item. Thus items which are otherwise deductible are deductible notwithstanding the provisions of this section, and items which are otherwise treated as capital items are to be so treated. Similarly, an item not otherwise deductible is not made deductible by this section. Nor is the absence of a provision in this section for treating a given item as a capital item to be construed as withdrawing or modifying the right now given to the taxpayer under any other provisions of subtitle A of the Code, or of the regulations thereunder, to elect to capitalize or to deduct a given item.

(c) Election to charge taxes and carrying charges to capital account. *(1)* If for any taxable year there are two or more items of the type described in paragraph (b)(1) of this section, which relate to the same project to which the election is applicable, the taxpayer may elect to capitalize any one or more of such items even though he does not elect to capitalize the remaining items or to capitalize items of the same type relating to other projects. However, if expenditures for several items of the same type are incurred with respect to a single project, the election to capitalize must, if exercised, be exercised as to all items of that type. For purposes of this section, a "project" means, in the case of items described in paragraph (b)(1)(ii) of this section, a particular development of, or construction of an improvement to, real property, and in the case of items described in paragraph (b)(1)(iii) of this section, the transportation and installation of machinery or other fixed assets.

(2) (i) An election with respect to an item described in paragraph (b)(1)(i) of this section is effective only for the year for which it is made.

(ii) An election with respect to an item described in—

(a) Paragraph (b)(1)(ii) of this section is effective until the development or construction work described in that subdivision has been completed;

(b) Paragraph (b)(1)(iii) of this section is effective until the later of either the date of installation of the property described in that subdivision, or the date when such property is first put into use by the taxpayer;

(c) Paragraph (b)(1)(iv) of this section is effective as determined by the Commissioner. Thus, an item chargeable to capital account under this section must continue to be capitalized for the entire period described in this subdivision applicable to such election although such period may consist of more than one taxable year.

(3) If the taxpayer elects to capitalize an item or items under this section, such election shall be exercised by filing with the original return for the year for which the election is made a statement indicating the item or items (whether with respect to the same project or to different projects) which the taxpayer elects to treat as chargeable to capital account. Elections filed for taxable years beginning before January 1, 1954, and for taxable years ending before August 17, 1954, under section 24(a)(7) of the Internal Revenue Code of 1939, and the regulations thereunder, shall have the same effect as if they were filed under this section. See section 7807(b)(2).

(d) The following examples are illustrative of the application of the provisions of this section:

Example (1). In 1956 and 1957 A pays annual taxes and interest on a mortgage on a piece of real property. During 1956, the property is vacant and unproductive, but throughout 1957 A operates the property as a parking lot. A may capitalize the taxes and mortgage interest paid in 1956, but not the taxes and mortgage interest paid in 1957.

Example (2). In February 1957, B began the erection of an office building for himself. B in 1957, in connection with the erection of the building, paid $6,000 social security taxes, which in his 1957 return he elected to capitalize. B must continue to capitalize the social security taxes paid in connection with the erection of the building until its completion.

Example (3). Assume the same facts as in example (2) except that in November 1957, B also begins to build a hotel. In 1957 B pays $3,000 social security taxes in connection with the erection of the hotel. B's election to capitalize the social security taxes paid in erecting the office building started in February 1957 does not bind him to capitalize the social security taxes paid in erecting the hotel; he may deduct the $3,000 social security taxes paid in erecting the hotel.

Example (4). In 1957, M Corporation began the erection of a building for itself, which will take three years to complete. M Corporation in 1957 paid $4,000 social security taxes and $8,000 interest on a building loan in connection with this building. M Corporation may elect to capitalize the social security taxes although it deducts the interest charges.

Example (5). C purchases machinery in 1957 for use in his factory. He pays social security taxes on the labor for transportation and installation of the machinery, as well as interest on a loan to obtain funds to pay for the machinery and for transportation and installation costs. C may capitalize either the social security taxes or the interest, or both, up to the date of installation or until the machinery is first put into use by him, whichever date is later.

(e) Allocation. If any tax or carrying charge with respect to property is in part a type of item described in paragraph (b) of this section and in part a type of item or items with respect to which no election to treat as a capital item is given, a reasonable proportion of such tax or carrying charge, determined in the light of all the facts and circumstances in each case, shall be allocated to each item. The rule of this paragraph may be illustrated by the following example:

Example. N Corporation, the owner of a factory in New York on which a new addition is under construction, in 1957 pays its general manager, B, a salary of $10,000 and also pays a New York State unemployment insurance tax of $81 on B's salary. B spends nine-tenths of his time in the general business of the firm and the remaining one-tenth in supervising the construction work. N Corporation treats as expenses $9,000 of B's salary, and charges the remaining $1,000 to capital account. N Corporation may elect to capitalize $8.10 of the $81 New York State unemployment insurance tax paid in 1957 since such tax is deductible under section 164.

T.D. 6313, 9/16/58, amend T.D. 6380, 5/26/59, T.D. 8584, 12/28/94.

§ 1.267(a)-1 Deductions disallowed.

Caution: The Treasury has not yet amended Reg § 1.267(a)-1 to reflect changes made by P.L. 100-647, P.L. 99-514, P.L. 98-369, P.L. 97-354, P.L. 95-628.

(a) Losses. Except in cases of distributions in corporate liquidations, no deduction shall be allowed for losses arising from direct or indirect sales or exchanges of property between persons who, on the date of the sale or exchange, are within any one of the relationships specified in section 267(b). See § 1.267(b)-1.

(b) Unpaid expenses and interest. *(1)* No deduction shall be allowed a taxpayer for trade or business expenses otherwise deductible under section 162, for expenses for production of income otherwise deductible under section 212, or for interest otherwise deductible under section 163—

(i) If, at the close of the taxpayer's taxable year within which such items are accrued by the taxpayer or at any time within 2½ months thereafter, both the taxpayer and the payee are persons within any one of the relationships specified in section 267(b) (see § 1.267(b)-1); and

(ii) If the payee is on the cash receipts and disbursements method of accounting with respect to such items of gross income for his taxable year in which or with which the taxable year of accrual by the debtor-taxpayer ends; and

(iii) If, within the taxpayer's taxable year within which such items are accrued by the taxpayer and 2½ months after the close thereof, the amount of such items is not paid and the amount of such items is not otherwise (under the rules of constructive receipt) includible in the gross income of the payee.

(2) The provisions of section 267(a)(2) and this paragraph do not otherwise affect the general rules governing the allowance of deductions under an accrual method of accounting. For example, if the accrued expenses or interest are paid after the deduction has become disallowed under section 267(a)(2), no deduction would be allowable for the taxable year in which payment is made, since an accrual item is deductible only in the taxable year in which it is properly accruable.

(3) The expenses and interest specified in section 267(a)(2) and this paragraph shall be considered as paid for purposes of that section to the extent of the fair market value on the date of issue of notes or other instruments of similar effect received in payment of such expenses or interest if such notes or other instruments were issued in such payment by the taxpayer within his taxable year or within 2½ months after the close thereof. The fair market value on the date of issue of such notes or other instruments of similar effect is includible in the gross income of the payee for the taxable year in which he receives the notes or other instruments.

(4) The provisions of this paragraph may be illustrated by the following example:

Example. A, an individual, is the holder and owner of an interest-bearing note of the M Corporation, all the stock of which was owned by him on December 31, 1956. A and the M Corporation make their income tax returns for a calendar year. The M Corporation uses an accrual method of accounting. A uses a combination of accounting methods permitted under section 446(c)(4) in which he uses the cash receipts and disbursements method in respect of items of gross income. The M Corporation does not pay any interest on the note to A during the calendar year 1956 or within 2½ months after the close of that year, nor does it credit any interest to A's account in such a manner that it is subject to his unqualified demand and thus is constructively received by him. M Corporation claims a deduction for the year 1956 for the interest accruing on the note in that year. Since A is on the cash receipts and disbursements method in respect of items of gross income, the interest is not includible in his return for the year 1956. Under the provisions of section 267(a)(2) and this paragraph, no deduction for such interest is allowable in computing the taxable income of the M Corporation for the taxable year 1956 or for any other taxable year. However, if the interest had actually been paid to A on or before March 15, 1957, or if it had been made available to A before that time (and thus had been constructively received by him), the M Corporation would be allowed to deduct the amount of the payment in computing its taxable income for 1956.

(c) Scope of section. Section 267(a) requires that deductions for losses or unpaid expenses or interest described therein be disallowed even though the transaction in which such losses, expenses, or interest were incurred was a bona fide transaction. However, section 267 is not exclusive. No deduction for losses or unpaid expenses or interest arising in a transaction which is not bona fide will be allowed even though section 267 does not apply to the transaction.

T.D. 6312, 9/10/58.

§ 1.267(a)-2T Temporary regulations; questions and answers arising under the Tax Reform Act of 1984 (temporary).

Caution: The Treasury has not yet amended Reg § 1.267(a)-2T to reflect changes made by P.L. 100-647, P.L. 99-514.

(a) Introduction. *(1) Scope.* This section prescribes temporary question and answer regulations under section 267(a) and related provisions as amended by section 174 of the Tax Reform Act of 1984, Pub. L. No. 98-369.

(2) Effective date. Except as otherwise provided by Answer 2 or Answer 3 in paragraph (c) of this section, the effective date set forth in section 174(c) of the Tax Reform Act of 1984 applies to this section.

(b) Questions applying section 267(a)(2) and (b) generally. The following questions and answers deal with the application of section 267(a)(2) and (b) generally:

Question 1: Does section 267(a)(2) ever apply to defer the deduction of an otherwise deductible amount if the person to whom the payment is to be made properly uses the completed contract method of accounting with respect to such amount?

Answer 1: No. Section 267(a)(2) applies only if an otherwise deductible amount is owed to a related person under whose method of accounting such amount is not includible in income unless paid to such person. Regardless of when payment is made, an amount owed to a contractor using the completed contract method of accounting is includible in the income of the contractor in accordance with § 1.451-3(d) in the year in which the contract is completed or in which certain disputes are resolved.

Question 2: Does section 267(a)(2) ever apply to defer the deduction of otherwise deductible original issue discount as defined in sections 163(e) and 1271 through 1275 ("the OID rules")?

Answer 2. No. Regardless of when payment is made, an amount owed to a lender that constitutes original issue discount is included in the income of the lender periodically in accordance with the OID rules. Similarly, section 267(a)(2) does not apply to defer an otherwise deductible amount to the extent section 467 or section 7872 requires periodic inclusion of such amount in the income of the person to whom payment is to be made, even though payment has not been made.

Question 3: Does section 267(a)(2) ever apply to defer the deduction of otherwise deductible unstated interest determined to exist under section 483?

Answer 3: Yes. If section 483 recharacterizes any amount as unstated interest and the other requirements of section 267(a)(2) are met, a deduction for such unstated interest will be deferred under section 267.

Question 4: Does section 267(a)(2) ever apply to defer the deduction of otherwise deductible cost recovery, depreciation, or amortization?

Answer 4: Yes, in certain cases. In general, section 267(a)(2) does not apply to defer the deduction of otherwise deductible cost recovery, depreciation, or amortization. Notwithstanding this general rule, if the other requirements of section 267(a)(2) are met, section 267(a)(2) does apply to defer deductions for cost recovery, depreciation, or amortization of an amount owed to a related person for interest or rent or for the performance or nonperformance of services, which amount the taxpayer payor capitalized or treated as a deferred expense (unless the taxpayer payor elected to capitalize or defer the amount and section 267(a)(2) would not have deferred the deduction of such amount if the taxpayer payor had not so elected). Amounts owed for services that may be subject to this provision include, for example, amounts owed for acquisition, development, or organizational services or for covenants not to compete. In applying this rule, payments made between persons described in any of the paragraphs of section 267(b) (as modified by section 267(3)) will be closely scrutinized to determine whether they are made in respect of capitalized costs (or costs treated as deferred expenses) that are subject to deferral under section 267(a)(2), or in respect of other capitalized costs not so subject.

Question 5: If a deduction in respect of an otherwise deductible amount is deferred by section 267(a)(2) and, prior to the time the amount is includible in the gross income of the person to whom payment is to be made, such person and the payor taxpayer cease to be persons specified in any of the paragraphs of section 267(b) (as modified by section 267(e)), is the deduction allowable as of the day on which the relationship ceases?

Answer 5: No. The deduction is not allowable until the day as of which the amount is includible in the gross income of the person to whom payment of the amount is made, even though the relationship ceases to exist at an earlier time.

Question 6: Do references in other sections to persons described in section 267(b) incorporate changes made to section 267(b) by section 174 of the Tax Reform Act of 1984?

Answer 6: Yes. References in other sections to persons described in section 267(b) take into account changes made to section 267(b) by section 174 of the Tax Reform Act of 1984 (without modification by section 267(e)(1)). For example, a transfer after December 31, 1983 (the effective date of the new section 267(b)(3) relationship added by the Tax Reform Act of 1984) of section 1245 class property placed in service before January 1, 1981, from one corporation to another corporation, 11 percent of the stock of which is owned by the first corporation, will not constitute recovery property (as defined in section 168) in the hands of the second corporation by reason of section 168(e)(4)(A)(i) and (D).

(c) Questions applying section 267(a) to partnerships. The following questions and answers deal with the application of section 267(a) to partnerships:

Question 1: Does section 267(a) disallow losses and defer otherwise deductible amounts at the partnership (entity) level?

Answer 1: Yes. If a loss realized by a partnership from a sale or exchange of property is disallowed under section 267(a)(1), that loss shall not enter into the computation of the partnership's taxable income. If an amount that otherwise would be deductible by a partnership is deferred by section 267(a)(2), that amount shall not enter into the computation of the partnership's taxable income until the taxable year of the partnership in which falls the day on which the amount is includible in the gross income of the person to whom payment of the amount is made.

Question 2: Does section 267(a)(1) ever apply to disallow a loss if the sale or exchange giving rise to the loss is between two partnerships even though the two partnerships are not persons specified in any of the paragraphs of section 267(b)?

Answer 2: Yes. If the other requirements of section 267(a)(1) are met, section 267(a)(1) applies to such losses arising as a result of transactions entered into after December 31, 1984 between partnerships not described in any of the paragraphs of section 267(b) as follows, and § 1.267(b)-1(b) does not apply. If the two partnerships have one or more common partners (i.e., if any person owns directly, indirectly, or constructively any capital or profits interest in each of such partnerships), or if any partner in either partnership and one or more partners in the other partnership are persons specified in any of the paragraphs of section 267(b) (without modification by section 267(e)), a portion of the selling partnership's loss will be disallowed under section 267(a)(1). The amount disallowed under this rule is the greater of: (1) The amount that would be disallowed if the transaction giving rise to the loss had occurred between the selling partnership and the separate partners of the purchasing partnership (in proportion to their respective interests in the purchasing partnership); or (2) the amount that would be disallowed if such transaction had occurred between the separate partners of the selling partnership (in proportion to their respective interests in the selling partnership) and the purchasing partnership. Notwithstanding the general rule of this paragraph (c) Answer 2, no disallowance shall occur if the amount that would be disallowed pursuant to the immediately preceding sentence is less than 5 percent of the loss arising from the sale or exchange.

Question 3: Does section 267(a)(2) ever apply to defer an otherwise deductible amount if the taxpayer payor is a partnership and the person to whom payment of such amount is to be made is a partnership even though the two partnerships are not persons specified in any of the paragraphs of section 267(b) (as modified by section 267(e))?

Answer 3: Yes. If the other requirements of section 267(a)(2) are met, section 267(a)(2) applies to such amounts arising as a result of transactions entered into after December 31, 1984 between partnerships not described in any of the paragraphs of section 267(b) (as modified by section 267(e)) as follows, and § 1.267(b)-1(b) does not apply. If the two partnerships have one or more common partners (i.e., if any person owns directly, indirectly, or constructively any capital or profits interest in each of such partnerships), or if any partner in either partnership and one or more partners in the other partnership are persons specified in any of the paragraphs of section 267(b) (without modification by section 267(e)), a portion of the payor partnership's otherwise allowable deduction will be deferred under section 267(a)(2). The amount deferred under this rule is the greater of: (1) The amount that would be deferred if the transaction giving rise to the otherwise allowable deduction had occurred between the payor partnership and the separate partners of the payee partnership (in proportion to their respective interests in the payee partnership); or (2) the amount that would be deferred if such transaction had occurred between the separate partners of the payor partnership (in proportion to their respective interests in the payor partnership) and the payee partnership. Notwithstanding the general rule of this paragraph (c) Answer 3, no deferral shall occur if the amount that would be deferred pursuant to the immediately preceding sentence is less than 5 percent of the otherwise allowable deduction.

Example. On May 1, 1985, partnership AB enters into a transaction whereby it accrues an otherwise deductible amount to partnership AC, AC is on the cash receipts and disbursements method of accounting. A holds a 5 percent capital and profits interest in AB and a 49 percent capital and profits interest in AC, and A's interest in each item of the income, gain, loss, deduction, and credit of each partnership is 5 percent and 49 percent, respectively. B and C are not related. Notwithstanding that AB and AC are not persons specified in section 267(b), 49 percent of the deduction in respect of such amount will be deferred under section 267(a)(2). The result would be the same if A held a 49 percent interest in AB and a 5 percent interest in AC. However, if A held more than 50 percent of the capital or profits interest of either AB or AC, the entire deduction in respect of such amount would be deferred under section 267(a)(2).

Question 4: What does the phrase "incurred at an annual rate not in excess of 12 percent" mean as used in section 267(e)(5)(C)(ii)?

Answer 4: The phrase refers to interest that accrues but is not includible in the income of the person to whom payment is to be made during the taxable year of the payor. Thus, in determining whether the requirements of section 267(e)(5) (providing an exception to certain provisions of section 267 for certain expenses and interest of partnerships owning low income housing) are met with respect to a transaction, the requirement of section 267(e)(5)(C)(ii) will be satisfied, even though the total interest (both stated and unstated) paid or accrued in any taxable year of the payor taxpayer exceeds 12 percent, if the interest in excess of 12 percent per annum, compounded semi-annually, on the outstanding loan balance (principal and accrued but unpaid interest) is includible in the income of the person to whom payment is to be made no later than the last day of such taxable year of the payor taxpayer.

T.D. 7991, 11/29/84.

---

§ 1.267(a)-3 Deduction of amounts owed to related foreign persons.

Caution: The Treasury has not yet amended Reg § 1.267(a)-3 to reflect changes made by P.L. 108-357.

(a) Purpose and scope. This section provides rules under section 267(a)(2) and (3) governing when an amount owed to a related foreign person that is otherwise deductible under Chapter 1 may be deducted. Paragraph (b) of this section provides the general rules, and paragraph (c) of this section provides exceptions and special rules.

(b) Deduction of amount owed to related foreign person. *(1) In general.* Except as provided in paragraph (c) of this section, section 267(a)(3) requires a taxpayer to use the cash method of accounting with respect to the deduction of amounts owed to a related foreign person. An amount that is owed to a related foreign person and that is otherwise deductible under Chapter 1 thus may not be deducted by the taxpayer until such amount is paid to the related foreign person. For purposes of this section, a related foreign person is any person that is not a United States person within the meaning of section 7701(a)(30), and that is related (within the meaning of section 267(b)) to the taxpayer at the close of the taxable year in which the amount incurred by the taxpayer would otherwise be deductible. Section 267(f) defines "controlled group" for purposes of section 267(b) without regard to the limitations of section 1563(b). An amount is treated as paid for purposes of this section if the amount is considered paid for purposes of section 1441 or section 1442 (including an amount taken into account pursuant to section 884(f)).

(2) Amounts covered. This section applies to otherwise deductible amounts that are of a type described in section 871(a)(1)(A), (B) or (D), or in section 881(a)(1), (2) or (4). The rules of this section also apply to interest that is from sources outside the United States. Amounts other than interest that are from sources outside the United States, and that are not income of a related foreign person effectively connected with the conduct by such related foreign person of a trade or business within the United States, are not subject to the rules of section 267(a)(2) or (3) or this section. See paragraph (c) of this section for rules governing the treatment of amounts that are income of a related foreign person effectively connected with the conduct of a trade or business within the United States by such related foreign person.

(3) Change in method of accounting. A taxpayer that uses a method of accounting other than that required by the rules of this section must change its method of accounting to conform its method to the rules of this section. The taxpayer's change in method must be made pursuant to the rules of section 446(e), the regulations thereunder, and any applicable administrative procedures prescribed by the Commissioner. Because the rules of this section prescribe a method of accounting, these rules apply in the determination of a taxpayer's earnings and profits pursuant to § 1.1312-6(a).

(4) Examples. The provisions of this paragraph (b) may be illustrated by the following examples:

Example (1). (i) FC, a corporation incorporated in Country X, owns 100 percent of the stock of C, a domestic corporation. C uses the accrual method of accounting in computing its income and deductions, and is a calendar year taxpayer. In Year 1, C accrues an amount owed to FC for interest. C makes an actual payment of the amount owed to FC in Year 2.

(ii) Regardless of its source, the interest owed to FC is an amount to which this section applies. Pursuant to the rules of this paragraph (b), the amount owed to FC by C will not be allowable as a deduction in Year 1. Section 267 does not preclude the deduction of this amount in Year 2.

Example (2). (i) RS, a domestic corporation, is the sole shareholder of FSC, a foreign sales corporation. Both RS and FSC use the accrual method of accounting. In Year 1, RS accrues $z owed to FSC for commissions earned by FSC in Year 1. Pursuant to the foreign sales company provisions, sections 921 through 927, a portion of this amount, $x, is treated as effectively connected income of FSC from sources outside the United States. Accordingly, the rules of section 267(a)(3) and paragraph (b) of this section do not apply. See paragraph (c) of this section for the rules governing the treatment of amounts that are effectively connected income of FSC.

(ii) The remaining amount of the commission, $y, is classified as exempt foreign trade income under section 923(a)(3) and is treated as income of FSC from sources outside the United States that is not effectively connected income. This amount is one to which the provisions of this section do not apply, since it is an amount other than interest from sources outside the United States and is not effectively connected income. Therefore, a deduction for $y is allowable to RS as of the day on which it accrues the otherwise deductible amount, without regard to section 267(a)(2) and (a)(3) and the regulations thereunder.

(c) Exceptions and special rules. *(1) Effectively connected income subject to United States tax.* The provisions of section 267(a)(2) and the regulations thereunder, and not the provisions of paragraph (b) of this section, apply to an amount that is income of the related foreign person that is effectively connected with the conduct of a United States trade or business of such related foreign person. An amount described in this paragraph (c)(1) thus is allowable as a deduction as of the day on which the amount is includible in the gross income of the related foreign person as effectively connected income under sections 872(a)(2) or 882(b) (or, if later, as of the day on which the deduction would be so allowable but for section 267(a)(2)). However, this paragraph (c)(1) does not apply if the related foreign person is exempt from United States income tax on the amount owed, or is subject to a reduced rate of tax, pursuant to a treaty obligation of the United States (such as under an article relating to the taxation of business profits).

(2) Items exempt from tax by treaty. Except with respect to interest, neither paragraph (b) of this section nor section 267(a)(2) or (a)(3) applies to any amount that is income of a related foreign person with respect to which the related foreign person is exempt from United States taxation on the amount owed pursuant to a treaty obligation of the United States (such as under an article relating to the taxation of business profits). Interest that is effectively connected income of the related foreign person under sections 872(a)(2) or 882(b) is an amount covered by paragraph (c)(1) of this section. Interest that is not effectively connected income of the related foreign person is an amount covered by paragraph (b) of this section, regardless of whether the related foreign person is exempt from United States taxation on the amount owed pursuant to a treaty obligation of the United States.

(3) Items subject to reduced rate of tax by treaty. Paragraph (b) of this section applies to amounts that are income of a related foreign person with respect to which the related foreign person claims a reduced rate of United States income tax on the amount owed pursuant to a treaty obligation of the United States (such as under an article relating to the taxation of royalties).

(4) Amounts owed to a foreign personal holding company, controlled foreign corporation, or passive foreign investment company. (i) Foreign personal holding companies. If an amount to which paragraph (b) of this section otherwise applies is owed to a related foreign person that is a foreign personal holding company within the meaning of section 552, then the amount is allowable as a deduction as of the day on which the amount is includible in the income of the foreign personal holding company. The day on which the amount is includible in income is determined with reference to the method of accounting under which the foreign personal holding company computes its taxable income and earnings and profits for purposes of sections 551 through 558. See section 551(c) and the regulations thereunder for the reporting requirements of the foreign personal holding company provisions (sections 551 through 558).

(ii) Controlled foreign corporations. If an amount to which paragraph (b) of this section otherwise applies is owed to a related foreign person that is a controlled foreign corporation within the meaning of section 957, then the amount is allowable as a deduction as of the day on which the amount is includible in the income of the controlled foreign corporation. The day on which the amount is includible in income is determined with reference to the method of accounting under which the controlled foreign corporation computes its taxable income and earnings and profits for purposes of sections 951 through 964. See section 6038 and the regulations thereunder for the reporting requirements of the controlled foreign corporation provisions (sections 951 through 964).

(iii) Passive foreign investment companies. If an amount to which paragraph (b) of this section otherwise applies is owed to a related foreign person that is a passive foreign investment company within the meaning of section 1296, then the amount is allowable as a deduction as of the day on which amount is includible in the income of the passive foreign investment company. The day on which the amount is includible in income is determined with reference to the method of accounting under which the earnings and profits of the passive foreign investment company are computed for purposes of sections 1291 through 1297. See sections 1291 through 1297 and the regulations thereunder for the reporting requirements of the passive foreign investment company provisions. This exception shall apply, however, only if the person that owes the amount at issue has made and has in effect an election pursuant to section 1295 with respect to the passive foreign investment company to which the amount at issue is owed.

(iv) Examples. The rules of this paragraph (c)(4) may be illustrated by the following examples. Application of the provisions of sections 951 through 964 are provided for illustration only, and do not provide substantive rules concerning the operation of those provisions. The principles of these examples apply equally to the provisions of paragraphs (c)(4)(i) through (iii) of this section.

Example (1). P, a domestic corporation, owns 100 percent of the total combined voting power and value of the stock of both FC1 and FC2. P is a calendar year taxpayer that uses the accrual method of accounting in computing its income and deductions. FC1 is incorporated in Country X, and FC2 is incorporated in Country Y. FC1 and FC2 are controlled foreign corporations within the meaning of section 957, and are both calendar year taxpayers. FC1 computes its taxable income and earnings and profits, for purposes of sections 951 through 964, using the accrual method of accounting, while FC2 uses the cash method. In Year 1 FC1 has gross income of $10,000 that is described in section 952(a) ("subpart F income"), and which includes interest owed to FC1 by P that is described in paragraph (b) of this section and that is otherwise allowable as a deduction to P under chapter 1. The interest owed to FC1 is allowable as a deduction to P in Year 1.

Example (2). The facts are the same as in Example 1, except that in Year 1 FC1 reports no subpart F income because of the application of section 954(b)(3)(A) (the subpart F de minimus rule). Because the amount owed to FC1 by P is includible in FC1's gross income in Year 1, the interest owed to FC1 is allowable as a deduction to P in Year 1.

Example (3). The facts are the same as in Example 1. In Year 1, FC1 accrues interest owed to FC2 that would be allowable as a deduction by FC1 under chapter 1 if FC1 were a domestic corporation. The interest owed to FC2 by FC1 is paid by FC1 in Year 2. Because FC2 uses the cash method of accounting in computing its taxable income for purposes of subpart F, the interest owed by FC1 is allowable as a deduction by FC1 in Year 2, and not in Year 1.

(d) Effective date. The rules of this section are effective with respect to interest that is allowable as a deduction under chapter 1 (without regard to the rules of this section) in taxable years beginning after December 31, 1983, but are not effective with respect to interest that is incurred with respect to indebtedness incurred on or before September 29, 1983, or incurred after that date pursuant to a contract that was binding on that date and at all times thereafter (unless the indebtedness or the contract was renegotiated, extended, renewed, or revised after that date). The regulations in this section issued under section 267 apply to all other deductible amounts that are incurred after July 31, 1989, but do not apply to amounts that are incurred pursuant to a contract that was binding on September 29, 1983 and at all times thereafter (unless the contract was renegotiated, extended, renewed, or revised after that date).

T.D. 8465, 12/31/92.

§ 1.267(b)-1 Relationships.

Caution: The Treasury has not yet amended Reg § 1.267(b)-1 to reflect changes made by P.L. 105-34, P.L. 99-514, P.L. 98-369, P.L. 97-354, P.L. 95-628.

(a) In general. *(1)* The persons referred to in section 267(a) and § 1.267(a)-1 are specified in section 267(b).

(2) Under section 267(b)(3), it is not necessary that either of the two corporations be a personal holding company or a foreign personal holding company for the taxable year in which the sale or exchange occurs or in which the expenses or interest are properly accruable, but either one of them must be such a company for the taxable year next preceding the taxable year in which the sale or exchange occurs or in which the expenses or interest are accrued.

(3) Under section 267(b)(9), the control of certain educational and charitable organizations exempt from tax under section 501 includes any kind of control, direct or indirect, by means of which a person in fact controls such an organization, whether or not the control is legally enforceable and regardless of the method by which the control is exercised or exercisable. In the case of an individual, control possessed by the individual's family, as defined in section 267(c)(4) and paragraph (a)(4) of § 1.267(c)-1, shall be taken into account.

(b) Partnerships. *(1)* Since section 267 does not include members of a partnership and the partnership as related persons, transactions between partners and partnerships do not come within the scope of section 267. Such transactions are governed by section 707 for the purposes of which the partnership is considered to be an entity separate from the partners. See section 707 and § 1.707-1. Any transaction described in section 267(a) between a partnership and a person other than a partner shall be considered as occurring between the other person and the members of the partnership separately. Therefore, if the other person and a partner are within any one of the relationships specified in section 267(b), no deductions with respect to such transactions between the other person and the partnership shall be allowed—

(i) To the related partner to the extent of his distributive share of partnership deductions for losses or unpaid expenses or interest resulting from such transactions, and

(ii) To the other person to the extent the related partner acquires an interest in any property sold to or exchanged with the partnership by such other person at a loss, or to the extent of the related partner's distributive share of the unpaid expenses or interest payable to the partnership by the other person as a result of such transaction.

(2) The provisions of this paragraph may be illustrated by the following examples:

Example (1). A, an equal partner in the ABC partnership, personally owns all the stock of M Corporation. B and C are not related to A. The partnership and all the partners use an accrual method of accounting, and are on a calendar year. M Corporation uses the cash receipts and disbursements method of accounting and is also on a calendar year. During 1956 the partnership borrowed money from M Corporation and also sold property to M Corporation, sustaining a loss on the sale. On December 31, 1956, the partnership accrued its interest liability to the M Corporation and on April 1, 1957 (more than 2½ months after the close of its taxable year), it paid the M Corporation the amount of such accrued interest. Applying the rules of this paragraph, the transactions are considered as occurring between M Corporation and the partners separately. The sale and interest transactions considered as occurring between A and the M Corporation fall within the scope of section 267(a) and (b), but the transactions considered as occurring between partners B and C and the M Corporation do not. The latter two partners may, therefore, deduct their distributive shares of partnership deductions for the loss and the accrued interest. However, no deduction shall be allowed to A for his distributive shares of these partnership deductions. Furthermore, A's adjusted basis for his partnership interest must be decreased by the amount of his distributive share of such deductions. See section 705(a)(2).

Example (2). Assume the same facts as in example (1) of this subparagraph except that the partnership and all the partners use the cash receipts and disbursements method of accounting, and that M Corporation uses an accrual method. Assume further, that during 1956 M Corporation borrowed money from the partnership and that on a sale of property to the partnership during that year M Corporation sustained a loss. On December 31, 1956, the M Corporation accrued its interest liability on the borrowed money and on April 1, 1957 (more than 2½ months after the close of its taxable year) it paid the accrued interest to the partnership. The corporation's deduction for the accrued interest it not allowed to the extent of A's distributive share (one-third) of such interest income. M Corporation's deduction for the loss on the sale of the property to the partnership is not allowed to the extent of A's one-third interest in the purchased property.

T.D. 6312, 9/10/58.

§ 1.267(c)-1 Constructive ownership of stock.

(a) In general. *(1)* The determination of stock ownership for purposes of section 267(b) shall be in accordance with the rules in section 267(c).

(2) For an individual to be considered under section 267(c)(2) as constructively owning the stock of a corporation which is owned, directly or indirectly, by or for members of his family it is not necessary that he own stock in the corporation either directly or indirectly. On the other hand, for an individual to be considered under section 267(c)(3) as owning the stock of a corporation owned either actually, or constructively under section 267(c)(1), by or for his partner, such individual must himself actually own, or constructively own under section 267(c)(1), stock of such corporation.

(3) An individual's constructive ownership, under section 267(c)(2) or (3), of stock owned directly or indirectly by or for a member of his family, or by or for his partner, is not to be considered as actual ownership of such stock, and the individual's constructive ownership of the stock is not to be attributed to another member of his family or to another partner. However, an individual's constructive ownership, under section 267(c)(1), of stock owned directly or indirectly by or for a corporation, partnership, estate, or trust shall be considered as actual ownership of the stock, and the individual's ownership may be attributed to a member of his family or to his partner.

(4) The family of an individual shall include only his brothers and sisters, spouse, ancestors, and lineal descendants. In determining whether any of these relationships exist, full effect shall be given to a legal adoption. The term "ancestors" includes parents and grandparents, and the term "lineal descendants" includes children and grandchildren.

(b) Examples. The application of section 267(c) may be illustrated by the following examples:

Example (1). On July 1, 1957, A owned 75 percent, and AW, his wife, owned 25 percent, of the outstanding stock of the M Corporation. The M Corporation in turn owned 80 percent of the outstanding stock of the O Corporation. Under section 267(c)(1), A and AW are each considered as owning an amount of the O Corporation stock actually owned by M Corporation in proportion to their respective ownership of M Corporation stock. Therefore, A constructively owns 60 percent (75 percent of 80 percent) of the O Corporation stock and AW constructively owns 20 percent (25 percent of 80 percent) of such stock. Under the family ownership rule of section 267(c)(2), an individual is considered as constructively owning the stock actually owned by his spouse. A and AW, therefore, are each considered as constructively owning the M Corporation stock actually owned by the other. For the purpose of applying this family ownership rule, A's and AW's constructive ownership of O Corporation stock is considered as actual ownership under section 267(c)(5). Thus, A constructively owns the 20 percent of the O Corporation stock constructively owned by AW, and AW constructively owns the 60 percent of the O Corporation stock constructively owned by A. In addition, the family ownership rule may be applied to make AWF, AW's father, the constructive owner of the 25 percent of the M Corporation stock actually owned by AW. As noted above, AW's constructive ownership of 20 percent of the O Corporation stock is considered as actual ownership for purposes of applying the family ownership rule, and AWF is thereby considered the constructive owner of this stock also. However, AW's constructive ownership of the stock constructively and actually owned by A may not be considered as actual ownership for the purpose of again applying the family ownership rule to make AWF the constructive owner of these shares. The ownership of the stock in the M and O Corporations may be tabulated as follows:

Person	Stock ownership in M Corporation		Total under Section 267	Stock ownership in O Corporation		Total under Section 267
	Actual	Constructive		Actual	Constructive	
	Percent	Percent	Percent	Percent	Percent	Percent
A	75	25	100	None	60 20	80
AW (A's wife)	25	75	100	None	20 60	80
AWF (AW's father)	None	25	25	None	20	20
M Corporation				80	None	80
O Corporation	None	None	None			

Assuming that the M Corporation and the O Corporation make their income tax returns for calendar years, and that there was no distribution in liquidation of the M or O Corporation, and further assuming that either corporation was a personal holding company under section 542 for the calendar year 1956, no deduction is allowable with respect to losses from sales or exchanges of property made on July 1, 1957, between the two corporations. Moreover, whether or not either corporation was a personal holding company, no loss would be allowable on a sale or exchange between A or AW and either corporation. A deduction would be allowed, however, for a loss sustained in an arm's length sale or exchange between A and AWF, and between AWF and the M or O Corporation.

Example (2). On June 15, 1957, all of the stock of the N Corporation was owned in equal proportions by A and his partner, AP. Except in the case of distributions in liquidation by the N Corporation, no deduction is allowable with respect to losses from sales or exchanges of property made on June 15, 1957, between A and the N Corporation or AP and the N Corporation since each partner is considered as owning the stock owned by the other; therefore, each is considered as owning more than 50 percent in value of the outstanding stock of the N Corporation.

Example (3). On June 7, 1957, A owned no stock in X Corporation, but his wife, AW, owned 20 percent in value of the outstanding stock of X, and A's partner, AP, owned 60 percent in value of the outstanding stock of X. The partnership firm of A and AP owned no stock in X Corporation. The ownership of AW's stock is attributed to A, but not that of AP since A does not own any X Corporation stock either actually, or constructively under section 267(c)(1). A's constructive ownership of AW's stock is not the ownership required for the attribution of AP's stock. Therefore, deductions for losses from sales or exchanges of property made on June 7, 1957, between X Corporation and A or AW are allowable since neither person owned more than 50 percent in value of the outstanding stock of X, but deductions for losses from sales or exchanges between X Corporation and AP would not be allowable by section 267(a) (except for distributions in liquidation of X Corporation).

T.D. 6312, 9/10/58.

§ 1.267(d)-1 Amount of gain where loss previously disallowed.

(a) General rule. *(1)* If a taxpayer acquires property by purchase or exchange from a transferor who, on the transaction, sustained a loss not allowable as a deduction by reason of section 267(a)(1) (or by reason of section 24(b) of the Internal Revenue Code of 1939), then any gain realized by the taxpayer on a sale or other disposition of the property after December 31, 1953, shall be recognized only to the extent that the gain exceeds the amount of such loss as is properly allocable to the property sold or otherwise disposed of by the taxpayer.

(2) The general rule is also applicable to a sale or other disposition of property by a taxpayer when the basis of such property in the taxpayer's hands is determined directly or indirectly by reference to other property acquired by the taxpayer from a transferor through a sale or exchange in which a loss sustained by the transferor was not allowable. Therefore, section 267(d) applies to a sale or other disposition of property after a series of transactions if the basis of the property acquired in each transaction is determined by reference to the basis of the property transferred, and if the original property was acquired in a transaction in which a loss to a transferor was not allowable by reason of section 267(a)(1) (or by reason of section 24(b) of the Internal Revenue Code of 1939).

(3) The benefit of the general rule is available only to the original transferee but does not apply to any original transferee (e.g., a donee) who acquired the property in any manner other than by purchase or exchange.

(4) The application of the provisions of this paragraph may be illustrated by the following examples:

Example (1). H sells to his wife, W, for $500, certain corporate stock with an adjusted basis for determining loss to him of $800. The loss of $300 is not allowable to H by reason of section 267(a)(1) and paragraph (a) of § 1.267(a)-1. W later sells this stock for $1,000. Although W's realized gain is $500 ($1,000 minus $500, her basis), her recognized gain under section 267(d) is only $200, the excess of the realized gain of $500 over the loss of $300 not allowable to H. In determining capital gain or loss W's holding period commences on the date of the sale from H to W.

Example (2). Assume the same facts as in example (1) except that W later sells her stock for $300 instead of $1,000. Her recognized loss is $200 and not $500 since section 267(d) applies only to the nonrecognition of gain and does not affect basis.

Example (3). Assume the same facts as in example (1) except that W transfers her stock as a gift to X. The basis of the stock in the hands of X for the purpose of determining gain, under the provisions of section 1015, is the same as W's, or $500. If X later sells the stock for $1,000 the entire $500 gain is taxed to him.

Example (4). H sells to his wife, W, for $5,500, farmland, with an adjusted basis for determining loss to him of $8,000. The loss of $2,500 is not allowable to H by reason of section 267(a)(1) and paragraph (a) of § 1.267(a)-1. W exchanges the farmland, held for investment purposes, with S, an unrelated individual, for two city lots, also held for investment purposes. The basis of the city lots in the hands of W ($5,500) is a substituted basis determined under section 1031(d) by reference to the basis of the farmland. Later W sells the city lots for $10,000. Although W's realized gain is $4,500 ($10,000 minus $5,500), her recognized gain under section 267(d) is only $2,000, the excess of the realized gain of $4,500 over the loss of $2,500 not allowable to H.

(b) Determination of basis and gain with respect to divisible property. *(1) Taxpayer's basis.* When the taxpayer acquires divisible property or property that consists of several items or classes of items by a purchase or exchange on which loss is not allowable to the transferor, the basis in the taxpayer's hands of a particular part, item, or class of such property shall be determined (if the taxpayer's basis for that part is not known) by allocating to the particular part, item, or class a portion of the taxpayer's basis for the entire property in the proportion that the fair market value of the particular part, item, or class bears to the fair market value of the entire property at the time of the taxpayer's acquisition of the property.

(2) Taxpayer's recognized gain. Gain realized by the taxpayer on sales or other dispositions after December 31, 1953, of a part, item, or class of the property shall be recognized only to the extent that such gain exceeds the amount of loss attributable to such part, item, or class of property not allowable to the taxpayer's transferor on the latter's sale or exchange of such property to the taxpayer.

(3) Transferor's loss not allowable. (i) The transferor's loss on the sale or exchange of a part, item, or class of the property to the taxpayer shall be the excess of the transferor's adjusted basis for determining loss on the part, item, or class of the property over the amount realized by the transferor on the sale or exchange of the part, item, or class. The amount realized by the transferor on the part, item, or class shall be determined (if such amount is not known) in the same manner that the taxpayer's basis for such part, item, or class is determined. See subparagraph (1) of this paragraph.

(ii) If the transferor's basis for determining loss on the part, item, or class cannot be determined, the transferor's loss on the particular part, item, or class transferred to the taxpayer shall be determined by allocating to the part, item, or class a portion of his loss on the entire property in the proportion that the fair market value of such part, item, or class bears to the fair market value of the entire property on the date of the taxpayer's acquisition of the entire property.

(4) Examples. The application of the provisions of this paragraph may be illustrated by the following examples:

Example (1). During 1953, H sold class A stock which had cost him $1,100, and common stock which had cost him $2,000, to his wife W for a lump sum of $1,500. Under section 24(b)(1)(A) of the 1939 Code, the loss of $1,600 on the transaction was not allowable to H. At the time the stocks were purchased by W, the fair market value of class A stock was $900 and the fair market value of common stock was $600. In 1954, W sold the class A stock for $2,500. W's recognized gain is determined as follows:

Amount realized by W on sale of class A stock		$2,500
Less: Basis allocated to class A stock— $900/$1,500 × $1,500		900
Realized gain on transaction		1,600
Less: Loss sustained by H on sale of class A stock to W not allowable as a deduction:		
Basis to H of class A stock	$1,100	
Amount realized by H on class A stock—$900/$1,500 × $1,500	900	
Unallowable loss to H on sale of class A stock		200
Recognized gain on sale of class A stock by W		1,400

Example (2). Assume the same facts as those stated in example (1) of this subparagraph except that H originally purchased both classes of stock for a lump sum of $3,100. The unallowable loss to H on the sale of all the stock to W is $1,600 ($3,100 minus $1,500). An exact determination of the unallowable loss sustained by H on sale to W of class A stock cannot be made because H's basis for class A stock cannot be determined. Therefore, a determination of the unallowable loss is made by allocating to class A stock a portion of H's loss on the entire property transferred to W in the proportion that the fair market value of class A stock at the time acquired by W ($900) bears to the fair market value of both classes of stock at that time ($1,500). The allocated portion is $900/$1,500 × $1,600, or $960. W's recognized gain is, therefore, $640 (W's realized gain of $1,600 minus $960).

(c) Special rules. *(1)* Section 267(d) does not affect the basis of property for determining gain. Depreciation and other items which depend on such basis are also not affected.

(2) The provisions of section 267(d) shall not apply if the loss sustained by the transferor is not allowable to the transferor as a deduction by reason of section 1091, or section 118 of the Internal Revenue Code of 1939, which relate to losses from wash sales of stock or securities.

(3) In determining the holding period in the hands of the transferee of property received in an exchange with a transferor with respect to whom a loss on the exchange is not allowable by reason of section 267, section 1223(2) does not apply to include the period during which the property was held by the transferor. In determining such holding period, however, section 1223(1) may apply to include the period during which the transferee held the property which he exchanged where, for example, he exchanged a capital asset in a transaction which, as to him, was nontaxable under section 1031 and the property received in the exchange has the same basis as the property exchanged.

T.D. 6312, 9/10/58.

§ 1.267(d)-2 Effective date; taxable years subject to the Internal Revenue Code of 1939.

Caution: The Treasury has not yet amended Reg § 1.267(d)-2 to reflect changes made by P.L. 100-647, P.L. 99-514, P.L. 98-369, P.L. 97-354, P.L. 95-628.

Pursuant to section 7851(a)(1)(C), the regulations prescribed in § 1.267(d)-1, to the extent that they relate to determination of gain resulting from the sale or other disposition of property after December 31, 1953, with respect to which property a loss was not allowable to the transferor by reason of section 267(a)(1) (or by reason of section 24(b) of the Internal Revenue Code of 1939), shall also apply to taxable years beginning before January 1, 1954, and ending after December 31, 1953, and taxable years beginning after December 31, 1953, and ending before August 17, 1954, which years are subject to the Internal Revenue Code of 1939.

T.D. 6312, 9/10/58.

§ 1.267(f)-1 Controlled groups.

(a) In general. *(1) Purpose.* This section provides rules under section 267(f) to defer losses and deductions from certain transactions between members of a controlled group (intercompany sales). The purpose of this section is to prevent members of a controlled group from taking into account a loss or deduction solely as the result of a transfer of property between a selling member (S) and a buying member (B).

(2) Application of consolidated return principles. Under this section, S's loss or deduction from an intercompany sale is taken into account under the *timing* principles of § 1.1502-13 (intercompany transactions between members of a consolidated group), treating the intercompany sale as an intercompany transaction. For this purpose:

(i) The matching and acceleration rules of § 1.1502-13(c) and (d), the definitions and operating rules of § 1.1502-13(b) and (j), and the simplifying rules of § 1.1502-13(e)(1) apply with the adjustments in paragraphs (b) and (c) of this section to reflect that this section—

(A) Applies on a controlled group basis rather than consolidated group basis; and

(B) Generally affects only the *timing* of a loss or deduction, and not its *attributes* (e.g., its *source* and *character*) or the holding period of property.

(ii) The special rules under § 1.1502-13(f) (stock of members) and (g) (obligations of members) apply under this section only to the extent the transaction is also an intercompany transaction to which § 1.1502-13 applies.

(iii) Any election under § 1.1502-13 to take items into account on a separate entity basis does not apply under this section. See § 1.1502-13(e)(3).

(3) Other law. The rules of this section apply in addition to other applicable law (including nonstatutory authorities). For example, to the extent a loss or deduction deferred under this section is from a transaction that is also an intercompany transaction under § 1.1502-13(b)(1), attributes of the loss or deduction are also subject to recharacterization under § 1.1502-13. See also, sections 269 (acquisitions to evade or avoid income tax) and 482 (allocations among commonly controlled taxpayers). Any loss or deduction taken into account under this section can be deferred, disallowed, or eliminated under other applicable law. See, for example, section 1091 (loss eliminated on wash sale).

(b) Definitions and operating rules. The definitions in § 1.1502-13(b) and the operating rules of § 1.1502-13(j) apply under this section with appropriate adjustments, including the following:

(1) Intercompany sale. An intercompany sale is a sale, exchange, or other transfer of property between members of a controlled group, if it would be an intercompany transaction under the principles of § 1.1502-13, determined by treating the references to a consolidated group as references to a controlled group and by disregarding whether any of the members join in filing consolidated returns.

(2) S's losses or deductions. Except to the extent the intercompany sale is also an intercompany transaction to which § 1.1502-13 applies, S's losses or deductions subject

to this section are determined on a separate entity basis. For example, the principles of § 1.1502-13(b)(2)(iii) (treating certain amounts not yet recognized as items to be taken into account) do not apply. A loss or deduction is from an intercompany sale whether it is directly or indirectly from the intercompany sale.

(3) Controlled group; member. For purposes of this section, a controlled group is defined in section 267(f). Thus, a controlled group includes a FSC (as defined in section 922) and excluded members under section 1563 (b)(2), but does not include a DISC (as defined in section 992). Corporations remain members of a controlled group as long as they remain in a controlled group relationship with each other. For example, corporations become nonmembers with respect to each other when they cease to be in a controlled group relationship with each other, rather than by having a separate return year (described in § 1.1502-13(j)(7)). Further, the principles of § 1.1502-13(j)(6) (former common parent treated as continuation of group) apply to any corporation if, immediately before it becomes a nonmember, it is both the selling member and the owner of property with respect to which a loss or deduction is deferred (whether or not it becomes a member of a different controlled group filing consolidated or separate returns). Thus, for example, if S and B merge together in a transaction described in section 368(a)(1)(A), the surviving corporation is treated as the successor to the other corporation, and the controlled group relationship is treated as continuing.

(4) Consolidated taxable income. References to consolidated taxable income (and consolidated tax liability) include references to the combined taxable income of the members (and their combined tax liability). For corporations filing separate returns, it ordinarily will not be necessary to actually combine their taxable incomes (and tax liabilities) because the taxable income (and tax liability) of one corporation does not affect the taxable income (or tax liability) of another corporation.

(c) Matching and acceleration principles of § 1.1502-13. *(1) Adjustments to the timing rules.* Under this section, S's losses and deductions are deferred until they are taken into account under the timing principles of the matching and acceleration rules of § 1.1502-13(c) and (d) with appropriate adjustments. For example, if S sells depreciable property to B at a loss, S's loss is deferred and taken into account under the principles of the matching rule of § 1.1502-13(c) to reflect the difference between B's depreciation taken into account with respect to the property and the depreciation that B would take into account if S and B were divisions of a single corporation; if S and B subsequently cease to be in a controlled group relationship with each other, S's remaining loss is taken into account under the principles of the acceleration rule of § 1.1502-13(d). For purposes of this section, the adjustments to § 1.1502-13(c) and (d) include the following:

(i) Application on controlled group basis. The matching and acceleration rules apply on a controlled group basis, rather than a consolidated group basis. Thus if S and B are wholly-owned members of a consolidated group and 21% of the stock of S is sold to an unrelated person, S's loss continues to be deferred under this section because S and B continue to be members of a controlled group even though S is no longer a member of the consolidated group. Similarly, S's loss would continue to be deferred if S and B remain in a controlled group relationship after both corporations become nonmembers of their former consolidated group.

(ii) Different taxable years. If S and B have different taxable years, the taxable years that include a December 31 are treated as the same taxable years. If S or B has a short taxable year that does not include a December 3l, the short year is treated as part of the succeeding taxable year that does include a December 31.

(iii) Transfer to a section 267(b) or 707(b) related person. To the extent S's loss or deduction from an intercompany sale of property is taken into account under this section as a result of B's transfer of the property to a nonmember that is a person related to any member, immediately after the transfer, under sections 267(b) or 707(b), or as a result of S or B becoming a nonmember that is related to any member under section 267(b), the loss or deduction is taken into account but allowed only to the extent of any income or gain taken into account as a result of the transfer. The balance not allowed is treated as a loss referred to in section 267(d) if it is from a sale or exchange by B (rather than from a distribution).

(iv) B's item is excluded from gross income or noncapital and nondeductible. To the extent S's loss would be redetermined to be a noncapital, nondeductible amount under the principles of § 1.1502-13 but is not redetermined because of paragraph (c)(2) of this section, then, if paragraph (c)(1)(iii) of this section does not apply, S's loss continues to be deferred and is not taken into account until S and B are no longer in a controlled group relationship. For example, if S sells all of the stock of corporation T to B at a loss and T subsequently liquidates into B in a transaction qualifying under section 332, S's loss is deferred until S and B (including their successors) are no longer in a controlled group relationship. See § 1.1502-13(c)(6)(ii).

(v) Circularity of references. References to deferral or elimination under the Internal Revenue Code or regulations do not include references to section 267(f) or this section. See, e.g., § 1.1502-13(a)(4) (applicability of other law).

(2) Attributes generally not affected. The matching and acceleration rules are not applied under this section to affect the attributes of S's intercompany item, or cause it to be taken into account before it is taken into account under S's separate entity method of accounting. However, the attributes of S's intercompany item may be redetermined, or an item may be taken into account earlier than under S's separate entity method of accounting, to the extent the transaction is also an intercompany transaction to which § 1.1502-13 applies. Similarly, except to the extent the transaction is also an intercompany transaction to which § 1.1502-13 applies, the matching and acceleration rules do not apply to affect the timing or attributes of B's corresponding items.

(d) Intercompany sales of inventory involving foreign persons. *(1) General rule.* Section 267(a)(1) and this section do not apply to an intercompany sale of property that is inventory (within the meaning of section 1221(1)) in the hands of both S and B, if—

(i) The intercompany sale is in the ordinary course of S's trade or business;

(ii) S or B is a foreign corporation; and

(iii) Any income or loss realized on the intercompany sale by S or B is not income or loss that is recognized as effectively connected with the conduct of a trade or business within the United States within the meaning of section 864 (unless the income is exempt from taxation pursuant to a treaty obligation of the United States).

(2) Intercompany sales involving related partnerships. For purposes of paragraph (d)(1) of this section, a partnership and a foreign corporation described in section 267(b)(10) are treated as members, provided that the income or loss of the

foreign corporation is described in paragraph (d)(1)(iii) of this section.

(3) Intercompany sales in ordinary course. For purposes of this paragraph (d), whether an intercompany sale is in the ordinary course of business is determined under all the facts and circumstances.

(e) Treatment of a creditor with respect to a loan in nonfunctional currency. Sections 267(a)(1) and this section do not apply to an exchange loss realized with respect to a loan of nonfunctional currency if—

(1) The loss is realized by a member with respect to nonfunctional currency loaned to another member;

(2) The loan is described in § 1.988-1(a)(2)(i);

(3) The loan is not in a hyperinflationary currency as defined in § 1.988-1(f); and

(4) The transaction does not have as a significant purpose the avoidance of Federal income tax.

(f) Receivables. If S acquires a receivable from the sale of goods or services to a nonmember at a gain, and S sells the receivable at fair market value to B, any loss or deduction of S from its sale to B is not deferred under this section to the extent it does not exceed S's income or gain from the sale to the nonmember that has been taken into account at the time the receivable is sold to B.

(g) Earnings and profits. A loss or deduction deferred under this section is not reflected in S's earnings and profits before it is taken into account under this section. See, e.g., §§ 1.312-6(a), 1.312-7, and 1.1502-33(c)(2).

(h) Anti-avoidance rule. If a transaction is engaged in or structured with a principal purpose to avoid the purposes of this section (including, for example, by avoiding treatment as an intercompany sale or by distorting the timing of losses or deductions), adjustments must be made to carry out the purposes of this section.

(i) [Reserved]

(j) Examples. For purposes of the examples in this paragraph (j), unless otherwise stated, corporation P owns 75% of the only class of stock of subsidiaries S and B, X is a person unrelated to any member of the P controlled group, the taxable year of all persons is the calendar year, all persons use the accrual method of accounting, tax liabilities are disregarded, the facts set forth the only activity, and no member has a special status. If a member acts as both a selling member and a buying member (e.g., with respect to different aspects of a single transaction, or with respect to related transactions), the member is referred as to M (rather than as S or B). This section is illustrated by the following examples.

Example (1). Matching and acceleration rules. (a) Facts. S holds land for investment with a basis of $130. On January 1 of Year 1, S sells the land to B for $100. On a separate entity basis, S's loss is long-term capital loss. B holds the land for sale to customers in the ordinary course of business. On July 1 of Year 3, B sells the land to X for $110.

(b) Matching rule. Under paragraph (b)(1) of this section, S's sale of land to B is an intercompany sale. Under paragraph (c)(1) of this section, S's $30 loss is taken into account under the timing principles of the matching rule of § 1.1502-13(c) to reflect the difference for the year between B's corresponding items taken into account and the recomputed corresponding items. If S and B were divisions of a single corporation and the intercompany sale were a transfer between the divisions, B would succeed to S's $130 basis in the land and would have a $20 loss from the sale to X in Year 3. Consequently, S takes no loss into account in Years 1 and 2, and takes the entire $30 loss into account in Year 3 to reflect the $30 difference in that year between the $10 gain B takes into account and its $20 recomputed loss. The attributes of S's intercompany items and B's corresponding items are determined on a separate entity basis. Thus, S's $30 loss is long-term capital loss and B's $10 gain is ordinary income.

(c) Acceleration resulting from sale of B stock. The facts are the same as in paragraph (a) of this *Example 1,* except that on July 1 of Year 3 P sells all of its B stock to X (rather than B's selling the land to X). Under paragraph (c)(1) of this section, S's $30 loss is taken into account under the timing principles of the acceleration rule of § 1.1502-13(d) immediately before the effect of treating S and B as divisions of a single corporation cannot be produced. Because the effect cannot be produced once B becomes a nonmember, S takes its $30 loss into account in Year 3 immediately before B becomes a nonmember. S's loss is long-term capital loss.

(d) Subgroup principles applicable to sale of S and B stock. The facts are the same as in paragraph (a) of this *Example 1,* except that on July 1 of Year 3 P sells all of its S and B stock to X (rather than B's selling the land to X). Under paragraph (b)(3) of this section, S and B are considered to remain members of a controlled group as long as they remain in a controlled group relationship with each other (whether or not in the original controlled group). P's sale of their stock does not affect the controlled group relationship of S and B with each other. Thus, S's loss is not taken into account as a result of P's sale of the stock. Instead, S's loss is taken into account based on subsequent events (e.g., B's sale of the land to a nonmember).

Example (2). Distribution of loss property. (a) Facts. S holds land with a basis of $130 and value of $100. On January 1 of Year 1, S distributes the land to P in a transaction to which section 311 applies. On July 1 of Year 3, P sells the land to X for $110.

(b) No loss taken into account. Under paragraph (b)(2) of this section, because P and S are not members of a consolidated group, § 1.1502-13(f)(2)(iii) does not apply to cause S to recognize a $30 loss under the principles of section 311(b). Thus, S has no loss to be taken into account under this section. (If P and S were members of a consolidated group, § 1.1502-13(f)(2)(iii) would apply to S's loss in addition to the rules of this section, and the loss would be taken into account in Year 3 as a result of P's sale to X.)

Example (3). Loss not yet taken into account under separate entity accounting method. (a) Facts. S holds land with a basis of $130. On January 1 of Year 1, S sells the land to B at a $30 loss but does not take into account the loss under its separate entity method of accounting until Year 4. On July 1 of Year 3, B sells the land to X for $110.

(b) Timing. Under paragraph (b)(2) of this section, S's loss is determined on a separate entity basis. Under paragraph (c)(1) of this section, S's loss is not taken into account before it is taken into account under S's separate entity method of accounting. Thus, although B takes its corresponding gain into account in Year 3, S has no loss to take into account until Year 4. Once S's loss is taken into account in Year 4, it is not deferred under this section because B's corresponding gain has already been taken into account. (If S and B were members of a consolidated group, S would be treated under § 1.1502-13(b)(2)(iii) as taking the loss into account in Year 3.)

Example (4). Consolidated groups. (a) Facts. P owns all of the stock of S and B, and the P group is a consolidated group. S holds land for investment with a basis of $130. On January 1 of Year 1, S sells the land to B for $100. B holds the land for sale to customers in the ordinary course of business. On July 1 of Year 3, P sells 25% of B's stock to X. As a result of P's sale, B becomes a nonmember of the P consolidated group but S and B remain in a controlled group relationship with each other for purposes of section 267(f). Assume that if S and B were divisions of a single corporation, the items of S and B from the land would be ordinary by reason of B's activities.

(b) Timing and attributes. Under paragraph (a)(3) of this section, S's sale to B is subject to both § 1.1502-13 and this section. Under § 1.1502-13, S's loss is redetermined to be an ordinary loss by reason of B's activities. Under paragraph (b)(3) of this section, because S and B remain in a controlled group relationship with each other, the loss is not taken into account under the acceleration rule of § 1.1502-13(d) as modified by paragraph (c) of this section. See § 1.1502-13(a)(4). Nevertheless, S's loss is redetermined by § 1.1502-13 to be an ordinary loss, and the character of the loss is not further redetermined under this section. Thus, the loss continues to be deferred under this section, and will be taken into account as ordinary loss based on subsequent events (e.g., B's sale of the land to a nonmember).

(c) Resale to controlled group member. The facts are the same as in paragraph (a) of this *Example 4,* except that P owns 75% of X's stock, and B resells the land to X (rather than P's selling any B stock). The results for S's loss are the same as in paragraph (b) of this *Example 4.* Under paragraph (b) of this section, X is also in a controlled group relationship, and B's sale to X is a second intercompany sale. Thus, S's loss continues to be deferred and is taken into account under this section as ordinary loss based on subsequent events (e.g., X's sale of the land to a nonmember).

Example (5). Intercompany sale followed by installment sale. (a) Facts. S holds land for investment with a basis of $130x. On January 1 of Year 1, S sells the land to B for $100x. B holds the land for investment. On July 1 of Year 3, B sells the land to X in exchange for X's $110x note. The note bears a market rate of interest in excess of the applicable Federal rate, and provides for principal payments of $55x in Year 4 and $55x in Year 5. Section 453A applies to X's note.

(b) Timing and attributes. Under paragraph (c) of this section, S's $30x loss is taken into account under the timing principles of the matching rule of § 1.1502-13(c) to reflect the difference in each year between B's gain taken into account and its recomputed loss. Under section 453, B takes into account $5x of gain in Year 4 and in Year 5. Therefore, S takes $20x of its loss into account in Year 3 to reflect the $20x difference in that year between B's $0 loss taken into account and its $20x recomputed loss. In addition, S takes $5x of its loss into account in Year 4 and in Year 5 to reflect the $5x difference in each year between B's $5x gain taken into account and its $0 recomputed gain. Although S takes into account a loss and B takes into account a gain, the attributes of B's $10x gain are determined on a separate entity basis, and therefore the interest charge under section 453A(c) applies to B's $10x gain on the installment sale beginning in Year 3.

Example (6). Section 721 transfer to a related nonmember. (a) Facts. S owns land with a basis of $130. On January 1 of Year 1, S sells the land to B for $100. On July 1 of Year 3, B transfers the land to a partnership in exchange for a 40% interest in capital and profits in a transaction to which section 721 applies. P also owns a 25% interest in the capital and profits of the partnership.

(b) Timing. Under paragraph (c)(1)(iii) of this section, because the partnership is a nonmember that is a related person under sections 267(b) and 707(b), S's $30 loss is taken into account in Year 3, but only to the extent of any income or gain taken into account as a result of the transfer. Under section 721, no gain or loss is taken into account as a result of the transfer to the partnership, and thus none of S's loss is taken into account. Any subsequent gain recognized by the partnership with respect to the property is limited under section 267(d). (The results would be the same if the P group were a consolidated group, and S's sale to B were also subject to § 1.1502-13.)

Example (7). Receivables. (a) Controlled group. S owns goods with a $60 basis. In Year 1, S sells the goods to X for X's $100 note. The note bears a market rate of interest in excess of the applicable Federal rate, and provides for payment of principal in Year 5. S takes into account $40 of income in Year 1 under its method of accounting. In Year 2, the fair market value of X's note falls to $90 due to an increase in prevailing market interest rates, and S sells the note to B for its $90 fair market value.

(b) Loss not deferred. Under paragraph (f) of this section, S takes its $10 loss into account in Year 2. (If the sale were not at fair market value, paragraph (f) of this section would not apply and none of S's $10 loss would be taken into account in Year 2.)

(c) Consolidated group. Assume instead that P owns all of the stock of S and B, and the P group is a consolidated group. In Year 1, S sells to X goods having a basis of $90 for X's $100 note (bearing a market rate of interest in excess of the applicable Federal rate, and providing for payment of principal in Year 5), and S takes into account $10 of income in Year 1. In Year 2, S sells the receivable to B for its $85 fair market value. In Year 3, P sells 25% of B's stock to X. Although paragraph (f) of this section provides that $10 of S's loss (i.e., the extent to which S's $15 loss does not exceed its $10 of income) is not deferred under this section, S's entire $15 loss is subject to § 1.1502-13 and none of the loss is taken into account in Year 2 under the matching rule of section § 1.1502-13(c). See paragraph (a)(3) of this section (continued deferral under § 1.1502-13). P's sale of B stock results in B becoming a nonmember of the P consolidated group in Year 3. Thus, S's $15 loss is taken into account in Year 3 under the acceleration rule of § 1.1502-13(d). Nevertheless, B remains in a controlled group relationship with S and paragraph (f) of this section permits only $10 of S's loss to be taken into account in Year 3. See § 1.1502-13(a)(4) (continued deferral under section 267). The remaining $5 of S's loss continues to be deferred under this section and taken into account under this section based on subsequent events (e.g., B's collection of the note or P's sale of the remaining B stock to a nonmember).

Example (8). Selling member ceases to be a member. (a) Facts. P owns all of the stock of S and B, and the P group is a consolidated group. S has several historic assets, including land with a basis of $130 and value of $100. The land is not essential to the operation of S's business. On January 1 of Year 1, S sells the land to B for $100. On July 1 of Year 3, P transfers all of S's stock to newly formed X in exchange for a 20% interest in X stock as part of a transaction to which section 351 applies. Although X holds many other assets, a principal purpose for P's transfer is to accelerate taking S's $30 loss into account. P has no plan or intention to dispose of the X stock.

(b) Timing. Under paragraph (c) of this section, S's $30 loss ordinarily is taken into account immediately before P's transfer of the S stock, under the timing principles of the acceleration rule of § 1.1502-13(d). Although taking S's loss into account results in a $30 negative stock basis adjustment under § 1.1502-32, because P has no plan or intention to dispose of its X stock, the negative adjustment will not immediately affect taxable income. P's transfer accelerates a loss that otherwise would be deferred, and an adjustment under paragraph (h) of this section is required. Thus, S's loss is never taken into account, and S's stock basis and earnings and profits are reduced by $30 under §§ 1.1502-32 and 1.1502-33 immediately before P's transfer of the S stock.

(c) Nonhistoric assets. Assume instead that, with a principal purpose to accelerate taking into account any further loss that may accrue in the value of the land without disposing of the land outside of the controlled group, P forms M with a $100 contribution on January 1 of Year 1 and S sells the land to M for $100. On December 1 of Year 1, when the value of the land has decreased to $90, M sells the land to B for $90. On July 1 of Year 3, while B still owns the land, P sells all of M's stock to X and M becomes a nonmember. Under paragraph (c) of this section, M's $10 loss ordinarily is taken into account under the timing principles of the acceleration rule of § 1.1502-13(d) immediately before M becomes a nonmember. (S's $30 loss is not taken into account under the timing principles of § 1.1502-13(c) or § 1.1502-13(d) as a result of M becoming a nonmember, but is taken into account based on subsequent events such as B's sale of the land to a nonmember or P's sale of the stock of S or B to a nonmember.) The land is not an historic asset of M and, although taking M's loss into account reduces P's basis in the M stock under § 1.1502-32, the negative adjustment only eliminates the $10 duplicate stock loss. Under paragraph (h) of this section, M's loss is never taken into account. M's stock basis, and the earnings and profits of M and P, are reduced by $10 under §§ 1.1502-32 and 1.1502-33 immediately before P's sale of the M stock.

(k) Cross-reference. For additional rules applicable to the disposition, deconsolidation, or transfer of the stock of members of consolidated groups, see §§ 1.337(d)-2, 1.1502-13(f)(6), 1.1502-35, and 1.1502-36.

(l) Effective dates. *(1) In general.* This section applies with respect to transactions occurring in S's years beginning on or after July 12, 1995. If both this section and prior law apply to a transaction, or neither applies, with the result that items are duplicated, omitted, or eliminated in determining taxable income (or tax liability), or items are treated inconsistently, prior law (and not this section) applies to the transaction.

(2) Avoidance transactions. This paragraph (l)(2) applies if a transaction is engaged in or structured on or after April 8, 1994, with a principal purpose to avoid the rules of this section (and instead to apply to prior law). If this paragraph (l)(2) applies, appropriate adjustments must be made in years beginning on or after July 12, 1995, to prevent the avoidance, duplication, omission, or elimination of any item (or tax liability), or any other inconsistency with the rules of this section.

(3) Prior law. For transactions occurring in S's years beginning before July 12, 1995 see the applicable regulations issued under sections 267 and 1502. See, e.g., §§ 1.267(f)-1, 1.267(f)-1T, 1.267(f)-2T, 1.267(f)-3, 1.1502-13, 1.1502-13T, 1.1502-14, 1.1502-14T, and 1.1502-31 (as contained in the 26 CFR part 1 edition revised as of April 1, 1995).

T.D. 8400, 3/16/92, amend T.D. 8597, 7/12/95, T.D. 8660, 3/13/96, T.D. 9048, 3/11/2003, T.D. 9187, 3/2/2005, T.D. 9254, 3/9/2006, T.D. 9424, 9/10/2008.

§ 1.268-1 Items attributable to an unharvested crop sold with the land.

In computing taxable income no deduction shall be allowed in respect of items attributable to the production of an unharvested crop which is sold, exchanged, or involuntarily converted with the land and which is considered as property used in the trade or business under section 1231(b)(4). Such items shall be so treated whether or not the taxable year involved is that of the sale, exchange, or conversion of such crop and whether they are for expenses, depreciation, or otherwise. If the taxable year involved is not that of the sale, exchange, or conversion of such crop, a recomputation of the tax liability for such year shall be made; such recomputation should be in the form of an "amended return" if necessary. For the adjustments to basis as a result of such disallowance, see section 1016(a)(11) and the regulations thereunder.

T.D. 6252, 9/12/57.

§ 1.269-1 Meaning and use of terms.

Caution: The Treasury has not yet amended Reg § 1.269-1 to reflect changes made by P.L. 98-369.

As used in section 269 and §§ 1.269-2 through 1.269-7—

(a) Allowance. The term "allowance" refers to anything in the internal revenue laws which has the effect of diminishing tax liability. The term includes, among other things, a deduction, a credit, an adjustment, an exemption, or an exclusion.

(b) Evasion or avoidance. The phrase "evasion or avoidance" is not limited to cases involving criminal penalties, or civil penalties for fraud.

(c) Control. The term "control" means the ownership of stock possessing at least 50 percent of the total combined voting power of all classes of stock entitled to vote, or at least 50 percent of the total value of shares of all classes of stock of the corporation. For control to be "acquired on or after October 8, 1940", it is not necessary that all of such stock be acquired on or after October 8, 1940. Thus, if A, on October 7, 1940, and at all times thereafter, owns 40 percent of the stock of X Corporation and acquires on October 8, 1940, an additional 10 percent of such stock, an acquisition within the meaning of such phrase is made by A on October 8, 1940. Similarly, if B, on October 7, 1940, owns certain assets and transfers on October 8, 1940, such assets to a newly organized Y Corporation in exchange for all the stock of Y Corporation, an acquisition within the meaning of such phrase is made by B on October 8, 1940. If, under the facts stated in the preceding sentence, B is a corporation, all of whose stock is owned by Z Corporation, then an acquisition within the meaning of such phrase is also made by Z Corporation on October 8, 1940, as well as by the shareholders of Z Corporation taken as a group on such date, and by any of such shareholders if such shareholders as a group own 50 percent of the stock of Z on such date.

(d) Person. The term "person" includes an individual, a trust, an estate, a partnership, an association, a company, or a corporation.

T.D. 6595, 4/13/62, amend T.D. 8388, 12/31/91.

§ 1.269-2 Purpose and scope of section 269.

Caution: The Treasury has not yet amended Reg § 1.269-2 to reflect changes made by P.L. 98-369.

(a) General. Section 269 is designed to prevent in the instances specified therein the use of the sections of the Internal Revenue Code providing deductions, credits, or allowances in evading or avoiding Federal income tax. See § 1.269-3.

(b) Disallowance of deduction, credit, or other allowance. Under the Code, an amount otherwise constituting a deduction, credit, or other allowance becomes unavailable as such under certain circumstances. Characteristic of such circumstances are those in which the effect of the deduction, credit, or other allowance would be to distort the liability of the particular taxpayer when the essential nature of the transaction or situation is examined in the light of the basic purpose or plan which the deduction, credit, or other allowance was designed by the Congress to effectuate. The distortion may be evidenced, for example, by the fact that the transaction was not undertaken for reasons germane to the conduct of the business of the taxpayer, by the unreal nature of the transaction such as its sham character, or by the unreal or unreasonable relation which the deduction, credit, or other allowance bears to the transaction. The principle of law making an amount unavailable as a deduction, credit, or other allowance in cases in which the effect of making an amount so available would be to distort the liability of the taxpayer, has been judicially recognized and applied in several cases. Included in these cases are Gregory v. Helvering (1935) (293 U.S. 465; Ct. D. 911, C.B. XIV-1, 193); Griffiths v. Helvering (1939) (308; U.S. 355; Ct. D. 1431, C.B. 1940-1, 136); Higgins v. Smith (1940) (308 U.S. 473; Ct. D. 1434, C.B. 1940-1, 127); and J.D. & A.B. Spreckles Co. v. Commissioner (1940) (41 B.T.A. 370). In order to give effect to such principle, but not in limitation thereof, several provisions of the Code, for example, section 267 and section 270, specify with some particularity instances in which disallowance of the deduction, credit, or other allowance is required. Section 269 is also included in such provisions of the Code. The principle of law and the particular sections of the Code are not mutually exclusive and in appropriate circumstances they may operate together or they may operate separately. See, for example, § 1.269-6.

T.D. 6595, 4/13/62.

§ 1.269-3 Instances in which section 269(a) disallows a deduction, credit, or other allowance.

(a) Instances of disallowance. Section 269 specifies two instances in which a deduction, credit, or other allowance is to be disallowed. These instances, described in paragraphs (1) and (2) of section 269(a), are those in which—

(1) Any person or persons acquire, or acquired on or after October 8, 1940, directly or indirectly, control of a corporation, or

(2) Any corporation acquires, or acquired on or after October 8, 1940, directly or indirectly, property of another corporation (not controlled, directly or indirectly, immediately before such acquisition by such acquiring corporation or its stockholders), the basis of which property in the hands of the acquiring corporation is determined by reference to the basis in the hands of the transferor corporation.

In either instance the principal purpose for which the acquisition was made must have been the evasion or avoidance of Federal income tax by securing the benefit of a deduction, credit, or other allowance which such person or persons, or corporation, would not otherwise enjoy. If this requirement is satisfied, it is immaterial by what method or by what conjunction of events the benefit was sought. Thus, an acquiring person or corporation can secure the benefit of a deduction, credit, or other allowance within the meaning of section 269 even though it is the acquired corporation that is entitled to such deduction, credit, or other allowance in the determination of its tax. If the purpose to evade or avoid Federal income tax exceeds in importance any other purpose, it is the principal purpose. This does not mean that only those acquisitions fall within the provisions of section 269 which would not have been made if the evasion or avoidance purpose was not present. The determination of the purpose for which an acquisition was made requires a scrutiny of the entire circumstances in which the transaction or course of conduct occurred, in connection with the tax result claimed to arise therefrom.

(b) Acquisition of control; transactions indicative of purpose to evade or avoid tax. If the requisite acquisition of control within the meaning of paragraph (1) of section 269(a) exists, the transactions set forth in the following subparagraphs are among those which, in the absence of additional evidence to the contrary, ordinarily are indicative that the principal purpose for acquiring control was evasion or avoidance of Federal income tax:

(1) A corporation or other business enterprise (or the interest controlling such corporation or enterprise) with large profits acquires control of a corporation with current, past, or prospective credits, deductions, net operating losses, or other allowances and the acquisition is followed by such transfers or other action as is necessary to bring the deduction, credit, or other allowance into conjunction with the income (see further § 1.269-6). This subparagraph may be illustrated by the following example:

Example. Individual A acquires all of the stock of L Corporation which has been engaged in the business of operating retail drug stores. At the time of the acquisition, L Corporation has net operating loss carryovers aggregating $100,000 and its net worth is $100,000. After the acquisition, L Corporation continues to engage in the business of operating retail drug stores but the profits attributable to such business after the acquisition are not sufficient to absorb any substantial portion of the net operating loss carryovers. Shortly after the acquisition, individual A causes to be transferred to L Corporation the assets of a hardware business previously controlled by A which business produces profits sufficient to absorb a substantial portion of L Corporation's net operating loss carryovers. The transfer of the profitable business, which has the effect of using net operating loss carryovers to offset gains of a business unrelated to that which produced the losses, indicates that the principal purpose for which the acquisition of control was made is evasion or avoidance of Federal income tax.

(2) A person or persons organize two or more corporations instead of a single corporation in order to secure the benefit of multiple surtax exemptions (see section 11(c)) or multiple minimum accumulated earnings credits (see section 535(c)(2) and (3)).

(3) A person or persons with high earning assets transfer them to a newly organized controlled corporation retaining assets producing net operating losses which are utilized in an attempt to secure refunds.

(c) Acquisition of property; transactions indicative of purpose to evade or avoid tax. If the requisite acquisition of property within the meaning of paragraph (2) of section 269(a) exists, the transactions set forth in the following subparagraphs are among those which, in the absence of additional evidence to the contrary, ordinarily are indicative that the principal purpose for acquiring such property was evasion or avoidance of Federal income tax:

(1) A corporation acquires property having in its hands an aggregate carryover basis which is materially greater than its aggregate fair market value at the time of such acquisition and utilizes the property to create tax-reducing losses or deductions.

(2) A subsidiary corporation, which has sustained large net operating losses in the operation of business X and which has filed separate returns for the taxable years in which the losses were sustained, acquires high earning assets, comprising business Y, from its parent corporation. The acquisition occurs at a time when the parent would not succeed to the net operating loss carryovers of the subsidiary if the subsidiary were liquidated, and the profits of business Y are sufficient to offset a substantial portion of the net operating loss carryovers attributable to business X (see further example (3) of § 1.269-6).

(d) Ownership changes to which section 382 § 1.269-3(l)(5) applies; transactions indicative of purpose to evade or avoid tax. *(1) In general.* Absent strong evidence to the contrary, a requisite acquisition of control or property in connection with an ownership change to which section 382(l)(5) applies is considered to be made for the principal purpose of evasion or avoidance of Federal income tax unless the corporation carries on more than an insignificant amount of an active trade or business during and subsequent to the title 11 or similar case (as defined in section 382(l)(5)(G)). The determination of whether the corporation carries on more than an insignificant amount of an active trade or business is made without regard to the continuity of business enterprise requirement set forth in § 1.368-1(d). The determination is based on all the facts and circumstances, including, for example, the amount of business assets that continue to be used, or the number of employees in the work force who continue employment, in an active trade or business (although not necessarily the historic trade or business). Where the corporation continues to utilize a significant amount of its business assets or work force, the requirement of carrying on more than an insignificant amount of an active trade or business may be met even though all trade or business activities temporarily cease for a period of time in order to address business exigencies.

(2) Effective date. The presumption under paragraph (d) of this section applies to acquisitions of control or property effected pursuant to a plan of reorganization confirmed by a court in a title 11 or similar case (within the meaning of section 368(a)(3)(A)) after August 14, 1990.

(e) **Relationship of section 269 to 11 U.S.C. 1129(d).** In determining for purposes of section 269 of the Internal Revenue Code whether an acquisition pursuant to a plan of reorganization in a case under title 11 of the United States Code was made for the principal purpose of evasion or avoidance of Federal income tax, the fact that a governmental unit did not seek a determination under 11 U.S.C. 1129(d) is not taken into account and any determination by a court under 11 U.S.C. 1129(d) that the principal purpose of the plan is not avoidance of taxes is not controlling.

T.D. 6595, 4/13/62, amend T.D. 8388, 12/31/91.

§ 1.269-4 Power of district director to allocate deduction, credit, or allowance in part.

Caution: The Treasury has not yet amended Reg § 1.269-4 to reflect changes made by P.L. 98-369, P.L. 94-455.

The district director is authorized by section 269(b) to allow a part of the amount disallowed by section 269(a), but he may allow such part only if and to the extent that he determines that the amount allowed will not result in the evasion or avoidance of Federal income tax for which the acquisition was made. The district director is also authorized to use other methods to give effect to part of the amount disallowed under section 269(a), but only to such extent as he determines will not result in the evasion or avoidance of Federal income tax for which the acquisition was made. Whenever appropriate to give proper effect to the deduction, credit, or other allowance, or such part of it which may be allowed, this authority includes the distribution, apportionment, or allocation of both the gross income and the deductions, credits, or other allowances the benefit of which was sought, between or among the corporations, or properties, or parts thereof, involved, and includes the disallowance of any such deduction, credit, or other allowance to any of the taxpayers involved.

T.D. 6595, 4/13/62.

§ 1.269-5 Time of acquisition of control.

Caution: The Treasury has not yet amended Reg § 1.269-5 to reflect changes made by P.L. 94-455.

(a) In general. For purposes of section 269, an acquisition of control occurs when one or more persons acquire beneficial ownership of stock possessing at least 50 percent of the total combined voting power of all classes of stock entitled to vote or at least 50 percent of the total value of shares of all classes of stock of the corporation.

(b) Application of general rule to certain creditor acquisitions. *(1)* For purposes of section 269, creditors of an insolvent or bankrupt corporation (by themselves or in conjunction with other persons) acquire control of the corporation when they acquire beneficial ownership of the requisite amount of stock. Although insolvency or bankruptcy may cause the interests of creditors to predominate as a practical matter, creditor interests do not constitute beneficial ownership of the corporation's stock. Solely for purposes of section 269, creditors of a bankrupt corporation are treated as acquiring beneficial ownership of stock of the corporation no earlier than the time a bankruptcy court confirms a plan of reorganization.

(2) The provisions of this section are illustrated by the following example.

Example. Corporation L files a petition under chapter 11 of the Bankruptcy Code on January 5, 1987. A creditor's committee is formed. On February 22, 1987, and upon the request of the creditors, the bankruptcy court removes the debtor-in-possession from business management and operations and appoints a trustee. The trustee consults regularly with the creditors' committee in formulating both short-term and long-term management decisions. After three years, the creditors approve a plan of reorganization in which the outstanding stock of Corporation L is cancelled and its creditors receive shares of stock constituting all of the outstanding shares. The bankruptcy court confirms the plan of reorganization on March 23, 1990, and the plan is put into effect on May 25, 1990. For purposes of section 269, the creditors acquired control of Corporation L no earlier than March 23, 1990. Similarly, the determination of whether the creditors acquired control of Corporation L with the principal purpose of evasion or avoidance of Federal income tax is made by reference to the creditors' purposes as of no earlier than March 23, 1990.

T.D. 6595, 4/13/62, amend T.D. 8388, 12/31/91.

§ 1.269-6 Relationship of section 269 to section 382 before the Tax Reform Act of 1986.

Section 269 and §§ 1.269-1 through 1.269-5 may be applied to disallow a net operating loss carryover even though such carryover is not disallowed (in whole or in part) under section 382 and the regulations thereunder. This section may be illustrated by the following examples:

Example (1). L Corporation has computed its taxable income on a calendar year basis and has sustained heavy net operating losses for a number of years. Assume that A purchases all of the stock of L Corporation on December 31, 1955, for the principal purpose of utilizing its net operating loss carryovers by changing its business to a profitable new business. Assume further that A makes no attempt to revitalize the business of L Corporation during the calendar year 1956 and that during January 1957 the business is changed to an entirely new and profitable business. The carryovers will be disallowed under the provisions of section 269(a) without regard to the application of section 382.

Example (2). L Corporation has sustained heavy net operating losses for a number of years. In a merger under State law, P Corporation acquires all of the assets of L Corporation for the principal purpose of utilizing the net operating loss carryovers of L Corporation against the profits of P Corporation's business. As a result of the merger, the former stockholders of L Corporation own, immediately after the merger, 12 percent of the fair market value of the outstanding stock of P Corporation. If the merger qualifies as a reorganization to which section 381(a) applies, the entire net operating loss carryovers will be disallowed under the provisions of section 269(a) without regard to the application of section 382.

Example (3). L Corporation has been sustaining net operating losses for a number of years. P Corporation, a profitable corporation, on December 31, 1955, acquires all the stock of L Corporation for the purpose of continuing and improving the operation of L Corporation's business. Under the provisions of sections 334(b)(2) and 381(a)(1), P Corporation would not succeed to L Corporation's net operating loss carryovers if L Corporation were liquidated pursuant to a plan of liquidation adopted within two years after the date of the acquisition. During 1956, P Corporation transfers a profitable business to L Corporation for the principal purpose of using the profits of such business to absorb the net operating loss carryovers of L Corporation. The transfer is such as to cause the basis of the transferred assets in the hands of L Corporation to be determined by reference to their basis in the hands of P Corporation. L Corporation's net operating loss carryovers will be disallowed under the provisions of section 269(a) without regard to the application of section 382.

T.D. 6595, 4/13/62, amend T.D. 8388, 12/31/91.

§ 1.269-7 Relationship of section 269 to sections 382 and 383 after the Tax Reform Act of 1986.

Section 269 and §§ 1.269-1 through 1.269-5 may be applied to disallow a deduction, credit, or other allowance notwithstanding that the utilization or amount of a deduction, credit, or other allowance is limited or reduced under section 382 or 383 and the regulations thereunder. However, the fact that the amount of taxable income or tax that may be offset by a deduction, credit, or other allowance is limited under section 382(a) or 383 and the regulations thereunder is relevant to the determination of whether the principal purpose of an acquisition is the evasion or avoidance of Federal income tax.

T.D. 8388, 12/31/91.

Proposed § 1.269A-1 Personal service corporations. [*For Preamble, see ¶ 150,847*]

(a) In general. Section 269A permits the Internal Revenue Service to reallocate income and tax benefits between personal Service corporations and their employee-owners to prevent evasion or avoidance of Federal income taxes or to reflect clearly the income of the personal service corporation or any of its employee-owners, if:

(1) Substantially all of the services of the personal service corporation are performed for or on behalf of one other entity, and

(2) The principal purpose for which the corporation was formed or availed of is the evasion or avoidance of Federal income tax. Such purpose is evidenced when use of the corporation either reduces the income of any employee-owner, or secures for any employee-owner one or more tax benefits which would not otherwise be available.

(b) Definitions. For purposes of section 269A and the regulations thereunder, the following definitions will apply:

(1) Personal service corporation. The term "personal service corporation" means a corporation the principal activity of which is the performance of personal services that are substantially performed by employee-owners.

(2) Employee-owner. The term "employee-owner" means an employee who owns, directly or indirectly, on any day of the corporation's taxable year, more than 10 percent of the outstanding stock of the personal service corporation. Section 318 will apply to determine indirect stock ownership, except that "5 percent" is to be substituted for "50 percent" in section 318(a)(2)(C).

(3) Entity. The term "entity" means a corporation, partnership, or other entity. All persons related to such entity will be treated as one entity. A related person is a related person within the meaning of section 103(b)(6)(C).

(4) Not otherwise be available. The term "not otherwise be available" refers to any tax benefit that would not be available to an employee-owner had such employee-owner performed the personal services in an individual capacity.

(5) Qualified employer plan. The term "qualified employer plan" means a qualified employer plan as defined in section 219(e)(3).

(6) Tax benefits. The term "tax benefits" means any expense, deduction, credit, exclusion or other allowance which would not otherwise be available. The term includes, but is not limited to: multiple surtax exemptions being claimed by the owners of a single integrated business operation conducted through multiple corporate entities, accumulation of income by the corporation, the corporate dividends received

deduction under section 243, deferral of income of an employee-owner through the use of a corporation with a fiscal year or accounting method differing from that of such employee-owner, the use of multiple classes of stock to deflect income to taxpayers in lower tax brackets, group-term life insurance (section 79), certain accident and health plans (section 105 and 106), certain employee death benefits (section 101), meals and lodging furnished for the convenience of the employer (section 119), and qualified transportation expenses (section 124). Except as otherwise provided in paragraph (d)(2)(ii) of this section, the term "tax benefits" does not include contributions to a qualified employer plan.

(c) Safe harbor. In general, a personal service corporation will be deemed not to have been formed or availed of for the principal purpose of avoiding or evading Federal income taxes if the Federal income tax liability of not employee-owner is reduced in a 12 month period by more than the lesser of (1) $2,500 or (2) 10 percent of the Federal income tax liability of the employee-owner that would have resulted in that 12 period had the employee-owner performed the personal services in an individual capacity. For purposes of the computation required by this paragraph, and current corporate tax liability incurred for that 12 month period by the personal service corporation will be considered to be the tax liability of the employee-owners in proportion to the employee-owners' stock holding in the personal service corporation.

(d) Special rules relating to qualified employer plans. *(1) In general.* Contributions to, and benefits under, qualified employer plans will not be taken into account in determining the presence or absence of a principal purpose of the personal service corporation for purposes of paragraph (c) of this section, except as provided in this paragraph.

(2) Taxable years beginning before January 1, 1984. For taxable years beginning before January 1, 1984.

(i) Corporations in existence on or before September 3, 1982. For corporations in existence on or before September 3, 1982, the general rule provided in paragraph (d)(1) of this section will apply unless:

(A) The corporation adopts a new qualified employer plan after September 3, 1982, that has a plan year differing from either the taxable year of the corporation or the calendar year; or

(B) The corporation changes the plan year of an existing qualified employer plan, or its taxable year, after September 3, 1982, in a manner that would extend the period during which section 416 (relating to restrictions on "top heavy" plans), or section 269A (if this (B) did not apply) would be inapplicable to such corporation.

If (A) or (B) applies, the corporation will be treated as a corporation formed after September 3, 1982 for purposes of this paragraph.

(ii) Corporations formed after September 3, 1982. For corporations formed after September 3, 1982, contributions to, and benefits under, a qualified employer plan that are in excess of those that would have been available to an employee-owner performing the personal services in an individual capacity are to be taken into account in determining the principal purpose of the personal service corporation and will be considered to be tax benefits.

(e) Effective dates. *(1) In general.* In general, section 269A and this section are effective for taxable years of personal service corporations beginning after December 31, 1982. Taxable years of employee-owners generally are not considered for purposes of this paragraph.

(2) Exceptions. If a personal service corporation changes its taxable year or qualified employer plan year after September 3, 1982, in a manner that would delay the effective date of section 416 (relating to restrictions on top-heavy plans), or section 269A (but for this (2)), section 269A will be applied to the corporation and its employee-owners on the earlier of the first day of the first taxable year of the corporation or any of its employee-owners beginning after December 31, 1982.

(f) Effect on section 269A on other sections. Nothing in section 269A or the regulations thereunder, including the safe harbor provided in paragraph (c) of this section, precludes application with respect to personal service corporations or their employee-owners of any other Code section (*e.g.*, sections 61 or 482) or tax law principle (*e.g.*, assignment of income doctrine) to reallocate or reapportion income, deductions, credits, etc., so as to reflect the true earner of income.

§ 1.269B-1 Stapled foreign corporations.

(a) Treatment as a domestic corporation. *(1) General rule.* Except as otherwise provided, if a foreign corporation is a stapled foreign corporation within the meaning of paragraph (b)(1) of this section, such foreign corporation will be treated as a domestic corporation for U.S. Federal income tax purposes. Accordingly, for example, the worldwide income of such corporation will be subject to the tax imposed by section 11. For application of the branch profits tax under section 884, and application of sections 871(a), 881, 1441, and 1442 to dividends and interest paid by a stapled foreign corporation, see §§ 1.884-1(h) and 1.884-4(d).

(2) Foreign owned exception. Paragraph (a)(1) of this section will not apply if a foreign corporation and a domestic corporation are stapled entities (as provided in paragraph (b) of this section) and such foreign and domestic corporations are foreign owned within the meaning of this paragraph (a)(2). A corporation will be treated as foreign owned if it is established to the satisfaction of the Commissioner that United States persons hold directly (or indirectly applying section 958(a)(2) and (3) and section 318(a)(4)) less than 50 percent of the total combined voting power of all classes of stock entitled to vote and less than 50 percent of the total value of the stock of such corporation. For the consequences of a stapled foreign corporation becoming or ceasing to be foreign owned, therefore converting its status as either a foreign or domestic corporation within the meaning of this paragraph (a)(2), see paragraph (c) of this section.

(b) Definition of a stapled foreign corporation. *(1) General rule.* A foreign corporation is a stapled foreign corporation if such foreign corporation and a domestic corporation are stapled entities. A foreign corporation and a domestic corporation are stapled entities if more than 50 percent of the aggregate value of each corporation's beneficial ownership consists of interests that are stapled. In the case of corporations with more than one class of stock, it is not necessary for a class of stock representing more than 50 percent of the beneficial ownership of the foreign corporation to be stapled to a class of stock representing more than 50 percent of the beneficial ownership of the domestic corporation, provided that more than 50 percent of the aggregate value of each corporation's beneficial ownership (taking into account all classes of stock) are in fact stapled. Interests are stapled if a transferor of one or more interests in one entity is required, by form of ownership, restrictions on transfer, or other terms or conditions, to transfer interests in the other entity. The determination of whether interests are stapled for this purpose is based on the relevant facts and circumstances, including, but not limited to, the corporations' bylaws, articles of incorporation or association, and stock certificates, shareholder agreements, agreements between the corporations, and voting trusts with respect to the corporations. For the consequences of a foreign corporation becoming or ceasing to be a stapled foreign corporation (e.g., a corporation that is no longer foreign owned) under this paragraph (b)(1), see paragraph (c) of this section.

(2) Related party ownership rule. For purposes of determining whether a foreign corporation is a stapled foreign corporation, the Commissioner may, at his discretion, treat interests that otherwise would be stapled interests as not being stapled if the same person or related persons (within the meaning of section 267(b) or 707(b)) hold stapled interests constituting more than 50 percent of the beneficial ownership of both corporations, and a principal purpose of the stapling of those interests is the avoidance of U.S. income tax. A stapling of interests may have a principal purpose of tax avoidance even though the tax avoidance purpose is outweighed by other purposes when taken together.

(3) Example. The principles of paragraph (b)(1) of this section are illustrated by the following example:

Example. USCo, a domestic corporation, and FCo, a foreign corporation, are publicly traded companies, each having two classes of stock outstanding. USCo's class A shares, which constitute 75% of the value of all beneficial ownership in USCo, are stapled to FCo's class B shares, which constitute 25% of the value of all beneficial ownership in F Co. USCo's class B shares, which constitute 25% of the value of all beneficial ownership in USCo, are stapled to FCo class A shares, which constitute 75% of the value of all beneficial ownership in FCo. Because more than 50% of the aggregate value of the stock of each corporation is stapled to the stock of the other corporation, USCo and FCo are stapled entities within the meaning of section 269B(c)(2).

(c) Changes in domestic or foreign status. The deemed conversion of a foreign corporation to a domestic corporation under section 269B is treated as a reorganization under section 368(a)(1)(F). Similarly, the deemed conversion of a corporation that is treated as a domestic corporation under section 269B to a foreign corporation is treated as a reorganization under section 368(a)(1)(F). For the consequences of a deemed conversion, including the closing of a corporation's taxable year, see §§ 1.367(a)-1T(e), (f) and 1.367(b)-2(f).

(d) Includible corporation. *(1)* Except as provided in paragraph (d)(2) of this section, a stapled foreign corporation treated as a domestic corporation under section 269B nonetheless is treated as a foreign corporation in determining whether it is an includible corporation within the meaning of section 1504(b). Thus, for example, a stapled foreign corporation is not eligible to join in the filing of a consolidated return under section 1501, and a dividend paid by such corporation is not a qualifying dividend under section 243(b), unless a valid section 1504(d) election is made with respect to such corporation.

(2) A stapled foreign corporation is treated as a domestic corporation in determining whether it is an includible corporation under section 1504(b) for purposes of applying §§ 1.904(i)-1 and 1.861-11T(d)(6).

(e) U.S. treaties. *(1)* A stapled foreign corporation that is treated as a domestic corporation under section 269B may not claim an exemption from U.S. income tax or a reduction in U.S. tax rates by reason of any treaty entered into by the United States.

(2) The principles of this paragraph (e) are illustrated by the following example:

Example. FCo, a Country X corporation, is a stapled foreign corporation that is treated as a domestic corporation under section 269B. FCo qualifies as a resident of Country X pursuant to the income tax treaty between the United States and Country X. Under such treaty, the United States is permitted to tax business profits of a Country X resident only to the extent that the business profits are attributable to a permanent establishment of the Country X resident in the United States. While FCo earns income from sources within and without the United States, it does not have a permanent establishment in the United States within the meaning of the relevant treaty. Under paragraph (e)(1) of this section, however, FCo is subject to U.S. Federal income tax on its income as a domestic corporation without regard to the provisions of the U.S.-Country X treaty and therefore without regard to the fact that FCo has no permanent establishment in the United States.

(f) Tax assessment and collection procedures. *(1) In general.* (i) Any income tax imposed on a stapled foreign corporation by reason of its treatment as a domestic corporation under section 269B (whether such income tax is shown on the stapled foreign corporation's U.S. Federal income tax return or determined as a deficiency in income tax) shall be assessed as the income tax liability of such stapled foreign corporation.

(ii) Any income tax assessed as a liability of a stapled foreign corporation under paragraph (f)(1)(i) of this section shall be considered as having been properly assessed as an income tax liability of the stapled domestic corporation (as defined in paragraph (f)(4)(i) of this section) and all 10-percent shareholders of the stapled foreign corporation (as defined in paragraph (f)(4)(ii) of this section). The date of such deemed assessment shall be the date the income tax liability of the stapled foreign corporation was properly assessed. The Commissioner may collect such income tax from the stapled domestic corporation under the circumstances set forth in paragraph (f)(2) of this section and may collect such income tax from any 10-percent shareholders of the stapled foreign corporation under the circumstances set forth in paragraph (f)(3) of this section.

(2) Collection from domestic stapled corporation. If the stapled foreign corporation does not pay its income tax liability that was properly assessed, the unpaid balance of such income tax or any portion thereof may be collected from the stapled domestic corporation, provided that the following conditions are satisfied—

(i) The Commissioner has issued a notice and demand for payment of such income tax to the stapled foreign corporation in accordance with § 301.6303-1 of this Chapter;

(ii) The stapled foreign corporation has failed to pay the income tax by the date specified in such notice and demand;

(iii) The Commissioner has issued a notice and demand for payment of the unpaid portion of such income tax to the stapled domestic corporation in accordance with § 301.6303-1 of this Chapter.

(3) Collection from 10-percent shareholders of the stapled foreign corporation. The unpaid balance of the stapled foreign corporation's income tax liability may be collected from a 10-percent shareholder of the stapled foreign corporation, limited to each such shareholder's income tax liability as determined under paragraph (f)(4)(iv) of this section, provided the following conditions are satisfied—

(i) The Commissioner has issued a notice and demand to the stapled domestic corporation for the unpaid portion of the stapled foreign corporation's income tax liability, as provided in paragraph (f)(2)(iii) of this section;

(ii) The stapled domestic corporation has failed to pay the income tax by the date specified in such notice and demand;

(iii) The Commissioner has issued a notice and demand for payment of the unpaid portion of such income tax to such 10-percent shareholder of the stapled foreign corporation in accordance with § 301.6303-1 of this Chapter.

(4) Special rules and definitions. For purposes of this paragraph (f), the following rules and definitions apply:

(i) Stapled domestic corporation. A domestic corporation is a stapled domestic corporation with respect to a stapled foreign corporation if such domestic corporation and the stapled foreign corporation are stapled entities as described in paragraph (b)(1) of this section.

(ii) 10-percent shareholder. A 10-percent shareholder of a stapled foreign corporation is any person that owned directly 10 percent or more of the total value or total combined voting power of all classes of stock in the stapled foreign corporation for any day of the stapled foreign corporation's taxable year with respect to which the income tax liability relates.

(iii) 10-percent shareholder in the case of indirect ownership of stapled foreign corporation stock. [Reserved].

(iv) Determination of a 10-percent shareholder's income tax liability. The income tax liability of a 10-percent shareholder of a stapled foreign corporation, for the income tax of the stapled foreign corporation under section 269B and this section, is determined by assigning an equal portion of the total income tax liability of the stapled foreign corporation for the taxable year to each day in such corporation's taxable year, and then dividing that portion ratably among the shares outstanding for that day on the basis of the relative values of such shares. The liability of any 10-percent shareholder for this purpose is the sum of the income tax liability allocated to the shares held by such shareholder for each day in the taxable year.

(v) Income tax. The term income tax means any income tax liability imposed on a domestic corporation under title 26 of the United States Code, including additions to tax, additional amounts, penalties, and interest related to such income tax liability.

(g) Effective dates. *(1)* Except as provided in this paragraph (g), the provisions of this section are applicable for taxable years that begin after July 29, 2005.

(2) Paragraphs (d)(1) and (f) of this section (except as applied to the collection of tax from any 10-percent shareholder of a stapled foreign corporation that is a foreign person) are applicable beginning on—

(i) July 18, 1984, for any foreign corporation that became stapled to a domestic corporation after June 30, 1983; and

(ii) January 1, 1987, for any foreign corporation that was stapled to a domestic corporation as of June 30, 1983.

(3) Paragraph (d)(2) of this section is applicable for taxable years beginning after July 22, 2003, except that in the case of a foreign corporation that becomes stapled to a domestic corporation on or after July 22, 2003, paragraph (d)(2) of this section applies for taxable years ending on or after July 22, 2003.

(4) Paragraph (e) of this section is applicable beginning on July 18, 1984, except as provided in paragraph (g)(5) of this section.

(5) In the case of a foreign corporation that was stapled to a domestic corporation as of June 30, 1983, which was entitled to claim benefits under an income tax treaty as of that date, and which remains eligible for such treaty benefits, paragraph (e) of this section will not apply to such foreign corporation and for all purposes of the Internal Revenue Code such corporation will continue to be treated as a foreign entity. The prior sentence will continue to apply even if such treaty is subsequently modified by protocol, or superseded by a new treaty, so long as the stapled foreign corporation continues to be eligible to claim such treaty benefits. If the treaty benefits to which the stapled foreign corporation was entitled as of June 30, 1983, are terminated, then a deemed conversion of the foreign corporation to a domestic corporation shall occur pursuant to paragraph (c) of this section as of the date of such termination.

T.D. 9216, 7/28/2005.

§ 301.269B-1 Stapled foreign corporations.

In accordance with section 269B(a)(1), a stapled foreign corporation is subject to the same taxes that apply to a domestic corporation under Title 26 of the Internal Revenue Code. For provisions concerning taxes other than income for which the stapled foreign corporation is liable, apply the same rules as set forth in § 1.269B-1(a) through (f)(1)(i), and (g) of this Chapter, except that references to income tax shall be replaced with the term tax. In addition, for purposes of collecting those taxes solely from the stapled foreign corporation, the term tax means any tax liability imposed on a domestic corporation under Title 26 of the United States Code, including additions to tax, additional amounts, penalties, and interest related to that tax liability.

T.D. 9216, 7/28/2005.

§ 1.271-1 Debts owed by political parties.

(a) General rule. In the case of a taxpayer other than a bank (as defined in section 581 and the regulations thereunder), no deduction shall be allowed under section 166 (relating to bad debts) or section 165(g) (relating to worthlessness of securities) by reason of the worthlessness of any debt, regardless of how it arose, owed by a political party. For example, it is immaterial that the debt may have arisen as a result of services rendered or goods sold or that the taxpayer included the amount of the debt in income. In the case of a bank, no deduction shall be allowed unless, under the facts and circumstances, it appears that the bad debt was incurred to or purchased by, or the worthless security was acquired by, the taxpayer in accordance with its usual commercial practices. Thus, if a bank makes a loan to a political party not in accordance with its usual commercial practices but solely because the president of the bank has been active in the party no bad debt deduction will be allowed with respect to the loan.

(b) Definitions. *(1) Political party.* For purposes of this section and § 1.276-1, the term "political party" means a political party (as commonly understood), a National, State, or local committee thereof, or any committee, association, or organization, whether incorporated or not, which accepts contributions (as defined in subparagraph (2) of this paragraph) or makes expenditures (as defined in subparagraph (3) of this paragraph) for the purpose of influencing or attempting to influence the election of presidential or vice-presidential electors, or the selection, nomination, or election of any individual to any Federal, State, or local elective public office, whether or not such individual or electors are selected, nominated, or elected. Accordingly, a political party includes a committee or other group which accepts contributions or makes expenditures for the purpose of promoting the nomination of an individual for an elective public office in a primary election, or in any convention, meeting, or caucus of a political party. It is immaterial whether the contributions or expenditures are accepted or made directly or indirectly. Thus, for example, a committee or other group, is considered to be a political party, if, although it does not expend any funds, it turns funds over to another organization, which does expend funds for the purpose of attempting to influence the nomination of an individual for an elective public office. An organization which engages in activities which are truly nonpartisan in nature will not be considered a political party merely because it conducts activities with respect to an election campaign if, under all the facts and circumstances, it is clear that its efforts are not directed to the election of the candidates of any particular party or parties or to the selection, nomination or election of any particular candidate. For example, a committee or group will not be treated as a political party if it is organized merely to inform the electorate as to the identity and experience of all candidates involved, to present on a nonpreferential basis the issues or views of the parties or candidates as described by the parties or candidates, or to provide a forum in which the candidates are freely invited on a nonpreferential basis to discuss or debate the issues.

(2) Contributions. For purposes of this section and § 1.276-1, the term "contributions" includes a gift, subscription, loan, advance, or deposit, of money or anything of value, and includes a contract, promise, or agreement to make a contribution, whether or not legally enforceable.

(3) Expenditures. For purposes of this section and § 1.276-1, the term "expenditures" includes a payment, distribution, loan, advance, deposit, or gift, of money or anything of value, and includes a contract, promise, or agreement to make an expenditure, whether or not legally enforceable.

T.D. 6996, 1/17/69.

§ 1.272-1 Expenditures relating to disposal of coal or domestic iron ore.

(a) Introduction. Section 272 provides special treatment for certain expenditures paid or incurred by a taxpayer in connection with a contract (hereafter sometimes referred to as a "coal royalty contract" or "iron ore royalty contract") for the disposal of coal or iron ore the gain or loss from which is treated under section 631(c) as a section 1231 gain or loss on the sale of coal or iron ore. See paragraph (e) of § 1.631-3 for special rules relating to iron ore. The expenditures covered by section 272 are those which are attributable to the making and administering of such a contract or to the preservation of the economic interest retained under the contract. For examples of such expenditures, see paragraph (d) of this section. For a taxable year in which gross royalty income is realized under the contract of disposal, such expenditures shall not be allowed as a deduction. Instead, they are to be added to the adjusted depletion basis of the coal or iron ore disposed of in the taxable year in computing gain or loss under section 631(c). However, where no gross royalty income is realized under the contract of disposal in a particular taxable year, such expenditure shall be treated without regard to section 272.

(b) In general. *(1)* Where the disposal of coal or iron ore is covered by section 631(c), the provisions of section 272 and this section shall be applicable for a taxable year in which there is income under the contract of disposal. (For purposes of section 272 and this section, the term "income" means gross amounts received or accrued which are royalties or bonuses in connection with a contract to which section 631(c) applies.) All expenditures paid or incurred by the taxpayer during the taxable year which are attributable to the making and administering of the contract disposing of the coal or iron ore and all expenditures paid or incurred during the taxable year in order to preserve the owner's economic interest retained under the contract shall be disallowed as deductions in computing taxable income for the taxable year. The sum of such expenditures and the adjusted depletion basis of the coal or iron ore disposed of in the taxable year shall be used in determining the amount of gain or loss with respect to the disposal. See § 1.631-3. For special rule in case of loss, see paragraph (c) of this section. Section 272 and this section do not apply to capital expenditures, and such expenditures are not taken into account in computing gain or loss under section 631(c) except to the extent they are properly part of the depletable basis of the coal or iron ore.

(2) The expenditures covered under section 272 and this section are disallowed as a deduction only with respect to a taxable year in which income is realized under the coal royalty contract (or iron ore royalty contract) to which such expenditures are attributable. Where no income is realized under the contract in a taxable year, these expenditures shall be deducted as expenses for the production of income, or as a business expense, or they may be treated under section 266 (relating to taxes and carrying charges) if applicable.

(3) The provisions of section 272 and this section apply to a taxable year in which income from the disposal by the owner of coal or iron ore held by him for more than 1 year (6 months for taxable years beginning before 1977; 9 months for taxable years beginning in 1977) is subject to the provisions of section 631(c) even though the actual mining of coal or iron ore under the coal royalty contract (or iron ore royalty contract) does not take place during the taxable year. Where the right under the contract to mine coal or iron ore for which advance payment has been made expires, terminates, or is abandoned before the coal or iron ore is mined, and paragraph (c) of § 1.631-3 requires the owner to recompute his tax with respect to such payment, the recomputation must be made without applying the provisions of section 272 and this section.

(c) Losses. If, in any taxable year, the expenditures referred to in section 272 and this section plus the adjusted depletion basis (as defined in paragraph (b)(2) of § 1.631-3) of the coal or iron ore disposed of during the taxable year exceed the amount realized under the contract which is subject to section 631(c) during the taxable year, such excess shall be considered under section 1231 as a loss from the sale of property used in the trade or business and, to the extent not availed of as a reduction of gain under that section, shall be a loss deductible under section 165(a) (relating to the deduction of losses generally).

(d) Examples of expenditures. *(1)* The expenditures referred to in section 272 include, but are not limited to, the following items, if such items are attributable to the making or administering of the contract or preserving the economic interest therein: Ad valorem taxes imposed by State or local authorities, costs of fire protection, costs of insurance (other than liability insurance), costs incurred in administering the contract (including costs of bookkeeping and technical supervision), interest on loans, expenses of flood control, legal and technical expenses, and expenses of measuring and checking quantities of coal or iron ore disposed of under the contract. Whether the interest on loans is attributable to the making or administering of the contract or preserving the economic interest therein will depend upon the use to which the borrowed monies are put.

(2) Any expenditure referred to in this section which is applicable to more than one coal royalty contract or iron ore royalty contract shall be reasonably apportioned to each of such contracts. Furthermore, if an expenditure applies only in part to the making or administering of the contract or the preservation of the economic interest, then only such part shall be treated under section 272. The apportionment of the expenditure shall be made on a reasonable basis. For example, where a taxpayer has other income (such as income from oil or gas royalties, rentals, right of way fees, interest, or dividends) as well as income under section 631(c), and where the salaries of some of its employees or other expenses relate to both classes of income, such expenses shall be allocated reasonably between the income subject to section 631(c) and the other income. Where a taxpayer has more than one coal royalty contract or iron ore royalty contract, expenditures under this section relating to a contract from which no income has been received in the taxable year may not be allocated to income from another contract from which income has been received in the taxable year.

(3) The taxpayer may have expenses which are not attributable even partly to making and administering a coal royalty contract or iron ore royalty contract or to the preservation of the economic interest retained under the contract and, accordingly, are not included in the expenditures described in section 272. These include such items as ad valorem taxes imposed by State or local authorities on property not covered by the contract, salaries, wages, or other expenses entirely incident to the ownership and protection of such property and depreciation of improvements thereon, fire insurance on such property, charitable contributions, and similar expenses unrelated to the making or to the administering of coal royalty contracts or iron ore royalty contracts or preserving the taxpayer's economic interest retained therein.

(e) Nonapplication of section. For purposes of section 543, the provisions of section 272 shall have no application. For example, the taxpayer may, for the purposes of section 543(a)(3)(C) or the corresponding provisions of prior income tax laws, include in the sum of the deductions which are allowable under section 162 an amount paid to an attorney as compensation for legal services rendered in connection with the making of a coal royalty contract or iron ore royalty contract (assuming the expenditure otherwise qualifies under section 162 as an ordinary and necessary expense incurred in the taxpayer's trade or business), even though such expenditure is disallowed as a deduction under section 272.

T.D. 6281, 12/20/57, amend T.D. 6841, 7/26/65, T.D. 7728, 10/31/80.

§ 1.273-1 Life or terminable interests.

Amounts paid as income to the holder of a life or a terminable interest acquired by gift, bequest, or inheritance shall not be subject to any deduction for shrinkage (whether called by depreciation or any other name) in the value of such interest due to the lapse of time. In other words, the holder of such an interest so acquired may not set up the value of the expected future payments as corpus or principal and claim deduction for shrinkage or exhaustion thereof due to the passage of time. For the treatment generally of distributions to beneficiaries of an estate or trust, see subparts A, B, C, and D (section 641 and following), subchapter J, chapter 1 of the Code, and the regulations thereunder. For basis of property acquired from a decedent and by gifts and transfers in trust, see sections 1014 and 1015, and the regulations thereunder.

T.D. 6313, 9/16/58.

§ 1.274-1 Disallowance of certain entertainment, gift and travel expenses.

Section 274 disallows in whole, or in part, certain expenditures for entertainment, gifts and travel which would otherwise be allowable under chapter 1 of the Code. The requirements imposed by section 274 are in addition to the requirements for deductibility imposed by other provisions of the Code. If a deduction is claimed for an expenditure for entertainment, gifts, or travel, the taxpayer must first establish that it is otherwise allowable as a deduction under chapter 1 of the Code before the provisions of section 274 become applicable. An expenditure for entertainment, to the extent it is lavish or extravagant, shall not be allowable as a deduction. The taxpayer should then substantiate such an expenditure in accordance with the rules under section 274(d). See § 1.274-5. Section 274 is a disallowance provision exclusively, and does not make deductible any expense which is disallowed under any other provision of the Code. Similarly, section 274 does not affect the includability of an item in, or the excludability of an item from, the gross income of any taxpayer. For specific provisions with respect to the deductibility of expenditures: for an activity of a type generally considered to constitute entertainment, amusement, or recreation, and for a facility used in connection with such an activity, as well as certain travel expenses of a spouse, etc., see § 1.274-2; for expenses for gifts, see § 1.274-3; for expenses for foreign travel, see § 1.274-4; for expenditures deductible without regard to business activity, see § 1.274-6; and for treatment of personal portion of entertainment facility, see § 1.274-7.

T.D. 6659, 6/24/63, amend T.D. 8666, 5/29/96.

PAR. 5.

Section 1.274-1 is amended by removing everything after the word "business" in the last sentence of paragraph (d) and adding in its place "activity, see § 1.274-6,"; revising paragraph (e) and adding paragraph (f) to read as follows:

Proposed § 1.274-1 [Amended] [*For Preamble, see ¶ 151,137*]

(e) treatment of personal portion of entertainment facility, see § 1.274-7, and

(f) employee achievement awards, see § 1.274-8.

§ 1.274-2 Disallowance of deductions for certain expenses for entertainment, amusement, recreation, or travel.

Caution: The Treasury has not yet amended Reg § 1.274-2 to reflect changes made by P.L. 108-357, P.L. 100-647, P.L. 99-514.

(a) General rules. *(1) Entertainment activity.* Except as provided in this section, no deduction otherwise allowable under chapter 1 of the Code shall be allowed for any expenditure with respect to entertainment unless the taxpayer establishes—

(i) That the expenditure was directly related to the active conduct of the taxpayer's trade or business, or

(ii) In the case of an expenditure directly preceding or following a substantial and bona fide business discussion (including business meetings at a convention or otherwise), that the expenditure was associated with the active conduct of the taxpayer's trade or business.

Such deduction shall not exceed the portion of the expenditure directly related to (or in the case of an expenditure described in subdivision (ii) of this subparagraph, the portion of the expenditure associated with) the active conduct of the taxpayer's trade or business.

(2) Entertainment facilities. (i) Expenditures paid or incurred after December 31, 1978, and not with respect to a club. Except as provided in this section with respect to a club, no deduction otherwise allowable under chapter 1 of the Code shall be allowed for any expenditure paid or incurred after December 31, 1978, with respect to a facility used in connection with entertainment.

(ii) Expenditures paid or incurred before January 1, 1979, with respect to entertainment facilities, or paid or incurred before January 1, 1994, with respect to clubs. (a) Requirements for deduction. Except as provided in this section, no deduction otherwise allowable under chapter 1 of the Internal Revenue Code shall be allowed for any expenditure paid or incurred before January 1, 1979, with respect to a facility used in connection with entertainment, or for any expenditure paid or incurred before January 1, 1994, with respect to a club used in connection with entertainment, unless the taxpayer establishes—

(1) That the facility or club was used primarily for the furtherance of the taxpayer's trade or business; and

(2) That the expenditure was directly related to the active conduct of that trade or business.

(b) Amount of deduction. The deduction allowable under paragraph (a)(2)(ii)(a) of this section shall not exceed the portion of the expenditure directly related to the active conduct of the taxpayer's trade or business.

(iii) Expenditures paid or incurred after December 31, 1993, with respect to a club. (a) In general. No deduction otherwise allowable under chapter 1 of the Internal Revenue Code shall be allowed for amounts paid or incurred after December 31, 1993, for membership in any club organized for business, pleasure, recreation, or other social purpose. The purposes and activities of a club, and not its name, determine whether it is organized for business, pleasure, recreation, or other social purpose. Clubs organized for business, pleasure, recreation, or other social purpose include any membership organization if a principal purpose of the organization is to conduct entertainment activities for members of the organization or their guests or to provide members or their guests with access to entertainment facilities within the meaning of paragraph (e)(2) of this section. Clubs organized for business, pleasure, recreation, or other social purpose include, but are not limited to, country clubs, golf and athletic clubs, airline clubs, hotel clubs, and clubs operated to provide meals under circumstances generally considered to be conducive to business discussion.

(b) Exceptions. Unless a principal purpose of the organization is to conduct entertainment activities for members or their guests or to provide members or their guests with access to entertainment facilities, business leagues, trade associations, chambers of commerce, boards of trade, real estate boards, professional organizations (such as bar associations and medical associations), and civic or public service organizations will not be treated as clubs organized for business, pleasure, recreation, or other social purpose.

(3) Cross references. For definition of the term "entertainment", see paragraph (b)(1) of this section. For the disallowance of deductions for the cost of admission to a dinner or program any part of the proceeds of which inures to the use of a political party or political candidate, and cost of admission to an inaugural event or similar event identified with any political party or political candidate, see § 1.276-1. For rules and definitions with respect to—

(i) "Directly related entertainment", see paragraph (c) of this section,

(ii) "Associated entertainment", see paragraph (d) of this section,

(iii) "Expenditures paid or incurred before January 1, 1979, with respect to entertainment facilities or before January 1, 1994, with respect to clubs", see paragraph (e) of this section, and

(iv) "Specific exceptions", to the disallowance rules of this section, see paragraph (f) of this section.

(b) Definitions. *(1) Entertainment defined.* (i) In general. For purposes of this section, the term "entertainment" means any activity which is of a type generally considered to constitute entertainment, amusement, or recreation, such as entertaining at night clubs, cocktail lounges, theaters, country clubs, golf and athletic clubs, sporting events, and on hunting, fishing, vacation and similar trips, including such activity relating solely to the taxpayer or the taxpayer's family. The term "entertainment" may include an activity, the cost of which is claimed as a business expense by the taxpayer, which satisfies the personal, living, or family needs of any individual, such as providing food and beverages, a hotel suite, or an automobile to a business customer or his family. The term "entertainment" does not include activities which, although satisfying personal, living, or family needs of an individual, are clearly not regarded as constituting entertainment, such as (a) supper money provided by an employer to his employee working overtime, (b) a hotel room maintained by an employer for lodging of his employees while in business travel status, or (c) an automobile used in the active conduct of trade or business even though used for routine personal purposes such as commuting to and from work. On the other hand, the providing of a hotel room or an automobile by an employer to his employee who is on vacation would constitute entertainment of the employee.

(ii) Objective test. An objective test shall be used to determine whether an activity is of a type generally considered to constitute entertainment. Thus, if an activity is generally considered to be entertainment, it will constitute entertainment for purposes of this section and section 274(a) regardless of whether the expenditure can also be described otherwise, and even though the expenditure relates to the taxpayer alone. This objective test precludes arguments such as that "entertainment" means only entertainment of others or that an expenditure for entertainment should be characterized as an expenditure for advertising or public relations. However, in applying this test the taxpayer's trade or business shall be considered. Thus, although attending a theatrical performance would generally be considered entertainment, it would not be so considered in the case of a professional theater critic, attending in his professional capacity. Similarly, if a manufacturer of dresses conducts a fashion show to introduce his products to a group of store buyers, the show would not be generally considered to constitute entertainment. However, if an appliance distributor conducts a fashion show for the wives of his retailers, the fashion show would be generally considered to constitute entertainment.

(iii) Special definitional rules. (a) In general. Except as otherwise provided in (b) or (c) of this subdivision, any expenditure which might generally be considered either for a gift or entertainment, or considered either for travel or entertainment, shall be considered an expenditure for entertainment rather than for a gift or travel.

(b) Expenditures deemed gifts. An expenditure described in (a) of this subdivision shall be deemed for a gift to which this section does not apply if it is:

(1) An expenditure for packaged food or beverages transferred directly or indirectly to another person intended for consumption at a later time.

(2) An expenditure for tickets of admission to a place of entertainment transferred to another person if the taxpayer does not accompany the recipient to the entertainment unless the taxpayer treats the expenditure as entertainment. The taxpayer may change his treatment of such an expenditure as either a gift or entertainment at any time within the period prescribed for assessment of tax as provided in section 6501 of the Code and the regulations thereunder.

(3) Such other specific classes of expenditure generally considered to be for a gift as the Commissioner, in his discretion, may prescribe.

(c) Expenditures deemed travel. An expenditure described in (a) of this subdivision shall be deemed for travel to which this section does not apply if it is:

(1) With respect to a transportation type facility (such as an automobile or an airplane), even though used on other occasions in connection with an activity of a type generally considered to constitute entertainment, to the extent the facility is used in pursuit of a trade or business for purposes of transportation not in connection with entertainment. See also paragraph (e)(3)(iii)(b) of this section for provisions covering nonentertainment expenditures with respect to such facilities.

(2) Such other specific classes of expenditure generally considered to be for travel as the Commissioner, in his discretion, may prescribe.

(2) Other definitions. (i) Expenditure. The term "expenditure" as used in this section shall include expenses paid or incurred for goods, services, facilities, and items (including items such as losses and depreciation).

(ii) Expenses for production of income. For purposes of this section, any reference to "trade or business" shall include any activity described in section 212.

(iii) Business associate. The term "business associate" as used in this section means a person with whom the taxpayer could reasonably expect to engage or deal in the active conduct of the taxpayer's trade or business such as the taxpayer's customer, client, supplier, employee, agent, partner, or professional adviser, whether established or prospective.

(c) Directly related entertainment. *(1) In general.* Except as otherwise provided in paragraph (d) of this section (relating to associated entertainment) or under paragraph (f) of this section (relating to business meals and other specific exceptions), no deduction shall be allowed for any expenditure for entertainment unless the taxpayer establishes that the expenditure was directly related to the active conduct of his trade or business within the meaning of this paragraph.

(2) Directly related entertainment defined. Any expenditure for entertainment, if it is otherwise allowable as a deduction under chapter 1 of the Code, shall be considered directly related to the active conduct of the taxpayer's trade or business if it meets the requirements of any one of subparagraphs (3), (4), (5), or (6) of this paragraph.

(3) Directly related in general. Except as provided in subparagraph (7) of this paragraph, an expenditure for entertainment shall be considered directly related to the active conduct of the taxpayer's trade or business if it is established that it meets all of the requirements of subdivisions (i), (ii), (iii) and (iv) of this subparagraph.

(i) At the time the taxpayer made the entertainment expenditure (or committed himself to make the expenditure), the taxpayer had more than a general expectation of deriving some income or other specific trade or business benefit (other than the goodwill of the person or persons entertained) at some indefinite future time from the making of the expenditure. A taxpayer, however, shall not be required to show that income or other business benefit actually resulted from each and every expenditure for which a deduction is claimed.

(ii) During the entertainment period to which the expenditure related, the taxpayer actively engaged in a business meeting, negotiation, discussion, or other bona fide business transaction, other than entertainment, for the purpose of obtaining such income or other specific trade or business benefit (or, at the time the taxpayer made the expenditure or committed himself to the expenditure, it was reasonable for the taxpayer to expect that he would have done so, although such was not the case solely for reasons beyond the taxpayer's control).

(iii) In light of all the facts and circumstances of the case, the principal character or aspect of the combined business and entertainment to which the expenditure related was the active conduct of the taxpayer's trade or business (or at the time the taxpayer made the expenditure or committed himself to the expenditure, it was reasonable for the taxpayer to expect that the active conduct of trade or business would have been the principal character or aspect of the entertainment, although such was not the case solely for reasons beyond the taxpayer's control). It is not necessary that more time be devoted to business than to entertainment to meet this requirement. The active conduct of trade or business is considered not to be the principal character or aspect of combined business and entertainment activity on hunting or fishing trips or on yachts and other pleasure boats unless the taxpayer clearly establishes to the contrary.

(iv) The expenditure was allocable to the taxpayer and a person or persons with whom the taxpayer engaged in the active conduct of trade or business during the entertainment or with whom the taxpayer establishes he would have engaged in such active conduct of trade or business if it were not for circumstances beyond the taxpayer's control. For expenditures closely connected with directly related entertainment, see paragraph (d)(4) of this section.

(4) Expenditures in clear business setting. An expenditure for entertainment shall be considered directly related to the active conduct of the taxpayer's trade or business if it is established that the expenditure was for entertainment occurring in a clear business setting directly in furtherance of the taxpayer's trade or business. Generally, entertainment shall not be considered to have occurred in a clear business setting unless the taxpayer clearly establishes that any recipient of the entertainment would have reasonably known that the taxpayer had no significant motive, in incurring the expendi-

ture, other than directly furthering his trade or business. Objective rather than subjective standards will be determinative. Thus, entertainment which occurred under any circumstances described in subparagraph (7)(ii) of this paragraph ordinarily will not be considered as occurring in a clear business setting. Such entertainment will generally be considered to be socially rather than commercially motivated. Expenditures made for the furtherance of a taxpayer's trade or business in providing a "hospitality room" at a convention (described in paragraph (d)(3)(i)(b) of this section) at which goodwill is created through display or discussion of the taxpayer's products, will, however, be treated as directly related. In addition, entertainment of a clear business nature which occurred under circumstances where there was no meaningful personal or social relationship between the taxpayer and the recipients of the entertainment may be considered to have occurred in a clear business setting. For example, entertainment of business representatives and civic leaders at the opening of a new hotel or theatrical production, where the clear purpose of the taxpayer is to obtain business publicity rather than to create or maintain the goodwill of the recipients of the entertainment, would generally be considered to be in a clear business setting. Also, entertainment which has the principal effect of a price rebate in connection with the sale of the taxpayer's products generally will be considered to have occurred in a clear business setting. Such would be the case, for example, if a taxpayer owning a hotel were to provide occasional free dinners at the hotel for a customer who patronized the hotel.

(5) Expenditures for services performed. An expenditure shall be considered directly related to the active conduct of the taxpayer's trade or business if it is established that the expenditure was made directly or indirectly by the taxpayer for the benefit of an individual (other than an employee), and if such expenditure was in the nature of compensation for services rendered or was paid as a prize or award which is required to be included in gross income under section 74 and the regulations thereunder. For example, if a manufacturer of products provides a vacation trip for retailers of his products who exceed sales quotas as a prize or award which is includible in gross income, the expenditure will be considered directly related to the active conduct of the taxpayer's trade or business.

(6) Club dues, etc., allocable to business meals. An expenditure shall be considered directly related to the active conduct of the taxpayer's trade or business if it is established that the expenditure was with respect to a facility (as described in paragraph (e) of this section) used by the taxpayer for the furnishing of food or beverages under circumstances described in paragraph (f)(2)(i) of this section (relating to business meals and similar expenditures), to the extent allocable to the furnishing of such food or beverages. This paragraph (c)(6) applies to club dues paid or incurred before January 1, 1987.

(7) Expenditures generally considered not directly related. Expenditures for entertainment, even if connected with the taxpayer's trade or business, will generally be considered not directly related to the active conduct of the taxpayer's trade or business, if the entertainment occurred under circumstances where there was little or no possibility of engaging in the active conduct of trade or business. The following circumstances will generally be considered circumstances where there was little or no possibility of engaging in the active conduct of a trade or business:

(i) The taxpayer was not present;

(ii) The distractions were substantial, such as—

(a) A meeting or discussion at night clubs, theaters, and sporting events, or during essentially social gatherings such as cocktail parties, or

(b) A meeting or discussion, if the taxpayer meets with a group which includes persons other than business associates, at places such as cocktail lounges, country clubs, golf and athletic clubs, or at vacation resorts.

An expenditure for entertainment in any such case is considered not to be directly related to the active conduct of the taxpayer's trade or business unless the taxpayer clearly establishes to the contrary.

(d) Associated entertainment. *(1) In general.* Except as provided in paragraph (f) of this section (relating to business meals and other specific exceptions) and subparagraph (4) of this paragraph (relating to expenditures closely connected with directly related entertainment), any expenditure for entertainment which is not directly related to the active conduct of the taxpayer's trade or business will not be allowable as a deduction unless—

(i) It was associated with the active conduct of trade or business as defined in subparagraph (2) of this paragraph, and

(ii) The entertainment directly preceded or followed a substantial and bona fide business discussion as defined in subparagraph (3) of this paragraph.

(2) Associated entertainment defined. Generally, any expenditure for entertainment, if it is otherwise allowable under chapter 1 of the Code, shall be considered associated with the active conduct of the taxpayer's trade or business if the taxpayer establishes that he had a clear business purpose in making the expenditure, such as to obtain new business or to encourage the continuation of an existing business relationship. However, any portion of an expenditure allocable to a person who was not closely connected with a person who engaged in the substantial and bona fide business discussion (as defined in subparagraph (3)(i) of this paragraph) shall not be considered associated with the active conduct of the taxpayer's trade or business. The portion of an expenditure allocable to the spouse of a person who engaged in the discussion will, if it is otherwise allowable under chapter 1 of the Code, be considered associated with the active conduct of the taxpayer's trade or business.

(3) Directly preceding or following a substantial and bona fide business discussion defined. (i) Substantial and bona fide business discussion. (a) In general. Whether any meeting, negotiation or discussion constitutes a "substantial and bona fide business discussion" within the meaning of this section depends upon the facts and circumstances of each case. It must be established, however, that the taxpayer actively engaged in a business meeting, negotiation, discussion, or other bona fide business transaction, other than entertainment, for the purpose of obtaining income or other specific trade or business benefit. In addition, it must be established that such a business meeting, negotiation, discussion, or transaction was substantial in relation to the entertainment. This requirement will be satisfied if the principal character or aspect of the combined entertainment and business activity was the active conduct of business. However, it is not necessary that more time be devoted to business than to entertainment to meet this requirement.

(b) Meetings at conventions, etc. Any meeting officially scheduled in connection with a program at a convention or similar general assembly, or at a bona fide trade or business meeting sponsored and conducted by business or professional organizations, shall be considered to constitute a substantial and bona fide business discussion within the meaning of this section provided—

(1) Expenses necessary to taxpayer's attendance. The expenses necessary to the attendance of the taxpayer at the convention, general assembly, or trade or business meeting, were ordinary and necessary within the meaning of section 162 or 212;

(2) Convention program. The organization which sponsored the convention, or trade or business meeting had scheduled a program of business activities (including committee meetings or presentation of lectures, panel discussions, display of products, or other similar activities), and that such program was the principal activity of the convention, general assembly, or trade or business meeting.

(ii) Directly preceding or following. Entertainment which occurs on the same day as a substantial and bona fide business discussion (as defined in subdivision (i) of this subparagraph) will be considered to directly precede or follow such discussion. If the entertainment and the business discussion do not occur on the same day, the facts and circumstances of each case are to be considered, including the place, date and duration of the business discussion, whether the taxpayer or his business associates are from out of town, and, if so, the date of arrival and departure, and the reasons the entertainment did not take place on the day of the business discussion. For example, if a group of business associates comes from out of town to the taxpayer's place of business to hold a substantial business discussion, the entertainment of such business guests and their wives on the evening prior to, or on the evening of the day following, the business discussion would generally be regarded as directly preceding or following such discussion.

(4) Expenses closely connected with directly related entertainment. If any portion of an expenditure meets the requirements of paragraph (c)(3) of this section (relating to directly related entertainment in general), the remaining portion of the expenditure, if it is otherwise allowable under chapter 1 of the Code, shall be considered associated with the active conduct of the taxpayer's trade or business to the extent allocable to a person or persons closely connected with a person referred to in paragraph (c)(3)(iv) of this section. The spouse of a person referred to in paragraph (c)(3)(iv) of this section will be considered closely connected to such a person for purposes of this subparagraph. Thus, if a taxpayer and his wife entertain a business customer and the customer's wife under circumstances where the entertainment of the customer is considered directly related to the active conduct of the taxpayer's trade or business (within the meaning of paragraph (c)(3) of this section) the portion of the expenditure allocable to both wives will be considered associated with the active conduct of the taxpayer's trade or business under this subparagraph.

(e) Expenditures paid or incurred before January 1, 1979, with respect to entertainment facilities or before January 1, 1994, with respect to clubs. *(1) In general.* Any expenditure paid or incurred before January 1, 1979, with respect to a facility, or paid or incurred before January 1, 1994, with respect to a club, used in connection with entertainment shall not be allowed as a deduction except to the extent it meets the requirements of paragraph (a)(2)(ii) of this section.

(2) Facilities used in connection with entertainment. (i) In general. Any item of personal or real property owned, rented, or used by a taxpayer shall (unless otherwise provided under the rules of subdivision (ii) of this subparagraph) be considered to constitute a facility used in connection with entertainment if it is used during the taxable year for, or in connection with, entertainment (as defined in paragraph (b)(1) of this section). Examples of facilities which might be used for, or in connection with, entertainment include yachts, hunting lodges, fishing camps, swimming pools, tennis courts, bowling alleys, automobiles, airplanes, apartments, hotel suites, and homes in vacation resorts.

(ii) Facilities used incidentally for entertainment. A facility used only incidentally during a taxable year in connection with entertainment, if such use is insubstantial, will not be considered a "facility used in connection with entertainment" for purposes of this section or for purposes of the recordkeeping requirements of section 274(d). See § 1.274-5(c)(6)(iii).

(3) Expenditures with respect to a facility used in connection with entertainment. (i) In general. The phrase "expenditures with respect to a facility used in connection with entertainment" includes depreciation and operating costs, such as rent and utility charges (for example, water or electricity), expenses for the maintenance, preservation or protection of a facility (for example, repairs, painting, insurance charges), and salaries or expenses for subsistence paid to caretakers or watchmen. In addition, the phrase includes losses realized on the sale or other disposition of a facility.

(ii) Club dues. (a) Club dues paid or incurred before January 1, 1994. Dues or fees paid before January 1, 1994, to any social, athletic, or sporting club or organization are considered expenditures with respect to a facility used in connection with entertainment. The purposes and activities of a club or organization, and not its name, determine its character. Generally, the phrase *social, athletic, or sporting club or organization* has the same meaning for purposes of this section as that phrase had in section 4241 and the regulations thereunder, relating to the excise tax on club dues, prior to the repeal of section 4241 by section 301 of Public Law 89-44. However, for purposes of this section only, clubs operated solely to provide lunches under circumstances of a type generally considered to be conducive to business discussion, within the meaning of paragraph (f)(2)(i) of this section, will not be considered social clubs.

(b) Club dues paid or incurred after December 31, 1993. See paragraph (a)(2)(iii) of this section with reference to the disallowance of deductions for club dues paid or incurred after December 31, 1993.

(iii) Expenditures not with respect to a facility. The following expenditures shall not be considered to constitute expenditures with respect to a facility used in connection with entertainment—

(a) Out of pocket expenditures. Expenses (exclusive of operating costs and other expenses referred to in subdivision (i) of this subparagraph) incurred at the time of an entertainment activity, even though in connection with the use of facility for entertainment purposes, such as expenses for food and beverages, or expenses for catering, or expenses for gasoline and fishing bait consumed on a fishing trip;

(b) Non-entertainment expenditures. Expenses or items attributable to the use of a facility for other than entertainment purposes such as expenses for an automobile when not used for entertainment; and

(c) Expenditures otherwise deductible. Expenses allowable as a deduction without regard to their connection with a taxpayer's trade or business such as taxes, interest, and casualty losses. The provisions of this subdivision shall be applied in the case of a taxpayer which is not an individual as if it were an individual. See also § 1.274-6.

(iv) Cross reference. For other rules with respect to treatment of certain expenditures for entertainment-type facilities, see § 1.274-7.

(4) Determination of primary use. (i) In general. A facility used in connection with entertainment shall be considered as used primarily for the furtherance of the taxpayer's trade or business only if it is established that the primary use of the facility during the taxable year was for purposes considered ordinary and necessary within the meaning of sections 162 and 212 and the regulations thereunder. All of the facts and circumstances of each case shall be considered in determining the primary use of a facility. Generally, it is the actual use of the facility which establishes the deductibility of expenditures with respect to the facility; not its availability for use and not the taxpayer's principal purpose in acquiring the facility. Objective rather than subjective standards will be determinative. If membership entitles the member's entire family to use of a facility, such as a country club, their use will be considered in determining whether business use of the facility exceeds personal use. The factors to be considered include the nature of each use, and frequency and duration of use for business purposes as compared with other purposes, and the amount of expenditures incurred during use for business compared with amount of expenditures incurred during use for other purposes. No single standard of comparison, or quantitative measurement, as to the significance of any such factor, however, is necessarily appropriate for all classes or types of facilities. For example, an appropriate standard for determining the primary use of a country club during a taxable year will not necessarily be appropriate for determining the primary use of an airplane. However, a taxpayer shall be deemed to have established that a facility was used primarily for the furtherance of his trade or business if he establishes such primary use in accordance with subdivision (ii) or (iii) of the subparagraph. Subdivisions (ii) and (iii) of this subparagraph shall not preclude a taxpayer from otherwise establishing the primary use of a facility under the general provisions of this subdivision.

(ii) Certain transportation facilities. A taxpayer shall be deemed to have established that a facility of a type described in this subdivision was used primarily for the furtherance of his trade or business if—

(a) Automobiles. In the case of an automobile, the taxpayer establishes that more than 50 percent of mileage driven during the taxable year was in connection with travel considered to be ordinary and necessary within the meaning of section 162 or 212 and the regulations thereunder.

(b) Airplanes. In the case of an airplane, the taxpayer establishes that more than 50 percent of hours flown during the taxable year was in connection with travel considered to be ordinary and necessary within the meaning of section 162 or 212 and the regulations thereunder.

(iii) Entertainment facilities in general. A taxpayer shall be deemed to have established that—

(a) A facility used in connection with entertainment, such as a yacht or other pleasure boat, hunting lodge, fishing camp, summer home or vacation cottage, hotel suite, country club, golf club or similar social, athletic, or sporting club or organization, bowling alley, tennis court, or swimming pool, or,

(b) A facility for employees not falling within the scope of section 274(e)(2) or (5) was used primarily for the furtherance of his trade or business if he establishes that more than 50 percent of the total calendar days of use of the facility by, or under authority of, the taxpayer during the taxable year were days of business use. Any use of a facility (of a type described in this subdivision) during one calendar day shall be considered to constitute a "day of business use" if the primary use of the facility on such day was ordinary and necessary within the meaning of section 162 or 212 and the regulations thereunder. For the purposes of this subdivision, a facility shall be deemed to have been primarily used for such purposes on any one calendar day if the facility was used for the conduct of a substantial and bona fide business discussion (as defined in paragraph (d)(3)(i) of this section) notwithstanding that the facility may also have been used on the same day for personal or family use by the taxpayer or any member of the taxpayer's family not involving entertainment of others by, or under the authority of, the taxpayer.

(f) Specific exceptions to application of this section. *(1) In general.* The provisions of paragraphs (a) through (e) of this section (imposing limitations on deductions for entertainment expenses) are not applicable in the case of expenditures set forth in subparagraph (2) of this paragraph. Such expenditures are deductible to the extent allowable under chapter 1 of the Code. This paragraph shall not be construed to affect the allowability or nonallowability of a deduction under section 162 or 212 and the regulations thereunder. The fact that an expenditure is not covered by a specific exception provided for in this paragraph shall not be determinative of the allowability or nonallowability of the expenditure under paragraphs (a) through (e) of this section. Expenditures described in subparagraph (2) of this paragraph are subject to the substantiation requirements of section 274(d) to the extent provided in § 1.274-5.

(2) Exceptions. The expenditures referred to in subparagraph (1) of this paragraph are set forth in subdivisions (i) through (ix) of this subparagraph.

(i) Business meals and similar expenditures paid or incurred before January 1, 1987. (a) In general. Any expenditure for food or beverages furnished to an individual under circumstances of a type generally considered conducive to business discussion (taking into account the surroundings in which furnished, the taxpayer's trade, business, or income-producing activity, and the relationship to such trade, business or activity of the persons to whom the food or beverages are furnished) is not subject to the limitations on allowability of deductions provided for in paragraphs (a) through (e) of this section. There is no requirement that business actually be discussed for this exception to apply.

(b) Surroundings. The surroundings in which the food or beverages are furnished must be such as would provide an atmosphere where there are no substantial distractions to discussion. This exception applies primarily to expenditures for meals and beverages served during the course of a breakfast, lunch or dinner meeting of the taxpayer and his business associates at a restaurant, hotel dining room, eating club or similar place not involving distracting influences such as a floor show. This exception also applies to expenditures for beverages served apart from meals if the expenditure is incurred in surroundings similarly conducive to business discussion, such as an expenditure for beverages served during the meeting of the taxpayer and his business associates at a cocktail lounge or hotel bar not involving distracting influences such as a floor show. This exception may also apply to expenditures for meals or beverages served in the taxpayer's residence on a clear showing that the expenditure was commercially rather than socially motivated. However, this exception, generally, is not applicable to any expenditure for meals or beverages furnished in circumstances where there are major distractions not conducive to business discussion, such as at night clubs, sporting events, large cocktail parties, sizeable social gatherings, or other major distracting influences.

(c) Taxpayer's trade or business and relationship of persons entertained. The taxpayer's trade, business, or income-producing activity and the relationship of the persons to whom the food or beverages are served to such trade, business or activity must be such as will reasonably indicate that the food or beverages were furnished for the primary purpose of furthering the taxpayer's trade or business and did not primarily serve a social or personal purpose. Such a business purpose would be indicated, for example, if a salesman employed by a manufacturing supply company meets for lunch during a normal business day with a purchasing agent for a manufacturer which is a prospective customer. Such a purpose would also be indicated if a life insurance agent meets for lunch during a normal business day with a client.

(d) Business programs. Expenditures for business luncheons or dinners which are part of a business program, or banquets officially sponsored by business or professional associations, will be regarded as expenditures to which the exception of this subdivision (i) applies. In the case of such a business luncheon or dinner it is not always necessary that the taxpayer attend the luncheon or dinner himself. For example, if a dental equipment supplier purchased a table at a dental association banquet for dentists who are actual or prospective customers for his equipment, the cost of the table would not be disallowed under this section. See also paragraph (c)(4) of this section relating to expenditures made in a clear business setting.

(ii) Food and beverages for employees. Any expenditure by a taxpayer for food and beverages (or for use of a facility in connection therewith) furnished on the taxpayer's business premises primarily for his employees is not subject to the limitations on allowability of deductions provided for in paragraphs (a) through (e) of this section. This exception applies not only to expenditures for food or beverages furnished in a typical company cafeteria or an executive dining room, but also to expenditures with respect to the operation of such facilities. This exception applies even though guests are occasionally served in the cafeteria or dining room.

(iii) Certain entertainment and travel expenses treated as compensation. (A) In general. Any expenditure by a taxpayer for entertainment (or for use of a facility in connection therewith) or for travel described in section 274(m)(3), if an employee is the recipient of the entertainment or travel, is not subject to the limitations on allowability of deductions provided for in paragraphs (a) through (e) of this section to the extent that the expenditure is treated by the taxpayer—

(1) On the taxpayer's income tax return as originally filed, as compensation paid to the employee; and

(2) As wages to the employee for purposes of withholding under chapter 24 (relating to collection of income tax at source on wages).

(B) Expenses includible in income of persons who are not employees. Any expenditure by a taxpayer for entertainment (or for use of a facility in connection therewith), or for travel described in section 274(m)(3), is not subject to the limitations on allowability of deductions provided for in paragraphs (a) through (e) of this section to the extent the expenditure is includible in gross income as compensation for services rendered, or as a prize or award under section 74, by a recipient of the expenditure who is not an employee of the taxpayer. The preceding sentence shall not apply to any amount paid or incurred by the taxpayer if such amount is required to be included (or would be so required except that the amount is less that $600) in any information return filed by such taxpayer under part III of subchapter A of chapter 61 and is not so included. See section 274(e)(9).

(C) Example. The following example illustrates the provisions this paragraph (f):

Example. If an employer rewards the employee (and the employee's spouse) with an expense paid vacation trip, the expense is deductible by the employer (if otherwise allowable under section 162 and the regulations thereunder) to the extent the employer treats the expenses as compensation and as wages. On the other hand, if a taxpayer owns a yacht which the taxpayer uses for the entertainment of business customers, the portion of salary paid to employee members of the crew which is allocable to use of the yacht for entertainment purposes (even though treated on the taxpayer's tax return as compensation and treated as wages for withholding tax purposes) would not come within this exception since the members of the crew were not recipients of the entertainment. If an expenditure of a type described in this subdivision properly constitutes a dividend paid to a shareholder or if it constitutes unreasonable compensation paid to an employee, nothing in this exception prevents disallowance of the expenditure to the taxpayer under other provisions of the Internal Revenue Code.

(iv) Reimbursed entertainment expenses. (a) Introductory. In the case of any expenditure for entertainment paid or incurred by one person in connection with the performance by him of services for another person (whether or not such other person is an employer) under a reimbursement or other expense allowance arrangement, the limitations on allowability of deductions provided for in paragraphs (a) through (e) of this section shall be applied only once, either (1) to the person who makes the expenditure or (2) to the person who actually bears the expense, but not to both. For purposes of this subdivision (iv), the term "reimbursement or other expense allowance arrangement" has the same meaning as it has in section 62(2)(A), but without regard to whether the taxpayer is the employee of a person for whom services are performed. If an expenditure of a type described in this subdivision properly constitutes a dividend paid to a shareholder, unreasonable compensation paid to an employee, or a personal, living or family expense, nothing in this exception prevents disallowance of the expenditure to the taxpayer under other provisions of the Code.

(b) Reimbursement arrangements between employee and employer. In the case of an expenditure for entertainment paid or incurred by an employee under a reimbursement or other expense allowance arrangement with his employer, the limitations on deductions provided for in paragraphs (a) through (e) of this section shall not apply—

(1) Employees. To the employee except to the extent his employer has treated the expenditure on the employer's income tax return as originally filed as compensation paid to the employee and as wages to such employee for purposes of withholding under chapter 24 (relating to collection of income tax at source on wages).

(2) Employers. To the employer to the extent he has treated the expenditure as compensation and wages paid to an employee in the manner provided in (b)(1) of this subdivision.

(c) Reimbursement arrangements between independent contractors and clients or customers. In the case of an expenditure for entertainment paid or incurred by one person (hereinafter termed "independent contractor") under a reimbursement or other expense allowance arrangement with another person other than an employer (hereinafter termed "client or customer"), the limitations on deductions provided for in paragraphs (a) through (e) of this section shall not apply—

(1) Independent contractors. To the independent contractor to the extent he accounts to his client or customer within the meaning of section 274(d) and the regulations thereunder. See § 1.274-5.

(2) Clients or customers. To the client or customer if the expenditure is disallowed to the independent contractor under paragraphs (a) through (e) of this section.

(v) Recreational expenses for employees generally. Any expenditure by a taxpayer for a recreational, social, or similar activity (or for use of a facility in connection therewith), primarily for the benefit of his employees generally, is not subject to the limitations on allowability of deductions provided for in paragraphs (a) through (e) of this section. This exception applies only to expenditures made primarily for the benefit of employees of the taxpayer other than employees who are officers, shareholders or other owners who own a 10-percent or greater interest in the business, or other highly compensated employees. For purposes of the preceding sentence, an employee shall be treated as owning any interest owned by a member of his family (within the meaning of section 267(c)(4) and the regulations thereunder). Ordinarily, this exception applies to usual employee benefit programs such as expenses of a taxpayer (a) in holding Christmas parties, annual picnics, or summer outings, for his employees generally, or (b) of maintaining a swimming pool, baseball diamond, bowling alley, or golf course available to his employees generally. Any expenditure for an activity which is made under circumstances which discriminate in favor of employees who are officers, shareholders or other owners, or highly compensated employees shall not be considered made primarily for the benefit of employees generally. On the other hand, an expenditure for an activity will not be considered outside of this exception merely because, due to the large number of employees involved, the activity is intended to benefit only a limited number of such employees at one time, provided the activity does not discriminate in favor of officers, shareholders, other owners, or highly compensated employees.

(vi) Employee, stockholder, etc., business meetings. Any expenditure by a taxpayer for entertainment which is directly related to bona fide business meetings of the taxpayer's employees, stockholders, agents, or directors held principally for discussion of trade or business is not subject to the limitations on allowability of deductions provided for in paragraphs (a) through (e) of this section. For purposes of this exception, a partnership is to be considered a taxpayer and a member of a partnership is to be considered an agent. For example, an expenditure by a taxpayer to furnish refreshments to his employees at a bona fide meeting, sponsored by the taxpayer for the principal purpose of instructing them with respect to a new procedure for conducting his business, would be within the provisions of this exception. A similar expenditure made at a bona fide meeting of stockholders of the taxpayer for the election of directors and discussion of corporate affairs would also be within the provisions of this exception. While this exception will apply to bona fide business meetings even though some social activities are provided, it will not apply to meetings which are primarily for social or nonbusiness purposes rather than for the transaction of the taxpayer's business. A meeting under circumstances where there was little or no possibility of engaging in the active conduct of trade or business (as described in paragraph (c)(7) of this section) generally will not be considered a business meeting for purposes of this subdivision. This exception will not apply to a meeting or convention of employees or agents, or similar meeting for directors, partners or others for the principal purpose of rewarding them for their services to the taxpayer. However, such a meeting or convention of employees might come within the scope of subdivisions (iii) or (v) of this subparagraph.

(vii) Meetings of business leagues, etc. Any expenditure for entertainment directly related and necessary to attendance at bona fide business meetings or conventions of organizations exempt from taxation under section 501(c)(6) of the Code, such as business leagues, chambers of commerce, real estate boards, boards of trade, and certain professional associations, is not subject to the limitations on allowability of deductions provided in paragraphs (a) through (e) of this section.

(viii) Items available to the public. Any expenditure by a taxpayer for entertainment (or for a facility in connection therewith) to the extent the entertainment is made available to the general public is not subject to the limitations on allowability of deductions provided for in paragraphs (a) through (e) of this section. Expenditures for entertainment of the general public by means of television, radio, newspapers and the like, will come within this exception, as will expenditures for distributing samples to the general public. Similarly, expenditures for maintaining private parks, golf courses and similar facilities, to the extent that they are available for public use, will come within this exception. For example, if a corporation maintains a swimming pool which it makes available for a period of time each week to children participating in a local public recreational program, the portion of the expense relating to such public use of the pool will come within this exception.

(ix) Entertainment sold to customers. Any expenditure by a taxpayer for entertainment (or for use of a facility in connection therewith) to the extent the entertainment is sold to customers in a bona fide transaction for an adequate and full consideration in money or money's worth is not subject to the limitations on allowability of deductions provided for in paragraphs (a) through (e) of this section. Thus, the cost of producing night club entertainment (such as salaries paid to employees of night clubs and amounts paid to performers) for sale to customers or the cost of operating a pleasure cruise ship as a business will come within this exception.

(g) Additional provisions of section 274—travel of spouse, dependent or others. Section 274(m)(3) provides that no deduction shall be allowed under this chapter (except section 217) for travel expenses paid or incurred with respect to a spouse, dependent, or other individual accompanying the taxpayer (or an officer or employee of the taxpayer) on business travel, unless certain conditions are met. As provided in section 274(m)(3), the term *other individual* does not include a business associate (as defined in paragraph (b)(2)(iii) of this section) who otherwise meets the requirements of sections 274(m)(3)(B) and (C).

T.D. 6659, 6/24/63, amend T.D. 6996, 1/17/69, T.D. 8051, 9/6/85, T.D. 8601, 7/18/95, T.D. 8666, 5/29/96.

§ 1.274-3 Disallowance of deduction for gifts.

Caution: The Treasury has not yet amended Reg § 1.274-3 to reflect changes made by P.L. 104-188.

(a) In general. No deduction shall be allowed under section 162 or 212 for any expense for a gift made directly or indirectly by a taxpayer to any individual to the extent that such expense, when added to prior expenses of the taxpayer for gifts made to such individual during the taxpayer's taxable year, exceeds $25.

(b) Gift defined. *(1) In general.* Except as provided in subparagraph (2) of this paragraph the term "gift", for purposes of this section, means any item excludable from the gross income of the recipient under section 102 which is not excludable from his gross income under any other provision of chapter 1 of the Code. Thus, a payment by an employer to a deceased employee's widow is not a gift, for purposes of this section, to the extent the payment constitutes an employee's death benefit excludable by the recipient under section 101(b). Similarly, a scholarship which is excludable from a recipient's gross income under section 117, and a prize or award which is excludable from a recipient's gross income under section 74(b), are not subject to the provisions of this section.

(2) Items not treated as gifts. The term "gift", for purposes of this section, does not include the following:

(i) An item having a cost to the taxpayer not in excess of $4.00 on which the name of the taxpayer is clearly and permanently imprinted and which is one of a number of identical items distributed generally by such a taxpayer.

(ii) A sign, display rack, or other promotional material to be used on the business premises of the recipient, or

(iii) In the case of a taxable year of a taxpayer ending on or after August 13, 1981, an item of tangible personal property which is awarded before January 1, 1987, to an employee of the taxpayer by reason of the employee's length of service (including an award upon retirement), productivity, or safety achievement, but only to the extent that—

(A) The cost of the item to the taxpayer does not exceed $400; or

(B) The item is a qualified plan award (as defined in paragraph (d) of this section); or

(iv) In the case of a taxable year of a taxpayer ending before August 13, 1981, an item of tangible personal property having a cost to the taxpayer not in excess of $100 which is awarded to an employee of the taxpayer by reason of the employee's length of service (including an award upon retirement) or safety achievement.

For purposes of paragraphs (b)(2)(iii) and (iv) of this section, the term "tangible personal property" does not include cash or any gift certificate other than a nonnegotiable gift certificate conferring only the right to receive tangible personal property. Thus, for example, if a nonnegotiable gift certificate entitles an employee to choose between selecting an item of merchandise or receiving cash or reducing the balance due on his account with the issuer of the gift certificate, the gift certificate is not tangible personal property for purposes of this section. To the extent that an item is not treated as a gift for purposes of this section, the deductibility of the expense of the item is not governed by this section, and the taxpayer need not take such item into account in determining whether the $25 limitation on gifts to any individual has been exceeded. For example, if an employee receives by reason of his length of service a gift of an item of tangible personal property that costs the employer $450, the deductibility of only $50 ($450 minus $400) is governed by this section, and the employer takes the $50 into account for purposes of the $25 limitation on gifts to that employee. The fact that an item is wholly or partially excepted from the applicability of this section has no effect in determining whether the value of the item is includible in the gross income of the recipient. For rules relating to the taxability to the recipient of any item described in this subparagraph, see sections 61, 74, and 102 and the regulations thereunder. For rules relating to the deductibility of employee achievement awards awarded after December 31, 1986, see section 274(j).

(c) Expense for a gift. For purposes of this section, the term "expense for a gift" means the cost of the gift to the taxpayer, other than incidental costs such as for customary engraving on jewelry, or for packaging, insurance, and mailing or other delivery. A related cost will be considered "incidental" only if it does not add substantial value to the gift. Although the cost of customary gift wrapping will be considered an incidental cost, the purchase of an ornamental basket for packaging fruit will not be considered an incidental cost of packaging if the basket has a value which is substantial in relation to the value of the fruit.

(d) Qualified plan award. *(1) In general.* Except as provided in subparagraph (2) of this paragraph the term "qualified plan award," for purposes of this section, means an item of tangible personal property that is awarded to an employee by reason of the employee's length of service (including retirement), productivity, or safety achievement, and that is awarded pursuant to a permanent, written award plan or program of the taxpayer that does not discriminate as to eligibility or benefits in favor of employees who are officers, shareholders, or highly compensated employees. The "permanency" of an award plan shall be determined from all the facts and circumstances of the particular case, including the taxpayer's ability to continue to make the awards as required by the award plan. Although the taxpayer may reserve the right to change or to terminate an award plan, the actual termination of the award plan for any reason other than business necessity within a few years after it has taken effect may be evidence that the award plan from its inception was not a "permanent" award plan. Whether or not an award plan is discriminatory shall be determined from all the facts and circumstances of the particular case. An award plan may fail to qualify because it is discriminatory in its actual operation even though the written provisions of the award plan are not discriminatory.

(2) Items not treated as qualified plan awards. The term "qualified plan award," for purposes of this section, does not include an item qualifying under paragraph (d)(1) of this section to the extent that the cost of the item exceeds $1,600. In addition, that term does not include any items qualifying under paragraph (d)(1) of this section if the average cost of all items (whether or not tangible personal property) awarded during the taxable year by the taxpayer under any plan described in paragraph (d)(1) of this section exceeds $400. The average cost of those items shall be computed by dividing (i) the sum of the costs for those items (including amounts in excess of the $1,600 limitation) by (ii) the total number of those items.

(e) Gifts made indirectly to an individual. *(1) Gift to spouse or member of family.* If a taxpayer makes a gift to the wife of a man who has a business connection with the taxpayer, the gift generally will be considered as made indirectly to the husband. However, if the wife has a bona fide business connection with the taxpayer independently of her relationship to her husband, a gift to her generally will not be considered as made indirectly to her husband unless the gift is intended for his eventual use or benefit. Thus, if a taxpayer makes a gift to a wife who is engaged with her husband in the active conduct of a partnership business, the gift to the wife will not be considered an indirect gift to her husband unless it is intended for his eventual use or benefit. The same rules apply to gifts to any other member of the family of an individual who has a business connection with the taxpayer.

(2) Gift to corporation or other business entity. If a taxpayer makes a gift to a corporation or other business entity intended for the eventual personal use or benefit of an individual who is an employee, stockholder, or other owner of the corporation or business entity, the gift generally will be considered as made indirectly to such individual. Thus, if a taxpayer provides theater tickets to a closely held corporation for eventual use by any one of the stockholders of the corporation, and if such tickets are gifts, the gifts will be considered as made indirectly to the individual who eventually uses such ticket. On the other hand, a gift to a business organization of property to be used in connection with the business of the organization (for example, a technical manual) will not be considered as a gift to an individual, even though, in practice, the book will be used principally by a readily identifiable individual employee. A gift for the eventual personal use or benefit of some undesignated member of a large group of individuals generally will not be considered as made indirectly to the individual who eventually uses, or benefits from, such gifts unless, under the circumstances of the case, it is reasonably practicable for the taxpayer to ascertain the ultimate recipient of the gift. Thus, if a taxpayer provides several baseball tickets to a corporation for the eventual use by any one of a large number of employees or customers of the corporation, and if such tickets are gifts, the gifts generally will not be treated as made indirectly to the individuals who use such tickets.

(f) Special rules. *(1) Partnership.* In the case of a gift by a partnership, the $25 annual limitation contained in paragraph (a) of this section shall apply to the partnership as well as to each member of the partnership. Thus, in the case of a gift made by a partner with respect to the business of the partnership, the $25 limitation will be applied at the partnership level as well as at the level of the individual partner. Consequently, deductions for gifts made with respect to partnership business will not exceed $25 annually, for each recipient, regardless of the number of partners.

(2) Husband and wife. For purposes of applying the $25 annual limitation contained in paragraph (a) of this section, a husband and wife shall be treated as one taxpayer. Thus, in the case of gifts to an individual by a husband and wife, the spouses will be treated as one donor; and they are limited to a deduction of $25 annually for each recipient. This rule applies regardless of whether the husband and wife file a joint return or whether the husband and wife make separate gifts to an individual with respect to separate businesses. Since the term "taxpayer" in paragraph (a) of this section refers only to the donor of a gift, this special rule does not apply to treat a husband and wife as one individual where each is a recipient of a gift. See paragraph (d)(1) of this section.

(g) Cross reference. For rules with respect to whether this section or § 1.274-2 applies, see § 1.274-2(b)(1)(iii).

T.D. 6659, 6/24/63, amend T.D. 8230, 9/19/88.

PAR. 6. Section 1.274-3 is amended as follows:

(a) The last sentence of paragraph (b)(1) is amended by substituting "subsections (b) and (c) of section 74" for "section 74(b)".

(b) The language "recipient, or" at the end of paragraph (b)(2)(ii) is replaced by the language "recipient."

(c) Subdivisions (iii) and (iv) of paragraph (b)(2) are removed.

(d) The first, second, and fourth sentences of the flush material immediately following subdivision (iv) are removed and the last sentence is amended by substituting "sections 61, 74, 102, and 132" for "sections 61, 74, and 102".

(e) Paragraph (d) is removed and paragraphs (e), (f), and (g) are redesignated as paragraphs (d), (e), and (f).

Proposed § 1.274-3 [Amended] [*For Preamble, see ¶ 151,137*]

§ 1.274-4 Disallowance of certain foreign travel expenses.

Caution: The Treasury has not yet amended Reg § 1.274-4 to reflect changes made by P.L. 100-647, P.L. 99-514, P.L. 99-44, P.L. 98-369, P.L. 98-67, P.L. 97-424, P.L. 97-34, P.L. 96-608, P.L. 96-605, P.L. 96-222, 95-600, 94-455.

(a) Introductory. Section 274(c) and this section impose certain restrictions on the deductibility of travel expenses incurred in the case of an individual who, while traveling outside the United States away from home in the pursuit of trade or business (hereinafter termed "business activity"), engages in substantial personal activity not attributable to such trade or business (hereinafter termed "nonbusiness activity"). Section 274(c) and this section are limited in their application to individuals (whether or not an employee or other person traveling under a reimbursement or other expense allowance arrangement) who engage in nonbusiness activity while traveling outside the United States away from home, and do not impose restrictions on the deductibility of travel expenses incurred by an employer or client under an advance, reimbursement, or other arrangement with the individual who engages in nonbusiness activity. For purposes of this section, the term "United States" includes only the States and the District of Columbia, and any reference to "trade or business" or "business activity" includes any activity described in section 212. For rules governing the determination of travel outside the United States away from home, see paragraph (e) of this section. For rules governing the disallowance of travel expense to which this section applies, see paragraph (f) of this section.

(b) Limitations on application of section. The restrictions on deductibility of travel expenses contained in paragraph (f) of this section are applicable only if—

(1) The travel expense is otherwise deductible under section 162 or 212 and the regulations thereunder,

(2) The travel expense is for travel outside the United States away from home which exceeds 1 week (as determined under paragraph (c) of this section), and

(3) The time outside the United States away from home attributable to nonbusiness activity (as determined under paragraph (d) of this section) constitutes 25 percent or more of the total time on such travel.

(c) Travel in excess of 1 week. This section does not apply to an expense of travel unless the expense is for travel outside the United States away from home which exceeds 1 week. For purposes of this section, 1 week means 7 consecutive days. The day in which travel outside the United States away from home begins shall not be considered, but the day in which such travel ends shall be considered, in determining whether a taxpayer is outside the United States away from home for more than 7 consecutive days. For example, if a taxpayer departs on travel outside the United States away from home on a Wednesday morning and ends such travel the following Wednesday evening, he shall be considered as being outside the United States away from home only 7 consecutive days. In such a case, this section would not apply because the taxpayer was not outside the United States away from home for more than 7 consecutive days. However, if the taxpayer travels outside the United States away from home for more than 7 consecutive days, both the day such travel begins and the day such travel ends shall be considered a "business day" or a "nonbusiness day", as the case may be, for purposes of determining whether nonbusiness activity constituted 25 percent or more of travel time under paragraph (d) of this section and for purposes of allocating expenses under paragraph (f) of this section. For purposes of determining whether travel is outside the United States away from home, see paragraph (e) of this section.

(d) Nonbusiness activity constituting 25 percent or more of travel time. *(1) In general.* This section does not apply to any expense of travel outside the United States away from home unless the portion of time outside the United States away from home attributable to nonbusiness activity constitutes 25 percent or more of the total time on such travel.

(2) Allocation on per day basis. The total time traveling outside the United States away from home will be allocated on a day-by-day basis to (i) days of business activity or (ii) days of nonbusiness activity (hereinafter termed "business days" or "nonbusiness days" respectively) unless the taxpayer establishes that a different method of allocation more clearly reflects the portion of time outside the United States away from home which is attributable to nonbusiness activity. For purposes of this section, a day spent outside the United States away from home shall be deemed entirely a business day even though spent only in part on business activity if the taxpayer establishes—

(i) Transportation days. That on such day the taxpayer was traveling to or returning from a destination outside the United States away from home in the pursuit of trade or business. However, if for purposes of engaging in nonbusiness activity, the taxpayer while traveling outside the United States away from home does not travel by a reasonably direct route, only that number of days shall be considered business days as would be required for the taxpayer, using the same mode of transportation, to travel to or return from the same destination by a reasonably direct route. Also if, while so traveling, the taxpayer interrupts the normal course of travel by engaging in substantial diversions for nonbusiness reasons of his own choosing, only that number of days shall be considered business days as equals the number of days required for the taxpayer, using the same mode of transportation, to travel to or return from the same destination without engaging in such diversion. For example, if a taxpayer residing in New York departs on an evening on a direct flight to Quebec for a business meeting to be held in Quebec the next morning, for purposes of determining whether nonbusiness activity constituted 25 percent or more of his travel time, the entire day of his departure shall be considered a business day. On the other hand, if a taxpayer travels by automobile from New York to Quebec to attend a business meeting and while en route spends 2 days in Ottawa and 1 day in Montreal on nonbusiness activities of his personal choice, only that number of days outside the United States shall be considered business days as would have been required for the taxpayer to drive by a reasonably direct route to Quebec, taking into account normal periods for rest and meals.

(ii) Presence required. That on such day his presence outside the United States away from home was required at a particular place for a specific and bona fide business purpose. For example, if a taxpayer is instructed by his employer to attend a specific business meeting, the day of the meeting shall be considered a business day even though, because of the scheduled length of the meeting, the taxpayer spends more time during normal working hours of the day on nonbusiness activity than on business activity.

(iii) Days primarily business. That during hours normally considered to be appropriate for business activity, his principal activity on such day was the pursuit of trade or business.

(iv) Circumstances beyond control. That on such day he was prevented from engaging in the conduct of trade or business as his principal activity due to circumstances beyond his control.

(v) Weekdays, holidays, etc. That such day was a Saturday, Sunday, legal holiday, or other reasonably necessary standby day which intervened during that course of the taxpayer's trade or business while outside the United States away from home which the taxpayer endeavored to conduct with reasonable dispatch. For example, if a taxpayer travels from New York to London to take part in business negotiations beginning on a Wednesday and concluding on the following Tuesday, the intervening Saturday and Sunday shall be considered business days whether or not business is conducted on either of such days. Similarly, if in the above case the meetings which concluded on Tuesday evening were followed by business meetings with another business group in London on the immediately succeeding Thursday and Friday, the intervening Wednesday will be deemed a business day. However, if at the conclusion of the business meetings on Friday, the taxpayer stays in London for an additional week for personal purposes, the Saturday and Sunday following the conclusion of the business meeting will not be considered business days.

(e) Domestic travel excluded. *(1) In general.* For purposes of this section, travel outside the United States away from home does not include any travel from one point in the United States to another point in the United States. However, travel which is not from one point in the United States to another point in the United States shall be considered travel outside the United States. If a taxpayer travels from a place within the United States to a place outside the United States, the portion, if any, of such travel which is from one point in the United States to another point in the United States is to be disregarded for purposes of determining—

(i) Whether the taxpayer's travel outside the United States away from home exceeds 1 week (see paragraph (c) of this section),

(ii) Whether the time outside the United States away from home attributable to nonbusiness activity constitutes 25 percent or more of the total time on such travel (see paragraph (d) of this section), or

(iii) The amount of travel expense subject to the allocation rules of this section (see paragraph (f) of this section).

(2) Determination of travel from one point in the United States to another point in the United States. In the case of the following means of transportation, travel from one point in the United States to another point in the United States shall be determined as follows—

(i) Travel by public transportation. In the case of travel by public transportation, any place in the United States at which the vehicle makes a scheduled stop for the purpose of adding or discharging passengers shall be considered a point in the United States.

(ii) Travel by private automobile. In the case of travel by private automobile, any such travel which is within the United States shall be considered travel from one point in the United States to another point in the United States.

(iii) Travel by private airplane. In the case of travel by private airplane, any flight, whether or not constituting the entire trip, where both the takeoff and the landing are within the United States shall be considered travel from one point in the United States to another point in the United States.

(3) Examples. The provisions of subparagraph (2) may be illustrated by the following examples:

Example (1). Taxpayer A flies from Los Angeles to Puerto Rico with a brief scheduled stopover in Miami for the purpose of adding and discharging passengers and A returns by airplane nonstop to Los Angeles. The travel from Los Angeles to Miami is considered travel from one point in the United States to another point in the United States. The travel from Miami to Puerto Rico and from Puerto Rico to Los Angeles is not considered travel from one point in the United States to another point in the United States and, thus, is considered to be travel outside the United States away from home.

Example (2). Taxpayer B travels by train from New York to Montreal. The travel from New York to the last place in the United States where the train is stopped for the purpose of adding or discharging passengers is considered to be travel from one point in the United States to another point in the United States.

Example (3). Taxpayer C travels by automobile from Tulsa to Mexico City and back. All travel in the United States is considered to be travel from one point in the United States to another point in the United States.

Example (4). Taxpayer D flies nonstop from Seattle to Juneau. Although the flight passes over Canada, the trip is considered to be travel from one point in the United States to another point in the United States.

Example (5). If in example (4) above, the airplane makes a scheduled landing in Vancouver, the time spent in traveling from Seattle to Juneau is considered to be travel outside the United States away from home. However, the time spent in Juneau is not considered to be travel outside the United States away from home.

(f) Application of disallowance rules. *(1) In general.* In the case of expense for travel outside the United States away from home by an individual to which this section applies, except as otherwise provided in subparagraph (4) or (5) of this paragraph, no deduction shall be allowed for that amount of travel expense specified in subparagraph (2) or (3) of this paragraph (whichever is applicable) which is obtained by multiplying the total of such travel expense by a fraction—

(i) The numerator of which is the number of nonbusiness days during such travel, and

(ii) The denominator of which is the total number of business days and nonbusiness days during such travel.

For determination of "business days" and "nonbusiness days", see paragraph (d)(2) of this section.

(2) Nonbusiness activity at, near, or beyond business destination. If the place at which the individual engages in nonbusiness activity (hereinafter termed "nonbusiness destination") is at, near, or beyond the place to which he travels in the pursuit of a trade or business (hereinafter termed "business destination"), the amount of travel expense referred to in subparagraph (1) of this paragraph shall be the amount of travel expense, otherwise allowable as a deduction under section 162 or section 212, which would have been incurred in traveling from the place where travel outside the United States away from home begins to the business destination, and returning. Thus, if the individual travels from New York to London on business, and then takes a vacation in Paris before returning to New York, the amount of the travel expense subject to allocation is the expense which would have been incurred in traveling from New York to London and returning.

(3) Nonbusiness activity on the route to or from business destination. If the nonbusiness destination is on the route to or from the business destination, the amount of the travel expense referred to in subparagraph (1) of this paragraph shall be the amount of travel expense, otherwise allowable as a deduction under section 162 or 212, which would have been incurred in traveling from the place where travel outside the United States away from home begins to the nonbusiness destination and returning. Thus, if the individual travels on business from Chicago to Rio de Janeiro, Brazil with a scheduled stop in New York for the purpose of adding and discharging passengers, and while en route stops in Caracas, Venezuela for a vacation and returns to Chicago from Rio de Janeiro with another scheduled stop in New York for the purpose of adding and discharging passengers, the amount of travel expense subject to allocation is the expense which would have been incurred in traveling from New York to Caracas and returning.

(4) Other allocation method. If a taxpayer establishes that a method other than allocation on a day-by-day basis (as determined under paragraph (d)(2) of this section) more clearly reflects the portion of time outside the United States away from home which is attributable to nonbusiness activity, the amount of travel expense for which no deduction shall be allowed shall be determined by such other method.

(5) Travel expense deemed entirely allocable to business activity. Expenses of travel shall be considered allocable in full to business activity, and no portion of such expense shall be subject to disallowance under this section, if incurred under circumstances provided for in subdivision (i) or (ii) of this subparagraph.

(i) Lack of control over travel. Expenses of travel otherwise deductible under section 162 or 212 shall be considered fully allocable to business activity if, considering all the facts and circumstances, the individual incurring such expenses did not have substantial control over the arranging of the business trip. A person who is required to travel to a business destination will not be considered to have substantial control over the arranging of the business trip merely because he has control over the timing of the trip. Any individual who travels on behalf of his employer under a reimbursement or other expense allowance arrangement shall be considered not to have had substantial control over the arranging of his business trip, provided the employee is not—

(a) A managing executive of the employer for whom he is traveling (and for this purpose the term "managing executive" includes only an employee who, by reason of his authority and responsibility, is authorized, without effective veto procedures, to decide upon the necessity for his business trip), or

(b) Related to his employer within the meaning of section 267(b) but for this purpose the percentage referred to in section 267(b)(2) shall be 10 percent.

(ii) Lack of major consideration to obtain a vacation. Any expense of travel, which qualifies for deduction under section 162 or 212, shall be considered fully allocable to business activity if the individual incurring such expenses can establish that, considering all the facts and circumstances, he did not have a major consideration, in determining to make the trip, of obtaining a personal vacation or holiday. If such a major consideration were present, the provisions of subparagraphs (1) through (4) of this paragraph shall apply. However, if the trip were primarily personal in nature, the traveling expenses to and from the destination are not deductible even though the taxpayer engages in business activities while at such destination. See paragraph (b) of § 1.162-2.

(g) Examples. The application of this section may be illustrated by the following examples:

Example (1). Individual A flew from New York to Paris where he conducted business for 1 day. He spent the next 2 days sightseeing in Paris and then flew back to New York. The entire trip, including 2 days for travel en route, took 5 days. Since the time outside the United States away from home during the trip did not exceed 1 week, the disallowance rules of this section do not apply.

Example (2). Individual B flew from Tampa to Honolulu (from one point in the United States to another point in the United States) for a business meeting which lasted 3 days and for personal matters which took 10 days. He then flew to Melbourne, Australia where he conducted business for 2 days and went sightseeing for 1 day. Immediately thereafter he flew back to Tampa, with a scheduled landing in Honolulu for the purpose of adding and discharging passengers. Although the trip exceeded 1 week, the time spent outside the United States away from home, including 2 days for traveling from Honolulu to Melbourne and return, was 5 days. Since the time outside the United States away from home during the trip did not exceed 1 week, the disallowance rules of this section do not apply.

Example (3). Individual C flew from Los Angeles to New York where he spent 5 days. He then flew to Brussels where he spent 14 days on business and 5 days on personal matters. He then flew back to Los Angeles by way of New York. The entire trip, including 4 days for travel en route, took 28 days. However, the 2 days spent traveling from Los Angeles to New York and return, and the 5 days spent in New York are not considered travel outside the United States away from home and, thus, are disregarded for purposes of this section. Although the time spent outside the United States away from home exceeded 1 week, the time outside the United States away from home attributable to nonbusiness activities (5 days out of 21) was less than 25 percent of the total time outside the United States away from home during the trip. Therefore, the disallowance rules of his section do not apply.

Example (4). D, an employee of Y Company, who is neither a managing executive of, nor related to, Y Company within the meaning of paragraph (f)(5)(i) of this section, traveled outside the United States away from home on behalf of his employer and was reimbursed by Y for his traveling expense to and from the business destination. The trip took more than a week and D took advantage of the opportunity to enjoy a personal vacation which exceeded 25 percent of the total time on the trip. Since D, traveling under a reimbursement arrangement, is not a managing executive of, or related to, Y Company, he is not considered to have substantial control over the arranging of the business trip, and the travel expenses shall be considered fully allocable to business activity.

Example (5). E, a managing executive and principal shareholder of X Company, travels from New York to Stockholm, Sweden, to attend a series of business meetings. At the conclusion of the series of meetings, which last 1 week, E spends 1 week on a personal vacation in Stockholm. If E establishes either that he did not have substantial control over the arranging of the trip or that a major consideration in his determining to make the trip was not to provide an opportunity for taking a personal vacation, the entire travel expense to and from Stockholm shall be considered fully allocable to business activity.

Example (6). F, a self-employed professional man, flew from New York to Copenhagen, Denmark, to attend a convention sponsored by a professional society. The trip lasted 3 weeks, of which 2 weeks were spent on vacation in Europe. F generally would be regarded as having substantial control over arranging this business trip. Unless F can establish that obtaining a vacation was not a major consideration in determining to make the trip, the disallowance rules of this section apply.

Example (7). Taxpayer G flew from Chicago to New York where he spent 6 days on business. He then flew to London where he conducted business for 2 days. G then flew to Paris for a 5 day vacation after which he flew back to Chicago, with a scheduled landing in New York for the purpose of adding and discharging passengers. G would not have made the trip except for the business he had to conduct in London. The travel outside the United States away from home, including 2 days for travel en route, exceeded a week and the time devoted to nonbusiness activities was not less than 25 percent of the total time on such travel. The 2 days spent traveling from Chicago to New York and return, and the 6 days spent in New York are disregarded for purposes of determining whether the travel outside the United States away from home exceeded a week and whether the time devoted to nonbusiness activities was less than 25 percent of the total time outside the United States away from home. If G is unable to establish either that he did not have substantial control over the arranging of the business trip or that an opportunity for taking a personal vacation was not a major consideration in his determining to make the trip, 5/9ths (5 days devoted to nonbusiness activities out of a total 9 days outside the United States away from home on the trip) of the expenses attributable to transportation and food from New York to London and from London to New York will be disallowed (unless G establishes that a different method of allocation more clearly reflects the portion of time outside the United States away from home which is attributable to nonbusiness activity).

(h) Cross reference. For rules with respect to whether an expense is travel or entertainment, see paragraph (b)(1)(iii) of § 1.274-2.

T.D. 6659, 6/24/63, amend T.D. 6758, 9/9/64.

§ 1.274-5 Substantiation requirements.

(a) and (b) [Reserved]. For further guidance, see § 1.274-5T(a) and (b).

(c) Rules of substantiation. *(1) [Reserved].* For further guidance, see § 1.274-5T(c)(1).

(2) Substantiation by adequate records. (i) and (ii) [Reserved].

For further guidance, see § 1.274-5T(c)(2)(i) and (ii).

(iii) Documentary evidence. (A) Except as provided in paragraph (c)(2)(iii)(B), documentary evidence, such as receipts, paid bills, or similar evidence sufficient to support an expenditure, is required for—

(1) Any expenditure for lodging while traveling away from home, and

(2) Any other expenditure of $75 or more except, for transportation charges, documentary evidence will not be required if not readily available.

(B) The Commissioner, in his or her discretion, may prescribe rules waiving the documentary evidence requirements in circumstances where it is impracticable for such documentary evidence to be required. Ordinarily, documentary evidence will be considered adequate to support an expenditure if it includes sufficient information to establish the amount, date, place, and the essential character of the expenditure. For example, a hotel receipt is sufficient to support expenditures for business travel if it contains the following: name, location, date, and separate amounts for charges such as for lodging, meals, and telephone. Similarly, a restaurant receipt is sufficient to support an expenditure for a business meal if it contains the following: name and location of the restaurant, the date and amount of the expenditure, the number of people served, and, if a charge is made for an item other than meals and beverages, an indication that such is the case. A document may be indicative of only one (or part of one) element of an expenditure. Thus, a cancelled check, together with a bill from the payee, ordinarily would establish the element of cost. In contrast, a cancelled check drawn payable to a named payee would not by itself support a business expenditure without other evidence showing that the check was used for a certain business purpose.

(iv) and (v) [Reserved]. For further guidance, see § 1.274-5T(c)(2)(iv) and (v).

(3) through *(7)* [Reserved]. For further guidance, see § 1.274-5T(c)(3) through (7).

(d) and (e) [Reserved]. For further guidance, see § 1.274-5T(d) and (e).

(f) Reporting and substantiation of expenses of certain employees for travel, entertainment, gifts, and with respect to listed property. *(1) through (3) [Reserved].* For further guidance, see § 1.274-5T(f)(1) through (3).

(4) Definition of an adequate accounting to the employer. (i) In general. For purposes of this paragraph (f) an adequate accounting means the submission to the employer of an account book, diary, log, statement of expense, trip sheet, or similar record maintained by the employee in which the information as to each element of an expenditure or use (described in paragraph (b) of this section) is recorded at or near the time of the expenditure or use, together with supporting documentary evidence, in a manner that conforms to all the adequate records requirements of paragraph (c)(2) of this section. An adequate accounting requires that the employee account for all amounts received from the employer during the taxable year as advances, reimbursements, or allowances (including those charged directly or indirectly to the employer through credit cards or otherwise) for travel, entertainment, gifts, and the use of listed property. The methods of substantiation allowed under paragraph (c)(4) or (c)(5) of this section also will be considered to be an adequate accounting if the employer accepts an employee's substantiation and establishes that such substantiation meets the requirements of paragraph (c)(4) or (c)(5). For purposes of an adequate accounting, the method of substantiation allowed under paragraph (c)(3) of this section will not be permitted.

(ii) Procedures for adequate accounting without documentary evidence. The Commissioner may, in his or her discretion, prescribe rules under which an employee may make an adequate accounting to an employer by submitting an account book, log, diary, etc., alone, without submitting documentary evidence.

(iii) Employer. For purposes of this section, the term employer includes an agent of the employer or a third party payor who pays amounts to an employee under a reimbursement or other expense allowance arrangement.

(5) [Reserved]. For further guidance, see § 1.274-5T(f)(5).

(g) Substantiation by reimbursement arrangements or per diem, mileage, and other traveling allowances. *(1) In general.* The Commissioner may, in his or her discretion, prescribe rules in pronouncements of general applicability under which allowances for expenses described in paragraph (g)(2) of this section will, if in accordance with reasonable business practice, be regarded as equivalent to substantiation by adequate records or other sufficient evidence, for purposes of paragraph (c) of this section, of the amount of the expenses and as satisfying, with respect to the amount of the expenses, the requirements of an adequate accounting to the employer for purposes of paragraph (f)(4) of this section. If the total allowance received exceeds the deductible expenses paid or incurred by the employee, such excess must be reported as income on the employee's return. See paragraph (j)(1) of this section relating to the substantiation of meal expenses while traveling away from home, and paragraph (j)(2) of this section relating to the substantiation of expenses for the business use of a vehicle.

(2) Allowances for expenses described. An allowance for expenses is described in this paragraph (g)(2) if it is a—

(i) Reimbursement arrangement covering ordinary and necessary expenses of traveling away from home (exclusive of transportation expenses to and from destination);

(ii) Per diem allowance providing for ordinary and necessary expenses of traveling away from home (exclusive of transportation costs to and from destination); or

(iii) Mileage allowance providing for ordinary and necessary expenses of local transportation and transportation to, from, and at the destination while traveling away from home.

(h) [Reserved]. For further guidance, see § 1.274-5T(h).

(i) [Reserved].

(j) Authority for optional methods of computing certain expenses. *(1) Meal expenses while traveling away from home.* The Commissioner may establish a method under which a taxpayer may use a specified amount or amounts for meals while traveling away from home in lieu of substantiating the actual cost of meals. The taxpayer will not be relieved of the requirement to substantiate the actual cost of other travel expenses as well as the time, place, and business purpose of the travel. See paragraphs (b)(2) and (c) of this section.

(2) Use of mileage rates for vehicle expenses. The Commissioner may establish a method under which a taxpayer may use mileage rates to determine the amount of the ordinary and necessary expenses of using a vehicle for local transportation and transportation to, from, and at the destination while traveling away from home in lieu of substantiating the actual costs. The method may include appropriate limitations and conditions in order to reflect more accurately vehicle expenses over the entire period of usage. The taxpayer will not be relieved of the requirement to substantiate

the amount of each business use (i.e., the business mileage), or the time and business purpose of each use. See paragraphs (b)(2) and (c) of this section.

(3) Incidental expenses while traveling away from home. The Commissioner may establish a method under which a taxpayer may use a specified amount or amounts for incidental expenses paid or incurred while traveling away from home in lieu of substantiating the actual cost of incidental expenses. The taxpayer will not be relieved of the requirement to substantiate the actual cost of other travel expenses as well as the time, place, and business purpose of the travel.

(k) and (l) [Reserved]. For further guidance, see § 1.274-5T(k) and (l).

(m) Effective date. This section applies to expenses paid or incurred after December 31, 1997. However, paragraph (j)(3) of this section applies to expenses paid or incurred after September 30, 2002.

T.D. 8864, 1/21/2000, amend T.D. 9020, 11/8/2002, T.D. 9064, 6/30/2003.

PAR. 3. Section 1.274-5 paragraphs (k) and (l) and the last sentence of paragraph (m) are revised to read as follows:

Proposed § 1.274-5 Substantiation requirements. [*For Preamble, see ¶ 153,001*]

* * * * *

(k) Exceptions for qualified nonpersonal use vehicles. *(1) In general.* The substantiation requirements of section 274(d) and this section do not apply to any qualified nonpersonal use vehicle (as defined in paragraph (k)(2) of this section).

(2) Qualified nonpersonal use vehicle. (i) In general. For purposes of section 274(d) and this section, the term qualified nonpersonal use vehicle means any vehicle which, by reason of its nature (that is, design), is not likely to be used more than a de minimis amount for personal purposes.

(ii) List of vehicles. Vehicles which are qualified nonpersonal use vehicles include the following:

(A) Clearly marked police, fire, and public safety officer vehicles (as defined and to the extent provided in paragraph (k)(3) of this section).

(B) Ambulances used as such or hearses used as such.

(C) Any vehicle designed to carry cargo with a loaded gross vehicle weight over 14,000 pounds.

(D) Bucket trucks (cherry pickers).

(E) Cement mixers.

(F) Combines.

(G) Cranes and derricks.

(H) Delivery trucks with seating only for the driver, or only for the driver plus a folding jump seat.

(I) Dump trucks (including garbage trucks).

(J) Flatbed trucks.

(K) Forklifts.

(L) Passenger buses used as such with a capacity of at least 20 passengers.

(M) Qualified moving vans (as defined in paragraph (k)(4) of this section).

(N) Qualified specialized utility repair trucks (as defined in paragraph (k)(5) of this section).

(O) Refrigerated trucks.

(P) School buses (as defined in section 4221(d)(7)(c)).

(Q) Tractors and other special purpose farm vehicles.

(R) Unmarked vehicles used by law enforcement officers (as defined in paragraph (k)(6) of this section) if the use is officially authorized.

(S) Such other vehicles as the Commissioner may designate.

(3) Clearly marked police, fire, or public safety officer vehicles. A police, fire, or public safety officer vehicle is a vehicle, owned or leased by a governmental unit, or any agency or instrumentality thereof, that is required to be used for commuting by a police officer, fire fighter, or public safety officer (as defined in section 402(l)(4)(C) of this chapter) who, when not on a regular shift, is on call at all times, provided that any personal use (other than commuting) of the vehicle outside the limit of the police officer's arrest powers or the fire fighter's or public safety officer's obligation to respond to an emergency is prohibited by such governmental unit. A police, fire, or public safety officer vehicle is clearly marked if, through painted insignia or words, it is readily apparent that the vehicle is a police, fire, or public safety officer vehicle. A marking on a license plate is not a clear marking for purposes of this paragraph (k).

(4) Qualified moving van. The term qualified moving van means any truck or van used by a professional moving company in the trade or business of moving household or business goods if—

(i) No personal use of the van is allowed other than for travel to and from a move site (or for de minimis personal use, such as a stop for lunch on the way between two move sites);

(ii) Personal use for travel to and from a move site is an irregular practice (that is, not more than five times a month on average); and

(iii) Personal use is limited to situations in which it is more convenient to the employer, because of the location of the employee's residence in relation to the location of the move site, for the van not to be returned to the employer's business location.

(5) Qualified specialized utility repair truck. The term qualified specialized utility repair truck means any truck (not including a van or pickup truck) specifically designed and used to carry heavy tools, testing equipment, or parts if—

(i) The shelves, racks, or other permanent interior construction which has been installed to carry and store such heavy items is such that it is unlikely that the truck will be used more than a de minimis amount for personal purposes; and

(ii) The employer requires the employee to drive the truck home in order to be able to respond in emergency situations for purposes of restoring or maintaining electricity, gas, telephone, water, sewer, or steam utility services.

(6) Unmarked law enforcement vehicles. (i) In general. The substantiation requirements of section 274(d) and this section do not apply to officially authorized uses of an unmarked vehicle by a "law enforcement officer". To qualify for this exception, any personal use must be authorized by the Federal, State, county, or local governmental agency or department that owns or leases the vehicle and employs the officer, and must be incident to law-enforcement functions, such as being able to report directly from home to a stakeout or surveillance site, or to an emergency situation. Use of an unmarked vehicle for vacation or recreation trips cannot qualify as an authorized use.

(ii) Law enforcement officer. The term law enforcement officer means an individual who is employed on a full-time basis by a governmental unit that is responsible for the prevention or investigation of crime involving injury to persons or property (including apprehension or detention of persons for such crimes), who is authorized by law to carry firearms, execute search warrants, and to make arrests (other than merely a citizen's arrest), and who regularly carries firearms (except when it is not possible to do so because of the requirements of undercover work). The term "law enforcement officer" may include an arson investigator if the investigator otherwise meets the requirements of this paragraph (k)(6)(ii), but does not include Internal Revenue Service special agents.

(7) Trucks and vans. The substantiation requirements of section 274(d) and this section apply generally to any pickup truck or van, unless the truck or van has been specially modified with the result that it is not likely to be used more than a de minimis amount for personal purposes. For example, a van that has only a front bench for seating, in which permanent shelving that fills most of the cargo area has been installed, that constantly carries merchandise or equipment, and that has been specially painted with advertising or the company's name, is a vehicle not likely to be used more than a de minimis amount for personal purposes.

(8) Examples. The following examples illustrate the provisions of paragraphs (k)(3) and (6) of this section:

Example (1). Detective C, who is a "law enforcement officer" employed by a state police department, headquartered in City M, is provided with an unmarked vehicle (equipped with radio communication) for use during off-duty hours because C must be able to communicate with headquarters and be available for duty at any time (for example, to report to a surveillance or crime site). The police department generally has officially authorized personal use of the vehicle by C but has prohibited use of the vehicle for recreational purposes or for personal purposes outside the state. Thus, C's use of the vehicle for commuting between headquarters or a surveillance site and home and for personal errands is authorized personal use as described in paragraph (k)(6)(i) of this section. With respect to these authorized uses the vehicle is not subject to the substantiation requirements of section 274(d) and the value of these uses is not included in C's gross income.

Example (2). Detective T is a "law enforcement officer" employed by City M. T is authorized to make arrests only within M's city limits. T, along with all other officers of the force, is ordinarily on duty for eight hours each work day and on call during the other sixteen hours. T is provided with the use of a clearly marked police vehicle in which T is required to commute to his home in City M. The police department's official policy regarding marked police vehicles prohibits personal use (other than commuting) of the vehicles outside the city limits. When not using the vehicle on the job, T uses the vehicle only for commuting, personal errands on the way between work and home, and personal errands within City M. All use of the vehicle by T conforms to the requirements of paragraph (k)(3) of this section. Therefore, the value of that use is excluded from T's gross income as a working condition fringe and the vehicle is not subject to the substantiation requirements of section 274(d).

Example (3). Director C is employed by City M as the director of the City's rescue squad and is provided with a vehicle for use in responding to emergencies. The City's rescue squad is not a part of City M's police or fire departments. The director's vehicle is a sedan which is painted with insignia and words identifying the vehicle as being owned by the City's rescue squad. C, when not on a regular shift, is on call at all times. The City's official policy regarding clearly marked public safety officer vehicles prohibits personal use (other than for commuting) of the vehicle outside of the limits of the public safety officer's obligation to respond to an emergency. When not using the vehicle to respond to emergencies, City M authorizes C to use the vehicle only for commuting, personal errands on the way between work and home, and personal errands within the limits of C's obligation to respond to emergencies. With respect to these authorized uses, the vehicle is not subject to the substantiation requirements of section 274(d) and the value of these uses is not includable in C's gross income.

(l) Definitions. For purposes of section 274(d) and this section, the terms automobile and vehicle have the same meanings as prescribed in §§ 1.61-21(d)(1)(ii) and 1.61-21(e)(2), respectively. Also, for purposes of section 274(d) and this section, the terms employer, employee and personal use have the same meanings as prescribed in § 1.274-6T(e).

(m) * * * However, paragraph (j)(3) of this section applies to expenses paid or incurred after September 30, 2002, and paragraph (k) applies to clearly marked public safety officer vehicles, as defined in 1.274-5(k)(3), only with respect to uses occurring after January 1, 2009.

§ 1.274-5A Substantiation requirements.

Caution: The Treasury has not yet amended Reg § 1.274-5A to reflect changes made by P.L. 100-647, P.L. 99-514, P.L. 99-44.

(a) In general. No deduction shall be allowed for any expenditure with respect to—

(1) Traveling away from home (including meals and lodging) deductible under section 162 or 212,

(2) Any activity which is of a type generally considered to constitute entertainment, amusement, or recreation, or with respect to a facility used in connection with such an activity, including the items specified in section 274(e), or

(3) Gifts defined in section 274,

unless the taxpayer substantiates such expenditure as provided in paragraph (c) of this section. This limitation supersedes with respect to any such expenditure the doctrine of Cohan v Commissioner (C.C.A. 2d 1930) 39 F. 2d 540. The decision held that where the evidence indicated a taxpayer incurred deductible travel or entertainment expenses but the exact amount could not be determined, the court should make a close approximation and not disallow the deduction entirely. Section 274(d) contemplates that no deduction shall be allowed a taxpayer for such expenditures on the basis of such approximations or unsupported testimony of the taxpayer. For purposes of this section, the term "entertainment" means entertainment, amusement, or recreation, and use of a facility therefor; and the term "expenditure" includes expenses and items (including items such as losses and depreciation).

(b) Elements of an expenditure. *(1) In general.* Section 274(d) and this section contemplate that no deduction shall be allowed for any expenditure for travel, entertainment, or a gift unless the taxpayer substantiates the following elements for each such expenditure:

(i) Amount;

(ii) Time and place of travel or entertainment (or use of a facility with respect to entertainment), or date and description of a gift;

(iii) Business purpose; and

(iv) Business relationship to the taxpayer of each person entertained, using an entertainment facility or receiving a gift.

(2) Travel. The elements to be proved with respect to an expenditure for travel are—

(i) Amount. Amount of each separate expenditure for traveling away from home, such as cost of transportation or lodging, except that the daily cost of the traveler's own breakfast, lunch, and dinner and of expenditures incidental to such travel may be aggregated, if set forth in reasonable categories, such as for meals, for gasoline and oil, and for taxi fares;

(ii) Time. Date of departure and return for each trip away from home, and number of days away from home spent on business;

(iii) Place. Destinations or locality of travel, described by name of city or town or other similar designation; and

(iv) Business purpose. Business reason for travel or nature of the business benefit derived or expected to be derived as a result of travel.

(3) Entertainment in general. Elements to be proved with respect to an expenditure for entertainment are—

(i) Amount. Amount of each separate expenditure for entertainment, except that such incidental items as taxi fares or telephone calls may be aggregated on a daily basis;

(ii) Time. Date of entertainment;

(iii) Place. Name, if any, address or location, and designation of type of entertainment, such as dinner or theater, if such information is not apparent from the designation of the place;

(iv) Business purpose. Business reason for the entertainment or nature of business benefit derived or expected to be derived as a result of the entertainment and, except in the case of business meals described in section 274(e)(1), the nature of any business discussion or activity;

(v) Business relationship. Occupation or other information relating to the person or persons entertained, including name, title, or other designation, sufficient to establish business relationship to the taxpayer.

(4) Entertainment directly preceding or following a substantial and bona fide business discussion. If a taxpayer claims a deduction for entertainment directly preceding or following a substantial and bona fide business discussion on the ground that such entertainment was associated with the active conduct of the taxpayer's trade or business, the elements to be proved with respect to such expenditure, in addition to those enumerated in subparagraph (3)(i), (ii), (iii), and (v) of this paragraph, are—

(i) Time. Date and duration of business discussion;

(ii) Place. Place of business discussion;

(iii) Business purpose. Nature of business discussion, and business reason for the entertainment or nature of business benefit derived or expected to be derived as the result of the entertainment;

(iv) Business relationship. Identification of those persons entertained who participated in the business discussion.

(5) Gifts. Elements to be proved with respect to an expenditure for a gift are—

(i) Amount. Cost of the gift to the taxpayer;

(ii) Time. Date of the gift;

(iii) Description. Description of the gift;

(iv) Business purpose. Business reason for the gift or nature of business benefit derived or expected to be derived as a result of the gift; and

(v) Business relationship. Occupation or other information relating to the recipient of the gift, including name, title, or other designation, sufficient to establish business relationship to the taxpayer.

(c) Rules for substantiation. *(1) In general.* A taxpayer must substantiate each element of an expenditure (described in paragraph (b) of this section) by adequate records or by sufficient evidence corroborating his own statement except as otherwise provided in this section. Section 274(d) contemplates that a taxpayer will maintain and produce such substantiation as will constitute clear proof of an expenditure for travel, entertainment, or gifts referred to in section 274. A record of the elements of an expenditure made at or near the time of the expenditure, supported by sufficient documentary evidence, has a high degree of credibility not present with respect to a statement prepared subsequent thereto when generally there is a lack of accurate recall. Thus, the corroborative evidence required to support a statement not made at or near the time of the expenditure must have a high degree of probative value to elevate such statement and evidence to the level of credibility reflected by a record made at or near the time of the expenditure supported by sufficient documentary evidence. The substantiation requirements of section 274(d) are designed to encourage taxpayers to maintain the records, together with documentary evidence, as provided in subparagraph (2) of this paragraph. To obtain a deduction for an expenditure for travel, entertainment, or gifts, a taxpayer must substantiate, in accordance with the provisions of this paragraph, each element of such an expenditure.

(2) Substantiation by adequate records. (i) In general. To meet the "adequate records" requirements of section 274(d), a taxpayer shall maintain an account book, diary, statement of expense or similar record (as provided in subdivision (ii) of this subparagraph) and documentary evidence (as provided in subdivision (iii) of this subparagraph) which, in combination, are sufficient to establish each element of an expenditure specified in paragraph (b) of this section. It is not necessary to record information in an account book, dairy, statement of expense or similar record which duplicates information reflected on a receipt so long as such account book and receipt complement each other in an orderly manner.

(ii) Account book, diary, etc. An account book, diary, statement of expense or similar record must be prepared or maintained in such manner that each recording of an element of an expenditure is made at or near the time of the expenditure.

(a) Made at or near the time of the expenditure. For purposes of this section, the phrase "made at or near the time of the expenditure" means the elements of an expenditure are recorded at a time when, in relation to the making of an expenditure, the taxpayer has full present knowledge of each element of the expenditure, such as the amount, time, place and business purpose of the expenditure and business relationship to the taxpayer of any person entertained. An expense account statement which is a transcription of an account book, diary, or similar record prepared or maintained in accordance with the provisions of this subdivision shall be considered a record prepared or maintained in the manner prescribed in the preceding sentence if such expense account statement is submitted by an employee to his employer or by an independent contractor to his client or customer in the regular course of good business practice.

(b) Substantiation of business purpose. In order to constitute an adequate record of business purpose within the meaning of section 274(d) and this subparagraph, a written statement of business purpose generally is required. However, the degree of substantiation necessary to establish business purpose will vary depending upon the facts and circumstances of each case. Where the business purpose of an expenditure is evident from the surrounding facts and circumstances, a written explanation of such business purpose will not be required. For example, in the case of a salesman calling on customers on an established sales route, a written explanation of the business purpose of such travel ordinarily will not be required. Similarly, in the case of a business meal described in section 274(e)(1), if the business purpose of such meal is evidence from the business relationship to the taxpayer of the persons entertained and other surrounding circumstances, a written explanation of such business purpose will not be required.

(c) Confidential information. If any information relating to the elements of an expenditure, such as place, business purpose or business relationship, is of a confidential nature, such information need not be set forth in the account book, diary, statement of expense or similar record, provided such information is recorded at or near the time of the expenditure and is elsewhere available to the district director to substantiate such element of the expenditure.

(iii) Documentary evidence. Documentary evidence, such as receipts, paid bills, or similar evidence sufficient to support an expenditure shall be required for—

(a) Any expenditure for lodging while traveling away from home, and

(b) Any other expenditure of $25 or more, except, for transportation charges, documentary evidence will not be required if not readily available. Provided, however, that the Commissioner, in his discretion, may prescribe rules waiving such requirements in circumstances where he determines it is impracticable for such documentary evidence to be required. Ordinarily, documentary evidence will be considered adequate to support an expenditure if it includes sufficient information to establish the amount, date, place, and the essential character of the expenditure. For example, a hotel receipt is sufficient to support expenditures for business travel if it contains the following: name, location, date, and separate amounts for charges such as for lodging, meals, and telephone. Similarly, a restaurant receipt is sufficient to support an expenditure for a business meal if it contains the following: name and location of the restaurant, the date and amount of the expenditure, and, if a charge is made for an item other than meals and beverages, an indication that such is the case. A document may be indicative of only one (or part of one) element of an expenditure. Thus, a cancelled check, together with a bill from the payee, ordinarily would establish the element of cost. In contrast, a cancelled check drawn payable to a named payee would not by itself support a business expenditure without other evidence showing that the check was used for a certain business purpose.

(iv) Retention of documentary evidence. The Commissioner may, in his discretion, prescribe rules under which an employee may dispose of documentary evidence submitted to him by employees who are required to, and do, make an adequate accounting to the employer (within the meaning of paragraph (e)(4) of this section) if the employer maintains adequate accounting procedures with respect to such employees (within the meaning of paragraph (e)(5) of this section).

(v) Substantial compliance. If a taxpayer has not fully substantiated a particular element of an expenditure, but the taxpayer establishes to the satisfaction of the district director that he has substantially complied with the "adequate records" requirements of this subparagraph with respect to the expenditure, the taxpayer may be permitted to establish such element by evidence which the district director shall deem adequate.

(3) Substantiation by other sufficient evidence. If a taxpayer fails to establish to the satisfaction of the district director that he has substantially complied with the "adequate records" requirements of subparagraph (2) of this paragraph with respect to an element of an expenditure, then, except as otherwise provided in this paragraph, the taxpayer must establish such element—

(i) By his own statement, whether written or oral, containing specific information in detail as to such element; and

(ii) By other corroborative evidence sufficient to establish such element.

If such element is the description of a gift, or the cost, time, place, or date of an expenditure, the corroborative evidence shall be direct evidence, such as a statement in writing or the oral testimony of persons entertained or other witness setting forth detailed information about such element, or the documentary evidence described in subparagraph (2) of this paragraph. If such element is either the business relationship to the taxpayer of persons entertained or the business purpose of an expenditure, the corroborative evidence may be circumstantial evidence.

(4) Substantiation in exceptional circumstances. If a taxpayer establishes that, by reason of the inherent nature of the situation in which an expenditure was made—

(i) He was unable to obtain evidence with respect to an element of the expenditure which conforms fully to the "adequate records" requirements of subparagraph (2) of this paragraph,

(ii) He is unable to obtain evidence with respect to such element which conforms fully to the "other sufficient evidence" requirements of subparagraph (3) of this paragraph, and

(iii) He has presented other evidence, with respect to such element, which possesses the highest degree of probative value possible under the circumstances, such other evidence shall be considered to satisfy the substantiation requirements of section 274(d) and this paragraph.

(5) Loss of records due to circumstances beyond control of taxpayer. Where the taxpayer establishes that the failure to produce adequate records is due to the loss of such records through circumstances beyond the taxpayer's control, such as destruction by fire, flood, earthquake, or other casualty, the taxpayer shall have a right to substantiate a deduction by reasonable reconstruction of his expenditures.

(6) Special rules. (i) Separate expenditure. (a) In general. For the purposes of this section, each separate payment by the taxpayer shall ordinarily be considered to constitute a separate expenditure. However, concurrent or repetitious expenses of a similar nature occurring during the course of a single event shall be considered a single expenditure. To illustrate the above rules, where a taxpayer entertains a business guest at dinner and thereafter at the theater, the payment for dinner shall be considered to constitute one expenditure and the payment for the tickets for the theater shall be considered to constitute a separate expenditure. Similarly, if during a day of business travel a taxpayer makes separate payments for breakfast, lunch, and dinner, he shall

be considered to have made three separate expenditures. However, if during entertainment at a cocktail lounge the taxpayer pays separately for each serving of refreshments, the total amount expended for the refreshments will be treated as a single expenditure. A tip may be treated as a separate expenditure.

(b) Aggregation. Except as otherwise provided in this section, the account book, diary, statement of expense, or similar record required by subparagraph (2)(ii) of this paragraph shall be maintained with respect to each separate expenditure and not with respect to aggregate amounts for two or more expenditures. Thus, each expenditure for such items as lodging and air or rail travel shall be recorded as a separate item and not aggregated. However, at the option of the taxpayer, amounts expended for breakfast, lunch, or dinner, may be aggregated. A tip or gratuity which is related to an underlying expense may be aggregated with such expense. For other provisions permitting recording of aggregate amounts in an account book, diary, statement of expense or similar record see paragraph (b)(2)(i) and (b)(3) of this section (relating to incidental costs of travel and entertainment).

(ii) Allocation of expenditure. For purposes of this section, if a taxpayer has established the amount of an expenditure, but is unable to establish the portion of such amount which is attributable to each person participating in the event giving rise to the expenditure, such amount shall ordinarily be allocated to each participant on a pro rata basis, if such determination is material. Accordingly, the total number of persons for whom a travel or entertainment expenditure is incurred must be established in order to compute the portion of the expenditure allocable to each such person.

(iii) Primary use of a facility. Section 274(a)(1)(B) and (2)(C) denies a deduction for any expenditure paid or incurred before January 1, 1979, with respect to a facility, or paid or incurred at any time with respect to a club, used in connection with an entertainment activity unless the taxpayer establishes that the facility (including a club) was used primarily for the furtherance of his trade or business. A determination whether a facility before January 1, 1979, or a club at any time was used primarily for the furtherance of the taxpayer's trade or business will depend upon the facts and circumstances of each case. In order to establish that a facility was used primarily for the furtherance of his trade or business, the taxpayer shall maintain records of the use of the facility, the cost of using the facility, mileage or its equivalent (if appropriate), and such other information as shall tend to establish such primary use. Such records of use shall contain—

(a) For each use of the facility claimed to be in furtherance of the taxpayer's trade or business, the elements of an expenditure specified in paragraph (b) of this section, and

(b) For each use of the facility not in furtherance of the taxpayer's trade or business, an appropriate description of such use, including cost, date, number of persons entertained, nature of entertainment and, if applicable, information such as mileage or its equivalent. A notation such as "personal use" or "family use" would, in the case of such use, be sufficient to describe the nature of entertainment.

If a taxpayer fails to maintain adequate records concerning a facility which is likely to serve the personal purposes of the taxpayer, it shall be presumed that the use of such facility was primarily personal.

(iv) Additional information. In a case where it is necessary to obtain additional information, either—

(a) To clarify information contained in records, statements, testimony, or documentary evidence submitted by a taxpayer under the provisions of paragraph (c)(2) or (c)(3) of this section, or

(b) To establish the reliability or accuracy of such records, statements, testimony, or documentary evidence,

the district director may, notwithstanding any other provision of this section, obtain such additional information as he determines necessary to properly implement the provisions of section 274 and the regulations thereunder by personal interview or otherwise.

(7) Specific exceptions. Except as otherwise prescribed by the Commissioner, substantiation otherwise required by this paragraph is not required for—

(i) Expenses described in section 274(e)(2) relating to food and beverages for employees, section 274(e)(3) relating to expenses treated as compensation, section 274(e)(8) relating to items available to the public, and section 274(e)(9) relating to entertainment sold to customers, and

(ii) Expenses described in section 274(e)(5) relating to recreational, etc., expenses for employees, except that a taxpayer shall keep such records or other evidence as shall establish that such expenses were for activities (or facilities used in connection therewith) primarily for the benefit of employees other than employees who are officers, shareholders or other owners (as defined in section 274(e)(5)), or highly compensated employees.

(d) Disclosure on returns. The Commissioner may, in his discretion, prescribe rules under which any taxpayer claiming a deduction for entertainment, gifts, or travel or any other person receiving advances, reimbursements, or allowances for such items, shall make disclosure on his tax return with respect to such items. The provisions of this paragraph shall apply notwithstanding the provisions of paragraph (e) of this section.

(e) Reporting and substantiation of expenses of certain employees for travel, entertainment, and gifts. *(1) In general.* The purpose of this paragraph is to provide rules for reporting and substantiation of certain expenses paid or incurred by taxpayers in connection with the performance of services as employees. For purposes of this paragraph, the term "business expenses" means ordinary and necessary expenses for travel, entertainment, or gifts which are deductible under section 162, and the regulations thereunder, to the extent not disallowed by section 274(c). Thus, the term "business expenses" does not include personal, living or family expenses disallowed by section 262 or travel expenses disallowed by section 274(c), and advances, reimbursements, or allowances for such expenditures must be reported as income by the employee.

(2) Reporting of expenses for which the employee is required to make an adequate accounting to his employer. (i) Reimbursements equal to expenses. For purposes of computing tax liability, an employee need not report on his tax return business expenses for travel, transportation, entertainment, gifts, and similar purposes, paid or incurred by him solely for the benefit of his employer for which he is required to, and does, make an adequate accounting to his employer (as defined in subparagraph (4) of this paragraph) and which are charged directly or indirectly to the employer (for example, through credit cards) or for which the employee is paid through advances, reimbursements, or otherwise, provided that the total amount of such advances, reimbursements, and charges is equal to such expenses.

(ii) Reimbursements in excess of expenses. In case the total of the amounts charged directly or indirectly to the employer or received from the employer as advances, reimbursements, or otherwise, exceeds the business expenses paid or incurred by the employee and the employee is required to, and does, make an adequate accounting to his employer for such expenses, the employee must include such excess (including amounts received for expenditures not deductible by him) in income.

(iii) Expense in excess of reimbursements. If an employee incurs deductible business expenses on behalf of his employer which exceed the total of the amounts charged directly or indirectly to the employer and received from the employer as advances, reimbursements, or otherwise, and the employee wishes to claim a deduction for such excess, he must—

(a) Submit a statement as part of his tax return showing all of the information required by subparagraph (3) of this paragraph, and,

(b) Maintain such records and supporting evidence as will substantiate each element of an expenditure (described in paragraph (b) of this section) in accordance with paragraph (c) of this section.

(3) Reporting of expenses for which the employee is not required to make an adequate accounting to his employer. If the employee is not required to make an adequate accounting to his employer for his business expenses or, though required, fails to make an adequate accounting for such expenses, he must submit, as a part of his tax return, a statement showing the following information:

(i) The total of all amounts received as advances or reimbursements from his employer, including amounts charged directly or indirectly to the employer through credit cards or otherwise; and

(ii) The nature of his occupation, the number of days away from home on business, and the total amount of business expenses paid or incurred by him (including those charged directly or indirectly to the employer through credit cards or otherwise) broken down into such categories as transportation, meals and lodging while away from home overnight, entertainment, gifts, and other business expenses. In addition, he must maintain such records and supporting evidence as will substantiate each element of an expenditure (described in paragraph (b) of this section) in accordance with paragraph (c) of this section.

(4) Definition of an "adequate accounting" to the employer. For purposes of this paragraph an adequate accounting means the submission to the employer of an account book, diary, statement of expense, or similar record maintained by the employee in which the information as to each element of an expenditure (described in paragraph (b) of this section) is recorded at or near the time of the expenditure, together with supporting documentary evidence, in a manner which conforms to all the "adequate records" requirements of paragraph (c)(2) of this section. An adequate accounting requires that the employee account for all amounts received from his employer during the taxable year as advances, reimbursements, or allowances (including those charged directly or indirectly to the employer through credit cards or otherwise) for travel, entertainment, and gifts. The methods of substantiation allowed under paragraph (c)(4) or (c)(5) of this section also will be considered to be an adequate accounting if the employer accepts an employee's substantiation and establishes that such substantiation meets the requirements of such paragraph (c)(4) or (c)(5). For purposes of an adequate accounting the method of substantiation allowed under paragraph (c)(3) of this section will not be permitted.

(5) Substantiation of expenditures by certain employees. An employee who makes an adequate accounting to his employer within the meaning of this paragraph will not again be required to substantiate such expense account information except in the following cases:

(i) An employee whose business expenses exceed the total of amounts charged to his employer and amounts received through advances, reimbursements or otherwise and who claims a deduction on his return for such excess;

(ii) An employee who is related to his employer within the meaning of section 267(b) but for this purpose of percentage referred to in section 267(b)(2) shall be 10 percent; and

(iii) Employees in cases where it is determined that the accounting procedures used by the employer for the reporting and substantiation of expenses by such employees are not adequate, or where it cannot be determined that such procedures are adequate. The district director will determine whether the employer's accounting procedures are adequate by considering the facts and circumstances of each case, including the use of proper internal controls. For example, an employer should require that an expense account must be verified and approved by a responsible person other than the person incurring such expenses. Accounting procedures will be considered inadequate to the extent that the employer does not require an adequate accounting from his employees as defined in subparagraph (4) of this paragraph, or does not maintain such substantiation. To the extent an employer fails to maintain adequate accounting procedures he will thereby obligate his employees to separately substantiate their expense account information.

(f) Substantiation by reimbursement arrangements or per diem, mileage, and other traveling allowances. The Commissioner may, in his discretion, prescribe rules under which—

(1) Reimbursement arrangements covering ordinary and necessary expenses of traveling away from home (exclusive of transportation expenses to and from destination),

(2) Per diem allowances providing for ordinary and necessary expenses of traveling away from home (exclusive of transportation costs to and from destination), and

(3) Mileage allowances providing for ordinary and necessary expenses of transportation while traveling away from home,

will, if in accordance with reasonable business practice, be regarded as equivalent to substantiation by adequate records or other sufficient evidence for purposes of paragraph (c) of this section of the amount of such traveling expenses and as satisfying, with respect to the amount of such traveling expenses, the requirements of an adequate accounting to the employer for purposes of paragraph (e)(4) of this section. If the total travel allowance received exceeds the deductible traveling expenses paid or incurred by the employee, such excess must be reported as income on the employee's return. See paragraph (h) of this section relating to the substantiation of meal expenses while traveling.

(g) Reporting and substantiation of certain reimbursements of persons other than employees. *(1) In general.* The purpose of this paragraph is to provide rules for the reporting and substantiation of certain expenses for travel, entertainment, and gifts paid or incurred by one person (hereinafter termed "independent contractor" in connection with services performed for another person other than an employer (hereinafter termed "client or customer") under a reimbursement or other expense allowance arrangement with such client or customer. For purposes of this paragraph, the term "business expenses" means ordinary and necessary expenses for travel, entertainment, or gifts which are deductible under section 162, and the regulations thereunder, to the extent not disallowed by section 274(c). Thus, the term "business expenses" does not include personal, living or family expenses disallowed by section 262 or travel expenses disallowed by section 274(c), and reimbursements for such expenditures must be reported as income by the independent contractor. For purposes of this paragraph, the term "reimbursements" means advances, allowances, or reimbursements received by an independent contractor for travel, entertainment, or gifts, in connection with the performance by him of services for his client or customer, under a reimbursement or other expense allowance arrangement with his client or customer, and includes amounts charged directly or indirectly to the client or customer through credit card systems or otherwise.

(2) Substantiation by independent contractors. An independent contractor shall substantiate, with respect to his reimbursements, each element of an expenditure (described in paragraph (b) of this section) in accordance with the requirements of paragraph (c) of this section; and, to the extent he does not so substantiate, he shall include such reimbursements in income. An independent contractor shall so substantiate a reimbursement for entertainment regardless of whether he accounts (within the meaning of subparagraph (3) of this paragraph) for such entertainment.

(3) Accounting to a client or customer under section 274(e)(4)(B). Section 274(e)(4)(B) provides that section 274(a) (relating to disallowance of expenses for entertainment) shall not apply to expenditures for entertainment for which an independent contractor has been reimbursed if the independent contractor accounts to his client or customer to the extent provided by section 274(d). For purposes of section 274(e)(4)(B), an independent contractor shall be considered to account to his client or customer for an expense paid or incurred under a reimbursement or other expense allowance arrangement with his client or customer if, with respect to such expense for entertainment, he submits to his client or customer adequate records or other sufficient evidence conforming to the requirements of paragraph (c) of this section.

(4) Substantiation by client or customer. A client or customer shall not be required to substantiate, in accordance with the requirements of paragraph (c) of this section, reimbursements to an independent contractor for travel and gifts, or for entertainment unless the independent contractor has accounted to him (within the meaning of section 274(e)(4)(B) and subparagraph (3) of this paragraph) for such entertainment. See paragraph (h) of this section relating to the substantiation of meal expenses while traveling.

(h) Authority for an optional method of computing meal expenses while traveling. The Commissioner may establish a method under which a taxpayer may elect to use a specified amount or amounts for meals while traveling in lieu of substantiating the actual cost of meals. The taxpayer would not be relieved of substantiating the actual cost of other travel expenses as well as the time, and business purpose of the travel. See paragraph (b)(2) and (c) of this section.

(i) Effective date. *(1) In general.* Section 274(d) and this section apply with respect to taxable years ending after December 31, 1962, but only with respect to period after that date.

(2) Certain meal expenses. Paragraph (h) of this section is effective for expenses paid or incurred after December 31, 1982.

T.D. 6630, 12/27/62, amend T.D. 7226, 12/14/72, T.D. 7909, 9/6/83, T.D. 8051, 9/6/85, T.D. 8715, 3/24/97.

---

§ 1.274-5T Substantiation requirements (temporary).

(a) In general. For taxable years beginning on or after January 1, 1986, no deduction or credit shall be allowed with respect to—

(1) Traveling away from home (including meals and lodging),

(2) Any activity which is of a type generally considered to constitute entertainment, amusement, or recreation, or with respect to a facility used in connection with such an activity, including the items specified in section 274(e),

(3) Gifts defined in section 274(b), or

(4) Any listed property (as defined in section 280F(d)(4) and § 1.280F-6T(b)),

unless the taxpayer substantiates each element of the expenditure or use (as described in paragraph (b) of this section) in the manner provided in paragraph (c) of this section. This limitation supersedes the doctrine founded in *Cohan v. Commissioner,* 39 F.2d 540 (2d Cir. 1930). The decision held that, where the evidence indicated a taxpayer incurred deductible travel or entertainment expenses but the exact amount could not be determined, the court should make a close approximation and not disallow the deduction entirely. Section 274(d) contemplates that no deduction or credit shall be allowed a taxpayer on the basis of such approximations or unsupported testimony of the taxpayer. For purposes of this section, the term "entertainment" means entertainment, amusement, or recreation, and use of a facility therefor; and the term "expenditure" includes expenses and items (including items such as losses and depreciation).

(b) Elements of an expenditure or use. *(1) In general.* Section 274(d) and this section contemplate that no deduction or credit shall be allowed for travel, entertainment, a gift, or with respect to listed property unless the taxpayer substantiates the requisite elements of each expenditure or use as set forth in this paragraph (b).

(2) Travel away from home. The elements to be proved with respect to an expenditure for travel away from home are—

(i) Amount. Amount of each separate expenditure for traveling away from home, such as cost of transportation or lodging, except that the daily cost of the traveler's own breakfast, lunch, and dinner and of expenditures incidental to such travel may be aggregated, if set forth in reasonable categories, such as for meals, for gasoline and oil, and for taxi fares;

(ii) Time. Dates of departure and return for each trip away from home, and number of days away from home spent on business;

(iii) Place. Destinations or locality of travel, described by name of city or town or other similar designation; and

(iv) Business purpose. Business reason for travel or nature of the business benefit derived or expected to be derived as a result of travel.

(3) Entertainment in general. The elements to be proved with respect to an expenditure for entertainment are—

(i) Amount. Amount of each separate expenditure for entertainment, except that such incidental items as taxi fares or telephone calls may be aggregated on a daily basis;

(ii) Time. Date of entertainment;

(iii) Place. Name, if any, address or location, and designation of type of entertainment, such as dinner or theater, if such information is not apparent from the designation of the place;

(iv) Business purpose. Business reason for the entertainment or nature of business benefit derived or expected to be derived as a result of the entertainment and, except in the case of business meals described in section 274(e)(1), the nature of any business discussion or activity;

(v) Business relationship. Occupation or other information relating to the person or persons entertained, including name, title, or other designation, sufficient to establish business relationship to the taxpayer.

(4) Entertainment directly preceding or following a substantial and bona fide business discussion. If a taxpayer claims a deduction for entertainment directly preceding or following a substantial and bona fide business discussion on the ground that such entertainment was associated with the active conduct of the taxpayer's trade or business, the elements to be proved with respect to such expenditure, in addition to those enumerated in paragraph (b)(3)(i), (ii), (iii), and (v) of this section are—

(i) Time. Date and duration of business discussion;

(ii) Place. Place of business discussion;

(iii) Business purpose. Nature of business discussion, and business reason for the entertainment or nature of business benefit derived or expected to be derived as the result of the entertainment;

(iv) Business relationship. Identification of those persons entertained who participated in the business discussion.

(5) Gifts. The elements to be proved with respect to an expenditure for a gift are—

(i) Amount. Cost of the gift to the taxpayer;

(ii) Time. Date of the gift;

(iii) Description. Description of the gift;

(iv) Business purpose. Business reason for the gift or nature of business benefit derived or expected to be derived as a result of the gift; and

(v) Business relationship. Occupation or other information relating to the recipient of the gift, including name, title, or other designation, sufficient to establish business relationship to the taxpayer.

(6) Listed property. The elements to be proved with respect to any listed property are—

(i) Amount. (A) Expenditures. The amount of each separate expenditure with respect to an item of listed property, such as the cost of acquisition, the cost of capital improvements, lease payments, the cost of maintenance and repairs, or other expenditures, and

(B) Uses. The amount of each business/investment use (as defined in § 1.280F-6T(d)(3) and (e)), based on the appropriate measure (i.e., mileage for automobiles and other means of transportation and time for other listed property, unless the Commissioner approves an alternative method), and the total use of the listed property for the taxable period.

(ii) Time. Date of the expenditure or use with respect to listed property, and

(iii) Business or investment purpose. The business purpose for an expenditure or use with respect to any listed property (see § 1.274-5T(c)(6)(i)(B) and (C) for special rules for the aggregation of expenditures and business use and § 1.280F-6T(d)(2) for the distinction between qualified business use and business/investment use).

See also § 1.274-5T(e) relating to the substantiation of business use of employer-provided listed property and § 1.274-6T for special rules for substantiating the business/investment use of certain types of listed property.

(c) Rules of substantiation. *(1) In general.* Except as otherwise provided in this section and § 1.274-6T, a taxpayer must substantiate each element of an expenditure or use (described in paragraph (b) of this section) by adequate records or by sufficient evidence corroborating his own statement. Section 274(d) contemplates that a taxpayer will maintain and produce such substantiation as will constitute proof of each expenditure or use referred to in section 274. Written evidence has considerably more probative value than oral evidence alone. In addition, the probative value of written evidence is greater the closer in time it relates to the expenditure or use. A contemporaneous log is not required, but a record of the elements of an expenditure or of a business use of listed property made at or near the time of the expenditure or use, supported by sufficient documentary evidence, has a high degree of credibility not present with respect to a statement prepared subsequent thereto when generally there is a lack of accurate recall. Thus, the corroborative evidence required to support a statement not made at or near the time of the expenditure or use must have a high degree of probative value to elevate such statement and evidence to the level of credibility reflected by a record made at or near the time of the expenditure or use supported by sufficient documentary evidence. The substantiation requirements of section 274(d) are designed to encourage taxpayers to maintain the records, together with documentary evidence, as provided in paragraph (c)(2) of this section.

(2) Substantiation by adequate records. (i) In general. To meet the "adequate records" requirements of section 274(d), a taxpayer shall maintain an account book, diary, log, statement of expense, trip sheets, or similar record (as provided in paragraph (c)(2)(ii) of this section), and documentary evidence (as provided in paragraph (c)(2)(iii) of this section) which, in combination, are sufficient to establish each element of an expenditure or use specified in paragraph (b) of this section. It is not necessary to record information in an account book, diary, log, statement of expense, trip sheet, or similar record which duplicates information reflected on a receipt so long as the account book, etc. and receipt complement each other in an orderly manner.

(ii) Account book, diary, etc. An account book, diary, log, statement of expense, trip sheet, or similar record must be prepared or maintained in such manner that each recording of an element of an expenditure or use is made at or near the time of the expenditure or use.

(A) Made at or near the time of the expenditure or use. For purposes of this section, the phrase "made at or near the time of the expenditure or use" means the elements of an expenditure or use are recorded at a time when, in relation to the use or making of an expenditure, the taxpayer has full present knowledge of each element of the expenditure or use, such as the amount, time, place, and business purpose of the expenditure and business relationship. An expense account statement which is a transcription of an account book, diary, log, or similar record prepared or maintained in accordance with the provisions of this paragraph (c)(2) (ii) shall be considered a record prepared or maintained in the manner prescribed in the preceding sentence if such expense account statement is submitted by an employee to his employer or by an independent contractor to his client or customer in the regular course of good business practice. For example, a log maintained on a weekly basis, which accounts for use during the week, shall be considered a record made at or near the time of such use.

(B) Substantiation of business purpose. In order to constitute an adequate record of business purpose within the meaning of section 274(d) and this paragraph (c)(2), a written statement of business purpose generally is required. However, the degree of substantiation necessary to establish business purpose will vary depending upon the facts and circumstances of each case. Where the business purpose is evident from the surrounding facts and circumstances, a written explanation of such business purpose will not be required. For example, in the case of a salesman calling on customers on an established sales route, a written explanation of the business purpose of such travel ordinarily will not be required. Similarly, in the case of a business meal described in section 274(e)(1), if the business purpose of such meal is evident from the business relationship to the taxpayer of the persons entertained and other surrounding circumstances, a written explanation of such business purpose will not be required.

(C) Substantiation of business use of listed property. (1) Degree of substantiation. In order to constitute an adequate record (within the meaning of section 274(d) and this paragraph (c)(2)(ii)), which substantiates business/investment use of listed property (as defined in § 1.280F-6T(d)(3)), the record must contain sufficient information as to each element of every business/investment use. However, the level of detail required in an adequate record to substantiate business/investment use may vary depending upon the facts and circumstances. For example, a taxpayer who uses a truck for both business and personal purposes and whose only business use of a truck is to make deliveries to customers on an established route may satisfy the adequate record requirement by recording the total number miles driven during the taxable year, the length of the delivery route once, and the date of each trip at or near the time of the trips. Alternatively, the taxpayer may establish the date of each trip with a receipt, record of delivery, or other documentary evidence.

(2) Written record. Generally, an adequate record must be written. However, a record of the business use of listed property, such as a computer or automobile, prepared in a computer memory device with the aid of a logging program will constitute an adequate record.

(D) Confidential information. If any information relating to the elements of an expenditure or use, such as place, business purpose, or business relationship, is of a confidential nature, such information need not be set forth in the account book, diary, log, statement of expense, trip sheet, or similar record, provided such information is recorded at or near the time of the expenditure or use and is elsewhere available to the district director to substantiate such element of the expenditure or use.

(iii) [Reserved]. For further guidance, see § 1.274-5(c)(2)(iii).

(iv) Retention of written evidence. The Commissioner may, in his discretion, prescribe rules under which an employer may dispose of the adequate records and documentary evidence submitted to him by employees who are required to, and do, make an adequate accounting to the employer (within the meaning of paragraph (f)(4) of this section) if the employer maintains adequate accounting procedures with respect to such employees (within the meaning of paragraph (f)(5) of this section).

(v) Substantial compliance. If a taxpayer has not fully substantiated a particular element of an expenditure or use, but the taxpayer establishes to the satisfaction of the district director that he has substantially complied with the "adequate records" requirements of this paragraph (c)(2) with respect to the expenditure or use, the taxpayer may be permitted to establish such element by evidence which the district director shall deem adequate.

(3) Substantiation by other sufficient evidence. (i) In general. If a taxpayer fails to establish to the satisfaction of the district director that he has substantially complied with the "adequate records" requirements of paragraph (c) (2) of this section with respect to an element of an expenditure or use, then, except as otherwise provided in this paragraph, the taxpayer must establish such element—

(A) By his own statement, whether written or oral, containing specific information in detail as to such element; and

(B) By other corroborative evidence sufficient to establish such element.

If such element is the description of a gift, or the cost or amount, time, place, or date of an expenditure or use, the corroborative evidence shall be direct evidence, such as a statement in writing or the oral testimony of persons entertained or other witnesses setting forth detailed information about such element, or the documentary evidence described in paragraph (c)(2) of this section. If such element is either the business relationship to the taxpayer of persons entertained, or the business purpose of an expenditure, the corroborative evidence may be circumstantial evidence.

(ii) Sampling. (A) In general. Except as provided in paragraph (c)(3)(ii)(B) of this section, a taxpayer may maintain an adequate record for portions of a taxable year and use that record to substantiate the business/investment use of listed property for all or a portion of the taxable year if the taxpayer can demonstrate by other evidence that the periods for which an adequate record is maintained are representative of the use for the taxable year or a portion thereof.

(B) Exception for pooled vehicles. The sampling method of paragraph (c)(3)(ii)(A) of this section may not be used to substantiate the business/investment use of an automobile or other vehicle of an employer that is made available for use by more than one employee for all or a portion of a taxable year.

(C) Examples. The following examples illustrate this paragraph (c)(3) (ii).

Example (1). A, a sole proprietor and calendar year taxpayer, operates an interior decorating business out of her home. A uses an automobile for local business travel to visit the homes or offices of clients, to meet with suppliers and other subcontractors, and to pick up and deliver certain items to clients when feasible. There is no other business use of the automobile but A and other members of her family also use the automobile for personal purposes. A maintains adequate records for the first three months of 1986 that indicate that 75 percent of the use of the automobile was in A's business. Invoices from subcontractors and paid bills indicate that A's business continued at approximately the same rate for the remainder of 1986. If other circumstances do not change (e.g., A does not obtain a second car for exclusive use in her business), the determination that the business/investment use of the automobile for the taxable year is 75 percent is based on sufficient corroborative evidence.

Example (2). The facts are the same as in example (1), except that A maintains adequate records during the first week of every month, which indicate that 75 percent of the use of the automobile is in A's business. The invoices from A's business indicate that A's business continued at the same rate during the subsequent weeks of each month so that A's weekly records are representative of each month's business use of the automobile. Thus, the determination that the business/investment use of the automobile for the taxable year is 75 percent is based on sufficient corroborative evidence.

Example (3). B, a sole proprietor and calendar year taxpayer, is a salesman in a large metropolitan area for a company that manufactures household products. For the first three weeks of each month, B uses his own automobile occasionally to travel within the metropolitan area on business. During these three weeks, B's use of the automobile for business purposes does not follow a consistent pattern from day to day or week to week. During the fourth week of each month, B delivers to his customers all the orders taken during the previous month. B's use of his automobile for business purposes, as substantiated by adequate records, is 70 percent of the total use during that fourth week. In this example, a determination based on the records maintained during that fourth week that the business/investment use of the automobile for the taxable year is 70 percent is not based on sufficient corroborative evidence because use during this week is not representative of use during other periods.

(iii) Special rules. See § 1.274-6T for special rules for substantiation by sufficient corroborating evidence with respect to certain listed property.

(4) Substantiation in exceptional circumstances. If a taxpayer establishes that, by reason of the inherent nature of the situation—

(i) He was unable to obtain evidence with respect to an element of the expenditure or use which conforms fully to the "adequate records" requirements of paragraph (c)(2) of this section,

(ii) He is unable to obtain evidence with respect to such element which conforms fully to the "other sufficient evidence" requirements of paragraph (c)(3) of this section, and

(iii) He has presented other evidence, with respect to such element, which possesses the highest degree of probative value possible under the circumstances, such other evidence shall be considered to satisfy the substantiation requirements of section 274(d) and this paragraph.

(5) Loss of records due to circumstances beyond control of the taxpayer. Where the taxpayer establishes that the failure to produce adequate records is due to the loss of such records through circumstances beyond the taxpayer's control, such as destruction by fire, flood, earthquake, or other casualty, the taxpayer shall have a right to substantiate a deduction by reasonable reconstruction of his expenditures or use.

(6) Special rules. (i) Separate expenditure or use. (A) In general. For the purposes of this section, each separate payment or use by the taxpayer shall ordinarily be considered to constitute a separate expenditure. However, concurrent or repetitious expenses or uses may be substantiated as a single item. To illustrate the above rules, where a taxpayer entertains a business guest at dinner and thereafter at the theater, the payment for dinner shall be considered to constitute one expenditure and the payment for the tickets for the theater shall be considered to constitute a separate expenditure. Similarly, if during a day of business travel a taxpayer makes separate payments for breakfast, lunch, and dinner, he shall be considered to have made three separate expenditures. However, if during entertainment at a cocktail lounge the taxpayer pays separately for each serving of refreshments, the total amount expended for the refreshments will be treated as a single expenditure. A tip may be treated as a separate expenditure.

(B) Aggregation of expenditures. Except as otherwise provided in this section, the account book, diary, log, statement of expense, trip sheet, or similar record required by paragraph (c)(2) (ii) of this section shall be maintained with respect to each separate expenditure and not with respect to aggregate amounts for two or more expenditures. Thus, each expenditure for such items as lodging and air or rail travel shall be recorded as a separate item and not aggregated. However, at the option of the taxpayer, amounts expended for breakfast, lunch, or dinner, may be aggregated. A tip or gratuity which is related to an underlying expense may be aggregated with such expense. In addition, amounts expended in connection with the use of listed property during a taxable year, such as for gasoline or repairs for an automobile, may be aggregated. If these expenses are aggregated, the taxpayer must establish the date and amount, but need not prove the business purpose of each expenditure. Instead, the taxpayer may prorate the expenses based on the total business use of the listed property. For other provisions permitting recording of aggregate amounts in an account book, diary, log, statement of expense, trip sheet, or similar record, see paragraphs (b)(2)(i) and (b)(3) of this section (relating to incidental costs of travel and entertainment).

(C) Aggregation of business use. Uses which may be considered part of a single use, for example, a round trip or uninterrupted business use, may be accounted for by a single record. For example, use of a truck to make deliveries at several different locations which begins and ends at the business premises and which may include a stop at the business premises in between two deliveries may be accounted for by a single record of miles driven. In addition, use of a passenger automobile by a salesman for a business trip away from home over a period of time may be accounted for by a single record of miles traveled. De minimis personal use (such as a stop for lunch on the way between two business stops) is not an interruption of business use.

(ii) Allocation of expenditure. For purposes of this section, if a taxpayer has established the amount of an expenditure, but is unable to establish the portion of such amount which is attributable to each person participating in the event giving rise to the expenditure, such amount shall ordinarily be allocated to each participant on a pro rata basis, if such determination is material. Accordingly, the total number of persons for whom a travel or entertainment expenditure is incurred must be established in order to compute the portion of the expenditure allocable to each such person.

(iii) Primary use of a facility. Section 274(a)(1)(B) and (2)(C) deny a deduction for any expenditure paid or incurred before January 1, 1979, with respect to a facility, or paid or incurred before January 1, 1994, with respect to a club, used in connection with an entertainment activity unless the taxpayer establishes that the facility (including a club) was used primarily for the furtherance of the taxpayer's trade or business. A determination whether a facility before January 1, 1979, or a club before January 1, 1994, was used primarily for the furtherance of the taxpayer's trade or business will depend upon the facts and circumstances of each case. In order to establish that a facility was used primarily for the furtherance of his trade or business, the taxpayer shall maintain records of the use of the facility, the cost of using the facility, mileage or its equivalent (if appropriate), and such other information as shall tend to establish such primary use. Such records of use shall contain—

(A) For each use of the facility claimed to be in furtherance of the taxpayer's trade or business, the elements of an expenditure specified in paragraph (b)(3) of this section, and

(B) For each use of the facility not in furtherance of the taxpayer's trade or business, an appropriate description of such use, including cost, date, number of persons entertained, nature of entertainment and, if applicable, information such as mileage or its equivalent. A notation such as "personal use" or "family use" would, in the case of such use, be sufficient to describe the nature of entertainment.

If a taxpayer fails to maintain adequate records concerning a facility which is likely to serve the personal purposes of the taxpayer, it shall be presumed that the use of such facility was primarily personal.

(iv) Additional information. In a case where it is necessary to obtain additional information, either—

(A) To clarify information contained in records, statements, testimony, or documentary evidence submitted by a taxpayer under the provisions of paragraph (c)(2) or (c)(3) of this section, or

(B) To establish the reliability or accuracy of such records, statements, testimony, or documentary evidence,

the district director may, notwithstanding any other provision of this section, obtain such additional information by personal interview or otherwise as he determines necessary to implement properly the provisions of section 274 and the regulations thereunder.

(7) Specific exceptions. Except as otherwise prescribed by the Commissioner, substantiation otherwise required by this paragraph is not required for—

(i) Expenses described in section 274(e)(2) relating to food and beverages for employees, section 274(e)(3) relating to expenses treated as compensation, section 274(e)(8) relating to items available to the public, and section 274(e)(9) relating to entertainment sold to customers, and

(ii) Expenses described in section 274(e)(5) relating to recreational, etc., expenses for employees, except that a taxpayer shall keep such records or other evidence as shall establish that such expenses were for activities (or facilities used in connection therewith) primarily for the benefit of employees other than employees who are officers, shareholders or other owners (as defined in section 274(e)(5)), or highly compensated employees.

(d) Disclosure on returns. *(1) In general.* The Commissioner may, in his discretion, prescribe rules under which any taxpayer claiming a deduction or credit for entertainment, gifts, travel, or with respect to listed property, or any other person receiving advances, reimbursements, or allowances for such items, shall make disclosure on his tax return with respect to such items. The provisions of this paragraph shall apply notwithstanding the provisions of paragraph (f) of this section.

(2) Business use of passenger automobiles and other vehicles. (i) On returns for taxable years beginning after December 31, 1984, taxpayers that claim a deduction or credit with respect to any vehicle are required to answer certain questions providing information about the use of the vehicle. The information required on the tax return relates to mileage (total, business, commuting, and other personal mileage), percentage of business use, date placed in service, use of other vehicles, after-work use, whether the taxpayer has evidence to support the business use claimed on the return, and whether or not the evidence is written.

(ii) Any employer that provides the use of a vehicle to an employee must obtain information from the employee sufficient to complete the employer's tax return. Any employer that provides more than five vehicles to its employees need not include any information on its return. The employer, instead, must obtain the information from its employees, indicate on its return that it has obtained the information, and retain the information received. Any employer—

(A) That can satisfy the requirements of § 1.274-6T(a)(2), relating to vehicles not used for personal purposes,

(B) That can satisfy the requirements of § 1.274-6T(a)(3), relating to vehicles not used for personal purposes other than commuting, or

(C) That treats all use of vehicles by employees as personal use

need not obtain information with respect to those vehicles, but instead must indicate on its return that it has vehicles exempt from the requirements of this paragraph (d)(2).

(3) Business use of other listed property. On returns for taxable years beginning after December 31, 1984, taxpayers that claim a deduction or credit with respect to any listed property other than a vehicle (for example, a yacht, airplane, or certain computers) are required to provide the following information:

(i) The date that the property was placed in service,

(ii) The percentage of business use,

(iii) Whether evidence is available to support the percentage of business use claimed on the return, and

(iv) Whether the evidence is written.

(e) Substantiation of the business use of listed property made available by an employer for use by an employee. *(1) Employee.* (i) In general. An employee may not exclude from gross income as a working condition fringe any amount of the value of the availability of listed property provided by an employer to the employee, unless the employee substantiates for the period of availability the amount of the exclusion in accordance with the requirements of section 274(d) and either this section or § 1.274-6T.

(ii) Vehicles treated as used entirely for personal purposes. If an employer includes the value of the availability of a vehicle (as defined in § 1.61-21(e)(2)in an employee's gross income without taking into account any exclusion for a working condition fringe allowable under section 132 and the regulations thereunder with respect to the vehicle, the employee must substantiate any deduction claimed under §§ 1.162-25 and § 1.162-25T for the business/investment use of the vehicle in accordance with the requirements of section 274(d) and either this section or § 1.274-6T.

(2) Employer. (i) In general. An employer substantiates its business/investment use of listed property by showing either—

(A) That, based on evidence that satisfies the requirements of section 274(d) or statements submitted by employees that summarize such evidence, all or a portion of the use of the listed property is by employees in the employer's trade or business and, if any employee used the property for personal purposes, the employer included an appropriate amount in the employee's income, or

(B) In the case of a vehicle, the employer treats all use by employees as personal use and includes an appropriate amount in the employees' income.

(ii) Reliance on employee records. For purposes of substantiating the business/investment use of listed property that an employer provides to an employee and for purposes of the information required by paragraph (d)(2) and (3) of this section, the employer may rely on adequate records maintained by the employee or on the employee's own statement if corroborated by other sufficient evidence unless the employer knows or has reason to know that the statement, records, or other evidence are not accurate. The employer must retain a copy of the adequate records maintained by the employee or the other sufficient evidence, if available. Alternatively, the employer may rely on a statement submitted by the employee that provides sufficient information to allow the employer to determine the business/investment use of the property unless the employer knows or has reason to know that the statement is not based on adequate records or on the employee's own statement corroborated by other sufficient evidence. If the employer relies on the employee's statement, the employer must retain only a copy of the statement. The employee must retain a copy of the adequate records or other evidence.

(f) Reporting and substantiation of expenses of certain employees for travel, entertainment, gifts, and with respect to listed property. *(1) In general.* The purpose of this paragraph is to provide rules for reporting and substantiation of certain expenses paid or incurred by employees in connection with the performance of services as employees. For purposes of this paragraph, the term "business expenses" means ordinary and necessary expenses for travel, entertainment, gifts, or with respect to listed property which are deductible under section 162, and the regulations thereunder, to the extent not disallowed by sections 262, 274(c), and 280F. Thus, the term "business expenses" does not include personal, living, or family expenses disallowed by section 262, travel expenses disallowed by section 274(c), or cost recovery deductions and credits with respect to listed property disallowed by section 280F(d)(3) because the use of such property is not for the convenience of the employer and required as a condition of employment. Except as provided in paragraph (f)(2), advances, reimbursements, or allowances for such expenditures must be reported as income by the employee.

(2) Reporting of expenses for which the employee is required to make an adequate accounting to his employer. (i) Reimbursements equal to expenses. For purposes of computing tax liability, an employee need not report on his tax return business expenses for travel, transportation, entertainment, gifts, or with respect to listed property, paid or incurred by him solely for the benefit of his employer for which he is required to, and does, make an adequate accounting to his employer (as defined in paragraph (f)(4) of this section) and which are charged directly or indirectly to the employer (for example, through credit cards) or for which the employee is paid through advances, reimbursements, or otherwise, provided that the total amount of such advances, reimbursements, and charges is equal to such expenses.

(ii) Reimbursements in excess of expenses. In case the total of the amounts charged directly or indirectly to the employer or received from the employer as advances, reimbursements, or otherwise, exceeds the business expenses paid or incurred by the employee and the employee is required to, and does, make an adequate accounting to his employer for such expenses, the employee must include such excess (including amounts received for expenditures not deductible by him) in income.

(iii) Expenses in excess of reimbursements. If an employee incurs deductible business expenses on behalf of his employer which exceed the total of the amounts charged directly or indirectly to the employer and received from the employer as advances, reimbursements, or otherwise, and the employee makes an adequate accounting to his employer, the employee must be able to substantiate any deduction for such excess with such records and supporting evidence as will substantiate each element of an expenditure (described in paragraph (b) of this section) in accordance with paragraph (c) of this section.

(3) Reporting of expenses for which the employee is not required to make an adequate accounting to his employer. If the employee is not required to make an adequate accounting to his employer for his business expenses or, though required, fails to make an adequate accounting for such expenses, he must submit, as a part of his tax return, the appropriate form issued by the Internal Revenue Service for claiming deductions for employee business expenses (e.g., Form 2106, Employee Business Expenses, for 1985) and provide the information requested on that form, including the information required by paragraph (d)(2) and (3) of this section if the employee's business expenses are with respect to the use of listed property. In addition, the employee must maintain such records and supporting evidence as will substantiate each element of an expenditure or use (described in paragraph (b) of this section) in accordance with paragraph (c) of this section.

(4) [Reserved]. For further guidance, see § 1.274-5(f)(4).

(5) Substantiation of expenditures by certain employees. An employee who makes an adequate accounting to his employer within the meaning of this paragraph will not again be required to substantiate such expense account information except in the following cases:

(i) An employee whose business expenses exceed the total of amounts charged to his employer and amounts received through advances, reimbursements or otherwise and who claims a deduction on his return for such excess,

(ii) An employee who is related to his employer within the meaning of section 267(b), but for this purpose the percentage referred to in section 267(b)(2) shall be 10 percent, and

(iii) Employees in cases where it is determined that the accounting procedures used by the employer for the reporting and substantiation of expenses by such employees are not adequate, or where it cannot be determined that such procedures are adequate. The district director will determine whether the employer's accounting procedures are adequate by considering the facts and circumstances of each case, including the use of proper internal controls. For example, an employer should require that an expense account be verified and approved by a reasonable person other than the person incurring such expenses. Accounting procedures will be considered inadequate to the extent that the employer does not require an adequate accounting from his employees as defined in paragraph (f)(4) of this section, or does not maintain such substantiation. To the extent an employer fails to maintain adequate accounting procedures he will thereby obligate his employees to substantiate separately their expense account information.

(g) [Reserved]. For further guidance, see § 1.274-5(g).

(h) Reporting and substantiation of certain reimbursements of persons other than employees. *(1) In general.* The purpose of this paragraph is to provide rules for the reporting and substantiation of certain expenses for travel, entertainment, gifts, or with respect to listed property paid or incurred by one person (hereinafter termed "independent contractor") in connection with services performed for another person other than an employer (hereinafter termed "client or customer") under a reimbursement or other expense allowance arrangement with such client or customer. For purposes of this paragraph, the term "business expenses" means ordinary and necessary expenses for travel, entertainment, gifts, or with respect to listed property which are deductible under section 162, and the regulations thereunder, to the extent not disallowed by sections 262 and 274(c). Thus, the term "business expenses" does not include personal, living, or family expenses disallowed by section 262 or travel expenses disallowed by section 274(c), and reimbursements for such expenditures must be reported as income by the independent contractor. For purposes of this paragraph, the term "reimbursements" means advances, allowances, or reimbursements received by an independent contractor for travel, entertainment, gifts, or with respect to listed property in connection with the performance by him of services for his client or customer, under a reimbursement or other expense allowance arrangement with his client or customer, and includes amounts charged directly or indirectly to the client or customer through credit card systems or otherwise. *See* paragraph (j) of this section relating to the substantiation of meal expenses while traveling away from home.

(2) Substantiation by independent contractors. An independent contractor shall substantiate, with respect to his reimbursements, each element of an expenditure (described in paragraph (b) of this section) in accordance with the requirements of paragraph (c) of this section; and, to the extent he does not so substantiate, he shall include such reimbursements in income. An independent contractor shall so substantiate a reimbursement for entertainment regardless of whether he accounts (within the meaning of paragraph (h)(3) of this section) for such entertainment.

(3) Accounting to a client or customer under section 274(e)(4)(B). Section 274(e)(4)(B) provides that section 274(a) (relating to disallowance of expenses for entertainment) shall not apply to expenditures for entertainment for which an independent contractor has been reimbursed if the independent contractor accounts to his client or customer, to the extent provided by section 274(d). For purposes of section 274(e)(4)(B), an independent contractor shall be considered to account to his client or customer for an expense paid or incurred under a reimbursement or other expense allowance arrangement with his client or customer if, with respect to such expense for entertainment, he submits to his client or customer adequate records or other sufficient evidence conforming to the requirements of paragraph (c) of this section.

(4) Substantiation by client or customer. A client or customer shall not be required to substantiate, in accordance with the requirements of paragraph (c) of this section, reimbursements to an independent contractor for travel and gifts, or for entertainment unless the independent contractor has accounted to him (within the meaning of section 274(e)(4)(B) and paragraph (h)(3) of this section) for such entertainment. If an independent contractor has so accounted to a client or customer for entertainment, the client or customer shall substantiate each element of the expenditure (as described in paragraph (b) of this section) in accordance with the requirements of paragraph (c) of this section.

(i) [Reserved]

(j) [Reserved]. For further guidance, see § 1.274-5(j).

(k) Exceptions for qualified nonpersonal use vehicles. *(1) In general.* The substantiation requirements of section 274(d) and this section do not apply to any qualified nonpersonal use vehicle (as defined in paragraph (k)(2) of this section).

(2) Qualified nonpersonal use vehicle. (i) In general. For purposes of section 274(d) and this section, the term "qualified nonpersonal use vehicle" means any vehicle which, by reason of its nature (i.e., design), is not likely to be used more than a de minimis amount for personal purposes.

(ii) List of vehicles. Vehicles which are qualified nonpersonal use vehicles include the following—

(A) Clearly marked police and fire vehicles (as defined and to the extent provided in paragraph (k)(3) of this section),

(B) Ambulances used as such or hearses used as such,

(C) Any vehicle designed to carry cargo with a loaded gross vehicle weight over 14,000 pounds,

(D) Bucket trucks ("cherry pickers"),

(E) Cement mixers,

(F) Combines,

(G) Cranes and derricks,

(H) Delivery trucks with seating only for the driver, or only for the driver plus a folding jump seat,

(I) Dump trucks (including garbage trucks),

(J) Flatbed trucks,

(K) Forklifts,

(L) Passenger buses used as such with a capacity of at least 20 passengers,

(M) Qualified moving vans (as defined in paragraph (k)(4) of this section),

(N) Qualified specialized utility repair trucks (as defined in paragraph (k)(5) of this section),

(O) Refrigerated trucks,

(P) School buses (as defined in section 4221(d)(7)(C)),

(Q) Tractors and other special purpose farm vehicles,

(R) Unmarked vehicles used by law enforcement officers (as defined in paragraph (k)(6) of this section) if the use is officially authorized, and

(S) Such other vehicles as the Commissioner may designate.

(3) Clearly marked police or fire vehicles. A police or fire vehicle is a vehicle, owned or leased by a governmental unit, or any agency or instrumentality thereof, that is required to be used for commuting by a police officer or fire fighter who, when not on a regular shift, is on call at all times, provided that any personal use (other than commuting) of the vehicle outside the limit of the police officer's arrest powers or the fire fighter's obligation to respond to an emergency is prohibited by such governmental unit. A police or fire vehicle is clearly marked if, through painted insignia or words, it is readily apparent that the vehicle is a police or fire vehicle. A marking on a license plate is not a clear marking for purposes of this paragraph (k).

(4) Qualified moving van. The term "qualified moving van" means any truck or van used by a professional moving company in the trade or business of moving household or business goods if—

(i) No personal use of the van is allowed other than for travel to and from a move site (or for de minimis personal use, such as a stop for lunch on the way between two move sites),

(ii) Personal use for travel to and from a move site is an irregular practice (i.e., not more than five times a month on average), and

(iii) Personal use is limited to situations in which it is more convenient to the employer, because of the location of the employee's residence in relation to the location of the move site, for the van not to be returned to the employer's business location.

(5) Qualified specialized utility repair truck. The term "qualified specialized utility repair truck" means any truck (not including a van or pickup truck) specifically designed and used to carry heavy tools, testing equipment, or parts if—

(i) The shelves, racks, or other permanent interior construction which has been installed to carry and store such heavy items is such that it is unlikely that the truck will be used more than a de minimis amount for personal purposes, and

(ii) The employer requires the employee to drive the truck home in order to be able to respond in emergency situations for purposes of restoring or maintaining electricity, gas, telephone, water, sewer, or steam utility services.

(6) Unmarked law enforcement vehicles. (i) In general. The substantiation requirements of section 274(d) and this section do not apply to officially authorized uses of an unmarked vehicle by a "law enforcement officer". To qualify for this exception, any personal use must be authorized by the Federal, State, county, or local governmental agency or department that owns or leases the vehicle and employs the officer, and must be incident to law-enforcement functions, such as being able to report directly from home to a stakeout or surveillance site, or to an emergency situation. Use of an unmarked vehicle for vacation or recreation trips cannot qualify as an authorized use.

(ii) Law enforcement officer. The term "law enforcement officer" means an individual who is employed on a full-time basis by a governmental unit that is responsible for the prevention or investigation of crime involving injury to persons or property (including apprehension or detention of persons for such crimes), who is authorized by law to carry firearms, execute search warrants, and to make arrests (other than merely a citizen's arrest), and who regularly carries firearms (except when it is not possible to do so because of the requirements of undercover work). The term "law enforcement officer" may include an arson investigator if the investigator otherwise meets the requirements of this paragraph (k)(6)(ii), but does not include Internal Revenue Service special agents.

(7) Trucks and vans. The substantiation requirements of section 274(d) and this section apply generally to any pickup truck or van, unless the truck or van has been specially modified with the result that it is not likely to be used more than a de minimis amount for personal purposes. For example, a van that has only a front bench for seating, in which permanent shelving that fills most of the cargo area has been installed, that constantly carries merchandise or equipment, and that has been specially painted with advertising or the company's name, is a vehicle not likely to be used more than a de minimis amount for personal purposes.

(8) Examples. The following examples illustrate the provisions of paragraph (k)(3) and (6) of this section:

Example (1). Detective C, who is a "law enforcement officer" employed by a state police department, headquartered in city M, is provided with an unmarked vehicle (equipped with radio communication) for use during off-duty hours because C must be able to communicate with headquarters and be available for duty at any time (for example, to report to a surveillance or crime site). The police department generally has officially authorized personal use of the vehicle by C but has prohibited use of the vehicle for recreational purposes or for personal purposes outside the state. Thus, C's use of the vehicle for commuting between headquarters or a surveillance site and home and for personal errands is authorized personal use as described in paragraph (k)(6)(i) of this section. With respect to these authorized uses, the vehicle is not subject to the substantiation requirements of section 274(d) and the value of these uses is not included in C's gross income.

Example (2). Detective T is a "law enforcement officer" employed by city M. T is authorized to make arrests only within M's city limits. T, along with all other officers on the force, is ordinarily on duty for eight hours each work day and on call during the other sixteen hours. T is provided with the use of a clearly marked police vehicle in which T is required to commute to his home in city M. The police department's official policy regarding marked police vehicles prohibits personal use (other than commuting) of the vehicles outside the city limits. When not using the vehicle on the job, T uses the vehicle only for commuting, personal errands on the way between work and home, and personal errands within city M. All use of the vehicle by T conforms to the requirements of paragraph (k)(3) of this section. Therefore, the value of that use is excluded from T's gross income as a working condition fringe and the vehicle is not subject to the substantiation requirements of section 274(d).

(l) Definitions. For purposes of section 274(d) and this section, the terms "automobile" and "vehicle" have the same meanings as prescribed in § 1.61-21(d)(1)(ii) and § 1.61-21(e)(2), respectively. Also, for purposes of section 274(d) and this section, the terms "employer," "employee," and "personal use" have the same meanings as prescribed in § 1.274-6T(e).

(m) Effective date. Section 274(d), as amended by the Tax Reform Act of 1984 and Public Law 99-44, and this section (except as provided in paragraph (d)(2) and (3) of this section) apply with respect to taxable years beginning after December 31, 1985. Section 274(d) and this section apply to any deduction or credit claimed in a taxable year beginning after December 31, 1985, with respect to any listed property, regardless of the taxable year in which the property was placed in service. However, except as provided in § 1.132-5(h) with respect to qualified nonpersonal use vehicles, the substantiation requirements of section 274(d) and this section do not apply to the determination of an employee's working condition fringe exclusion or to the determination under § 1.162-25(b) of an employee's deduction before the date that those requirements apply, under this paragraph (m), to the employer, if the employer is taxable. Paragraph (j)(3) of this section applies to expenses paid or incurred after September 30, 2002.

T.D. 7986, 10/19/84, amend T.D. 8009, 2/15/85, T.D. 8061, 11/1/85, T.D. 8063, 12/18/85, T.D. 8276, 12/7/89, T.D. 8451, 12/4/92, T.D. 8601, 7/18/95, T.D. 8715, 3/24/97, T.D. 8864, 1/21/2000, T.D. 9020, 11/8/2002, T.D. 9064, 6/30/2003.

PAR. 4. Section 1.274-5T is revised by amending paragraphs (k) and (l) as follows:

Proposed § 1.274-5T Substantiation requirements (temporary). [*For Preamble, see ¶ 153,001*]

* * * * *

(k) and (l) [Reserved]. For further guidance, see §§ 1.274-5(k) and (l).

* * * * *

§ 1.274-6 Expenditures deductible without regard to trade or business or other income producing activity.

The provisions of §§ 1.274-1 through 1.274-5, inclusive, do not apply to any deduction allowable to the taxpayer without regard to its connection with the taxpayer's trade or business or other income producing activity. Examples of such items are interest, taxes such as real property taxes, and casualty losses. Thus, if a taxpayer owned a fishing camp, the taxpayer could still deduct mortgage interest and real property taxes in full even if deductions for its use are not allowable under section 274(a) and § 1.274-2. In the case of a taxpayer which is not an individual, the provisions of this section shall be applied as if it were an individual. Thus, if a corporation sustains a casualty loss on an entertainment facility used in its trade or business, it could deduct the loss even though deductions for the use of the facility are not allowable.

T.D. 6659, 6/24/63, amend T.D. 8051, 9/6/85.

§ 1.274-6T Substantiation with respect to certain types of listed property for taxable years beginning after 1985 (temporary).

(a) Written policy statements as to vehicles. *(1) In general.* Two types of written policy statements satisfying the conditions described in paragraph (a)(2) and (3) of this section, if initiated and kept by an employer to implement a policy of no personal use, or no personal use except for commuting, of a vehicle provided by the employer, qualify as sufficient evidence corroborating the taxpayer's own statement and therefore will satisfy the employer's substantiation requirements under section 274(d). Therefore, the employee need not keep a separate set of records for purposes of the employer's substantiation requirements under section 274(d) with respect to use of a vehicle satisfying these written policy statement rules. A written policy statement adopted by a governmental unit as to employee use of its vehicles is eligible for these exceptions to the section 274(d) substantiation rules. Thus, a resolution of a city council or a provision of state law or a state constitution would qualify as a written policy statement, as long as the conditions described in paragraph (a)(2) and (3) of this section are met.

(2) Vehicles not used for personal purposes. (i) Employers. A policy statement that prohibits personal use by an employee satisfies an employer's substantiation requirements under section 274(d) if all the following conditions are met—

(A) The vehicle is owned or leased by the employer and is provided to one or more employees for use in connection with the employer's trade or business,

(B) When the vehicle is not used in the employer's trade or business, it is kept on the employer's business premises, unless it is temporarily located elsewhere, for example, for maintenance or because of a mechanical failure,

(C) No employee using the vehicle lives at the employer's business premises,

(D) Under a written policy of the employer, neither an employee, nor any individual whose use would be taxable to the employee, may use the vehicle for personal purposes, except for de minimis personal use (such as a stop for lunch between two business deliveries), and

(E) The employer reasonably believes that, except for de minimis use, neither the employee, nor any individual whose use would be taxable to the employee, uses the vehicle for any personal purpose.

There must also be evidence that would enable the Commissioner to determine whether the use of the vehicle meets the preceding five conditions.

(ii) Employees. An employee, in lieu of substantiating the business/investment use of an employer-provided vehicle under § 1.274-5T, may treat all use of the vehicle as business/investment use if the following conditions are met—

(A) The vehicle is owned or leased by the employer and is provided to one or more employees for use in connection with the employer's trade or business,

(B) When the vehicle is not used in the employer's trade or business, it is kept on the employer's business premises, unless it is temporarily located elsewhere, for example, for maintenance or because of a mechanical failure,

(C) No employee using the vehicle lives at the employer's business premises,

(D) Under a written policy of the employer, neither the employee, nor any individual whose use would be taxable to the employee, may use the vehicle for personal purposes, except for de minimis personal use (such as a stop for lunch between two business deliveries), and

(E) Except for de minimis personal use, neither the employee, nor any individual whose use would be taxable to the employee, uses the vehicle for any personal purpose.

There must also be evidence that would enable the Commissioner to determine whether the use of the vehicle meets the preceding five conditions.

(3) Vehicles not used for personal purposes other than commuting. (i) Employers. A policy statement that prohibits personal use by an employee, other than commuting, satisfies an employer's substantiation requirements under section 274(d) if all the following conditions are met—

(A) The vehicle is owned or leased by the employer and is provided to one or more employees for use in connection with the employer's trade or business and is used in the employer's trade or business,

(B) For bona fide noncompensatory business reasons, the employer requires the employee to commute to and/or from work in the vehicle,

(C) The employer has established a written policy under which neither the employee, nor any individual whose use would be taxable to the employee, may use the vehicle for personal purposes, other than for commuting or de minimis personal use (such as a stop for a personal errand on the way between a business delivery and the employee's home),

(D) The employer reasonably believes that, except for de minimis personal use, neither the employee, nor any individual whose use would be taxable to the employee, uses the vehicle for any personal purpose other than commuting,

(E) The employee required to use the vehicle for commuting is not a control employee (as defined in § 1.61-2T(f)(5) and (6)) required to use an automobile (as defined in § 1.61-2T(d)(1)(ii)), and

(F) The employer accounts for the commuting use by including in the employee's gross income the commuting value provided in § 1.61-2T(f)(3) (to the extent not reimbursed by the employee).

There must be evidence that would enable the Commissioner to determine whether the use of the vehicle met the preceding six conditions.

(ii) Employees. An employee, in lieu of substantiating the business/investment use of an employer-provided vehicle under § 1.274-5T, may substantiate any exclusion allowed under section 132 for a working condition fringe by including in income the commuting value of the vehicle (determined by the employer pursuant to § 1.61-2T(f)(3) if all the following conditions are met:

(A) The vehicle is owned or leased by the employer and is provided to one or more employees for use in connection with the employer's trade or business and is used in the employer's trade or business,

(B) For bona fide noncompensatory business reasons, the employer requires the employee to commute to and/or from work in the vehicle,

(C) Under a written policy of the employer, neither the employee, nor any individual whose use would be taxable to the employee, may use the vehicle for personal purposes, other than for commuting or de minimis personal use (such as a stop for a personal errand on the way between a business delivery and the employee's home),

(D) Except for de minimis personal use, neither the employee, nor any individual whose use would be taxable to the employee, uses the vehicle for any personal purpose other than commuting,

(E) The employee required to use the vehicle for commuting is not a control employee (as defined in § 1.61-2T(f)(5) and (6)) required to use an automobile (as defined in § 1.61-2T(d)(1)(ii)), and

(F) The employee includes in gross income the commuting value determined by the employer as provided in § 1.61-2T(f)(3) (to the extent that the employee does not reimburse the employer for the commuting use).

There must also be evidence that would enable the Commissioner to determine whether the use of the vehicle met the preceding six conditions.

(b) Vehicles used in connection with the business of farming. *(1) In general.* If, during a taxable year or shorter period, a vehicle, not otherwise described in section 274(i), § 1.274-5T(k), or paragraph (a)(2) or (3) of this section, is owned or leased by an employer and used during most of a normal business day directly in connection with the business of farming (as defined in paragraph (b)(2) of this section), the employer, in lieu of substantiating the use of the vehicle as prescribed in § 1.274-5T(b)(6)(i)(B), may determine any deduction or credit with respect to the vehicle as if the business/investment use (as defined in § 1.280F-6T(d)(3)(i)) and the qualified business use (as defined in § 1.280F-6T(d)(2)) of the vehicle in the business of farming for the taxable year or shorter period were 75 percent plus that percentage, if any attributable to an amount included in an employee's gross income. If the vehicle is also available for personal use by employees, the employer must include the value of that personal use in the gross income of the employees, allocated among them in the manner prescribed in § 1.132-5T(g).

(2) Directly in connection with the business of farming. The phrase "directly in connection with the business of farming" means that the vehicle must be used directly in connection with the business of operating a farm (i.e., cultivating land or raising or harvesting any agricultural or horticultural commodity, or the raising, shearing, feeding, caring for, training, and management of animals) or incidental thereto (for example, trips to the feed and supply store).

(3) Substantiation by employees. If an employee is provided with the use of a vehicle to which this paragraph (b) applies, the employee may, in lieu of substantiating the business/investment use of the vehicle in the manner prescribed in § 1.274-5T, substantiate any exclusion allowed under section 132 for a working condition fringe as if the business/investment use of the vehicle were 75 percent, plus that percentage, if any, determined by the employer to be attributable to the use of the vehicle by individuals other than the employee, provided that the employee includes in gross income the amount determined by the employer as includible in the employee's gross income. See § 1.132-5T(g)(3) for examples illustrating the allocation of use of a vehicle among employees.

(c) Vehicles treated as used entirely for personal purposes. An employer may satisfy the substantiation requirements under section 274(d) for a taxable year or shorter period with respect to the business use of a vehicle that is provided to an employee by including the value of the availability of the vehicle during the relevant period in the employee's gross income without any exclusion for a working condition fringe with respect to the vehicle and, if required, by withholding any taxes. Under these circumstances, the employer's business/investment use of the vehicle during the relevant period is 100 percent. The employer's qualified business use of the vehicle is dependent upon the relationship of the employee to the employer (see § 1.280F-6T(d)(2)).

(d) Limitation. If a taxpayer chooses to satisfy the substantiation requirements of section 274(d) and § 1.274-5T by using one of the methods prescribed in paragraphs (a)(2) or (3), (b), or (c) of this section and files a return with the Internal Revenue Service for a taxable year consistent with such choice, the taxpayer may not later use another of these methods. Similarly, if a taxpayer chooses to satisfy the substantiation requirements of section 274(d) in the manner prescribed in § 1.274-5T and files a return with the Internal Revenue Service for a taxable year consistent with such choice, the taxpayer may not later use a method prescribed in paragraph (a)(2) or (3), (b), or (c) of this section. This rule applies to an employee for purposes of substantiating any working condition fringe exclusion as well as to an employer. For example, if an employee excludes on his federal income tax return for a taxable year 90 percent of the value of the availability of an employer-provided automobile on the basis of records that allegedly satisfy the "adequate records" requirement of § 1.274-5T(c)(2), and that requirement is not satisfied, then the employee may not satisfy the substantiation requirements of section 274(d) for the taxable year by any method prescribed in this section, but may present other corroborative evidence as prescribed in § 1.274-5T(c)(3).

(e) Definitions. *(1) In general.* The definitions provided in this paragraph (e) apply for purposes of section 274(d), § 1.274-5T, and this section.

(2) Employer and employee. The terms "employer" and "employee" include the following:

(i) A sole proprietor shall be treated as both an employer and employee,

(ii) A partnership shall be treated as an employer of its partners, and

(iii) A partner shall be treated as an employee of the partnership.

(3) Automobile. The term "automobile" has the same meaning as prescribed in § 1.61-2T(d)(1)(ii).

(4) Vehicle. The term "vehicle" has the same meaning as prescribed in § 1.61-2T(e)(2).

(5) Personal use. "Personal use" by an employee of an employer-provided vehicle includes use in any trade or business other than the trade or business of being the employee of the employer providing the vehicle.

(f) Effective date. This section is effective for taxable years beginning after December 31, 1985.

T.D. 8009, 2/15/85, amend T.D. 8061, 11/1/85, T.D. 8063, 12/18/85.

§ 1.274-7 Treatment of certain expenditures with respect to entertainment-type facilities.

If deductions are disallowed under § 1.274-2 with respect to any portion of a facility, such portion shall be treated as an asset which is used for personal, living, and family purposes (and not as an asset used in trade or business). Thus, the basis of such a facility will be adjusted for purposes of computing depreciation deductions and determining gain or loss on the sale of such facility in the same manner as other property (for example, a residence) which is regarded as used partly for business and partly for personal purposes.

T.D. 6659, 6/24/63.

§ 1.274-8 Effective date.

Except as provided in § 1.274-2(a) and (e), §§ 1.274-1 through 1.274-7 apply with respect to taxable years ending after December 31, 1962, but only in respect of periods after such date.

T.D. 6659, 6/24/63, amend T.D. 8051, 9/6/85.

PAR. 7.

Section 1.274-8 is redesignated as § 1.274-9 and a new § 1.274-8 is added immediately following § 1.274-7 to read as set forth below.

Proposed § 1.274-8 [Redesignated as § 1.274-9]. [*For Preamble, see ¶ 151,137*]

Proposed § 1.274-8 Disallowance of certain employee achievement award expenses. [*For Preamble, see ¶ 151,137*]

(a) In general. No deduction is allowable under section 162 or 212 for any portion of the cost of an employee achievement award (as defined in section 274(j)(3)(A)) in excess of the deduction limitations of section 274(j)(2).

(b) Deduction limitations. The deduction for the cost of an employee achievement award made by an employer to an employee: (1) Which is not a qualified plan award, when added to the cost to the employer for all other employee achievement awards made to such employee during the taxable year which are not qualified plan awards, shall not exceed $400, and (2) which is a qualified plan award, when added to the cost to the employer for all other employee achievement awards made to such employee during the taxable year (including employee achievement awards which are not qualified plan awards), shall not exceed $1,600. Thus, the $1,600 limitation is the maximum amount that may be deducted by an employer for all employee achievement awards granted to any one employee during the taxable year.

(c) Definitions. *(1) Employee achievement award.* The term "employee achievement award", for purposes of this section, means an item of tangible personal property that is transferred to an employee by reason of the employee's length of service or safety achievement. The item must be awarded as part of a meaningful presentation, and under conditions and circumstances that do not create a significant likelihood of the payment of disguised compensation. For purposes of section 274(j), an award made by a sole proprietorship to the sole proprietor is not an award made to an employee.

(2) Tangible personal property. For purposes of this section, the term "tangible personal property" does not include cash or a certificate (other than a nonnegotiable certificate conferring only the right to receive tangible personal property). If a certificate entitles an employee to receive a reduction of the balance due on his account with the issuer of the certificate, the certificate is a negotiable certificate and is not tangible personal property for purposes of this section. Other items that will not be considered to be items of tangible personal property include vacations, meals, lodging, tickets to theater and sporting events, and stocks, bonds, and other securities.

(3) Meaningful presentation. Whether an award is presented as part of a meaningful presentation is determined by a facts and circumstances test. While the presentation need not be elaborate, it must be a ceremonious observance emphasizing the recipient's achievement in the area of safety or length of service.

(4) Disguised compensation. An award will be considered disguised compensation if the conditions and circumstances surrounding the award create a significant likelihood that it is payment of compensation. Examples include the making of employee achievement awards at the time of annual salary adjustments or as a substitute for a prior program of awarding cash bonuses, the providing of employee achievement awards in a manner that discriminates in favor of highly paid employees, or, with respect to awards the cost of which would otherwise be fully deductible by the employer under the deduction limitations of section 274(j)(2), the making of an employee achievement award the cost of which to the employer is grossly disproportionate to the fair market value of the item.

(5) Qualified plan awards. (i) In general. Except as provided in paragraph (c)(5)(ii) of this section, the term "qualified plan award" means an employee achievement award that is presented pursuant to an established written plan or program that does not discriminate in terms of eligibility or benefits in favor of highly compensated employees. See section 414(q) of the Code for the definition of highly compensated employees. Whether an award plan is established shall be determined from all the facts and circumstances of the particular case, including the frequency and timing of any changes to the plan. Whether or not an award plan is discriminatory shall be determined from all the facts and circumstances of the particular case. An award plan may fail to qualify because it is discriminatory in its actual operation even though the written provisions of the award plan are nondiscriminatory.

(ii) Items not treated as qualified plan awards. No award presented by an employer during the taxable year will be considered a qualified plan award if the average cost of all employee achievement awards presented during the taxable year by the taxpayer under any plan described in paragraph (c)(5)(i) of this section exceeds $400. The average cost of employee achievement awards shall be computed by dividing (A) the sum of the costs to the employer for all employee achievement awards (without regard to the deductibility of those costs) by (B) the total number of employee achievement awards presented. For purposes of the preceding sentence, employee achievement awards of nominal value shall not be taken into account in the computation of average cost. An employee achievement award that costs the employer $50 or less shall be considered to be an employee achievement award of nominal value.

(d) Special rules. *(1) Partnerships.* Where employee achievement awards are made by a partnership, the deduction limitations of section 274(j)(2) shall apply to the partnership as well as to each member thereof.

(2) Length of service awards. An item shall not be treated as having been provided for length of service achievement if the item is presented for less than 5 years employment with the taxpayer or if the award recipient received a length of service achievement award (other than an award excludable under section 132(e)(1)) during that year or any of the prior 4 calendar years. An award presented upon the occasion of a recipient's retirement is a length of service award subject to the rules of this section. However, under appropriate circumstances, a traditional retirement award will be treated as a de minimis fringe. For example, assume that an employer provides a gold watch to each employee who completes 25 years of service with the employer. The value of the gold watch is excluded from gross income as a de minimis fringe. However, if the employer provides a gold watch to an employee who has not completed lengthy service with the employer or on an occasion other than retirment, the value of the watch is not excludable from gross income under section 132(e).

(3) Safety achievement awards. (i) In general. An item shall not be treated as having been provided for safety achievement if—

(A) During the taxable year, employee achievement awards (other than awards excludable under section 132(e)(1)) for safety achievement have previously been awarded by the taxpayer to more than 10 percent of the eligible employees of the taxpayer, or

(B) Such item is awarded to a manager, administrator, clerical employee, or other professional employee.

(ii) "Eligible employee" defined. An eligible employee is one not described in paragraph (d)(3)(i)(B) of this section and who has worked in a full-time capacity for the taxpayer for a minimum of one year immediately preceding the date on which the safety achievement award is presented.

(iii) Special rules. Where safety achievement awards are presented to more than 10 percent of the taxpayer's eligible employees, only those awards presented to eligible employees before 10 percent of the taxpayer's eligible employees are exceeded shall be treated as having been provided for safety achievement. Where the only safety achievement awards presented by an employer consist of items that are presented at one time during the calendar year, then, if safety achievement awards are presented to more than 10 percent of the taxpayer's eligible employees, the taxpayer may deduct an amount equal to the product of the cost of the item (subject to the applicable deduction limitation) and 10 percent of the taxpayer's eligible employees. Except as provided in the preceding sentence, no award shall be treated as having been provided for safety achievement except to the extent that it can be reasonably demonstrated that that award was made before the 10 percent limitation was exceeded.

§ 5e.274-8 Travel expenses of members of Congress.

(a) In general. Members of Congress (including any Delegate and Resident Commissioner) who are away from home within the meaning of section 162(a), in the Washington, D.C. area, may elect in accordance with paragraph (f) of this section to deduct an amount described in paragraph (c) of this section as living expenses, without substantiation. A Member who elects under this section may not deduct any amount for the living expenses described in paragraph (b). A Member who does not make an election under this section must substantiate his expenses for living in Washington, D.C. in accordance with section 274 and § 1.274-5.

(b) Living expenses covered. The amount allowed to be deducted without substantiation, pursuant to this section, for costs incurred for living in the Washington, D.C. area represents amounts expended for meals, lodging, and other incidental expenses. Meals include the actual cost of the food and expenses incident to the preparation and serving thereof. Lodging includes amounts paid for rent, care of premises, utilities, insurance and depreciation of household furnishings owned by the Member. In the case of a Member who lives in a residence owned by him in the Washington, D.C. area, the cost of lodging also includes depreciation on such residence. Other incidental expenses include laundry, cleaning, and local transportation. Local transportation includes travel within a 50 mile radius of Washington, D.C., whether by private automobile, taxicab or other transportation for hire. Interest and taxes on personal property will not be considered expenses to be included within this paragraph.

(c) Amounts allowed without substantiation. *(1)* The amount that may be deducted pursuant to section 162 and these regulations is an amount equal to the product of the number of Congressional days in the taxable year, multiplied by the designated amount. The designated amount is—

(i) In the case of a Member who deducts interest and taxes attributable to the ownership of a personal residence in the Washington, D.C. area, two-thirds of the maximum amount of actual subsistence for Washington, D.C. payable pursuant to 5 U.S.C. 5702(c), or

(ii) In the case of a Member not described in paragraph (c)(1)(i), the maximum amount of actual subsistence for Washington, D.C. Payable pursuant to 5 U.S.C. 5702(c).

A Member who incurs interest and taxes on his residence in the Washington, D.C. area may forego the deduction of such amounts and use the designated amount prescribed by paragraph (c)(1)(ii).

(2) If a Member, who lives in a residence owned by him in the Washington, D.C. area, chooses to deduct amounts prescribed in paragraph (c)(1) of this section, the Member must treat as an adjustment to the basis of such residence an amount equal to 20 percent of the maximum amount of actual subsistence multiplied by the number of Congressional days. Such adjustments will be considered a proper adjustment for exhaustion, wear, and tear under this subtitle.

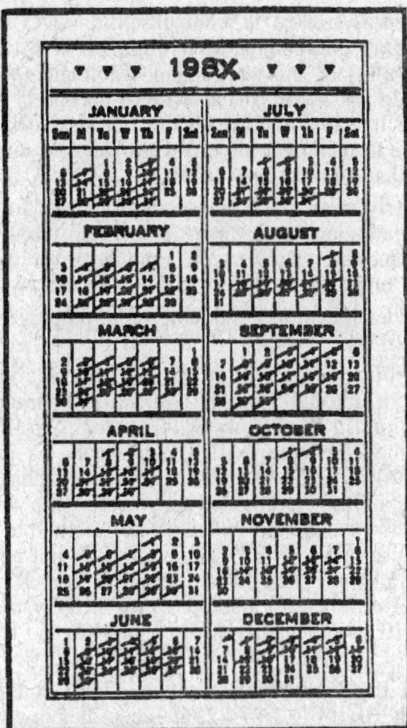

(d) Congressional days. The number of Congressional days with respect to a Member is the number of days in the taxable year less the number of days in periods in which the Member's Congressional chamber was not in session for 5 consecutive days or more (including Saturday and Sunday). The number of days with respect to a Member is determined without regard to whether or not the Member was in the Washington, D.C. area on such days.

(e) Other deductible amounts. This section does not preclude the deduction of otherwise allowable expenses for travel fares (other than local travel in the Washington, D.C.), long distance telephone and telegraph, and travel expenses incurred other than in the Washington, D.C. area. However, such expenses are subject to the substantiation requirements of section 274.

(f) Election. To elect to deduct the amounts prescribed by this section, a Member must attach to his return for the taxable year a statement indicating, (1) that the deduction for travel expenses while living in the Washington, D.C. area are computed pursuant to § 5e.274-8, and (2) whether a separate deduction is being taken for interest and taxes paid or incurred with respect to the personal residence of the Member if in the Washington, D.C. area.

(g) Effective date. This section is effective for taxable year beginning after December 31, 1980.

(h) Examples. The following examples are based on a calendar from a Final Edition of the Calendar of the United States, House of Representatives and History of Legislation. The marked days indicate days the House of Representatives was in session.

Example (1). In determining the number of Congressional days for 198X for which the designated amount may be computed, the number of days in such year is reduced by 125 days determined as follows:

	Days
Feb. 14–18	5
Apr. 3–14	12
May 23–27	5
July 3–20	18
Aug. 2–17	16
Aug. 29–Sept. 2	5
Oct. 3–Nov. 11	40
Nov. 22–Nov. 30	9
Dec. 17–Dec. 31	15
Total	125

Thus for 198X (a leap year) a typical Member of the House of Representatives will have 241 (366 – 125) Congressional days.

Example (2). On August 1, Z a calendar year taxpayer is elected to the Congress to fill the unexpired term of Member Y. In determining the number of Congressional days, Z may only consider the number of days during the year for which he was a Member of Congress. For Z the number of Congressional days is 68.

Example (3). Member X, a calendar year taxpayer, owns his own home in Washington, D.C., where he lives with his family. While in Washington, D.C., Member X is away from home within the meaning of section 162(a). X maintains no records attributable to his expenses in Washington, D.C. X has been a Member of Congress for the entire year. The maximum amount of subsistence for Washington, D.C. for 198X is $75. X may deduct for 198X $18,075 (241 days × $75) attributable to expenses while away from home in Washington, D.C. Even if X maintained records as to living expenses in Washington, D.C., X may choose to deduct $18,075 as the total amount attributable to living expenses in Washington, D.C. If X deducts $18,075 X may not deduct any interest and taxes under section 163 or 164 attributable to the residence in Washington, D.C.

Example (4). Member C, a calendar year taxpayer owns his own home in Washington, D.C., where he lives with his family. While in Washington, D.C. Member C is away from home within the meaning of section 162(a). C can establish that he paid $12,000 as interest on a mortgage and $3,000 in local real estate taxes. C has been a Member of Congress for the entire year. C may choose to deduct $12,050 (241 days Washington, D.C. Further, C may deduct under sections 163 and 164 $12,000 of interest and $3,000 of taxes respectively.

Example (5). Assume the same facts as in Example (4). In addition, on March 15, 16, and 17, Member C travels to New York City to deliver a speech for which he receives an honorarium which he includes in income. C receives no additional amounts for travel reimbursement. While in New York City C incurs $350 for 3 nights lodging at a hotel and $150 for meals. In addition to the amounts deductible pursuant to this section, C may deduct the $500 as a travel expenses. Such deduction is subject to the substantiation rules of section 274.

Example (6). Assume the same facts as example (5). Member C receives, in addition to the honorarium, $600 reimbursement for travel expenses. C must include the $600 in income and may deduct the travel expenses he incurred.

T.D. 7802, 1/15/82.

Proposed § 1.274-9 Entertainment provided to specified individuals. [*For Preamble, see ¶ 152,867*]

(a) In general. No deduction is allowed for expenses for entertainment provided to a specified individual (as defined in paragraph (b) of this section) except to the extent that the expenses do not exceed the amount of the expenses treated as compensation to the specified individual, as provided in section 274(e)(2)(B) and (9) and § 1.274-10. The amount disallowed is reduced by any amount that the specified individual reimburses a taxpayer for the entertainment.

(b) Specified individual defined. *(1)* A specified individual is an individual who is subject to section 16(a) of the Securities Act of 1934 with respect to the taxpayer, or an individual who would be subject to section 16(a) if the taxpayer were an issuer of equity securities referred to in that section. Thus, for example, a specified individual is an officer, director, or more than 10 percent owner of a corporation taxed under subchapter C or subchapter S, or a personal service corporation. A specified individual includes every individual who-

(i) Is the direct or indirect beneficial owner of more than 10 percent of any class of any registered equity (other than an exempted security);

(ii) Is a director or officer of the issuer of the security;

(iii) Would be the direct or indirect beneficial owner of more than 10 percent of any class of a registered security if the taxpayer were an issuer of equity securities; or

(iv) Is comparable to an officer or director of an issuer of equity securities.

(2) For partnership purposes, a specified individual includes any partner that holds more than a 10 percent equity interest in the partnership, or any general partner, officer, or managing partner of a partnership.

(3) For purposes of this section, officer has the same meaning as in 17 CFR § 240.16a-1(f).

(4) A specified individual includes a director or officer of a tax-exempt entity.

(5) A specified individual of a taxpayer includes a specified individual of a party related to the taxpayer within the meaning of section 267(b) or section 707(b).

(6) For purposes of section 274(a), a specified individual is treated as the recipient of entertainment provided to a spouse or family member of the specified individual or to another individual because of the relationship of the spouse, family member or other individual to the specified individual. Thus, expenses allocable to entertainment provided to the spouse, family member, or other individual are attributed to the specified individual for purposes of determining the amount of disallowed expenses.

(c) Entertainment use of aircraft by specified individuals. For rules relating to entertainment use of aircraft by specified individuals, see § 1.274-10.

(d) Effective/applicability date. This section applies to taxable years beginning after the date these regulations are published as final regulations in the Federal Register.

Proposed § 1.274-10 Special rules for aircraft used for entertainment. [*For Preamble, see ¶ 152,867*]

(a) Use of an aircraft for entertainment. *(1) In general.* Under section 274(a) and this section, no deduction otherwise allowable under chapter 1 is allowed for expenses for the use of a taxpayer-provided aircraft for entertainment, except as provided in paragraph (a)(2) of this section.

(2) Exceptions. (i) In general. Paragraph (a)(1) of this section does not apply to deductions for expenses for business entertainment air travel or to deductions for expenses that meet the exceptions of section 274(e), § 1.274-2(f), and this section.

(ii) Expenses treated as compensation. (A) Employees. Section 274(a), paragraphs (a) through (d) of § 1.274-2, and paragraph (a)(1) of this section, in accordance with section 274(e)(2), do not apply (in the case of specified individuals, as provided in paragraph (a)(2)(ii)(C) of this section), to expenses for entertainment air travel provided to employees to the extent that a taxpayer—

(1) Properly treats the expenses with respect to the recipient of entertainment as compensation to an employee under chapter 1 and as wages to the employee for purposes of chapter 24; and

(2) Includes the proper amount in the employee's income under § 1.61-21.

(B) Persons who are not employees. Section 274(a), paragraphs (a) through (e) of § 1.274-2, and paragraph (a)(1) of this section, in accordance with section 274(e)(9), do not apply (in the case of specified individuals, as provided in paragraph (a)(2)(ii)(C) of this section), to expenses for entertainment air travel provided to persons who are not employees to the extent the expenses are includible in the income of those persons. This exception does not apply to any amount paid or incurred by the taxpayer that is required to be included in any information return filed by the taxpayer under part III of subchapter A of chapter 61 and is not so included.

(C) Specified individuals. Section 274(a) and paragraphs (a) through (d) of § 1.274-2, in accordance with section 274(e)(2)(B), do not apply to expenses for entertainment air travel of a specified individual to the extent that the expenses do not exceed the sum of—

(1) The amount treated as compensation under paragraph (a)(2)(ii)(A) of this section or reported as income under paragraph (a)(2)(ii)(B) of this section to the specified individual; and

(2) Any amount the specified individual reimburses the taxpayer.

(b) Definitions. The definitions in this paragraph (b) apply for purposes of this section.

(1) Entertainment. For the definition of entertainment for purposes of this section, see § 1.274-2(b)(1). Entertainment does not include personal travel that is not for entertainment purposes. For example, travel to attend a family member's funeral is not entertainment.

(2) Entertainment air travel. Entertainment air travel is any travel aboard a taxpayer-provided aircraft for entertainment purposes.

(3) Business entertainment air travel. Business entertainment air travel is any entertainment air travel aboard a taxpayer-provided aircraft that is directly related to the active conduct of the taxpayer's trade or business or related to an expenditure directly preceding or following a substantial and bona fide business discussion and associated with the active conduct of the taxpayer's trade or business. See § 1.274-2(a)(1)(i) and (ii). Air travel is not business entertainment air travel merely because a taxpayer-provided aircraft is used for the travel as a result of a bona fide security concern under § 1.132-5(m).

(4) Taxpayer-provided aircraft. A taxpayer-provided aircraft is any aircraft owned by, leased to, or chartered to, a taxpayer or any party related to the taxpayer (within the meaning of section 267(b) or section 707(b)).

(5) Specified individual. For rules relating to the definition of a specified individual, see § 1.274-9.

(c) Amount disallowed. The amount disallowed under this section for an entertainment flight by a specified individual is the amount of expenses allocable to the entertainment flight of the specified individual under paragraph (e)(2)(ii)(D), (e)(3)(ii), or (f)(3) of this section, reduced (but not below zero) by the amount the taxpayer treats as compensation under paragraph (a)(2)(ii)(A) of this section or reports as income under paragraph (a)(2)(ii)(B) of this section to the specified individual, plus any amount the specified individual reimburses the taxpayer.

(d) Expenses taken into account under this section. *(1) Definition of expenses.* In determining the amount of expenses taken into account under this section, a taxpayer must take into account all of the expenses of operating the aircraft, including all fixed and variable expenses the taxpayer deducts in the taxable year. These expenses include, but are not limited to, salaries for pilots, maintenance personnel, and other personnel assigned to the aircraft; meal and lodging expenses of flight personnel; take-off and landing fees; costs for maintenance flights; costs of on-board refreshments, amenities and gifts; hangar fees (at home or away); management fees; costs of fuel, tires, maintenance, insurance, registration, certificate of title, inspection, and depreciation; and all costs paid or incurred for aircraft leased, or chartered, to or by the taxpayer.

(2) Leases or charters to third parties. Expenses allocable to a lease or charter of a taxpayer's aircraft to an unrelated third-party in a bona-fide business transaction for adequate and full consideration are not taken into account for purposes of the definition of expenses in paragraph (d)(1) of this section. Only expenses allocable to the charter period are not taken into account under this paragraph (d)(2).

(3) Straight-line method permitted for determining depreciation disallowance under this section. (i) In general. In lieu of the amount of depreciation deducted in the taxable year, solely for purposes of paragraph (d)(1) of this section, a taxpayer may elect to treat as its depreciation deduction the amount that would result from using the straight-line method of depreciation over the class life (as defined by section 168(g)(2) and taking into account the applicable convention under section 168(d)) of an aircraft, although the taxpayer uses another methodology to calculate depreciation for the aircraft under other sections of the Internal Revenue Code (for example, section 168). If the property is qualified property or 50-percent bonus depreciation property under section 168(k), qualified New York Liberty Zone property under section 1400L(b), or qualified Gulf Opportunity Zone property under section 1400N(d), depreciation for purposes of this straight-line election is determined on the unadjusted depreciable basis of the property. For purposes of this section, a taxpayer that elects to use the straight-line method and class life under this paragraph (d)(3) for any aircraft it operates must use that method for all taxpayer-provided aircraft it operates and must continue to use the method for the entire period the taxpayer uses any taxpayer-provided aircraft.

(ii) Aircraft placed in service in earlier taxable years. If the taxpayer elects to use this paragraph (d)(3) with respect to aircraft placed in service in taxable years before the current taxable year, the amount of depreciation is determined by applying the straight-line method of depreciation to the original cost (or, for property acquired in an exchange to which section 1031 applies, the basis of the aircraft as determined under section 1031(d)) and over the class life (taking into account the applicable convention under section 168(d)) of the aircraft as though the taxpayer used that methodology from the year the aircraft was placed in service.

(iii) Manner of making and revoking election. A taxpayer makes the election under this paragraph (d)(3) by filing an income tax return for the taxable year that determines the taxpayer's expenses for purposes of paragraph (d)(1) of this section by including depreciation as determined under this paragraph (d)(3). An election may be revoked only for compelling circumstances upon consent of the Commissioner by private letter ruling.

(4) Aggregation of aircraft. (i) In general. A taxpayer may aggregate the expenses of aircraft of similar cost profiles for purposes of calculating disallowed expenses under paragraph (c) of this section.

(ii) Similar cost profiles. Aircraft are of similar cost profiles if their operating costs per mile or per hour of flight are comparable. Aircraft must have the same engine type (jet or propeller) and the same number of engines to have similar cost profiles. Other factors to be considered in determining whether aircraft have similar cost profiles include, but are not limited to, payload, passenger capacity, fuel consumption rate, age, maintenance costs, and depreciable basis.

(e) Allocation of expenses. *(1) General rule.* For purposes of determining the expenses allocated to entertainment air travel of a specified individual under paragraph (a)(2)(ii)(C) of this section, a taxpayer must use either the occupied seat hours or miles method of paragraph (e)(2) of this section or the flight-by-flight method of paragraph (e)(3) of this section. A taxpayer must use the chosen method for all flights of all aircraft for the taxable year.

(2) Occupied seat hours or miles method. (i) In general. The occupied seat hours or miles method determines the amount of expenses allocated to a particular entertainment flight of a specified individual based on the occupied seat hours or miles for an aircraft for the taxable year. Under this method, a taxpayer may choose to use either occupied seat hours or miles for the taxable year to determine the amount of expenses allocated to entertainment flights of specified individuals, but must use occupied seat hours or miles consistently for all flights for the taxable year.

(ii) Computation of the occupied seat hours or miles method. The amount of expenses allocated to an entertainment flight taken by a specified individual is determined under the occupied seat hours or miles method by—

(A) Determining the total expenses for the year under paragraph (d)(1) of this section for the aircraft or group of aircraft (as determined under paragraph (d)(4) of this section), as applicable;

(B) Determining the total number of occupied seat hours or miles for the taxable year for the aircraft or group of aircraft by totaling the occupied seat hours or miles of all flights in the taxable year flown by the aircraft or group of aircraft, as applicable. The occupied seat hours or miles for a flight is the number of hours or miles flown for the flight multiplied by the number of seats occupied on that flight. For example, a flight of six hours with three passengers results in 18 occupied seat hours;

(C) Determining the cost per occupied seat hour or mile for the aircraft or group of aircraft, as applicable, by dividing the total expenses in paragraph (e)(2)(ii)(A) of this section by the total number of occupied seat hours or miles determined in paragraph (e)(2)(ii)(B) of this section; and

(D) Determining the amount of expenses allocated to an entertainment flight taken by a specified individual by multiplying the number of hours or miles of the flight by the cost per occupied hour or mile for that aircraft or group of aircraft, as applicable, as determined in paragraph (e)(2)(ii)(C) of this section.

(iii) Allocation of expenses of multi-leg trips involving both business and entertainment legs. A taxpayer that uses the occupied seat hours or miles allocation method must allocate the expenses of a trip by a specified individual that involves at least one segment for business and one segment for entertainment purposes between the business travel and the entertainment travel unless none of the expenses for the entertainment segment are disallowed. The entertainment cost of a multi-leg trip is the total cost of the flights (by occupied seat hours or miles) over the cost of the flights that would have been taken without the entertainment segment or segments.

(iv) Examples. The following examples illustrate the provisions of this paragraph (e)(2):

Example (1). (i) A taxpayer-provided aircraft is used for Flights 1, 2, and 3, of 5 hours, 5 hours, and 4 hours, respectively, during the Taxpayer's taxable year. On Flight 1, there are four passengers, none of whom are specified individuals. On Flight 2, passengers A and B are specified individuals traveling for entertainment purposes and passengers C and D are not specified individuals. Taxpayer treats $1,200 as compensation to A, and B reimburses Taxpayer $500. On Flight 3, all four passengers (A, B, E, and F) are specified individuals traveling for entertainment purposes. The Taxpayer treats $1,300 each as compensation to A, B, E, and F. Taxpayer incurs $56,000 in expenses for the operation of the aircraft for the taxable year. The aircraft is operated for 56 occupied seat hours for the period (four passengers times 5 hours or 20 occupied seat hours for Flight 1, plus four passengers times 5 hours or 20 occupied seat hours for Flight 2, plus four passengers times 4 hours or 16 occupied seat hours for Flight 3). The cost per occupied seat hour is $1,000 ($56,000/56 hours).

(ii) For purposes of determining the amount disallowed (to the extent not treated as compensation or reimbursed), $5,000 ($1,000 x 5 hours) each is allocable with respect to A and B for Flight 2, and $4,000 ($1,000 x 4 hours) each is allocable with respect to A, B, E, and F for Flight 3.

(iii) For Flight 2, because Taxpayer treats $1,200 as compensation to A, and B reimburses Taxpayer $500, Taxpayer may deduct $1,700 of the cost of Flight 2 allocable to A and B. The deduction for the remaining $8,300 cost allocable to entertainment provided to A and B on Flight 2 is disallowed (with respect to A, $5,000 less the $1,200 treated as compensation, and with respect to B, $5,000 less the $500 reimbursed).

(iv) For Flight 3, because Taxpayer treats $1,300 each as compensation to A, B, E, and F, Taxpayer may deduct $5,200 of the cost of Flight 3. The deduction for the remaining $10,800 cost allocable to entertainment provided to A, B, E, and F on Flight 3 is disallowed ($4,000 less the $1,300 treated as compensation to each specified individual).

Example (2). (i) G, a specified individual, is the sole passenger on an aircraft on a two-hour flight from City A to City B for business purposes. G then travels on a three-hour flight from City B to City C for entertainment purposes, and returns from City C to City A on a four-hour flight. G's flights have resulted in nine occupied seat hours (two for the first segment, plus three for the second segment, plus four for the third segment). If G had returned directly to City A from City B, the flights would have resulted in four occupied seat hours.

(ii) Under paragraph (e)(2)(iii) of this section, five occupied seat hours are allocable with respect to G's entertainment (nine total occupied seat hours minus the four occupied seat miles that would have resulted if the travel had been a roundtrip business trip without the entertainment segment). If Taxpayer's cost per occupied seat hour for the year is $1,000, $5,000 is allocated with respect to G's entertainment use of the aircraft ($1,000 x five occupied seat hours). The amount disallowed is $5,000 minus any amount the Taxpayer treats as compensation to G or that G reimburses Taxpayer.

(3) Flight-by-flight method. (i) In general. The flight-by-flight method determines the amount of expenses allocated to a particular entertainment flight of a specified individual on a flight-by-flight basis by allocating expenses to individual flights and then to a specified individual traveling for entertainment purposes on that flight.

(ii) Allocation of expenses. A taxpayer using the flight-by-flight method must aggregate all expenses (as defined in paragraph (d)(1) of this section) for the taxable year for the aircraft or group of aircraft (as determined under paragraph (d)(4) of this section), as applicable, and divide the total amount of expenses by the number of flight hours or miles for the taxable year for that aircraft or group of aircraft, as applicable, to determine the cost per hour or mile. Expenses are allocated to each flight by multiplying the number of miles or hours for the flight by the cost per hour or mile. The expenses for the flight are then allocated to the passengers on the flight per capita. Thus, if three of five passengers are traveling for business and two passengers are specified individuals traveling for entertainment purposes, and the total expense allocated to the flight is $10,000, the expense allocable to each specified individual is $2,000.

(f) Special rules. *(1) Determination of basis.* If an amount disallowed is allocable to depreciation under paragraph (f)(2) of this section, the rules of § 1.274-7 apply. In that case, the basis of an aircraft is not reduced for the amount of depreciation disallowed under this section.

(2) Pro rata disallowance. The expense disallowance provisions of this section are applied on a pro rata basis to all of the expenses disallowed by this section.

(3) Deadhead flights. (i) For purposes of this section, an aircraft returning without passengers after discharging passengers or flying without passengers to pick up passengers (deadheading) is treated as having the same number and character of passengers as the leg of the trip on which passengers are aboard for purposes of the allocation of expenses under paragraphs (e)(2) or (e)(3) of this section. For example, when an aircraft travels from point A to point B and then back to point A, and one of the legs is a deadhead flight, for determination of disallowed expenses, the aircraft is treated as having made both legs of the trip with the same passengers aboard for the same purposes.

(ii) When a deadhead flight does not occur within a roundtrip flight, but occurs between two unrelated flights involving more than two destinations (such as an occupied flight from point A to point B, followed by a deadhead flight from point B to point C, and then an occupied flight from point C to point A), the allocation of passengers and expenses to the deadhead flight occurring between the two occupied trips is based on the number of passengers on board for the two occupied legs of the flight, the character of the passengers on board (entertainment or nonentertainment purpose) and the length in hours or miles of the two occupied legs of the flight.

(g) Effective/applicability date. This section applies to taxable years beginning after the date these regulations are published as final regulations in the Federal Register.

§ 1.275-1 Deduction denied in case of certain taxes.

For description of the taxes for which a deduction is denied under section 275, see paragraphs (a), (b), (c), (d), (e) and (h) of § 1.164-2.

T.D. 6780, 12/21/64, amend T.D. 7767, 2/3/81.

§ 1.276-1 Disallowance of deductions for certain indirect contributions to political parties.

Caution: The Treasury has not yet amended Reg § 1.276-1 to reflect changes made by P.L. 93-443.

(a) In general. Notwithstanding any other provision of law, no deduction shall be allowed for income tax purposes in respect to any amount paid or incurred after March 15, 1966, in a taxable year of the taxpayer beginning after December 31, 1965, for any expenditure to which paragraph (b)(1), (e), (d), or (e) of this section is applicable. Section 276 is a disallowance provision exclusively and does not make deductible any expenses which are not otherwise allowed under the Code. For certain other rules in respect of deductions for expenditures for political purposes, see §§ 1.162-15(b), 1.162-20, and 1.271-1.

(b) Advertising in convention program. *(1) General rule.* (i) Except as provided in subparagraph (2) of this paragraph, no deduction shall be allowed for an expenditure for advertising in a convention program of a political party. For purposes of this subparagraph it is immaterial who publishes the convention program or to whose use the proceeds of the program inure (or are intended to inure). A convention program is any written publication (as defined in paragraph (c) of this section) which is distributed or displayed in connection with or at a political convention, conclave, or meeting. Under certain conditions payments to a committee organized for the purpose of bringing a political convention to an area are deductible under paragraph (b) of § 1.162-15. This rule is not affected by the provisions of this section. For example, such payments may be deductible notwithstanding the fact that the committee purchases from a political party the right to publish a pamphlet in connection with a convention and that the deduction of costs of advertising in the pamphlet is prohibited under this section.

(ii) The application of the provisions of this subparagraph may be illustrated by the following example:

Example. M Corporation publishes the convention program of the Y political party for a convention not described in subparagraph (2) of this paragraph. The corporation makes no payment of any kind to or on behalf of the party or any of its candidates and no part of the proceeds of the publication and sale of the program inures directly or indirectly to the benefit of any political party or candidate. P Corporation purchases an advertisement in the program. P Corporation may not deduct the cost of such advertisement.

(2) Amounts paid or incurred on or after January 1, 1968, for advertising in programs of certain national political conventions. (i) Subject to the limitations in subdivision (ii) of this subparagraph, a deduction may be allowed for any amount paid or incurred on or after January 1, 1968, for advertising in a convention program of a political party distributed in connection with a convention held for the purpose of nominating candidates for the offices of President and Vice President of the United States, if the proceeds from the program are actually used solely to defray the costs of conducting the convention (or are set aside for such use at the next convention of the party held for such purpose) and if the amount paid or incurred for the advertising is reasonable. If such amount is not reasonable or if any part of the proceeds is used for a purpose other than that of defraying such convention costs, no part of the amount is deductible. Whether or not an amount is reasonable shall be determined in light of the business the taxpayer may expect to receive either directly as a result of the advertising or as a result of the convention being held in an area in which the taxpayer has a principal place of business. For these purposes, an amount paid or incurred for advertising will not be considered as reasonable if it is greater than the amount which would be paid for comparable advertising in a comparable convention program of a nonpolitical organization. Institutional advertising (e.g., advertising of a type not designed to sell specific goods or services to persons attending the convention) is not advertising which may be expected to result directly in business for the taxpayer sufficient to make the expenditures reasonable. Accordingly, an amount spent for institutional advertising in a convention program may be deductible only if the taxpayer has a principal place of business in the area where the convention is held. An official statement made by a political party after a convention as to the use made of the proceeds from its convention program shall constitute prima facie evidence of such use.

(ii) No deduction may be taken for any amount described in this subparagraph which is not otherwise allowable as a deduction under section 162, relating to trade or business expenses. Therefore, in order for any such amount to be deductible, it must first satisfy the requirements of section 162, and, in addition, it must also satisfy the more restrictive requirements of this subparagraph.

(c) Advertising in publication other than convention program. No deduction shall be allowed for an expenditure for advertising in any publication other than a convention program if any part of the proceeds of such publication directly or indirectly inures (or is intended to inure) to or for the use of a political party or a political candidate. For purposes of this paragraph, a publication includes a book, magazine, pamphlet, brochure, flier, almanac, newspaper, newsletter, handbill, billboard, menu, sign, scorecard, program, announcement, radio or television program or announcement, or any similar means of communication. For the definition of inurement of proceeds to a political party or a political candidate, see paragraph (f)(3) of this section.

(d) Admission to dinner or program. No deduction shall be allowed for an expenditure for admission to any dinner or program, if any part of the proceeds of such event directly or indirectly inures (or is intended to inure) to or for the use of a political party or a political candidate. For purposes of this paragraph, a dinner or program includes a gala, dance, ball, theatrical or film presentation, cocktail or other party, picnic, barbecue, sporting event, brunch, tea, supper, auction, bazaar, reading, speech, forum, lecture, fashion show, concert, opening, meeting, gathering, or any similar event. For the definition of inurement of proceeds to a political party or a political candidate and of admission to a dinner or program, see paragraph (f) of this section.

(e) Admission to inaugural event. *(1)* No deduction shall be allowed for an expenditure for admission to an inaugural ball, inaugural gala, inaugural parade, or inaugural concert, or to any similar event (such as a dinner or program, as defined in paragraph (d) of this section), in connection with the inauguration or installation in office of any official, or any equivalent event for an unsuccessful candidate, if the event is identified with a political party or a political candidate. For purposes of this paragraph, the sponsorship of the event and the use to which the proceeds of the event are or may be put are irrelevant, except insofar as they may tend to identify the event with a political party or a political candidate. For the definition of admission to an inaugural event, see paragraph (f)(4) of this section.

(2) The application of the provisions of this paragraph may be illustrated by the following example:

Example. An inaugural reception for A, a prominent member of Y party who has been recently elected judge of the municipal court of F city, is held with the proceeds going to the city treasury. The price of admission to such affair is not deductible.

(f) Definitions. *(1) Political party.* For purposes of this section the term "political party" has the same meaning as that provided for in paragraph (b)(1) of § 1.271-1.

(2) Political candidate. For purposes of this section, the term "political candidate" is to be construed in accordance with the purpose of section 276 to deny tax deductions for certain expenditures which may be used directly or indirectly to finance political campaigns. The term includes a person who, at the time of the event or publication with respect to which the deduction is being sought, has been selected or nominated by a political party for any elective office. It also includes an individual who is generally believed, under the facts and circumstances at the time of the event or publication, by the persons making expenditures in connection therewith to be an individual who is or who in the reasonably foreseeable future will be seeking selection, nomination, or election to any public office. For purposes of the preceding sentence, the facts and circumstances to be considered include, but are not limited to, the purpose of the event or publication and the disposition to be made of the proceeds. In the absence of evidence to the contrary it shall be presumed that persons making expenditures in connection with an event or publication generally believe that an incumbent of an elective public office will run for reelection to his office or for election to some other public office.

(3) Inurement of proceeds to political party or political candidate. (i) In general. Subject to the special rules presented in subdivision (iii) of this subparagraph (relating to a political candidate), proceeds directly or indirectly inure to or for the use of a political party or a political candidate (a) if the party or candidate may order the disposition of any part of such proceeds, regardless of what use is actually made thereof, or (b) if any part of such proceeds is utilized by any person for the benefit of the party or candidate. These conditions are equally applicable in determining whether the proceeds are intended to inure. Accordingly, it is immaterial whether the event or publication operates at a loss if, had there been a profit, any part of the proceeds would have inured to or for the use of a political party or a political candidate. Moreover, it shall be presumed that where a dinner, program, or publication is sponsored by or identified with a political party or political candidate, the proceeds of such dinner, program, or publication directly or indirectly inure (or are intended to inure) to or for the use of the party or candidate. On the other hand, proceeds are not considered to directly or indirectly inure to the benefit of a political party or political candidate if the benefit derived is so remote as to be negligible or merely a coincidence of the relationship of a political candidate to a trade or business profiting from an expenditure of funds. For example, the proceeds of expenditures made by a taxpayer in the ordinary course of his trade or business for advertising in a publication, such as a newspaper or magazine, are not considered as inuring to the benefit of a political party or political candidate merely because the publication endorses a particular political candidate or candidates of a particular political party, the publisher independently contributes to the support of a political party or candidate out of his own personal funds, or the principal stockholder of the publishing firm is a candidate for public office.

(ii) Proceeds to political party. If a political party may order the disposition of any part of the proceeds in paragraph (c) or (d) of this section, such proceeds inure to the use of the party regardless of what the proceeds are to be used for or that their use is restricted to a particular purpose unrelated to the election of specific candidates for public office. Accordingly, where a political party holds a dinner for the purpose of raising funds to be used in a voter registration drive, voter education program, or nonprofit political research program, partisan or nonpartisan, the proceeds are considered to directly or indirectly inure to or for the use of the political party. Proceeds may inure to or for the use of a political party even though they are to be used for purposes which may not be directly related to any particular election (such as to pay office rent for its permanent quarters, salaries to permanent employees, or utilities charges, or to pay the cost of an event such as a dinner or program as defined in paragraph (d) of this section).

(iii) Proceeds to political candidate. Proceeds directly or indirectly inure (or are intended to inure) to or for the use of a political candidate if, in addition to meeting the conditions described in subdivision (i) of this subparagraph, (a) some part of the proceeds is or may be used directly or indirectly for the purpose of furthering his candidacy for selection, nomination, or election to any elective public office, and (b) they are not received by him in the ordinary course of a trade or business (other than the trade or business of holding public office). Proceeds may so inure whether or not the expenditure sought to be deducted was paid or incurred before the commencement of political activities with respect to the selection, nomination, or election referred to in (a) of this subdivision, or after such selection, nomination, or election has been made or has taken place. For example, proceeds of an event which may be used by an individual who, under the facts and circumstances at the time of the event, the persons making expenditures in connection therewith generally believe will in the reasonably foreseeable future run for a public office, and which may be used in furtherance of such individual's candidacy, generally will be deemed to inure (or to be intended to inure) to or for the use of a political candidate for the purpose of furthering such individual's candidacy. Or, as another example, proceeds of an event occurring after an election, which may be used by a candidate in that election to repay loans incurred in directly or indirectly furthering his candidacy, will be deemed to directly or indirectly inure (or to be intended to inure) to or for the use of a political candidate for the purpose of furthering his candidacy. For purposes of this subdivision, if the proceeds received by a candidate exceed substantially the fair market value of the goods furnished or services rendered by him, the proceeds are not received by the candidate in the ordinary course of his trade or business.

(iv) The application of the provisions of this subparagraph may be illustrated by the following examples:

Example (1). Corporation O pays the Y political party $100,000 per annum for the right to publish the Y News, and retains the entire proceeds from the sale of the publication. Amounts paid or incurred for advertising in the Y

News are not deductible because a part of the proceeds thereof indirectly inures to or for the use of a political party.

Example (2). The X political party holds a highly publicized ball honoring one of its active party members and admission tickets are offered to all. The guest of honor is a prominent national figure and a former incumbent of a high public office. The price of admission is designed to cover merely the cost of entertainment, food, and the ballroom, and all proceeds are paid to the hotel where the function is held, with the political party bearing the cost of any deficit. No deduction may be taken for the price of admission to the ball since the proceeds thereof inure to or for the use of a political party.

Example (3). Taxpayer A, engaged in a trade or business, purchases a number of tickets for admission to a fundraising affair held on behalf of political candidate B. The funds raised by this affair can be used by B for the purpose of furthering his candidacy. These expenditures are not deductible by A notwithstanding that B donates the proceeds of the affair to the charitable organization.

Example (4). A, an individual taxpayer who publishes a newspaper, is a candidate for elective public office. X Corporation advertises its products in A's newspaper, paying substantially more than the normal rate for such advertising. X Corporation may not deduct any portion of the cost of that advertising.

(4) Admission to dinners, programs, inaugural events. For purposes of this section, the cost of admission to a dinner, program, or inaugural event includes all charges, whether direct or indirect, for attendance and participation at such function. Thus, for example, amounts spent to be eligible for door prizes, for the privilege of sitting at the head table, or for transportation furnished as part of such an event, or any separate charges for food or drink, are amounts paid for admission.

T.D. 6996, 1/17/69, amend T.D. 7010, 4/30/69.

§ 1.278-1 Capital expenditures incurred in planting and developing citrus and almond groves.

Caution: The Treasury has not yet amended Reg § 1.278-1 to reflect changes made by P.L. 99-514, P.L. 94-455.

(a) General rule. *(1)* (i) Except as provided in subparagraph (2)(iii) of this paragraph and paragraph (b) of this section, there shall be charged to capital account any amount (allowable as a deduction without regard to section 278 or this section) which is attributable to the planting, cultivation, maintenance, or development of any citrus or almond grove (or part thereof), and which is incurred before the close of the fourth taxable year beginning with the taxable year in which the trees were planted. For purposes of section 278 and this section, such an amount shall be considered as "incurred" in accordance with the taxpayer's regular tax accounting method used in reporting income and expenses connected with the citrus or almond grove operation. For purposes of this paragraph, the portion of a citrus or almond grove planted in 1 taxable year shall be treated separately from the portion of such grove planted in another taxable year. The provisions of section 278 and this section apply to taxable years beginning after December 31, 1969, in the case of a citrus grove, and to taxable years beginning after January 12, 1971, in the case of an almond grove.

(ii) The provisions of this subparagraph may be illustrated by the following examples:

Example (1). T, a fiscal year taxpayer plants a citrus grove 5 weeks before the close of his taxable year ending in 1971. T is required to capitalize any amount (allowable as a deduction without regard to section 278 or this section) attributable to the planting, cultivation, maintenance, or development of such grove until the close of his taxable year ending in 1974.

Example (2). Assume the same facts as in example (1), except that T plants one portion of such grove 5 weeks before the close of his taxable year ending in 1971 and another portion of such grove at the beginning of his taxable year ending in 1972. The required capitalization period for expenses attributable to the first portion of such grove shall run until the close of T's taxable year ending in 1974. The required capitalization period for expenses attributable to the second portion of such grove shall run until the close of T's taxable year ending in 1975.

(2) (i) For purposes of section 278 and this section a "citrus grove" is defined as one or more trees of the rue family, often thorny and bearing large fruit with hard, usually thick peel and pulpy flesh, such as the orange, grapefruit, lemon, lime, citron, tangelo, and tangerine.

(ii) For purposes of section 278 and this section, an "almond grove" is defined as one or more trees of the species *Prunus amygdalus.*

(iii) An amount attributable to the cultivation, maintenance, or development of a citrus or almond grove (or part thereof) shall include, but shall not be limited to, the following developmental or cultural practices expenditures: Irrigation, cultivation, pruning, fertilizing, management fees, frost protection, spraying, and upkeep of the citrus or almond grove. The provisions of section 278(a) and this paragraph shall apply to expenditures for fertilizer and related materials notwithstanding the provisions of section 180, but shall not apply to expenditures attributable to real estate taxes or interest, to soil and water conservation expenditures allowable as a deduction under section 175, or to expenditures for clearing land allowable as a deduction under section 182. Further, the provisions of section 278(a) and this paragraph apply only to expenditures allowable as deductions without regard to section 278 and have no application to expenditures otherwise chargeable to capital account, such as the cost of the land and preparatory expenditures incurred in connection with the citrus or almond grove.

(iv) For purposes of section 278 and this section, a citrus or almond tree shall be considered to be "planted" on the date on which the tree is placed in the permanent grove from which production is expected.

(3) (i) The period during which expenditures described in section 278(a) and this paragraph are required to be capitalized shall, once determined, be unaffected by a sale or other disposition of the citrus or almond grove. Such period shall, in all cases, be computed by reference to the taxable years of the owner of the grove at the time that the citrus or almond trees were planted. Therefore, if a citrus or almond grove subject to the provisions of section 278 or this paragraph is sold or otherwise transferred by the original owner of the grove before the close of his fourth taxable year beginning with the taxable year in which the trees were planted, expenditures described in section 278(a) or this paragraph made by the purchaser or other transferee of the citrus or almond grove from the date of his acquisition until the close of the original holder's fourth such taxable year are required to be capitalized.

(ii) The provisions of this subparagraph may be illustrated by the following example:

Example. T, a fiscal year taxpayer, plants a citrus grove at the beginning of his taxable year ending in 1971. At the beginning of his taxable year ending in 1972, T sells the grove to X. The required period during which expenditures described in section 278(a) are required to be capitalized runs from the date on which T planted the grove until the end of T's taxable year ending in 1974. Therefore, X must capitalize any such expenditures incurred by him from the time he purchased the grove from T until the end of T's taxable year ending in 1974.

(b) Exceptions. *(1)* Paragraph (a) of this section shall not apply to amounts allowable as deductions (without regard to section 278 or this section) and attributable to a citrus or almond grove (or part thereof) which is replanted by a taxpayer after having been lost or damaged (while in the hands of such taxpayer) by reason of freeze, disease, drought, pests, or casualty.

(2) (i) Paragraph (a) of this section shall not apply to amounts allowable as deductions (without regard to section 278 or this section), and attributable to a citrus grove (or part thereof) which was planted or replanted prior to December 30, 1969, or to an almond grove (or part thereof) which was planted or replanted prior to December 30, 1970.

(ii) The provisions of this subparagraph may be illustrated by the following examples:

Example (1). T, a fiscal year taxpayer with a taxable year of July 1, 1969, through June 30, 1970, plants a citrus grove on August 1, 1969. Since the grove was planted prior to December 30, 1969, no expenses incurred with respect to the grove shall be subject to the provisions of paragraph (a).

Example (2). Assume the same facts as in example (1), except that T plants the grove on March 1, 1970. Since the grove was planted after December 30, 1969, all amounts allowable as deductions (without regard to section 278 or this section) and attributable to the grove shall be subject to the provision of paragraph (a). However, since paragraph (a) applies only to taxable years beginning after December 31, 1969, T must capitalize only those amounts incurred during his taxable years ending in 1971, 1972, and 1973.

T.D. 7098, 3/17/71, amend T.D. 7136, 8/10/71.

§ 1.279-1 General rule; purpose.

An obligation issued to provide a consideration directly or indirectly for a corporate acquisition, although constituting a debt under section 385, may have characteristics which make it more appropriate that the participation in the corporation which the obligation represents be treated for purposes of the deduction of interest as if it were a stockholder interest rather than a creditors interest. To deal with such cases, section 279 imposes certain limitations on the deductibility of interest paid or incurred on obligations which have certain equity characteristics and are classified as corporate acquisition indebtedness. Generally, section 279 provides that no deduction will be allowed for any interest paid or incurred by a corporation during the taxable year with respect to its corporate acquisition indebtedness to the extent such interest exceeds $5 million. However, the $5 million limitation is reduced by the amount of interest paid or incurred on obligations issued under the circumstances described in section 279(a)(2) but which are not corporate acquisition indebtedness. Section 279(b) provides that an obligation will be corporate acquisition indebtedness if it was issued under certain circumstances and meets the four tests enumerated therein. Although an obligation may satisfy the conditions referred to in the preceding sentence, it may still escape classification as corporate acquisition indebtedness if the conditions as described in sections 279(d)(3), (4), and (5), 279(f), or 279(i) are present. However, no inference should be drawn from the rules of section 279 as to whether a particular instrument labeled a bond, debenture, note, or other evidence of indebtedness is in fact a debt. Before the determination as to whether the deduction for payments pursuant to an obligation as described in this section is to be disallowed, the obligation must first qualify as debt in accordance with section 385. If the obligation is not debt under section 385, it will be unnecessary to apply section 279 to any payments pursuant to such obligation.

T.D. 7262, 3/2/73.

§ 1.279-2 Amount of disallowance of interest on corporate acquisition indebtedness.

(a) In general. Under section 279(a), no deduction is allowed for any interest paid or incurred by a corporation during the taxable year with respect to its corporate acquisition indebtedness to the extent that such interest exceeds—

(1) $5 million, reduced by

(2) The amount of interest paid or incurred by such corporation during such year on any obligation issued after December 31, 1967, to provide consideration directly or indirectly for an acquisition described in section 279(b)(1) but which is not corporate acquisition indebtedness. Such an obligation is not corporate acquisition indebtedness if it—

(i) Was issued prior to October 10, 1969, or

(ii) Was issued after October 9, 1969, but does not meet any one or more of the tests of section 279(b)(2), (3), or (4), or

(iii) Was originally deemed to be corporate acquisition indebtedness but is no longer so treated by virtue of the application of paragraphs (3) or (4) of section 279(d), or

(iv) Is specifically excluded from treatment as corporate acquisition indebtedness by virtue of sections 279(d)(5), (f), or (i).

The computation of the amount by which the $5 million limitation described in this paragraph is to be reduced with respect to any taxable year is to be made as of the last day of the taxable year in which an acquisition described in section 279(b)(1) occurs. In no case shall the $5 million limitation be reduced below zero.

(b) Certain terms defined. When used in section 279 and the regulations thereunder—

(1) The term "issued" includes the giving of a note or other evidence of indebtedness to a bank or other lender as well as an issuance of a bond or debenture. In the case of obligations which are registered with the Securities and Exchange Commission, the date of issue is the date on which the issue is first offered to the public. In the case of obligations which are not so registered, the date of issue is the date on which the obligation is sold to the first purchaser.

(2) The term "interest" includes both stated interest and unstated interest (such as original issue discount as defined in paragraph (a)(1) of § 1.163-4 and amounts treated as interest under section 483).

(3) The term "money" means cash and its equivalent.

(4) The term "control" shall have the meaning assigned to such term by section 368(c).

(5) The term "affiliated group" shall have the meaning assigned to such term by section 1504(a), except that all corporations other than the acquired corporation shall be treated as includible corporations (without any exclusion under section 1504(b)) and the acquired corporation shall not be treated as an includible corporation. This definition shall apply whether or not some or all of the members of the affiliated group file a consolidated return.

(c) Examples. The provisions of paragraph (a) of this section may be illustrated by the following examples:

Example (1). On March 4, 1973, X Corporation, a calendar year taxpayer, issues an obligation which satisfies the test of section 279(b)(1) but fails to satisfy either of the tests of section 279(b)(2) or (3). Since at least one of the tests of section 279(b) is not satisfied the obligation is not corporate acquisition indebtedness. However, since the test of section 279(b)(1) is satisfied, the interest on the obligation will reduce the $5 million limitation provided by section 279(a)(1).

Example (2). On January 1, 1969, X Corporation, a calendar year taxpayer, issues an obligation, which satisfies all the tests of section 279(b), requiring it to pay $3.5 million of interest each year. Since the obligation was issued before October 10, 1969, the obligation cannot be corporate acquisition indebtedness, and a deduction for the $3.5 million of interest attributable to such obligation is not subject to disallowance under section 279(a). However, since the obligation was issued after December 31, 1967, in an acquisition described in section 279(b)(1), under section 279(a)(2) the $3.5 million of interest attributable to such obligation reduces the $5 million limitation provided by section 279(a)(1) to $1.5 million.

Example (3). Assume the same facts as in example (2). Assume further that on January 1, 1970, X Corporation issues more obligations which are classified as corporate acquisition indebtedness and which require X Corporation to pay $4 million of interest each year. For 1970 the amount of interest paid or accrued on corporate acquisition indebtedness, which may be deducted is $1.5 million ($5 million maximum provided by section 279(a)(1) less $3.5 million, the reduction required under section 279(a)(2)). Thus, $2.5 million of the $4 million interest incurred on a corporate acquisition indebtedness is subject to disallowance under section 279(a) for the taxable year 1970.

Example (4). Assume the same facts as in example (3). Assume further that on the last day of each of the taxable years 1971, 1972, and 1973 of X Corporation neither of the conditions described in section 279(b)(4) was present.

Under these circumstances, such obligations for all taxable years after 1973 are not corporate acquisition indebtedness under section 279(d)(4). Therefore, the $2.5 million of interest previously not deductible is now deductible for all taxable years after 1973. Although such obligations are no longer treated as corporate acquisition indebtedness, the interest attributable thereto must be applied in further reduction of the $5 million limitation. The $5 million limitation of section 279(a)(1) is therefore reduced to zero. While the limitation is at the zero level any interest paid or incurred on corporate acquisition indebtedness will be disallowed.

T.D. 7262, 3/2/73.

§ 1.279-3 Corporate acquisition indebtedness.

(a) Corporate acquisition indebtedness. For purposes of section 279, the term "corporate acquisition indebtedness" means any obligation evidenced by a bond, debenture, note, or certificate or other evidence of indebtedness issued after October 9, 1969, by a corporation (referred to in section 279 and the regulations thereunder as "issuing corporation") if the obligation is issued to provide consideration directly or indirectly for the acquisition of stock in, or certain assets of, another corporation (as described in paragraph (b) of this § 1.279-3), is "subordinated" (as described in paragraph (c) of this § 1.279-3), is "convertible" (as described in paragraph (d) of this § 1.279-3), and satisfies either the ratio of debt to equity test (as described in paragraph (f) of § 1.279-5) or the projected earnings test (as described in paragraph (d) of § 1.279-5).

(b) Acquisition of stock or assets. *(1)* Section 279(b)(1) describes one of the tests to be satisfied if an obligation is to be classified as corporate acquisition indebtedness. Under section 279(b)(1), the obligation must be issued to provide consideration directly or indirectly for the acquisition of—

(i) Stock (whether voting or nonvoting) in another corporation (referred to in section 279 and the regulations thereunder as "acquired corporation"), or

(ii) Assets of another corporation (referred to in section 279 and the regulations thereunder as "acquired corporation") pursuant to a plan under which at least two-thirds (in value) of all the assets (excluding money) used in trades or businesses carried on by such corporation are acquired.

The fact that the corporation that issues the obligation is not the same corporation that acquires the acquired corporation does not prevent the application of section 279. For example, if X Corporation acquires all the stock of Y Corporation through the utilization of an obligation of Z Corporation, a wholly owned subsidiary of X Corporation, this section will apply.

(2) Direct or indirect consideration. Obligations are issued to provide direct consideration for an acquisition within the meaning of section 279(b)(1) where the obligations are issued to the shareholders of an acquired corporation in exchange for stock in such acquired corporation or where the obligations are issued to the acquired corporation in exchange for its assets. The application of the provisions of this subsection relating to indirect consideration for an acquisition of stock or assets depends upon the facts and circumstances surrounding the acquisition and the issuance of the obligations. Obligations are issued to provide indirect consideration for an acquisition of stock or assets within the meaning of section 279(b)(1) where (i) at the time of the issuance of the obligations the issuing corporation anticipated the acquisition of such stock or assets and the obligations would not have been issued if the issuing corporation had not so anticipated such acquisition, or where (ii) at the time of the acquisition the issuing corporation foresaw or reasonably should have foreseen that it would be required to issue obligations, which it would not have otherwise been required to issue if the acquisition had not occurred, in order to meet its future economic needs.

(3) Stock acquisition. (i) For purposes of section 279, an acquisition in which the issuing corporation issues an obligation to provide consideration directly or indirectly for the acquisition of stock in the acquired corporation shall be treated as a stock acquisition within the meaning of section 279(b)(1)(A). Where the stock of one corporation is acquired from another corporation and such stock constitutes at least two-thirds (in value) of all the assets (excluding money) of the latter corporation, such acquisition shall be deemed an asset acquisition as described in section 279(b)(1)(B) and subparagraph (4) of this section. If the issuing corporation

acquires less than two-thirds (in value) of all the assets (excluding money) used in trades or businesses carried on by the acquired corporation within the meaning of section 279(b)(1)(B) and subparagraph (4) of this paragraph and such assets include stock of another corporation, the acquisition of such stock is a stock acquisition within the meaning of section 279(b)(1)(A) and of this subparagraph. In such a case the amount of the obligation which is characterized as corporate acquisition indebtedness shall bear the same relationship to the total amount of the obligation issued as the fair market value of the stock acquired bears to the total of the fair market value of the assets acquired and stock acquired, as of the date of acquisition. For rules with respect to acquisitions of stock, where the total amount of stock of the acquired corporation held by the issuing corporation never exceeded 5 percent of the total combined voting power of all classes of stock of the acquired corporation entitled to vote, see § 1.279-4(b)(1).

(ii) If the issuing corporation acquired stock of an acquired corporation in an acquisition described in section 279(b)(1)(A), and liquidated the acquired corporation under section 334(b)(2) and the regulations thereunder before the last day of the taxable year in which such stock acquisition is made, such obligation issued to provide consideration directly or indirectly to acquire such stock of the acquired corporation shall be considered as issued in an acquisition described in section 279(b)(1)(B).

(4) Asset acquisition. (i) For purposes of section 279, an acquisition in which the issuing corporation issues an obligation to provide consideration directly or indirectly for the acquisition of assets of an acquired corporation pursuant to a plan under which at least two-thirds of the gross value of all the assets (excluding money) used in trades and businesses carried on by such acquired corporation are acquired shall be treated as an asset acquisition within the meaning of section 279(b)(1)(B). For purposes of section 279(b)(1)(B), the gross value of any acquired asset shall be its fair market value as of the day of its acquisition. In determining the fair market value of an asset, no reduction shall be made for any liabilities, mortgages, liens, or other encumbrances to which the asset or any part thereof may be subjected. For purposes of this subparagraph, an asset which has been actually used in the trades and businesses of a corporation but which is temporarily not being used in such trades and businesses shall be treated as if it is being used in such manner. For purposes of this paragraph, the day of acquisition will be determined by reference to the facts and circumstances surrounding the transaction.

(ii) For purposes of the two-thirds test described in section 279(b)(1)(B), the stock of any corporation which is controlled by the acquired corporation shall be considered as an asset used in the trades and businesses of such acquired corporation.

(5) Certain nontaxable transactions. (i) Under section 279(e), an acquisition of stock of a corporation of which the issuing corporation is in control in a transaction in which gain or loss is not recognized shall be deemed an acquisition described in section 279(b)(1)(A) only if immediately before such transaction the acquired corporation was in existence, and the issuing corporation was not in control of such corporation. If the issuing corporation is a member of an affiliated group, then in accordance with section 279(g), the affiliated group shall be treated as the issuing corporation. Thus, any stock of the acquired corporation, owned by members of the affiliated group, shall be aggregated in determining whether the issuing corporation was in control of the acquired corporation.

(ii) The $5 million limitation provided by section 279(a)(1) is not reduced by the interest on an obligation issued in a transaction which, under section 279(e), is deemed not to be an acquisition described in section 279(b)(1).

(iii) The provisions of this subparagraph may be illustrated by the following examples:

Example (1). On January 1, 1973, W Corporation, a calendar year taxpayer, issues to the public 10,000 10 year convertible bonds each with a principal of $1,000 for $9 million. On June 6, 1973, W Corporation transfers the $9 million proceeds of such bond issue to X Corporation in exchange for X Corporation's common stock in a transaction that satisfies the provisions of section 351(a). On December 31, 1973, W Corporation's ratio of debt to equity is 1½ to 1 and its project earnings exceed three times the annual interest to be paid or incurred. Immediately prior to the transaction between the two corporations W Corporation owned no stock in X Corporation which had been in existence for several years. However, immediately after this transaction W Corporation is in control of X Corporation. Since X Corporation, the acquired corporation, was in existence and W Corporation, the issuing corporation, was not in control of X Corporation immediately before the section 351 transaction (a transaction in which gain or loss is not recognized) and since W Corporation is now in control of X Corporation, the acquisition of X Corporation's common stock by W Corporation is not protected from treatment as an acquisition described in section 279(b)(1)(A). However, the obligation will not be deemed to be corporate acquisition indebtedness since the test of section 279(b)(4) is not met. The interest on the obligation will reduce the $5 million limitation of section 279(a).

Example (2). Assume the facts are the same as described in example (1), except that X Corporation was not in existence prior to June 6, 1973, but rather is newly created by W Corporation on such date. Since X Corporation, the acquired corporation, was not in existence before June 6, 1973, the date on which W Corporation, the issuing corporation, acquired control of X Corporation in a transaction on which gain or loss is not recognized, the acquisition is not deemed to be an acquisition described in section 279(b)(1)(A). Thus, under the provisions of subdivision (ii) of this subparagraph, the $5 million limitation provided by section 279(a)(1) will not be reduced by the yearly interest incurred on the convertible bonds issued by W Corporation.

Example (3). Assume that the facts are the same as described in example (1), except that W Corporation was in control of X Corporation immediately before the transaction. Since W Corporation was in control of X Corporation immediately before the section 351(a) transaction and is in control of X Corporation after such transaction, the result will be the same as in example (2).

(c) Subordinated obligation. *(1) In general.* An obligation which is issued to provide consideration for an acquisition described in section 279(b)(1) is subordinated within the meaning of section 279(b)(2) if it is either—

(i) Subordinated to the claims of trade creditors of the issuing corporation generally, or

(ii) Expressly subordinated in right of payment to the payment of any substantial amount of unsecured indebtedness, whether outstanding or subsequently issued, of the issuing corporation, irrespective of whether such subordination relates to payment of interest, or principal, or both. In applying section 279(b)(2) and this paragraph in any case where the issuing corporation is a member of an affiliated group of corporations, the affiliated group shall be treated as the issuing corporation.

(2) Expressly subordinated obligation. In applying subparagraph (1)(ii) of this paragraph, an obligation is considered expressly subordinated whether the terms of the subordination are provided in the evidence of indebtedness itself, or in another agreement between the parties to such obligation. An obligation shall be considered to be expressly subordinated within the meaning of subparagraph (1)(ii) of this paragraph if such obligation by its terms can become subordinated in right of payment to the payment of any substantial amount of unsecured indebtedness which is outstanding or which may be issued subsequently. However, an obligation shall not be considered expressly subordinated if such subordination occurs solely by operation of law, such as in the case of bankruptcy laws. For purposes of this paragraph, the term "substantial amount of unsecured indebtedness" means an amount of unsecured indebtedness equal to 5 percent or more of the face amount of the obligations issued within the meaning of section 279(b)(1).

(d) Convertible obligation. An obligation which is issued to provide consideration directly or indirectly for an acquisition described in section 279(b)(1) is convertible within the meaning of section 279(b)(3) if it is either—

(1) Convertible directly or indirectly into stock of the issuing corporation, or

(2) Part of an investment unit or other arrangement which includes, in addition to such bond or other evidence of indebtedness, an option to acquire directly or indirectly stock in the issuing corporation. Stock warrants or convertible preferred stock included as part of an investment unit constitute options within the meaning of the preceding sentence. Indebtedness is indirectly convertible if the conversion feature gives the holder the right to convert into another bond of the issuing corporation which is then convertible into the stock of the issuing corporation.

In any case where the corporation which in fact issues an obligation to provide consideration for an acquisition described in section 279(b)(1) is a member of an affiliated group, the provisions of section 279(b)(3) and this paragraph are deemed satisfied if the stock into which either the obligation or option which is part of an investment unit or other arrangement is convertible, directly or indirectly, is stock of any member of the affiliated group.

(e) Ratio of debt to equity and projected earnings test. For rules with respect to the application of section 279(b)(4) (relating to the ratio of debt to equity and the ratio of projected earnings to annual interest to be paid or incurred), see paragraphs (d), (e), and (f) of § 1.279-5.

(f) Certain obligations issued after October 9, 1969. *(1) In general.* Under section 279(i), an obligation shall not be corporate acquisition indebtedness if such obligation is issued after October 9, 1969, to provide consideration for the acquisition of—

(i) Stock or assets pursuant to a binding written contract which was in effect on October 9, 1969, and at all times thereafter before such acquisition, or

(ii) Stock in any corporation where the issuing corporation, on October 9, 1969, and at all times thereafter before such acquisition, owned at least 50 percent of the total combined voting power of all classes of stock entitled to vote of the acquired corporation.

Subdivision (ii) of this subparagraph shall cease to apply when (at any time on or after October 9, 1969) the issuing corporation has acquired control of the acquired corporation. The interest attributable to any obligation which satisfies the conditions stated in the first sentence of this subparagraph shall reduce the $5 million limitation of section 279(a)(1).

(2) Examples. The provisions of this paragraph may be illustrated by the following examples:

Example (1). On September 5, 1969, M Corporation, a calendar year taxpayer, entered into a binding written contract with N Corporation to purchase 20 percent of the voting stock of N Corporation. The contract was in effect on October 9, 1969, and at all times thereafter before the acquisition of the stock on January 1, 1970. Pursuant to such contract M Corporation issued on January 1, 1970, to N Corporation an obligation which satisfies the tests of section 279(b) requiring it to pay $1 million of interest each year. However, under the provisions of subparagraph (1)(i) of this paragraph, such obligation is not corporate acquisition indebtedness since it was issued to provide consideration for the acquisition of stock pursuant to a binding written contract which was in effect on October 9, 1969, and at all times thereafter before such acquisition. The $1 million of yearly interest on the obligation reduces the $5 million limitation provided for in section 279(a)(1) to $4 million since such interest is attributable to an obligation which was issued to provide consideration for the acquisition of stock in an acquired corporation.

Example (2). On October 9, 1969, O Corporation, a calendar year taxpayer, owned 50 percent of the total combined voting power of all classes of stock entitled to vote of P Corporation. P Corporation has no other class of stock. On January 1, 1970, while still owning such voting stock O Corporation issued to the shareholders of P Corporation to provide consideration for an additional 40 percent of P Corporation's voting stock an obligation which satisfied the tests of section 279(b) requiring it to pay $4 million of interest each year. Hence, O Corporation acquired control of P Corporation, and the provisions of subparagraph (1)(ii) of this paragraph ceased to apply to O Corporation. Thus, 75 percent of the obligation issued by O Corporation to provide consideration for the stock of P Corporation is not corporate acquisition indebtedness (that is, of the 40 percent of the voting stock of P Corporation which was acquired, only 30 percent was needed to give O Corporation control). Since 25 percent of the obligation is corporate acquisition indebtedness, $1 million of interest attributable to such obligation is subject to disallowance under section 279(a) for the taxable year 1970. The remaining $3 million of interest attributable to the obligation will reduce the $5 million limitation provided by in section 279(a)(1).

(g) Exemptions for certain acquisitions of foreign corporations. *(1) In general.* Under section 279(f), the term "corporate acquisition indebtedness" does not include any indebtedness issued to any person to provide consideration directly or indirectly for the acquisition of stock in, or assets of, any foreign corporation substantially all the income of which, for the 3-year period ending with the date of such acquisition or for such part of such period as the foreign corporation was in existence, is from sources without the United States. The interest attributable to any obligation excluded from treatment as corporate acquisition indebtedness by reason of this paragraph shall reduce the $5 million limitation of 279(a)(1).

(2) Foreign corporation. For purposes of this paragraph, the term "foreign corporation" shall have the same meaning as in section 7701(a)(5).

(3) Income from sources without the United States. For purposes of this paragraph, the term "income from sources without the United States" shall be determined in accordance with sections 862 and 863. If more than 80 percent of a foreign corporation's gross income is derived from sources without the United States, such corporation shall be considered to be deriving substantially all of its income from sources without the United States.

T.D. 7262, 3/2/73.

§ 1.279-4 Special rules.

(a) Special 3-year rule. Under section 279(d)(4), if an obligation which has been deemed to be corporate acquisition indebtedness for any taxable year would not be such indebtedness for each of any 3 consecutive taxable years thereafter if the ratio of debt to equity and the ratio of projected earnings to annual interest to be paid or incurred of section 279(b)(4) were applied as of the close of each of such 3 years, then such obligation shall not be corporate acquisition indebtedness for any taxable years after such 3 consecutive taxable years. The test prescribed by section 279(b)(4) shall be applied as of the close of any taxable year whether or not the issuing corporation issues any obligation to provide consideration for an acquisition described in section 279(b)(1) in such taxable year. Thus, for example, if a corporation, reporting income on a calendar year basis, has an obligation outstanding as of December 31, 1975, which was classified as a corporate acquisition indebtedness as of the close of 1972 and such obligation would not have been classified as corporate acquisition indebtedness as of the close of 1973, 1974, and 1975 because neither of the conditions of section 279(b)(4) were present as of such dates, then such obligation shall not be corporate acquisition indebtedness for 1976 and all taxable years thereafter. Such obligation shall not be reclassified as corporate acquisition indebtedness in any taxable year following 1975, even if the issuing corporation issues more obligations (whether or not found to be corporate acquisition indebtedness) in such later years to provide consideration for the acquisition of additional stock in, or assets of, the same acquired corporation with respect to which the original obligation was issued. The interest attributable to such obligation shall reduce the $5 million limitation provided by section 279(a)(1) for 1976 and all taxable years thereafter.

(b) Five percent stock rule. *(1) In general.* Under section 279(d)(5), if an obligation issued to provide consideration for an acquisition of stock in another corporation meets the tests of section 279(b), such obligation shall be corporate acquisition indebtedness for a taxable year only if at sometime after October 9, 1969, and before the close of such year the issuing corporation owns or has owned 5 percent or more of the total combined voting power of all classes of stock entitled to vote in the acquired corporation. If the issuing corporation is a member of an affiliated group, then in accordance with section 279(g) the affiliated group shall be treated as the issuing corporation. Thus, any stock of the acquired corporation owned by members of the affiliated group shall be aggregated to determine if the percentage limitation provided by this subparagraph is exceeded. Once an obligation is deemed to be corporate acquisition indebtedness such obligation will continue to be deemed corporate acquisition indebtedness for all taxable years thereafter unless the provisions of section 279(d)(3) or (4) apply, notwithstanding the fact that the issuing corporation owns less than 5 percent of the combined voting power of all classes of stock entitled to vote of the acquired corporation in any or all taxable years thereafter.

(2) Examples. The provisions of this paragraph may be illustrated by the following examples:

Example (1). Corporation Y uses the calendar year as its taxable year and has only one class of stock outstanding. On June 1, 1972, X Corporation which is also a calendar year taxpayer and which has never been a shareholder of Y Corporation acquires from the shareholders of Y Corporation 4 percent of the stock of Y Corporation in exchange for obligations which satisfy the conditions of section 279(b). At no time during 1972 does X Corporation own 5 percent or more of the stock of Y Corporation. Accordingly, under the provisions of subparagraph (1) of this paragraph, for 1972 the obligations issued by X Corporation to provide consideration for the acquisition of Y Corporation's stock do not constitute corporate acquisition indebtedness.

Example (2). Assume the same facts as in example (1). Assume further that on February 24, 1973, X Corporation acquires from the shareholders of Y Corporation an additional 7 percent of the stock of Y Corporation in exchange for obligations which satisfy all of the tests of section 279(b). On December 28, 1973, X Corporation sells all of its stock in Y Corporation. For 1973, the obligations issued by X Corporation in 1972 and in 1973 constitute corporate acquisition indebtedness since X Corporation at some time after October 9, 1969, and before the close of 1973 owned 5 percent or more of the voting stock of Y Corporation. Furthermore, such obligations shall be corporate acquisition indebtedness for all taxable years thereafter unless the special provisions of section 279(d)(3) or (4) could apply.

(c) Changes in obligation. *(1) In general.* Under section 279(h), for purposes of section 279—

(i) Any extension, renewal, or refinancing of an obligation evidencing a preexisting indebtedness shall not be deemed to be the issuance of a new obligation, and

(ii) Any obligation which is corporate acquisition indebtedness of the issuing corporation is also corporate acquisition indebtedness of any corporation which in any transaction or by operation of law assumes liability for such obligation or becomes liable for such obligation as guarantor, endorser, or indemnitor.

(2) Examples. The provisions of this paragraph may be illustrated by the following examples:

Example (1). On January 1, 1971, X Corporation, which files its return on the basis of a calendar year, issues an obligation, which satisfies the tests of section 279(b), and is deemed to be corporate acquisition indebtedness. On January 1, 1973, an agreement is concluded between X Corporation and the holder of the obligation whereby the maturity date of such obligation is extended until December 31, 1979. Under the provisions of subparagraph (1)(i) of this paragraph such extended obligation is not deemed to be a new obligation, and still constitutes corporate acquisition indebtedness.

Example (2). On June 12, 1971, X Corporation, a calendar year taxpayer, issued convertible and subordinated obligations to acquire the stock of Z Corporation. The obligations were deemed corporate acquisition indebtedness on December 31, 1971. On March 4, 1973, X Corporation and Y Corporation consolidated to form XY Corporation in accordance with State law. Corporation XY is liable for the obligations issued by X Corporation by operation of law and the obligations continue to be corporate acquisition indebtedness. In 1975 XY Corporation exchanges its own nonconvertible obligations for the obligations X Corporation issues. The obligations of XY Corporation issued in exchange for those of X Corporation will be deemed to be corporate acquisition indebtedness.

T.D. 7262, 3/2/73.

---

§ 1.279-5 Rules for application of section 279(b).

(a) Taxable years to which applicable. *(1) First year of disallowance.* Under section 279(d)(1), the deduction of interest on any obligation shall not be disallowed under section 279(a) before the first taxable year of the issuing corporation as of the last day of which the application of either section 279(b)(4) (A) or (B) results in such obligation being classified as corporate acquisition indebtedness. See section 279(c)(1) and paragraph (b)(2) of this section for the time when an obligation is subjected to the test of section 279(b)(4).

(2) General rule for succeeding years. Under section 279(d)(2), except as provided in paragraphs (3), (4), and (5) of section 279(d), if an obligation is determined to be corporate acquisition indebtedness as of the last day of any taxable year of the issuing corporation, such obligation shall be corporate acquisition indebtedness for such taxable year and all subsequent taxable years.

(b) Time of determination. *(1) In general.* The determination of whether an obligation meets the conditions of section 279(b) (1), (2), and (3) shall be made as of the day on which the obligation is issued.

(2) Ratio of debt to equity, projected earnings, and annual interest to be paid or incurred. (i) Under section 279(c)(1), the determination of whether an obligation meets the conditions of section 279(b)(4) is first to be made as of the last day of the taxable year of the issuing corporation in which it issues the obligation to provide consideration directly or indirectly for an acquisition described in section 279(b)(1) of stock in, or assets of, the acquired corporation. An obligation which is not corporate acquisition indebtedness only because it does not satisfy the test of section 279(b)(4) in the taxable year of the issuing corporation in which the obligation is issued for stock in, or assets of, the acquired corporation may be subjected to the test of section 279(b)(4) again. A retesting will occur in any subsequent taxable year of the issuing corporation in which the issuing corporation issues any obligation to provide consideration directly or indirectly for an acquisition described in section 279(b)(1) with respect to the same acquired corporation, irrespective of whether such subsequent obligation is itself classified as corporate acquisition indebtedness. If the issuing corporation is a member of an affiliated group, then in accordance with section 279(g) the affiliated group shall be treated as the issuing corporation. Thus, if any member of the affiliated group issues an obligation to acquire additional stock in, or assets of, the acquired corporation, this paragraph shall apply.

(ii) For purposes of section 279(b)(4) and this paragraph, in any case where the issuing corporation is a member of an affiliated group (see section 279(g) and § 1.279-6 for rules regarding application of section 279 to certain affiliated groups) which does not file a consolidated return and all the members of which do not have the same taxable year, determinations with respect to the ratio of debt to equity of, and projected earnings of, and annual interest to be paid or incurred by, any member of the affiliated group shall be made as of the last day of the taxable year of the corporation which in fact issues the obligation to provide consideration for an acquisition described in section 279(b)(1).

(3) Redetermination where control or substantially all the properties have been acquired. Under section 279(d)(3), if an obligation is determined to be corporate acquisition indebtedness as of the close of a taxable year of the issuing corporation in which section 279(c)(3)(A)(i) (relating to the projected earnings of the issuing corporation only) applied, but would not be corporate acquisition indebtedness if the determination were made as of the close of the first taxable year of such corporation thereafter in which section 279(c)(3)(A)(ii) (relating to the projected earnings of both the issuing corporation and the acquired corporation) could apply, such obligation shall be considered not to be corporate acquisition indebtedness for such later taxable year and all taxable years thereafter. Where an obligation ceases to be corporate acquisition indebtedness as a result of the application of this paragraph, the interest on such obligation shall not be disallowed under section 279(a) as a deduction for the taxable year in which the obligation ceases to be corporate acquisition indebtedness and all taxable years thereafter. However, under section 279(a)(2) the interest paid or incurred on such obligation which is allowed as a deduction will reduce the $5 million limitation provided by section 279(a)(1).

(4) Examples. The provisions of this paragraph may be illustrated by the following examples:

Example (1). In 1971, X Corporation, which files its Federal income tax return on the basis of a calendar year, issues its obligations to provide consideration for the acquisition of 15 percent of the voting stock of both Y Corporation and Z Corporation. Y Corporation and Z Corporation each have only one class of stock. When issued, such obligations satisfied the tests prescribed in section 279(b) (1), (2), and (3) and would have constituted corporate acquisition indebtedness but for the test prescribed in section 279(b)(4). On December 31, 1971, the application of section 279(b)(4) results in X Corporation's obligations issued in 1971 not being treated as corporate acquisition indebtedness for that year.

Example (2). Assume the same facts as in example (1), except that in 1972, X Corporation issues more obligations which come within the tests of section 279(b) (1), (2), and (3) to acquire an additional 10 percent of the voting stock of Y Corporation. No stock of Z Corporation is acquired after 1971. The application of section 279(b)(4)(B) (relating to the projected earnings of X Corporation) as of the end of 1972 results in the obligations issued in 1972 to provide consideration for the acquisition of the stock of Y Corporation being treated as corporate acquisition indebtedness. Since X Corporation during 1972 did issue obligations to acquire more stock of Y Corporation, under the provisions of section 279(c)(1) and subparagraph (2) of this paragraph the obligations issued by X Corporation in 1971 to acquire stock in Y Corporation are again tested to determine whether the test of section 279(b)(4) with respect to such obligations is satisfied for 1972. Thus, since such obligations issued by X Corporation to acquire Y Corporation's stock in 1971 previously came within the provisions of section 279(b) (1), (2), and (3) and the projected earnings test of section 279(b)(4)(B) is satisfied for 1972, all of such obligations are to be deemed to constitute corporate acquisition indebtedness for 1972 and subsequent taxable years. The obligations issued in 1971 to acquire stock in Z Corporation continue not to constitute corporate acquisition indebtedness.

Example (3). Assume the same facts as in examples (1) and (2). In 1973, X Corporation issues more obligations which come within the tests of section 279(b) (1), (2), and (3) to acquire more stock (but not control) in Y Corporation. On December 31, 1973, it is determined with respect to X Corporation that neither of the conditions described in section 279(b)(4) are present. Thus, the obligations issued in 1973 do not constitute corporate acquisition indebtedness. However, the obligations issued in 1971 and 1972 by X Corporation to acquire stock in Y Corporation continue to be treated as corporate acquisition indebtedness.

Example (4). Assume the same facts as in example (3), except that X Corporation acquires control of Y Corporation in 1973. Since X Corporation has acquired control of Y Corporation, the average annual earnings (as defined in section (c)(4)) of both X Corporation and Y Corporation under section 279(c)(3)(A)(ii) are taken into account in computing for 1973 the ratio of projected earnings to annual interest to be paid or incurred described in section 279(b)(4)(B). Assume further that after applying section 279(b)(4)(B) the obligations issued in 1973 escape treatment as corporate acquisition indebtedness for 1973. Under section 279(d)(3), all of the obligations issued by X Corporation to acquire stock in Y Corporation in 1971 and 1972 are removed from classification as corporate acquisition indebtedness for 1973 and all subsequent taxable years.

Example (5). In 1975, M Corporation, which files its Federal income tax return on the basis of a calendar year, issues its obligations to acquire 30 percent of the voting stock of N Corporation. N Corporation has only one class of stock. Such obligations satisfy the tests prescribed in section 279(b) (1), (2), and (3). Additionally, as of the close of 1975, M Corporation's ratio of debt to equity exceeds the ratio of 2 to 1 and its projected earnings do not exceed three times the annual interest to be paid or incurred. The obligations issued by M Corporation are corporate acquisition indebtedness for 1975 since all the provisions of section 279(b) are satisfied. In 1976 M Corporation issues its obligations to acquire from the shareholders of N Corporation an additional 60 percent of the voting stock of N Corporation, thereby acquiring control of N Corporation. However, with respect to the obligations issued by M Corporation in 1975, there is no redetermination under section 279(d)(3) and subparagraph (3) of this paragraph as to whether such obligations may escape classification as corporate acquisition indebtedness because in 1975 it was the ratio of debt to equity test which caused such obligations to be corporate acquisition indebtedness. If in 1975, M Corporation met the conditions of section 279(b)(4) solely because of the ratio of projected earnings to annual interest to be paid or incurred described in section 279(b)(4)(B), its obligation issued in 1975 could be retested in 1976.

(c) Acquisition of stock or assets of several corporations. An issuing corporation which acquires stock in, or assets of, more than one corporation during any taxable year must apply the tests described in section 279(b) (1), (2), and (3) separately with respect to each obligation issued to provide consideration for the acquisition of the stock in, or assets of, each such acquired corporation. Thus, if an acquisition is made with obligations of the issuing corporation that satisfy the tests described in section 279(b) (2) and (3) and obligations that fail to satisfy such tests, only those obligations satisfying such tests need be further considered to determine whether they constitute corporate acquisition indebtedness. Those obligations which meet the test of section 279(b)(1) but which are not deemed corporate acquisition indebtedness shall be taken into account for purposes of determining the reduction in the $5 million limitation of section 279(a)(1).

(d) Ratio of debt to equity and projected earnings. *(1) In general.* One of the four tests to determine whether an obligation constitutes corporate acquisition indebtedness is contained in section 279(b)(4). An obligation will meet the test of section 279(b)(4) if, as of a day determined under section 279(c)(1) and paragraph (b)(2) of this section, either—

(i) The ratio of debt to equity (as defined in paragraph (f) of this section) of the issuing corporation exceeds 2 to 1, or

(ii) The projected earnings (as defined in subparagraph (2) of this paragraph) of the issuing corporation, or of both the issuing corporation and acquired corporation in any case where subparagraph (2)(ii) of this paragraph is applicable, do not exceed three times the annual interest to be paid or incurred (as defined in paragraph (e) of this section) by such issuing corporation, or, where applicable, by such issuing corporation and acquired corporation. Where paragraphs (d)(2)(ii) and (e)(1)(ii) of this section are applicable in computing projected earnings and annual interest to be paid or incurred, 100 percent of the acquired corporation's projected earnings and annual interest to be paid or incurred shall be included in such computation, even though less than all of the stock or assets of the acquired corporation have been acquired.

(2) Projected earnings. The term "projected earnings" means the "average annual earnings" (as defined in subparagraph (3) of this paragraph) of —

(i) The issuing corporation only, if subdivision (ii) of this subparagraph, does not apply, or

(ii) Both the issuing corporation and the acquired corporation, in any case where the issuing corporation as of the close of its taxable year has acquired control, or has acquired substantially all of the properties, of the acquired corporation.

For purposes of subdivision (ii) of this subparagraph, an acquisition of "substantially all of the properties" of the acquired corporation means the acquisition of assets representing at least 90 percent of the fair market value of the net assets and at least 70 percent of the fair market value of the gross assets held by the acquired corporation immediately prior to the acquisition.

(3) Average annual earnings. (i) The term "average annual earnings" referred to in subparagraph (2) of this paragraph is, for any corporation, the amount of its earnings and profits for any 3-year period ending with the last day of a taxable year of the issuing corporation in which it issues any obligation to provide consideration for an acquisition described in section 279(b)(1), computed without reduction for—

(a) Interest paid or incurred,

(b) Depreciation or amortization allowed under chapter 1 of the Code,

(c) Liability for tax under chapter 1 of the Code, and

(d) Distributions to which section 301(c)(1) apply (other than such distributions from the acquired corporation to the issuing corporation),

and reduced to an annual average for such 3-year period. For the rules to determine the amount of earnings and profits of any corporation, see section 312 and the regulations thereunder.

(ii) Except as provided for in subdivision (iii) of this subparagraph, for purposes of subdivision (i) of this subparagraph in the case of any corporation, the earnings and profits for such 3-year period shall be reduced to an annual average by dividing such earnings and profits by 36 and multiplying the quotient by 12. If a corporation was not in existence during the entire 36-month period as of the close of the taxable year referred to in subdivision (i) of this subparagraph, its average annual earnings shall be determined by dividing its earnings and profits for the period of its existence by the number of whole calendar months in such period and multiplying the quotient by 12.

(iii) Where the issuing corporation acquires substantially all of the properties of an acquired corporation, the computation of earnings and profits of such acquired corporation shall be made for the period of such corporation beginning with the first day of the 3-year period of the issuing corporation and ending with the last day prior to the date on which substantially all of the properties were acquired. In determining the number of whole calendar months for such acquired corporation where the period for determining its earnings and profits includes 2 months which are not whole calendar months and the total number of days in such 2 fractional months exceeds 30 days, the number of whole calendar months for such period shall be increased by one. Where the number of days in the 2 fractional months total 30 days or less such fractional months shall be disregarded. After the number of whole calendar months is determined, the calculation for average annual earnings shall be made in the same manner as described in the last sentence of subdivision (ii) of this subparagraph.

(e) Annual interest to be paid or incurred. *(1) In general.* For purposes of section 279(b)(4)(B), the term "annual interest to be paid or incurred" means—

(i) If subdivision (ii) of this subparagraph does not apply, the annual interest to be paid or incurred by the issuing corporation only, for the taxable year beginning immediately after the day described in section 279(c)(1), determined by reference to its total indebtedness outstanding as of such day, or

(ii) If projected earnings are determined under paragraph (d)(2)(ii) of this section, the annual interest to be paid or incurred by both the issuing corporation and the acquired corporation for 1 year beginning immediately after the day described in section 279(c)(1), determined by reference to their combined total indebtedness outstanding as of such day. However, where the issuing corporation acquires substantially all of the properties of the acquired corporation, the annual interest to be paid or incurred will be determined by reference to the total indebtedness outstanding of the issuing corporation only (including any indebtedness it assumed in the acquisition) as of the day described in section 279(c)(1).

The term "annual interest to be paid or incurred" refers to both actual interest and unstated interest. Such unstated interest includes original issue discount as defined in paragraph (a)(1) of § 1.163-4 and amounts treated as interest under section 483. For purposes of this paragraph and paragraph (f) of this section (relating to the ratio of debt to equity), the indebtedness of any corporation shall be determined in accordance with generally accepted accounting principles. Thus, for example, the indebtedness of a corporation includes short-term liabilities, such as accounts payable to suppliers, as well as long-term indebtedness. Contingent liabilities, such as those arising out of discounted notes, the assignment of accounts receivable, or the guarantee of the liability of another, shall be included in the determination of the indebtedness of a corporation if the contingency is likely to become a reality. In addition, the indebtedness of a corporation includes obligations issued by the corporation, secured only by property of the corporation, and with respect to which the corporation is not personally liable. See section 279 (g) and § 1.279-6 for rules with respect to the computation of annual interest to be paid or incurred in regard to members of an affiliated group of corporations.

(2) Examples. The provisions of these paragraphs may be illustrated by the following examples:

Example (1). Corporation X's earnings and profits calculated in accordance with section 279(c)(3)(B) for 1972, 1971, and 1970 respectively were $29 million, $23 million, and $20 million. The interest to be paid or incurred during the calendar year of 1973 as determined by reference to the issuing corporation's total outstanding indebtedness as of December 31, 1972, was $10 million. By dividing the sum of the earnings and profits for the 3 years by 36 (the number of whole calendar months in the 3-year period) and multiplying the quotient by 12, the average annual earnings for X Corporation is $24 million. Since the projected earnings of X Corporation do not exceed by three times the annual interest to be paid or incurred (they exceed by only 2.4 times), one of the circumstances described in section 279(b)(4) is present.

Example (2). On March 1, 1972, W Corporation acquires substantially all of the properties of Z Corporation in exchange for W Corporation's bonds which satisfy the tests of section 279(b) (2) and (3). W Corporation files its income tax returns on the basis of fiscal years ending June 30. Z Corporation, which was formed on September 1, 1969, is a calendar year taxpayer. The earnings and profits of W Corporation for the last 3 fiscal years ending June 30, 1972, calculated in accordance with the provisions of section 279(c)(3)(B) were $300 million, $400 million, and $380 million, respectively. The average annual earnings of W Corporation is $360 million ($1,080 million ÷ 36 × 12). The earnings and profits of Z Corporation calculated in accordance with the provisions of section 279(c)(3)(B) were $4 million for the period of September 1, 1969 to December 31, 1969, $10 million and $14 million for the calendar years of 1970 and 1971, respectively, and $2 million for the period of January 1, 1972, through February 29, 1972, or a total of $30 million. To arrive at the average annual earnings, the sum of the earnings and profits, $30 million, must be divided by 30 (the number of whole calendar months that Z Corporation was in existence during W Corporation's 3-year period ending with the day prior to the date substantially all the assets were acquired) and the quotient is multiplied by 12, which results in an average annual earnings of $12 million ($30 million ÷ 30 × 12) for Z Corporation. The combined average annual earnings of W Corporation and Z Corporation is $372 million. The interest for the fiscal year ending June 30, 1973, to be paid or incurred by W Corporation on its outstanding indebtedness as of June 30, 1972, is $110 million. Since the projected earnings exceed the annual interest to be paid or incurred by more than three times, the obligation will not be corporate acquisition indebtedness, unless the issuing corporation's debt to equity ratio exceeds 2 to 1.

(f) Ratio of debt to equity. *(1) In general.* The condition described in section 279(b)(4)(A) is present if the ratio of debt to equity of the issuing corporation exceeds 2 to 1. Under section 279(c)(2), the term "ratio of debt to equity" means the ratio which the total indebtedness of the issuing corporation bears to the sum of its money and all its other assets (in an amount equal to adjusted basis for determining gain) less such total indebtedness. For the meaning of the term "indebtedness", see paragraph (e)(1) of this section. See section 279(g) and § 1.279-6 for rules with respect to the computation of the ratio of debt to equity in regard to an affiliated group of corporations.

(2) Examples. The provisions of section 279(b)(4)(A) and this paragraph may be illustrated by the following example:

Example (1). On June 1, 1971, X Corporation, which files its federal income tax returns on a calendar year basis, issues an obligation for $45 million to the shareholders of Y Corporation to provide consideration for the acquisition of all of the stock of Y Corporation. Such obligation has the characteristics of corporate acquisition indebtedness described in section 279(b) (2) and (3). The projected earnings of X Corporation and Y Corporation exceed 3 times the annual interest to be paid or incurred by those corporations and, accordingly, the condition described in section 279(b)(4)(B) is not present. Also, on December 31, 1971, X Corporation has total assets with an adjusted basis of $150 million (including the newly acquired stock of Y Corporation having a basis of $45 million) and total indebtedness of $90 million. Hence, X Corporation's equity is $60 million computed by subtracting its $90 million of total indebtedness from its $150 million of total assets. Since X Corporation's ratio of debt to equity of 1.5 to 1 ($90 million of total indebtedness over $60 million equity) does not exceed 2 to 1, the condition described in section 279(b)(4)(A) is not present. Therefore, X Corporation's obligation for $45 million is not corporate acquisition indebtedness because on December 31, 1971, neither of the conditions specified in section 279(b)(4) existed.

(g) Special rules for banks and lending or finance companies. *(1) Debt to equity and projected earnings.* Under section 279(c)(5), with respect to any corporation which is a bank (as defined in section 581) or is primarily engaged in a lending or finance business, the following rules are to be applied:

(i) In determining under paragraph (f) of this section the ratio of debt to equity of such corporation (or of the affiliated group of which such corporation is a member), the total indebtedness of such corporation (and the assets of such corporation) shall be reduced by an amount equal to the total indebtedness owed to such corporation which arises out of the banking business of such corporation, or out of the lending or finance business of such corporation, as the case may be;

(ii) In determining under paragraph (e) of this section the annual interest to be paid or incurred by such corporation (or by the issuing corporation and acquired corporation referred to in section 279(c)(4)(B) or by the affiliated group of corporations of which such corporation is a member), the amount of such interest (determined without regard to this subparagraph) shall be reduced by an amount which bears the same ratio to the amount of such interest as the amount of the reduction for the taxable year under subdivision (i) of this subparagraph bears to the total indebtedness of such corporation; and

(iii) In determining under section 279(c)(3)(B) the average annual earnings, the amount of the earnings and profits for the 3-year period shall be reduced by the sum of the reductions under subdivision (ii) of this subparagraph for such period.

For purposes of this paragraph, the term "lending or finance business" means a business of making loans or purchasing or discounting accounts receivable, notes, or installment obligations. Additionally, the rules stated in this paragraph regarding the application of the ratio of debt to equity, the determination of the annual interest to be paid or incurred, and the determination of the average annual earnings also apply if the bank or lending or finance company is a member of an affiliated group of corporations. However, the rules are to be applied only for purposes of determining the debt, equity, projected earnings and annual interest of the bank or lending or finance company which then are taken into account in determining the debt to equity ratio and ratio of projected earnings to annual interest to be paid or incurred by the affiliated group as a whole. Thus, these rules are to be applied to reduce the bank's or lending or finance corporation's indebtedness, annual interest to be paid or incurred, and average annual earnings which are taken into account with respect to the group, but are not to reduce the indebtedness of, annual interest to be paid or incurred by, and average annual earnings of, any corporation in the affiliated group which is not a bank or a lending or finance company. In determining whether any corporation which is a member of an affiliated group is primarily engaged in a lending or finance business, only the activities of such corporation, and not those of the whole group, are to be taken into account. See § 1.279-6 for the application of section 279 to certain affiliated groups of corporations.

(2) Examples. The provisions of this paragraph may be illustrated by the following examples:

Example (1). As of the close of the taxable year, X Bank has a total indebtedness of $100 million, total assets of $115 million, and $80 million is owed to X Bank by its customers. Bank X's indebtedness is $20 million ($100 million total indebtedness less $80 million owed to the X Bank by its customers) and its assets are $35 million ($115 million total assets less $80 million owed to the bank by its customers). If its annual interest to be paid or incurred is $5 million, such amount is reduced by $4 million

$$\$5 \text{ million interest to be paid or incurred} \times \frac{\$80 \text{ million owed to X Bank by its customers}}{\$100 \text{ million total indebtedness}}$$

Thus, X Bank's annual interest to be paid or incurred is $1 million.

Example (2). Assume the same facts as in example (1). X Bank has earnings and profits of $23 million for the 3-year period used to determine projected earnings. In computing the average annual earnings, the $23 million amount will be reduced by $12 million (three times the $4 million reduction of interest in example (1), assuming that the reduction was the same for each year). Thus X Bank's earnings and profits for such 3-year period are $11 million ($23 million total earnings and profits less $12 million reduction).

T.D. 7262, 3/2/73, amend T.D. 9264, 5/26/2006.

---

§ 1.279-6 Application of section 279 to certain affiliated groups.

(a) In general. Under section 279(g), in any case in which the issuing corporation is a member of an affiliated group, the application of section 279 shall be determined by treating all of the members of the affiliated group in the aggregate as the issuing corporation, except that the ratio of debt to equity of, projected earnings of, and the annual interest to be paid or incurred by any corporation (other than the issuing corporation determined without regard to this paragraph) shall be included in the determinations required under section 279(b)(4) as of any day only if such corporation is a member of the affiliated group on such day, and, in determining projected earnings of such corporation under section

279(c)(3), there shall be taken into account only the earnings and profits of such corporation for the period during which it was a member of the affiliated group. The total amount of an affiliated member's assets, indebtedness, projected earnings, and interest to be paid or incurred will enter into the computation required by this section, irrespective of any minority ownership in such member.

(b) Aggregate money and other assets. In determining the aggregate money and all the other assets of the affiliated group, the money and all the other assets of each member of such group shall be separately computed and such separately computed amounts shall be added together, except that adjustments shall be made, as follows:

(1) There shall be eliminated from the aggregate money and all the other assets of the affiliated group intercompany receivables as of the date described in section 279(c)(1);

(2) There shall be eliminated from the total assets of the affiliated group any amount which represents stock ownership in any member of such group;

(3) In any case where gain or loss is not recognized on transactions between members of an affiliated group under paragraph (d)(3) of this section, the basis of any asset involved in such transaction shall be the transferor's basis;

(4) The basis of property in a transaction to which § 1.1502-13 applies is the basis of the property determined under that section; and

(5) There shall be eliminated from the money and all the other assets of the affiliated group any other amount which, if included, would result in a duplication of amounts in the aggregate money and all the other assets of the affiliated group.

(c) Aggregate indebtedness. For purposes of applying section 279(c), in determining the aggregate indebtedness of an affiliated group of corporations the total indebtedness of each member of such group shall be separately determined, and such separately determined amounts shall be added together, except that there shall be eliminated from such total indebtedness as of the date described in section 279(c)(1)—

(1) The amount of intercompany accounts payable,

(2) The amount of intercompany bonds or other evidences of indebtedness, and

(3) The amount of any other indebtedness which, if included, would result in a duplication of amounts in the aggregate indebtedness of such affiliated group.

(d) Aggregate projected earnings. In the case of an affiliated group of corporations (whether or not such group files a consolidated return under section 1501), the aggregate projected earnings of such group shall be computed by separately determining the projected earnings of each member of such group under paragraph (d) of § 1.279-5, and then adding together such separately determined amounts, except that—

(1) A dividend (a distribution which is described in section 301(c)(1) other than a distribution described in section 243 (c)(1)) distributed by one member to another member shall be eliminated, and

(2) In determining the earnings and profits of any member of an affiliated group, there shall be eliminated any amount of interest income received or accrued, and of interest expense paid or incurred, which is attributable to intercompany indebtedness,

(3) No gain or loss shall be recognized in any transaction between members of the affiliated group, and

(4) Members of an affiliated group who file a consolidated return shall not apply the provisions of § 1.1502-18 dealing with inventory adjustments in determining earnings and profits for purposes of this section.

(e) Aggregate interest to be paid or incurred. For purposes of section 279(c)(4), in determining the aggregate annual interest to be paid or incurred by an affiliated group of corporations, the annual interest to be paid or incurred by each member of such affiliated group shall be separately calculated under paragraph (e) of § 1.279-5, and such separately calculated amounts shall be added together, except that any amount of annual interest to be paid or incurred on any intercompany indebtedness shall be eliminated from such aggregate interest.

T.D. 7262, 3/2/73, amend T.D. 8560, 8/12/94, T.D. 8597, 7/12/95.

---

§ 1.279-7 Effect on other provisions.

Under section 279(j), no inference is to be drawn from any provision in section 279 and the regulations thereunder that any instrument designated as a bond, debenture, note, or certificate or other evidence of indebtedness by its issuer represents an obligation or indebtedness of such issuer in applying any other provision of this title. Thus, for example, an instrument, the interest on which is not subject to disallowance under section 279 could, under section 385 and the regulations thereunder, be found to constitute a stock interest, so that any amounts paid or payable thereon would not be deductible.

T.D. 7262, 3/2/73.

PARAGRAPH 1.

Section 1.280A-1, as proposed, is amended as follows:

1. Paragraph (d)(1) is amended by removing the word "calendar" in the last sentence.

2. Paragraphs (f) and (g) are redesignated as paragraphs (i) and (j) respectively.

3. Paragraphs (c) and (e) are revised and new paragraphs (f), (g) and (h) are added to read as set forth below.

Proposed § 1.280A-1 Limitations on deductions with respect to a dwelling unit which is used by the taxpayer during the taxable year as a residence. [*For Preamble, see ¶ 150,873*]

* * * * *

(c) Dwelling unit. *(1) In general.* For purposes of this section and §§ 1.280A-2 and 1.280A-3, the term "dwelling unit" includes a house, apartment, condominium, mobile home, boat, or similar property, which provides basic living accommodations such as sleeping space, toilet, and cooking facilities. A single structure may contain more than one dwelling unit. For example, each apartment in an apartment building is a separate dwelling unit. Similarly, if the basement of a house contains basic living accommodations, the basement constitutes a separate dwelling unit. All structures and other property appurtenant to a dwelling unit are considered part of the unit. For example, an individual who rents to another person space in a garage which is appurtenant to a house which the individual owns and occupies may claim deductions with respect to that rental activity only to the extent allowed under section 280A, paragraph (b) of this section, and § 1.280A-3.

(2) Exception. Notwithstanding the provisions of paragraph (c)(1) of this section, the term "dwelling unit" does not include any unit or portion of a unit which is used exclusively as a hotel, motel, inn, or similar establishment. Property is so used only if it is regularly available for occupancy by paying customers and only if no person having an interest in the property is deemed under the rules of this section to have used the unit (or the portion of the unit) as a residence during the taxable year. Thus, this exception may apply to a portion of a home used to furnish lodging to tourists or to long-term boarders such as students. This exception may also apply to a unit entered in a rental pool (see § 1.280A-3(e)) if the owner of the unit does not use it as a residence during the taxable year.

* * * * *

(e) Personal use of dwelling unit. *(1) General rule.* For purposes of this section and §§ 1.280A-2 and 1.280-3, a taxpayer shall be deemed to have used a dwelling unit for personal purposes on any day on which, for any part of the day, any portion of the unit is used—

(i) For personal purposes by the taxpayer or any other person who has an interest in the unit;

(ii) By a brother or sister (whether by the whole or half blood), spouse, ancestor, or lineal descendant of the taxpayer or of any other person who has an interest in the unit;

(iii) By any individual who uses the unit under an arrangement which enables the taxpayer to use some other dwelling unit for any period of time, whether or not a rental is charged for the use of the other unit and regardless of the length of time that the taxpayer uses the other unit; or

(iv) By any individual, other than an employee with respect to whose use section 119 (relating to meals or lodging furnished for the convenience of the employer) applies, unless for such day the dwelling unit is rented for a rental which, under the facts and circumstances, is fair rental.

For purposes of this paragraph, a person is considered to have an interest in a dwelling unit if that person holds any interest in the unit (other than a security interest or an interest under a lease for a fair rental) even if there are no immediate rights to possession and enjoyment under the interest.

(2) Rental at fair rental to other persons for use as principal residence. Notwithstanding paragraph (e)(1) of this section, a taxpayer shall not be treated as using a dwelling unit for personal purposes by reason of a rental arrangement for any day on which the taxpayer rents the dwelling unit at a fair rental to any person for use as that person's principal residence. If a taxpayer actually makes personal use of a unit on any such day, however, that personal use is taken into account because it arises other than "by reason of a rental arrangement." For purposes of the preceding sentence, a brief visit during which the taxpayer is a guest of the occupant of the unit shall not be considered personal use by the taxpayer. For the meaning of the term "principal residence," see section 1034 and § 1.1034-1(c)(3).

(3) Rental to persons having interest in the unit. (i) In general. Paragraph (e)(2) of this section shall apply in the case of a rental of a unit to a person who has an interest in the unit only if the rental is pursuant to a shared equity financing agreement.

(ii) Shared equity financing agreement. A shared equity financing agreement is any written agreement under which—

(A) Two or more persons acquire qualified ownership interests in the dwelling unit, and

(B) A person (or persons) holding one or more of the interests is—

(1) Entitled to occupy the dwelling unit for use as a principal residence, and

(2) Required to pay rent to one or more persons holding a qualified ownership interest in the unit.

(iii) Fair rental. For purposes of paragraph (e)(3) of this section, the determination whether a unit is rented at a fair rental (within the meaning of paragraph (g) of this section) shall be made in light of all the facts and circumstances that existed at the time the agreement was entered into. The totality of rights and obligations of all parties under the agreement is taken into account in determining fair rental.

(iv) Qualified ownership interest. For purposes of this paragraph (e)(3), the term "qualified ownership interest" means an undivided interest for more than 50 years in the entire dwelling unit and appurtenant land being acquired in the transaction to which the shared equity financing agreement relates.

(v) Not necessary that all owners charge fair rental. A shared equity financing arrangement may exist even if one or more of the owners does not charge the occupant fair rental for use of the unit. Paragraph (e)(2) of this section, however, applies only to those owners who do charge fair rental.

(4) Special rule for "qualified rental period." For purposes of determining whether section 280A (c)(5) and § 1.280A-3(d) limit deductions for expenses allocable to a "qualified rental period," a taxpayer shall not be considered to have used the rental unit for personal purposes on any day during the taxable year before or after a "qualified rental period" described in paragraph (e)(4)(i) of this section, or before a "qualified rental period" described in paragraph (e)(4)(ii) of this section, if the rented unit was the principal residence of the taxpayer with respect to that day. The use of the unit for personal purposes shall, however, be taken into account for all other purposes of section 280A. A "qualified rental period" is a consecutive period of—

(i) 12 or more months which begins or ends during the taxable year, or

(ii) less than 12 months which begins in the taxable year and at the end of which the rented unit is sold or exchanged, and for which the unit is rented, or is held for rental, at a fair rental. For the meaning of the term "principal residence," see section 1034 and § 1.1034-1(c)(3).

(5) Dwelling units in which a partnership, a trust, an estate, or an electing small business corporation has an interest. (i) In general. This paragraph (e)(5) sets out special rules for purposes of applying paragraph (e)(1) and (2) of this section to a dwelling unit in which a partnership, a trust, an estate, an electing small business corporation (as defined in section 1371(b), as it read before the enactment of the Subchapter S Revision Act of 1982), or an S corporation (as defined in section 1361(a)) has an interest. For purposes of this paragraph (e)(5), these entities shall be referred to as pass-through entities, and any partner, beneficiary, or shareholder that owns an interest in such an entity shall be referred to as a beneficial owner of the entity.

(ii) Personal use under paragraph (e)(1). For purposes of paragraph (e)(1) of this section, a pass-through entity shall be considered to have made personal use of a dwelling unit on any day on which any beneficial owner of the entity would be considered to have made personal use of the unit. Personal use under the preceding sentence shall be determined as if each beneficial owner had an interest in the unit. Thus, for example, personal use by a sister of a partner is considered personal use by the partnership.

(iii) Personal use under paragraph (e)(2). (A) In general. For purposes of applying the second sentence of paragraph (e)(2) of this section to a dwelling unit in which a pass-through entity has an interest, actual personal use by any beneficial owner of that pass-through entity shall be treated as personal use by the entity. Deemed personal use by a beneficial owner under paragraph (e)(1), for example, by reason of the personal use of the unit by a sister of the beneficial owner, shall not be treated as personal use by the entity.

(B) Exception for certain partnerships. If—

(1) A partnership owns an interest in a dwelling unit,

(2) A partner rents the unit from the partnership at a fair rental for use as the partner's principal residence, and

(3) The items of income, gain, loss, deduction or credit of the partnership related to the unit are allocated among the partners in accordance with their percentage ownership interest in the partnership, use of the unit by that partner as that partner's principal residence shall not be treated as personal use of the unit by the partnership for purposes of paragraph (e)(2). The partner actually making use of the unit, however, is subject to the limitations of section 280A (c)(5) with respect to items related to the unit that are allocated to that partner.

(C) Example. The provisions of paragraph (e)(5)(iii)(B) of this section may be illustrated by the following example.

Example. A, B, and C form partnership P, in which each holds a one-third interest. P acquires a dwelling unit that C rents from P at fair rental for use as C's principal residence. All items of income, gain, loss, deduction, or credit of P that are related to the unit are allocated one-third to each partner. Under these circumstances, the personal use of the unit by C is not treated as personal use by P. Consequently, the use of the unit by C does not subject A and B to the limitations of section 280A(c)(5) with respect to their shares of the items related to the unit. C, however, is subject to the limitations of section 280A (c) (5) with respect to C's share of those items.

(6) Use of the unit for repairs and maintenance. Notwithstanding the provisions of paragraph (e)(1) of this section, a dwelling unit shall not be deemed to have been used by the taxpayer for personal purposes on any day on which the principal purpose of the use of the unit is to perform repair or maintenance work on the unit. Whether the principal purpose of the use of the unit is to perform repair or maintenance work shall be determined in light of all the facts and circumstances including, but not limited to, the following: The amount of time devoted to repair and maintenance work, the frequency of the use for repair and maintenance purposes during a taxable year, and the presence and activities of companions. In no case, however, shall a day on which the taxpayer enganges in repair and maintenance of the unit on a substantially full-time basis be considered a day of personal use by the taxpayer.

(7) Examples. The provisions of this paragraph (e) may be illustrated by the following examples:

Example (1). B owns a vacation home which B rents to S, B's sister, at fair rental for 10 days. B also rents the home to C at fair rental for 11 days as a part of an arrangement whereby B is entitled to use D's home for 6 days. As a favor, B rents the home to F at a discount rate for 15 days. On the basis of the rental activity described, B is deemed to have used the home for personal purposes for 36 days.

Example (2). X Inc., an electing small business corporation in which A and B are shareholders, is the owner of a fully equipped recreational vehicle. During the month of July, the vehicle is used by three individuals. A uses the vehicle on a 7-day camping trip. D, who is B's daughter, rents the vehicle from X Inc. at fair rental for 10 days. E rents the vehicle at fair rental for 12 days under an arrangement whereby B is entitled to use an apartment owned by F, a friend of E, for 9 days. X Inc. is deemed to have used the dwelling unit for personal purposes on any day on which any of its shareholders would be deemed to have so used the unit. Therefore, X Inc. is deemed to have used the recreational vehicle for personal purposes on 29 days.

Example (3). A owns a lakeside cottage which A rents during the summer. A and B, A's spouse, arrive late Thursday evening after a long drive to prepare the cottage for the rental season. A and B prepare dinner but do no work on the unit that evening. A spends a normal work day working on the unit on Friday and Saturday; B helps for a few hours each day but spends most of the time relaxing. By Saturday evening, the necessary maintenance work is complete. Neither A nor B works on the unit on Sunday; they depart shortly before noon. The principal purpose of the use of the unit from Thursday evening through Sunday morning is to perform maintenance work on the unit. Consequently, the use during this period will not be considered personal use by A.

Example (4). C owns a mountain cabin which C rents for most of the year. C spends a week at the cabin with family members. C works on maintenance of the cabin 3 or 4 hours each day during the week. C spends the rest of the time fishing, hiking, and relaxing. C's family members, however, work substantially fulltime on the cabin on each day during the week. The principal purpose of the use of the cabin is to perform maintenance work. Therefore, the use during this period will not be considered personal use by C.

Example (5). B, an individual whose taxable year is the calendar year, uses a dwelling unit as a principal residence from January 1, 1978, to June 30, 1978. On July 1, 1978, B rents the unit at a fair rental to D, an unrelated individual, for a two-year period beginning immediately. In determining whether section 280A(c)(5) and § 1.280A-3(d) limit deductions for expenses allocable to this "qualified rental period," B is not considered to have used the unit for personal purposes from January 1, 1978, to June 30, 1978. Note, however, that section 280A(e) and § 1.280A-3(c) limit the portion of the total 1978 expenses with respect to the unit which may be attributed to the "qualified rental period." B's personal use of the unit is similarly taken into account in applying section 280A(c)(5) to any other use of the unit during the taxable year, e.g., the use of a portion of the unit as a place of business.

(f) "Day" defined. For purposes of section 280A, this section, and § 1.280A-3, the term "day" means generally the 24-hour period for which a day's rental would be paid. Thus, a person using a dwelling unit from Saturday afternoon through the following Saturday morning would generally be treated as having used the unit for 7 days even though the person was on the premises on 8 calendar days.

(g) Fair rental in the case of co-owners. *(1) In general.* For purposes of sections 280A, this section, and § 1.280A-3, a co-owner of a dwelling unit shall be treated as renting the unit at a fair rental if the co-owner charges an amount that is equal to the fair rental of the entire unit multiplied by that co-owner's fractional interest in the unit.

(2) Example. The provisions of this paragraph may be illustrated by the following example:

Example. B and C own undivided one-half interest in a dwelling unit, fair rental for which would be $100x per month. D rents the unit from B and C for a month. B charges D $50x for the month's rental, but C charges D only $20x. B is treated as renting the unit at a fair rental for that month because B charges D $50x, which is equal to the fair rental of the entire unit ($100x), multiplied by B's one-half interest in the unit.

(h) Coordination with section 162(a)(2). Nothing in section 280A or this section shall be construed to disallow any deduction allowable under section 162(a)(2) (or any deduction which meets the tests of section 162(a)(2) but is allowable under another provision of the Internal Revenue Code) by reason of the taxpayer's being away from home in pursuit of a trade or business (other than the trade or business of renting dwelling units).

* * * * *

Proposed § 1.280A-1 Limitations on deductions with respect to a dwelling unit which is used by the taxpayer during the taxable year as a residence. [*For Preamble, see ¶ 150,615*]

Caution: The Treasury has not yet amended Reg § 1.280A-1 to reflect changes made by P.L. 100-647, P.L. 99-514.

(a) General rule. In the case of an individual, a partnership, a trust an estate, or an electing small business corporation (as defined in section 1371(b)), no deductions which would otherwise be allowable under chapter 1 of the Code shall be allowed with respect to the use of a dwelling unit used by such person during the taxable year as a residence except as provided in section 280A and in §§ 1.280A-1 through 1.280A-3. The requirements imposed by section 280A are in addition to the requirements imposed by other provisions of the Code. If a deduction is claimed for an item attributable to a dwelling unit used by the taxpayer during the taxable year as a residence, the taxpayer must first establish that it is otherwise allowable as a deduction under chapter 1 of the Code before the provisions of section 280A become applicable. Section 1.280A-2 sets forth the rules relating to the deductibility of expenses attributable to the rental of a dwelling unit used as a residence. Note that the allocation rule of section 280A(e) and § 1.280A-3(c) applies to expenses attributable to any dwelling unit used by the taxpayer for personal purposes on any day during the taxable year, whether or not the taxpayer is treated as using the unit as a residence.

(b) Deductions allowable without regard to any connection with a trade or business or an income-producing activity. Deductions which are allowable without regard to any connection with a trade or business or an income-producing activity are allowed with respect to the use of dwelling units. Such deductions include the deduction for interest under section 163, the deduction for taxes under section 164, and the deduction for casualty losses under section 165.

(c) Dwelling unit. *(1) In general.* For purposes of this section and §§ 1.280A-2 and 1.280A-3, the term "dwelling unit" includes a house, apartment, condominium, mobile home, boat, or similar property, which provides basic living accommodations such as sleeping space, toilet, and cooking facilities. All structures and other property appurtenant to a dwelling unit which do not themselves constitute dwelling units are considered part of the unit. For example, an individual who rents to another person space in a garage which is appurtenant to a house which the individual owns and occupies may claim deductions with respect to that rental activity only to the extent allowed under section 280A, paragraph (b) of this section, and § 1.280A-3.

(2) Exception. Notwithstanding the provisions of paragraph (c)(1) of this section the term "dwelling unit" does not include any portion of a unit which is used exclusively as a hotel, motel, inn, or similar establishment. Property is so used only if it is regularly available for occupancy by paying customers and only if no person having an interest in the property is deemed under the rules of this section to have used the unit as a residence during the taxable year. For example, this exception will apply to a unit entered in a rental pool (see § 1.280A-3(e)) only if the owner of the unit does not use it as a residence during the taxable year.

(d) Use as residence. *(1) In general.* For purposes of this section and §§ 1.280A-2 and 1.280A-3, a taxpayer uses a dwelling unit during the taxable year as a residence if the taxpayer uses the unit for personal purposes for a number of days which exceeds the greater of—

(i) 14 days, or

(ii) 10 percent of the number of days during the year for which the unit is rented at a fair rental. For purposes of this determination, a unit shall not be treated as rented at fair rental for any calendar day on which it is used for personal purposes.

(2) Examples. The provisions of this paragraph (e) may be illustrated by the following examples:

Example (1). B owns a boat suitable for overnight use. B is deemed, under paragraph (d) of this section, to have used the boat for personal purposes for 16 days during B's taxable year. B rents the boat at fair rental for 163 days during B's taxable year. B is not deemed to have used the boat for personal purposes on any of the 163 days for which it is rented at fair rental. Since the number of days on which B used the boat for personal purposes does not exceed 16.3 (10 percent of 163, the number of days on which the boat is treated as rented at a fair rental for purposes of this determination), B has not used the boat as a residence for the taxable year.

Example (2). Assume the same facts as in example (1) of this subparagraph, except that 5 of the 16 days on which B is deemed to have used the boat for personal purposes were included in the 163 days on which the boat was rented at fair rental. On those 5 days the boat is not treated as rented at a fair rental for purposes of this paragraph. Since the number of days on which B used the boat for personal purposes exceeds 15.8 (10 percent of 158, the number of days on which the boat is treated as rented at a fair rental for purposes of this determination), B has used the boat as a residence for the taxable year.

(e) Personal use of dwelling unit. *(1) General rule.* For purposes of this section and §§ 1.280A-2 and 1.280A-3, a taxpayer shall be deemed to have used a dwelling unit for personal purposes for a calendar day if, for any part of such day, any portion of the unit is used—

(i) For personal purposes by the taxpayer or any other person who has an interest in the unit;

(ii) By a brother or sister (whether by the whole or half blood), spouse, ancestor, or lineal descendant of the taxpayer or of any other person who has an interest in the unit;

(iii) By any individual who uses the unit under an arrangement which enables the taxpayer to use some other dwelling unit for any period of time, whether or not a rental is charged for the use of the other unit and regardless of the length of time that the taxpayer uses the other unit; or

(iv) By any individual, other than an employee with respect to whose use section 119 (relating to meals or lodging furnished for the convenience of the employer) applies, unless for such day the dwelling unit is rented for a rental which, under the facts and circumstances, is fair rental.

For purposes of this paragraph, a person is considered to have an interest in a dwelling unit if that person holds any interest in the unit (other than a security interest or an interest under a lease for a fair rental) even if there are no immediate rights to possession and enjoyment under the interest.

(2) Special rule for "qualified rental period". For purposes of determining whether section 280A(c)(5) and § 1.280A-3(d) limit deductions for expenses allocable to a "qualified rental period", a taxpayer shall not be considered to have used the rented unit for personal purposes on any day during the taxable year before or after a "qualified rental period" described in paragraph (e)(2)(ii) of this section, or before a "qualified rental period" described in paragraph (e)(2)(ii) of this section, if the rented unit was the principal residence of the taxpayer with respect to that day. The use of the unit for personal purposes shall, however, be taken into account for all other purposes of section 280A. A "qualified rental period" is a consecutive period of—

(i) 12 or more months which begins or ends during the taxable year, or

(ii) less than 12 months which begins in the taxable year and at the end of which the rented unit is sold or exchanged, and

for which the unit is rented to a person other than a member of the family of the taxpayer, or is held for rental, at a fair rental. For purposes of the preceding sentence, the family of the taxpayer includes the brothers and sisters (whether by the whole or half blood), spouse, ancestors, and lineal descendants of the taxpayers. For the meaning of the term "principal residence", see section 1034 and § 1.1034-1(c)(3).

(3) Dwelling units in which a partnership, a trust, an estate, or an electing small business corporation has an interest. For purposes of applying the provisions of paragraph (e)(1) of this section to a dwelling unit in which a partnership, a trust, an estate, or an electing small business corporation (as defined in section 1371(b)) has an interest, the entity shall be considered to have made personal use of the unit on any calendar day on which any member of the partnership, beneficiary of the trust or estate, or shareholder in the corporation would be considered to have made personal use of the unit if that member, beneficiary, or shareholder had an interest in the dwelling unit.

(4) Use of the unit for repairs and maintenance. For purposes of applying the provisions of paragraph (e)(1) of this section, the use of a dwelling unit by any individual on any calendar day shall be disregarded if on that calendar day that individual is engaged in repair or maintenance work on the unit on a substantially full-time basis. An individual will be deemed to have satisfied this condition on any calendar day on which the individual works on the unit for the lesser of 8 hours or 2/3 of the time that the individual is present on the premises. If all individuals on the premises on a calendar day who are capable of working do work on the unit on a substantially full-time basis, incidental use of the unit on the same day by other individuals incapable of working, e.g., small children, shall be disregarded for purposes of paragraph (e)(1) of this section.

(5) Examples. The provisions of this paragraph (e) may be illustrated by the following examples:

Example (1). B owns a vacation home which B rents to S, B's sister, at a fair rental for 10 days. B also rents the home to C at fair rental for 11 days as a part of an arrangement whereby B is enable to use D's home for 6 days. As a favor, B rents the home to F at a discount rate for 15 days. On the basis of the rental activity described, B is deemed to have used the home for personal purposes on 36 days.

Example (2). X Inc., an electing small business corporation in which A and B are shareholders, is the owner of a fully equipped recreational vehicle. During the month of July, the vehicle is used by three individuals. A uses the vehicle on a 7-day camping trip. D, who is B's daughter, rents the vehicle from A and B at fair rental for 10 days. E rents the vehicle at fair rental for 12 days under an arrangement whereby B is enabled to use an apartment owned by F, a friend of E, for 9 days. X Inc. is deemed to have used the dwelling unit for personal purposes on any day on which any of its shareholders would be deemed to have so used the unit if each shareholder had an interest in the unit.

Example (3). A owns a lakeside cottage which A rents during the summer. A arrives at the cottage alone at 8 p.m. on a Thursday to prepare it for the summer season. A works on the cottage for 3 hours that evening and for 10 hours on Friday. B, A's spouse, joins A at the cottage at noon on Saturday. A works on the cottage for 9 hours that day, and B works on the cottage for 4 hours. On Sunday A and B work on the cottage for one hour and then return home. A and B ate their meals in the cottage and slept there during the time that they were present. A will be deemed to have used the cottage for personal purposes on Saturday because B, who made personal use of the cottage on that day, did not work on the cottage on a substantially full-time basis. A also made personal use of the cottage on Sunday on which A worked only briefly. A will not be deemed to have used the cottage for personal purposes on Thursday or Friday because the use by A, the only person making use of the cottage on those days, is disregarded since A was engaged in repair and maintenance work on the unit for more than 2/3 of the time that A was on the premises on Thursday and for more than 8 full hours on Friday.

Example (4). A owns a mountain cabin which A rents for most of the year. A works on maintenance of the cabin on a substantially full-time basis for several days. A's four-year old son, S, accompanies A to the cabin and plays while A works. The personal use of the cabin by S is disregarded since S, who is incapable of working is accompanying A, who is working on a substantially full-time basis. If S were 16 years old and otherwise capable of working, however, A would be deemed to have used the cottage for personal purposes unless S worked on the cabin on a substantially full-time basis.

Example (5). B, an individual whose taxable year is the calendar year, uses a dwelling unit as a principal residence from January 1, 1978, to June 30, 1978. On July 1, 1978, B rents the unit at a fair rental to D, an unrelated individual, for a two-year period beginning immediately. In determining whether section 280A(c)(5) and § 1.280A-3(d) limit deductions for expenses allocable to this "qualified rental period", B is not considered to have used the unit for personal purposes from January 1, 1978, to June 30, 1978. Note, however, that section 280A(e) and § 1.280A-3(c) limit the portion of the total 1978 expenses with respect to the unit which may be attributed to the "qualified rental period." B's personal use of the unit is similarly taken into account in applying section 280A(c)(5) to any other use of the unit during the taxable year, e.g., the use of a portion of the unit as a place of business.

(f) Coordination with section 183. If a dwelling unit is used by the taxpayer during the taxable year as a residence, section 183 (relating to activities not engaged in for profit) shall not apply with respect to the unit for the taxable year. The taxable year shall, however, be taken into account as a taxable year for purposes of determining whether the presumption described in section 183(d) applies.

Example. B owns a cottage which B rents for part of the summer in 1976, 1977, and 1978. B also uses the cottage as a residence in 1976 and 1977, but not in 1978. B's rental income for 1976 exceeds the expenses allocable to the rental activity, but in 1977 the expenses exceed the rental income. In determining whether B may claim for 1978 the benefit of the presumption described in section 183(d), the rental activity in 1976 and 1977 is taken into account even though section 183 did not apply with respect to the cottage for those years.

(g) Effective date. This section and §§ 1.280A-2 and 1.280A-3 apply to taxable years beginning after December 31, 1975.

PAR. 2. Section 1.280A-2, as proposed, is amended by revising paragraphs (b), (c), (g)(1) and (i)(2) to read as set forth below.

Proposed § 1.280A-2 Deductibility of expenses attributable to business use of a dwelling unit used as a residence. [*For Preamble, see ¶ 150,873*]

* * * * *

(b) Use as the taxpayer's principal place of business. *(1) In general.* Section 280A(c)(1)(A) provides an exception to the general rule of section 280A(a) for any item to the extent that the item is allocable to a portion of the dwelling unit which is used exclusively and on a regular basis as the principal place of business for any trade or business of the taxpayer.

* * * * *

(c) Use by patients, clients, or customers in meeting or dealing with the taxpayer in the normal course of business. Section 280A(c)(1)(B) provides an exception to the general rule of section 280A for any item to the extent the item is allocable to a portion of the dwelling unit which is used exclusively and on a regular basis as a place of business in which patients, clients, or customers meet or deal with the taxpayer in the normal course of the taxpayer's business. Property is so used only if the patients, clients, or customers are physically present on the premises; conversations with the taxpayer by telephone do not constitute use of the premise by patients, clients or customers. This exception applies only if the use of the dwelling unit by patients, clients, or customers is substantial and integral to the conduct of the taxpayer's business. Occasional meetings are insufficient to make this exception applicable.

* * * * *

(g) Exclusive use requirement. *(1) In general.* Paragraph (b), (c), or (d) of this section may apply to the use of a portion of a dwelling unit for a taxable year only if there is no use of that portion of the unit at any time during the taxable year other than for business purposes. For purposes of section 280A(c)(1) and this section, the phrase "a portion of the dwelling unit" refers to a room or other separately identifiable space; it is not necessary that the portion be marked off by a permanent partition. Paragraph (b), (c), or (d) of this section may apply to a portion of a unit which is used for more than one business purpose. Necessary repair or maintenance does not constitute use for purposes of this paragraph.

* * * * *

(i) Limitation on deductions. * * *

(2) Gross income derived from use of unit. (i) Only income from qualifying business use to be taken into account. For purposes of section 280A and this section, the taxpayer shall take into account, in applying the limitation on deductions, only gross income from a business use described in section 280A(c). For example, a taxpayer who teaches at school may also be engaged in a retail sales business. If the taxpayer uses a home office on a regular basis as the principal place of business for the retail sales business (a use described in section 280A(c)(1)(A)) and makes no non-business use of the office, the taxpayer shall take the gross income from the use of the office for the retail sales business into account in applying the limitation on deductions. Even if the taxpayer also corrects student papers and prepares class presentations in the home office (not a use described in section 280A(c)), no portion of the taxpayer's gross income from teaching may be taken into account in applying the limitation on deductions.

(ii) More than one location. If the taxpayer engages in a business in the dwelling unit and in one or more other locations, the taxpayer shall allocate the gross income from the business to the different locations on a reasonable basis. In making this determination, the taxpayer shall take into account the amount of time that the taxpayer engages in activity related to the business at each location, the capital investment related to the business at each location, and any other facts and circumstances that may be relevant.

(iii) Exclusion of certain amounts. For purposes of section 280A(c)(5)(A) and this section, gross income derived from use of a unit means gross income from the business activity in the unit reduced by expenditures required for the activity but not allocable to use of the unit itself, such as expenditures for supplies and compensation paid to other persons. For example, a physician who uses a portion of a dwelling unit for treating patients shall compute gross income derived from use of the unit by subtracting from the gross income attributable to the business activity in the unit any expenditures for nursing and secretarial services, supplies, etc.

* * * * *

Proposed § 1.280A-2 Deductibility of expenses attributable to business use of a dwelling unit used as a residence. [*For Preamble, see ¶ 150,615*]

Caution: The Treasury has not yet amended Reg § 1.280A-2 to reflect changes made by P.L. 105-34, P.L. 104-188, P.L. 100-647.

(a) Scope. This section describes the business uses of a dwelling unit used as a residence for which items may be deductible under an exception to the general rule of section 280A and explains the general conditions for the deductibility of items attributable to those uses. Deductions are allowable only to the extent provided in section 280A(c)(5) and in paragraph (i) of this section. See § 1.280A-1 for the general rules under section 280A.

(b) Use as the taxpayer's principal place of business. *(1) In general.* Section 280A(c)(1)(A) provides an exception to the general rule of section 280A(a) for any item to the extent the item is allocable to a portion of the dwelling unit which is used exclusively and on a regular basis as the taxpayer's principal place of business.

(2) Determination of principal place of business. For purposes of section 280A(c)(1)(A) and this section, a taxpayer may have only one principal place of business regardless of the number of business activities in which the taxpayer may be engaged. When a taxpayer engages in business activities at more than one location, it is necessary to determine the principal place of the taxpayer's overall business activity in light of all the facts and circumstances. Among the facts and circumstances to be taken into account in determining an individual's principal place of business are the following:

(i) The portion of the total income from business activities which is attributable to activities at each location;

(ii) The amount of time spent in business activities in each location; and

(iii) The facilities available to the taxpayer at each location.

For example, a home office in which a taxpayer engages in business as a self-employed person would rarely qualify as the taxpayer's principal place of business if the taxpayer's primary source of income is wages for services performed in another business on the employer's premises. On the other-hand, if an outside salesperson has no office space except at home and spends a substantial amount of time on paperwork at home, the office in the home may qualify as the salesperson's principal place of business.

(c) Use by patients, clients, or customers in meeting or dealing with the taxpayer in the normal course of business. Section 280A(c)(1)(B) provides an exception to the general rule of section 280A(a) for any item to the extent the item is allocable to a portion of the dwelling unit which is used exclusively and on a regular basis as a place of business in which patients, clients, or customers meet or deal with the taxpayer in the normal course of the taxpayer's business. This exception applies only if the use of the dwelling unit by patients, clients, or customers is substantial and integral to the conduct of the taxpayer's business. Occasional meetings are insufficient to make this exception applicable.

(d) Use of a separate structure not attached to the dwelling unit in connection with the taxpayer's trade or business. Section 280A(c)(1)(C) provides an exception to the general rule of section 280A(a) for any item to the extent that the item is allocable to a separate structure which is appurtenant to, but not attached to, the dwelling unit and is used exclusively and on a regular basis in connection with the taxpayer's trade or business. An artist's studio, a florist's greenhouse, and a carpenter's workshop are examples of structures that may be within the description of this paragraph.

(e) Use as a storage unit for taxpayer's inventory. Section 280A(c)(2) provides an exception to the general rule of section 280A(a) for any item to the extent such item is allocable to space within the dwelling unit which is used on a regular basis as a storage unit for the inventory of the taxpayer held for use in the taxpayer's trade or business of selling products at retail or wholesale. The storage unit includes only the space actually used for storage; thus, if a taxpayer stores inventory in one portion of a basement, the storage unit includes only that portion even if the taxpayer makes no use of the rest of the basement. The exception provided under section 280A(c)(2) applies only if—

(1) The dwelling unit is the sole fixed location of that trade or business, and

(2) The space used is a separately identifiable space suitable for storage.

(f) Use in providing day care services. *(1) In general.* Section 280A(c)(4) provides an exception to the general rule of section 280A(a) for any item to the extent that the item is allocable to the use of any portion of the dwelling unit on a regular basis in the taxpayer's trade or business of providing day care services for children, for individuals who have attained age 65, or for individuals who are physically or mentally incapable of caring for themselves.

(2) Day care services. Day care services are services which are primarily custodial in nature and which, unlike foster care, are provided for only certain hours during the day. Day care services may include educational, developmental, or enrichment activities which are incidental to the primary custodial services. If the services performed in the home are primarily educational or instructional in nature, however, they do not qualify as day care services. The determination whether particular activities are incidental to the primary custodial services generally depends upon all the facts and circumstances of the case. Educational instruction to children of nursery school age shall be considered incidental to the custodial services. Further, educational instruction to children of kindergarten age would ordinarily be considered incidental to the custodial services if the instruction is not in lieu of public instruction under a State compulsory education requirement. In addition, enrichment instruction in arts and crafts to children, handicapped individuals, or the elderly would ordinarily be considered incidental to the custodial services rendered.

(3) State law requirements. This paragraph applies to items accruing after August 31, 1977, only if the owner or operator of the day care business is, at the time the item accrues, acting in accordance with the applicable State law relating to the licensing, certification, registration, or approval of day care centers or family or group day care homes. A person satisfies the condition stated in the preceding sentence for any period for which—

(i) There is no applicable State law of the type described;

(ii) The person is exempt from the requirements of the applicable State law;

(iii) The person has whatever license, etc., is required under the applicable State law; or

(iv) The person has applied for whatever license, etc., is required under the applicable State law, provided, that the application has not been rejected, and provided that the person has corrected or removed any deficiencies that resulted in the revocation of any previous license, etc., or in the rejection of any previous application.

(g) Exclusive use requirement. *(1) In general.* Paragraph (b), (c), or (d) of this section may apply to the use of a portion of a dwelling unit for a taxable year only if there is no use of that portion of the unit at any time during the taxable year other than for business purposes. Paragraph (b), (c), or (d) may apply to a portion of a unit which is used for more than one business purpose. Necessary repair or maintenance does not constitute use for purposes of this paragraph.

(2) Convenience of the employer. In the case of an employee, paragraph (b), (c), or (d) shall apply to a use of a

portion of a dwelling unit only if that use is for the convenience of the employer.

(h) Use on a regular basis. The determination whether a taxpayer has used a portion of a dwelling unit for a particular purpose on a regular basis must be made in light of all the facts and circumstances.

(i) Limitation on deductions. *(1) In general.* The deductions allowable under chapter 1 of the Code for a taxable year with respect to the use of a dwelling unit for one of the purposes described in paragraphs (b) through (f) of this section shall not exceed the gross income derived from such use of the unit during the taxable year, as determined under subparagraph (2) of this paragraph. Subparagraphs (3) and (4) of this paragraph provide rules for determining the expenses allocable to the business use of a unit. Subparagraph (5) of this paragraph prescribes the order in which deductions are allowable.

(2) Gross income derived from use of unit. (i) More than one location. If the taxpayer engages in a business in the dwelling unit and in one or more other locations, the taxpayer shall determine the portion of the gross income from the business that is attributable to business activity in the unit. In making this determination, the taxpayer shall take into account the amount of time that the taxpayer engages in business activity at each location, and any other facts and circumstances that may be relevant.

(ii) Exclusion of certain amounts. For purposes of section 280A and this section, gross income derived from use of a unit means gross income from the business activity in the unit reduced by expenditures required for the activity but not allocable to the use of the unit itself, such as expenditures for supplies and compensation paid to other persons. For example, a physician who uses a portion of a dwelling for treating patients shall compute gross income derived from use of the unit by subtracting from the gross income attributable to the business activity in the unit any expenditures for nursing and secretarial services, supplies, etc.

(3) Expenses allocable to portion of unit. The taxpayer may determine the expenses allocable to the portion of the unit used for business purposes by any method that is reasonable under the circumstances. If the rooms in the dwelling unit are of approximately equal size, the taxpayer may ordinarily allocate the general expenses for the unit according to the number of rooms used for the business purpose. The taxpayer may also allocate general expenses according to the percentage of the total floor space in the unit that is used for the business purpose. Expenses which are attributable only to certain portions of the unit, e.g., repairs to kitchen fixtures, shall be allocated in full to those portions of the unit. Expenses which are not related to the use of the unit for business purposes, e.g., expenditures for lawn care, are not taken into account for purposes of section 280A.

(4) Time allocation for use in providing day care services. If the taxpayer uses a portion of a dwelling unit in providing day care services, as described in paragraph (f) of this section, and the taxpayer makes any use of that portion of the unit for non-business purposes during the taxable year, the taxpayer shall make a further allocation of the amounts determined under subparagraph (3) of this paragraph to be allocable to the portion of the unit used in providing day care services. The amounts allocated to the business use of the unit under this subparagraph shall bear the same proportion to the amounts determined under subparagraph (3) of this paragraph as the length of time that the portion of the unit is used for day care services bears to the length of time that the portion of the unit is available for all purposes. For example, if a portion of the unit is used for day care services for an average of 36 hours each week during the taxable year, the fraction to be used for making the allocation required under this subparagraph is 36/168, the ratio of the number of hours of day care use in a week to the total number of hours in a week.

(5) Order of deductions. Business deductions with respect to the business use of a dwelling unit are allowable in the following order and only to the following extent:

(i) The allocable portions of amounts allowable as deductions for the taxable year under chapter 1 of the Code with respect to the dwelling unit without regard to any use of the unit in trade or business, e.g., mortgage interest and real estate taxes, are allowable as business deductions to the extent of the gross income derived from use of the unit.

(ii) Amounts otherwise allowable as deductions for the taxable year under chapter 1 of the Code by reason of the business use of the dwelling unit (other than those which would result in an adjustment to the basis of property) are allowable to the extent the gross income derived from use of the unit exceeds the deductions allowed or allowable under subdivision (i) of this subparagraph.

(iii) Amounts otherwise allowable as deductions for the taxable year under chapter 1 of the Code by reason of the business use of the dwelling unit which would result in an adjustment to the basis of property are allowable to the extent the gross income derived from use of the unit exceeds the deductions allowed or allowable under subdivisions (i) and (ii) of this subparagraph.

(6) Cross reference. For rules with respect to the deductions to be taken into account in computing adjusted gross income in the case of employees, see section 62 and the regulations prescribed thereunder.

(7) Example. The provisions of this subparagraph may be illustrated by the following example:

Example. A, a self-employed individual, uses an office in the home on a regular basis as a place of business for meeting with clients of A's consulting service. A makes no other use of the office during the taxable year and uses no other premises for the consulting activity. A has a special telephone line for the office and occasionally employs secretarial assistance. A also has a gardener care for the lawn around the home during the year. A determines that 10% of the general expenses for the dwelling unit are allocable to the office. On the basis of the following figures, A determines that the sum of the allowable business deductions for the use of the office is $1,050.

Gross income from consulting services	$1,900
Expense for secretary	500
Business telephone	150
Supplies	200
Total expenditures not allocable to use of unit	850
Gross income derived from use of unit	1,050
Deductions allowable under subparagraph (5)(i) of this paragraph:	
Mortgage interest (total $5,000)	500[1]
Real estate taxes (total $2,000)	200[1]
Amount allowable	700

Limit on further deductions	350
Deductions allowable under subparagraph (5)(ii) of this paragraph:	
Insurance (total $600)	$ 60[1]
Utilities, other than residential telephone (total $900)	90[1]
Lawn care (total $500)	0[1]
Amount allowable	150
Limit on further deductions	200
Deductions allowable under subparagraph (5)(iii) of this paragraph:	
Depreciation (total $3,200)	320[1]
Amount allowable	200

[1] Allocable to office.

No portion of the lawn care expense is allocable to the business use of the dwelling unit. A may claim the remaining $6,300 paid for mortgage interest and real estate taxes as itemized deductions.

PAR. 3. Section 1.280A-3, as proposed, is amended as follows:

1. Paragraph (c)(1) is amended by removing "§ 1.280A-1(e)(4)" and inserting in lieu thereof "§ 1.280A-1(e)(6)" and by removing the word "calendar" wherever it appears.

2. Paragraph (d)(1) is amended by removing "section 280A(d)(3) and § 1.280A-1(e)(2)" and inserting in lieu thereof "section 280A(d)(4) and § 1.280A-1(e)(4)."

3. Paragraph (e)(5) is redesignated as paragraph (e)(6).

4. Paragraph (f)(5) is amended by adding "(determined without regard to the provisions of § 1.280A-1(g)" after the words "fair rental" in the second sentence.

5. Paragraph (e)(4) is revised and paragraph (e)(5) is added to read as set forth below:

Proposed § 1.280A-3 Deductibility of expenses attributable to the rental of a dwelling unit used as a residence. [*For Preamble, see ¶ 150,873*]

* * * * *

(e) Application of the provisions of § 1.280A-1 and this section to rental pools. * * *

(4) Determination of use when averaging is not elected. (i) Applicability. This paragraph (e)(4) applies with respect to a rental pool unit only for periods for which the unit is not subject to paragraph (e)(5) of this section.

(ii) Actual use rule. For purposes of § 1.280A-1(d)(1) and paragraph (c) of this section, the number of days on which the unit is rented at fair rental and the number of days on which the unit is used for any purpose shall be determined by reference to the actual use of the unit. Availability for rental through the rental pool does not constitute rental at a fair rental or use of the unit for any purpose. If the taxpayer's unit is actually rented at a fair rental on any day during the taxpayer's participation in the rental pool, the taxpayer may count that day as a day on which the unit is rented at a fair rental although the taxpayer receives only a portion of the rent paid.

(iii) Furnishing information. The rental agency managing the rental pool shall furnish the taxpayer within 60 days after the end of the pool season a written statement indicating the number of days the taxpayer's unit was actually rented at fair rental and the number of days the unit was used for any other purpose (other than repair and maintenance) during the pool season.

(5) Election to average rental use. (i) Applicability. This paragraph (e)(5) applies to a taxpayer with respect to participation in a rental pool season only if—

(A) The taxpayer signs and furnishes to the pool management a document stating that the taxpayer irrevocably consents to the application of this paragraph (e)(5) for that pool season, and

(B) the pool management sends to the taxpayer a written notice stating that there has been unanimous consent by all pool participants to the application of this paragraph (e)(5) for the pool season and providing the taxpayer with the information necessary to enable the taxpayer to comply with the rules of this paragraph (e)(5).

It is not necessary that the taxpayer furnish a separate consent for each pool season; a consent may provide that it applies to more than one pool season. If the Commissioner determines that there has not been unanimous consent to the application of this paragraph (e)(5) or that the pool management has failed to provide the required notice to pool participants, the Commissioner may require all pool participants to determine the use of their units under paragraph (e)(4) of this section.

(ii) General rules. All taxpayers with interests in units participating in a rental pool during a pool season with respect to which this paragraph (e)(5) applies shall determine the number of days that the unit is rented at fair rental during its participation in a rental pool in that pool season under paragraph (e)(5)(iii) of this section. All use of the unit on days other than participation days and all use of the unit on participation days other than use at fair rental shall be determined by reference to actual use of the unit. These determinations are for purposes of applying § 1.280-1(d)(1) and paragraph (c) of this section.

(iii) Averaging formula. The aggregate number of days that units in the rental pool were rented at fair rental during the pool season shall be apportioned among the units in the pool according to the following ratio:

$$\frac{\text{number of participation days of a particular unit}}{\text{aggregate number of participation days of all units}}$$

Thus, if the aggregate number of days of rental at fair rental for all units in a pool were 300, the number of participation days of a particular unit were 80, and the aggregate number of participation days of all units in the pool were 480, the number of days of rental at fair rental to be allocated to the particular unit would be 50, computed as follows:

$$\frac{80}{480} \times 300 = 50$$

(iv) When pool season overlaps 2 taxable years. If a pool season with respect to which this paragraph (e)(5) applies overlaps 2 taxable years of a person with an interest in a unit participating in the rental pool during that pool season, that person shall apportion the number of days of fair rental allocated to that unit for that season under paragraph (e)(5)(iii) of this section between the taxable years according to the following ratio:

$$\frac{\text{number of participation days of the unit during the pool season that fall in the taxable year}}{\text{number of participation days of the unit during the pool season}}$$

(v) "Participation day" defined. A "participation day" of a unit is a day for which that unit is entered in the rental pool.

* * * * *

Proposed § 1.280A-3 Deductibility of expenses attributable to the rental of a dwelling unit used as a residence. [*For Preamble, see ¶ 150,615*]

Caution: The Treasury has not yet amended Reg § 1.280A-3 to reflect changes made by P.L. 100-647, P.L. 99-514.

(a) Scope. This section provides rules for determining the deductibility of expenses attributable to the rental of a dwelling unit used as a residence. Note that paragraph (c) of this section applies to any dwelling unit used by the taxpayer for personal purposes on any day during the taxable year, whether or not the taxpayer is treated as using the unit as a residence. See § 1.280A-1 for the general rules under section 280A.

(b) Short rental period. If a dwelling unit used by the taxpayer as a residence during the taxable year is actually rented for less than 15 days during the taxable year,

(1) No deduction otherwise allowable because of the rental use shall be allowed, and

(2) The rental income shall not be included in gross income.

(c) Allocation. *(1) In general.* If a taxpayer uses a dwelling unit for personal purposes on any day during the taxable year, the amount deductible by reason of the rental use of the unit during the taxable year shall not exceed an amount which bears the same relationship to the total expenses paid or incurred with respect to the unit during the taxable year as the number of calendar days on which the unit is rented at fair rental during the year bears to the total number of calendar days that the unit is used for any purpose during the taxable year. For purposes of section 280A(e) and this section, the fact that a unit is deemed to be used for personal purposes on a particular day does not prevent that day from being counted as a day on which the unit is rented at fair rental. Use of a unit for repair and maintenance which is disregarded under § 1.280A-1(e)(4) shall be disregarded for purposes of this paragraph.

(2) Portion of unit rented. If the taxpayer rents only a portion of the dwelling unit, the rule prescribed in subparagraph (1) of this paragraph shall be applied to the expenses attributable to that portion of the unit, and the days to be taken into account shall be the days on which that portion of the unit is rented at fair rental during the taxable year and the days on which that portion of the unit is used for any purpose during the taxable year. The expenses attributable to any portion of a unit shall be determined in accordance with the rules prescribed in § 1.280A-2(i)(3).

(3) Deductions allowable without regard to rental use. This paragraph shall not disallow any part of those deductions with respect to a dwelling unit which are allowable without regard to the rental use of the unit.

(4) Example. The provisions of this paragraph may be illustrated by the following example:

Example. A, an individual, owns a cottage which A rents to vacationers at fair rental for 120 days during the taxable year. A is deemed to have made personal use of the cottage on 15 of those 120 days. The unit is used for one or more purposes (other than repair or maintenance) on 160 days during the taxable year. The amount that A may claim as rental expenses may not exceed 120/160 of the total expenses paid or incurred with respect to the unit during the taxable year. If A itemizes deductions, A may claim the remaining 40/160 of items, such as mortgage interest and taxes, which are deductible without regard to the rental use of the unit.

(d) Limitation on deductions if taxpayer has used dwelling unit as a residence. *(1) In general.* The deductions allowable under chapter 1 of the Code for a taxable year with respect to the rental use of a dwelling unit which the taxpayer is treated as having used as a residence during such year shall not exceed the gross rental income from the unit for such year. See section 280A(d)(3) and § 1.280A-1(e)(2) for special rules affecting the determination whether the taxpayer has used a unit as a residence if any day during the taxable year is part of a "qualified rental period."

(2) Gross rental income. For purposes of section 280A and this section gross rental income from a unit equals the gross receipts from rental of the unit reduced by expenditures to obtain tenants for the unit, such as realtor's fees and advertising expense. The gross rental income from a unit for a taxable year includes rental income for periods during which the unit is rented at less than a fair rental as well as rental income for periods during which the unit is rented at fair rental.

(3) Order of deductions. Deductions with respect to the rental use of a dwelling unit are allowable in the following order and only to the following extent:

(i) The allocable portions of amounts otherwise allowable as deductions for the taxable year under chapter 1 of the Code with respect to the dwelling unit without regard to the rental use of the unit, e.g., mortgage interest and real estate taxes, are deductible as rental expenses to the extent of the gross rental income from the unit.

(ii) The allocable portions of amounts otherwise allowable as deductions for the taxable year under chapter 1 of the Code by reason of the rental use of the dwelling unit (other than those which would result in an adjustment to the basis of property) are allowable to the extent the gross rental income exceeds the deductions allowed or allowable under subdivision (i) of this subparagraph.

(iii) The allocable portions of amounts otherwise allowable as deductions for the taxable year under chapter 1 of the Code by reason of the rental use of the dwelling unit which would result in an adjustment to the basis of property are allowable to the extent the gross rental income exceeds the deductions allowed or allowable under subdivisions (i) and (ii) of this subparagraph.

For purposes of this subparagraph, the portion of any item which is allocable to the rental use of a unit during a taxable year shall be that amount which bears the same relationship to the total amount of the item as the number of days on which the unit is rented at a fair rental during the taxable year bears to the number of days on which the unit is used for any purpose (other than repair or maintenance) during the taxable year.

(4) Example. The provisions of this paragraph may be illustrated by the following example:

Example. B owns a lakeside home which B rents at a fair rental for 90 days during the taxable year. B uses the home for personal purposes on 20 other days during the taxable year and also rents it to a friend at a discount for 10 days. Thus, the home is used for some purpose (other than repair or maintenance) on 120 days during the taxable year, and the rental allocation fraction may not exceed 90/120. On the basis of the following figures, B determines that the sum of the rental expenses for the home for the taxable year that are deductible under subparagraph (3) of this paragraph is $2,200. The advertising expense and the realtor's fee are also deductible.

Gross receipts from rental:	
90 days at $25 per day	$2,250
10 days at $15 per day	150
Total	2,400
Computation of gross rental income:	
Gross receipts from rental	2,400
Less: Advertising and realtor's fee	200
Gross rental income	2,200

	Total	Allocable to rental
Deductions allowable under subparagraph (3)(i) of this paragraph:		
Mortgage interest	$1,000	$ 750
Real estate taxes	800	600
Amount allowable		1,350
Limit on further deductions		850
Deductions allowable under subparagraph (3)(ii) of this paragraph:		
Insurance	400	300
Utilities	600	450
Amount allowable		750
Limit on further deductions		100
Deductions allowable under subparagraph (3)(iii) of this paragraph:		
Depreciation	1,500	1,125
Amount allowable		100

NOTE. —If B itemizes deductions, B may claim the other $250 in mortgage interest and the other $200 in real estate taxes as itemized deductions.

(e) Application of the provisions of § 1.280A-1 and this section to rental pools. *(1) In general.* In the case of a dwelling unit which is entered in a rental pool, as defined in subparagraph (2) of this paragraph, during the taxable year, the provisions of § 1.280A-1 and this section shall be applied in accordance with this paragraph.

(2) Rental pool. For purposes of this section, the term "rental pool" means any arrangement whereby two or more dwelling units are made available for rental and those persons with interests in the units agree to share at least a substantial part of the rental income from the units without regard to the actual use of the various units. The fact that those persons with interests in a particular unit are entitled to an occupancy fee or other payment for the actual use of the unit does not prevent the arrangement from constituting a rental pool if the percentage of the rental income in which the participants in the arrangement share is substantial.

(3) Gross rental income of participants. Participants in a rental pool shall include in gross rental income all amounts received or accrued by reason of participation in the rental pool (including payments such as occupancy fees) except amounts which are clearly not rental income, e.g., interest earned on deposits held in escrow on behalf of the rental pool participants. Thus, a taxpayer who participates in a rental pool may have gross rental income although the unit in which the taxpayer has an interest is not actually rented during the taxable year.

(4) Determination of use. For purposes of § 1.280A-1(d)(1) and paragraph (c) of this section, the number of days on which the unit is rented at fair rental and the number of days on which the unit is used for any purpose shall be determined by reference to the actual use of the unit. Availability for rental through the rental pool does not constitute rental at a fair rental or use of the unit for any other purpose. If the taxpayer's unit is actually rented at a fair rental on any day during the taxpayer's participation in the rental pool, the taxpayer may count that day as a day on which the unit is rented at a fair rental although the taxpayer receives only a portion of the rental paid.

(5) Reciprocal arrangements. If the rental pool agreement provides that a participant whose unit is rented on a given day may make use of another unit in the pool on that day, a taxpayer who has an interest in a unit so used by another participant shall be deemed to have used the unit for personal purposes on any day on which another participant uses the unit under that provision of the agreement.

(f) Application of the rules of § 1.280A-1 and this section to time sharing arrangement. *(1) In general.* In the case of a dwelling unit which is used during the taxable year under a time sharing arrangement, as defined in subparagraph (2) of this paragraph, the provisions of § 1.280A-1 and this section shall be applied in accordance with this paragraph.

(2) Time sharing arrangement. For purposes of this section, the term "time sharing arrangement" means any arrangement whereby two or more persons with interests in a dwelling unit agree to exercise control over the unit for different periods during the taxable year. For example, an arrangement under which each of twelve persons with interests in a unit is entitled to exercise control over the unit for one month during the taxable year is a time sharing arrangement. Whether all twelve persons have undivided interests in the unit for the entire year or each has the sole interest in the unit for a single month during the year is immaterial.

(3) Use for personal purposes. For purposes of § 1.280A-1(d) and (e), each of the persons with an interest in the unit subject to the time sharing arrangements shall be considered to have a continuing interest in the unit regardless of the terms of the interest under local law.

(4) Short rental period. The provisions of paragraph (b) of this section shall be applied on the basis of the number of days that the unit is actually rented during the entire taxable year.

(5) Allocation rule. The provisions of paragraph (c) of this section shall apply if any person with an interest in the unit is deemed to use the unit for personal purposes on any day during the taxable year. The provisions of paragraph (c) of this section shall be applied on the basis of the taxpayer's expenses for the unit, the number of days during the taxable year that the unit is rented at a fair rental, and the number of days during the taxable year that the unit is used for any purpose.

(6) Limitation on deductions. The provisions of paragraph (d) of this section shall be applied on the basis of the taxpayer's rental income and expenses with respect to the unit.

§ 1.280B-1 Demolition of structures.

Caution: The Treasury has not yet amended Reg § 1.280B-1 to reflect changes made by P.L. 109-135.

(a) In general. Section 280B provides that, in the case of the demolition of any structure, no deduction otherwise allowable under chapter 1 of subtitle A shall be allowed to the owner or lessee of such structure for any amount expended for the demolition or any loss sustained on account of the demolition, and that the expenditure or loss shall be treated as properly chargeable to the capital account with respect to the land on which the demolished structure was located.

(b) Definition of structure. For purposes of section 280B, the term *structure* means a building, as defined in § 1.48-1(e)(1), including the structural components of that building, as defined in § 1.48-1(e)(2).

(c) Effective date. This section is effective for demolitions commencing on or after December 30, 1997.

T.D. 8745, 12/29/97.

§ 1.280C-1 Disallowance of certain deductions for wage or salary expenses.

Caution: The Treasury has not yet amended Reg § 1.280C-1 to reflect changes made by P.L 105-277, P.L. 104-188, P.L. 98-369.

If an employer elects to claim the targeted jobs credit under section 44B (as amended by the Revenue Act of 1978), or elects to claim the new jobs credit under section 44B (as in effect prior to enactment of the Revenue Act of 1978), the employer must reduce its deduction for wage or salary expenses paid or incurred in the year the credit is earned by the amount allowable as credit (determined without regard to the provisions of section 53). In the case in which wages and salaries are capitalized the amount subject to depreciation must be reduced by an amount equal to the amount of the credit (determined without regard to the provisions of section 53) in determining the depreciation deduction. In the case of an employer who uses the full absorption method of inventory costing under § 1.471-11, the portion of the basis of the inventory attributable to the wage or salary expenses giving rise to the credit and paid or incurred in the year the credit is earned must be reduced by the amount of the credit allowable (determined without regard to the provisions of section 53). If the employer is an organization that is under common control (as described in § 1.52-1), it must reduce its deduction for wage or salary expenses by the amount of the credit apportioned to it under § 1.52-1(a) or (b). The deduction for wage and salary expenses must be reduced in the year the credit is earned, even if the employer is unable to use the credit in that year because of the limitations imposed by section 53.

T.D. 7553, 7/20/78, amend T.D. 7921, 11/18/83.

§ 1.280C-3 Disallowance of certain deductions for qualified clinical testing expenses when section 28 credit is allowable.

(a) In general. If a taxpayer is entitled to a credit under section 28 for qualified clinical testing expenses (as defined in section 28(b)), it must reduce the amount of any deduction for qualified clinical testing expenses paid or incurred in the year the credit is earned by the amount allowable as credit for such expenses (determined without regard to section 28(d)(2)).

(b) Capitalization of qualified clinical testing expenses. In a case in which qualified clinical testing expenses are capitalized, the amount chargeable to the capital account for a taxable year must be reduced by the excess of the amount of the credit allowable for the taxable year under section 28 (determined without regard to section 28(d)(2)) over the amount allowable as a deduction for qualified clinical testing expenses (determined without regard to paragraph (a) of this section) for the taxable year. See section 174 and the regulations thereunder.

(c) Controlled group of corporations; organizations under common control. In the case of a taxpayer described in paragraph (d)(5) of § 1.28-1 of this chapter (relating to controlled groups of corporations and organizations under common control), paragraphs (a) and (b) of this section shall be applied in accordance with the rules prescribed for aggregation of expenditures under that paragraph.

(d) Example. The following example illustrates the application of paragraphs (a) and (b) of this section:

Example. A incurs $1,000 in clinical testing expenses for which a $500 credit is allowable under section 28. A also elects under section 174 of the Code to amortize these expenses over a 5-year period beginning in the year the credit is claimed. Under paragraph (a), the current year amortization deduction of $200 ($1,000 ÷ 5) is disallowed. Moreover, the amount which would otherwise be capitalized, $800, is reduced by the excess of the amount of the section 28 credit claimed for the taxable year over the amount of the allowable section 174 amortization deduction for the taxable year, or $300 ($500 – $200). Thus, the amount chargeable to the capital account for the taxable year is $500 ($800 – $300). A is entitled to amortize $500 over the remaining amortization period resulting in a deduction of $125 for each of the remaining four years.

T.D. 8232, 9/30/88.

§ 1.280C-4 Credit for increasing research activities.

(a) In general. The election under section 280C(c)(3) to have the provisions of section 280C(c)(1) and (2) not apply shall be made by claiming the reduced credit under section 41(a) determined by the method provided in section 280C(c)(3)(B) on an original return for the taxable year, filed at any time on or before the due date (including extensions) for filing the income tax return for such year. An election, once made for any taxable year, shall be irrevocable for that taxable year.

(b) Transition rule. *(1) In general.* In the case of a taxable year beginning after December 31, 1988, for which the due date (including extensions) for filing the return is on or before March 4, 1990, the election under section 280C(c)(3) shall be made by claiming the reduced credit under section 41(a) determined by the method provided in section 280C(c)(3)(B) on an original or amended return for such taxable year filed on or before March 3, 1990.

(2) Taxpayers who made an election under former section 41(b). If a taxpayer—

(i) Prior to December 19, 1989, made an election for a taxable year described in paragraph (b)(1) of this section under section 41(h) (as it existed before it was repealed by section 7814(e) of the Revenue Reconciliation Act of 1989) by not claiming any credit allowable under section 41(a), and

(ii) Has not filed an amended return on or before March 3, 1990 claiming the full credit allowable under section 41(a),

the taxpayer will be treated as having made an election under section 280C(c)(3). Therefore, the provisions of section 280C(c)(1) and (2) shall not apply in such taxable year. However, in order to obtain the benefit of the reduced credit under section 41(a) determined by the method provided in section 280C(c)(3)(B), such a taxpayer must claim the reduced credit on an amended return filed before the expiration of the period prescribed in section 6511 for filing a claim for credit or refund of the tax imposed by chapter 1 of the Code.

(c) Effective date. The provisions of this section are effective for taxable years beginning after December 31, 1988.

T.D. 8282, 1/23/90.

§ 1.280F-1T Limitations on investment tax credit and recovery deductions under section 168 for passenger automobiles and certain other listed property; overview of regulations (temporary).

Caution: The Treasury has not yet amended Reg § 1.280F-1T to reflect changes made by P.L. 108-27, P.L. 107-147, P.L. 105-34, P.L. 101-508, P.L. 100-647.

(a) In general. Section 280F(a) limits the amount of investment tax credit determined under section 46(a) and recovery deductions under section 168 for passenger automobiles. Section 280F(b) denies the investment tax credit and requires use of the straight line method of recovery for listed property that is not predominantly used in a qualified business use. In certain circumstances, section 280F(b) requires the recapture of an amount of cost recovery deductions previously claimed by the taxpayer. Section 280F(c) provides that lessees are to be subject to restrictions substantially equivalent to those imposed on owners of such property under section 280F(a) and (b). Section 280F(d) provides definitions and special rules; note that section 280F(d)(2) and (3) apply with respect to all listed property, even if the other provisions of section 280F do not affect the treatment of the property.

(b) Key to Code provisions. The following table identifies the provisions of section 280F under which regulations are provided, and lists each provision below with its corresponding regulation section:

Section 1.280F-2T	Section 1.280F-3T	Section 1.280F-4T	Section 1.280F-5T and 1.280F-7	Section 1.280F-6
(a)	(b)	(d)(2)	(c)	(d)(3)
(d)(1)	(d)(1)			(d)(4)
(d)(8)				(d)(5)
(d)(10)				(d)(6)

Sections 1.280F-2T(f) and 1.280F-4T(b) also provide special rules for improvements to passenger automobiles and other listed property that qualify as capital expenditures.

(c) Effective dates. *(1) In general.* This section and §§ 1.280F-2T through 1.280F-6 apply to property placed in service or leased after June 18, 1984, in taxable years ending after that date. Section 1.280F-7 applies to property leased after December 31, 1986, in taxable years ending after that date.

(2) Exception. This section and §§ 1.280F-2T through 1.280F-6 shall not apply to any property—

(i) Acquired pursuant to a binding contract in effect on June 18, 1984, and at all times thereafter, or under construction by the taxpayer on that date, but only if the property is placed in service before January 1, 1985 (January 1, 1987, in the case of 15-year real property), or

(ii) Leased pursuant to a binding contract in effect on June 18, 1984, and at all times thereafter, but only if the lessee first uses such property under the lease before January 1, 1985 (January 1, 1987, in the case of 15-year real property).

(3) Leased passenger automobiles. Section 1.280F-5T(e) generally applies to passenger automobiles leased after April 2, 1985, and before January 1, 1987, in taxable years ending after April 2, 1985. Section 1.280F-5T(e) does not apply to any passenger automobile that is leased pursuant to a binding contract, which is entered into no later than April 2, 1985, and which is in effect at all times thereafter, but only if the automobile is used under the lease before August 1, 1985. If § 1.280F-5T(e) does not apply to a passenger automobile, *see* paragraph (c)(1) and (2) of this section. Section 1.280F-7(a) applies to passenger automobiles leased after December 31, 1986, in taxable years ending after that date.

T.D. 7986, 10/19/84, amend T.D. 8061, 11/1/85, T.D. 8218, 8/5/88, T.D. 8473, 4/9/93, T.D. 9133, 6/24/2004.

§ 1.280F-2T Limitations on recovery deductions and the investment tax credit for certain passenger automobiles (temporary).

Caution: The Treasury has not yet amended Reg § 1.280F-2T to reflect changes made by P.L. 108-27, P.L. 107-147, P.L. 105-206, P.L. 105-34, P.L. 101-508, P.L. 100-647, P.L. 99-514, P.L. 99-44.

(a) Limitation on amount of investment tax credit. *(1) General rule.* The amount of the investment tax credit determined under section 46(a) for any passenger automobile shall not exceed $1,000. For a passenger automobile placed in service after December 31, 1984, the $1,000 amount shall be increased by the automobile price inflation adjustment (as defined in section 280F(d)(7)) for the calendar year in which the automobile is placed in service.

(2) Election of reduced investment tax credit. If the taxpayer elects under section 48(q)(4) to reduce the amount of the investment tax credit in lieu of adjusting the basis of the passenger automobile under section 48(q)(1), the amount of the investment tax credit for any passenger automobile shall not exceed two-thirds of the amount determined under paragraph (a)(1) of this section.

(b) Limitations on allowable recovery deductions. *(1) Recovery deduction for year passenger automobile is placed in service.* For the taxable year that a taxpayer places a passenger automobile in service, the allowable recovery deduction under section 168(a) shall not exceed $4,000. See paragraph (b)(3) of this section for the adjustment to this limitation.

(2) Recovery deduction for remaining taxable years during the recovery period. For any taxable year during the recovery period remaining after the year that the property is placed in service, the allowable recovery deduction under section 168(a) shall not exceed $6,000. See paragraph (b)(3) of this section for the adjustment to this limitation.

(3) Adjustment to limitation by reason of automobile price inflation adjustment. The limitations on the allowable recovery deductions prescribed in paragraph (b)(1) and (2) of this section are increased by the automobile price inflation adjustment (as defined in section 280F(d)(7)) for the calendar year in which the automobile is placed in service.

(4) Coordination with section 179. For purposes of section 280F(a) and this section, any deduction allowable under section 179 (relating to the election to expense certain depreciable trade or business assets) is treated as if that deduction were a recovery deduction under section 168. Thus, the amount of the section 179 deduction is subject to the limitations described in paragraph (b)(1) and (2) of this section.

(c) Disallowed recovery deductions allowed for years subsequent to the recovery period. *(1) In general.* (i) Except as otherwise provided in this paragraph (c), the "unrecovered basis" (as defined in paragraph (c)(1)(ii) of this section) of any passenger automobile is treated as a deductible expense in the first taxable year succeeding the end of the recovery period.

(ii) The term "unrecovered basis" means the excess (if any) of—

(A) The unadjusted basis (as defined in section 168(d)(1)(A), except that there is no reduction by reason of an election to expense a portion of the basis under section 179) of the passenger automobile, over

(B) The amount of the recovery deductions (including any section 179 deduction elected by the taxpayer) which would have been allowable for taxable years in the recovery period (determined after the application of section 280F (a) and paragraph (b) of this section and as if all use during the recovery period were used described in section 168(c)(1)).

(2) Special rule when taxpayer elects to use the section 168(b)(3) optional recovery percentages. If the taxpayer elects to use the optional recovery percentages under section 168(b)(3) or must use the straight line method over the earnings and profits life (as defined and described in § 1.280F-3T(f), the second succeeding taxable year after the end of the recovery period is treated as the first succeeding taxable year after the end of the recovery period for purposes of this paragraph (c) because of the half-year convention. For example, assume a calendar-year taxpayer places in service on July 1, 1984, a passenger automobile (i.e., 3-year recovery property) and elects under section 168(b)(3) to recover its cost over 5 years using the straight line optional percentages. Based on these facts, calendar year 1990 is treated as the first succeeding taxable year after the end of the recovery period.

(3) Deduction limited to $6,000 for any taxable year. The amount that may be treated as a deductible expense under this paragraph (c) in the first taxable year succeeding the recovery period shall not exceed $6,000. Any excess shall be treated as an expense for the succeeding taxable years. However, in no event may any deduction in a succeeding taxable year exceed $6,000. The limitation on amounts deductible as an expense under this paragraph (c) with respect to any passenger automobile is increased by the automobile price inflation adjustment (as defined in section 280F(d)(7)) for the calendar year in which such automobile is placed in service.

(4) Deduction treated as a section 168 recovery deduction. Any amount allowable as an expense in a taxable year after the recovery period by reason of this paragraph (c) shall be treated as a recovery deduction allowable under section 168. However, a deduction is allowable by reason of this paragraph (c) with respect to any passenger automobile for a taxable year only to the extent that a deduction under section 168 would be allowable with respect to the automobile for that year. For example, no recovery deduction is allowable for a year during which a passenger automobile is disposed of or is used exclusively for personal purposes.

(d) Additional reduction in limitations by reason of personal use of passenger automobile or by reason of a short taxable year. See paragraph (i) of this section for rules regarding the additional reduction in the limitations prescribed by paragraphs (a) through (c) of this section by reason of the personal use of a passenger automobile or by reason of a short taxable year.

(e) Examples. The provisions of paragraphs (a) through (c) of this section may be illustrated by the following examples. For purposes of these examples, assume that all taxpayers use the calendar year and that no short taxable years are involved.

Example (1). (i) On July 1, 1984, B purchases for $45,000 and places in service a passenger automobile which is 3-year recovery property under section 168. In 1984, B does not elect under section 179 to expense a portion of the cost of the automobile. The automobile is used exclusively in B's business during taxable years 1984 through 1990.

(ii) The maximum amount of B's investment tax credit is $1,000 (i.e., the lesser of $1,000 or .06 × $45,000). B's unadjusted basis for purposes of section 168 is $44,500 (i.e., $45,000 reduced under section 48(q)(1) by $500). B selects the use of the accelerated recovery percentages under section 168(b)(1).

(iii) The maximum amount of B's recovery deduction for 1984 is $4,000 (i.e., the lesser of $4,000 or .25 × $44,500); for 1985, $6,000 (i.e., the lesser of $6,000 or .38 × $44,500); and for 1986, $6,000 (i.e., the lesser of $6,000 or .37 × $44,500).

(iv) At the beginning of taxable year 1987, B's unrecovered basis in the automobile is $28,500 (i.e., $44,500 − $16,000). Under paragraph (c) of this section, B may expense $6,000 of the unrecovered basis in the automobile in 1987. This expense is treated as a recovery deduction under section 168. For taxable years 1988 through 1990. B may deduct $6,000 of the unrecovered basis per year. At the beginning of 1991, B's unrecovered basis in the automobile is $4,500. During that year, B disposes of the automobile. B is not allowed a deduction for 1991 because no deduction would be allowable under section 168 based on these facts.

Example (2). (i) On July 1, 1984, C purchases for $50,000 and places in service a passenger automobile which is 3-year recovery property under section 168. The automobile is used exclusively in C's business during taxable years 1984 through 1992. In 1984, C does not elect under section 179 to expense a portion of the automobile's cost. C elects under section 48(q)(4) to take a reduced investment tax credit in lieu of the section 48(q)(1) basis adjustment.

(ii) The maximum amount of C's investment tax credit is $665.67 (i.e., the lesser of ⅔ of $1,000 or .04 × $50,000). C's unadjusted basis for purposes of section 168 is $50,000. C elects to use the optional recovery percentages under section 168(b)(3) based on a 5-year recovery period.

(iii) The maximum amount of C's recovery deduction for 1984 is $4,000 (i.e., the lesser of $4,000 or .10 × $50,000); for taxable years 1985 through 1988, $6,000 per year (i.e., the lesser of $6,000 or .20 of $50,000). C's recovery deduction for 1989 is $5,000 (i.e., the lesser of .10 × $50,000 or $6,000).

(iv) At the beginning of taxable year 1990, C's unrecovered basis in the automobile is $17,000. Under paragraph (c) of this section, C may expense $6,000 of the unrecovered basis in the automobile in 1990, this expense is treated as a recovery deduction under section 168. For taxable years 1991 and 1992, C may deduct $6,000, and $5,000, respectively of the unrecovered basis per year.

Example (3). Assume the same facts as in example (2), except that C disposes of the passenger automobile on July 1, 1990. Under paragraph (c) of this section, C is not allowed a deduction for 1990 or for any succeeding taxable year because no deduction would be allowable under section 168 based on these facts.

Example (4). (i) On July 1, 1984, G purchases for $15,000 and places in service a passenger automobile which is 3-year recovery property under section 168. The automobile is used exclusively in G's business during taxable years 1984 through 1987. In 1984, G elects under section 179 to expense $5,000 of the cost of the property.

(ii) The maximum amount of G's investment tax credit is $600 (i.e., the lesser of .06 × $10,000 or $1,000).

(iii) G's unadjusted basis for purposes of section 168 is $9,700 (i.e., $15,000 minus the sum of $5,000 (the amount of the expense elected under section 179) and $300 (one-half of the investment tax credit under section 48(q)(1))). Under paragraph (b)(4) of this section, the allowable deduction under section 179 is treated as a recovery deduction under section 168 for purposes of this section. Thus, the maximum amount of G's section 179 deduction is $4,000 (i.e., the lesser of $4,000 or $5,000 + .25 × $9,700). G is entitled to no further recovery deduction under section 168 for 1984. The amount of G's 1985 and 1986 recovery deductions are $3,666 (i.e., the lesser of .38 × $9,700 or $6,000) and $3,589 (i.e., the lesser of .37 × $9,700 or $6,000), respectively. At the beginning of 1987, G's unrecovered basis in the automobile is $3,425 (i.e., $14,700 – $11,275). Under paragraph (c) of this section, G may expense the remaining $3,425 in 1987.

Example (5). (i) On July 1, 1984, D purchases for $55,000 and places in service a passenger automobile which is 3-year recovery property under section 168. The automobile is used exclusively in D's business during taxable years 1984 through 1993. In 1984, D elects under section 179 to expense $5,000 of the cost of the property.

(ii) The maximum amount of D's investment tax credit is $1,000 (i.e., the lesser of $1,000 or .06 × $50,000).

(iii) D's unadjusted basis for purposes of section 168 is $49,500 (i.e., $55,000 minus the sum of $5,000 (the amount of the expense elected under section 179) and $500 (one-half of the investment tax credit under section 48(q)(1))). Under paragraph (b)(4) of this section, the allowable deduction under section 179 is treated as a recovery deduction under section 168 for purposes of this section. Thus, the maximum amount of D's section 179 deduction is $4,000 (i.e., the lesser of $4,000 or $5,000 + .25 × $40.500). D is entitled to no further recovery deduction under section 168 for 1984. The maximum amount of D's 1985 recovery deduction is $6,000 (i.e., the lesser of $6,000 or .38 × $49,500); and for 1986, $6,000 (i.e., the lesser of $6,000 or .37 of $49,500).

(iv) At the beginning of 1987, D's unrecovered basis is $38,500. D may expense the remaining unrecovered basis at the rate of $6,000 per year through 1992 and $2,500 in 1993.

Example (6). Assume the same facts as in example (5), except that in 1993, D uses the automobile only 60 percent in his business. Under paragraph (c)(4) of this section for 1993, D may expense $1,500 (i.e., .60 × $2,500). D is entitled to no further deductions with respect to the automobile in any later year.

Example (7). (i) On July 1, 1984, F purchases for $44,500 and places in service a passenger automobile which is 3-year recovery property under section 168. The automobile is used exclusively in F's business during taxable years 1984 through 1992. In 1984, F elects under section 179 to expense $5,000 of the cost of the property.

(ii) F elects under section 48(q)(4) to take a reduced investment tax credit in lieu of the section 48(q)(1) basis adjustment. The maximum amount of F's investment tax credit is $666.67 (i.e., the lesser of ⅔ of $1,000 or .04 × $39,500).

(iii) F's unadjusted basis for purposes of section 168 is $39,500 (i.e., $44,500 – $5,000 (the amount of the expense elected under section 179)). F elects to use the optional recovery percentage under section 168(b)(3) based on a 5-year recovery period. Under paragraph (b)(4) of this section, the allowable section 179 deduction is treated as a recovery deduction under section 168 for purposes of this section. Thus, the maximum amount of F's section 179 deduction is $4,000 (i.e., the lesser of $4,000 or $5,000 + .10 × $39,500). F is entitled to no further recovery deduction under section 168 for 1984. The maximum amounts of F's recovery deductions for 1985 through 1988 are $6,000 per year (i.e., the lesser of $6,000 or .20 × $39,500). F's recovery deduction for 1989 (the first taxable year after the 5-year recovery period but the sixth recovery year for purposes of section 168) is $3,950 (i.e., the lesser of .10 × $39.500 or $6,000).

(iv) Under paragraph (c), taxable year 1990 is considered to be the first taxable year succeeding the end of the recovery period. At the beginning of taxable year 1990, F's unrecovered basis in the automobile is $12,550 (i.e., $44,500 – $31,950). Under paragraph (c), F may expense $6,000 of his unrecovered basis in the automobile in 1990 and in 1991. This expense is treated as a recovery deduction under section 168. For taxable year 1992, F may expense the remaining $550 of his unrecovered basis in the automobile.

(f) Treatment of improvements that qualify as capital expenditures. An improvement to a passenger automobile that qualifies as a capital expenditure under section 263 is treated as a new item of recovery property placed in service in the year the improvement is made. However, the limitations in paragraph (b) of this section on the amount of recovery deductions allowable are determined by taking into account as a whole both the improvement and the property of which the improvement is a part. If that improvement also qualifies as an investment in new section 38 property under section 48(b) and § 1.48-2(b)(2), the limitation in paragraph (a)(1) of this section on the amount of the investment tax credit for that improvement is determined by taking into account any investment tax credit previously allowed for the passenger automobile (including any prior improvement considered part of the passenger automobile). Thus, the maximum credit allowable for the automobile (including the improvement) will be $1,000 (or ⅔ of $1,000, in the case of an election to take a reduced credit under section 48(q)(4)) (adjusted under section 280F(d)(7) to reflect the automobile price inflation adjustment for the year the property of which the improvement is a part is placed in service).

(g) Treatment of section 1031 or section 1033 transactions. *(1) Treatment of exchanged passenger automobile.* For a taxable year in which a transaction described in section 1031 or section 1033 occurs, the unadjusted basis of an exchanged or converted passenger automobile shall cease to be taken into account in determining any recovery deductions allowable under section 168 as of the beginning of the taxable year in which the exchange or conversion occurs. Thus, no recovery deduction is allowable for the exchanged or converted automobile in the year of the exchange or conversion.

(2) Treatment of acquired passenger automobile. (i) In general. The acquired automobile is treated as new property placed in service in the year of the exchange (or in the replacement year) and that year is its first recovery year.

(ii) Limitations on recovery deductions. If the exchanged (or converted) automobile was acquired after the effective date of section 280F (as set out in § 1.280F-1(c)), the basis of that automobile as determined under section 1031(d) or section 1033(b) (whichever is applicable) must be reduced for purposes of computing recovery deductions with respect to the acquired automobile (but not for purposes of determining the amount of the investment tax credit and gain or loss on the sale or other disposition of the property) by the excess (if any) of—

(A) The sum of the amounts that would have been allowable as recovery deductions with respect to the exchanged (or converted) automobile during taxable years preceding the year of the exchange (or conversion) if all of the use of the automobile during those years was use described in section 168(c), over

(B) The sum of the amounts allowable as recovery deductions during those years.

(3) Examples. The provisions of this paragraph (g) may be illustrated by the following examples:

Example (1). (i) In 1982, F purchases and places in service a passenger automobile which is 3-year recovery property under section 168. The automobile is used exclusively in F's business.

(ii) On July 1, 1984, F exchanges the passenger automobile and $1,000 cash for a new passenger automobile ("like kind" property). Under paragraph (g)(1) of this section, no recovery deduction is allowed in 1984 for the exchanged automobile. Any investment tax credit claimed with respect to that automobile is subject to recapture under section 47.

(iii) F's basis in the acquired property (as determined under section 1031(d) and F's qualified investment are $20,000. Under the provisions of paragraph (g)(2)(i) of this section, the acquired property is treated as new recovery property placed in service in 1984 to the extent of the full $20,000 of basis. The maximum amount of F's investment tax credit is limited to $1,000 (i.e., the lesser of $1,000 or .06 × $20,000). Cost recovery deductions are computed pursuant to paragraph (b) of this section.

Example (2). (i) On July 1, 1984, E purchases for $30,000 and places in service a passenger automobile which is 3-year recovery property under section 168. In 1984, E's business use percentage is 80 percent and such use constitutes his total business/investment use.

(ii) E elects under section 48(q)(4) to take a reduced investment tax credit in lieu of the section 48(q)(1) basis adjustment. The maximum amount of E's investment tax credit is $533.33 (i.e., the lesser of ⅔ of $1,000 × .80 or .80 × .04 × $30,000).

(iii) E's unadjusted basis for purposes of section 168 is $30,000. E selects the use of the accelerated recovery percentages under section 168(b)(1). The maximum amount of E's recovery deduction for 1984 is $3,200 (i.e., the lesser of .80 × $4,000 or .80 × .25 × $30,000).

(iv) On June 10, 1985, E exchanges the passenger automobile and $1,000 cash for a new passenger automobile ("like kind" property). Under paragraph (g)(1) of this section, no recovery deduction is allowable in 1985 for the exchanged automobile. The investment tax credit claimed is subject to recapture under section 47. Under paragraph (g)(2)(ii) of this section, E's basis in the acquired property for purposes of computing recovery deductions under section 280F is $27,000 (i.e., $27,800 (section 1031(d) basis) − $800). The acquired automobile is used exclusively in F's business during taxable years 1985 through 1988. Under paragraph (g)(2) of this section, the acquired property is treated as new recovery property placed in service in 1985. Assume that the automobile price inflation adjustment (as described under section 280F(d)(7)) is zero. E's qualified investment in the property, as determined under § 1.48-3(c)(1), is $27,800. The maximum amount of E's investment tax credit is $1,000 (i.e., the lesser of $1,000 or .06 × $27,800). E's unadjusted basis for purposes of section 168 is $26,500 (i.e., $27,000 reduced under section 48(q)(1) by $500). Cost recovery deductions are computed pursuant to paragraph (b) of this section.

(h) Other nonrecognition transactions. [Reserved]

(i) Limitation under this section applies before other limitations. *(1) Personal use.* The limitations imposed upon the maximum amount of the allowable investment tax credit and the allowable recovery deductions (as described in paragraphs (a) through (c) of this section) must be adjusted during any taxable year in which a taxpayer makes any use of a passenger automobile other than for business/investment use (as defined in § 1.280F-6(d)(3)). The limitations on the amount of the allowable investment tax credit (as described in paragraph (a) of this section) and the allowable cost recovery deductions (as described in paragraphs (b) and (c) of this section) are redetermined by multiplying the limitations by the percentage of business/investment use (determined on an annual basis) during the taxable year.

(2) Short taxable year. The limitations imposed upon the maximum amount of the allowable recovery deductions (as described in paragraphs (a) through (c) of this section) must be adjusted during any taxable year in which a taxpayer has a short taxable year. In this case, the limitation is adjusted by multiplying the limitation that would have been applied if the taxable year were not a short taxable year by a fraction, the numerator of which is the number of months and part-months in the short taxable year and the denominator of which is 12.

(3) Examples. The provisions of this paragraph (i) may be illustrated by the following examples:

Example (1). On July 1, 1984, A purchases and places in service a passenger automobile and uses it 80 percent for business/investment use during 1984. Under paragraph (i)(1) of this section, the maximum amount of the investment tax credit that A may claim for the automobile is $800 (i.e., .80 × $1,000).

Example (2). Assume the same facts as in example (1), except that A elects under section 48(q)(4) to take a reduced investment tax credit in lieu of the section 48(q)(1) basis adjustment. Under paragraph (i)(1) of this section, the maximum amount of the investment tax credit that A may claim for the automobile is $533.33 (i.e., .80 × ⅔ × $1,000).

Example (3). On July 1, 1984, B purchases and places in service a passenger automobile and uses it 60 percent for business/investment use during 1984. Under paragraph (i)(1) of this section, the maximum amount of the investment tax credit that B may claim for the automobile is $600 (i.e., .60 × $1,000). B uses the car 70 percent for business/investment use during 1985 and 80 percent during 1986. Under paragraph (i)(1) of this section, the maximum amount of recovery deductions that B may claim for 1984, 1985, and 1986 are $2,400 (i.e., .60 × $4,000), $4,200 (i.e., .70 × $6,000), and $4,800 (i.e., .80 × $6,000), respectively.

Example (4). Assume the same facts as in example (3) with the added facts that B's unrecovered basis at the beginning of 1987 is $6,000 and that B uses the automobile 85 percent for business/investment use during 1987. Under paragraph (i)(1) of this section, the maximum amount that B may claim as an expense for 1987 is $5,000 (i.e., .85 × $6,000).

Example (5). On August 1, 1984, C purchases and places in service a passenger automobile and uses it exclusively for business. Taxable year 1984 for C is a short taxable year which consists of 6 months. Under paragraph (i)(2) of this section, the maximum amount that C may claim as a recovery deduction for 1984 is $2,000 (i.e., 6/12 × $4,000).

Example (6). Assume the same facts as in example (5), except that C uses the passenger automobile 70 percent for business/investment use during 1984. Under paragraph (i)(1) and (2) of this section, the maximum amount that C may claim as a recovery deduction for 1984 is $1,400 (i.e., .70 × 8/12 × $4,000).

T.D. 7986, 10/19/84, amend T.D. 9133, 6/24/2004.

§ 1.280F-3T Limitations on recovery deductions and the investment tax credit when the business use percentage of listed property is not greater than 50 percent (temporary).

Caution: The Treasury has not yet amended Reg § 1.280F-3T to reflect changes made by P.L. 108-27, P.L. 107-147, P.L. 101-508, P.L. 100-647, P.L. 99-514, P.L. 99-44.

(a) In general. Section 280F(b), generally, imposes limitations with respect to the amount allowable as an investment tax credit under section 46(a) and the amount allowable as a recovery deduction under section 168 in the case of listed property (as defined in § 1.280F-6(b)) if certain business use of the property (referred to as "qualified business use") does not exceed 50 percent during a taxable year. "Qualified business use" generally means use in a trade or business, rather than use in an investment or other activity conducted for the production of income within the meaning of section 212. See § 1.280F-6(d) for the distinction between "business/investment use" and "qualified business use."

(b) Limitation on the amount of investment tax credit. *(1) Denial of investment tax credit when business use percentage not greater than 50 percent.* Listed property is not treated as section 38 property to any extent unless the business use percentage (as defined in section 280F(d)(6) and § 1.280F-6(d)(1)) is greater than 50 percent. For example, if a taxpayer uses listed property in a trade or business in the taxable year in which it is placed in service, but the business use percentage is not greater than 50 percent, no investment tax credit is allowed for that listed property. If, in the taxable year in which listed property is placed in service, the only business/investment use (as defined in § 1.280F-6(d)(3)) of that property is qualified business use (as defined in § 1.280F-6(d)(2)(i)), and the business use percentage is 55 percent, the investment tax credit is allowed for the 55 percent of the listed property that is treated as section 38 property. The credit allowed is unaffected by any increase in the business use percentage in a subsequent taxable year.

(2) Recapture of investment tax credit. Listed property ceases to be section 38 property to the extent that the business/investment use (as defined in § 1.280F-6(d)(3)) for any taxable year is less than the business/investment use for the taxable year in which the property is placed in service. See § 1.47-2(c). If the business use percentage (as defined in § 1.280F-6(d)(1)) of listed property is greater than 50 percent for the taxable year in which the property is placed in service, and less than or equal to 50 percent for any subsequent taxable year, that property ceases to be section 38 property in its entirety in that subsequent taxable year. Under § 1.47-1(c)(1)(ii)(b), the property (or a portion thereof) is treated as ceasing to be section 38 property on the first day of the taxable year in which the cessation occurs.

(c) Limitation on the method of cost recovery under section 168 when business use of property not greater than 50 percent. *(1) Year of acquisition.* If any listed property (as defined in § 1.280F-6(b)) is not predominantly used in a qualified business use (as defined in § 1.280F-6(d)(4)) in the year it is acquired, the recovery deductions allowed under section 168 for the property for that taxable year and for succeeding taxable years are to be determined using the straight line method over its earnings and profits life (as defined in paragraph (f) of this section). Additionally, the taxpayer is not entitled to make any election under section 179 with respect to the property for that year.

(2) Subsequent years. If any listed property is not subject to paragraph (c)(1) of this section because such property is predominantly used in a qualified business use (as defined in § 1.280F-6(d)(4)) during the year it is acquired but is not predominantly used in a qualified business use during a subsequent taxable year, the rules of this paragraph (c)(2) apply. In such a case, the taxpayer must determine the recovery deductions allowed under section 168 for the taxable year that the listed property is not predominantly used in a qualified business use and for any subsequent taxable year as if such property was not predominantly used in a qualified business use in the year in which it was acquired and there had been no section 179 election with respect to the property. Thus, the recovery deductions allowable under section 168 for the remaining taxable years are computed by determining the applicable recovery percentage that would apply if the taxpayer had used the straight line method over the property's earnings and profits life beginning with the year the property was placed in service.

(3) Effect of rule on recovery property that is not listed property. The mandatory use of the straight line method over the property's earnings and profits life under paragraphs (d)(1) and (2) of this section does not have any effect on the proper method of cost recovery for other recovery property of that same class placed in service in the same taxable year by the taxpayer and does not constitute an election to use an optional recovery period under section 168(b)(3).

(d) Recapture of excess recovery deductions claimed. *(1) In general.* If paragraph (c)(2) of this section is applicable, any excess depreciation (as defined in paragraph (d)(2) of this section) must be included in the taxpayer's gross income and added to the property's adjusted basis for the first taxable year in which the property is not predominantly used in a qualified business use (as defined in § 1.280F-6(d)(4)).

(2) Definition of "excess depreciation". For purposes of this section, the term "excess depreciation" means the excess (if any) of—

(i) The amount of the recovery deductions allowable with respect to the property for taxable years before the first taxable year in which the property was not predominantly used in a qualified business use, over

(ii) The amount of the recovery deductions which would have been allowable for those years if the property had not been predominantly used in a qualified business use for the year it was acquired and there had been no section 179 election with respect to the property.

For purposes of paragraph (d)(2)(i), any deduction allowable under section 179 (relating to the election to expense certain depreciable trade or business assets) is treated as if that deduction was a recovery deduction under section 168.

(3) Recordkeeping requirement. A taxpayer must be able to substantiate the use of any listed property, as prescribed in section 274(d)(4) and § 1.274-5T or § 1.274-6T, for any taxable year for which recapture under section 280F(b)(3) and paragraph (d)(1) and (2) of this section may occur even if the taxpayer has fully depreciated (or expensed) the listed property in a prior year. For example, in the case of 3-year recovery property, the taxpayer shall maintain a log, journal, etc. for six years even though the taxpayer fully depreciated the property in the first three years.

(e) Earnings and profits life. *(1) Definition.* The earnings and profits life with respect to any listed property is generally the following:

In the case of—	The applicable recovery period is—
3-year property	5 years
5-year property	12 years
10-year property	25 years
18-year real property and low-income housing	40 years
15-year public utility property	35 years

However, if the recovery period applicable to any recovery property under section 168 is longer than the above assigned recovery period, such longer recovery period shall be used. For example, generally, the recovery period for recovery property used predominantly outside the United States is the property's present class life (as defined in section 168(g)(2)). In many cases, a property's present class life is longer than the recovery period assigned to the property under the above table. Pursuant to this paragraph (e)(1), the property's recovery period is its present class life.

(2) Applicable recovery percentages. If the applicable recovery period is determined pursuant to the table prescribed in paragraph (e)(1) of this section, the applicable recovery percentage is:

(i) For property other than 18-year real property or low-income housing:

If the recovery year is—	And the recovery period is— 5	12	25	35
1	10	4	2	1
2	20	9	4	3
3	20	9	4	3
4	20	9	4	3
5	10	8	4	3
7		8	4	3
8		8	4	3
9		8	4	3
10		8	4	3
11		8	4	3
12		8	4	3
13		4	4	3
14			4	3
15			4	3
16			4	3
17			4	3
18			4	3
19			4	3
20			4	3
21			4	3
22			4	3
23			4	3
24			4	3
25			4	3
26			2	3
27				3
28				3
29				3
30				3
31				3
32				2
33				2
34				2
35				2
36				1

(ii) For 18-year real property: [Reserved]

(iii) For low-income housing: [Reserved]

(f) Examples. The provisions of this section may be illustrated by the following examples. For purposes of these examples, assume that all taxpayers use the calendar year and that no short taxable years are involved.

Example (1). On July 1, 1984, B purchases for $50,000 and places in service an item of listed property (other than a passenger automobile) which is 3-year recovery property under section 168. For the first taxable year that the property is in service, B used the property 40 percent in a trade or business, 40 percent for the production of income, and 20 percent for personal purposes. Although B's total business/investment use is greater than 50 percent, the business use percentage for that taxable year is only 40 percent. Under paragraph (b)(1) of this section, no investment tax credit is allowed for the property.

Example (2). (i) On January 1, 1985, C purchases for $40,000 and places in service an item of listed property (other than a passenger automobile) that is 3-year recovery property under section 168. Seventy percent of the use of the property is in C's trade or business and 30 percent of the use is for personal purposes. C does not elect a reduced investment tax credit under section 448(q)(4). The amount of C's investment tax credit is $1,680 (i.e., $40,000 × .60 × .10 × .70).

(ii) In addition, in 1986, only 55 percent of the use of the property is in C's trade or business and 45 percent of the use is for personal purposes. Under paragraph (b)(2) of this section, the property ceases to be section 38 property to the extent that the use in a trade or business decreased below 70 percent. As a result, a portion of the investment tax credit must be recaptured as an increase in tax liability for 1986 under the rules of section 47 (relating to the recapture of investment tax credit). See section 47(a)(5) and § 1.47-2(e) for rules relating to the computation of the recapture amount.

Example (3). On July 1, 1984, B purchases and places in service an item of listed property (other than a passenger automobile) that is 3-year recovery property. B elects to take a reduced investment tax credit under section 48(q)(4). In 1984, B uses the property exclusively in his business. Assume that B's 1984 allowable recovery deduction is $12,500. In 1985 and 1986, the property is not predominantly used in a qualified business use. The investment tax credit claimed is subject to recapture in full under section 47 in 1985 since the property ceases to be section 38 property in its entirety on January 1, 1985. Under paragraph (c)(2) of this section, B must treat the property for 1985 and subsequent taxable years as if he recovered its cost over a 5-year recovery period (i.e., its earnings and profits life) using the straight line method (with the half-year convention) from the time it was placed in service. Therefore, taxable year 1985 is treated as the property's second recovery year (of its 5-year recovery period) and the applicable recovery deduction using the straight line method must be used to determine the recovery deduction. Under paragraph (d) of this section, B must recapture any excess depreciation claimed for taxable year 1984. If B had used the straight line method over a 5-year recovery period his recovery deduction for 1984 would have been $5,000. Under paragraph (d)(2) of this section, B's excess depreciation is $7,500 (i.e., $12,500 − $5,000) and that amount must be included in B's 1985 gross income and added to the property's basis. The taxable years 1986 through 1989 are the property's second through sixth recovery years, respectively, of such property's 5-year recovery period.

Example (4). Assume the same facts as in example (3), except that in 1986 B used the property exclusively in his business. B is entitled to no investment tax credit with respect to the property in 1986 and must continue to recover the property's cost over a 5-year recovery period using the straight line method.

Example (5). On July 1, 1984. H purchases and places in service listed property (other than a passenger automobile) which is 3-year recovery property under section 168. H selects the use of the accelerated recovery percentages under section 168. In 1984 through 1986, H uses the property exclusively for business. In 1987, the property is not predominantly used in a qualified business use. Under paragraph (c)(2) of this section, H must compute his 1987 and subsequent taxable year's recovery deductions using the straight line method over a 5-year recovery period with 1987 treated as the fourth recovery year. Under paragraph (d) of this section, H must recapture any excess depreciation claimed for taxable years 1984 through 1986 even though by 1987 the full cost of the property had already been recovered.

Example (6). Assume the same facts as in example (5), except that H uses the property exclusively for personal purposes in 1987. Under paragraph (d) of this section, H must recapture any excess depreciation claimed for taxable years 1984 through 1986. H is entitled to no cost recovery deduction under the 5-year straight line method for 1987. Assume further that in 1988 H uses the property 70 percent in his business. Thus, H's business use percentage for that year is 70 percent. Under paragraph (c)(2) of this section, H must compute his 1988 cost recovery deduction using the straight line method over a 5-year recovery period with 1988 treated as the fifth recovery year.

Example (7). (i) On July 1, 1984, F purchases for $70,000 and places in service listed property (other than a passenger automobile) which is 3-year recovery property under section 168. F's business use percentage for 1984 through 1986 is 60 percent. F elects under section 179 to expense $5,000 of the cost of the property.

(ii) F elects a reduced investment tax credit under section 48(q)(4). The maximum amount of F's investment tax credit is $1,560 (i.e., $65,000 × .04 × .60).

(iii) F's unadjusted basis for purposes of section 168 is $65,000 (i.e., $70,000 reduced by the $5,000 section 179 expense). F selects the use of the accelerated recovery percentages under section 168(b)(1). F's recovery deduction for 1984 is $9,750 (i.e., $65,000 × .25 × .60).

(iv) In 1985, the property is not predominantly used in a qualified business use. The investment tax credit claimed is subject to recapture in full under section 47 in 1985 since the property ceases to be section 38 property in its entirety on January 1, 1985. Under paragraph (c)(2) of this section, F must treat the property for 1985 and subsequent taxable years as if he recovered its cost over a 5-year recovery period (i.e., its earnings and profits life) using the straight line method (with the half year convention) from the time it was placed in service. Under paragraph (d) of this section, F must recapture any excess depreciation claimed for taxable year 1984. F's excess depreciation is $10,550 [i.e., ($65,000 × .25 × .60 + $5,000) − ($70,000 × .10 × .60)). This amount must be included in F's 1985 gross income and added to the property's adjusted basis.

Example (8). (i) On July 1, 1984, G purchases for $60,000 and places in service a passenger automobile which is 3-year recovery property under section 168.

(ii) In 1984, G's business use percentage is 80 percent and such use constitutes his total business/investment use. G elects under section 48(q)(4) to take a reduced investment tax credit in lieu of the basis adjustment under section 48(q)(1). The maximum amount of G's investment tax credit is $533.33 (i.e., the lesser of .80 × 2/3 × $1,000 or $60,000 × .80 × .04).

(iii) In 1984, G does not elect under section 179 to expense a portion of the automobile's cost. G selects the use of the accelerated recovery percentages under section 168. G's unadjusted basis for purposes of section 168 is $60,000. The maximum amount of G's 1984 recovery deduction is $3,200 (i.e., the lesser of .80 × $4,000 or .80 × .25 × $60,000).

(iv) In 1985, G's business use percentage is 80 percent and such use constitutes his total business/investment use. The maximum amount of G's 1985 recovery deduction is $4,800 (i.e., the lesser of .80 × $6,000 or .80 × .38 × $60,000).

(v) In 1986, G's business use percentage is 45 percent and such use constitutes his total business/investment use. Under paragraph (b)(2) of this section, as a result of the decline in the business use percentage to 50 percent or less, the automobile ceases to be section 38 property in its entirety and G must recapture (pursuant to §§ 1.47-1(c) and 1.47-2(e)) the investment tax credit previously claimed. Since G's business use percentage in 1986 is not greater than 50 percent, under the provisions of paragraph (d) of this section, G must recompute (for recapture purposes) his recovery deductions for 1984 and 1985 using the straight line method over a 5-year recovery period (i.e., earnings and profits life for 3-year recovery property using the half-year convention) to determine if any excess depreciation must be included in his 1986 taxable income. G's recomputed recovery deductions for 1984 and 1985 are $3,200 (i.e., the lesser of .80 × $4,000 or .80 × .10 × $60,000), and $4,800 (i.e., the lesser of .80 × $6,000 or .80 × .20 × $60,000), respectively. G does not have to recapture any excess depreciation since his recovery deductions for 1984 and 1985 computed using the straight line method over a 5-year recovery period are the same as the amounts actually claimed during those years.

(vi) Under paragraph (c)(2) of this section, for 1986 and succeeding taxable years G must compute his remaining recovery deductions using the straight line method over a 5-year recovery period beginning with the third recovery year. The maximum amount of G's 1986 recovery deduction is $2,700 (i.e., the lesser of .45 × $6,000 or .45 × .20 × $60,000). For taxable years 1987 through 1993, G's business use percentage is 55 percent and such use constitutes his total business/investment use. G's 1987 and 1988 recovery deductions are $3,300 per year (i.e., the lesser of .55 × $6,000 or .55 × .20 × $60,000). For taxable year 1989 (the last recovery year), G's recovery deduction is $3,300 (i.e., .55 × .10 × $60,000 or .55 × $6,000).

(vii) As of the beginning of 1990, G will have claimed a total of $20,600 of recovery deductions. Under § 1.280F-2T(c), G may expense his remaining unrecovered basis (up to a certain amount per year) in the first succeeding taxable year after the end of the recovery period and in taxable years thereafter. If G had used his automobile for 100 percent business use in taxable years 1984 through 1989, G could have claimed a recovery deduction of $4,000 in 1984 and a recovery deduction of $6,000 in each of those remaining years. At the beginning of 1990, therefore, G's unrecovered basis (as defined in section 280F(d)(8)) is $26,000 (i.e., $60,000 − $34,000). The maximum amount of G's 1990 recovery deduction is $3,300 (i.e., .55 × $6,000). At the beginning of 1991, G's unrecovered basis is $20,000 (i.e., $26,000 adjusted under section 280F(d)(2) and § 1.280F-4T(a) to account for the amount that would have been claimed in 1990 for 100 percent business/investment use during that year). The maximum amount of G's 1991 recovery deduction is $3,300 (i.e., .55 × $6,000), and his unrecovered basis as of the beginning of 1992 is $14,000 (i.e., $20,000 − $6,000). In 1992, G disposes of the automobile. G is not allowed a recovery deduction for 1992.

T.D. 7986, 10/19/84, amend T.D. 8061, 11/1/85, T.D. 9133, 6/24/2004.

§ 1.280F-4T Special rules for listed property (temporary).

Caution: The Treasury has not yet amended Reg § 1.280F-4T to reflect changes made by P.L. 108-27, P.L. 107-147, P.L. 105-34, P.L. 100-647, P.L. 99-514, P.L. 99-44.

(a) Limitations on allowable recovery deductions in subsequent taxable years. *(1) Subsequent taxable years affected by reason of personal use in prior years.* For purposes of computing the amount of the recovery deduction for "listed property" for a subsequent taxable year, the amount that would have been allowable as a recovery deduction during an earlier taxable year if all of the use of the property was use described in section 168(c) is treated as the amount of the recovery deduction allowable during that earlier taxable year. The preceding sentence applies with respect to all earlier taxable years, beginning with the first taxable year in which some or all use of the "listed property" is use described in section 168(c). For example, on July 1, 1984, B purchases and places in service listed property (other than a passenger automobile) which is 5-year recovery property under section 168. B selects the use of the accelerated percentages under section 168. B's business/investment use of the property (all of which is qualified business use as defined in section 280F(d)(6)(B) and § 1.280F-6(d)(2)) in 1984 through 1988 is 80 percent, 70 percent, 60 percent, and 55 percent, respectively, and B claims recovery deductions for those years based on those percentages. B's qualified business use for the property for 1989 and taxable years thereafter increases to 100 percent. Pursuant to this rule, B may not claim a recovery deduction in 1989 (or for any subsequent taxable year) for the increase in business use because there is no adjusted basis remaining to be recovered for cost recovery purposes after 1988.

(2) Special rule for passenger automobiles. In the case of a passenger automobile that is subject to the limitations of § 1.280F-2T. the amount treated as the amount that would have been allowable as a recovery deduction if all of the use of the automobile was use described in section 168(c) shall not exceed $4,000 for the year the passenger automobile is placed in service and $6,000 for each succeeding taxable year (adjusted to account for the automobile price inflation adjustment, if any, under section 280F(d)(7) and for short taxable year under § 1.280F-2T(i)(2)). See. § 1.280F-3T(g). *Example (8).*

(b) Treatment of improvements that qualify as capital expenditures. *(1) In general.* In the case of any improvement that qualifies as a capital expenditure under section 263 made to any listed property other than a passenger automobile, the rules of this paragraph (b) apply. See § 1.280F-2T(f) for the treatment of an improvement made to a passenger automobile.

(2) Investment tax credit allowed for the improvement. If the improvement qualifies as an investment in new section 38 property under section 48(b) and § 1.48-2(b), the investment tax credit for that improvement is limited by paragraph (b)(1) of § 1.280F-3T, as applied to the item of listed property as a whole.

(3) Cost recovery of the improvement. The improvement is treated as a new item of recovery property. The method of cost recovery with respect to that improvement is limited by § 1.280F-3T(c), as applied to the item of listed property as a whole.

T.D. 7986, 10/19/84, amend T.D. 9133, 6/24/2004.

§ 1.280F-5T Leased property (temporary).

Caution: The Treasury has not yet amended Reg § 1.280F-5T to reflect changes made by P.L. 108-27, P.L. 107-147, P.L. 101-508, P.L. 100-647.

(a) In general. Except as otherwise provided in this section, the limitation on cost recovery deductions and the investment tax credit provided in section 280F(a) and (b) and §§ 1.280F-2T and 1.280F-3T do not apply to any listed property leased or held for leasing by any person regularly engaged in the business of leasing listed property. If a person is not regularly engaged in the business of leasing listed property, the limitations on cost recovery deductions and the investment tax credit provided in section 280F and §§ 1.280F-2T and 1.280F-3T apply to such property leased or held for leasing by such person. The special rules for lessees set out in this section apply with respect to all lessees of listed property, even those whose lessors are not regularly engaged in the business of leasing listed property. For rules on determining inclusion amounts with respect to passenger automobiles, see paragraphs (d), (e) and (g) of this section, and see § 1.280F-7(a). For rules on determining inclusion amounts with respect to other listed property, see paragraphs (f) and (g) of this section, and see § 1.280F-7(b).

(b) Section 48(d) election. If a lessor elects under section 48(d) with respect to any listed property to treat the lessee as having acquired such property, the amount of the investment tax credit allowed to the lessee is subject to the limitation prescribed in § 1.280F-3T(b)(1) and (2). If a lessor elects under section 48(d) with respect to any passenger automobile to treat the lessee as having acquired such automobile, the amount of the investment tax credit allowed to the lessee is also subject to the limitations prescribed in § 1.280F-2T(a) and (i).

(c) Regularly engaged in the business of leasing. For purposes of paragraph (a) of this section, a person shall be considered regularly engaged in the business of leasing listed property only if contracts to lease such property are entered into with some frequency over a continuous period of time. The determination shall be made on the basis of the facts and circumstances in each case, taking into account the nature of the person's business in its entirety. Occasional or incidental leasing activity is insufficient. For example, a person leasing only one passenger automobile during a taxable year is not regularly engaged in the business of leasing automobiles. In addition, an employer that allows an employee to use the employer's property for personal purposes and charges such employee for the use of the property is not regularly engaged in the business of leasing with respect to the property used by the employee.

(d) Inclusions in income of lessees of passenger automobiles leased after June 18, 1984, and before April 3, 1985. *(1) In general.* If a taxpayer leases a passenger automobile after June 18, 1984, but before April 3, 1985, for each taxable year (except the last taxable year) during which the taxpayer leases the automobile, the taxpayer must include in gross income an inclusion amount (prorated for the number of days of the lease term included in that taxable year), determined under this paragraph (d)(1), and multiplied by the business/investment use (as defined in § 1.280F-6(d)(3)(i)) for the particular taxable year. The inclusion amount—

(i) Is 7.5 percent of the excess (if any) of the automobile's fair market value over $16,500 for each of the first three taxable years during which a passenger automobile is leased.

(ii) Is 6 percent of the excess (if any) of the automobile's fair market value over $22,500 for the fourth taxable year during which a passenger automobile is leased.

(iii) Is 6 percent of the excess (if any) of the automobile's fair market value over $28,500 for the fifth taxable year during which a passenger automobile is leased.

(iv) Is 6 percent of the excess (if any) of the automobile's fair market value over $34,500 for the sixth taxable year during which a passenger automobile is leased.

For the seventh and subsequent taxable years during which a passenger automobile is leased, the inclusion amount is 6 percent of the excess (if any) of the automobile's fair market value over the sum of (A) $16,500 and (B) $6,000 multiplied by the number of such taxable years in excess of three years. See paragraph (g)(2) of this section for the definition of fair market value.

(2) Additional inclusion amount when less than predominant use in a qualified business use. (i) If a passenger automobile, which is leased after June 18, 1984, and before April 3, 1985, is not used predominantly in a qualified business use during a taxable year, the lessee must add to gross income in the first taxable year that the automobile is not so used (and only in that year) an inclusion amount determined under this paragraph (d)(2). This inclusion amount is in addition to the amount required to be included in gross income under paragraph (d)(1) of this section.

(ii) If the fair market value (as defined in paragraph (h)(2) of this section) of the automobile is greater than $16,500, the inclusion amount is determined by multiplying the average of the business/investment use (as defined in paragraph (h)(3) of this section) by the appropriate dollar amount from the table in paragraph (d)(2)(iii) of this section. If the fair market value (as defined in paragraph (h)(2) of this section) of the automobile is $16,500 or less, the inclusion amount is the product of the fair market value of the automobile, the average business/investment use, and the applicable percentage from the table in paragraph (d)(2)(iv) of this section.

(iii) The dollar amount is determined under the following table:

If a passenger automobile is not predominantly used in a qualified business use during—	The dollar amount Lease term (years)			
	1	2	3	4 or more
The first taxable year of the lease term	$350	$700	$1,350	$1,850
The second taxable year of the lease term			$ 650	$1,250
The third taxable year of the lease term				$ 650

(iv) The applicable percentage is determined under the following table:

If a passenger automobile is not predominantly used in a qualified business use during—	The applicable percentage Lease term (years)			
	1	2	3	more
The first taxable year of the lease term	3.0	6.0	10.2	13.2
The second taxable year of the lease term		1.25	6.2	10.4
The third taxable year of the lease term			2.25	6.5
The fourth taxable year of the lease term				1.7
The fifth taxable year of the lease term				0.5

(e) Inclusions in income of lessees of passenger automobiles leased after April 2, 1985, and before January 1, 1987. *(1) In general.* For any passenger automobile that is leased after April 2, 1985, and before January 1, 1987, for each taxable year (except the last taxable year) during which the taxpayer leases the automobile, the taxpayer must include in gross income an inclusion amount determined under subparagraphs (2) through (5) of this paragraph (e). Additional inclusion amounts when a passenger automobile is not used predominantly in a qualified business use during a taxable year are determined under paragraph (e)(6) of this section. See paragraph (h)(2) of this section for the definition of fair market value.

(2) Fair market value not greater than $50,000: years one through three. For any passenger automobile that has a fair market value not greater than $50,000, the inclusion amount for each of the first three taxable years during which the automobile is leased is determined as follows:

(i) For the appropriate range of fair market values in the table in paragraph (e)(2)(iv) of this section, select the dollar amount from the column for the quarter of the taxable year in which the automobile is first used under the lease,

(ii) Prorate the dollar amount for the number of days of the lease term included in the taxable year, and

(iii) Multiply the prorated dollar amount by the business/investment use for the taxable year.

(iv) Dollar amounts: Years 1-3:

Dollar Amounts: Years 1-3

Fair market value		Taxable year quarter			
Greater than—	But not greater than—	4th	3d	2d	1st
$11,250	$11,500	$ 8	$ 7	$ 6	$ 6
11,500	11,750	24	21	19	17
11,750	12,000	40	35	32	29
12,000	12,250	56	49	44	40
12,250	12,500	72	64	57	52
12,500	12,750	88	78	70	63
12,750	13,000	104	92	83	75
13,000	13,250	120	106	95	86
13,250	13,500	144	128	115	104
13,500	13,750	172	153	137	124
13,750	14,000	200	177	159	145
14,000	14,250	228	202	182	165
14,250	14,500	256	227	204	185
14,500	14,750	284	252	226	206
14,750	15,000	312	277	249	226
15,000	15,250	340	302	271	246
15,250	15,500	369	327	293	266
15,500	15,750	397	352	316	287
15,750	16,000	425	377	336	307
16,000	16,250	453	402	360	327
16,250	16,500	481	426	383	348
16,500	16,750	509	451	406	368
16,750	17,000	537	476	426	388
17,000	17,500	579	514	461	419
17,500	18,000	635	563	506	459
18,000	18,500	691	613	550	500
18,500	19,000	748	663	595	541
19,000	19,500	804	713	640	581
19,500	20,000	860	783	685	622
20,000	20,500	916	812	729	662
20,500	21,000	972	862	774	703
21,000	21,500	1,028	912	819	744
21,500	22,000	1,064	962	863	784
22,000	23,000	1,169	1,036	930	845
23,000	24,000	1,281	1,136	1,020	926
24,000	25,000	1,393	1,236	1,109	1007
25,000	26,000	1,506	1,335	1,199	1,089
26,000	27,000	1,618	1,435	1,288	1,170
27,000	28,000	1,730	1,534	1,377	1,251
28,000	29,000	1,842	1,634	1,467	1,332
29,000	30,000	1,955	1,734	1,556	1,413
30,000	31,000	2,067	1,833	1,646	1,495
31,000	32,000	2,179	1,933	1,736	1,576
32,000	33,000	2,292	2,032	1,824	1,657
33,000	34,000	2,404	2,132	1,914	1,736
34,000	35,000	2,516	2,232	2,003	1,819
35,000	36,000	2,629	2,331	2,093	1,901
36,000	37,000	2,741	2,431	2,182	1,962
37,000	38,000	2,853	2,530	2,271	2,063
38,000	39,000	2,965	2,630	2,361	2,144
39,000	40,000	3,078	2,730	2,450	2,225
40,000	41,000	3,190	2,829	2,540	2,307
41,000	42,000	3,302	2,929	2,629	2,388
42,000	43,000	3,415	3,028	2,718	2,469
43,000	44,000	3,527	3,128	2,808	2,550
44,000	45,000	3,639	3,228	2,897	2,631
45,000	46,000	3,752	3,327	2,987	2,713
46,000	47,000	3,864	3,427	3,076	2,794
47,000	48,000	3,976	3,526	3,165	2,875
48,000	49,000	4,088	3,626	3,255	2,956
49,000	50,000	4,201	3,726	3,344	3,037

(3) Fair market value not greater than $50,000: years four through six. For any passenger automobile that has a fair market value greater than $18,000, but not greater than $50,000, the inclusion amount for the fourth, fifth, and sixth taxable years during which the automobile is leased is determined as follows:

(i) For the appropriate range of fair market values in the table in paragraph (e)(3)(iv) of this section, select the dollar amount from the column for the taxable year in which the automobile is used under the lease,

(ii) Prorate the dollar amount for the number of days of the lease term included in the taxable year, and

(iii) Multiply this dollar amount by the business/investment use for the taxable year.

(iv) Dollar Amounts: Years 4-6:

Dollar Amounts: Years 4-6

Fair market value		Year		
Greater than—	But not greater than—	4	5	6
$18,000	$18,500	$ 15		
18,500	19,000	45		
19,000	19,500	75		
19,500	20,000	105		
20,000	20,500	135		
20,500	21,000	165		
21,000	21,500	195		
21,500	22,000	225		
22,000	23,000	270		
23,000	24,000	330	$ 42	
24,000	25,000	390	102	
25,000	26,000	450	162	
26,000	27,000	510	222	
27,000	28,000	570	282	
28,000	29,000	630	342	$ 54
29,000	30,000	690	402	114
30,000	31,000	750	462	174
31,000	32,000	810	522	234
32,000	33,000	870	582	294
33,000	34,000	930	642	354
34,000	35,000	990	702	414
35,000	36,000	1,050	762	474
36,000	37,000	1,110	822	534
37,000	38,000	1,170	862	594
38,000	39,000	1,230	942	654
39,000	40,000	1,290	1,002	714
40,000	41,000	1,350	1,062	774
41,000	42,000	1,410	1,122	834
42,000	43,000	1,470	1,162	894
43,000	44,000	1,530	1,242	954
44,000	45,000	1,590	1,302	1,014
45,000	46,000	1,650	1,362	1,074

46,000	47,000	1,719	1,422	1,134
47,000	48,000	1,770	1,482	1,194
48,000	49,000	1,830	1,542	1,254
49,000	50,000	11,890	1,602	1,314

(4) Fair market value greater than $50,000: years one through six. (i) For any passenger automobile that has a fair market value greater than $50,000, the inclusion amount for the first six taxable years during which the automobile is leased is determined as follows:

(A) Determine the dollar amount by using the appropriate formula in paragraph (e)(4)(ii) of this section,

(B) Prorate the dollar amount for the number of days of the lease term included in the taxable year, and

(C) Multiply this dollar amount by the business/investment use for the taxable year.

(ii) The dollar amount is computed as follows:

(A) If the automobile is first used under the lease in the fourth quarter of a taxable year, the dollar amount for each of the first three taxable years during which the automobile is leased is the sum of—

(1) $124, and

(2) 11 percent of the excess of the automobile's fair market value over $13,200.

(B) If the automobile is first used under the lease in the third quarter of a taxable year, the dollar amount for each of the first three taxable years during which the automobile is leased is the sum of—

(1) $110, and

(2) 10 percent of the excess of the automobile's fair market value over $13,200.

(C) If the automobile is first used under the lease in the second quarter of a taxable year, the dollar amount for each of the first three taxable years during which the automobile is leased is the sum of—

(1) $100, and

(2) 9 percent of the excess of the automobile's fair market value over $13,200.

(D) If the automobile is first used under the lease in the first quarter of a taxable year, the dollar amount for each of the first three taxable years during which the automobile is leased is the sum of—

(1) $90, and

(2) 8 percent of the excess of the automobile's fair market value over $13,200.

(E) For the fourth taxable year during which the automobile is leased, the dollar amount is 6 percent of the excess of the automobile's fair market value over $18,000.

(F) For the fifth taxable year during which the automobile is leased, the dollar amount is 6 percent of the excess of the automobile's fair market value over $22,800.

(G) For the sixth taxable year during which the automobile is leased, the dollar amount is 6 percent of the excess of the automobile's fair market value over $27,600.

(5) Seventh and subsequent taxable years. (i) For any passenger automobile that has a fair market value less than or equal to $32,400, the inclusion amount for the seventh and subsequent taxable years during which the automobile is leased is zero.

(ii) For any passenger automobile that has a fair market value greater than $32,400, the inclusion amount for the seventh and subsequent taxable years during which the automobile is leased is 6 percent of—

(A) The excess (if any) of the automobile's fair market value, over

(B) The sum of—

(1) $13,200 and

(2) $4,800 multiplied by the number of taxable years in excess of three years.

(6) Additional inclusion amount when less than predominant use in a qualified business use. (i) If a passenger automobile, which is leased after April 2, 1985, and before January 1, 1987, is not predominantly used in a qualified business use during a taxable year, the lessee must add to gross income in the first taxable year that the automobile is not so used (and only in that year) an inclusion amount determined under this paragraph (e)(6). This inclusion amount is in addition to the amount required to be included in gross income under paragraph (e)(2), (3), (4), and (5) of this section.

(ii) If the fair market value (as defined in paragraph (h)(2) of this section) of the automobile is greater than $11,250, the inclusion amount is determined by multiplying the average of the business/investment use (as defined in paragraph (h)(3) of this section) by the appropriate dollar amount from the table in paragraph (e)(6)(iii) of this section. If the fair market value of the automobile is $11,250 or less, the inclusion amount is the product of the fair market value of the automobile, the average business/investment use, and the applicable percentage from the table in paragraph (e)(6)(iv) of this section.

(iii) The dollar amount is determined under the following table:

If a passenger automobile is not predominantly used in a qualified business use during—	Lease term (years)— The dollar amount is:			
	1	2	3	4 or more
The first taxable year of the lease term	$350	$700	$1,150	$1,500
The second taxable year of the lease term		150	700	1,200
The third taxable year of the lease term			250	750

(iv) The applicable percentage is determined under the following table:

If a passenger automobile is not predominantly used in a qualified business use during—	Lease term (years)— The applicable percentage:			
	1	2	3	4 or more
The first taxable year of the lease term	3.0	6.0	10.2	13.2
The second taxable year of the lease term		1.25	6.2	10.4
The third taxable year of the lease term			2.25	6.5
The fourth taxable year of the lease term				1.7
The fifth taxable year of the lease term				0.5

(f) Inclusions in income of lessees of listed property other than passenger automobiles. *(1) In general.* If listed property other than a passenger automobile is not used predominantly in a qualified business use in any taxable year in which such property is leased, the lessee must add an inclusion amount to gross income in the first taxable year in which such property is not so predominantly used (and only in that year). This inclusion amount is determined under paragraph (f)(2) of this section for property leased after June 18, 1984, and before January 1, 1987. The inclusion amount is determined under § 1.280F-7(b) for property leased after December 31, 1986.

(2) Inclusion amount for property leased after June 18, 1984, and before January 1, 1987. The inclusion amount for property leased after June 18, 1984, and before January 1, 1987, is the product of the following amounts:

(i) The fair market value (as defined in paragraph (h)(2) of this section) of the property.

(ii) The average business/investment use (as defined in paragraph (h)(3) of this section), and

(iii) The applicable percentage (as determined under paragraph (f)(3) of this section).

(3) Applicable percentages. The applicable percentages for 3-, 5-, and 10-year recovery property are determined according to the following tables:

(I) In the case of 3-year recovery property:

	For the first taxable year in which the business use percentage is 50 percent or less, the applicable percentage for such taxable year is—					
Taxable year during lease term	1	2	3	4	5	6 and later
For a lease term of						
1 year	3.0					
2 years	6.0	1.25				
3 years	10.2	6.2	2.25			
4 or more years	13.2	10.4	6.5	1.7	0.5	0

(II) In the case of 5-year recovery property:

	For the first taxable year in which the business use percentage is 50 percent or less the applicable percentage for such taxable year is—											
Taxable year during lease term	1	2	3	4	5	6	7	8	9	10	11	12
For a lease term of:												
1 year	2.7											
2 years	5.3	1.2										
3 years	9.9	6.1	1.6									
4 years	14.4	11.1	7.3	2.3								
5 years	18.4	15.7	12.4	8.2	3.0							
6 or more years	21.8	19.6	16.7	13.5	9.6	5.25	4.4	3.6	2.8	1.8	1.0	0

(III) In the case of 10-year recovery property:

	For the first taxable year on which the business use percentage is 50 pct or less the applicable percentage for such taxable year is—														
Taxable year during lease term	1	2	3	4	5	6	7	8	9	10	11	12	13	14	15
For a lease term of:															
1 year	2.5														
2 years	5.1	.6													
3 years	9.8	5.6	1.0												
4 years	14.0	10.3	6.2	1.4											
5 years	17.9	14.5	10.9	6.7	1.8										
6 years	21.3	18.3	15.1	11.4	7.1	2.1									
7 years	21.9	19.0	15.9	12.4	8.4	3.9	2.4								
8 years	22.4	19.6	16.7	13.4	9.7	5.5	4.5	2.7							
9 years	22.9	20.2	17.4	14.3	10.9	7.0	6.4	5.1	3.0						
10 years	23.5	20.9	18.2	15.2	11.9	8.3	8.1	7.2	5.7	3.3					
11 years	23.9	21.4	18.8	16.0	12.8	9.3	9.4	8.9	7.7	5.9	3.1				
12 years	24.3	21.9	19.3	16.5	13.4	10.1	10.3	10.0	9.3	7.8	5.5	2.9			
13 years	24.7	22.2	19.7	16.9	14.0	10.7	11.1	11.0	10.4	9.2	7.4	5.2	2.7		
14 years	25.0	22.5	20.1	17.3	14.4	11.1	11.6	11.7	11.3	10.3	8.8	6.9	4.8	2.5	
15 years or more	25.3	22.8	20.3	17.5	14.7	11.5	12.0	12.2	11.9	11.1	9.8	8.2	6.5	4.5	2.3

(g) Special rules applicable to inclusions in income of lessees. This paragraph (g) applies to the inclusions in gross income of lessees prescribed under paragraphs (d)(2), (e)(6), or (f) of this section, or prescribed under § 1.280F-7(b).

(1) Lease term commences within 9 months of the end of lessee's taxable year. If—

(i) The lease term commences within 9 months before the close of the lessee's taxable year,

(ii) The property is not predominantly used in a qualified business use during that portion of the taxable year, and

(iii) The lease term continues into the lessee's subsequent taxable year, then the inclusion amount is added to gross income in the lessee's subsequent taxable year and the amount is determined by taking into account the average of the business/investment use for both taxable years and the applicable percentage for the taxable year in which the lease term begins (or, in the case of a passenger automobile with a fair market value greater than $16,500, the appropriate dollar amount for the taxable year in which the lease term begins).

(2) Lease term less than one year. If the lease term is less than one year, the amount which must be added to gross income is an amount that bears the same ratio to the inclusion amount determined before the application of this paragraph (g)(2) as the number of days in the lease term bears to 365.

(3) Maximum inclusion amount. The inclusion amount shall not exceed the sum of all deductible amounts in connection with the use of the listed property properly allocable to the lessee's taxable year in which the inclusion amount must be added to gross income.

(h) Definitions. *(1) Lease term.* In determining the term of any lease for purposes of this section, the rules of section 168(i)(3)(A) shall apply.

(2) Fair market value. For purposes of this section, the fair market value of listed property is such value on the first day of the lease term. If the capitalized cost of listed property is specified in the lease agreement, the lessee shall treat such amount as the fair market value of the property.

(3) Average business/investment use. For purposes of this section, the average business/investment use of any listed property is the average of the business/investment use for the first taxable year in which the business use percentage is 50 percent or less and all preceding taxable years in which such property is leased. See paragraph (g)(1) of this section for special rule when lease term commences within 9 months before the end of the lessee's taxable year.

(i) Examples. This section may be illustrated by the following examples.

Example (1). On January 1, 1985, A, a calendar year taxpayer, leases and places in service a passenger automobile with a fair market value of $55,000. The lease is to be for a period of four years. During taxable years 1985 and 1986, A uses the automobile exclusively in a trade or business. Under paragraph (d)(1) of this section, A must include in gross income in both 1985 and 1986, $2,887.50 (i.e., ($55,000 − $16,500) × 7.5%).

Example (2). The facts are the same as in example (1), and in addition, A uses the automobile only 45 percent in a trade or business during 1987. Under paragraph (d)(1) of this section for 1987, A must include in gross income $1,299.38 (i.e., ($55,000 − $16,500) × 7.5% × 45%). In addition, under paragraph (d)(2) of this section, A must also include in gross income in 1987, $530.85 (i.e., $650 × 81.67%, average business/investment use).

Example (3). On August 1, 1985, B, a calendar year taxpayer, leases and places in service an item of listed property which is 5-year recovery property, with a fair market value of $10,000. The lease is to be for a period of 5 years. B's qualified business use of the property is 40 percent in 1985, 100 percent in 1986, and 90 percent in 1987. Under paragraphs (f)(1) and (g)(1) of this section, before the application of paragraph (g)(3) of this section, B must include in gross income in 1986, $1,288.00 (i.e., $10,000 × 70% × 18.4%, the product of the fair market value, the average business use for both taxable years, and the applicable percentage for year one from the table in paragraph (f)(3)(ii) of this section).

Example (4). On October 1, 1985, C, a calendar year taxpayer, leases and places in service an item of listed property which is 3-year recovery property with a fair market value of $15,000. The lease term is 6 months (ending March 31, 1986) during which C uses the property 45 percent in a trade or business, the only business/investment use. Under paragraphs (f)(1) and (g)(1) and (2) of this section, before the application of paragraph (g)(3) of this section. C must include in gross income in 1986, $100.97 (i.e., $15,000 × 45% × 3% × 182/365, the product of the fair market value, the average business use for both taxable years, and the applicable percentage for year one from the table in paragraph (f)(3)(i) of this section, prorated for the length of the lease term).

Example (5). On July 15, 1985, A, a calendar year taxpayer, leases and places in service a passenger automobile with a fair market value of $45,300. The lease is for a period of 5 years, during which A uses the automobile exclusively in a trade or business. Under paragraph (e)(2) and (3) of this section, for taxable years 1985 through 1989, A must include the following amounts in gross income:

Taxable year	Dollar amount	Proration	Business use (percent)	Inclusion
1985	$3,327	170/365	100	$1,550
1986	3,327	365/365	100	3,327
1987	3,327	365/365	100	3,327
1988	1,650	366/366	100	1,650
1989	1,362	365/365	100	1,362
1990	1,074	196/365	100	577

Example (6). The facts are the same as in example (1), except that A uses the automobile only 45 percent in a trade or business during 1987 through 1990. Under § 1.280F-5T(e)(6), A must include in gross income for taxable year 1987, the first taxable year in which the automobile is not used predominantly in a trade or business, an additional amount based on the average business/investment use for taxable years 1985 through 1987. For taxable years 1985 through 1989, A must include the following amounts in gross income:

Taxable year	Dollar amount	Proration	Business use (percent)	Inclusion
1985	$3,327	170/365	100	$1,550
1986	3,327	365/365	100	3,327
1987	3,327	365/365	45	1,497
	750		81.67	612
1988	1,650	366/366	45	743
1989	1,362	365/365	45	613
1990	1,074	196/365	45	260

T.D. 7986, 10/19/84, amend T.D. 8061, 11/1/85, T.D. 8218, 8/5/88, T.D. 8473, 4/9/93, T.D. 9133, 6/24/2004.

§ 1.280F-6 Special rules and definitions.

Caution: The Treasury has not yet amended Reg § 1.280F-6 to reflect changes made by P.L. 108-27, P.L. 107-147, P.L. 105-34, P.L. 101-239, P.L. 100-647, P.L. 99-44.

(a) Deductions of employee. *(1) In general.* Employee use of listed property shall not be treated as business/investment use (as defined in paragraph (d)(3) of this section) for purposes of determining the amount of any recovery deduction allowable (including any deduction under section 179) to the employee unless that use is for the convenience of the employer and required as a condition of employment.

(2) "Convenience of the employer" and "condition of employment" requirements. (i) In general. The terms "convenience of the employer" and "condition of employment" generally have the same meaning for purposes of section 280F as they have for purposes of section 119 (relating to the exclusion from gross income for meals or lodging furnished for the convenience of the employer).

(ii) "Condition of employment." In order to satisfy the "condition of employment" requirement, the use of the property must be required in order for the employee to perform the duties of his or her employment properly. Whether the use of the property is so required depends on all the facts and circumstances. Thus, the employer need not explicitly require the employee to use the property. Similarly, a mere statement by the employer that the use of the property is a condition of employment is not sufficient.

(iii) "Convenience of employer". [Reserved]

(3) Employee use. For purposes of this section, the term "employee use" means any use in connection with the performance of services by the employee as an employee.

(4) Examples. The principles of this paragraph are illustrated in the following examples:

Example (1). A is employed as a courier with W, which provides local courier services. A owns and uses a motorcycle to deliver packages to downtown offices for W. W does not provide delivery vehicles and explicitly requires all of its couriers to own a car or motorcycle for use in their employment with the company. A's use of the motorcycle for delivery purposes is for the convenience of W and is required as a condition of employment.

Example (2). B is an inspector for X, a construction company with many construction sites in the local area. B is required to travel to the various construction sites on a regular basis: B uses her automobile to make these trips. Although X does not furnish B an automobile, X does not explicitly require B to use here own automobile. However, X reimburses B for any costs she incurs in traveling to the various job sites. B's use of here automobile in here employment is for the convenience of X and is required as a condition of employment.

Example (3). Assume the same facts as in example (2), except that X makes an automobile available to B who chooses to use her own automobile and receive reimbursement, B's use of her own automobile is not for the convenience of X and is not required as a condition of employment.

Example (4). C is a pilot for Y, a small charter airline. Y requires its pilots to obtain x hours of flight time annually in addition to the number of hours of flight time spent with the airline. Pilots can usually obtain these hours by flying with a military reserve unit or by flying part-time with another airline. C owns his own airplane. C's use of his airplane to obtain the required flight hours is not for the convenience of the employer and is not required as a condition of employment.

Example (5). D is employed as an engineer with Z, an engineering contracting firm. D occasionally takes work home at night rather than working late in the office. D owns and uses a computer which is virtually identical to the one she uses at the office to complete her work at home. D's use of the computer is not for the convenience of here employer and is not required as a condition of employment.

(b) Listed property. *(1) In general.* Except as otherwise provided in paragraph (b)(5) of this section, the term "listed property" means—

(i) Any passenger automobile (as defined in paragraph (c) of this section).

(ii) Any other property used as a means of transportation (as defined in paragraph (b)(2) of this section),

(iii) Any property of a type generally used for purposes of entertainment, recreation, or amusement, and

(iv) Any computer or peripheral equipment (as defined in section 168(i)(2)(B)), and

(v) Any other property specified in paragraph (b)(4) of this section.

(2) "Means of transportation". (i) In general. Except as otherwise provided in paragraph (b)(2)(ii) of this section, property used as a "means of transportation" includes trucks, buses, trains, boats, airplanes, motorcycles, and any other vehicles for transporting persons or goods.

(ii) Exception. The term "listed property" does not include any vehicle that is a qualified nonpersonal use vehicle as defined in section 274(i) and § 1.274-5T(k).

(3) Property used for entertainment, etc. (i) In general. Property of a type generally used for purposes of entertainment, recreation, or amusement includes property such as photographic, phonographic, communication, and video recording equipment.

(ii) Exception. The term "listed property" does not include any photographic, phonographic, communication, or video recording equipment of a taxpayer if the equipment is use either exclusively at the taxpayer's regular business establishment or in connection with the taxpayer's principal trade or business.

(iii) Regular business establishment. The regular business establishment of an employee is the regular business establishment of the employer of the employee. For purposes of this paragraph (b)(3), a portion of a dwelling unit is treated as a regular business establishment if the requirements of section 280A(c)(1) are met with respect to that portion.

(4) Other property. [Reserved]

(5) Exception for computers. The term "listed property" shall not include any computer (including peripheral equipment) used exclusively at a regular business establishment. For purposes of the preceding sentence, a portion of a dwelling unit shall be treated as a regular business establishment if (and only if) the requirements of section 280A(c)(1) are met with respect to that portion.

(c) Passenger automobile. *(1) In general.* Except as provided in paragraph (c)(3) of this section, the term "passenger automobile" means any 4-wheeled vehicle which is—

(i) Manufactured primarily for use on public streets, roads, and highways, and

(ii) Rated at 6,000 pounds gross vehicle weight or less.

(2) Parts, etc. of automobile. The term "passenger automobile" includes any part, component, or other item that is physically attached to the automobile or is traditionally included in the purchase price of an automobile. The term

does not include repairs that are not capital expenditures within the meaning of section 263.

(3) Exception for certain vehicles. The term "passenger automobile" shall not include any—

(i) Ambulance, hearse, or combination ambulance-hearse used by the taxpayer directly in a trade or business,

(ii) Vehicle used by the taxpayer directly in the trade or business of transporting persons or property for compensation or hire, or

(iii) Truck or van that is a qualified nonpersonal use vehicle as defined under § 1.274-5T(k).

(d) Business use percentage. *(1) In general.* The term "business use percentage" means the percentage of the use of any listed property which is qualified business use as described in paragraph (d)(2) of this section.

(2) Qualified business use. (i) In general. Except as provided in paragraph (d)(2)(ii) of this section, the term "qualified business use" means any use in a trade or business of the taxpayer. The term "qualified business use" does not include use for which a deduction is allowable under section 212. Whether the amount of qualified business use exceeds 50 percent is determinative of whether the investment tax credit and the accelerated percentages under section 168 are available for listed property (or must be recaptured). See § 1.280F-3T.

(ii) Exception for certain use by 5-percent owners and related persons)

(A) In general. The term "qualified business use" shall not include—

(1) Leasing property to any 5-percent owner or related person,

(2) Use of property provided as compensation for the performance of services by a 5-percent owner or related person, or

(3) Use of property provided as compensation for the performance of services by any person not described in paragraph (d)(2)(ii)(A)(2) of this section unless an amount is properly reported by the taxpayer as income to such person and, where required, there was withholding under chapter 24.

Paragraph (d)(2)(ii)(A)(1) of this section shall apply only to the extent that the use of the listed property is by an individual who is a related party or a 5-percent owner with respect to the owner or lessee of the property.

(B) Special rule for aircraft. Paragraph (d)(2)(ii)(A) of this section shall not apply with respect to any aircraft if at least 25 percent of the total use of the aircraft during the taxable year consists of qualified business use not described in paragraph (d)(2)(ii)(A).

(C) Definitions. For purposes of this paragraph—

(1) 5-percent owner. The term "5-percent owner" means any person who is a 5-percent owner with respect to the taxpayer (as defined in section 416(i)(1)(B)(i)).

(2) Related person. The term "related person" means any person related to the taxpayer (within the meaning of section 267(b)).

(3) Business/investment use. (i) In general. The term "business/investment use" means the total business or investment use of listed property that may be taken into account for purposes of computing (without regard to section 280F(b)) the percentage of cost recovery deduction for a passenger automobile or other listed property for the taxable year. Whether the accelerated percentages under section 168 (as opposed to use of the straight line method of cost recovery) are available with respect to listed property or must be recaptured is determined, however, by reference to qualified business use (as defined in paragraph (d)(2) of this section) rather than by reference to business/investment use. Whether a particular use of property is a business or investment use shall generally be determined under the rules of section 182 or 212.

(ii) Entertainment use. The use of listed property for entertainment, recreation, or amusement purposes shall be treated as business use to the extent that expenses (other than interest and property tax expenses) attributable to that use are deductible after application of section 274.

(iii) Employee use. See paragraph (a) of this section for requirements to be satisfied for employee use of listed property to be considered business/investment use of the property.

(iv) Use of taxpayer's automobile by another person. Any use of the taxpayer's automobile by another person shall not be treated, for purposes of section 280F, as use in a trade or business under section 162 unless that use—

(A) Is directly connected with the business of the taxpayer,

(B) Is properly reported by the taxpayer as income to the other person and, where required, there was withholding under chapter 24, or

(C) Results in a payment of fair market rent. For purposes of this paragraph (d)(4)(iv)(C), payment to the owner of the automobile in connection with such use is treated as the payment of rent.

(4) Predominantly used in qualified business use. (i) Definition. Property is predominantly used in a qualified business use for any taxable year if the business use percentage (as defined in paragraph (d)(1) of this section) is greater than 50 percent.

(ii) Special rule for transfers at death. Property does not cease to be used predominantly in a qualified business use by reason of a transfer at death.

(iii) Other dispositions of property. [Reserved]

(5) Examples. The following examples illustrate the principles set forth in this paragraph.

Example (1). E uses a home computer 50 percent of the time to manage her investments. The computer is listed property within the meaning of section 280F(d)(4) E also uses the computer 40 percent of the time in her part-time consumer research business. Because E's business use percentage for the computer does not exceed 50 percent, the computer is not predominantly used in a qualified business use for the taxable year. Her aggregate business/investment use for purposes of determining the percent of the total allowable straight line depreciation that she can claim is 90 percent.

Example (2). Assume that E in example (1) uses the computer 30 percent of the time to manage her investments and 60 percent of the time in her consumer research business. E's business use percentage exceeds 50 percent. Her aggregate business/investment use for purposes of determining her allowable investment tax credit and cost recovery deductions is 90 percent.

Example (3). F is the proprietor of a plumbing contracting business. F's brother is employed with F's company. As part of his compensation, F's brother is allowed to use one of the company automobiles for personal use. The use of the company automobiles by F's brother is not a qualified business use because F and F's brother are related parties within the meaning of section 267(b).

Example (4). F, in example (3), allows employees unrelated to him to use company automobiles as part of their compensation. F, however, does not include the value of these automobiles in the employees' gross income and F does not withhold with respect to the use of these automobiles. The use of the company automobiles by the employees in this case is not business/investment use.

Example (5). X Corporation owns several automobiles which its employees use for business purposes. The employees are also allowed to take the automobiles home at night. However, the fair market value of the use of the automobile for any personal purpose, e.g., commuting to work, is reported by X as income to the employee and is withheld upon by X. The use of the automobile by the employee, even for personal purposes, is a qualified business use the respect to X.

(e) Method of allocating use of property. *(1) In general.* For purposes of section 280F, the taxpayer shall allocate the use of any listed property that is used for more than one purpose during the taxable year to the various uses in the manner prescribed in paragraph (e)(2) and (3) of this section.

(2) Passenger automobiles and other means of transportation. In the case of a passenger automobile or any other means of transportation, the taxpayer shall allocate the use of the property on the basis of mileage. Thus, the percentage of use in a trade or business for the year shall be determined by dividing the number of miles the vehicle is driven for purposes of that trade or business during the year by the total number of miles the vehicle is driven during the year for any purpose.

(3) Other listed property. In the case of other listed property, the taxpayer shall allocate the use of that property on the basis of the most appropriate unit of time the property is actually used (rather than merely being available for use). For example, the percentage of use of a computer in a trade or business for a taxable year is determined by dividing the number of hours the computer is used for business purposes during the year by the total number of hours the computer is used for any purpose during the year.

(f) Effective date. *(1) In general.* Except as provided in paragraph (f)(2) of this section, this section applies to property placed in service by a taxpayer on or after July 7, 2003. For regulations applicable to property placed in service before July 7, 2003, see § 1.280F-6T as in effect prior to July 7, 2003 (§ 1.280F-6T as contained in 26 CFR part 1, revised as of April 1, 2003).

(2) Property placed in service before July 7, 2003. The following rules apply to property that is described in paragraph (c)(3)(iii) of this section, was placed in service by the taxpayer before July 7, 2003, and was treated by the taxpayer as a passenger automobile under § 1.280F-6T as in effect prior to July 7, 2003 (pre-effective date vehicle):

(i) Except as provided in paragraphs (f)(2)(ii), (iii), and (iv) of this section, a pre-effective date vehicle will be treated as a passenger automobile to which section 280F(a) applies.

(ii) A pre-effective date vehicle will be treated as property to which section 280F(a) does not apply if the taxpayer adopts that treatment in determining depreciation deductions on the taxpayer's original return for the year in which the vehicle is placed in service.

(iii) A pre-effective date vehicle will be treated, to the extent provided in this paragraph (f)(2)(iii), as property to which section 280F(a) does not apply if the taxpayer adopts that treatment on an amended Federal tax return in accordance with this paragraph (f)(2)(iii). This paragraph (f)(2)(iii) applies only if, on or before December 31, 2004, the taxpayer files, for all applicable taxable years, amended Federal tax returns (or qualified amended returns, if applicable (for further guidance, see Rev. Proc. 94-69 (1994-2 C.B. 804) and § 601.601(d)(2)(ii)(b) of this chapter)) treating the vehicle as property to which section 280F(a) does not apply. The applicable taxable years for this purpose are the taxable year in which the vehicle was placed in service by the taxpayer (or, if the period of limitation for assessment under section 6501 has expired for such year or any subsequent year (a closed year), the first taxable year following the most recent closed year) and all subsequent taxable years in which the vehicle was treated on the taxpayer's return as property to which section 280F(a) applies. If the earliest applicable taxable year is not the year in which the vehicle was placed in service, the adjusted depreciable basis of the property as of the beginning of the first applicable taxable year is recovered over the remaining recovery period. If the remaining recovery period as of the beginning of the first applicable taxable year is less than 12 months, the entire adjusted depreciable basis of the property as of the beginning of the first applicable taxable year is recovered in that year.

(iv) A pre-effective date vehicle will be treated, to the extent provided in this paragraph (f)(2)(iv), as property to which section 280F(a) does not apply if the taxpayer adopts that treatment on Form 3115, Application for Change in Accounting Method, in accordance with this paragraph (f)(2)(iv). The taxpayer must follow the applicable administrative procedures issued under § 1.446-1(e)(3)(ii) for obtaining the Commissioner's automatic consent to a change in method of accounting (for further guidance, for example, see Rev. Proc. 2002-9 (2002-1 C.B. 327) and § 601.601(d)(2)(ii)(b) of this chapter). If the taxpayer files a Form 3115 treating the vehicle as property to which section 280F(a) does not apply, the taxpayer will be permitted to treat the change as a change in method of accounting under section 446(e) of the Internal Revenue Code and to take into account the section 481 adjustment resulting from the method change. For purposes of Form 3115, the designated number for the automatic accounting method change authorized for this paragraph (f)(2)(iv) is 89.

T.D. 7986, 10/19/84, amend T.D. 8009, 2/15/85, T.D. 8061, 11/1/85, T.D. 9069, 7/3/2003, T.D. 9133, 6/24/2004.

PAR. 5. Section 1.280F-6 is amended by revising paragraph (b)(2)(ii) to read:

Proposed § 1.280F-6 Special rules and definitions. [*For Preamble, see ¶ 153,001*]

* * * * *

(b) * * *

(2) * * *

(ii) Exception. The term "listed property" does not include any vehicle that is a qualified nonpersonal use vehicle as defined in section 274(i) and § 1.274-5(k).

* * * * *

§ 1.280F-7 Property leased after December 31, 1986.

Caution: The Treasury has not yet amended Reg § 1.280F-7 to reflect changes made by P.L. 108-27, P.L. 107-147, P.L. 105-34.

(a) Inclusions in income of lessees of passenger automobiles leased after December 31, 1986. *(1) In general.* If a taxpayer leases a passenger automobile after December 31, 1986, the taxpayer must include in gross income an inclusion amount determined under this paragraph (a), for each taxable year during which the taxpayer leases the automobile. This paragraph (a) applies only to passenger automobiles for which the taxpayer's lease term begins after December 31, 1986. See §§ 1.280F-5T(d) and 1.280F-5T(e) for rules on determining inclusion amounts for passenger automobiles for which the taxpayer's lease term begins before January 1, 1987. See § 1.280F-5T(h)(2) for the definition of fair market value.

(2) Inclusion amount. For any passenger automobile leased after December 31, 1986, the inclusion amount for each taxable year during which the automobile is leased is determined as follows:

(i) For the appropriate range of fair market values in the applicable table, select the dollar amount from the column for the taxable year in which the automobile is used under the lease (but for the last taxable year during any lease that does not begin and end in the same taxable year, use the dollar amount for the preceding taxable year).

(ii) Prorate the dollar amount for the number of days of the lease term included in the taxable year.

(iii) Multiply the prorated dollar amount by the business/investment use (as defined in § 1.280F-6(d)(3)(i)) for the taxable year.

(iv) The following table is the applicable table in the case of a passenger automobile leased after December 31, 1986, and before January 1, 1989:

DOLLAR AMOUNTS FOR AUTOMOBILES WITH A LEASE TERM BEGINNING IN CALENDAR YEAR 1987 OR 1988

Fair market value of automobile		Taxable year during lease				
Over	Not over	1st	2nd	3rd	4th	5 and later
$ 12,800—	$ 13,100	$ 2	$ 5	$ 7	$ 8	$ 9
13,100—	13,400	6	14	20	24	28
13,400—	13,700	10	23	34	41	47
13,700—	14,000	15	32	47	57	65
14,000—	14,300	19	41	61	73	84
14,300—	14,600	23	50	74	89	103
14,600—	14,900	27	59	88	105	122
14,900—	15,200	31	68	101	122	140
15,200—	15,500	35	77	115	138	159
15,500—	15,800	40	87	128	154	178
15,800—	16,100	44	96	142	170	196
16,100—	16,400	48	105	155	186	215
16,400—	16,700	52	114	169	203	234
16,700—	17,000	56	123	182	219	253
17,000—	17,500	62	135	200	240	277
17,500—	18,000	69	150	223	267	309
18,000—	18,500	76	166	246	294	340
18,500—	19,000	83	181	268	321	371
19,000—	19,500	90	196	291	348	402
19,500—	20,000	97	211	313	375	433
20,000—	20,500	104	226	336	402	465
20,500—	21,000	111	242	358	429	496
21,000—	21,500	117	257	381	456	527
21,500—	22,000	124	272	403	483	558
22,000—	23,000	135	295	437	524	605
23,000—	24,000	149	325	482	578	667
24,000—	25,000	163	356	527	632	729
25,000—	26,000	177	386	572	686	792
26,000—	27,000	190	416	617	740	854
27,000—	28,000	204	447	662	794	917
28,000—	29,000	218	477	707	848	979
29,000—	30,000	232	507	752	902	1,041
30,000—	31,000	246	538	797	956	1,104
31,000—	32,000	260	568	842	1,010	1,166
32,000—	33,000	274	599	887	1,064	1,228
33,000—	34,000	288	629	933	1,118	1,291
34,000—	35,000	302	659	978	1,172	1,353
35,000—	36,000	316	690	1,023	1,226	1,415
36,000—	37,000	329	720	1,068	1,280	1,478
37,000—	38,000	343	751	1,113	1,334	1,540

Fair market value of automobile		Taxable year during lease				
Over	Not over	1st	2nd	3rd	4th	5 and later
38,000—	39,000	357	781	1,158	1,388	1,602
39,000—	40,000	371	811	1,203	1,442	1,665
40,000—	41,000	385	842	1,248	1,496	1,727
41,000—	42,000	399	872	1,293	1,550	1,789
42,000—	43,000	413	902	1,338	1,604	1,852
43,000—	44,000	427	933	1,383	1,658	1,914
44,000—	45,000	441	963	1,428	1,712	1,976
45,000—	46,000	455	994	1,473	1,766	2,039
46,000—	47,000	468	1,024	1,518	1,820	2,101
47,000—	48,000	482	1,054	1,563	1,874	2,164
48,000—	49,000	486	1,085	1,608	1,928	2,226
49,000—	50,000	510	1,115	1,653	1,982	2,288
50,000—	51,000	524	1,146	1,698	2,036	2,351
51,000—	52,000	538	1,176	1,743	2,090	2,413
52,000—	53,000	552	1,206	1,788	2,144	2,475
53,000—	54,000	566	1,237	1,834	2,198	2,538
54,000—	55,000	580	1,267	1,879	2,252	2,600
55,000—	56,000	594	1,297	1,924	2,306	2,662
56,000—	57,000	607	1,328	1,969	2,360	2,725
57,000—	58,000	621	1,358	2,014	2,414	2,787
58,000—	59,000	635	1,389	2,059	2,468	2,849
59,000—	60,000	649	1,419	2,104	2,522	2,912
60,000—	62,000	670	1,465	2,171	2,603	3,005
62,000—	64,000	698	1,525	2,262	2,711	3,130
64,000—	66,000	726	1,586	2,352	2,819	3,255
66,000—	68,000	753	1,647	2,442	2,927	3,379
68,000—	70,000	781	1,708	2,532	3,035	3,504
70,000—	72,000	809	1,768	2,622	3,143	3,629
72,000—	74,000	837	1,829	2,712	3,251	3,753
74,000—	76,000	865	1,890	2,802	3,359	3,878
76,000—	78,000	892	1,951	2,892	3,468	4,003
78,000—	80,000	920	2,012	2,982	3,576	4,128
80,000—	85,000	969	2,118	3,140	3,765	4,346
85,000—	90,000	1,038	2,270	3,365	4,035	4,658
90,000—	95,000	1,108	2,422	3,590	4,305	4,969
95,000—	100,000	1,177	2,574	3,816	4,575	5,281
100,000—	110,000	1,282	2,802	4,154	4,980	5,749
110,000—	120,000	1,421	3,105	4,604	5,520	6,372
120,000—	130,000	1,560	3,409	5,055	6,060	6,996
130,000—	140,000	1,699	3,713	5,505	6,600	7,619
140,000—	150,000	1,838	4,017	5,956	7,140	8,243
150,000—	160,000	1,977	4,321	6,406	7,680	8,866
160,000—	170,000	2,116	4,625	6,857	8,221	9,490
170,000—	180,000	2,255	4,929	7,307	8,761	10,113
180,000—	190,000	2,394	5,232	7,758	9,301	10,737
190,000—	200,000	2,533	5,536	8,208	9,841	11,360

(v) The applicable table in the case of a passenger automobile first leased after December 31, 1988, will be contained in a revenue ruling or revenue procedure published in the Internal Revenue Bulletin.

(3) Example. The following example illustrates the application of this paragraph (a):

Example. On April 1, 1987, A, a calendar year taxpayer, leases and places in service a passenger automobile with a fair market value of $31,500. The lease is to be for a period of three years. During taxable years 1987 and 1988, A uses the automobile exclusively in a trade or business. During 1989 and 1990, A's business/investment use is 45 percent. The appropriate dollar amounts from the table in paragraph (a)(2)(iv) of this section are $260 for 1987 (first taxable year during the lease), $568 for 1988 (second taxable year during the lease), $842 for 1989 (third taxable year during the lease), and $842 for 1990. Since 1990 is the last taxable year during the lease, the dollar amount for the preceding year (the third year) is used, rather than the dollar amount for the fourth year. For taxable years 1987 through 1990, A's inclusion amounts are determined as follows:

Tax year	Dollar amount	Proration	Business use (percent)	Inclusion amount
1987	$260	275/365	100	$196
1988	568	366/366	100	568
1989	842	365/365	45	379
1990	842	90/365	45	93

(b) Inclusion in income of lessees of listed property (other than passenger automobiles) leased after December 31, 1986. *(1) In general.* If listed property other than a passenger automobile is not used predominantly in a qualified business use in any taxable year in which such property is leased, the lessee must add an inclusion amount to gross income in the first taxable year in which such property is not so predominantly used (and only in that year). This year is the first taxable year in which the business use percentage (as defined in § 1.280F-6(d)(1)) of the property is 50 percent or less. This inclusion amount is determined under this paragraph (b) for property for which the taxpayer's lease term begins after December 31, 1986 (and under § 1.280F-5T(f) for property for which the taxpayer's lease term begins before January 1, 1987). See also § 1.280F-5T(g).

(2) Inclusion amount. The inclusion amount for any listed property (other than a passenger automobile) leased after December 31, 1986, is the sum of the amounts determined under subdivisions (i) and (ii) of this subparagraph (2).

(i) The amount determined under this subdivision (i) is the product of the following amounts:

(A) The fair market value (as defined in § 1.280F-5T(h)(2)) of the property,

(B) The business/investment use (as defined in § 1.280F-6(d)(3)(i)) for the first taxable year in which the business use percentage (as defined in § 1.280F-6(d)(1)) is 50 percent or less, and

(C) The applicable percentage from the following table:

	First taxable year during lease in which business use percentage is 50% or less											
Type of property	1	2	3	4	5	6	7	8	9	10	11	12 and Later
Property with a recovery period of less than 7 years under the alternative depreciation system (such as computers, trucks and airplanes)	2.1	−7.2	−19.8	−20.1	−12.4	−12.4	−12.4	−12.4	−12.4	−12.4	−12.4	−12.4
Property with a 7 to 10-year recovery period under the alternative depreciation system (such as recreation property)	3.9	−3.8	−17.7	−25.1	−27.8	−27.2	−27.1	−27.6	−23.7	−14.7	−14.7	−14.7
Property with a recovery period of more than 10 years under the alternative depreciation system (such as certain property with no class life)	6.6	−1.6	−16.9	−25.6	−29.9	−31.1	−32.8	−35.1	−33.3	−26.7	−19.7	−12.2

(ii) The amount determined under this subdivision (ii) is the product of the following amounts:

(A) The fair market value of the property,

(B) The average of the business/investment use for all taxable years (in which such property is leased) that precede the first taxable year in which the business use percentage is 50 percent or less, and

(C) The applicable percentage from the following table:

	First taxable year during lease in which business use percentage is 50% or less											
Type of property	1	2	3	4	5	6	7	8	9	10	11	12 and Later
Property with a recovery period of less than 7 years under the alternative depreciation system (Such as computers, trucks and airplanes)	0.0	10.0	22.0	21.2	12.7	12.7	12.7	12.7	12.7	12.7	12.7	12.7
Property with a 7 to 10-year recovery period under the alternative depreciation system (such as recreation property)	0.0	9.3	23.8	31.3	33.8	32.7	31.6	30.5	25.0	15.0	15.0	15.0

Property with a recovery period of more than 10 years under the alternative depreciation system (such as certain property with no class life)	0.0	10.1	26.3	35.4	39.6	40.2	40.8	41.4	37.5	29.2	20.8	12.5

(3) Example. The following example illustrates the application of this paragraph (b):

Example. On February 1, 1987, B, a calendar year taxpayer, leases and places in service a computer with a fair market value of $3,000. The lease is to be for a period of two years. B's qualified business use of the property, which is the only business/investment use, is 80 percent in taxable year 1987, 40 percent in taxable year 1988, and 35 percent in taxable year 1989. B must add an inclusion amount to gross income for taxable year 1988, the first taxable year in which B does not use the computer predominantly for business *(i.e.,* the first taxable year in which B's business use percentage is 50 percent or less). Since 1988 is the second taxable year during the lease, and since the computer has a 5-year recovery period under the General and Alternative Depreciation Systems, the applicable percentage from the table in subdivision (i) of paragraph (b)(2) is – 7.2%, and the applicable percentage from the table in subdivision (ii) is 10%. B's inclusion amount is $154, which is the sum of the amounts determined under subdivisions (i) and (ii) of subparagraph (b)(2) of this paragraph. The amount determined under subdivision (i) is – $86 [$3,000 × 40% × (– 7.2%)], and the amount determined under subdivision (ii) is $240 [$3,000 × 80% × 10%].

There is a need for immediate guidance with respect to the provisions contained in this Treasury decision. For this reason, it is found impracticable to issue it with notice and public procedure under subsection (b) of section 553 of Title 5 of the United States Code or subject to the effective date limitation of subsection (d) of this section.

T.D. 8218, 8/9/88, amend T.D. 8298, 4/11/90, T.D. 8473, 4/9/93, T.D. 9133, 6/24/2004.

§ 1.280G-1 Golden parachute payments.

The following questions and answers relate to the treatment of golden parachute payments under section 280G of the Internal Revenue Code of 1986, as added by section 67 of the Tax Reform Act of 1984 (Pub. L. No. 98-369; 98 Stat. 585) and amended by section 1804(j) of the Tax Reform Act of 1986 (Pub. L. No. 99-514; 100 Stat. 2807), section 1018(d)(6)-(8) of the Technical and Miscellaneous Revenue Act of 1988 (Pub. L. No. 100-647; 102 Stat. 3581), and section 1421 of the Small Business Job Protection Act of 1996 (Pub. L. No. 104-188; 110 Stat. 1755). The following is a table of subjects covered in this section:

Overview:
- Effect of section 280G Q/A-1
- Meaning of "parachute payment" Q/A-2
- Meaning of "excess parachute payment" Q/A-3
- Effective date of section 280G Q/A-4

Exempt Payments:
- Exempt payments generally Q/A-5
- Exempt payments with respect to certain corporations Q/A-6
- Shareholder approval requirements Q/A-7
- Exempt payments under a qualified plan Q/A-8
- Exempt payments of reasonable compensation Q/A-9
- Payor of Parachute Payments Q/A-10

Payments in the Nature of Compensation:
- The nature of compensation Q/A-11
- Property transfers Q/A-12
- Stock options Q/A-13
- Reduction of amount of payment by consideration paid Q/A-14

Disqualified Individuals:
- Meaning of "disqualified individual" Q/A-15
- Personal service corporation treated as individual Q/A-16
- Meaning of "shareholder" Q/A-17
- Meaning of "officer" Q/A-18
- Meaning of "highly-compensated individual" Q/A-19
- Meaning of "disqualified individual determination period" Q/A-20
- Meaning of "compensation" Q/A-21

Contingent on Change in Ownership or Control:
- General rules for determining payments contingent on change Q/A-22
- Payments under agreement entered into after change Q/A-23
- Amount of payment contingent on change Q/A-24
- Presumption that payment is contingent on change Q/A-25, 26
- Change in ownership or control Q/A-27, 28, 29

Three-Times-Base-Amount Test for Parachute Payments:
- Three-times-base-amount test Q/A-30
- Determination of present value Q/A-31, 32, 33

Meaning of "base amount" Q/A-34
Meaning of "base period" Q/A-35
Special rule for determining base amount Q/A-36
Securities Violation Parachute Payments Q/A-37
Computation and Reduction of Excess Parachute Payments:
Computation of excess parachute payments Q/A-38
Reduction by reasonable compensation Q/A-39
Determination of Reasonable Compensation:
General criteria for determining reasonable compensation Q/A-40
Types of payments generally considered reasonable compensation Q/A-41, 42, 43
Treatment of severance payments Q/A-44
Miscellaneous rules:
Definition of corporation Q/A-45
Treatment of affiliated group as one corporation Q/A-46
Effective date:
General effective date of section 280G Q/A-47
Effective date of regulations Q/A-48

Overview

Q-1. What is the effect of Internal Revenue Code section 280G?

A-1. (a) Section 280G disallows a deduction for any excess parachute payment paid or accrued. For rules relating to the imposition of a nondeductible 20-percent excise tax on the recipient of any excess parachute payment, see Internal Revenue Code sections 4999, 275(a)(6), and 3121(v)(2)(A).

(b) The disallowance of a deduction under section 280G is not contingent on the imposition of the excise tax under section 4999. The imposition of the excise tax under section 4999 is not contingent on the disallowance of a deduction under section 280G. Thus, for example, because the imposition of the excise tax under section 4999 is not contingent on the disallowance of a deduction under section 280G, a payee may be subject to the 20-percent excise tax under section 4999 even though the disallowance of the deduction for the excess parachute payment may not directly affect the federal taxable income of the payor.

Q-2. What is a parachute payment for purposes of section 280G?

A-2. (a) The term parachute payment means any payment (other than an exempt payment described in Q/A-5) that—

(1) Is in the nature of compensation;

(2) Is made or is to be made to (or for the benefit of) a disqualified individual;

(3) Is contingent on a change—

(i) In the ownership of a corporation;

(ii) In the effective control of a corporation; or

(iii) In the ownership of a substantial portion of the assets of a corporation; and

(4) Has (together with other payments described in paragraphs (a)(1), (2), and (3) of this A-2 with respect to the same disqualified individual) an aggregate present value of at least 3 times the individual's base amount.

(b) Hereinafter, a change referred to in paragraph (a)(3) of this A-2 is generally referred to as a change in ownership or control. For a discussion of the application of paragraph (a)(1), see Q/A-11 through Q/A-14; paragraph (a)(2), Q/A-15 through Q/A-21; paragraph (a)(3), Q/A-22 through Q/A-29; and paragraph (a)(4), Q/A-30 through Q/A-36.

(c) The term parachute payment also includes any payment in the nature of compensation to (or for the benefit of) a disqualified individual that is pursuant to an agreement that violates a generally enforced securities law or regulation. This type of parachute payment is referred to in this section as a securities violation parachute payment. See Q/A-37 for the definition and treatment of securities violation parachute payments.

Q-3. What is an excess parachute payment for purposes of section 280G?

A-3. The term excess parachute payment means an amount equal to the excess of any parachute payment over the portion of the base amount allocated to such payment. Subject to certain exceptions and, limitations, an excess parachute payment is reduced by any portion of the payment which the taxpayer establishes by clear and convincing evidence is reasonable compensation for personal services actually rendered by the disqualified individual before the date of the change in ownership or control. For a discussion of the nonreduction of a securities violation parachute payment by reasonable compensation, see Q/A-37. For a discussion of the computation of excess parachute payments and their reduction by reasonable compensation, see Q/A-38 through Q/A-44.

Q-4. What is the effective date of section 280G and this section?

A-4. In general, section 280G applies to payments under agreements entered into or renewed after June 14, 1984. Section 280G also applies to certain payments under agreements entered into on or before June 14, 1984, and amended or supplemented in significant relevant respect after that date. This section applies to any payment that is contingent on a change in ownership or control and the change in ownership or control occurs on or after January 1, 2004. For a discussion of the application of the effective date, see Q/A-47 and Q/A-48.

Exempt Payments

Q-5. Are some types of payments exempt from the definition of the term parachute payment?

A-5. (a) Yes, the following five types of payments are exempt from the definition of parachute payment—

(1) Payments with respect to a small business corporation (described in Q/A-6 of this section);

(2) Certain payments with respect to a corporation no stock in which is readily tradeable on an established securities market (or otherwise) (described in Q/A-6 of this section);

(3) Payments to or from a qualified plan (described in Q/A-8 of this section);

(4) Certain payments made by a corporation undergoing a change in ownership or control that is described in any of the following sections of the Internal Revenue Code: section 501(c) (but only if such organization is subject to an express statutory prohibition against inurement of net earnings to the benefit of any private shareholder or individual, or if the organization is described in section 501(c)(1) or section 501(c)(21)), section 501(d), or section 529, collectively referred to as tax-exempt organizations (described in Q/A-6 of this section); and

(5) Certain payments of reasonable compensation for services to be rendered on or after the change in ownership or control (described in Q/A-9 of this section).

(b) Deductions for payments exempt from the definition of parachute payment are not disallowed by section 280G, and such exempt payments are not subject to the 20-percent excise tax of section 4999. In addition, such exempt payments are not taken into account in applying the 3-times-base-amount test of Q/A-30 of this section.

Q-6. Which payments with respect to a corporation referred to in paragraph (a)(1), (a)(2), or (a)(4) of Q/A-5 of this section are exempt from the definition of parachute payment?

A-6. (a) The term parachute payment does not include—

(1) Any payment to a disqualified individual with respect to a corporation which (immediately before the change in ownership or control) would qualify as a small business corporation (as defined in section 1361(b) but without regard to section 1361(b)(1)(C) thereof), without regard to whether the corporation had an election to be treated as a corporation under section 1361 in effect on the date of the change in ownership or control;

(2) Any payment to a disqualified individual with respect to a corporation (other than a small business corporation described in paragraph (a)(1) of this A-6) if—

(i) Immediately before the change in ownership or control, no stock in such corporation was readily tradeable on an established securities market or otherwise; and

(ii) The shareholder approval requirements described in Q/A-7 of this section are met with respect to such payment; or

(3) Any payment to a disqualified individual made by a corporation which is a tax-exempt organization (as defined in paragraph (a)(4) of Q/A-5 of this section), but only if the corporation meets the definition of a tax-exempt organization both immediately before and immediately after the change in ownership or control.

(b) For purposes of paragraph (a)(1) of this A-6, the members of an affiliated group are not treated as one corporation.

(c) The requirements of paragraph (a)(2)(i) of this A-6 are not met with respect to a corporation if a substantial portion of the assets of any entity consists (directly or indirectly) of stock in such corporation and any ownership interest in such entity is readily tradeable on an established securities market or otherwise. For this purpose, such stock constitutes a substantial portion of the assets of an entity if the total fair market value of the stock is equal to or exceeds one third of the total gross fair market value of all of the assets of the entity. For this purpose, gross fair market value means the value of the assets of the entity, determined without regard to any liabilities associated with such assets. If a corporation is a member of an affiliated group (which group is treated as one corporation under A-46 of this section), the requirements of paragraph (a)(2)(i) of this A-6 are not met if any stock in any member of such group is readily tradeable on an established securities market or otherwise.

(d) For purposes of paragraph (a)(2)(i) of this A-6, the term stock does not include stock described in section 1504(a)(4) if the payment does not adversely affect the redemption and liquidation rights of any shareholder owning such stock.

(e) For purposes of paragraph (a)(2)(i) of this A-6, stock is treated as readily tradeable if it is regularly quoted by brokers or dealers making a market in such stock.

(f) For purposes of paragraph (a)(2)(i) of this A-6, the term established securities market means an established securities market as defined in § 1.897-1(m).

(g) The following examples illustrate the application of this exemption:

Example 1. A small business corporation (within the meaning of paragraph (a)(1) of this A-6) operates two businesses. The corporation sells the assets of one of its businesses, and these assets represent a substantial portion of the assets of the corporation. Because of the sale, the corporation terminates its employment relationship with persons employed in the business the assets of which are sold. Several of these employees are highly-compensated individuals to whom the owners of the corporation make severance payments in excess of 3 times each employee's base amount. Since the corporation is a small business corporation immediately before the change in ownership or control, the payments are not parachute payments.

Example 2. Assume the same facts as in Example 1, except that the corporation is not a small business corporation within the meaning of paragraph (a)(1) of this A-6. If no stock in the corporation is readily tradeable on an established securities market (or otherwise) immediately before the change in ownership or control and the shareholder approval requirements described in Q/A-7 of this section are met, the payments are not parachute payments.

Example 3. Stock of Corporation S is owned by Corporation P, stock in which is readily tradeable on an established securities market. The Corporation S stock equals or exceeds one third of the total gross fair market value of the assets of Corporation P, and thus, represents a substantial portion of the assets of Corporation P. Corporation S makes severance payments to several of its highly-compensated individuals that are parachute payments under section 280G and Q/A-2 of this section. Because stock in Corporation P is readily tradeable on an established securities market, the payments are not exempt from the definition of parachute payments under this A-6.

Example 4. A is a corporation described in section 501(c)(3), and accordingly, its net earnings are prohibited from inuring to the benefit of any private shareholder or individual. A transfers substantially all of its assets to another corporation resulting in a change in ownership or control. Contingent on the change in ownership or control, A makes a payment that, but for the potential application of the exemption described in A-5(a)(4), would constitute a parachute payment. However, one or more aspects of the transaction that constitutes the change in ownership or control causes A to fail to be described in section 501(c)(3). Accordingly, A fails to meet the definition of a tax-exempt organization both immediately before and immediately after the change in ownership or control, as required by this A-6. As a result, the payment made by A that was contingent on the change in ownership or control is not exempt from the definition of parachute payment under this A-6.

Example 5. B is a corporation described in section 501(c)(15). B does not meet the definition of a tax-exempt organization because section 501(c)(15) does not expressly prohibit inurement of B's net earnings to the benefit of any private shareholder or individual. Accordingly, if B has a change in ownership or control and makes a payment that would otherwise meet the definition of a parachute payment, such payment is not exempt from the definition of the term parachute payment for purposes of this A-6.

Q-7. How are the shareholder approval requirements referred to in paragraph (a)(2)(ii) of Q/A-6 of this section met?

A-7.

(a) General rule. The shareholder approval requirements referred to in paragraph (a)(2)(ii) of Q/A-6 of this section are met with respect to any payment if—

(1) Such payment is approved by more than 75 percent of the voting power of all outstanding stock of the corporation entitled to vote (as described in this A-7) immediately before the change in ownership or control; and

(2) Before the vote, there was adequate disclosure to all persons entitled to vote (as described in this A-7) of all material facts concerning all material payments which (but for Q/A-6 of this section) would be parachute payments with respect to a disqualified individual.

(b) Voting requirements.

(1) General rule. The vote described in paragraph (a)(1) of this A-7 must determine the right of the disqualified individual to receive the payment, or, in the case of a payment made before the vote, the right of the disqualified individual to retain the payment. Except as otherwise provided in this A-7, the normal voting rules of the corporation are applicable. Thus, for example, an optionholder is generally not permitted to vote for purposes of this A-7. For purposes of this A-7, the vote can be on less than the full amount of the payment(s) to be made. Shareholder approval can be a single vote on all payments to any one disqualified individual, or on all payments to more than one disqualified individual. The total payment(s) submitted for shareholder approval, however, must be separately approved by the shareholders. The requirements of this paragraph (b)(1) are not satisfied if approval of the change in ownership or control is contingent, or otherwise conditioned, on the approval of any payment to a disqualified individual that would be a parachute payment but for Q/A-6 of this section.

(2) Special rule. A vote to approve the payment does not fail to be a vote of the outstanding stock of the corporation entitled to vote immediately before the change in ownership or control merely because the determination of the shareholders entitled to vote on the payment is based on the shareholders of record as of any day within the six-month period immediately prior to and ending on date of the change in ownership or control, provided the disclosure requirements described in paragraph (c) of this A-7 are met.

(3) Entity shareholder. (i) Approval of a payment by any shareholder that is not an individual (an entity shareholder) generally must be made by the person authorized by the entity shareholder to approve the payment. See paragraph (b)(4) of this A-7 if the person so authorized by the entity shareholder is a disqualified individual who would receive a parachute payment if the shareholder approval requirements of this A-7 are not met.

(ii) However, if a substantial portion of the assets of an entity shareholder consists (directly or indirectly) of stock in the corporation undergoing the change in ownership or control, approval of the payment by that entity shareholder must be made by a separate vote of the persons who hold, immediately before the change in ownership or control, more than 75 percent of the voting power of the entity shareholder entitled to vote. The preceding sentence does not apply if the value of the stock of the corporation owned, directly or indirectly, by or for the entity shareholder does not exceed 1 percent of the total value of the outstanding stock of the corporation undergoing a change in ownership or control. Where approval of a payment by an entity shareholder must be made by a separate vote of the owners of the entity shareholder, the normal voting rights of the entity shareholder determine which owners shall vote. For purposes of this (b)(3)(ii), stock represents a substantial portion of the assets of an entity shareholder if the total fair market value of the stock held by the entity shareholder in the corporation undergoing the change in ownership or control is equal to or exceeds one third of the total gross fair market value of all of the assets of the entity shareholder. For this purpose, gross fair market value means the value of the assets of the entity, determined without regard to any liabilities associated with such assets.

(4) Disqualified individuals and attribution of stock ownership. In determining the persons entitled to vote referred to in paragraph (a)(1) or (b)(3) of this A-7, stock that would otherwise be entitled to vote is not counted as outstanding stock and is not considered in determining whether the more than 75 percent vote has been obtained under this A-7 if the stock is actually owned or constructively owned under section 318(a) by or for a disqualified individual who receives (or is to receive) payments that would be parachute payments if the shareholder approval requirements described in paragraph (a) of this A-7 are not met. Likewise, stock is not counted as outstanding stock if the owner is considered under section 318(a) to own any part of the stock owned directly or indirectly by or for a disqualified individual described in the preceding sentence. In addition, if the person authorized to vote the stock of an entity shareholder is a disqualified individual who would receive a parachute payment if the shareholder approval requirements described in this A-7 are not met, such person is not permitted to vote such shares, but the entity shareholder is permitted to appoint an equity interest holder in the entity shareholder, or in the case of a trust another person eligible to vote on behalf of the trust, to vote the otherwise eligible shares. However, if all persons who hold voting power in the corporation undergoing the change in ownership or control are disqualified individuals or related persons described in this paragraph (b)(4), then such stock is counted as outstanding stock and votes by such persons are considered in determining whether the more than 75 percent vote has been obtained.

(c) Adequate disclosure. To be adequate disclosure for purposes of paragraph (a)(2) of this A-7, disclosure must be full and truthful disclosure of the material facts and such additional information as is necessary to make the disclosure not materially misleading at the time the disclosure is made. Disclosure of such information must be made to every shareholder of the corporation entitled to vote under this A-7. For each disqualified individual, material facts that must be disclosed include, but are not limited to, the event triggering the payment or payments, the total amount of the payments that would be parachute payments if the shareholder approval requirements described in paragraph (a) of this A-7 are not met, and a brief description of each payment (e.g., accelerated vesting of options, bonus, or salary). An omitted fact is considered a material fact if there is a substantial likelihood that a reasonable shareholder would consider it important.

(d) Corporation without shareholders. If a corporation does not have shareholders, the exemption described in Q/A-6(a)(2) of this section and the shareholder approval requirements described in this A-7 do not apply. Solely for purposes of this paragraph (d), a shareholder does not include a member in an association, joint stock company, or insurance company.

(e) Examples. The following examples illustrate the application of this A-7:

Example 1. Corporation S has two shareholders--Corporation P, which owns 76 percent of the stock of Corporation S, and A, a disqualified individual who would receive a parachute payment if the shareholder approval requirements of this A-7 are not met. No stock of Corporation P or S is readily tradeable on an established securities market (or otherwise). The value of the stock of Corporation S equals or exceeds one third of the gross fair market value of the assets of Corporation P, and thus, represents a substantial portion of the assets of Corporation P. All of the stock of Corporation S is sold to Corporation M. Contingent on the change in ownership of Corporation S, severance payments are made to certain officers of Corporation S in excess of 3 times each officer's base amount. If the payments are approved by a separate vote of the persons who hold, immediately before the sale, more than 75 percent of the voting power of the outstanding stock entitled to vote of Corporation P and the disclosure rules of paragraph (a)(2) of this A-7 are complied with, the shareholder approval requirements of this A-7 are met, and the payments are exempt from the definition of parachute payment pursuant to A-6 of this section.

Example 2. (i) Stock of Corporation X, none of which is traded on an established market, is acquired by Corporation Y. In the voting ballot concerning the sale, the Corporation X shareholders are asked to vote either "yes" on the sale and "yes" to paying parachute payments to A, a disqualified individual with respect to Corporation A, or "no" on the sale and "no" to paying parachute payments to A.

(ii) Because the approval of the change in ownership or control is conditioned on the approval of the payments to A, the shareholder approval requirements of this A-7 are not satisfied. If the payments are made to A, the payments are not exempt from the definition of parachute payment pursuant to Q/A-6 of this section.

(iii) Assume the same facts as in paragraph (i) of this Example 2, except that the acquisition agreement between Corporation X and Corporation Y states that the acquisition is approved only if there are no parachute payments made to A. If the shareholder approval and the disclosure requirements described in this A-7 are met, the payments will not be parachute payments. Alternatively, if the shareholders do not approve the payments, the payments cannot be made (or retained). Thus, the transaction is not conditioned on the approval of the parachute payments. If the payments are made and the requirements of this A-7 are met, the payments are exempt from the definition of parachute payment pursuant to Q/A-6 of this section.

Example 3. Corporation M is wholly owned by Partnership P. No interest in either M or P is readily tradeable on an established securities market (or otherwise). The value of the stock of Corporation M equals or exceeds one third of the gross fair market value of the assets of Partnership P, and thus, represents a substantial portion of the assets of Partnership P. Corporation M undergoes a change in ownership or control. Partnership P has one general partner and 200 limited partners. The general partner is not a disqualified individual. None of the limited partners are entitled to vote on issues involving the management of the partnership investments. If the payments that would be parachute payments if the shareholder approval requirements of this A-7 are not met are approved by the general partner and the disclosure rules of paragraph (a)(2) of this A-7 are complied with, the shareholder approval requirements of this A-7 are met, and the payments are exempt from the definition of parachute payment pursuant to A-6 of this section.

Example 4. Corporation A has several shareholders including X and Y, who are disqualified individuals with respect to Corporation A and would receive parachute payments if the shareholder approval requirements of this A-7 are not met. No stock of Corporation A is readily tradeable on an established securities market (or otherwise). Corporation A undergoes a change in ownership or control. Contingent on the change in ownership or control, severance payments are payable to X and Y that are in excess of 3 times each individual's base amount. To determine whether the shareholder approval requirements of paragraph (a)(1) of this A-7 are satisfied regarding the payments to X and Y, the stock of X and Y is not considered outstanding, and X and Y are not entitled to vote.

Example 5. Assume the same facts as in Example 4, except that after adequate disclosure of all material facts (within the meaning of paragraph (a)(2) of this A-7) to all shareholders entitled to vote, 60 percent of the shareholders who are entitled to vote approve the payments to X and Y. Because more than 75 percent of the shareholders holding outstanding stock who were entitled to vote did not approve the payments to X and Y, the payments cannot be made.

Example 6. Assume the same facts as in Example 4 except that disclosure of all the material facts (within the meaning of paragraph (a)(2) of this A-7) regarding the payments to X and Y is made to two of Corporation A's shareholders, who collectively own 80 percent of Corporation A's stock entitled to vote and approve the payment. Both shareholders approve the payments. Assume further that no adequate disclosure of the material facts regarding the payments to X and Y is made to other Corporation A shareholders who are entitled to vote within the meaning of this A-7. Notwithstanding that 80 percent of the shareholders entitled to vote approve the payments, because disclosure regarding the payments to X and Y is not made to all of Corporation A's shareholders who were entitled to vote, the disclosure requirements of paragraph (a)(2) of this A-7 are not met, and the payments are not exempt from the definition of parachute payment pursuant to Q/A-6.

Example 7. Corporation C has three shareholders—Partnership, which owns 20 percent of the stock of Corporation C; A, an individual who owns 60 percent of the stock of Corporation C; and B, an individual who owns 20 percent of Corporation C. Stock of Corporation C does not represent a substantial portion of the assets of Partnership. No interest in either Partnership or Corporation C is readily tradeable on an established securities market (or otherwise). P, a one-third partner in Partnership, is a disqualified individual with respect to Corporation C. Corporation C undergoes a change in ownership or control. Contingent on the change, a severance payment is payable to P in excess of 3 times P's base amount. To determine the persons who are entitled to vote referred to in paragraph (a)(1) of this A-7, one-third of the stock held by Partnership is not considered outstanding stock. If P is the person authorized by Partnership to approve the payment, none of the shares of Partnership are considered outstanding stock. However, Partnership is permitted to appoint an equity interest holder in Partnership (who is not a disqualified individual who would receive a parachute payment if the requirements of this A-7 are not met), to vote the two-thirds of the shares held by Partnership that are otherwise entitled to be voted.

Example 8. X, Y, and Z are all employees and disqualified individuals with respect to Corporation E. No stock in Corporation E is readily tradeable on an established securities market (or otherwise). Each individual has a base amount of $100,000. Corporation E undergoes a change in ownership or control. Contingent on the change, a severance payment of $400,000 is payable to X; $600,000 is payable to Y; and $1,000,000 is payable to Z. Corporation E provides each Corporation E shareholder entitled to vote (as determined under this A-7) with a ballot listing and describing the payments of $400,000 to X; $600,000 to Y; and $1,000,000 to Z and the triggering event that generated the payments. Next to each name and corresponding amount on the ballot, Corporation E requests approval (with a ''yes'' and ''no'' box) of each total payment to be made to each individual and states that if the payment is not approved the payment will not be made. Adequate disclosure, within the meaning of this A-7 is made to each shareholder entitled to vote under this A-7. More than 75 percent of the Corporation E shareholders who are entitled to vote under paragraph (a)(1) of this A-7 approve each payment to each individual. The shareholder approval requirements of this A-7 are met, and the payments are exempt from the definition of parachute payment pursuant to A-6 of this section.

Example 9. Assume the same facts as in Example 8 except that the ballot does not request approval of each total payment to each individual separately. Instead, the ballot states that $2,000,000 in payments will be made to X, Y, and Z and requests approval of the $2,000,000 payments. Assuming the triggering event and amount of the payments to X, Y, and Z are separately described to the shareholders entitled to vote under this A-7, the shareholder approval requirements of paragraph (a)(1) of this A-7 are met, and the payments are exempt from the definition of parachute payment pursuant to A-6 of this section.

Example 10. B, an employee of Corporation X, is a disqualified individual with respect to Corporation X. Stock of Corporation X is not readily tradeable on an established securities market (or otherwise). Corporation X undergoes a change in ownership or control. B's base amount is $205,000. Under B's employment agreement with Corporation X, in the event of a change in ownership or control, B's stock options will vest and B will receive severance and bonus payments. Contingent on the change in ownership or control, B's stock options with a fair market value of $500,000 immediately vest, $200,000 of which is contingent on the change, and B will receive a $200,000 bonus payment and a $400,000 severance payment. Corporation X distributes a ballot to every shareholder of Corporation X who immediately before the change is entitled to vote as described in this A-7. The ballot contains adequate disclosure of all material facts and lists the following payments to be made to B: The contingent payment of $200,000 attributable to options, a $200,000 bonus payment, and a $400,000 severance payment. The ballot requests shareholder approval of the $200,000 bonus payment to B and states that whether or not the $200,000 bonus payment is approved, B will receive $200,000 attributable to options and a $400,000 severance payment. More than 75 percent of the shareholders entitled to vote as described by this A-7 approve the $200,000 bonus payment to B. The shareholder approval requirements of this A-7 are met, and the $200,000 payment is exempt from the definition of parachute payment pursuant to A-6 of this section.

Q-8. Which payments under a qualified plan are exempt from the definition of parachute payment?

A-8. The term parachute payment does not include any payment to or from—

(a) A plan described in section 401(a) which includes a trust exempt from tax under section 501(a);

(b) An annuity plan described in section 403(a);

(c) A simplified employee pension (as defined in section 408(k)); or

(d) A simple retirement account (as defined in section 408(p)).

Q-9. Which payments of reasonable compensation are exempt from the definition of parachute payment?

A-9. Except in the case of securities violation parachute payments, the term parachute payment does not include any payment (or portion thereof) which the taxpayer establishes by clear and convincing evidence is reasonable compensation for personal services to be rendered by the disqualified individual on or after the date of the change in ownership or control. See Q/A-37 of this section for the definition and treatment of securities violation parachute payments. See Q/A-40 through Q/A-44 of this section for rules on determining amounts of reasonable compensation.

Payor of Parachute Payments

Q-10. Who may be the payor of parachute payments?

A-10. Parachute payments within the meaning of Q/A-2 of this section may be paid, directly or indirectly, by—

(i) The corporation referred to in paragraph (a)(3) of Q/A-2 of this section;

(ii) A person acquiring ownership or effective control of that corporation or ownership of a substantial portion of that corporation's assets; or

(iii) Any person whose relationship to such corporation or other person is such as to require attribution of stock ownership between the parties under section 318(a).

Payments in the Nature of Compensation

Q-11. What types of payments are in the nature of compensation?

A-11.

(a) General rule. For purposes of this section, all payments—in whatever form—are payments in the nature of compensation if they arise out of an employment relationship or are associated with the performance of services. For this purpose, the performance of services includes holding oneself out as available to perform services and refraining from performing services (such as under a covenant not to compete or similar arrangement). Payments in the nature of compensation include (but are not limited to) wages and salary, bonuses, severance pay, fringe benefits, life insurance, pension benefits, and other deferred compensation (including any amount characterized by the parties as interest thereon). A payment in the nature of compensation also includes cash when paid, the value of the right to receive cash (including the value of accelerated vesting under Q/4-24(c)), or a transfer of property. However, payments in the nature of compensation do not include attorney's fees or court costs paid or incurred in connection with the payment of any amount described in paragraphs (a)(1), (2), and (3) of Q/A-2 of this section or a reasonable rate of interest accrued on any amount during the period the parties contest whether a payment will be made.

(b) When payment is considered to be made. Except as otherwise provided in A-11 through Q/A-13 of this section, a payment in the nature of compensation is considered made (and is subject to the excise tax under section 4999) in the taxable year in which it is includible in the disqualified individual's gross income or, in the case of fringe benefits and other benefits excludible from income, in the taxable year the benefits are received.

(c) Prepayment rule. Notwithstanding the general rule described in paragraph (b) of this A-11, a disqualified individual may, in the year of the change in ownership or control, or any later year, prepay the excise tax under section 4999, provided that the payor and disqualified individual treat the payment of the excise tax consistently and the payor satisfies its obligations under section 4999(c) in the year of prepayment. The prepayment of the excise tax for purposes of section 4999 must be based on the present value of the excise tax that would be due in the year the excess parachute payment would actually be paid (calculated using the discount rate equal to 120 percent of the applicable Federal rate (determined under section 1274(d) and regulations thereunder; see Q/A-32)). For purposes of projecting the future value of a payment that provides for interest to be credited at a variable interest rate, it is permissible to make a reasonable assumption regarding this variable rate. A disqualified individual is not required to adjust the excise tax paid under this paragraph (c) merely because the interest rates in the future are not the same as the rate used for purposes of projecting the future value of the payment. However, a disqualified individual may not apply this paragraph (c) of this A-11 to a payment to be made in cash if the present value of the payment would be considered not reasonably ascertainable under section 3121(v) and § 31.3121(v)(2)-1(e)(4) of this Chapter or to a payment related to health benefits or coverage. The Commissioner may provide additional guidance regarding the applicability of this paragraph (c) to certain payments in published guidance of general applicability under § 601.601(d)(2) of this Chapter.

(d) Transfers of property. Transfers of property are treated as payments for purposes of this A-11. See Q/A-12 of this section for rules on determining when such payments are considered made and the amount of such payments. See Q/A-13 of this section for special rules on transfers of stock options.

(e) The following example illustrates the principles of this A-11:

Example. D is a disqualified individual with respect to Corporation X. D has a base amount of $100,000 and is entitled to receive two parachute payments, one of $200,000 and the other of $400,000. A change in ownership or control of Corporation X occurs on May 1, 2005, and the $200,000 payment is made to D at the time of the change in ownership or control. The $400,000 payment is to be made on October 1, 2010. Corporation X and D agree that D will prepay the excise tax and X will satisfy its obligations under section 4999(c) with respect to the $400,000 payment. Using discount rate determined under Q/A-32, Corporation X and D determine that the present value of the $400,000 payment is $300,000 on the date of the change in ownership or control. The portions of the base amount allocated to these payments are $40,000 (($200,000/$500,000) x $100,000) and $60,000 (($300,000/$500,000 x $100,000), respectively. Thus, the amount of the first excess parachute payment is $160,000 ($200,000-$40,000) and that of the second excess parachute payment is $340,000 ($400,000-$60,000). The excise tax on the $400,000 payment is $68,000 ($340,000 x 20 percent). Assume the present value (calculated in accordance with paragraph (c) of this A-11) of $68,000 is $50,000. To prepay the excise tax due on the $400,000 payment, Corporation X must satisfy its obligations under section 4999 with respect to the $50,000, in addition to the $32,000 withholding required with respect to the $200,000 payment.

Q-12. If a property transfer to a disqualified individual is a payment in the nature of compensation, when is the payment considered made (or to be made), and how is the amount of the payment determined?

A-12. (a) Except as provided in this A-12 and Q/A-13 of this section, a transfer of property is considered a payment made (or to be made) in the taxable year in which the property transferred is includible in the gross income of the disqualified individual under section 83 and the regulations thereunder. Thus, in general, such a payment is considered made (or to be made) when the property is transferred (as defined in § 1.83-3(a)) to the disqualified individual and becomes substantially vested (as defined in § 1.83-3(b) and (j)) in such individual. The amount of the payment is determined under section 83 and the regulations thereunder. Thus, in general, the amount of the payment is equal to the excess of the fair market value of the transferred property (determined without regard to any lapse restriction, as defined in § 1.83-3(i)) at the time that the property becomes substantially vested, over the amount (if any) paid for the property.

(b) An election made by a disqualified individual under section 83(b) with respect to transferred property will not apply for purposes of this A-12. Thus, even if such an election is made with respect to a property transfer that is a payment in the nature of compensation, for purposes of this section, the payment is generally considered made (or to be made) when the property is transferred to and becomes substantially vested in such individual.

(c) See Q/A-13 of this section for rules on applying this A-12 to transfers of stock options.

(d) The following example illustrates the principles of this A-12:

Example. On January 1, 2006, Corporation M gives to A, a disqualified individual, a bonus of 100 shares of Corporation M stock in connection with the performance of services to Corporation M. Under the terms of the bonus arrangement A is obligated to return the Corporation M stock to Corporation M unless the earnings of Corporation M double by January 1, 2009, or there is a change in ownership or control of Corporation M before that date. A's rights in the stock are treated as substantially nonvested (within the meaning of § 1.83-3(b)) during that period because A's rights in the stock are subject to a substantial risk of forfeiture (within the meaning of § 1.83-3(c)) and are nontransferable (within the meaning of § 1.83-3(d)). On January 1, 2008, a change in ownership or control of Corporation M occurs. On that day, the fair market value of the Corporation M stock is $250 per share. Because A's rights in the Corporation M stock become substantially vested (within the meaning of § 1.83-3(b)) on that day, the payment is considered made on that day, and the amount of the payment for purposes of this section is equal to $25,000 (100 x $250). See Q/A-38 through 41 for rules relating to the reduction of the excess parachute payment by the portion of the payment which is established to be reasonable compensation for personal services actually rendered before the date of a change in ownership or control.

Q-13. How are transfers of statutory and nonstatutory stock options treated?

A-13. (a) For purposes of this section, an option (including an option to which section 421 applies) is treated as property that is transferred when the option becomes vested (regardless of whether the option has a readily ascertainable fair market value as defined in § 1.83-7(b)). For purposes of this A-13, vested means substantially vested within the meaning of § 1.83-3(b) and (j) or the right to the payment is not otherwise subject to a substantial risk of forfeiture within the meaning of section 83(c). Thus, for purposes of this section, the vesting of such an option is treated as a payment in the nature of compensation. The value of an option at the time the option vests is determined under all the facts and circumstances in the particular case. Factors relevant to such a determination include, but are not limited to: The difference between the option's exercise price and the value of the property subject to the option at the time of vesting; the probability of the value of such property increasing or decreasing; and the length of the period during which the option can be exercised. Thus, an option is treated as a payment in the nature of compensation on the date of grant or vesting, as applicable, without regard to whether such option has an ascertainable fair market value. For purposes of this A-13, valuation may be determined by any method prescribed by the Commissioner in published guidance of general applicability under § 601.601(d)(2) of this Chapter.

(b) Any money or other property transferred to the disqualified individual on the exercise, or as consideration on the sale or other disposition, of an option described in paragraph (a) of this A-13 after the time such option vests is not treated as a payment in the nature of compensation to the disqualified individual under Q/A-11 of this section. Nonetheless, the amount of the otherwise allowable deduction under section 162 or 212 with respect to such transfer is reduced by the amount of the payment described in paragraph (a) of this A-13 treated as an excess parachute payment.

Q-14. Are payments in the nature of compensation reduced by consideration paid by the disqualified individual?

A-14. Yes, to the extent not otherwise taken into account under Q/A-12 and Q/A-13 of this section, the amount of any payment in the nature of compensation is reduced by the amount of any money or the fair market value of any property (owned by the disqualified individual without restriction) that is (or will be) transferred by the disqualified individual in exchange for the payment. For purposes of the preceding sentence, the fair market value of property is determined as of the date the property is transferred by the disqualified individual.

Disqualified Individuals

Q-15. Who is a disqualified individual?

A-15. (a) For purposes of this section, an individual is a disqualified individual with respect to a corporation if, at any time during the disqualified individual determination period (as defined in Q/A-20 of this section), the individual is an employee or independent contractor of the corporation and is, with respect to the corporation—

(1) A shareholder (but see Q/A-17 of this section);

(2) An officer (see Q/A-18 of this section); or

(3) A highly-compensated individual (see Q/A-19 of this section).

(b) For purposes of this A-15, a director is a disqualified individual with respect to a corporation if, at any time during the disqualified individual determination period, the director is, with respect to the corporation, a shareholder (see Q/A-17 of this section), an officer (see Q/A-18 of this section), or a highly-compensated individual (see Q/A-19 of this section).

(c) For purposes of this A-15, an individual who is an employee or independent contractor of a corporation other than the corporation undergoing a change in ownership or control is disregarded for purposes of determining who is a disqualified individual if such individual is employed by the corporation undergoing the change in ownership or control only on the last day of the disqualified individual determination period. Thus, for example, assume that E is an employee of Corporation X, that Y is acquired by Corporation X, and that Y undergoes a change in ownership or control. If E becomes an employee of Y on the date of the acquisition, in determining the disqualified individuals with respect to Y, E is disregarded under this paragraph (c).

Q-16. Is a personal service corporation treated as an individual?

A-16. (a) Yes. For purposes of this section, a personal service corporation (as defined in section 269A(b)(1)), or a noncorporate entity that would be a personal service corporation if it were a corporation, is treated as an individual.

(b) The following example illustrates the principles of this A-16:

Example. Corporation N, a personal service corporation (as defined in section 269A(b)(1)), has a single individual as its sole shareholder and employee. Corporation N performs personal services for Corporation M. The compensation paid to Corporation N by Corporation M puts Corporation N within the group of highly-compensated individuals of Corporation M as determined under A-19 of this section. Thus, Corporation N is treated as a highly-compensated individual with respect to Corporation M.

Q-17. Are all shareholders of a corporation considered shareholders for purposes of paragraphs (a)(1) and (b) of Q/A-15 of this section?

A-17. (a) No. Only an individual who owns stock of a corporation with a fair market value that exceeds 1 percent of the fair market value of the outstanding shares of all classes of the corporation's stock is treated as a disqualified individual with respect to the corporation by reason of stock ownership. An individual who owns a lesser amount of stock may, however, be a disqualified individual with respect to the corporation if such individual is an officer (see Q/A-18) or highly-compensated individual (see Q/A-19) with respect to the corporation.

(b) For purposes of determining the amount of stock owned by an individual for purposes of paragraph (a) of this A-17, the constructive ownership rules of section 318(a) apply. Stock underlying a vested option is considered owned by an individual who holds the vested option (and the stock underlying an unvested option is not considered owned by an individual who holds the unvested option). For purposes of the preceding sentence, however, if the option is exercisable for stock that is not substantially vested (as defined by § § 1.83-3(b) and (j)), the stock underlying the option is not treated as owned by the individual who holds the option. Solely for purposes of determining the amount of stock owned by an individual for purposes of this A-17, mutual and cooperative corporations are treated as having stock.

(c) The following examples illustrates the principles of this A-17:

Example 1. E, an employee of Corporation A, received options under Corporation A's Stock Option Plan. E's stock options vest three years after the date of grant. E is not an officer or highly compensated individual during the disqualified individual determination period. E does not own, and is not considered to own under section 318, any other Corporation A stock. Two years after the options are granted to E, all of Corporation A's stock is acquired by Corporation B. Under Corporation A's Stock Option Plan, E's options are converted to Corporation B options and the vesting schedule remains the same. Under paragraph (b) of this A-17, the stock underlying the unvested options held by E on the date of the change in ownership or control is not considered owned by E. Because E is not considered to own Corporation A stock with a fair market value exceeding 1 percent of the total fair market value of all of the outstanding shares of all classes of Corporation A and E is not an officer or highly-compensated individual during the disqualified individual determination period, E is not a disqualified individual within the meaning of Q&A-15 of this section with respect to Corporation A.

Example 2. Assume the same facts as in Example 1, except that Corporation A's Stock Option Plan provides that all unvested options will vest immediately on a change in ownership or control. Under paragraph (b) of this A-17, the stock underlying the options that vest on the change in ownership or control is considered owned by E. If the stock considered owned by E exceeds 1 percent of the total fair market value of all of the outstanding shares of all classes of Corporation A stock (including for this purpose, all stock owned or constructively owned by all shareholders, provided that no share of stock is counted more than once), E is a disqualified individual within the meaning of Q/A-15 of this section with respect to Corporation A.

Example 3. Assume the same facts as in Example 1 except that E received nonstatutory stock options that are exercisable for stock subject to a substantial risk of forfeiture under section 83. Assume further that under Corporation A's Stock Option Plan, the nonstatutory options will vest on a change in ownership or control. Under paragraph (b) of this A-17, E is not considered to own the stock underlying the options that vest on the change in ownership or control because the options are exercisable for stock subject to a substantial risk of forfeiture within the meaning of section 83. Because E is not considered to own Corporation A stock with a fair market value exceeding 1 percent of the total fair market value of all of the outstanding shares of all classes of Corporation A stock and E is not an officer or highly compensated individual during the disqualified individual determination period, E is not a disqualified individual within the meaning of Q/A-15 of this section with respect to Corporation A.

Q-18. Who is an officer?

A-18. (a) For purposes of this section, whether an individual is an officer with respect to a corporation is determined on the basis of all the facts and circumstances in the particular case (such as the source of the individual's authority, the term for which the individual is elected or appointed, and the nature and extent of the individual's duties). Any individual who has the title of officer is presumed to be an officer unless the facts and circumstances demonstrate that the individual does not have the authority of an officer. However, an individual who does not have the title of officer may nevertheless be considered an officer if the facts and circumstances demonstrate that the individual has the authority of an officer. Generally, the term officer means an administrative executive who is in regular and continued service. The term officer implies continuity of service and excludes those employed for a special and single transaction.

(b) An individual who is an officer with respect to any member of an affiliated group that is treated as one corporation pursuant to Q/A-46 of this section is treated as an officer of such one corporation.

(c) No more than 50 employees (or, if less, the greater of 3 employees, or 10 percent of the employees (rounded up to the nearest integer)) of the corporation (in the case of an affiliated group treated as one corporation, each member of the affiliated group) are treated as disqualified individuals with respect to a corporation by reason of being an officer of the corporation. For purposes of the preceding sentence, the number of employees of the corporation is the greatest number of employees the corporation has during the disqualified individual determination period (as defined in Q/A-20 of this section). If the number of officers of the corporation exceeds the number of employees who may be treated as officers under the first sentence of this paragraph (c), then the employees who are treated as officers for purposes of this section are the highest paid 50 employees (or, if less, the greater of 3 employees, or 10 percent of the employees (rounded up to the nearest integer)) of the corporation when ranked on the basis of compensation (as determined under Q/A-21 of this section) paid during the disqualified individual determination period.

(d) In determining the total number of employees of a corporation for purposes of this A-18, employees are not counted if they normally work less than 17½ hours per week (as defined in section 414(q)(5)(B) and the regulations thereunder) or if they normally work during not more than 6 months during any year (as defined in section 414(q)(5)(C) and the regulations thereunder). However, an employee who is not counted for purposes of the preceding sentence may still be an officer.

Q-19. Who is a highly-compensated individual?

A-19. (a) For purposes of this section, a highly-compensated individual with respect to a corporation is any individual who is, or would be if the individual were an employee, a member of the group consisting of the lesser of the highest paid 1 percent of the employees of the corporation (rounded up to the nearest integer), or the highest paid 250 employees of the corporation, when ranked on the basis of compensation (as determined under Q/A-21 of this section) earned during the disqualified individual determination period (as defined in Q/A-20 of this section). For purposes of the preceding sentence, the number of employees of the corporation is the greatest number of employees the corporation has during the disqualified individual determination period (as defined in Q/A-20 of this section). However, no individual whose annualized compensation during the disqualified individual determination period is less than the amount described in section 414(q)(1)(B)(i) for the year in which the change in ownership or control occurs will be treated as a highly-compensated individual.

(b) An individual who is not an employee of the corporation is not treated as a highly-compensated individual with respect to the corporation on account of compensation received for performing services (such as brokerage, legal, or investment banking services) in connection with a change in ownership or control of the corporation, if the services are performed in the ordinary course of the individual's trade or business and the individual performs similar services for a significant number of clients unrelated to the corporation.

(c) The total number of employees of a corporation for purposes of this A-19 is determined in accordance with Q/A-18(d) of this section. However, an employee who is not counted for purposes of the preceding sentence may still be a highly-compensated individual.

Q-20. What is the disqualified individual determination period?

A-20. The disqualified individual determination period is the twelve-month period prior to and ending on the date of the change in ownership or control of the corporation.

Q-21. How is compensation defined for purposes of determining who is a disqualified individual?

A-21. (a) For purposes of determining who is a disqualified individual, the term compensation means the compensation which was earned by the individual for services performed for the corporation with respect to which the change in ownership or control occurs (changed corporation), for a predecessor entity, or for a related entity. Such compensation is determined without regard to sections 125, 132(f)(4), 402(e)(3), and 402(h)(1)(B). Thus, for example, compensation includes elective or salary reduction contributions to a cafeteria plan, cash or deferred arrangement or tax-sheltered annuity, and amounts credited under a nonqualified deferred compensation plan.

(b) For purposes of this A-21, a predecessor entity is any entity which, as a result of a merger, consolidation, purchase or acquisition of property or stock, corporate separation, or other similar business transaction transfers some or all of its employees to the changed corporation or to a related entity or to a predecessor entity of the changed corporation. The term related entity includes—

(1) All members of a controlled group of corporations (as defined in section 414(b)) that includes the changed corporation or a predecessor entity;

(2) All trades or businesses (whether or not incorporated) that are under common control (as defined in section 414(c)) if such group includes the changed corporation or a predecessor entity;

(3) All members of an affiliated service group (as defined in section 414(m)) that includes the changed corporation or a predecessor entity; and

(4) Any other entities required to be aggregated with the changed corporation or a predecessor entity pursuant to section 414(o) and the regulations thereunder (except leasing organizations as defined in section 414(n)).

(c) For purposes of Q/A-18 and Q/A-19 of this section, compensation that was contingent on the change in ownership or control and that was payable in the year of the change is not treated as compensation.

Contingent on Change in Ownership or Control

Q-22. When is a payment contingent on a change in ownership or control?

A-22. (a) In general, a payment is treated as contingent on a change in ownership or control if the payment would not, in fact, have been made had no change in ownership or control occurred, even if the payment is also conditioned on the occurrence of another event. A payment generally is treated as one which would not, in fact, have been made in the absence of a change in ownership or control unless it is substantially certain, at the time of the change, that the payment would have been made whether or not the change occurred. (But see Q/A-23 of this section regarding payments under agreements entered into after a change in ownership or control.) A payment that becomes vested as a result of a change in ownership or control is not treated as a payment which was substantially certain to have been made whether or not the change occurred. For purposes of this A-22, vested means the payment is substantially vested within the meaning of § 1.83-3(b) and (j) or the right to the payment is not otherwise subject to a substantial risk of forfeiture as defined by section 83(c).

(b)(1) For purposes of paragraph (a), a payment is treated as contingent on a change in ownership or control if—

(i) The payment is contingent on an event that is closely associated with a change in ownership or control;

(ii) A change in ownership or control actually occurs; and

(iii) The event is materially related to the change in ownership or control.

(2) For purposes of paragraph (b)(1)(i) of this A-22, a payment is treated as contingent on an event that is closely associated with a change in ownership or control unless it is substantially certain, at the time of the event, that the payment would have been made whether or not the event occurred. An event is considered closely associated with a change in ownership or control if the event is of a type often preliminary or subsequent to, or otherwise closely associated with, a change in ownership or control. For example, the following events are considered closely associated with a change in the ownership or control of a corporation: The onset of a tender offer with respect to the corporation; a substantial increase in the market price of the corporation's stock that occurs within a short period (but only if such increase occurs prior to a change in ownership or control); the cessation of the listing of the corporation's stock on an established securities market; the acquisition of more than 5 percent of the corporation's stock by a person (or more than one person acting as a group) not in control of the corporation; the voluntary or involuntary termination of the disqualified individual's employment; a significant reduction in the disqualified individual's job responsibilities; and a change in ownership or control as defined in the disqualified individual's employment agreement (or elsewhere) that does not meet the definition of a change in ownership or control described in Q/A-27, 28, or 29 of this section. Whether other events are treated as closely associated with a change in ownership or control is based on all the facts and circumstances of the particular case.

(3) For purposes of determining whether an event (as described in paragraph (b)(2) of this A-22) is materially related to a change in ownership or control, the event is presumed to be materially related to a change in ownership or control if such event occurs within the period beginning one year before and ending one year after the date of the change in ownership or control. If such event occurs outside of the period beginning one year before and ending one year after the date of change in ownership or control, the event is presumed not materially related to the change in ownership or control. A payment does not fail to be contingent on a change in ownership or control merely because it is also contingent on the occurrence of a second event (without regard to whether the second event is closely associated with or materially related to a change in ownership or control). Similarly, a payment that is treated as contingent on a change in ownership or control because it is contingent on a closely associated event does not fail to be treated as contingent on a change in ownership or control merely because it is also contingent on the occurrence of a second event (without regard to whether the second event is closely associated with or materially related to a change in ownership or control).

(c) A payment that would in fact have been made had no change in ownership or control occurred is treated as contingent on a change in ownership or control if the change in ownership or control (or the occurrence of an event that is closely associated with and materially related to a change in ownership or control within the meaning of paragraph (b)(1) of this A-22), accelerates the time at which the payment is made. Thus, for example, if a change in ownership or control accelerates the time of payment of deferred compensation that is vested without regard to the change in ownership or control, the payment may be treated as contingent on the change. See Q/A-24 of this section regarding the portion of a payment that is so treated. See also Q/A-8 of this section regarding the exemption for certain payments under qualified plans and Q/A-40 of this section regarding the treatment of a payment as reasonable compensation.

(d) A payment is treated as contingent on a change in ownership or control even if the employment or independent contractor relationship of the disqualified individual is not terminated (voluntarily or involuntarily) as a result of the change.

(e) The following examples illustrate the principles of this A-22:

Example 1. A corporation grants a stock appreciation right to a disqualified individual, A, more than one year before a change in ownership or control. After the stock appreciation right vests and becomes exercisable, a change in ownership or control of the corporation occurs, and A exercises the right. Assuming neither the granting nor the vesting of the stock appreciation right is contingent on a change in ownership or control, the payment made on exercise is not contingent on the change in ownership or control.

Example 2. A contract between a corporation and B, a disqualified individual, provides that a payment will be made to B if the corporation undergoes a change in ownership or control and B's employment with the corporation is terminated at any time over the succeeding 5 years. Eighteen months later, a change in the ownership of the corporation occurs. Two years after the change in ownership, B's employment is terminated and the payment is made to B. Because it was not substantially certain that the corporation would have made the payment to B on B's termination of employment if there had not been a change in ownership, the payment is treated as contingent on the change in ownership under paragraph (a) of this A-22. This is true even though B's termination of employment is presumed not to be, and in fact may not be, materially related to the change in ownership or control.

Example 3. A contract between a corporation and C, a disqualified individual, provides that a payment will be made to C if C's employment is terminated at any time over the succeeding 3 years (without regard to whether or not there is a change in ownership or control). Eighteen months after the contract is entered into, a change in the ownership or control of the corporation occurs. Six months after the change in ownership or control, C's employment is terminated and the payment is made to C. Termination of employment is considered an event closely associated with a change in ownership or control. Because the termination occurred within one year after the date of the change in ownership or control, the termination of C's employment is presumed to be materially related to the change in ownership or control under paragraph (b)(3) of this A-22. If this presumption is not successfully rebutted, the payment will be treated as contingent on the change in ownership or control under paragraph (b) of this A-22.

Example 4. A contract between a corporation and a disqualified individual, D, provides that a payment will be made to D upon the onset of a tender offer for shares of the corporation's stock. A tender offer is made on December 1, 2008, and the payment is made to D. Although the tender offer is unsuccessful, it leads to a negotiated merger with another entity on June 1, 2009, which results in a change in the ownership or control of the corporation. It was not substantially certain, at the time of the onset of the tender offer, that the payment would have been made had no tender offer taken place. The onset of a tender offer is considered closely associated with a change in ownership or control. Because the tender offer occurred within one year before the date of the change in ownership or control of the corporation, the onset of the tender offer is presumed to be materially related to the change in ownership or control. If this presumption is not rebutted, the payment will be treated as contingent on the change in ownership or control. If no change in ownership or control had occurred, the payment would not be treated as contingent on a change in ownership or control; however, the payment still could be a parachute payment under Q/A-37 of this section if the contract violated a generally enforced securities law or regulation.

Example 5. A contract between a corporation and a disqualified individual, E, provides that a payment will be made to E if the corporation's level of product sales or profits reaches a specified level. At the time the contract was entered into, the parties had no reason to believe that such an increase in the corporation's level of product sales or profits would be preliminary or subsequent to, or otherwise closely associated with, a change in ownership or control of the corporation. Eighteen months later, a change in the ownership or control of the corporation occurs and within one year after the date of the change of ownership or control, the corporation's level of product sales or profits reaches the specified level. Under these facts and circumstances (and in the absence of contradictory evidence), the increase in product sales or profits of the corporation is not an event closely associated with the change in ownership or control of the corporation. Accordingly, even if the increase is materially related to the change in ownership or control, the payment will not be treated as contingent on a change in ownership or control.

Q-23. May a payment be treated as contingent on a change in ownership or control if the payment is made under an agreement entered into after the change?

A-23. (a) No. Payments are not treated as contingent on a change in ownership or control if they are made (or are to be made) pursuant to an agreement entered into after the change (a post-change agreement). For this purpose, an agreement that is executed after a change in ownership or control pursuant to a legally enforceable agreement that was entered into before the change is considered to have been entered into before the change. (See Q/A-9 of this section regarding the exemption for reasonable compensation for services rendered on or after a change in ownership or control.) If an individual has a right to receive a payment that would be a parachute payment if made under an agreement entered into prior to a change in ownership or control (pre-change agreement) and gives up that right as bargained-for consideration for benefits under a post-change agreement, the agreement is treated as a post-change agreement only to the extent the value of the payments under the agreement exceed the value of the payments under the pre-change agreement. To the extent payments under the agreement have the same value as the payments under the pre-change agreement, such payments retain their character as parachute payments subject to this section.

(b) The following examples illustrate the principles of this A-23:

Example 1. Assume that a disqualified individual is an employee of a corporation. A change in ownership or control of the corporation occurs, and thereafter the individual enters into an employment agreement with the acquiring company. Because the agreement is entered into after the change in ownership or control occurs, payments to be made under the agreement are not treated as contingent on the change.

Example 2. Assume the same facts as in Example 1, except that the agreement between the disqualified individual and the acquiring company is executed after the change in ownership or control, pursuant to a legally enforceable agreement entered into before the change. Payments to be made under the agreement may be treated as contingent on the change in ownership or control pursuant to Q/A-22 of this section. However, see Q/A-9 of this section regarding the exemption from the definition of parachute payment for certain amounts of reasonable compensation.

Example 3. Assume the same facts as in Example 1, except that prior to the change in ownership or control, the individual and corporation enter into an agreement under which the individual will receive parachute payments in the event of a change in ownership or control of the corporation. After the change, the individual agrees to give up the right to payments under the pre-change agreement that would be parachute payments if made, in exchange for compensation under a new agreement with the acquiring corporation. Because the individual gave up the right to parachute payments under the pre-change agreement in exchange for other payments under the post-change agreement, payments in an amount equal to the parachute payments under the pre-change agreement are treated as contingent on the change in ownership or control under this A-23. Because the post-change agreement was entered into after the change, payments in excess of this amount are not treated as parachute payments.

Q-24. If a payment is treated as contingent on a change in ownership or control, is the full amount of the payment so treated?

A-24.

(a)(1) General rule. Yes. If the payment is a transfer of property, the amount of the payment is determined under Q/A-12 or Q/A-13 of this section. For all other payments, the amount of the payment is determined under Q/A-11 of this section. However, in certain circumstances, described in paragraphs (b) and (c) of this A-24, only a portion of the payment is treated as contingent on the change. Paragraph (b) of this A-24 applies to a payment that is vested, without regard to the change in ownership or control, and is treated as contingent on the change in ownership or control because the change accelerates the time at which the payment is made. Paragraph (c) of this A-24 applies to a payment that becomes vested as a result of the change in ownership or control if, without regard to the change in ownership or control, the payment was contingent only on the continued performance of services for the corporation for a specified period of time and if the payment is attributable, at least in part, to services performed before the date the payment becomes vested. Paragraph (b) or (c) does not apply to any payment (or portion thereof) if the payment is treated as contingent on the change in ownership or control pursuant to Q/A-25 of this section. For purposes of this A-24, vested has the same meaning as provided in Q/A-22(a).

(2) Reduction by reasonable compensation. The amount of a payment under paragraph (a)(1) of this A-24 is reduced by any portion of such payment that the taxpayer establishes by clear and convincing evidence is reasonable compensation for personal services rendered by the disqualified individual on or after the date of the change of control. See Q/A-9 and Q/A-38 through 44 of this section for rules concerning reasonable compensation. The portion of an amount treated as contingent under paragraph (b) or (c) of this A-24 may not be reduced by reasonable compensation.

(b) Vested payments. This paragraph (b) applies if a payment is vested, without regard to the change in ownership or control, and is treated as contingent on the change in ownership or control because the change accelerates the time at which the payment is made. In such a case, the portion of the payment, if any, that is treated as contingent on the change in ownership or control is the amount by which the amount of the accelerated payment exceeds the present value of the payment absent the acceleration. If the value of such a payment absent the acceleration is not reasonably ascertainable, and the acceleration of the payment does not significantly increase the present value of the payment absent the acceleration, the present value of the payment absent the acceleration is treated as equal to the amount of the accelerated payment. If the value of the payment absent the acceleration is not reasonably ascertainable, but the acceleration significantly increases the present value of the payment, the future value of such payment is treated as equal to the amount of the accelerated payment. For rules on determining present value, see paragraph (e) of this A-24, Q/A-32, and Q/A-33 of this section.

(c)(1) Nonvested payments. This paragraph (c) applies to a payment that becomes vested as a result of the change in ownership or control to the extent that—

(i) Without regard to the change in ownership or control, the payment was contingent only on the continued performance of services for the corporation for a specified period of time; and

(ii) The payment is attributable, at least in part, to the performance of services before the date the payment is made or becomes certain to be made.

(2) The portion of the payment subject to paragraph (c) of this A-24 that is treated as contingent on the change in ownership or control is the amount described in paragraph (b) of this A-24, plus an amount, as determined in paragraph (c)(4) of this A-24, to reflect the lapse of the obligation to continue to perform services. In no event can the portion of the payment treated as contingent on the change in ownership or control under this paragraph (c) exceed the amount of the accelerated payment, or, if the payment is not accelerated, the present value of the payment.

(3) For purposes of this paragraph (c) of this A-24, the acceleration of the vesting of a stock option or the lapse of a restriction on restricted stock is considered to significantly increase the value of a payment.

(4) The amount reflecting the lapse of the obligation to continue to perform services (described in paragraph (c)(2) of this A-24) is 1 percent of the amount of the accelerated payment multiplied by the number of full months between the date that the individual's right to receive the payment is vested and the date that, absent the acceleration, the payment would have been vested. This paragraph (c)(4) applies to the accelerated vesting of a payment in the nature of compensa-

tion even if the time at which the payment is made is not accelerated. In such a case, the amount reflecting the lapse of the obligation to continue to perform services is 1 percent of the present value of the future payment multiplied by the number of full months between the date that the individual's right to receive the payment is vested and the date that, absent the acceleration, the payment would have been vested.

(d) Application of this A-24 to certain payments.

(1) Benefits under a nonqualified deferred compensation plan. In the case of a payment of benefits under a nonqualified deferred compensation plan, paragraph (b) of this A-24 applies to the extent benefits under the plan are vested without regard to the change in ownership or control. Paragraph (c) of this A-24 applies to the extent benefits under the plan become vested as a result of the change in ownership or control and are attributable, at least in part, to the performance of services prior to vesting. Any other payment of benefits under a nonqualified deferred compensation plan is a payment in the nature of compensation subject to the general rule of paragraph (a) of this A-24 and the rules in Q/A-11 of this section.

(2) Employment agreements. The general rule of paragraph (a) of this A-24 (and not the rules in paragraphs (b) or (c)) applies to the payment of amounts due under an employment agreement on a termination of employment or a change in ownership or control that otherwise would be attributable to the performance of services (or refraining from the performance of services) during any period that begins after the date of termination of employment or change in ownership or control, as applicable. For purposes of this paragraph (d)(2) of this A-24, an employment agreement means an agreement between an employee or independent contractor and employer or service recipient which describes, among other things, the amount of compensation or remuneration payable to the employee or independent contractor. See Q/A-42(b) and 44 of this section for the treatment of the remaining amounts of salary under an employment agreement.

(3) Vesting due to an event other than services. Neither paragraph (b) nor (c) of this A-24 applies to a payment if (without regard to the change in ownership or control) vesting of the payment depends on an event other than the performance of services, such as the attainment of a performance goal, and the event does not occur prior to the change in ownership or control. In such circumstances, the full amount of the accelerated payment is treated as contingent on the change in ownership or control under paragraph (a) of this A-24. However, see Q/A-39 of this section for rules relating to the reduction of the excess parachute payment by the portion of the payment which is established to be reasonable compensation for personal services actually rendered before the date of a change in ownership or control.

(e) Present value. For purposes of this A-24, the present value of a payment is determined as of the date on which the accelerated payment is made.

(f) Examples. The following examples illustrate the principles of this A-24:

Example 1. (i) Corporation maintains a qualified plan and a nonqualified supplemental retirement plan (SERP) for its executives. Benefits under the SERP are not paid to participants until retirement. E, a disqualified individual with respect to Corporation, has a vested account balance of $500,000 under the SERP. A change in ownership or control of Corporation occurs. The SERP provides that in the event of a change in ownership or control, all vested accounts will be paid to SERP participants.

(ii) Because E was vested in $500,000 of benefits under the SERP prior to the change in ownership or control and the change merely accelerated the time at which the payment was made to E, only a portion of the payment, as determined under paragraph (b) of this A-24, is treated as contingent on the change. Thus, the portion of the payment that is treated as contingent on the change is the amount by which the amount of the accelerated payment ($500,000) exceeds the present value of the payment absent the acceleration.

(iii) Assume the same facts as in paragraph (i) of this Example 1, except that E's account balance of $500,000 is not vested. Instead, assume that E will vest in E's account balance of $500,000 in 2 years if E continues to perform services for the next 2 years. Assume further that the SERP provides that all unvested SERP benefits vest immediately on a change in ownership or control and are paid to the participants. Because the vesting of the SERP payment, without regard to the change, depends only on the performance of services for a specified period of time and the payment is attributable, in part, to the performance of services before the change in ownership or control, only a portion of the $500,000 payment, as determined under paragraph (c) of this A-24, is treated as contingent on the change. The portion of the payment that is treated as contingent on the change is the lesser of the amount of the accelerated payment or the amount by which the accelerated payment exceeds the present value of the payment absent the acceleration, plus an amount to reflect the lapse of the obligation to continue to perform services.

(iv) Assume the same facts as in paragraph (i) of this Example 1, except that in addition to the pay out of the vested account balance of $500,000 on the change in ownership or control, an additional $70,000 will be credited to E's account and included in the payment to E. Because the $500,000 was vested without regard to the change in ownership or control, paragraph (b) of this A-24 applies to the $500,000 payment. Because the $70,000 is not vested, without regard to the change, and is not attributable to the performance of services prior to the change, the entire $70,000 payment is contingent on the change in ownership or control under paragraph (a) of this A-24.

(v) Assume the same facts as in paragraph (i) of this Example 1, except that the benefit under the SERP is calculated using a percentage of final average compensation multiplied by years of service. If, contingent on the change in ownership or control, E is credited with additional years of service, an adjustment to final average compensation, or an increase in the applicable percentage, any increase in the benefit payable under the SERP is not attributable to the performance of services prior to the change, and the entire increase in the benefit is contingent on the change in ownership or control under paragraph (a) of this A-24.

Example 2. As a result of a change in the effective control of a corporation D, a disqualified individual with respect to the corporation, receives accelerated payment of D's vested account balance in a nonqualified deferred compensation account plan. Actual interest and other earnings on the plan assets are credited to each account as earned before distribution. Investment of the plan assets is not restricted in such a manner as would prevent the earning of a market rate of return on the plan assets. The date on which D would have received D's vested account balance absent the change in ownership or control is uncertain, and the rate of earnings on the plan assets is not fixed. Thus, the amount of the payment absent the acceleration is not reasonably ascertainable. Under these facts, acceleration of the payment does not significantly increase the present value of the payment absent the acceleration, and the present value of the payment absent the acceleration is treated as equal to the amount of the accelerated payment. Accordingly, no portion of the payment is treated as contingent on the change.

Example 3. (i) On January 15, 2006, a corporation and a disqualified individual, F, enter into a contract providing for a retention bonus of $500,000 to be paid to F on January 15, 2011. The payment of the bonus will be forfeited by F if F does not remain employed by the corporation for the entire 5-year period. However, the contract provides that the full amount of the payment will be made immediately on a change in ownership or control of the corporation during the 5-year period. On January 15, 2009, a change in ownership or control of the corporation occurs and the full amount of the payment ($500,000) is made on that date to F. Under these facts, the payment of $500,000 was contingent only on F's performance of services for a specified period and is attributable, in part, to the performance of services before the change in ownership or control. Therefore, only a portion of the payment, as determined under paragraph (c) of this A-24 is treated as contingent on the change. The portion of the payment that is treated as contingent on the change is the amount by which the amount of the accelerated payment (i.e., $500,000, the amount paid to the individual because of the change in ownership) exceeds the present value of the payment that was expected to have been made absent the acceleration (i.e., $406,838, the present value on January 15, 2009, of a $500,000 payment on January 15, 2011), plus $115,000 (1 percent x 23 months x $500,000) which is the amount reflecting the lapse of the obligation to continue to perform services. Accordingly, the amount of the payment treated as contingent on the change in ownership or control is $208,162, the sum of $93,162 ($500,000-$406,838) + $115,000). This result does not change if F actually remains employed until the end of the 5-year period.

(ii) Assume the same facts as in paragraph (i) of this Example 3, except that the retention bonus will vest on the change in ownership or control, but will not be paid until January 15, 2011 (the original date in the contract). Because the payment of $500,000 was contingent only on F's performance of services for a specified period and is attributable, in part, to the performance of services before the change in ownership or control, only a portion of the $500,000 payment is treated as contingent on the change in ownership or control as determined under paragraph (c) of this A-24. Because there is accelerated vesting of the bonus, the portion of the payment treated as contingent on the change is the amount described in paragraph (b) of this A-27, which is $0 under these facts, plus an amount reflecting the lapse of the obligation to continue to perform services which is $93,573 (1 percent x 23 months x $406,838 (the present value of a $500,000 payment).

Example 4. (i) On January 15, 2006, a corporation gives to a disqualified individual, in connection with her performance of services to the corporation, a bonus of 1,000 shares of the corporation's stock. Under the terms of the bonus arrangement, the individual is obligated to return the stock to the corporation if she terminates her employment for any reason prior to January 15, 2011. However, if there is a change in the ownership or effective control of the corporation prior to January 15, 2011, she ceases to be obligated to return the stock. The individual's rights in the stock are treated as substantially nonvested (within the meaning of § 1.83-3(b) and (j)) during that period. On January 15, 2009, a change in the ownership of the corporation occurs. On that day, the fair market value of the stock is $500,000.

(ii) Under these facts, the payment was contingent only on performance of services for a specified period and is attributable, in part, to the performance of services before the change in ownership or control. Thus, only a portion of the payment, as determined under paragraph (c) of this A-24, is treated as contingent on the change in ownership or control. The portion of the payment that is treated as contingent on the change is the amount by which the present value of the accelerated payment on January 15, 2009 ($500,000), exceeds the present value of the payment that was expected to have been made on January 15, 2011, plus an amount reflecting the lapse of the obligation to continue to perform services. At the time of the change, it cannot be reasonably ascertained what the value of the stock would have been on January 15, 2011. The acceleration of the lapse of a restriction on stock is treated as significantly increasing the value of the payment. Therefore, the value of such stock on January 15, 2011, is deemed to be $500,000, the amount of the accelerated payment. The present value on January 15, 2009, of a $500,000 payment to be made on January 15, 2011, is $406,838. Thus, the portion of the payment treated as contingent on the change is $208,162, the sum of $93,162 ($500,000-$406,838), plus $115,000 (1 percent x 23 months x $500,000), the amount reflecting the lapse of the obligation to continue to perform services.

Example 5. (i) On January 15, 2006, a corporation grants to a disqualified individual nonqualified stock options to purchase 30,000 shares of the corporation's stock. The options will be forfeited by the individual if he fails to perform personal services for the corporation until January 15, 2009. The options will, however, vest in the individual at an earlier date if there is a change in ownership or control of the corporation. On January 16, 2008, a change in the ownership or control of the corporation occurs and the options become vested in the individual. The value of the options on January 16, 2008, determined in accordance with Q/A-13, is $600,000.

(ii) The payment of the options to purchase 30,000 shares was contingent only on performance of services for the corporation until January 15, 2009, and is attributable, in part, to the performance of services before the change in ownership or control. Therefore, only a portion of the payment is treated as contingent on the change. The portion of the payment that is treated as contingent on the change is the amount by which the accelerated payment on January 16, 2008 ($600,000) exceeds the present value on January 16, 2008, of the payment that was expected to have been made on January 15, 2009, absent the acceleration, plus an amount reflecting the lapse of the obligation to continue to perform services. At the time of the change, it cannot be reasonably ascertained what the value of the options would have been on January 15, 2009. The acceleration of vesting in the options is treated as significantly increasing the value of the payment. Therefore, the value of such options on January 15, 2009, is deemed to be $600,000, the amount of the accelerated payment. The present value on January 16, 2008, of a $600,000 payment to be made on January 15, 2009, is $549,964. Thus, the portion of the payment treated as contingent on the change is $116,036, the sum of $50,036 ($600,000-$549,964), plus an amount reflecting the lapse of the obligation to continue to perform services which is $66,000 (1 percent x 11 months x $600,000).

Example 6. (i) Assume the same facts as in Example 5, except that the options become vested periodically (absent a change in ownership or control), with one-third of the options vesting on January 15, 2007, 2008, and 2009, respectively. Thus, options to purchase 20,000 shares vest independently of the January 16, 2008, change in ownership or control and the options to purchase the remaining 10,000 shares vest as a result of the change in ownership or control.

(ii) The payment of the options to purchase 10,000 shares was contingent only on performance of services for the corporation until January 15, 2009, and is attributable, in part, to the performance of services before the change in ownership or control. Therefore, only a portion of the payment as determined under paragraph (c) of this A-24 is treated as contingent on the change in ownership or control. The portion of the payment that is treated as contingent on the change in ownership or control is the amount by which the accelerated payment on January 16, 2008 ($200,000) exceeds the present value on January 16, 2008, of the payment that was expected to have been made on January 15, 2009, absent the acceleration, plus an amount reflecting the lapse of the obligation to perform services. At the time of the change in ownership or control, it cannot be reasonably ascertained what the value of the options would have been on January 15, 2009. The acceleration of vesting in the options is treated as significantly increasing the value of the payment. Therefore, the value of such options on January 15, 2009, is deemed to be $200,000, the amount of the accelerated payment. The present value on January 16, 2008, of a $200,000 payment to be made on January 15, 2009, is $183,328.38. Thus, the portion of the payment treated as contingent on the change is $38,671.62, the sum of $16,671.62 ($200,000-$183,328.38), plus an amount reflecting the lapse of the obligation to continue to perform services which is $22,000 (1 percent x 11 months x $200,000).

Example 7. Assume the same facts as in Example 5, except that the option agreement provides that the options will vest either on the corporation's level of profits reaching a specified level, or if earlier, on the date on which there is a change in ownership or control of the corporation. The corporation's level of profits do not reach the specified level prior to January 16, 2008. In such case, the full amount of the payment, $600,000, is treated as contingent on the change in ownership or control under paragraph (a) of this A-24. Because the payment was not contingent only on the performance of services for the corporation for a specified period, the rules of paragraph (b) and (c) of this A-24 do not apply. See Q/A-39 of this section for rules relating to the reduction of the excess parachute payment by the portion of the payment which is established to be reasonable compensation for personal services actually rendered before the date of a change in ownership or control.

Example 8. On January 1, 2005, E, a disqualified individual with respect to Corporation X, enters into an employment agreement with Corporation X under which E will be paid wages of $200,000 each year during the 5-year employment agreement. The employment agreement provides that if a change in ownership or control of Corporation X occurs, E will be paid the present value of the remaining salary under the employment agreement. On January 1, 2006, a change in ownership or control of Corporation X occurs, E is terminated, and E receives a payment of the present value of $200,000 for each of the 4 years remaining under the employment agreement. Because the payment represents future salary under an employment agreement (i.e., amounts otherwise attributable to the performance of services for periods that begin after the termination of employment), the general rule of paragraph (a) of this A-24 applies to the payment and not the rules of paragraphs (b) and (c) of this A-24. See Q/A-42(c) and 44 of this section for the treatment of the remaining payments under an employment agreement.

Presumption That Payment Is Contingent on Change

Q-25. Is there a presumption that certain payments are contingent on a change in ownership or control?

A-25. Yes, for purposes of this section, any payment is presumed to be contingent on such a change unless the contrary is established by clear and convincing evidence if the payment is made pursuant to—

(a) An agreement entered into within one year before the date of a change in ownership or control; or

(b) An amendment that modifies a previous agreement in any significant respect, if the amendment is made within one year before the date of a change in ownership or control. In the case of an amendment described in paragraph (b) of this A-25, only the portion of any payment that exceeds the amount of such payment that would have been made in the absence of the amendment is presumed, by reason of the amendment, to be contingent on the change in ownership or control.

Q-26. How may the presumption described in Q/A-25 of this section be rebutted?

A-26. (a) To rebut the presumption described in Q/A-25 of this section, the taxpayer must establish by clear and convincing evidence that the payment is not contingent on the change in ownership or control. Whether the payment is contingent on such change is determined on the basis of all the facts and circumstances of the particular case. Factors relevant to such a determination include, but are not limited to, the content of the agreement or amendment and the circumstances surrounding the execution of the agreement or amendment, such as whether it was entered into at a time when a takeover attempt had commenced and the degree of likelihood that a change in ownership or control would actually occur. However, even if the presumption is rebutted with respect to an agreement, some or all of the payments under the agreement may still be contingent on the change in ownership or control pursuant to Q/A-22 of this section.

(b) In the case of an agreement described in Q/A-25 of this section, clear and convincing evidence that the agreement is one of the three following types will generally rebut the presumption that payments under the agreement are contingent on the change in ownership or control—

(1) A nondiscriminatory employee plan or program as defined in paragraph (c) of this A-26;

(2) A contract between a corporation and an individual that replaces a prior contract entered into by the same parties more than one year before the change in ownership or control, if the new contract does not provide for increased payments (apart from normal increases attributable to increased responsibilities or cost of living adjustments), accelerate the payment of amounts due at a future time, or modify (to the individual's benefit) the terms or conditions under which payments will be made; or

(3) A contract between a corporation and an individual who did not perform services for the corporation prior to the one year period before the change in ownership or control occurs, if the contract does not provide for payments that are significantly different in amount, timing, terms, or conditions from those provided under contracts entered into by the corporation (other than contracts that themselves were entered

into within one year before the change in ownership or control and in contemplation of the change) with individuals performing comparable services.

(c) For purposes of this section, the term nondiscriminatory employee plan or program means: a group term life insurance plan that meets the requirements of section 79(d); a self insured medical reimbursement plan that meets the requirements of section 105(h); a cafeteria plan (within the meaning of section 125); an educational assistance program (within the meaning of section 127); a dependent care assistance program (within the meaning of section 129); a no-additional-cost service (within the meaning of section 132(b)) or qualified employee discount (within the meaning of section 132(c)); a qualified retirement planning services program under section 132(m); an adoption assistance program (within the meaning of section 137); and such other items as provided by the Commissioner in published guidance of general applicability under § 601.601(d)(2). Payments under certain other plans are exempt from the definition of parachute payment under Q/A-8 of this section.

(d) The following examples illustrate the application of the presumption:

Example 1. A corporation and a disqualified individual who is an employee of the corporation enter into an employment contract. The contract replaces a prior contract entered into by the same parties more than one year before the change in ownership or control and the new contract does not provide for any increased payments other than a cost of living adjustment, does not accelerate the payment of amounts due at a future time, and does not modify (to the individual's benefit) the terms or conditions under which payments will be made. Clear and convincing evidence of these facts rebuts the presumption described in A-25 of this section. However, payments under the contract still may be contingent on the change in ownership or control pursuant to Q/A-22 of this section.

Example 2. Assume the same facts as in Example 1, except that the contract is entered into after a tender offer for the corporation's stock had commenced and it was likely that a change in ownership or control would occur and the contract provides for a substantial bonus payment to the individual upon his signing the contract. The individual has performed services for the corporation for many years, but previous employment contracts between the corporation and the individual did not provide for a similar signing bonus. One month after the contract is entered into, a change in the ownership or control of the corporation occurs. All payments under the contract are presumed to be contingent on the change in ownership or control even though the bonus payment would have been legally required even if no change had occurred. Clear and convincing evidence of these facts rebuts the presumption described in A-25 of this section with respect to all of the payments under the contract with the exception of the bonus payment (which is treated as contingent on the change). However, payments other than the bonus under the contract still may be contingent on the change in ownership or control pursuant to Q/A-22 of this section.

Example 3. A corporation and a disqualified individual, who is an employee of the corporation, enter into an employment contract within one year of a change in ownership or control of the corporation. Under the contract, in the event of a change in ownership or control and subsequent termination of employment, certain payments will be made to the individual. A change in ownership or control occurs, but the individual is not terminated until 2 years after the change in ownership or control. If clear and convincing evidence does not rebut the presumption described in A-25 of this section, because the payment is made pursuant to an agreement entered into within one year of the date of the change in ownership or control, the payment is presumed contingent on the change under A-25 of this section. This is true even though A's termination of employment is presumed not to be materially related to the change in ownership or control under Q/A-22 of this section.

Change in Ownership or Control

Q-27. When does a change in the ownership of a corporation occur?

A-27. (a) For purposes of this section, a change in the ownership of a corporation occurs on the date that any one person, or more than one person acting as a group (as defined in paragraph (b) of this A-27), acquires ownership of stock of the corporation that, together with stock held by such person or group, has more than 50 percent of the total fair market value or total voting power of the stock of such corporation. However, if any one person, or more than one person acting as a group, is considered to own more than 50 percent of the total fair market value or total voting power of the stock of a corporation, the acquisition of additional stock by the same person or persons is not considered to cause a change in the ownership of the corporation (or to cause a change in the effective control of the corporation (within the meaning of Q/A-28 of this section)). An increase in the percentage of stock owned by any one person, or persons acting as a group, as a result of a transaction in which the corporation acquires its stock in exchange for property will be treated as an acquisition of stock for purposes of this section. This A-27 applies only when there is a transfer of stock of a corporation (or issuance of stock of a corporation) and stock in such corporation remains outstanding after the transaction. (See Q/A-29 for rules regarding the transfer of assets of a corporation).

(b) For purposes of paragraph (a) of this A-27, persons will not be considered to be acting as a group merely because they happen to purchase or own stock of the same corporation at the same time, or as a result of the same public offering. However, persons will be considered to be acting as a group if they are owners of a corporation that enters into a merger, consolidation, purchase or acquisition of stock, or similar business transaction with the corporation. If a person, including an entity shareholder, owns stock in both corporations that enter into a merger, consolidation, purchase or acquisition of stock, or similar transaction, such shareholder is considered to be acting as a group with other shareholders in a corporation only with respect to the ownership in that corporation prior to the transaction giving rise to the change and not with respect to the ownership interest in the other corporation.

(c) For purposes of this A-27 (and Q/A-28 and 29), section 318(a) applies to determine stock ownership. Stock underlying a vested option is considered owned by the individual who holds the vested option (and the stock underlying an unvested option is not considered owned by the individual who holds the unvested option). For purposes of the preceding sentence, however, if the option is exercisable for stock that is not substantially vested (as defined by sections 1.83-3(b) and (j)), the stock underlying the option is not treated as owned by the individual who holds the option. In addition, mutual and cooperative corporations are treated as having stock for purposes of this A-27.

(d) The following examples illustrate the principles of this A-27:

Example 1. Corporation M has owned stock with a fair market value equal to 19 percent of the value of the stock of Corporation N (an otherwise unrelated corporation) for many years prior to 2006. Corporation M acquires additional stock with a fair market value equal to 15 percent of the value of the stock of Corporation N on January 1, 2006, and an additional 18 percent on February 21, 2007. As of February 21, 2007, Corporation M has acquired stock with a fair market value greater than 50 percent of the value of the stock of Corporation N. Thus, a change in the ownership of Corporation N is considered to occur on February 21, 2007 (assuming that Corporation M did not have effective control of Corporation N immediately prior to the acquisition on that date).

Example 2. All of the corporation's stock is owned by the founders of the corporation. The board of directors of the corporation decides to offer shares of the corporation to the public. After the public offering, the founders of the corporation own a total of 40 percent of the corporation's stock, and members of the public own 60 percent. If no one person (or more than one person acting as a group) owns more than 50 percent of the corporation's stock (by value or voting power) after the public offering, there is no change in the ownership of the corporation.

Example 3. Corporation P merges into Corporation O (a previously unrelated corporation). In the merger, the shareholders of Corporation P receive Corporation O stock in exchange for their Corporation P stock. Immediately after the merger, the former shareholders of Corporation P own stock with a fair market value equal to 60 percent of the value of the stock of Corporation O, and the former shareholders of Corporation O own stock with a fair market value equal to 40 percent of the value of the stock of Corporation O. The former shareholders of Corporation P will be treated as acting as a group in their acquisition of Corporation O stock. Thus, a change in the ownership of Corporation O occurs on the date of the merger. See Q/A-29, Example 3, regarding whether there is a change in ownership or control of P.

Example 4. Assume the same facts as in Example 3, except that immediately after the change, the former shareholders of Corporation P own stock with a fair market value of 51 percent of the value of Corporation O stock and the former shareholders of Corporation O own stock with a fair market value equal to 49 percent of the value of Corporation O stock. Assume further that prior to the merger several Corporation O shareholders also owned Corporation P stock (overlapping shareholders). In the merger, those O shareholders received additional O stock by virtue of their ownership of P stock with a fair market value of 5 percent of the value of Corporation O stock. Including the O stock attributable to the P shares, the O shareholders hold 54 percent of O after the transaction. However, those overlapping shareholders that owned both Corporation O stock and Corporation P stock prior to the merger are treated as acting as a group with the Corporation O shareholders only with respect to their ownership interest in Corporation O prior to the transaction. Therefore, because the Corporation O shareholders owned 49 percent of the value of Corporation O stock, a change in the ownership of Corporation O occurs on the date of the merger. See Q/A-29, Example 3, regarding whether there is a change in ownership or control of P.

Example 5. A, an individual, owns stock with a fair market value equal to 20 percent of the value of the stock of Corporation Q. On January 1, 2007, Corporation Q acquires in a redemption for cash all of the stock held by shareholders other than A. Thus, A is left as the sole shareholder of Corporation O. A change in ownership of Corporation O is considered to occur on January 1, 2007 (assuming that A did not have effective control of Corporation Q immediately prior to the redemption).

Example 6. Assume the same facts as in Example 5, except that A owns stock with a fair market value equal to 51 percent of the value of all the stock of Corporation Q immediately prior to the redemption. There is no change in the ownership of Corporation Q as a result of the redemption.

Q-28. When does a change in the effective control of a corporation occur?

A-28. (a) Notwithstanding that a corporation has not undergone a change in ownership under Q/A-27, for purposes of this section, a change in the effective control of a corporation is presumed to occur on the date that either—

(1) Any one person, or more than one person acting as a group (as determined under paragraph (e) of this A-28), acquires (or has acquired during the 12-month period ending on the date of the most recent acquisition by such person or persons) ownership of stock of the corporation possessing 20 percent or more of the total voting power of the stock of such corporation; or

(2) A majority of members of the corporation's board of directors is replaced during any 12-month period by directors whose appointment or election is not endorsed by a majority of the members of the corporation's board of directors prior to the date of the appointment or election.

(b) The presumption of paragraph (a) of this A-28 may be rebutted by establishing that such acquisition or acquisitions of the corporation's stock, or such replacement of the majority of the members of the corporation's board of directors, does not transfer the power to control (directly or indirectly) the management and policies of the corporation from any one person (or more than one person acting as a group) to another person (or group). For purposes of this section, in the absence of an event described in paragraph (a)(1) or (2) of this A-28, a change in the effective control of a corporation is presumed not to have occurred.

(c) In no event does a change in effective control under this A-28 occur in any transaction in which either of the two corporations involved in the transaction has a change in ownership or control under Q/A-27 or 29 of this section. Thus, for example, assume Corporation P transfers more than one-third of the total gross fair market value of its assets to Corporation O in exchange for 20 percent of O's stock. Because P has undergone a change in ownership of a substantial portion of its assets under Q/A-29 of this section, O does not have a change in effective control under Q/A-28.

(d) If any one person, or more than one person acting as a group, is considered to effectively control a corporation (within the meaning of this A-28), the acquisition of additional control of the corporation by the same person or persons is not considered to cause a change in the effective control of the corporation (or to cause a change in the ownership of the corporation within the meaning of Q/A-27 of this section).

(e) For purposes of this A-28, persons will not be considered to be acting as a group merely because they happen to purchase or own stock of the same corporation at the same time, or as a result of the same public offering. However, persons will be considered to be acting as a group if they are owners of a corporation that enters into a merger, consolidation, purchase or acquisition of stock, or similar business transaction with the corporation. If a person, including an entity shareholder, owns stock in both corporations that enter into a merger, consolidation, purchase or acquisition of stock, or similar transaction, such shareholder is considered to be acting as a group with other shareholders in a corporation only with respect to the ownership in that corporation prior to the transaction giving rise to the change and not with respect to the ownership interest in the other corporation.

(f) For purposes of determining stock ownership, see Q/A-27(c).

(g) The following examples illustrate the principles of this A-28:

Example 1. Shareholder A acquired the following percentages of the voting stock of Corporation M (an otherwise unrelated corporation) on the following dates: 16 percent on January 1, 2005; 10 percent on January 10, 2006; 8 percent on February 10, 2006; 11 percent on March 1, 2007; and 8 percent on March 10, 2007. Thus, on March 10, 2007, A owns a total of 53 percent of M's voting stock. Because A did not acquire 20 percent or more of M's voting stock during any 12-month period, there is no presumption of a change in effective control pursuant to paragraph (a)(1) of this A-28. In addition, under these facts there is a presumption that no change in the effective control of Corporation M occurred. If this presumption is not rebutted (and thus no change in effective control of Corporation M is treated as occurring prior to March 10, 2007), a change in the ownership of Corporation M is treated as having occurred on March 10, 2007 (pursuant to Q/A-27 of this section) because A had acquired more than 50 percent of Corporation M's voting stock as of that date.

Example 2. A minority group of shareholders of a corporation opposes the practices and policies of the corporation's current board of directors. A proxy contest ensues. The minority group presents its own slate of candidates for the board at the next annual meeting of the corporation's shareholders, and candidates of the minority group are elected to replace a majority of the current members of the board. A change in the effective control of the corporation is presumed to have occurred on the date the election of the new board of directors becomes effective.

Q-29. When does a change in the ownership of a substantial portion of a corporation's assets occur?

A-29. (a) For purposes of this section, a change in the ownership of a substantial portion of a corporation's assets occurs on the date that any one person, or more than one person acting as a group (as determined in paragraph (c) of this A-29), acquires (or has acquired during the 12-month period ending on the date of the most recent acquisition by such person or persons) assets from the corporation that have a total gross fair market value equal to or more than one-third of the total gross fair market value of all of the assets of the corporation immediately prior to such acquisition or acquisitions. For this purpose, gross fair market value means the value of the assets of the corporation, or the value of the assets being disposed of, determined without regard to any liabilities associated with such assets. This A-29 applies in any situation other than one involving the transfer of stock (or issuance of stock) in a parent corporation and stock in such corporation remains outstanding after the transaction. Thus, this A-29 applies to the sale of stock in a subsidiary (when that subsidiary is treated as a single corporation with the parent pursuant to Q/A-46) and to mergers involving the creation of a new corporation or with respect to the corporation that is not surviving entity.

(b)(1) There is no change in ownership or control under this A-29 when there is a transfer to an entity that is controlled by the shareholders of the transferring corporation immediately after the transfer, as provided in this paragraph (b). A transfer of assets by a corporation is not treated as a change in the ownership of such assets if the assets are transferred to—

(i) A shareholder of the corporation (immediately before the asset transfer) in exchange for or with respect to its stock;

(ii) An entity, 50 percent or more of the total value or voting power of which is owned, directly or indirectly, by the corporation;

(iii) A person, or more than one person acting as a group, that owns, directly or indirectly, 50 percent or more of the total value or voting power of all the outstanding stock of the corporation; or

(iv) An entity, at least 50 percent of the total value or voting power is owned, directly or indirectly, by a person described in paragraph (b)(1)(iii) of this A-29.

(2) For purposes of paragraph (b) and except as otherwise provided, a person's status is determined immediately after the transfer of the assets. For example, a transfer to a corporation in which the transferor corporation has no ownership interest in before the transaction, but which is a majority-owned subsidiary of the transferor corporation after the transaction is not treated as a change in the ownership of the assets of the transferor corporation.

(c) For purposes of this A-29, persons will not be considered to be acting as a group merely because they happen to purchase assets of the same corporation at the same time, or as a result of the same public offering. However, persons will be considered to be acting as a group if they are owners of a corporation that enters into a merger, consolidation, purchase or acquisition of assets, or similar business transaction with the corporation. If a person, including an entity shareholder, owns stock in both corporations that enter into a merger, consolidation, purchase or acquisition of stock, or similar transaction, such shareholder is considered to be acting as a group with other shareholders in a corporation only to the extent of the ownership in that corporation prior to the transaction giving rise to the change and not with respect to the ownership interest in the other corporation.

(d) For purposes of determining stock ownership, see Q/A-27(c).

(e) The following examples illustrate the principles of this A-29:

Example 1. Corporation M acquires assets having a gross fair market value of $500,000 from Corporation N (an unrelated corporation) on January 1, 2006. The total gross fair market value of Corporation N's assets immediately prior to the acquisition was $3 million. Since the value of the assets acquired by Corporation M is less than one-third of the total gross fair market value of Corporation N's total assets immediately prior to the acquisition, the acquisition does not represent a change in the ownership of a substantial portion of Corporation N's assets.

Example 2. Assume the same facts as in Example 1. Also assume that on November 1, 2006, Corporation M acquires from Corporation N additional assets having a fair market value of $700,000. Thus, Corporation M has acquired from Corporation N assets worth a total of $1.2 million during the 12-month period ending on November 1, 2006. Since $1.2 million is more than one-third of the total gross fair market value of all of Corporation N's assets immediately prior to the earlier of these acquisitions ($3 million), a change in the ownership of a substantial portion of Corporation N's assets is considered to have occurred on November 1, 2006.

Example 3. (i) All of the assets of Corporation P are transferred to Corporation O (an unrelated corporation). In exchange, the shareholders of Corporation P receive Corporation O stock. Immediately after the transfer, the former shareholders of Corporation P own 60 percent of the fair market value of the outstanding stock of Corporation O and the former shareholders of Corporation O own 40 percent of the fair market value of the outstanding stock of Corporation O. Because Corporation O is an entity more than 50 percent of the fair market value of the outstanding stock of which is owned by the former shareholders of Corporation P (based on ownership of Corporation P prior the change), the transfer of assets is not treated as a change in ownership of a substantial portion of the assets of Corporation P. However, a change in the ownership (within the meaning of Q/A-27) of Corporation O occurs.

(ii) The result in paragraph (i) would be the same if immediately after the change, the former shareholders of Corporation P own stock with a fair market value of 51 percent of the value of Corporation O stock because Corporation O is an entity more than 50 percent of the fair market value of the outstanding stock of which is owned by the former shareholders of Corporation P. See Q/A-27, Example 4, regarding whether there is a change in ownership or control of O.

Example 4. Corporation P sells all of the stock of its wholly-owned subsidiary, S, to Corporation Y. The fair market value of the affiliated group, determined without regard to its liabilities, is $210 million. The fair market value of S, determined without regard to its liabilities, is $80 million. Because there is a change in more than one-third of the gross fair market value of the total assets of the affiliated group, there is a change in the ownership of a substantial portion of the assets of the affiliated group.

Three-Times-Base-Amount Test for Parachute Payments

Q-30. Are all payments that are in the nature of compensation, are made to a disqualified individual, and are contingent on a change in ownership or control, parachute payments?

A-30. (a) No. To determine whether such payments are parachute payments, they must be tested against the individual's base amount (as defined in Q/A-34 of this section). To do this, the aggregate present value of all payments in the nature of compensation that are made or to be made to (or for the benefit of) the same disqualified individual and are contingent on the change in ownership or control must be determined. If this aggregate present value equals or exceeds the amount equal to 3 times the individual's base amount, the payments are parachute payments. If this aggregate present value is less than the amount equal to 3 times the individual's base amount, no portion of the payment is a parachute payment. See Q/A-31, Q/A-32, and Q/A-33 of this section for rules on determining present value. Parachute payments that are securities violation parachute payments are not included in the foregoing computation if they are not contingent on a change in ownership or control. See Q/A-37 of this section for the definition and treatment of securities violation parachute payments.

(b) The following examples illustrate the principles of this A-30:

Example 1. A is a disqualified individual with respect to Corporation M. A's base amount is $100,000. Payments in the nature of compensation that are contingent on a change in the ownership or control of Corporation M totaling $400,000 are made to A on the date of the change in ownership or control. The payments are parachute payments because they have an aggregate present value at least equal to 3 times A's base amount of $100,000 (3 x $100,000 = $300,000).

Example 2. Assume the same facts as in Example 1, except that the payments contingent on the change in the ownership or control of Corporation M total $290,000. Because the payments do not have an aggregate present value at least equal to 3 times A's base amount, no portion of the payments is a parachute payment.

Q-31. As of what date is the present value of a payment determined?

A-31. (a) Except as provided in this section, the present value of a payment is determined as of the date on which the change in ownership or control occurs, or, if a payment is made prior to such date, the date on which the payment is made.

(b)(1) For purposes of determining whether a payment is a parachute payment, if a payment in the nature of compensation is the right to receive payments in a year (or years) subsequent to the year of the change in ownership or control, the value of the payment is the present value of such payment (or payments) calculated in accordance with Q/A-32 of this section and based on reasonable actuarial assumptions.

(2) If the payment in the nature of compensation is an obligation to provide health care, then for purposes of this A-31 and for applying the 3-times-base-amount test under Q/A-30 of this section, the present value of such obligation should be calculated in accordance with generally accepted accounting principles. For purposes of Q/A-30 and this A-31, the obligation to provide health care is permitted to be measured by projecting the cost of premiums for purchased health care insurance, even if no health care insurance is actually purchased. If the obligation to provide health care is made in coordination with a health care plan that the corporation makes available to a group, then the premiums used for this purpose may be group premiums.

Q-32. What discount rate is to be used to determine present value?

A-32. For purposes of this section, present value generally is determined by using a discount rate equal to 120 percent of the applicable Federal rate (determined under section 1274(d) and the regulations thereunder) compounded semiannually. The applicable Federal rate to be used for this purpose is the Federal rate that is in effect on the date as of which the present value is determined, using the period until the payment would have been made without regard to the change in ownership or control as the term of the debt instrument under section 1274(d). See Q/A-24 and 31 of this section. However, for any payment, the corporation and the disqualified individual may elect to use the applicable Federal rate that is in effect on the date that the contract which provides for the payment is entered into, if such election is made in the contract.

Q-33. If the present value of a payment to be made in the future is contingent on an uncertain future event or condition, how is the present value of the payment determined?

A-33. (a) In certain cases, it may be necessary to apply the 3-times-base-amount test of Q/A-30 of this section, or to allocate a portion of the base amount to a payment described in paragraphs (a)(1), (2), and (3) of Q/A-2 of this section, at a time when the aggregate present value of all such payments cannot be determined with certainty because the time, amount, or right to receive one or more such payments is contingent on the occurrence of an uncertain future event or condition. For example, a disqualified individual's right to receive a payment may be contingent on the involuntary termination of such individual's employment with the corporation. In such a case, it must be reasonably estimated whether the payment will be made. If it is reasonably estimated that there is a 50-percent or greater probability that the payment will be made, the full amount of the payment is considered for purposes of the 3-times-base-amount test and the allocation of the base amount. Conversely, if it is reasonably estimated that there is a less than 50-percent probability that the payment will be made, the payment is not considered for either purpose.

(b) If the estimate made under paragraph (a) of this A-33 is later determined to be incorrect, the 3-times-base-amount test described in Q/A-30 of this section must be reapplied (and the portion of the base amount allocated to previous payments must be reallocated (if necessary) to such payments) to reflect the actual time and amount of the payment. Whenever the 3-times-base-amount test is applied (or whenever the base amount is allocated), the aggregate present value of the payments received or to be received by the disqualified individual is redetermined as of the date described in A-31 of this section, using the discount rate described in A-32 of this section. This redetermination may affect the amount of any excess parachute payment for a prior taxable year. Alternatively, if, based on the application of the 3-times-base-amount test without regard to the payment described in paragraph (a) of this A-33, a disqualified individual is determined to have an excess parachute payment or payments, then the 3-times-base-amount test does not have to be reapplied when a payment described in paragraph (a) of this A-33 is made (or becomes certain to be made) if no base amount is allocated to such payment.

(c) To the extent provided in published guidance of general applicability under § 601.601(d)(2) of this Chapter, an initial estimate of the value of an option subject to Q/A-13 of this section is permitted to be made, with the valuation subsequently re-determined, and the 3-times-base-amount test reapplied.

(d) The following examples illustrate the principles of this A-33:

Example 1. A, a disqualified individual with respect to Corporation M, has a base amount of $100,000. Under A's employment agreement with Corporation M, A is entitled to receive a payment in the nature of compensation in the amount of $250,000 contingent on a change in ownership or control of Corporation M. In addition, the agreement provides that if A's employment is terminated within 1 year after the change in ownership or control, A will receive an additional payment in the nature of compensation in the amount of $150,000, payable 1 year after the date of the change in ownership or control. A change in ownership or control of Corporation M occurs and A receives the first payment of $250,000. Corporation M reasonably estimates that there is a 50-percent probability that, as a result of the change, A's employment will be terminated within 1 year of the date of the change. For purposes of applying the 3-times-base-amount test (and if the first payment is determined to be a parachute payment, for purposes of allocating a portion of A's base amount to that payment), because M reasonably estimates that there is a 50-percent or greater probability that, as a result of the change, A's employment will be terminated within 1 year of the date of the change, Corporation M must assume that the $150,000 payment will be made to A as a result of the change in ownership or control. The present value of the additional payment is determined under Q/A-31 and Q/A-32 of this section.

Example 2. Assume the same facts as in Example 1, except that Corporation M reasonably estimates that there is a less than 50-percent probability that, as a result of the change, A's employment will be terminated within 1 year of the date of the change. For purposes of applying the 3-times-base-amount test, because Corporation M reasonably estimates that there is a less than 50-percent probability that, as a result of the change, A's employment will be terminated within 1 year of the date of the change, Corporation M must assume that the $150,000 payment will not be made to A as a result of the change in ownership or control.

Example 3. B, a disqualified individual with respect to Corporation P, has a base amount of $200,000. Under B's employment agreement with Corporation P, if there is a change in ownership or control of Corporation P, B will receive a severance payment of $600,000 and a bonus payment of $400,000. In addition, the agreement provides that if B's employment is terminated within 1 year after the change, B will receive an additional payment in the nature of compensation of $500,000. A change in ownership or control of Corporation P occurs, and B receives the $600,000 and $400,000 payments. At the time of the change in ownership or control, Corporation P reasonably estimates that there is a less than 50-percent probability that B's employment will be terminated within 1 year of the change. For purposes of applying the 3-times-base-amount test, because Corporation P reasonably estimates that there is a less than 50-percent probability that B's employment will be terminated within 1 year of the date of the change, Corporation P assumes that the $500,000 payment will not be made to B. Eleven months after the change in ownership or control, B's employment is terminated, and the $500,000 payment is made to B. Because B was determined to have excess parachute payments without regard to the $500,000 payment, the 3-times-base-amount test is not reapplied and the base amount is not reallocated to include the $500,000 payment. The entire $500,000 payment is treated as an excess parachute payment.

Q-34. What is the base amount?

A-34. (a) The base amount of a disqualified individual is the average annual compensation for services performed for the corporation with respect to which the change in ownership or control occurs (or for a predecessor entity or a related entity as defined in Q/A-21 of this section) which was includible in the gross income of such individual for taxable years in the base period (including amounts that were excluded under section 911), or which would have been includible in such gross income if such person had been a United States citizen or resident. See Q/A-35 of this section for the definition of base period and for examples of base amount computations.

(b) If the base period of a disqualified individual includes a short taxable year or less than all of a taxable year, compensation for such short or incomplete taxable year must be annualized before determining the average annual compensation for the base period. In annualizing compensation, the frequency with which payments are expected to be made over an annual period must be taken into account. Thus, any amount of compensation for such a short or incomplete taxable year that represents a payment that will not be made more often than once per year is not annualized.

(c) Because the base amount includes only compensation that is includible in gross income, the base amount does not include certain items that constitute parachute payments. For example, payments in the form of excludible fringe benefits are not included in the base amount but may be treated as parachute payments.

(d) The base amount includes the amount of compensation included in income under section 83(b) during the base period. See Q/A-35 for the definition of base period.

(e) The following example illustrates the principles of this A-34:

Example. A disqualified individual, D, receives an annual salary of $500,000 per year during the 5-year base period. D defers $100,000 of D's salary each year under the corporation's nonqualified deferred compensation plan. D's base amount is $400,000 ($400,000 x (5/5)).

Q-35. What is the base period?

A-35. (a) The base period of a disqualified individual is the most recent 5 taxable years of the individual ending before the date of the change in ownership or control. For this purpose, the date of the change in ownership or control is the date the corporation experiences one of the events described in Q/A-27, Q/A-28, or Q/A-29 of this section. However, if the disqualified individual was not an employee or independent contractor of the corporation with respect to which the change in ownership or control occurs (or a predecessor entity or a related entity as defined in Q/A-21 of this section) for this entire 5-year period, the individual's base period is the portion of such 5-year period during which the individual performed personal services for the corporation or predecessor entity or related entity.

(b) The following examples illustrate the principles of Q/A-34 of this section and this Q/A-35:

Example 1. A disqualified individual, D, was employed by a corporation for 2 years and 4 months preceding the taxable year in which a change in ownership or control of the corporation occurs. D's includible compensation income from the corporation was $30,000 for the 4-month period, $120,000 for the first full year, and $150,000 for the second full year. D's base amount is $120,000, ((3 x $30,000) + $120,000 + $150,000)/3.

Example 2. Assume the same facts as in Example 1, except that D also received a $60,000 signing bonus when D's employment with the corporation commenced at the beginning of the 4-month period. D's base amount is $140,000, (($60,000 + (3 x $30,000)) + $120,000 + $150,000) / 3. Since the bonus will not be paid more often than once per year, the amount of the bonus is not increased in annualizing D's compensation for the 4-month period.

Example 3. E is a disqualified individual with respect to Corporation X who was not an employee or independent contractor for the full 5-year base period. In 2004 and 2005, E is a director of X and receives $30,000 per year for E's services. In 2006, E becomes an officer of X. E's includible compensation from Corporation X is $250,000 for 2006 and 2007, and $300,000 for 2008. In 2008, X undergoes a change in ownership or control. E's base amount is $140,000 ((2 x $250,000) + (2 x $30,000)/4).

Q-36. How is the base amount determined in the case of a disqualified individual who did not perform services for the corporation (or a predecessor entity or a related entity as defined in Q/A-21 of this section), prior to the individual's taxable year in which the change in ownership or control occurs?

A-36. (a) In such a case, the individual's base amount is the annualized compensation for services performed for the corporation (or a predecessor entity or related entity) which—

(1) Was includible in the individual's gross income for that portion, prior to such change, of the individual's taxable year in which the change occurred (including amounts that were excluded under section 911), or would have been includible in such gross income if such person had been a United States citizen or resident;

(2) Was not contingent on the change in ownership or control; and

(3) Was not a securities violation parachute payment.

(b) The following examples illustrate the principles of this A-36:

Example 1. On January 1, 2006, A, an individual whose taxable year is the calendar year, enters into a 4-year employment contract with Corporation M as an officer of the corporation. A has not previously performed services for Corporation M (or any predecessor entity or related entity as defined in Q/A-21 of this section). Under the employment contract, A is to receive an annual salary of $120,000 for each of the 4 years that he remains employed by Corporation M with any remaining unpaid balance to be paid immediately in the event that A's employment is terminated without cause. On July 1, 2006, after A has received compensation of $60,000, a change in the ownership or control of Corporation M occurs. Because of the change, A's employment is terminated without cause, and he receives a payment of $420,000. It is established by clear and convincing evidence that the $60,000 in compensation is not contingent on the change in ownership or control, but the presumption that the $420,000 payment is contingent on the change is not rebutted. Thus, the payment of $420,000 is treated as contingent on the change in ownership or control of Corporation M. In this case, A's base amount is $120,000 (2 x $60,000). Since the present value of the payment which is contingent on the change in ownership of Corporation M ($420,000) is more than 3 times A's base amount of $120,000 (3 x $120,000 = $360,000), the payment is a parachute payment.

Example 2. Assume the same facts as in Example 1, except that A also receives a signing bonus of $50,000 from Corporation M on January 1, 2006. It is established by clear and convincing evidence that the bonus is not contingent on the change in ownership or control. When the change in ownership or control occurs on July 1, 2006, A has received compensation of $110,000 (the $50,000 bonus plus $60,000 in salary). In this case, A's base amount is $170,000 ($50,000 + (2 x $60,000)). Because the $50,000 bonus will not be paid more than once per year, the amount of the bonus is not increased in annualizing A's compensation. The present value of the potential parachute payment ($420,000) is less than 3 times A's base amount of $170,000 (3 x $170,000 = $510,000), and therefore no portion of the payment is a parachute payment.

Securities Violation Parachute Payments

Q-37. Must a payment be contingent on a change in ownership or control in order to be a parachute payment?

A-37. (a) No, the term parachute payment also includes any payment (other than a payment exempted under Q/A-6 or Q/A-8 of this section) that is in the nature of compensation and is to (or for the benefit of) a disqualified individual, if such payment is a securities violation payment. A securities violation payment is a payment made or to be made—

(1) Pursuant to an agreement that violates any generally enforced Federal or state securities laws or regulations; and

(2) In connection with a potential or actual change in ownership or control.

(b) A violation is not taken into account under paragraph (a)(1) of this A-37 if it is merely technical in character or is not materially prejudicial to shareholders or potential shareholders. Moreover, a violation will be presumed not to exist unless the existence of the violation has been determined or admitted in a civil or criminal action (or an administrative action by a regulatory body charged with enforcing the particular securities law or regulation) which has been resolved by adjudication or consent. Parachute payments described in this A-37 are referred to in this section as securities violation payments.

(c) Securities violation parachute payments that are not contingent on a change in ownership or control within the meaning of Q/A-22 of this section are not taken into account in applying the 3-times-base-amount test of Q/A-30 of this section. Such payments are considered parachute payments regardless of whether such test is met with respect to the disqualified individual (and are included in allocating base amount under Q/A-38 of this section). Moreover, the amount of a securities violation parachute payment treated as an excess parachute payment shall not be reduced by the portion of such payment that is reasonable compensation for personal services actually rendered before the date of a change in ownership or control if such payment is not contingent on such change. Likewise, the amount of a securities violation parachute payment includes the portion of such payment that is reasonable compensation for personal services to be rendered on or after the date of a change in ownership or control if such payment is not contingent on such change.

(d) The rules in paragraph (b) of this A-37 also apply to securities violation parachute payments that are contingent on a change in ownership or control if the application of these rules results in greater total excess parachute payments with respect to the disqualified individual than would result if the payments were treated simply as payments contingent on a change in ownership or control (and hence were taken into account in applying the 3-times-base-amount test and were reduced by, or did not include, any applicable amount of reasonable compensation).

(e) The following examples illustrate the principles of this A-37:

Example 1. A, a disqualified individual with respect to Corporation M, receives two payments in the nature of compensation that are contingent on a change in the ownership or control of Corporation M. The present value of the first payment is equal to A's base amount and is not a securities violation parachute payment. The present value of the second payment is equal to 1.5 times A's base amount and is a securities violation parachute payment. Neither payment includes any reasonable compensation. If the second payment is treated simply as a payment contingent on a change in ownership or control, the amount of A's total excess parachute payments is zero because the aggregate present value of the payments does not equal or exceed 3 times A's base amount. If the second payment is treated as a securities violation parachute payment subject to the rules of paragraph (b) of this A-37, the amount of A's total excess parachute payments is 0.5 times A's base amount. Thus, the second payment is treated as a securities violation parachute payment.

Example 2. Assume the same facts as in Example 1, except that the present value of the first payment is equal to 2 times A's base amount. If the second payment is treated simply as a payment contingent on a change in ownership or control, the total present value of the payments is 3.5 times A's base amount, and the amount of A's total excess parachute payments is 2.5 times A's base amount. If the second payment is treated as a securities violation parachute payment, the amount of A's total excess parachute payments is 0.5 times A's base amount. Thus, the second payment is treated simply as a payment contingent on a change in ownership or control.

Example 3. B, a disqualified individual with respect to Corporation N, receives two payments in the nature of compensation that are contingent on a change in the control of Corporation N. The present value of the first payment is equal to 4 times B's base amount and is a securities violation parachute payment. The present value of the second payment is equal to 2 times B's base amount and is not a securities violation parachute payment. B establishes by clear and convincing evidence that the entire amount of the first payment is reasonable compensation for personal services to be rendered after the change in ownership or control. If the first payment is treated simply as a payment contingent on a change in ownership or control, it is exempt from the definition of parachute payment pursuant to Q/A-9 of this section. Thus, the amount of B's total excess parachute payment is zero because the present value of the second payment does not equal or exceed 3 times B's base amount. However, if the first payment is treated as a securities violation parachute payment, the amount of B's total excess parachute payments is 3 times B's base amount. Thus, the first payment is treated as a securities violation parachute payment.

Example 4. Assume the same facts as in Example 3, except that B does not receive the second payment and B establishes by clear and convincing evidence that the first payment is reasonable compensation for services actually rendered before the change in the control of Corporation N. If the payment is treated simply as a payment contingent on a change in ownership or control, the amount of B's excess parachute payment is zero because the amount treated as an excess parachute payment is reduced by the amount that B establishes as reasonable compensation. However, if the payment is treated as a securities violation parachute payment, the amount of B's excess parachute payment is 3 times B's base amount. Thus, the payment is treated as a securities violation parachute payment.

Computation and Reduction of Excess Parachute Payments

Q-38. How is the amount of an excess parachute payment computed?

A-38. (a) The amount of an excess parachute payment is the excess of the amount of any parachute payment over the portion of the disqualified individual's base amount that is allocated to such payment. For this purpose, the portion of the base amount allocated to any parachute payment is the amount that bears the same ratio to the base amount as the present value of such parachute payment bears to the aggregate present value of all parachute payments made or to be made to (or for the benefit of) the same disqualified individual. Thus, the portion of the base amount allocated to any parachute payment is determined by multiplying the base amount by a fraction, the numerator of which is the present value of such parachute payment and the denominator of which is the aggregate present value of all such payments. See Q/A-31, Q/A-32, and Q/A-33 of this section for rules on determining present value and Q/A-34 of this section for the definition of base amount.

(b) The following example illustrates the principles of this A-38:

Example. An individual with a base amount of $100,000 is entitled to receive two parachute payments, one of $200,000 and the other of $400,000. The $200,000 payment is made at the time of the change in ownership or control, and the $400,000 payment is to be made at a future date. The present value of the $400,000 payment is $300,000 on the date of the change in ownership or control. The portions of the base amount allocated to these payments are $40,000 (($200,000/$500,000) x $100,000) and $60,000 (($300,000/$500,000) x $100,000), respectively. Thus, the amount of the first excess parachute payment is $160,000 ($200,000-$40,000) and that of the second is $340,000 ($400,000-$60,000).

Q-39. May the amount of an excess parachute payment be reduced by reasonable compensation for personal services actually rendered before the change in ownership or control?

A-39. (a) Generally, yes. Except in the case of payments treated as securities violation parachute payments or when the portion of a payment that is treated as contingent on the change in ownership or control is determined under paragraph (b) or (c) of Q/A-24 of this section, the amount of an excess parachute payment is reduced by any portion of the payment that the taxpayer establishes by clear and convincing evidence is reasonable compensation for personal services actually rendered by the disqualified individual before the date of the change in ownership or control. Services reasonably compensated for by payments that are not parachute payments (for example, because the payments are not contingent on a change in ownership or control and are not securities violation parachute payments, or because the payments are exempt from the definition of parachute payment under Q/A-6 through Q/A-9 of this section) are not taken into account for this purpose. The portion of any parachute payment that is established as reasonable compensation is first reduced by the portion of the disqualified individual's base amount that is allocated to such parachute payment; any remaining portion of the parachute payment established as reasonable compensation then reduces the excess parachute payment.

(b) The following examples illustrate the principles of this A-39:

Example 1. Assume that a parachute payment of $600,000 is made to a disqualified individual, and the portion of the individual's base amount that is allocated to the parachute payment is $100,000. Also assume that $300,000 of the $600,000 parachute payment is established as reasonable compensation for personal services actually rendered by the disqualified individual before the date of the change in ownership or control. Before the reasonable compensation is taken into account, the amount of the excess parachute payment is $500,000 ($600,000--$100,000). In reducing the excess parachute payment by reasonable compensation, the portion of the parachute payment that is established as reasonable compensation ($300,000) is first reduced by the portion of the disqualified individual's base amount that is allocated to the parachute payment ($100,000), and the remainder ($200,000) then reduces the excess parachute payment. Thus, in this case, the excess parachute payment of $500,000 is reduced by $200,000 of reasonable compensation.

Example 2. Assume the same facts as in Example 1, except that the full amount of the $600,000 parachute payment is established as reasonable compensation. In this case, the excess parachute payment of $500,000 is reduced to zero by $500,000 of reasonable compensation. As a result, no portion of any deduction for the payment is disallowed by section 280G, and no portion of the payment is subject to the 20-percent excise tax of section 4999.

Determination of Reasonable Compensation

Q-40. How is it determined whether payments are reasonable compensation?

A-40. (a) In general, whether payments are reasonable compensation for personal services actually rendered, or to be rendered, by the disqualified individual is determined on the basis of all the facts and circumstances of the particular case. Factors relevant to such a determination include, but are not limited to, the following—

(1) The nature of the services rendered or to be rendered;

(2) The individual's historic compensation for performing such services; and

(3) The compensation of individuals performing comparable services in situations where the compensation is not contingent on a change in ownership or control.

(b) For purposes of section 280G, reasonable compensation for personal services includes reasonable compensation for holding oneself out as available to perform services and refraining from performing services (such as under a covenant not to compete).

Q-41. Is any particular type of evidence generally considered clear and convincing evidence of reasonable compensation for personal services?

A-41. Yes. A showing that payments are made under a nondiscriminatory employee plan or program (as defined in Q/A-26 of this section) generally is considered to be clear and convincing evidence that the payments are reasonable compensation. This is true whether the personal services for which the payments are made are actually rendered before, or are to be rendered on or after, the date of the change in ownership or control. Q/A-46 of this section (relating to the treatment of an affiliated group as one corporation) does not apply for purposes of this A-41. No determination of reasonable compensation is needed for payments under qualified plans to be exempt from the definition of parachute payment under Q/A-8 of this section.

Q-42. Is any particular type of evidence generally considered clear and convincing evidence of reasonable compensation for personal services to be rendered on or after the date of a change in ownership or control?

A-42. (a) Yes, if payments are made or to be made to (or on behalf of) a disqualified individual for personal services to be rendered on or after the date of a change in ownership or control, a showing of the following generally is considered to be clear and convincing evidence that the payments are reasonable compensation for services to be rendered on or after the date of the change in ownership or control—

(1) The payments were made or are to be made only for the period the individual actually performs such personal services; and

(2) If the individual's duties and responsibilities are substantially the same after the change in ownership or control, the individual's annual compensation for such services is not significantly greater than such individual's annual compensation prior to the change in ownership or control, apart from normal increases attributable to increased responsibilities or

cost of living adjustments. If the scope of the individual's duties and responsibilities are not substantially the same, the annual compensation after the change is not significantly greater than the annual compensation customarily paid by the employer or by comparable employers to persons performing comparable services. However, except as provided in paragraph (b) and (c) of this A-42, such clear and convincing evidence will not exist if the individual does not, in fact, perform the services contemplated in exchange for the compensation.

(b) Generally, an agreement under which the disqualified individual must refrain from performing services (e.g., a covenant not to compete) is an agreement for the performance of personal services for purposes of this A-42 to the extent that it is demonstrated by clear and convincing evidence that the agreement substantially constrains the individual's ability to perform services and there is a reasonable likelihood that the agreement will be enforced against the individual. In the absence of clear and convincing evidence, payments under the agreement are treated as severance payments under Q/A-44 of this section.

(c) If the employment of a disqualified individual is involuntarily terminated before the end of a contract term and the individual is paid damages for breach of contract, a showing of the following factors generally is considered clear and convincing evidence that the payment is reasonable compensation for personal services to be rendered on or after the date of change in ownership or control—

(1) The contract was not entered into, amended, or renewed in contemplation of the change in ownership or control;

(2) The compensation the individual would have received under the contract would have qualified as reasonable compensation under section 162;

(3) The damages do not exceed the present value (determined as of the date of receipt) of the compensation the individual would have received under the contract if the individual had continued to perform services for the employer until the end of the contract term;

(4) The damages are received because an offer to provide personal services was made by the disqualified individual but was rejected by the employer (including involuntary termination or constructive discharge); and

(5) The damages are reduced by mitigation. Mitigation will be treated as occurring when such damages are reduced (or any payment of such damages is returned) to the extent of the disqualified individual's earned income (within the meaning of section 911(d)(2)(A)) during the remainder of the period in which the contract would have been in effect. See Q/A-44 of this section for rules regarding damages for a failure to make severance payments.

(d) The following examples illustrate the principles of this A-42:

Example 1. A, a disqualified individual, has a three-year employment contract with Corporation M, a publicly traded corporation. Under this contract, A is to receive a salary for $100,000 for the first year of the contract and, for each succeeding year, an annual salary that is 10 percent higher than the prior year's salary. During the third year of the contract, Corporation N acquires all the stock of Corporation M. Prior to the change in ownership, Corporation N arranges to retain A's services by entering into an employment contract with A that is essentially the same as A's contract with Corporation M. Under the new contract, Corporation N is to fulfill Corporation M's obligations for the third year of the old contract, and, for each of the succeeding years, pay A an annual salary that is 10 percent higher than A's prior year's salary. Amounts are payable under the new contract only for the portion of the contract term during which A remains employed by Corporation N. A showing of the facts described above (and in the absence of contradictory evidence) is regarded as clear and convincing evidence that all payments under the new contract are reasonable compensation for personal services to be rendered on or after the date of the change in ownership. Therefore, the payments under this agreement are exempt from the definition of parachute payment pursuant to Q/A-9 of this section.

Example 2. Assume the same facts as in Example 1, except that A does not perform the services described in the new contract, but receives payment under the new contract. Because services were not rendered after the change, the payments under this contract are not exempt from the definition of parachute payment pursuant to Q/A-9 of this section.

Example 3. Assume the same facts as in Example 1, except that under the new contract A agrees to perform consulting services to Corporation N, when and if Corporation N requires A's services. Assume further that when Corporation N does not require A's services, the contract provides that A must not perform services for any other competing company. Corporation N previously enforced similar contracts against former employees of Corporation N. Because A is substantially constrained under this contract and Corporation N is reasonably likely to enforce the contract against A, the agreement is an agreement for the performance of services under paragraph (b) of this A-42. Assuming the requirements of paragraph (a) of this A-42 are met and there is clear and convincing evidence that all payments under the new contract are reasonable compensation for personal services to be rendered on or after the date of the change in ownership, the payments under this contract are exempt from the definition of parachute payment pursuant to Q/A-9 of this section.

Example 4. Assume the same facts as in Example 1, except that instead of agreeing not to compete with Corporation N, under the new agreement A agrees not to disparage either Corporation M or Corporation N. Because the nondisparagement agreement does not substantially constrain A's ability to perform services, no amount of the payments under this contract are reasonable compensation for the nondisparagement agreement.

Example 5. Assume the same facts as in Example 1, except that the employment contract with Corporation N does not provide that amounts are payable under the contract only for the portion of the term for which A remains employed by Corporation N. Shortly after the change in ownership, and despite A's request to remain employed by Corporation N, A's employment with Corporation N is involuntarily terminated. Shortly thereafter, A obtains employment with Corporation O. A commences a civil action against Corporation N, alleging breach of the employment contract. In settlement of the litigation, A receives an amount equal to the present value of the compensation A would have received under the contract with Corporation N, reduced by the amount of compensation A otherwise receives from Corporation O during the period that the contract would have been in effect. A showing of the facts described above (and in the absence of contradictory evidence) is regarded as clear and convincing evidence that the amount A receives as damages is reasonable compensation for personal services to be rendered on or after the date of the change in ownership. Therefore, the amount received by A is exempt from the definition of parachute payment pursuant to Q/A-9 of this section.

Q-43. Is any particular type of payment generally considered reasonable compensation for personal services actually rendered before the date of a change in ownership or control?

A-43. Yes, payments of compensation earned before the date of a change in ownership or control generally are considered reasonable compensation for personal services actually rendered before the date of a change in ownership or control if they qualify as reasonable compensation under section 162.

Q-44. May severance payments be treated as reasonable compensation?

A-44. (a) No, severance payments are not treated as reasonable compensation for personal services actually rendered before, or to be rendered on or after, the date of a change in ownership or control. Moreover, any damages paid for a failure to make severance payments are not treated as reasonable compensation for personal services actually rendered before, or to be rendered on or after, the date of such change. For purposes of this section, the term severance payment means any payment that is made to (or for the benefit of) a disqualified individual on account of the termination of such individual's employment prior to the end of a contract term, but does not include any payment that otherwise would be made to (or for the benefit of) such individual on the termination of such individual's employment, whenever occurring.

(b) The following example illustrates the principles of this A-44:

Example. A, a disqualified individual, has a three-year employment contract with Corporation X. Under the contract, A will receive a salary of $200,000 for the first year of the contract, and for each succeeding year, an annual salary that is $100,000 higher than the previous year. In the event of A's termination of employment following a change in ownership or control, the contract provides that A will receive the remaining salary due under the employment contract. At the beginning of the second year of the contract, Corporation Y acquires all of the stock of Corporation X, A's employment is terminated, and A receives $700,000 ($300,000 for the second year of the contract plus $400,000 for the third year of the contract) representing the remaining salary due under the employment contract. Because the $700,000 payment is treated as a severance payment, it is not reasonable compensation for personal services on or after the date of the change in ownership or control. Thus, the full amount of the $700,000 is a parachute payment.

Miscellaneous Rules

Q-45. How is the term corporation defined?

A-45. For purposes of this section, the term corporation has the meaning prescribed by section 7701(a)(3) and § 301.7701-2(b) of this Chapter. For example, a corporation, for purposes of this section, includes a publicly traded partnership treated as a corporation under section 7704(a); an entity described in § 301.7701-3(c)(1)(v)(A) of this Chapter; a real estate investment trust under section 856(a); a corporation that has mutual or cooperative (rather than stock) ownership, such as a mutual insurance company, a mutual savings bank, or a cooperative bank (as defined in section 7701(a)(32)), and a foreign corporation as defined under section 7701(a)(5).

Q-46. How is an affiliated group treated?

A-46. For purposes of this section, and except as otherwise provided in this section, all members of the same affiliated group (as defined in section 1504, determined without regard to section 1504(b)) are treated as one corporation. Rules affected by this treatment of an affiliated group include (but are not limited to) rules relating to exempt payments of certain corporations (Q/A-6, Q/A-7 of this section (except as provided therein)), payor of parachute payments (Q/A-10 of this section), disqualified individuals (Q/A-15 through Q/A-21 of this section (except as provided therein)), rebuttal of the presumption that payments are contingent on a change (Q/A-26 of this section (except as provide therein)), change in ownership or control (Q/A-27, 28, and 29 of this section), and reasonable compensation (Q/A-42, 43, and 44 of this section).

Effective Date

Q-47. What is the general effective date of section 280G?

A-47. (a) Generally, section 280G applies to payments under agreements entered into or renewed after June 14, 1984. Any agreement that is entered into before June 15, 1984, and is renewed after June 14, 1984, is treated as a new contract entered into on the day the renewal takes effect.

(b) For purposes of paragraph (a) of this A-47, a contract that is terminable or cancellable unconditionally at will by either party to the contract without the consent of the other, or by both parties to the contract, is treated as a new contract entered into on the date any such termination or cancellation, if made, would be effective. However, a contract is not treated as so terminable or cancellable if it can be terminated or cancelled only by terminating the employment relationship or independent contractor relationship of the disqualified individual.

(c) Section 280G applies to payments under a contract entered into on or before June 14, 1984, if the contract is amended or supplemented after June 14, 1984, in significant relevant respect. For this purpose, a supplement to a contract is defined as a new contract entered into after June 14, 1984, that affects the trigger, amount, or time of receipt of a payment under an existing contract.

(d)(1) Except as otherwise provided in paragraph (e) of this A-47, a contract is considered to be amended or supplemented in significant relevant respect if provisions for payments contingent on a change in ownership or control (parachute provisions), or provisions in the nature of parachute provisions, are added to the contract, or are amended or supplemented to provide significant additional benefits to the disqualified individual. Thus, for example, a contract generally is treated as amended or supplemented in significant relevant respect if it is amended or supplemented—

(i) To add or modify, to the disqualified individual's benefit, a change in ownership or control trigger;

(ii) To increase amounts payable that are contingent on a change in ownership or control (or, where payment is to be made under a formula, to modify the formula to the disqualified individual's advantage); or

(iii) To accelerate, in the event of a change in ownership or control, the payment of amounts otherwise payable at a later date.

(2) For purposes of paragraph (a) of this A-47, a payment is not treated as being accelerated in the event of a change in ownership or control if the acceleration does not increase the present value of the payment.

(e) A contract entered into on or before June 14, 1984, is not treated as amended or supplemented in significant relevant respect merely by reason of normal adjustments in the terms of employment relationship or independent contractor relationship of the disqualified individual. Whether an adjustment in the terms of such a relationship is considered normal for this purpose depends on all of the facts and circumstances of the particular case. Relevant factors include, but are not limited to, the following—

(1) The length of time between the adjustment and the change in ownership or control;

(2) The extent to which the corporation, at the time of the adjustment, viewed itself as a likely takeover candidate;

(3) A comparison of the adjustment with historical practices of the corporation;

(4) The extent of overlap between the group receiving the benefits of the adjustment and those members of that group who are the beneficiaries of pre-June 15, 1984, parachute contracts; and

(5) The size of the adjustment, both in absolute terms and in comparison with the benefits provided to other members of the group receiving the benefits of the adjustment.

Q-48. What is the effective date of this section?

A-48. This section applies to any payments that are contingent on a change in ownership or control if the change in ownership or control occurs on or after January 1, 2004. Taxpayers may rely on these regulations after August 4, 2003, for the treatment of any parachute payment.

T.D. 9083, 8/1/2003.

§ 1.280H-0T Table of contents (temporary).

This section lists the captions that appear in the temporary regulations under section 280H.

§ 1.280H-1T Limitation on certain amounts paid to employee-owners by personal service corporations electing alternative taxable years (temporary).

(a) Introduction.

(b) Limitations on certain deductions of a personal service corporation.

(1) In general.

(2) Carryover of nondeductible amounts.

(3) Disallowance inapplicable for certain purposes.

(4) Definition of applicable amount.

(i) In general.

(ii) Special rule for certain indirect payments.

(iii) Examples.

(c) Minimum distribution requirement.

(1) Determination of whether requirement satisfied.

(i) In general.

(ii) Employee-owner defined.

(2) Preceding year test.

(i) In general.

(ii) Example.

(3) 3-year average test.

(i) In general.

(ii) Applicable percentage.

(iii) Adjusted taxable income.

(A) In general.

(B) Determination of adjusted taxable income for the deferral period of the applicable election year.

(C) NOL carryovers.

(D) Examples.

(d) Maximum deductible amount.

(1) In general.

(2) Example.

(e) Special rules and definition.

(1) Newly organized personal service corporations.

(2) Existing corporations that become personal service corporations.

(3) Disallowance of NOL carryback.

(4) Deferral period.

(5) Examples.

(f) Effective date.

T.D. 8205, 5/24/88.

§ 1.280H-1T Limitation on certain amounts paid to employee-owners by personal service corporations electing alternative taxable years (temporary).

Caution: The Treasury has not yet amended Reg § 1.280H-1T to reflect changes made by P.L. 100-647.

(a) Introduction. This section applies to any taxable year that a personal service corporation has a section 444 election in effect (an "applicable election year"). For purposes of this section, the term "personal service corporation" has the same meaning given such term in § 1.441-3(c).

(b) Limitation on certain deductions of personal service corporations. *(1) In general.* If, for any applicable election year, a personal service corporation does not satisfy the minimum distribution requirement in paragraph (c) of this section, the deduction otherwise allowable under chapter 1 of the Internal Revenue Code of 1986 (the Code) for applicable amounts, as defined in paragraph (b) (4) of this section, shall not exceed the maximum deductible amount, as defined in paragraph (d) of this section.

(2) Carryover of nondeductible amounts. Any amount not allowed as a deduction in an applicable election year under paragraph (b) (1) of this section shall be allowed as a deduction in the succeeding taxable year.

(3) Disallowance inapplicable for certain purposes. The disallowance of deductions under paragraph (b)(1) of this section shall not apply for purposes of subchapter G of chapter 1 of the Code (relating to corporations used to avoid income tax on shareholders) nor for determining whether the compensation of employee-owners is reasonable. Thus, for example, in determining whether a personal service corporation is subject to the accumulated earnings tax imposed by section 531, deductions disallowed under paragraph (b)(1) of this section are treated as allowed in computing accumulated taxable income.

(4) Definition of applicable amount. (i) In general. For purposes of section 280H and the regulations thereunder, the term "applicable amount" means, with respect to a taxable year, any amount that is otherwise deductible by a personal service corporation in such year and includible at any time, directly or indirectly, in the gross income of a taxpayer that during such year is an employee-owner. Thus, an amount includible in the gross income of an employee-owner will be considered an applicable amount even though such employee owns no stock of the corporation on the date the employee

includes the amount in income. See example (1) in paragraph (b)(4)(iii) of this section.

(ii) Special rule for certain indirect payments. For purposes of paragraph (b)(4)(i) of this section, amounts are indirectly includible in the gross income of an employee-owner of a personal service corporation that has made a section 444 election (an electing personal service corporation) if the amount is includible in the gross income of—

(A) The spouse (other than a spouse who is legally separated from the partner or shareholder under a decree of divorce or separate maintenance) or child (under age 14) of such employee-owner, or

(B) A corporation more than 50 percent (measured by fair market value) of which is owned in the aggregate by employee-owners (and individuals related under paragraph (b)(4)(ii)(A) of this section to such employee-owners), of the electing personal service corporation, or

(C) A partnership more than 50 percent of the profits and capital of which is owned by employee-owners (and individuals related under paragraph (b)(4)(ii)(A) of this section to such employee-owners) of the electing personal service corporation, or

(D) A trust more than 50 percent of the beneficial ownership of which is owned in the aggregate by employee-owners (and individuals related under paragraph (b)(4)(ii)(A) of this section to any such employee-owners), of the electing personal service corporation.

For purposes of this paragraph (b)(4)(ii), ownership by any person described in this paragraph (b)(4)(ii) shall be treated as ownership by the employee-owners of the electing personal service corporation. Paragraph (b)(4)(ii)(B) of this section will not apply if the corporation has made a section 444 election to use the same taxable year as that of the electing personal service corporation. Similarly, paragraph (b)(4)(ii)(C) of this section will not apply if the partnership has made a section 444 election to use the same taxable year as that of the electing personal service corporation. Notwithstanding the general effective date provision of paragraph (f) of this section, this paragraph (b)(4)(ii) is effective for amounts deductible on or after June 1, 1988.

(iii) Examples. The provisions of paragraph (b)(4) of this section may be illustrated by the following examples.

Example (1). A is an employee of P, an accrual basis personal service corporation with a taxable year ending September 30. P makes a section 444 election for its taxable year beginning October 1, 1987. On October 1, 1987, A owns no stock of P; however, on March 31, 1988, A acquires 10 of the 200 outstanding shares of P stock. During the period October 1, 1987 to March 31, 1988, A earned $40,000 of compensation as an employee of P. During the period April 1, 1988 to September 30, 1988, A earned $60,000 of compensation as an employee-owner of P. If paragraph (b) of this section does not apply, P would deduct for its taxable year ended September 30, 1988 the $100,000 earned by A during such year. Based upon these facts, the $100,000 otherwise deductible amount is considered an applicable amount under this section.

Example (2). I1 and I2, calendar year individuals, are employees of PSC1, a personal service corporation that has historically used a taxable year ending January 31. I1 and I2 also own all the stock, and are employees, of PSC2, a calendar year personal service corporation. For its taxable years beginning February 1, 1987, 1988, and 1989, PSC1 has a section 444 election in effect to use a January 31 taxable year. During its taxable years beginning February 1, 1986, 1987, and 1988, PSC1 deducted $10,000, $11,000, and $12,000, respectively, that was included in PSC2's gross income. Furthermore, of the $12,000 deducted by PSC1 for its taxable year beginning February 1, 1988, $7,000 was deducted during the period June 1, 1988 to January 31, 1989. Pursuant to paragraph (b)(4)(ii)(B) of this section, the $7,000 deducted by PSC1 on or after June 1, 1988, and included in PSC2's gross income is considered an applicable amount for PSC1's taxable year beginning February 1, 1988. Amounts deducted by PSC1 prior to June 1, 1988, are not subject to paragraph (b)(4)(ii)(B) of this section.

Example (3). The facts are the same as in example (2), except that for its taxable years beginning February 1, 1987, 1988, and 1989, PSC2 has a section 444 election in effect to use a January 31 taxable year. Since both PSC1 and PSC2 have the same taxable year and both have section 444 elections in effect, paragraph (b)(4)(ii)(B) of this section does not apply to the $7,000 deducted by PSC1 for its taxable year beginning February 1, 1988.

(c) Minimum distribution requirement. *(1) Determination of whether requirement satisfied.* (i) In general. A personal service corporation meets the minimum distribution requirement of this paragraph (c) for an applicable election year if, during the deferral period of such taxable year, the applicable amounts (determined without regard to paragraph (b)(2) of this section) for all employee-owners in the aggregate equal or exceed the lesser of—

(A) The amount determined under the "preceding year test" (see paragraph (c)(2) of this section), or

(B) The amount determined under the "3-year average test" (see paragraph (c)(3) of this section).

The following example illustrates the application of this paragraph (c)(1)(i).

Example. Q, an accrual-basis personal service corporation, makes a section 444 election to retain a year ending January 31 for its taxable year beginning February 1, 1987. Q has 4 employee-owners, B, C, D, and E. For Q's applicable election year beginning February 1, 1987 and ending January 31, 1988, B earns $6,000 a month plus a $45,000 bonus on January 15, 1988; C earns $5,000 a month plus a $40,000 bonus on January 15, 1988; D and E each earn $4,500 a month plus a $4,000 bonus on January 15, 1988. Q meets the minimum distribution requirement for such applicable election year if the applicable amounts during the deferral period (i.e., $220,000) equal or exceed the amount determined under the preceding year test or the 3-year average test.

(ii) Employee-owner defined. For purposes of section 280H and the regulations thereunder, a person is an employee-owner of a corporation for a taxable year if—

(A) On any day of the corporation's taxable year, the person is an employee of the corporation or performs personal services for or on behalf of the corporation, even if the legal form of that person's relationship to the corporation is that of an independent contractor, and

(B) On any day of the corporation's taxable year, the person owns any outstanding stock of the corporation.

(2) Preceding year test. (i) In general. The amount determined under the preceding year test is the product of—

(A) The applicable amounts during the taxable year preceding the applicable election year (the "preceding taxable year"), divided by the number of months (but not less than one) in the preceding taxable year, multiplied by

(B) The number of months in the deferral period of the applicable election year.

(ii) Example. The provisions of paragraph (c)(2) of this section may be illustrated by the following example.

Example. R, a personal service corporation, has historically used a taxable year ending January 31. For its taxable year beginning February 1, 1987, R makes a section 444 election to retain its January 31 taxable year. R is an accrual basis taxpayer and has one employee-owner, F. For R's taxable year ending January 31, 1987, F earns $5,000 a month plus a $40,000 bonus on January 15, 1987. The amount determined under the preceding year test for R's applicable election year beginning February 1, 1987 is $91,667 ($100,000, the applicable amounts during R's taxable year ending January 31, 1987, divided by 12, the number of months in R's taxable year ending January 31, 1987, multiplied by 11, the number of months in R's deferral period for such year).

(3) 3-year average test. (i) In general. The amount determined under the 3-year average test is the applicable percentage multiplied by the adjusted taxable income for the deferral period of the applicable election year.

(ii) Applicable percentage. The term "applicable percentage" means the percentage (not in excess of 95 percent) determined by dividing—

(A) The applicable amounts during the 3 taxable years of the corporation (or, if fewer, the taxable years the corporation has been in existence) immediately preceding the applicable election year, by

(B) The adjusted taxable income of such corporation for such 3 taxable years (or, if fewer, the taxable years of existence).

(iii) Adjusted taxable income. (A) In general. The term "adjusted taxable income" means taxable income determined without regard to applicable amounts.

(B) Determination of adjusted taxable income for the deferral period of the applicable election year. Adjusted taxable income for the deferral period of the applicable election year equals the adjusted taxable income that would result if the personal service corporation filed an income tax return for the deferral period of the applicable election year under its normal method of accounting. However, a personal service corporation may make a reasonable estimate of such amount.

(C) NOL carryovers. For purposes of determining adjusted taxable income for any period, any NOL carryover shall be reduced by the amount of such carryover that is attributable to the deduction of applicable amounts. The portion of the NOL carryover attributable to the deduction of applicable amounts is the difference between the NOL carryover computed with the deduction of such amounts and the NOL carryover computed without the deduction of such amounts. For purposes of determining the adjusted taxable income for the deferral period, an NOL carryover to the applicable election year, reduced as provided in this paragraph (c)(3)(iii)(C), shall be allowed first against the income of the deferral period.

(D) Examples. The provisions of this paragraph (c)(3)(iii) may be illustrated by the following examples.

Example (1). S is a personal service corporation that has historically used a taxable year ending January 31. For its taxable year beginning February 1, 1987, S makes a section 444 election to retain its taxable year ending January 31. S does not satisfy the minimum distribution requirement for its first applicable election year, and the applicable amounts for that year exceed the maximum deductible amount by $54,000. Under paragraph (b)(2) of this section, the $54,000 excess is carried over to S's taxable year beginning February 1, 1988. Furthermore, if S continues its section 444 election for its taxable year beginning February 1, 1988, and desires to use the 3-year average test provided in this paragraph for such year, pursuant to paragraph (c)(3)(iii)(A) of this section the $54,000 will not be allowed to reduce adjusted taxable income for such year. See also section 280H (e) regarding the disallowance of net operating loss carrybacks to (or from) any taxable year of a corporation personal service election under section 444 applies.

Example (2). T, a personal service corporation with a section 444 election in effect, is determining whether it satisfies the 3-year average test for its second applicable election year. T had a net operating loss (NOL) for its first applicable election year of $45,000. The NOL resulted from $150,000 of gross income less the sum of $96,000 of salary, $45,000 of other expenses, and $54,000 of deductible applicable amounts. Pursuant to paragraph (c)(3)(iii)(C) of this section, the entire amount of the $45,000 NOL is attributable to applicable amounts since the applicable amounts deducted in arriving at the NOL (*i.e.,* $54,000) were greater than the NOL (*i.e.,* $45,000). Thus, for purposes of computing the adjusted taxable income for the deferral period of T's second applicable election year, the NOL carryover to that year is $0 ($45,000 NOL less $45,000 amount of NOL attributable to applicable amounts).

(d) Maximum deductible amount. *(1) In general.* For purposes of this section, the term "maximum deductible amount" means the sum of—

(i) The applicable amounts during the deferral period of the applicable election year, plus

(ii) An amount equal to the product of—

(A) The amount determined under paragraph (d)(1)(i) of this section divided by the number of months in the deferral period of the applicable election year, multiplied by

(B) The number of months in the nondeferral period of the applicable election year. For purposes of the preceding sentence, the term "nondeferral period" means the portion of the applicable election year that occurs after the portion of such year constituting the deferral period.

(2) Example. The provisions of paragraph (d)(1) of this section may be illustrated by the following example.

Example. U, an accrual basis personal service corporation with a taxable year ending January 31, makes a section 444 election to retain a year ending January 31 for its taxable year beginning February 1, 1987. For its applicable election year beginning February 1, 1987, U does not satisfy the minimum distribution requirement in paragraph (c) of this section. Furthermore, U has 3 employee-owners, G, H, and I. G and H have been employee-owners of U for 10 years. Although I has been an employee of U for 4 years, I did not become an employee-owner until December 1, 1987, when I acquired 5 of the 20 outstanding shares of U stock. For U's applicable election year beginning February 1, 1987, G earns $5,000 a month plus a $40,000 bonus on January 15, 1988, and H and I each earn $4,000 a month plus a $32,000 bonus on January 15, 1988. Thus, the total of the applicable amounts during the deferral period of the applicable election year beginning February 1, 1987 is $143,000. Based on these facts, U's deduction for applicable amounts is limited to $156,000, determined as follows—$143,000 (applicable amounts during the deferral period) plus $13,000 (applicable amounts during the deferral period, divided by the number of months in the deferral period, multiplied by the number of months in the nondeferral period).

(e) Special rules and definition. *(1) Newly organized personal service corporations.* A personal service corporation is deemed to satisfy the preceding year test and the 3-year average test for the first year of the corporation's existence.

(2) Existing corporations that become personal service corporations. If an existing corporation becomes a personal service corporation and makes a section 444 election, the determination of whether the corporation satisfies the preceding year test and the 3-year average test is made by treating the corporation as though it were a personal service corporation for each of the 3 years preceding the applicable election year.

(3) Disallowance of NOL carryback. No net operating loss carryback shall be allowed to (or from) any applicable election year of a personal service corporation.

(4) Deferral period. For purposes of section 280H and the regulations thereunder, the term "deferral period" has the same meaning as under § 1.444-1T(b)(4).

(5) Examples. The provisions of this paragraph (e) may be illustrated by the following examples.

Example (1). V is a personal service corporation with a taxable year ending September 30. V makes a section 444 election for its taxable year beginning October 1, 1987, and incurs a net operating loss (NOL) for such year. Because an NOL is not allowed to be carried back from an applicable election year, V may not carry back the NOL from its first applicable election year to reduce its 1985, 1986, or 1987 taxable income.

Example (2). W, a personal service corporation, commences operations on July 1, 1990. Furthermore, for its taxable year beginning July 1, 1990, W makes a section 444 election to use a year ending September 30. Pursuant to paragraph (e)(1) of this section, W satisfies the preceding year test and the 3-year average test for its first year in existence. Thus, W may deduct, without limitation under this section, any applicable amounts for its taxable year beginning July 1, 1990.

Example (3). The facts are the same as in example (2). For its taxable year beginning October 1, 1990, W incurs an NOL and is not a personal service corporation. Furthermore, W desires to carry back the NOL to its preceding taxable year (a year that was an applicable election) year). Pursuant to paragraph (e)(3) of this section, W may not carry back an NOL "to" its taxable year beginning July 1, and ending September 30, 1990, because such year was an applicable election year.

(f) Effective date. The provisions of this section are effective for taxable years beginning after December 31, 1986.

T.D. 8205, 5/24/88, amend T.D. 8996, 5/16/2002.

Proposed § 1.280H-1T [*For Preamble, see ¶ 152,177*]

§ 1.281-1 In general.

Caution: The Treasury has not yet amended Reg § 1.281-1 to reflect changes made by P.L. 95-473, P.L. 94-455.

Section 281 provides special rules for the computation of the taxable incomes of a terminal railroad corporation and its shareholders when the terminal railroad corporation, as a result of taking related terminal income into account, reduces a charge which was made or which would be made for related terminal services furnished to a railroad corporation. Section 281 and paragraphs (a) and (b) of § 1.281-2 provide that the "reduced amount" described in paragraph (c) of § 1.281-2 is not includable in gross income of the terminal railroad corporation, is not treated as a dividend or other distribution to its railroad shareholders, and is not treated as an amount paid or incurred by the railroad shareholders to the terminal railroad corporation. Section 281 and paragraph (a)(2) of § 1.281-2 provide that no deduction otherwise allowable to a terminal railroad corporation shall be disallowed as a result of the "reduced amount" described in paragraph (c) of § 1.281-2. Section 1.281-3 defines the terms "terminal railroad corporation", "related terminal income", "related terminal services", "agreement", and "railroad corporation", Section 1.281-4 describes the effective dates and special rules for application of section 281 to taxable years ending before October 23, 1962.

T.D. 7356, 5/30/75.

§ 1.281-2 Effect of section 281 upon the computation of taxable income.

Caution: The Treasury has not yet amended Reg § 1.281-2 to reflect changes made by P.L. 95-473, P.L. 94-455.

(a) Computation of taxable income of terminal railroad corporations. *(1) Income not considered received or accrued.* A terminal railroad corporation (as defined in paragraph (a) of § 1.281-3) shall not be considered to have received or accrued the "reduced amount" described in paragraph (c) of this section in the computation of its taxable income. Thus, income is not to be considered accrued or actually or constructively received by a terminal railroad corporation where, in the manner described in paragraph (c) of this section, (i) a charge which would be made to any railroad corporation for related terminal services is not made, or (ii) a portion of any liability payable by any railroad corporation with respect to related terminal services is discharged.

(2) Deduction not disallowed. In the computation of the taxable income of a terminal railroad corporation, a deduction relating to a "reduced amount", described in paragraph (c) of this section, which is otherwise allowable to it under chapter 1 of the Code (without regard to sec. 277) shall not be disallowed by reason of section 281. Thus, deductions for expenses attributable to services rendered to a shareholder are not to be disallowed to a terminal railroad corporation merely because, in the manner described in paragraph (c) of this section, (i) a charge which would be made to any railroad corporation for related terminal services is not made, or (ii) a portion of any liability payable by any railroad corporation with respect to related terminal services is discharged. To the extent that section 281 applies to a deduction relating to a "reduced amount", such deduction shall not be disallowed under section 277.

(b) Computation of taxable income of shareholders. *(1) Income not considered received or accrued.* A shareholder of a terminal railroad corporation shall not be considered to have received or accrued any "reduced amount" (described in paragraph (c) of this section) in the computation of the shareholder's taxable income. Thus a dividend is not to be considered actually or constructively received by a shareholder of a terminal railroad corporation merely because, in the manner described in paragraph (c) of this section, (i) a charge which would be made to the shareholder or any other railroad corporation for related terminal services is not made, or (ii) a portion of any liability payable by it or any other railroad corporation with respect to related terminal services is discharged.

(2) Expenses not considered paid or incurred. In the computation of the taxable income of a shareholder of a terminal railroad corporation, the shareholder shall not be considered to have paid or incurred any "reduced amount" (described in paragraph (c) of this section). Thus, a shareholder of the terminal railroad corporation may not deduct as an expense for related terminal services (as defined in paragraph (c) of § 1.281-3) an amount in excess of the net cost to it of such services.

(c) Amounts to which section 281 applies. *(1) Reduced amount.* For purposes of this section, the term "reduced amount" means, subject to the limitation of paragraph (c)(4) of this section, the amount by which—

(i) A charge which would be made by a terminal railroad corporation for its taxable year for related terminal services provided to a railroad corporation; or

(ii) A liability of a railroad corporation, resulting from a charge made by a terminal railroad corporation for its taxable year, with respect to related terminal services provided by the terminal railroad corporation,

is reduced by reason of the terminal railroad corporation's taking into account, pursuant to an agreement (as defined in paragraph (d) of § 1.281-3), related terminal income (as defined in paragraph (b) of § 1.281-3) received or accrued (without regard to section 281) during such taxable year.

(2) Charge which would be made. For purposes of this section, a "charge which would be made" by a terminal railroad corporation is the amount that would be charged to any railroad corporation for related terminal services provided if the terminal railroad corporation made the charge without taking related terminal income into account.

(3) Reduction resulting from related terminal income. For purposes of subparagraph (1) of this section, a charge or a liability is reduced by taking related terminal income into account to the extent that—

(i) Related terminal income is received or accrued (without regard to section 281) by the terminal railroad corporation for its taxable year in which the charge or liability is reduced; and

(ii) The charge or liability in question would have been larger than it is had such income not been received or accrued (without regard to section 281).

The reduction must be made (directly or indirectly) on the books of the terminal railroad corporation, and in fact, for the same taxable year for which the charge would be made or for which the liability is incurred. The reduction of the charge or liability must be taken into account by the terminal railroad corporation in ascertaining the income, profit, or loss for such taxable year for the purpose of reports to shareholders and the Interstate Commerce Commission, and for credit purposes.

(4) Limitation. To the extent that a reduced amount (as described in paragraph (c)(1) of this section but without regard to the limitation under this subparagraph) would operate either to create or to increase a net operating loss for the terminal railroad corporation, this section shall not apply. Therefore, if a portion of a liability is discharged (in the manner described in this paragraph) and the discharged portion of the liability exceeds an amount equal to the terminal railroad corporation's gross income minus the deductions allowed by chapter 1 of the Code (computed with regard to the modifications specified in section 172(d) but without regard to section 281 and this section), then section 281 and this section shall not apply to such excess. The limitation described in this subparagraph shall apply only to taxable years of terminal railroad corporations ending after October 23, 1962.

(d) Examples. The provisions of this section may be illustrated by the following examples. In these examples, references to "before the application of section 281", "after the application of section 281", "taxable income", and "allowable deductions" take no account of section 277, which may apply to deductions to which section 281 does not apply.

Example (1). (i) Facts. The T Company is a terminal railroad corporation which charges its three equal shareholders, the X, Y, and Z railroad corporations, a rental calculated monthly on a wheelage or user basis for the use of its services and facilities. The T Company and each of its shareholders report income on the calendar year basis. A written lease agreement to which all of the shareholders were parties was entered into in 1947. The agreement provides that at the end of each year the liabilities of each of the shareholders resulting from charges for rental obligations with respect to related terminal services shall be reduced by the shareholder's one-third share of the net income from each source of revenue that produced income (computed before reduction for Federal income taxes). For the calendar year 1973, the T Company's charges to its shareholders include the following charges for related terminal services: $35,000 to the X Company, $25,000 to the Y Company, and $20,000 to the Z Company. Thus, prior to reduction, total shareholder liabilities to the T Company for related terminal services are $80,000 at the end of 1973. The T Company's net income from all sources (before reduction of liabilities pursuant to the 1947 agreement and before reduction for Federal income taxes) and its taxable income, before the application of section 281, for 1973 are $36,000 determined as follows:

Source	Gross income	Allowable deductions	Income (or loss)
Related terminal services performed:			
For shareholders	$ 80,000	$ 65,000	$15,000
For nonshareholders	46,000	37,000	9,000
Related terminal income ...	126,000	102,000	24,000
Nonrelated terminal income................	30,000	18,000	12,000
Total	156,000	120,000	36,000

The liability of each shareholder is, pursuant to the agreement, discharged in part by the T Company crediting $12,000 against the rental due from each shareholder for a total discharge of liabilities of $36,000 (the net income from all sources), resulting in net shareholder liabilities owing to the T Company at the end of 1973 of $44,000 ($80,000 less $36,000): $23,000 from the X Company, $13,000 from the Y Company, and $8,000 from the Z Company.

(ii) Effect on terminal railroad corporation. The reduced amount to which this section applies is $24,000 (related terminal income of $9,000 from nonshareholders and $15,000 from shareholders). Thus, to the extent of $24,000, the T Company is not considered to have received or accrued income from the discharged liabilities of $36,000. Similarly, to the extent of the same $24,000, the T Company is not disallowed deductions for expenses merely by reason of the discharge. The T Company's taxable income for 1973 after application of section 281 is $12,000, computed as follows:

Gross income ($156,000 less $24,000)	$132,000
Less allowable deductions	120,000
Taxable income	12,000

(iii) Effect on shareholders. The reduced amount of $24,000 shall not be deemed to constitute either a dividend to the shareholders of the T Company or an expense paid or incurred by them. Thus, under the facts described, neither the X Company, the Y Company, nor the Z Company shall be considered to have received or accrued a dividend of $8,000, or to have paid or incurred an expense of $8,000. Assuming the X Company's taxable income for 1973 before the application of section 281 would have been $43,200, computed in the following manner, its taxable income for 1973 after the application of section 281 is $50,000, determined as follows:

	Before the application of sec. 281	After the application of sec. 281
Gross income:		
From sources other than T Co	$146,000	$146,000
Dividend considered received because of T Co.'s discharge of liabilities of $12,000	12,000	4,000
Total	158,000	150,000
Less allowable deductions:		
From sources other than T Co	69,600	69,600
85 percent dividend received deduction under sec. 243 attributable to dividend considered received because of T Co.'s discharge of liabilities	10,200	3,400
Expenses for accrued charges for related terminal services performed by T Co	35,000	27,000
	114,800	100,000
Taxable income	43,200	50,000

Example (2). Assume the same facts as in example (1), except that the charges to each of the shareholders for related terminal services for 1973 were as follows: $35,000 to the X Company, $40,000 to the Y Company, and $5,000 to the Z Company. Assume further that the Z Company, prior to the reduction in liabilities at the end of 1973, owed the T Company an additional $4,000 resulting from charges for 1972 for related terminal services and $6,000 resulting from the purchase of equipment. Since only $21,000 (X Company $8,000, Y Company $8,000, Z Company $5,000) of the liabilities which were discharged resulted from charges made for 1973 for related terminal services, the reduced amount to which this section applies is $21,000 (instead of $24,000 as in example (1)). Thus, the T Company's taxable income for 1973 would be $15,000 ($36,000 less $21,000 reduced amount) and the amount which shall be considered not to have been received or accrued as a dividend nor paid or incurred as an expense of each shareholder is $8,000 for the X Company, $8,000 for the Y Company, and $5,000 for the Z Company.

Example (3). Assume the same facts as in example (1), except that the allowable deductions with respect to nonrelated terminal activities were $39,000 instead of $18,000. The T Company's net income from all sources (before reduction for Federal income taxes) and its taxable income, before the application of section 281, is therefore $15,000, determined as follows:

Source	Gross income	Allowable deductions	Income (or loss
Related terminal income ...	$126,000	$102,000	$24,000
Nonrelated terminal income	30,000	39,000	(9,000)
Total	156,000	141,000	15,000

The liability of each shareholder is nevertheless discharged in part, pursuant to the agreement, by the T Company crediting $8,000 against the rental due from each shareholder for a total discharge of liabilities of $24,000 (the net income from each source of revenue that produced income). Assume further that none of the modifications specified in section 172(d) apply. If the limitation under paragraph (c)(4) of this section were not applied, the reduced amount for the purposes of this section would be $24,000, and the operation of this section would result in a net operating loss of $9,000, since the allowable deductions of $141,000 would exceed the gross income of $132,000 ($156,000 less discharged liabilities of $24,000) by that amount. Because of the limitation under paragraph (c)(4) of this section, however, $9,000 is not included in the reduced amount to which this section applies. Accordingly, the reduced amount is $15,000 (instead of $24,000 as in example (1)). Thus, the T Company's taxable income for 1973 would be zero ($15,000 less the $15,000 reduced amount), and the amount which each shareholder shall be considered not to have received or accrued as a dividend nor paid or incurred as an expense is $5,000.

Example (4). Assume the same facts as in example (1), except that under the agreement income from the terminal parking lot would not reduce the shareholders' liabilities. Assume further that such income amounted to $3,000 of the total related terminal income of $24,000 for the taxable year 1973. The liability of each shareholder therefore is discharged by crediting $11,000 against its rental due for a total discharge of liabilities of $33,000. The reduced amount to which this section applies is $21,000 ($24,000 less $3,000) since only to the extent of $21,000 would there have been no such reduction under the agreement if there were no related terminal income.

Example (5). Assume the same facts as in example (1), except that, pursuant to the agreement, the A Company, a nonshareholder railroad corporation, is to have its liabilities resulting from charges for rental obligations reduced equally with each of the shareholders. Assume further that the T Company's charges to the A Company for the calendar year 1973 included $15,000 for related terminal services and that the liability of each shareholder and the A Company is discharged in part pursuant to the agreement by the T Company crediting $9,000 against the rental due from each. The reduced amount to which this section applies is $24,000. Thus, the T Company's taxable income for 1973 is $12,000, and each shareholder shall not be considered to have received or accrued as a dividend nor paid or incurred as an expense $6,000 ($24,000/$36,000 × $9,000) merely because of the discharge of its own liability. Similarly, each shareholder shall not be considered to have received or accrued as a dividend nor paid or incurred as an expense $2,000 (⅓ × ($24,000/$36,000 × $9,000)) merely because of the discharge of the liability of the A Company. Section 281 does not apply to the determination of the tax consequences of the transaction to the A Company. Similarly, the section does not apply to the determination of the tax consequences to the shareholders resulting from that portion of the discharge of the liability of the A Company which is not related terminal income $3,000). Hence, such consequences shall be determined under the sections of the Internal Revenue Code which govern in the absence of section 281.

Example (6). (i) Facts. The TR Company is a terminal railroad corporation with three equal shareholders, the M, N, and O Railroad Corporations. The TR Company and each of its shareholders report income on the calendar year basis. Pursuant to a written agreement entered into in 1947 to which all shareholders were parties, the TR Company makes one annual charge to each of the three shareholders at the end of each year for the difference between the cost of operations, allocated on a wheelage or user basis for the use of its services and facilities provided to the shareholder during the year, and one-third of its net income from all other sources (computed before reduction for Federal income taxes). The TR Company's taxable income, before the application of section 281, for 1973 is $21,000 determined as follows:

Source	Gross income	Allowable deductions	Income (or loss)
Related terminal services performed:			
For shareholders	$ 65,000	$ 65,000	0
For nonshareholders	46,000	37,000	$ 9,000
Related terminal income ...	111,000	102,000	9,000
Nonrelated terminal income from nonshareholders....	30,000	18,000	12,000
Total	141,000	120,000	21,000

For the calendar year 1973, the TR company's charges to its shareholders are $23,000 ($30,000 less $7,000) to the M company, $13,000 ($20,000 less $7,000) to the N company, and $8,000 ($15,000 less $7,000) to the O company for a total of $44,000 for related terminal services.

(ii) Effect on terminal railroad corporation. The reduced amount to which this section applies is $9,000. The TR company is not considered to have received or accrued income of $9,000 (related terminal income) merely because the charge of $21,000 (net income from all sources other than shareholders) was not made. Similarly, to the extent of $9,000, the TR company is not disallowed deductions for expenses merely because the full cost of services was not for 1973 after application of section 281, is $12,000, computed as follows:

Gross income ($141,000 less $9,000 charges not made)..	$132,000
Less allowable deductions	120,000
Taxable income...........................	12,000

(iii) Effect on shareholders. Neither the M company, the N company, nor the O company shall be considered to have received or accrued a dividend of $3,000 nor to have paid or incurred an expense of $3,000 merely by reason of the reduced charges. Thus, assuming the M company's taxable income for 1973 before the application of section 281 would have been $47,450, computed in the following manner, its taxable income for 1973 after the application of section 281 is $50,000, determined as follows:

	Before the application of sec. 281	After the application of sec. 281
Gross income:		
From sources other than TR Co	$146,000	$146,000
Dividend considered received because of TR Co.'s reduction of charges	7,000	4,000
Total	153,000	150,000
Less allowable deductions:		
From sources other than ETR Co	69,600	69,600
85 percent dividend received deduction under sec. 243 attributable to dividend considered received because of TR Co.'s reduction of charges....................	5,950	3,400
Expenses for accrued charges for related terminal services performed by TR Co	30,000	27,000
	105,550	100,000
Taxable income..................	47,450	50,000

T.D. 7356, 5/30/75.

§ 1.281-3 Definitions.

Caution: The Treasury has not yet amended Reg § 1.281-3 to reflect changes made by P.L. 95-473, P.L. 94-455.

(a) Terminal railroad corporation. The term "terminal railroad corporation" means a corporation which, in the taxable year, meets all of the following conditions:

(1) The corporation and each of its shareholders must be domestic corporations. Thus, all of the shareholders of the corporation, as well as the corporation itself, must be corporations which were organized or created in the United States, including only the States and the District of Columbia, or under the law of the United States or of any State or territory.

(2) All of the shareholders must be railroad corporations which are subject to part I of the Interstate Commerce Act. Thus, if any shareholder of the corporation, regardless of the class or percentage of stock owned, is not subject to the jurisdiction of the Interstate Commerce Commission under part I of that Act, the corporation cannot qualify as a terminal railroad corporation.

(3) The corporation must not be a member of an affiliated group of corporations (as defined in section 1504), other than as a common parent corporation. For this purpose it is immaterial whether or not the affiliated group has ever made a consolidated income tax return. Thus, if the X railroad corporation owns 80 percent of all of the outstanding stock of the Y railroad corporation, the X railroad corporation may qualify, but the Y railroad corporation cannot qualify, as a terminal railroad corporation.

(4) The primary business of the corporation must be that of providing to domestic railroad corporations subject to part I of the Interstate Commerce Act and to the shippers and passengers of such railroad corporations one or more of the following facilities or services: (i) Railroad terminal facili-

ties, (ii) railroad switching facilities, (iii) railroad terminal services, or (iv) railroad switching services. The designated facilities and services include the furnishing of terminal trackage, the operation of stockyards or a union passenger or freight station, and the operation of railroad bridges and ferries. The providing of the designated facilities includes the leasing of those facilities. A corporation shall be considered as having established that its primary business is that of providing the designated facilities and services if more than 50 percent of its gross income (computed without regard to section 281, and excluding dividends and gains and losses from the disposition of capital assets or property described in section 1231(b)) for the taxable year is derived from those sources. The fact that income from a service or facility is included within the definition of related terminal income is immaterial for purposes of determining whether that service or facility is one which is designated in this subparagraph. Thus, although income from the operation of a commuter railroad line may be related terminal income, a corporation whose primary business is the operation of that facility is not a terminal railroad corporation, since its primary business is not the providing of the designated facilities or services.

(5) A substantial part of the services rendered by the corporation for the taxable year must be rendered to one or more of its shareholders. For purposes of this requirement, providing the use of facilities shall be considered the rendering of services.

(6) Each shareholder of the corporation must compute its taxable income on the basis of a taxable year which either begins or ends on the same day as the taxable year of the corporation.

(b) Related terminal income. *(1) In general.* Related terminal income is, generally, the type of income normally earned from the operation of a railroad terminal. The term "related terminal income" means the taxable income (computed without regard to sections 172, 277, or 281) which the terminal railroad corporation derives for the taxable year from the sources enumerated in paragraph (b)(2) of this section. Related terminal income must be derived from direct provision of the specified facilities or services by the terminal corporation itself. Thus, income consisting of rent from a lease of a terminal facility by a terminal corporation to a railroad user would qualify; but dividends from a corporation in which the terminal corporation owned stock and which provided such facilities or services to others would not qualify. The term does not include gain or loss derived from the sale, exchange, or other disposition of capital assets or section 1231 assets, whether or not section 1245 or section 1250 applies to part or all of that gain. For example, the term does not apply to gain from the sale of a terminal building or terminal equipment. All direct and indirect expenses and other deductible items attributable to related terminal services or facilities shall be deducted in determining related terminal income. Attribution shall be determined in accordance with customary railroad accounting practices accepted by the Interstate Commerce Commission, except that interest paid with respect to the indebtedness of a terminal railroad corporation shall be deducted from related terminal income to the extent that the proceeds from the indebtedness were directly or indirectly applied to facilities or activities producing such income. The district director may either accept the use of the taxpayer's method of determining the application of the proceeds of all indebtedness of such corporation or prescribe the use of another method which, under all the facts and circumstances, appears to reflect more accurately the probable application of such proceeds.

(2) Sources of related terminal income. The term "related terminal income" includes only income derived from one or more of the following sources:

(i) From services or facilities of a character ordinarily and regularly provided by terminal railroad corporations for railroad corporations or for the employees, passengers, or shippers of railroad corporations. Whether the services or facilities are of a character ordinarily and regularly provided by terminal railroad corporations is to be determined by accepted industry practice. The fact that nonterminal businesses may also provide such services or facilities is immaterial. However, there must be a direct relationship between the service or facility provided and the operation of the terminal, including the operation of its trackage and switching facilities. Thus, the term "related terminal income" includes income derived from operating or leasing switching facilities and terminal facilities, such as income from charges to railroad corporations for the use of a union passenger or freight station. Also included for this purpose is income derived from charges to railroad shippers, including express companies and freight forwarders, for the use of sheds or warehouses, even though not directly intended for railroad use. The term includes income derived from leasing or operating restaurants, drugstores, barbershops, newsstands, ticket agencies, banking facilities, car rental facilities, or other similar facilities for passengers, in waiting rooms or along passenger concourses. Similarly, the term includes income derived from operating or leasing passenger parking facilities, and from renting taxicab space, located on or adjacent to the terminal premises. Although the term does include income derived from the operation of a small hotel operated primarily for and usually occupied primarily by the employees of the railroad corporations, it does not include income derived from the operation of a hotel for passengers or other persons.

(ii) From any railroad corporation for services or facilities provided by the terminal railroad corporation in connection with railroad operations. A service or a facility is provided in connection with railroad operations if it is of a character ordinarily and regularly availed of by railroad corporations. For purposes of this subdivision, the income must be derived from railroad corporations. Thus, in addition to the income derived from sources described in paragraph (b)(2)(i) of this section, the term "related terminal income" includes income derived from switching facilities or leasing to any railroad corporation, or operating for the benefit of such corporation, a beltline or bypass railroad leading to or from the terminal premises. Also included are income derived from the rental of office space (whether or not services are provided to the occupants) in the terminal building to any railroad corporation for that corporation's administrative or operating divisions, and income derived from tolls charged to any railroad corporation for the use of a railroad bridge or ferry.

(iii) From the use by persons other than railroad corporations of a portion of a facility, or of a service, which is used primarily for railroad purposes. A facility or service is used primarily for railroad purposes if the predominant reason for its continued operation or provision is the furnishing of facilities or services described in either subdivision (i) or (ii) of this subparagraph. The determination required by this subdivision is to be made independently for each separate facility or service. Two substantial portions of a single structure may be considered separate facilities, depending upon the respective uses made of each. Moreover, any substantial addition, constructed after October 23, 1962, to a facility shall be considered a separate facility.

The term "related terminal income" includes income produced by operating a commuter service or by renting tracks and facilities for a commuter service to an independent operator. The term also includes the sale or rental of advertising space at a terminal facility. If the conditions described in this subdivision are satisfied, the term "related terminal income" may include income which has no connection with the operation of the terminal. Thus, if a terminal railroad corporation operates a railroad bridge primarily to provide railroad corporations a means of crossing a river and the lower level of the bridge contains a roadway for similar use by automobiles, the term includes income derived from the tolls charged to the automobiles for the use of the bridge roadway. However, upon the discontinuance of operations of the railroad level of the bridge, the term would cease to include the automobile tolls. If excess steam from a steam plant operated primarily to supply steam to the terminal is sold to another business in the neighborhood, the term would include the income derived from such sale. However, because an oil or gas well or a mine constitutes a separate facility, the term "related terminal income" does not include income derived in any form from a deposit of oil, natural gas, or any other mineral located on property owned or leased by the terminal railroad corporation.

Similarly, while the term includes income derived from the rental of a small number of offices located in the terminal building (whether or not the lessees are railroad corporations), it does not include income derived from the leasing or operation, for the use of the general public, of a large number of offices or a large number of rooms for lodging, whether or not the space is physically part of the same structure as the terminal. Moreover, the term does not include income derived from the rental of offices to the general public in an addition to the terminal building constructed after October 23, 1962, unless the addition is primarily used for railroad purposes and the offices rented to the general public do not constitute a separate facility in the addition. Whether or not income from the addition is determined to be related terminal income, the income from the small number of offices which were included in the terminal building before the addition was constructed shall continue to be related terminal income.

(iv) From the United States in payment for facilities or services in connection with mail handling. The income must be derived directly from the U.S. Government, or any agency thereof (including for this purpose the U.S. Postal Service), through the receipt of payments for mail-handling facilities or services. Thus, the term would include income derived from the rental of space for a post office for use by the general public on the terminal premises or from the sorting of mail in a railroad box car.

(3) Illustration. The provisions of this paragraph may be illustrated by the following example:

Example. For its calendar year 1973, the R Company, a terminal railroad corporation, has taxable income of $36,000, before the application of section 281 and taking no account of section 277, determined as follows:

Gross income:		
Switching charges		$ 50,000
Express companies		2,000
Commuter line		4,000
U.S. mail handling		4,000
Railroad bridge tolls:		
From railroads	2,000	
From automobiles	1,000	
Total		3,000
Station and train charges		47,000
Terminal parking lot		4,000
Rent from terminal building:		
Passenger facilities (ground level)	8,000	
Offices leased to railroads (2d floor)	3,000	
Offices leased to others (2d floor)	1,000	
Hotel open to public (3d through 6th floors)	14,000	
Total		26,000
Interest received from bond investments		1,500
Dividends received from wholly owned subsidiary		10,000
Amount realized from sale of equipment	6,000	
Less:		
Adjusted basis	1,000	
Expenses of sale	500	
	1,500	
		4,500
		156,000
Allowable deductions:		
Dividend received deduction		8,500
Interest paid:		
On loan for hotel furnishings	1,500	
On loan for rolling stock	2,000	
		3,500
Maintenance, depreciation, management and other expenses:		
Attributable to hotel	3,000	
Attributable to parking lot	1,000	
Attributable to U.S. mail handling	1,000	
All other	98,000	
		103,000
Loss from sale of securities		3,000
Charitable contribution		500
Net operating loss deduction		1,500
		120,000
Taxable income before the application of sec. 281		36,000

The R Co.'s related terminal income for 1973 is $24,000 computed as follows:

Taxable income (before the application of sec. 281)		$36,000
Less:		
Dividend received	10,000	
Minus dividend received deduction	8,500	
		1,500
Interest received		1,500
Amount realized from sale of equipment	6,000	
Less:		
Adjusted basis	1,000	
Expense of sale	500	
	1,500	
		4,500
Hotel income	14,000	
Less:		
Interest paid on loan for hotel	1,500	
Other hotel expenses	3,000	
	4,500	
		9,500

	17,000
	19,000
Add:	
Loss from sale of securities	3,000
Charitable contribution	500
Net operating loss deduction	1,500
	5,000
Related terminal income	24,000

(c) Related terminal services. The term "related terminal services" means only the services or the use of facilities, provided by the terminal railroad corporation, which are taken into account in computing related terminal income. Thus, the term includes the providing of terminal and switching services, the furnishing of terminal and switching facilities including the furnishing of terminal trackage, and the operation of bridges and ferries for railroad purposes. For example, upon the facts of the example in the preceding paragraph, the charges for related terminal services are $126,000, determined as follows:

Switching charges	$ 50,000
Express companies	2,000
Commuter line	4,000
U.S. mail handling	4,000
Railroad bridge tolls	3,000
Station and train charges	47,000
Terminal parking lot	4,000
Rent from:	
Passenger facilities	8,000
Offices	4,000
Total	126,000

(d) Agreement. As used in section 281 and § 1.281-2 the term "agreement" means a written contract, entered into before the beginning of the terminal railroad corporation's taxable year in question, to which all shareholders of the terminal railroad corporation are parties. The fact that other railroad corporations or persons are also parties will not disqualify an agreement. Section 281 applies only if, and to the extent that, the reduction of the liability or charge that would be made, as described in paragraph (c) of § 1.281-2, results from the agreement. Thus, where the other conditions of the statute are met, section 281 applies if a written agreement, to which all of the shareholders were parties and which was entered into prior to the beginning of the terminal railroad corporation's taxable year, provides that the net revenues of the terminal railroad corporation are to be applied as a reduction of what would otherwise be the charge for the taxable year for related terminal services provided to the shareholders. Similarly, section 281 applies, where its other requirements are fulfilled, if the agreement provides that the net revenues are to be credited against rental obligations resulting from related terminal services furnished to shareholders. However, section 281 does not apply where the agreement provides that the net revenues are to be divided among the shareholders and distributed to them in cash or held subject to their unconditional right of withdrawal instead of being applied to the computation of charges, or in reduction of liabilities incurred, for related terminal services.

(e) Railroad corporation. For purposes of section 281, § 1.281-2, and this section, the term "railroad corporation" means any corporation (regardless of whether it is a shareholder of the terminal railroad corporation) that is engaged as a common carrier in the furnishing or sale of transportation by railroad, or is a lessor of railroad equipment or facilities. For purposes of the preceding sentence, a corporation is a lessor of railroad equipment or facilities only if (1) it is subject to part I of the Interstate Commerce Act, (2) substantially all of its railroad properties have been leased to a railroad corporation or corporations, (3) each lease is for a term of more than 20 years, and (4) 80 percent or more of its gross income for the taxable year is derived from such lease.

T.D. 7356, 5/30/75.

§ 1.281-4 Taxable years affected.

Caution: The Treasury has not yet amended Reg § 1.281-4 to reflect changes made by P.L. 99-514.

(a) In general. Except as provided in paragraph (b) of this section, the provisions of section 281 and §§ 1.281-2 and 1.281-3 shall apply to all taxable years to which either the Internal Revenue Code of 1954 or the Internal Revenue Code of 1939 apply.

(b) Taxable years ending before October 23, 1962. *(1)* (i) In the case of a taxable year of a terminal railroad corporation ending before October 23, 1962, section 281(a) shall apply only to the extent that the terminal railroad corporation (a) computed its taxable income on its return for such taxable year as if the "reduced amount", described in paragraph (c) of § 1.281-2, were not received or accrued, and (b) did not decrease its otherwise allowable deductions for such taxable year on account of that "reduced amount". Similarly, in the case of a taxable year of a shareholder of a terminal railroad corporation ending before October 23, 1962, section 281(b) shall apply only to the extent that such shareholder computed its taxable income on its return for such taxable year as if the shareholder had neither received or accrued as a dividend nor paid or incurred as an expense the "reduced amount" described in paragraph (c) of § 1.281-2. Such return must have been filed on or before the due date (including the period of any extension of time) for filing the return for the applicable taxable year. The fact that an amended return or claim for refund or credit of overpayment was subsequently filed, or a deficiency subsequently assessed, based upon a computation of taxable income which is inconsistent with the manner in which the taxable income was computed on the timely filed return, is immaterial.

(ii) The provisions of this paragraph may be illustrated by the following examples:

Example (1). The G Company is a terminal railroad corporation which in 1960 reduced the liabilities resulting from charges to its shareholders, pursuant to a 1947 written agreement, by its income from nonshareholder sources. For the calendar year 1960, the G Company's related terminal income was $24,000, of which $3,000 is attributable to income from the United States in payment for facilities and services in connection with mail handling. Although the shareholders' liabilities were reduced by $24,000 as a result of taking related terminal income earned during the taxable year into account, on its timely filed 1960 income tax return the G Company treated the $3,000 of liabilities which were reduced on account of income from mail handling as gross income received or accrued during the year. Assuming that the provisions of § 1.281-2 otherwise apply, their application to the determination of the 1960 tax liability of the G Company shall not extend to the entire "reduced amount" of $24,000, but shall be limited to $21,000 of that amount.

Example (2). Assume the same facts as in example (1), and the following additional facts. The G Company had three shareholders in 1960, and an equal discharge of liability of $8,000 resulted for each of them on account of related terminal income. Each shareholder treated, on its timely filed 1960 income tax return, $1,000 of its liabilities, which were so reduced and were attributable to income from the United States in payment for facilities and services in connection with mail handling, as if it had received $1,000 from the G Company as a dividend and paid that $1,000 to the G Company for services. Each shareholder treated the remaining $7,000 of its liabilities which were so reduced as if the liabilities which were reduced had never been incurred. Assuming that the provisions of § 1.281-2 otherwise apply, each shareholder shall not be considered to have received or accrued as a dividend, nor to have paid or incurred as an expense $7,000 (instead of $8,000).

(2) For any taxable year of a terminal railroad corporation ending before October 23, 1962, a claim for refund or credit of overpayment of income tax based upon section 281 may be filed, even though such refund or credit of overpayment was otherwise barred by operation of any law or rule of law on October 23, 1962, subject to the conditions set forth in paragraph (b)(2)(i) through (v) of this section.

(i) The claim for refund or credit of overpayment must not have been barred by a closing agreement (under either section 3760 of the Internal Revenue Code of 1939 or section 7121 of the Internal Revenue Code of 1954), or by a compromise (under section 3761 of the Internal Revenue Code of 1939 or section 7122 of the Internal Revenue Code of 1954);

(ii) The claim for refund or credit of overpayment shall be allowed only to the extent that the overpayment of income tax results from the recomputation of the terminal railroad corporation's taxable income in the manner described in paragraph (a) of § 1.281-2;

(iii) The claim for refund or credit of the overpayment must have been filed prior to October 23, 1963;

(iv) The claim for refund or credit of overpayment shall be allowed only to the extent that the manner in which the terminal railroad corporation's taxable income is recomputed is the manner in which the terminal railroad corporation's taxable income was computed on its timely filed income tax return for such taxable year; and

(v) Each railroad corporation which was a shareholder of the terminal railroad corporation during such taxable year must consent in writing to the assessment, within such period as may be agreed upon with the district director, of any deficiency for any year (even though assessment of the deficiency would otherwise be prevented by the operation of any law or rule of law at the time of filing the consent) to the extent that—

(A) The deficiency is attributable to the recomputation of the shareholder's taxable income in the manner described in paragraph (b) of § 1.281-2, and

(B) The deficiency results from the shareholder's allocable portion of the "reduced amount" (described in paragraph (c) of § 1.281-2) which gives rise to the refund or credit granted to the terminal railroad corporation under this subparagraph.

T.D. 7356, 5/30/75.